A CHRONOLOGY OF AMERICAN MUSICAL THEATER

A CHRONOLOGY OF
AMERICAN
MUSICAL THEATER

Richard C. Norton

VOLUME 2

OXFORD
UNIVERSITY PRESS
2002

OXFORD
UNIVERSITY PRESS

Oxford New York
Auckland Bangkok Buenos Aires Cape Town Chennai
Dar es Salaam Delhi Hong Kong Istanbul Karachi Kolkata
Kuala Lumpur Madrid Melbourne Mexico City Mumbai Nairobi
São Paulo Shanghai Singapore Taipei Tokyo Toronto
and an associated company in Berlin

Copyright © 2002 by Oxford University Press

Published by Oxford University Press, Inc.
198 Madison Avenue, New York, New York 10016
www.oup.com

Oxford is a registered trademark of Oxford University Press

Library of Congress Cataloging-in-Publication Data
Norton, Richard C., 1953-
A chronology of American musical theater / Richard C. Norton
Includes indexes
ISBN 0-19-508888-3 (set: cloth : alk. paper) – ISBN 0-19-515565-3 (v. 1: cloth : alk. Paper)
1. Musical theater—New York (State)—New York—Chronology. I. Title.
ML 1711.8.N3 N67 2002
782.1'4'097471—dc21   2001055710

EDITORIAL AND PRODUCTION STAFF
Project Editor: Mark Mones
Production Director: John Sollami
Indexes: Prepared by Magic Fingers
Manufacturing Controller: Ben Lee
Book Designer: Joan Greenfield
Composition: General Meador, Inc.
Publisher: Karen Day

1 3 5 7 9 8 6 4 2
Printed in the United States of America
on acid-free paper

CONTENTS

A CHRONOLOGY OF AMERICAN MUSICAL THEATER

A CHRONOLOGY OF AMERICAN MUSICAL THEATER

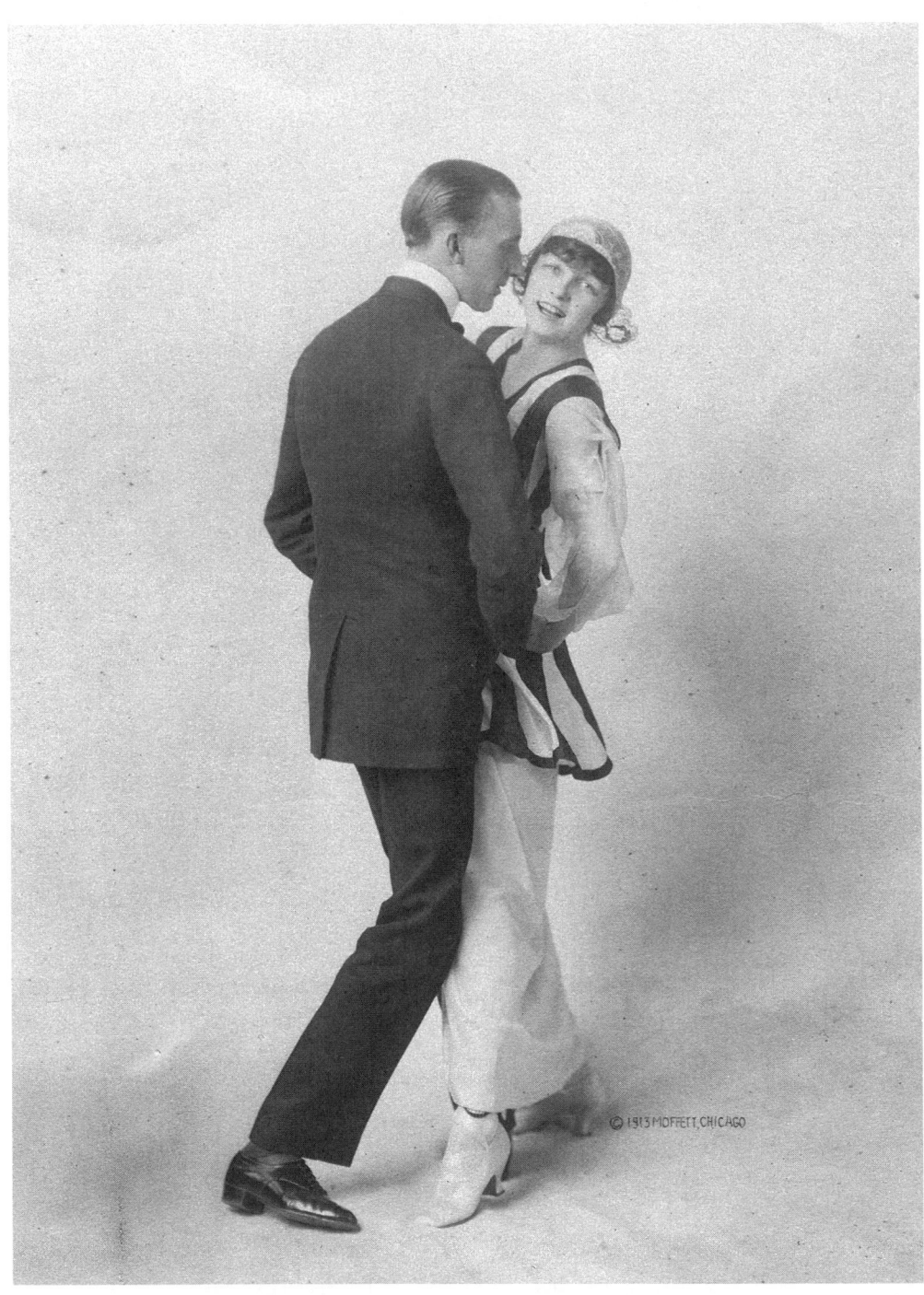

Vernon and Irene Castle in THE SUNSHINE GIRL (Photo: Moffett)
Billy Rose Theatre Collection, New York Public Library for the Performing Arts

1912–1913 SEASON

THE PIRATES OF PENZANCE,
1912.21   or The Slave of Duty

An Elaborate Star Revival of the Comic Opera in Two Acts[1]. Libretto by William S. Gilbert and Arthur Sullivan. Staged under the direction of William J. Wilson. Scenery by H. Robert Law. Costumes by Max & Mahieu. Orchestra under the direction of Clarence Rogerson. Produced by the Messrs. Shubert and William A. Brady. Opened 3 June 1912 at the Casino Theatre and closed 26 June 1912 after 28 performances.

CAST: *Richard*, a Pirate Chief: EUGENE COWLES. *Samuel*, His Lieutenant: RICHARD W. TEMPLE. *Frederic*, a Pirate Apprentice: ARTHUR ALDRIDGE. *Major-General Stanley* of the British Army: GEORGE J. MacFARLANE. *Edward*, a Sergeant of Police: DeWOLF HOPPER. *General Stanley's Daughters (4): Mabel*: BLANCHE DUFFIELD. *Kate*: ALICE BRADY. *Edith*: VIOLA GILLETTE. *Isabel*: Louise Barthell. *Ruth*, a Piratical Maid of All Work: JOSEPHINE JACOBY.

Chorus of General Stanley's Daughters: Misses Fern Hollis, Margaret Morrison, Ruth Bonner, Nora McClory, Alice Stratton, Marion George, Loretta Doyle, Rose Wertz, Nathalie Saymore, Annette Herbert, Flora Lyons, Josephine DeNoville, Dorothy Cassel, Caro DuBurgho, Florence Sommerville, May von Summerfield, Edith Buell, Sara Meredith, Harriett DeNorma, Florence Harris, Edna Lee, Marie Corty, Helen Starr, Pauline Sterling, Leonora Guest. *Pirates, Policemen*: Messrs. Henry Holt, J. Barbara, Joseph Galton, Frank Mirose, Louis Derman, Jose Pepe, John C. Cryan, George Williams, Irving Lavitz, Lew Graham, Fred Walker, J. Leonard Feiner, L. Williams, Tom Bryan, Jack Evans, Parker Leonard, David Heilbron, Herbert Hall, John E. Reese, Alex. Keene, William Baumann, Lew Litchfield.

H.M.S. PINAFORE,
1912.22   or The Lass That Loved a Sailor

A Revival of the Comic Opera in Two Acts.[2] Libretto by William S. Gilbert. Music by Arthur Sullivan. Entire production staged by W. G. Stewart. Settings by H. Robert Law. Costumes by Max & Mahieu. Orchestra under the direction of Clarence Rogerson. Produced by the Messrs. Shubert and William A. Brady. Opened 27 June 1912 at the Casino Theatre and closed 28 June 1912 after 2 performances.

CAST: *The Rt. Hon. Sir Joseph Porter, K.C.B.*, First Lord of the Admiralty: ARTHUR CUNNINGHAM. *Captain Corcoran*, Commander of the *H.M.S. Pinafore*: GEORGE G. MacFARLANE. *Rackstraw*, Able Seaman: ARTHUR ALDRIDGE. *Dick Deadeye*, Able Seaman: DeWOLF HOPPER. *Bill Bobstay*, Boatswain: Eugene Cowles. *Josephine*, the Captain's Daughter: BLANCHE DUFFIELD. *Hebe*, Sir Joseph's First Cousin: ALICE BRADY. *Little Buttercup*, Mrs. Cripps, a Portsmouth bum-boat woman: VIOLA GILLETTE. *First Lord's Sisters, His Aunts, His Cousins, His Middies, Marine Band, Marine Drum Corps, Marine Guard, Sailors.*

THE MIKADO,
1912.23   or The Town of Titipu

A Revival of the Comic Opera in Two Acts.[3] Libretto by William S. Gilbert. Music by Arthur Sullivan. Staged by W. G. Stewart. Settings by H. Robert Law. Costumes by Max & Mahieu. Orchestra under the direction of Clarence Rogerson. Produced by the Messrs. Shubert and William A. Brady. Opened and closed 29 June 1912 at the Casino Theatre after 2 performances.

CAST: *The Mikado of Japan*: GEORGE J. MacFARLANE. *Nanki-Poo*, his son: ARTHUR ALDRIDGE. *Ko-Ko*, Lord High Executioner of Titipu: DeWOLF HOPPER. *Pooh-Bah*, Lord High Everything Else: EUGENE COWLES. *Pish-Tush*, a Noble

---

[1]First presented in New York 31 December 1879 at the Fifth Avenue Theatre for 91 performances in two engagements. For Synopsis of Scenes and Musical Numbers, see original 1879 production.
[2]Originally presented in New York 15 January 1879 at the Standard Theatre for 175 performances. For Synopsis of Scenes and Musical Numbers, see original 1879 production.
[3]First presented in New York 20 July, 10-29 August 1885 at the Union Square and People's Theatres for 22 performances. First authorized production presented 19 August 1885 at the Fifth Avenue Theatre by Richard D'Oyly Carte for 250 performances. For Synopsis of Scenes and Musical Numbers, see 19 August 1885 D'Oyly Carte production.

Lord: ARTHUR CUNNINGHAM. *Three Sisters, Wards of Ko-Ko: Yum-Yum*: BLANCHE DUFFIELD. *Pitti-Sing*: ALICE BRADY. *Peep-Bo*: LOUISE BARTHEL. *Katisha*, an Elderly Lady in love with Nanki-Poo: KATE CONDON. *School Girls, Nobles and Attendants.*

THE PASSING SHOW OF 1912/
1912.24   THE BALLET OF 1830

A Double Bill of a Kaleidoscopic Almanac (Musical Revue) in Two Acts, 7 Scenes,[4] preceded by a Ballet in 3 Scenes. Sketches and lyrics by George Bronson-Howard and Harold Atteridge. Music by Louis A. Hirsch, (Earl Carroll, Harry Orlob, Irving Berlin). Entire production staged by Ned Wayburn. Dances arranged by Ned Wayburn. Ballet choreographed by Theodore Kosloff. Costumes designed by Melville Ellis. Scenery painted by John Y. Young, Louis Young. Orchestra under the direction of Samuel Lehman. Orchestrations by Oscar Radin, Frank Saddler. Produced by the Winter Garden Company (Messrs. Shubert). Opened 22 July 1912 at the Winter Garden and closed 16 November 1912 after 136 performances.

CAST: TRIXIE FRIGANZA, EUGENE HOWARD, WILLIE HOWARD, JOBYNA HOWLAND, CHARLOTTE GREENWOOD, SIDNEY GRANT, ANNA WHEATON, HARRY FOX, ERNEST HARE, ROGER DAVIS, SHIRLEY KELLOGG, OSCAR SCHWARTZ [SHAW], CHARLES J. ROSS, CLARENCE HARVEY, DANIEL MORRIS, GEORGE MOON, ADELAIDE AND HUGHES, EMILE AGOUST, EMIL ZAJAH, Edward Cutler, L'Aerolia, Albert S. Howson, Kitty Kyle, Fanny Kidston, Helen Claggette, Clara Lloyd, May Dealy, Florence Cable, Olga Hempstone, Winona Wilkins, Isabelle Jason, Hilarion Ceballos, Rosalie Ceballos, Nellie Brown, Greville Moore, F. Zanfretta.

Personnel of the Chorus: Trans-Atlantic Passengers, etc.: Misses Betty Scott, Mae Dealy, Lillian Harris, Fanny Kidston, Clara Stanton, Vivian MacDonald, Edith Whitney, Louise MacFarlane, Ethel Dennison, Mae Tormey, Lola Taylor, Olga Hempstone, Clara Lloyd, Helen Claggette, Frances Morris, Winona Wilkins, Kitty Kyle, Kathryn Humphreys, Margie Herman, Bertie Britton, Celeste Campbell, Dorothy Barnette, Elinore Dell, Marie Corty. *Jockeys, Hieland Lassies, Quaker Boys, etc.*: Misses Billie Townley, Alleyne Pickard, Gertrude Rutland, Connie Magnett, Maud Worden, Fannie Grant, Alma Braham, Helen Lloyd, Lottie Franklin, Lotta Morse, Ester Shannon, Etta Franklin, Bessie Shannon, Marie Wallace, Mabel Beck, Isabel Barclay, Agnes Hall, Grace Hall, Ester Pierce, Charlotte Cushman, Hazel Mooney, Maurice Madison, Bessie Gray, Marie Earle, Isabelle Jason. *Reporters, Inspectors, Policemen, Pirates, etc.*: Messrs. Henry Holt, Harry Sulkins, Stanley Vickers, Herbert Hall, Fred Bates, A. Keene, Edward Gordon, Austin Clark, Raymond Strath, Roger Davis, Jack Laughlin, Edward Scanlin, Ralph O'Brien, Jerry Childs, Edward Grant. *The Bathers*: Misses Mae Dealy, Winona Wilkins, Bertie Britton, Bessie Gray, Connie Magnett, Alma Braham, Hazel Mooney, Ettie Franklin, Mabel Beck, Billie Townley, Ester Pierce, Alleyne Pickard.

BALLET

The Ballet of 1830, a mimo-dramatic ballet in 3 Scenes. Scenario by Maurice Volny. Music from French composers adapted by George Bing. Scenery by T. Ryan. Costumes by C. Alias. Pantomime action and dances incidental to this ballet staged by Emile Agoust.

CAST: *Rodolphe*: EMILE AGOUST. *Mariette*: ENIL ZAJAH. *The Vampire Girl*: Greville Moore. *The Baron*: E. Zanfretta. *Painters, Midinettes, Members of the Wedding Party, Flower Girls, etc.*

Scene 1: The Studio. *Scene 2*: Restaurant de Nuit. *Scene 3*: Jardin des Amoureux. followed by

THE PASSING SHOW OF 1912, a kaleidoscopic almanac in 7 Scenes, presenting the comic aspect of many important events, political, theatrical, and otherwise embracing the sunny side of "Bought and Paid For," "Bunty Pulls the Strings," "A Butterfly on the Wheel," "Kismet," "The Typhoon," "The Quaker Girl," "The Pirates of Penzance," "Oliver Twist," etc.

ACT 1
Scene 1

    "We've Been to Europe" (Opening Chorus)
      Entire Chorus
    "There You Have (Old) New York Town"
      S. Kellogg, Show Girls
      (*Lyrics by* Louis Hirsch.)
    "(The) Rag Time Jockey Man"
      W. Howard, Chorus
      (*Music and Lyrics by* Irving Berlin.)

---

[4]The second in the annual series of Passing Show revues which began in 1894, and the first edition produced by the Messrs. Shubert. The Ballet of 1830 was billed as having "played for 8 months at the Alhambra Theatre, London."

"Handy Andy"
C. Harvey, Dancers
"Pirates and Quaker Girl"
A. Wheaton, Male Chorus
"The Wedding Glide"
S. Kellogg, O. Schwarz, Chorus
(*Lyrics by Louis A. Hirsch.*)
Scene: Pier of the *S. S. Cleveland*.
Lady Fluff-Bored 'un: J. Howland. *Porters*: D. Moon, G. Morris. *Collector of the Port*: E. Howard. *A Johnnie in captivity*: R. Davis. *Zorah Tourraine*: S. Kellogg. *Tony, alias Lord Arthur Plantaget Pantalette*: H. Fox. *Boldenstein, his valet*: W. Howard. *Bunty*: S. Kellogg. *Wealum*: O. Schwarz. *The Strenuous Citizen*: C. J. Ross. *Carnegie*: C. Harvey. *The Quaker Girl*: A. Wheaton. *Customs Inspector*: E. Cutler.
Scene 2[5]
"Ida"
H. Fox
"Modern Love"
C. Greenwood, S. Grant
"Girlish Laughter"
C. Greenwood
Scene: Greeley Square, New York.
Officer 666: E. Hare. *Tony*: H. Fox. *Jimmy Gilley*: S. Grant. *Fanny Silly*: C. Greenwood.
Scene 3
"When Was There Ever a Night Like This"
E. Hare
(*Lyrics by Louis A. Hirsch.*)
"All the World Is Madly Prancing"
T. Friganza, G. Moon, D. Morris, Dancers
"The Spark of Life" (Descriptive Dance)
Adelaide and Hughes
Mahaba, a Hindoo sorcerer, fascinated by the grace and beauty of a dancing girl, carries her captive to his palace, where she is held under his magic spell. Nypah, in a trance, and dressed as a Buddha goddess, is brought into the presence of the sorcerer. Being that she is a slave to the influence of Mahaba, he causes her to be awakened and commands her to dance. During the dance she becomes weak and falls. Mahaba, after much effort, restores her and commands that she continue to dance. He then loses his head and embraces her, and the sorcerer falls backward on his neck, which is all but broken. He staggers to his feet, making a last attempt to overcome Nypah, when a mysterious power from heaven, showering its rays, protects her from malign influence. Mahaba drops dead. The spell is broken and Nypah falls on the throne lifeless.
"The Bacchanal Rag"
A. Wheaton, W. Howard, Chorus
(*Lyrics by Louis A. Hirsch.*)
Scene: The Harem of Sewer-Man.
First Eunuch: E. Hare. *Murah*: I. Jason. *Zarah, a diving girl*: L'Aerolia. *Ferusah, queen of the harem*: J. Howland. *Amarsah*: S. Kellogg. *Chief Eunuch*: S. Grant. *Mahaba, a sorcerer*: J. J. Hughes. *Nypah, the favorite dancer*: Adelaide. *What-Fur*: O. Schwarz. *The Oldest Eunuch*: E. Cutler. *Maid of the Harem*: C. Greenwood. *Sewer-Man*: A. S. Howson. *The Quaker Girl*: A. Wheaton. *Keokuk*: T. Friganza. *Teddy Hadj*: C. J. Ross. *Tony*: H. Fox. *Peter Grimm*: W. Howard. *David Belasco*: E. Howard.

ACT 2[6]
Scene 1
"A Policeman's Lot Is a Happy One"
E. Hare, Male Chorus
"You Never Could Tell We Were Married"
T. Friganza

---

[5]For subsequent national tour, "Ida," "Modern Love" and "Girlish Laughter" were dropped and replaced by:
"Foolishness"
T. Friganza
[6]Added to Act 2, Scene 3 for subsequent national tour were:
"(That) Haunting Melody" (from VERA VIOLETTA)
C. Harvey, E. Hare
(*Music and Lyrics by George M. Cohan.*)
"Rum, Tum, Fidele" (Rum, Tum, Tiddle)(from VERA VIOLETTA)
C. Harvey, E. Hare
(*Music by Jean Schwartz. Lyrics by Edward Madden.*)

"My Reuben Girlie"
J. J. Hughes, Dancers
(*Lyrics by Louis A. Hirsch.*)
A Japanese Valet: W. Howard. *Miss Taken*: K. Kyle. *Miss Fortune*: F. Kidston. *Miss Deed*: H. Claggette. *Miss Believe*: C. Lloyd. *Miss Understood*: M. Dealy. *Miss Demeanor*: F. Cable. *Miss Informed*: O. Hempstone. *Miss Calculate*: W. Wilkins. *Officer 666*: E. Hare. *The Quaker Girl*: A. Wheaton. *Robert Stafford*: C. J. Ross. *Julia Scream*: T. Friganza. *Bridget*: I. Jason. *Broadway Billy*: J. J. Hughes. *Tony*: H. Fox.
Scene 2[7]
"It's All Over Now"
S. Grant, C. Greenwood
"The Kangaroo Hop"
C. Greenwood
"Cohen's (Yiddisha) Band"
W. Howard, E. Howard
(*Music by Al Piantadosi. Lyrics by Ballard Macdonald.*)
The Quaker Girl: A. Wheaton. *Fanny*: C. Greenwood. *Jimmy*: S. Grant. *Cabaret Manager*: E. Howard. *A Waiter*: W. Howard.
Scene 3
"Always Together"
G. Moon, D. Morris
The American Dancers
Adelaide and Hughes
"The Philadelphia Drag"
S. Grant, A. Wheaton, Dancers
(*Music and Lyrics by Harold Orlob.*)
The Fearless Waltz[8]
H. Ceballos, R. Ceballos
"The Metropolitan Squawk-tette"
T. Friganza, W. Howard, E. Howard, E. Hare
Mutt: D. Morris. *Jeff*: G. Moon. *Guests of Honor*: Adelaide and Hughes. *Jimmy Gilley*: S. Grant. *The Quaker Girl*: A. Wheaton. *Nancy Sykes*: T. Friganza. *Bill Sykes*: C. J. Ross. *Fanny Silly*: C. Greenwood. *A Cabaret Dancer*: H. Ceballos. *His Partner*: R. Ceballos.
Scene 4
"In 2010"
S. Kellogg, Chorus
Finale
Company
Scene: The Birth of the 21st Century. (*Drum effects by* John E. Lyneham.)

1912.25   # HANKY PANKY

A Jumble of Jollification in Two Acts, 3 Scenes.[9] Book by Edgar Smith. Music by A. Baldwin Sloane. Lyrics by E. Ray Goetz. Staged by Gus Sohlke. Costumes designed by Cora MacGeachy. Orchestra under the direction of Paul Schindler. Orchestrations by Hilding Anderson. Produced by Lew Fields. Opened 5 August 1912 at the Broadway Theatre and closed 2 November 1912 after 104 performances.

CAST (in order of appearance): *Cutie Wriggle, Dotie Wriggle, known as "The Wriggle Sisters" in vaudeville*: FLO MAY, MYRTLE GILBERT. *Ponsonby*: Byrd Goolsby. *Sir J. Rufus Wallingford, a recent addition to the British peerage*: HUGH CAMERON. *Herman Bierheister, partner and financial guide to Rausmitt*: BOBBY NORTH. *Wilhelm Rausmitt, a capitalist*: MAX ROGERS. *Solomon Bumpski, an angel*: HARRY COOPER. *Clorinda Scribblem, Wallingford's typewriter, with literary aspirations*: FLORENCE MOORE. *Iona Carr, "formerly of the Lunch Counter Girl Company and now of the Peerage"*: VIRGINIA EVANS. *Blackie Daw, Wallingford's former pal, but present foe*: CARTER DeHAVEN. *Cleopatra, who has been in cold storage for a matter of two thousand years*: CHRISTINE NIELSEN. *Harry Manleigh, a divinity student*: HUGH CAMERON. *Hiney Rausmitt, a college boy*: William Montgomery.
Peeresses: Gracia Hammond, Tess Allen, Mabel Allen, Gladys Breston, Billie DeHon, Estella Frazer, Viola Williams, Louise Cameron, Halle Crouse, Sadie Mullen. *Tennis Girls*: Sally Daly, Ruth Hanson, Zoe Brown, Belle Snow, Grace Russell, Eva Burnettt, Gertie O'Connor, Lillian Elliott, Isabella Burnside, Gertie Hudson. *Tea Girls*: Celie Pink, Nellie Crawford, Ara Martin, Blanche Barnes, Opal Flynn, Maude Powell, Lee Leontine, Pease Diehl, Margie Cogan, Neinda Snow.

---

[7]For subsequent national tour, "It's All Over Now," "The Kangaroo Hop" and "Cohen's Band" were dropped and replaced by:
"Mr. Pagliacci"
E. Howard, W. Howard
[8]Dropped for subsequent national tour.
[9]Billed as Lew Fields' Midsummer Production.

Tennis Boys: Philip Sohlke, Percy M. Weller, Edward Stokem, Jack Rice, Jay Melville, Louis Strangard, Charles Miller, Milton Silsbe, Joe Rogers, Victor Bozart.

Act 1: Wallingford's Villa at Bilgewater on Thames.

Act 2, Scene 1: University of Chicago College Campus. *Scene 2*: Cleopatra's Lodge, Wallingford's Chicago Residence.

ACT 1[10]

    Opening Chorus
        Ensemble
    "Tennis"
        F. May, M. Gilbert, Ensemble
    "The Dollar Bill's the Flag That Rules the World"
        H. Cameron, Ensemble
    "Where the Edelweiss Is Blooming"
        B. North, M. Rogers, F. May, M. Gilbert
    "My Hero" (parody on "The Chocolate Soldier")
        H. Cooper, F. Moore
    "(Under) The Ragtime Flag"
        C. DeHaven, Ensemble
    "Rose of Pyramid Land"
        C. Nielsen, Ensemble
    "Ragtime Opera" (burlesque on the Sexette from Lucia)
        F. Moore, C. Nielsen, H. Cooper, B. North, M. Rogers, H. Cameron
        (*Music [adaptation] and Lyrics by* Irving Berlin.)
    "The Lyre Bird and the Jay"
        C. DeHaven, M. Gilbert
    "Where the Edelweiss Is Blooming" (Finale)
        Company

ACT 2

    "College Days" (Opening)
        Ensemble
    "The Minstrel Man"[11] (Here Comes My Minstrel Man)(Duet)
        W. Montgomery, F. Moore
    "Meet Me at the Stage Door To-night"
        Ensemble
    "Dixie Love" (Song)
        C. Nielsen, Ensemble
    "The Million Dollar Ball" (Song and Dance)
        C. DeHaven, V. Evans, Ensemble
        (*Music and Lyrics by* Irving Berlin, E. Ray Goetz.)
    "The Hanky Panky Glide" (Song)
        H. Cooper, Ensemble
        (*Music by* Harry Cooper, Joe Cooper. *Lyrics by* Ballard Macdonald.)
    "Boola Boola" (Finale)
        Company

THE GIRL FROM MONTMARTRE

1912.26

A Farce with Music in Three Acts, 5 Scenes. American book by Harry B. Smith and Robert B. Smith. Based on a French operette 'Das Mädel von Montmartre' by Rudolph Schanzer adapted from the French farce "La Dame de chez Maxim" [The Girl from Maxim's'] by Georges Feydeau. Music by Henry Berény, (Jerome Kern). Produced (staged) by Thomas L. Reynolds. Scenery designed by Homer Emens. Costumes by Lord & Taylor; Kurtman. Orchestra under the direction of Harold Vicars. Presented by Charles Frohman. Opened 5 August 1912 at the Criterion Theatre and closed 28 September 1912 after 64 performances.[12]

---

[10]As per published sheet music, the following were interpolated:
    "That Baboon Baby Dance'
        H. Cooper
        (*Music by* Joe Cooper. *Lyrics by* Dave Oppenheim.)
    "Somebody's Coming to Town (from Dixie)"
        (*Music by* Henry Clay Smith. *Lyrics by* Raymond A. Browne.)
[11]Replaced during the run by:
    "Oh You Circus Day" (Duet)
        W. Montgomery, F. Moore
        (*Music by* James V. Monaco. *Lyrics by* Edith Maada Lessing.)
[12]Played a return engagement 7 April 1913 at the Grand Opera House for 8 performances.

CAST: *Dr. Pepyton*: RICHARD CARLE. *Gabrielle*, his wife: MARION ABBOTT. *Dr. Brumage*: WILLIAM DANFORTH. *General Petypon*, Dr. Petypon's uncle: AL HART. *Clementine*, his niece: MOYA MANNERING. *Lieutenant Corignon*: GEORGE LYDECKER. *Andre*: ALAN MUDIE. *Duchess de Valmonte*: Bertha Holly. *Loulou*, her son: LENNOX PAWLE. *Abbe*: Percy F. Leach. *Mme. Sauverel*: Mercita Esmond. *Mme. Hautignol*: Louise Donovan. *Mme. De Claux*: Dai Turgeon. *Mme. Vautier*: Lela Lee. *Mme. Veron*: Hazel Troutman. *Mme. King*: Clara Eckstrom. *Baroness de Granelle*: Mary Gilmore. *Baron de Granelle*: George T. Chance. *Monsieur Sauverel*: John Hamilton. *Mme. Ottalie*: Alice Carrington. *Etienne*, Dr. Petypon's servant: RALPH NAIRN. *Footman*: George R. Lynch. *Praline*: HATTIE WILLIAMS. (*Dance Specialty*: Joseph C. Smith. *Act 3*: Trixie Wilson.)

Debutantes: Lillian Rice, Angie Weimers, Ida Howe, Grace Beaumont, Marion Miller, Helene Lucas, Dolly Filley, Katherine Daly. *Bridesmaids*: Jeanette Greene, Geraldine Taylor, Audrey Burton, Lillian Davis, Cissie Sewall, May Sheldon, Viola Harty. *Maids*: Marie Rose, Natalie Burr, Frances Carter, Maud Clare, Hazel Flint.

Act 1: Dr. Petypon's Study. Paris.

Act 2: General Petypon's Chateau at Touraine.

Act 3, 1: Dr. Petypon's Drawing Room. Paris. *2*: The Chase. *3*: Gardens near Paris.

ACT 1

    "Serenade"
        W. Danforth, R. Nairn, Servants
    "Bohemia" (Recitative and Song)
        H. Williams
        (*Music by* Jerome Kern. *Lyrics by* Robert B. Smith.)
    "Ghost Quintette"
        H. Williams, R. Carle, M. Abbott, W. Danforth, R. Nairn
    "Half-Past Two" (Duet)
        A. Mudie, M. Mannering
        (*Music by* Howard Talbot. *Lyrics by* Percy Greenbank, Arthur Wimperis.)
    "Don't Turn My Picture to the Wall" (Duet)
        H. Williams, G. Lydecker
        (*Music by* Jerome Kern. *Lyrics by* Robert B. Smith.)
    Finale

ACT 2[13]

    Opening
    "Something Like This" (Trio)
        H. Williams, A. Mudie, M. Mannering
        (*Music by* Franz Wagner. *Lyrics by* Harry B. Smith.)
    "Hoopla, Father Doesn't Care" (Hoop-La-La Papa!)(Song)
        H. Williams, Chorus, Sextette
        (*Music by* Jerome Kern. *Lyrics by* M. E. Rourke.)
    "I've Taken Such a Fancy to You"
        R. Carle
        (*Music by* Jerome Kern. *Lyrics by* Clifford Harris.)
    "I'll Be True to You"[14] (Duet)
        A. Mudie, M. Mannering
    "Vienna Roll" (Dance)
        Ensemble
    "Love Will Win"[15] (Song)(from THE ARCADIANS)
        G. Lydecker, Chorus
        (*Music by* Lionel Monckton. *Lyrics by* Arthur Wimperis.)
    Finale

ACT 3[16]

    "Oh Doctor" (Double Octette)
        Misses Donovan, Turgeon, Lee, Carrington, Troutman, Eckstrom, T. Wilson; Messrs. Hamilton, Rogers, Vandeveer, Bryant, Olney, Carpenter, Gilbert, J. Smith.

---

[13]Performed in Act 2 was:
    Specialty Dance (The Sandwich Drag)
        J. Smith, L. Rice, A. Weimers
During the run, producer inserted the following in Act 2: "A Slice of Life," a skit on the problem play by J. M. Barrie. *Mr. Hyphen-Brown*: R. Carle. *Mrs. Hyphen Brown*: H. Williams. *Frederik*, their butler: W. Danforth. *Scene*: The Hyphen-Brown's Drawing Room. *Time*: The present. [This was retained for the tour.]
[14]Dropped during the run.
[15]For subsequent tour, replaced by:
    "Myrella" (Song)
        G. Lydecker, Chorus
[16]Added during the run to Act 3:
    Specialty Dance (The Tango)
        J. Smith, assisted by Veola Harty

"One of the Boys"[17] (Song)
  L. Pawle
"Popsey Wopsey"[18] (Trio)
  R. Carle, H. Williams, A. Hart
Song
  R. Carle
"Ooo-ooo Lena"[19] (Song)
  H. Williams
  (*Music by* Jerome Kern. *Lyrics by* John Golden.)
Finale

1912.27 THE MERRY COUNTESS

A Comic Opera in Three Acts.[20] Book by Gladys Unger. Based on the comic operette "Die Fledermaus", (libretto by Carl Haffner and Richard Genée, based on "Le Réveillon" by Henri Meilhac and Ludovic Halévy). Music by Johann Strauss. Lyrics by Arthur Anderson. Stage director, Charles A. Maynard. Dances[21] arranged by Emile Agoust. Settings by McCleery and Terraine. Costumes by Melville Ellis. Orchestra under the direction of Oscar Radin. Play produced under the personal supervision of Melville Ellis. Produced by the Messrs. Shubert. Opened 20 August 1912 at the Casino Theatre and closed 14 December 1912 after 135 performances.

CAST (in order of appearance): *Ilka*, a Parlormaid: FRITZIE VON BÜSING. *Gabor Szabo*, a Hungarian: MAURICE FARKOA. *Leopold*, Tiger to Prince Orloffsky: Robert Feuhrer. *Countess Rosalinda Cliquot*: JOSÉ COLLINS. *Dr. Berncastler*: CLAUDE FLEMMING. *Count Max Cliquot*: FORREST HUFF. *Hochheimer*, Governor of the New Age Prison: TOM A. SHALE. *Adele*: YANCSI DOLLY. *Felice*: ROSZIKA DOLLY. *Minna* of Prince Orloffsky's Private Ballet, Ilka's Sister: Mabel Burnege. *Prince Orloffsky*: MARTIN BROWN. *Inspector of Police*: Frank Ross. *Neirstiner*, Deputy Governor: Frank Farrington. *A Warden*: George Lyman. *Mattoni*: ARTHUR W. BASCOMB. (*Premiere Danseuse*: Mlle. DAZIE.) *Sidi*: Josephine Brandell. *Irma*: Evelyn Provost. *Melanie*: Ninon Dudley.
  The Front Row of Prince Orloffsky's Ballet (7): *Faustine*: Vyvyan Danner. *Natalie*: Estelle Grayce. *Felicita*: Marion George. *Fritzie*: Juanita Russell. *Doreen*: Sue Young. *Sabine*: C. Peckard. *Hermine*: Violet Lorraine. *Guests of the Prince* (7): *Alfred*: Frank Ross. *Franz*: George Lyman. *Ernest*: Arthur Miller. *Joseph*: J. Georgi. *Wilhelm*: Arthur Pepe. *Oscar*: B. Nodraer.
  Personnel of Chorus: *Show Girls*: Arthur, Dudley, B. Berry, Donner, DeAragon, Frain, Fonteny, George, Grayce, Hall, Jewell, B. Lang, Lawlor, Lorraine, Russell, Stone Sommerfield, Young, Lyons, MacDonald, C. Peckard. *Dancers*: Misses Lorraine Bright, Mildred Bright, Corgene Dare, Miuller, Murrie, Randolph, Sartoris, Scherer, Sayce, J. Collins, Dunn, M. Peckard, H. Collins, Summerville, Raymond, Young. *Men*: Messrs. Pepe, Trentini, O'Rourke, Diamond, Sacks, Frenac, Dunlap, Miller, H. Brown, Hanft, Whitcomb, Gault, Klein, Bogart, Lavitz, F. Brown, Ross, Holmer, Feiner, Nodraer.

The action takes place at a fashionable watering place in Austria.

Act 1: At Count Cliquot's Villa. Rosalinda's Boudoir. 6 P.M. (McCleery.)
Act 2: At the Arum Lily Club. Prince Orloffsky's Ball. 6 A.M. (Terraine.)
Act 3: The Governor's House in the New Age Prison. 10 A.M. (McCleery.)

ACT 1[22]
  Serenade
    M. Farkoa

---

[17]Dropped during the run.
[18]Replaced during the run by:
  "In Spirit Land" (Duet)
    R. Carle, W. Danforth
[19]During the run, moved to follow "Oh Doctor" in Act 3; new song added prior to Finale:
  "I'll Be Waiting at the Window" (I'll Be Waiting 'Neath Your Window)(Duet)
    M. Mannering, A. Mudie
    (*Music by* Jerome Kern. *Lyrics by* James Duffy.)
[20]This adaptation previously produced in London as NIGHT BIRDS.
[21]The dance music has been selected and arranged by Melville Ellis from other operas and pianoforte compositions by Johann Strauss.
[22]Individual songs were not listed in the New York program. Above song list prepared from subsequent tour programs and published musical score. Other possible interpolations not in published score: "Oh! What a Night," "Homeland," The Tango Dance (*Music by* Melville Ellis.), "Just That You Are You," and "Tis You I Love for Aye" (*Music by* Napoleon Laubelet. *Lyrics by* Arthur Cleveland.)

"Letter Song"
  F. von Busing
Duet
  J. Collins, F. von Busing
Duet
  C. Flemming, F. Huff
Trio
  J. Collins, F. von Busing, F. Huff
Finale
  J. Collins, M. Farkoa, T. A. Shale
ACT 2
  Opening Chorus
    Ensemble
  Specialty
    M. Brown
  Song
    F. von Busing, Chorus
  (Prince Orloffsky's) Ballet
    (Mlle. Dazie, Ballet)
  Czardas
    J. Collins
  Finale
    (Ensemble)
ACT 3
  "Jail Birds"
    (R. Dolly, Chorus)
    (*Music by* Melville Ellis. *Lyrics by* Martin Brown.)
  "The Blue Danube" (Just That You Are You)
    M. Farkoa, A. W. Bascomb
  "Must We Say Goodbye?" (Duet)
    J. Collins, M. Farkoa
    (*Music and Lyrics by* Joseph H. McKeon and Arthur Gutman.)
  Finale

1912.28 THE PINK LADY

A Return Engagement of the Musical Comedy Deluxe in Three Acts.[23] Book and lyrics by C. M. S. McClellan. Based on the French play "Le Satyr" Georges Berr and Marcel Guillemaud. Music by Ivan Caryll. Staged by Herbert Gresham. Musical numbers staged by Julian Mitchell. Costumes by F. Richard Anderson. Settings designed by Ernest Albert. Lighting by Frank Detering. Orchestra under the direction of Watty Hydes. Produced by (Marc) Klaw and (Abraham L.) Erlanger. Opened 26 August 1912 at the New Amsterdam Theatre and closed 14 September 1912 after 24 performances.

CAST (in order of appearance): *Serpolette Pochet*: Flora Crosbie. *Desirée*: FRANCES GORDON. *A Photographer*: Henry M. Johnson. *Pochet*: F. Newton Lindo. *The Hungry Man*: Joseph Carey. *Annette*: Ida Gabriel [Gabrielle]. *Gilberte*: Mae Carmen. *Gabrielle*: Teddy Hudson. *Raymonde*: Violet McKnight. *Minette*: Minerva Walton. *Sophie*: Jean Barnette. *Benevol*: WILLIAM CLIFTON. *Lucien Garidel*: JACK HENDERSON. *Julie*: Violet Zell. *Nini*: Julie Eastman. *Suzanne*: Kitty Graham. *Angele*: ALICE DOVEY. *Maurice D'Uzac*: CRAUFURD KENT. *Bebe Guingolph*: JED PROUTY. *The Girl from Saskatchewan*: Queenie Stair. *Claudine, The Pink Lady*: HAZEL DAWN. *Crapote*: Edward Morris. *Madame Dondidier*: ALICE HEGEMAN. *Philippe Dondidier*: FRANK LALOR. *Theodore Lebec*: A. S. Humerson. *Comtesse de Montavert*: LOUISE KELLEY. *Rouget*: Henry M. Johnson. *Dr. Mazou*: Maurice Hegeman. *Pan*: W. Jackson Sadler. *Ywaxy*, a violinist: Benjamin Lissit. *Chorus*.

1912.29 THE GIRL FROM BRIGHTON

A Hodge, Podge of Jest and Nonsense (Musical Comedy) in Two Acts. Book and lyrics by Jean C. Havez, (Aaron Hoffmann[24]). Music by William Becker [George Botsford]. Staged by Jack Mason. Costumes by Paul Arlington. Orchestra under the direction of William Becker. Produced by William Fox.

---

[23]First produced in New York 13 March 1911 at the New Amsterdam Theatre for 312 performances. For Synopsis of Scenes and Musical Numbers, see original 1911 production.
[24]Hoffmann's name appears in reviews as co-librettist, but not in the opening night program.

Opened 31 August 1912 at the Academy of Music and closed 28 September 1912 after 49 performances.[25]

CAST: *Rudolph Bock*, a promoter with business instinct: AL RAYMOND. *Otto Heinz*, anxious to buy a summer hotel: FRANK CAVERLY. *George M. Cohen*, Landlord of Little Pigs' Hotel, Sheepshead Bay: Harry First. *Dr. Burg* of Pittsburgh, instructor of turkey trotting: ROBERT DAILEY. *Sarsfield O'Brien*, a retired plumber visiting on Long Island: MARK HART. *Montgomery Worries*, son of a New York millionaire: CLAY SMITH. *Jimmy Dodson*, his secretary, in love with Gertie Dewdrop: NED NORTON. *Oliver Fitznoodle*, Amuses by himself: HENRY LEWIS. *Smoke*, a porter: Harry Lander. *Chauffeur*: Roy Torrey. *Duchess "Ivy Bigroll,"* head of a matrimonial agency: MAUDE ROCKWELL. *Honora O'Brien*, daughter of Sarsfield O'Brien, anxious to go on stage: Sophia Petrayer. *Margie and Gertie Dewdrop*, the Dewdrop Sisters in vaudeville: KITTY FLYNN, ANNA ORR. *Miss Snowball*, a dusky belle of Brighton: KITTY FLYNN. (*Specialties*: The Skatells (skating act), Keno and Greene (dance), Burns and Fulton.) *Quartette, Waiters, Summer Girls, Students, Bathers, etc.*

The action takes place on Long Island in June.

Act 1: Little Pigs' Hotel, Sheepshead Bay.

Act 2: Brighton Beach.

ACT 1

Opening Chorus
    Entire Company
"I Want to Go Back to New York"
    M. Hart, Chorus
"Melody Man"
    C. Smith, K. Flynn, A. Orr
    (*Music by* Les Copeland.)
"After Vespers"
    M. Rockwell, Chorus
    (*Music by* Neil Moret.)
Specialty
    Burns and Fulton
"Keep Away from the Fellow Who Owns an Automobile"
    C. Smith, Chorus
"Since You Said You Loved Me"
    A. Orr, Chorus
"Get Rich Quick Wallingford"
    F. Caverly, A. Raymond
    (*Music by* Raymond Walker. *Lyrics by* William Tracey.)
"The Turkey Trot"/
    "The Academy Rag" (That Academy Rag)
    K. Flynn, Chorus
"Jingle Bells" (Oh, You Silv'ry Bells)
    Entire Chorus
    (*Music by* George Botsford.)
ACT 2

Opening Chorus
    Entire Company
"The Brighton Beach Rag"
    A. Orr, Chorus
    (*Music and Lyrics by* William Becker.)
"Minstrel Tune"
    K. Flynn, H. Lander
"Honeymoon Days"
    N. Norton, A. Orr, Chorus
    (*Music by* Les Copeland.)
Specialty
    H. Lewis
"I Wonder Where I Met You"
    R. Dailey, K. Flynn
    (*Music by* George Botsford.)
"A Brand New Soldier Tune"
    M. Rockwell, Chorus
    (*Music by* George Botsford.)
"(Waiting for the) Robert E. Lee"
    M. Rockwell, Chorus
    (*Music by* Lewis F. Muir. *Lyrics by* L. Wolfe Gilbert.)
Finale
    Entire Company

---

[25]Settings uncredited. Performed with a schedule of daily matinees.

1912.30

UNDER MANY FLAGS

A Musical Spectacle in Three Acts, 13 Scenes. Drama (book) by Carroll Fleming. Music and lyrics by Manuel Klein. Staged by Carroll Fleming. Stage groupings and musical numbers arranged and staged by William J. Wilson. Scenery designed by Arthur Voegtlin. Orchestra under the direction of Manuel Klein. Produced by the Messrs. Shubert. Opened 31 August 1912 at the Hippodrome and closed 17 May 1913 after 445 performances.[26]

CAST: ALBERT PELLATON, Leonard Kirtley, ALBERT FROOM, Harry Truax, H. A. Barstar, Harry Jackson, Joseph Redman, Jack Warren, E. PERCY PARSONS, SABERY DORSELL, EDITH SINGLETON, ELSIE BAIRD, Irene Ward, Mildred Flora, Helen Gilmore, Angel Barbara, Georgia Russell, BLANCHE BOONE, Harry LaPearl, George W. Duncan, J. H. Taylor, Leo Van Dell, John Cheviot, Tommy Mullens, James R. Adams, Little Nan Turner, Emme Fette, GEORGE W. DUNSTAN, Fred Levine, John Wood Charles, Frank Hanson, The Great Clivette, Gwilyn Edwards, G. Anspake, Harry E. Cluett, John Haydock, Sandy Ferguson, Edward Austin, John Pritchard, R. C. Carlisle, Fred Cox, Claudia Scott, Morris Fertel, Jeanne Ribierre, Charlotte Davies.

ACT 1
Scene 1
"Sweetheart, Let's Go a Walking"
    E. Singleton, Chorus
"(The) Dear Old White House"
    A. Pellaton
    Scene: Washington, D.C. Lawn of the White House.
        Major General Edmund Fitzhugh, retired, Secretary of War: A. Pellaton. *Captain Alan Strong*, Military Attaché, Designer of the Airship "The Peacemaker": L. Kirtley. *Lord Angus Gordon*, British Ambassador to the U.S.: A. Froome. *Lieutenant Frank Searle*, Naval Attaché: H. Truax. *Admiral Surridge*, U.S. Navy: H. A. Barstar. *James Barclay*, Promoter of the firm Barclay & Grotch: H. Jackson. *Peter Grotch*, Builder of "The Peacemaker": J. Redman. *Colonel Zach Ryder*, Member of Congress from Arizona: J. Warren. *Monsieur Delapasse*, Ambassador from France: E. P. Parsons. *Jasper*, Body Servant to General Fitzhugh: J. H. Taylor. *Ambassador from Germany*: S. Ferguson. *Ambassador from Russia*: L. Van Dell. *Ambassador from Austria*: J. Cheviot. *Ambassador from Persia*: A. Barbara. *Ambassador from China*: F. Hanson. *Officers Moody, Brown*, in charge of the White House grounds: G. II. Adams, T. Mullens. *Civil War Veterans*: F. Reno, G. Anspake, H. Gennard, J. A. Adams, H. LaPearl, S. Miaco, R. Flight. *Eleanor Fitzhugh*, Daughter of General Fitzhugh: S. Dorsell. *Janet Gordon*, Daughter of Lord Gordon: E. Singleton. *Mrs. Beverly Carrington*, a society leader: E. Baird. *Mrs. Zach Ryder*: I. Ward. *Jess Ryder*, Her Daughter: M. Flora. *Ambassadors, Members of Congress and Their Families, Visitors, Officers, Tourists, Newspaper Reporters, etc.*
Scene 2
"(The) Youngsters of the Navy" (Song)
    G. W. Dunstan, Chorus
    Scene: Annapolis. Parade Grounds of the Naval Academy.
        Additional Characters: John Brand, Chief of the U.S. Secret Service: G. H. Adams. *Commandant of Midshipmen*: G. H. Dunstan. *Midshipmen, Officers, Summer Girls, Visitors, etc.*
            During this scene will be introduced the review of the Midshipmen by the Admiral and His Staff, the Signal Drill, and Exercises with Mounted Guns.
Scene 3
"Once a Fisherman Went to Sea" (Legend of Brittany)
"Fishing" (Song)
    S. Dorsell, Chorus
    Scene: Brittany. A Fishing Village on the Coast.
        Additional Characters: Mother Bouchard: H. Gilmore. *Pere Rennard*: A. Barbara. *Baptiste*, a Village Lad: G. Russell. *Recruiting Sergeant*: J. Warren. *Clotilde*: B. Boone. *Net Menders (4): Margot*: J. Cowen. *Chevettte*: M. Neilson. *Nanette*: I. Spellman. *Babette*: M. Addison. *Dancing Clown*: H. LaPearl. *Fun on a See-Saw*: S. Miaco, D. Diers, S. Ferguson. *Fisherman, Fish Wives, Villagers, etc.*
            During this scene Messrs. Patrick and Francesco will appear in their famous comedy specialty 'The Tumbling Haymakers.'
Scene 4
    Scene. The Airship. Passing over a City at Night.
        The Passengers in the Airship are those who entered it during the naval manoeuvres at Annapolis.
Scene 5
"Home Is Where the Heart Is"

---

[26]Costumes uncredited.

"Old Rhine Wine"
> Scene: Germany. A Berlin Summer Garden.
> Additional Characters: Sergeant Major of Dragoons: H. A. Barstar. Lieutenant of Infantry: G. W. Dunstan. Franz, Head Waiter: J. H. Taylor. Leader of the Street Band: S. Miaco. Emil, Fritz, Comedy Waiters: J. A. Adams, H. LaPearl. Student Corps, Military Officers, Pedestrians, Frauleins, Kellners, Madchens, etc, etc.
> During this scene the Six Brachs, foremost Risley artists, will present their latest gymnastic conceit. Also Dippy Diers will appear in his Break Neck Table Act, assisted by Steve Miaco and the Hippodrome Clowns.

Scene 6
Finale:
"Tis Summer"
Visitors
"Tulips with Your Color So Bright"
> Scene: Holland. Canal Side at Utrecht.
> Additional Characters: Mynheer Maartens, the Burgomaster: H. A. Barstar. Neeltje, His Daughter: B. Boone. Killieen, a Dandy: L. Van Dell. Diedrich, a Vegetable Peddler: A. Barbara. Maarten, a Milk Seller: J. Cheviot. Annatja, a Cheese Merchant: T. Mullens. Pedrus, a Tulip Vendor: J. R. Adams. Canal Boatmen (4): Hendrik: S. Miaco. Johannes: D. Diers. Myndert: S. Ferguson. Gerritt: F. Hanson. Jan, an Ox Driver: Little N. Tanner. Vrou van Deense, the School Mistress: H. Gilmore. Hucksters, Windmill Tenders, Tulip Growers, Seminary Girls, Villagers, Marketmen, Housewives, Dogcart Drivers, etc.

ACT 2
Scene 1
"Wedding Procession"
> Scene: Russia. Public Square in Moscow.
> Additional Characters: Prince Dimitri: H. A. Barstar. Chief of Military Police: H. Truax. Captain of Cossacks: J. Warren. Ivan Ivanowitch, a Merchant: J. H. Taylor. Olga, His Daughter, a Bride: E. Fette. Petrov Petrovich, a Silversmith, the Bridegroom: G. W. Dunstan. Mikel, a Gossip: G. H. Adams. Sergeant of Cossacks: L. Van Dell. High Priest: A. Barbara. Minor Priest: J. Cheviot. Zara, an Old Woman: H. Gilmore. Droski Driver: R. C. Carlisle. Cossacks, Guards, Wedding Guests, Acolytes, Street Merchant, Moujiks, Siberian Prisoners, etc, etc.
> During the action of this scene the celebrated Mazetti Troupe will present their marvelous acrobatic posings and grouping on horseback while riding at full speed.

Scene 2
"Scotland Forever" (Song)
E. P. Parsons, Chorus
> Scene: Scotland. A Highland Glen.
> Additional Characters: Roy Roy, Chief of the MacGregor Clan: E. P. Parsons. Janie, Maid Servant: B. Boone. Sandy McNabb: H. Gennard. Betsey McNabb: I. Burt. Highland Drummer: J. W. Charles. Rab, Dugald, Drummer Boys: J. White, J. Fleming. Aleck, Ewan, Gillies: F. Hanson, J. Pritchard. Highland Dancers: J. D. Williamson, Annie Fraser, Aleck Fraser, N. K. Fraser. Highland Pipers: R. K. Ireland, A. M. Fraser, J. Dow, J. MacCaskill, P. K. McHardie, D. Graham. Donald Douglass, a Flag Bearer: G. Quay. Men of the Clans MacGregor, McLeod o'Lewes, McIntosh, Gordon, Highlanders, Deer Stalkers, Gun Bearers, Gamekeepers, Servants, Gillies, etc.

Scene 3
Melodramatic Opening (China)
"Pretty Little Maiden on the Screen" (Song)
March of the Dragon
> Scene: China. A Street in Peking.
> Additional Characters: Ling Hi, a wealthy merchant: F. Hanson. Kwang Su, Magician: The Great Clivette. Chang See, Keeper of the Sacred Dragon: A. Froome. Ming Fu, Hop Sing, Revolutionists: G. Edwards, G. Anspake. Song Chow, High Priest: H. E. Cluett. Mong Gow, High Priest: J. Haydock. Yo Min, Merchant's Daughter: B. Boone. Screen Sellers (8). Su Ling: M. Carlisle. Fan To: N. Donner. Man Kee: K. Drolet. Soy Sin: B. McLean. Tow San: E. Scott. Chu Long: M. O'Keefe. Toi Din: M. Tobin. Ho Joy: S. Martelle. Revolutionaries, Fanatics, Screen Girls, Masqueraders, Beggars, Europeans, Coolies, Merchants, Dragon Worshippers.
Festival of the Sacred Dragon

Scene 4
> Scene: Arizona. Main Street in Rydersville.
> Additional Characters: Bill Jordan, the Sheriff: A. Pellaton. Jim Cusack, Deputy Sheriff: J. H. Taylor. Ike Massy, Deputy Sheriff: J. Cheviot. Bill Sanders, Proprietor of Sanders' Hotel: S. Ferguson. Jinny Sanders, His Daughter: G. Russell. Side Winder Sam, a Half-Breed: E. Austin. Cochise, an Apache Chief: A. Barbara. Lew Diamond, a Gambler: H. Jackson. Wahnahtee, the Chief's Squaw: H. Gilmore. Jerry Simpson, Barkeeper at the Hotel: J. Pritchard. Sam Lee, a Chinese Laundryman: F. Hanson. Daredevil Dixon, Boss of the Diamond R Ranch: R. C. Carlisle. Half Breeds: J. R. Adams, G. Anspake. Slim Jim, a Broncho Buster: F. Cox. Four from the Diamond R Outfit: Bandy Pete: C. Bennett. Shorty: B. Harder. Luke Martin:

J. O'Rourke. Big Bill Rickerts: W. Patrick. Bess: L. Carlisle. Nell: M. Cox. Fan: L. Vandreau. Liza: E. Gothals. Molly: L. Severin. Mamie: E. Gruwell. Callie: L. Robb. Belle: A. Nasfield. Boston Joe, a Drummer: T. Mullens. Pedro, Manuel, Joe, Mexican Cattle Thieves: J. Moore, S. Lutz, J. Dismuke. Rydersville Glee Club (9): Dave: E. Griffin. Sam: T. White. Jack: J. Pittschaw. Tom: M. O'Brien. Pete: W. J. Sullivan. Dan: A. Wyart. Aleck: J. Carbona. Dick: G. Newman. Phil: A. Renton. Broncho Busters, Cattle Rangers, Horse Traders, Ranchmen, Cowgirls, Rustlers, Half-breeds, Gamblers, Loungers, Cowboys, Indians, Squaws, Papooses, etc., etc.
> Part 1: During this scene R. C. Carlisle's Wild West Company will present their sensational act, exploiting expert lariat throwing, lariat spinning, fancy foot roping, trick riding, trick roping, equestrian quadrille by Cowboys and Girls. The Carlisles in their specialty, Australian Bull-whip manipulation, Miss Myrtle Cox presenting her remarkable exhibition of riding on a bucking horse. Part 2: The Tornado. Part 3: The Prairie Fire. The Stampede.

Scene 5
"Temple Bells (in the Soft Moonlight)" (Quartette and Ensemble)
> Scene: Persia. A Plaza in Teheran.
> Additional Characters: Muley Affid, the Grand Wizier: E. P. Parsons. Ben Sudi Bey, His Major Domo: L. Van Dell. Bul-Bul, His Favorite: C. Scott. Muley Hafiz, Master of the Chimes: M. Fertel. Zuleika, High Priestess of the Sacred Dance: J. Ribierre. Zenobeia, Keeper of the Sacred Fire: C. Davies. Wives of the Wizier (3): Zadi: M. Carlisle. Nadja: I. Brown. Sobeide: K. Carter. High Priests, Minor Priests, Court Officals, Bell Ringers, Worshippers, Altar Tenders, Train Bearers, Mendicants, Vestals, etc.
> During this scene the marvelous Florence Family will give an exhibition of athletic exercises, including a triple somersault from shoulder to shoulder, a feat unequaled by any other acrobats.

Scene 6
Flowers of the Nations (Ballet)
"Every Nation Has a Flower That It Loves the Best"
B. Boone, Girls
> Tableau 1: Old Gaffer's Cottage in Devonshire, England
> Tableau 2: . The Peach Orchard.
> Gaffer Jones, Master of the Peach Orchard: G. H. Adams. Richard, His Son: E. P. Parsons. Daisy, His Granddaughter: B. Boone. Schoolgirls, Friends of Daisy, etc..
> Premiere Danseuses: Austria: P. Whiteside. Spain: H. Sullivan. Russia: D. Smythe. Italy: S. Mordecai. Germany: M. Joost. France: J. Ribierre. England: N. Doner. America: E. Warren.

ACT 3
Part 1
The Magic City of Golden Palms
> The King: E. P. Parsons. The Queen: E. Baird. Princess Irma: S. Dorsell. Princess Myra: E. Singleton. Prince Rolando: H. Truax. A Herald: I. Spellman. Court Sages, King's Philosophers, King's Messengers, Pages, Trumpeters, Foresters, Sylvan Dwellers, Flower Bearers, etc.

Part 2
The Silver Palace of Universal Peace
> Grand Finale Tableau (Song and Change of Scene)
> The Court of the Crystal Fountains

1912.31

MY BEST GIRL

A Musical Play in Three Acts. Book and lyrics by Channing Pollock and Rennold Wolf. Music by Augustus Barratt and Clifton Crawford. Staged by Sydney Ellison. Scenery painted by H. Robert Law. Costumes by Schneider-Anderson Company. Orchestra under the direction of Augustus Barratt. Produced by Henry B. Harris. Opened 12 September 1912 at the Park Theatre and closed 9 November 1912 after 68 performances.

CAST (in order of appearance): Police Officers: Jack Potter, James O'Neill. Harry Perkins, an automobile salesman: Harrison Garrett. Mrs. Wellington Bollivar: Florence Edney. Colonel Wellington Bollivar, of the 50th Infantry, U. S. A.: HARRY DAVENPORT. Beatrice, his daughter: OLIVE ULRICH. Samuel Brown, a chauffeur: EDWIN NICANDER. Captain Robert Denton, U.S.A.: HARRY FAIRLEIGH. Gus Bludge, a private soldier: FRANK H. BELCHER. Daphne Follette, of the Moulin Rouge: HARRIET BURT. The Little Stranger: Coralinn Waide. Richard Venderfleet (Dickie): CLIFTON CRAWFORD. Dora Lane: RITA STANWOOD. Private Stuart: John Fitzhugh. A Sergeant: Louis Baum. Tommy Langham: Willard Louis. Grace Carr: Bessie Bell. Gwendoline Le Monde, formerly of the Moulin Rouge: Eileene Marshall.

Shoppers, Moulin Rouge Girls, Salesmen, Soldiers, etc.: Misses Jean Brae, Rose Huber, Marie Brandon, Adele Davidson, Aileen Leftwich, Catherine Halstone, Annette Jordan, Ruth Crawford, Helen Randolph, Edna Fitzhugh, Paula Leslie, Betty White, Margaret Vinton, Mildred Goodyear, Rose Leslie, Gertrude Thurston, Minnie Higgins, Katherine Foster, Ethel Russell, Violet Mack, Katherine Stoessel, Antoinette Fisher, Harriet Kendall, Marion Mosby, Madge Harman, Betty Meers, Libby Rae,

Anna Abbott, Natalie Saymore, Elleene Marshall, Vinnie Mason, Meta Weidlich, Sis Sheldon, Hazel Robertson, Viola Cain, Pam Boise, Kathleen Hitchens, Vivian Rogers, Evelyn Smith, Sally Ronayne. Messrs. Jack Squire, Albert Baron, Maurice Levov, William Leonard, Jack Fitzhugh, C. E. Walt, David Christy, Jack Gibson, Fred Guertier, Irving Finn, Dick Stuart, Lee Carrier, M. Miller, G. A. Dolan, Frank Silberman, Raymond Hancock, O. John Markle, Robert Waite.

Act 1: An Automobile Salesroom, New York. September.

Act 2: Colonel's Row, Governor's Island, New York. November.

Act 3: Cherry Tree Inn, near New York. December.

ACT 1[27]

Opening Chorus

"Love and the Automobile" (Quartette)
H. Davenport, H. Fairleigh, H. Garrett, O. Ulrich

"I Love My Art"[28] (Song)
H. Burt, Girls

"If the Morning After Were the Night Before" (Song)
C. Crawford
(*Music and Lyrics by* C. Crawford.)

"I Do Like Your Eyes" (Duet)
R. Stanwood, C. Crawford
(*Music and Lyrics by* Clifton Crawford.)

Finale

ACT 2

Opening Chorus

"I'm Smiling at the Moon That Smiles at You"
(I'm Smiling at de Moon Dat Smiles at You)
J. Fitzhugh

"Mr. Schnoodle"
C. Waide

"Howdy Do" (Ensemble)
H. Davenport, F. Edney, O. Ulrich, H. Fairleigh, Guests

"The Missionary Maids" (Double Octette)
Guests, Officers

"Catamaran"[29]
C. Crawford

"The Regular Army Man" (Song)
F. H. Belcher

"The Language of Lovers' Smiles"[30] (Song)
O. Ulrich

"Come / Take a Dance with Me" (Duet)
C. Crawford, R. Stanwood

Finale

ACT 3[31]

Opening Chorus

---

[27]Added during the run to Act 1 before Finale:
"A Treasure of a Girl" (Song)
O. Ulrich
Added to Act 1 for subsequent tour:
"The Bogie Boo" (That Syncopated Bogie Boo)
Maud Raymond (Daphne)
(*Music by* George W. Meyer. *Lyrics by* Sam M. Lewis.)
[28]Replaced during the run by:
"Follow Me Around" (Song)
H. Burt or M. Raymond, Girls
(*Music and Lyrics by* Irving Berlin.)
[29]Replaced during the run by: (but later restored for tour, following "Henry Clay"):
"Henry Clay" (When the Henry Clay Comes Steaming into Mobile Bay)(Song)
O. Ulrich
(*Music by* Jean Schwartz. *Lyrics by* Grant Clarke, William Jerome.)
[30]Replaced during the run by:
"I Can't Do Without the Men" (Song)(dropped for tour)
O. Ulrich
[31]During the run, the show was revised from 3 Acts into 2. Act 3 Opening Chorus was dropped, "Soft Shoes" and "My Best Girl" were inserted before the Act 2 Finale, and the Act 3 set was discarded.

"Soft Shoes"[32] (Duet)
H. Burt, E. Nicander

"My Best Girl" (Song)
C. Crawford
(*Music and Lyrics by* Clifton Crawford.)

Finale

1912.32 AN AZTEC ROMANCE

A Romantic Spectacular Play in Four Acts. Play by Orestes Bean. Music by Harold Orlob. Produced under the stage direction of Charles B. Hanford. Scenery by Young Brothers. Costumes by Eaves Company. Musical director, Harold Orlob. Produced by O. U. Bean & Company. Opened 16 September 1912 at the Manhattan Opera House and closed 21 September 1912 after 8 performances.[33]

CAST: *Corianton*, wayward priest of High Priest Alma: ROBERT WARWICK. *Seantum*, Prince of Antionum: EDWIN ARDEN. *Shiblon*, righteous son of High Priest Alma: J. ARTHUR YOUNG. *Alma*, High Priest of Zarahemla: CHARLES B. HANFORD. *Korihor*, the Blasphemer: R. D. MacLEAN. *Nephiah*, Chief Judge of Zarahemla: George C. Gunther. *Laman*, Seantum's second in command: Douglas Graves. *Amuloki*, a traitor, in league with Seantum: William A. Evans. *Lamarck*, one of Amuloki's confederates: Frederick Guest. *Zenos*, a loyal citizen: Thomas O'Malley. *Nehama*, officer in charge of Korihor: James Forbes. *Zebu*, captain of Seantum's guard: Frank Bunting. *Bastol*, the jester: Clifford Leigh. *Relia*, plighted wife of Shiblon: Louise Hamilton. *Manetah*, the siren's slave: Josephine Bowers. *Zean Ze Isobel*, the siren: MISS TITTEL-BRUNE. *Choir*.

Act 1: Temple of Justice, Zarahemla.

Act 2: Seantum's Garden at Antionum.

Act 3: Zoan's Palace at Siron.

Act 4: Home of High Priest Alma overlooking the city of Zarahemla.

1912.33 THE COUNT OF LUXEMBOURG

A Musical Romance in Two Acts. (Original Viennese operette libretto, 'Der Graf von Luxembourg' by Robert Bodansky and A. M. Willner, adapted from Willner and Bernard Buchbinder's libretto 'Die Göttin der Vernunft.') American libretto by Glen MacDonough. Music by Franz Lehár. Lyrics by Adrian Ross and Basil Hood. Staged by Herbert Gresham. Musical numbers staged by Julian Mitchell. Costumes by Comelli. Lighting by Frank Detering. Orchestra under the direction of Anton Heindl. Produced by (Marcus) Klaw & (Abraham L.) Erlanger. Opened 16 September 1912 at the New Amsterdam Theatre and closed 28 December 1912 after 120 performances.

CAST (in order of appearance): *Juliette*: FRANCES CAMERON. *Pierre, Raymond*, artists: A. Percy Woodley, William L. Hobart. *Brissard*, an artist: FRED WALTON. *Foyot*, money lender: Russell Simpson. *Nicholai*, poet: Harold J. Rehill. *Sidonie*: Ida Van Tine. *Coralie*: Evelyn Westbrook. *Count Rene of Luxembourg*: GEORGE LEON MOORE. *Pelegrin, Mentschikoff, Paulovitch*, the Grand Duke's Attendants: F. S. Humphrey, William C. Reid, Harry W. Smith. *Grand Duke Rutzinov*: FRANK MOULAN. *Angele Didier*: ANN SWINBURNE. *Registrar*: Fred Bishop. *M. Valmont*: A. Percy Woodley. *M. DeTressac*: Harry Johnson. *Minette*: Bessie Gross. *Lisette*: Eleanor Scott. *Eleurette*: Dottie Wang. *Clairette*: Beth Harrison. *Princess Kokozeff*: Gladys Homfrey.

Act 1: Brissard's Studio, Paris.

Act 2: Reception Hall at the Grand Duke Rutzinov's, Paris.

ACT 1

"Carnival! Make the Most of Carnival!" (Opening Chorus)

"Land of Make Believe" (Song)
F. Cameron, Chorus

"Love Spats" (Love Duet)
F. Cameron, F. Walton

"Make the Most of Carnival!" (Entrance of Chorus)

"The Count of Luxembourg" (Song)
G. L. Moore

---

[32]For subsequent tour, moved to Act 1 after "I Do Like Your Eyes." New song inserted in its place:
"Back to Broadway"
C. Crawford, Ensemble
[33]No musical numbers listed in programs.

Entrance Chorus and Dance
"A Carnival for Life" (Duet)
   F. Cameron, F. Walton, Chorus
"I Am in Love' (Song)
   F. Moulan
"Cousins of the Czar" (Duet)
   A. Swinburne, F. Moulan
Finale
   G. L. Moore, A. Swinburne, F. Moulan, Attendants, Chorus

ACT 2
Opening Scene and Dance
   Chorus
"Hail, Angele, Our Nightingale" (Entrance Chorus)
   Chorus
"Day Dreams" (Solo)
   A. Swinburne, Chorus
"In Society" (Duet)
   F. Cameron, F. Walton
"Say Not Love Is a Dream" (Duet)
   A. Swinburne, G. L. Moore
"Rootsie-Pootsie" (Song)
   F. Moulan, Girls
"Are You Going to Dance?" (Duet)
   F. Cameron, F. Walton
"The Wedding March" (Song)
   F. Moulan, F. Cameron, Chorus
Finale

1912.34   OH! OH! DELPHINE

A Musical Comedy in Three Acts. Book and lyrics by C. M. S. McLellan. Based on the French farce "La Grimpette" ["Villa Primrose"] by Georges Berr and Marcel Guillemaud. Music by Ivan Caryll. Staged by Herbert Gresham. Ensembles by Julian Mitchell. Settings by Homer Emens, Edward G. Unitt and Joseph Wickes. Costumes designed by F. Richard Anderson. Musical conductor, Frederick Solomon. Produced by (Marc) Klaw and (Abraham L.) Erlanger. Opened 30 September 1912 at the Knickerbocker Theatre, moved 3 February 1913 to the New Amsterdam Theatre and closed 2 May 1913 after 258 performances.[34]

CAST (in order of appearance): *Colonel Pomponnet*: Frank Doane. *Fernande*: Lila Benton. *Blum*, a hotel manager: G. Clennett Glass. *A Hall Porter*: John Fairbanks. *Victor Jobileau*: SCOTT WELSH. *Models (6)*: *Jacqueline*: Florence Geneva. *Tutu*: Dolly Alwin. *Antoinette*: Edythe Taylor. *Amandine*: May Day. *Lulu*: Dorothy Quintette. *Distinguette*: Eunice Mackay. *Louis Gigoux*: George Stuart Christie. *Alphonse Bouchotte*: FRANK McINTYRE. *Delphine (Jobileau)*: GRACE EDMOND. *Finette*, a flower vendor: Mildred Manning. *Bimboula*, a Persian woman: OCTAVIA BROSKE. *Uncle Noel Jolibeau*: George A. Beane. *Pluchard*, a lawyer: Alfred Fisher. *Simone*: STELLA HOBAN. *Madame Bax*: Helen Raymond. *Louise*: Polly Bowman. *Lucie*: Jessie Howe. *Jeanne*: Ethel Millard. *Blanche*: DOROTHY LANGDON. Army Officers, Officers' Wives, Midinettes, Jewelers, Shop Messengers, Hotel Guests, Porters, Waiters, Housemaids, etc. Chorus.

Act 1: The Entrance Hall and Lounge of the Hotel Beau Rivage, at Brest, France.

Act 2: The Veranda and Rose Gardens of the Villa Primrose.

Act 3: A Grand Reception Hall opening into the Ballroom, Hotel Beau Rivage.

ACT 1
Opening Chorus (If the Colonel Wasn't Coming)
   F. Doane, Officers, Wives
"Please Turn Your Backs"
   F. Doane
"Posing for Venus" (Song)
   S. Welsh
"Oh! Oh! Delphine" (Duet)
   G. Edmond, F. McIntyre
"Allaballa Goo-Goo" (Duet)
   F. Doane, O. Broske

"Why Shouldn't You Tell Me That?" (Trio)
   G. Edmond, S. Welsh, F. McIntyre
Finale

ACT 2
Opening Chorus (Oh, Gifted Master Sleep!)
   M. Manning, Models
"Hush! Hush! Hush!"
   G. Edmond, F. Doane, G. A. Beane, Housemaids, Models
"Oh — P-p-p-poor Bouchotte" (Ensemble)
   G. A. Beane, F. Doane, G. S. Christie
"Can We E'er Forget?" (Waltz Duet)
   G. Edmond, G. A. Beane
"The Maxim Girl" (Song)
   S. Hoban, Chorus
"Everything's at Home Except Your Wife" (Song)
   F. McIntyre, Housemaids
"The Quarrel" (Duet)
   G. Edmond, S. Hoban
Finale
   Principals, Chorus

ACT 3
Opening Chorus (Pavlova)
Officers' Chorus[35]
   F. Doane, Officers
"The Venus Waltz"
   S. Welsh, O. Broske
"Then All Come Along" (Song)
   F. McIntyre, Chorus
Finale

1912.35   TANTALIZING TOMMY

A Musical Comedy in Three Acts. Book by Michael Morton and Paul Gervault. (Based on their English play of the same name, adapted from the French play "La Petite Chocolatière"[36] by Paul Gervault.) Music by Hugo Felix. Lyrics by Adrian Ross. Staged by George Marion. Settings designed by Percy Anderson. Costumes by Frances; Russell Uniform Company. Orchestra under the direction of Hans S. Linné. Produced by A. H. Woods. Opened 1 October 1912 at the Criterion Theatre and closed 26 October 1912 after 31 performances.

CAST: *Paul Normand*, a clerk in the Ministry of Fine Arts: GEORGE ANDERSON. *Gaston Berolle*, a painter, his friend: JOHN PARK. *Louis Camelot*, a rich manufacturer of candies: ROBERT PITKIN. *Aristide Mingassol*, Under Secretary in the Ministry of Fine Arts: DALLAS WELFORD. *Biff*, a chauffeur: HARRY CLARKE. *Lord Hector de Souzac Ipecac*: Donald Hall. *Toupet, Bergere*, clerks in the Ministry of Fine Arts: Gilbert Tennant, Bobby Newman. *Casimir*, doorkeeper at the Ministry of Fine Arts: Jack Sayre. *"Tommy,"* Camelot's daughter: ELIZABETH BRICE. *Julie*, Normand's servant: DOROTHY WEBB. *Cecile*, Berolle's wife: Peggy Forsyth. *Florisse*, Mingassol's daughter: Valleaux Elliott. *Zizi of the Follies Bergère*: FRANCES RICHARDS. *Annik*, a fisher girl: Madeline Harrison. *Celeste*, classique dancer: Breton Fishermen and Girls, Clerks and Revue Girls, Society Men and Women, etc.

Fisher Girls: Elsa Bernard, Valleaux Elliott, Alice Fitch, Billie Francis, Grace Lloyd, Birdie McLaughlin, Marjorie Purcell, Evelyn Shaw, Lillian Howell, Isabelle Bradley, Margaret Landon, Gertrude Davis, Marie Baren, Gladys Clifton, Annita Francesca, Carolyn Landers, Isabelle McLeod, Bettina Touraine, Billie Ward, Jean Slater, Ada Welford, Margaret Langdon. *Fisher Men*: Bobby Newman, William Springer, Billy Gibbon, Gilbert Tennant, Norman Haywood, Charles Williams, Ferdinand Turner, Edgar Evans, Ralph Irving, Jay C. McCormack, William Quimby, Peter Canova, William P. Collins, Jack Sayre, Guy Premo, Glen Cushing. *Folies Bergère Girls*: Elsa Bernard, Valleaux Elliott, Grace Lloyd, Birdie McLaughlin, Margaret Langdon, Marie Baren, Annita Francesca, Bettina Touraine. *Clerks*: Bobby Newman, William Springer, Gilbert Tennant, Charles Williams, Ferdinand Turner, Edgar Evans, William Quimby, Glen Cushing. *Society Ladies and Men*: Elsa Bernard, Valleaux Elliott, Alice Fitch, Billie Francis, Grace Lloyd, Birdie McLaughlin, Marjorie Purcell, Evelyn Shaw, Lillian Howell, Isabelle Bradley, Margaret Langdon, Gertrude Davis, Marie Baren, Fladys Clifton, Anita Francis, Carolyn Lander, Isabelle McLeod, Bettina Touraine, Billie Ward, Jean Slater, Ada Welford, Robert Newman, William Springer, Billy Gibbon, Gilbert Tennant, Edward

---

[34]Played a return engagement 15 September 1913 at the Grand Opera House for 8 performances.

[35]Dropped late in subsequent national tour.
[36]This play was previously adapted into English and performed in New York as "The Richest Girl."

Kennedy, Charles Williams, Ferdinand Turner, Edgar Evans, Ralph Irving, Jay C. McCormack, William Quimby, Peter Canova, William P. Collins, Jack Sayre, Guy Premo, Glen Cushing.

Act 1: Chateau de Polpendolmen-Kerlaniac. Brittany. Night into morning.

Act 2: The Ministry of Fine Arts. Paris.

Act 3: Camelot's Park, near Paris.

ACT 1

    Introduction; Opening Chorus; Ballad of the Seigneur
        P. Forsyth, M. Langdon, Chorus

    "I Am a Tom-Boy" (Song)
        E. Brice, D. Webb, G. Anderson, J. Park, H. Clarke

    Musical Clock

    "A Tandem" (Duet)
        D. Webb, H. Clarke

    Intermezzo and Chorus
        G. Anderson, Chorus

    "Just Like You" (Duet)
        E. Brice, G. Anderson

    "Oh, Go Away" (Song)
        D. Webb, J. Park, G. Anderson

    Dance
        R. Pitkin

    Finale

ACT 2

    Opening Chorus

    "Zizi" (Song)
        F. Richards, Chorus

    "You Don't Know"
        J. Park

    "Fairy Bells" (Song)
        E. Brice

    "Irish Stew" (Duet)
        E. Brice, G. Anderson

    "Tie Song"
        R. Pitkin, Girls

    Finale

ACT 3

    Opening Chorus and Dance
        M. Harrison, Chorus

    "Cupid's Car" (Duet)
        D. Webb, H. Clarke

    "This and That and the Other" (Song)
        J. Park, Girls

    Scena—Duet
        E. Brice, G. Anderson

    Finale

1912.36   THE CHARITY GIRL

An American Musical Play in Three Acts, 6 Scenes. Libretto and lyrics by Edward Peple. Music by Victor Holländer. Added lyrics by Melville Alexander. Staged by George W. Lederer. Musical director, Albert Krause. Produced by the George W. Lederer Producing Company. Opened 2 October 1912 at the Globe Theatre and closed 19 October 1912 after 21 performances.

CAST (in order of appearance): *Becky,* a lady of the East Side: BLOSSOM SEELEY. *Moe,* a gent of the East Side: HENRY FINK. *Mrs. Jeremiah Hopping,* wife of the clairvoyant: RAY COX. *Detective French:* Herbert Denton. *Timothy Van Hoden,* a lawyer: D. L. Don. *"Billy" Brant,* a friend of the clairvoyant: C. MORTON HORNE. *Rosemary,* the crusader: MARIE FLYNN. *Officer 666:* Edward Baker. *The Guardian of the Portal:* Herbert Denton. *Vesta Virga,* a spinster: Olive Fargo. *Harry Hooligan,* a taxi-cab driver: HARRY TURPIN. *Kaluka,* the clairvoyant's charming assistant: Annabelle Whitford. *Tetah,* an Egyptian palmist: Ethel Douras. *Charmian,* a Romany crystal-gazer: Velma Roberts. *Aouwaya,* a Turkish medium: Nathalie Dana. *Vardi,* an Assyrian hypnotist: Vera Lawrence. *Madame Bowwowski,* a Russian seeress: Gladys Benjamin. *Olga,* a gypsy fortune-teller: Minnie Monroe. *Yengi Sin,* a Chinese prophetess: Rosamund Miller. *Fanchon,* a Parisian phrenologist: Augusta Behrens. *Nona,* an Italian mind-reader: Reina Jones. *Argol,* an astrologer: HARRY TURPIN. *Kismet,* the Slave at the Shrine: Edgar Connor. *Jeremiah Hopping,* the clairvoyant: RALPH HERZ. *Cherub, Seraph,* two heavenly twins: Masters Alfred Turner, Allan Turner. *Mumbo,*

Jumbo, two Gold Dust Twins: FLOURNOY MILLER, AUBREY LYLES. (*Specialty:* The Marvelous Millers.) *Crusaders, Little Fawns, Seeresses, "Gents" of the Ghetto, etc.*

    Crusaders: Misses May Fields, Lea Lature, Pansy LeRoy, Mazona Bradcome, Irma Flynn, Mabel Gebeau, Leota Sinclair, Meri Meredith. *The Little Fawns:* Misses Margaret Taylor, Jennie Praeger, Miriam Sanford, Veva DeFord, Ella Ray, Bessie Oliver, Harriet Wright, Annette Woodman. *Seeresses:* Misses Coleman, Hilda Peters, Olive Fargo, Cecelia Conway. *Gents of the Ghetto:* Messrs. Potts, Kusky, Thompson, Peel, Polen, Kugler, Hope, O'Donnell, Hagner, Cooley, Rice, Nauman, Fishman, Hearts, Ryder.

The action takes place in New York and Atlantic City just about now.

Act 1, Scene 1: Rutger's Square in the Ghetto, New York. *Scene 2:* Entrance to Jeremiah Hopping's Residence adjoining the St. Regis Hotel, New York. *Scene 3:* The Clairvoyant's luxurious Parlors of Polite Deception.

Act 2: The Beach and the Board-walk. Atlantic City.

Act 3: The Black and Gold Reception Hall in Mrs. Hopping's Residence.

MUSICAL NUMBERS

    "Come, Come" (Come and Let Us Rock You in the Cradle of Our Hearts)

    "I'd Rather Be a Chippie Than a Charity Bum"

    "Motif Lilt"

    "When the Parlor Clock Strikes"
        C. M. Horne, M. Flynn

    "Angel Rag"
        B. Seeley

    "Rosemary"

    "The Ghetto Glide"
        B. Seeley

    "Yum Yum Time"

    "Champagne Song"

    "Every Fellow Loves a Pretty Girl"

    "Just We Two Dear"

    "The Magic Kiss"

    "Things Unfeminine"

    "Charity"

    "There Never Was a White Hope Whose Christian Name Was Cohen"
        H. Fink
        (*Music by* Phil Schwartz. *Lyrics by* Irving Lee.)

    "Keep On Lovin'"
        H. Fink, E. Douras
        (*Music by* Ernest Breuer. *Lyrics by* M. Gunsky.)

    "Those Ragtime Melodies"
        (*Music and Lyrics by* Gene Hodgkins.)

    "The Belle of the Beach"

    "When Texas Tommy Did the Turkey Trot"
        (*Music and Lyrics by* Billy Gaston and Edgar Selden.)

1912.37   THE WOMAN HATERS

An Operetta in Three Acts. American book and lyrics by George V. Hobart. Based on the Viennese operette 'Der Frauenfresser,' libretto by Leo Stein and Karl [Carl] Lindau. Music by Edmund Eysler. Staged by George Marion. Settings by Dodge & Castle, Walter Burridge. Costumes by Mme. Francis. Orchestra under the direction of John Lund. Produced by A. H. Woods. Opened 7 October 1912 at the Astor Theatre and closed 2 November 1912 after 32 performances.[37]

CAST (in order of appearance): *Tilly von Eberhardt:* DOLLY CASTLES. *Baroness von Eberhardt,* her mother: MRS. STUART ROBSON. *Frau von Kreger:* Jane Bliss. *Jennie, Nellie,* her daughters: Amelia Rose, Helen Latten. *Frau von Aullander:* Elsa Ward. *Kitty, May,* her daughters: Grace Robinson, Adele Remington. *Frau von Babst:* Kitty Baldwin. *Jessie, Ada,* her daughters: Gladys Carroll, Casmo Lane. *Lina,* Tilly's maid: Gwendoline Coate. *Spitzki,* the Major's servant: Dan Marble. *Colonel Liebwohl,* Vice President, Woman Haters' Club: Charles W. Kaufman. *Captain Schnepp,* Secretary Woman Haters' Club: Snitz Edwards. *Herr Pfhiger,* Treasurer Woman Haters' Club: Albert Macklin. *Baron Sileer:* Bert Crossman. *Herr Zimmer:* Herbert Connop. *Lieutenant Wagner:* Arthur J. Snyder. *Herr Obermiller:* Harry Levian. *Herr Krupp:* Walter P. Hearne. *Major John von Essenburg:* WALTER LAWRENCE. *Camillo,* his

---

[37]Toured subsequently under the title THE WOMAN HATER'S CLUB; alternate title THE PRETTY LITTLE WIDOW.

nephew: JOSEPH SANTLEY. *Lord Everbee*: Leslie Kenyon. *Marie Wilton*: SALLIE FISHER.

Opposition to the Club: Misses Eugenie Alba, Edna Hale, Gladys Carroll, Adele Remington, Grace Robinson, Amelia Rose, Florence Hastings, Naomi Malone, Catherine Urspring, Marion Down, Antonnette deGerbeau, Kathryn Melton, Peggy O'Neil, Helen Latten, Alice M. Gibbons, Mabel Benelisha, Edna M. Houck. *Members of the Club*: Messrs. Thomas, Shannon, Albert Macklin, Arthur J. Snyder, Robert Landsdown, Joseph Wells, Ernest Murray, Sam Silvers, Bert Crossman, John W. Walker, Jack Carleton, Herbert Connop, LeGrange Abbott, Henry Dyer, William Frazer.

Act 1: Castle of Prezlau, twenty miles north of Berlin. First week in August, last summer. (Dodge & Castle.)

Act 2: The conservatory in the home of Marie Wilton in Berlin. (Dodge & Castle.)

Act 3: The terraced garden near the Castle. Three days later. (Burridge.)

ACT 1
  "Love Is the Joy of Living"
    D. Castles
  "Woman Haters' Club Hymn"
    Chorus
  "It Was Marie"
    W. Lawrence
  "Little Girl Come Back to Me" (Duet)
    D. Castles, J. Santley
    (*Lyrics by* M. E. Rourke.)
  "He Will Take Me to His Heart"
    S. Fisher
    (*Lyrics by* M. E. Rourke.)
  Finale

ACT 2
  "The Letters That Never Were Written" (Duet)
    S. Fisher, W. Lawrence
  "Come On Over Here"
    D. Castles, J. Santley
    (*Music by* Walter Kollo. *Lyrics by* George V. Hobart, Jerome Kern.)
  "Comes a Feeling"
    W. Lawrence
  "The Racing Quartette"
    S. Fisher, D. Castles, J. Santley, L. Kenyon
  The Dance Polka (Dance the Polka)
    D. Castles, W. Lawrence
  Finale

ACT 3
  Opening Chorus
  "Love's Alphabet"
    D. Castles, J. Santley
  "The Jag of Joy"
    S. Fisher, D. Castles, J. Santley
  Finale

1912.38 ZIEGFELD FOLLIES OF 1912

A Musical Revue in Two Acts, 10 Scenes.[38] Words (book and lyrics) by Harry B. Smith. Music by Raymond Hubbell. Staged by Julian Mitchell. Settings designed by Ernest Albert. Costumes by Callot. Orchestra under the direction of Frank Darling. Orchestrations by Frank Saddler. Produced by Florenz Ziegfeld. Opened 21 October 1912 at the Moulin Rouge and closed 4 January 1913 after 88 performances.

<u>CAST</u> (in order of appearance): *A Manager*: LEON ERROL. *A Theatre-goer*: Charles Scribner. *Song and Dance Men*: MAX SCHECK, CHARLES GILMORE. *A Gallery Boy*: HARRY WATSON, JR. *M. Poulet from Paris*: CHARLES JUDELS. *Mam'selle Paree*: IDA ADAMS. *Mam'selle Maxime*: Evelyn Carlton. *Mr. Knox Freely*, a first nighter: Charles Gilmore. *Mrs. Freely*: Grace DuBoise. *Howell Noyes*, carriage caller: BERT WILLIAMS. *Mr. Knight Byrd*: BERNARD GRANVILLE. *Stage Door Keeper*: Harry Luck. *Soubrettes* (6): *Floretta*: Margaret Morris. *Mazie*: Adele LaPierre. *Lillian*: Hazel Lewis. *Adelo*: Frances Leslie. *Hazel*: Zaina Curzon. *Eleanor*: Dorothy Godfrey. *Chappies* (6): *Jefferson*: Eleanor St. Claire. *Jerry*: Ruby Lewis. *Clarence*: Daisy Virginia. *Flo*: Lola Hilton. *Percival*: Jesse Lewis. *Alexander*: Ella Warner. *Maggie Muggins of the Chorus*: May Leslie. *Cheatham Daly*:

LEON ERROL. *Skinner Lamb*: Clifford Saum. *Doolittle Goode*: Charles Gilmore. *Gideon Olde*: HARRY WATSON, JR. *Flossie*: IDA ADAMS. *"Mother"*: JOSIE SADLER. *Cabman*: BERT WILLIAMS. *Mr. Bounder*: LEON ERROL. *Nicodemus*, a race horse: LeBrun and Queen. *A Summer Girl*: LILLIAN LORRAINE. *Reggie Boardwalk*: BERNARD GRANVILLE. *Walker Foote*, a roller chair man: BERT WILLIAMS. *Flora Footlight*: IDA ADAMS. *Uncle*: MAX SCHECK. *Lotta Ginger*: RAY [Rae] SAMUELS. *Bonnie*: LILLIAN LORRAINE. *Billy*: LEON ERROL. *Harlequin*: Evelyn Carlton. *An Ethiopian Slave*: Flo Hart. *Venus*: Elise Hamilton. *Marguerite*: Madeline Howard. *Duchess of Devonshire*: Marie Baxter. *La Pompadour*: Marion Hale. *Cleopatra*: Catheryn Peters. *Scheherazade*: Jane Warrington. *Madame Recamier*: Katheryn Smyth. *Queen Louise of Prussia*: Olga Hempstone. *Pocahontas*: May Leslie. *Carmen*: Eleanor Christy. *Joan of Arc*: Beatrice Allen. *Greek Statues*: Bessie Fennell, Vivian MacDonald. *Salome*: IDA ADAMS. *The 20th Century Girl*: LILLIAN LORRAINE. *Dusty Bob, Weary Flo, Hoboes*: LEON ERROL, HARRY WATSON, JR. *Circus Barker*: Peter Swift. *A Colored Party*: BERT WILLIAMS. *Uncle Sam*: Clifford Saum. *Mons. Theodore*: HARRY WATSON, JR. *Mons. Princeton*: LEON ERROL. *A Suffragette*: Natalie Dagwell. *A Circus Queen*: LILLIAN LORRAINE. *Commerce*: IDA ADAMS. *The Donkey*: LeBrun and Queen. *The Bull Mouse*: John G. Schrode. *The Elephant*: Fred Woodward.

Act 1, Scene 1: A Bill Board. *Scene 2*: Exterior of a Theatre. *Scene 3*: Stage Door of a Broadway Theatre. *Scene 4*: A Cottage. *Scene 5*: Herald Square.

Act 2, Scene 1: A Palace of Beauty. *Scene 2*: A Cottage. *Scene 3*: Boardwalk, Atlantic City. *Scene 4*: Exterior of a Circus Tent. *Scene 5*: Interior of a Circus Tent.

ACT 1
  "Hurry, Little Children"
    M. Scheck, C. Gilmore
  Yodel Song
    B. Granville
  "You Might As Well Stay on Broadway"
    I. Adams, C. Judels, Girls
  "Romantic Girl"
    L. Lorraine, H. Watson
  "You Got to Keep a' Moving" and Dance (You Gotta Keep A' Going)
    B. Granville, Chorus
  "Stage Door Number"
    Millionaires, Girls, Chappies
  "Mother Doesn't Know"[39]
    Misses I. Adams, E. Carlton, J. Sadler; Messrs. H. Watson, L. Errol, B. Granville
  "Row, Row, Row"
    L. Lorraine
    (*Music by* James V. Monaco. *Lyrics by* William Jerome.)
  "The Broadway Glide" (Finale)
    C. Judels, Company
    (*Music by* Bert Grant. *Lyrics by* A. Seymour Brown.)

ACT 2[40]

[38]The Sixth in the annual series of musical revues produced by Florenz Ziegfeld which began in 1907.

[39]Dropped for subsequent tour.
[40]Act 2 was revised in the second week, and the following were added after "Pretty Little White House:"
  "Dip, Dip, Dip"
    B. Granville, Bathing Girls
  "In a Pretty Little Cottage"
    L. Lorraine, L. Errol

In the third week, the following was added, preceding Rae Samuels Specialty:
  "Louisiana"
    Elizabeth Brice

Late in the run this was replaced by:
  "(There's) One in a Million Like You"
    E. Brice, Male Chorus
    (*Music by* Jean Schwartz. *Lyrics by* Grant Clarke.)
  "The Million" (added before Bert Williams Specialty)
    E. Brice

Late in the New York run, the following Specialty was added, next to finale, Act 2:
  Argentinian Dance of the Concourse—The Tango
    Senorita Eloise Gabbi, Senor Bendito Bianquetti

For subsequent tour, the following was added:
  "Great Big Blue-eyed Baby"
    E. Brice, Male Chorus

"Beautiful, Beautiful Girl"[41]
    B. Granville, L. Lorraine, I. Adams, Chorus
    (*Lyrics by* John E. Hazzard.)
Pierrot and Pierette Dance
    L. Errol, S. Chatelaine
Songs
    R. Samuels
"The Boardwalk Parade"
    B. Granville, Chorus
"In a Pretty Little White House of Our Own"
    L. Lorraine, B. Granville
    (*Music by* Leo Edwards. *Lyrics by* Blanche Merrill.)
Songs
    B. Williams
    ["My Landlady"
        (*Music and Lyrics by* Bert Williams.)
    "(You're) On the Right Road"
    "Borrow from Me"
        (*Music and Lyrics by* Bert Williams.)]
"Good Old Circus Band"[42]
    L. Lorraine, B. Granville, H. Watson, L. Errol, C. Judels, Chorus
Finale
    Company

THE LADY OF THE SLIPPER,
1912.39   or A Modern Cinderella

A Musical Fantasy in Three Acts, 5 Scenes. Book by Anne Caldwell and Lawrence McCarty.[43] Music by Victor Herbert. Lyrics by James O'Dea. Staged by R. H. Burnside. Settings designed by Homer Emens. Costumes designed by Wilhelm, London. Orchestra under the direction of William E. McQuinn. Produced by Charles B. Dillingham. Opened 28 October 1912 at the Globe Theatre and closed 17 May 1913 after 232 performances.

CAST: *The Crown Prince Maximilian:* DOUGLAS STEVENSON. *Prince Ulrich,* his brother: Eugene Revere. *Captain Ladislaw,* aide-de-camp to Maximilian: JAMES G. REANEY. *Baron von Nix,* Cinderella's father: Charles A. Mason. *Atzel,* the Baron's butler: VERNON CASTLE. *Mouser,* the Baron's cat: David Abrahams. *Albrecht,* a shoemaker: Samuel Burbank. *Louis,* his assistant: Harold Russell. *Joseph,* a milliner: Edgar L. Hay. *Matthias,* a furrier: Ed Randall. *Punks, Spooks,* from the Cornfield: DAVE MONTGOMERY, FRED STONE. *Cinderella:* ELSIE JANIS. *Romneya:* ALLENE CRATER. *Dollbabia, Freakette,* Cinderella's step-sisters: Lillian Lee, Queenie Vassar. *The Fairy Godmother:* VIVIAN RUSHMORE. *Valerie,* maid at the Baron's: Peggy Wood. *Sophia,* Albrecht's wife: Florence Williams. *Irma,* Joseph's wife: Edna Bates. *Clara,* Louis' wife: Helen Falconer. *Ludovica,* Matthias' wife: Gladys Zell. *Maida:* Lillian Rice. *Gretchen:* Angie Weimers. *Première danseuse:* LYDIA LOPOKOVA.
    Courtiers, soldiers, ladies in waiting, Oriental women of the harem, etc: Misses Marie Gordon, Marion Henry, Estelle Richmond, Marguerite St. Clair, Carol Lynn, Claire Bertrand, Gladys Feldman, Selma Mantell, Esther Lee, Kathryn Daly, Lola Curtis, Isabel Falconer, Olive Carr, Edna Dana, Evelyn Conway, Alice Keese, Anna Stone, Mazie LeRoy, Dolly Filly. Messrs. R. C. Bosch, R. C. Bell, Harry Silvey, John Roberts, Paul Franac, Frank Wayne, J. F. Johnson, Joseph Donnelly. *Dancing Girls:* Ethel Rosebud, Lottie Grossland, Maud Grossland, Phyllis Erroll, Violet Horlock, Nellie Kelly, Bertha Williams, Marjory Graham, Mattie Cronin, Annie Ray. *Corps de Ballet:* Marie Walsh, Helen Shea, Irene Kearney, Alice Moriarty, Marion O'Neill, Myrtle Ziegler, Adelaide Ziegler, Josephine Taylor, Sadie Howard, Margie Moriarty, Ida Goldstein, Emily Callen, Helen Ward, Helen Ellsworth, Mazie Goss, Jeanette Wollenberg. *Halloween Kiddies:* Agnes McCarthy, Marie Moore, Kathleen Carroll, Marie Carroll, Joe Quinn, George Phelps, Charles Jackson, Herbert Ziegler.

Time: Once Upon a Time—

Act 1, Scene 1: Kitchen in the Palace of Baron von Nix. *Scene 2:* On the Way to the Palace.

Act 2: Ball-room in the Palace of Prince Maxmilian.

Act 3, Scene 1: The Baron's Kitchen. *Scene 2:* Throne Room of the Prince's Palace.

ACT 1
Scene 1

    (Opening) Chorus
        Tradesmen, their wives and Assistants

"Fond of the Ladies"
    V. Castle, F. Williams, E. Bates, H. Falconer, G. Zell, L. Rice, A. Weimers, Chorus
"Meow! Meow! Meow!"
    E. Janis, D. Abrahams
"Love Me Like a Real, Real Man"
    E. Janis, D. C. Montgomery, F. Stone
"All Hallowe'en"[44]
    E. Janis, Kiddies
Witch Ballet
    Dancing Girls

ACT 2
    "At the Bal Masque," introducing the French Quadrille
        Dancing Girls
    "Princess of Far Away"
        E. Janis, D. Stevenson, Chorus
    "Them Was the Childhood Days"[45]
        D. C. Montgomery, F. Stone
    "Youth" (Ballet)[46]
        L. Lupokova, Corps de Ballet
    "Bagdad"
        D. C. Montgomery, Chorus
        (*Lyrics by* Anne Caldwell.)
    "(A) Little Girl at Home"
        D. Stevenson, E. Janis
    "Punch Bowl Glide"
        F. Stone
    "The Drums of the Nations"
        Presenting the drums of the Crown Prince, the Drums of Leipzic, of Napoleon, of Britain, of North America, of Young America and of Dixie.

ACT 3
Scene 1

    Harlequinade
        Harlequinade: D. C. Montgomery, F. A. Stone. *Harlequin:* L. Rice. *Columbine:* H. Falconer. *Cat:* D. Abrahams. *Policemen:* G. Melville, E. L. Hay, G. Phelps.
    "The Lady of the Slipper" (March)
        J. G. Reaney, Chorus
    "Cinderella's Dream"
        E. Janis
Scene 2
    "Put Your Best Foot Forward, Little Girl"
        D. Stevenson, Court Ladies, Pages
    Finale (And They Lived Happily Ever Afterwards)

THE DOVE OF PEACE
1912.40

A Comic Opera in Three Acts, 6 Scenes. Dramatic plot by Wallace Irwin and Walter Damrosch. Book and lyrics by Wallace Irwin. Music by Walter Damrosch. Staged by William J. Wilson and R. H. Burnside. Scenery painted by H. Robert Law. Costumes designed by Will R. Barnes. Orchestra under the direction of Max Hirschfeld. Produced by Walter Damrosch. Opened 4 November 1912 at the Broadway Theatre and closed 16 November 1912 after 16 performances.

CAST: *Hon. Terence Donnybrook,* a professional peace agitator: ARTHUR DEAGON. *Willie Petruchio Perkins,* the unkissed child of peace: FRANK POLLOCK. *Hildegarde Tyler,* a college girl (in Winter): ALICE YORKE. *Sir Hannibal Hobbs,* British Ambassador to Guam: ERNEST TORRENCE. *Arabella Smithson,* a waitress (in Summer): JESSIE BRADBURY. *Captain Paul Jones,* U.S. Navy, a hero: THOMAS HARDIE. *Saffron Kidd,* editor, New York Daily Chanticleer: William Welp. *Juanita Mendoza,* a Spanish exile at Guam: HENRIETTA WAKEFIELD. *Don Ramon Casava,* Crown Governor of Guam: Frederick Waelder. *McGinnis,* a bos'n, U.S. Navy: Jack Henderson. *General Cortez,* official clock-winder of Guam: William Welp. *Hoppy Toddy,* an Igarotte head-hunter: George Burke Scott.
    Summer Girls, Tennis Girls, Waitresses, Red Cross Nurses, Suffragettes, Igarotte Brides, etc.: Anna Estelle Wolcott, Paule Hummel, Vera Velmont, Marjorie Gateson,

---

[41]For the second week, moved to "next-to-closing" spot before finale.
[42]After opening, moved to follow Pierrot and Pierrette Dance in Act 2.
[43]Based on the traditional Cinderella story originated by Charles Perrault.

[44]Dropped during subsequent tour.
[45]Travesty on the old-fashioned song and dance and burlesquing the first song and dance ever done by Montgomery and Stone.
[46]For subsequent tour, the ballet was titled "Sweet Sixteen."

Amy Wallace, Blanche Scott, Violet Kingston, Cleo Henderson, Denise Morris, Doris Easton, Beatrice Rogers, Nell Pierpont, Peggy Dee, Minnie Wiegel, Grace Emmens, Nancy Clayborne, Louise Hollis, Eleanor Doherty, Luella Gateson, Patricia O'Connor, Leonore Torriani, Emma Bell, Anna Bankson, Inka Kolar, Ethel Fellen, Alma Buol, Miriam Arndt, Margaret Smith, Anette Black, Helen Elkas, Anita Ryan, Dixie Ewald, Eva Lane. *U.S. Sailors, Waiters, Spanish Soldiers, Tennis Men, Golfers, Senators, Diplomats, etc.*: Burton Lenihan, Martin Conroy, Edward Erick, Ralph Brainard, Walter Zachs, Frederick Jupraner, Arthur Bruno, Carl Otto, Lew Nickolson, Briggs French, H. P. Wagner, George Anderson, J. P. Allen, Charles McCarthy, F. W. Wyatt, Harry Stapleton, Gustave Dahlgren, Oswald Conti, August Brodie, John Koch, Clayton Hillard, Harvey Weitzer, George Price, F. G. Bowling, Glenmore Shepherd, Fred Kuhn, Alexander Dorfman.

Time: Early Summer, 1898.

Act 1: Veranda of the Fashionable Hotel Spendmore, Portsmouth, New Hampshire.

Act 2, Scene 1: Ramparts on the Island of Guam. *Scene 2*: The Dream of Universal Peace.

Act 3, Scene 1: Ramparts on the Island of Guam, one day later. *Scene 2*: Tropical Jungle, Island of Guam. *Scene 3*: United States Chamber at Washington, D.C., after the dream of Universal Peace has settled over the World.

ACT 1

"Empty Hours of Summer Chatter" (The Hen Chorus)
 E. Torrence, Chorus of Women

"Mark His Bright and Flashing Eye" (Ensemble)
 A. Deagon, F. Pollock, E. Torrence, Chorus of Women

"What Lips Are Made For—Eve Came to Adam's Paradise" (Song)
 A. Yorke, Chorus of Women

"Dove of Peace" (Song and Chorus)
 A. Deagon, Chorus

"Step By Step" (Duet)
 F. Pollock, A. Yorke

"Blood Is Thicker Than Water" (Duet and Chorus)
 J. Bradbury, E. Torrence, Chorus

"You Show Some Surprise" (Sailor's Fake Walk)
 F. Pollock, Chorus

"O, Thank You Kindly, My Pretty Dears" (Finale)
 T. Hardie, All Soloists, Chorus

ACT 2

"Was Ever Maid of Spain" (Song)
 H. Wakefield

"The Brag and Bluster—It's Painful to the Yankee Soul" (Ensemble)
 A. Yorke, J. Bradbury, F. Pollock, A. Deagon, T. Hardie, Full Chorus

"Your Eyes Have Told Me and My Heart Has Heard" (Duet)
 H. Wakefield, T. Hardie

"Prince of My Dreams" (Duet)
 A. Yorke, F. Pollock

"Behold the Dove!" (Finale)
 All Soloists, Chorus

ACT 3

"Oh! the World of Peace" (Song and Dance)
 A. Deagon, Soloists, Chorus

"Pre-Historic Man" (Song)
 J. Bradbury, G. B. Scott, F. Waedler, E. Torrence

"The Cave-man and the Cave-woman" (Dance Pantomime)
 A. Deagon, J. Bradbury

"Woman, How Dare You!" (Ensemble)

"Ochone! Far, Oh Far is the Mango Island" (Song)
 A. Deagon, Chorus of Women

"March of the Militant Suffragettes" (Intermezzo)
 Orchestra

"At Last Has Downtrod Woman" (Song of the Crowing Hens)
 A. Yorke, Chorus of Women

"Prisoners, Stand Up!"
 All Soloists, Chorus

"Two Little Cannibal Ladies" (Song)
 A. Deagon, Chorus of Women

"As Long as Men Love Women" (Choral)
 Soloists

"Dove of Peace" (Finale)
 Soloists

1912.41

THE RED PETTICOAT

A Musical Comedy in Three Acts. Book and lyrics by Rida Johnson Young and Paul West. Based on the play 'Next' by Rida Johnson Young. Music by Jerome D. Kern. Produced (staged) by Joseph W. Herbert. Orchestra under the direction of Clarence West. Orchestrations by Frank Saddler. Presented by the Messrs. Shubert. Opened 13 November 1912 at Daly's Theatre, moved 16 December 1912 to the Broadway Theatre and closed 4 January 1913 after 61 performances.

CAST: *Sophie Brush*: HELEN LOWELL. *Phyllis Oldham*, Brick's sister: LOUISE MINK. *Dora Warner*, Jack's sister: GRACE FIELD. *"Sage Brush" Kate*: FRANCES KENNEDY. *Otto Schmaltz*: JAMES B. CARSON. *Jack Warner*: JOSEPH PHILLIPS. *Brick Oldham*: DONALD MacDONALD. *Bad Jake*: E. L. Fernandez. *Barney Barnes*: Henry Norman. *Long Jim*: Wallace Owen. *Swat Rogers*: George Neville. *Sam Small*: Charles MacDonald. *Rig Regan*: WILLIAM PRUETTE. *"Slim"*: Allen Kearns. *A Chinaman*: Thomas Fulton. *Parrot*: KATHERINE BELKNAP. *Indian*: Joseph Maloney.

Manicure Girls: Misses Betty LaBoulaye, Millie Dupree, Catherine Milligan, Helen Lee, Geraldine Lameer, Mildred Barret, Anita Barretto, Lillian Lawrence. *Concert Hall Girls*: Misses Gladys Meyrick, Jane Barry, Sally Ronanyne, Madge Griffin, Dorothy Stevens, Marjorie Barnes, Marah Vivien, Louise Grant. *Eastern Boys*: Messrs. F. Carey, V. Carey, Leon Rosenthal, J. Carey, Allen Kearns, Mack Brown, F. Moore, Harry Seid. *Miners*: Messrs. J. Maloney, George Averill, F. Fabri, A. Allenmang, A. Stuart, Joseph B. Marvyn, Gerlad Murphy, J. Mills, Rober Fay.

Act 1: Office of the Up-to-date Real Estate and Investment Company, Lost River, Nevada.

Act 2: Same. One week later.

Act 3: Main Street. Lost River.

ACT 1

Opening Chorus
 Miners

"Sing, Sing, You Tetrazinni!"
 F. Kennedy, Chorus

"I Wonder" (Duet)
 L. Mink, J. Phillips

"The Correspondence School"
 H. Lowell, Chorus

"Dance, Dance, Dance"
 D. MacDonald, A. Kearns, Manicure Girls

"Little Golden Maid" (Duet)
 G. Field, D. MacDonald

Finale

ACT 2

Opening Chorus
 F. Kennedy, J. B. Carson, Chorus

"Oh You Beautiful Spring" (Oh You Wonderful Spring)
 G. Field, Chorus
 (*Lyrics by* M. E. Rourke.)

"Where Did the Bird Hear That?" (Trio)
 H. Lowell, J. B. Carson, K. Belknap

"(My) Peaches and Cream" (Ensemble)
 L. Mink, J. Phillips, Chorus

"The Ragtime Restaurant"
 D. MacDonald, Chorus

"A Prisoner of Love" (Trio)
 H. Lowell, L. Mink, G. Field

Finale

ACT 3

"Walk, Walk, Walk"
 D. MacDonald, Chorus

"The Joy of That Kiss" (Duet)
 L. Mink, J. Phillips

"Oo-Oo-Oo"
 J. B. Carson, Girls

"Since the Days of Grandmamma"
 H. Lowell, Girls

"The Waltz Time Girl"
 L. Mink, D. MacDonald

Finale

1912.42

THE GYPSY

A Romantic Operetta in Two Acts. Book and lyrics by Frank Pixley. Music by Gustav Luders. Staged by A. M. Holbrook. Orchestra under the direction of Hilding Anderson. Produced by John Cort. Opened 14 November 1912 at the Park Theatre and closed 23 November 1912 after 12 performances.[47]

<u>CAST</u>: *Lord Stanhope*, owner of Stanhope Hall and large estates surrounding it: RONALD HAMILTON EARLE. *Lord Kyddlehurst*, a young gentleman of leisure in love with Lady Lucy: ERNEST LAMBERT. *Count von Sternberg*, a Austrian fortune hunter, paying court to Lady Alicia: JOHN HAZZARD. *Paulo*, a gypsy chieftain, in command of the gypsy camp: FRANCIS LIEB. *Bago*, a gypsy, second in command: WILLIAM SELLERY. *Phipps*, assistant to Lord Stanhope's gardener; afterwards a "buttons" boy in Stanhope Hall: FORREST WINANT. *Lady Alicia*, heiress to the Stanhope Estates: VIOLET SEATON. *Lady Lucy*, her cousin, visiting at the Hall: ELEANOR KENT. *Agra*, Queen of the Gypsies: Josephine Morse. *Clytie*, a gypsy girl, pet of the camp: Blanche West. *Sophie*, daughter of Lord Stanhope's gardener, afterwards ladies' maid at the Hall: ANNA WILKES. *Chorus*.

The action takes place in rural England near Salisbury at the present time.

Act 1: Camp of the Gypsies. A summer afternoon and evening.

Act 2: Stanhope Hall. Two weeks later.

ACT 1

"What Else Can a Gypsy Do?" (Opening Chorus)
   W. Sellery (Solo), Chorus
"Sing a Song of Sixpence" (Duet)
   A. Wilkes, F. Winant
"Disappear"
   E. Lambart, Girls
"Daffy" (My Daffydil)
   V. Seaton, Chorus
"Gems of the Night"
   V. Seaton, F. Lieb
"Flirting"
   E. Kent, J. Hazzard
"The Tale of the Tadpole"
   V. Seaton, E. Kent, F. Lieb, W. Sellery, Chorus
"The Gypsy Rover"
   B. West, F. Lieb, Gypsy Boys
Czardas; "The Gypsy's Good-night" (Finale)

ACT 2

"The Chaperone" (Opening Chorus)
   E. Kent (Solo), Chorus
"Isn't It Delicious" (Ain't That Delicious)
   J. Hazzard
"I Love You As You Are"
   F. Winant, A. Wilkes
"Every Year Is Leap Year"
   V. Seaton, Chorus
"We Know, Sweetheart, We Know"
   F. Lieb
"Trail Along"
   A. Wilkes, J. Hazzard, E. Lambart
"The Girl I Can't Forget"
   E. Lambart, Girls
"Auf Wiedersehn"
   V. Seaton, F. Lieb
Finale

1912.43

(FROM) BROADWAY TO PARIS

A Musical "Causerie" (Revue) in Two Acts, 12 Scenes. Book and lyrics by George Bronson-Howard and Harold Atteridge. Music by Max Hoffmann. Additional numbers by Anatol Friedland. Production and dances staged by Ned Wayburn. Settings by John and Louie Young. Costumes by Melville Ellis, Robert Jones. Orchestra under the direction of Max Hoffmann. Produced under the direction of Morris Gest. Produced by the Winter Garden Company (Messrs. Shubert). Opened 20 November 1912 at the Winter Garden and closed 25 January 1913 after 77 performances.

---

[47]Settings, costumes uncredited.

<u>CAST</u>: GERTRUDE HOFFMANN, GEORGE BICKEL, GEORGE AUSTIN MOORE, IRENE BORDONI, MR. MAURICE, FLORENCE WALTON, JAMES C. DUFFY, MARION SUNSHINE, SAM MANN, LOUISE DRESSER, BARNEY BERNARD, Ralph Austin, James Carmody [C.] Morton, James C. Harris, Harry F. Gilbert, Henry Awd, Milbury Ryder, Lee Chapin, A. C. Gilman, Joseph C. Schrode, Cordelia Haager, Laura Hill, Ethel Hopkins, Pernikoff, Pierce and Macon, M. Pietro, the Skateles, CHARLES AHEARN AND THE AHEARN TROUPE (of Cyclists).

Show Girls: Misses Elizabeth Francis, Rosa Delomare, Edith Whitney, Beatrice Bentley, Inez Courtez, May Morrell, Kathryn Cullen, Julia Carle. *Dancers*: Misses Gladys Smith, Emma Cunningham, Mabel Grete, Margery Ward, Jeannette Cooke, Katheryn Perry, Flo Summerville, Lucille Kavanaugh, Gertrude Roland, Matilda Boss, Margery Miller, Mabel Martin, Bessie Harris, Dorothy Thomas, Lillian Broderick, Marguerette Fenton, Elsie Frohlich, Laura Hill, Marion Hopkins, Marion Mooney, Marion Werner, Anabelle Jeanette, Alice Van Ryker, Mabel Hill, Nellie Castleman, Florence McNally, Elsie Lanice, Dorothy Keeran, Rose Quint, Hattie Gray, Margery Powell, Esther Gruber, Marguerette Koehl, Olga Zaizef, Eleanor Jackson. *Chorus Boys*: Messrs. Ellis Burge, John Roland, Henry Awd, Walter Haynes, Syd Ayers, Hugh Southgate, Thomas O'Brien, Harry Pierce, Charles Yorkshire, Harry Hamilton, Leslie Raleigh, Lee Chapin, Jack Stone, Billy Macon, Pierre Lafayette, Thomas McCormick, Leo Howe.

ACT 1

Scene 1

"Let Me Show You Paris"
   E. Hopkins, Chorus
   Scene: Proem—Outside Olympus.
      Lao Tsen, the Fountain of All Wisdom: H. F. Gilbert. *Venus*: E. Hopkins. *Apollo*: G. A. Moore. *Momus*: H. Awd. *Stuyvesant Van Cortlandt*, a rich man's son: J. C. Duffy. *Isabelle Montclair*, a New Jersey heiress: M. Sunshine. *Lafe Sherlock, Rafe Holmes*, Employees of Burns' Detective Agency: R. Austin, J. C. Morton. *Mr. Cohan* from Newark: B. Bernard.

Scene 2

Opening Chorus
   Ensemble
"Dance Dracula"
   G. Hoffmann, assisted by L. Chapin
   Scene: At the Theatre Olympia.
      Anne Trelawney: G. Hoffman. *Mr. Hilary Ravenshaw*: L. Chapin.

Scene 3

"Paree's a Branch of Broadway"
   G. A. Moore
   (*Music and Lyrics by* Max Hoffmann.)
"The Eye That Never Sleeps"
   R. Austin, J. C. Morton
   (*Music and Lyrics by* Max Hoffmann.)
"(Hello Cupid,) Send Me a Fellow"
   M. Sunshine
"The Gertrude Hoffmann Glide"
   R. Austin, J. C. Morton, G. Hoffmann, Chorus
   (*Music and Lyrics by* Max Hoffmann.)
"Everybody Loves a Chicken"
   Chorus
   (*Music and Lyrics by* Bobby Jones.)
   Scene: In the Champs Elysées.
      Diane Danon, Heinri Hyacinthe, Official Guides: E. Hopkins, G. A. Moore. *"Stuyvie" Van Cortlandt*: J. C. Duffy. *A Gendarme*: M. Ryder. *Isabel Montclair*: M. Sunshine. *Mildred Vincent*, Isabel's companion: C. Haager. *Lafe Sherlock*: R. Austin. *Rafe Holmes*: J. C. Morton. *A Runaway Horse*: J. Harris, J. C. Schrode. *Anne Trelawney*, Star Artiste of the Theatre Olympia: G. Hoffmann.

Scene 4

"Life Is a Game of Chance"
   Chorus
"(Take Me to That) Swanee Shore"
   G. A. Monroe, Chorus
   (*Music by* Lewis F. Muir. *Lyrics by* L. Wolfe Gilbert.)
   Scene: A Street in Enghein, near Paris.
      Henri, the Guide: G. A. Moore. *Montague Potach*, seeing Paris: S. Mann. *Leonora Longacre*, formerly of New York: L. Dresser.

Scene 5

An Artist from the Folies Marigny (Specialty)
   I. Bordoni
Specialty
   L. Dresser

15

Dream Waltz; Tango Argentino; Society Glide
   M. Pernikoff
"(Mr.) Yankee Doodle"
   E. Hopkins, Chorus
   Scene: The Casino at Enghein.
   Henri: G. A. Moore. *Mildred:* C. Haager. *Mons. Fouche,* an old roué: M.
   Ryder. *"Stuyvie":* J. C. Duffy. *Mlle. Bordoni,* an Artist from the Theatre
   Capucines: I. Bordoni. *Heinrich:* B. Bernard. *Isabelle:* M. Sunshine. *Diane:*
   E. Hopkins. *Miss Longacre:* L. Dresser. *Mr. Potash:* S. Mann. *Lafe:* R. Austin.
   Rafe: J. C. Morton. *An Entertainer:* Pernikoff.

ACT 2
Scene 1
"The Garden of Girls" (Dance)
   G. Hoffmann, Ballet
(Specialties)
   Pernikoff, Pierce, Macon
Nymphs by the Royal Ballet.
   Scene: During a matinee performance at the Theatre Olympia.
Scene 2
   Scene: Behinds the Scenes at the Olympia.
   The Stage Manager: H. F. Gilbert. *A Stage Door Johnnie,* Stuyvie Van
   Cortlandt: J. C. Duffy.
Scene 3
"The New Leader"
   S. Mann, Company
Specialty (Violinist)
   Pietro
   Scene: Stage of the Theatre Olympia during a rehearsal after a Matinee.
   Props: J. C. Schrode. *The New Leader:* S. Mann, *A Vaudeville Performer:* G.
   A. Moore. *Three American Beauties:* Misses Carle, French, Wilson.
Scene 4
"The Merry, Merry Maidens of the Old Front Row"
   Ensemble
"I'll Find a Girl" (I'll Find a Boy)
   J. C. Duffy, M. Sunshine
   Scene: The Cafe American.
   American Dancers: Doyle and Dickson.
Scene 5
"Roller Rinkers"
   The Skatells
   Scene: Exterior of Motordome, Paris.
   Isabelle: M. Sunshine. *Stuyvie:* J. C. Duffy. *Roller Rinkers:* The Skatells.
Scene 6
"Ride Me Around with You, Dearie"
   G. Hoffmann, Chorus
"The Rag-Time Boxing Match"
   E. Hopkins, G. A. Moore, Ensemble
The Ahearn Troupe (Bicycle Specialty)
   C. Ahearn, Company
Finale
   Ensemble
   Scene: Arena of the Paris Motordome.
   Young Montgomery, alias "Fighting Dave": R. Austin. *"Old" Stone,* champion
   actor-pugilist: J. C. Morton. *Referee:* J. C. Schrode. *A Second:* L. Chapin.
   Another: J. Harris. *Percival Whirlwind,* the bicycle champion: C. Ahearn.
   Contestants: The Ahearn Troupe. *Show Girls, Dancers, Chorus Boys.*

1912.44

ROLY POLY

Weber & Fields' All Star Stock Company in A More or Less Digestible
Dramatic Dessert (Double-Bill of a Vaudeville and a Travesty. Burlesque)
mixed by Edgar Smith. Lyriced and Tuned by E. Ray Goetz and A. Baldwin
Sloane. Staged by Gus Sohlke. Scenery painted by John Young. Costumes
by Cora MacGeachy. Orchestra under the direction of DeWitt C.
Coolman. (Produced by [Joseph] Weber and [Lew] Fields.) Opened 21
November 1912 at the Weber and Fields' Theatre and closed 11 January
1912 after 60 performances.

CAST [in order of appearance]: *Reuben Hayes,* a stranded disciple of Cook: Arthur
Aylsworth. *Molly Maguire* of the souvenir booth: Helena Collier Garrick. *Percy
Fitzsimmons,* Hiram's college-bred son: JACK NORWORTH. *Hiram Fitzsimmons,* pro-
moter and mercantile soldier of misfortune, familiarly known as "Doc": FRANK

DANIELS. *Bijou Fitzsimmons* with an eye on Schmaltz and Grand Opera: MARIE
DRESSLER. *Michael Schmaltz,* seeking health in the waters at Raatenbad: JOE
WEBER. *Meyer Talzmann,* his friend and general adviser: LEW FIELDS. *La Frolique,*
a cosmopolitan queen of vaudeville: NORA BAYES. *Cerita,* a dancer: BESSIE CLAY-
TON. *Katrina,* a bier stube divinity: HAZEL KIRKE. *Herr Blotz,* proprietor of the
Hotel Raatenbad: Thomas Beauregard. *Dancers from St. Petersburg:* Sascha Piatov,
Ethel Hartla. *Heidelberg Students (4): Niersteiner:* Patrick Hanley. *Hocheimer:* James
Lum. *Pilsener:* Charles Doll. *Hofbrauer:* Augustus Wicke. *Spring Maids (4): Dolores:*
Alleyne Pickard. *Nella:* Verna Arnold. *Rhoda:* Marcelle Hontabat. *Fifine:* Mabel
Taylor. *A Newsboy:* Gertrude Moyer. *A Flower Girl:* Edna Chase. *A Bootblack:* Hazel
Rosewood. *A Grisette:* Margaret Cassidy. *A Senorita:* Inez Borrero. *Drum Major:*
Adelaide Mason. *A Tourist:* Evelyn Westbrook.
   Incidental to a perversion of WITHIN THE LAW (the thriller by Bayard Veiller)
under the caption of WITHOUT THE LAW:[48] *Act 2, Scenes 2-4: Snarah,* a private
secretary: NORA BAYES. *Swipeson,* a floor walker: Thomas Beauregard. *Richard Pilfer:*
JACK NORWORTH. *Edward Pilfer,* proprietor of the "Scamporium": FRANK
DANIELS. *George Damnrascal,* a lawyer: Arthur Aylesworth. *Inspector Bunk,* of the
Police: JOE WEBER. *Merry Urner,* a victim of honesty: MARIE DRESSLER. *Jagnes,* a
servant lady: HELENA COLLIER GARRICK. *Joke Arson,* forger: LEW FIELDS.
Pearline, a maid: HAZEL KIRKE. *Chicago Red,* a burglar: Thomas Beauregard.
English Eddie, a crook: George Dowling.
   Personnel of the Chorus: Tourists, Military Maids, etc.: Misses Elsa Reinhardt,
Harriet Leidy, May Willard, Emily Monte, Edith Offut, Maidie Burker, Evelyn
Westbrook, May Hopkins, Mabel Ray, Lee Wyant, Eloise Rowe, Sue Duval, Mary
Ellison, Carrie Monroe, Maureau Huban, Grace Williams, Frances Ramey, Lousie
Wilson, Katheryn Kirwan, Helen Neilsen. *Hussars, Gypsies, etc.:* Misses Vonnie
Hoyt, Marie LaChere, Violet Jewell, Gladys Ingraham, Kathleen Allen, Norma
Phillips, Tao Howard, Verna Arnold, Laura Hoffman, Lu Taylor, Margie DeGrasse,
Eileen Kramer, Eugenie Miller, Alleyne Pickard, Marcelle Hontabat, Dorothy
Bertrand, Mabel Taylor, Gertie DeVere, Inez Borrero, Margaret Cassidy, Lilette Boyes.
Chappies, Dutch Girls, etc.: Misses Claire Aldwyn, Eva Ray, Ethel Ray, Nellie Moyse,
Marian Sanford, May Hatherley, Mabel Farber, Margaret Taylor. *Spring Maids, etc.:*
Misses Adelaide Mason, Bertha Lovelace, Sylvia Clark, Bessie Clark, Gertrude
Rutland, Josephine Fields, Myrtle Mayer, Marie Sherwood, Myrtle Ross, Lotta Morse,
Lillian Hazel, Gertie Moyer, Hazel Rosewood, Edna Chase. Drum effects by John
E. Lynehan.

Act 1, Scene 1: The Spring at Raatenbad. *Scene 2:* A Stream near Raatenbad. *Scene 3:*
The Palace of Dance, Berlin.

Act 2, Scene 1: The terrace of the Hotel Raatenbad. *Scene 2:* Private office of the
"Scamporium." *Scene 3:* Merry Urner's Flat. *Scene 4:* The Reconstructed Tombs.

ACT 1
"At Gay Raatenbaad" (Opening Ensemble)
   Entire Chorus
"Dear Old Heidelberg"
   J. Norworth, Chorus
"I'm a Lonseome Romeo"
   F. Daniels, Chorus
"The Prima Donnas"
   M. Dressler
"(Way Down in) Cuba"
   N. Bayes, Chorus
   (*Music and Lyrics by* Jack Norworth, Nora Bayes, Antonio Torroella Chijo.)
"Die Neue Art" von Munich (Dance of the New Art)
   B. Clayton, Ballet
"In My Birch Canoe (with Emmy Lou)"[49]
   N. Bayes, J. Norworth
"Steinland"
   H. Kirke, Chorus
"I Cannot Drink the Old Drinks"[50]
   F. Daniels
"Nobody Knows What We Girls Go Through"[51]
   N. Bayes
"The Zingaras" (Finale)
   M. Dressler, F. Daniels, Chorus

ACT 2:
"When I'm Waltzing" (Opening Ensemble)
   H. Kirke, Chorus

---

[48]Dropped by early December, along with the musical numbers
"Brooklyn," "The Pinkerton Detective" and "The Burglar's Ball."
[49]By early December, moved to the Opening of Act 2.
[50]By early December, moved to the middle of Act 2.
[51]Dropped during the run.

Incidental Dance
S. Piatov, E. Hartla
"(When It's) Apple Blossom Time in Normandy"
N. Bayes, J. Norworth
(*Music and Lyrics by* Tom Mellor, Harry Gifford and Huntley Trevor.)
"The Stair Dance"[52]
B. Clayton, Ballet
"The Regimental Roly Poly Girl"
(B. Clayton, Ballet)
"Brooklyn" (He Believes I'm in Brooklyn Tonight)
N. Bayes
"The Pinkerton Detective (Moon)"
J. Norworth, H. Kirke
(*Music and Lyrics by* Jack Norworth and Nora Bayes.)
"The Burglar's Ball"
N. Bayes, Chorus
Finale
Entire Company

1912.45

THE SUN DODGERS

A Fanfare of Frivolity in Two Acts. Book by Edgar Smith. Music by A. Baldwin Sloane. Lyrics by E. Ray Goetz. Additional songs by Irving Berlin, Ben Jerome and Jean Schwartz. Staged by Ned Wayburn. Scenery painted by John Young. Costumes by Cora MacGeachy. Orchestra under the direction of August Kleinecke. Orchestrations by Hilding Anderson, William Redfield. Produced by Lew Fields. Opened 30 November 1912 at the Broadway Theatre and closed 14 December 1912 after 18 performances.

CAST: *Praline Nutleigh* a footlight goddess of the vaudeville persuasion, to whom sunshine is a novelty: BESSIE WYNN. *Mrs. Honoria O'Day*, Wakeleigh Knight's wealthy widowed aunt, with a desire to live down her daylight past in the far West: GEORGE W. MONROE. *P. V. Hawkins*, of Lonesome Falls, Montana, fiancé and business advisor of the Widow O'Day: HARRY FISHER. *Rose Hubbs*, a rural bud, whose experience in life has been confined to the daylight hours at Reubenville Corners, Long Island: ANN TASKER. *Wakeleigh Knight*, a gilded youth of the metropolis, and a leading spirit of the Sun Dodgers, a coterie devoted to the night life of the great city: HAROLD CRANE. *Hiram Hubbs*, a Long Island Nurseryman, proprietor of the site for Sunless City: Nat Fields. *Todd Hunter*, who moves along the line of least resistance: Denman Maley. *Sam Porter*, Wakeleigh Knight's colored valet, who works while his master sleeps: Jerry Hart. (*Dance Specialties*: Madeline Harrison, Cartmell, Harris and Miller, Mark Whiting, Edith Abbott.)

Of the Sun Dodgers Coterie: Vera Light, a show girl: NAN BRENNAN. *Trixie Turner*, a "broiler": MAUD GRAY. *A. Goode Lamb*, man about town: HARRY CLARK. *Y. DeWake Taylor*, another: JACK JARROTT. *I. M. Stude*, another still: James C. Breese.

Officer Muldoon: James Dyso. *A Cab Driver*: Fred Duffy.

Personnel of Chorus: Misses Naomi Dale, Marie Berdine, Elsie Markert, Florence Kern, Gray Stowe, Ida Doerge, Mabel d'Elmar, Billie DeHon, Gladys Breston, Lillian Baker, Minnie Monroe, Bertie Britton, Olive Horner, Ethel Fuller, Nelia Hadley, Louise Jackson, Grace Sholholm, Edna Fenton, Burns Parish, Jennie Cannar, Geraldine Taylor, Grace Williams, Beatrice Dakin, Lee Leontine, Vinnie Mason, Pearl Diehl, Ethel Wheeler, Laura Gaynelle, Helen Mooney, Fannie Grant, Alma Braham, Helen Williams, Catherine Sinclair. Messrs. Bert Devlin, Frank Gilbert, Charles Van, James Breese, Joseph Hadley, Henry Goulett, John Shanks, Frank McAvoy, Clyde Hall, James Barry.

Act 1, Scene 1: The Beefsteak Cellar of the Sun Dodgers Club. *Scene 2*: Exterior of the Sun Dodgers Club. *Scene 3*: The Country Club at Reubenville Corners, Long Island.

Act 2, Scene 1: The Main Plaza of "Sunless City," the New Community Settlement of the Sun Dodgers. *Scene 2*: Exterior of the Automat Cafe. *Scene 3*: Interior of the Automat.

ACT 1[53]

Scene 1

"Down in the Old Rathskeller" (Opening Chorus)
J. Jarrott, Chorus

---

[52]Dropped during the run; "Regimental Roly Poly Girl" retained.
[53]For a subsequent tour, the book was revised by Mark Swan, uncredited; Jack Norworth and Nora Bayes joined the cast, assuming the roles of Wakeleigh Knight and Praline Nutleigh; Kitty Flynn assumed the role of Peaceful Knight, and Nan Brennan played Rose Hubbs, and the musical score was revised as follows:

"Rag Me Around"
M. Gray, N. Brennan, J. Jarrott, H. Clark
"Song of the Cocktail"
H. Crane, Chorus
La Danse a Pieds Nus
M. Harrison
"You're My Baby"
B. Wynn, Chorus
"Ginger"
M. Gray, Chorus

ACT 1
"Down in the Old Rathskeller" (Opening Chorus)
Chorus
"Take Me to the Chicken Ball" (Act 1)
H. Clark, Chorus
(*Music by* O. E. Story. *Lyrics by* Bobby Jones.).
"Beautiful Spring"
K. Flynn
"I Am Crazy About Somebody (and That Somebody Is You)"
J. Norworth, N. Bayes
(*Music by* Dave Stamper. *Lyrics by* Gene Buck.)
"Poor Old Cow" (The Night the Old Cow Died)
G. W. Monroe, H. E. Fisher, J. Norworth
"Ginger"
M. Gray, Chorus
"(When You Said) How Do You Do"
H. Clark, N. Brennan
"How Can They Tell That I'm Irish?"
N. Bayes
(*Music and Lyrics by* Nora Bayes and Jack Norworth.)
"In the Garden of Your Heart"
Chorus
"The Sunshine Girl"
K. Flynn, Chorus
"(When It's) Apple Blossom Time in Normandy" (from ROLY POLY)
N. Bayes, J. Norworth
(*Music and Lyrics by* Harry Gifford, Tom Mellor, Huntley Trevor.)
Finale: "Old-Home Week"/"The Night Brigade"
Principals

ACT 2
"Dixie Love"
H. Clark, Chorus
"Keep on Looking Up"
N. Bayes
"Down on Uncle Jerry's Farm"
K. Flynn, Chorus
"I'd Like an Introduction to You, Dearie"
Chorus
"At the Picture Show"
H. Clark, M. Gray, Chorus
(*Music and Lyrics by* Irving Berlin, E. Ray Goetz.)
Melodrama
G. W. Monroe, H. E. Fisher
"Pinkerton Detective Moon" (from ROLY POLY)
J. Norworth, N. Bayes
(*Music and Lyrics by* Nora Bayes and Jack Norworth.)
Finale
Later interpolations, as per published sheet music:
"Way Down in Cuba" (from ROLY POLY)
J. Norworth, N. Bayes
(*Music by* Antonio Torella Chijo. *American version and lyrics by* Jack Norworth and Nora Bayes.)
"She Believes I'm in Brooklyn Tonight"
"Nobody Knows What We Girls Go Through"
"In My Birch Bark Canoe (with Emmy Lou)" (from ROLY POLY)
(*Music by* A. Baldwin Sloane. *Lyrics by* E. Ray Goetz.)

Scene 2

Dance
Cartmell and Miller

"When You Said How Do You Do"
B. Wynn, H. Clark

Scene 3

"The Garden of Flowers"
Ensemble

"Every Flower Has a Melody"
B. Wynn
(*Music by* Orean Smith. *Lyrics by* Earl Carroll.)

"Marry a Sunshine Girl"
A. Tasker, H. Crane, Chorus

"The Night Brigade"
N. Brennan, Chorus

ACT 2

Scene 1

"Good Morning" (Opening Chorus)
Ensemble

"Two Heads Are Better Than One"
J. Dyso

"Society" (I Never Would Do It in Society)
B. Wynn, Chorus

"Dixie Love"
H. Clark, Chorus

Lariat Dance
M. Whiting, E. Abbott

Specialty Dance
Cartmell and Harris

Scene 2

"What Happened to Mary?"
B. Wynn
(*Music by* Orean Smith. *Lyrics by* Earl Carroll.)

Scene 3

"At the Automat"
Ensemble

"At the Picture Show"
M. Gray, H. Clark, Chorus
(*Music and Lyrics by* Irving Berlin, E. Ray Goetz.)

Burlesque Drama
G. W. Monroe, H. Fisher

Finale
Ensemble

1912.46   THE FIREFLY

A Comedy Opera in Three Acts. Book and lyrics by Otto Hauerbach [Harbach]. Music by Rudolf Friml. Staged by Frederick G. Latham. Incidental dances arranged by Signor Albertieri. Special dances arranged by Sammy Lee. Scenery by Theodore Reisig Dove Studios, P. Dodd Ackerman Studios. Costumes designed by W. Matthews. Orchestra under the direction of Gaetano Merola. Produced by Arthur Hammerstein. Opened 2 December 1912 at the Lyric Theatre, moved 30 December 1912 to the Casino Theatre and closed 15 March 1913 after 120 performances.

CAST (in order of appearance): *Sybil Vandare*: Vera DeRosa. *Suzette*: RUBY NORTON. *Pietro*: SAMMY LEE. *Geraldine Vandare*: AUDREY MAPLE. *Jack Travers*: CRAIG CAMPBELL. *John Thurston*: MELVILLE STEWART. *Mrs. Oglesby Vandare*: Katherine Stewart. *Jenkins*: ROY ATWELL. *Herr Franz*: HENRY VOGEL. *Nina Corelli*, (alias Antonio Columbo): EMMA TRENTINI. *Antonio Columbo*: Irene Cassini. *Corelli*: George Williams.
Other characters: Misses Virginia Steinhardt, Eileen Gerald, Belle Anderson, Mona Harmon, Hulda Morton, Violette von Nichols, Mattie Vance, Dorothy Walmer, Alvina Dare, Marion Lee, Marie Granville, Grace Noble, Louie Ducey, .Bessie Bourne, Neva Cassini, Bessie Stivers, Frankie Farrell, Marie Melvin, Vera Ling, Florence Reed, Irene Samson, Katherine Ardavini, Viola Garrick, Amelia Wurtz, Katherine Hauser, Edith Bonnett, Florence Williams, Alice Rose. Messrs. Stanley Sobelson, Edward Agnini, William Stanz, William Brown, Max Silver, James Johnson, Robert Odierno, Walter Burke, George Bruger, Robert Halstead, Edwin Archer, Arthur Spencer, Alex. Sparks, Russell Brown, Ernest Band, Bernard Tieman, Louie Linton.

Act 1: Recreation Pier, Foot of 23rd Street, New York. Present time. (Dove.)

Act 2: The Vandare Estate, Bermuda. Three weeks later. (Ackerman.)

Act 3: The Vandare Home, New York. Three years later. (Ackerman.)

ACT 1

"A Trip to Bermuda" (Opening Chorus)
V. DeRosa, R. Norton, S. Lee, Chorus

"He Says Yes, She Says No!"
A. Maple, C. Campbell, Chorus

"Call Me Uncle"
M. Stewart, V. DeRosa, Chorus

"Love Is Like a Firefly"
E. Trentini

"Something"
R. Norton, R. Atwell

"Giannina (Mia)" (Italian Street Song)
E, Trentini

Finale
Ensemble

ACT 2

"(In) Sapphire Seas" (Opening Chorus)
V. DeRosa, Ensemble

"Tommy Atkins (on a Dress-Parade)" (I Want to be a Jolly Soldier)
E. Trentini, Ensemble

"Sympathy"
A. Maple, M. Stewart

"A Woman's Smile"
C. Campbell

"De Trop"
R. Atwell, S. Lee, R. Norton, Chorus

"We're Going to Make a Man of You"
E. Trentini, H. Vogel, C. Campbell, M. Stewart, R. Atwell

"The Beautiful Ship from Toyland"
H. Vogel, Male Chorus

"When a Maid Comes Knocking at Your Heart"
E. Trentini, C. Campbell, H. Vogel

Finale
Ensemble

ACT 3

Opening Chorus
Ensemble

"An American Beauty Rose"
M. Stewart, Ensemble

"The Latest Thing from Paris"
S. Lee, R. Norton

"Kiss Me and 'Tis Day"[54] (The Dawn of Love)
E. Trentini

Finale
Ensemble

1912.47   MISS PRINCESS

An American Operetta in Two Acts. Book by Frank Mandel. Music by Alexander Johnstone. Lyrics by Will B. Johnstone. Costumes by Elsie DeWolfe, Wachner & Company; Mme. Abarbanell's gowns by Lucile. Orchestra under the direction of Max Bendix. Produced by John Cort. Opened 23 December 1912 at the Park Theatre and closed 4 January 1913 after 16 performances.[55]

CAST (in order of appearance): *Senator Caldwell*: Charles P. Morrison. *Baron Gustav von Vetter*, Ambassador to the United States: Ben Hendricks. *Baroness von Vetter*, his wife: Isabel C. Francis. *Hypatia Caldwell*, the Senator's daughter: MARGARET [Marguerite] FARRELL. *Prince Alexis*: HENRI LEONI. *Countess Matilda*, Polonia's chaperon: Louise Foster. *Frau Kattrina De Creusi*, known as the Human Spider: JOSEPHINE WHITTELL. *Lincoln T. Creery*, Assistant U.S. Secretary of War: John H. Pratt. *Princess Polonia*: LINA ABARBANELL. *Captain Merton Raleigh*, 16th United States Cavalry: ROBERT WARWICK. *Sergeant Tim McGrew*, 16th United States

---

[54]Dropped for subsequent national tour.

[55]Direction, settings uncredited.

Cavalry: FELIX HANEY. *Corporal Stephens, 16th United States Cavalry:* Donald Buchanan. *Private Ryan, 16th United States Cavalry:* Albert Borneman.

Debutantes: Misses Gladys Fox, Anna Breucher, Bessie Clyne, Billie Francis, Edith Allen, Irma Bertrand, Billie Wood, Anna McConville. *Society Girls:* Misses Doris DeWilde, Edith Hardlow, Beatrice Bertrand, Lulu Strater, Dorothy Honey, Evelyn Smith, Catherine McMahon, Gwen Sears. *Matrons:* Misses Mellis Merrill, Margaret Gordon, Grace Lavelle, May Stockton, Fanny Hasbrouck, Paula Keane, Maybelle Pratt, Violet Whitney. *Ambassadors:* Messrs. Richad King, Emmet McDonald, Frank O'Neil, Bernard Ravage, Thomas Lee, Frank Mullen, Manny Duprez, Billy Cohen. *Guests:* Messrs. Charles Sloane, Nathan Lawson, Robert Prein, John Hope, Ralph Raymond, Thomas Fudger, George Sawyer.

Act 1: Garden of the Ambassador in Washington. An afternoon in May. Present time.

Act 2: United States Reservation on the Mexican Border in Southern California. A morning in September.

ACT 1

Opening Ensemble

"I Never Had a Kiss" (Duet)
H. Leon, J. Whittell

"Give Me Love, Love, Love"
L. Abarbanell, Ensemble

"Ay Oomps"
F. Haney, Ensemble

"The Wireless Way" (Duet)
L. Abarbanell, H. Leon

"Humpty Dumpty"
R. Warwick, Ensemble

"It Might Have Been" (Duet)
L. Abarbanell, R. Warwick

"Behind the Scenes" (Sextette)
J. Whittell, M. Farrell, L. Foster, H. Leon, B. Hendricks, F. Haney

Finale
Entire Company

ACT 2

"The Galloping Cavalree"
R. Warwick, Soldiers

"A Little Red Book and a Five Cent Bag"
F. Haney, Soldiers
(*Lyrics by* Hiram E. Russell.)

"Come My Sweetheart"
L. Abarbanell, Ensemble
(*Music by* Johan Strauss.)

"Temperamental Dances"
M. Farrell, Ensemble
With F. Hale, assisted by S. Paterson.

"Queen Thou Art: (Duet)
L. Abarbanell, H. Leon

"The Princess Can't Be Found, Sir"
Ensemble

"Pillow Number"
L. Abarbanell, H. Leon, Ensemble

Finale

EVA

1912.48

A Musical Play in Three Acts. Book and lyrics by Glen MacDonough. (Based on the original Viennese operetta 'Eva,' ['Das Fabriksmädel'] by Robert Bodanzky and A. M. Willner.) Music by Franz Lehár. Staged by Herbert Gresham. Dances arranged by Julian Mitchell. Costumes by F. Richard Anderson. Lighting by Frank Detering. Orchestra under the direction of Hugo Reisenfeld. Produced by (Marc) Klaw and (Abe) Erlanger. Opened 30 December 1912 at the New Amsterdam Theatre and closed 18 January 1913 after 24 performances.

CAST (in order of appearance): *Larousse,* foster-father of Eva and foreman of the factory: T. J. McGRANE. *Antoine,* private secretary: WALLACE McCUTCHEON, JR. *Voisin,* manager of the factory: JOHN DALY MURPHY. *Dagobert Millefleurs,* Octave's butterfly uncle, whom he struggles to reform: WALTER LAWRENCE. *Pipsi Paquerette,* a Parisienne in search of adventure: ALMA FRANCIS. *Eva,* an apprentice at the Flaubert glass-factory: SALLIE FISHER. *Octave Flaubert,* a young Parisian man

about town, who falls heir to the factory: WALTER PERCIVAL. *Ellie,* of the Folies Bergère: Marie Ashton. *Friends of Octave (4): Lizette:* Marie Vernon. *Freddie:* Alden MacClaskie. *Edmond:* William T. Ford. *Hortense:* Fawn Conway. *Matthew,* a porter: John Gibson. *A Maid:* Viola Cain. *Yvonne:* Edna Broderick.

Act 1: Main office of the Flaubert glass-factory at Montarlier, Belgium. A summer morning.

Act 2: Garden of the mansion of the owner of the factory. Night.

Act 3: Ellie's apartment, overlooking the Bois de Boulogne, Paris. A winter afternoon, five months later.

ACT 1[56]

Opening Chorus ("We'll the new master greet)

"The Voice of Paris" (Duet)(A country mouse I ne'er could be)
A. Francis, W. Lawrence

"Vision Song" (The night winds were sighing)
S. Fisher

"Love is a Pilgrim"
S. Fisher

"Joy and Glass" (Trio)(Glass like this)
W. Percival, J. D. Murphy, W. Lawrence

Finale (You are the foster father)
W. Percival, S. Fisher, T. J. McGrane

ACT 2

Opening Chorus (Let us whirl, swirl, twirl)

"The Starlight Guards" (March Octette)(We Starlight Guards)
A. Francis, W. Percival, Double Octette

"Life Is a masquerade" (Trio)(If to Paris I should go)
S. Fisher, W. Lawrence, W. McCutcheon

"Cinderella" (Duet)(So unreal does this seem)
W. Percival, S. Fisher

Finale (To what I say, attention pay)
W. Lawrence, W. Percival, S. Fisher, A. Francis, etc.

ACT 3

"The Unrepentant Butterfly" (In gold and purple)
W. Lawrence, Chorus

"The Imp of Montmartre" (Duet)(When comes the time of night)
A. Francis, W. Percival

"Love is a Pilgrim" (Waltz Song)(Nevermore we'll meet)
S. Fisher

"The Quarrel Duet" (Do you really dare to face me)
A. Francis, W. Lawrence

Finale (Octave, I love you so!)
S. Fisher, W. Percival

ALL FOR THE LADIES

1912.49

A Farce with Music in Two Acts. Book and lyrics by Henry Blossom. Based on the French farce "Aime des Femmes" by Maurice Hennequin. Music by Alfred G. Robyn. Scenery by D. Frank Dodge and William Castle. Costumes by Melville Ellis. Orchestra under the direction of John Lund. Produced by the Messrs. Shubert. Opened 30 December 1912 at the Lyric Theatre and closed 5 April 1913 after 112 performances.[57]

CAST: *Marie,* a typewriter: LOUISE MEYERS. *Alphonse Clemente:* GEORGE A. SCHILLER. *Georgette Clemente:* ALICE GENTLE. *Ernest Panturel:* TEDDY WEBB. *Nancy Panturel:* ADELE RITCHIIE. *Charles:* Max d'Arcy. *Hector Renaud:* STEWART BAIRD. *Leon von Laubenheim,* of Pantural, Clemente & Co.: SAM BERNARD. *Madam Suzette,* Leo's assistant: Margery Pearson. *Models (3): Finette:* Lillie Leslie. *Blanche:* Marta Spears. *Augusta:* Maxie MacDonald. *Baroness des Herbettes:* Amy Leicester. *Marquis de Calvados:* Edna Carruthers. *General Villefranche:* Jerome Uhl. *Gaston LeBlanc:* Arthur Webner. *Grand Duchess Alexia of Russia:* Lena Robinson. *Francois,* a valet: Henry M. Holt.

---

[56]Musical numbers prepared from published piano vocal score (G. Schirmer, New York, 1912). Two musical numbers identified by reviewers, but not contained in published score:

"On the Day I Marry"

"The Up-to-Date Troubadour"
W. Lawrence, A. Francis

[57]Direction and dances uncredited.

Personnel of Chorus: Attendants: Misses Helen Knight, Paula Leslie, Gladys Clifton, Jean Brae, Rose Huber, Vivian Rogers. *A la Mode Girls*: Misses Nathalie Saymore, Margaret Vinton, Birdie Sargeant, Viola Ford, Anita Tremper, Gladys Benjamin. *Shoppers*: Misses Rose Leslie, Sue Young, Anna Berg, Florence Bowers, Hazel Sexton, Camille Irving, May Allen, Winnie Munroe. *Models as They Appear*: Misses Anna Berg, Sue Young, Helen Knight, Nathalie Saymore, Birdie Sergeant, Gladys Benjamin, Viola Ford, Rose Leslie. *Johnnies*: Messrs. Daniel Piel, Hery Ward, Homer Potts, Charles Williams, Edward Myers, William Brandell. *Flunkies*: Messrs. Robert Newman, William Nau, Arthur Wells, Frank Meyrose, Henry M. Holt. *Floor Walker*: Harry Semels.

Prologue: Office of Pantural, Clemente & Co., in the Rue Vigon. Present time.

Act 1: "The Fitting Parlors" in the Rue de la Paix. Six weeks later.

Act 2: Living room in Leo's home.

PROLOGUE
"If You Love Me, Marry Me" (Song)
    L. Meyers
"I'd Like a Girl Like You To Like Me" (Duo)
    S. Baird, L. Meyers
"The Sunday Dress Parade" (Trio)
    A. Ritchie, A. Gentle, S. Baird

ACT 1
"What a Change" (Opening Chorus)
    Ensemble
"Cupid is a Cruel Master"[58] (Trio)
    M. Spears, M. MacDonald, L. Leslie
"A la Parisienne"[59] (Song)
    L. Meyers, Models
"It's Permissible" (Song)
    S. Bernard
Finale
    Ensemble

ACT 2
"Paris, Paris" (Opening Chorus)
    Leo's Guests
"Women, Women" (Song)
    S. Baird, Male Chorus
"(I Live But) In Dreams Alone" (Song)
    A. Gentle
Finale
    Ensemble

1913.01 SOMEWHERE ELSE

A Musical Fantasy in Two Acts. Book and lyrics by Avery Hopwood. Music by Gustav Luders. Staged by Frank Smithson. Dances arranged by David Marion. Scenery painted by Ernest Gros. Costumes by Freisinger, J. Weiner, Boinet & Hirsig, Mme. Zimmerman. Lighting by Joseph Wilson. Conductor, George A. Nichols. Produced by Henry W. Savage. Opened 20 January 1913 at the Broadway Theatre and closed 25 January 1913 after 8 performances.

CAST: *Mary VII*, Queen of Somewhere Else: CECIL CUNNINGHAM. *Villainus*, step-uncle of the Queen: WILL PHILBRICK. *Chloe*, cousin of the Queen: ELENE LESKA. *Billy Getaway*, of New York City: TAYLOR HOLMES. *Rocky Rixon*, cousin of Gettaway: FRANKLYN FARNUM. *Hepzibah Dodds*, Gettaway's step-daughter: Catherine Hayes. *The Cheerful Executioner*: Donald Chalmers. *Teddy Wood*, Rocky's best friend: BURTON LENIHAN. *Deputy Chief Boy Scouts*: Marion Whitney.
Chloe's Friends, who believe that the proper study of Womankind is Man: *Hebe*: Helene W. Davis. *Rilda*: Edith Warren. *Daphne*: Ellen Evans. *Phoebe*: Florida Bellaire. *Cynthia*: Rita Bellaire. *Gloria*: Blixie Murrie. *Sophia*: Alys Baldwin. *Penelope*: Susie McChroan.
Rocky's College Chums, who are taking a post-graduate course in Feminology: *Tommy Wade*: H. R. Haskell. *Jimmy Parker*: Maxwell Kennedy. *Freddy Truesdale*: Martin Conroy. *Larry Deane*: Richard Hall. *Johnny Williams*: Briggs French. *Charlie Hunt*: Dick Stewart. *Billy Wright*: Fred M. Fisher. *Roddy Reilly*: H. P. Wagner.

---
[58]Replaced during the run by:
    "If I Were Only a Man" (Song)
        A. Ritchie, Chorus
[59]Dropped during the run.

Young Cousins of the Queen: Mo Mo: Mabel Callon. *To To*: Daisy McNally. *Bo Bo*: Perry Alvarez. *Tondi*: Devor Alvarez. *Peepo*: Doris Ferges. *Dadee*: Mildred Lawrence.
Truth: Ednah Bernard. *The Messenger of Dawn*: Edith Thayer. *A Lad Named Cupid*: Violet DeBiccai. *Guards*: Melville Anderson, George Healy. *Palace Girls*: Misses Billie St. Clair, Marion Whitney, Dorothy Carrigne, Cecil Thackara, Leslie Wilson, Estelle Francesca, Ethel West, Sally Berch, Pauline Winters. *Maids*: Misses Monte Grayce, Mabel Gebeau, Naidene Parker, Hilda Peters, Helene Davis, Helen Kent. *Somewhere Else Boys*: Messrs. Melville Anderson, Shephard Garretson, W. C. Stanley, H. T. McCoy, Frank Wayne, W. A. Healey.

The action takes place Somewhere Else, at the present time, with inclinations towards the future.

Act 1: The Palace Garden of the Queen. On a morning in late spring.

Act 2: The Nursery of the Royal Children. Evening of the same day.

ACT 1
Opening Number
    E. Thayer
Cupid's Entrance
"How Do You Do"
    T. Holmes, Chorus
"Well Fellows, I Guess We're Here"
    F. Farnum, College Men
"As Birds Greet Morning Skies"
    E. Leska, Full Chorus
Queen's Entrance (Chorus)
"Love at First Sight"
    C. Cunningham, Full Chorus
"Forget Me Not"
    E. Leska, B. Lenihan, Chorus
"Can You Do This?"
    C. Cunningham, E. Leska, T. Holmes, F. Farnum, W. Philbrick, D. Chalmers
Finale
    Ensemble
ACT 2
"Wake Up, Little Hepzibah" (Opening Number)
"For You, Dear Heart"
    E. Leska, Chorus
"Somebody's Eyes"
    C. Cunningham
"The Boy Scouts"
    W. Philbrick, Chorus
Dance d'Amour
    F. Farnum, E. Leska, Chorus
"B-a-b-e-e"
    Ensemble
"Dingle Dangle" (Finale)

1913.02 THE MAN WITH THREE WIVES

An Operetta in Three Acts. Book by Agnes Bangs Morgan, Paul M. Potter and Harold R. Atteridge. (Based on the Viennese original 'Der Mann mit den drei Frauen,' libretto by by Julius Bauer.) Music by Franz Lehár. (Lyrics by Harold R. Atteridge and Paul M. Potter.) Staged by William J. Wilson, J. C. Huffman. Costumes by Melville Ellis. Orchestra under the direction of Oscar Radin. Produced by the Messrs. Shubert. Opened 23 January 1913 at Weber and Fields' 44th Street Theatre and closed 8 March 1913 after 52 performances.

CAST (in order of appearance): *First Clerk*: Jack McCoy. *Second Clerk*: Robert Ranier. *Third Clerk*: Walter Smith. *Franz*, Zifler's secretary: ROBERT G. PITKIN. *Rosa*, Lori's maid: Dorothy Webb. *Baron Pickford*, English director of the Pickford Tourist Agency: LESLIE KENYON. *Captain Adhemar*, Third Hussars: STEWART BAIRD. *Lieutenant Loriot*, Third Hussars: Arthur Geary. *Marie*, Flix's wife: Katheryn Sainpolis. *Flix*, tourist: Harold Robe. *Blix*, tourist: James Billings. *Anna*, tourist: Marah Vivian. *Hans Zifler*, courier of the agency: CECIL LEAN. *Wendelin*, a country bridegroom: SYDNEY GRANT. *Lori*, Hans Zifler's wife: ALICE YORKE. *Sidonie*, a flirtatious bride: CHARLOTTE GREENWOOD. *Colette*, instructress of ballet school: SOPHYE BARNARD. *Blanche*, a pupil in school: Marguerite LaPierie. *Suzette*, Colette's maid: Ida Jeanne. *Olivia*, proprietress of the Geranium Inn: DOLLY

CASTLES. *Alice*, Olivia's maid: CLEO MAYFIELD. *Cabby*: Frank Hart. *Tourists, Clerks, Officers, Pupils, etc.*

Personnel of the Chorus: Dancers: Eva Burnett, Mabel Beck, Alice Burns, Dolly Gray, Edna Hettler, Marie Hannon, Fanny Ide, Ida Kramer, Trixie Lakewood, Leafy Walker, Billie Ward, Esther Gruber, Maurie Maidson, Clara Floyd, Flo Summerville, Marion Mooney, Lillian Broderick, Marjory Ward. *Show Girls*: Annette Herbert, Mary Casell, Beatrice Purcell, Marguerite LaPierre, Edythe Whitney, Sandra Kerwin, Gertrude Braun, Katheryn Sainpolis, Marah Vivien, Mae Paul, Edith Brown, Vyvyen Donner Annette Louis. *Clerks, Tourists and Officers*: James Billings, Fred Shaw, Fred Foyn, John Foyn, Jack McCoy, Robert Rainer, George Robinson, Harry Hamft, Walter Smith, Peter George, Joseph Breslaw, Fred Bradbury, Michael Wagmar, Gwilyn Edwards, Thomas Doolan, Max Dorftman, Kenneth Cooley, Stephen Gillie, Starret Howard, Robert Page.

Act 1: Office of Pickford Tourist Agency, Vienna.

Act 2: Garden of Colette's ballet school, Paris

Act 3: The Geranium Inn, suburb of London.

ACT 1

Opening Chorus
Tourists
"Love's Fairy Tales" (Duet)
D. Webb, R. G. Pitkin
"There's Always a Girl Who is Waiting"
S. Baird, Girls
"The Temporary Widow" (Quartette)
A. Yorke, C. Lean, D. Webb, R. G. Pitkin
"The Vale of Dreaming" (Lullaby)
A. Yorke, C. Lean
"When You're Traveling"
C. Lean, Girls
"Tootsie Wootsie" (Duet)
C. Greenwood, S. Grant
"Man Is Faithful Till He's Caught" (Duet)
A. Yorke, L. Kenyon
"Vengeance" (Trio)
A. Yorke, D. Webb, L. Kenyon
"Paris, Oh Festive Land" (Finale)
Tourists

ACT 2

Ballet
Ballet Girls
"The Poor Cadets"
Ballet Girls
"Rose of Yesterday"
S. Barnard
"Kisses That I Have Missed" (Duet)
S. Barnard, S. Baird
"Tempo Di Gavotte" (Ballet Rehearsal)
Scholars
"Lullaby"
S. Barnard
"Woman of Temperament" (Trio)
A. Yorke, S. Barnard, C. Lean
Entrance of Ballet
S. Barnard, Scholars
"To London" (Grand Finale)
Company

ACT 3

"All in a Little Dance"
D. Castles, Maids
"Hello, Hello" (Duet)
C. Greenwood, S. Grant
(*Music by* Al W. Brown. *Lyrics by* Harold Atteridge.)
"Love's Flower Is Always Blooming" (Trio)
A. Yorke, S. Barnard, D. Castles
"We Are Free" (Sextette)
A. Yorke, S. Barnard, D. Castles, C. Lean, S. Baird, L. Kenyon
"Cupids Soldiers" (Finale)
Company

1913.03

THE ISLE O' DREAMS

A Play with Music in Four Acts. Play by Rida Johnson Young. Music by Ernest Ball. Lyrics by Chauncey Olcott, George Graff, Rida Johnson Young. Staged by Henry Miller. Scenery painted by Homer F. Emens. Musical director, Edwin F. Kendall. Incidental music by Edwin F. Kendall. Produced by Henry Miller. Opened 27 January 1913 at the Grand Opera House and closed 22 February 1913 after 32 performances.[60]

CAST (in order of appearance): *Lanty Madden*: M. Tello Webb. *Mother Kelway*, (Ivor's foster mother): MRS. JENNIE LAMONT. *Phelim O'Flynn*: John Sheehan. *An Old Fisherman*: Robert Watt. *Mona*: AGNES HERON MILLER. *Ivor Kelway*: CHAUNCEY OLCOTT. *Father John*: Alfred Moore. *Colonel McFarlan*: DAVID GLASSFORD. *Lieutenant John Martin*: Walter Colligan. *Kathleen O'Doon*: EDITH BROWNING. *Robert O'Doon*: J. C. King. *Old Padrig*: Frederick Roberts. *Lieutenant Grey*: George Ahearn. *Lieutenant Forbes*: Thomas R. Slicer. *Lieutenant Elliott*: Oscar Lambert. *Lieutenant Warren*: Maurice Handy. *Sergeant Fennel*: Julian Ross. *Pere Baret*: Everett Lansing. *Major Ross*: Brian Darley. *Captain Dawes*: Arthur C. Laylin. *Big Hallam*: William R. Gleason.

The action of the play takes place in 1799, at the time of the threatened invasion of Ireland by the Emperor Napoleon.

Act 1: Mother Kelway's Tap Room, located on a small island off the South Coast of Ireland, known as The Isle o' Dreams.

Act 2: A Steep Cliff overhanging the Sea. On the Island.

Act 3: Fergus Castle, mutilated by the British Forces. On the Mainland.

Act 4: On Board the "*Sea Gull*."

MUSICAL NUMBERS[61]

"The Isle o' Dreams"
(*Music by* Ernest R. Ball. *Lyrics by* George Graff, Jr. and Chauncey Olcott.)
"Mother Machree"
(*Music by* Ernest R. Ball. *Lyrics by* George Graff, Jr. and Chauncey Olcott.)
"When Irish Eyes Are Smiling"
(*Music by* Ernest R. Ball. *Lyrics by* George Graff, Jr. and Chauncey Olcott.)
"Kathleen Aroon"
(*Music by* Ernest R. Ball. *Lyrics by* Louis Weslyn and Chauncey Olcott.)

1913.04

THE SUNSHINE GIRL

A Musical Play in Two Acts. Book by Paul Rubens and Cecil Raleigh. Music by Paul Rubens. Lyrics by Arthur Wimperis and Paul Rubens. Staged by J. A. E. Malone. Scenery designed by Ernest Albert and Homer Emens. Gowns by Lord & Taylor; men's uniforms and clothes by Russell Uniform Company. Musical director, Augustus Barratt. Produced by Charles Frohman. Opened 3 February 1913 at the Knickerbocker Theatre, closing for summer vacation 21 June 1913; re-opened 1 September 1913 at the Knickerbocker Theatre and closed 20 September 1913 after a total of 181 performances.

CAST: *Lord Bicester*, known as "Bingo," a young stockbroker: VERNON CASTLE. *Vernon Blundell*: ALAN MUDIE. *Schlump*, an ex-four-wheeler driver, now tramping from Land's End to John O'Groats: JOSEPH CAWTHORN. *Steve Daly*, an American, in the advertising department: TOM LEWIS. *Hudson*, Chief Manager of the Works at Soaptown: E. [Edward] Soldene Powell. *Stepnyak*, Manager of the Continental Department: J. J. Horwitz. *Whitney*, Manager of the British Department: Edward C. Yeager. *Dever*, Manager of the Manufacturing Department: Joseph Tullar. *Wears*, Manager of the Colonial Department: Edwin Stone. *Dora Dale*: JULIA SANDERSON. *Lady Rosabelle Merrydew*, Lord Bicester's fiancée: EILEEN KEARNEY. *Mrs. Blacker*, Schlump's wife, calling herself by her maiden name: EVA DAVENPORT. *Marie Silvaine*, head of the Packing Department at the Works: FLOSSIE HOPE. *Lady Mary*: Ruth Thorpe. *Heads of Various Departments (5)*: *Kate*: Florence Deshon. *Alice*: Eleanor Rasmussen. *Sybil*: Irene Hopping. *Violet*: Constance Hunt. *Lily*: Dorothy Berry. *Boggs*, photographer: Dickson Elliott. *Williams*, solicitor: Russell Griswold. *Swell*: Harry Law. *Suffragette*: *Policemen*: Lew Leroy, William T. Francis, Jr. *Flunkeys*: Charles L. McGee, Owen Jones. (*Dance Specialty*: Mrs. VERNON [Irene] CASTLE.)

Act 1: Port Sunshine. (Albert.)

Act 2: Mr. Blundell's Private House at Port Sunshine. (Emens.)

---

[60]Costumes uncredited.
[61]Not in performance order. All songs were performed by Chauncey Olcott.

ACT 1

Opening Chorus (When You Want a Cake of Soap)

"Get a Move On"
F. Hope, Factory Girls

"Josephine"
V. Castle, Chorus

"You and I" (Duet)
J. Sanderson, A. Mudie

"(The) Kitchen Range" (Duet)
T. Lewis, E. Davenport
(Lyrics by Paul Rubens.)

"Chorus of Welcome"
Ensemble

"Ladies'" (Duet)
V. Castle, J. Sanderson
(Lyrics by Arthur Wimperis.)

"Nuts"
F. Hope, J. Cawthorn

"(A) Tiny Touch" (Song)
J. Sanderson, Factory Girls

Finale

ACT 2

Opening Chorus

"Here's to Love"
R. Thorpe, Chorus
(Lyrics by Arthur Wimperis.)

"The Butler" (Sextette)
F. Hope, E. Davenport, E. Kearney, T. Lewis, V. Castle, J. Cawthorn

"Take Me For—"[62] (Song)
J. Sanderson, Chorus
(Lyrics by Paul Rubens.)

"You Can't Play Every Instrument in the Band"
J. Cawthorn
(Music by John Golden. Lyrics by Joseph Cawthorn.)

"Little Girl, Mind How You Go" (Song)
V. Castle, Chorus
(Lyrics by Paul Rubens.)

"Little Girl" (Dance)
I. Castle

"Who's the Boss" (Quartette)
A. Mudie, V. Castle, T. Lewis, J. Cawthorn

"Miss Blush" (Song)
J. Sanderson, Chorus

Musical Selection
J. Cawthorn

"In Your Defense"
V. Castle, J. Cawthorn

"I've Been to America" (Song)
E. Davenport, Chorus

"(The Argentine) Tango" (Duet)
A. Mudie, J. Sanderson

Finale

1913.05 THE HONEYMOON EXPRESS

A Spectacular Farce with Music in Two Acts, 6 Scenes. Book by Joseph W. Herbert. Music by Jean Schwartz. Lyrics by Harold Atteridge. Staged by Ned Wayburn. Scenery by Theodore Reisig, William Little. Costumes designed by Melville Ellis. Orchestra under the direction of Oscar Radin. Orchestrations by Frank Saddler. Produced by the Winter Garden Company. (Messrs. Shubert.) Opened 6 February 1913 at the Winter Garden and closed 14 June 1913 after 156 performances. (Second edition opened 28 April 1913)

CAST: Henri Dubonet: ERNEST GLENDINNING. Pierre, his friend: HARRY FOX. Baudry, a lawyer: HARRY PILCER. Gardonne, hotel keeper at Arignon: Lou Anger.

---

[62]Replaced early in the run by:
"Good-Bye to Flirtation" (Song)
J. Sanderson, Male Chorus

Gus, butler at Dubonet's: AL JOLSON. Doctor D'Zuvay: MELVILLE ELLIS. Bachelor Friends of Henri Dubonet (6): Achille: Frank Holmes. Eduard: Robert Hastings. Gautier: Gerald McDonald. Constant: Jack Carleton. Paul: Henry Dyer. Guillaume: Clint Russell. Felix, a gateman: Harry Wardell. Alfonse, Gaston, Expressmen: HARLAND DIXON, JAMES DOYLE. Maurice, a poster painter: Owen Baxter. Yvonne, wife of Henri: GABY DESLYS. Mme. de Bressie, Yvonne's aunt: ADA LEWIS. Marguerite, Gardonne's daughter: YANCSI DOLLY. Marcelle, a domestic: FANNIE BRICE. Marcus, a waiter: Gilbert Watson. Noelie, a maid: Marjorie Lane.

Personnel of the Chorus: Misses Kelcey Staunton, Jane Arrol, Dorothy Page, Jeanette Murray, Helen Broderick, Marjorie Lane, Frankie Lee, Sadie Carr, Lillian West, Lillian Baker, Laura Hastings, Gladys Breston, Florence Kern, Noelie Dolores, Catherine Hurst, Mabel d'Elmar, Maudie Worden, Peggy Whitney, Ella Vincent, Geraldine Taylor, Grace Henry, Dorothy Armstrong, Nan Fredericks, Madeline Frain, Stella Brindley, Lois Moncrief, Oliver Horner, Mignon Rozelle, Louise Owen, Florence Coleman, Ethel Wheeler, Minerva Walton, Alma Braham, Madelein Russe, Helen Mooney, Bobbie Roberts, Clara Whiteford, Agnes Richter, Bessie Burch, Babe Dakin, Heloise Sheppard, Marie Leonard, Gracie Falk, Bessie Shannon, Veva DeFord, Laura Gaynelle, Tao Howard, Bessie Holbrook. Messrs. Sven Erick, Clint Russell, Paul Moore, Gerald McDonald, Jack Carleton, Henry Dyer, Robert Hastings, Howard Stevens, Louis Van Blake, Gilbert Wilson, Harry Wilcox, Frank Holmes, Toby Lyons, John Kusky, Dave Marshall.

Act 1, Scene 1: Grounds of Cercle du Sports, at rear of Dubonet's Villa. Scene 2: Railway Station at Etretat. (Little.) Scene 3: The Junction at Rouen.

Act 2, Scene 1: Henri's Apartments, Paris. Scene 2: Corridor leading to Henri's Apartments. Scene 3: Lobby of the Grand Opera House, Paris.

ACT 1[63]

Scene 1

"Tennis Tournament" (Opening Chorus)
Entire Chorus

"That Is the Life for Me"[64] (This Is the Life for Me)
H. Fox, Chorus

"The Moving Man" (Don't Take My Baby Grand)
J. Doyle, H. Dixon, Chorus
(Music by Al W. Brown.)

"When the Honey Moon Stops Shining"
G. Deslys, Show Girls

"Syncopatia Land"
F. Brice, Chorus

"You'll Call the Next Love the First"
G. Deslys, H. Pilcer

"I Want the Strolling Good"
Y. Dolly, Male Chorus

"The Rag Time Express"
E. Glendinning, Chorus

Scene 2

"That Gal of Mine"
A. Jolson

"Up on the Hudson Shore" (Give Me the Hudson Shore)
A. Jolson
(Music by Al Jolson.)

ACT 2

Scene 1

"Coco-Cola Belle"[65] (My Cocoa-Cola Belle)
F. Brice

"The Same One They Picked for Me"[66] (You Are the Someone)
H. Fox, Y. Dolly

Pianologue
M. Ellis

---

[63]Interpolated as per published sheet music:
"On the Honeymoon Express"
Artie Mehlinger
(Music by James Kendis and Frank Stillwell. Lyrics by Lou Klein.)
"You're a Good Little Devil"
G. Deslys, H. Pilcer
(Music by Joe Cooper. Lyrics by Edgar Leslie and Lew Cooper.)

[64]Dropped for subsequent tour.

[65]Replaced for subsequent tour by:
"I Haven't Seen the Little Fellow Since"
Rae Samuels (Marcelle)

[66]Dropped for subsequent tour.

Scene 2

"I Want a Toy Soldier Man"
    J. Doyle, H. Dixon, Chorus
"A Little Cabaret at Home"[67] (Our Little Cabaret Up Home)
    H. Fox

Scene 3

"The Oriental Bacchanale" [Egyptian Ballet]
    H. Pilcer, Y. Dolly, Chorus
    (*Music by* Alexander Borodin. *Staged by* Theodore Kosloff. *Costumes designed by* Robert Edmond Jones.)
"Bring Back Your Love"[68]
    G. Deslys, E. Glendinning, M. Ellis
"My Raggydore"
    F. Brice, Chorus
"(My) Yellow Jacket Girl"[69]
    A. Jolson, M. Hill, Chorus
"When Gaby Did the Gaby Glide"
    G. Deslys, H. Pilcer, Chorus
Finale
    Ensemble

1913.06 THE AMERICAN MAID

A Comic Opera in Three Acts. Book (and lyrics) by Leonard Liebling. Music by John Philip Sousa. Staged by George Marion. Scenery painted by Homer F. Emens. Costumes by Elsie DeWolfe, Wachner and Company. Orchestra under the direction of Herbert Kerr. Produced by John Cort. Opened March 3 1913 at the Broadway Theatre and closed 15 March 1913 after 16 performances.

CAST: *Jack Bartlett*: JOHN PARK. *Duke of Branford*: CHARLES BROWN. *Silas Pompton*: Edward Wade. *Stumpy*: GEORGIE MACK. *Colonel Vandeveer*: George O'Donnell. *Lefty McCarty*: JOHN G. SPARKS. *Annabel Vandeveer*: LOUISE GUNNING. *Geraldine Pompton*: DOROTHY MAYNARD. *Mrs. Pompton*: Maude Turner Gordon. *Mrs. Vandeveer*: ADELE ARCHER. *Rose Green*: MARGUERITE FARRELL. *Nellie Brown*: Mary Smith. *Hans Hippel*: H. Hooper. *Pietrio Nuttino*: Pietro Canova. *Cawkins*: J. Kern.

    Receiving at Mrs. Vandeveer's: Gladys: Katherine Stossel. *Helen*: Julia Bruns. *Alice*: Amy Russell. *Veronica*: Nellie Could. *Hazel*: Marie Elliott. *Madge*: Marjorie Edwards. *Edith*: Neomi Sumers. *Mabel*: Marie Dolber. *Beatrice*: Irma Bertrand. *Irene*: Carrie Lauders.

    Footman: Albert Sachs. *First Glassblower*: James Yunch. *Second Glassblower*: Ella Yunch. *A Batchman*: George Wilson. *Six Maids*: Misses McKay, Barnban, Sullivan, Jordan, M. Sullivan, Brown. *Factory Girls, Boys, Glassblowers, Teasers, Batchmen, Cuban Girls, Red Cross Nurses, United States Volunteers.*

---

[67]Replaced for subsequent tour by:
    "Adam and Eve"
        R. Samuels
[68]Replaced for subsequent tour by:
    "Where the Red, Red Roses Grow"
        A. Wheaton (Marguerite), Earl Benham (Eaudry)
[69]Jolson's Specialty Songs included:
    "The Spaniard That Blighted My Life"
        (*Music and Lyrics by* Billy Merson.)
    For the Second Edition:
    "You Made Me Love You" (also in THE PASSING SHOW OF 1913)
        (*Music by* James V. Monaco. *Lyrics by* Joseph McCarthy.)
    "Good-Bye, Boys"
        (*Music by* Harry Von Tilzer. *Lyrics by* Andrew B. Sterling, William Jerome.)
    "I Love Her (Oh! Oh! Oh!)"
        (*Music by* James V. Monaco. *Lyrics by* Joseph McCarthy, E. P. Morgan.)
    "Down Where the Tennessee Flows"
        (*Music by* Bert L. Rule. *Lyrics by* Ray Sherwood.)
    And for the subsequent national tour they included:
    "He's Have to Get Under—Get Out and Get Under" (introduced in THE PLEASURE SEEKERS)
        (*Music by* Maurice Abrahams. *Lyrics by* Grant Clarke and Edgar Leslie.)
    "I'm on My Way to Mandalay"
    "Who Paid the Rent for Mrs. Rip Van Winkle?"
        (*Music by* Fred Fisher. *Lyrics by* Alfred Bryan.)
    "While They Were Dancing Around"
        (*Music by* James V. Monaco. *Lyrics by* Joseph McCarthy.)

Act 1: Reception at Mrs. Vandeveer's, upper Fifth Avenue, New York. 1898.

Act 2: The Consolidated Glass Works, Greenpoint, Long Island.

Act 3: Camp Jackson, near Santiago, Chile.

ACT 1

Reception Scene at the Vandeveer's
    "Cleopatra's a Strawb'ry Blonde" (Song)
        D. Maynard, C. Brown, Chorus
    "The Matrimonial Mart" (Recitative, Trio and Ensemble)
        L. Gunning, G. O'Donnell, A. Archer
    "This Is My Busy Day" (Vocal Scherzo)
        J. Park, L. Gunning, D. Maynard, C. Brown, A. Archer, Receiving Girls
    "Nevermiore" (Duet)
        J. Park, G. Mack
    "Most Omniscient Maid" (Finale)
        Ensemble

ACT 2

Factory Scene
    "We Chant a Song of Labor"/
    "My Love Is a Blower"
        M. Farrell, M. Smith, G. Mack
    "Cheer Up" (Sextette)
        L. Gunning, D. Maynard, M. Farrell, J. Park, C. Brown, G. Mack
    "The Dinner Pail" (Song)
        J. Park, Male Chorus
    "With Pleasure" (Dance Hilarious)
        J. Park, J. G. Sparks, M. Farrell, Factory Girls
    "The Crystal Lute" (Valse Song)
        L. Gunning
    "The American Girl" (Song and Dance)
        D. Maynard, C. Brown, Chorus
    "From Maine to Oregon (March)" (Finale)
        Ensemble

ACT 3

Orchestra Description:
    "The Bivouac" (Dream Picture)
    "I Can't Get 'Em Up" (Song—Reveille)
        J. Park, Male Chorus
    "When You Change Your Name to Mine" (Song)
        M. Farrell, G. Mack
    "Sweetheart" (Song and Scene)
        L. Gunning, D.Maynard, A. Archer, J. Park, C. Brown, Chorus
    Battle Scene[70] and Ensemble
    Finale

1913.07 MARIE DRESSLER'S ALL STAR GAMBOL

An Entertainment Revue in Two Acts, 11 Scenes. Sketches arranged and compiled by Marie Dressler. Music by A. Baldwin Sloane. Staged by Marie Dressler. Dances arranged by Lester Swerd. Curtains, decorations, costumes designed by Marie Dressler. Orchestra under the direction of Frederick Schwartz. Opened 10 March 1913 at Weber and Fields' Music Hall and closed 15 March 1913 after 8 performances.

CAST: MARIE DRESSLER, CHARLES E. EVANS, JEFFERSON DeANGELIS, ROBERT DROUET, MLLE. YORSKA, May Hopkins, Ethel Fairbanks, Mina Schall, Madge Voe, Frederick Hastings, Arthur Row, Hooper L. Atchley, Harry Weber, Ethel Wilson, Amy Hamlin, Helena Phillips, Mary Desmond, Mlle. Techita, Mlle. Prager, Dorothy Toye, Louise Skillman.

ACT 1

Scene 1

Prologue—Introducing the Heralds of the Muses
    Music: M. Hopkins. *Dance*: E. Fairbanks. *Drama*: M. Schall. *Comedy*: M. Voe.

---

[70]The battle scenes incidental to this production, portraying the Battle of Santiago, were made by the Kalem Company of New York from historical data.

Scene 2

Eddie Rowley (The Greatest Buck and Wing Dancer That Ever Lived)

Scene 3

All at Sea (A Farcical Skit with the comic opera star Jefferson DeAngelis)

Time: Saturday afternoon.

Jack Wall, a broker: J. DeAngelis. *Mrs. Jack Wall,* his wife: M. Voe. *Joseph Newman,* an Alaska mine owner: D. Jarret, Jr. *Captain Shark,* owner of the Yacht "*Nugent*": M. Harlan. *Percy*: H. Weber.

Scene 4

Frederick Hastings (Baritone) in costume arias from "Pagliacci" and other standard operas. Mr. Hastings appeared earlier this season as co-star with Tetrazzinni.

Scene 5

Harry Weber and Ethel Wilson (Sensational Dancers, in a series of original novelties in Terpsichore)

Scene 6

Songs and Recitations:

M. Dressler

"A Great Big Girl Like Me" (Song)(*Lyrics by* Edgar Smith.)

"The Glove" (Recitation with incidental music)

The Prima Donnas of Grand Opera (Burlesque)

ACT 2

Scene 1

The Outpost (A One-Act Military Drama by J. F. Archibald.)

Scene: Jungle in the Philippine Islands.

Jeff: M. Harlan. *Billy*: D. Jarrett, Jr.

Scene 2

Miss Mary Desmond, Contralto, of the Covent Garden Theatre, London

"My Heart Is Weary" (Aria from NADESCHDA)(*Music by* Goring-Thomas.)

"The Silver Ring" (*Music by* Chaminade.)

"Come Back to Erin" (*Music by* Claribel.)

Scene 3

Evolution of Dancing (*Conceived and arranged by* Marie Dressler)

Ancient Greek Dancing

M. Hopkins

Old Fashioned Step Dancing

E. Fairbanks

Original Spanish Dancing

Mlle. Tencita

Classic Toe Dancing

Mlle. Prager

Eccentric Dancing

E. Rowley

Lightning Turkey-Trot

E. Wilson, H. Weber

N.B.: Miss Wilson and Mr. Weber, who were the originators of the Texas Tommy Dance, will introduce that form of cabaret terpsichore in the symposium.

Scene 4

Clam-Ille (A Burlesque on Camille, absolutely conceded to be the funniest bit of nonsense ever presented on the American stage.)

M. Dressler, J. DeAngelis

Scene 5

"Good Night Madrigal"

Entire Company

1913.08 THE BEGGAR STUDENT

A Revival of the Comic Opera in Three Acts, 5 Scenes.[71] (Original Viennese libretto, "Der Bettelstudent," by F. Zell and Richard Genée, based

on Fernande by Victorien Sardou and "The Lady of Lyons" by Edward Bulwer-Lytton.[72]) Music by Carl Millöcker. Staged by William J. Wilson. Dances arranged by Emile Agoust. Scenery by H. Robert Law. Costumes designed by Melville Ellis. Orchestra under the direction of Frank M. Paret. Produced by the Messrs. Shubert and William A. Brady. Opened 22 March 1913 at the Casino Theatre and closed 19 April 1913 after 33 performances.

CAST (in order of appearance): *Puffke, Piffke,* Turnkeys: Harry Smith, Parker Leonard. *Enterich,* a jailer: Arthur Cunningham. *Alexis,* a prisoner: Leo Frankel. *Olga,* his wife: Adelaide Robinson. *Lieutenant Wangerheim*: Paul Farnac. *Major Schweinitz*: Joseph P. Galton. *Major Holzhoff*: Jack Evans. *Captain Henrici*: Robert Millikin. *Ensign Richtofen*: C. A. Hughes. *Lieutenant Poppenburg*: Viola Gillette. *General Ollendorf,* Governor of Cracow: DeWOLF HOPPER. *Symon Symonovicz,* the Beggar Student: GEORGE MacFARLANE. *Janitsky,* a Polish noble: ARTHUR ALDRIDGE. *Mayor of Cracow*: David Heilbrunn. *Countess of Palmatica*: KATE CONDON. *Laura, Bronislava,* her daughters: BLANCHE DUFFIELD, ANNA WHEATON. *Onouphrie,* their servant: OLIN HOWLAND. *Sitzka,* innkeeper: Louis Derman. *Cousins to Palmatica (2): Bogumil*: Charles W. Meyers. *Eva,* his wife: Louise Barthel. *Maid of Honor*: Nina Napier. *Special Dances in Act 2*: Rozsika Dolly, Emile Agoust.

Chorus of prisoners' wives, peasants, noble ladies, pages, merchants' wives, etc.: Cecile Mayo, Trixie Moore, Grace Moore, Betty Marshall, Marion Earle, Elisabeth Warde, Lucille Monroe, Ethel Roslyn, Mildred Jackson, Dorothy Duncan, Nemo Ormston, Violet Lawson, Constance Talbot, Nellie DeGrossart, Elsie Mitchell, Gladys Macdonald, Helen Steele, Ella Evans, Millie Dupree, Anna Savce, Maude Preston, Eva McKenzie, Lavinia Miller, Bessie Fisher, Rosamund Rankin, Janette Cook, Florence Hart, Bessie Nelligan, Anita Baretto, Marjory Purcell, Shirley Love, Helen Marche, Helen Neilsen. *Chorus of prisoners, soldiers, merchants, officers, etc.*: Messrs. Litchfield, Derman, Stein, Smith, Rose, Curran, William, Reyborn, Hamilton, Jaffe, Walker, Clay, Mack, Frankel, Heilbrunn, Mayer, Shannon, Dolan, Cody, Cronan, Rice, Zerbee, Max, Edwin, Bryant, M. Rose, Stuart, Hart, Warshaw, Benedict, Bendall.

Dancers: Premiere Dancers: EMILE AGOUST, ROZSIKA DOLLY. *Ballet*: Cecile Mayo, Eva McKenzie, Millie Dupree, Nellie DeGrossart, Ella Evans, Mildred Jackson, Nemo, Ormston. Messrs. Edwin, Stein, Williams, Curran, Mack, Hamilton, Cody, Smith.

1913.09 THE GEISHA

A Revival of the Japanese Musical Play (Musical Comedy) in Two Acts.[73] Book by Owen Hall. Music by Sidney Jones. Lyrics by Henry Greenbank. Production staged by Edwin T. Emery. Scenery by Theodore Reisig. Costumes by Melville Ellis. Musical director, Gaetano Merola. Produced by Arthur Hammerstein and the Messrs. Shubert. Opened 27 March 1913 at the 44th Street Theatre and closed 10 May 1913 after 52 performances.

CAST (in order of appearance): *Wun Hi,* Proprietor of the Tea House: JAMES T. POWERS. *Arthur Brownville*: Bert Young. *Officers of the H.M.S. Turtle (3): Tommy Stanley,* Midshipman: Cecil Renard. *Dick Cunningham*: CHARLES KING. *Reginald Fairfax*: CARL GANTVOORT. *Nami,* Wave of the Sea: Irene Cassini. *Juliet,* French interpreter attendant: GEORGIA CAINE. *Marquis Imari,* Governor of the Province and Chief of Police: EDWIN STEVENS. *Takemini,* his attendant: George Williams. *Guests of Lady Constance (3): Ethel Hurst*: Florence Topham. *Mabel Grant*: Jane Burdett. *Marie Worthington*: Grace Bradford. *Lady Constance Wynne,* travelling in her yacht: PAULINE HALL. *O Mimosa San,* Chief Geisha: ALICE ZEPPILLI. *Churia,* Coolie of the Rickshaw: Eugene Roder. *Captain Katana* of the Governor's Guard: FRANK POLLOCK. *Molly Seamore*: LINA ABARBANELL. *Geishas (4): Blossom*: Zetta Metchik. *Golden Harp*: Olga Harting. *Chrysanthemum*: Alice Baldwin. *Little Violet*: Edith Thayer. *Attendants (4): Koko San*: Anna Ailion. *Hanna San*: Amelia Rose. *Reto San*: Suzanne Douglas. *Saki San*: Nellie Ford.

English Girls: Vilma Roberts, Elsie Waller, Grace Williams, Marion Thompson, Berdice McLaughlin, Jeanne Daws, Blanche Netta. *Coolie Dancing Girls*: Ruby Lewis, Ethel Merrillies, Emily Saunders, Marjorie Cummer, Jessie Lewis, Elizabeth West. *Tea Girls*: Lily Norton, Blanche, Blanche Barnes, Gladys Coleman, May Whitney, Nellie Chick, Austina Mason, Helena Baird, Louise Chanfrau, Marie Heutte, Nel Jenkins, Alberta Masters, Alice Evanston, Hortense Ireland, Lucy Todd. *Officers*: Ted Sullivan, Arthur Spencer, Robert Harberson, Fred Bradbury,

---

[71]Originally produced in New York in German 19 October 1883 at the Thalia Theatre, and in English 29 October 1883 at the Casino Theatre for 107 performances. For Synopsis of Scenes and Musical Numbers, see original 29 October 1883 production. Musical numbers not listed in program; Dances in Act 2:

Polka Mazurka

Corps de Ballet

Valse Ennivrante

R. Dolly, E. Agoust

March of the Tambourines

Corps de Ballet; R. Dolly, E. Agoust (solos)

[72]English libretto adaptation uncredited.

[73]First presented in New York 9 September 1896 at Daly's Theatre for 161 performances. For Synopsis of Scenes and Musical Numbers, see original 1896 production.

Nat Webster, A. H. McCurdy. *Coolie Men: Noblemen and Soldiers*: Max Dorfman, Jack Howard, Harry Sachs, N. Agnini, Sol Singlust, Arthur Stapleton, Frank Wayne, Eugene Podget, S. Annisman, W. Wagman, Harry Erschof, Ed. Wheelahan.

1913.10

THE PURPLE ROAD

An Operatic Romance in Two Acts and an Epilogue. Book and lyrics by Fred deGrésac [Mme. Victor Maurel] and William Cary Duncan. (Based on the original Viennese singspiel 'Napoleon und die Frauen,' libretto by Heinrich Reinhardt.) Music by Heinrich Reinhardt and William Frederick Peters.[74] Directed by E. P. Temple and George Marion. Scenery designed by Walter H. Harvey, P. Dodd Ackerman. Costumes by the Orange Manufacturing Company. Orchestra under the direction of Gustave Salzer. Produced by Joseph M. Gaites. Opened 7 April 1913 at the Liberty Theatre, moved 16 June 1913 to the Casino Theatre and closed 2 August 1913 after 136 performances.

CAST: *Act 1: Napoleon*: HARRISON BROCKBANK. *Colonel Stappe*, an Austrian patriot: EDWARD MARTINDEL. *French Officers (3): Major*: Horace J. Hain. *Captain*: Jerome Van Norden. *Lieutenant*: John Maddern. *Bridegrooms (3): Pappi*: HAROLD H. FORDE [Hal Forde]. *Bisco*: CLIFTON WEBB. *Franz*: Frank Grom. *Rouston*, The Marmeluke: Robert Smith. *A Soldier*: B. Brennan. *Wanda*: VALLI VALLI. *Frau Stimmer*: ELITA PROCTOR OTIS. *Eight Brides: Kathi*: EVA FALLON. *Lori*: Anna Wilkes. *Ophelia*: Mabel Parmalee. *Paula*: Annabelle Dennison. *Theresa*: Elsa Lynn. *Bertha*: Evelyn Grahme. *Mitzi*: Elsie Braun. *Stephanie*: Winnie Brandon. *Chorus of Bridegrooms, Porters, Austrian Soldiers, Peasants, etc.*.

ACT 2: *Napoleon*: HARRISON BROCKBANK. *Talleyrand*: EDWARD MARTINDEL. *Fouche*: William J. Ferguson. *Murat*: John Maddern. *Bernadotte*: John Ward. *Constant*, valet to Napoleon: Horace J. Hain. *Vestris*, dancing master: CLIFTON WEBB. *Pappi*: HAROLD H. FORDE. *Constant*, valet to Napoleon: Horace J. Hain. *The Empress Josephine*: JANET BEECHER. *The Princess Lugano*: Annabelle Dennison. *The Duchess of Dantzic*: Harriet Burt. *Wanda*: VALLI VALLI. *Kathi*: EVA FALLON. *Page to the Empress*: Anna Wilkes. *Anita Carina*, prima ballerina: Emilie Lea. *Chorus of Grand Dames, Diplomats, Officers, Pages, Courtiers and Servants.*

Epilogue: Richard: Jerome Van Norden. *Sidney*: EDWARD MARTINDEL. *Wanda*: VALLI VALLI.

Act 1: Courtyard of The Cloister Inn (formerly a monastery), in the Village of Schonbrun, near Vienna. 1808. (Harvey.)

Act 2: A Room in the Tuilleries—Napoleon's Palace, Paris. 1809. (Harvey.)

Epilogue: The Island of St. Helena. 1821. (Ackerman.)

ACT 1

"When Someone Marries Me" (Opening Ensemble)
    E. Fallon, Brides, E. P. Otis
    (*Music by* William Frederick Peters.)

"March of the Bridegrooms"
    Ensemble
    (*Music by* William Frederick Peters.)

"The Mysterious Kiss" (Aria and Scene)
    V. Valli, Ensemble
    (*Music by* William Frederick Peters.)

"Feed Me with Love" (Duo)
    H. Forde, E. Fallon
    (*Music by* Heinrich Reinhardt.)

"The Love Spell" (Duo)
    H. Brockbank, V. Valli

"Austrian Patrol"
    Orchestra
    (*Music by* William Frederick Peters.)/

"I Am All Alone"
    V. Valli
    (*Music by* Heinrich Reinhardt.)

ACT 2

Opening Ensemble
    C. Webb, E. Lea, A. Dennison

"The Break-Neck Quadrille"
    Entire Ensemble
    (*Music by* William Frederick Peters.)/

"A Hit in Paris" (To Make a Hit in Par-ee)
    (Musical Scene and Dance)

---

[74]Reinhardt composed the original score, and Peters provided the American interpolations.

H. Burt, Ensemble
    (*Music by* William Frederick Peters.)

"Diplomacy" (Song)
    E. Martindel, Ensemble
    (*Music by* William Frederick Peters. *Lyrics by* William Cary Duncan.)

"Pretty Little Chichis" (Wicked Little Chichis)
    E. Fallon, Ensemble
    (*Music by* William Frederick Peters.)

"Be Mine, Be Mine"[75] (Duo)
    V. Valli, H. Brockbank

"Dear Little Pages" (Five Little Pages)
    A. Walker, Pages
    (*Music by* William Frederick Peters. *Lyrics by* William Cary Duncan.)

"Irresistible" Soliloquy[76] (I Am Simply Irresistible)
    H. Forde

Specialty Dance[77]
    E. Lea

Finale
    H. Brockbank, J. Beecher, V. Valli, All Principals, Ensemble
    (*Music by* William Frederick Peters.)

EPILOGUE

Intermezzo

"The Reaper's Chorus" (Song of the Reapers)
    Ensemble
    (*Music by* William Frederick Peters.)

"He Is Gone"
    V. Valli

1913.11

THE MIKADO,
or The Town of Titipu

A Revival of the Comic Opera in Two Acts.[78] Libretto by William S. Gilbert. Music by Arthur Sullivan. Staged by William G. Stewart. Scenery by H. Robert Law. Costumes by Mme. Ripley, Max & Mahieu. Orchestra conducted by Frank M. Paret. Produced by William A. Brady and the Messrs. Shubert. Opened 21 April 1913 at the Casino Theatre and closed 3 May 1913 after 16 performances.

CAST: *The Mikado of Japan*: GEORGE MacFARLANE. *Nanki-Poo*, his son disguised as a wandering minstrel, in love with Yum-Yum: ARTHUR ALDRIDGE. *Ko-Ko*, Lord High Executioner of Titipu: DeWOLF HOPPER. *Pooh-Bah*, Lord High Everything Else: ARTHUR CUNNINGHAM. *Pish-Tush*, a Noble Lord: WILLIAM G. STEWART. *Three Sisters, Wards of Ko-Ko: Yum-Yum*: GLADYS CALDWELL. *Pitti-Sing*: ANNA WHEATON. *Peep-Bo*: LOUISE BARTHEL. *Katisha*, an Elderly Lady in love with Naki-Poo: KATE CONDON.

School Girls: Misses Cecile Mayo, Trixie Moore, Grace Moore, Betty Marshall, Adelaide Robinson, Marion Earle, Elizabeth Warde, Lucille Monroe, Ethel Duffield, Mildred Jackson, Dorothy Duncan, Nemo Ormston, Violet Lawson, Constance Talbot, Nellie DeGrossart, Laverne Miller, Bessie Nelligan, Marjory Purcell. *Nobles and Attendants*: Messrs. Litchfield, Derman, Stein, Rose, S. Smit Curran, Leonard, Williams, Millikin, Shannon, Dolan, MacSorley, M. Rose, Evans, Hamilton, Frankee, Hughes, Clay, Jeffe, Bryant, Masour, Mack, Heilbrun, Patterson, Reyborn.

1913.12

H.M.S. PINAFORE,
or The Lass That Loved a Sailor

A Revival of the Comic Opera in Two Acts.[79] Libretto by William S. Gilbert. Music by Arthur Sullivan. Staged by William J. Wilson. Scenery by H.

---

[75]Replaced during the run by:
    "In the Valley of Beautiful Dreams"
        V. Valli

[76]Dropped for subsequent tour.

[77]Dropped for subsequent tour.

[78]First presented in New York 20 July, 10-29 August 1885 at the Union Square and People's Theatres for 22 performances. First authorized production presented 19 August 1885 at the Fifth Avenue Theatre by Richard D'Oyly Carte for 250 performances. For Synopsis of Scenes and Musical Numbers, see 19 August 1885 D'Oyly Carte production.

[79]Originally presented in New York 15 January 1879 at the Standard Theatre for 175 performances. For Synopsis of Scenes and Musical Numbers, see original 1879 production.

Robert Law. Costumes designed by Melville Ellis. Orchestra under the direction of Frank M. Paret. Produced by William A. Brady and the Messrs. Shubert. Opened 5 May 1913 at the Casino Theatre and closed 10 May 1913 after 8 performances.

CAST: *The Rt. Hon. Sir Joseph Porter, K.C.B.*, First Lord of the Admiralty: RICHARD TEMPLE. *Captain Corcoran*, Commander of the *H.M.S. Pinafore*: GEORGE MacFARLANE. *Ralph Rackstraw*, Able Seaman: ARTHUR ALDRIDGE. *Dick Deadeye*, Able Seaman: DeWOLF HOPPER. *Bill Bobstay*, Boatswain: Arthur Cunningham. *Josephine*, the Captain's Daughter: JOSEPHINE DUNFEE. *Little Buttercup*, Mrs. Cripps, a Portsmouth bum-boat woman: VIOLA GILLETTE. *Hebe*, Sir Joseph's First Cousin: Louise Barthel.

Roster of Chorus: Girls: Misses Cecile Mayo, Betty Marshall, Elsie Mitchell, Lucille Monroe, Camille Truesdale, Nemo Ormston, Violet Lawson, Adele DePerrier, Mildred Jackson, Nellie DeGrossart, Ethel Duffield, Adelaide Robinson, Marian Earle, Dorothy Duncan, Marie Parkes, Valoise Drew, Elmo Carroll, Edna Lee, Ethel Earle, Constance Talbot, Lillian Dirkin, Gladys MacDonald, Elizabeth Ward. *Men*: Messrs. Louis Derman, Billy Williams, Harry Rose, James Curran, Harry Smith, John Cryan, Lew Litchfield, Teddy Stein, Robert Millikin, Lawrence Mack, Stanley Rayborn, Robert Hamilton, Leo Frankel, David Heilbrunn, Albert Masour, Leslie Clay, Jack Evans, Fred Walker, Samuel Glaser, Parker Leonard, Louis Jaffee, Paul Hall, Frank Wilson.

IOLANTHE,
1913.13   or The Peer and the Peri

A Revival of the Comic Opera in Two Acts.[80] Libretto by William S. Gilbert. Music by Arthur Sullivan. Staged by William J. Wilson. Settings by H. Robert Law. Costumes designed by Melville Ellis. Orchestra under the direction of Frank M. Paret. Produced by the Messrs. Shubert and William A. Brady. Opened 12 May 1913 at the Casino Theatre and closed 14 June 1913 after 40 performances.

CAST: *Strephon*, an Arcadian Shepherd: GEORGE MacFARLANE. *The Earl of Mount Ararat*: ARTHUR CUNNINGHAM. *The Earl of Tolloller*: ARTHUR ALDRIDGE. *Private Willis* of the Grenadier Guards: JOHN HENDRICKS. *The Train-Bearer*: Henry Smith. *The Lord Chancellor*: DeWOLF HOPPER. *Iolanthe*, a Fairy, Strephon's Mother: VIOLA GILLETTE. *The Fairy Queen*: KATE CONDON. *Celia*: Anna Wheaton. *Leila*: Louise Barthel. *Fleta*: Nina Napier. *Phyllis*, an Arcadian Shepherdess and Ward in Chancery: CECIL CUNNINGHAM.

Chorus of Fairies: Misses Cecile Mayo, Betty Marshall, Elsie Mitchell, Lucille Monore, Camille Truesdale, Nemo Ormston, Violet Lawson, Adele DePerrier, Mildred Jackson, Nellie DeGrossart, Ethel Duffield, Adelaide Robinson, Marian Earle, Dorothy Duncan, Marie Parkes, Valoise Dre, Elmo Carroll, Edna Lee, Ethel Clarle, Constance Talbot, Lillian Dirkin, Gladys MacDonald, Elizabeth Ward. *Chorus of Peers*: Louis Derman, Billy Williams, Harry Rose, James Curran, Harry Smith, John Cryan, Lew Litchfield, Teddy Stein, Robert Millikin, David Heilbrunn, Albert Masour, Leslie Clay, Jack Evans, Fred Walker, Samuel Glaser, Parker Leonard, Louis Jaffe, Paul Hall, Frank Wilson.

1913.14   MY LITTLE FRIEND

A Musical Farce in Two Acts and a Prologue. From the German (original Viennese book, 'Die kleine Freudlin') by Dr. A. M. Willner and Leo Stein. American adaptation by Harry B. Smith. Music by Oscar Straus. Lyrics by Robert B. Smith. Staged by Herbert Gresham. Dance numbers arranged by Joseph C. Smith. Scenery by D. Frank Dodge and William Castle. Miss Dale's costumes designed by Schneider-Anderson Company. Orchestra under the direction of Antonio DeNovellis. Produced by the Whitney Opera Company (Direction, F. C. Whitney). Opened 19 May 1913 at the New Amsterdam Theatre and closed 7 June 1913 after 24 performances.

CAST: *Count Henry Artois*, a nobleman, heavily mortgaged: FRED WALTON. *Fernand*, his son: CRAUFURD [Crawford] KENT. *Barbasson*, self-made, and proud of it: WILLIAM PRUETTE. *Mme. Barbasson*, with social aspirations: EDITH SINCLAIR. *Claire*, their daughter, in love with Dr. LaFleur: JUANITA FLETCHER. *Louison*, an artist's model: REBA DALE. *Philine*, a florist, secretly married to Fernand: LEILA HUGHES. *Saturnin*, a Latin Quarter poet, in love with Louison: CHARLES ANGELO. *Mouchon*, valet to Barbasson: HARRY MACDONOUGH. *Dr. la Fleur*, Egyptologist: LIONEL HOGARTH. *Margot*, maid to Mme. Barbasson: Mattie Hartz.

Piperlin, a chauffeur: Harry Macdonough, Jr. *Gaby*: Marcia Lawson. *Paulette*: Hallie de Young.

Wedding Guests of the Provincial Aristocracy: Dr. Calineau: Richard M. Simson. *Mme. Calineau*: Grace Bishop. *The Mayor of Mironville*: Maurice Cass. *De Polichard*: Harry Nelson. *Mme. De Polichard*: Cora Williams. *Baron DuBois*: Harold Merriam. *Baroness DuBois*: Helen Gilmore. *Mme. DeBergerac*: Violet McKay. *Colonel De Bergerac*: Harry Lang. *M. Fortune*: Earl Craddock. *The Misses Fortune*: Grace Irving, Harriet de Norma. *Landlord*: Byron Russell. *His Daughters*: Bettie Martin, Delia Hunt, Luella Gateson. *General Duclos*: Elmer Layton. *M. Dupont*: Eugene Padgett. *Mme. Dupont*: Blanche Rice. *Bridesmaids*: Martha Johnson, Irene Palmer, Maude Christie, Violet Whiting, Adelaide Hall, Viola Cain. *School Girls*: Kathryn Sinclair, Vera Chenet, Edna Lee, Vera Pearsall, Irene St. Clair, Rose Baraban, Marie Dobler, Eileine Marshall. *Casino Girls*: Isabel MacLeod, Florence Norman, Lila Holden, Dorothy Stevens, Ethel Thompson, Marcia Hutt. *Wedding Guests, Servants, Villagers, Singers, Poets, Artists*.

Prologue: The Dining-room of Barbasson's Villa at Mironville.

Act 1: Fernand's Bachelor Apartment in the Latin Quarter, Paris.

Act 2: A Villa in the Suburbs of Paris. Six months later.

PROLOGUE
   "The Fast Express" (Sextet)
      F. Walton, W. Pruette, E. Sinclair, J. Fletcher, L. Hogarth,
      H. Macdonough
   "When I Was Young" (Song)
      F. Walton, Ensemble
   "When Cupid Entertains" (Duet and Ensemble)
      J. Fletcher, L. Hogarth, Wedding Guests
   "The Betrothal Kiss" (Finale)

ACT 1
   "Music Hath Charms" (Opening Ensemble)
   "With All Your Faults, We Love You Still" (Duet)
      C. Angelo, R. Dale
   "No Journey's Too Far for a Lover" (Duet)
      L. Hughes, C. Kent
   "Never Take a Step Too Far" (Trio)
      R. Dale, C. Kent, F. Walton
   "My Little Friend" (Solo)
      L. Hughes
   "What You Don't Know Will Do You No Harm" (What You Never Knew)(Duet)
      R. Dale, F. Walton
   "A Bachelor's Song" (Finale and Song)
      C. Kent, L. Hughes, Ensemble

ACT 2
   Opening Reminiscence
      R. Dale, C. Angelo, Chorus
   "Spring Song" (Trio)
      R. Dale, C. Angelo, F. Walton
   "Love the World Over Is Much the Same" (Duet)
      L. Hughes, C. Kent
   "Marriage Is Not What It Used to Be" (Quartet)
      L. Hughes, R. Dale, C. Kent, C. Angelo
   "Advice" (March Sextet)
      F. Walton, H. Macdonough, W. Pruette, C. Kent, C. Angelo,
      L. Hogarth
   Finale

1913.15   MLLE. MODISTE

A Revival of the Comic Opera in Two Acts, 3 Scenes.[81] Book and lyrics by Henry Blossom. Music by Victor Herbert. Staged by Fred G. Latham. Scenery by E. Van Ackerman. Costumes by Adler; Miss Scheff's gowns by Henri Bendel; evening gowns by Stern Brothers. Orchestra under the direction of John Lund. Produced by the Fritzi Scheff Opera Company.

---

[80]First presented in New York 25 November 1882 at the Standard Theatre for 105 performances. For Synopsis of Scenes and Musical Numbers, see original 1882 production.

[81]Originally produced 25 December 1905 at the Knickerbocker Theatre for 202 performances. Musical Numbers not listed in program. For Synopsis of Scenes and Musical Numbers, see original 1905 production.

1913–1914 SEASON

Alma Francis performing "This Gay Paree" in THE LITTLE CAFÉ (Photo: White Studio)
Billy Rose Theatre Collection, New York Public Library for the Performing Arts

Opened 26 May 1913 at the Globe Theatre and closed 14 June 1913 after 24 performances.

CAST (in order of appearance): *Mme. Cecile's Daughters (2)*: *Fanchette*: Maxie McDonald. *Nanette*: Peggy Wood. *Bebe*, Dancer at the Folies Bergère: Inez Bauer. *General Le Marquis de Villefranche*: Gilbert Clayton. *Mrs. Hiram Bent*: BERTHA HOLLY. *Mme. Cecile*, Proprietress of a Parisian hat-shop: MME. GAILLARD. *François*, Porter at Mme. Cecile's: Henry Holt. *Captain Étienne de Bouvray*, his nephew: C. MORTON HORNE. *Lieutenant Rene La Motte*, engaged to Marie Louise: Karl Stall. *Marie Louise de Bouvray*, Étienne's Sister: Florence Martin. *Henry de Bouvray*, Comte de St. Mar: Henry Leone [HENRI LEONI]. *Fifi*: FRITZI SCHEFF. *Hiram Bent*, an American Millionaire: CLAUDE GILLINGWATER. *Gaston*, an Artist, Mme. Cécile's Son: LEO WHITE. *Milliners, Guests, Dancers, Soldiers, Servants.*

Ladies of the Chorus: Misses Jean Brae, Isabella Falconer, Marguerite St. Clair, Dorothy St. Clair, Margaret Vinton, Florence Bowers, Maud LeRoy, Rose Leslie, Lou Donovan, Marjorie Edwards, Lillian Smith, Dolores Parquette, Bettie Cottrell, Minnie Martrit, Grace Hevenor, Annie Boye, Ethel Robbins, Violet Drew, Marie Francis. *Gentlemen of the Chorus*: Messrs. Jack Rose, Irving Finn, William Nau, Fred Hudler, Andrew Guise, Homer Potts, Frank Meyrose, Robert Newman, Charles Williams, Harold Russel, Morris Avery.

1913–1914 SEASON

1913.16

ALL ABOARD

A Musical Comedy in Two Acts, 10 Scenes. Book by Mark Swan. Music by E. Ray Goetz and Malvin Franklin. Lyrics by E. Ray Goetz. Staged by William J. Wilson and W. H. Post. Stage business, dances and effects used in the numbers devised and staged by William J. Wilson. Costumes designed by Melville Ellis. Scenery designed by H. Robert Law. Lighting by David Atchison. Orchestra under the direction of DeWitt C. Coolman. Produced by Lew Fields. Opened 5 June 1913 at Lew Fields' 44th Street Roof Garden Theatre and closed 6 September 1913 after 108 performances.

CAST:[1] *Jan Van Haan*, an old sailor: LEW FIELDS. *Nancy Lee*: GEORGE W. MONROE. *Captain of the ship*: LAWRENCE D'ORSAY. *Marime Sinkavitch*: ZOE BARNETT. *Dick, Mary*, an engaged couple: CARTER DeHAVEN, FLORA PARKER DeHAVEN. *Hook*, a stoker: Nat Fields. *Russell*, a customs officer: WILL PHILBRICK. *Alice Brown*, a traveler: VENITA FITZHUGH. *Tillie Whiteway*: DOLLY CONNELLY. *Mrs. Van Haan*, Jan's wife: Marcia Harris. *Mr. Smooth*, a bunco man: Stephen Maley. *Mr. Ruff*, his pal: RALPH RIGGS. *Purser*: Juan Villasana. *Mr. Scoot*: Arthur Hartley. *Jones*, information clerk: James Grant. *A Bridegroom*: Malcolm Grindell. *Fourth Mate*: Olin Howland. *Carmen*, a Cubist model: Natalie Holt. *Margot*, a dancer: KATHRYN WITCHIE. *Nellie, Nettie*, friends of Alice: Nellie DeGrasse, Emily Miles. *Poor Little Rich Girl*: Pattie Rose. *Florence DeForrest*, candidate for Mayoress (with a past): ZOE BARNETT. *Boss Mahoney*, political leader: GEORGE W. MONROE. *Cyril Mahoney*, the boss' fatherless child: CARTER DeHAVEN. *Harold Hargreaves*, a wronged man: LEW FIELDS.

Personnel of the Chorus: Misses Elsa Reinhardt, Harriet Leidy, Edith Offurt, May Willard, Elaine Hall, Grace Grindell, Nellie DeGrasse, Emily Miles, Florence Cable, Kathryn Peters, Anna Bruecher. Misses Dorothy Bertrand, Marie Milo, Laura Hoffman, Ida Doerge, Inez Borrero, Eunice Hamilton, Carrie Monroe, Hazel Rosewood, Margie Herman, Edna Fenton. Misses Gertrude Rutland, Patricia DeForrest, Adelaide Mason, Myrtle Mayer, Eileen Kreimeier, Pattie Rose, Josephine Fields, Allene Pickard, Esther Rutland, Helen Stewart. Messrs. Van Sand, Luiz, Rush, Hamilton, Goodsby, Hadley, Baun, Gilbert, Cohan.

Act 1, Scene 1: Office of the Around the World Tours Company. *Scene 2*: The Dock. *Scene 3*: Jan dreams of a voyage. *Scene 4*: Jan dreams of Spain. *Scene 5*: Jan dreams of the Sierras.

Act 2, Scene 1: Jan dreams of Holland. *Scene 2*: When Women Rule (by Ned Joyce Heaney): Office of Florence DeForrest, candidate for Mayoress, on the eve of election, year 2013. *Scene 3*: Jan dreams of Cubist art. *Scene 4*: Jan dreams of China. *Scene 5*: Jan wakes up.

ACT 1
"All Aboard" (Opening Chorus)
    Chorus
"Good-Bye, Poor Old Manhattan"
    D. Connelly, Chorus
"Monkey Doodle"[2] (The Monkey Doodle Doo)
    W. Philbrick, Chorus
    (*Music and Lyrics by* Irving Berlin.)
"Mr. Broadway, U.S.A."
    C. DeHaven, Chorus
"Captain Kidd" (Hornpipe)
    R. Riggs, Chorus
"Over the Ocean"
    V. Fitzhugh, Male Chorus
"Honey You Were Made for Me"
    C. DeHaven, F. Parker-DeHaven
    (*Music by* Jack Glogau. *Lyrics by* Earl Carroll.)
"Serafina"
    Z. Barnett, A. Hartley, Chorus
    (*Music by* Joaquin Valverde.)
Dance
    R. Riggs, K. Witchie
"Ragtime Yodeling Man"
    W. Philbrick, Chorus
Finale—Musical Pantomime

---

[1]These characters appear in Jan's dream in various guises.
[2]Replaced during the run by:
    "Wriggly Rag"
        W. Philbrick, Chorus

ACT 2
"Tulip Time"
    V. FitzHugh, Chorus
"In a Garden of Eden for Two"
    C. DeHaven, F. Parker-DeHaven
    (*Music and Lyrics by* E. Ray Goetz.)
"Love Is Just the Same Old Game (in Every Land)"
    F. Parker-DeHaven, Chorus
"(My) Cubist Girl"
    R. Riggs, K. Witchie, N. Holt, Models
Monologue
    G. W. Monroe
"Under the China Moon" (Under the Eastern Moon)
    Z. Barnett, Chorus
    (*Music and Lyrics by* E. Ray Goetz.)
Finale

1913.17

ZIEGFELD FOLLIES OF 1913

A Musical Revue in Two Acts, 14 Scenes.[3] Words (sketches and lyrics) by George V. Hobart. Music by Raymond Hubbell. Additional songs by Gene Buck and Dave Stamper. Staged by Julian Mitchell. Scenery designed by Ernest Albert, Frank Gates, Edward A. Morange, John H. Young. Costumes by Schneider & Anderson. Lighting by Frank Detering. Orchestra under the direction of Frank Darling. Produced by Florenz Ziegfeld. Opened 16 June 1913 at the New Amsterdam Theatre and closed 6 September 1913 after 108 performances.

CAST: ANNA [Ann] PENNINGTON, FRANK TINNEY, LEON ERROL, ELIZA-BETH BRICE, NAT M. WILLS, JOSÉ COLLINS, MAX SCHECK, IAN MacLAREN, MARTIN BROWN, BERNARD DYLLYN, MAY LESLIE, ETHEL AMORITA KELLY, EVELYN CARLTON, FLORENCE NUGENT JEROME, CHARLES PURDY, CHARLES GILMORE, ARTHUR WOODLEY, PETER SWIFT, ERNEST WOODS, WILLIAM LeBRUN, STELLA CHATELAINE, ROSE DOLLY, Murray Queen.

Ladies of the Ensemble: Misses LaPierre, Jessie Crane, Jean Crane, Jessie Lewis, Gabrielle, Virginia, Hennessy, ZaBelle, Howe, Wardell, Marsden, Gros, Wendell, Beverly, Cooke, Barnette, Morris, Hazel Lewis, Ruby Lewis, St. Clair, Hamilton, Harriman, Carmen, Day, Bowman, Hilton, Thompson, Daly, Christy.

ACT 1
Scene 1
    Scene: New York at Night from the Hotel McAlpin Roof.
        Hawkeye, an Indian Chief: I. MacLaren.
Scene 2
"You Must Have Experience"
"Katie Rooney"
    F. N. Jerome, Company
"New York, What's the Matter with You?" (Good Bye My Tango)
    N. M. Wills
"Just You and I and the Moon"
    J. Collins
    (*Music by* Dave Stamper. *Lyrics by* Gene Buck.)
    Scene: The Public Library.
        William Satan: M. Brown. *McSweeney*: B. Dyllyn. *May*: M. Leslie.
        Knowledge Seekers: Misses Lapierre, Jessie Crane, Jean Crane, J. Lewis,
        Gabrielle, Virginia, Hennessy, ZaBelle, Howe, Wardell, Marsden, Gros,
        Wendell, Beverly, Cooke, Barnette. *Knowledge*: E. A. Kelley. *Experience*: E.
        Carlton. *Rosemary Lee*: F. N. Jerome. *Jones*, a citizen: C. Purdy. *Gladys
        Canby*: A. Pennington. *Van Chappington*: N. M. Wills. *Good Little Devils*:
        Misses Morris, H. Lewis, R. Lewis, St. Clair, Hamilton, Harriman, Carmen,
        Day, Bowman, Hilton, Thompson, Daly. *First Waiter*: M. Sheck. *Second
        Waiter*: C. Gilmore. *Mrs. Playfair*: J. Collins.
Scene 3
"Going There"[4] (Going Some)
    E. Brice
    Scene: A Street.

---

[3]The seventh in the annual series of revues produced by Florenz Ziegfeld beginning in 1907. Songs by Hubbel and Hobart except as noted.
[4]Replaced for subsequent tour by:
    "(You're) Never Too Old to Love"
        E. Brice
        (*Music by* Albert Gumble. *Lyrics by* Alfred Bryan, William Jerome.)

Scene 4

   "The Ragtime Suffragette"
     N. Wills, Chorus
   "Everybody Sometime Must Love Someone"[5]
     J. Collins
     (*Music by* Dave Stamper. *Lyrics by* Gene Buck.)
     Scene: Bryant Park.
     Joan of Arc: E. Carlton. *Rafferty*: A. Woodley. *Saul Wright*: L. Errol. *Mac Sweeney*: B. Dyllyn. *Mrs. Playfair*: J. Collins. *Asthma*, a horse: W. LeBrun, M. Queen.

Scene 5

   "If a Table at Rector's Could Talk"[6]
     N. M. Wills
     (*Lyrics by* Will D. Cobb.)
     Scene: September Morn.
     Miss September: A. Pennington.

Scene 6

   Scene: The Subway Station at Steenth Street.
     Ticket Chopper: C. Gilmore. *Saul Wright*: L. Errol. *Ticket Seller*: P. Swift. *Buddy*: F. Tinney. *B. Durham*: E. Woods.

Scene 7

   Dance[7]
     E. A. Kelley
     Scene: The Olio Drop.

Scene 8

   "Panama" (Finale)
     J. Collins, Company
     Scene The Opening of the Panama Canal.

ACT 2

Scene 1

   "Hello, Honey"
     E. Brice
     Scene: Short Circuits on the Telephone.
     Mame, an operator: E. Brice. *Kitty*, another operator: E. A. Kelley. *Secretary Bryan*: P. Swift. *President Wilson*: E. Wood. *A Japanese*: W. LeBrun. *William Satan*: M. Brown. *Rosemary Lee*: F. N. Jerome. *Winifred Fewclose*: E. Carlton. *Mrs. Lushington*: L. Vernon. *John Lushington*: C. Gilmore.

Scene 2

   "Sleep Time, My Honey"
     J. Collins
     Scene: L'Amour, or The Psychological Moment.
     Marie, the wife: J. Collins. *Pierre*, the husband: F. Tinney. *Henri*, the friend: M. Brown. *Fanchon*, the servant: E. Carlton.

Scene 3

   "(I Can Live) Without You"[8]

---

[5]Replaced after opening by:
   "Just a Little Love" (A Little Love, a Little Kiss)
     J. Collins
     (*Music by* Leo Silesu. *Lyrics by* Nilson Fysher, Adrian Ross.)
   For subsequent tour, replaced by:
   "Bye Bye" (Bye and Bye You Will Miss Me)
     J. Collins
     (*Music by* Dave Stamper. *Lyrics by* Gene Buck.)
   Which was later replaced by:
   "Peggy of My Heart" (Peg o' My Heart)
     J. Collins
     (*Music by* Fred Fisher. *Lyrics by* Alfred Bryan.)
[6]For subsequent tour, the following was added to this scene, following "If a Table at Rector's Could Talk":
   Song, Selection from Grand Opera
     N. M. Wills
[7]During the run, this dance was retitled and reset in Spring:
   "Cupid's Dart" (*Music by* Louis Dannenberg)
     E. A. Kelley
[8] Late in the subsequent tour, replaced by:
   "In the Cradle of Love"
     E. Brice, Male Chorus
     (*Music and Lyrics by* J. Leubrie Hill.)

     E. Brice, Male Chorus
     (*Music by* David Stamper. *Lyrics by* Harry Ruby.)
     Scene: Exterior of the French Theatre.[9]

Scene 4

   "Tangoitis" (Dance)
     Tangomaniacs
   "Turkish Trottishness"
     L. Errol, S. Chatelaine
   "(Dance) Classiceccentrique"
     R. Dolly, M. Brown
   "You're Some Girl" (Girls)
     N. M. Wills, Ensemble
     Tangomaniacs: Misses Morris, H. Lewis, Leslie, Christy, St. Clair, R. Lewis, Hamilton, Harriman, Thompson, Carmen, Day, LaPierre, Bowman, Hennessy, Daly, Hilton.

Scene 5

   Specialty
     F. Tinney
     Scene: Theatre Rabelais.

Scene 6

   "Isle d'Amour"[10]
     J. Collins
     (*Music by* Leo Edwards. *Lyrics by* Earl Carroll.)
   Grand Finale
     Company
     Scene: A Room in the Satanic Cabaret.

1913.18   # THE PASSING SHOW OF 1913

A Musical Revue in Two Acts, 12 Scenes. Dialogue (sketches) and lyrics by Harold Atteridge. Music by Jean Schwartz and Albert W. Brown. Staged by Ned Wayburn. Scenery by H. Robert Law. Costumes by Melville Ellis. Orchestra under the direction of Oscar Radin. Orchestrations by Frank Saddler. Produced by the Winter Garden Company (Sam S. and Lee Shubert Inc.). Opened 24 July 1913 at the Winter Garden; Second Edition opened 29 September 1913; production closed 1 November 1913 after 116 performances.

CAST: First Edition: BESSIE CLAYTON, LAURA HAMILTON, WELLINGTON CROSS, LOIS JOSEPHINE, MOLLIE KING, CHARLES KING, GEORGE LeMAIRE, FREDDIE NICE, CHARLES DeHAVEN, GRACE KIMBALL, MAY BOLEY, HERBERT CORTHELL, LEW BRICE, EDWARD BEGLEY, HARRY GIL-FOIL, SYDNEY GRANT, LILLIAN GONNE, FRANK CONROY, TONY HUNT-ING, CORINNE FRANCES, JOHN CHARLES THOMAS, GEORGE HANLON, GEORGE FORD, CHARLOTTE GREENWOOD.

Personnel of the Chorus: Misses Gladys Leroy, Virginia Gunther, Edith Whitney, Clara Stanton, Fay Pulsifer, Blanche Marr, Nell Carrington, Nell Howard, Grace DuBois, Zounie Maury, Mae Dealey, Irene Markey, Carel Orr, Daisy Delmar, Katherine Talbot, Mary Ellison, Muriel Magill, Evelyn Hall, Rose Wertz, Mae Parker, Beatrice Garland, Nina DuBal, Blanche Leslie, Marie Caldwell, Georgica Storm, Dorothy Moran, Marion Mooney, Anna Sayce, Katherine Perry, Margie Dayton, Elsie Froehlich, Alice Van Ryker, Vera Tirrell, Mabel Hill, Rose Quinn, Grace Williams, Vinnie Mason, Georgia Moore, Bessie Shannon, Bessie Gray, Nina Goulette, Lucile Cavanaugh, Gladys Smith, Evelyn Phillips, Irene Spencer, Violet Delmar, Dotty Mantell, Fannie Grant, Helen Lloyd, Jeanette Alpine, Ruth Heil, Mabel Grete, Agnes Hall, Ethel Faber, Clara Aldwyn, Mirian Sanford, Eve Ray, Ethel Ray, Nellie Moyse. Messrs. Al Knight, Andrew Harper, Allen Fagan, Carle Hall, Kenneth Cooley, Ed Campbell, Arthur Whitman, John Kusky, Dudley Farnworth, Ray Strath, Ted Wing, Edgar Pierce, Dick Dickinson, Leslie Powers, Alex Gibson, Henry Detloff.

Second Edition: Mlle. ANNE DANCREY, ARTIE MEHLINGER, HENRY NOR-MAN, HERBERT CORTHELL, FREDDIE NICE, CHARLES DeHAVEN, WELLINGTON CROSS, LOIS JOSEPHINE, MAY BOLEY, MOLLIE KING, CHARLES KING, JOHN CHARLES THOMAS, LAURA HAMILTON, ETHEL HOPKINS, SADIE BURT, GEORGE WHITING, CORINNE FRANCES, BESSIE CLAYTON, EDWARD BEGLEY, HENRY DETLOFF, GEORGE LeMAIRE, FRANK CONROY, SWAN WOOD, GEORGE HANLON, GEORGE FORD.

Personnel of the Chorus: Clara Stanton, Nell Carrington, Katherine Sainpolis, Irene Markey, etc.

---

[9]Later in the run reset in an Italian Garden.
[10]For subsequent tour, replaced by (see footnote above):
   "A Little Love, a Little Kiss" (Just a Little Love)
     J. Collins

FIRST EDITION

ACT 1

Scene 1

Prologue

> The Usher: T. Hunting. The Tired Business Man. Baron Sands: H. Gilfoil. A Modern Poet: H. Corthell.

Scene 2

Opening Chorus
> Chorus

"My Cinderella Girl"
> L. Hamilton, C. DeHaven, F. Nice

"It Won't Be the Same Old Broadway"
> W. Cross, L. Josephine, Chorus

"My Irish Romeo"
> M. King, Chorus
> (Music by Albert W. Brown.)

"When I Want to Settle Down"
> C. King, Chorus

"Ragging the Nursery Rhymes"
> L. Gonne, E. Begley, Chorus
> (Music by Albert W. Brown.)

"(That) Good Old-Fashioned Cakewalk"
> T. Hunting, C. Frances, Principals, Chorus
> (Music by Albert W. Brown, Jean Schwartz.)
> Scene: Tango Square.
>> Charles McNance, A Poor Little Devil: T. Hunting. Bully Billie Burke, who loves the Poor Little Devil: C. Frances. Cinderella Janis: L. Hamilton. Scarecrow Stone: F. Nice. Punkinhead Montgomery: C. DeHaven. Never-Say-Die-Collier: W. Cross. The Sunshine Girl: L. Josephine. The Fair Lillian, who knows how to live 100 years: G. Kimball. Mrs. Potiphar, a Militant Suffragette: M. Boley. Joseph Asche Rayton, the Chrysanthemum Detective: H. Corthell. Parcel Postman: L. Brice. Peg o' My Heart, an Importation: M. King. Michael Rab, a non-talking dog: Himself. An Ex-President: E. Begley. The Man Who Makes Noises: H. Gilfoil. "Woody", the Alleged President: S. Grant. Gaby Gwendolyn, the Fresh Little Rich Girl: L. Gonne. Joe Garson. Always Within the Law: G. LeMaire. Conspiracy Bill, From the Underworld. F. Conroy.

Scene 3

> Scene: Somewhere Else.
>> Joe Garson: G. LeMaire. Conspiracy Bill: F. Conroy. Peg o' My Heart: M. King. Charles McNance: T. Hunting. Bully Billie Burke: C. Frances.

Scene 4

"Reflections"
> G. Hanlon, G. Ford
> Scene: Mrs. Potiphar's Boudoir.
>> Mrs. Potiphar: M. Boley. Mulette, her maid: L. Hamilton. Joseph Asche Rayton: H. Corthell. Her Butler: G. Hanlon. His Reflection: G. Ford.

Scene 5

"Won't You Come Into My Playhouse?"
> C. King, W. Cross

"I Must Have My Way"
> C. Greenwood, S. Grant

"The Working Girl"
> C. Greenwood
> Scene: Incandescent Lane, Broadway.
>> Broadway Jones: C. King. Never-Say-Die-Collier: W. Cross. Baron Sands: H. Gilfoil. A Bell Hop: L. Hamilton. The Underpaid Working Girl, Mary Turner: C. Greenwood. The Fifth Frankforter: S. Grant.

Scene 6

"North, East, G.A.R., South and West"
> Chorus

"The White House Glide"
> B. Clayton, Ballet

"Zatun" (Zatuma)
> S. Wood

"The Golden Stairs of Love"
> W. Cross, L. Josephine, Chorus
> (Music by Jean Schwartz.)

"Tangle Footed Monkey Wrench Dance"
> C. DeHaven, F. Nice

"Inauguration Day"
> C. Frances, Chorus

> Scene: The Capitol Steps. (Scenery conceived by Ned Wayburn.)
>> Joe Garson: G. LeMaire. Conspiracy Bill: F. Conroy. Pavlovnaperdansky: B. Clayton. Fairy Queen Gab, Thought from A-far: C. Greenwood. The Sunshine Girl: L. Josephine. Never-Say-Die-Collier: W. Cross. Office Seekers: C. DeHaven. F. Nice. Zatuma: S. Wood. Mrs. George Monroe Potiphar: M. Boley. A Flying Messenger: G. Kimball. Marc Anthony: H. Corthell. King's English: H. Gilfoil.

ACT 2

Scene 1

"In Romance Land" (Romance Land)
> C. Frances, Chorus
> (Music by Albert W. Brown.)

"Whistling Cowboy Joe"
> L. Gonne, L. Brice, Chorus
> (Music by Albert W. Brown.)

"Strongheart"
> J. C. Thomas, Chorus
> (Music by Albert W. Brown.)

"He Blew on His Bugle-E-OO"
> C. King, Chorus
> Scene: Along the Rio Grande.
>> Bonita from Arizona: C. Frances. Captain Mary Turner of the Suffragette Army: C. Greenwood. 6 from the Suffragette Army: Lieutenant Agnes Lynch Nash: L. Hamilton. Private Maggie Pepper: V. Gunther. Private Patricia Paprika: N. Carrington. Private Letty Lettuce: N. Howard. Private Olive Oil: I. Markey. Peg o' My Heart: M. King. Broadway Jones: L. Brice. Colonel Madras, in command of the Mexican Army: H. Corthell. His Orderly: S. Grant. A Seventh Avenue Barber: L. Brice. The "Sassy Little" Rich Girl: L. Gonne. Joe Garson: G. LeMaire. Conspiracy Bill: F. Conroy. An Indian Brave: J. C. Thomas. Mosquito. in charge of Mexican Army: H. Gilfoil. Merkle McGraw, a Runner: C. DeHaven. Mathewson Meyers, another: F. Nice. Dusty Farnum: E. Begley. Jane, the two-faced nurse: M. Boley.

Scene 2

"Florodora Slide"
> Chorus
> Scene: The Passers-by.
>> Pretty Maidens: Show Girls. Perfect Nuts: Male Chorus.

Scene 3

"Lights and Shadows"
> W. Cross, L. Josephine
> Never-Say-Die-Collier: W. Cross. The Sunshine Girl: L. Josephine.

Scene 4

"The Old Stuff"
> The Phony Ballet
> Scene: A Railway Siding.
>> Joe Garson: G. LeMaire. Conspiracy Bill: F. Conroy. Mrs. Potiphar: M. Boley. Railroad Official: T. Hunting. Chicago Red, His Assistant: H. Dettloff. Slim-String-Bean, alias "English Eddie": E. Begley. Peg o' My Heart: M. King.

Scene 5

"The Dance of the Perfume"
> B. Clayton, Chorus
> Scene: The Indigo Harem.
>> Majah. A Eunuch: J. C. Thomas. The Favorite Dancer: B. Clayton.

Scene 6

> Scene: The Silver Palace.

Finale
> Entire Company

SECOND EDITION

ACT 1[11]

Scene 1

Prologue—Before the Show
> The Usher: A. Mehlinger. The Tired Business Man. Baron Sands: H. Norman. A Modern Poet: H. Corthell.

Scene 2

"Florodora Slide"
> Male Chorus, Show Girls

---

[11]Added for subsequent tour:
> "Winter Garden Girl"
>> C. King, M. King
>> (Music and Lyrics by Bobby Jones.)

"My Irish Romeo"
M. King, Chorus
(*Music by* Albert W. Brown.)
"Ragging the Nursery Rhymes"
L. Hamilton, E. Begley, Chorus
(*Music by* Albert W. Brown.)
Scene: Central Park.
Parcel Postman: C. DeHaven. *Peg o' My Heart,* an Importation: M. King. *Michael Rab,* a non-talking dog: Himself. *The Fair Lillian,* who knows how to live 100 years: G. Kimball. *Mrs. Potiphar,* a Militant Suffragette: M. Boley. *Joseph Asche Rayton,* the Chrysanthemum Detective: H. Corthell. *"Woody",* the Alleged President: A. Mehlinger. *The Man Who Makes Noises:* H. Norman. *Gaby Gwendolyn,* the Fresh Little Rich Girl: L. Hamilton.

Scene 3

Scene: Somewhere Else.
Gaby Gwendolyn: L. Hamilton.

Scene 4

"Reflections"
G. Hanlon, G. Ford
Scene: Mrs. Potiphar's Boudoir.
Mrs. Potiphar: M. Boley. *Mulette,* her maid: E. Hopkins. *Joseph Asche Rayton:* H. Corthell. *Her Butler:* G. Hanlon. *His Reflection:* G. Ford.

Scene 5

"How Do' Do"
G. Whiting, S. Burt
"If You Don't Love Me Why Do You Hang Around?"
G. Whiting, S. Burt
Scene: Incandescent Lane. Broadway.
Broadway Jones: C. King. *Never-Say-Die-Collier:* W. Cross. *Buster Collier:* L. Hamilton. *The Underpaid Working Girl.* Mary Turner: S. Burt. *The Fifth Frankforter:* G. Whiting.

Scene 6

"Oh. You Tango"
Chorus
"Midnight Masquerade"
A. Mehlinger
"When I Want to Settle Down"
C. King, M. King, Chorus
(*Music by* Jean Schwartz.)
"My Cinderella Girl" (Foolish Cinderella Girl)
L. Hamilton, C. DeHaven, F. Nice
"Le Paradis de Mohamet"
A. Dancrey
"It Won't Be the Same Old Broadway"
W. Cross, L. Josephine, Chorus
"(That) Good Old-Fashioned Cakewalk"
Principals, Chorus
(*Music by* Albert W. Brown, Jean Schwartz.)
Scene: Tango Square (*Devised by* Ned Wayburn.)
The Good Little Devil: A. Mehlinger. *Inspector Burke,* alias "Stop Thief": J. C. Thomas. *Broadway Jones:* C. King. *Peg o' My Heart:* M. King. *Cinderella Janis:* L. Hamilton. *Punkinhead Montgomery:* C. DeHaven. *Scarecrow Stone:* F. Nice. *A Famous French Actress* (First American Appearance): A. Dancrey. *The Sunshine Girl:* L. Josephine. *Never-Say-Die-Collier:* W. Cross. *Joe Garson.* Always Within the Law: G. LeMaire. *Conspiracy Bill.* From the Underworld: F. Conroy. *Mrs. Potiphar:* M. Boley.

ACT 2

Scene 1

"The Dance of the Perfume"
W. Cross, B. Clayton, Chorus
Scene: The Indigo Harem.
Majah. A Eunuch: J. C. Thomas. *The Favorite Dancer:* B. Clayton.

Scene 2

"The Butterfly and the Rose"
C. King, M. King
(*Music by* Jean Schwartz.)
Scene: The Passers-by.
Broadway Jones: C. King. *Peg o' My Heart:* M. King.

Scene 3

"Chiffons! Frou Frous!"
A. Dancrey, Chorus
"I'm Looking for a Sweetheart"
A. Dancrey, C. King

"Strongheart"
J. C. Thomas, Chorus
(*Music by* Albert W. Brown.)
Scene: The Mexican Border.
Bonita from Arizona: E. Hopkins. *Captain Mary Turner* of the Suffragette Army: M. Boley. *6 from the Suffragette Army: Lieutenant Agnes Lynch Nash:* L. Hamilton. *Private Maggie Pepper:* C. Stanton. *Private Patricia Paprika:* N. Carrington. *Private Letty Lettuce:* K. Sainpolis. *Private Olive Oil:* I. Markey. *Peg o' My Heart:* M. King. *Bronco Billy:* L. Brice. *The Famous French Actress:* A. Dancrey. *Broadway Jones:* C. King. *Joe Garson:* G. LeMaire. *Conspiracy Bill:* F. Conroy. *Merkle McGraw,* a Runner: C. DeHaven. *Mathewson Meyers,* another: F. Nice. *Madero,* A Knife Thrower: H. Dettloff.

Scene 4

"High Lights"
W. Cross, L. Josephine
Never-Say-Die-Collier: W. Cross. *The Sunshine Girl:* L. Josephine.

Scene 5

"On the Boat"
A. Mehlinger
Scene: A Persian Garden.
The Good Little Devil: A. Mehlinger.

Scene 6

"German Cooking"
G. Whiting
"Love Me While the Lovin' Is Good"
G. Whiting, S. Burt
(*Music by* Harry Von Tilzer. *Lyrics by* Stanley Murphy.)
"Tangle Footed Monkey Wrench Dance"
C. DeHaven, F. Nice
"Zatuma"
S. Wood
"Inauguration Day"
Chorus

Finale

Ensemble
Scene: The Capitol Steps. (*Scenery conceived by* Ned Wayburn.)
Pavlovnaperdansky: B. Clayton. *The Fifth Frankforter:* G. Whiting. *The Underpaid Working Girl:* S. Burt. *Office Seeker:* F. Nice. *Office Seeker:* C. DeHaven. *Zatuma:* S. Wood. *Marc Anthony:* H. Corthell.

1913.19   WHEN DREAMS COME TRUE

A Musical Comedy of Youth in Three Acts, 4 Scenes. Book and lyrics by Philip Bartholomae. Music by Silvio Hein. Staged by Frank Smithson under the personal supervision of Philip Bartholomae. Mr. Santley's dances invented and arranged by Joseph Santley. Scenery by Frank Gates & E. A. Morange. Costumes by B. Altman & Co., Ford Uniform Co., Orange Co., Siedle Studio. Musical director, Hilding Anderson. Produced by Philip Bartholomae. Opened 18 August 1913 at the Lyric Theatre, moved 15 September 1913 to the 44th Street Theatre, and closed 11 October 1913 after 64 performances.

CAST (in order of appearance): *A Sailor:* Thomas Aiken. *Hermann,* a steward: Otto Schrader. *Saranoff:* Saranoff. *Mrs. Hopkins-Davis-Story:* ANN MOONEY. *Hercules Strong,* a detective: EDWARD GARVIE. *Kean Hedges:* JOSEPH SANTLEY. *Beth,* his dream girl: MARIE FLYNN. *Mrs. William Smith:* AMELIA SUMMERVILLE. *Margaret Smith,* her daughter: ANNA WHEATON. *Griggs,* a butler: Clyde Hunnewell. *Jerome K. Hedges,* Kean's father: Frazer Coulter. *Denny,* in love with Margaret: DONALD MACDONALD. *Matilda,* who has a "Black-on-White": MAY VOKES.
Emigrants, Sailors, Policemen, Bridesmaids, Flower Girls, Maids, Ushers, etc.
Personnel of the Chorus: Misses Callahan, Cripps, Fox, Gilmore, Gordon, Hanley, Hastings, Leroy, Kernel, Macy, Mason, Randal, Smith, Stenman, Wolf, Zabelle. Messrs. Clarke, Edwards, George, Gillespie, Murray, Seaton, Squires, Summerville.

Act 1, Scene 1: The emigrant deck of steamship *"Kaiser"* bound for New York. Late afternoon. *Scene 2:* Pier No. 3, North River. Midnight.

Act 2: Hall of Home of Jerome K. Hedges. An hour later.

Act 3: Ballroom in home of Jerome K. Hedges. That evening.

ACT 1

"America"
Emigrants
"It's Great to be a Wonderful Detective"
A. Mooney, E. Garvie, O. Shrader
"The Town That Grows Where the Hudson Flows"

J. Santley, Stewardesses, Sailors

"Dear World"
M. Flynn

"When Dreams Come True"
J. Santley, Saranoff
(*Music by* Silvio Hein, Roy Webb.)

"Y-O-U, Dear, Y-O-U"
M. Flynn, J. Santley

ACT 2

"Wedding Rehearsal"
A. Wheaton, D. Macdonald, Ensemble

"Love Is Such a Funny Little Feeling"
M. Vokes, E. Garvie

"Giddy Up, Giddy Up, Dearie"
M. Flynn, A. Wheaton, J. Santley, D. Macdonald

Finale
Ensemble

ACT 3

"O.K. Two-Step"
Ensemble

"When the Clock Strikes One"
A. Wheaton, D. Macdonald

"Who's the Little Girl?"
M. Flynn, J. Santley, Debutantes
(Introducing the Santley Tango[12] with Miss Randall.)

"There Ain't No Harm in What You Do"
M. Vokes

"The Boy with the Violin"
Saranoff, Violinettes

Waltz
A. Mooney, J. Santley

"Come Along to the Movies"
M. Vokes, A. Wheaton, A. Mooney, J. Santley, E. Garvie, D. Macdonald

"Auction Dance"[13]
Ensemble
"Laughing Water Ripple"
A. Wheaton, J. Santley
"Minnie-Ha-Ha"
M. Vokes, E. Garvie
"Dream Waltz"
M. Flynn, J. Santley

1913.20

THE DOLL GIRL

A Musical Play in Three Acts. Original Viennese ("Das Puppenmädel") libretto by Leo Stein and A. M. Willner, adapted from a play ("Riquette et Sa Mere") by Gaston deCaillavet and Robert deFlers. English book and lyrics by Harry B. Smith. Music by Leo Fall. Dances arranged by Edward Royce; incidental dances in Act 3 by Mazie King. Costumes designed by Comelli. Orchestra under the direction of Gustave Salzer. Produced by Charles Frohman. Opened 25 August 1913 at the Globe Theatre and closed 8 November 1913 after 88 performances.

CAST: *Marquis de la Tourelle*: RICHARD CARLE. *Tiborius*, his nephew: ROBERT EVETT. *Romeo Talmi*, a theatrical manager: WILL WEST. *Buffon*: CHARLES McNAUGHTON. *Daudalon*: Ralph Nairn. *Marcel*, a head waiter: Carl C. Judd. *Pierre*: Victor LeRoy. *Mme. Prunier*: CHERIDAH SIMPSON. *Yvette*: DOROTHY WEBB. *Mlle. Poche*: Emily Francis. *Madame Merlin*: Clara Eckstrom. *Madame Bichon*: Letha Walters. *Mme. Laurent*: Marion Mosby. *Toto*: Veronique Banner. *Heloise*: Veola Harty. *Cora*: Florence Brodbelt. *Belle*: Helen Dudley. *Francine*: Barbara Bel Babas. *Suzette*: Alice Palmer. *Lily*: Lilian Leroy. *Perinne*: Edith Hardlow. (*Dance Specialty*: Mazie King.)
Other characters by Misses Edith P. Allen, Edith Burch, Alice Carrington, Constance Crane, Selma Mantell, Edith Barr. Ethel Milton, Laura Harland, Louise Astor, Maude Christy, Carolyn Burke, Anna Monette, Adelaide Hall, Mabel Gebeau, Dency Watson, Fannie Hasbrouck, Helen Fell, Adrienne Allen, Blanche Lipton. Messrs. Roger Davis, Victor LeRoy, Radford D'Orsay, Theodore Stein, John W.

Walker, David Romaine, W. G. Freeman, James A. Smith, Charles Hartman, David Heilbrun, M. A. Carpenter, Edward Coleman, Matthew Crosson, Carl C. Judd, Eugene Shepherd, James B. O'Reilly.

Act 1: Chateau Bercy, a small city in Picardy, France.

Act 2: In Paris, at the Palace of the Marquis de la Tourelle.

Act 3: Exterior of a Restaurant in the Bois de Boulogne.

ACT 1[14]

Opening Chorus

"Now and Then" (Song)
C. Simpson

"What Do They Say, Dolly Dear?" (Song)
D. Webb

"Come On Over Here" (Song)
H. Williams, Chorus
(*Music by* Walter Kollo. *Lyrics by* Jerome Kern and Harry B. Smith.)

"Brittany" (Song)
D. Webb, Chorus

"Will It All End in Smoke?"
R. Evett
(*Music by* Jerome Kern.)

"(If We Were) On Our Honeymoon" (Railway Duet)
D. Webb, D. Evett
(*Music by* Jerome Kern.)

"A Little Thing Like a Kiss" (Song)
R. Carle, Girls
(*Music by* Jerome Kern.)

"Come On Over Here" (Duet, reprise)
H. Williams, R. Carle

Finale

ACT 2

Opening Chorus (Russian Dance)
(*Music by* Jerome Kern.)

"Papa" (Duet)
D. Webb, R. Carle

"You're So Fascinating" (Song)
H. Williams

"Rosalilla of Seville" (Trio)
H. Williams, R. Carle, R. Evett

"I'm Going Away" (Song)
W. West
(*Music by* Jerome Kern.)

Serenade (Song)
R. Evett, Chorus

"When You're on the Stage" (Quartette)
D. Webb, C. Simpson, R. Carle, R. Evett

Finale

ACT 3

Opening Chorus

"That Ragtime Dinner Band" (Song)
C. McNaughton, Girls
(*Music by* Will E. Haines. *Lyrics by* Wilfred Chandler.)

Dance
M. King

"(That's) Love with a Capitol L" (Song)
H. Williams, the 14 Club
(*Music by* P. H. Christine.)

"At Night" (Trio)
R. Carle, H. Williams, W. West

"When Three Is Company" (Cupid Song)(Duet)
D. Webb, R. Evett
(*Music by* Jerome Kern. *Lyrics by* M. E. Rourke.)

"It Is I" (Song)
R. Evett

Finale

---

[12]For subsequent tour, additional dance specialties, "Triple Trot" and "Cubist Glide" were added.
[13]For subsequent tour, an additional dance specialty, "Tangoitis" was added, replacing "Laughing Water Ripples" and "Minnie-Ha-Ha."

---

[14]Interpolated for subsequent tour, as per published sheet music:
"The Futurist" (Hesitation Waltz)
(*Music by* Edwin Burch.)

1913.21

ADELE

A Musical Comedy in Three Acts. Original French libretto by Paul Hervé.[15] English adaptation by Adolf Philipp and Edward A Paulton. Music by Jean Briquet. Staged by Ben Teal. Scenery designed by Edward G. Unitt and Joseph Wickes. Dresses by B. Altman & Co. Light effects by Kliegl Brothers. Orchestra under the direction of Arthur Weld. Produced by New Era Producing Company (Joseph P. Bickerton, Jr. Managing Director). Opened 28 August 1913 at the Longacre Theatre, moved 29 December 1913 to the Harris Theatre and closed 14 February 1914 after 196 performances.

<u>CAST:</u> *Baron Charles de Chantilly*: HAL FORDE. *Robert Friebur*: CRAUFURD KENT. *Henri Parmaceau*: WILL DANFORTH. *Alfred Friebur*: Dallas Welford. *Jacques*: HARRY C. BRADLEY. *Louis Papricot*: Michael Ring. *Gaston Neuilly*: E. H. Barlab. *Armond Cartouche*: Henry Ward. *Francois*: Charles Frye. *Pierre*: Edward Wooster. *Adele*: NATALIE ALT. *Mme. Myrianne de Neuville*: GEORGIA CAINE. *Babiole*: EDITH BRADFORD. *Violette*: Jane Hall. *Germaine*: Betty Brewster. *Gabrielle*: Grace Walton. *Faustine*: Jane Warrington. *Therese*: Estelle Richmond. *Pauline*: Helen May. *Henriette*: Edna Doddsworth. *Georgette*: Alice York.

Act 1: Bachelor Apartment of the Baron Charles de Chantilly, Paris.

Act 2: Adele's Boudoir. Trouville. One week later.

Act 3: Garden surrounding the hotel. Trouville. One night later.

ACT 1

Opening Number (Solo and Ensemble)
H. Forde, H. C. Bradley, Girls, Men

Quartette and Solo:
"It's Love" (Quartette)
N. Alt, W. Danforth, E. Bradford, H. C. Bradley
"Is It Worth While?" (Solo)
N. Alt

"Adele" (Song)
N. Alt

"Like Swallow Flying" (Duet)
G. Caine, H. Forde

"(A) Honeymoon with You" (Duet)
G. Caine, H. Forde

Finale
"Paris! Good-Bye!" (Solo)
H. Forde
"Adele" (Ensemble)
H. Forde, Girls

ACT 2

"Wedding Bells" (Opening Number)
E. Bradford, H. C. Bradley, Bridesmaids, Ushers

"Yours for Me, and Mine for You" (Quartette and Ensemble)
N. Alt, H. Forde, G. Caine, C. Kent, E. Bradford, H. C. Bradley, Bridesmaids, Ushers

"Matter of Opinion" (Trio)
G. Caine, H. Forde, C. Kent

"Close Your Eyes" (Duet)
H. Forde, N. Alt

"When the Little Birds Are Sleeping" (Duet)
C. Kent, N. Alt

"The Clock Is Striking Ten" (Concerted Number and Solo)
N. Alt, H. Forde, G. Caine, C. Kent, E. Bradford, W. Danforth, D. Welford, H. C. Bradley, Bridesmaids, Ushers

"Yesterday" (Song)
N. Alt

Finale
N. Alt, H. Forde, G. Caine, C. Kent

ACT 3

"You Are a Very Nice Boy"[16] (Song)
G. Caine, C. Kent, Girls, Boys

"Strawberries and Cream" (Duet)
H. Forde, N. Alt

"My Long Lost Love, Lenore" (Song)
W. Danforth

---

[15]So far as Kurt Gänzl (Encyclopedia of Musical Theatre) and this editor can determine, neither Paul Hervé nor Jean Briquet appear to have existed; most likely they are nom de plumes for Adolf Phillipp. Nor does it appear that "Adele" was previously produced in France.
[16]Dropped during the run and replaced by "Gay Soldier Boy."

"Gay Soldier Boy" (Song)
E. Bradford, H. C. Bradley, Girls, Boys

"A Waste of Time to Plan"[17] (Quartette)
N. Alt, H. Forde, G. Caine, C. Kent

Finale

1913.22

AMERICA

A Musical Spectacle in Three Acts, a Prologue and 15 Scenes. Conceived and invented by Arthur Voegtlin. Drama written by John P. Wilson. Music and lyrics by Manuel Klein. Staged by William J. Wilson. Scenic effects by Arthur Voegtlin. Costumes designed by William R. Barnes, Cora MacGeachy, P. J. Mathews. Musical director, Manuel Klein. Produced by the Messrs. Shubert. Opened 30 August 1913 at the Hippodrome and closed 28 March 1914 after 360 performances.

<u>CAST:</u> *Macklin Haywood, an Underground Spy*: ALBERT FROOME. *"Slippery Sam" Croker, Haywood's Pal*: JOSEPH REDMAN. *Lieut. Frank Forsythe, of the U.S. Engineers*: WILLIAM C. REID. *Captain Wilkes, of the U.S. Cavalry*: HARRY L. JACKSON. *Vivian Phillips, Forsythe's Sweetheart*: MAYBELLE McDONALD. *Jason Sellers, a Farm Boy*: FELIX HANEY. *A Yokel*: HARRY LA PEARL. *Sallie Perkins, a Milkmaid*: NELLIE DONER. *Lucy Mortimer, Haywood's Accomplice*: ELSIE BAIRD. *Samantha Stubbs, a Housekeeper*: IRENE WARD. *John Strong, a New England Farmer*: JOHN FOSTER. *Detective Scalds of the Secret Service*: JACK WARREN. *John, the Blacksmith*: E. PERCY PARSONS. *Manager of the Ponce de Leon Hotel*: JOHN FOSTER. *Mrs. Beacon-Hill, a Chaperone*: MARGARET CRAWFORD. *Train Caller*: ALEX CRAIG. *"Cherokee Bill" Phelps, a Western Sheriff*: JOHN FOSTER. *"The Colonel," Commandant at Panama*: E. PERCY PARSONS. *Professor Strunz, an Ethical Instructor*: HAROLD A. ROBE.

(*Other Featured Roles:*) GEORGE ADAMS, SA KO EN TE THA, NINA CHAPMAN, TOMMY MULLINS, ANGEL BARBARA. *Men of the Ensemble*: Eddie Russell, Harry Taylor, John Fleming, Spook Hanson, Jack Pritchard, John Lovely, James Smith, Stanley Ferguson, Harry LaPearl. *Solo Dancers*: Daisy Smythe, Fib Whiteside, Jeanne Ribierre, Von Schettka. *Specialties*: The Wonderful Woodchoppers, The Phyllis Equestrians, The Walthours (Bicyclists), Equila Brothers (Ladder Act).

ACT 1

Prologue

The Landing of Columbus
Columbus: G. Adams. *Priest*: E. P. Parsons. *Indian Chief*: Sa Ko En Te Tha.

Scene 1

Opening
Porters, Callers, Travelers, Chauffeurs, Station Police, Messengers

"Though Hearts We May Secure"
M. Crawford, H. A. Robe

"Good-Bye, Hiram"
College Boys

"My Wife's Gone"
Men

"A Gay Excursion"
M. Crawford, H. A. Robe
Plot to Steal the Fortification Plans by Haywood and Sam. Forsythe to go to the Farm. Haywood on the Trail. Arrival of a Great Excursion Party.

"The U.S.A. Limited"
W. C. Reid, Entire Ensemble

(The Parasol Number)
To East, West, North and South
Scene: Railway Station, Afternoon. In which is depicted with musical accompaniment the Daily Occurrences in a Great Starting Point of Country-Wide Travel.
Chaperone: M. Crawford. *Professor*: H. A. Robe.

Scene 2

"The Girl in the Gingham (Gown)"
E. P. Parsons, M. McDonald, Haywagon Girls, Milkmaids, Haymakers, Farms Hands, etc.
Scene: New England Farm. Dawn.
John: E P. Parsons. *Vivian*: M. McDonald.

Scene 3

Melodies of the Sunny South
Double Quartette

---

[17]Replaced during subsequent tour by:
"Disappointed Love" (Quartette)
Carolyn Thomson (Adele), John Park (Charles), Mae Phelps (Myrianne), Stephen Stott (Robert)

Dancing Ensemble

Overseers

Haywood Pursued. Forsythe and Detective Scalds Arrive. Arrest of Haywood and Sam. The Escape in the Red Auto. The Chase Again.

"Dark Eyes (Am Now A Shinin' for You)"

The Overseers

(*Lyrics by* John P. Wilson.)

With Negroes, Mammies, Swell Colored Folks, Creoles, Cakewalkers, Pickaninnies.

Scene: Levee at New Orleans.

The Overseers: E. Russell, H. Taylor, J. Fleming, S. Hanson, J. Pritchard, J. Lovely, J. Smith, S. Ferguson, H. LaPearl.

Scene 4

Public Plaza and the Historic Alamo. Captain Wilkes ordered to help Forsythe. Episode of Mexican Guide and Chicago Millionaire. Jason and the Peppers. Haywood and Sam to secure Vivian. 'I Will Hold Her as A Club Over Forsythe's Head.'

"Mister Soldier Man" (Everybody Loves a Soldier)

Sextette, Ensemble

Scene: San Antonio.

Millionaire: T. Mullins. *His Wife*: I. Ward. *Guide*: J. Foster. *Con Carne Vendor*: A. Barbara. *Shellfish Vendor*: H. LaPearl.

Scene 5

"Ragtime in the Air"

(Entire Hippodrome Company)

A Typical East Side Street, with its great variety of characters. Jason and Sallie as Detectives. 'We must find Miss Vivian.' Vivian brought to the rendezvous. Jason and Sallie on hand. Multiplicity of humorous and characteristic events in which the entire Hippodrome Company participates. Pushcart Men, White Wings, Shirtwaist Girls, Settlement Workers, East Side Boys and Girls, Country Visitors, Tradesmen, Policemen, Nurses and Interns, Fakirs, Carts and Horses affected by the Turkey Trot Craze.

Scene: A New York Street.

Scene 6

The Suffrage Parade (Replica of the Parade held recently in New York)

Haywood confronted by Forsythe. 'We've found Miss Vivian.' The getaway of Haywood and Lucy in Hansom.

Scene: Another New York Street. Typical fashionable hotel.

Scene 7

General Fire Alarm

Wonderful effect of racing horses pulling complete fire-fighting apparatus.

Scene 8

Fighting the Flames.

Forsythe breaks through cordon of Police and Firemen. Vivian saved by Firemen. Reunion of the lovers.

ACT 2

Scene 1

"Lola (, the Fairest Daughter of Panama)"

Quintette

The Tango

Native Dancers

Great Celebration Parade

(Hippodrome Company)

The Town on the Pacific side of the Isthmus, whose name will ever be associated with the greatest engineering and industrial achievement that the World has ever known. Eve of the Opening of the Great Canal. The Colonel: "The Government trusts you, Mr. Forsythe, as I do." Forsythe to take up the chase again. Message from the President: "The Great Canal to be officially opened." Parade with the Colonel and Staff, Foreign Ambassadors, Military and Naval Attachés, Canal Commission and Their Ladies, Members of Congress, Soldiers, Jackies, Marines, Zone and Panama Police, Senors and Senoritas, Dancers, Fiesta Participants, etc.

Scene: Panama.

Pedro, a Panama swell: J. Redman. *Lola*, the Pearl of Panama: M. McDonald. A *Vaquero*: E. Percy Parsons. *Inez*, Lola's friend: M. Crawford. *Ysabel*, Lola's friend: I. Ward. *Panamanians, Senoritas, Flower Girls, Soldiers*, etc.

Scene 2

First Passage of American Merchant Vessel through the Canal at the Famous Man-Made Gorge of Culebra Cut.

Scene: The Culebra Cut.

Scene 3

("Merry Little Chop Chop"

The Wonderful Woodchoppers)

View of the Great National Reservation in Wyoming, Montana and Idaho. The Encampment. Uncle Sam's Cavalry. The Wonderful Woodchoppers. The Phyllis Equestrians. Arrival of Tourists. Haywood is at the Ponce de Leon, posing as an English Lord. Forsythe and his friends off for Florida.

Scene: The National Park in Three States.

Scene 4

(Aeroplane Number, Fencing Girls, Football Number, Basketball Girls, Baseball Number, Boxing Number, Golf Girls)

Realistic picture of the Famous Resort. The Walthours, Bicyclists. Haywood ejected for cheating at cards. National Sports: Golf, Bicycling, Canoeing, Aviation, Swimming, Yachting, Basket Ball, Foot Ball, Tennis, Boxing, Riding and Baseball.

Scene: Ponce de Leon Hotel, Florida.

Solo Dancers: Smythe, Whiteside, Ribierre, Von Schettka.

Scene 5

The Harvest Dance

Indians, assisted by their Native Band

Invocation to the Spirits

M. Crawford, Spirits, Indian Dancers

Showing Real Indians (Chief Joe White Eagle) of the Southwest at Home. Their Varied Industries. Pottery Making and Painting, Basketmaking, Blanket Weaving, Corn Grinding and Tending Their Flocks and Herds. Their Curious Ceremonial Customs and Dances are also shown, the whole forming an exhibition of exceptional educational value. The Harvest Dance. Gathering the Corn. Grinding the Corn. The Feast. The Bird Mask Clowns. The Touring Party. Haywood and Sam in Flight. Forsythe and Cherokee Bill Phelps pursue. Equilla Brothers (Wonderful Ladder Act).

Scene 6

The Most Awe-inspiring Scene on the American Continent. The Indian, the Real American, oblivious to the strife of Civilization. The Prospectors, Forsythe and Cherokee Bill on the Trail. The Red Auto is seen circling around the precipitous cliffs. It grows in size as it approaches nearer and nearer to the brink of the Great River. With its swift currents and treacherous whirlpools, the Red Auto becomes unmanageable and plunges into the torrent.

Scene: Grand Canyon of the Colorado River.

ACT 3

Court of Honor

(Entire Company)

1913.23   LIEBER AUGUSTIN

An Operetta in Three Acts.[18] Original German libretto ("Der liebe Augustin") by Rudolf Bernauer and Ernest Welisch.[19] American version and lyrics by Edgar Smith. Music by Leo Fall. Staged by J. C. Huffman and Al. Holbook. Dances staged by Julian Alfred. Settings by H. Robert Law and Lee Lash Studios. Costumes designed by Melville Ellis. Orchestra under the direction of John Lund. Produced by the Messrs. Shubert. Opened 3 September 1913 at the Casino Theatre and closed 4 October 1913 after 37 performances.

CAST (in order of appearance): *Jasomir*: Arthur Cunningham. *Sigilioff*: Wilmuth Merkyl. *Anna*: GRACE FIELD. *Marguerita*: Vera Dunn. *Gretchen*: Peggy Caudrey. *Ursula*: Mona Sartoris. *Lisbeth*: Edna Stillwell. *Juro*: Frank Farrington. *Bogumil*: DeWOLF HOPPER. *Augustin Hoffer*: GEORGE MacFARLANE. *Princess Helen*: MAY DeSOUSA. *Captain Pips*: Viola Gillette. *Prince Nikola*: FRED LESLIE. *Clementine*: ROSZIKA DOLLY. *Colonel Burko*: Jack Evans. *Mattoeus*: Wilmuth Merkyl.

Maids at the Palace: Lorraine Bright, Alta Young, Mae Pickard, Corrine Pickard, Ester Channon, Claire Pearl, Gertrude Davenport, Dorothy Scherer, Emma Mcgrath, Marjory Warde, Helen Marche, Catherine Humphrey, Rose Bennett, Blanche Toole, Mildred Jackson, Nellie Degrossart, Maude Crockett, Muroff Allo, Peggy O'Neill, Helen Longfellow, Lucille Monroe, May Tomey, Doris Jeffrey, Edith Hollar, Bessie Hollar, Bessie Barclay, Florence Davidson. *Court Ladies*: Florence Davidson, Bessie Barclay, Lucille Monroe, Doris Jeffrey, Rose Bennett, Helen Marche, Maude Crockett, Blanche Toole, Corinne Pickard, Helen Longfellow, May Tomey, Catherine Humphrey, Mona Sartoris, Mildred Jackson, Edith Hollar, Marjory Warde. *Clementine Girls*: Vera Dunn, Mona Sartoris, Peggy Coudrey, Edna Stillwell, Muroff Allo, Emma McGrath, Alta Young, Mae Pickard, Clare Pearl, Dorothy Scherer, Lorraine Bright, Dixie O'Neill. *Pages*: Mae Pickard, Dixie O'Neill, Dorothy Scherer, Alta Young.

---

[18]Title changed during the run and for subsequent tour to MISS CAPRICE. The original title remained as a subtitle on programs late in the New York run.

[19]"Der liebe Augustin" was a revised version of an earlier failure "Der Rebell" (1905) by Messrs. Bernauer, Welisch and Fall.

Bridesmaids: Misses Allo, Pearl McGrath, Davenport, Young, Coudrey, O'Neill, Bright, Scherer, Pickard. *Male Chorus*: Messrs. Evans, Sullivan, Mack, Centor, Shannon, Dolan, Mason, Hyman, Harvey, Townsend, Williamson, Phillips, M. Rose, H. Rose, Bryant, Reyborn.

Act 1: A room in the Palace of Thessalia. (Law.)

Act 2: Throne room of the Palace. (Lash.)

Act 3: Gateway and Courtyard of the Monastery. (Law.)

ACT 1

Opening Chorus

"Anna"

    G. Field, Chorus

"I'm the Patsy Bolivar of the World"

    D. Hopper

Song ("Take Your Time")

    G. MacFarlane

    (*Lyrics by* Harry Beswick.)

Piano Duet

    M DeSousa, G. MacFarlane

"Why Do They All Make Love to Me?"

    V. Gillette, Chorus

Ensemble

Finale

    M. DeSousa, G. MacFarlane

ACT 2

Opening Ensemble

"Lieber Augustin"

    M. DeSousa

"Clementine"

    R. Dolly, Chorus

"Look in Her Eyes"

    G. MacFarlane, Chorus

"Anna, What's Wrong?" (Trio)

    G. Field, G. MacFarlane, A. Cunningham

Coquetterie Waltz

    R. Dolly, F. Leslie

"If You Were Mine" (Duet)

    M. DeSousa, G. MacFarlane

Finale

ACT 3

Prelude—Angelus

Wedding Bells

    R. Dolly, G. Field, Chorus

"The Truth Must Come Out Some Day"

    D. Hopper

"Do You Like Me Best?" (Trio)

    M. DeSousa, G. Field, A. Cunningham

Finale

1913.24

SWEETHEARTS

A Musical Play in Two Acts. Book by Harry B. Smith and Fred de Grésac.[20] Music by Victor Herbert. Lyrics by Robert B. Smith. Staged by Frederick Latham. Ensemble and dances by Charles S. Morgan, Jr. Scenery painted by D. Frank Dodge and William Castle. Costumes by William Adler and Max & Mahieu. Orchestra under the direction of Charles McGhie. Orchestrations by Victor Herbert. Produced by Louis A. Werba and Mark A. Luescher.[21] Opened 8 September 1913 at the New Amsterdam Theatre, moved 10 November 1913 to the Liberty Theatre, and closed 3 January 1914 after 136 performances.

CAST: The story of the opera is founded on the adventures of Princess Jeanne, daughter of the King Rene of Naples, who reigned in the fifteenth century. Time has been changed to the present, and the locale to the ancient city of Bruges, to which the little princess is carried for safety in time of war, and is given the name of *Sylvia*; CHRISTIE MacDONALD. As an infant she is found in the tulip garden one morning by *Dame Paula*: ETHEL DU FRE HOUSTON who conducts the Laundry of the White Geese, and who is known as "Mother Goose." Sylvia is brought up as the daughter of Paula,

although the latter has six daughters of her own, known as the White Geese: *Lizette*: Nellie McCoy. *Clairette*: Cecilia Hoffman. *Babette*: Edith Allen. *Jeannette*: Gertrude Rudd. *Toinette*: Gene Peltier. *Manette*: Gretchen Hartman. *Mikel Mikeloviz*: TOM McNAUGHTON, who disguised as a monk, left Sylvia when an infant in Dame Paula's care. Knowing that Sylvia is the Crown Princess of the little kingdom of Zilania, Mikel is conspiring to restore her to the throne, which is about to be offered to *Franz*, the heir presumptive: THOMAS CONKEY, who, in traveling incognito, has fallen in love with Sylvia, and who finds a rival in *Lieutenant Karl*: EDWIN WILSON, a military Lothario, betrothed to Sylvia. Mikel's plans are endangered by the schemes of *Hon. Percy Algernon Slingsby*: LIONEL WALSH, *Petrus Van Tromp*: FRANK BELCHER, *Aristide Caniche*: ROBERT O'CONNOR, who wish to purchase, for their own purposes, Prince Franz's estates in Zilania. *Liane*, a milliner: HAZEL KIRKE has sought temporary employment in the Laundry of the White Geese, and is mistaken by Mikel and Slingsby for the lost Princess. Other characters introduced are *Captain Lorent*: Briggs French. *First Footman*: Edward Crawford. *Second Footman*: William Wilder.

    Ladies of the Court, Laundry Girls, Peasants, Soldiers, etc: Misses Laura Thaler, Louise Squires, Louise Havele, Grace Williams, Beth Grant, Jeanne Jack, Lou Wilson, Elma Decker, Anna Christopher, Tempe Evans, Eunice Breach, Margaret Livingstone, Alberta Brittain, Alma Morrison, Margaret Walsingham, Margaret Braun, Sallie Roming, Delia Burton, Landince Meers, Alma Picard, Betty Elkins, Olga Harding, Babe Langdon, Irma Bertrand, Dorothy Garrique, Jane Delbes, Jane Lovell, Lexi Muro, Gertrude Davis, Mae Heagney. Messrs. Roland St. John, James Hope, James Whelan, William Lassen, Henry Mack, William Kline, Garrett Carroll, Mad. Wilson, Ernest Crawford, Broggs French, Gus Kennedy, Jack Hagner, Roscoe Gibson, Richard Anderson, Louis Walters, Martin Baltz, William Jakob.

Act 1: The Laundry of the White Geese in Bruges. Present time.

Act 2: The Chateau of Prince Franz in Zilania.

ACT 1

Opening Chorus ("Iron! Iron! Iron!")

"On Parade"

    Ensemble

"Smiles"

    H. Kirke, Ensemble

"Sweethearts" (If You Ask Where Love Is Found)

    C. MacDonald, Ensemble

"For Every Lover (Must Meet His Fate)"

    T. Conkey, Ensemble

"Mother Goose"

    C. MacDonald, Ensemble

"Angelus"

    C. MacDonald, T. Conkey

"Sabot Dance" (Jeannette and Her Little Wooden Shoes)(Clip Clop Clop)

    H. Kirke, L. Walsh, R. O'Connor, F. Belcher

Finale

ACT 2

Opening Chorus ("Waiting for the Bride")

    Male Chorus

Dance Eccentrique

    R. O'Connor

"Pretty as a Picture"

    F. Belcher, Male Chorus

"In the Convent They Never Taught Me That"

    C. MacDonald, Ensemble

"Game of Love"

    E. Wilson, Six Daughters

"I Don't Know How I Do It But I Do"

    L. Walsh

    (*Lyrics by* Harry B. Smith.)

"Cricket on the Hearth"

    C. MacDonald, T. Conkey

"The Monks' Quartette"

    T. McNaughton, F. Belcher, L. Walsh, R. O'Connor

Finale

1913.25

ROB ROY

The DeKoven Opera Company in a Revival of the Comic Opera in Three Acts.[22] Book by Harry B. Smith. Music by Reginald DeKoven. Staged by

---

[20]Fréderique de Grésac was Mrs. Victor Maurel.
[21]During the run the producers' billing was changed to read "Werba-Luescher Opera Co., Inc."

[22]Originally produced in New York 29 October 1894 at the Herald Square Theatre for 253 performances. For Synopsis of Scenes and Musical Numbers, see original 1894 production.

Daniel V. Arthur. Scenery by Frank Gates and Edward A. Morange. Costumes designed by Will R. Barnes. Orchestra under the direction of Frank E. Tours. Produced by Daniel V. Arthur. Opened 15 September 1913 at the Liberty Theatre and closed 4 October 1913 after 24 performances.

CAST: *Rob Roy MacGregor*, a Highland Chief: JAMES STEVENS. *Janet*, daughter of the Mayor: BESSIE ABOTT. *Prince Charles Edward Stuart*, called "The Young Pretender": FRANK POLLOCK. *Flora MacDonald*, heiress of a chief of the Clan MacDonald, a partisan of the Pretender: HENRIETTE WAKEFIELD. *Dugald MacWheeble*, Mayor of Perth: JEFFERSON DeANGELIS. *Lochiel*, a Highlander, otherwise Donald Cameron, of the Cameron Clan: HERBERT WATEROUS. *Captain Ralph Sheridan*, of King George's Grenadiers: RALPH BRAINARD. *Sandy MacSherry*, town crier: SIDNEY BRACY. *Tammas MacSorlie*, the Mayor's henchman: Fred Frear. *Lieutenant Cornwallis of King George's Grenadiers*: Mary Bennett. *Lieutenant Clinton*: Frances Burress. *Nellie, Millie*, barmaids of "The Crown and Thistle": Betty McNeel, Mary Carroll. *Jamie MacDougal*, the Mayor's stable boy: Joseph A. Tinsley. *Jamie MacLeod*, the Mayor's cook: John Daniels. *Jamie MacAllister*, the Mayor's valet: Eugene Elliott. *Jamie MacTavish*, the Mayor's coachman: Manny Worth. *Jamie MacLean*, the Mayor's gardener: Raymond Hancock.

Dancers: Misses Ada Fuld, Sadie Chester, May Chester, Florence Harden, Sylvia Saunders, Billie Wilburn, Mae Borden, Annette Joarden, Gladys Spuler, Camille Truesdale, Sadie Anken, Fayles Hilton. *Ladies and Gentlemen of the Chorus* (representing the Highlanders of the Clans MacPherson, Cameron, MacGregor, Campbell, MacDonald, and Moray, English Grenadiers, Lowland Folk, Drummer Boys, Watchmen): Misses Margaret Smith, Isabelle MacLeod, Pauline Hendricks, Jane Nash, Mattie Vance, Hazel Linden, Olga Boehm, Della Hunt, Isabelle Burnside, Nona Clifford, Naomi Raiss, May Collier, Jeanette Thurber, Edith Herrmann, Anna Fielding, Jeanette Fielding, Edna Orth, Augusta Dauche, Mina Manley, Catherine Scott, Sophia Mossell, Margaret Weidman, Hazel Kingdon, Cherie Bonnar, Hazel Kingdon, Cherie Bonnar. Messrs. J. F. McKinnon, H. Eugene, R. J. Courcell, Ralph Walton, Lewis Anismann, H. Eugene, Sherman Miller Charles Cook, Alfred Sappio, Lewis Hermann, Albert Baron, Irving LaPato, Barney Goldie, Louis Maniero, Ollie Vanderberg, Paul Curtis, Gene Francis, I. Bienfast, Robert White, Emanuel Tirnauer, Loring Merritt, William Collins, William Anismann.

Time: 1745.

Act 1: An open place before the house of the Mayor of Perth.

Act 2: Culloden, Rob Roy's retreat in the Highlands.

Act 3: Sterling Castle by moonlight.

ACT 1

Introduction—Opening Scene and Ensemble
"Hunting Song"
    Chorus
Duet
    Prince
"Town Crier's Song"
    Chorus
Entrance
Song and Chorus
    English Soldiers
Chorus of Hughlanders/Song of Rob Roy
Scene and Duet
    Rob Roy, Janet
"My Name Is Where the Heather Blooms"
    Janet
"My Hairt Is in the Highlands" (Song)
    Mayor, Servant
Finale

ACT 2

Introduction and Opening Scene
"The Merry Miller"
    Chorus
Scene and Concerted Number
"Dearest Heart of My Heart" (Romanza)
"My True Love Is a Shepherdess" (Quintet and Chorus)
Scotch Ballet
"Love Land" (Waltz Song)
Finale

ACT 3

March
    Chorus
Chansonette and Duet

"Song of the Turnkey"
Serenade
"Rustic Song"
Finale

1913.26 # THE MARRIAGE MARKET

A Musical Play in Three Acts. Original Hungarian libretto ('Leányvásár') by Max (Miksa) Bródy and Franz [Ferenc] Martos. American adaptation by Gladys Unger. Music by Victor [Viktor] Jacobi. Lyrics by Arthur Anderson and Adrian Ross. Staged by Edward Royce. Scenery by Homer F. Emens. Costumes designed by Comelli. Orchestra under the direction of Harold Vicars. Produced by Charles Frohman. Opened 22 September 1913 at the Knickerbocker Theatre and closed 29 November 1913 after 80 performances.[23]

CAST: *Edward Fleetwood*, know as "Tulare Teddy": DONALD BRIAN. *Senator Abe K. Gilroy*: GEORGE T. MEECH. *Bald-Faced Sandy*, Sheriff of Mendocino Bluff and Proprietor of the Palace Hotel: GUY NICHOLS. *Cowboys (4): Mexican Bill*: C. Vandiveer. *Shorty*: Winship Fink. *Tabasco Ned*: Arthur Dauche. *Cheyenne Harry*: Arthur Metcalf. *Hi-Ti*, a Chinese barkeeper: Edwin Burch. *Captain on the "Mariposa"*: Frank Adair. *Lord Hurlingham*: PERCIVAL KNIGHT. *Blinker*, valet to Lord Hurlingham: ARTHUR REYNOLDS. *Mariposa Gilroy*: VENITA FITZHUGH. *A Middy*: Cissie Sewell. *Emma*, maid to Mariposa: MOYA MANNERING. *Guests on the Yacht (4): Dolly*: Irene Hopping. *Pansy*: Elizabeth Wood. *Peach*: Viola Cain. *Dora*: Gene Cole. *Dolores*: Marie Annis. *Kitty Kent*: CARROLL McCOMAS. *Spanish and American Cowboys, Spanish and American Girls, Miners, Sailors, Guests, Middles, Footmen, etc.*

Act 1: Mendocino Bluff, Southern California. Present time.

Act 2: The yacht "*Mariposa*," anchored in the Bay of San Francisco.

Act 3: Senator Gilroy's Palace, San Francisco.

ACT 1

"Over the Hills in Monterey" (Scene and Song)
    Chorus
"Never Count Your Chicks Before They're Hatched" (Duet)
    M. Mannering, A. Reynolds
"The Mendocino Stroll"
    D. Brian, Cowboys
    (*Music and Lyrics by* Donald Brian.)
"Compliments" (Trio)
    D. Brian, V. Fitzhugh, C. McComas
"American Courtship" (Song)
    C. McComas
"The One I Love" (Waltz Duet)
    D. Brian, V. Fitzhugh
    (*Lyrics by* Adrian Ross.)
"The Marriage Market"
    Chorus
"Hand in Hand" (Quartette)
    D. Brian, V. Fitzhugh, C. McComas, P. Knight
Finale

ACT 2[24]

Opening Chorus
"All the Little Ladies Love a Sailor Man"[25] (Song)
    F. Adair, Chorus
"Oh, How Near and Yet How Far" (Duet)
    D. Brian, V. Fitzhugh
"Naval Manoeuvres" (Song)
    D. Brian, Chorus

---

[23]Played a return engagement at the Grand Opera House 8 December 1913 for 8 performances.
[24]Added to Act 2, after "Money in The Bank" for subsequent tour:
    "Very Little Time for Loving Nowadays" (Song)
      A. Reynolds, Chorus
      (*Music by* Pedro de Zulueta.)
[25]Dropped for subsequent tour.

"(I've Got) Money in the Bank"
  M. Mannering, A. Reynolds
  (*Music by* Jerome Kern. *Lyrics by* M. E. Rourke.)
"June Is in the Air" (Duet)
  D. Brian, V. Fitzhugh
"A Little Bit of Silk"[26]
  M. Mannering
  (*Music by* Jerome Kern. *Lyrics by* M. E. Rourke.)
"Boys" (Whistling Song)
  C. McComas
  (*Music by* Edwin Burch. *Lyrics by* Edwin Burch and M. E. Rourke.)
Finale

ACT 3[27]

Opening Chorus
"Little Grey Home in the West"[28] (Song)
  V. Fitzhugh
"(I'm Looking for) An Irish Husband"[29]
  D. Brian, Chorus
  (*Music by* Jerome Kern. *Lyrics by* M. E. Rourke.)
"I Always Come Back to You"[30] (Duet)
  C. McComas, P. Knight
"The Futurist Twirl" (Song)
  D. Brian, assisted by Misses Sewell, Harriman, Raynham, Sinclair
  (*Music by* Edwin Burch. *Lyrics by* Edwin Burch and M. E. Rourke.)
Finale

1913.27
HER LITTLE HIGHNESS

A Musical Play in Three Acts. Book and lyrics by Channing Pollock and Rennold Wolf, based on Channing Pollock's comedy "Such a Little Queen." Music by Reginald DeKoven. Staged by George Marion. Dances arranged by Julian Mitchell. Scenery painted by D. Frank Dodge and William Castle. Costumes by the Orange Manufacturing Company; sketches by William Matthews. Orchestra under the direction of Max Bendix. Produced by (Louis F.) Werba and (Mark A.) Luescher. Opened 13 October 1913 at the Liberty Theatre and closed 25 October 1913 after 16 performances.

CAST: *Hertzegovinians: Anna Victoria,* Queen of Herzogovina: MIZZI [Mitzi] HAJÓS. *Baron Cosaca,* Her Prime Minister: ALLAN POLJÓCS. *General Myrza,* Commanding the Army: WILLIAM STRUNZ. *Herr Rumler,* Lord Mayor of Mostar: WILLIAM J. McCARTHY. *The Lord Chamberlain:* Francis J. Tyler. *A Captain of the Guard:* George Dunston. *Princess Louise,* First Lady in Waiting: May Emory. *Princess Marion,* First Mistress of the Wardrobe: May McCarthy. *Princess Evelyn,* First Lady of the Bedchamber: Jane Elliott.
  Bosnians: Stephen IV, King of Bosnia: WILMUTH MERKYL. *Prince Niklas:* Holton Herr. *The Duke of Ravanica:* Francis Bolger.
  Americans: Adolph Lauman of Lauman & Son: WILLARD LOUIS. *Elizabeth Lauman,* His Daughter: LOUISE KELLY. *Robert Trainor,* General Manager for Lauman & Son: WALLACE McCUTCHEON. *Friends of Elizabeth (2): Madeline Schuyler:* Ethel May Davis. *Eleanor Winton:* Mae Murray. *Nathaniel Quigg:* William J. McCarthy. *Mary Ann:* Anna Boyd.
  Officials of the Court of Herzegovina, Flunkeys, Soldiers, Peasants, Tourists, Shop Girls, Draymen, A Messsenger, Neighbors of the Queen, Friends of Lauman, etc.: Leigh Buchanan, Adele Meeker, Kathryn Florence, Adrienne Dillon, Maude Sterling, Millie Murray, Vivian DuBois, Leah Griffith, Grace Langdon, Luella Gateson, Lillian Tashman, Marie Hill, Violet McKay, Blanche Nesbiitt, Jean Knight, Madeline Dupont, Jean Hill, Bess Hardy, Gertrude Barnes, Lillian Harrison, Irene Mitchell, Mabel Leon, Jeanne Crane, Jennie Canaan, Louise Hardy, Beatrice McKay, Amelia Rose, Marguerite Pates, Hilda Peters, Virginia Calvert, Madeline Dailey, Mae Heagney, Fifi Parfrey, Jane Delles. Messrs. Carl Porter, Al Racklin, William Connell, Ord Bohannon, William Mack, Dane Piel, Wells McClelland, Arthur Bedell, Francis Schultze, Dean Crary, Kirk Bride, Lovay Wilder, Herbert Weir, Harry Wagner, Gus

Minton, Ben Rogers, Al Johnson, Max Zipp, Frank Horley, Gus Schultz, Mell Hecht, Ed Jacobs.

Act 1: Throne Room of the Palace at Mostar, Herzegovina.

Act 2: Living Room of an Apartment in Amsterdam Avenue, New York. Two months later.

Act 3: Grounds of the Lauman Residence, Irvington-on-Hudson. The following evening.

ACT 1
"When the Queen Wakes Up in the Morning" (Opening Chorus)
"The Practical Patriots"
  W. Strunz, W. M. McCarthy, H. Herr, F. Bolger
Folk Song; "When You're Sweet Sixteen"
  M. Hajós
"A Self Made Man"
  W. Louis, L. Kelly, E. M. Davis, M. Murray
"My Fairy Prince"
  M. Hajós
"Ancient Rules of Observing Etiquette"
  M. Hajós, W. Merkyl, Courtiers
Finale

ACT 2
"Mary Ann" (Opening Number)
  A. Boyd, A. Pollock, Chorus
"C.O.D."
  M. Hajós, A. Pollock, Shop Girls
"One Little Girl"
  L. Kelley, Friends
"When the Landlord Comes a-Knocking at the Door"
  M. Hajós, W. Merkyl, A. Pollock, W. McCarthy, Draymen
Finale

ACT 3
Opening Chorus
"(Ancient Rules of Observing) Etiquette" (reprise)
  W. Louis, L. Kelley
"Romanza Heimweh"
  M. Hajós
"Czardas"
  M. Hajós, W. McCutcheon
Dances (The Tango; Turkey Trot; Waltz; Brazilian)
  W. McCutcheon, assisted by M. Murray, E. M. Davis, G. Langdon
"The Ladies"
  A. Pollock, Chorus
"Drink and Be Merry"
  W. McCutcheon, W. Strunz, W. J. McCarthy, Male Chorus
Finale

A GLIMPSE OF THE
GREAT WHITE WAY/
1913.28   ## THE MODISTE SHOP

An Innovation (Double Bill of a Musical Entertainment followed by a Comedy with Music). Produced by Lew Fields. Opened 27 October 1913 at the 44th Street Music Hall and closed 1 November 1913 after 12 performances.

ACT 1: A GLIMPSE OF THE GREAT WHITE WAY

CAST: *Archie Piccadilly, Bertie Strand,* two pleasure-seekers: ROBERT WARD, LAWRENCE WARD. *Miss Manhattan,* a "show-you-around" showgirl: FRANCES DEMAREST. *Mr. Church-Mountain,* a restaurant owner: MILBURY RYDER. *L'Abbaye,* Apache dancers: DELLARIO and LOUIS. *Gus,* an entertainer: HARRY ROSE. *Jacques Serviette:* EMIL AGOUST. *Rastus Uptown, Ophelia Harlem,* two colored swells: ALEXANDER and SCOTT. *Pro, Con:* SCHWARTZ BROTHERS. *Forest Casino:* FOREST HUFF. *Fritzi Lyric:* FRITZI von BUSING. *Hammerstein Harmony:* ARTHUR ALBRO. *The Spider:* MADO MINTY.
  Note: The Spider awakens. She cares not for the fly nor the morning butterfly, which are too easy a prey for her. She is only fascinated by the pursuit of the beautiful moth and displays all her elegance to fascinate the moth. At the end, the Spider is victorious. She drags her prey into her web and kills. Tired soon after her triumph, she cares no more for her victim.

---

[26]Dropped during the run.
[27]Added to Act 3 [before "I Always Come Back"/"It Might Be an Oomps"] for subsequent tour:
  "Honeymoon" (Song)
  D. Brian, V. Fitzhugh, C. McComas, M. Mannering, A. Reynolds, Chorus
[28]Dropped during the New York run, but reinstated for subsequent tour.
[29]Dropped for subsequent tour.
[30]Replaced during tour by:
  "It Might Be an Oomps Sight Worse"
  C. McComas, P. Knight

LE VISITEUR, a play in One act in French,[31] by arrangement with F. Ray Comstock and Morris Gest, from the Vaudeville Theatre, Paris.

CAST: *The Actress*: Mlle. POLAIRE. *The Visitor*: Mons. Edgar Becmann. *A Maid*: Mlle. Clasis.

Scene: The Boudoir of a famous Parisian star. 3 A.M.

ACT 2

"The 44th Street Music Hall March" (*Music by* Herbert Kerr.)

Spanish Dances and Songs
  Tortajada

An Everyday Occurrence in Central Park
  Mack & Walker

Billy McDermott (Comedian)

THE MODISTE SHOP,[32] a comedy with music in 1 scene. Book and lyrics by Henry Blossom. Music by Alfred G. Robyn. Stage direction by William G. Stewart, Emil Agoust. Tango dance number caught by Joseph C. Smith. Scenery by D. Frank Dodge and William Castle. Costumes by Melville Ellis. Orchestra under the direction of Herbert Kerr.

CAST: *Leo van Laubenheim*: SAM BERNARD. *Marie, a typewriter*:[33] Louise Meyers. *Alphonse Clemente*: GEORGE A. SCHILLER. *Georgette Clemente, his wife*: EDITH LOWE. *Ernest Panturel*: TEDDY WEBB. *Nancy Panturel, his wife*: FRANCES DEMAREST. *François, a valet*: Henry M. Holt. *Madame Suzette, Leo's assistant*: Amy Leicester. *Finette, Helene, Augusta, models*: Vivian Lawrence, Rose Huber, Lillian Howell. *Marquise de Calvados*: Ethel Russell. *Grand Duchess Alexia of Russia*: Lena Robinson.

Personnel of Chorus: Attendants: Rose Huber, Emma Prager, Lillian Howell, Marjorie Cook, Lydia Scott, Billy Ward. *A la Mode Girls*: Misses Camille Irving, Gladys Benjamin, Lydia Scott, Ethel Barry, Helene Laurence, Eleanor Ryley. *Shoppers*: Misses Bessie Cortell, Ella Ray, Elsa Schumann, Genevieve Tucker, Florence Hart, Florence Holmes. *Models as they appear on miniature stage*: Misses Elsa Schumann, Marjorie Cook, Rose Huber, Eleanor Ryley, Helen Glenmore, Lydia Scott, Vivian Lawrence, Camille Irving, Ethel Barry, Gladys Benjamn, Florence Holmes. *Johnnies*: Messrs. Fred H. Marshall, Homer Potts, Harry Saunders, Joseph Starr, Robert Newmann, Bert Lawrence. *Flunkies*: Messrs. Frank Meyrose, William Nau, Jack Mehl, J. Arthur Kelle, Guy Collins, James Anderson.

Scene: Living room in Leo's home.

MUSICAL NUMBERS

"What a Change" (Opening Chorus)
  Ensemble

"If I Were Only a Man"
  F. Demarest, Chorus

The Tango Dance
  F. Demarest, Chorus

"I'll Marry Him for Love"
  L. Meyers, R. Huber, L. Howell

"Permissable"
  S. Bernard

Finale
  Ensemble

OH, I SAY!

1913.29

A Musical Comedy in Three Acts. Book by Sidney Blow and Douglas Hoare. Based on English play of the same name adapted from the French farce ("Une nuit de noces") by Henri Kéroul and Albert Barré. Music by Jerome D. Kern. Lyrics by Harry B. Smith. Staged by J. C. Huffman. Dances arranged by Julian Alfred. Scenery painted by Lee Lash Studios. Costumes by Melville Ellis. (Orchestra under the direction of Alfred Bendell. Orchestrations by Frank Saddler.) Produced by the Messrs. Shubert. Opened 30 October 1913 at the Casino Theatre and closed 27 December 1913 after 68 performances.[34]

CAST (in order of appearance): *Baptiste, hotel proprietor*: Dick Temple. *Count Buzot*: JOSEPH W. HERBERT. *Julie, Member of Sydonie's Company*: LOIS JOSEPHINE. *Gabrielle, Member of Sydonie's Company*: NELLIE KING. *Hugo, Member of Sydonie's Company*: WELLINGTON CROSS. *Madam Portal, Suzette's mother*: Jeffreys Lewis. *Jules Portal, Suxette's Father*: WALTER JONES. *Marcel Durand*: CHARLES MEAKINS. *Suxette, Marcel's Bride*: ALICE YORKE. *Henri, Marcel's Best Man*: JOSEPH PHILLIPS. *Langely, Member of Sydonie's Company*: Ray Dodge. *Sydonie de Mornay*: CECIL CUNNINGHAM. *Waiter*: James Notos. *Madeline, Suzette's Bridesmaid*: Olga Hempstone. *Fifi, Suxette's Bridesmaid*: Marjory Lane. *Mimi, Suxette's Bridesmaid*: Marion George. *Elsie, Suxette's Bridesmaid*: Anna Berg. *Claudine, Sydonie's Maid*: CLARA PALMER. *Madam Pigache, a Housekeeper*: Elizabeth Arians. *Joseph, Sydonie's Footman*: Tyler Brooks. *Jacques Laverdo*: Dick Temple.

Act 1: At Portal's Hotel, Beauvais.

Act 2: Sydonie's Apartment in Paris.

Act 3: Sydonie's Villa on the Outskirts of Paris.

ACT 1

Opening Chorus
  Guests of Hotel

Dance Duet[35]
  L. Josephine, W. Cross, N. King

"Each Pearl a Thought"[36] (Scene)
  A. Yorke

"I Know and She Knows" (Trio)
  W. Jones, J. Phillips, C. Meakins

Ensemble
  C. Cunningham, Chorus

"Well This Is Jolly" (Trio)
  C. Cunningham, J. Phillips, C. Meakins

"Each Pearl a Thought" (Reprisal)
  W. Jones

Finale

ACT 2

Opening Chorus
  Servants

"The Old Clarinet" (Dance Duet)
  C. Palmer, T. Brooks
  (*Music by* Jean Gilbert.)

"Alone at Last" (Duet)
  C. Meakins, A. Yorke

"A Woman's Heart" (Terzette)
  C. Cunningham, W. Jones, J. W. Herbert

"Katy-did" (Duet)
  L. Josephine, W. Cross

Supper Scene
  Chorus

Finaletto
  C. Meakins, W. Jones, C. Cunningham, J. Phillips, J. W. Herbert, Chorus

ACT 3

Opening Chorus
  Guests of Laverdo

"I Can't Forget Your Eyes" (Song)
  C. Palmer, W. Cross

"A Wife of Your Own" (Duettino)
  J. Phillips, A. Yorke

Duel Bouffe
  W. Jones, J. W. Herbert

Finaletto—"Alone at Last"

THE PLEASURE SEEKERS

1913.30

An Entirely New Jumble of Jollification (Musical Revue) in Two Acts. Book by Edgar Smith. Music and lyrics by E. Ray Goetz. Staged by William J.

---

[31]Authorship uncredited.
[32]A revised and shortened version of ALL FOR THE LADIES, which was previously produced in New York 30 December 1912 at the Lyric Theatre for 112 performances. Also titled MY PARTNER'S WIVES.
[33]In program for MY PARTNER'S WIVES, *Hector Renaud*: Robert Newman. The character of Louise is identified as his sweetheart.
[34]Toured subsequently as OH, I SAY!, or The Wedding Night, and then as THEIR WEDDING NIGHT.

---

[35]Replaced during the run by:
  "How Do You Do?" (Dance Octette)
  W. Cross, Ballet
[36]Replaced during the run by:
  "Suzanne"
  A. Yorke

Wilson. Scenery designed by Arthur Voegtlin. Costumes designed by Cora MacGeachy, William Henry Matthews. Orchestra under the direction of Oscar Radin. Produced by the Messrs. Shubert. Opened 3 November 1913 at the Winter Garden and closed 3 January 1914 after 72 performances.[37]

CAST (in order of appearance): *Isaac Googenheimer*, president of The Pleasure Seekers, an organization of Hebrew commercial drummers:[38] HUGH CAMERON. (*Headliners of the Pleasure Seekers*, 2): *Isidore Eisenstein*: HARRY COOPER. *Max Rosenberg*: BOBBY NORTH. *M'lle Marcelle*, in vaudeville: DOROTHY JARDON. *Heinrich Brobschloff*, a silent partner in the firm of Mannheimer, Limited: MAX ROGERS. *Heine Brobschloff*, his good-for-nothing son: WILLIAM MONTGOMERY. *Limousine Panhard*, a footlight divinity: VIRGINIA EVANS. *Jack Hemingway*, a night owl: GEORGE WHITE. *George Bliffkins*, a western ranch owner: HUGH CAMERON. *Maria Bliffkins*, his wife: SALLY DALY. *Violet Bliffkins*, his daughter: FLORENCE MOORE. *Butterflies of Broadway* (2): *Marcelline*: MYRTLE GILBERT. *Vera*: FLO MAY.

Members of the Chorus: Ladies: Shirley Forsyth, Rita Bates, Lillian Harris, M. Hoban, Bessie Hoban, Marie Olcott, Dorothy Landers, May Morrell, Mabel Landers, Edna Britton, Maud LeRoy, Nona Clifford, Harriott Miller, Nora May, Mary Murrell, Lillian Elliott, Ruth Harris, Gertie O'Connor, Bermah Brokaw, Lillian Heim, Irma Dixon, Alice Statten, Annie Russell, Kittie Carpenter, Olive Forgo, Minna Kaufman, Adele Clark, Elizabeth Young, Lara Hastings, Violet DeVon, M. Foltz, Minnie Monroe, Marie Berdean, Edith Parfrey, Alice Fitch, Mary Purcell, L. Taylor, Marie Parton, Daisy Lovell, Ruth Copeley, Maud Estee, Daisy Statton, Mazie Keane, Blanche Barnes, Helen Paine, Maud Powell, May Francis, Ada Holt, Margie Cogan, Myrtle Ross, Florence Cripps, Ara Martin, Grace Falk, Florence Dean, Edna Moore. *Gentlemen:* Jay Melville, Milton Silbe, Eric Krebs, August Reese, Joe Rogers, Ben Kinngoff, Frank Wayne, Bernard Edwards, James Coer, Joe McGrath, Irwin Gruhl, Philip Sohlke, Sherman Miller, John Weldon, Victor Bozart, Rogers McKenna, Howard Murrell, Tom Doolan, Charles Miller, William Wilson, Harry Stephenson, Thoams Stevens, Ed Stokes, Robert Dillon, Lew Turner, Thomas Hawmer, Geoge Borowsky, Fred Baekman, Will McElhenny, Walter Fiske, Gustave Wargans, Charles Butler, Arthur Beach, William Snyder, Paul DeMonde, Fred Barnes.

Act 1, Scene 1: Banquet Room of the Ritz-Carlton Hotel, New York. *Scene 2:* Exterior of the Ritz-Carlton. *Scene 3:* Aboard the *Imperator*. *Scene 4:* Switzerland. *Scene 5:* The Alps.

Act 2, Scene 1: A Paris Boulevard. *Scene 2:* Interlude. *Scene 3:* A Studio Apartment in the Latin Quarter. *Scene 4:* A Cafe on the Seine. *Scene 5:* M'lle. Marcelle's modiste establishment.

ACT 1[39]

Opening Chorus
    Ensemble
"Levi Is a Grand Old Name"
    B. North, H. Cooper, Chorus
"Follow the Midnight Girl"
    D. Jardon, Chorus
    (*Music by* Bert Grant and E. Ray Goetz.)
"Don't Blame It All on Broadway"
    G. White, W. Montgomery
    (*Music by* Bert Grant. *Lyrics by* Henry Williams, Joe Young.)
"They're on Their Honeymoon" (Ensemble)
    Chorus
"My Arverne Rose"
    H. Cooper, Chorus
    (*Music by* Bert Grant.)
Medley
    D. Jardon, M. Rogers
"Give Me Something in a Uniform of Blue"[40]
    F. Moore, Chorus
"I Have a Little Chalet in the Valley" (Quartet)(I've Got a Little Chalet in the Valley)
    M. Rogers, B. North, M. Gilbert, F. May
    (*Music by* Bert Grant and E. Ray Goetz.)
"Ski Song" and Specialty Dance
    G. White, Chorus
Finale: "Switzerland"
    "The Alpine Girl"
        Chorus
    (*Music by* Bert Grant.)

───────────

[37]Settings uncredited.
[38]For subsequent tour this was revised to read "an organization of Commercial Salesmen."
[39]After the opening, the running order was revised, and the following was added before Ski Song:
    "The Monte Carlo Glide"
        H. Cooper, Chorus
[40]Dropped during the run, but restored for subsequent tour.

ACT 2[41]

Ensemble; "There's a Lot of Pretty Little Things in Paris"
    G. White, M. Gilbert, Chorus
"Get Out and Get Under" (He'd Have to Get Under, Get Out and Get Under)
    B. North
    (*Music by* Maurice Abrahams. *Lyrics by* Grant Clarke and Edgar Leslie.)
"Une Nuit Paris" (Pantomime Dance)
    Ensemble
"The Serpentine" (Song and Specialty Dance)
    V. Evans, G. White, Chorus
"Faust Up to Date"
    D. Jardon, B. North, H. Cooper
"(At That Bully) Woolly Wild West Show"[42]
    F. Moore, W. Montgomery
    (*Music by* Maurice Abrahams. *Lyrics by* Grant Clarke and Edgar Leslie.)
"Love Me in a Viennese Melody" (Love Me to a Viennese Melody)
    D. Jardon, Chorus
Finale
    Entire Company

1913.31 THE LITTLE CAFÉ

A Musical Comedy in Three Acts. Book and lyrics by C. M. S. McLellan. Based on the French farce "Le Petit Café" by Tristan Bernard. Music by Ivan Caryll. Dialogue staged by Herbert Gresham. Ensemble numbers staged by Julian Mitchell. Scenery by Edward G. Unitt and Joseph Wickes. Costumes designed by F. Richard Anderson. Orchestra under the direction of Anton Heindl. Produced by Marc Klaw and A. L. Erlanger. Opened 10 November 1913 at the New Amsterdam Theatre and closed 14 March 1914 after 144 performances.

CAST (in order of appearance): *Veauchenu*, an old café lounger: Joseph Monahan. *Celeste*, cashier in The Little Café: Marjorie Gateson. *Philibert*, proprietor of The Little Café: HAROLD VIZARD. *Gaston*, an artist: H. P. Woodley. *Yvonne*, Philibert's daughter: ALMA FRANCIS. *Albert Loriflan*, waiter in The Little Café: JOHN E. YOUNG. *Katziolinka*, a Hungarian singer: GRACE LEIGH. *Six Belles of Hungary: Ilsa:* Eleanor St. Clair. *Alma:* Ethel Davies. *Louka:* Trixie Whiteford. *Zora:* Lillian Rice. *Thyrza:* Alys Belga. *Oola:* Lorayne Leslie. *Isabel*, a midinette: Charlotte Carter. *Bigredon*, a promoter: Tom Graves. *Postman:* Maurice Cass. *Adolphe*, glass washer in The Little Café: Harry Depp. *Anatol:* Albert Stuart. *Marcel:* John H. Roberts. *Maurice:* Maurice Cass. *Durand*, a detective: William Doyle. *Edmond*, a young man about town: H. R. Woodley. *Gaby Gaufrette*, Queen of the Night Restaurants: HAZEL DAWN. *Loulou Millefleurs*, her friend: Marie Empress. *Leonce*, head waiter at the Restaurant Grand Gala: Eddie Morris. *Baron Tombola*, Major Domo of Prince Max: FRED GRAHAM. *Prince Max* of Galmania: John Deverell. *Colonel Klink*, his aide-de-camp: F. STANTON HECK. *Godinard*, a notary: Joseph Monahan. *Nina:* Marjorie Gateson. *Zaza:* Charlotte Carter.

Act 1: The Little Café, Paris

Act 2: The Restaurant Grand Gala, Paris

Act 3: The Gardens of the Chateau San Souci, Marly.

ACT 1

"My Pretty Little Family of One" (Opening Chorus—Song)
    H. Vizard, Chorus
"I Wonder Whom I'll Marry" (Song)
    A. Francis, Chorus
"I'm a Hunting Jaguar" (Song)
    G. Leigh, Belles of Hungary, Chorus
"You Little Café, Good-day" (Song)
    J. E. Young, Chorus
Finale
    Principals, Chorus

ACT 2

"So I Smile" (Opening Chorus—Song)
    H. Dawn, Chorus

───────────

[41]Added to Act 2, after "Get Out and Get Under" for subsequent tour:
    "Sit Down, You're Rocking the Boat" (Stop Rocking the Boat)
        F. Moore, W. Montgomery
        (*Music by* Jean Schwartz. *Lyrics by* William Jerome and Grant Clarke.)
[42]Also known as "At That Bully Woolly Wild West Show." Dropped during the run.

"Do You Call That Dancing?" (Song)
G. Leigh, Chorus
"Serve the Caviar" (Song)
J. E. Young, Chorus
"The Best Queen of All" (Chorus)
Chorus
"This Gay Paree" (Song)
A. Francis, Chorus
"Thy Mouth Is a Rose" (Song)
H. Dawn, Chorus
Finale
Principals, Chorus

ACT 3
"The Beauty Contest" (Opening Chorus)
F. Graham, F. S. Heck, Chorus
"Just Because It's You" (Waltz Song)
H. Dawn, G. Leigh, J. E. Young, Chorus
"They Found Me" (Song)
J. E. Young, Chorus
Finale
Principals, Chorus

1913.32 THE MADCAP DUCHESS

A Comic Opera in Two Acts. Book and lyrics by David Stevens and Justin Huntly McCarthy. Based on the novel "Seraphica" by Justin Huntley McCarthy. Music by Victor Herbert. Staged by Fred G. Latham. Dances arranged by Gilbert Clayton. Scenery painted by D. Frank Dodge and William Castle. Costumes by W. H. Matthews, Jr. Orchestra under the direction of Robert Hood Bowers. Orchestrations by Victor Herbert. Produced by H. H. Frazee. Opened 11 November 1913 at the Globe Theatre and closed 10 January 1914 after 71 performances.[44]

CAST: *Renaud*, Prince of St. Pol in Artois: GLENN HALL. *Guardians of Seraphina* (2): *Vidame de Bethune*: Russell Powell. *M. de Secherat*: Gilbert Clayton. *Master Hardi*, Manager of the Regent's Players: HARRY MACDONOUGH. *Louis* XV, King of France: Master Percy Helton. *Philip of Orleans*, the Regent: FRANCIS K. LIEB. *Watteau*, Court Painter: David Andrada. *Duc de Pontsable*, Marshall of France: Edmund Mulcahy. *Canillac*, Captain of the King's Musketeers: HENRY VINCENT. *Panache*, Sergeant of the King's Musketeers: Herman Holland. *Stephanie*, Marquise de Phalaris: JOSEPHINE WHITTELL. *Gillette*, Serving Maid at the Windmill Inn: PEGGY WOOD. *Seraphina*, Duchess of Bapaume in Artois: ANN SWINBURNE. *(4) of the Regent's Players*: *Spavento*: Mario Rogati. *Tartaglia*: Alexander Gibson. *Coraline*: Virginia Carewe-Carvel. *Zerbine*: Virginia Allen. *Watteau Shepherdesses and Shepherds*: Misses Kathleen Breen, Billie Williamson, Glen Ellis, Minna Martrit, Messrs. Morris Avery, J. Elliott, Sven Erick, H. B. Foster.

Musketeers, Players, Courtiers, etc.: Misses Alice Kingsley, Anna Powell, Mabel Allen, Katherine Stoessel, Grace Russell, Natalie Saymore, Olive Osborn, Ethel Hendricks, Margaret Andrews, Nora Gourley, Grace Loker, Evelyn Raymond, Jessie Goldie, Jane Gilroy, Laura Wentworth, Nell Donohue. Messrs. E. L. Mosher, Horace Valianti, Neil Walton, J. Kusky, Martin Cox, Ed Schroff, O. L. Love, B. Foster, R. S. Mosher.

Act 1: Garden of "The Windmill Inn." Autumn, 1720. Early Morning.

Act 2: Watteau's Theatre in the Garden of Versailles. Evening.

ACT 1
Opening Ensemble
P. Wood, H. Holland, Chorus
"Aurora Blushing Rosily" (Entrance of Renaud—Romanza)
G. Hall, Male Chorus
"Love and I Are Playing" (Entrance of Seraphina Aria)
A. Swinburne
"The Deuce, Young Man" (Scene and Duo)
A. Swinburne, G. Hall
"Tweedle-dee and Tweedle-dum" (Duo and Dance)
G. Clayton, R. Powell
"Oh, Up! It's Up!" (Hunting Song)
F. K. Lieb, J. Whittell, Chorus

"Love Is a Story That's Old" (Song)
A. Swinburne
"That Is Art" (Character Song)
H. Macdonough, Players
"Companions, I Have Summoned You" (Scene and Ensemble)
A. Swinburne, H. Macdonough, Chorus
"To Paris" (Finale)
Ensemble

ACT 2
"Now Is the South-Wind Blowing" (Ensemble)
A. Swinburne, G. Hall, H. Macdonough, Chorus
Intermezzo
"Babette of Beaujolais" (Madrigal)
A. Swinburne, Chorus
"Goddess of Mine"[45] (Star of Love)(Canzonetta)
G. Hall
"Winged Love" (Duo)
J. Whittell, H. Macdonough
"Far Up the Hill" (Duo and Shepherd Dance)
A. Swinburne, D. Andrada, Chorus
"Do You Know?"
A. Swinburne, G. Hall
"Love Is a Story That's Old" (Finale)
Ensemble

1913.33 HOP O' MY THUMB

A Fairy Tale (Pantomime) in Two Acts, 12 Scenes. Book by George R. Sims, Frank Dix and Arthur Collins. American version by Sydney Rosenfeld. Music composed and arranged by Manuel Klein. Ballet music by J. M. Glover. Staged by Ernest D'Auban. Ballets by Maude Crompton; incidental dances arranged by Ernest D'Auban. Scenery by Henry Emden, C. Formilli, R. McCleary, Joseph Harker, Bruce Smith. Dresses by Alias, Fisher, Simmons, Angel, Hannam, Orange Company. Orchestra under the direction of Manuel Klein. Produced by the Drury Lane Company of America (William Brady, Morris Gest, F. Ray Comstock, Managers) by arrangement with Arthur Collins. Opened 26 November 1913 at the Manhattan Opera House and closed 3 January 1914 after 46 performances.

CAST: *King Mnemonica*: DeWOLF HOPPER. *Tango*: RALPH AUSTIN. *Trotter*: WALTER S. WILLS. *The Kow Zebra*: Messrs. Schrode, Harris. *Datas*: Neal McNeal. *Joseph*, Ogre's Chef: Neal McNeal. *Ogre*: ALBERT HART. *John*: Charles M. Hinton. *Hilario*: VIOLA GILETTE. *Mirabelle*: EVA FALLON. *Zaza*, the Queen: TEXAS GUINAN. *Jenny*, Woodcutter's Wife: Marie Clifford. *Marie*, Ogre's Housekeeper: Marie Clifford. *Baroness Chicot*: Ross Snow. *Hop o' my Thumb*: IRIS HAWKINS.

Hop's Brothers (6): *John Henry*: Martha Ehrlich. *Arthur Herbert*: Winnie Ritchie. *George Frederick*: Leah dePiean. *Richard Arthur*: Lillian Barry. *Joseph James*: Caroline Duffy. *Walter William*: Runie Farrington. *The Six Princesses*: Misses Shields, Truppel, M. Leishman, A. Leishman, Rogers, Crook. *Living Statues*: The DeSerris.

Immortals: *Amber Witch*: FLAVIA ARCARO. *Fairy Forget-me-not*: Bertha Delmonte. *Voice of the Night*: Edith Gordon. *Fairy Love*: Edna Fenton.

Outlaws: Misses Morris, French, Bonnan, Harmon, Saunders, Andree, Knight, Lee, Bollow, Meyer, Denken, Hall. *Fairies, Court Ladies, Hussars, Cuirassiers, Dances, Pages, Heralds, etc.*

Act 1, Scene 1: Woodcutter's Hut. Summer. *Scene 2*: The Forest. *Scene 3*: Entrance to Castle Grim. *Scene 4*: Hall of Castle Grim. *Scene 5*: The Secret Passage. *Scene 6*: The Garden of Statues.

Act 2, Tableau: The Hole in the Rock. *Scene 1*: The King's Palace. *Scene 2*: Forget-me-not's Bower. *Scene 3*: Land of Lost Memories. *Scene 4*: Terrace of the Palace. *Scene 5*: Woodcutter's Hut. Winter. *Scene 6*: Goodwill to Men; Entrance to Fairyland.

ACT 1
Speaking Fairies
"A Happy, Noble Outlaw Band" (Song)
V. Gilette
"Bird Talk" (Duet)
R. Austin, W. S. Wills
"The Date Tree" (Quartette)
R. Snow, A. Hart, R. Austin, W. S. Wills
"The Forest Bird" (Song)
E. Fallon

---

[44]Played a return engagement 9 March 1914 at the Grand Opera House for 8 performances.

[45]Revised after opening under the new title "Star of Love."

"Come and Watch the Moon with Me" (Duet)
V. Gilette, E. Fallon
"Hop, Hop, Hop" (Song)
I. Hawkins
"Fee Fi Fo Fum" (Song)
A. Hart
"Run Along, Mr. Ogre Man" (Quartette)
R. Snow, A. Hart, R. Austin, W. S. Wills
Ballet of Living Statues
The DeSerris

ACT 2
"Here You See Eight Ladies of Quality" (Opening Chorus)
"No Damaged Goods" (Song)
D. Hopper, Chorus
"Those Seven League Boots" (Song, Solo)
D. Hopper
"For a Girl Has Her Living to Make"[46] (Song)
T. Guinan
Dancing Duet
D. Hopper, I. Hawkins
"Those Days of Long Ago" (Duet)
E. Fallon, V. Gilette
"Love Me, Love Me, Won't You?" (Song)
F. Arcaro
Bacchanalian Chorus
Specialty Dance
R. Austin, W. S. Wills
"Take a Little Perfume" (Solo)
E. Fallon, Chorus
"Salute to the King"
Chorus
Christmas Carol and Finale

1913.34 ## HIGH JINKS

A Musical Jollity (Comedy) in Three Acts. Book by Leo Dietrichstein and Otto Hauerbach [Harbach]. Based on Leo Ditrichstein's farce "Before and After," (adapted from the French farce 'Les Dragées d'Hercule' by Maurice Hennequin and Paul Bilhaud). Music by Rudolf Friml. Lyrics by Otto Hauerbach [Harbach]. Staged by Frank Smithson. Scenery by Theodore Reisig Scenic Studio. Gowns, costumes by B. Altman. Orchestra under the direction of Paul Schindler. Produced by Arthur Hammerstein. Opened 10 December 1913 at the Lyric Theatre, moved 12 January 1914 to the Casino Theatre, and closed 13 June 1914 after 213 performances.

CAST (in order of appearance): *Dr. Gaston Thorne*, a fashionable Parisian neurologist: ROBERT PITKIN. *Florence*: Elaine Hammerstein. *Monsieur Jacques Rabelais*: IGNACIO MARTINETTI. *Mme. Rabelais*: EDITH GARDINER. *Maid*: Blanche Field. *Dick Wayne*, an explorer: BURRELL BARBARETTO. *Mrs. Marion Thorne*: ADA MEADE. *Fritz Denkmahl*: SNITZ EDWARDS. *Mr. J. J. Jeffreys*, an American lumber king: TOM LEWIS. *Sylvia Dale*, Wayne's girl friend: MANA ZUCCA. *Adelaide Fontaine*, a runaway wife: ELIZABETH MURRAY. *Chi-Chi*: EMILIE LEA. *Garçon*: Augustus Schultz. *Page*: Elsie Gergley. *Mrs. Thorne's Companion*: Gladys Feldman.
Visiting Girls: Helen Sinclair, Yewell Fields, Gladys Feldman, Mazie Hartford, Henrietta Hosford, Grace Hoey, Alberta DeVere, Siegrid Oleson, Naomie Dale, May Dougherty, Fern Kenney, Hulda Morton, Violet Armstrong, Valla Dares, Eileen Gerald. *Housemaids*: May Dougherty, Marion Brown, Maggie Melvin, Anna McConnville, Bessie Skeet, Bessie Brown, Fern Kenney. *Nurses*: Florence Lee, Lola Edwards, Edna St. Claire, Billy Blane, Ethel Powell. *Guest Girls*: Misses St. Claire, Hartford, Field, Feldman, Fields. *Summer Girls*: Misses Hosfeldt, DeVoe, St. Claire, Brown, Edwards, Hoey, Dale. *French Shop Girls*: Misses Morgan, McConnville, Skeet, Brown, Melvin. *Bathing Girls*: Misses DeVere, Blane, Gleson, Lee, Powell. *Promenade Girls*: Misses Sinclair, Hartford, Field, Feldman, Fields, Dougherty, Dale. *Seaside Girls*: Misses Hosfeldt, Lee, Edwards, St. Claire, Blane, Brown, Devere, Melville, McConnville, Gleason, DeVoe, Skeet, Brown, Powell, Hoey. *Guest Boys*: Messrs. Wise, Watson, Vessey, Davis, Page, Clifford, Harley, Cooper, Nelson, Sharp, Forbes. *Frenchmen*: Messrs. Cantry, Protas, Levine, Vessey, Hoeckner. *Guest Men*: Messrs. Wise, Hoeckner, Watson, Vessey, Davis, Page. *Waiters*: Messrs. Cantry, Protas, Levine, Hoeckner.

Act 1: Dr. Thorne's Flower Garden near Paris. Afternoon.

Act 2: Hotel DePavillion. At a French bathing resort. Forenoon, following day.

Act 3: Same as Act 2. Evening of the same day.

---

[46]Dropped late in the run.

ACT 1[47]
"High Jinks"[48]
B. Barbaretto, E. Hammerstein, Visitors
"Jim"
E. Murray, Chorus
"Is This Love at Last?"[49]
M. Zucca, B. Barbaretto
Finale
Ensemble
ACT 2[50]
Opening Chorus
Ensemble
"I'm Through with Roaming Romeos"
E. Murray
"Chi-Chi"
E. Lea, B. Barbaretto
"Come Hither, Eyes" (Duet)
E. Murray, T. Lewis
"I Know Your Husband Very Well"
S. Edwards, A. Meade, Visitors
Finale[51]
Ensemble
ACT 3
Opening Chorus
Ensemble
"Bubbles"
E. Lea, B. Barbaretto, M. Zucca
"When Sammy Sang the Marseillaise"
A. Meade, Chorus
"All Aboard for Dixie(land)"[52]
E. Murray
(*Music by* George L. Cobb. *Lyrics by* Jack Yellen.)
Finale
Ensemble
Concluding with famous "High Jinks Tangle"

1913.35 ## ANNA HELD'S ALL STAR VARIETÉ JUBILEE

A Vaudeville Revue in One Act, 7 Scenes. Orchestra under the conductorship of Ernest Bial. Produced by John Cort. Opened 29 December 1913 at the Casino Theatre and closed 3 January 1914 after 8 performances.

CAST: ANNA HELD, GEORGE BEBAN, FRANCIS and FLORETTE, [Frank 'Pop'] WARD and [John 'P.'] CURRAN, CHARLES JUDELS, HIRSCHEL HENDLER, CHARLES AHEARN, IMPERIAL PEKINESE ACROBATS (6 Mongolian Gymnasts), Samuel J. Murphy, Frank Lynch, Pearl Cook, Richard Bartlett, Edith MacBride, Florence Daniels, Roland Bottomly, Jean L'Estrange, Charles H. Yorkshire, Harry T. Belmont, Victor Snyder, Felix F. McCabe, Les Raleigh, Leslie Jones, Nellie Crawford, Sadie Carr, Julia Sullivan, Eileen Adair, Marion Roth, Gladys Fox.

---

[47]Added to Act 1 for subsequent tour (preceding title song):
Opening Chorus
"Dr. Grouch is Going Away"
E. Hammerstein, Girls
[48]Added to this scene after opening:
"Something Seems Tingle-Ingle-ing"
B. Barbaretto, E. Hammerstein, Visitors
[49] Replaced after opening by:
"Love's Own Kiss"
M. Zucca, B. Barbaretto
[50]Added during the run to Act 2, following "Chi-Chi":
"Not Now But Later" (Duet)
I. Martinetti, M. Zucca
[51]Added during the run to the Finale:
[52]Replaced during the run by:
"(The) Dixiana Rise"
E. Murray

ACT 1[53]

Scene 1

Mlle. Baby (a musical playlet in 2 scenes)
Book and lyrics by Stanley Murphy. Music by Henry I. Marshall. Staged by Frank Smithson.

Mlle. Baby: A. Held. *Jack*, her fiancée: R. Bottomly. *Francois Vlobert*, her guardian: C. Judels. *Lewis*, the waiter: J. L'Estrange. *Raoul Berton*: C. H. Yorkshire. *Gaston Duval*: H. T. Belmont. *Jose Romaine*: V. Snyder. *Armand DeGrasac*: F. F. McCabe. *Henri L'Almont*: L. Raleigh. *Jean Biquet*: L. Jones. *Patrons of the Café Paris (6)*: *Fifi*: N. Crawford. *Babette*: S. Carr. *Toto*: J. Sullivan. *Adele*: E. Adair. *Alma*: M. Roth. *Jule*: G. Fox.

Scene a: Outside the "Jardin des Fleurs," Nice. *Scene b*: Interior of Cafe Paris-Nice, Nice.

Scene a

"I Want a Boy to Love Me" (I Want a Girl to Love Me)
R. Bottomly, Boys
"I'm Goin' to Go, Go, Go"
A. Held, Girls
"Roll Those Eyes"
A. Held
(*Lyrics by Henry Marshall.*)

Scene b

"Drink, Drink, Drink"
Ensemble
"Dinah"
C. Judels, Chorus
"Je Suis Gris"
A. Held
"When It's Buzz, Buzz, Buzzin' Time in Bee, Bee, Bee Town"
A. Held, R. Bottomly, Chorus
Medley (Finale)
A. Held, C. Judels, R. Bottomly, Chorus

Scene 2

The Sign of the Rose (*by* George Beban)
G. Beban, S. J. Murphy, P. Cook, company of 10

Scene 3

Francis and Florette
(Ball-room dance specialty: The Tango; The Beverly; The Shadow; The Manchester; The Slide Drop Glide; The Sensational Scroll; The Hesitation Waltz)

Scene 4

Andrew Mack (Irish ballads)

Scene 5

Hirschel Hendler
(Virtuoso pianist: impressions of Paderewski, Lhevinne, Godowski, d'Albert, etc.)

Scene 6

Charles Ahearn and His 10 'speed-burners' in a "Speed Mania"
Burlesque: Wheels within Wheels (Bicycle-automobile act)

Scene 7

Ward and Curran: The Stage Door-Tender, or The Terrible Judge (comedy and songs)
Imperial Pekinese Acrobats

1913.36 THE GIRL ON THE FILM

A Musical Farce in Three Acts.[54] Book by James T. Tanner. Based on the original German musical comedy (Filmzauber) by Rudolf Bernauer and Rudolf Schanzer. Music by Walter Kollo, Willy Bredschneider and Albert Sirmay. Lyrics by Adrian Ross. Production staged by Harry B. Burcher. Settings by Alfred Terraine, E. Ryan. Costumes designed by Comelli. Orchestra under the direction of Leonard Hornsbee. Produced by the Messrs. Shubert. Opened 29 December 1913 at the 44th Street Theatre and closed 21 February 1914 after 64 performances.

CAST: *Cornelius Clutterbuch*, a miller, Linda's Uncle: John McArdle. *Valentine Twiss*, an old college friend of Max's, in love with Linda: PAUL PLUNKETT. *Daudet*, prompter at the Vioscope office: Grafton Williams. *General Fitzgibbon*, V.C., D.S.O., of the War Office: Percy Terriss. *Sergeant Tozer*, Commissionaire of the Vioscope Offices: John Western. *Lord Ronny*, Secretary of the Army League: Lord Dangan [Arthur Wellesley]. *Tom Brown*, the defeated candidate: Milbury Ryder. *Max Daly*, a

Cinema author, actor and producer, the leading spirit of the Vioscope: GEORGE GROSSMITH. *Winifred*, Freddy, General Fitzgibbon's daughter: EMMY WEHLEN. *Linda*, Clutterbuck's niece, secretary to Max at the Vioscope: MADELEIN SEYMOUR. *Signora Maria Gesticulata*, an Italian Cinema actress: MARY ROBSON. *Friends of Freddy (3)*: *Viola*: Blanche Stocker. *Olivia*: Vere Sinclair. *Portia*: Gertie Birch. *An Officer*: C. P. Galton. *Mrs. Clutterbuch*: Hattie Arnold. *Macawber*: Edward Cutler. *Euphemia Knox*, Manageress of the Vioscope: CONNIE EDISS. *Specialty Dancers*: Oy-Ra, Dorma Leigh. *Girls, Men, Society People, Girl Typists, Actresses, Actors of the Cinema, Country Folk*: (Ensemble).

Act 1: The Offices of the Vioscope. (Terraine.)

Act 2: The Mill, Poggleford, Lincolnshire. (Ryan.)

Act 3: The Army League Soirée. (Terraine.)

ACT 1

Opening Chorus
"Correspondence" (Song)
M. Seymour, Chorus
"I Heard That Tale Before" (Duet)
M. Seymour, P. Plunkett
"You Don't See It But It's There" (Song)
C. Ediss, E. Wehlen
"In Bond Street" (Song)
E. Wehlen, G. Grossmith
Finale
Principals, Chorus

ACT 2

Opening Chorus
"On the Ground" (Song)
C. Ediss
"Song of the Mill"(The Good Old Mill)(Song)
M. Seymour
(*Music by* Willy Bredschneider.)
"Down By the Country Side" (Song)
G. Grossmith, Chorus
"Won't You Come and Waltz with Me" (Song)
M. Seymour, P. Plunkett
(*Music by* Albert Sirmay.)
"Ah! Che Vedo" (Scena Italiana)
M. Robson, G. Grossmith
"Oh! If You Were a Girl" (Duet)
E. Wehlen, G. Grossmith

ACT 3

Introduction and Dance
"Tommy Won't You Teach Me How to Tango" (Tango Song)
G. Grossmith, Chorus
Tango Dance
G. Grossmith, G. Birch
"Won't You Come and Waltz with Me" (Song, reprise)
M. Seymour, P. Plunkett
Finale
Principals, Chorus

1913.37 IOLE

A Musical Comedy in Two Acts. Book and lyrics by Robert W. Chambers and Ben Teal. Based on the novel of the same name by Robert W. Chambers. Music by William Frederick Peters. Staged by Ben Teal. Scenery designed by Ernest Albert. Orchestra under the direction of John McGhie. Produced by Harry H. Frazee. Opened 29 December 1913 at the Longacre Theatre and closed 17 January 1914 after 24 performances.

CAST (under the Sign of Mars): *Clarence Guilford*, the poet: FRANK LALOR. *Lionel Frawley*, the cubist poet: STEWART BAIRD. *George Wayne*, the broker: CARL GANTVOORT. *Harrow*, the real artist: Rexford Kendrick. *Lethbridge*, the real sculptor: Roydon Keith. *Stuyvesant Briggs*, the lawyer: LESLIE GASE. *Hiram*, the gardener: George Gorman. *Archibald Bunn*, a Cubist painter: Craig Lee. *Rawley Bunn*, a Cubist sculptor: W. E. Hovell. *Virgil Bunn*, a Cubist poet: Augustus Minton. *A Clergyman*: George O'Connor. *A Florist*: R. Flower. *A Jeweler*: G. Diamond. *Four Mentals*: *Brown*: Edward Dunn. *Black*: Jack Newton. *Green*: Ben Rogers. *White*: Lloyd Montgomery.
(Under the Sign of Venus): *The Eight Daughters of Guilford*: *Iole*: FERN ROGERS. *Vanessa*: HAZEL KIRKE. *Dione*: Mary Allison. *Lissa*: Marta Spears. *Philodice*: Edna Pendleton. *Chlorippe*: Edna Temple. *Cybele*: Anna Vane. *Aphrodite*: Gretchen Eastman. *Mrs. Bunn*: Lena Robinson.

---

[53]Not in performance order.
[54]Billed as Mr. George Edwardes' production from the London Gaiety.

Act 1: Peach and Plum Orchard in Blossom and Fruit, adjacent to the House Beautiful of Guilford, the Poet.

Act 2: A Simple Hallway in a Mansion of Manhattan, occupied by Frawley. Six weeks later.

ACT 1

"Back to Nature" (Opening Chorus)
Eight (Guilford) Daughters

"Oh Precious Thought" (Song)
F. Lalor, Eight Daughters

"I Wonder Why" (Duet)
H. Kirke, L. Briggs

"If Dreams Come True" (Octette)
F. Rogers, H. Kirke, M. Allison, M. Spears, C. Gantvoort, L. Gaze, R. Kendrick, R. Keith

"Comes an Exquisite Sensation" (Quartette)
F. Rogers, H. Kirke, M. Allison, M. Spears

"Amo"
F. Rogers

"To Rent, To Let" (Trio)
F. Lalor, L. Gaze, C. Gantvoort

"Why Do You Think I Love You So"[55] (Duet)
F. Rogers, C. Gantvoort

Finale
Ensemble

ACT 2

"Think of That" (Opening Chorus)
M. Allison, M. Spears, G. Eastman, A, Vane, E. Pendleton, E. Temple

"Time Is Flying" (Song)
H. Kirke, Daughters

"Like a Shepherdess" (Song)
F. Rogers

"Nude Descending a Staircase" (Song)
F. Lalor, Daughters

"And That Is All" (Song)
S. Baird

"Take It from Me" (Duet)
F. Lalor, S. Baird

"Iole" (Duet)
C. Gantvoort, F. Rogers

"None But the Brave Deserve the Fair" (Song)
F. Rogers, H. Kirke, M. Allison, M. Spears, E. Pendleton, E. Temple, C. Gantvoort, L. Gaze, R. Kendrick, R. Keith

"Oh, What's the Use?" (Song)
F. Lalor, Miss King

Finale
Ensemble

1914.01 THE WHIRL OF THE WORLD

A Delirious Dance Craze (Musical Revue) in Two Acts, 12 Scenes. Dialogue (sketches) and lyrics by Harold Atteridge. Music by Sigmund Romberg. Staged by William J. Wilson. Settings designed by Young Brothers. Costumes by Melville Ellis. Orchestra under the direction of Oscar Radin. Produced by the Winter Garden Company (Messrs. Shubert). Opened 10 January 1914 at the Winter Garden and closed 30 May 1914 after 161 performances.

CAST: *Jacques*: GEORGE MOON. *Beppo*: DANIEL MORRIS. *Viola*: MAY BOLEY. *Steward of the Amber Club*: EUGENE HOWARD. *Sammy Meyers*: WILLIE HOWARD. *M. Archambault*: Louis J. Cody. *Marquis Tullyrand*: RALPH HERZ. *Claudie*: Arthur Welsley. *Jack Phillips*: BERNARD GRANVILLE. *General Pavlo*: Laurence Grant. *The Virginia Judge*: WALTER C. KELLY.
   Members of the Amber Club: *Archie Piccadilly*: Lawrence Ward. *Bertie Strand*: Robert Ward. *Pierre*: Harry Delf. *Francois*: Lester Sheehan.
   Ladies of the Amber Club: *Fifi*: LILLIAN LORRAINE. *Olivia*: ROSIKA DOLLY. *Nanette*: JULIETTE LIPPE. *Annette*: TRIXIE RAYMOND. *Babette*: Dorothy Barnett. *Marguerite*: Elita Sherman. *Adele*: Liana Lorelly. *Elise*: June Eldridge. *Clarice*: Marie Salisbury. *Louise*: Emily Ross. *Lorette*: Lillian Howell.
   Footman: Jean Leprince. *Captain of the Police*: Earle Talbot. *Sergeant of the Police*: George Hanlon. *A Gendarme*: Felix Patty. *A Gendarme*: Harry Weber. *Captain of "La*

France" Purser of "La France": EUGENE HOWARD. *A Wireless Operator*: Louis J. Cody. *Ahmed*: George Moon. *Hassan*: Daniel Morris. *The Mysterious Arabian*: EUGENE HOWARD. *Cleopatra II*: LILLIAN LORRAINE. (*Dance Specialty*: LYDIA KYASHT, SERGE LITAVKIN.)
   Personnel of the Chorus: Misses Rena Markey, Florence Kern, Lois Stowe, Dorothy Landers, Marie Salisbury, Anna Perine, June Eldridge, Dot Page, Grace Dubois, Lillian Parrish, Emily Russ, Liani Lorrelli, Evelyn Hall, Grace Georgian, Marion McDonald, Myrtle Bauer, Paulita Sherman, Helen Glenmore, Lillian Howell, Dorothy Barnette, Helen Marche, Ruth Carberry, Elinore Ryley, Lucile Cavanaugh, Jennie Callen, Lena Betts, Vivian Lawrence, Vera Tirrell, Ethel Wheeler, Dorothy Moran, Dot Rozell, Trixie Raymond, Vera Dunn, Rosa Huber, Mazie Lawless, Muroff Allo, Elinor Wallace, Mabel Benelisha, Pearl Betts, Edna Hettler, Nellie Pennington, Follie Faulkner, Mazie Gilmore, Alice Eldon, Virginia Shelby, Claire Pearl, Rena Pelham, Rossella Meyers, Bobbie Roberts. Messrs. Winnie Parker, Fred Bates, Allan Fagan, Art Garvey, Charles Townshend, Larry Mac, Irving Jackson, Ray Goodrich, William Wilder, Irving Finn, Stanley Rayburn, Arthur Kelly.

Act 1, Scene 1: Maxixe Restaurant, Paris. *Scene 2*: Rue de Tango, Paris. *Scene 3*: The Amber Club, Paris. *Scene 4*: A Street in Havre. (H. Robert Law.) *Scene 5*: Rue de Tango. *Scene 6*: The Dock in Havre.

Act 2, Scene 1: Lounge on "La France." *Scene 2*: The Wireless Room. *Scene 3*: Off the Coast of Nova Scotia. *Scene 4*: Exterior of the Century Opera House, New York. *Scene 5*: The Arabian Night Ball at Madison Square Garden, New York.

ACT 1

Scene 1

"Come On In, the Dancing's Fine"
Guests at the Maxixe Restaurant

"A Broadway in Paree" (Paree, Paree,)
M. Boley, Chorus
(*Staged by* Henry Lehman.)

"Nobody Was in Love with Me" (Nobody's in Love with Me)
W. Howard, Chorus

Scene 2

"The Whirl of the World"
R. Herz

Scene 3

"The Amber Club"
Members of the Club

"A Dancing Romeo"
B. Granville, T. Raymond, Chorus

"Life's (Just) a Dress Parade"
J. Lippe, Chorus

"Hello, Little Miss U.S.A." (Hallo! Little Miss U.S.A.)
L. Lorraine, Chorus
(*Music and Lyrics by* Harry Gifford and Fred Godfrey.)

"The Dance of the Fortune Wheel"
R. Dolly, Chorus

"The Dolly Maxixe"
R. Dolly, L. Sheehan

"The Twentieth Century Rag"
B. Granville, Chorus
(*Staged by* Henry Lehman.)

"The Noble Cause of Art"[56]
R. Herz

Scene 5

"We Forgot the Number of the House"
R. Ward, L. Ward

Scene 6

"All Aboard"
The Travelers

"The Ragtime Pinafore"[57]
W. Howard, Chorus

"How D'you Do, Goodbye"
J. Lippe

"Everybody Means It When They Say Goodbye"
Principals, Chorus

---

[55]Dropped after opening, and replaced by "Iole," moved from Act 2.

[56]Briefly replaced during the run by (then later restored):
   "What We Want and What We Get" (from DR. DELUXE)
      R. Herz
   (*Music and Lyrics by* Edward Laska.)

[57]Dropped after opening.

ACT 2
Scene 1

"A Lovely Trip"
The Travelers

"I'll Come Back to You"[58]
R. Dolly

"Early Hours of the Morn"
B. Granville

"This Is the Life for Me"[59]
L. Lorraine

"Goodbye, London Town"[60]
R. Ward, L. Ward

Scene 4

"The Whirl of the Opera"
W. Howard, E. Howard

Scene 5

"Oh, Allah"
The Arabian Masqueraders

Harlequin and Bluebird[61] (Dance Divertissement arranged by Lydia Kyasht.)
Bluebird: L. Kyasht. *Harlequin*: S. Litavkin. *Pierrots*: Winter Garden Corps de Ballet.

Dance Eccentric[62]
G. Moon, D. Morris

"My Cleopatra Girl"
L. Lorraine, Chorus

"The Pavlowa Gavotte"
R. Dolly, L. Sheehan

"Ragtime Arabian Nights"
E. Howard, Chorus
(*Staged by* Henry Lehman.)

Finale
Arabian Masqueraders

1914.02 THE QUEEN OF THE MOVIES

A Musical Comedy in Three Acts. Book by Glen MacDonough. Based on the German musical 'Die Kino Königin' by Julius Freund and George Okonowski [Georg Okonkowski]. Music by Jean Gilbert. Lyrics by Edward E. Paulton. Dialogue rehearsed by Herbert Gresham. Ensemble numbers by Julian Mitchell. Scenery and costumes from the studio of Hugo Baruch. Orchestra under the direction of Hugo Riesenfeld. Produced by Thomas W. Ryley. Opened 12 January 1914 at the Globe Theatre and closed 11 April 1914 after 104 performances.

CAST (in order of appearance): *Mrs. Clutterbuck*, the second wife of Professor Josias Clutterbuck, founder of the Anti Moving-Picture League of America: JEANETTE HORTON. *Anne Clutterbuck*, daughter of Professor Clutterbuck's first wife: ALICE DOVEY. *Professor Josias Clutterbuck*, a rich and famous inventor of artificial foods, known as 'The Wizard of the Market Basket': FRANK MOULAN. *Baron Victor de Gardennes*, a titled Frenchman, employed at the Biograph Studio: JOHN H. GOLDSWORTHY. *Celia Gill*, a prominent moving-picture actress, known as "The Queen of the Movies": VALLI VALLI. *Croker*, an old school comedian, now acting as assistant to Billy Hilton: DAN COLLYER. *Louise*, maid at Miss Gill's: Flora Crosbie. *Elevator Boy*: Dorothy St. Clair. *Bell Boy*: June White. *Moving Picture Actresses (4)*: *May*: Diane Oste. *Bijou*: Mildred Richardson. *Agnes*: Jean Tyne. *Maude*: Alma Harrison. *Mr. and Mrs. Leightlywedd*: Fred Jones, Jean Tyne. *Greene*, a biograph operator: J. Estevan.
Dancing Ladies: Selma Mantell, Lydia Scott, May Leslie, Hazel Lewis, Marguerite St. Claire, Nancy Poole, Truly Ewers, Elsie Hamilton, Margaret Morris, Lillian West. *Pages*: Dorothy St. Claire, Teresa Hendricks, Eleanor Boise, June White, June Dodson, Marie Arment. *Ladies of the Ensemble*: Marie Wallace, Pauline Sterling, Isabel McLeod, Olga Boehm, Violet McKay, Helen O'Day, Dorothy Betts, Hazel Kingdon.

Gentlemen of the Ensemble: Messrs. Chapman, Pierce, Hartman, Nau, Sheridan, Wienpahl, Bryant, Faye, Lynwood, Cornish.

The action takes place in Washington at the present time.

Act 1: An entrance hall in the New Hotel.

Act 2: Drawing-room in the home of Celia Gill.

Act 3: Exterior of the Celia Moving-Picture Theatre.

ACT 1[63]

Opening Chorus

"Whistle"
A. Dovey, Boys
(*Music by* Leslie Stuart.)

"Pardon Me If I Stutter"
F. Adler

"Who Is to Know?"
J. H. Goldsworthy, A. Dovey, Chorus

"Follow the Crowd"
F. Moulan, Chorus
(*Music and Lyrics by* Irving Berlin.)

Trio
V. Valli, J. Redmond, F. Adler

Finale

ACT 2

Opening Chorus

"Forgive and Forget"
J. H. Goldsworthy, V. Valli

"Oh, Cecilia"
V. Valli, F. Moulan

"Girls, Run Along"
F. Adler, Chorus

Finale

ACT 3

Opening Chorus

"When the Moon Slyly Winks in the Night" (In the Night)
F. Adler, Chorus

"Cutie"
V. Valli, F. Moulan

Finale

1914.03 SÁRI

An Operetta in Two Acts.[64] English book and lyrics by C. C. S. Cushing and E. P. Heath. Based on the Viennese original 'Der Zigeunerprimás' by Julius Wilhelm and Fritz Grünbaum. Music by Emmerich Kálmán. Staged by George Marion. Scenery designed by Ernest Gros and Ronsin. Costumes by A. R. Wheelan; Miss Hajos' costumes by Maison Berkovitz and Frances, Inc. Conductor, Max Bendix. Produced by Henry W. Savage. Opened 13 January 1914 at the Liberty Theatre, moved 13 April 1914 to the New Amsterdam Theatre, and closed 23 May 1914 after 151 performances.

CAST: *Pali Racz*, the Gypsy Leader: VAN RENSSELAER WHEELER. *His Children (3)*: *Laczi*: J. HUMBIRD DUFFEY. *Sari*: MIZZI [Mitzi] HAJÓS. *Klari*: EVA BALL. *Joska Fekete*, his friend: Karl Stall. *Juliska Fekete*, his daughter: Blanche Duffield. *Gaston*, Count Irini: CHARLES MEAKINS. *Cadeaux*, his Shadow: HARRY DAVENPORT. *Count Estragon*, H. R. H. King of Massilia: Wilmuth Merkyl. *Count Mustari*, his Master of Ceremonies: Eugene Roder. *Pierre*: Harry Crapo.
Other Children of Racz: Misses Bush, Baldwin, Borden, Brooks, Merritt, Watkins; Eva and Madeline Ball, Lillian Fuchs, Ethel Baedor, Julius Scheinkman. *Gypsy Musicians*: Bernard Schmidt, Peter Eisenberg, John Berger, John Schildkret, Joseph Keckniger, M. Holland. *Postman*: Edward Smith. *Peasant Women*: Misses DeLome, Dettling, Vance, Schneider, Buress, Francesca, Sheridan, Church, Hall, Held, Moeller, Hendricks, Hunt, Lee. *Buds*: Misses Bush, Baldwin, Borden, Brooks, Merritt, Watkins. *Guests*: Misses DeLome, Dettling, Vance, Schneider, Buress, Francesca, Sheridan, Church, Hall, Held, Moeller, Hendricks, Hunt, Watkins and Lee. Messrs. Haberson, Murphy, McAvoy, Smith, Buchanan, Hahn, Miller, Francis, Calvin, Cook.

---

[58]Dropped after opening.
[59]Replaced during the run by (then dropped late in the run):
The Virginia Judge
W. C. Kelly
[60]Dropped late in the run.
[61]Dropped late in the run.
[62]Dropped late in the run.

---

[63]Interpolated as per published sheet music:
"Mootching Along (at the Cotton Ball)"
(*Music by* Lewis F. Muir. *Lyrics by* L. Wolfe Gilbert.)
[64]"Victorious Ever Is Youth" billed below the title.

Act 1: Courtyard of Pali Racz's Home. Lorinczfalva, Hungary. (Gros.)

Act 2: Paris Home of Count Irini. (Ronsin.)

ACT 1

"Stop It, Stop It"
V. R. Wheeler, Children

"Time, Oh, Time"
V. R. Wheeler

"Marry Me"
V. R. Wheeler, B. Duffield

"Pick a Husband"
M. Hajós, Children

"Paris? Oh, My! Yes, Dear"
H. Davenport, Village Maids

"Love Has Wings"
B. Duffield, J. H. Duffey

"Hazaza" (Ha-za-za)
M. Hajós, C. Meakins

"Triumphant Youth"
J. H. Duffey, B. Duffield, V. R. Wheeler, M. Hajós

Finale

ACT 2

"With Lowered Head" (Opening Chorus0

"Follow Me"
W. Merkyl, Chorus

"There's No Place Like Home for You"
M. Hajós, Guests

"My Faithful Stradivari"
V. R. Wheeler, W. Merkyl, C. Meakins, E. Roder

"Softly Through the Summer Night"
B. Duffield, J. H. Duffey

"Long Live the King" (Vive le Roi)
V. R. Wheeler, M. Hajós, B. Duffield, W. Merkyl

"Love's Own Sweet Song"
M. Hajós, C. Meakins

"The Contest"
Entire Company

Finale

1914.04   THE LAUGHING HUSBAND

A Musical Comedy in Three Acts. Book (and lyrics) by Arthur Wimperis adapted from the German (original 'Der lachende ebemann' by Julius Brammer and Alfred Grünwald). Music by Edmund Eysler. Ladies' dresses and costumes designed by Henri Bendel. Musical director, Gustave Selzer. Produced under the stage direction of Edward Royce. Produced by Charles Frohman. Opened 2 February 1914 at the Knickerbocker Theatre and closed 14 March 1914 after 48 performances.[65]

CAST: *Ottokar Bruckner*, a retired confectioner: COURTICE POUNDS. *Hella Bruckner*, his wife: BETTY CALLISH. *Andreas Pipelhuber*, his friend, alias Arnold Bentz, the famous novelist: FRED WALTON. *Dolly*, his niece: VENITA FITZHUGH. *Lucinda*, his cousin: JOSIE INTROPODI. *Mr. Rosenrot*, his lawyer: WILLIAM NORRIS. *Count Selztal*: GUSTAVE WERNER. *Herr von Basewitz*, a rich Berlin publisher: JOHN DALY MURPHY. *Etelka*, his wife: FRANCES DEMAREST. *Lutz Nachtigall*, a poetaster in love with Etelka: ROY ATWELL. *Hans Zimt*, an architect: Nigel Barrie. *Wiedehopf*, Majordomo at Buchenau: Bert D. Melville. *Baldrian*, footman: Leonard Feiner. *Juliette*, typist to Mr. Rosenrot: Irene Palmer. *Marie*, maid at Buchenau: Dorothy Chesmond. *Dancers*: Josephine Harriman, Genevieve O'Hara, Quentin Tod.

Guests: Evelyn Turner, Constance Hunt, Florence Moll, Gertrude Wilson, Gertrude Andea, Beatrice Percell, Marie George, Beatrice Hoover, Dorothy West, Marguerete Milford, Jessie Crane, Jeanne Crane, Yetla Nicoll, Evelyn Wildner, Marie Barbara, Margaret P. Langdon, Regina Knott, Frank Kenny, George Mortimer, William Gibney, Paul Pollock, Jack Mehl, George Fredericks, Oswald Love, Kenneth Munro.

Act 1: Reception Room in Ottokar Bruckner's Residence in Berlin. Present time.

Act 2: Shooting Box at Buchenau.

Act 3: In Mr. Rosenrot's Law Office. A year later.

ACT 1

Scene Music; Tango Eduard
G. O'Hara, Q. Tod

---

[65]Settings uncredited.

"Just a Little Gossip"[66] (Song)
B. Callish, Chorus

"Forbidden Fruit" (Duet)
R. Atwell, F. Demarest

"A Husband in Love with His Wife"[67] (Song)
C. Pounds

"In Beautiful Italiano" (Duet)
F. Walton, J. Intrpodi

"Little Miss Understood"
G. Werner, B. Callish

"Bought and Paid For" (Duet)
N. Barrie, V. Fitzhugh
(*Music by* Jerome Kern. *Lyrics by* Harry B. Smith.)

Finale

ACT 2[68]

Opening Chorus; "A Heart Will Fall" (Song)
G. Werner, Chorus

"Love Is Like a Violin" (Song)
B. Callish
(*Music by* Jerome Kern. *Lyrics by* Harry B. Smith.)

"Wine Song"
C. Pounds

"You're Here and I'm Here" (Duet)
V. Fitzhugh, N. Barrie
(*Music by* Jerome Kern. *Lyrics by* Harry B. Smith.)

"Take a Step with Me"[69] (Song)
F. Demarest, Chorus
(*Music by* Jerome Kern. *Lyrics by* Harry B. Smith.)

"Away from Thee" (Duet Bouffe)
C. Pounds, B. Callish

"Since Grandpa Learned to Tango" (Dance Quartette)
R. Atwell, J. D. Murphy, B. D. Melville, F. Walton
(*Music by* Pedro de Zulueta. *Lyrics by* L. Williams.)

"Silken Screen" (Duet)
G. Weerner, B. Callish

Finale

ACT 3

"Marital Malignity" (Opening Chorus)

"You're Here and I'm Here" (reprise)
G. Werner, V. Fitzhugh

"Lizette"[70] (Song)
C. Pounds

"Telephone Duet"
C. Pounds, B. Callish

Finale

1914.05   SHAMEEN DHU

A Play with Music in Three Acts. Play by Rida Johnson Young. Incidental music by Cassius Freeborn. Orchestra under the direction of Cassius Freeborn. Produced under the direction of Henry Miller. Opened 2 February 1914 at the Grand Opera House and closed 28 February 1914 after 32 performances.[71]

CAST (in order of appearance): *Peggy O'Dea*: CONSTANCE MOLINEAUX. *Sheila Farrell*: BETH FRANKLYN. *Lanty*: ROBERT WATT. *Norah*: Maribel Seymour. *Betsy*

---

[66]Replaced after opening by:
"Go To Paris or Vienna"
B. Callish, Chorus

[67]Dropped after opening.

[68]Added after opening, after "Since Grandpa Learned to Tango":
"The Futurist" (Hesitation Waltz/Dance)
J. Harriman, Q. Tod
(*Music by* Edwin Burch.)
(also used in THE DOLL GIRL and THE MARRIAGE MARKET on tour)

[69]Dropped after opening.

[70]After opening, move to Act 1 to follow "Bought and Paid For."

[71]Settings, costumes uncredited.

Bowers: Jennie Lamont. *Andy Bowers*: JOHN G. SPARKS. *Martin McGleash*: David Glassford. *Dare O'Donnell*:[72] CHAUNCEY OLCOTT. *Edward O'Dea*: ARTHUR MAITLAND. *Tim*: John Sheehan. *Flynn*: Walter Colligan. *Waters*: Frederick Roberts. *McPhatter*: MAURICE DREW.

The action takes place in the village of Kilcannon, Ireland, in about 1779.

Act 1: Mrs. Farrell's Sitting Room.

Act 2: The Pipe Room of the Green Dragon Inn.

Act 3: Mrs. Farrell's Garden.

MUSICAL NUMBERS[73]
  "Yankee Doodle"
    C. Olcott
  "My Little Dhudeen"
    C. Olcott
    (*Music by* Ernest R. Ball. *Lyrics by* George Graff, Jr.)
  "Dream Girl o' Mine"
    C. Olcott
    (*Music by* Cassius Freeborn. *Lyrics by* Chauncey Olcott.)
  "I Never Before Met a Girl Like You"
    C. Olcott
    (*Music by* Cassius Freeborn, Chauncey Olcott. *Lyrics by* George Graff, Jr.)
  "Peggy Darlin'"
    C. Olcott
  "Too Ra, Loo Ra, Loo Ra, Ly, That's an Irish Lullaby"
    C. Olcott
    (*Music and Lyrics by* James Royce Shannon.)
  "My Wild Irish Rose" (from ROMANCE OF ATHLONE)
    C. Olcott
    (*Music and Lyrics by* Chauncey Olcott.)

1914.06   WHEN CLAUDIA SMILES

A Farce with Songs in Three Acts. Play and lyrics by Anne Caldwell. Devised from the basic material contained in a play by Leo Ditrichstein. Music by Jean Schwartz. Directed by Charles J. Winninger. Scenery painted by H. Robert Law. Gowns and costumes by Maison Bernard, Max and Mayhieu, B. Altman. Orchestra under the direction of Al Ellis. Produced by Frederic E. McKay. Opened 2 February 1914 at the 39th Street Theatre, moved 23 February 1914 to the Lyric Theatre, and closed 21 March 1914 after 56 performances.

CAST: *Frederick W. Walker*, from Chicago: HARRY CONOR. *Chester D. Hoffman*, of Meadowbrook Hunt Club: Mahlon Hamilton. *Charles D. Hoffman*, Attorney at Law, and Chester's uncle: CHARLES J. WINNINGER. *"Bunny" Van Tyne*, only a millionaire's son: JOHN J. SCANNELL. *Saladillo Escalada Del Mendoza*, a tango teacher: R. M. Dolliver. *"Johnny" Rogers*, agent for Green Seal champagne: HARRY HILLIARD. *Albert*, a head-waiter at the Ritz-Carlton: William Keller. *Jingle Bells*, a bell boy: Charles Silber. *Elevator Attendant*: James Minnehan. *Officers Casey, Nolan* of the Jefferson Market Police Station: Albert Byrnes, Peter Donovan. *Alice Hoffman*, Chester Hoffman's wife, and daughter of Mr. Walker: BERTHA MANN. *Kate Walker*, Alice's sister: ANNA LAUGHLIN. *Mme. Verdier*, who adores society and the stage: FLORENCE EDNEY. *Cynthia*, Claudia's colored maid: Nellie Fillmore.
  Ornaments of the Stage: Daisy Tottenham: Cleo LeMoyne. *Belle Nesville*: Claire Bertrand. *Blanche DeFontenoy*: Rae Daly. *Cleo Berode*: Eva Stuart. *Angie DuPont*: Dolores Parquette. *Clara Rockaway*: Gladys Breston.
  The Merry Madcaps: Lily Atlanta: Pearl Evans. *Violet Richmond*: Marie Callahan. *Rose Reno*: Claire Weston. *Hyacinth Hartford*: Peggy Coudray. *Daisy Denver*: Evelyn Mead. *Pansy Portland*: Emma McGrath.
  Boys About Town: Reggie Renfrew: Harry Delmar. *Willie Wilbur*: Harry Wesner. *Percy Plimpton*: Harry Rensler. *Billy Bender*: Edwin H. Weihe. *Jimmy Jansen*: Edward Clyne. *Bertie Billings*: Jack Costello.
  And *Claudia Rogers*, a show girl, recently divorced from Johnny Rogers: BLANCHE RING.

Act 1: Foyer of the Ritz-Carlton Hotel, New York. Afternoon.

Act 2: Claudia Rogers' Boudoir in East 46th Street, New York. The same evening.

Act 3: Same as Act 1. The following night.

ACT 1[74]
  "Boys, Boys, Boys"
    A. Laughlin, Boys
  "(It's a) Grand Old Life"
    B. Ring, Show Girls
    (*Lyrics by* William Jerome.)
  "I've Got Everything I Want But You"
    J. J. Scannell, A. Laughlin
    (*Music by* Henry I. Marshall. *Lyrics by* Marion Sunshine.)
  "The Flower Garden Ball"
    B. Ring, Chorus
    (*Lyrics by* William Jerome.)
ACT 2
  "If They'd Only Move Old Ireland Over Here"
    B. Ring
    (*Music by* Frank Gillen. *Lyrics by* Jamie Kelly and Lou Klein.)
  "(Dear Old) Dinah"
    J. J. Scannell, A. Laughlin, Girls
    (*Music by* Henry I. Marshall. *Lyrics by* Stanley Murphy.)
  "(He's a) Dear Old Pet"
    B. Ring, H. Conor
    (*Lyrics by* William Jerome.)
ACT 3
  "Everybody (Sometime) Must Love Someone"
    B. Ring, Ensemble
    (*Music by* Dave Stamper. *Lyrics by* Gene Buck.)
  "You're My Boy"
    A. Laughlin, J. J. Scannell
    (*Music by* Henry I. Marshall. *Lyrics by* Marion Sunshine.)
  "Why Is the Ocean So Near the Shore?" (Why, Why, Why)
    B. Ring
    (*Music by* Clarence Jones. *Lyrics by* Arthur Weinberg.)

1914.07   THE MIDNIGHT GIRL

A Musical Comedy in Three Acts. Original German book ('Das Mitternacht Mädel'[75]) by Paul Hervé. English version by Adolf Philipp and Edward A. Paulton. Music by Jean Briquet and Adolf Philipp. Staged by Ben Teal. Musical numbers staged by Jack Mason. Costumes designed by Melville Ellis. Orchestra under the direction of Herbert Kerr. Produced by the Messrs. Shubert. Opened 23 February 1914 at the 44th Street Theatre and closed 23 May 1914 after 104 performances.[76]

CAST (in order of appearance): *Clarisse*: Fremont Benton. *Pierre*: DENMAN MALEY. *Mme. Gimblette*: Amy Leicester. *Dr. Benoit*: GEORGE A. SCHILLER. *Mme. Benoit*: LOUISE KELLEY. *General Chambert*: TEDDY WEBB. *Lucille*: EVA FALLON. *Gustave Criquet I*: GEORGE MacFARLANE. *Francois*: HARRY DELF. *Helene*: MARGARET ROMAINE. *Guiseppe*: Paul Ker. *Babette*: Margaret Brunelle. *Gustave Criquet II*: CLARENCE HARVEY. *Maurice*: Edouard Durand. *Heloise*: ZOE BARNETT. *Alfons*: Madison Smith. *Charles*: Harold Nelson. *Josef*: Stanley Vickers. *Gustave Criquet III*: Lionel Belmore. *Marcel*, a page: Kathryn Robertson.

The action takes place in Chantilly, France at the present time.

Act 1: Criquet's salon. Late afternoon.

Act 2: Honeymoon Hall, Pyrénées Mountains. Next evening.

Act 3: Gardens of Honeymoon Hall. Next morning.

ACT 1
  "Decorations" (Opening Chorus)
    Ensemble

---

[72]Shameen Dhu is Gaelic for Black Jamie, whose name Dare O'Donnell uses to hide his own.
[73]Not necessarily in performance order. Not listed in program, but prepared from press notices. Olcott freely reprised additional song hits from his earlier shows.

[74]Musical numbers not listed in opening night program, but contained in later programs from the Lyric Theatre engagement. Also performed as per published sheet music, or perhaps dropped before the New York opening:
  "Sweetheart, Let Us Dance the Boston"
    B. Ring
    (*Music and Lyrics by* George A. Spink.)
[75]Previously produced in New York in German and English 1 September 1913 at Adolf Philipp's 57th Street Theatre for 100 performances.
[76]Settings uncredited.

Concerted Entrance
  T. Webb, G. A. Schiller, L. Kelley, A. Leicester, E. Fallon
"Dolly" (Solo)
  E. Fallon
"Burglars" (Trio, descriptive)
  G. MacFarlane, F. Benton, D. Maley
"Love and Victory" (Song)
  H. Delf, Officers
"A Lesson in Love"[77] (duet)
  H. Delf, E. Fallon
"The Midnight Girl"
  M. Romaine, Nurses
"Come Back to the (Old) Cabaret" (Duetto)
  P. Ker, M. Romaine, Nurses
"I've Waited Long for You, Dear"[78] (Duet)
  G. MacFarlane, M. Romaine
"Ten O'Clock"
  G. MacFarlane, M. Romaine, T. Webb, G. A. Schiller, Nurses
"When the Band Begins to Play" (Finale)

ACT 2
"Honeymoon Hall" (Opening Chorus)
  P. Ker, Waiters
"Oh, Gustave" (Duetto)
  M. Romaine, G. MacFarlane
"We Will Ramble (You and I, Dear)"[79] (Duet)
  H. Delf, E. Fallon
"The Midnight Girl"[80] (Solo, reprise)
  G. MacFarlane, Guests
"The Midnight Cabaret"
  M. Romaine, Ensemble
The Maxixe[81] (Dance)
  H. Delf, E. Fallon
Finale

ACT 3
Opening Chorus
  M. Romaine, Officers, Guests, Peasants
"On the Lonely Lagoon"[82]
  M. Romaine, Chorus
  (Music by Sigmund Romberg.)
"Oh, You John"[83]
  E. Fallon, Ensemble
  (Music by Sigmund Romberg.)
"Good Night Love"
  G. MacFarlane
  (Music and Lyrics by Will Anderson.)
Finale
  Full Company

---

[77]Replaced during the run by:
  "Cure of Love" (Duetto)
    H. Delf, E. Fallon
[78]Replaced during the run by:
  "The Path to Honeymoon Land" (Duetto)
    G. MacFarlane, M. Romaine
[79]Replaced during the run by:
  "A Certain Something About You" (Song)
    Z. Barnett, G. MacFarlane, C. Harvey, Chorus
[80]Replaced for subsequent national tour by:
  "Look in Her Eyes" (Solo)(from LIEBER AUGSTIN; MISS CAPRICE)
    G. MacFarlane, Waiters
  (Music by Jerome Kern. Lyrics by M. E. Rourke.)
[81]Dropped during the run.
[82]Dropped during the run.
[83]Replaced during the run by:
  "The Path to Honeymoon Land"(reprise)
    M. Romaine, G. MacFarlane, Full Chorus
  Which was replaced for subsequent tour by:
  "Won't You Waltz With Me?"
    H. Delf, Dolly Castles (Lucille)

1914.08

THE CRINOLINE GIRL

A Farcical Melodramatic Comedy with Songs in Three Acts. Book by Otto Hauerbach [Harbach]. Music by Percy Wenrich. Lyrics by Julian Eltinge. Staged by John Emerson. Scenery painted by D. Frank Dodge and William Castle. Costumes by Julian Eltinge. Orchestra under the direction of J. Albert Browne. Produced by A. H. Woods. Opened 16 March 1914 at the Knickerbocker Theatre and closed 30 May 1914 after 88 performances.[84]

CAST (in order of appearance): *Dorothy Ainsley*, daughter of Richard Ainsley, a wealthy American: HELEN LUTTRELL. *Lord Robert Bromleigh*: Herbert McKenzie. *Smith*, butler to Richard Ainsley: Joseph S. Marba. *Marie*, a maid: Augusta Scott. *Richard Ainsley*: CHARLES P. MORRISON. *Jerry Ainsley*, his nephew: HERBERT CORTHELL. *Alice Hale*, a wealthy American girl: Maidel Turner. *Tom Hale*, brother of Alice Hale: JULIAN ELTINGE. *Charles Griffith*, a newspaper correspondent: James C. Spottswood. *John Lawton*, a detective: Walter Horton. *Rosalind Bromleigh*, sister of Lord Bromleigh (The Crinoline Girl): EDNA WHISTLER. *William*: Edwin Cushman.

Act 1: Sitting-room of the Ainsley Suite in the Hotel de Beau Rivage, Lausanne, Switzerland. 8:30 P.M.

Act 2: A corner of the Palm Room, same hotel. Ten minutes later.

Act 3: Same as Act 2. Five minutes later.

ACT 1[85]
  "In My Dream of You"
    J. Eltinge
ACT 2
  "When Martha Was a Girl"
    J. Eltinge
ACT 3
  "That Tempting Tango"
    J. Eltinge

1914.09

MAIDS OF ATHENS

A Comic Opera in Two Acts and a Prologue. English version by Carolyn Wells. Based on the Viennese original ('Die ideale Gattin'[86]) by Victor Léon. (Founded on Edmond About's classic "Le Roi de Montagne.") Music by Franz Lehár. Staged by George Marion. Orchestra under the direction of John McGhie. Produced by Henry W. Savage. Opened 18 March 1914 at the New Amsterdam Theatre and closed 4 April 1914 after 22 performances.

CAST: *Prince of Parnes*: ALBERT PELLATON. (*Hadschi Stavros*, King of the Mountain Bandits: ALBERT PELLATON.) *Captain William Penn Harris*: ELBERT FRETWELL. *Princess Photini*: CECIL CUNNINGHAM. *Mary Louise*: LEILA HUGHES. *Van Green, Dyke Green*, from Scotland Yard: BERT GILBERT, W. S. PERCY. *Mrs. Rosamund Barley*: Marie Horgan. *Christodolus*: Charles Meyer. *Pericles*: James Davis. *Marula*: Jennie Dickerson. *Atalanta*: Retta Bellaire. *Aeeta*: Florida Bellaire. *Tamburis*: Albert Hedge. *Spiro*: Harry Hamilton. *Lieutenant Morris*: Russell Griswold. *Guide*: Allan Forbes.
  Greek Maidens: Misses Calame, St. Claire, Nash, Margrave, Albertus, West, Gilkinson, Hill, Harris, Baker, Duffield, Warren, Toole, Merlau, Carroll, Lang, Rowena, Gypsy Bellaire, Douglas, Lipton, LeBrun, Thebaud, Richards, Graham, Fisher, White, Elton, Call. *Firebrands of Hellas*: Messrs. Chadwick, Hawsley, White, Sansiper, Mulvey, Clark, McGurgan, Gibney, Hedge, Forbes, Fletcher, Hamilton, Griswold, Stewart, Gibson, Cox, Waite, Lee, Rankin, Carlos. *Nurses*: Misses Harris, Warren, Carroll, Merlau, Duffield, Baker. *Suffragettes*: Misses Nash, Gilkinson, Calame, Magrave, Albertus, Hill, West, St. Claire.

Prologue: Palace of the Prince of Parnes in Athens.

Act 1: Mountain Home of "Firebrands of Hellas."

Act 2: On Board the U. S. S. *Oklahoma*.

PROLOGUE
  "Ah, Yes, I Am in Love"
    C. Cunningham, E. Fretwell

---

[84]Played a return engagement 14 December 1914 at the Standard Theatre for 8 performances.
[85]Added to Act 1 in fourth week of the run, after "In My Dream of You":
  "(The) Game of Eyes"
    J. Eltinge
[86]"Die ideale Gattin" itself was a revised version of an earlier Lehár operetta "Der Göttergate" (1904).

"The Girl He Couldn't Kiss"
 L. Hughes, A. Pellaton
"The Clever Detective"
 B. Gilbert, W. S. Percy
 (*Music by* Charles J. Anditzer.)
Finale
 Ensemble

ACT 1
"The Brigands' Chorus"
 Chorus
"Life Is Lonely"
 A. Pellaton, Brigands
"Nurse, Nurse, Nurse"
 Sextette
 (*Music by* Arthur Lange and Felix Arndt.)
"When the Heart Is Young"
 L. Hughes
"Heavenly Ladies"
 A. Pellaton
"Rosie"
 M. Horgan, B. Gilbert, W. S. Percy
 (*Music by* Frederic Norton.)
"Bid Me Forget"
 C. Cunningham, E. Fretwell
Finale
 Ensemble

ACT 2
"Old Sea Songs" (Chanties—Arranged)
"Our Glorious Stripes and Stars"
 E. Fretwell, Male Chorus
 (*Music by* Paul Kerr.)
"One or Another"
 B. Gilbert, W. S. Percy, M. Horgan
 (*Music by* Oscar Haase.)
"Waltz, You Siren of Melody"
 Principals, Chorus
Finale
 Ensemble

1914.10 THE BELLE OF BOND STREET

A Musical Play in Three Acts. Book by Owen Hall and Harold Atteridge, adapted as an up-to-date version of the musical "The Girl from Kay's." Music by Ivan Caryll and Lionel Monckton. Lyrics by Adrian Ross and Claude Aveling. Staged by Edwin T. Emery. Dances arranged by Jack Mason. Settings by H. Robert Law. Costumes by Melville Ellis. Orchestra under the direction of Leonard Hornsey. Produced by the Messrs. Shubert. Opened 30 March 1914 at the Sam S. Shubert Theatre and closed 9 May 1914 after 48 performances.

CAST (in order of appearance): *James*, the butler: Joseph P. Galton. *Ellen*, the maid: Lottie Collins. *Norah*, the bride: FRITZI VON BUSING. *Harry Gordon:* FORREST HUFF. *Jack Richley*, a friend: HARRY PILCER. *Mrs. Chalmers*, Norah's mother: Alice Gordon. *Mr. Chalmers*, the father: Charles Burrows. *Theodore Quench, K.C.*, the uncle: Jere McAuliffe. *Hon. Percy Fitzthistle*, a friend of "Piggy": LAWRENCE D'ORSAY. *Max Hoggenheimer:* SAM BERNARD. *Winnie Harborough*, the Belle of Bond Street: GABY DESLYS. *Joseph*, the hall porter: Grafton Williams. *Pepper*, the head waiter: Norman A. Blume. *Miss Slender:* Grace Orr.

 The Girls from Bond Street: Nancy: Marjory Lane. *Hilda:* Gladys Benjamin. *Clara:* Harriet Leidy. *Mary:* Adelaide Wilson. *Cora:* Edith Offut. *Mabel:* Marie Maury. *The Brides Maids: Rodha:* Vera Cameron. *Ella:* Ida Prosser. *Maud:* Emily Burnham. *Gertrude:* Natalie Saymore. *Olive:* Olive Tremper. *Joan:* Bille DeHon. *Belle:* Shirley Love. *Gladys:* Marjory Fischer. *Elsie:* Mabel Carrouthers. *Sonia:* Anita Delories. *The Hat Box Girls:* Winona Wilkins, Mabel Hill, Babe Dakin, Lillian Broderick, Ruby Lewis, Millie Dupree, Gladys Clifton, Edna Stillwell, Della Hunt, Emily Hall. *Gentlemen Guests:* Messrs. Firwen, Mantiel, Rockwell, Spaulding, Smith, Gibbon, Russell, Phelps, Potts, Brennan.

Act 1: The Sitting-room in Mr. Chalmer's Villa, Kensington.

Act 2: His Majesty's Hotel, Flacton-on-the-Sea. England.

Act 3: Corridor of the Hotel Carlton, London.

ACT 1

Opening Interlude
 Guests at Breakfast
"The Bridal Bevy"
 Bridesmaids
"As I Came Down the Aisle"
 F. von Busing
"We've Come for You Ladies"
 Guests, Bridesmaids
 (*Music by* Harry Carroll. *Lyrics by* Harold Atteridge.)
"The Tango Maid" (A Little Tango Maid)
 L. Collins, Chorus
 (*Music by* Harry Carroll. *Lyrics by* Harold Atteridge.)
"That Hat and Not the Girl" (It's the Hat and Not the Girl)
 G. Deslys, Maids
"They Say I'm Frivolous"
 G. Deslys, H. Pilcer
"Too Many Cooks"
 F. Huff
Finale
 Ensemble

ACT 2
"Flacton-On-Sea"
 Guests, Girls
"A Honeymoon Trip All Alone"
 F. Huff, F. von Busing
"The Tango Dip"
 G. Deslys, H. Pilcer, Chorus
 (*Music by* Harry Carroll. *Lyrics by* Harold Atteridge.)
"Pierrotland"
 L. Collins, Girls
"Prunella"
 H. Pilcer
 (*Music by* Harry Carroll. *Lyrics by* Harold Atteridge.)
Finale
 Entire Company

ACT 3
Opening Chorus
 Ensemble
"Sufficiency"[87]
 S. Bernard
"My Turkey Trotting Boy" (The Turkey Totting Boy/Oh! You Turkey Trotter)
 G. Deslys, H. Pilcer
 (*Music by* Harry Carroll. *Lyrics by* Harold Atteridge.)
"Hoggenheimer of Park Lane"
 G. Deslys, S. Bernard
Finale
 Concerted Ensemble

**1914.11 H.M.S. PINAFORE,
or, The Lass That Loved a Sailor**

A Revival of the Comic Opera in Two Acts.[88] Libretto by William S. Gilbert. Music by Arthur Sullivan. Production staged by William J. Wilson. Scenic investiture and marine accessories by Arthur Voegtlin. Costumes designed

---

[87]Replaced after the opening by:
 "Who Paid the Rent for Mrs. Rip Van Winkle? (When Rip Van Winkle Was Away)"
 S. Bernard
 (*Music by* Fred Fisher. *Lyrics by* Alfred Bryan.)

[88]Originally presented in New York 15 January 1879 at the Standard Theatre for 175 performances. For Synopsis of Scenes and Musical Numbers, see original 1879 production. To allow the two performances per day schedule at the Hippodrome, two full casts were given. Members of the principal cast are listed first, alternate cast listed second. The following were interpolated into this production: Gavotte from RUDDIGORE; March Entrance from IVANHOE; Hornpipe from RUDDIGORE; Opening: Introduction from YEOMEN OF THE GUARD.

by William H. Matthews, Jr. Musical conductors, Manuel Klein and Selli Simonson. Produced by the Messrs. Shubert. Opened 9 April 1914 at the Hippodrome and closed 23 May 1914 after 77 performances.

CAST: *The Rt. Hon. Sir Joseph Porter, K.C.B.*: HARRISON BROCKBANK, WILLIAM G. GORDON. *Captain Corcoran, Commander of H.M.S. Pinafore*: WILLIAM HINSHAW, BERTRAM PEACOCK. *Ralph Rackstraw, Able Seaman*: VERNON DALHART, JOHN BARDSLEY. *Dick Deadeye, Able Seaman*: ALBERT HART, E. PERCY PARSONS. *Bill Bobstay*, Boatswain: Earl W. Marshall, Eugene Cowles. *Bob Becket*, Sergeant of Marines: ??. *Tom Tucker*, Midshipmite: ??. *Tom Bowlin*, Boatswain's Mate: ??. *Josephine*, the Captain's Daughter: Ruby Cutter Savage, Helen Heinemann. *Little Buttercup*, Mrs. Cripps, a Portsmouth Bum-Boat Woman: JOSEPHINE JACOBY, MARIE HORGAN. *Hebe*, Sir Joseph's First Cousin: Elise Marryett, Grace Camp.

Officer of the Deck: P. A. Young. *Senior Lieutenant*: J. Carey. *Junior Lieutenant*: William Belton. *Sergeant of Marines*: Harry Millirns. *Quartermaster*: L. Litchfield. *Coxswain*: John Pritchard. *Carpenter*: Daniel Dawson. *Boatswain's Mates*: C. Bendette, R. DeCendre. *Petty Officers*: Harry Cluett, George Warner, Harry Dale, Manuel Valles. *Midshipmites*: E. Hope, C. Welford, Frances Okey, Lilyan Jones, M. Mitchell, B. Hope, Gwen Jack, A. Hart. *First Lord's Sisters, his Cousins and his Aunts*: Ladies of the Chorus. *Commissioned Offciers, Marines, Drummers, Topmen, Sailors*: Gentlemen of the Chorus.

1914.12   THE RED CANARY

A Musical Play in Two Acts. Book by William LeBaron and Alexander Johnstone. Music by Harold Orlob. Lyrics by Will B. Johnstone. Staged by Ben Teal. Orchestra under the direction of Dewitt C. Coolman. Costumes by B. Altman & Co. Produced by the Mackay Production Company (under the personal direction of J. C. Rigby). Opened 13 April 1914 at the Lyric Theatre and closed 25 April 1914 after 16 performances.[89]

CAST (in order of appearance): *Marie*, Saleswoman at Donnet's: Cecile Renard. *Lois*, Principal Saleswoman at Donnet's: ADELE ROWLAND. *Jacques*, Principal Salesman at Donnet's: E. M. Foley. *Archibald Speed*, a wealthy Yankee: PHIL RYLEY. *Mrs. Kirk*, a widow and Mother of Jane: Ida Waterman. *Gustave Donnet*, Scarf Merchant and Colorist: NEAL McCAY. *Trixie Turner*, Ward of Archibald Speed: Nita Allen. *Jane*, an American Buyer: LEILA HUGHES. *Hunter Upjohn*, an American "Mixer": T. ROY BARNES. *Chauffeur*: Charles Prince. *Baron de Treville*: DAVID REESE. *Gaston Philippe*, Proprietor of "The Garden of Birds": Arthur Lipson. *Alice Vail*, Companion to Mrs. Kirk: Dorothy Wilcox. (*Dance Specialty*: Rosita Mantilla, B. Lloyd.)

Flower Girls: Misses Cadiz, DeForest, Maier, Renard. *Saleswomen*: Misses Trixie Cadiz, Buddie Callahan, Florence Coleman, Patsie DeForest, Hazel Maier, Ada Meade, Hilda Packard, Marjorie Purcell, Margaret Ward, Cecile Renard. *Customers*: Misses June Buckingham, Ethel Clayton, Maude Crockett, Gertrude Fayot, Eveyln Fulton, Grace Grindell, Anna Hall, Helen Longfellow, Madeleine Frain, Elsie Marquette, Bettie Martin, Corrinne Picard, Dorothy Wilcox. *Shop Assistants*: Messrs. Timothy O'Rourke, Jean DeHeck, Walter Mozee, H. S. Palmer. *Buyers*: Messrs. James Black, Gene Elliott, Frank Kingsley, James Egan, Victor Munro, Jay McCormack, Billy Gibney, Jack Mann.

The action takes place at the present time in Paris.

Act 1: Scarf Shop of Gustave Donnet. Afternoon.

Act 2: The Garden of Birds, a Parisian Café. Same evening.

ACT 1

Opening Chorus

"Donnet's Color Scheme" (Donnet Does the Trick)
  A. Rowland, P. Ryley, E. M. Foley

"The Call of Love"
  N. McCay, Chorus

"Come to Paris"
  L. Hughes, Chorus

"Color Blind" (Colors Mean Nothing to Me)
  T. R. Barnes

"Buy, Buy, Baby"
  A. Rowland, Chorus

"The Color Mixing Scheme"
  L. Hughes, N. McCay, D. Reese

"I'm So Weary"
  L. Hughes, T. R. Barnes, Chorus

"The Canary's Escape" — Finale
  Ensemble

ACT 2

Opening:
  "The Garden of Birds" (Pantomimic Chorus)
    Ensemble

---

[89]Settings uncredited.

"The Globe-Trotter"
  P. Ryley, A. Rowland, Chorus

Specialty Dances
  R. Mantilla, B. Lloyd

"The Blue Bell and the Rose"
  L. Hughes, Chorus

"Simply Looking Around"
  N. Allen

"(Since) Diaphanous Diana (is Back in Town)"
  A. Rowland, Chorus
  (*Music by* Raymond Walker. *Lyrics by* Thomas Gray.)

"Next"
  T. R. Barnes

"Goodbye to Blue"
  D. Reese

"The Kiss"
  L. Hughes, D. Reese

"The Cabaret Siren"
  L. Hughes, Company

Finale
  Ensemble

1914.13   THE BEAUTY SHOP

A Musical Comedy in Three Acts. Book and lyrics by Channing Pollock and Rennold Wolf. Music by Charles J. Gebest. Staged by R. H. Burnside. Costumes by Max & Mahieu. Settings by Edward G. Unitt and Joseph Wickes. Orchestra under the direction of Charles J. Gebest. Produced by George M. Cohan and Sam Harris. Opened 13 April 1914 at the Astor Theatre and closed 27 June 1914 after 88 performances.

CAST (in order of appearance): *Vivian*: ANNA ORR. *Gladys*: Christine Mangasarian. *Hiram Sharp*, representing a Committee of Creditors: Harry Hermsen. *Anna Budd*, ward of Dr. Budd: TESSA KOSTA. *Phil Farady*: JOSEPH W. HERBERT, JR. *Daniel Webster Briggs*: LAWRENCE WHEAT. *Doctor Arbutus Budd*: RAYMOND HITCHCOCK. A *Chauffeur*: George E. Mack. *Miss Montmorency*: Gertrude Aldrich. A *Stout Party*: Agnes Gildea. *Sigfried Schmalz*, a Band Master: Harry Hermsen. *Garibaldi Panatella*, Lardlord of the Inn: Edward Metcalfe. *Lola*, a Spanish Dancer: MARION SUNSHINE. *Logubrio Sobini*, an Undertaker: George E. Mack. *Caramba Maldanado*, a Corsican Duelist: George Romaine. *Natalie Panatella*: Bernice Buck. *The Souvenir Girl*: Margaret Henry. *Chorus of Customers, Hairdressers, Manicures, Society Ladies, Johnnies, Creditors, Corsican Girls, Peasants, Fishermen, Fisher Girls, Fisher Boys and Tourists*.

Chorus: Act 1, *The Ladies*: *Customers*: Misses Hastings, Crane, Markusson, Aldrich, Bell, Tennis, Newell, E. Clifford. *Wives*: Misses Farnsworth, Goulette, Lockard, Young, Reeves, Pinder, Donn, O'Kane. *Society Ladies*: Misses Richmond, Newell, Markusson, Henry. *Manicures*: Misses Wallace, Crane, Poir, Wendell, Nolan, Ellsworth, M. Gildea, DeVere. *Pages*: Misses Ellsworth, Poir. *The Gentlemen*: *Hairdressers*: Messrs. Kelly, Hessong, Morrison, Cody, Enwright, Macrossan, Montgomery, Geyer. *Business Men*: Messrs. Brusch, McShane, Piper, Johnson, Ross, Lafferty, Emerson, Rowe.

Act 2, The Ladies: *Corsican Boys*: Misses Pinder, Goulette, Hastings, O'Kane, Markusson, Bell, Tennis, E. Clifford. *Corsican Wives*: Misses Aldrich, Richmond, Newell, Pinder, Lockard, Reeves, Donn, Farnsworth. *Bar Maids*: Misses Richmond, Newell, Young, Henry. *Waitresses*: Misses Wendell, Poir, Wallace, Crane, M. Gildea, DeVere. *The Gentlemen*: *Corsican Peasants*: Messrs. Kelly, Hessong, Morrison, Cody, Enwright, Macrossan, Montgomery. *Tourist Boys*: Messrs. Morrison, Cody, Enright, Montgomery. *Corsican Johnnies*: Messrs. Johnson, McShane, Brusch, Piper, Ross, Lafferty, Emerson, Rowe. *The Band*: Messrs. Wagner, Verdi, Meyerbeer, Sousa.

Act 3, The Ladies: *Fisher Girls*: Misses Aldrich, Hastings, Tennis, O'Kane, Markusson, Bell, E. Clifford. *Fisher Wives*: Misses Goulette, Lockard, Reeves, Pinder, Donn, A. Gildea. *Fisher Boys*: Misses Wendell, Wallace, Crane, Nolan, Ellsworth, Poir, Gildea, DeVere. *The Gentlemen*: *Corsicans*: Messrs. Kelly, Hessong, Morrison, Cody, Enwright, Macrossan, Montgomery, Geyer. *Fishermen*: Messrs. Johnson, McShane, Brusch, Piper, Ross, Lefferty, Emerson, Rowe.

Act 1: Reception Room of Dr. Budd's Beauty Parlors in Fifth Avenue, New York City.

Act 2: Interior of Panatella's Hotel, Omessa in Corsica. Ten days later.

Act 3: On the Beach at Ajaccio, Corsica. The following day.

ACT 1

"In a Beauty Shop" (Opening Chorus)
  Ensemble

"I Want to Look Like Lillian Russell"
  A. Orr, Chorus

"Come Along, Little Girl, Come Along"
  A. Orr, T. Kosta, J. Herbert, L. Wheat

"Saturday Afternoon on Broadway"
R. Hitchcock, Chorus

"Love's Hesitation"
T. Kosta, J. Herbert
(*Lyrics by* Maurice E. Marks.)

"When the Creditor Comes to Call"
R. Hitchcock, Chorus

"(When You're) All Dressed Up and No Place to Go"
R. Hitchcock
(*Music by* Silvio Hein. *Lyrics by* Benjamin Hapgood Burt.)

"Poor Uncle Gasazus" (Finale)
Ensemble

ACT 2

"In Corsica" (Opening Chorus)
Ensemble

"I Love All the Boys in the World"
M. Sunshine, Chorus

"The Sunshine Maxixe"
M. Sunshine, J. Herbert

"'Twas in September"
A. Orr, L. Wheat
(*Music by* Silvio Hein. *Lyrics by* Benjamin Hapgood Burt.)

"I Love You Just the Same"
M. Sunshine, R. Hitchcock
(*Music by* Dave Stamper. *Lyrics by* Gene Buck.)

"Ring Out, Glad Bells"
Ensemble

ACT 3

"The Tale of a Mermaid"
T. Kosta, Chorus

"The Fishing Fleet is Homeward Bound"
Ensemble

"My Tango Queen"
M. Sunshine, Chorus

"Give Us Your Kind Applause"
R. Hitchcock, L. Wheat, J. Herbert, T. Kosta, A. Orr, M. Sunshine

"We Will Sail Back Home" (Finale)
Entire Company

1914.14   MADAM MOSELLE

A Musical Play in Three Acts. Book and lyrics by Edward A. Paulton, adapted from the French. Music by Ludwig Engländer. Staged by George W. Lederer. Dances arranged by Allan K. Foster. Costumes by Samuel Zalud. Orchestra under the direction of August Kleinecke. Produced by George W. Lederer. Opened 23 May 1914 at the Sam S. Shubert Theatre and closed 30 May 1914 after 9 performances.[90]

CAST: *Gabriel Smudge*, Secretary, etc. of the Vane Charities: RALPH HERZ. *Ms. Vane*, a rich widow: JOSIE INTROPODI. *Nina*, her daughter, educated in France: DIANE D'AUBREY. *Fred Corson*, engaged to Mrs. Vane: JACK HENDERSON. *Eva Moselle*, directress of the Moselle Academy: OCTAVIA BROSKE. *Harry Boland*, an English art instructor at the Moselle Academy: ERNEST LAMBART. *Matthew*, hand man at the Moselle Academy: HALLEN MOSTYN. *Kerrazzo*, a 'near' Turk: WILLIAM PRUETTE. *Betty*, housemaid at Mrs. Vane's: Jessie Duncan. *Mortimer*, butler at Mrs. Vane's: Royal Cutter. *La Petite Adele*: Helene Novita.

Art Students: *Doris*: Ethel Osterheld. *Irene*: Kathleen Allen. *Ivy*: Olive Osborne. *Mabel*: Florence Normand. *Myrtle*: Billie Wood. *Lottie*: Kathleen Erroll. *Fern*: Marie Finney. *Gladys*: Adele Carroll. *Florine*: Ethel Davies.

Act 1: Garden of Mrs. Vane's Villa in New Rochelle. Afternoon.

Act 2: The Moselle Academy. Class room and studio.

Act 3: Mrs. Vane's Garden—En fête. Evening.

ACT 1

"Back Out While the Backing Out is Good" (Duet)
J. Henderson, E. Lambart

"Students of Art Are We" (Entrance of Students)
Girls

"Everybody Knows Madame Moselle"
O. Broske, Students

"I'll Be There" (Song)
D. d'Aubrey

"What Are We Going to Do About It?"[91] (Song)
R. Herz

"Ding Dong" (Duet)
D. d'Aubrey, J. Henderson

"Is That All?" (Trio)
O. Broske, J. Henderson, E. Lambart

Finale
Company

ACT 2

"The (Live) Model" (Art Students' Song)(Chorus)
H. Mostyn

"If I Should Lose My Only Girl"
J. Henderson, Students
(*Music and Lyrics by* William P. Chase.)

"Tell Me the French Word for Squeeze Me"
D. d'Aubrey, J. Henderson

"Constantinople" (Song and Chorus)
W. Pruette, Girls

"El Bruta" (*Dance created by* A. Foster)
J. Henderson, H. Novita

"Rosie of Palermo" (Song)
D. d'Aubrey

Finale
Company

ACT 3

"Good-bye, Little Girl" (Duet)
D. d'Aubrey, J. Henderson

"(By Tumna's) Rolling Waters" (Song)
O. Broske, H. Mostyn, Girls

Finale
Ensemble

---

[90]Settings uncredited.

[91]Published as "What Are You Going to Do About It?"

1914–1915 SEASON

Fred Stone and David Montgomery in CHIN-CHIN (Photo: White Studio)
Billy Rose Theatre Collection, New York Public Library for the Performing Arts

1914–1915 SEASON

1914.15 ZIEGFELD FOLLIES OF 1914

A Musical Revue in Two Acts, 16 Scenes.[1] Devised and produced under the personal direction of Florenz Ziegfeld. Book (sketches) and lyrics by George V. Hobart. Music by Raymond Hubbell. Special numbers by Dave Stamper. Additional lyrics by Gene Buck. Staged by Leon Errol. Costumes designed by Cora MacGeachy. Scenery designed by William H. Matthews. Orchestra under the direction of Frank N. Darling. Produced by Florenz Ziegfeld. Opened 1 June 1914 at the New Amsterdam Theatre and closed 5 September 1914 after 112 performances.

CAST: VERA MICHELENA, ANN [Anna] PENNINGTON, LEON ERROL, BERT WILLIAMS, ARTHUR DEAGON, GEORGE McKAY, ED WYNN, J. BERNARD DYLLYN, HERBERT CLIFTON, LOUISE MEYERS, R. MORTON HORNE, RITA GOULD, Addison Young, Henry Lutz, Dorothy Newell, Gladys Feldman, Dal Vayne, William Greenlaw, Gertrude Vanderbilt, Kay Laurell, Ruby Lewis, Hilda Hirsch, Freda Hirsch, Freda Hirsch, May Carmen, Vivian Rogers, Rose Wertz, Bessie Gross, Jean Barnette, Stella Chatelaine, May Leslie, Miss Ardine.

ACT 1[2]

Scene 1[3]

"Be Careful What You Do"
V. Michelena, Chorus

"I'm a Statesman"
A. Deagon

Tango Brazilian Dreams
V. Michelena, G. Feldman

"My Little Pet Chicken"
A. Deagon
(*Lyrics by* George V. Hobart.)
Scene: The Reception Hall in Hell.
Satan: V. Michelena. *Benzina*: A. Pennington. *Izrafel*: G. Vanderbilt. *Salamander*, elevator boy: G. McKay. *September Morn*: K. Laurell. *I. Holduppe*: A. Young. *Officer Keegan*: J. B. Dyllyn. *Jennings B. Bryan*: A. Deagon. *Peter Peroxide*, the eugenic groom: H. Lutz. *Sal Hepatica*, the eugenic bride: D. Newell. *Geraldine*, a show girl: M. Leslie. *The Spirit of the Tango*: G. Feldman. *The Chicken*: A. Pennington. *Joe King*, the joke king: E. Wynn. *The Executioner*: W. Greenlaw. *Satan's Royal Chef*: A. Deagon.

Scene 2

"I Love That Man"[4]
R. Gould, Chorus
Scene: Broadway and 42nd Street.

Scene 3

"The Hurdy Gurdy Man" (Goodnight, Mr. Hurdy-Gurdy Man)
L. Meyers, Chorus

"I'm Cured"
B. Williams
(*Music by* Bert Williams. *Lyrics by* Jean C. Havez.)

---

[1]The eighth in the annual series of revues produced by Florenz Ziegfeld beginning in 1907.

[2]All musical numbers by Hubbell and Hobart except as noted. For subsequent tour, Scenes 2 and 3 were combined, and the following was added:
"Underneath a Japanese Moon"
R. H. Horne, L. Meyers, Chorus
(*Music by* Walter Gustave Haenschen. *Lyrics by* Gene Buck.)(Billed in its published sheet music as the vocal version of the Moorish Glide)

[3]Added to this scene late in the run:
"A Nut Sundae"
Kitty Doner (Hazel Nut)

[4]Replaced after opening by: (Scene later dropped altogether.)
"I've Got Him Now"
R. Gould
(*Music by* Dave Stamper.)
Which was then later replaced by:
"Wonderful (Garden of) Love"
Whitney and Burt
(*Music by* Dave Stamper.)

Scene: Broadway and Fifth Avenue, five days after a snowstorm.
Honest Bill, a policeman: G. McKay. *Onyx*, a member of the Alimony Club: B. Williams.

Scene 4

"Poppy"[5]
V. Michelena, Chorus

Dance
A. Pennington

The Tango Lesson
L. Errol, Misses R. Lewis, H. Hirsch, F. Hirsch, M. Carmen, V. Rogers, R. Wertz, B. Gros, J. Barnette
Scene: The Tango Palace.
Joe King, the Tango Teacher: E. Wynn. *I. Bragg*, the manager: J. B. Dyllyn. *A. Bunn*, who wants to learn: L. Errol. *A. Nutt*, who can't learn: G. McKay.

Scene 5

"Because I Can't Tango"
G. McKay
Scene: A Street.

Scene 6

"Prunella (Mine)"
L. Meyers, R. M. Horne, Chorus
(*Music by* Dave Stamper. *Lyrics by* Gene Buck.)
Scene: Prunella.

Scene 7

Medley
V. Michelena, A. Deagon
Scene: Ziegfeld Danse de Follies.

Scene 8

"The Ragtime Regiment" (When the Ragtime Army Goes Away to War)
G. McKay, A. Pennington, 16 Ziegfeld Girls
(*Music and Lyrics by* A. Seymour Brown.)

"The Lone Star Girl" (The Lone Star Boy)
V. Michelena, Entire Company, Military Band, Drum Corps
Scene: The Border Line between Texas and Mexico.
Captain Coldslaw, a golfist: L. Errol. *MacTavish*, a caddy: B. Williams. *The Governor of Texas*: J. B. Dyllyn. *Lieutenant Turkey*: A. Pennington. *Captain Ragtime*: G. McKay.
Historical Characters in Final Tableau: The Revolutionary War: General Mad Anthony Wayne, General Israel Putnam, General George Washington, General Lafayette, Paul Revere. The Mexican War of 1849: Davy Crockett, Sam Houston, General Winfield Scott, General Zachary Taylor. The Civil War: General Phil Sheridan, General Hancock, General Ulysses S. Grant, General Meade, General Sherman.

ACT 2

Scene 1

"There's Something in the Air in Springtime"[6]
G. Vanderbilt, a Half Dozen Peaches
(*Music by* Dave Stamper. *Lyrics by* Gene Buck.)
Scene: In Peachland.

Scene 2

Song
H. Clifton
Scene: Olio Drop.

Scene 3

"The Futurist Girl" (Song)
V. Michelena, Chorus
(*Music by* Dave Stamper. *Lyrics by* Gene Buck.)

"Good Night" (Duet)
L. Meyers, R. M. Horne
(*Music by* Dave Stamper.)

The Tangomaniacs
L. Errol, S. Chatelaine

"Night Life in Old Manhattan"
A. Deagon, Chorus
Scene: In a Mansion à la Mode.

---

[5]Dropped after opening.

[6]Replaced after opening by:
"Save Your Love for Me" (Keep Your Love for Me)(Duet)
Whitney and Burt, Six Peaches
(*Music by* Raymond Hubbell.)

Scene 4[7]

"Nothing to Wear" (Song)
L. Meyers
(*Music by* Dave Stamper.)
Scene: A Street.
Miss Minus: L. Meyers. *Tessie Easygo*: D. Newell. *Gladys Kanbee*: Miss Vernon.

Scene 5

On the 1313 Story in Course of Construction
Scene: The Skyscraper.
Slim: L. Errol. *Henry Onyx*: B. Williams.

Scene 6

"Rock Me in the Cradle of Love"[8]
R. Gould, Male Chorus
(*Music and Lyrics by* J. Leubrie Hill.)
Scene: A Street.

Scene 7

Songs
B. Williams
["The Darktown Poker Club"
(*Music and Lyrics by* Bert Williams, Will Vodery and Jean Havez.)
"The Man Who Wrote 'The Vampire' Must Have Known My Wife"
(*Music by* Bert Williams. *Lyrics by* Gene Buck and Earle C. Jones.)]
Scene: Ziegfeld Danse de Follies.

Scene 8

The One Step; The Dancing Contest (for the Palm Beach Cup)
"Tangorilla"[9]
G. McKay, Miss Ardine, Chorus
Scene: Palm Beach.
Mrs. Gotrox: V. Michelena. *D.J. Braydaydy*: A. Deagon. *Charlie Champney*: G. McKay. *Lord Fizzington*: R. M. Horne. *Miss Plus*: L. Meyers.

1914.16 # THE PASSING SHOW OF 1914

A Musical Revue in Two Acts, 14 Scenes.[10] Dialogue and lyrics by Harold Atteridge. Music by Sigmund Romberg and Harry Carroll. Staged by J. C. Huffman. Dances and musical numbers arranged by Jack Mason. Scenery painted by Young Brothers, Robert Law and William Rising. Trans-Atlantic Flight and Burning of San Francisco effects by Frank D. Thomas. Costumes designed by Melville Ellis. Lighting by Nick Kronyack. Incidental ballet music selected and arranged by Melville Ellis. Orchestra under the direction of Oscar Radin. Produced by the Winter Garden Company (Messrs. Shubert). Opened 10 June 1914 at the Winter Garden and closed 3 October 1914 after 133 performances.

CAST [in order of appearance]: *Deuce Baggot*: John Freeman. *Mary Packard*: MURIEL WINDOW. *A Camera Man*: William Dunham. *Miss High Jinks*: ETHEL AMORITA KELLY. *The Midnight Girl*: FRANCES DEMAREST. *Rip Van Winkle Roosevelt*: ROBERT EMMETT KEANE. *Little Buttercup*, the Queen of the Movies: GEORGE W. MONROE. *Huerta*: LEW BRICE. *Sari*: Elsie Pilcer. *A Gypsy Fiddler*: IVAN BANKOFF. *Lady Windermere*: Bessie Crawford. *The Misleading Nut*: T. Roy Barnes. *First Attendant*: Joseph P. Galton. *Second Attendant*: Parker Lesard. *Jarrold McGee*: BERNARD GRANVILLE. *Panthea*: FRANCES DEMAREST. *Kitty MacKay*: JOSÉ COLLINS. *Baron Criquet*: HARRY FISHER. *Miss Jerry*: MURIEL WINDOW. *Leonora*: FRANCES DEMAREST. *Mr. Varenka*: HARRY FISHER. *Mr. Manhattan*: ROBERT EMMETT KEANE. *Pierrot*: Stafford Pemberton. *Prunella*: ETHEL AMORITA KELLY. *Omar Khayyam*: BERNARD GRANVILLE. *Shireen*: JOSÉ COLLINS. *Imam Allafake*: ROBERT EMMETT KEANE. *Zarah*: FRANCES DEMAREST. *Turkey Trot*: IVAN BANKOFF. *Tango*: Winifred Gilrain. *Maxixe*: Elsie Pilcer. *Nizam*: John Freeman. *A Priest*: LEW BRICE. *A Priest*: William Dunham. *The Crinoline Girl*: T. Roy Barnes. *An Aviator*: Jack Evans. *Joe Oswald*: LEW BRICE. *William Bulldoon*: ROBERT EMMETT KEANE. *Mr. Gymnast*: Nat Nazarro. *Mr. Handspring*: J. Edward Nazarro. *Miss Flip*: Erman Nazarro. *Mr. Hoops*: Frank L.

Gregory. *Mr. Roller*: Thomas Allen. *Miss Twist*: Nellie Gilman. *Mr. Circle*: Julian Gilman. *Mr. Bar*: Frank Warnick. *Mr. Pulley*: William Green. *Miss Trapeze*: Rupert Gregory. *Conductor*: Jack Evans. *Mlle. Genée*: MARILYNN MILLER. *Salvation Nell*: MURIEL WINDOW. *Miss Glasgow*: Winona Wilkins. *Miss Leeds*: June Elvidge. *Miss Edinburgh*: Thelma Hoeffle. *Miss Henrietta*: Florence Averell.

Personnel of the Chorus: Adele Christy, Estelle Christy, Raye Shirley, Mae Tarmey, Ida Scaife, Betty Berry, Edna Wentworth, Fife Lissier, Dorothy Landers, Helen Carrington, Rene Markey, Carrie Hahn, Daisy Lovell, Nita Lamadrid, Vivian Gardon, Barbara Clark, Irene Hutchins, Elfreda Hanswarth, Dolly Grey, Miriam McDonald, Mae Marrell, Blanche Marr, Carrine Pickard, Emily Monte, Emily Miles, Helen West, Dorothy Cameron, Alice Randolph, Josephine Raye, Georgie Moore, Ida Kramer, Ethel DuBois, Gertrude Foy, Eunice Hamilton, Emma McGrath, Cecil Carter, Virginia June, Marie Gray, Anna Pauly, Anna Waywood, Margarite Carmen, Bobbie Roberts, Lauretta Grant, Lottie Franklyn, Marion Mooney, Irene Mitchell, Lucy Maurelli, Grace Robinson, Hazel Black, Margarite Ward, Gertrude Mackey, Jeanne Dare. Edward Gardon, Fred Hudler, Dave Marshall, James Curran, Bob Wynne, Arthur Whitman, Frank Durand, Bob Hastings, William Young, Robert Gilbert, Charles Turner, Walter Smith.

Act 1, Scene 1: The Moving Picture Studio of the "Famous Players." *Scene 2*: The Private Office of the Queen of the Movies. *Scene 3*: Divertissement. *Scene 4*: A Persian Garden "A Thousand Years Ago." *Scene 5*: Aviation Field at Hempstead. *Scene 6*: The Trans-Atlantic Flight.

Act 2, Scene 1: Bulldoon's Eugenic Gymnasium. *Scene 2*: The Railroad Station at Noplace. *Scene 3*: The Sloping Path. *Scene 4*: A Street Scene. *Scene 5*: The Palace Hotel, San Francisco. *Scene 6*: A Street in Chinatown. *Scene 7*: The Burning of "Old San Francisco." *Scene 8*: The Dawn of the "New San Francisco" at the Panama Pacific Exposition.

ACT 1

"Working for the Pictures"
The Famous Players
"The Maude Adams of the Screen"
M. Window, Chorus
"The Midnight Girl at the Midnight Cabaret"
F. Demarest, Chorus
The "Sari" Dance
E. Pilcer, I. Bankoff, W. Gilrain, Chorus
"Kitty MacKay"
J. Collins, Chorus
(*Music by* Harry Carroll.)
"You're Just a Little Bit Better" (Than the One I Thought Was Best)
J. Collins, B. Granville
(*Music by* Harry Carroll.)
"The Moving Picture Glide"
E. Kelly, J. Freeman, W. Dunham, Chorus
(*Music by* Harry Carroll.)
Divertissement
E. A. Kelly, S. Pemberton, I. Bankoff, M. Miller, E. Pilcer, W. Gilrain
"Omar Khayyam"
B. Granville, Chorus
"Dreams of the Past"
J. Collins
"Way Down East"[11]
F. Demarest, Chorus
"The Crinoline Girl"[12]
T. R. Barnes, Chorus

ACT 2

"Eugenic Girls"
Ensemble
"The Girl of To-day"
J. Collins, Chorus
"On a Modern Wedding Day"
M. Window, R. E. Keane, Chorus
"(That) Bohemian Rag"
J. Collins, Men
(*Music by* Gus Edwards and Louis Silvers. *Lyrics by* Jean C. Havez.)
"The Sloping Path"
E. A. Kelly, Chorus
"Don't Hesitate With Me"[13]
B. Crawford

---

[7]Added to this scene after opening, following "Nothing to Wear":
"Nobody Seems to Know" (Song)
E. Wynn
[8]Dropped for subsequent tour.
[9]Replaced after opening by:
"At the Ball" (Finale)
V. Michelena, Entire Chorus
(*Music and Lyrics by* J. Leubrie Hill.)
[10]Billed as the Third Annual Revue in the series which began in 1912 under the auspices of the Messrs. Shubert, inspired by the original Passing Show of 1894.

[11]Dropped after opening and for subsequent tour.
[12]Dropped after opening and for subsequent tour.
[13]For subsequent tour, replaced by:

"Good Old Levee Days"
  B. Granville, E. A. Kelly, M. Miller, L. Brice, Chorus
  (*Music by* Harry Carroll.)
"(Out) In 'Frisco Town"
  F. Demarest, Chorus
  (*Music by* Harry Carroll.)
"Impressions"
  M. Miller
"The Eagle Rock"
  B. Granville, E. A. Kelly, Chorus
  (*Music by* Harry Carroll.)
"The Grape Dance"
  B. Granville, L. Brice
"You Can't Go Wrong with Us"
  M. Window, Chorus
"California"
  J. Collins, Ensemble

1914.17   THE DANCING DUCHESS

A Musical Comedy in Two Acts. Book and lyrics by C. V. Kerr and R. H. Burnside. Music by Milton Lusk. Staged by R. H. Burnside. Dances arranged by Vera Maxwell, Wallace McCutcheon. Costumes by Will R. Barnes, Arthur D. Brooks. Settings designed by H. Robert Law. Orchestra under the direction of John McGhie. Orchestrations by Otto C. A. Meorz, Frank Saddler. Produced by the Dancing Duchess Company (Messrs. Shubert). Opened 19 August 1914 at the Casino Theatre and closed 29 August 1914 after 13 performances.

<u>CAST:</u> *Countess Pauline von Bereny,* a society leader: DOROTHY JARDON. *Rosalie,* niece to the Countess: LEILA McINTYRE. *Tilly,* a housemaid: ADA LEWIS. *Count Gabor von Bereny,* who likes a little fling now and then: JOHN HYAMS. *Max Tokay,* Gabor's friend in joy and sorrow: HARRY DAVENPORT. *Captain Carl Czardis,* who is suitor for Rosalie's hand: JOHN H. GOLDSWORTHY. *Richter,* a very superior butler: OTIS HARLAN. *Baron Felix Puppchen,* who likes the ladies: Mark Smith. *Herr Picklesnits,* a celebrated dancing master: Jack Story. *Celestine,* the pet of Vienna (the Duchess of Darmia): LAURA HAMILTON. *Lieutenant Bonn,* a young army officer: Carl Porter: *Adolphus Spiggott,* a skilled artisan: William Burress. *Fritz,* steward at the Cage Budapesth: R. M. Dolliver. *Emil,* a waiter at Cafe Budapesth: Fred Russell.

Venus Girls: Elaine French, Helen Guarino, Marjorie Cook, Fanny Kidston, Mary Peyton, Betty Grant, Bertha Siple, Frances Sherman. *Show Girls:* Ella Alexander, Helen O'Dea, Helen Longfellow, Helen Ames, Katherine Johnson, H. Lind, Iris Gilbert, Bertha Bemidette, Patricia Berrian, Eva Hanthorpe. *Debutantes and Hungarian Girls:* Nellie Castleman, Goldie Foley, Mabel Hill, Dixie O'Neil, Loraine Bright, Florence Dean, Helen Mordecai, Evelyn Mitchell, Rose Baraban, Grace Bird, Poney Cantor, Nella Hadley. *Viennese Johnnies:* Clarence Rockwell, Lee Phelps, H. Johnson, F. Osborn, Jack Dillon, Carl Porter, M. Duprez, Irving Finn. *Army Officers:* H. Rose, E. Elliott, J. Egan, P. O'Neill, I. Lavitt, Harry Sulken, D. Bogart, G. Hall. *Waiter:* P. O'Neill, D. Bogart, I. Lavitt, T. Fast.

The action takes place somewhere in Vienna at the present time.

Act 1: Music Room at the von Bereny's Villa on the Outskirts of Vienna. Morning.

Act 2: The Terrace of the Cafe Budapesth overlooking the Danube. Evening.

ACT 1

"With Joy That Is Ecstatical" (Opening)
  Ensemble
"The Tango Breakfast" (Song)
  D. Jardon, Chorus
"Never Worry" (Duet)
  J. Hyams, H. Davenport
"Love Is a Summer's Morning" (Waltz Duet)
  J. H. Goldsworthy, L. McIntyre
"(I'm) Looking for a Girl Like Venus" (Song)
  O. Harlan, Chorus
  (*Lyrics by* R. H. Burnside.)
"That's the Kind of Man You Ought to Marry" (Trio)
  J. Hyams, D. Jardon, L. McIntyre
"Celestine" (Entrance)
  L. Hamilton, Male Chorus

"The American Englishman"
  R. E. Keane
Which was later replaced by:
"Here We Are"
  Boyle and Brazil

"The Bumble Bee and the Butterfly" (Duet)
  J. Hyams, L. McIntyre
Finale: "Everybody's Happy in Vienna"
  Ensemble
"We're Off for Budapesth"
  Ensemble

ACT 2
  Opening
    Ensemble
      "Danube So Blue" (Solo)
        J. H. Goldsworthy, Chorus
      Hungarian Dance
        Hungarian Girls
      "On With the Dance" (Solo)
        L. Hamilton, Chorus
  "I've Been Looking for You" (Duet)
    O. Harlan, A. Lewis
    (*Lyrics by* R. H. Burnside.)
  "That's the Way to Win a Girl" (Song)
    J. Hyams, Chorus
  "Fol-de-rol-lol" (Trio)
    J. Hyams, H. Davenport, W. Burress
  "The Song of Songs" (Song)
    D. Jardon
  "It's the Girls" (Trio)
    J. Hyams, H. Davenport, Chorus
  "Nay, Nay Pauline"
    M. Smith, D. Jardon, J. H. Goldsworthy, L. McIntyre
  "(Do You Like Me?) I Like You" (Duet)
    J. H. Goldsworthy, L. McIntyre, Ensemble
  "The Tango Contest"
    Ensemble
    Quadrille; Maxixe; Hesitation; Tango.
  "The Ragtime Whirl" (Song)
    L. Hamilton, Ensemble
  Finale

1914.18   THE GIRL FROM UTAH

A Musical Comedy in Two Acts, an Introductory and 4 Scenes. Book by James T. Tanner. Music by Paul Rubens and Sydney Jones. Additional numbers by Jerome D. Kern. Lyrics by Percy Greenbank and Adrian Ross. Staged by J. A. E. Malone. Gowns and costumes by Schneider-Anderson Company. Orchestra under the direction of Gustave Salzer. Produced by Charles Frohman. Opened 24 August 1914 at the Knickerbocker Theatre and closed 5 December 1914 after 120 performances.

<u>CAST:</u> *Una Trance,* The Girl from Utah: JULIA SANDERSON. *Sandy Blair,* leading man at the Gaiety Theatre: DONALD BRIAN. *Trimpel,* of Brixton Rest: JOSEPH CAWTHORN. *Lord Amersham:* George Bishop. *Policeman P. R. 38:* Edgar Dickson. *Colonel Oldham-Pryce:* George Grundy. *Page:* Master Michael Mathews. *Commissionaire:* William Francis, Jr. *Detective Shooter* of Scotland Yard: Walter S. Wills. *Lord Orpington:* Harry Law. *Archie Tooth:* George Wharton. *Douglas Noel:* Russell Griswold. *Bobbie Longshot:* Dickson Elliott. *Dora Manners,* leading lady of the Gaiety Theatre: VENITA FITZHUGH. *Lady Amersham,* Lord Amersham's mother: QUEENIE VASSAR. *Clancy* Miss Manners' maid: Renee Reel. A *Flapper:* Jessie Crane. *Actresses at the Gaiety Theatre (5): Miss Mona West:* Diane Oste. *Miss Sylvia Paget:* Dorothy Wilcock. *Miss Lydia Saville:* Mabel Gibson. *Miss Violet Vesey:* Alma Harrison. *Miss Rosie Jocelyn:* Louise Donovan. A *Waitress:* Eunice MacKay. *Lady Muriel Chepstone:* Clara Eckstrom. *Honorable Miss St. Auburn:* Alice Palmer. *Lady Mary Nowell:* Irene Palmer. *Mrs. Ponsonby:* Veronique Banner.

Waitresses: Eunice Mackay, Violet Marsden, Margaret Langdon, Kathleen Hitchens, Louise Worthington, Edith Barr. *Matinee Girls:* Caroline Oden, Irene Palmer, Edith Hordlow, Kathleen Erroll, Frances Burress, Gladys Siddons, Zamora Pierce, Lorraine Waters, Edith Allen, Dorothy Erhard, Olga Markuson, Irene Enright, Fannie Hasbrouck, Marie Francis, Jacque Hastings, Catharine Hurst, Marie McCullough. *Matinee Boys:* Edward C. Yeager, William L. Hobart, Radford D'Orsay, F. S. Foley, William W. Fink, Charles E. Vandiver, Lester Ostrander, Frank Snyder, Walter Gilbert, James O'Neill, Jack Potter, A. Von Bereghy.

Introductory: "To the Land of Let's Pretend."

Act 1: Rumpelmeyers, St. James Street, London. Present day.

Act 2, Scene 1: A Street in Brixton, suburb of London. *Scene 2:* A Mormon's House, Brixton. *Scene 3:* The Arts Ball, London. The Land of Let's Pretend.

ACT 1

Opening Chorus ("Land of Let's Pretend")
(*Music by* Jerome D. Kern. *Lyrics by* Harry B. Smith.)

"Mother Will Be Pleased" (Song)
G. Bishop

Entrance of Actresses

"Only to You" (Song)
V. Fitzhugh, Chorus
(*Music and Lyrics by* Paul Rubens.)

"Gilbert the Filbert"[15] (Song)
D. Brian, Chorus
(*Music by* Herman Finck. *Lyrics by* Arthur Wimperis.)

"Follow Me" (D'Ye Folly Me)(Duet)
R. Reel, J. Cawthorn

"(A) Girl from Utah" (Song)
J. Sanderson, Chorus
(*Music by* Sidney Jones. *Lyrics by* Percy Greenbank.)

"When We Meet the Mormon" (Quartette)
J. Sanderson, V. Fitzhugh, R. Reel, D. Brian

"We're Getting On Very Well" (Duet)
J. Sanderson, J. Cawthorn

"The Girl in the Clogs and Shawl" (Trio)
J. Sanderson, J. Cawthorn, D. Brian
(*Music and Lyrics by* Harry Castling and C. W. Murphy.)

Finale

ACT 2

Scene 1

"Where Has Una Gone?" (Quintette)
V. Fitzhugh, R. Reel, G. Bishop, J. Cawthorn, D. Brian
(*Music by* Paul Rubens. *Lyrics by* Percy Greenbank.)

Scene 2

"Call Right Here"[16] (Song)
J. Sanderson, Actresses
(*Music by* Paul Rubens. *Lyrics by* Percy Greenbank.)

"Same Sort of Girl" (Duet)
J. Sanderson, D. Brian
(*Music by* Jerome D. Kern. *Lyrics by* Harry B. Smith.)

"Florrie the Flapper" (Song)
J. Cawthorn
(*Music by* Herman Finck. *Lyrics by* Arthur Wimperis.)

"Garden Gate" (Trio)
J. Sanderson, D. Brian, J. Cawthorn

Scene 3

Opening Chorus

"Nothing at All" (Song)
R. Reel
(*Music and Lyrics by* Paul Rubens.)

"The Music of Love" (Duet)
V. Fitzhugh, G. Bishop
(*Music by* Paul Rubens. *Lyrics by* Percy Greenbank.)

"You Never Can Tell"[17] (Song)
J. Sanderson, Men
(*Music by* Jerome D. Kern. *Lyrics by* Harry B. Smith.)

---

[15]Also in THE PASSING SHOW OF 1914 (USA), and THE PASSING SHOW (1914) in London. Dropped for subsequent tour and replaced by:
"Step This Way"
D. Brian, Chorus

[16]Replaced during run, or for tour by:
"(I'd Like to Wander with) Alice in Wonderland"
J. Sanderson, Chorus
(*Music by* Jerome D. Kern. *Lyrics by* Harry B. Smith.)

[17]Replaced during run, or for tour by:
Julia Sanderson's Popular Songs
J. Sanderson, Men
Which was then replaced by:
"Molly Dear, It's You I'm After"
J. Sanderson, Men
(*Music by* Henry E. Pether. *Lyrics by* Frank Wood.)

"They Didn't Believe Me" (Duet)
J. Sanderson, D. Brian
(*Music by* Jerome D. Kern. *Lyrics by* Herbert Reynolds.)

"(At Our) Tango Tea (Last Week)" (Song)
J. Cawthorn
(*Music by* Worton David. *Lyrics by* Bert Lee.)

"(Why Don't They Dance) the Polka (Anymore?)" (Song)
D. Brian, Chorus
(*Music by* Jerome D. Kern. *Lyrics by* Harry B. Smith.)

Dance ["Ballin' the Jack," *Music by* Chris Smith.]
D. Brian, C. Sewell

Sketch[18]
J. Sanderson, D. Brian, J. Cawthorn

Concerted Number
Q. Vassar, R. Reel, V. Fitzhugh, Men

Finale ("Land of Let's Pretend" reprise)

1914.19   WARS OF THE WORLD

A Musical Extravaganza in Three Acts, 16 Scenes. Conceived and invented by Arthur Voegtlin. Dialogue written by John P. Wilson. Music and lyrics by Manuel Klein. Staged by William J. Wilson. Resident stage director, William G. Stewart. Scenic effects by Arthur Voegtlin. Costumes by Max & Mahieu, Frances M. Ziebarth. Lighting by Joseph Elsner. Orchestra conducted by Manuel Klein. Produced by the Messrs. Shubert. Opened 5 September 1914 at the Hippodrome and closed 16 January 1915 after 229 performances.

CAST: LAWRENCE GRANT, ADELE ARCHER, WILLIAM C. GORDON, GEORGE O'DONNELL, STANLEY FERGUSON, JAMES DAVIS, DORA KUMERFELT, JOHN P. WILSON, HARRY JACKSON, JOHNNY FLEMING, DAN DAWSON, GRACE CAMP, HARRY CLUETT, ALBERT FROOM, GEORGE ADAMS, JOHN GIBSON, H. C. EASTMAN, IRENE WARD, JACK PRITCHARD, NELLIE DONER, MARCELINE, PETER YOUNG, TOMMY DOWD, HARRY DALE, DAISY SMYTHE, JEANNE RIBIERRE, FIB WHITESIDE, Ensemble.

ACT 1

Prologue

History: L. Grant.

Scene 1

The War for Existence and Conquest:

When the Earth Was Young—Dawn of Civilization

First Tableau: The Jungle People, Tree and Cave People

Second Tableau: Romans and Barbarians—Rome, Mistress of the World

Scene 2

Wars for Religion

Ave Maria
G. Camp (solo), Chorus of Nuns

The Morris Dance

"Death to the Infidel!" (Finale)

The Joust
H. Jackson, J. Fleming
Scene: An Abbey in the Forest.—The Crusaders.
The Abbess: A. Archer. *Robin Hood*: W. C. Gordon. *Will Scarlet*: G. O'Donnell. *Friar Tuck*: S. Ferguson. *The Prince*: J. Davis. *The Princess*: D. Kumerfelt. *King's Herald*: J. P. Wilson. *Sir Modred*: H. Jackson. *Sir Silvester*: J. Fleming. *Principal Templar*: D. Dawson. *Archers, Knights, Templars, Knights of Malta, Hospitalers, Ladies of Honor, Nuns, Retainers, Esquires, Priests, Beggars, Yeomen and Morris Dancers*: (Ensemble).

Scene 3

War of Mass Against Class

The Minuet; Watteau Dance
Smythe, Ribierre (solo dancers), (Company)
Scene: Gardens of Versailles, Period French Revolution.
Marquis de Frontenac: W. C. Gordon. *Marchioness de Frontenac*: A. Archer. *Count de Charny*: H. Cluett. *Member Committee of Public Safety*: A. Froom. *Marie Antoinette*: G. Camp. *Priest*: G. Adams. *Nobles, Ladies, Lackeys, Dancers, Republican Soldiers, San Culottes*: (Ensemble).

---

[18]Replaced after the opening by:
"In the Movies"
J. Sanderson, D. Brian, J. Cawthorn

Scene 4

War of Brother Against Brother

"When You Come Home Again Johnny!"
 G. Camp, J. Davis, Cadets, Girls

The March to the Front

Finale
 Scene: The South—Typical Southern Mansion and Grounds.
 General Hope: J. Gibson. *General Price*: G. O'Donnell. *Major St. John*: W. C. Gordon. *Major Conklin*: H. C. Eastman. *Dick Talbot*: J. Davis. *Lieutenant Frank Clayton*: H. Jackson. *Mollie Clayton*: G. Camp. *Mrs. Clayton*: I. Ward. *Confederate Picket*: G. Adams. *Uncle Benny*: J. Pritchard. *Aunt Keziah*: S. Ferguson. *Confederate Solders, Southern Belles, Darkies, Officers, Cadets, Crinoline Girls*: (Ensemble).

Scene 5

The Price of War
 Tableau: After the Battle.

Scene 6

The War of Sport

Showing an English Roadside Fair, with its characteristic life and attractions.

Introduction of the Popular Hippodrome Clown, Marceline.

"The Road to Henley"
 Costers, Bicyclists, Nigger Minstrels, Coaching Party, Crew

"Dear Old Fashioned Henley"
 A. Archer, G. Camp, I. Ward, J. Davis, W. C. Gordon
 Scene: The Road to Henley.
 Bill Jenks, a Fair Proprietor: A. Froom. *Dan Deucace*, a Gambler: W. C. Gordon. *Jed Hawkins*, a Coster: D. Dawson. *Jack Morton*, Stroke of Harvard: H. Jackson. *Clara Carden*: G. Camp. *Matilda Stubbs*, Jed's sweetheart: N. Doner. *Alice Arbuckel*: A. Archer. *Nancy Elliott*: D. Kumerfelt. *Novelty Acrobats*: Anza and Lorella.

Scene 7

War of Sport
 Scene: Henley, the Famous Scene of English and International Regattas

"Henley on a Summer Day"
 Picnic Party (Ensemble)

"(You're) Just the One I've Waited For"
 A. Archer, J. Davis, Picnic Party

The Race between Leander and Harvard: Harvard Wins!
 Characters as in Scene 6 with Additional: *John Henry Bullock*, an American Plunger: G. O'Donnell. *A Betting Commissioner*: G. Adams.

Scene 8

Algiers—War of Races

Dance of the Bayadères
 Carmen, Smythe, Whiteside, Ribierre and Belles of Seville

Attack of the French, and Flight of the Caravan

Rifle Drill by Spahis
 Scene:
 Sheik Ibrihim: A. Froom. *Chief Selim*: W. C. Gordon. *Arab Soldiers, Caravan Men and Camp Followers, Arab Musicians, Bayaderes, French Spaahis, Officers*: (Ensemble).

Scene 9

The Carnival—War of Pleasure

Opening
 Farmers, Carters, Peasants

Gathering of the Maskers

Grand March

"Baby Eyes"
 N. Doner, D. Dawson, A. Archer, G. O'Donnell, Carnival Chorus

Dance of Pierrots

Grand Finale
 Scene: Italian Village in the Riviera.
 Mephisto: J. P. Wilson. *King Pleasure*: : Marceline. *Queen Folly*: A. Archer. *Peasants, Carters, Farmers, Maskers, Bicyclists, Lanterns, Animal Sets, Confetti Sets, Ribbon Sets, Columbines, Harlequins, Giants, Pierrots, etc.*: (Ensemble).

ACT 2

Scene 1

The Elements

Adoration of Buddha

"In Siam"
 A. Archer, G. Camp, G. O'Donnell, J. Davis, Chorus

Pageant of the Coronation

The Weises Perch Act
 Scene: Square in Siamese City.
 The Regent: A. Froom. *Princess Hinda*: G. Camp. *Chamberlain*: G. O'Donnell. *Royal Magician*: W. C. Gordon. *Nobles, Warriors, Priests, Fan Bearers, Dancers, Camel Men, Elephant Men, Bowmen, Spearmen, Tartar Chiefs, Siamese Citizens, Councillors, Umbrella Bearers, Maids of Honor, etc.*: (Ensemble).

Scene 2

The Elements (Flame and Veil Effects by Ida Fuller.)

Scene 3

War for Equal Rights
 Scene: Street in City of Tampico, Mexico.
 Ramon Blake, a Texan: H. Jackson. *Arthur Stryker*, U.S. Consul: G. O'Donnell. *Colonel Vargas*, a Federal: A. Froom. *Texas Castillo*, Ramon's Sweetheart: A. Archer. *Her Duenna*: I. Ward. *Captain Garcia*, a Federal: W. C. Gordon. *Lieutenant Gonzales*, a Federal: D. Dawson. *Sergeant Chao*, a Federal: P. Young. *Quartermaster*, U. S. Cruiser: H. C. Eastman. *A Mexican Spy*: T. Dowd. *Peons, Mexican Soldiers, Vaqueros, Senoritas, Venders, Citizens, Waiters, U. S. Jackies, etc.*: (Ensemble).

"Under a Gay Sombrero"
 Soldiers, Vaqueros, Senoritas, Cigar Girls

Mexican Tango
 The Belles of Seville

Carl Eugenie Troupe of Acrobats

Scene 4

War on the Ocean: Sea Pictures

Scene 5

War for Equal Rights (conclusion)
 Burt Shepherd, the Whip King and Company
 Frank L. Gregory and Troupe
 Hoop Rollers
 Scene: Same as Scene 3.
 Additional characters: *General Maas*, in command at Tampico: J. P. Wilson. *An American Refugee*: J. Gibson. *An English Refugee*: H. Dale. *A Woman Refugee*: S. Ferguson. *A Toreador*: Marceline. *Refugees, Bull Fighters, The Bull Populace, Soldiers, etc.*: (Ensemble).

Scene 6

War for Humanity
 Coming of the American Fleet
 The Attack on the City
 Taking of Vera Cruz by the Americans
 Parade of the Occupying Forces and the Raising of the Flag
 Scene: Square in Vera Cruz.

ACT 3

Terrace of Fountains

1914.20   MISS DAISY

A Play with Music in Three Acts. Book and lyrics by Philip Bartholomae. Music by Silvio Hein. Staged by J. C. Huffman. Dances and ensembles arranged by Jack Mason. Scenery designed by Frank Gates, Edward A. Morange. Costumes designed by Orange. Orchestra under the direction of August Kleinecke. Produced by Philip Bartholomae. Opened 9 September 1914 at the Sam S. Shubert Theatre, moved 28 September 1914 to the Lyric Theatre and closed 3 October 1914 after 29 performances.

CAST (in order of appearance): *Daisy Hollister*: FLORENCE MACKIE. *Elvira Walsh*: HELEN LEE. *Maisie Dearborn*: Gwennllyan Jocelyn. *Fern Randolph*: Elsie Hitz. *Edna Barber*: Molly Chrysty. *Dolly Sweet*: Gladys Zell. *Huggins*, a butler: John E. Wheeler. *Walter Hollister*: DONALD MacDONALD. *Frederic*: ALLEN KEARNS. *Billy*: John Boyle. *Joe*: Charles Murray. *John*: Frank Parker. *Elsie Swigget*: ANNA WHEATON. *The Duke of Tormina*: JOSEPH LERTORA. *Mrs. Swigget*: EVELYN CARTER CARRINGTON. *Anastasia*: ALICE HEGEMAN. *Josie*: Rae Bowdin. *Sally Smith*: Claiborne Foster. *Pierrete*: Mae Murray.

Act 1: Bedroom of Daisy Hollister. A day in June.

Act 2: Home of Mrs. Swigget. A few days later.

Act 3, Scene 1: Kitchen of Mrs. Swigget. Next day. *Scene 2*: Ball of the Pierrots. A little later.

ACT 1

"Dream! Oh, Dream!"
 Dream Maiden: C. Foster. *Nightmare*: F. Parker.

"Won't You Dance?"
　Misses Hitz, Jocelyn, Lee, Chrysty, Zell; Messrs. Boyle, Kearns, Macdonald, Murray, Parker
"I Adore the American Girl!"
　J. Lertora, Mesrrs. Boyle, Kearns, Murray, Parker
"I Love You, Dear, I Love But You"
　A. Wheaton, J. Lertora, D. Macdonald
"If You Propose to Propose"
　F. Mackie, D. Macdonald
"My Little Queen Bee"
　D. Macdonald, Misses Foster, Hitz, Lee, Chrysty, Zell
"Tea Leaves"
　H. Lee, Misses Foster, Hitz, Jocelyn, Mackie, Chrysty, Zell
"Weave From Your Loom"
　J. Lertora

ACT 2
"Youth"
　J. Lertora, Misses Foster, Hitz, Jocelyn, Chrysty, Wheaton, Zell; Messrs. Boyle, Kearns, Murray, Parker
"You Can't Stop Me from Thinking"
　A. Hegeman
"The Race of Life"
　D. Macdonald, A. Kearns, J. Boyle
"Cheer Up"
　A. Wheaton, D. Macdonald, Messrs. Boyle, Kearns, Murray, Parker
"You Were Made for Love"
　J. Lertora
"Interruptions"
　F. Mackie, D. Macdonald; Misses Hegeman, Wheaton, Carrington; J. Lertora
"Melodrama"
　Hero: C. Murray. Heroine: A. Hegeman. Villain: J. Lertora. Lady All Forlorn: H. Lee. Juveniles: A. Wheaton, A. Kearns. Chorus: Misses Foster, Hitz, Jocelyn, Chrysty, Zell; Messrs. Boyle, Parker.
"Gentle Moon"
　F. Mackie
"Shadows"
　F. Mackie, J. Lertora

ACT 3
"Kissing"
　E. Hitz, A. Kearns, Misses Foster, Jocelyn, Lee, Chrysty, Zell; Messrs. Boyle, Murray, Parker
"Cherries Are Ripe"
　A. Wheaton, D. Macdonald
"Little Girl, What Have You Done to Me?"
　F. Mackie, J. Lertora
Pierrot and Pierrette
　G. Zell, F. Parker
　Mae Murray as "Pierrette"
"Pierrot's Ball"
　Misses Foster, Hitz, Lee, Chrysty, Wheaton; Messrs. Boyle, Kearns, Macdonald, Murray
"Weave From Your Loom" (reprise)
　J. Lertora

1914.21　PRETTY MRS. SMITH

A Comedy with Music in Three Acts.[19] Book by Oliver Morosco and Elmer Harris. Music by Henry James and Alfred Robyn. Lyrics by Earl Carroll. Staged by T. Daniel Frawley. Scenery designed by Robert Brunton, Homer Emens, Kellam. Costumes designed by Melville Ellis, Lucille (F. Scheff), Clarice (C. Greenwood). Musical director, John Lund. Produced by Oliver Morosco. Opened 21 September 1914 at the Casino Theatre and closed 31 October 1914 after 48 performances.

CAST: Drucilla Smith, the cause: FRITZI SCHEFF. Letititia Proudfoot, her ally: CHARLOTTE GREENWOOD. Bobby Jones, an eugenic hotel clerk: SYDNEY GRANT. Frank Smith, Drucilla's present: CLAUDE FLEMMING. Ferdinand Smith, her first past: THEODORE BABCOCK. Forest Smith, her second past: CHARLES PURCELL. Myrtle Adair, contender for her present: Lillian Tucker. George, a watchful

---

[19]For subsequent tour, the show was revised and presented under the title LONG LEGGED LETTY.

waiter: James A. Gleason. Mrs. Marian Dalzell, who is: Grace Shaw. Mrs. Tom Wilson, who was: Daisy Burton. Mrs. Waldemar Hayes, who might be: Ocie Williams. Miss Prudence Morris, who will be: Dolores Parquette. Miss Helen Partington, who is to be: Louise Cook. Miss Phoebe Snow, who is willing to be: Marie de Marquis. Tim Wilson, a jollier: J. Richard Ryan. Dick Potter, a philanderer: J. Van Ryan. Paul Hunter, a trifler: J. H. Childs. Hal Dorsey, a punter: Harold Proctor. Henriette, "who knows": Mlle. Marcelle.
　Morosco California Quartette: J. Richard Ryan, Harold Proctor, J. Van Ryan, J. H. Childs.

The action takes place in Palm Beach, Florida, at the present time.

Act 1: Hotel Benedict, Palm Beach.

Act 2: Frank Smith's Suite.

Act 3: Same as Act 2.

ACT 1
"Drucilla"
　L. Tucker, Ladies
　(Music by Alfred G. Robyn.)
"The Bensonhurst Gavotte"
　C. Greenwood, S. Grant
　(Music by Alfred G. Robyn.)
"The Plain Ol' Name o' Smith"
　C. Flemming, C. Purcell, T. Babcock, S. Grant
　(Music by Alfred G. Robyn.)
"Love Has Come to Live in Our House"
　C. Flemming, F. Scheff, Ladies, Gentlemen
　(Music by Henry James.)

ACT 2
"Let Bygones Be Bygones"[20]
　F. Scheff, C. Flemming
　(Music by Alfred G. Robyn.)
"Mississippi, You're a Grand Old Girl"
　C. Greenwood, S. Grant
　(Music and Lyrics by Billy Gould and Ashlyn.)
"Pretty Mrs. Smith"[21]
　F. Scheff, Quartette, Ladies
　(Music by Henry James.)

ACT 3[22]
"Dawn in Florida"
　Guests
　(Music by Henry James.)
"My Dream of Dreams"
　F. Scheff, Quartette
　(Music by Alfred G. Robyn.)
"Long, Lean, Lank Letty"
　C. Greenwood
　(Music and Lyrics by Sydney Grant.)

1914.22　DANCING AROUND

A Modern Musical Spectacle in Two Acts, 12 Scenes.[23] Dialogue and lyrics by Harold Atteridge. Music by Sigmund Romberg and Harry Carroll. Staged by J. C. Huffman. Dances arranged by Jack Mason. Scenery by P. Dodd Ackerman, H. Robert Law, George Williams, James Surridge. Train effect by Lincoln J. Carter and Thomas A. Morris. Costumes designed by Melville Ellis. Lighting by Nick Kronyack. All ballet and dance music selected and arranged by Melville Ellis. Orchestra under the direction of Oscar Radin. Orchestrations by Oscar Radin, Frank Saddler. Produced by the Winter Garden Company (Messrs. Shubert). Opened 10 October 1914 at the Winter Garden and closed 13 February 1915 after 145 performances.

---

[20]Dropped for subsequent tour as PRETTY MRS. SMITH.
[21]Dropped for subsequent tour as PRETTY MRS. SMITH.
[22]For subsequent PRETTY MRS. SMITH tour, "Dawn in Florida" and "Melody Lane" were replaced by:
　"Can't You Hear Me Calling, Caroline?"
　　Quartette
　　(Music by Caro Roma. Lyrics by William H. Gardner.)
　"Melody Lane"
　　S. Grant
[23]Billed as the Winter Garden's Annual Fall Production.

<u>CAST</u> (in order of appearance): *Lieutenant Larry*: James Doyle. *Lieutenant Tommy*: HARLAND DIXON. *Lieutenant Hartley*: BERNARD GRANVILLE. *Clarice*: Aimee Dalmores. *Shirley*: Eleanor Brown. *Dora*: Olga Hempstone. *Pinky Roberts*: KITTY DONER. *Lieutenant Harry Graham*: FRANK CARTER. *Annettte Truesdale*: LUCY WESTON. *Lieutenant Robert*: Earl Fox. *Tillie*, a telephone operator: Georgie O'Ramey. *Clarence*: CLIFTON WEBB. *Gus*, a man of many parts: AL JOLSON. *Mlle. Mitzi*, of the Frivolity: Mary Robson. *Ethel*: Eileen Molyneux. *Beulah Elliott*, prima donna: CECIL CUNNINGHAM. *Lord Graham*: FRED LESLIE. *Fireman*: Phil Branson. *Train Announcer*: Harold Robe. *John Elliott*: Melville Ellis. *Messenger Boy*: Mabel Hill. *Patricia*: Mildred Manning. *Lucy*: May Dealy. *Butler*: Phil Branson. *Miss Thames*: Effie Graham. *Maid*: Georgie O'Ramey. *Miss Gerard*: Katherine Hill. *Miss Social Leader*: Lucy Weston. *Monsieur Jean*: AL JOLSON.

Personnel of the Chorus: Misses Olga Hempstone, Eleanor Brown, Violet Rochlitz, Catherine Perry, Helen Marche, Katherine Johnson, Peggy Whitney, Effie Graham, Marion MacDonald, Marjorie Palmer, Agnes Hall, Mabel Hill, Dorothy Nita, Gladys Lang, Estelle Hadden, Dorothy Cameron, Joy Gardner, Rita Bates, Doris Easton, Katheryn Hill, Berti Burwell, Natalie Holt, Olive Dale, Helen Lorraine, Mary McDonald, Jean Crane, Bessie Gray, Grace Hall, Queenie Queenen, Dorothy Moran, Ethel Kinley, Lotta Morse, Rauth Maybee, Marion Mooney, Alice Van Ryker, Mae Dealy, Ethel Dennison, Helen O'Day, Margie Kivel, Hazel Cameron, Mai Poth, Marie Caldwell, Lester Lewis, La Vina, Gladys Smith, Mabel Grete, Ruth Heil, Genevieve Wilmont, Caroline Hennessy, Jeanne Dare, Rita Hernbrook, Dorothy Quinn. Messrs. Harry Wilcox, Verne Fitzpatrick, Jack Carlton, Irwin Hardy, Harry Davis, Clint Russell, Bert Dunlap, Charles Wilson, Howard Johnson, Peter O'Neill, Fred Bates, Lee Phelps, Ted Doner, Al Walton, Raymond Smith, James Simpson.

Act 1, Scene 1: The Lounge of the Army Club, London. *Scene 2*: In front of Lieutenant Hartley's Home. *Scene 3*: The Gold Room of the Army Club. *Scene 4*: Stage Door of the Frivolity Theatre. *Scene 5*: A Railway Waiting Room. *Scene 6*: The Pursuit of the Edinburgh Express.

Act 2, Scene 1: Hotel Lavender. *Scene 2*: Lobby of the Hotel Lavender. *Scene 3*: Jean's Dressmaking Shop. *Scene 4*: The Song Shop. *Scene 5*: A Waterway in Venice. *Scene 6*: A Venetian Carnival.

ACT 1[24]

"The Army Club"
    Officers
"When Tommy Atkins Smiles at All the Girls"
    J. Doyle, H. Dixon, Chorus
"Never Trust a Soldier Man"
    L. Weston, Chorus
"When an Englishman Marries a Parisian"
    M. Robson, Chorus
"My Rainbow Beau"
    B. Granville, E. Molyneux, Chorus
"The Army Club Foxtrot"
    Officers, Ladies
"It's a Long, Long Way to Tipperary"[25]
    B. Granville, Chorus
    (*Music by* Jack Judge. *Lyrics by* Harry Williams.)
"I Was Born on the Isle of Man"
    C. Cunningham, Men
"There's Something About You"
    F. Carter, Chorus

_____

[24]Harry Carroll's songs not identified. Jolson's Specialty Songs included:
"When Grown Up Ladies Act Like Babies (I've Gotta Love 'Em, That's All)"
    (*Music by* Maurice Abrahams. *Lyrics by* Joe Young, Edgar Leslie.)
"Tennessee, I Hear You Calling"
    (*Music by* Harry Robe. *Lyrics by* Jeff Godfrey.)
"Sister Susie's Sewing Shirts for Soldiers"
    (*Music by* Herman Darewski. *Lyrics by* R. P. Weston.)
"Everybody Rag With Me"
    (*Music by* Grace LeRoy. *Lyrics by* Gus Kahn.)
"When I Leave the World Behind"
    (*Music and Lyrics by* Irving Berlin.)
"Bring Along Your Dancing Shoes"
    (*Music by* Grace LeRoy. *Lyrics by* Gus Kahn.)
"I'm Glad My Wife's in Europe"
    (*Music by* Archie Gottler. *Lyrics by* Howard Johnson and Coleman Goetz.)
"Virginia Lee"
    (*Music by* Arthur Lange. *Lyrics by* Jeff T. Branen.)
[25]Replaced for subsequent tour by:
"Irish and Proud of It, Too"
    Frank Carter (Lieut. Hartley), Chorus

"My Lady of the Telephone"
    B. Granville, Chorus
    (*Music by* Jean Gilbert.)
Dance Eccentrique
    B. Granville, K. Doner
"I Want to Be in Norfolk"
    A. Jolson
"The Shepherd Gavotte"
    C. Webb, E. Molyneux
"The Call of the Colors"
    B. Granville, Ensemble
"Somebody's Dancing with My Girl"
    K. Doner
Silhouette Ballet
"Oh, You John"[26]
    B. Granville, F. Carter, J. Doyle, H. Dixon

ACT 2

"An Afternoon Tea"[27]
    M. Manning, Ensemble
"I'm Seeking for Siegfried"
    A. Jolson
Dance Conceptions[28]
    J. Doyle, H. Dixon
"A Fashion's Slave"
    C. Cunningham, Chorus
"The Dancing Maniacs"[29]
    F. Carter, K. Doner, Chorus
(Specialty)[30]
    M. Ellis, His Eight Fashion Plates
"The Broadway Triangle"[31]
    M. Ellis, C. Cunningham, B. Granville
"A Dance Study"[32]
    B. Granville, M. Ellis
"Venetia"[33]
    A. Jolson
"The Venetian Carnival"
    C. Webb, E. Molyneux, Ensemble
"He Is Sweet, He Is Good"[34]
    C. Cunningham
"By the Grand Canal"[35]
    B. Granville, Ensemble
"The Shuffling Shiveree"[36]
    A. Jolson, Chorus

CHIN-CHIN,
1914.23   or, A Modern Aladdin

A Musical Fantasy in Three Acts, 7 Scenes. Book by Anne Caldwell and R. H. Burnside. Music by Ivan Caryll. Lyrics by Anne Caldwell and James O'Dea. Staged by R. H. Burnside. Scenery designed by Homer Emens. Costumes by Wilhelm. Motion picture effect by Lubin. Musical director, William E. MacQuinn. Produced by Charles Dillingham. Opened 20 October 1914 at the Globe Theatre and closed 3 July 1915 after 295 performances.

<u>CAST</u>: *Chin Hop Lo, the Widow, Coolie, Clown, Gendarme*: DAVE MONT-GOMERY. *Chin Hop Hi, Paderewski, Ventriloquist, Mlle. Fallosffski, Gendarme*: FRED STONE. *Aladdin*: DOUGLAS STEVENSON. *Abanazar*: CHARLES T.

_____

[26]Dropped for subsequent national tour.
[27]Dropped for subsequent national tour.
[28]Dropped for subsequent national tour.
[29]Dropped for subsequent national tour.
[30]Dropped for subsequent national tour.
[31]Dropped for subsequent national tour.
[32]Dropped for subsequent national tour.
[33]Dropped for subsequent national tour.
[34]Dropped for subsequent national tour.
[35]Dropped during the run.
[36]Replaced for subsequent national tour by:
"(Bring Along Your) Dancing Shoes"
    A. Jolson, Chorus
    (*Music by* Grace LeRoy. *Lyrics by* Gus Kahn.)

ALDRICH. *Cornelius Bond*: R. E. GRAHAM. *Tzu Yung*: Eugene Revere. *Li-Dragon Face*: Edgar Lee Hay. *Ring Master*: Charles Mast. *Violet Bond*: HELEN FALCONER. *Goddess of the Lamp*: BELLE STORY. *Widow Twankey*: ZELMA RAWLSTON. *Sen-Sen*: Juliette Day. *Fan-Tan*: Violet Zell. *Silver Ray*: Marjorie Bentley. *Moon Blossom*: Lola Curtis. *Lily Petal*: Evelyn Conway. *Lotus Leaf*: Hazel Lewis. *Cherry Bloom*: Lorayne Leslie. *Little Wing Wu*: Agnes McCarthy. *Little Lee Toy*: George Phelps. *The Four Bears*: Misses Breen. *Spirit of New Year*: Mildred Richardson. *Poppy Bud*: Eleanor St. Clair. *Spring Flower*: Tot Qualters. *Wistaria*: Margaret St. Clair. *Honeysuckle*: Lillian Rice.

Other Members of the Company: Misses Hilda Allison, Claire Bertrand, Cecil Conway, Harriet Leidy, Cassie Qualters, Dorothy Richardson, Grace Beaumont, Bessie Burch, Olive Carr, Marion Davies, Isabel Falconer, Anna Ford, Marjorie Graham, Mazie Leroy, Loretta McDonald, Selma Mantell, Lydia Scott, Dorothy St. Clair, Marguerite St. Clair, Janet Wollenburg, Anna Berry, Julia Berry, Sarah Berry, Andrea Cresson, Rose Douglas, Helen Ellsworth, Esther Herrick, Irene Kearney, Marie Kennedy, Victoria Meyers, Vivian Morrison, Margaret O'Neill, Marion O'Neill, Josephine Taylor, Betty Wales, Helen Ward. Messrs. R. C. Bosch, Martin Cox, Roger Davis, Joseph Gormley, Jack Hagner, J. F. Johnson, Arthur Kuesta, Peter Page, H. S. Palmer, E. H. Randall, Harold Russell, Harry Silvey.

Act 1, Scene 1: The Toy Bazaar. *Scene 2*: The Way to the Tea Shop. *Scene 3*: The Tea Shop.

Act 2, Scene 1: The Palace Terrace. *Scene 2*: Outside the Dressing Tent. *Scene 3*: Inside the Circus.

Act 3: In the Park.

ACT 1
Scene 1
"Quaint Toys"
    Chorus
"Shopping in the Orient"
    J. Day, E. Revere
Teddy Bear Dance
    Misses Breen
"The Chinese Honeymoon"
    D. Montgomery, F. Stone
    (*Lyrics by* Bryan Williams.)
Scene 2
"Chipper China Chaps" (The Pekin Patrol)
    Chorus
"Goodbye Girls, I'm Through"
    D. Stevenson, Blossom Girls
    (*Lyrics by* John Golden.)
"Go Gar Sig Gong-Jue"
    D. Montgomery, F. Stone
Scene 3
"In an Oriental Way"
    Chorus
"Violet"
    B. Story
    (*Lyrics by* Anne Caldwell.)
"(Ragtime) Temple Bells"
    F. Stone
    (*Lyrics by* James O'Dea.)
Finale
ACT 2
Scene 1
"Will o' the Wisp"[37] (Dance)
    M. Bentley, Ballet (Ensemble)
Lighning Changes[38]
    C. T. Aldrich
"Wedding Gifts of Silver"
    Chorus
"The Grey Dove"
    B. Story
    (*Lyrics by* Anne Caldwell.)
Fred Stone at the piano ["The Rag of Rags (syncopater)"[39]]
    (*Music by* William E. MacQuinn.)
"Love Moon"
    D. Stevenson, H. Falconer

Danse Poetique
    F. Stone, V. Zell
The Flight of the Pagoda
Scene 2
The Ventriloquist
    F. Stone, "Eddie"
The Clown Band
    Six Brown Brothers
    ["Pretty Baby"/"Chin-Chin"]
Scene 3
The Breen Family[40]
Mlle. Falloffski
    F. Stone
Clown[41]
    D. Montgomery
ACT 3
"Strollers"
    Chorus
"Little Deeds of Kindness"[42]
    B. Story
"It's a Long, Long Way to Tipperary"[43]
    D. Montgomery, F. Stone
    (*Music by* Jack Judge. *Lyrics by* Harry Williams.)
"Chin-Chin" (Open Your Heart and Let Me In)(Finale)
    (*Music and Lyrics by* A. Seymour Brown.)

1914.24

EXPERIENCE

A (Morality) Play with Songs in Three Acts, 10 Scenes. Play by George V. Hobart.[44] Incidental music by Max Bendix. Songs and cabaret music by Silvio Hein. Staged by George V. Hobart and J. C. Huffman. Scenery by Reisig. Costumes designed by Melville Ellis. Orchestra under the direction of Carlo Edwards. Produced by William Elliott. Opened 27 October 1914 at the Booth Theatre, moved 11 January 1915 to the Casino Theatre, moved 3 May 1915 to the Maxine Elliott Theater and closed 5 June 1915 after 255 performances.

CAST [in order of appearance]: *Love*: MIRIAM COLLINS. *Hope*: May McManus. *Youth*: WILLIAM ELLIOTT. *Ambition*: Wallace Worsley. *Experience*: Ben Johnson. *Pleasure*: ROXANE BARTON. *Opportunity*: Adele Holt. *Excitement*: Eleanore Christy. *Travel*: Walter Kingsford. *Song*: Frances Richards. *Sport*: Joseph McManus. *Fashion*: Bess Ryan. *Blueblood*: Elyston Morris. *Style*: Julian Little. *Frivolity*: Marion Whitney. *Conceit*: Edmund Roth. *Snob*: Duncan Harris. *Pride*: Elizabeth West. *Beauty*: MADELINE HOWARD. *Deceit*: Dorothy Parker. *Slander*: Frances Richards. *Wealth*: CHARLES A. STEVENSON. *Waiter*: Ralph H. Jones. *Waiter*: George Berliner. *Intoxication*: Margot Williams. *Passion*: Florence Short. *Good Nature*: Duncan Harris. *Superstition*: Joseph McManus. *System*: Edmund Roth. *Stupid*: Walter Kingsford. *Despair*: Harry Lane. *Chance*: George T. Meech. *Careless*: Thomas Herbert. *Thoughtless*: Edwin Silton. *Roulette Dealer*: Billy [William] Betts. *Waiter*: David Bryant. *Stool Pigeon*: Ralph H. Jones. *Work*: WILLARD BLACKMORE. *Grouch*: BILLY [William] BETTS. *Frailty*: MARGOT WILLIAMS. *Make-shift*: George T. Meech. *Rogue*: Thomas Herbert. *Dissolute*: Dorothy Parker. *Sneak*: Edwin Silton. *Illiterate*: Frances Richards. *Indolence*: Eleanore Christy. *Rascal*: Joseph McManus. *Reckless*: Elizabeth West. *Cheat*: Edmund Roth. *Waiter*: Ralph H. Jones. *Poverty*: Harry J. Lane. *Law*: FRANCIS BRANDON. *Delusion*: HARRY BUCHANAN. *Habit*: ALBA DeANCHORIZ. *Degradation*: MARION HOLCOMBE. *Crime*: FRANK McCORMACK.

Act 1, Scene 1: In the Land Where Dreams Begin. *Scene 2*: In the Street of Vacillation. *Scene 3*: The Primrose Path.

Act 2, Scene 1: In the Corridors of Chance. *Scene 2*: The Street of Disillusion. *Scene 3*: In the House of Last Resort.

---

[37]Dropped for subsequent tour.
[38]Dropped for subsequent tour.
[39]Piano specialty identified in Boston and Philadelphia tour programs.

[40]Dropped for subsequent tour.
[41]Dropped for subsequent tour.
[42]Dropped during the run.
[43]Subsequently replaced on tour by:
    "Bally Mooney (and Biddy McGee)"
        D. Montgomery, F. Stone
        (*Music and Lyrics by* Terence Lowry.)
[44]Adapted from a shorter One-Act, 7 Scene version which formed the closing portion of a Lamb's Club Gambol 1 March 1914.

Act 3, Scene 1: The Street of Remorse. *Scene 2*: The House of Lost Souls. *Scene 3*: The Street of Forgotten Days. *Scene 4*: In the Land Where the Dreamer Wakens. The End of the Pilgrimage.

MUSICAL NUMBERS[45]

Act 1, Scene 3

"The Primrose Path"

"The Experience One-Step"

"The Experience Fox-Trot"

"The Modern Song"

1914.25
THE LILAC DOMINO

An Operetta in Three Acts, 4 Scenes. Original German book ("Der lila Domino") and lyrics by Emerich von Gatti and Béla Jenbach. Music by Charles Cuvillier. English book by Harry B. Smith. English lyrics by Robert B. Smith. Produced (staged) by Sydney Ellison. Costumes by Ludwig Zwieback and Brother, Vienna; B. Altman & Co, New York; E. L. Freisinger, A. Uzel & Son, New York. Scenery by Kautsky and Rottonara, Vienna. Orchestra under the direction of Anselm Goetzl. Presented by the Dippell Opera Comique Company (Andreas Dippel, director). Opened 28 October 1914 at the 44th Street and closed 30 January 1915 after 109 performances.

CAST: *Vicomte de Brissac*: GEORGE CURZON. *Georgine, his daughter*: ELEANOR PAINTER. *Elledon, his nephew*: JAMES HARROD. *Leonie D'Andorcet*: RENÉ DETLING. *Count André de St. Amand*: WILFRID DOUTHITT. *Prosper, Casimir, his friends*: JOHN E. HAZZARD, ROBERT O'CONNOR. *Baroness de Villiers, Georgine's governess*: JEANNE MAUBOURG. *Istvan, leader of a gypsy orchestra*: Harry Hermsen. *Fifi*: Anita Andrews. *Mimi*: Jane E. Miller. *Mariette*: Marie Hamilton. *Suzanne*: Chrisie D'Allott. *Celeste*: Gertrude Grossberg. *Florette*: Julie Cahill. *Jean, lackey of the Vicomte*: Leicester Parker. *Frederic, valet to Count André*: Maxwell Olney. *Max, a waiter at the Casino*: Robert Terrill. *Henry, Maurice, attendants at the Casino*: Louis Burke, H. B. Boell. *Antoine, butler at Vicomte's residence*: John Fielderhof. *Stage Orchestra and Gypsy Musicians, Guests, Dominos, Officers, Attendants, etc*

Dominos: Misses Evelyn Bohlman, Genevieve Forbes, Edna Goldsberry, Margaret Hussar, Ora L. Keeler, Augusta Leeper. *Guests*: Misses Anita Andrews, Angelica Berrenberg, Evelyn Bohleman, Helen Curtis, Chrisie D'Allott, Julie Cahill, Irma Case, Lyn Donaldson, Frances DuBarry, Calvine Emery, Marjorie Foley, Genevieve Forbes, Myrta Gilkinson, Edna Goldsburry, Gertrude Grossberg, Rose Held, Margaret Hussar, May Johnson, Ora L. Keeler, Frances Kennedy, Martha Krambach, Eleanor Lemdorfer, Augusta Leeper, Daisy Marshall, Norah May, Helen Merriman, Harriet Miller, Jane E. Miller, Madeleine Mitten, Adele Raynor, May Robbins, Helen Tashman, Mattie Vance, Irene Walters, Anna Week, Onor Winer. *Gentlemen Guests, Officers and Attendants*: Messrs. Arthur Ballance, H. B. Boell, Bernard Brown, Bruce Brown, L. Burgstaller, Louis Burke, John Feilderhof, A. R. Gilchrist, George Gordon, S. Grundgeard, R. A. Harbeson, Brodford Kirkbride, Mario Laurenti, Frederick Manley, Mario Rogati, Maxwell Olney, Leicester Parker, Robert Terrill, Karl Van Holland.

The action takes place in Nice at the present time.

Act 1: Bal Masqué at the Casino.

Act 2: Exterior of Vicomte de Brissac's Residence.—Thé Dansant.

Act 3, Scene 1: Library in the Home of Count André. *Scene 2*: Square of Prefecture at Nice.

ACT 1[46]

Opening Chorus

G. Curzon, J. Harrod, R. Detling, Ensemble

"True Love Will Find a Way"

R. Detling, J. Harrod

"Let the Music Play"

W. Douthitt, Chorus

"When Love Is Waiting" (Where Love Is Waiting)

E. Painter, J. Maubourg

"The Lilac Domino"

E. Painter, J. Harrod, G. Curzon

Finale

E. Painter, W. Douthitt, J. Harrod, J. E. Hazzard, R. O'Connor, H. Hermsen, G. Curzon, Chorus

ACT 2

Opening Chorus

R. Detling, J. Harrod, J. Maubourg, Chorus

"The Lilac Domino" (reprise)

W. Douthitt, R. Detling, J. E. Hazzard, R. O'Connor, E. Painter, G. Curzon, Chorus

"What Every Woman Knows"[47] (Frocks and Frills)

E. Painter, R. Detling, J. Maubourg

"Song of the Chimes" (Bim Bam)

E. Painter, W. Douthitt

"Ladies' Day"

R. Detling, J. Harrod, J. E. Hazzard, R. O'Connor, G. Curzon

"What is Done You Can Never Undo"

E. Painter, W. Douthitt

Finale

Company

ACT 3[48]

"Carnival at Nice"—Intermezzo

Chorus

"I Call You Back to Me"[49]

W. Douthitt

(*Music by* Ellen Tuckfield. *Lyrics by* Wilfrid Douthitt.)

"(But) Still We Smile"

J. E. Hazzard, R. O'Connor

"Cupid Keeps the Love Light Burning"[50]

E. Painter, H. Hermsen

Ensemble

W. Douthitt, J. Harrod, G. Curzon, J. E. Hazzard, R. O'Connor, H. Hermsen, Guests

Transformation and Coriandoli Song

Chorus

Finale

Entire Company

1914.26
PAPA'S DARLING

A Musical Comedy in Three Acts. Book and lyrics by Harry B. Smith. Based on the French comedy 'Le fils surnaturel' by Grenet d'Ancourt and Maurice Vaucaire. Music by Ivan Caryll. Ensemble numbers staged by Julian Mitchell. Scenery painted by Unitt & Wickes, Ernest Albert. Costumes designed by Schneider-Anderson Company. Lighting by Tony Greshoff. Musical director, Anton Heindl. Produced by (Marc) Klaw and (Abraham L.) Erlanger. Opened 2 November 1914 at the New Amsterdam Theatre and closed 5 December 1914 after 40 performances.[51]

CAST: *Achile Petipas, Professor of Experimental Moral Psychology*: FRANK LALOR. *Sophie Petipas, his wife, head of the famous Petipas Feminist Academy*: Octavia Broske. *Germaine Petipas, their daughter, with her own ideas on the bringing up of parents*: ALICE DOVEY. *Mayor Le Blanc, Mayor of Epinal, a mere husband*: FRED WALTON. *Yolande, his wife*: Georgia Harvey. *Zozo, a music hall singer, "The Countess"*: DOROTHY JARDON. *Colonel du Parvis, an Algerian veteran, sane on several subjects*: FRANK DOANE. *Marcel du Parvis, his son, in love with Germaine*: Jack Henderson. *Dorine, pupil at Mme. Petipas's school, cousin of Germaine*: Edna Hunter. *Mme. du Parvis*: Lucille Saunders. *Lieutenant Maurice*: Horace G. Davenport. *First Deputy*: Albert C. Davis. *Second Deputy*: Peter Swift. *School Girls at Mme. Petipas's (3): Marguerite*: Bertha Blake. *Celeste*: Flora Crosbie. *Justine*: Kathleen Vesey. *Mignon*: Polly Bowman. *Florine*: Teddy Hudson. *Fifine*: Elise Murray. *Paulette*: Millicent Murray. *Guide*: E. K. Edwards. *Cupid*: Polly Bowman.

---

[45]Musical Numbers not listed in program, but taken from production typescript. Two songs by Hein and Hobart were published: "Call Me Baby" and "The Road to Home Sweet Home."

[46]For subsequent national tour, the song order was revised. "But Still We Smile" moved from Act 3 to Act 1 prior to the Finale. Added to Act 2 replacing the title song reprise:

"The Sunny Riviera"

Amparito Farrar (Leonie), Chorus

(*Music by* Malvin M. Franklin. *Lyrics by* L. Wolfe Gilbert.)

---

[47]Dropped for subsequent national tour.

[48]Between Acts 2 and 3 a Musical Intermezzo will be rendered with Kinemacolor Pictures: (a) Battle of Flowers, (b) Carnival Scenes at Nice.

[49]Dropped for subsequent national tour.

[50]Dropped for subsequent national tour.

[51]Played a return engagement 28 December 1914 at the Grand Opera House for 8 performances.

"Midnight Sun Girls": Flora Crosbie, Polly Bowman, Teddy Hudson, Ida Howe, Ethel Delmar, Millicent Murray, Muriel Martin, Kathleen Vesey, Sadie Livermore, Bertha Blake, Alice Carington, Edna Hettler.

Act 1: Grounds of Madame Petipas' Advanced Feminist Academy. (Unitt & Wickes.)

Act 2: Reception in the Exhibition Room of Madame Petipas's Academy. Unitt & Wickes.)

Act 3: Café de Boheme. (Albert.)

ACT 1
   Musical Exercise
      Chorus
   March Song
      O. Broske, Chorus
   "A Touch of Spring"
      F. Lalor, F. Walton
   "Edelweiss" (Song)
      A. Dovey, Chorus
   "A Certain Little Way of Mine" (Song)
      D. Jardon, Chorus
   "Who Cares?" (Duet)
      A. Dovey, J. Henderson
   Finale

ACT 2
   Opening Chorus
      D. Jardon, Chorus
   "The Land of the Midnight Sun"
      J. Henderson, P. Bowman, T. Hudson, Chorus
   "Sparkling Moselle" (Song)
      D. Jardon, Chorus
   "(Where Shall We Go for) Our Honeymoon"
      A. Dovey, J. Henderson
   "Finale
      Principals, Chorus

ACT 3
   "Dolores" (Opening Song)
      D. Jardon, Chorus
   "The Popular Pop" (Song)
      F. Lalor, F. Walton, P. Bowman, T. Hudson, Chorus
   "Oh, This Love" (Waltz Song)
      A. Dovey, O. Broske, D. Jardon, Chorus
   Finale
      Principals, Chorus

THE ONLY GIRL

1914.27

A Musical Farcical Comedy in Three Acts. Book (and lyrics) by Henry Blossom. (Based on the play 'Our Wives' by Frank Mandel and Helen Kraft,[52] adapted from the German "Jugendfreunde" by Ludwig Fulda.) Music by Victor Herbert. Staged by Fred G. Latham. Dances arranged by Joseph C. Smith. Scenery by Dodge & Castle. Ladies dresses by Bendel.[53] Orchestra under the direction of Robert Hood Bowers. Orchestrations by Victor Herbert. Produced by Joseph Weber. Opened 2 November 1914 at the 39th Street Theatre, moved 16 November 1914 to the Lyric Theatre and closed 5 June 1915 after 240 performances.

CAST: *Alan Kimbrough*, "Kim," a librettist: THURSTON HALL. *Sylvester Martin*, "Corksey," a broker: RICHARD BARTLETT. *John Ayre*, "Fresh," a lawyer: JED PROUTY. *Andrew McMurray*, "Bunkie," a painter: ERNEST TORRENCE. *Ruth Wilson*, a composer: WILDA BENNETT. *Saunders*, Kimbrough's valet: John Findlay. *Birdie Martin*: Louise Kelley. *Margaret Ayre*: Josephine Whittell. *Jane McMurray*: Vivian Wessell. *Patrice LaMontrose*, "Patsy," a soubrette: ADELE ROWLAND. *Ruby*: Estelle Richmond. *Violet*: Marjorie Oviatt. *Viola*: Jane Hilbert. *Paula*: Claire Standish. *Perle*: Gladys Schultz. *Renee*: Jeanne Darys.

Time: The present.

Act 1: The Living Room of Kimbrough's Apartment, New York.

---

[52]"Our Wives" source appears in touring programs, but not in the Broadway run.
[53]For subsequent tour, design of all gowns and hats were credited to Lucile, Ltd.

Act 2: The same. Six weeks later.

Act 3: The Dining Room. Same evening.

ACT 1
   "The More I See of Others, Dear, the Better I Love You" (Song)
      A. Rowland
   "When You're Away" (Song)
      W. Bennett
   "Be Happy, Boys, Tonight" (Quartette)
      T. Hall, E. Torrence, J. Prouty, R. Bartlett
   "The Compact" (Finale, Duo)
      W. Bennett, T. Hall

ACT 2
   "Personality" (Song)
      A. Rowland, Friends
   "Antoinette" (Song)
      J. Darys
   "Here's to the Land We Love, Boys" (Duo March)
      T. Hall, A. Rowland, Friends
   "Tell It All Over Again" (Song)
      V. Wessell
   "Connubial Bliss" (Sextette)
      E. Torrence, J. Prouty, R. Bartlett, V. Wessell, J. Whittell, L. Kelley

ACT 3
   "Here's How" (Opening Chorus)
      A. Rowland, Chorus
   "You Have to Have a Part to Make a Hit"
      A. Rowland, Friends
   "When Your Ankle Wears the Ball and Chain" (Trio)
      J. Prouty, E. Torrence, R. Bartlett
      (*Lyrics by* Harry B. Smith.)
   "Equal Rights" (Why Should We Stay at Home and Sew?)(Trio)
      J. Whittell, V. Wessell, L. Kelley
   "You're the Only One for Me"[54] (Duo)
      W. Bennett, T. Hall
   Finale

SUZI

1914.28

A Comedy Operetta in Three Acts. (English) Book and lyrics by Otto Hauerbach [Harbach]. Founded on a Hungarian operetta (libretto, 'A kis gróf') by Franz [Ferenc] Martos. Music by Aladár Rényi. Staged by George Marion. Scenery by Young Brothers and H. Robert Law. Ladies' costumes by B. Altman & Company. Lighting by David Atchison. Orchestra under the direction of Gaetano Merola. Produced by Lew Fields, Inc. by arrangement with Edward F. Rush. Opened 3 November 1914 at the Casino Theatre, moved 30 November 1914 to the Sam S. Shubert Theatre, and closed 19 December 1914 after 55 performances.[55]

CAST (in order of appearance): *Joseph*, head waiter at the Sans Souci Gardens: Juan Villasana. *A. Page*: Gertrude Rutland. *B. Page*: Adelaide Mason. *Magda*, a waitress: Laura Hoffman. *Signor Piglioni*, a composer: Arthur Lipson. *Count Emerich*: MELVILLE STEWART. *Countess Rosetti*: FRITZI VON BUSING. *Stephan*, Emerich's son: ROBERT EVETT. *Dr. Herring*. Stephan's tutor: TOM McNAUGHTON. *Suzi*. prima donna at the Sans Souci Theatre: JOSÉ COLLINS. *Herr Horn*, a director: LEW HEARN. *Lina Balzer*, a stage mother: CONNIE EDISS. *Chef de Reception*: Gilbert Clayton. *Marie*: Gene Peltier. *Celeste*: Pauline DeLorme. *Gabrielle*: Adelaide Vernon. *A Maid*: Esther Rutland. *Wilma, Tina*, Sorrento Butterflies: Elsa Reinhardt, Georgie Cummings. *Dancers at the Sans Souci Gardens*: Doris LaFrance, Howell Benham. *A Sorrento Waiter*: Walter Peck.

   Waitresses: Esther Rutland, Laura Hoffman, Dorothy Bertrand, Louise Hardy, Marie Hampton, Ara Martin, Adele Christy. *Ladies*: Carrie Monroe, Adelaide Vernon, Gene Drake, Lillian Francis, Pauline DeLorme, Elsa Reinhardt, Georgie Cummings, Natalie Vincent. *Guests*: Bertha Stock, Fifi Hanswirth, Ethel Betterton, Helen Bonnot, Virginia Roydon, Mignon Ranseer, Marie Benedict, Jean White. *Gentlemen*: Alexander Gibson, Walter Briggs, Harry Miller, Willie Mack, Edwin McEnery, Morris Sacks, Harry Polk, Sidney Smith, Bernard Milton, Simeon Jurist, Ted Andrews, Jack Polen, David Heilbrunn.

Time: The present.

---

[54]Alternate title: "You're the One Girl for Me."
[55]Played a return engagement 25 January 1915 at the Standard Theatre for 8 performances.

Act 1: Sans Souci Summer Gardens, Buda Pesth, Hungary. Matinee time.

Act 2: A Hotel at Sorrento, Italy. Late in the afternoon. One week later.

Act 3: Same as Act 1. Night. Two weeks later.

ACT 1[56]

    Overture
        Chorus of the Sans Souci Theatre Company

    "I Love You, Marina"[57]
        A. Lipson, L. Hearn, Chorus

    "The (Gallant) Brave Huzzar"
        M. Stewart, F. von Busing

    "Life Is a Garden"
        J. Collins, M. Stewart, Chorus

    "Secrets"[58] (Quintette)
        J. Collins, F. von Busing, M. Stewart, C. Ediss, L. Hearn

    "Oh, Fascinating Night"
        J. Collins, R. Evett

ACT 2

    "Marina" (Opening Chorus)

    "The Match Makers" (Quartette)
        F. von Busing, C. Ediss, L. Hearn, T. McNaughton

    "It Trills! It Thrills!"
        J. Collins, R. Evett

    "The Ocean, The Ocean"
        F. von Busing, M. Stewart, Chorus

    "Heaven Measured You for Me"
        J. Collins, L. Hearn

    "'Twas in a Garden" (Trio)
        R. Evett, F. von Busing, J. Collins

    "The Engagement" (Finale)
        Company

ACT 3

    Opening

    "Teenie, Eenie, Weenie" (Duet)
        L. Hearn, C. Ediss
        (*Music by* Paul Lincke.)

    "Venus Calls and I'll Obey"[59]
        R. Evett, Chorus

    "Tick-a-Tick" (Suzi, I'm Ticking Love Taps)
        J. Collins, T. McNaughton, Chorus
        (*Music by* Max Perschk.)

    "The Best Toast of All" (Kiss Her and Look in Her Eyes)
        J. Collins, Chorus
        (*Music by* Franz Lehár.)

    Finaletto

1914.29 THE HEART OF PADDY WHACK

An Irish Drama in Three Acts. Play by Rachel Crothers. Music by Ernest R. Ball. Lyrics by J. Keirn Brennan. Staged by Henry Miller. Musical director, George Lyding. Produced by Henry Miller. Opened 23 November 1914 at the Grand Opera House and closed 5 December 1914 after 17 performances.

CAST: *Michael*: Little STEPHEN DAVIS. *Granny*: Jessie Crommette. *Bridget O'Riley*: Jennie Lamont. *Miss Margaret Flinn*: Maud Hosford. *Mona Cairn*: EDITH LUCKETT. *Dennis O'Malley*: CHAUNCEY OLCOTT. *Squire Linnering*: CHARLES E. VERNER. *Lawrie Linnering*: FLEMING WARD. *Mr. O'Dowd*:

Richard Quilter. *Mrs. O'Dowd*: Bessie LeaLestina. *Mrs. McGinniss*: Nina Seville. *Mr. McGinniss*: Walter Colligan.

Scene: Ireland, 1830.

Act 1: Living-room of Dennis O'Malley's home.

Act 2: Garden of Dennis O'Malley.

Act 3: Living-room of Dennis O'Malley's home.

MUSICAL NUMBERS[60]

    "A Broth of a Boy"
        (C. Olcott)

    "The Heart of Paddy Whack"
        (C. Olcott)

    "A Little Bit of Heaven (Sure They Call It Ireland)"
        (C. Olcott)

    "Who Knows" (Act 3)
        (C. Olcott)
        (*Lyrics by* Paul Lawrence Dunbar.)

    "Irish Eyes of Love"
        (C. Olcott)
        (*Lyrics by* J. Edward Killalea.)

1914.30 THE DÉBUTANTE

An Operetta (Musical Comedy) in Two Acts. Book by Harry B. Smith and Robert B. Smith. Music by Victor Herbert. Lyrics by Robert B. Smith. Staged by George Marion. Dances arranged by Allan K. Foster. Scenery painted by Edward G. Unitt and Joseph Wickes. Costumes designed by William Henry Matthews, Cora MacGeachy, William Henry Matthews. Orchestra under the direction of Carlo Edwards. Orchestrations by Victor Herbert. Produced by John C. Fisher. Opened 7 December 1914 at the Knickerbocker Theatre and closed 16 January 1915 after 48 performances.

CAST (in order of appearance): *The Honorable Spencer Mainwaring Cavendish, Midshipman*: SYLVIA JASON. *An Old Sailor*: Cyril Smith. *Bo'sun, H.M.S. Scorpion*:: Thomas Reynolds. *The Cook, H.M.S. Scorpion*: J. Abbott Worthley. *Lieutenant Larry Sheridan, British Navy*: ROBERT G. PITKIN. *Mildred*: Dolly Alwin. *Annabel*: Peggy Parker. *Mrs. Zenobia Bunker, wife of Ezra Bunker*: MAUDE ODELL. *Ezra Bunker, composer of the music of the future*: WILL WEST. *Godfrey Frazer, an American captain of industry*: WILLIAM DANFORTH. *Wiggins*: Jack Hall. *Elaine, daughter of Sir Francis Vane*: HAZEL DAWN. *School Girl Companions of Elaine (8)*: *Marie*: Marie Baxter. *Elsie*: Elsie Schneider. *Dorothy*: Dorothy Landers. *Irene*: Irene Hopping. *Harriet*: Harriet Dubarry. *Mae*: Mae Doherty. *Eva*: Eva Stuart. *Frances*: Frances Ramey. *Armand, Marquis de Frontenac*: STEWART BAIRD. *Philip Frazer, son of Godfrey*: WILMUTH MERKYL. *Irma, a Russian dancer*: ZOE BARNETT. *Teslavitz, a famous violoncellist*: Theodore Heinroth. *Nina, a future ballet girl*: Sylvia Jason. *Paul Masson, a famous sculptor*: J. Abbott Worthley. *English Ambassador*: Frank Travers. *German Ambassador*: Jack Heisler. *French Ambassador*: William Gibney. *Footmen*: Robert Waite, Owen Jones. *Midshipmen*: Misses Mae Hennessy, Fritzie Smith, Kitty Carmen, Eleanor Matthewson, Lottie Harvey, Evelyn Rosewood, Helen Walsh, Florence Walsh. *Society Buds, Masqueraders*: Misses Anna George, Fanchon Haywood, Teresa Hendricks, Beatrice McKay, Harriet DeNorma, Helen Hardick, Gertrude Thurston, Adelaide Murray, Florence Flandreaux, Isabel MacLeod, Anna Howard, May Allen, Marion Dale, Mary Howard, Dorothy Whiting, Gladdie MacDonald, Irma Bertrand, Violet McKay, May Thompson, Blye Brown, Peggy Parker. *Officers, Sailors, Masqueraders*: Messrs. James H. Hager, Theodore Stein, William Izzard, Arthur Kugler, Hal Peel, Fred Hudler, E. G. Elliott, Bert McCarthy, Victor LeRoy, Carl C. Judd, Cyril Smith, Frank Travers, Jack Heisler, William Gibney, Robert Waite, Owen Jones. *"Call Around Again" Girls*: Misses Dolly Alwin, Anna Howard, Blye Brown, (Fay) Fanchon Haywood, May Thompson, Mary Howard, Peggy Parker, Helen Hardick.

Act 1: Godfrey Frazer's Villa, Mt. Edgecombe, near Plymouth, England.

Act 2: The Reception Room of Paul Masson's studio in Paris.

ACT 1

    Opening Chorus

    "Love Is a Battle"
        R. G. Pitkin, Chorus

    "On a Sunny Afternoon"
        W. West, S. Jason, R. G. Pitkin

    "Take Me Home with You"
        H. Dawn, Chorus

---

[56]Added during the run:
    "I'll Not Let Love Disparage Marriage" (Act 1, after "I Love You, Marina")
        M. Stewart, F. von Busing, R. Evett
        Hungarian Dance (Act 3, after Opening)
For subsequent tour, the running order was revised, and the following added:
    "Angling" (Act 1)
        J. Collins, R. Evett
[57]Dropped for subsequent tour.
[58]Dropped for subsequent tour.
[59]Revised as "Venus and I Are Pals" for subsequent tour.

[60]Not in performance order.

"All for the Sake of a Girl"
  S. Baird, Girls
"The Golden Age"
  H. Dawn, W. Merkyl
"The Love of the Lorelei"
  H. Dawn, R. G. Pitkin, W. Merkyl
"Peggy's a Creature of Moods"
  R. G. Pitkin, Male Chorus
"Never Mention Love When We're Alone"
  H. Dawn, S. Baird
Finale
  Ensemble
ACT 2[61]
"The Lorelei Waltz" (Love Theme)
  T. Heinroth (cello solo)
"When I Played Carmen"
  Z. Barnett, Chorus
"Call Around Again"
  H. Dawn, Chorus
"The Gay Life"
  W. West, S. Baird, R. G. Pitkin, W. Merkyl, J. A. Worthley
"The Will o' the Wisp"
  S. Baird, M. Hennessy
"The Dancing Lesson"
  W. Danforth, M. Odell
Sextette ("The Face Behind the Mask")
  H. Dawn, Z. Barnett, M. Odell, W. West, R. G. Pitkin, W. Merkyl
"The Baker's Boy and the Chimney Sweep"
  S. Jason, R. G. Pitkin, C. C. Judd
Burlesque of Modern Opera
  W. West, Chorus
Violin Solo
  H. Dawn
Finale Ultimo
  Ensemble

1914.31

WATCH YOUR STEP

A Syncopated Musical Show (Revue) in Three Acts, 7 Scenes. Made in America. Plot (book) if any by Harry B. Smith. Music and lyrics by Irving Berlin. Staged by R. H. Burnside. Scenery designed by Helen Dryden and Robert McQuinn. Costumes designed by Helen Dryden. Musical director, DeWitt Coolman. Produced by Charles Dillingham. Opened 8 December 1914 at the New Amsterdam Theatre and closed 8 May 1915 after 175 performances.

CAST: *Willie Steele*, a tango lawyer: Sam Burbank. *Silas Flint*, a maxixe lawyer: William J. Halligan. *Estelle*, a hesitating typewriter: JUSTINE JOHNSTONE. *Ebeneezer Hardacre*, a thrifty sport: HARRY KELLY. *Birdie O'Brien*, of the Comedie Francise, Dublin: ELIZABETH MURRAY. *Ernesta Hardacre*, too good to be true: SALLIE FISHER. *Joseph Lilyburn*, who invented the steps you watch: VERNON CASTLE. *Algy Cuffs*, a matinee idol: CHARLES KING. *Iona Ford*: Dama Sykes. *Stella Spark*: ELIZABETH BRICE. *Mrs. Vernon Castle*: MRS. VERNON [Irene] CASTLE. *Anne Marshall*, the lovely laundress: Harriet Leidy. *The Ghost of Verdi*: Harry Ellis. *A Carriage Caller at the Opera, a Pullman Porter, a Coat Room Boy*: FRANK TINNEY. *Denny*: Irving J. Carpenter. *Josiah Jay*: Gus Minton. *Samantha Jay*: Dorothy Morosco. *Opera Box Holders (5)*: *Mrs. Swift*: Julia Beaubien. *Mrs. Bright*: Mabel Callahan. *Mrs. Gay*: Natalie Saymore. *Mrs. Smart*: Gladys Sykes. *Mrs. Climber*: Ethel Sykes. *The Man in Box 51*: C. L. Kelley. *A Professional Escort*: Rokey Johnson. *A Young Chappy*: Charles Swan. *An Old Chappy*: Max Scheck. *An Impressario*: Terry Starwer. *An Usher*: W. M. Holbrook.
  Other Members of the Company: Misses Rose Leslie, Marie Dana, Flo Hart, Esther Lee, Dorothy Banks, Helen Barnes, Leila Benton, Christyne Bowers, Barbara Clark, Ethel Davies, Rose Davies, Phyllis Munday, Billie Norton, Virginia Shelby, Annette Simonet, Trixie Smith, Paula Sterling, Marie Walsh, Libbian Diamond, Marcel Earl, Jessie Holbrook, Alleyne Pickard, Nancy Poole, Myrtle Ross, Edna Stilwell, Bunny Wendell, Olive Birt, Gwendoline DeBraw, Ethel Hobart, May Homer, Maud Homer, Violet Pardue, Violet Sydney, Peggy Trevor. Messrs. John Q. Adams, Earl Amos, M. G.

Avery, C. T. Beanie, James Black, Richard Dickinson, Joseph Hadley, H. Hoey, W. M. Holbrook, Fred Rockwell.

Act 1, Scene 1: Law Office de Danse. *Scene* 2: The Old Stage Door. *Scene* 3: The Palais de Fox-Trot.

Act 2, Scene 1: The Foyer of the Metropolitan Opera House. *Scene* 2: The Opera House.

Act 3, Scene 1:A Pullman Sleeper. *Scene* 2: A Fifth Avenue Cabaret, or "Home Life in New York."

ACT 1
Scene 1
  "Office Hours" (Opening Chorus)
    Chorus
  "What Is Love"[62]
    S. Fisher
  "The Dancing Teacher"
    V. Castle
  "The Minstrel Parade"
    E. Murray
  "Around the Town" (Let's Go 'Round the Town)
    Entire Company
Scene 2
  "They (Always) Follow Me Around"
    C. King, Matinee Girls
Scene 3
  "Show Us How to Do the Fox-Trot"
    I. Castle, Pupils
  "When I Discovered You"
    E. Brice, C. King, Dancing Teachers
    (*Music and Lyrics by* Irving Berlin and E. Ray Goetz.)
  "The Syncopated Walk"
    Entire Company
ACT 2[63]
Scene 1
  "Metropolitan Nights"
    Chorus
  "I Love to Have the Boys Around Me"
    E. Brice, Chappies
  "Settle Down in a One-Horse Town"
    E. Brice, C. King
  Polka (Specialty)
    V. Castle, I. Castle
Scene 2
  "Chatter Chatter"
    Chorus
  "Old Operas in a New Way" (Ragtime Opera Medley)
    Entire Company
ACT 3
Scene 1
  "Move Over"[64]
    E. Brice
Scene 2
  The High Steppers

---

[62]Replaced late in the run and for subsequent tour by:
  "Lead Me to Love"
    Edna Bates (Ernesta Hardacre)
    (*Music by* Ted Snyder.)
[63]The following were added for the national tour:
  "What is Love?" (reinstated after "One Horse-Town")
    Belle Rutland (Ernesta Hardacre)
  "(I've Gotta Go Back to) Texas" (Act 1)
    Bernard Granville (Joseph Lilyburn)
  "I'm Sober" (Act 2)
    B. Granville
[64]Replaced late in the run and for subsequent tour by:
  "Homeward Bound"
    E. Brice, C. King, Chorus

---

[61]After opening, the running order of "Call Around Again" and "The Gay Life" were reversed.

"Play a Simple Melody" (Simple Melody)
    S. Fisher, C. King
The One-Step
    V. Castle, I. Castle
"Look at Them Doing It"
    Entire Company

1914.32 ## TO-NIGHT'S THE NIGHT

A Musical Comedy in Two Acts, 4 Scenes.[67] Book by Fred Thompson. (Based on "Les Dominos Roses" by Maurice Hennequin and Alfred Delacour.) Music by Paul Rubens. (Lyrics by Paul Rubens and Percy Greenbank. Additional music by Jerome Kern, additional lyrics by Desmond Carter.) Staged by Austen Hurgon. Settings by Joseph and Phil Harker, Alfred Craven, Brunskill. Costumes by Maison Lucile, B. J. Simmons, Mme. Fisher. Orchestra under the direction of Frank E. Tours. Produced by the Messrs. Shubert. Opened 24 December 1914 at the Sam S. Shubert Theatre and closed 27 March 1915 after 112 performances.

CAST: *Montagu Lovitt-Lovitt:* JAMES BLAKELEY. *Henry,* his nephew: LAURI DeFRECE. *Pedro,* a tango teacher: MAURICE FARKOA. *Robin Carraway:* David Burnaby. *Archibald,* head waiter at Covent Garden: Robert Nainby. *Albert:* LESLIE HENSON. *Lord Ridgmount:* LAURIE DESMOND. *Tolly Beauchamp:* Stanley Brightman. *Policeman:* Frank Smythe. *The Honorable Dudley Mitten:* GEORGE GROSSMITH. *Beatrice Carraway,* Robin's wife: Iris Hoey. *Victoria,* her maid: FAY COMPTON. *Daisy de Monthe,* of the Piccadilly Theatre: Madge Saunders. *Angela Lovitt-Lovitt,* Montagu's wife: Gladys Homfrey.
    Guests at the Carraways: Lady Kitty Preston: Peggy Kurton. *Lady Edith Taplow:* Hon. Helen Cecil Douglas-Scott-Montagu. *Mimi Skeats:* Gertrude Laarhoven. *Honorable Baby Vereker:* Doris Stocker. *Avice Carlton:* Grace Riopelle. *Yvette la Plage:* Adrah Fair. *Lil Vincent:* Barbara Dunbar. *Irene Goodson:* Mabel Twemlow. *Alice,* maid at Daisy's: Gipsy O'Brien. *June:* EMMY WEHLEN.
    Ensemble: Mabel Woof, Gladys Tree, Edith Hanbury, Kitty Lindley, Mabel Twemlow, Glen Hawthorne, Prudence O'Shea, Winifred Green, Gypsy O'Brien, Cynthia Murray, Marlah Blanchard, Olive Branch, Susanne Losanne, Connie Guy, Marie Guy, Nellie Laurette, Ethel Baird, Beryl Stackard, Vivienne Storia, Dorothy Way, Herbert Standing, Oliver Smith, Philip Travers, Michael Raven, Robert Whitehouse, Wilson Pembroke, Albert Gater, Frank Smythe, Cecil Clovelly, Gerrard Freeman, Stanley Brightman.

Act 1: The Carraway's House at Maidenhead.

Act 2, Scene 1: Foyer of the Boxes, Royal Opera House. *Scene 2:* Covent Garden Market. *Scene 3:* Daisy's Flat in Mount Street.

ACT 1[66]
    Opening Chorus
    "When the Boys Come Home to Tea" (Song)
        D. Burnaby
    "Too Particular" (Trio)
        I. Hoey, L. DeFrece, J. Blakeley
    "You Must Not Flirt with Me" (Please Don't Flirt with Me)(Duet)
        E. Wehlen, M. Farkoa
    "The Only Way" (Song)
        G. Grossmith
    "Land and Water" (Duet)
        F. Compton, L. DeFrece
    "To-Night's the Night"[67] (Song)
        J. Blakeley
    Finale

ACT 2
Scene 1
    Opening Chorus

"Round the Corner"[68] (Duet)
    E. Wehlen, D. Burnaby
"I'd Like to Bring My Mother" (Song)
    F. Compton
"I'm a Millionaire" (Song)
    M. Farkoa
"Boots and Shoes" (Duet)
    G. Grossmith, I. Hoey
"Dancing Mad" (Trio)
    G. Grossmith, D. Burnaby, L. DeFrece
Finale
Scene 2
    "Stars"[69] (Song)
        E. Wehlen
Scene 3
    Opening Chorus
    "Pink and White" (Song)
        M. Farkoa
    Duet
        E. Wehlen, L. DeFrece
    "I Could Love You If I Tried"[70] (Song)
        G. Grossmith
    Finale

1914.33 ## LADY LUXURY

A Musical Comedy in Two Acts. Book and lyrics by Rida Johnson Young. Music by William Schroeder. Production staged by J. H. Benrimo. Dances arranged by Charles S. Morgan, Jr. Gowns by Lucile. Orchestra under the direction of Arthur F. Kautzenbach. Opened 25 December 1914 at the Casino Theatre, moved 11 January 1915 to the Comedy Theatre, and closed 23 January 1915 after 35 performances.[71]

CAST (in order of appearance): *Edward Van Cuyler,* a common-sense man, sir,—without frills, ma'am—whose home and ideals are a generation old, as is his butler: HARRY CONOR. *Harper,* Van Cuyler's butler who, however, adores his young mistress, Eloise: FRANK ANDREWS. *Eloise Van Cuyler,* an American heiress whose fortune has been held in trust for her until the hour the play opens: INA CLAIRE. *Jimmy,* Eloise's brother, who has been spending his share, and is just home from abroad on the same boat with Mrs. Draper-Cowles: ALAN MUDIE. *Mrs. Draper-Cowles,* an English chaperone, who comes to assume charge of Eloise's social campaign, accompanied by her daughter Maude: EMILY FITZROY. *Maude Draper-Cowles,* her daughter, destined for a rich marriage, but secretly in love with a very different type of man: ALICE MOFFAT. *Sam Warren* from Texas—not used to modern girls but anxious to learn from Eloise: FOREST HUFF. *Madame Mischkowa,* a Russian dancer, engaged by Eloise to appear during the birthday festivities with her partner, Monsieur Ivan: EMILIE LEA. *Monsieur Ivan,* who becomes frantic over the loss of the dancer's jewel case that resembles one carried by Count Pisianelli: FRANCIS BRYAN. *Count Pisianelli,* who own losses make him fear the coming of Detective Scatro: Arthur Albro. *Detective Scatro,* who endeavors to solve the mystery before the fall of the final curtain with the aid of (everyone else): E. H. CRAWFORD. *Debutantes and Other Guests, Dancers, etc.:* Misses Dorothy Fitch, Loretta Wilson, Louise Morris, Alice Elden, Dorothy Honey, Lee Buchanan, Frances Mink, Kathryn Andrews, Catherine Taggert, Katherine Grant, Elsie Comerford, Georgia Dawson, Carolyn Burke, Dorothy Betts, Gladys Wilson, Marie Barbara, Lauretta Grant, Naomi Waldron, Ethel Russell, Billie Woods, Grace Byron, Ruth Tate. Messrs. James Whelan, Carl Porter, Garrett Carroll, William Kline, Alfred Maxwell, John Bryant, Roscoe Saunders, Curtis Dunham, George Forrest, Herbert Noll, Stuart Fisher, William Wilder, Herbert Paul, Harry Nelson.

Act 1: Living Room of the Van Cuyler Residence, on the Hudson.

Act 2: The Living Room and Garden—Five days later.

---

[65]Billed as a presentation of Theatrical Attractions, Ltd., of London (Messrs. Grossmith & Laurillard, Managing Directors) All-Star Company direct from the Gaiety Theatre, London.
[66]Added to Act 2 after "I'm a Millionaire" for subsequent tour:
    "Wonderful Thing They Call Love" (Song)
        F. Compton
[67]Dropped for subsequent tour.

[68]Replaced during the run and for subsequent tour by:
    "Play Me That Tune" (Song)
        E. Wehlen
[69]Replaced during the run and for subsequent tour by:
    "Murders" (Song)
        G. Grossmith
[70]Dropped during the run.
[71]Produced prior to New York by F. C. Whitney; subsequent tour produced by Charles H. Wuerz.

ACT 1[72]

Opening Chorus
Ensemble

"Those Awful Tattle-tales"
I. Claire

"I'll Take You All"
A. Mudie, Girls

"Lady Luxury" (Ensemble)
I. Claire, Chorus

"Hi There, Buddy"
F. Huff, Boys

"Kiss Me Once More"
A. Albro, A. Moffat

"Whistle When You Want Me" (Whistle and I'll Come to You)[73]
Boys, Girls

"Dream On (My Princess)"
F. Huff

"Birthday Ensemble"
I. Claire, Ensemble

Danse Climatique
E. Lea, F. Byan

"Longing (Just) for You"[74]
F. Huff

Finale
I. Claire, F. Huff, Chorus

ACT 2

Opening Chorus

"(Pick, Pick,) Pick-a-Pickaninny"[75]
I. Claire

Poster Dance
E. Lea, F. Bryan

"Don't You Really Think I'll Do?"
A. Mudie, A. Moffat

"(It's) Written in the Book of Destiny"
I. Claire, F. Huff

"When I Sing in Grand Opera"
A. Albro, A. Moffat, F. Huff, H. Conor

"Longing for You"
I. Claire

"(Oh My, How He Loves) That Rag-tag Dance"
A. Mudie, E. Lea

Finale

1914.34   HELLO, BROADWAY!

A Musical Crazy Quilt (Revue) in Two Acts, 13 Scenes. Sketches, music and lyrics by George M. Cohan. Staged by George M. Cohan. Dances arranged by James Gorman, Ned Wayburn.[76] Scenery by Edward G. Unitt and Joseph Wickes. Costumes by Cora MacGeachy. Orchestra under the direction of Charles J. Gebest. Produced by George M. Cohan and Sam Harris. Opened 25 December 1914 at the Astor Theatre and closed 10 April 1915 after 123 performances.[77]

CAST: *George Babbitt*, The Millionaire Kid: GEORGE M. COHAN. *Bill Shaverfam*, The Hawk: WILLIAM COLLIER. *Bolivar Babbit*, the soap king: Charles Dow Clark. *Ambrose Deming*, the advertising nut: LAWRENCE WHEAT. *Kick in McCluskey*, the stage policeman: SYDNEY JARVIS. *Bum Lung*, the dancing slave: MARTIN

BROWN. *Mr. Wu*, a Chinese playwright: JOHN HENDRICKS. *Victor*, the butler: Charles Dow Clark. *Daddy Long Beard*, The Miracle Man: TOM DINGLE. *His Brother*: Jack Corcoran. *Judge Reizenstein*: WILLIAM COLLIER. *The Defensive Attorney*: GEORGE M. COHAN. *The Offensive Attorney*: LAWRENCE WHEAT. *Leo Getrichstein*: GEORGE M. COHAN. *Innocent*: WILLIAM COLLIER. *Uncle Malcolm*, Innocent's Guide: SYDNEY JARVIS. *The Man from Knoblacks's*: Charles Dow Clark. *Starter* for Cohan's Theatre: Jack Corcoran. *Starter* for Collier's Theatre: Tom Dingle. *Patsy Pygmalion*, a flower girl: LOUISE DRESSER. *Ruth Chatterbox*, a Gaiety girl: BELLE BLANCHE. *Chin Chin*, Mr. Wu's daughter: ROZSIKA DOLLY. *Elsie Workingson*, an outcast: PEGGY WOOD. *Aunt Laura*, Innocent's Aunt: LOUISE DRESSER. *A Maid*: PEGGY WOOD. *Officer Flynn*: Florence Moore. *Officer O'Malley*: Thelma Pinder.

Act 1, Patch 1: Outside the Soap Factory and Reform School, Jersey City. (Touching on "It Pays to Advertise."[78]) *Patch 2*: Mr. Wu's Home in Hong Kong. (Touching on "Mr. Wu.") *Patch 3*: George Babbit's Apartment, Riverside Drive. (Touching on "Outcast.") *Patch 4*: On the Sidewalk. (A Bit of Old-Time Song and Dance.) *Patch 5*: New York's Chinatown. (Touching on "Chin Chin.") *Patch 6*: Another Sidewalk. (Touching on Advance Playwriting.) *Patch 7*: Ballroom in a New York Hotel. (A Bit of the Rag Craze.)

Act 2, Patch 1: In Front of the Hippodrome. (Showing How Popular Songs Are Made.) *Patch 2*: On the Sidewalk. (Touching on Popular Actors.) *Patch 3*: In the Court House. (Touching on the Big Hit, "On Trial.") *Patch 4*: Innocent's Home. (Bits of "Innocent," "My Lady's Dress" and "Phantom Rival.") *Patch 5*: In Front of Two New York Theatres. (Touching on Personalities.) *Patch 6*: Overlooking New York Bay. (The Patriotic Stuff.)

ACT 1[79]

"It Pays to Advertise"
G. M. Cohan, S. Jarvis, L. Wheat, Chorus

"Pygmalion Roses"
L. Dresser, Chorus

"My Miracle Man"
B. Blanche, Chorus

"Hello, Broadway"
G. M. Cohan, W. Collier, Chorus

"Look Out for Mr. Wu"
J. Hendricks, Chorus

"I Wanted to Come to Broadway"
P. Wood

"Two Dandy Darkies"
G. M. Cohan, W. Collier

"Chinese Celebration"
Chorus

Characteristic Dance
M. Brown, R. Dolly

"Sneaky Steps"
T. Dingle

"Broadway Tipperary"
S. Jarvis, Chorus

"The Irving Berlin Melodies" (Those Berlin Melodies)
G. M. Cohan, Chorus

ACT 2

"Hippodrome Folks"
Chorus

"The Barnum and Bailey Rag"
L. Wheat, Chorus

Tango[80]
M. Brown, R. Dolly

"Down By the Erie Canal"
L. Dresser, Chorus

---

[72]Added for second week of the run:
"Life Is Just a Joke" (Act 1, after "Hi There, Buddy")
F. Huff, Boys
[73]Dropped second week of the run.
[74]Dropped for second week of the run, but Act 2 reprise was retained.
[75]Replaced in second week of the run by:
"Moon, Moon"
I. Claire
[76]Ned Wayburn staged "Berlin Melodies," "Erie Canal," and "My Flag."
[77]Toured with a subtitle: HELLO BROADWAY! or the Mystery of the Hat Box.

---

[78]These parenthetical remarks [Touching on. ., Bits of. .] were added to the program during the show's run.
[79]Dance music in the Chin Chin numbers composed by Jerome Schwartz. During the run, the show was revised from 13 to 16 Scenes, 3 of which were added after Act 2, Scene 4: On the Sidewalk (Touching on Susie Songs); The Music House (Touching on the Big Hit, "Song of Songs"); Castle Square (Touching on "Watch Your Step").
[80]Dropped early in the run and replaced by:
"Old-Fashioned Cakewalk"
W. Collier, R. Dolly, G. M. Cohan, M. Brown, Chorus

"Imitations"
   B. Blanche
"Fool Dance"
   G. M. Cohan, W. Collier
"The Carriage Starters' Glide"[81]
   J. Corcoran, T. Dingle
"The Two Playhouses"
   G. M. Cohan, W. Collier
"Parodies"
   G. M. Cohan, W. Collier
"My Flag"
   P. Wood, Chorus
Finale
   Entire Company

1915.01   90 IN THE SHADE

A Musical Play in Two Acts. Book by Guy Bolton. Music by Jerome Kern. Lyrics by Harry B. Smith. Production staged by Robert Milton. Dances and ensembles by Julian Alfred. Scenery by D. Frank Dodge and William Castle. Costumes by Hilarie Mahieu & Co. Orchestra under the direction of John McGhie. Produced by Daniel V. Arthur. Opened 25 January 1915 at the Knickerbocker Theatre and closed 27 February 1915 after 40 performances.

CAST (in order of appearance): *Coolie*: Willard Reynolds. *Bolo*, Parker's native servant: Philip Sheffield. *Bob Mandrake*, owner and skipper of the schooner *"Double Cross"*: EDWARD MARTINDEL. *Willoughby Parker*, agent of the Manilla Hemp Company: RICHARD CARLE. *Captain Jerry Carvel*, U.S. Marine Corps: VICTOR MORLEY. *Polly Bainbridge*: MARIE CAHILL. *Madge Splint*: ELENOR HENRY. *Dot Splint*: Dorothy Arthur. *Peter Thompson*: Rollin Grimes. *Judge Splint*, father of Madge and Dot: FRED WALTON. *Hodgins*, Judge Splint's secretary: Ralph Nairn. *Bridesmaids (8)*: *Rose Carter*: May Thompson. *Lilly Whitehead*: Jeanne Crane. *Pansy Whitehead*: Bettie Best. *Daisy Hammond*: Jessie Crane. *Clover Royce*: Alice Carrington. *Myrtle Wattersen*: Alma Braham. *Violet Fuller*: Madeline Fliege. *Lettice Romaine*: Amperito Ferrer. *Sergeant McGinn*: Murray D'Arcy. *Mozi*, an educated Filipino: Pedro de Cordoba. *Catti*, his wife: Florence Dillon. *Hai-cho*, a Filipino chief: Abbott Adams. *Donna Estrada*: JEAN NEWCOMBE. *Marines*, *Natives*.

The action takes place at the present time on Amorillo Island, Philippine Archipelago.

Act 1: Terrace outside Willoughby Parker's Bungalow.

Act 2: Interior of Willoughby Parker's Bungalow.

ACT 1[82]

Scene Music
"Where's the Girl for Me?"
   V. Morley
"Jolly Good Fellow"
   R. Carle, V. Morley, E. Martindel
   (*Lyrics by* Clare Kummer.)
"Lonely in Town"
   M. Cahill
   (*Music and Lyrics by* Clare Kummer.)
"I Have Been About a Bit"
   E. Henry, V. Morley
"Rich Man, Poor Man"
   Girls
   (*Lyrics by* Clare Kummer.)
"A Regular Guy"
   F. Walton, Girls
"Human Nature"
   M. Cahill, R. Carle, F. Walton
"Whistling Dan"
   M. Cahill, Company

---

[81]Dropped during the run. Later replaced by:
   "The Jesse James Glide"
      T. Dingle, Irene Enwright (Vernon and Irene Castle)
[82]Added after opening:
   "It Isn't Your Fault"
      (*Lyrics by* M. E. Rourke.)

"Where's the Girl for Me?" [reprise]
   E. Martindel
Finale
ACT 2
Chant
   F. Dillon, Natives
"(A) Package of Seeds"
   R. Carle, Girls
"Courtship de Dance"
   E. Henry, V. Morley, D. Arthur, R. Grimes
"My Lady's Dress"
   M. Cahill
"Foolishness"
   R. Carle
"Peter Pan"
   D. Arthur, R. Grimes
"The Triangle"
   M. Cahill, R. Carle
   (*Lyrics by* Guy Bolton.)
"Wonderful Days"
   E. Henry, R. Carle, Girls
   (*Lyrics by* Clare Kummer.)
"My Mindanao Chocolate Soldier"
   M. Cahill
   (*Music by* P. H. Christine. *Lyrics by* Clare Kummer.)
Finale

1915.02   MAID IN AMERICA

A Revusical Production (Musical Revue) in Two Acts, 12 Scenes. Song Cues (sketches) and lyrics by Harold Atteridge. All kinds of music rewritten by Sigmund Romberg and Harry Carroll. Staged by J. C. Huffman. Musical numbers staged by Jack Mason. Settings designed by H. Robert Law. Costumes by Melville Ellis. Orchestra under the direction of Oscar Radin. Produced by the Winter Garden Company (Messrs. Shubert). Opened 18 February 1915 at the Winter Garden and closed 22 May 1915 after 108 performances.

CAST (in order of appearance): *The Made in America Song Writer*: HARRY CARROLL. *The Made in America Chorus Girl*: MINERVA COVERDALE. *The Made in America French Actress*: Belle Ashlyn. *Made in America Man from Home*: John Sparks. *An American Made Coat Room Boy*: LEW BRICE. *The Made in America Cabaret Entertainer*: YVETTE. *Ignatz*, a Waiter, Made in America: Sam Adams. *Ignatz the Second*, also Made in America: Carl Dellorto. *An American Made Diner*: Will Stanton. *Frederick*, an American Waiter: JAMES CLEMONS. *Another America Made Diner*: Harold Robe. *The Made in America English Lord*: BERT CLARK. *George Rival*, her former lover, re-made in America: CHARLES J. ROSS. *Anna Gray*, his American wife: MAUD LAMBERT. *John Gray*, a Jealous Husband, Made in America: HAL FORDE. *The Made in America Society Lady*: BLOSSOM SEELEY. *The American Made Comedian*: HARRY FOX. *Nettie*, Belle of "The Broadway Knitting Club," Made Over Here: NORA BAYES. *An American "Souse"*: Sam Adams. *The American Made Bride*: YANCSI DOLLY. *Gaby*, Made in America: YANCSI DOLLY. *The American Made Vagabond*: Joe Jackson. *Miss Wise-Un*, Home-Grown: Belle Ashlyn. *Appolonora*, Bottled in the U.S.A.: BLOSSOM SEELEY. *Charmion*, Made in America: Belle Ashlyn. *Sorry They Were Not Made in America (6)*: *Caesar*: BERT CLARKE. *Alexandra*: Ruby Helder. *Ftatateeta*: NORA BAYES. *Cleopatra*: NORA BAYES. *Marc Anthony*: CHARLES J. ROSS. *Romanca*, an American Made Dancer: MLLE. DAZIE. *David Belasco*, Made in U.S.A.: CHARLES J. ROSS. *The Belasco Girl*: Lois Whitney. *Miss Soubrette*: NORA BAYES. *Miss Moving Pictures*: Belle Ashlyn. *The Rathskeller Trio*: BERT CLARK, HARRY FOX, HAL FORDE. *A Chorus Girl*: Eleanor Brown. *Stage Manager*: John Sparks. *Dorziat*: Belle Ashlyn. *Mr. Fliversham*: HAL FORDE. *Mr. Legit*: CHARLES J. ROSS. *The Hero*: HARRY FOX. *The Heroine*: MAUD LAMBERT. *The Villain*: BERT CLARKE. *The Property Man*: Sam Adams. *The Stage Hand*: Harold Robe. *The Villainess*: BLOSSOM SEELEY. *The Friend*: MINERVA COVERDALE. *Nora Bayes*: NORA BAYES. *Harry Fox*: HARRY FOX. *Socrates*: CHARLES J. ROSS. *The Modern New Yorker*: HARRY CARROLL. *Touchstone*: HAL FORDE. *The Vaudevillians*: HARRY FOX, JOHN SPARKS. *The Spirit of Song*: MAUD LAMBERT. *The Spirit of Ragtime*: BLOSSOM SEELEY. *Diana*: Marguerite Beriza. *The Old-Fashioned Woman*: MINERVA COVERDALE. *The Modern Woman*: Belle Ashlyn.

Winter Garden Corps de Ballet: Emma McGrath, Grace Robinson, Bly Brown, Ethel Edison, Marion Mooney, Mabel Van Ryker, Jean White, Bobbie Roberts, Mertha Erlich, Katheryne Andrews, Rose Quinn, Lucy Lakewood, Ruth Mayne, Matt Riordan, Van Beck, William Kinlee, Guy Collins, Glen Roberts, Ray Conlin, Frank Crawford,

Frank Durand. (*Ballet Soloists*: Mlle. DAZIE, Leo Pernikoff, Mabel Hill, Dot Roselle, Marguerite Carmen, Mabel Grete.)

Winter Garden Chorus: Misses Baldwin, Cameron, Waters, Eugene, Holt, Cullen, Glennon, West, Vincent, Freuen, Montigue, Hill, Bates, DeHon, Marchea, Brady, Neat. Misses Rose, Christy, Faulkner, Willa, Winters, Nash, E. LeRoy, Harrington, M. LeRoy, Ethel Courtney, Nella Hadley, Jean White, Ralita Whitmore, Dolly Douglas, Vin Stevens, Agnes Jepson, Ethel Edison, Emmie Hastings. Misses Trixie Lakewood, Viola Quinn, Marion Mooney, Ruth Maybe, Rose Quinn, Mabel Hill, Mabel Grete, Bobby Roberts, Dot Rozelle, Emma McGrath, Vera Pearselle, Grace Reade, Daisy DeVere, Pony Canton, M. Carmen, Van Ryker, Grace Robinson, Hazel Black, K. Andrews, B. Brown, Rose Hubert, Peggy Hudson. Messrs. David Rudnick, Henry Ward, Leo Nashetier, Miles Carpenter, Jim Smith, Frank Durand, Frank Crawford, Charles Starr, Henry Beck, Guy Collins, Talbot Vaughn, Prothel Binns, Jack Naldrett, George Stevens, Ray Conlin, Glen Roberts, Matt Riordan, Fred Osborn, Ted Andrews, Jack Kelly, Eddy Dolly, Andrew Harper, H. W. Scott, William Kinley, Jack Murry.

Act 1, Scene 1: Made in America Exhibition. Madison Square Garden. *Scene 2*: The American Made Restaurant. *Scene 3*: John Gray's Home. *Scene 4*: The Boardwalk at Times Square. *Scene 5*: In Front of Experience — Casino Theatre. *Scene 6*: In Front of the War Map, Times Square. *Scene 7*: Egypt, near Alexandria.

Act 2, Scene 1: The Ballet of Color and Motion — The Orgie. *Scene 2*: In Front of a Billboard. *Scene 3*: Behind the Scenes of the Melodrama Theatre. *Scene 4*: An Idealized Ballroom. *Scene 5*: Grecian Gardens.

ACT 1[83]

"The Typical Opening Chorus"
  M. Coverdale, Chorus
"Made in the U.S.A."
  H. Carroll, Chorus
  (*Music by* Harry Carroll.)
"Here's a Bale of Cotton for You"
  M. Coverdale, Chorus
  (*Music by* Harry Carroll.)
"Have a Restaurant of Your Own"
  Yvette, Chorus
"The Ragtime Dinner Order"[84]
  C. J. Ross, M. Lambert, H. Forde, H. Carroll, J. Clemons, Ragtime Waiters
"Sister Susie's Started Syncopation"
  B. Seeley, Chorus
  (*Music by* Sigmund Romberg.)
"It Is All for You" (Only for You)
  H. Forde
  (*Music by* Sigmund Romberg.)
"The Times Square Arguments"
  H. Carroll, L. Brice, Chorus
"There's a Little Bit of Everything on Broadway"
  N. Bayes, Chorus
  (*Music and Lyrics by* Leo Edwards.)
"Manhattan Mad"
  Y. Dolly, Chorus
  (*Music by* Sigmund Romberg.)
"Everyone's Moving Up Town" (Everyone's Moving Up on Broadway)
  Yvette, M. Coverdale, J. Clemons, L. Brice, H. Carroll, Chorus
"The Stolen Melody"
  N. Bayes
  (*Music by* Nora Bayes. *Lyrics by* Phil Schwartz.)

[83]The show was rewritten after the opening; in particular Act 2 was shortened, characters dropped, songs reassigned. The show was revised for subsequent national tour, and the following were added:
  "You Can't Get Away from Tipperary" (Act 1)
    Florence Moore
  "When Grandma Was a Girl" (Act 2)
    M. Coverdale
  "Ha, Ha, Ha" (Act 2)
    F. Moore
  "The Olympian Glide" (Act 2)
    Louise Mink
  Balloon Number (Act 2)
    M. Coverdale
[84]Replaced after opening by:
  "The Girlie from the Cabaret"
    Y. Dolly, J. Clemons, M. Coverdale, L. Brice, Chorus
    (*Music by* Sigmund Romberg.)

"Let's Bungalow"[85]
  H. Fox, Y. Dolly
"Garden of Paradise"
  Mme. Beriza, H. Forde
  (*Music by* Sigmund Romberg.)
"Oh, Those Days"
  B. Seeley, Chorus
  (*Music by* Sigmund Romberg.)
ACT 2
  The Ballet of Color and Motion — The Orgie (*Staged by* Theodore Kosloff.)
    Mlle. Dazie, L. Pernikoff, M. Hill, D Roselle, M. Carmen, M. Grete
    Soprano: Mlle. M. Beriza. *Contralto*: R. Helder. *Basso*: Monsieur Sparr. And the Winter Garden Chorus, Corps de Ballet. *Satyrs*: L. Brice, J. Clemons.
"The Rathskeller Trio"[86]
  B. Clark, F. Fox, H. Forde
"Whistle and I'll Come to You"[87]
  N. Bayes
  (*Music by* Leo Edwards. *Lyrics by* Blanche Merrill.)
"I'm Looking for Someone's Heart"
  M. Lambert, Chorus
  (*Music by* Sigmund Romberg.)
"Castles in the Air"[88]
  Y. Dolly, J. Clemons, L. Brice, Chorus
"Suzi Ann" (Susie Ann)[89]
  N. Bayes, H. Fox
  (*Music and Lyrics by* Nora Bayes, Tom Mellor, and Harry Gifford.)
"Diana"[90]
  Mme. Beriza, Chorus
  (*Music by* Sigmund Romberg.)
"Mr. Tosti, Good-Bye"[91]
  B. Seeley, Chorus
"(At) The Fox Trot Ball" — Finale
  Ensemble
  (*Music and Lyrics by* Joe Jordan.)

1915.03   JACK'S ROMANCE

An Irish Comedy Drama in Four Acts. Play by Augustus Pitou, Sr. Music by Linda Bloodgood. Lyrics by Fiske O'Hara. Produced under the personal direction of Augustus Pitou, Jr. Musical director, Linda Bloodgood. Produced by Augustus Pitou, Jr. Inc. Opened 22 February 1915 at the Grand Opera House and closed 27 February 1915 after 8 performances.[92]

CAST: *Jack*: FISKE O'HARA. *James Butler, Duke of Ormonde*: James E. Miller. *Sir Thomas Connolly, of Castletown Manor*: DON MERRIFIELD. *Edmund Farley*, secretary to Sir Thomas: Daniel Lawler. *Sandy McFarland*, a cattle buyer: J. P. SULLIVAN. *Phadrig Mulhall*, a stock raiser: William T. Sheehan. *Hugh Barton*: Gerald McCoy. *Myles Dowling*: Charles McHenry. *Constable*: Morey Hanta. *Servant*: P. J. Burke. *Lady Constance Butler*: ETHEL VON WALDREN. *Lady Elizabeth Connolly*: Elizabeth Paige. *Kathleen Mulhall*: MARIE QUINN. *Mrs. Bridget Muldoody*: Lou Ripley. *Mary Burke*: Lisle Bloodgood. Constables, Peasants, etc.

The action takes place at Castletown, County Kildare, the seat of Sir Thomas Connolly.

Act 1: Phadrig Mulhall's Home.

Act 2: The Gardens of Castletown Manor.

[85]Replaced after opening by [later dropped altogether]:
  "There Was a Time"
    H. Fox, Y. Dolly
    (*Music by* Harry Carroll. *Lyrics by* Alfred Bryan.)
[86]Dropped after opening.
[87]Dropped after opening.
[88]Dropped for subsequent national tour.
[89]Replaced after opening by:
  "Dancing Around the U.S.A."
    H. Carroll, Helen Rook, Chorus
    (*Music by* Harry Carroll, George L. Cobb. *Lyrics by* Jack Yellen.)
[90]Dropped late in the New York run.
[91]Dropped after opening.
[92]Scenery and costumes uncredited.

Act 3: The Shooting Lodge.

Act 4: A Room in the Manor.

MUSICAL NUMBERS

"The Highwayman"
F. O'Hara

"You and I"
F. O'Hara

"Colleen Machree"
F. O'Hara

"Killarney"
F. O'Hara
(*Music by* Michael Balfe.)

1915.04 ## THE PEASANT GIRL

A Musical Play in Three Acts. (Original Viennese) Book ("Polenblut") by Leo Stein, adapted by Edgar Smith. Music by Oskar Nedbal. Additional music by Rudolf Friml. Lyrics by Herbert Reynolds and Harold Atteridge. Entire production staged by J. C. Huffman and J. H. Benrimo. Ensembles arranged by Jack Mason. Scenery by Ackerman Brothers. Costumes designed by Melville Ellis. Orchestra under the direction of Gaetano Merola. Produced by the Messrs. Shubert, in association with Messrs. Ray Comstock and Morris Gest. Opened 2 March 1915 at the 44th Street Theatre and closed 5 June 1915 after 111 performances.

CAST (in order of appearance): *Von Mirski*, friend of Bolo's: ERNEST HARE. *Countess Napolska*: EDITH KINGDON HALLOR. *Pan Jan Zarémba*, owner of an estate: FRANCIS J. BOYLE. *Jadwiga Pawlowa*, Wanda's mother: Ethel Houston. *Wanda Kwadinskaja*, dancer at the Opera: LETTY YORKE. *Bronio Von Popiel*, Bolo's friend: CLIFTON CRAWFORD. *Count Bolo Baránksi*: JOHN CHARLES THOMAS. *Hélena*, Zaremba's daughter: EMMA TRENTINI. *Wlatek*, butler to Bolo: Henry Mack. *Von Gorski*: Charles Guidon. *Companion's of Bolo's* (4): Von Senovica: Stanley Henry. *Celeste*: FRANCES PRITCHARD. *Baroness Petroffski*: Lucille Blair. *Fraulein Drygalska*: Karen Krischner.

Frauleins, Admirers of Wanda: Margot: Miss Davidson. *Babette*: Miss Berg. *Marcel*: Miss Gordon. *Toinette*: Miss Evon. *Doris*: Miss Babbit. *Angelique*: Miss Lucey. *Mellina*: Miss Harrison. *Violetta*: Miss Flood. *Dancer with Mr. Crawford*: FRANCES PRITCHARD.

Members of the Ballet of the Opera: Misses Mitchell, Berry, Stallman, DeForest, Perle, Watson, Alexander, Bright, Lawlor, Harriman, Spencer, Raye, Paula, Wolf, Franklin. *Ensemble*: Misses Reynolds, Kline, Ehilid, Berg, Dayton, Cedar, Sutton, Siple, Clayton, Challenger, Werner, Estey, Horn, Tappen, Flood, Gordon, Taylor, Harrison, Davidson, Lampe, Crockett, Boyd, Maury. *Companions of Von Mirski*: Messrs. Everts, Hall, Henry, Singlust, Wagner, Fest, Allison, Croft, Hamilton, Warren, Kessler, Miller, Lee, Smith. *Bailiffs, Peasants, Guests, Servants, etc.*

Act 1: Conservatory in adjoining Ballroom.

Act 2: Hall in the Castle of Count Baranski.

Act 3: The Park before the Castle.

ACT 1

Opening Mazurka
Chorus

"Advice to the Young"
E. K. Hallor, E. Houston, F. J. Boyle, E. Hare

"Wanda"
L. Yorke, Chorus

"One and Only" (Duet)
C. Crawford, J. C. Thomas

"The Best Waltz of All"
L. Yorke, J. C. Thomas

"Love Is the Reason"
E. Trentini

"Love Is Like a Butterfly"[93]
C. Crawford, F. Pritchard
(*Music by* Rudolf Friml. *Lyrics by* Herbert Reynolds.)

"On to Conquer" (Finale)
E. Trentini, C. Crawford, J. C. Thomas, Ensemble

---

[93]Added after opening to "Love Is Like a Butterfly:"
Danse Poetique
C. Crawford, F. Pritchard
(*Music by* Rudolf Friml.)

ACT 2

"A Game of Cards"
Male Chorus

"Native Women" (March)
J. C. Thomas, Male Chorus

"Childhood Lessons"
E. Trentini, C. Crawford

"The Flame of Love"
E. Trentini, J. C. Thomas
(*Music by* Rudolf Friml. *Lyrics by* Harold Atteridge.)

"The Heart of the Rose"
E. Trentini
(*Music by* Rudolf Friml *Lyrics by* Herbert Reynolds.)

"The Gypsy Dance"
F. Pritchard, Chorus
(*Staged by* Theodore Kosloff.)

"Love's Awakening" (Finale)
E. Trentini, J. C. Thomas, E. Hare, L, Yorke, E. Houston, F. J. Boyle, Chorus
(*Music by* Oskar Nedbal and Rudolf Friml. *Gypsy Dance staged by* Theodore Kosloff.)

ACT 3

"Prosperity"
Ensemble

"After the Rain—Sunshine"
E. Trentini
(*Music by* Rudolf Friml.)

"Mary Had a Lamb" (That Little Lamb Was Me)
C. Crawford, F. Pritchard, Chorus
(*Music and Lyrics by* Clifton Crawford.)

Finale
Entire Company

1915.05 ## FADS AND FANCIES

Klaw and Erlanger's Entertainers in a Musical Medley (Revue) in Two Acts, 14 Scenes. Book (sketches) and lyrics by Glen MacDonough. Music by Raymond Hubbell. Dialogue directed by Herbert Gresham. Musical numbers arranged by Julian Mitchell. Scenery painted by John Young. Costumes designed by F. Richard Anderson and Cora MacGeachy. Electrical effects by Tony Greshoff. Orchestra under the direction of Raymond Hubbell. Produced by (Marc) Klaw and (Abraham L.) Erlanger. Opened 8 March 1915 at the Knickerbocker Theatre and closed 17 April 1915 after 48 performances.

CAST: *Professor Glum*, a happiness-hating magician: FRANK MOULAN. *Chase Clews*, an income-tax collector, in search of the missing $24,000,000: TOM McNAUGHTON. *Ayling Harte*, a lawyer, who makes sentimental troubles his specialty: Paul Morton. *Leicester Square*, of one of the oldest English families in Boston: FRANK DOANE. *Alan*, a country boy, employed by Professor Glum: TYLER BROOKE. *Phoebe*, his sweetheart: STELLA HOBAN. *Mrs. Hunter-Rumpuss*, whose life is equally divided between her search for a thrill and her devotion to her pet dog: MADGE LESSING. *Sir Giovanni Gasolini*, an Italian automobile dealer: LEO CARRILLO. *The Spirit of Pleasure*: LYDIA LOPOKOVA. *Sally Mander*, a thoroughly respectable adventuress: LAURA HAMILTON. *Sally's Six dearest friends*: Gladys: Evelyn Wildner. *Ethylle*: A. Howard. *Lucille*: Elise Hamilton. *Myrtle*: Teddy Hudson. *Mabelle*: Ethel Delmar. *Elsie*: Dottie Wang. *James Henry George, Sylvester Nightingale*, 2 soldiers of misfortune: Frank Conroy, George Lemaire. *Hawkshaw Holmes, Sherlock Pinkerton*, aides to Clews: JOHN MILLER, JAMES MACK. *Miss Murgatroyd*, cashier at the Mylaminitt Inn: Maude Grey. *Mrs. Wadburner*, an average New Yorker: Daisy Hudd. *Musharoogoo*, Mrs. Rumpuss' pet dog: David Abrahams. *Fido*, his yellow dog friend: David Abrahams, Jr. *An Irish Geisha*: Elise Murray. *A Cabaret Dancer*: Dorothy Quinnette. *Another*: G. Davenport. *Two Country Girls*: June White, Dorothy Quinnette.

Act 1, Scene 1: In the Mountains at the End of the Rainbow. *Scene 2*: In the Foothills. *Scene 3*: New York Salesroom of the Prestissimo Automobile Company. *Scene 4*: Another Part of the Salesroom. *Scene 5*: The Birthday Party of Mrs. Hunter-Rumpuss' Pet Dog. *Scene 6*: Riverside Drive near Claremont. *Scene 7*: Mrs. Hunter-Rumpuss' Tea House at Lenox. *Scene 8*: In the Foothills. *Scene 9*: The Hunt Ball.

Act 2, Scene 1: Main Room of the Mylaminitt Inn on the Electric Speedway. *Scene 2*: Neversink Terrace, the Venice of Long Island. *Scene 3*: The Gasoline Divorce Trial in the Court of Sentimental Relations. *Scene 4*: Piazza of the Imperial Palm Hotel. *Scene 5*: Ballroom of the Imperial Palm Hotel.

ACT 1
    "Come Across"
        T. McNaughton, J. Miller, J. Mack
    "In Search of a Thrill" (I'm Seeking a Thrill)
        M. Lessing, Men
    "Automobilia" (March)
        Chorus
    "Love Me, Love My Dog"
        Chorus
    "It is Heaven to Boheme"
        L. Hamilton, Chorus
    "Honey" (Duet)
        M. Lessing, T. McNaughton
    "I'm Still Single" (The Single Man)
        P. Morton, Chorus
    "I'm Lonely For Only One"
        S. Hoban, Male Chorus
    "Mary Ann O'San"
        L. Hailton, Chorus
    "The Hunt Ball" (Finale)
        Company
ACT 2
    "Music With Meals" (Opening—Dance)
        Chorus
    "We'll Take Care of You All" (Refugee Song)
        M. Lessing, Little Refugees, Chorus
        (*Music by* Jerome Kern. *Lyrics by* Harry B. Smith.)
    "Past and Present" (Dancing Specialty)
        T. Brooke, L. Lopokova
    "Those Girls of Long Ago"
        T. McNaughton, Company
    "They Do You Much Better at Home"
        P. Morton, Chorus
    "Never Again"
        F. Moulan, J. White, D. Quinnette
    Dance
        T. Brooke, J. White, D. Quinnette
    "Alimony Alley"
        P. Morton, Chorus
    "The Yuca Tango"
        M. Lessing, Chorus
    Finale
        Company

THE YEOMEN OF THE GUARD,
1915.06   or, The Merryman and His Maid

A Revival of the Comic Opera in Two Acts.[94] Libretto by by William S. Gilbert. Music by Arthur Sullivan. Stage director, Herbert Cripps. Musical director, Clarence West. Produced by William A. Brady. Opened 19 April 1915 at the 48th Street Theatre and closed 8 May 1915 after 24 performances in repertory.

CAST: *Sir Richard Cholmondeley*: John Willard. *Colonel Fairfax*: ARTHUR ALDRIDGE. *Sergeant Meryll*: HERBERT L. WATEROUS. *Leonard Meryll*: HUGH DWYER *Jack Point*: DE WOLF HOPPER. *Wilfred Shadbolt*: WILLIAM DANFORTH. *The Headsman*: James Hughes. *First Yeoman*: Frank Clarke. *Second Yeoman*: George Abbott. *First Citizen*: William Quimby. *Second Citizen*: Henry Smith. *Elsie Maynard*: NATALIE ALT. *Phoebe Meryll*: Gladys Caldwell. *Dame Carruthers*: Marie Horgan. *Kate*: Alice McComb. *Chorus of Yeomen of the Guard, Gentlemen, Citizens, etc.*

1915.07   # NOBODY HOME

A Musical Play in Two Acts. Book by Guy Bolton, Paul Rubens (based on the libretto by Joseph W. Herbert for the English musical "Mr. Popple

of Ippleton"). Music by Jerome Kern, (Otto Motzan, others. Lyrics by Herbert Reynolds, Schuyler Greene, Harry B. Smith.) Directed by J. H. Benrimo. Dances arranged by Dave Bennett. Settings designed by Elsie deWolfe. Gowns from Hickson's; men's clothes from R. B. Fashion Clothes. Orchestra under the direction of Max Hirschfeld. Orchestrations by Frank Saddler. Produced by Elisabeth Marbury and F. Ray Comstock. Opened 20 April 1915 at the Princess Theatre, moved 7 June 1915 to the Maxine Elliott Theatre and closed 7 August 1915 after 135 performances.

CAST (in order of appearance):[95] *Regan Terry*, Assistant Manager, Hotel Blitz: J. Abbott Worthley. *An Unknown*: Tom Graves. *Bellboy*, at the Blitz: QUENTIN TOD. *Rolando D'Amorini*: CHARLES JUDELS. *Mrs. D'Amorini*, his wife: MAUDE ODELL. *Vernon Popple*, a society dancer: GEORGE ANDERSON. *Violet Brinton*, Mrs. D'Amorini's niece: ALICE DOVEY. *Barmaid* at the Blitz: Della Connor. *The Pippin*, a show girl: Louise White. *Lucille*, Tony Miller's personal manager: Lillian Tucker. *Jack Kenyon*, a jealous admirer of Tony: GEORGE LYDECKER. *Miss "Tony" Miller*, prima donna at the Winter Garden: ADELE ROWLAND. *Dolly Dip*, a dancer: HELEN CLARKE. *Freddy Popple*, of Ippleton, England: LAWRENCE GROSSMITH. *Platt*, an ex-groom, Freddy's man-servant: Carl Lyle. *An Interior Decorator*: Tom Graves. *Havelock Page*, easily elevated to society overnight by his dancing: QUENTIN TOD.

    Guests at the Blitz Hotel: *Veroniva Vandelier*: Lillian Gaylor. *Edna Esmelton*: Cleo Carter. *Beatrice Beresford*: Winifred Browne. *Patricia Parkington*: Helen O'Day. *Violet Vivienne*: Elizabeth Moore. *Clarice Carrington*: Ethel Clayton.

    Dancers from the Winter Garden: *Maria Maxixe*: Vera Vendome. *Tessie Trot*: Gertrude Waixel. *Hilda Hesitation*: Mona Sartoris. *Polly Polka*: Marion Davis [Davies]. *Gertie Gavotte*: Flora Fredericks. *Trilby Tango*: Marion Dale.

    Devotess of the Stage Door: *Splendor Colgate*: Lester Greenwood. *Roger Gallet*: Frank Ross. *Edward Pinaud*: Byrd Coolsby. *Riker Hegeman*: Irving Kreuder. *Daggett Ramsdell*: Theodore Buerk.

Act 1: Entrance Lounge, Hotel Blitz, New York, Evening.

Act 2: Tony Miller's Apartment, Central Park West. Afternoon of the next day.

ACT 1[96]
    Opening Chorus
        Ensemble
    "You Know and I Know (and We Both Understand)" (Duet)
        A. Dovey, G. Anderson
        (*Lyrics by* Schuyler Greene.)
    "Cupid at the Plaza"[97]
        G. Anderson, Chorus
    "In Arcady"
        G. Lydecker
        (*Lyrics by* Herbert Reynolds.)
    "The Magic Melody"
        A. Rowland, Chorus
        (*Lyrics by* Schuyler Greene.)
    Military Dance
        Q. Tod, H. Clarke
    "Ten Little Bridesmaids"[98]
        A. Dovey, Chorus
    Finale
        Ensemble
ACT 2[99]
    Opening Chorus and Cakewalk

---

[94]First presented in New York 17 October 1888 at the Casino Theatre for 100 performances. For Synopsis of Scenes and Musical Numbers, see original 1888 production. Settings, costumes uncredited.

[95]After the opening, revisions in the text and cast list:
    Added: *Maurice*, assistant manager, Hotel Blitz: Tom Graves.
    Dropped: *Regan Terry*, Assistant Manager, Hotel Blitz: J. Abbott Worthley. *An Unknown*: Tom Graves.

[96]Added to Act 1 after opening chorus in second week of run:
    "Why Take a Sandwich to a Banquet"
        C. Judels
        (*Music by* Worton David. *Lyrics by* J. P. Long.)

[97]Replaced later in the run by:
    "Keep Moving" (from A MODERN EVE)

[98]Replaced during the run by:
    "The Chaplin Walk"
        A. Dovey, Chorus
        (*Music by* Otto Motzan, Jerome Kern. *Lyrics by* Schuyler Greene.)

[99]Added to subsequent tour (Boston, October 1915) to Act 2, after "Another Little Girl":
    "Hands Up"
        A. Rowland

Q. Tod, H. Clarke, Chorus
(*Music for 'Cakewalk' by* Otto Motzan.)

"Bed, Wonderful Bed" (Bed, Beautiful Bed)
L. Grossmith
(*Music by* C. W. Murphy, Dan Lipton. *Lyrics by* Lawrence Grossmith.)

"Another Little Girl" (Duet)
A. Dovey, G. Anderson
(*Lyrics by* Herbert Reynolds.)

"Any Old Night (Is a Wonderful Night)"
A. Rowland, Chorus
(*Music by* Otto Motzan, Jerome Kern. *Lyrics by* Schuyler Greene, Harry B. Smith.)

Dance
Q. Tod, H. Clarke

"The San Francisco Fair" (At That San Francisco Fair)
A. Rowland, Chorus
(*Music by* Jerome Kern (verse only), Ford Dabney, James Reese Europe. *Lyrics by* Schuyler Greene.)

Finale
Ensemble

1915.08   A MODERN EVE

A Musical Comedy in Two Acts. (Original German libretto, "Die moderne Eva," by George Okonkowski and A. Schönfeld.) American adaptation by William M. Hough. Music by Jean Gilbert and Victor Hollaender. Lyrics by Benjamin Hapgood Burt. Dance numbers arranged by Julian Alfred. Costumes by William H. Matthews. Orchestra under the direction of Ben M. Jerome. Orchestrations by Charles Miller. (Produced by John Cort.) Opened 3 May 1915 at the Casino Theatre and closed 19 June 1915 after 56 performances.[100]

CAST (in order of appearance): *Baroness de la Roche Taille*: HAZEL COX. *Count Castell-Vajour*: ALEXANDER CLARK. *Justin Pontgirard*: ERNEST GLENDINNING. *Dickey Rutherford*, barrister: CYRIL CHADWICK. *Renée Cascadier*: LEILA HUGHES. *Camille Cascadier*: DOROTHY WEBB. *Madame Niniche-Cascadier*: Georgie Drew Mendum. *Casimir Cascadier*: WILLIAM NORRIS. *Secretary*: Ailene Boley. *Minister*: Herbert Salinger. *Ponette*: Billie Wilkens. *Marguerite*: Tracy Elbert. *The International Dancers*: Frank Hale, Signe Patterson. *Modern Girls, Sirens, Pages, Bridesmaids and Attendants*.

The action takes place at the present time.

Act 1: Summer Residence of the Cascadiers, Aix Les Bains.

Act 2: Garden in House of the Pontgirards. One year later.

ACT 1

"The Song of the Sirens" (Opening Chorus)
Ensemble

"That's the Lesson I'm Teaching to You"
H. Cox, Sirens

"I'm Waiting for You" (I've Just Been Waiting for You)
L. Hughes, E. Glendinning, Chorus
(*Music by* Jerome Kern. *Lyrics by* Harry B. Smith.)

"Good-Bye Everybody"
D. Webb, F. Hale
(*Music by* Jean Gilbert. *Lyrics by* Will Hough.)

"When Love Comes Stealing In"
L. Hughes, Chorus

"When the Madame Goes Away"
W. Norris, Chorus
(*Music by* Ben M. Jerome. *Lyrics by* Benjamin Hapgood Burt.)

Wedding Finale
Ensemble

ACT 2

"Won't You Smile?"
H. Cox, L. Hughes, Chorus

"A Quiet Evening at Home"
E. Glendinning
(*Music by* Ben M. Jerome. *Lyrics by* Benjamin Hapgood Burt.)

"Keep Moving"
W. Norris, Chorus
(*Music by* Otto Motzan. *Lyrics by* Benjamin Hapgood Burt and Stanley Murphy.)

"Excuse Me? Certainly!"
D. Webb, C. Chadwick, A. Clark
(*Music by* Victor Hollaender. *Lyrics by* Charles Brown.)

"Is the Girl You Married Still the Girl You Love?"
L. Hughes, Chorus
(*Music by* Victor Hollaender. *Lyrics by* Will Hough.)

The International Dancers
F. Hale, S. Patterson

Finale—"Good-Bye, Everybody"
Entire Company

1915.09   THE MIKADO, or, The Town of Titipu

A Revival of the Comic Opera in Two Acts.[101] Libretto by William S. Gilbert. Music by Arthur Sullivan. Stage director, Herbert Cripps. Music director, Clarence West. Produced by William A. Brady. Opened 10 May 1915 at the 48th Street Theatre and closed 19 June 1915 after 20 performances total in repertory.

CAST: *The Mikado of Japan*: WILLIAM DANFORTH. *Nanki-Poo*, his son, disguised as a wandering minstrel, and in love with Yum-Yum: ARTHUR ALDRIDGE. *Ko-Ko*, Lord High Executioner of Titipu: DeWOLF HOPPER. *Pooh-Bah*, Lord High Everything Else: HERBERT L. WATEROUS. *Pish-Tush*, a Noble Lord: John Willard. *Three Sisters, Wards of Ko-Ko*: *Yum-Yum*: NATALIE ALT. *Pitti-Sing*: Gladys Caldwell. *Peep-Bo*: Alice McComb. *Katisha*, an elderly lady, in love with Nanki-Poo: MARIE HORGAN. *Chorus of School Girls, Nobles, Guards and Coolies*: Ensemble.

1915.10   THE SORCERER

A Revival of the Comic Opera in Two Acts.[102] Libretto by William S. Gilbert. Music by Arthur Sullivan. Stage director, Herbert Cripps. Musical director, Clarence West. Produced by William A. Brady. Opened 24 May 1915 at the 48th Street Theatre and closed 5 June 1915 after 16 performances in repertory.

CAST: *Sir Marmaduke Pointdextre*, an elderly Baronet: HERBERT WATEROUS. *Alexis*, of the Grenadier Guards, his son: ARTHUR ALDRIDGE. *Doctor Daly*, Vicar of Ploverleigh, specially engaged: DIGBY BELL. *Notary*: Henry Smith. *John Wellington Wells*, of J. Wells & Co., Family Sorcerers: DE WOLF HOPPER. *Lady Sangazure*, a lady of ancient lineage: MARIE HORGAN. *Aline*, her daughter, betrothed to Alexis: NATALIE ALT. *Mrs. Partlett*, a pew opener: Alice McComb. *Constance*, her daughter: GLADYS CALDWELL. *Hercules*, a page: May Arnold. *Chorus of Peasantry*: Ensemble.

followed by

TRIAL BY JURY, or, Love and Duty. A Revival of the Comic Opera in One Act.[103] Libretto by William S. Gilbert. Music by Arthur Sullivan. Stage director, Herbert Cripps. Musical director, Clarence West. Produced by William A. Brady.

---

[100]Staging, uncredited in New York programs, credited to Frank Smithson, on sheet music. Settings uncredited.

[101]First presented in New York 20 July, 10-29 August 1885 at the Union Square and People's Theatres for 22 performances. First authorized production presented 19 August 1885 at the Fifth Avenue Theatre by Richard D'Oyly Carte for 250 performances. For Synopsis of Scenes and Musical Numbers, see 19 August 1885 D'Oyly Carte production. Settings, costumes uncredited.

[102]First presented in New York 21 February 1879 at the Broadway Theatre for 20 performances. For Synopsis of Scenes and Musical Numbers, see original 1879 production. Settings, costumes uncredited.

[103]First presented in New York 15 November 1875 at the Eagle Theatre for 8 performances. For Synopsis of Scenes and Musical Numbers, see original 1875 production. Settings, costumes uncredited. Beginning the week of 7 June 1915, TRIAL BY JURY was paired with H.M.S. PINAFORE.

CAST: *The Judge*: DeWOLF HOPPER. *The Defendant*: ARTHUR ALDRIDGE. *Counsel for the Plaintiff*: JOHN WILLARD. *Usher*: WILLIAM DANFORTH. *Foreman of the Jury*: HERBERT L. WATEROUS. *Plaintiff*: GLADYS CALDWELL. *First Bridesmaid*: Alice McComb.

Jurymen: Messrs. Hall, Averill, Flynn, Thayman, Wood, Annison, Annisman, West, Dupont, Soyer, Barrett. *Bridesmaids*: Misses Brooks, Maudant, Allen, Flynn, Kurrier, Mar, Tucket, Price, Grosberg, Stratton, Paine.

1915.11 # THE PASSING SHOW OF 1915

A Musical Revue in Two Acts, 13 Scenes.[104] Dialogue (sketches) and lyrics by Harold Atteridge. Music by Leo Edwards, W. F. Peters and J. Leubrie Hill. Staged by J. C. Huffman. Dances arranged by Jack Mason. Ballets by Theodor Kosloff. Settings by P. Dodd Ackerman, H. Robert Law, Mettenleiter. Costumes by Mrs. J. J. Shubert. Orchestra under the direction of Oscar Radin. Produced by the Winter Garden Company (Messrs. Shubert). Opened 29 May 1915 at the Winter Garden and closed 2 October 1915 after 145 performances.

CAST [in order of appearance]: *First Love*: MARILYN MILLER. *Everywoman*: FRANCES DEMAREST. *Youth*: JOHN CHARLES THOMAS. *Gay Life*: JULIETTE LIPPE. *Woman's Intuition*: Helen Ely. *Miss Manhattan*: Frances Pritchard. *Mocha*: John Boyle. *Java*: Walter Brazil. *Experience*: John T. Murray. *Ruby, a modern working girl*: DAPHNE POLLARD. *R.J.*: EUGENE HOWARD. *Sammy*: WILLIE HOWARD. *Lily*: GEORGE MONROE. *Roughy Raffles*: ERNEST HARE. *Daniel Calkins*: HARRY FISHER. *Calkin's Three Wives: Elsie Outcast*: Eleanor Pendleton. *Ethel Shadow*: Olga Hempstone. *Ruth Chatterteeth*: Kitty Hill. *Miss Intoxication*: Eleanor Brown. *A Police Commissioner*: EUGENE HOWARD. *Belascoa Odile*: Bessie Morin. *Anglina Tarrymore*: Zena Morin. *A Ballet Master*: THEODOR KOSLOFF. *The Bird Man*: RODION MENDELVITCH. *Miss Terpsichore*: Mme. Baldina. *Peasant Girl*: Helen Ely. *Clifton Crawford*: MARILYN MILLER. *Trilby*: WILLIE HOWARD. *Svengali*: EUGENE HOWARD. *Gecko*: Sam Hearne. *Miss Baseball*: Rosie Quinn. *Wine*: Eleanor Brown. *Dance*: Frances Pritchard. *Passion*: Eleanor Pendleton. *Fortune*: Helen Ely. *Frailty*: GEORGE MONROE. *Beauty*: Harry Fisher. *Lou Telegram*: WILLIE HOWARD. *Louis J. Stonehead*: John T. Murray. *Hamlet*: WILLIE HOWARD. *Macbeth*: EUGENE HOWARD. *Androcles*: WILLIE HOWARD. *The Lion*: Arthur Hill. *Hawaiian Serenaders*: IRENE WEST'S ROYAL HAWAIIAN SEXTETTE. (*Featured Dancer*: Alexis Kosloff.)

Show Girls: Misses Margie Lane, Kathleen Cullen, Frances Henrich, Edna Waddell, Adrienne Dillon, Rene Smythe, Helena Hudson, Helen Carrington, Ivy Sherer, Claire Mullin, Emily Miles, Helen Cameron, Margie Moore, Helen Neat, Betty Randolph, Marie Salisbury, Sue Brett, Helen Marche, Louise Mayorga, Belle Whitney, Florence Boyd, Henrietta Bordeau, Ruth Cooper, Lorraine Waters, Kathryn Brady, Jean Forrest, Frances Whalen, Elsie Durant, Vivien Darville. *Dancers*: Misses Rosie Quinn, Marion Mooney, Alice Van Riker, Viola Quinn, Pearl Franklyn, Irene Mitchell, Betty Brown, Cecille Markels, Margaret Warde, Ruth Harris, Georgia Moore, Betty Hardgrove, Dorothy Charleston, Ethel French, Vera Delatour, Lorraine Delatour, Sylvia Dietz, Martha Ehrlich, Frieda Hoffman, Violet Lester, Rheba Stewart, Georgina Schram, Viola Watson, Fib Whiteside, Genevieve Willment, Ella Alexander, Olga Zicerva, Muriel Dewey, Dorothy Phillips. *Boys*: Messrs. Clarence Rockwell, Jack Laughlin, Roy Goodrich, Austin Clarke, Gus Martial, Ted Sullivan, Harry Russell, Charles Wilson, Dudley Farnworth, Jacque Stone, William Warren, George Collins, Philip Gilpin, Barnard Druce, Harry Bostock.

Act 1, Scene 1: Youth's home in the country. "In the land where musical shows begin." (Ackerman.) *Scene 2*: The City from a roof garden. "In the street of Vacillating Plots." (Ackerman.) *Scene 3*: Oriental Bazaar Shop, Atlantic City. "The Bored Walk." (Law.) *Scene 4*: Daniel Calkins' home. "The usual triangle parlor scene." (Law.) *Scene 5*: Floral Ball. "The last resort of librettists." (Ackerman)

Act 2, Scene 1: Corridor of chance. "The land of forgotten jokes." (Ackerman). *Scene 2*: Interior of a hotel parlor. "The abode of disillusioned actors." (Mettenleiter) *Scene 3*: Twin Beds Apartment. "A polygamist's life is not a happy one." (Law) *Scene 4*: Polo Field, near Ippleton. "The land of lost plots." (Ackerman) *Scene 5*: Aeroplane Invasion. "The home of scenic affects." (Law) *Scene 6*: Typical Musical Comedy Interior. "Where Beauty Congregates." (Mettenleiter) *Scene 7*: Arena at Wallack's Theatre. "Shaw in the Winter Garden" (Law) *Scene 8*: Hawaiian Baths. "The land where the audience awakes." (Ackerman)

ACT 1

"Spring Time in the Country"
Ensemble

"First Love Is the Best Love of All"
J. C. Thomas
(*Music by* Leo Edwards.)

"Every Small Town Girlie Has a Big Town Way"
M. Miller, Country Lassies
(*Music by* Leo Edwards.)

"I Will Follow Her" (Silk Stockings)
F. Pritchard, J. Boyle, W. Brazil, Ensemble
(*Music by* William F. Peters.)

"There's Something Missing in the Movies"
J. T. Murray

"Shopping"
Ensemble
(*Music by* William F. Peters.)

"(Take Me to) The Midnight Cakewalk Ball"
D. Pollard, Chorus
(*Music and Lyrics by* Maurice Abrahams, Eddie Cox and Arthur Jackson.)

"Broadway Sam"[105]
W. Howard
(*Music by* Leo Edwards. *Lyrics by* Blanche Merrill.)

"My Trombone Man" (Trombone Man)
M. Miller, Ensemble
(*Music by* J. Leubrie Hill.)

"I Don't Like the Sea"
F. Demarest, Ensemble
(*Music by* William F. Peters.)

"The Primrose Way"
J. Lippe, Ensemble
(*Music by* Leo Edwards.)

"(You'd Better See) America First"[106]
F. Demarest, Ensemble
(*Music by* Phil Schwartz.)

"The Peasant Girl"[107]
H. Ely, J. C. Thomas
(*Music by* Leo Edwards.)

Hungarian Dance
M. Miller, A. Kosloff
(*Conceived by* Theodor Kosloff.)

"The Spanish Fandango"
J. T. Murray

"My Trilby Maid"
E. Howard, Ensemble
(*Music and Lyrics by* Harold Atteridge, Bobby Jones and Will Morrissey.)

"Ragtime Overtures (of Grand Operas)"[108]
E. Howard, W. Howard, E. Hare, J. C. Thomas, F. Demarest, J. Lippe, H. Eley, L. Lucy, E. Pendleton, C. Starr
(*Music by* Leo Edwards.)

The Spring Ballet
Adagio
M. Baldina, T. Kosloff, Corps de Ballet
Classical Variations
M. Miller, Corps de Ballet
Variations–The Nightingale
M. Baldina
(*Composed and played by* Rodion Mendelvitch.)
Theodore Kosloff
M. Miller, Mme. Baldina, T. Kosloff

ACT 2[109]

"Gamble on Me"
H. Eley
(*Music by* Leo Edwards.)

"My Brother Bill"
D. Pollard

---

[104]The Fifth in the annual series of revues, produced since 1912 by the Messrs. Shubert, which began in 1894. Billed as the Winter Garden's Annual Revue.

[105]Replaced for subsequent tour by: ("Broadway Sam" moved to Act 2)
"Rosie Rosenblott"
W. Howard
[106]Dropped for subsequent tour.
[107]Dropped after opening.
[108]Dropped after opening.
[109]During the run, the running order to Act 2 was revised.

"The Shakespearian Rag" (Billy Shakespeare)[110]
    W. Howard, E. Howard
    (*Music by* Leo Edwards.)

"Flower of My Heart"
    J. C. Thomas
    (*Music by* Lee Edwards. *Lyrics by* Leo Wood.)

Specialty
    J. Boyle. W. Brazil

"Summer Sports"
    E. Pendleton, R. Quinn, L. Lucey

"Any Old Time with You"
    M. Miller, J. C. Thomas
    (*Music by* Leo Edwards.)

"My Hula Maid"
    F. Demarest, E. Hare, Royal Hawaiians
    (*Music by* Leo Edwards.)

"Panama Pacific Drag"
    Ensemble
    (*Music by* Leo Edwards.)

Finale
    Ensemble

---

[110]Replaced during the run by:
"Isle d'Amour" (from ZIEGFELD FOLLIES OF 1913)
    W. Howard, E. Howard
Which was replaced by a medley of 2 songs for the subsequent tour:
"Sing Me to Sleep with an Old-Fashioned Melody"
    W. Howard, E. Howard
"Broadway Sam"
    W. Howard

1915–1916 SEASON

Al Jolson as Good Friday in ROBINSON CRUSOE, JR. (Photo: White Studio)
Billy Rose Theatre Collection, New York Public Library for the Performing Arts

1915–1916 SEASON

THE PIRATES OF PENZANCE,
1915.12   or, The Slave of Duty

A Revival of the Comic Opera in Two Acts[1]. Libretto by William S. Gilbert. Music by Arthur Sullivan. Stage director, Herbert Cripps. Musical director, Clarence West. Produced by William A. Brady. Opened 7 June 1915 at the 48th Street and closed 18 June 1915 after 4 performances in repertory[2].

CAST: *The Pirate King:* HERBERT L. WATEROUS. *Frederick:* ARTHUR ALDRIDGE. *Samuel:* John Willard. *Major General Stanley:* WILLIAM DANFORTH. *Sergeant of Police:* DeWOLF HOPPER. *Mabel:* ALICE BRADY. *Edith:* Alice McComb. *Kate:* Una Brooks. *Isabel:* Maude Mordaunt. *Ruth:* MARIE HORGAN. *Chorus of Policemen, Pirates, etc.*

H.M.S. PINAFORE,
1915.13   or, The Lass That Loved a Sailor

A Revival of the Comic Opera in Two Acts[3]. Libretto by William S. Gilbert. Music by Arthur Sullivan. Stage director, Herbert Cripps. Musical director, Clarence West. Produced by William A. Brady. Opened 10 June 1915 (matinee) at the 48th Street Theatre and closed 17 June 1915 (matinee) after 3 performances in repertory (followed by TRIAL BY JURY with same cast and credits as previously presented with THE SORCERER, 24 May 1915)[4].

CAST: *The Rt. Hon. Sir Joseph Porter, K.C.B.,* First Lord of the Admiralty: WILLIAM DANFORTH. *Captain Corcoran,* Commander of H.M.S. Pinafore: GEORGE MacFARLANE. *Ralph Rackstraw,* Able Seaman: ARTHUR ALDRIDGE. *Dick Deadeye,* Able Seaman: DeWOLF HOPPER. *Bill Bobstay,* Boatswain's Mate: HERBERT L. WATEROUS. *Josephine,* the Captain's Daughter: ALICE BRADY. *Hebe,* Sir Joseph's First Cousin: Alice McComb. *Little Buttercup,* Mrs. Cripps, a Portsmouth Bum-Boat Woman: MARIE HORGAN. *First Lord's Sisters, His Cousins, His Aunts, Sailors, Marines.*

IOLANTHE,
1915.14   or, The Peer and the Peri

A Revival of the Comic Opera in Two Acts[5]. Libretto by William S. Gilbert. Music by Arthur Sullivan. Stage director, Herbert Cripps. Musical director, Clarence West. Produced by William A. Brady. Opened 10 June 1915 at the 48th Street Theatre and closed 17 June 1915 after 4 performances in repertory[6].

CAST: *The Lord Chancellor:* DeWOLF HOPPER. *Earl of Mountararat:* RICHARD TEMPLE. *Earl Tolloler:* ARTHUR ALDRIDGE. *Private Willis* of the Grenadier Guards: HERBERT L. WATEROUS. *Strephon,* an Arcadian shepherd: JOHN WILLARD. *Queen of the Fairies:* MARIE HORGAN. *Iolanthe,* a fairy—Strephon's mother: GLADYS CALDWELL. *Three Fairies: Celia:* Alice McComb. *Leila:* Una Brooks. *Fleta:* Maude Mordaunt. *Phyllis,* an Arcadian shepherdess and ward in chancery: ALICE BRADY. *Chorus of Fairies, Earls, Viscounts, Lords, Peers.*

ZIEGFELD FOLLIES OF 1915
1915.15

A Musical Revue in Two Acts, 21 Scenes[7]. Lines (sketches) and lyrics by Channing Pollock, Rennold Wolf and Gene Buck. Music by Louis Hirsch

and Dave Stamper. Staged by Julian Mitchell and Leon Errol. Settings designed by Joseph Urban. Costumes designed by Lady Duff-Gordon. Orchestra under the direction of Frank Darling. Devised and produced under the personal direction of Florenz Ziegfeld. Opened 21 June 1915 at the New Amsterdam Theatre and closed 18 September 1915 after 104 performances.

CAST: BERNARD GRANVILLE, BERT WILLIAMS, GEORGE WHITE, INA CLAIRE, LEON ERROL, CARL RANDALL[8], MELVILLE STEWART, HELEN ROOK, ED WYNN, ANN PENNINGTON[9], JUSTINE JOHNSTONE, KAY LAURELL, EMIL DWYER, MAE MURRAY, WILL WEST, OAKLAND SISTERS (Vivian, Dagmar), W. C. FIELDS, LUCILLE CAVANAUGH, PHIL DWYER, LOTTIE VERNON, MAY HENNESSY, John Ryan.
Follies Girls: Misses OLIVE THOMAS, Gladys Feldman, Dorothy Godfrey, Dottie Wang, Flo Hart, Ethel Davies, Marcelle Earle, Dorothy St. Clair, Margaret St. Clair, Helen Barnes, Buny Wendell, Peggy Dana, Muriel Martin, Nancy Wallace, Rose Werts, Edith Whitney, May Paul, Gladys Loftus, Evelyn Kerner, Wilson, Touraine.

ACT 1
Scene 1
"Under the Sea"
    Channel Belle: K. Laurell. *Submarine Pilot:* M. Stewart. *Mermaids:* Misses E.
    Kerner, Hart, Feldman, Wilson, Touraine.
Scene 2
"Hold Me in Your Loving Arms" (Song)
    H. Rook, Chorus
    (*Music by* Louis A. Hirsch. *Lyrics by* Gene Buck.)
    Scene: Home of the Sun.
Scene 3
"My Zebra Lady Fair" (Zebra Girl)(Song)
    G. White, Zebra Girls
    (*Music by* Dave Stamper. *Lyrics by* Gene Buck.)
    Scene: The Silver Forest.
Scene 4
Dance
    Dwarf Girls
"I Can't Do Without Girls" (Song)
    C. Randall, Country Girls
"Twenty Years Ago" (Trio)
    L. Errol, W. West, E. Wynn
    Scene: The Catskill Mountains.
    Ralph Van Winkle, Jr.: C. Randall. *Ralph Van Winkle:* L. Errol. *Jennings B.
    Ryan:* W. West. *Nut Sundae:* E. Wynn.
Scene 5
"The Birth of a Chicken" (Dance)
    A. Pennington
    Scene: Barker's Jungle.
    O. Shaw Androcles: B. Williams. *Professor Alsoranville Barker:* W. West. *The
    Lion:* P. Dwyer.
Scene 6
"My Radium Girl"
    B. Granville, Radium Girls
    (*Music by* Louis A. Hirsch. *Lyrics by* Gene Buck.)
    Scene: Radiumland.
Scene 7
Commotion Picture
    Director: E. Wynn. *Merry Pickem:* M. Murray.
Scene 8
"Hello Frisco" (I Called You Up to Say Hello)
    B. Granville, I. Claire
    (*Music by* Louis A. Hirsch. *Lyrics by* Gene Buck.)
    Scene: Across the Continent.
Scene 9
'Some' Midnight Cabaret
    Al A. Cart: E. Wynn. *The Onion Sisters:* Oakland Sisters. *A Pool Player:* W. C.
    Fields.
Scene 10
"I'll Build a Home in the U.S.A." (We'll Build a Little Home in the U.S.A.)
    B. Granville
    (*Music by* Charles Elbert. *Lyrics by* Ward Wesley.)
    'Honor': B. Granville.

---

[1]First presented in New York 31 December 1879 at the Fifth Avenue Theatre for a total of 91 performances in two engagements. For Synopsis of Scenes and Musical Numbers, see original 1879 production.
[2]Settings, costumes uncredited.
[3]Originally presented in New York 15 January 1879 at the Standard Theatre for 175 performances. For Synopsis of Scenes and Musical Numbers, see original 1879 production.
[4]Settings, costumes uncredited.
[5]First presented in New York 25 November 1882 at the Standard Theatre for 105 performances. For Synopsis of Scenes and Musical Numbers, see original 1882 production.
[6]Settings, costumes uncredited.
[7]The ninth in the annual series of revues produced by Florenz Ziegfeld beginning in 1907.

---

[8]Billed throughout the program as Carl Randell.
[9]Billed throughout the program as Anna Pennington.

Scene 11
America
Dance
Cotton Girls
Major Domo: L. Cavanaugh. *Navy*: A. Pennington, G. White. *Army*: M. Murray, C. Randall.Rulers of the World: Servia, Austria, Russia, Japan, Turkey, Belgium, France, England, Italy, Germany, United States. The Wealth of the World—Gold Girl—Silver Girl—Copper Girl—Coal Girl. *Aide to the President*: O. Thomas. *Consort*: B. Granville. *Dove of Peace*: K. Laurell. *Columbia*: J. Johnstone.
Finale

ACT 2[10]
Scene 1
"I'll Be a Santa Claus to You"
W. West
(*Music by* Louis A. Hirsch. *Lyrics by* Gene Buck.)
Scene: A Christmas Eve Fantasy.
Santa Claus: W. West. *Cinderella*: M. Murray. *Nightie Girls*: O. Thomas, D. Wang, H. Barnes, N. Wallace. *Sprites*: M. Earle, M. St. Claire, D. Godfrey, R. Werts. *Christmas Trees*: G. Feldman, M. Paul, E. Whitney, G. Loftus.
Scene 2
Himself
W. C. Fields
Scene: Home of the Sun.
Scene 3
Flirtation Medley Dance
A. Pennington, G. White
Scene: A 57th Street Shop.
Scene 4
"If the Girlies Could Be Soldiers"[11]
M. Murray, C. Randall, Chorus
(*Music by* Dave Stamper. *Lyrics by* Gene Buck.)
Scene: The Silver Forest.
Scene 5
"Marie Odile"
I. Claire
(*Music by* Louis A. Hirsch. *Lyrics by* Channing Pollock, Rennold Wolf.)
Scene: Belasco Theatre. *David Belasco*: M. Stewart.
Scene 6
"Go to Sleep, My Baby"
W. West, Brady Girls
(*Music and Lyrics by* Irving Berlin.)
Scene: Hallway of the Bunkem Court Apartments.
Thomas, the hall boy: B. Williams. *Sammy*, a messenger boy: A. Pennington. *Adam Fargo*: W. C. Fields. *Lotta Pep*: L. Cavanaugh. *A Tenant*: L. Vernon. *A Waiter*: J. Ryan. *Gladiolo*: J. Johnstone. *Constant Bunn*: L. Errol. *The Midnight Girl*: O. Thomas.
Scene 7
Ed Wynn
Scene: A 57th Street Shop.
Scene 8
Dance
M. Murray, C. Randall
"A Girl for Each Month in the Year"
B. Granville, Month Girls
(*Music by* Louis A. Hirsch. *Lyrics by* Channing Pollock and Rennold Wolf.)
Dance Egyptienne
L. Errol, M. Hennessy
Scene: Elysium.
The Lady on the Wall: K. Laurell.
Scene 9
Songs:
B. Williams
["I'm Neutral"(*Music and Lyrics by* Bert Williams.)
"Indoor Sports" (*Music and Lyrics by* Seymour Furth and ?.)]
Scene: Home of the Sun.
Scene 10
Ziegfeld Danse de Follies
Dance
L. Cavanaugh, C. Randall

---

[10]During the run, the running order of Act 2 was revised.
[11]Dropped during the run.

Dance
A. Pennington, G. White
"The Midnight Frolic Glide"
H. Rook, Chorus
(*Music by* Dave Stamper, Will Vodery. *Lyrics by* Gene Buck.)
Finale

1915.16

HANDS UP

A Musico-Comico-Filmo-Melo-Drama in Two Acts, 11 Scenes. Book by Edgar Smith. Music by E. Ray Goetz and Sigmund Romberg. Lyrics by E. Ray Goetz. Staged by J. H. Benrimo. Dances and ensembles arranged by Jack Mason. All modern dances arranged by Monsieur Maurice. Polish Ballet in Act 2 arranged by Theodore Kosloff. Settings designed by H. Robert Law, Mark Lawson, P. Dodd Ackerman, Ernest Albert, F. D. Thomas. Orchestra under the direction of William Daly. Orchestrations by Frank Saddler. Produced by the Messrs. Shubert. Opened 22 July 1915 at the 44th Street Theatre and closed 3 September 1915 after 52 performances.

CAST (in order of appearance): *Strong Arm Steve*, a star of the underworld: GEORGE HASSELL. *Helene Fudge*, daughter of a retired bank wrecker: ALICE DOVEY. *Percy Bonehead*, Helene's steady company: ARTIE MEHLINGER. *Mlle. Marcelle*, a tango pal of Helene's: EMILIE LEE [Lea]. *Obadiah Fudge*, a retired bank wrecker: Willard Louis. *Waltz King*, a millionaire "Maitre de Dance": MONSIEUR MAURICE. *La Belle Claire*, Waltz King's fiancée: FLORENCE WALTON. *Ingersoll*, a police dog: Alfred Latell. *Simp Watson*, assistant to Fake Kennedy: BOBBIE NORTH. *Fake Kennedy*, an amateur scientific detective: RALPH HERZ. *Violet Lavender*: IRENE FRANKLIN. *Lindy*: Adele Jason. *Sergeant Murphy*, a veteran roundsman: Peter Swift. *Cow-Boy Will*: WILL ROGERS. *Mr. Need-in-time*: BURTON GREEN. *Harry Lightfoot*: Donald Macdonald. *F. C. Centric*: A. Robbins. *Ignatz*, the chef: Henry Mack.

Maurice's Dancing Men: Sedgewick Draper, Stewart Gilmore, Vincent Cassidy, James Gillespie. *Kiddies*: Adelaide Lawrence, Margaret Satler, Dorothy Strong, Sunshine Jarmin, Clarice Snyder.

Act 1, Scene 1: The Orange Grove. (Lawson). Scene 2: Office of Fake Kennedy. Scene 3: The Animated Screen. (Ackerman). Scene 4: Exterior of the Tango Dental Parlor. (Ackerman). Scene 5: Tango Dental Parlor. Scene 6: Baliffe Beach, Bilkmore by the Sea. Scene 7: The Bathing Machines at Bilkmore. (Thomas). Scene 8: Boardwalk at the Bilkmore. (Ackerman).

Act 2, Scene 1: The Dansant at Sing Sing. (Law). Scene 2: A Room in Fudge's House. Scene 3: Dancing Curtains. (Arranged and executed by Baron Adolph DeMeyer.) Scene 4: The Ball Room in Fudge's House. (Albert).

ACT 1
"Orange Girl" (Opening Chorus)
E. Lee, Chorus
"Ginger"
A. Mehlinger, Chorus
"I"m Simply Crazy Over You"
A. Mehlinger, A. Dovey, Chorus
(*Music by* E. Ray Goetz and Jean Schwartz. *Lyrics by* William Jerome.)
"Cling a Little Closer"
M. Maurice, F. Walton, A. Mehlinger, A. Dovey
"Ting-a-Ling"
Principals, Chorus
"It's a Clue"
R. Herz
"(On) The Levee Along Broadway"
D. Macdonald, E. Lee, Chorus
Song[12]
I. Franklin
"Come On In, the Water's Fine" (Scene)
F. Walton, A. Mehlinger

---

[12]Irene Franklin's specialties here and in Act 2 included:
"You Can't Fool a New York Kid"
(*Music by* Burton Green. *Lyrics by* Irene Franklin.)
"All Wrong" (The Wail of a Chorus Lady)
"Dimples"
"Red-Head" (from THE SUMMER WIDOWERS)
(*Music by* Burton Green. *Lyrics by* Irene Franklin.)

"The Best Little Sweetheart of All"
    M. Maurice, Kiddies

Specialty
    A. Robbins

"Opening of Atlantic City"
    Chorus

"(Cute Little) Summery Time"
    A. Dovey, Chorus

"How Do You Do, Good-bye"
    A. Dovey, A. Mehlinger

"Esmeralda"
    M. Maurice, F. Walton
    (*Music and Lyrics by* Cole Porter.)

"Way Down on Honolulu Bay"
    B. North, Chorus

Number
    I. Franklin, A. Latell

"Evolution of Ragtime" (Evolution of a Rag)(Finale)
    Entire Company

ACT 2
Opening Chorus
"(The) Pirate's Rag"
    A. Mehlinger
    (*Music by* Bert Grant, Joe Young. *Lyrics by* Grant Clarke, E. Ray Goetz.)

Specialty
    I. Franklin, B. Green

Parody on "Crazy Over You"
    B. North, Girl

"(Sing Sing) Tango Tea"
    M. Maurice, F. Walton
    (*Music by* Sigmund Romberg. *Lyrics by* Harold Atteridge.)

Specialty
    W. Rogers

(Polish) Ballet
    M. Maurice, F. Walton, Ballet

Opening Chorus
    Chorus

"Tiffany Girl"
    A. Dovey, Male Chorus

Waltz
    M. Maurice, F. Walton

Finale
    Entire Company

1915.17   THE BLUE PARADISE

A Musical Play in a Prologue and Two Acts. (American) Book by Edgar Smith. Based on the Viennese original ("Ein Tag im Paradies") by Leo Stein and Béla Jenbach. Music by Edmund Eysler. Additional numbers by Sigmund Romberg. Lyrics by Herbert Reynolds. Staged by J. H. Benrimo. Musical numbers, ensembles and dances staged by Ed Hutchinson. Gowns by Joseph, Francis. Scenes designed by J. H. Benrimo, painted by Sundquist Studio. Orchestra under the direction of Herbert Kerr. Produced by the Messrs. Shubert. Opened 5 August 1915 at the Casino Theatre, moved 29 May 1916 to the 44th Street Theatre and closed 10 June 1916 after 356 performances.

CAST (in order of appearance): *Mizzi*, flower girl at the Blue Paradise Inn: VIVI-ENNE SEGAL. *An Officer*: James Billings. *The Meister*: William Belton. *A Lady*, guest at the Blue Paradise Inn: Carolyn Burke. *A Diner*, guest at the Blue Paradise Inn: Eugene Hohenwart. *Franz*, a waiter: Otto Schrader. *Josef Stransky*: WALTER ARMIN. *Hans Walther*: ROBERT G. PITKIN. *Justus Hampel*: TEDDY WEBB. *Rudolph Stoeger*: CECIL LEAN. *A Tourist*: James Billings. *Head Waiter*: Charles Holly. *Head Porter*: Otto Schrader. *Second Porter*: William Belton. *Hazel James*: CLEO MAYFIELD. *Gaby*: VIVIENNE SEGAL. *Rudolph Oberdorher* [Rudy]: TED LORRAINE. *Director of Hotel*: Joseph Dillon. *Second Tourist*: Frank Wayne. *Third Tourist*: Richard Melbourne. *The Eight Chaperons*: Misses Barclay, O'Shea, George, Blanchard, Harrison, Davidson, O'Brien, Burk. *Mrs. Gladys Wynne*: FRANCES DEMAREST. *Page Boy*: Carrie DeNoville. *Vera*, an actress from the Hoff Theatre: HATTIE BURKS. *Baron von Schlegan*: James Billings. *Chef*: Eugene Hohenwart. *Baroness von Schlegan*: Carolyn Burk. *Countess von Schwartzkoff*: Bunty Davidson. *Countess von Houssnan*: Betty Barclay. *Baroness von Hahn*: Gertrude Harrison. *Waitress*: Gypsy O'Brien. *Flower Girls, Fruit Vendors, Cabaret Dancers, Students,*

Officers and Guests in the Blue Paradise Garden, Porters, Bell Boys, Maids, Guests and Tourists in the Ring Hotel.

    Members of the Chorus: Misses Helen Arlington, Monna Blanchard, Betty Barclay, Carolyn Burke, Bunty Davidson, Mary Finney, Marion George, Gertrude Harrison, Kitty Kerwin, Gypsy O'Brien, Prudence O'Shea, Alice Randolph, Winnifred Dunn, Carrie DeNoville, Mabel DeBahlul, Lottie Franklyn, Lucille Martin, Elsa Mitchener, Mona Sartoris, Ruby Simpson, Camille Truesdale, Alta Young, Josephine Ray, Joan Butlin, Sydelle Seit, Rose Gibson, Mary Moriarty, Betty Grant. Messrs. Joseph Dillon, Ray Dodge, Bernard Fritzie, Charles Holly, Richard Melbourne, Stanley Rayburne, Charles Starr, Dick Stewart, Nat Sanders, Edward Smith, Charles Townshend, Frank Wayne, Charles Weston, Jack Birkson.

The action is set in Vienna. *Prologue*: Blue Paradise Inn.

Act 1: The Ring Hotel. 24 years later. *Act 2*: Blue Paradise Inn.

ACT 1
"A Toast to Women's Eyes" (Opening Ensemble)
    Ensemble
    (*Music by* Sigmund Romberg.)

"Here's to You, My Sparkling Wine" (Drinking Song)
    C. Lean, R. G. Pitkin, T. Webb, W. Armin
    (*Music by* Leo Edwards. *Lyrics by* Blanche Merrill.)

"To Paradise We'll Gaily Trip"
    C. Lean, assisted by R. G. Pitkin, T. Webb, W. Armin, Chorus
    (*Music by* Edmund Eyssler.)

"Auf Wiedersehn"
    C. Lean, V. Segal
    (*Music by* Sigmund Romberg.)

ACT 2
"We Wish You a Pleasant Journey" (Opening Chorus)
    Tourists, Guests, Attachés
    (*Music by* Sigmund Romberg.)

Duet and Dance
    T. Lorraine, V. Segal

"There's Only One Who Rules My House"
    T. Webb, V. Segal, T. Lorraine

"Vienna, Vienna"
    C. Lean, assisted by R. G. Pitkin, T. Lorraine, T. Webb
    (*Music by* Edmund Eysler.)

"I'm from Chicago"
    F. Demarest, Chaperones
    (*Music by* Sigmund Romberg.)

"If Central Should Talk in Her Sleep"[13]
    C. Lean

"Just Win a Pretty Widow"
    C. Lean, F. Demarest, Ensemble
    (*Music by* Edmund Eysler.)

"One Step into Love"
    F. Demarest, R. G. Pitkin
    (*Music by* Sigmund Romberg.)

"Vienna, How D'ye Do" (Tutti Ensemble)
    C. Lean, Company
    (*Music by* Edmund Eysler.)

ACT 3
"Why Are We Invited Here?" (Opening Chorus)
    Ensemble
    (*Music by* Sigmund Romberg.)

"Old Blue Paradise"
    Ensemble

"I Had a Dog" (Comedy Song)
    T. Lorraine, T. Webb
    (*Music by* Leo Edwards.)

Folk Song and Yodel
    F. Demarest
    (*Music by* Leo Edwards.)

"Waltz of the Season" (Classic Dance)
    T. Lorraine, H. Burks
    (*Music by* Edmund Eysler.)

"My Model Girl"
    C. Mayfield, R. G. Pitkin
    (*Music by* Sigmund Romberg. *Lyrics by* Harold Atteridge.)

[13]Dropped after opening.

"(The Tune) They Croon in the U.S.A."
C. Lean, Dancers
(*Music and Lyrics by* Cecil Lean.)

"I'm Dreaming of a Wonderful Night"
C. Lean, F. Demarest
(*Music by* Edmund Eysler.)

"Auf Wiedersehn" (Reminiscence)
C. Lean, V. Segal
(*Music by* Sigmund Romberg.)

Finale
Company

THE GIRL WHO SMILES

1915.19

A Musical Comedy in Three Acts. Original version by Paul Hervé. Music by Jean Briquet and Adolf Philipp. English version by Edward A. Paulton and Adolf Philipp. Staged by Ben Teal. Scenery designed by Edward G. Unitt and Joseph Wickes. Costumes by Dazian; Miss Alt's gowns by Frances, Lucile. Orchestra under the direction of Augustus Barratt. Produced by the Times Producing Corporation. Opened 9 August 1915 at the Lyric Theatre, moved 30 August 1915 to the Longacre Theatre, and closed 6 November 1915 after 104 performances.

CAST (in order of appearance): *Paul Fabre,* impatient: WILLIAM DANFORTH. *Anatole,* his son, imperturbable: PAUL DECKER. *Marie,* Paul's daughter, imaginative: NATALIE ALT. *Pauline Legarde,* her maid, impulsive: MARIE FANCHONETTI. *Madame Bouliere,* imperious: JENNIE DICKERSON. *Theodore,* her son, immature: RALPH BUNKER. *Henriette,* her daughter, impressionable: Lillian Spencer. *Alphonse Duttier,* the chef, impracticable: FRED WALTON. *Francois Déchanelle,* an artist, impecunious: GEORGE BALDWIN. *Rudolf Tapine,* a sculptor, improvident: Joseph Phillips. *Pierre Renauld,* a composer, impoverished: PAUL HYDE DAVIES. *Clarisse Luniere,* an actress, impertinent: Grace Leigh. *Fogère,* a landlord, implacable: Nace Nonville. *Paul Dechanelle,* last and least important: ??[14].

Models (4), immune: *Yvonne:* Elsa Garrette. *Madeline:* Irene Hopping. *Modiste:* Grace deWolfe. *Grisettes (5),* immaterial: *Suzanne:* Dorothy Dunn. *Lucille:* Marie McDonald. *Celeste:* Eva Stuart. *Elaine:* Lillian Starr. *Josephine:* Natalie Vincent. *Art Students (4),* impossible: *Jacques:* Jack Sears. *Henri:* John Young. *Louis:* James Whelan. *Gaston:* C. Dunham, Jr. *Maids (2),* immovable: *Janette:* Claire Lawrence. *Lizette:* ??. *Servants (4),* impervious: *Jules:* Jack Sears. *Adolf:* John Young. *Philippe:* James Whelan. *Edouard:* C. Dunham, Jr.

Act 1: Country Home of Paul Fabre at Argenteuil—not far from Paris. May, in the immediate past. *Act 2*: A Studio in the Latin Quarter, Paris Five weeks later. *Act 3*: Same as Act 1. 18 months later, and in the time of falling leaves.

ACT 1[15]

"A Little Difference at Breakfast"[16] (Opening Chorus)
W. Danforth, P. Decker, Serving Men and Women

"Life Has Just Begun" (Song)
N. Alt

"Join the Familee"[17] (Sextette)
P. Decker, N. Alt, R. Bunker, L. Spencer, J. Dickerson, W. Danforth

"Dance Me Good-bye" (Duet)
F. Walton, M. Fanchonetti

---

[14]Mystery character was played by "Rag Baybee" on tour.
[15]Following its New York run, the show was revised as a vehicle for Eva Tanguay in the added role of Phonette Duttier, the cook, inimitable. Songs were dropped and the following songs were added:

"I'm Built for Speed"
E. Tanguay

"Father Never Raised Any Foolish Children"
E. Tanguay

"I Forgot the Number of the House"
Robert and Lawrence Ward [Bertie, Archie, new characters]

"Have You Heard the Scandal"
R. Ward. L. Ward

"Dance Me Good-Bye"
E. Tanguay, R. Ward, L. Ward

"Cozey Corner"
Elsa Garrette [Marie], Charles Morrison [Paul], James Whelan [Rudolf], Victor Bozart [Pierre]

[16]Dropped during subsequent tour.
[17]Dropped during subsequent tour.

"Teach Me to Smile" (Duet)
G. Baldwin, N. Alt

"The Story of a Sparrow" (Song)
W. Danforth

Finale

ACT 2

"A Breath from Bohemia" (Opening Number)
J. Phillips, G. deWolfe, I. Hopping, E. Garrette, G. Baldwin, P. H. Davies

"I Whispered It to the Rose"[18] (Song)
P. H. Davies

Solo and Concerted Number
N. Alt, F. Walton, J. Phillips, P. H. Davies, G. Baldwin, I. Hopping, G. deWolfe, E. Garrette

"You Are My Little Cupid" (Duet)
F. Walton, G. Leigh

"Oh! Pauline" (My Pauline)(Trio)
G. Leigh, F. Walton, M. Fanchonetti

"Your Picture" (Song)
G. Baldwin

"We're Looking for Marie" (Oh Dear Marie)(Concerted Number)
Everybody

"Temptation Waltz" (Let Us Dance)
G. Leigh, G. Baldwin, J. Phillips, P. H. Davies, Girls, Boys

"A Girl from Paree" (Song and Chorus)
N. Alt, Everybody

Finale

ACT 3[19]

"When Labor Comes into Its Own" (Opening Chorus)
F. Walton, Serving Men and Women

"(A) Honeymoon in May"[20] (Duet)
F. Walton, M. Fanchonetti

"Baby Mine" (Sextette)
N. Alt, G. Baldwin, J. Phillips, F. Walton, P. H. Davies, M. Fanchonetti

Finale

THE GIRL FROM UTAH

1915.18

A Return Engagement of the Musical Comedy in Two Acts, an Introductory and 4 Scenes[21]. Book by James T. Tanner. Music by Paul Rubens and Sydney Jones. Additional numbers by Jerome D. Kern. Lyrics by Percy Greenbank and Adrian Ross. Staged by J. A. E. Malone. Gowns and

---

[18]Replaced during the run by:

"At Last United"
P. H. Davies

Which was replaced for subsequent tour by:

Specialty Dance of the Incas
Dottie King (Fleurette, a new character)

[19]Added for tour in 1916-17 season to Act 3, following opening chorus:

"Not Yet, But Soon"
Clara Thropp (Madame Boulière)

[20]Replaced during the run by:

"A Trip Abroad" (Duet)
F. Walton, M. Fanchonetti

[21]First produced in New York 24 August 1914 at the Knickerbocker Theatre for 120 performances. For Synopsis of Scenes and Musical Numbers, see original 1914 production. For this engagement, previous changes were retained, and the following changes in the score were made. "Garden Gate" (Act 2, Scene 2) was replaced by:

"I Want to Be the Captain"
J. Sanderson, D. Brian, J. Cawthorn

"The Music of Love" (Act 3) was replaced by:

"Dance With Me"
E. Henry, A. DeManby

Dance, Act 3 was replaced by:

"Ferban" (Waltz)
D. Brian, C. Sewell

costumes by Schneider-Anderson Company. Orchestra under the direction of Theodore Stearns. Produced by Charles Frohman. Opened 9 August 1915 at the Knickerbocker Theatre and closed 28 August 1915 after 24 performances.[22]

CAST: *Una Trance*, The Girl from Utah: JULIA SANDERSON. *Sandy Blair*, leading man at the Gaiety Theatre: DONALD BRIAN. *Trimpel*, of Brixton Rest: JOSEPH CAWTHORN. *Lord Amersham*: Alfred DeManby. *Policeman P. R. 38*: Frank Markham. *Colonel Oldham-Pryce*: George Grundy. *Page*: Robert Slattery. *Commissionaire*: William Francis, Jr. *Detective Shooter* of Scotland Yard: Walter Gilbert. *Lord Orpington*: George Wharton. *Archie Tooth*: Frank Snyder. *Douglas Noel*: William Hobart. *Bobbie Longshot*: Winship Fink. *Dora Manners*, leading lady of the Gaiety Theatre: Eleanor Henry. *Lady Amersham*, Lord Amersham's mother: QUEENIE VASSAR. *Clancy* Miss Manners' maid: Renee Reel. *A Flapper*: Katherine Murray. *Actresses at the Gaiety Theatre* (5): Miss *Mona West*: Clara Eckstrom. Miss *Sylvia Paget*: Mabel Gibson. Miss *Lydia Saville*: Dorothy Dumont. Miss *Violet Vesey*: Dolly Wilmot. Miss *Rosie Jocelyn*: Gene Cole. Miss *Alma Cavendish*: Helen Allen. *Lady Muriel Chepstone*: Anita McCloskey. *Honorable Miss St. Auburn*: Mabel Landers. *Lady Mary Nowell*: Pauline Hendrix. *Mrs. Ponsonby*: Lillian Clifford.

1915.20   COUSIN LUCY

A Comedy (with Music) in Three Acts. Book by Charles Klein. Music by Jerome Kern. Lyrics by Schuyler Greene. Staged by Robert Milton. Dances by Dave Bennett. Scenes painted by Homer Emens. Costumes designed by Melville Ellis. Orchestra under the direction of August Kleinecke. Orchestrations by Frank Saddler. Produced by A. H. Woods. Opened 27 August 1915 at the George M. Cohan Theatre and closed 2 October 1915 after 43 performances[23].

CAST (in order of appearance): *Bister*: DALLAS WELFORD. *Klayburgh*: Leo Donnelly. *Horace Holden*: Austin Webb. *Mrs. Hillary Bronson*: MARIE CHAMBERS. *Hillary Bronson*: Mark Smith. *Jerry Jackson*, (alias Cousin Lucy): JULIAN ELTINGE. *Chauffeur*: James Budd. *Queeny*: JANE OAKER. *James Baldwin*: Ned Barton. *Angela Baldwin*: OLIVE TELL. *Dorothy Walbrook*: CLAIBORNE FOSTER. *Miss Henshaw*: Edith Hanbury. *Della*: Irene Palmer. *Mrs. Wallingford*: Mrs. Stuart Robson. *Broad*: J. W. Ashley. *Policeman*: Henry Friend. *Expressman*: Frank Stevens.

Ladies in Madame Lucette's Dressmaking Establishment: Ethel Russell, Claudia Carlstead, Elsie Weller, Irene Palmer, Alice Palmer, Grace Walton, Lillian Ormonde, Elsie Marquette, Edna Stilwell, Grace Russell.

Time: Present. *Place*: New York. *Act 1*: Gerald Jackson's Apartment. *Act 2*: Madame Lucette's Dressmaking Establishment. Two months later. *Act 3*: Gerald Jackson's Apartment. The same evening.

ACT 1[24]

"Those 'Come Hither' Eyes"
   J. Eltinge

---

[22]Settings uncredited.
[23]Played a touring engagement at the Standard Theatre, New York, 10 January 1916 for 8 performances.
[24]For subsequent tour, the music was at times variously credited to Percy Wenrich, Edward Madden and Kern; at other times to Ted Ward and Kern, with lyrics by Ed. Grossmith. Toured following its Broadway engagement, retaining only "Two Heads Are Better than One." Added at different times were:

"Cheer Up, Eat and Grow Thin" (Act 1)
   J. Eltinge
   (*Music by* E. Ray Goetz. *Lyrics by* Julian Eltinge.)
"I've Loved Only Once and the Girl Was You" (Act 2)
   M. Smith
   (*Music by* Percy Wenrich. *Lyrics by* Carl Randall.)
"Call on Me" (I'm at Your Service, Girls)(Act 2)
   J. Eltinge
   (*Music and Lyrics by* Ted Ward and Edward Crossmith.)
"The Things They Say and the Things They Do" (Act 2)
   Elsie Weller (Miss Henshaw) assisted by D. Welford, Maybelle Cedars (Angela), Carrie Reynolds (Mrs. Bronson), M. Smith
"Sweetheart" (Act 2)
   M. Cedars
   (*Music by* Percy Wenrich. *Lyrics by* Edward Madden.)
"Two Heads Are Better than One" (Act 3)
   J. Eltinge, M. Cedars

ACT 2
"Mam'selle Lucette"
   J. Eltinge
   (*Music by* Percy Wenrich. *Lyrics by* Edward Madden.)
ACT 3
"Two Heads Are Better Than One"
   J. Eltinge
   (*Lyrics by* Jerome Kern and Schuyler Greene.)
"Society" (Song)
   J. Eltinge, Ensemble
"Keep Going" (Specialty Dance)
   C. Foster, G. Russell, G. Eastman
   (*Music by* August Kleinecke.)

1915.21   TWO IS COMPANY

A Musical Comedy[25] in Three Acts. (American) Book and lyrics by Edward A. Paulton and Adolf Philipp. Adapted from the French 'Mon Ami Emile' of Paul Hervé. Music by Jean Briquet and Adolf Philipp. Staged by Adolf Philipp. Scenery designed by Young Brothers. Dresses designed by Gallois; Darci; B. Altman & Co.; Orange Manufacturing Co. Orchestra under the direction of C. von Wegern. Produced by the Savoy Producing Company (Paul Philipp, Adolf Philipp). Opened 22 September 1915 at the Lyric Theatre and closed 16 October 1915 after 29 performances.

CAST: *Henri* Baron d'Heurville: CLAUDE FLEMMING. *Heloise*, his wife: GEORGIA CAINE. *Emile*, Baronde Solanger, their best friend: ROYDON KEITH. *Lulu LaGrange*, an actress: MAY DeSOUSA. *Max*, Henri's valet: Victor LeRoy. *Annette*, Heloise's maid: Gwendolyn Lowrey. *Dubois*, *Duprè*, divorce detectives, partners and rivals: RALPH NAIRN, CLARENCE HARVEY. *Comte de Perigord*: HAROLD VIZARD. *Clarisse*, Lulu's maid: Lyda Carlisle.

The Ette Girls: *Babette*: Rosel Frey. *Fleurette*: Frances Chase. (*Jealousy rousers in the employ of Dubois:*) *Georgette*: Harriet duBarry. *Janette*: Cleo LeMoyne. *Lizette*: Alice Leslie. *Manette*: Gertrude Grossberg. *Pierette*: Frances duBarry. *Suzette*: Barberra Coulon. *Fanchette*: Betty Clark. *Clarette*: Kitty Lawrence.

The Boulevard Boys: *Charles*: Sidney Myers. *Etienne*: Carl Judd. *Gustave*, *Armand*, home wreckers in the employ of Dupre: John Varnell, Harry Smithfield. *Leon*: Charles Yorkshire. *Gaston*: William Kline.

The entire action of this play takes place between the hours of 8:30 P.M. and 2:30 A.M.
Act 1: Country Home of Henri, Baron d'Heurville. A Suburb of Paris. *Act 2*: Summer Home of Lulu LaGrange. *Act 3*: Same as Act 1.

ACT 1
"A Family Quarrel"
   C. Flemming, G. Caine, V. LeRoy, G. Lowrey
"If You But Knew What I Know"
   R. Keith, G. Caine
"At the Telephone" (Trio)
   C. Flemming, R. Keith, G. Caine
"Back to Lotusland" (Lotusland)(Song)
   C. Flemming
Concerted Number
   R. Nairn, Ette Girls
"Free as Air" (Song)
   G. Caine
Concerted Number
   C. Harvey, Home Wreckers

"Everybody Do the Hula" (Act 3)
   J. Eltinge
   (*Music and Lyrics by* Percy Wenrich.)
Specialty Dance (Act 3)
   Dorothy Waldbrook
"Call on Me" (Act 2)
   J. Eltinge
"Sometimes the Dream Comes True" (Act 2)
   Nina Melville (Miss Henshaw)
   (*Music by* Ted Ward. *Lyrics by* Edward Grossmith.)
"Summertime" (Act 3)
   J. Eltinge, Ensemble
   (*Music by* Howard Patrick. *Lyrics by* Weston Williams.)
[25]Billed as the Parisian Musical Novelty.

"La Belle Lulu" (Song)
  M. DeSousa
"Two Is Company" (Song)
  G. Caine
Finale

ACT 2

"You Were Charming" (Opening Number)
  M. DeSousa, Boulevard Boys, Matinee Girls
Concerted Number
  C. Harvey, M. DeSousa, Girls
"In the Land of Lorraine" (Song)
  G. Caine
"The Footman and the Maid" (Duet)
  G. Caine, R. Keith
"(A) Stamp (Is) Enclosed" (Quartette)
  G. Caine, M. DeSousa, C. Flemming, R. Keith
"Come with Me to Paree" (Duet)
  G. Caine, C. Flemming
"We Like to Whirl" (Trio)
  R. Nairn, C. Harvey, H. Vizard
"The Lure of the Waltz" (Concerted Number)
  M. DeSousa, Officers, Girls
Finale

ACT 3

Introduction
  G. Caine, C. Flemming, V. LeRoy, G. Lowrey
"I Prefer the Cat" (Duet)
  G. Caine, C. Flemming
"Free! (Free!)" (Concerted Number)
  C. Flemming, R. Nairn, Girls
"Who Says So" (Duet)
  R. Nairn, C. Harvey
Finale

(NED WAYBURN'S)
TOWN TOPICS

1915.22

A Musical Comedy Spectacle (Revue) in Two Acts, 21 Scenes. Book and lyrics by Harry B. Smith, Thomas J. Gray and Robert B. Smith[26]. Music by Harold Orlob. Entire production conceived and staged by Ned Wayburn. Scenery by H. Robert Law, John Young, Seidle Studio, Edward G. Unitt and Joseph Wickes. Costumes by Cora MacGeachy. Orchestra under the direction of Hilding Anderson. Orchestrations by Frank Saddler. Produced by Ned Wayburn[27]. Opened 23 September 1915 at the Century Theatre and closed 20 November 1915 after 68 performances.

CAST: WILL ROGERS, TRIXIE FRIGANZA, ADELAIDE (Hughes) and (Johnny) HUGHES, WELLINGTON CROSS, EILEEN MOLYNEUX, CLIFTON WEBB, BERT LESLIE, MANA ZUCCA, DOROTHY CAMERON, MADELINE CAMERON, MARIE LAVARRE, GUS SHY, EDWARD FLANAGAN, NEALY EDWARDS, LEW HEARN, BLOSSOM SEELEY, VERA MICHELENA, Peter Page, Mabel Elaine, Carbrey Brothers (John, Douglas), James Fox, Lois Josephine, Jacob P. Adler, Jr., Baby Bartlett, Stafford Pemberton. (*Specialty*: Will Vodery's Ragphony Orchestra.)
The Fairly Tall Girls: Misses Natalie Holt, Harriet Leidy, Frances Thompson, Ethel Tennis, Paula Leslie, Elaine French, Fannie Kidston, Virginia Steinhardt, Laura Hastings, Jacques Pardica, Emily Monte, Ethel Denison, Lillian LeRoy, Barbara Davenport, Jennie Cannar, Helen Bletterman, Mabel Godding. *The Not Quite So Tall Girls*: Misses Alberta Turner, Vera Mercer, Ruth Harris, Florence Flandreaux, Beth O'Sullivan, Marjorie Herman, Charlotte Marmont, Vinnie Mason, Ethel Bletterman, Cecil Boylan, Florence Challenger, Jane Roberts, Grace Jones, Hazel Coulter, Mabel Taylor, Hazel Frisbie. *The Just a Little Bit Smaller Girls*: Misses Flora Lea, Gertrude Roland, Marie Klein, Alice Gordon, Eileen Rooney, Mildred Chandler, Winnie Hunter, Eileen Clark, Lucille Wolf, Rose LaPlace, Peggy Bell, Dorothy Cort, Edna

Alford, Elsie Wolf, Effie Allan, Millicent Earl. *The Bob Up and Down Girls*: Misses Adelaide Mason, Connie Magnet, Monica Boulais, Rose Boulais, Euice Hamilton, Alma Braham, Pearl Betts, Jane Gill, Evelyn Rosewood, Hazel Ellswoth Bessie Shanon, Bessie Burch, Violet Prager, Esther Shannon, Cecile Stahl, Heloise Sheppard. *The Male Vocal and Terpsichorean Assistants*: Messrs. Fred Bates, Stanley Vickers, James Templeton, W. B. Taylor, Warren Jaxon, Frank Ellis, Clarence Lutz, James Curran, Jr., Arthur Stapleton, Melville Henderson, Gerald MacDonald, Carl Hall, Harry Cahill, John Kusky, Armand King, Everett Albin, Arthur Gross, William Matthews, John Ellis, Joseph Marriott, Edward Fitzgerald, Eddie Sims, Alexander Edwards, George Cavanagh, James Monahan, Charles McNally.

ACT 1[28]
Scene 1
  "Town Topics"
    Carbrey Brothers, Misses Cameron, Chorus
    Scene: Hotel de Gink. (Law)
    Bill Daily, hotel clerk: J. Fox. *Rip*, *Tip*, hotel porters: J. Carbrey, D. Carbrey. *Rosie and Posie Century*, musical comedy sisters: D. Cameron, M. Cameron. *Ophelia Nichols*, news-counter girl: M. Lavarre. *Tired Tuttle*, a gink: J. P. Adler, Jr.
  "All Full of Ginger"[29]
    M. Lavarre, Dancers
    (*Lyrics by* Thomas J. Gray.)
    Sheriff Zack Doolittle, a rural Sherlock: L. Hearn. *Molly R. Motion*, a café canary: B. Seeley.
Scene 2
  "The Keystone Glide"
    B. Seeley, Chorus
    (*Lyrics by* Thomas J. Gray.)
    Scene: A Ballroom. (Law)
Scene 3
  "The Idol of Eyes"[30]
    V. Michelena, Chorus
    (*Lyrics by* Robert B. Smith.)
    Fritzi Flirt, a beauty doctor: V. Michelena.
Scene 4
  "It's the Gown That Makes the Girl"[31]
    Misses Cameron, Chorus
  "The Old Are Getting Younger Every Day"
    T. Friganza
    (*Lyrics by* Robert B. Smith.) *Scene*: A Dancing Pavilion. (Painted by Grinager and Beardsley of Lee Lash Studio)
    Fuller Hopps, a dancing instructor: P. Page. *Constance Spinner*, his assistant: E. Molyneux. *Hardy Able*, a pupil: G. Shy. *Steve Hogan*, a professor of languages: B. Leslie. *David Dansant*, who trips the light fantastic: C. Webb. *Mrs. Albany Dayline*, an ambitious actress: T. Friganza.
Scene 5
  "The Oskaloosa Pets"
    E. Flanagan, N. Edwards
    (*Lyrics by* Robert B. Smith.)
  "Take It From Me"
    M. Zucca, W. Cross, Boutonniere Girls
    (*Lyrics by* Robert B. Smith.)
    Scene: A Theatre Lobby. (Law) *Car Bona*, a vaudeville actor: E. Flanagan. *Ben Zine*, his partner: N. Edwards. *Brighton Early*, publicity promoter for Mrs. Albany Dayline: W. Cross. *Will Rogers*: W. Rogers. *Lillian Love*: L. Josephine. *Dorothy Doolittle*, a city bred country girl: M. Zucca.

---

[26]Contrary to the program credit, Harry B. Smith did not write any lyrics, nor did Messrs. R. B. Smith and Gray collaborate on lyrics. Credit for book is at it appears in the opening night playbill.
[27]For subsequent tour, Ned Wayburn's name was dropped altogether from the credits as its producer and director. Messrs. Shubert presented the tour and J. H. Benrimo was credited with the direction. Dances were credited to Allan K. Foster.

---

[28]After opening, the running order was revised. Added to Act 1 for subsequent tour:
  "Paprica"
    J. Johnston, A. Mehlinger, Chorus
    Scene: A Theatre Lobby.
    Brighton Early, publicity promoter for Mrs. Dayline: W. Cross. *Dorothy Doolittle*, a city bred country girl: L. Josephine. *Car Bona*, a vaudeville actor: J. Johnston. *Ben Zine*, his partner: A. Mehlinger.
  "What a Beautiful Baby You Are"
    L. Hearn
    Scene: Warships on the Hudson.
    The Sheriff: L. Hearn. *Miss Green*: Miss Bonita. *Flower Vendor*: J. Carbrey.
[29]Dropped during the run.
[30]Replaced during the run by: (but re-instated for subsequent tour)
  Dance Medley
    C. Webb, E. Molyneux
[31]Dropped for subsequent tour.

Scene 6

"I Want Someone Who's Lonesome"
M. Elaine

"Walking on the Lake"
E. Flanagan, N. Edwards

"I'll Get You Yet, Cigarette"
V. Michelena, "Cigarettes"
(*Lyrics by* Thomas J. Gray.)

"The Melody of the Century"
B. Seeley, Chorus
(*Lyrics by* Thomas J. Gray.)
Scene: Behind the Scenes. (Law)
A *Benefit Fiend*, David Dansant, box party: M. Lavarre, C. Webb. *Steve*, the stage manager: B. Leslie. *Fuller Hopps*, the announcer: P. Page. *The Great Goatee*, a magician: J. P. Adler, Jr. *Four Kings of Melody*: Messrs. Kern, Ellis, Vickers, Henderson. *Jennie the Juggler*: A. Gordon. *Gertie Gorgonzola*, a small timer: M. Elaine. *Draw M. Inn*, a cartoonist: C. Hall. *Fritzi Flirt*, a prima donna in this scene: V. Michelena. *Car Bona, Ben Zine*, showing their act: E. Flanagan, N. Edwards.

Scene 7

"The Indian Suffragette" (Heap Big Suffragette)
T. Friganza

Tone Pictures (Orchestra conducted by Harold Orlob.)
Scene: A Prairie.

Scen (Scenes 8-11[32])

Tone Pictures to exploit America's representative dancers, Adelaide and Hughes

Scene 8

"Midsummer Waltz"
Adelaide and Hughes
Scene: Summer. (Unitt & Wickes)
Picnicers, Campers, and Sun Beams: Tone Expessionists. *Summer Girl*: Miss Adelaide. *Summer Boy*: Mr. Hughes. *Cupid*: B. Bartlett. *Spirit of Evil*: S. Pemberton.

Scene 9

Dance of Joy
Adelaide and Hughes

Dance of Bewilderment
Adelaide and Hughes
Scene: Autumn. (Unitt & Wickes)
Wood Nymphs, Hunters, Harvesters: (Ensemble). *Dryad*: Miss Adelaide. *Summer Boy*: Mr. Hughes. *Spark*: F. Lea. *Smokes and Flames*: (Ensemble). *Myth*: J. Kusky.

Scene 10

Skating Waltz
Miss Cameron
Scene: Winter. (Unitt & Wickes)
Tobogganners, Skiiers, Blackbirds, Snowflakes, Hail and Skaters: (Ensemble). *Spirit of Winter*: Miss Adelaide. *Mercury*: Mr. Hughes.

Scene 11

Butterfly Dance

"The Triumph of Love"[33]
Scene: Spring. (Unitt & Wickes)
Zephyrs and Morning Glories: (Ensemble). *Robin*: F. Lea. *Violets and Roses*: (Ensemble). *Spring's Messenger*: Mr. Hughes. *A Butterfly*: Miss Adelaide. *Lightning*: J. Templeton. *Umbrellas, Bridesmaids, Rainbows*: (Ensemble).

ACT 2

Scene 1

"Subway Love"
(*Lyrics by* Robert Smith.)
Scene: In the Subway[34]. (Siedle Studios)
Subway Guard: B. Leslie. *Mr. Harlem Bronx*: J. Fox. *Mrs. Harlem Bronx*: B. Calla. *Car Bona, Ben Zine*, the morning after: E. Flanagan, N. Edwards. *Brighton Early*: W. Cross. *Fritzi Flirt*: V. Michelena. *David Dansant, Constance Spinner*, slumming: C. Webb, E. Molyneux.

Scene 2

"(Riff-Raff) Rafferty"[35]
M. Lavarre, Dancers
(*Lyrics by* Robert B. Smith.)

"You've Got the Style and the Smile"
Misses Cameron, Messrs. E. Flannigan, N. Edwards, Chorus
(*Lyrics by* Thomas J. Gray.)

Eccentric Footery
Carbrey Brothers
Scene: Outside the Polo Grounds, New York. (John Young)
Give, Take, doortenders: J. Carbrey, D. Carbrey. *Fuller Hopps*: P. Page. *An Office Boy*, the original baseball joke: J. Fox. *Brighton Early*, a business man in this scene: W. Cross. *Rose Century, Posie Century*, Lady fans: D. Cameron, M. Cameron. *Car Bona, Ben Zine*, baseball bugs: E. Flanagan, N. Edwards, . *Right Score*, a reporter: J. Adler, Jr. *Will Play*, a baseball player: G. Shy. *Sheriff Doolittle*: L. Hearn. *A Policeman*, played by that rising young chorus boy: S. Vickers. *Harlem Bronx*: J. Fox.

Scene 3

(Will) Vodery's Ragphony Orchestra[36]

"Put It Over"
T. Friganza, Fan-Semble
(*Lyrics by* Robert B. Smith.)
Scene: Interior of the Polo Grounds. (John Young)
Captain of the Home Team: B. Leslie. *Jiggler*, the umpire: P. Page. *Captain of the Lady Giants*: B. Seeley. *Catcher of the Lady Giants*: T. Friganza. *Score Card Boy*: J. Fox. *Will Rogers*: W. Rogers. *Ty Cobb*, F.O.B. Detroit, first on base: E. Flanagan. *Hans Wagner*, a perpetual youth: N. Edwards. *A Fan*: L. Hearn.

Scene 4

"An Old-Fashioned Groom and an Up-to-Date Bride"
W. Cross, L. Josephine
(*Lyrics by* Robert B. Smith.)

Shop Talk
W. Rogers

"Barcarole"[37]
Misses Cameron
Scene: Exterior of a Fashion Shop.

Scene 5[38]

Dance
E. Molyneux, C. Webb

"The Marionettes"
Adelaide and Hughes
(*Lyrics by* Frank M. Stammers.)
Scene: Madame Flair's Emporium of Chic.
Madame Flair: V. Michelena. *Cocktail Maids*: Misses F. Challenger, Turner, Flandreaux, O'Sullivan, Harris, Coulter. *Ponies*: Misses Magnet, Roland, Lea, Rooney. *Bird-Cage Girls*: Misses Prager, Rosewood, Hamilton, Burch. *Pajama Girls*: Misses Betts, A. Mason. *Shoppers*: Misses Monte, Marmont, Steinhardt. *Stars*: Misses Thompson, Holt, Babbitt, Leslie, Leidy. *Artless Flower*: Miss H. Sheppard. *The Siren*: Miss G. Jones. *I Am It*: Miss F. Kidston. *The Slav*: Miss E. French. *The Cocktail Maid*: Miss J. Cannar. *Gwendolyn*: Miss B. Davenport. *Lady Goit*: Miss E. Dennison. *The Unknown*: Miss J. Pardica. *Thelma Ibsen*: Miss L. Hastings. *Mrs Rolly Rags*: E. Molyneux.

Scene 6

"Brazilian Jubilee"[39]
T. Friganza
Scene: Exterior of a Fashion Shop.
Steve: B. Leslie. *Albany*: T. Friganza.

Scene 7

"Cotton Blossom Time" (Cotton Blossom Serenade)
M. Elaine, Chorus
(*Lyrics by* Thomas J. Gray.)

"The Musical Mokes"[40]-
E. Flanagan, N. Edwards
Scene: Newport Transformed to the Sunny South. On the Mississippi.

---

[32]Dropped for subsequent tour.
[33]Dropped for subsequent tour.
[34]Scene dropped during the run.
[35]Both "Rafferty" and "You've Got the Style and the Smile" were dropped during the run.

[36]Dropped during the run.
[37]Dropped during the run.
[38]Added briefly to this scene during the run:
"I Wonder Who She Spoons with Now"
V. Michelena, Chorus
Which was later replaced by:
"Idol of Eyes" (previously in Act 1)
V. Michelena
[39]Dropped for subsequent tour. May also be known as "Brazilian Nut."
[40]Dropped during the run.

Scene 8

"Wake Up! It's Cake Walk Day" (Cake Walk Days)
  B. Seeley, Chorus
  (*Lyrics by* Thomas J. Gray.)
  Scene: A Cotton Plantation.

Scene 9

Siamese Dance
  Carbrey Brothers
Lariat Dance
  Miss Josephine and W. Rogers
"In Time of Peace Prepare for War"
  Finale Ensemble
  (*Lyrics by* Robert B. Smith.)
  Scene: On the Hudson.

Scene 10

Finale
  Scene: A Hot Time in Times Square.

1915.23   THE PRINCESS PAT

A Comic Opera in Three Acts. Book and lyrics by Henry Blossom. Music by Victor Herbert. Staged by Fred G. Latham. Dances arranged by Bena Hoffman. Scenery painted by Homer F. Emens. Gowns by Hickson, Inc. Orchestra under the direction of Gustave Salzer. Orchestrations by Victor Herbert. Produced by John Cort. Opened 29 September 1915 at the Cort Theatre and closed 12 February 1916 after 158 performances.

CAST (in order of appearance): *Marie*: Leonora Novasio. *Thomas*: Martin Haydon. *Bob Darrow*: Sam B. Hardy. *Tony Schmalz, Jr.*: ROBERT OBER. *Si Perkins*: Alexander Clark. *Grace Holbrook*: EVA FALLON. *General John Holbrook*: LOUIS CASAVANT. *Anthony Schmalz*: AL SHEAN. *Princess de Montaldo, née Patrice O'Connor*: ELEANOR PAINTER. *Prince Antonio di Montaldo, Prince Toto*: JOSEPH R. LERTORA. *Bertie Ashland*: Ralph Riggs. *Gabrielle Fourneaux*: Katherine Witchie. *Anne Winthrop*: Clare Freeman. *Bella Wells*: Charlotte LaGrande. *Coralie Bliss*: Doris Kenyon. *Dorothy Pryme*: Lyn Donaldson. *Elsie Smith*: Kathleen Erroll. *Frances Hedges*: Una Brooks. *Hester Lisle*: Clara Taylor. *Maude Van Cortlandt*: Lilian Charles. *Reggie Calthorpe*: Este Morrison. *Sidney Gray*: Jack Hagner. *Duncan Arthur*: Sven Eric. *Teddy Thorne*: William Quinby. *Lee Bainbridge*: Carl Drury. *Jack Wickham*: William Collins. *Nat Franklin*: Irving Fast. *Achille Mazetti*: Mario Rogati.

The action takes place on Long Island at the present time.

Act 1: Garden of General Holbrook's Home. Forenoon.

Act 2: Living Room in General Holbrook's Home. Evening of same day.

Act 3: Smoking Room at the Westmoreland Hunt Club. The following night.

ACT 1

"Allies" (Duet)
  L. Novasio, M. Haydon
"Make Him Guess"
  E. Fallon, Ladies
"I'd Like to Be a Quitter, But I Find It Hard to Quit"
  R. Ober
Arrival of the Princess Pat
  Ensemble
"Love Is the Best of All"
  E. Painter, Ensemble
"For Better or For Worse" (Sunshine)(Duet)
  E. Painter, E. Fallon
Finale Act 1:
"When a Girl's About to Marry" (Trio)
  E. Fallon, L. Casavant, A. Shean
(Finale)
  Ensemble

ACT 2

"Estellita" (Opening)
  Ensemble
"Neapolitan Love Song" (T'amo![41])(Sweet One How My Heart Is Yearning)
  J. R. Lertora

---

[41]Italian adaptation (lyrics) by Max Villani.

"I Wish I Was an Island in an Ocean of Girls"
  A. Shean, Girls
"I Need Affection"[42]
  E. Painter
Dance—Fox Trot
  Ensemble
"All for You" (Duet)
  E. Painter, J. R. Lertora
Finale
  Ensemble

ACT 3

Opening Chorus
  L. Casavant, A. Shean, S. B. Hardy, R. Ober, J. Lertora, Male Chorus
Dance Divertissement
  K. Witchie, R. Riggs
"In a Little World for Two"
  E. Painter, S. B. Hardy, E. Fallon, R. Ober
"The Shoes of Husband Number One Are Worn by Number Two"
  A. Clark
"Two Laughing Irish Eyes"
  Ensemble
Finale Ultime
  Ensemble

1915.24   HIP-HIP-HOORAY

A Musical Revue in Three Acts. Book by R. H. Burnside. Music by Raymond Hubbell. Lyrics by John L. Golden. Staged by R. H. Burnside. Dances arranged by Mariette Lorette. Settings designed by Homer Emens, Mark Lawson, Frank Gates and Edward A. Morange, Ernest Albert. Costumes designed by William H. Matthews, Robert McQuinn, Frances Zelbarth. Lighting by Joseph Ellsner. Orchestra under the direction of Raymond Hubbell. Produced by Charles Dillingham. Opened 30 September 1915 at the Hippodrome; second edition opened 1 May 1916 and closed 3 June 1916 after 425 performances.

CAST: *The Ambitious Actor, in love with the innocent ingenue*: JOSEPH PARSONS. *The Innocent Ingenue*: ANNA MAY ROBERTS. *The Jaunty Juvenile, in love with the saucy soubrette*: HARRY GRIFFITHS. *The Saucy Soubrette*: BETH SMALLEY. *The Chubby Comedian, in love with the artful adventuress*: ARTHUR DEAGON. *The Vicious Villain, also in love with the artful adventuress*: JAMES REANEY. *The Artful Adventuress*: LESLIE LEIGH. *The Happy Hobo*: NAT M. WILLS. *The Hero*: ORVILLE HARROLD. *The Heroine*: BELLE STOREY. *Toto, the Mischief-maker*: Himself. And DAVE ABRAHAMS, AL GRADY, TOMMY COLTON, DIPPY DIERS, EDDIE RUSSELL, CHARLES T. ALDRICH, JOHN PHILIP SOUSA AND HIS BAND, KATE SCHMIDT, HILDA RUCKERTS, ALFRED NAESSE, ELLEN DALLERUP, MALLIA, BART and MALLIA, THE GLORIAS, THE AMARANTHS, SOLTI DUO, HALE and PATTERSON, BENTLEY and TAYLOR, POPE and KERNER, STEELE and WINSLOW, CHARLOTTE, THE MARIMBA GUATE-MALAN (String) BAND, THE BOGANNY TROUPE OF ACROBATS, POWERS' ELEPHANTS.
  Ensemble: Marjory Bentley, Alberta Randle, Helen Williams, Willa Delle, Marie Cullen, Dora Wischer. *Ballet*: Poldy Kollhofa, Margaret Wrusch, Rosa Gebauer, Irmgard Markel, Elsa Prenslow, Martha Kollett, Martha Georges, Alice Weisemann, Elsie Schaefer, Martha Weidemann, Hanny Frick, Reta Walter, Johanna Worm, Martha Schmidt, Margaretta Muller, Lotta Werkusat, Erna Voigt. *Ski Jumpers*: Sigard Loiten, George Andresan, Raeder Anderson, Hakon Hansen, Ola Kristeansean, Andreas Ronneng.

Act 1: In and About New York.

Act 2: At the Panama Exposition.

Act 3: Lake St. Moritz the Engadine, Switzerland.

ACT 1[43]

Scene 1

"The Kat Cabaret"
  Scene: On the Roofs. (Lawson)

---

[42]Replaced during the run by:
  "Flirting"
  E. Painter
[43]Added in late February 1916 to Act 2

Flossie, the flirt: D. Abrahams. *Thomas*: A. Grady. *Maria*, his spouse: T. Colton. *Pucky*: Toto. *Toby*: D. Diers. *Tabby*: E. Russell. *Kittens*: Misses M. Bentley, A. Randle, H. Williams, W. Delle, M. Cullen.

Specialties

The Amaranths; the Romanos; 5 Tornados

Scene 2

Scene: Grand Central Station. (Emens)

The Baggage Smashers: Mallia, Bart and Mallia. *Some Detective*: C. T. Aldrich.

Scene 3

"How D'ye Do, Fifth Avenue?"

"(My) Fox Trot Wedding Day"

N. M. Wills

(*Music and Lyrics by* Benjamin Hapgood Burt.)

"My Land, My Flag"

O. Harrold

(*Music by* Zoel J. Parenteau. *Lyrics by* Marcus C. Connelly [Marc Connelly].)

Scene: On Fifth Avenue. (Lawson)

Scene 4

Dancing Carnival

Les Glorias, The Solti Duo, The Amaranths, The Solti Duo, Toto and Gloria, Bentley and Taylor

Selections

Guatemala Marimba Band

"The Flower Garden Ball"

B. Storey

(*Music by* Jean Schwartz. *Lyrics by* William Jerome.)

"The Land of Love and Roses"[44]

J. Parsons

Scene: The Cascades at the Biltmore Hotel.

"America First" (March)

(*Music by* John Philip Sousa.)

Beginning 1 May 1916, advertised as Second Edition. Changes included:

"The Cute Little Beau Called Anna" (replaced "Fox Trot Wedding Day")

(*Music and Lyrics by* Benjamin Hapgood Burt.)

"Everything in America Is Ragtime" (replaced The Flower Garden Ball")

(*Music and Lyrics by* Irving Berlin.)

"San San Soo" or "In a Sampan for Two" (replaced "Chin Chin, I Love You")

(*Music by* Raymond Hubbell. *Lyrics by* John L. Golden.)

(Sheet music credits Alf. J. Lawrence with music, Percy Edgar with lyrics.)

"The Pathfinder of Panama" (replaced "The New York Hippodrome March")

(*Music by* John Philip Sousa.)

Also added were:

"A Day in Camp"

(*Music by* John Philip Sousa.)

"Dance Oriental"

(*Music by* Raymond Hubbell.)

"Moth and the Flame" (Waltz)

(*Music by* Raymond Hubbell)

Added 19 May 1916:

"For the Honor of the Flag"

Arthur Aldridge

(*Music by* Raymond Hubbell. *Lyrics by* R. H. Burnside.)

Added to Act 1 (after On Fifth Avenue scene) during the run and for subsequent tour:

Here the plot will be interfered with for a few minutes by

A Politician: Lou Anger.

Scene: Lobby of the National Reprogressive Democratic Club.

[44]Replaced during the run with:

"The Ladder of Roses"

H. Griffiths

(*Lyrics by* R. H. Burnside.)

ACT 2

Scene 1

"The Wedding of Jack and Jill"

A. Deagon

Specialties

Powers' Elephants, Milton Mooney's Blue Ribbon Horses

Scene: Toyland in the Zone. (Emens)

Scene 2

The Boganny Troupe

Scene: Chinatown. (Gates and Morange)

"Chin-Chin, I Love You" (Chin-Chin, Open Your Heart and Let Me See In)

O. Harrold, B. Storey

(*Music and Lyrics by* A. Seymour Brown.)

Scene 3

"The Lamp-Posts of Old Broadway"[45]

(N. M. Wills)

(*Music and Lyrics by* Benjamin Hapgood Burt.) *Scene*: Moving Picture Street. (Lawson)

The Messenger Boy: N. M. Wills.

Scene 4

Sousa and His Band (John Philip Sousa, Conductor):

"The New York Hippodrome March"

(*Music by* John Philip Sousa.)

"The Cabaret Dancers" from the Suite, Impressions at the Movies (Ballet Ensemble)

(*Music by* John Philip Sousa.)

"The March of the States" (Ballet of the States/Sisterhood of the States)

(*Music by* John Philip Sousa.)

Scene: The Tower of Jewels.

("Stars and Stripes Forever")

ACT 3

"Flirting at St. Moritz" (Ballet Extraordinary Direct from Admiral's Palace, Berlin)

Book by Leo Bartuschek. Music by Julius Einodshofer. Dances arranged by Mme. Mariette Lorette. Scene by Ernest Albert.

CAST: *Kitty Goldbird*, a rich widow: K. Schmidt. *Maud Wilson*, her sister: H. Ruckerts. *Oluf Jacobsen*, a sportsman: A. Naesse. *Alex Rasmussen*, a government attaché: E. Dallerup. *Lehmann*, a would-be sportsman: Toto. *First Dandy*: D. Wischer. *Other Dandies*: P. Kollhofa, M. Wruch, R. Gebauer. *Polish Ladies and Gentlemen*: I. Markel, E. Prenslow, M. Kollett, M. Georges, A. Weidemann, E. Schaefer, M. Weidemann, H. Frick. *Tourists*: R. Walter, J. Worm, M. Schmidt, M. Muller, L. Werkusat, M. Werkusat, E. Voigt. *Ski Jumpers*: S. Loiten, G. Andresan, R. Anderson, H. Hansen, O. Kristeansan, A. Ronneng. *Skating Divertissements*: The Naesses, Pope and Kerner, Toto and Steele and Winslow (ice comedians), Charlotte.

1915.25 ## MISS INFORMATION

A Little Comedy with a Little Music in Three Acts. Play by Paul Dickey and Charles W. Goddard. Music by Jerome Kern. Lyrics by Elsie Janis. Staged by Robert Milton. Costumes designed by Melville Ellis. Musical director, Harold Vicars. Produced by Charles Dillingham. Opened 5 October 1915 at the George M. Cohan Theatre and closed 13 November 1915 after 47 performances.[46]

CAST: *Mrs. Cadwalder*: ANNIE ESMOND. *Joan*, her daughter: Vivian Rushmore. *Jack Cadwalder*, her son: HOWARD ESTABROOK. *Bob Dunstan*, an American novelist: Eugene Revere. *Ewing Francis*, a book-sleuth: David Todd. *Dennis Gillicuddy*, an insurance detective: Francis D. McGinn. *Michael Breschnehan*, a police inspector: Frank Rainger. *Benny*, the valet: Leavitt James. *Marie*, a maid: Julia Bruns. *Messenger Boy*: Albert Lamson. *Jules Bancourt*, pianist from Fychère's: MELVILLE ELLIS. *Francois Fychère*: MAURICE FARKOA. *Elaine Foazane*: IRENE BORDONI. *The Crystal Reader*, the Lady of the Black Mask: Paulette Antoine. *Radeau*: Thomas DeVassey. *Dorothy Marsden*, from Poughkeepsie: Diane Oste. *Bob's Bohemian Army* (3): *A Poet*: Reynolds Sweetland. *An Artist*: Albert Stuart. *A Sculptor*: Frank Furlong. *A Nihilist*: Sinead Alvord. *Dot*, from Nowhere: ELSIE JANIS.

Visitors at Fychère's: Misses Julia Beaubien, Lorayne Leslie, Hazel Lewis, Nan Carter, Marion Davies, Eleanor St. Clair. *The American Band at Fychère's*: Mel Craig, Harry Ward, Rodger Perry, Harry Lewis, Harry Pooley, Irving Levy.

---

[45]Dropped during the run.

[46]Settings uncredited.

Act 1: The Cadwalder Home, New York City.

Act 2: Bob's Apartment in Paris.

Act 3: At Fychère's Midnight Restaurant, Paris.

ACT 2

"Two Big Eyes"
  I. Bordoni
  (*Music and Lyrics by* Cole Porter[47].)

"(The) Banks of the Wye"
  M. Farkoa
  (*Music by* Frank Tours. *Lyrics by* Fred E. Weatherly.)

ACT 3

Pianologue
  M. Ellis

"A Little Love (But Not for Me)"
  I. Bordoni

"Some Sort of Somebody (All of the Time)"
  E. Janis, M. Farkoa

Dance Eccentrique
  E. Janis

"Constant Lover"[48]
  M. Farkoa, Guests
  (*Music by* Herman Finck. *Lyrics by* Arthur Wimperis.)

"The Mix-up Rag"[49]
  The American Band

"Drigo Serenade"[50] (Waltz)
  E. Janis
  (*Music by* Riccardo Drigo.)

1915.26   A WORLD OF PLEASURE

A Musical Revue in Two Acts, 11 Scenes. Dialogue and lyrics by Harold Atteridge. Music by Sigmund Romberg. Entire production staged by J. C. Huffman. Dances by Jack Mason. Ballets by Theodore Kosloff. Settings by P. Dodd Ackerman Studio, H. Robert Law. Costumes by Mrs. J. J. Shubert. Orchestra under the direction of Oscar Radin. Produced by the Winter Garden Company (Messrs. Shubert). Opened 14 October 1915 at the Winter Garden and closed 22 January 1916 after 116 performances.

CAST (in order of appearance): *Scene 1*: A *Policeman*: Dwight Dana. *First Club Man*: Jack Bick. *Second Club Man*: Gilbert Wells. *Dick Grayson*: William L. Gibson. *The Strollers*: Collins and Hart. *A Chauffeur*: Dan Healey. *A Pedestrian*: Bud Murray. *Tony Van Schuyler*: CLIFTON CRAWFORD. *Dorothy Gates*: VENITA FITZHUGH. *Annette Gates*: ADA MEADE. *James*, a waiter: Gustave Schult. *Sim Slim*: Daniel Morris. *Oliver Short*: George Moon. *Scene 2*: *Sam*: LEW [Lou] HOLTZ. *Blinker*, manager of the Progressive Employment Agency: FRANKLYN BATIE. *Hector Walnut*: Edward Aveling. *Wilbur Chestnut*: Albert S. Lloyd. *V. Gates*: Sydney Greenstreet. *Tessie*, a stenographer: Jack Wilson. *Tom Collins*: Jack Wilson. *Marjorie*: Eleanor Brown. *Vera*: Olga Hempstone. *Nellie*: Marie Salisbury. *Lucy*: Lois Whitney. *Sylvia Stone*: KITTY GORDON. *Violet*: Frances Pritchard. *Mr. Whirlwind*: Maurice Diamond. *Miss Hesitation*: Helen McMahon. *Miss Fox Trot*: Rene Chaplow. *Scene 3*: *Dick Bird*: William Banfield Talor. *Yvette*, a flirtatious widow: STELLA MAYHEW. *The Dancing Diners*: CHARLES and LOUIS MOSCONI. *Scene 4*: *A Ballet Master*: THEODORE KOSLOFF. *Rosebud*: ROSIE QUINN. *Scene 5*: *Miss Gotham*: ROSIE QUINN. *Toymaker*: Dwight Dana. *French Doll*: Olga Hempstone. *Giggling Doll*: Eleanor Brown. *The Acrobatic Dolls*: Collins and Hart. *Rag Doll*: Kittie Hill. *Clown Doll*: Lois Whitney. *First Spy*: William Banfield Taylor. *Second Spy*: STELLA MAYHEW. *Third Spy*: VENITA FITZHUGH. *Act 2, Scene 1*: *The Arabian Dancer*: Sahary Djeli.

Act 1, Scene 1: The Good Fellows' Club. (Ackerman) *Scene 2*: The Progressive Employment Agency. (Law) *Scene 3*: Exterior of the Lobster Square Restaurant. (Ackerman) *Scene 4*: A Japanese Tea Room. (Ackerman) *Scene 5*: Exterior of Tea Room. (Ackerman) *Scene 6*: A Toy Shop. (Law)

Act 2, Scene 1: The Enchanted Roof Garden. (Ackerman) *Scene 2*: Riverside Drive. (Ackerman) *Scene 3*: The Fleet Review. (Law) *Scene 4*: The Daisy Field. (Ackerman) *Scene 5*: An Oriental Ballroom. (Ackerman)

ACT 1

"The Good Fellows' Club"[51]
  O. Taylor

"Fifth Avenue"[52]
  W. L. Gibson, Chorus

"The Dance of the Midnight Sons"[53]
  G. Moon, D. Morris

"The Employment Agency"
  J. Wilson

"In My War Against Men"
  K. Gordon, Ensemble

"Miss Innovation"
  F. Batie, H. McMahon, M. Diamond, R. Chaplow, Ensemble

"Girlies Are Out of My Life"
  C. Crawford, F. Pritchard, Ensemble

"I'll Make You Like the Town"
  L. Holtz, Ensemble

Danse Eccentrique
  Mosconi Brothers

Japanese Ballet
  T. Kosloff, R. Quinn

"I Could Go Home to a Girl Like You"
  C. Crawford, V. Fitzhugh

"Down in Cattycorner"[54]
  K. Gordon, Ensemble

"Syncopation"[55]
  L. Holtz, F. Pritchard, Ensemble
  (*Music and Lyrics by* J. Leubrie Hill.)

"At the Toy Shop"
  E. Brown, Ensemble

"Dance of the Square Heads"
  Messrs. Moon, Morris, Healy, Wells, Diamond, Grant, Manning, Roland, Roberts, Stoker, Bick, Murray

The Doll Dance
  F. Pritchard

"Reminiscent Rosy-Posy" (Rosey Posey)[56]
  R. Quinn, Ensemble

Flights of Fancy
  Collins and Hart

"Mechanical Soldiers"
  Mosconi Brothers

"The Melting Pot"
  A. Meade

ACT 2

"The Ragtime Pipe of Pan"
  F. Batie

"In Arabia"[57]
  S. Djeli

"The Wop Cabaret (Song)"[58]
  S. Mayhew
  (*Music and Lyrics by* John L. Golden.)

"The Girl of the Fan" (The Girl and the Fan)
  K. Gordon, F. Batie, Ensemble

"Take Me Home (with You)"[59]
  V. Fitzhugh

---

[47]Lyrics also ascribed to John Golden.
[48]Late in the run replaced by:
  "Grammatical Grievances"
  M. Farkoa
[49]Late in the run replaced by Melville Ellis' Pianologue.
[50]Replaced after opening by:
  Waltz, Chopin A-Minor
  E. Janis

---

[51]Dropped for subsequent tour.
[52]Dropped for subsequent tour.
[53]Dropped for subsequent tour.
[54]Dropped for subsequent tour.
[55]Dropped for subsequent tour.
[56]Dropped for subsequent tour.
[57]Dropped for subsequent tour.
[58]Dropped for subsequent tour.
[59]Dropped for subsequent tour.

"I Played My Concertina"[60]
C. Crawford
"Fascination"[61]
K. Gordon, F. Batie
"The Greatest Battle Song of All"[62]
J. Wilson
(*Lyrics by* Harold Atteridge and Jack Wilson.)
"Ragtime Carnival"
S. Mayhew, Ensemble
The Dancing Carnival
Mosconi Brothers, Moon and Morris, McMahon, Diamond and Chaplow, Healey, Wells, Murray, B. Dakin
"The Jigaree"
Ensemble

1915.27   ALONE AT LAST

An Operette in Three Acts, 5 Scenes. (Original) Viennese book ('Endlicht Allein') by Dr. A. M. Willner and Robert Bodanzky. Music by Franz Lehár. American adaptation by Edgar Smith and Joseph Herbert. Additional lyrics by Matthew C. Woodward. Staged by J. H. Benrimo. Dances arranged by Allan K. Foster. Scenery built by James Surridge; John Young Studio. Gowns by Josephs; Frances; J. M. Gidding & Co. Lighting by John Whelen. Orchestra under the direction of Gaetano Merola. Produced by the Messrs. Shubert. Opened 19 October 1915 at the Sam S. Shubert Theatre and closed 18 March 1916 after 180 performances[63].

CAST (in order of appearance): *Morel*, hotel manager: S. Paul Veron. *Hans Ketterer*, a veteran Swiss guide: Edmond Mulcahy. *A Waiter*: James Georgi. *A Guide*: Frank C. Sparling. *Count Max Splenningen*: HARRY CONOR. *Count Willigard*: ROY ATWELL. *Dolly Cloverdale*, an American heiress: MARGUERITE NAMARA, (BETH LYDY, alt). *Mrs. Phoebe Cloverdale*, a wealthy American widow: ELIZABETH GOODALL. *Baron Franz von Hansen*: JOHN CHARLES THOMAS. *Tilly Dachau*, of the Hoff Theatre, Vienna: JOSÉ COLLINS. *von Flamberg*: Herold Everts. *Rudiman*: Walter Croft. *Bondi*: Gene Hamilton. *Yvonne Everett*, an American girl: Barbara Schaefer. *Mrs. Jeffry*, an American tourist: Mildred Bronell. *von Mannheim*, a German tourist: George Vogner. *Professor Dinglebender*, geologist: Charles Gnidion. *Head Porter*, Grand Hotel: S. Paul Veron. *Hotel Porter*: Harold Wright. *A Waiter*: Sol Singlust. *Guides, Tourists, Pesants, Hotel Guests, Maids, Porters, Waiters*, etc.

Show Girls: Olga Britton, Mildred Bronell, Miriam Folger, Eleanor Dayne, Lillian Horne, Helen Glenmore, Helen Mesereau, Eleanor Ryley, Gladys Siddons, Margaret Vingut. *Mediums*: Marie Blucher, Clara DeBeers, Ann Delmore, Maud Florenz, Virginia Lee, Vivian Macdonell, Helen Ray, Mildred Stokes, Alice Stratton, Constance Werner. *Dancers*: Mabel Blake, Tracy Elbert, Blanche Georgi, Mazie Gilmore, Mazie Lyon, Marie Mann, Lucy Maurelli, Lili Patay, Lillie Simpson, Ethel Stuart, Vivian White, Adele Christy. *Men*: Ernest Brunniviora, Walter Croft, Eugene Elliot, Harold Everts, Rudolph Fink Maurice Gardener, Gene Hamilton, Gursham Hall, Harry Rose, Henry Schiff, Julius Schwartz, Frank Sheppard, Sol Singlust, Frank Sparling, William Warren, George Wagner, Robert Whitehouse, Harold Wright.

Act 1: Garden of the Hotel Victoria, Interlaken, Switzerland. Late afternoon. (Surridge.)

Act 2, Scene 1: The Terrace of the Grand Hotel, Kurhaus, Murren. Sunrise, the next morning. *Scene 2*: On the Trail of the Jungfrau. Afternoon. *Scene 3*: The Summit of the Peak. Sunset. (Young.)

Act 3: Lounge of the Hotel Victoria, Interlaken. The following evening. (Surridge.)

ACT 1

Opening Chorus (The Peasant Wedding Party)
Ensemble
"One in the Game of Love"
M. Namara, Entire Chorus
"Thy Heart (Is) My Prize"
J. C. Thomas
(*Lyrics by* Matthew C. Woodward.)
"Oh, My Darling Tilly"
J. Collins, R. Atwell
(*Lyrics by* Joseph W. Herbert.)

"Nature Divine"
M. Namara, J. C. Thomas
(*Lyrics by* Matthew C. Woodward.)
"Waltz Entrancing"
J. Collins, Men
(*Lyrics by* Joseph W. Herbert.)
Finale
M. Namara, J. C. Thomas, J. Collins, R. Atwell, Chorus

ACT 2
Scene 1

Opening Chorus
"Bright Morning Star"
B. Schaefer, Chorus
"Pretty Edelweiss"
M. Namara
(*Lyrics by* Matthew C. Woodward.)
"Not Now, But By the Moon"
J. Collins, R. Atwell
(*Lyrics by* Matthew C. Woodward.)
"Picnic in the Sky" (Finaletto)
J. Collins, R. Atwell, H. Conor, E. Goodall, E. Mulcahy, Chorus
(*Music by* Gaetano Merola.)

Scene 2
"This Is My World"[64]
M. Namara, J. C. Thomas
"Some Little Bug Will Find You Some Day"
R. Atwell
(*Music by* Silvio Hein. *Lyrics by* Roy Atwell and Benjamin Hapgood Burt.)

Scene 3
Scene: Duet—Finale
M. Namara, J. C. Thomas

ACT 3
"Scandals in the Air" (Opening Chorus)
"Return to Warm My Heart Again"[65]
J. Collins, Chorus
(*Music by* Gaetano Merola.)
Reminiscences[66]
M. Namara, J. C. Thomas
Finale

1915.28   AROUND THE MAP

A Musical Globe Trot (Revue) in Three Acts, 13 Scenes. Book and lyrics by C. M. S. McLellan. Music by Herman Finck. Dialogue directed by Herbert Gresham. Musical numbers staged by Julian Mitchell. Scenery by Joseph Urban. Costumes designed by Cora MacGeachy, Avon and F. Richard Anderson, O'Kane Conwell (last scene), Dazian (mens'). Orchestra under the direction of Charles Previn. Produced by Marc Klaw and Abe L. Erlanger. Opened 1 November 1915 at the New Amsterdam Theatre and closed 29 January 1916 after 104 performances.

CAST: Act 1: *Impikoff; Maharajah of Gginggs Gaboo*: WILLIAM NORRIS. *Count (Georgie) de Gai; Champion Amateur Boxer*: ROBERT PITKIN. *Ludovici Sacarappa*: Arthur Klein. *Toto de Beers*: P. O'Malley Jennings. *Pearly Rheinstein*: TYLER BROOKE. *Hoppolyte Boun*: Irving Brooks. *Pierre*: Edwin Wilson. *M. Alphonse*: Freddy Nice. *M. Gustave*: Bob C. Adams. *Boy and Page Boy*: Irving Gross. *Jacqueline Bonheur*, familiarly known as "Tootsi": ELSE ADLER. *Lulu Cachou*: GEORGIA O'RAMEY. *Madame Kapinski*: HAZEL COX. *Louisette*: Marjorie Gateson. *Phrynette*: Flora Crosbie. *Gladiola*: LOUISE GROODY. Act 2: *Count de Pompon; Impikoff; Prince Nippa*: WILLIAM NORRIS. *Count Georgie de Gai; Tannhowski*: ROBERT PITKIN. *Ludovici Sacarappa*: Arthur Klein. *Toto de Beers*: P. O'Malley Jennings.

---

[60]Dropped for subsequent tour.
[61]Dropped for subsequent tour.
[62]Dropped for subsequent tour.
[63]Later played a New York area return engagement for one week 12 February 1917 at the Standard Theatre.

---

[64]Replaced after the opening by:
"Victory to the Bold"
M. Namara, J. C. Thomas
[65]For subsequent tour, replaced by:
"We Don't Know Why We Love"
Letty Yorke (Tilly), Chorus
(*Music by* Gaetano Merola. *Lyrics by* Darl MacBoyle.)
[66]Later billed as "Pretty Edelweiss;" "Thy Heart, My Prize" (reprise).

Pearly Rheinstein: TYLER BROOKE. *Meyer; Blum*: Irving Brooks. *Schwartz; Blumski*: James MacElhern. *Pierre*: Edwin Wilson. *Gideon U. Conn*: Freddy Nice. *Leonardo*: Bob C. Adams. *A Pixie*: Sylvia deFrankie. *"Tootsi"* : ELSE ADLER. *Lulu Cachou*: GEORGIA O'RAMEY. *Madame Kapinski*: HAZEL COX. *Hortense*: Belle D'Aube. *Venus Lova*: Prudence O'Shea. *First Constant Luncher*: Teddy Hudson. *First Constant Diner*: Anna Howard. *First Constant Dancer*: Ada Weeks. *First Constant Kisser*: Edna Chase. *The Right Girl*: May Day. *Another One*: June White. *Act 3: Sheik Hoora Al Radish; Dr. Billy Bullamore; Impikoff*: WILLIAM NORRIS. *Count (Georgie) de Gai*: ROBERT PITKIN. *Baptiste*: Arthur Klein. *Peter Squibb*: P. O'Malley Jennings. *Pearly Rheinstein*: TYLER BROOKE. *Pierre*: Edwin Wilson. *Nosuf; Freddy*: Freddy Nice. *Yusuf; Henri*: Bob C. Adams. *Page Boy*: Albert James. *"Tootsi"* : ELSE ADLER. *Lulu Cachou*: GEORGIA O'RAMEY. *Madame Kapinski*: HAZEL COX. *Doorkeeper*: W. W. Jones.

Act 1, Scene 1: The Roof of Count de Gai's House. *Scene 2*: Rue Caumartin. *Scene 3*: Tootsi's Bedroom. *Scene 4*: The Bar in the Club House of "The Discontented Lulus."

Act 2, Scene 1:Unter Den Linden, Berlin. *Scene 2*: The Boundary Line Between Germany and Russia. *Scene 3*: Tootsi's Dream. *Scene 4*: Reception Room at Impikoff's Petrograd Establishment. *Scene 5*: The Japanese Jockey Club at Port Arthur.

Act 3, Scene 1: At the San Francisco Exposition. *Scene 2*: Georgie's Sitting Room in a San Francisco Hotel. *Scene 3*: Exterior of "The Red Hot Stove Cabaret," New York. *Scene 4*: Interior of "The Red Hot Stove Cabaret," New York.

ACT 1
Scene 1

   Opening Chorus
      Chorus
   "I'm the Boom, Boom, Boomer" (Song)
      I. Brooks, Chorus
   "I Don't Know Her Name Yet" (Song)
      R. Pitkin, Chorus

Scene 2

   "I'm Madame Kapinski" (Song)
      H. Cox, Chorus
   "Here Comes Tootsi" (Song)
      E. Adler, R. Pitkin, E. Wilson, P. O. Jennings, Chorus
   "Lazy Lulu" (Duet)
      G. O'Ramey, R. Pitkin

Scene 3

   "Little Maud Isn't Meant for You" (Song)
      E. Adler, Others

Scene 4

   "There's (Only) One Thing a Coon Can Do" (Song)
      L. Groody, Chorus
      (*Music by* Louis A. Hirsch.)
   Finale
      Principals, Chorus

ACT 2
Scene 1

   Chorus of Nurses
      Chorus
   "When the Right Girl Comes Along" (Song)
      R. Pitkin, Chorus
   "Some Girl Has Got to Darn His Socks" (Song)
      E. Adler, Others
      (*Music by* Herman Finck and Louis A. Hirsch[67].)
   "Take Me a Ride of Joy" (Song)
      G. O'Ramey, Chorus

Scene 2

   "Katie Clancy" (Song)
      H. Cox, Chorus
      (*Music by* Louis A. Hirsch.)

Scene 3

   Chorus of "Constant Lunchers, Constant Diners, Constant Dancers and Constant Kissers"
      Chorus
      (*Music by* Louis A. Hirsch.)

Scene 4

   "Goodness, Ain't You Glad?" (Duet)
      W. Norris, H. Cox, Chorus

Scene 5

   Opening Chorus
      Chorus
   "It's a Very Fine World" (Song)
      E. Adler, Chorus
   Finale
      Principals, Chorus

ACT 3
Scene 1

   Opening Chorus
      Chorus
   "Let Us Stay Where the Crowd Is" (Song)
      E. Adler, W. Norris, Others
      (*Music by* Louis A. Hirsch.)

Scene 2

   "Dolly Dear" (Song)
      E. Adler

Scene 3

   "Billy the Bubbler" (Song)
      W. Norris, Chorus
      (*Music by* Louis A. Hirsch.)

Scene 4[68]

   "The Dear Old Fighting Boys" (Song)
      R. Pitkin, Chorus
   Waltz Song
      G. O'Ramey, E. Adler, Chorus
   Finale
      Principals, Chorus

1915.29   # KATINKA

A Musical Play in Three Acts. Book and lyrics by Otto Hauerbach [Harbach]. Music by Rudolf Friml. Staged by Frank Smithson. Scenery painted by Edward Sundquist. Costumes by Paul Arlington, Inc.; men's clothes by Brook's Uniform Company. Orchestra under the direction of John McGhie. Produced by Arthur Hammerstein. Opened 23 December 1915 at the 44th Street Theatre, moved 3 April 1916 to the Lyric Theatre, and closed 1 July 1916 after 220 performances.

CAST (in order of appearance): *Varenka*: Nina Napier. *Petrov*: Albert Sackett. *Ivan Dimitri*: SAMUEL ASH. *Boris Strogoff*: COUNT (LORRIE) GRIMALDI. *Katinka*: MAY NAUDAIN. *Tatiana*: Norma Mendoza. *Thaddeus Hopper*: FRANKLYN ARDELL. *Russian Dancers*: May Thompson, Edmund Makalif. *Herr Kopf*: W. J. McCARTHY *Abdul*: Daniel Baker. *Arif Bey*: EDWARD DURAND. *Halif*: A. Robins. *Olga Nashan*: EDITH DECKER. *Mrs. Helen Hopper*: ADELE ROWLAND. *A Spy*: Harry Cinton. *Pierre*: Gustav Schultz. *Bell Boy*: Helen Kroner.

   Guests, Travelers, American Girls, Bridesmaids: Blanche Betters, Juanita MacGergor, Jane Fielding, Ethel Hendricks, Abbie Stewart, Christine Von Holt, Marie Duchette, Rosalie Malette, Louise Bardusch, Cynthia Kellogg, Vera Fromm, Betty Brooke, Violette Armstrong, Bess Arlington, May Farrar. *Visitors, Turkish Girls, Flower Girls, Barmaids*: Charlotte Arkell, Ellis Graves, Edith Oakley, Camilla Elkjaer, Mary Bacile, Yetta Metchik, Marietta Servain, Etta Bellaire. *Serving Maids, Slave Girls, Vienna Dancers*: Gypsy Bellaire, Reta Delmar, Kathryn Sinclair, Irene Lamal, Helen Kroner, Violet Delmar, Mildred Franklyn, Genevieve Jewett, Etta Bellaire. *Guests, American Men, Russian Officers, Flunkies*: Frank Harley, Karle Nelson, Jerry Childs, Neil Moore, Billy Budd, Charles Frey, Harry Cinton, Al Racklin, Edward Foley, Fred Nerret. *Austrian Officers, Servants, Waiters*: A. Novick, William Onisman, Louis Jacobs, B. Opatowski, George St. John, Lester Smith.

The action takes place just before the war.

Act 1: Villa of Boris Strogoff at Yalta, Russia, on the Black Sea. Late afternoon and evening of a summer day.

Act 2: A Street in Old Stamboul, Turkey.

Act 3: (Herr Knopf's) Cafe, Turkoise-in-Vienna, Austria. Three weeks later.

---

[67]Hirsch elsewhere credited with sole authorship of music.

---

[68]Added to Act 3, Scene 4, opening the scene, for subsequent tour:
   "Walking Step Walkover" (Dance)
      F. Nice, A. Weeks

ACT 1

Opening Chorus
N. Napier, Chorus

"In Vienna"
S. Ash, Chorus

Russian Wedding March
L. Grimaldi, M. Naudain, N. Mendoza, Chorus

"One Who Will Understand"
M. Naudain, Chorus

"Katinka"
S. Ash, L. Grimaldi, Male Chorus

"In a Hurry"
F. Ardell, Chorus

"Tis the End"[69]
S. Ash, M. Naudain

Russian Dance
M. Thompson, E. Makalif

Finale
Company

ACT 2

"Stamboul"
E. Decker, Chorus

"Hidden Charms" (Charms Are Fairest When They're Hidden)[70]
E. Decker, Chorus

"Your Photo"
A. Rowland, Boys

"Allah's Holiday"[71]
E. Decker, Chorus

"The Weekly Wedding"
A. Rowland, F. Ardell

"I Want All the World to Know"[72]
S. Ash

"Rackety Coo!"[73]
M. Naudain, S. Ash

Finale
Company

ACT 3[74]

Divertissement:

Waltz
M. Thompson

"The Walking Music Store"[75]
A. Robins

"Mignonette"[76]
H. Kroner, E. Makalif

"I Want to Marry a Male Quartette"[77]
A. Rowland, Boys

---

[69]Replaced after opening by:
"Rackety Coo!" (from Act 2)
M. Naudain, S. Ash
[70]Dropped after opening.
[71]Dropped during the New York run, but reinstated for the tour as the Act 2 opening, replacing "Stamboul" and "Hidden Charms."
[72]After opening, moved to Act 3 before "Skidiskiscatch" and replaced in Act 2 by:
Circassian Dance
M. Thompson, E. Makalif
"The Walking Music Store"
A. Robins
[73]After opening, moved to Act 1, after "In a Hurry."
[74]Added to opening of Act 3 after opening:
"My Paradise"
M. Naudain, Chorus
[75]After opening, moved to Act 2, before Finale.
[76]Dropped after opening.
[77]After opening, the running order of "I Want to Marry a Male Quartette" and " I Can Tell By the Way You Dance, Dear" was reversed. The latter was reassigned as a Duet between A. Rowland, E. Makalif.

"Skidiskiscatch"[78]
F. Ardell, M. Naudain, S. Ash, W. J. McCarthy, E. Durand, E. Decker

"I Can Tell By the Way You Dance, Dear"
A. Rowland, Girls

Finale
Company

1915.30   VERY GOOD EDDIE

A Musical Play in Two Acts, 3 Scenes. Book by Philip Bartholomae and Guy Bolton. Based on the farce "Over Night" by Philip Bartholomae. Music by Jerome Kern. Lyrics by Schuyler Greene, (Herbert Reynolds). (Staged by Frank McCormick.) Dances arranged by David Bennett. Scenery (Act 2) by Elsie DeWolfe. Costumes by Melville Ellis. Orchestra under the direction of Max Hirschfield. Orchestrations by Frank Saddler. Produced by the (Elisabeth) Marbury-(Ray) Comstock Company. Opened 23 December 1915 at the Princess Theatre, moved 29 May 1915 to the Casino Theatre, moved 11 September 1916 to the 39th Street Theatre, moved 2 October 1916 to the Princess Theatre, and closed 14 October 1916 after 341 performances.

CAST (in order of appearance): *Steward on The Catskill*: Benjamin F. Wright. *Monsieur de Rougemont*: James Lounsbery. *Purser on The Catskill*: Lew Fullerton. *Dick Rivers*: OSCAR SHAW. *Madame Matroppo*: ADA LEWIS. *Elsie Lilly*: ANN ORR. *Eddie Kettle*: ERNEST TRUEX. *Georgina Kettle*, his wife: HELEN RAYMOND. *Magazine Girl*: Georgia Spelvin. *Percy Darling*: JOHN WILLARD. *Elsie Darling*, his wife: ALICE DOVEY. *West Point Cadet*: Kuy Kendall. *Al Cleveland*, clerk at the Rip Van Winkle Inn: JOHN E. HAZZARD. *Victoria Lake*: Julia Mills. *Chrystal Poole*: Tess Mayer. *Lily Pond*: Bessie Kelly. *Belle Fontaine*: Arline Chase. *Flo Tide*: Helene Bond. *Virginia Spring*: Dorothy Silvia. *Miss Always Innit*: Helen O'Day. *Miss Carrie Closewell*: Genevieve Willment. *Miss Funnie Rekkod*: Louise Cook. *Miss Munnie Duzzyt*: Mary Louise Morrison. *Miss Gay Ann Giddy*: Dorothy Nita. *Miss E. Z. Morrels*: Katherine Rahn. *Mr. Tayleurs Dummie*: Carl Wadsworth. *Mr. Fullern A. Goat*: Morton Wood. *Mr. Dyer Thurst*: Herbert Hoey. *Mr. Rollo Munn*: Sedgewick Draper. *Mr. Watt Pumkyns*: Stuart Gillmore. *Mr. Dustin Stacks*: Harry McKenna.

Act 1: Deck of the Hudson River Boat, *The Catskill*. One summer afternoon.

Act 2, Scene 1: The Rip Van Winkle Inn. That evening. *Scene 2*: The same, the next morning.

ACT 1[79]

"We're on Our Way" (Opening)
J. Mills, Ensemble

"The Same Old Game" (Song)
O. Shaw, Girls

"Some Sort of Somebody (All the Time)" (Duet)(from MISS INFORMATION)
O. Shaw, A. Orr
(*Lyrics by* Elsie Janis.)

"Isn't It Great To Be Married?" (Quartet)
E. Truex, A. Dovey, J. Willard, H. Raymond

"Wedding Bells Are Calling Me" (from NOBODY HOME) (Finaletto)
(*Lyrics by* Harry B. Smith.)

ACT 2

Scene 1

"On the Shore at Le Lei Wi"[80] (Opening)
A. Orr, O. Shaw, Ensemble
(*Music by* Jerome Kern (verse), Henry Kailimai (chorus), *Lyrics by* Herbert Reynolds.)

"If I Find the Girl" (Song)
O. Shaw, Ensemble
(*Lyrics by* Herbert Reynolds, John E. Hazzard.)

---

[78]After opening this song became a duet for F. Ardell, W. J. McCarthy.
[79]Added after opening:
"Old Bill Baker (Undertaker)"
E. Truex
(*Lyrics by* Ring Lardner.)
[80]Variation on the popular Hawaiian song "On the Beach at Waikiki," music by Henry Kailimai, lyrics by G. H. Stover.

"When You Wear a 13 Collar" (Thirteen Collar)(Song)
E. Truex
"Old Boy Neutral" (Duet)
A. Orr, O. Shaw, Ensemble
"Babes in the Wood" (Duettino)
E. Truex, A. Dovey
(*Lyrics by* Jerome Kern, Schuyler Greene.)
Scene 2
"The Fashion Show" (Song)
J. Mills, Ensemble
"I Wish I Had a Million" (I'd Like to Have a Million in the Bank)(Song)
J. E. Hazzard, Girls
(*Lyrics by* Herbert Reynolds.)
"Nodding Roses" (Duet)
A. Orr, O. Shaw
(*Lyrics by* Herbert Reynolds, John, E. Hazzard.)
Finale
Ensemble

1915.31
STOP! LOOK! LISTEN!

A Musical Comedy in Three Acts, 8 Scenes. Book by Harry B. Smith. Music and lyrics by Irving Berlin. Staged by R. H. Burnside. Scenery and costumes designed by Robert McQuinn. Orchestra under the direction of Robert Hood Bowers. Orchestrations by Frank Saddler. Produced by Charles Dillingham. Opened 25 December 1915 at the Globe Theatre and closed 25 March 1916 after 105 performances.

CAST (in order of appearance): *Owen Coyne:* WALTER WILLS. *Members of Frivolity Theatre Company* (6): *Iona Carr:* Olga Olonova. *Nora Marks:* Tot Qualters. *Gladys Canby.* Helen Winter: Julia Beaubien. *May Knott:* Flo Hart. *Carrie Waite:* Ethel Sykes. *Gideon Gay,* a tired business man: FRANK LALOR. *Page Boy:* Helen Ellsworth. *Mary Singer,* a comic opera star: JUSTINE JOHNSTONE. *Mrs. Singer,* her ma: Florence Morrison. *Rob Ayers,* a librettist: JAMES DOYLE. *Frank Steele,* a composer: HARLAND DIXON. *Gaby,* only a chorus girl now, but just wait: GABY DESLYS. *Abel Connor,* a press agent: HARRY FOX. *Lotta Nichols,* a saleslady at newspaper stand: Helen Barnes. *Van Cortland Parke,* who wants to do people good: JOSEPH SANTLEY. *Deserving Poor Protegés of Van Cortland Parke* (5): *A Country Girl:* Claire Bertrand. *A Flower Girl:* Lillian Rice. *Salvation Sal:* Anna Stone. *An Irish Girl:* Grace Beaumont. *An Italian Girl:* Bobbie Reed. *The Magazine Girls* (4): *Spring:* Eleanor St. Clair. *Summer:* Marion Davies. *Autumn:* Evelyn Conway. *Winter:* Hazel Lewis. *Willie Chase:* FLORENCE TEMPEST. *Vera Gay:* MARION SUNSHINE. *Anthony St. Anthony,* a leading man: HARRY PILCER. *Lilla Kiliana,* a Hula Hula girl: BLOSSOM SEELEY. *Steward:* James Curran. *Violinist:* Charles Tucker.
Ensemble: *Hawaiian Octette:* E. K. Miller, Henry N. Clark, R. Kuaha, Dan C. Makaena, Robert Kaawa, James K. Ahloy, James I. Kamakani, James Ii, Al Kalani. *Soubrettes:* Misses Kathleen Cullen, Rose Leslie, Trixie Wilson, Neil Bertrand, Dorothy Clifford, May Clark, Fifi Hansworth, Julie Newell. *Lucile Girls:* Katherine Mack, Carolyn Heinz, Kitty Mahoney, Grace Williams, Elsie Lewis, Effie Wheeler, Bobbie Reed, Phyllis Munday. *Dancing Girls:* Grace Beaumont, Anna Stone, Cecil Markles, Madeline Dare, Evelyn LeRoy, Flo Lawlor, Lola Curtis, Lillian Rice. *Pages:* Rose Burns, Eileen Percy, Helen Ellsworth, Dorothy Davenport. *Bathing Girls:* Claire Bertrand, Iva Sherer, Tot Qualters, Flo Hart, Olga Olonova, May Clark, Dorothy Clifford, Neil Bertrand, Kathryn Wilson, Kathleen Cullen. *Pianists:* Messrs. Cliff Hess, James Curran, Henry Santley, Jack Stanley, William Noll, Sam Fineberg. *Designers:* William Mack, Leo Howe, Franz Kellar, Harry McMasters, Dan Bryant, Ken Griffin, Frank Gillespie, William Dunn. *Johnnies:* James Curran, Clyde Miller, Harry Vale, Roy Hoyer, D. Heilbrunn, Charles Hartmann, Herbert Goff, W. R. Gault.

Act 1, Scene 1: At the Costumer's. *Scene 2:* At the Railroad Station. *Scene 3:* At the Big Shop, Musical Department.

Act 2, Scene 1: At Honolulu. *Scene 2:* At Honolulu. *Scene 3:* On the Beach of Waikiki. *Scene 4:* At the Farm

Act 3: Gold Room of the 'All Night' Club.

ACT 1
Scene 1
Opening Chorus
Ensemble
"Blow Your Horn"
W. Wills, Girls
"Give Us a Chance"
G. Deslys, Girls

"I Love to Dance"
G. Delsys, H. Pilcer, Chorus
Scene 2
"And Father Wanted Me to Learn a Trade"
H. Fox
"The Girl on the Magazine"
J. Santley, Magazine Girls (4 Seasons)
Scene 3
"I Love a Piano"
H. Fox, Ensemble
Finale
Principals, Ensemble
ACT 2
Scene 1
Opening Chorus
Tourists, Natives
"The Hula Hula" (That Hula Hula)
T. Kosta, Ensemble
"A Pair of Ordinary Coons"
J. Doyle, H. Dixon
"When I'm Out with You"
G. Deslys, J. Santley, Ensemble
Scene 2
"On the Beach at Waiki-ki"[81]
Hawaiian Octette
(*Music by* Henry Kailimai. *Lyrics by* G. H. Stover.)
"One-Two-Three-Four"
Hawaiian Octette
(*Music by* Jack Alau. *Lyrics by* S. Kalama.)]
Scene 3
"Take Off a Little Bit"
G. Deslys, Girls
Scene 4
"Teach Me How to Love"[82]
F. Tempest, M. Sunshine
"The Law Must Be Obeyed"
J. Doyle, H. Dixon
"Ragtime Melodrama" (Finale)
Principals, Ensemble
ACT 3
"When I Get Back to the U.S.A."
J. Santley, Ensemble
"Stop! Look! Listen!" (Sexette)
W. Wills, F. Lalor, J. Doyle, H. Dixon, H. Fox, J. Santley
"I'll Be Coming Home with a Skate On"
H. Pilcer
"Everything in America Is Ragtime"
G. Deslys
Finale
Entire Company

1915.32
RUGGLES OF RED GAP

A Comedy in Four Acts (with Music). Play by Harrison Rhodes. Based on the Saturday Evening Post story of the same name by Harry Leon Wilson. Incidental music by Sigmund Romberg. Lyrics by Harold Atteridge. Staged by J. H. Benrimo. Costumes by the Shubert Costuming Company. Produced by the Messrs. Shubert. Opened 25 December 1915 at the Fulton Theatre and closed 22 January 1916 after 33 performances.[83]

---

[81]Replaced during the run by:
   "(Snooky) Ookums"
      F. Lalor, F. Morrison
[82]Moved during the run to Act 3, following "When I Get Back to the U.S.A.," where it was reassigned to G. Deslys and H. Fox.
[83]Settings and musical direction uncredited.

CAST (in order of appearance): *Mrs. Floud*, (Mrs. Effie): LOUISE CLOSSER HALE. *Mrs. Charles Belknap-Jackson*: LUCILE DALBERG. *Mr. Charles Belknap-Jackson*: Lynn Pratt. *Mr. Egbert Floud*, (Cousin Egbert): FREDERICK BURTON. *Waiter at Hotel Castiglione*: Jack Kelly. *The Honorable George Vane-Baseingwell*: GEORGE HASSELL. *Senator James Knox Floud*: James C. Malaidy. *Manager of Hotel Castiglione*: Frederick Osborne. *Mrs. Kenner*, (Klondike Kate): JOBYNA HOWLAND. *Alfred Ruggles*: RALPH HERZ. *The Earl of Brinstead*: Arthur Laceby. *Messenger from High-Life Tailor*: Irving Jackson. *A Girl Helper*: Ray Hartley. *A Messenger from the Shirtmaker's*: Dickie Kendall. *A Messenger from Cravat Dealer's*: Alma Hawly. *A Girl Helper*: Kittie Berg. *A Barber*: Gus Verace. *Proprietor of Booth*: John Hamilton. *Waiter at "Au Rendezvous des Cochers Fideles"*: Adrian H. Rosley. *Flower Girl*: Marie Vernon. *First French Soldier*: Billy Groves. *Second French Soldier*: Homer Potts. *A Cabman*: Francis Gaillard. *Jeff Tuttle*: Fred W. Strong. *Post Card Seller*: Austin Miller. *Street Singer*: Harriet Kneitel. *Girl Selling Songs*: Minnie Hart. *Watterman*: Philip Dunning. *Mrs. Pettingill*, (The Mixer): Jessie Ralph. *Mrs. Judge Ballard*: Adelaide Cumming. *Miss Beryl Mae Watson*: Viola Bowers. *Mrs. Henry P. Hartman*: Marion Fuller. *Mr. Henry P. Hartman*: Louis Arno. *Ed Perkins*, Society Reporter of the Red Gap Reporter: James Boyle. *Miss Frances Coolbrith*: Caroline Oden. *Mrs. Elmer J. Brown*: Leslie Marion. *Mrs. Dawson*: Grace Newton. *Hat Boy at the United States Grill*: Harold Nelson.

Act 1: Sitting Room of Mrs. Floud's Apartment, Hotel Castiglione, Paris.

Act 2: An Open Place, Montmarte, Paris.

Act 3: Library in Senator Floud's House, Red Gap.

Act 4: Lounge Room at the United States Grill, Red Gap.

MUSICAL NUMBERS[84]

"Beware of Love"

"Everybody Hum with Me"

"The Imp of Montmartre"

"Sing Me a Song of Love"

"When the Colored Regiment Goes Off to War"

1916.01   SYBIL

A Musical Comedy in Three Acts. Based on the original (Hungarian) operett 'Szibill' by Max Brody [Miksa Bródy] and Frank Martos [Ferenc Martos]. American version by Harry Graham and Harry B. Smith. Music by Victor Jacobi [Viktor Jacobi]. Produced under the stage direction of Fred G. Latham. Musical numbers staged by Julian Mitchell and Jack Mason. Scenery by Homer Emens. Costumes by Schneider-Anderson Company (ladies); Bendal (Miss Sanderson), Dazian (men). Orchestra under the direction of Harold Vicars. Produced by Charles Frohman. Opened 10 January 1916 at the Liberty Theatre and closed 3 June 1916 after 168 performances.

CAST: *Sybil Renaud*, Opera Singer: JULIA SANDERSON. *The Grand Duke Constantine*: DONALD BRIAN. *Otto Spreckles*, Impressario: JOSEPH CAWTHORN. *The Grand Duchess Anna Pavlovna*: JOSEPHINE WHITTELL. *The Governor of Bomsk*: GEORGE E. MACK. *Captain Paul Petrow*, Officer of the Guard: STEWART BAIRD. *The Duke's Aides-de-camp (2): Captain Dologow*: Walter Gilbert. *Lieutenant Koyander*: William Francis. *Count Milowski*, Court Courier: Jackson Hines. *Lieutenant Zelenoy*: Charles Lester. *Margot*, Spreckles' wife: MAISIE GAY. *Bortschakow*, Hotel Manager: Charles Hampden. *A Schoolmaster*: Clyde Crawford. *Cossack Officer*: Frank Markham. *Page Boy*: Master Statzes. *First Waiter*: Edward G. Yeager. *Second Waiter*: George Wharton. *Mr. Crighton*, tourist: Robert Markwell. *Mrs. Crighton*, tourist: Cynthia Latham. (*Dance Specialty*: Cissy Sewell.)

Waiters: Messes. Edward Yeager, William Hobart, George Wharton, Lester Ostrander, Joseph Tullar, Frank Snyder. *Waitresses*: Misses Eleanor Scott, Eunice MacKay, Millie Murray, Kathleen Lindley, Goldie Redding, Lillian Lavone. *Hotel Guests*: Misses Cynthia Latham, Clara Eckstrom, Emily Monte, Kathleen Edwards, Lenora Greenwood, Dorothy Banks, Prudence O'Shea, Marna Blanchard, Dorothy Banks, Yetla Nicholl, Louise Ward. Messrs. Frank Markham, George Ross, Russell Griswold, Charles Kamp, William Doyle, Clarence Lutz, Arthur Kugler, A. von Bereghy, Owen Jones, Frank Kenny. *Orphans*: Misses Gene Cole, Marie Francis, Helen Rintelen, Edith Allen, Helen Trainor, Dorice Wingrove, Alice Carrington, Frances Ceratt, Katherine Rodgers, Leona Francis. *Hussars*: Messrs. Frank Markham, Edward Yeager, William Hobart, Joseph Fuller, Owen Jones, William Kenny.

Act 1: The Office of the Grand Hotel, Bomsk, Russia.

Act 2: Room in the Governor's Palace.

Act 3: Entresol of the Grand Hotel.

ACT 1

Opening Chorus[85] (Politeness Pays, or All Hearts With a Keen Curiosity Burn)
 (C. Hampden)
 (*Lyrics by* Harry Graham.)

Chorus of Orphans
 (Orphans)

"At a Grand Hotel" (Duet)
 M. Gay, J. Cawthorn

"Letter Duet" (My Dearest Paul)(Duet)
 J. Sanderson, S. Baird

"Good Advice" (Duet)
 J. Sanderson, J. Cawthorn
 (*Lyrics by* Harry B. Smith.)

"The Colonel of the Crimson Hussars" (Song)
 J. Sanderson, Chorus

Finale (Sybil, Sybil! Your highness, I Should Say)

ACT 2

Opening Chorus (We're Feeling Overcome)

"A Cup of Tea"
 M. Gay

"Lift Your Eyes to Mine" (Duet)
 J. Sanderson, D. Brian, Chorus

"Following the Drum" (Song)
 M. Gay, Chorus

"Love May Be a Mystery" (Duet)
 J. Sanderson, D. Brian
 (*Lyrics by* Harry Graham.)

"I Can Dance with Everybody But My Wife" (Song)
 J. Cawthorn
 (*Music by* John Golden. *Lyrics by* John Golden and Joseph Cawthorn.)

"I Like the Boys" (Song)
 J. Sanderson, Chorus
 (*Lyrics by* Harry B. Smith.)

Finale (My wife! Good heavens!)

ACT 3

Opening Chorus (Goodnight, goodnight)

"Two Can Play at That Game" (Quartette)
 J. Sanderson, J. Whittell, D. Brian, S. Baird
 (*Lyrics by* Harry B. Smith.)

"Girls, You Are Such Wonderful Things" (Song)
 D. Brian, Ladies
 (*Lyrics by* Harry B. Smith.)

Dance
 D. Brian, C. Sewell

"When Cupid Calls" (The Rat-Tat-Tat Song)(Trio)
 J. Sanderson, D. Brian, J. Cawthorn
 (*Lyrics by* Harry B. Smith.)

Finale

1916.02   THE COHAN REVUE OF 1916

A Musical Crazy-Quilt, Patched Together, Threaded (Revue) in Two Acts, 14 Scenes. Book (sketches), music and lyrics by George M. Cohan. Staged by George M. Cohan. Costumes by Cora MacGeachy; Avon; Max Marx (men's). Scenery by Edward G. Unitt and Joseph Wickes. Orchestra under the direction of Charles J. Gebest. Produced by George M. Cohan and Sam H. Harris. Opened 9 February 1916 at the Astor Theatre and closed 1 July 1916 after 165 performances.

CAST: *The Jester*: JOHN HENDRICKS. *Captain Jones*, of the Salvation Army: WALTER BRAZIL. *Colonel Smith*, also of the Salvation Army: JOHN BOYLE. *Andrew Overdraft*, cannonball: JAMES C. MARLOWE. *H. H. Hobson*, boot maker: JAMES C. MARLOWE. *Mrs. Andrew Overdraft*, Andrew's wife: ELIZABETH M. MURRAY. *R. J. Carroll*, detective: PERCY AMES. *Major Barbara*, Overdraft's daughter: LILA RHODES. *Stephen Overdraft*, the son: FREDERICK SANTLEY. *Billy Holliday*, the bartender: HARRY DELF. *Dr. Booberang*, the love cure man: RICHARD CARLE. *Ed. Dundreary*, his valet: JOHN HENDRICKS. *Jane Clay*, the crying servant: VALLI VALLI. *Emily Stevenson*, the unchased woman: MISS JULIET. *Jean Paurel*,

[84]Musical numbers not listed in programs; list prepared from published sheet music (Schirmer, New York, 1915).

[85]Dropped for subsequent tour.

89

the great lover: CHARLES WINNINGER. *Young America*, a vagabond: LITTLE BILLY. *Jasper*, his dog: Alfred Latell. *Emma McChesney*, a saleswoman: MISS JULIET. *Sadie Love*, another saleswoman: ALICE HARRIS. *Gaby DeLys*, actress: MISS JULIET. *Bill Bones*, a pirate: JOHN HENDRICKS. *A Dancing Pirate*: JOHN BOYLE. *Another Dancing Pirate*: WALTER BRAZIL. *Flanigan*, an Irish guardsman: JAMES C. MARLOWE. *Manager of the Opera House*: JAMES C. MARLOWE. *Potter*, Paurel's dresser: HARRY DELF. *Basso*, of the Metropolitan: JOHN HENDRICKS. *Madam Sabattini*, also of the Metropolitan: LITTLE BILLY. *Judge Kinkead*: RICHARD CARLE. *B.P.O.E. Mason*: JAMES C. MARLOWE. *Mrs. Clay*: ELIZABETH M. MURRAY. *Owen Kildara*: FREDERICK SANTLEY. *Joe Silver*, a copper: HARRY BULGER. *Soldier*: Harry Delf. *Victory*: Dorothy Jane Londoner. *Defeat*: Anita Elson. *Soldier*: Harry Delf. *The God of War*: George Fredericks.

Members of the Chorus: Misses Thelma Pinder, Kitty deVere, Clara Whitford, Connie Magnet, Reba Kent, Marion Carroll, Hilda Smith, Lillian Johnson, Emily Morrison, Pearl Gabrielle, Florence Sandford, Catherine Grant, Grace Nolan, Goldie Foley, Grace Russell, Mathield Rodriguez, Dorothy Whitford, Gladdie McDonald, Gladys Siddons, Jeannie Dare, Virginia Allen, Hazel Frisbie, Martha Dean, Jean Murray, Josephine Rhodes, Billy Wilkins, Marjory Grace, Hazel Coulter, Dazie Burton, Virginia Steinhardt, Hazel Ellsworth, Florence Moore, Catherine Brady, Bobby Bertrand, Gertrude Harrison, Mabel Allen, Helen Learning. Messrs. John Rowe, Edward Geer, Charles Hessong, Arthur Engel, Walter Baker, Frank Duball, James O'Brien, Jack Brusch, Willard Barger, John Silbe, John Blue, Harry Rose, Bernard Druce, Burrell Rhodes, Frank Goldie, Murray Evans. *Boy Scouts*: George Lydiate, Daniel Hickey, John Kearney, John Lawless, Bert Roberts, Eugene Armento, Charles Impartore, Frank Griffiths, Thomas Deeby, Francis Armento, Richard Backman, George Bastedl, William Sample, John Kelly, Gardner James, Joseph Lycett.

The action takes place somewhere in Rhode Island at 8 o'clock.

Act 1, Scene 1: The Salvation Army Barracks. (Touching on "Major Barbara" and "Fair and Warmer.") *Scene 2*: Hobson's Boot Store. (Touching on Hobson's Choice.") *Scene 3*: Dr. Booberang's Office. (Touching on "The Booberang" and "The House of Glass.") *Scene 4*: In front of the Harvard Club. (Touching on "Young America.") *Scene 5*: Abe and Mawruss's Costume Establishment. (Touching on "Mrs. McChesney" and "Hit-the-Trail Holiday.") *Scene 6*: In front of the Punch and Judy Theatre (Touching on "Treasure Island.") *Scene 7*: Overdraft's Cannon Plant. (Touching on "Under Fire.")

Act 2, Scene 1: Interior of the Vanderbilt Hotel (Touching on "Sanderson, Brian and Cawthorne" and the Hippodrome.) *Scene 2*: In front of the Metropolitan Opera House. (Touching on Current Topics.) *Scene 3*: Jean Paurel's Dressing Room. (Touching on "The Great Lover.") *Scene 4*: In front of the Republic Theatre (Touching on Cohan Melodies.) *Scene 5*: The Common Clay Court Room. (Touching on "Common Clay.") *Scene 6*: Riverside Drive (Touching on Personalities.) *Scene 7*: Roof Garden. (Touching on Ziegfeld's Roof.)

ACT 1

Opening Chorus
  J. Hendricks, L. Rhodes, W. Brazil, J. Boyle, H. Bulger, Chrous

"He Can Cure You of Love"
  R. Carle, Chorus

"Crying Jane"
  V. Valli, Chorus

"The Fair and Warmer Cocktail"
  H. Delf, Chorus

"(It's a Long Way) From Broadway to Edinboro Town"
  J. C. Marlowe, Chorus

"(We'll Be) Alone at Last"
  V. Valli, C. Winninger

"You Can Tell That I'm Irish"
  E. M. Murray, Chorus

"Busy, Busy, Busy"
  A. Harris, Miss Juliet, Chorus

"My Musical Comedy Maiden"
  L. Rhodes, R. Carle

"Gaby"
  Miss Juliet, Chorus

"Running Around with the Chorus Girls"
  F. Santley, Chorus

"The Dancing Pirates"
  J. Boyle, W. Brazil

The "Under Fire" Dance
  H. Delf, D. J. Londoner, A. Elson

March
  Chorus

Boy Scouts' Drill[86]
  Boy Scouts

"Young America"
  Little Billy, Chorus

ACT 2

Opening Chorus
  J. Hendricks, Chorus

"Julia and Donald and Joe"[87]
  R. Carle, V. Valli, C. Winninger

Sousa Melodies
  Boys of the Chorus

A Harry Bulger Song
  H. Bulger

Dance Reminiscent
  J. Boyle, W. Brazil

Imitations
  Miss Juliet

"The Ziegfeld Rag"
  F. Santley, Chorus

"The 'Frisco Melody"
  A. Harris, Chorus

"The Balloon Girls"
  Chorus

Finale
  Entire Company

1916.03 ROBINSON CRUSOE, JR.

An Original Musical Extravaganza in Two Acts, 10 Scenes. Book and lyrics by Harold Atteridge and Edgar Smith. Music by Sigmund Romberg and James Hanley. Entire production staged by J. C. Huffman. Musical numbers staged by Allan K. Foster. Scenery designed by P. Dodd Ackerman, H. Robert Law, John Young. Costumes designed by Aloys Bohnen, Faibsey. Orchestra under the direction of Oscar Radin. Orchestrations by Oscar Radin and Frank Saddler. Produced by the Winter Garden Company (Messrs. Shubert.) Opened 17 February 1916 at the Winter Garden and closed 10 June 1916 after 139 performances.

CAST (in order of appearance): *Poindexter*: Lee Phelps. *Frank Speed*: Frank Holmes. *Bob Van Astor*: JOHNNY BERKES. *Jack Jitney*: FRANK GRACE. *Gladys Brookville*: Wanda Lyons. *Dorothy Hempstead*: Louisa Conti. *Hiram Westbury*: CLAUDE FLEMMING. *Captain Chichester*: LAWRENCE D'ORSAY. *Diana Westbury*: HELEN SHIPMAN. *Suzie Westbury*: KITTY DONER. *Mazie Underwood*: Rae Bowdin. *Howell Louder*, director of "The Shameless Players' Film Co.": BARRY LUPINO. *The Leading Lady* of "The Shameless Players' Film Co.": Jean Forbes. *The Soubrette* of "The Shameless Players' Film Co.": Eleanor Brown. *Miss Reel* of "The Shameless Players' Film Co.": Lois Whitney. *The Leading Man* of "The Shameless Players' Film Co.": Harry Wilcox. *The Star Feature* of "The Shameless Players' Film Co.": Mme. Comont. *The Camera Man* of "The Shameless Players' Film Co.": Bert Dunlap. *A Movie Actor* of "The Shameless Players' Film Co.": George Lavender. *Dick Hunter*, a 'speed bug': FRANK CARTER. *Gus Jackson*, his chauffeur: AL JOLSON. *First Constable*: Edward Bowers. *Second Constable*: Alfred Crocker. *Third Constable*: Frank Walters. *Robinson Crusoe*: CLAUDE FLEMMING. *Good Friday*: AL JOLSON. *Happy*: JOHNNIE BERKES. *Hotten*: FRANK GRACE. *Tot*: George Lavender. *A Cannibal*: Edward Bowers. *Chief Boola*: Alfred Crocker. *Zoola*: Frank Walters. *A Goat*: George Thornton. *Sailor Jim*: KITTY DONER. *Lady Diana*: HELEN SHIPMAN. *The Spaniard*: LAWRENCE D'ORSAY. *Captain Dick*, the pirate: FRANK CARTER. *The Spirit of Captain Kidd*: Frank Holmes. *The Voodoo Lady*: Ada Androva. *Flip*: FRANK GRACE. *Trip*: JOHNNIE BERKES. *A Pirate*: James Conners. *Sailor Frank*: FRANK GRACE. *Sailor Johnnie*: JOHNNIE BERKES. *Liverpool Jake*: Edward Bowers. *Boozey Bill*: Alfred Crocker. *Shanghai Joe*: Frank Walters. *José*: FRANK CARTER. *Manuel*: KITTY DONER. *Vanilla*: HELEN SHIPMAN. *Slave Girls*: Wanda Lyons, Louisa Conti, Eleanor Brown, Lois Whitney. *Tuffghi*: BARRY LUPINO. *Coco Cola*: Rae Bowdin. *Sailor*: Lee Phelps. *Bamboozla*: Lawrence D'Orsay. *Bacnumber*: Mme. Comont. *Fatima*: AL JOLSON. *Lillian*: Eleanor Brown. *Louisa*: Lois Whitney. *Rosita*, a Spanish dancer: Isabel Rodriguez.

---

[86]Renamed during the run:
  Cohan Cadet Drill
    Cohan Cadets

[87]A Burlesque on the trio of stars of SYBIL, Donald Brian, Joseph Cawthorn and Julia Sanderson.

Papita: Dot Rozelle. *Carlo*: BARRY LUPINO. *Gladys*: Wanda Lyons. *Helen DeHazzard*: Mme. Comont.

Personnel of the Chorus: Misses Helen Hudson, Elizabeth Drew, Helen Carrington, Helen Neat, Sue Nally, Peggy Loris, Florence Nelson, Phyllis Grey, Alice Humphries, Ruth Christie, Gladys Benjamin, Florence Elmore, Carroll Beerd, Marie Wiereman, Evelyn Carberry, Vivian Darville, May Poth, Dorothy Barnet, Kathryn Perry, Martha Ehrlich, Betty Randolph, Jean White, Rae Hartley, Mildred Stokes, Cecele Arno, Kathryn Perry, Mabel Hill, Marion Mooney, Pearl Weber, Fay Arthur, Kathryn Johnson, Mabel Booth, Peggy Smith, Marie Leonard, Elino Wallace, Laura McLure, Margaret Carmen, Marjorie Dayton, Irene Mitchell, Mae Chesterly, Ethel Kinley, Caroline Maywood, Faye Atkins, Pearl Eaton, Edna Eaton, Agnes Hall, Grace Hall, Ona Hamilton, Viola Watson, Mabel Grete, Viola Quinn, Jean Hackett, Dot Rozelle, Gladys Turner, Mildred Simon, Babe Dakin, Agnes Richter, Mabel Winters, Ruth Maybee. Messrs. Peter O'Neill, Harry Nelson, Al Watson, Harry Davis, Bert Dunlap, Clint Russell, Leon Shack, Harry Cohen, Harry Wilcox, William Morris, Homer Potts, James Conners.

Act 1, Scene 1: Hiram Westbury's Summer Home, Westbury Towers, Westbury Road, Long Island. *Scene 2*: The Arbor on Westbury's Grounds. *Scene 3*: Robinson Crusoe's Island. *Scene 4*: The Haunted Forest. *Scene 5*: Another Part of the Island. *Scene 6*: Cabin of the Pirate Ship, *Skull and Bones*. *Scene 7*: The Deck of the Pirate Ship.

Act 2, Scene 1: The Silver City, Ragmachottschie. *Scene 2*: The Arbor on Westbury's Grounds. *Scene 3*: The Ballroom at Westbury Towers.

ACT 1[88]

Scene 1

Opening Chorus
    Entire Chorus
"Simple Life"
    C. Flemming, Chorus
    (*Music by* Sigmund Romberg.)
"(You'll Have to) Gallop Some"
    K. Doner, Chorus
    (*Music by* Sigmund Romberg.)
"When You're Starring in the Movies"
    B. Lupino, J. Forbes, Chorus
    (*Music by* Sigmund Romberg.)
"(Go Ahead and) Dance a Little More"
    F. Carter, K. Doner, B. Lupino, J. Berkes, F. Grace, Chorus
    (*Music by* James F. Hanley.)

Scene 2

"Way Down Upon the Suwanee River" (Down Where the Swanee River Flows)
    A. Jolson
    (*Music by* Albert von Tilzer. *Lyrics by* Charles S. Alberte and Charles McCarron.)
"Now He's Got a (Beautiful) Girl"
    A. Jolson
    (*Music by* Ted Snyder. *Lyrics by* Edgar Leslie and Grant Clarke)
"(Pretty Little) Mayflower Girl"
    F. Carter, H. Shipman
    (*Music by* James F. Hanley.)

Scene 3

"Happy Hottentots"
    F. Grace, J. Berkes, Chorus
    (*Music by* Sigmund Romberg.)
Song[89]
    A. Jolson

Scene 4

"My Voodoo Lady" (My Voodoo Maiden)
    A. Androva, Chorus
    (*Music by* Sigmund Romberg.)

---

[88]All Lyrics by Harold Atteridge except as noted.
[89]Jolson's Specialty Songs:
    "Where Did Robinson Crusoe Go with Friday on Saturday Night?"
        (*Music by* George W. Meyer. *Lyrics by* Sam M. Lewis and Joe Young.)
    "I Sent My Wife to the Thousand Isles"
    "You're a Dangerous Girl"
        (*Music by* James V. Monaco. *Lyrics by* Grant Clarke.)
    Added Jolson Specialty during subsequent National Tour:
    "Where the Black-Eyed Susans Grow"
        (*Music by* Richard A. Whiting. *Lyrics by* Dave Radford.)

Scene 5

Fast Steppers
    F. Grace, J. Berkes
Scene 6

"Don't Be a Sailor"
    K. Doner, F. Grace, J. Berkes, Chorus
    (*Music by* Sigmund Romberg.)
"Sailor's Fling"
    E. Bowers, A. Crocker, F. Walters
"(My) Pirate Lady"
    F. Carter, Chorus
    (*Music by* Sigmund Romberg.)
Scene 7

Finale
    Entire Company
ACT 2

Scene 1

Opening Number
    Entire Chorus
"Robinson Crusoe"
    C. Flemming
    (*Music by* Sigmund Romberg and James F. Hanley.)
Scene 2

"Spinning a Yarn"
    W. Lyons, Chorus
    (*Music and Lyrics by* John Golden.)
"Yaaka Hula Hickey Dula" (Yacki Hicki Doola)
    A. Jolson
    (*Music by* Pete Wendling. *Lyrics by* E. Ray Goetz and Joe Young)
"Tillie Titwillow"
    A. Jolson
    (*Music by* Phil Schwartz. *Lyrics by* Harold Atteridge.)
Scene 3

The Spanish Ballet
    Mlle. Rodriguez, B. Lupino, Ensemble
"Hunter's Fox-Trot Ball"
    F. Carter, Girls
A Dance
    B. Lupino
"Minstrel Days"
    K. Doner, (Chorus)
    (*Music by* Phil Schwartz.)
Finale
    Entire Ensemble

POM-POM

1916.04

A Comic Opera in Two Acts. Book and lyrics by Anne Caldwell. (Based on the libretto for the Hungarian operett 'Csibészkirály' by Lajos Széll and Akos Buttykay.) Music by Hugo Felix. Staged by George Marion. Scenery designed by Joseph Urban. Gowns from DeWolfe Wachner Company; Freisinger; Frances, Inc (Miss Hajos). Orchestra under the direction of Max Bendix. Produced by Henry W. Savage. Opened 28 February 1916 at the George M. Cohan Theatre and closed 17 June 1916 after 128 performances.

CAST (in order of appearance): *Count de Joie*: George Brugger. *Manager of the Olympia*: Eric Campbell. *Evelyn, Paulette's maid*: EDITH DAY. *Policeman No. 13*: TOM McNAUGHTON. *Secretary to Manager of the Olympia*: Allan Kelly. *The Author*: Charles Angelo. *Paulette, first appearance as Pom-Pom, the pickpocket*: MITZI HAJOS. *A Critic*: Ben Lewin. *Stage Carpenter of the Olympic*: Thomas Wood. *Bertrand, Chief of Municipal Detectives*: CARL GANTVOORT. *Grolmus, Burglar-in-Chief*: Thomas Walsh. *Macache, a burglar*: William Eville. *Bidage, a burglar*: Harry Childs. *Therese, a confidence woman*: RITA DANE. *Cina, a thief*: EDITH DAY. *Jean, a hold-up man*: Thomas Wood. *Papa Chapelle, Sanctimonious Thief*: George Brugger. *Big Biassou, Colossus of Thieves*: DETMAR POPPEN. *Ballet Girls at the Olympia (3)*: *Lucie*: Marion Owen. *Gabriella*: Eleanor Williams. *Rosa*: Blanche Terrill. *A Policeman*: Victor LeRoy. *A Detective*: Rupert Greenlaw. *The Dummy*: Phyllis Davis. *Crevette*: Signe Paterson. *Gigolo*: Frank Hale. *Flic*: Carl Judd.

Evelyn Girls: Misses Mathewson, Temple, Robinson, Page, Livingston, Harvey, Williams, Borden. *Shop Lifters*: Misses Mellette, Forbes, Calame, Frances, McFarland, Thaler. *Women with Babies*: Misses Borden, Hamlin, Heylman, Terrill, Graves,

Williams. *Apaches*: Misses Flandreaux, LaMoyne, Owen, Quiller. Messrs. Murphy, Dickson, Greenlaw, Jurist. *Blind Men*: Messrs. McShane, Ritter, LeRoy, Judd.

The action takes place in Nice at the present time.

Act 1, Scene 1: Green Room, Olympia Theatre. *Scene 2*: Foyer of the Olympia Theatre. *Scene 3*: Yard of the Police Precinct Station.

Act 2: At the Black Elephant.

ACT 1
Opening Chorus
"Come and Cuddle Me"
    T. McNaughton, E. Day
"Only One Hour"
    C. Gantvoort
"Pom-Pom"
    M. Hajos, Chorus
"Zim-Zim"
    T. Walsh, W. Eville, H. Childs
"She's Gone"
    Ensemble
"Mon Désir"
    R. Dane, C. Gantvoort
"In the Dark"
    M. Hajos, Male Chorus

ACT 2
Opening Chorus
"The Army of Crooks"
    Ensemble
Tornado Dance
    F. Hale, S. Paterson
"Evelyn"
    M. Hajos, Chorus
"I'm Unlucky"
    T. McNaughton
    (*Music by* Jean Schwartz. *Lyrics by* William Jerome.)
"Mister Love"
    E. Day, S. Patterson, F. Hale, C. Judd
"Ships in the Night"
    C. Gantvoort, R. Dane
"The Circus in the Moon"
    M. Hajos, T. McNaughton
"Kiss Me"
    M. Hajos, C. Gantvoort
"You Shall Not Go"
    M. Hajos, Principals, Chorus
Finale

1916.05   THE ROAD TO MANDALAY

A Comic Opera in Two Acts. Book by W. H. Post. Music by Oreste Vessella. Lyrics by William McKenna. Staged by William J. Wilson. Gowns (for Misses. Lucey, Kirke and Eastman) by Miss Tafel. Orchestra under the direction of Antonio DeNovellis. Produced by the Orella Producing Co., Inc. Opened 1 March 1916 at the Park Theatre and closed 18 March 1916 after 21 performances.[90]

CAST (in order of appearance): *Ensign Tom Ballantine*: John Roberts. *Lieutenant Steve North*: Stanley C. Ridges. *Alphonse Vivani, proprietor of the Rising Moon Tea House*: EDDIE "Cupid" MORRIS. *Mrs. Everleigh Fitzhugh, a globe-trotter*: MARIE HORGAN. *Yvette, wife of Alphonse*: GRETCHEN EASTMAN. *Rose Montgomery*: HAZEL KIRKE. *Lily Montgomery*: LEOLA LUCEY. *Lieutenant Jack Poindexter*: FRANK POLLOCK. *Hiram Montgomery, a retired molasses manufacturer*: HERBERT CORTHELL. *Singh Poontano, Boom and Chief of Police of Rangoon*: LAWRENCE GRANT. *Mharajah's Dancer*: Doraldina. *Tourists, Naval Officers, Sailors, Natives, Guards, Eunuchs, Waiters, Ladies of the Harem, Fan Bearers, etc.*: (unidentified).

The action takes place at the present time in Rangoon, India.

---

[90]Settings uncredited.

Act 1: Exterior of the Rising Moon Tea House, Rangoon. Afternoon.

Act 2: Gardens of Hiram Montgomery's residence in the suburbs of Rangoon. One week later.

ACT 1
"Tourists" (Opening)
    G. Eastman, Officers
"Sail Away"
    F. Pollock
"Shadows" (Solo)
    G. Eastman, E. Morris
"Looking for a Girl My Size"
    H. Corthell, Chorus
"You'll Find the Party Isn't There" (Song)
    E. Morris
"Heart of My Heart" (Duet)
    L. Lucey, F. Pollock
"Arrival of the Boom" (Ensemble)
    Company
"Imagination" (Trio)
    L. Grant, E. Morris, G. Eastman
"(The) Road to Mandalay" (Finale)
    H. Kirke, Company

ACT 2
"Moonlight Gavotte"
    Company
"Waltz" (Dance)
    S. C. Ridges, V. Gauran
"(The) Firefly"
    L. Lucey, Chorus
"Father's Whiskers" (Song)
    H. Corthell
"Bright Day's Dawning" (Trio)
    L. Lucey, H. Kirke, M. Horgan
"Till You Try" (Duet)
    H. Corthell, M. Horgan
"(The) Ocean of Dreams" (Waltz Song)
    F. Pollock, L. Lucey, Company
"Back to Paris" (Duet)
    G. Eastman, E. Morris
Oriental Dance
    Doraldina
"See America First" (Finale)
    H. Corthell, Company

1916.06   SEE AMERICA FIRST

A Comic Opera in Two Acts. Book by T. Lawrason Riggs. Music and lyrics Cole Porter. Staged by J. H. Benrimo. Dances arranged by Edward Hutchinson. Dances arranges by Edward Hutchinson and Theodore Kosloff. Costumes designed by Homer Conant and Melville Ellis. Settings designed by Frank Gates and E. A. Morange. Orchestra under the direction of Clarence West. Produced by Elisabeth Marbury. Opened 28 March 1916 at the Maxine Elliott Theatre and closed 8 April 1916 after 15 performances.

CAST (in order of appearance): *Lo, The Poor Indian*: Henry Red Eagle. *Notonah*: JEANNE CARTIER. *Percy*: CLIFTON WEBB. *Guy*: Leo Gordon. *Marmaduke*: Lloyd Carpenter. *Cecil, Duke of Pendragon*: JOHN GOLDSWORTHY. *Sarah*: CLARA PALMER. *Algernon*: Algernon Greig. *Chief Blood-in-His-Eye*: FELIX ADLER. *Ethel*: Roma June. *Gwendolyn*: Betty Brewster. *Muriel*: Gypsy O'Brien. *Polly Higgens*: DOROTHIE BIGELOW. *Senator Huggins*: SAM EDWARDS. *Dancing with Clifton Webb*: JEANNE CARTIER.

American Buds: Adele Christy, Bettina Best, Dorothy Mead, Alice Yorke, Ruth Darby, Mary Howard, Margaret MacKenzie, Lucine Paula, Edna Coigne, Helen Herendeen, Irma Chase, Daisy Rudd. *Younger Sons of Peers*: Ernest Clarke, Jack Bohn, Robert Casey, William Warren, Eric Block, Don Seaton, Jack Hagner, Perry C. Smith, Harry Pahl, Ray Klages, Jack Varnell, Frank Shephard.

Act 1: On the Mesa.

Act 2: In the Forest.

ACT 1

Dawn Music

"Indian Girls' Chant"

"Badmen" [Opening Chorus]
    Ensemble

"To Follow Every Fancy"
    J. Goldsworthy, Younger Sons

"Indian Maidens' Chorus"
    R. June, B. Brewster, G. O'Brien, Buds

"Something's Got to Be Done"
    F. Adler, C. Palmer

"I've (Got) an Awful Lot to Learn"
    D. Bigelow, Buds

"Beautiful, Primitive Indian Girls"
    C. Webb, R. June, B. Brewster, G. O'Brien, Younger Sons, Buds

"Hold-Up Ensemble"
    J. Goldsworthy, S. Edwards, Younger Buds

"See America First"
    S. Edwards

"The Language of Flowers"
    C. Webb, J. Cartier

"Damsel, Damsel" (Prithee Come Crusading with Me)
    J. H. Goldsworthy, D. Bigelow

"The Lady I've Vowed to Wed"
    Principals, Ensemble

Finale (Hail the Female Relative)
    Principals, Ensemble

ACT 2

Opening Chorus (Mirror, Mirror)
    Chorus

"Ever and Ever Yours"
    D. Bigelow, J. Goldsworthy

"Lima"
    C. Palmer

"Will You Love Me (When My Flivver Is a Wreck)?" (Ballade)
    F. Adler

Woodland Dance[91]
    C. Webb, J. Cartier

"Buy Her a Box at the Opera"
    D. Bigelow, Younger Sons

"I've a Shooting Box in Scotland"
    J. Goldsworthy, D. Bigelow, Younger Sons

"When I Used to Lead the Ballet"
    F. Adler, Younger Songs, Buds

Finale
    Principals, Chorus

1916.07 ## COME TO BOHEMIA

A Story of the Latin Quarter (Musical Play) in Two Acts, 6 Scenes. Book and lyrics by George S. Chappell. Music by Kenneth M. Murchison, (Raymond Hubbell). Produced under the direction of Jacques Coini. Scenery designed by Rockwell Kent. Girls' costumes desiged by O'Kane Conwell; men's costumes by Mahieu and Lanzilotti. Music director, Theodore Stier. Produced by the Stuyvesant Producing Company. Opened 27 April 1916 at the Maxine Elliott Theatre and closed 13 May 1916 after 20 performances.

CAST: *Madeleine D'Orsay*: NATALIE ALT. *Gaston D'Orsay*: WILLIAM DANFORTH. *Andre LeGrand*: WALTER PERCIVAL. *Mme. Zenobie D'Orsay*: CLARA PALMER. *Jean Paul Marinarde*: DENMAN MALEY. *Dustin Banks*: FRITZ WILLIAMS. *Mimi Clairon*: OLIVE REEVES-SMITH. *Baux*: Donald MacMillan. *Mazet*: Joseph Harris. *Count de LaTour*: Percy Woodley. *Charvet*, lawyer: Gilbert Clayton. *Pierre*, headwaiter: Henry Watson. *Louis*: Paisley Noon. *François*: Richard Hall. *Gendarme*: Malcolm Barrett. *Guy*: Max Scheck. *Julie*: Loretta Brady. *Helene*: Diane Lemee. *Ernestine*: Edna Kraft. *Christine*: Violette von Nickol.

Yvonne: Ora Keeler. *Melisande*: Ruth Price. *Marthe*: Lilian Baker *Gabrielle*: Helen Dentler. *Angele*: Billie Vernon. *Leontine*: Harriet DuBarry. *Georgette*: Betty Millar. *Marguerite*: Bessie Carey. *Berthe*: June White. *Francine*: TEDDY HUDSON. *Lili*: Edna Stillwell. *Marie*: Helen Larkins. *Jeanne*: Olive Massey. *Venus*: Thyra von Ulm.

Dancers: Fred J. Nice, Ada Mae Weeks. *Students*: Messrs. Gibson, Kavanaugh, Coombs, Paulaney, St. John, Barlow.

The action takes place in Paris in 1912.

Act 1: Studio of Mme. D'Orsay, 5 Rue St. Benoit. 10 o'clock on a May morning.

Act 2, Scene 1: American Bar. Bal des Quat'z' Arts. *Scene 2*: Stage Door. Theatre de la Gaieté Montparnasse. *Scene 3*: Interior. Theatre de la Gaieté Montparnasse. *Scene 4*: Same as Scene 2. *Scene 5*: Exterior. Café des Deux Magots, Place St. Germain-des-Prés.

ACT 1

Opening Chorus
    Chorus

"Any Time, Any Place, Anywhere"
    T. Hudson, Chorus

"Sounds from Home"
    W. Danforth, Chorus

"Deep in the Heart"
    N. Alt

"(In) Poster-land"
    N. Alt, W. Percival
    (*Music by* Raymond Hubbell. *Lyrics by* Glen MacDonough.)

"Friendship"
    W. Percival, Students

"Fashionable Life"
    N. Alt, C. Palmer, W. Danforth, P. Woodley

"Come and Fuss with Me"
    T. Hudson, Students

Finale

ACT 2

Scene 1

Opening Chorus

"The Big Brass Band"
    T. Hudson, Chorus

"She Doesn't Exist at All"
    W. Percival, Chorus
    (*Music by* Raymond Hubbell. *Lyrics by* Glen MacDonough.)

"The Shimmering Nile" (On the Shimmering, Glimmering Nile)
    W. Danforth, C. Palmer, Chorus
    (*Music by* Raymond Hubbell. *Lyrics by* Glen MacDonough.)

"Marche des Pompiers"
    Chorus

"When Somebody Isn't There"
    N. Alt, Students
    (*Music by* Raymond Hubbell. *Lyrics by* Glen MacDonough.)

"The Walking Walkover"
    F. J. Nice, A. M. Weeks

"The Days of Romance"
    N. Alt, W. Percival

"Bohemia"
    T. Hudson, Ensemble

Scene 2

"High Art"
    C. Palmer, F. Williams

Scene 4

"Run Along, Little Man"
    T. Hudson, Messrs. Noon, Scheck

Scene 5

"Has Anybody Seen the Waiter?"
    P. Woodley, P. Noon, R. Hall, Chorus

Specialty Dance
    F. J. Nice, A. M. Weeks

"Come to Bohemia"
    N. Alt, Chorus

Finale

---

[91]Woodland Dance arranged by Theodore Kosloff.

1916.08

MOLLY O'

An Operetta in Two Acts. Book and lyrics by Harry B. Smith and Robert B. Smith. Based on a story of Giovanni Boccaccio. Music by Carl Woess. Produced under the stage direction of George Marion. Scenery designed by H. Robert Law. Orchestra under the direction of Clarence West. Orchestrations by Clarence West. Produced by John Cort. Opened 17 May 1916 at the Cort Theatre and closed 24 June 1916 after 45 performances.

CAST (in order of appearance): *Mrs. Kean*, who introduces the O'Malley's into society: AUDREY MAPLE. *Princess DeTogueville*: Mabel Josephine Harris *Prince deTogueville*: Count deVassey. *Hiram J. Kidder*, Dan O'Malley's social Guide: DAN QUINLAN. *Freddy Sands*, a little brother of the rich: JOHN E. YOUNG. *Mrs. Prunella O'Malley*, with social aspirations: JOSIE INTROPODI. *Dan O'Malley*, self-made and proud of the job: TOM LEWIS. *Josette*, a Viennese artist: GRACE FIELD. *Hal Rutherford*, in love with Josette: DONALD MACDONALD. *Count Walter von Walden*: THOMAS CONKEY. *Molly O'Malley*: KATHERINE GALLOWAY. *Dance Specialty in State and Flirtation Dance*: Weily and Ten Eyck. *Bridesmaids (6): Prudence Page*: Elizabeth Hines. *Sylvia Shaw*: Estelle Francesca. *Helen Butler*: Anita Francesca. *Laura Putnam*: Ray Lloyd. *Agnes Fielding*: Helen Hillarde. *Louise Darling*: Marion Comfort. *Daisy, Rose*, flower girls: Hilda Hand, Florence Cassidy. *Willie Speed*: Trixie Warren. *Georgette*: Vivian Morrison. *Victor*: Joseph Miller. *Mariette*: Anita Francesca. *Gaston*: James Whelan. *Manuel*: Donald Crane. *Wedding Guests, Maskers, Students, etc.*

Act 1: The O'Malley Villa, Newport.

Act 2: Students' Ball, Vienna.

ACT 1[92]

>   Opening Chorus
>>   Ensemble
>
>   "Anna of Havana"
>>   J. E. Young
>
>   "Marry Me and See" (Duet)
>>   G. Field, D. Macdonald
>
>   "The Right Girl"
>>   T. Conkey, Chorus
>
>   "Love Is an Art"
>>   K. Galloway, Chorus
>
>   "The Girl That Wins My Heart"
>>   J. E. Young, Chorus
>
>   "When Fortune Smiles (on You)"
>>   K. Galloway
>
>   "The Voice of Love"
>>   T. Conkey, K. Galloway
>
>   "One Way of Doing It" (Trio)
>>   J. E. Young, D. Macdonald, G. Field
>
>   Finale
>>   Ensemble

ACT 2

>   Opening Chorus
>>   Ensemble
>
>   "Isn't That Like a Man"
>>   D. Macdonald, G. Field
>
>   "Aesop Was a Very Moral Man"
>>   A. Maple, Girls
>
>   "Marionettes"
>>   J. E. Young, G. Field, D. Macdonald, A. Maple
>
>   "Champagne and Laughter"
>>   K. Galloway
>
>   Dance
>>   G. Field, D. Crane
>
>   Auction Scene
>>   Ensemble
>
>   "Little Women" (Quartette)
>>   T. Conkey, T. Lewis, J. E. Young, D. Macdonald

---

[92]Lyrics in piano vocal score credited to Robert B. Smith.

>   Finale
>>   Ensemble

1916.09

STEP THIS WAY

A Musical Production (Comedy) in Two Acts. Book by Edgar Smith. Based on his libretto for the musical "The Girl Behind the Counter." Music by E. Ray Goetz and Bert Grant. Lyrics by E. Ray Goetz. Production staged by Frank McCormack. Musical ensembles and dances by Jack Mason. Settings by (Edward) Sundquist Studio, P. Dodd Ackerman. Gowns and costumes by Orange; Mme. Kahn. Orchestra under the direction of Frank E. Tours. Orchestrations by Frank Saddler. Produced by Lew Fields. Opened 29 May 1916 at the Sam S. Shubert Theatre, moved 10 July 1916 to the Astor Theatre, and closed 12 August 1916 after 88 performances.

CAST (in order of appearance): *Maggie* at the wrapping desk: Fannie Hasbrouck. *Mitzi Gossard*: Louise Clark. *Miss Billings*: Virginia Richardson. *Mrs. M. Whittington*: Martha Erlich. *Henri Duval*, a Parisian expert in millinery and lingerie, and general manager of the "Universal,' an American department store in London: CHARLES JUDELS. *Mrs. Crossleigh Shoppington*: Nan J. Brennan. *Ninette Valois* of the millinery department: LAURA HAMILTON. *Susie Scraggs*, assistant cashier of the "Universal': GLADYS CLARK. *Dudley Cheatham*, cashier of the 'Universal' and imbued with the American idea of high finance: HENRY BERGMAN. *Millie Mostyn*, "overlady" at the "Universal,' with a tender spot in her heart for Gussie: MARGUERITE FARRELL. *Mrs. Henry Schniff*, a former landlady, in whom the sudden accession of wealth has awakened a desire for social preferment: Alice Fischer. *Winnie Willoughby*, Mrs. Schiff's daughter, who has been under the refining influences of boarding school, but has nevertheless sound ideal concerning life in general and matrimony in particular: BETH LYDY. *Henry Schniff*, a soldier of misfortune, dazzled by the sudden transition from life in a boarding house in Gower Street to a butterfly existence in Easy Street: LEW FIELDS. *Charles Chetwynd*, a self-made young millionaire: JOHN CHARLES THOMAS. *Lord Augustus Gushington*, familiarly known as 'Gussie,' the proprietor of an empty title, an empty purse and an equally empty head: ERNEST TORRENCE. *The Honorable Bertie Epsom*: LEW BRICE. *Willard Fitzcorbett*, a waiter: Charles Mitchell. *Hawaiian Dancer*: DORALDINA.

Models, Customers, etc.: Misses Dorothy Leeds, Edna Rochelle, Virginia Taylor, Margaret Vingut, Gladys Dupell, Faun Conway, Selma Morris, Frances Morris, Harriet Gustin, Perle Germonde, Esther Solon, Virginia Richardson, Hortense Taylor, Mabel Godding. *Salesladies, etc.*: Misses Nancy Smith, Maida Burka, Mildred Keenan, Inez Borrero, Bobbie McCormack, Louise Clark, Bessie Gray, Lolita Whitmore. *Cash Girls, etc.*: Misses Betty Hamilton, Alice Van Ryker, Trixie Smith, Betty Brown, Adele Christie, Betty Shannon, Violet Marsden, Frances Mink, Jean Russell, Kitty Mahoney. *Elevator Boys, etc.*: Misses Esther Shannon, Lotta Morse, Cecile Carter, Dorothy Flamm. *The High Steppers*: Misses Violet Pardue, Gwendolyn Pardue, Ethel Hobart, Ethel Rosebud, Peggy Trevor, Maud Homer, May Homer, Kitty Donnelly. *Floorwalker, etc.*: Messrs. James Clark, William Kinley, Kenneth Christy, Walter Mozee, Joseph McGurgan, Jock Donnelly, Lionel Spencer, James Smith, George O'Donnell, Al Cooper.

Act 1: Interior of the 'Universal,' a department store in London on the American plan with unlimited scope and ability to furnish everything from a spool of thread to a swell society function. (Sundquist.)

Act 2: The garden of the 'Jardin de Paris' at Hammersmith, devoted to the first class entertainment of second class people. (Ackerman.)

ACT 1

>   "Keep Up the Pace" (Opening Chorus)
>>   Ensemble
>
>   "Step This Way"
>>   C. Judels, Chorus
>
>   "Romany" (When the Sun Goes Down in Romany)
>>   G. Clark, H. Bergman
>>   (*Music by* Bert Grant. *Lyrics by* Sam M. Lewis, Joe Young.)
>
>   "The Heart of the Golden West"
>>   J. C. Thomas
>
>   "Kelly" (If I Knock the 'L' Out of Kelly)
>>   M. Farrell, Chorus
>>   (*Music by* Bert Grant. *Lyrics by* Sam M. Lewis, Joe Young.)
>
>   "You Ought To Go to Paris"
>>   L. Hamilton, Rumbo and the High Steppers
>
>   "Won't You Buy?"
>>   B. Lydy, J. C. Thomas

Finale
  Ensemble

ACT 2[93]

Opening Chorus
  Ensemble
"Frivolity" (dance)
  Eight High Steppers
"Love Me at Twilight"
  B. Lydy, Chorus
  (*Music by* Bert Grant. *Lyrics by* William Jerome, Joe Young.)
"I've Got a Sweet Tooth (Bothering Me)"
  G. Clark, H. Bergman
  (*Music and Lyrics by* Irving Berlin.)

"Cairo" (When You Drop Off at Cairo, Illinois)
  M. Farrell, Chorus
  (*Music and Lyrics by* Cliff Hess and E. Ray Goetz.)
"By the Sad Luana Shore"
  G. Clark, H. Bergman, Chorus
  (*Music and Lyrics by* E. Ray Goetz.)
Hawaiian Dance
  Doraldina and Her Hawaiian Band
"All for You"
  B. Lydy, J. C. Thomas
Finale
  Ensemble

---

[93]Added during the run to Act 2, after "I've Got a Sweet Tooth":
  "The Call of Love"
    J. C. Thomas

Anna Held in FOLLOW ME (Photo: White, 1916)
Museum of the City of New York, Gift of Miss Leonie Sigrist, 46.404.66

1916–1917 SEASON

1916.10 ZIEGFELD FOLLIES OF 1916

A Musical Revue in Two Acts, 22 Scenes[1]. Sketches by George V. Hobart and Gene Buck. Music by Louis A. Hirsch, Irving Berlin, Jerome Kern, Dave Stamper. Lyrics by Gene Buck. Staged by Ned Wayburn. Scenery designed by Joseph Urban. Costumes designed by Lady Duff-Gordon, Cora MacGeachy, Alice O'Neil. Orchestra under the direction of Frank Darling. Produced by Florenz Ziegfeld. Opened 12 June 1916 at the New Amsterdam Theatre and closed 16 September 1916 after 112 performances.

CAST: FANNIE BRICE, BERT WILLIAMS, W. C. FIELDS, INA CLAIRE, ANN PENNINGTON, FRANCES WHITE, BERNARD GRANVILLE, EMMA HAIG, JUSTINE JOHNSTONE, DON BARCLAY, SAM B. HARDY, MARION DAVIES, ALLYN KING, TOT QUALTERS, CARL RANDALL, WILLIAM ROCK, LILYAN TASHMAN, Gertrude Scott, Hazel Lewis, Gladys Loftus, Grace Jones, May Carmen, Helen Barnes, Gladys Feldman, Evelyn Conway, Ethel Callahan, Arthur Whitman, Clay Hill, Peter Swift, Norman Blume, Bird Millman, Misses Gunther, Paul, Hart.

ACT 1[2]

Scene 1

Prologue: The Birth of Elation

Scene: In the Park of Phantasy.
Puck: E. Haig. *William Shakespeare*: W. Rock. *George M. Cohan*: C. Randall. *Follies Girl of 1907*: G. Scott. *Follies Girl of 1908*: H. Lewis. *Follies Girl of 1909*: G. Loftus. *Follies Girl of 1910*: G. Jones. *Follies Girl of 1911*: M. Carmen. *Follies Girl of 1912*: T. Qualters. *Follies Girl of 1913*: H. Barnes. *Follies Girl of 1914*: G. Feldman. *Follies Girl of 1915*: E. Conway. *Follies Girl of 1916*: A. King.

Scene 2

The Street of Masks and Faces

Mark Antony: B. Granville. *A Roman Woman*: E. Callahan. *A Man*: A. Whitman. *Julius Caesar*: D. Barclay.

Scene 3

"(There's) Ragtime Is in the Air"
D. Barclay, Toga Girls and Boys
(*Music by* Dave Stamper.)
Scene: The Forum in Rome.
Julius Caesar: D. Barclay.

Scene 4

"The Six Little Wives of the King"
S. B. Hardy, Misses M. Davies, E. Conway, H. Lewis, G. Feldman, Tuey, T. Qualters

"I've Saved All My Lovin' for You"
F. White, W. Rock, Male Chorus
(*Music by* Dave Stamper.)
Scene: In the Golden Corridor.
King Henry VIII: S. B. Hardy. *William Shakespeare*: W. Rock. *Ann Hathaway*: F. White.

Scene 5

Travesty of Romeo and Juliet

"If You Were the Only Girl (in the World)"
I. Claire, B. Granville
(*Music by* Nat D. Ayer. *Lyrics by* Clifford Grey.)
Scene: In the Backyard of the Capulets.
Friar Lawrence: C. Hill. *Romeo*: B. Granville. *Juliet*: I. Claire. *Nurse*: J. Johnstone.

Scene 6

Escaping the Movies (Dance)
A. Pennington

"Somnambulistic Melody" (Somnambulistic Tune)
F. White, Sparkling Girls
(*Music by* Dave Stamper.)

Scene 7

Travesty of Othello

Scene: The Bedroom in Mr. and Mrs. Othello's Apartment.
Emilia: H. Barnes. *Iago*: S. B. Hardy. *Othello*: B. Williams. *Desdemona*: D. Barclay.

Scene 8

"When the Lights Are Low"
I. Claire
(*Music by* Jerome Kern.)

Scene 9

"My Lady of the Nile"
B. Granville, Ensemble
(*Music by* Jerome Kern.)
Scene: On the Banks of the Nile.
Antony: B. Granville. *Shakespeare*: W. Rock. *Cleopatra*: A. King. *Ladies from Shakespeare's Plays* (10): *Lady Macbeth*: G. Loftus. *Viola*: L. Tashman. *Mistress Page*: G. Feldman. *Rosalind*: E. Conway. *Ophelia*: T. Qualters. *Desdemona*: Miss Gunther. *Juliet*: M. Davies. *Miranda*: Miss Paul. *Katherine*: Miss Hart. *Portia*: H. Lewis. Shakespeare's Finish.

Scene 10

Unpreparedness[3]

Scene: A Room in the Home of the Original Optimist.
Uncle Sam: S. B. Hardy. *Columbia, his daughter*: J. Johnstone. *God of War*: P. Swift. *Common People*: B. Granville.

Defenseless America[4]

Venus: A. King.

Scene 11

Somewhere in the North Seas (Modern Naval Warfare)
(Illusion invented by Frank C. Thomas.)

Scene 12

Specialty[5]
W. Rock, F. White

Scene 13

Songs
B. Williams

"The Lee Family"
(*Music by* Will Vodery. *Lyrics by* Alex Rogers.)

"I'm Gone Before I Go"
(*Music by* Harry Carroll. *Lyrics by* Ballard Macdonald.]

Scene 14

"I Left Her on the Beach at Honolulu"
B. Granville, Hawaiian Girls
(*Music by* Louis Hirsch.)
Scene: In Far Hawaii.
A Yankee Tourist: B. Granville. *A Hula Dancer*: A. Pennington. *Ukalili Lou*: B. Williams. *A Hawaiian Lady*: I. Claire. And the Royal Hawaiian Players.

ACT 2

Scene 1

The Blushing Ballet: Dance
E. Haig, 'Sylphides' Girls
Scene: The Ante-Room of the Harem.

A Suggestion of "La Spectre de la Rose"
(C. Randall)
Nijinski: C. Randall.

Travesty of 'Sheherazade'
"Nijinski"
F. Brice, Male Chorus
(*Music by* Dave Stamper.)
The Sultan: S. B. Hardy. *O. Shaw*: W. C. Fields. *Zobeide*: D. Barclay. *Eunuch*: N. Blume. *Nijinski*: B. Williams.

Scene 2

"Ain't It Funny What a Difference Just a Few Drinks Make?"[6]
I. Claire, S. B. Hardy
(*Music by* Jerome Kern.)

---

[1]The tenth in the annual series of revues produced by Florenz Ziegfeld beginning in 1907.
[2]The running order was revised after the opening. Added after opening:
Will Rogers and His Educated Ropes (Specialty)(Act 1)
Recruiting (Act 1)
Hazza Gun: N. Blume. *Spickan Spann*: S. B. Hardy. *Suffern Smith*: W. Rock. *Reddan Greene*: W. C. Fields. *Will Jessard*: P. Swift. *Upall Day*: D. Barclay. *Maybee Knott*: B. Williams.

[3]Dropped after opening.
[4]Dropped after opening.
[5]Replaced during the run or for subsequent tour by:
A Girl's Trousseau
Mr. Modiste: S. B. Hardy. *His Customer*: N. Blume. And the Misses G. Feldman, Kern, H. Lewis, E. Conway, G. Loftus.
[6]Dropped after opening.

Scene 3

"Good Bye, Dear Old Bachelor Days" (Bachelor Days)
B. Granville
Assisted by Miss J. Johnstone, Bachelor Girls.
(*Music by* Louis Hirsch.)

Scene 4

"I Want That Star"
I. Claire, Eight Little Billies
(*Lyrics by* George V. Hobart.)
Scene: Puck's Pictorial Palace.
Oberon: A. King. *Moonlight:* H. Barnes. *Peaseblossom:* M. Davies *Moth:* T. Qualters. *Cobweb:* G. Feldman. *Mustardseed:* H. Lewis. *Josephus Daniels:* W. C. Fields. *Jane Cowl:* I. Claire. *William Jennings Bryan:* D. Barclay. *Mary Pickford:* A. Pennington. *Lou-Tellegen:* S. B. Hardy. *Geraldine Farrar:* I. Claire. *Teddy Roosevelt:* W. C. Fields. *John D. Rockefeller:* W. Rock. *Theda Bara:* F. Brice. *Villa:* B. Williams. *Billie Burke:* I. Claire.

Scene 5

A Croquet Game
Scene: On the Lawn at Lallypoosa.
Miss Zipp, a croquet player: W. C. Fields. *Mr. Zupp, a waiter:* S. B. Hardy.

Scene 6

"Stop and Go"
C. Randall, Avenue Girls
Scene: Fifth Avenue.
Stop-Go Girl: T. Qualters. *Traffic Cop:* C. Randall. *Miss Believe:* M. Davies. *Miss Understood:* E. Conway. *Miss Hap:* H. Lewis. *Miss Behave:* M. Carmen.

Scene 7

"Beautiful Island of Girls"
A. King, Nature Girls
(*Music by* Franz Lehár, adapted from GYPSY LOVE.)
"I've Said Good Bye to Broadway"
F. White, Broadway Girls
(*Music by* Dave Stamper.)
Scene: The Island of Girls.
A Modern Eve: A. King. *Miss Manhattan:* F. White.

Scene 8

Songs
F. Brice
["The Dying Swan"
(*Music by* Leo Edwards. *Lyrics by* Blanche Merrill.)
"The Hat"
(*Music by* Leo Edwards. *Lyrics by* Blanche Merrill.)]

Scene 9

"The Midnight Frolic Rag"[7] (Song)
F. White, Chorus
Scene: Ziegfeld Danse de Follies.
In the Air: B. Millman.

Finale
Company

1916.11   THE PASSING SHOW OF 1916

A Musical Revue in Two Acts, a Prologue and 16 Scenes[8]. Book (sketches) and lyrics by Harold Atteridge. Music by Sigmund Romberg and Otto Motzan. Staged by J. C. Huffman. Dances arranged by Allan K. Foster. Settings by Sundquist & Street, P. Dodd Ackerman, Dodge & Castle, Unitt & Wickes, Pelzon & Carson. Costumes designed by Faibsey, Mme. Kahn, Mahieu & Co., Homer Conant. Orchestra under the direction of Oscar Radin. Produced by Messrs. Shubert. Opened 22 June 1916 at the Winter Garden and closed 21 October 1916 after 140 performances.

CAST: ED WYNN, HERMAN TIMBERG, FLORENCE MOORE, STELLA HOBAN, WILLIAM H. PHILBRICK, FRANCES DEMAREST, JAMES HUSSEY, FRED WALTON, JACK BOYLE, JAMES CLEMONS, CHARLES MACK, JOHN SWOR, HATTIE DARLING, GEORGE BALDWIN, DOLLY HACKETT, ELIDA

MORRIS, William Dunn, Guy Collins, William Harper, Billie DeHon, Bly Brown, William Healy, Peggy Eleanor, Mabel Kelly, Peggy Smith, Grace Keeshon, Ruth Randall, Saranoff, Dorothy Godfrey, Grace Langdon, Ford Sisters (Mabel, ??), Adolf Blome, Ruth Murphy, Vera Roehm, Bud Murray. *Premiere Danseuses:* THAMARA SWIRSKAIA, MA-BELLE. *Violin Girls:* Misses Leonore Puron, Marion Glover, Mazibelle Valeta, Mizzi Nada, Mona Mahler, Mildred Anderson.

Personnel of the Chorus: Misses Adele Forrest, Blanche Parks, Barbara McCree, Marie Coghlan, Millie Carlson, Elsie Durant, Charlotte Cushman, Betty Gans, Abby Stewart, Leila Von Holk, Charlotte Marmont, Eleanor Franko, Elsie Bambrick, Peggy Smith, Ethel Dennison, Henrietta Faust, Beryl Mobis, Dorothy West, Madeline LeVine, Jane Angardi, Adrien Hayes, Ann Delmore, Emily Miles, Mabelle Kelly, Peggy Eleanor, Evelyn Parks, Marion Parks, Ethel Westie, Crissie Joss, Muriel Greil, Polly Lorimer, Esther Pierce, Trixie Raymond, Julia Bozzo, Jane Barton, Grace Kushan, Gussie Berg, Ada Ful, Dorothy Godfrey, Flo Howe, Wilma Garrison, Sophie Mills, Gertie Neilan, Pearl Eaton, Agnes Richter, Margerie Dayton, Gladys Turner, Grace Hall, Agnes Hall, Ona Hamilton, Mae Vaughan, Delores Mandez, Mabel Hill, Mabel Grete, Anna Pauly, Nancy Everett. Messrs. Harry McMasters, Frank McMasters, Clyde Miller, Charles Wilson, Matt Riordan, Bob Gilbert, Harry DeWitt, David Brown, Ted Andrews, Clarence Rockwell, Bert Clark, Guy Collins, George Collins, Harold Healy, Andrew Demarest, Lovitt Wilder.

ACT 1

Prologue

"Wine, Woman and Song"
G. Baldwin
Father Time: J. Clemons. *Year 1916:* F. Walton. *Justice:* B. DeHon. *Year 1917:* G. Baldwin. *The Devil:* W. Dunn. *War:* G. Collins. *Uncle Sam:* W. Harper. *Chorus Girl:* B. Brown. *The High Brow Dramatist:* W. Healy. *Charlie Chaplin:* B. Murray. *Woman:* P. Eleanor. *Wine:* M. Kelly. *Song:* P. Smith. *The Lass of the Cocktail Glass:* G. Keeshon.

Scene 1

"Ragging the Apache"
E. Morris, R. Randall, J. Clemons, Chorus
(*Music by* Otto Motzan.)
"So This Is Paris!"
F. Demarest, Chorus
(*Music by* Harry Tierney.)
Violin Solo
Saranoff
"Play My Melody"
H. Darling, H. Timberg, Violin Girls
Scene: Montmartre. (Sundquist & Street)
La Cherie: E. Morris. *An Apache:* J. Clemons. *A Grisette:* R. Randall. *Rudolph:* G. Baldwin. *Mizzi:* S. Hoban. *A Chauffeur:* J. Hussey. *Guy Speeder:* J. Boyle. *Lady Style:* F. Demarest. *Ed Wynn:* Himself. *Jean:* Saranoff. *Fiffi:* D. Godfrey. *Mimi:* G. Langdon. *Paganinni:* H. Timberg. *His Subject:* H. Darling. *Violin Girls:* Misses L. Puron, M. Glover, M. Valeta, M. Nada, M. Mahler, M. Anderson.

Scene 2

Scene: Plaza Circle. (Ackerman)
Ed Wynn: Himself. *An Actor:* J. Boyle.

Scene 3[9]

"Sweet and Pretty"
E. Morris, Chorus
(*Music by* Otto Motzan.)
"How to Make a Pretty Girl"
D. Hackett, Chorus
"Around the Town"
F. Moore
"Roosevelt, Wilson and Hughes"
W. H. Philbrick, F. Walton, A. Harper
"Let Cupid In"
F. Demarest, Chorus
(*Music by* Otto Motzan.)
Scene: Madame Faibisie's Dressmaking Establishment (Unitt & Wickes)
Lady Bluff Gordon: F. Moore. *Monsieur Tappan:* J. Boyle. *Roosevelt:* W. H. Philbrick. *Wilson:* F. Walton. *Hughes:* A. Harper. *Miss Nomination:* F. Demarest.

---

[7]Replaced during the run and for subsequent national tour by:
"In Florida Among the Palms"
B. Granville, Chorus
(*Music and Lyrics by* Irving Berlin.)
[8]The Sixth in the annual series of revues, produced since 1912 by the Messrs. Shubert, which began in 1894. Billed as the Winter Garden's Annual Revue.

---

[9]Late in the subsequent national tour, the following song was added to this scene:
"Faces"
B. Ashlyn (Lady Bluff Gordon)

Scene 4
    "Your Auto Ought To Get Girls"
        Ford Sisters, Chorus
        Scene: Columbus Circle. (Ackerman)
        Miss Auto, Miss Mobile: Ford Sisters.
Scene 5
        Scene: A Modern Garage. (Ackerman)
        Ed Wynn: Himself. *High Speed*: J. Boyle. *Miss Bly*: B. Brown. *Mizzi*: S. Hoban. *Lady Style*: F. Demarest. *An Auto Buyer*: B. Murray. *A Blind Man*: J. Clemons.
Scene 6
    Burlesque on The Heart of Wetona, and Rio Grande[10].
        Scene: On the Rio Grande. (Pelzon & Carson)
        Bill Hicks: J. Hussey. *Wetona*: F. Moore. *Big Chief Meyers*: F. Walton.
Scene 7[11]
    "Pretty Baby"
        D. Hackett, Chorus
        (*Music by* Egbert Van Alstyne. *Lyrics by* Gus Kahn.)
    "What's the Matter With You?"
        G. Baldwin
        (*Music and Lyrics by* Clifton Crawford.)
        Scene: On the Border. (Ackerman)
        Sergeant Ellsworth: G. Baldwin. *Private Smith*: B. Murray. *Villa*: J. Clemons. *Carranza*: A. Harper. *Roosevelt*: W. H. Philbrick.
Scene 8
    Charge of the U.S. Cavalry
        The Cavalry Charge invented by Lincoln J. Carter and built under his personal supervision.
ACT 2
Scene 1
    An Olympian Ballet
        Scene: A Grecian Bath. (Ackerman)
        Helen, a Grecian slave: T. Swirskaia. *Troilus*: W. Dunn. *Keeper of the Baths*: F. Walton. *Perfect*: J. Clemons. *Cressida*: Ma-Belle. And the Winter Garden Corps de Ballet.
Scene 2
    "Any Night on Broadway"
        J. Clemons, Boys
        Scene: Any Night. (Ackerman)
        Mr. Late-Up: J. Clemons.
Scene 3
    Burlesque of Potash and Perlmutter
        Scene: Potash and Perlmutter's Loan Shop. (by P. Dodd Ackerman)
        Mr. Nut: E. Wynn. *Abe Potash*: B. Murray. *Maurice Perlmutter*: J. Hussey. *Mr. Conn*: W. H. Philbrick. *Henry*: C. Mack. *Alexander*: J. Swor.
Scene 4
        Scene: A Modern Shakespearean Street. (Dodge & Castle)
        Alexander: J. Swor. *Henry*: C. Mack.
Scene 5
    "Broadway School Days"
        H. Timberg, H. Darling, R. Randall, S. Jackson, Chorus
        Scene: Schooldays on Broadway. (Ackerman)
Scene 6
    "Romeo and Juliet"
        G. Baldwin, S. Hoban, Chorus
        (*Music by* Sigmund Rombers.)
        Scene: Capulet's Garden. (Sundquist & Street)
        Romeo: G. Baldwin. *Juliet*: S. Hoban. *Rosalind*: D. Hackett. *Shakespeare*: F. Walton. *Clerk of the Court*: A. Harper. *Shylock*: H. Timberg. *Portia*: F. Moore. *Henry*: C. Mack.
Scene 7
    Travelogues
        E. Wynn

─────────

[10]The Heart of Wetona (Melodrama by George Scarborough); Rio Grande (Play by Augustus Thomas).
[11]Late in the subsequent tour, "Pretty Baby" and "What's the Matter with You" were replaced by:
    "Nothing's Too Good For a Good Little Girl"
        S. Hoban, Chorus
    "Yours Sincerely U.S.A."
        William Arnold

Scene 8
    Ballet
        Ma-Belle, Winter Garden Corps de Ballet
    "Ragtime Calisthenics"
        V. Roehm, R. Murphy, Athletic Girls
        Scene: Eat and Grow Thin Parlors. (Ackerman)
        The Ballet Master: A. Blome. *The Athletic Girl*: R. Murphy. *The Boxing Girl*: V. Roehm. *Mr. Rest Cure*: J. Clemons.
    "That's Called Walking the Dog" (Walking the Dog)
        H. Darling, H. Timberg, Chorus
    Finale

1916.12   YVETTE

A Musical Production in Two Acts. Book by Benjamin Thorne Gilbert. Music and lyrics by Frederick Herendeen. Interpolations by James Hanley and Arthur Jackson[12]. Production staged by M. Ring. Entire production designed by Janet E. Fox, Inc. Orchestra under the direction of Arthur H. Gutman. Orchestrations by Arthur Gutman. Produced by Paul Benedek (Inc.). Opened 10 August 1916 at the 39th Street Theatre and closed 12 August 1916 after 4 performances.

CAST (in order of appearance): *Paullette*: E. MARIE DAY. *Francois*: Eugene Redding. *August Schmitz*: JOHN W. RANSOME. *Countess Rochebaron*: ROSE LAHARTE. *Robert DeVilloc*: CRAWFURD KENT. *Yvette*: CYRIL CHADWICK. *Billy Usefulle*: Wolf DeWolf. *Lord Silverhampton*: CYRIL CHADWICK. *Senator Brown*: C. Welch Homer. *Marion Brown*: Gertie Merrod. *Cupid*: Effie Allan. (*Dance Specialty*: ROSHANARA.)
    Bathing Girls: Violet Bristow, Queenie Stair, Adele Rudolph, Rose LaPlace, Dorothy Hunt, Adah Baker, Effie Allan. *Guests*: Clara Stanton, Grace Williams, Vivian Webb, Constance Melvin, Corine Lincoln, Elsie Ross, Peggy Cameron, Louise Astor, Frances Bradford, Dorothy Stevens. *St. Cyr Cadets*: Jack Roberts, B. G. Shean, L. Clarke, H. Goulden, F. Stanton, D. J. Carew, Lawrence Shean, H. R. Butler, A. Phillips, Chris Dahl, E. McEnery, A. Lambert.

ACT 1
    Opening Chorus
        Ensemble
    "Wimmens"
        J. W. Ransone
    "St. Cyr's March"
        St. Cyr Cadets
    "Love's Serenade"
        C. Kent
    "Love Holds Sway"
        Chapine
    "Some Girls"
        C. Kent, Chapine, Ensemble
    "Tick-Tick"
        Chapine, J. W. Ransone, C. Chadwick
    "I Want All of the Boys"
        E. M. Day, W. Dewolf
    "I Love You So"
        Chapine
    "(The) Galloping Major"
        C. Chadwick, Ensemble
    "Just One More Kiss" (Finale)
        Chapine
ACT 2
    "Summer Night" (Opening Chorus)
        Ensemble
    "American Beauties"
        R. Laharte, Ensemble
    "Wonderful Kiss"
        E. M. Day, W. Dewolf, Ensemble
    "Someone Just Like You"
        C. Kent
    "Love Letters"
        Chapine, C. Kent
    Specialty
        Roshanara

─────────

[12]Interpolations not specified in programs.

"Silly Ass"
  C. Chadwick
"Since I Met You"
  Chapine, C. Kent
"Modern Melody"
  Ensemble
Finale
  Chapine, Ensemble

1916.13 BROADWAY AND BUTTERMILK

A Comedy with Songs in Three Acts[13]. Play by Willard Mack. Music by Charles N. Grant. Lyrics by Schuyler Greene. Staged by Ben Teal. Orchestra under the direction of John R. Britz. Produced by Frederic McKay. Opened 15 August 1916 at the Maxine Elliott's Theatre and closed 2 September 1916 after 23 performances.[14]

CAST (in order of appearance): *Mrs. Mary Denby*: Helen Lowell. *Mrs. Amanda Hodge*: Josephine Morse. *Ruth Denby*: Fayette Perry. *Asa Denby*: Tommy Meade. *Major Dunworthy Hawes*: Erville Alderson. *Eldridge Pickens*: Knute Erickson. *Madame Nadine (Jane O'Day)*: BLANCHE RING. *Harry White*: CHARLES WALTON. *Hank Woolwine*: CHARLES WITHERS. *Celia Hodge*: Rea Martin. *Tom Burrows*: William P. Carleton. *Franklyn Abbott*: Calvin Thomas.

Act 1: The Denby Home, Killimuck Falls, Maine.

Act 2: Exterior of the Denby Home. The afternoon of the following day.

Act 3: Same as Act 2. 8 P.M. of the same day.

MUSICAL NUMBERS[15]
  "Girls, If You Ever Get Married"
  "Pickin' 'Em Up and Layin' 'Em Down"
  "I Have Always Been the Patsy"
    (*Music by* Dave Stamper)

1916.14 THE GIRL FROM BRAZIL

A Musical Comedy in Three Acts. Book by Edgar Smith. Adapted from the Viennese original ('Die schöne Schwedin') by Julius Brammer and Alfred Grünwald, music by Robert Winterberg. Music by Sigmund Romberg and Robert Winterberg. Lyrics by Matthew Woodward. Staged by J. H. Benrimo. Dances arranged by Allan K. Foster. Settings designed by Homer Conant. Gowns designed by Homer Conant. Orchestra under the direction of Gaetano Merola. Under the personal direction of J. J. Shubert. Produced by Messrs. Shubert. Opened 30 August 1916 at the 44th Street Theatre, moved 9 October 1916 to the Sam S. Shubert Theatre, and closed 21 October 1916 after 61 performances.

CAST (in order of appearance): *Colonel Zamzelius*, friend of Baron Heinz: CLARENCE HARVEY. *Nancy*: Betty Brown. *Swanhilda*, Cederstol's aunt: MAUDE ODELL. *Lieutenant Olaf Nansen*: STEWART JACKSON. *Lona Cedarstrom*, an actress: DOROTHY MAYNARD. *Billings*: Eric Van Dyck. *Footmen*: Jack Kelly, Earl Farlow. *Carl Cederstol*, a banker of Stockholm: HAL FORDE. *Hilma*, his sister: BETH LYDY. *Azel*, his secretary: Louis Simon. *Herr Torkel*, creditor of Cederstol: GEORGE HASSELL. *Baron Heinz von Reedigan*, a nobleman: JOHN H. GOLDSWORTHY. *Gerda*, a friend of Hilma: Nora White. *Edith Lloyd*, of Lloyd & Co., Rio de Janeiro: FRANCES DEMAREST. *Carfuso*: Lester Schurff. *Lissla*: Dorothy Wahl. *Cariboca*: Winthrop Chamberlain. *Guests of Cederstol, Brazilians, etc..*
  Personnel of the Chorus: *Show Girls*: Anita Baldwin, Eleanor Leigh, Kitty Astra, Nita Lamadrid, Rose Gibson, Betty Brown, Florence Collier, Rena Manning, Ida Evon, Judith Voss, Olga Britton, Ethel Seeley. *Dancers*: Vera Pearsall, Helen Meher, Marie Varella, Pearl Betts, Edith Pierce, Lilly Patay, Jessie Ruddock, Mazie Lyon, Jeannette McManus, Nellie Crawford, Bessie Burch, Dorothy Pond, Doris Lohr. *Boys*: Jack Stone, Wycliff Parker, Jack Kane, Frank Carroll, Henry Schiff, Girard Gardner, Earl Farlow, Don Seaton, Lester Scharff, Harry Edwards, Henry Dempsey, Wesley Morris.

Act 1: Piazza and Garden of Cederstol's residence. Afternoon. (Conant.)

Act 2: Reception Room, Cederstol's Residence, Stockholm. Evening. (Conant.)

Act 3: Villa of Senor Camberito, near Rio de Janeiro. Morning.

---

[13]Subsequently toured under the title JANE O'DAY OF BROADWAY.
[14]Settings, costumes uncredited.
[15]Additional songs interpolated for subsequent tour, as per published sheet music:

  "My Grandfather's Girl"
    (*Music and Lyrics by* Will A. Dillon.)

ACT 1
  Opening Chorus
  "The Financial Viking"
    H. Forde
  "Childhood Days"
    B. Lydy
    (*Music by* Sigmund Romberg.)
  "I Want to Be a Romeo" (I'll Be Your Own Romeo)
    J. H. Goldsworthy
    (*Music by* Robert Winterberg.)
  "Stolen Kisses"
    J. H. Goldsworthy, B. Lydy
    (*Music by* Sigmund Romberg.)
  "Darling, I Love You So"
    D. Maynard, S. Jackson
    (*Music by* Robert Winterberg.)
  "Ivy and the Oak"
    M. Odell, G. Hassell
    (*Music by* Sigmund Romberg.)
  Finale

ACT 2
  Opening Chorus
    N. White
  "The Right Brazilian Girl"
    F. Demarest
    (*Music by* Sigmund Romberg.)
  "Come Back, Sweet Dreams"
    B. Lydy
    (*Music by* Sigmund Romberg.)
  "Oh, You Lovely Ladies!"
    S. Jackson, J. H. Goldsworthy, H. Forde, L. Simon, G. Hassell, C. Harvey
  "Heart to Heart"[16]
    F. Demarest, H. Forde
    (*Music by* Robert Winterberg.)
  "Bachelor Girl and Boy"
    D. Maynard, S. Jackson
    (*Music by* Sigmund Romberg.)
  "Ski-ing"
    D. Maynard
  Finale

ACT 3
  Opening Chorus
  Baccarole[17]
    D. Maynard, S. Jackson
  "My Señorita"
    J. H. Goldsworthy, B. Lydy
    (*Music by* Sigmund Romberg.)
  Finale

1916.15 THE BIG SHOW

A Musical Spectacle in Three Acts. Sketches by R. H. Burnside. Music by Raymond Hubbell. Lyrics by John Golden. Entire production staged by R. H. Burnside. Sleeping Beauty Ballet arranged by Ivan Clustine. Ice ballet dances arranged by Mariette Loretta. Scenery designed by Ernest Albert, Leon Bakst, Mark Lawson. Costumes designed by Mme. Francis, Robert McQuinn. Lighting by Joseph Ellsner. Orchestra under the direction of Raymond Hubbell. Produced by Charles Dillingham. Opened 31 August 1916 at the Hippodrome and closed 5 May 1917 after 425 performances.

CAST: ANNA PAVLOVA, HENRY TAYLOR, DIXIE GIRARD, Otto, Leon, Albert, Sylvester and Charles Metzetti; Dippy Diers, Charles Ravel, Stanley Ferguson, Bob Reano, Dave Rosen, John Miller, James Mack, Paul Briant, Walter Briant, John Tweedley, Fred Sweeney, 'TOTO', Robert Gross, Emil Davis, Peter Ladella, Tony Ladella, W. G. Ladella, Walter Nelson, Howard Nichols, Norman Nichols, Jack Bart, Millard Nichols, THE SIX BROWN BROTHERS, EDDIE RUSSELL, ROBERT ROSAIRE, BOBBY HALE, JOHNNY DAVIS, FRED GREGORY, Matt Keefe, William Maxwell, Gus Wicke, Gus Proppe, Al Silverman, Happy Milke, Charles Ahearn, Harry Wardell, George Davis, Billy Woolfe, William Lorrimer, James Carty, Enzo Bozano, David Irwin, J. P. COOMBS, Austin Walsh, George Hermann, Joseph Parsons, Emanuel List, W. C. Reid, Letty Yorke, Blanche Marci, Adelaide Clark,

---

[16]Dropped during the run.
[17]Dropped during the run.

Adelaide Lorrett, Georges Marck, Yvonne Marck, Emma Kiyo, Yoshie and Nobu, HARU ONUKI, B. K. Okita, THE ELM CITY FOUR, the Four Singers, THE BROTHERS LEIGHTON (Bert, Frank), George Wilson, W. G. Stewart, Natalie Dagwell, ALEXANDRE VOLININE, M. Vajinski, M. Domislavski, M. Hubart, Katie Schmidt, Ellen Dallerup, Cathleen Pope, George Kerner, Hilda Rückerts, Mariette Loretta, Frank Scalish, Max Aronson, J. R. Proctor, James Graham, the El Rey Sisters (Claire, Zoe).

Ballet Ensemble: Stefa S. Plaskovietyka, Mlles. Butzova, Lindovskaja, Collinet, Griffova, Leggierova, Shelton, Courtnowa, Tastova, Brunova, Verins, Doganova, Moskvina, Myersa, Stuart, Smallers, Grassova. Messrs. Zalewski, Montes, Parker, Poppelow, Radezki, Bain, Veseloff, Oliveroff. *Ice Ballet Ensemble*: Misses Sully, M. Weikusat, Walters, C. Weikusat, Weideman, Gebauer, Wruck, Mullar, Welden, Anderson, Merkel, Kollhofer, Worm, Schaefer, Georges, Frick, Moore, Overlack, Norman, Margaret O'Neill, Marion O'Neill, Beverly Miller, Phylis Miller, Caine, Melville, Meerest, Johnson, Moran, Pritchard, Frederick, Dix and Corty.

ACT 1[18]

Scene 1

"The Hippodrome Street Parade"
  A. Walsh, Four Singers, Entire Company
  Milton Mooney's Horses
  Powers' Elephant
  Scene: Outside the Hippodrome. (Lawson.)

Scene 2

The Revenge of the Lions[19] (*by Georges Marck*)
  The Countess de Kerny: B. Marci. *Her Friends*: A. Lorrett, A. Clarke. *Gaston Derives*: G. Marck. *His Adopted Daughter*: V. Marck. *The Maid*: E. Fette. *The Butler*: F. Scherman. *The Organ Grinder*: A. Byrne.
  Scene: Somewhere in France. *Part 1*: Cinemagraphic Picture. *Part 2*: Exterior of the Countess' Villa near Paris.

Scene 3

Dancing Specialty
  G. Herman
"Toto"
Specialty
  Volant
  Scene: Somewhere in Spiritland. (Lawson.)

Scene 4

A few minutes with Frank Fogarty[20]
  Scene: Somewhere in Ireland.

Scene 5

"We'll Stand By Our Country"
  H. Taylor, D. Girard, Hippodrome Company
  Scene: Somewhere in America. (Lawson.)
    Tableau One: *West Point Officers*: O. Metzetti, L. Metzetti, A. Metzetti, S. Metzetti, C. Metzetti, D. Diers, C. Ravel, S. Ferguson, B. Reano, D. Rosen, J. Tweedley, "Toto," R. Gross, J. Miller, J. Mack, E. Davis, P. Ladella, T. Ladella, W. G. Ladella, W. Nelson, H. Nichols, N. Nichols, J. Bart. *Tableau Two*: *Captain*: E. Russell. *Officers*: R. Rosaire, B. Hale. *Midshipmen*: J. Davis, F. Gregory. *Naval Officers*: M. Keefe, W. Maxwell, G. Wicke, G. Proppe, A. Silverman, H. Milke, C. Ahearn, J. Davis, G. Davis, W. Ladella, W. Briant, B. Woolfe, W. Lorrimer, J. Carty, D. Irwin, J. P. Coombs, A. Walsh, G. Hermann, J. Parsons, E. List, W. C. Reid. *Cadets and Sailors*: Hippodrome Company.

Scene 6

Japanese Dance
  Misses Kiyo, Yoshie, Nobu; B. K. Okita
"Poor Butterfly" (Song)
  H. Onuki, assisted by the Four Singers, Elm City Four, Hippodrome Chorus
  (*Scenery and Costumes designed by* Robert McQuinn.)

Scene 7

The Six Brown Brothers[21]
  Scene: Somewhere in Chinchinland.

_____

[18]Added to the show during the run:
  "Hello! I've Been Looking for You" (added 18 October 1916)
    J. Parsons, Chorus
  "The Good Ship Honeymoon"
    (added 9 November 1916)
  A Little Surprise from the Front: "Ushing Ain't the Only Thing We Do"
    (added 23 November 1916)
    Uniformed Chorus of Hippodrome Ushers
[19]Dropped early in the run.
[20]Dropped early in the run.
[21]Replaced early in the run by The Ahearn Troupe (Bicycle Act).

Scene 8

The Mammoth Minstrels (400—Count 'Em—400)
"Come On Down to Rag-time Town" (Song)
  H. Wardell
Dance[22]
  J. Miller, J. Mack
"On the Mountain" (Song)
  M. Keefe, asssited by the Four Singers, Elm City Four
Song and Dance[23]
  The Brothers Leighton
["Steamboat Bill"
  (*Music by* Bert and Frank Leighton. *Lyrics by* Ren Shields.)]
Medley Finale
  Entire Company
  End Men: C. Ahearn, G. Wilson. *Interlocutor*: W. G. Stewart. *Pages*: J. Miller, J. Mack. *Assisted by* "Toto," M. Keefe, H. Taylor, J. Parsons, E. List, H. Wardell, B. Hale, W. C. Reid, D. Irwin, J. Byrne, A. Walsh, S. Ferguson, C. Ravel, The Four Singers, R. Rosaire, The Elm City Four, W. Briant, P. Briant, H. Milke, J. Tweedley, F. Gregory, D. Rosen, F. Sweeney, R. Gross, A. Silvermann, W. Nelson, W. Ladella, P. Ladella, T. Ladella, W. G. Ladella, H. Nichols, M. Nichols, N. Nichols, J. Bart, G. Davis, John Davis, E. Davis, Johnny Davis, L. Metzetti, C. Metzetti, A. Metzetti, O. Metzetti, S. Metzetti, D. Diers.
  Scene: Somewhere in Minstreland. (Lawson.)

ACT 2

Anna Pavlova in THE SLEEPING BEAUTY, a Ballet in Four Tableaux[24]. From the fairy tale of Charles Perrault, arranged by R. H. Burnside. Music by Pyotr Ilyich Tchaikovsky. Scenery and costumes designed by Leon Bakst. Dances arranged by Ivan Clustine, Ballet Master of the Russian Imperial Theatre.

CAST: *The King*: J. P. Coombs. *The Queen*: N. Dagwell. *The Princess Aurora*: A. PAVLOWA. *The Prince Desiré, A Ventian Prince*: A. Volinine. *A Spanish Prince*: M. Vajinski. *An Italian Prince*: M. Domislavski. *An Oriental Prince*: M. Hubart. *Lilas, the Good Fairy*: L. Yorke. *Carrabosse, the Bad Fairy*: H. Taylor. *The Major-Domo*: E. Bozano. *The Herald*: W. C. Reid. *Companions of the Princess Aurora, Ladies of Honor, Cavaliers, of the Court, Pages, Suite of the Good Fairy, Suite of the Bad Fairy, Peasant Men and Women, Guards, etc.*

Tableau 1

Prologue:
  Reception in the palace of the King and Queen to celebrate the birthday of their first child, the Princess Aurora.

Tableau 2

The Gardens of the King's Palace.
  Sixteen years have passed. The King and Queen are giving a grand festival in honor of the birthday of Princess Aurora and the various princes who have come to ask for the hand of their daughter.
  Grand Valse: S. Plaskovietyka, Mlles. Butzova, Lindovskaja, Collinet, Griffova, Leggierova, Shelton, Courtnowa, Tastova, Brunova, Verins, Doganova, Moskvina, Myersa, Stuart, Smallers, Grassova. Messrs. Zalewski, Montes, Parker, Poppelow, Radezki, Bain, Veseloff, Oliveroff, Corps du Ballet.
Entrance of Princess Aurora
  Adagio: A. Pavlova, A. Volinine. M. Vajinski, Domislavski, Hubart.
Dance of the Princess' Companions
  Pas de cinq: Mlles. Butzova, Collinet, Griffovaa, Leggierova, Doganova.
  Variations: A. Pavlova, A. Volinine.
  Coda General.

Tableau 3

A forest in which a young Prince, Desiré, with his suite is hunting.
  Arrival of the Prince and his suite. Appearance of the Good and the Bad Fairies.
  The Vision: Grand pas d'action. A. Volinine, A. Pavlova. And Ballet of Nymphs.

Tableau 4

The Palace of the King. Awakening of Princess Aurora.
  Grand Festival in honor of the engagement of the Princess Aurora and Prince Desiré.
  Gavotte: A. Pavlova, A. Volinine.
  Gallop Finale. Apotheosis. Entire Hippodrome Chorus.

_____

[22]Dropped early in the run.
[23]Dropped early in the run.
[24]THE SLEEPING BEAUTY Ballet replaced 27 November 1916 by A Program of Request Numbers selected from Anna Pavlova's repertory of divertissements. This was replaced 22 January 1917 by an Aquatic Spectacle, THE QUEEN OF THE MERMAIDS. Music by Raymond Hubbell. Lyrics by Anne Caldwell. Directed by R. H. Burnside. Principals included Annette Kellerman, Toto, Thomas Keenan.

ACT 3

THE MERRY DOLL, the new Ice Ballet, direct from the Admiral's Palast, Berlin. Book by Leo Bartuschek. Music by Julius Einedshofer and Raymond Hubbell. Lyrics by John L. Golden. Dances arranged by Mme. Mariette Loretta. Scenery by Mark Lawson. Costumes by Mme. Freisinger, Franes M. Ziebarth.

Scene: Somewhere in Germany.

MUSICAL NUMBERS

"Queen of the Land of Snow" (Waltz and Song)
    H. Taylor, K. Schmidt, Chorus
    (*Music by* Raymond Hubbell.)

Duet, Pierrot and Pierrette
    K. Schmidt, E. Dallerup

Solo, The Merry Doll
    H. Rückerts

March of the Masqueraders
    Toy Soldiers: W. Briant, P. Briant, W. G. Ladella, P. Ladella. *Langermann*: A. Walsh. *Happy Hooligan*: F. Scalish. *Tramp*: C. Ahearn. *Dude*: H. Wardell. *Scotchman*: B. Hale. *Sandow*: D. Irwin. *Friar*: J. P. Coombs. *Chinaman*: M. Aronson. *Kaiser*: G. Wicke. *Simple Simon*: D. Rosen. *Stan*: S. Matzetti. *Arab*: M. Keefe. *Turk*: J. J. Daly. *Russian Soldier*: F. Sweeney. *French Soldier*: J. Graham. *John Bull*: J. R. Proctor. *Austrian Soldier*: D. Diers. *Fat Boy*: S. Ferguson.

Dance of the Dolls
    Chemise Dolls: Misses Sully, M. Weikusat, Walters, C. Weikusat. *Clown Dolls*: Misses Weideman, Gebauer, Wruck, Mullar. *Japanese Dolls*: Misses Welden, Anderson, Merkel, Kollhofer. *French Dolls*: Misses Worm, Schaefer, Georges, Frick. *Jumping Dolls*: Misses Moore, Overlack, Norman, Margaret O'Neill, Marion O'Neill, B. Miller, P. Miller, Caine, Melville, Meerest, Johnson, Moran, Pritchard, Frederick, Dix and Corty.

Dance, Max and Moritz
    J. Miller, J. Mack

Specialty
    Nichols-Nelson Troupe

Waltz Duet
    C. Pope, G. Kerner

"Toto" (the Clown)
    Butterfly Ballet
    Misses Wruck, Gebauer, Mullar, Werkel, Weideman, Kollhofer, Walters, C. Weikusat, M. Weikusat, Weldon, Anderson, Sully, Frick, Schaefer, Worm, Georges

Oriental Dance
    Charlotte

The Fastest Skaters in the World
    Lamy Brothers

"My Skating Girl" (Finale)
    Elm City Four, El Rey Sisters, Company
    (*Music by* Raymond Hubbell and Max Darewski. *Lyrics by* John L. Golden and C. A. Bovill.)

1916.16   PIERROT THE PRODIGAL

A Revival of the Pantomime with Music in Three Acts[25]. Story (Original French play without words 'L'enfant prodigue') by Michel Carré. Music by André Wormser. Staged by Louis Fournier. Scenes by Edward G. Unitt and Joseph Wickes. Costumes by Pope and Bradley, London; Lucile, Ltd. Conductor, Elliott Schenck. Produced by Winthrop Ames and Walter Knight. Opened 6 September 1916 at the Booth Theatre, moved 6 November 1916 to the Little Theatre, and closed 27 January 1917 after 165 performances.

CAST (in order of appearance): *Pierrot's Father*: PAUL CLERGET. *Pierrot's Mother*: GABREILLE PERRIER. *Pierrot*: MARJORIE PATTERSON. *Phrynette*: MARGOT KELLY. *A Servant*: Charles Dubuis. *Monsieur le Baron*: EMILE J. deVARNEY.
    Solo Pianist: Aloys Friedheim-Kremer.

ACT 1

Father Pierrot and his kind old wife are troubled. Their only son is moody and depressed. In vain they tempt him to eat, to drink, to laugh. His youthful jollity is gone. In truth the boy is sick with love. He has lost his heart to a laundress of the village—

Phrynette, with the sparkling, naughty eyes. But Phrynette has no notion of marrying a poor country lad. Her dreams are of quite another color. So mad is poor Pierrot to posses her, at whatever the cost, that while his parents are asleep he steals his father's savings, and with Phrynette flies from the little town.

ACT 2

The first mad revel over, Pierrot and his mistress find themselves in debt and harassed with bills. Phrynette makes it clear that she is to be held by luxury, not love; and Pierrot, still infatuated with the little jade, takes another downward step. By gambling with false cards he hopes to win enough to keep her yet a little longer. Meantime Phrynette has been coquetting with a richer lover—the dissolute Monsieur le Baron. Satisfied that he will gild life for her again, she flies with him. Pierrot returns with his ill-won gold, only to find his mistress gone.

ACT 3

Pierrot's Father is heartbroken. Daily his mother prays the Virgin to restore their erring son. At last her prayer is answered. A ragged beggar knocks at the door. It is the Prodigal come home. Instantly the Mother takes the penitent into her arms. The father cannot so soon forgive the sin against his name. Martial music sounds in the village street. A regiment is passing. Pierrot seizes the chance to redeem himself. He will enlist, and in his country's service win honor back again. And so, his Mother smiling on him through her tears, and with his Father's blessing, he marches off to War.

1916.17   FLORA BELLA

An Operetta in Three Acts. (Original German) Book by Felix Dörmann, (adapted from André Barde), revised and adapted by Cosmo Hamilton and Dorothy Donnelly. Music by Charles Cuvillier and Milton Schwarzwald[26]. Lyrics by Percy Waxman. Staged by Richard Ordynski. Dances by Carl Randall. Scenery by Joseph Urban. Costumes by Mme. Kerner. Orchestra under the direction of Gustave [Gus] Salzer. Produced by John Cort. Opened 11 September 1916 at the Casino Theatre, moved 27 November 1916 to the 44th Street Theatre and closed 16 December 1916 after 112 performances[27].

CAST (in order of appearance): *Ludovic*, the butler: Gilbert Clayton. *Baron Tigo Oblonsky*: MORTIMER H. WELDON. *Countess Ola Drubetzkoy*: MURIEL HUDSON. *Count Sergiey Weronzeff*: LAWRENCE GROSSMITH. *Princess Manja Demidoff*, (alias Flora Bella): LINA ABARBANELL. *Sophie*, the maid: Kate Stout. *Prince Nicholas Demidoff*: CHARLES PURCELL. *Kosonoff*: Adolph Link. *Madame Vera Ludoffska*: JULIETTE LIPPE. *Rosset*, manager of "The Sign of the Golden Calf": ROBERT O'CONNOR. (*Dance Specialties*: Grant and Wing, Hilda Blyar.) Peasants, Servants, Dancers, Members of "The Sign of the Golden Calf".

The action takes place in Russia at the present time.

Act 1: The House of Prince Nicholas in the country.

Act 2: "The Sign of the Golden Calf" in Petrograd.

Act 3: The House of Prince Nicholas in the country.

ACT 1

Procession of Peasants
    Chorus
    (*Music by* Charles Cuvillier.)

"Good-Day, Good-Night" (Quarrel Duet)
    M. Hudson, M. H. Weldon
    (*Music by* Milton Schwarzwald.)

Floral Offering
    Chorus
    (*Music by* Milton Schwarzwald.)

"Blossom of My Own"
    L. Abarbanell, Chorus

"It Is Very Hard to Bring Up Father"
    L. Abarbanell, Male Chorus
    (*Music by* Milton Schwarzwald.)

"Young Men Take a Tip from Me"
    C. Purcell
    (*Music by* Charles Cuvillier.)

"Cat and Mouse" (Cat, You Can't Leave Mice Alone)(Duet)
    M. Hudson, C. Purcell
    (*Music by* Charles Cuvillier.)

---

[25]First produced in New York 7 March 1891 at Daly's Theatre as THE PRODIGAL SON for 7 performances, and 21 August 1893 at Daly's Theatre as L'ENFANT PRODIGUE for 49 performances. For Synopsis of Scenes, see original 1891 production.

[26]Cuvillier composed the original score, and Schwarzwald provided the American interpolations.
[27]Played a subsequent touring week at the Standard Theatre, Broadway at 90th Street, 18 December 1916.

"Love Is a Dance" (Waltz)
L. Abarbanell
(*Music by* Charles Cuvillier.)

"On to Petrograd" (Finale)
L. Abarbanell, M. Hudson, C. Purcell, M. H. Weldon, L. Grossmith
(*Music by* Charles Cuvillier.)

ACT 2

"Hail to the Golden Calf"
R. O'Connor, Chorus
(*Music by* Milton Schwarzwald.)

Dance Divertissements
Grant and Wing

Bacchanale
H. Blyar

"We'll Dance Till Dawn of Day"
J. Lippe

"Flora Bella" (March)
L. Abarbanell, Chorus
(*Music by* Milton Schwarzwald. *Lyrics by* Earl Carroll.)

"You're the Girl"
C. Purcell, Girls
(*Music by* Milton Schwarzwald. *Lyrics by* Victor Schertzinger.)

"Give Me All of You" (Waltz Duet)
L. Abarbanell, C. Purcell
(*Music by* Milton Schwarzwald. *Lyrics by* Earl Carroll.)

"Adam" (Quartette)
C. Purcell, L. Grosmith, R. O'Connor, M. H. Weldon
(*Music by* Charles Cuvillier.)

"Hypnotizing" (Duet)
L. Abarbanell, M. H. Weldon
(*Music by* Charles Cuvillier.)

Finale
Entire Company
(*Music by* Charles Cuvillier.)

ACT 3

"Creep, Creep, the World's Asleep"
J. Lippe, L. Grossmith, M. H. Weldon, M. Hudson, R. O'Connor, Chorus
(*Music by* Milton Schwarzwald. *Lyrics by* Victor Schertzinger.)

Finale
L. Abarbanell, C. Purcell
(*Music by* Milton Schwarzwald.)

1916.18   THE AMBER EMPRESS

An Operatic Comedy (Musical Play) in Two Acts. Book and lyrics by Marcus [Marc] C. Connelly. Music by Zoel Parenteau, (Robert Planquette). Staged by George Marion. Scenery painted by D. Frank Dodge and William Castle. Medieval costumes designed by Raymond Newton Hyde; modern costumes designed by Mrs. O'Kane Conwell. Orchestra under the direction of Max Bendix. Produced by Madison Carey and Joseph Riter. Opened 19 September 1916 at the Globe Theater and closed 30 September 1916 after 15 performances.

CAST (in order of appearance): *Tom Brenner,* a motion-picture director: DONALD MACDONALD. *Pete,* a camera-man: Colin Campbell. *Carl Lumleigh,* an exchange manager: Maurice Boddington. *Trixie Scott,* Ms. Scott's daughter: LOUISE ALLEN. *Sheldon Scott,* Mrs. Scott's son: THOMAS CONKEY. *Count Ruffano:* Lew Christy. *Sam Lewis,* a money-lender: John Daly Murphy. *Mrs. Harriet Scott,* of New York: EMMA JANVIER. *Percival Hopkins,* a New York promoter: FRANK LALOR. *Beverly Mason,* an American singer, "in pictures": MABEL WILBER. *The Doge of Venice* in pictures: Ronald Green. *Giovanni,* the lover in the pictures: Paul Pollock. *The Pages* in the pictures: Florida Bellaire, Rita Bellaire. *Harry Austin,* of London: Andrew Higginson. *Liza Jones,* of London: Daisy Revett. *A Waiter:* Jack Pratos. *The Premiere Danseuse:* CLAIRE LORRAINE.

Mrs. Scott's Guests: Elma Decker: Elma Decker. *Anita Francesca:* Anita Francesca. *Estelle Francesca:* Estelle Francesca. *Jane Gilroy:* Jane Gilroy. *Phyllis Grey:* Phyllis Grey. *Madge North:* Madge North. *Edna Waddell:* Edna Waddell. *Kathryn Bauer:* Kathryn Bauer. *Maud Leroy:* Maud Leroy. *Marguerite Agniel:* Marguerite Agniel.

The Serenaders: Irene Audrey, Madge North, Elma Decker, Estelle Thebaud. *Coster Boys and Girls: Characters in the Picture, Gendarmes, Tourists, Carnival Characters, Musicians, Gondoliers:* Misses Mary Sullivan, Clara Bruce, Blanche Terrell, Irene Doten, Florida Bellaire, Rita Bellaire, May Elsie, Marie Macdonald, Dodo Bernard, Mignon Sydney, Marion Comfort, Tillie Patterson, Aimee Chappelle, Dorothy Veron, Ena Westcott, Billy Francis, Louise Adams, Lucille Moore, Marjorie Shields, Laura Terrell, Alice Ford, Lillian Heiss, Inez Sebring, Helen Driscoll, Olive Kellogg, Alice Clifford, Estelle Thebaud, Muriel Foley. Messrs. Edward Donnelly, Frank Binns, Ronald Green, W. Hovel, Edwin Leech, George Mortimer, Paul Pollock, Jack Pratos, Frank Sheppard, Franklin Feeney, Hilliard Hudson Jr., Teddy Shelby, Maurice Boddington, George Allen.

Act 1: St. Mark's Square, Venice.

Act 2: Mrs. Scott's Villa and Garden, adjoining that of Count Ruffano, Venice.

ACT 1

Opening Chorus:
"King Carnival"
Ensemble

"With Militant Stride"
Ensemble

"Don't Lose Your Way, Little Boy"
L. Allen, D. Macdonald

"(Her) Cannonading Eyes"
T. Conkey, Chorus

"They Can't Run Off the Reels Too Fast for Me"
F. Lalor

"Gossip"
E. Janvier

"You're a Hero" (Trio)
F. Lalor, D. Revett, A. Higginson

"The Arrival of the Amber Empress"
Pantomime
M. Wilber, Chorus

"Open Your Heart to Love"

"There's Always One You Can't Forget" (Duet)
M. Wilber, T. Conkey
(*Lyrics by* Marcus Connelly and Robert B. Smith.)

Finale

ACT 2

"The Serenade" (Opening Chorus)
Ensemble

Divertissement
C. Lorraine

"Melody Will Keep You Young" (Duet)
M. Wilber, L. Allen

"A Kiss Affects Me Most of All" (Duet)
D. Macdonald, Chorus

"Palace or Cot"
T. Conkey

"Love Flies Everywhere" (Duet)
M. Wilber, T. Conkey

"There's Nothing So Uncertain as a Dead Sure Thing"
F. Lalor

"It's the Only One for Me"/The Chinese Fox Trot
D. Macdonald, L. Allen

Finale

1916.19   MISS SPRINGTIME

A Musical Comedy in Three Acts. Book by Guy Bolton. (Based on the Hungarian operetta 'Zsuzsi kisasszony' with libretto by Miksa Bródy and Ferenc Martos.) Music by Emmerich Kálmán. Lyrics by P. G. Wodehouse and Herbert Reynolds. Staged by Herbert Gresham. Ensemble numbers staged by Julian Mitchell. Scenery by Joseph Urban. Costumes designed by F. Richard Anderson and Alice O'Neil. Lighting by Ben Beerwald. Orchestra under the direction of Charles Previn. Produced by Marc Klaw and Abe Erlanger. Opened 25 September 1916 at the New Amsterdam Theatre and closed 7 April 1917 after 224 performances.

CAST (in order of appearance): *Paul Pilgrim,* editor of the Pilota Gazette: CHARLES MEAKINS. *Michael Robin,* assistant editor: JOHN E. HAZZARD. *Katski Schmiidt,* Rosi's maiden aunt: JOSIE INTROPODI. *Henry Wenzel,* druggist and postmaster: Nick Burnham. *Hugo Knaus,* 'native son' of Pilota: Maurice Cass. *Rosika Wenzel,* Wenzel's daughter: SARI PETRASS. *Jo Varady,* a gypsy photographer: GEORGE MacFARLANE. *Maimie Stone,* from New York: GEORGIA O'RAMEY. *Dustin Stone,* a rich American: JED PROUTY. *Officer:* William Cohan. *Inspector Block:* Percy Woodley. *Secretary to Rudolfo Marto:* Wayne Nunn. *Maitre de Ballet:* Fred Nice. *Premiere Danseuse:* Ada Weeks. *Russie:* Audrey Burton. *Cessie:* Billie Vernon. *Marto*

Reception Committee: Misses Teddy Hudson, Edna Stillwell, June White, Cap Storer, Joyce Linden, Helen Kroner.

Act 1: Old Home Week in the Village of Pilota.

Act 2: Wenzel's Apothecary Shop, Pilota.

Act 3: The Stage of the Budapest Opera House.

ACT 1

"Throw Me a Rose" (Duet)
    C. Meakins, J. E. Hazzard
    (*Lyrics by* P. G. Wodehouse and Herbert Reynolds.)

"Sunrise" (Intermezzo)
    "This Is the Existence" (Song)
    J. E. Hazzard, Committee of Six
    (*Lyrics by* P. G. Wodehouse.)

"Once Upon a Time" (Song)
    S. Petrass
    (*Lyrics by* P. G. Wodehouse.)

"Life Is a Game of Bluff" (Duet)
    J. E. Hazzard, G. MacFarlane
    (*Lyrics by* Herbert Reynolds.)

"A (Little) Bid for Sympathy" (Duet)
    C. Meakins, S. Petrass
    (*Lyrics by* Herbert Reynolds.)

Finale

ACT 2

Opening
    Ensemble

"The Love Monopoly" (Song)
    G. MacFarlane, Girls
    (*Lyrics by* Herbert Reynolds.)

"My Castle in the Air" (Song)
    S. Petrass, Men
    (*Music by* Jerome Kern. *Lyrics by* P. G. Wodehouse.)

"A Very Good Girl on Sunday" (Saturday Night)(Song)
    G. O'Ramey, Misses T. Hudson, C. Storer, E. Stillwell, J. White, J. Linden, H. Kroner
    (*Music by* Jerome Kern. *Lyrics by* P. G. Wodehouse.)

"Some One" (Song)
    S. Petrass
    (*Music by* Jerome Kern. *Lyrics by* Herbert Reynolds.)

"The Oold-Fashioned Drama" (Burletta)
    G. O'Ramey, J. Prouty, J. E. Hazzard

"(In) The Garden of Romance" (Duet)
    G. MacFarlane, S. Petrass
    (*Lyrics by* Herbert Reynolds.)

Finale

ACT 3

Opening Ballet:
    The Dance of Isis
    Ensemble

Dance Eccentrique
    F. Nice, A. Weeks

"A (Little) Country Mouse" (Song)
    S. Petrass, Ensemble
    (*Lyrics by* Herbert Reynolds.)

"When You're Full of Talk" (All Full of Talk)(Song)
    J. E. Hazzard
    (*Music by* Jerome Kern. *Lyrics by* P. G. Wodehouse.)

"Some One" (Reminiscence)
    G. MacFarlane, C. Meakins, S. Petrass
    (*Music by* Jerome Kern. *Lyrics by* Herbert Reynolds.)

Finale

1916.20   # BETTY

A Musical Play in Three Acts. Book by Gladys Unger and Frederick Lonsdale. Music by Paul A. Rubens. Lyrics by Adrian Ross and Paul A. Rubens. Additional numbers by Ernest Steffan and Merlin Morgan. Staged by Edward Royce. Scenery designed by Homer Emens. Costumes designed by Mme. Freisinger. Orchestra under the direction of William J. Daly. Produced by Charles Dillingham. Opened 3 October 1916 at the Globe Theatre and closed 25 November 1916 after 63 performances.

CAST: *Duke of Crowborough*: JOSEPH HERBERT. *Gerard, The Earl of Beverly*: JOSEPH SANTLEY. *Lord D'Arcy Playne*: RAYMOND HITCHCOCK. *David Playne*: Master (Arthur) Lowrie. *The Hon. Victor Halifax*: Henry Vincent. *Achille Jotte*, a dressmaker: Peter Page. *Hillier*, a butler: Sam Burbank. *Alf*, a page: Master Crumpton. *Cedric*: Alan Fagan. *Lathers (Tregellan)*, a valet: Eugene Revere. *Dora*, Countess of Playne: Katherine Stewart. *Chicquette*: JUSTINE JOHNSTONE. *Estelle*: Eileen Dennes. *Mrs. Rawlins*: Verda Shelberg. *Jane*: Marion Davies. *Betty*: IVY SAWYER. *Lady Charlotte Knowles*: Edna Bates. *Hon. Mrs. Partarlington*: Elinor St. Clair. *Lady Cholmondley*: Bunny Wendell. *Lady Majoribanks*: Florence Cripps. *Lady Paula Colquhuoun*: Prudence O'Shea. *Lady Violet Chichester*: Marna Blanchard. *Hon. Patience Pemberton*: Dorothy Germaine. *Lady Mary Manzies*: Lydia Scott. *Pansy*: Lillian Rice. *Daisy*: Anna Stone. *Lily*: Marie Benedict.

    Ensemble: *Jotte Girls*: Isabel Adams, Gertrude Roland, Ethel Burke, Mona Sartoris, Marie Benedict, Dorothy Harrigan, Mildred St. Clair, A. Roland, Peggy Dana, Anna Stone, Louise Worthington, Lotta Morse, Jean White, Jessie Howe, Ida Howe, Dorothy Duncan, Lillian Rice. *Smart Set Girls*: Kitty Lindley, Opal Essent, Virginia Taylor, Annette Herbert, Peggy Williamson, Grace Ford, Alice Roberts, Marie Baxter, Cecile Conway, Esther Lee, Prudence O'Shea, Marna Blanchard, Lydia Scott, Isabel Falconer, Dorothy Germaine, Jacquelin Woods. *Their Friends*: Messrs. J. Black, J. Brush, Doc Donnelly, Herbert Goff, A. Homme, Roy Hoyer, Rokey Johnson, Frank Keller, Walter Mozee, Fred Rockwell, Joseph Tierney, William Holbrook.

Act 1: Beverly Home, Regent's Park, London.

Act 2: The Garden of Beverly House.

Act 3: Bal Chinoise at Lord Playne's House.

ACT 1[28]

"High Life Down Stairs" (Opening Chorus)
    Butlers, Maids

"The Duchess of Dreams"
    I. Sawyer, A. Lowrie

"I Love the Girls"
    J. Santley, J. Johnstone, M. Davies, Chorus
    (*Lyrics by* Adrian Ross.)

"Some Time"
    R. Hitchcock
    (*Music by* Harry Tierney. *Lyrics by* William Jerome.)

"When I Am Twenty-One"
    J. Santley, Boys
    (*Music by* Jean Schwartz. *Lyrics by* Edgar Leslie.)

"Cinderella"
    I. Sawyer
    (*Lyrics by* Adrian Ross.)

Finale

ACT 2

"We've Got Some Work to Do" (Madrigal)
    House Servants

"I'm Jotte, the Dressmaker"
    P. Page, Midinettes

"Eyes Have a Language"
    J. Santley, Girls
    (*Music by* Silvio Hein. *Lyrics by* Benjamin Hapgood Burt.)

"I Feel So Happy"
    I. Sawyer, R. Hitchcock, M. Crumpton
    (*Lyrics by* Adrian Ross.)

"On a Saturday Afternoon"
    E. Dennes, A. Lowrie
    (*Lyrics by* Adrian Ross.)

---

[28]Act 1 was totally revised for subsequent tour (Chicago, April 1917) as follows:

"I Love the Girls" (Opening Chorus)
    Chorus

"The Girls I'd Like to Love"
    J. Santley, Chorus
    (*Music and Lyrics by* Joseph Santley.)

"Some Time"
    R. Hitchcock

"Poor Butterfly" (from THE BIG SHOW)
    I. Sawyer
    (*Music by* Raymond Hubbell. *Lyrics by* John Golden.)

"When You Grow To Be Twenty-One" (When I Was Twenty-One)
    J. Santley, M. Davies, Boys
    (*Music by* Jean Schwartz. *Lyrics by* Edgar Leslie.)

Finale

"If It Were True"
 I. Sawyer, J. Santley
 (*Music by* Ernest Steffan. *Lyrics by* Merlin Morgan.)
"Here Comes the Groom"
 R. Hitchcock
 (*Music and Lyrics by* Benjamin Hapgood Burt.)
Finale
ACT 3
 Opening Chorus
 Dance
 Misses St. Clair, Bates, Cripps, Wendell; Messrs. Fagan, Hoyer, Johnson, Goff
 "Dance With Me" (Waltz Duet)
 I. Sawyer, J. Santley
 (*Lyrics by* Percy Greenbank.)
 "The Little Harlequin"
 M. Davies, Chorus
Finale

1916.21 SO LONG LETTY

A Musical Farce in Two Acts, 3 Scenes. Book by Oliver Morosco and Elmer Harris. Music and lyrics by Earl Carroll. Book staged by Oliver Morosco. Dances and ensembles arranged by Julian Alfred. Orchestra under the direction of Harry James. Staged under the personal direction of Oliver Morosco. Produced by Oliver Morosco. Opened 23 October 1916 at the Sam S. Shubert Theatre and closed 13 January 1917 after 96 performances.[29]

CAST: *Letty Robbins*: CHARLOTTE GREENWOOD. *Grace Miller*: MAY BOLEY. *Tommy Robbins*: SYDNEY GRANT. *Harry Miller*: WALTER CATLETT. *Mrs. Cease*: Vera Doria. *Chita Alvarez*: FRANCES CAMERON. *Sadie McQuiggle*: WINNIE BALDWIN. *Philip Brown*: PERCEY BRONSON. *Billy Monday*: BEN LINN. *Chauffeur*: Robert Calley. *Dancers from the Casino*: DOROTHY CAMERON, MADELINE CAMERON.

 Personnel of the Chorus: Misses Gertrude Reynolds, Kay Beach, Muriel Griel, Ethel Westie, Marie Cattell, Murry Lavone, Margaret App, Betty Calais, Vera Mercer, Jennie Cannar, Margaret Moll, Betty Parker, Florence Flandreaux, Pauline DeLorme, Hazel Ellsworth, Jessie Reynolds. Messrs. Grover Franke, Wesley Spears, Jack Birkson, William McGuire, Frank O'Neil, Jack Wells, Roy Adams, Frank Leslie.

The action takes place in San Francisco at the present time.

Act 1: Trolley-Car Colony, Golden Gate Beach. Homes of Robbins and Miller. Saturday afternoon.

Act 2, Scene 1: Exterior of Robbins' Car. Evening. *Scene 2*: Interior of Robbins' Car. One week later.

ACT 1[30]
 Opening[31]
 Chorus
 "Letter Trio"
 V. Doria, F. Cameron, P. Bronson
 "All the Comforts of Home"
 M. Boley, Girls
 "So Long, Letty" (Duet)
 C. Greenwood, S. Grant
 Bathing Ensemble
 Ensemble
 "Pass Around the Apples Once Again"[32]
 W. Baldwin, P. Bronson

---

[29]Settings, costumes uncredited.
[30]Added to Act 1 for subsequent tour (April 1918), after "All the Comforts of Home":
 "Aloha"
 S. Grant, Boys
[31]Subsequent touring programs (May 1918) identified the opening chorus as a medley: "The Busiest Week" and "Cab Arabian Nights," followed by Dances from Casino and Chorus.
[32]Replaced for subsequent tour at various times by the following:
 "Let's Not Have a Kissless Day"
 Tyler Brooke (Philip), Halle Manning (Chita)
 "I've Got Enough to Marry You"
 W. Baldwin, P. Bronson, Boys
 "I've Got the Nicest Little Home in Dixie"
 Arthur Hartley (Philip), Muriel Greil (Chita), Chorus

"Blame It (All) on the Girls"[33]
 W. Catlett, Cameron Sisters, Chorus
"If I Could Read the Kisses Others Printed on Your Lips"[34]
 F. Cameron, P. Bronson, Chorus
Finale
 C. Greenwood, W. Catlett, S. Grant, M. Boley
ACT 2
 "(On a) Beautiful Beach" (Opening)
 W. Baldwin, Chorus, C. Greenwood
 "Mr. Patrick Henry Must Have Been a Married Man"[35]
 B. Linn
 Valse Poinsettia—Specialty Dance[36]
 Cameron Sisters
 Quarrel Duet[37]
 C. Greenwood, W. Catlett
 Specialty Dance[38]: Old Masters Fox Trot; Butterflies
 Cameron Sisters
 Southern and Hawaiian: (Specialty)
 F. Cameron, P. Bronson, Chorus, Musicians
 "Play Me a Ukelele" (Hawaiian)
 "When Jackson Moans on His Saxophone"[39] (Southern)
 "(Here Come the) Married Men"[40]
 C. Greenwood
 Finale
 Ensemble, Principals, Chorus

1916.22 GO TO IT

A Musical Play in Two Acts[41]. Book by John L. Golden. Based on the play "A Milk White Flag" by Charles Hoyt. Music by John Golden. Lyrics by John L. Golden, John E. Hazzard and Anne Caldwell. Staged by Frank Smithson. Dances and ensembles by David Bennett. Scenery designed by Elsie deWolfe. Gowns by Faibsey; men's clothes designed by Finchley. Orchestra under the direction of Max Hirschfeld. Produced by the Comstock-Elliott Company (F. Ray Comstock, William Elliott). Opened 24 October 1916 at the Princess Theatre and closed 11 November 1916 after 23 performances.

CAST: *The Colonel*: CHARLES JUDELS. *The Captain*: WELLINGTON CROSS. *The Private*: PERCIVAL KNIGHT. *The Bandmaster*: Will Archie. *The Lieutenant*: TYLER BROOKE. *Piggott Luce, the dear departed*: WILL DEMING. *Mr. Graves*: Dan Marble. *Mrs. Piggott Luce*: EMMA JANVIER. *Lucy, her daughter*: LOIS JOSEPHINE. *Vera Courtney*: ETHEL PETTIT. *Grape Juice*: Helen Bond. *Ginola*: Gertrude Waixel. *Rye*: Cecil Markel. *Winnie Wood*: Jeanette Cooke. *Sal Vation*: Betty Shannon. *Cara Mell*: Helen Francis. *Daisy Queen*: Gladys Clifton. *Sarah Nade*: Ethel Ford. *Seema Curves*: Alice Rodier. *Annie Mosity*: Lillian Galer. *Jessie Mine*: Marguerite Mason. *Annie Mation*: Bessie Sessions. *Myra Gard*: Katherine Hurst. *Molly Fie*: Helen O'Day. *Ella May*: Anne Kelly. *Katy Did*: Alice York. *Lizzie Wood*: Louise Cook. *Milly Tarry*: Lillian Lavonne. *Willie Fall*: Charles Yorkshire. *O. B. Gentle*: Wilbur Stutz. *Ruffan Reddy*: Leo Howe. *E. Z. Pickens*: Charles Hartmann. *Cuttan Splash*: Austin Clark. *Rising Stox*: Harry Davis. *Bull Marquette*: Jack Leslie. *Billy B. Good*: Arthur Whitman.

"After You've Gone"
 A. Hartley, M. Greil, Chorus
 (*Music by* Turner Layton. *Lyrics by* Henry Creamer.)
[33]Replaced first by "Do You Believe Me," then dropped during subsequent national tour.
[34]Replaced late in subsequent tour by:
 "I Showed That I Know Something When I Fell in Love with You"
 A. Hartley, M. Greil, Chorus
[35]Replaced for subsequent tour (later dropped):
 "When They Start to Yodel Ragtime Songs in Tennessee"
 S. Grant
[36]Replaced for subsequent tour by another dance specialty (later dropped):
 "Chasing the Squirrel"
 The Three DuFors
[37]Replaced during the run by "If the Good Die Young" which may be the same song. Dropped late in subsequent tour.
[38]Dropped during subsequent national tour.
[39]Variously titled "When You Hear Jackson Moan on His Saxophone."
[40]Replaced late in subsequent tour by:
 "I Am Going to Follow the Boys"
 C. Greenwood
[41]Billed as the Third Annual Princess Theatre Musical Production.

Act 1: Private Quarters of the Officers of the Corsican Blues.

Act 2: Reception Room at the Home of Mrs. Piggott Luce.

ACT 1

"Ladies Day"
Ensemble

"Kiss Your Soldier Boy (Au Revoir)"
E. Pettit, Ensemble

"Come Along Little Girls"
G. Waixel, C. Markel, T. Brooke, Ensemble

"When You're in Love You'll Know"
L. Josephine, W. Cross, Ensemble
(*Music by* Jerome Kern and John Golden. *Lyrics by* John Golden.)

"Where's the Little Boy for Me?"
E. Pettit, Boys
(*Music by* Charles N. Grant. *Lyrics by* Schuyler Greene.)

"Girls, If You Ever Get Married"
P. Knight, W. Cross, C. Judels, W. Archie, T. Brooke

"Every Little While"
L. Josephine, W. Cross, Ensemble
(*Music by* John L. Golden, James W. Tate. *Lyrics by* Clifford Harris.)

"Extra!"
E. Janvier, H. Bond, P. Knight

"Go To It"
Company
(*Music by* Raymond Hubbell. *Lyrics by* Max Darewski, John L. Golden.)

ACT 2

"Languanay"
E. Pettit, Ensemble

"Doesn't Anybody Want Me?"
Widows

"Love Me Just a Little Bit"
L. Josephine, W. Cross, Ensemble

"London Taps" (The Broken Doll)
E. Pettit

"A Little World of Our Own"
E. Pettit, T. Brooke, Ensemble
(*Lyrics by* John L. Golden.)

"There's Something About You (Dear That Appeals to Me)"
H. Bond, P. Knight
(*Music by* Silvio Hein and John Golden. *Lyrics by* Frank Craven.)

"You're the Girl That Sets Me Stuttering"
L. Josephine, W. Cross, Ensemble
(*Music and Lyrics by* Charles N. Grant and John L. Golden.)

"Little By Little (and Bit By Bit)"
P. Knight
(*Music and Lyrics by* Worton David, William Hargreaves, Schuyler Greene.)

Finale
Company

1916.23 THE SHOW OF WONDERS

A Musical Revue in Two Acts, 14 Scenes[43]. Dialogue (sketches) and lyrics by Harold Atteridge. Music by Sigmund Romberg, Otto Motzan and Herman Timberg. Staged by J. C. Huffman. Musical numbers arranged by Allan K. Foster. Scenery by H. Robert Law and John H. Young. Costumes designed by Homer Conant. Orchestra under the direction of Oscar Radin.

---

[43]A Second Edition was introduced 12 February 1917; most musical numbers remained intact, but the following new scenes were introduced:

"A Bit of Opera" (replacing "Mendelssohn and Liszt", Act 2)
Amato: W. Howard. *Tamato*: E. Howard.

Submarine F.7 (*by* James MacQueen)(Act 2, after "A Bit of Opera")

A Representation correct in every detail of a real submarine in action. Invented by Henri de Vries.

Lieutenant Hardy, commander of submarine F.7: Arthur Davis. *Ensign Yates*, second in command: Nathan Anderson. *Kelly*, chief machinist mate: Louis Alter. *Barry*, seaman at helm: William A. Evans. *Toomey*, torpedo man: Frank L. Hall. *Smith*, seaman at diving wheel bow: Gerard Arbous. *Hackford*, torpedo man: Joseph Costigan. *Guilbert*, torpedo man: Frank Dale.

Produced by the Winter Garden Company (Messrs. Shubert). Opened 26 October 1916 at the Winter Garden and closed 21 April 1917 after 209 performances[44].

CAST: WILLIE HOWARD, EUGENE HOWARD, ERNEST HARE, WALTER C. KELLY, MARILYNN [Marilyn] MILLER, JAMES McINTYRE, J. K. HEATH, SAMMY WHITE, LEW [Lou] CLAYTON, TOM LEWIS, GEORGE MONROE, JOHN T. MURRAY, EDMUND MULCAHY, MARIE LAVARRE, GEORGE BALDWIN, ELEANOR BROWN, GRACE FISHER, DAISY IRVING, SIDNEY PHILLIPS, IRENE ZOLAR, MYRTLE VICTORINE, ALEXIS KOSLOFF, DAISIE IRVING, JAMES A. WATTS, Dan Quinlan, James Grant, Jimmy Fox, Otto Johnson, Arthur Becker, Mabel Elaine, Doris Lloyd.

Ladies of the Ensemble: Helen Neat, Shirley Forsythe, Nell Carrington, Florence Elmore, Barbara McCree, Peggy Eleanor, Emily Miles, Alice Tabor, Margaret Hoban, Ivy Sherer, Madge Quest, Ada Winegard, Louise Mayorga, Clementine Clayman, Peggy Smith, Frances Whelean, Thea Thompson, May Belle, Dorothy Scofield, Dorothy Lloyd, Lillian Stein, Pearl Weber, Elizabeth Drew, Lucille Fletcher, Florence Shortell, Noel Woodward, Mabel Andrews, Mary Booth, Virginia May, Pauline Carlton, Phyliss Furcella, Luciel Peacock, Frances Veer, Dorothy Godfrey, Trixie Raymond, Agnes Richter, Grace Keeshon, Marion Mooney, Agnes Hall, Grace Hall, Peggie Dempsey, Effie Allan, Inez Francis, Dot Rozelle, Babe Dakin, Violet Watson, Flo Howe, Aileen Rooney, Lillian Lester, Elvira Kramer, Fay Tunis, Ethel Wallis, Nancy Everett, Orilla Mars, Virginia Smith, Halle Graham. *Gentlemen of the Ensemble*: Harry Bostack, Graham Wynn, Art Becker, Larry Mack, Dudley Farnsworth, Syd Meyers, Bob Casey, George Bayer, Walter Blair, Tex Turner, Ted Andrews, Harry Wilcox, Clyde Miller, Andrew Demarest, Phil Henry.

ACT 1

Scene 1

"Back to Nature"
D. Irving, Back-to-Nature Girls

"Wedding Bells"
M. Miller, G. Baldwin, J. T. Murray

"When Pavlowa Starts Bucking and Winging"
M. Lavarre, World's Greatest Dancers
Scene: Somewhere in the Adirondacks.
Hermit Joe: E. Mulcahy. *Eve*: M. Miller. *Iona Richley*: D. Irving. *Laura*: M. Lavarre. *Vivian*: E. Brown. *Jack Christopher*: G. Baldwin. *George Gloomy*: J. T. Murray.

Scene 2

"Hicky Do"[45]
W. Howard
Scene: The Deer Trail.
A Hunter: E. Howard. *Sammy*: W. Howard. *A Constable*: D. Quinlan. *Hermit Joe*: E. Mulcahy. *A Bear*: J. Grant. *Pietro*: E. Hare. *Vivian*: E. Brown.

Scene 3

"Girls Prepare"
G. Fisher, M. Victorine, I. Zolar, Fencing Girls

"Angels"[46]
J. T. Murray, D. Lloyd

"Aladdin"
E. Howard, Entire Ensemble
Scene: The Oriental Bazaar.
Henrietta: G. Fisher. *Miss Parry*: M. Victorine. *Miss Thrust*: I. Zolar. *Iona Richley*: D. Irving. *George Gloomy*: J. T. Murray. *Jack Christopher*: G. Baldwin. *Pansy*: G. Monroe. *Hermit Joe*: E. Mulcahy. *Eve*: M. Miller. *Modern Cleopatra*: D. Lloyd. *Mr. Edgeon*: D. Quinlan. *Hector*: T. Lewis. *Aladdin*: E. Howard.

Scene 4

"Girl on the Square"
S. Phillips, Girls from Different Climes
Scene: The Squares, New York City.
Mr. Manhattan: S. Phillips.

Scene 5

Scene: Gambling House.
Henry: J. H. Heath. *Alexander*: J. McIntyre. *The Gambling-House Owner*: O. Johnson. *Lucinda Morgan*: P. Eleanor.

---

[44]Running order revised for tour. Scenery uncredited; on subsequent tour it was credited to (H. Robert) Law and John H. Young.
[45]Replaced for subsequent tour by:
"My Yiddisha Butterfly"
W. Howard, E. Howard
[46]Dropped for subsequent tour.

Scene 6

"Louisiana"[47]

M. Lavarre, Cute Girlies, White and Clayton
Scene: At the Railroad Station.

Scene 7

"Pajama Girlie"

G. Baldwin, E. Brown, Pajama Girlies
Scene: In a Pullman Car.
Pansy: G. Monroe. *Conductor*: D. Quinlan. *Nip*: S. White. *Tuck*: L. Clayton.
Jack: G. Baldwin. *Hector*: T. Lewis. *Mr. Newlywed*: J. Fox. *Mrs. Newlywed*: G.
Fisher. *Hermit Joe*: E. Mulcahy. *Eve*: M. Miller. *George*: J. T. Murray. *A Kidnapper*: E. Hare.

Scene 8

"Get a Girlie"

G. Fisher, Winter Garden Peaches
Scene: The Garden of Peaches.

ACT 2

Scene 1

A Burmese Ballet (*Staged by* Allan K. Foster.)

A. Kosloff, M. Miller, D. Irving, Entire Ensemble
Scene: A Burmese Temple.
The Great Lover of the World: A. Kosloff. *Tamoura*: M. Miller. *Sanchea*: D.
Irving. *Harp Girls*: M. Wall, M. Swiler, M. McClintock, P. DeFontenry, R.
Masurette, I. Shepherd, B. Oliver (oboe).

Scene 2

"Mendelssohn and Liszt"

E. Howard, W. Howard
Scene: The Lane of Mystic Spirits.
Mendelssohn: W. Howard. *Liszt*: E. Howard.

Scene 3

The Virginia Judge[48]

W. C. Kelly
Scene: A Virginia Court Room.

Scene 4

"Naughty! Naughty! Naughty!"[49]

G. Fisher, Naughty Naughty Naughty Girls

"Wedding By the Sea"

D. Irving, Bathing Girls

"Diabolo"

M. Miller, A. Kosloff, Diabolo Girls and Boys
Scene: On the Beach.
Iona: D. Irving. *Eve*: M. Miller. *Hermit Joe*: E. Mulcahy. *George*: J. T.
Murray. *Miss Long Beach*: D. Lloyd. *Miss Atlantic City*: F. Elmore. *Miss
Deal Beach*: I. Sherer. *Miss Rye Beach*: H. Neat. *Mermaid*: V. Smith. *Beach
Guard*: D. Quinlan. *Old Salt*: A. Becker. *Hector*: T. Lewis. *Pansy*: G.
Monroe. *Henrietta*: G. Fisher.

Scene 5

"Medley of Song"[50]

W. Howard, E. Howard
Scene: The Lobby of the Giltmore Hotel.
Sammy: W. Howard. *Elevator Boy*: A. Demarest. *Jean*: E. Howard. *Eleanor*:
E. Brown. *Waiter*: J. Grant.

Scene 6

Italian Ballet Miniature[51]

M. Miller, A. Kosloff, Troubadour Boys, Masked Girlies

"Slavlova"[52]

J. A. Watts

"Zoo" (The Zoo Step)

M. Lavarre, S. White, Winter Garden Steppers

---

[47]Dropped for subsequent tour.
[48]Dropped for subsequent tour.
[49]Replaced for subsequent tour by:
"Love Is a Bubble"
Adele Ardsley, Bubble Girls
[50]Replaced for subsequent tour by:
"The Ghost of the Ukelele"
W. Howard, E. Howard
[51]Solo dances arranged by Alexis Kosloff.
[52]Dropped during the run.

Finale

Entire Ensemble
Scene: The Masked Ball.
Jack: G. Baldwin. *Pansy*: G. Monroe. *Miss Topnote*: J. A. Watts. *George*: J. T.
Murray. *Iona*: D. Irving. *Hector*: T. Lewis. *Eleanor*: E. Brown. *Hermit Joe*: E.
Mulcahy. *Eve*: M. Miller. *Jean*: E. Howard. *Sammy*: W. Howard.

1916.24 # THE CENTURY GIRL

A Musical Entertainment (Revue) in Three Acts, 19 Scenes. Music by
Victor Herbert, Irving Berlin. Lyrics by Irving Berlin, (Henry Blossom).
Staged by Edward Royce, Leon Errol. Scenes (designed) by Joseph Urban.
Costumes designed by Lucille, Marie Cook, Raphaël Kirchner, Cora
MacGeachy, William H. Matthews. Orchestra under the direction of Louis
Gottschalk, Max Hoffmann. Produced by Charles Dillingham and Florenz
Ziegfeld. Opened 6 November 1916 at the Century Theatre and closed 28
April 1917 after 200 performances.

CAST: ELSIE JANIS, SAM BERNARD, MARIE DRESSLER, HAZEL DAWN,
(Gus) VAN and (Joe) SCHENCK, LEON ERROL, IRVING FISHER, LILLIAN
TASHMAN, FRANK TINNEY, JOHN SLAVIN, (James) DOYLE and (Harland)
DIXON, FLORENCE WALTON and MAURICE, May Leslie, Marjorie Cassidy,
Semone D'Herlys, Hazel Lewis, Margaret Morris, Flo Hart, Evelyn Conway, Arthur
Cunningham, John Slavin, The Barr Twins, Vera Maxwell, Billie Allen, Harry Kelly,
Yvonne Shelton, Gus Minton, Myles McCarthy, Dave Abrams.
Century Girls: Misses Delmar, Erlich, Mack, Gardener, Mackenzie, DeBeera,
Montague, Logan, Marion Fairbanks, James, Broden, Colby, Irving, Watson,
Bruce, Donaldson, Baker, Madeline Fairbanks. *Girls of the Ensemble*: Misses Chase,
Hirsch, Leeds, R. Lewis, Curtis, Errol, Bade, Loring, Adair, Field, Alexander,
Hirsch, Shelton, Jeppson, LeGrande, Ellison, Magnus, Elsworth, Fisher, Carr,
M. Fisher, Wallace, Perry, Greete, Kohler, Kerner, Dewey, Feltes, Daintry, Hart,
Logan, Kohler, Kerner, Conway, Baker, Reeves, Colby, Montague, Leslie, Morris,
Borden, Whitney, Marjorie Cassidy, Delmar, H. Lewis, Erlich, James, Fisher,
Magnus, Greete, Alexander, Leeds, Field, Perry, Loring, C. Carroll, Kerstein, Dillon,
Murphy, Gray, Godins, Roberts, Gumport, Brown, Daly, Richter, Cronan, Murphy,
Stone, Owen.

ACT 1

Scene 1

"The Birth of the Century Girl"

(*Music by* Victor Herbert. *Lyrics by* Henry Blossom. *Staged by* Edward Royce.)
Scene: The Celestial Staircase.
Women of the Ages: *Queen Boadicea*: M. Leslie. *Helen of Troy*: M. Cassidy.
Cleopatra: S. D'Herlys. *Joan of Arc*: H. Lewis. *Catherine of Russia*: M.
Morris. *Marie Antoinette*: F. Hart. *Empress Josephine*: L. Tashman. *Barbara
Fritchie*: E. Conway. *The Century Girl*: H. Dawn. *The Butterflies*: Sunshine
Girls. *Century Girls*: Misses Delmar, Erlich, Mack, Gardener, Mackensie,
DeBeera, Montague, Logan, Madeline Fairbanks, James, Broden, Colby,
Irving, Watson, Bruce, Donaldson, Baker, Marion Fairbanks.

"The Century Girl" (Song)

H. Dawn, Chorus
(*Music by* Victor Herbert. *Lyrics by* Henry Blossom.)

Dance

A. Bell

Scene 2

"Opportunity"

M. Dressler
(*Music and Lyrics by* Helen Trix.)

"You Belong to Me" (Duet)

H. Dawn, I. Fisher
(*Music by* Victor Herbert. *Lyrics by* Harry B. Smith.)
Scene: Garden of a Modern Girls' School.
Marie Young, the Schoolmistress: M. Dressler. *Emil Klutz*: S. Bernard. *Eva
Brown*: H. Dawn. *Howell Lauder, a singing teacher*: I. Fisher. *School Girls*:
Misses Chase, Hirsch, Leeds, R. Lewis, Curtis, Errol, Bade, Loring, Adair,
Field, Alexander, Hirsch, Shelton, Jeppson, LeGarnde, Ellison, Magnus,
Elsworth, Fisher, Carr, M. Fisher, Wallace, Perry, Greete, Kohler, Kerner,
Dewey, Feltes, Daintry.

"The Music Lesson"

(*Music and Lyrics by* Irving Berlin.)
Victor Herbert: A. Cunningham. *Irving Berlin*: J. Slavin.

Scene 3

Eccentric Dance

L. Errol, G. Rutland
Scene: A Garden.

Scene 4

"It Takes an Irishman to Make Love" (Trio)
E. Janis, J. Doyle, H. Dixon
(*Music by* Irving Berlin. *Lyrics by* Irving Berlin, Elsie Janis.)
Scene: The Grand Central Station.
Peggy O'Brien: E. Janis. *Will B. Rich*: J. Doyle. *Wood B. Rich*: H. Dixon.
Marie Young: M. Dressler. *Emil Klutz*: S. Bernard.

Songs
G. Van, J. Schenck
["My Hawaiian Sunrise"
(*Music and Lyrics by* L. Wolfe Gilbert and Carey Morgan.)
"He Likes Their Ukelele"
(*Music and Lyrics by* James Kendis)]

Scene 5

Hunting for a New Dance—Finale
"The Chicken Walk" (That Broadway Chicken Walk)
(*Music and Lyrics by* Irving Berlin. *Staged by* Leon Errol.)
Scene: The Forest Glade.
The Lion: A. Cunningham. *The Lame Duck*: H. Dawn. *The Grizzly Bears*: J. Doyle, H. Dixon. *The Turkey*: M. Dressler. *The Fox*: H. Kelly. *The Two Foxesses*: The Barr Twins. *The Cub Fox*: J. Slavin. *The Hunter*: I. Fisher. *The Huntresses*: B. Allen, V. Maxwell. *The Rooster*: L. Errol. *The Chicken*: E. Janis. *The Lame Ducks*: Misses Hart, Mackenzie, Logan, Kohler, Kerner, Conway, Bruce, Baker, Errol, Reeves, Colby, Montague, LeGrande, Ellison, Tashman. *The Turkeys*: The Sunshine Girls. *The Foxes*: Misses Leslie, Morris, Mack, Borden, Hirsch, Whitney, Cassidy, Delmar, Gardner, Chase, Wallace, H. Lewis, Erlich, James, Fisher, Magnus. *The Chickens*: Madeleine Fairbanks, Marion Fairbanks, Y. Shelton, R. Lewis, Greete, Bade, Dewey, Feltes, Alexander, Leeds, Field, Perry, Jeppson, Curtis, Loring, Elsworth, Adair, Carr.

ACT 2
Scene 1

The Ballet Loose
Scene: The Stone Age.
(*Music by* Victor Herbert. *Staged by* Edward Royce and Leon Errol.)
Waldorf Dryginski: Leon Errolovitch. *Mike Debitesky*: Hary Kelloski. *Petite Publicbuildingski*: M. Dressleroff. *Cave Ladies*: B. Allen, V. Maxwell. And Ensemble.

Scene 2

"The Toy Soldiers" (Duet and Dance)
J. Doyle, H. Dixon
(*Music by* Victor Herbert. *Staged by* Edward Royce.)

Scene 3

Dance
Maurice and Walton
Scene: The Long Vue Restaurant.

Scene 4

"Alice in Wonderland" (Duet)
H. Dawn, I. Fisher
(*Music and Lyrics by* Irving Berlin. *Staged by* Edward Royce.)
Scene: Alice in Wonderland.
Eva Brown: H. Dawn. *Howell Lauder*: I. Fisher. *Alice*: Y. Shelton. *The Mad Hatter*: L. Errol. *The Carpenter*: L. Errol. *The Walrus*: H. Kelly. *The Dormouse*: L. Errol. *The Six Oysters*: Kisses Kerstein, Dillon, Murphy, Gray, Godins, Roberts. *Ace of Hearts*: Miss Erlich. *Ace of Diamonds*: Miss Delmar. *Ace of Clubs*: Miss Mack. *Ace of Spades*: Miss Gardner. *The King of Hearts*: Miss Tashman. *The King of Diamonds*: Miss Conway. *The King of Clubs*: Miss Hart. *The King of Spades*: Miss Baker. *The Queen of Hearts*: Miss Mackensie. *The Queen of Diamonds*: Miss Colby. *The Queen of Clubs*: Miss Kohlor. *The Queen of Spades*: Miss Donaldson. *The Jack of Hearts*: Miss Leeds. *The Jack of Diamonds*: Miss Marion Fairbanks. *The Jack of Clubs*: Miss Madeleine Fairbanks. *The Jack of Spades*: Miss Jeppson. *The Ten of Hearts*: Miss Hirsch. *The Ten of Diamonds*: Miss Fisher. *The Ten of Clubs*: Miss Borden. *The Ten of Spades*: Miss Chase. *The Nine of Hearts*: Miss Whitney. *The Nine of Diamonds*: Miss James. *The Nine of Clubs*: Miss Magnus. *The Nine of Spades*: Miss Perry. *The Eight of Hearts*: Miss Wallace. *The Eight of Diamonds*: Miss Curtis. *The Eight of Clubs*: Miss Elsworth. *The Eight of Spades*: Miss Field. *The Seven of Hearts*: Miss Carr. *The Seven of Diamonds*: Miss Bade. *The Seven of Clubs*: Miss Adair. *The Seven of Spades*: Miss Loring. *The Joker*: Miss C. Carroll. *The Children*: Misses Gumport, Brown, Daly, Richter, Cronan, Murphy, Stone, Owen.

Scene 5

Frank Tinney (Monologue)

Scene 6

"They've Got Me Doing It Too"
E. Janis, Sunshine Girls

(*Music and Lyrics by* Irving Berlin.)
Scene: Stage Door of the Frivolity Theatre.
Peggy O'Brien: E. Janis. *Emile Klutz*: S. Bernard. *Mr. Will B. Rich*: J. Doyle. *Mr. Wood B. Rich*: H. Dixon. *Stage Door Keeper of the Frivolity*: G. Minton.

Scene 7

(A Political Speech)
Scene: Outside the Union League Club.
Emil Klutz: S. Bernard. *A Club Member*: M. McCarthy.

Scene 8

"When Uncle Sam Rules the Wave" (When Uncle Sam Is Ruler of the Sea)
I. Fisher
(*Music by* Victor Herbert. *Lyrics by* Henry Blossom. *Staged by* Ned Wayburn.)
Scene: Uncle Sam's Children.
Columbia: H. Dawn. *Alaska*: E. Conway. *Porto Rico*: M. Morris. *The Philippines*: H. Lewis. *Hawaii*: M. Leslie. *The First American*: M. Cassidy. And the American Triple Tap Dancers.

ACT 3
Scene 1

"Under the Sea"
(*Music by* Victor Herbert. *Staged by* Edward Royce.)
The Queen Mermaid: V. Maxwell. *A Mermaid*: S. D'Herlys. *Another Mermaid*: Miss Mayfield. *The Diver*: L. Errol. *Corals and Lobsters*: The Sunshine Girls. *Anemones*: Misses Delmar, Mack, James, Mackensie, Bade, Erlich, Gardner, DeBeers. *Turtles*: Misses Hirsch, Greete, Beele, Feltes, Perry, Dewey, Elsworth, Daintry.

Scene 2

Marie Dressler[52a]

Scene 3

Elsie Janis

Scene 4

"Jumping Jacks" (The Romping Red Heads)(Song and Dance)
L. Errol, Sunshine Girls
(*Music by* Victor Herbert. *Lyrics by* Henry Blossom. *Staged by* Edward Royce.)

Scene 5

A Street in New York
A Traffic Policeman: F. Tinney. *A Traffic Sergeant*: M. McCarthy. *An Old Man*: D. Abrams.

Scene 6

Procession of the Laces of the World
(*Staged by* Edward Royce.)
Scene: The Crystal Palace.
French Lace: S. D'Herlys. *English Lace*: Miss Erlich. *Spanish Lace*: Miss Cassidy. *Belgian Lace*: Miss Leslie. *Italian Lace*: L. Tashman. *Irish Lace*: Miss Conway. *American Silver*: H. Lewis. *American Gold*: Miss Morris. *Columbine*: B. Allen. *Harlequin*: V. Maxwell.

"On the Train of a Wedding Gown"
H. Dawn, I. Fisher; J. Doyle, H. Dixon, Barr Twins; B. Allen, H. Kelly; M. Dressler, L. Errol; E. Janis, S. Bernard
(*Music and Lyrics by* Irving Berlin.)

1916.25

FOLLOW ME

A Musical Comedy in Three Acts. Based on an original (Viennese musical 'Was tut man nicht alles aus Liebe,') with music by Leo Ascher and libretto by Felix Dörmann. Music by Sigmund Romberg, (Harry Tierney). Lyrics by Robert B. Smith, (Alfred Bryan). Staged by J. K. Benrimo. Dances arranged by Jack Mason and Allan K. Foster. Scenery by P. Dodd Ackerman, H. Robert Law Studio. Costumes designed by Homer Conant. Orchestra under the direction of Frank Tours. Produced by Messrs. Shubert. Opened 29 November 1916 at the Casino Theatre and closed 3 February 1917 after 78 performances.[53]

CAST (in order of appearance): *Denise*, fortune teller at a charity bazaar: EDITH DAY. *Louis*, page boy: Wilmer Bentley. *Worth Muchmore*, American millionaire: HARRY TIGHE. *Laura*, Marquise de Lunay: LETTY YORKE. *Hector*, Marquis de Lunay: WILLIAM P. CARLTON. *Fresco*, a waiter from Maxime's: P. Paul Porcasi. *Jeweler*: George Egan. *Dr. Jolivet*: Robert Capron. *Alphonse*, call boy: Wilmer Bentley. *Claire LaTour* of the Theatre Varieties: ANNA HELD. *Ninon*, *Babette*, attendants at the bazaar: Gladys Sykes, Ethel Sykes. *Slavlova and Marcheesi*: James Watts. *Adolph Knutt*,

---

[52a]Miss Dressler's specialty was withdrawn after 3 performances, ostensibly because the production was overlong.
[53]Book adaptation uncredited.

poet at large: HENRY LEWIS. *Miss Watchcharm:* SYLVIA JASON. (*Dancers to the Spanish Court, Act 1:* EDUARDO AND ELISA CANSINO. *Ballet Specialty:* MARY EATON. *Violin Specialty:* Betsy Duncan.)

Personnel of the Chorus: Anna Held Girls: Anna Berg, Perle Germond, Mildred LeGue, Rena Manning, Edna Rochelle, Laura Hastings, Gertrude Harrison, Betsy Duncan, Carrol Ashley. *Show Girls:* Volga Hayworth, Marcie Hawley, Mae Manning, Caroline Roland, Leila Van Holk, Grace Langdon, Gladys Dupell, Emeline Emerson. *Mediums:* Beatrice Cloak, Helen Lane, Madeline Levene, Evelyn LeRoy, Ruth Miller, Florence Sommerville, Minna Whitmore, Sylvia Casel. *Dancers:* Grace Williams, Alice Van Ryker, Kittie Mahoney, Ruth Maybe, Eleanor Matthewson, Emily Morrison, Frances Mink, Dorothy Pond. (*Men of the Chorus*): George Collins, Stanley Dixon, Henry Ward, Lovett Wilder, Edmund Kaeding, Frank Binns, Alfred Opler, Walter Paustian, Frank Shepard, Norman Charles.

Act 1: Garden of a Villa near Paris. Charity Bazaar in Aid of Wounded Soldiers on a July Afternoon. (Ackerman.)

Act 2: Green Room at Theatre. Benefit performance. Evening. (Ackerman.)

Act 3: Les Ambassadeurs' Restaurant, Bois de Boulogne, Paris. Evening. (Law.)

ACT 1[54]

Opening Chorus

"We Always Take Them Home" (I Always See Them Safely Home)
H. Tighe, Chorus
(*Music by* Jack Galon. *Lyrics by* Howard Johnson.)

"Two Happy Tadpoles"[55]
E. Day, H. Tighe

"When a Man Is Single"
W. P. Carlton, G. Sykes, E. Sykes, Chorus
(*Music by* Frank E. Tours. *Lyrics by* Robert B. Smith.)

"A Tête à Tête with You"
L. Yorke, W. P. Carlton

"Follow Me"
A. Held, Boys
(*Music and Lyrics by* Helen Trix.)

"(Oh) I Want to Be Good But My Eyes Won't Let Me"
A. Held, H. Tighe
(*Music by* Harry Tierney. *Lyrics by* Anna Held and Alfred Bryan.)

"The Girls Are Getting Wiser"
H. Tighe, S. Jason
(*Music by* Harry Tierney. *Lyrics by* Anna Held and Alfred Bryan.)

Quartette
L. Yorke, E. Day, H. Tighe, W. P. Carlton

Finale

ACT 2[56]

Opening Chorus

Rose Ballet[57]
M. Eaton, Chorus

Classical Dance[58] (Burlesque)
J. Watts

---

[54]Added to Act 1 after "The Girls Are Getting Wiser" during the run:
"(There's Just) A Little Bit of Monkey (Still Left in You and Me)"
H. Lewis
(*Music by* James Monaco. *Lyrics by* Grant Clarke.)

A subsequent tour presented by Anna Held but starring Liane Carriere featured a much revised score; new songs included: "Kiss at Auction," "I Like It," "When I First Knew You," "When Yankee Doodle Learns to Parlez Vous," "Fool Me," "Yum, Yum, Yum," "I Am Not So Different," "Raggy Ragtime Train," "Darling of the Gods," "O, Marie," "La Parisienne Girl."

[55]Dropped after opening.

[56]Added to Act 2 after "Milady's Toilette Set" in second week of the run:
"It's the Little Things That Count"
S. Jason
(*Music by* Harry Tierney. *Lyrics by* Alfred Bryan.)

Added to Act 2 after "It's a Cute Little Way of My Own" in second week of run:
"What Do You Want to Make Those Eyes at Me For (When They Don't Mean What They Say)?"
H. Lewis
(*Music by* James V. Monaco. *Lyrics by* Howard Johnson, Joseph McCarthy.)

[57]Dropped during the run.

[58]Dropped during the run.

"Milady's Toliette Set"
E. Day, Milady Girls[59]
(*Music by* Harry Tierney. *Lyrics by* Alfred Bryan.)

"It's a Cute Little Way of My Own"
A. Held, Chorus
(*Music by* Harry Tierney. *Lyrics by* Anna Held and Alfred Bryan.)

"Adam Was the Only Lover"
A. Held, L. Yorke

"The Violin Song"[60]
L. Yorke, B. Duncan (violin)

"A Little Bit of Nonsense"[61]
H. Lewis

"I Am True to All"[62]
H. Tighe, Girls

Finale

ACT 3[63]

Opening Chorus

"Happy Land" (Happyland)
S. Jason, Chorus
(*Music by* Harry Tierney. *Lyrics by* Alfred Bryan.)

"How Would You Like to Bounce a Baby on Your Knee?"
E. Day, Dancing Girls
(*Music by* Harry Tierney. *Lyrics by* Alfred Bryan.)

"My Bohemian Fashion Girl"[64]
A. Held, Anna Held Girls, Chorus
(*Music by* Harry Tierney. *Lyrics by* Alfred Bryan.)

"Stop Tickling Me"
A. Held

(Finale)

1916.26   # HER SOLDIER BOY

A Musical Play in Two Acts. Book and lyrics by Rida Johnson Young. Adapted from a Viennese original ('Gold gab' ich für Eisen'), libretto by Victor Léon. Music by Sigmund Romberg and Emmerich Kálmán. Staged by J. J. Shubert. Dances arranged by Jack Mason. Scenery designed by P.

---

[59]Opening night playbill incorrectly assigned this song to James Watts.
[60]Replaced in second week of run by:
"A Word of Love"
L. Yorke, B. Duncan (violin)
(*Music by* Frank E. Tours. *Lyrics by* Robert B. Smith.)
"When They Grow Older"
H. Tighe, Girls
(*Music by* George Meyer. *Lyrics by* Sam Lewis.)
[61]Additional songs performed by Henry Lewis in his Specialty Spot in New York and on tour:
"Love Is a Wonderful Thing"
(*Music by* Anatole Friedland. *Lyrics by* L. Wolfe Gilbert.)
"Lily of the Valley" (The Nut Song)
(*Music by* Anatole Friedland. *Lyrics by* L. Wolfe Gilbert.)
"Where the Black-Eyed Susans Grow" (from ROBINSON CRUSOE, JR.)
(*Music by* Richard A. Whiting. *Lyrics by* Dave Radford.)]
[62]Dropped in the second week of run.
[63]Added to Act 3 after "Happy Land" during the run:
Specialty Dance
Cansinos
"A Little More Nonsense"
H. Lewis
Added to Act 3 for subsequent tour, after "Happyland":
Dance Flirtation
Seabury and Shaw
"(Oh, Johnny!) Oh, Johnny, Oh!"
H. Lewis
(*Music by* Abe Olman. *Lyrics by* Ed Rose.)
"What Did Eve Give Adam for Christmas?"
H. Lewis
(*Music and Lyrics by* Henry Lewis.)
[64]Dropped during the run and for subsequent tour.

Dodd Ackerman and Edward Sundquist. Costumes designed by Mme. Kahn; Miss Rowland's gowns by Faibsey. Orchestra under the direction of Augustus Barratt. Produced by the Messrs. Shubert. Opened 6 December 1916 at the Astor Theatre, moved 30 April 1917 to the Lyric Theatre, moved 14 May 1917 to the Sam S. Shubert Theatre, and closed 26 May 1917 after 198 performances.

CAST (in order of appearance): *In the Prologue: Alfred Appledorp:* Ward DeWolfe. *A Dancer:* Helen Hyde. *Frantz Delaunay:* FRANK RIDGE. *Alain Teniers:* JOHN CHARLES THOMAS. *Sergeant:* Earl Brunswick.

In the Play: Marlene Delaunay: BETH LYDY. *Boy:* Clarice Snyder. *Elsje:* Eliz Gergely. *Teddy McLane:* CLIFTON CRAWFORD. *Monty Mainwaring:* Cyril Chadwick. *Desiree:* Mildred Richardson. *Vitus Appledorp:* HAROLD VIZARD. *Baron von Artveldt:* GEORGE SCHILLER. *Alma:* Dorothy Flam. *Alfred Appledorp:* Ward DeWolfe. *Amy Lee:* ADELE ROWLAND. *Madame Karoline Delainay:* Ethel Brandon. *Alain Teniers:* JOHN CHARLES THOMAS. *Sergeant:* Earl Brunswick. *A Private:* Owen Hervey. *First Sergeant:* Ralph J. Herbert. *Martin von Artveldt:* Byrd Goolsby. *Frantz Delaunay:* FRANK RIDGE.

Personnel of the Chorus: Peasant Girls: Ethel Van Arsdale, Florence Vinsen, Violet Marsden, Dorothy Flam, Sydelle Seit, Camille Truesdale, Nellie Mallin, Helen Hyde, Jane Gray, Marjorie Taylor, Nan Bryce. *American Girls:* Lillian Horn, Katherine Vincent, Frances Hendricks, Dorothy Schaefer, Chloe Richter, Bessie Hoban, Paula Leslie, Doris Sheerin, Mabel Henry, Rosina Timponi, Dolly Dempsey, Peggy Whitney. *Soldiers:* F. D. Henry, Fred Hoag, Sol Singlust, Owen Hervey, John Bilham, H. Grady Miller, Walter Mahoney, William Tillett, Dan MacNeil, Paul Burtnett, Irving Jackson, Fred Williams, Albert McWilliams, John Walsh, Byrd Goolsby, Dan Sparks.

Prologue: Behind the Lines. Somewhere in Belgium.

Act 1: Chateau Delaunay; the Village of Ghistelle. (Sundquist.)

Act 2: A Room in the Chateau. (Ackerman.)

PROLOGUE

  Opening
    W. DeWolfe, Soldiers
  "Mother"[65]
    F. Ridge
  "Song of Home"
    F. Ridge, J. C. Thomas
    (*Music by* Emmerich Kálmán.)

ACT 1

  "Fairy Song"[66]
    B. Lydy
  "All Alone in a City of Girls"
    C. Crawford, Peasant Girls
    (*Music by* Sigmund Romberg.)
  "I Want to Go Home"[67]
    A. Rowland, Chorus
  "He's Coming Home"
    B. Lydy
    (*Music by* Sigmund Romberg.)
  "Song of Home"
    J. C. Thomas
    (*Music by* Emmerich Kálmán.)
  Finale

ACT 2

  "I'd Be Happy Anywhere with You"
    W. DeWolfe, M. Richardson, Chorus
    (*Music by* Sigmund Romberg.)
  "Smile, Smile, Smile" (Pack Up Your Troubles in Your Old Kit Bag)
    A. Rowland, Boys
    (*Music by* Felix Powell. *Lyrics by* George Asaf.)

---

[65]Two songs with the same name "Mother" were written for the show:
    (*Music by* Emmerich Kálmán. *Lyrics by* Darl MacBoyle.)
    (*Music by* Sigmund Romberg.)
  Which was performed on opening night is not known; most likely Romberg's replaced Kálmán's.
[66]Replaced after opening by:
  "The Sleeping Princess" (The Lonely Princess)
    B. Lydy
    (*Music by* Sigmund Romberg.)
[67]Replaced after opening by:
  "Home Again"
    A. Rowland, Chorus
    (*Music by* Sigmund Romberg. *Lyrics by* Augustus Barratt.)

"Slavery"
    C. Crawford
    (*Music and Lyrics by* Clifton Crawford.)
"Golden Sunshine"
    B. Lydy, J. C. Thomas
    (*Music by* Emmerich Kálmán.)
"Amsterdam"
    E. Gergely
    (*Music and Lyrics by* Augustus Barratt.)
"Kiss Waltz"
    B. Lydy, J. C. Thomas
    (*Music by* Sigmund Romberg.)
"History"
    C. Crawford
    (*Music and Lyrics by* Clifton Crawford.)
"Military Stamp"
    C. Crawford, A. Rowland, Chorus
    (*Music and Lyrics by* Clifton Crawford.)
Finale

1917.01   HAVE A HEART

A Musical Comedy in Two Acts, 3 Scenes. Book and lyrics by Guy Bolton and P. G. Wodehouse. Music by Jerome Kern. Staged by Edward Royce. Scenery designed by Henry Ives Cobb, Jr. Costumes designed by Frances, Inc. Lighting by Joseph Wilson. Orchestra under the direction of Gus Salzer. Orchestrations by Frank Saddler. Produced by Henry W. Savage. Opened 11 January 1917 at the Liberty Theatre and closed 17 March 1917 after 76 performances.

CAST (in order of appearance): *Henry*, the elevator boy at Schoonmakers': BILLY B. VAN. *Ted Sheldon:* DONALD MACDONALD. *Lizzie O'Brien:* MARJORIE GATESON. *Detective Baker*, of the Blueport Police: Eugene Keith. *Rutherford Schoonmaker*, proprietor of the Schoonmaker Department Store (Ruddy): THURSTON HALL. *Captain Charles Owen:* Roy Gordon. *Peggy Schoonmaker:* EILEEN VAN BIENE. *Mrs. Pyne*, Peggy's Aunt: FLAVIA ARCARO. *Matthew Pyne:* James Bradbury. *Dolly Brabazon:* LOUISE DRESSER. *Yussuf*, the entertainer: JOSEPH DEL PUENTE. *Maitre d'Hotel:* Eugene Revere. *Georgia:* PEGGY FEARS.

Shoppers: Misses Rosalie Mellette, Helen Eby, Charmion Furlong, Dazie Burton, Anne Sands, Grace DuBois, Annette Besuden, Margaret Fritts. *Salesgirls:* Misses Doris Predo, Martha Parsons, Alice Maurice, Mabel Guilford, Marie Hollywell, Helen Lane, Belle Bowman, Helen Donohue. *Men:* Messrs. William Deacon, Will Smith, Paul Mountaney, Bert Pullaney, Roy Wells, Will Cobb, Earl Jordon, Walter Burke, Jules Rigoni, Arthur Eley.

The action takes place in Blueport, Rhode Island, at the present time.

Act 1: Lingerie Room at Schoonmaker's.

Act 2, Scene 1: Lounge of the Ocean View Hotel. Night. *Scene 2:* The same. Next morning.

ACT 1[68]

  "Shop" (Entrance)
    Salesgirls
  "I'm So Busy" (Duet)
    M. Gateson, D. Macdonald
    (*Lyrics by* P. G. Wodehouse and Schuyler Greene.)
  "Have a Heart" (Musical Scene)
    T. Hall
  "(And) I Am All Alone" (Duo)
    T. Hall, E. Van Biene
    (*Lyrics by* P. G. Wodehouse and Jerome Kern.)
  "I'm Here, Little Girl, I'm Here" (Song)
    D. Macdonald, Girls
  "Bright Lights" (Dance Duet)
    L. Dresser, B. B. Van

---

[68]Added after the opening:
  "Look in His Eyes" (from LIEBER AUGUSTIN and MISS CAPRICE, revised)
    Margaret Romaine (Peggy)
    (*Lyrics by* Herbert Reynolds [M. E. Rourke].)
  Added for subsequent tour:
  "What Would You Do for $50,000"
    (*Music by* Harry Tierney. *Lyrics by* Alfred Bryan.)
  "Reminiscences" (reprise of "And I Am All Alone")
    Orchestra

"The Road That Lies Before" (Musical Scene)
T. Hall, E. Van Biene

Finale
Ensemble

ACT 2[69]

Opening Chorus
Guests

"Samarkand"
J. del Punte, Ensemble

"Honeymoon Inn" (Song)
E. Van Biene, Ensemble

"Come Out of the Kitchen"[70] (Song)
L. Dresser
(*Music and Lyrics by* James Kendis and Charles Bayha.)

"My Wife—My Man" (Duet)
E. Van Biene, T. Hall

"You Said Something" (Duo)
D. Macdonald, M. Gateson, Ensemble
(*Lyrics by* P. G. Wodehouse and Jerome Kern.)

Dance Duet
D. Macdonald, P. Fears

"Napoleon" (Song)
B. B. Van, Flunkeys, Girls

"Peter Pan"[71] (Song)
E. Van Biene

Finale
Ensemble

LOVE O' MIKE

1917.02

A Comedy with Music in Two Acts and a Prologue. Book by Thomas Sydney [Sydney Smith and Augustus Thomas, Jr.]. Music by Jerome Kern. Lyrics by Harry B. Smith. Staged by J. H. Benrimo. Scenery designed by Robert McQuinn. Gowns designed by Faibsey. Orchestra under the direction of Frank Tours. Orchestrations by Frank Saddler. Produced by Elisabeth Marbury and Lee Shubert. Opened 15 January 1917 at the Sam S. Shubert Theatre, moved 19 March 1917 to Maxine Elliott's Theatre, and closed 30 June 1917 after 192 performances; re-opened 27 August 1917 at the Casino Theatre and closed 29 September 1917 after 41 additional performances. Total: 233 performances.

CAST (in order of appearance): *Betty,* a maid: Katherine Rodgers. *Mrs. Allison Marvin,* the hostess: Allison McBain. *Bif Jackson,* the butler, a moving picture fan: GEORGE HASSELL. *Leone:* Leone Morgan. *Molly:* MOLLY McINTYRE. *Vivian:* VIVIAN WESSELL. *Luella:* LUELLA GEAR. *Helen:* Helen Clarke. *Peggy:* PEGGY WOOD. *Bruce Grant:* Alan Edwards. *Jack Vaughn:* DONALD ROBERTS. *Lieutenant Stafford,* Kildare's secretary: Rollin Grimes. *Captain Lord Michael Kildare:* LAWRENCE GROSSMITH. *Alonzo Bird:* CLIFTON WEBB. *Phil Marvin:* QUENTIN TOD. *Ted Watson:* John Bohm. *Mrs. O'Rourke:* Annie Lydiate. *Mrs. Schmaltz:* Lillian Devere. *Hilda:* Hilda Pentland. *Gloria,* a dancer: GLORIA GOODWIN. *Boys Scouts, Camp Fire Girls, and the Bronxville Volunteer Fire Department.*

Prologue: Bedroom in Mrs. Marvin's Country House, Bronxville, New York. 2 A.M.

Act 1: Living-room in Mrs. Marvin's House. 9 A.M.

Act 2: The same. 8:30 P.M.

---

[69]Dance specialty for 2 new characters added late in the New York run and for tour to Act 1, after "My Wife—My Man":
"Whirlwind Trot"
Marguerite MacCarton (Daddeane), John Marrone (Frances)
[70]Replaced during the New York run by:
"It's a Sure, Sure Sign"
Flora Zabelle (Dolly)
Which was then replaced for subsequent tour by:
"Polly Believes in Preparedness"
F. Zabelle, Girls
Which was then dropped and replaced by:
"Can the Cabaret"
F. Zabelle, Billy Kent (Henry), Ernie S. Adams (Maitre D'hotel)
[71]Replaced late in the run and for subsequent tour by:
"Daisy"
Margaret Romaine (Peggy)

PROLOGUE

Scene Music

"Drift With Me"
L. Morgan, M. McIntyre, V. Wessell, L. Gear, H. Clarke, P. Wood

Scene Music

ACT 1[72]

"Tell Me"[73]
D. Roberts, M. McIntyre

"It Wasn't Your Fault" (It Wasn't My Fault)[73a]
V. Wessell, L. Grossmith
(*Lyrics by* Herbert Reynolds.)

"Don't Tempt Me"
M. McIntyre, V. Wessell, L. Morgan, H. Clarke, P. Wood, A. Edwards, J. Bohn, Q. Tod, D. Roberts, C. Webb

"We'll See"
P. Wood, A. Edwards

Dance
Q. Tod, H. Clarke

"I Wonder Why"
V. Wessell

Finale

ACT 2[74]

Scene Music

"Moo Cow"
L. Grossmith, Ensemble

"Life's a Dance"
H. Clarke, Q. Tod, L. Morgan, C. Webb

"A Lonesome Little Tune" (Simple Little Tune)[75]
P. Wood

"Hoot Mon"
M. McIntyre, Men

"It's in the Book" (Look in the Book)
C. Webb, G. Goodwin

"Lulu"[76]
D. Roberts, C. Webb, A. Edwards, J. Bohm, L. Grossmith, C. Goodwin

Finale

DANCE AND GROW THIN

1917.03

A Midnight (Musical) Revue in Two Acts, 14 Scenes. Music and lyrics by Irving Berlin, Blanche Merrill. Staged by Leon Errol. Decorations and scenery by Joseph Urban. Costumes sketches by Mr. Kirchner, Misses Cook and O'Neill. Musical director, Max Hoffmann. Produced by Charles Dillingham and Florenz Ziegfeld. Opened 18 January 1917 at the Coconut Grove (Century Roof) and closed 2 June after (117) performances[77].

CAST: LEON ERROL, JOE JACKSON, (Gus) VAN and (Joe) SCHENCK, IRVING FISHER, EDITH HALLOR, GERTRUDE HOFFMAN, ARTHUR CUNNINGHAM, THE BROTHERS LEIGHTON, BLUE AND WHITE MARIMBA BAND, Rita Boland, Dolly Hackett, Vera Maxwell, Mlle. Veronica, Coconut Grove Orchestra.

---

[72]Added to Act 1 after the Dance, for the return engagement:
"It Can't Be Done"
C. Webb, H. Pentland, L. Gear, Clare Stratton (Clare), A. McBain
[73]Replaced after opening by:
"How Was I To Know"
M. McIntyre
[73a]Previously used as "It Isn't Your Fault" in 90 IN THE SHADE.
[74]Added during the run to Act 2 after "Hoot Mon":
"The Baby Vampire" (Poor Little Baby Vampire)
V. Wessell
[75]Replaced for return engagement by:
"Who Cares?"
Mabel Weeks (Mabel), A. Edwards
[76]Dropped for return engagement.
[77]Sometimes titled merely MIDNIGHT REVUE. Performed 6 times weekly at midnight with much of the same talent appearing downstairs in THE CENTURY GIRL. Following the wartime New York City limit on the sale of liquor after 1 A.M. effective 1 May 1917, the curtain was moved back to 11 P.M. The Ethical Culture Society successfully sought an injunction against the service of any spirits at the Cocoanut Grove on 1 June 1917 thereby precipitating the show's closing.

Ensemble: Misses Dorothy Leeds, Evelyn Conway, Ethel Davies, Rosa Davies, Brown, I. Falconer, Lilyan Tashman, Florence Cripps, Geraldine Alexander, Edna Chase, Drange, Borden, Eileen Percy, Beatrice Hughes, Marie Wallace, Leonora Kohler, C. Conway, M. Falconer, Agnes Jepson, Lee, Yvonne Shelton, Mlle. Semone, Charline Mayfield, Allison Worth, Billie Allen, Quinette.

ACT 1[78]

Scene 1

"Way Down South" (There's Something Nice About the South)

    G. Van, J. Schenck

    (*Music and Lyrics by* Irving Berlin.)

        Southern Girls: Misses D. Leeds, E. Conway, E. Davies, R. Davies, Brown, I. Falconer, L. Tashman, F. Cripps, G. Alexander, E. Chase, Drange, Borden, E. Percy, B. Hughes, M. Wallace, L. Kohler.

Scene 2

Dance

    L. Errol, Misses Maxwell, Mayfield, Shelton

Scene 3

"Birdie" (Song)

    (*Music and Lyrics by* Irving Berlin.)

        The Parrot: E. Hallor. *The Cardinal*: Misses G. Alexander, Borden, F. Cripps, E. Chase, B. Hughes, E. Percy, Ellsworth, A. Worth, Drange, C. Conway, B. Allen, Falconer, I. Falconer, A. Jepson, M. Wallace, Lee.

Scene 4

Songs

    G. Van, J. Schenck

    ["Cinderella Lost Her Slipper"

    (*Music and Lyrics by* Irving Berlin.)

    "For Me and My Gal"

    (*Music by* George W. Meyer. *Lyrics by* Edgar Leslie and E. Ray Goetz.)

    "Mary Brown"

    (*Music and Lyrics by* Irving Berlin.)]

Scene 5

The Dance of Arabia

    M. Edwards

Danse Blue Danube

    M. Edwards

    Assisted by Misses M. Falconer, Lee, B. Hughes, Ellsworth, A. Worth, Fisher, Drange, Borden, LeRoy, B. Allen, E. Percy.

ACT 2

Scene 1

"The Kirchner Girls"

    I. Fisher

    The Gibson Girl: L. Kohler. *The Brinkley Girl*: F. Cripps. *The Harrison Fisher Girl*: E. Davies.

    The Kirchner Girls: *Merry Christmas*: L. Tashman. *Through the Heart*: E. Conway. *Hatched*: G. Alexander. *A Feather in Her Hat*: C. Mayfield. *Rosalba*: Y. Shelton. *Morning Call*: M. Wallace. *Pierrot*: B. Hughes. *The Scout Girl*: A. Jepson. *Little Sister*: D. Leeds. *Intermezzo*: E. Percy. *Sailor Boy*: E. Chase. *Innocence*: R. Davies. *Spoils of the Chase*: A. Worth. *Temptation Eve*: Mlle. Semone. *Shopping*: V. Maxwell.

Scene 2

The Brothers Leighton

Scene 3

The Sunshine Girls

Scene 4

"Don't Look at Me"

    Y. Shelton, Mises Drange, A. Worth, Borden, E. Percy

Scene 5

"Letter Boxes" (Just Placed in New York)

    R. Boland

    (*Music and Lyrics by* Irving Berlin.)

    (*Assisted by*) Misses LeRoy, G. Alexander, E. Chase, Quinette, F. Cripps, Ellsworth, I. Falconer, A. Jepson, M. Falconer, B. Allen.

Scene 6

Telepathy

    V. Maxwell, L. Errol

Scene 7

Dance

    Mlle. Veronica

Scene 8

"Dance and Grow Thin"

    G. Van, J. Schenck, Chorus

    (*Music by* Irving Berlin and George W. Meyer. *Lyrics by* Irving Berlin.)

Scene 9

"Let's All Be Americans Now"

    A. Cunningham, Entire Company

    (*Music and Lyrics by* Irving Berlin, Edgar Leslie and George W. Meyer.)

1917.04   CANARY COTTAGE

A Musical Farce in Two Acts, 4 Scenes. Book by Oliver Morosco and Elmer Harris. Music and lyrics by Earl Carroll. Book staged by Oliver Morosoco. Musical numbers staged by Frank Stammer and Frank Rainger. Scenery designed by Robert McQuinn. Gowns designed by Madame Keeler. Orchestra under the direction of Alfred Goodman. Produced by Oliver Morosco. Opened 5 February 1917 at the Morosco Theatre and closed 12 May 1917 after 112 performances.

CAST (in order of appearance): *Michael O'Finnegan*: CARL McCULLOUGH. *Sam Asbestos Hicks*: Hugh Cameron. *Mrs. Hugg*: Grace Ellsworth. *Pauline Hugg*: REINE DAVIES. *Jerry Summerfield*: CHARLES RUGGLES. *Betty Fair*: DOROTHY WEBB. *Billy Moss*: HERBERT CORTHELL. *Nip and Tuck*, Billy's Imagination: Ergotti Lilliputians. *Blanche Moss*: TRIXIE FRIGANZA. *Mitzie*: Hazel Purdy. *Mabel*: Virginia Tavares. *Hal*: Louis Natheaux. *Ostrich*, Still Billy's Imagination: Elsie Gordon. *Maid to the Cook*: Olga Marwig. (*Dance Specialty*: Melissa Ten Eyck, Max Weiley.)

    Guests at Canary Cottage: Helen Higgins, Nan Baker, Hazel Purdy, Babette Busey, Jessie Pollard, Ruth Reavis, Barbara Guillan, Virginia Tavares, Christine Malcolm, Marion Thompson, Edward Bolles, Arthur Price, Jack Rogers, Roy Wissing, Edwin Loweree, Deney Davidson, William Taylor, Charles Newton.

Act 1: Canary Cottage, 5 o'clock in the afternoon.

Act 2, Scene 1: Upstairs Sleeping Porch of Canary Cottage. 10 minutes before the end of Act 1. *Scene 2*: A Scene in California. (McQuinn's Impression.) *Scene 3*: An Orange Grove in California. (McQuinn's Impression.)

ACT 1[79]

Opening Chorus

    C. McCullough, Chorus

"Such a Chauffeur"

    G. Ellsworth, R. Davies

"Old Man Methuselah"

    C. Ruggles, Boys

"I Never Knew"

    C. Ruggles, D. Webb

"But in the Morning"

    H. Corthell

Billy's Imagination

    Ergotti Lilliputians

"(The) Canary Cottage"

    C. Ruggles, D. Webb, Chorus

Fire Ensemble

    Principals, Chorus

"(That) Syncopated Harp"

    R. Davies, C. McCullough, Chorus

"Follow the Cook"

    T. Friganza, Chorus

Finale with Quartette

    D. Webb, T. Friganza, C. Ruggles, R. Davies

ACT 2

Opening Ensemble

Classic (Statue) Dance[80]

    M. Ten Eyck, M. Weiley

---

[78]Added during the run:

    Legerdemania

        Ching Ling Foozie: L. Errol.

[79]Added during the run to Act 1 after Billy's Imagination: (retained for tour)

    "It Ruined Marc Anthony"

        H. Cameron

[80]Dropped during the run.

"The More I See of Men (The More I Love My Dog)"
T. Friganza, Chorus

Fantasie L'Ostriche
E. Gordon

"As Long as I Have You"
D. Webb, Chorus

"It's Always Orange Day in California"
R. Davies, C. McCullough, Chorus

Finale
Entire Company

1917.05 YOU'RE IN LOVE

A Musical Play in Two Acts. Book and lyrics by Otto Hauerbach [Harbach] and Edward Clark. Music by Rudolf Friml. Staged by Edward Clark. Dances and ensembles arranged by Robert Marks. Scenery painted by Edward Sundquist Scenic Studio. Costumes by Paul Arlington, Inc. Orchestra under the direction of John McGhie. Produced by Arthur Hammerstein. Opened 6 February 1917 at the Casino Theatre and closed 30 June 1917 after 167 performances.

CAST (in order of appearance): *Judge Brewster:* JACK RAFFAEL. *Lacey Hart:* LAURENCE WHEAT. *Dorothy:* MAY THOMPSON. *Mrs. Payton:* FLORINE ARNOLD. *Georgianna:* MARIE FLYNN. *Hobby Douglas:* HARRY CLARKE. *Mr. Wix:* AL ROBERTS. *Captain:* ALBERT PELLATON. *Passengers:* Barbara Valdini, M. Cunningham, Hazel Clements. *Sailors:* C. Balfour Lloyd, Gilbert Wells. *Deck Steward:* George Pierpont. *Stewardess:* Virginia Wynn. *Dancers:* Cunningham and Clements, (Lloyd and Wells).

Guests and Friends: Lillian Cullen, June Delight, Frances Jordan, Adele Christy, Edna Coigne, Betty Stivers, Florence Wilson, Irma Marwick, Nancy Griffith, Emily Monte, Lillian Gilford, Ethel Clayton, Helen O'Day, Estelle Francesca, Violet Armstrong, Anita Francesca, Flora Hollister, Mildred Stevens, Carolyn Diehl, Harry Murray, Kenneth Christy, George Pierpont, H. Forbes, Howard Smith, Jacque Stone, Harry Wild, Harry Cornell.

Act 1: Sun Parlor, Santa Monica Hotel, Southern California.

Act 2: On board the S. S. "High Hope." Three days out.

ACT 1

Opening
J. Raffael, Chorus

"Married Life"
L. Wheat, M. Thompson, Chorus

"You're in Love"
L. Wheat, M. Flynn, Chorus

"Keep Off the Grass"
F. Arnold

"He Will Understand"
L. Wheat, M. Thompson, M. Flynn, Chorus

"The Dance of the Rose"
M. Thompson

"Buck Up"
H. Clarke, Chorus

"Things You Must Not Do"
M. Flynn, F. Arnold, J. Raffael, H. Clarke

"Snatched from the Cradle"
A. Roberts

Finale
Company

ACT 2[81]

Opening ("We'll Drift Along")
B. Valdini, Chorus

"Be Sure It's Light"
L. Wheat, Chorus

Eccentric Sailor Dance
Lloyd and Wells

---

[81]Added during the run to Act 2, after Dancing on Deck:
"That's the Place Where Our Flag Shall Fly"
A. Pellaton, Chorus
For subsequent tour, this was replaced by:
Impersonations
Carl McCullough {Lacey Hart}

"A Year Is a Long (Long) Time"
M. Flynn, H. Clarke

"Boola Boo"
A. Roberts, Chorus
(*Lyrics by* Otto Harbach.)

"Loveland"
M. Flynn, A. Pellaton, Male Chorus
(*Lyrics by* Otto Harbach.)

"The Musical Snore"
M. Thompson, F. Arnold, A. Roberts, L. Wheat

Dancing on Deck
Mr. Lloyd and Miss M. Thompson, Mr. Cunningham and Miss Clements

"I Am Only Dreaming"
M. Flynn, Chorus

Finale
Company

1917.06 OH, BOY!

A Musical Play in Two Acts, 3 Scenes. Book and lyrics by Guy Bolton and P. G. Wodehouse. Music by Jerome Kern. Staged by Edward Royce. Scenery designed by D. M. Aiken. Costumes designed by Faibsey. Orchestra under the direction of Max Hirschfield. Orchestrations by Frank Saddler. Produced by the Comstock-Elliott Company (F. Ray Comstock, William Elliott). Opened 20 February 1917 at the Princess Theatre, moved 19 November 1917 to the Casino Theatre, and closed 30 March 1918 after 463 performances.

CAST (in order of appearance): *Briggs,* George Budd's valet: Carl Lyle. *Friends of Jim Marvin* (2): *Jane Packard:* MARION DAVIES. *Polly Andrus:* JUSTINE JOHNSTONE. *Jim Marvin:* HAL FORDE. *George Budd:* TOM POWERS. *Lou Ellen Carter:* MARIE CARROLL. *Jackie Simpson,* playing 'Modesty' in "Experience": ANNA WHEATON. *Constable Simms:* Stephen Maley. *Judge Daniel Carter:* FRANK McGINN. *Mrs. Carter:* Augusta Haviland. *Miss Penelope Budd:* EDNA MAY OLIVER. *A Club Waiter:* Jack Merritt. *Miss Lottie Limmut:* Jeannette Cooke. *Miss Iona Saxon:* Patrice Clarke. *Miss Rhoda Byke:* Evelyn Grieg. *Miss Sheila Ryve:* Margaret Mason. *Miss Inna Ford:* Anna Stone. *Miss Georgia Spelvin:* Florence McGuire. *Miss Wanda Farr:* Katherine Hurst. *Miss Anna Thorpe:* Ethel Forde. *Miss Billie Dew:* Lillian Rice. *Miss Lotta Noyes:* Kathryn Rahn. *Miss Annie Olde-Knight:* Lillian Lavonne. *Miss B. Ava Little:* Marjorie Rolland. *Mr. Olaf Lauder:* Austin Clark. *Mr. Ivan L. Ovanerve:* Alden Glover, Jr. *Mr. Will Hooper Rupp:* Joseph Hadley. *Mr. Phil Ossify:* Charles Yorkshire. *Mr. Phelan Fyne:* Ralph O'Brien. *Mr. Hugo Chaseit:* Clarence Lutz. (*Dance Specialty:* Dorothy Dickson, Carl Hyson.)

Act 1, Scene 1: The Bachelor Apartment of George Budd, at Meadowsides, Long Island. Night. *Scene 2:* The same. Next morning.

Act 2: The Meadowsides Country Club. Afternoon of the same day.

ACT 1[82]

Scene 1

Scene Music
"Let's Make a Night of It" (Ensemble)
H. Forde, Ensemble

"You Never Knew About Me" (Duet)
M. Carroll, T. Powers

"A Package of Seeds" (Song)(from 90 IN THE SHADE)
H. Forde, M. Davies, J. Johnstone, Girls
(*Lyrics by* Herbert Reynolds, P. G. Wodehouse)

"An Old-Fashioned Wife" (Song)
M. Carroll, Girls

"A Pal Like You" (We're Going to Be Pals)(Duet)
A. Wheaton, H. Forde

"Till the Clouds Roll By" (Duet)
A. Wheaton, T. Powers
(*Lyrics by* P. G. Wodehouse, Jerome Kern.)

Scene 2

"A Little Bit of Ribbon" (Song)
M. Davies, Girls

"The First Day of May" (Trio)
A. Wheaton, H. Forde, T. Powers

Finale
Company

ACT 2

"Koo-La-Loo" (Opening)
H. Forde, Ensemble

---

[82]Wodehouse wrote the lyrics alone except as noted.

Dance
    D. Dickson, C. Hyson
"Rolled into One" (Song)
    A. Wheaton
"Oh, Daddy, Please!" (Trio)
    M. Carroll, T. Powers, F. McGinn
"Nesting Time (in Flatbush)" (Duet)
    A. Wheaton, H. Forde
    (*Lyrics by* P. G. Wodehouse, Jerome Kern.)
"Words Are Not Needed (Every Day)" (Song)
    M. Carroll, Boys
"Flubby Dub, the Cave-Man" (Trio)
    A. Wheaton, H. Forde, T. Powers
Finale
    Company

1917.07   EILEEN

A Comic Opera in Three Acts. Book and lyrics by Henry Blossom. Music by Victor Herbert. Book staged by Fred G. Latham. Dances arranged by George Marion. Scenery by H. Robert Law Studios. Costumes designed by Raymond Newton Hyde. Orchestra under the direction of Arthur Kautzenbach. Concert master, Harold Sanford. Produced by Joseph Weber. Opened 19 March 1917 at the Sam S. Shubert Theatre and closed 12 May 1917 after 64 performances.

CAST: *Captain Barry O'Day*: WALTER SCANLAN [Walter Van Brunt]. *Sir 'Reggie' Stribling*: ALGERNON GRIEG. *Dinny Doyle*: SCOTT WELSH. *Lanty Hackett*: Harry Crosby. *'Humpy' Grogan*: John B. Cooke. *Shaun Dhu*: GREEK EVANS. *Mickey O'Brien*: Joseph Dillon. *Colonel Lester*: EDWARD MARTINDEL. *Biddy Flynn*: Josie Claflin. *Rosie Flynn*: LOUISE ALLEN. *Lady Maude Estabrooke*: OLGA ROLLER. *Eileen Mulvaney*: GRACE BREEN. *Marie*, her maid: Paulette Antoine. *Myles*, a footman: Lewis Ayer. *Peter*, the piper: Francis X. Hennessy. *Sergeant*: Roger McKenna. *Corporal*: Eric Block. *Fisherman, Redcoats, Smugglers, Guests, Tenantry, Servants, etc.*

Ladies of the Chorus: Margaret Chandler, Carolyn Birch, Samice Burdette, Madeline Couple, Ethyl Charles, Margaret Cusack, Martha Jarden, Marie Dillon, Adele Fielder, Frances Fielder, Phyllis Gill, Fanchon Haywood, Virginia Hilton, Suzanne Jenkins, Susie McCrohan, Peggy Merritt, Ruth Dean, Mary Stuart, Janet Reid, Edna Mae, Gail Webster, Beatrix Young, Grace DuBois. *Gentlemen of the Chorus*: Ben Berison, Frank Crawford, Samuel Casper, William Attell, Eric Block, Joseph Dillon, Kirby Ellis, Jack Hagner, Roy McKenna, Michael Kavannaugh, Este Morrison, Wilbur Hamilton, Maurice Robertson. *Soldiers*: W. J. Barry, Herbert Smith, Joseph Gildman, Edward Gobber, Charles McLoughlin, George B. Sopher, Arthur C. Tenneson, Thomas McHough, H. Pall, Thomas Allins.

The action takes place on the Western coast of Ireland in 1798.

Act 1: At the Sign of the Black Bull. Morning.

Act 2: Interior of the Castle. Afternoon.

Act 3: Gardens of the Castle. Evening.

ACT 1
"Free Trade and a Misty Moon" (Opening Chorus)
    G. Evans, Smuggler Chorus
"My Little Irish Rose"
    L. Allen
"Ireland, My Sireland" (When Shall I Again See Ireland)
    W. Scanlan
Finale:
    Ensemble
"Glad, Triumphant Hour"
    W. Scanlan, Chorus

ACT 2
"Too-re-loo-re" (Opening Chorus)
    G. Breen, Chorus
"Eileen, Alanna, Asthore"
    W. Scanlan
"If Eve Had (Only) Left the Apple on the Bough"
    A. Grieg
"I'd Love to be a Lady (Someday)"
    S. Welsh, L. Allen
"When Love Awakes!"
    G. Breen, Girls
"Life's a Game at Best"
    O. Roller, E. Martindel

Finale
    Ensemble
ACT 3
Opening Chorus:
    Jig
Song of the Acolytes
Serenade
    S. Welsh
"In Erin's Isle" (Song)
    O. Roller, Ensemble
"Thine Alone" (Duet)
    W. Scanlan, G. Breen
"The Irish Have a Great Day To-night"
    S. Welsh, Male Chorus
"When Ireland Stands Among the Nations of the World"
    W. Scanlan, Ensemble

1917.08   THE PASSING SHOW OF 1917

A Musical Revue in Two Acts, 21 Scenes[83]. Dialogue (sketches) and lyrics by Harold Atteridge. Music by Sigmund Romberg and Otto Motzan[84]. Staged by J. C. Huffman. Musical numbers staged by Allan K. Foster. Orchestra under the direction of Oscar Radin. Produced under the personal direction of J. J. Shubert by the Winter Garden Company (Messrs. Shubert). Opened 26 April 1917 at the Winter Garden and closed 13 October 1917 after 196 performances.

CAST: DeWOLF HOPPER, JEFFERSON DeANGELIS, MARIE NORDSTROM, TOM LEWIS, CHIC SALE, IRENE FRANKLIN, JOHNNY DOOLEY, DOLLY CONNOLLY, YVETTE RUGEL, FRANKLYN BATIE, JOHN T. MURRAY, EFFIE WESTON, DONALD KERR, WANDA LYON, (John) MILLER and (James) MACK, (Gladys) CLARK and (Henry) BERGMAN, GEORGE SCHILLER, ROSIE QUINN, ALICE VAN RYKER, BURTON GREEN, ZEKE COLVAN, John Crone, Emily Miles, Muriel Dae, Claude Allen, Fred J. Ardath, William Singer, Stafford Pemberton, Marion Mooney, Caroline Maywood, Yvonne Gouraud, Mlle. Swirskaia, O. E. Patapovitch, Nat Carr, Murray Evans, William Singer.

Personnel of the Chorus Misses Dorothy Godfrey, Babe Dakin, Marion Mooney, Grace Hall, Agnes Hall, Effie Allen, Peggie Dempsey, Nancy Everett, Grace Keeshon, Trixie Raymond, Inez Francis, Elsie Froehlich, Edith Pierce, Jean Staples, Vera Pearsal, Delores Mendez, Gussie Berg, Alvira Kramer, Carolyn Maywood, Lois Leigh, Lillian Griffith, Bobbie Gaylor, Viola Quinn, Hazel Black, Ada Fuld, Louise Dale, Reba Stewart, Mildred LaGue, Dorothy Scofield, Irene Wallace, Elinore Leigh, Gladys Kelley, Helen Kelley, Adrienne Dillon, Jessie Reed, Nora Reed, Evelyn Leroy, Tess Rubin, Betty Brown, Edna May Russell, Fay Tunis, Lorraine Waters, Glory Mora, Lenora Greenwood, Marjory Lane, Emily Miles, Nell Carrington, Ray Shirley, Rae Hartley, Frances Ramey, Kitty Berg, Bobbie McCree, Flow Elmore, Mabel Leila Von Holk, Helen Montague. Messrs. Andrew Demarest, Ted Andrews, Dudley Farnsworth, Ed. McHenry, Murray Evans, Clyde Miller, Clay Stearns, Charles Thatcher, John Mills, Dan Sparks, John Thomas, John Ross.

ACT 1
Scene 1
"Father Knickerbocker"
    F. Batie
    (*Music by* Sigmund Romberg.)
    Scene: Trinity Church.
        Ruth Law: M. Nordstrom. *Policeman*: F. Batie. *Father Knickerbocker*: J. T. Murray.
Scene 2
    Scene: A Flight Over New York.
        Father Knickerbocker: J. T. Murray. *Ruth Law*: M. Nordstrom.
Scene 3
    Finale—"The Passing Show"
        Winter Garden Shirt Front Girls
        Scene: The Finale of a Winter Garden Show.
        The Soubrette: E. Weston. *First Principal*: D. Kerr. *First Lady Principal*: W. Lyon. *Rosie*: R. Quinn. *Violet*: A. Van Ryker. *Miss Broadway*: M. LaGue.

---

[83]The Seventh in the annual series of revues, produced since 1912 by the Messrs. Shubert, which began in 1894. Billed as the Winter Garden's Annual Revue. Settings and costumes uncredited.
[84]Motzan is not credited with individual musical numbers either in programs or published sheet music.

Scene 4

Scene: After the First Performance of a Winter Garden Show in front of the Curtain.
First Critic: G. Schiller. Second Critic: J. Crone. Musical Director: B. Green. Stage Director: J. T. Murray.

Scene 5

"Same Old Song"

D. Kerr, E. Weston, I. Franklin, Winter Garden Girls in practice clothes
Scene: Back Stage after the Curtain Falls.
Stage Director: J. T. Murray. First Principal: D. Kerr. First Lady Principal: W. Lyon. The Soubrette: E. Weston. Rosie: R. Quinn. Violet: A. Van Ryker. Stage Manager: Z. Colvan. Dance Director: F. Batie. Author: H. Bergman. Miss Clark: G. Clark. Miss Rugel: Y. Rugel. Chorus Girl: I. Franklin.

Scene 6

"Faster and Faster"

J. Miller, J. Mack, Winter Garden Triple Steppers
Scene: The Wanderer.
Stage Director: J. T. Murray. Dance Director: F. Batie. Stage Manager: Z. Colvan. Two Sheep: Miller and Mack. Father: J. Crone. Jester: J. Dooley. Naomie: D. Connolly. Mrs. Jesse: M. Nordstrom. The Wandering Daughter: I. Franklin. Author: H. Bergman.

Scene 7

"Won't You Write to Me" (Won't You Send a Letter to Me?)

W. Lyon, Love Letter Girls
(Music by Sigmund Romberg.)

"America's Fighting Jack"[85]

F. Batie, Winter Garden Jackies
(Music and Lyrics by Clifton Crawford.)

"Meet Me at the Station"[86]

G. Clark, H. Bergman
(Music by Ted Snyder. Lyrics by Sam M. Lewis, Joe Young.)

"(I've) A Little Bit of Scotch (in Me)"[87]

J. Dooley, R. Quinn, A. Van Ryker, Hieland Lassies
(Music by Sigmund Romberg.)
Scene: A Drug Store.
Jack: F. Batie. Myrtle: E. Miles. Mrs. Uptown: M. Dae. Frances Starr: W. Lyon. Ruth: Y. Rugel. Cinderella: C. Clark. Joe: H. Bergman. Hank: C. Allen. Zeke: F. J. Ardath. Bud: W. Singer. Mr. Uptown: T. Lewis. Mack: J. Dooley. Manager: G. Schiller.
Famous American Winter Garden Beauties: Mildred: M. LaGue. Helen: H. Carrington. Emily: E. Miles. Rae: R. Hartley. Jessie: J. Reed. Grace: G. Keeshon. Marion: M. Mooney.

Scene 8

"(The) Dancing Family"

M. Nordstrom

Dances, Past and Present

M. Nordstrom, assisted by S. Pemberton, A. Demarest
Scene: Out Front.

Scene 9

"Pierrot"

D. Connolly, Pierrots
Animated Pierrots: J. Miller and J. Mack, D. Kerr and Weston, R. Quinn, M. LaGue, A. Van Ryker, M. Mooney, I. Frances, T. Raymond, G. Keeshon, C. Maywood.

Scene 10

"My Bedouin Girl" (Bedouin Girl)

F. Batie, Bedouin Girls
(Music by Sigmund Romberg.)

"The Ready-Made Sandwich"

D. Hopper

"Ruth St. Denis"

J. Dooley

"Orgy"

Mlle. Swirskaia, Assisted by S. E. Potapovitch, Harem Girls
Scene: Harem Scene—Wanderer.
Nadino: J. T. Murray. The Wandering Daughter: I. Franklin. Tush: D. Hopper. The Lady Jeweller: V. Quinn. Lady Sea Captainess: M. Nordstrom. First Mate: R. Quinn. Second Mate: Y. Gouraud. Billy Sunday: G. Schiller. Bedouin Girl: Mlle. Swirskaia. Slave: O. E. Potapovitch.

Scene 11

"The Awkward Age"[88]

I. Franklin
(Music by Burton Green. Lyrics by Burton Green and Irene Franklin.)
Scene: In Black and Blue.
Miss Sixteen: I. Franklin.

Scene 12

"The Golden West"

D. Connolly, Lasso Lassies
Scene: Somewhere Out West.
Miss Lasso: D. Connolly.

Scene 13

"(I'll Be a) College Boy's Dear"

W. Lyon, College Boy Girlies
(Music by Sigmund Romberg.)
Scene: Just Outside the Yale Bowl.
Percival English: N. Carr. Miss Rooter: W. Lyon. Mack: J. Dooley. Cinderella: G. Clark. Miss Yale: M. Nordstrom. Head Coach: G. Schiller. Violet: A. Van Ryker. Grace: Y. Gouraud. Agnes: D. Connolly. Marion: E. Weston. Fred: D. Kerr. Joe: H. Bergman.

Scene 14

The Football Game between Yale and Harvard
Scene: Yale Bowl.

ACT 2

Scene 1

"Under the Willow Tree"

Y. Rugel
(Music by Sigmund Romberg.)

"My Yokohama Girl"

G. Clark, H. Bergman, Butterfly Girls
(Music by Harry Tierney. Lyrics by Alfred Bryan.)
Scene: The Willow Tree.
Peach Blossom: G. Clark. Lotus Eyes: W. Lyon. Coolie: D. Farnsworth. Mr. Rounder: T. Lewis. Jap: J. Mack. Japanese: J. Miller. John Charles Toggs: J. DeAngelis. He Lee: H. Bergman. Mr. Manhattan: G. Schiller. Miss New York: D. Connolly. Gilly: J. T. Murray. Mack: J. Dooley. Tacky, the Image Maker: D. Hopper. Image Girl: M. Nordstrom. Bird Seller: M. Evans.

Scene 2

The Rural Sunday School Benefit[89]

C. Sales
Scene: Sunday Morning; 7:30 Friday Evening.

Scene 3

"Won't You Be My Daddy?"

R. Quinn, Beau Girls
(Music by Sigmund Romberg.)
Rosie: R. Quinn.
And Daddy Girls.

Scene 4

Scene: A Dining Car.
The Cook: F. J. Ardath. The Stove: C. Allen. Mr. Rube: W. Singer. Mack: J. Dooley. Gilly: J. T. Murray. Joe: H. Bergman. Cinderella: G. Clark. Sam: T. Lewis. Conductor: F. Batie. Mr. English: N. Carr. Mr. Commuter: J. Mack. Waiter: J. Miller. Ruth: Y. Rugel.

Scene 5

"(The Wail of) The Chorus Girl"[90]

I. Franklin

"The Telephone Girl"

I. Franklin
(Music and Lyrics by Benjamin Hapgood Burt.)
Scene: A Telephone Exchange.
The Operator: I. Franklin. Mr. Madison: B. Green. Miss Schuyler: W. Lyon.

---

[88]Replaced for subsequent tour by:
"Please Don't Say There Isn't Any Santa Claus"
(Music and Lyrics by Irene Franklin and Burton Green.)
At the Piano: Burton Green.
[89]Dropped for subsequent tour.
[90]Both songs and scene replaced for subsequent tour by:
"The Girl from Rector's"/"Broadway Isn't Broadway Since They Close at One O'Clock"
(Music and Lyrics by Irene Franklin and Burton Green.)
At the Piano: Burton Green.

---

[85]Dropped late in the New York run.
[86]Dropped for subsequent tour.
[87]Dropped for subsequent tour.

Scene 6

"Language of the Fan"
D. Connolly, Fan Girls of All Nations

"A Table for Two"
D. Clark, H. Bergman, Table Girls

"The Girl Who Drinks Champgane"
J. Dooley, Y. Rugel, Cocktail Girls
Scene: The Fountain Room.
Cinderella: G. Clark. *Jo*: H. Bergman. *The Love Triangle* (3): *Husband*: D. Hopper. *Wife*: M. Nordstrom. *Chorus Girl*: I. Franklin. *Mack*: J. Dooley. *Ruth*: Y. Rugel.

Scene 7

"(That) Peach-a-reen-o Phil-a-peen-o Dance"
D. Connolly, D. Kerr and E. Weston, J. Miller and J. Mack, R. Quinn, A. Van Ryker, Peechareena Girls

"Ring Out (the)Liberty (Bell)"
Y. Rugel, F. Batie, American Girls
(*Music by* Sigmund Romberg.)

Finale[91]

1917.09   HIS LITTLE WIDOWS

A Comedy with Music in Three Acts. Book and lyrics by Rida Johnson Young and William Cary Duncan. Music by William Schroeder. Book staged by Frank Stammers. Dances arranged by David Bennett. Scenes designed by D. Frank Dodge and William Castle, Edward G. Unitt and Joseph Wickes. Ensemble gowns by Harry Collins, J. M. Giddings & Co., Lizzie Cummins, Inc. Men's furnishings by Nat Lewis. Orchestra under the direction of Silvio Hein. Orchestrations by Silvio Hein. Produced by G. M. Anderson and L. Lawrence Weber. Opened 30 April 1917 at the Astor Theatre and closed 30 June 1917 after 72 performances.[92]

CAST (in order of appearance): *Brokers of the Firm of Lloyd, Grayson & Hale* (3): *Jack Grayson*: ROBERT EMMETT KEANE. *'Bif' Hale*: HARRY TIGHE. *'Pete' Lloyd*: CARTER DeHAVEN. *Hotel Manager*: Dwight Dana. *Abijah Smith*: FRANK LALOR. *Blanche Hale*: FRANCES CAMERON. *Harry Jolson*: Charles Prince. *Sandy Barr*: John Robb. *Lucinda Lloyd*: Julia Ralph. *Annabelle Lloyd*: FLORA PARKER. *Murilla Lloyd*: HATTIE BURKS. *Officiating Elder*: Wallace Camp. *Lily*: GRACE HALEY. *Dahlia*: Bernice Haley. *Tulip*: Lucile Haley. *Rose*: Mabel Haley. *Pansy*: Alma Pickard. *Mignon-ette*: Violette Strathmore. *Hyacinthe*: Lucile Zintheo. *Narcissus*: Irma von Nagy. *Guards*: Walter Rowley, Frank Young. (*Dance Specialty*: Evelyn Cavanaugh, Richard Doré.)
Girls of 'The Sorceress' Company: Virginia Gunther, Doris Lloyd, Irene Held, Virginia Lillard, Lillian Galer, Ivy Sherer, May Manning, Fifi Hansworth, Jean Voltaire, Mae Clark, Rene Manning, Helen Hastings. *Boys of 'The Sorceress' Company*: Harry Dempsey, Louis Strangard, Bernard Druce, Frank Aberwald, Wilfred Shepard, James Brannon. *The Latter Day Saints*: James Nichols, Sol Solomon, Walter Coupe, Carl Gordon.

Act 1: Private Suite in Hotel Ridgemonte, New York. Evening. (Dodge & Castle.)

Act 2: Home of the Widows in Salt Lake City. Four days later. (Dodge & Castle.)

Act 3: Rotunda in the Lloyd Residence. The same evening. (Unitt & Wickes.)

ACT 1

"When You Waltz With Me"
Ensemble

"Oh, You Girls!"
H. Tighe

"Saints of the Latter Day"
F. Lalor, Elders

"My Love Is a Secret"
C. DeHaven, F. Cameron
(*Lyrics by* Rida Johnson Young.)

"Johnny Come Follow Me"
F. Cameron, Ensemble

ACT 2

"This Is the Best We Ever Struck"
F. Lalor, Elders, Ensemble

"I'm Wondering"[93]
F. Parker

"I Need Someone's Love"
H. Burks

"(What Are You Going To Do) When the Animals Are Gone"
Haley Sisters
(*Music by* Malvin F. Franklin. *Lyrics by* Thomas J. Gray.)

"A Wife For Each Day in the Week"
F. Lalor, C. DeHaven, R. E. Keane

"That Weepy Creepy Feeling" (I Loved You the Moment We Met)
H. Tighe, R. E. Keane, H. Burks, F. Parker
(*Lyrics by* Rida Johnson Young.)

Finale

ACT 3

"I Want Them All (to Leave Me Alone)"
C. DeHaven Widows

"In Cabaret-Land"
F. Cameron, Ensemble

Dance Divertissement[94]
E. Cavanaugh, R. Doré

"Salt Lake City"[95]
F. Lalor

"Love Me Best of All"
C. DeHaven, Widows

The Guards[96]
W. Rowley, F. Young

Finale

1917.10   THE HIGHWAYMAN

A Revival of the Romantic Comic Opera in Three Acts[97]. Book and lyrics by Harry B. Smith. Music by Reginald DeKoven. Staged by Edward P. Temple. Scenery by Robert Law Studios (Acts 1 and 3), P. Dodd Ackerman (Act 2). Costumes by Adler Costume Company. Orchestra under the direction of Frank Tours. Produced by Messrs. Shubert. Opened 2 May 1917 at the 44th Street Theatre and closed 19 May 1917 after 22 performances.

CAST: *Dick Fitzgerald* (Captain Scarlet), an Irish "soldier of fortune": JOHN CHARLES THOMAS. *Lady Constanze Sinclair*, in love with Dick: BIANCA SAROYA. *Sir Godfrey Beverly*, a country baronet: STANLEY FORDE. *Lady Pamela*, his daughter: GRACE FJORDE. *Lieutenant Rodney*, a young naval officer: SAM ASH. *Foxy Quiller*, a Bow Street Constable: JEFFERSON DeANGELIS. *Dolly Primrose*, with a romantic nature: LETTY YORKE. *Toby Winkle*, "Boots" of "The Cat and the Fiddle": TEDDY WEBB. *Lieutenant Lovelace*, a militia officer: LAWRENCE CAMERON. *Lord Phelim Kilkenny*: J. Sylvester Murray. *Sir John Hawkhurst*: Osborne Clemson. *The Landlord*: James Murry. *The Constables*: Harry Bulger, Jr., Will Montgomery, A. Carbone, H. Rollands. *An Old Soldier*: Richard Coombs.
Ladies of the Chorus: Margela Boudreau, Ira Bertrand, Billie Davenport, Bertha Pyle, Rose Cooper, Louise Dupont, Janet Marsh, Ann Claire Page, Betty Martin, Lillian Beaudett, Clara Koeniges, Bessie Hoban, Verra Ferrier, Rose Gibson, Jean Wells, Lulette Adrienne, Norma Day, Dorothy Hartig, Zetta Metchik, Olive Prouser, Barbara Stedman, Dorothy Hellis, Vera Fromm, Billie Martells, Ellen Crane, Lydia Crane, Marfant Haven, Florence Vinson, Constance Paulton, Felicia Sprague, Evelyn Deverell, Mynna Estey, Cleo Deschamps, Marion Howard, Blanch Marr, Pearl Weber, Gladys Dupell, Nita Lamdrid, Mildred Garrison, Mae Jiron, Ruth Malcolm, Alice Gordon. *Men of the Chorus*: William Plummer, Churchill Goar, Lee Campbell, Lloyd Montgomery, Harry Bulger (Jr.), Joseph Tierney, John Seaton, Marins Carbone, Fred Steinman, Harry Coombs, Herman Steinman, Joseph Toner, Barton Isboll, Lawrence Smith, Arthur Ridell, Harry Rolland, Al Baron, George Rove, Samuel Laderman, Ben Wells, William Anisman, Dave Klein, Martin Liberfeld.

ACT 1

Prelude and Opening Ensemble

"Bread, Cheese and Kisses" (Duet)
L. Yorke, T. Webb

"Marching Away" (Song and Chorus)
L. Cameron

---

[91]Added to Finale during the run:
"Goodbye Broadway, Hello France"
(*Music by* Billy Baskette. *Lyrics by* Benny Davis, C. Francis Reisner.)
[92]Costumes uncredited; prior to New York, gowns were credited to Pauline Elliott Thacker.

[93]Dropped during the run.
[94]Dropped during the run.
[95]Dropped during the run.
[96]Dropped during the run.
[97]Originally produced 13 December 1897 at the Broadway Theatre for 144 performances. For Synopsis of Scenes, see original 1897 production.

"The Highwayman" (Song)
  J. C. Thomas, Chorus
"In London Town" (Gavotte Quintette)
  G. Fjorde, S. Forde, T. Webb, L. Yorke, Chorus
"Viva la Bagatelle" (Ensemble and Song)
  B. Saroya
"Gretna Green" (Song)
  S. Ash
Finale

ACT 2
Kitty O'Brien" (Song)
  J. C. Thomas
Chorus of Villagers
"The Farmer and the Scarecrow" (Duet and Chorus)
  T. Webb, J. DeAngelis, Chorus
"Do You Remember, Love?" (Duet)
  B. Saroya, J. C. Thomas
"Gipsy Song" (Song)
  J. DeAngelis, Constables
Finale

ACT 3
Opening Chorus and Dance
"While the Four Winds Blow" (Sea Song)
  S. Ash
"For This" (Song)
  B. Saroya
  (Lyrics by Leontine Stanfield.)
"On the Track" (Song)
  J. DeAngelis, Constables
"Farewell to the King's Highway" (Song)
  J. C. Thomas
Finale

WHEN JOHNNY COMES MARCHING HOME

1917.11

A Revival of the Patriotic Military Opera in Three Acts, 4 Scenes[98]. Book (and lyrics) by Stanislaus Stange. Music by Julian Edwards. Book staged by Fred Bishop. Military pageant staged by R. H. Burnside. Scenery by D. Frank Dodge and William Castle, Robert Law. Costumes by Freisinger. Musical director, Antonio DeNovellis. Brass Band and Fife and Drum Corps under the direction of Paul R. Doti. Entire production under the personal direction of F. C. Whitney. Produced by F. C. Whitney. Opened 7 May 1917 at the New Amsterdam Theatre, moved 28 May 1917 to the Manhattan Opera House and closed 16 June 1917 after 48 performances.

CAST: *General William Allen*, of the Federal Army: ARTHUR CUNNINGHAM. *Cordelia Allen*, his daughter: JUANITA FLETCHER. *Felix Graham*, a Southern planter: PERCY PARSONS. *Colonel John Graham*, his son, of the Federal Army, alias John Johnson, "Johnny": EDWARD BASSE. *Mrs. Constance Pemberton*, a widow, cousin of Felix: BONNIE BOYCE. *Kate Pemberton*, her niece: NANETTE FLACK. *Amelia Thropp, Susan Clay*, also nieces: Elsa Garrette, Aimee Torriani. *Robert Pemberton*, Kate's brother: Julia Gifford. (Three of the Federal Army:) *Captain Geoffry Martin*: Harrison Garret. *Major George Buckle*: George Burns. *Major William Walker*: Roy Raymond. *Jonathan Phoenix*, a ne'er-do-well: Maurice Darcy. *Uncle Tom*, an old slave: Wilbur Cox.
  Southern Belles: Marie Tracy: Harriet Springer. *Minnie Cortney*: Wreathe McIntyre. *Mary Rivers*: Claire Hill. *Jessie Fairfax*: Cecil Corry. *Nellie Jefferson*: Helen Fox. *Bella Montrose*: Clara Taylor. *Lottie Allyn*: Anita Corradi. *Bessie Beauregard*: Lillian Flower. *Honie Chisholm*: Gertrude Hogan. *Carrie Sadler*: Helen Burke. *Fannie Ludlow*: Rena Brown. *Jennie Holly*: Bonnie Lorraine. *Fanny Seabright*: Roberta Kennedy. *Mary Rogers*: Edith Lenox. *Bertha Wilbur*: Jeannette Hill. *Loretta Stair*: Gwen Canfield. *Sarah Abbott*: Marie Finney.
  Federal Officers: Captain Mate: George Vanduzer. *Captain Kellard*: James Lawrence. *Captain Hume*: Charles Catterson. *Captain Vaughn*: Pedro Montalto. *Captain Mawin*: Morris Saks. *Captain Anderson*: Mark Truscott. *Captain Totten*: Henry Kessler. *Captain Hopkinson*: Frank Snyder. *Captain Hunter*: Perry Higgins. *Captain Summers*: V. J. Barlow. *Lieutenant Byrne*: Frank Lambert. *Lieutenant Briggs*:

Joseph Sherry. *Lieutenant Phillips*: Vernon Struppa. *Lieutenant Prince*: Leon Litchfield. *Lieutenant Battell*: Harry Strawbridge. *Lieutenant Grant*: Bernard Fritzie. *Lieutenant Rhodes*: Charles Weston. *Lieutenant Fields*: Garret Carrol.
  Plantation Darkies: Chloe: Lillian Franko. *Mandy*: Ethel Young. *Eliza*: Ida Dodge. *Harriet*: Florence Lee. *Rebecca*: Carrie Sager. *Matilda*: Jennie Faas. *Susannah*: Lillian Chambers. *Lindy*: Ethel Phillips. *Ephraim*: Harry Leclair. *Chan*: Ed Douglass. *Marmaduke*: Jack Roberts. *Rastus*: Albert Wyatt. *Jefferson Clay*: Kris Dahl. *Washington Clay*: David Adler. *Nick Bomby*: Ben Tillson. *Abraham*: Marshall Stone.

Act 1: General Allen's Headquarters. Cordelia's Birthday Party. (Dodge & Castle.)

Act 2: Felix Graham's Plantation. On the Banks of the Mississippi. (Dodge & Castle.)

Act 3, Scene 1: Encampment of the Federal Army. Prior to Declaration of Peace. (Robert Law.) *Scene 2*: Grand Finale, Gathering of the Allies. (Robert Law.)

ACT 1
"Hurrah! Hurrah!" (Opening Chorus)
  Federal Officers
"My Father Fights for Uncle Sam"[99]
  J. Fletcher, Officers
"I Could Waltz On Forever with You"
  J. Fletcher, E. Garrette, A. Torriani, G. Burns, R. Raymond, Officers
"My Own United States"
  E. Basse
"(Just) Marry the Man and Be Merry"
  B. Boyce, Chorus
"When Our Lips in Kisses Met"
  A. Cunningham, B. Boyce
"Fairyland"
  N. Flack
"Who Knows?"
  E. Basse, N. Flack
"While You're Thinking"
  J. Fletcher, Chorus
"The Suwanee River"
  N. Flack, B. Boyce, J. Gifford, A. Cunningham, E. Basse
Finale
  Entire Company

ACT 2
"Sing, Darkies, Sing!"
  Plantation Darkies
"Ma Honeysuckle Gal" (My Honeysuckle Girl)
  W. Cox, Darkies
"Love's Night"
  E. Basse, N. Flack
"Really Upset"[100] (I Was Quite Upset)
  M. Darcy
"Spring, Sweet Spring"
  B. Boyce
"(Katie,) My Southern Rose"
  E. Basse, B. Boyce, Chorus
"(Twas Down in the) Garden of Eden"
  H. Garrett, J. Fletcher
"Years Touch Not the Heart"
  B. Boyce
"The Spy" (Finale)
  Entire Company

ACT 3
"Flag of My Country"
  E. Basse, Chorus
"But They Didn"'t"
  J. Fletcher, Chorus
"The Drums"
  Chorus
Finale
  Entire Company

---

[98]Originally produced in New York 16 December 1902 at the New York Theatre for 71 performances. Dropped for this production: "Good Day, Yankees" (Act 2). Song order was revised.

[99]Not in original production.
[100]Not in original production.

Sam B. Hardy and Juliette Day in THE RIVIERA GIRL (Photo: White Studio)
Billy Rose Theatre Collection, New York Public Library for the Performing Arts

1917–1918 SEASON

1917.12 ## HITCHY-KOO (1917)

An Intimate (Musical) Revue in Two Acts, 14 Scenes[1]. Book (sketches) and lyrics by Glen MacDonough and E. Ray Goetz. Music by E. Ray Goetz. Staged by Julian Mitchell and Leon Errol. Scenery designed by the Washington Square Players. Costumes by Freisinger, Dazian, Willy Pogany, Robert E. Locher, W. H. Mathews. Orchestra under the direction of William M. Daly. Orchestrations by Frank Saddler. Produced by Raymond Hitchcock and E. Ray Goetz. Opened 7 June 1917 at the Cohan and Harris Theatre, moved 27 August 1917 to the Liberty Theatre, moved 24 September 1917 to the 44th Street Theatre, and closed 15 December 1917 after 220 performances.

CAST: RAYMOND HITCHCOCK, IRENE BORDONI, LEON ERROL, GRACE LaRUE, FRANCES WHITE, WILLIAM ROCK, ADELAIDE WINTHROP, ALFRED NEWMAN, TEDDY HUDSON, GEORGE MOORE, FLORENZ AMES, Cissie Sewell, Florence Ware, Trixie Whiteford, William Holbrook, Felix Rush, William Galpen, Florence Cripps, Frank Kellar, Roy Hoyer, Helen Bond, Eleanor Sinclair, Dorothy Klewer.

ACT 1[2]

Scene 1

A Summer Evening at San Sebastian, Spain

Baron de Marron, a roué: W. Rock. *Claire de Bouillon*: I. Bordoni. *Gladys Brown*, an American heiress: G. LaRue. *Captain* Pimento, of the 23rd Frijoles: R. Hoyer. *Lizzie Brown*, Gladys' sister: F. White. *Hiram Brown*, the Mayor of Ashtabula: L. Errol.

Scene 2

Le Compere: R. Hitchcock.
Scene: Tableau Curtain.

Scene 3

"Somewhere on Broadway"
Scene: The Lobby of the Theatre.
My Soldier Boy: G. Moore. *Miss Springtime*: E. Sinclair. *The Century Girl*: F. Cripps. *A Kiss for Cinderella*: T. Hudson. *Out There*: T. Whiteford, R. Hoyer, W. Holbrook, F. Kellar.

Scene 4

"The Baldwin Corners' Brass Band"
Opry House Orchestra

Specialty
L. Errol, Jass Band, Chorus
Scene: A Country Store.
Silas Pringle, Chief of Baldwin Corners' Fire Department: R. Hitchcock. *Mrs. Pringle*, his wife: A. Winthrop. *George Bassett*, Mrs. Pringle's brother: F. Ames. *Jim Hastings*, representing the Eureka Home Building Company: L. Errol. *The Storekeeper*: F. Rush. *The Sheriff*: W. Galpin.

Scene 5

"Chinese Letter Song"[3]
W. Rock, F. White
(*Music by* William White. *Lyrics by* E. Ray Goetz.)
Scene: Tableau Chinois.

Scene 6

Caught in a Jamb
Skatewell Looseways: F. Ames. *Maria Falsdeen*: A. Winthrop.

---

[1]Raymond Hitchcock claimed in print that his show was based on the London revue SOME. Reviewers also credited Harry Grattan with additional sketches.
[2]Added after opening to Act 1, after Caught in a Jamb:
A Photograph Gallery
The Photographer: R. Hitchcock. *The Commuter*: L. Errol.
[3]During the run, Frances White also introduced 2 other songs:
"M-I-S-S-I-S-S-I-P-P-I" (also used in the ZIEGFELD MIDNIGHT FROLIC)
F. White
(*Music by* Harry Tierney. *Lyrics by* Bert Hanlon and Benny Ryan.)
"I'd Like to Be a Monkey in the Zoo" (I Wish I Was a Monkey in the Zoo)(Act 2)
F. White
(*Music by* William White. *Lyrics by* Bert Hanlon.)

Scene 7

"When You've Picked Your Basket of Peaches"/
"The Girls of Home, Sweet Home" (Finale)
G. LaRue, R. Hitchcock, Chorus
Scene: A Photograph Gallery.
The Photographer: R. Hitchcock. *The Commuter*: L. Errol. *The Bride of 1860*: I. Bordoni. *The Groom of 1860*: G. Moore. *The Bride of 1870*: A. Winthrop. *The Groom of 1870*: F. Ames. *The Bride of 1880*: C. Sewell. *The Groom of 1880*: L. Errol. *The Bride of 1890*: F. White. *The Groom of 1890*: W. Rock. *The Spirits of the Album*: E. Sinclair, F. Cripps.

ACT 2

Scene 1[4]

"The Ragtime Alphabet"
H. Bond, Chorus

Piano Specialty
A. Newman

Songs
I. Bordoni
Scene: The Modern School.
Walsingham Glider: F. Ames. *Professor Castlemaurice*: W. Rock. *Violette*: I. Bordoni. *Mrs. Prime*: A. Winthrop. *Emily Prime*: F. Ware. *Professor Twinkle*: G. Moore. *Handel Keys*: A. Newman. *Rose*: T. Hudson. *Pansy*: H. Bond. *Lily*: T. Whiteford. *Marigold*: D. Klewer.

Scene 2

"Six-Times-Six Is Thirty-Six"[5]
F. White
(*Music by* William White. *Lyrics by* Bert Hanlon.)
Scene: Kiddieland.

Scene 3

The Manager
R. Hitchcock
Scene: Tableau Curtain.

Scene 4

"Ghosts"[6]
L. Errol, Chorus
Scene: The Haunted Bedroom.
The Composer: L. Errol. *The Butler*: G. Moore. *The Ghost Girl*: E. Sinclair.

Scene 5

"The Pill-Box Revue"
W. Rock, F. White

Scene 6

Songs
"I May Be Gone for a Long Long Time"
(*Music by* Albert Von Tilzer. *Lyrics by* Lew Brown.)
G. LaRue
Scene: Tableau Curtain.
Manager: R. Hitchcock.

Scene 7

"Beautiful Lady of the Sea"[7] (Lady of the Sea)
I. Bordoni, Chorus
Scene: The Beach at San Sebastian.
The Proprietor: R. Hitchcock. *The Waiter*: L. Errol. *The Heiress*: G. LaRue. *Armand*: W. Rock. *The Cocotte*: F. White. *Le Jeune Premier*: I. Bordoni. *The Gendarme*: G. Moore.

---

[4]For the Second edition, this scene was replaced by:
"The Dreamy Parisian Coon"
Josephine Whittell
Songs
I. Bordoni
"The Lady and the Ship"
W. Rock, F. White
Scene: The Chorus Girls' Lounge.
Mlle. Fifi: I. Bordoni. *The Prima Donna*: J. Whittell. *Herman Louder*, the stage manager: G. Moore. *George Gagwell*, a comedian: L. Errol. *Philbert Nutt*: W. Rock. *Lucy Nutt*: F. White. *Cleo, Pansy, Gladys, Helen*, chorus girls: Misses Sinclair, Whitford, Hudson, Cripps.
[5]Dropped for subsequent tour.
[6]Song replaced for Second edition , but dropped for subsequent tour; scene retained:
"Jim Jams Gems"
L. Errol. Chorus
[7]Replaced late in the New York run and for tour by:
"Isle of Lost Romance"

Finale
Company

1917.13 ZIEGFELD FOLLIES OF 1917

A Musical Revue in Two Acts, 19 Scenes[8]. Sketches by Gene Buck and George V. Hobart. Music by Raymond Hubbell and Dave Stamper. Lyrics by Gene Buck. Staged by Ned Wayburn. Scenery designed by Joseph Urban. Costumes by Lady Duff-Gordon. Orchestra under the direction of Frank Darling. Produced by Florenz Ziegfeld. Opened 12 June 1917 at the New Amsterdam Theatre and closed 4 September 1917 after 111 performances.

CAST: WILL ROGERS, BERT WILLIAMS, IRVING FISHER, ALLYN KING, FANNY [Fannie] BRICE, WALTER L. CATLETT, W. C. FIELDS, THE FAIRBANKS TWINS (Madeline, Marion), EDDIE CANTOR, RUSSELL VOKES, DON BARCLAY, PEGGY HOPKINS, TOM RICHARDS, EDITH HALLOR, DOLORES, Dorothy Dickson, Carl Hyson, Lilyan Tashman, Gus Minton, Clay Hill, Malcolm Hicks, Peter Ostrander, Fred Heider, Helen Barnes, Bruce McKay, Charles Scribner.

Ensemble: Misses Florence Kern, Doris Lloyd, Dorothy Leeds, Betty Browne, Gladys Loftus, Margaret St. Clair, Ethel Delmar, Emily Drange, Marie Wallace, Mary Arthur, Edythe Whitney, Alexander, Marcelle Earle, Carr, Bowman, Mary Arthur, Cecile Markle, Barnett, May Carmen, F. Hirsch, Dewey, Eberts, Palfer, Walsh, D. Allen, M. Falconer, Calais, Ellsworth, Nelligan, Worth, H. Hirsch, Claremont Carroll.

ACT 1
Scene 1

The Episode of an Arabian Night in New York
"My Arabian Maid" (Song)
I. Fisher, A. King, Chorus
(*Music by* Raymond Hubbell.)
"The Arabian Fox Trot" (Ensemble Dance)
D. Lloyd, Arabian Dancers
Shaharazad: A. King. *Dinozad:* P. Hopkins. *Dick Burton:* I. Fisher. *John Vanburnen:* G. Minton. *The Grand Vizier:* T. Richards.
(*Costumes created by* Lady Duff Gordon, excepting Dancers.)

Scene 2

The Episode of the Purse
A. Jay: W. Catlett. *Aileen Jing:* A. King. *Joe Doakes:* C. Hill. *Patrolman:* M. Hicks. *Traffic Cop:* R. Vokes. *A Pedestrian:* P. Ostrander.

Scene 3

The Episode of the Garden of Girls
The Spirit of the Garden
E. Drange
(*Scene Music by* Victor Herbert.)
"(In the) Beautiful Garden of Girls"
E. Hallor
(*Music by* Raymond Hubbell.)
Pansy: F. Kern. *Forget-Me-Not:* M. St. Clair. *Poppy:* D. Lloyd. *Cornflower:* M. Earle. *Daisy:* E. Delmar. *Golden Rod:* L. Tashman. *Violet:* M. Wallace. *Lily:* D. Leeds. *Orchid:* B. Browne. *Rose:* G. Loftus. *Bubbles:* A. King, E. Lang.

Scene 4

The Episode of the Dog
Don, the inebriated canine: Himself. *Policeman:* R. Vokes.

Scene 5

The Episode of the Tennis Match
Rufus Racket: W. C. Fields. *Willie Love:* W. Catlett. *Allyn:* A. King. *Flo:* P. Hopkins.

Scene 6

The Episode of the Ziegfeld Follies Rag
"Ziegfeld Follies Rag"
F. Brice, Follies Dancers
(*Music by* Dave Stamper.)

Scene 7

The Episode of the Information Bureau
"The Potato Bug"[9]
F. Heider
(*Music by* Dave Stamper.)
Ichabod, the information clerk: G. Minton. *Mr. Pelham:* F. Heider. *Miss Mamaroneck:* M. Carmen. *Murgatroyd Jones,* a Red-cap: B. Williams. *Miss*

Punxsutawney: H. Barnes. *Teenie:* Marion Fairbanks. *Weenie:* Madeline Fairbanks. *Their Father:* R. Vokes. *Beatrice Bogey,* a golf enthusiast: L. Tashman. *Her Caddie:* B. McKay. *Virginia,* a train-misser: A. King. *Mildred,* another: P. Hopkins. *Abner Jones:* E. Cantor.

Scene 8

The Episode of the Telephone Wires
"Hello, (My) Dearie"
E. Hallor
(*Music by* Dave Stamper.)
At the Club: I. Fisher. *In the Trenches somewhere in France:* T. Richards.

Scene 9

The Episode of the Eddiecantor
Songs and Observations[10]
E. Cantor
"(The Modern) Maiden's Prayer"
(*Music by* James Hanley. *Lyrics by* Ballard Macdonald.)
"(That's) The Kind of a Baby for Me"
(*Music by* Jack Egan. *Lyrics by* Alfred Harriman.)

Scene 10

The Episode of Patriotism
Grand Finale: "Can't You Hear Your Country Calling?"
(*Music by* Victor Herbert.)
Tableaux: *Paul Revere's Ride:* T. Richards. *President Washington:* J. Kilgour. *President Lincoln:* (J. Barrett). *Our President:* W. Catlett.

Scene 11

The Episode of the American Eagle
"The March of the Continentals"
The Spirit of the North: L. Tashman. *The Spirit of the East:* G. Loftus. *The Spirit of the South:* M. Arthur. *The Spirit of the West:* H. Barnes. *Resources of the North, East, South, West:* Children. *The Navy:* Marion Fairbanks. *The Army:* Madeline Fairbanks. *Belgium:* D. Leeds. *Russia:* E. Delmar. *Japan:* C. Markle. *Italy:* E. Whitney. *Canada:* M. Carmen. *Scotland:* M. St. Clair. *Ireland:* M. Wallace. *England:* P. Hopkins. *France:* D. Lloyd. *America:* A. King.
Our Flag, Our Navy (Battleship effect by Langdon MacCormick.)

ACT 2[11]
Scene 1

The Episode of the Wedding Morning
"Because You Are Just You"[12] (Just Because You're You)
I. Fisher, "Mawrasette"
(*Music by* Jerome Kern.)
The Bride: "Mawrasette." *The Friend:* "Phyllis." *The Other Friend:* "Marma." *The Little Sister:* C. Carroll. *The Maid:* "Ruby."
The Episode of Chiffon
"Jealous Moon"
E. Hallor
Ladies of Fashion: Terrible Temptation: P. Hopkins *A Symbol of Change and Emotion:* L. Tashman. *A New Sensation:* D. Leeds. *Enchantment:* G. Loftus. *Lonely Loveliness Means Danger:* M. St. Clair. *Hope Deferred:* M. Wallace. *Impassionate Sensation:* E. Whitney. *The Call of the Wild:* M. Arthur. *Nights of Gladness:* C. Markle. *The Joy of Living:* B. Brown. *Going Some:* D. Lloyd. *The Discourager of Hesitancy:* Miss Dolores, the Empress of Fashion.

Scene 2

"The Episode of Williamswarbles
Songs:
B. Williams
"Home, Sweet Home" (No Place Like Home)
(*Music and Lyrics by* Ring Lardner.)
"Unhappy" (I'm So Happy)
(*Music by* Turner Layton. *Lyrics by* Henry Creamer.)

---

[8]Eleventh in the annual series of revues produced by Florenz Ziegfeld which began in 1907. During the run, the running order of Act 2 was revised, and Act 2, Scene 1 divided into 2 scenes.
[9]Dropped during the New York run.

[10]Introduced by Eddie Cantor during subsequent tour, as per sheet music and biography:
"The Dixie Volunteers"
E. Cantor
(*Music and Lyrics by* Edgar Leslie and Harry Ruby.)
[11]Added during the run:
Dance (Act 2, after The Episode of Williamwarbles)
Ann Pennington
[12]Replaced during the run by:
"Beautiful Girl, Good-Bye"
T. Richards
(*Music by* Dave Stamper.)

["I Ain't Married No More"
  (*Music by* Les Copeland. *Lyrics by* Rennold Wolf.)
"Everybody's Crazy 'Bout the Doggone Blues but I'm Happy"
  (*Music by* Turner Layton. *Lyrics by* Henry Creamer.)]

Scene 3

The Episode of the Mississippi Levee

"Just You and Me"
  F. Brice, E. Cantor
  (*Music by* Dave Stamper.)

Dance
  H. Wilson
  The Ante-Bellum Girls: Misses Braham, M. Boulais, R. Boulais, Rosewood, S. Howard, H. Lloyd, Heil, Gill, E. Young. *The Dandies of 1859:* Messrs. Cavanaugh, Simms, Evans, Baker, Nevins, Burggraf, Newsome, Mathews, Barrett.

Scene 4

The Episode of New York Streets and Subways

Dance[13]
  D. Dickson, C. Hyson
  Adolphus, an Alpine Guide: F. Heider. *Amy:* A. King. *Betty:* P. Hopkins *Clara:* L. Tashman. *Emma:* M. Carmen. *Mr. Wooley,* from the West: W. Catlett. *Jerry,* a policeman: C. Scribner. *Tom,* a taxi-driver: R. Vokes. *Bill,* a newsboy: K. Perry. *Jessie,* a cloakroom girl: H. Barnes. *Sammy,* a friend of hers: M. Hicks. *Wise Acres,* the peanut man: W. C. Fields. *Pasquale,* an animal trainer: T. Richards. *Grizzly Bear:* B. Williams. *Finnegan,* a foreman: G. Minton. *Bob,* a workman: D. Barclay. *Mike,* another: C. Hill.

Scene 5

The Episode of the Fannybriceisms

Songs
  F. Brice
  ["Egyptian"
  (*Music by* Leo Edwards. *Lyrics by* Blanche Merrill.)]

Scene 6

The Episode of the Chinese Lacquer

"Chu Chin Chow"
  A. King
  (*Music by* Dave Stamper.)
  Fanbearers: Fairbanks Twins. *The Parasol Girls:* Misses L. Tashman, G. Loftus, D. Leeds, Browne, Kern, Markle, St. Clair, D. Lloyd.

Scene 7

The Episode of the Willrogersayings
  Will Rogers (He is liable to talk about anything or anybody.)

Scene 8

The Episode of 'An Arabian Night' (3 hours later)

Finale Ensemble
  Entire Company

1917.14 ## MY LADY'S GLOVE

An Operetta in Three Acts. Book and lyrics by Edgar Smith and Edward A. Paulton. (Based on the Viennese operette 'Die schöne Unbekannte' [The Beautiful Unknown], libretto by Leopold Jacobson and Leo Stein.) Music by Oscar Straus; additional musical numbers by Sigmund Romberg. Staged by J. C. Huffman. Dances and ensembles by Allan K. Foster. Costumes designed by Mme. Kahn, Adler Costume Company. (Orchestra under the direction of Gaetano Merola.) Produced under the personal direction of J. J. Shubert. Produced by Messrs. Shubert. Opened 18 June 1917 at the Lyric Theatre and closed 30 June 1917 after 16 performances.[14]

<u>CAST:</u> *Colonel Bombarde,* the martinet commander of the 25th Regiment: CHARLES JUDELS. *Captain Poildeau,* of the 25th, familiarly known as "Poldi": CHARLES PURCELL. *M. Theodore Lampelle,* of Lampelle's Soups, his uncle: CHARLES McNAUGHTON. *Antoine,* "Toni," Captain Poildeau's orderly: Ned Monroe. *Lieutenant Ponsonby,* British military attaché: HORACE SINCLAIR. *Lieutenant Jureau,* bandmaster of the 25th: ARTHUR GEARY. *Lieutenants Victorien, Conde,* sub-officers: Paul Burtnett, J. W. Kelly. *Elaine,* "Elly," the Colonel's young daughter: VIVIENNE SEGAL. *Lydia Petrowska,* a popular actress: FRANCES DEMAREST. *Mme. Fifi,* a rich widow: MAUDE ODELL. *Charlotte:* Grace Daniels. *Mimi:* Doris Marvin. *Mlle. Montmartre:* Virgnia Fissinger. *Ladies, Debutantes, Officers, Guests, etc.* (*Opera Specialty:* Mme. Nadina Tagelli.)

---

[13]Dropped during the run.
[14]Settings uncredited.

Personnel of the Chorus: Show Girls: Silvia Wood, Helen Rintelen, Mabel Godding, Gladys Logan, Grace Burton, Katherine Kildare, Florence Shortelle, Suzanna Collingwood, Rose Timble, Beatrice Cloak, Nita Lamadrid, Anna Delmore, Eleanor Fox, Fay King. *Dancers:* Isabelle Adams, Helen Berkeley, Josephine Raye, Florence Challenger, Madelyne LaVene, Pearl Baremore, Pearl Weber, Joan Butlin, Lottie Franklyn, Sylvia Cassell, Mareta George, Rebekah Cauble, Faye Atkins. *Men:* Gene Aubrey, Kenneth Tudor, Herman Fink, Joe Stenton, Ray Moore, Teddy Stevens, Alex Morrissey, C. L. Henderson, C. H. Gilbert, Harold Rolland, C. H. Miller N. Walton, Jack Donelly, Larry Mulvaney.

The action takes place at the Barracks of the 25th Regiment at Chantilly, near Paris, France, in 1913.

Act 1: Officers' Mess Room at Chantilly.

Act 2: The Regimental Bazaar.

Act 3: Garden of Colonel Bombarde's Residence.

ACT 1[14a]

"Officers of the 25th" (Opening)
  H. Sinclair, A. Geary
  (*Music by* Sigmund Romberg.)

"Keep Repeating It" (March)
  A. Geary, Chorus
  (*Music by* Sigmund Romberg.)

"I'll Hate to Leave the Boys"
  C. Purcell, G. Daniels, D. Marvin, Officers' Daughters

"Foolish Little Maiden, I" (Solo)
  V. Segal
  (*Music by* Sigmund Romberg.)

"(Woman's Said to Be) The Fickle Sex" (Duet)
  V. Segal, C. Purcell
  (*Music by* Sigmund Romberg and Oscar Straus.)

Finale
  C. Purcell, A. Geary, H. Sinclair, C. McNaughton, Officers

ACT 2

Opening Chorus and Ensemble

Concerted Song
  Mme. N. Tagelli

Valse Classique
  V. Fissinger

"I'm Madly in Love with a Dream Girl"
  C. Purcell

"Amorous Rose" (Auction Ensemble)
  F. Demarest, C. Judels, H. Sinclair, A. Geary, C. Purcell, Chorus
  (*Music by* Oscar Straus.)

"Do Buy Some Candy, Sir"
  V. Segal, A. Geary, H. Siclair, Chorus
  (*Music by* Sigmund Romberg.)

"Secrecy" (Sextette)
  V. Segal, F. Demarest, M. Odell, C. Purcell, C. McNaughton, H. Sinclair
  (*Music by* Oscar Straus.)

"I Mean to be Married as Soon as I Can" (Duet and Pantomime)
  M. Odell, C. Judels
  (*Music by* Oscar Straus.)

"Prudence Has Fled" (Love Is For Youth) (Duet)
  F. Demarest, C. Purcell
  (*Music by* Oscar Straus.)

Finale
  Entire Company

ACT 3

"Since To-day Our Colonel's Mating" (Opening)
  A. Geary, N. Monroe, Chorus
  (*Music by* Oscar Straus.)

"No More Girls for Me"
  C. Purcell, Girls

"An-ti-ci-pa-tion" (Duet)
  F. Demarest, C. McNaughton

Wedding March (Bridal March)
  Ensemble
  (*Music by* Oscar Straus.)

"Look Before You Leap" (Sextette)
  C. Judels, C. Purcell, A. Geary, H. Sinclair, C. McNaughton, N. Monroe
  (*Music by* Sigmund Romberg.)

Finale
  Entire Company

[14a]All lyrics by Edward Paulton.

1917.15

MAYTIME

A Play with Music in Four Acts. Book and lyrics by Rida Johnson Young. (Based on the libretto to the German musical comedy "Wei einst im Mai", libretto by Rudolf Bernauer and Rudolf Schanzer. Music by Walter Kollo and Willy Bredschneider.) Music by Sigmund Romberg. Staged by Edward P. Temple. Dances arranged by Allan K. Foster. All scenery and costumes designed by Homer Conant. Orchestra under the direction of Frank Tours. Orchestrations by Sandar Harmathy and Kiefert. Entire production under the supervision of J. J. Shubert. Produced by Messrs. Shubert. Opened 16 August 1917 at the Sam S. Shubert Theatre, moved 18 February 1918 to the 44th Street Theatre, moved 1 April 1918 to the Broadhurst Theatre, moved 5 August 1918 to the Lyric Theatre, moved 9 September 1918 to the Broadhurst Theatre, and closed 19 October 1918 after 492 performances.

CAST (in order of appearance): *Act 1: John Wayne:* Richard Morgan. *Colonel Van Zandt:* CARL [Karl] STALL. *Ottillie, his daughter:* PEGGY WOOD. *Richard Wayne, an apprentice:* CHARLES PURCELL. *Matilda Van Zandt:* Edith Wright. *Alice Tremaine:* Laura Arnold. *Matthew Van Zandt:* WILLIAM NORRIS. *Claude Van Zandt:* DOUGLAS J. WOOD. *Maria:* Grace Daniels. *Rudolfo:* ARTHUR ALBRO. *Ensemble of Apprentices, Young Ladies, Gypsies, etc.*

Act 2: Madame Delphine: Rose Winter. *Hannaford:* Gene Aubrey. *Stuyvesant:* C. H. Miller. *Doorman:* Frank Sidney. *Claude Van Zandt:* DOUGLAS J. WOOD. *Angelica, Matthew's second wife:* Pearl Barimore. *Matthew Van Zandt:* WILLIAM NORRIS. *P. T. Barnum:* Edward F. Nannary. *Estrella Amorita:* Minna Valieri. *Signor Vivalla:* Arthur Albro. *Ottilie Van Zandt:* PEGGY WOOD. *Alice Tremaine:* Laura Arnold. *Richard Wayne:* CHARLES PURCELL. *Ensemble of Guests, Servants, etc.*

Act 3: Madame Delphine: Rose Winter. *Matthew Van Zandt:* WILLIAM NORRIS. *Lizzie,* Matthew's third wife: MAUDE ODELL. *Little Dick Wayne,* age 5: Warner Anderson. *Richard Wayne:* CHARLES PURCELL. *John Rutherford:* Ralph J. Herbert. *Mr. Hicks,* auctioneer: Teddy Webb. *Algernon:* R. Melbourn. *Ottilie Van Zandt:* PEGGY WOOD. *Ensemble of Bidders.*

Act 4: Ottilie Van Zandt, known as Mlle. Brown: PEGGY WOOD. *Hortense, a model:* Eleanor B. Fox. *Letty:* Rose Timble. *Estelle* forewoman: Janet Kenny. *Ermintrude D'Albert:* GERTRUDE VANDERBILT. *Winifred St. Albans:* Florence Bruce. *Matthew Van Zandt:* WILLIAM NORRIS. *Dicky Wayne:* CHARLES PURCELL. *Ensemble of Models, Dressmakers, etc.*

Ensemble: Ladies: Ann Delmore, Rena Manning, Helen Cameron, Adele LeRoy, Pearl Barrymore, Rose Timble, Virginia Heffren, Edna Rochelle, Eleanor Fox, Pearl Germonde, Jane Russell. *Gentlemen:* Jack Harvey, Fred Williams, C. H. Miller, George Allen, Teddy Stevens, R. Melbourn, Bud Davidson, Teddy Shelber, Henry Ward, Burt Hall.

Act 1: The Van Zandt Home in Washington Square, New York City. 1840.

Act 2: Mme. Delphine's Night Club. 1855.

Act 3: Back Parlor of the Van Zandt House in Washington Square. In the 1880s.

Act 4: Same location as Act 3, now Mlle. Brown's Dressmaking Establishment. Twentieth Century.

ACT 1

Opening Ensemble
  Apprentices
"In Our Little Home, Sweet Home"
  P. Wood, C. Purcell
"It's a Windy Day at the Battery"
  W. Norris, L. Arnold, Girls
"Gypsy Song"
  A. Albro
"Will You Remember (Sweet heart)?"
  P. Wood, C. Purcell

ACT 2

Opening Mazurka
  Chorus
"Jump Jim Crow"
  W. Norris, Chorus
"The Road to Paradise"
  P. Wood, W. Norris
Spanish Dance
  M. Valieri
"Will You Remember (Sweetheart)?" (reprise)
  A. Albro

ACT 3

Auction Chorus ("Odd Lots, Job Lots")(Opening)
  Ensemble
"Reminiscence"
  W. Anderson

ACT 4

"Selling Gowns"
  P. Wood, Girls
  (*Lyrics by* Cyrus Wood.)
"Dancing Will Keep You Young"
  G. Vanderbilt, W. Norris
  (*Lyrics by* Cyrus Wood.)
"Only One Girl for Me"
  C, Purcell, Girls
"Will You Remember (Sweetheart)?" (reprise)
  P. Wood, C. Purcell

1917.16

CHEER UP

A Musical Revue in Three Cheers (Acts), 11 Scenes. Sketches by R. H. Burnside. Music by Raymond Hubbell. Lyrics by John L. Golden. Entire production staged by R. H. Burnside. Scenery designed by H. Robert Law and Mark Lawson. Costumes designed by Robert McQuinn, Katherine H. Lovell, Gladys Monkhouse, William H. Matthews, Willard Barnes. Orchestra under the direction of Raymond Hubbell. Produced by Charles Dillingham. Opened 23 August 1917 at the Hippodrome and closed 11 May 1918 after 456 performances.

CAST: NAT M. WILLS, HARRY HOUDINI, JOHN HENDRICKS, Sophye Bernard, Joseph Frohoff, HELEN GLADINGS, Ethel Lorraine, RHEA NORTON, GUADALUPE MELENDEZ, J. P. Coombs, Nancy Keay, Matty O'Brien, Eddie Russell, James J. Doherty, Harry Ward, James Byrne, Andrew Byrne, Charles Ravel, John Abbott, FRANCES ROEDER, HENRY TAYLOR, FLORA E. MERRILL, Albert Froom, Ethel Hopkins, Nellie Doner, Mirano Brothers, (Maud) MALLIA, BART and MALLIA, BUD SNYDER Trio, George Powers (and His Elephants), TOZART, THE BRIGHTONS, The Soltis, Mark Freeman, Steve Miaco, The Four Amaranths, Ladella Comiques, George Davis Family, ELM CITY FOUR, Tommy Colton, Major Johnson, Billy Pandur, The Bogannys, JOHN BYRNE, THE BERLO SISTERS (Twinnie, Pauline, Lillian, Madeline, Florence), Arthur Hill, Stanley Ferguson, Bob Reano, Robert Rosaire, Thomas Keenan, Bill Caress, Adolph Adams, Claire Rochester, The Grigolettos, Edward Wirth, Lou Lorrimer, Myer Swirse, Charles Melody, Angel Barbara, George Fleming, William Stanley, Kris Dahl, James Carty, Phil Gilpin, Aaron Beers, A. Rees, May Smith, Herman Smith, Dan Carew, Johnny Davis, C. K. Kessler, Eugene Diers, Peter Young, Marie De Young, William DuPont, Robert Flynn, Helen Osborne, Emma Dickson, Louise Owen, FRED WALTON, DIPPY DIERS.

CHEER 1 (ACT 1)[15]

Scene 1

Opening Chorus
  Entire Company
"One—Two—Three"
  R. Norton, Entire Company
Divertissements
  The Soltis, The Hippodrome Clowns
"The Blushing Bride and Groom"
  Elm City Four
  (*Music by* Milton Ager. *Lyrics by* William Jerome.)
  Scene: The Hippodrome Workshop. (*Painted by* Mark Lawson.)
    The Wizard of Hippodrome: J. Hendricks. *The Messenger Boy:* W. Evans. *'Poor Butterfly':* E. Hopkins. *John Philip Sousa:* J. Frohoff. *The Dancing Doll:* H. Gladings. *Charlotte:* E. Lorraine. *Anna Pavlova:* R. Norton. *Annette Kellerman:* G. Melendez. *The Villain:* J. P. Coombs. *Belle Story:* N. Keay. *Toto:* M. O'Brien. *Marcelline:* E. Russell. *Minstrel Man:* J. J. Doherty. *Joe Jackson:* H. Ward. *Arnaut Brothers:* J. Byrne, A. Byrne. *Minister:* C. Ravel.
    From HIP, HIP, HOORAY: *The Ambitious Actor:* J. Abbott. *The Innocent Ingenue:* F. Roeder. *The Jaunty Juvenile:* H. Taylor. *The Saucy Soubrette:* H. Gladings. *The Chubby Comedian:* A. Froom. *The Artful Adventuress:* N. Doner. *The Toy Soldier:* F. Walton. *Other Characters:* Mallia, Bart and Mallia, Mirano Brothers, Bud Snyder Trio, G. Powers, The Soltis, Tozart, The Brightons, M. Freeman, S. Miaco, Four Amaranths, Ladella Comiques,

---

[15]Added to production during the run:
  "Miss Liberty" (added 4 September 1917)
    S. Barnard, Ensemble
    (*Music by* Raymond Hubbell. *Lyrics by* John L. Golden.)
  "Columbus March" (added 12 October 1917)
    (*Music by* John Philip Sousa.)
  "Polly Poll" (added 18 March 1918)
    (*Music by* Raymond Hubbell. *Lyrics by* John L. Golden.)

George Davis Family, Elm City Four, Slayman Ali Troupe, T. Colton, Major Johnson, B. Pandur, J. Byrne, A. Hill, S. Ferguson, D. Diers, B. Reano, R. Rosaire, T. Keenan, B. Caress, A. Adams.

Scene 2

John Byrne (Portraits and Painting)
Tozart (Lightning Landscape Artist)
The Brightons (Artistic Rag Pickers)
Scene: Along Broadway. (*Painted by* Mark Lawson.)

Scene 3

"(Gee!) What a Wonderful Mate You'll Be"
E. Hopkins, Chorus

Specialties

Powers' Elephants (Jennie, Lena, Roxie, Julia); The Four Amaranths
Scene: The Jungle. (*Painted by* Mark Lawson.)
The Ape: H. Ward. *The Gorilla*: A. Hill. *The Hunter*: F. Walton. *Mr. Cockatoo*: E. Hopkins. *Miss Cockatoo*: E. Gladings. *The Girl on the Wire*: M. Mallia.

Specialty[16]

Houdini offers his latest creation, "The Vanishing Elephant." The Most Colossal Disappearing Mystery that History Records. Dissolving into thin air, on the largest stage in the world, an elephant weighing 10,000 pounds. Before one's very eyes, in a blaze of light, with bewildering rapidity, this pachyderm monster suddenly eludes the vision.

Scene 4

"When Old New York Goes Dry"
N. M. Wills
(*Music and Lyrics by* Benjamin Hapgood Burt.)
Scene: The Country Station. (*Painted by* Mark Lawson.)
The Furniture Movers: Mallia, Bart and Mallia.

Scene 5

"Melody Land"
J. Hendricks, Hippodrome Chorus
Scene: The Music Shop. (*Painted by* Mark Lawson and H. Robert Law.)
The Pierrot: J. Hendricks. *The Soldier*: F. Walton. *The Music Maid*: H. Gladings.

CHEER 2 (ACT 2)

Scene 1

The Happy Hobo
N. M. Wills

Medley

W. Evans, Elm City Four, A. Froom, J. P. Coombs, Hippodrome Company

"My Bridal Rose" (Song)
H. Taylor, Chorus
Scene: The Farm. (Lawson.)

Scene 2

Specialties

F. Walton; The Merano Brothers

"Cheer Up, 'Liza!"
J. Hendricks, Entire Company

Off to France (Tableau)
Scene: The Recruiting Station. (Lawson.)

Scene 3

Bud Snyder and Company
Scene: Inside the Hippodrome. (Law.)

Scene 4

"(Beautiful) Queen of the Nile"
E. Hopkins, Chorus
Scene: The Sphinx. (Lawson.)
Arab Chief: J. P. Coombs. *Arabians*: Elm City Four. And the Berber Troupe, the Slayman Ali Troupe, The Tzigane Troupe.

Scene 5

"The Land of Liberty"
(*Music arranged and compiled by* John Philip Sousa. *Scene painted by* Mark Lawson. *Costumes by* Mme. Freisinger.)
1492: Columbus: A. Froom.
1497-1499: Cabot: R. Reano. *Vespucci*: L. Lorrimer.
1501-1539: De Leon: M. Swirse. *De Soto*: W. Ladella. *Balboa*: W. Caress.
1534-1668: Cartier: C. Melody. *Ribault*: P. Ladella. *DeChamplain*: E. Russell. *LaSalle*: H. Ward. *Marquette*: A. Hill.
1524: Verrazano: A. Barbara.

1607-1620: Captain John Smith: G. Fleming. *Pocahontas*: G. Melendez. *Miles Standish*: J. P. Coombs. *Priscilla*: R. Norton. *John Alden*: J. Abbott.
1631-1732: George Calvert: W. Stanley. *Carteret*: G. Davis. *William Penn*: A. Byrne. *Roger Williams*: T. Colton. *Oglethorpe*: K. Dahl.
1608-1647: Hendrick Hudson: S. Miaco. *Peter Stuyvesant*: J. Frohoff.
1776: George Washington: H. Taylor. *Lafayette*: J. Carty. *Paul Jones*: E. Brennan. *Paul Revere*: E. Wirth. *DeKalb*: L. Lazerin. *Molly Pitcher*: N. Doner. *Betsy Ross*: M. Mallia. *Benjamin Franklin*: C. Ravel. *Thomas Jefferson*: S. Ferguson. *John Hancock*: P. Gilpin. *John Adams*: J. Byrne. *Nathan Hale*: J. Davis. *Israel Putnam*: A. Beers. *Spirit of 1776*: A. Rees, R. Rosaire, T. Ladella.
1861-1865: Abraham Lincoln: D. T. Carew. *Slaves*: T. Keenan, J. Davis, M. Smith. *Grant*: H. Smith. *Lee*: C. K. Kessler. *Sherman*: E. Diers. *Sheridan*: M. Truscott. *Farragut*: J. Masters. *Stonewall Jackson*: P. Young. *Barbara Freitchie*: M. DeYoung.
1898-1917: Dewey: J. Byrne. *Sampson*: W. DuPont. *Schley*: R. Flynn. *Theodore Roosevelt*: J. Hendricks. *Miss Liberty*: E. Hopkins. *Incidental to the finale*: The Four Amaranths, The Soltis, H. Gladings, F. E. Merrill. Other characters by the Hippodrome Company.

CHEER 3 (ACT 3)

The Submarine Belles

"Joy Town"
Elm City Four, assisted by Misses Merrill, Keay, Carter, Hippodrome Company
Scene: Joytown. (Lawson.)

The Disappearing Divers—Where Do They Go?

Diving Specialty

The Girl in Red: H. Osborne. *The Girl in Blue*: E. Dickson. *The Girl in Lavender*: M. DeYoung. *The Girl in Green*: G. Melendez. *The Girl in Orange*: L. Owen. *The Girl in Purple*: M. Smith.

Gorman's Diving Horse—Queen

Specialty[17]

Exclusive engagement of the world-famous Houdini. Introducing at every performance his original, uncanny and perilous feat of extrication. The Submersible Iron-Bound Box Mystery. Manacled and roped, Houdini will be nailed into an iron-bound box burdened with 300 pounds of weights, and the box lowered into a tank containing 500,000 gallons of water. The box, being perforated, will fill with water within twenty seconds. To escape drowning, Houdini must therefore release himself while submerged. A committee of investigation is invited on the stage at every performance.

The Berlo Sisters—Champion Divers

Finale

1917.17

LEAVE IT TO JANE

A Musical Comedy in Two Acts, 3 Scenes. Book by P. G. Wodehouse and Guy Bolton. Based on the comedy "The College Widow" by George Ade. Music by Jerome Kern. Lyrics by P. G. Wodehouse. Staged by Edward Royce. Dances and ensembles by David Bennett. Scenery designed by D. M. Aiken. Costumes by Collins, Finchley, Spaulding. Orchestra under the direction of John McGhie. Orchestrations by Frank Saddler. Produced by William Elliott, F. Ray Comstock and Morris Gest. Opened 28 August 1917 at the Longacre Theatre and closed 19 January 1918 after 167 performances.

CAST (in order of appearance): *Ollie Mitchell*, a sophomore: RUDOLF CUTTEN. *Matty McGowan*, a trainer: Dan Collyer. *'Stub' Talmadge*, a busy undergraduate: OSCAR SHAW. *'Silent' Murphy*, a center rush: Thomas Delmar. *Bessie Tanner*, an athletic girl: ANN ORR. *Sally Cameron*, a co-ed: JANE CARROLL. *Town Girls (4)*: *Bertha Tyson*: Lillian Cullen. *Cora Jenks*: Catherine Mack. *Martha Abbott*: Marie King. *Josephine Barclay*: Frances Burns. *Dancers (3)*: *Louella Banks*: Arlene Chase. *Marion Mooney*: Helen Rich. *Cissie Summers*: Tess Mayer. *Peter Witherspoon*, A.M., Ph. D., President of Atwater College: Frederic Graham. *Howard Talbot*, a tutor: Algernon Grieg. *Jane Witherspoon*, daughter of Peter Witherspoon: EDITH HALLOR. *Jimsey Hopper*, a student: Harry Forbes. *Dick McAllister*, another student: D. E. Charles. *Flora Wiggins*, a prominent waitress: GEORGIA O'RAMEY. *Hiram Bolton*, D.D., L.L.D.: Will C. Crimans. *Billy Bolton*, a halfback: ROBERT G. PITKIN. *Honorable Elam Hicks* of Squantumville: Allan Kelly. *Harold 'Bub' Hicks*, a freshman: OLIN HOWLAND. *College students, co-eds, town girls, etc.*

Act 1, Scene 1: Atwater College. The Terrace of Memorial Hall on the opening day of the fall term. Late afternoon. *Scene 2*: Night.

Act 2: Outside the Football Field.

---

[16]Houdini departed early in the show's run.

[17]Houdini departed early in the show's run.

ACT 1[18]

Scene 1

Atwater College Songs ("Good Old Atwater")
Male Ensemble

"A Peach of a Life" (Duet)
O. Shaw, A. Orr

"Wait Till Tomorrow" (Song)
E. Hallor, Boys

"(Just You) Watch My Step" (Song)
O. Shaw, A. Chase, Girls

"Leave It to Jane" (Trio)
E. Hallor, O. Shaw, A. Orr, Girls

"The Crickets Are Calling" (Duet)
E. Hallor, R.G. Pitkin

Scene 2

Medley of College Songs[19]
Principals, Ensemble

"When the Orchestra's Playing Your Favorite Waltz" (There It Is Again)(Song)
R. G. Pitkin, Town Girls

"Cleopatterer" (Song)
G. O'Ramey

"Something to Say" (What I'm Longing to Say) (Duet)
E. Hallor, R. G. Pitkin

Finale

ACT 2

"Football Song"
A. Orr, Ensemble

"The Days of Chivalry" (Sir Galahad) (Trio)
O. Shaw, G. O'Ramey, O. Howland

"Football Song" (reprise)
Ensemble

"The Sun Shines Brighter" (I'm So Happy)(Duet)
A. Orr, O. Shaw

"The Siren's Song" (Duet)
E. Hallor, A. Orr, Girls

"I'm Going to Find a Girl (Someday)" (Trio)
O. Shaw, O. Howland, R. Cutten, A. Chase, H. Rich, T. Mayer

Finale

1917.18   GOOD NIGHT PAUL

A Musical Farce in Three Acts. Book and lyrics by Roland Oliver and Charles Dickson. Music by Harry B. Olsen. Gowns by Lucile. Staged by J. H. Benrimo. Produced by Ralph Herz. Opened 3 September 1917 at the Hudson Theatre and closed 6 October 1917 after 40 performances.[20]

CAST: *Mrs. Audrey Heywood*: AUDREY MAPLE. *Madame Louise*, modiste on the ground floor: LOUISE KELLY. *Robert Hayward*: BURRELL BARBARETTO. *Paul Forster*: RALPH HERZ. *Frank Forster*: FRANK LALOR. *Elizabeth M. O'Brien*: ELIZABETH M. MURRAY.

Models from Madame Louise: Misses Trimponi, Gladys Smith, Jene Glening, Marjorie Stevens, Betty Gram, Julie Ross.

The action takes place in Paris at the present time.

Act 1: Living-room in the Hayward Apartment.

Act 2: Mrs. Hayward's Apartment. Evening.

Act 3: Same as Act 1. Following morning.

ACT 1[20a]

"Gowns"
L. Kelley, Girls

"Eenie Weenie (Lovey Dovey)"
A. Maple, B. Barbaretto

"(Nothing Seems Right, Oh!) The World Is All Wrong"
R. Herz, B. Barbaretto, A. Maple

"(Poor) Mary Ann O'Shea"
E. Murray
(*Music by* Arthur E. Aerseth. *Lyrics by* George C. Mack.)

ACT 2

"Constancy"
A. Maple

"Sailing (Away) on the Henry Clay"
E. Murray
(*Music by* Egbert Van Alstyne. *Lyrics by* Gus Kahn.)

"Flattery"[21]
E. Murray, A. Maple

"Serenade"
B. Barbaretto, A. Maple

ACT 3

"I've Given My Heart to You, Dear"
A. Maple, B. Barbaretto

"(Eenie Weenie) Lovey Dovey"
E. Murray, R. Herz

"Purity"[22]
L. Kelley, E. Murray, R. Herz, F. Lalor

"I Like You"
L. Kelley, F. Lalor

Finale
Company

1917.19   RAMBLER ROSE

A Musical Comedy in Three Acts. Book and lyrics by Harry B. Smith. Music by Victor Jacobi. Staged by W. H. Bentley. Dances and groupings arranged by Jack Mason. Scenery designed by Homer Emens; Act 2 designed by Baron Voruz de Vaux. Ladies' gowns and costumes by Schneider-Anderson Company; Miss Sanderson's gowns by Henri Bendel. Men's clothes by Russell Uniform Co. Orchestra under the direction of Harold Vicars. Produced by Charles Frohman. Opened 10 September 1917 at the Empire Theatre and closed 10 November 1917 after 72 performances.

CAST: *Rosamund Lee*, an American girl: JULIA SANDERSON. *Joseph Guppy*: JOSEPH CAWTHORN. *Gerald Morton*, a painter: JOHN GOLDSWORTHY. *Marcel Petipas*, a sculptor: STEWART BAIRD. *Timothy Briggs*, Guppy's uncle from Brazil: GEORGE E. MACK. *Willis*, a chauffeur: George Egan. *A Farmer's Boy*: W. H. Bentley. *Angele*, an actress: ADE MEADE. *Lady Cloverdale*. directress of a school for girls: KATE SERGEANTSON. *Schoolgirls (3)*: *Claire*: Ethel Boyd. *Blanche*: Doris Predo. *Dora*: Wilma Walton. *Tita*: Gladys Siddons.

Pupils at Lady Cloverdale's School: Helen Trainor, Anita Wood, Doris Sheerin, Eileen Clinton, Clara K. Taylor, Dot Nichols, Helen Maillard, Hilda Allison, Selma Morris, Florence Lee, Muriel Parker, Harriet Gustin, Betty Berry, Marion George, Olga Ziceva, Betty Shannon, Marie Francis, Helen Hyde, Ella Foster, Murray Lavone, Frances Mink, Marie Gray, Camille Truesdale, Jean Burke. *Guests at Gerald's Studio*: Camille Truesdale, Frances Mink, Ella Foster, Marie Francis, Olga Ziceva, Betty Berry, Muriel Parker, Selma Morris, Helen Maillard, Clara K. Taylor, Doris Sheerin, Helen Trainor, Garrett Carroll, Alexander Morrissey, William Plummer, Frank Snyder, Kenneth Tudor, Sidney Ayres, George Wharton. *The Schools of Painting*: *Flemish (Rubens)* Doris Sheerin; *Byzantine (Russo)* Marion George; *Roman (Raphael)* Dot Nichols; *Venetian (Carpaccio)* Selma Morris; *Spanish (Velasquez)* Helen Maillard; *Florentine (Purists)* Helen Trainor; *German (Durer)* Harriet Gustin; *French (Vigee Le Brun)* Eileen Clinton; *German (Holbein)* Betty Berry; *French (Watteau)* Hilda Allison; *The Futurists*, Doris Predo, Ethel Boyd, Wilma Walton, Anita Wood; *Gothic*, Marie Francis, Helen Hyde, Ella Foster, Murray Lavone, Frances Mink, Marie Gray, Camille Truesdale, Jean Burke. *Visitors at Deauville*: Marie Gray, Jean Burke, Murray Lavone, Helen Hyde, Betty Shannon, Marion George, Harriet Gustin, Florence Lee, Hilda Allison, Dot Nichols, Eileen Clinton, Anita Wood, Peggy Higgins, Malcolm Murray, Russell Griswold, Jack Bick, Bernard Fritze, Clarence Rockwell, Jack Donnelly.

Act 1: Lady Cloverdale's School, near Plymouth, England.

Act 2: Marcel and Gerald's Studio in Paris.

Act 3: The Casino Garden at Deauville, France.

---

[18]Late in the run, the song order was revised. "The Siren's Song" was moved to end Act 1, Scene 1; "Something to Say" was dropped, and "The Crickets Are Calling" closed Act 1.
[19]Medley included "Boola-Boola," "Seeing Nellie Home," and "My Bonnie."
[20]Settings, musical director uncredited.
[20a]Roland Oliver alone is credited with lyrics on all published sheet music.

[21]Dropped during the run.
[22]Dropped during the run.

ACT 1

Opening Chorus

"Just a Little Bit in Love"
S. Baird, E. Boyd, D. Predo

"Rambler Rose"
J. Sanderson, Chorus

"Dream! Dream!"
J. Sanderson, J. Goldsworthy

"Smile a Little, Smile for Me"
J. Sanderson, J. Cawthorn

Finale

ACT 2

Opening Chorus

"The Land of the Midnight Sun"
A. Meade, Chorus

Valse—Quartette
A. Meade, E. Boyd, J. Goldsworthy, S. Baird

"Whenever I Think of You"
J. Sanderson
(*Music by* Charles N. Grant. *Lyrics by* Schuyler Greene.)

"Bundle of Nerves"
J. Cawthorn

"I Know You"
A. Meade, G. E. Mack

"Come to Gypsy Land" (Gypsy Song)
J. Sanderson, Chorus

Finale

ACT 3

Opening Chorus

"One Look, One Word"
J. Sanderson, Male Chorus

"Poor Little Rich Girl's Dog"
J. Cawthorn
(*Music and Lyrics by* Irving Berlin.)

"I Might Say Yes"
S. Baird, A. Meade

"But Not for You"
J. Cawthorn, J. Sanderson

Finale

1917.20 THE RIVIERA GIRL

A Musical Comedy in Three Acts. Book by Guy Bolton and P. G. Wodehouse. (Based on the Viennese operette 'Die Csárdásfürstin' [Gypsy Princess], libretto by Leo Stein and Béla Jenbach.) Music by Emmerich Kálmán. Lyrics by P. G. Wodehouse. Dialogue directed by Herbert Gresham. Dances arranged by Julian Mitchell. Scenery by Joseph Urban. Costumes designed by Alice O'Neil. Lighting by Ben Beerwald. Orchestra under the direction of Charles Previn. Produced by (Joseph) Klaw and (Abraham L.) Erlanger. Opened 24 September 1917 at the New Amsterdam Theatre and closed 15 December 1917 after 100 performances.

CAST (in order of appearance): *Sylva Vareska,* a vaudeville singer: WILDA BENNETT. *Baron Ferrier,* an Ex Ambassador: J. CLARENCE HARVEY. *Charles Lorenz:* Arthur Burckley. *Gustave,* proprietor of the Côte d'Azur: EUGENE LOCKHART. *Anatole* (English), a waiter: Frank Farrington. *Sam Springer* of Fishburg, Illinois: SAM HARDY. *Birdie Springer,* his wife: JULIETTE DAY. *Count Michael Lorenz:* LOUIS CASAVANT. *Cleo:* Bessie Gros. *Julie:* Florence Delmar. *Lucile:* Mae Carmen. *Babette:* Ethel Delmar. *Victor de Berryl:* CARL GANTVOORT. *Old Rigg,* a broken-down lawyer: William Sadler. *Claire Ferrier:* Viola Cain. *The Butterfly:* Marjorie Bentley. *Daisy:* Marjorie Bentley. *Paul:* J. Lowe Murphy. *The New Star:* Louise Evans.

Ensemble: [Misses Richardson, Crosbie, Winaut, Fielder, Rentelen, Cotton, Edith Callan, Julia Callan, Edwardy, Alwyn, Delmar, Coigne, Christy, Field, James, Redding, K. Carmen, Gertie Rial. Messrs. Aubrey Burton, Billy Vernon.]

Act 1: Garden Theatre of the Côte d'Azur, Theatre of Variéties, Monte Carlo. Night.

Act 2: Flower Fête in the Garden of Ferrier's Villa, Monte Carlo. Afternoon. A few weeks later.

Act 3: A Revue, 'Nights Revelries' in the Rotunda of the Côte d'Azur, Theatre of Varieties, Monte Carlo. Night. A few weeks later.

ACT 1

Opening Song and Chorus
W. Bennett, Chorus

"Sometimes I Feel Just Like Grandpa"
S. Hardy, Girls

"The Fall of Man"
W. Bennett, A. Burckley

"There'll Never Be Another Girl Like Daisy"
L. Casavant, J. C. Harvey, Male Chorus

"Life's a Tale" (Duet)
W. Bennett, C. Gantvoort

Finale
Principals, Chorus

ACT 2

Opening Chorus
M. Bentley, Chorus

"Just a Voice to Call Me Dear"
W. Bennett, Men

"Half a Married Man"
C. Gantvoort, Girls

"Man, Man, Man" (Quartette)
C. Gantvoort, W. Bennett, V. Cain, A. Burckley

"Let's Build a Little Bungalow in Quogue" (The Bungalow in Quogue)
S. Hardy, J. Day
(*Music by* Jerome Kern.)

"Will You Forget" (Duet)
W. Bennett, C. Gantvoort

Finale
Principals, Chorus

ACT 3

Opening
Characters in the Revue: *Two Rascals:* M. Carmen, B. Gross. *Spirit of Night:* Miss Richardson. *Good Luck:* A. Burton. *Bad Luck:* B. Vernon. *Candelabra Girls:* Misses Crosbie, Winaut, Fielder, Rentelen. *Flower Girls:* Misses Cotton, E. Callan, J. Callan, Edwardy. *Four Innocents:* Misses Alwyn, Delmar, Coigne, Christy. *Little Devils:* Misses Field, James, Redding, K. Carmen. *Queen of Night:* G. Rial.

"Why Don't They Hand It to Me?"
S. Hardy, Girls

"Gypsy, Bring Your Fiddle"
W. Bennett, Chorus

Finale
Principals, Chorus

1917.21 FURS AND FRILLS

A Musical Farce in Two Acts. Book and lyrics by Edward Clark. (Based on his comedy "Coat Tales.") Music by Silvio Hein. Staged by Edward Clark[23]. Dances and ensembles arranged by Robert Marks. Stage decorations by P. Dodd Ackerman. Costumes designed by Harry Collins and L. Wenzelberg; Croydon, Ltd. (men's). Orchestra under the direction of Herbert Stothart. Produced under the personal direction of Arthur Hammerstein. Produced by Arthur Hammerstein[24]. Opened 9 October 1917 at the Casino Theatre and closed 3 November 1917 after 32 performances.

CAST (in order of appearance): *Jones,* assistant music teacher: Charles Angelo. *Clyde Macey,* librettist: GEORGE ANDERSON. *William MacTavish,* composer: ERNEST TORRENCE. *Polly,* MacTavish and Macey's stenographer: RUBY NORTON. *"Wally,"* Mrs. Macey's brother: WARD DeWOLFE. *Mrs. Macey,* Macey's wife: BEATRICE ALLEN. *Mrs. MacTavish,* MacTavish's wife: FRANCES DEMAREST. *Butler:* Ben Wells. *Mr. Manheimer,* pawnbroker: Harry Miller. *Deputy Sheriff:* Ernest Carr. *Guests:* Ethel Sykes, Gladys Sykes.

Scholars, Visitors: Misses Ivy Scherer, Charlotte Buckman, Mildred Renard, Gladys Alexander, Marie Milburne, Frances Schofield, Flora Hollister, Betty Stivers, Ruth Vale, Frances Grant. Messrs. Harold Raymond, Harold Williams, Frank Rowe, Gerald Eton, Paul Cordes, Francis Murphy. *Violinists:* Misses Sylvia Hurd, Alice Kane, Grace

---

[23]For subsequent tour, direction credited to Lew Morton.

[24]Subsequent tour presented under the auspices of Adeline Amusement Company Max and Edward Spiegel).

Livingston, Ida Diggs, Margaret Carhart, Violet Horning, Henrietta Fields, Flo Richardson.

The action takes place in New York two days before Christmas.

Act 1: MacTavish and Macey's Conservatory of Music atop the Wellworth Building.

Act 2: The MacTavish Apartment. Washington Square.

ACT 1[25]

Opening
C. Angelo, Violinists, Chorus

"When My Wife Returns"
G. Anderson, Chorus

"You Can't Take It With You When You Die"
E. Torrence, G. Anderson

"Does Polly Want Wally"
R. Norton, W. DeWolfe

"Furs and Frills"
B. Allen Chorus

"It's Easy to Lie to Your Husband"
F. Demarest, Chorus

"A Short Farewell Is Best"
R. Norton, W. DeWolfe

"Heart of My Heart"
R. Norton

ACT 2[26]

"Make Yourselves at Home" (Make Yourself at Home)(Opening)
Chorus
(*Lyrics by* Oscar Hammerstein II.)

Dancing Specialty
B. Allen, A. Niemeyer

"Always Take Mother's Advice"
E. Torrence, R. Norton

"The Yuletide Spirit"
F. Demarest, Chorus

"The Tale of a Coat"
E. Torrence, F. Demarest, G. Anderson, B. Allen

"This Is My Lucky Day" (Gee! But This Sure Is My Lucky Day)
R. Norton, W. DeWolfe
(*Music by* Claude E. MacArthur.)

"Pot-Pouri" (Finale)
Entire Company

1917.22   # JACK O' LANTERN

A Musical Extravaganza in Two Acts, 8 Scenes. Book and lyrics by Anne Caldwell and R. H. Burnside. Music by Ivan Caryll. Staged by R. H. Burnside. Scenery designed by Ernest Albert, Homer Emens, Joseph Urban[27]. Costumes designed by Helen Dryden, Robert MacQuinn, and Gladys Monkhouse. Musical director, William Macquinn. Produced by Charles Dillingham. Opened 16 October 1917 at the Globe Theatre and closed 1 June 1918 after 265 performances.

CAST: *Jack O'Lantern* (John Obadiah Lantern): FRED STONE. *Paul*: Douglas Stevenson. *Henry Tripp*: CHARLES T. ALDRICH. *Bobbie*: Harold West. *Uncle George*: OSCAR RAGLAND. *Vilanessa*: ALLENE CRATER. *Cicely*: HELEN FALCONER. *Lady of Dreams*: Margaret Irving. *Zingarella*: TERESA VALERIO.

[25]Added for subsequent tour, after "It's Easy to Lie to Your Husband:"
"You Can't Think of Everything"
C. Angelo

[26]Added for subsequent tour before "Always Take Mother's Advice":
"The Highland Kiltie Rag"
E. Torrence, Chorus
Which was later replaced by:
"Love-Love"
Ferne Rogers (Mrs. Macey)
Added during the run, but dropped for subsequent tour (after "This Is My Lucky Day"):
"We're So Happy"
E. Torrence, F. Demarest, G. Anderson, B. Allen

[27]All Scenes by Joseph Urban except Act 2, Scenes 1 and 5 (Homer Emens) and Scene 7 (Ernest Albert).

Babby: Kathleen Robinson. *Janet*: EDNA BATES. *Polly*: Bunny Wendell. *Rosie*: Frances Jordan. *Posie*: Beatrice Hughes. *May*: Marcelle Earl. *Gladys*: Lydia Scott. *Bessie*: Lola Curtis. *Tessie*: Evelyn Conway. *King Jujube*: Lord Robert. *Princess Nougat*: Anna. Hoy. *Countess Caramel*: Marietta Hoy. *Duchess of Marshmallow*: Mary Hoy. *Susie Sasfras*: VIOLET ZELL. *Gerald*: John Byrne. *Percy*: William Caress. *Eugene*: Frank Herbert. *Peter*: Coly Lorella.

Other Characters by Helen Arlington, Veronique Banner, Carolyn Burke, Cecile Conway, Isabelle Adams, Dorothy Duncan, Alice Earl, Isabel Bruce, Victoria Meyers, Vera Olcott, Nancy Wallace, Marie Walsh, Kathleen Errol, Lulu Everett, Grace Flemming, Peggy Williams, Marguerite Falconer, Dorothy Francis, Ida Howe, Mazie Leroy, Mona Sartoris, Jet Stanley.

The Sunshine Girls: Madge Reyner, Ada Mitchell, Jackie Hart, Hetty Ward, Cissie Bell, Aggie Dawnsby, Janie Hughes, Chrissie Stahler, Dolly Masley, Dolly Maxted, Eileen Rogan, Elsie Cliffe, Dorothy Sabin, Ida Calva, Ethel Glaster, Mary Read.

Act 1: Appledale Farm.

Act 2, *Scene 1*: Banquet Hall in Jack's Villa. *Scene 2*: The Cave of Dreams. *Scene 3*: Candyland. *Scene 4*: Outside the Lines. *Scene 5*: Camp Nowhere. *Scene 6*: Clowntown. *Scene 7*: The Ice Carnival.

ACT 1[28]

"Hear the Bell" (Opening)

Gyspy Music
Marconi Brothers

"Wait Till the Cows Come Home"
H. Falconer, D. Stevenson
(*Lyrics by* Anne Caldwell.)

"(The) Girls I've Met"
F. Stone, Sunshine Girls
(*Lyrics by* Louis Harrison.)

"Knit, Knit, Knit"
A. Crater, H. Falconer, E. Bates
(*Lyrics by* Anne Caldwell.)

"I'll Take You Back to Italy"
F. Stone, T. Valerio
(*Music and Lyrics by* Irving Berlin.)

"The Kidnapper" (Finale)

ACT 2

Scene 2
"Take a Trip to Candyland" (Candyland)
H. West, K. Robinson
(*Lyrics by* Anne Caldwell.)

Scene 3
"Oh, Papa!"
Hoy Sisters

"A Sweetheart of My Own"
H. Falconer

Drum Dance
H. Falconer, D. Stevenson

Nightmare Dance
F. Stone, V. Zell

Scene 4
"Along Came Another Little Girl"
D. Stevenson
(*Lyrics by* Benjamin Hapgood Burt.)
Assisted by Misses Scott, Jordan, Hughes, Conway, Earl, Curtis, Irving, Wendell.

Scene 5
Signal Corps March
A. Crater, Sunshine Girls

The Man with a Hundred Faces (Specialty)
C. Aldrich

"Follow the Girls (Around)"
F. Stone
(*Lyrics by* Anne Caldwell.)

Scene 6
Six Brown Brothers (Specialty)

["Darktown Strutters' Ball"
(*Music and Lyrics by* Shelton Brooks.)

[28]Added after opening to Act 1, after "Hear the Bell" (Opening):
"Take a Swing With Me" (Come and Have a Swing with Me)
D. Stevenson
(*Lyrics by* Anne Caldwell.)

"Comedy Tom"
(*Music by* Gus King.)]
Scene 7
  Skating Octette
  Charlotte Russe
    F. Stone
  Finale

1917.23

DOING OUR BIT

A Musical Revue in Two Acts, 16 Scenes. Dialogue (sketches) and lyrics by Harold Atteridge. Music by Sigmund Romberg and Herman Timberg. Staged by J. C Huffman. Musical numbers arranged by Allan K. Foster. Scenery designed by Joseph Physioc and John Young. Costumes designed by Homer Conant. Orchestra under the direction of Oscar Radin. Produced under the personal direction of J. J. Shubert. Produced by Messrs. Lee and J. J. Shubert. Opened 18 October 1917 at the Winter Garden and closed 9 February 1918 after 130 performances.

CAST: HENRY LEWIS, SAM ASH, JAMES J. CORBETT, THE DUNCAN SISTERS (Rosetta, Vivian), ADA LEWIS, HERMAN TIMBERG, FRANK TINNEY, ED WYNN, CHARLES JUDELS, CHILSON OHRMAN, VIRGINIA FISSINGER, LEAH NORAH, FRANK CARTER, THE CANSINOS (Eduardo, Elisa), JAMES CLEMONS, SYLVIA JASON, Andrew Harper, Bud Murray, Vera Roehm, Roma June.
Violin Girls: Miriam Glover, Mazibelle Glover, Helen Pennell, Mitza Nada, Leonora Puron, Midred Coughlan, Rose Birdenfild, Lucile Panteloff, Hattie Rand, Augusta Pessman, Hilda Major, Edna Commerford, Katherine Stang, Rose Goldhair, Anna DeLaurentis, Ruby Whitney, Ethel Sturges, Gwendolyn LeMassena, Helen DeSeife, Fay Teller, Sheila Goffe, Ingrid Slettengren.
Show Girls: Mildred LaGue, Rae Hartley, Florence Elmore, Kittie Berg, Vera Mercer, Beatrice DeRoe, Jessie Reed, Nora Reed, Lela Von Holk, Mabel Kelly, Barbara McCreee, Adrian Dillon, Mary Pell, Billie Sheridan, Winona Wilkins, Lola Taylor, Helen Montague, Charlotte Marmont, Millie Carlson, Beatrice Cloak, Virginia May, Fay Tunis, Elsie Bambrick, Mildred Holliday, Aieda Crucini, Helen Leonard, Gertrude Blake. *Dancers*: Beatrice Dakin, Grace Keeshon, Edith Pierce, Marion Mooney, Marion Parks, Evelyn Parks, Blanche Parks, Nancy Everette, Reba Stewart, Anna Paula, Gladys Turner, Elsie LaMont, Jean Staples, Sophie Mills, Inez Francis, Ailene Wilmer, Marie Kennedy, Henrietta Wall, Ilene Edwards, Jeane Fowler, Ailene Rooney, Edna Whitney, Viola Clarens, Florence Wilde, Irene Mitchell, Mattie Gromley, Carolyn Maywood, Rebekah Corbel, Rose Coyle, Dorothy Coyle, Dorothy Court, Eugene White, Dolly Wallace, Allison King, Nida Rose, Rose Villa, Mildred Symons, Adele Rudolph, Corinne Jackson, Tina Bidekoff. Messrs. Floyd Snyder, Joe Evans, George Coogan, C. L. Henderson, Ed McHenry, Clyde Miller, Dave Brown, Frank McMasters, Harry DeWitt, Ed Stokem, James Monohan.

ACT 1
Scene 1
  Scene: At the Farnsbee's.
    Sally Farnsbee: C. Ohrman. *Bud Travers*: F. Carter. *Sylvia Farnsbee*: S. Jason. *The Clergyman*: A. Harper. *The Bridesmaids*: G. Blake, B. DeRoe, M. Kelly, M. Pell. *Dr. Jim*: J. J. Corbett. *Annabelle Lee*: A. Lewis. *John Lee*: C. Judels.
Scene 2
  Scene: Justine Johnstone Club.
    Annabelle: A. Lewis. *Sylvia Farnsbee*: S. Jason. *Willie*: H. Timberg. *Dr. Jim*: J. J. Corbett. *Hat Check Boy*: B. Murry. *Bud Travers*: F. Carter. *John Lee*: C. Judels. *Grace Steven*: V. Duncan. *Olive Warren*: L. Norah. *Mildred*: M. LaGue. *Ray*: R. Hartley. *Jesse*: J. Reed. *Vera*: V. Mercer. *Mabel*: M. Kelly. *Beatrice*: B. DeRoe. *A Waiter*: A. Harper. *Edwin Nichols*: E. Wynn. *A Guest*: J. Clemons. *A Peach*: V. Roehm. *Miss U.S.A.*: G. Keeshon. *Violin Girls*: Ensemble.
Scene 3
  Scene: In front of the 44th Street Theatre.
    Edwin Nicols: E. Wynn. *Grace Stevens*: V. Duncan. *Lillian Stevens*: R. Duncan. *Bud Travers*: F. Carter. *Dr. Jim*: J. J. Corbett. *Olive Warren*: L. Norah. *Frank*: F. Tinney. *Telegraph Boy*: F. Wilde.
Scene 4
  Scene: White Sulphur Springs.
    Olive Warren: L. Norah. *Mr. Resorter*: J. Clemons. *Willie*: H. Timberg. *Grace*: V. Duncan. *Dr. Jim*: J. J. Corbett. *Bud*: F. Carter. *Frank*: F. Tinney. *Sylvia*: S. Jason. *Annabelle*: A. Lewis. *Sally*: C. Ohrman. *John Lee*: C. Judels. *Olive Warren*: L. Norah. *Virginia Spring*: V. Fissinger. *A Nurse*: V. Roehm.
Scene 5
  The Lightning Calculator
    Edwin Nicols: E. Wynn. *The Butler*: A. Harper. *Sylvia*: S. Jason.
Scene 6
  Scene: Near the Pyramids[29]
    Mr. Egyptian: J. Clemons. *Miss Glide*: B. Dakin.

Scene 7
  Scene: McDougal's Alley
    Bud: F. Carter. *Mr. Smile*: S. Ash. *Sally*: C. Ohrman. *John Leo*: C. Judels. *Edwaurdo*: E. Cansino. *Elisa*: E. Cansino. *Virginia*: V. Fissinger.
Scene 8
  Scene: Registration Station
    Olive: L. Norah. *Sylvia*: S. Jason. *Mr. Army Man*: S. Ash. *Mr. Exempt*: H. Timberg. *Bud*: F. Carter. *Sally*: C. Ohrman. *Dr. Jim*: J. J. Corbett. *Frank*: F. Tinney.
Scene 9
  Scene: Aboard the Troop Ship
Scene 10
  Soldier's Dream
Scene 11
  Dis-embarkation American Troops in France.
    (*Invented by* Lincoln J. Carter and J.J. Shubert. *Painted by* John Young. All rights owned by J.J. Shubert.)

ACT 2
Scene 1
  Scene: Colonial Observatory.
    The Master: S. Ash. *Miss Ballet*: V. Fissinger. *Miss Old-Fashion*: R. Duncan. *Miss Fourteen*: V. Duncan. *Annabelle*: A. Lewis. *Maid*: V. Roehm. *John Lee*: C. Judels. *Olive*: L. Norah.
Scene 2
  Scene: Girls' Hotel.
    Edwin Nicols: E. Wynn. *Miss Bell*: B. Dakin. *Miss A. Picture*: L. Norah. *Miss White*: V. Duncan. *Miss Frills*: W. Wilkins. *Miss Green*: R. Corbel. *Miss Black*: G. Turner.
Scene 3
  Scene: Out front.
    Sylvia: S. Jason. *Henry*: H. Lewis.
Scene 4
  Scene: Jewels in Velvet.
    Olive: L. Norah.
Scene 5
  Scene: Monte Carlo.
    Sally: C. Ohrman. *Frank*: F. Tinney. *Dr. Jim*: J. J. Corbett. *Bud*: F. Carter. *Virginia*: V. Fissinger. *Eduardo*: E. Cansino. *Elisa*: E. Cansino.

MUSICAL NUMBERS

ACT 1
  "Orange Blossoms"
    C. Ohrman, Bridesmaids
  "Mr. Rag and I"
    V. Fissinger, J. Clemons, Rag and I Girls
  "(Oh, You) Sweeties"
    V. Duncan, Bon Bon Girls
  "Doing My Bit"
    L. Norah, V. Duncan, G. Keeshon, E. Pierce, Allied Girls
  Violin Ensemble
    H. Timberg, Violin Girls
  Millinery Number
    R. Duncan, Hat Box Girls
  "A Loving Daddy"[30]
    S. Jason, Daddy Girls
  "Egyptian Rag"
    J. Clemons, B. Dakin, Winter Garden Girls
  "Nothing on Today"
    L. Norah, Hot Day Girls
  "Let Her Go"
    F. Carter, Carnival Girls
  "Phantom of Your Smile"
    S. Ash
  "Fashion Show"
    C. Judels
  Castinet Dance
    The Cansinos
  "Festa"
    V. Fissinger, Festa Girls

---

[29]Scene not listed in some programs

[30]Dropped during the run.

"Dance, Dance, Dance"[31]
  H. Timberg
"Sally (Down Our Alley)"[32]
  C. Ohrman, F. Carter
"For the Sake of Humanity"[33]
  S. Ash
ACT 2[34]
Colonial Ballet
  S. Ash, V. Fissinger, Colonial Girls
"Old-Fashioned Girls"
  Duncan Sisters
"Fine Feathers"
  L. Norah, Fine Feather Girls
"I May Be Small, But I Have Big Ideas"[35]
  S. Jason
Some Songs
  H. Lewis
["I'm the Brother of the Lily of the Valley"
  (Music by Anatole Friedland. Lyrics by L. Wolfe Gilbert, Henry Lewis.)
"The Wild, Wild Women (Are Making a Wild Man of Me)"
  (Music by Al Piantadosi. Lyrics by Henry Lewis and Al Wilson.)
"When I'm Making Love to You"
  (Music by Fred Fisher. Lyrics by Alfred Bryan, Henry Lewis, Joseph McCarthy.)
"If They Ever Put a Tax on Love"
  (Music by Nat Osborne. Lyrics by Sam Ehrlich.)
"I'd Like to See the Kaiser with a Lily in His Hand"
  (Music and Lyrics by Billy Frisch, Howard Johnson, Henry Leslie.)]
"Perfect Jewels"
  S. Ash, Jewel Girls
"Roses"
  C. Ohrman
"Hello, Miss Tango"
  F. Carter, V. Fissinger, The Cansinos, Tango Girls
Spanish Cloak Dance
  The Cansinos

1917.24

CHU CHIN CHOW

A Musical Tale of the East in Three Acts, 13 Scenes. Told (book and lyrics) by Oscar Asche. Set to Music by Frederick Norton. Staged by E. Lyall Swete. Dances arranged by Mlle. Guida and Alexis Kosloff. Scenery designed by Joseph Harker and Phil Harker. Costumes designed by Percy Anderson. Orchestra under the direction of Gustave Ferrari. Orchestrations by Percy Fletcher. Produced by William Elliott, E. Ray Comstock and Morris Gest. Opened 22 October 1917 at the Manhattan Opera House, moved 14 January 1918 to the Century Theatre, and closed 27 April 1918 after 208 performances.

CAST: *Abu Hassan, The Shayk of the Robbers:* TYRONE POWER. *Members of His Band (2): Khuzymah:* Albert Moore. *Musab:* Robert Lee Hill. *Kasim Baba:* ALBERT HOWSON. *Alcolom, Kasim Baba's Head Wife:* KATE CONDON. *Abdullah, Kasim's Steward:* FRANCIS J. BOYLE. *Marjanah, Kasim's Singing Slave:* TESSA KOSTA. *Zahrat-Al-Huda, Kasim's Head Slave:* FLORENCE REED. *Ali Baba, Kasim's Poor Brother:* HENRY DIXEY. *Mabubah, Ali Baba's Wife:* LUCY BEAUMONT. *Nur-Al-Huda, Ali's Son:* GEORGE RASELY. *Bostan, Ali's Servant:* Matty Thomas. *Mukbill, an Auctioneer:* Frank McCormack. *Zatel-Demaki, a Slave Buyer:* Ida Mulle. *A Dancer:* Katherine Galanta. *The Woman in Green:* Harda Daube. *The Stranger:* Gordon Staples. *The Fortune Teller:* Olive Prosser. *The Son of the Bean Seller:* George Bell. *The Lady in the Pantomime:* Josephine Emery. *The Husband:* Robert Lee Hill. *The Lover:* Lester Sweyd. *Baba Mustafa, a Cobbler:* Felice DeGregorio. *Otbah, Keeper of the Silk Stall:* Richie Ling.

[31]Moved to the Act 2 after one month and for subsequent tour.
[32]Dropped for subsequent tour.
[33]Moved to the Act 2 Finale after one month and for subsequent tour.
[34]The running order of Act 2 was totally revised after the first month. Added later in the run:
  "Adopt a Pretty Baby"
    V. Duncan, Baby Girls
[35]Dropped for subsequent tour.

Jaavanese Fanners: Gladys Earlcott, Adele Meeker, Olga Merville, Lillian Neilson, Mary Reilly, Rosita Khoury, Beatrice Steiner, Gabrielle Pitcher. *Javanese Dancers:* Helen LaTour, Dolores Brune, Louise Blanid, Joan Remville, Margerita Patti, Edith Barr, Ethel Mae Whitely. *Nile Girls:* Inez Borrero, Sallie Roumayne, Eleanor Hargrave, Hazel M. Robertson, Mai Poth, Helen Fox. *Ballet (Desert Dancers, Jewel Dancers, Dervish Dancers):* Dorothy Lee, Leonore Thompson, Stella Rothacker, Rita Fanning, Berta Knight, Claire Boyd, Nina Artska, Adele Stollman, Jessie Lorraine, Alma Rosine, Ann Linn, Dorothy Butler. *Extra Dancers:* Jeannette Kayton, Irene Sparry, Ethel Mae Whitely, Pauline Williams, Claire Daste, Louise Rothacker. *Circassian Slave:* Frances Hendricks. *Turkestan Slaves:* Claire Burton, Olga Merville. *Pot Girls:* Clara Vedera, Marion Gray, Mai Poth, Claire Burton, Dorothy Butler, May Copeland. *Washer Women:* Suzanne Renard, Beatrice Steiner, Minnie Meyers, Gladys Earlcott. *Fruit Girls:* Lillian Neilson, Adele Meeker, Mercedes DeCordoba, Annabelle Hennessey, Clara Vedera, Dolores Brune, Claire Boyd, Marion Gray, Suzanne Renard, Olga Merville, Gladys Earlcott, Helen LaTour, Rosita Khoury. *Mannequins: Group One:* Helen Fox, Mai Poth, Hazel M. Robertson, Beatrice Steiner. *Group Two:* Eleanor Hargrave, Gabrielle Pitcher, Sallie Roumayne, Inez Borrero, Minnie Meyers. *Group Three:* Bertha Knight, Louise Blanid, Adele Stollman, Ann Linn. *Group Four:* Lenore Thompson, Claire Burton, Joan Remville, Kiyo Okita, Nobu Watuma. *Carrier Girls:* Ethel Mae Whitely, Pauline Williams, Alma Rosine, Irene Sparry, Jessie Lorraine, Jeannette Kayton, Claire Daste, Nan Rainsforth. *Ensemble of Robbers, Peddlers, Water Carriers, Pedestrians, Wedding Guests, etc.*

Act 1, Scene 1: Kasim Baba's Palace in Bagdad. A thousand years ago. *Scene 2:* At Marjanah's Window. *Scene 3:* A Cactus Grove. *Scene 4:* Entrance to the Cave. *Scene 5:* The Slave Market of El Kabar.

Act 2, Scene 1: A Mean Street in Bagdad. *Scene 2:* At a Silk Stall. *Scene 3:* The Blue Hall in Kasim's Palace. *Scene 4:* In Kasim's Harem. *Scene 5:* The Cave (of Abu Hassan).

Act 3, Scene 1: A Bazaar (of Bagdad). *Scene 2:* On the Rose Terrace. *Scene 3:* The Orchard by Moonlight.

ACT 1[36]
Scene 1
"Here Be Oysters Stewed in Honey" (Opening Chorus)
  F. J. Boyle, Chorus
"I Am Chu Chin Chow" (Entrance of Chu Chin Chow)
  T. Power, Chorus
Javanese Dance
  "Cleopatra's Nile" (Marjanah's Song)
  T. Kosta, Chorus
"I'll Sing and Dance" (Act 1 Finale)
  (H. Dixey, Entire Company)
Scene 2
"Corraline"
  G. Rasely
Scene 3
"When a Pullet Is Plump" (Song)
  H. Dixey
"We Are the Robbers of the Woods"
  Robbers' Chorus
Scene 4
"I Shiver and Shake with Fear" (Trio)
  H. Dixey, T. Kosta, G. Rasely
Scene 5
"Behold"
  F. J. Boyle
ACT 2
Scene 1
"Beans, Beans, Beans" (Introduction and Song)
  L. Beaumont
(Finale)
  (H. Dixey, G. Rasely, T. Kosta)
Scene 2
"All My Days Till End of Life" (Duet)
  T. Kosta, H. Dixey
Scene 3
"At Siesta Time" (Song)
  T. Kosta, Chorus
  (Music by Grace Torrens. Lyrics by Arthur Anderson.)

[36]No song list appeared in the program for the first month's run.

128

Scene 4

"Any Time's Kissing Time" (Song)
K. Condon
(*Music and Lyrics by* Frederick Norton.)

Scene 5

"If I Liken Thy Shape" (Duet)
T. Kosta, G. Rasely

"The Song of The Scimitar"
T. Power, Chorus

ACT 3

Scene 1

"The Cobbler's Song" (Song)
F. DeGregorio

"We Bring Ye Fruits" (Song)
Fruit Girls

"From Cairo, Bagdad, Khorasan" (Song and Mannequin Parade)
R. Ling

Scene 2

"How Dear Is Our Day" (Duet)
K. Condon, H. Dixey

(Finale Trio)
(F. J. Boyle, H. Dixey, K. Condon)

Scene 3

"(Sweet) Olive Oil" (Song)
F. J. Boyle, Chorus

"Wedding Procession" (Finale)
Ensemble

1917.25 ## THE LAND OF JOY

A Spanish-American Fantastic (Musical) Review in Two Acts, a Prologue and 11 Scenes. (Original Spanish[37]) Book and lyrics by J. F. Elizonda and Eulogio Velasco. (English book) Adaptation by Ruth Boyd Ober[38]. Music by Quinito Valverde. Staged by Eulogio Velasco and Alonzo Price[39]. Scenery by Tarazona Brothers. Costumes by Schneider-Anderson (New York), Grand Gerard, Vde Peris, Mme. Balbina Juan Valencia. Orchestra under the direction of Julian Benloch. Produced by Valverde Musical Enterprises, Inc. Opened 31 October 1917 at the Park Theatre, moved 14 January 1918 to the Knickerbocker Theatre under the auspices of William Morris[40], and closed 26 January 1918 after 100 performances.

CAST (American Characters): *Mercedes*: NANETTE FLACK. *Schuyler Wrightwell*: GEORGE LYDECKER. *Charles Seek*: IRVING BROOKS. *Foxwell Hunt*: MATT HANLEY. *Chevy Chase*: MATT HANLEY. *Dolores*: RUTH BOYD OBER.
(Spanish Characters): *Valencienne, Holy Week, Maja de Goya, La Guitarra*: MARIA MARCO. *Zobeida, Fair of Seville, Torerito, La Tirana, Serafina, Cucu*: LUISITA PUCHOL. *The Gypsy, Marchosito, Torerito, Maja Moderna, Cucu*: AMPARO SAUS. *Jerezano, Torerito, Cucu*: CARMEN LOPEZ. *Almanzor*: MANUEL VILLA. *Toreador, the Bullfighter*: ANTONIO BILBAO. *Gypsy Dancers*: DOLORETES MANZANTI-NITA. *Pepe Hillo*: JESUS NAVARRO. *Classic Dancer*: L'ARGENTINA. (LACALLE's SPANISH ORCHESTRA).
Spanish Gypsies, Dancers, Chorus: Misses Maria Sinovas, Concha Tomas, Julia Garcia, Emilia Usatorre, Amelia Lahoz, Francisca Gil, Anita Juan, Carmen J. Espazza, Luisa Espazza, Maria Verdiales, Julia Verdiales, Mercedes Zunen, Maria Carrascal, Margaritta Tregant, Pia San Cristobal, Maria Martinez, Emilia Falagan, Teresa Cervera, Nilda Hanez, Enriqueta Pareda, Angeles L. Sinovas, Carmen Fernandez, Isabel Jimenez, Antonia Ramos, Cristina Aragon. Messrs. Francisco Viveros, Vincente Galindo, Jose V. Maldonado, Alfonso Martinez, Manuel Esparante, Ramon Rey, Homero Menendez, Vincente Pastor, Manuel Verdiales, Vincente Molina, Antonio Ramos, Jose F. Perez.

Prologue: Wrightwell's Office, New York.

Act 1, Scene 1: Valencia. *Scene 2*: Granada. *Scene 3*: Court of the Lions, Alhambra. *Scene 4*: The Posters. *Scene 5*: Seville.

---

[37]World premiere of THE LAND OF JOY was 6 October 1917 in Havana.
[38]After the transfer to the Knickerbocker, Julius Tannen was retained as conferencier, and a new English book was credited to Montague Glass and C. A. deLima.
[39]During the run Alonzo Price's name was withdrawn as co-director.
[40]Subsequent tour presented by Marc Klaw and Abraham L. Erlanger.

Act 2, Scene 1: Exterior Plaza de Toros. *Scene 2*: Interior of same. *Scene 3*: The Tapestries. *Scene 4*: Madrid, Centennial of Goya. *Scene 5*: A Roadway. *Scene 6*: The Dancing Academy.

PROLOGUE[41]

Opening Chorus
Stenographers

"Love Is Very Different"
G. Lydecker, Girls

"Come With Me"
N. Flack

"Off to Spain"
G. Lydecker, N. Flack, Girls

ACT 1[42]

Scene 1

A Wedding Song
M. Marco

A Wedding Dance
Ensemble of Valencians

Scene 2

"Garotin Song" and Dance
I. Brooks

Spanish Bear Dance
I. Brooks, Girls

Scene 3

Serenade
M. Villa

Moorish Dance
L. Puchol, Doloretes, Spanish Ensemble

Gypsy Dance
A. Saus, Spanish Dancing Girls

Scene 4

"Holy Week" (Song)
M. Marco

Table Dance (Alegrias)
A. Bilbao

"Ay! Que Rico"
L. Puchol, Chorus

"New York, U.S.A."[43] (Duet)
N. Flack, G. Lydecker

Scene 5

"Jerezanos" (Song)
C. Lopez, Chorus

"Marchosito" (Song)
A. Saus, Chorus

---

[41]After the opening, the prologue was revised and recast as follows:
John Fieldstone, a Theatrical Manager: JOHN DALY MURPHY. *Goldie Fieldstone*, His Wife, a Primadonna: EDNA MUNSEY. *George C. George*, a Librettist: JULIUS TANNEN. *Somerville Ross*, a Composer: THOMAS CONKEY. *Pedro Estilocalido*, an Actor: JESUS NAVARRO. *Pedro's Daughter*: VIOLETA.
Scene: Fieldstone' Office, New York.
"La Solea Yel Jaleo"
Violeta
"Come With Me"
E. Munsey
"Off to Spain"
E. Munsey, T. Conkey, J. D. Murphy
Later in the run, when the Americans had departed the cast, the Prologue was reconceived:
"Basilia" (Song)
A. Saus
Farruca (Dance)
Doloretes
[42]Also performed in the show:
"Los Crotolos" (Tambourine Dance)
[43]Dropped late in the run.

Bulerias (Dance)
  Doloretas, Mazantinita, Dancing Girls
Heel Dance[44]
  A. Bilbao, Doloretas, Mazantinita, Dancing Girls
ACT 2
Scene 1
  "To te quiero"[45] (Song)
    N. Flack, Chorus
  Beggar Dance
    Violeta, Doloretes, Mazantinita
Scene 2
  Pasa calle (Parade of the Bullfighters)
  "Torerito Torerazo" (Song)
    L. Puchol, A. Saus, C. Lopez, Chorus
Scene 3
  "Can This Be Love"[46]
    N. Flack
Scene 4
  "Pepe Hillo" (Song)
    J. Navarro, Chorus
  "Maja de Goya" (Song)
    M. Marco, Chorus
  "Maja Modernia" (Song)
    A. Saus, Chorus
  Serafina
    L. Puchol
  Cymbal Dance
    Spanish Dancing Girls
Scene 5
  "There's a Chapter"[47]
    N. Flack, G. Lydecker
Scene 6
  La Guitarre[48]
    M. Marco
  "Schottiss del Cucu" (Trio)
    L. Puchol, A. Saus, C. Lopez
  Dancing Competition
    Doloretes, A. Bilbao, Mazantinita, Mari-Jule, Mari-Pia, Falagan, Sevillanito, E. Pereda, Spanish Dancing Girls
  Finale
    Entire Company

---

[44]Replaced late in the run by:
  Fatima (Dance)
    Mari-Jule Sisters
  Cucu Schotis
    A. Saus, L. Puchol, C. Lopez
  Salvage (Dance)
    A. Bilbao, Spanish Dancing Girls
[45]Dropped late in the run.
[46]Replaced late in the run by:
  Batiburrillo (Dance)
    Violeta
  "La Tirana" (Song)
    L. Puchol
[47]Replaced late in the run by:
  Pensamiento Enamorado
    M. Marco, M. Villa
[48]Both La Guitarre and "Schottiss del Cucu" were replaced late in the run by:
  Mantilla Espanola (Trio)
    L. Puchol, A. Saus, C. Lopez
  Panaderos (Dance)
    A. Bilbao, Doloretes

1917.26 # MISS 1917

A Musical Revue in Two Acts, 18 Scenes. Book[49] (sketches) by P. G. Wodehouse and Guy Bolton. Music by Jerome Kern and Victor Herbert. Sketches staged by Ned Wayburn. Dances arranged by Adolph Bohm. Scenery designed by Joseph Urban. Costumes designed by Paul Chaflin, Dazian, Faibsey, Lady Duff-Gordon, Cora MacGeachy, Phelps, Willy Pogany, Max Weldy. Orchestra under the direction of Robert Hood Bowers. Produced by Charles B. Dillingham and Florenz Ziegfeld. Opened 5 November 1917 at the Century Theatre and closed 5 January 1918 after 72 performances.

CAST: LEW FIELDS, BESSIE McCOY DAVIS, (Elizabeth) BRICE & (Charles) KING, (Gus) VAN & (Joe) SCHENCK, IRENE CASTLE, VIVIENNE SEGAL, MARION DAVIES, ANN PENNINGTON, CECIL LEAN, CLEO MAYFIELD, (Bert) SAVOY & (Joe) BRENNAN, HARRY KELLY, GEORGE WHITE, LILYAN TASHMAN, ANDREW TOMBES, EMMA HAIG, ZITELKA DOLORES, VERA MAXWELL, Dorothy Klewer, Yvonne Shelton, Albertine Marlowe, Flora Revalles, Adolf Bohm, Arthur Cunningham, Leavitt James, Joseph Sparks, Eugene Revere, Olive Osborne, William Fuller, Gus Stevenson, Louis Baum, Dolores Rose, Margaret Morris, May Leslie, Tot Qualters, Marshall Hall, Ivan Tarasov, Alexander Umanski, Juana Sheppard, Hilda Hirsch, Kathryn Perry, Leonore Korhler, Flo Hart, Semone D'Herlys, Mlle. Phyllis, Mlle. Dolores, Mlle. Mauresette, Gladys Coburn, Elizabeth Morton, Irene Hayes, Stephen O'Rourke, Cecile Markle, Pauline Hall, Albertine Marlowe, Herbert Fields. *Dance Specialty:* TORTOLA VALENCIA.
Ladies of the Ensemble: Misses Margaret Morris, May Leslie, Flo Hart, Peggy Dana, May Borden, Betty Hamilton, Pollie Bowman, Diana Allen, Agnes Jepson, Anna Stone, Betty Hale, Geraldine Alexander, Kathryn Perry, Amelia Johnson, Evangeline Marshalck, Lois Leigh, Mauresett, Gladys Coburn, Gladys Loftus, Lilyan Tashamn, Juana Sheppard, Olive Osborne, Kitty Boylan, Rene Braham, Marie Frawley, Myrtle King, Ethel Rough, Winnie Ward, May Irving, Irene Spencer, Helen Mooney, Rosella Myers, Edith Warren, Emeline Gorman, Effie Allen, Pearl Franklin, Cecilia Cullen, Lottie Franklin, Alma Braham, Martha Wood, Mildred Shelly, Minnie Harrison, Margie Bell, Vivian Morrison, Ruth Heil, Ruby Wilbur. *Men of the Ensemble:* Mike Bell, Dan Gordon, James Quinn, Jack Lynch, Walter Baker, James Marr, Frank Sharp, Mark White, Fred Duhall, Frank Duball, Charles Root, Joe Knoffer, Charles Jones, Lawrence Clark, John Parks, Mack Williams, William Shelly, Emmet Grant, John Warren, Nicholas Kane, Emil Barth, Addison Mead, Murray Starr, Arthur Elson, Paul Briant, William Briant. *Century Male Octette:* Messrs. Frank Leonard, James Bradley, Gus Stevenson, Ray Klages, Leonard Howard, Paul M. Bell, William Fuller, Louis Baum. *Ballet Dancers:* Margit Leeraas, Rita Leeraas, Rita Zalmani, Elizabeth Gardiner, Natasha Stephanova, Misses Selskaya, Sterling, Vernon, Nova, Uhr.

ACT 1[50]
Scene 1
  "The Mosquitos Frolic"
    Farmshands, Mosquitos, Vegetables
    (*Music by* Victor Herbert.)
    Scene: The "Turn to the Right" Pickle Farm.
      Hiram Askem: L. Fields. *Joe Askem,* one of the Askem Pickled Onions—Sing Sing Class of 1917: A. Tombes. *Deacon Stillinger*—he holds the mortgage: A. Cunningham. *Polly-with-a-past,* his daughter: V. Segal. *Fellow classmates of Joe Askem* (2): *Buggs,* a pickpocket: C. Lean. *Willy,* an eggman: H. Kelly. *The Hired Man:* L. James. *The Other Hired Man:* J. Sparks. *Mr. Reggie Starr,* a moving picture director: E. Revere. *Miss Celia Lloyd,* a movie actress: *Miss Ina Fillum,* a movie actress: D. Klewer. *Miss Erna Pyle,* a movie actress: Z. Dolores. *Miss Wanda Farr,* a movie actress: O. Osborn.
  "The Society Farmerettes" (Song)
    V. Segal, Farmerettes
    (*Music by* Victor Herbert.)
      Farmerettes: Misses M. Morris, M. Leslie, F. Hart, P. Dana, M. Borden, B. Hamilton, P. Bowman, D. Allen, A. Jepson, A. Stone, B. Hale, G. Alexander, K. Perry, A. Johnson, E. Marshalck, L. Leigh.
  "(We're) Crooks" (Duet)
    C. Lean, H. Kelly
    (*Music by* Jerome Kern.)
  "Papa Would Persist in Picking Peaches" (Peaches)(Song)
    A. Tombes, Z. Dolores, Y. Shelton, Peaches
    (*Music by* Jerome Kern.)
      Peaches: Misses Mauresette, G. Coburn, G. Loftus, L. Tashman, J. Shepherd, O. Osborne.

---

[49]Wodehouse biographies credit him alone, and not Bolton, with the lyrics.
[50]Added during the run:
  Impressions
    Elsie Janis

Scene 2

"A Dancing M. D." (Song)

G. White, V. Maxwell, M. Davies, E. Haig

(*Music by* Jerome Kern.)

Scene: The Skyline of New York, from Brooklyn Bridge, looking toward New York. *Dr. George W. Lightfoot*, a dancing doctor: G. White. A *Dance-Craze Victim*: M. Davies. *Another*: V. Maxwell. *One More*: E. Haig. *Polly*: V. Segal. *Ferdinand*, Polly's grizzle hound: Himself. *Willy*: H. Kelly. *Lizzie*, the marvelous trained dog: Herself.

Travesty

H. Kelly, V. Segal

"That's the Picture I Want to See" (The Picture I Want to See)(Duet)

E. Brice, C. King, E. Allen, A. Marlowe, the Century Male Octette

(*Music by* Jerome Kern.)

Scene 3

"The Honor System" (A Movie Melodrama)

(*Music by* Jerome Kern.)

Scene: Interior (of a) Motion-Picture Studio.

The Butler: H. Kelly. *The Villain*: A. Tombes. *The Hero*: G. White. *The Child*: A. Pennington. *The Heroine*: V. Maxwell. *The Keystone Kops*: Misses K. Boylan, R. Braham, M. Frawley, M. King, E. Rough, W. Ward, M. Irving, I. Spencer, H. Mooney, R. Myers, E. Warren, E. Gorman, E. Allen, P. Franklin, C. Cullen, L. Franklin, A. Braham, M. Wood, M. Shelly, M. Harrison, M. Bell, V. Morrison, R. Heil, R. Wilbur. Messrs. M. Bell, D. Gordon, J. Quinn, J. Lynch, W. Baker, J. Marr, F. Sharp, M. White, F. Duhall, F. Duball, C. Root, J. Knoffer, C. Jones, L. Clark, J. Parks, M. Williams, W. Shelly, E. Grant, J. Warren, N. Kane, E. Barth, A. Mead, M. Starr, A. Elson.

Scene 4

"Good-bye Broadway, (Hello France)" (from PASSING SHOW OF 1917)

C. Lean, C. Mayfield

(*Music by* Billy Baskette. *Lyrics by* Benny Davis and C. Francis Reisner.)

Scene 5

"(I'm) The Old Man in the Moon" (Song and Dance)

B. M. Davis

(*Music by* Jerome Kern.)

Scene 6

A Chance Meeting

Savoy & Brennan

Scene 7

"The Land Where Good Songs Go"

E. Brice, C. King

(*Music by* Jerome Kern.)

The Stage-Door Keeper: A. Cunningham. *Charlie*: C. King. *Bessie*: E. Brice.

Miss Edna May's "Follow On" (They All Follow Me)(from THE BELLE OF NEW YORK)

M. Davies, Double Octette

(*Music by* Gustave Kerker. *Lyrics by* Hugh Morton.)

(b) Miss Blanche Ring's "In the Good Old Summertime" (from THE DEFENDER)

C. Mayfield, Summer Time Girls

(*Music by* George Evans. *Lyrics by* Ren Shields.)

(c) Mr. Peter F. Dailey's "Dinah" (from HURLY-BURLY)

C. Lean, E. Haig, Y. Shelton, Dinah Girls

(*Music by* John Stromberg. *Lyrics by* Edgar Smith and Harry B. Smith.)

(d) Cole and Johnson's "Under the Bamboo Tree" (from SALLY IN OUR ALLEY)

G. Van, J. Schenck

(*Music and Lyrics by* Bob Cole and J. Rosamond Johnson.)

(e) Bessie McCoy's "(The) Yama Yama (Man)" (from THREE TWINS)

B. M. Davis, Yama Yama Girls

(*Music by* Karl Hoschna. *Lyrics by* Otto Harbach.)

Scene 8

(f) Mabel Barrison's "Sammy" (from THE WIZARD OF OZ)

P. Hopkins, T. Qualters, D. Klewer, H. Kelly

(*Music by* Edward Hutchinson. *Lyrics by* James O'Dea.)

(g) Fritzi Scheff's "Kiss Me Again" (from MLLE. MODISTE)

V. Segal

(*Music by* Victor Herbert. *Lyrics by* Henry Blossom.)

(h) Bring & King's "(Be My Little Baby) Bumble Bee"

E. Brice, C. King

(from ZIEGFELD FOLLIES OF 1911, A WINSOME WIDOW)

(*Music by* Henry I. Marshall. *Lyrics by* Stanley Murphy.)

(i) Herbert's "March of the Toys" (from BABES IN TOYLAND)

(*Music by* Victor Herbert.)

(j) "Toy Clog Dance"

(*Music by* Jerome Kern. Staircase dance effect devised by Ned Wayburn.)

ACT 2

Scene 1

Falling Leaves (A Poem-Choreographic conceived and staged by Adolf Bohm)

(*Music by* Victor Herbert.)

The Spirit of the Wind: A. Bohm. *The Golden Birch*: F. Revalles. *The Shepherd*: M. Hall. *The Old Satyr*: I. Tarasov. *The Young Satyr*: A. Umanski. *Nymphs*: M. Leeraas, R. Leeraas, R. Zalamani, E. Gardiner, N. Stephanova, Misses Selskaya, Sterling, Vernon, Nova, Uhr. Dancers represent Dryads, Trees, Leaves and the Golden Autumn.

Argument: The trees and shrubs of the forest, clinging to their autumnal raiment, are fearful of the advent of the Wind. They bask happily in the warm, still air of late October, while Dryads and Satyrs disport themselves through the glades of the wood and a shepherd boy plays on his Pan pipes. A nymph imprisoned by a charm in the body of a Golden Birch Tree longs to be free, and calls to her lover, who has also been turned into a tree that grows near by. The Wind, hearing the whispered appeal of the Golden Birch, comes to her rescue and liberates her, but in so doing he scatters all the silver leaves, and himself enamoured of her beauty, he pursues her through the wood. Finally realizing that she longs to return to her lover, he frees them both, and himself goes on his way, scattering the leaves of the forest as he departs.

Scene 2

The Singing Blacksmith of Curriclough

Irish Jig

S. O'Rourke, Century Double Octette

(*Music arranged by* Victor Herbert from songs by his grandfather, Samuel Lover)

Scene 3

"We Want to Laugh" (Song)

B. M. Davis, K. Perry, M. Leslie, L. Tashman, T. Qualters

(*Music by* Jerome Kern.)

Blutch: K. Perry. *Eddie Foy*: M. Leslie. *Frank Tinney*: L. Tashman. *Fred Stone*: T. Qualters. *Jos Jackson*: B. M. Davis.

Scene 4

The Deluge Saloon

Hiram Askem: L. Fields. *Joe Askem*, his son: A. Tombes. *Willy*: H. Kelly. *Mr. Reggie Starr*, the movie director: E. Revere. *The Champagne Chameleon*: J. Sparks. *The Waiter*: L. James. *A Cabaret Sister Act*: Y. Shelton, E. Haig. *Horace*: P. Briant. *Special Officer*: W. Briant.

Scene 5

The Midnight Frolic Cabaret: The Blue and White Marimba Band

Maja Dance

T. Valencia

"A Dancing Courtship" (Duet)

G. White, A. Pennington

Dance

I. Castle

"Who's Zoo in Girl Land"

A. Tombes, M. Morris, Mlle. Dolores, C. Markle, M. Leslie, P. Hopkins, D. Klewer

(*Music by* Jerome Kern.)

The Tiger: M. Morris. *The Serpent*: Mlle. Dolores. *The Cat*: C. Markle. *The Butterfly*: M. Leslie. *The Peacock*: P. Hopkins. *The Bear*: D. Klewer.

Scene 6

Songs

G. Van, J. Schenck

["Midnight in Dreamy Spain"

(*Music and Lyrics by* Joseph McCarthy, Gus Van and Joseph Schenck.)

"Oh What a Beautiful Baby"

(*Music by* Harry Tierney. *Lyrics by* Stanley Murphy.)]

Scene 7

The Beauty Shop in the Hotel Blitz

Hiram Askem: L. Fields. *News Girl*: L. McKenzie. *Manager*: C. King. *Miss Claire Ridge*: V. Maxwell. *Miss Cherie Delmonica*: S. D'Herlys. *Miss Rita Carlton*: P. Hopkins. *Miss Claire Mont*: D. Klewer. *Miss Sybil St. Regis*: Mlle. Phyllis. *Miss Sallie Shelbourne*: Mlle. Dolores. *Miss Bertie Bellevue*: Mlle. Mauresette. *Miss Lotta Noyes*: B. Savoy. *Models*: G. Loftus, O. Osborne, E. Morton, I. Hayes.

Scene 8

Dancing Specialty

A. Pennington

Scene 9

"The Palm Beach Girl"

C. Lean, C. Mayfield

(*Music by* Jerome Kern.)

The Pajama Girl: Mlle.Mauresette. *The Bicycle Girl*: Y. Shelton. *The Tennis Girl*: Z. Dolores. *The Bathing Girl*: D. Klewer. *The Cocktail Girl*: Miss Phyllis. *The Fishing Girl*: L. Tashman. *The One-step Girl*: C. Markle. *The Roulette Girl*: Mlle. Dolores. *The Palm-Beacher*: E. Revere.

Scene 10

Finale
    Scene: The Seashore at Palm Beach.

1917.27

KITTY DARLIN'

A Musical Romance in Three Acts. Book and lyrics by Otto Harbach. Based on the play "Sweet Kitty Bellairs" by David Belasco and the novel (on which it was based) by Edgerton Castle. Music by Rudolf Friml. Staged by Edward Royce. Scenery by P. H. Reisig. Ladies' gowns by Harry Collins. Miss Nielsen's gowns by Mme. Julie. Orchestra under the direction of William P. Axt. Produced by William Elliott, F. Ray Comstock and Morris Gest. Opened 7 November 1917 at the Casino Theatre and closed 17 November 1917 after 14 performances.

CAST: *Sir Jasper Standish*, a baronet living in Bath: JACKSON HINES. *Colonel the Honorable Henry Villiers*, commanding the 51st: EDWIN STEVENS. *Captain Spicer*, of the 51st Regiment: FRANK WESTERTON. *Lieutenant Lord Verney*, of the 51st Regiment: GLEN HALL. *Gandy*, the Colonel's orderly: H. Jess Smith. *Colonel Kimby McFinton*, commanding the 6th (Inniskilling) Regiment of Dragoons: GEORGE CALLAHAN. *Captain Dennis O'Hara*, of the 6th Inniskillings: WORTHE FAULKNER. *Mallow*, Lord Verney's man: Frank Bradley. *Lady Julia Standish*, wife of Sir Jasper: JUANITA FLETCHER. *Lady Bab Flyte*, the late Belle of Bath: SIDONIE ESPERO. *Lydie*, Mistress Kitty's Maid: Eleanor Daniels *Lady Beaufort*: Patricia Frewen. *Mistress Kitty Bellairs*, a young widow: ALICE NIELSEN.
    Ladies of Bath: Misses Erna Steinway, Yettla Nicoll, Gertrude Hogan, Peggy Troland, Jane Buchanan, Doris Faithful, Charlotte Lenox, Margaret May, Ruby Thomas, Shirley Love, Jeanne Sparry, Grace Dean, Clare King, Mary Lee Stevens, Peggy Brandon, Edith Appleton. *Debutantes of Bath*: Misses Olive Kingston, Rose Benedict, Molly Christie, Helen Christie, Mary Comerford, Fayette Howard, Josephine Bryan, Ann Page, Muril Smither, Florence Haynes. *Officers of the 51st Regiment (English)*: Messrs. Bert Clark, Benjamin Rogers, R. St. John, Louis LaVie, Edward Watson, R. G. Elliott, S. Critcheson, Albert Noome. *Officers of the Inniskillings (Irish)*: Messrs. H. Clark, Anton Ingaroa, B. Tieman, Walter Palm, N. P. Bryan, Frank P. Sparling, C. Enisman, William Hovel.

Act 1: The Garden at Prideaux Hall. The temporary quarters of the 51st Regiment and their guests, the Inniskillings, during their stay in Bath. The Regiment has a Ladies' Day.

Act 2: Lord Verney's Lodgings. Three o'clock in the morning.

Act 3: The Great Gallery at Prideaux Hall. The Regimental Ball of the 51st.

ACT 1[50a]

"Dear Bath"
    Ensemble
"My Father's Sword"
    G. Hall, E. Stevens, Officers
"Kitty Darlin'"
    W. Faulkner, Ensemble
"Love's Own Call"
    A. Nielsen, Ensemble
"Am I to Blame?"
    F. Westerton, J. Hines, A. Nielsen
"You're Plenty of a Lady as You Are"
    E. Daniels, F. Bradley
"You'll See"
    A. Nielsen, J. Fletcher, Ladies
"When She Gives Him a Shamrock Bloom"
    A. Nielsen, Ensemble
Finale
    Ensemble

ACT 2
"Kitty Darlin'" (reprise)
    G. Hall
"Noah"
    E. Stevens, Officers
    (*Lyrics by* P. G. Wodehouse.)

[50a]Wodehouse's lyrics appear to have been retained from a failed Buffalo tryout from September 1917, inasmuch as the song titles, vocal attributions and placement are nearly identical. Harbach assumed all program credit from Guy Bolton and P. G. Wodehouse's previous book and lyrics.

"Peggy's Leg"
    Officers
    (*Lyrics by* P. G. Wodehouse.)
"Just We Two"
    G. Hall, A. Nielsen
ACT 3
"The Ball of the Fifty-First"
    Ensemble
"Spread the News"
    S. Espero, Ladies
"Dear Old Dublin"
    W. Faulkner, G. Callahan, Officers
    (*Lyrics by* P. G. Wodehouse.)
"I Want a Man Who's Gentle"
    S. Espero, F. Westerton, J. Hines, Ensemble
"'Twas Pretense"
    A. Nielsen, G. Hall, Ensemble
Finale

1917.28

HER REGIMENT

An Operetta in Three Acts. Book and lyrics by William Le Baron. Music by Victor Herbert. Staged by Fred G. Latham. Scenery by D. Frank Dodge and William Castle. Costumes by Schneider-Anderson; Croyden, Ltd. Orchestra under the direction of Fritz Stahlberg. Produced by Joseph Weber. Opened 12 November 1917 at the Broadhurst Theatre, moved 10 December 1917 to the Knickerbocker Theatre and closed 29 December 1917 after 56 performances.

CAST: *Colonel Ponstable*: Hugh Chilvers. *André de Courcy*: DONALD BRIAN. *Blanquet*: FRANK MOULAN. *Eugene de Merriame*: SIDNEY JARVIS. *Sergeant Sabretache*: Frederick Manatt. *Carabine*: George Averill. *François*: Frank Meyers. *Estelle Duvernay*: AUDREY MAPLE. *Lisette Berlier*: JOSIE INTROPODI. *Madame Guerriere*: Paulina French. *Jeanette*: Norma Brown. *Georgette*: Cissie Sewell. *Fifi*: Edythe Mason. *Soldiers, Peasants, Girls, Guests, Servants, etc.*
    Ladies of the Chorus: Clara Eckstrom, Alice Leslie, Phyllis Curl, Lillian Ring, Virginia O'Brien, Beryl Gwynne, Mina Davis, Elizabeth Young, Elaine Landau, Norma Day, Florence Jay, Ethyl Tennis, Alice Maurice, Betty Diggott. *Gentlemen of the Chorus*: Charles Hessong, Arthur Kinney, William Kline, P. McShane, George Avery, August Shelthrope, P. Scott Paton, D. Peel, G. Arnold, J. Preslow, Jack Sparley, Harry Bostock, Ben Rogers, Lionel Chalmers, George Averill.

The action takes place at a French Military encampment in Normandy, June 1914.

Act 1: Outside the "Pomme d'Or."

Act 2: Reception Room of the Chateau Belleville.

Act 3: Officers' Quarters at the Barracks.

ACT 1
Opening Ensemble
"You Never Can Tell How a Marriage Will Take"
    F. Moulan, J. Intropodi
"Oh, My!" (Entrance)
    D. Brian, Soldiers
"Soldier Men"
    A. Maple, Chorus
"(A) Little Farm in Normandie"
    A. Maple, D. Brian
"'Twixt Love and Duty"
    D. Brian, Chorus
Finale
ACT 2
(Opening Chorus)
"(The) American Serenade"
    A. Maple, Chorus
Dance
    D. Brian, C. Sewell
"Art" (The Art Song)
    S. Jarvis, Girls
"Some Day"
    A. Maple, D. Brian
Finale
ACT 3
(Opening Chorus)
"The Devil and the Deep Sea"
    F. Moulan, J. Intropodi, Soldiers

"Superlative Love"
  A. Maple, D. Brian
"As the Years Roll By"
  F. Moulan
"Vive la France!"
  (D. Brian, Company)

1917.29 ## ODDS AND ENDS OF 1917

A Chummy Musical Revue in Two Acts, 28 Scenes. Book (sketches) by Bide Dudley and John Godfrey. Music and lyrics by Bide Dudley, John Godfrey and James Byrnes[51]. Interpolated songs by R. P. Weston and Bert Lee. Production staged by Julian Alfred. Scenery by H. Robert Law Studios. Costumes designed by Yetta Kiviat [Kiviette]. Orchestra under the direction of James Byrnes. Produced by Jack Norworth and Samuel Shannon. Opened 19 November 1917 at the Bijou Theatre, moved 28 January 1918 to the Norworth Theatre and closed 23 February 1918 after 112 performances.

CAST: JACK NORWORTH, PAUL FRAWLEY, LILLIAN LORRANE, LAURA HAMILTON, [Sergeant] HARRY WATSON, JR., JOSEPH HERBERT, JR., JACK EDWARDS, YOUNG KID BATTLING DUGAN, Georgia Manatt, Maxine Brown, Joseph Madden, John Birch, Lola Hilton, James C. Lane, Upert Carlton, Marjorie Poir, Mlle. Aquateeta, Professor Kamo, Joseph Hart, Jr., Norma Phillips.

  Girls: Misses Hilton, Dunn, Randall, Doyle, Pond, Benelisha, Cattel, Williams, Dayne, Simpson, Hazel Flint, Hazel Squires, Weber, Holtz, Smith, Crawford, Reba Kent. *Men:* Messrs. Baker, Cohen, Paige, Wendell, LeVoy, King, Pollock, Finn.

ACT 1
Scene 1
  "(There's) A Lovely Crop of Girls (This Year)"
    J. Herbert, Girls
    (*Music by* Jack Norworth. *Lyrics by* R. P. Weston.)
      Girls: Misses Hilton, Dunn, Randall, Doyle, Pond, Benelisha, Cattel, Williams.
        Here the Plot Beginneth, Here the Plot Endeth
Scene 2
  "Bravo, Antonio!"
    G. Manatt, 8 Bersagleri Girls
Scene 3
  "The Dove Dance"
    N. Phillips, 8 Girls
    (*Music by* Jack Norworth.)
      Girls: Misses Dayne, Simpson, Flint, Weber, Holtz, Smith, Crawford, Kent.
        At this point, Miss Lorraine will make her appearance and tell you why Rosie went back home.
  "Dear Old Bronx"
    L. Lorraine, Girls
Scene 4
  Direct from the Alhambra, London, Captain Lionel Flounder presents Mlle. Aquateeta, the little Water Nymph, in a series of novel and artistic amphibious poses.
Scene 5
  Dance
    L. Hamilton, J. Herbert, Jr
Scene 6
  Some Military Manoeuvres
    Sergeant H. Watson, Men
      Men: Messrs. Baker, Cohen, Paige, Wendell, LeVoy, King, Pollock, Finn. And R. Kent.
Scene 7
  "Give Me an Old-Fashioned Girlie" (Give Me an Old-Fashioned Melody)
    P. Frawley, Girls
Scene 8
  A Fireside, a Sofa, Two Sweethearts, and One Song:
  "Fancy You Fancying Me"[52]
    L. Lorraine, J. Norworth
    (*Music and Lyrics by* Nora Bayes and Jack Norworth.)
Scene 9
  (Scene)
    J. Madden, J. Birch, J. Edwards, P. Frawley, L. Hamilton, J. Herbert, Jr.

Scene 10
  "Where Did You Get Those Irish Eyes?"[53]
    M. Brown, L. Hilton, U. Carlton
Scene 11
  Young Kid Battling Dugan (First Stage Appearance)
Scene 12
  Song
    J. Norworth
  ["Ten Little Bridesmaids"
  "There's a Lovely Crop of Girls This Year"
    (*Music by* Jack Norworth. *Lyrics by* R. P. Weston.)]
Scene 13
  "Sister Susie Glide"
    L. Lorraine, J. Herbert, All the Girls
Scene 14
  Grand Spectacular Finale
    Entire Company
    (*Conceived and designed by* Samuel Shannon.)
ACT 2
Scene 1
  Opening Chorus
    G. Manatt, J. Hart, Jr., 8 Little Maids
  "My Lady's Clothes"
    L. Hamilton, H. Squires, H. Flint, the girl in the tub, 8 Assisters
    Scene: A Beauty Shop.
Scene 2
  "Hector"
    L. Lorraine, J. Norworth
Scene 3
  Impersonations
    Professor Kamo
Scene 4
  Dancing Lesson
    L. Hamilton, J. Edwards
Scene 5
  Dance of the Marionettes
    M. Brown
    Assisted by Misses Kent, Cornell, Cattell, Williams.
Scene 6
  Somewhere with Pershing
  "The Further It Is from Tipperary"
    J. Norworth
      A Private: U. Carlton. *A Corporal:* J. Birch. *A Sergeant:* J. Norworth. *A Major:* J. Madden. *A Red Cross Nurse:* M. Poir.
Scene 7
  "The Vampire Maids"
  Look out, movie stars! Here come the 8 Vampire Maids, namely—oh, by this time surely you know them
    P. Frawley, N. Phillips, 8 Vampire Maids
Scene 8
  Song[54]
    L. Lorraine
Scene 9
  Jack Edwards will try and break his ankles
Scene 10
  "The Voice with the Smile Wins"
    L. Hamilton, N. Phillips
    Two Smiling Voices: Misses Hamilton, Phillips. *Another Smiling Voice:* J.

---

[51]In published sheet music James A. Byrnes does not share credit for the book.
[52]Ascribed to R. P. Weston and Bert Lee in published sheet music.

---

[53]Replaced late in the run by (but reinstated for subsequent tour):
  "Every Girl Is Doing Her Bit" (also in EVERYTHING; ZIEGFELD MIDNIGHT FROLIC)
    Dolly Connolly
    (*Music by* James Tate. *Lyrics by* Clifford Harris.)
[54]Replaced late in the run by:
  "Blues"
    D. Connolly

Herbert, Jr. *A Voice with a Grouch*: H. Watson, Jr.

Scene 11

"The Eternal Triangle Blues"
L. Lorraine, H. Watson, J. Norworth

Scene 12

"When I Wave My Flag"[55]
P. Frawley, Chorus
(*Music by* Jack Norworth. *Lyrics by* R. P. Weston.)

Scene 13

"We've Got to Put Up with It"
J. Norworth

Scene 14

Finale Episode
(Wait for this ladies. It's not like the Finale of Part I. Au Revoir!)

1917.30

THE STAR GAZER

A Comedy with Music in Three Acts. (American) Book by Cosmo Hamilton (based on the Viennese original 'Der Sturngucker' by Fritz Löhner-Beda and A. M. Willner). Music by Franz Lehár. Lyrics by Matthew C. Woodward. Staged by Edward P. Temple. Orchestra under the direction of Gaetano Merola. Produced under the personal direction of J. J. Shubert. Produced by the Messrs. Shubert. Opened 26 November 1917 at the Plymouth Theatre and closed 1 December 1917 after 8 performances.[56]

CAST: *Peter Blunt Esq.*, an enthusiast on astronomy: JOHN T. MURRY. *Kitty*, his sister: CAROLYN THOMSON. *Peckham*, Mr. Blunt's confidential servant: John Harwood. *Arthur Howard*, a young gallant: JOHN CHARLES THOMAS. *Sir Joshua Puddifant*, Master of fox hounds: Alfred Hemming. *Lady Puddifant*: Jeanne Belyea. *Rebecca Puddifant*, another daughter: EDNA TEMPLE. *Elizabeth Puddifant*, his daughter: Carolyn Duffy. *Alderman Hornblower*: George Harcourt. *Mrs. Hornblower*: Catherine Manning. *Martha Hornblower*, their daughter: WANDA LYON. *Squire Trendlecome*: Theodore F. Reynolds. *Mrs. Trendlecome*: Elizabeth Goodall. *Anne*, their daughter: JENNETTA METHVEN[57]. *Lieutenant Claydown*, His Majesty's 10th Regiment of Foot: Arthur Geary. *Horace Howyer, Esp.*, a young fop: Billy Lynn. *Nicholas Finchley, Esq.*: Jack Paulton. *Miss Honora Titterton*, principal of the ladies' seminary: Isabel Vernon. *Mr. Percy Ebblewhite*, teacher of music: Paul Irving. *Mr. Ollyffe* of the Official Information Bureau of the City of Bath: Herbert Salinger. *Footman* at Miss Titterton's School: Owen Hervey. *Maid*: Elizabeth Harcourt.

The action takes place in Bath, England, in 1830.

Act 1: The Lecture Room in Miss Titterton's Seminary for the Daughters of Gentlemen.

Act 2: The Parlor in Peter Blunt's House. The following afternoon.

Act 3: The Garden of Same. Two weeks later.

ACT 1

"While All Are Asleep"
C. Thomson

"We Loved and We Lost, Good-Bye!" (Duet)
J. C. Thomas, J. Methven

"Twinkle, Twinkle" (Quartette)
C. Thomson, J. Methven, W. Lyon, E. Temple

"Butterfly" (Quartette)
C. Thomson, J. Methven, E. Temple, W. Lyon

"My Heart Is Like a Bird in May" (Duet)
C. Thomson, J. C. Thomas

"You, You, You!" (Trio)
C. Thomson, J. Methven, J. C. Thomas

"You My Sweetheart Will Have to Be"
E. Temple, J. T. Murry

Finale
C. Thomson, J. T. Murry, J. C. Thomas, E. Temple, J. Methven, A. Hemming, J. Belyea, G. Harcourt, K. Manning, T. F. Reynolds, E. Goodall

ACT 2

"If You Only Knew" (Solo)
C. Thomson
(*Music by* Albert Von Tilzer. *Lyrics by* Neville Fleeson.)

"When You Are Mine, All Mine" (Duet)
J. C. Thomas, C. Thomson

"If a Bachelor in Love Should Fall" (Trio)
C. Thomson, J. T. Murry, J. Harwood

"Won't You Come Up to the Table?" (Quartette)
J. Methven, E. Temple, W. Lyon, J. T. Murry

"Rhyming for a Dance" (Quintette)
J. Methven, E. Temple, W. Lyon, J. T. Murry, C. Thomson

"Star Gazer (Star Gazer)" (Duet)
J. Methven, J. T. Murry

"But You Alone" (Solo)
J. C. Thomas

Finale
J. C. Thomas, C. Thomson, J. T. Murry, J. Methven

ACT 3

"A Bachelor's Button" (Song)
J. Harwood

"Drink Some Tea" (Duet)
J. Methven, J. T. Murry

"As the Butterfly Sips the Roses" (Quartette)
C. Thomson, J. C. Thomas, J. Methven, J. T. Murry

"My Heart Is Like a Bird in May"—Finale (Reminiscence)
C. Thomson, J. C. Thomas, E. Temple, B. Lynn, W. Lyon, A. Geary, J. Methven, J. T. Murry

1917.31

OVER THE TOP

A Musical Revue in Two Acts, 15 Scenes. Words (sketches) by Philip Bartholomae and Harold Atteridge. Music by Sigmund Romberg; additional tunes by Herman Timberg. Lyrics by Matthew C. Woodward and Charles Manning. Staged by J. C. Huffman. Dances arranged by Allan K. Foster. Stage decorations (Scenery) by P. Dodd Ackerman Studios. Costumes designed by Homer Conant; gowns and dresses by Joseph, Madame Kahn. Orchestra under the direction of Frank Tours. Produced by Messrs. Lee and J. J. Shubert. Opened 28 November 1917 at the 44th Street Roof Theatre and closed 2 February 1918 after 78 performances[58].

CAST [in order of appearance]: *Justine*: JUSTINE JOHNSTONE. *Maggie*: Aleen Bronson. *Sammy*: JOE LAURIE. *Mrs. Brown*: Emma Sharrock. *Fred*: CRAIG CAMPBELL. *Madame Celeste*: VIVIEN OAKLAND. *Nellie*: Beatrice Little. *Mlle. Lingerie*: Phyllis Prince. *Mlle. Gown*: Anna Berg. *Mlle. Souliers*: Molly Moore. *Mlle. Corset*: Anita Baldwin. *Mlle. Stocking*: Beatrice Sommers. *Mlle. Bonneterie*: Bly Brown. *M. Auguste*: FRED ASTAIRE. *Adele*: ADELE ASTAIRE. *Mr. Plot*: T. ROY BARNES. *Floor Walker*: TED LORRAINE. *Betty*: Betty Pierce. *Salesladies*: Misses Russell, Dale, Herman, Comboy, Carroll, Green, J. Carroll, Powell, Little, Murray, Wright, Fuld. *Patrons of Mme. Celeste's Shop*: Misses Prince, Berg, Moore, Baldwin, Sommers, Brown. *Teddy*: TED LORRAINE. *Sadie*: DAGMAR OAKLAND. *Queen of the Billboard*: JUSTINE JOHNSTONE. *Shayne Fur Poster Girl*: Phyllis Prince. *Elcaya Cream Poster Girl*: Jean Carroll. *Clysmic Ginger Ale Poster Girl*: Jean Rebeera. *Pacific Coast Borax Poster Girl*: Muriel Barnes. *Frederic Pearl Poster Girl*: Anna Berg. *Milo Cigarette Poster Girl*: Hilda Wright. *Rubberset Toothbrush Poster Girl*: Edna Russell. *Drednaught Tire Poster Girl*: Aileen French. *Pinaud's Eau de Quinine Poster Girl*: Molly Moore. *Crown Veil Poster Girl*: Nina Whittmore. *Photo Poster Girl*: Clara Carroll. *Hygenol Powder Puff Poster Girl*: Beatrice Little. *The Sculptor*: CRAIG CAMPBELL. *The Aviator*: TED LORRAINE. *Myrtle*: VIVIEN OAKLAND. *Ivy*: Dagmar Oakland. *Galatéa*: JUSTINE JOHNSTONE. *Mark Anthony*: ROLANDA. *Colonel Von Spitzer*: Harry Sharrock. *Private Bauer*: Hal Taggart. *Boxholders*: OAKLAND SISTERS, TED LORRAINE, JOE LAURIE, AILEEN BRONSON. *Pages*: Misses Carroll, Little. *The Minstrel*: CRAIG CAMPBELL. *The Golden Pheasants*: Misses Collier, Berg, Baldwin, Prince, Morre, Whittmore. *Chanticleer Pheasant*: Ma-Belle. *Hen Pheasant* MARY EATON. *Princess of the Rising Sun*: VIVIEN OAKLAND. *Odalisques*: Misses Sommers, Dale, Brown, Eden, Levine, Russell, Challenger, Summerville, Palmer, Powell, Rebeera, Knight, Barnes, Carroll. *Marjorie*: JUSTINE JOHNSTONE. *Her Brother*: JOE LAURIE. *Her Sister*: Aleen Bronson. *The Yogi*: T. ROY BARNES. *The Lover*: CRAIG CAMPBELL. *The Beautiful Slave*: JUSTINE JOHNSTONE. *Zaza*, the mystic: EMMA SHARROCK. *Chu Chin Chow*: HARRY SHARROCK. *Attendant*: Hal Taggart.

Rolanda's Neo-Classical Dancers: Misses Rook, Cassidy, Forbes, Arnold, Edward, Lorber, Sortelle, Youde, Warwick.

---

[55]Replaced late in the run by: (reinstated for subsequent tour)
"The Navy of To-day's All Right"
D. Connolly

[56]Settings, costumes uncredited.

[57]Several reviewers saw Sidonie Espero in this role.

[58]Toured subsequently under the title OH, JUSTINE! for which a new title song was written:
"Oh, Justine!"
(*Music by* Sigmund Romberg and Herman Timberg. *Lyrics by* Charles Manning.)

Act 1, Scene 1: Somewhere in New Jersey. *Scene 2*: Land of Frocks and Frills. *Scene 3*: The Girl for Me. *Scene 4*: At the Railroad Station. *Scene 5*: Posterland. *Scene 6*: A Studio in Greenwich Village. *Scene 7*: An Aviation Camp. *Scene 8*: In the Trenches.

Act 2, Scene 1: A Theatre. *Scene 2*: The Golden Forest; In Algeria. *Scene 3*: A Little Flirtation. *Scene 4*: The Eyes of Youth. *Scene 5*: In Chu Chin Chow's Cave. *Scene 6*: The Mystifying Harry and Emma Sharrock. *Scene 7*: Justine Johnstone's Little Club.

ACT 1
Scene 1
  Opening Chorus
    (Ensemble)
Scene 2
  "Frocks and Frills"
    V. Oakland, Chorus
  Gown Dance
    F. Astaire, A. Astaire
  "My Rainbow Girl"
    J. Johnstone, C. Campbell
Scene 3
  "The Girl for Me"
    Oakland Sisters, T. Lorraine
Scene 4
  Specialty
    J. Laurie, A. Bronson
Scene 5
  "Posterland"
    J. Johnstone, Chorus
Scene 6
  The Gladiator Dance
    Rolanda's Neo-Classical Dancers
  "That Airship of Mine"
    T. Lorraine, Chorus
  "Greenwich Village Belle"
    Oakland Sisters, T. Lorraine, Chorus
  "Oh, Galatéa!" (Song)
    C. Campbell
    (*Music by* Sigmund Romberg and Herman Timberg. *Lyrics by* Philip Bartholomae.)
  Dance
    J. Johnstone, T. Lorraine
Scene 7
  "Over the Top"[59]
    T. Lorraine
  A Bit of Airy Camouflage[60]
    T. R. Barnes
Scene 8
  (The aeroplane invasion effect invented by Lincoln J. Carter.)

ACT 2
Scene 1
  "Golden Pheasant"
    C. Campbell
    (*Music by* Sigmund Romberg and Herman Timberg. *Lyrics by* Matthew C. Woodward.)
  Pas de Deux (Dance)
    Ma-Bell, M. Eaton
  "Algerian Girl"
    V. Oakland, Chorus
Scene 3
  "Where Is the Language to Tell?"
    F. Astaire, A. Astaire
Scene 5
  Jewel Dance
    Rolanda's Neo-Classical Dancers
Scene 6
  The Mystifying Sharrocks[61]
    E. Sharrock, H. Sharrock

[59]Dropped after the opening.
[60]Some programs from the opening week place this specialty in Act 2 after "The Justine Johnstone Rag."
  Dropped by the end of the New York run.
[61]Dropped for subsequent tour.

Scene 7
  "The Justine Johnstone Rag"
    F. Astaire, A. Astaire, Oakland Sisters, B. Pierce, T. Lorraine
    (*Music by* Frank Carter, Sigmund Romberg, Herman Timberg. *Lyrics by* Charles Manning.)
  Dance
    F. Astaire, A. Astaire
  Finale
    Ensemble

1917.32 ## THE GRASS WIDOW

A Musical Play in Three Acts. Book and lyrics by Channing Pollock and Rennold Wolf. Basd on the play "Le Péril Jaune" [The Yellow Peril] by Bisson and St. Albin. Music by Louis A. Hirsch. Staged by George Marion. Produced by Madison Corey. Opened 3 December 1917 at the Liberty Theatre, moved 24 December 1917 to the Princess Theatre, and closed 5 January 1918 after 43 performances.

CAST: *An Ill-Humored Man*: J. C. Klein. *Annette*, the cashier: HELEN LOWELL. *Vincent*, the head-waiter: Tom O'Hare. *Anatol Pivert*, the proprietor: GEORGE MARION. *Larry Doyle*, 'Aunt Abigail' on the Wilmington Whisper: ROBERT EMMET KEANE. *Four Delaware Peaches: Dorothy*: Irene Dixon. *Florence*: Edna Waddell. *Betty*: Marion Ford. *Angie*: May Hopkins. *Denise*, a waitress: NATALIE ALT. *Colette*, of the Candy Shop: GRETCHEN EASTMAN. *Fernand Dore*: VICTOR MORLEY. *Fanchon*, waitress: Marion Pollard. *Claire*, waitress: Anita Francesca. *Jacques*, the Count of Cluny: HOWARD MARSH. *Lucille*, his sister: Marguerite L. Fritts. *Monsieur Faverau*, the Minister of Foreign Affairs: Leon E. Brown.
  The Grass Widow Jazz Band: Joseph H. Woodward (pianist), Harry Davis (banjoist), Saxi Holstworth (saxophonian).
  The action takes place in France during the summer of 1912.

Act 1: The Railway Station Restaurant at Tours.

Act 2: The Home of the Count de Cluny, Paris. Three months later.

Act 3: The Inn of the Golden Pheasant, Fontainebleau. Just before night of the same day.

ACT 1
  "Soup" (Opening Chorus)
    H. Lowell, T. O'Hare, Ensemble
  "C.D.Q."
    R. Keane, E. Waddell, M. Hopkins, M. Ford, E. Stede, Ensemble
  "Dance with Me"
    G. Eastman, Ensemble
  "(The) Song of Love"
    N. Alt
    (*Music by* Louis Hirsch and Digby Latouche.)
  "Farewell" (Letter Song)
    N. Alt, H. Marsh
  "You Can't Be a Husband To-day" (Finale)
    Ensemble

ACT 2
  Opening Chorus
    M. L. Fritts, V. Morley, Ensemble
  "The Grass Widow"
    N. Alt, G. Eastman, M. L. Fritts, H. Marsh, V. Morley, Ensemble
  "Somewhere There's Someone for Me"
    G. Eastman, V. Morley
  "Just You and Me"
    N. Alt, H. Marsh
  "All the Girls Have Got a Friend in Me"
    R. E. Keane, E. Waddell, M. Hopkins, M. Ford, E. Stede, Ensemble
  Finale

ACT 3
  "The Whirlwind Whirl" (Opening Number, Dance Specialty)
    S. Leyman, S. Chaulsae
  "When the Saxophone Is Playing"
    G. Eastman, Ensemble
  "What's the Use of Loving Only One Girl?"
    V. Morley
  Finale
    Ensemble

1917.33 A NIGHT IN SPAIN

A Midnight (Musical) Revue in Two Acts, 16 Scenes. Music by Quinito Valverde. Assembled and produced by Charles Dillingham and Florenz Ziegfeld by arrangement with the Velasco Brothers. Scenery by Tarazona Brothers. Costumes by Messrs. Schneider, Anderson, Calzado. Orchestra under the direction of Julian Benloch. Opened 6 December 1917 at the Cocoanut Grove Roof (atop the Century Theatre) and closed 12 January 1918 after 33 performances.

CAST: RAYMOND HITCHCOCK (compère), DOLORETES, VIOLETA, MANUEL VILLA, MAZZANTINITA JESUS NAVARRO, AMPARO SAUS, MARIA MARCO, LUISITA PUCHOL, CARMEN LOPEZ, ANTONIO de BILBAO, PENTENERAS and SEVILLANAS.

Ensemble: Falagan, Mari, Julis, Mari, Pias, Flores de Mayo, Hermanas Pereda.

ACT 1
Scene 1
  "El Tango del Molinillo" (The Molinillo Tango)
    L. Puchol, A. Saus, Mazzantinita
Scene 2
  Los Boleros (Dance)
    Doloretes, Violeta, A. Bilbao, Ensemble
Scene 3
  "Serenata de Achares" (Serenade of Achares)(Song)
    M. Villa
Scene 4
  "La Mantilla Espanola" (The Spanish Mantilla)(Dance with song)
    L. Puchol, A. Saus, C. Lopez
Scene 5
  La Reina de Aragon (The Queen of Aragon)(Dance)
    Mazzantinita
Scene 6
  Como Tamba Rumba (Rumba Dance)
    Violeta, J. Navarro
Scene 7
  "Espanola Moderna" (Modern Spanish)(Song)
    A. Saus, Ensemble
Scene 8
  "Espanola Antigua" (Antique Spanish)(Song)
    M. Marco, Ensemble
Scene 9
  "La Tirana" (Song)
    L. Puchol, Ensemble
ACT 2
Scene 1
  "Cancion del Minino" (Minino Song)
    L. Puchol, A. Saus, C. Lopez, Bailarinas, Ensemble
Scene 2
  "Torerito" (Song)
    L. Puchol, A. Saus, C. Lopez
Scene 3
  Alegrias Flamencas (Dance)
    A. de Bilbao
Scene 4
  "Duo de la Capa" (Duet)
    M. Marco, M. Villa
Scene 5
  Zambra Granadina (Dance)
    Doloretes, Violeta, Mazzantinita, Falagan, C. Lopez, Mari, Julis, Pias, Flores de Mayo, H. Pereda, A. de Bilbao, Sevillanito, Chorus
Scene 6
  "Claveles de Espana" (Song)
    A. Saus, L. Puchol
Scene 7
  Concurso de bailes (Dance)
    Peteneras, Sevillanas, Entire Company

1917.34 FLO-FLO

A Musical Comedy in Two Acts. Book by Fred de Grésac.[62] (Based on a vaudeville skit known as "The Bride Shop.") Music by Silvio Hein. Lyrics by Edward Paulton and Fred de Gresac. Staged by Walter Brooks. Dances arranged by David Bennett. Scenery by H. Robert Law Studios. Costumes designed by R. Kerner. Orchestra under the direction of Theodore Stearns. Produced by John Cort. Opened 20 December 1917 at the Cort Theatre and closed 29 June 1918 after 220 performances.

CAST: Flo-Flo, a deluxe show girl looking for fame and fortune: VERA MICHELENA. Isidor Mooser: JAMES B. CARSON. Robert Simpson, his partner and owner of "The Bride Shop": OSCAR FIGMAN. Billy Cope from Oshkosh: LEON LEONARD. Angelina Stokes: RUBY NORTON. Mrs. R. G. Stokes, her chaperoning mother: LOUISE BEAUDET. Count Pedro deSeguilla: George Renavent. Carmen Carassa, a Spanish girl: FINITA deSORIA. Pink: THOMAS HANDERS. Mudd, his partner, handy in picking up things: ARTHUR MILLIS. Officer Casey: William Hugh Mack. Maid: Marie Hollywell. Counter Girls: Bella: Blanche Bellaire. Cora: Esther Ingham. Rosa: Anna Sands. Mona: Kate Stout.

Shop Girls: Helen Allan, Helen Rintelen, Nell O'Connell, Flora Hollister, Virginia Badger, Alice Taber, Edna St. Clair, Virginia Wynn, Lou Adami, Blanche Terrell, Lillian Browning, Ethel Phillips.

The action takes place at the present time .

Act 1: The Bride Shop, Fifth Avenue, New York City.

Act 2: Conservatory in Mrs. Stokes' Country Residence, Long Island.

ACT 1
  Opening Chorus
    Ensemble
  "A Wonderful Creature"
    O. Figman, J. B. Carson, V. Michelena
  "There's Only One Little Girl"
    L. Leonard, Girls
    (Lyrics by Edward Paulton.)
  "Business Is Business"
    O. Figman, J. B. Carson, L. Leonard
  "Good-Bye, Happy Days"
    R. Norton
  "In Spain"
    F. deSoria
  "Lingerie"
    O. Figman, Girls
  "When a Small Town Girl Meets a Small Town Boy"[63]
    L. Leonard, R. Norton
    (Lyrics by George Edwards.)
  "Sarah from Sahara"[64]
    J. B. Carson, Girls
    (Music by Hugo Frey. Lyrics by George Edwards.)
  "Would You Say No?"
    V. Michelena, L. Leonard
ACT 2[65]
  Opening
    G. Renavent, R. Norton, L. Beaudet, Chorus
  "If It Wasn't for My Wife and Family"
    O. Figman, J. B. Carson
  "I Don't Know What You See in Me"
    L. Leonard, Girls
  "That's the Kind of a Boy for Me"[66]
    V. Michelena
  "Don't Trust Them"
    O. Figman, J. B. Carson, T. Handers, A. Millis
  Eccentric Dance
    T. Handers, A. Millis

---

[62]Fréderique de Grésac was Mrs. Victor Maurel.

[63]A Boston touring program dated 28 April 1919 credits these lyrics to George E. Stoddard.
[64]Replaced for subsequent tour by:
  "On the River Nile"
    Andrew Tombes (Simpson)
    (Lyrics by George E. Stoddard.)
[65]Added for subsequent tour to Act 2:
  "O Paradise of Love" (after Opening)
    Edna Morn (Angelina)
    (Lyrics by George E. Stoddard.)
  "Would You Love Me?" (after "If It Wasn't for My Wife")
    Rean Parker (Flo-Flo), A. Tombes
    (Lyrics by George E. Stoddard.)
[66]Dropped for subsequent tour.

"The Ziegfeld Girl"
V. Michelena, Chorus
Finale

1917.35 WORDS AND MUSIC

A Snappy (Musical) Revue in Two Acts, 10 Scenes. Words said to be by William Shakespeare and music by Ludwig Beethoven. (Sketches by Raymond Hitchcock. Music and lyrics by E. Ray Goetz.) Staged by Leon Errol. Produced by Raymond Hitchcock and E. Ray Goetz. Opened 24 December 1917 at the Fulton Theatre and closed 12 January 1918 after 24 performances.

CAST: *A Yogi, a Husband, a Lieutenant, a Toy Soldier*: WELLINGTON CROSS. *A Distinguished Playwright*, (William Shakespeare): FRANK MAYNE. *A Famous Composer*, (Ludwig Beethoven): Ben Hendricks. *The Yogi's Assistant*: Harry Seymour. *A Commuter*: Gladys Logan. *A Stenographer, an Usheress*: ANNA MAY SEYMOUR. *A Gambler*: Jay Wilson. *A Theatrical Manager, an Electrician, a Poet, A Starter*: RICHARD CARLE. *Eve*: Mildred Colby. *Helen of Troy*: Ellen Cassidy. *Circe*: Edythe Whitney. *Delilah*: Evelyn Monte. *Lucretia Borgia*: Lillian Davis. *Madamella Pompadour*: Dorothy Koffee. *Lola Montez*: Evelyn Kerner. *Cora Pearl*: Flo Hart. *Gaby Delsys, a Geisha, a French Doll*: MARION DAVIES. *A Plain Clothes Man*: Harry Tanner. *Mrs. Billings F. Cooings*, a bride: ELIZABETH BRICE. *Katie*: Dorothy Herman. *Gazzolean*, an unhappy bridesmaid: RAY DOOLEY. *Al Radish*, her second husband: WILLIAM DOOLEY. *Inbad*, a sailor: GORDON DOOLEY. *Some Others*: Jeanne Dare, Annette Bade, Mauri Madison, Martine Burnley, Dot Quintette. *A Commuteress*: Edna Aug. *Three Whirlwinds*: THE DOOLEYS (Ray, William, Gordon).

ACT 1(no complete program available; not in performance order)
Scene 1
Russian Ballet (Burlesque)
The Dooleys
Scene: A Villa on the Banks of the Oesophagus.
Scene
Drugless Drugstore
Artistic Commuter: E. Aug.
Scene 3
A Oriental Seance
Scene 4
"First Nighters"
Scene: A Theatre Lobby.
Scene 5
A Newly-Weds Apartment
Scene 6
A Street in Tokio
Scene 7
"Christmastide Love"
(*Music by* William White.)
Scene : A Nursery with Christmas Tree
ACT 2
Scene 1
An Express Elevator
Starter: R. Carle.
Scene 2
"Stop Your Camouflaging with Me" (Camouflaging)
(*Music by* Jean Schwartz.)
Scene: The Camouflage Café
Scene 3
Jass Dance
Frisco
Scene 4
"New York, What's Become of You?"
R. Carle
Scene 5
Scene 6
"Brickerty-Brackerty—Tootsies"
"Call on Rag Doll"
(*Music by* William White.)
"Everything Looks Rosy and Bright"
"Ginger"
"I May Stay Away a Little Longer"
(*Music by* Albert Von Tilzer. *Lyrics by* Lew Brown.)

"If You Hadn't Answered No"
(*Music by* Harry Ruby. *Lyrics by* Bert Kalmar, Edgar Leslie.)
"It's All Right If You Love (One Another)"
(*Music by* Harry Ruby. *Lyrics by* Edgar Leslie.)
"The Ladies"
"Lady Romance"
"March of the Enchantress"
"My Broadway Butterfly"
(*Music by* William White.)
"Nonsense"
Oriental Prelude
"They'll Be Whistling It All Over Town"
(*Music by* Jean Schwartz.)
"Wait Till the Silver Moon Rolls By"
"Walk Down the Avenue with Me"

1917.36 GOING UP

A Musical Farce in Three Acts, 6 Scenes. Book and lyrics by Otto Harbach. Based on the comedy "The Aviator" by James Montgomery. Music by Louis A. Hirsch. Staged by Edward Royce and James Montgomery. Scenery painted by Edward G. Unitt and Joseph Wickes. Ladies' gowns by Harry Collins, Lucile; men's attire by Max Marx. Orchestra under the direction of Gus Salzer. Orchestrations by Frank Saddler. Produced by George M. Cohan and Sam Harris. Opened 25 December 1917 at the Liberty Theatre and closed 26 October 1918 after 351 performances.

CAST (in order of appearance): *Miss Zonne*, a telephone girl: Ruth Donnelly. *John Gordon*, manager of the Gordon Inn: JOHN PARK. *F. H. Douglas*, a chronic bettor: DONALD MEEK. *Mrs. Douglas*, his wife: Grace Peters. *Jules Gaillard*, their prospective son-in-law, (French aviator): JOSEPH LERTORA. *Grace Douglas*, his fiancée: EDITH DAY. *Madeline Manners*, her chum: MARION SUNSHINE. *Hopkinson Brown*, her fiancé: Frank Otto. *Robert Street* author of 'Going Up': FRANK CRAVEN. *James Brooks*, his publisher: Arthur Stuart Hull. *Sam Robinson*, a mechanician: Edward Begley. *Louis*, Gaillard's mechanician: Francois Vaulry.
Pages, Ladies, Gentlemen, Guests at Gordon Inn: Miss Eleanor Pendleton, Vivian May, Mary Ward, Nancy Griffith, Helen Miller, Neida Snow, Beatrice Dwight, Catherine O'Neil, Emily Russ, Phoebe Crossley, Kitty Mahoney, Louise Kelly, Lillian Gurley, Josephine McNichol, Jeanette Cook, Eunice Sizer, Helen Neary, Virginia Watson, Messrs. Harold Grau, Edgar Gates, Charles Andrews, Maurice Walker, Willard Barger, Alexander Morrissey, Henry Dempsey, Thomas Maynard, Paul Lester, Allen K. Fagen, Richard Weeman, Lee Campbell.

Act 1: Lounging Room at Gordon Inn, Lenox, Massachusetts. (Mr. Douglas makes a bet.)

Act 2: Sitting room of Robert Street's apartment at the Inn, same evening. (Grace Douglas makes a bet.)

Act 3, Scene 1: A field near Gordon Inn, six o'clock the next afternoon. *Scene 2*: Another portion of the field. *Scene 3*: In the air, an hour later. *Scene 4*: Exterior of the hotel, one hour later.

ACT 1
Opening Number ("Paging Mr. Street")
R. Donnelly, Ensemble
"I'll Bet You"
J. Park, Ensemble
"I Want a Determined Boy" (I Want a Boy Who's Determined to Do What I Say)
M. Sunshine, F. Otto
"If You Look in Her Eyes"
E. Day, M. Sunshine
"Going Up"
J. Lertora, Ensemble
"First Act, Second Act, Third Act"[67]
F. Craven, E. Day
Finale
Entire Company
ACT 2
"The Touch of a Woman's Hand"
E. Day, Girls

---

[67]Replaced during the run by:
"When the Curtain Falls"
F. Craven, E. Day
(*Music and Lyrics by* Irving Berlin.)

"Up, Down, Left, Right"
F. Craven, F. Otto, A. S. Hull, E. Begley
"Do It for Me"
F. Otto, M. Sunshine
"(Everybody Ought To Know How to Do) The Tickle Toe"
E. Day, Ensemble
"Kiss Me"
E. Day, J. Lertora
Finale
Company

ACT 3

"There's a Brand New Hero" (Opening Chorus)
J. Lertora, M. Sunshine, Ensemble
"Here's to the Two of You"
E. Day, Ensemble
Finale
Company

1917.37   THE COHAN REVUE OF 1918

A Musical Conglomeration (Hit and Run Play Batted Out) by George M. Cohan. (A Musical Comedy in Two Acts, 15 Scenes.) Music (and lyrics) by Irving Berlin and George M. Cohan. Staged by George M. Cohan. Musical numbers staged by Jack Mason, James Gorman, George M. Cohan. Ladies' costumes by Schneider-Anderson Company; Miss Bayes' hats and gowns designed by Lucile, Ltd.; men's costumes by Eaves Costume Company; men's modern clothes by Max Marx. Orchestra under the direction of Charles J. Gebest. Orchestrations by Frank Saddler. Produced by George M. Cohan and Sam Harris. Opened 31 December 1917 at the New Amsterdam Theatre and closed 23 March 1918 after 96 performances.

CAST [in order of appearance]: *Belasco*: Charles Dow Clark. *Belasco's Office Boy*: Al Stedman. *Jazbo, the Hindoo*: IRVING FISHER. *Polly of the Follies*: NORA BAYES. *Miss Maytime*: Lila Rhodes. *Mr. Maytime*: Lou Lockett. *Miss 1918*: Lucille Romain. *Jack O'Lantern*: Hansford Wilson. *Bessie McCoy*: Jessica Brown. *Tiger Rose*: Eleanor Henry. *Bill McDevlin*: Sydney Jarvis. *Zeigfeld*: Paul Nicholson. *Potash*: Phil White. *Perlmutter*: Paul E. Burns. *Rosie Potash*: Fanny Stedman. *A Regular Tiger*: Arthur Hill. *A Spanish Bull*: Arthur Hill. *A Newsboy*: Neil Kelly. *John Paul Bart*, a tailor's hand: FREDERIC SANTLEY. *Hitchy-Koo*: Paul Nicholson. *Blond*, the King's detective: Al Stedman. *King Leo*, of Moldavia: CHARLES WINNINGER. *The King's Attendant*: John B. Dyllyn. *Tanya Huber*, the Tailor's daughter: Lila Rhodes. *Count Zucco*, the King's chamberlain: Al Stedman. *Frank Tinney*: Bert Dunlap. *Bluch*: Edward Gepp. *Frank Craven*: Murray Evans. *Jack Ibbetson*: Paul Nicholson. *Lionel Ibbetson*: Sydney Jarvis. *Marjorie Rambeau*: Sydney Jarvis. *Madame Sand*: NORA BAYES. *The He Dancer*: Lou Lockett. *The She Dancer*: Jessica Brown. *Miss Melody*: Eleanor Henry. *Mr. Words*: FREDERIC SANTLEY. *Miss Harmony*: Lila Rhodes. *Music Butler*: Al Stedman. *Music Minister*: John B. Dyllyn. *Music Writer*: Sydney Jarvis. *Music Memory*: NORA BAYES. *The Dancing Slave*: Jessica Brown. *A Slave Auctioneer*: FREDERIC SANTLEY. *Chu Chin Chow*: John B. Dyllyn. *Florence Reed*: NORA BAYES. *A Soldier Boy*: IRVING FISHER. *Corbett*: Paul Nicholson. *Bosco from the Globe*: Arthur Hill. *Tailor-Made Mitchell*: FREDERIC SANTLEY. *His Stenographer*: Sydney Jarvis. *His Secretary*: CHARLES WINNINGER. *Nathan*, his boss: Paul Nicholson. *Labor Union Men* (3): *Russell*: Sydney Jarvis. *Flynn*: Paul E. Burns. *Hart*: Phil White. *Another Minister*: Al Stedman.

Act 1, Scene 1: A Manager's Office. Scene 2: In front of the Office. Scene 3: Theatre Alley. Scene 4: In front of the Alley. Scene 5: Tailor Shop and Picture Studio. Scene 6: In front of the Tailor Shop. Scene 7: Potash and Perlmutter's Home. Scene 8: In front of their home. Scene 9: The Music Room.

Act 2, Scene 1: The Slave Market. Scene 2: In front of the Market. Scene 3: Outside the Winter Garden. Scene 4: Grant Mitchell's Office. Scene 5: In front of his office. Scene 6: The Red Cross Pavilion.

ACT 1

"(Polly) Pretty Polly" (Polly with a Past)
(*Music by* Irving Berlin. *Lyrics by* George M. Cohan.)
"Show Me the Way"
(*Music and Lyrics by* Irving Berlin.)
Ensemble
(*Music and Lyrics by* George M Cohan.)
"When Ziegfeld's Follies Hit the Town"
(*Music and Lyrics by* George M Cohan.)
"Our Acrobatic Melodramatic Home"
(*Music and Lyrics by* George M Cohan.)
"Spanish"
(*Music by* Irving Berlin. *Lyrics by* George M Cohan.)
"The Eyes of Youth See the Truth"
(*Music and Lyrics by* George M Cohan.)

"All Dresseed Up in a Tailor-Made"
(*Music and Lyrics by* George M Cohan.)
"The Potash and Perlmutter Ball"
(*Music and Lyrics by* George M Cohan.)
"A Man Is Only a Man"
(*Music and Lyrics by* Irving Berlin.)
"King of Broadway"
(*Music and Lyrics by* Irving Berlin.)
Pipes of Pan Dance
"The Wedding of Words and Music" (Fox Trot)
(*Music and Lyrics by* Irving Berlin.)

ACT 2

"The Gathering of the Slaves"
The Slave Dance
"A Bad Chinaman from Shanghai"
(*Music and Lyrics by* Irving Berlin.)
"Down Where the Jack O'Lanterns Grow"
(*Music and Lyrics by* Irving Berlin, George M. Cohan.)
Songs:
"The Old Maid Blues"
N. Bayes
(*Music by* David W. Guion. *Lyrics by* Web Maddox.)
"Who Do You Love?"
N. Bayes
(*Music by* James Brockman. *Lyrics by* Ed Moran.)
["Regretful Blues"
(*Music by* Cliff Hess. *Lyrics by* Grant Clarke.)
"The Man Who Put the Germ in Germany"]
"Their Hearts Are Over Here" I. Fisher
(*Music and Lyrics by* George M Cohan.)
Finale (Entire Company)

1918.01   EXPERIENCE

A Revival of the (Morality) Play with Music in Three Acts, 10 Scenes[68]. Play by George V. Hobart[69]. Incidental music by Max Bendix. Songs and cabaret music by Silvio Hein. Staged by George V. Hobart and J. C. Huffman. Gowns by Bendel[70]. Musical director, Jack LeBowitz. Produced by William Elliott, F. Ray Comstock and Morris Gest. Opened 22 January 1918 at the Manhattan Opera House and closed 9 February 1918 after 23 performances.[71]

CAST [in order of appearance]: *Love*: FLOY MURRAY. *Hope*: May McManus. *Youth*: RAYMOND VAN SICKLE. *Ambition*: John Todd. *Experience*: William Ingersoll. *Pleasure*: MARIE HORNE. *Opportunity*: Marion Holcombe. *Excitement*: Ebba Andrus. *Sport*: George Seybold. *Travel*: Phil M. Sheridan. *Dance*: James Bradbury, Jr. *Song*: Mary Comerford. *Fashion*: Claudia Wheeler. *Blueblood*: Guy Collins. *Style*: Courtney White. *Frivolity*: Dodo Bernard. *Conceit*: Charles Haskins. *Snob*: Duncan Harris. *Beauty*: JEAN DOWNS. *Deceit*: Blanche Crossan. *Slander*: Doris Hardy. *Pride*: Emma Wey. *Drivel*: Frank Rhoades. *Wealth*: Frazer Coulter. *Ambition*: John Todd. *Waiter*: Chet Huffman. *Intoxication*: Ada Wingard. *Passion*: Dorothy Newell. *Good Nature*: Duncan Harris. *Superstition*: Frank Rhoades. *System*: George Seybold. *Stupid*: Phil Sheridan. *Temptation*: Dodo Bernard. *Caution*: Mary Comerford. *Venture*: Doris Hardy. *Despair*: Harry J. Lane. *Chance*: George T. Meech. *Careless*: James Bradbury, Jr. *Thoughtless*: Courtney White. *Roulette Dealer*: William Betts. *Stool Pigeon*: Charles Haskins. *Waiter*: Irving Wood. *Faro Dealer*: James Paskman. *Work*: JOHN TODD. *Grouch*: WILLIAM BETTS. *Frailty*: EBBA ANDRUS. *Makeshift*: George T. Meech. *Rogue*: James Badbury, Jr. *Dissolute*: Dorothy Newell. *Sneak*: Phil M. Sheridan. *Illiterate*: Doris Hardy. *Indolence*: Ada Wingard. *Rascal*: Charles Haskins. *Waiter*: James Paskman. *Law*: GEORGE SEYBOLD. *Poverty*: Harry J. Lane. *Delusion*: PHIL M. SHERIDAN. *Habit*: EBBA ANDRUS. *Degradation*: MARION HOLCOMBE. *Crime*: GEORGE T. MEECH. *Organist*: Frank Rhoades. *Choir Singer*: Dorothy Newell.

1918.02   GIRL O' MINE

A Musical Comedy in Two Acts, 3 Scenes. Book and lyrics by Philip Bartholomae. Music by Frank Tours. Produced (staged) by Clifford Brooke

---

[68]Originally produced 27 October 1914 at the Booth Theatre for 255 performances. For Synopsis of Scenes and Musical Numbers, see original 1914 production.
[69]Adapted from a shorter One-Act, 7 Scene version which formed the closing portion of a Lamb's Club Gambol 1 March 1914.
[70]Original production credited costume design to Melville Ellis.
[71]Settings uncredited; original production credited scenery by Theodore Reisig.

and Edward P. Temple. Dancing numbers by Edward Hutchinson and Allan K. Foster. Scenery designed by Watson Barratt. Gowns, dresses and clothes by Zarah, Henri Bendel, Lucile Ltd., Mme. Kahn, S. R. Kerner Co., Finchley (men's). Orchestra under the direction of Frank Tours. Presented by Elisabeth Marbury in association with Messrs. Lee and J. J. Shubert. Opened 28 January 1918 at the Bijou Theatre and closed 9 March 1918 after 48 performances.

CAST (in order of appearance): *Chef de Gare*: Ernest Perrin. *Duc de Bouvais*: James Lounsbery. *Toby*: CARL HYSON. *Betty*: DOROTHY DICKSON. *Lulu*: EDNA WALLACE HOPPER. *Charlie*: BARRATT GREENWOOD. *Teddy*: DAVID QUIXANO. *Lily*: MARIE NORDSTROM. *Jack*: FRANK FAY. *Mildred*: HELEN LEE. *A Waiter*: Charles Burrows. *Greene*: Carlton Macy. *Maître d'Hotel*: Ernest Perrin.

All Important to Plot: Misses Elizabeth Moffat, Clarissa Stem, Cynthia Randolph, Virginia Curtis, Charlotte Wakefield, Carolyn Nunder. *Equally Important*: Misses Charlotte Stevenson, Kathryn Rahn, Kathleen Quain, Ruth Rollins, Sylvia Cassell, Virginia Gunther. *Also*: Messrs. Robert H. Casey, Irving Carter, Leo Howe, Joseph McCallion, Stanley Rayburn, Frank Ervin.

Act 1, Scene 1: Railway Station in Paris. *Scene 2*: Winter Garden of a Fashionable Hotel in Paris. Three days later.

Act 2: Café in the same hotel. Three days later.

ACT 1[72]

"The Winning Race" (Trio)
B. Greenwood, C. Hyson, J. Lounsbery

"Not So Fast" (Duet)
D. Dickson, B. Greenwood

"The Birdies in the Trees" (Duet)
M. Nordstrom, F. Fay

"Love Is Just a Fairy Tale"[73] (Song)
H. Lee

Dancing Lesson[74]
C. Hyson, Ensemble

"The Woman Pays" (It's the Woman Who Pays)(Trio)
M. Nordstrom, B. Greenwood, F. Fay

"I Like to Play with the Boys" (Song)
D. Dickson, Ensemble

"A Comic Camouflage"
F. Fay

"Girl o' Mine"[75] (Duet, a novelty)
H. Lee, D. Quixano

Dance
D. Dickson, C. Hyson

"Shrug Your Shoulders"[76] (Song)
E. W. Hopper, Girls

"Every Cloud Is Silver-Lined" (Duet)
D. Dickson, B. Greenwood

ACT 2

"Rug, Snug"[77] (Quartette)
M. Nordstrom, E. W. Hopper, F. Fay, J. Lounsbery

"Telephone Song" (Duet)
H. Lee, D. Quixano

Dance
D. Dickson, C. Hyson

"To-day Is the Day"[78] (Duet)
M. Nordstrom, F. Fay

"Omar Khayyam" (Song)
D. Quixano

"Changing Styles" (Song)
M. Nordstrom

"Saturday Night"[79] (Ensemble)
B. Greenwood, Ensemble

Finale
Entire Company

"My Service Flag"
E. W. Hopper, Ensemble

1918.03

OH, LADY! LADY!

A Musical Comedy in Two Acts[80]. Book and lyrics by Guy Bolton and P. G. Wodehouse. Music by Jerome Kern. Staged by Robert Milton and Edward Royce. Costumes designed by Harry Collins. Scenery designed by Clifford Pember. Orchestrations by Frank Saddler. Produced by F. Ray Comstock and William Elliott. Opened 1 February 1918 at the Princess Theatre, moved 17 June 1918 to the Casino Theatre and closed 10 August 1918 after 219 performances.

CAST (in order of appearance): *Parker*: CONSTANCE BINNEY. *Mollie Farrington*: VIVIENNE SEGAL. *Mrs. Farrington*: Margaret Dale. *Willoughby Finch*: CARL RANDALL. *Hale Underwood*: HARRY C. BROWNE. *Spike Hudgins*, Willoughby Finch's valet: EDWARD ABELES. *Fanny Welch*: FLORENCE SHIRLEY. *May Barber*: CARROLL McCOMAS. *Cyril Twombley*: Reginald Mason. *William Watty*: Harry Fisher. *Miss Lettice Romayne*: Lois Whitney. *Miss Lotta Pommery*: Bobby Brewster. *Miss Della Catessen*: May Elsie. *Miss Hallie Butt*: Elsie Lewis. *Miss Sal Munn*: Dorothy Allan. *Miss Marie Schino*: Billie Booker. *Miss Mollie Gatawney*: Mildred Fisher. *Miss Marion Etta Herring*: Edna Hettler. *Miss C. Ella Rhy*: Gipsey Mooney. *Miss Barbara O'Rhum*: Mildred Roland. *Miss Clarette Cupp*: Jeanne Sparry. *Miss May Anne Ayes*: Mabel Stanford. *Miss Cassie Roll*: Janet Velie. *Miss Virginia Hamm*: Bettie Gereaux. *Mr. Artie C. Hoke*: William Walsh. *Mr. B. Russell Sprout*: Charles Hartman. *Mr. C. Ollie Flower*: Charles Columbus. *Mr. H. Ash-Brown*: J. Randall Phelan. *Mr. Stewart Prune*: Jack Vincent. *Mr. Con Kearney*: Irving Jackson.

Act 1: Living Room of the Farrington Place at Hempstead, Long Island.

Act 2: Roof Garden of Willoughby Finch's Studio in Waverly Mews.

ACT 1

Scene Music (Wedding Day)

"I'm To Be Married Today"
V. Segal, Girls

"Not Yet" (Duet)
V. Segal, C. Randall

"Do It Now" (Trio)
H. C. Browne, E. Abeles, C. Randall

"Our Little Nest"
E. Abeles, F. Shirley

"Do Look at Him!"[81]
V. Segal, Girls

"Oh, Lady! Lady!"
C. Randall, Girls

"You Found Me and I Found You"
C. McComas, H. C. Browne

Finaletto
Company Ensemble

ACT 2

"Moon" (The Moon Song)(Opening)
J. Sparry, Ensemble

Dance
C. Binney, J. R. Phelan

"Waiting Around the Corner"
C. McComas, Boys

"Little Ships Come Sailing Home"[82] (When the Ships Come Home)
V. Segal, Girls

"Before I Met You"
C. Randall, V. Segal

---

[72]The running order of songs was revised during the run.

[73]Dropped during the run and replaced by "Omar Khayyam" from Act 2.

[74]Dropped during the run.

[75]During the run moved to Act 2 before "Changing Styles."

[76]Dropped during the run and replaced by:

[77]Dropped during the run and replaced by "To-day Is the Day."

[78]After opening, moved to open Act 2 and replaced by:

"Fatal Step"
B. Greenwood, Ensemble

[79]Replaced during the run by:

"Toddler's Ball"
E. W. Hopper

[80]Billed as the fifth New York Princess Theatre Musical Production.

[81]Replaced second month after opening by:

"Little Ships Come Sailing Home" (When the Ships Come Home)
V. Segal, Girls

[82]Replaced second month after opening by:

"The Sun Starts to Shine Again"
V. Segal, Girls

"Greenwich Village" (Trio)
C. Randall, E. Abeles, F. Shirley
"Wheatless Days"[83] (Duet)
H. C. Browne, C. McComas
"It's a Hard, Hard World for a Man"
C. Randall, H. C. Browne, R. Mason
Finale
Ensemble

1918.04

THE LOVE MILL

A Musical Comedy in Two Acts. Book and lyrics by Earl Carroll. (Based on a German farce 'Training for the Marriage Market' by Envel and Stobitzer.) Music by Alfred Francis. Staged by Mack Whiting. Scenery painted by Joseph Physioc. Orchestra under the direction of Louis Kroll. Presented by Andreas Dippel. Opened 7 February 1918 at the 48th Street Theatre and closed 23 March 1918 after 52 performances.[84]

CAST: *Mrs. Carter Beaumont*: GRACE FISHER. *Mrs. Thompson*: JEANNETTE LOWRIE. *Their Daughters (3)*: *Millie Thompson*: CARRIE McMANUS. *Lucille Thompson*: EMILIE LEA. *Peggy Thompson*: YOLANDE PRESBURY. *Count Aladair Calman Maria Przeaprodensky*: AL ROBERTS. *George Dodge*: HARRY TIGHE. *William King*: VICTOR MORLEY. *Tom Morris*: CLARENCE NORDSTROM. *James*: Edward Richards. *Henry*: Joseph Bennett. *Fifi*: Frances Fielder. *Peggy's Friends (8)*: *Laura*: Daisy Burton. *Olive*: Addie Clark. *Vivian*: Lillian Daley. *Elsie*: Helen Borden. *Marcelle*: Pauline Carlton. *Ida*: Frances Fielder. *Lillian*: Adele Fielder. *Lauretta*: Dorothy Clay. *Friends of Mrs. Carter Beaumont (4)*: *Mrs. Bellemill*: Valerie Clark. *Mrs. Vandermill*: Irene Hayes. *Mrs. Crownmill*: Tessie Hammer. *Mrs. Doughmill*: Eileen Clinton. *Dance Specialties*: Cortez and Peggy, Vera Meyers, Margaret Philpot.

Little Girls from Department Stores: Vera Meyers, Dency Davidson, Margaret Philpot, Juliet Strahl, Adrienne Allen, Gertrude Mansfield. *Tennis Boys*: Joe Miller, G. L. Mortimer, George Ross, W. Deacon, F. H. Hagenmeyer, Fred Jones.

Act 1: The Drawing Room of the Thompson House. Mt. Vernon. Summer.

Act 2: The Thompson Rose Garden and Patio. One year later.

ACT 1

Opening Chorus
"(I May Look Strong, But) I'm Far from Healthy"
C. McManus
"Follow Mamma's Advice"
J. Lowrie, C. McManus, E. Lea, Y. Presbury
"When You Feel a Little Longing (in Your Heart)"
Y. Presbury, C. Nordstrom, Girls, Boys
"Przeaprodensky" (Prseprodensky)
A. Roberts, Girls
"Down the Bridal Path of Love"
G. Fisher
"The Seaside Buccaneer"
A. Roberts, Boys, Girls
"In the State of Matrimony"
Y. Presbury, C. Nordstrom, Boys, Girls
"The Love Mill"
G. Fisher
Finale
Entire Company

ACT 2
"Every Flower Has a Melody"
Ensemble
"Why Can't It All Be a Dream?"
G. Fisher
"Where the Cotton Blossoms Grow"
Y. Presbury, C. Nordstrom, Boys, Girls
"Watch the Things You Eat"
E. Lea, H. Tighe

---

[83]Replaced second month after opening by:
"A Picture I Want to See" (from MISS 1917)
H. C. Browne, C. McComas
[84]Costume design uncredited. Credited to Harry Collins prior to New York.

"We Must Hooverize"
C. McManus, V. Morley
"I Loved Him for He Loved (the Love) that I Loved"
G. Fisher
"It's the Women" (Trio)
A. Roberts, V. Morley, H. Tighe
"Q.T.U.C.I.M.4.U." (Cutie, You See I Am For You)
Y. Presbury, C. Nordstrom, Ensemble
Finale
Entire Company

1918.05

SINBAD

A Musical Extravaganza in Two Acts, 14 Scenes. Book and lyrics by Harold Atteridge. Music by Sigmund Romberg, (Al Jolson, Jean Schwartz, Harry Tierney, Turner Layton, Albert Gumble). (Additional lyrics by Buddy G. DeSylva, Gus Kahn, Alfred Bryan, Jack Yellen, Sam Lewis, Joe Young, Henry Creamer, Irving Caesar.) Staged by J. C. Huffman and J. J. Shubert. Dances arranged by Jack Mason. Scenery designed by Watson Barratt. Costumes designed by Homer Conant, Cora MacGeachy, S. Zalud. Orchestra under the direction of Oscar Radin. Produced by Messrs. Lee and J. J. Shubert. Opened 14 February 1918 at the Winter Garden and closed 6 July 1918 after 164 performances; re-opened 2 September 1918 at the Century Theatre, moved 14 October 1918 to the Casino Theatre, moved 11 November 1918 to the Winter Garden, moved 10 February 1919 to the 44th Street Theatre, and closed 29 March 1919 after 240 additional performances. Total for all engagements: 404 performances.

CAST (in order of appearance): *Harriet*: Grace Washburn. *Mildred*: Nora White. *Marcelle*: Beth Young. *Doris*: Doris Benham. *Pearl*: Pearl Germond. *Gertrude*: Gertrude Doyle. *Marian*: Marian Stokes. *Beatrice*: Beatrice Cloak. *Grace*: Grace Langdon. *Jack*: F. A. BATIE. *Harry*: Frank Holmes. *Gus*: AL JOLSON. *Mildred*: Nora White. *Mack*: Bob McClellan. *Betty*: Jessie Reed. *Vivian*: Florence Elmore. *Isabel*: Pearl Germond. *Florence*: Mildred LaGue. *Helen*: Vera Mercer. *Beatrice*: Thelma Turnball. *Nan*: Virginia Fox Brooks. *Tony*: Harry Kearley. *A Yogi*: John Kearney. *A Cobbler*: FRANKLYN A. BATIE. *A Slave Girl*: Virginia Fox Brooks. *The King of Serendib*: LAWRENCE D'ORSAY. *The Queen of Serendib*: FRITZI VON BUSING. *A Court Lady*: Grace Washburn. *Prince Stubb*: KITTY DONER. *Princess Audrey*: MABEL WITHEE. *Inbad, the Porter*: AL JOLSON. *Emil, Inbad's donkey*: George Thornton. *Kassin*: EDGAR ATCHISON ELY. *Amina*: HAZELL COX. *Geni*: John Kearney. *A Servant*: Harry Kearley. *Kickem*: Frank Grace. *Tapem*: Johnny Berkes. *Tessie*: CONSTANCE FARBER. *Jeanette*: IRENE FARBER. *El Orient*: ALEX KOSLOFF. *Queen Butterfly*: Mlle. Rita (Zalmani). *Fareast*: Roshanara. *Ali Baba*: Florence Elmore. *Wine*: Grace Keeshon. *Song*: Marian Mooney *Beauty*: JESSIE REED. *Style*: Thelma Turnball. *Inspiration*: Rae Hartley. *Vampire*: Grace Washburn. *Modesty*: Jean Thomas. *Passion*: Mildred LaGue. *Devotion*: Marian Stokes. *Goodfellowship*: CONSTANCE FARBER. *Love*: HAZELL COX. *Leonora*: Beth Young. *Patricia*: HAZELL COX. *Van*: FORREST HUFF. *Stephen*: LAWRANCE D'ORSAY. *Mrs. Van Decker*: FRITZI VON BUSING. *Professor Graves*: EDGAR ATCHISON ELY. *Johnny*: Johnny Berkes. *Frank*: Frank Grace.

Winter Garden Blue Ribbon Girls: *Margaret*: Margaret Ferguson. *Dorothy*: Dorothy Bruce. *Charlotte*: Charlotte Marmont. *Rae*: Rae Hartley. *Beatrice*: Beatrice Seymour. *May*: May Bell. *Doris*: Doris Benham. *Jean*: Jean Morgan. *Betty*: Betty Touraine. *Eleanor*: Eleanor Franko. *Beatrice*: Beatrice Cloak. *Grace*: Grace Langdon.

Ladies of the Ensemble: *Show Girls*: Jessie Reed, Florence Elmore, Mildred LaGue, Rae Hartley, Vera Mercer, Marian Mooney, Grace Keeshon, Barbara McCree, Pearl Germond, Marian Stokes, Isabel Whitney, Eleanor Leigh, Thelma Turnball, Mabel Cloud, Marie Lorillard, Flo Landreaux, Evangeline Murray, Eleanor Franke, Jean Troutman, Jane Adams, Fay Tunis, Beatrice Cloak, Doris Benham, Jean Morgan, Gertrude Doyle, Grace Langdon, Alice Van Ryker, Billie Sheridan. *Dancers*: Viola Clarens, Inez Frances, Elsie LaMont, Irene Mitchell, Edith Pierce, Florence Wilde, Trixie Raymond, Monica Boulais, Rose Boulais, Rheba Stewart, Edna Whitney, Ona Hamilton, Gertrude Reynolds, Lois Leigh, Jean Thomas, Ella Foster, Mattie Gormley, Laralda Poppany, Yvette Reals, Kitty Holton, Peggy Purtell, Dot Bryant, Mae Terresfield, Mildred Kaye. *Gentlemen of the Ensemble*: Jack Laughlin, Chandler Waldo, Milus Carpenter, Van Buren Hartman, Richard Warner, Billy Marr, Henry LeVoy, Wade Riesemy, George Baker.

Act 1, Scene 1: North Shore Country—Amateur Dog Show. *Scene 2*: Golf Shelter. *Scene 3*: A Street in Bagdad. *Scene 4*: In the Perfumed East. *Scene 5*: The Palace of Sinbad. *Scene 6*: Cabin of the Good Ship *Whale*. *Scene 7*: Deck of the *Whale*. *Scene 8*: A Raft on the Briny Deep.

Act 2, Scene 1: Grotto of the Valley of Diamonds. *Scene 2*: Hindu Snake Dance. *Scene 3*: Somewhere on the Isle of Eternal Youth. *Scene 4*: The Island of Eternal Youth. *Scene 5*: Golf Shelter. *Scene 6*: Garden of the North Shore Country Club.

ACT 1[85]

"On Cupid's Green"
N. White, Boy and Girl Golfers

"A Little Bit of Every Nationality"
H. Cox, Our Allied Beauties

"Our Ancestors"
K. Doner, M. Withee, Cave Men and Girls

"A Thousand and One Arabian Nights"
F. A. Batie, V. F. Brooks, F. Huff

"Where Do They Get Those Guys?"[86]
C. Farber

"Beauty and Beast"
G. Washburn, Blue Ribbon Girls, Meehan's Leaping Hounds

"Rock-a-Bye Your Baby with a Dixie Melody"
A. Jolson
(*Music by* Jean Schwartz. *Lyrics by* Joe Young, Sam Lewis.)

"(Why Do They All Take the) Night Boat to Albany?"
A. Jolson
(*Music by* Jean Schwartz. *Lyrics by* Joe Young, Sam Lewis.)

"Bagdad"
F. A. Batie, Arabian Desert Girls

"The Rag Lad of Bagdad"
K. Doner, M. Withee, F. Grace, J. Berkes, Rag Lad Girls
(*Music by* Al Jolson, Sigmund Romberg.)

"A Night in the Orient"
H. Cox, Oriental Dancers

"Cleopatra"
A. Jolson
(*Music by* Harry Tierney. *Lyrics by* Alfred Bryan.)

(Selection, see footnote below
A. Jolson)

"I Hail from Cairo"
C. Farber, Cairo Girls

Guests Ballet
Roshanara, A. Kosloff, Magic Lamp Dancers

"Love Ahoy!"
I. Farber, F. Grace, J. Berkes, Love Ahoy Sailor Girls

ACT 2[87]

"The Bedalumbo"
K. Doner, F. Grace, J. Berkes, Yama Yama Girls
(*Music by* Al Jolson.)

Butterfly Ballet
A. Kosloff, Mlle. Rita, Butterfly Girls

Snake Dance
Roshanara, E. West, P. Dale, H. Link, J. Rhys, A. D'Walle, M. Palya

"Isle of Youth"
H. Cox, Beauties of Greece

"I'll Tell the World"
F. Huff, Isle of Youth Dreams
(*Music and Lyrics by* Buddy G. DeSylva and Harold Atteridge.)

---

[85]Specialty also performed during the New York run:
"How'd You Like to Be My Daddy?"
Farber Sisters
(*Music by* Ted Snyder. *Lyrics by* Sam M. Lewis, Joe Young.)
"I'm Not Jealous (But I Just Don't Like It)"
Farber Sisters
(*Music by* Ed. G. Nelson and Fred Mayo. *Lyrics by* Harry Pease.)
[86]Dropped for subsequent national tour.
[87]Added for national tour following final New York engagement:
"Everybody Wonders Why They Love Me?" (Philadelphia, October 1919)
Farber Sisters
Alexander's Band
Farber Sisters
"Hold Me" (tour, n.d.)
Virginia Smith, Hold Me Girls
"Rose" (Los Angeles, April 1921)
V. Smith, Rose Girls

Selections[88]
A. Jolson

"It's Wonderful"
M. Withee, Some Wonderful Girls

"Raz-Ma-Taz"
K. Doner, F. Grace, J. Berkes, Jazz Girls
(*Music by* Al Jolson. .)

1918.06   # FOLLOW THE GIRL

A Musical Comedy in Three Acts, 4 Scenes. Book and lyrics by Henry Blossom. Music by Zoel Parenteau, (Sigmund Romberg. Additional lyrics by Harold Atteridge.) Staged by J. C. Huffman. Dances arranged by Walter Brooks. Scenery by Edward G. Unitt and Joseph Wickes. Dresses by Joseph. Orchestra under the direction of Frank Tours. Produced by Raymond Hitchcock and E. Ray Goetz. Opened 2 March 1918 at the 44th Street Roof Theatre, moved 18 March 1918 to the Broadhurst Theatre and closed 23 March 1918 after 25 performances.

CAST: *T. Lyman Niles*, banker and broker: WILLIAM DANFORTH. *Mrs. Niles*, his wife: JOBYNA HOWLAND. *Gladys Niles*, his daughter: EILEEN VAN BIENE. *Fifine*, Mrs. Niles' maid: Alice Ryan. *Senor Guillereno Barbarento*, an Argentine: ROBERT O'CONNOR. *Edwina Blake*, known as Teddy: MERCEDES LORENZE. *Alfred Vanderveer*, known as Freddy: HARRY FENDER. *Buck Sweeney*, his friend: WALTER CATLETT. *Brophy*, head bell man: Richard Tabor. *Hotel Clerk*: Claude E. Archer. *Albert Vanderveer*, known as Bertie: Charles Clear. *Mrs. Vanderveer*, his mother: Ann Warrington. *Rev. Jonas Tod, D.D.*: Ralph Nairne. *William Tell*, proprietor of "Come On Inn": GEORGE L. BICKEL. *Mademoiselle Anna*, modiste: Louise White. *Washington*, colored bell boy: William Everett. *Mlle. Rizpaz*, a dancer: Ernestine Myers.

Guests at the Hotel: *Tennis Girls*: Nancy Everett, Peggy Dempsey, Aileen Rooney, Dorothy Godfrey. *Motor Girls*: Rita Faust, May Jennings. *Ouja Girls*: Ethel Rinehart, Marie Stone. *Yachting Girls*: Frances Ross, Claire Vernon, Courtney Palmer, Bessie Gross, Maurie Madison, Jean Rebara. *Bathing Girls*: Louise Saunders, Anna Berg, Helen O'Day, Ivy Sherer, Jane Berlyn, Phyllis Prince, Grace Weeks, Nonita Naldi. *Gentlemen Guests*: Arthur Wilson, Byrd Goolsby, Tom Doolan, Frank Peters, Roy Adams, Albert Shrubb.

Act 1: Piazza of the Grand View Hotel, Maine. Forenoon.

Act 2, Scene 1: Same as Act 1. Evening of the same day. *Scene 2*: The Lake.

Act 3: At the "Come On Inn." Later the same evening.

ACT 1

Opening Chorus
Ensemble

---

[88]Jolson's Specialty Songs included:
"I Wonder Why She Kept on Saying 'Si, Si, Si, Si, Senor'"
(*Music by* Ted Snyder. *Lyrics by* Sam Lewis, Joe Young.)
"'N Everything" (And Everything)
(*Music by* Al Jolson. *Lyrics by* Buddy G. DeSylva, Gus Kahn.)
"Tell That to the Marines"
(*Music by* Jean Schwartz and Al Jolson. *Lyrics by* Harold Atteridge.)
Following the summer 1918 layoff, his specialties included:
"Hello Central! Give Me No Man's Land"
(*Music by* Jean Schwartz. *Lyrics by* Sam Lewis, Joe Young.)
"I'll Say She Does"
(*Music by* Al Jolson. *Lyrics by* Buddy G. DeSylva, Gus Kahn.)
"On the Road to Calais"
(*Music by* Jean Schwartz, Al Jolson. *Lyrics by* Alfred Bryan.)
Later on national tour, the specialties included:
"By the Honeysuckle Vine"
(*Music by* Al Jolson. *Lyrics by* Buddy G. DeSylva.)
"I Gave Her That"
(*Music by* Al Jolson. *Lyrics by* Buddy G. DeSylva.)
"Chloe"
(*Music by* Al Jolson. *Lyrics by* Buddy G. DeSylva.)
"Swanee"
(*Music by* George Gershwin. *Lyrics by* Irving Caesar.)
"Avalon"
(*Music and Lyrics by* Al Jolson, Buddy G. DeSylva, Vincent Rose.)
"My Mammy"
(*Music by* Walter Donaldson. *Lyrics by* Sam Lewis, Joe Young.)
"You're a Better Man Than I Am Gungadin"
(*Music by* Nat Osborne. *Lyrics by* Sam Ehrlich.)

"Follow the Girl" (Duet)
R. Tabor, A. Ryan
"I Like the Boys" (Song)
M. Lorenze, Chorus
"I Can't Love One and All" (Song)
E. Van Biene, Chorus
"Easy Come, Easy Go" (Trio)
W. Catlett, M. Lorenze, H. Fender
"There's Always One You Can't Forget" (Duet)
E. Van Biene, H. Fender
"Everything Is Rosy Now" (Duet)
M. Lorenze, W. Catlett, Chorus
(*Music by* Buddy G. DeSylva. *Lyrics by* Harold Atteridge.)

ACT 2
"Swing Song" (Duet)
E. Van Biene, H. Fender
"I Wish That Girls Could Go to War" (Song)
M. Lorenze, Chorus
"Ever By Your Side" (Duet)
E. Van Biene, H. Fender
(*Music by* Sigmund Romberg. *Lyrics by* Harold Atteridge.)
"Women, Wine and Jazz" (Duet)
M. Lorenze, W. Catlett, Chorus

ACT 3
Opening Chorus
Ensemble
Specialty Dance
E. Myers
"Honeymoon Land" (Duet)
E. Van Biene, H. Fender
(*Music by* Sigmund Romberg. *Lyrics by* Harold Atteridge.)
"I'm Through With Girls" (Song)
H. Fender, Girls
"You're the Only One for Me" (Chinese Fox Trot)
W. Catlett, M. Lorenze, Ensemble
"I'm Married, I'm Single, I'm Divorced and I'm in Love" (Quartette)
R. Nairne, W. Catlett, R. O'Connor, H. Fender
Finale

1918.07

OH, LOOK!

A Musical Comedy in Two Acts, 3 Scenes. Book by James Montgomery, suggested by his farce "Ready Money." Music by Harry Carroll. Lyrics by Joseph McCarthy. Dances arranged by David Bennett. Scenery by H. Robert Law. Costumes by Faibsey and Paul Arlington, Inc. Orchestra under the direction of Theodore Stearns. Produced by Harry Carroll and William Sheer. Opened 7 March 1918 at the Vanderbilt Theater and closed 4 May 1918 after 68 performances.[89]

CAST: *Stephen Baird*: HARRY FOX. *Sidney Rosenthal*: George Sidney. *Sam Welch*: ALFRED KAPPELER. *William Stewart*: CLARENCE NORDSTROM. *James E. Morgan*: Alexander F. Frank. *Hon. John H. Tyler*: Albert Sackett. *Jackson Ives*, an international character: Frederick Burton. *Captain West*, a detective: HARRY KELLY. *Neil*: Charles Mussett. *James Clark*: Ted Wing. *Grace Tyler*: LOUISE COX. *Genevieve Tyler*: GENEVIEVE TOBIN. *Mrs. John H. Tyler*: Amelia Gardner. *Margy Elliott*: Florence Bruce. *Bertha Smith*: Betty Hope Hale. *Peggy Warburton*: Mildred Sinclair. *Frances Huntley*: Betty Hamilton. *Ethel Bennett*: Francis Grant. *Maud Reid*: Elsie Gordon *Marion Brokaw*: Elsa Thomas. *Ruth Francis*: Emily Morrison.
Girls: Julia Ross, Gertrude Hamilton, Allison Worth, Lillian McKenzie, Ethel Kinley, Dolly Griffith, Laura Hastings, Ruth Sawyer, Genevieve Markham, Dorothy Harrigan, Beatrice Burrows, Florence Lee, Doris Sheerin. *Boys*: Stanley Dale, Alfred Waldon, Al Eley, George Griffin, Jack Gulick, Carl Meeker, Frank Rowe, Jack Rogers.

Act 1: The Home of Sam Welch, Long Island. The day before the Fourth.

Act 2: The Conservatory. The night of the Fourth.

ACT 1[90]
Opening
Ensemble
"I Know"[91]
G. Tobin, C. Nordstrom
"(Wherever There's Music and) Beautiful Girls"
G. Sidney, A. Kappeler, C. Nordstrom
"I'm Always Chasing Rainbows"[92]
H. Fox
"The Good Little Things We Do"[93]
L. Cox
"I Think She's Absolutely Wonderful"[94] (What Do You Think of Me)
G. Tobin, H. Fox
"Far Apart Still You're in My Heart"[95]
L. Cox
"You're a Young Little Old-Fashioned Girl" (An Old-Fashioned Girl)
G. Tobin, C. Nordstrom
Finale
Ensemble

ACT 2
"Changeable Girls"[96]
L. Cox, Chorus
"Typical Topical Tunes"
H. Fox
"A Kiss for Cinderella"
L. Cox, H. Fox
"I'm Just a Good Man"[97]
H. Kelly
"It's a Long Way to Tiffany's"[98]
G. Tobin, C. Nordstrom
"Moonbeams"[99]
Grant and Wing
"(We Will Live for) Love and Love Alone"[100]
L. Cox, H. Fox

[90]The production was revised around the talents of the Dolly Sisters for its subsequent tour under the auspices of producers F. Ray Comstock and Morris Gest. Added were:
"I Want to Marry" (Act 1)
Roszika and Yancsi Dolly (Grace and Genevieve), Male Ensemble
"Tell Me Why" (Act 1)
R. Dolly, Ben Harrison (Steven Baird), Y. Dolly, Hal Van Rensselaer (William Stewart)
(*Music by* Vincent Rose. *Lyrics by* Richard Coburn.)
"Sweethearts" (Act 2)
Robert Ames (Welch), Ensemble
"The Dolly Twinkle" (Act 2)
Dolly Sisters
(*Lyrics by* Joseph McCarthy, Edward Royce.)
"(My) Isle of Golden Dreams" (Act 2)
Dolly Sisters, Ensemble
(*Music by* Walter Blaufuss. *Lyrics by* Gus Kahn.)
"Vamp a Little Lady" (The Vamp)(Act 2, before Finale)
Dolly Sisters, Ensemble
(*Music and Lyrics by* Byron Gay.)
[91]Dropped for national tour with the Dolly Sisters.
[92]Music based on Chopin's "Fantasie Impromptu in C Sharp Minor."
[93]Dropped for national tour with the Dolly Sisters.
[94]Revised for tour as "I Think You're Absolutely Wonderful."
[95]In the second month of the run, "Far Apart Still You're in My Heart" and "You're a Young Little Old-Fashioned Girl" were replaced by:
"These Colors Will Not Run" (dropped for Dolly Sisters tour)
C. Nordstrom
[96]Dropped for national tour with the Dolly Sisters.
[97]Dropped for national tour with the Dolly Sisters.
[98]Dropped for national tour with the Dolly Sisters.
[99]Dropped for national tour with the Dolly Sisters.
[100]Dropped for national tour with the Dolly Sisters.

[89]No directorial credits appear in programs or reviews for the New York engagement. Subsequent Comstock-Gest tour credits Robert Milton and Edward Royce as co-directors

"Sunkissed Land"[101]
Ensemble
Finale
Ensemble

1918.08

LET'S GO

A Costless, Castless, Careless (Musical) Revue in Two Acts, a Prologue and 19 Scenes[102]. (Staged by William Rock.) Musical director, Ernest Golden. (Produced by William Rock and Frances White.) Opened 9 March 1918 at the Fulton Theatre and closed 30 March 1918 after 25 performances.[103]

CAST: WILLIAM ROCK, FRANCES WHITE, BEATRICE HERFORD, FRANK DOANE, BOBBY EDWARDS, Yvonne Garrick, Jack Magee, Beatrice Palmer, Dorothy Ellsworth, Loretta McDermott, Gick Watson, New York Clef Club (Singers and Players), SMITH and AUSTIN.

Chorus: Misses Martine Burnley, Emma Dare, Jean Dare, Sadie Howard, Betty Fratini, Dorothy Bailey, Ethel Deane, Monte Walsh, Elsie Lewis.

ACT 1[104]
Prologue
 Scene: Office of Robert Fulton, Theatrical Manager.
  Robert Fulton, a manager: J. Magee. *A Stenographer*: G. Watson. *William Rock*, an actor: W. Rock. *Frances White*, his partner: F. White.
Scene 1
 "The Newspaper Girl"
  (*Music and Lyrics by* E. Ray Goetz.)
  D. Ellsworth, Hooverized Chorus
  Scene: Newspaper Row.
  Note—Average cost of costumes, 10¢. Scenery, $11.50.
Scene 2
 Old Songs and New
  W. Rock, F. White
  (a) W. Rock, F. White
 Fern Song from THE ORCHID
  W. Rock
 "Flower Garden Ball"
  F. White
 "I'm Only a Poor Little Kid"
  W. Rock, F. White
  Note—Scene rented for $25 per week.
Scene 3
 Smith and Austin will hold the stage for a few moments.
  Note—Drop discovered in an alley.
Scene 4
 A Denatured Sister Act
  D. Ellsworth, B. Palmer
  Note—Scenery and furniture rented for $25 a week, payable in advance.
Scene 5
 New Dances to Old Tunes
  W. Rock, F. White
  Note—Scenery rented for $25 a week.

Scene 6
 Miss Beatrice Herford
  Note—Scene loaned; table and chair built by Miss Herford. Cost of lumber, 67¢.
Scene 7
 "Since Daddy's Gone Away"[105]
  F. White
 "Dictionary Song"
  W. Rock, F. White
  Scene: A Nursery.
  Note—Furniture rented, $10 a week.
Scene 8
 A Few Minutes of Vaudeville
  Smith and Austin
  Note—Scenery you have seen before.
Scene 9
 The Old First Nighter
 "The Land of Yesteryear"
  (*Music and Lyrics by* E. Ray Goetz.)
  Old First Nighter: W. Rock. *The Waiter*: B. Edwards. *Delehanty and Dengler*: Smith and Austin. *Lotta Faust*: F. White. *Richard Mansfield*: W. Rock. *Pete Dailey*: J. Magee. *Fritzi Scheff*: F. White. *The Rogers Brothers*: Smith and Austin. __: G. Watson. __: M. Walsh.
  Note—Cost of Properties and Stereopticon, $100. Principals' costumes, $100. Chorus Costumes, $80.

After the Intermission, The Clef Club Singers and Players will entertain you (with Spirituals and Plantation Songs). The members of The Clef Club do not use Mennen's Talcum Powder.

ACT 2
Scene 1
 "Swede Song"[106]
  W. Rock, F. White
 "The Pessimist"
  W. Rock
 "What Do I Care?"
  F. White
  Scene: A Railroad Station.
  Note—Scene used in Act 1. Properties, $8.
Scene 2
 "Why Can't a Girl Be a Soldier?"[107]
  G. Watson, Smith and Austin, Chorus
  Scene: A Military Tableau.
  Note—Cost of properties, $24. Scenery used in Act 1.
Scene 3
 Miss Beatrice Herford
  Note—Scenery and properties used in Act 1.
Scene 4
 "The Inevitable"[108] (Pantomime Dance)
  W. Rock, F. White
  Note—Scenery used in Act 1. Furniture rented.
Scene 5
 Professor J. Edmund Magee, A Scientific Demonstrator of Hypnotism and Levitation.
  Note—Scenery used in Act 1.
Scene 6
 "The Flower Garden Girls"
  D. Ellsworth, B. Palmer, Chorus
  Note—Scenery rented, $25 a week. Costumes of costumes, $25 each.
Scene 7
 Smith and Austin's Canines in a Day in Curville[109]
  Note—Scene used in Act 1. Cost of Properties, $40.

---

[101]Dropped for national tour with the Dolly Sisters.
[102]The following note appears on the title page of the program: In keeping with the spirit of the times this Hooverized Revue has been produced at a total cost of $996.20 for costumes and scenery. This establishes a new record in producing a complete evening's musical entertainment on Broadway. All costumes worn by Mr. Rock and Miss White throughout the entertainment are selected from their personal wardrobes. Miss White is indebted to Mr. DeSoto for discovering the Mississippi River.
[103]Sketches, music and lyrics uncredited. Scenery on rental; costumes from personal wardrobe of the players.
[104]Added for second week of the run:
 The Infernal Triangle (A Vaudeville Travesty by George Abbott and Frederick Wallace) *Scene*: A luxuriously furnished apartment on Riverside Drive. *Husband*: F. Doane. *Wife*: Y. Garrick. Note—Cost of scenery, $24.50.
 Twelve Feet of Drama (sketch)
 "Have You Seen the Ducks Go By" (from HITCHY-KOO, 1917) F. White, Chorus (*Music by* Felix Powell. *Lyrics by* E. Ray Goetz.) *Scene*: On the Farm. Note—Cost of costumes, $100.

---

[105]"Since Daddy's Gone Away" and "Dictionary Song" dropped for second week.
[106]Scene dropped for second week of the run, and replaced by:
 Ketcham and Cheatem in "A Breeze from the West"
  Note—Scenery used in Act 1.
[107]Scene dropped for second week of run.
[108]Dropped for second week of run.
[109]Dropped for second week of run.

Scene 8

Kid Songs

F. White

["M-I-S-S-I-S-S-I-P-P-I" (from HITCHY-KOO OF 1917)
(*Music by* Harry Tierney. *Lyrics by* Bert Hanlon and Benny Ryan.)

"Six-Times-Six Is Thirty-Six" (from HITCHY-KOO OF 1917)
(*Music by* William White. *Lyrics by* Bert Hanlon.)

"Gozinto" (also used in ZIEGFELD MIDNIGHT FROLIC)
(*Music and Lyrics by* Phil Ponce.)]
Scene: Outside the Schoolhouse.
Note—Scene designed and painted by Miss Frances White. Cost of material, $37.

Scene 9

As no Revue is complete without a cabaret scene, for its final episode we have chosen Polly's Greenwich Village Inn for our closing scene.

(a) With no trouble at all we have engaged Mr. Bobby Edwards, the Greenwich Village Troubadour and his tame ukulele to appear in his native lair. The supernumeraries in this scene are warranted genuine Greenwich Villagers.

(b) An Impression of a Popular Dance Favorite
L. McDermott

(c) A Few Moments of Jazz
D. Ellsworth, B. Palmer

(d) Specialty
W. Rock, F. White

Finale

Entire Company
Note—Scene same as used in prologue. Furniture and properties rented, $10 a week. Chorus costumes, $6 each. Principals' costumes from personal wardrobe. Mr. Edwards' ukulele studio made at cost of 17¢.

1918.09   TOOT-TOOT!

A Train of Mirth and Melody (Musical Comedy) in Two Acts, 4 Scenes. Book by Edgar Allan Woolf. Based on the farce 'Excuse Me' by Rupert Hughes. Music by Jerome Kern. Lyrics by Berton Braley. Staged by Edgar Allan Woolf and Edward Rose. Dances and ensembles arranged by Robert Marks. Scenery designed by Clifford Pember. Costumes designed by Faibsey. Lighting by Joseph Wilson. Orchestra under the direction of Anton Heindl. Produced by Henry W. Savage. Opened 11 March 1918 at the George M. Cohan Theatre and closed 13 April 1918 after 40 performances.

CAST (in order of appearance): *Lieutenant Shaw*: Louis A. Templeton. *Lieutenant Hudson*: Anthony Hughes. *Porter*: Harry Fern. *Mr. James Wellington*: EDWARD GARVIE. *Mrs. James Wellington*: FLORA ZABELLE. *Mr. Walter Colt, D. D.*: EARL BENHAM. *Mrs. Walter Colt*: LOUISE GROODY. *Captain Jones*: GREEK EVANS. *Lieutenant Flint*: NORMAN BRYAN. *Lieutenant Harry Mallory*: DONALD MacDONALD. *Marjorie Newton*: LOUISE ALLEN. *Snoozelums*: Himself. *Messenger Boy*: Lew Renard. *A Ballyhoo*: Alonzo Price. *Pandora Buncombe*: Florence Johns. *Hyperion Buncombe*: BILLY [William] KENT. *Train Butcher*: Ernie Adams. *Conductor*: Ben Hendricks. *Gambler*: Alonzo Price. *Minister*: Louis A. Templeton. *Indian Chief*: Oskenonton. *Peter Deerfoot*: GREEK EVANS. *Karontowanen*: Albert Racklin.

Female Passengers: *Classic Dancers*: Irma Marwick, Hazel O'Brien, Mlle. Madriene, Dorothy McCord, Helen Ukers, Ruth Caplan, Daphne Prince, Jean Anthony. *Marjorie's Friends*: Alma Claussen, Mary Lee Webb, Clothilde Woods, Marguerite La Pierre, Hazel Fox, Helen Donohue, Jean Fair, Daisy MacGlashan. *Mrs. Wellington's Friends*: Nina Calame, Bunola Loraine, Annette Besuden, Marie Ahern, Irene Smythe, Dorice Wingrove, Helen Holcomb, Mabel Cox.

Act 1: Railway Terminal of a Western City.

Act 2, Scene 1: Observation and smoking compartment car of the Overland Limited. *Scene 2*: Exterior of sleeping car of the Overland Limited. *Scene 3*: Open country in the Rockies.

ACT 1

Scene Music

"Toot-Toot!"
Ensemble

"Quarrel and Part"
E. Garvie, F. Zabelle, Ensemble

"Runaway Colts"
E. Benham, L. Groody

"Kan the Kaiser"
Military Ensemble

"Every Girl in All America"
D. MacDonald, L. Allen, Ensemble

"Show of Rice"
Ensemble

"Let's Go"
D. MacDonald, L. Allen

"It's Greek to Me"
F. Johns, B. Kent, Pupils

"The Last Long Mile" (Plattsburg Marching Song, 1917)
G. Evans, Ensemble
(*Music and Lyrics by* Lieutenant Emil Breitenfeld.)

ACT 2

Scene Music

"When You Wake Up Dancing"
Ensemble

"Girlie"
D. MacDonald, L. Allen

"Smoke"
Ensemble

"Cute Soldier Boy"
F. Zabelle, Military Ensemble
(*Music by* Anatol Friedland. *Lyrics by* Edgar Allan Woolf.)

"It's Immaterial to Me"
H. Fern

"If (Only You Cared for Me)"
D. MacDonald, L. Allen, B. Kent, Sally

"Indian Folk Song"
Oskenonton

"Indian Fox Trot"
G. Evans, Ensemble

Finale

1918.10   GETTING TOGETHER

A Play with Music in Three Acts, 6 Scenes. Play by Major Beith (Ian Hay), J. Hartley Manners and Percival Knight. Songs (music, lyrics) by Lieutenant Gitz Rice. Staged by Holbrook Blinn and Frederick Stanhope. Scenery designed by Clifford Pember. Costumes by Eaves. Orchestra under the direction of Manuel Klein[110]. Presented under the auspices of the British-Canadian Recruiting Mission, and with the cooperation of the United States Military and Naval Forces[111] (Representative, Major Wallace McCutcheon, English Army). Opened 18 March 1918 at the Lyric Theatre and closed 23 March 1918; re-opened 3 June 1918 at the Sam S. Shubert Theatre and closed 31 August 1918 after 104 performances. Total: 112 performances.

CAST (in order of appearance): *Orrin Palmer*: HOLBROOK BLINN. *A Servant*: Edwin Taylor. *Mrs. Palmer*: BLANCHE BATES. *Edward Wadsworth*: William Roselle. *First Recruit*: Leonard Barry. *Second Recruit*: William Rowland. *Third Recruit*: James Flint. *First Spectator*: E. J. Kennedy. *Second Spectator*: John Thorne. *Third Spectator*: W. J. O'Neill. *Fourth Spectator*: Timothy Conway. *Fifth Spectator*: Edwin Taylor. *Warrant Officer*: HARRISON BROCKBANK. *Lieutenant Gitz Rice*: LIEUTENANT GITZ RICE (First Canadian Contingent). *A Retired Bellhop*: Harry Blakemore. *A Woman*: Harriet Sterling. *British Sergeant*: Sergeant L. Shannon Cormack. *British Soldier*: Private Charles Francis. *A Poilu*: Gustave Rolland. *Sergeant Atkins*: PERCIVAL KNIGHT. *Santa Claus*: HARRISON BROCKBANK. *Death*: Private Charles Francis. *Sergeant Jennings, U. S. Army*: JOHN THORNE. *First British Soldier*: Edwin Taylor. *First American Soldier*: Arthur Ray. *Second American Soldier*: E. J. Kennedy. *War Tank Officer*: Sergeant L. Shannon Cormack. *British Surgeon*: Private Charles Francis. *Miss Fletcher*: Dorothy Knight. *A Waitress*: Suzanne Feday. *A Refugee*: Ruth Benson.

Act 1, Scene 1: Mrs. Palmer's Drawing Room in New York City. *Scene 2*: A Recruiting Station in New York City.

Act 2, Scene 1: A Trench Fantasy (Palmer's Dream). *Scene 2*: A First Line Trench.

Act 3, Scene 1: No Man's Land. *Scene 2*: A French Village.

---

[110]For return engagement, Howard A. Cook was musical director.
[111]For the return engagement, "and the Tank "Britannia" was added to the list of presenters.

ACT 1[112]

Scene 2

"Who Carries the Gun?"[113]
H. Brockbank
(*Lyrics by* Rudyard Kipling.)

"You've Got to Go In or Go Under"
Lieut. G. Rice
(*Music by* Lieutenant Gitz Rice. *Lyrics by* Percival Knight.)

"Come My Lad and Be a Soldier"[114]
H. Brockbank
(*Music and Lyrics by* Harrison Brockbank.)

"We Stopped Them on the Marne"
Lieut. G. Rice
(*Music and Lyrics by* Lieutenant Gitz Rice.)

ACT 2

Scene 1

Overture and Incidental Music to "A Trench Fantasy" by Roy Webb.

ACT 3

"(Dear) Old Pal of Mine"
Sgt. J. Thorne
(*Music by* Lieutenant Gitz Rice. *Lyrics by* Harold Robe.)

"Little Lad"[115]
H. Brockbank

"I Want To Go Home"
Sgt. P. Knight
(*Music and Lyrics by* Lieutenant Gitz Rice.)
(*Music and Lyrics by* C. W. Murphy and Worton David.)

1918.11   THE RAINBOW GIRL

A Musical Play in Three Acts, 4 Scenes. Book and lyrics by Renold Wolf. Based on the comedy 'Lady Fanny and the Servant Problem' [The New Lady Bantock] by Jerome K. Jerome. Music by Louis A. Hirsch. Staged by Julian Mitchell and Herbert Gresham. Scenes (designed) by Joseph Urban. Costumes designed by Marie Cook and Alice O'Neil; men's clothes designed by Croydon, Ltd. Lighting by Tony Greshoff. Orchestra under the direction of Max Steiner. Produced by Marc Klaw and Abraham L. Erlanger. Opened 1 April 1918 at the New Amsterdam Theatre, moved 17 June 1918 to the Gaiety Theatre, and closed 17 August 1918 after 160 performances[116].

CAST (in order of appearance): *Daisy Meade, a soubrette:* LAURA HAMILTON. *Frank Scudder, a stage manager:* William Clifton. *Buck Evans, a comedian:* BILLY B. VAN. *Gus Norton, a New York theatrical manager:* ROBERT G. PITKIN. *The Four Pippins: Newtown:* Polly Bowman. *Russet:* Ethel Delmar. *Jonathan:* Dorothy St. Clair. *Baldwin:* Edna Stillwell. *Robert Vernon Dudley, Lord Wetherell:* HARRY BENHAM. *Mollie Murdock of "The Rainbow Girl":* BETH LYDY. *Miss Terris:* Miriam Medie. *Miss Gwendolin:* Marguerite St. Clair. *Clergyman:* Frederic Solomon. *Miss Dudley, the elder (spinster):* Jane Burby. *Miss Dudley, the younger (spinster):* Margaret Merriman. *Girl in Blue:* Florence Ware. *Electric Light Inspector:* William Clifton.

The Bennett Family—12 of Them: Martin Bennett, a butler: Sydney Greenstreet. *Susannah Bennett, a housekeeper:* Claire Grenville. *Honoria Bennett, a lady's maid:* Kathleen Lindley. *Ernest Bennett, a footman:* HARRY DELF. *Jane Bennett, a housemaid:* LENORA NOVASIO. *Matilda Bennett, a kitchen maid:* Jane Callan. *Mary Anne Bennett, a scullery maid:* Marion Sitgreaves. *Simeon Bennett, a gardener:* Jessie Willingham. *Charles Bennett, a cook:* Charles Fulton. *Anastasia Bennett, a laundry maid:* Julie Eastman. *James Bennett, a coachman:* Charles Hall. *John Bennett, a flunkey:* Carlisle Blackton.

---

[112]Added for tour following return engagement (Act 1, after "You've Got to Go In or Go Under"):
"Road That Leads Back Home"
J. Thorne

[113]Replaced for subsequent tour and return engagement by:
"Keep Your Head Down, Fritzie Boy"
Lieut. G. Rice
(*Music and Lyrics by* C. W. Murphy and Worton David.)

[114]Replaced for subsequent tour and return engagement by:
"Liberty Bell" (Till the Liberty Bell Rings Out)
J. Thorne
(*Music by* Halsey K. Mohr. *Lyrics by* Joe Goodwin.)

[115]Dropped for subsequent tour and return engagement.

[116]Later played a return engagement at the Standard Theatre, New York 22 September 1919 for 1 week.

Ladies of the Rainbow Company Chorus: Misses Mann, Dana, Mantell, Beach, Roche, Callon, Livermore, Barry, Daly, Day, Woodworth.

Act 1, Scene 1: The Green Room of the Frivolity Theatre, London. *Scene 2:* Boudoir in Wetherell Hall, near Manchester, England. One week later.

Act 2: Drawing room. in Wetherell Hall. The following afternoon.

Act 3: Modern sun parlor and breakfast room in Wetherell Hall. The following morning.

ACT 1

Scene 1

"Rainbow Girl" (Opening)
B. Lydy

"Won't Some Nice Boy Marry Me?" (Song)
L. Hamilton, Girls

"Just You Alone" (Duet)
B. Lydy, H. Benham

"Alimony Blues" (Song)
B. B. Van
Assisted by Misses Ware, Delmar, Bowman, D. St. Clair, Stillwell.

"The Wedding Ceremony" (Finale)
Principals, Ensemble

Scene 2

"In a Month or Two" (Song)
H. Benham
Assisted by M. St. Clair, M. Medie, Girls.

"My Rainbow Girl" (Duet)
B. Lydy, H. Benham

"We Fear You Will Not Do, Lady Wetherell"
B. Lydy, Bennett Family

ACT 2

"Let's Go Down to the Shop" (Opening)
H. Delf
Assisted by M. St. Clair, M. Medie, Girls.

"Love's Ever New" (Duet)
B. Lydy, H. Benham

"I'll Think of You" (Duet)
L. Novasio, H. Delf

"Mister Drummer Man" (Song)
L. Hamilton, Girls

Finale
Principals, Ensemble

ACT 3

"I Wonder" (Opening)
L. Hamilton, the Pippins, Girls

"Soon We'll All Be Seen Upon the Screen" (Duet)
L. Novasio, H. Delf

"Beautiful Lady (Tell Me)" (Song)
B. Lydy

Finale
Principals, Ensemble

1918.12   FANCY FREE

A Musical Play in Three Acts. Book by Dorothy Donnelly. Music and lyrics by Augustus Barratt. Clifton Crawford's songs written by himself. Staged by J. C. Huffman. Musical numbers and dances arranged by Jack Mason. Stage decorations by P. Dodd Ackerman. Orchestra under the direction of Augustus Barratt. Produced by Messrs. Lee & J. J. Shubert. Opened 11 April 1918 at the Astor Theatre, moved 20 May 1918 to the Casino Theatre, moved 17 June 1918 to the Bijou Theatre and closed 20 July 1918 after 116 performances.

CAST (in order of appearance): *Lady Guests of the Hotel (8): Grace Cornell:* Rena Manning. *Mae LaRue:* Virginia Lee. *Nita Bernstein:* Mae Posner. *Newberry Adams:* Mae Manning. *Vera La Mont:* Ethel Clayton. *Genevieve Willett:* Leila Von Holk. *Violet Ring:* Dorothy Miller. *Gertrude Hemming:* Helen Marche. *Elevator Boy:* Alton Weber. *Hotel Clerk:* William Tillett. *Bell Boy:* Joe Tinsley. *Hotel Manager:* John E. Wheeler. *Yvette:* YVONNE D'ARLE. *Philip Pike:* RAY RAYMOND. *Betty Pestlewaite:* MARILYNN MILLER. *Albert Van Wyck:* CLIFTON CRAWFORD. *Flower Girl:* Regina Crawford. *The Bridegroom:* Hal Peel. *The Bride:* Tim Poni. *Professor Hybrower:* CHARLES BROWN. *Pinkie Pestlewaite:* MARJORIE GATESON. *The Manicurist:*

Yvonne Gouraud. *The Mysterious One*: Harold Evarts. *Benjamin Pestlewaite*: HARRY CONOR. *Peter Pope*: ROBINSON NEWBOLD. *Gussie Pope*: Violet Englefield. *Mr. Lajoie*: Francis Murphy.

    Guests and Friends of Captain Pope (5): *Mr. W. Van*: James Smith. *Mr. H. F. A. Willis*: Joseph Spence. *Mr. Charles Brown Newton*: Clyde Miller. *Mr. Frank Nollis*: Edward Wynn. *Mr. Billy Woods*: Albert Williams.

    Maids of the Hotel: Misses Carrie DeNoville, Clara Carroll, Jeanette Carroll, Jean Campbell, Ethel Hart, Marion Loomis, Nancy Everett, Nan Bryce.

Act 1: Public Lounge and office of Hotel at Palm Beach, Florida. About noon.

Act 2: Same as Act 1. Later.

Act 3: Palm Gardens of Hotel. Evening.

ACT 1

  "Pretty Baby Doll from Paree" (Duet)
    Y. D'arle, R. Raymond, Chorus
  "Tinkle-inkle-inkle" (Duet)
    M. Gateson, Chorus
  "If You're Crazy About the Women" (Song)
    C. Crawford, Girls
    (*Music and Lyrics by* Clifton Crawford.)
  "My Bibliophile" (Duet)
    M. Miller, C. Brown
  "Rat-tat-a-tat" (Duet)
    M. Miller, C. Crawford, Chorus

ACT 2

  "When I Came to America" (Song)
    Y. D'arle, Chorus
  "Someone Has Your Number" (Trio)
    M. Miller, H. Conor, R. Raymond
  "Love Comes A-Stealing" (Song and Dance)
    M. Miller
  "A Cocktail of Flowers" (Song)
    R. Raymond, Chorus
  "The Road to Anywhere"[117] (Song)
    Y. D'arle, Chorus

ACT 3[118]

  "When the Moon Shines Down" (Song)
    R. Raymond, Chorus
  "Give Me the Moonlight" (Song)
    H. Conor, Chorus
  "Sweet Seventeen" (Dance)
    M. Miller
  "Eve" (Song)
    C. Crawford
    (*Music and Lyrics by* Clifton Crawford.)
  Finale
    Entire Company

1918.13   YOU KNOW ME AL!

A Farce with Music in Three Acts. Book by Privates W. Anson Hallahan, Hugh Stanislaus Stange and Stannard Mears. Music by Private Burton Hamilton. Lyrics by Lieutenant William A. Halloran, Jr. Interpolated numbers by Sergeant Leon DeCosta. Staged by Private Harry (Wagstaff) Gribble. Dances arranged by Trumpeter Stanley Hughes. Art director, C. C. Beall. Entire production under the direction of Lieutenant William A. Halloran, Jr. Musical director, Sergeant Leon DeCosta. Produced by the New York Division (27th U.S. Army). Opened 11 April 1918 at the Lexington Theatre and closed 27 April 1918 after 22 performances.

CAST: *Al Carleton*, alias Livewire Al: Pvt. RUSSELL BROWN. *Bill McGraw*, alias Brightlights: Pvt. SIDNEY MARION. *Tom Brush*, alias Reddycash: Pvt. CURT KARPE. *Amos Bronson*, a retired merchant: Pvt. Harry (Wagstaff) Gribble. *Barrington Booth*, an actor: Pvt. Stanley G. Wood. *Primrose Tinney Jolson*, a black-face comedian: Pvt. JACK MAHONEY. *A Cabaret Singer*: Pvt. JACK ROCHE. *A Dancer*: Trumpeter Stanley Hughes. *A Vaudevillian*: Pvt. Andrew Kennedy. *Another Actor*: Pvt. J. R. McDonald. *And One More*: Pvt. H. M. Cundy. *Himself*: Pvt. Harvey Brooks. *Arline*

Bronson, a Society Bud: Pvt. WALTER ROBERTS. *Sally LaBergere*, a Camouflaged Actress: Pvt. E. ALBERT CRAWFORD. *Knotta Soude, Lotta Noyes*, a brace of chickens: Pvt. W. Pauly, Pvt. Dan Burns.

    Female Chorus: Pvts. Dan Burns, W. Pauly, H. Plassman, G. Carr, W. M. Bramman, I. R. Waite, J. J. Sullivan, D. Mitchell, R. Hilton, J. McNally, R. M. Heft, R. Sentenne, Corp. A. V. Streat. *Male Chorus*: Pvts. A. A. Jarrett, R. J. Timmins, H. Dougherty, H. M. Cundy, LeRoy Beers, E. H. Downey, A. Cooper, C. Lacey, R. E. Nelson, J. Johannes, H. A. Unger, O. Kuhl, Sergeant E. H. O'Leary. *Dancers*: Pvts. S. Scammace, J. Clooney, C. Fleming, E. Tierney, A. Fitzpatrick, G. Downey, S. Ahearn, Corp. J. A. Donnelly.

The action takes place at the present time.

Act 1: The Lobby of the Pineland Inn, Cloud Mountains, Adirondacks—Twilight.

Act 2: The same evening.

Act 3: Pineland Terrace. Midnight—The Bal Masqué.

ACT 1

  "Broadway Girl"
    C. Karpe, Girls
    (*Music and Lyrics by* Eric Krebs.)
  "Spoons" (Specialty)
    A. Kennedy
  "My Little Loving Baby Mine"
    J. Mahoney, Quartette
    (*Music by* William A. Halloran, Jr.)
  "They've Completely Camouflaged Me"
    E. A. Crawford
  "My Heart Belongs to the U.S.A."
    R. Brown, Chorus
  "When the Right Man Comes Along"
    W. Roberts, R. Brown
    (*Music and Lyrics by* Leon DeCosta.)

ACT 2

  "Sweetness"
    J. Mahoney, Six Dancers
  "Bring Back That (Old) Yama Dance to Me"
    R. Brown, Chorus
    (*Lyrics by* Russell Brown.)
  "I'm Old Enough for a Little Loving"
    E. A. Crawford
  "(In My) Garden of Love for 2"
    J. Roche, W. Pauly
  "I Want the Boys Around Me"
    W. Brooks, Boys
    (*Music by* Sidney Marion and Burton Hamilton.)

ACT 3

  "Frenchie" (Opening Chorus)
    Ensemble
    (*Music and Lyrics by* Leon DeCosta.)
  Quartet
    Pvts. Mahoney, Johannes, Wittman, Unger
  Specialty
    J. Fallon
  "Let Me Have a Corner of Your Heart"
    W. Brooks, R. Brown
    (*Music and Lyrics by* Leon DeCosta.)
  Specialty
    S. Hughes
  "Visions at Twilight"
    J. Roche
    (*Music and Lyrics by* Leon DeCosta.)
  "I'm Going Back to Mobile, Alabam'"
    J. Mahoney, Chorus
  Finale
    Entire Company

1918.14   GOOD-BYE, BILL

A Play with Music in Three Acts[119]. Book and lyrics by Sgt. Richard B. Fechheimer. Music by Pvt. William B. Kernell. Produced under the direc-

---

[117]Dropped after opening.
[118]Shortly after the opening, the following was added to open Act 3:
  "Honeymoon Land" (Song)
    Y. Darle, Chorus

---

[119]Previously presented for two benefit performances in March 1918 at the 48th Street Theatre.

tion of Lieut. Edwin R. Wolfe. Costumes supplied by Eves. Costume Company. Chorus and ensembles under the direction of Pvt. Calvin M. King. Musical director, Edward Mellon. Musical arrangements by Edward Mellon. Produced by the U.S. Ambulance Service. Opened 22 April 1918 at the 44th Street Roof Theatre and closed 5 May 1918 after 17 performances.

CAST (in order of appearance): *Prologue*: Pvt. George W. Kowalski. *Caesar Charlemagne Pershing Lee*: Pvt. Robert Covington. *Joseph Jackson Joffre Jones*: Pvt. Charles Hamp. *A Sergeant*: Pvt. Carle V. Middleton. *Another Sergeant*: Pvt. Edward Bonoff. *Still Another Sergeant*: Sgt. Richard B. Fechheimer. *Mitzy McFagin*: Pvt. Charles Kirk. *Bud Weizer*: Sgt. F. Turley. *A Policeman*: Pvt. Paul McCoy. *Hardluck Himself*: Pvt. Charles Lawrence. *Tom Collins*: Pvt. William A. McMichaels. *Basil B. Vedeer, Harvard '17*: Pvt. Edward Bunting. *Bernice Buttercup*: Pvt. Charles H. Giradeau. *Lieut. Allen Towne*: Pvt. Milton E. Claypoole. *A Messenger Boy*: Pvt. William Adriance. *A Gate Guard*: Pvt. George Kowalski. *Another Gate Guard*: Pvt. William A. McMichaels. *A Usaac*: Sgt. W. Baron. *Taps*: Corp. Raymond Clarke. *Miss Franco-American*: Pvt. Charles Keck. *Flivver Pilot No. 1*: Pvt. Edward Bonoff. *Flivver Pilot No. 2*: Pvt. Charles Lawrence. *A Tommy*: Pvt. Edward Bunting. *A Spy*: Pvt. William M. Michaels. *A Poilu*: Pvt. Allen E. Mattox. *Mr. Dreams*: Lieut. Hubert Linscott. *Ober General Harsenpfeffer*: Sgt. Richard Fechheimer. *The Kaiser*: Pvt. George W. Kowalski. *Henry Ford*: Pvt. Ira Hidden.

Red Cross Nurses: Patrick Walsh, Edward E. Glenn, Clifford Crowthers, Justin Langville, Harold Conklin, Marshall Allen. *Last Aid Crew*: Charles Hamp, Lee Parker, Frank Morin, Paul McCoy, Robert Tanner, Charles Pawlick, Charles E. Johnson. *Personnel of the Chorus*: Edward E. Glenn, Donald A. McInnes, Frank B. Ryan, Patrick Walsh, Henry Carr, Henry Fry, William J. Rehr, Edward Saunders, Clifford Crowthers, Marshall Allen, Justin Langville, Harold Conklin, William Adriance, Winfield Dougherty, Norman Toohey, Thomas H. Elliott, Clarence W. Heisse, Allen E. Mattox, Richard McCarl, Edward Hohman, John S. Saunders.

Act 1: A Recruiting Station in New York, about nine months ago.

Act 2: The gate at the U.S.A. Ambulance Camp, Allentown, Pennsylvania. Four months later.

Act 3: A Forest Spot, somewhere over there, about nine months from today.

ACT 1[120]

    "The Whitewings Marimba"
        Opening Chorus
    "(We're) Recrootin'"
        R. Fechheimer, C. V. Middleton
    "Buy a Bond"
        C. Hamp, Chorus

ACT 2

    "Boys, Be Proud You're a USAAC"
        Ensemble
    "Patsy Bolivar"
        C. Lawrence
    "I'm the Guy"
        G. W. Kowalski, M. E. Claypoole
    "Just a Little After Taps"
        R. Clarke
    "Bring Me a Blonde"[121]
        Pvt. Schmidt
    "Good-Bye Bill"
        C. Kirk, M. E. Claypoole, G. W. Kowalski

ACT 3

    "The Ladies of London and Paris"
        E. Bunting
    "A Jazz Band Am the Firstest Aid for Me"
        E. Bonoff
        (*Music and Lyrics by* Pvt. Louis Duggan.)
    "'Till I Come Home to You"
        H. Linscott, R. Clarke
    "USAAC—Good-Bye Bill" Finale
        (Company)

---

[120]Added during the New York run or tour:
    "I Didn't Hesitate' Cause I Knew That I Was Lost" (Act 1)
        C. Hamp
    "The Old Camp Chef" (Act 2)
        C. Hamp
    "Je ne parle pas Anglais" (Act 3)
        E. Bonoff, C. Keck
        (*Music and Lyrics by* Pvt. Louis Duggan.)
[121]Dropped during the run.

1918.15

THE KISS BURGLAR

A Musical Romance in Two Acts, 5 Scenes. Book and lyrics by Glen MacDonough. Music by Raymond Hubbell. Staged by Julian Mitchell and Edgar MacGregor. Scenes designed by Clifford Pember. Costumes by W. H. Matthews and Helene Price, Inc. Orchestra under the direction of Leo Merriman. Produced by William P. Orr (Direction of John M. Welch). Opened 9 May 1918 at the George M. Cohan Theatre, moved 1 July 1918 to the Eltinge Theatre and closed 3 August 1918 after 100 performances.[122]

CAST: *Aline, Grand Duchess of Orly*: FAY BAINTER. *Mr. E. Chatteron-Pym*: CYRIL CHADWICK. *Mrs. E. Chatteron-Pym*: GRACE FIELD. *Miss Harte*: JANET VELIE. *Bert DuVivier, The Kiss Burglar*: ARMAND KALISZ. *Tommy Dodd*: HARRY CLARKE. *Oswald Gayly*: DENMAN MALEY. *Colonel Trotovitch*: E. Payton Gibbs. *First Aide to General Trotovitch*: H. Morrison. *Second Aide to General Trotovitch*: George Otto. *A Detective*: A. Settle. *Miss Tinkle*: Evelyn Cavanaugh. *Mr. Toby*: Richard Dore. *Proprietor of Pennington Inn*: Paul Dulzell. *Waiter*: H. Coughlan. *Pinkie Doolittle*: Gertrude Harrison. *Tissie Baltimore*: June White. *Rose, maid to the Duchess*: Virginia Richmond. *Natalie, maid to the Duchess*: Betty Dodsworth. *Page*: Peggy Ellis.

Miss Stuyvesant: Margaret Cusak. *Miss Greeley*: Eleanor Scott. *Miss Morrisana*: Marie Baxter. *Miss Yonkers*: Dot Nichols. *Miss Hastings*: Evelyn Koerner. *Miss Dobbs*: Virginia Richmond. *Miss Tarrytown*: Helen Trainor. *Miss Irvington*: Emily Monte. *Miss Peekskill*: Margaret Healey. *Miss Albany*: Louise Moran. *Miss Poughkeepsie*: Carol Rutter. *Miss Troy*: Bessie Gros. *Miss Amsterdam*: Fritzie Smith. *Miss Rochester*: Marjorie Whiteford. *Miss Oneida*: Marion Phillips. *Miss Schenectady*: Nell Edwardy. *Miss Canojoharie*: Marie McConnell. *Miss Beacon*: Dot Quinette.

Act 1, Scene 1: Room in the law office of Ayling Harte & Company. *Scene 2*: Humming Bird Alley in the Hotel St. George. *Scene 3*: Bedroom o'top of the Chatterton-Pym mansion on Fifth Avenue.

Act 2, Scene 1: The Della Robbia room at the Pennington Inn, in the Berkshire Hills. Night. *Scene 2*: The same afternoon of the next day.

ACT 1

    "He Loved, He Loves Me Not" (Opening)
        J. Velie, E. Cavanaugh, Chorus
    "A Little Class of One" (Duet)
        J. Velie, H. Clarke
    "Since I Met Wonderful You" (Song)
        A. Kalisz
    "One Day" (Song)
        G. Field
    "The Mantlepiece Tragedy"
        F. Bainter

ACT 2

    "The Shimmering, Glimmering Nile" (Opening Song)
        H. Clarke
    "The Little Black Sheep" (Song)
        G. Field
    "The Girl I Can't Forget" (Song)
        A. Kalisz
    "I Want to Learn to Dance" (Song)
        F. Bainter, C. Chadwick
    "Because You Do Not Know" (Duet)
        F. Bainter, A. Kalisz
    "The Rose" (Song)
        Ensemble
    Dance[123]
        R. Dore, E. Cavanuagh
    "Your Kiss Is Champagne"[124] (Song)
        A. Kalisz

1918.16

ROCK-A-BYE BABY

A Musical Comedy in Three Acts. Book by Edgar Allan Woolf and Margaret Mayo. Based on the farce "Baby Mine" by Margaret Mayo. Music by Jerome Kern. Lyrics by Herbert Reynolds. Staged by Edward Royce. Dances arranged by Robert Marks. Scenery designed by Joseph Physioc. Costumes

---

[122]Played a return engagement under the auspices of the Messrs. Shubert 17 March 1919 for 24 performances. See separate entry in 1918-1919 season.
[123]Dropped during the run.
[124]Dropped during the run, and replaced by Finale for tour.

designed by Lucille [Lady Duff-Gordon]. Orchestra under the direction of Frank Tours. Produced by Selwyn & Company (Arch, Edgar Selwyn). Opened 22 May 1918 at the Astor Theatre and closed 3 August 1918 after 85 performances.

CAST: *Pasquale*: ARTHUR LIPSON. *Waiters*: Phil Stanton, Bert Pullaney. *Evelyn*: Evelyn Ferris. *Frances*: Frances Kaufman. *Norah*: Norah Sprague. *Florence*: Florence Eldridge. *Charlotte*: Charlotte Wakefield. *Janet*: Janet McIlwaine. *Albertine*: Albertine Marlowe. *Gladys*: Gladys White. *Lilyan*: Lilyan White. *Clothilde*: Clothilde Woods. *Olive*: Olive Jacqueline. *Constance*: Constance Carper. *Archie Drummond*: CARL HYSON. *Monte Laidlaw*: ALAN HALE. *George Westbury*: EDDY MEYERS. *Madam Tentelucci*: EDNA MUNSEY. *Bellboy*: S. Sydney Chon. *Alfred Hardy*: FRANK MORGAN. *Zoie Hardy*: EDNA HIBBARD. *Jimmy Jinks*: Walter Jones. *Chauffeur*: Frank Derr. *Aggie Jinks*: LOUISE DRESSER. *Dorothy Manners*: DOROTHY DICKSON. *Maid*: Claire Nagle. *Weenie*: Mae Carmen. *Finnegan*: Gus Baci. *Weenie's Father*: H. Nelson Dickson. *The Kiddies*: Ruth Collins, Claire Hillier.

Act 1: Rock-a-Bye Baby Inn, on the Albany Post Road on a summer night.

Act 2: The Boudoir in Zoie's new home. Afternoon.

Act 3: The Nursery in Zoie's Home. Evening.

ACT 1[125]

"Bella Mia"[126]
  A. Lipson, G. Baci, B. Pullaney
"Hurry Now" (Ensemble)
  Girls
"Motoring Along the Old Post Road"
  C. Hyson, Girls
"One, Two, Three" (Song)
  D. Dickson, C. Hyson, A. Hale, E. Meyers, Girls
"I Never Thought" (Duet)
  E. Hibbard, F. Morgan
"I Believed All She Said" (I Believed All They Said)(Trio)
  A. Hale, C. Hyson, E. Meyers, Girls
"A Kettle Is Singing" (The Kettle Song)
  L. Dresser

ACT 2

"Stitching, Stitching" (Ensemble)
  L. Dresser, E. Hibbard, A. Hale, Girls
"Rock-a-Bye Baby Dear"[127] (Song)
  E. Munsey, Girls
"Little Tune Go Away" (Song)
  L. Dresser, Girls
"According to Dr. Holt" (Quartette)
  L. Dresser, E. Hibbard, W. Jones, F. Morgan
"There's No Better Use for Time than Kissing" (Trio and Dance)
  E. Hibbard, D. Dickson, C. Hyson
"The Real Spring Drive" (The Big Spring Drive)(Song)
  E. Hibbard, A. Hale, C. Hyson, E. Meyers, Girls
Finaletto
  Ensemble

ACT 3

"My Own Light Infantry" (Song)("Nursery Fanfare")
  E. Hibbard, Kiddies
"I Can Trust Myself with a Lot of Girls" (Song)
  A. Hale, C. Hyson, E. Meyers, Ensemble
Finale
  Ensemble

1918.17   # BIFF-BANG!

A Song and Dance Revue in Three Acts, 9 Scenes, by and with the sailors from Pelham Naval Training Camp. Book (sketches) by Philip Dunning. Music by William Schroeder. Lyrics by Philip Dunning, Robert D. Cohen, Frank Mills and Joseph Fields. Stage director, Philip Dunning. Dances by Dinnie MacDonald. Bandmaster, William Schroeder. Produced by the U.S.

Navy. Opened 30 May 1918 at the Century Theatre and closed 5 June 1918 after 10 performances.[128]

CAST: Georgie Lane, Frank Meehan, Samuel Baumel, Alonzo King, George Robinson, George Wulfing, Jimmie Fox, John J. Byrnes, Arthur Leydecker, Willis Claire, William Israel, Robert D. Cohen, Harry Davies, Hugh Dillman, Alexander Hyde, Bob Fischer, Frank Mills, Edmund Culleton, Edward Costello, Jim Ellins, Richard Brown, D. Cifarelli, Roy Duck, Valentine Nierle, Raymond Schuster, Ray E. McKimmey, Henry Levy, E. M. Kyte, H. D. Scofield. (Sailors of the Naval Training Camp).

Show Girls: Joe Fields, Robert B. Mantell, C. V. Farley, W. D. Connors, J. W. Sears, W. Romer, B. Chambers, J. S. McCauley, L. Mooney, F. Landers, R. I. Platou, H. Levey, F. Huckersmith, P. J. Waldron, W. Haffer, C. B. Walker, W. F. McCoy, D. A. Dawson, G. Purce, H. S. Terhune, A. Senecal, G. G. Tuthill, E. M. Kyte, H. G. Spielburger, F. C. Hagerty, O. S. Wishert, F. Matthews, T. J. Kenny, R. Fekete, G. A. Chapman. *Waiters*: J. Barrett, William Hesser, S. G. Levy, W. H. Lewis, W. L. Valentine, S. O'Hanna, J. J. Hallacy, E. F. Logan, H. Kaufman. *Ponies*: A. T. Knight, C. J. Murry, C. A. Fitzsimmons, O. R. Washburn, E. Thayer, L. Cavanaugh, G. H. Smith, A. Pringle, J. Wirricks, W. E. McCaulcy, A. E. Hogan, W. A. Duggan, J. J. Lamont, J. Costello, E. Keese, C. Cuningham. *Sailors and Persian Men*: E. J. Culleton, J. B. Stevens, J. E. Dalton, J. R. Burke, D. E. Murphy, W. E. Munkelwitz, T. Isherwood, G. C. Harrison, O. B. Swenson, A. T. Leonard, J. T. Boyle, J. R. Brendes, A. W. Simpson, J. H. White, F. C. Wood, R. F. White, E. T. Cassidy, A. Romano, F. F. Dunberg, E. D. Powers, J. J. McNamara, R. L. Pendleton, P. J. Donnelly, L. Eichenbaum, W. C. Krohne, A. C. Parker, G. J. Miller, M. Lehr, M. S. Brown, E. M. Kelly, J. J. Knudsen, J. S. Green, J. H. Mirrian, J. W. Scannell, J. J. Cummings, E. Talbot, J. W. Burke, H. Van Hutchler, H. D. Scofield, W. Hill, C. W. Root, M. G. Eckberg, M. M. Schwerin, J. J. Dunseath, J. A. Goffigan, L. A. Johnson, R. M. DeGrilla, G. R. Gaston, L. Colan, T. M. Quinn, I. A. Kuntz, A. W. Cook, H. A. Watson, R. T. Fairbrother, B. L. Burman.

ACT 1

Scene 1

Opening Chorus
  Entire Chorus
"Corner in My Heart"
  H. Dillman, Show Girls
"Come Along, Little Girl"
  F. Mills, Ponies
Waltz Specialty
  Pringle and Levy
"Love, Love, Love"
  The Actress, Entire Chorus
  Scene: The Hunter Island Inn.
    The Hat Boy: G. Lane. *The First Waiter*: S. Baumel. *The Second Waiter*: F. Meehan. *The Sailor*: G. Robinson. *The Girl*: A. King. *The Kid Brother*: J. Fox. *The Mother*: G. Wulfing. *The Chicago Millionaire*: J. J. Byrnes. *The Gypsy King*: A. Lydecker. *The First Gypsy Girl*: W. Claire. *The Second Gypsy Girl*: B. Davies. *The Cabaret Queen*: H. Dillman. *The Two Detectives*: W. Israel, R. D. Cohen. *The Cafe Manager*: F. Mills.

ACT 2

Scene 1

"Things We Pay Money to See"
  Entire Cast
  Characters at the Movies: Entire Cast.
  Scene: The Movie Theatre.

Scene 2

The Wild, Wild West
  The Widow: W. Claire. *The Baby*: J. Fox. *The Villain*: J. J. Byrnes. *The Cowboy Hero*: E. Culleton.

Scene 3

The Circus
  Characters in the Circus: Entire Cast.

Scene 4

"The Rendezvous Waltz"
  E. Costello, H. Davies
  Scene: The Vogue Cover.
    The Lady: E. Costello. *The Gentleman*:
Skating Number (Dance)
  Skating Girls and Boys

---

[125]Following the opening, the running order of songs was radically revised.
[126]Dropped after opening and for subsequent tour.
[127]Dropped for subsequent national tour.

[128]Scenery donated by Messrs. Shubert, New York Hippodrome, Comstock & Gest, Metropolitan Opera Co. Gowns donated by Hickson, Inc., Best & Co., Stern Bros., B. Altman & Co. Saks & Co., Henri Bendel, Oppenheim-Collins; character costumes by Eaves Costume Company.

Skating Girls: Messrs. Wishert, Duggan, Haffer, Costello, Conner, Sears.
Skating Boys: Messrs. Hesser, Hogan, Lamont, Mathews, DeGrilla, Waldron.

Scene 5

Violin Solo

"That Gypsy Rag"

Four Gypsies

(*Lyrics by* William Israel, Robert Cohen)
Scene: The Road near Whispering Brook.
The First Gypsy Girl: W. Claire. *The Gypsy King*: A. Leydecker. *The Second Gypsy Girl*: H. Davies. *The Sailor*: G. Robinson. *The Girl*: A. King. *The Chicago Millionaire*: J. J. Byrnes. *The Mother*: G. Wulfing. *The Kid Brother*: J. Fox. *The Two Detectives*: W. Israel, R. D. Cohen.

Scene 6

The Gypsy Camp

The Gypsy Boy: A. Hyde. *The First Gypsy Girl*: W. Claire. *The Two Detectives*: W. Israel, R. D. Cohen. *The Gypsy King*: A. Lydecker. *The Baby Snatcher*: B. Fisher. *The Horse Thief*: G. Lane. *The Jewel Robber*: J. Ellins. *The Second Gypsy Girl*: H. Davies. *The Sailor*: G. Robinson. *The Girl*: A. King. *Eli the Second*: Himself.

Scene 7

(a) Paul Revere

(b) Three Letters from Home

(c) On the Way to Waikiki

(d) Pussyfoot

Over There

Six Funny Sailors
Scene: The Road near the Camp.

Six Funny Sailors: R. Brown, D. Cifarelli, R. Duck, V. Nierle, R. Schuster, R. E. McKimmey.

Scene 8

"The Sailors' Fox Trot Wedding"

Entire Company
The Girl: A. King. *The First Bridesmaid*: H. Levy. *The Second Bridesmaid*: E. M. Kyte. *The Minister*: H. D. Scoffield. *The Chicago Millionaire*: J. J. Byrnes. *The Mother*: G. Wulfing. *The Kid Brother*: J. Fox. *The Two Detectives*: W. Israel, R. D. Cohen. *Girls and Boys at the Wedding*: Entire Chorus.

ACT 3

Scene 1

"Persian Love Song"

B. Fisher, Entire Chorus

"I Like 'Em Wild"

J. Fox, the Beauty

"The Sport"

J. J. Byrnes, Sport Girls

"We're Going Across"

G. Robinson, Entire Chorus

Grand Finale

Entire Company
Scene: The Persian Garden at the Hotel Commodore.
The Persian: B. Fisher. *The Two Detectives*: W. Israel, R. D. Cohen. *The Mayor of City Island*: J. Fox. *The Harlem Vampire*: G. Wulfing. *The Chicago Millionaire*: J. J. Byrnes. *The Girl*: A. King. *The Sailor*: G. Robinson. *The Kid Brother*: J. Fox. *The Hunter Island Inn Hat Boy*: G. Laine.

1918–1919 SEASON

Joseph Santley and Ivy Sawyer in SHE'S A GOOD FELLOW (Photo: White Studio)
Billy Rose Theatre Collection, New York Public Library for the Performing Arts

1918–1919 SEASON

1918.18 ## HITCHY-KOO OF 1918

A Summer (Musical) Revue in Two Acts, 14 Scenes[1]. Sketches and lyrics by Glen MacDonough and E. Ray Goetz. Music by Raymond Hubbell. Staged by Leon Errol. Scenery designed by H. Robert Law. Costumes by Arlington and Mary Blackburn; men's modern clothing by Nat Lewis. Orchestra under the direction of Oscar Radin. Orchestrations by Maurice DePackh and Frank Saddler. Produced by Raymond Hitchcock. Opened 6 June 1918 at the Globe Theatre and closed 3 August 1918 after 68 performances.

CAST: RAYMOND HITCHCOCK, LEON ERROL, IRENE BORDONI, GEORGE MOORE, ROY CUMMINGS, WARREN JACKSON, WILLIAM HOL-BROOK, ROY BINDER, THE KOUNS SISTERS (Sara, Nellie), THE MILLER QUARTETTE, EARL BENHAM, RAY DOOLEY, FELIX RUSH, ELEANOR SIN-CLAIR, CHARLES CARTMELL, LAURA HARRIS, James Miller, Frank Bessinger, Ivan Arbuckle, Frank Matier, Louise Saunders.
Chorus of Forty under Twenty: Elsie Lawson, Grace Russell, Gertrude Rial, Evelyn Des Roches, Laura Maverick, June Roberts, Lillian Fermoyle, Edith Stockham, FLORENCE O'DENISHAWN, Ruth Mitchell, Emma Haig, Elsie Lawson, Lucille Darling, June Gill, Misses R. Fermoyle, J. Dare, Lancier, Howard, Murray, Curtiss, Markham.

ACT 1[2]
Scene 1
The Miller's Daughter
Leonardo, Diego, two bandits: R. Hitchcock, L. Errol. *Tobasco*, the miller of Madajos: G. Moore. *Don Oleo*, her accepted suitor: R. Cummings. *Lorenzo*, her rejected suitor: W. Jackson. *Pepita*, the miller's daughter: W. Jackson. *Dolores*, a steed: R. Mitchell. *Carmen, Jacinta*, friends of Pepita: N Couns, S. Kouns. *Carmencita*, a dancer: J. Roberts. *Four Toreadors*: The Miller Quartette. *Villagers, Toreadors, Dancing Girls, etc.*
Scene 2
Two Minutes with Leon and Hitchy
(L. Errol, R. Hitchcock)
Scene 3
"Hitchy Koo Girl"
E. Benham
(*Music by* Percy Wenrich.)
Dance
C. Cartmell and Harris
Scene: The Golden Glades. *Southern Girl*: E. Lawson. *Northern Girl*: G. Russell. *Eastern Girl*: G. Rial. *Western Girl*: E. Des Roches. *Hitchy Koo Girl*: L. Maverick.
Scene 4
The Small Town Fireman's Ball
"It Will All End Up with the Right End Up"[3]
R. Hitchcock, Firemen
(*Music and Lyrics by* Henry Marshall.)

---

[1]The second of four in the annual series of musical revues produced by Raymond Hitchcock.
[2]Added to Act 1 for subsequent tour:
The Vendue
Cyrus Baxter, the auctioneer: R. Hitchcock. *Perce Baxter*, his assistant: Charles Howard. *Lydia Hatch*: E. Sinclair. *Captain Potter*, the town oracle: G. Moore. *Rufus Sprague*, the town sport: Jack Donahue. *Angustoria baxter*, only child of Baxter: R. Dooley. *Ethel*, a steed: Henri Lingen (fore), Al Holbrook (aft).
"How Can You Tell?"
Jean Tyne, E. Benham, assisted by Mr. Averacher
(*Music by* Harold Orlob.)
The Flower Shop
"Where Do They Come From?"
G. Moore Chorus
(*Music by* Harold Orlob. *Lyrics by* Fred Herendeen.)
George Gladiolies, a florist: R. Hitchcock. *Vincent Geranium*, head sales-man: G. Moore. *Mrs. Chestnut Hill*, a suburbanite: R. Mitchell. *Percy Penwiggle*, an author: C. Howard.
[3]Dropped for tour.

Jazz Dancing Number[4]
Misses Rial, Roberts, Lawson, Mitchell, Messrs. Holbrook, Lingen, Cartmell, Cummings, Chorus
Scene: Engine House in a New England Town.
Chief Silas Pringle of Alert Hose Company No. 1: R. Hitchcock. *Chauncey Nightingale*, town photographer: L. Errol. *Lem*, Captain of Hose Company, No. 1: F. Rush. *Martha Pringle*: R. Dooley. *Firemen, Guests*: (Ensemble).
Scene 5
"Se Saran Rose"[5] (Melba Waltz)
(*Music by* Luigi Arditi. *Italian Lyrics by* Pietro Mazzini.)/
"Echo Duet"[6] (In the Alps/Swiss Echo Song)
The Kouns Sisters
(*Music by* Carl Eckert.)
Scene 6
Somewhere in Brooklyn[7] (A Drama)
Song
R. Hitchcock
Horace Plunkett: R. Hitchcock. *Angy*, his only child: R. Dooley. *Verbena*, the Flatbush vampire: L. Harris.
Scene 7
Japanese Song
E. Benham, E. Sinclair
"The Lily of Longacre Square"
Misses Gill, J. Dare, Lancier, Howard, Murray, Curtiss
Scene: Japan.
Scene 8
A Music Store
A Salesman: R. Hitchcock. *Another Salesman*: L. Errol. *Irene La Nuisance*: I. Bordoni. *Percy Penwiggle*: R. Cummings. *"Clara"*: I. Bordoni.
Scene 9
The Trap
"Resurrection Rag"
E. Benham
Scene: Somewhere in the Wildest West.
Jack Rancid: R. Hitchcock. *Peublo Pete*, a bad man: L. Errol. *Cash Dawkins*: E. Benham. *Brass-Knuckle Bessie*: G. Moore. *Muck-a-Weena*, an Indian princess: E. Sinclair. *Agony Al*, a piano player: C. Cartmell. *Big Bill*: J. Miller. *Small Change*: R. Cummings. *Loose Cash*: F. Bessinger. *Cow Gentlemen*: (Ensemble). *Mag*: J. Roberts. *Mary*: G. Rial. *Tilly*: E. Haig. *Kate*: R. Dooley. *Flo*: R. Mitchell.

ACT 2[8]
Scene 1
One Arabian Night

---

[4]Replaced for subsequent tour by:
"Jazz-a-Muh-Jazz"
R. Mitchell, J. Donahue, Ensemble
(*Music by* Harold Orlob.)
[5]Dropped for tour.
[6]Dropped for tour.
[7]Added to this scene for tour:
"Ten Dirty Little Fingers"
R. Hitchcock
[8]Added to Act 2 for tour:
"Oh, What a Beautiful Baby You Turned Out To Be"
R. Hitchcock, Girls
(*Music by* Harry Tierney. *Lyrics by* Stanley Murphy and Ned Wayburn.)
"Underneath a Parasol"
Misses M. Benedict, E. Kearns, D. Welford, G. Rutland, L. Michaels, C. Welford
Music by Harold Orlob, Earl Benham and Eleanor Sinclair.)
Scene: Tokio.
"Come Dance with Me"
Juanita Means
Dance
F. O'Denishawn, E. Benham, Polka Girls
(*Music by* Harold Orlob.)
"The Devil Dog Marines"
G. Tyne, Chorus
"Here Come the Yanks with Their Tanks"
R. Mitchell
(*Music by* Harold Orlob. *Lyrics by* Ned Wayburn.)

Dance (Duet)
 L. Errol, E. Haig
Dance (Solo)
 F. O'Denishawn
  Ali Pasha, Vali of Babylone: G. Moore. *Selim Bey, Kadri Bey,* his aides: C.
  Cartmell, I. Arbuckle. *Essad Pasha,* the traitor: F. Matier. *"Erb Higgins":* R.
  Hitchcock. *'Harry Arrison:* L. Errl. *Aysha:* E. Lawson. *Hatidja:* L. Darling.
  Kondjeh: E. Des Roches. *Pervin:* G. LaRue. *Saidah:* E. Stockham. *Zuleika:*
  G. Russell. *Narifa,* a dancer: E. Haig. *Dancing Girls, Favorites, etc.:*
  (Ensemble).
Scene 2
 Raymond Hitchcock and Irene Bordoni
Scene 3
 Dinner Is Served[9]
  Scene: Kitchen in a Country Residence.
   Mr. Skillet, a chef: L. Errol. *Elizabeth,* a kitchen maid: R. Dooley.
   Pauncefort, a butler: G. Moore.
Scene 4
 One Afternoon
 Gold Dance
  C. Cartmell, L. Harris
 "When the Girls Get Wise"[10]
  R. Cummings, Girls
   Basil Beaver: R. Cummings. *Mignonette Murgatroyd:* R. Mitchell. *Girls:*
   Misses L. Fermoyle, R. Fermoyle, Lawson, Markham, Lancier, E. Des Roches.
Scene 5
 The Peace Maker[11]
 "Let's Play Hookie"[12]
  R. Dooley, Girls
   The Curate: E. Benham. *The Curate's Wife:* L. Saunders. *Ronald MacGreel:*
   R. Hitchcock. *His Brood (5): Christie MacGreel:* F. O'Denishawn. *Jamas
   MacGreel:* J. Gill. *Kathie MacGreel:* E. Sinclair. *Mary MacGreel:* J. Roberts.
   Davey MacGreel: C. Cartmell. *Georgie MacTavish:* L. Errol. *His Clan (5):
   Maggie MacTavish:* R. Dooley. *Sandy MacTavish:* G. Moore. *Jeannie
   MacTavish:* R. Mitchell. *Nan MacTavish:* L. Fermoyle. *Agnes MacTavish:* E.
   Haig. *Walking Delegate:* I. Arbuckle.
Finale
 (Entire Company)

1918.19 ZIEGFELD FOLLIES OF 1918

A Musical Revue in Two Acts, 26 Scenes[13]. Lines (sketches) and lyrics by
Rennold Wolf and Gene Buck. Music by Louis A. Hirsch and Dave
Stamper. Interpolations by Irving Berlin and Victor Jacobi. Staged by Ned
Wayburn. Scenic decorations by Joseph Urban. Costumes designed by
Schneider-Anderson Artists. Lighting by Ben Beerwald. Orchestra under the
direction of Frank Darling. Produced by Florenz Ziegfeld, Jr. Opened 18
June 1918 at the New Amsterdam Theatre and closed 14 September 1918
after 105 performances.

CAST: EDDIE CANTOR, ANN PENNINGTON, WILL ROGERS, MARILYN
MILLER, W.C. FIELDS, FRANK CARTER, THE FAIRBANKS TWINS (Madeleine,
Marion), ROSE DOLORES, JOE FRISCO, HARRY KELLY, ALLYN KING, KAY
LAURELL, LILLIAN LORRAINE, BILLIE RITCHIE, BERT SAVOY, JAY BREN-
NAN, GUS MINTON, BEE PALMER, Sylvia Ellias, Pauline Hall, John Blue, Marie
Wallace, Dorothy Leeds, Leonard Barton, Muriel Miles, Martha Mansfield, Gladys
Feldman, Kathryn Perry, Olive Osborne, Florence Cripps, Clay Hill.

"Good-bye, France (You'll Never Be Forgotten by the U.S.A)"
 R. Mitchell
 (*Music and Lyrics by* Irving Berlin.)
 Scene: The Beachwood Inn.
  Horace Plunkett: R. Hitchcock. *Dorothy Doolittle:* Gene Tyne. *Mr. Jobings,* a
  first nighter: E. Benham. *Miss Billings,* his fiancée: Anne Murray. *Henri,* a
  waiter: H. Lingen. *Captain of Tank Corps:* E. Sinclair.
[9]Revised for tour as Dinner at Seven for subsequent tour, reset at Golter,
Long Island (near Great Neck).
[10]Dropped for tour.
[11]The Peace Maker and "Let's Play Hookie" were replaced during the New
York run by:
 A Dream
  First Nighter: E. Benham. *His Wife:* Eslie Lawson.
[12]Dropped for tour.
[13]The twelfth in the annual series of musical revues which began in 1907
under the auspices of Florenz Ziegfeld.

Ladies of the Ensemble: Ruth Taylor, Hazel Washburn, Nancy Larned, Edith Hawes,
Irene Nilson, Dorothy Richardson, Gladys Zielian, Muriel Miles, Annette Herbert,
Carol Young, Theresa Rubins, Miles Rubins, Florence Atkinson, Charlotte LaGrande,
Julie Ross, Minnie Harrison, Martha Wood, Carrol Young, Addie Young, Virginia
Young, Katherine Brady, Agnes Virginia, Helen Lloyd, Misses V. Taylor, McKenzie,
Barnes, Robinson, Morton, Ullman, Mack, Masso, Fiore, Pompan, Reed, Poole,
LaBarre, Reynolds, Jordan, Savage, D. Miller, Ahearn, Braham, Baron, Walsh, Swayne,
Perry, Sheppard, Allo, M. Washburn, Vernon, Thropp, Erwin, Blue, Farnworth,
Mathewes, Barrett, Shelly, Baker, Evans, Mildred Richardson, Bell, Betts, Leisy,
Clarens. *Male Chorus:* Messrs. Cody, Hicks, Young, Rogers, Vickers, Hill, Kelly,
Ostrander, Davis, Smith.

ACT 1[14]
Scene 1
 The Warring World
  Spirit of the Follies: K. Laurell.
Scene 2
 The Folly of Speed: O. Osborne. *The Folly of Dance:* J. Ross. *The Folly of Drink:*
 F. Cripps. *The Folly of Fame:* G. Zielian. *The Folly of Vanity:* F. Atkinson. *The
 Folly of Bluff:* G. Feldman. *The Folly of Love:* D. Leeds. *The Folly of Clothes:* R.
 Dolores. *Herald:* S. Ellias.
Scene 3
 The Peaches of 1918: R. Taylor, H. Washburn, N. Larned, E. Hawes, I. Nilson,
 D. Richardson, M. Miles, A. Herbert, C. Young, T. Rubins, C. LaGrande. *The
 Follies Girl of 1918:* A King.
Scene 4
 A Patent Attorney's Office
  Bunkus Munyan, a patent attorney: W. C. Fields. *George Trimmer,* his clerk: F.
  Carter. *Clarence,* an office boy: E. Cantor. *Henry Nutt,* gun inventor: G.
  Minton. *Bill Auburn,* chair inventor: H. Kelly.
Scene 5
 Indian Dance[15]
  A. Pennington
Scene 6
 "Starlight"
  L. Lorraine
  (*Music by* Dave Stamper.)
   Evening Star: L. Lorraine. *Other Stars:* McKenzie, Barnes, Robinson,
   Morton, Brady, Ullman, Virginia, Mack, Ross, Masso, Pompan, Reed, Poole,
   LaBarre, Reynolds, Jordan, Savage, D. Miller, Ahearn, Braham, Baron,
   Walsh, Harrison, Wood, Swayne, Perry, Sheppard, Allo, M. Washburn,
   Vernon, Thropp.
Scene 7
 "In Old Versailles"
  (*Music by* Louis A. Hirsch.)
   Billie Burke: A. King. *Henry Miller:* F. Carter. *Millers:* Misses G. Feldman, F.
   Cripps, A. Virginia, K. Brady. *Burkes:* Misses R. Taylor, C. Young, H.
   Washburn, O. Osborne.
 "(When I Hear a) Syncopated Tune"
  M. Miller
  (*Music by* Louis A. Hirsch.)
Scene 8
 Camouflage as devised and written by Will Rogers[16]
  H. Kelly
Scene 9
 A Miniature: "When I'm Looking at You" L. Lorraine, M. Wallace,
 Fairbanks Twins
  (*Music by* Dave Stamper.)
Scene 10
 Timely Topics (He is liable to talk about anything or anybody.)
  W. Rogers
 "A Prairie Frolic"
  A. Pennington

---

[14]Interpolated for subsequent tour, as per published sheet music:
 "If She Means What I Think She Means"
  Frank Carter
  (*Music and Lyrics by* Buddy G. DeSylva and Arthur Jackson.)
 "The Navy Will Bring Them Back!"
  Frank Carter
  (*Music by* Ira Schuster. *Lyrics by* Howard Johnson.)
[15]Replaced for subsequent tour by a Dance performed by Frank Carter.
[16]Replaced after opening by:
 The Original Joe Frisco, Creator of Jazz Dancing

Scene 11

Finale

"I'll Pin My Medal on the Girl I Left Behind"
(*Music and Lyrics by* Irving Berlin.)
A Private: F. Carter. *A General*: G. Minton. [*The Girl I Left Behind*: M. Mansfield.] *Our Boys*: Male Chorus (all rejected).

"We're Busy Building Boats"
(*Music by* Louis A. Hirsch.)
Ship Builders: A. Young, Misses LeGrande, Herbert, Osborne, V. Taylor, R. Taylor, Larned, Hogan, Flore, Miles, Rubens, Richardson, H. Washburn, Barnes, Erwin, Atkinson.

Aviators' Parade
Girl Chorus
Red Cross: E. Hawes.

"A Yankee Doodle Dance"
M. Miller
Assisted by Misses M. Wood, Blue, Farnworth, H. Lloyd, Mathewes, Barrett, M. Harrison, Williams, M. Shelly, Baker, Evans.
Allied Color Bearers United: *America*: M. Mansfield. *France*: G. Feldman. *England*: R. Taylor. *Belgium*: H. Washburn. *Cuba*: F. Cripps. *Italy*: Miss Atkinson. *Portugal*: M. Richardson. *China*: M. Miles. *Japan*: M. Wallace. *Servia*: Miss Larned. *Greece*: O. Osborne. *Montenegro*: C. Young. *Victory*: A. King.

Scene 12

Forward, Allies! (A Picture arranged and staged by Ben Ali Haggin.)
France: K. Laurel. *Red Cross Nurse*: P. Hall. *Children*: Fairbanks Twins. *America*: Dolores. *England*: D. Leeds. *Allied Soldiers, etc.*

ACT 2[17]

Scene 1

The Lower Regions
His Satanic Majesty (added lines written by himself): W. Rogers. *Head Clerk*: F. Carter. *The Girl in Hell*: A. King. *Bell Boy*: K. Perry. *A Profiteer*: H. Kelly. *New York Society Woman*: Dolores. *A Dancing Girl*: A. Pennington. *Eve*: K. Laurel. *Twin Imps*: Fairbanks Twins. *Liberty Loan Slacker*: C. Hill. *Somebody's Sweetheart*: D. Leeds. *Senator La Follette*: W. C. Fields. *The Czar*: A. Youngs. *The Kaiser*: G. Minton. *Imps*: Wood, Poole, Harrison, Braham, Bell, Shelly, Betts, Lloyd. *She Devils*: Virginia, Robinson, Morton, Brady, Leisy, Richardson, Ullman, Erwin. *Demons*: Male Dancers.

Scene 2

"Mine Was a Marriage of Convenience"
M. Miller
(*Music by* Louis A. Hirsch.)
Billie Burke: M. Miller.

Scene 3

"The Blue Devils (of France)"
L. Lorraine
(*Music and Lyrics by* Irving Berlin.)
(*Assisted by*) Misses R. Taylor, Eaton, Virginia, Brady, Larned, Perry, Westcott, Ross, Masso, Wallace, LaBarre, Ahearn, Reed, Savage, Baron, Sheppard, Jordan, Miller, Braham, Wood, Harrison, Washburn, Clarens.

Scene 4

A Game of Golf (by W. C. Fields)
Colonel Bogie: W. C. Fields. *Brassie*, his caddy: H. Kelly. *Another Caddy*: J. Blue. *Miss Green*, his opponent: A. King. *Miss Bride L. Path*: D. Leeds. *Miss Hope I. Shootem*: M. Mansfield. *Miss Dunwoodie*: G. Feldman. *Ignatz*, her little brother: K. Perry.

Scene 5

"Poor Little Me"
M. Miller

Scene 6

The Aviator's Test
Percival Johnson, the Applicant: E. Cantor. *Recruiting Officer*: F. Carter. *His Assistant*: G. Minton. *Asylum Attendant*: H. Kelly.

Scene 7

"Since the Men Have Gone to War"
A. King
Fire-Miss: R. Taylor. *Conductorette*: J. Ross. *Police-MAM*: K. Perry.

---

[17]For subsequent tour, the following was added to Act 2:
A Syncopated Frolic
A. Pennington
Added after opening to Act 2, Scene 1, end:
Inventor of Comedy Bicycles (Scene 1, end)
Billie Ritchie, assisted by Male Principals

Messengeress: M. Wallace. *Mail-miss*: F. Cripps. *Chauffeurette*: L. Baron. *Bell-Hop*: G. Feldman.

Scene 8

"Any Old Time at All"
L. Lorraine, Male Chorus
(*Music by* Louis A. Hirsch.)

Scene 9

"A Dream" (*Scene music by* Victor Jacobi.)
The Premiere: M. Miller. *Her Rival*: D. Miller. *The Dreamer*: F. Carter. *Coryphees*: Misses Braham, Alls, Baron, Savage, LaBarre, Walsh, Clarens, Reed, Vernon, L. Lorraine, D. Miller, Sheppard, Swayne, Westcott, M. Washburn, Jordan.

Scene 10

Fresh from the Bronx[18]
E. Cantor

["But After the Ball Was Over! (Then He Made Up for Lost Time)"
(*Music and Lyrics by* Buddy G. DeSylva and Arthur Jackson.)

"If She Means What I Think She Means"
(*Music by* Buddy G. DeSylva. *Lyrics by* Buddy G. DeSylva and Arthur Jackson.)

"Oh How I Hate to Get Up in the Morning"[19]
(*Music and Lyrics by* Irving Berlin.)

"Broadway's Not a Bad Place After All"
(*Music and Lyrics by* Harry Ruby and Eddie Cantor.)

"Would You Rather Be a Soldier with an Eagle on Your Shoulder, or a Private with a Chicken on Your Knee?"
(*Music by* Archie Gottler. *Lyrics by* Sidney D. Mitchell.)

"Roaming Romeo"

"You Keep Sending 'Em Over and We'll Keep Knocking 'Em Down"

"Come On Papa"
(*Music and Lyrics by* Edgar Leslie and Harry Ruby.)]

Scene 11

"The Garden of Your Dreams" (The Garden of My Dreams)
L. Lorraine, F. Carter
(*Music by* Louis A. Hirsch, Dave Stamper.)
Assisted by M. Brady, U. Barnes, McKenzie, LeGrande, Fiore, R. Taylor, Osborne, Larned, Rubins, Herbert, V. Taylor, H. Washburn, V. Young, Male Chorus.

Scene 12

Getting Acquainted
B. Savoy and J. Brennan

Scene 13

"I Want to Learn (How) to Jazz Dance"
B. Palmer
(*Music by* Dave Stamper.)
Dance
A. Pennington
Assisted by 'Frisco." *Frisco Girls*: Misses Ross, Dunn, Jordan, Bell, M. Washburn, Poole, Shelley, Harrison, Wood, Braham, Westcott, D. Miller, Reynolds, Baron, Voltaire, Perry. *Cabaret Girls*: Misses Hawes, Robinson, Zielian, Erwin, Nielson, Atkinson, Richardson, Hagan, Fiore, V. Taylor, Herbert, LaGrande, Barnes, Morton, McKenzie.

Scene 14

Finale
Everybody

1918.20   THE PASSING SHOW OF 1918

A Musical Revue in Two Acts, 13 Scenes[20]. Sketches and lyrics by Harold Atteridge. Music by Sigmund Romberg and Jean Schwartz. Staged by J. C. Huffman. Musical numbers and ballet staged by Jack Mason. Scenery designed by Watson Barratt. Orchestra under the direction of Charles Previn. Entire production under the personal supervision of J.J. Shubert. Produced by Messrs. Shubert. Opened 25 July 1918 at the Winter Garden and closed 9 November 1918 after 142 performances[21].

---

[18]Later billed as "The Apostle of Pep."
[19]Introduced in YIP YIP YAPHANK in August 1918 and added later by Eddie Cantor to the FOLLIES.
[20]The Eighth in the annual series of revues, produced since 1912 by the Messrs. Shubert, which began in 1894. Billed as the Winter Garden's Annual Revue.
[21]Costumes uncredited.

CAST: GEORGE HASSELL, WILLIE HOWARD, EUGENE HOWARD, SAM WHITE, LOU CLAYTON, AILEEN ROONEY, ADELE ASTAIRE, FRED ASTAIRE, FRANK FAY, ISABEL LOWE, JESSIE REED, VIOLET ENGLEFIELD, CHARLES RUGGLES, VIRGINIA FOX BROOKS, NELL CARRINGTON, ISABEL RODRIGUEZ, EMILY MILES, OLGA ROLLER, LOUISE CONTI, DAVID DREYER, ARTHUR ALBRO, GEORGE SCHILLER, Florence Elmore, Dorsha, Edward Basse.

Personnel of the Chorus: Show Girls: Grace Keeshon, Marion Mooney, Marie Stafford, Fawn Conway, May Booth, Nita Naldi, Betty Fitch, Barbara McCree, Mary Rinehart, Adrienne Dillon, Beatrice DeRoe, Kitty Astra, Betty Palmer, Lillian Stone, Trixie Brunette, Peggy Mitchell, Loretta Harris, Grace Lee, Dorothy Clay, Grace Rivers, Ethel Walsh, Mae Moore, Nan Valentine, Arline Page, Peggy Radford, Elsie Young, Ruth Coster, Marion Harley. *Dancers:* Edith Pierce, Inez Francis, Elsie LaMont, Florence Wilde, Trixie Raymond, Edna Whitney, Ella Foster, Aileen Rooney, Rose Coyle, Helen Edward, Irene Held, Weedie Furlong, Dorothy Pond, Lotta Morse, Alice Elliott, Billie Elliott, Gypsy Mooney, Peggy Pendleton, Frances Hudson, Helen Neary, Ann Mason, Dolores Mendez, Dolly Wallace, Mary Gray, Orilla Smith, Mona Lorraine, Peggy Dixon. *Men:* Messrs. George Barnum, Channing Hare, Lare Benson, Harry Homan, Jack Hall, Frank Hall, Jay Lindsay, Stanley Rayburn, Ralph Symington, Teddy Stevens.

ACT 1[22]

Scene 1

"I (Really) Can't Make My Feet Behave"
    A. Astaire, a Bouquet of Winter Garden Steppers

"War Stamps" (Won't You Buy a War Stamp?)
    I. Lowe, C. Ruggles, Thrift Stamp Beauties
    (*Music by* Ray Perkins.)

"My Baby Talking Girl" (My Baby-Talk Lady)
    F. Fay, C. Ruggles, I. Lowe, Baby Talking Girls
    (*Music by* Sigmund Romberg.)

"Go West, Young Girl"
    V. F. Brooks, some queens of the East and West
    (*Music by* Russell Tarbox.)

"Trombone Jazz"
    S. White, L. Clayton, Winter Garden Jazz Dancers
    (*Music by* Jean Schwartz.)
        Scene: Hotel Giltmore.
        Miss Song: O. Roller. *Miss Dansant:* A. Astaire. *Miss Flirt:* F. Elmore.
        John Paul Bart: C. Ruggles. *William Baxter:* F. Fay. *Miss Louise:* L. Conti.
        Lola Pratt: I. Lowe. *Head Porter:* S. White. *Another Porter:* L. Clayton.
            A Bouquet of Winter Garden Beauties: Jessie: J. Reed. *Marian:* M.
        Stafford. *Fawn:* F. Conway. *Nita:* N. Naldi. *Grace:* G. Keeshon. *Marion:*
        M. Mooney. *Mary:* M. Booth. *Betty:* B. Fitch. *Loretta:* L. Harris. *Beatrice:*
        B. DeRoe. *Virginia:* V. F. Brooks. *William:* F. Fay. *John:* C. Ruggles. *Victor
        Gates:* G. Hassell. *Michael Devlin:* E. Basse. *Mr. Sleuth:* D. Dreyer.

Scene 2

"My Vampire Girl" (Oh, You Vampire Girls)(Oh Those Vampire Girls)
    A. Albro, Alluring Vampire Girls
        Scene: Artland.
            An Artist: A. Albro.

Scene 3

"Squab Farm"
    F. Astaire, a Nest of Milk Fed Squabs
    (*Music by* Sigmund Romberg.)

"The Shimmy Sisters"
    E. Pierce, A. Rooney, F. Fay

"I'll Make an Angel Out of You"
    F. Fay, I. Lowe
    (On the Level, You're a Devil, But I'll Soon Make an Angel Out of You)
    (*Music by* Jean Schwartz. *Lyrics by* Joe Young.)

"(That Soothing) Serenade"
    E. Howard, W. Howard
    (*Music and Lyrics by* Harry DeCosta.)

---

[22]Added for subsequent tour after "Bring on the Girls", before Ballet (Act 1):
    "Merely Passing Through"
        Irene Franklin
    Added for subsequent tour, as per published sheet music:
    "Peachie"
        E. Miles
        (*Music by* Albert Gumble. *Lyrics by* Jack Yellen.)

"Bring on the Girls"
    E. Miles, N. Carrington, A. Astaire, F. Astaire, Clayton & White, Some Beautiful Girls
        Scene: Excelsior Moving Picture Studio.
        The Steno: E. Miles. *Mr. Chicadee:* F. Astaire. *John:* C. Ruggles. *William:*
        F. Fay. *Harriet:* F. Conway. *Rena:* L. Conti. *The Shimmy Sisters:* E.
        Pierce, A. Rooney. *Lola:* I. Lowe. *Sammy:* W. Howard. *The Director:* E.
        Howard. *Miss Jambo:* N. Carington. *Miss Homely:* F. Elmore. *Mr. Pistol:*
        G. Schiller. *Victor Gates:* G. Hassell. *Virginia:*

Scene 4
    Scene: Courtyard of the Palace of Americus.
    Nubian Slave: Dorsha.

Scene 5

Ballet (Salome)[23]
    Narcissa: A. Albro. *Admiration:* E. Basse. *A Page:* F. Fay. *Cabaretta:* B. DeRoe.
    Rowena: F. Conway. *Walza:* M. Stafford. *Fox Trotta:* P. Germond. *Jazza:* J. Reed.
    Salome: V. F. Brooks. *Samnicus:* W. Howard. *Genicus:* E. Howard. *The Prophet:*
    G. Schiller. *Gay Life:* V. Englefield. *Americus:* G. Hassell. *Dance:* I. Rodriquez.

ACT 2[24]

Scene 1

"Twit, Twit, Twit"
    F. Astaire, A. Astaire, a flock of dancing birds

"My Holiday Girls"
    C. Ruggles, a girl for every month
    (*Music by* Augustus Barratt.)

"Quick Service"
    F. Astaire, A. Astaire
        Scene: Birdland.
        Miss Robin: A. Astaire. *Chanticleer:* F. Astaire.

Scene 2

A Listening Post on the Shore of England

Scene 3

A London Air Raid

Scene 4
    Scene: Somewhere in the Arbor.
    Lou: L. Clayton. *Sam:* S. White.

Scene 5

"(The) Galli Curci Rag"
    W. Howard, E. Howard, V. Englefield
    (*Music by* Sigmund Romberg.)

"Smiles"
    N. Carrington, some smiling girls
    (*Music by* Lee S. Roberts. *Lyrics by* J. Will Callahan.)
        Scene: Child's, at 59th Street.
        The Butler: J. Hall. *Miss Wheatcakes:* E. Miles. *The Oriental Kid:* L.
        Benson. *The Jolly Sisters:* K. Astra, P. Mitchell. *The Shimmy Sisters:* E.
        Pierce, A. Rooney. *Mrs. Reizenweber:* A. Astaire. *A Waiter:* F. Astaire.
        Mary Ryan: M. Booth. *Nazimova:* L. Stone. *Frances Black:* P. Purtell. *Ina
        Claire:* M. Rinehart. *Jessie Reed:* Herself. *John:* C. Ruggles. *Miss
        Meadowbrook:* N. Carrington. *Clarence:* F. Fay. *Yeggman Jim:* G. Hassell.
        Ethel Barrymore: V. F. Brooks. *Mr. Grapefruit:* D. Dreyer. *The Chief:* W.
        Howard. *Lady Style:* J. Belyea. *Galli Curci:* V. Englefield. *Caruso:* E.
        Howard. *Police Captain:* E. Basse.

Scene 6

A Marriage of Inconvenience

"My Duchess of the Long Ago"
    O. Roller, some wonderful girls
        Marton: V. F. Brooks. *Jessamina:* N. Carrington. *Mme. le Comte Billie Burke:*
        I. Lowe. *Peter:* E. Basse. *William:* F. Fay. *John:* C. Ruggles. *Rowbez:* A. Albro.
        Victor Gates: G. Hassell. *Comte D'Candle:* G. Schiller.

Scene 7

Some Songs
    E. Howard, W. Howard
    ["Boots"]

---

[23]A burlesque on Oscar Wilde's 'Salome.'

[24]Added for subsequent tour after "Twit, Twit, Twit" in Act 2:
    "Sammie"
        I. Franklin
    "When the Kaiser's Mother Called Him Little Willie"
        I. Franklin
        At the Piano: Burton Green.

Scene: A Telegraph Office.
  Sammy: W. Howard. *Eugene*: E. Howard. *Flo*: F. Elmore.
Scene 8[25]
  "Dress, Dress, Dress"
    O. Roller, a few Winter Garden Models
    (*Music by* Sigmund Romberg.)
  Spanish Ballet
    I. Rodriquez, Spanish Dancing Girls and Boys
    Scene: The Gold Room.
      A *Spanish Girl*: I. Rodriquez. *Virginia*: V. F. Brooks. *Charles*: C. Ruggles.
      Nell: N. Carrington. *Emily*: E. Miles. *Frank*: F. Fay. *George*: G. Hassell.
      Isabel: I. Lowe. *Fred*: F. Astaire. *Adele*: A. Astaire. *Violet*: V. Englefield.

1918.21

YIP YIP YAPHANK

A Musical 'Mess' Cooked up by the Boys of Camp Upton (Musical Revue) in Two Acts, 8 Scenes. Music and lyrics by Sergeant Irving Berlin. Staged by Private Will H. Smith. Authorized and given through the courtesy and cooperation of Major-General J. Franklin Bell. Band under the direction of Sergeant Dan Castler. Produced by Uncle Sam. Opened 19 August 1918 at the Century Theatre, moved 2 September 1918 to the Lexington Theatre and closed 14 September 1918 after 32 performances[26].

CAST: Sergeant IRVING BERLIN, Q. M. Sergeant Major WILLIAM BAUMAN, Pvt. DANNY [DAN] HEALY, SAMMY LEE, KUY KENDALL, Pvt. BOB HIGGINS, BENNY LEONARD, HOWARD FRIEND, LOUIS GAUT, Pvt. GORDAN NEWMAN, Captain PAUL McALLISTER, Pvts. SOLLY CUTNER, HUGHIE L. CLARK, JAMES REILLY, HARRY GREEN, Brennan, Brenna, Phillips, Snyder, Schor, Ward, Johnson, Kline, Jorn, Murphy, Ferreriar, Grey, Glander, Sheridan, Miglion, B. Collins, J. White, C. Cahn, William Dale, Matt Feiber, Jack Farley, F. Hamburger, H. Bowen, F. DeMatthews, Ed Astroff, L. Lohr, P O'Neill, D. Miglinio, J. Rothaug, B. Marcus, Milt Geiber.

Chorus: Privates Abbott, Breen, G. Becker, Brennick, Bjornquist, Breslin, Balling, Barnett, J. Barsalion, B. Brown, Bragg, Bolton, D. Brown, A. Brown, Boyle, Bolles, Buckley, P. J. Burns, Borgraff, Burett, Breyer, Bryde, Campbell, Colando, Cullen, Conden, Conway, Cline, Cronin, Haggerty, M. Clark, Churchill, Cahill, Conden, Dermody, Degnan, Deick, Dinan, Davison, Donaldson, Ellis, Epstein, Ewell, Francois, Frederich, Feilberman, Fitzpatrick, Frost, Gedney, Gold, Gaulen, Grossman, Garblick, Ginsberg, Gigli, Gorman, Goldoff, Gray, Golenski, Gillen, Downey, Gilman, Hayes, Herman, Heim, Hill, Holly, Jorgas, Jacobs, Johnson, Johnston, Jonas, Kouch, Kruger, Kader, Karsch, Jack Kelly, Sgt. Joe Kelly, J. Kelly, First Sergeant E. Kelly, Kime, Kubler, Long, Lederer, Langdon, Lyons, Lynch, LaGleur, Meyers, McEnaney, Meidel, Mathias, McCrystal, Mitchell, Mullins, Murray, Mahoney, McNamara, McMahan, J. O. Martin, Sgt. Miller, Mantia, McNeil, Mintz, Moffat, J. Moran, McGuiness, Nacht, Nelson, Newman, Nelve, J. A. O'Brien, Orlando, W. O'Brien, Osterweil, J. O'Brien, Patton, Pakulski, Podmar, Robinson, Rosenberg, Reidler, Anderson, Rosenblum, Randal, Reiss, Rothang, Reiss, Sgt. Richard, Rosenthal, Syester, Scheedy, Seigel, Stenworth, Schlomchug, Scarpellas, Stengel, Stover, Schwimmer, Steffin, Stark, Schonfeld, Strohm, Schreenan, Tassimero, Talbot, Turner, Welch, Walsh, Woodward, Walderman, White, Weissberg, York.

ACT 1
Scene 1

  Upton Military Minstrels
    In Command: Captain P. McAllister. *Interlocutor*: Q. M. Sergeant Major W. Bauman. *End Men*: Privates H. L. Clarke, J. Reilly, H. Green, S. Cutner.
  Tamborine Drill
    Entire Company
  "Hello, Hello, Hello" (Opening Chorus)
    Entire Company
  Solos
    Pvts. Brennan, Brenna, Phillips, Snyder, Schor, Ward
  The Captain's Address to the Company
  "Bevo"
    Pvt. Schor, Company

---

[25] Added during the run to this scene before the Spanish Ballet:
  "Messenger Boy"
    W. Howard
[26] Scenery donated by Cohan & Harris, Elliott, Comstock and Gest, Messrs. Shubert, J. H. Beaumont, C. B. Dillingham, Dodge & Castle. Costumes donated by Cohan & Harris, Florenz Ziegfeld, Snyder Anderson & Company, C. B. Dillingham. Individual costumes donated by Mme. Alda, Norma Talmadge, Alice Joyce, Ann Pennington, Lillian Lorraine, Marilynn Miller, and the Dolly Sisters.

"Silver Threads (Among the Gold)"
  Pvts. Johnson, Brenna, Kline, Jorm, Chorus
  (*Music by* H. P. Danks. *Poem [lyrics] by* Eben Rexford.)
"What a Difference a Uniform Will Make"(Ever Since I Put on a Uniform)
  Pvt. Clark, Chorus
"Mandy" (Sterling Silver Moon)
  Pvt. Murphy, Pickininnies, Chorus
    Mandy: Pvt. D. Healy. *Pickininnies*: *Girls*: Pvts. B. Collins, J. White, C. Cahn, W. Dale, M. Feiber, J. Farley. *Boys*: Pvts. Hamburger, H. Bowen, F. D. Mathews, F. D. Matthews, E. Astroff, L. Loehr, P. O'Neill.
"Ragtime Razor Brigade"
  Pvts. Clark, Snyder, Reilly, Chorus
The Court Martial
  The Prisoner: Pvt. B. Higgins. *Firing Squad*: Heim, Padmore, Schreenan, Sheridan.
"Ding Dong"
  Pvt. Higgins, Chorus
    The Bride: H. Friend. *The Preacher*: L. Gaut. *Four Bridesmaids*: (Themselves).
Scene 2
  Killing Time
    K. Kendall, S. Lee
      The Bicycle Rider: Pvt. Downey. *The Juggler*: Pvt. Ferreriar. *The Acrobats*: Pvts. D. Miglinio, J. Rothaug, G. Becker, J. Tassinero, W. Lynch, J. Martin, J. Bassilion.
Scene 3
  "Come Along, Come Along, Come Along"
    Boys, Girls
      Girls: L. Gaut, Fleeson, H. L. Clarke, T. Ward, D. Healy, J. Kelly, Moffet, Fielberman, J. Reilly, Cline, Schongold, G. Newman. *Boys*: Pvts. Murphy, Astroff, Goldorff, Snyder, Turner, Schor, Conway, Talbot, Haggerty, Stover, O'Neill, Hamburger.
Scene 4
  "Love Interest" (Duet)
    Brennan, B. Higgins
      The Boy: Pvt. Brennan. *The Girl*: Pvt. B. Higgins. *The Mother*: Pvt. Grey.
Scene 5
  "Jazz Land" (Send a Lot of Jazz Bands Over There)
    Entire Company
ACT 2
Scene 1
  Company Street, Camp Upton
    The Sergeant: Pvt. B. Higgins. *The Corporal*: Pvt. H. Clark.
  "(Dream On, Little) Soldier Boy"
    Pvt. Glander, Chorus
  The Dancing Drill
    Sgt. B. Higgins, (Privates)
    (*Staged by* Pvts. Murphy and Healy.)
      Privates: M. Geiber, L. Lohr, J. Farley, B. Marcus, H. Bowen, J. White, C. Cahn, F. Hamburger, P. J. Burns, P. O'Neill, F. DeMatthews, W. Dale, F. Gaulter, P. Cahill, M. Frederick, J. E. O'Brien.
  "(Oh,) How I Hate to Get Up in the Morning"
    Sgt. I. Berlin
    Down from the Follies:
      Ponies: (Pvts.) D. Brown, Steffen, Osterweil, Rickards, McNeill, Dale, Stark, LaFleur, Ginsburg, Godney, Brenneck, Rosenthal, Meyers, Boyle, Burnett, Gilman. *Show Girls*: Pvts. Dieck, Jorges, Breslin, Mahoney, Degnon, Mahoney, Ellis, Patton, H. Friend. *Principals*: *Lillian Lorraine*: Pvt. Snyder. *W.C. Fields*: Pvt. Ferrerier. *Will Rogers*: Pvt. G. Newman. *Marilynn Miller*: Pvt. Belles. *Eddie Cantor*[27]: Pvt. S. Cutner. *(Joe) Frisco*: Pvt. Lohr. *Ann Pennington*: Pvt. K. Kendall. *The Military Police*: Pvts. Seyster, McCrystal, Barnett, White, Martin, Bryde, W. O'Brien, Meidel. *The Army Cooks*: Pvts. Ward, Schor, J. Kelly, York, Brennan, Johnson, Weisberg, Brenna. *The Army Doctors*: Pvts. Cline, Bolton, Cronin, Welsh, A. Kelly, Talbot, Schonegold, Reiss. *Prisoners*: Pvts. Turner, Rosenberg, Moon, McEnaney, Johnston, Nacht, A. Brown, Philips. *Buglers*: Pvts. J. O'Brien, Robinson, A. Clark, Grossman, Fields, McGuiness, McNamara, Ewell.
  "Kitchen Police" (Poor Little Me, I'm on K.P.)
    Sgt. I. Berlin, Chorus

---

[27] Singing "Baby" per Variety review.

Scene 2

Killing More Time

Savoy & Brennan: Sgt. Bauman, Pvt. Fitzpatrick.

Specialty

Dolly Sisters: K. Kendall, S. Lee.

Scene 3

"(I Can Always Find a Little Sunshine in) The Y.M.C.A."

Pvt. Johnson, Chorus

Scene: Interior of the Y.M.C.A. Hut.

Boxing Exhibition

Instructor B. Leonard, Pvt. Miglion

"We're on Our Way to France"

Pvt. Brennan, Entire Company

Finale

1918.22   HE DIDN'T WANT TO DO IT

A Play with Music in Three Acts. Book and lyrics by George Broadhurst. Music by Silvio Hein. Based on the farce of the same name by Walter Hackett and George Broadhurst. Staged by Clifford Brook. Dances and musical numbers staged by Bert French. Scenery painted by D. Frank Dodge and William Castle. Gowns, costumes and hats designed by Henri Bendel. Orchestra under the direction of Theodore Stearns. Produced by George Broadhurst. Opened 20 August 1918 at the Broadhurst Theatre and closed 7 September 1918 after 23 performances.

CAST: *Alexander McPherson*: ERNEST TORRENCE. *O. Vivian Smith*: PERCY AMES. *Washington Demming*: CHARLES MEAKINS. *Detective*: NED. A. SPARKS. *Manager of the Hotel*: Alexander Frank. *Waiter*: Robert O'Connor. *Lieutenant Rodgers*: JOSEPH WILMOT. *Paula Wainwright*: KATHERINE GALLOWAY. *Marjorie Thompson*: HELEN SHIPMAN. *Norma Wallace*: Adele Blood. *Mary Manners*: Elsa Thomas. *Wilda Wood*: Elsie Gordon. *Bertha Barrison*: Natalie Bates. *Constance Conover*: Helen Pierre. *Roberta Runyon*: Edna Pierre. *Francis Farrington*: Mary Cunningham. *Neva Norcross*: Carrie DeNoville. *Gertrude Glover*: Florence Collier. *Dorothy Daniels*: Anna Toddings. *Kate Carley*: Mary McDonald. *Henrietta Hadley*: Jean Carroll. *Janice Godfrey*: Clara Carroll. *Katherine Kollis*: Ona Hamilton. *Marie Melton*: Dorothy LaRue. *Leonore Leonard*: Gladys Clifton. *Nanette Norris*: Ida Ross.

The action takes place in the Lounge Room of a Hotel on the Riviera at the present time.

Act 1: Morning.

Act 2: Afternoon.

Act 3: Evening.

ACT 1

"What Mother Used to Say to Me" (Song)

H. Shipman, Chorus

"What Would You Do in a Case Like That?" (Trio)

E. Torrence, P. Ames, C. Meakins

"The Song of the Trees" (Song)

K. Galloway, Chorus

"I'm Dying to Dance with Oscar" (Song)

H. Shipman, assisted by J. Wilmot, R. O'Connor, Chorus

Finale

ACT 2

"Everyone He Swear at the Waiter" (Song)

R. O'Connor, assisted by E. Thomas, E. Gordon, N. Bates, Chorus

"I'm Only a Girl from the City" (Ballad)

E. Torrence, H. Pierre

"The Song of the World" (Song)

K. Galloway, Ensemble

"It's the Scotch" (Quartette)

E. Torrence, P. Ames, K. Galloway, H. Shipman

"Nothing Escapes Me" (Song)

N. A. Sparks, Ensemble

ACT 3

"The Spirit of the Carnival"

J. Wilmot, E. Thomas, E. Gordon, E. Pierre, Chorus

"I'm Fond of the Girls" (Song)

C. Meakins, Chorus

"You're the Only One for Me" (Duet)

H. Shipman, N. A. Sparks, J. Wilmot, E. Thomas, E. Gordon

Finale

1918.23   EVERYTHING

A Musical Spectacle in Three Acts, 15 Scenes. Book by R. H. Burnside. Music by John Philip Sousa, Irving Berlin, and others (William Daly, Harry Tierney, Raymond Hubbell, J. M. Rumshinsky, Percy Wenrich). Lyrics by John L. Golden, others (Irving Berlin, Joseph McCarthy, R. H. Burnside, Daniel McBoyle, Jack F. Mahoney). Staged by R. H. Burnside. Costumes designed by Will R. Barnes, William H. Matthews, Robert McQuinn, Gladys Monkhouse. Scenery by Mark Lawson, Tarrazona Brothers, Robert McQuinn. Lighting by Joseph Elsner. Orchestra under the direction of William M. Daly. Produced by Charles Dillingham. Opened 22 August 1918 at the Hippodrome and closed 17 May 1919 after 461 performances.

CAST: DeWOLF HOPPER, CHARLES T. ALDRICH, HARRY HOUDINI, BELLE STORY, ARTHUR HILL, WILL J. EVANS, ALBERT FROOM, 'BLUCH', PEGGY H. BARNSTEAD, TOMMY COLTON, WILLIAM A. WESTON, J. PARKER COOMBS, ALBERT ALBERTO, TOM BROWN'S CLOWN BAND[28], THE BREEN FAMILY (Nellie, John, Inez, Catherine), MARION SAKI, J. NELSON, ADOLPH, THE YOSCAROS (Herman, Adolph, Fernando), ADA LaSHAN, OCTAVIO TAY, ARTHUR GEARY, ALBERT JOHNSON, JAMES JOHNSON, JOHN ABBOTT, WILL STANLEY, MADGE LOOMIS, LOUISE BEAUTORA, DANIEL [Dippy] DIERS, JOSEPH FROHOFF, CHARLES RAVEL, E. BRENNAN, MALLIA & BART, J. F. CARTY, J. LORIMER, H. WARD, THE BYRNE BROTHERS (James, Andrew, John) and Zip, EDDIE RUSSELL, ROBERT ROSAIE, A. REES, THE FOUR LADELLAS (Will, George, Chester, ??), THE ELM CITY FOUR, SLAYMAN'S ALI ARABS, THE FOUR AMARANTHS (Jennie, Tina, Mary, Hannah), THE FOUR GUINTINIS (Poppy, Camile, ??, ??), THE MUSICAL JOHNSTONS, THE TWO GAUDSMITHS, ROBERT REANO, GEORGE GIFFORD, The EL REY SISTERS, HELEN REYNOLDS, EARL REYNOLDS, STEELE and WINSLOW, James Cheviot, Leo and George Davis, D. J. Carew, P. Smith, Thomas Colton, Charles Melody, Max Aaronson, Phil Gilpin, William Morgan, Stanley Clarke, Bernard Milton, Eugene Vary, Angel Barbara, John Aspe, Charles Floyd, William Unangst, John Davis, A. Davis.

Dancers: DESIREE LUBOVSKA, GERDA GULDA, STELLA NORELLE, HELEN PATTERSON, Peggy H. Barnstead, Inez Bauer, Daisy Smyth, Marion Saki, Anita Carlton, Margaret Millard, Minna Clifton, Cissie Hayden, Louise Cardone, Ethel Clarke, Loretta Mack, Cissie Osborn, Lillian Quinn, Lillian Carena, Sophie Mordecai, Kate Mordecai, Anna Carter, Nellie Melville, Lee Losch, Louise Cardone, Jessie Nelson, Florence Phelps, Poppy Guintini, Genevieve Dix, Marjorie Kelly, Bertha Moore, Camile Guintini, Margaret Leon, Jeanne Schreiver, Helen Ward, Catherine Huth, F. Clarke, Edna Nash, Barbara Harwood, Jessie Nelson, Alice Nash, Netta Russell, Margaret Nugent.

ACT 1[29]

Scene 1 (1st Thing)

The Beginning of the World[30] (Ballet)

Night: D. Lubovska. *The Moon*: P. H. Barnstead. *The Rainbow*: G. Gulda. *Her Attendants*: I. Bauer, H. Patterson, M. Saki, N. Breen, K. Breen, C. Hayden. *The Sun*: S. Norelle. *Rainbow Ballet*: D. Smyth, A. Carlton, M. Millard, L. Carena, M. Clifton, E. Clarke, L. Mack, C. Osborn, L. Quinn, S. Mordecai, K. Mordecai, A. Carter, N. Melville, L. Losch, L. Cardone, J. Nelson, F. Phelps, P. Guintini, G. Dix, M. Kelly, B. Moore, C. Guintini, M. Leon, J. Schreiver.

(*Painted by* Mark Lawson.)

Scene 2 (2nd Thing)

The Country Circus

"The Circus Is Coming to Town"

W. J. Evans

(*Music and Lyrics by* Irving Berlin.)

The Village Constable: A. Froom. *The Village Postmaster*: T. Colton. *Weary Willie*: W. J. Evans. *Lazy Luke*: W. A. Weston. *John Jingling*, the circus proprietor: D. Hopper. *Jack Rough*, the boss canvasman: J. P. Coombs. *Mr. Smart*: A. Alberto. *Specialties*: The Four Amaranths, Power's Elephants, Slayman Ali's Arabs, 60 Clowns—Count 'Em—60!!

(*Painted by* Mark Lawson.)

Scene 3 (3rd Thing)

The Two Gaudsmiths

---

[28]Also known as the Six Brown Brothers.

[29]Added to the show 9 September 1918:

"Along the Hudson"

A. Geary, B. Storey, Chorus

Added to the show 5 May 1919:

"The Land of Romance"

A. Geary, J. Mai

(*Music by* William M. Daly. *Lyrics by* John L. Golden.)

[30]Dropped during the run.

Scene 4 (4th Thing)

Toy Factory

"Come Along to Toytown"

B. Story

(*Music and Lyrics by* Irving Berlin.)

The Toymaker: D. Hopper. *The Amateur Magician*: C. T. Aldrich. *The Little Stranger*: H. Patterson. *The Good Fairy*: B. Story. *The Terrible Tiger*: A. Hill. *The Rag Doll*: W. J. Evans. *The Tin Soldier*: A. Froom. *Specialties*: C. T. Aldrich, The Four Amaranths, Sisters Breen, G. Gifford, Mallia & Bart, D. Diers and E. Russell, The Two Nelsons, The Four Ladellas, The Davis Family, Byrne Brothers and "Zip."

(*Painted by* Mark Lawson.)

Scene 5 (5th Thing)

The Artist's Studio: A Few Pictures by Bert Levy (cartoonist)

Scene 6 (6th Thing)

France—Then and Now

First Tableau: Chateau-Thierry—July, 1914.

Second Tableau: Chateau-Thierry—March, 1918.

"A Rainbow from the U.S.A."

D. Hopper, B. Story

(*Music by* Percy Wenrich. *Lyrics by* William Jerome, J. F. Mahoney.)

Uncle Sam: D. Hopper. *Columbia*: B. Story. *France*: S. Norelle.

(*Painted by* the Tarrazona Brothers.)

ACT 2[31]

Scene 1 (7th Thing)

On the Beach at Atlantic City

"On Atlantic City Beach" (Opening Chorus)

Elm City Quartette, Chorus

(*Music by* Harry Tierney. *Lyrics by* Joseph McCarthy.)

Mr. Boardwalk: D. Hopper. *Miss Boardwalk*: B. Story. *Jimmie Tough*, a newsboy: W. J. Evans. *John Strong*, a policeman: A. Froom. *Specialties*: C. T. Aldrich and "Bluch," assisted by the Davis Family.

(*Painted by* Mark Lawson.)

Scene 2 (8th Thing)

Along the Hudson

"You're the Very Girl I've Looked For"[32] (Song)

A. Geary, B. Story, Chorus

(*Music by* William M. Daly. *Lyrics by* John Golden.)

The Dashing Hero: A. Geary. *The Dainty Heroine*: B. Story.

(*Painted by* Mark Lawson.)

Scene 3 (9th Thing)

Houdini[33]

Scene 4 (10th Thing)

Arrival of the Bad Ship "*Bolsheviki*" in New York

"I Like New York"[34]

D. Hopper, Hippodrome Company

(*Music by* James Tate. *Lyrics by* John L. Golden.)

Nicholas Getfullovitch: A. Froom. *Boris Grabthecoinsky*: J. P. Coombs. *Captain Inbadsky*: "Bluch." *Ivan Outforthestuffsky*: D. Hopper. *Specialty*: The Three Yoscaros.

---

[31]Added to Act 2, 25 November 1918:

Ten Minutes with Gilbert and Sullivan: Miniature version of "H.M.S. Pinafore"

(*Music by* Arthur Sullivan. *Lyrics by* W. S. Gilbert.)

Right Honorable Sir Joseph Porter, K.C.B., First Lord of the Admiralty: W. T. Carleton. *Captain Corcoran*, commanding H.M.S. Pinafore: A. Froom. *Ralph Rackstraw*, seaman: A. Geary. *Dick Deadeye*, seaman: J. P. Coombs. *Josephine*: B. Story. *Little Buttercup*: V. Bailey. *Hebe*: Sir Joseph's first cousin: J. Mai. *First Lord's Sisters, his cousins and his aunts, etc.*: Full Hippodrome Chorus.

Scene: Deck of H.M.S. Pinafore, of Portsmouth, England.

(*Painted by* Mark Lawson.)

The Great Hanneford Family (First time in any American theatre)

England's most thrilling bareback riders, including the foremost bareback riders in the world. An entirely new idea in equestrianism, and introducing for the first time here Edward Hanneford "Poodles," the World's Greatest Comedian on Horseback, who combines sensational horsemanship with an unerring sense of comedy.

[32]Dropped during the run.

[33]Departed after 10 weeks.

[34]Dropped during the run.

Scene 5 (11th Thing)

Somewhere on the East Side

"Sunshine Alley"[35]

Hippodrome Company

(*Music by* William M. Daly. *Lyrics by* John L. Golden.)

"(Everything Is Hunky Dory Down in) Honky Tonky Town"

W. J. Evans, Entire Hippodrome Company

(*Music by* Harry Tierney. *Lyrics by* Joseph J. McCarthy.)

Johnny Green: W. Wolf. *Jenny Jones*: A. LaShan. *Ephraham Jasbo*: W. A. Weston. *Musical Specialties*: The Four Guintinis, O. Tay, The Musical Johnstons, W. A. Weston.

(*Painted by* Mark Lawson.)

Scene 6 (12th Thing)

Tom Brown's Clown Band

Leader: J. Thomas.

Scene 7 (13th Thing)

In Lampland (*Painted by* Mark Lawson.)

(Music compiled and arranged by Lieutenant John Philip Sousa.)

"Come to the Land of Romance" (The Land of Romance)

A. Geary, Entire Chorus

(*Music by* William M. Daly. *Lyrics by* John L. Golden and R. H. Burnside.)

The Bridegroom: A. Geary. *The Bride*: S. Norelle. *Grecian Dancers*: I. Bauer, P. H. Barnstead, C. Hayden. *French Dancer*: N. Breen. *Snake Dancer*: H. Patterson. *Japanese Dancer*: M. Saki. *Egyptian Dancer*: D. Lubovska. *Burmese Dancers*: The Four Amaranths. *Danish Dancer*: G. Gulda. *Statue Dancers*: L. Cardone, A. Carlton, H. Ward, M. Collins, C. Huth, F. Clarke, L. Carena, E. Nash, D. Smythe, B. Harwood, J. Nelson, A. Nash, N. Russell, M. Nugent, F. Phelps, N. Melville. "*Liberty*": B. Story.

Waltz Song ("Liberty")

(*Music by* J. M. Rumshinsky. *Lyrics by* Darl MacBoyle.)

Grand Finale: March of the Lamps of the World

ACT 3

Scene 1 (14th Thing)

Somewhere in the Gay City

"Roll Along" (Opening Number)

Elm City Four, Hippodrome Chorus

(*Music by* William M. Daly. *Lyrics by* John L. Golden.)

(*Scenery and costumes designed by* Robert McQuinn.)

[Roller Skating] *Specialties*: The Two Nelsons, M. Mallia, El Rey Sisters, E. Reynolds, N. Donegan, Steele and Winslow.

Scene 2 (15th Thing)

The Hall of History

"Follow the Flag"

A. Geary, Entire Hippodrome Chorus

(*Music by* Raymond Hubbell. *Lyrics by* R. H. Burnside.)

Uncle Sam: D. Hopper. *Columbia*: B. Story. *La Belle France*: S. Norelle. *Britannia*: M. Loomis. *Italy*: L. Beautora. *U.S.A. Officer*: A. Geary. *U.S.N. Officer*: W. Ladella. *President Wilson*: C. T. Aldrich. *Columbus*: A. Froom. *Lord Kitchener*: J. P. Coombs. *General Sherman*: D. Diers. *Peter Stuyvesant*: J. Frohoff. *John Paul Jones*: E. Brennan. *Lafayette*: F. C. Carty. *Garibaldi*: L. Lorimer. *Lord Nelson*: H. Ward. *Admiral Dewey*: John Byrne. *William Penn*: A. Byrne. *John Adams*: James Byrne. *General Grant*: E. Russell. *Spirit of '76*: R. Rosaie, A. Rees, G. Ladella. *Nathan Hale*: L. Davis. *George Calvert*: G. Davis. *Sebastian Cabot*: R. Reano. *Benjamin Franklin*: C. Ravel. *George Carteret*: W. Stanley. *George Washington*: J. Carty. *Oliver Cromwell*: J. Abbott. *Henry VIII*: A. Alberto. *Julius Caesar*: J. Breen. *Abraham Lincoln*: D. J. Carew. *Louis XIV*: A. Johnson. *Louis XVI*: J. Johnson. *Napoleon*: J. Nelson. *Victor Emanuel*: A. Yoscaro. *Alexander*: H. Yoscaro. *General Foch*: F. Yoscaro. *General Petain*: J. Cheviot. *General Joffre*: P. Smith. *General Diaz*: T. Colton. *General Pershing*: C. Melody. *Sir Douglas Haig*: M. Aaronson. *Hendrik Hudson*: P. Gilpin. *Paul Revere*: W. Morgan. *General Sheridan*: S. Clarke. *Admiral Farragut*: B. Milton. *Stonewall Jackson*: E. Vary. *Admiral Sampson*: A. Barbara. *Admiral Schley*: J. Aspe. *Duke of Wellington*: C. Floyd. *Buffalo Bill*: W. Unangst. *Marc Anthony*: J. Davis. *Herod*: G. Ladella. *Sir Walter Raleigh*: C. Ladella. *Sir Philip Sidney*: A. Davis. *Cardinal Mercier*: O. Tay. *King Arthur*: W. A. Weston. *Alfred the Great*: W. J. Evans. *Catherine of Russia*: P. H. Barnstead. *Barbara Freitchie*: I. Bauer. *Molly Pitcher*: K. Breen.

---

[35]Sheet music for "Sunshine Alley" credits Music by R. P. Weston and Bert Lee, Lyrics by R. H. Burnside and John L. Golden. "Sunshine Alley" and "Honky Tonky Town" were dropped during the run and replaced by:

"Everything Is Hunky Dory"

H. Lambert, Elm City Four, Entire Hippodrome Company

(*Music by* Harry Tierney. *Lyrics by* Joseph McCarthy.)

Betsy Ross: M. Mallia. *Cleopatra*: D. Lubovska. *Queen Elizabeth*: J. Amaranth. *Helen of Troy*: C. Hayden. *Pocahontas*: T. Amaranth. *Marie Antoinette*: N. Breen. *Josephine Bonaparte*: E. Amaranth. *Joan of Arc*: G. Gulda.
(*Painted by* Mark Lawson.)

1918.24 WHY WORRY?

A Melodramatic Farce in Three Acts. Play by Montague Glass and Jules Eckert Goodman. Staged by George Marion. Produced by A. H. Woods. Opened 23 August 1918 at the Harris Theatre and closed 14 September 1918 after 27 performances[36].

CAST (in order of appearance): *Dora*: FANNIE BRICE. *Stella*: MAY BOLEY. *Mrs. Harris*: VERA GORDON. *Shapiro*: Ezra C. Walck. *Felix Noblestone*: GEORGE SIDNEY. *Louis*: Carl Dietz. *Steffens*: Edwin Maxwell. *Wolter*: Harry Dumont. *David Meyer*: CHARLES TROWBRIDGE. *Devlin*: Jack Sharkey. *Thorpe*: John Wallace. *Dan*: Ralf Belmont. *A Lady*: Francesca Rotoli. *A Gentleman*: True S. James. *Rashkind, Margolius, Dubin, November*, the Avon Comedy Four: JOE SMITH, CHARLES DALE, IRVING KAUFMAN, HARRY GOODWIN. *Flo*: Frances Richards. *Frost*: Kalman Matus. *Bedell*: James Cherry. *Guests, etc.*

Act 1: Fischbein & Blintz's Ideal Restaurant and Lunch Room, Harris & Joseph, Successors, Second Avenue, New York.

Act 2: The Ivy Leaf Inn, Boston Post Road, Larchmont. One week later.

Act 3: Same as Act 2. Evening of the same day.

MUSICAL NUMBERS[37]
"I'm an Indian"
F. Brice
(*Music and Lyrics by* Blanche Merrill.)
"I'm Bad"
F. Brice
(*Music and Lyrics by* Blanche Merrill.)
Tosti's Goodbye (Burlesque)
Avon Comedy Four
Hungarian Restaurant Scene
Avon Comedy Four

1918.25 HEAD OVER HEELS

A Play with Music in Two Acts, 3 Scenes. Book by Edgar Allan Woolf. Suggested by Lee Arthur's dramatization of Nalbro Bartley's story "Shadows." Music by Jerome Kern. Lyrics by Edgar Allan Woolf. Staged by George Marion. Musical numbers staged by Julian Mitchell. Settings by Frank Gates and Edward A. Morange (Act 1), Joseph Urban (Act 2). Costumes by William H. Matthews, Madame Frances, Madame Faibsey. Orchestra under the direction of Harold Levey. Produced by Henry W. Savage. Opened 29 August 1918 at the George M. Cohan Theatre and closed 23 November 1918 after 100 performances.

CAST: *Stenographers* (4): *Miss Graham*: Fan Haggerty. *Miss Wentworth*: Martha Bowes. *Miss Collins*: Florence Browne. *Miss Hammond*: Eleanor Livingston. *Messenger Girl* (4): *Elsie Van Pelt*: Edan Hyatt. *Anita Vanderhayden*: Marion Earle. *Luella Vanderwater*: Dorothy Smoller. *Wanda Van Zandt*: Adelaide Fiset. *Elevator Girls* (4): *Fanchon Van Twiller*: Marie Hollywell. *Delia Van Maarck*: Marion Phillips. *Zoie Van Puyster*: Irma Marwick. *Lorine Vandusen*: Niobe Marwick. *Telephone Girls* (4): *Marcine Vanbaar*: Martha Voight. *Diane Van Renssaler*: Dorothy Gilbert. *Philene Van Strooch*: Angele Baber. *Dijonne Van Piet*: Ruth Parker. *Miss Muriel Sterling*: DOROTHY MACKAYE. *Office Boy*: Lambert Terry. *Mr. Robert Lawson*: BOYD MARSHALL. *Mr. Edward Sterling*: IRVING BEEBE. *Mr. T. Anthony Squibbs*: ROBERT EMMETT KEANE. *Mitzi Bambinetti*: MITZI [HAJOS]. *Signor Bambinetti*: CHARLES JUDELS. *Miss Edith Penfield*: JEAN MANN. *Mrs. Sarah Montague*: MARGARET LINDEN. *Baron Everard Cesare D'Oultremont*: PAUL OSCARD. *Jarvis of the Ritz*: Edmund Gurney. *Molly, Wardrobe Mistress*: Carrie McManus. *Bambinetti troupe* (4): *Toni*: Joseph Dunn. *Oscar*: James Oliver. *Buxaume*: Andy Bennett. *Henri*: Edward Mathews.

ACT 1
Scene 1
"With Type a-Ticking" (Opening)
F. Haggerty, M. Bowes, F. Browne, E. Livingston

"Today Is Spring" (Spring)
D. Mackaye, Girls
"Any Girl"
I. Beebe, Girls
"Mitzi's Lullaby"
Mitzi
"The Big Show"
Mitzi, Girls
"The Moments of the Dance"
J. Mann, M. Linden, D. Mackaye, B. Marshall, I. Beebe, P. Oscard
"Head Over Heels"
Mitzi, B. Marshall
Scene 2
"At the Thé Dansant"[38]
M. Linden, D. Mackaye, J. Mann, P. Oscard, Girls
"Vordeveele"
Mitzi, R. E. Keane
"All the World Is Swaying"
Mitzi, Girls
"Me"
C. Judels, J. Dunn, J. Oliver, A. Bennett
Finale (Houp-La)

ACT 2
"The Charity Bazaar" (Opening)
M. Linden, D. Mackaye, J. Mann, P. Oscard, Girls
"Every Bee Has a Bud of Its Own"
Mitzi
(*Music by* Harold A. Levey.)
"Ladies, Have a Care!"
R. E. Keane, B. Marshall, I. Beebe, Girls
"I Was Lonely"
J. Mann, I. Beebe
"Funny Little Something"
Mitzi, R. E. Keane, D. Mackaye
Finale

1918.26 FIDDLERS THREE

A Modern Operetta in Two Acts, 3 Scenes. Book and lyrics by William Cary Duncan. Music by Alexander Johnstone. Staged by Clifford Brooke. Dances by Carl Randall. Costumes designed by Mary Blackburn, H. Mahieu & Company; men's clothes designed by Finchley. Scenery by H. Robert Law Studios. Orchestra under the direction of Eugene Salzer. Orchestrations by Domenico Sodero. Produced by John Cort. Opened 3 September 1918 at the Cort Theatre and closed 16 November 1918 after 87 performances.

CAST (in order of appearance): *Gilda Varelli*: LOUISE GROODY. *Carlo Andreani*: HENRY LEONI. *Reginald Denby, Lord Duffer*: ECHLIN GAYER. *Sam Wigglesbury*: HAL SKELLEY. *Rosa*: Betty Dodsworth. *Nicolo Colona*: THOMAS CONKEY. *Giuseppe*: Joseph Miller. *Suzanne Foppitt*: JOSIE INTROPODI. *Bernice Brockway*: HAZEL KIRKE. *Anina Andreani*: TAVIE BELGE. *Beppo*: Antonio Salerno. *Paganini*: Gilbert Clayton. *Kubelik*: Antonio Salerno. *Giorgio*: Tempe Evans. *Master-Violinisy*: J. Rabilino. *Dance Divertissement*: Layman and Kling.
Pages: Misses May, Dwight, Rosewood, Lane, Savoy. *Judges of Violins*: Messrs. Joslyn, Mangione, Palm, Rogati, Miller, Russell, Griswold. *Peasants, Citizens of Cremona, Revelers, Tourists, etc.*

Time: Present. *Place*: Cremona, the "Violin City" in Lombardy.

Act 1: A Public Square in Cremona.

Act 2, Scene 1: An Ante-Room in Count Valdo's Palace in Cremona. *Scene 2*: The Grand Palace in the Ballroom.

ACT 1
"Rap, Rap, Rap"
L. Groody, Ensemble

---

[36]Scenery, costumes and musical director uncredited.
[37]Not in performance order. Musical numbers and comedy sketches not listed in program, but taken from reviews, biographical materials.

---

[38]For subsequent tour, the following number was added before "At the Thé Dansant":
"Oriental Tea Song"
Ruth Oswald (Edith), Girls
(*Music by* Harold A. Levey.)

"When the Fiddler's Bow Begins to Fly"
 H. Leoni, Girls
"Don't You Think You'll Miss Me?"
 L. Groody, E. Gayer
"As the Flitting Swallows Fly"
 T. Conkey
"It Was All on Account of Nipper"
 J. Intropodi, H. Kirke, E. Gayer
"Can It Be Love at Last?"
 T. Belge, Ensemble
Shadow Dance
 H. Skelley
"One Hour, Sweetheart, with You!"
 T. Conkey
Finale
 T. Belge, T. Conkey, H. Leoni, Company

ACT 2
Scene 1
Carnival Music
"Proud Little Pages"
 T. Evans, Pages
"Virtuosos Great Are We"
 Judges of Violins
Intermezzo
Scene 2
Carnival Dance
 L. Groody, Girls
Dance Divertissement
 Layman and Kling
"Just a Slip of the Tongue"
 E. Gayer
"For Love"
 L. Groody, H. Skelley
"(My) Love of a Day"
 T. Belge
Throne Scene
 T. Belge, T. Conkey, Ensemble
Finale
 Entire Company

1918.27 THE MAID OF THE MOUNTAINS

A Musical Play in Three Acts. Book by Frederick Lonsdale. Music by Harold Fraser-Simpson. Lyrics by Harry Graham. Additional music by James W. Tate, Lieutenant Gitz Rice; additional lyrics by F. Clifford Harris and (Arthur) Valentine. Staged by Captain J. A. E. Malone. Dances arranged by Bert French. Scenery by Edward G. Unitt and Joseph Wickes. Costumes by Dazian, Schneider-Anderson. Orchestra under the direction of John McGhie. Produced by William Elliott, F. Ray Comstock and Morris Gest. Opened 11 September 1918 at the Casino Theatre and closed 12 October 1918 after 37 performances.

CAST: *Baldassare*, the Brigand Chief: WILLIAM COURTENAY. *Members of Baldassare's Band (3): Tonio:* BERT CLARK. *Beppo:* CARL GANTVOORT. *Carlo:* Jackson Hines. *Andrea:* M. LaPrade. *Pietro:* Victor Leroy. *General Malona, Governor of Santo:* WILLIAM DANFORTH. *Crumpet,* the Governor's aide: Al Roberts. *Lieutenant Rugini:* JOHN STEEL. *Mayor of Santo:* William Reid. *Zacchi:* Louis Le Vie. *Teresa,* the maid of the mountains: SIDONIE ESPERO. *Vittoria,* Tonio's widow: MIRIAM DOYLE. *Angela,* daughter of the Governor: Evelyn Egerton. *Friends of Angela (5): Gianetta:* Gertrude Hamilton. *Maria:* Mina Davis. *Marietta:* Marguerite May. *Beppira:* Eva Newton. *Pepita:* Patricia Frewen.
 Dancers: Margaret Morris (solo). Olive Kingston, Charlotte Lennox, Jean Rebera, Merle Smither, May Borden, Gladys Slater. *Ladies of the Court:* Gertrude Hogan, Shirley Love, Regna Ahlstrom, Peggy Hansel, Helen Mayo, Annette Besudin, Dolres Brune, Yetla Nicoll, Erna Steinway, Elsa Criag, Jeanne Bayne, Gabrielle Pitcher, Mary Lee Stevens, Bess Arlington. *Guardsmen:* M. St. John, Basil Spirdelli, M. Boris, Eugene Elliott, William Altwell, A. Gibson, Bernard Tieman, Antone Ingrao, M. Robinson, Harry Clark, William Hovel, Ben Rogers, Ralph Walker, James Harley.

Act 1: In the Mountains of a Country in Southern Europe.

Act 2: Courtyard of the Governor's Palace.

Act 3: On an Island.

ACT 1[39]
"Friends Have to Part" (Opening Chorus)
 Bandits
"Live for Today" (Song)
 C. Gantvoort, Bandits
"My Life Is Love" (Song)
 S. Espero, C. Gantvoort, Bandits
 (*Music by* James W. Tate. *Lyrics by* F. Clifford Harris and Arthur Valentine.)
Nocturne (instrumental)
"Farewell" (Song)
 S. Espero
"Dividing the Spoil"
 C. Gantvoort, J. Hines, B. Clark, W. Courtenay, Bandits
"Tho' Curs May Quail" (Finale)
 C. Gantvoort, Bandits
ACT 2
"We're Gathered Here" (Opening Chorus)
 Ensemble
"For Many a Year" (Governor's Song)
 W. Danforth, Ensemble
"Love Will Find a Way" (Song)
 S. Espero
Laughing Chorus
"Dirty Work" (Duet)
 W. Danforth, B. Clark
"A Paradise for Two" (Duet)
 S. Espero, C. Gantvoort
 (*Music by* James W. Tate. *Lyrics by* F. Clifford Harris and Arthur Valentine.)
"Husbands and Wives" (Duet)
 M. Doyle, B. Clark
"I Don't Care" (Song)
 C. Gantvoort, Girls
Finale—Dramatic
 (W. Courtenay, S. Espero)
ACT 3
"When Each Day" (Chorus of Fisherfolk)
 (Ensemble)
"Waiting (for You)" (Song)
 J. Steel
 (*Music by* Lieutenant Gitz Rice. *Lyrics by* Marc Connelly.)
"Good People, Gather Round" (Solo and Chorus)
 W. Danforth, Ensemble
"When You're in Love" (Duet)
 S. Espero, W. Danforth
 (*Music by* James W. Tate. *Lyrics by* F. Clifford Harris and Arthur Valentine.)
"Over There and Over Here" (Duet)
 M. Doyle, B. Clark
Finale
 (Entire Company)

1918.28 THE GIRL BEHIND THE GUN

A Musical Comedy (Play) in Three Acts[40]. Book and lyrics[41] by Guy Bolton and P. G. Wodehouse. (Based on the French farce "Madame et son filleul" [Madame and her Godson] by Maurice Hennequin and Pierre Veber.) Music by Ivan Caryll. Dialogue directed by Edgar MacGregor. Ensembles arranged by Julian Mitchell. Scenery designed by Clifford Pember. Costumes designed by Schneider-Anderson Company; men's clothes designed by Croydon, Ltd. . Orchestra under the direction of Charles Previn. Produced by (Marc) Klaw and (Abraham L.) Erlanger. Opened 16 September 1918 at the New Amsterdam Theatre and closed 1 February 1919 after 160 performances.

---

[39]For the American production, "For Many a Year," "Waiting for You," and "I Don't Care" (replacing "I Understood") were added; "A Bachelor Gay" was dropped.
[40]Subsequently produced in London under the title KISSING TIME.
[41]Contrary to the program billing, Guy Bolton is not credited with any lyrics in published sheet music.

CAST: *Robert Lambrissac*: DONALD BRIAN. *Pierre Breval*: JACK [John E.] HAZZARD. *Georgette Breval*: ADA MEADE. *Colonel Servan*: FRANK DOANE. *Lucienne Lambrissac*: WILDA BENNETT. *Harper Wentworth*: Bert Gardner. *Eileen Moore*: Eva Francis. *Brichoux*: John E. Young. *Zellie*: Virginia O'Brien. *American Girls* (4): *Edna*: Florence Delmar. *Pollie*: Elaine Palmer. *Margie*: Cissie Sewell. *Carrie*: June White. *Ensemble*.

Act 1: Garden of Georgette's Villa. Fontainebleu.

Act 2: Porch of Georgette's House.

Act 3: Interior of Pavilion.

ACT 1
  Opening Chorus
  "Godsons and Grandmothers" (Song)
    A. Meade, Chorus
  "True to Me" (Song)
    J. E. Young, 4 American Girls
  "Happy Family" (Trio)
    F. Doane, A. Meade, D. Brian
  "Some Day Waiting Will End" (Song)
    W. Bennett, Girls
  "I Like It" (Quartette)
    J. Hazzard, D. Brian, F. Doane, A. Meade
  Ensemble

ACT 2
  Opening Chorus
  "(Oh,) How Warm It is Today" (Trio)
    D. Brian, F. Doane, A. Meade
  "The Girl Behind the Gun" (Song)
    W. Bennett, Chorus
  "Women Haven't Any Mercy on a Man" (Song)
    J. Hazzard
  "Life in the Old Dog Yet" (Duet)
    D. Brian, W. Bennett
  Finale—"Flags of Allies"
    Tout Ensemble

ACT 3
  Opening Chorus
  "Back to the Dear Old Trenches" (Trio)
    D. Brian, J. Hazzard, J. E. Young
  "There's a Light in Your Eyes" (Song)
    D. Brian, W. Bennett
  Finale

1918.29

SOME NIGHT!

A Delirious Comedy with Music and Surprise in Three Acts. Story (book), music and words (lyrics) by Harry Delf. Staged by W. H. Post. Dances arranged by Julian Mitchell. Orchestra under the direction of Hilding Anderson. Produced by Joseph Klaw. Opened 16 September 1918 at the Harris Theatre and closed 5 October 1918 after 24 performances.

CAST (in order of appearance): *John Hardy*: FORREST WINANT. *Robert*: Charles Welsh-Homer. *Mrs. Hardy*: Camilla Crume. *Marjorie*: Grace Edmond. *Daisy*: ANNA FREDRICKS. *Bobby*: HARRY LAMBERT. *Joe*: LOUIS SIMON. *Dorothy Wayne*: ROMA JUNE. *Madden*: Thomas H. Walsh. *Joe Scanlon*: JAMES C. MARLOWE. *Henry Spiffens*: Charles W. Meyer. *Constables*: Charles Hall, Jesse W. Willingham, Charles Fulton.

Neighbors: Elaine Landau, Lindley Lenton, Jeanne Dare, Virginia Roche, Dolly Alwin, Helen Halpren, Edna Richmond, Laura Lyle, Billy Vernon, Catherine Hurst, Blanche Terrell.

Act 1: Forethought. A Summer Day. Living Room in the home of the Hardys.

Act 2: That same summer day. An hour later in the same room.

Act 3: Still that same summer day. The room above Somewhere.

ACT 1[42]
  "Forethought!"[43]

[42]For subsequent tour, the running order was revised, and added was:
  "The Snap of the Whip"
    Robert E. James (Bobby), Olive Wright (Daisy), Joe Fields (Johnny), Neighbors
[43]Dropped for subsequent tour.

"Something That Money Can't Buy"
    F. Winant, G. Edmond, C. Crume, A. Fredricks, H. Lambert
"Send Me a Real Girl"
    F. Winant, C. Welsh-Homer, Neighbors
"When We Are Married"
    A. Fredricks, H. Lambert
"All Night"[44]
    T. H. Walsh, F. Winant, R. June
"Alone in a Great Big World"
    R. June
ACT 2[45]
  "Once Upon a Time"
    R. June, F. Winant
  "(By My Window) I'll Be Waiting for You"
    A. Fredricks, H. Lambert, Neighbors
  "With the Boy I Love"
    Neighbors
  "Look Before You Leap"[46]
    J. C. Marlowe, T. H. Walsh, C. Welsh-Homer
  "Some Night"
    Ensemble
ACT 3
  "Can't You See" (Can't You Tell by the Look in His Eyes)
    G. Edmond, Neighbors
  "Everything Is Going Higher"[47]
    A. Fredricks, H. Lambert
  "Painting My Picture of You" (While I Paint My Picture of You)
    R. June, F. Winant
  "Somewhere!"[48]

1918.30

SOMETIME

A Musical Romance in Two Acts, 9 Scenes[49]. Book and lyrics by Rida Johnson Young. Music by Rudolf Friml. Additional lyrics by Ed Wynn. Staged by Oscar Eagle. Dances arranged by Allan K. Foster. Costumes by Orange Manufacturing Company; Miss Ford's dresses by Lucile; men's clothes by Croydon, Ltd. Orchestra under the direction of Herbert Stothart. Produced by Arthur Hammerstein. Opened 14 October 1918 at the Sam S. Shubert Theatre, moved 11 November 1918 to the Casino Theatre, and closed 7 June 1919 after 283 performances.

CAST (in order of appearance): *Mayme Dean*: MAE WEST. *Phyllis*: Beatrice Summers. *Henry Vaughn*: HARRISON BROCKBANK. *Loney Bright*: ED WYNN. *Enid Vaughn*: FRANCINE LARRIMORE. *Dressing Room Girls*: Betty Silvers, Virginia Lee. *Joe Allegretti*: Charles DeHaven. *Mike Mazetti*: Fred Nice. *Richard Carter*: JOHN MERKYL. *Sylvia DeForrest*: FRANCES CAMERON. *Argentine Dancer*: Mildred LeGue. *Argentine Singer*: William Dorrian. *Apthorp*: Albert Sackett. *George Gray*: Harold Williams. *Roof Garden Manager*: Francis Murphy. *Mr. Jones*: George Gaston.
  Girls: Marie Astor, Anna Stone, Ann Toddings, Josie Carmen, Renee Hughes, Nan Bainford, Loretta Morgan, Roberta Lomax, Beatrice Summers, Kewpie Collier, Virginia Lee. Irma Coigne, Edna Coigne, Helen O'Day, Genevieve Ullman, Lucile Williams, Nancy Griffith, Mary McDonald. *Boys*: Harold Williams, Jerome Kirkland, Arnold Gluck, Leo Howe, Stanley Rayburn, Francis Murphy.

Act 1, Scene 1: Stage of a New York Theatre. Present time. *Scene 2*: Enid's Dressing Room. Present time. *Scene 3*: Room in Actor's Boarding House, Five years earlier. *Scene 4*: Enid's Dressing Room. Present time. *Scene 5*: Garden of Racing Club in Buenos Aires. Four years earlier.

Act 2, Scene 1: Enid's Dressing Room. Present time. *Scene 2*: Roof Garden of Gotham Theatre. One year earlier. *Scene 3*: Enid's Dressing Room. Present time. *Scene 4*: "Somewhere."

[44]Dropped for subsequent national tour.
[45]Added for subsequent tour, before "Look Before You Leap":
  "Some Day, Some How, Some Where"
    J. Fields, Gayle Wendell (Dorothy)
[46]Dropped after opening, but reinstated for tour.
[47]Dropped after opening, but reinstated for tour.
[48]Replaced for tour by:
  Finale
    Entire Company
[49]Scenery uncredited.

ACT 1

"What Do You Have To Do?"
  M. West
"Picking Peaches"
  H. Brockbank, Girls
"Sometime"
  F. Larrimore, Girls
"Keep on Smiling"
  F. Cameron, J. Merkyl, Girls
"Sometime" (reprise)
  F. Larrimore, J. Merkyl
"Spanish Maid" (Nina Espagnola)
  W. Dorrian
Dance
  C. DeHaven, F. Nice
Argentine Dance
  M. LeGue
"The Tune You Can't Forget"
  F. Cameron, Chorus
"Oh! Argentine"
  E. Wynn
  (*Lyrics by* Ed Wynn.)
Finale

ACT 2

"Beautiful Night"
  F. Cameron, H. Williams, Chorus
"Baby Doll"
  F. Larrimore, Boys
"Any Kind of Man"
  M. West
Finale

THE BETTER 'OLE,
1918.31 or, The Romance of Old Bill

Fragment from France in Two Explosions, Seven Splinters and a Short Gas Attack. (Comedy with music in Two Acts, 7 Scenes and an Epilogue). Book by Captain Bruce Bairnsfather and Captain Arthur Elliott. Music composed, selected and arranged by Herman Darewski, and (with lyrics by) Percival Knight, James Heard. Staged by Percival Knight. Dances arranged by Lily Leonora. Scenery designed by Ernest Albert. Costumes designed by Madame Broich, Christie and Co. Orchestra under the direction of Eliott Schenck. Produced by Mr. and Mrs. Charles Coburn. Opened 19 October 1918 at the Greenwich Village Theatre, moved 18 November 1918 to the Cort Theatre, moved 16 June 1919 to the Booth Theatre; suspended performances 21 August 1918 for the Actors' Equity strike, resumed 8 September 1919 and closed 4 October 1919 after 353 performances.

CAST (in order of appearance): *The Sergeant Major*: Edwin Taylor. *Angèle*: Gwen Lewis. *Bert*: CHARLES McNAUGHTON. *Alf*: COLIN CAMPBELL. *Old Bill*: CHARLES COBURN. *Rachel*: Eugenie Young. *The Colonel*: Henry Warwick. *A Spy*: Lark Taylor. *Suzette*: Mona Desmond. *A Tommy*: Albert Kenway. *Victoire*: MRS. CHARLES COBURN. *Captain of the Women's Workers' Camp*: Lillian Spencer. *The Women War Workers* (8): *Mollie from Ireland*: Marguerite Torrey. *Suzette from France*: Hazel O'Brien. *Maggie from Scotland*: Athalie Jenkins. *Helene from Belgium*: Mollie Carroll. *Nancy from England*: Eugenie Young. *Mary Brown from America*: Ruth Urban. *Rosa from Italy*: Therese Josephs. *Peg from Canada*: Theodora Keene. *Military Postman*: Nevin Clark. *Captain Milne*: Lark Taylor. *Berthe*: Helen Tilden. *A French Officer*: Howard Taylor. *A French Porter*: Eugene Borden. *Maggie, Mrs. Bill Busby*: Kenyon Bishop. *Kate, Old Bill's Niece*: Ruth Vivian. *The Vicar*: George Logan. *An Old Villager*: Nevin Clark.

Tommies: Albert Kenway, Rene Wren, J. M. Deeter, Charles Engels, William Swayne, Henry Ward, Vincenze Ioucelli, William Fish, Nevin Clark, George Logan.

The action takes place before 10 November 1918 somewhere in France and somewhere in England.

Explosion I, Splinter 1: "The Gaff" near the base, somewhere in France. *Splinter 2*: Outside the Cafe des Oiseaux, nearer the Front. *Splinter 3*: "Billets" just behind the front.

Explosion II, Splinter 4: The Way In." *Splinter 5*: In." *Splinter 6*: "Headquarters." *Splinter 7*: The Leave Train." A railway siding near Boulogne.

A short gas attack: "The Better 'Ole," an English village.

MUSICAL NUMBERS

"Tommy"
  M. Desmond, Tommies
  (*Lyrics by* James Heard.)
"(When You Take) That Trip Across the Rhine"
  L. Spencer, Women War Workers
  (*Music and Lyrics by* Percival Knight.)
"(My Word! Ain't We) Carrying On"
  C. McNaughton, C. Campbell, C. Coburn
  (*Lyrics by* Melville Gideon, James Heard, Percival Knight, Herman Darewski.)
"We Wish We Was in Blighty" (I Wish I Was in Blighty)
  C. McNaughton, C. Campbell, C. Coburn
  (*Lyrics by* W. R. Titterton.)
"When You Look in the Heart of a Rose"
  L. Taylor
  (*Music by* Florence Methven. *Lyrics by* Marion Gillespie)
"(She's)Venus de Milo (to Me)"
  C. Coburn
  (*Music and Lyrics by* Peter Bernard, Oliver DeGerde.)
"Je sais que vous êtes gentil" (It's Our Wedding Day)
  H. Tilden, C. McNaughton
  (*Music by* P. H. Christiné, Percival Knight. *Lyrics by* Grant Stewart, Percival Knight.)
"(Have a Little) Regiment of Our Own" (A Little Regiment of Our Own)
  C. McNaughton, French Girls
  (*Music and Lyrics by* Percival Knight.)
"Regiment of Our Own" (dance)
  C. McNaughton, M. Torrey

LADIES FIRST
1918.32

A Musical Play in Three Acts. Book and lyrics by Harry B. Smith. Based on the play "A Contented Woman" by Charles H. Hoyt. Music by A. Baldwin Sloane, (Nora Bayes, Harry Akst, George Gershwin, Seymour B. Simons, Harry Clarke). (Additional lyrics by Irving Fisher, Seymour Simons, Ira Gershwin, Schuyler Greene, Harry Clarke.) Book staged by Frank Smithson. Scenery designed by D. Frank Dodge & William Castle. Orchestra under the direction of Oscar Radin. Produced by H. H. Frazee. Opened 24 October 1918 at the Broadhurst Theatre, moved 30 December 1918 to the Nora Bayes Theatre, and closed 15 March 1919 after 164 performances.[50]

CAST: *Uncle Tody*: WILLIAM KENT. *Brighton Betts*: STANLEY H. FORDE. *Lefty McGuirk*: Paul E. Burns. *Larry Burt*: CHARLES OLCOTT. *Benton Holmes*: IRVING FISHER. *Betty Burt*: NORA BAYES. *Aunt Jim*: FLORENCE MORRISON. *Little Jack*: CLARENCE NORDSTROM. *D. C. Washington*: LEW COOPER. *Edith*: Florence Lee. *Jane*: Elsie Shaw. *Laura*: Henriette Wilson. *Martha*: Martha Dean. *Kate*: Doris Sheerin. *Stella*: Elma Decker. *Belle*: Jane Conrad. *Hattie*: May Brooks. *Ada*: Lottie Tyler. *Mrs. Ebbsmith*: Jane Elliott.

Act 1: Uncle Tody's House.

Act 2: The adjoining gardens of Benny and Benton.

Act 3: Betty Burt's House.

ACT 1[51]

"Happy Days"
  W. Kent, C. Olcott, S. H. Forde
"(I'm Always Happy with a) Crowd of Girls"
  C. Olcott, Girls

---

[50]Costumes uncredited.

[51]For subsequent tour, Act 1 was revised by November 1919. All 4 songs were replaced by the following:
"I Cannot Drink the Cold Drinks" (from ROLY POLY)
  Al Roberts (Tody), Arthur Stuart Hall (Larry), J. W. Ashley (Mac), Jerome Bruner (Betts)
"What Could Be Sweeter Than You?"
  A. S. Hall, Girls
"Just Like a Gypsy"
  N. Bayes
  (*Music and Lyrics by* Seymour Simons.)
"Just the Two of Us"
  N. Bayes, I. Fisher
  (*Music and Lyrics by* Seymour Simons.)

"Without You"
N. Bayes
(*Music by* Irving Fisher. *Lyrics by* Nora Bayes.)
"(When I) Build a Home"
N. Bayes, I. Fisher
(*Music by* Irving Fisher. *Lyrics by* Nora Bayes.)

ACT 2[52]
"The Tea Party"
N. Bayes, Girls
"Spanish"[53]
N. Bayes
(*Music and Lyrics by* Harry Clarke.)
"(Just) What a Girl Can Do"
N. Bayes, Girls
"The Older They Get the Harder They Fall"[54]
W. Kent
(*Music and Lyrics by* James Kendl, James Brockmann and Nat Vincent.)
Duet
W. Kent, F. Morrison
"What a Man Can Do" (Just What a Girl Can Do)
I. Fisher, W. Kent, S. H. Forde, C. Clausland, L. Cooper
"On to Victory"
Ensemble

ACT 3[55]
"(The Real) American Folk Song (is a Rag)"
C. Olcott, Girls
(*Music by* George Gershwin. *Lyrics by* Ira Gershwin.)
"All My Life"
I. Fisher
(*Music and Lyrics by* Harry Akst, Nora Bayes, Irving Fisher.)
Songs
I. Fisher, L. Cooper
"Me and You"
I. Fisher, N. Bayes
(*Music by* Harry Akst, Irving Fisher. *Lyrics by* Nora Bayes.)
"Good-bye France (You'll Never Be Forgotten by the U.S.A.)"
N. Bayes
(*Music and Lyrics by* Irving Berlin.)

GLORIANNA

1918.33

A Play with Music in Three Acts. Book and lyrics by Catherine Chisholm Cushing, based on her play "A Widow by Proxy." Music by Rudolf Friml. Staged by Clifford Brooke. Dances by Bert French. Scenery designed by Joseph Urban. Costumes designed by Harry Collins and Mme. Kerner. Miss Painter's costumes by Mary Blackburne. Orchestra under the direction of Milan Roder. Produced by John Cort. Opened 28 October 1918 at the Liberty Theatre and closed 18 January 1919 after 96 performances.

---

[52]Added for subsequent tour, after "The Older They Are:"
"What Could Be Fairer Than That?"
N. Bayes, I. Fisher
[53]Dropped during subsequent tour.
[54]Dropped during subsequent tour.
[55]For the subsequent tour (April 1919), the Act 3 was discarded and replaced by the following:
"Caroline"
I. Fisher
"Zing Boom Bah"
I. Fisher
"Maybe" (M-A-Y-B-E)
N. Bayes
(*Music and Lyrics by* Edgar Leslie and Harry Ruby.)
"Prohibition Blues"
N. Bayes
(*Music by* Nora Bayes. *Lyrics by* Ring Lardner.)
"What Will We Do on a Saturday Night When the Town Goes Dry?"
N. Bayes
Finale
N. Bayes, I. Fisher

CAST: *Glorianna Grey*: ELEANOR PAINTER. *Dolores Pennington*: DOROTHY SOUTH. *Therese, Ltd.*: JOSEPHINE WHITTELL. *Tonio*: Curtis Karpe. *Mrs. Saphronica Pennington*: Ursula Ellsworth. *Miss Angelica Pennington*: Marion Sitgreaves. *Lieutenant "Dick" Pennington*: JOSEPH LERTORA. *Jonathan Pennington*: Ralph Whitehead. *Alexander Galloway*: ALEXANDER CLARK. *Robbins*: James Joseph Dunn. *Nenette, Rintintin*: Ergotti Twins. *Jessica*: EMILIE LEA. *Porters*: Gilbert Wells, C. Balfour Lloyd. *Maids*: Marguerite St. Clair, Elsie Lawson. *Ring Bearer*: Vera Dunn. *Dolores' Dancing Class of Debutantes and Maids*: Miss Stout, Wynn, O'Connell, Merode, Redding, Burton, Bowhan, White, Sharp, Sitgraves, Smith, Stevens, Hall, Foreman, Scott, Haddone, Warren.

The action takes place in New York City and Boston at the present time.

Act 1: Glorianna's Studio Apartment, New York City. A Monday afternoon in September.

Act 2: The Pennington Sun Parlor, Boston, Massachusetts. Friday evening.

Act 3: The same. A few minutes later.

ACT 1[56]
"The Dancing Lesson" (Opening Number)
D. South, Dancing Class
"Frocks and Frills"
J. Whittell, "Midinette"
"Just a Little Laughter"[57]
E. Painter
"Nenette and Rintintin"
D. South, assisted by Ergotti Twins
"When a Girl"
J. Lertora

ACT 2[58]
Dance of the Porters
C. B. Lloyd, G. Wells
"Why Don't You Speak for Yourself, John?"
E. Painter, Dancing Class
"Dance of the Servants"
J. J. Dunn, Maids
"Love, Love"[59] (Love! Love! Love!)
E. Painter, J. Lertora
"Toodle 'oo!"[60]
E. Lea, Dancing Class
Finale

ACT 3[61]
"Chianti"
E. Lea, C. B. Lloyd, G. Wells
Finale
(Entire Company)

THE CANARY

1918.34

A Musical Comedy in Three Acts. (Book by Harry B. Smith.) Based on the (unproduced) French (scenario) by Louis Verneuil and Georges Barr (adapted from a novel "Le Coffre-fort vivant" by Frédéric Mauzens). Music

---

[56]The show was revised to suit the talents of Fritzi Scheff for national tour the following season. Added to close Act 1 was:
"My Climbing Rose"
Al H. Wilson (Galloway)
[57]Dropped for subsequent national tour.
[58]Added during run (after Why Don't You Speak for Yourself):
"The Best Man Never Gets the Worst of It"
Herbert Corthell (Galloway)
[59]"Replaced for the subsequent national tour by:
"(Tell Me,) Crystal Ball"
F. Scheff
[60]Replaced for subsequent national tour by:
"Tea in the Orient" (Oriental Song)
Edith Abbott (Dolores), Dancing Class
[61]Added during the run (before "Chianti"):
"Every Day Will Be Sunday When the Town Goes Dry"
H. Corthell

by Ivan Caryll, Irving Berlin, (Jerome Kern, William B. Kernell, Harry Tierney). (Lyrics by P. G. Wodehouse, Anne Caldwell, Richard Fechheimer, Harry Clarke, Benjamin Hapgood Burt, Clifton Crawford). Produced [staged] by Fred G. Latham and Edward Royce. Scenery designed by Joseph Urban. Costumes designed by Gladys Monkhouse (Act 2), Schneider-Anderson and Brooks Uniform Company; modern dresses by Dowling and Griffiths. Orchestra under the direction of Harold Vicars. Presented by Charles Dillingham. Opened 4 November 1918 at the Globe Theatre and closed 15 March 1919 after 152 performances.

CAST (in order of appearance): *Eugenie*: Doris Faithful. *Mrs. Beasley*: Edna Bates. *Ned Randolph*: Sam Hardy. *Mr. Trimmer*: GEORGE E. MACK. *Dr. Dippy*: LOUIS HARRISON. *Dodge*: JAMES DOYLE. *Fleece*: HARLAND DIXON. *Timothy*: JOSEPH CAWTHORN. *Julie*: JULIA SANDERSON. *Rico*: WILMER BENTLEY. *Mary Ellen*: MAUDE EBURNE. *A Minister*: George Egan.

Other Characters: Pauline Hall, Mildred Sinclair, Elsa Thomas, Kay Beach, Peggy Williams, Lillian White, Clare Vernon, Peg Raymond, Evelyn Conway, Peggy Eleanor, Mary Phillips, Evelyn Des Roches, Muriel Riley, Jean White, Martine Burnley, Dorothy Harrigan, Dorothy Duncan, Florence Bruce, Charlotte Wakefield, Elsie Gordon, Albertine Marlowe, Helen Lovett, Lorrayn Nelson, Peggy Dana, Gladys White, Shelagh Courtney, Marietta O'Brien, Mona Sartoris, Esther Worth, Peggy Smith, Isabel Adams. Frank Snyder, Sidney Ayres, Lester Ostrander, George Wharton.

Act 1: Trimmer's Antique Shop.

Act 2: Dr. Dippy's Sanitorium.

Act 3: Ned's Party.

ACT 1
    Opening
        Ensemble
        (*Music by* Ivan Caryll.)
    "That's What Men Are For"
        E. Bates, Chorus
        (*Music by* Ivan Caryll. *Lyrics by* P. G. Wodehouse.)
    "This Is the Time"
        S. Hardy, Chorus
        (*Music and Lyrics by* Clifton Crawford.)
    Burglar Dance
        J. Doyle, H. Dixon
        (*Music by* Harold Vicars.)
    "Love Me in the Spring"
        J. Sanderson, J. Cawthorn
        (*Music by* William B. Kernell. *Lyrics by* Richard Fechheimer.)
    "Thousands of Years Ago"
        J. Sanderson, Chorus
        (*Music by* Ivan Caryll. *Lyrics by* P. G. Wodehouse.)
    "Only in Dreams"
        S. Sanderson, S. Hardy
        (*Music by* Ivan Caryll. *Lyrics by* Harry B. Smith.)
    Finale
        (*Music by* Ivan Caryll.)

ACT 2
    Opening
        Ensemble
        (*Music by* Ivan Caryll.)
    "Hunting Song"
        J. Sanderson, Chorus
        (*Music by* Ivan Caryll. *Lyrics by* Anne Caldwell.)
    "You're So Beautiful"
        M. Eburne, J. Cawthorn
        (*Music and Lyrics by* Irving Berlin.)
    "Take a Chance (Little Girl and Learn to Dance)"
        J. Doyle, H. Dixon, Chorus
        (*Music by* Jerome Kern. *Lyrics by* Harry B. Smith.)
    "I Have Just One Heart (for Just One Boy)"
        J. Sanderson, F. Bruce, E. Conway, P. Hall, D. Faithful, A. Marlowe, M. Sinclair
        (*Music and Lyrics by* Irving Berlin.)
    Finale: "Ding Dong" (from YIP YIP YAPHANK)
        (*Music and Lyrics by* Irving Berlin.)

ACT 3
    Opening
        Ensemble
        (*Music by* Ivan Caryll.)

Dance
    E. Gordon, E. Thomas
Dance
    H. Dixon, M. Callahan
"That Little German Band"[62]
    J. Cawthorn
    (*Music by* Ivan Caryll. *Lyrics by* Benjamin Hapgood Burt.)
"I Wouldn't Give That for the Man Who Couldn't Dance"
    J. Sanderson, J. Doyle, H. Dixon, Chorus
    (*Music and Lyrics by* Irving Berlin.)
Finale
    (*Music by* Ivan Caryll.)

1918.35   LITTLE SIMPLICITY

A Play with Music in Three Acts. Book and lyrics by Rida Johnson Young. Music by Augustus Barratt. Production staged by Edward P. Temple. Dances by Jack Mason. Dances for the Cameron Sisters arranged by Alexis Kosloff. Scenery designed by Watson Barratt. Costumes designed by S. Zalud. Orchestra under the direction of Augustus Barratt. Produced by Messrs. Lee and J.J. Shubert. Opened 4 November 1918 at the Astor Theatre, moved 23 December 1918 to the 44th Street Theatre, and closed 8 February 1919 after 112 performances.

CAST (in order of appearance): *Jezirah*, *Zillah*, Native dancers: THE CAMERON SISTERS. *The Sheik of Kudah*, an Arabian noble: Ben Hendricks. *Joseph*, a waiter: PHIL RYLEY. *Clavelin*, proprietor of restaurant: Eugene Redding. *Lulu Clavelin*: MARJORIE GATESON. *Professor Erasmus Duckworth* of Troy, New York: CHARLES BROWN. *Pierre Lefebre*, a French student: PAUL PORCASI. *Jack Sylvester*, an American student: STEWART BAIRD. *Philip Dorrington*, an English student: HENRY VINCENT. *Alan Van Cleeve*, a rich young American: CARL GANTVOORT. *Irene*, a native flower girl: Polly Pryer. *Veronique*: CAROLYN THOMSON. *Mr. Morgan Van Cleeve*, Alan's father: Robert Lee Allen. *Messenger Boy*: Allan McDonald. *A Young Officer*: Samuel Critcherson. *Maude McCall*, a canteen 'hostess': FLORENCE BERESFORD.

Ladies of the Ensemble: Beatrice Little, Esther Small, Helene Douglass, Marie Vogel, Jane Scott, Rose Burdick, Ethel Hart, Hilda Wright, Alice Vely, Ella Evans, Jean Allen, Madeline Smith, Camille Truesdale, Nan Hope, Lucille Conroy, Madeline Dare, Betty Byrnes, Marjorie Hawman, Beatrice Knight, Bobby Watts, Blanche Gillmore, Lyola Whyte, Jean Brown, Marie Wilson, Marie Sorley. *Gentlemen of the Ensemble*: M. Swirse, Sam Critcherson, A. McDonald, George Rove.

Act 1: A French Café in Tunis, Africa. 1912.

Act 2: In the Latin Quarter, Paris. Three months later.

Act 3: With the Y.M.C.A. 'somewhere in France,' 1917.

ACT 1
    Opening
        Ensemble
    Oriental Dance
        Cameron Sisters
    "Women"[63] (Song)
        P. Ryley
    "Days of Youth"
        M. Gateson, C. Gantvoort, S. Baird, P. Porcasi, H. Vincent, P. Ryley
    "National Airs"
        M. Gateson, C. Gantvoort, S. Baird, P. Porcasi, H. Vincent, C. Brown
    "My Caravan"
        S. Baird, Chorus
    "Flower Song"
        C. Thomson
    "My Lulu" (Trio)
        M. Gateson, C. Brown, S. Baird
    "You Don't Know"[64]
        C. Gantvoort, C. Thomson

---

[62]Replaced for subsequent tour by:
    "They're Getting Away with Murder"
        J. Cawthorn
        (*Music by* William B. Kernell. *Lyrics by* Richard Fechheimer.)
[63]Dropped after opening.
[64]Dropped for subsequent tour.

"First Love"
P. Porcasi, S. Baird, H. Vincent

ACT 2[65]

"Just a Little Sunshine" (Song)
C. Thomson

"Hush! Hush!" (Sextette)
C. Thomson, C. Gantvoort, P. Porcasi, H. Vincent, S. Baird, Grisettes

"Maybe You'll Look Good to Me"
M. Gateson, C. Brown, Girls

"Learning to Love" (Trio)
C. Thomson, C. Gantvoort, C. Brown

Dance
Cameron Sisters

"Boomerang"
C. Thomson, P. Porcasi

"I Cannot Leave You Now" (Love Duet)
C. Gantvoort, C. Thomson

ACT 3[66]

Song and Dance
Cameron Sisters

"Voice Calling Me"
C. Gantvoort

Reminiscence
C. Thomson

"Fox Trot Military Tune"
F. Beresford, Girls, Cameron Sisters

"Same Old Way"
S. Baird

"March No."[67]
M. Gateson, C. Brown, Girls

Finale

1918.36 **GOOD LUCK, SAM!**

A Picture of Soldier Life in a Musical Comedy Frame, in Three Acts, 4 Scenes. Book and lyrics by Sergeant Edward Anthony. Music by Sergeant Louis G. Merrill. Produced by, of and for the Boys of Camp Merritt, New Jersey, under the direction of Frank Lea Short. Dances and ensembles by Michael Ring. Orchestrations by Gene Rawtenbury. Scenery and costumes by Robert Edmund Jones. Authorized and given through the courtesy and co-operation of Lieut. Colonel John Fawcett. Big Brothered by George M. Cohan. Opened 25 November 1918 at the Lexington Theatre, moved 9 December 1918 to the Knickerbocker Theatre and closed 21 December 1918 after 32 performances.

CAST (in order of appearance): *Viola Dell*: CHRISTOPHER HAYES. *Mrs. Mabel Marshmallow*: LEO HERRUP. *Second Lieutenant Fred Andrews*: LORENZO GILLETTE. *Ulysses S. Grant Johnson*: N. D. Cohen. *Private Sam Easterbrook*: JOSEPH LEGRANGE ABBOTT. *Martha Walters*: Corporal F. H. Healy. *General Goff*, the Judge: JOHN P. STACK. *The Colonel*, Attorney for the Defense: M. T. Collins. *The Major*: W. J. Dunn. *The Captain*, Prosecuting Attorney: Joseph R. Flick. *The First Lieutenant*: Robert L. Hamilton. *The Second Lieutenant*: Robert A. Blackburne. *The Orderly*: James J. Sullivan. *Entertainment Captain*: Joseph R. Flick. *The Bugler*: Lorenzo W. Brown. *Alexander*: George Tripler. *Mrs. George Washington Cackle*: George Rubin. *Mrs. Larson*: J. W. Wujcik. *Wireless Operator*: Lew Berk.

Specialties in Act 2: *Buck Dancers*: Frank Byrne, Frank Gill, Jack Lynch, Lorenzo D. Brown, C. Andrew Tuttle. *Prisoners*: Leo E. Knoblauch, Jerry Crowther, Leo Solomon, Edwin Brehme, Thomas Sullivan, James R. Dixon, Louis H. Schmidt, George Lawson. *Double Quartette*: E. J. Cote, James J. Luby, John W. Coakley, William J. Timmerman, Eugene R. Cohn, George Hackett, George Rubin, Isaac McCrum, Albert Pfeifer. *The*

Jazz Band: Sergeant Joseph W. Sheer (in charge), Ralph Harper, J. T. Brunette, R. J. Vachon, E. D. Westland, Thomas Prince, John F. McLaughlin, Fred Mangels, Thomas J. Mathews, Francis E. Walker, J. T. Wicker, Hugh King, Scott Hamilton, Ted Finder, Raymond Paul. *Strong Man*: Sergeant Edward R. Christman. *Handcuff King*: W. H. Vuylsteke. *The Magician*: Corporal Anthony Parini. *Cartoonists*: Ed Dillon, Jack Rosenberg. *Trick Ropers*: Sergeant Jack Fretz, Joseph Gulager. *The Isadora Duncan Dancers* (7): *Irma*: Patrick Kiley. *Erica*: Glenn Van Nauker. *Gretel*: Frank Butler. *Temple*: Eugene Bass. *Teresa*: George Rasmussen. *Anna*: Allison Rhue. *Lisel*: Sam Robinson.
Ponies: Roy P. Argenbright, Eugene Bass, Frank Butler, Arthur Batho, Samuel Congress, Henry Ezorsky, Albert Feinstein, Lorenzo W. Brown, Patrick Kiley, Benjamin Lustberg, Saul Mattus, George Rasmussen, Sam Robinson, Allison Rhue, Glen Van Nauker, Sidney Ward, William Walsh. *Butlers*: George Coberg, James J. Connolly, G. H. Martin, Patrick F. Brannan, Benjamin J. Levine, J. W. Wujcik, F. V. Witte, Randolph Kudile, B. J. Rafferty, Robert A. Hamilton, John W. Coakley, Lorenzo W. Brown. *Washerwomen*: W. F. Conway, Henry Friedman, A. J. O'keefe, N. A. Pomfret, G. F. Harrington, G. M. Scheetz, Jerry Crowther, E. H. Brehme, George Tripler, H. R. Harrell, Leo E. Knoblauch, W. J. Funsch. *Dishwashers*: J. H. Edsall, L. H. Schmidt, W. W. Schmidt, Courtney D. Krook, Albert Pfeiffer, Samuel Riber, Thomas Sullivan, James J. Sullivan, Leo Solomon, James J. O'Brien, Edward Wolz, Benjamin Katz. *Belle Girls*: Sidney Ward, Albert Feinstein, William Walsh, Henry Ezorsky, Samuel Congress, Roy P. Argenbright, Saul Mattus, Arthur Batho. *Belle Boys*: G. M. Martin, Patrick F. Brannan, F. V. Witte, Edward Marceau, Randolph Kudile, Edward L. Wolz, W. F. Conway, Benjamin J. Rafferty. *Male Chorus*: 106 Men.

Act 1: Reception Hall, Mrs. Mabel Marshmallow's School for Girls.

Act 2, Scene 1: Exterior of Guard House. *Scene 2*: Interior of Guard House, exactly as it is NOT.

Act 3: The Court Martial.

ACT 1

Opening Chorus
Men Returning to Camp

"Knitting Chorus"
Ponies

"Song of the Pictures"
C. Hayes

Duet
C. Hayes, L. Gillette

"Fred's Farewell"
L. Gillette

"O Need I Speak"
J. L. Abbott

"There's a Trace of the War in Everyone's Home"
L. Herrup, Chorus

"Into the Kitchen Boy"
J. L. Abbott, Chorus

"Good Luck, Sam!" (Finale)
L. Herrup, Entire Company

ACT 2

Opening Choruses:

Prisoners Chorus
Prisoners

Belle Boys Chorus
Belle Boys

Belle Girls Chorus
Belle Girls

"Watermelon and a Pair o' Dice"
N. D. Cohen, Chorus

"Good Luck, Sam!" (Finale)
J. P. Stack, Entire Company

ACT 3

Opening Chorus
Double Quartette

"(Oh!) It's Nice to Get Money from Home"
J. L. Abbott, Chorus

"Floorflushers" (Topical Song)
J. P. Stack

A Love's Sextette
J. P. Stack, L. Herup, L. Gillette, F. H. Healy, J. L. Abbott, C. Hayes

"Prisoner, Prisoner, Run Along"
Jury

"It's the Same Old Chow"
L. Gillette, Chorus

[65]Added during the run after "Hush! Hush!":
"It's Worth While Waiting for Someone Worth While"
M. Gateson, S. Baird
[66]Running order of songs in Act 3 was revised after opening. Added to Act 3, Opening, for tour:
"When the Whistle Blows"
S. Baird
[67]Replaced for subsequent tour by:
"Follow the Boys"
M. Gateson, Girls

"Good Luck, Sam!" (Finale)
 C. Hayes, Entire Company

1918.37

OH, MY DEAR!

A Musical Comedy in Two Acts[68]. Book and lyrics by Guy Bolton and P. G. Wodehouse. Music by Louis A. Hirsch, (Jean Schwartz). Staged by Robert Milton. Scenery designed by Robert Milton and Edward Royce. Gowns by Harry Collins; men's clothes designed by Croyden, Ltd. Orchestra under the direction of Max Hirschfield. Produced by William Elliott and F. Ray Comstock. Opened 27 November 1918 at the Princess Theatre, moved 21 April 1919 to the 39th Street Theatre, and closed 10 May 1919 after 189 performances[69].

<u>CAST</u> (in order of appearance): *Hazel*: Evelyn Dorn. *Dr. Rockett*: FREDERICK GRAHAM. *Broadway Willie Burbank*: ROY ATWELL. *Grace Spelvin*: Marjorie Bentley. *Bagshott*: Joseph Allen. *Bruce Allenby*: JOSEPH SANTLEY. *Hilda Rockett*: IVY SAWYER. *Georgie Van Alstyne*: Helen Barnes. *Pickles*: Miriam Collins. *Babe*: Helen Clarke. *Mrs. Rockett*: GEORGIA CAINE. *Jennie Wren*: JULIETTE DAY. *Joe Plummer*: Francis X. Conlan. *Nan Hatton*: Florence McGuire.
 Miss Lennox: Miss Clara Carroll. *Miss Bryant*: Dorothy LaRue. *Miss Schuyler*: Gene Carroll. *Miss Stuyvesant*: Frances Chase. *Miss Rhinelander*: Victoria Miles *Miss Greeley*: Jennifer Sinclair. *Miss Beekman*: Dorothy Bailey. *Miss Cortlandt*: Bessie More. *Miss Franklin*: Rene Manning. *Miss Audubon*: Alfa Lanee. *Miss Barclay*: Patricia Gordon. *Neal Clarke*: Sven Eric. *Harry Coppins*: Robert Gebhardt. *Willie Love*: Victor LeRoy. *Frank Lynn*: Jacque Stone.

Act 1: An Open Portico at the Rockett Health Farm. Afternoon.

Act 2, Scene 1: In front of the Portico. Night. *Scene 2*: The same. Early morning.

ACT 1[70]
 "I Shall Be All Right Now"
  R. Atwell, Girls
 "I Wonder Whether (I've Loved You All My Life)"
  J. Santley, I. Sawyer
 "Ask Dad"[71]
  H. Barnes, R. Atwell, F. Graham, M. Collins, H. Clarke
 "Our City of Dreams"
  I. Sawyer, Girls
 "Come Where Nature Calls"
  G. Caine, J. Santley, I. Sawyer, F. Graham, Girls
 "Phoebe Snow"
  J. Day, Girls
 Finale

ACT 2
Scene 1
 "Go, Little Boat" (Boat Song)(Opening)
  I. Sawyer, Boys, Girls
  (*Music by* Jerome Kern.)
 "You Never Know"
  J. Santley, I. Sawyer, H. Clarke, Girls, Boys
 "Try Again"[72]
  J. Santley, I. Sawyer, J. Day

---

[68]Billed as the sixth annual New York Princess Theatre Musical Comedy.
[69]For subsequent tour, the additional musical numbers were staged by David Bennett. The following songs were dropped: "The Train That Leaves for Town," "What's the Use?," "Ask Dad." "It Makes a Fellow Stop and Think" (title revised) was restored.
[70]Added to Act 1 for subsequent tour prior to the Finale:
 "Isn't It Wonderful?"
  J. Santley, I. Sawyer
[71]Replaced for subsequent tour by:
 "Now and Then" (Quartette)
  Hal Forde (Willie), Evelyn Macvey (Georgia), Rene Manning (Babe), Jennifer Sinclair (Pickles)
  (*Music by* Jean Schwartz. *Lyrics by* Alfred Bryan.)
[72]Dropped for subsequent tour and replaced by:
 "If You Only Know the Way"
  Lorraine Manville (Hilda), Douglas Stevenson (Bruce), J. Day
 "(I Love a) Musical Comedy Show"
  D. Stevenson, J. Day
  (*Music by* Jean Schwartz. *Lyrics by* Alfred Bryan.)

"It Sort of Makes a Fellow Stop and Think"[73]
 R. Atwell
 (*Music by* Benjamin Hapgood Burt. *Lyrics by* Roy Atwell.)
"Childhood Days"[74]
 J. Santley, F. Graham, J. Allen, H. Barnes, H. Clarke, M. Collins
Finaletto ("Oh, My Dear")
Scene 2
 "I'd Ask No More"[75]
  I. Sawyer, J. Day, Boys
 "If They Ever Parted Me from You"
  R. Atwell, J. Day
 Finale

1918.38

ATTA BOY

A Musical Comedy (Revue) in Two Acts, 6 Scenes[76]. Book and lyrics for Act 1 by Andre Sherri. (Music uncredited.) Additional musical numbers by Lieutenant Ballard Macdonald and Nat Osborne. Staged by Jack Mason. Scenery designed by Charles LeMaire (Act 1). Costumes designed by Andre Sherri. Musical direction by First Lieutenant P. O. Potts, Nat Osborne and Arthur Guttman. Authorized and given through the courtesy of Colonel William A. Phillips. Produced by the Soldiers of Aberdeen Proving Ground, Maryland. Opened 23 December 1918 at the Lexington Theatre and closed 11 January 1919 after 24 performances.

CAST: *Madame Sherri*, of the Maison Andre Millinery Shop: Pvt. GEORGE L. GAUDER. *Andre Sherri*, her son: Pvt. THOMAS FAIRCLOUGH. *Nanette*, his sweetheart: Corp. GEORGE GUNN. *Hiram Hicks*, an American millionaire: Pvt. Marty Maley. *Florizell Flushing Hicks*, his wife: Sgt. WILLIAM K. MEANS. *Pierre Poux Poux*, infamous detective: Pvt. B. GRINNEL. *Mr. Marshall*: Corp. J. M. Cohen. *Babette*: Sgt. Oliver Hunter. *Annie*: Sgt. Earl W. Spencer. *Right Reverend Tweedledum*: Pvt. Sam Cella. *Himself*: Capt. FRANK TINNEY. *The Music Masters*: Sgt. JAMES DUFFY, Pvt. FRED SWEENEY. *Milliners, Salesgirls, Customers*: (Ensemble).
 Chorus: Ponies: Sgt. Thomas F. Swick, Sgt. Oliver Hunter, Sgt. Earl W. Spencer, Cook Valentine V. Simon, Corp. John Voll, Corp. Isadore Cion, Pvt. William W. Richards, Pvt. Harry Mahan, Pvt. Carl Limon, Pvt. I. Leonard Kunis, Pvt. John J. Shea, Pvt. Maurice J. Dunn, Pvt. Harry A. Foster, Pvt. Howard M. Perrin, Pvt. LeRoy Dontigne, Pvt. Murry Rosenfeld. *First Show Girls*: Sgt. Walter J. Johnson, Corp. Frank Cox, Pvt. Paul R. Maley, Pvt. Paul R. Mealey, Pvt. Michael K. Schappert, Pvt. Roebrt B. Goodwin, Pvt. Edward A. Walker, Pvt. Guido Vogel, Pvt. Joseph p. Lavelle. *Second Show Girls*: Corp. Frank J. Lawlor, Pvt. Albert R. Morgan, Pvt. James Kearns, Pvt. George Ross, Pvt. Irving H. Engber, Pvt. Walter Miller, Pvt. John Castle, Corp. Harold Cogley. *Men*: Sgt. Isadore Sunberg, Corp. John F. Hughes, Pvt. John J. Hughes, Corp. Terry J. McHugh, Pvt. Edward A. Fennell, Pvt. Edward Dawson.

Act 1: The Millinery Shop of Madame Sherri.

Act 2, Scene 1: The Post Exchange. *Scene 4*: The Trench.

ACT 1
 Opening Ensemble
  G. Gunn, G. L. Gaunder, Chorus
 "Elephant Skid"
  G. L. Gaunder, Chorus
 "Hold Me in Your Arms"
  T. Fairclough, Chorus
 "I Love Her and She Loves Me"
  M. Maley, W. K. Means

---

[73]Previously used under the title "It's an Awful Thing Not to Know Where You Are" in ALL OVER TOWN which closed prior to New York in 1915. Replaced during the run by: (but reinstated for tour)
 "A Moment of Peace"
  R. Atwell, E. Dorn, H. Clarke, M. Collins, H. Barnes, Girls
[74]Replaced during the run by: (dropped for tour)
 "What's the Use?"
  F. Graham, J. Santley, J. Allen, Girls
 Dance
  A. H. Fagan, H. Clarke
[75]Replaced during the run by: (later dropped)
 "The Train That Leaves for Town"
  J. Day, A. H. Fagan, Girls
[76]Reconceived and recast as a revue with many different songs for subsequent tour under the direction of Dan Dody.

"Strolling 'round the Camp with Mary"
J. Duffy, F. Sweeney
(*Music by* Nat Osborne. *Lyrics by* Ballard Macdonald.)
"Ragtime Wedding"
T. Fairclough, G. Gunn, S. Cella, Chorus
Melodrama
G. Gunn, G. L. Gaunder, T. Fairclough, B. Grinnel, Chorus
"The Worst Is Yet to Come"
W. K. Means
"The Stars in the Service Flag" (Finale)
T. Fairclough, Chorus

ACT 2
Scene 1
Opening Ensemble
Pony Ballet
The Captain: Sgt. J. Duffy. *The Waiter*: Capt. F. Tinncy.
Private Maley and His Instrumentalists
Ballet
G. Gunn, Pony Ballet
Scene 2
Not Will Rogers, But Corp. Alfred Harris
Salvation Army Girls
Scene 3
The Rookie Squad
Scene 4
Behind the Front
The Captain: Sgt. J. Duffy. *The Private*: Capt. F. Tinney.
Scene 5
"Angel Child"
E. W. Spencer, O. Hunter, Chorus
Finale
R. Faulkner, Entire Company

1918.39 LISTEN LESTER

A Musical Entertainment in Two Acts. Book and lyrics by Harry L. Cort and George E. Stoddard. Music by Harold Orlob. Staged by Robert Marks. Scenery designed by H. Robert Law Studios. Costumes by H. Mahieu & Company. Orchestra under the direction of Gus Salzer. Produced by John Cort. Opened 23 December 1918 at the Knickerbocker Theatre, suspended performances 6-11 August 1919 for the Actors' Equity strike, and closed 16 August 1919 after 272 performances.

CAST (in order of appearance): *Miss Down*: Mary Milburn. *Miss Upp*: Irma Marwick. *Miss Belle*, a phone girl: Esther Ingham. *Colonel Rufus Dodge*, a dodger: EDDIE GARVIE. *Miss Pink*, a detective: Ruth Mabee. *William Penn, Jr.*, a fixer: JOHNNY DOOLEY. *Jack Griffin*, a fiancé: CLIFTON WEBB. *Miss Mary Dodge*, a sweetheart: ADA MAE WEEKS. *Mrs. Tillie Mumm*, a widow: ADA LEWIS. *Lester Lite*, a porter: HANSFORD WILSON. *Miss Arbutus Quilty*, a live one: GERTRUDE VANDERBILT. *Harmony by* the Four Entertainers.
Ladies of the Ensemble: Agnes Hall, Grace Hall, Nella Kline, Lucille Constante, Jean Troupman, Neida Snow, Marguerite Francisco, Yvette Reals. *Guests*: Ethel Whiteley, Irene Smythe, Gertrude Bullock, Juana Ward, Beth Hardy, Florence McKenna, Nina Calame, Helen Wynn, Margaret Curtiss, Dorothy Scott.

Act 1: The Gold Room of the Hotel Ritz, Palm Beach. Afternoon.

Act 2: The Supper Porch, same hotel. Evening.

ACT 1[77]
"Show a Little Something New"
J. Dooley, Girls
"When Things Come Your Way"
J. Dooley, C. Webb, Girls
"Feather Your Nest"
A. M. Weeks, Girls
"Waiting for You"
A. M. Weeks, C. Webb, Girls
"Two is Company"
A. M. Weeks, C. Webb, J. Dooley

"(I Was) A Very Good Baby in the Daytime"
G. Vanderbilt, H. Wilson
ACT 2[78]
"When the Shadows Fall" (Opening)
M. Milburn, Entertainment Quartette
B. Valse
R. Mabee, C. Webb
"I'd Love To"
G. Vanderbilt, J. Dooley, Girls
Dance Eccentric
H. Wilson
"For a Girl Like You"
C. Webb, A. M. Weeks
"(Oh! You) Sweet Stuff"
J. Dooley, Girls
Dance
C. Webb, G. Vanderbilt
"Who Was the Last Girl (You Called By Her First Name)?" (Mock Duet)
J. Dooley, E. Garvie
"See Her First"
G. Vanderbilt, Girls
Finale
Company

1918.40 SOMEBODY'S SWEETHEART

A Musical Play in Two Acts. Book and lyrics by Alonzo Price. Music by Antonio Bafunno. Staged by Alonzo Price. Orchestra under the direction of Herbert Stothart. (Settings) Designed by Homer Conant. Gowns by Paul Arlington, Inc, Brooks Uniform Co. (Men's), Collins (Nonette's). Produced under the personal direction of Arthur Hammerstein. Produced by Arthur Hammerstein. Opened 23 December 1918 at the Central Theatre, moved 9 June 1919 to the Casino Theatre, and closed 5 July 1919 after 224 performances.

CAST (in order of appearance): *A Troubador*: Rose deGranada. *Andrews*: Bernard Gorcey. *Colonel Williams*, U.S. Consul to Seville: ALBERT SACKETT. *Harry Edwards*: WALTER SCANLAN. *Helen Williams*: EVA FALLON. *Roderic*, Spanish Prince: Arthur Klein. *Bessie Williams*: LOUISE ALLEN. *Sam Benton*: WILLIAM KENT. *Machaquito*, Consul's Secretary: Chester Brown. *Dolores*, a Water Girl: Carmen Granada. *Zaida*: NONETTE. *Ben Hud*: JOHN DUNSMURE. *Scipio*: Basil Stratti. *Oriental Dancer*: VERONICA. *Matadors, Water Girls, American Tourists, etc.*
Ensemble: Blanche Stanhope, Elinor Cullen, Natalie Bates, Rose deGranada, Elsie Shaw, Ruth Young, Nellie Crawford, Adeah Wise, Helen Doring, M. Madison, Neysa Huben, Billie Fisher, Nita Chandos, Marion Simpson, Louise Clarke, Dorothy Donlon, Marie Duchette, Julie Hoey, Dorothy Vernon, Sybil Bethel, Gilman M. Williams, B. Spirdelli, B. Scott, William C. Hovel, B. Caplan, William Altwell, Michael Kosker, John St. John, Wiliam Feistel.

Act 1: A Square in Seville, Spain.

Act 2: Garden of the U.S. Consulate.

ACT 1
Opening Chorus:
"Serenade"/"Viva la Toreador"
R. deGranada, Ensemble
"Spain"
E. Fallon, A. Klein, Chorus
(*Music and Lyrics by* Arthur Hammerstein and Herbert Stothart.)
"Girl of My Heart"
W. Scanlan, L. Allen
"Somebody's Sweetheart"
W. Kent, L. Allen
"Follow Me"/"It Gets Them All"
Nonette, J. Dunsmure, Chorus
(*Music and Lyrics by* Arthur Hammerstein and Herbert Stothart.)
"On Wings of Doubt"
Nonette, J. Dunsmure
"What Shall We Sing?"
W. Scanlan, Chorus

---

[77]Running order revised after opening. "Show a Little Something New" moved to follow "Waiting for You."

[78]Running order revised after opening. "Who Was the Last Girl" moved to follow "I'd Love To."

"Twinkle"
  W. Kent, W. Scanlan, Chorus
ACT 2
Prelude and Recitative
  W. Scanlan
"Sultana"
  J. Dunsmure
Oriental Dance
  Veronica
"Gypsy Melodies"
  Nonette
"The Old Fashion Way" (In the Old Fashioned Way)
  W. Scanlan, E. Fallon, Chorus
  (*Music and Lyrics by* Arthur Hammerstein and Herbert Stothart.)
"Then I'll Marry You"
  W. Kent, L. Allen
"Is It Your Smile?"
  W. Kent, Nonette
Finale
  Company

1918.41 THE VOICE OF McCONNELL

A Comedy with Songs in Three Acts. Play, music and lyrics by George M. Cohan. (Staged by George M. Cohan, Sam Forrest.) Musical director, George Lydwig. Produced by George M. Cohan and Sam Harris. Opened 25 December 1918 at the Manhattan Opera House and closed 18 January 1919 after 30 performances.[79]

CAST (in order of appearance): *Hendricks*: Roy Cochrane. *Bell Boy*: Arthur Shields. *J. Austin Severard*: EDWARD FIELDING. *Waiter*: H. P. Woodley. *Tom O'Connell*: CHAUNCEY OLCOTT. *Miss Giles*: Edna Leslie. *Miss Hemingway*: Agnes Gildea. *Mr. Jackson*: Fletcher Harvey. *Mr. Sullivan*: David V. Wall. *Miss Embree*: Wilda Marie Moore. *Mrs. Dwight McNamara*: Mrs. Alice Chapin. *Evelyn McNamara*: GILDA LEARY. *Barry*: Edward O'Connor. *Susan*: Elsie Lyding. *Harry McNamara*: RICHARD TABER. *Douglas Graham*: HAROLD deBECKER. *Miss Collinsby*: CONSTANCE BEAUMAR. *Mr. Smithers*: Bert Dunlap. *Miss Drake*: Mae Jennings. *Miss Copeland*: Ruth Price.

Guests in the McNamara Home: Misses Manning, Ruth Price, Richmond, Jepp, Gassel, Clark, Rogers, Mae Jennings. Messrs. Clarke, Arthur Shields, Ross, Rogers, Grant, Harper.

Act 1: McConnell's Apartment in a New York Hotel.

Act 2: The McNamara Home the following evening.

Act 3: Same as Act 1, two days later.

MUSICAL NUMBERS[80]
"Ireland, My Land of Dreams"
  C. Olcott
"You Can't Deny You're Irish"
  C. Olcott
"When I Look in Your Eyes, Mavourneen"
  C. Olcott
"Mother Machree" (from BARRY OF BALLYMORE; ISLE O' DREAMS)
  C. Olcott
  (*Music by* Ernest R. Ball, Chauncey Olcott. *Lyrics by* Rida Johnson Young.)
"That Tumble Down Shack in Athlone"
  (*Music by* Monte Carlo and Alma Sanders. *Lyrics by* Richard W. Pascoe.)

1918.42 THE MELTING OF MOLLY

A Musical Comedy in a Prologue and Three Acts. Book by Maria Thompson Davies, based on her novel of the same name. Musical adaptation by Edgar Smith. Music by Sigmund Romberg. Lyrics by Cyrus Wood. Staged by Oscar Eagle. Dances arranged by Allan K. Foster. Scenery designed by Watson Barratt. Costumes by Adler Costume Company and Arlington Company. Orchestra under the direction of Victor Baravalle.

Produced under the personal direction of J. J. Shubert. Produced by Messrs. Lee and J. J. Shubert. Opened 30 December 1918 at the Broadhurst Theatre and closed 15 March 1919 after 88 performances.

CAST (in order of appearance): Prologue: *Miss Proctor*: Betty Carter. *Miss Pearl*: Gladys Miller. *Miss Pierce*: Gladys Turner Walton. *Mrs. Carter*: Maude Turner Gordon. *Judge Wade*: Frank Kingdon. *Judy*: Mrs. Charles G. Craig. *Dot Carter*: GLORIA GOODWIN. *Tom Morgan*: TED LORRAINE. *Molly Carter*: ISABELLE LOWE. *John Moore*: CHARLES PURCELL. *Alfred Bennett*: Robert Bentley. *Guests of Mrs. Carter*.
  Play: *Judy*: Mrs. Charles G. Craig. *Mrs. Carter*: Maude Turner Gordon. *Dot Carter*: GLORIA GOODWIN. *Molly Carter*: ISABELLE LOWE. *Tom Morgan*: TED LORRAINE. *Ethel Morgan*: Marjorie Dunbar Pringle. *Judge Wade*: Frank Kingdon. *Doctor Moore*: CHARLES PURCELL. *Athletic Instructor*: Vera Roehm. *St. Clair McTabb*: EDGAR NORTON. *Miss Chester*: Alison McBain. *Guest*: George S. Trimble. *Collectors, Guests, Sanitarium Patients, etc.*
  Ensemble: Misses Regina Lorraine, Mabel Roberts, May McHale, Cecilia North, Toots Bryce, Flo Summerville, Carolyn Arnold, Ingeborg Christensen, Dorothy Chappell, Helen Cressman, Dorothy Clifton, Ann Swann, Virginia Huntington. Messrs. George Schall, Clarence Hansen, George Baker, Farrell Fitzpatrick.

Prologue: Lawn of the Carter Residence.

Act 1: Living Room of the Carter Residence. Four years later.

Act 2: The Sanitarium of Dr. Moore. Three months later.

Act 3: Same as Prologue.

PROLOGUE
Opening
  Entire Chorus
"Dancing School"
  G. Goodwin, T. Lorraine
"Darling"
  C. Purcell, I. Lowe
"Reminiscence"
  C. Purcell, I. Lowe
ACT 1
"Bills" (Opening)
  Mrs. C. G. Craig, Boys
"Dear Old Gown"
  I. Lowe
"Jazz, How I Love to Hear It"
  T. Lorraine, G. Goodwin, M. D. Pringle, Chorus
"Lodger"
  I. Lowe, C. Purcell
"Jazz All Your Troubles Away"
  I. Lowe, T. Lorraine, G. Miller, G. Walton, M. D. Pringle, G. Goodwin, Chorus
  (*Lyrics by* Augustus Barratt.)
"Oh! Doctor, Doctor"
  C. Purcell, G. Walton, G. Miller, Girls
"Reminiscence" (reprise)
  C. Purcell, Ensemble
ACT 2
"You Win"
  V. Roehm, Girls
"Floating Down a Moonlight Stream"
  T. Lorraine, G. Goodwin, Girls
"You Remember Me"
  I. Lowe, C. Purcell
"Rolling Exercise"
  Mrs. C. G. Craig, I. Lowe
ACT 3
"Bridesmaids"/"Wedding by Proxy"
  T. Lorraine, G. Miller, G. Walton, Chorus
"I Want My Husband When I'm Wed"
  G. Goodwin, T. Lorraine, Chorus
Finale
  Ensemble

1919.01 THE VELVET LADY

A Musical Comedy in Three Acts. Book by Fred Jackson, based on Fred Jackson's farce "A Full House." Music by Victor Herbert. Adaptation and

---

[79]Settings, costumes uncredited.
[80]Not in performance order.

lyrics by Henry Blossom. Book staged by Edgar MacGregor. Dances arranged by Julian Mitchell. Scenery designed by H. Robert Law Scenic Studios. Costumes designed by Schneider-Anderson Company, Mary Blackburn; Croydon, Ltd. (men's). Orchestra under the direction of Frederic Stalberg. Orchestrations by Victor Herbert. Produced by Marc Klaw and Abe L. Erlanger. Opened 3 February 1919 at the New Amsterdam Theatre and closed 31 May 1919 after 136 performances.

CAST (in order of appearance): *Parks:* ERNEST TORRENCE. *Bridesmaids (9): Una:* Una Fleming. *Teddy:* Teddie Hudson. *Janet:* Janet McIlwaine. *Lucine:* Lucine Paula. *Florence:* Florence Crips. *Dolly:* Dolly Alwyn. *Helen:* Helen Borden. *Mignon:* MIGNON REED. *Tess:* Tess Mayer. *Ottilie Howell,* a Bride: MARIE FLYNN. *Susie,* the Howell's Maid: GEORGIA O'RAMEY. *Miss Winnacker,* Auntie: Eleanor Gordon. *Bubbles,* Ottilie's sister: MINERVA COVERDALE. *Nicholas King:* JED PROUTY. *Ned Pembroke:* ALFRED GERRARD. *George Howell:* RAY RAYMOND. *Sergeant:* Daniel Sullivan. *Mooney,* a new cop: EDDIE DOWLING. *"Spookie Ookum":* Janet McIlwaine. *Verna Vernon,* The Velvet Lady: FAY MARBE. *Mrs. Pembroke:* Edna von Buelow.

Guests: Marjorie Lee, Trixie Bush, Gladys Jordan, Marie Finney, Henriett Brewster, Elsie Malstad, Billie Vernon, Eleanor Innes. *Policemen:* Gene Richard, Jack Whalen, Roy Lewis, Clyde Miller.

Act 1: The Library of Howell's house on Riverside Drive. Late afternoon.

Act 2: The Living Hall of Howell's house. Early the same evening, Halloween.

Act 3: The Living Room in Howell's House. An hour later.

ACT 1

"Tonight's the Night" (Opening Chorus)
Girls

"Come Be My Wife"
M. Flynn, Girls

Duet ("Scandal")
E. Torrence, G. O'Ramey

"Little Boy and Girl"
A. Gerrard, M. Coverdale, Girls

"Fair Honeymoon"
R. Raymond, A. Gerrard, M. Flynn, M. Coverdale

"Any Time New York Goes Dry"[81]
J. Prouty

"There's Nothing Too Fine for the Finest"
R. Raymond, J. Prouty, E. Dowling, D. Sullivan, 4 Cops

ACT 2

Opening:
"Way Down in Yucatan"
E. Malstad, H. Brewster

"Bubbles"
M. Coverdale, Girls

"Spooky Ookum"
R. Raymond, J. McIlwaine, Girks

"Policeology"[82]
E. Dowling, Cops, U. Fleming, T. Hudson, J. McIlwaine

"I've Danced to Beat the Band"
A. Gerrard, F. Crips, D. Alwyn, U. Fleming, T. Hudson, M. Coverdale

"Logic"
E. Dowing, E. Torrence

"Life and Love"
R. Raymond

Dance
R. Raymond, U. Fleming

"What a Position for Me"
G. O'Ramey

Finale
Company

ACT 3

"Wedding Bells" (Opening)
Girls

---

[81]Dropped after opening.
[82]Dropped after opening.

"Dancing at the Wedding"
M. Coverdale, Bridesmaids

"Throwing the Bull"
F. Marbe, A. Gerrard, R. Raymond, M. Flynn, M. Coverdale, E. Gordon

Finale
Company

1919.02 GOOD MORNING, JUDGE

A Musical Play in Two Acts, 4 Scenes. Book by Frederick Thompson. Based on [the English musical "The Boy," founded upon] the play "The Magistrate" by Arthur Wing Pinero. Music by Lionel Monckton and Howard Talbot. Lyrics by Adrian Ross and Percy Greenbank. Staged by Wybert Stamford. Musical numbers arranged by Jack Mason. Scenery designed by D. Frank Dodge and William Castle. Costumes designed by S. Zalud. Orchestra under the direction of Frank Paret. Produced by the Messrs. Shubert. Opened 6 February 1919 at the Sam S. Shubert Theatre and closed 6 June 1919 after 140 performances.

CAST (in order of appearance): *Lyall Heeson-Gallway,* guest at the Meebles: Raymond Oakes. *Elsie Erskine:* Helene Shaw. *Cuthbert Sutten:* Cecil Clovelly. *Rose Ingleby:* Katherine Alexander. *Joy Chatterton,* Hughie's music mistress: MOLLIE KING. *Cash,* butler at the Meebles: Robert Vivian. *Hughie Cavanaugh,* Mrs. Cavanaugh's son: CHARLES KING. *Katie Muirhead,* Mrs. Meebles' niece: Betty Pierce. *An Elderly Lady:* Nellie Graham-Dent. *Turner,* a maid to the Meebles: Eileen Cotty. *Diana Fairlie,* Mrs. Meebles' sister: GRACE DANIELS. *Albany Pope,* of Lloyd's: Harold Crane. *Margaret Hayes:* Georgine Baker. *Winnie Sweet:* Nellie King. *Mr. Burridge,* chief magistrate of Bromley Street Police Court: Shep Camp. *Millicent Meebles,* late Cavanaugh: Margaret Dale. *Horatio Meebles,* a magistrate of the Bromley Street Police Court: GEORGE HASSELL. *Napoleon,* a waiter: Alfred Hessé. *Adelphi Artists:* Cunningham and Clements. *Colonel Bagot* from Bengal, retired: EDWARD MARTINDEL. *Jené,* a dancer: Emily Lea. *Juniori Fratti,* proprietor of the Cosmos: Jean De La Valle. *Attendant:* Ellyn Harcourt. *Inspector Eason:* Frederick Annerley. *Constable Styles:* Robert McClellan. *Sergeant Dix* of the Metropolitan Police: Charles M. Hinton. *Mr. Honeyball,* chief clerk of Bromley Street: Ashton Tonge. (*Dance Specialty:* Aleta Doré.)

Chorus Girls: Betty Marshall, Edith Pollack, Dorothy Flamm, Peggie Hansel, Gene Fleming, Jesse Phillip, Eva Rutherford, Mae Borden, Lola Joyce, Harriete Gustine, Laila Stanley, Constance Huntington, Josephine Ray, Sadye Everett, Helen Trainor, Peggy Radford, Elma Gylden, Mary Brittain, Peggy Dempsey, Glada Davis, Claire Benedict, Norma Dale. *Chorus Men:* Robert Hurst, L. R. Nelson, William Raymond, Hal Peel, S. Harvey.

Act 1: Mr. Meebles' House in West Hampstead.

Act 2, Scene 1: The Cosmos Hotel, Verrey Street, W.C. *Scene 2:* The Magistrate's Room, Bromley Street. *Scene 3:* Garden at Mr. Meebles' Home.

ACT 1

Opening Chorus
Ensemble

"A Game That Ends with a Kiss" (Song)
M. King, Girls

"That Has Nothing to Do with You" (It's Nothing to Do with You)(Trio)
M. King, C. King, B. Pierce
(*Music by* Lionel Monckton. *Lyrics by* Percy Greenbank.)

"Make Hay (Little Girl)" (Song)
G. Daniels, Girls
(*Music by* Lionel Monckton. *Lyrics by* Percy Greenbank.)

"Young Folks and Old Folks" (Quintet)
M. Dale G. Daniels, C. King, S. Camp, G. Hassell

"(I've Got a Pair of) Swinging Doors (That Lead Right into My Heart)" (Song)
C. King, Girls
(*Music by* Bert Grant. *Lyrics by* Sam M. Lewis, Joe Young.)

"Oh, That We Two Were Maying" (Duet)
M. Dale, G. Hassell
(*Music by* Lionel Monckton. *Lyrics by* Percy Greenbank.)

"I Am So Young and You Are So Beautiful" (Song)
M. King, C. King
(*Music by* George Gershwin. *Lyrics by* Alfred Bryan, Irving Caesar.)

Finale

ACT 2

Scene 1

Introduction and Dance

Dance Specialty
Cunningham and Clements
Special Dance
E. Lea
"Sporty Boys" (Duet)
C. King, G. Hassell
(*Music by* Lionel Monckton. *Lyrics by* Percy Greenbank.)
"Dinky Doodle Dicky" (Song)
M. King, C. King, Ensemble
(*Music by* Howard Talbot. *Lyrics by* Percy Greenbank.)
"I Am the Boy (and I Am the Girl)"[83] (Dance)
M. King
(*Music by* Louis Silvers. *Lyrics by* Buddy G. DeSylva.)
"Midnight Cabaret" (Scene)
Ensemble
Scene 3
"Pansy Day" (Opening Chorus and Solo)
B. Pierce, Ensemble
(*Music by* Lionel Monckton. *Lyrics by* Percy Greenbank.)
Dance Specialty
A. Doré
Dance Specialty[84]
Cunningham and Clements
"I Want To Go Bye-Bye"[85] (Song)
G. Hassell, Girls
(*Music by* Lionel Monckton. *Lyrics by* Percy Greenbank.)
Imitations
M. King
Finale
Ensemble

MONTE CRISTO, JR.

1919.03

A Musical Extravaganza in Two Acts, 18 Scenes[86]. Dialogue (book) and lyrics by Harold Atteridge. Music by Sigmund Romberg and Jean Schwartz. Staged by J. C. Huffman. Musical numbers arranged by Allan K. Foster. Stage settings by Watson Barratt; Roman scene by P. Strahlendorff. Costumes designed by Kiviette and S. Zalud. Orchestra under the direction of Frank Tours. Produced by Messrs. Lee and J. J. Shubert. Opened 12 February 1919 at the Winter Garden; suspended performances 6 August 1919 for the Actors' Equity strike; resumed performances 8 September 1919 and closed 4 October 1919 after 254 performances.

CAST (in order of appearance): *Harry Sterling*: SYDNEY JARVIS. *Annette*: Helen Patterson. *Grace*: Grace Keeshon. *Florence*: Fawn Conway. *Mack*: Tom Lewis. *Julian*: SAM ASH. *Matilda*: Muriel Tindal. *Mercedes*: AUDREY MAPLE. *Monte*: CHARLES PURCELL. *Florence*: Katherine Van Pelt. *Maisie, Helen*: WATSON SISTERS (Kitty, Fanny). *Wilbur*: GORDON DOOLEY. *Clarence*: WILLIAM DOOLEY. *A Waiter*: Anthony Jochim. *Yvonne*: Flore Revalles. *Gladys*: Gladys Buckridge. *The Bride*: ADELAIDE. *The Groom*: J. J. HUGHES. *The Minister*: Jack Manning. *Zeke*: Anthony Hughes. *Jefferson Sap, Jr.*: CHIC SALE. *Hector*: Mart Fuller-Golden. *Shirley*: Shirley Sherman. *Virginia*: Virginia Fissinger. *Fernand*: SYDNEY JARVIS. *Danglers*: SAM ASH. *Jameson*: RALPH HERZ. *Dantes*: CHARLES PURCELL. *Morell*: Anthony Hughes. *Haydee*: Flore Revalles. *Maizdes, Constantinopla*: WATSON SISTERS. *Toy Dance*: ADELAIDE and HUGHES. *Vampa*: TOM LEWIS. *Magistrate*: James Daley. *Gendarmes*: Mart Fuller-Golden, Anthony Jochim. *The Jailer*: Mart Fuller-Golden. *A Keeper*: Arthur Cardinal. *Abe Faria*: Anthony Jochim. *Pierre DeTay*: James Daley. *Edward Francois*: John Kearns. *Gaston*: Roger Little. *The Governor*: Anthony Hughes. *Reverend Fluffy Ruff*: RALPH HERZ. *Chief Zalay*: James Daley. *Tarzan the Ape*: Anthony Hughes. *Diamonda*: Flore Revalles. *King Love*: Rose Rolanda. *Emerald*: Shirley Sherman. *Sapphire*: Virginia

Fissinger. *Ruby*: Jean Thomas. *Topaz*: Trixie Jennery. *Festal*: Gladys Buckridge. *A Roman*: Rose Rolanda. *Danseuse*: Virginia Fissinger. *Queen Josephine, Constantinopla*: WATSON SISTERS. *Napoleon*: TOM LEWIS. *The Count of Monte Cristo*: CHARLES PURCELL. *An Apache*: WILLIAM DOOLEY. *A Grizette*: GORDON DOOLEY. *Countess of Shamokin*: ADELAIDE. *A Servant*: Anthony Jochim. *Daisy*: ESTHER WALKER.

Winter Garden Beauties (Show Girls): Grace Keeshon, Alfa Lanee, Jeane Thomas, Adele ReRoy, Hellen Marche, Mildred Johnson, Muriel Seeley, Beatrice Benton, Margaret Green, Betty Brown, DeOearia Anguillar, Ella Darcy, Louise Atkinson, Gladys Gray, Harriett Jacobs, Marion Haslop, Dorothy Bruce, Myrtle Riggs, Mabel Allen, Lola Taylor, Mary Rinehart, Virginia Kimber, Beth Pitt, Fawn Conway, Betty Francisco, Lorraine Clarke, Dorothy Dentone, Florence Elmore, Pearl Germonde, Helene Neary, Myrtle McLindon, Ruth Coster, Patricia Gordon, Catherine Wyley, Helen Patterson. *Dancers*: Ella Foster, Aileen Rooney, Hazel Frisby, Dolores Mendez, Lorrelda Poppanny, Edith Pierce, Sylvia Forde, Jeane Cameron, Gertrude Raye Kossar, Dorothy Bryant, Viola Watson, Orilla Smith, Julia Grant, Mazie Elliott, Virginia Allen, Mabel Munson, Jeanne Berkley, Anna Berry, Jewel Berry, Eva Fuller, Beverley Miller, Phyllis Miller, Flo Howard, Alice Wagner.

ACT 1[87]
"Just My Type" (They're All My Type)
S. Jarvis, Winter Garden Types
"Sentimental Knights"
A. Maple, S. Ash, S. Jarvis, a few pictures of long ago
"Mi Lady's Dress"[88]
S. Ash, Winter Garden Beauties
"Fiji"
F. Watson, K. Watson
"Broadway Butterfly"
C. Purcell, Broadway Butterflies
"Military Glide"
G. Buckridge, Brides, Marines, Adelaide and Hughes
"Stepping Out To-night"
W. Dooley, G. Dooley, F. Watson, K. Watson
"Monte Cristo"
C. Purcell, S. Sherman, V. Fissinger
"Marseilles"
M. Tindal, Flower Girls, Coquettes
"Girl in Every Port"
C. Purcell, Girls from Every Port
"Woman and Light"
R. Herz
(*Music and Lyrics by* Earl Carroll.)
"Nanette and Rin Tin Tin"
Nanettes and Rin Tin Tin
"Toy Dance"
Adelaide and Hughes
"Jazz Marimba" (Dance)
K. Watson, Entire Ensemble
"Fast Steppers"
Winter Garden Fast Steppers
"Jewel Ballet"
Jewel Girls, Misses R. Rolando, V. Fissinger, T. Jennery, S. Sherman, J. Thomas, F. Revalles, Adelaide and Hughes
ACT 2
"Festive Nights"
R. Rolando, V. Fissinger, G. Buckridge, Roman Dancers
"(Who Played Poker with) Pocahontas"
F. Watson
(*Music by* Fred E. Alhert. *Lyrics by* Sam. M. Lewis, Joe Young.)
"Vampire Dance"
W. Dooley, G. Dooley
"Carnival Times"
S. Jarvis, Carnival Girls
Songs
K. Watson, F. Watson
["I Always Think I'm in Heaven When I'm Down in Dixieland"
(*Music by* Maurice Abrahams. *Lyrics by* Sam M. Lewis, Joe Young.)]

[83]Published as "I'm the Boy and I'm the Girl." Replaced for subsequent tour by:
"One Night, One Waltz, One Girl"
A. Kearns {Hughie Cavanaugh}, Mercedes Lorenze {Joy Chatterton}
[84]Dropped after opening and replaced by:
"Little Miss Melody"
G. Daniels, Ensemble
(*Music by* Lionel Monckton. *Lyrics by* Percy Greenbank.)
[85]Dropped for subsequent tour.
[86]Billed as the Winter Garden's Annual Mid-Winter Extravaganza.

[87]The running order of songs was revised during the run.
[88]Dropped during the run.

Dance
  Adelaide
"Empire Days"
  F. Revalles, Court Boys, Girls
"World of Beauty"[89]
  C. Purcell, Beauties of History
"Sugar Baby"
  E. Walker, Winter Garden Sugar Babies
"Indoor Sports"
  S. Jarvis, Sports Girls

1919.04   THE ROYAL VAGABOND

A Cohanized Opéra-Comique in Three Acts. Book by Stephen Ivor-Szinnyey and William Cary Duncan. (Based on an unproduced operetta "Cherry Blossoms" by Messrs. Ivor-Szinnyey, Duncan and Goetzl.) Music by Dr. Anselm Goetzl. Lyrics by William Cary Duncan. (Additional numbers by George M. Cohan.) Staged by Julian Mitchell, Sam Forrest. Costumes designed by Alice O'Neil. Scenery designed by Edward G. Unitt and Joseph Wickes. Orchestra under the direction of Gus Salzer. Entire production under the direction of George M. Cohan. Produced by George M. Cohan and Sam Harris. Opened 17 February 1919 at the Cohan and Harris Theatre and suspended performances 6 August 1919 for the Actor's Equity strike; resumed 8-15 August 1919; resumed 8 September 1919 and closed 3 January 1920 after 348 performances.

CAST: *Chefcheck*, the Inn Keeper: Charles Wayne. *Marcel*, the Barber: Roger Gray. *Janku*, the Apothecary: Louis Simon. *Anitza Chefcheck*, the Milliner: TESSA KOSTA. *Colonel Ivan Petroff:* John Goldsworthy. *Sixtus*, an Officer: Julian Winters. *Prince Stephan*, Crown Prince of Bargravia: FREDERICK SANTLEY. *Professor Robert Aubrey Montague Hopkins*, his tutor: ROBINSON NEWBOLD. *Princess Violetta*, First Lady of the Bath: FRANCES DEMAREST. *Princess Helena*: Grace Fisher. *Queen of Bargravia*: Winifred Harris. *Wanda*: Gladys Zell. *Josette*: Edna Pierre. *Carlotta*: DOROTHY DICKSON. *Captain Dantzig*: CARL HYSON. *Drodono*, Gypsy Chief: Walter Palm. (*Rozello*, the charming Gypsy: MARY EATON.) *The Messenger*: Helen Pierce. *The Queen's Guard*: Jack Connors, Charles Callahan, John Ross, Edward Ryan.
  Ladies of the Ensemble: Gladys Coleman, Louise Gumpricht, Dorothy Norwood, Vera Bayles, Kittie Collier, Aimee Torriani, Blanche Terrel, Gladys Stone, Betty Dair, Annette Weber, Ethel Duffield, Beatrice Swanson, Jane Augarde, Effie Shelley, Sonia Tamora, Reba Kent. *Dancers*: Jessie Howe, Ida Howe, Sadie Livermore, D. Whiteford, M. Whiteford, Marion Phillipa, Edna Hyat, Norma Grave, Frances Mink, Mae Terrifield, Murray Lavone, Janet Deitrich. *Court Ladies*: Billie Huntington, Marie Halpern, Catherine Hurst, Clara Taylor, Marion Grey, Alberta Turner. *Gentlemen of the Ensemble*: Alfred Hardy, Maxwell Spencer, Ainsley Lambert, Eugene Elliott, Walter Palm, Harry Bolton, John Ellis, Harry Walters, Irving Clair, Ed Sheldon, Howard McCreary, Walter Blair, H. M. Arden, Boris Meilman, Harry Wilde, Ralph LeFree.

The action takes place in Bargravia.

Act 1: At the Kings Head Inn.

Act 2: In the Royal Palace Courtyard.

Act 3: In the Throne Room.

ACT 1
"Opera, Comic Opera" (Opening Ensemble)
  R. Gray, C. Wayne, L. Simon, Ensemble
  (*Music and Lyrics by* George M. Cohan.)
"Love of Mine"
  T. Kosta
  (*Music by* Anselm Goetzl. *Lyrics by* William Cary Duncan.)
"Here Come the Soldiers"
  C. Callahan, J. Ross, J. Connors, E. Ryan, Ensemble
  (*Music and Lyrics by* George M. Cohan.)
"Democracy"
  F. Santley, R. Newbold, Chorus
  (*Music by* Anselm Goetzl. *Lyrics by* William Cary Duncan.)

"A Wee Bit of Lace"
  F. Demarest, G. Zell, E. Pierre, Chorus
  Introducing D. Dickson, C. Hyson.
  (*Music by* Harry Tierney. *Lyrics by* George M. Cohan.)
"Love Is Love" (Where the Cherry Blossoms Fall)
  J. Goldsworthy, G. Fisher, T. Kosta
  (*Music by* Anselm Goetzl. *Lyrics by* William Cary Duncan.)
Finale
  Entire Company
ACT 2
Opening Ensemble
  (*Music and Lyrics by* George M. Cohan.)
"Royalty"
  G. Fisher, Chorus
  (*Music by* Anselm Goetzl. *Lyrics by* George M. Cohan.)
"What You Don't Know Won't Hurt You"
  F. Santley, R. Newbold, G. Zell, E. Pierre
  (*Music by* Anselm Goetzl. *Lyrics by* William Cary Duncan.)
"Messenger"
  F. Demarest, H. Pierre, Queen's Guard, Chorus
  (*Music by* Anselm Goetzl. *Lyrics by* George M. Cohan.)
"In a Kingdom of Our Own"
  G. Fisher, J. Goldsworthy
  (*Music and Lyrics by* George M. Cohan.)
"Charming"
  D. Dickson, Chorus
  Introducing M. Eaton.
  (*Music by* Harry Tierney. *Lyrics by* Joseph McCarthy.)
ACT 3
"Coronation Rehearsal"
  D. Dickson, C. Hyson, Ensemble
  (*Music by* Anselm Goetzl.)
"The Mikado" (Specialty)
  R. Newbold
  (*Music by* Arthur Sullivan. *Lyrics by* William S. Gilbert.)
"Talk, Talk, Talk"[90]
  F. Santley, R. Newbold, R. Gray, L. Simon, T. Kosta
  (*Music by* Anselm Goetzl. *Lyrics by* William Cary Duncan.)
"Goodbye, Bargravia"
  F. Santley, T. Kosta, Chorus
  (*Music and Lyrics by* George M. Cohan.)
Finale
  (*Music and Lyrics by* George M. Cohan.)

1919.05   THE KISS BURGLAR

A Revival of the Musical Romance in Two Acts, 4 Scenes[91]. Book and lyrics by Glen MacDonough. Music by Raymond Hubbell. Staged by Edward P. Temple. Dance numbers staged by Murray Queen. Scenery designed by Clifford F. Pember. Orchestra under the direction of Leo Merriman. (Produced by the Messrs. Lee and J. J. Shubert.) Opened 17 March 1919 at the Broadhurst Theatre, moved 31 March 1919 to the Nora Bayes Theatre and closed 5 April 1919 after 24 performances.[92]

CAST: *Aline*, Grand Duchess of Orly: MARIE CARROLL. *Mr. E. Chatterton-Pym*: OLIVER SMITH. *Mrs. E. Chatterton-Pym*: LOUISE MINK. *Miss Harte*: ANNE SANDS. *Bert Duvivier*: GEORGE LEON MOORE. *Tommy Dodd*: HARRY CLARKE. *Oswald Gayly*: DENMAN MALEY. *Colonel Trotovitch*: EMMETT SHACKLE-FORD. *First Aide to Colonel Trotovitch*: Louis Brown. *Second Aide to Colonel Trotovitch*: Robert Norman. *A Detective*: W. J. Barry. *Proprietor of Pennington Inn*: William Caryl. *Waiter*: Muray Queen. *Raffels*: Harry Belmont. *Pinkie Doolittle*: Vera

---

[89]During the run, replaced by: (dropped for subsequent tour)
"Sahara (Now We're as Dry as You)"
  E. Walker
  (*Music by* Jean Schwartz. *Lyrics by* Alfred Bryan.)

[90]Dropped during the run.
[91]First produced in New York 9 May 1918 at the George M. Cohan Theatre for 100 performances. For Synopsis of Scenes and Musical Numbers, see original 1918 production. For this revival, the running order of songs in Act 2 was revised, Act 2 was reduced from 2 Scenes to 1, and "Your Kiss Is Champagne" was dropped, and the following was added:
  "Temperament" (Duet and Dance)
    D. Maley, H. Clarke
[92]Costumes uncredited.

Grosse. *Tissie Baltimore*: Bessie Gray. *Rose*, maid to the Duchess: Ruby Rosalie. *Natalie*, maid to the Duchess: Jeannette Cooke. *Page*: Mary Gleason.

Miss Stuyvesant: Evelyn Paul. *Miss Greeley*: Lucille Dawson. *Miss Morrisana*: Larilla Russell. *Miss Yonkers*: Jere Fitzgerald. *Miss Hastings*: Edna Kuehne. *Miss Dobbs*: Ruth Carberry. *Miss Tarrytown*: Gladys Fisher. *Miss Irvington*: Marie Hebold. *Miss Peekskill*: Libyon Frank. *Miss Poughkeepsie*: Margaret King. *Miss Albany*: Mae DeVaul. *Miss Troy*: Ester Fair.

1919.06   TUMBLE IN

A Comic Rhapsody in Two Raps and Four Taps (Musical Comedy in Two Acts, 4 Scenes). Book and lyrics by Otto Harbach. Based on the farce comedy ("Seven Days") by Mary Roberts Rinehart and Avery Hopwood. Music by Rudolf Friml. Book staged by Bertram Harrison. Musical numbers staged by Bert French. Costumes designed by Bert French. Scenery by (Joseph) Physioc. Orchestra under the direction of Herbert Stothart. Produced under the personal direction of Arthur Hammerstein. Produced by Arthur Hammerstein in conjunction with Selwyn & Company. Opened 24 March 1919 at the Selwyn Theatre and closed 12 July 1919 after 128 performances.

CAST (in order of appearance): *The Burglar*: Johnny Ford. *Helen*: Helen Lyons. *Jim Wilson*: HERBERT CORTHELL. *Claire*: CLAIRE NAGLE. *Dallas Brown*: CHARLES RUGGLES. *Kitty McNair*: EDNA HIBBARD. *Anne Wilson*: PEGGY O'NEIL. *Tom Harbison*: ARTHUR SWANSTONE. *Bella Knowles*: Virginia Hammond. *Aunt Selina*: Zelda Sears. *Flannigan*: Fred Lennox. *Nicholas*, a footman: Ivan Strogoff. *Olga*, a maid: Olga Mishka. *Isabel*: Isabel Adams. *Beatrice*: Beatrice Summers. *Dorothy*: Dorothy Taylor. *Kathryn*: Kathryn Yates. *Alice*: Alice Van Buren. *Courtney*: Courtney Collins. *Ruth*: Ruth Harrington. *Marietta*: Marietta O'Brien. *Maxine*: Maxine Robinson. *Edna*: Edna Hettler. *Babe*: Babe Marlowe. *Kitty*: Kitty Berg. *Jane*: Jane Cobb. *Emily*: Emily Russ. *Hortense*: Hortense Alden. *Guards*: George Bingham, Nick Wilson, Dudley Farnsworth, Harry Pollard.

Time: Present—until June 30.

Act 1: The Drawing Room in James Wilson's Home on Riverside Drive.

Act 2, Scene 1: The Kitchen. *Scene 2*: The Roof Coping. *Scene 3*: The Roof. Seven days later.

ACT 1
  Burglar Pantomime
    J. Ford
  "Trousseau Waltz"
    C. Nagle
  "Gowns, Soft and Clingy"
    Girls, Boys
  "You'll Do It All Over Again"
    C. Ruggles, H. Corthell, Chorus
  "I've Told My Love"
    E. Hibbard, Girls
  "The Wedding Blues"
    P. O'Neil, E. Hibbard, C. Ruggles, H. Corthell, Chorus
  "Limbo Land"
    P. O'Neil, C. Ruggles, Chorus
  "The Thoughts that I Wrote on the Leaves of My Heart"
    E. Hibbard, A. Swanstone
  "Snuggle and Dream"
    P. O'Neil, Girls
  Finale
    Ensemble
ACT 2[93]
  "A Little Chicken Fit for Old Broadway"
    C. Ruggles, C. Nagle, O. Mishka, Chorus
  "Serve It Only for Two"[94]
    R. Hogue, E. Hibbard

---

[93]Added for subsequent national tour to Act 2 after "Valse au L'Air":
  "The Argentines, the Portuguese and Greeks" (from FIFTY-FIFTY, LTD.)
    H. Corthell
  (*Music by* Carey Morgan. *Lyrics by* Arthur Swanstrom.)
[94]Dropped during the run and for subsequent tour.

  "The Laugh"
    E. Hibbard, P. O'Neil, C. Ruggles, H. Corthell
  "Won't You Help Me Out?"
    C. Nagle, Girls
  "Valse au L'Air"
    I. Strogoff, O. Mishka
  Burglar Dance[95]
    J. Ford
  "The Trousseau Ball"
    P. O'Neil, C. Ruggles, O. Mishka, Girls
  Finale
    Ensemble

1919.07   TAKE IT FROM ME

A Musical Play in a Prologue and Two Acts. Book and lyrics by Will B. Johnstone. Music by Will R. Anderson. Book staged by Fred A. Bishop and Joe C. Smith. Costumes designed by S. Zalud. Stage decorations designed by P. Dodd Ackerman. Orchestra under the direction of Ted Coleman. Orchestrations by George Trinkhaus. Produced by Joseph M. Gaites. Opened 31 March 1919 at the 44th Street Theatre, moved 9 June 1919 to the Central Theatre and closed 21 June 1919 after 96 performances.

CAST (in order of appearance): *Vernon Van Dyke*: FRED HILLEBRAND. *Barney*: Charles Welsh Homer. *Dick Roller*: A. DOUGLAS LEAVITT. *Gwendolyn Forsythe*: Helen Raftery. *Tom Eggett*: JACK McGOWAN. *Sheriff 'Biff' Doyle*: John C. Lamont. *Horace Turner*: HAROLD VIZARD. *Ella Abbott*: ALICE HILLS. *Wilkins*: HARRY BURNHAM. *Cyrus Crabb*: WILLIAM BALFOUR. *Grace Gordon*: GEORGIA MANATT. *Queenie LaBelle*: VERA MICHELENA. *Miss DeWitt Buttler*: Dorothy Betts. *Harmon*: Ed Leech. *Judson*: George Mortimer. (*Specialty Dances*: The Gardiner Trio. [Edgar, Arline, Helen])

Leah: Leah Griffith. *Marienne*: Marienne Taylor. *Florence*: Florence Grove. *Teressa*: Teressa Wardell. *Mildred*: Mildred Thompson. *Bernice*: Bernice Frank. *Lucretia*: Lucretia Craig. *Estelle*: Estelle White. *Maudie*: Maudie Clifton. *Marion*: Marion Comfort. *Brownie*: Brownie Ross. *Ruth*: Ruth Sawyer. *Betty*: Btty DeGrasse. *Belle*: Belle Sawyer. *Carrie*: Carrie DeNoville. *Cecil*: Cecil Renaud. *Peggy*: Peggy Ellis.

Prologue: Tom's Bachelor Apartment. Early spring.

Act 1: Executive Offices of the Eggett Company. A week later.

Act 2: Tom's 'Cozy Corner' on the Steenth Floor of Eggett Company. One year later.

PROLOGUE
  "Tip-Toe"
    F. Hillebrand, Girls
  "The Tanglefoot"
    F. Hillebrand, Girls
  "Tomorrow"
    J. McGowan, A. D. Leavitt, F. Hillebrand, Girls
ACT 1
  "It's Different Now"
    A. Hills, H. Burnham, Girls
  "Explanations"[96]
    J. McGowan, G. Manatt
  "Take It from Me"
    V. Michelena, J. McGowan, Girls
  "The Tanglefoot Trot" (Dance Specialty)
    G. Manatt, F. Hillebrand
  "The Call of the Cozy Little Home"
    J. McGowan, G. Manatt, Girls
  "I Like to Linger in the Lingerie"
    A. D. Leavitt, Girls
ACT 2
  "From Then and Now"
    The Girls
  Dance Divertissement
    Gardiner Trio

---

[95]Dropped during the run and for subsequent tour.
[96]Replaced for subsequent tour by:
  Egyptian Dance
    Helen Gardiner, Girls

Skating Waltz
    E. Gardiner, A. Gardiner
"The Kiss"
    A. Hills
"To Have and To Hold"
    V. Michelena
Pantomimic impression of Rudyard Kipling's 'A Fool There Was" conceived by Joseph C. Smith
    V. Michelena, F. Hillebrand
"Good, Bad, Beautiful Broadway"[97]
    J. McGowan, A. D. Leavitt, F. Hillebrand, Girls
"Camouflage"
    V. Michelena, Girls
Dance of the Marines
    Gardiner Trio
Finale
    Company

COME ALONG

1919.08

A Musical Comedy in a Prologue and Two Acts. Book by Bide Dudley. Music and lyrics by John Louw Nelson. Staged by Edward Royce. Dances arranged by Jack Mason. Scenery designed by Homer Emens, Frank Gates and Edward A. Morange. Costumes by William H. Matthews, Milgrim Brothers, Lucille, H. R. Mallinson, Brooks Uniform Company (men). Orchestra under the direction of Milan Roder. Produced under the direction of Frank Jackson. Produced by Marne Productions, Inc. Opened 8 April 1919 at the Nora Bayes Theatre and closed 17 May 1919 after 47 performances.

CAST: PROLOGUE: *Jim Doolittle*: HARRY TIGHE. *Barbara Benton*: REGINA RICHARDS. *Tom McManus*: PAUL FRAWLEY. *Frank Marshall*: CHARLES STANTON. *John Phillips*: Irving Rose. *Charles Williams*: Edward Bailey. *Salvation Army Girls* (3): *Corporal Sue Taylor*: Connie Madison. *Private Jane Miller*: Ellen King. *Private Louise Brown*: Ellen Best.
    PLAY: *Major Barbara Benton*: REGINA RICHARDS. *Mess Sergeant Doolittle*: HARRY TIGHE. *Lieutenant Frank Marshall*: CHARLES STANTON. *Sergeant Tom McManus*: PAUL FRAWLEY. *Private Peanuts Barker*: ALLEN KEARNS. *Madelon*: MARCELLE CARROLL. *Mrs. Crosby*: ETHEL DU FRE HOUSTON. *Peggy Penny*: Patsie DeForest. *Mme. Juliet*: JULIA KELETY. *Private Jeff Scroggins*: Billy Clark. *Sergeant Chauncey Holmes*: Dan Dawson. *General Baker, A. E. F.*: Ernest E. Pollack. *Colonel Mitchell, S. A.*: John Holden. *Algerian*: Robert Milasch. *Cuckoo*: Marian Lytle. *Alouette*: Marjorie Lytle. *Corporal Sue Taylor*: Connie Madison. *Private Jane Miller*: Ellen King. (*Specialty Dances*: Jessica Brown.)
    Ensemble; Connie Madison, Ellen King, Grace Evans, Betty Burch, Hazel Morgan, Dorothy Beattie, Rose Maynard, Merrill Ross, May Weston, Emma Smith, Margaret Daniels, Anna Best. *Male Ensemble*: Messrs. Page, Reisnay, Henry, Bailey, Joe Page, Allen, Chase, Alter, LeRoy, Smythe, Vanard, Bartles, Fatovsky.

Prologue: St. James Club, New York City. 1918.

Act 1: Aviation Billet, Chateau in Alsace. Six weeks later.

Act 2: Alsatian Village Street, near Chateau. The following day.

ACT 1
"(It's a) Long Long Time (Before Pay Day Comes 'Round)"
    D. Dawson, Male Chorus
"Rolling de Bones at Coblenz on de Rhine"
    B. Clark, Male Chorus
    (*Music by* John Louw Nelson. *Lyrics by* Bide Dudley.)
"Doughnuts for Doughboys"[98]
    E. D. F. Houston, H. Tighe, D. Dawson
    (*Music by* John Louw Nelson. *Lyrics by* Bide Dudley.)
"Yankee Land"
    A. Kearns, Ensemble
"(She's) Salvation Sal"
    R. Richards, Salvation Army Girls
    (*Music by* Fred Watson. *Lyrics by* Bide Dudley.)
"Gas (Mask)"
    A. Kearns, Ensemble
    (*Music by* John Louw Nelson. *Lyrics by* Bide Dudley.)

"When They're Beautiful"
    H. Tighe, Motor Corps Girls
"When You Are Happy"
    R. Richards, P. Frawley, Ensemble
"Mother Dear"
    P. Frawley
Finale
    Entire Company
ACT 2[99]
"Cuckoo"
    M. Carroll, Ensemble
"K. P."
    A. Kearns, Ensemble
"Big Drum, Little Drum"[100]
    R. Richards, H. Tighe
    (*Music by* John Louw Nelson. *Lyrics by* Bide Dudley.)
"Thoughts"
    R. Richards, P. Frawley
"But You Can't Believe Them"
    P. DeForest, A. Kearns
    (*Music and Lyrics by* Blanche Merrill.)
"Big Offensive"[101]
    H. Tighe, M. Carroll
Specialties
    J. Brown

SHE'S A GOOD FELLOW

1919.09

A Musical Comedy in Three Acts. Book and lyrics by Anne Caldwell. Music by Jerome Kern. Staged by Fred G. Latham and Edward Royce. Scenery designed by D. Frank Dodge and William Castle. Costumes designed by Gladys Monkhouse. Orchestra under the direction of William Daly. Orchestrations by Frank Saddler. Produced by Charles Dillingham. Opened 5 May 1919 at the Globe Theatre and closed 16 August 1919 after 120 performances.

CAST: *Robert McLane*: JOSEPH SANTLEY. *Admiral Franklin*: James C. Marlowe. *Horatio Pollard*: Alexander Clark. *Chester Pollard*: OLIN HOWLAND. *Billy Hopkins*: SCOTT WELSH. *McVey*: Jay Wilson. *Jacqueline Fay*: IVY SAWYER. *Lavinia Lee*: ANN ORR. *Zizi Sumarez*: Elsie Lawson. *Mrs. Franklin*: Gertrude Maitland. *Mazie Moore*: ROSETTA DUNCAN. *Betty Blair*: VIVIAN DUNCAN. *Miss Busby*: Florence Edney. *Geranium White*: Nellie Fillmore. *Gladys Grace*: Arline Chase.
    Pupils at Roselawn Academy and Friends of Jacqueline and Lavinia: Misses Helen Allen, Marie Ayres, Martine Burnley, Lucile Darling, Pauline Hall, Beatrice Hughes, Dorothy Hollis, Helen Lovett, Florence Martin, Eleanor Mathison, Phyllis Munday, Grace O'Connor, Hilah Reeder, Genevieve Willment, Irene Wilson, Lillian White, Alice Earle.

Time: The Present.

Act 1: The Franklin Home, Down South.

Act 2: Roselawn Academy.

Act 3: The Garden of the Franklin Home.

ACT 1
"Some Party" (Ensemble and Song)
    A. Orr, Girls
"The Navy Foxtrot Man"
    S. Welsh, Girls
"The First Rose of Summer"
    I. Sawyer, J. Santley, Girls

---

[97]For subsequent tour, moved to Act 1 Finale.
[98]Dropped during the run.

---

[99]Added to Act 2 during the run:
    Specialty (following Jessica Brown's Specialty)
        J. Kelety
[100]Replaced during the run by:
    "Cupid" (When Cupid Flies)
        R. Richards, Ensemble
    "Prohibition Ball"
        B. Clark, Ensemble
        (*Music by* Abner Silver. *Lyrics by* Alex Gerber.)
[101]Dropped during the run.

"A Happy Wedding Day"
    I. Sawyer, A. Orr, S. Welsh, J. Santley, J. C. Marlowe
"Jubilo"
    A. Orr, Girls
    (Music and lyric founded on "Kingdom Comin'" by Henry Clay Work.)
Finale

ACT 2
"Faith, Hope and Charity" (Opening Chorus)
    Ensemble
"Just a Little Line"[102]
    I. Sawyer, A. Orr
"Teacher, Teacher!"
    A. Orr, S. Welsh
"Bullfrog Patrol" and Songs
    Duncan Sisters
"Oh, You Beautiful Person!"
    J. Santley, O. Howland
"Snip, Snip, Snip" (Finale)
    I. Sawyer, J. Santley, J. Wilson

ACT 3
"I Want My Little Gob"
    A. Orr, Girls
"The Bumble Bee"
    O. Howland, Girls
"I've Been Waiting for You All the Time"
    I. Sawyer, J. Santley, S. Welsh, A. Orr, O. Howland, Duncan Sisters, Chorus
Finale

1919.10   TOOT SWEET

An Overseas (Musical) Revue in a Prologue and Two Offensives (Acts), 12 Scenes[103]. Book (sketches) by Everybody (Will Morrissey). Music by Richard A. Whiting. Lyrics by Raymond B. Egan. Staged by Will Morrissey. Orchestra under the direction of Hilding Anderson. Produced by Will Morrissey. Opened 7 May 1919 at the Princess Theater, moved 12 May 1919 to the Nora Bayes Theatre, and closed 14 June 1919 after 45 performances.[104]

CAST (in order of appearance): *Mlle. Jeanette Tourneur*: Mlle. JEANETTE TOURNEUR. *Thomas Penfold*: THOMAS PENFOLD. *Edward Miller*: EDWARD MILLER. *Clarence Nordstrom*: CLARENCE NORDSTROM. *Lieutenant McPherson*: LIEUTENANT McPHERSON. *Lon Hascall*: LON HASCALL. *Will Morrissey*: WILL MORRISSEY. *Harry Miller*: HARRY MILLER. *Sam Ward*: SAM WARD. *May Boley*: MAY BOLEY. *Corporal Fenley*: Corporal Fenley. *Elizabeth Brice*: ELIZABETH BRICE. *Little Norma Gallo*: Little Norma Gallo. *Evelyn Downing*: Evelyn Downing. *Virginia Lancier*: Virginia Lancier. *Babe Bayer*: Babe Bayer., *Bess Arlington*: Bess Arlington. *Wilma Bruce*: Wilma Bruce. *Lloyd Bruce*: Lloyd Bruce. *Ruth Sterling*: Ruth Sterling. *Alice Hascall*: Alice Hascall. *Elsie Young*: Elsie Young. *Henrietta Merriman*: Henrietta Merriman. *Elsie Wheeler*: Elsie Wheeler. *Clarice Spaulding*: Clarice Spaulding. *Soldiers, Villagers, Aviators, Second Lieutenants, Gendarmes, Gobs, Nurses and such as that.*

First Offensive, Scene 1: READY. Public Square in a French Village, near the town of (censored). *Scene 2*: AIM. On the road to Rouen. (Written by Roy K. Moulton.) *Scene 3*: BARRAGE. Any Hut, Part of the original performance as presented by Elizabeth Brice and her company in the Argonne Forest.
    Second Offensive, Scene 1: ARMISTICE. Cafe Trescher, Paris. (Mustered out.) *Scene 2*: FIRE. "Remember Lizzie" (Dance) "What Our Girls Can Do" *Scene 3*: VERDUN. The Poilu and the Refugee. "On ne passe pas" (they shall not pass). *Scene 4*: ZERO HOUR. The Song Brigade. (Awkward Squad.) *Scene 5*: BAYONET ASSAULT. Miner's cabin on the breast of a mountain near Brest, one thousand miles from anywhere. *Scene 6*: ON LEAVE. The dancing Gobs in a cheerful mood. *Scene 7*: BARRAGE. He and She meet. *Scene 8*: TANK ATTACK. Humoresque. French Concert Company. *Scene 9*: CANONADE. L'Elefant Skeed—Finale—REMEMBER LIZZIE.

---

[102]Dropped during the run and for subsequent tour.
[103]Billed also as "a Franco-American Revue depicting the humorous side of the war, with satires on things observed at the front by Miss Brice and Mr. Morrissey, who have only recently returned from France."
[104]Settings, costumes uncredited.

ACT 1
"Preliminary Skirmish"
    E. Miller, Squad
"Eyes of the Army"
    C. Nordstrom, Aviators
"Tout Suite"
    W. Morrissey, M. Boley, L. Hascall
"French Soldiers on Leave" (Dance)
    H. Miller, S. Ward
"Je ne sais pas"
    C. Nordstrom, H. Miller, S. Ward
"America's Answer"
    E. Brice, Squad
"One of the Ruins of France"
    M. Boley
    (*Music and Lyrics by* Roy K. Moulton.)
"Madelon" (The French Tipperary)
    E. Miller, Squad
    (*Music by* Camille Robert. *French lyrics by* Louis Bousquet; *English lyrics by* Alfred Bryan.)
"Salvation Sal"
    E. Brice, Trench Angels
Original Shock Unit Show (Art Smith at the piano)
"Baby Vampire"
    M. Boley
    (*Music and Lyrics by* Roy K. Moulton.)
"Blighty Bound"
    C. Nordstrom
Recitation
    L. Hascall
"You'll Never Get a Whimper Out of Me"
    W. Morrissey
    (*Music and Lyrics by* Will Morrissey)
At Your Service—"Give Him Back His Job"
    E. Brice
Finale of the First Offensive
    Entire Company

ACT 2
"Carolina" and Dance Deluxe
    E. Brice, C. Nordstrom
Dance Eccentrique
    E. Brice, C. Nordstrom, H. Miller
Dance Eccentrique
    M. Boley, W. Morrissey, L. Hascall
Jazzical Moments
    H. Miller, S. Ward, Misses Lancier, Merriman, Young, Downing
"Rose of Verdun"
    E. Miller, Belgian Refugee
"Charge of the Song Brigade"
    T. Penfold, Awkward Squad
Dance of the Nautica Americaine
    H. Miller, S. Ward
"Just Around the Corner from Easy Street"
    E. Brice, C. Nordstrom
Specialty by the French Concert Company
    M. Boley, W. Morrissey, L. Hascall, H. Miller, T. Penfold
"L'Elefant Skeed" (Elephant Skid)
    Entire Company
"Remember Lizzie"

1919.11   THE LADY IN RED

A Musical Comedy in Three Acts. Book and lyrics by Anne Caldwell. (Adapted from the German 'Die Dame in Rot' of Julius Brammer and Alfred Grünwald.) Music by Robert Winterberg. Staged by Frank Smithson. Scenery designed by Joseph Physioc Studio. Costumes by Hickson, Inc., Lady Duff Gordon, H. Mahieu Co, Inc., Maison Andre Sherri, Nat Lewis. Orchestra under the direction of J. Albert Browne. Produced by John P. Slocum. Opened 12 May 1919 at the Lyric Theatre and closed 21 June 1919 after 48 performances.

CAST (in order of appearance): *Wright*: Louis Christy. *Colonel Prince*: Neil Moore. *Marjorie Cole*: Dorothy Godfrey. *Muriel Dean*: Gladys Miller. *Mabel Kirkpatrick*: Ruth Mitchell. *Maude Langoon*: Irene Corlett. *Tony Stafford*: DONALD MacDONALD. *Kitty St. Claire*: ADELE ROWLAND. *Darius Dirks*: FRANKLYN ARDELL. *Sylvia Stafford*, Tony's cousin: RUTH MacTAMMANY. *Bruce Vernon*: Tom Richards. *Peppina Cattaneo*: BERTEE BEAUMONTE. *Dick Carrington*: Harry Turpin. *Attendant*: Donald Roberts. *Percy*: William Warren. *Butler*: Walter Croft. *Celloist*: Edmund Makalif. (*Dance Specialty*: The Glorias.)

Ladies and Gentlemen of the Ensemble: Audrey Burton, Lillian Stewart, Vonda Marine, Marcelle Swanson, Jean Hamilton, Helen Coles, Francesca Devens, Lucie Inge, May Sheldon, Selwa Sheldon, Alice Gordon, Dora Duby. Harry Williams, William Warren, Dana Maiyo, Walter Croft, Donald Roberts, Robert Casey, George Elsing, John Kenyon.

Act 1: An Art Gallery, New York.

Act 2: Home of Darius Dirks, New York City.

Act 3: Studio Apartment of Vernon.

ACT 1[105]

Opening Chorus
  Ensemble
"Pretty Little Girls Like You" (Quintet)
  D. MacDonald, D. Godfrey, G. Miller, R. Mitchell, I. Corlett
"Family Faces" (Trio)
  A. Rowland, D. MacDonald, F. Ardell
"Beautiful Lady in Red" (Song)
  R. MacTammany
"Chinese Dragon Blues" (Song)
  A. Rowland
  (*Music by* Walter Donaldson. *Lyrics by* Irving Caesar.)
"My Own California" (Song)
  H. Turpin, Girls, Boys
"Ships (That Pass) in the Night" (Duet)
  R. MacTammany, T. Richards
Finale
  Ensemble

ACT 2

Opening Chorus
  Ensemble
"I'd Rather Dance Here Than Hereafter" (Song)
  T. Richards
Dance Specialty
  The Glorias
"Something About Love" (Song)
  A. Rowland, D. MacDonald
  (*Music by* George Gershwin. *Lyrics by* Lou Paley.)
"I Can't Forget Your Eyes" (Duet)
  R. MacTammany, T. Richards
"Play Me That Tune" (Ya-Da-De-Dum-Dum) (Song)
  A. Rowland
  (*Music by* Walter Donaldson. *Lyrics by* Irving Caesar.)
"Garibaldi Band" (Song)
  B. Beaumonte, D. Godfrey, G. Miller, R. Mitchell, I. Corlett, Boys, Girls
Finale
  R. MacTammany, A. Rowland, T. Richards, H. Turpin

ACT 3

Opening Chorus
  Ensemble, The Glorias[106]
"I Want Somebody" (Song)
  R. Mitchell, F. Ardell
"A Little Bit of Scotch" (Song)
  R. MacTammany, D. MacDonald, D. Godfrey, G. Miller, R. Mitchell, I. Corlett, Boys, Girls

---

[105]Toured the following season with a wholly new cast and many new songs including:
  "Mr. Love Will Get You"
  "Tumble El Toro"
  "Reconciliation"
[106]Billed as the originators of the world's famous skating imitation dance.

"I Want to Be Like Cleo" (Song)
  B. Beaumonte, E. Makalif

1919.12

LA-LA-LUCILLE!

A Farce with Music in Three Acts. Book by Fred Jackson. Music by George Gershwin. Lyrics by Arthur J. Jackson, B. G. DeSilva [Buddy G. DeSylva]. Staged by Herbert Gresham and Julian Alfred. Scenery by H. Robert Law Studios. Gowns designed by Mark Blackburn; men's clothes designed by Croydon, Ltd. Orchestra under the direction of Charles Previn. Produced by Alex A. Aarons and George B. Seitz. Opened 26 May 1919 at Henry Miller's Theatre, suspended performances 19 August 1919 for the Actors' Equity strike; resumed 8 September 1919 at the Criterion Theatre and closed 11 October 1919 after 104 performances.

CAST: *Johnathon Jaynes*, an ex-juggler: J. Clarence Harvey. *Lucille Jaynes Smith*, his daughter: JANET VELIE. *John Smith*, her husband, a dentist: JOHN E. HAZZARD. *Oyama*, a Japanese butler: M. Rale. *Nicholas Grimsby*, a lawyer: Maurice Cass. *Thomas Brady*: Sager Midgely. *Mrs. Thomas Brady*: Cordelia MacDonald. *Allan Brady*: JOHN LOWE. *Reginald Blackwood*, another lawyer: Alfred Hall. *Fanny*, a janitress: Eleanor Daniels. *Mlle. Victorine*, a cabaret dancer: MARJORIE BENTLEY. *Britton Hughes*, a Romeo from the South: LORIN RAKER. *Mrs. Britton Hughes* (Peggy), his Juliet: HELEN CLARK. *A Bellboy*: Edward DeCamp. *A Waiter*: Harold D. Millar. *Dufey*, house detective: George W. Callahan. *Colonel Marrion*, Peggy's father: STANLEY H. FORDE. *A Stranger*: Estar Banks.

Bill Collectors, Heiresses, etc.: The Misses Morgan, Jarvis, Hamilton, Devere, Irving, Miles, Wilson, Harden, Harrison, Cotton, Cullen, Edwards. *Heirs, etc.*: Misses DeCamp, Joslyn, Millar, Daly.

The action of the play occurs between the hours of 5 P.M. and 2 A.M. the same night.

Act 1: Living room of John Smith's apartment, New York.

Act 2: Bridal Suite of the Hotel Philadelphia, New York.

Act 3: The same.

ACT 1

Opening Chorus (Kindly Pay Us)
  J. C. Harvey, Chorus
"When You Live in a Furnished Flat"
  J. Velie, J. C. Harvey, M. Rale
"The Best of Everything"
  J. E. Hazzard, Chorus
"From Now On"
  J. Velie, J. E. Hazzard
"Money, Money, Money"[107]
  J. Velie, J. E. Hazzard, J. C. Harvey, S. Midgely, C. MacDonald, M. Cass, Chorus
Specialty Dance
  M. Bentley, J. Lowe
"Tee Oodle Um Bum Bo"
  J. Velie, J. C. Harvey, Chorus
Specialty Dance
  M. Bentley
Finale

ACT 2[108]

Opening Chorus (Hotel Life)

---

[107]Replaced late in the run by: (also for subsequent tour, dropped in 1922)
  "It's Hard To Tell"
    J. Velie, J. E. Hazzard, J. Lowe, C. MacDonald, M. Cass, Chorus
[108]Once LA, LA, LUCILLE reached San Francisco under the auspices of Oliver Morosco on its national tour in the summer of 1922, the following interpolations had been added: (Gone are the hyphens and exclamation point in the title)
  "My Dream of Love Is You" (Act 2)
    Roy Giusti (Britton)
  "It Sort Makes a Fellow Stop and Think" (Act 2)(from OH, MY DEAR)
    Roy Atwell (Jonathan)
    (*Music by* Benjamin Hapgood Burt. *Lyrics by* Roy Atwell.)
  "Reputation" (Act 2)
    Marjorie Leach (Fanny), R. Atwell

"(Oo, How) I Love to Be Loved by You"[109]
L. Raker, H. Clark, Chorus
(*Lyrics by* Lou Paley.)
"It's Great To Be in Love"
H. Clark, J. Lowe, Chorus
Specialty Dance
M. Bentley
Finale

ACT 3
"Kisses" (There's More to a Kiss than the Sound)
H. Clark, Chorus
(*Lyrics by* Irving Caesar.)

"It Seldom Comes True"
J. Velie
"Tee Oodle Um Bum Bo" (reprise)
J. Velie, S. H. Forde
"The Ten Commandments of Love"
J. E. Hazzard, J. Velie, Chorus
Specialty Dance
M. Bentley, J. Lowe
Finale
Entire Company

"Some Sunny Day" (Act 2)
Winnie Baldwin (Peggy), Percy Bronson (John Smith)
(*Music and Lyrics by* Irving Berlin.)
"Yodel O" (Act 2)
P. Bronson
(*Music and Lyrics by* Bryan Foy.)
"My Fannie" (Act 3)
James Dunn (Tony
"All the While" (Act 3)
W. Baldwin, P. Bronson
(*Music and Lyrics by* Constance Uhl.)
"Golden Days"
R. Giusti, Alma Francis (Lucille)
(*Music and Lyrics by* Nat Goldstein.)
"Un peu d'Amour"
George Baldwin (Brady)
Opera Burlesque (Act 3)
The program also carried the note "all extra lyrics sung by Percy Bronson,
written and arranged by George Baldwin."
[109]Replaced late in the run by: (also for subsequent tour)
"Nobody But You"
L. Raker, H. Clark, Chorus

1919–1920 SEASON

Ed Wynn and Lillian Fitzgerald in ED WYNN CARNIVAL (Photo: White Studio)
Billy Rose Theatre Collection, New York Public Library for the Performing Arts

1919–1920 SEASON

GEORGE WHITE'S SCANDALS OF 1919

1919.13

A Modern Musical Revue in Two Acts, 15 Scenes[1]. Book (sketches) and lyrics by Arthur Jackson and George White. Music by Richard A. Whiting, (Herbert Spencer). Directed by Edgar MacGregor. (Dances) Staged by George White. Scenes by H. Robert Law Studios; Herbert Ward, art director. Costumes by Paul Arlington, Inc. Orchestra under the direction of Julius Lenzberg. Produced by George White. Opened 2 June 1919 at the Liberty Theatre, suspending performances 23 August 1919 for the Actors' Equity strike, resumed 6 September 1919 and closed 11 October 1919 after 128 performances.

CAST: *The Little Leading Lady*: ANN PENNINGTON. *The Little Prima Donna*: MABEL WITHEE. *The Littler Prima Donna*: YVETTE RUGEL. *The Class(y)ic Dancer*: LA SYLPHE. *The Soubrette*: ETHEL DELMAR. *Another Soubrette*: DOROTHY ST. CLAIR. *Another Soubrette*: LOIS LEIGH. *Another Soubrette*: ONA MUNSON. *The Dancing Leading Man*: GEORGE WHITE. *The Comedian*: GEORGE BICKEL. *The Specialist*: LESTER ALLEN. *The Singing Juvenile*: AL SEXTON. *The Dancing and Singing Men*: (Joseph) BENNETT and (Edward) RICHARDS. *The Juvenile Comedian*: LOWELL B. DREW. *The Talking Comedian*: BURT HANLON. *The Character Man*: LARRY BECK. *The Rube Comedian*: JAMES MILLER.

Ensemble: Misses Kerr, Viola Mattison, Knight, Dolan, Chase, Christie, Welford, Ashton, Dale.

Act 1, Scene 1: Playground of the Immortals on the Planet Mars. *Scene 2*: In Front of Rector's. *Scene 3*: The "Three Mile Limit" Cafe. *Scene 4*: I Could Be Happy. *Scene 5*: Bennett and Richards. *Scene 6*: The Shimmy Shop. *Scene 7*: All Stretch!

Act 2, Scene 1: An Overcrowded Hotel. *Scene 2*: Girls Are Like the Weather to Me. *Scene 3*: Hospital de Luxe. *Scene 4*: Broadway Belles. *Scene 5*: A Long Island Bed-Room. *Scene 6*: At the Old Court House. *Scene 7*: Yvette Rugel. *Scene 8*: Specialties. *Scene 9*: Finale.

ACT 1[2]

Scene 1

"Land of My Heart's Desire"
M. Withee
(*Music by* Richard A. Whiting. *Lyrics by* Arthur Jackson.)
A Scientist: L. Beck.

"Up Above the Stars"
Y. Rugel
(*Music by* Herbert Spencer. *Lyrics by* Arthur Jackson.)

Scene 2

A Slicker: G. Bickel. *An Incident*: L. Allen.

"I'll Be There"
M. Withee, A. Sexton, Chorus

"Scandalous One-Step"
LaSylphe

Scene 3

Wireless Operator: L. Beck. *Proprietor*: L. B. Drew. *Head Waiter*: L. Beck. *Messenger*: V. Mattison.

"The Three Mile Limit Cafe"
M. Withee, Chorus
(*Music by* Richard A. Whiting. *Lyrics by* Arthur Jackson.)

"Suwanee River"[3] in Minor
Y. Rugel
A Slicker: G. Bickel. *A Vampire*: La Sylphe. *A Musician*: L. Allen. *A Dancer*: G. White. *His First Partner*: L. Allen. *His Second Partner*: E. Delmar. *Partners for* "*The Evolution of Dixie*": L. Leigh, R. Savoy, D. St. Clair, O. Munson.

Dance Flirtation
G. White, A. Pennington

---

[1]Advertised its "Second edition" in the fifth week of its run. This was the first in the annual series of revues produced by George White, which continued for 13 editions ending in 1939.

[2]The running order was revised after the opening. Lou Holtz joined the cast; added to Act 1 was:

An Interruption
Lou Holtz

[3]Dropped after opening.

Scene 4

"I Could Be Happy (With One Little Boy)"[4]
M. Withee, Chorus

Scene 5

(Specialty)
Bennett and Richards

Scene 6

"Step This Way"
A. Pennington, G. White
(*Music by* Richard A. Whiting. *Lyrics by* Arthur Jackson.)
The Proprietor: G. White. *A Hanger On*: L. Allen. *A Model*: E. Delmar. *A Pumpkin*: La Sylphe. *A Customer*: M. Withee. *A Shopper*: A. Pennington. *A Vampire*: La Sylphe. *Milliners*: Little Girls. *Swell Heads*: Show Girls. *Johns*: The Boys. *Models*: Misses Kerr, V. Mattison, Knight, Dolan, Chase, Christie. *Ensemble*: Entire Company.

Scene 7

All Stretch!

ACT 2

Scene 1

"Peacock Alley" (The Peacock Parade)
Y. Rugel, Girls
(*Music by* Richard A. Whiting. *Lyrics by* Arthur Jackson.)
Telephone Fanny: E. Delmar. *An Accomodating Clerk*: L. B. Drew. *A Hotel Pest*: L. Allen. *A Guest*: Y. Rugel. *Another Guest*: J. Miller. *Another Guest*: G. Bickel. *Maitre d'Hotel*: L. Beck. *A Page*: Miss Welford. *Six Royal Bell Hops*: The Boys. *A Guest*: G. White.

"Girls in My Address Book" (My Little Address Book)
G. White and the Misses
(*Music by* Richard A. Whiting. *Lyrics by* Arthur Jackson.)
The Riverside Drive Girl: Miss Dale. *The Washington Square Girl*: Miss Mattison. *The Harlem Girl*: Miss Howard. *The Fifth Avenue Girl*: Miss Christie. *The Fort Lee Girl*: Miss Savoy. *The Pelham Girl*: Miss Hamilton. *The Brooklyn Girl*: O. Munson. *The Reformer*: M. Withee. *Porters*: Bennett and Richards.

Peacock Dance
La Sylphe

Scene 2

"Girls Are Like the Weather to Me"
A. Sexton
(*Music by* Herbert Spencer. *Lyrics by* Arthur Jackson.)
A Fair Girl: Miss Ashton. *A Stormy Girl*: Miss Kerr. *A Warm Girl*: V. Mattison. *A Mild Girl*: Miss Christie. *A Rainy Girl*: Miss Knight. *A Cold Girl*: Miss Dale. *A Cloudy Girl*: Miss Chase. *A Hot Girl*: Miss Welford.

Scene 3

Hospital de Luxe[5]
A Patient: ?. *Another Patient*: ?. *Another Patient*: ?. *Another Patient*: ?. *Dr. Two-Step*: G. White. *Nurse*: M. Withee. *A Sleepy Guy*: L. B. Drew. *A Stuttering Girl*: D. St. Clair. *A Lover of Horses*: E. Delmar.

Scene 4

"Broadway Belles"
A. Sexton, Chorus
(*Music by* Herbert Spencer. *Lyrics by* Arthur Jackson.)

Scene 5

The Innocent Wife: M. Withee. *The Virtuous Husband*: G. White. *The Villanous Suitor*: L. Allen. *The Other Innocent Wife*: D. St. Clair.

Scene 6

The Stern Judge: G. Bickel. *A Terrible District Attorney*: L. B. Drew. *The Defenseless Attorney*: L. Allen. *A Sharp-Shooting Wife*: M. Withee. *An Eavesdropping Maid*: A. Pennington. *A Weeping Court Crier*: L. Beck. *Stenographers*: E. Delmar, L. Leigh, D. St. Clair. *Reporters, Jury, Spectators*: The Merry Merry. *Aesthetic Jazz*: A. Pennington.

Scene 7

Specialty
Y. Rugel

Scene 8

Aesthetic Jazz
A. Pennington

Dance Picturesque
L. Allen

---

[4]Dropped after opening.

[5]Dropped after opening and replaced by:

A Nuisance
L. Holtz

Between the Scenes
  B. Hanlon
Scene 9
  An Operatic Fan Fan: G. White. *More Fans*: E. Delmar, L. Leigh, D. St. Clair, O. Munson, the Girls.
Finale
  Entire Company

1919.14

A LONELY ROMEO

A Musical Comedy in Three Acts, 5 Scenes. Book by Harry B. Smith and Lew Fields. Music by Malvin M. Franklin and Robert Hood Bowers. Lyrics by Robert B. Smith. Book produced (staged) by W. H. Post. Musical numbers and dances by Jack Mason. Stage decorations (scenery) by P. Dodd Ackerman. Costumes by Cora MacGeachy. Orchestra under the direction of Robert Hood Bowers. Orchestrations (for Malvin Franklin's numbers) by Charles Grant. Produced by Messrs. Shubert, (Lew Fields). Opened 10 June 1919 at the Sam S. Shubert Theatre, moved 28 July 1919 to the Casino Theatre, suspending performances 23 August 1919 for the Actors' Equity strike; resumed 8 September 1919 and closed 11 October 1919 after 128 performances.

CAST (in order of appearance): *Ananias Beebe*: WILLIE SOLAR. *Tessie*, a cabaret girl: Nellie St. Clair. *Archie*, of the cabaret: Willie St. Clair. *Augustus Tripp*: LEW FIELDS. *Mazie Gay*: FRANCES CAMERON. *Marcelle Wave*: Catherine Van Pelt. *Tom Thomas*: Jack Kellar. *Freddy Sharp*: Artie Leeming. *Kitty Blythe*: ELEANOR HENRY. *Gilbert Grant*: ALAN HALE. *Sybil Tripp*: VIOLETTE WILSON. *Alexina Tripp*: OCTAVIA BROSKE. *Daisy Cloak*, a shop girl: Fay Tunis. *Larry Tripp*: HARRY CLARKE. *Milton*: Herbert Fields. *Madame Flambauex*: Muriel Lodge. *Francois*: Pauline Garon. *Jimmy Lock*, a Locksmith: Charlie Mitchell. *Ichabod Wintergreen*: FRANK DOANE. *Candy Salesgirls (6)*: *Julie Bonbon*: Catherine Van Pelt. *Tutti Frutti*: Virginia DeLillies. *Minte Drop*: Louise Dale. *Cerisse Wilde*: Elsie Lange. *Dorothy Marshmallow*: Marion Dorr. *Marjorie Fudge*: Louise Strong. *Meeda Tharra*: Helen Fox. *Bessie Bonstella*: Muriel Lodge. *Sadie Little*, cashier in candy store: Pauline Garon. *Rider Lott*, a candy salesman: Frank Cornell. *Professor Ketchem*, a vocal teacher: WILLIE SOLAR.
  Specialty Artists: Jessica Brown, Joe Wilmot Niemeyer, Willie and Nellie St. Clair, Artie Leeming, and the PENN FOUR (Arthur Ball, Clarence Levy, Richard Russ, Jack Keller).
  Ensemble: *Customers in Tripp's Hat Store*: *Mrs. Stuyvesant*: Catherine Van Pelt. *Mrs. Livingston*: Virginia DeLillies. *Mrs. Van Duzen*: Helen Fox. *Mrs. Van Cortlandt*: Louise Strong. *Mrs. Astorbilt*: Marion Dorr. *Mrs. Bleecker*: Elsie Lange. *Mrs. Murray Hill*: Louise Dale. *Mrs. Lenox*: Muriel Lodge.
  Salesgirls in Tripp's Hat Store (8): *Cleo*: Fay Tunis. *Diana*: Helene Blake. *Hebe*: Marjorie Day. *Minerva*: Ruth Reavis. *Psyche*: Gladys Fisher. *Thais*: Ellen Best. *Portia*: Nan Hope. *Leila*: Edna Chase.
  Tripp's Pages in Hat Store (4): *Algie*: Lauretta Stanley. *Reggie*: Hazel Bowman. *Percy*: Jeanette Cooke. *Clarence*: Gypsy Mooney.
  Friends of Sybil (6): *Rose*: Margaret Finley. *Violet*: Gladys Lang. *Pansy*: Julia Barnette. *Daisy*: Toots Bryce. *Cherry*: Jeanne Carrol. *Lily*: Clara Carrol.
  Customers in Hat Store (6): *Mr. Bunker*: Frank Billings. *Mr., Kidder*: Jim Dalton. *Mr. Connor*: Alton Weber. *Mr. Cheatham*: Frank Binns. *Mr. Cooker*: Robert Calley. *Mr. Tooker*: George Coogan.
  Salesgirls in Candy Shop (6): *Viola*: Catherine Van Pelt. *Rosalind*: Virginia DeLillies. *Ophelia*: Louise Strong. *Gwendolen*: Elsie Lange. *Pauline*: Louise Dale. *Clarisse*: Marion Dorr.
  Salesmen in Tripp's Hat Store (4): *Billie Williams*: Arthur Ball. *Jimmy James*: Clarence Levy. *Harry Harrison*: Richard Russ. *Phil Fillmore*: Jack Keller.
  Customers in Candy Shop: Misses Muriel Lodge, Helen Fox, Fay Tunis, Marjorie Day, Ruth Reavis, Helene Blake, Gladys Fisher, Nan Hope, Ellen Best, Clarke, Margaret Finley, Gladys Lang, Lauretta Stanley, Julia Barnette, Hazel Bowman, Toots Bryce, Jeanette Cooke, Clara Carrol, Jeanne Carrol, Mooney.

Act 1, Scene 1: In front of the Shimmering Pheasant Restaurant, 4 A.M. *Scene 2*: Interior of Tripp's Hat Store, Fifth Avenue, 10 minutes later. *Scene 3*: The same— 10 A.M.

Act 2: Gilbert Grant Ice Cream and Candy Emporium. The same afternoon.

Act 3: House and Garden at Pelham Manor. A few hours later.

ACT 1[6]
  "Influenza Blues"
    W. Solar
    (*Music by* Malvin M. Franklin.)
  "Underneath a Big Umbrella"
    C. Van Pelt, J. Kellar
    (*Music by* Malvin M. Franklin.)

[6]Added to the show 26 August 1919:
  "I Guess I'm More Like Mother Than Like Father"
    (*Music by* Richard A. Whiting. *Lyrics by* Raymond B. Egan.)

Slumber Music[7]
"Opening of Hat Store"[8]
  Chorus
  (*Music by* Robert Hood Bowers.)
"Leave It to Your Milliner"[9]
  E. Henry, Chorus
  (*Music by* Robert Hood Bowers.)
"You Never Can Tell"
  A. Hale, V. Wilson, Penn Four
  (*Music by* Robert Hood Bowers.)
"Save a Little Daylight (for Me)"
  F. Cameron, Girls
  (*Music by* Robert Hood Bowers.)
"Jolly Me"
  A. Hale, E. Henry, H. Clarke
  (*Music by* Robert Hood Bowers.)
"Wait for Me"
  F. Cameron, Penn Four, Boys
  (*Music by* Robert Hood Bowers.)
"Let's Go"—Finale
  Ensemble
  (*Music by* Robert Hood Bowers.)

ACT 2
  Opening Chorus
    Chorus
  "Sweets to the Sweet"
    V. Wilson, J. W. Niemeyer, Chorus, Kiddies
    (*Music by* Malvin M. Franklin.)
  "One I Love, Two I Love"
    E. Henry, J. W. Niemeyer, Chorus
    (*Music by* Robert Hood Bowers.)
  "Don't Do Anything 'Till You Hear from Me"
    L. Fields, F. Cameron, A. Hale, F. Doane, E. Henry, O. Broske
    (*Music by* Malvin M. Franklin.)
  "Flirtation Fantasies" (Flirtation Fantasy)
    J. Brown, J. W. Niemeyer
    (*Music by* Malvin M. Franklin.)
  "The Candy Jag"
    N. St. Clair, W. St. Clair, J. Brown, W. Solar
    (*Music by* Malvin M. Franklin.)

ACT 3
  Opening (Singing and Dancing School)
    Chorus
  "Will o' Wisp"
    F. Cameron, Penn Four, Chorus
    (*Music by* Malvin M. Franklin, Otis Spencer.)
  "(I Want a) Lonely Romeo"
    V. Wilson, J. Kellar, Ponies
    (*Music by* Malvin M. Franklin.)
  Jazz Dance[10]
    A. Leeming
  Finale
    Entire Company

1919.15

ZIEGFELD FOLLIES OF 1919

A Musical Revue in Two Acts, 23 Scenes[11]. Sketches by Dave Stamper, Gene Buck and Rennold Wolf. Music and lyrics by Irving Berlin, Gene Buck, Rennold Wolf, Dave Stamper, (Joseph McCarthy, Harry Tierney).

[7]Dropped during the New York run.
[8]Dropped for subsequent tour. The interpolations below were likewise dropped, and the song order revised.
[9]"Leave It to Your Milliner" and "You Never Can Tell" dropped in late August 1919, and replaced by:
  "Any Old Place with You"
    H. Clarke, E. Lynn, Penn Four
    (*Music by* Richard Rodgers. *Lyrics by* Lorenz Hart.)
[10]Dropped after opening.
[11]The thirteenth in the annual series of musical revues which began in 1907 under the auspices of Florenz Ziegfeld.

Ballet composed by Victor Herbert. Staged by Ned Wayburn. Scenery designed by Joseph Urban. Costumes designed by Lady Duff-Gordon and Mme. Francis. Musical director, Frank Darling. Orchestrations (for Buck and Stamper songs) by Stephen Jones. Produced by Florenz Ziegfeld. Opened 16 June 1919 at the New Amsterdam Theatre, suspending performances 12 August 1919 for the Actors' Equity strike; resumed 10 September 1919 and closed 6 December 1919 after 171 performances.

CAST: MARILYN MILLER, EDDIE CANTOR, JOHNNY DOOLEY, RAY DOOLEY, (Gus) VAN and (Joe) SCHENCK, BERT WILLIAMS, JOHN STEEL, DELYLE ALDA, EDDIE DOWLING, THE FAIRBANKS TWINS (Madeleine, Marion), JESSIE REED, PHIL DWYER, GEORGE LEMAIRE, the Follies Kiddies.

Follies Girls: Mildred Sinclair, Marcelle Earle, Mauresette, Kathryn Perry, Lucille Levant, Mary Hay, Florence Ware, Hazel Washburn, Martha Pierre, Bernice Dewey, Margaret Irving, Ethel Hallor, Ruth Taylor, Florence Crane, Betty Morton, Corone Paynter, Mary Washburn, Nan Larned, Simone D'Herlys, Betty Francesco, Monica Boulais, Martha Wood, Lois Davison, Mabel Hastings, Madeline Wales, Minnie Harrison, Viola Clarens, Helen Shea, Olive Vaughn, Edna Lindsey, Carolyn Erwin, Ruth Foster, Edna Rochelle, Lillian McKenzie, Helen Jesmer, Beulah McFarland, Edith Hawes, Peggy Dana, Edith Kessler, Laura Maverick, Grace Jones, Elsie Westcott, Ruth Taylor, Alma Braham, Amy Frank, Mildred Shelly, Margie Bell, Winnie Dunn, Gene Garrick, May Graney, Fay West, Peggy Smith, Margaret John, Virginia Lyon, Heloise Sheppard, Felise Lomont. *Gentlemen of the Ensemble*: Wesley Pierce, Lee LaBlanc, Jack Waverly, Harry Meyers, Jack Natter, Peter McArthur, Jerry Childs, Kenneth Lawrence, Bernard Carples, Thomas Howard, William Conrad, Ray Klages, George Otis, Bruce Douglas, Hubert Butler, Willie Newsome, Walter Baker, George Burggraf, Fred DuBall, Jack Lynch, Joe Evans, Eddie Sims, William Mathews.

ACT 1

Scene 1

"The Follies Salad"

E. Dowling

(*Music by* Dave Stamper. *Lyrics by* Gene Buck.)
Lettuce: M. Sinclair. *Spice*: M. Earle. *Oil*: Mauresette. *Sugar*: K. Perry. *Paprika*: L. Levant. *Chicken*: M. Hay. *Salt and Pepper*: Fairbanks Twins. *Follies Girl of 1919*: F. Ware.

Scene 2

Hail to the Thirteenth Folly (An arrangement {tableau} by Ben Ali Haggin)
The New Folly: J. Reed. *Her Twelve Sisters*: H. Washburn, M. Pierre, B. Dewey, M. Irving, E. Hallor, R. Taylor, F. Crane, B. Morton, C. Paynter, M. Washburn, N. Larned, S. D'Herlys.

Scene 3

A Pet

M. Hay, P. Dwyer

Scene 4

A Spanish Frolic (*by* Rennold Wolf)
Toreador: J. Dooley. *Carmen*: R. Dooley. *Announcer*: E. Dowling. *Matador*: W. Pierce. *Picador*: J. Lynch. *The Bull* (2): *Fore*: P. Dwyer. *Aft*: W. Newsome.

Scene 5

"My Baby's Arms"

D. Alda

(*Music by* Joseph Tierney. *Lyrics by* Joseph McCarthy.)
Assisted by L. Levant, K. Perry, M. Hay, F. Ware, Fairbanks Twins.

Scene 6

"Sweet Sixteen"

M. Miller

(*Music by* Dave Stamper. *Lyrics by* Gene Buck.)
Assisted by M. Sinclair, B. Dewey, M. Washburn, M. Earle, M Wood, L. Davison, C. Paynter, L. Lorraine, M. Boulais, M. Hastings, M. Wales, M. Harrison, V. Clarens, H. Shea, O. Vaughn, E. Lindsey.

Scene 7

"The Popular Pests"

(*Music by* Dave Stamper. *Lyrics by* Gene Buck.)
Waiter: E. Dowling. *Janitor*: B. Williams. *The Motorman*: G. Van. *The Hall Boy*: J. Schenck. *Hat Check Boy*: J. Dooley. *Taxi Driver*: E. Cantor. *Servant Girl*: R. Dooley.

Scene 8

"Tulip Time"

J. Steel, D. Alda

(*Music by* Dave Stamper. *Lyrics by* Gene Buck.)
Assisted by C. Erwin, R. Foster, E. Rochelle, B. Francesco, L. McKenzie, H. Jesmer, B. McFarland, E. Hawes, P. Dana, E. Kessler, B. Morton, L. Davison, L. Maverick, G. Jones, E. Westcott, R. Taylor, the Follies Kiddies.

Scene 9

He Seldom Misses (*by* Rennold Wolf and George Lemaire)
Sure-Shot Dick: G. Lemaire. *Jasper Slocum*: B. Williams. *Prairie Nell*: J. Reed.

Scene 10

"Shimmy Town" (Shimmee Town)

J. Dooley, R. Dooley

(*Music by* Dave Stamper. *Lyrics by* Gene Buck.)
Assisted by the Shimmie Girls and the Follies Pickaninnies.

Scene 11

The Epostle of Pep

E. Cantor

["You'd Be Surprised"
(*Music and Lyrics by* Irving Berlin.)
"How Ya' Gonna Keep 'Em Down on the Farm (After They've Seen Paree)?"
Music by Walter Donaldson. *Lyrics by* Sam M. Lewis, Joe Young.)
"You Don't Need the Wine to Have a Wonderful Time"
(*Music by* Harry Akst. *Lyrics by* Howard Rogers.)
"I've Got My Captain Working for Me Now"
(*Music and Lyrics by* Irving Berlin.)
"When They're Old Enough to Know Better"
(*Music by* Harry Ruby. *Lyrics by* Sam Lewis and Joe Young.)
"(Oh! She's the) Last Rose of Summer"
(*Music and Lyrics by* Harry Ruby and Eddie Cantor.)]

Scene 12

"I Love a Minstrel Show" (I Want to See a Minstrel Show/I'd Rather See a Minstrel Show)

J. Dooley

(*Music and Lyrics by* Irving Berlin.)

Scene 13

"The Follies Minstrels"

Entire Company

(*Music and Lyrics by* Irving Berlin.)
Tambo: E. Cantor. *Bones*: B. Williams. *Middle Man*: G. Lemaire. *Quartette*: *First Tenor*: J. Schenck. *Second Tenor*: J. Steel. *Baritone*: E. Dowling. *Bass*: G. Van.

"Mandy" (from YIP YIP YAPHANK)

G. Van, J. Schenck

(*Music and Lyrics by* Irving Berlin.)
George Primrose: M. Miller. *Mandys*: L. Levant, M. Hay, A. Braham, A. Frank, M. Shelly, M. Harrison, M. Bell, W. Dunn, O. Vaughn, G. Garrick. *Dandys*: W. Baker, G. Burggraf, F. DuBall, J. Lynch, J. Evans, E. Sims, W. Mathews, W. Newsome. *Mandy*: R. Dooley. Accompanied by the Follies Pickaninnies.

Grand Finale

Entire Aggregation

ACT 2

Scene 1

"Harem Life" (Outside of That Every Little Thing's All Right)

H. Washburn

(*Music and Lyrics by* Irving Berlin.)
Ladies of the Harem: Mauresette, M. Graney, H. Jesmer, E. Kessler, L. MacKenzie, B. Morton, F. Crane. *Cleopatra*: M. Pierre. *Favorite Wives* (in order of their appearance): J. Reed, C. Erwin, A. King, H. Washburn, E. Hallor, R. Taylor, N. Larned, M. Irving. *Dancers of the Harem*: B. Dewey, K. Perry, M. Washburn, M. Sinclair, A. Braham, M. Earl. *A Dancer*: L. Levant.

Scene 2

"I'm the Guy Who Guards the Harem (and My Heart's in My Work)"

J. Dooley

(*Music and Lyrics by* Irving Berlin.)

Scene 3

Songs

B. Williams

["When the Moon Shines on the Moonshine"
(*Music by* Robert Hood Bowers. *Lyrics by* Francis DeWitt.)
"Bring Back Those Wonderful Days"
(*Music and Lyrics by* Nat Vincent and Darl MacBoyle.)
"It's Nobody's Business But My Own"
(*Music and Lyrics by* Will E. Skidmore and Marshall Walker.)
"Somebody (Else, Not Me)"
(*Music by* James Hanley. *Lyrics by* Ballard Macdonald.)]

Scene 4

"The Circus Ballet"

Danced by M. Miller

(*Music by* Victor Herbert.)

Ringmaster: M. Sinclair. *Clowns*: G. Garrick, F. West, K. Mahoney, B. Dewey, L. Lorraine, M. Shelley, L. Maverick, E. Kessler, B. McFarland, C. Paynter, M. Harrison, E. Westcott, M. Bell, P. Smith, M. John, W. Dunn. *Bare Back Riders*: M. Earl, O. Vaughn, V. Clarens, M. Hastings, H. Shea, A. Frank, E. Lindsey, H. Jesmer, V. Lyon, M. Wales, G. Jones, A. Braham, M. Boulais, H. Sheppard, L. Davison, M. Wood.

Scene 5

"A Pretty Girl Is Like a Melody"
J. Steel, accompanied by M. Washburn
(*Music and Lyrics by* Irving Berlin.)
Humoresque: Mauresette. *Spring Song*: H. Washburn. *Elegy*: M. Pierre. *Barcarolle*: J. Reed. *Serenade*: A. King. *Traumeri*: M. Irving.

Melody, Fantasy and Folly of Years Gone By (A Picture by Ben Ali Haggin)
The Lady of Coventry: S. D'Herlys. *Her Handmaidens*: K. Perry, C. Erwin, R. Foster, B. Morton, F. Lamont, O. Vaughn, M. Harrison, W. Dunn. *The Heralds*: Fairbanks Twins. *The Jester*: A. Young. *The Guards*: W. Baker, G. Burggraf, F. DuBall, J. Lynch, J. Evans, E. Sims, W. Mathews, W. Newsome, Follies Kiddies.

Scene 6

At the Osteopath's (*by* Rennold Wolf and Eddie Cantor)
Dr. Cheeseboro Simpson: G. Lemaire. *Percival Fingersnapper*: E. Cantor. *Orchid Swan*, a stenographer: K. Perry. *A Visitor*: H. Washburn.

Scene 7

"Prohibition"
(*Music and Lyrics by* Irving Berlin.)
Father Time: E. Dowling. *Mourners*: E. Westcott, P. Dana, E. Rochelle, E. Hawes, L. McKenzie, B. Morton. *Liquor Lovers*: W. Pierce, L. LaBlanc, J. Waverly, H. Meyers, J. Natter, P. McArthur, J. Childs, K. Lawrence. *Bartenders*: G. Van, J. Schenck, and W. Baker, G. Burggraf, F. DuBall, J. Lynch, J. Evans, E. Sims, W. Mathews, W. Newsome. *Chorus Girls*: M. Irving, N. Larned, F. Crane, M. Pierre, A. King, R. Foster, R. Taylor, C. Erwin. *The Working Man*: A. Young. *Our Boys from Over There*: B. Carpies, H. Butler, R. Klages, T. Howard, W. Conrad, B. Douglas, G. Otis.

"You Cannot Make Your Shimmy Shake on Tea"
B. Williams
(*Music by* Irving Berlin. *Lyrics by* Irving Berlin and Rennold Wolf.)

"The Near Future"
(*Music and Lyrics by* Irving Berlin.)
Scene: A Saloon of the Future.
A Customer: J. Steel. *The Waiter*: E. Cantor. *Coca Cola*: E. Hallor. *Sarsparilla*: J. Reed. *Grape Juice*: B. Francesco. *Lemonade*: H. Washburn. *Bevo*: Mauresette. *Lady Alcohol*: D. Alda.

"A Syncopated Cocktail"
M. Miller
(*Music and Lyrics by* Irving Berlin.)
China Dolls: M. Wood, M. Earle, M. Washburn, V. Clarens, M. Wales, M. Hastings, M. Boulais, L. Davison, M. Sinclair, A. Braham, O. Vaughn, K. Mahoney, L. Lorraine, H. Sheppard, H. Shea, E. Lindsey.

Scene 8

Song
G. Van, J. Schenck
["Sweet Kisses (That Came in the Night)"
(*Music by* Albert Von Tilzer. *Lyrics by* Lew Brown and Eddie Buzzell.)
"They're All Sweeties"
(*Music by* Harry Von Tilzer. *Lyrics by* Andrew Sterling.)
"Oh, How She Can Sing"
(*Music and Lyrics by* Gus Van, Joe Schenck and Jack Yellen.)]

Scene 9

"My Tambourine Girl"
J. Steel
(*Music and Lyrics by* Irving Berlin.)
The Girl: J. Reed. *Salvation Lassies*: H. Washburn, B. Morton, E. Hallor, C. Erwin, A. King, M. Pierre, F. Crane, M. Irving. *Officers Chorus*: W. Pierce, L. LaBlanc, J. Waverly, H. Meyers, J. Natter, P. McArthur, J. Childs, K. Lawrence, B. Carples, T. Howard, W. Conrad, R. Klages, G. Otis, B. Douglas, H. Butler.

Scene 10

"We Made the Doughnuts Over There"
(*Music and Lyrics by* Irving Berlin.)
Scene: Victory Arch.
Salvation Army Girls: R. Taylor, B. Francesco, E. Rochelle, E. Hawes, P. Dana, L. McKenzie, M. Sinclair, M. Wood, M. Washburn, M. Earle, C. Paynter, M. Wales, K. Mahoney, H. Shea, E. Lindsey, L. Lorraine, P. Smith, M. Boulais, H. Sheppard, V. Clarens, M. Hastings, L. Maverick, E. Westcott, B. McFarland, H. Jesmer, L. Davison, E. Kessler, G. Jones, A. Braham, M. Shelley, M. Bell, B. Dewey.

THE SHUBERT GAIETIES
OF 1919

1919.16

A Musical Revue in Two Acts, 22 Scenes. Dialogue by Edgar Smith. Ed Wynn's scenes by Harold Atteridge and Ed Wynn. Music by Jean Schwartz. Lyrics by Alfred Bryan. Additional songs by Blanche Merrill. Staged by J. C. Huffman. Dances arranged by Allan K. Foster and Kuy Kendall. Art director (scenic design), Watson Barratt. Costumes under the personal direction of Romayne Simmons. Costumes designed by Homer Conant. Orchestra directed by Oscar Radin. Orchestrations supervised by J. Bodewalt Lampe. Produced by the Messrs. Lee and J. J. Shubert. Opened 7 July 1919 at the 44th Street Theatre, suspending performances 9 August 1919 for the Actors' Equity strike; resumed 8 September 1919, moved 6 October 1919 to the Winter Garden and closed 18 October 1919 after 87 performances.

CAST: ED WYNN, HENRY LEWIS, GLADYS WALTON, GILDA GRAY, STEWART BAIRD, LLORA HOFFMAN, HARRY FENDER, CLAYTON and WHITE, MARGUERITE FARRELL, THE GLORIAS, INA WILLIAMS, TED LORRAINE, GLADYS WALTON, AUGUSTUS [Gus] MINTON, MARJORIE GATESON, GEORGE HASSELL, WILLIAM KENT, JACK BOHM, JULIE BALLEW, KUY KENDALL, JIMMIE FOX, Olga Hempstone, Freda Leonard, Kathryn Hart, Billy Wagner.
Ladies of the Ensemble: Muriel Sharp, Perle Germonde, Florence Elmore, Mabel Cloud, Doris Benham, Marie Stafford, Gertrude Doyle, Dorothy Snyder, Mildred Soper, Mabel Roberts, Doris Cameron, Roberta Lomax, Alice Humphries, Ruth Moore, Juliette Rooke, Virginia Weyman, Josie Carmen, Margaret Maloney, Margaret Mack, Ruth Alexander, Daphne Hicks, Gene Cleveland, Polly Pryor, Hilda Smith Fischer, Frances Richards, Elsie Bambrick, Alice Velie, Lillian Brand, Hermosa Jose, Bert Best, Peggy Hart, Ruby Wilbur, Gene Gordon, Estelle Haddon, Rose Light, Alice Parry, Peggy O'Neil, Poppy Morton, Margery Hope, Rena Brown, Betty Connelly, Alice Monroe, Madeleine Dare, Kitty Fallon, Billie Williams, Gene Danjou, Billy Wagner, Phyllis Cameron. *Gentlemen of the Ensemble*: James Monahan, Frank McMasters, Edward Schanol, George Hale, Arthur Freeman, John Stone, Joseph Fields, Philip Gerold.

ACT 1[12]

Before the Curtain
E. Wynn

Scene 1

"Coat o' Mine" (Coat of Mine)
S. Baird, Girls
(*Music by* M. K. Jerome. *Lyrics by* Blanche Merrill.)

"A Maid Like You" (I've Made Up My Mind to Mind a Maid Made Up Like You)
S. Baird, M. Gateson

_____

[12]Added after the opening:
"You'd Be Surprised" (also in ZIEGFELD FOLLIES OF 1919)
George Jessel
(*Music and Lyrics by* Irving Berlin.)

The running order was revised for subsequent tour; added were:
"Everybody Shimmies (Now)"
Sophie Tucker
(*Music by* Joe Gold and Edmund J. Porray. *Lyrics by* Eugene West.)

"(At the) Jazz Babies' Ball"
S. Tucker
(*Music by* Maceo Pinkard. *Lyrics by* Charles Bayha.)

"You'll See the Day"
S. Tucker
(*Music and Lyrics by* Bud Green, Charlie Pierce and Ted Fiorito.)

George Jessel sings his own songs (Specialty)
"And He'd Say "Oo-La-La! Wee-Wee"
(*Music by* Harry Ruby. *Lyrics by* George Jessel.)

"You Know What I Mean" (from ZIEGFELD GIRLS OF 1920)
(*Music by* Dave Stamper. *Lyrics by* Gene Buck.)

"Girl You Marry" (added late in tour)
S. Baird, Chorus

Specialty
Klein Brothers (Harry, Al)
["She Was Bred in Old Kentucky"
(*Music by* Stanley Carter. *Lyrics by* Harry Braisted.)

"He Went in Like a Lion and Came Out Like a Lamb"
(*Music by* Harry Von Tilzer. *Lyrics by* Andrew B. Sterling.)

"They're All Sweeties"
(*Music by* Harry Von Tilzer. *Lyrics by* Andrew B. Sterling.)]

Scene: Lounging Room in the Suburban Mansion of Jack Potter
Hobson: F. McMasters. *Major Flittington*: A. Minton. *Jack Potter*: S. Baird. *Tom Brush*: H. Fender. *The Shepherdess*: M. Gateson.

Scene 2

"Baby Vampire (Land)"
J. Ballew, some other Baby Vampires
Scene: In Baby Vampire Land.

Scene 3

"Vamp a Little Lady"
F. Leonard, K. Hart, Girls

Song
M. Farrell

"(Please) Don't Take Away the Girls"
W. Kent, Chorus
Scene: The Gardens at Jack Potter's Home.
The Blond Vamp: F. Leonard. *The Brunette Vamp*: K. Hart. *The Cabaret Dancers*: The Glorias. *Violet*: M. Gateson. *Tom Brush*: H. Fender. *Major Flittington*: A. Minton. *Mrs. Flittington*: M. Farrell. *John Dough*: G. Hassell. *Lina*: O. Hempstone. *Daisy*: P. Germonde. *Pansy*: F. Elmore. *Pearl*: M. Cloud. *Myrtle*: M. Stafford. *Ruth*: G. Doyle. *Annabelle*: M. Soper. *Corabelle*: D. Snyder. *Gabrielle*: M. Sharp. *Mabelle*: M. Roberts. *Dorothy*: D. Benham. *A Rounder*: W. Kent.

Scene 4

Ed Wynn

Scene 5

"Crazy Quilt" (Dippy-Doodle-um) (Song)
I. Williams, Chorus (some other patches)
Scene: A Crazy Quilt.
(*Music by* M. K. Jerome. *Lyrics by* Blanche Merrill.)

Scene 6

"(For) the Freedom of the C's"
H. Fender, Chorus (Gaiety Girls)
Tom Brush: H. Fender.

Scene 7

Scene: Hotel in Paris.
Mr. Dough: G. Hassell. *Mr. Swift*: W. Kent. *Girl*: O. Hempstone. *Stage Manager*: A. Minton.

Scene 8

White and Clayton

Scene 9

Chanson Apache
T. Lorraine, G. Walton

"Beautiful American Girl"
S. Baird, Chorus

Selection
L. Hoffman

"Beale Street Blues"[13]
G. Gray
(*Music and Lyrics by* W. C. Handy.)
Scene: In a Greenwich Village Restaurant.
Monsieur Le Chanteur: T. Lorraine. *Mademoiselle La Danseuse*: G. Walton. *Waiter*: J. Fox. *Flimflaminetti*: W. Kent. *Jack Potter*: S. Baird. *The Shepherdess*: M. Gateson. *Major Flittington*: A. Minton. *The Cabaret Artist*: G. Gray. *The Singer*: L. Hoffman. *Greenwich Village Beauties*: M. Sharp, M. Soper, P. Germonde, F. Elmore, M. Cloud, M. Stafford, V. Weyman, G. Doyle, O. Hempstone, D. Benham, D. Snyder.

Scene 10

Ed Wynn

Scene 11

"Rainbow Ball"
K. Hart, K. Kendall, H. Jose, Chorus

Imitation of Ann Pennington[14]
K. Kendall

The Fox Trot
T. Lorraine, G. Walton

Buck and Wing
White and Clayton

One Step Eccentrique à la Russe
The Glorias

"What Are We Going To Do?"[15]
M. Gateson

Finale: "(Let Us Keep) The Shimmy"
(Company)
Scene: The Trial of the Shimmy.
The Judge: W. Kent. *Prosecutor*: G. Hassell. *District Attorney*: S. Baird. *The Clerk*: J. Bohm. *The Minister*: J. Fox. *Foreman of the Jury*: A. Minton. *The Defendant*: M. Gateson. *Exhibits at the Trial*: K. Kendall, Lorraine and Walton, Clayton and White, The Glorias.

ACT 2[16]

Scene 1

"Cherry Blossom (Lane)"
S. Baird, M. Gateson, Chorus
Scene: The Cherry Blossom Grove.
The Shepherdess: M. Gateson. *Jack Potter*: S. Baird.

Scene 2

"(Little) Boy Blue"
I. Williams, White and Clayton
Scene: In the Country.
Boy Blue: I. Williams. *Scare Crows*: White and Clayton.

Scene 3

The Trans-Atlantic Flight
The Aviator: E. Wynn. *The Navigator*: A. Minton. *First Trainer*: G. Hale. *Second Trainer*: J. Fields. *A Visitor*: J. Fox. *First Mechanic*: F. McMasters. *Second Mechanic*: J. Monahan. *Mary*: B. Wagner.

Scene 4

"Cozy Corner"
J. Ballew, K. Kendall, Chorus
Scene: In a Cozy Corner.
Molly: J. Ballew. *Cholly*: K. Kendall.

Scene 5

"The Lamp of Love"
L. Hoffman, T. Lorraine, G. Walton
The Moth: G. Walton. *The Flame*: T. Lorraine.

Scene 6

At Tom Brush's Studio
Tom Brush: H. Fender. *Miss Revue*: J. Ballew. *Major Flittington*: A. Minton. *Mrs. Flittington*: M. Farrell. *Mr. Dough*: G. Hassell. *Parisian Models*: M. Sharp, M. Soper, F. Elmore, M. Cloud, M. Stafford, D. Snyder, P. Germonde, G. Doyle, D. Benham.

Scene 7

The Revels of Neptune

Scene 8

"My (Beautiful) Tiger Girl"
H. Fender, Chorus
Scene: In the Tiger's Cage.
The Lover: H. Fender. *The Beautiful Tigress*: P. Germonde.

Scene 9

The Auction
E. Wynn

Scene 10

"This Is the Day"
S. Baird, M. Gateson
(*Music by* M. K. Jerome. *Lyrics by* Blanche Merrill.)
Scene: Lounging Room in the Suburban Mansion of Jack Potter.
Jack Potter: S. Baird. *The Shepherdess*: M. Gateson.

Scene 11

Roller Skating Waltz
The Gloria

---

[15]For subsequent tour, moved to Act 2 Finale; later in tour moved back to Act 1 Finale.
[16]The running order was revised for subsequent tour; added to Act 2 were:
Sophie Tucker and Her 7 Kings of Syncopation (Specialty)
"Mouthfull of Kisses" (added late in tour)
Janet Adair, Chorus

---

[13]Dropped for subsequent tour, then later restored for Sophie Tucker.
[14]Dropped for subsequent tour.

Military Decorations (Dance)
> J. Ballew, I. Williams, G. Walton, P. Germonde, H. Fender, T. Lorraine, K. Kendall, F. McMasters

Grand Finale
> *Scene*: The Ballroom at the Potters.
>> *Mr. Dough*: G. Hassell. *Tom Brush*: H. Fender. *Major Flittington*: A. Minton. *Mrs. Flittington*: M. Farrell. *Violet*: M. Gateson. *Charlie Swift*: W. Kent. *Jack Potter*: S. Baird.

THE OLD LADY/ DREAMS OF THREE

1919.17

A Double Bill of a Light Operas (Zarzuelas) in Two Acts, in Spanish. Directed and produced by Leoncia Mosquera. Opened 14 July 1919 at the Cort Theatre and closed 26 July 1919 after 16 performances.

ACT 1

LA VIEJECITA (The Old Lady), a Zarzuela in One Act, 2 Scenes. Libretto by Miguel Echegaray. Music by Manuel Fernández Caballero (and Mariano Hermoso).

CAST: *Carlos*: CONSUELO BAILLO. *Lucia*: ADELINA VEHI. *Sir George*: Miguel Pros. *The Marquis*: Leandro Diaz. *Don Manuel*: Manuel Noriega. *Fernando*: CARLOS VILLARIAS. *Federico*: Jose Tamargo. *Officer*: Pepe Luis. *Ujier*: Jose Abeytua. *Officers, Dragoons, Ladies, General Chorus of 50.*

ACT 2

DREAMS OF THREE (Las Musas Latinas), a Zarzuela in One Act, 5 Scenes. (Libretto by M. Moncayo. Music by M. Panella.)

CAST: *Spanish Painter*: Miguel Pros. *French Painter*: Miguel Santascam. *Italian Painter*: Carlos Villarias. *The Landlady*: Juana Andres. *The Spanish Muse*: CARMEN LOPEZ. *The French Muse*: ADELINA VEHI. *The Italian Muse*: CONSUELO BAILLO. *General Chorus of 50.*

THE GREENWICH VILLAGE FOLLIES (1919)

1919.18

A Revusical Comedy of New York's Latin Quarter (A Musical Revue) in Two Acts, a Prologue and 13 Scenes[17]. Sketches by Philip Bartholomae and John Murray Anderson. Music by A. Baldwin Sloane. Lyrics by Arthur Swanstrom and John Murray Anderson. Staged by John Murray Anderson. Scenes designed by Charles B. Falls. Costumes designed by Shirley Barker. Musical director, Hilding Anderson. Orchestrations by Hilding Anderson. Produced by the Bohemians, Inc. Opened 15 July 1919 at the Greenwich Village Theatre, moved 9 September 1919 to the Nora Bayes Theatre, and closed 31 January 1920 after 232 performances.

CAST: TED LEWIS, SUSANNE MORGAN, CHARLES DERICKSON, BESSIE McCOY DAVIS, AL HERMAN, WILLIAM FORAN, IRENE OLSEN, ROBERT [Bobby] EDWARDS, RITA ZALMANI, JAMES WATTS, IRENE S. MATHEWS, JANE CARROLL, HOMER ROSINE, WILLARD WARD, REX STORY, HARRY DELF, ADA FORMAN, CECIL CUNNINGHAM, CYNTHIA PEROT, WARNER GAULT, EDMOND MAKALIF, EDGAR THORNTON, OLGA ZICEVA.

Ladies of the Ensemble: Arjamand, Dorothy Clay, Anna Mae Clift, Doris Faithful, Alden Gay, Virginia Lee, Rita Marshall, Irene Marcellus, Billie Weston, Babette Busey, Virginia Curtis, Jacqueline Delaine, Helen Frances, Ruth Weeks.

ACT 1[18]

Prologue

The Green Line[19]
> A *Ticket Chopper*: S. Morgan. A *Juvenile*: C. Derickson. A *Thief*: W. Foran. A *Bobby Edwards*: R. Edwards. *June Day*: J. Watts.

Before the Curtain
> A *Village Belle*: J. Carroll. A *Painter*: H. Rosine. A *Poet*: W. Ward. A *Musician*: W. Gault. *An Artist*: E. Thornton.

Scene 1
> *Scene*: The Greenwich Village Theatre.
>> *The Art Director*: H. Delf. *Villagers*: Ladies of the Ensemble. *Pansy Jewel*: B. M. Davis.

"The Stolen Melody"
> B. M. Davis, H. Delf
>> *The Juvenile*: C. Derickson. *The Ingenue*: I. Olsen.

"I Want a Daddy (Who Will Rock Me to Sleep)"
> I. Olsen, C. Derickson
>> (*Lyrics by* John Murray Anderson and Philip Bartholomae.)
>> *The Dancer*: R. Zalmani.

Scene 3
A Street in Greenwich Village
> *June Day*: J. Watts. A *Johnnie*: R. Story.

Scene 4
"My Little Javanese"
> J. Carroll
>> (*Lyrics by* John Murray Anderson and Philip Bartholomae.)
>> *Scene*: In Java.
>> *The Dancer*: A. Forman. And Ladies of the Ensemble.

Scene 5
Ted Lewis, the Jazz King:
["When My Baby Smiles at Me"
> (*Music by* Bill Munro. *Lyrics by* Ted Lewis, Andrew B. Sterling.)

"The Vamp"
> (*Music and Lyrics by* Byron Gay.)

"I Know Why (Because I'm in Love with You)"
> (*Music by* Ted Lewis, Jimmy Morgan. *Lyrics by* Benny Davis.)

"I'll See You in C-U-B-A"
> (*Music and Lyrics by* Irving Berlin.)]

Scene 6[20]
"Red, Red As the Rose"
> C. Derickson
>> (*Lyrics by* John Murray Anderson and Philip Bartholomae.)
>> *Scene*: Godiva's Gambol.
>>> *Patsy*: I. Olsen. *The Gold Columbine*: C. Perot. *The Silver Harlequin*: E. Makilif. *The Master of Ceremonies*: R. Edwards. *The Widow of Haig and Haig*: S. Morgan. *The Widow's Mite*: H. Delf. *Lady Godiva*: J. Watts.

Danse Classique "Adagio"
> J. Watts
>> *Ava Phalova*: J. Watts. *Cissinsky*: R. Story.

"Tony Sarg" (My Marionette)
> I. Olsen
>> *The Marionette*: B. M. Davis. *The Singer*: I. Olsen. Ladies of the Ensemble, the Greenwich Village Quartet. *The Thief*: W. Foran. *The Doctor*: R. Edwards. A *Newsboy*: E. Makilif. A *Newsgirl*: R. Zalmani.

"The Critic's Blues"
> H. Delf
>> (*Lyrics by* John Murray Anderson and Philip Bartholomae.)

ACT 2
Scene 1
"I've a Sweetheart in Each Star"
> C. Derickson
>> (*Lyrics by* John Murray Anderson and Philip Bartholomae.)
>> *Scene*: Up in the Air.
>>> *The Aviator*: C. Derickson. *Mercury*: E. Makilif. *The Signs of the Zodiac*: Ladies of the Ensemble. *The Girl in the Star*: O. Ziceva. *Night*: I. Mathews.

Scene 2
Cecil Cunningham[21]

Scene 3
"The Message of the Cameo"[22]
> B. M. Davis
>> (*Lyrics by* John Murray Anderson and Philip Bartholomae.)

The Dream Lovers
> E. Thornton, H. Rosine, W. Ward, W. Gault, B. Busey, J. Delaine, H. Frances, V. Lee, R. Marshall, R. Weeks

---

[17]The first in the annual series of revues which continued for eight editions ending in 1928.
[18]Added after opening:
Our Foreign Bad Relations (*by* John Murray Anderson)
[19]Later known on tour as In the New York Subways.

[20]Added for subsequent tour to this scene, before Danse Classique:
"Such a Little Queen"
> Frances White
>> (*Music by* Earnie Golden. *Lyrics by* John Henry Mears.)
[21]Replaced for subsequent tour by:
"Ding Toes"
> F. White
>> (*Music and Lyrics by* "Jack" Caddigan and "Chick" Story.)]
>> *Scene*: Before the Curtain. *At the Piano*: E. Golden.
[22]Dropped for subsequent tour.

Passe-Pied
O. Ziceva, V. Curtis, E. Makalif
Scene: The Cameo.

Scene 4

Bobby Edwards

Scene 5

Marguerite's Back Yard
Siebel: S. Morgan. *Faust:* W. Foran. *Mephisto:* E. Thornton. *Marguerite:* J. Watts.

Scene 6

Specialty[23]
A. Herman

["Moonshine (Is in the Mountain Still)"
(*Music by* A. Behr. *Lyrics by* Al Herman.)

"True Blue Sal"
(*Music and Lyrics by* Al Herman, Alex Gerber, Abner Silver.)

"All That I Need Is a Hallway"
(*Music by* Abner Silver. *Lyrics by* Alex Gerber.)

"Give Me the Sultan's Harem" (Won't You Give That Harem to Me)
(*Music by* Abner Silver. *Lyrics by* Alex Gerber.)]

Scene 7

The Floating Cabaret (Three Miles Out)
The Hostess: B. M. Davis. *The Proprietor:* H. Delf. *The Waiter:* W. Foran.

"I'm the Hostess of a Bum Cabaret"[24]
B. M. Davis
(*Lyrics by* John Murray Anderson and Philip Bartholomae.)
Mr. O'Hearn: H. Delf. *Mrs. O'Hearn:* S. Morgan. *Patsy:* I. Olsen. *Jack:* C. Derickson. *A Guest:* R. Edwards.

"I Am Ashamed to Look the Moon in the Face"
H. Delf, Ensemble
(*Lyrics by* John Murray Anderson and Philip Bartholomae.)
A Dancer: C. Perot.

Finale
Entire Company

1919.19

OH, WHAT A GIRL!

A Musical Farce in Two Acts, 4 Scenes. Book and lyrics by Edgar Smith and Edward Clark. Music by Charles Jules and Jacques Presburg. Staged by Edward Clark. Settings designed by Watson Barratt. Orchestra under the direction of Fred Walz. Orchestrations by Jacques Presburg. Produced by Messrs. Lee and J.J. Shubert. Opened 28 July 1919 at the Sam S. Shubert Theatre, suspending performances 6 August 1919 for the Actors' Equity strike; resumed 15 September 1919, moved 6 October 1919 to the Central Theatre and closed 1 November 1919 after 68 performances[25].

CAST (in order of appearance): *Jack's Friends* (6): *Downes:* Larry Francis. *Carr:* Mat Murphy. *Taylor:* George Stifter. *Smathers:* William Zinnel. *Holmes:* Harold Hulen. *Williams:* William Barry. *Ross at the piano:* Dave Dreyer. *Washington,* Jack's valet: Lew Cooper. *Bill Corcoran,* Jack's chum: FRANK FAY. *Jack Rushton,* a young student: SAM ASH. *Margot Merrivale,* a cabaret singer: HAZEL KIRKE. *Lola Chappelle,* Fravola's wife: VERA GROSET. *Luigi Fravola,* a composer: IGNACIO MARTINETTI. *Deacon Amos Titmouse,* Jack's uncle: HARRY KELLY. *Perkins,* a country yokel: Sam Curtis. *Susie Smith,* a country girl: Nancy Fair. *Amanda Titmouse,* uncle's wife: ELIZABETH MOFFAT. *Cinderella:* Clarice Snyder. *Prince Charming:* Ethel Mary Oakland. *Fairy Godmother:* Ma-Belle. *Headwaiter:* Lester Scharff. *Guests, Actresses, Dairy Maids, Farmers,* etc. (Specialty Dancers: Renee Adore, Lewis Sloden, Kathleen O'Hanlon, Theo Zambouni, Veronica Marquise.)

―――――――

[23]In programs for the tour, this specialty was listed as "Not That I Care But—."
[24]For subsequent tour, "I'm the Hostess of a Bum Cabaret" and "I'm Ashamed to Look the Moon in the Face" replaced by:
   "I'm Just a Lonesome Vampire"
   F. White
   Another Frances White specialty interpolated, as per published sheet music (1920):
   "Gee! I Wish I Was a Caveman's Kid"
   F. White
   (*Music by* Earnie Golden. *Lyrics by* Phil Ponce.)
[25]Presented in a condensed version on the Shubert Vaudeville Circuit with a wholly different cast October 1921 at the 44th Street Theatre. Few of the original songs were retained.

Chorus: Misses Billie Andrews, Phoebe Appleton, Diana Peyton, Agnes Allen, Evelyn Clifford, Florence Darling, Ella Evans, Margaret Ferguson, Bessie Gray, Kitty Holten, Margaret King, Clarice Miller, Pauline Markham, Florence Nelson, Agnes Shiedell, Elizabeth Treep, Elizabeth West, Bobbie Watts, Lillian Wilson, Kitty Astra. Messrs. Frank Crawford, George Stifter, Harold Hulen, William Barry, Jack Polen, Mat Murphy.

Act 1: Jack Rushton's Apartment, Riverside Drive, New York,

Act 2, Scene 1: Lawn of Uncle's Home, Cemetery Corners, New Jersey. Next morning. *Scene 2:* A Country Lane. That night. *Scene 3:* Century Midnight Whirl. That night.

ACT 1[26]

"Musical Poker Game"
Jack's Friends

"Gimme (This—Gimme This—Gimme That)"
L. Cooper
(*Music and Lyrics by* L. Wolfe Gilbert, Alex Sullivan and Nat Vincent.)

"Oh, What a Girl!"
S. Ash, Boys
(*Lyrics by* Edgar Smith.)

"A Nice Sweet Kiss"[27]
H. Kirke, S. Ash, F. Fay, Chorus
(*Lyrics by* Edgar Smith.)

Fox Trot[28]
R. Adoree, L. Sloden

Dance
Ma-Belle

"Oh, That Shimmy"
F. Fay, Chorus

"Travesty Opera"
Entire Company

ACT 2

Scene 1

Medley of Old Songs
Manhattan Comedy Four

"Prince Charming"
N. Fair, Chorus
(*Lyrics by* Edward Clark.)

"Get Him Up" (Ensemble)
F. Fay, H. Kirke, V. Groset, I. Martinetti, Chorus

"Dainty Little Girl (Like You)"
F. Fay, N. Fair
(*Lyrics by* Edgar Smith.)

Scene 2

"Breeze in the Trees" (The Breeze Through the Trees)
S. Ash, H. Kirke
(*Lyrics by* Edgar Smith.)

"Could You Teach Me?"
F. Fay, E. Moffat, I. Martinetti

Scene 3

(Toe) Dance
V. Marquise

"I've Got My Captain Working for Me Now"[29] (from ZIEGFELD FOLLIES OF 1919)
L. Cooper
(*Music and Lyrics by* Irving Berlin.)

Specialty
K. O'Hanlon, T. Zambouni

"(Such a) Baby"
N. Fair
(*Music by* Egbert Van Alstyne. *Lyrics by* Gus Kahn.)

Specialty
F. Fay

"Pot Pourri"
Entire Company

―――――――

[26]The running order and cast were revised following the strike.
[27]Dropped after opening.
[28]Dropped after opening.
[29]Replaced after strike settlement by:
   "You'd Be Surprised" (Specialty)
   L. Cooper, S. Ash
   (*Music and Lyrics by* Irving Berlin.)

CHU CHIN CHOW

1919.20

A New Costume Edition (Revival) of the Musical Tale of the East in Three Acts, 13 Scenes[30]. Book and lyrics by Oscar Asche. Music by Frederick Norton. Staged by E. Lyall Swete. Dances arranged by Alexis Kosloff. New dances arranged by Mlle. Guida. Scenery designed by Joseph Harker and Phil Harker. Costumes designed by Percy Anderson. Orchestra under the direction of Gustave Ferrari. Orchestrations by Percy E. Fletcher. Produced by William Elliott, E. Ray Comstock and Morris Gest. Opened 8 August 1919 at the Century Theatre, suspending performances 15 August 1919 for the Actors' Equity strike; reopened 6 September 1919 and closed 27 September 1919 after 33 performances.

CAST: *Abu Hassan*, the robber sheyk, alias *Chu Chin Chow*: LIONEL BRAHAM. *Members of His Band (2)*: *Khuzymah*: Thoral Lake. *Musab*: Tex Rogers. *Kasim Baba*, the richest and meanest man in Bagdad: Albert Howson. *Abdullah*, steward for Kasim Baba: EUGENE COWLES. *Zahrat-Al-Kalub*, the Desert Woman: MARJORIE WOOD. *Alcolom*, head wife in Kasim's harem: Adelaide Mesmer. *Ali Baba*, Kasim's poor brother, a wine bibber: DON W. FERRANDOU. *Nur-Al-Huda*, his son: GEORGE RASELY. *Marjanah*, the singing slave girl: HELEN GUNTHER. *Mukbill*, auctioneer in the slave market: Robert Merriman. *Zatel-Demaki*, a woman slave buyer: Hattie Carmontel. *Mahbubah*, the shrewish wife of Ali Baba: Gladys Earlcott. *Bostan*, her hlaf-witted servant: Tina Russell. *Son of the Bean Seller*: Charles Foster. *The Lady in Green*: Clara Burton. *The Stranger* in the Mean Street: Roy Tracy. *Dancers in Kasim's Palace*: Mlle. Guida, Martha Lorber. *In the Pantomime (3)*: *The Lady*: Hattie Carmontel. *The Lover*: Milton Stiefel. *The Husband*: Thoral Lake. *Baba Mustafa*, a cobbler of Bagdad: Felice DeGregorio. *Otbah*, a silk merchant: Christopher Hayes. *The Peddler* in the Bazaar: Roy Tracy.

Ensemble: *Javanese Fanners*: May Copeland, Suzanne Renard, Irene Mesmer, Margaret Wimer, Evelyn Richmond, Violet Kingston, Edna Moore, Virginia Chakair. *Burmese Dancers*: Joan Renville, Estelle Granau, Helen Trevor, Bessie Rice, Mimi Ormston, Olive Kingston, Bertha Knapp, Masie Thomas. *Nile Girls*: Vanda Tirindelli, Mae Poth, May Irwin, Lorraine Wimer, Clara Burton, Elsie Graham. *Ballet (Desert Dancers, Jewel Dancers, Dervish Dancers)*: Louise Blanid, Carmen Vasylvia, Jeannette Kayton, Margaret Kline, Anna Kronberg, Helen Rickeby, Helen Lee, Edith LeRoy, Hazel Jones, Lillian Kayton, Anna Boronsky, Alma Rosine, Mabel Freeman, Helen Bowers, Louise Potter, Vanda Tirindelli. *Circassian Slave*: Clara Burton. *Turkestan Slaves*: Lorraine and Margaret Wimer. *Pot Girls*: Vanda Tirindelli, Elsie Graham, Lorraine Wimer, Evelyn Richmond, Louise Potter, Anna Zanders, May Irwin. *Fruit Girls*: Irene Mesmer, Louise Potter (Soloists). Elsie Graham, May Copeland, Virginia Chakair, Margaret Wimer, Evelyn Richmond, Estelle Granau, Helen Trevor, Bessie Rice, Olive Kingston, Maisie Thomas, Bertha Knapp.

Mannequins in the Fashion Show: *Dusters*: Margaret Kline, Anna Borousky. *Group 1*: Agnes Tate, Mabel Freeman, May Poth, Irene Mesmer, Gertrude Royal. *Group 2*: Lorraine Wimer, Anna Kronberg, Evelyn Richmond, Suzanne Renard, Violet Kingston. *Group 3*: Alma Rosine, Margaret Wimer, Louise Blanid, May Copeland, Vanda Trindelli. *Group 4*: Martha Lorber, Helen Lee, Carmen Vasylvioa, Joan Renville, Clara Burton, Bertha Knapp, May Irwin, Edna Moore. *Carrier Girls*: Anna Borousky, Lillian Kayton, Edith LeRoy, Helen Rickebey, Margaret Kline, Jeannete Kayton, Hazel Jones, Mimi Ormston. *Ensemble of Robbers, Peddlers, Water Carriers, Wedding Guests, etc.*

Premier Dancers: *Yellow Dancer in Slave Market*: Martha Lorber. *Dancer in Mean Street*: Mlle. Guida. *Dancer in Dervish Number*: Mlle. Guida. *Diamond Dancer in Cave Scene*: Martha Lorber. *Dancer in Wedding Scene*: Martha Lorber.

Act 1, Scene 1: At Kasim Baba's Palace in Bagdad. A thousand years ago. The Feast in honor of Chu Chin Chow. *Scene 2*: By Marjanah's Window. Nur-al-huda sings his love. *Scene 3*: A Cactus Grove near the City. The robbers' cave. *Scene 4*: Entrance to the cave. *Scene 5*: The Slave Market of Bagdad. The raid of Chu Chin Chow and His Band of Forty Thieves.

Act 2, Scene 1: A Mean Street in Bagdad. Ali Baba's sudden wealth. *Scene 2*: At a Silk Stall. Ali Baba purchases fine raiment. *Scene 3*: The Blue Hall in Kasim's Palace. The Entertainment for Kasim-Baba. *Scene 4*: In Kasim's Harem. Ali Baba frolics while Kasim goes to the robbers' cave. *Scene 5*: The Cave of Abu Hasan. The end of Kasim Baba.

Act 3, Scene 1: A Bazaar of Bagdad. The Fashion Display of the Mannequins. *Scene 2*: On the Rose Terrace. Ali Baba and Alcolom are happy. *Scene 3*: The Orchard by Moonlight. The end of Abu Hasan.

ACT 1
"Here Be Oysters Stewed by Honey" (Song)
 E. Cowles, Chorus
"I Am Chu Chin Chow of China" (Entrance of Chu Chin Chow)
 Javanese Dance
"Cleopatra's Nile" (Song)
 H. Gunther
"I'll Sing and Dance" (Finale, Scene 1)
 D. H. Ferrandou

"Corraline" (Serenade)
 G. Rasely
"When a Pullet Is Plump, It's Tender" (Song)
 D. H. Ferrandou
"Only a Slave"[31] (Song)
 G. Rasely, H. Gunther
"We Are the Robbers of the Woods"
 Robbers' Chorus
"I Shiver and Shake with Fear" (Trio)
 D. H. Ferrandou, H. Gunther, G. Rasely
"Behold" (Song)
 E. Cowles

ACT 2
"Beans, Beans, (Beans)" (Introduction and Song)
 G. Earlcott
"I Love You So"[32] (Song)
 G. Rasely
 (*Lyrics by* Hartley Carrick.)
"All My Days Till End of Life" (Duet)
 H. Gunther, D. W. Ferrandou
"At Siesta Time"[33] (Song)
 H. Gunther, Chorus
 (*Music by* Grace Torrens. *Lyrics by* Arthur Anderson.)
"Any Time's Kissing Time" (Song)
 A. Mesmer
 (*Lyrics by* Frederick Norton.)
"My Fairy Castle in the Air"[34] (Duet)
 G. Rasely, H. Gunther
"The Song of the Scimitar" (Song)
 L. Braham, Chorus

ACT 3
"The Cobbler's Song" (Song)
 F. DeGregorio
"We Bring Ye Fruits" (Song)
 Fruit Girls
"From Cairo, Bagdad, Khorasan" (Song and Mannequin Parade)
 C. Hayes
"How Dear Is Our Day" (Song)
 A. Mesmer, D. W. Ferrandou
"Olive Oil" (Song)
 E. Cowles
Finale, Wedding Procession

PEEK-A-BOO

1919.21

A Musical Revue in Two Acts, 9 Scenes[35]. Book (sketches) by Jean Bedini. Music and lyrics by Michael Zelenko. Staged by Larry Ceballos. Scenery designed by Lee Lash Studios. Costumes designed by William H. Barnes. Produced by Jean Bedini. Opened 11 August 1919 at the Central Theatre and closed 23 August 1919 after 16 performances[36].

CAST: *Count Rolling Stone No Moss*: BOBBY CLARK. *Duke Few Clothes*: PAUL McCULLOUGH. *French Girl*: LALA SELBINI. *Buncum*, proprietor of the circus: JOE KELSO. *Ezra Grunt*, proprietor of the health farm: Jim DeForest. *Josh*, the village cut-up: HARRY KELSO. *Tom, Dick, Harry*, Sports of the Town: Peek-a-Boo Trio. *Count Bon Frit*: BEN GRINNELL. *Dolly Varden*, pet of the farm: MAY MYERS. *Beauty Fairfax*, queen of the circus: FRANKIE JAMES. *Tootsie*, the girl with a kick: Lillian McNeil. *Daisy*, the fashion-plate girl: EMMY BARBIER. *Country Girls and Boys*,

---

[30]Originally produced in New York 22 October 1917 at the Manhattan Opera House for 208 performances.

[31]Added for this revival.
[32]Added for this revival.
[33]Added for this revival.
[34]Not in 1917 Broadway production, though performed in London. Added for this revival.
[35]Originally produced under a vaudeville contract at the Columbia Theatre, New York 19 May-9 August 1919, but moved to a Broadway house to take advantage of the Actors' Equity strike. Many popular song interpolations not by Zelenko are included in the score, uncredited.
[36]Toured with Clark & McCullough as late as 1921 with a different score by Harry Archer and P. D. Cook.

Bridesmaids, Guests, Clowns, Gymnasts, Minstrels, Fashion-Plate Girls, Slave Girls, Nautch Girls and Tourists.

Act 1, Scene 1: The Health Farm, Down East. *Scene 2*: Outside of the Buncum Circus. *Scene 3*: The Circus Zoo. *Scene 4*: Interior of Circus. *Scene 5*: The Phonograph. *Scene 6*: Milday's Boudoir.

Act 2, Scene 1: Interior of the Gymnasium on the Health Farm. *Scene 2*: Deck of the Good Ship, "All Wet." *Scene 3*: A "Persian Garden."

ACT 1

"Our Health Farm" (Opening Chorus)
    Ensemble
"Circus Comes to Town"[37]
    Principals, Girls
"When the Preacher Makes You Mine"
    Peek-a-Boo Trio, F. James, Miss Drew, E. Barbier
"Baby Blue"
    E. Barbier, Girls
    (*Music by* Jean Schwartz. *Lyrics by* William Jerome.)
A Song
    B. Clark, P. McCullough
Revival of "Robert E. Lee"
    M. Myers, Girls
The Village Band
    Village Cut-Ups
Specialty
    F. James
Wedding Medley
    Bridesmaids, Grooms
"Rube Wedding"
    M. Myers, Company
Fun with Dice
    B. Clark, P. McCullough, J. Kelso
"Dixie Jubilee"
    M. Myers, Miss Drew, Girls
A Bit of Harmony
    Peek-a-Boo Trio
"Milady's Boudoir"
    The Four Little Maids
Specialty
    The Three Rosebuds
"Floating Down the Amazon"
    E. Barbier
"Vanities" (Finale)
    Entire Company
ACT 2
"Physical Culture Girls" (Opening Chorus)
    Ensemble
Yodeling Specialty
    M. Myers
Specialty
    Kelso Brothers
"The Old Light"
    B. Grinnell
"Bon Jour, Marie"
    F. James, Girls
Specialty
    B. Clark, P. McCullough
"(Take Me to) The Land of Jazz"
    L. McNeil, Girls
    (*Music by* Pete Wendling. *Lyrics by* Bert Kalmar and Edgar Leslie.)
"In a Persian Garden"
    Ensemble
Dance D'Orient
    L. McNeil
"Ramtah"
    Vernie
"Peek-a-Boo" (Finale)
    Entire Company

---

[37]Most likely the same as "Circus Is Coming to Town," Music and Lyrics by Irving Berlin, introduced in EVERYTHING, 1918.

1919.22

HAPPY DAYS

A Mammoth Musical Spectacle in Three Acts, 16 Scenes. Book (sketches) and lyrics by R. H. Burnside. Music by Raymond Hubbell. Entire production staged under the personal direction of R. H. Burnside. Costumes designed by Will R. Barnes and Marie Cook. Lighting by Joseph Elsner. Orchestra conducted by Raymond Hubbell. Musical director, A. J. Garing. Orchestrations by Frank Saddler. Produced by Charles Dillingham. Opened 23 August 1919 at the Hippodrome, suspending performances 28 August 1919 for the Actors' Equity strike; resumed performances 1 September 1919 and closed 15 May 1920 after 452 performances.

CAST: BELLE STORY, ALBERT FROOM, VERA BAILEY, JOSEPH PARSONS, ARTHUR GEARY, HENRY MALLIA, MAUDE MALLIA, CLYDE COOK, CHARLES BART, BERT NAGLE, WILLIAM WILLIAMS, THOMAS COLTON, JOSEPH FROHOFF, ARTHUR HILL, BERT BOWLEN, ALICE NASH, EDNA NASH, CHINCO and KAUFMAN, ELIZABETH COYLE, THE AGOUSTS (Alfred, Alice, Emile, Louise, Paul), 'HAPPY' JACK LAMBERT, VALODIA VESTOFF, BERT LEVY, HATTIE TOWNE, THE GREAT HANNEFORD FAMILY (Edwin "Poodles," Grace, etc.), THE FOUR AMARANTHS (Mary, Tina, Jennie, Hannah), LALLA SELBINI, HARTLEY, THE PEREZOFFS, MINNIE KAUFMAN, DANE CLAUDIUS, LILLIAN SCARLET, VENETIAN QUARTETTE, WILLIAM A. WESTON, MAY GERALD, HELEN CARR and DOROTHY GATES (World's Most Daring Diving Venuses).

Eddie Russell, Misha Fremzo, Alfred Harrison, Sylvia Stone, Cissie Hayden, Frances Mann, Inez Bauer, William Ricardo, Harry Ward, Andrew Byrne, James Byrne, John Byrne, Charles Ravel, Thomas Keenan, Steve Miaco, Albert Alberto, Bobbie Hale, Charles Oro, Benjamin Lewis, Helen Shoreits, Florence Pray, Gertrude Meek, Emma Christy, Louise Beautora, Mattie Vance, Fritzie deRoss, Alice Poole, Marie DeYoung, Adele Hart, Effie Langill, Ethel Whitney, Ethel McCarthy, Stella Clare, Bert Moore, John Abbott.

Act 1, Scene 1: The Kiddies' Dormitory. *Scene 2*: Fairyland. *Scene 3*: When We Were Kids. *Scene 4*: At the Circus. *Scene 5*: A Book Store. *Scene 6*: The Artists Studio. *Scene 7*: The World's Derby.

Act 2, Scene 1: A Flower Store. *Scene 2*: A Street Scene. *Scene 3*: A Chinese Cabaret Restaurant. *Scene 4*: Inside the Hippodrome. *Scene 5*: In Any Community. *Scene 6*: Somewhere in Songland. *Scene 7*: The Hall of Colors.

Act 3, Scene 1: The Golden City. *Scene 2*: The Magic Grotto.

ACT 1
Scene 1
"Let's Go to Fairyland" (Song)
    A. Nash, E. Nash, Pajama Girls
"Jazz-time City" (Song)
    J. Frohoff, B. Bowlen, A. Froom, W. Williams, Chorus
    A Nurse: V. Bailey. *Puck*: C. Cook. *Mr. Calico*, a visitor: B. Nagle. *Maria*: T. Colton. *Thomas*: A. Hill. *The Little Singer*: A. Nash. *Another Little Singer*: E. Nash. *Mr. Sand Man*: J. Lambert. *Mr. Dream Man*: V. Vestoff. (And) All the Children.
Scene 2
"Love Is Very Wonderful" (Song)
    B. Story
"Be a Party at the Party Tonight" (Song)
    J. Lambert, Chorus
Specialties
    The Four Amaranths, C. Cook, M. Mallia, L. Selbini, M Kaufman
    The Fairy Queen: B. Story. *Puck*: C. Cook. *Mr. Sand Man*: : J. Lambert. *Mr. Dream Man*: : V. Vestoff. *Cupid*: H. Towne. And Fairies, Elves, Sprites, Animals, Fliers, etc.
Scene 3
"Don't You Remember Those School Days?" (Song)
    J. Parsons, M. Gerald, Chorus
Scene 4
Powers' Performing Elephants
Scene 5
Opening Chorus to Scene
    W. Williams, C. Cook, A. Froom, Chorus
"Happy Days"
    J. Lambert, Chorus
    Puck, the Mischief Maker: C. Cook. *The Pied Piper*: A. Geary. *Mr. Shakespeare*: A. Froom. *The Mad Hatter*: H. Mallia. *Simple Simon*: C. Bart. *Peck's Bad Boy*: J. Lambert. *The Watchman*, Father Time: W. Williams. *Uncle Tom*: J. Frohoff. *The Fat Boy*: B. Bowlen. And Heroes, Heroines, Villains, Adventuresses, Fairytales.
        Storybook Characters: The Tin Woodman: E. Russell. *Robin Hood*: M. Fremzo. *Uncle Tom*: J. Frohoff. *Abanazer*: A. Harrison. *Red Riding Hood*: S. Stone. *Fairies from Midsummer Night's Dream*: E. Coyle, C. Hayden,

F. Mann, I. Bauer. *Cinderella*: M. Amaranth. *Evangeline*: T. Amaranth. *Little Eva*: J. Amaranth. *Polly of the Circus*: H. Amaranth. *Rip Van Winkle*: W. Ricardo. *Lord Nelson*: H. Ward. *William Penn*: A. Byrne. *John Quincy Adams*: James Byrne. *Admiral Dewey*: John Byrne. *Benjamin Franklin*: C. Ravel. *Richard III*: W. Weston. *Tom Thumb*: T. Keenan. *Hendrik Hudson*: S. Miaco. *Henry VIII*: A. Alberto. *Père Marquette*: A. Hill. *Rob Roy*: B. Hale. *Napoleon*: A. Agoust. *Abraham Lincoln*: C. Oro. *Robinson Crusoe*: B. Lewis. *DuBarry*: H. Shoreits. *Cleopatra*: V. Bailey. *Sappho*: F. Pray. *Salome*: E. Christy. *Thelma*: L. Beautora. *Charlotte Corday*: M. Vance. *Helen of Troy*: F. de Ross. *Ophelia*: A. Poole. *Juliet*: M. DeYoung. *Dolly Varden*: A. Hart. *Tess of the D'Urbervilles*: E. Langill. *Cigarette*: E. Whitney. *Lady Jane Grey*: E. McCarthy. *Marie Antoinette*: S. Clare. *Mme. Butterfly*: B. Moore. *Oliver Twist*: J. Abbott.

Scene 6

One Minute Sketches

B. Levy

Scene 7

"Life's a Race"

J. Lambert, Entire Chorus

ACT 2

Scene 1

"The Stately American Rose" (Song)

J. Parsons, Chorus

Specialties

The Four Amaranths, V. Vestoff, C. Hayden, D. Smyth, E. Coyle, F. Mann, S. Stone, I. Bauer

"The Marriage of the Lily and the Rose" (The Lily and the Rose)(Song)

B. Story, Chorus

Scene 2

Dancing Specialty

C. Cook

Scene 3

The Chinese Jazz Band

Specialties

Chinco & Kaufman, The Agousts, Selbini, Hartley, The Perezoffs, W. A. Weston

"My Sing Song Girl" (Song)

B. Story, A. Geary, Entire Chorus

Scene 4

The Great Hanneford Family of thrilling bareback riders, introducing Edwin Hanneford—"Poodles"

Scene 5

"The Call of the Sixties"

D. Claudius, L. Scarlet

Scene 6

"Somewhere There's Some Girl" (Somewhere There's a Girl)(Song)

A. Geary, Chorus

Scene 7

"I've Found the Girl That I've Been Looking For" (Song)

J. Parsons, Entire Company

ACT 3

Scene 1

"Beautiful Golden Land" (Song)

B. Story, Chorus

Specialties

Venetian Quartette, Disappearing Divers and the Wonderful Water Girls, H. Carr, D. Gates

Scene 2

Grand Finale

B. Story, Entire Company

1919.23   SEE-SAW

A Musical Comedy in Two Acts, 3 Scenes. Book and lyrics by Earl Derr Biggers. Music by Louis A. Hirsch. Staged by John McKee. Dances arranged by Julian Alfred. Scenery designed by Frank Gates and Edward A. Morange. Costumes by Madame Faibisy, Spencer & Co., Finchley (men's). Lighting by Joseph P. Wilson. Orchestra under the direction of Max Steiner. Produced by Henry W. Savage. Opened 23 September 1919 at the George M. Cohan Theatre and closed 29 November 1919 after 89 performances.

CAST (in order of appearance): *Helen*: ELIZABETH HINES. *Billy Meyrick*: GUY ROBERTSON. *Captain Starboard*: Horace M. Gardner. *Harkins*: FREDERICK GRAHAM. *Lord Harrowby*: CHARLIE BROWN. *Kinkaid*: John H. McKenna. *Cleo Ray*: Helen Bolton. *Spencer Meyrick*: George Barbier. *Aunt Mary*: Jeanette Lowrie. *Cynthia Meyrick*: DOROTHEA MACKAYE. *Jephson* (of Lloyds): Charles Esdale. *Richard Minot*: FRANK CARTER. *Henry Trimmer*: CHARLES MEAKINS. *Bell Boy*: Jimmie Parker. *Bird Byron*: Byron Hallstead.

Ella, Lindley, Dancers: Ella Danaher, Dorothy Smoller. *Girls of the Wedding Party* (12): *Dorothy*: Dorothy Whitmore. *Eleanor*: Eleanor Livingstone. *Ruth*: Ruth Parker. *Kathleen*: Kathleen Carroll. *Sydney*: Sydney Reynolds. *Florence*: Florence Brown. *Dorothy*: Dorothy Gilbert. *Rose*: Rose Stone. *Helen*: Helene Travis. *Gwen*: Gwen Monteir. *Marie*: Marie Boulais. *Connie*: Connie Madison. *Boys of the Wedding Party* (5): *Walter*: Walter Bellinger. *Theodore*: Theodore Bellinger. *Wesley*: Wesley Totten. *Jerry*: Jerry Walsh. *Fred*: Fred Ryker.

Act 1: On board the steam yacht "*Lilith. .*"

Act 2, Scene 1: Courtyard of Florida Hotel. Five days later. *Scene 2*: The same, next morning.

ACT 1

"This Is the Life"

Ensemble

"A World Full of Girls"

E. Hines, G. Robertson, Girls

"When You Come Near Me, I Feel All of a Ooh!"[38]

H. Bolton, F. Graham

"Join the Navy"

G. Robertson, Sailors

"You'll Have to Find Out"

D. Mackaye, C. Brown, Girls

"I'll Take Care of Him"

F. Carter, C. Brown, C. Esdale

"Happiest Moments" (The Happiest Moment I've Ever Known)

D. Mackaye, F. Carter

Finale

Entire Company

ACT 2

Scene 1

"See-Saw"

D. Whitmore, Company

"Good-bye—Hello"

C. Meakins, Girls

"When Two Hearts Discover"

D. Mackaye, F. Carter

"Senorita—Senorita"

H. Bolton, E. Hines, C. Meakins, G. Robertson

"When You Dance"

D. Mackaye, Company

Finale

Entire Company

Scene 2

"Southern Melody"

Twentieth Century Four

"I Just Want Jazz"

J. Parker

"Peep-Peep"

E. Hines, G. Robertson, Girls

Dancer: E. Danaher. *Bird Voices*: B. Hallstead.

Finale

Entire Company

1919.24   ROLY-BOLY EYES

A Musical Comedy in Three Acts. Book and lyrics by Edgar Allan Woolf. Music by Eddy Brown and Louis Gruenberg. Staged by Will H. Smith. Production built by James Van Sickler, painted by Beaux Arts Studio. Costumes by Paul Arlington Inc., H. Mahieu & Co.[39] Dances by Margaret Edwards. Musical director, Gene Salzer. Produced by John Cort. Opened 25 September 1919 at the Knickerbocker Theatre and closed 27 December 1919 after 108 performances.

---

[38]Dropped for subsequent tour.

[39]Mahieu's costumes were for Act 3.

CAST: *Judge Robert Warren:* Hugh Chilvers. *Mrs. Robert Waren:* Adora Andrews. *Ida Loring:* QUEENIE SMITH. *Myron S. Rentham,* junior member of law firm of Warren and Rentham: Harry Anson Truax. *Mrs. Penelope Giddings,* three times merrily widowed: Maud Leone. *Dorothy Giddings,* her daughter by the first: Kate Pullman. *Buddie Montrose,* for whom no dancing steps are too difficult: EARL GATES. *Michael Fiachetti,* an inventor: Frank Martins. *Peter,* the old gardener of Warren Estate: H. D. Blakemore. *Dances by* Margaret Edwards. *Billy Emerson,* the singer: EDDIE LEONARD. *Billy Rice,* the comic: EDDIE MAZIER. *Billy West,* the female impersonator: BERT McGARVEY. *Fred W. Wambold,* the manager: G. Clayton Frye. *Kitty Rice,* wife of the troupe: MAY BOLEY. (*Specialty:* Honeydew Octette.)

Ensemble: Misses Peggy Wilson, Neida Snow, Grace Hall, Agnes Hall, Anita Francesca, Estelle Francesca, Jean Troupman, Beth Hardy, Florence McKenna, Hazel Hammond, Tempe Evans, Blanche Terrell, Jessie Lorraine, Fay Celeste, Aileen White, Cecil Harrington, Helen Dale, Louise Mayorga.

Act 1: Garden of Judge Warren's country home. Apple Blossom Time in the Berkshires.

Act 2: Sleeping porch of the same. Seven o'clock the next morning.

Act 3: Sleeping porch of the same. Autumn.

ACT 1

Opening Chorus
"When Dancing's a Profession"
E. Gates, Chorus
"Old Fashioned Flowers"
Q. Smith, Girls
"Ain't It Sweet"
Ensemble
"Biddle-be-boo"
E. Mazier, Chorus
"The Blushing, Gushing Widow"
B. McGarvey
"That Minstrel Man"
E. Leonard, Company
"Just a Girl, Just a Boy"
Q. Smith, E. Leonard
"When They Do the Dippy Dooliums"
E. Gates, Girls
"Minstrel Serenade"—Finale
E. Leonard

ACT 2

"A Matron's Good Night's Sleep" (Introduction and Song)
M. Leone, Girls
"I Want a Man"
K. Pullman, E. Gates
"All Washed Up"
M. Boley
"Your Voice I Hear"
Q. Smith, E. Leonard, Chorus
Finale—The Rehearsal—
Ida's Dance
(Q. Smith)
"Spring"
M. Boley
Arabian Eccentrique (dance)
M. Edwards
Billy Emerson's Songs:
(E. Leonard)
["(Roll Dem) Roly Boly Eyes"
(*Music and Lyrics by* Eddie Leonard.)]
"Ida! Sweet as Apple Cider"
(*Music by* Eddie Munson. *Lyrics by* Eddie Leonard.)]

ACT 3

"Harvesters' Song"
Honeydew Octette
"Where Is She?"
Ensemble
"A Bungalow for Two"
K. Pullman, E. Gates, Chorus
"(Ida, Sweet as) Apple Cider" (reprise)
Honeydew Octette
Finale

1919.25

HITCHY-KOO OF 1919

A Musical Revue in Two Acts, 15 Scenes[40]. Book (sketches) by George V. Hobart. Music and lyrics by Cole Porter. Staged by Julian Alfred. Orchestrations by Stephen Jones. Scenery by H. Robert Law Studios and Joseph Urban. Costumes by Paul Arlington, Inc., Brooks Uniform Company, Anna Spencer and J. M. Gidding & Company. Orchestra under the direction of Cassius M. Freeborn. Produced by Raymond Hitchcock. Opened 6 October 1919 at the Liberty Theatre and closed 22 November 1919 after 56 performances.

CAST: RAYMOND HITCHCOCK, LUCILLE AGER, SYLVIA CLARK, CHARLES HOWARD, WANETA MEANS, RUTH MITCHELL, CHARLES WITZELL, MAURICE BLACK, MARK SULLIVAN, JOSEPHINE MacNICOLL, JAMES J. DOHERTY, ELAINE PALMER, JOSEPH [Joe] COOK, LILLIAN KEMBLE COOPER, URSULA O'HARE, HENRI LINGEN, CHIEF EAGLE HORSE, PRINCESS WHITE DEER, CHIEF OS-KO-MON, BLANCHE GERVAIS, BETTY (Dopey) BRAUN.

Ballet: Ruth Valle, Peggy Ellis, Betsy Ross, Flo Howard, May Rowan, Mildred Mann. *Pierrots:* Arvis Smith, Edith Howard, (Zuleika) Anastasia Reilly, Marie (Babe) Stanton, Darry Welford, Marie Clare. *Soubrettes:* Mabel Martin, Catherine Byron, Alice Earl, Viola Kane, Violet Francis, Frances Ney. *Lorgnettes:* Emlee Haddone, Victoria Gale, Phoebe Crossley, Lillian Martin, Sascha Beaumont, Edith Lindholme. *Pull-Backs:* Viola Degnon, Phyllis Hooper, Gladys Harrison, Asta Valle, Gertrude Miller, Florence Stone. *High Hats:* Pauline Delorme, Myrtle Stuart, Hazel Purdy, Ann Walsh, Mae Green, Ursula Dale. *Principal Dancers:* Mildred Keats, ELEANOR SINCLAIR, FLORENCE O'DENISHAWN, BILLY HOLBROOK, Simone Cochet, Aleta Dove. *Joeys:* Charles Howard, Joseph Cook, Mark Sullivan, James J. Doherty, Maurice Black, Henri Lingen, James Duffy, Fred Sweeney, Chief Eagle Horse. *The Boys:* Harry Edwards, Dan Brennan, Donald Roberts, Charles Witzel, Edward Garrett, Roger Davis.

Act 1, Scene 1: Introduction. *Scene 2:* Hitchy's Garden of Roses. *Scene 3:* Reubenville. In front of the grocery store, now. *Scene 4:* Waiting. *Scene 5:* Steamship Office, London—A Passenger to India. *Scene 6:* Pocahontas. A Woodland Glade in Virginia.

Act 2, Scene 1: A Temple in India—A Jade Phantasy. *Scene 2:* A Temple in. . . . . ?? *Scene 3:* A Corner in the Ritz. *Scene 4:* A Telephone Threnody. *Scene 5:* Old New York—Time 1850. *Scene 6:* The Barber Shop. *Scene 7:* Modes, Past and Present. *Scene 8:* Touching On and Appertaining To. *Scene 9:* Hitchy's Home in Great Neck, Long Island.

ACT 1[41]

Scene 1

Introduction
Proprietor of Hitchy Koo 1919: R. Hitchcock. *Stage Manager:* C. Howard. *His Daughter:* J. MacNicoll. *Ballet, Pierrots, Soubrettes, Lorgnettes, Pull-Backs, High Hats, Principal Dancers, Joeys, The Boys.*
"Pagliacci"[42] (Song)
L. K. Cooper, E. Palmer, U. O'Hare
"When Black Sallie Sings Pagliacci" (Song)
R. Mitchell, Chorus
"I Introduced" (Presentation Song)
R. Hitchcock
Introducing for the first time: W. Means, B. Gervais, U. O'Hare, B. Braun.

Scene 2

"Hitchy's Garden of Roses" (In Hitchy's Garden)(Song)
L. K. Cooper
Wild Rose: P Delorme. *White Rose:* J. MacNicoll. *Yellow Rose:* E. Palmer. *Killarney Rose:* M. Keats. *Japanese Tea Rose:* E. Sinclair. *American Beauty Rose:* F. O'Denishawn. *Lightning Bugs:* S. Cochet, A. Dore. *Hitchy's Rose Buds.*

Scene 3

"When I Had a Uniform On"[43] (Demobilization Song)
J. Cook, E. Sinclair, Cirls
Emsden Doolittle, postmaster, supervisor, mayor, etc.: R. Hitchcock. *Citronella,* his daughter: S. Clark. *Petroleum,* his son: C. Howard. *Hannah,* their aunt: W. Means. *Ezra Poindexter,* the grocer: C. Witzell. *Selvage Higginbottom,* a fire fighter: M. Black. *Marcy Greenbrier,* a citizen: M. Sullivan. *Seth Peters,* a citizen: J. J. Doherty. *I. Golightly,* a stranger: J. Cook. *City Girls:* B. Gervais, B. Braun, U. O'Hare. *Ethel:* A steed, formerly a circus performer, now retired. *Fore:* B. Holbrook. *Aft:* H. Lingen.

---

[40]The third in the annual series of revues produced by Raymond Hitchcock beginning in 1917.
[41]Added to the show for subsequent tour:
  Specialty
    Bert Savoy and Jay Brennan
[42]Dropped for subsequent tour.
[43]Dropped for subsequent tour.

Scene 4

"I've Got Somebody Waiting" (Song)

R. Mitchell

Assisted by Misses R. Valle, M. Mann, A. Reilly, V. Degnon, M. Stanton, M. Rowan, B. Ross, A. Smith.

Scene 5

Lord Bridgewalters, a tourist: R. Hitchcock. *Clerk*: J. Cook. *French Tourists*: E. Sinclair, B. Gervais. *Commissionaires*: M. Sullivan, D. Roberts.

Scene 6

"Song of the Sun"[44]

Chief Eagle Horse

Characteristic Indian Dance

Princess White Deer, E. Sinclair

Indian Jazz Dance

Princess White Deer

Assisted by Indian Maidens, Bluebird, Moonlight, Chasing Rainbow.

Dance of the Five Senses

Chief Os-Ko-Mon

(Assisted by) Chorus of Indians, Pirates, More Indians, More Pirates.

"Peter Piper" (Song)

R. Hitchcock, Ensemble

"The Sea Is Calling" (Song)

R. Mitchell, Pirates

Prince Opodildoc, the chief's son: C. Howard. *Kod-Liv-Royl*, a medicine Man: M. Sullivan. *Sault-Sen-Senna*, another: J. J. Doherty. *A Warrior*: Chief Eagle Horse. *Rock-in-the Head*, historian of the Tuscaroras: J. Cook. *Flappers from Tuscarora's Fashionable Finishing School* (4): *Cute-As-Kanbe*, *Luv-Lee_Kretta*, *Oso-Bew-Full*, *Lum-Pa-Shuga*: L. Ager, E. Sinclair, W. Means, U. O'Hare. *H. J. Powhatan*, king of the Tuscaroras: M. Black. *Princess Pocahontas*, his daughter: S. Clark. *Willie Growbig*, a midshipman: R. Mitchell. *Captain John Smith* of Merrie England: R. Hitchcock.

ACT 2

Scene 1

A Jade Phantasy

The Jade Goddess: F. O'Denishawn. *The Vandal*: B. Holbrook. *The Beggar Girl*: E. Sinclair. *The Priestesses*: J. MacNicoll, E. Palmer. *Priestesses, Worshippers, etc.*

Scene 2

"I'm an Anaesthetic Dancer"[45]

S. Clark

Scene 3

"My Cosy Little Corner in the Ritz" (My Cozy Little Corner. .)

R. Hitchcock

Guests at the Ritz: W. Means, M. Keats, E. Palmer, B. Gervais, B. Braun, J. MacNicoll.

Scene 4

In the Ritz[46]

Mazie, an operator: R. Mitchell. *An Operator*: U. O'Hare. *Page Boy*: C. Witzell. *Harvey Windsor*, a number seeker: J. Cook.

Scene 5

"An Old-Fashioned Garden"

L. K. Cooper

Dance

L. K. Cooper, J. MacNicoll, E. Palmer

Old-Fashioned Misses: V. Degnon, P. Hooper, V. Gale, F. Stone, A. Valle, G. Miller. *Old-Fashioned Beaux*: H. Edwards, D. Brennan, R. Davis, H. Lingen, E. Garrett, C. Witzel.

Scene 6

Melville, the Barber: R. Hitchcock. *Murphy*, the bootblack: J. Cook. *Madge*, the manicure: S. Clark. *Marie*, the sister: L. K. Cooper. *Mr. Moose*, the customer: C. Howard. *Mickey*, the brush boy: E. Sinclair. *Monsieur O'Hair*, in a big hurry: M. Sullivan.

Scene 7

"A Little Bear" (My Little Bear Skin)(Song)

R. Mitchell

(*Music by* Neysa McMein. *Lyrics by* Sally J. Farnum.)

Dance

R. Mitchell, M. Stanton, R. Valle, Girls

Stone Age Modes: *Beaver*: A. Valle. *Ermine*: B. Braun. *Rabbit*: V. Gale. *Sables*: P. Delorme. *Lynx*: A. Reilly. *Fox*: S. Beaumont. *Bear*: M. Stanton. *Modes of Today*: *Tailored*: G. Harrison. *Negligee*: G. Miller. *Tennis*: D. Welford. *Chiffon*: B. Gervais. *Riding Habit*: M. Stuart. *Motor Coat*: A. Walsh. *Mole*: R. Valle.

Scene 8

Mr. Brush, chairman and president: M. Black. *A Moving Picture*: J. Cook. *Prof. Reigndroppe*, prohibitionist: R. Hitchcock. *Percy Penpoint*, a playwright: C. Howard. *Three Buck Dancers*: B. Holbrook, Princess White Deer, D. Brennan. *Signor Tincanni*, who must-a seeng-a: J. J. Doherty.

Scene 9

"Bring (Me) Back My Butterfly"

L. K. Cooper, Entire Chorus

Dance

M. Keats, Girls

Hitchy Koo 1919 Medley

Entire Company

1919.26 # HELLO, ALEXANDER

A Musical Extravaganza in Two Acts, 9 Scenes. Book by Edgar Smith and Emily M. Young. (Based on the musical farce "The Ham Tree," book by George V. Hobart, Music and lyrics by Jean Schwartz and William Jerome.) Music by Jean Schwartz. Lyrics by Alfred Bryan. Dance numbers staged by Allan. K. Foster. Costumes designed by S. Zalud. Orchestra under the direction of Samuel Lehman. Produced by the Messrs. Shubert. Opened 7 October 1919 at the 44th Street Theatre and closed 22 November 1919 after 56 performances[47].

CAST: *Colonel Winslow*, a railway magnate of New York and New Orleans: DAN QUINLAN. *Lieutenant Jack Winslow*, his son, of U.S. Air Service: JACK CAGWIN. *Aunt Kittie*, the Jazz Queen: SOPHIE TUCKER. *Ethel Winslow*, his daughter: JEAN TYNE. *Captain Chomendley*, of the British Air Service: EARL RICKARD. *"Toots" McSwat*, bush leaguer and casual vaudevillian: FRANK WESTPHAL. *Joe*, a servant: Joe Hamilton. *Simons and Slocum*, minstrels: BOYLE and BRAZIL. *Officers in the U.S. Service* (4): *Lieutenant Clay*: Fred Bliss. *Lieutenant Allen*: Murray Salet. *Lieutenant Gordon*: Harry Forsyeth. *Lieutenant Jackson*: Martin Griffin. *"Muggs" Casey*: Charles Judson. *Spike Murphy*, a minstrel: Eddie Flynn. *Jim Delilly*, a minstrel: Larry Clifford. *Bull Conners*, mate of *The Crescent City*: Joe Hamilton. *Leader of Crowd*: Milton Pohs. *Maude Bradbury*, friend of Ethel: ROSIE QUINN. *Mrs. Carter*: Gabriel Grey. *Gloria Carter*: Chick Barrymore. *Eczema Johnson*, Mulatto manicurist in hotel barber shop: MABEL ELAINE. *Red Cross Workers* (3): *Susie Folsom*: Lottie Reick. *Mary Lawton*: Peggy Dempsey. *Mollie Bragg*: Dot Mantell. *Aunt Jeminma*: VIVIAN HOLT. *Mammy Chloe*: LILLIAN ROSEDALE. *Alexander*, man of all work and former minstrel: JAMES McINTYRE. *Henry Clay Jones*, proprietor of the Ever-Ready Colored Minstrels: THOMAS K. HEATH.

Ladies of the Ensemble: Peggy Dempsey, Esther Miller, Marjorie Bush, Trixie Warren, May Battie, Helen McCarthy, Evelyn Sintae, Catherine Rich, Kitty Boylan, Mollie McCabe, May Irving, Esther Shannon, Pearle Betts, Pearle Matthews, Winnie Ward, Bertine Farnsworth, Florence Winn, Lillian Simms, Marie Valerio, Marty Lee, Jean Lee, Marie Nason, Florence DeBard, Elinore Rosedale, Helen DeWitt, Renee Genere, Betty Squire, Marion Comfort, Marion Stockwell, Edith Mainard, Irmelda LaMort, Edith Rook, Beth McKendry, Mae Millar. *Gentlemen of the Ensemble*: Charles Judson, Joe Mullen, Eddie Scanlon, Sid Williams, John Golden, Al Ladden, John Mills, Jack Fleming.

Act 1, *Scene 1*: Tampa Bay Hotel. *Scene 2*: Exterior of Aviation Camp. *Scene 3*: Grand Minstrel First Part. Jones' Ever-Ready Minstrels.

Act 2, *Scene 1*: Levee, on the Mississippi. *Scene 2*: At the Drug Store. *Scene 3*: Villa of Colonel Winslow. *Scene 4*: In New Orleans. *Scene 5*: Jazz Valley. *Scene 6*: Ballroom, Colonel Winslow's Mansion, New Orleans.

ACT 1

Scene 1

"Tampa Bay" (Opening Ensemble)

Boyle and Brazil, Ensemble

"Up in the Air"

J. Tyne, R. Quinn, J. Cagwin, E. Rickard

"Baseball"

C. Barrymore, Baseball Players

"Pantomime Baseball"

F. Westphal, C. Judson, E. Flynn

---

[44]Music and lyrics not by Cole Porter.
[45]Dropped for subsequent tour.
[46]For subsequent tour, scene moved to Act 1, and the following song added:

"Sentimental Song and Dance"

George Moore, E. Palmer, F. O'Denishawn, B. Holbrook

---

[47]Direction uncredited; subsequent tour first credits Jack Bell as Stage Director, then later Allan K. Foster as Director. Settings uncredited.

"Why Are Chickens So High?"[48]
S. Tucker
(*Music and Lyrics by* Carey Morgan.)
"(Those) Dixie Melodies" (Minstrel Parade)
Boyle and Brazil, Ensemble

Scene 2
"Give Me the South (All the Time)"
R. Quinn, J. Cagwin

Scene 3
Opening Introduction
Entire Company
"Glad I'm from Dixie"
L. Clifford
"Tell Me"
J. Cagwin, Quartette
"(Sweet) Hawaiian Moonlight"[49]
V. Holt, L. Rosedale
(*Music and Lyrics by* Harold G. Frost and F. Henri Klickmann.)
"Roses of Picardy"
V. Holt, L. Rosedale
(*Music by* Haydn Wood. *Lyrics by* Frederick E. Weatherley.)
"Rock-a-Bye Baby"
E. Rickard
Introduction of Alexander and Henry Jones (MacIntyre & Heath)
"At the High Brown Baby's Ball"[50]
S. Tucker
And Her Seven Kings of Syncopation: Pete Quinn, Gus Arronheim [Arnheim],
Dan Alvin, Bobby Jobes, Irving Rothschild, Joe Gold, Ben Shapiro.
"(When Those) Mason and Dixon Minstrels (Hit Town)"
Boyle and Brazil, Entire Company

ACT 2
Scene 1
"Ma Curly Headed Baby"
V. Holt, L. Rosedale
(*Music and Lyrics by* G. H. Clutsam.)
"Ghost of Old Black Joe"
M. Elaine, Boyle and Brazil, Ensemble
"Swanee Glide"
M. Elaine, Ensemble

Scene 2
Specialty
Boyle and Brazil

Scene 3
"Two Lips from Georgia"
J. Cagwin
"Old Fashioned Rag"
J. Tyne, R. Quinn, J. Cagwin, E. Rickard, Ensemble

---

[48]Replaced for subsequent tour by:
"Everybody Is Crazy About Dixie"
Esther Walker (Aunt Kittie)
(*Music by* Will Donaldson and Rubey Cowan. *Lyrics by* Bobby Jones.)
[49]Holt & Rosedale's specialties varied during the run and tour to include:
"That Naughty Waltz"
(*Music by* Sol Levy. *Lyrics by* Edwin Stanley.)
"Hiawatha's Melody of Love"
(*Music by* George W. Meyer. *Lyrics by* Alfred Bryan and Artie Mehlinger.)
"Sweet and Low"
[50]Replaced during the New York run by: (reinstated for tour)
"Beale Street Blues" (from SHUBERT GAIETIES OF 1919)
Gilda Gray (Gloria Carter)
(*Music and Lyrics by* W. C. Handy.)
"Yazoo Rag"
M. Elaine, Boyle and Brazil
Later in the tour, a new song replaced "At the High Brown Baby's Ball":
"I Am Always Falling in Love with the Other Fellow's Girl"
Gracie Deagon (Aunt Kitty)
(*Music by* George W. Meyer. *Lyrics by* Irving Caesar.)

Scene 4
"(Pretty Up, Pretty Up,) Pretty Baby"
R. Quinn, Ensemble
Scene 5
Specialty[51]
S. Tucker
["Oh How Much Good He Does Me"
"When It Comes to Lovin' the Girls I'm Way Ahead of the Times"
(*Music by* Jack Glogau. *Lyrics by* Murray Kissen and Joe Burns.)]
Scene 6
"Yip! Yip! (Mardi Gras Ball)"
Ensemble
Grand Finale
Company

APPLE BLOSSOMS

1919.27

An Operetta in a Prologue and Two Acts. Book and lyrics by William LeBaron. (Based on the novel 'Un Mariage sous Louis XV' by Alexandre Dumas.) Music by Fritz Kreisler and Victor Jacobi. Staged by Fred G. Latham and Edward Royce. Settings designed by Joseph Urban. Costumes designed by Lichtenstein, Brooks Uniform Company. Orchestra under the direction of William Daly. Produced by Charles Dillingham. Opened 7 October 1919 at the Globe Theatre and closed 24 April 1920 after 256 performances.

CAST (in order of appearance): *Julie*: Rena Parker. *Polly*: Juanita Fletcher. *Molly*: ADELE ASTAIRE. *Johnny*: FRED ASTAIRE. *Nancy*: WILDA BENNETT. *Lucy Fielding*: Pauline Hall. *Anabel Mason*: Hilah Reeder. *Richard (Dickey) Stewart*: PERCIVAL KNIGHT. *Mail Carrier*: Frank Snyder. *Chauffeur*: George Fordyce. *George Winthrop Gordon*: HARRISON BROCKBANK. *Harvey*: ROY ATWELL. *Phillip Campbell*: JOHN CHARLES THOMAS. *Mrs. Anne Merton*: FLORENCE SHIRLEY. (*Dance Specialty*: Alan Fagan.)
School Girls, Bridesmaids, etc.: Misses Helen Arlington, Pauline Hall, Helene Allen, Genevieve Willament, Lillian White, Gladys White, Ruth White, Grace O'Connor, Hilah Reeder, Phyllis Munday, Marie Ayres, Kathleen Conway, Peggy Parmalee, Edna Wheaton, Marie Walsh, Kathleen Errol, Veronique Banner, Loraine Nelson, Peggy Williams, Dorothy Harrigan, Eleanor Mathison, Esther Worth, Ruth Lee, Brenza Dugro. Messrs. Frank Snyder, H. Cornell, Edward Smith, C. Townshend, W. D. Smith, W. Dennis, I. Carter, L. Kristel, A. Blair, E. Barlab, B. Sheldon, H. Starrett.

The action takes place at the present time.

Prologue: Garden of Castle Hall School, Clifton-on-Hudson.

Act 1: At Phillip Campbell's House, near Fifth Avenue.

Act 2: The Ball Room.

PROLOGUE
Opening Chorus
J. Fletcher, Girls
(*Music by* Fritz Kreisler.)
"Brothers"
R. Parker, J. Fletcher, Girls
(*Music by* Victor Jacobi.)
"Who Can Tell?"
W. Bennett, Girls
(*Music by* Fritz Kreisler.)
"When You Are Mine"
W. Bennett, P. Knight
(*Music by* Victor Jacobi.)
"On the Banks of the Bronx"[52]
R. Parker, P. Knight
(*Music by* Victor Jacobi.)
Dance
F. Astaire, A. Astaire
(*Music by* Victor Jacobi.)
Finale:
Ensemble and Duet[53]
(*Music by* Victor Jacobi.)

---

[51]6 songs per opening night reviews.
[52]Dropped for subsequent tour. The Dance by Astaires was retained.
[53]Replaced during the run by:
"I'll Be True to You" (Ensemble and Song)
W. Bennett
(*Music by* Victor Jacobi.)

"Nancy's Farewell"
W. Bennett, J. Fletcher, R. Parker, H. Brockbank, P. Knight, Company
(*Music by* Fritz Kreisler.)

ACT 1

"The Marriage Knot"
R. Parker, R. Atwell
(*Music by* Fritz Kreisler.)

"When the Wedding Bells Are Ringing"
W. Bennett, Girls
(*Music by* Victor Jacobi.)

Dance
W. Bennett, A. Fagan

"Little Girls, Goodbye"
J. C. Thomas, Men
(*Music by* Victor Jacobi.)

"You Are Free"
W. Bennett, J. C. Thomas
(*Music by* Victor Jacobi.)

Finale:

Quintette and Phillip's Story
(*Music by* Fritz Kreisler.)

Ensemble
Company
(*Music by* Fritz Kreisler and Victor Jacobi.)

ACT 2

Ensemble
Chorus
(*Music by* Fritz Kreisler.)

"Star of Love"
W. Bennett, Girls
(*Music by* Fritz Kreisler.)

"A Girl, a Man, a Night, a Dance"
F. Shirley, Men
(*Music by* Fritz Kreisler.)

Dance [Tambourin Chinois]
F. Astaire, A. Astaire
[*Music by* Fritz Kreisler.]

"I Am in Love"
J. C. Thomas
(*Music by* Fritz Kreisler.)

"The Second Violin"
F. Shirley, P. Knight
(*Music by* Fritz Kreisler.)

Finale
Entire Company
(*Music by* Fritz Kreisler and Victor Jacobi.)

1919.28   THE LITTLE WHOPPER

A Musical Comedy Exquisite in Two Acts, 5 Scenes. Book by Otto A. Harbach. (Based on the film "Miss George Washington."[54]) Music by Rudolf Friml. Lyrics by Bide Dudley and Otto A. Harbach. Book staged by Oscar Eagle. Musical numbers staged by Bert French. Costumes by Harry Collins, Inc. under the personal supervision of Bert French. Stage settings painted by (Edward G.) Unitt and (Joseph) Wickes. Orchestra under the direction of Anton Heindl. Produced by Abraham Levy. Opened 13 October 1919 at the Casino Theatre and closed 3 April 1920 after 204 performances.

CAST (in order of appearance): *Janet MacGregor:* MILDRED RICHARDSON. *Miss Granville:* Nellie Graham-Dent. *Kitty Wentworth:* VIVIENNE SEGAL. *George Emmett:* SYDNEY GRANT. *John Harding:* HARRY C. BROWNE. *Harry Hayward:* Albert Obler. *James Martin:* Sidney Hall. *Oliver Butts:* W. J. Ferguson. *William, Robert:* WILTON SISTERS (Rose, May). *Judge MacGregor:* DAVID TORRENCE. *Mrs. MacGregor:* Lotta Linthicum. *Frances:* Lucille Williams. *Teenty:* ROSE WILTON. *Tonty:* MAY WILTON. *Jack Dodge:* Edward Tierney. *Edward Penfield:* Louis Coombs. *Fred Hood:* Birnie Prevost.
Ensemble: Inez Courtney, Florence Courtney, Irma Coigne, Edna Coigne, Norma Dale, Marie Astor, Vivian White, Florence Doran, Josie Carman, Tess Mayer, Lillian Drewry, Irene Duffy, Victoria Gardner, Hazel Flint, Doris Marquette, Eunice Sizer, Mabel Grete, Jean Rhodes.

[54]Released in November 1916 by Paramount. Authorship uncredited.

Act 1, Scene 1: Grounds of the Arlington Academy. Thursday, 11:00 A.M. *Scene 2:* Corridor of Blenheim Hotel, Philadelphia. Same day, 1:45 P.M. *Scene 3:* Harding's Rooms at The Blenheim. Same day, 2:00 P.M.

Act 2, Scene 1: The MacGregor Drawing Room, Baltimore. Next night, 10:00 P.M. *Scene 2:* The same. The following morning, 9:00 A.M.

ACT 1

"Oh, You Major Scales" (Opening Chorus)
M. Richardson, V. Segal, Ensemble
(*Lyrics by* Otto Harbach.)

"Twinkle Little Star"
V. Segal, Ensemble
(*Lyrics by* Otto Harbach.)

"Oh, What a Little Whopper"
N. Graham-Dent, Ensemble
(*Lyrics by* Otto Harbach.)

"'Round the Corner"
W. J. Ferguson, Wilton Sisters
(*Lyrics by* Otto Harbach.)

"I Have a Date"
S. Grant, H. C. Browne, Boys

"It Can't Be Wrong"
M. Richardson, V. Segal, H. C. Browne

"It's Great To Be Married"
V. Segal, H. C. Browne
(*Lyrics by* Otto Harbach.)

"Oh, What a Little Whopper"[55] (reprise)
D. Torrence

"I've Got to Leave You"
V. Segal, H. C. Browne, Ensemble

Finaletto
H. C. Browne

ACT 2

"I'm Lonely When I'm Alone"
R. Wilton, M. Wilton
(*Lyrics by* Otto Harbach.)

"The Kiss"
V. Segal, L. Linthicum, D. Torrence, H. C. Browne

"Snap Your Fingers"
S. Grant, R. Wilton, Ensemble
(*Lyrics by* Otto Harbach.)

"We May Meet Again" (reprise?)
S. Grant, V. Segal

"Sweet Dreams"
D. Torrence, Ensemble
(*Lyrics by* Otto Harbach.)

"There's Only One Thing to Do"
M. Richardson, H. C. Browne
(*Lyrics by* Otto Harbach.)

"Let It Be Soon"
R. Wilton, M. Wilton
(*Lyrics by* Otto Harbach.)

"Good Morning, All"
M. Richardson, Ensemble

Finale
Entire Company

1919.29   NOTHING BUT LOVE

A Smart Musical Comedy in Three Acts and a Prologue. Book and lyrics by Frank Stammers. Score (music) by Harold Orlob. Play staged by Frank Stammers. Musical ensembles arranged by David Bennett. Scenery designed by John Dudley. Gowns by Homer Conant; Miss Sunshine's costumes by Hickson. Orchestra under the direction of Max Hirschfield. Produced by Charles B. Maddock and Max Hart. Opened 14 October 1919 at the Lyric Theatre, moved 24 November 1919 to the 44th Street Theatre, and closed 6 December 1919 after 64 performances.

[55]Replaced for subsequent tour by:
"It's a Lie"
D. Torrence, L. Linthicum, V. Segal, Laura Arnold (Janet), H. C. Browne

CAST (in order of appearance): *Billy Marbury*: Easton Yonge. *Lucy Cotton*: MARION SUNSHINE. *June Marbury*: RUBY NORTON. *Allyn Hicks*: ANDREW TOMBES. *Doctor Tibbetts*: DONALD MEEK. *"His Majesty"*: Millicent Gleeman. *Drake*: ROBERT WOOLSEY. *Bella*, a maid: Florence Enright. *Mrs. Maud Winchester*: Arline Fredericks. *Teddy Winchester*: CLARENCE NORDSTROM. *Brooks*: Philip Bishop. *Stacey Adams*: John Roche. *Commodore Marbury*: STANLEY H. FORDE. *Fleming*: Jack McSorley. *Mignon*: Mignon Reed.

Friends of June Marbury: *Muriel*: Muriel Reilly. *Luvah*: Luvah Roberts. *Grace*: Grace Weeks. *Nell*: Nell Hall. *Rose*: Rose DeVere. *Jere*: Jere Fitzgerald. *Elizabeth*: Elizabeth Darling. *Gracie*: Gracie LaRue. *Josephine*: Muriel Wilson. *Betty*: Betty Warlow. *Alice*: Alice Fessenden. *Claire*: Claire Stevens. *Dorothea*: Dorothea King. *Beatrice*: Beatrice Darling. *Florence*: Florence Allen. *Kathryn*: Kathryn Kelly.

The action takes place in Miami, Florida, at the present time.

Prologue: Living Room of the Marburys.

Act 1: Same as Prologue. Six hours later.

Act 2: At the Yacht Club.

Act 3: Plaza Mrs. Winchester's Home.

ACT 1

"Dawn"

"Wonderful Man"
 A. Fredericks, R. Woolsey, Girls

"I'll Remember You"
 R. Norton

"Beware"
 A. Tombes, Girls

"When I Walk Out with You"
 M. Sunshine, C. Nordstrom

"Ask the Stars"
 A. Tombes, R. Norton, Girls

"When I Walk Out with You" (reprise)
 R. Norton

ACT 2

"Stop Waltz"
 J. Roche, M. Reed, E. Yonge, M. Sunshine, C. Nordstrom, Girls
 (*Staged by* J. J. Hughes.)

"It's Not What You Say"
 A. Tombes, C. Nordstrom, P. Bishop, S. H. Forde, D. Meek, R. Woolsey

"Some Other Time"
 R. Norton, J. Roche

"Ask the Stars" (reprise)
 R. Norton, A. Tombes

Finale
 Entire Company

ACT 3

"Moonbeams"
 R. Norton, Girls

"At the Shore"
 A. Tombes, Girls

Dance Eccentrique
 R. Woolsey

Finale
 Entire Company

1919.30   THE PASSING SHOW OF 1919

A Musical Revue in Two Acts, 14 Scenes[56]. Dialogue (sketches) and lyrics by Harold Atteridge. Music by Jean Schwartz, (Sigmund Romberg). Staged by J. C. Huffman. Dance numbers arranged by Allan K. Foster. Art director (settings design), Watson Barratt. Costumes designed by Cora MacGeachy, Homer Conant. Orchestra under the direction of Oscar Radin. Orchestrations by J. Bodewalt Lampe, James C. McCabe, Oscar Radin, Frank Tours. Produced under the personal direction of J. J. Shubert. Produced by the Messrs. Shubert. Opened 23 October 1919 at the Winter Garden and closed 5 June 1920 after 280 performances.

CAST: WALTER WOOLF, JACK DONNELLY, HARRY TURPIN, FRANK MARTIN, AVON COMEDY FOUR (Joe Smith, Charles Dale, E. Rash, Charles Adams), FRANKIE HEATH, LON HASCALL, JAMES BARTON, HAZEL COX, TILLIE BARTON, CHARLES ADAMS, KATHERINE WITCHIE, EDDIE MILLER, THE FOUR HALEY SISTERS (Grace, Bernice, Mabel, Lucille), RALPH RIGGS, JOHN CRONE, JOE OPP, GRACE KEESHON, OLGA COOK, BLANCHE RING, RATH BROTHERS [George, Dick], JAMES GRANT, CHARLES WINNINGER, REGINALD DENNY, Mlle. MADGE DERNY.

Show Girls: Dorothy Bruce, Mae Dealy, DeVeara Anguillira, Lola Taylor, Mildred Soper, Mabel Griswold, Madge McCarthy, Phoebe Lee, Helen Dempsey, Beatrice Lancois, Madeline Lombard, Virginia O'Sullivan, Carolyn Roland, Violet Weber, Mae Guiran, Muriel Knowles, Beth Elliott, Gertrude Lane, Ann Delmore, Helen Crawford, Betty Durland, Doris Evans, Kittens Moore, Margaret Hansel, Louise Wayne, Mary Kissell, Trixie Brunette, Peggy Merrimont, Bernice Page, Bobbie McCree, Maxine Robinson, Thea Thompson. *Dancing Girls*: Orilla Smith, Phyllis Miller, Beverly Miller, Anna Berry, Jewel Berry, Dolores Mendez, Jean Cameron, Maisie Elliott, Hazel Frisbie, Ella Foster, Irene Held, Flo Summerville, Pauline Dakla, Isabel Holland, Beatrice Jennings, Adele Devereaux, Marie Gray, Yvette Reals, Marion Dunham, Dorothy Jackson, Violet Ayres, Jean Woods, Josephine Kernan, Lucille Pryor, Juliet Strahl, Isabel McLaughlin, Ruby Howard, Polly Mayer, Burtress Dietch, Peggy Furst, Shirley Gallop, Mary Eaton, Regina Lorraine, Millie Edwards, Marie LeMar, Pearl Seeton. *Gentlemen*: Jack Donnell, Billy Creedon, Julian Martin, Roland Woodruff, George Schall, Arthur Becker, Ray Oddo, Walter Baker, Nicholas Kane, Jegger Marr, Jack Jerome, James Nichols, Ralph Roehm.

Act 1, Scene 1: Mount Olympus—The Home of the Gods. *Scene 2*: The Border Lying Between Canada and America. *Scene 3*: Back in Salem—During the Puritanical Days. *Scene 4*: Mischief in Your Eyes. *Scene 5*: The Road to Destiny. *Scene 6*: In Florence à la Jest. *Scene 7*: King Solomon's Kitchen. *Scene 8*: The Court of King Solomon.

Act 2, Scene 1: Water Lily. *Scene 2*: A Love Boat in China. *Scene 3*: The Doctor Shop. *Scene 4*: A Summer Garden. *Scene 5*: The Melting Pot of America's Popular Tunes. *Scene 6*: Ball Room.

ACT 1[57]

Scene 1

Prologue:

"Wine Ballet"
 V. Burke, Grecian Girls

Opening Chorus
 Mellette Sisters, Ensemble

"Seven Ages of Women"
 L. Hascall, Seven Ages
  Bacchus: W. Woolf. *Zeus*: H. Turpin. *Hestia*: B. Elliott. *Falstaff*: L. Hascall. *Robin Hood*: H. Cox. *Rip Van Winkle*: C. Adams. *Omar Khyaam*: E. Miller. *Neptune*: R. Riggs. *Bevo*: J. Crone.

Scene 2

"Molly Malone"
 O. Cook, Some Irish Beauties
 (*Music by* Chris Schonberg. *Lyrics by* Hale Byers.)

"Tumble Inn" (Tumble In)
 W. Woolf, F. Heath, 4 Haley Sisters, Tumble Inn Girls
 (*Music by* Jean Schwartz. *Lyrics by* Harold Atteridge.)

"Good-bye"
 Avon Comedy Four
  Lightning Bill Mahoney: J. Opp. *Molly*, his daughter: O. Cook. *Bill*: L. Hascall. *Alf*: R. Woodruff. *Bert*: J. Grant. *William Prince*: R. Denny. *Photographer*: J. Donnelly. *Waiter*: F. Martin. *Comfort*: F. Heath. *Mr. Comeon*: J. Barton. *Miss Flirt*: T. Barton. *Four Haley Sisters*: Grace, Bernice, Lucille, Mabel Haley. *Dick*: W. Woolf. *Avon Comedy Four*: *Isadore*: J. Smith. *Herman*: C. Dale. *James*: E. Rash. *Henry*: C. Adams. *Constable*: J. Crone. *First Gent*: G. Schall. *Second Gent*: J. Donnelly. *Third Gent*: R. Woodruff. *Fourth Gent*: N. Kane.

Scene 3

"In Salem"
 W. Woolf, R. Riggs, K. Witchie, Witch Dancers
  Mrs. Spritely: K. Witchie. *Mr. Sprite*: R. Riggs. *A Witch*: B. Elliott

Scene 4

"(You've Got) Mischief in Your Eyes"
 O. Cook, Some Mischievous Girls
 (*Music and Lyrics by* Benjamin Hapgood Burt.)

---

[56]The Ninth in the annual series of revues which began in 1894, produced since 1912 by the Messrs. Shubert. Billed as the Winter Garden's Annual Revue.

---

[57]Specialty interpolated during the run or tour as per published sheet music:

"Honolulu Eyes"
 Avon Comedy Four
 (*Music by* Violinsky. *Lyrics by* Howard Johnson.)

Scene 5

"Road to Destiny"

R. Denny, M. Haley, G. Haley, B. Hale

William Prince: R. Denny. *Spirit of the Left Road*: G. Haley. *Spirit of the Main Road*: B. Haley. *Spirit of the Right Road*: M. Haley.

Scene 6

"Dreamy Florence"

H. Cox, Florentine Beauties

(*Music by* Jean Schwartz and Sigmund Romberg. *Lyrics by* Harold Atteridge.)

"Neapolitan Jazz"

E. Miller, Mellette Sisters, Some Neapolitan Beautie

William Prince: R. Denny. *Spirit*: B. Elliott. *Madonna*: G. Keeshon. *John Giametto*: B. Ring. *Fatchio*: R. Oddo. *Lionel Neri*: C. Winninger. *Callandra*: W. Woolf. *Doctor*: R. Riggs.

Scene 7

Plate Dance

Winter Garden Oriental Chefs

"Orient"

O. Cook, Winter Garden Chorus

(*Music by* Jean Schwartz. *Lyrics by* Alfred Bryan.)

[Hungarian Restaurant Scene]

Major Domo: J. Opp. *Avon Comedy Four*: *Chef*: J. Smith. *High Chef*: C. Dale. *First Chef*: C. Adams. *Second Chef*: E. Rash.

Scene 8

"The King's Favorite"

M. Derny

"Shimmy à la Egyptian"[58]

J. Barton, Winter Garden Company

The King's Favorite: M. Derny. *Spirit of the Main Road*: B. Haley. *William Prince*: R. Denny. *Rosie*: G. Keeshon. *First Wife*: F. Heath. *Second Wife*: T. Barton. *Page*: B. Elliott. *Ephraim*: L. Hascall. *King Solomon*: C. Winninger. *Courier*: J. Crone. *The Queen of Sheba*: B. Ring. *A Hand Maiden*: V. Burke. *The King's Dancers*: R. Mellette, H. Mellette. *Mr. Who's This*: J. Barton.

ACT 2

Scene 1

"Water Lily"

H. Cox, Water Lilies

Scene 2

"Love Boat" (In a Love Boat with You)

E. Miller, O. Cook, R. Riggs, K. Witchie

(*Music by* Jean Schwartz and Sigmund Romberg. *Lyrics by* Harold Atteridge.)

"Miss Unruly"

B. Ring

"Sing Song Girl"

W. Woolf, F. Heath, Some Sing Song Girls

(*Music by* Sigmund Romberg.)

An Idol: K. Witchie. *The Idol's Worshipper*: R. Riggs. *Oolong Toy*: E. Miller. *Molly*: O. Cook. *William Prince*: R. Denny. *Spirit of the Right Road*: M. Haley. *Lo San Kee*: L. Hascall. *Auctioneer*: H. Turpin. *First Merchant*: J. Crone. *Second Merchant*: J. Grant. *First Slave*: B. Elliott. *Second Slave*: M. Knowles. *Ming Toy*: B. Ring. *Charlie Young*: C. Winninger. *Me So Kee*: W. Woolf. *Sing Song*: F. Heath.

Scene 3

The Doctor Shop (Doctor Kronkheit sketch)

Avon Comedy Four

Scene 4

America's Popular Athletes

G. Rath, D. Rath

"(It's Always) Summertime at the Winter Garden"

B. Ring, C. Winninger, Skating Girls

(*Music by* Jean Schwartz. *Lyrics by* Alfred Bryan.)

Albert: R. Denny. *Jack*: W. Woolf. *Josephine*: F. Heath. *Kid Sponge*: J. Barton. *Charlie*: J. Opp. *Kid Bucket*: L. Hascall.

Scene 5

"America's Popular Tune" (America's Popular Song)

E. Miller, Winter Garden High Steppers

(*Music by* Jean Schwartz and Sigmund Romberg. *Lyrics by* Harold Atteridge.)

[58]Replaced for subsequent tour by:

"(You Can't Get into Heaven Unless You Have a) Jazz Band"

J. Barton, Winter Garden Company

Scene 6

"Lovable Moon"

Avon Comedy Four, 4 Haley Sisters

(*Music by* Jean Schwartz. *Lyrics by* Harold Atteridge.)

"A la Hockey"

J. Barton

Ignatz: L. Hascall. *Jim*: J. Barton. *William Prince*: R. Denny. *Molly*: O. Cook. *Jack*: W. Woolf. *Josephine*: F. Heath. *Lionel Neri*: C. Winninger. *John Giametto*: B. Ring.

1919.31

BUDDIES

A Comedy of Quaint Brittany (with Music) in Two Acts and an Epilogue. Book by George V. Hobart. Music and lyrics by B. C. Hilliam. Orchestra under the direction of B. C. Hilliam. Produced by Arch Selwyn and Edgar Selwyn. Opened 27 October 1919 at the Selwyn Theatre and closed 12 June 1920 after 259 performances[59].

CAST (in order of appearance): *Biff*, the sergeant: Robert Middlemas. *Buddy*: Bert Melville. *Hank*: George B. George. *Abie*: Adrian H. Rosley. *Johnny*: Horace A. Ruwe. *Pete*: Frank R. Woods. *Rube*: Richard Cramer. *Babe*: ROLAND YOUNG. *Sonny*: DONALD BRIAN. *Orderly*: Douglas Newbury. *Madame Benoit*: CAMILLE DALBERG. *Marie*: ANNETTE MONTEIL. *Babette*: PAULINE GARON. *Julie*: PEGGY WOOD. *Alphonse Pettibois*: EDOUARD DURAND. *Louise Maitland*: MAXINE BROWN.

Act 1: The courtyard of the home of Madame Benoit, somewhere in Brittany.

Act 2: Same as Act 1. The same afternoon.

Epilogue: Interior of the barn of Madame Benoit's place. The evening of the same day.

ACT 1

"Italie"

A. Monteil, P. Garon, Buddies

"Please Learn to Love"

P. Wood

"The Wail of the Tale of the Long Long Trail"

D. Brian

"Darling I—"[60]

R. Young, D. Brian, Buddies

ACT 2

"My Indispensable Girl"[61]

M. Brown, D. Brian

"Fairy Tales" (Cinderella Tale)

P. Wood

EPILOGUE

"Twilight Song"[62]

H. A. Ruwe, Buddies

"Hello Home!" (Hullo Home)

P. Wood, Buddies

"To Be Together is the Thing"[63]

M. Brown, D. Brian

1919.32

FIFTY-FIFTY, LTD.

A Musical Comedy in Three Acts. Book by Margaret Michael and William Lennox. Based on the farce 'All the Comforts of Home' by William Gillette.

[59]Stage direction, settings, costumes uncredited. For subsequent tour, stage direction credited to Richard Pitman.

[60]Replaced for subsequent tour (1921) by:

"I Never Realized"

Wallace Eddinger [Babe], D. Brian, Buddies

(*Music and Lyrics by* Melville Gideon [and Cole Porter].)

[61]Replaced for subsequent tour (1921) by:

"Altogether Too Fond of You"

Maxine Brown, D. Brian

(*Music and Lyrics by* Melville Gideon.)

[62]Replaced for subsequent tour (1921) by:

"Buddies Ensemble"

Buddies

[63]Replaced for subsequent tour (1921) by:

"We'll Settle Down in Washington Square"

M. Brown, D. Brian

(*Music and Lyrics by* Melville Gideon.)

Music and lyrics by Leon DeCosta. Interpolated numbers by Arthur Swanstrom and Carey Morgan. Staged by Walter Brooks. Settings designed by Mabel A. Buell. Gowns, costumes designed by Akramere, Inc. Orchestra under the direction of George Hirst. Produced under the personal supervision of Anton F. Scibilia. Produced by the Scibilia Theatrical Enterprises. Opened 27 October 1919 at the Comedy Theatre and closed 29 November 1919 after 40 performances.

CAST (in order of appearance): *Phyllis Wyndham*: Marguerite McNulty. *Rosabelle Wyndham*: Elsie Douglas. *Katy*: Margaret Michael. *Monty*: WILLIAM LENNOX. *Judge Geoffrey Wyndham*: LYNN PRATT. *Kenneth Patterson*: BARRETT GREENWOOD. *Fluffy LaGrange*: GERTRUDE VANDERBILT. *Marian Carter*: Norma Hark. *Poultney Steele*: Frank Bernard. *Professor Josephus Dabney*: JOHN SLAVIN. *Cornwallis Crosby*: HERBERT CORTHELL. *Phineas Tanner*: Frank Walsh. *Minerva Crosby*: Jean Newcombe. *Claire Crosby*: DORIS ARDEN. *Dolly Manners, Angelica Manners*: Gosman Twins. (*Specialty*: Dorothy Quintette.)

Girls of Midnight Scrambles: *Toodles Gray*: Alice Cavanaugh. *Miss Debath*: Ann Lemeau. *Giovannina Yon*: Elsie Young. *Tommy Gallagher*: Wilma Bruce. *Pauline Bell*: Lillian Lee. *Betty Roberts*: Beatrice Moran. *Claire Campbell*: Kathryn Richards. *Frederica Ashton*: Rose King. *Polly Leeds*: Fannie Driscoll. *Cissie Merideth*: Marian Driscoll.

The action takes place at Judge Wyndham Home, New York City, at the present time.

Act 1: Reception Room. A summer afternoon.

Act 2: Second Floor. Late the same summer. Morning.

Act 3: Reception Room. Evening.

ACT 1
"Daddy" (Any Kind of a Daddy Will Do)
G. Vanderbilt, Girls
(*Music by* Carey Morgan. *Lyrics by* Arthur Swanstrom.)
"Along the Hudson"
J. Slavin, B. Greenwood, W. Lennox
(*Music by* Carey Morgan. *Lyrics by* Arthur Swanstrom.)
"Girls"
H. Corthell, Girls
"Silence of Love"
B. Greenwood, D. Arden

ACT 2
"Spooky Nights"
G. Vanderbilt, Girls
Dance Specialty
F. Bernard
"Fifty-Fifty" (I'll Fifty-Fifty With You)
H. Corthell, G. Vanderbilt
(*Music by* Carey Morgan. *Lyrics by* Arthur Swanstrom.)
"Honeybunch" (Honey Bunch)
B. Greenwood, D. Arden, Girls
"(Is It) the Girl or Is It the Gown?"
G. Vanderbilt, Girls
Ensemble
Company
(*Music by* Carey Morgan. *Lyrics by* Arthur Swanstrom.)

ACT 3
"Nanette"
N. Hark
"Persia" (Dance Specialty)
Dorothy Quintette, B. Greenwood
"(Home Is Never Home, Sweet Home) Without a Beautiful Girl"
B. Greenwood, D. Arden
(*Music by* Carey Morgan. *Lyrics by* Arthur Swanstrom.)
"The Argentines, the Portuguese and the Greeks"
H. Corthell
(*Music by* Carey Morgan. *Lyrics by* Arthur Swanstrom.)
"(I'm a) Jazz Vampire"
G. Vanderbilt, Girls
(*Music by* Carey Morgan. *Lyrics by* Arthur Swanstrom.)
"Every Little Girlie Has a Way All Her Own"[64]
B. Greenwood, Gosman Twins
Finale
Entire Company

---

[64]Also known as "Every Little Girl Has a Way of Her Own."

1919.33   JUST A MINUTE

A Musical Entertainment (Comedy) in Two Acts. Book and lyrics by Harry L. Cort, George E. Stoddard and Harold Orlob. Music by Harold Orlob. Staged by Robert Marks. Scenery painted by H. Robert Law Studios. Costumes designed by Paul Arlington, Inc. Orchestra under the direction of Arthur H. Gutman. Produced by John Cort. Opened 27 October 1919 at the Cort Theatre and closed 29 November 1919 after 40 performances.

CAST (in order of appearance): *The Song Girls*: Niobe Warwick, Mae Terresfield. *The Saleslady, Miss Noyes*: MERLE HARTWELL. *The Demonstrators, The Monarck Four*: Messrs. Green, Murphy, Fenn, Curren. *The Girl, Dorothy May*: MABEL WITHEE. *The Other Girl, Margaret Gibson*: MONA CELETE. *The Porter, Earl*: Billy Clark. *The Aunt, Mrs. Tom Collins*: MAY VOKES. *The Executor, Robert Fulton*: WELLINGTON CROSS. *The Trouble, Will Tell*: GEORGE F. MOORE. *The Pilot, Captain Ebb Tide*: PERCY POLLOCK. *The Bathing Girl, Miss Dippe*: Virginia Clark. *The Dancers*: Morin Sisters.

Ladies of the Ensemble: Misses Niobe Marwick, Mae Terresfield, Virginia Clark, Cecil Boylan, Dorothy Donlon, Gertrude Defour, Agatha DeBussy, Lu Leathers, Marie Bellaire, Mildred Stevens, Jean Berkly, Phyllis Edwards, Christine Adair, Anna Hartwig, Alice Lallor, Mildred Kay.

Act 1: The Boardwalk, Atlantic City.

Act 2: Private Yacht "*Sweet Stuff*." Evening.

ACT 1[65]
Scene Music
Types
"Some Other Girl" (Song)
M. Hartwell
"Some Other Girl" (Refrain)
M. Withee, M. Celete
"(I'm Going To Be) Lonesome" (Song)
G. M. Moore, M. Withee
"Wonderful Day" (Song)
G. M. Moore, Girls
"Because You're Different" (Duet)
M. Celete, W. Cross
"Roll Me" (Double Octette)
Girls
Specialty Dance
Miss Morin
Eccentric Dance
Miss Morin
"No Birdie Ever Flew So High" (Song)
M. Vokes, P. Pollock
"Grandfather's Clock" (Duet)
M. Withee, W. Cross
Finale—Scenic Music—"Some Other Girl," "Lonesome"

ACT 2
Opening—Melody
Guests
"Some Other Girl" (Refrain)
M. Withee, W. Cross
"Just Imagine" (Song)
G. F. Moore, M. Withee

---

[65] Song order was revised after opening. "No Birdie Ever Flew So High" moved to follow Eccentric Dance. For subsequent tour, Act 1 was totally revised, and the following were added, replacing "Lonesome," "Because You're Different" and "Grandfather's Clock":
Opening, On the Boardwalk
Types
"The Five Profiteers"
Pearl Evans, Helen Lowe, Irma Marwick, Beatrice Darling, Delano Dell
"The One You've Been Waiting For"
M. Withee, Grace Moore (Margaret), Tom Dingle (Fulton), Arthur Millar (Tell)
"Little By Little"
M. Withee, A. Millar, Company
"When You Dance with a Certain Girl"
M. Withee, A. Millar, Company

"To Make Them Fall" (Song)
  M. Vokes
"I'll Say I Will" (Song)
  M. Withee, W. Cross, M. Celete
Specialty Dance
  Morin Sisters
"Girl I Want to Call Wife" (Song)
  W. Cross, Girls, M. Celete
"Over and Over Again" (Trio)
  P. Pollock, W. Cross, G. F. Moore
Finale
  Company

1919.34 ## THE LITTLE BLUE DEVIL

Musical Farce in Three Acts. Book and lyrics by Harold Atteridge. (Based on the play 'The Little Blue Mouse' by Clyde Fitch, adapted from Julius Horst and Alexander Engel's comedy "Der blaue Maus"). Music by Harry Carroll. Staged by Oscar Eagle. Ensembles and numbers (staged) by Bert French. Scenery by (D. Frank) Dodge and (William E.) Castle. Miss Lorraine's gowns by Henri Bendel. Orchestra under the direction of Eugene Salzer. Produced by Joe Weber. Opened 3 November 1919 at the Central Theatre and closed 3 January 1920 after 74 performances.

CAST (in order of appearance): *Tom, Dick, Harry*, Bookkeepers: Jack Geier, Edward Bisland, James Buckley. *Billie*, an Office Boy: Eddie Cox. *Freddie*, an Elevator Boy: James Wheeler. *Mary*, Head Office Stenographer: Eleanor Griffith. *Stella*, a Stenographer: Frances Dunlop. *Pansy*, wife of Augustus Rollett: Anne Sands. *Augustus Rollett*, secretary to Mr. Lewellyn: BERNARD GRANVILLE. *Paulette Divine*, The Little Blue Devil: LILLIAN LORRAINE. *Mrs. Lewellyn*: Eleanor Gordon. *Mr. Lewellyn*, President of the Inter-County Railroad: Wilfred Clarke. *Philip Scarsdale*: JACK McGOWAN. *George Wallus*, Mrs. Rollet's Father: EDWARD MARTINDEL. *Lizzie*, Paulette's maid: Marion Mosby. *Purkiss*, an Auctioneer: W. H. Powers. *Moss*, Assistant to Purkiss: Eddie Cox. *Tiney*, a dancer: Katherine Hatfield. *An Old Man*, one of the buyers: Jack Geier. *A Maid*: Elsie Lange. *First Porter*: James Buckley. *Second Porter*: Edward Bisland. *Annie*. Maid to Mrs. Rollett: Eleanor Griffith. *Police Officer*: W. H. Powers. (*Dance Specialty*: Donald Kerr, Effie Weston.)

Paulette's Friends: Miss Dac Crandall, Jule Anderson, Florence Dixon, Kathleen Kendall, Elsie Lange, Anita Mason, Billie Stone, Marienne Taylor. *Little Blue Devils*: Alice Ridnor, Jea Thomas, Winnie Dunne, Frances Dunlop. *The Typewriters*: Carroll Shirley, Dorothy Harrison, Betty Brown, Frances Dunlop, Alice Ridnor, Winnie Dunn, Jean Thomas, Virginia Lee.

Act 1: Office of the New York Inter-County Railroad. 9:30 A.M.

Act 2: "The Little Blue Devil's" Apartment. Evening. Same day.

Act 3: The Home of Augustus Rollett. Evening. Next day.

ACT 1
  "The Office Blues"
    E. Cox, Employees
  "Hello, Everybody"
    L. Lorraine, Her Friends
  "Just a Kiss"
    B. Granville, L. Lorraine
  "I'm So Sympathetic"
    J. McGowan
  "Shimmy—Shaking—Love"
    B. Granville, L. Lorraine, W. Clarke, E. Gordon, Ensemble
ACT 2
  "The Secret Service Club"
    Ensemble
  "The Little Blue Devil" (You Little Blue Devil)
    J. McGowan, L. Lorraine, Blue Devils
  "Reprise Sympathetic"
    L. Lorraine, J. McGowan
  "A Stroller in Dreamland"
    B. Granville
  "Cuckoo Town"
    B. Granville, K. Hatfield, Girls
  "Dancing Shoes"
    L. Lorraine, Ensemble
  "Auction Rag"
    E. Cox, W. H. Powers, Ensemble

ACT 3
  "The Butler's Fox Trot"
    White Way Trio, Servants
  Dance Specialty
    D. Kerr, E. Weston
  "Peter Pan"
    J. McGowan, A. Sands
  "Omar Khayyam"
    B. Granville
  Finale
    Company

1919.35 ## THE MAGIC MELODY

A Romantic Musical Play in Two Acts and a Prologue. Book and lyrics by Frederic Arnold Kummer. Music by Sigmund Romberg. Staged by J. C. Huffman and J. Clifford Brooke. Musical numbers staged by Allan K. Foster. Art director, (scenery and costume design by) Willy Pogany. Orchestra under the direction of Charles Previn. Orchestrations by Oscar Radin. Produced by Max R. Wilner and Sigmund Romberg. Opened 11 November 1919 at the Sam S. Shubert Theatre and closed 17 March 1920 after 143 performances.

CAST (in order of appearance): Prologue: *Anita*: Jeannette Kahn. *Delarose*: Marie McConnell. *Teresa*: Adele Freeman. *Salvatore*: Walter Armin. *Pietro*: Gus Stevenson. *Antonio*: Louis Morrell. *Beppo Corsini*: CHARLES PURCELL. *Lisa*: Bertee Beaumonte. *Gianina*: Julia Dean. *Beppino*: Billie Roth. *Postman*: Jack Manning. *Bianca*: Jean Rebera. *Maria*: Nellie Crawford.
The Play: *Carmencita*: FAY MARBE. *Prince Vladimir*: ROBERT BENTLEY. *Lady Chester*: AILEEN POE. *Captain Arthur Stanley*: CHARLES PURCELL. *Isabel de Vernon*: RENEE DELTING. *Richard Palmer Adams*: EARL BENHAM. *Mrs. Fishbacker*: FLAVIA ARCARO. *Sophie*, her daughter: CARMEL MYERS. *Sir Reggie Chester*: TOM McNAUGHTON. *Lulu*: Dorothy Wallace. *Cluclu*: Marie McConnell. *Madame Jessonda*: JULIA DEAN. *Marquis de Vernon*: Emile de Varny. *Fifine*: BERTEE BEAUMONTE. *Melody of Dance*: LOIS LEIGH. *Lola Winwood*: FAY MARBE. *Salvatore*: Walter Armin. *Mademoiselle Cherie*: Legotie Hoover. *Mademoiselle Nitouche*: Marion Dixon. *Mademoiselle Fleurie*: Claire Hodgson. *Mademoiselle Marguerite*: Mary Cunningham. *Mademoiselle Yvonne*: Eleanor Leigh.

Guests of Madame Jessonda: Misses Mary Cunningham, Eleanor Leigh, Harriet Gustine, Vivian Ward, Elizabeth Drew, Estelle Garry, Kathryn Gobet, Billy Sheridan, Frances Broeker, Helen French. *Guests of Prince Vladimir*: Misses Eleanor Tierney, Jean Rogers, Fina Orloff, Marion Ward, Eileen Adair, Beatriz Nisbet, Jean Riley, Grace Moore, Ruth Henry. *Dancers from the Marigny Theatre*: Misses Frisco DeVere, Loretta Morgan, Jean Rebera, Billy Fisher, Sylvia Ford, Billy Booker, Alma Morrison, Madeline LeVene, Nellie Crawford, Dorothy Wallace, Lucille Moore, Marie Bernard, Claire Benedict, Adele Freeman. *Gentlemen in Waiting*: Gus Stevenson, Harry Burdick, Herbert Carleton, Joseph Carleton, Charles Wallace, Charles Schilling, Jack Dewey, Charles Gilbert, Leonard Feiner, Charles Lauben.

Prologue: A Sicilian Fishing Village. Twenty years ago.

Act 1: Reception Room in Prince Vladimir Potemsky's House, Paris. The present time.

Act 2: Garden of Madame Jessonda's Villa, Versailles, France. Afternoon of the day following.

PROLOGUE
  Opening
    J. Kahn, M. McConnell, A. Freeman, J. Rebera, N. Crawford, Ensemble
  "Love Makes the World Go Round"
    C. Purcell
  Dance
    B. Beaumonte
  "Gianina"
    C. Purcell
ACT 1[66]
  Opening Chorus
    Ensemble
  Dance Session[67]
    F. Marbe

---

[66]For subsequent tour, Dance Session, "Melody of Dance," Dance Eccentrique and "Night of Love" were dropped, and the latter replaced by:
  "Come on and Dance With Me"
    T. McNaughton, F. Arcaro
  "When You're in Right with the Right Little Girl"
    Emma Haig (Mademoiselle Claire)
[67]Dropped late in the run.

"Lips, Lips, Lips"
  C. Purcell, R. Delting, A. Poe
"Two's Company, Three's a Crowd"
  C. Purcell, R. Delting, E. Benham, C. Myers
"I Am the Pasha"
  T. McNaughton, D. Walalce, M. McConnell, Ensemble
"Melody of Dance"
  L. Leigh
  (*Lyrics by* Alex Gerber.)
Dance Eccentric
  L. Leigh, E. Benham
"Night of Love"
  R. Delting
"Down by the Nile"
  B. Beaumonte
Dance Orientale
  B. Beaumonte
"Once Upon a Time" (The Magic Melody)
  C. Purcell, R. Delting
Finale
  C. Purcell, R. Delting, Ensemble
ACT 2[68]
"We Are the Fixers"
  E. Benham, D. Wallace, M. McConnell, L. Hoover, M. Dixon, C. Hodgson, Ensemble
Waltz Fantastic[69]
  F. Marbe
"Dream Girl Give Back My Dream (to Me)"
  C. Purcell, R. Delting
"Melody of Dance"[70] (reprise)
  L. Leigh
"We Take It, Just Take It from You"[71]
  F. Marbe
  (*Lyrics by* Alex Gerber.)
Dance Vampire
  B. Beaumonte
"The Little Church Around the Corner"
  E. Benham, C. Myers, Ensemble
  (*Lyrics by* Alex Gerber.)
"Once Upon a Time" (reprise)
  C. Purcell, Ensemble
Finale
  Ensemble

1919.36 # IRENE

A Musical Comedy in Two Acts, 7 Scenes. Book by James Montgomery. (Based on the play "Irene O'Dare" by James Montgomery.) Music by Harry Tierney. Lyrics by Joseph McCarthy. Staged by Edward Royce. Ladies costumes designed by Lucille, Ltd.; men's costumes designed by Finchley. Scenery by H. Robert Law Studios, Clifford Pember. Orchestra under the direction of Gus Salzer. Produced by the Vanderbilt Producing Company (Carle Carleton). Opened 18 November 1919 at the Vanderbilt Theatre and closed 18 June 1921 after 675 performances.

CAST: *Donald Marshall*: WALTER REGAN. *Robert Harrison*: Hobart Cavanaugh. *J. P. Bowden*: ARTHUR BURCKLY. *Lawence Hadley*: John B. Litel. *Clarkson*: Walter Croft. *Irene O'Dare*: EDITH DAY. *Helen Cheston*: EVA PUCK. *Jane Gilmour*: Gladys Miller. *Mrs. Marshall*: FLORENCE MILLS. *Eleanor Worth*: Bernice McCabe. *Mrs. O'Dare*: DOROTHY WALTERS. *Mrs. Cheston*: Lillian Lee. *Madame Lucy*: BOBBIE WATSON.
  Ladies of the Ensemble: Constance Melville, Josephine Kernell, Vivian Davidson, Ethel Kinley, Adele Ormiston, Marion Dockerill, Erica Mackay, Margaret Moore,

Betty DeGrasse, Helen Miller, Arden Benlian, Dorothy Whitmore, Cornelia Burchell, Irene Enright, Edna Ross. *Gentlemen of the Ensemble*: George Eising, Abner Barnhart, Robert Burns, John McSorley, Harry Blake, Alfred Watson, Al Watson, Austin Clarke.

Act 1, *Scene 1*: The Veranda, Donald Marshall's Home, Long Island. *Scene 2*: The O'Dare Home, New York City. *Scene 3*: The Veranda. Two days later. (Law.)
Act 2, *Scene 1*: The Tenement. Two months later. *Scene 2*: The Garden of Bowden's Home, New York City. *Scene 3*: The Tenement. After midnight. *Scene 4*: The Garden of Bowden's Home. (Pember.)

ACT 1
  Opening
    Ensemble
  "Hobbies"
    B. McCabe, Ensemble
  "Alice Blue Gown"
    E. Day
  "Castle of Dreams"
    B. McCabe, Ensemble
  "The Talk of the Town"
    B. Watson, E. Puck, G. Miller
  "To Be Worthy (of You)"
    E. Day, Ensemble
  Finale
    Company
ACT 2
  Opening
    A. Burckly, Ensemble
  "We're Getting Away With It"
    B. Watson, W. Regan, H. Cavanaugh, E. Puck, G. Miller
  "Irene"
    E. Day, Ensemble
  "To Love You"
    A. Burckly, E. Day
  "Sky Rocket" (Skyrocket)
    E. Day, Ensemble
  "(The) Last Part of Any Party" (The Last Part of Ev'ry Party)
    E. Puck, G. Miller, Ensemble
  "There's Something in the Air"
    Ensemble
  Finale

1919.37 # LINGER LONGER LETTY

A Comedy with Music in Three Acts. Book by Anna Nichols. Music by Alfred Goodman. Lyrics by Bernard Grossman. Musical numbers staged by Will H. Smith. Costumes by Schneider-Anderson. Orchestra under the direction of Alfred Goodman. Produced under the personal supervision of Oliver Morosco[72]. Produced by Oliver Morosco. Opened 20 November 1919 at the Fulton Theatre and closed 21 January 1920 after 69 performances.[73]

CAST: *Letty*: CHARLOTTE GREENWOOD. *Nancy*: Eleanor Henry. *Mayme*: Olga Roller. *Juliet*: MARJORIE McCLINTOCK. *Mrs. Brewster*: Louise Mink. *Ethelmay*: Bernice Hirsch. *Roberta*: Frances Victory. *Marie*: Virginia Travares. *Jim*: OLIN HOWLAND. *Walter*: ARTHUR HARTLEY. *Colonel*: Cyril Ring. *Lazelle*: France Bendsten. *Father*: Oscar Figman. (*Specialty Dancer*: Marguerite Severn.)
  Ensemble: Misses Edna Renard, Alice Knowlton, Margaret Kearns, Faith Belmont, Marjorie Wall, Polly Watkins, Ann Greenway, Dora Duby, Halcyon Chambers, Vera Bradley, Mary Shepard, Marjorie Clements, Helen Trainor, Myra Lane, Eva Warrington, Ethel Hobart, Virginia Lancier, Sadie Howe. Messrs. Robert Cowles, Boris Scott, Harold Williams, Frank Brooks, Roule Wilder, Jack Grieves, Harold Abbey.

Act 1: Kitchen of the Larkin Home.
Act 2: Letty's Boudoir.
Act 3: Lawn Fete and Dance at the Larkin Home.

ACT 1
  "Ssh!—Ssh!—Ssh!"
    B. Hirsch, F. Victory

---

[68]Added for subsequent tour (after "The Little Church Around the Corner"):
  "The Three Trees"
    T. McNaughton
    (*Music and Lyrics by* Tom McNaughton.)
[69]Dropped late in the run.
[70]Dropped late in the run.
[71]Dropped late in the run.

---

[72]No director was credited for the Broadway production, apart from Morosco himself. For subsequent tour, Frank McCormick was credited with direction, and Joseph Smith with staging of the musical numbers.
[73]Scenery uncredited.

"The Twentieth Century Lullaby"
   C. Greenwood, B. Hirsch, F. Victory
   (*Music by* Alfred Goodman and W. Frisch. *Lyrics by* Bernard Grossman and George Yoerger.)
"Did You, My Boy, Did You?"
   E. Henry, A. Hartley
"Let's Pretend"
   C. Greenwood, O. Howland
"Strawberry Festival" (Strawberry Glide)
   M. McClintock, Ensemble
"Linger Longer Letty"
   C. Greenwood, O. Howland
   (*Lyrics by* Oliver Morosco.)

ACT 2[74]
   Opening Chorus
      Ensemble
   "Parisienne Mechanical Models" (Mechanical Doll)
      F. Bendsten, Models
   "Movements"
      O. Howland
   "Slow Town Is a Jazz Town Now"
      A. Hartley, Chorus
      (*Lyrics by* Bernard Grossman and George Yoerger.)
   Finale
      Company

ACT 3[75]
   "(Climbing) the Ladder of Love"
      O. Roller, Chorus
   Specialty Dance[76]
      M. Severn
   "Denishawn" (Nature Dance)[77]
      C. Greenwood
   Finale
      Entire Company

1919.38

APHRODITE

A Romance of Manners from ancient Egypt in Three Acts, 7 Scenes. Play by Pierre Frondaie and George C. Hazelton. Based on the novel by Pierre Louÿs. Music by Henri Fevrier and Anselm Goetzl. (Lyrics by Arthur A. Penn, E. Lyall Swete.) Staged by E. Lyall Swete. Ballets arranged by Michel

---

[74]For subsequent tour, the show was revised repeatedly. The first four numbers in Act 2 were replaced by:
   "My Lady Fair"
      L. Mink, Chorus
   Which was later replaced by:
   "What's the Matter with Letty?"
      Jack Raffael (Father), Ensemble
   Also added was:
   "Maid to Order Maid"
      A. Hartley, Chorus
[75]For subsequent tour, Act 3 was repeatedly revised. "Two to One" and "Oh By Jingo" in Act 3 were replaced, respectively, by:
   "My Little Highland Highball"
      George Sweet (Walter), Curtyne Englar (Juliet), Chorus
   "Denishawn"
      C. Greenwood
   Also added was:
   "Luck"
      O. Howland
[76]After the opening, Miss Severn's specialty was moved to Act 2 and replaced by:
   "Two to One" (Ten to One You Fall)
      C. Ring, M. McClintock, Chorus
      (*Music by* Alfred Goodman. *Lyrics by* Bernard Grossman and George Yoerger.)
[77]Replaced after the opening by:
   "Oh! By Jingo! (Oh By Gee, You're the Only Girl for Me)"
      C. Greenwood
      (*Music by* Albert Von Tilzer. *Lyrics by* Lew Brown.)

Fokine. Scenery designed by Joseph Harker and Phil Harker. Costumes designed by Percy Anderson; additional costumes by Leon Bakst. Properties designed by Percy Anderson and Carl Link. Orchestra under the direction of William Axt. Entire production under the personal supervision of Morris Gest. Produced by F. Ray Comstock and Morris Gest. Opened 24 November 1919 at the Century Theatre and closed 3 April 1920 after 148 performances.

CAST (in order of appearance): *Timon*, a Greek Gallant: Frederick Macklyn. *Phrasilas*, a Courtier: RICHARD HALE. *Horatius*, a Roman Poet: Mayne Linton. *Naukrates*, Physician to the Queen: ETIENNE GIRARDOT. *Theoxenes*, Minister of State: Robert Ayrton. *His Spies*: William Gedney, Edward Nacht, William Holly, Wallace Jackson. *Bubastic*, a Court Chamberlain: William McNeill. *Berenike*, Queen of Egypt: HAZEL ALDEN. *Officer of the Guard*: Nikolai Glovatski. *Demetrios*, a Greek Sculptor: McKAY MORRIS. *Ampelis*: Rita Gould. *A Beggar*: Renwick Roget. *A Donkey Boy*: Basil Smith. *Korine, Ioessa*, Votaries of the Temple: Suzette Gordon, Mabel Allan. *Fruit Peddler*: Arnold Van Leer. *Fish Peddler*: Lester Sweyd. *A Young Sailor*: Richard Schwendler. *A Snake Peddler*: William McNeal. *A Youth*: Edward Howell. *Harhingir Khyam*, an Asiatic Prince: Mark Loebell. *Myrtis, Rhodocleia*, Sisters: Annette Bade, Carolyn Nunder. *City Girls*: Hazel Miller, Louise Blanid, Mai Poth, Agnes Tate, Gladys Morrison, Augusta Magruder. *Bacchys*, Mistress to Naukrates: Maude Odell. *Chrysis* of Galilee: DOROTHY DALTON. *Aphrodite*, the Goddess of Love: MILDRED WALKER.
   The Queen's Ladies: Phoenike: Estelle Paul. *Eirene*: Winifred Hampton. *Daphne*: Dottie Edwards. *Faustina*: Ann. Lyall. *Elena*: Lina Toselli. *Sena*: Kay MacCausland. *Mysiennes*: Louise Adams. *Ghadames*: Hattie Simms. *Doryclas*: Katherine Turner. *Hermia*: Anita Corraldi. *Diala*: Julia Carroll. *Heliope*: Kitty Gilbert.
   Courtiers (6): Bathyllos: William Grieg. *Damon*: Carl Linke. *Myxaros*: John Triefalt. *Lysander*: J. Stafford. *Gadales*: Al Ojeman. *Hector*: Clinton Russell. *Jester*: Henry Cline. *Votaries of the Temple of Aphrodite (4): Mnais*: Vera Leonard. *Moussarian*: Shirley Warde. *Theano*: PATTERSON DIAL. *Melitta*: Lucille LaVerne. *Chimeris*, a Greek Sybil: Hope Sutherland. *Touni*, the High Priestess: Judith M. Voselli. *Melitta's Mother*, a Priestess: Hazel Woodhull. *Eunike*, another Priestess: Genevieve Dolaro. *Singer*: Martin Breval. *Chief Butler*: Clarence Redd. *Female Slaves to Bacchys (2) Djala*: Paori Arendine. *Bamshi*: Lorna Mayer. *Aphrodasia*, a Dancing Slave: Mlle. DAZIE. *Old Sailor*: William McNeal. *High Priest*: Guy Collins.
   Ladies of the Chorus: Valerie Sergeant, Hattie Arnold, Adele Lacy, Billie Wedgewood, Ila Jewell, Isabel Stone, Gladys Fisher, Alola Yates, Erna Steinway, Gladys Leigh, Geina Genova, H. DeWitt. *Gentlemen of the Chorus*: Edward Howell, Rene de la Chapele, Hugh Reed, Wallace King, Lionel Velky, Leo Collins, W. Perloff, H. Arden, Daniel Quimby, John Surra, A. Frank, Francis Murphy. *Ladies of the Ballet*: Betty Wayne, Ann Smith, Kathleen Lowry, Oriole Maude, Dorothy Scoville, Helen Lyons, Margaret Mangan, Dorinda Bradley, Edith Maude, Ermina Mathews, Mildred Marsh, Dorothy Chesmond, Louise Romaine, Georgia Poutch, Nancy Cobhan, Myrna Reeves, Margaret Mackenzie, Elvira Berti, Dorothy Lee, Irene Van Cleef, Peggy Raymond, Nelly Savage, Alice Wayne, Marion O'Neill, Estelle Gray, Betty Linn, Billie Wilcox, Gae Foster, Violante Francelli, Anita Gay, Virginia McDonald, Violette de Chevier, Rhoda Sylvane, Estelle Penning. *Others in the Play*: Temple Votaries, the Queen's Guard, Litter Bearers, Priests, Chanters, Incense Bearers, Phoenician Sailors, Chinese and Jewish Merchants, Camel Drivers, Arab Horsemen, Peddlers, Fruit and Flower Sellers, Asiatic Attendants, Guests of Bacchys, People of the City, etc.

Act 1: The Port of Alexandria, B.C. 56. The Fore-Court of Queen Berenike's Palace.

Act 2, Scene 1: The Grove of Aphrodite. Two hours later. *Scene 2*: Interior of the Temple of Aphrodite. The next morning. *Scene 3*: On the road to the House of Bacchys. Evening. *Scene 4*: The Feast of Bacchys. One hour later.

Act 3, Scene 1: The Studio of Demetrios. The same hour as the Feast. (The Dream.) *Scene 2*: The Beacon of Alexandria. Next morning. (The Prophecy.)

ACT 1
   Opening Ensemble
      R. Hale, Male Chorus
      (*Music by* Anselm Goetzl. *Lyrics by* E. Lyall Swete.)
   Entrance of Queen Berenike
      (*Music by* Anselm Goetzl.)
   Berenike Motif
      (*Music by* Henri Fevrier.)
   Demetrios Motif
      (*Music by* Anselm Goetzl.)
   Chrysis Motif—"Aphrodite Waltz"
      (*Music by* Anselm Goetzl.)

ACT 2
   "Eros, Eros"
      P. Dial, Male Chorus
      (*Music by* Anselm Goetzl. *Choreography by* Michel Fokine.)
   "Alexandria"
      M. Breval
      (*Music by* Anselm Goetzl. *Lyrics by* Arthur A. Penn.)
   "Bacchanale" (Ballet)
      (*Music by* Modest Moussorgsky. *Choreography by* Michel Fokine.)

Dance Aphrodasia
Mlle. Dazie
(*Music by* Alexander Glazunov. *Choreography by* Michel Fokine.)

ACT 3

"The Dream of Demetrios"
(*Music by* Anselm Goetzl.)

1919.39 THE ROSE OF CHINA

A Musical Comedy in Three Acts. Book by Guy Bolton. (Based on the play "East Is West" by Samuel Shipman.) Music by Armand Vecsey. Lyrics by P. G. Wodehouse. Staged by Robert Milton and Julian Mitchell. Scenery designed by Joseph Urban. Costumes designed by Alice O'Neil; Miss Richardson's costumes designed by Helen Dryden. Orchestra under the direction of Frank Tours. Produced by F. Ray Comstock and Morris Gest. Opened 25 November 1919 at the Lyric Theatre and closed 7 January 1920 after 47 performances.

CAST (in order of appearance): *Dum Tong*, Gardener: Paul Irving. *Ton Ka*, a Chinese Dancer: Louise Brownel. *Ling Tao*, Tsao Ling's daughter: JANE RICHARDSON. *Ting-Fang-Lee*: STANLEY RIDGES. *Tsao Ling*: WILLIAM H. PRINGLE. *Tommy Tilford*: OSCAR SHAW. *Wilson Peters*: Frank McIntyre. *Polly Baldwin*: Cecil Cunningham. *Priest*: Leo Dwyer. *Chung*, Tommy's Servant: Thomas E. Jackson. *Grace Hobson*: Cynthia Perot. *Mrs. Hobson*, Her Mother: EDNA MAY OLIVER. (*Dance Specialty*: Swan Wood.)

Chinese Dancers: Misses Beatrice Singer, Marie Hebold, Jane Brown, Georgie Decker, Virginia Richmond, Mona Sartoris, Madelaine Hurlock, Mary Scott, Olive O'Brien, Gene Billington, Virginia Roche, Georgie Scott, Nelly Day, Mabelle Elliott, Marion Cushion, Grace West, Thelma Richards, Blanche Christen. *American Girls*: Misses Jean Barnett, Marjorie Bailey, Dolly Alwin, Bessie Mulligan, Eleanore Scott, Bessie More. *Guards*: Messrs. Billy Izzard, Larry Mack, Robert Morey, Gus Richton, Perry Lindbloom, Percy Davenport, Ed. Pierce, Ed Dwyer.

Act 1: The Garden of Tsao Ling.

Act 2: Tommy Tilford's Bungalow. A few hours later.

Act 3: The Terrace outside the Bungalow. A few hours later.

ACT 1

Opening—
Sunrise Intermezzo
"Hymn to the Sun"
Ensemble
Dance
L. Brownel, Girls
"Yale" (Song)
S. Ridges, Chinese Girls
"Bunny Dear" (Song)
J. Richardson, Chinese Girls
"The Legend of the Tea Tree" (Duet)
J. Richardson, O. Shaw
"College Spirit" (Trio)
O. Shaw, F. McIntyre, S. Ridges
"What! What! What!"[78]
C. Cunningham, O. Shaw
Finale
Company

ACT 2

"Little Bride"[79] (Opening)
J. Richardson, Ensemble
"Our Chinese Bungalow" (In Our Bungalow) (Duet)
J. Richardson, O. Shaw
(*Lyrics by* Oscar Shaw and P. G. Wodehouse.)
"Proposals" (Trio)
C. Cunningham, F. McIntyre, O. Shaw

---

[78]Replaced during the run by:
"Romeo and Juliet" (Duet)
C. Cunningham, O. Shaw
[79]Replaced during the run by:
"My Bridal Day" (Opening)
J. Richardson, Girls
Then later replaced by "Yesterday" from later in Act 2.

"When You Are in China" (Quartet)
J. Richardson, O. Shaw, C. Perot, E. M. Oliver
"Yesterday"[80] (Duet)
J. Richardson, O. Shaw
Finale
Company

ACT 3

"The Spirit of the Drum" (Opening)
L. Brownel, Girls
"(Down) On the Banks of the Subway"[81] (Duet)
C. Cunningham, F. McIntyre
"My China Rose"[82] (Song)
O. Shaw, Girls
"Broken Blossoms"[83] (Song)
J. Richardson
Finale
Company

1919.40 ELSIE JANIS AND HER GANG

A Bomb Proof Revue in Two Acts, 8 Scenes. Book (sketches) by Elsie Janis. Jokes by Everybody. Songs by William B. Kernell and B. C. Hilliam (music), Richard Fechheimer and Elsie Janis (lyrics), etc. Staged by Elsie Janis. Costumes designed by Charles LeMaire. Orchestra under the direction of William Schroeder. Produced by Charles Dillingham and Florenz Ziegfeld. Opened 1 December 1919 at the George M. Cohan Theatre and closed 17 January 1920 after 55 performances.

CAST: *The Gang*: ELSIE JANIS, BILL KERNELL, CHICK DEVEAU, EDDIE HAY, RICHARD RYAN, BRADLEY KNOCHE, BILL REARDON, JERRY HOEKSTRA, HENRY JANSWICK [Harry Jans], JACK BRANT, SAM BURBANK, CHARLES LAWRENCE, FRANK MILLER, HERBERT GOFF.
Six Rather Nice Accessories: *The Parisienne*: EVA LeGALLIENNE. *The Y.M.C.A. Girl*: RUTH WELLS. *The K. of C. Girl*: HENRIETTE ORVILLE. *The Ambulance Service Girl*: MARGARET SOUSA. *The Motor Transport Girl*; LILLIAN CULLEN. *The Red Cross Nurse*; MARY BALFOUR.
The Jazz Band: Ewart Allen, Harry Berger, Norman Merleton, Joe Wise, Howard Johnson, Nat Martin, Edward W. Reno, B. Romolo.

Act 1, Scene 1: Anywhere in France—before November, 1918. *Scene 2*: Any street in Paris—same epoch. *Scene 3*: A cheap restaurant in Paris. (We never found one!) *Scene 4*: Any park in Paris—where they have benches.

Act 2, Scene 1: Anywhere in Coblenz, Germany—after the occupation. *Scene 2*: Anywhere, any time. *Scene 3*: Anywhere in New York. *Scene 4*: Anywhere in America.

ACT 1

"Let's Go"
E. Janis, Gang
(*Music by* William B. Kernell. *Lyrics by* Richard Fechheimer.)
"Somewhere in America"
J. Hoekstra, Gang
(*Music by* William B. Kernell. *Lyrics by* Richard Fechheimer.)
Songs We Sang
E. Janis, Gang
["Smiles" (FROM PASSING SHOW OF 1918)
(*Music by* Lee Roberts. *Lyrics by* Will Callahan.)
"The Darktown Strutters' Ball"
(*Music and Lyrics by* Shelton Brooks.)
"Along the Rocky Road to Dublin"
(*Music by* Bert Grant. *Lyrics by* Joe Young.)]

---

[80]Replaced during the run by:
"Love Is a Wonderful Feeling" (Duet)
F. McIntyre, O. Shaw, Girls
"The American Jazz"
O. Shaw, F. McIntyre, Jean Barnett {Grace Hobson}, Ensemble
[81]During the run, title listed as "Banks of the Subway."
[82]Replaced during the run by:
"Lovely Ladies" (Song)
O. Shaw, Girls
[83]Replaced during the run by:
"Never More" (Song)
J. Richardson

"The M. P. Song" (Ah, Oui!)
  J. Brant, C. Lawrence, S. Burbank
  (*Music by* William B. Kernell. *Lyrics by* Richard Fechheimer.)
"In the Latin Quarter"
  J. Hoekstra, H. Janswick, B. Knoche
  (*Music by* William B. Kernell. *Lyrics by* Richard Fechheimer.)
"It's My Temperament" (My Artistic Temperament)
  C. Lawrence
  (*Music by* William B. Kernell. *Lyrics by* Richard Fechheimer.)
"Gee, But It's Great to Meet a Girl from Home"
  H. Goff, R. Wells, Accomplices
  (*Music by* William B. Kernell. *Lyrics by* Richard Fechheimer.)
"Just a Little Touch of Paris"
  E. Janis, E. Hay
  (*Music by* William B. Kernell. *Lyrics by* Richard Fechheimer.)
"I Love Them (All), Just a Little Bit" (from HULLO, AMERICA!;
London revue)
  E. Janis, Ladies
  (*Music by* Dan Kildare.)
"Après la Guerre" (from HULLO, AMERICA!; London revue)
  H. Goff, B. Reardon, H. Janswick, E. Janis
  (*Music by* B. C. Hilliam. *Lyrics by* B. C. Hilliam and Clifford Grey.)
Finale
  The Whole Gang

ACT 2
"The Heinie Fiftette"
  The Pursued: C. Deveau, C. Lawrence, H. Janswick, B. Reardon, E. Hay. *The Pursuers*: M. Balfour, M. Sousa, H. Orville, L. Cullen, R. Wells. *M.P.s*: B. Knoche, R. Ryan, N. Merleton, J. Brant, H. Goff.
"Just a Little After Taps"
  J. Dykstra, M. Balfour
  (*Music by* William B. Kernell. *Lyrics by* Richard Fechheimer.)
Jazz Band (They will play as many as you can stand!)
  Themselves
Rank (Just an Idea in One Scene)
  Johnny Cotton, erstwhile Private U. S. Infantry: C. Deveau. *James Steele*, erstwhile Captain U. S. Artillery: J. Hoekstra. *Stenographer*: E. LeGallienne.
Miss Janis
  No telling what she will do
["Give Me the Moonlight" (from HULLO, AMERICA!; London revue)
  (*Music by* Albert Von Tilzer. *Lyrics by* Lew Brown.)]
"When I Took My Jazz Band to the Fatherland"
  E. Janis, Gang
Finale
  Gang

1919.41   MISS MILLIONS

A Comedy with Music in Three Acts. Book and lyrics by R. H. Burnside. Music by Raymond Hubbell. Produced under the stage direction of the author. Scenery designed by Mark Lawson. Costumes designed by Gladys Monkhouse and Will R. Barnes. Musical director, Victor Baravalle. Orchestrations by Frank Sadler. A. H. Canby, Management. Opened 9 December 1919 at the Punch and Judy Theatre and closed 21 January 1920 after 47 performances.

CAST: *Mary Hope*: VALLI VALLI. *Horace Honeydew*, a Coffee Broker: RAPLEY HOLMES. *Timothy Bond*, his partner: CLAYTON WHITE. *Jack Honeydew*, his nephew: VINTON FREEDLEY. *Ephraim Tutt* from New Jersey: WILLIAM BURRESS. *John J. Hawkins*: JOHN HENDRICKS. *Mr. Sharpe*, a lawyer: Harry Hermsen. *Willie Lightfoot*, the Dancing Teacher: Lewis Sloden. *Bates*, a Butler: Frank Farrington. *Waiter*: Walter Coupe. *Percy*: Frank Slater. *Reggie*: Alfred Siegler. *Ezra Tucker*: George Stuart. *Silas Dingley*: B. J. Tieman. *Tobias Wilkins*: Harry Smith. *Hiram Jones*: William Duane. *Mrs. Honeydew*: LOUISE MACKINTOSH. *Ethel Bradley Smith*: VERA ROSANDER. *Julia Joyce*, Proprietress of Tea Shop: Jessie Standish. *Peggy*, a maid: CISSIE SEWELL. *Waitresses at the Tea Shop* (7): *Mamie*: Carrie Reynolds. *Rosie*: Gertrude Early. *Sophie*: Sophie Brenner. *Eleanor*: Eleanor Masters. *Kathryn*: Kathryn Yates. *Edna*: Edna Fenton. *Marie*: Marie Sewell. *Tabitha Tutt*, Ephraim's wife: Mrs. William Pruette. *Aunt Miranda*, Her Sister: Genevieve Tucker. *Cynthia*, Her Little Daughter: Bonnie Murray. *Matilda*: Amy Scott. *Martha*: Gladys White.
(*Ensemble*): Misses Georgie Kay, Thelma Keough, Belle Waters, Bobbie Galvin, Nan Ashe, Dorothy Barkman, Joan Broadhurst, Elsie Ashforth, Marie Clifford, Frances Halliday, Marie Moore, Ione Richie; Messrs. W. Douglas, Otto Graff, Eddie Edwards, Stewart Duane. *The California Four*: William Quimby, L. R. Montsanto, Harold Goulden, Grady Miller.

Time: The present.
Act 1: A Tea Shop on Fifth Avenue.
Act 2: The Reception Room of "Mary's" Residence, New York City. Five days later.
Act 3: Down on the Farm in Jersey. Ten days later.

ACT 1
Opening Chorus (Tea Shop Scandal)
  J. Standish, Chorus
"Just Laugh"
  C. Reynolds, Girls
"Mary" (Entrance Song)
  V. Valli, Boys
"I'm in Love with You" (Duet)
  V. Freedley, V. Valli
"My Advice" (Solo)
  R. Holmes
"Don't Say Good-bye" (Finale)
  Ensemble

ACT 2
"Hustle and Bustle Around"
  F. Farrington, C. Sewell, G. Early, Chorus
"Cutest Little House" (Duet)
  F. Farrington, C. Sewell
"The Kind of Man I Want to Marry" (Ensemble)
  J. Standish, C. Reynolds, Girls
"Down on the Farm"
  V. Valli, Relations
"The Dancing Lesson"
  V. Valli, C. Sewell, L. Sloden
"Dreams" (Quartette)
  R. Holmes, C. White, J. Standish, V. Valli
"If You'll Just Wait a Little While" (Duet)
  V. Freedley, V. Valli
Finale ("Toast")
  Ensemble

ACT 3
"Farming Life" (Quartette)
  California Four
"She Was Only a Farmer's Daughter"
  J. Standish, Girls
"Since Hiram Came Back (from the War)"
  W. Burress, Chorus
"Letter Song" (Solo)
  V. Valli
Finale
  Ensemble

1919.42   MONSIEUR BEAUCAIRE

A Romantic Opera in Three Acts and a Prologue. Libretto by Frederick Lonsdale. Based on the novel of the same name by Booth Tarkington (and the play by Booth Tarkington and Evelyn Greenleaf Sutherland). Music by André Messager. Lyrics by Adrian Ross. Directed by J. A. E. Malone. Costumes designed by Percy Anderson. Orchestra under the direction of Charles Previn. Produced by Gilbert Miller, under the management of Abraham L. Erlanger. Opened 11 December 1919 at the New Amsterdam Theatre and closed 3 April 1920 after 143 performances.[84]

CAST: *Monsieur Beaucaire* (Duc d'Orleans/de Châteaurien): MARION GREEN. *Philip Molyneux*: JOHN CLARKE. *Frederick Bantison*: LENNOX PAWLE. *Rakell*: Spencer Trevor. *Francois*: Yvan Servais. *Duke of Winterset*: ROBERT PARKER. *Beau Nash*: Robert Cunningham. *Townbrake*: Andre Brouard. *Captain Badger*: Percy Carr. *Joliffe*: Harry Frankiss. *Bicksitt*: Eric Snowden. *Marquis de Mirepoix*: Yvan Servais. *Lucy*: MARJORIE BURGESS. *Countess of Greenbury*: Barbara Esme. *A Girl* (in Act 1): Ellen Grubb. *Lady Mary Carlisle*: BLANCHE TOMLIN.
Dancers: Misses Gladys Burgess, Kathleen Davennon, Pat Newell, Dieudonne Donaldson, Patricia Hare, Lillie Rennie, Barbara Esme, Elaine Maureen, Olive Barlee, Kitty Malone, Elsie Kennedy. *Guests*: Misses Florence de Barde, Evelyn Claire, Freda Williams, Rosatta Chandler, Myrtle Leonard, Helen Arden, Jean Hill, Helen

---

[84]Gilbert Miller's London production was brought to New York intact; scenery was uncredited both in New York and London.

Marting, Helen Isensee, Lora Sonderson, Henrietta Brewster. *Soldiers*: Messrs. Herbert Edwards, Ian Alexander, William Phillips, Brewster Meadows, James Alderman, Cyril Edgar. *Courtiers*: Messrs. Anthony Thane, Gordon Baskerville, William Murray, Harry Harrington, Alex McNulty, Fred Molyneux.

Prologue: Monsieur Beaucaire's Lodgings in Bath. Early evening.

Act 1: Lady Rellerton's Ballroom. Same evening.

Act 2: At Mr. Bantison's Park, outside Bath. Three weeks later.

Act 3: Assembly Room at Bath. One week later.

PROLOGUE

"Voyageur's Song"
    Chorus
"Red Rose" (Song)
    M. Green
"Going to the Ball" (Trio)
    J. Clarke, M. Green, R. Parker

ACT 1[85]

"The Beaux and the Belles of Bath" (Opening Chorus)
    Chorus
"A Little More" (I Love You a Little) (Duet)
    M. Burgess, J. Clarke
"Come With Welcome"
    Chorus
"I Do Not Know" (Song)
    B. Tomlin
"Who Is This?"
    Chorus
"English Maids" (Song)
    M. Green
"Lightly, Lightly"
    B. Tomlin, M. Green
"No Offence" (Quartette)
    J. Clarke, M. Green, P. Carr, R. Parker
Rose Minuet and Finale, Act 1
    B. Tomlin, M. Green

ACT 2

Pastoral Fête (Chorus and Dance)
"When I Was King of Bath" (Song)
    R. Cunningham
"That's a Woman's Way" (Song)
    M. Burgess
"Philomel" (Song)
    B. Tomlin
"Honor and Love" (Song)
    J. Clarke
"Say No More" (Duet)
    B. Tomlin, M. Green
Finale, Act 2
    B. Tomlin, M. Green

ACT 3

"Have You Heard?" (Opening Chorus)
    Chorus
"The Honours of War" (Sextette)
    S. Trevor, A. Brouard, H. Frankiss, P. Carr, L. Pawle, E. Snowden
"We Are Not Speaking Now" (Duet)
    M. Burgess, J. Clarke
"Under the Moon" (Song)
    M. Green
"What Are Names?" (Solo)
    B. Tomlin, M. Green
"Way for the Ambassador"
    Chorus

---

[85]Musical Numbers do not appear in the program. Above list is prepared from the published piano vocal score (Ascherberg, Hopwood & Crew, London, 1919). An additional song from the score which was recorded in London and may have been preformed in New York:
"Gold and Blue and White"
    M. Green

"A Son of France" (Song)
    Y. Servais
Finale Act 3

MORRIS GEST'S
MIDNIGHT WHIRL

1919.43

A Musical Revue in Two Acts, 13 Scenes[86]. Sketches and lyrics by Buddy G. DeSylva and John Henry Mears. Music by George Gershwin. Staged by Julian Mitchell and David Bennett. Scenery designed by Joseph Urban. Costumes by Schneider-Anderson. Orchestra under the direction of Frank Tours. Produced by Morris Gest[87]. Opened 27 December 1919 at the Century Grove (atop the Century Theatre) and closed 13 March 1920 after 68 performances.

CAST: HELEN SHIPMAN, BERNARD GRANVILLE, BESSIE McCOY DAVIS, ANNETTE BADE, JAMES WATTS, (Joseph) BENNETT and (Edward) RICHARDS, THE RATH BROTHERS (George, Dick), LESLIE BURNETT, KATHRYN HATFIELD, Rex Story. *Century Trio*: S. Falke, W. Woods, H. Tinner.

Ensemble: Grace Beaumont, Jean Fair, Gertrude Coates, Betty Brae, Annette Weber, May Leslie, Gladys Zelian, Pearl Weber, Madeline Hurlock, Margaret Morris, Carolyn Erwin, Bess Fuller, Fay King, Helen Lovett, Betty Squires, Eliane Dore, Lillian Littell, Jane Berlyn, Gladys Dale, Lee Smith, Clara Carroll, Floret Duval, Peggy Bell, Minnie Harrison, Billie Carmen, Dorinda Bradley, Lillian Pompan, Gertrude Miller, Peggy Mitchell, Peggy Fears, May Hennessey.

ACT 1[88]

Scene 1
    Toil: H. Shipman.
Scene 2
    Life: B. Granville.
    ("I'll Show You a Wonderful World"
        H. Shipman, B. Granville)
Scene 3
    "The League of Nations (Depends on Beautiful Clothes)"
        B. Granville
            Mannikins: G. Beaumont, J. Fair, G. Coates, B. Brae, A. Weber, M. Leslie, G. Zelian, P. Weber, M. Hurlock, M. Morris, C. Erwin. *Patrons*: B. Fuller, F. King, H. Lovett, B. Squires, E. Dore, L. Littell, J. Berlyn, G. Dale. *Model*: L. Burnett.
Scene 4
    "Doughnuts"
        A. Bade
            Salvation Doughnuts from Cushman's: L. Smith, C. Carroll, F. Duval, P. Bell, M. Harrison, B. Carmen, D. Bradley, L. Pompan.
Scene 5
    Dance
        B. Granville
Scene 6
    Eviction
        J. Watts
            Assisted by R. Story, G. Miller, P. Mitchell, E. Dore, B. Fuller.
Scene 7
    "Poppyland"
        B. Granville, H. Shipman
        (*Music by* George Gershwin. *Lyrics by* John Henry Mears and Buddy G. DeSylva.)
            Assisted by Misses Harrison, Carmen, Brae, Mitchell, Yates, Smith, Bell, Miller, Dore, Littell, Pompan, Duval, Carroll, Hurlock, Bradley, King, Dale, Fuller, berlyn, Squires, Burnett, A. Weber, Fair, Coates.

---

[86]Billed as "Third of the Series."
[87]Subsequent tour presented by John Henry Mears under the title THE CENTURY MIDNIGHT WHIRL, using material from all previous editions of THE MIDNIGHT WHIRL.
[88]The running order was revised after the opening. Additional songs which may have been interpolated during the New York run, or added for the tour, as per published sheet music:
"Care-Free Cairo Town"
    (*Music and Lyrics by* John Wolcott.)
"Peggy"
    Dorothy Dickson, Carl Hyson
    (*Music by* Neil Moret. *Lyrics by* Harry Williams.)
"Your Baby For All the Time"
    (*Music and Lyrics by* John Woolcott.)

"Limehouse Nights"
   B. M.Davis
   (*Music by* George Gershwin. *Lyrics by* John Henry Mears and Buddy G. DeSylva.)
   Assisted by Misses M. Leslie, M. Morris, P. Fears, H. Lovett.
"Aphronightie"[89] (Parody on Fokine's Bacchanal from "Aphrodite")
   J. Watts

ACT 2
Scene 1
"Let Cutie Cut Your Cuticle"
   A. Bade
   Assisted by Misses P. Weber, A. Weber, G. Miller, B. Brae, H. Lovett, P. Fears, A. Yates, M. Harrison.
Scene 2
America's Athletes in a Study of Endurance
   Rath Brothers
Scene 3
"Baby Dolls"
   H. Shipman
   Cavalier: M. Leslie. *Leonora Ulric*: M. Morris. *Telephone*: G. Zelian. *Bob-Bon*: G. Beaumont. *English*: G. Miller. *Baby*: M. Harrison. *French*: L. Smith. *Kewpie*: P. Fears. *Splash Me*: J. Fair. *Topsie*: M. Hennessey.
Scene 4
Dark Clouds
   Bennett and Richards
Scene 5
Profiteers
   A *Gold Digger*: H. Shipman. *Coal*: M. Morris. *Milk*: G. Coates. *Sugar*: G. Zelian. *Other Gold Diggers*: H. Lovett, P. Mitchell, G. Beaumont, P. Fears, M. Harrison, C. Carroll.
Scene 6
Carnival
Dance
   B. Granville, K. Hatfield
   The Good Little Fairy: H. Shipman.
"East Indian Maid"
   B. M. Davis, Bennett and Richards
Snake Dance
   J. Watts
Finale
   Entire Company

1919.44   ANGEL FACE

A Musical Play in Three Acts. Book by Harry B. Smith[90]. (Based on the play "The Elixir of Love" by Zellah Covington and Jules Simonson, produced in New York as "Some Baby.") Music by Victor Herbert. Lyrics by Robert B. Smith. Staged by George W. Lederer. Musical numbers staged by Julian Alfred. Scenery designed by Herbert Moore. Costumes designed by O'Kane Conwell. Lighting by Tony Greshoff. Orchestra under the direction of Harold Vicars. Produced by George W. Lederer. Opened 29 December 1919 at the Knickerbocker Theatre and closed 14 February 1920 after 57 performances.

CAST: *Tom Larkins*, a rich young man, whose fad is musical comedy, composer of "The Lemon Girl": JOHN E. YOUNG. *Arthur Griffin*, a sculptor, Tom's friend who shares his apartment: TYLER BROOKE. *Friends of Tom and Arthur (3)*: *Sandy Sharp*: RICHARD PYLE. *Hugh Fairchild*: JOHN REINHARD. *Rockwell Gibbs*: HOWARD JOHNSON. *Professor Barlow*, an eccentric scientist: GEORGE SCHILLER. *Ira Mapes*, a student of entomology: Bernard Thornton. *Slooch*, a correspondence school detective: JACK DONAHUE. *Irving*, Tom's servant: William Cameron. *Mrs. Zenobia Wise*: Edna von Buelow. *Betty*, her youngest daughter, aged 17: MARGUERITE ZENDER. *Vera*, her eldest daughter, aged 28: MINERVA GREY. *Completing the Quintet of*

Mrs. Wise's daughters (3): *Paula*: MARY MILBURN. *Lily*: Marguerite St. Clair. *Pearl*: Gertrude Wadelle. *Mrs. Larkins*, Tom's grandmother from Keokuk: Sarah McVicker. *Tessie Blythe*. Tom's fiancée: EMILY LEA. *Moya*, a friend of Tessie: May Thompson. *Members of a Musical Comedy Company*: *Kitty*: Georgie Sewell. *Mary*: Miriam Medie. *Cissie*: June White. *Geraldine*: Audrey Burton. *Mabel*: Flora Crosbie. *Tottie*: Virginia Eastman. *Dottie*: Lucille Kent. *Pearl*: Edna Stillwell. *Evangeline*: Irene Wylie. *Beatrice*: Lillian Young. *Letty*: Anita Walton. *Ruby*: Muriel Manners.

Act 1: Bachelor Apartment shared by Arthur Griffin and Tom Larkins.

Act 2: The Same.

Act 3: The Hotel Lounge across the street.

ACT 1[91]
"I Might Be Your Once-in-a-While"
   J. E. Young, E. Lea, Ensemble
"Sow Your Wild Oats Early"
   J. E. Young, T. Brooke, J. Reinhard, H. Johnson, R. Pyle
"Everybody's Crazy Part of the Time" (Everybody's Crazy Half of the Time)
   R. Pyle, Ensemble
"I Might Be Your Once-in-a-While" (reprise)
   M. Zender
"Someone Like You"
   M. Milburn, R. Pyle
"How Do You Get That Way?"
   H. Johnson, G. Wadelle, R. Pyle, M. Milburn, J. E. Young

ACT 2
"A Man Should Have a Double When He's Single"
   T. Brooke, Girls
"Say When"
   J. E. Young, E. Lea
Dance Eccentrique
   J. Donahue
"Lullaby" (Bye Bye Baby)
   J. E. Young
"I Don't Want to Go Home"
   E. Lea, Girls
Finale
   Ensemble

ACT 3
Ensemble and Incidental Dance
   M. Medie, G. Sewell
"Tip Your Hat to Hatty"
   E. Lea
Herbert Potpourri
"My Idea of Something to Go Home To"
   R. Pyle, M. Milburn, J. Reinhard, M. St. Claire, H. Johnson, G. Wadelle
"Those Since I Met You Days"
   M. Milburn, T. Brooke, M. Zender
"Why Do They Make Them So Beautiful?"
   J. E. Young, Girls
   (*Lyrics by* Melville Alexander and Robert B. Smith.)
"Topsy Turvy"[92]
   J. Donahue
"If You Can Love Like You Can Dance"
   T. Brooke, M. Thompson
Finale
   Ensemble

1920.01   ALWAYS YOU

A Musical Comedy in Two Acts and a Prologue. Book and lyrics by Oscar Hammerstein II. Music by Herbert P. Stothart. Directed by Arthur Hammerstein. Dances arranged by Robert Marks. Scenery designed by Julius Dove. Costumes designed by Homer Conant. Orchestra under the

---

[89]Also known as "You Have to Put a Nightie on Aphrodite."

[90]The following note appears on the program's title page: "Taking a gland from a young and vigorous chimpanzee I grafted it onto a man 80 years old who was virtually in a state of decrepitude. The patient showed a complete change. His shoulders became upright, he walked straighter and seemed to enjoy the physical and mental powers of a young man of 30."—Dr. Serge Voronoff, head of the physiological laboratories of the College de France.

[91]Added after opening to Act 1, after "Everybody's Crazy Part of the Time":
   "Angel Face"
      E. Lea

[92]Dropped after opening.

direction of Herbert P. Stothart. Produced by Arthur Hammerstein. Opened 5 January 1920 at the Central Theatre, moved 26 January 1920 to the Lyric Theatre, and closed 28 February 1920 after 66 performances.

CAST (in order of appearance): *Toinette Fontaine*: HELEN FORD. *Bruce Nash*: WALTER SCANLAN. *An East Indian Peddler*: EDOUARD CIANNELLI. *Julie Fontaine*: JULIA KELETY. *Charlie Langford*: RUSSELL MACK. *Montmorency Jones*: RALPH HERZ. *A Mysterious Conspirator*: Bernard Gorcey. *Joan Summers*: ANNA SEYMOUR. *Thomas*: Joseph Barton. *A Waitress*: Emily Russ. *Dancers*: Cortez and Peggy. (*Pianist*: Burton Green.)

Girls of the Ensemble: Marietta O'Brien, Beatrice Summers, Virginia Clark, Irma Marwick, Emily Russ, Memphis Russell, Mildred Rowland, Helen Neff, Rose Cardiff, Jose Carmen, Marvee Snow, Lillian Held, Elinore Cullen, Gene Morrison. *Boys*: Jacque Stone, Leo Howe, George Hale, Jack Zambouli.

Prologue: Trouville, France. August 1918.

Act 1: The Grounds of a Hotel in Trouville. August 1919.

Act 2: The Lounge of the Trouville Casino. Late evening the same day.

PROLOGUE
"Always You"
  H. Ford, W. Scanlon

ACT 1
"The Voice of Bagdad"
  E. Ciannelli
"A Wonderful War"
  J. Kelety, Chorus
"Always You" (reprise)
  H. Ford
"I Never Miss"
  R. Mack, Girls
"Syncopated Heart"
  H. Ford, R. Mack
"Same Old Places"
  H. Ford, W. Scanlon
"Some Big Something"
  A. Seymour
"Mysterioso"
  R. Herz, J. Barton, B. Gorcey
"My Pousse-café" (Pousse Café)
  J. Kelety, R. Herz
Finale
  Ensemble

ACT 2
"I'll Say So"[93]
  R. Mack, A. Seymour
"Do You Remember?"
  J. Kelety, H. Ford
"Woman"
  R. Herz
"Always You" (reprise)
  W. Scanlon
Dance Divertissement
  Cortez and Peggy
"Drifting (On)"
  W. Scanlon
"The Tired Business Man"
  A. Seymour, R. Mack
Finale
  Company

1920.02   FRIVOLITIES OF 1920

A Musical Revue in Two Acts, 21 Scenes[94]. Sketches by William Anthony McCuire. Music and lyrics by William B. Friedlander. Additional songs by Harry Auracher [Archer] and Tom Johnstone. Directed by William Anthony McCuire. Dances arranged by Edward Bower, Allan K. Foster. Musical num-

bers staged by William B. Friedlander. Scenery designed by (D. Frank) Dodge and (William E.) Castle Studio, Tarazona Brothers. Costumes by Andre Sherri, Mahieu & Co., Behrens Costume Co., E. Nussbaum & Co., Brooks Uniform Co., Baron de Meyer. Orchestra under the direction of Harry Auracher. Produced under the personal direction of G. M. Anderson and J. C. Huffman. Produced by G. M. Anderson. Opened 8 January 1920 at the 44th Street Theatre and closed 28 February 1920 after 61 performances.

CAST: HENRY LEWIS, RICHARD BOLD, NELLIE and SARA KOUNS, FLORENZ AMES, ADELAIDE WINTHROP, DORALDINA, EDWARD GALLAGHER, JOSEPH ROLLEY, THE BARR TWINS, TOM NIP, (Arthur) MOSS and (Ed) FRYE, CHARLES O'BRIEN, FRANK DAVIS, DELLE DARNELL, ZELDA SANTLEY, ALFRED GIRARD, MARIE STAFFORD, IRENE DELROY, John Flynn, Colin Chase, Fletcher Norton, Will Goodal.

Ladies of the Ensemble: Evelyn Downing, Vivian West, Marie Messier, Grace Lee, Josie McRae, Rae Fields, Billy Bryant, Muriel Cort, Fay Franklin, Helen Jackson, Helen Crewe, Anita Nenci, May Keefe, Frances Ney, Peggy Purtell, Betty Wright, Agnes Frawley, Helen Neary, Alice Winters, Marie Grenville, Peggy Van, Ruby Hart, Bernice Frank, May Lockwood, Margaret Clayton, Emily Proctor, Dorothy Parker, Mildred Kay, Ruth Kraft, Mercedes Desmordant, Miriam Breen, Alice Lawlor, Dolly Best, Jeanne Voltaire, Victorine Voltaire, Carol Haydon, Adele Kane, Mabel Roberts, Irma King, Doris Lloyd, Vesta Wallace.

ACT 1[95]
Scene 1
  Hell-O (*by William Anthony McGuire*)
    A Clubman: C. Chase. *Satan*: F. Norton. *Sorrow*: D. Lloyd. *Happiness*: M. Roberts. *Beauty*: V. Voltaire. *Clothes*: J. Voltaire. *Lingerie*: D. Best. *Dance*: I. Delroy. *Age*: M. Grenville. *Youth*: G. Lee. *Song*: M. Hartwell. *Minnie Shimmy*: T. Carlton.
Scene 2
  "My Frivolity Girl"
    F. Norton
    (*Music and Lyrics by* Harry Auracher and Tom Johnstone.)
      Follies: H. Neary. *Hitchy Koo*: B. Wright. *Gaieties*: R. Hart. *Greenwich Village*: R. Craft. *Scandals*: E. Proctor. *Winter Garden*: A. Winters. *Cohan Revue*: D. Parker. *Frivolities*: M. Stafford.
Scene 3
  "Jazz Up Jasper"
    Z. Santley, Country Girls
    (*Music and Lyrics by* Harry Auracher and Tom Johnstone.)
      Scene: The Country Fair.
  "Farmer's Band"
    7 Musical Nosses
      Country Girls: E. Downing, V. West, M. Messier, G. Lee, J. McRae, R. Fields, B. Bryant, M. Lockwood, M. Cort, F. Franklin, H. Jackson, H. Crewe, A. Nenci, M. Keefe, F. Ney, P. Purtell.
  The Race[96]
    Horse Owner: E. Gallagher. *Jockey*: J. Rolley.
    Dancing Specialty: Barr Twins.
  "The Farmerettes"
    Themselves[97]
      Farmerettes: B. Wright, A. Frawley, H. Neary, A. Winters, M. Grenville, R. Hart, B. Frank, P. Van, E. Proctor, D. Parker, M. Kay, R. Kraft, M. Desmordant, M. Breen, A. Lawlor.
  Two Rubes
    T. Nip, C. O'Brien
Scene 4
  How High Is Up?[98]
    Moss and Fry

[93]During the run, replaced by:
  "Let's Marry" ("I'll Say So" reinstated for tour.)
[94]Prematurely billed as "the first of an annual series."

[95]The running order was revised after the opening. Added during the run:
  Massaging the Depot (Act1)
    Glenn and Jenkins
  The Battle of What's the Use (Act 1)
    Edward Gallagher, Joseph Rolley
  Also performed by the Kouns Sisters during the run:
  "Pretty Little Cinderella"
    Kouns Sisters
    (*Music by* Nat Vincent. *Lyrics by* Blanche Franklin.)
[96]Dropped during the run.
[97]Later in the run reassigned vocally to T. Nip, C. O'Brien.
[98]Replaced during the run by:
  The Battle of What's the Use
    E. Gallagher, J. Rolley

Scene 5
  "Pretty Polly"
    A. Girard
    (*Music and Lyrics by* Harry Auracher and Tom Johnstone.)
  Dance
    T. Nip, V. Wallace, Z. Santley
    Pollys: M. Cort, H. Jackson, F. Franklin, F. Ney, R. Fields, B. Bryant, R. Craft, A. Nenci. *Crackers*: E. Downing, H. Crewe, G. Lee, M. Messier, J. McRae, A. Frawley, M. Keefe, V. West.
Scene 6
  Peacock Allies (*by* William Anthony McGuire)
    Scene: The Alley of the Hotel Astor.
    Bell Boy: H. Lewis. *Lobby Hound*: W. Goodal. *Man-About-Town*: F. Davis. *Mr. Madden*: C. Chase. *Guests*: M. Stafford, J. Voltaire, V. Voltaire, M. Roberts.
  "Squidgulums"
    H. Lewis
  "In Peacock Alley"
    S. Kouns
    Peacock Alley Girls: D. Lloyd, J. Voltaire, V. Voltaire, M. Roberts, D. Best, C. Haydon, A. Kane, M. Clayton.
Scene 7
  "On a Moonlit Night"
    M. Hartwell
    Scene: At the Beach.
  Dances
    I. Delroy, Z. Santley, V. Wallace, T. Nip, C. O'Brien, Whiting
    Bathing Beauties: R. Hart, P. Van, D. Parker, A. Winters, B. Wright, E. Downing, M. Messier, M. Lockwood, M. Cort, A. Frawley, J. McRae, F. Franklin, R. Fields, F. Ney, M. Keefe, H. Neary, A. Nenci, B. Bryant.
Scene 8
  Birdseed
    F. Davis, D. Darnell
Scene 9
  "What is Love?"[99]
    N. Kouns, S. Kouns
  Minuet
    The Soltis
    Period 1500 Girl: H. Neary. *Period 1500 Boy*: M. Kay. *Period 1600 Girl*: P. Van. *Period 1600 Boy*: M. Cort. *Period 1700 Girl*: E. Proctor. *Period 1700 Boy*: A. Winters. *Period 1800 Girl*: B. Wright. *Period 1800 Boy*: R. Hart.
Scene 10
  Sandals (*Written and staged by* William Anthony McGuire.)
    (A satire on the play 'Scandal' by Cosmo Hamilton.)
    The Maid: Z. Santley. *Brownie*: H. Lewis. *Francine Larrimore*: D. Darnell. *Charles Cherry*: E. Gallagher.
Scene 11
  The Court of Public Opinion[100]
    F. Ames, A. Winthrop
Scene 12
  Omar, the Wine-Maker (*by* William Anthony McGuire)
    Scene: Arabia.
    An Important Mogul: F. Norton. *A Slave Girl*: D. Lloyd. *Three American Tourists*: F. Davis, C. Chase, T. Nip. *Another Slave Girl*: M. Stafford. *Royal Interpreter*: J. Rolley. *Omar Khayyam*: E. Gallagher. *The Dancer*: Doraldina.
  "Araby"
    H. Antrim
  Dances
    Doraldina
    Arabian Girls: E. Downing, G. Lee, J. McRae, M. Messier, F. Franklin, M. Keefe, A. Frawley, A. Nenci. *East Indian Girls*: A. Lawler, B. Wright, D. Parker, P. Van, M. Cort. *Persian Girls*: R. Fields, H. Crewe, A. Winters, H. Neary, R. Craft. *Chinese Girls*: B. Bryant, M. Grenville, P. Purtell, M. Lockwood, F. Ney, M. Kay. *Turkish Girls*: E. Proctor, M. Desmordant, M. Clayton, V. West, R. Hart, M. Breen. *Egyptian Princesses*: D. Lloyd, B. Frank, A. Kane, S. Shaffer, C. Haydon. *Arabian Princesses*: D. Best, V. Voltaire, M. Roberts, J. Voltaire. *Favorites of Omar*: H. Jackson, V. Wallace, Z. Santley, I. Delroy.

ACT 2
Scene 1[101]
  Spanish Aria
    N. Kouns
    Scene: Spain.

The Guide and the Tourists
    A Tourist: F. Davis. *Another Tourist*: M. Stafford. *Guide*: J. Rolley.
  A Spanish Movement
    Barr Twins
  "The Cuddle-Uddle"
    A. Girard
  Dance
    The Soltis
    Spanish Girls and Boys: V. Voltaire, D. Lloyd, C. Haydon, S. Shafer, M. Roberts, A. Kane, B. Frank, M. Clayton, M. Grenville, M. Lockwood, M. Breen, D. Parker, M. Desmordant, A. Winters, V. West, P. Van. *Spanish Dancers*: R. Caft, B. Wright, F. Franklin, H. Neary, H. Jackson, H. Crewe, E. Proctor, R. Hart, E. Downing, M. Messier, J. McRae, R. Fields, M. Keefe, G. Lee, A. Frawley, A. Nenci.
Scene 2
  Promiscuous Frivols
    H. Lewis
  ["Oh How I Love You"
    (*Music and Lyrics by* Andrew B. Sterling, Henry Lewis and Dave Dreyer.)]
Scene 3
  "(Swiss) Echo Song"
    N. Kouns, S. Kouns
    (*Music by* Carl Eckert.)
    Scene: In the Swiss Alps.
Scene 4
  At Eton College, England
  Dance
    T. Nip, C. O'Brien
    Eton Boys: B. Wright, M. Desmordant, R. Craft, E. Proctor, E. Downing, V. West, F. Ney, M. Messier, G. Lee, J. McRae, R. Fields, B. Bryant, M. Cort, F. Franklin, H. Jackson, H. Crewe, M. Keefe, A. Frawley.
Scene 5
  "Music"
    R. Bold
    Rigoletto: V. Voltaire. *La Boheme*: D. Best. *Faust*: M. Roberts. *Madame Butterfly*: Z. Santley. *Thais*: J. Voltaire. *Aida*: D. Lloyd. *Tales of Hoffman*: I. Delroy.
Scene 6
  "Peachy" (Peachie)[101a]
    I. Delroy
    (*Music by* Albert Gumble. *Lyrics by* Jack Yellen.)
Scene 7
  An Indian Flirtation[102]
    F. Ames, A. Winthrop
Scene 8
  In Frivolities Garden (Dancing Specialty)
    Barr Twins
  "In a Garden of Eden for Two"[103]
    I. Delroy
  Creation Dance[104]
    Doraldina
    Adam and Eve Girls: E. Downing, V. West, M. Messier, G. Lee, J. McRae, R. Fields, B. Bryant, M. Lockwood, F. Franklin, H. Jackson, H. Crewe, A. Nenci, M. Keefe, A. Frawley, F. Ney, P. Purtell, M. Cort, R. Hart, P. Van, R. Craft, E. Proctor, M. Kay, M. Desmordant, A. Lawlor.
Scene 9
  The Battle of Bay Rum
    Admiral: E. Gallagher. *Sailor*: H. Lewis.
  Grand Final Frivol: "Military Wedding of the Nations" (Military Marches)
    Entire Company
    Scene: The League of Nations.

1920.03   # AS YOU WERE

A Fantastic Musical Revue in Two Acts, 6 Scenes. Book and lyrics by Arthur Wimperis. (Based on the French revue 'Plus Ça Change' by Rip.) Music by

---

"Saxophones"
    7 Musical Nosses

[99] Dropped during the run.
[100] Dropped after opening.
[101] Added to Act 2, Scene 1 after opening:
[101a] Previously introduced in THE PASSING SHOW OF 1918, on tour.
[102] Dropped after opening.
[103] Dropped after opening.
[104] Dropped after opening.

Herman Darewski. American version by Glen MacDonough. Additional music and lyrics by E. Ray Goetz, (Melville Gideon, Cole Porter). Staged by George Marion. Musical numbers by Julian Mitchell. Costumes designed by Homer Conant, Dorothy Armstrong, Pieter Meyer, Mme. Pascaud, Paul Poiret, Anna Spencer. Scenery designed by H. Robert Law Studios, Withald Gordon. Art director, Herbert Ward. Orchestra under the direction of Louis Silvers. Produced by E. Ray Goetz, by arrangement with Charles B. Cochran of the London Pavilion. Opened 27 January 1920 at the Central Theatre and closed 29 May 1920 after 143 performances.

CAST: SAM BERNARD, IRENE BORDONI, CLIFTON WEBB, HUGH CAMERON, VIOLET STRATHMORE, STANLEY HARRISON, FRANK MAYNE, RUTH DONNELLY, Pat Walshe, William Ward, Irwin Emmer. *Specialty Dancers*: Sascha Piatov, Mlle. Moskovina, Helen Kroener.

Ladies of the Ensemble: Misses Grace Jones, May Carmen, Olive Brown, Lucille Gordon, Jeanette Cook, Peggy Tomson, Betty Hamilton, Marilyn Martin, Effie Smith, Mae Terrisfield.

Act 1, Scene 1: A House Party at Wolfie Wafflestein's Country House, Vanilla Villa, Westchester, A.D. 1920. *Scene 2*: The Royal Gardens at Versailles, A.D. 1650. *Scene 3*: Egypt. The Terrace of Cleopatra's Palace. B.C. 49.

Act 2, Scene 1: In Athens. B.C. 68-7? *Scene 2*: A Primeval Forest. B.C. ?? *Scene 3*: Vanilla Villa. A.D. 1920.

ACT 1

Scene 1

"Saturday Afternoon Till Monday Morning"
V. Strathmore
(*Music and Lyrics by* E. Ray Goetz.)

"Washington Square"[105]
C. Webb, R. Donnelly, Misses Carmen, Godfrey, Terresfield, Watson, Chorus
(*Music by* Melville Gideon. *Lyrics by* E. Ray Goetz, Cole Porter.)

"If You Could Care for Me"
I. Bordoni
(*Music by* Herman Darewski. *Lyrics by* Arthur Wimperis.)
Chase Clews: H. Cameron. *Ethel Nutt*: R. Donnelly. *Pinkie Smith*: V. Strathmore. *Cuthbert*: S. Harrison. *Wolfie Wafflestein*: S. Bernard. *Ki Ki*: C. Webb. *Gervaise*: I. Bordoni. *Professor Filbert*: F. Mayne.

Scene 2

"Follow Mr. Watteau"
V. Strathmore
(*Music by* Herman Darewski. *Lyrics by* Arthur Wimperis.)

"Ninon Was a Naughty Girl"
I. Bordoni
(*Music by* Herman Darewski. *Lyrics by* Arthur Wimperis.)
A Marquis: V. Strathmore. *Henri, Comte de Belamy*: C. Webb. *Ninon de l'Enclos*: I. Bordoni. *De La Reynie*: F. Mayne. *Wolfie Wafflestein*: S. Bernard. *Nicole*: R. Donnelly.

Scene 3

Specialty Dance
S. Piatov, Mlle. Moscovina, H. Kroener

"I Am Cleopatra"
I. Bordoni

Finale
(*Music and Lyrics by* E. Ray Goetz.)
The Court Dancers: S. Piatov, Mlle. Moscovina, H. Kroener. *Charmion*: R. Donnelly. *Captain Hodgkins*: S. Harrison. *Wolfie Wafflestein*: S. Bernard. *The Man from Cooks*: H. Cameron. *A Royal Slave*: F. Mayne. *Cleopatra*: I. Bordoni. *Mark Antony*: C. Webb.

ACT 2

Scene 1

"Under Grecian Skies"
V. Strathmore
(*Music and Lyrics by* E. Ray Goetz.)

Danse Pastorelle[106]
S. Piatov, Mlle. Moscovina

"Helen of Troy"
I. Bordoni
(*Music by* Herman Darewski. *Lyrics by* Arthur Wimperis.)
An Athenian Serenader: V. Strathmore. *A Sergeant in the Military Police*: S. Harrison. *Thermos*: H. Cameron. *Wolfie Wafflestein*: S. Bernard. *Diogenes*: F. Mayne. *Paris*: C. Webb. *Helen of Troy*: I. Bordoni.

---

[105]Performed as "In Chelsea Somewhere" in THE ECLIPSE, London.
[106]Dropped during the run.

Scene 2

"Who Ate Napoleons with Josephine (When Napoleon Was Away?)"
S. Bernard
(*Music by* E. Ray Goetz. *Lyrics by* Alfred Bryan.)
A Primeval Husband: P. Walshe. *A Prehistoric Wife*: W. Ward. *Wolfie Wafflestein*: S. Bernard. *An Antediluvian Friend of the Family*: I. Emmer.

Scene 3

"(When You're Dancing in) A Nightie on the Lawn"
C. Webb
(*Music and Lyrics by* E. Ray Goetz.)

Specialty Dance
C. Webb, H. Kroener

"If You Could Care for Me" (reprise)
I. Bordoni

Finale
Gervaise: I. Bordoni. *Wolfie Wafflestein*: S. Bernard. *Cuthbert*: S. Harrison. *KiKi*: C. Webb. *Mr. Clews*: H. Cameron. *Ethel Nutt*: R. Donnelly. *Pinkie Smith*: V. Strathmore. *Professor Filbert*: F. Mayne.

1920.04 THE NIGHT BOAT

A Musical Comedy in Three Acts. Book and lyrics by Anne Caldwell. Based on a farce ('Le Contrôleur de wagons-lits') by Alexandre Bisson. Music by Jerome Kern. Play staged by Fred G. Latham. Musical numbers staged by Ned Wayburn. Costumes designed by O'Kane Conwell. Orchestra under the direction of Victor Baravelle. Orchestrations by Frank Saddler. Produced by Charles Dillingham. Opened 2 February 1920 at the Liberty Theatre and closed 30 October 1920 after 313 performances.

CAST (in order of appearance): *Minnie, a maid*: Marie Reagan. *A Workman*: Irving Carpenter. *Mrs. Maxim*: ADA LEWIS. *Barbara, her younger daughter*: LOUISE GROODY. *Mrs. Hazel White, her elder daughter*: STELLA HOBAN. *Freddie Ides*: HAL SKELLY. *Inspector Dempsey*: John Scannell. *Bob White*: JOHN E. HAZZARD. *Captain Robert White*: ERNEST TORRENCE. *The Steward*: HANSFORD WILSON. *Dora DeCosta*: Lillian Kemble Cooper. *Florence DeCosta*: Betty Hale. *Ladies' Maids (6)*: *Betty*: Arline Chase. *Susan*: Lois Leigh. *Molly*: Mildred Sinclair. *Jane*: Bunny Wendell. *Alice*: Geraldine Alexander. *Polly*: Lydia Scott. *Mrs. de Costa*: Mrs. John Findlay. (*Dance Specialty*: Cansino Brothers.) Other characters played by:
Ensemble: Misses Babz Fowler, Evelyn Conway, Cecile Conway, Irene Wilson, Lola Curtis, Jeanette MacDonald, Beatrice Hughes, Isabel Falconer, Phoebe Appleton, Janet Carleton, Mildred Sinclair, Helen Gates, Marie Cavanagh, Peggy Craven, Agnes Allen, Daisy Daniels, Mae LeRoy, Dorothy Hollis, Gene Fleming, Evelyn Plumadore, Marie Benedict. Messrs. Paul Lester, Gordon Kyle, Jack Hughes, Ray Moore, Ralph O'Brien, Frank Rowan, Dan Sparkes, Kay Tudor.

Act 1: At the White's.

Act 2: The Night Boat.

Act 3: At the DeCosta's.

ACT 1

"Some Fine Day"
L. Groody, Ensemble

"Whose Baby Are You?"
L. Groody, H. Skelly

"Left All Alone Again Blues"
S. Hoban, Ensemble

"Good Night Boat"
J. E. Hazzard, S. Hoban, L. Groody, H. Skelly, A. Lewis, Ensemble
(*Lyrics by* Anne Caldwell and Frank Craven.)

Plot Demonstrators
Ladies' Maids

"I'd Like a Lighthouse"
L. Groody, H. Skelly

Buffo Finale

ACT 2

"Catskills, Hello" (Opening)
Ensemble

Jug Band and Dance
H. Wilson, Jug Band

Maid's Sextette
Ladies' Maids

"Don't You Want to Take Me?"
L. Groody, H. Skelly

"I Love the Lassies" (I Love Them All)
  E. Torrence, A. Chase, L. Leigh, Misses B. Wendell, Curtis, Sinclair, Hollis, Alexander, Wilson, Conway, Gates, Daniels, Cavanagh, Appleton, Burns
River Song Medley[107]:
"The Quadalquiver"
  Dances by the Cansino Brothers
"(By the) Saskatchewan" (from THE PINK LADY)
  (Music by Ivan Caryll. Lyrics by C. M. S. McLellan.)
"On the Banks of the Wabash (Far Away)"
  (Music and Lyrics by Paul Dresser.)
"Congo Love Song" (from NANCY BROWN)
  (Music by J. Rosamond Johnson. Lyrics by Bob Cole.)
"Row, Row, Row" (from ZIEGFELD FOLLIES OF 1912)
  (Music by James Monaco. Lyrics by William Jerome.)
"Down by the Erie" (from HELLO, BROADWAY)
  (Music and Lyrics by George M. Cohan.)
"M-i-s-s-i-s-s-i-p-p-i" (from ZIEGFELD'S MIDNIGHT REVUE, 1916, and HITCHY-KOO OF 1917)
  (Music by Harry Tierney. Lyrics by Bert Hanlon and Benny Ryan.)
"Good Night, Boat" (reprise)

ACT 3
Plot Demonstrators
  Ladies' Maids
Laundry Duet
  J. E. Hazzard, L. K. Cooper
"A Heart for Sale"
  L. Groody, Boys
"Girls Are Like a Rainbow"
  H. Skelly, Misses Chase, L. Leigh, Sinclair, Wendell, Chorus
Finale
  Ensemble

1920.05   MY GOLDEN GIRL

A Comedy with Music in Two Acts. Book and lyrics by Frederic Arnold Kummer. Music by Victor Herbert. Directed by J. Clifford Brooke. Dances arranged by Julian Alfred. Orchestra under the direction of Philip James. Produced by Harry Wardell. Opened 2 February 1920 at the Nora Bayes Theatre, moved 5 April 1920 to the Casino Theatre, and closed 1 May 1920 after 105 performances.[108]

CAST (in order of appearance): *Wilson*, the Mitchell's butler: ROBERT O'CONNOR. *Blanche*, the maid: DOROTHY TIERNEY. *Kitty Mason*, a friend of Mrs. Mitchell: EVELYN CAVANAUGH. *Captain Paul de Bazin*, her fiancé: RICHARD DORE. *Arthur Mitchell*, a dissatisfied young man: VICTOR MORLEY. *Peggy Mitchell*, his wife, equally dissatisfied: MARIE CARROLL. *Martin*, the Mitchell's chauffeur: Raymond Barrett. *Mr. Hanks*, Mrs. Mitchell's lawyer: NED A. SPARKS. *Mr. Pullinger*, Mr. Mitchell's lawyer: EDWARD SEE. *Helen Randolph*, Mr. Mitchell's affinity: HELEN BOLTON. *Howard Pope*, Mrs. Mitchell's affinity: GEORGE TRABERT. *Mrs. Judson Mitchell*, Mr. Mitchell's mother: EDNA MAY OLIVER. *Mr. Clarence Swan*, Mrs. Mitchell's father: HAROLD VIZARD. *Friends of Kitty (2): Mildred Ray*: Victoria White. *Lois Booth*: Adele Boulais.
Ensemble: Trixie Packard, Yvonne LaGrange, Gladys Hart, Eileen Adaire, Caroline Holton, Viola Degnan, Flo Howard, Jeannette Dietrich, Robina Davidson, Peggy Schramm, Marcia White, Loretta Walsh, Norma Eve Warrington, Robert Archibald, Eastman McRoy, William Strubain.

The action takes place at the present time on a Saturday afternoon in June.

Act 1, Scene 1: Main Hall of the Mitchell's Country Home on Long Island. *Scene 2*: The same. That evening before dinner.

Act 2: The Mitchell's Private Bathing Beach. That night,

ACT 1
Scene 1
"The Jazzy-Jaz—Dancing Lesson"
  R. O'Connor
"A Little Nest for Two"
  E. Cavanaugh, R. Dore, Chorus

Basson Solo
  V. Morley
"Darby and Joan"[109]
  V. Morley, M. Carroll
"Variety"
  V. Morley, M. Carroll, E. See, N. A. Sparks
"Name the Day"
  E. Cavanaugh, R. Dore, Chorus
Finale
Scene 2
"I Want You"
  V. Morley, Chorus
"My Golden Girl"
  G. Trabert
"A Song Without (Many) Words"
  V. Morley, H. Bolton, Chorus
"Ragtime Terpsichore"
  R. O'Connor, D. Tierney
"If We Had Met Before"
  H. Bolton, G. Trabert
Finale
ACT 2[110]
"Shooting Star"
  M. Carroll, Chorus
"My Golden Girl" (reprise)
  G. Trabert
"Change Partners"
  V. Morley, M. Carroll, G. Trabert, E. Cavanaugh, R. Dore, Chorus
Specialty
  R. Dore, E. Cavanaugh
"I'd Like a Honeymoon with You"
  M. Carroll
"Think It Over"
  N. A. Sparks, E. See, H. Vizard
"What Shall We Do If the Moon Goes Out"
  E. Cavanaugh, R. Dore, Chorus
Finale

1920.06   TICK-TACK-TOE

The Latest and Brightest Musical Outburst (a Musical Revue) in Two Acts, 12 Courses (scenes). Sketches, music and lyrics by Herman Timberg. Settings designed by Watson Barratt. Costumes designed by Homer Conant. Orchestra under the direction of William A. Krauth. Produced by Herman Timberg. Opened 23 February 1920 at the Princess Theatre and closed 20 March 1920 after 32 performances.[111]

CAST: FLO LEWIS, JAY GOULD, HERMAN TIMBERG, DORA HILTON, C. LELAND MARSH, BILLY DREYER, LAURA DREYER, PEARL EATON, GEORGE MAYO, HATTIE DARLING, J. GUILFOYLE, (Arthur) MOSS and (Ed) FRYE, Eddie Frankel, Charles Senft.
Ladies of the Ensemble: C. Loralda Poppenay, Carmen Hayes, Helen Lewis, Mabel Benelesha, Marjorie Drury, Dotty Bryant, Elsie Frank, Amy Frank, Gloria Mason, Beth Carpenter, Marie Gilmore, Pearl Mathews, Ruby Smith, Willa Lorena, Sally Barry, Dorothy Lewis.

---

[107]With the exception of "Good Night Boat," the popular songs in the medley are not by Jerome Kern.
[108]No credit in programs for scenery or costumes.

---

[109]Dropped during the run.
[110]Added late in the run to Act 2, after the Specialty:
  "Hobbies"
    V. Morley
[111]Subsequently toured in the fall of 1920 in a revised form under the auspices of Arthur Klein, restaged by Edwin T. Emery, starring Sophie Tucker, and featuring Eddie Foley. As per published sheet music, specialties introduced included:
  "Sweet Mamma (Papa's Getting Mad)" (also in PASSING SHOW OF 1920)
    S. Tucker
    (Music and Lyrics by Peter L. Frost.)
  "The Dardanella Blues"
    S. Tucker
    (Music by John S. Black. Lyrics by Fred Fisher.)

ACT 1

Scene 1

Another Prologue
J. Gould

Scene 2

Exterior of Stove

Scene 3

"A Double Order of Chicken"
P. Eaton, Chickens
Scene: Interior of Stove.
Some Chicken: P. Eaton. *First Chick*: C. L. Poppenay. *Second Chick*: C. Hayes.
Third Chick: H. Lewis. *Fourth Chick*: M. Benelesha. *Fifth Chick*: M. Drury.
Sixth Chick: D. Bryant. *Seventh Chick*: E. Frank. *Eighth Chick*: A. Frank.

Scene 4

"(Love Is) A Game of Cards"
H. Timberg, J. Gould
Scene: Song Writer's Workshop.
Joe Lyric: J. Gould. *Fuller Melody*: H. Timberg.

Scene 5

"Chinese-American Rag"
D. Hilton, Chinese Maids

Specialty
E. Frankel

Specialty
B. Dreyer

"Take Me Back to Philadelphia, Pa." (I Want to Go Back to Philadelphia, Pa.)
F. Lewis, Dream Stars

Violin Specialty and Dance
H. Timberg

Hop Recitation
F. Lewis, J. Gould

"Hoppy Poppy Queen"
J. Gould, H. Darling, Poppy Queens

Shimmy Lesson
H. Timberg, G. Mayo, P. Eaton, Shimmy Pupils

"(I'd Like to Know Why) I Fell in Love with You"
J. Gould, F. Lewis, H. Darling

"A Lesson in Love"
H. Timberg, H. Darling

Specialty
B. Dreyer, L. Dreyer

"Shimmy All the Blues Away"
J. Gould, F. Lewis

"Playing for the Girl"
J. Gould, C. L. Marsh, Girls

Finale
Scene: Stu-Hi's Chinese-American Restaurant.
Stu-Hi: W. Bence. *Stu Lo*, his daughter: D. Hilton. *Flo*, fresh from
Philadelphia: F. Lewis. *Jay*, fresh from the same place: J. Gould. *Jim*, fresh
from anywhere: C. L. Marsh. *Stu Mutch* (should have more to do): C. Senft.
Sho Mee, a celestial dancing master: B. Dreyer. *Kik Lo*, his pupil: L. Dreyer.
Sing Hi (a Chinese vamp): D. Hilton. *Ni No* (knows nothing): E. Frankel.
Celestial Maids: M. Drury, G. Mason, B. Carpenter. *Dream Stars*: *Lillian
Lorraine*: C. Hayes. *Frisco*: M. Benelesha. *Dolly Sisters*: A. Frank, E. Frank.
Ann Pennington: C. L. Popenay. *Al Jolson*: H. Lewis. *Frances White*: D.
Bryant. *Ethel Barrymore*: M. Gilmore. *Julius* (nothing to do with the plot): H.
Timberg. *Pearl* (just a girl): P. Eaton. *Meyer* (everything to do with the plot):
G. Mayo. *Like Me* (she loves the boys): H. Darling. *Sight Seers*: P. Mathews,
R. Smith, W. Lorena, S. Barry, D. Lewis.

ACT 2

Scene 1

Scene: Manager's Office.
Mr. Two Bit (he hires and fires): J. Guilfoyle. *Author* (the usual struggle):
J. Gould. *Messenger Boy* (working for himself): E. Frankel. *Letter Carrier*
(working for the Government): C. Senft. *Chorus Girl* (with a gift of gab):
P. Eaton. *Another Chorus Girl* (also gifted): A. Frank.

Scene 2

"Girls, Girls, Girls"
H. Darling, Soubrettes

"My Manicure Maids"
J. Gould, F. Lewis, G. Mayo, P. Eaton, Manicure Maids

Scene: A Rehearsal.
Hallie Primma (she opens the show): H. Darling. *Joe* (he produces the show):
J. Gould. *Max* (he stages the dances): C. L. Marsh. *Minnie* (she shouldn't
worry): C. Hayes. *Lillie* (she doesn't care either): M. Drury. *Dotty* (always out
of step): D. Bryant. *Elssie* (there's a nail in her shoe): E. Frank. *Willa* (full of
dates): W. Lorena.

Scene 3

Scene: Room in a Hotel.
First Guest: G. Mayo. *Second Guest*: J. Guilfoyle. *Third Guest*: J. Gould.
Fourth Guest: D. Hilton. *Bell-Boy*: E. Frankel. *Miss Trimmer*: F. Lewis.
Second Trimmer: P. Eaton.

Scene 4

"Tell Me, Kind Spirit"
P. Eaton, Ouija Girls

"Where's My Sweet and Pretty Man?"
F. Lewis

Novelty Number

"Dance Mad"
H. Darling, C. L. Marsh
Scene: The Drawing Room Upstairs.
Miss Seance: P. Eaton. *Marjorie* (full of spirits?): M. Drury. *Joe* (Johnny
Walker): J. Gould. *Flo* (where's her sweet and pretty man?): F. Lewis. *Meyer*
(he's in and he's seen too): G. Mayo. *Leland* (Gee! what a name): C. L.
Marsh. *Carmen* (visitor): C. Hayes. *Helen* (visitor): H. Lewis. *Svengali*: H.
Timberg. *Trilby*: H. Darling.

Scene 5

Scene: The Automat in 1940.
Cashier: C. L. Marsh. *Julius*: H. Timberg. *Meyer*: G. Mayo. *Joe*: J. Gould.

Scene 6

Important Chatter
Moss and Frye
Scene: Times Square, 7 A.M.

Scene 7

Joe's Novelty Punch Scene

Finale
Entire Company

1920.07 LOOK WHO'S HERE

A Musical Farce in Two Acts, 5 Scenes. Book by Frank Mandel. Music by
Silvio Hein. Lyrics by Edward Paulton; travesties, additional dialogue and
lyrics by Cecil Lean. Production staged by Edwin T. Emery. Dances by
Edward Hutchinson. Scenery by H. Robert Law Studio. Costumes by
Mahieu; Miss Mayfield's Costumes by Joseph. Orchestra under the direc-
tion of William Howard. Produced by Spiegel's Productions, Inc. (Max
Spiegel). Opened 2 March 1920 at the 44th Street Theatre and closed 22
May 1920 after 87 performances.

CAST (in order of appearance): *James Saunders*, Proprietor of Dreamer's Inn: GEORGE
R. Lynch. *May*, Clerk of Dreamer's Inn: MADGE RUSH. *Bell Boys (2)*: *Flo*: ALICIA
McCARTHY. *Jo*: MARY McCARTHY. *Caroline Holmes*: LOUISE KELLEY. *Carlos
Del Monte*, an Art Critic: DAVE QUIXANO. *Robert W. Holmes*, Famous American
Novelist: CECIL LEAN. *Rosamond Purcell*, Matrimonial Expert: CLEO
MAYFIELD. *Horace Bream*: GEORGIE MACK. *Dorothy Chase*: SYLVIA DeFRANKIE. *Daniel V.
Chase*, Her Father: JOHN F. MORRISSEY.

Ladies of the Ensemble: Georgia Empey, Gayle Friegel, Adelarie Starr, Burnic
Cantor, Lispa Taft, Alice Biglow, Millicent Fillat, Lillian Dennis, Florence Haynes,
Dorothy Neill, Ruth Thomas, Harriette Munson.

Act 1: The Lobby of the Dreamer's Inn, Catskill Mountains. Early evening.

Act 2, Scene 1: The Balcony Hallway, after midnight. *Scene 2*: Interior of Holmes'
Room in the Hotel. 3 A.M. *Scene 3*: The Balcony Hallway. *Scene 4*: Interior of Holmes'
Room.

ACT 1

Opening Ensemble
G. R. Lynch, A. McCarthy, M. McCarthy, Sport Girls

"My Night in Venice"[112]
D. Quixano, Girls

"If I Had Only Met You, Dear"
L. Kelley, D. Quixano

---

[112]For subsequent tour replaced by:
"I Love Beauty"

"I Know and You Know"
  C. Lean
  (*Lyrics by* Cecil Lean, Edward Paulton.)
"(I'll Make) Bubbles"
  C. Lean, C. Mayfield
"Love, Love, Love"
  L. Kelley
"I Wonder What She's Thinking of Now"
  G. Mack, M. Rush
"Love Never Changes"
  C. Lean, C. Mayfield
  (*Lyrics by* Cecil Lean, Edward Paulton.)
Finale
  Principals, Chorus
ACT 2
"The Bell Hop Blues"
  A. McCarthy, M. McCarthy
  (*Music and Lyrics by* Frank Goodman and Al Piantadosi.)
"Give Me a Little Cosey Corner"[113]
  C. Mayfield
"Look Who's Here"[114]
  C. Lean, S. DeFrankie
"The Turk Has the Right Idea"
  C. Lean, C. Mayfield, Chorus
  (*Lyrics by* Cecil Lean, Edward Paulton.)
"I Cannot Understand"
  L. Kelley, D. Quixano
Dance
  M. Rush
"When a Wife Gets Fat" (Since My Wife Got Fat)
  C. Lean
  (*Lyrics by* Cecil Lean, Edward Paulton.)
Finale
  Company

1920.08   WHAT'S IN A NAME?

A Musical Revue in Two Acts, 17 Scenes. Book and lyrics by John Murray Anderson, in collaboration with Anna Wynne O'Ryan and Jack Yellen. Music by Milton Ager. Entire production devised and staged by John Murray Anderson. Dances arranged by Michio Ito. Costumes designed by Robert E. Locher, Kay Turner. Settings designed by James Reynolds. Orchestra under the direction of Augustus Barratt. Orchestrations by Maurice DePackh and Arthur Lange. Produced by John Murray Anderson, Inc. Opened 19 March 1920 at the Maxine Elliott's Theatre, moved by 19 April 1920 to the Lyric Theatre, and closed 26 June 1920 after 115 performances.

CAST: PHIL WHITE, HERBERT WILLIAMS, ALICE HEGEMAN, EDWARD E. FORD, CHARLES DERICKSON, ROSALIND FULLER, ALLYN [Allen] KEARNS, MARY LANE, REX DANTZLER, SHEILA COURTNEY, THOMAS MORGAN, ETHEL SINCLAIR, MARIE GASPAR, JOE BURROUGHS, BEATRICE HERFORD, HONEY KAY, VIVIAN CONNORS, OLIN HOWLAND, ROBERT MANNING, JOHN ALEXANDER, THOMAS MORGAN, GLORIA FOY, Frank Parker, Margaret Petit, Joseph Palkowitch, Dick Dolliver, (Herbert) Williams and (Hilda) Wolfus.

Ladies of the Ensemble: Virginia Lee, Constance Barnes, Olive Brower, Beatrice Milner, Olive LaVaine, Gertrude Alces, Muriel Manners, Dorothy Utley, Sallie Yarrow, Hildred, Helen Lee Worthing, Arjamond, Juliette Compton, Dorothy Smoller, Zola Terryl, Olive Brower, Corone Paynter, June Korle. *Dancers:* Mildred Mann, Grace DeCarlton, Dorothy Loveclark, Carol Miller, Emilie Haddone, Jessie Loraine, Christine Bernsman, Mimi Youde, Zola Terryl, Yasu Katayama, Vera Myers, Sara Crewe, Loretta Morgan, Flora Keane, Dorothy DeVinna. *Gentlemen of the Ensemble:* A. M. Gowing, H. Glenn Gamble, Lane McLeod, Willard Eldridge.

---

[113]Replaced for subsequent tour by:
"Somebody's Eyes"
  C. Mayfield, Chorus
  (*Music by* Herbert Clair and Frank Goodman. *Lyrics by* Bud Green.)
[114]Replaced for subsequent tour by:
"There's a Romeo for Every Girl I Know"
  C. Lean, Viola Frayne (Dorothy)
  (*Music by* Sam H. Stept. *Lyrics by* Cecil Lean and Bud Green.)

ACT 1[115]
Prologue
  The Boss: P. White. *Martin:* H. Williams. *Drama:* A. Hegeman. *The Tired-Business-Man:* E. E. Ford. *Opportunity:* C. Derickson.
Scene 1
"The Theatrical Blues"
  Scene: The Outer Stage.
  The Little Blue Girl: R. Fuller. *The Juvenile:* A. Kearns. *The Soprano:* M. Lane. *The Tenor:* R. Dantzler. *The Leading Lady:* S. Courtney. *The Composer:* T. Morgan. *The Chorus Girl:* E. Sinclair. *The Old-Timer:* P. White.
Scene 2
  The Optimist: M. Gaspar.
  Scene: The Inner Stage.
Scene 3
"Rap-Tap-a-Tap" (Rap Tap, a Tap)
  M. Gaspar, Girls, Boys
  The Ouija Girls: V. Lee, C. Barnes, O. Brower, B. Milner, O. LaVaine, G. Alces, M. Manners, D. Utley. *The Blue Girls:* S. Yarrow, J. Loraine, Do. DeVinna, L. Morgan, D. Loveclark, F. Keane, C. Miller, E. Haddone. *Blue Boys:* A. M. Gowing, H. Glenn Gamble, L. McLeod, W. Eldridge.
The Seance
  Bolivar Podge: J. Burroughs. *Madame Albino,* a medium: A. Hegeman.
Danse Planchette
  G. Foy
  Commére: B. Herford. *The Critic:* H. Kay. *The Ballerina:* V. Connors. *The Toe Dancers:* M. Mann, G. DeCarlton, M. Youde, C. Bernsman. *Columbine:* M. Petit. *Harlequin:* F. Parker. *Light:* Hildred. *Colour:* H. L. Worthing. *Architecture:* Arjamond. *Dress:* J. Compton.
Scene 4
"What's in a Name?" (Love Is Always Love)
  R. Dantzler
  Romeo: C. Derickson. *Juliet:* M. Lane. Ladies in the Polonaise.
Scene 5
Divertissement
  O. Howland
  Scene: The Outer Stage.
Scene 6
"The Jewels of Pandora"
  M. Lane
  Scene: The Inner Stage.
  The Bearer of the Lamp of Life: D. Smoller. *The Bearer of the Mirror:* S. Courtney. *The Bearer of Pandora's Box:* Z. Terryl. *The Harpist:* O. Brower. *Pandora:* Hildred. *Jewels: The White Pearl:* H. L. Worthing. *The Amethyst:* C. Barnes. *The Scarab:* D. Utley. *The Sapphire:* M. Manners. *The Coral:* O. LaVaine. *The Jade:* Arjamond. *The Sardonyx:* C. Paynter. *The Topaz:* S. Yarrow. *The Ruby:* B. Milner. *The Black Pearl:* J. Compton. *The Turquoise:* G. Alces. *The Diamond:* V. Lee. *The Dancer:* M. Holiday.
Scene 7
Highlowbrow (*by* S. Jay Kaufman)
  Tom: P. White. *Bill:* E. E. Ford. *An Elderly Gentleman:* O. Howland. *An Elderly Lady:* M. Lane. *A Waiter:* L. McLeod. *A Gentleman:* O. Howland. *A Doctor:* R. Manning. *Lamia:* J. Alexander. *Pilate:* T. Morgan. *A Brakeman:* A. Kearns. *His Wife:* E. Sinclair.
Scene 8
"A Young Man's Fancy" (Music Box Song)
  R. Fuller
  Scene: The Inner Stage.
  The Shepherdess: J. Korle. *The Shepherd:* F. Parker. *The Dancer:* M. Petit. *Eliza Jane:* V. Connors. *The Antiquarian:* H. Kay. *Corps de Ballet:* M. Youde, C. Bernsman, D. Loveclark, J. Loraine, G. DeCarlton, M. Mann.
Scene 9
"Strike!"
  G. Foy, A. Kearns
Dance
  D. Smoller, J. Vincent; V. Lee, L. McLeod; S. Courtney, A. M. Gowing; S. Crewe, W. Eldredge; G. Foy, O. Howland
Scene 10
Divertissement
  Williams and Wolfus
  Scene: The Inner Stage.

---

[115]Added to Act 1:
  The Intruders (after Scene 3)
    Billy B. Van, James J. Corbett
  Dance
    Nirska

Scene 11

"The Valley of Dreams"[116]
  C. Derickson
    Inspiration: M. Petit. *Elo*: D. Smoller. *Echo*: S. Courtney.
    The Muses: Erato: Hildred. *Euterpe*: M. Manners. *Eurania*: D. Utley. *Thalia*:
    G. Alces. *Clio*: B. Milner. *Calliope*: Arjamond. *Polymia*: V. Lee. *Terpsichore*:
    H. L. Worthing. *Melpomene*: J. Compton. *Athena*: M. Lane.
    The Graces: M. Petit, Z. Terryl, J. Loraine. *Chorus*: C. Paynter. *Coryphees*:
    M. Youde, G. DeCarlton, F. Keane, M. Mann, D. Loveclark, C.
    Bersman, E. Haddone.

Scene 12

"The Evolution of the Finale"
    1900: *The Musical Director*: J. Palkowitch. *First Student*: D. Dolliver. *Second
    Student*: T. Morgan. *Elsa*: A. Hegeman. *Captain Ralph*: P. White. *The Youngest
    Villager*: H. Kay. *A Herald*: D. Loveclark. *The Duke of Mordeaux*: O. Howland.
    The Duchess: B. Herford. *Their Daughter*: V. Myers. *The Inn-Keeper*: E. E. Ford.
    The Captain of the Guards: J. Burroughs. *The Army*: L. McLeod. *The Gypsy
    Queen*: S. Courtney.
    1910: *Georgem*: A. Kearns. *Miss Manhattan*: E. Sinclair. *Liberty*: G. Alces. *The
    C.H.I.L.D.*: V. Connors. And the Georgem Girls.
    1920: *The Author*: J. Alexander. *The Composer*: T. Morgan. *The Singer*: M.
    Lane. *The Juvenile*: C. Derickson. *The Ingenue*: M. Gaspar. *The Comedian*: H.
    Williams. *The Soubrette*: G. Foy. *The Costumer*: C. Paynter. *The Angel*: P.
    White. *Mr. Shubert*: A. Kearns. *The Scrubwoman*: A. Hegeman. And Ensemble.

ACT 2
Scene 1

"In Fair Japan"
  V. Myers
    The Musician: Z. Terryl. *The Story-Teller*: C. Derickson. *The Princess*: D.
    Smoller. *The Prince*: F. Parker. *The Dancer*: K. Kimuar. *The Goose Girl*: Y.
    Katayama.
    Dancers: Spring: M. Mann, G. DeCarlton, D. Loveclark, C. Miller, E.
    Haddone, J. Loraine, C. Bernsman, M. Youde. *Summer*: Z. Terryl, Y.
    Katayama, V. Myers. *Autumn*: E. Haddone, S. Crewe, J. Loraine, C.
    Bernsman. *Winter*: L. Morgan, M. Youde, F. Keane, C. Miller, D.
    Loveclark, D. DeVinna. *Attendants*: W. Eldridge, L. McLeod, A. M.
    Gowing. (*Native dances arranged by* Michio Itow.)

Scene 2

"Without Kissing, Love Isn't Love"
  G. Foy, A. Kearns

Scene 3

"That Reminiscent Melody"
  M. Gaspar, R. Fuller, V. Myers, H. Kay, G. Foy, M. Lane, G. Alces, J. Korie, V.
  Lee, T. Morgan, A. M. Gowin, J. Vincent, J. Burroughs, W. Eldridge, L.
  McLeod, A. Kearns, R. Dantzler, C. Derickson
    Scene: The Outer Stage. At the piano: H. Williams.

Scene 4

Beatrice Herford

Scene 5

"The Bridal Veil"
    Scene: The Inner Stage.
    The Bride-to-Be: R. Fuller. *The Page*: M. Petit.
    Her Ancestors: Medieval Bride: J. Compton.
    Her Maids: G. Alces, O. Browe, R. Sharpe, C. Barnes. *Elizabethan Bride*: M.
    Lane. *Dancers of the "Passe-de-la-Rene"*: S. Courtney, D. Smoller. *Louis XVI
    Bride*: H. L. Worthing. *The Flower Bride*: V. Connors. *Dancers in the "Menuet
    de la Coeur"*: J. Loraine, D. Loveclark, C. Bernsman, M. Youde. *The Empire
    Bride*: V. Lee. *Her Maids*: Hildred, B. Milner, D. Utley, M. Manners. *1870
    Bride*: C. Paynter. *Her Maids*: L. Morgan, S. Crewe. *1870 Bridegroom*: J.
    Vincent.

"The Chelsea Reach"
    Wedding Guests and Dancers: A. Hegeman, G. Foy, V. Myers, B. Herford, A.
    Kearns, E. E. Ford, O. Howland, J. Burroughs. *Dana Gibson Bride*: O. LaVaine.
    Flower Girls: G. DeCarlton, M. Mann. *1930 Bride*: Arjamond. *Her Maids*: F.
    Keane, E. Haddone, D. DeVinna, C Miller.

Epilogue

1920.09 # FLORODORA

A Revival of the Musical Play in Two Acts, 3 Scenes[117]. Book by Owen
Hall. (Revised by Harry B. Smith.) Music by Leslie Stuart. Lyrics by Ernest

---

[116]Added to this scene late in the run was a dance solo:
  The Dance of the Silver Bubble
    Grace Christie
[117]Originally produced 12 November 1900 at the Casino Theatre for 505
performances.

Boyd-Jones and Paul Rubens. Staged by Lewis Morton. Musical numbers
staged by Allan. K. Foster and Lewis Hooper. Scenes designed by Watson
Barratt. Costumes designed by Cora MacGeachy. Orchestra under the
direction of Charles Drury. Produced by Messrs. Lee and J. J. Shubert.
Opened 5 April 1920 at the Century Theatre and closed 14 August 1920 after 150
performances.

CAST (in order of appearance): *Marquita*: Marie Wells. *Paquita*: Perle Germonde.
Leandro, Overseer at the Farm: Nace Bonville. *Frank Abercoed*, Confidential Clerk to
Gilfain and Manager of the Island: WALTER WOOLF. *English Clerks to Mr. Griffin
(6): Pym*: Minor McLain. *Langdale*: George Ellison. *Symes*: Lucius Metz. *Allen*: Lewis
Christy. *Scott*: Allen C. Jenkins. *Grogan*: William Lillite. *Anthony Tweedlepunch*,
Showman, Hypnotist, Palmist and Phrenologist: GEORGE HASSELL. *Cyrus Gilfain*,
Proprietor of the Island of Florodora, and Owner of the Famous Florodora Perfume:
JOHN T. MURRAY. *Lady Hollyrood*, a Widow, Arthur Donegal's Sister: CHRISTIE
MacDONALD. *Angela Gilfain*, Cyrus Gilfain's Daughter: MARGOT KELLY. *Captain
Arthur Donegal* of the Fourth Royal Life Guards, and Lady Hollyrood's
Brother: HARRY FENDER. *English Girls (Sextette) (6): Claire*: Dama Sykes. *Bernice*:
Dorothy Leeds. *Mabel*: Fay Evelyn. *Lucille*: Beatrice Swanson. *Alice*: Marcella
Swanson. *Daisy*: Muriel Lodge. *Dolores*, a Girl on Gilfain's Farm: ELEANOR
PAINTER. *Juanita*: ISABELLE RODRIGUEZ. *Valeda*, a Maid at Abercoed Castle:
Muriel de Forest. *Spanish Farm Hands, Flower Girls, Porters, Guests, etc.*

Spanish Girls: Misses Billy Andrews, Bernice Dewey, Margaret Grace, Adelina
Thomason, Blue Cloud, Betty Dair, Elizabeth Darling, Beatrice Darling, Jacqueline
Logan, Rheba Stewart, Helen O'Day, Bunny Stuart. *Perfume Bearers*: Misses Hannah
Krum, Helen Weber, Dorothy Johnson, Gypsy Mooney, Ellen Este, Hilda Wright,
Madeline Laurell, Margaret Adair, Edna Rodet, Natalie Graves, Olive Channing,
Frances Dunlap. *Guests*: Misses Anna Berg, Peggy Holmes, Estelle Langner, Imelda
LaMorte, Leila Van Holk, Helen Sovrani, Betty Palmer, Ethel Loris, Ruth Hervey,
Elizabeth Walsh, Camilla Lyon, Eleanor Grover. *Overseers at the Farm*: Misses Idamae
Oderlin, Elaine Hall, June Kellard, Helen Adams, Mona Mode, Trixie Stegman.
Laborers, Farm Hands, Guests: Messrs. Conroy, Miller, Harvey, Christy O'Donnell,
Packard, Dillon, Tillett, Steele, Johnson. *Sextette Understudies*: Misses Vera Gibson,
Madelene Richers.

Act 1: The Island of Florodora.

Act 2, Scene 1: The Garden at Abercoed Castle. *Scene 2*: The Ball Room at Abercoed
Castle.

ACT 1
Opening Chorus

"We Are the Clerks"[118]
    6 English Clerks, Dancing Girls

"Chorus of Welcome to Gilfain"[119]
    Ensemble of Natives, Flower Girls
    (*Lyrics by* Ernest Boyd-Jones.)

"Come and See Our Island"
    Six English Girls, 6 English Clerks

"When I Leave Town"
    C. MacDonald
    (*Lyrics by* Paul Rubens.)

"Hello, People"[120] (from HAVANA)
    M. Kelly, Girls
    (*Lyrics by* George Arthurs.)

"The Fellow Who Might Be"/"Galloping"
    M. Kelly, H. Fender
    (*Lyrics by* Ernest Boyd-Jones.)

"Love's a Game"[121] (Song)
    E. Painter

"Somebody"
    E. Painter, W. Woolf

"I Want to Marry a Man, I Do"
    G. Hassell, C. MacDonald, J. T. Murray
    (*Lyrics by* Paul Rubens.)

"Phrenology"
    J. T. Murray, Ensemble
    (*Lyrics by* Ernest Boyd-Jones.)

Dance
    I. Rodriguez

---

[118]Interpolated for this revival.
[119]Interpolated for this revival.
[120]Interpolated for this revival.
[121]Interpolated for this revival. Replaced during the run by:
  "Caramba!" (Spanish Song)
    E. Painter
    (*Music by* Milan Roder. *Lyrics by* Harry B. Smith.)

"(Under the) Shade of the Sheltering Palms"
W. Woolf
(*Music and Lyrics by* Leslie Stuart.)
Finale
Entire Company
ACT 2
Opening Chorus
Ensemble
"The Millionaire"[122]
J. T. Murray, Ensemble
"Tact"
C. MacDonald
(*Lyrics by* Paul Rubens.)
"Love Will Find You"[123]
E. Painter
(*Music by* P. Tirindelli. *Lyrics by* Harry B. Smith.)
"Tell Me, Pretty Maiden" (Florodora Sextette)
Sextette Girls, Clerks
(*Lyrics by* Leslie Stuart.)
"I Want to Be a Military Man"
H. Fender, Chorus
(*Lyrics by* Frank Clement.)
"Come to St. George's"[124] (from THE BELLE OF MAYFAIR)
C. MacDonald, M. Kelly, H. Fender, W. Woolf
(*Lyrics by* Leslie Stuart.)
Finale
Entire Company

1920.10 THE ED WYNN CARNIVAL

An Entertainment (Musical Revue) in Two Acts, 13 Scenes. Dialogue, music and lyrics by Ed Wynn. Directed by Ned Wayburn. Scenery designed by Joseph Physioc. Costumes designed by Schneider and Anderson. Orchestra under the direction of Antonio Bafunno. Orchestrations by Stephen Jones and Frank Saddler. Produced by B. C. Whitney. Opened 5 April 1920 at the New Amsterdam Theatre, moved 21 June 1920 to the Selwyn Theatre, and closed 14 August 1920 after 150 performances.

CAST: ED WYNN, LILLIAN FITZGERALD, TED ROBERTS, FRANK RIDGE, THE MEYAKOS, RICHIE LING, LILLIAN WOODS, LILLIAN DURKIN, FAY WEST, HERBERT RUSSELL, HENRY REGAL, SIMEON MOORE, MARION DAVIES, EARL BENHAM, RAY MILLER'S BLACK AND WHITE MELODY BOYS, Evan Burrows Fontaine, Orville Fisher, Arthur Williams, Trixie Jennery.
Ensemble: Carol Young, Caroline Erwin, Buelah McFarland, Dorothy Dean, Edith Rook, Dade Winlack, Ida Gerber, Margaret Hoban, Jane Bowen, Ursula Dale, Violet Bristow, Lillian Woods, Fay West, Gladys Lee, Sadie Howe, Catherine Doyle, Joan Butlin, Florence Quarters, Bessie Hoban, Ann Greenway, Elizabeth Chatterton, Olga Kale.

ACT 1
Scene 1
Prologue
Pierre: It. *Pierette*: She. *Pierot*: He. *Pierrat*: Him. *Pierrata*: Her. *Pierrento*: Who. *Proprietor*: Himself.
Scene 2
"(March of the) Gladiators"
F. Ridge
Scene: The Amphitheatre. (*Painted by* Joseph Physioc.)
The Lion: T. Roberts. *The Gladiator*: F. Ridge. *The King*: R. Ling. *The King's Daughter*: L. Durkin. *The Slave*: H. Russell.
"When I Was Small"
L. Durkin
The Walking Delegate: H. Regal. *The Wrestler*: S. Moore. *Roman Soldiers, Gladiators, Wrestlers, etc.*
Scene 3
Plot-Land
The Playwright: E. Wynn. *Real Japanese*: The Meyakos.
Scene 4
"In Old Japan"
F. Ridge
(*Music and Lyrics by* Ed Wynn and Alfred Bryan.)

Scene: Japanella. (*Painted by* Joseph Physioc.)
Nanki-Pooh-Pooh: F. Ridge. *Yum-Yum-Sing*: L. Wood. *Yum-Yum-Sang*: F. West. *Geisha Girls*: All of Them.
Scene 5
A Little Parisian Atmosphere
"C'est Toi"[125]
L. Fitzgerald
Himself: E. Wynn. *The Atmosphere*: L. Fitzgerald.
Scene 6
"Good-Bye Sunshine, Hello Moon"
M. Davies, E. Benham
(*Music by* William Eckstein. *Lyrics by* Gene Buck.)
Scene: At the Cottage Gate. (*Painted by* Triangle Scenic Studios.)
Scene 7
Himself: E. Wynn. *A Little Cutie*: F. West. *A Carnival Performer*: H. Regal. *Another*: S. Moore.
Scene: Main-Entrance to Carnival.
Scene 8
"Come Along (to the Carnival)"
Ensemble (*Music and Lyrics by* Ed Wynn.)
Scene: The Carnival Grounds.
Jazzy Melodies
Carnival Band (Ray Miller's Black and White Melody Boys)
["Underneath the Dixie Moon"
(*Music and Lyrics by* Ray Miller, Billy Fazioli and Raymond Klages.)
"Can You Tell"
(*Music by* Lou Handman and Ray Miller. *Lyrics by* Alex Sullivan.)
"Molly"
(*Music and Lyrics by* Ray Miller and Ring Hager.)
"Rose of Spain"
(*Music by* Tom Brown, Billy Fazioli and Ray Miller. *Lyrics by* Fred Fisher.)
"The Irish Were Egyptians Long Ago"
(*Music by* Chris Smith. *Lyrics by* Alfred Bryan.)
"Down in Honeymoon Town"
(*Music and Lyrics by* Alex Sullivan, Ray Miller and Clarence Seena.)]
Bally-Hoo Bill: H. Russell. *Lightning Calculator*: E. Wynn. *Eccentric Toe-Dance*: T. Jennery.
Acrobats
Regal and Moore
A Juggler: E. Wynn.
Finale: "I Love the Land of Old Black Joe"
M. Davies
(*Music by* Walter Donaldson. *Lyrics by* Grant Clarke.)
ACT 2
Scene 1
"Sphinx of the Desert"
L. Durkin
(*Music and Lyrics by* Ed Wynn.)
Scene: The Lady of the Pyramids.
"My Sahara Rose"
E. Benham
(*Music by* Walter Donaldson. *Lyrics by* Grant Clarke.)
Egyptian Dance[126]
Shadow of Nekatross
Incidental Music arranged by O. Lifshey.
Queen of the Nile: E. B. Fontaine. *Attendants*: O. Fisher, A. Williams.
Scene 2
"The Palmy Days"
E. Wynn, L. Fitzgerald
Page: F. West. *Mr. Lea*: E. Wynn. *Mrs. Perrin*: L. Fitzgerald.
Scene: Vaudeville Atmosphere.
Scene 3
"My Log-Fire Girl"
F. Ridge
(*Music and Lyrics by* Ed Wynn.)
Visions of Loveliness: *The Bathing Girl*: M. Hoban. *The Savannah Girl*: C. Young. *The Autumn Girl*: C. Erwin. *The Boating Girl*: I. Gerber. *The Springtime Girl*: E. Rook. *The Winter Girl*: D. Winlack. *The Logfire Girl*: U. Dale. *Himself*: E. Wynn. *The Girl of His Wish*: L. Woods.

---

[122]Interpolated for this revival.
[123]Interpolated for this revival.
[124]Interpolated for this revival.

---

[125]Very likely performed in this spot was the published song "It Must Be You" with music and lyrics by Ed Wynn, credited to this show.
[126]Dropped late in the run.

Scene 4

"Americanisms"

The Meyakos

Himself: E. Wynn. *The Atmosphere*: The Violin.

Scene 5

"I'd Rather Not See You at All (Rather Than See You Once in a While)"[127]

M. Davies, E. Benham

(*Music by* Walter Donaldson. *Lyrics by* Grant Clarke.)

Scene: The Palace of Nowhere.

Himself: E. Wynn. *The Heroine*: M. Davies. *The Hero*: E. Benham. *The Mimic*: L. Fitzgerald.

Finale

Ensemble

3 SHOWERS

1920.11

A Comedy with Music in Two Acts, 3 Scenes. Book by William Cary Duncan. Music by Turner Layton. Lyrics by Henry Creamer. Directed by Oscar Eagle. Musical numbers staged by Edward P. Bower. Costumes designed by Irma Campbell (women's), Finchley (men's). Scenery designed by Frank Gates and Edward A. Morange. Orchestra under the direction of Ivan Rudisill. Orchestrations by Will H. Vodery. Produced by Mr. and Mrs. Charles Coburn. Opened 5 April 1920 at the Harris Theatre, moved 26 April 1920 to the Plymouth Theatre and closed 15 May 1920 after 48 performances.

CAST: *Colonel John White*, owner of the Longview Farm: WALTER WILSON. *His Daughters (3)*: *Anna Mobberly*: VERA ROSS. *Roberta Lee White* ('Bob'): ANNA WHEATON. *Ray White*: EDNA MORN. *Willie Mobberly*: ANDREW J. LAWLOR, JR. *Peter Fitzhugh*: PAUL FRAWLEY. *Hudson Gatling*: William Winter Jefferson. *'Rastus Redmond Reynolds* (Red): LYNN STARLING. *Riley*, a camera man: Wilbur Cox. *Bruce Payne*: Norman Jefferson.

Weekend Visitors at Longview Farms: *Virginia May Gordon*: Ruth Urban. *Mary Love Burgess*: Lulu May Hubbard. *Patsy Ann Pritchard*: Daisy MacGlashan. *Maria Allan Morgan*: Margaret Fitch. *Alice Dean Lowe*: Lillian Wagner. *Penelope Dangerfield*: Doris Wingrove. *Lida Belle Norwood*: Frances M. Halliday. *Sally May Blaine*: Mildred Mason. *Bruce Payne*, a neighbor's son: Norman Jefferson.

Members of the Country Club: *Clarence Melton*: Ralph Deist. *William Henry Fish*: Russell Griswold. *Robinson Tucker*: James McKenzie. *Ward Allan Yancy*: H. M. Arden. *Byron Habersham*: Carl Rose. *Kinsey McAllister*: Henry Ward. *Stuart Thompson*: Alfred Siegler. *Norman Castleman*: Frank Slater.

"Worthless" Akers: *Farm-Hands at Longview*: *Jackson Gray*: Arthur Porter. *Lincoln Brown*: Richard Cooper. *Harrison Green*: Charles B. Foster.

The action takes place somewhere in Virginia at the present time.

Act 1: "Longview," Colonel White's Farm. Morning.

Act 2, Scene 1: Interior of the Barn. Afternoon. *Scene 2*: The same, 3 hours later. Evening.

ACT 1

Shower

Orchestra

Work Chant

Farm Quartette

"Open Your Heart"

A. Wheaton

"One of the Boys"

A. Wheaton, Ensemble

"B. Is the Note"

L. Starling, A. Lawlor, Jr.

"It Must Be Love"

P. Frawley, A. Wheaton

"I'll Have My Way"

W. Wilson

"Love Me, Sweetheart Mine"

V. Ross

"Where Is the Love?"

P. Frawley, A. Wheaton, Ensemble

"Open Your Heart"

P. Frawley, A. Wheaton, Ensemble

---

[127]Replaced for subsequent tour by:

"You Look Much Better Now"

M. Harrison, E. Benham

(*Music and Lyrics by* Earl Benham.)

"Love Me, Sweetheart Mine" (Finale)

A. Wheaton, Ensemble

ACT 2

Scene 1

"Pussyfoot"

E. Morn, Ensemble

"If, And, and But" (If and But)

A. Wheaton

"How Wonderful You Are"

P. Frawley, A. Wheaton

"He Raised Everybody's Rent but Katie's"

L. Starling, Quartette

Scene 2

"There's a Way Out"

Double Octette

Dance

J. McKenzie, D. MacGlashan

"The Old Love Is the True Love"

V. Ross, Ensemble

"Dancing Tumble Tom"

A. Wheaton, Ensemble

Finale

Entire Company

LASSIE

1920.12

A Musical Comedy in Three Acts. Book and lyrics by Catherine Chisholm Cushing, based on her play 'Kitty MacKay.' Music by Hugo Felix. Directed by Edward Royce. Scenery built by William Kellam. Costumes by Schneider-Anderson, Brooks, and Russell Uniform Company. Orchestra under the direction of Erno Rapee. Produced by Lassie, Inc. Opened 6 April 1920 at the Nora Bayes Theatre, moved 2 August 1920 to the Casino Theatre, and closed 21 August 1920 after 159 performances.

CAST (in order of appearance): *Lily*, daughter of Mrs. McNab: Miriam Collins. *Mrs. McNab*, a shrewish Scotch woman: LOUIE EMERY. *Winkie*, a shepherd boy who can read the stars: COLIN O'MORE. *Sandy*, the drunken husband of Mrs. McNab: RALPH NAIRN. *Jean MacGregor*, a neighbor: Alma Mara. *MacGregor*, Jean's husband and Sandy's boon companion: PERCIVAL VIVIAN. *Meg Duncan*, Kitty's bosom friend: MOLLY PEARSON. *Kitty MacKay*, an orphan who lives with the McNabs: TESSA KOSTA. *Lieutenant The Honorable David Graham* of the Coldstream Guards: ROLAND BOTTOMLEY. *Philip Grayson*, David's cousin: CARL HYSON. *Lady Gwendolyn Spencer-Hill*, Philip's fiancée: DOROTHY DICKSON. *Lord Inglehart*, David's father: DAVID GLASSFORD. *Mrs. Grayson*, Philip's mother: ADA SINCLAIR. *Robbins*, His Lordship's servant: Robert Smythe.

Ladies of the Ensemble: Agatha DeBussy, Hazel O'Brien, Elsie Craig, Julia Silvers, Lucille Marion, Edna Richmond, Elsie Frolick, Olive Hammond, Julie Collins, Virginia Richmond, Laura Hastings, Polly Shorreck, Violet McCabe, Ruth Allison, Madelaine Dare, Ethel Hobart, Marjorie Wall, Polly Watkins, Alice Gordon. *Gentlemen of the Ensemble*: Arthur Green, Harold Williams, Boris Scott, Charles Mansfield, Mack Ruber, Louis Laub, Harold Abbey, Let K. Thompson.

The action takes place in Scotland and London in the 1860's.

Act 1: Juniper Green, on the Banks of the Waters of Leith. A summer morning.

Act 2: Lond Inglehart's Town House in Berkley Square, London. An afternoon, one year later.

Act 3: Juniper Green. An autumn sunset.

ACT 1

The Opening

"Piper o' the Dundee" (The Piper of Dundee)

M. Collins, Ensemble

"Barrin'-o'-th'-Door, -O'"

R. Nairn, P. Vivian, L. Emery

"Echo"

T. Kosta

"Boo-Hoo"

D. Dickson, C. Hyson

"Fairy Whispers"

C. O'More, T. Kosta

Finale

T. Kosta, C. O'More, Ensemble

ACT 2

The Opening

D. Glassford, A. Sinclair, Ensemble

"Lady Bird"
  D. Dickson, C. Hyson, Ensemble
"Lovely Corals"
  T. Kosta, R. Bottomley
"Lassie"
  R. Bottomley, Ladies of the Ensemble
"Under the Jessamine"[128]
  T. Kosta
"A Teacup and a Spoon" (The Tea Cup and the Spoon)
  T. Kosta, R. Bottomley, D. Dickson, C. Hyson, M. Pearson, A. Sinclair
Finale
  T. Kosta, C. O'More

ACT 3
The Opening
  P. Vivian, Ensemble
"Kitty of Juniper Green" (Bonnie Sweet Kitty)
  C. O'More
"Skeletons"
  D. Dickson, R. Bottomley, C. Hyson, A. Sinclair, D. Glassford
"Flirting"
  C. Hyson, D. Dickson
Finale
  Entire Company

THE GIRL FROM HOME

1920.13

A Farce with Music in Three Acts. Book and lyrics by Frank Craven. Based on the farce ("The Dictator") by Richard Harding Davis. Music by Silvio Hein. Staged by R. H. Burnside. Costumes designed by O'Kane Conwell. Settings painted by (D. Frank) Dodge and (William) Castle, Tarrazona Brothers, Mark Lawson. Orchestra under the direction of Anton Heindl. Produced by Charles Dillingham. Opened 3 May 1920 at the Globe Theatre and closed 22 May 1920 after 24 performances.

CAST: *Brook Travers*, alias Steve Hill: FRANK CRAVEN. *Simpson*, alias Jim Dodd: JED PROUTY. *Charles Hyne*, wireless operator for the Red D Line: RUSSELL MACK. *Colonel John T. Bowie*, U.S. Consul to Porto Banos: John Parks. *Duffy*, a detective: Charles Mitchell. *General Santos Campos*, President of San Manana: William Burress. *Reverend Arthur Bostick*: Walter Coupe. *Lieutenant Victor, U.S.S. Pennsylvania*: Sam Burbank. *Dr. Vasquez*, health officer at Porto Banos: GEORGE E. MACK. *Jose Dravo*, proprietor of the Hotel del Prado: John Hendricks. *Senor Hoakumo*: Jose Vallhonrat. *Lucy Sheridan*: Gladys Caldwell. *Merci Hope*: MARION SUNSHINE. *Senora Juanita Arguilla*: FLORA ZABELLE. *Sister Agnes*: Virginia Shelby. *Sister Eleanor*: Eleanor Masters. *Sister May*: Sophie Brenner. *Sister Marie*: Marie Sewell. *Sister Isabel*: Edna Fenton. *Sister Helen*: Kathryn Yates. *Sister Mabel*: Janet Megrew. *Sister Clara*: Clara Carroll. (*Dance Specialties*: Jessica Brown, Margarita Flora DeMayo, Eduardo and Elisa Cansino.) *Passengers, Missionaries, Soldiers, Residents of Porto Banos, etc.*

Other characters by the Misses Estelle MacIntosh, Ann Poulson, Jean Carroll, Dorothy Haighton, Marie Fredericks, Arline Mason, Hazel G. Webb, Ione Ritchie, Doris Landy, Peggy Dana, Alma Braham, Elizabeth Reed, Mayre Morris, Mary Ellen Capers, Bonnie Murray, Dorothy Grace; Messrs. Tom Maynard, Harry King, John Allan, Robert Norman, Charles Kirby, Harry Pierce, Joe Qualters, William Boren.

Act 1: Deck of the Steamship *Bolivar*, Harbor of Porto Banos. Republic of San Manana, Central America. (Dodge & Castle.)

Act 2: The Exterior of the Hotel Del Prado, and Consulate of the United States at Porto Banos. Three hours later. (Tarrazona.)

Act 3: The Interior of the Consulate. Two hours later. (Lawson.)

ACT 1
"All Ashore" (Opening)
  Ensemble
"Nine Little Missionaries"
  G. Caldwell, Missionaries
"Just Say Good-Bye"
  M. Sunshine, R. Mack, Ensemble
"Ocean Blues"
  R. Mack, Ensemble
"Bit o' Breeze" (Dance Specialty)
  J. Brown
Finale
  Principals, Ensemble

ACT 2
"Porto Banos" (Opening)
  Ensemble
Dance
  M. F. DeMayo
"Our Presidents"
  J. Hendricks, Ensemble
"Sometime"
  F. Zabelle
"Vanity" (Dance)
  J. Brown
"Manana"
  G. Caldwell, Boys
"The Wireless Heart"
  M. Sunshine, R. Mack, Ensemble
"El Presidente"
  W. Burress, Ensemble
"I'll Be Dictator"
  Principals, Chorus

ACT 3
Opening
  F. Craven, His Army
"(It's) A Wonderful Spot"
  F. Craven, J. Prouty
"By the Palmist Tree"
  G. Caldwell
"Mirimba" (Marimba)
  M. Sunshine, R. Mack
Specialty
  The Cansinos
Finale
  Principals, Ensemble

HONEY GIRL

1920.14

A Musical Comedy in Three Acts. Book by Edward Clark. Based on the comedy 'Checkers' by Henry Blossom. Music by Albert Von Tilzer. Lyrics by Neville Fleeson. Staged by Bert French and Sam Forrest. Scenery designed by (Edward G.) Unitt and (Joseph) Wickes. Costumes by Henri Bendel, Arlington, Schneider-Anderson, Brooks Uniform Co.[129]. Orchestra under the direction of Eugene Salzer. Produced by Sam H. Harris. Opened 3 May 1920 at the Cohan and Harris Theatre and closed 4 September 1920 after 142 performances.

CAST (in order of appearance): *Judge Martin*: Peter Lang. *Cynthia*: RENE RIANO. *Honora Parker* (Honey): EDNA BATES. *Lucy Martin*: LOUISE MEYERS. *David Graham* (Checkers): LYNNE OVERMAN. *Orville Bryan*: Robert Armstrong. *Timothy Smiley* (Tip): GEORGE McKAY. *G. W. Parker*: DODSON MITCHELL. *Sol Frankenstein*: William Mortimer. *Carmencita*: SIDONIE ESPERO. *Jim Hayward*: Edmund Elton. *Charles Hawkins*: MERCER TEMPLETON. *Marion Rose*: Cissie Sewell. *Thomas Lyons*: Charlie Yorkshire. *Esther Blake*: Ottie Ardine.

Ladies of the Ensemble: Betty Shannon, Florence Ashton, Lucretia Craig, Kay Mahoney, Francis Mink, Helen Berkley, Beth Fowne, Patricia Mayer, Marie DuChette, Hazel Purcy, Fern Collier, Annette Gardner, Tess Mayer, Helen Trainor, Harriet Gustin, Katherine Wilson, Bert Alden, Virginia Allen, Mabel Allen, Beatrice Anderson, Louise Mallory, Ann Ross, Florence Rush, Grace Elliott, Marie Wallace. *Gentlemen of the Ensemble*: Leo Howe, Allan Blair, Harold Brady, Clifford Daly, Lou Sears, Walter Mayo, William Wilder, Bill Bailey.

Act 1: Parkerstown, Louisiana.

Act 2: At New Orleans, Louisiana. One year later.

Act 3: G. W. Parker's Home. Same evening.

ACT 1
"Shopping" (Opening Chorus)
  P. Lang, Ensemble
"Small Town Girl"
  L. Meyers, Chorus
"I'm Losing My Heart to Someone"
  L. Overman, Chorus

---

[128]Dropped after opening.

[129]Costumes by Henri Bendel (principals), Arlington, Schneider-Anderson (Blue-bird number), Brooks (men's).

"It's a Very Easy Matter" (It's a Very Simple Matter)
G. McKay, L. Meyers, Chorus
"Anything You Liked"
E. Bates, L. Meyers, Chorus
"Close to Your Heart"
E. Bates, L. Overman
ACT 2
Opening
Ensemble
"Racing Blues"
M. Templeton, Chorus
"Can I Find a Toreador"
S. Espero, Chorus
"I'd Place a Bet"
C. Sewell, M. Templeton, Chorus
"You're Just the Boy for Me"
L. Meyers, G. McKay, O. Ardine, Chorus
"Why Worry?"
R. Riano
"I'm Trying"
L. Overman
ACT 3
Opening
"MYLTIL and TYLTIL" (The Bluebird Song)
E. Bates, S. Espero, Children
Bluebird Ballet: Good Fairy: S.Espero. *Berylune:* L. Craig. *Fire:* H. Gustin.
Water: G. Elliott. *Light:* C. Wilson. *Night:* H. Trainer. *Bluebird:* C. Sewell.
Tyltil: M. Templeton.
"I Love to Fox Trot"
L. Meyers
Specialty Dances
M. Templeton, C. Sewell, O. Ardine, L. Craig
"I'm the Fellow"
G. McKay, R. Riano
Finale
Cast, Ensemble

1920.15 BETTY, BE GOOD

A Musical Farce in Three Acts. Book and lyrics by Harry B. Smith. Based on a French vaudeville by Scribe. Music by Hugo Reisenfeld. Staged by David Bennett. (Scenic) Production by P. Dodd Ackerman Studios. Costumes designed by Yvette Kiviat [Kiviette]. Orchestra under the direction of Ross Mobley. Produced by Charles G. Stewart and Lee Morrison. Opened 4 May 1920 at the Casino Theatre and closed 26 June 1920 after 63 performances.

CAST (in order of appearance): *First Bridesmaid:* Grace Hallam. *First Guest:* Gladys Elliott. *Second Guest:* Louise Hersey. *Page:* Frances Grant. *Somers Short,* hotel clerk: Raymond Oswald. *Philip Fuller,* an amateur impressario: WORTHINGTON ROMAINE. *Girls in Betty's Company* (2): *Maggie:* Jeanette Wilson. *Bernice:* Thy Daly. *Colonel Ichabod Starkweather:* EDDIE GARVIE. *Mrs. Starkweather,* his wife: JOSIE INTROPODI. *Tom Price,* the bridegroom: IRVING BEEBE. *Amy Starkweather:* GEORGIA HEWITT. *Sam Kirby,* the best man: FRANK CRUMIT. *Betty Lee,* musical comedy star: JOSEPHINE WHITTELL. *Marion Love,* cabaret dancer: VIVIENNE OAKLAND. *Madame O'Toole:* Lucille Manion. *Guy:* Raymond Oswald. *Percy:* Peter Mott.
Members of Betty's Company (6): *Laura:* Grace Duncan. *Cora:* Millie Fillat. *Nora:* Mabel Benelisha. *Dora:* Pauline Delmore. *Flora:* Betty Raedel. *Moira:* Jess Fay. *Muriel:* Frances Romana. *Amy's Bridesmaids* (7): *Gwendoline:* Thy Daly. *Eulalie:* Bobbie Rait. *Annabel:* Grace Duncan. *Belinda:* Grace Hallam. *Clarissa:* Betty Raedel. *Diana:* Thelma Holiday. *Imogene:* Dore Leighton. *Dance Specialties in Acts 2 and 3:* Frances Grant, Ted Wing.

Act 1: Exterior of Bon Ton Hotel, Lenox, Massachusetts. Noon.

Act 2: Living Room of Betty's Apartment, New York City. Evening of the same day.

Act 3: Exterior of Betty's Country Home, Kew Gardens, Long Island. Later that same evening.

ACT 1
"Let's Pretend We're Free"[130]
W. Romaine, Girls

[130]Replaced during the run by:
"Ahead of the Times"
W. Romaine, Girls

"Where Shall We Go"
I. Beebe, G. Hewitt
"Tell Me, Daisy"
G. Hewitt, Bridesmaids
"Betty, Be Good" (Betty Behave)
J. Whittell, Girls
"You Must Be Good, Girls"
F. Crumit, Girls
"Keep the Love Lamp Burning (in the Windows of Your Eyes)"
J. Whittell, I. Beebe
Finale
ACT 2
"Keep Them Guessing"
V. Oakland, Girls
Dance Unique
F Grant, T. Wing
"Listen to My Heart Beat"
I. Beebe, G. Hewitt, Girls
"'Tis in Vain (That I Try to Forget You)"[131]
J. Whittell
"The End of a Perfect Night"
J. Whittell, E. Garvie, W. Romaine
"I'd Like to Take You Away"
V. Oakland, F. Crumit
Finale
ACT 3
Moonlight Dance
F. Grant, T. Wing
"Temptation"
V. Oakland, P. Mott, R. Oswald, Girls
"Same Old Stars, (Same Old Moon)"
V. Oakland, F. Crumit, Girls
"Keep The Love Lamp Burning" (reprise)
J. Whittell
Finale

1920.16 MACUSHLA

A Revival of the Beautiful Irish Comedy (Pulse of My Heart) in Four Acts[132]. Play by Rida Johnson Young. Music by Ernest R. Ball. Lyrics by J. Keirn Brennan. Staged by William Henry Miller. Musical director, Al. Terry. Produced by Abraham L. Erlanger. Opened 17 May 1920 at the Park Theatre and closed 5 June 1920 after 24 performances.

CAST: *Sir Brian Fitzgerald:* CHAUNCEY OLCOTT. *Warren Fairchild:* LEO STARK. *Thomas Wiggins:* John Todd. *Dinny O'Mara,* the 'Ostler: JOHN HAMILTON. *Sandy McNab,* Overseer: JOE KENNEDY. *Dawkins,* a Jockey: J. Arthur O'Brien. *Patricia Boyer:* ALLYN GILLYN. *Mrs. Boyer:* JOSIE CLAFLIN. *Gwendolin Fairchild:* Nellie Strong. *Lady Dorothy Hammond:* Louise Francis. *A Bookmaker:* James Marr.

MUSICAL NUMBERS[133]
"That's How the Shannon Flows"
C. Olcott
"Macushla Asthore" (Pulse of My Heart)
C. Olcott
"I'll Miss You, Old Ireland (God Bless You, Goodbye)"
C. Olcott
"'Tis an Irish Girl I Love, and She's Just Like You"
C. Olcott
(*Music by* Ernest R. Ball. *Lyrics by* J. Keirn Brennan, Al Dubin.)

[131]Replaced during the run by:
"Don't Blame Me"
J. Whittell
[132]First produced 5 February 1912 at the Grand Opera House for 24 performances. For Synopsis of Scenes, see original 1912 production. No program found for New York engagement.
[133]No New York program found. All new songs not in original 1912 production.

1920–1921 SEASON

Donald Kerr and Elise Bonwit in POOR LITTLE RITZ GIRL (Photo: White Studio)
Billy Rose Theatre Collection, New York Public Library for the Performing Arts

1920–1921 SEASON

GEORGE WHITE'S SCANDALS (1920)

1920.17

A Modern Musical Revue in Two Acts, 18 Scenes[1]. Book (sketches) by Andy Rice and George White. Music by George Gershwin. Lyrics by Arthur Jackson. Staged by George White. Book directed by William Collier. Scenes by H. Robert Law Studios; Herbert Ward, Art director. Costume sketches by Cook and Fields; costumes by Schneider-Anderson, Paul Arlington, Inc. Orchestra under the direction of Alfred Newman. Orchestrations by Frank Saddler. Produced by George White. Opened 7 June 1920 at the Globe Theatre and closed 2 October 1920 after 134 performances.

CAST: ANN PENNINGTON, LESTER O'KEEFE, LOU HOLTZ, GEORGE ['Doc'] ROCKWELL, AL FOX, LA SYLPHE, LESTER ALLEN, ETHEL DELMAR, GEORGE BICKEL, GEORGE WHITE, Jack Rose, Myra Cullen, Lloyd Garrett, Peggy Dolan, James Miller, Frances Arms, Ruth Savoy, Christine Welford, Darry Welford, Sascha Beaumont, James Steiger, Dorothy Buckley, Betty Marshall, YERKES HAPPY SIX.

Ladies of the Ensemble: Misses Peggy First, Kathryn Mannion, Frances Ney, Jacqueline Bond, Ona Hamilton, Lou Martell, Lucille Cook, Anna Spelton, Sophie Howard, Flo Howard, Winnie Dunn, Eleanor Dana, G. Moore, Marie Cattell, Grace Reade, Gertrude McGushion, Marion Ward, Anna Green, Adele Christie, Louise Mayorga, Vera Colburn, Ruth Grey.

ACT 1[2]

Scene 1

A Modern Pandora's Box
  Pages: C. Welford, P. First, K. Manion. F. Ney.
  They Introduce Misses J. Bond, O. Hamilton, L. Martell, L. Cook, A. Spelton, S. Howard, F. Howard, W. Dunn, E. Dana, G. Moore, M. Cattell, G. Reade, G. McGushion, M. Ward, A. Green, A. Christie.

They Tell About Our:
  Songs: S. Beaumont. *Costumes*: V. Colburn. *Comedy*: P. Dolan. *Surprise*: B. Marshall. *Drama*: L. Mayorga. *Miss Dance*: La Sylphe.
  (Pandora *Costumes by* Arlington.)

Scene 2

"My Lady"
  L. O'Keefe

"Everybody Swat the Profiteer"
  Misses Cullen, Green, Schramm, Grey, Christie, Colburn
  Paint Girls: Misses C. Welford, D. Welford, First, Howard, Ward, Martell, Ney.
    Scene: Any Old Street.
      Silks: B. Marshall. *Cotton*: M. Cullen. *Wool*: V. Colburn. *Seals*: D. Buckley. *Sables*: P. Dolan *Dummies*: G. Rockwell, A. Fox. *Bryan*: G. Bickel. *A Good Girl*: C. Welford. *A Bad Boy*: L. Allen. *A Shop Lifter*: D. Welford. *Another Lifter*: R. Savoy. *A Female Detective*: E. Delmar. *A Copper*: J. Miller.
      (*Costumes by* Schneider-Anderson.)

Scene 3

Three Miles Up
  Porter: L. Holtz. *A Drunk*: L. Allen. *News Butcher*: J. Rose. *Purser*: L. Garrett. *Captain*: L. O'Keefe. *Cabin Boy*: C. Welford. *Musicians*: Yerkes Jazz Band. *Passengers*: J. Miller, F. Arms, B. Marshall, P. Dolan, S. Beaumont, D. Buckley, R. Grey.

The Poor Old Road House (Recitation)
  L. Holtz
  (*Costumes by* Schneider-Anderson.)

Scene 4

Some Place in Mexico
  Mexican Bandits: Girls. *Mexican Bandit Captain*: A. Pennington. *Soldiers of Misfortunes*, who are after the Mexican Bandits: G. Bickel, J. Rose, G. Rockwell, L. Garrett, J. Miller, J. Steiger, L. Holtz. *Their Unfortunate Captain*: L. Allen. *Dry Oil Well Promoters*: G. Rockwell, J. Rose, G. Bickel. *Villa*: A. Fox.

A Mexican Cigarette Dance
  E. Delmar, Girls

---

[1]The Second in the annual series of musical revues produced by George White beginning in 1919.
[2]Added during the run:
  "Rock the Baby to Sleep"

(*Costumes by* Schneider-Anderson, except Bandit Girl Costumes by Arlington.)

Scene 5

The Painted Girls
"On My Mind the Whole Night Long"
  L. Garrett
  The Girl in Green Paint: V. Colburn. *Orange*: P. Dolan. *Black*: B. Marshall. *Blue*: D. Buckley. (The girls in this number are covered with a special preparation of real paint. *Costumes by* Schneider-Anderson.)

Scene 6

The Mechanical Piano Doll ("On My Mind the Whole Night Long" reprise)
  A. Pennington
  (The Piano is played by a Mel-O-Dee Roll made specially by the Aeolian Company.)

Scene 7

Lou Holtz (Specialty)
["O-H-I-O"
  (*Music by* Abe Olman. *Lyrics by* Jack Yellen.)
"You've Got to Give the Babies a Bottle"
  (*Music and Lyrics by* Howard Johnson and Milton Ager.)]

Scene 8

"Scandal Walk"
  A. Pennington, Girls
  Scene: A Presidential Convention.
    Chairman Bryan: G. Bickel. *The Common People*: L. Allen. *Sergeant-at-Arms*: J. Rose. *Sleeping Candidate*: J. Steiger. *Next Candidate*: L. Garrett. *Next*: J. Miller. *Next*: G. Rockwell. *Next*: Yerkes Jazz Band. *Female Candidate*: A. Pennington.
    (*Costumes by* Schneider-Anderson.)

Scene 9

All Stretch

ACT 2

Scene 1

The Spider Ballet
  Scene: A Hawaiian Beach.
    The Spider: La Sylphe. *A Grasshopper*: A. Spelton. *Glow Worms*: C. Welford, P. First, C. Manion, F. Ney. *Caterpillars*: W. Dunn, A. Christie. *Blue Flies*: M. Cullen, R. Savoy. *Butterflies*: V. Colburn, D. Buckley. *Beetles*: P. Dolan, R. Grey.

Scene 2

Lou Holtz

Scene 3

The Kiss Me Dolls
"Come On and Kiss Me" (Tum On and Tiss Me)
  A. Pennington, Girls
  (*Costumes by* Arlington.)

Scene 4

Palisade Bluff Apartments
  The Landlord: G. Bickel. *A Tenant*: L. Allen. *His Wife*: F. Arms. *A Tenant*: J. Miller. *His Boarder*: J. Rose. *A Tenant*: L. Garrett. *His Wife*: E. Delmar. *Ice Man*: S. Ledner. *Laundry Man*: L. O'Keefe.

Scene 5

I Love the Old Songs: "The Songs of Long Ago"
  L. O'Keefe
  Home Sweet Home: D. Welford. *Hiawatha*: M. Cullen. *Silvery Bell*: S. Beaumont. *Silver Threads Among the Gold*: C. Welford.
  (*Costumes by* Schneider-Anderson.)

Scene 6

Russian Drama
  The Mansky: L. Allen. *The Other Mansky's Wifesky*: F. Arms. *The Husbandsky, Off Stagesky*: S. Ledner. *The Guy That Got in First*: J. Miller. *Translated Bysky*: L. Holtz.

Scene 7

A Piece of Carved Jade: "Idle Dreams"
  L. Garrett
  And the Girls: The Girls. *The Idol*: A. Pennington.
  (*Costumes by* Schneider-Anderson.)

Scene 8

(George) Rockwell and (Al) Fox

Scene 9

"The Lattice Room Number"
  G. White, Some of the Girls

Parade
    Scandals of 1920
Good Night

1920.18   ZIEGFELD FOLLIES OF 1920

A Musical Revue in Two Acts, 25 Scenes[3]. Music and lyrics by Irving Berlin. Additional music and lyrics by Dave Stamper, Gene Buck, Joseph McCarthy, Harry Tierney. Special music by Victor Herbert. Staged by Edward Royce. Scenes by Joseph Urban. Costumes designed by Lady Duff-Gordon, Alice O'Neil. Orchestra under the direction of Frank Tours. Orchestrations by Maurice DePackh, Charles Grant, Stephen Jones, Frank Saddler. Tableaux by Ben Ali Haggin. Produced under the personal direction of Florenz Ziegfeld. Opened 22 June 1920 at the New Amsterdam Theatre and closed 16 October 1920 after 123 performances.

CAST: EDDIE CANTOR, RAY DOOLEY, CARL RANDALL, FANNIE BRICE, JOHN STEEL, W. C. FIELDS, MARY EATON, DORIS EATON, JACK DONO-HUE, DeLYLE ALDA, CHARLES WINNINGER, JANE CARROLL, BERNARD GRANVILLE, (Gus) VAN and (Joe) SCHENCK, JEROME & HERBERT, (George) MORAN and (Charles) MACK, LILLIAN BRODERICK, OLIVE CORNELL, OLIVE VAUGHN, FLORENCE WARE, JESSIE REED, HELEN SHEA, Addison Young, William Blanche, Jack Mahan, (ART HICKMAN ORCHESTRA).

Follies Girls: Margaret Irving, Gladys Loftus, Eleanor Dell, Albertine Marlowe, Juliet Compton, Alta King, Eva Grady, Betty Morton, Ethel Hallor, Beatrice Milner, Charlotte Wakefield, Avonne Taylor, Emily Drange, Phebe Lee, Margaret Morris, Edna French.

ACT 1

Scene 1

Opening ("Come Along")
    Follies Boys
    (*Music and Lyrics by* Irving Berlin.)

Scene 2

"Creation" (*by* James Montgomery. *Music by* Victor Herbert.)
    The Slenderness of the Reed: M. Irving. *The Bloom of the Flower:* G. Loftus. *The Timidity of the Hare:* E. Dell. *The Vanity of the Peacock:* J. Reed. *The Softness of the Parrot's Bosom:* A. Marlowe. *The Cruelty of the Tiger:* J. Compton. *The Warm Glow of Fire:* A. King. *The Coldness of Snow:* E. Grady. *The Wooing of the Dove:* B. Morton. *The Chattering of the Jay:* E. Hallor. *The Hypocrisy of the Crane:* B. Milner *The Fidelity of the Pelican:* C. Wakefield. *Eve:* A. Taylor.

Scene 3

"(They're) So Hard to Keep When They're Beautiful"[4]
    C. Randall, and Misses O. Vaughn, F. Ware, H. Shea, D. Eaton.
    (*Music by* Harry Tierney. *Lyrics by* Joseph McCarthy.)

Scene 4

"Sunshine and Shadows"[5]
    J. Steel, J. Carroll
Colonial Dance
    E. Drange, J. Reed
    (*Music by* Dave Stamper. *Lyrics by* Gene Buck.)
        Scene: A Room at the Mt. Vernon.
            George: J. Steel. *Martha:* J. Carroll. *George Washington:* B. Granville. *Martha Washington:* D. Alda.

Scene 5

Chiffon Fantasie: "When the Right One Comes Along"
    M. Eaton, Boys
    (*Music by* Victor Herbert. *Lyrics by* Gene Buck.)

Scene 6

Here's a Go (*by* George V. Hobart)
    Scene: In the Park.
        The Baby: R. Dooley. *The Man:* C. Winninger. *The Nurse:* M. Irving. *The Flirt:* A. Young.

Scene 7

"I'm a Vamp from East Broadway"
    F. Brice

(*Music and Lyrics by* Irving Berlin, Bert Kalmar and Harry Ruby.)

Scene 8

"(The) Girls of My Dreams"
    J. Steel, Cloud Girls
    (*Music and Lyrics by* Irving Berlin.)
        Scene: Up in the Clouds.

Scene 9

Specialty
    G. Moran, C. Mack

Scene 10

Truly Rural[6]:
    (a) "Any Place Would Be Wonderful with You" B. Granville, D. Eaton, Haystack Girls
        (*Music by* Dave Stamper. *Lyrics by* Gene Buck.)
    (b) "Mary and Doug"
        M. Eaton, C. Randall
        (*Music by* Dave Stamper. *Lyrics by* Gene Buck.)
    (c) "Where Do Mosquitos Go (in the Wintertime)?"[7]
        G. Van, J. Schenck
        (*Music by* Harry Tierney. *Lyrics by* Joe McCarthy.)
    (d) Dance
        J. Donohue
    (e) The Family Ford (*Conceived, written and staged by* W. C. Fields.)
        George Fliverton: W. C. Fields. *Baby Rose Fliverton:* R. Dooley. *Mrs. Fliverton:* F. Brice. *Elsie May:* J. Reed. *Henry Steel:* W. Blanch. *James Cunningham:* J. Cahan. *Miss Rose:* B. Marlow. *Jack Rose:* Miss Rolph. *Adel Smith:* E. Grady. *Officer Burns:* A. Young.

Scene 11

Specialty
    Jerome & Herbert

Scene 12

"Bells"
    B. Granville
    (*Music and Lyrics by* Irving Berlin.)
        Scene: The Land of Bells.
            The Groom: B. Granville. *The Bride:* J. Carroll. *The Bishop:* C. Winninger. *The Story Tellers:* G. Van, J. Schenck. *Bridesmaids:* H. Shea, D. Eaton, Bell Girls.

Finale

ACT 2

Scene 1

The Little Follies Theatre during Intermission (*by Irving Berlin*)
    (a) In the Lobby:
        The First Nighter: B. Granville. *Between the Actors:* Follies Boys.
    (b) In the Theatre
        The Tired Business Man: C. Randall. *The Lady with Him:* D. Alda. *The Water Girls:* 6 Little Follies Girls. *Just a Husband:* W. C. Fields. *His Wife:* F. Brice. *A Critic:* C. Winninger. *A Fellow Who Paid to Get In:* J. Donohue. *A Lover:* J. Steel. *His Sweetheart:* M. Eaton. And a Follies Audience.
        (*Dresses designed by* Madame Francis, under the supervision of Ben Ali Haggin.)

Scene 2

Songs
    G. Van, J. Schenck
["Green River"
    (*Music by* Eddie Cantor. *Lyrics by* Gus Van and Joe Schenck.)
"All She'd Say Was Um Hum"
    (*Music and Lyrics by* Gus Van, Joe Schenck, Mac Emery and King Zany.)
"Everybody Tells It to Sweeney (And Sweeney Tells It to Me)"
    (*Music by* George Fairman. *Lyrics by* Sidney D. Mitchell.)
"My Home Town is a One Horse Town (But It's Big Enough for Me)"
    (*Music by* Abner Silver. *Lyrics by* Alex Gerber.)]
        Scene: The Follies Curtains.

---

[3]The Fourteenth in the annual series of musical revues produced by Florenz Ziegfeld beginning in 1909. Billed as "a national institution."
[4]Replaced during the run and for subsequent national tour by:
    "Hold Me"
        C. Randall, O. Vaughn, F. Ware, H. Shea, D. Eaton
        (*Music and Lyrics by* Ben Black and Art Hickman.)
[5]Song and scene were dropped for subsequent national tour, but the dance was retained.

[6]Added to Truly Rural Scene for subsequent national tour:
    "I'm a Terrible Squaw" (I'm an Indian)
        F. Brice
        (*Music by* Leo Edwards. *Lyrics by* Blanche Merrill.)
[7]Replaced for subsequent tour by a specialty sketch that encompassed songs:
    Two Rubes
        G. Van, J. Schenck

Scene 3

Her First Lesson (*Music by* Victor Herbert.)

Scene: The Dancing School.

The Pupil: M. Eaton. *The Master*: C. Winninger. *The New Pupil*: F. Brice.

Scene 4

"The Leg of Nations"

C. Randall

(*Music and Lyrics by* Irving Berlin.)

Scene 5

"The Ziegfeld Sextette" (Come Along Sextette)

(*Music and Lyrics by* Irving Berlin.)

"Poor Florodora Girl"[8]

F. Brice

(*Music and Lyrics by* Irving Berlin.)

Scene: On Fifth Avenue.

Ziegfeld Follies Girls: B. Morton, A. King, M. Irving, J. Reed, C. Wakefield, E. Hallor. With Sextette Boys, The Rolls Royce Chauffeurs.

Scene 6

"Chinese Fantasy: "Chinese Firecrackers" (Chinese Fireworks)

G. Van, J. Schenck, Firecracker Girls

(*Music and Lyrics by* Irving Berlin.)

Scene 7

Chappie Dance

B. Granville, D. Eaton

Scene 8

"Tell Me, Little Gypsy"

J. Steel, D. Alda

(*Music and Lyrics by* Irving Berlin.)

Scene: The Gypsy Trail.

France: D. Marlowe. *Spain*: J. Compton. *Japan*: G. Loftus. *Hawaii*: P. Lee. *Turkey*: M. Morris.

Scene 9

Dance

L. Broderick, C. Randall

Scene 10

The Golden Gates

Jackson Lee: Mack. *St. Peter*: B. Granville. *A Girl*: M. Irving.

Scene 11

"The Love Boat"

(J. Steel)

(A Pictorial Fantasy of Romantic Venice by Ben Ali Haggin.)

(*Music by* Victor Herbert. *Lyrics by* Gene Buck. *Orchestrations by* Victor Herbert.)

The Troubadour: J. Steel. *Ladies of Venice*: M. Morris, A. King, M. Irving, B. Morton, E. Hallor. *Catherine*: J. Reed. *Margherita*: C. Wakefield. *Antonetta*: E. Drange. *Lucrezia*: E. Dell. *Antice*: A. Marlowe. *Leonida*: B. Milner. *Teresita*: E. Grady. *Gina*: A. Taylor. *Simonetta*: M. Morris. *The Figure Head*: E. French. *Paula*: G. Loftus.

Scene 12

A Surprise[9]:

["Every Blossom I See Reminds Me of You"

E. Cantor

(*Music and Lyrics by* Eddie Cantor.)

"I Found a Baby on My Door Step"

(*Music and Lyrics by* Eddie Cantor.)

"O-H-I-O"

(*Music by* Abe Olman. *Lyrics by* Jack Yellen.)

"Noah's Wife Lived a Wonderful Life"

(*Music by* Ernie Erdman and Abe Olman. *Lyrics by* Jack Yellen and Roger Lewis.)]

Scene 13

The Midnight Frolic:

"The Syncopated Vamp"[10]

---

[8]Replaced later in the run and for tour by:

"I Was a Florodora Baby" (from ZIEGFELD MIDNIGHT FROLIC of 1920)

F. Brice

(*Music by* Harry Carroll. *Lyrics by* Ballard Macdonald.)

[9]Cantor's specialty was billed as "A Surprise" in the program.

[10]Replaced late in the run and for subsequent tour by:

"My Midnight Frolic Girl"

B. Granville, C. Randall, J. Donohue, L. Broderick, F. Ware, R. Dooley, All the Little Vamps, Art Hickman's Famous Midnight Frolic Orchestra

(*Music and Lyrics by* Irving Berlin.)

Finale

1920.19 CINDERELLA ON BROADWAY

A (Musical) Fantasy of the Great White Way in Two Acts, 21 Scenes[11]. Dialogue and lyrics by Harold Atteridge. Music by Bert Grant. Incidental music by Al Goodman. Staged by J. C. Huffman. Dance numbers staged by Allan K. Foster. Scenery designed by Watson Barratt. Costumes designed by Homer Conant, Madame Haverstick, Cora MacGeachy, S. Zalud. Orchestra under the direction of Oscar Radin. Produced under the personal direction of J. J. Shubert. Produced by Lee and J. J. Shubert. Opened 24 June 1920 at the Winter Garden and closed 25 September 1920 after 126 performances.

CAST: AL SEXTON, AL [El] BRENDEL, JOE NIEMEYER, SHIRLEY ROYCE, GEORGIE PRICE, RENEE DENTLING, EILEEN VAN BIENE, LLORA HOFFMAN, ROGER LITTLE, STEWART BAIRD, CONSTANTIN KOBELEFF, JESSICA BROWN, THE GLORIAS (Adelaide and Albert DiNovaloff), JOHN T. MURRAY, AL SHAYNE, HOMER DICKINSON, GRACE DEAGON, WILLIAM KINLEY, FLO BERT, NORMA GALLO, JAMES DALY, ARTHUR CARDINAL, JOHN KEARNS, BYRON HALSTEAD, THE PURCELLA BROTHERS (Frank, Raymond), Walter Brower, Vadie Kobeleff, Felix Patty, Marion Vadie, Grace Keeshon.

Winter Garden Types: Dorothy Bruce, Mae Dealy, De Anguilliar, Madge McCarthy, Mildred Soper, Muriel Knowles, Louise Wayne, Lola Taylor, Ann Whitehill, Gene Gray, Lyola Whyte, Mae Devereaux, Anita Miramar, Margie Clayton, Gertrude Doyle, Marie Walker, Charlotte Sprague, Marie Farrell, Doris Lloyd, Marie Stafford, Gertrude Lang, Birdie Burwell, Violet Gleason, Ginette Derval, Elaine Thompson, Violet Ayres, Florence Wayne, Lois Huggins, Flo Summerville, Isabelle Holland, Phyllis Miller, Beverly Miller, Juliet Strahl, Burtress Dietch, Shirley Gallop, Dorothy Jackson, Alice Monroe, Dolores Mendez, Marie Gray, Yvette Reals, Beatrice Jennings, Josephine Kernan, Ruby Howard, Jean Woods, Lucille Pryor, Stella Hadden, Marjorie Hope, Betty MacDonald, Vivien Bartlett, Thelma Johns, Annabelle Whitney, Eve Fuller, Polly Mayer, Loralda Poppany, Gene Danjou, Bert Best, Evelyn Rosewood, Hermosa Jose, Billy Wagner.

ACT 1[12]

Scene 1

Prologue

Boy: B. Dietch. *Girl*: D. Mendez. *Peter Pan*: N. Gallo. *Broadway*: A. Sexton.

Scene 2

Chair Ballet

Chair Sprites

"Old King Cole"

S. Royce, Winter Garden Toys

Toy Dance[13]

J. Niemeyer

"(Just Like) The House That Jack Built"[14]

E. Van Biene, S. Baird, Girls of the Beauty Union

The Glorias (Specialty)[15]

Themselves

B. Granville, Frolic Girls

(*Music and Lyrics by* Ben Black, Art Hickman.)

Dance

R. Dooley, J. Donohue

Grand Finale

Entire Company, Art Hickman's Famous Midnight Frolic Orchestra

[11]Billed as the Winter Garden's annual revue.

[12]Added to Act 1 in second month:

"(Wild) Romantic Blues" (after "My Phantom Loves")

Jane Green, Purcella Brothers

(*Music by* Jean Schwartz. *Lyrics by* Alfred Bryan.)

Added to Act 1 late in the run (before "Wheel of Fate"):

"Old Gentleman's Jazz"

Marie Dressler

Added for subsequent tour, after "Cindy"

"I Have Somebody's Heart"

R. Delting, Some Sweeties

"Three Musketeers of Broadway"

Marie Dressler, J. T. Murray, Ernest F. Young

[13]Dropped during the run, but restored late in run and for tour.

[14]Dropped during the run, but restored late in run and for tour.

[15]Dropped during the run, but restored late in run and for tour.

"Fairy Tales"[16]
   H. Dickinson, Deagon
"Jazzing the Alphabet"[17]
   G. Price, Alphabet Girls
"(The Land) Beyond the Candle Light"
   E. Van Biene, Some Sweet Dream Girls
      Scene: A Top Shop and a Book Store.
         Peter Pan: N. Gallo. *Simple Simon*: S. Royce. *Old King Cole*: J. Daly. *Jack
         Horner*: A. Cardinal. *Santa Claus*: J. Kearns. *Jack in the Box*: R. Little.
         Whistle: B. Halsted. *A Toy*: J. Niemeyer. *Tad*: G. Price. *Cindy*: E. Van Biene.
         Tarzan: Himself. *Keeper*: F. Patty. *Prince Charming*: S. Baird. *Joy*: J. Brown.
         Gloom: J. T. Murray. *The Glorias*: Themseves. *Hal*: H. Dickinson. *Chummy
         Four*: Marie: M. Stafford. *Charlotte*: C. Sprague. *Mildred*: M. Soper. *Lyola*:
         L. White. *Mrs. Content*: M. Farrell.
Scene 3
   "All the Little Glooms Start Dancing"
      J. T. Murray, Eight Little Glooms
         Scene: Gloomland.
            Gloom: J. T. Murray. *Prince Charming*: S. Baird.
Scene 4
   "(My) Phantom Loves"
      S. Baird, Loves of Bygone Days
         Prince Charming: S. Baird.
Scene 5
      Scene: Cafe de Paris.
         Artie: W. Brower. *Broadway*: A. Sexton. *Hal*: H. Dickinson. *Miss Pretty*: G.
         Keeshon. *Miss Homely*: M. Farrell. *Beauty*: R. Dentling. *Prince*: S. Baird.
Scene 6
   "Whistle (and I'll Come to Meet You)"
      F. Burt, Whistling Girls
   "Cindy"
      E. Van Biene, G. Deagon, G. Price, S. Royce, J. Niemeyer, A. Sexton, A.
      Brendel
   "Why Don't You Get a Sweetie?"
      S. Royce, Some Sweeties
         Scene: Humpty Dumpty Lane.
            Miss Moffet: F. Burt. *Yonson*: A. Brendel. *Cindy*: E. Van Biene. *Simon*: G.
            Price. *Mary Jane*: G. Deagon. *Jack*: J. Niemeyer. *Jill*: A. Sexton. *Susie*: S.
            Royce. *Mrs. Content*: M. Farrell.
Scene 7
   The Husband and the Friend
      Broadway: A. Sexton. *Peter Pan*: N. Gallo. *The Husband*: J. Daly. *The Friend*: H.
      Dickinson. *The Wife*: R. Dentling. *The Other Man*: W. Brower.
Scene 8
      Scene: Anywhere.
         Artie: W. Brower.
Scene 9
   The Devil Examines His Accounts
      Gloom: J. T. Murray. *Prince*: S. Baird. *Beauty*: R. Dentling.
Scene 10
   "Wheel of Fate"
      L. Hoffman
   Roulette Dance
      M. Vadie, C. Kobeleff, Black and Red Girls
         Scene: The Top of the World.
            A Vampire: D. Bruce. *The Joker*: F. Summerville. *Dice*: I. Holland.
            Another: V. Gleason. *Queen of Hearts*: G. Keeshon. *Jack of Hearts*: M.
            Devereaux. *Ace of Diamonds*: L. White. *Ace of Spades*: B. Burwell. *Queen
            of Spades*: A. Delmore. *Misfortune*: M. Dealy. *Poverty*: L. Wayne. *Hope
            Abandoned*: De Anguilliar. *Vice*: M. McCreary. *Shame*: M. McCarthy.
            Degradation: M. Farrell. *Hope Gone Wrong*: M. Soper. *Voice*: L.
            Hoffman. *Laughter*: R. Little. *Dance*: C. Kobeleff.
Scene 11
   Honeymoon Cottage[18]
   Minuet
      F. Burt, A. Brendel
      Miss Moffet: F. Burt. *Yonson*: A. Brendel.
Scene 12
   "The Last Waltz I Had with You"
      L. Hoffman, a Group of Winter Garden Beauties

---

[16]Dropped during the run.
[17]Dropped during the run.
[18]Sketch with songs.

"Cinderella on Broadway"
   G. Price, G. Deagon, a Few Broadway Cinderellas
Joy Dance
   J. Brown
"Any Little Melody"
   F. Burt, A. Sexton, The Glorias, J. Brown, J. Niemeyer, Purcella Brothers
      Scene: The Silver Slipper Ball
         Miss Waltz: L. Hoffman. *Butler*: R. Little. *Tad*: G. Price. *Joy*: J. Brown.
         Hal: H. Dickinson. *Artie*: W. Brower. *Beauty*: R. Dentling. *Prince*: S.
         Baird. *Maid*: F. Wagner. *Cindy*: E. Van Biene. *Gloom*: J. T. Murray. *Miss
         Moffet*: F. Burt. *The Glorias*: Themselves. *Jack*: J. Niemeyer. *Purcella
         Brothers*: Themselves.
ACT 2[19]
Scene 1
   "The Old Music Masters"
      M. Vadie, The Glorias, C. Kobeleff
         Prince: S. Baird. *Mendelssohn*: A. Howson. '*Spring Song*': M. Vadie.
         Paderewski: R. Little. '*Minuet*': The Glorias. *Liszt*: J. Daly. '*Hungarian
         Rhapsodies*': Mlle. Vadie-Kubeleff.
Scene 2
   "Lady of Mars"
      G. Price, Some Aviator Beauties
         Scene: Caproni Station.
            Inventor: J. T. Murray. *Cindy*: E. Van Biene. *Broadway*: A. Sexton. *Hal*:
            H. Dickinson. *Mary*: G. Deagon. *Tad*: G. Price. *Yonson*: A. Brendel. *First
            Mate*: F. Burt.
Scene 3
   At the Circus
      Cindy: E. Van Biene. *The Ring Master*: J. T. Murray. *Tarzan*: Himself. *The
      Keeper*: F. Patty. *Mijares and Brother*: Themsleves.
Scene 4
   Waiting Room, Ritz-Plaza Hotel, New York City.
      Peter Pan: N. Gallo. *Broadway*: A. Sexton. *Edith*: E. Van Biene. *Ralph*: H.
      Dickinson. *Tommy*: S. Baird. *Amy*: F. Burt.
Scene 5
   "The Primrose Path" (Primrose Ways)
      R. Dentling, S. Baird, a Bouquet of Beautiful Girls
         Beauty: R. Dentling. *Prince*: S. Baird.
Scene 6
   Out Front
      Gloom: J. T. Murray. *An Opera Singer*: A. Shayne. *A Musician*: W. Kinley.
Scene 7
   "Naughty Eyes"
      S. Royce, Some Naughty Girls
      (*Music and Lyrics by* Cliff Friend and Harry Richman.)
   "Girl Belongs to You"
      J. Brown, J. Niemeyer, A. Sexton
         Scene: Watteau Land.
            Susie: S. Royce. *Joy*: J. Brown. *Folly*: J. Niemeyer. *Broadway*: A. Sexton.
            Yonson: A. Brendel. *Miss Moffet*: F. Burt. *Minister*: A. Howson. *Gloom*: J.
            T. Murray.
Scene 8
   On Broadway
      Broadway: A. Sexton. *Tad*: G. Price.
Scene 9
   "Precious Jewels"
      Tiffany Girls
         Scene: The Jewelled Castle

---

[19]Added to Act 2 at end of New York run and for tour:
   "Rolling Up the Barcarolle"
      F. Burt
   "Rock Me in Your Loving Arms"
      O. Cook, Some Naughty Girls
   Added to Act 2 for subsequent tour:
   "Hold Me" (from ZIEGFELD FOLLIES of 1920)
      Vivian Oakland
   "The Labor Agitator"
      J. T. Murray
   "Theda Bara"
      M. Dressler
   Rigoletto Quartette
      M. Dressler, J. T. Murray, L. Hoffman, A. Cardinal

1920.20

BUZZIN' AROUND

Will Morrissey's Comiques offer their Annual Revuesque (Musical Revue) in Two Acts, 7 Scenes. Book (sketches) and lyrics by William Morrissey and Edward Madden. Music by William Morrissey. Staged under the personal direction of Will Morrissey. Dances arranged by Ernest F. Young. Costumes worn by Miss Brice from designs by Margery Brice and Mme. Pulliche. Orchestra under the direction of Ivan Rudisill. Produced by Will Morrissey. Opened 6 July 1920 at the Casino Theatre and closed 24 July 1920 after 23 performances[20].

CAST: *Betty Barrett*: ELIZABETH BRICE. *Walter Barrett*, her father: WALTER WILSON. *Minerva*, her cousin: Priscilla Parker. *La Belle Violet*: VIOLET INGLEFIELD. *Donald*, her son: DONALD ROBERTS. *Ernest F. Keene*, a tragedian: ERNEST F. YOUNG. *Billy Hope*, an actor, author, manager: WILL MORRISSEY. *Big Harry and Little Jack*: HARRY MASTERS, JACK KRAFT. *Henry*: Henry Rigoletto. *Charlie*: Charlie Rigoletto. *The Duke of Mixture*: Robert Milo. *Property Man*: Jack Ingliss. *Pinky*, a dancer: Helen Gladdings. *Clara*, a dancer: Clara Carroll. *Aleta* on her toes: ALETA.

The Dancing Ponies: Peggy Ellis, Lillian May, Maron Stanford, Gladys Nagle, Bobbie Burns, Julie Barnette. *The Prima Donnas*: Betty Lewis, Ruth Carbery, Margaret Fry, Emilie Spalding, Oretta Lewis, Mary Cassel. *Show Girls*: Rena Manning, May Manning, Adele LeRoy, Ann Swan, Nella Neslon, Adele Kelly, Linnea Theorin, Nan Hope. (*Boys*): Tom Smith, Charles Lincoln, Joe Fields, Roy Vernon, Hal Devine, Carl Rose, Harry Bolton.

Act 1: Front of Betty's Bungalow. Mortgageville, Long Island.

Act 2, Scene 1: Backstage of Mortgageville Opera House. *Scene 2*: French Theatre. *Scene 3*: Courtyard of the Barrymores' Home. *Scene 4*: Chinese Wedding Procession. *Scene 5*: "The Hatchett Man," Chinese Fantasy. *Scene 6*: "Mikado" Travesty, Apartment District, Japan.

ACT 1

 Opening Ensemble

 "Pip Pip? Toot Toot"
  V. Inglefield, W. Wilson

 "Buzzin' Around"
  E. Brice, Boys

 Specialty Dance
  H. Gladdings

 "I'll Be Just the Same"
  E. Brice, D. Roberts

 Dance
  G. Nagle, C. Carroll

 "Poor Winter Garden Girl"
  W. Morrissey, Girls

 Solos
  B. Lewis, M. Fry, P. Parker

 Dance
  Aleta

 Sword Dance
  E. F. Young

 Russian Dance
  H. Masters, J. Kraft

 "O.I.L. Spells Oil"
  W. Morrissey, V. Inglefield, D. Roberts

 "Good-Night, Dear" (Finale)

ACT 2

Scene 1

 Opening Chorus—The Revuesque
  Entire Company

 "Every Nation Has a Broadway of Its Own"
  D. Roberts, Girls

Scene 2

 Waltz
  R. Manning, E. F. Young

 "How Could She Love Me Like That?"
  W. Morrissey

 "Voulez Vous"
  E. Brice, H. Masters, J. Kraft

 Dance
  Aleta

Scene 3

 Lionel: W. Wilson. *Ethel*: E. Brice. *John*: W. Morrissey. *Butler*: E. F. Young.

Scene 4

 Chinese Wedding Procession

Scene 5

 The Hatchet Man by Pinkie and Ernest

 "Ching-Aling-Fling"
  E. Brice, W. Morrissey

 Dance Eccentrique
  H. Masters, J. Kraft

 The Son-Daughter: E. Brice. *Theda Bara*: V. Inglefield. *Dr. Ding Dong*: W. Wilson. *The Gambler*: E. F. Young. *Tom Lee*: W. Morrissey.

Scene 6

 Mikado Travesty

 Wandering Minstrel: D. Roberts. *Yum Yum*: E. Brice. *Lord High Profiteer*: E. F. Young. *Ko Ko*: W. Morrissey. *Kokoette*: Aleta. *Katisha*: V. Inglefield.

 "Will You Forgive Us?"
  Comiques

 Finale

1920.21

THE GIRL IN THE SPOTLIGHT

An Operetta in Two Acts, 5 Scenes. Book and lyrics by Richard Bruce [Robert B. Smith]. Music by Victor Herbert. Staged by George W. Lederer. Musical numbers staged by Julian Alfred. Scenery designed by Triangle Scenic Studio. Costumes designed by William H. Matthews. Lighting by Tony Greshoff. Musical conductor, Harold Vicars. (Orchestrations by Victor Herbert.) Produced by the George W. Lederer Producing Company. Opened 12 July 1920 at the Knickerbocker Theatre and closed 28 August 1920 after 56 performances.

CAST [in order of appearance]: *Tom Fielding*, a young musician whose great future always keeps just ahead of him, and who shares an apartment with Bill and Ned: JOHN REINHARD. *Bill Weed*, a poet, misfortune's favorite son: JOHNNY DOOLEY. *Ned Brandon*, an artist: Richard Pyle. To their humble abode comes *Max Preiss*, who has made a fortune in the fur business, which he has invested in the Frivolity Theatre: JAMES B. CARSON. *Molly Shannon*, house-maid at Mrs. Todgers' lodging house: MARY MILBURN. Where the smallest hall-room is occupied by *Frank Marvin*, formerly of the A.E.F., but just a man out of a job: BEN FORBES. *Bess*: Minerva Grey. *Clare*: Jessie Lewis. *June*: Agnes Patterson. Each of who hopes to make a conquest of *Watchem Tripp*, stage manager, who is putting on the dances in the new opera: HAL SKELLEY. In which the star is *Nina Romaine*, leading lady of the Frivolity Theatre: JUNE ELVIDGE. *John Rawlins*, Nina Romaine's most constant admirer, a western mine owner: John Hendricks. *Principal Dancers in Preiss' Company*: *Margot*: Ruby Lewis. *Julie*: Lucille Kent. *Laurette*: Lillian Young.

Ensemble: *Ethel*: Flora Crosbie. *Margery*: June White. *Kitty*: Gertrude Reynolds. *Dorothy*: Evelyn Greig. *Mabelle*: Helen Gates. *Estelle*: Geneva Mitchell. *Berenice*: Helen March. *Audrey*: Ann Milburn. *Clarice*: Elizabeth Chase. *Jean*: Margaret Kerr. *Leila*: Georgie Prentice. *Natalie*: Dorothy Barth. *Olivia*: Marguerite Daniels. *Rosina*: Gladys Hart. *Stella*: Ly Wirth.

Act 1, Scene 1: The Sky Parlor of Mrs. Todgers' Lodging House, near Washington Square. *Scene 2*: The Rehearsal Hall of Max Priess' Frivolity Theatre Company, across the court from Mrs. Todgers.

Act 2, Scene 1: The Green Room of the Frivolity Theater, converted into a Chorus Dressing Room for the first night of a new Operetta. *Scene 2*: A Corridor in the Theater. *Scene 3*: The Garden of Orchids, the last scene of Max Priess' Opera, set for an Impromptu Supper after the Performance.

ACT 1[21]

 "I Knew Him When"[22] (Trio)
  J. Dooley, J. Reinhard, R. Pyle

 "I Cannot Sleep Without Dreaming of You" (Song)
  M. Milburn, B. Forbes, Ensemble

 "Come Across" (Sextette)
  M. Grey, J. Lewis, A. Patterson, R. Pyle, J. Reinhard, J. Dooley

 "It Would Happen Anyway" (Duet)
  M. Milburn, B. Forbes

 Intermezzo

---

[20]Settings uncredited.

[21]For subsequent tour, the running order of songs was revised. Added to Act 1 after "Come Across":
 "Where Were You?"
  M. Grey, June White (June), James J. Dunn (Bill), Girls

[22]Dropped during subsequent tour.

"'Twas in the Month of June" (Song)
  J. Dooley, Ensemble
"Catch 'Em Young, Treat 'Em Rough, Tell 'Em Nothing" (Song)
  J. B. Carson, R. Lewis, Girls
"Somewhere I Know There's a Girl for Me" (Song)
  B. Forbes
Dancing Lesson
  H. Skelley, Girls
Finale

ACT 2
Opening Ensemble
  Company
"In My Looking Glass"
  J. Lewis, A. Patterson, Girls
"I'll Be There"[23] (Sextette)
  J. Dooley, M. Grey, J. B. Carson, J. Lewis, H. Skelley, A. Patterson
"I Love the Ground You Walk On"[24] (Song)
  J. Elvidge, Girls
"Oo La La" (Song)
  J. Dooley
"I Cannot Sleep Without Dreaming of You" (reprise)
  B. Forbes
"(There's a) Tender Look in Your Eyes" (Duet)
  M. Milburn
Ensemble
  Company
"A Savage I Remain"[25] (Song)
  J. Hendricks
"I Learned About Women (from Her)" (Song and Dance)
  H. Skelley, Girls
Finale

1920.22 THE CENTURY REVUE

A Musical Revue in Two Acts, 20 Scenes[26]. Book (sketches) by Howard E. Rogers. Music by Jean Schwartz. Lyrics by Alfred Bryan. Staged by Lew Morton. Musical numbers staged by Jack Mason. Orchestra under the direction of Oscar Radin. Entire production staged under the personal directon of J. J. Shubert. Produced by the Messrs. Shubert, Morris Gest, William Elliott and F. Ray Comstock. Opened 12 July 1920 at the Century Promenade (atop the Century Theatre) and closed 1 January 1921 after 150 performances.

CAST: LEO BEERS, MURIEL DeFORREST, HAL HIXON, MADELON LaVARRE, JOHN BYAM, (Vivian) HOLT and (Lillian) ROSEDALE, JOHN LOWE, JESSICA BROWN, (Jane) GREEN and (Jimmie) BLYLER, ROSIE QUINN, VIVIAN OAKLAND, (Bickie) FORD and (Ruth) HAZELTON, MAY THOMPSON, MILO, TOT QUALTERS, INA WILLIAMS, (Ted) LORRAINE and (Grace) WALTON, VERA ROEHM, GEORGE HALE, JACK STRAUSS, THE PURCELLA BROTHERS (Frank, Raymond), THEODORE ZAMBOUNI, KATHLEEN O'HANLON, (Frank) GRACE and (Johnny P.) BERKES, THE FRANK SISTERS.
The Girls: Beth Benton, Florence Darling, Jewel Jordon, Evan Iinard, Thelma Turnbull, Frances Whitmore, Fay Celeste, Clarice Miller, Alberta Harrison, Mildred Seals, Molly Boulais, Jean Carroll, Elizabeth Darling, Dorothy Flamm, Jene Gordon, Cecil Hannon, Norma Simpson, Babette Wood, Mildred Soper, Florence Moore, Violet Bennett, Lorrette Harris, Grace Langdon, Barbara McCree, Elinore Taylor, Ingrid Zanders, Ruth Coster, Pauline Leland, Sydney Nelson, Jean Troupman, Rose Boulais, Olive Channing, Amy Frank, Norma Gould, Kitty Holton, Viola Weller, DeVeaera Anguilliar, Marie Stafford, Anna May Dennehy, Evelyn Jack, Sally Long, Betty Pecan, Nina Whitmore, Frances Dunlap, Bernice Dewey, Leonore Lukens, Elizabeth Reed, Mary Arlington, Mildred Burton, Beatrice Darling, Marie Forbes, Elsie Frank, Gertrude Hartman, Mabel Olson, Jeannette Deitrich, Marie Whitmore, Charlotte Sprague.

---

[23]Dropped during subsequent tour, and replaced by:
  "Stage Life"
    Eunice Vane (Nina), Girls
[24]Dropped during subsequent tour, and replaced by:
  "Let's Pretend"
    M. Milburn, H. Skelley
[25]Dropped during subsequent tour, and replaced by:
  "The Night Time"
    M. Grey, J. J. Dunn, Paul Burns (Preiss)
[26]Presented 6 nights a week at 8:30 P.M., to be followed by THE MID-NIGHT ROUNDERS at 11:30 P.M.

ACT 1
Scene 1
  At the Club
Scene 2
  "Millions of Tunes"
    J. Blyler (piano)
    Scene: In front of the Century Promenade.
    The Man at the 'Phone: L. Beers. *First Rounder*: H. Hixon. *Second Rounder*: J. Byam. *Third Rounder*: J. Lowe. *Fourth Rounder*: J. Blyler. *The Deceiver*: V. Oakland. *The Bluffer*: M. Thompson. *The Fibber*: T. Qualters. *Muriel*: M. DeForrest.
Scene 3
  "Shine On, Little Son"
    Century Promenade Girls, Grace and Berkes
    Scene: The Futurist Bootblack Parlor.
Scene 4
  Some Nonsense
    J. Strauss
Scene 5
  The Heart Burglars: "Shimmy Valentine"
    Frank Sisters, Girls
Scene 6
  The Evolution of a Girl: "Marcelle"
    L. Beers, M. LaVere, Debutantes
Scene 7
  Musical Fantasy: "Hiawatha's Melody of Love"[26a]
    V. Holt, L. Rosedale
    (*Music by* George W. Meyer. *Lyrics by* Alfred Bryan and Artie Mehlinger.)
Scene 8
  "Fig Leaf Number"
    M. DeForrest, Girls
  Dance
    R. Quinn, G. Hale
    Scene: Garden of Eden.
Scene 9
  Just Clothes: "Symphony in Dress" (dance)
    M. LaVarre, Girls
Scene 10
  Black and White Ballet (*Staged by* Alexis Kosloff.)
    Premier Dancers: B. Ford, R. Hazelton.

ACT 2[27]
Scene 1
  Conscience (A dramatic pantomime staged by Allan K. Foster.)
    The Apache: T. Zambouni. *The Girl*: K. O'Hanlon.
      An apache returns to his garret abode with loot that has necessitated a murder. Whilst washing the blood stains from his arms, his partner, a girl of the streets, enters. He displays contempt at her small earnings and shows her the jewels. From the street, far below, a murder extra is shouted. The girl recognizes the blood stains on the apache's clothes and is horrified to learn that the jewels belonged to her sister. She goes to the window to scream, but the murderer strangles her before she can raise an alarm. He crams her into a trunk-like box and returns to the loot. His conscience rebels, however, and he is tormented by the spirit of the girl which rises from the box and pursues him. Finally he commits suicide by leaping from the window.
Scene 2
  Specialty
    L. Beers
    Scene: Around the Baby Grand.
Scene 3
  "Keep Your Weight Down"
    V. Roehm, Purcella Brothers, Girls
    Scene: At the Gymnasium.
Scene 4
  At the Metropolitan: The Singer
    Milo
    (*Gowns by* Rabinoff. *Shoes by* Curzon. *Hats by* Fervous.)

[26a]Previously interpolated by Holt & Rosedale into HELLO, ALEXANDER.
  Mijares and Brother
[27]Added to Act 2 during the run:
  Wire Specialty (High Above You)
  Mijares and Brother

Scene 5

Extra Dry: "Bottle Up a Pretty Girl"
M. Thompson, Girls

Specialty
I. Williams, Grace and Berkes

Scene 6

The Lamp of Love (Dance Novelty)
T. Lorraine, G. Walton, Love Lamp Girls

Scene 7

Musical Moments
J. Green, J. Blyler

["Wild Romantic Blues"
(*Music by* Jean Schwartz. *Lyrics by* Alfred Bryan.)]

Scene 8

Scene Oriental: "The Sphinx"
V. Oakland, Girls

Scene 9

Dance[28]
J. Brown

Scene 10

"Hold Me"
T. Qualters, Hugging Girls

THE MIDNIGHT
ROUNDERS (1920)

1920.23

A Musical Revue in Two Acts, 28 Scenes[29]. Book (sketches) by Howard E. Rogers. Music by Jean Schwartz. Lyrics by Alfred Bryan. Staged by Lew Morton. Musical numbers staged by Jack Mason. Costumes and scenery designed by Homer Conant. Orchestra under the direction of Oscar Radin. Entire production staged under the personal direction of J. J. Shubert. Produced by the Messrs. Shubert. Opened 12 July 1920 at the Century Promenade (atop the Century Theatre) and closed 27 November 1920 after 120 performances.

CAST: JOHN WHEELER, MURIEL DeFORREST, VIVIEN OAKLAND, THE PURCELLA BROTHERS, GRACE ELLSWORTH, INA WILLIAMS, JOE OPP, MADELON LaVARRE, LEW HEARN, (Ted) LORRAINE and (Gladys) WALTON, HAL HIXON, JOHN BYAM, HARRY KELLY, LEO BEERS, (Jane) GREEN and (James) BLYLER, ROSIE QUINN, TOT QUALTERS, MAY THOMPSON, WALTER WOOLF, JACK STRAUSS, (Vivian) HOLT and (Lillian) ROSEDALE, JESSICA BROWN, JOHN LOWE, GEORGE HALE, KATHLEEN O'HANLON, THEODORE ZAMBOUNI, PANDORA, INGRID SOLFENG. The Girls.[30]

ACT 1[31]

Scene 1

"Who Cares?"[32]
V. Oakland, H. Hixon
(*Music by* Leo Edwards. *Lyrics by* Howard Rogers.)
Scene: The Garden of Deacon Pepper's Home
The Butler: J. Wheeler. *Grace Pepper:* V. Oakland. *Mrs. Pepper:* G. Ellsworth. *Dr. Bull:* J. Opp. *Mr. Amon Crabapple:* L. Hearn. *Ralph:* H. Hixon. *The Deacon:* H. Kelly.

Scene 2

"The Valley of Romance
"(Wild) Romantic Blues"
J. Green, Girls
(*Music by* Jean Schwartz. *Lyrics by* Alfred Bryan.)

---

[28]Replaced after opening by:
Inebriated Acrobation
H. Hixon
[29]Billed as "the Greatest Late Night Entertainment ever staged." Presented 6 nights a week at 11:30PM, following THE CENTURY REVUE at 8:30. Subsequently toured with radically revised cast, content and running order.
[30]Same as in THE CENTURY REVUE above.
[31]Added to Act 1 for tour:
"Just Clothes" (from THE CENTURY REVUE)
M. LaVarre, Girls
Symphony and Dress: Helen Bolton, Girls. *More Clothes:* Nan. Halperin.
Toyland: "Rattle Rattle"
F. Dunlap, Girls
[32]Contrary to the program, published sheet music credits music to Milton Ager, and lyrics to Jack Yellen.

Scene 3

When Time Flies
"Clock Song"
T. Qualters, Purcella Brothers, Girls

Scene 4

The Nymph: Danse Jazzique
M. DeForrest

Scene 5

"The Rag Doll"
I. Williams, Girls
(*Music by* Jean Schwartz. *Lyrics by* E. Ray Goetz.)
Scene: At the Seminary.
The Deacon: H. Kelly. *The Butler:* J. Wheeler. *Amon Crabapple:* L. Hearn. *'Tiny' Tot:* I. Williams.

Scene 6

"Je'ne com prom pa" (Je ne comprends pas)
M. LaVarre
Scene: Stage Door at the Winter Garden.
The Deacon: H. Kelly. *Crabapple:* L. Hearn. *Mlle. La La:* M. LaVarre. *Peggy:* Pandora. *Dolly Dimple:* C. Wyley. *Joan:* A. M. Dennehy. *Helen:* F. Celeste. *Bernice:* E. Reed. *Celeste:* B. Pecan. *Jeannette:* G. Langdon. *Lorette:* J. Troupman. *Babette:* B. Dewey. *Marie:* P. Leland.

Scene 7

"The Mansion of Roses"
T. Lorraine, G. Walton
Scene: Roseland.

Scene 8

The Willing Widows: "Heartbreakers"
J. Byam, Girls

Scene 9

"The Story of the Waltz"
(*Music by* Leo Edwards. *Lyrics by* Howard Rogers.)
At the piano: L. Beers. *The Blue Danube:* R. Quinn, G. Hale. *The Chocolate Soldier:* M. Thompson, J. Lowe. *The Merry Widow:* V. Oakland, H. Hixon. *The Pink Lady:* T. Lorraine, N. Rouskaya. *The Count of Luxembourg:* J. Byam, M. DeForrest. *Sari:* K. O'Hanlon, T. Zambouni.

Scene 10

A Bunch of Sweets
"A Mouthful of Kisses"
R. Quinn, Girls

Scene 11

"Chanson"
M. LaVarre, T. Lorraine
(*Music by* Leo Edwards. *Lyrics by* Howard Rogers.)
"Shimmy Nods" (from Chaminade)
T. Qualters, Girls
Scene: Café de la Paix.
The Deacon: H. Kelly. *Crabapple:* L. Hearn. *The Manager:* J. Opp. *A Midnight Rounder:* G. Price. *A Man About Town:* J. Byam. *A Man from Home:* T. Lorraine. *A Mlle. La La:* M. LaVarre. *The Quiet Man:* J. Strauss.

Scene 12

A Few Songs
J. Green, J. Blyler

Scene 13

More Dance
I. Williams, Burns and Foren

Scene 14

A Fantastic Conception of Twenty-Four Hours (The Wedding of the Sun and Moon)
C. Bronner, (I. Solfeng), Company
(*Conceived and staged by* Cleveland Bronner.)
The Norwegian Beauty: I. Solfeng.
Mr. Bronner interprets, through the poetry of motion and color, the passing of twenty-four hours. Inspiration arises, leaving behind the terrors of the night. The moonbeams are visualized in human form as are the sun rays. The Lord of the Sun pays court to the Queen of the Moon. Their union marks the coming of perfect day. Hours pass and nightfall approaches. The Medicine Man appears to warn of the close of day. The followers of the Lord of the Sun attempt to slay him, but find that he is their own chieftain. Night comes and ends the cycle of twenty-four hours.

ACT 2

Scene 1

Loveland

"The Swing" (Swing Song)
  M. Thompson, J. Lowe, Girls
Scene 2
  The Lockstep: Just Out[33]
  Purcella Brothers
Scene 3
  "Beauty Is Like a Rose"[34]
  W. Woolf, Girls
Scene 4
  The Simple Maiden: "Josephine"
  M. LaVarre
Scene 5
  "Three Little Marys"
  T. Lorraine, M. Thompson, R. Quinn, T. Qualters
  Scene: In Normandy.
Scene 6
  Dance
  J. Brown, J. Lowe
Scene 7
  A Few Intimate Moments
  "Whisper in My Ear" (Let Me Whisper in Your Ear)
  R. Quinn, Whispering Girls
Scene 8
  "(O, You) Heavenly Body"
  W. Woolf
  Scene: In the Clouds.
  The Girl: S. Long.
Scene 9
  The Duel
  The Deacon: H. Kelly. *Crabapple:* L. Hearn. *The Doctor:* J. Opp. *Mrs. Pepper:* G. Ellsworth. *Mrs. Trouble:* T. Qualters.
Scene 10
  Les Espagnoles:
  "La Veda"
  V. Holt, L. Rosedale
  Violin
  N. Rouskaya
  Dance
  M. Thompson, J. Lowe
  Tango
  K. O'Hanlon, T. Zambouni
Scene 11
  "William Tell It to Me" (William Tell Me)
  T. Qualters, Grace and Berkes
Scene 12
  Looking Backwards
  "Beautiful Shoulders"
  V. Oakland, Girls
Scene 13
  Inebriated Acrobation[35]
  H. Hixon
Scene 14
  "(My) Lady of the Cameo"
  N. Halperin, J. Byam, Cameo Girls
Scene 15
  "The Century Promenade"
  Entire Company

1920.24   SILKS AND SATINS

A Musical Revue in Two Acts, 28 Scenes. Book (sketches) by Thomas Duggan. Music by Leon Rosebrook. Lyrics by Louis Weslyn. (Staged by William Rock.) Dances and ensemble numbers staged by Earl Lindsay.

---

[33]Dropped during the New York run.
[34]Dropped during the New York run.
[35]Dropped during the New York run.

Scene painting by Bergmann-Nayan Studios. Costumes by Kiviette. Orchestra under the direction of Leon Rosebrook. Orchestrations by Alfred Delby and Leon Rosebrook. Produced by William Rock. Opened 15 July 1920 at the George M. Cohan Theatre and closed 4 September 1920 after 60 performances.

CAST: WILLIAM ROCK, AILEEN STANLEY, THOMAS DUGGAN, WILLIAM DEMAREST, IRENE and BERNICE HART, RUDY WIEDOFT, BABETTE RAYMOND, ERNESTINE MYERS, DELPHIE DAUGHN, JAY M. REGAN, HAZEL WEBB, HARRY HINES, DENNIS O'NEIL, HELYN EBY, WEST AVEY, GEORGE SHELLY, ROBERT DALE, LOUISE and NORMA DALE, JOHNNY DALE, JUE QUON TAI, ESTELLE COLLETTE, CONSTANTINE PERMANE.
Chorus: PHOEBE KING, Ursula Dale, Zenia Fedova, Virginia Lee, Elsie Westcott, Marcelle Barnes, Marjorie Flynn, Jean Thomas, Babette Busey, Daisy Watson, Connie Madison, Irene Mayberry, Orilla Smith, Betty Brown, Blanche Clarke, Carolyn Maywood, Betty Stewart, Elsie Held.

ACT 1[36]
Scene 1
  Opening Chorus
  H. Eby, Chorus
  The girl who starts the show: H. Eby. *The young ladies who have consented to be in the opening chorus:* P. King, U. Dale, Z. Fedova, V. Lee, E. Westcott, M. Barnes, M. Flynn.
Scene 2
  A Bit of Militarism
  "Tommy Atkins"
  H. Webb
  Officers (2 generals): L. Dale, N. Dale. *Rookies:* J. Thomas, B. Busey, D. Watson, C. Madison, I. Mayberry, O. Smith, B. Brown, B. Clarke, C. Maywood, M. Flynn, B. Stewart, E. Held. *A Tommy:* H. Webb.
Scene 3
  A Word from the Bolsheviki
  H. Hines, D. O'Neil, J. Regan, W. Demarest, W. Avey, G. Shelly, C. Permane, H. Harrington
Scene 4
  Just—Johnny Dale
Scene 5
  Behind the Scenes (all in this scene you have seen before)
  "(At) That Colored Jassboray" (That Colored Jazzoray)
  A. Stanley, Ensemble
  (*Music by* Oliver G. Wallace. *Lyrics by* Arthur Freed.)
Scene 6
  "I've Got a Sentry" (I'm Just a Sentry)
  J. M. Regan
  (*Music by* Oliver G. Wallace. *Lyrics by* Arthur Freed.)
  The Prisoner: J. M. Regan. *The Jailer:* P. King. *The Guard:* H. Eby. And Misses Westcott, Barnes, Fedova, Busey, Held, Stewart.
Scene 7
  Danse Orientale
  E. Myers
  Assisted by Misses Thomas, Madison, Smith, N. Dale, Maywood and Smith.
Scene 8
  Rudy Wiedoeft will play on his saxophone, and then comes Aileen Stanley
  Saxophone Solo
  R. Wiedoft
  "I've Shaken Everything I've Got"
  A. Stanley
Scene 9
  Old Age and Youth: "Sunday's Child"
  W. Rock, assisted by I. Hart, B. Hart
  "Life Was Worth While"
  W. Rock
  And Misses King, Eby, Flynn, L. Dale, Clark, U. Dale, Mayberry.
Scene 10
  "Around the Town"
  D. Daughn
  Assisted by Misses Maywood, Madison, Hatfield, Thomas, Webb, N. Dale, Smith, Busey.

---

[36]The running order was changed during the run.

Scene 11

Ace in the Hole
T. Duggan, B. Raymond
The Butler: H. Harrington.

Scene 12

A Little Harmony: "I Want to Be Somebody's Baby"
I. Hart, B. Hart
(*Music and Lyrics by* Jesse Greer and Ed Smalle.)

Scene 13

A Suggestion in Dancing
W. Rock
The Polonaise Girl: V. Lee. *Eccentric Girl*: D. Daughn. *Spanish Girl*: P. King.
Waltz Step: H. Eby. *One Step Girl*: J. Thomas. *Crinoline Girl*: H. Webb. And
L. Dale, R. Dale.

Scene 14

A Study in Black Art
W. Avey, D. O'Neil

Scene 15

Ancient China Ultra Modern: "Nanking Blues"
Jue Quon Tai, Ensemble
(*Music by* Leon Rosebrook. *Lyrics by* Louis Weslyn and William Rock.)
The Princess: Jue Quon Tai. And Entire Company.

ACT 2

Scene 1

Midnight at Reisenrobbers[37]

Scene 2

"Step Along (with Me)"
A. Stanley, Girls

Scene 3

Musical Variety
W. Demarest, E. Collette

Scene 4

"My Rose of Memory"
J. M. Regan
(*Music by* Leon Rosebrook. *Lyrics by* Lloyd Garrett.)
Poppy: H. Eby. *Violet*: L. Dale. *Black-eyed Susan*: I. Maywood. *Pansy*: H.
Webb. *Marigold*: U. Dale. *Daisy*: J. Thomas. *Water Lily*: P. King. *Blue-bell*:
M. Flynn. And the American Beauties.

Scene 5

The Bowery Swell and the Bowery Bum
T. Duggan, W. Rock
We leave you to decide which is which.

Scene 6

"Annie Laurie"[38]
Jue Quon Tai

Scene 7

A Midsummer's Maid: "Midsummer Maiden"
H. Webb
Standing: Misses U. Dale, Westcott, Flynn, Thomas, Lee, Held. *Seated*:
Misses Madison, Mayberry, Smith, Watson, Clark, Maywood.

Scene 8

Danse Eccentrique
E. Meyers, J. Dale

Scene 9

"They Auto Know Better"[39]
T. Duggan, B. Raymond

Scene 10

"Chili Bean"[40] (Eenie-Meenie-Minie-Mo)
A. Stanley
(*Music by* Albert Von Tilzer. *Lyrics by* Lew Brown.)

---

[37]Dropped during the run.
[38]Dropped during the run.
[39]Dropped during the run.
[40]Also performed in this specialty spot:
"My Little Bimbo (Down on the Bamboo Isle)"
A. Stanley
(*Music by* Walter Donaldson. *Lyrics by* Grant Clarke.)

"Alibi Blues"[41]
A. Stanley
(*Music and Lyrics by* Arthur Swanstrom.)

Scene 11

The Mirror of Life
The Singer: J. M. Regan. *The Boy*: R. Dale. *The Butler*: G. Shelley. *The
Cosmopolite*: W. Rock. *Extravagance*: P. King. *The Flirt*: L. Dale. *The Woman of
Scarlet*: Z. Fedova. *Vanity*: V. Lee. *The Children*: I. Hart, B. Hart.

Scene 12

Harry Hines: The 58th Variety:
"He Went in Like a Lion"[42] (from SHUBERT GAIETIES OF 1919)
H. Hines
(*Music by* Harry Von Tilzer. *Lyrics by* Andrew Sterling.)

Scene 13

"I'm Glad to Be Back Again"[43]
J. M. Regan

Finale

Scene: The National Woman's Sporting Club

1920.25 ## POOR LITTLE RITZ GIRL

An Original Musical Novelty (Comedy) in Two Acts, 9 Scenes. Book by
George Campbell and Lew Fields. Music by Richard C. Rodgers, Sigmund
Romberg. Lyrics by Lorenz M. Hart, Alex Gerber. Entire production staged
by Ned Wayburn. Dances arranged by David Bennett. Settings designed by
H. Robert Law. Transformation scene effects and lighting devised by Ned
Wayburn. Costumes designed by Cora MacGeachy, Marie Cook, Anna
Spencer. Lighting by Ned Wayburn. Orchestra under the direction of
Charles Previn. Musical director, Pierce de Reeder. Produced by Lew
Fields. Opened 28 July 1920 at the Central Theatre and closed 16 October
1920 after 93 performances.

CAST (in order of appearance): *From the "Poor Little Ritz Girl" Company (4)*:
Barbara Allen: ELEANOR GRIFFITH. *Madge Merrill*: LULU McCONNELL.
Lillian Lawrence: Aileen Poe. *Annie Farrell*, Sweetie: FLORENCE WEBBER.
William Pembroke, Billy, a wealthy bachelor: CHARLES PURCELL. *Dr. Russell
Stevens*, his bachelor pal: ANDREW TOMBES. *Dorothy Arden*, Barbara's sister:
Ardelle Cleaves. *Jane DePuyster*, Billy's aunt: Eugenie Blair. *From the "Poor Little Ritz
Girl" Company (6)*: *Teddie Burns*, a leading juvenile: Donald Kerr. *Helen Bond*, a
dancer: Elsie Bonwit. *Marguerite*, another (dancer)[44]: Ruth Hale. *Mlle. Lova*, premiere
danseuse: Dolly Clements. *Mons. Mordky*, her partner: Michael Cunningham. *Stage
Manager*: Grant Simpson.
Ensemble: Muriel Manners, Bobbie Beckwith, Julie Anderson, Madeline Smith,
DeSacia Crandell, Dore Leighton, Frisco Devere, Mabel Pearson, Nan Phillips, Betty
Warlow, Vivian White, Mary Phillips, Josephine Rolfe, Peggy Walsh, Mabel Hastings,
Lee Smith.

Act 1, Scene 1: Stage of the Frivolity Theatre, Broadway. During a Dress Rehearsal.
Midnight. *Scene 2*: Apartment of William Pembroke, Riverside Drive, New York. 1
A.M. *Scene 3*: Stage of the Frivolity Theatre. During any performance of "Poor Little
Ritz Girl." *Scene 4*: The Apartment.

Act 2, Scene 1: The Apartment. 10 A.M. the next morning. *Scene 2*: Stage Door of the
Frivolity Theatre. During a Rehearsal, 11:15 A.M. *Scene 3*: The Apartment. *Scene 4*:
Stage of the Frivolity Theatre. During the Opening Performance in New York City.
Scene 5: The Apartment. After the Performance.

ACT 1

Scene 1

"Poor Little Ritz Girl"
Ensemble
(*Music by* Sigmund Romberg. *Lyrics by* Alex Gerber.)
"Mary, Queen of Scots"
L. McConnell
(*Music by* Richard Rodgers. *Lyrics by* Herbert Fields.)

Scene 2

"Love Will Call"
E. Griffith
(*Music by* Richard Rodgers. *Lyrics by* Lorenz Hart.)

---

[41]Replaced during the run by:
"(I'll Be with You in) Apple Blossom Time"
A. Stanley
(*Music by* Albert Von Tilzer. *Lyrics by* Neville Fleason.)
[42]Dropped during the run.
[43]Dropped during the run.
[44]The characters of Marguerite, Mlle. Lova and Mons. Mordky were eliminated in September 1920.

Scene 3

"Pretty Ming Toy"

F. Webber, Ensemble

(*Music by* Sigmund Romberg. *Lyrics by* Alex Gerber.)

Scene 4

"I Love to Say Hello to the Girls (I Hate to Say Goodbye)"

A. Tombes

(*Music by* Sigmund Romberg. *Lyrics by* Alex Gerber.)

"When I Found You"

C. Purcell

(*Music by* Sigmund Romberg. *Lyrics by* Alex Gerber.)

ACT 2[45]

Scene 1

"You Can't Fool Your Dreams"

E. Griffith, C. Purcell, A. Tombes

(*Music by* Richard Rodgers. *Lyrics by* Lorenz Hart.)

Scene 2

"What Happened Nobody Knows"

L. McConnell, A. Poe, F. Webber

(*Music by* Richard Rodgers. *Lyrics by* Lorenz Hart.)

"My Violin"

A. Cleaves

(*Music by* Sigmund Romberg. *Lyrics by* Alex Gerber.)

Scene 3

"All You Need To Be a Star"

E. Griffith, A. Cleaves, C. Purcell, A. Tombes

(*Music by* Richard Rodgers. *Lyrics by* Lorenz Hart.)

"Love's Intense in Tents"

A. Cleaves, A. Tombes

(*Music by* Richard Rodgers. *Lyrics by* Lorenz Hart.)

Scene 4

"The Daisy and the Lark"

F. Webber, E. Bonwit, Ensemble

(*Music by* Richard Rodgers. *Lyrics by* Lorenz Hart.)

"In the Land of Yesterday"

A. Cleaves, E. Bonwit, Ensemble

(*Music by* Sigmund Romberg. *Lyrics by* Alex Gerber.)

"The Phantom Waltz"

Danced by D. Clements, M. Cunningham

(*Music by* Sigmund Romberg.)

"The Bombay Bombashay"

D. Kerr, E. Bonwit, R. Hale, Ensemble

(*Music by* Sigmund Romberg[46]. *Lyrics by* Alex Gerber.)

Scene 5

Finale

Company

1920.26

GOOD TIMES

A Monster Musical Spectacle in Three Acts, 15 Scenes. Book and lyrics by R. H. Burnside. Music by Raymond Hubbell. Entire production staged by R. H. Burnside. Dances arranged by Cissie Hayden. Scenery designed by H. Robert Law and Mark Lawson. Costumes designed by Will R. Barnes and Gladys Monkhouse. Orchestra under the direction of A. J. Garing. Orchestrations by Frank Saddler. Produced by Charles Dillingham. Opened 9 August 1920 at the Hippodrome and closed 30 April 1921 after 456 performances.

CAST: BELLE STORY, NANETTE FLACK, "HAPPY" [Jack] LAMBERT, THE HANNEFORD FAMILY (Edwin "Poodles," Grace, etc.), ARTHUR GEARY, JOSEPH PARSONS, JOE JACKSON, ROBERT MacCLELLAN, VIRGINIA FUTRELLE, THE PENDER TROUPE, THE BERLO SISTERS (Kittie, Madeline, Dora, Lillian), MARCELINE, ALICE and EDNA NASH, GLADYS COMERFORD, FERRY CORWEY, William Williams, Al Harrison, Four Madcaps, Sascha Piatov, William Weston, Lee Gross, Bobby Rosaire, Charles Revell, Eddie Russell, Albert Alberto, Mike Morris, Bobby Riano, George Bleasdale, the Four Nelsons (Rozina, Carmincita, Estrella, ?), Billy Pandor, William Stanley.

---

[45]Added in second week to Act 2, after "What Happened Nobody Knows":

"Dear Heart My Heart Sweetheart"

C. Purcell

(*Music and Lyrics by* Bide Dudley and Fred [Ted] Barron.)

[46]Sheet music credits the music to Ray Perkins.

Premiere Danseuses: MIRIAM MILLER, DAISY SMYTH, MLLE. NATALIE, MAUDIE MALLIA, FLORENCE GAST, ELIZABETH COYLE, THE ROSE SISTERS (Emma, Louise, Bertha, Elsie). *Ensemble*: (300 Unidentified including) Olive Love Clark, Winifred Wood, Mollie Wood, Bobbie Kern, Iase Nelson, Florence Phelps, Minnie Clifton, Nellie Melville, Ethel Whitney, Alice Poole, Hattie Towne, Helda Strauss, Florence Pray, Maude Mallia, Vera Bailey, Violette Beasey, Lillian Carena, Madge Loomis. *High Divers*: Dorothy Gates, Agnes Mack.

ACT 1

Scene 1

Shadowland (*Invented and arranged by* Max Teuber. *Music by* Max Steiner.)

The Statue of Light: E. Coyle. *Her Shadow*: D. Smythe. *Irridescent Shadows*: M. Miller, O. Clark, W. Wood, M. Wood, B. Kern, I. Nelson, F. Phelps, M. Clifton, N. Melville. *Shadows of Long Ago. Bubbles.*

Scene 2

"(Down in the) Valley of Dreams" (Solo)

J Parsons

"Sunbeams" (Song)

A. Nash, E. Nash

"Morning" (Adagio)

Mlle. Natalie

Entrance of the Flowers (Specialty)

Four Madcaps

"Youth and Truth" (Duet)

B. Story, N. Flack

"Wake Up Father Time" (Song)

H. Lambert, Entire Company

Scene: The Valley of Dreams.

Imagination: H. Lambert. *Time*: W. Williams. *Adventure*: A. Froom. *Ambition*: A. Harrison. *Hope*: R. MacClellan. *Courage*: J. Parsons. *Happiness*: G. Comerford. *Justice*: E. Whitney. *Romance*: A. Poole. *Love*: H. Towne. *Sunbeam*: D. Smythe. *Moonbeam*: E. Coyle. *Dawn*: L. Rose. *Wisdom*: J. Frohoff. *Spring*: F. Gast. *Summer*: H. Strauss. *Autumn*: O. Clark. *Winter*: M. Miller. *Truth*: B. Story. *Youth*: N. Flack. *Night*: S. Piatov. *Morning*: Mlle. Natalie. *First Rainbow*: A. Nash. *Second Rainbow*: E. Nash. *Rainbows, Sunbeams, Nymphs, Fairies, Butterflies, Bees, etc.*: (Hippodrome Company).

Scene 3

Music and Fun

F. Corwey

Scene 4

March of International Produce

Entrance of the United States

Entrance of Truth, with Liberty, Peace and Columbia

"The Land I Love" (Finale)

B. Story, A. Geary, Hippodrome Chorus

Scene: The Hall of Commerce.

Japan and China: O. Clark, H. Towne. *Holland*: E. Coyle. *Russia*: H. Strauss. *Poland*: F. Pray. *India*: D. Smythe. *Greece*: A. Poole. *Egypt*: M. Mallia. *Spain*: V. Bailey. *Belgium*: V. Beasey. *Italy*: L. Carena. *France*: Mlle. Natalie. *England*: G. Comerford. *Scotland*: E. Nash. *Wales*: A. Nash. *Ireland*: F. Gast. *Hawaii*: M. Miller. *Philippines*: E. Rose. *Panama*: L. Rose. *Porto Rico*: B. Rose. *Samoa*: E. Rose. *America*: M. Loomis. *An American*: A. Geary. *Truth*: B. Story. *Liberty*: N. Flack. *Columbia*: V. Futrelle.

ACT 2[47]

Scene 1

"The Wedding of the Dancing Doll"

B. Story, Hippodrome Chorus

Specialty

Four Roses

---

[47]Added during the run to Act 2:

The Racing Sensation, depicting "Man 'o War's" Victory in the Futurity Race at Belmont Park (Entry, Number, Owner, Colors, Jockey)

Man o' War, 8, Samuel D. Riddle; black, yellow sash, yellow bars on sleeves, black cap; Loftus. *John F. Grier*, 9, H. P., Whitney; light blue jacket, brown cap; Ambrose. *Dominique*, 2, S. C. Hildreth; black, white sash, blue sleeves; Kummer. *Cleopatra*, 3, W. R. Coe; green, white polka dots, white sleeves, green cap; McAtee. *Upset*, 6, H. P. Whitney; light blue jacket, brown cap; Rice. *On Watch*, 10, G. W. Loft; gold and maroon stripes, maroon cap; Kelsey. *Paul Jones*, 1, Ral Parr; blue and white stripes, red sash, black cap; Butwell. *Dr. Clark*, 4, H. P. Whitney; light blue jacket, brown cap; Johnson. *Captain Alcock*, 5, J. E. Madden; scarlet, maroon sleeves, blue cap; Ensor. *Miss Jemima*, 7, C. E. Rowe; light green, blue cap; Buxton.

Specialty
  Four Nelsons
"You Can't Beat the Luck of the Irish" (Solo)
  A. Geary, Hippodrome Chorus
Dance—Harlequin and Columbine
  S. Piatov, Mlle. Natalie
"Hands Up" (Song)
  H. Lambert
Abdallah's Arabs
  Scene: A Toy Store.
    The Musical Dolly: B. Story. *The Tin Soldier*: R. MacClellan. *The Dancing Doll*: G. Comerford. *The Minister*: C. Strong. *Harlequin*: S. Piatov. *Columbine*: Mlle. Natalie. *Italian Doll*: W. Weston. *Magic Doll*: A. Harrison. *Tramp Doll*: L. Gross. *Jack in the Box*: B. Rosaire. *French Doll*: M. Miller. *Pierette*: H. Strauss. *Spanish Doll*: O. Clark. *Egyptian Doll*: E. Coyle. *Irish Dolls*: Nash Sisters. *Clown Dolls*: C. Revell, E. Russell, J. Russell, A. Alberto, M. Morris, B. Riano, G. Bleasdale, Four Nelsons, B. Pandor, W. Stanley. *Fat Doll*: J. Frohoff. *Rag Doll*: G. Davis. *Dog*: T. Colton. *Monkey*: H. Ward. *Lion*: A. Hill.

Scene 2
  Specialty
    The Pender Troupe
      Scene: Outside the Hippodrome.
Scene 3
  Return of Marcelline
    Scene: Inside the Hippodrome.
Scene 4
  The Hanneford Family, introducing Edwin Hanneford—"Poodles," the World's Leading Comedian-Equestrian.
Scene 5
  At the Circus
    Powers' Performing Elephants
Scene 6
  "(You're) Just Like a Rose" (Duet)
    N. Flack, J. Parsons
      Scene: The Garden of Flowers.
Scene 7
  "Hello Imagination" (Song)
    H. Lambert, Hippodrome Chorus
      Scene: Anywhere in America.
Scene 8
  Specialty
    J. Jackson
      Scene: On the Boardwalk.
Scene 9
  "I Want to Show You Colorland" (Colorland)
    B. Story, A. Geary, Hippodrome Chorus
      Scene: On the Road to Colorland.
ACT 3
Scene 1
  "Sing a Serenade" (Solo)
    N. Flack
      Scene: The Magic Grotto.
Scene 2
  "Welcome Truth" (Solo)
    J. Parsons
  March of the Water Guards (where do they go?)
  Specialty (Swimmers)
    Berlo Sisters
  The Twelve Disappearing Diving Girls
  High Divers
    D. Gates, A. Mack
  "Truth Reigns Supreme" (Finale)
    B. Story, Hippodrome Chorus

1920.27   TICKLE ME

A Musigirl Comedy (Musical Comedy) in Two Acts, 9 Scenes. Book and lyrics by Otto Harbach, Oscar Hammerstein II and Frank Mandel[48]. Music

---

[48]Contrary to program billing, Frank Mandel did not write lyrics.

by Herbert Stothart. Staged by William Collier. Dances and ensembles by Bert French. Scenery designed by Joseph Physioc. Costumes designed by Charles LeMaire. Orchestra under the direction of Herbert Stothart. Produced under the personal direction of Arthur Hammerstein. Produced by Arthur Hammerstein. Opened 17 August 1920 at the Selwyn Theatre and closed 12 February 1921 after 207 performances.

CAST (in order of appearance): *Mary Fairbanks*: LOUISE ALLEN. *Jack Barton*: ALLEN KEARNS. *Marcel Poisson*: VIC CASMORE. *Frank Tinney*: FRANK TINNEY. *Alice West*: MARGUERITE ZENDER. *Customs Inspector*: Benjamin Mulvey. *A Native Boatman*: William Dorriani. *Dance Specialties*: Olga and Mishka, Frances Grant and Ted Wing. *A Slave*: Jack Heisler. *The Tongra*: Marcel Rousseau. *Blah Blah*: Harry Pearce. *Keeper of the Sacred Horse*: Tex Cooper.
Girls of the Ensemble: Betty Nevins, Ruby Nevins, Marietta O'Brien, Sunshine Heyerdahl, Rose Cardiff, Memphis Russell, Emma Pesh, Alys Roby, Josie Carmen, Constance Reed, Laura Maverick, Mildred Mason, Ruth Andrews, Rheba Stewart, Muriel Graham, Florence Dixon, Muriel Reed. *Boys of the Ensemble*: George Griffin, Bobbie Culbertson, Jerome Kirkland, Jack O'Brien, Arnold Gluck, Harry Pearce, Gerard Gardner, Arthur Conway.

Act 1, Scene 1: Studio of Poisson Pictures Corporation, Hollywood, California. *Scene 2*: Customs House, Calcutta, India. *Scene 3*: Garden of Paradise, Thibet. *Scene 4*: The Veil of Mystery. *Scene 5*: Ceremony of the Sacred Bath.

Act 2, Scene 1: The Bower of Temptation. *Scene 2*: Anywhere. *Scene 3*: Customs House at Calcutta. *Scene 4*: Aboard the S.S. *Tickle Me*.

ACT 1
  Act 1
    "Safe in the Arms of Bill Hart"
      V. Casmore, Chorus
    "You're the Type"
      V. Casmore, Chorus
    "A Perfect Lover"
      A. Kearns, Chorus
    Finaletto
      L. Allen, M. Zender, A. Kearns, Chorus
  Act 2
    "I Don't Laugh at Love Anymore"
      A. Kearns, M. Zender
  Act 3
    "The Sun Is Nigh"
      W. Dorriani
    Adagio
      Olga and Mishka
    "Then Love Began"
      A. Kearns, L. Allen
    "Play a Little Hindoo" (Little Hindoo Man)
      A. Kearns, L. Allen, Chorus
  Act 5
    "Ceremony of the Sacred Bath"
      White Lama, Olga and Mishka, F. Grant, T. Wing, Chorus
ACT 2
  Act 1
    "Until You Say Goodbye"
      A. Kearns, M. Zender
    "Temptation"
      A. Kearns, Chorus
  Act 3
    "Until You Say Goodbye" (reprise)
      M. Zender
  Act 4
    Valse du Salon
      Olga and Mishka
    "We've Got Something"
      M. O'Brien, Chorus
    Bagpipe Specialty
      F. Tinney
    "Tickle Me"
      L. Allen, Chorus
    "If a Wish Could Make It So"
      M. Zender, A. Kearns, Chorus
    "Broadway Swell and Bowery Bum"
      F. Tinney, L. Allen
    Finale

THE GREENWICH VILLAGE FOLLIES OF 1920

1920.28

A Revusical Comedy (Musical Revue) of New York's Latin Quarter in Two Acts, a Prologue and 6 Scenes[49]. Dialogue (sketches) by Thomas J. Grey. Music by A. Baldwin Sloane. Lyrics by John Murray Anderson and Arthur Swanstrom. Entire production devised and staged by John Murray Anderson. Costumes and scenery designed by Robert E. Locher. Persian setting and costumes, 14th century Russian costumes by James Reynolds. Orchestra under the direction of Charles Previn. Orchestrations by A. C. Columbo and Mornay D. Helm. Produced by The Bohemians, Inc. (A. L. Jones, Morris Green, Managing directors) Opened 30 August 1920 at the Greenwich Village Theatre, moved 20 September 1920 to the Sam S. Shubert Theatre, and closed 5 March 1921 after 217 performances.

CAST: FRANK CRUMIT, HARRIET GIMBEL, AGNES BRADY, MARGARET DAVIES, DORIS GREEN, JANET STONE, MARGARET SEVERN, PEE WEE MEYERS, FORD HANFORD, HOWARD MARSH, BERT SAVOY, JAY BRENNAN, JAMES CLEMONS, HAP HADLEY, IVAN BANKOFF, Mlle. PHEBE, (Sim) COLLINS and HART, CONSTANCE FARBER, IRENE FARBER, MARY LEWIS, Martha Throop, Dorothy Arnold, Mona Celeste, Maurice Quinlivan, Olive Brower, Florence Browne, Heléne Jesmer, Marie Voorhees, Helen Lee Worthing, Alden Gay, Anna Mae Clift, Lou Gorey, Florence Elmore, Eugene Fosdick, Edward Graham, Allen Joslyn, Florence Normand, Peggy Mathews, Betty Linn, Sybil Stokes, Elizabeth North. *Dancers*: Cyrena Dahl, Marie Tudar, Olga Ziceva, Mary Bay, Frances Mann, Mildred Mann.

PROLOGUE

The Village Pawn Shop

The Pawnbroker: M. Quinlivan. *His Daughter*: H. Gimbel. *The Singer*: M. Lewis. *Her Voice*: O. Brower. *The Poet*: H. Marsh. *His Rhymes*: F. Browne. *The Comedian*: J. Clemons. *His Sense of Humor*: H. Jesmer. *The Dancer*: S. Clark. *Her Technique*: D. Green. *The Manager*: F. Crumit. *His Money*: M. Voorhees. *The Follies of the Village*: L. Gorey, A. Gay, H. L. Worthing, A. M. Clift.

ACT 1

Scene 1

'Set' in Silver: "The Naked Truth"

F. Crumit

The Compére: F Crumit.

Scene: A Studio.

The Models: 130 West 26th Street: ?. 125 Sixth Avenue: ?. 212 West 57th Street: ?. Formerly Philadelphia: ?. 244 Mulberry Street: ?. Address Unknown: ?. 0 Gay Street: ?. c/o Smith, 37 East 18th Street: ?. c/o Flo, 214 West 42nd Street: ?. 200 MacDougal Alley: ?. Hotel Beau Sejour, Staten Island: ?. *The Art Students*: E. Fosdick, E. Graham, M. Quinlivan, A. Joslyn. *A Beginner*: H. Gimbel. *The Batik Girls*: S. Stokes, E. North. *The Botticelli Girl*: A. Brady. And H. Hadley.

Le Torso: Arms: H. Jesmer, F. Browne. *Neck and Shulders*: A. M. Clift, M. Voorhees. *Waist Line*: O. Brower, B. Linn. *Knees*: L. Gorey, D. Arnold. *Ankles and Feet*: H. L. Worthing, D. Green. *The Greenwich Village Follies Girl*: A. Gay. *A Sculptor*: J. Brennan. *His Inspiration*: B. Savoy.

"Just Sweet Sixteen"

H. Marsh, M. Celeste

The Birthday Girls: P. Matthews, A. Brady, E. North, F. Browne, H. Jesmer, M. Stokes, B. Linn, M. Voorhees. *The Dancers*: J. Stone, M. Davies. *The Birthday Cake*: H. L. Worthing, A. M. Clift, D. Green, L. Gorey. *The 'Baby' Years* (One to Four): M. Tudar, C. Dahl. *The 'Doll-Time' Years* (Four to Eight): M. Mann, M. Bay. *The 'School-Girl' Years* (Eight to Twelve): F. Mann, O. Ziceva. *The Years of the Cake* (Twelve to Sweet Sixteen): M. Celeste, H. Marsh. *'Set' in Silver*: C. Farber, I. Farber. *The Claque*: F. Crumit, S. Clark.

Scene 2

The Valentine: "I'll Be Your Valentine"

M. Lewis

The Cupids: M. Mann, H. Gimbel. *The Belle*: M. Davies. *The Beau*: J. Stone. *Terminal Ornaments*: P. Matthews, B. Linn. *The Postman*: F. Mann. *The Valentine Girls*: M. Tudar, C. Dahl, M. Bay, O. Ziceva. *The True Lovers*: I. Bankoff, Mlle. Phebe. *Adagio*: I. Bankoff, Mlle. Phebe. *The Coquette*: D. Green. *Beaux*: A. Joslyn, E. Fosdick. (Ballet Music for the Valentine Pas de Deux by Charles Previn.)

Before the 'Rural Motif': *The Rube-o-hemians*: P. W. Meyers, F. Hanford.

["Old Black Joe"; "My Old Kentucky Home"; "Down in Arkansas"]

Meyers, Hanford

Scene 3[50]

The Hell Hole: "Come to Bohemia"

H. Marsh

The Villagers: *The Black Cat*: F. Normand. *The Green Witch*: A. M. Clift. *The Purple Pup*: L. Gorey. *The Vermillion Hound*: P. Mathews. *The Polly Girl*: H. Jesmer. *The Pirates Den Girl*: O. Brower. *Mlle. Lafayette*: H. L. Worthing. *The Rogues Tavern Girl*: M. Voorhees. *Mlle. Brevort*: D. Green. *The Treasure Box Girl*: B. Linn. *The Greenwich Village Inn Girl*: A. Gay. *The Jekyll and Hyde Girl*: D. Arnold. *An Organ Grinder*: H. Gimbel. *A Singing Waitress*: S. Clark. *An Apache*: J. Brennan. *Lady Nicotine* (A Cigarette Girl): B. Savoy. *The Mad Hatters*: J. Stone, M. Davies.

"(Just) Snap Your Fingers at Care"

F. Crumit

(*Music by* Louis Silvers. *Lyrics by* Buddy G. DeSylva.)

Dance

J. Clemons

"Murder in My Heart"

S. Clark

"The Song of the Samovar"

H. Marsh

The Woman of the Samovar: M. Throop. *The Torch Bearers*: E. Fosdick, E. Graham, M. Quinlivan, A. Joslyn.

Pas de Deux

I. Bankoff, Mlle. Phebe

The Dancers: C. Dahl, M. Tudar, O. Ziceva, F. Mann, M. Bay, M. Mann. *The Princess*: A. Gay. *The Ladies of the Court*: H. Jesmer, F. Browne.

"Tam" (Tam, Tam, Tam, Tam, Tam)

F. Crumit, Ensemble

ACT 2

In Front of the Screens

Le Diseur: H. Marsh. *The Cartoonist*: H. Hadley. *The Sandwich Girls*: S. Stokes, F. Browne, M. Voorhees, P. Mathews, B. Linn, E. North.

"(At the) Krazy Kat's Ball"

H. Gimbel, J. Stone, M. Davies

Divertissement

The Ho Bohemians, Collins and Hart

Before the Music Motif Curtain

F. Crumit

Scene 1

The Sin Shop: "Tsin"

H. Marsh

The Adolescent Boys: B. Linn, S. Stokes, E. North, M. Voorhees. *The Adolescent Girls*: A. Brady, P. Mathews, H. Jesmer, F. Browne.

"Parfum d'Amour" (Perfume of Love)

M. Lewis

The Slave to Perfume: E. Graham. *Les Parfums*: *Violet de Parme*: O. Brower. *Attar des Roses*: D. Green. *Sandalwood*: D. Arnold. *Cypres*: H. L. Worthing. *Arête*: L. Gorey. *Elange-Elange*: A. Gay. *Tsin*: F. Normand. *Peau d'Orange*: A. M. Clift.

The Dance

M. Severn

Before the Music Motif Curtain

F. Crumit

["I'm a Lonesome Little Raindrop"

(*Music by* James Hanley. *Lyrics by* Joe Goodwin and Murray Roth.)

"Wait Until You See My Madeleine"

(*Music by* Albert Von Tilzer. *Lyrics by* Lew Brown.)

"Marimba"

(*Music by* Johnny Black. *Lyrics by* Howard Johnson and Cliff Hess.)]

'Set' in Silver

B. Savoy, J. Brennan

Scene 2[51]

The Golden Carnival:

---

[49]The second in the annual series of revues which began in 1919 under the auspices of The Bohemians, transferring from Off-Broadway to Broadway.

---

[50]Added during Broadway run after "(Just) Snap Your Fingers at Care":

"A Broadway Cinderella"

C. Farber

(*Music by* Harry Carroll. *Lyrics by* Ballard Macdonald.)

[51]Added after Valse Empire during Broadway run:

"The Greenwich Village Carnival"

M. Throop, H. Marsh

Valse Empire
    B. Linn, A. Joslyn; M. Lewis, E. Fosdicks; P. Mathews, E. Graham; F. Browne, M. Quinlivan
An Episode with Benda Masks (Masks by W. J. Benda)
    M. Severn
Dance Guignole
    J. Clemons
Resume by Everybody (Finale)

1920.29   THE SWEETHEART SHOP

A Musical Comedy in Three Acts. Book and lyrics by Anne Caldwell. Music by Hugo Felix. Entire production staged by Edgar J. MacGregor. Musical numbers staged by Julian Alfred. Scenery designed by Herbert Moore. Costumes by S. Strauss, Inc. Lighting by Tony Greshoff. Orchestra under the direction of Hilding Anderson. Produced by Edgar J. MacGregor and William Moore Patch. Opened 31 August 1920 at the Knickerbocker Theatre and closed 16 October 1920 after 55 performances.

CAST (in order of appearance): *Gideon Blount*: Roy Gordon. *Freddie*: DANIEL HEALY. *Peggy*: UNA FLEMING. *Julian Lorimer*: JOSEPH LERTORA. *Mildred Blount*: MARY HARPER. *Peter Potter*: HARRY K. MORTON. *Minerva Butts*: ESTHER HOWARD. *Natalie Blythe*: HELEN FORD. *Daphne*: Zela Russell. *Mr. Hylo*: Clay Hill.
    Bridesmaids in the Sweetheart Shop: *Grace*: Irma Irving. *Teddy*: Teddy Hudson. *Iona*: Dorothy Irving. *Mary*: Marie Brady.
    Artist's Models: *Amaranth*: Charlotte Taylor. *Clarinda*: Jane Arrol. *Timandra*: Mary O'Brien.
    Attendants: *Tom*: Ralph Derst. *Jerry*: Thomas Malaney. *Harry*: Alfred Opler. *Jack*: Clay Hill. *Bill*: Jack Scheidel. *Pete*: William Strahlman.
    Patronesses: Mary O'Brien, Martha Parsons, Frankie Dawn, Charlotte Starbuck, Charlotte Taylor, Jane Arrol, Bobbie Renys, Virginia Taylor, Kathryn Fallon, Lucille Poirier, Wilma Busey, Doris Irving, Dot Tosbelle, Teddy Hudson, Irma Irving, Marie Brady, Dorothy Irving, Rhea Norton. *Attendants*: Gene Martinette, Al Knight.

Act 1: The Sweetheart Shop. Late afternoon.

Act 2: Lorimer's Studio. Evening.

Act 3: A Fifth Avenue Auction Room.

ACT 1
    Opening:
    Pantomime Dance
        U. Fleming, Boys
    "As We Go Out Walking"
        The Sweethearts
    "The Sweetheart Shop"
        R. Gordon, M. Harper, Sweethearts
    "Oh, Mister Postman"
        D. Healy, Girls
    "Is There Any Little Thing I Can Do For You?"
        H. K. Morton, Bridesmaids
    "I Want to Be a Blooming, Blushing Bride"
        E. Howard, Boys
    "Didn't You?"
        J. Lertora, H. Ford
    "A Sweetheart Shop Wedding" (Finale)
        Company
ACT 2
    Opening:
    "The Glow of the Cigarette"
        C. Taylor, Models
    Dance Divertissement
        U. Fleming
    "June Bells"[52]
        D. Healy, T. Hudson, Models
    "She's Artistic"
        E. Howard, Boys
    "Waiting for the Sun to Come Out"
        H. Ford, J. Lertora, Boys
        (*Music by* George Gershwin. *Lyrics by* Arthur Francis [Ira Gershwin].)
    "My Caravan"
        J. Lertora, E. Howard, Oriental Chorus

"(I'd Like to Teach You the) A-B-C of Love"
    H. K. Morton, Z. Russell
Finale
    Company
ACT 3
    Opening:
    "The Dresden China Belle"
        U. Fleming, Chorus
    Dance Eccentrique
        U. Fleming, D. Healy
    "Life Is a Carousal"
        J. Lertora, Company
    Finale
        Company

1920.30   LITTLE MISS CHARITY

The 1921 Model Musical Comedy in Two Acts, 4 Scenes[53]. Book and lyrics by Edward Clark. Based on a short story by Edgar S. Franklin (and Edward Clark's farce 'Not with My Money'). Music by S. R. Henry and M. Savin. Staged by Alfred Hickman and C. A. deLima. Dances staged by Sammy Lee. Scenery designed by P. Dodd Ackerman. Costumes by Schneider-Anderson Company (gowns), Finchley (men's clothes). Orchestra under the direction of Gus Salzer. Orchestrations by Arthur Lange and M. Savin. Produced by Richard G. Herndon. Opened 2 September 1920 at the Belmont Theatre and closed 6 November 1920 after 77 performances.

CAST (in order of appearance): *Rosalie, Angel's maid*: Lucille Williams. *"Dickey" Foster, alias J. Robert Fulton, a confidence man*: FREDERICK RAYMOND, JR. *Graham, Fulton's valet*: Henry Vincent. *"Fingers" Clay, alias Reverend Dr. Clayton, Fulton's associate*: FRANK MOULAN. *Amy Shirley, another of Fulton's associates*: MARJORIE GATESON. *Angel Butterfield, known as Little Miss Charity*: JUANITA FLETCHER. *Miss Wheeler, her aunt*: EDNA SHAW. *Woodruff Porter, her fiancé*: Bernard Wells. *Mortimer Gayling, her attorney*: Jere McAuliffe. *Billikins, the office boy*: Lillian White.
    Applicants and friends of Angel Butterfield: Eddie Pierce, James Healy, Jacques Stone, Charles Mansfield, Betty Mack, Marcia Joy, Laurette Stanley, Grace Bonney, Ruth Mansfield, Victoria Gardner, Beth Meakins, Amata Grassi, Helen Fleming, Mildred Quinn.

Act 1, Scene 1: Exterior of Angel Butterfield's Country Home. Scene 2: Interior of Same.

Act 2, Scene 1: Offices of the Butterfield Society. Three days later. Scene 2: The same. Two days later.

ACT 1
Scene 1
    "Little Miss Charity"
        A. Mayo, Applicants
    "That Certain Something"
        M. Gateson, F. Moulan
    "Little Miss Charity" (reprise)
        F. Raymond, Jr.
    "Step Inside"
        J. Fletcher, E. Shaw, Girls
Scene 2
    "That Certain Something" (reprise)
        J. Fletcher, Ensemble
    "Crinoline Girl"
        J. Fletcher, E. Shaw, Girls
    "I Think So, Too"
        F. Raymond, Jr., J. Fletcher, E. Shaw, J. McAuliffe, B. Wells
    "Revenge"
        M. Gateson, F. Moulan
    Finale
        Entire Company
ACT 2
Scene 1
    "A Woman's Touch"
        J. Fletcher, E. Shaw, M. Gateson, Ensemble

---
[52]Dropped for subsequent tour.

---
[53]Subtitled 'A New Inspiration for Old New York.'

"Eyes of Youth"[54]
  F. Raymond, Jr., J. Fletcher, Ensemble
"Poor Workingman"
  M. Gateson, F. Moulan, F. Raymond, Jr.
"Angel Town"
  F. Raymond, Jr., Entire Company
"When Loves Comes to Your Heart"
  J. Fletcher, F. Raymond, Jr.
Scene 2
"When Love Comes to Your Heart" (dance)
  A. Mayo
"Dance Me Around"
  M. Gateson, Ensemble
Finale
  Ensemble

1920.31   HONEYDEW

A Play with Music in Two Acts, 3 Scenes. Book and lyrics by Joseph W. Herbert (based on his play 'The Scourge of the Sea'). Music by Efrem Zimbalist, Sr. Staged by Hassard Short. Dances arranged by Kuy Kendall. Settings designed by Hassard Short. Gowns and costumes designed by Ralph Mulligan. Orchestra under the direction of Max Hirschfeld. Orchestrations by Carl Kiefert, J. Bodewalt Lampe and James McCabe. Produced by Joseph Weber. Opened 6 September 1920 at the Casino Theatre, closing 19 February 1921 after 200 performances; re-opened 16 May 1921 at the Casino Theatre[55] and closed 25 June 1921 after 49 additional performances. Total: 249 performances.

CAST: *Henry Honeydew*: HAL FORDE. *Sylvester Adams*: JOHN PARK. *Howard Taylor*: SAM ASH. *Captain Dick*: JOHN DUNSMURE. *Jack*: KUY KENDALL. *Pedro*: FRANK GILL. *Chanser*: Fred Manatt. *Timothy Hay*: Gordon Spelvin. *Mrs. Vanoni*: THERESA MAXWELL CONOVER. *Lenore*: DOROTHY FOLLIS. *Muriel*: ETHELIND TERRY. *Penelope*: Marie Hall. *Conchita*: MLLE. MARGUERITE. *Daisy*: Evelyn Earle. *Sing Loo*: Helen Long.

  Young Ladies of the Glee Club: *Miss Japonica*: Dorothy Powers. *Miss Rosemary*: Aldian Hudson. *Miss Jonquil*: Adele Sanderson. *Miss Nasturtium*: Betty Hill. *Miss Violet*: Margaret Arthur. *Miss Dahlia*: Victoria Wallace. *Miss Azalea*: Doris Benham. *Miss Orchid*: Margaret Leona. *Miss Hollyhock*: Dorothy Neill. *Miss Columbine*: Alice Purcell. *Miss Gardenia*: Betty DeGrasse. *Chinese Servants*: Misses Pauline, Catherine Lee, Adeline Lee, May Moy.

Act 1: The Studio of Henry Honeydew at Pelham.

Act 2, Scene 1: Henry Honeydew's New Home at Larchmont. Afternoon, a year later. *Scene 2*: Same, a few hours later.

ACT 1
  "Slaves of the Demon King"
    H. Forde, Ladies
  "My Husband's Dearest Friend"
    D. Follies, S. Ash
  "The June Bug"
    H. Forde
  Entrance of Fairies
    H. Forde, E. Herbert, Ladies
  "The Morals of a Sailor"
    J. Dunsmure, Ladies
  "Oh, How I Long for Someone!"
    D. Follies, S. Ash
  "A Cup of Tea"
    E. Terry, H. Forde, J. Park
  Chinese Fantasy—
    The Maid: Mlle. Marguerite. *The Mandarin*: J. Dunsmure. *The Coolie*: F. Gill.
  "Drop Me a Line"
    E. Terry, H. Forde
  Finale
    Ensemble
ACT 2
  Dance
    M. Hall, K. Kendall

Entrance of the Bridesmaids
  Ladies
"Spanish Song"
  Mlle. Marguerite, Ladies
"Your Second Wife"[56]
  E. Terry
"Time to Take a Drink"
  Mlle. Marguerite, M. Hall, M. Leona, D. Neill, F. Gill, K. Kendall
Polka
  M. Hall, K. Kendall
"Honeydew Waltz"
  Mlle. Marguerite, F. Gill
"Unrequited Love"
  D. Follis, T. M. Conover, J. Park
"Believe Me, Beloved"[57]
  S. Ash
"Sunshine of Love"
  E. Terry, H. Forde
"The Sound of the Sound"
  E. Terry, M. Hall, A. Cavanaugh, Ladies
"A la Minute" (Dance)
  K. Kendall
"A Fast Step Creation"
  Mlle. Marguerite, F. Gill
"It's a Small, Small World"
  H. Forde, S. Ash, J. Park, J. Dunsmure
"Morning Glories"
  E. Terry, Ladies
Finale
  Ensemble

1920.32   PITTER PATTER

A Musical Comedy in Three Acts, 5 Scenes. Book by Will M. Hough. Based on the farce 'Caught in the Rain' by William Collier and Grant Stewart. Music and lyrics by William B. Friedlander. Dances and ensembles staged by David Bennett. Scenery painted by (D. Frank) Dodge and (William E.) Castle. Costumes by Paul Arlington, Inc. Orchestra under the direction of Harry Archer. Produced by William B. Friedlander[58]. Opened 28 September 1920 at the Longacre Theatre and closed 1 January 1921 after 111 performances[59].

CAST (in order of appearance): *Bob Livingston*: JOHN PRICE JONES. *Bryce Forrester*: JACK SQUIRES. *Violet Mason*: MILDRED KEATS. *Mrs. George Meriden*: HELEN BOLTON. *James Maxwell*: Frederick Hall. *Muriel Mason*: JANE RICHARDSON. *"Dick Crawford"*: WILLIAM KENT. *George Thompson*: Albert Warner. *Howard Mason*: HUGH CHILVERS. *Proprietor of Candy Shop*: George Smithfield. *Street Car Conductor*: George Spelvin. *Butler*: Arthur Greeter.

  The Girls: Elsa Dawn, Dawn Renard, Anne Foose, Billie Vernon, Rae Fields, Hazel Rix, Aileen Grenier, Alice Norris, Florence Davis, Mabel Benelisha, Georgie Cable, Katherine Powers, Sunny Harrison, Estelle Callen, Gertrude Morgan, Florence Carroll, Pearl Crossman, Violet Hazel. *The Boys*: Messrs. Fields, Cagney, LeVoy, Grager, Maclyn, Smith, Jackson, Mayo.

Act 1: A Street in Colorado Springs, Colorado.

Act 2, Scene 1: Drawing Room of the Mason Home. Afternoon. *Scene 2*: At the Bottom of a Mine Shaft. *Scene 3*: Drawing Room of the Mason Home. Evening.

Act 3: Exterior of Hotel Miramar, Havana, Cuba.

ACT 1
  "I'm a Bachelor"
    J. P. Jones, J. Squires, M. Keats, Ensemble
  "Since You Came into My Life"
    J. P. Jones, Ensemble

---

[54]Dropped during the run.
[55]Return engagement had the following cast change: *Daisy*: Helen Robinson.

---

[56]Replaced after opening by:
  "Sunshine of Love"
    E. Terry, H. Forde
[57]Replaced during the run by:
  "The Eyes of the Girl I Love"
    S. Ash
[58]Subsequently toured under the auspices of Edmond Plohn.
[59]Direction uncredited.

"Send for Me"
 H. Bolton, M. Keats, J. P. Jones, J. Squires
 (*Music and Lyrics by* William Friedlander and Will M. Hough.)
"Somebody's Waiting for Me"
 J. Richardson, Ensemble
"Wedding Blues"
 H. Bolton, J. P. Jones, J. Squires, Ensemble
"Pitter Patter"
 J. Richardson
 (*Lyrics by* Will M. Hough.)

ACT 2
"Any Afternoon"[60]
 H. Bolton, M. Keats, J. P. Jones, J. Squires, Ensemble
"You Never Can Tell"
 M. Keats, J. P. Jones
"Pitter Patter" (reprise)
 J. Richardson
"True Love" (Meet Your True Love Half Way)
 J. Richardson, W. Kent
"Bagdad on the Subway"
 J. P. Jones, Ensemble
"I Saved a Waltz for You"
 J. Richardson
 (*Lyrics by* Will M. Hough.)
Finale
 Ensemble

ACT 3
Wedding Chorus, including "Love Me Tonight"
 H. Bolton, J. Squires, Ensemble
"A Man, a Maid"[61]
 J. Richardson
"They're Jazzing It Up in Havana"
 J. P. Jones, Ensemble
Finale
 J. Richardson, W. Kent

1920.33 BROADWAY BREVITIES OF 1920

An Entertainment with Music, Comedy and Dancing (Musical Revue) in Two Acts, 22 Scenes. Sketches by George LeMaire. Music by Archie Gottler. Lyrics by Blair Traynor. Additional numbers by Bert Kalmar and Harry Ruby, Irving Caesar, Irving Berlin, George Gershwin, Arthur Jackson. Directed by J. C. Huffman. Dances and ensembles staged by Jack Mason. Scenery designed by Herbert Ward. Costumes designed by Charles LeMaire. Orchestra under the direction of Louis Gress. Orchestrations by Stephen Jones and Will Vodery[62]. Produced by George LeMaire. Opened 29 September 1920 at the Winter Garden and closed 18 December 1920 after 105 performances.

CAST: EDDIE CANTOR, BERT WILLIAMS, GEORGE LeMAIRE, HAL VAN RENSELLAER, ULA SHARON, EDDIE BUZZELL, ALEXIS KOSLOFF, PEGGY PARKER, EDITH HALLOR, PAUL VAN DYKE, TECK MURDOCK, WILLIAM SULLY, VERA GROSSET, NATALIE KINGSTON, GENEVIEVE HOUGHTON, Jay Dillon.
 Ladies of the Ensemble: Ethel Callhan, Florence Kerns, Marcelle Barnes, Beverly Worth, Helen LeVon, Renee Hughes, Kitty Berg, Alva Fenton, Ona Hamilton, Alma Drange, Estelle Penning, Peggy Mitchell, Jan Jarvis, Mercedes Desmordant, Virginia Roche, Norma Waterman, Elsie Westcott, Wilma Bruce, Catharine Flynn, Dorothy Stokes, Carol Miller, Alice Haynes, Dorothy King, Hilda Wright, Delphine Deery, Phyllis Blair, Patricia Parker, Emlee Haddone, Anna Paulson, Edith Pollack, Dorothy Hall, Virginia Dixon, Flora Keene.

ACT 1[63]

---

[60]Dropped late in the run.
[61]Dropped early in the run.
[62]For Bert Williams' songs.
[63]Added for subsequent tour to Act 1:
 "My Broadway Chorus Girl"
  Maurice Diamond, Virginia Roche
  (*Music and Lyrics by* Con Conrad.)
 "Bright Eyes"
  Mildred Richardson, Bob Nelson
  (*Music and Lyrics by* Con Conrad.)

Scene 1
 Prologue
  The Author: H. Van Rensellaer. *The Producer*: G. LeMaire.
Scene 2
 Times Square
 "The Usual Opening Chorus"
  Entire Ensemble
 "I Love to Dance"[64]
  T. Murdock, V. Roche, P. Mitchell, A. Fenton, O. Hamilton
Scene 3
 A Will and a Way
  E. Buzzell, P. Parker
  Peggy Parker's Friend: G. Houghton, B. Parker. *Messenger Boy*: J. Dillon.
 "(I'm Going to) Love, Honor and O'Baby"
  E. Buzzell, P. Parker
  (*Music by* Archie Gottler. *Lyrics by* Blair Treynor.)
Scene 4
 "That Means Home to Me"[65]
  G. Houghton, M. Francis
 Spring Dance
  N. Kingston, Girls
 The Dance of the Nymphs
  U. Sharon
  Scene: The Birch Forest
Scene 5
 Ninety Days from Broadway
  Al Johnson: B. Williams. *Stonewall Jackson*: G. LeMaire. *The Warden*: T. Murdock.
Scene 6
 "Spanish Love"
  (*Music by* George Gershwin. *Lyrics by* Irving Caesar.)
 Dance
  Brevity Girls
  In the Aisles: H. Van Rensselaer, M. Francis. *The Lady Beautiful*: E. Hallor.
Scene 7
 "(We've Got) The Stage Door Blues"
  Misses F. Kerns, K. Berg, R. Hughes, E. Callahan, H. LaVon, E. Westcott, B. Worth, M. Barnes
  (*Music and Lyrics by* Bert Kalmar and Harry Ruby.)
Scene 8
 Songs[66]
  B. Williams
 ["The Moon Shines on the Moonshine"
  (*Music by* Robert Hood Bowers. *Lyrics by* Frances DeWitt.)
 "I Want to Know Where Tosti Went"
  (*Music and Lyrics by* Chris Smith.)
 "I Makes Mine Myself"
  (*Music by* Robert Hood Bowers. *Lyrics by* Frances DeWitt.)
 "You'll Never Need a Doctor No Mo'"
  (*Music and Lyrics by* Chris Smith.)
 "Save a Little Dram for Me"
  (*Music and Lyrics by* Will E. Skidmore and Marshall Walker.)
 "Eve Cost Adam Just One Bone"
  (*Music and Lyrics by* Charles Bayha.)

 "Anna in Indiana"
  B. Nelson
  (*Music and Lyrics by* Billy and Eddie Gorman, Harry Rose.)
 "Rose of Old Seville"
  M. Richardson
  (*Music and Lyrics by* J. Russel Robinson and Con Conrad.)
 "Rainy Afternoons"
  M. Richardson, Frank Bernard, Ensemble
  (*Music and Lyrics by* Con Conrad.)
[64]Dropped during the run.
[65]Dropped during the run.
[66]According to published sheet music, the last three of these songs were performed in the show's third edition, on tour. The first three are credited to the first edition.

""Somebody (Else, Not Me)" (from ZIEGFELD FOLLIES OF 1919)
(*Music by* James Hanley. *Lyrics by* Ballard Macdonald.)
"Get Up"[67]
(*Music and Lyrics by* Robert Hood Bowers.)]
Scene 9
"Wonderful"[68]
P. Parker, Girls
Scene 10
At the Dentist's[69]
A Patient: E. Cantor. *Dr. Pain*: G. LeMaire.
Scene 11
"Love Me While the Snow Flakes Fall" (Snow Flakes)
E. Hallor, H. Van Rensellaer
(*Music by* George Gershwin. *Lyrics by* Arthur Jackson.)
The Swiss Mountain Climbers: W. Sully, T. Murdock. *The Yodler*: P. Van Dyke.
Finale
Entire Ensemble
ACT 2[70]
Scene 1
The Kiss (*Pantomime and Music conceived by* Bert Williams. *Staged by* Alexis Kosloff.)
Youth: U. Sharon. *The Officer*: A. Kosloff.
An Officer of the Guards craves the Kiss of Youth, but she hides from him. Insensate, he invades the sanctuary, coaxes, pleads, implores, but Youth defeats even force, seeking revenge on an outer balcony. Mad with desire, he drags her back and ravishes the Kiss from Youth. Defiled, Youth, with unconscious courage, drives to his base heart the pin from her corsage. He will never kiss again.
Scene 2
Between Dances: "A Housetop of Our Own"
W. Sully, G. Houghton
Scene 3
"Won't You Let Me Take a Picture of You?"
V. Grosset, Kodak Girls
Scene 4
"Beautiful Faces Need Beautiful Clothes"
E. Hallor, Girls
(*Music and Lyrics by* Irving Berlin.)
Scene: A Fifth Avenue Shop Window.
Scene 5
The Usual Thing
Mr. Moe Goldfarb: E. Cantor. *Mr. Ponzi Dough*: G. LeMaire. *The Ladies*: P. Parker, G. Houghton.
Scene 6
"I'm a Dancing Fool"[71]
W. Sully, Girls
(*Music by* George Gershwin. *Lyrics by* Arthur Jackson.)

---

[67]May have been dropped before New York opening or early in the run.
[68]Dropped during the New York run.
[69]Dropped during the New York run.
[70]Added to Act 2 for subsequent tour:
"Choo-Choo Blues"
M. Diamond
Reconciliation Polka
U. Sharon
"I've Got the Blues for My Kentucky Home"
B. Nelson & Cronin
(*Music and Lyrics by* Clarence Gaskill.)
"Kentucky Blues"
B. Nelson & Cronin
(*Music and Lyrics by* Clarence Gaskill.)
"In Cherry Blossom Time with You"
D. Jardon
(*Music by* Dorothy Jardon and Joseph Daly. *Lyrics by* Blair Treynor.)
"Blow, Blow, Blow"
M. Richardson, Ensemble
(*Music and Lyrics by* Con Conrad.)
[71]Replaced during the run by:
"Darling"
P. Parker, H. Van Rensellaer

A Typical Restaurant Revue Scene
E. Cantor, G. LeMaire, V. Grosset, P. Parker, M. Barnes, F. Kern
"Drigo's Polka"
U. Sharon
Scene: A Roof Garden of a Modern Apartment.
Scene 7
"Stolen Sweets"[72]
E. Hallor, H. Van Rensellaer
Scene 8
The Smart Bootery
(*Music by* Joseph M. Daly. *Dance music by* Maurie Rubens.)
A Customer: B. Williams. *The Proprietor*: G. LeMaire. *The Shoppers*: K. Berg, D. King, N. Waterman, M. Barnes, E. Westcott, R. Hughes. *The Clerks*: O. Hamilton, P. Mitchell, J. Jarvis, V. Roche, A. Drange, A. Fenton.
Scene 9
"Lu-Lu"
E. Hallor, Girls
(*Music by* George Gershwin. *Lyrics by* Arthur Jackson.)
Lindy: W. Sully. *Mandy*: E. Buzzell. *Carolina*: H. Van Rensellaer. *Mary*: M. Francis.
Scene 10
Eddie Cantor[73]
["I Wish That I'd Been Born in Borneo"
(*Music by* Walter Donaldson. *Lyrics by* Grant Clarke.)
"Palesteena" (Lena is the Queen of Palesteena")
(*Music and Lyrics by* Con Conrad, J. Russel Robinson.)
"Margie"
(*Music by* Con Conrad, J. Russel Robinson. *Lyrics by* Benny Davis.)]
Scene 11
Finale[74]
E. Cantor, G. LeMaire, B. Williams, Entire Ensemble
Scene: The Marble Steps

1920.34 **MECCA**

A Mosaic in Music and Mime (Musical Spectacle) in Three Acts, 13 Scenes. Book and lyrics by Oscar Asche. Music by Percy E. Fletcher. Dances and choreography by Michel Fokine. Staged by E. Lyall Swete. Scenery designed by Joseph Harker and Philip Harker. Costumes designed by Percy Anderson; additional costumes by Leon Bakst. Properties designed by Carl Link. Orchestra under the direction of Frank Tours. Entire production produced under the personal direction of Morris Gest. Produced by F. Ray Comstock and Morris Gest. Opened 4 October 1920 at the Century Theatre and closed 22 January 1921 after 130 performances.

CAST (in order of appearance): *Officer of the Guard*: Richard Henry. *Gate Keeper* of Cairo: Arthur Barron. *Abdullah, Chief Steward of the Sultan*: John Nicholson. *Kataf*, a Mute in the Service of the Prince: Robert Rhodes. *Orange Seller*: Julian Winters. *Prince Nur Al-Din*, Pretender to the Throne: Herbert Grimwood. *An Old Wazir*: Lionel Chalmers. *The Sultan, Al Malik Al-Nasir*: ORVILLE R. CALDWELL. *An Old Woman*: Genevieve Dolaro. *The Blind Man*: Basil Smith. *Ali Shar*, the Wrestler of Al-Yamamah: LIONEL BRAHAM. *Zammurud, His Daughter*: HANNAH TOBACK. *Abu Yaksan*, His Clown: JOHN DORAN. *Zarka*, His Keeper of Pots and Pans: Kate Mayhew. *Zaid*, His Juggler: Edward Watson. *Zan*, His Tumbler: Thomas Merryman. *Conspirators serving Prince Nur Al-Din* (2): *Wazir Al Khasib*: Harold Skinner. *Wazir Abu Shamar*: John Pierson. *Sharazad*, Widow of the Late Sultan and Sister of the Prince Nur Al-Din: GLADYS HANSON. *Wei San Wei*, a Chinese Gambler: THOMAS LEARY. *Wei Wa Shi*, His Wife: IDA MÜLLE. *The Patriarch of the Pilgrims*: Richard Henry. *A Singer of the Pilgrims*: Harry L. Reese. *Dancing Girl* in Nur Al-Din's Harem: Martha Lorber. *Ayesha*, ex-favorite of Nur Al-Din's Harem: Audrey Anderson. *Inmates of Nur Al-Din's Harem* (2): *Zobeide*: Elizabeth Talma. *Nazida*: Helen Zorn. *Abram*, Keeper of the Slave Market: Walter Lane. *Buyers in the Slave Market* (2): *Lamra*: Margaret Brodnax. *Mirza*: Mai Poth.
Sharazad's Women: Georgia Lane, Elizabeth West, Lily Lubell, Billie Wilcox, Dorothy Lee, Florence Chandler, Nellye Savage, Dorothy Durland, Dorothy Johnson, Phyllis Sydney, Nesha Medwin, Sybil Gunn. *Ladies of the Ensemble*: Suzanne Rennard, Beulah Berson, Esther Brankin, Alice Cole, Evelyn Farrar, Viola Green, Harriet Hicklin, Gabrielle Pitcher, Florence Loeb, Edwina Oliver, Hildreth Keehner, Irene Titus, Erna Steinway, Virginia Richardson. *Gentlemen of the Ensemble*: Messrs.

---

[72]Dropped during the New York run.
[73]Cantor's specialty songs compiled by Herbert G. Goldman in his biography of Eddie Cantor, "Banjo Eyes" (Oxford University Press, 1997).
[74]Later identifed in programs as or else replaced by "All for a Girl."

Bowlan, Boughman, Conroy, Lawrence, Nash, Hoppe, Gray, Fitzpatrick, Oliver. *Fruit Vendors, Merchants, Dancing Girls, Pilgrims, Slaves, Buyers, others.*

Act 1, Scene 1: The Gates of Cairo. About a thousand years ago. *Scene 2*: Ali Shar's Dwelling, later the same day. *Scene 3*: The Sultan's Palace. The Feast of Rhamazan. *Scene 4*: Wei San Wei's Gaming House by the Eastern Gate. The same night. *Scene 5*: The Garden's of the Sultan's Palace. The next day.

Act 2, Scene 1: The Encampment of the Pilgrims by the Nile. *Scene 2*: The Harem of Prince Nur Al-Din. *Scene 3*: An old Egyptian Palace.

Act 3, Scene 1: The Slave Market of El-Taban. *Scene 2*: Wei San Wei's Dwelling. *Scene 3*: The Ruined Temple of Askabar. *Scene 4*: Another Part of the Ruins, 1 year later. *Scene 5*: The Gates of Cairo.

ACT 1

Scene 1

"The Gates of Cairo" (Descriptive Song)

"From Bagdad We Come" (Entrance Song)`
    L. Braham, Troupe

"My King of Love" (Song)
    H. Toback

Scene 2

"A Fool There Was" (Song)
    J. Doran

Scene 3

"The Sultan's March"
    Sharazad's Theme

"When Love Knocked Upon the Door" (Song)
    H. Toback

"Allah Guard Thee" (Bridal Chorus)
    Ensemble

Scene 4

"Me Welly Poor Old Chinaman" (The Chinaman's Song)
    T. Leary

Scene 5

"In the Palace Gardens" (Descriptive Interlude)
    Entrance of Singers and Dancers

Finale, Act 1

ACT 2

Scene 1

Intermezzo

The Pilgrim's Prayer

"Hast Thou Been to Mecca?" (Song)
    J. Doran

Dance Poem
    G. Hanson, Desert Dancers

"The Kin of Nur Al-Din" (March Chorus)

Scene 2

"In the Harem" (Interlude)

"Love in My Breast"
    H. Toback
    (*Lyrics freely adapted from* Sir Richard Burton.)

Scene 3

Procession and Ballet "Memories of the Past" (*Arranged by* Michel Fokine.)
    Isis, Goddess of Love: Rita Hall. *Triumphant Love*: M. Lorber. *Plaintive Love*: D. Durland. *Combative Love*: Martha Bellack. *Jealous Love*: Grace Segal. *Arabian Group*: Helen Talmar, Rosalind Clark, Dorothy Lee, Billie Wilcox, Nellye Savage. *Fantastic Arabian Group*: Elizabeth West, Nennette Conigere, Lily Lubell, Margaret Waldron. *Egyptian Group*: Rena Wilde, Sybil Gunn, Phyllis Sydney, Nesha Medwin, Dorothy Johnson, Phyllis Renolds, Millicent Bishop, Margaret Chandler.

Bacchanale (*Arranged by* Michel Fokine; *Costumes by* Alice O'Neil.)
    Premier Dancers: M. Lorber, Sergei Pernikoff; and Ina Seligman, Olga Krogal, Agnes Arlova, Helen Rose, Frances Lee, Terry Bauer, May Savage, Marion O'Neil, Constance Joscelyn, Julia Dorian, Corneile Niles, Dorothy Calnan, Florence Martin, D. Durland, M. Bellack, G. Segal, R. Clark, D. Lee, B. Wilcox, N. Savage, E. West, N. Conigere, M. Waldron, Georgia Lane, Clair Bruce, Doris Renolds, Tanya Salovy, Anna Case, Wiona McFarlaine, Wilmer Engles, Lillian Lane, Evrena Weaver, R. Wilde, S. Gunn, P. Sydney, N. Medwin, D. Johnson, P. Renolds, M. Bishop, M. Chandler, Edna Sortelle, Anita Barlow, Felicia Axelrod, Grace Fiala, Adele Stollman, Irene Van Cleve, Messrs. English, Gardner, Bland, Fisher, Merriman, Roth, Talmand.

ACT 3

Scene 1

"The Slave Market" (Descriptive Scene)

Scene 2

Chinese Interlude

Scene 3

Finale

1920.35

JIM JAM JEMS

A Musical Pastime (Comedy) in Two Acts, 6 Scenes[75]. Book and lyrics by Harry L. Cort and George E. Stoddard. Music by James Hanley. Staged under the supervision of Edgar MacGregor. Dances and ensembles by Robert Marks. Scenery designed by Beaux Art Studio. Costumes by H. Mahieu Company. Orchestra under the direction of Gus Salzer. Produced by John Cort. Opened 4 October 1920 at the Cort Theatre and closed 1 January 1921 after 105 performances.

CAST (in order of appearance): *Cyrus Ward*, a careful uncle: STANLEY FORDE. *June Ward*, a watched niece: ADA MAE WEEKS. *Annette*, a maid: Irma Marwick. *Philip Quick*, a busy butler: JOE E. BROWN. *Johnny Case*, a Jim Jam Jems reporter: FRANK FAY. *James*, a chauffeur: Harry Langdon. *Geraldine McCann*, a wise one: Kathryn Miley. *Archie Spotter*, a detective: NED SPARKS. *Birdie McIntyre*, a flapper: Virginia Clark. *Murphy*, a dancing cop: GATTISON JONES. *Minnie*, a jazz servant: Miss Gay. *O'Ryan*, another cop: JOE E. MILLER. *Miss Flip*, a general understudy: Irma Marwick. *Mr. Jazz*, a cabaret star: Roscoe Ails. *Miss Jazz*, a dancing partner: Midgie Miller. *Rosie Robbins*, a hostess: Zoe Barnett. *Harry Judson*, a good fellow: Paul McCarty. *Miss Pad, Miss Pencil*, Jim Jam Jems workers: The King Sisters. *Miss High*, a lift girl: Cecelia Edwin. *Miss Lowe*, another: Viola Duval. *Miss Sextette*, a Florodora girl: Madge Lawrence. *The Temple Four*: Arthur Brooks, Thomas E. Woods, Harry R. Maurer, Murray Hart. (*Specialties*: Cecil Langdon, R. Langdon, Saxi Holtsworth Harmony Hounds.) *Guests, Cabaret Performers, Policemen, etc.*

    Ladies of the Ensemble: Misses Eleanore Matthewson, Grace Hall, Agnes Hall, Sybil Gould, Bessie Gray, Margaret Fitzgerald, Lurleen Garrison, Irene Medora, Ella Ewen, Pauline LaGrail, Gertrude Farrell, Diana St. Guye, Viola Duval, Elsie Elliott, Claire St. Claire, Winifred Mitchell. *Gentlemen of the Ensemble*: Messrs. D. C. Winne, N. H. Miller, Paul Pollock, Robert Rolem, Jack Sloat, R. L. Ridgeley, Fred Hamilton, W. H. Muller.

Act 1, Scene 1: Reception Room of Cyrus Ward's Residence. 9:45 P.M. *Scene 2*: Exterior of Ward's Residence, 23 East 65th Street, (New York City). 10:15 P.M. *Scene 3*: Fifth Avenue Fronting Plaza Hotel, 10:45 P.M. *Scene 4*: Atop the Astorbilt Hotel, 11 P.M.

Act 2, Scene 1: Lounge Promenade, Hotel Astorbilt, 11:30 P.M. *Scene 2*: Ball Room, Same Hotel, Midnight.

ACT 1[76]

Scene 1

"The Magic Kiss" (Opening)
    S. Forde

"Show Me the Town" (Ensemble)
    S. Forde, Chorus

"Poor Little Rich Little Me" (Song)
    A. M. Weeks

Ensemble
    Chorus

Dance
    G. Jones

Scene 2

Pantomime
    Types

Dance
    Miss Gay, G. Jones

Scene 3

Automobile Scene
    H. Langdon, assisted by R. Langdon, C. Langdon

Scene 4

Jazz Entertainment
    R. Ails, M. Miller, Saxi Holtsworth Harmony Hounds

---

[75]Titled changed for one week 27 November 1920 to HELLO LESTER before reverting back to JIM JAM JEMS.
[76]Added during run to Act 1 after Automobile Scene:
    "After To-night, Goodbye"
        P. McCarty, Girls

"Fond of Babies" (Song)
  S. Forde, Girls
Specialty Dance
  G. Jones
"Sweet Little Stranger"
  A. M. Weeks, P. McCarty
Eccentric Dance (Specialty)
  J. E. Brown
"Jim Jam Jems" (Trio)
  F. Fay, King Sisters
"Right Little Girl"[77] (Song)
  Z. Barnett, F. Fay
"Little Bo Peep" (Song)
  A. M. Weeks, Boys
Finale

ACT 2
Scene 1

"Just a Little Bit Behind the Times" (Opening)
  P. McCarty, King Sisters, Girls
"Poor Old Florodora Girl"[78] (Song)
  S. Forde, M. Lawrence, Chorus
  (Lyrics by Ballard Macdonald.)
"Right Little Girl"
  F. Fay, Z. Barnett, A. M. Weeks, P. McCarty
"Don't Let Me Catch You Falling in Love" (Song)
  F. Fay, A. M. Weeks
"Everybody's Got Somebody But Me"[79] (Ev'rybody But Me)(Song)
  K. Miley
  (Lyrics by Joe Goodwin.)
Scene 2

Opening—Ballet[80]
  Girls
Danse Pantomime
  A. M. Weeks
"Raggedy Ann" (Song)
  King Sisters, Girls
"They're Making Them Wonderful"[81] (Duet)
  P. McCarty, Z. Barnett
Finale (Ensemble)
  Company

1920.36   TIP-TOP

A Musical Extravaganza in Two Acts, 8 Scenes. Book and lyrics[82] by Anne Caldwell and R. H. Burnside. Music by Ivan Caryll. Staged by R. H. Burnside. Dances arranged by Charles Mast. Costumes designed by O'Kane Conwell and G. Wilhelm. Scenery built by T. B. MacDonald Company. Orchestra under the direction of William E. MacQuinn. Produced by Charles Dillingham. Opened 5 October 1920 at the Globe Theatre and closed 7 May 1921 after 246 performances.

CAST: *Judge Tiger*: OSCAR RAGLAND. *Lawyer Pussyfoot*: Dan Baker. *Lawyer Maltese*: Bert Jordan. *Miss Puff*: Lilyan White. *Charles Youngcat*: Tommy Bell. *Court Clerk*: Fred Brown. *Court Attendants*: Billy Brown, Harry Brown, Verne Brown, Alfred Brown. *Fairy Justicia*: HELEN RICH. *Jonas Barker*: OSCAR RAGLAND. *Dick*

----

[77]Replaced during the run by:
  "In a Cabaret"
    Marie Wells (Rosie)
[78]"Poor Old Florodora Girl"/"Right Little Girl" dropped during the run.
[79]Replaced during the run by:
  "Why We Ride in the Subway"
    Girls
[80]Opening—Ballet and Danse Pantomime dropped during the run. and replaced by:
  "Ding Dong Dell"
    F. Fay, Girls
[81]Dropped during the run.
[82]Contrary to program credit, R. H. Burnside wrote the book and Anne Caldwell the lyrics.

Derby: SCOTT WELSH. *Tipton Topping*: FRED STONE. *Lord Cyril Gower*: ROY HOYER. *Jinia Jones*: TERESA VALERIO. *Barker's Daughters (3)*: *Alice*: GLADYS CALDWELL. *Worse*: VIVIAN DUNCAN. *Nina*: MARIE SEWELL. *Adele*: PAULINE HALL. *Rosalie*: Ursula O'Hare. *Bertha*: Dorothy Clark. *The Mysterious Detectives (2)*: *Sharp*: Dan Butler. *Smart*: Bert Jordan. *I. Skinem, a lawyer*: Gus Minton. *Lizzie Cowface*: Charles Mast. *Sheriff*: Ray Talmage. *Wetonah*: PRINCESS WHITE DEER. *Judy*: VIOLET ZELL. *Fairy Caprice*: A. Ludmila. (*Specialty Dancer*: Anna Ludmila. *Specialty*: THE SIX BROWN BROTHERS.)

London Palace Girls: Jessie Wharton, Kitty Dolan, Minnie Shaw, Annie Lorraine, Teresa McSpirit, Hettie Ward, Rosa Swettenham, Ethel Swettenham, Minnie Gray, Dolly Thompson, Rosa Thompson, Elsie Thompson, Cissie Bailey, Violet Little, Dolly Pacy. *Other Characters*: Misses Peggy Williams, Marcelle Earle, Gladys White, Janet Megrew, Alida Middlecoat, Lola Curtis, Jet Stanley, Lillian Harrington, Adelaide Robinson, Leila Randall, Adeline Valerio, Mona Sartoris, Frances Margulies, Ruth White, Lilyan White, Corabelle Platt, Myrtle Miller, Phoebe Appleton, Dorothy Francis, Dolly Stanley, Peggy Dana, Kitty Conway, Margaret Taylor, Betty Mack, Elsie Elwell, Martha Elwell, Verna Burke, May Blythe, Marjorie Belle, Grace Duncan, Madge Reed, Evelyn Conway, Dorothy Duncan. Messrs. David Catlin, Peter Thompson, Eugene Ford.

Act 1, Scene 1: A Courtroom. *Scene 2*: Barker's Shop. *Scene 3*: Outside the School. *Scene 4*: School Room. *Scene 5*: The Red Canyon.

Act 2, Scene 1: On the Beach. *Scene 2*: Melodyville. *Scene 3*: Land of Heart's Desire.

ACT 1
Scene 1

Opening Chorus
  Ensemble
"Little Fairy in the Home"
  H. Rich, Girls
"Pussyfoot and Maltese" (Cat Dance)
  D. Baker, B. Jordan
Scene 2

"The Girl Who Keeps Me Guessing"
  R. Hoyer, M. Sewell
  (Music by Ivan Caryll. Lyrics by Anne Caldwell.)
"Wonderful Girl—Wonderful Boy"
  S. Welsh, G. Caldwell
  (Music by Ivan Caryll. Lyrics by Anne Caldwell.)
Shoppers' Dance
  London Palace Girls
Mysterious Detectives[83]
  D. Baker, B. Jordan
"I Want a Lily"
  F. Stone, Girls
  (Music by Ivan Caryll. Lyrics by Anne Caldwell.)
"Beautiful Booby Prize"[84]
  F. Stone, T. Valerio
"Give Me That Letter" (Ensemble)
  Company
Scene 3

Dance of the School Girls
  London Palace Girls
Scene 4

Pianologue
  D. Clark
Some Songs:
  Duncan Sisters
["Baby Sister Blues"
  (Music and Lyrics by Henry I. Marshall, Marion Sunshine.)
"Humming"
  (Music and Lyrics by Ray Henderson and Louis Breau.)
"When Shall We Meet Again"
  (Music by Richard Whiting. Lyrics by Raymond Egan.)]
Scene 5

Dance of the Young Warrior[85]
  Princess White Deer

----

[83]Dropped during the run.
[84]Replaced during the run by:
  "I Don't Belong on a Farm"
    F. Stone, T. Valerio
    (Music by Arthur Swanstrom. Lyrics by Dorothy Clark.)
[85]Dropped during the run.

"Keewa-Tak-e-Yaka-holo"
  F. Stone
  (*Lyrics by* Louis Harrison.)
Indian Ensemble and Finale

ACT 2[86]
Scene 1
  "In the Sea"[87]
    Bathing Girls
  "The Girl I Never Met"[88]
    S. Welsh, Duncan Sisters
    (*Music by* Ivan Caryll. *Lyrics by* Anne Caldwell.)
  Dance[89]
    Princess White Deer
  Mysterious Detectives[90]
    D. Baker, B. Jordan
  "What Makes the Wild Waves Wild?"[91]
    F. Stone, London Palace Girls
Scene 2
  Six Brown Brothers with Tom Brown (Saxophone Sextet):
  ["Wonderful Girl—Wonderful Boy"
  "Finders Is Keepers (And I Found You)"
    (*Music and Lyrics by* Tom Brown and Jack Frost.)
  "The Girl I Never Met" [reprise]
  "Don't Bring Me Posies (It's Shoesies That I Need)"
    (*Music by* Fred Rose. *Lyrics by* Billy McCabe, Clarence Jennings.)
  "Sweet Baby Mine"
    (*Music and Lyrics by* Tom Brown and Jack Frost.)]
Scene 3
  Valse Divertissement
    A. Ludmila
  "Life Is Like a Punch and Judy Show"
    R. Hoyer, M. Sewell, F. Stone, V. Zell
  Dance of the Valentines
    London Palace Girls
  "Tip-Top"
    H. Rich, Company
  Finale

1920.37 # KISSING TIME

A Musical Comedy in Two Acts, 3 Scenes. Book by George V. Hobart. (Based on the musical 'Mimi,' libretto by Adolf Philipp and Edward A. Paulton.) Music by Ivan Caryll. Lyrics by (George V. Hobart,) Philander Johnson, Irving Caesar and Clifford Grey. Staged by Edward Royce. Scenery by (D. Frank) Dodge and (William E.) Castle. Orchestra under the direction of Max Steiner. Orchestrations by Ivan Caryll and Claude MacArthur. Produced by the Empire Producing Corporation (Management, Robert Campbell). Opened 11 October 1920 at the Lyric Theatre, moved 8 November 1920 to the Astor Theatre, and closed 4 December 1920 after 65 performances.

---

[86]Added to Act 2, Scene 1, after "In the Sea:"
  "The Wireless Heart"
    R. Hoyer, M. Sewell, Girls
    (*Music by* Silvio Hein. *Lyrics by* Anne Caldwell.)
[87]During the run, replaced by: ("In the Sea" restored for part of tour.)
  "Sweet Dreams"
    R. Hoyer, M. Sewell, Girls
    (*Music by* Ivan Caryll. *Lyrics by* Anne Caldwell.)
[88]Dropped during the run and replaced by:
  "I Want To See My Ida Hoe (in Idaho)"
    S. Welsh, Duncan Sisters
    (*Music by* Bert Rule. *Lyrics by* Alex Sullivan.)
[89]Dropped during the run.
[90]Dropped during the run.
[91]Replaced late in the run by:
  'She Knows It"
    Harlan Dixon (Tipton Topping)

CAST (in order of appearance): *Tashi*, Mimi's assistant: Primrose Caryll. *Emile Grossard*, Mimi's secretary: Harry Coleman. *Mimi of the Maison Mimi*: DOROTHY MAYNARD. *Clarice*, the other Mimi: EDITH TALIAFERRO. *Polydore Cliquot*: WILLIAM NORRIS. *Robert Perronet*, admired by Mimi: PAUL FRAWLEY. *Armond Moulanger*, another Mimi admirer: FRANK DOANE. *Of the Banque Mayonnaise* (2): *Paul Pommery*: CARL HYSON. *Anatole Absinthe*: Charles Edwards. *Rose-Marie*: Georgia Lynne. *Virginia*: Eleanor Ladd. *Jeannette*: Cora d'Orsay. *Babette*: Jessie Lynne. *Suzanne*: Frances Chase. *Diane*: May Whitney. *Helene*: Margaret Green. *Vivienne*: Norma Warington. *Loie*: Shirley Latham. *Georgette*: Ellen Best. *Maxine*: Ruby Vernon. (*Specialty Dancer*: EVELYN CAVANAUGH.)
  Clerks of the Banque Mayonnaise: *Pierre Martini*: DeForrest Woolley. *George Bacardi*: Thomas Maynard. *Raphael Sauterne*: Fred Packard. *Francois Chandon*: Frank Bryant. *Henri Martel*: William McGurn. *Gaston Burgundy*: John Daly.

Act 1, Scene 1: The Maison Mimi, Paris; the Fitting Room. *Scene 2*: Reception Room of the Café Sylvaine, Paris. (That evening.)

Act 2: Mimi's Apartment, Paris. Later that night.

ACT 1
Scene 1
  "Custom-Made Maids" (Opening Chorus)
    Shoppers and Models
  "Bill and Coo"
    P. Caryll, H. Coleman
    (*Lyrics by* George V. Hobart.)
Scene 2
  "Temporary Wives" (Opening Chorus)
    Ensemble
  Specialty Dance
    C. Hyson, E. Cavanaugh
  "(It's) The Nicest Sort of Feeling" (Ting-a-ling-a-ling)
    P. Frawley, Ensemble
    (*Music by* William Daly. *Lyrics by* Irving Caesar.)
  "An Absolute Don of a Juan"
    W. Norris, E. Cavanaugh
  "Love's Telephone"
    E. Taliaferro, P. Frawley
  "Mimi"
    D. Maynard, the Boys
  "Keep a Fox-Trot for Me"[92]
    E. Cavanaugh, C. Hyson, P. Caryll, H. Coleman, Ensemble
  "Kikerikee"
    E. Taliaferro, D. Maynard, F. Doane, P. Frawley
    (*Lyrics by* George V. Hobart.)
  Finale
    Entrie Company

ACT 2
  Opening Chorus
    Ensemble
  "Bill and Coo" (reprise)
    P. Frawley, E. Taliaferro
  "So Long as the World Goes Round" (As Long as the World Goes Round)
    E. Taliaferro, D. Maynard, W. Norris, P. Frawley
    (*Lyrics by* George V. Hobart.)
  "Mimi Jazz"[93]
    D. Maynard, Ensemble, C. Hyson, E. Cavanaugh
  "Kissing Time"
    P. Frawley
    (*Lyrics by* Irving Caesar.)
  "Kissimee"[94]
    D. Maynard, W. Norris, Ensemble
    (*Lyrics by* George V. Hobart.)
  "Absolutely Certain"
    E. Taliaferro, P. Frawley
  Finale
    Entire Company

---

[92]Late in the run and for tour, moved to Act 2, before the title song.
[93]Dropped late in the run and for tour.
[94]Dropped late in the run and for tour.

MARY

1920.38

George M. Cohan's Comedians in a Musical Comedy in Two Acts[95]. Book by Otto Harbach and Frank Mandel. Music by Louis A. Hirsch. Lyrics by Otto Harbach. Staged by Julian Mitchell and Sam Forrest. Scenery painted by (Edward G.) Unitt and (Joseph) Wickes. Costumes by Mme. Francis, Schneider-Anderson Company, Finchley. Orchestra under the direction of Charles J. Gebest. Entire production under the personal direction of George M. Cohan. Produced by George M. Cohan. Opened 18 October 1920 at the Knickerbocker Theatre and closed 23 April 1921 after 220 performances.

CAST [in order of appearance]: *Jack Keene*: JACK McGOWAN. *Mrs. Keene*: GEORGIA CAINE. *Tommy Boyd*: ALFRED GERRARD. *Madeline Francis*: FLORRIE MILLERSHIP. *Mary Howells*: JANET VELIE. *Huggins*: Frederic Graham. *Gaston Marceau*: CHARLES JUDELS. *Mr. Goddard*: James C. Marlowe. *Deakon*: Gene Richards. *Meakon*: Wesley Totten. *Chicky*: Herself.

Guests: Golden Girl: Sibylla Bowhan. *Whirlwind Willie*: Si Layman. *Toddling Tessie*: Helen Kling. *Hotfoot Harry*: Bert Shadow. *Dancing Dora*: Lillian McNeil. *Two-Step Tom*: Lou Lockett. *Waltzing Winnie*: Edna Pierre. *Billy, Covey*: Themselves.

Ladies of the Chorus: Molly Christie, Helen Borden, Ruth Sawyer, Helen Jackson, Helen Christie, Edna Stilwell, Muriel Cort, Belle Gannon, Kitty Bird, Agnes Purtell, Kitty Dever, Dolly King, Loretta Ryan, Anna Christopher, Virginia Alves, Marion Baker. *Gentlemen of the Chorus*: Walter Blair, Jack Neilan, Harry Rose, Harold Jackson, Edward Grant, Walter Dodge, W. J. Hawkins, Harry Case, Harry Bolton, Gordon Bennett.

Act 1: Reception Hall in the Long Island Home of Mrs. Keene. A Night in January.

Act 2: An Exterior of Mrs. Keene's Home. The Garden. An Afternoon in June.

ACT 1

"That May Have Satisfied Grandma"
    J. McGowan, F. Millership, A. Gerrard, Chorus
"Down on That Old Kansas Farm" (That Farm Out in Kansas)
    J. Velie, J. McGowan
"Anything You Want to Do, Dear"
    A. Gerrard, F. Millership
"Every Time I Meet a Lady"
    C. Judels, Girls
"Tom, Tom, Toddle"
    A. Gerrard, F. Millership, S. Layman, H. Kling, Ensemble
"The Love Nest"
    J. Velie, J. McGowan
Reprise
    C. Judels, G. Caine
Finale
    Entire Company

ACT 2[96]

Opening Chorus
"Flirtation Dance"[97]
    L. Lockett, E. Pierre
"Mary"
    J. Velie, Boys
"When a Woman Exits Laughing"
    A. Gerrard, F. Millership
Reprise
    J. McGowan
"Don't Fall Until You've Seen Them All"
    A. Gerrard, F. Millership, Girls
"Waiting"
    J. Velie
"Money, Money, Money"
    J. C. Marlowe, A. Gerrard, C. Judels, J. McGowan
"We'll Give a Wonderful Party"
    A. Gerrard, F. Millership, B. Shadow, L. McNeil, S. Layman, H. Kling, L. Lockett, E. Pierre, Ensemble
Finale
    Entire Company

---

[95]Subtitled (Isn't It a Grand Old Name?)
[96]Added during the run after Act 2 reprise, then later dropped for tour:
    "Deeper"
        J. McGowan, Boys
[97]Replaced for subsequent tour:
    Golf Dance
        (Golden Girl, Whirlwind Willie)

(RAYMOND HITCHCOCK'S) HITCHY-KOO 1920

1920.39

A Musical Revue in Two Acts, 12 Scenes[98]. Book (sketches) by Glen MacDonough. Music by Jerome Kern. Lyrics by Glen MacDonough and Anne Caldwell. Staged by Ned Wayburn. Scenery painted by H. Robert Law Studios. Costumes by O'Kane Conwell, Mme B. Rasimi. Orchestra under the direction of Cassius Freeborn. (Orchestrations by Frank Saddler.) Produced by Raymond Hitchcock. Opened 19 October 1920 at the New Amsterdam Theatre and closed 18 December 1920 after 71 performances.

CAST: RAYMOND HITCHCOCK, JULIA SANDERSON, G. P. HUNTLEY, TYLER BROOKE, FLORENCE O'DENISHAWN, BILLY HOLBROOK, ANASTASIA REILLY, DOUGLAS STEVENSON, GRACE MOORE, MAURICE BLACK, MARION WILBANKS, CLAIRE MARTIN, BOBBY CONNOLLY, MOSCONI BROTHERS (Louis, Charles, Verna, Willie), HAL SANDS, ARTHUR CUNNINGHAM, JACK LYNCH, RUTH MITCHELL, HENRI LINGEN.

Ladies of the Ensemble: Beulah McFarland, Myrtle Stewart, Betty Palmer, Frances Tumulty, Vera Carlton, Beatrice Desahw, Vonda Case, Dorothy Harrigan, Virginia McDonald, Lucille Conboy, May Carlton, Fay West, Ruth Matthews, Pearl Bailey, Ann Mason, Helen Claire, Carolyn James, Laurette Fallon, Jacqueline Delaine, Alvira Yates, Phyllis Hooper, Rose Lockwood, Helen McDonald, Ruth Weeks, Dorothy Leeds, Peggy Underwood, Muriel Lodge, Inez Ford, Nettie Thomas, Patricia Clarke, Gracie Turner, Amelia Johnson, Corone Paynter, Virginia Lee. *Gentlemen of the Ensemble*: Messrs. Dan Brennan, Jack Lynch, Fred DuBall, James McKenzie, Joe Evans, Eddie Simms, D. Hennessy.

Act 1, Scene 1: At the Maison Daguerre. *Scene 2*: Hitchy-Koo Corridor. *Scene 3*: Love in Lavender. *Scene 4*: Moon of Love. *Scene 5*: The Owl Drug Store. *Scene 6*: Where Fifth Avenue Met Broadway.

Act 2, Scene 1: How Ethel Lost the Oaks. *Scene 2*: I Want to Marry. *Scene 3*: Her Wedding Cake. *Scene 4*: Interior of the "Opry" House. *Scene 5*: After the Show. *Scene 6*: Tryangett Inn.

ACT 1[99]

Scene 1

Dance
    M. Wilbanks, Girls
"The Millinery Mannequin" (Mannequin Dance)
    F. O'Denishawn
"I Am Daguerre"
    T. Brooke, Rainbow Girls
Old-Fashioned Dances:
Oriental
    Mosconi Brothers
The Levee
    M. Van, B. Holbrook
        Assisted by Messrs. Brennan, Lynch, DuBall, McKenzie, Evans, Simms.
The Serpentine
    F. O'Denishawn
"Sweetie"
    R. Mitchell, the Balloonatics
        Hitchy-Koo, an actor manager: R. Hitchcock. *Sir Ronald Roundhead* in search of an emotion: G. P. Huntley. *Theophile Daguerre*, founder of the Maison Daguerre: T. Brooke. *Annie Key*, America's premier rough-house soubrette, known as the "Radium Kid": R. Mitchell. *Ladies of the Ensemble* (4): *Iona Rolls*: D. Leeds. *Violet Ray*: I. Ford. *Maida Wood*: P. Clarke. *Heva Sigh*: N. Thomas. A *Millinery Mannequin*: F. O'Denishawn. *Octave Hyer*, a musical director: B. Holbrook. A *Nurse*: A. Reilly. *Dolores*, forelady at Daguerre's: M. Lodge. *Bohemian Boy*: V. Case. *Bohemian Girl*: C. Paynter. *An Italian Girl*: B. Palmer. *Another*: B. McFarland. *A Greek*: G. Turner. *The Same*: H. McDonald.

Scene 2

Introducing Charles Louis and Verna Mosconi

---

[98]The fourth and last (to reach New York) in the annual series of musical revues produced by Raymond Hitchcock beginning in 1917.
[99]Added during the run:
    "Ethel's Frolic" (Act 2, Scene 2)
    Added for subsequent tour:
    "Won't You All Fall in Love with Me?" (Act 1, Scene 1)
        J. Sanderson
    "When You're Safe in Bed at Night" (Act 2, Scene 1)
        R. Hitchcock

Scene 3

"Ding Dong, It's Kissing Time"[100]
  J. Sanderson, D. Stevenson
    Lorrequer, an ancient serving man: A. Cunningham. *Jackson*, a New York reporter: T. Brooke. *Lucy*, a belle of yesterday: J. Sanderson. *William*, a composer: D. Stevenson.

Scene 4

"Moon of Love"
  G. Moore, Chorus Girls

Scene 5

"Canajoharie"
  D. Stevenson, Chorus

"Buggy Riding"
  J. Sanderson, R. Hitchcock

"Old New York" (The Old Town)
  R. Hitchcock, C. Freeborn, G. Moore, A. Cunningham
    Noble Dubb, the popular druggist: R. Hitchcock. *Aubrey Pauncefort*: G. P. Huntley. *Basil Prune*, a reform detective: A. Cunningham. *Mrs. Prune*, his wife: G. Moore. *Handsome Harry*, an old-time New York bartender: M. Black. *Chester Coons*, the local sport: D. Stevenson. *Angie Baker*, the belle of the village: J. Sanderson. *Peggy*, the cashier: P. Underwood. *Louella*: A. Reilly. *Posey*: M. Wilbanks. *Mac*: J. McKenzie.

Scene 6

Flopper: C. Martin. *Peanut Vendor*: J. Evans. *Policeman*: A. Cunningham. *Hoffman House Cigar Man*: B. Connolly. *John L. Sullivan*: A. Cunningham. *Phil Casey*, Sullivan's trainer: F. DuBall. *Hot Corn Man*: H. Sands. *Volunteer Fireman*: M. Black. *Bicycle Rider*: T. Brooke. *Lamp Lighter*: J. Lynch. *Bowery Girls*: Misses Mosconi, Van, Mitchell, Reilly. *Bowery Boys*: Messrs. L. Mosconi, C. Mosconi, Holbrook, Lingen. *Fifth Avenue Belles*: F. O'Denishawn, G. Moore, D. Leeds. *Society Ladies*: Misses Underwood, Thomas, Ford, Lodge, Clark. *West Point Cadet*: D. Stevenson. *Shop Girls*: Ensemble. *Captain Busby*: G. P. Huntley. *The Jersey Lily*: J. Sanderson. A *Dude*: R. Hitchcock.

ACT 2

Scene 1

"We'll Make a Bet"
  Ensemble

Dance
  F. O'Denishawn, T. Brooke
    Plunger Dalton, Patron of the Turf and owner of Ethel: R. Hitchcock. *Ethel*, "The Grey Whirlwind": *Fore*: B. Holbrook. *Aft*: H. Lingen. *Dusty Miller*, Dalton's betting commissioner: M. Black. *Churchill Downs*, Dalton's trainer: A. Cunningham. *Henry Bone*, an English jockey: G. P. Huntley. *Miss Belmont*: D. Leeds. *Miss Jamaica*: N. Thomas. *Miss Havre de Grace*: I. Ford. *Miss Ascot*: M. Lodge. *Miss Saratoga*: P. Clarke. *Miss Longue Champs*: P. Underwood. *Miss Empire*: A. Reilly. *Jockeys*: Misses Turner, C. Paynter.

Scene 2

"I Want to Marry"[101]
  J. Sanderson

Scene 3

Her Wedding Cake
  Decorated by A. Reilly, V. Lee, M. Van, Messrs. D. Stevenson, T. Brooke, H. Lingen, B. Holbrook. *Parson*: B. Connolly.

Scene 4

For Pity's Sake (A travesty of the Old-Time Melodrama)
  Cy Splivers: C. Withers. *Bud Splivers*: A. James. *The Old Father*: W. Jones. *The Mother*: R. Burkhart. *Sally*: T. Dowling. *Clementine Hope*: V. Murray. *Claude Smith*: A. H. Hall. *The Sheriff*: J. M. Kelly. *Jack Harrington*: J. J. Kelly. *First Sailor*: P. Matthews. *Second Sailor*: F. L. Elliot. *Captain Submarine*: D. Hennessy.

Scene 5

After the Show
  C. Withers

Scene 6

"Treasure Island"
  G. Moore, Chorus

---
[100]Dropped for subsequent tour.
[101]Dropped for subsequent tour.

Dance
  F. O'Denishawn

"Bring 'Em Back"[102]
  D. Stevenson, J. Sanderson

Dance-o-Mania
  L. Mosconi, C. Mosconi, V. Mosconi, W. Mosconi

"The Star of Hitchy-Koo"
  J. Sanderson, G. P. Huntley, R. Hitchcock

Finale
  Ensemble

1920.40   THE HALF MOON

A Musical Play in Three Acts. Book and lyrics by William LeBaron. Music by Victor Jacobi. Staged by Fred G. Latham. Dances arranged by Allan K. Foster. Scenery painted by (D. Frank) Dodge and (William E.) Castle. Costumes designed by Lichtenstein's, Fifth Avenue. Orchestra under the direction of Harold Vicars. Produced by Charles Dillingham. Opened 1 November 1920 at the Liberty Theatre and closed 11 December 1920 after 48 performances.

CAST (in order of appearance): *Harkins*: Herbert Sparling. *Mrs. Francis Adams Jarvis*: EDNA MAY OLIVER. *Grace Bolton*: IVY SAWYER. *Joe Beckett*: Charles W. Lawrence. *Anne*: Virginia Shelby. *Mary Bolton*: May Thompson. *John Copley Adams*: William Ingersoll. *Henry Hudson Hobson*: JOSEPH CAWTHORN. *Bradford Adams*: OSCAR SHAW. *Charlie Hobson*: JOSEPH SANTLEY. *Estelle*: Elaine Palmer. *Maggie Green*: Maude Eburne.

Other Characters by Doris Landy, Pearl Bennett, May Morris, Daisy Daniels, Bobbie Rait, Betty Raedel, Madeline O'Brien, Caroline Burke, Sophie Brenner, Lucille Darling, Isabel Falconer, Jean Farrel, Peggie Smith, Migonne Reed, Lorraine Nelson, Rose Timponi, Sallie Everett, Ruth Appleton, Edna Wheaton, Sally Chester, Peggy Parmalee, Helen Allan, Mary Ellison, Betty Mack, Lucille Conboy.

Act 1: Garden of Mrs. Hobson's House. The present.

Act 2: At Mrs. Adams', Brookline, Massachusetts.

Act 3: 36 Lower Fifth Avenue, New York City. Six months later.

ACT 1

"Innocent Girls"
  I. Sawyer, Girls

"The Girls Along Fifth Avenue"
  J. Santley, O. Shaw, Girls

"When You Smile"
  J. Cawthorn, Girls

"The Little Book"
  I. Sawyer, M. Thompson, J. Santley, O. Shaw

Finale

ACT 2

Opening Chorus
  (Company)

Dance
  E. Palmer

"The Dancing Band"
  I. Sawyer, M. Thompson, J. Santley, O. Shaw, Girls

"Deep in Your Eyes"
  I. Sawyer, J. Santley

"What's the Matter with Women Now?"
  J. Cawthorn

"Half Moon!"
  M. Thompson, O. Shaw, E. Palmer

Finale: "Serenade"
  O. Shaw

Ensemble
  Company

ACT 3

"Days That Used To Be"
  J. Santley, O. Shaw

"Stay Awhile"
  I. Sawyer, M. Thompson, J. Santley, O. Shaw

---
[102]Dropped for subsequent tour.

Finale
Company

1920.41   AFGAR

An Intimate Extravaganza (Musical Spectacle) in Two Acts, 3 Scenes[103]. Book by Fred Thompson and Worton David. (Based on the French operette 'Afgar, ou Les Loisirs andalous,' libretto by André Barde and Michel Carré fils.) Music by Charles Cuvillier. Lyrics by Douglas Furber. Staged by Frank Collins. Scenery and costumes designed by Paul Poiret. Orchestra under the direction of Victor Baravalle. Produced by F. Ray Comstock and Morris Gest. Opened 8 November 1920 at the Central Theatre and closed 2 April 1921 after 168 performances.

CAST: *The Prologue: Wise Man of the East*: Guy Collins.
   The Play: Don Juan, Jr., a Spanish prisoner: IRVING BEEBE. *Coucourli*, his squire: LUPINO LANE. *Houssain*, Chief of the Abode of Felicity: PAUL IRVING. *Danasch*, Master of the Cates: Guy Collins. *Ciafar*, Master of the Sherberts: Phil M. Sheridan. *Khasan*, Chief Coffee Server: Glenn Gamble. *Lord Afgar*, a Rich Moor: W. H. RAWLINS. *Isilda*, a Spanish girl: FRANCES CAMERON.
   Wives of Lord Afgar: Messaouda: Violet Blythe. *Hanifa*: Fay Evelyn. *Amina*: Jean Casselle. *Badoura*: Gene Grey. *Morgiana*: Alyce Melzard. *Belbali*: Clara Burton. *Seraphine*: Vera Ruby. *Marrima*: Carolyn Reynolds. *Zarruda*: Oretta Lewis. *Delona*: Jacque Sage. *Sylphine*: Anna Milier. *Antilas*: Billie Dauscha. *Zaydée*: ALICE DELYSIA.
   Dancing Girls in Lord Afgar's Harem (3): Nissa: Betty Michaels. *Anneka*: Olga Harting. *Zubaydah*: Queenie Andrews. *Slave Girls in Lord Afgar's Harem (4): Elhawa*: Olga Nezzie. *Shayana*: Agnes D'Assia. *Nayhara*: Anna Fisher. *Kamarrah*: Betty Squiers. *Zaumiss*, the Flower Girl: Jean Barnette.
   Soldiers, Guards, Husbands, etc.: James Duffer, Edward Sheldon, Roy Fitzsimmons, Bertran Urrenne, Morris Milman, Alfred Frank. (*Le Conteur*, Act 2: William P. Adams.)

Act 1: Courtyard of the Palace of the Moor, Afgar.

Act 2, Scene 1: Interlogue before the Curtain. *Scene 2*: The Harem of the Palace.

ACT 1
  Chorus of Wives
  "Give the Devil His Due" (Song)
    I. Beebe
  Concerted Number
    L. Lane, W. H. Rawlins, F. Cameron, Chorus
  "Rose of Seville" (Song)
    F. Cameron
  "Live for Love" (Song)
    A. Delysia
  "Man from Mexico" (Song)
    L. Lane
  "Why Don't You?" (Duet)
    A. Delysia
    (*Music by* Harry Tierney. *Lyrics by* Joseph McCarthy.)
  Finale
    Entire Company
ACT 2
  Chorus of Husbands ("United We Stand")
    L. Lane, P. Irving, Chorus
  "We're the Gentlemen of the Harem" (Trio)
    L. Lane, W. H. Rawlins, I. Beebe, Chorus
  "Sunshine Valley" (Song)
    F. Cameron
  "Where Art Thou, Romeo?" (Song)
    A. Delysia
    (*Music by* Harry Tierney. *Lyrics by* Joseph McCarthy.)
  "Garden of Make Believe"[104] (Song)
    A. Delysia

---

[103]Advertised as Alice Delysia (from the London Pavilion, London) by arrangement with Charles B. Cohran, with Lupino Lane, in her London and Paris success.
[104]Replaced during the run by:
"Caresses"
  A. Delysia
  (*Music and Lyrics by* James Monaco.)
For subsequent tour, this was replaced by the following two songs:
"I Want Love"
  A. Delysia

"I Hate the Lovely Women" (Song)
  L. Lane
  (*Music by* Harry Tierney. *Lyrics by* Joseph McCarthy.)
"Ceremony of Veils" (Concerted Number)
  A. Delysia, F. Cameron, P. Irving, Chorus
Dance
  L. Lane
"'Neath Thy Casement" (Song)
  I. Beebe
Finale
  Entire Company

1920.42   JIMMIE

A Musicomedy (Musical Comedy) in Three Acts, 4 Scenes. Book by Otto Harbach, Oscar Hammerstein II and Frank Mandel. Music by Herbert Stothart. Lyrics by Otto Harbach and Oscar Hammerstein II. Book staged by Oscar Eagle. Dances arranged by Bert French. Scenery designed by Joseph Physioc. Costumes designed by Henri Bendel. Orchestra under the direction of Herbert Stothart. Produced by Arthur Hammerstein. Opened 17 November 1920 at the Apollo Theatre and closed 15 January 1921 after 71 performances.

CAST (in order of appearance): *Vincenzo Carlotti*: PAUL PORCASI. *Madame Gambetti*: Dee Loretta. *Beatrice*: HATTIE BURKS. *Jimmie*: FRANCES WHITE. *Tom O'Brien*: DON BORROUGHS. *Milton Blum*: HARRY DELF. *Jacob Blum*: Ben Welch. *Jerry O'Brien*: Howard Truesdell. *Watkins*: Tom O'Hare. *A Dancer*: Rita Owin. *A Violinist*: Irwin Rossa. *Peters*: Peter Mott. *Henri*: Raymond E. Oswald. *Giuseppi*: Jack Heisler. *Antonio*: George Clifford. *Wanda Holmes*: Betty Marshall. *Rose*: Mary Jane. *Henrietta*: Helen Neff. *Blanche*: Tess Mayer.
  Girls of the Ensemble: Tess Mayer, Mary Jane, Jessie Lorraine, Betty Marshall, Edna Fenten, Geraldine Burnhartt, Laura Maverick, Lottie Graham, Evelyn Palmer, Adelaide Starr, Dorothy Gilbert, Frances Lawrence, Marjorie Flynn, Helen Neff.

Act 1, Scene 1: Private Dining Room above Carlotti's Restaurant. Afternoon. *Scene 2*: Carlotti's Restaurant. Evening.

Act 2: Jacob Blum's Home. Eight months later.

Act 3: Apartment of "The Little Gray Kitten." A year later.

ACT 1[105]
Scene 1
  An Aria
    H. Burks, D. Loretta, P. Porcasi
  "Baby Dreams"
    F. White
Scene 2
  "Below the Macy-Gimbel Line"
    M. Jane, R. Owin, Chorus
  "In a Two by Four" (Cute Little Two by Four)
    F. White, T. Burroughs
  "All That I Want"
    H. Delf, Girls
  "Carlotti's"
    P. Porcasi, B. Welch, R. Owin, Chorus
  "Jimmie"
    F. White
  "She Alone Could Understand"
    H. Burks
  Finale
    (Company)

  (*Music by* Maurice Yvain. *Lyrics by* Irving Bibo and Cyrus D. Wood.)
"Eyes of Blue"
  A. Delysia
  (*Music by* Harry Tierney. *Lyrics by* Joseph McCarthy.)
The latter song was later replaced by:
"Julie" (Julie-Oolio-Oolio-oo)
  Tim O'Connor (Coucourli)
  (*Music by* Harry Archer. *Lyrics by* Irving Bibo and Cyrus D. Wood.)
[105]Added during the run:
"Rickety Crickety"

ACT 2

"Don' Yo' Want to See de Moon?"
    H. Burks, I. Rossa, Chorus

"It Isn't Hard to Do"[106]
    H. Delf, H. Neff, Girls

"Jimmie"[107] (reprise)
    D. Burroughs, Girls

"Just a Smile"
    D. Burroughs, Girls

"Do, Ra, Me" (Do, Re, Mi)
    F. White

"Some People Make Me Sick"
    F. White

"I Wish I Was a Queen"
    F. White

ACT 3

"Toodle Oodle Um"
    F. White, Girls

"A Little Plate of Soup"
    H. Delf

Fantasie
    F. White

Finale
    (Company)

LADY BILLY

1920.43

A Musical Romance in Three Acts. Book and lyrics by Zelda Sears. Music by Harold A. Levey. Book staged by John McKee. Dances arranged by Julian Alfred. Scenery designed by Arnold A. Kraushaar. Costumes by Bergdorf Goodman & Co; Mitzi's costumes by Frances, Inc. Lighting by Joseph Wilson. Orchestra under the direction of Harold A. Levey[108]. Produced by Henry W. Savage. Opened 14 December 1920 at the Liberty Theatre and closed 21 May 1921 after 188 performances.

CAST (in order of appearance): *The Billy Four*[109] (4): *Tom:* Harry Lang. *Dick:* Lawrence Lee. *Harry:* Harry R. Webster. *George:* Ted Weller. *Joe:* Mack Kennedy. *Anastasia Kosiankowski:* BEATRICE CONSTANCE. *Bateson:* SYDNEY GREENSTREET. *Mrs. Wallingford-Butler-Daventry:* JEAN NEWCOMBE. *Eloise:* JOSEPHINE ADAIR. *Octette of Singing Girls* (8): *Lucia:* Marion Barton. *Elsie:* Billie Wedgewood. *Gladys:* Harriet Arnold. *Helen:* Willa Renard. *Mildred:* Helen Halpren. *Muriel:* Betty Diggett. *Mildred:* Estella Birney. *Edith:* Gwendoline Lamb. *Señor Manuel Montijo:* ARTHUR UTTRY. *Mlle. Viorica:* Beatrice Collenette. *Dancing Quartette* (4): *Slavaka:* Babe Stanton. *Gaska:* Eleanor Livingston. *Mariaska:* Anita Monroe. *Vaska:* Helen Paine. *Countess Antonia Celestina-Elizabeta-Selana-Wilhelmina of Pardove* (alias Master Billy): MITZI (HAJOS). *John Smith:* BOYD MARSHALL. *Alphonse:* Charles Gay.

Act 1: The Castle of the Countess. Roumania.

Act 2: Studio of Madame Kosiankowski. Greenwich Village. Three months later.

Act 3: John Smith's Apartment. Downtown. Same evening.

ACT 1

Opening
    The Billy Four, M. Kennedy

"That's All He Wants"
    A. Uttry, Octette, Quartette, B. Collenette

"Just Plant a Kiss"
    Mitzi, Quartette, Octette

"The Legend" (Duet)
    Mitzi, B. Marshall

ACT 2

"Greenwich Village"
    J. Newcombe, J. Adair, Billy Four, Octette, Quartette, B. Collenette

"Love Comes Like a Butterfly" (Duet)
    J. Adair, B. Marshall

"The Futurist Rag"
    B. Constance, Billy Four, Octette, Quartette

"Come to Arcady (with Me)"
    Mitzi

"The Worm's Revenge"
    S. Greenstreet

"Historic Huzzies"
    Mitzi, S. Greenstreet, A. Uttry, B. Marshall, Billy Four

"Good-bye, Good-bye"
    Mitzi, B. Marshall

Finale

ACT 3

"If"
    Mitzi

"The Tune They Plug" (The Tune They Play)
    J. Adair, J. Newcombe, B. Marshall, Billy Four, Octette, Quartette

SALLY

1920.44

A Musical Comedy in Three Acts, 5 Scenes. Book by Guy Bolton. Music by Jerome Kern. Lyrics by Clifford Grey, (Anne Caldwell, P. G. Wodehouse, Buddy G. DeSylva). Butterfly Ballet Music by Victor Herbert. Production staged by Edward Royce. Settings designed by Joseph Urban. Costumes designed by Alice O'Neil. Orchestra under the direction of Gus Salzer. Produced by Florenz Ziegfeld, Jr. Opened 21 December 1920 at the New Amsterdam Theatre and closed 22 April 1922 after 561 performances.

CAST: *Pops*, Proprietor of the Alley Inn, New York: ALFRED P. JAMES. *Rosalind Rafferty*, a manicurist: MARY HAY. *Madame Nookerova's Maid:* MARY HAY. *Sascha*, Violinist at the Alley Inn: Jacques Rebiroff. *Otis Hooper*, a Theatrical Agent: WALTER CATLETT. *Mrs. Ten Broek*, a Settlement Worker: DOLORES. *Sally of the Alley*, a Foundling: MARILYN MILLER. *Madame Nookerova*, a Wild Rose: MARILYN MILLER. *Premier Star of the Follies:* MARILYN MILLER. *Connie*, a Waiter at the Alley Inn: LEON ERROL. *Duke of Czechogovinia:* LEON ERROL. *Miss New York*, a Niece: Agatha Debussy. *Admiral Travers*, a gay one: Phil Ryley. *Blair Farquar*, an Only Son: IRVING FISHER. *Jimmie Spelvin:* STANLEY RIDGES. *Alta:* Alta King. *Betty:* Betty Williams. *Barbara:* Barbara Dean. *Vivian:* Vivian Vernon. *Mary:* Mary McDonald. *Emily:* Emily Drange. *Richard Farquar:* Frank Kingdon. *Foundlings* (6): *Miss Rhinelander:* Miss Kingsley. *Miss Vanderbilt:* Miss Otis. *Miss Worth:* Miss Maide. *Miss Bryant:* Miss Henderson. *Miss Audubon:* Miss Freeland. *Miss Bowling Green:* Miss Vernon. *Billy Porter:* Wade Boothe. *Harry Burton:* Jack Barker. *Children:* Baby Dot, Dolly Tigue, Rita Murphy, Minerva Bartz. *Boy:* Frank Bages.

    Ensemble: Misses Mary McDonald, Barbara Dean, Alta King, Emily Drange, Vivian Vernon, Betty Williams, Hunter, DeBussy, Hanson, Platt, Wilson, Orville, LeRoy, Bowie, Lyle, Shand, Misses Donley, Mayer, Oliphant, Stanfield, Kingsley, Collings, Akers, Fenron, Otis, Parks, Closs, Maide, S. Vernon, Vreeland, Ford, Braham.

Act 1: The Alley Inn, New York.

Act 2: The Garden of Richard Farquar's Home, Long Island.

Act 3, Scene 1: The Land of Butterflies (Ballet) in the Ziegfeld Follies. *Scene 2:* Sally's Dressing Room at the Amsterdam Theatre after the Follies premiere. *Scene 3:* The Little Church Around the Corner.

ACT 1

Opening Ensemble

Violin Solo
    J. Rabinoff

"Way Down East"[110] (Song)
    M. Hay, Ensemble

"On with the Dance" (Song)
    W. Catlett, M. Hay, B. Williams, J. Barker

"This Little Girl"[111] (Song and Dance)
    Dolores, A. P. James, Foundlings

"Joan of Arc" (You Can't Keep a Good Girl Down) (Song)
    M. Miller, Foundlings

"Look for the Silver Lining" (Duet)
    M. Miller, I. Fisher
    (*Lyrics* by Buddy G. DeSylva.)

---

[106]Dropped for subsequent tour.
[107]Dropped for subsequent tour.
[108]During the tryout, the orchestrations were credited to Charles Sadler. For the New York run, they were not credited.
[109]Later billed as the Tip Top Four.

[110]Replaced after opening by:
    Song and Dance
        S. Ridges, Misses Akers, S. Vernon, Ensemble
[111]Dropped after opening and replaced by a dance for the Foundlings, then later M. Miller and Foundlings.

Dance
>M. Miller, L. Errol

"Sally" (Song)
>I. Fisher, Ensemble

Dance
>M. Miller

Finale
>M. Miller, L. Erroll, M. Hay, W. Catlett, Ensemble

ACT 2

"The Social Game" (Opening)
>S. Ridges, Ensemble

"The Wild Rose" (Song and Dance)
>M. Miller, Diplomats

"(On the Banks of) The Schnitza-Komisski" (Song)
>L. Errol, Ensemble

Schnitza Dance ("Pzchcrkatrotsky")
>L. Errol

"Whip-poor-Will" (Duet)
>M. Miller, I. Fisher
>(*Lyrics by* Buddy G. DeSylva.)

"The Lorelei" (Trio)
>W. Catlett, M. Hay, S. Ridges
>(*Lyrics by* Anne Caldwell.)

"Little Church Around the Corner" (Duet)
>M. Hay, W. Catlett
>(*Lyrics by* P. G. Wodehouse.)

Slavic Dance
>M. Miller

Finale
>Entire Company

ACT 3

Scene 1

"Land of Butterflies" Ballet (*Music by* Victor Herbert.)
>*Butterflies*: Misses M. McDonald, B. Dean, A. King, E. Drange, V. Vernon, B. Williams, Hunter, DeBussy, Hanson, Platt, Wilson, Orville, LeRoy, Bowie, Lyle, Shand. *Moths*: Misses Donley, Mayer, Oliphant, Stanfield, Kingsley, Collings, Akers, Fenron, Otis, Parks, Closs, Maide, S. Vernon, Vreeland, Ford, Braham. *The Bat*: Dolores. *Premiere Danseuse* (Sally's Debut in the Follies): M. Miller.

Scene 3

The Wedding Day: Finale
>*The Happy Pairs*: M. Miller, I. Fisher; Dolores, L. Errol; W. Catlett, M. Hay. *Bridesmaids*: Misses A. King, Drange, V. Vernon, MacDonald, Williams. *Little Bridesmaids*: Misses Vreeland, Otis, Henderson, Maide, S. Vernon, Kingsley. *Children*: Baby Dot, D. Tigue, R. Murphy, M. Bartz. *Boy*: F. Bages.

1920.45

HER FAMILY TREE

A Fantastic Play with Music in Two Acts, 11 Scenes. Book by Al Weeks and 'Bugs' Baer. Music and lyrics by Seymour Simons. Staged by Hassard Short. Dances arranged by Carl Randall. Scenery designed by P. Dodd Ackerman. Costumes designed by Shirley Barker. Julius Tannen's Scenes written by himself. Orchestra under the direction of Arthur Gutman. Orchestrations by Arthur Gutman. Produced by Nora Bayes. Opened 27 December 1920 at the Lyric Theatre, moved 7 March 1921 to the Sam S. Shubert Theatre, and closed 19 March 1921 after 90 performances.

CAST: NORA BAYES, JULIUS TANNEN, FRANK MORGAN, THE RANDALL SISTERS, AL ROBERTS, FLORENCE MORRISSON, THELMA CARLTON, JEROME BRUNER, MARGUERITE DANIELS, UNA FLEMING, ALAN EDWARDS, TOM BRYAN, DONALD SAWYER, HENRIETTE WILSON.
>*Ensemble*: Cecil Harrington, Helen McCarthy, Millie Oertel, Florence Brady, Evelyn Sintae, Grace Russell, Dorothy Morrison, Edith Rook, Betty Stewart, Ray Vance, Dudley Wilkinson, Polly Bowman, Cecile Lee, Estelle Nesbit, Grace Rivers, Earl Mossman.

ACT 1

Scene 1

"Ouija Board"
>N. Bayes

(Introducing Entire Company.)
>*Scene*: The Home of Nora Bayes overlooking New Jersey.

Scene 2
>*Scene*: Just around the corner.

Seeker After Truth: J. Tannen. *Scrya*: A. Fowler. *Muraffa*: E. Mossman. *Spirit of the Ages*: Randall Sisters.

Scene 3

"The Gold Diggers"
>A. Edwards, T. Carlton, Ensemble

Tango
>U. Fleming, T. Bryan

"No Other Gal" (No Other Girl)
>N. Bayes
>*Scene*: A Gambling Dive in California in 1849.
>*Tom Craddock*, the gambler: F. Morgan. *Jim Hilton*, a miner: J. Bruner. *Claude Hemingwater*, a rough cowboy: A. Edwards. *Pedro*, a greaser: A. Roberts. *Le Hi Lo*, a Chinese: R. Vance. *Chief Blah*, an Indian: E. Mossman. *Mr. Bumsteeple*, a waiter: D. Sawyer. *Sue*, the prairie flower: F. Morrison. *Favorita*: U. Fleming. *Nevada Nell*: N. Bayes.

Scene 4

The Light of Vishnu

Scene 5

"The Elevator Gavotte"
>T. Carlton, Ladies

"Boom Whee!"
>T. Bryan, Ladies

Trio
>T. Carlton, E. Sintae, D. Sawyer

Waltz
>U. Fleming

"Where Tomorrow Begins"[112]
>N. Bayes
>*Scene*: A Georgian Garden in England.
>*James*, the Duke of Westerham: A. Roberts. *Anne*, the Duchess of Westerham: F. Morrison. *The Lady Eleanor*, their niece: N. Bayes. *Sir Walter Trent*, Bart: F. Morgan. *Richard Manning*: A. Edwards. *Paul*, a dancing master: T. Bryan. *Page*: H. Wilson.

ACT 2

Scene 1

The Sacrificial Ballet:

Oranges
>T. Bryan

Silks
>T. Carlton
>*Scene*: The Story of a Chinese Parchment.
>*Tsao-Tung*, a Holy Man: F. Morgan. *San-Moy*, his daughter: N. Bayes. *Yang-sheng*, a Prince: A. Roberts. *Ming-Wu*: A. Edwards.

Scene 2

What Lies Around the Corner

Scene 3

"A Romantic Knight"
>A. Edwards, U. Fleming, T. Carlton, Ensemble

"As We Sow (So Shall We Reap)"
>N. Bayes, A. Edwards

"I Love You"
>U. Fleming, T. Bryan; N. Bayes, R. Vance
>*Scene*: The Day of Knights.
>*Sawful, Knight*: A. Roberts. *Beatrice*, his daughter: N. Bayes. *Ursula*, a lot more daughter: F. Morrison. *Sunday, Knight*: A. Edwards. *Smother, Knight*: F. Morgan.

Scene 4

The Heart of Scrya

Scene 5

"Why Worry"[113]
>N. Bayes
>*Scene*: Outside of Noah's Ark.

---

[112]Replaced during the run by:
>"Remember the Rose"
>>N. Bayes
>>(*Music by* Seymour Simons. *Lyrics by* Sidney Mitchell.)

[113]Late in the run this scene was reset at "The End of a Perfect Day at the Home of Nora Bayes." Featured in place of "Why Worry?" were:
>"The Broadway Blues" (and other popular songs to cheer you)

Noah: A. Roberts. *Mrs. Noah*: F. Morrison. *Ham*: F. Bruner. *Shem*: A. Edwards. *Japheth*: T. Bryan. *Mrs. Shem*: U. Fleming. *Mrs. Ham*: F. Brady. *Mrs. Japhet*: N. Bayes. *A Reporter*: F. Morgan.

Scene 6
  The Story
    N. Bayes

1920.46   WO DIE LERCHE SINGT

An Operetta in Three Acts, in German. Libretto by A. M. Willner and Heinz Reichert. Music by Franz Lehár. Stage director, Kurt Gordon. Ernst Knoch, Conductor. (Produced by Max Winter.) Opened 27 December 1920 at the Manhattan Opera House and closed 1 January 1921 after 5 performances in repertory.[114]

CAST: *Török Pál*, an old peasant: KURT GORDON. *Margit*, his granddaughter: MARTHA GANTZBERG. *Sándor Zápolja*, a painter: MAX BRATT. *Baron Árpád Ferenczy*, his friend: CHRISTIAN RUB. *Wilma Garamy*, Opera Singer: EVA LEONI. *Bodrogy Pista*, a young farmer: OSCAR HOFMANN. *Borcsa*, a servant: Maude Burk. *Kovács Lajos*, innkeeper: Julius Bayer. *János*, a helper: Alex Greenac. *Rezsö*, a painter: Louis Richling. *Painters, young farmers, farmerettes.*
   Dance Specialties: LOLA MENZELI (Prima Ballerina), Dorothy Mettke, Charlotte Mettke, Gertrude Schulz, Paula Schwenke, Frieda Coursen, Frieda Low.

Act 1: A little Hungarian village.

Act 2: Sandor's House in Budapest.

Act 3: Sandor's House in Budapest.

ACT 1[115]

  Introduktion (Es rötelt im Laube)
    C. Rub, L. Richling, J. Bayer, Chorus
  "Was geh'n mich an die Leute"
    K. Gordon
  "Ein Hauch, wie von Blüten" (Duettszene)
    E. Leoni, C. Rub
  "Durch die weiten Felder" (Entréelied)
    M. Gantzberg
  "Schöne Margit" (Duett)(Wo die Lerche singt, wo die Sichel klingt)
    M. Gantzberg, M. Bratt
  Reminiszenz (Schöne Margit, kleine Lerche, komm' und werde mein)
    M. Bratt
  "Auf dem Bankerl" (Terzett)(Bitte, nehmen S' doch Platz bei der Laube)
    E. Leoni, M. Gantzberg, K. Gordon
  "Ja, auf dem Land" (Duett)(Kein Theater und kein Kino)
    E. Leoni, L. Gordon
  "March und Palótas" (Kommen gradewegs vom Schnitt)
    M. Gantberg, O. Hofmann, Chorus
  Finale (Wie von ferne ruft es leise)
    E. Leoni, M. Gantzberg, M. Bratt, O. Hofmann, K. Gordon
  Ungarische Tänze (Hungarian Dance)

ACT 2
  "Sonntag kommt mein Schatz" (Ich, Du, Er, Wir, Ihr und Sie)
    M. Gantzberg
  "Wer ist denn der Mann mit der schönen Frau?" (Duett)
  (Bin ich erst der grosse Mann)
    M. Gantzberg, M. Bratt
  "Das Lied von Temesvár" (Pali, sagt' mir einst die Mutter)
    K. Gordon, Ladies' Chorus
  "Fern wie aus vergagng'nen Tagen" (Duet)
    E. Leoni, M. Bratt
  Reminiszenz (Was geh'n mich an die Leute)
    K. Gordon
  Finale (Du wilder Teufel, Du)
    M. Gantzberg, M. Burk, M. Bratt

ACT 3
  Reminiszenz (Keiner wichst Spitzeln vom Schnubart so ein)
    K. Gordon

"Nur Temp'rament" (Walzer-Duett)(Kühn zu neuem Leben)
    E. Leoni, M. Bratt
Reminiszenz (Fern wie aus vergang'nen Tagen)
    E. Leoni, M. Bratt
Finaletto (Sonne scheint und Himmel ist ganz blau)
    M. Gantzberg, M. Burk, O. Hofmann, K. Gordon, M. Bratt
ANHANG (Appendix)
  "Heut' is heut'!" (Was schert uns das?)
    C. Rub, Two Women
  "Jay, nagy a bay!"
    C. Rub és két hölgy
  "Introduktion, Walzer und Galopp" (Ensemble-Szene)
  (Trallala! Trallala!)
    E. Leoni, M. Bratt, L. Richling, C. Rub, Chorus
  "Golden Fox-Trot" (Tanz-Szene)
    E. Leoni, M. Bratt

1920.47   THE PASSING SHOW OF 1921

A Musical Revue in Two Acts, 26 Scenes[116]. Dialogue (sketches) and lyrics by Harold Atteridge. Music by Jean Schwartz; additional music by Lew Pollack; incidental music by Alfred Goodman. Staged by J. C. Huffman. Dance numbers staged by Max Scheck. Art director (scenery designed by) William Weaver. Costumes designed by Cora MacGeachy. Orchestra under the direction of Alfred Goodman. Orchestrations under the supervision of J. Bodewalt Lampe. Produced by Lee and J. J. Shubert. Opened 29 December 1920 at the Winter Garden and closed 28 May 1921 after 191 performances.

CAST: WILLIE HOWARD, EUGENE HOWARD, MARIE DRESSLER, HARRY WATSON, INA HAYWARD, JANET ADAIR, IRVING O'HAY, DOLLY HACKETT, ROSALIE MELLETTE, HELEN MELLETTE, FRANK GRACE, JOHNNY BERKES, GRACE KEESHON, EMILY MILES, RUTH MILES, J. HAROLD MURRAY, SAMMY WHITE, TOT QUALTERS, Harry C. Bannister, Juliet Strahl, Jeanette Dietrich, Frank Ridge, Kathleen O'Hanlon, Theo Zambouni, Robert Gilbert, Eileen Rooney, Jack E. Rice, Gene Martinette, Anthony Jochim, Joseph Schrode, Abe Aronson, Gaby Lorraine, Mildred LaGue, Mae Devereaux, W. H. Pringle, Perry Askam, Irving Mels, Francis X. Mahoney, Miles Mershon, Joseph Toner, Stephen Cortez, Miss Peggy, Violet Englefield, Adele Devereaux, Orilla Smith, (Cleveland Bronner, Iris Solfeng).
   Buds and Blossoms: Dorothy Bruce, Marie Stafford, Charlotte Sprague, Mildred Soper, Barbara McCree, Muriel Seeley, Lyola White, Helen Fox, Mona Mode, Louise Wayne, Hazel Flynn, Alice Rohrey, Maria Talwynne, Virginia Wilson, Lenore D'Arcy, Mary Clowes, Zillah Lenney, Anita Mirrarar, Madeline Smith, Emma James, Elsie May, Betty St. Clair, Flo Summerville, Violet Ayres, Violet Weber, Glada Davies, Elf Lorraine, Dixie O'Neil, Kitty Desmond, Edna Starch, Jean Fox, Estelle Lang, Jean Scott, Elfin Haye, Dorothy Daniels, Billie Davis, Louise Darcey, Ann Delmore, Ruth Newman, Edith Pierce, Sonia Fields, Ruby Howard, Jean Danjou, Dolores Mendez, Lucila Mendez, Laralda Popenny, Poppy Morton, Marjorie Hope, Shirley Gallop, Peggy Sletner, Kitty Holton, Ethel Baedor, Sophie Howard, Marion Joy, Evelyn Meade, Ruth Channing, Margaret Wood, Elaine Courtney, Mildred Lee, Orilla Smith, Marie Kane, (Miss Stryder).

ACT 1
Scene 1
  Prologue
  "Hello Miss Knickerbocker"
    I. Hayward, some New York girls
      Mrs. Knickerbocker: I. Hayward.
Scene 2
  A Book of New York History
    Stepen: J. Strahl. *Dancen*: J. Dietrich.
Scene 3
  "In Little Old New York" (Not So Long Ago)
    J. Adair, a group of old-fashioned sweets
    (Music by Jean Schwartz.)
      Mrs. Stuyvesant Knickerbocker: I. Hayward. *Irene*: J. Adair. *Bell*: J. Toner. *The James Boys*: I. O'Hay, P. Askam. *Black*: J. Schrode. *White*: A. Aronson. *Edison*: A. Jochim. *Heinz*: W H Pringle. *Tilford*: H. C. Bannister. *Park*: M. Mershon. *Mennen*: J. E. Rice. *Gillette*: R. Gilbert. *The Smith Brothers*: F. X. Mahoney, I. Mels. *Lydia Pinkham*: M. Devereaux.
Scene 4
  New York "1921"

---

[114]Literally translated, 'Where the Lark Sings.' No credits in program for producer, scenery or costumes.
[115]Musical numbers not listed in program. List prepared from published Viennese piano vocal score, (W. Karczag, Vienna, 1918).

---

[116]The Ninth in the annual series of revues which began in 1894, presented since 1914 by the Messrs. Shubert.

A Policeman: P. Askam. *Mr. Oppenheim*: H. C. Bannister. *Moe Levey*: J. E. Rice. *George Sidney Solomon*: W. H. Pringle. *The Stranger*: A. Jochim.

Scene 5

The Charm School:

"When There's No One to Love"
D. Hackett, Mellette Sisters, a few lonely girls
(*Music by* Jean Schwartz.)

"The Charm School"
J. H. Murray, some charming charmers
(*Music by* Jean Schwartz. *Lyrics by* Alfred Bryan.)
Lady Billy: D. Hackett. *Rosalie*: R. Mellette. *Helen*: H. Mellette. *Poor Little Ritz Girl*: M. Devereaux. *Mabel St. John*: E. Miles. *Lerry Jemare*: G. Keeshon. *Topsy Lemaire*: M. LaGue. *Miss Charity*: R. Mills. *Bevans*: J. H. Murray. "*Mary*": G. Lorraine. "*Irene*": J. Adair. *Dr. Noah Peach*: J. E. Rice. *Frances Belasco Starr*: M. Dressler.

Scene 6

"(Let's Have) A Rattling Good Time"
T. Qualters, Good Time Girlies
(*Music by* Jean Schwartz. *Lyrics by* Alfred Bryan.)
Miss Rattle: T. Qualters.

Scene 7

"Silks and Satins"
I. Hayward, A Few Winter Garden Beauties

Scene 8

The Desert Cafe—Times Square
Miss New York: G. Keeshon. *Mr. New Yorker*: F. Ridge.

Scene 9

Broadway to Sahara

Selections
W. Howard, E. Howard
["June Moon"
(*Music by* Frank Magine and Charley Straight. *Lyrics by* Joe Lyons.)
"When Caruso Comes to Town"
(*Music by* Lew Pollack. *Lyrics by* Sidney Mitchell and Sidney Clare.)
"When Shall We Meet Again"
(*Music by* Richard Whiting. *Lyrics by* Richard Egan.)
"Michigan"
(*Music by* Malvin Franklin. *Lyrics by* Alex Gerber.)
"Underneath Hawaiian Skies"
(*Music by* Ernie Erdman. *Lyrics by* Fred Rose.)
"Weep No More My Mammy"
(*Music by* Lew Pollack. *Lyrics by* Sidney Mitchell and Sidney Clare.)]
Sammy: W. Howard. *Jean*: E. Howard. *The Camel*: J. Schrode, A. Aronson. *Mr. Gray*: J. E. Rice. *Miss Nice*: E. Miles. *Miss Sweet*: D. Hackett. *Cowboy*: H. C. Bannister.

"She's the Mother of Broadway Rose"

Scene 10

"You May Be a Bad Man"
D. Hackett, Some Prairie Flowers, O'Hanlon and Zambounis

Scene 11

Lightning [A burlesque of the play by Winchell Smith and Frank Bacon]
Alfred: H. C. Bannister. *Josephine*: D. Hackett. *Frank Bacon*: W. Howard.

Scene 12

The Bat [A burlesque of the play by Mary Roberts Rinehart and Avery Hopwood]
May: J. Adair. *Mrs. Hopwood*: M. Dressler. *A Man*: R. Gilbert. *The Doctor*: H. C. Bannister. *Detective*: H. Watson. *Bijou*: I. Hayward. *Gardener*: A. Jochim. *Interpreter*: G. Martinette. *A Mysterious Person*: J. E. Rice.

Scene 13

Two of a Kind
Miss Strutter: E. Rooney. *Mr. Strutter*: S. White.

Scene 14

Chinese Mecca [A burlesque of the spectacle by Oscar Asche]
"My Wife"
W. Howard, E. Howard
"Ta Voo" (Ta-Hoo)
D. Hackett, J. Adair, TaVoo Girls
(*Music by* Jean Schwartz.)
"The Lady of the Lamp" (My Lady of the Lamp)
J. H. Murray, I. Hayward

Sing High: W. Howard. *Sing Low*: E. Howard. *Mr. White*: F. Ridge. *Bevans*: J. H. Murray. *Government Inspector*: R. Gilbert. *Chin See*: J. Adair. *La See*: D. Hackett. *The Lady of the Lamp*: I. Hayward.

Scene 15

Mecca [A burlesque of the spectacle by Oscar Asche]
"I'm Oriental"
J. Adair, F. Grace, J. Berkes, Mellette Sisters, Allah Jazzers
(*Music by* Lew Pollack.)
The Sultan: J. H. Murray. *Abdulla*: H. C. Bannister. *Zobeida*: J. Adair. *Merra*: K. O'Hanlon. *Selah*: T. Zambouni. *Fatima*: H. Mellette. *Kataf*: R. Mellette. *Fixerah*: F. Grace. *Ali Shah*: J. Berkes.

ACT 2

Scene 1

Dream Fantasies Ballet: "Dream Fantasies"
C. Bronner, some dreams

(A Series of Visualized Dreams, *conceived and executed by* Cleveland Bronner)
Spirits of Dreams: M. Mode, A. Rohrey, M. Talwynne. *Mystery*: C. Bronner. *The Moth and the Flame*: I. Solfeng, C. Bronner. *Spanish Visions*: E. May, M. Woods, F. Summerville, E. Pierce, O. Smith. *Love Phantoms*: I. Solfeng, C. Bronner. *Spirit of the Globe. Vanity*: C. Bronner, H. Flynn, L. White, L. Wayne, H. Fox, A. Mirrarar, L. D'Arcy. *The Dream Priestesses*: M. Clowes, Z. Lenney, A. Delmore, Stryder. *Dual Natures*: C. Bronner. *Spirit of the Orient*: I. Solfeng. *Fire Flies*: C. Bronner, Ensemble.

Scene 2

In the Dark
A Woman: M. Dressler. *A Man*: W. H. Pringle.

Scene 3

Out Front
Frankie: F. Grace. *Johnny*: J. Berkes. *Tot*: T. Qualters.

Scene 4

"Where Is the Beautiful Face?" (Beautiful Faces)
J. H. Murray
(*Music by* Lew Pollack.)

Scene 5

Versailles
"Becky from Babylon"
W. Howard
(*Music by* Abner Silver. *Lyrics by* Alex Gerber.)
Cortez: S. Cortez. *Peggy*: Miss Peggy. *Professor Strong*: I. O'Hay. *Miss Adams*: I. Hayward. *Miss Bates*: G. Keeshon. *Sammy*: W. Howard. *Jean*: E. Howard. *Matthew*: F. X. Mahoney. *Gaston*: H. C. Bannister. *Page*: I. Mels. *Mr. Masher*: R. Gilbert. *A Mysterious Person*: J. E. Rice.

Scene 6

"Smiling Sam"
S. White, a few strutting girlies
Mr. Strutter: S. White.

Scene 7

"Spanish Love"
(W. Howard, E. Howard)
(*Music and Lyrics by* the Howard Brothers, Alex Gerber and Abner Silver.)
"Tip Top Toreador"
I. Hayward, Spanish Love Girls
Rogue: R. Gilbert. *Chiquita*: M. LaGue. *Margueretta*: G. Keeshon. *Alvarez*: A. Jochim. *Domingo*: W. H. Pringle. *Furnsantra*: M. Devereaux. *Margals*: S. White. *An Usher*: J. Adair. *Romero*: P. Askam. *Marie Adel Carmen*: M. Dressler. *William*: H. Watson. *Java*: J. H. Murray. *Poncho*: H. C. Bannister. *Cortez*: S. Cortez. *Peggy*: Miss Peggy.

Scene 8

"Rigoletto Quartette" (A Bit of Opera)
W. Howard, E. Howard, V. Englefield, I. Hayward

Scene 9

An Egyptian Bath
"Rubyiats from the Rubyiat" (Sparkling Rubies from the Rubyiat)
T. Qualters, Sparkling Rubyiat Girls
(*Lyrics by* Alfred Bryan.)
Sultana: A. Devereaux. *Rubyiat*: T. Qualters.

Scene 10

Pennsylvania Station—At the Magazine Stand
"Sweetest Melody"
E. Howard, W. Howard

Gladys: O. Smith. *Sammy*: W. Howard. *Mama*: M. Devereaux. *Mr. Swain*: J. E. Rice. *Miss Maid*: E. Miles. *Jean*: E. Howard.

Scene 11

A Garden

"The Dancing Blues" (Dance Off the Blues)
F. Grace, J. Berkes, Mellette Sisters, S. Cortez and Peggy, Winter Garden Steppers
(*Music by* Lew Pollack.)

1921.01

ERMINIE

A Revival of the Comic Opera in Three Acts[117]. Book and lyrics by Harry Paulton, (Claxson Bellamy). (Based on the French melodrama 'L'Auberge des Adrets' and its sequel 'Robert Macaire' by Benjamin Antier, Saint-Amand and Paulyanthe.) Revisions by Marc Connelly. Music by Edward Jakobowski. Staged by Charles C. Fais. Scenery and costumes by Norman Bel Geddes. Musical director, Selli Simonson. Produced by George C. Tyler and William Farnum. Opened 3 January 1921 at the Park Theatre and closed 26 February 1921 after 64 performances.

CAST: *Cadeaux* (Caddy): FRANCIS WILSON[118]. *Ravennes* (Ravvy): DeWOLF HOPPER. *Marquis de Pomvert*: FRANCIS LIEB. *Chevalier de Brabazon*, Guest of the Marquis: ALEXANDER CLARK. *Eugene Marcel*, Secretary to the Marquis: Warren Proctor. *Captain Delauney*: MADGE LESSING. *Dufois*, Landlord of the Lion d'Or: Richard Malchien. *Simon*, Waiter at the Lion d'Or: Adrian Morgan. *Vicomte de Brissac*: E. John Kennedy. *Sergeant*: John H. Reed. *Benedict*: John E. Douglas. *Erminie*: IRENE WILLIAMS. *Princess de Gramponeur*: JENNIE WEATHERSBY[119]. *Cerise Marcel*, Erminie's companion: Alice Hanlon. *Marie*: Angela Warde. *Javotte*: ROSAMOND WHITESIDE. *Flower Girls, Soldiers, Peasants, Clowns, Lords and Ladies, etc.*

Act 1: Courtyard of the Lion d'Or.

Act 2: The Ballroom.

Act 3: The Corridor.

ACT 1

Opening Chorus
"Vive Le Marquis"
Chorus

"When Love Is Young"
I. Williams

"Past and Future"
I. Williams, W. Proctor

"Ohe Mama"[120]
R. Whiteside
(*Lyrics by* Marc Connelly.)

"All for Glory"
M. Lessing, Chorus

"Downy Jail Birds of a Feather"
F. Wilson, D. Hopper

"The Blissful Pleasure I Profess"
Ensemble

Finale

ACT 2

"Here on Lords and Ladies Waiting"
Chorus

"A Woman's Dress"
R. Whiteside

"Darkest the Hour"
W. Proctor

"Joy Attend on Erminie"
Chorus

"Lullaby"
I. Williams, Chorus

"What the Dicky Bird Says"[121]
F. Wilson
(*Additional Lyrics by* Marc Connelly and James T. Powers.)

Finale—Gavotte
Ensemble

ACT 3

"Good Night"
Ensemble

Finale
Ensemble

THE MIDNIGHT ROUNDERS OF 1921

1921.02

A Vaudeville Revue in Two Acts, 31 Scenes[122]. Sketches by Harold Atteridge. Music by Jean Schwartz; additional music by Lew Pollack. Lyrics by Alfred Bryan. Staged by Jack Mason. Scenery by William Weaver. Gowns by Madame Routon. Orchestra under the direction of Alfred Goodman. Produced under the supervision of J. J. Shubert. Produced by Messrs. Lee and J.J. Shubert. Opened 7 February 1921 at the Century Promenade and closed 2 April 1921 after 49 performances.

CAST: JOE BROWNING, GLADYS WALTON, TED LORRAINE, ARTHUR DONNELLY, J. HAROLD MURRAY, JOHN GUIRAN, FLORENCE RAYFIELD, TOT QUALTERS, JOHN LOWE, J. FRANCIS DOOLEY, BESSIE CLIFFORD, JESSICA BROWN, OLGA COOK, LA PETITE MARGUERITE, ADA FORMAN, CLEVELAND BRONNER, INGRID SOLFENG, CORINNE SALES, ETHEL DAVIS, LOU EDWARDS, Anna Maria DeMalita, David Gardner.

Ensemble: Florence Wilde, Amy Frank, Elsie Frank, Beatrice Jennings, Alva Fenton, Kitty Kelley, Bobby Lester, Thelma Johns, Phyllis Millar, Sidney Nelson, Anna Buckley, Helen Weber, Evelyn Rosewood, Billy Williams, Florence Moore, Bonna Odear, LaVerre DeMarr, Viola Votrouba, Virginia Allen, Anna Niebel, Edna Richmond, Virginia Richmond, Jean Troupman, Grace Langdon, Gladys Montgomery, Virginia Calmer, Marie Booth, Jewel Jordan, Peggy Hoffman, Georgia Empey, Helen Herendeen, Nan Rainsford, Viola Bennett, Margaret Kerns, Margaret Himes, Florence Darling, Muriel Manners, Margaret Menges, Virginia Fallon, Phoebe Lee, Jane Wyatt, Elinor Dell, Clare Hooper, Evon Linnard, Sally Long, Elsie Davenport, Loretta Harris, Pauline Dakla, Beatrice Jackson.

ACT 1[123]

Scene 1
Prologue
J. Browning

Scene 2
"Sprinkle Me with Diamonds"
G. Walton, T. Lorraine, Ensemble

Scene 3
Songs
O. Cook

Scene 4
He Talks with His Fingers (Shadow Box Specialty)
A. Donnelly

Scene 5
"You Tickle Me"
F. Rayfield, Ensemble
(*Music by* Lew Pollack. *Lyrics by* Sidney Clare.)

Scene 6
"La Vie Parisienne"
J. F. Dooley, C. Sales

Scene 7
"Blue Blondes"
O. Cook, E. Davis, Ensemble

Scene 8
Songs
E. Davis

---

[117]Originally produced in New York 10 May 1886 at the Casino Theatre for 571 performances.
[118]Recreating his original role.
[119]Recreating her original role.
[120]An interpolation for this revival; one critic remarked that the melody had been "filched" from Millöcker's THE BEGGAR STUDENT.

[121]An interpolation for this revival.
[122]This New York production subsequently toured as a vaudeville revue under a Shubert Vaudeville contract, returning briefly to the Winter Garden 20 February 1922 with revised cast, songs and sketches. An altogether different touring production entitled THE MIDNIGHT ROUNDERS starring Eddie Cantor toured profitably but did not play New York.
[123]The running order was subject to revision and frequent interpolations.

Scene 9
 "Passionettes"
  T. Qualters, Ensemble
Scene 10
 Harpist
  A. M. DeMalita
 The Florida Cracker
  A. Donnelly
Scene 11
 "Keep Them in a Golden Cage"
  J. H. Murray
Scene 12
 Eccentrique
  L. Edwards
Scene 13
 "Ballet of the Pyramids"
  (Ballet in 4 Scenes conceived, *staged and designed by* Cleveland Bronner.)
 A Spectacular Pageant with incidental dances depicting Worshippers of the Golden Moon and Sacred Serpents.
  Scene 1: The pilgrims enter the Temple of Tannit.
  Scene 2: Shrine of the Golden Moon.
   The Moon Goddesses: Misses E. Frank, A. Frank, Nelson, Moore, Fenton, Williams. *Moon Gods*: Misses Wilde, Odear, Lester, Johns, Jennings, Weber, Kelley, DeMarr. *Golden Ibis*: Misses Troupman, V. Richmond, E. Richmond, Allen, Lee, Menges, Rainsford, Himes.
  Scene 3: The Snake Worshippers. The Sacrifice—Each harvest the most beautiful maiden obtainable is sacrificed to the Sacred Serpent. We see her enter followed by the snake. To her hypnotized mind the snake appears to assume human form. As it circles about her, its shimmering skin seems like trailing robes of gold and silver. She struggles to break the spell. The serpent coils about her and the pagan god has claimed one more victim.
   High Priestess: Miss Herendeen. *Snake Girls*: Miss Langdon, Jackson, Votrouba, Buckley, Nebel, Rosewood, Hoffman, Dakla, Millar. *The Victim*: I. Solfeng. *The Spirit of the Snake*: C. Bronner.
  Scene 4: The Pageant in honor of the Sacrifice. Soft lamps glow in the darkness. The air becomes fragrant with the perfume of many flowers. The High Priestesses of the Temple appear, and the ceremony begins.

ACT 2[124]
Scene 1
 Poses Classique
  B. Clifford
Scene 2
 "Picket Fence"
  J. Brown, Ensemble
Scene 3
 "Perfume and Passion"
  O. Cook
 Dances
  J. Brown, J. Lowe, G. Walton, T. Lorraine
Scene 4
 A Few Moments with J. Francis Dooley and Corinne Sales
Scene 5
 "Take a Chance with Me"
  (O. Cook)
Scene 6
 Old Melodies
  O. Cook, J. H. Murray
 "Poor Butterfly" (from the BIG SHOW)
  La Petite Marguerite
  (*Music by* Raymond Hubbell. *Lyrics by* John Golden.)
 "Annie Laurie" (traditional, Scottish)
  F. Rayfield
 "(O) Solo Mio"
  A. Frank
  (*Music and Italian lyrics by* Ernesto DiCapua.)

---

[124]Added after opening:
 "The Lost Pocketbook"
  J. F. Dooley, C. Sales, assisted by L. Edwards
 Arabesque
  A. Forman
 Athletic Specialty (A Study in Endurance)
  Rath Brothers (George, Dick)

"Humoresque"
 G. Langdon, J. Lowe
 (*Music by* Anton Dvorák.)
"La Paloma" (traditional, Spanish)
 G. Walton, T. Lorraine
"Strauss Waltz"
 T. Johns, D. Gardner
 (*Music by* Johann Strauss.)
(Selection from) TALES OF HOFFMAN
 L. Duby
 (*Music by* Jacques Offenbach.)
"Mother Machree" (from BARRY OF BALLYMORE)
 K. Kelley
 (*Music by* Chauncey Olcott and Ernest R. Ball. *Lyrics by* Rida Johnson Young.)
"Roses of Picardy" (interpolated into HELLO, ALEXANDER)
 J. Brown
 (*Music by* Haydn Wood. *Lyrics by* Frederick E. Weatherley.)
Scene 7
 A Good Old-Fashioned Buck Dance
Scene 8
 A Few Remarks
  J. Browning
Scene 9
 "Gold Fish"
Scene 10
 Terpsichorean Novelties
  J. Guiran, La Petit Marguerite
Scene 11
 "Would You Like to Sleep Upon My Pillow?" (Pillow Song)
  F. Rayfield, Ensemble
Scene 12
 "Spirit of Java"
  A. Forman
Scene 13
 Pony Trot
  G. Walton, J. Lowe
Scene 14
 "Snap a Wishbone with Me"
  C. Sales, Ensemble
Scene 15
 "Beautiful Girls Are Like Opium"
  J. H. Murray
Scene 16
 Dance Eccentrique
  J. Brown, D. Duby
Scene 17
 "Sand Witches"
  E. Davis, Ensemble
Scene 18
 "Century Toddle"
  T. Qualters, Ensemble

1921.03   THE ROSE GIRL

A Play with Music in Two Acts. Book and lyrics by William Cary Duncan. Music by Anselm Goetzl. Production staged by Hassard Short. Special ballet conceived and staged by Michel Fokine. Dancing master, Max Scheck. Scenery designed by William Weaver. Costumes designed by Ralph Mulligan. Orchestra under the direction by Max Steiner. Produced by Anselm Goetzl (Goetzl Theatrical Enterprises Inc.) under the direction of Lee Shubert. Opened 11 February 1921 at the Ambassador Theatre and closed 7 May 1921 after 99 performances.

CAST (in order of appearance): *Filipard*, Overseer: David Andrada. *Fleurette*, a Flower Girl: MARJORIE GATESON. *Mme. Donay*, a Wealthy Parisienne: MAY BOLEY. *Her Four Protegés*: *Colette*: Beatrice Darling. *Denise*: Elizabeth Darling. *Felice*: Helen Lyons. *Suzette*: Virginia Wynn. *Filipe Telicot*, Manager for Poincier, Ltd.: FRED HILLEBRAND. *Count Henri de Guise*: STEWART BAIRD. *Adelle La Flamme*: MARCELLA SWANSON. *Jeanne Du Verne*: BEATRICE SWANSON. *Ambrose Lollypop*, a Would-Be Financier: Shep Camp. *Oswald Pettibone*, His Partner: Louis Simon. *Victor Marquis de la Roche*, Nephew of the Count: CHARLES PURCELL. *Mignon Latour*, the Rose Girl: MABEL WITHEE. *Nadine Bankoff*, the

Count's Fiancée: ZOE BARNETT. *A Gypsy Dancer*: Rose Rolando. *Louise*: Aleta. *Marie*: Florence Gast. (*Ballerina* in "The Ballet des Perfumes": LYDIA LOPOKOVA.) *Flower Girls, Shop Girls, Visitors.*

Flower Girls: Misses Charlotte Lowery, Lillian Sanger, Viola Allen, Helen Lockhart, Jean Woods, Marion Phillips, Thelma Parker, Alice Monroe, Billy Wagner, Constance Brady, Jean Goddard, Gladys Strother. *Guests and Visitors at Grasse*: Misses Rita Tracey, Elba Woods, Vivian Kelley, Helen O'Day, Dorothy Schaefer, Edith Scott, Florence Brandie, Marie Woods.

Act 1: The Rose Gardens of Poincier, Ltd., in Grasse, Riviera, France. Present time.

Act 2: The Perfume Salon of Poincier, Ltd., Paris Six months later.

ACT 1
Opening Chorus
 Ensemble
"The Protegés"
 M. Boley, Four Protegés
"Beauty's Candy Shop"
 S. Baird, M. Swanson, B. Swanson, Visitors
"When Our Sundays Are Blue"
 M. Gateson, F. Hillebrand
"There Comes a Some Day"
 M. Withee, C. Purcell
"Flirtation Quartette"
 Z. Barnett, M. Boley, S. Baird, F. Hillebrand
"Wondrous Midnight Eyes"
 R. Rolando, Ensemble
 (*Lyrics by* Kay Reese.)
"The Spanish Senorita"
 F. Hillebrand
"That's Me"
 M. Withee, M. Gateson, Z. Barnett, Ensemble
Finale

ACT 2
"The Ballet des Perfumes"[125]
 L. Lopokova, Corps de Ballet
 (*Ballet arranged by* Michel Fokine. *Waltz by* Johannes Brahams. "Some Day" *by* Anselm Goetzl.)
"Quarrel Number"
 M. Gateson, F. Hillebrand
"When That Somebody Comes"
 M. Gateson, Girls
"The Hour With You"[126]
 C. Purcell
"May and September"
 M. Withee, S. Baird
"My (Old) New Jersey Home"
 M. Gateson, F. Hillebrand
 (*Music by* Nat Vincent. *Lyrics by* Ballard Macdonald.)
"The Rose Girl Blues"
 M. Gateson, F. Hillebrand
"Lingerie"
 Z. Barnett, Girls
"Rose Girl Waltz"
 M. Withee, C. Purcell
Finale

1921.04   BLUE EYES

A Musical Comedy in Two Acts. Book and lyrics by Leon Gordon and LeRoy Clemens. (Based on their farce "Let Tommy Do It.") Music by Isidore Benjamin Kornblum. Lyrics by Z. Myers [Meyers]. Staged by Clifford Brooke. Ensembles and dances by Bert French. Orchestra under the direction of Eugene Salzer. Produced by Morris Rose, (Lew Fields). Opened 21 February 1921 at the Casino Theatre, moved 21 March 1921 to the Sam S. Shubert Theatre, and closed 10 April 1921 after 56 performances.

CAST (in order of appearance): *Dawson Ripley*: ANDREW TOMBES. *Fifi*: Dorothy Tierney. *Steinberg*: Philip White. *Peter Van Dam*: LEW FIELDS. *Dorothy Manners*: MOLLIE KING. *Bobby Brett*: RAY RAYMOND. *Kitty Higgins*: DELYLE ALDA. *Mr. Manners*: Carl Eckstrom. *Mrs. Manners*: Jessemine Newcombe. *Stranger*: Leo Frankel. *Specialty Dancers*: Inez Courtney, Aline McGill, Harry Pearce. *Artists, Models, Show Girls, Guests, etc.*

Chorus Ensemble: Inez Courtney, Florence Courtney, Laurette Stanley, Gypsy Mooney, Lucille Arden, Gertrude McDonald, Margaret Finlay, Mabel Grete, Clara K. Taylor, Helen Gates, Grace Hall, Gladys Langdon, Helen Rich, Eunice Barrington, Doris Marquette, Nancy Vaughn, Harry Pearce, Ted Wheeler, Ralph Robbins, Jacques Stone.

Act 1: Studio of Brett, Van Dam and Ripley. Gramercy Square.

Act 2: The Manners' Home at Great Neck, Long Island.

ACT 1
"In ze Park"
 D. Tierney, Ensemble
"Baby Walk"
 H. Gates, I. Courtney, L. Arden, G. McDonald, Girls, Boys
"Blue Eyes"
 M. King, R. Raymond
"Just Suppose"
 D. Alda, A. Tombes
"Danger Ahead"
 R. Raymond, A. Tombes, Ensemble
"Without a Girl Like You"
 M. King, D. Alda, R. Raymond, A. Tombes
Finale
 Entire Company

ACT 2
"Just Suppose" (Opening reprise)
 Ensemble
"So Long Jazz"
 A. Tombes, A. McGill, H. Pearce, I. Courtney, Ensemble
"When Gentlemen Disagree"
 A. Tombes, R. Raymond, L. Fields
"When Gramercy Square Was Uptown"
 M. King, R. Raymond, Ensemble
"Wanting You"
 A. Tombes, D. Alda, Ensemble
 (*Music by* George Gershwin. *Lyrics by* Irving Caesar.)
Specialty
 M. King
Finale
 Entire Company

1921.05   CHINESE LOVE

A Miniature Musical Comedy in One Act[127]. Book, music and lyrics by Clare Kummer. Stage direction by W. L. Gilmore. Produced by Clare Kummer. Opened 28 February 1921 at the Punch and Judy Theatre and closed 10 March 1921 after 12 matinee performances.

CAST (in order of appearance): *Mo Yen*, Emissary of the Law and Custodian of the Tea House: J. M. Kerrigan. *Ah Mee*, a dear lady friend of Chan Fah: Mary Ellison. *Chan Fah*, wife of Wing So: SALLIE FISHER. *Ming Too*, son of Wing So: Uarda Burnett. *Wing So*, a Chinese pirate: Stanley Howlett. *Hing Hi*, a Mandarin: James Lounsberry.

Scene: Garden of Mo Yen's Tea Home. A summer afternoon.

MUSICAL NUMBERS[128]
"Golden Love"
"See How It Sparkles"
followed by

---

[125]Dropped during the run and replaced by:
 Toe Dance
  Aleta
[126]Dropped during the run and replaced by:
"The One Girl Boy"
 A. Barbour Halliday (Victor Marquis)

---

[127]CHINESE LOVE and THE CHOIR REHEARSAL were preceded by a one-act comedy *Bridges*, and followed by a one-act comedy *The Robbery*, both by Clare Kummer, on the same program. In the evenings Clare Kummer's comedy *Rollo's Wild Oat* was played.
[128]No musical numbers listed. List prepared from published sheet music. Not in performance order.

THE CHOIR REHEARSAL
1921.05

A Miniature Musical Comedy in One Act[129]. Book, music and lyrics by Clare Kummer.

CAST: *William*: John Ryan. *Esmerelda*: SALLIE FISHER. *Reverend Alan Wylie*: Stanley Howlett. *Abigail*: Mary Ellison. *Amos*: James Lounsberry. *Enoch*: Walter Coupe.

Scene: The Living Room of Esmerelda's House, Tuckertown. Eight o'clock of a spring evening in the long ago.

MUSICAL NUMBER[130]

"A Wonderful Thing"
S. Fisher

LOVE BIRDS
1921.06

A Musical Comedy in Two Acts, 5 Scenes. Book by Edgar Allen Woolf. Music by Sigmund Romberg. Lyrics by Ballard Macdonald. Staged by Edgar MacGregor and Frank Smithson, and Julian Alfred. Scenery and lighting designed by P. Dodd Ackerman. Costumes designed by Mme. Gilman. Orchestra under the direction of J. Frank Cork. Produced by Max R. Wilner and Sigmund Romberg[131]. Opened 15 March 1921 at the Apollo Theatre and closed 11 June 1921 after 103 performances.

CAST (in order of appearance): *Arthur Harwood*: RICHARD BOLD. *A Shopper*: Betty Mack. *Violet Morely*: EVELYN CAVANAUGH. *Hal Sterling*: BARRETT GREENWOOD. *Jennie O'Hara*: ELIZABETH MURRAY. *A Shopper*: Edna Luce. *Mrs. Bronson Charteris*: GRACE ELLSWORTH. *Allene Charteris*: ELIZABETH HINES. *Mr. Bronson Charteris*: JAMES E. SULLIVAN. *Mamie O'Grady*: MARION BENT. *Mr. Johnson*: VINCENT LOPEZ. *Pat*: PAT ROONEY. *A Porter*: Tom Gott. *Mme. Delaunois*: EMILIE LEA. *Mons. Champvallon*: Ramsey DeMar. *Emir Nehmid Duckin*: HARRY MAYO. *Allene's Maid*: Patsy Delany. *Emir's Attendant*: Harold Gieser. *Velouka*: EMILIE LEA. *Warrington Knight*: TOM DINGLE. *Fatima*: Eva Davenport. *Saki*: Sylvia Ford.

Guards of the Palace of Emir Nehmid Duckim: Tom Gott, Bill Hamilton, Tom White. *Vincent Lopez and the Kings of Harmony*: Vincent Lopez (Piano), Bill Hamilton (Clarinet), Tom Gott (Cornet), Harold Gieser (Trombone), Tom White (Drums). *Futurity Chorus of Dancers and Singers*: Betty Mack, Betty Warlow, Lucille Prather, Betty Hamilton, Bobby Reed, Louise Segal, Lucille Gordon, Edna Luce, Marie Cattell, Patsy Delany, Peggy Dolan, Helen Johnson, Beverly Maude, Anna Hunkle, Rose Desmon, Wayne Dorel, Irma Coigne, Nerene Swinton, Celene Cravan, Edna Coigne.

Act 1, Scene 1: Stocking and Lingerie Department in a Fashionable Shop. *Scene 2*: Salon in the Charteris Home.

Act 1, Scene 1: The Garden of Emir Duckin's Palace, Persia. *Scene 2*: Fatima's Boudoir. *Scene 3*: The Garden on Carnival Night.

ACT 1
Scene 1
Opening Chorus
Ensemble
"Let's Pretend"
E. Cavanaugh, B. Greenwood
"The Trousseau Incomplete"
E. Hines, Girls
"Can Macy Do Without Me?"
P. Rooney, M. Bent, Girls
"Two Little Love Birds"
R. Bold, E. Hines
Finale
P. Rooney, M. Bent, E. Murray, J. E. Sullivan, R. Bold, E. Hines, Ensemble
Scene 2
"(Introducing the Futurity) Debutante Chorus"[132]
G. Ellsworth, Guests
(*Lyrics by* Edgar Allen Woolf.)
Specialty Dance
E. Lea

"Fat-Fat-Fatima"
H. Mayo, Guests
"Is It Hard to Guess?"
E. Hines, R. Bold, E. Cavanaugh, B. Greenwood
"Girl Like Grandma"
P. Rooney, M. Bent, Misses Mack, Reed, Craven, Gordon
"Murrayisms" (and "Down Around the River")[133]
E. Murray
"Rooneyisms" (and "Molly O'Malley and Me")
P. Rooney
[(*Music and Lyrics by* Pat Rooney, Jay Kendis and A. Brockman.)]
Finale
G. Ellsworth, E. Lea, P. Rooney, Ensemble

ACT 2[134]
Scene 1
Opening Chorus
Ensemble
"Persian Fantasy" (Persiana)
E. Lea
(*Lyrics by* Clarence Marks and Jack Stern.)
"When the Cat's Away"
T. Dingle, Harem Ladies
"A Little Dream That Lost Its Way"
H. Mayo, E. Hines
"I Love to Go Swimmin' with Wimmin'"
P. Rooney, Harem Girls
"Bokhara" (In Bokhara, Miss O'Hara?)
E. Murray
"(Two Little) Love Birds" (reprise)
R. Bold, E. Hines
"Love Will Always Find a Way" (Serenade)
R. Bold
Scene 3
"Carnival Night"
E. Cavanaugh, B. Greenwood, E. Lea, T. Dingle, Ensemble
Specialty
P. O'Brien
Finale
P. Rooney, M. Bent, Ensemble

THE RIGHT GIRL
1921.07

A Musical Comedy in Thee Acts. Book and lyrics by Raymond Peck. Music by Percy Wenrich. Staged by Walter Wilson. Dances by David Bennett. Settings by the Selwyn Studio, Servas. Costumes designed by Helen, Meyers, Bert French. Orchestra under the direction of J. Albert Browne. Orchestrations by Arthur Lange. Produced by the Gleerich Productions Inc.[135] Opened 15 March 1921 at the Times Square Theatre and closed 4 June 1921 after 98 performances[136].

CAST: *Anthony Stanton*, unlucky in love: EARLE BENHAM. *Henry Watkins*, his friend, a New Jersey judge: ROBERT WOOLSEY. *John Freeman*, his attorney: Frank Munnell. *Barry Darcy*, who tests Anthony's nerve: Rapley Holmes. *Dera Darcy*, his daughter: CAROLYN THOMSON. *Molly Darcy*, his niece: DOLLY CONNELLY. *Arthur Cadman*: Harry Redding. *Valera Valador*, a Spanish girl: Helen Montrose. A

[129]Previously produced in vaudeville at the Palace Theatre in 1917 with Sallie Fisher.
[130]No musical numbers listed. List prepared from published sheet music.
[131]Toured subsequently under the auspices of Pat Rooney, Inc.
[132]Replaced for the 1923-24 national tour by:
"The Prevalent Condition of the Mind"
E. Cavanaugh, B. Greenwood, Josephine Harmon (Mrs. Chateris), H. Mayo, E. Lea, T. Dingle, Ensemble

[133]For the 1923-24 national tour, "Murrayisms" and "Rooneyisms" were replaced by:
"Mind Your Own Business"
P. Rooney, M. Bent, E. Murray
[134]For the 1923-24 national tour, the following were added after "I Love to Go Swimmin' with Wimmin'":
"Laugh and Grow Fat"
E. Davenport
Septette
J. E. Sullivan, J. Harmon, H. Mayo, B. Greenwood, M. Bent, E. Cavanaugh, E. Murray
[135]During the run Virgil Randolph's name replaced Gleerich Productions Inc. as producer.
[136]Credits for settings, costumes and conductor did not appear in opening night programs.

Bootlegger: Louis F. Spaulding. *One of Anthony's Friends*: Elma Decker. *Messenger*: Frank Hope.

Friends, Guests, etc.: Misses Gertrude Bond, Leslie Grey, Ursula Ward, May Rushing, Mildred Mayo, Hazel Mack, Lucille Darling, Miriam Malloy, Jerry Trevor, Devah Worrell, Jean Farrell, Lela Norton, Beulah Clinton, Harriet Leslie, Mignon Reed, Moravia Loustanau. Messrs. Bud Davidson, Albert Barren, Jerry Child, Galem Graves, Joe Carey, Kenneth Smith, James Healy.

Act 1: Office of Anthony Stanton, New York City. About 5 P.M., Saturday afternoon, summer. (Selwyn.)

Act 2: Tea Garden of a Palm Beach Hotel. Afternoon, during the season. (Selwyn.)

Act 3: Living Room of Anthony's Palm Beach Home. 11 P.M. the same evening.(Servas.)

ACT 1

    "Cocktail Hour" (Opening)
        Girls, Boys

    "Things I Learned in Jersey"
        R. Woolsey, Girls

    "You'll Get Nothing from Me"
        D. Connolly

    "Girls All Around Me"
        E. Benham, Girls

    "Call of Love"
        C. Thomson

    "We Were Made to Love"
        Girls

    "Old Flames" (There's an Old Flame Burning)
        E. Benham, Girls

ACT 2

    "Rocking Chair Fleet"
        Girls, Boys

    "A Girl in Your Arms"
        C. Thomson, Boys

    "Love's Little Journey"
        D. Connolly

    "Harmony"
        C. Thomson, D. Connolly, E. Benham, R. Woolsey

    "Look for the Girl"
        R. Woolsey, Girls

    Finale
        Company

ACT 3

    "Aladdin"
        D. Connolly

    "Lovingly Yours"
        C. Thomson, E. Benham

    "Oriental Serenade"
        D. Connolly, C. Thomson

1921.08   # IT'S UP TO YOU

A Musical Girlicomedy (Musical Comedy) in Three Acts[137]. Book by Augustin McHugh and A. Douglas Leavitt. Music by John L. McManus and Manuel Klein. Lyrics by Edward Paulton and Harry Clarke. Staged by Frank Stammers. Dances arranged by David Bennett. Scenery designed by H. Robert Law. Costumes designed by Almerin Gowing. Orchestra under the direction of John L. McManus. Production under the personal direction of William Moore Patch. Produced by William Moore Patch. Opened 28 March 1921 at the Casino Theatre and closed 16 April 1921 after 24 performances.

CAST: *Three Modern Musketeers*: *Ned Spencer*: CHARLES KING. *Dick Dayton*: DOUGLAS LEAVITT. *Jim Duke*: HARRY SHORT. *Freddy Oliver*, in love with Harriet: Ray George. *Colonel Stephen Forrest*, with a lot of money: Albert Sackett. *A Collector*, who wants his money: Frank Michel. *Sheriff McCabe*, a legal persuader: Royal Cutter. *Harriet Hollistar*, in love with Ned Spencer: BETTY PIERCE. *Ethel Hollistar*, her sister: RUTH MARY LOCKWOOD. *Mrs. Van Lando Hollistar*, their mother: FLORENCE EARLE. *Lotta DeVere*, neglected musical comedy star: Norma Brown. *Hortense Gessitt*, a modern steno: Florence Hope. *Suzanne*, maid at the Hollistar's: Madeline Dare. *Russian Dancers*: Sacha Piatov, May Kitchen, Suzanne Rossi.

Guests at Mrs. Hollistar's Party: Pamelia Bradford, Lorraine Garrison, Thea Thompson, Ruby Hart, Marcia Byron, Belle Maycliff, Dorothy Selfridge, Gladys Dore. *At the Sale You Will Also Meet*: Majory Grant, Claire Daniels, Patricia Mayer, Violet Lobell, Madeleine Dare, Susanne Chase, Peggy Ellis, Phylis Reid. *Guests, Escorts, Clerks*: Thomas Dawber, Jack Andrews, Lawrence New, Harry Levoy, Leonard Mooney, George Carpentier, Almerin Gowing, Jack Clubly.

Act 1: At Mrs. Hollistar's Malba-on-the-Sound, Long Island. 11:30 P.M. on a May evening. "Laying the Foundation"

Act 2: Office of the Spencer Land & Realty Company, near Fairhaven, Long Island. Two months later in the Morning. "Building"

Act 3: The same, a year later. An evening late in August. "The House Warming"

ACT 1

    Opening
        Company

    "I Will, I Won't"
        R. M. Lockwood, R. George, Ensemble

    "Havana"
        D. Leavitt, C. King
        (*Music and Lyrics by* John L. McManus.)

    A Visualization
        N. Brown, Ensemble

    "Love Me"
        C. King, L. Rhodes
        (*Music and Lyrics by* Ray Perkins.)

ACT 2

    "I Want a Bungalow" (Opening)
        S. Rossi, M. Kitchen, Ensemble

    "When I Dance Alone"
        F. Hope, H. Short, Ensemble
        (*Music by* John L. McManus. *Lyrics by* Edward A. Paulton.)

    "Bee-Deedle Dee-Dum Dey"
        N. Brown, Ensemble, S. Piatov, M. Kitchen
        (*Music by* John L. McManus. *Lyrics by* Harry Clarke.)

    "Castles in the Air" (In Our Little Castle in Air)
        C. King, B. Pierce
        (*Music by* John L. McManus. *Lyrics by* Harry Clarke and John McManus.)

    "A Country Wife"
        B. Pierce, Ensemble

    "I Want a Home"
        R. M. Lockwood, D. Leavitt, Ensemble
        (*Music by* Manuel Klein. *Lyrics by* Edward A. Paulton.)

ACT 3

    "Dream Girl"
        B. Pierce, Ensemble

    Adagio Classique
        S. Piatov, M. Kitchen

    Pas de Trua
        S. Piatov, S. Rossi, M. Kitchen

    "After My Ship Comes In"
        C. King, Girls
        (*Music by* John L. McManus. *Lyrics by* Edward A. Paulton.)

    "I'll Tell the World"
        R. M. Lockwood, D. Leavitt
        (*Music by* John L. McManus. *Lyrics by* Edward A. Paulton.)

    "Those Oriental Blues"
        N. Brown, F. Hope, M. Kitchen, S. Rossi, Ensemble
        (*Music by* John L. McManus. *Lyrics by* Harry Clarke.)

    Finale
        Company

1921.09   # JUNE LOVE

A Musical Play in Two Acts. Book by Otto Harbach and W. H. Post. Based on a story ("In Search of a Sinner") by Charlotte Thompson. Music by Rudolf Friml. Lyrics by Brian Hooker. Production staged under the personal direction of George Vivian. Dance ensembles by David Bennett. Costumes designed by Bertha A. Fields. Orchestra under the direction of Gene Salzer. Produced by Sherman Brown. Opened 25 April 1921 at the Knickerbocker Theatre and closed 4 June 1921 after 48 performances[138].

---

[137]A revised version of the musical HI AND DRI which closed out of town in 1919.

[138]Settings uncredited.

CAST (in order of appearance): *Tiny Golden*: LOIS JOSEPHINE. *Mrs. Martia Golden*: Martha Mayo. *Bobbie Foster*, Tiny's caveman: CLARENCE NORDSTROM. *Geoffrey Love*, a wealthy sportsman: JAMES BILLINGS. *Jack Garrison*, amateur golf champion: W. B. DAVIDSON. *Eddie Evans*, a golf expert: JOHNNY DOOLEY. *Mrs. June Love*, Geoffrey's sister-in-law: ELSE ADLER. *Belle Bolton* of Broadway: BERTEE BEAUMONTE. *Thompson*, Garrison's valet: Lionel Pape. *Tiny's Friends (4)*: *Miss Summers*: Billie Shilling. *Miss Elisman*: Constance Madison. *Polly Smith*: Doris Landy. *Kitty Smith*: Alice Gordon. *Butler*: Robert Heft.

Ensemble: *Rita*: Rita Frederick. *Dorothy*: Dorothy Irving. *Irma*: Irma Irving. *Nancy*: Nancy Bateman. *Winifred*: Winifred Gibson. *Betty*: Betty Campbell. *Doris*: Doris Landy. *Billie*: Billie Shilling. *Dot*: Dorothy Tosbelle. *Bobbie*: Bobby Renys. *Martha*: Martha Wood. *Constance*: Constance Madison. *Lotta*: Lotta Corri. *Alice*: Alice Gordon. *Goldie*: Goldie Foley. *Mabel*: Mabel Grete. *Sopranos*: Caroline Cali, Eve Hackett, Mabel Taylor, Ann Greenway. *Tenors*: Tom Rice, Ralfe Manning, Paul Logan, Robert Heft, Leon Chrystal, Louis Laub. *Baritones*: Harrold Abbey, Harry Miller, Norman Williams. *Basses*: Boris Scott, Fred Grod, Sam Goodman.

Act 1: Porch and Garden at the Love's, somewhere near New York. The present.

Act 2: Reception Room in Geoffrey Love's Country Home.

ACT 1

　Opening Chorus
　　L. Josephine , Ensemble
　"Runaway Little Girl"
　　L. Josephine, C. Nordstrom, Ensemble
　"Keep Your Eye on the Ball"
　　J. Dooley, (assisted by)
　　　Misses D. Irving, I. Irving, C. Madison, B. Campbell, W. Gibson, M. Grete
　"Dear Love, My Love"
　　E. Adler, Ensemble
　"Don't Call Them Dearie" (Don't Keep Calling Me Dearie)
　　B. Beaumonte, C. Nordstrom
　"I'm Not in Love with You"
　　E. Adler, W. B. Davidson
　"Be Careful"
　　L. Josephine, B. Beaumonte, C. Nordstrom, J. Dooley
　Finale
　　E. Adler, Ensemble

ACT 2

　"The Harvest Moon"
　　C. Cali, Ensemble
　"The Egyptian Dance"
　　B. Beaumonte
　"The Spider's Web"
　　E. Adler, Girls
　"With a Woman You Never Can Tell"
　　J. Dooley, Specialty Six
　"Someone Like You" (Somebody Like You)
　　L. Josephine, W. B. Davidson, M. Wood, B. Renys, Ensemble
　"The Flapper and the Vamp"
　　B. Beaumonte
　"June Love"
　　E. Adler, W. B. Davidson
　"Comme Çi, Comme Ça"
　　L. Josephine, C. Nordstrom, Ensemble
　Finale

1921.10　TWO LITTLE GIRLS IN BLUE

A Musical Comedy in Three Acts, 4 Scenes. Book by Fred Jackson. Music by Paul Lannin and Vincent Youmans. Lyrics by Arthur Francis [Ira Gershwin]. Book and dances staged by Ned Wayburn. Scenery designed by H. Robert Law. Costumes designed by Shirley Barker, Iverson and Henneage. Orchestra under the direction of Charles Previn. Orchestrations by Stephen Jones and Paul Lannin. Produced by Abraham L. Erlanger. Opened 3 May 1921 at the George M. Cohan Theatre and closed 27 August 1921 after 135 performances.

CAST: *Dolly Sartoris*: MADELINE FAIRBANKS. *Polly Sartoris*: MARION FAIRBANKS. *Robert Barke*: OSCAR SHAW. *Jerry Lloyd*: FRED SANTLEY. *Morgan Atwell*: OLIN HOWLAND. *Hariette Neville*: EMMA JANVIER. *Ninon LaFleur*: JULIA KELETY. *Dudley La Fleur*: ETIENNE GIRARDOT. *Captain Morrow*: STANLEY JESSUP. *Jennings*, deck steward: Jack Tomson. *Kennedy*, library steward: Tommy Tomson. *Newton Canney*, a lawyer: Fred Hall. *Sammy Snipe*: Fred Hall. *Maid o' the Mist*: Vanda Hoff. *Orienta*, a Nautch girl: Vanda Hoff. *Cecile*, a ladies' maid: Vanda Hoff. *Margie*, a passenger: EVELYN LAW. *Ophelia*, a stewardess: Patricia Clarke. *Mary Bird*, a prima donna: Edith Decker. *The Bride*: Beulah McFarland.

Personality Contingent: Beulah McFarland, Peggy Underwood, Muriel Lodge, Caroline Erwin, Jacqueline Hunter, Margery Morrison, Kay Harrison, Rose Taylor, Edith Kessler, Helen Gates, Leonore Lukens, Rosemary Sill, Daisy Daniels, Dorothy Harrison, Jobyna Ralston, Fay West. *Male Ensemble*: Otis Harper, Fred Rogers, Harold Thompson, Frank Hall, Ellwood Gray, Paul Porter, Gayle Mays.

Act 1: S. S. *Empress* ready to sail for India.

Act 2, Scene 1: Main Saloon. *Scene 2*: Dolly's Cabin.

Act 3: Off the Indian Shore.

ACT 1

　"(We're Off on) A Wonderful Trip"
　　G. Mack, J. Tomson, T. Tomson, Ensemble
　　(*Music by* Vincent Youmans.)
　"(Your) Wonderful U.S.A."[139]
　　O. Howland, Ensemble
　　(*Music by* Paul Lannin.)
　"When I'm With the Girls"
　　O. Shaw, Chorus
　　(*Music by* Vincent Youmans.)
　"Two Little Girls in Blue"
　　Madeline Fairbanks, Marion Fairbanks
　　(*Music by* Vincent Youmans.)
　"The Silly Season"
　　E. Janvier, O. Shaw, F. Santley, E. Law, [Olive[140]], Chorus
　　(*Music by* Vincent Youmans.)
　"Oh Me, Oh My, Oh You"
　　O. Shaw, Marion Fairbanks
　　(*Music by* Vincent Youmans.)
　"You Started Something When You Came Along"
　　F. Santley, Madeline Fairbanks
　　(*Music by* Vincent Youmans.)
　Finale—"We're Off to India"
　　Ensemble
　　(*Music by* Vincent Youmans.)
　Maid of the Mist Ballet
　　(V. Hoff.)

ACT 2

　"Here, Steward"
　　J. Tomson, T. Tomson, P. Clarke, Chorus
　　(*Music by* Vincent Youmans.)
　"The Gypsy Trail"
　　J. Kelety, Male Chorus
　　(*Music by* Paul Lannin. *Lyrics by* Irving Caesar.)
　"Dolly"
　　O. Shaw, F. Santley, Chorus
　　(*Music by* Vincent Youmans. *Lyrics by* Arthur Francis [Ira Gershwin], Schuyler Greene.)
　"Who's Who With You?"
　　O. Shaw, Marion Fairbanks
　　(*Music by* Vincent Youmans.)
　"Just Like You"
　　F. Santley, Madeline Fairbanks, E. Decker, V. Hoff, J. Tomson, T. Tomson
　　(*Music by* Paul Lannin.)
　"There's Something About Me They Like"
　　O. Howland, E. Law, Girls
　　(*Music by* Vincent Youmans. *Lyrics by* Arthur Francis [Ira Gershwin], Fred Jackson.)
　"Rice and Shoes" (Sweetest Girl)
　　O. Shaw, F. Santley, Chorus
　　(*Music by* Vincent Youmans. *Lyrics by* Arthur Francis [Ira Gershwin], Schuyler Greene.)
　"She's Innocent" (Finale)
　　Ensemble

ACT 3

　"Honeymoon (When Will You Shine for Me?)"
　　J. Kelety, F. Santley, Chorus
　　(*Music by* Paul Lannin.)
　Dance
　　E. Law
　"I'm Tickled Silly" (Slapstick)
　　O. Howland, O. Shaw, F. Santley
　　(*Music by* Paul Lannin.)

---

[139]Dropped during the run.
[140]No character by the name of Olive appears in the cast list.

"Orienta"
  Ensemble
  (*Music by* Vincent Youmans.)
Nautch Dance
  V. Hoff
Reprise
  Ensemble

1921.11 PRINCESS VIRTUE

A Musical Comedy in Two Acts, 3 Scenes. Book, music and lyrics by B. C. Hilliam and (Lieutenant) Gitz Rice[141]. Staged by Leon Errol. Scenery by the P. Dodd Ackerman Studios. Gowns by Hickson, New York, under the supervision of Willie DeLignamare. Orchestra under the direction of Victor Baravalle. Produced by Gerald Bacon. Opened 4 May 1921 at the Central Theatre and closed 14 May 1921 after 13 performances.

CAST (in order of appearance): *Gautier, Proprietor of the Maison Gautier*: JULES EPAILLY. *Pierre, assistant to Gautier*: ALLEN FAGAN. *Francine, another assistant*: ALICE MAISON. *Mrs. Demarest from New York*: SARAH EDWARDS. *Miss Leadbeater, her companion*: Anne Page. *Bourbon, the Guide*: Hugh Cameron. *Bruce Crawford, an American*: BRADFORD KIRKBRIDE. *Carré, a Parisian dancer*: EARL A. FOX. *Hiram Demarest*: FRANK MOULAN. *Maxine, a Midinette*: Sylvia Elias. *Baron Transky*: ROBERT G. PITKIN. *Lane Demarest, "Princess Virtue"*: TESSA KOSTA. *Sir Arthur Gower, Liane's Step-father*: Frank Greene. *Claire Morin from the Moulin Rouge*: ZELLA RAMBEAU. *Francois, the Florist*: Charles Jerome. *Charlot, the Caterer*: Grady Miller. *Chic, the Costumier*: Leroy Montesanto. *Poisson, the Printer*: Harold Goulden.
  The Nobodies: Misses Penny Rowland, Sally Berry, Beth Meakins, Bessie Gross, Wilma Bruce, Marie Benedict, Grace Russell, Margaret Finley. *Shop Girls, Customers*: Misses Jessie Howe, Eleanor Wallace, Frances Stone, Arden Benlawin, Beth Carpenter, Alma Montefiore, Lucille Wallace, Hazel Mack, Elizabeth Cline, Jean Forsythe, Vera Rossander, Clare Burton, Katherine Valentine, Josephine Doane, Yvonne LaGrange, Dorothy Stokes, Opal Essent, Betty Palmer.

Act 1: The Maison Gautier, Paris.
Act 2, Scene 1: Sunken Garden adjoining the Chateau of Sir Arthur Gower at Deauville. *Scene 2*: The same. Evening.

ACT 1
  "When My Lady Goes in Quest of Finery" (Opening Ensemble)
    J. Epailly, Chorus
  Dear Sweet Eyes"
    B. Kirkbride
  Waltz
    A. Fagan, A. Maison
  "Eight Little Nobodys"
    E. A. Fox, Nobodies
  "The Modern Village Blacksmith"
    F. Moulan, Quartette
  "There's Something Irresistible About Me"
    R. Pitkin, Girls
  "Princess Virtue"
    T. Kosta, Ensemble
  "Life Is All Sunshine with You"
    E. A. Fox, Z. Rambeau, Ensemble
  Dance
    A. Fagan, A. Maison
  Quartette
    G. Miller, L. Montesano, H. Goulden, C. Jerome
  "Smoke Rings"
    T. Kosta, B. Kirkbride
  "Seeing Paris"
    Z. Rambeau, F. Moulan
  "Perfect Song of Love"[142] (Finale)
    Principals, Ensemble
ACT 2
Scene 1
  Opening Ensemble

"Voices of Youth"
  S. Edwards
Cane Dance (Specialty)
  A. Maison, A. Fagan
"While My Wife's Away"
  F. Moulan, Nobodies
"Clothes"
  F. Moulan, R. Pitkin, E. A. Fox, H. Cameron, J. Epailly
"(Little) Red Riding Hood"
  Z. Rambeau, F. Moulan, Chorus
"When I Meet Love"
  T. Kosta, Nobodies
"Quarreling Duet"
  T. Kosta, B. Kirkbride
Finale
  Principals, Ensemble
Front Scene
  Eight Nobodies
Scene 2
"Moonlight"
  S. Elias, Quartette, Ensemble
Pierrot Dance
  A. Fagan, A. Maison
"Bacchanale"
  Ensemble
"Toddling Along" (Specialty)
  Principals, Ensemble
Grand Finale
  Principals, Ensemble

1921.12 BIFF! BING! BANG!

The Dumbells[143] in Their Overseas (Musical) Revue in Two Acts (from Canada). Sketches by Jack McLaren. Dances arranged by Alan Murray. Gowns by Leonard Young. Musical director, Ivor E. Ayre. Produced by Captain M. W. Plunkett. Opened 9 May 1921 at the Ambassador Theatre and closed 9 July 1921 after 73 performances[144].

CAST: ROSS HAMILTON, "RED" NEWMAN, ALBERT PLUNKETT, JACK McLAREN, CAPTAIN M. W. PLUNKETT, ARTHUR (Jock) HOLLAND, FRED FENWICK, CHARLES McLEAN, TED CHARTERS, JIMMY GOODE, Bill Tennant, Frank Brayford, Tom Young, Jack Ayer, Leonard Young, Alan Murray, Ben Allen, Morley Plunkett, Bobby Scott, Bert Wilkinson, Percy Campbell, Arthur Witham, Arthur Nicholson.

ACT 1
Scene 1
  "Goodbye Khaki!" (Opening)
    F. Fenwick, Company
  "All the Girls Are Lovely By the Sea"
    J. McLaren, Company
Scene 2
  "A Little Nonsense"
    J. Goode
Scene 3
  Hi and Si's[145]
    R. Newman, C. McLean

---

[141]Tryout programs credit a story by Louise Winter as source material; advertising for the New York engagement credit "French sources." Management declined to divide authorship credit between Messrs. Hilliam and Rice.
[142]Adapted from Franz Lizst's Second Nocturne, known as Lizst's 'Love Dream.'

---

[143]Program note: The 'Dumbells' Company was the official entertainment corps of the third division of the Canadian Army in France and is composed entirely of men who have done their "bit" in the trenches. The average active service record of each man being eighteen months. After the war the organization was kept intact by Captain Plunkett and they have been appearing in England and Canada for the past two years as a regular theatrical attraction. This gives them a record of two years as entertainers in France, a season in London and eighty-four weeks in Canada—and now New York—?
[144]Settings uncredited.
[145]Replaced during the run by:
  "A Spanish Cocktail"
    R. Newman, C. McLean

Scene 4

    "Dreams of Delight!"

        Marjorie (R. Hamilton), Boys

Scene 5

    "I Know Where the Flies Go (on a Cold and Frosty Morning)"

        A. Plunkett

        (*Music by* Sam Mayo. *Lyrics by* Sam Mayo and John Harrington.)

Scene 6

    "Take a Look at Me Now"[146]

        A. Holland

Scene 7

    "What of the Night (Watchman)"

        Octette[147]

Scene 8

    "D. S. O."[148]

        R. Newman

Scene 9

    Behind the Lines

        Buddie: T. Young. *Madame*: C. McLean. *Marie*: F. Fenwick. *Poilu*: A. Murray. *Q. M. Sergeant*: J. McLaren. *Jerry*: F. Brayford. *Tanky*: T. Young. *Red*: R. Newman. *Soldiers*: Themselves.

            Note: To those at home who have so often wondered "what is he doing?" the Dumbells bring this picture of one side of life overseas. To those who were there, who found momentary forgetfulness of their troubles in the Estaminet's genial atmosphere, the picture will perhaps bring memories of some of the things that helped them forget what had been yesterday and what was to be tomorrow; memories of warmth and light; laughter and music; fun and fellowship of friends. This skit was first played in France by the original "Princess Pats" (P.P.C.L.I.) Party in 1916 and 1917.

    Finale

        Company

ACT 2

Scene 1

    Some Songs

        Octette

        At the Piano: Leon and Young. *Violin*: A. Witham.

Scene 2

    More Nonsense

        J. Goode

Scene 3

    "A Little Bit of Scotch"

        A. Holland, Chorus

Scene 4

    "Oh, Oh, Oh, It's a Lovely War"

        R. Newman

        (*Music and Lyrics by* J. P. Long and M. Scott.)

Scene 5

    "Some Day I'll Make You Love Me"

        Marjorie (R. Hamilton)

Scene 6

    "Just a Policeman"[149]

        T. Charters, assisted by A. Holland, J. McLaren

Scene 7

    "(Way) Down Texas Way"

        A. Plunkett

        (*Music and Lyrics by* Fred Godfrey, A. J. Mills and Bennett Scott.)

Scene 8

    The Duchess Entertains

---

[146]Replaced during the run by:

    "O, Cherie—La La"

        A. Holland

[147]Octette consisted of Messrs. Murray, Allen, Scott, Brayford, Tennent, Wilkinson, A. Plunkett, M. Plunkett, T. Young.

[148]Replaced during the run by:

    "Medals on My Chest" (*by* Waite)

        R. Newman

[149]Replaced during the run by:

    "Kit Inspection"

        T. Charters

    The Duchess: L. Young. *Mlle. Tres Moutarde*: C. McLean. *Flossy Fuclose*: A. Murray. '*Scotty*': J. McLaren. '*Strike Me Pink*': R. Newman.

Scene 9

    Finale

        Entire Company

1921.13   PHOEBE OF QUALITY STREET

A Comedy with Music in Two Acts and a Prologue. Adapted (book, lyrics) by Edward Delaney Dunn. Based on the play 'Quality Street' by Sir James M. Barrie (and its adaptation the German operette 'Drei alte Schachteln" with book by Hermann Haller, Lyrics by Rideamus). Music by Walter Kollo. Staged by W. H. Gilmore. Dances arranged by Max Scheck. Costumes designed by the Mode Costume Company. Orchestra under the direction of Max Steiner. Produced under the personal direction of J. J. Shubert. Produced by the Messrs. Lee and J. J. Shubert. Opened 9 May 1921 at the Sam S. Shubert Theatre and closed 21 May 1921 after 16 performances.

CAST: *Phoebe Throssel*: DOROTHY WARD. *Susan Throssel*: Jessamine Newcomb. *Valentine Brown*: WARREN PROCTOR. *Sergeant Terence O'Toole*: SHAUN GLENVILLE. *Patty*: GERTRUDE MUDGE. *Miss Willoughby*: Muriel Tindal. *Fanny Willoughby*: Mary McCord. *Henrietta Trumbull*: Marie Pettes. *Lieutanant Spier*: Lucius Metz. *Ensign Blades*: Joe Tinsley. *Charlotte*: Gertrude Blair. *Harriet*: Lillian Wilck. *Isabella*: Elaine McIntosh. *Elizabeth*: Marie Farrell. *Georgie*: Alfred Little. *William Smith*: Thomas Victory. *June*: Uarda Burnett. *Dancers*: THE GLORIAS.

    Ladies: Patricia Clifford, Catherine Frank, Beth Ormby, Florence Pettingill, Irene Gilmore, Kitty Leckie, Ethel Carlin, Elsie Clifton, Nancy Vaughn. *Officers*: James Smith, Minor McLain, Oliver Stewart, Arthur Cardinal, Jack Kearns, Ernest Miller, Dennis Murray, Thomas Manners. *Children*: Ruth Cloos, Dorothy Kitchen, Grace Durkin, James Coudert.

The action takes place in an English Country Town during the Napoleonic Wars.

Prologue: The Home of the Misses Throssel in Quality Street.

Act 1: Same as the Prologue. Five years later.

Act 2: At the Ball in the Regimental Barracks. Evening of the same day.

PROLOGUE

    Opening

        Ensemble

    "Dream of Joy"

        D. Ward

    Finale:

    Recitative; "You'll Find the Rainbow" (Promise of the Rainbow)

        W. Proctor

        (*Lyrics by* Mrs. Edward Delaney Dunn.)

ACT 1

    Gavotte

        D. Ward, Children

    March Incidental

    "(The) Autumn Sun" (Solo)

        W. Proctor

    "Dawn Turns to Morning" (Dawn Grows to Morning)(Duet)

        D. Ward, W. Proctor

    "It Is Safe to Depend on the Irish" (Duet)

        G. Mudge, S. Glenville

    "I Want To Be Merry" (Oh, Let Us Be Merry)(Solo)

        D. Ward

        (*Lyrics by* Mrs. Edward Delaney Dunn.)

ACT 2

    Dance

        The Glorias

    "Little Wallflowers" (Quintet)

        J. Newcomb, 4 Wallflowers

    "O'Toole" (Solo)

        S. Glenville, Girls

    "Waltzing Is Passing from Land to Land" (Waltzing Is Spreading from Land to Land)

        (Waltz Ensemble)

            D. Ward, W. Proctor, Ensemble

    "Let's Make Up" (Duet)

        G. Mudge, S. Glenville

        (*Lyrics by* Mrs. Edward Delaney Dunn.)

    Finale

1921.14 THE LAST WALTZ

An Operetta in Three Acts. (Original German book for "Der letzte Walzer" and lyrics by Julius Brammer and Alfred Grünwald.) English adaptation by Harold Atteridge and Edward Delaney Dunn. Music by Oscar Straus. Additional music by Alfred Goodman. Staged by J. C. Huffman and Frank Smithson. Musical numbers staged by Allan K. Foster and Jack Mason. Stage settings by Watson Barratt. Orchestra under the direction of Oscar Radin. Entire production under the personal direction of Mr. J. J. Shubert. Produced by the Messrs. Lee and J. J. Shubert and United Plays Company. Opened 10 May 1921 at the Century Theatre and closed 29 October 1921 after 185 performances[150].

CAST (in order of appearance): *General Miecu Krasian*: CLARENCE HARVEY. *Vandalian Officers (4)*: *Ensign Orsinski*: Rex Carter. *Captain Kaminski*: JOHN V. LOWE. *Lieutenant Matlain*: Ted Lorraine. *Adjutant Labinescue*: Irving Rose. *Mariette*: Ruth Mills. *Vladek*: Timothy Daly. *Lieutenant Jack Merrington, U.S.N.*: WALTER WOOLF. *Mat Maltby*, Lieutenant Merrington's orderly: JAMES BARTON. *Vera Lizaveta*: ELEANOR PAINTER. *Countess Alexandrowna Corpulinski*, her mother: Florence Morrison. *Other Daughters of the Countess (4)*: *Annuschka*: BEATRICE SWANSON. *Hannuschka*: MARCELLA SWANSON. *Petruschka*: GLADYS WALTON. *Babushka*: ELEANOR GRIFFITH. *Baron Ippolith*: HARRY FENDER. *Grand Duke Hubenstitch*: George Evans. *Carmenina*: Isabel Rodriguez. *Dancers*: (John) GIURAN and MARGUERITE. *Prince Paul*, Regent of Vandalia: HARRISON BROCKBANK. *Dancers at the Royal Opera (5)*: *Chochette*: Rena Manning. *Lolo*: Nan Rainsford. *Sylvette*: Helen Herendeen. *Babette*: Carolyn Reynolds. *Francine*: Jean Thomas. *Zadie*: Amelia Allen. *Ladies and Gentlemen, Dancers, Masqueraders, Soldiers, Servants*.

Ladies of the Ensemble: Nan Rainsford, Chase Herendeen, Helen Herendeen, Virginia Calmer, May Jennings, Betty Walsh, Carolyn Reynolds, Nita Miramar, Ann Delmore, Aquilla Sharpe, Adolphia Sharpe, Bruzilla Sharpe, Thelma Smith, Yvonne Linnard, Thelma Turnbull, Rena Manning, Anna May Dennehy, Florence Darling, Marjorie Muir, Ruth Shaw, Marie LaVon, Mary Kissel, Corine Jackson, Peggy Glendenning, May Beck, Jean Wallace, Bunny Castle, Sybil Morais, Clio Ayres, Jean Troupman, Jean Thomas, Gladys Davis, Dorothy Laudena, Donna Mobley, Peggy Brown, Catherine Flynn. *Gentlemen of the Ensemble*: William Tillet, Alfred Brauning, Harry Rosedale, John Castle, Max Rosenberg, Murray Minehart, John Miller, George Levoy, Walton Ford, Ben Jackson, Marc Roselle.

The action takes place in Vandalia, a Kingdom in the Balkans near the Russian Frontier, at the present.

Act 1: Drawing Room in the Castle of General Krasian, near the City of Vandalia.

Act 2: Ballroom in the Castle of General Krasian.

Act 3: Drawing Room in the Palace of Prince Paul, Regent of Vandalia.

ACT 1

  Opening Ensemble
  "Hail to Our General"
    Officers, Men
  "The Next Dance With You"
    J. V. Lowe, R. Carter, J. Thomas, R. Mills
    (*Music by* Alfred Goodman. *Lyrics by* Louis Friedman.)
  "Live for Today"
    W. Woolf, Officers, Men
    (*Music by* Alfred Goodman, A. Werau. *Lyrics by* Harold Atteridge.)
  "(The) Charming Ladies"
    J. Barton, Chorus
    (*Music by* Alfred Goodman, A. Werau. *Lyrics by* Harold Atteridge.)
  "My Heart Is Waking"
    E. Painter
  "Roses Out of Reach"
    E. Painter
  Dance Polka
    H. Fender, B. Swanson, M. Swanson, G. Walton
  "The Last Waltz"
    E. Painter, W. Woolf, Chorus
    (*Lyrics by* Edward Delaney Dunn.)
  Finale
    Ensemble

ACT 2

  Dance
    J. Giuran, Marguerite
  "Reminiscence"[151]
    E. Painter, W. Woolf

  "Ladies Choice"
    J. Barton, J. V. Lowe, I. Rose, R. Carter, B. Swanson, M. Swanson, G. Walton
  "Bring Him My Love Thoughts"[152]
    E. Painter, Ensemble
  "A Baby in Love"
    E. Griffith, H. Fender
    (*Music by* Ralph Benatzky, Alfred Goodman. *Lyrics by* Harold Atteridge.)
  "Fading Golden Love Dream" (Now Fades My Golden Love Dream)
    (*Lyrics by* Edward Delaney Dunn.)
    E. Painter, W. Woolf
  Balalaika Dance[153]
    J. Giuran
  Finale
    E. Painter, W. Woolf, Ensemble

ACT 3

  Egyptian Dance
    J. Guiran, Marguerite
  Dance Espagnol
    I. Rodriguez, J. Barton
  "The Whip Hand"
    H. Brockbank, Chorus
    (*Music by* Rudolf Nelson. *Lyrics by* Harold Atteridge.)
  "Oo-La-La"[154]
    E. Painter
    (*Lyrics by* Edward Delaney Dunn.)
  Finale
    Ensemble

1921.15 THE THREE MUSKETEERS

A Musical Costume Play (Operetta) in Two Acts, 8 Scenes. Book, music and lyrics by Richard W. Temple. (Adapted from the novel of the same name by Alexandre Dumas.) Staged by Richard W. Temple. Costumes by Eaves. Scenery built by Theodore Reisig. Musical director, Ernest Knoch. Produced by Richard W. Temple (for the Southern Light Opera Company). Opened 19 May 1921 at the Manhattan Opera House and closed 23 May 1921 after 5 performances.

CAST: *Louis XIII*, King of France and Poland: CHARLES ANGELO. *Anne of Austria*, Queen of France: PAULA TEMPLE. *Armand, Jean Duplesis, Duc de Richelieu* (Cardinal Richelieu): EDWARD EMERY. *Lady de Winter*, known as 'Miladi,' agent of the Cardinal: WINIFRED VERINA. *Constance Bonacieux*, seamstress to the Queen: JEAN WILKINS. *George Villiers, Duke of Buckingham*, Prime Minister to Charles I: B. N. Lewin. *Comte de Rochefort*, agent of the Cardinal: Leo Stark. *De Treville*, Captain of the Musketeers: LEONARD BOOKER. *The Three Musketeers*: *Athos*: PERCY CARR. *Porthos*: JOHN PARSONS. *Aramis*: J. HUMBIRD DUFFY. *D'Artagnan*: RICHARD W. TEMPLE. *Monsieur Bonacieux*, husband of Constance: EDWARD FAVOR. *De Jussac*, Captain of the Cardinal's Guards: Hedley Hall. *Cardinal's Guards (4)*: *Biscarat*: Frederick Saunders. *Bernajoux*: Gerald Ewing. *De Busigny*: Lionel Langtry. *Cahusac*: Hiram Murphy. *Ladies in Waiting (6)*: *Madame de Bois-Tracy*: Elsie Meyer. *Madame de Surgis*: Hilda Steiner. *Madame d'Aigullon*: Grace Wood. *Madame de Lannoy*: Ethel Cook. *Madame d'Estrees*: Edith Hughes. *Donna Estafania*: Annabel Grey. *Gabrielle*, a dancer: Beatrice Whitney. *Landlord of The Jolly Miller*: J. H. Kline. *A Waiter*: J. Perloff. *The Spanish Grandee*: Sidney Stone. *An Agent of the Cardinal*: Percy Richards. *Patrick*, valet to the Duke of Buckingham: J. H. Kline. *Secretary to the Duke of Buckingham*: Sidney Stone. *A Jeweler*: Hedley Hall. *A Chamberlain*: Lorenzo Vitale. *The Monk*: Frank Petell.

Peasants, Shopkeepers, Valets, Street Vendors, Musketeers, Cardinal's Guard, Ladies in Waiting.

Act 1, Scene 1: The Village of Meung, France. April 1625. *Scene 2*: Outside the Headquarters of the Musketeers, Paris. Two days later. *Scene 3*: The Boudoir of Queen Anne in the Palace of the Louvre, Paris. One week later.

Act 1, Scene 1: D'Artagnan's apartment in the House of Constance Bonacieux, Paris. *Scene 2*: The Ride from Paris to the Coast. *Scene 3*: The Port of Calais, France. *Scene 4*: Room in Buckingham Palace, London. *Scene 5*: Ball Room in the Hotel de Ville. Paris.

---

[150]Costumes uncredited.
[151]Dropped for subsequent tour.

---

[152]Replaced for subsequent tour by:
  "The Song of the Mirror" (The Mirror Song)
    E. Painter, Ensemble
    (*Lyrics by* Edward Delaney Dunn.)
[153]Dropped during the run.
[154]Dropped late in the run, then re-instated.

ACT 1
Scene 1
  "This Sleepy Old Village of Meung" (Opening Chorus)
  "I'm Going to Join the Musketeers" (Song)
    R. W. Temple
Scene 2
  "Paris! Paris!" (Opening Chorus)
  "Yes I Am Here" (Trio)
    P. Carr, J. Parsons, J. H. Duffy
  "Oh! Friendship!" (Quartette)
    P. Carr, J. Parsons, J. H. Duffy, R. Temple
Scene 3
  "Oh Lovely Star of Night" (Chorus of Ladies)
  "Venus and Mars" (Recitative—Song)
    P. Temple
  "But Put Thy Hand in Mine" (Song)
    P. Temple
  "Bold Musketeers" (Entrance of Musketeers)
  Finale
    Ensemble

ACT 2
Scene 1
  Opening Chorus
    Trades People of Paris
  "You'll Have to Find Another Girl" (Duet)
    J. Wilkins, R. W. Temple
  "Now Drink a Glass with Me My Friends" (Quintette)
    J. Wilkins, P. Carr, J. Parsons, J. H. Duffy, R. W. Temple
Scene 2
  "Riding Through the Mist and Mire" (Chorus)
Scene 4
  "Honour and Glory" (Chorus, Royal Anthem)
  Vocal March
    P. Carr, J. Parsons, J. H. Duffy, J. Wilkins, Ladies of Court, Musketeers
  "The Articles of Toilette for a Lady" (Song)
    J. H. Duffy
Scene 5
  "Oh! Who Will Be a Queen!"
    P. Temple, J. Wilkins, P. Carr, J. Parsons, J. H. Duffy, Chorus

1921.16   # SHUFFLE ALONG

An All-Negro Musical Comedy in Two Acts, 9 Scenes. Book by Flournoy Miller and Aubrey Lyles[155]. Music by Eubie Blake. Lyrics by Noble Sissle. Staged by Walter Brooks. Dances arranged by Charles Davis and Lawrence Deas. Orchestra under the direction of Eubie Blake. Musical arrangements by Will Vodery. Produced by Nikko Producing Company (John Scholl, Al Mayer, Flournoy Miller, Aubrey Lyles, Noble Sissle, Eubie Blake)[156]. Opened 23 May 1921 at the 63rd Street Music Hall and closed 15 July 1922 after 484 performances.

CAST (in order of appearance): *At the Piano:* EUBIE BLAKE. *Jim Williams,* Proprietor of Jimtown Hotel: Paul Floyd. *Jessie Williams,* His Daughter: LOTTIE GEE. *Ruth Little,* Her Chum: GERTRUDE SAUNDERS. *Harry Walton,* Candidate for Mayor: ROGER MATTHEWS. *Board of Aldermen (4):* Richard Cooper, Arthur Porter, Arthur Woodson, Snippy Mason. *Mrs. Sam Peck,* Suffragette: MATTIE WILKS. *Tom Sharper,* Political Boss: NOBLE SISSLE. *Steve Jenkins,* Candidate for Mayor: FLOURNOY E. MILLER. *Sam Peck,* Another Candidate for Mayor: AUBREY LYLES. *Jack Penrose,* Detective: Lawrence Deas. *Rufus Loose,* War Relic: C. Wesley Hill. *Soakum Flat,* Mayor's Bodyguard: A. E. Baldwin. *Strutt,* Jim Town Swell: Billy Williams. *Uncle Tom:* Charles Davis. *Old Black Joe:* Bob Williams. *Secretary to Mayor:* Ina Duncan.
Jazz Jasmines: Misses Goldie Cisco, Mildred Brown, Theresa West, Jennie Day, Adelaide Hall, Lillian Williams, Beatrice Williams, Evelyn Irving. *Happy Honeysuckles:* Misses Ruth Seward, Lucia Johnson, Marguerite Weaver, Bee Freeman, Marion Gee, Mamie Lewis, Marie Roberts. *Syncopating Sunflowers:* A. E. Baldwin,

Charles Davis, Bernard Johnson, Robert Lee, Snippy Mason, Miles Williams, Arthur Woodson, Bob Williams. *Majestic Magnolias:* Misses Edna Battles, Ina Duncan, Lula Wilson, Hazel Burke, Paula Sullican.

The action takes place on Election Day in Jimtown, in Dixieland.

Act 1, Scene 1: Exterior of Jimtown Hotel. *Scene 2:* Possum Lane. *Scene 3:* Jenkins' and Peck's Grocery Store. *Scene 4:* Public Square[157].

Act 2, Scene 1: Calico Corners. *Scene 2:* Possum Lane. *Scene 3:* The Mayor's Office. *Scene 4:* Saunders Lane. *Scene 5:* Ball Room of Jimtown's Hotel.

ACT 1[158]
  Opening Chorus
    Entire Company on Election Day
  "(I'm) Simply Full of Jazz"
    G. Saunders, Syncopation Steppers
  "Love Will Find a Way" (Duet)
    L. Gee, R. Matthews
  "Bandana Days"
    A. Porter, Company
  "Sing Me to Sleep, Dear Mammy"[159]
    R. Matthews, Board of Aldermen
  "(In) Honeysuckle Time (When Emmaline Said She'd Be Mine)"
    N. Sissle
  "Gypsy Blues"[160]
    L. Gee, G. Saunders, R. Matthews
  Grand Finale
    Entire Population of Jimtown
ACT 2
  "Shuffle Along"
    Jimtown Pedestrians, Traffic Cop
  "(I'm Just) Wild About Harry"
    L. Gee, Jimtown Sunflowers
  Jimtown's Fisticuffs
    F. E. Miller, A. Lyles
  "Syncopation Stenos"
    Mayor's Staff
  Selections ["Good Night Angeline"]
    Board of Aldermen
  "If You Haven't Been Vamped by a Brownskin, You Haven't Been Vamped at All"
    F. E. Miller, A. Lyles, Jimtown Vamps
  "Uncle Tom and Old Black Joe"
    C. Davis, B. Williams
  "Everything Reminds Me of You" (Duet)
    L. Gee, R. Matthews
  "Oriental Blues"
    N. Sissle, Oriental Girls
  "I Am Craving for That Kind of Love" (Kiss Me)/"Daddy (Won't You Please Come Home)"
    G. Saunders
  A Few Minutes with Sissle and Blake
    ["Serenade Blues," "Ain'tcha Comin' Back Mary Ann to Maryland," "Love Will Find a Way," "Lowdown Blues," "Pickaninny Shoes," "Out in No Man's Land," "Buzz Mirandy," "How Ya Gonna Keep 'Em Down on the Farm After They've Seen Paree?" (*Music by* Walter Donaldson, *Lyrics by* Sam M. Lewis and Joe Young.)]
  "Baltimore Buzz"
    N. Sissle, Jimtown's Jazz Steppers
  "African Dip"
    F. E. Miller, A. Lyles
  Finale by Entire Outfit
    Including You

---

[155]According to Henry T. Sampson in his book "Blacks in Blackface," Miller and Lyles based the story on two previous works, "Mayor of Dixie" (1905) and "Who's Stealing?" (1918).
[156]Later Shuffle Along, Inc. billed as producer.

[157]Scene dropped by February 1922.
[158]Added during run:
    "My Vision Girl" (from MIDNIGHT ROUNDERS OF 1920)
[159]During the run moved to Act 2 after "Jimtown's Fisticuffs" and replaced in Act 1 by:
    "Uncle Tom and Old Black Joe"
    C. Davis, B. Williams
[160]Later programs carried the note (with apologies to Victor Herbert).

1921.17

SUN-KIST

A Pacific Coast Musical Extravaganza (Revue) in Two Acts, 14 Scenes. Book, music and lyrics by Fanchon and Marco (Wolff). Scenery by Newby and Alexander, San Francisco. Gowns by Miss Fanchon (for herself), Eva Clark (all others). Orchestra under the direction of Reuben Wolff. Produced by Fanchon and Marco (Wolff). Opened 23 May 1921 at the Globe Theatre, moved 20 June 1920 to the Sam H. Harris Theatre, and closed 2 July 1921 after 48 performances.

CAST (in order of appearance): *Willie Logan*, an office boy: ARTHUR WEST. *Violet Ray*, a stenographer: DAISY DeWITTE. *Chester P. Hemingway*, a scenario writer: JOHN SHEEHAN. *Mack Phelan*, a motion picture director: JACK SQUIRE. *Gladys Sullivan*, a movie child actress: LUCILLE HARMON. *Annabelle Foster*, a social leader in the movies: EVA CLARK. *Two 'Nut' Applicants* trying to break into the movies: EDDIE NELSON, DELL CHAIN. *The Indian Idol*: MURIEL STRYKER. *Two Peppy Kids*: Ivanelle Ladd, Sybil Stuart. *Miss Smiles*: Marcia Adair. *The Dancers*: Wright Dancers. *Jeanette Dare*: MISS FANCHON (Wolff). *Jack Cartwright*: MR. MARCO (Wolff). *Assistant Director*: DONALD KERR. *Aspiring Movie Queens, Property Men, Carpenters, Gypsies, Indians, Race Track Hangerson, etc. etc.*

Ensemble: Sybil Stuart, Ferris Hallet, Lorena Hall, Martha Hicks, Nita Susoff, Dorothy Vardon, Rowena Ray, Merriam Wallace, Blanche Roberts, Evyleen Gerald, Edythe Marshall, Aileen Forbes, Olga Broadwell, Helen Gilmour.

The action takes place in Hollywood and Mexico at the present time.

Act 1, Scene 1: Interior, Rainbow Film Company's Office. *Scene 2*: En route to Gypsy location. *Scene 3*: Gypsy Life on location. *Scene 4*: Exterior Rainbow Film Company. *Scene 5*: Shooting a Scene at the Studio: A Trapper's Cabin in the Frozen Northwest. *Scene 6*: The I Dunno Wat. *Scene 7*: In California.

Act 2, Scene 1: Indian Location. The Shrine of the Zunis, etc. *Scene 2*: Shooting a Scene at Tiajuana. *Scene 3*: A Pretty Dance is Like a Violin. *Scene 4*: Exterior. Sunset Inn at Tiajuana, Mexico. *Scene 5*: Interior Sunset Inn, Tiajuana, Mexico. Banquet Scene. *Scene 6*: What the Critics Said. *Scene 7*: Fanchon's Fancies.

ACT 1[161]

Scene 1

"Breaking into the Movies"
Ensemble

"Bragging Song"
A. West

"My Sweetie's Smile"
J. Squire, D. DeWitte, Ensemble
Cameraman: M. Stryker. *Bride*: I. Ladd. *Groom*: E. Gerald. *Preacher*: H. Gilmour. *Other Queens*: Ensemble.

Scene 3

Dance by Gypsies
Wright Dancers

"The Love a Gypsy Knows"
E. Clark

Gypsy Dance
Miss Fanchon, Mr. Marco

Scene 4

"Use Your Judgement"
E. Nelson, D. Chain

Scene 5

"They Call Me Pollyana"
L. Herman
'Little Nell': Miss Fanchon. *'Big-Hearted Ned'*: Mr. Marco. *Ralph Stackpole*: A. West. *Director*: J. Squire. *Props*: Eph and Zeke. *Little Jasper*: Himself. *Glad Girls*: S. Stuart, I. Ladd, F. Hallett, D. Vardon, R. Ray, M. Hicks, A. Forbes, D DeWitte.

Scene 6

"The I Dunno Wat" (The I-Dun-No-Wat)
D. Kerr, assisted by D. DeWitte, L. Harmon

Scene 7

"I Want to Meet You (Some Day) in California"
Miss Fanchon

The Birth of Jazz
Mr. Marco

Finale
Entire Company

Intermission Specialty by Charles Seiger and Reuben Wolff

ACT 2

Scene 1

The Shrine of the Zunis:

Ceremonial Chant
Virgin Maidens

The Scalp Dance
Wright Dancers

The Dance
M. Stryker
The Bronze Image: M. Stryker. *High Priestess*: E. Clark.
The Legend of the Zuni Tribe tells of a young warrior turned to bronze, but none the less guardian of the Sacred Jewels of the ancestors, the belief being that at the approach of outside danger to the secret shrine where the jewels are hid, the deified warrior comes to life and relent-lessly takes to the trail, avenging the violation of the sacred precincts. The ceremonial worship is yearly conducted by the virgin maidens and priestesses.

Scene 2

Shooting a Scene at Tiajuana
J. Squire, D. Chain, A. West

Scene 3

"A Pretty Dance Is Like a Violin"
Mr. Marco

Song ["Comin' Through the Rye"]
E. Clark

Beethoven's Minuet
S. Stuart, E. Marshall

Souvenir Drdla
A. Forbes, H. Gilmour

Pizzicato Delibes
E. Gerald

Pierrot and Pierette
N. Susoff, I. Ladd

Orientale
M. Stryker

Drigo's Serenade
Miss Fanchon, Mr. Marco

Scene 4

"For No Reason Whatsoever"
E. Nelson, D. Chain

Scene 5

Hi Henry's Minstrels on Parade
D. Kerr, E. Nelson, Peaches

"Lo! Hear the Gentle Lark" (Solo)
E. Clark

Dance Impressions
Miss Fanchon, Mr. Marco

Scene 6

"What the Critics Said"
A. West

Scene 7

Fanchon's Fancies
D. Vardon, D. DeWitte, E. Gerald, H. Gilmour, A. Forbes, O. Broadwell, R. Ray, B. Roberts, M. Wallace

Misses Jazz
I. Ladd, S. Stuart, F. Hallett, M. Hicks, L. Hall, M. Stryker

---

[161] Also performed in the New York engagement, as per published sheet music:
"Ain't We Got Fun"
(*Music by* Richard Whiting. *Lyrics by* Gus Kahn and Raymond Egan.)

Charlotte Greenwood, Autographed Carte de Viste (Photo: Otto Sarony Co., Undated)
Museum of the City of New York

1921–1922 SEASON

(SELWYN'S) SNAPSHOTS OF 1921

1921.18

A Travesty Revue in Two Acts, 15 Scenes. Music by George Gershwin, Con Conrad, José Padilla, George Meyer, Malvin F. Franklin, Harry Ruby, James Monaco, Leopold Godowsky. Lyrics by E. Ray Goetz, Con Conrad, Frances Nordstrom, Alex Gerber, Bert Kalmar, Sidney Mitchell, Grant Clarke. Directed by Leon Errol. Musical director, Herbert Stothart. Produced by the Selwyns (Edgar, Arch) and Lew Fields. Opened 2 June 1921 at the Selwyn Theatre and closed 9 July 1921 after 44 performances; re-opened 25 July 1921 at the Selwyn Theatre and closed 6 August 1921 after 16 additional performances. Total: 60 performances.[1]

CAST: NORA BAYES, LEW FIELDS, DeWOLF HOPPER, LULU McCONNELL, GEORGE McKAY, ALAN EDWARDS, DELYLE ALDA, ERNEST LAMBART, PHIL WHITE, GILDA GRAY, Symplane, Leo Henning, Ruth White, Grant Simpson, Joe Torpy, Belle McEwan, Helen McMahon, Maurice Diamond, Bill Little, Berta Donn, Tommy Suyematsu, Ruth White.
Girls: Inez Courtney, Gypsey Mooney, Lucille Arden, Lauretta Stanley, Dolores Mendez, Grace Hall, Florence Courtney, Violet Vale, Mildred Quinn, Florence Challenger, Ursula Mack, Alice Fessenden, Eunice Barrington, Lillian Dawn, Marie Otto, Gertrude McDonald, Ruth Thomas, Alma Drange, Anita Furman, Barbara Brislaw, Virginia Dixon, Frances Stone.

ACT 1
Scene 1

"Dub-Derro" [A travesty of the Sacha Guitry play 'Deburau']
  L. Henning, R. White
Waltz Ballet (Deburau)
  (*Sketch by* Francis Nordstrom. *Music by* Malvin Franklin. *Lyrics by* Alex Gerber.)
  Deburau: D. Hopper. *The Son*: P. White.

Scene 2

The Hat Shop (*by* Glen MacDonough)
"Beautiful Feathers Make Beautiful Birds"
  B. McEwan, Girls
  (*Music by* George Meyers. *Lyrics by* E. Ray Goetz.)
"Rendezvous"[2]
  N. Bayes, A. Edwards
  (*Music by permission of* Leopold Godowsky. *Lyrics by* Sidney Mitchell.)
  Tony, a salesgirl: B. Donne. *Martelle*, a shop girl: R. White. *Florabelle*, a maid: F. Stone. *Annabelle*, a maid: C. Robbins. *Minnie Mink*, the bookkeeper: D. Alda. *Chase Cash*, an expert accountant: D. Hopper. *Van Dyke Brown*, a convulsionist painter: E. Lambert. *Louis Dinglebender*, owner of the shop: L. Fields. *Goldie Eckles*, a widow from Lemonhurst: L. McConnell.
"On the Brim of Her Old-Fashioned Bonnet"
  D. Alda, Girls
  (*Music by* George Gershwin. *Lyrics by* E. Ray Goetz.)

Scene 3

"Every Girlie Wants To Be a Sally"
  (*Music by* Malvin Franklin. *Lyrics by* Alex Gerber.)
  Leon Errol: G. McKay. *Six Marilyn Miller Girls*: I. Courtney, G. McDonald, F. Courtney, L. Dawn, U. Mack, M. Quinn.

Scene 4

The Eternal Triangles:
  (a) The American Conception of the English Triangle (*by* John Hastings Turner)
  Mr. Albert Brown: D. Hopper. *Mrs. Mary Brown*, his wife: N. Bayes. *Basil*: E. Lambert.
  (b) The English Conception of the American Triangle (*by* James Montgomery Flagg)
  Caleb F. VanDergulch: L. Fields. *Mrs. Caleb F. VanDergulch*: L. McConnell. *Lyman R. Spooner*: G. Simpson. *The Butler*: J. Torpy.

Scene 5

The Children's Hour in a Modern Nursery (*by* Glen MacDonough)
"Baby Dollie Walk"
  B. Donn, Children
  (*Music and Lyrics by* Con Conrad.)
"The Rag Doll"
  H. McMahon, M. Diamond
  Alva: D. Alda. *Ollie*: E. Lambert. *Billie Binks*: B. Donn. *Butler*: G. Simpson. *Bessie Bullion*: L. McConnell. *Mickey Bullion*: L. Fields. *Tiny*: P. White.
"Baby Blues"
  G. Gray, Children
  (*Music by* George Gershwin. *Lyrics by* E. Ray Goetz.)

Scene 6

Clara Da Loon (*by* H. I. Phillips)
  (a) The Parade of the Mountebanks
  D. Hopper, Followers
  (b) The Duchess' Bedroom
  Clara, Duchess of Worcestershire: L. McConnell. *Ursus*, a butler: G. McKay. *Symplane*: D. Hopper. *Blind Girls*: L. Fields. *The Queen*: N. Bayes. *The Prince*: A. Edwards. And *Ladies in Waiting*: (Ladies of the Ensemble).

Scene 7

"Memories"
  B. McEwan
  (*Music by* Harry Ruby. *Lyrics by* Bert Kalmar.)
  Assisted by the Snapshots Sextette.

Scene 8

An Iridescent Symphony: "The Bamboula" [El Relicario]
  D. Alda, Chorus
  (*Music by* José Padilla. *Lyrics by* E. Ray Goetz.)
Dance
  L. Henning, R. White

ACT 2
Scene 1

In the Garden[3]
"Futuristic Melody"
  L. Henning, R. White, G. McDonald, V. Vale, I. Courtney, F. Courtney
  (*Music by* George Gershwin. *Lyrics by* E. Ray Goetz.)
The Shimmy
  G. Gray
"Remember the Rose"
  N. Bayes
  (*Music by* Seymour Simons. *Lyrics by* Sidney Mitchell.)
Character Dance
  G. McKay, R. Hale

Scene 2

"Yokohama Lullaby"
  D. Alda
  Assisted by T. Suyematsu, R. White, B. McEwan, Girls.
  (*Music by* James V. Monaco. *Lyrics by* Grant Clarke.)

Scene 3

Who Done It? (*by* Frances Nordstrom)(A travesty on detective dramas. *Staged by* William Pinkham.)
  The Girl: N. Bayes. *Jimmie the Boy*: A. Edwards. *A Policeman*: L. Fields. *The Inspector*: D. Hopper. *Johnnie*: G. Simpson.

Scene 4

"Mother Dixie, the Flag and You"[4]
  L. McConnell, G. McKay
  (*Music by* George Meyer. *Lyrics by* E. Ray Goetz.)

---

[1]Prior to the opening, the book (sketches) was credited to Glen MacDonough and Francis Nordstrom. Joining the cast for the second engagement were the following featured performers: Betty Bond, Sylvia Chaulsae, Edward Kimmie, Otti Ardine, Jack Douglas, Ida Van Tine, Louise Kelley.
[2]Dropped for second engagement.

[3]Added to the scene In the Garden, which was moved to the Act 2 Finale for the show's second engagement:
"Happyland"
  Ensemble
  (*Music by* Malvin Franklin. *Lyrics by* Alex Gerber.)
[4]Replaced for second engagement by:
"Big Casino"
  G. McKay, The Little Casinos
  (*Music by* Louis Silvers. *Lyrics by* Buddy G. DeSylva.)
  Big Chief Firewater: G. McKay.

Scene 5

Nora Bayes in Songs, assisted by Alan Edwards[5]:
["Saturday"
(*Music by* Harry Brooks. *Lyrics by* Sidney D. Mitchell.)]

Scene 6

"Sky High Bungalow"[6]
D. Alda, L. Henning, Girls
(*Music by* George Meyer. *Lyrics by* E. Ray Goetz.)

Eccentric Dance
M. Diamond
Scene: Sky High Roof.
Mr. Daly Hunt, homeseeker: G. McKay. *Mrs. Daly Hunt*, his wife: L. McConnell. *George Restwell, a slave of toil*: G. Simpson.

Scene 7

Nora Bayes, Lew Fields, DeWolf Hopper

Finale
Ensemble

1921.19 # THE BROADWAY WHIRL[7]

A Five Star Musical Intoxicant (Musical Revue) in Two Acts, 20 Scenes. Sketches by Thomas J. Gray. Music by Harry Tierney, George Gershwin, (Ernie Golden). Lyrics by Joseph McCarthy, Richard Carle, Buddy G. DeSylva, John Henry Mears. Staged by Bert French. Scenery by Triangle Studios. Costumes by Anna Spencer, Inc. Musical director, William Loraine. Produced by Artists Producers' Corporation (John Henry Mears, Director). Opened 8 June 1921 at the Times Square Theatre, moved 8 August 1921 to the Selwyn Theatre, and closed 20 August 1921 after 85 performances.

CAST: RICHARD CARLE, BLANCHE RING, CHARLES WINNINGER, WINONA WINTER, JAY GOULD, (Ray) MAXSON and (Charles) BROWN, JANET SISTERS, Virginia Birmingham, Lucille Ballentine, Hallie Manning, Abbott Adams, Warner Gault, Eppa Mona.

Ladies of the Ensemble: Jean Barrett, Mabel Stanford, Sylvia Highton, Grace Cronin, Joan Broadhurst, Leslie Burnett, Norma Dale, Eleanor Reedy, Marjorie Finley, Mildred Brown, Agnes Morrissey, Carol Seidler, Marguerite Ross, Jean Benton, Dolly Casner, Dorothy Addison, Thelma Addison, Edith May Capes, Florence Kraemer.

ACT 1[8]

Scene 1

Toil [later Innocence]
W. Winter

Scene 2

Life [later Experience]
J. Gould

Scene 3

"From the Plaza to Madison Square"
J. Gould, W. Winter
(With) J. Barrett, M. Stanford, S. Highton, G. Cronin, J. Broadhurst, L. Burnett, N. Dale, E. Reedy, M. Finley, M. Brown, A. Morrissey, C. Seidler.

Dance
R. Maxson, C. Brown, Janet Sisters

Scene: Fifth Avenue Rendezvous:
Life: J. Gould. *Toil*: W. Winter. *Proprietor*: R. Carle. *Heza Short*: C. Brown. *Joe Neverdrink*: C. Winninger. *Belle Broadway*: B. Ring. *A Reformer*: R. Maxson.

"Button Me Up the Back"
H. Manning, L. Ballentine
(With) Misses V. Birmingham, M. Ross, J. Benton, N. Dale, D. Casner, D. Addison, T. Addison, E. M. Capes, F. Kramer, M. Finley, A. Morrissey, C. Seidler.

"You Can Tell By the Skies"[9]
B. Ring
(*Music and Lyrics by* Henry Burr and Ray Perkins.)

"Wood Alcohol Blues"
R. Carle, C. Winninger
(*Music by* E. S. Hutchinson. *Lyrics by* J. Hershkowitz.)

Scene 4[10]

"Oh, Babe"
Eight Little Home-Run Makers
(*Music by* F. Henri. *Lyrics by* Jack Frost.)

Scene 5[11]

"Three Little Maids"
Janet Sisters, V. Birmingham

Scene 6

"Oh, Dearie (You Must Come Over)"
B. Ring
(*Music by* Harry Tierney. *Lyrics by* Joseph McCarthy.)

Scene 7

"Stars of Broadway"
J. Gould
Star Girls: T. Addison, D. Addison. *Mary*: M. Stanford. *Mitzi*: J. Benton. *Bessie McCoy*: E. Reedy. *Dorothy Dickson*: J. Barrett. *Ann Pennington*: M. Finley. *Irene*: V. Birmingham. *Marilyn Miller*: L. Ballentine. *Two Little Girls in Blue*: Janet Sisters. *May Vokes*: M. Ross.

Scene 8

Something Different
W. Winter

Scene 9

Worries (A Dough-mestic Try-angle)
The Husband: C. Winninger. *The Wife*: B. Ring. *The Butler*: A. Adams. *The Worrier*: R. Carle. (The lights will be lowered to denote the lapse of one day.)

"The Husband, the Wife and Lover"
R. Carle, B. Ring, C. Winninger

Scene 10[12]

"Poppy Land"
W. Winter
(*Music by* George Gershwin. *Lyrics by* Buddy G. DeSylva, John Henry Mears.)
Assisted by Misses V. Birmingham, Cronin, Burnett, Highton, Stanford, Capes, Dale, Finley, Seidler, Kraemer, Morrissey, Reedy, Brown, Broadhurst, D. Addison, T. Addison J. Benton, Casner, Barrett, Ross.

Saxophone Solo[13]
C. Winninger

"Lime House Nights"
J. Gould
(*Music by* George Gershwin. *Lyrics by* Buddy G. DeSylva, John Henry Mears.)
Assisted by Misses Birmingham, Cronin, Barrett, Reedy.

Finale ("Poppy Land")

---

[5]When Nora Bayes departed the show, this scene was replaced for its second engagement by:
The Delicatessen Shoppe
Otto Know: L. Fields. *Game Hunter*: G. Simpson. *Con Conwell*: M. Diamond. *Isshe Cone*: P. White. *Haywood Hayseed*: D. Hopper. *Celia Clews*: L. McConnell. *Max Marks*: G. McKay. *Oxford Tighe*: E. Lambert. *Fritzi Fluff*: D. Alda. *Clerks*: J. Torpy, J. Douglas.
[6]Added to this scene for the second engagement:
"Irene Rosensteen"
(*Music by* Malvin Franklin. *Lyrics by* Alex Gerber.)
Irene: B. Bond.
Dance
S. Chaulsae, E. Kimmie, assisted by the Irene Girls.
[7]Toured under the title THE BROADWAY WHIRL OF 1921.
[8]Also performed in the show:
"There's a Typical Tipperary Over Here"
B. Ring
(*Music by* Abner Silver. *Lyrics by* Alex Gerber.)

[9]Replaced after opening by:
"Stand Up and Sing for Your Father"
B. Ring
(*Music and Lyrics by* Henry Burr and Ray Perkins.)
[10]Added to Act 1, Scene 4 for tour:
Dance Eccentrique
I. Courtney, G. McDonald
[11]Added to Act 1, Scene 5 for tour:
The Toddle Top
R. Maxson, C. Brown, Girls, N. Penn
[12]Added for Act 1 Finale during tour:
"Black-Eyed Susans"
W. Winter, Ladies of the Ensemble
(*Music by* Ernie Golden. *Lyrics by* John Henry Mears.)
[13]Dropped after opening.

ACT 2

Scene 1

"All Girls Are Like a Rainbow"
 W. Gault, Girls, introducing L. Ballentine
 (*Music by* Harry Tierney. *Lyrics by* Joseph McCarthy.)

Scene 2

A Condensed Comic Opera
 R. Carle, B. Ring

Scene 3

"Let Cutie Cut Your Cuticle"
 H. Manning, L. Ballentine
 (*Music by* George Gershwin. *Lyrics by* Buddy G. DeSylva, John Henry Mears.)
 (With) Misses Benton, Brown, Broadhurst, Barrett, Casner, Dale, Highton, Kraemer, Stanford, Finley, D. Addison, T. Addison.

Scene 4

Getting a Passport
 Passport Clerk: R. Carle. *Income Tax Clerk*: C. Winninger. *Mrs. John Smith*: W. Winter. *Mr. John Smith*: J. Gould.

Scene 5

"Baby Dolls"
 E. Mona, M. Ross
 (*Music by* George Gershwin. *Lyrics by* Buddy G. DeSylva, John Henry Mears.)
 Cavalier: G. Cronin. *Japanese*: J. Barrett. *Telephone*: E. Reedy. *Bon Bon*: F. Kraemer. *English*: D. Addison. *French*: J. Benton. *Baby*: D. Casner. *Kewpie*: T. Addison. *Splash Me*: J. Broadhurst. *Topsie*: V. Birmingham.

Scene 6

Dancing Shadows of the Past
 R. Maxson, C. Brown

Scene 7

Moves in the Movies[14]
 Director: J. Gould. *Props*: R. Maxson. *Assistant Props*: C. Brown. *Winners of Pikin, Ohio, Popularity Contest (2)*: *Elmer*: R. Carle. *Agatha*: W. Winter. *Max Fisher, a Musician*: C. Winninger. *Miss Pearl Greenford, a Movie Star*: B. Ring.

Scene 8

"Care Free Cairo Town"
 B. Ring, C. Winninger
 (*Music by* Wyman. *Lyrics by* Thomas.[15])

Scene 9

"(The) Broadway Whirl"
 J. Gould
 (*Music by* Harry Tierney. *Lyrics by* Joseph McCarthy.)

Scene 10

Finale
 Entire Company

1921.20 # THE WHIRL OF NEW YORK

A Musical Comedy in Two Acts, 7 Scenes. Book and lyrics by Hugh Morton and Edgar Smith, based on the musical comedy "The Belle of New York"[16]. Music by Gustav Kerker, Alfred Goodman and Lew Pollock. Additional music by Leo Edwards. Additional lyrics by Sidney D. Mitchell. Staged by Lew Morton. Musical numbers staged by Allan K. Foster. Scenes designed by Watson Barratt. Orchestra under the direction of Alfred Goodman. Entire production under the personal supervision of J.J. Shubert. Produced by the Messrs. Lee and J.J. Shubert. Opened 13 June 1921 at the Winter Garden and closed 17 September 1921 after 124 performances[17].

CAST (in order of appearance): *Twiddles*, Secretary to Harry Bronson: Carl Judd. *Fricot*, Chef at Bronson Home: Al Martin. *Fifi*: FLORENCE RAYFIELD. *Harry Bronson*: J. HAROLD MURRAY. *Cora Angelique*, the Queen of Comic Opera and Harry Bronson' fiancée: DOROTHY WARD. *Maid of Honor*: Grace Keeshon. *Doc Sniffkins*, Theatrical Manager and Cora Angelique's Personal Representative: Teddy Webb. *Count Rattsi, Count Tattsi*, Two Brazilian Nuts: FRANK PURCELLA,

RAYMOND PURCELLA. *Karl Bauer*, a Polite Lunatic: Louis Mann. *Blinky Bill*, a Young Man from East New York: JOE KENO. *Kissie Fitzgarter*, a Vaudeville Artist and Another Fiancée of Harry Bronson: Kitty Kelly. *Ichabod Bronson*, a Reformer who is in favor of Blue Sundays and all other days, from Cohoes, New York: JOHN T. MURRAY. *I. Ketchum, U. Cheatham*, Two Aspiring Detectives: JOE SMITH, CHARLES DALE. *Mingtoy, Ching Foo*, Chinese Entertainers: MLLE. ADELAIDE, JOHNNY HUGHES. *The Spirit of the Vase*: Kyra. *Violet Gray*, Captain of the Salvation Army: NANCY GIBBS. *John Blinkerton*: Al Martin. *Maxa*: Maxa McCree. *Mamie Clancy*, Blinky's Sweetheart: Rosie Green. *Bridesmaids to Cora Angelique (12)*: *Miss Whyte*: Charlotte Sprague. *Miss Gray*: Florence Elmore. *Miss Black*: May Dealy. *Miss Wilson*: Bobby McCree. *Miss Jones*: Dorothy Bruce. *Miss Frances*: Claire Hooper. *Miss Rivers*: Mariam Seeley. *Miss Lake*: Louise Whyte. *Miss Henry*: Fay Wayne. *Miss Walters*: Helen Fox. *Miss Page*: Florence Schubert. *Miss Brooks*: Mildred Soper. *Mamie Clancy, Jr.*: Miriam Batistta. *Blinky Bill, Jr.*: Junior Tiernan. (*Specialties*: Johnny McCree, Rath Brothers [George, Dick].)

Ensemble: Edith Pierce, Ruby Howard, Hermosa Jose, Orilla Smith, Ethel Bryant, Dolores Russelle, Flo Worth, Juliet Strahl, Viola Votruba, Beatrice Reiss, Poppy Morton, Benna Odear, Florence Wilde, Flore Moore, Pauline Dakla, Sidney Nelson, Beatrice Jackson, Lucille Mendez, Louise Stark, Grace Langdon, Edna Richmond, Georgia Empey, Dorothy Wegman, Mary Preston, Helen O'Brien, Anna A. Berry, Jule J. Berry, Marlyn Yates, Edna E. Stark, Irene Pierre, Louise L. McGovern, Irene I. McGovern, Emma James, Madaline M. Smith, Olive Clark, Anna Buckley, Margaret Menges, Virginia Richmond, Virginia Wilson, Nina Klau, Belle Mazelle, Maude Satterfield, Grace Hamilton, Gypsy Norman, Elizabeth Reynolds. *Chinese Children in Act 1, Scene 4*: Alice Wong, Edward Low, Margaret Low, Doris Lee, Catherine Lee, Evelyn Lee, Nellie Hor, Henry Chew.

Act 1, Scene 1: The Home of Harry Bronson, Riverside Drive, at 8 A.M. *Scene 2*: The Garden of Harry Bronson's Home. *Scene 3*: Old Curiosity Shop. The Spirit of the Vase. *Scene 4*: Chinese New Year in Chinatown.

Act 2, Scene 1: Sherries' Tiffin Shop, New York. *Scene 2*: The Rath Brothers. *Scene 3*: The Garden of the Sound Proof Country Club.

ACT 1

Opening Chorus
 J. H. Murray, Men

Dance
 Kyra

"The Queen of Musical Comedy" (Cora Angelique)
 D. Ward, Bridesmaids
 (*Music by* Lew Pollack. *Lyrics by* Sidney D. Mitchell.)

"Dancing Fools"
 K. Kelly, J. Keno, F. Purcella, R. Purcella, S. Glenville

"Teach Me How to Kiss"
 F. Rayfield, J. H. Murray

"From Far Cohoes"
 J. T. Murray, Ensemble

"Just One Good Time" (One Last Good Time)
 J. H. Murray, F. Rayfield, Chorus
 (*Music by* Lew Pollack and Alfred Goodman. *Lyrics by* Cyrus Wood.)

"Little Baby"
 J. T. Murray, D. Ward

"The Spirit of the Chinese Vase"
 Kyra

Chinese New Year's Ballet

Dance Divertissement[18]
 Adelaide and Hughes

"Follow On"
 N. Gibbs, Salvation Army Girls

"Mandalay"
 J. H. Murray

"The Belle of New York"
 R. Green, J. Keno, Chorus

"Molly, Molly" (Molly on a Trolley)
 D. Ward, Girls

Finale
 Company

ACT 2[19]

"Tiffin, Tiffin"
 Ensemble

---

[14]Miss Ring and Mr. Winninger acknowledge their indebtedness to Mr. Alexander Leftwich for their portion of this scene.
[15]Though credited to Messrs. Wyman and Thomas, this may be the same song as "Care Free Cairo Town" (*Music and Lyrics by* John Wolcott.) credited to MORRIS GEST'S MIDNIGHT WHIRL, 1919.
[16]Originally produced 28 September 1897 at the Casino Theatre for 56 performances.
[17]Costumes uncredited.

---

[18]Dropped late in the run.
[19]Added late in the run to Act 2, after "When We Are Married":
 "The Pastry Cooks"
 "Ginger Cake and Frosted Cake"
 Adelaide and Hughes

"Dance, Dance, Dance"[20]
  J. McCree
"Whistling (It All Over Town)"
  D. Ward, Chorus
"When We Are Married"
  F. Rayfield, J. H. Murray
Chain Dance
  F. Purcella, R. Purcella
"The Purity Brigadiers"
  N. Gibbs, Purity Brigade Girls
"I Know That I'm in Love"
  N. Gibbs, J. H. Murray
  (*Music by* Lew Pollack. *Lyrics by* Sidney D. Mitchell.)
"I Do So, There!"
  N. Gibbs, J. T. Murray, Chorus
The Rath Brothers[21]
"La Belle Parisienne"[22]
  F. Rayfield, French Girls
Dance
  Adelaide and Hughes
"Gee, I Wish I Had a Girl (Like You)"[23]
  N. Gibbs, J. H. Murray
  (*Music by* Lew Pollack and Alfred Goodman. *Lyrics by* Cliff Friend.)
Finale
  Company

1921.21 ZIEGFELD FOLLIES OF 1921

A Musical Revue in Two Acts, 27 Scenes[24]. Lines (sketches) and lyrics by Channing Pollock, Gene Buck, Willard Mack, Ralph Spence, Buddy G. DeSylva. Music by Victor Herbert, Rudolf Friml, Dave Stamper, (James Monaco, James Hanley). Staged by Edward Royce. Dialogue rehearsed by George Marion. Scenery by Joseph Urban. Costumes designed by James Reynolds and others. Orchestra under the direction of Frank Tours. Orchestrations by Maurice DePackh, Stephen Jones. Supervised by Florenz Ziegfeld. Produced by Florenz Ziegfeld. Opened 21 June 1921 at the Globe Theatre and closed 1 October 1921 after 119 performances.

CAST: RAYMOND HITCHCOCK, W. C. FIELDS, FANNIE BRICE, MARY EATON, (Gus) VAN and (Joe) SCHENCK, Mlle. GERMAINE MITTI, M. TILLIO, RAY DOOLEY, FLORENCE O'DENISHAWN, MARY MILBURN, JOHN CLARKE, VERA MICHELENA, JESSIE REED, MARIE ASTROVA, (Charles) O'Donnell and (Ethel) Blair, Mary Lewis, Margery Chapin, Peggy Davis, Consuelo Flowerton, Helen Lee Worthing, Phil Dwyer, Herbert Hoey, Mr. Payne, Diana Gordon, The Mandel Brothers (Joe, William), The Innez Brothers (Frank, Albert).
Follies Girls: Misses. Rolph, Hughes, Stohl, Flowerton, Chappel, Selden, Gordon, Leigh, French, Loftus, Chase, Barnett, Lomp, Campbell, The Keene Twins, Madilyn Morrissey, Albertine Marlowe, Betty Carsdale, Marguerite Falconer, Edna Wheaton, Irene Marcellus, Pearl Germonde, Doris Lloyd, Eva Brady, Edna French, Avonne Taylor, Emma Beresbach, Gertrude Seldon, Frances Reveaux, Beatrice Millner, Helen Hunt, Madelyn Lombard, Anastasia Reilly, Evelyn Campbell, The Darling Twins, Janet Stone, Geneva Mitchell.

ACT 1
Scene 1

The Statue of Liberty:
The Wail of the Common People (*by* Willard Mack)
  R. Hitchcock
Scene 2

Follies Mirror[25] (A Decoration by Ben Ali Haggin)
  Misses. J. Reed, M. Morrissey, A. Marlowe, B. Carsdale, M. Falconer, E. Wheaton, I. Marcellus, P. Germonde, D. Lloyd, G. Loftus, E. French, A. Taylor, E. Beresbach, M. Seldon

Scene 3
"Mr. Ziegfeld's Idea of Chorus Men"
  (*Music by* Rudolf Friml. *Lyrics by* Buddy G. DeSylva.)
Scene 4

The Professor (*by* Willard Mack and Raymond Hitchcock)
  The Deacon: W. C. Fields. *The Professor:* R. Hitchcock. *His Daughter:* R. Dooley.
Scene 5

"Strut Miss Lizzie"[26]
  G. Van, J. Schenck
  (*Music by* Turner Layton. *Lyrics by* Henry Creamer.)
  And J. Stone.
Scene 6

"The Legend of the Cyclamen Tree" (The Legend of the Golden Tree)
  (*Music by* Victor Herbert. *Lyrics by* Gene Buck. *Scenes and Costumes by* James Reynolds. *Part 2 [Scene] by* Joseph Urban.)
  The action takes place in Persia in the twelfth century.
    Part 1: The enclosed garden of the Princess Zenocrate. *Part 2:* In the Desert.
    Princess Zenocrate: J. Reed. *Two Suitors: A Prince from Arabia:* J. Clarke. *A Prince from Byzantium:* George Spelvin. *Two Litter Bearers:* Channing Pollocko. *Five Spear Bearers:* Jose Urbano. *A Soothsayer:* G. Van.
"Princess of My Dreams"
  J. Clarke
  (*Music by* Victor Herbert. *Lyrics by* Gene Buck.)
    Two Chamberlains to the Princess: (Ensemble.) *Eight Adolescent Dancers:* (Ensemble.) *Slave Women: A Slave from Greece:* G. Loftus. *A Slave from Asia:* P. Germonde. *A Slave from Tartary:* I. Marcellus. *A Slave from Persia:* M. Morrissey. *A Slave from Cythera:* A. Taylor. *A Slave from Sicily:* F. Reveaux. *A Slave from Egypt:* A. Marlowe. *A Slave from Tyre:* B. Millner. *The Spirit of the Cyclamen Tree:* F. O'Denishawn.
Scene 7

"Second Hand Rose"
  F. Brice
  (*Music by* James Hanley. *Lyrics by* Grant Clarke.)
Scene 8

The Piano Tuner
  The Piano Tuner: C. O'Donnell. *The Lady:* E. Blair.
Scene 9

The Rose Bower: "Bring Back My Blushing Rose"
  J. Clarke
  (*Music by* Rudolf Friml. *Lyrics by* Gene Buck. *Verses by* Brian Hooker.)
    The White Rose: M. Milburn. *The Yellow Rose:* F. O'Denishawn. *The Pink Rose:* M. Lewis. *The Red Rose:* V. Michelena. *The Rose Bud:* M. Eaton, Girls.
Scene 10

"Plymouth Rock"[27] (If Plymouth Rock Had Landed on the Pilgrims Instead of the Pilgrims Landing on the Rock)
  R. Hitchcock
  (*Music by* Dave Stamper. *Lyrics by* Channing Pollock.)
Scene 11

The Harem[28]
  J. Clarke
    Ladies of the Harem: G. Mitti, M. Tillio, from the Folies Bergere, Paris.
Scene 12

"Scotch Lassie" (Scotch Song)
  F. Brice
  (*Music by* Leo Edwards. *Lyrics by* Blanche Merrill.)
Scene 13

The Stage Door:
"Raggedy Rag"
  M. Milburn
  (*Music by* Dave Stamper. *Lyrics by* Gene Buck.)
"Sally Come Back to the Alley"
  J. Schenck
  (*Music by* Dave Stamper. *Lyrics by* Gene Buck.)
    With Ragamuffins, Alley Girls.

---

[20]Dropped late in the run.
[21]Dropped late in the run.
[22]Dropped late in the run.
[23]Replaced second week of the run by: (Also dropped late in the run.)
  "Take Me Down to Coney"
    R. Green, J. Keno
    (*Music and Lyrics by* Lew Pollack, Ed Rose, Richard A. Whiting.)
[24]The Fifteenth in the annual series of revues produced by Florenz Ziegfeld beginning in 1907.
[25]Dropped for subsequent tour.

---

[26]Dropped for subsequent tour. Later used by its authors in a musical of the same name 19 June 1922 at the Times Square Theatre for 96 performances.
[27]Dropped for subsequent tour.
[28]Dropped for subsequent tour.

Scene 14

Lionel, Ethel and Jack, with Camille Burlesque (*by* Channing Pollock and Dave Stamper[29])

Lionel: R. Hitchcock. *Ethel*: F. Brice. *Jack*: W. C. Fields.

Scene 15

"Our Home Town"

G. Van, J. Schenck

(*Music by* Harry Carroll. *Lyrics by* Ballard Macdonald.)

Scene 16

"The Championship of the World"

(*Music by* Victor Herbert. *Lyrics by* Gene Buck.)

George Carpentier: F. Brice. *Jack Dempsey*: R. Dooley. *The Announcer*: R. Hitchcock. *The Referee*: W. C. Fields. *The Fight Fans, Trainers, Seconds.*

Finale

ACT 2[30]

Scene 1

The Birthday of the Dauphin (*by* James Reynolds)

An Interlude at Versailles in the Reign of Louis XVI.

(*Music by* Victor Herbert. *Scenes by* Joseph Urban.)

Scene: A Terrace in the Garden of Versailles.

Cast (in order of appearance): *Master of Ceremonies*: V. Michelena. *The Dauphin of France*: C. Eaton. *Cardinal*: C. O'Donnell. *Mme. La Comtesse de Vergenne*: B. Millner. *A Cloaked Gallant*: D. Lloyd. *An Unknown Lady*: M. Morrison. *Two Chefs*: Coli: P. Davis. *Rene*: C. Flowerton. *The Veiled Marquise*, Marquise de Soveral: H. L. Worthing. *An Old Roué*, M. Le Duc de Chateau Briand: W. C. Fields. *A Coquette*: H. Hunt. *A Young Duc*, M. Le Duc de Villefranche: F. Reveaux. *Marquise de St. Chaumont*: G. Seldon. *Louis XVI*, Roi de France: R. Hitchcock. *Marie Antoinette*, Reine de France: B. Carsdale. *Mme. La Princesse de Chateau Rein*: G. Loftus. *Goli*: Miss Payne. *A Venetian Lady*: E. Wheaton. *A Fop*: P. Germond. *Angelique*, Mme. La Comtesse de Chartres: D. Gordon. *Another Fop*: M. Lombard. *Madeline de Beauharnais*: A. Marlowe. *Mme. La Duchesse de Chatillon*: I. Marcellus. *Mme. La Princesse de Lamballe*: J. Reed. *A Milliner's Mannequin*: F. O'Denishawn. *A Masked Marquis*: A. Reilly. *Mme. La Duchesse de Grammont*: E. Campbell. *Da Grammerci*, Harlequin and Columbine: The Darling Twins.

Scene 2

The Innez Brothers[31]

Scene 3

"My Man" (Mon Homme)

F. Brice

(*Music by* Maurice Yvain. *Original French Lyrics by* Albert Willemetz and Jacques Charles. *English Lyrics by* Channing Pollock.)

Scene: The Bridge on the Seine.

Burlesque Apache Dance

R. Dooley, C. O'Donnell

Scene 4

"Four Little Girls With a Future and Four Little Girls With a Past"

(*Music by* Rudolf Friml. *Lyrics by* Buddy G. DeSylva.)

Future Girls: J. Stone, M. Chapin, G. Mitchell, A. Reilly. *Past Girls*: J. Reed, H. L. Worthing, P. Germonde, M. Morrissey.

Scene 5

Off to the Country (*by* W. C. Fields)

Scene: The Subway.

The Fliverton: W. C. Fields. *Mrs. Fliverton*: F. Brice. *Sammy Sap Fliverton*: R. Hitchcock. *Ray Tut Fliverton*: R. Dooley. *A Ticket Chopper*: F. Innez. *White Wings*: P. Dwyer. *Passengers, etc.*: (Ensemble).

Scene 6

"Some Day the Sun Will Shine"[32]

M. Milburn

(*Music by* James V. Monaco[33]; Melody from Schubert's Unfinished Symphony. *Lyrics by* Grant Clarke.)

Scene 7

"Now I Know"[34]

M. Eaton, H. Hoey, Butterfly Girls

(*Music by* James V. Monaco. *Lyrics by* Grant Clarke.)

Scene 8

Passion's Altar[35] ([A Tableau] by Ali Ben Haggin)

Misses Rolph, Hughes, Stohl, Flowerton, Chappel, Selden, Gordon, Leigh, French, Loftus, Chase, Beresbach, Barnett, Lomp, Campbell, Keene Twins

Algerian Dance

G. Mitti, M. Tillio

Scene 9

"Allay Up"[36]

F. Brice

(*Music by* James Hanley. *Lyrics by* Ballard Macdonald.)

Scene 10

Songs

G. Van, J. Schenck

["In the Old Town Hall"

(*Music and Lyrics by* Harry Pease, Ed Nelson, Howard Johnson.)

"O'Reilly, I'm Ashamed of You"

(*Music and Lyrics by* Harry Pease, Ed Nelson, Elsie White.)

"Wang Wang Blues"

(*Music by* Henry Busse, Gus Mueller, Buster Johnson. *Lyrics by* Leo Wood.)

"Are You Coming Out Malinda?"

(*Music by* Harry Von Tilzer. *Lyrics by* Andrew B. Sterling and Edward P. Moran.)

"While Miami Dreams"

(*Music by* Richard A. Whiting. *Lyrics by* Raymond B. Egan.)

"What's A-Gonna Be Next?"]

Scene 11

"Every Time I Hear a Band Play"[37]

V. Michelena, F. O'Denishawn, Band Girls

(*Music by* Rudolf Friml. *Lyrics by* Gene Buck.)

Scene: The Blue Lagoon.

Scene 12

Finale

Ensemble

GEORGE WHITE'S SCANDALS OF 1921

1921.22

A Musical Revue in Two Acts, 19 Scenes[38]. Book (sketches) by "Bugs" Baer and George White. Music by George Gershwin. Lyrics by Arthur Jackson. Entire production staged by George White. Dialogue rehearsed by John Meehan. Art director, Herbert Ward. Costumes designed by Albertina Randall Wheelan, Alice O'Neil, Ada Fields, Gilbert Adrian. Orchestra under the direction of Alfred Newman. Produced by George White. Opened 11 July 1921 at the Liberty Theatre and closed 1 October 1921 after 97 performances.

---

[29]A Burlesque on the Barrymore family. Stamper's name in later credits replaced by Ned Joyce Heaning.

[30]Added for tour:

"Spring" (Act 2)

F. Brice

Added during the run of the show to Act 2, then dropped for subsequent tour:

"Rosemary"

John Steel, E. Wheaton

(*Music by* Dave Stamper. *Lyrics by* Buddy G. DeSylva.)

[31]Dropped for subsequent tour.

[32]Dropped during the run.

[33]ASCAP credits song to James Hanley.

[34]During the run the following was added to this scene:

Butterfly Dance

M. Eaton

[35]Dropped for subsequent tour.

[36]Dropped during the run.

[37]Replaced for tour by:

"My Midnight Frolic Girl"

G. Van, J. Schenck

(*Music by* Dave Stamper. *Lyrics by* Gene Buck.)

[38]The third in the annual series of musical revues produced by George White beginning in 1919.

CAST: ANN PENNINGTON, GEORGE WHITE, AUNT JEMIMA [Theresa or Tess Gardella], GEORGE LeMAIRE, OLIVE VAUGHN, LOU HOLTZ, VICTORIA HERBERT, LESTER ALLEN, GENE FORD, CHARLES KING, MYRA CULLEN, GEORGE BICKEL, CHRISTINE WELFORD, BERT GORDON, DARRY WELFORD, LLOYD GARRETT, GERALDINE ALEXANDER, JAMES MILLER, PHOEBE LEE, HARRY ROSE.

George White Girls: Misses Sybil Stokes, Dorothy Stokes, Helen Knight, Savoy, Hamilton, Ellsworth, Vera Colburn, Peggy Smith, Malvern, Turner, Roche, Michell, Cook, Mahoney, Helen LaVonne, Helen Cox, Yvette Currier, Hazel Dare, Bryant, Sanker, Martell, McGushion, Dunn, Marcelle Barnes, Hoffman, Dana, Ney, May Morris, McClure.

ACT 1[39]
Scene 1

Mrs. Grundy
The Scandalmongers: Misses S. Stokes, Cullen, Knight, Savoy, Hamilton, Dare, Ellsworth, C. Welford, Colburn, Smith, Malvern, Turner, Roche, Michell, Cook, Mahoney. *Divorce*: G. Alexander. *Style*: H. LaVonne. *Modesty*: P. Lee.

Scene 2

Broadway—A Hold-Up
The Singing Burglar: L. Holtz. *The Victim*: L. Allen. *The Shimmying Burglar*: O. Vaughn.

Scene 3

Don Juan
Olga: V. Herbert. *Zoe*: H. LaVonne. *Elevera*: G. Alexander. *Archangela Tarabotte*: P. Lee. *Esmerelda*: H. Knight. *Mercedes*: Y. Currier. *Zulma*: D. Stokes. *Aualle*: H. Cox. *Don Juan*: C. King.

Scene 4

A Dressing Room Back Stage
Ollie: O. Vaughn. *Margie*: H. LaVonne. *Crissie*: C. Welford. *Darry*: D. Welford. *Myra*: M. Cullen. *Hazel*: H. Dare. *Phoebe*: P. Lee. *Yvette*: Y. Currier. *Dorothy*: D. Stokes. *Sybil*: S. Stokes. *Geraldine*: G. Alexander. *Stage Manager*: S. Ledner.

Scene 5

The Winter Palace in Russia
The Girl on the Tambourine: A. Pennington. *Peasants*: Misses Ellsworth, Morris, Smith, Malvern, Turner, Mahoney, Michell, Cook, Roche, Bryant, Savoy, Hamilton, Sanker, Martell, McGushion, Dunn. *The Sentry*: L. Allen. *The General*: G. LeMaire. *The Man of Mystery*: G. Bickel. *The Sergeant*: C. King. *Totrotsky*: H. Rose. *Sam the Butcher*: B. Gordon. *Little Nellsky*: M. Barnes. *A Russian Fool*: J. Miller. *Prisoner*: L. Garrett. *Another Prisoner*: S. Gold. *Soldiers, etc.*

Scene 6

"I Love You"
A Love Bug: H. Rose. *Spanish Girl*: Y. Currier. *Swedish Girl*: H. Cox. *Italian Girl*: H. Knight. *Chinese Girl*: P. Lee.

A French Version
O. Vaughn

A Hebrew Version
V. Herbert

Scene 7

Samson and Delilah Ballet
Explained by L. Holtz. *Delilah*: A. Pennington. *Samson*: L. Allen. *Philistine Captain*: G. Bickel. *Philistine Guards*: H. LaVonne, M. Barnes. *Philistine Girls*: Misses Hamilton, Hoffman, Morris, Smith, Malvern, Mahoney, Martell, Colburn, Lande, Dana, D. Stokes.

Scene 8

A Vodeville Show
Pages: G. Alexander, S. Stokes. *Ventriloquists*: Misses Michell, Dunn, Bryant, Roche. *Magicians*: Misses Savoy, Dare, Turner, Sanker. *Quartette*: Misses C. Welford, Cullen, Malvern, D. Welford.

Scene 9

The Divorce Court
The Judge: G. Bickel. *Mr. Johnson*: L. Holtz. *Mrs. Johnson*: T. Gardela. *Court Crier*: D. Welford. *Morris Pest*: B. Gordon. *Henry Fliver*: J. Miller. *Pest's Attorney*: G. LeMaire. *Fliver's Attorney*: L. Allen. *Mrs. Sillyman*: O. Vaughn. *Mr. Sillyman*: L. Garrett. *Choruspondents*: Misses Alexander, LaVonne, Knight, Lee, Currier, D. Stokes.

[39]Added for subsequent tour:
Advice to the Lovelorn by George White (Act 1)
Stenographer: M. Cullen. *First Girl*: H. LaVonne. *Second Girl*: O. Vaughn. *Third Girl*: R. Savoy.

Scene 10

South Sea Isles: "Sunny South Sea Islands"
C. King

South Sea Dance
A. Pennington
South Sea Islanders: Misses S. Stokes, Cook, Hamilton, Turner, Mahoney, Michell, Cullen, Ellsworth, Dana, Martell, McGushion, Dunn, Dare, C. Welford, Bryant, Ney, McClure, Sanker, Savoy, Morris, Smith, Malvern, Roche, D. Welford, Colburn, Hoffman, Cox, Barnes. *South Sea Quartette*: H. Rose, L. Garrett, L. Allen, B. Gordon.

Scene 11

Specialty
L. Holtz

["Mother Eve"
(*Music by* James F. Hanley. *Lyrics by* Ballard Macdonald.)]

Scene 12

Panama: "Where East Meets West"
C. King, V. Herbert
Roosevelt: G. Bickel. *Goethals*: G. LeMaire. *The Laborers*: Misses Savoy, Hamilton, Dare, Ellsworth, Malvern, Roche, Mahoney, D. Welford. *The Mint: Gold*: H. LaVonne. *Silver*: M. Barnes. *Copper*: P. Lee. *The Common People*: L. Allen, Misses Michell, Turner, Cook, Dana, Sanker, Martell, McGushion, Dunn. *The Foreign Nations: England*: H. Cox. *France*: H. Knight. *Japan*: Y. Currier. *Belgium*: D. Stokes. *Italy*: V. Colburn. *Roumania*: G. Alexander. *Columbia*: A. Pennington. *East*: P. Smith. *West*: M. Morris. *South*: M. Cullen. *North*: S. Stokes. *Captain of the Cruiser*: G. White. *Lieutenant*: O. Vaughn. *Sailors*: Misses C. Welford, Ney, Bryant, McClure.

Finale

ACT 2
Scene 1

The School for Scandal
Teacher: G. Bickel. *Professor Sudds*: L. Allen. *Professor Wartax*: H. Rose. *Professor Thug*: G. LeMaire. *The Head of the Class*: O. Vaughn. *The Rest of the Class*: Misses S. Stokes, Knight, D. Stokes, Lee, Courier, Colburn, Alexander, LaVonne, Cullen, Smith, Dare, D. Welford, Malvern, Michell, Savoy.

Scene 2

A Singing Lesson
B. Gordon, G. Ford

Scene 3

The Flying Dutchman: "Drifting Along with the Tide"
L. Garrett, V. Herbert
Sailors: Misses S. Stokes, Knight, Dare, Morris, Smith, Malvern, Mahoney, Michell, Cook, Dunn, Colburn, D. Welford, Turner, McClure, McGushion, Sanker.

Scene 4

"(She's) Just a Baby"
A. Pennington
Babies: Misses C. Welford, Martell, Bryant, Sanker, Roche, Ney, Ellsworth, Hamilton.

Scene 5

The Gordon Gin-nasium
Mr. Gordon: G. LeMaire. *A Thin Customer*: L. Allen. *A Fat Customer*: G. Bickel. *Clients*: H. Rose, B. Gordon, J. Miller.

Scene 6

Jemima's Home Town (Specialty)
Aunt Jemima

Scene 7

The White Woods
Mushroom Girls: Misses Ellsworth, Morris, Malvern, Turner, Mahoney, Michell, Cook, Bryant, Ney, McClure, Dana, Sanker, Martell, McGushion, Dunn, Roche. *Rose Girls*: Misses Knight, D. Stokes, Cox, Alexander, Lee, Barnes, Colburn, Hoffman. *Tree Girls*: Misses LaVonne, Currier.

Recitation
G. White

Finale
Entire Company

1921.23

TANGERINE

A Musical Satire of the Sexes (Musical Comedy) in Two Acts, 4 Scenes. Book by Philip Bartholomae and Guy Bolton. (Based on a play by Lawrence

Langner and Philip Bartholomae.) Music by Monte Carlo and Alma Sanders. Lyrics by Howard Johnson. Staged by George Marion and Bert French. Scenery designed by P. Dodd Ackerman, Lee Simonson. Costumes designed by Dorothy Armstrong, Mme. Francis, Pieter Mayer. Orchestra under the direction of Gus Kleinecke. Produced by Carle Carlton. Opened 9 August 1921 at the Casino Theatre, closing 27 May 1922 for summer vacation after 337 performances; resumed 7 August 1922 at the Casino Theatre and closed 26 August 1922 after 24 additional performances. Total: 361 performances.

CAST: *A Warden*: P. A. Leonard. *Jack Floyd*: HARRY PUCK. *Lee Loring*: ALLEN KEARNS[40]. *Fred Allen*: JOSEPH HERBERT, JR. *Dick Owens*: FRANK CRUMIT. *Shirley Dalton*: JULIA SANDERSON. *Kate Allen*: MARTHA LORBER[41]. *Elsie Loring*: BECKY [Rebekah] CAUBLE. *Mildred Floyd*: GLADYS WILSON. *Noa*: Jeannetta Methven. *Clarence*: Wayne Nunn. *Joe Perkins*, the Easy Boss: JOHN E. HAZZARD. *Tangerine Police Force*: California Four.

Eight Little Wives: *Akamai*: Mary Collins. *Huhu*: Victoria Miles. *Kulikuli*: Helen Frances. *Pilikia*: Nerene Swinton. *Ukola*: Carolyn Hancock. *Polihu*: Ruth Rollins. *Aloha, Aloha Oe* (Twins): Hazel Wright, Grace DeCarlton. *Arameda, Oro*, 2 Native Dancers: Anna Ludmilla, Frank Holbrook.

Act 1, Scene 1: Alimony Jail, New York. *Scene 2*: Legend of the Tropic Sea. *Scene 3*: Lanai of the King.

Act 2: Main Street, Tangerine.

ACT 1
Scene 1

"It's Great to Be Married (and Lead a Single Life)"
  J. Herbert, Jr., A. Kearns, H. Puck
  (*Music by* Monte Carlo, Alma Sanders, Carle Carlton. *Lyrics by* Howard Johnson.)
"Love Is a Business"
  J. Sanderson, F. Crumit, J. Herbert, Jr., A. Kearns, H. Puck
"Isle of Tangerine"
  J. Sanderson, F. Crumit
Scene 2
"The Sea of the Tropics"[42] (dance)
  Holbrook and Ludmilla
Scene 3
"Ode and Sun Dance"
  J. Methven, Quartette, Eight Little Wives
  (*Music by* Monte Carlo, Alma Saunders, Carle Carlton. *Lyrics by* Howard Johnson.)
"Listen to Me"
  J. Sanderson, F. Crumit
"In Our Mountain Bower"
  J. Methven, Quartette, Eight Little Wives
"There's a Sunbeam for Every Drop of Rain"
  A. Kearns, B. Cauble
"Man Is the Lord of It All"
  J. Sanderson, G. Wilson, B. Cauble, M. Lorber, J. Herbert, Jr., A. Kearns, H. Puck
  (*Music by* Jean Schwartz.)
Finale
  J. Sanderson, F. Crumit
ACT 2[43]
"South Sea Island Blues"
  Quartette, F. Crumit, J. Herbert, Jr., A. Kearns, H. Puck

"Tropic Vamps" (Tropical Vamps)
  Eight Little Wives
"Sweet Lady"
  J. Sanderson, F. Crumit
  (*Music by* Dave Zoob and Frank Crumit. *Lyrics by* Howard Johnson.)
"Civilization"
  J. E. Hazzard, Eight Little Wives
"It's Your Carriage That Counts"
  J. Sanderson, Eight Little Wives
Dance Tangerine
  M. Lorber
"She Was Very Dear to Me"
  J. E. Hazzard
  (*Music and Lyrics by* Benjamin Hapgood Burt.)
"We'll Never Grow Old"[44]
  B. Cauble, A. Kearns
Finale

1921.24 # SONNY[45]

A Melody Play in Three Acts, 6 Scenes. Book and lyrics by George V. Hobart. Music by Raymond Hubbell. Staged by George V. Hobart. Dances arranged by Carl Randall. Scenery designed by Clifford F. Pember. Gowns by Bergdorf Goodman, Caroline Nunder. Orchestra under the direction of Mario Agnolucci. Orchestrations by Maurice DePackh. Produced by the Selwyns (Arch, Edgar). Opened 16 August 1921 at the Cort Theatre and closed 10 September 1921 after 31 performances.

CAST (in order of appearance): *Buddy*: CARL RANDALL. *James*: Russell Medcraft. *Florence*: BERTA DONNE. *Nora*: GEORGIE LAURENCE. *Harper Craig*: RICHIE LING. *Mrs. Crosby*: EMMA DUNN. *Charlie Crosby*: ERNEST GLENDINNING. *Madge*: ESTELLE HOWARD. *Jasper*: Bert Melville. *Henry*: Horace James. *Joe Marden*: ERNEST GLENDINNING. *Alicia*: MABEL WITHEE. *Thomas*: James Kilpatrick. *Zeke*: Jack Fox. *Zach*: Joseph Evans. *Dick*: Robert Pollock. *Harry*: William Meredith. *Martin*: Fred Grod. *Donald*: Nate Goodwin. *Rose*: Violet Gray. *Rosemary*: Dorothy Clark.

Act 1, Scene 1: The Exterior of the Home of the Crosbys in Pelham Manor. 1917. *Scene 2*: The Exterior of Joe Marden's Garage in Granby, Michigan. 1917. *Scene 3*: A Room in a Base Hospital in France. 1918. *Scene 4*: Part of the Deck of a Transport Homeward Bound. Spring, 1919.

Act 2: The Living Room in the Home of the Crosbys in Pelham Manor. Early Summer, 1919.

Act 3: Same as Act 2. Eight days later.

ACT 1
Scene 1
"I'm in Love, Dear"
  C. Randall, B. Donne, R. Medcraft
Scene 4
"Dream"
  E. Glendinning, M. Withee, Ensemble
ACT 2
"Sonny"
  M. Withee, Ensemble
"My Chum" (My Dear Old Chum)
  E. Glendinning, Ensemble
ACT 3
"Peaches"
  C. Randall, Ensemble

1921.25 # THE MIMIC WORLD OF 1921

An Intimate Revue in Two Acts, a Prologue and 27 Scenes. Book (sketches) and lyrics by Harold Atteridge, James Hussey and Owen Murphy. Music by

---

[40]Opening night programs notwithstanding, the New York Times and Billboard both reviewed Billy Rhodes in the role of Lee Loring.
[41]Opening night programs notwithstanding, the New York Times and Billboard both reviewed Edna Pierre in the role of Kate Allen.
[42]Scene and song dropped during the run.
[43]Act 2 running order revised, and added to Act 2, after "South Sea Island Blues" two months into the run:
Old Melodies
  F. Crumit, Quartette
Added briefly to Act 2 before "We'll Never Grow Old" in second month of run:
Dance Samoan
  Ludmilla and Holbrook
Added late in the run to Act 2, before "She Was Very Dear to Me:"

"(You and I) Atta Baby"
  R. Cauble, Joseph McCallion (Lee Loring)
[44]Dropped late in the run.
[45]Title changed to SONNY BOY shortly after the opening.

Jean Schwartz, Lew Pollack and Owen Murphy. Entire production staged by Allen K. Foster. Scenery and properties designed by Watson Barratt. Orchestra under the direction of Alfred Goodman. Produced by Messrs. Shubert. Opened 17 August 1921 at the Century Promenade (atop the Century Theatre) and closed 10 September 1921 after 26 performances[46].

CAST: JIMMY HUSSEY, (El) BRENDEL and (Flo) BERT, MAE WEST, CLARENCE HARVEY, CLIFF EDWARDS, ANN TODDINGS, LOU EDWARDS, GLADYS JAMES, (William) MORAN and (Albert) WISER, PEGGY BROWN, BETH STANLEY, EDDIE HICKEY, MARJORIE CARVILLE, Miriam Miller, Ruth Hazelton, Frank Hurst, Evelyn Martyn, Helen Nelidova, C. L. Henderson, Madeline Smith, Jimmy Kirk, Gene Delmont, Elizabeth Morgan, Gladys Blair.

Ensemble: Elaine Courtney, Jeanne Danjou, Marjorie Hope, Anita Miramar, Madeline Smith, Helen Armstrong, Ginnette Dorval, Lebanon Hoffa, Estelle Lang, Gladys Montgomery, Zella Lenney, Mae LeRoux, Betty Palmer, Dorothy McCarthy, Margaret McCarthy, May Sullivan, Margaret Wood, Alice Burton, Portland Hoffa, May Blair, Virginia Blair, Bert Best, Lucille Pryor, Thelma Johns, Hazel Rix, Vivian West, Jane Brown.

ACT 1

Prologue
> D. McCarthy

Scene 1

"Old Fashioned Sweetheart"
> F. Hurst, Colonial Belles
>> *Scene*: At the Club
>>> *Page*: P. Brown. *Tom*: L. Edwards. *Dick*: E. Hickey. *Harry*: A. Wiser. *John*: C. Harvey. *Howard Dashing*: F. Hurst. *Genevieve*: B. Palmer. *Gwendolyn*: G. Montgomery. *Annette*: A. Miramar.

Scene 2

"Any Night on Old Broadway"
> E. Hickey, Pedestrians
> (*Music by* Jean Schwartz. *Lyrics by* Harold Atteridge.)
>> *Scene*: Times Square at Midnight
>>> *John*: C. Harvey. *Howard Dashing*: F. Hurst. *Tom*: L. Edwards. *Dick*: E. Hickey. *Harry*: A. Wiser. *Genevieve*: B. Palmer. *Gwendolyn*: G. Montgomery. *Annette*: A. Miramar. *Cliff*: C. Edwards. *Mary*: H. Armstrong. *Officer*: E. Hickey. *Bootblack*: H. Nelidova. *Newsie*: E. Morgan. *Blind Man*: F. Masters. *Miriam*: M. Miller. *Madeline*: M. Smith. *Pickpocket*: C. Edwards. *Anita*: A. Miramar. *Anti-Volstead*: L. Edwards. *Yonson*: E. Brendel. *Evelyn*: E. Martyn. *James Bradstreet*: A. Wiser. *A Card Shark*: W. Moran. *Gunman*: L. Edwards. *Shifty Liz*: M. West. *Salvation Army Officer*: F. Masters.

Scene 3

"Broadway Pirates"
> G. James, P. Brown, Broadway Pirates
> (*Music by* Lew Pollack. *Lyrics by* Sidney Clare.)
>> *Captain Kid Up to Date*: G. James. *His First Mate*: P. Brown. *Twentieth Century Pirates (8)*: *Betty*: B. Palmer. *Gladys*: G. Montgomery. *Mae*: M. LeRoux. *Anita*: A. Miramar. *Ginette*: G. Dorval. *Lebanon*: L. Hoffa. *Estelle*: E. Lang. *Zella*: Z. Lenny.

Scene 4

"Weep No More, My Mammy"
> F. Burt
> (*Music by* Lew Pollack. *Lyrics by* Sidney Clare.)
>> *Scene*: An Elopement.
>>> *Yonson*: E. Brendel. *Hilda Swanson*: F. Burt.

Scene 5

"Bridget McShane"
> B. Stanley, Biddies, Jailors
>> *Scene*: A Hotel Corridor.
>>> *Bridget McShane*: B. Stanley.

Scene 6

Waiter's Dance
> F. Masters

"Gay Brazilian"
> M. West, C. Harvey, Brazilian Beauties
>> *Scene*: Cafe de Paris.
>>> *John*: C. Harvey. *Phil, a waiter*: W. Moran. *Louis*: A. Wiser. *An Entertainer*: F. Masters. *Miss Promenade*: G. James. *Madelon*: M. West.

Scene 7

A Few Moments with Ukelele Ike
> C. Edwards

---

[46]Costumes uncredited.

Scene 8

A Girl's Fancy
"Daddy Buy Me a Bow Wow"
> A. Toddings, Bow Wow Girls
> *Miss Bow Wow*: A. Toddings.

Scene 9

"Fine Feathers"
> F. Hurst, M. Carville, Mannikins

Hat Specialty
> W. Moran, A. Wiser
>> *Scene*: A Hat Store
>>> *Babbette*: M. Carville. *Howard Dashing*: F. Hurst. *Hats*: W. Moran, A. Wiser. *Lieutenant Black*: E. Hickey. *Miss Shopping*: A. Toddings. *A Bathing Girl*: M. Miller.

Scene 10

"A Posty and a Maid"
> P. Brown, F. Masters
>> *Scene*: On the Street.
>>> *Mail Man*: F. Masters. *Maid*: P. Brown.

Scene 11

"Moth and the Flame"
> A. Toddings, C. Edwards, L. Edwards

Knee Dance
> L. Edwards
>> *Agent*: L. Edwards. *Mary*: A. Toddings. *Jimmy*: C. Edwards.

Scene 12

"Rose of the Rotisserie"
> J. Hussey

"Mighty Like a Rosenbloom"
> J. Hussey
>> *Scene*: Exterior (of a) Police Station.
>>> *Mac*: C. Harvey. *O'Brien*: E. Hickey. *Nathan*: J. Hussey. *A Prisoner*: F. Masters.

Scene 13

"Chicago"
> M. West
> (*Music by* Lew Pollack. *Lyrics by* Sidney Clare.)

"Sidewalk"
> M. West, Ensemble
>> *Scene*: Interior (of a) Police Station.
>>> *A Prisoner*: A. Wiser. *His Buddie*: W. Moran. *A Jazz Cop*: B. Stanley. *Nathan*: J. Hussey. *O'Brien*: E. Hickey. *Miss Shimmy*: M. West. *Attorney*: C. Harvey.

ACT 2

Scene 1

"Tennis Terpsichorean"
> R. Hazelton, M. Miller, H. Nelidova, E. Martyn, E. Morgan, Old-Fashioned Belles

Scene 2

"Ma Femme"
> J. Hussey, A. Toddings, Apache Girls
> *Nathan*: J. Hussey. *Branny Frice*: A. Toddings.

Scene 3

> *Scene*: In Yonson's Drawing Room.
>> *Yonson*: E. Brendel. *His Wife*: F. Burt.

Scene 4

"Star of Love"
> F. Hurst, M. Miller
>> *Scene*: In the Clouds.
>>> *Howard Dashing*: F. Hurst. *Moon Maiden*: M. Miller.

Scene 5

"Jazzimova"
> M. West, Jazzimova Girls
> *Nazimova à la Jazz*: M. West.

Scene 6

At the Fight
> *Announcer*: L. Edwards. *A Girl Fan*: B. Stanley. *Eddie*: E. Hickey. *Gene Delmont*: Himself. *Jimmy Kirk*: Himself. *Referee*: C. Harvey.

Scene 7

Temptation
> *Dance*: M. Carville.

Scene 8

"(In) Watermelon Time"/"(Those) Mason and Dixon Blues"
F. Burt, Watermelon Girls, L. Edwards, F. Masters, G. James, C. Harvey
(*Music by* Archie Gottler. *Lyrics by* Howard Johnson.)
Scene: A Watermelon.
Miss Dixie: F. Burt. *Her Sisters* (4): H. Nelidova, E. Morgan, E. Martyn, M. Miller. *Kentucky:* F. Masters. *Alabama:* L. Edwards. *Mississippi:* C. Harvey. *Miss Virginia:* G. James.

Scene 9

"When the Statues Come to Life"
C. Edwards, Statues
Scene: At the Museum.
Watchman: C. Edwards. *Venus:* H. Nelidova. *Adonis:* E. Morgan. *Diana:* G. James. *Mercury:* M. Smith. *Apollo:* M. Miller. *Psyche:* E. Martyn. *Minerva:* R. Hazelton.

Scene 10

"My Screen Maid"
F. Hurst, Some Screen Favorites
Scene: At the Studio.
Director: F. Hurst. *Marguerite Clark:* J. Danjou. *Bebe Daniels:* L. Pryor. *Mae Marsh:* G. Blair. *Pola Negri:* V. West. *Corrinne Griffith:* E. Courtney. *Mary Pickford:* M. Wood. *Theda Bara:* A. Miramar.

Scene 11

An Interlude with Mae West

"Baby Vampire"
M. West
(*Lyrics by* Harold Atteridge, James Hussey, Owen Murphy.)

Scene 12

Scene: In Yonson's Kitchen.
Yonson: E. Brendel. *His Wife:* F. Burt.

Scene 13

"Daisy Days"
A. Toddings, Daisy Girls

Scene 14

"Shakespeare's Garden of Love"
A. Toddings, Ensemble
A Page: A. Toddings. *Shakespeare:* F. Hurst. *Hamlet:* L. Edwards. *Ophelia:* H. Nelidova. *Romeo:* C. L. Henderson. *Juliet:* M. Smith. *Othello:* C. Edwards. *Desdemona:* M. Carville. *Portia:* F. Burt. *Bassanio:* E. Hickey. *Shylock:* J. Hussey. *Anthony:* A. Wiser. *Cleopatra:* M. West. *Petruchio:* F. Masters. *Katherine:* E. Morgan. *Richard III:* C. Harvey. *Queene Anne:* G. James. *Henry VIII:* W. Moran. *His Wives:* J. Brown, M. Miller, B. Stanley, E. Martyn, P. Brown, H. Armstrong.

1921.26

PUT & TAKE

A Colorful Musical Revue in Two Acts, 11 Scenes. Sketches by Irvin C. Miller. Music (and lyrics) by Spencer Williams. Additional music by J. Tim Brymn and Perry Bradford. Staged by Irvin C. Miller. Costumes by Brownie. Scenery by Beaumont Studios. Orchestra under the direction of J. Tim Brymn. Produced by the McCormick Amusement Co./Irvin C. Miller. Opened 23 August 1921 at Town Hall and closed 17 September 1921 after 32 performances.

CAST: IRVIN C. MILLER, CORA GREEN, ANDREW TRIBBLE, HAMTREE HARRINGTON, EARL DANCER, EDITH WILSON, MILDRED SMALLWOOD, EMMETT ANTHONY, GEORGE BRAXTON, FRED LaJOY, JOE PETERSON, (Julius) FOXWORTH and FRANCES, FLORENCE PARHAM, Al Pizzaro, Lillian Goodner, Mae Crowder and Maxie, Berni Barber, Roscoe Wickham, John Roscoe, Percy William, Virgie Cousins, Tabor and Green.
Ladies of the Ensemble: Viola Branch, Alva Smith, Florence Brown, Agnes Anthony, Juanita Hunter, Lorabelle Wise, Anaconia Turner, Theresa West, Essie Worth, Halaria Friend, Theo. Washington, Blanche Jones, Willie Blackwell, Annie Cousins, Katherine Miller, Mary Wells, Dempey Braxton, Sarah Cooper, Carrie Braxton. *Gentlemen of the Ensemble:* Thomas Brooks, Hobart Shand, Joe Peterson, Dick Conway, Wilfred Blanks, Ed. Caldwell, Charles Lawrence, Archie Cross. *Tennessee Four:* Percy William, Walter Richardson, Claude Lawson, Arthur Ford.

FIRST SPIN (ACT 1)

Put 1

"(Way) Down in Dixieland" (Opening Chorus)
(*Music and Lyrics by* Berni Barber.)
Scene: Wedding Day in Georgia.
Uncle Plummer: H. Harrington. *John Hale:* E. Dancer. *Aunt Ophelia:* A.

Tribble. *Marie Norris:* C. Green. *Ethel Norris:* M. Smallwood. *Rastus Jones:* I. C. Miller. *Mose:* E. Anthony.

"Stop and Rest Awhile"
E. Dancer, C. Green, Chorus
(*Music by* J. Tim Brymn. *Lyrics by* L. Wolfe Gilbert.)

"Dog"
E. Anthony

"Wedding Bells"
Entire Company

"(My) June Love"
F. LaJoy, Girls
(*Music and Lyrics by* Spencer Williams.)

"Snag 'em Blues"
A. Tribble, Entire Company
(*Music and Lyrics by* Spencer Williams.)

Put 2

Specialty:[47]
F. Parham

["Strut Miss Lizzie" (from ZIEGFELD FOLLIES OF 1921)
(*Music by* Turner Layton. *Lyrics by* Henry Creamer.)]

Put 3

Land of Silence
Rastus: I. C. Miller. *Mose:* E. Anthony. *The Ghost:* H. Shand.

Put 4

"Separation Blues"[48]
L. Goodner, M. Crowder
(*Music and Lyrics by* Spencer Williams.)

Put 5

In Old Virginia
Rastus: I. C. Miller. *Mose:* E. Anthony. *Policeman:* F. LaJoy. *Little Girl:* V. Branch. *Vamps:* V. Cousins, E. Worth. *Criminal:* J. Peterson. *The Victim:* —.

"Beedle 'Em Boo"
H. Harrington, J. Foxworth, Boys
(*Music and Lyrics by* Spencer Williams.)

Dance
T. West

Put 6

One String Novelty
G. Braxton

Put 7

Circus Grounds
Rastus: I. C. Miller. *Mose:* E. Anthony. *Manager:* F. LaJoy.

Put All

Circus

Put and Take Tumblers
G. Braxton, A. Pizzaro, Company

Foreign Band
I. C. Miller, E. Anthony, J. Peterson, J. Roscoe, H. Harrington

"Put and Take"
J. Foxworth, Company
(*Music and Lyrics by* Spencer Williams.)

Dance
H. Harrington, A. Tribble, G. Braxton

SPIN TWO (ACT 2)

Take 1

Lincoln Stroll
Uncle Plummer: H. Harrington. *Aunt Ophelia:* A. Tribble. *Dick West:* E. Dancer. *Van Burtt:* F. LaJoy.

Song
J. Foxworth and Frances

"Creole Gal" (Creole Girls)
C. Green, Chorus
(*Music and Lyrics by* Spencer Williams.)

---

[47]Replaced during the run by:
"Nervous Blues"
E. Wilson
(*Music and Lyrics by* Perry Bradford.)
[48]Dropped during the run.

"Chocolate Brown"
> R. Wickham, Chorus
> (*Music and Lyrics by* Spencer Williams.)

Introducing The Put and Take Octette

Take 2

Specialty[49]
> C. Chappelle and J. Stinette

Take All

Bazaar
> *Uncle Plummer*: H. Harrington. *Rastus*: I. C. Miller. *Mose*: E. Anthony. *Aunt Ophelia*: A. Tribble. *Dick West*: E. Dancer. *Ethel Norris*: M. Smallwood.

Song
> Tennessee Four

Specialty
> Tabor & C. Green

"Yodel"/
> E. Anthony

"Georgia Rose"
> E. Anthony
> (*Music by* Harry Rosenthal. *Lyrics by* Jimmy Flynn, Alex Sullivan.)

Dance
> I. C. Miller, M. Smallwood

"Oldtime Blues"
> Company
> (*Music by* Johnny Dunn. *Lyrics by* Perry Bradford.)

Finale

THE GREENWICH VILLAGE
FOLLIES (1921)

1921.27

A Revusical Comedy (Musical Revue) of New York's Latin Quarter in Two Acts, a Prologue and 14 Scenes[50]. Sketches and lyrics by John Murray Anderson and Arthur Swanstrom. Music by Carey Morgan. Production devised and staged by John Murray Anderson. Incidental dances arranged by Madame Serova. Costumes by Robert Locher. Settings by Robert Locher and John Murray Anderson. Musical director, Victor Baravalle. Orchestrations by Morney D. Helm and Frank Barry. Produced by the Bohemians, Inc. (A. L. Jones, Morris Green, Managing directors) (Messrs. Shubert). Opened 31 August 1921 at the Sam S. Shubert Theatre and closed 21 January 1922 after 167 performances.

CAST: IRENE FRANKLIN, TED LEWIS, RICHARD BOLD, AL HERMAN, ROSALIND FULLER, JACK VINCENT, PEGGY HOPE, DONALD KERR, VALODIA VESTOFF, HILDRED, ADDIE ROLFE, ROBERT CASTLETON, DORÉ, MARGARET PETIT, ALDEN GAY, CORONE PAYNTER, GRETCHEN EASTMAN, HAMILTON CONDON, BASIL SMITH, JAMES WATTS, ROBERT PITKIN, GORDON THOMPSON.

Ensemble: Vildhelda, Betty Linn, Billie Weston, Dorothy Drew, Tarzanne, Florence Normand, Dolores Peters, Winifred Verina, Lou Gorey, Marguerite Young, Ada Forman, Evelyn Darville, Anna Mae Clift, Polly Platt, Jean Arundel, Devah Worrell, Julia Parker, Elizabeth North, Trilby Clarke, Louise Powell, Peggy Mathews, Charles Edmonds, Bird Millman.

ACT 1[51]

Prologue
> (a) On Earth
> *A Greenwich Village Follies Girl*: F. Normand. *A Stage Reformer*: R. Pitkin. *Two Messengers from the Beyond*: A. Rolfe, Doré.

> (b) A Courtroom in the Beyond
> *An Angel*: A. Herman. *The Judge*: R. Castleton. Lillian Owen's Marionettes. *Puppeteer*: H. Condon.
> (*Dialogue written by* Blanche Merrill.)

> (c) On Earth
> *Cerise Dome*: I. Franklin.

Scene 1:

"Broadway Wedding Bells"[52]
> I. Franklin

"When Dreams Come True"[53]
> R. Bold, R. Fuller

Pas de Trois
> D. Drew, V. Vestoff, W. Verina
> *Scene*: Madame Loose-Heel's Red Salon.
> *The Manageress*: E. Darville. *Buttons*: Doré. *A Customer*: A. Rolfe. *Her Escort*: J. Vincent. *The Midinettes*: L. Powell, Voldhelda, P. Matthews, D. Worrell, E. North, T. Clark.
> *The Mannequins: Hosiery*: C. Paynter. *Gloves*: B. Weston. *Furs*: M. Young. *Feathers*: D. Peters. *Shoes*: A. M. Clift. *Capes*: B. Linn. *Ball Gowns*: W. Verina. *Negligées*: Hildred. *Street Frocks*: P. Platt. *Hats*: F. Normand.

The Abstract Fashions of the Future
> *Concrete*: L. Gorey. *The Third Rail*: 'Tarzanne'.*Steel*: D. Drew. *The Fourth Dimension*: A. Gay.

Scene 2

Before the Venetian Blind[54]
> J. Watts

Scene 3

What Did Her Husband Say? (*by* H. F. Maltby)
> *Scene*: A Village Apartment House.
> *First Girl*: W. Verina. *Second Girl*: L. Gorey *The Janitor*: H. Condon. *The Wife*: I. Franklin. *The Friend*: R. Pitkin. *The Husband*: A. Herman. *The Girl Upstairs*: P. Hope. *The Boy Upstairs*: D. Kerr. *The Drunk*: T. Lewis.

Scene 4

"I Want a Picture of You"[55]
> D. Kerr, P. Hope
> (*Music and Lyrics by* Percy Wenrich.)
> *Scene*: Before the Venetian Blind.

Scene 5

"Snow Flake"
> R. Fuller
> (*[Conceived] by* John Murray Anderson from a synopsis by Charles Derickson)
> *Scene*: Under the Silver Dome.
> *Jack Frost*: V. Vestoff. *The Winter Night*: Hildred. *The North Star*: A. Rolfe. *The Aurora*: W. Verina. *The Herald*: R. Castleton. *King Winter*: J. Vincent. *The Jester*: Doré. *Moonbeams*: J. Arundel, Vildhelda, D. Worrell, J. Parker. *The Snowflake*: M. Petit.

Pas de Deux
> M. Petit, V. Vestoff
> *The Dawn*: A. Gay. *The Sun*: C. Paynter. *The Rays of the Sun*: E. North, T. Clarke, L. Powell, D. Peters, P. Matthews, B. Linn

Scene 6

Ted Lewis:

["Down the Old Church Aisle"
> (*Music and Lyrics by* Ray Perkins.)

"Fate" (It Was Fate When I Met You)
> (*Music and Lyrics by* Byron Gay.)

"(I'm Coming Back to You) Maybe"
> (*Music and Lyrics by* Ted Lewis and Earnest Golden.)

---

[49]Reviewers remarked that Chappy and Stinette failed to appear at opening. Replaced during the run by:
> Friends?
> A. Tribble, H. Harrington

[50]The third in the annual series of musical revues which began under the auspices of the Bohemians in 1919.

[51]Song and sketch order was revised for the tour. Added during the run to Act 1:
> "Miss Dooley and Mr. Brown"
> Joe E. Brown, G. Dooley
> (*Music by* J. Fred Coots. *Lyrics by* Edward Dowling and Raymond W. Klages.)
> *Scene*: Before the Purple Curtains.

---

[52]Added to Scene 1: "The Jewels of the Follies." Dropped for subsequent tour.
> G. Trabert
> *Light*: M. Baudaux. *Color*: D. Vanna. *Architecture*: N. Larned. *Dress*: B. Weston. *Turquoise*: H. Lesoir. *White Pearl*: A. Valle. *Amethyst*: J. Strong. *Jade*: P. Mathews. *Sapphire*: P. Platt. *Ruby*: D. Cadwell. *Coral*: B. Linn. *Black Pearl*: E. Gail. *Diamond*: C. Paynter. *The Dancer*: D. Drew.

[53]Dropped for subsequent tour.

[54]Dropped during the run.

[55]For subsequent tour, replaced by (later dropped):
> "I've Got My Habits On"
> D. Kerr
> (*Music by* Jimmie Durante. *Lyrics by* Chris Smith and Bob Schafer.)

"Unlucky Blues"
   (*Music and Lyrics by* Ted Lewis and J. Russel Robinson.)]
      Scene: Before the Venetian Blind.
Scene 7
  The Greenwich Village Fair[56]
    (a) "Oh-Heigh-Ho!"
      R. Fuller
        The Girl: M. Petit. *The Boy*: V. Vestoff. *The Village Gossip*: L. Gorey.
        The Village Belle: A. M. Clift. *The Village School Teacher*: W. Verina.
        The Vendor of Balloons: J. Vincent. *The Dairymaid*: P. Platt. *The Village*
        Vamp: B. Weston. *The Equestrienne*: D. Drew. *The Tom Boy*: Tarzanne.
        The Village Coquette: C. Paynter. *Jack*: Doré. *Jill*: A. Rolfe. *The Girl from*
        the Next Village: M. Young. *The Lady Who Came in a Carriage*: Hildred.
        The Gentleman Who Came in a Carriage: R. Castleton. *The Fortune*
        Teller: F. Normand. *The Lady from Afar*: A. Gay.
    (b) The Last Dance (*by* Gretchen Eastman)
        The Roughneck: D. Kerr. *The Dancer*: G. Eastman. *The Sneak*: H. London.
        The Jealous Lover: B. Smith.
    (c) "I'm Up in the Air Over You"
      R. Bold, B. Millman
    (d) Ballet Divertissements:
  A Dying Duck in a Thunder Storm (Solo)
  Love's Awakening (Adagio)
  "Pavlowa Song"
      (*Music and Lyrics by* Blanche Merrill.)
        Mutty: J. Watts. *Hillio*: D. Kerr.
    (e) "Bang! Bang!! Bang!!!"
      T. Lewis, Entire Company

ACT 2[57]
Scene 1
  Blue Law's Ninth Wife[58] (*by* Oliver Herford)
    Scene: Under the Silver Dome.
      An Author-Producer: R. Pitkin. *The Public*: I. Franklin. *The Headsman*:
      J. Vincent. *The Hanger of Heads*: B. Smith. *The Maker of Music*:
      G. Thompson. *Blue Law*: R. Castleton. *The Bean-Bearers*: A. Rolfe, Doré.
      Blue Law's Wives: *Playing Cards*: R. Pitkin. *Lady Nicotine*: B. Weston.
      The Spoken Drama: D. Drew. *The Silent Drama*: Tarzanne. *Loving Cup*:
      C. Paynter. *Sunday*: Hildred. *Art*: F. Normand. *Twinkletoes*: P. Hope.
      Piety: J. Watts. *Masks by* W. T. Benda.
Scene 2
  Irene Franklin (Songs)[59]
    (*Music by* Burton Green. *Lyrics by* Irene Franklin.)
      Scene: Before the Venetian Blind.
Scene 3
  "The Haunted Violin"[60] (*Invented by* Charles Edmonds)
    R. Bold
      Scene: In Green and Silver.
      The Violinist: C. Edmonds.

---

[56]Added during the run to this scene:
  Dance Eccentrique
    J. E. Brown
[57]Added during subsequent tour:
  "Strike" (Act 2, Scene 1)
    Marie Holly
  Dance Argentine
    Theo. Zambounis, Kathleen O'Hanlon, Ensemble
[58]Replaced during the run by:
  "The Reminiscent Melody"
    G. Miller, George Trabert, R. Fuller, G. Eastman, E. Darville, B. Linn, B.
    Smith, J. Vincent
    (*Music by* Milton Ager. *Lyrics by* John Murray Anderson and Jack Yellen.)
      Scene: Set in Green and Silver.
      At the piano: H. Condon. And P. Hope, D. Kerr.
[59]Dropped for subsequent tour.
[60]Replaced during the run by:
  Arrest Me
    Scene: Street in Greenwich Village.
      Down and Out: J. E. Brown. *The Friend*: F. Daniels. *Police Officer*: R. Pitkin.
      The Bum: B. Smith. *The Thief*: Albert Deano. *The Flirt*: B. Weston. *A Son-in-*
      Law: D. Kerr. *The Heiress*: A. Rolfe.

Scene 4
  "Ease Along"[61] (Easin' Along)
    D. Kerr
    (*Music and Lyrics by* Irving Bibo and Thomas Morris.)
      Scene: Before the Venetian Blind.
Scene 5
  Pay As You Enter, Madame[62] (*by* H. I. Phillips)
    Scene: A Prima Donna's Home.
      Flora: D. Peters. *Gerald*: R. Pitkin. *Valet*: G. Thompson. *Madame's Maid*: L.
      Gorey. *Madame's Doctor*: B. Smith. *Madame Yell-a-Gen*: J. Watts.
Scene 6
  'Set' in Black
    A. Herman
  ["Wha Wha" (That Imaginary Isle)
    (*Music by* Lester Stevens. *Lyrics by* Phil Furman.)
  "Moonshine Is in the Mountain Still"
    (*Music by* Allen Behr. *Lyrics by* Al Herman.
  "True Blue Sal"
    (*Music and Lyrics by* Al Herman, Alex Gerber, and Abner Silver.)]
Scene 7[63]
  The Beardsley Figures
    Scene: In Silver and Black.
      The Black Peacocks: H. Tatore, D. Drew. *Les Marquis*: G. Thompson, J.
      Vincent. *The Venetian Hat*: M. Young. *The Black Fan*: A. M. Clift. *The Abbé*:
      Robert Castleton. *The Masked Favorite*: A. Gay. *Honi-Soit-Qui-Mal-y-Pense*:
      F. Normand. *Black Wings*: L. Gorey. *La Belle Carlotta*: P. Platt. *Snare of*
      Vintage: W. Verina. *Fish Tails*: B. Weston. *The Jeune Fille*: C. Paynter.
      Fabulous Hat: Hildred. *The Mediums*: B. Linn, Vildhelda, T. Clarke, P.
      Mathews, L. Powell, D. Peters, E. North, D. Worrell. *The Silver Peacock*: A.
      Forman.
  "Three O'Clock in the Morning"
    R. Bold
    (*Music by* Julian Robledo. *Lyrics by* Dorothy Terriss.)
  The Chime Ringers
    M. Petit, V. Vestoff
  La Baronne de Table D'Hote
    J. Watts
  Resumé: The End

1921.28   # GET TOGETHER

An International Entertainment (Vaudeville Revue) in Two Acts, 9 Scenes.
Staged by R. H. Burnside. Costumes by Brooks Theatrical Costumers,
Madame Haverstick, Anna Spencer, Eaves Theatrical Costumes, Will R.
Barnes (Ice Ballet). Musical director, A. J. Garing. Produced by Charles
Dillingham. Opened 3 September 1921 at the Hippodrome and closed 22
April 1922 after 397 performances.

CAST: MICHEL FOKINE, VERA FOKINA, BERT LEVY, KATIE SCHMIDT,
PAUL KRECKOW, HOWARD NICHOLSON, FERRY CORWEY, EARL BARROY,
JACK HANLEY, FIVE KAETHS, THE THREE BOBS, MARCELLINE and
MORON, Mlle. CHARLOTTE, POWER'S PERFORMING ELEPHANTS,
ALFRED RENTON, FRANK HERBERT, ALBERT ALBERTO, GEORGE DAVIS.

---

[61]Replaced during the run by:
  "A Young Man's Fancy" (from WHAT'S IN A NAME)
    R. Fuller
    (*Music by* Milton Ager. *Lyrics by* John Murray Anderson and Jack Yellen.)
      Scene: Set in Purple and Green.
      The Shepherd: V. Vestoff. *The Shepherdess*: C. Paynter. *The Temptress*: M.
      Petit. *The Toe Dancers*: Misses Bizzette, Arudnel, Vildhelda, Worrell,
      Parker, Gaznowa. *Liza Jane*: A. Rolfe. *The Antiquarian*: A. Deano.
[62]Dropped during the run.
[63]Added to The Beardsley Figure Scene during the run:
  Finale: "The House That Jack Built"
    (*Music by* Milton Ager. *Lyrics by* John Murray Anderson and Jack Yellen.)
      The Author: J. E. Brown. *The Composer*: J. Vincent *The Soprano*: E. Darville.
      The Tenor: G. Trabert. *The Ingenue*: R. Fuller. *The Comedian*: A. Herman.
      The Soubrette: P. Hope. *The Angel*: D. Kerr. *Mr. Shubert*: R. Pitkin. *The*
      Scrubwoman: L. Gorey. *The Leader of the Chorus*: B. Weston. The Artist
      Models.
Finale (The End)

ACT 1[64]

Scene 1

Clyde Cook in his latest comedy picture, "The Toreador"[65]
> Exclusive pre-release public showing by arrangement with William Fox
> *Scene*: In Filmland.

Scene 2

Power's Performing Elephants[66] including Lena, Jennie, Roxy, Julia, together with a carnival of clowns including Marceline and Moron.
> *Scene*: At the Circus.

Scene 3

The Three Bobs with their wonderful dog and their marvelous crew
> *Scene*: At the Circus.

Scene 4

Ferry Corwey, the Merry Musical Clown
> *Scene*: On the Boardwalk.

Scene 5

The Thunder Bird[67], a Fantastic Ballet in One Act
> Book by Vera Fokina based upon an ancient Aztec legend. Dances and action composed and staged by Michel Fokine. Music composed by (Mily Alexeivich) Balakirev, (Alexander) Borodin, (Mikhail) Glinka, (Nikolai) Rimsky-Korsakov, (Pyotor Ilyich) Tchaichovsky. Conducted by Anselm Goetzl.
> *The Thunder Bird*: V. Fokina. *The Princess Nahua*: V. Fokina. *Aztjan*: M. Fokine. *The Master of Mystic Forces*: E. Barroy. *Wizards, Thunderbirds, Aztec Warriors, Aztec Wives, Aztec Girls, Bears, Tigers, Mask Aztlans, Attendants, Musicians, etc.*: (Ensemble).
> *Scene*: In a Peruvian Forest.

ACT 2

Scene 1

The Five Kaeths[68] with a Musical Offering (Their first appearance in the U.S.A.)
> *Scene*: Somewhere in Holland.

Scene 2

Bert Levey, International Artist and Entertainer
> *Scene*: In Cartoon.

Scene 3

"The Red Shoes," direct from the Admiral's Ice Palace, Berlin, by arrangement with Leo Bartuschek. Story by H. Regel. Music by Rasul Mader. Dances arranged by Mlle. Charlotte. Conducted by Anselm Goetz.

---

[64]Added to Act 1 during the run, after The Happy Hoboes sequence (see Scene 2 footnote):
> The Graf Trio (European Musical Novelty, first appearance in the USA)
> *Scene*: Somewhere in Switzerland.

[65]Replaced during the run by:
> "The Butterflies and the Bees" (Ballet)
> (*Music by* A. Ponchielli. Conducted by Dr. Anselm Goetzl.)
> *Scene*: Somewhere in the Land of the Imagination.
> "The Bumble Bee"
> H. Lambert
> (*Music by* Milton Lusk.)
> *The Queen of the Bees*: E. Hansen. *The Butterfly*: S. Gluckoff. *Bees, Butterflies*: Hippodrome Ensemble.

[66]Power's Elephants appeared as part of The Gathering of the Dolls (see Scene 5 footnote), and their Scene 2 spot was replaced during the run with:
> Medley
> Hippodrome Quartette (W. F. Williams, R. McClellan, J. J. Murphy, A. Brooks)
> The Happy Hoboes
> 'Spike' Davis, 'La La' Herbert, 'Tiger' Alberto, 'Cockney' Edwards, 'Dip' Reano, 'Kid' Ravel, 'Happy' Ward, 'Blinks' Becker, 'Hoofer' Russell, 'Stove' Byrne, 'Side' Byrne, 'Hoppie' Byrne, 'Rube' Corasire, 'Scotty' Doreto, 'Limey' Bleasdale, 'Curley' Colton, 'Hercules' Keenan

[67]Added during the run to close Act 1:
> The Gathering of the Toys, including a Carnival of Clowns
> *Dolls and Toys*: Ballet Dancing Doll: Elna Hansen. *Welsh Doll*: Albertina Vitak. *Fancy Dress Doll*: Gladys Waite. *French Doll*: Paul Truman. *Café Dancing Doll*: Lilly Lubell. *Pierette*: Agnes Hunter. *Pierrot*: Nellie Savage.

[68]Replaced during the run by:
> Memories of Minstrelsy
> *Scene*: In Melody Land.
> *Hippodrome Quartette*: W. F. Williams, R. McClellan, J. J. Murphy, A. Brooks.

Prince Ivan: P. Krechow. *Gregor*: A. Renton. *The Wounded Soldier*: F. Herbert. *Fedor*: A. Alberto. *Olga*: K. Schmidt. *Rozka*: H. Nicholson. *The Wandering Comedian*: G. Davis. *Darinka*: Charlotte. *Ivan's Friends, Pilgrims, Country People, Police, Soldiers, Cossacks, Russians, Kalmucks, Circassians, Musicians, etc.*: (Ensemble).
> *Scene*: Exterior of Fedor's Inn, near a small village in Southern Russia.

Scene 4

The Ice Palace of Prince Ivan. Specialties at the Inn:
> a) The Villagers at Play.
> b) Arrival of the Gypsies
> c) Katie Schmidt, solo.
> d) Howard Nicholson, assisted by Howard Nicholson.
> e) Arrival of Prince Ivan and His Friend.
> f) They tell the Innkeeper to send out his daughter Darinka to wait on them.
> g) Entrance of Darinka
> h) The Prince has flirtation with Darinka, who repulses him.
> i) The Prince points to the Red Shoes and tells Darinka that if she possessed them she would become a wonderful dancer. The prince leaves her with this thought in her mind, and presently Darinka, overcome by her desire to dance with the Prince takes the Red Shoes and finds after putting them on she can dance. The Villagers re-enter. They see Darinka has taken the Red Shoes and are horrified, and threatening Darinka, they chase her away.
> j) In the Palace, Opening Assembly of the Guests.
> k) Fast skating Solo, Howard Nicholson, the Douglas Fairbanks of the Ice.
> l) Gavotte by the Double Quartette (Misses E. Schaefer, I Schaefer, I. Merkle, M. Brewka, P. Kohlhoffer, T. Weideman, M. O'Neill, A. Mehlenberger).
> m) Entrance of the Prince.
> n) Entrance of Darinka, the Mysterious Guest, who is recognized by the Prince who offers her his hand in marriage.
> o) Steele & Winslow—The Ice Comedians
> p) Grand Finale

1921.29 THE MERRY WIDOW

A Revival of the Operetta in Three Acts[69]. (Original Viennese) Book ('Die Lustige Witwe') by Victor Léon and Leo Stein. after 'L'Attaché d'Ambassade' by Henri Meilhac. Music by Franz Lehár. Production staged by George Marion. Scenery designed by Joseph Urban. Costumes by Peggy Hoyt, E. S. Freisinger. Orchestra under the direction of Max Hirschfeld. Produced by Henry W. Savage. Opened 5 September 1921 at the Knickerbocker Theatre and closed 22 October 1921 after 56 performances.

CAST (in order of appearance): *Raoul de St. Brioche*: Ralph Soule. *Natalie*: Dorothy Francis. *Camille de Jolidon*: FRANK WEBSTER. *M. Khadja*, Counselor of Legation: Charles Angelo. *Nova Kovich*, of the Embassy: William H. White. *Olga*, his wife: Marie Wells. *General Nisch*, Messenger of the Embassy: JEFFERSON DeANGELIS. *Popoff*, Marsovian Ambassador: RAYMOND CRANE. *Prince Danilo*, Embassy Attaché: REGINALD PASCH. *Sonia*, a young widow: LYDIA LIPKOWSKA. *Marquis Cascada*: GEORGES DUFRANNE. *Melitza*, wife of Khadja: Margaret Schilling. *Little Willie*: Weslyn Hull. *Head Waiter*: John Yorke. *Orchestra Leader at Maxim's*: Bert V. Elias.
> *Girls at Maxim's*: Zo-Zo: Yvette DuBois. Fi-Fi: Peggy Arthur. Lo-Lo: Gwyn Stratford. Do-Do: Evelyn Dorn. Jou-Jou: Dorothy Gilbert. Frou-Frou: Margery Wall. Clo-Clo: Frances Romana. Margot: Esther Morris.
> *Guests*: Celeste Craven, Jeanne Stuart, Jean Ferguson, Kathleen Mayer, Blossom Churan, Elsie Bartlett, Dora Beck, Louise Rostrand, John Colvin, Edward Sheldon, Roscoe Snyder, Arthur Goodrich, Harry Parry, Robert Roberts, Herbert Heming, John Clark, John Yorke. *Hadjuk*: Charles Huston, Ad Meyer. *Marsovian Dancing Men*: Albert Bennet, Patrick Quinton, Horace R. Sisson, Albert Barber, Warren Bassette, Horace Milleron, Weslyn Hull, James Smith. *Marsovian Dancing Girls*: Dorothy Gilbert, Esther Morris, Gwyn Stratford, Francs Romana, Peggy Arthur, Yvette DuBois, Evelyn Dorn, Margery Wall. *Marsovian Troubadours*: Bert V. Elias, Blaz Tkalae, James Kovachevich, Joseph Huzar, Micha Vranasevich.

1921.30 MUSIC BOX REVUE (1921-22)

A Musical Revue in Two Acts, 23 Scenes and a Prologue[70]. Sketches by Willie Collier, T. J. Gray, Frances Nordstrom, George V. Hobart. Music and lyrics by Irving Berlin. Staged by Hassard Short. Dances arranged by Bert French, I Tarasoff. Scenery designed by Clark Robinson. Costumes

---

[69]First presented in New York 21 October 1907 at the New Amsterdam Theatre for 416 performances. For Synopsis of Scenes and Musical Numbers, see original 1907 production. English libretto, by Adrian Ross, uncredited.

[70]The first of four annual musical revues conceived by Irving Berlin and produced by Sam H. Harris.

designed by Ralph Mulligan, Cora MacGeachy, Alice O'Neil, Eaves (men's costumes). Lighting by John Brunton. Orchestra under the direction of Anton Heindl and Frank Tours. Orchestrations by Alfred Dalby, Maurice dePackh, Charles Grant, Stephen Jones, Oscar Radin and Frank Tours, under the supervision of Harry Akst. Produced by Sam H. Harris. Opened 22 September 1921 at the Music Box Theatre and closed 30 September 1922 after 440 performances.

CAST: WILLIAM COLLIER, SAM BERNARD, JOSEPH SANTLEY, IVY SAWYER, FLORENCE MOORE, PAUL FRAWLEY, RENE RIANO, THE BROX SISTERS (Kathlyn, Dagmar, Lorraine), WILDA BENNETT, IRVING BERLIN, EMMA HAIG, Mlle. MARGUERITE, ROSE ROLANDO, FRANK GILL, MAURICE QUINLIVAN, RICHARD W. KEENE, HUGH CAMERON, ALETA, ROBERT RHODES, Donald Hylan, George Mays, Edward Mendelsohn, Chester Hale, Ada Bochell, Joseph Bove.

Ladies of the Ensemble: Josephine Adair, Margaret Irving, Louise Bateman, Katherine Van Pelt, Elsie Sterling, Helen Rich, Clara Taylor, Helen Lyons, Lucretia Craig, Frances Mahan, Irene Duffy, Irene Wylie, Bert Foune, Dorothy Haver, Helen Shea, Misses Cox, Lowry. *Eight Little Notes*: Mary Beth Milford, Virginia Dixon, Helen Clare, Betsy Ross, Helen Newcombe, Claire Davis, Miriam Hopkins, Jeanne St. John.

ACT 1

Prologue

Scene 1

The Stranger Arrives
Scene: The Roof of the Music Box.

Scene 2

The Stage Hands ("What's in the Queer-looking Bundle?")
M. Quinlivan, D. Hylan, R. Rhodes, G. Maya, E. Mendelsohn
Scene: Exterior of the Music Box.

The Music Box Revue ("Where am I?")
Aleta

Scene 3

The Burglars ("We work while you sleep"/"We'll take the plot to Ziegfeld")
Misses Mahan, Duffy, Wylie, Foune, Haver, Meakins, Shea, Cox, Lowry

Eight Little Notes
M. Milford, V. Dixon, H. Clare, B. Ross, H. Newcombe, C. Davis, K. Mahoney, J. St. John

The Dancing Master
R. W. Keene
Scene: Interior of the Music Box.

Scene 4: The Revue

Under the Bed (*by* Frances Nordstrom, by arrangement with A. H. Woods. *Directed by* William Collier.)
The Wife: F. Moore. *Smith*: J. Santley. *Brown*: M. Quinlivan. *Jones*: P. Frawley. *Thompson*: H. Cameron.

Scene 5

"Dancing the Seasons Away" (Dance Your Troubles Away)
Behind the Counter: B. Meakins. *The Boy*: R. W. Keene. *The Girl*: E. Haig.

Scene 6

The Fan
The Lady of the Fan: W. Bennett. *The Tassels*: Mlle. Marguerite, F. Gill. *The Girls Behind the Fan*: J. Adair, M. Irving, L. Bateman, E. Sterling, K. Van Pelt, H. Rich, C. Taylor, H. Lyons.

"Behind the Fan"
W. Bennett

Scene 7

The Meeting
William Collier: W. Collier. *The Angel*: S. Ward.

Scene 8

Dining Out

"In a Cozy Kitchenette Apartment"
J. Santley, I. Sawyer
Scene: The Restaurant.
The Diners: I. Sawyer, J. Santley. *The Head Waiter*: H. Cameron. *The Coat Room Girl*: L. Craig. *The Coat Room Boy*: R. W. Keene. *The Oysters*: Misses Dixon, Clare, Davis, Ross, Newcombe, Mahan. *The Chicken*: E. Haig. *The Cauliflower*: M. Milford. *The Mushroom*: Aleta. *The French Pastry*: Mlle. Marguerite. *The Cigar*: R. Rolando. *The Check*: R. Riano. *The Tips*: Misses Duffy, Wylie, Foune, Meakins, Haver, Cox, Shea, Lowry. *The Waiters*: Messrs. Quinlivan, Hylan, Mays, Mendelsohn.

Scene 9

Nothing But Cuts (*by* William Collier. *Directed by* William Collier.)
The Director: W. Collier. *The Backer*: S. Bernard. *The Author*: M. Quinlivan. *The Leading Lady*: M. Irving. *The Leading Gentleman*: J. Santley. *The Friend of the Family*: R. Rhodes. *The Heavy Man*: H. Cameron. *The Chorus Girls*: Misses Wylie, Haver, Duffy, Meakins, Foune.

"My Ben Ali Haggin Girl"
R. Rhodes

Scene 10

"My Little Book of Poetry"
J. Santley, Girls
Anabel Lee: M. Irving. *The Vampire*: E. Haig. *Evangeline*: H. Lyons. *The Story Tellers*: The Eight Little Notes. *Paul Revere*: R. W. Keene. *Maud Muller*: B. Meakins. *Donga Ding*: F. Gill. *Hiawatha*: C. Hale. *The Raven*: I. Duffy. *The Bells*: Misses Aleta, D. Haver, B. Foune, I. Wylie, H. Shea.

Scene 11

"A Play Without a Bedroom"
F. Moore

Scene 12

"Say It With Music"
The Girl: W. Bennett. *The Man*: P. Frawley.

Scene 13

Finale: "Everybody Step"
Brox Sisters, Entire Company

ACT 2

Scene 1

The Fountain of Youth (*Dialogue by* Joseph Herbert.)
Scene: A Garden.
The Old Lady: A. Bochell. *The Child*: Aleta. *Ponce de Leon*: J. Santley. *The Statue*: C. Hale. *Faith*: M. Hopkins. *Hope*: M. B. Milford. *Ambition*: F. Mahan. *Love*: H. Newcombe. *The Fountain*: R. Rolanda. *The Water Lilies*: —.

Scene 2

"I Am a Dumbell" (I'm a Dumbell)
R. Riano

Scene 3

Words Mean Nothing (*by* George V. Hobart. *Directed by* William Collier.)
Scene: An Apartment in New York City.
The Butler: H. Cameron. *The Lover*: J. Santley. *The Wife*: W. Bennett. *The Husband*: W. Collier.

Scene 4

"The School House Blues"
Brox Sisters

Scene 5

Fair Exchange (At the Court Around the Corner)
Scene: An Obliging Court Room.
The Husband: J. Santley. *The Wife*: I. Sawyer. *The Judge*: H. Cameron. *The Attorney*: F. Moore. *Another Husband*: P. Frawley. *Another Wife*: W. Bennett.

Scene 6

"They Call It Dancing"
S. Bernard
Scene: The Ball Room.

The Dance
Ensemble

The Fox Trot
E. Haig, R. W. Keene

The Waltz
Mlle. Marguerite, F. Gill

Dancing That's All
R. Riano, S. Bernard

Scene 7

"The Legend of the Pearls"
The Pearl: W. Bennett. *Strings of Pearls*: Misses Adair, Irving, Bateman, Van Pelt, Rich, R. Taylor, Wylie, Sterling. *The Dancer*: H. Lyons.

Scene 8

House Hunting (*by* Thomas. J. Grey. *Directed by* William Collier.)
Scene: Streets in New York City.
The Janitor: W. Collier. *The Husband*: S. Bernard. *The Wife*: F. Moore. *The Girl*: R. Riano. *The Boy*: J. Bove.

Scene 9
"An Interview with Irving Berlin"
Scene: The Studio.
The Reporters: The Eight Little Notes.
Scene 10
Finale (Ladies and gentlemen, every revue)
W. Collier introducing the Entire Company

1921.31 BLOSSOM TIME

A Musical Play in Three Acts. Book and lyrics by Dorothy Donnelly. Adapted from the Viennese original ('Das Dreimäderlhaus') by A. M. Willner and Heinz Reichert, based on a novel 'Schwammerl' by Rudolf H. Bartsch. Music adapted and augmented by Sigmund Romberg from the melodies of Franz Schubert, selected and arranged by Heinrich Berté. Staged by J. C. Huffman. Dancing numbers arranged by Frank M. Gillespie. Scenery designed by Watson Barratt. Costumes designed by Mode Costume Company. Orchestra under the direction of Oscar Radin. Entire production under the personal direction of J. J. Shubert. Produced by the Messrs. Shubert. Opened 29 September 1921 at the Ambassador Theatre, closing 1 July 1922 after 319 performances for summer vacation. Reopened 7 August 1922 at the Ambassador Theatre, moved 2 October 1922 to Jolson's 59th Theatre, moved 23 October 1922 to the Century Theatre, and closed 27 January 1923 after a total of 516 performances.

CAST: *Mitzi*: OLGA COOK. *Bellabruna*: ZOE BARNETT. *Fritzi*: Dorothy Whitmore. *Kitzi*: Frances Halliday. *Mrs. Kranz*: ETHEL BRANDEN. *Greta*: EMMY NICLAS. *Baron Franz Schober*: HOWARD MARSH. *Franz Schubert*: BERTRAM PEACOCK. *Kranz*: WILLIAM DANFORTH. *Vogl*: ROY CROPPER. *Kupelweiser*: PAUL KER. *Von Schwind*: EUGENE MARTINET. *Binder*: Lucius Metz. *Erkman*: Perry Askam. *Count Sharntoff*: Yvan Servais. *Hansy*: Irving Mels. *Novotny*: Robert Payton Gibbs. *Rose*: Mildred Kay. *Mrs. Colburg*: Erba Robeson. *Waiter*: Howard A. Berman. *Dancer*: Burtress Deitch. *Four Guests*: Gotham City Four.
Ladies of the Ensemble: Norma Gould, Marie Gary, Juliet Strahl, Billy Williams, Dorothy Jackson, Mildred Soper, Bobbie McCree, Florence Elmore, Lyola Whyte, Dorothy Newell, Claire Hooper, Edith Holloway.

Act 1: The Prater in Vienna, 1826. An afternoon in May.

Act 2: Drawing room in the house of Kranz. Three months later.

Act 3: Schubert's lodgings. Two months later.

ACT 1
Opening
E. Niclas, P. Ker, E. Martinet, R. Cropper, Chorus
"Melody Triste"
Z. Barnett
"Three Little Maids"
O. Cook, D. Whitmore, F. Halliday, Chorus
"Serenade"
H. Marsh, B. Peacock, R. Cropper, P. Ker, E. Martinet, I. Mels
"My Springtime Thou Art"
H. Marsh, B. Peacock, R. Cropper, P. Ker, E. Martinet, Girls
"Song of Love"
B. Peacock, O. Cook
Finale
Ensemble

ACT 2
"Moment Musicale"
B. Peacock, I. Mels, B. Deitch
"Love Is a Riddle"
H. Marsh, L. Metz, P. Askam, O. Cook, D. Whitmore, F. Halliday, Girls
"Let Me Awake"
Z. Barnett, H. Marsh
"Tell Me Daisy"
O. Cook, B. Peacock
"Only One Love Ever Fills the Heart"
O. Cook, H. Marsh
Finale
O. Cook, B. Peacock, H. Marsh

ACT 3
Opening
E. Niclas
"Keep It Dark"
Z. Barnett, R. Cropper, E. Martinet, P. Ker
"Lonely Hearts"
O. Cook, D. Whitmore, F. Halliday, E. Niclas, B. Peacock
Finale
Ensemble

1921.32 THE O'BRIEN GIRL

George M. Cohan's Comedians in A Musical Comedy in Two Acts, 3 Scenes. Book by Otto Harbach and Frank Mandel. Music by Louis Hirsch. Lyrics by Frank Mandel. Staged by Julian Mitchell. Scenery designed by Edward G. Unitt and Joseph Wickes. Costumes designed by Alice O'Neil. Orchestra under the direction of Charles J. Gebest. Produced by George M. Cohan. Opened 3 October 1921 at the Liberty Theatre and closed 18 February 1922 after 164 performances.

CAST (in order of appearance): *Mrs. Hope*, an artist: Finita DeSoria. *Alice O'Brien*, the girl: ELIZABETH HINES. *Joe Fox*, an Indian guide: ALEXANDER YAKOVLEFF. *Lawrence Patten*, an art publisher: Edwin Forsberg. *Humphrey Drexel*, his partner: ROBINSON NEWBOLD. *Mrs. Drexel*, his wife: GEORGIA CAINE. *Eloise Drexel*, their daughter: ADA MAE WEEKS. *Larry Patten*, just out of college: TRUMAN STANLEY. *Wilbur Weathersby*, his chum: ANDREW TOMBES. *Gerald Morgan*, a dancing guest: CARL HEMMER. *Dancing Mad Maidens* (4): *Minerva*: Kitty Devere. *Lucille*: Vera O'Brien. *Aline*: Kathleen Mahoney. *Estelle*: Gretchen Grant. *Wolf*: Harry Rose. *Bear*: George Page. *Eagle*: Lou Lesser. *Owl*: George Hurd. *Mickey*: M. Cunningham. *Dickey*: Hazel Clements.
Ladies of the Chorus: Irene Regan, Alberta Tuttle, Kitty Devere, Vera O'Brien, Henrietta Morin, Marie Messier, Ethel Lyons, Louise Lyons, Helen Mann, Sylvia Carol, Florence Doherty, Dorothy Fuller, Lucille Wallace, Madeline Bailey, Gertrude Healey, Helen Menthe, Cecil Baisel, Abbie Harvey, Betty Wilson, Melba Pelleau. *Gentlemen of the Chorus*: Messrs. Ellison, Burke, Murray, Galivan, Cole, Rush, Vaughn, Downing, Ford, Drake, Stevens.

Act 1: The Exterior of a Fashionable Hotel on a Lake in the Adirondacks. Afternoon.

Act 2, Scene 1: A room adjoining the ballroom; same hotel. The same night. *Scene 2*: Exterior of Ballroom.

ACT 1
"Curiosity" (Pantomimic Opening)
"Give, Give"
G. Caine, A. M. Weeks, Chorus
"I'll Treat You Just Like a Sister"
A. M. Weeks, A. Tombes
"I Wonder How I Ever Passed You By"
E. Hines, T. Stanley
"Indian Prance"
A. Yakovleff, Chorus
"Learn to Smile"
F. DeSoria, E. Hines, C. Hemmer
"My Little Canoe"
A. M. Weeks, A. Tombes, Chorus
Finale
Entire Company

ACT 2
"Entrance of Dancers" (Opening)
G. Grant, A. Tuttle, K. Devere, V. O'Brien
Grotesque Dance
A. Yakovleff
"I'm So Excited"
E. Hines, A. Tombes, Boys
"Murder" (Specialty)
R. Newbold
"The Conversation Step"
A. M. Weeks, A. Tombes, Chorus
"The O'Brien Girl"
E. Hines, T. Stanley, C. Hemmer
"Partners"
A. M. Weeks, A. Tombes, M. Cunningham, H. Clements

Reprise
  E. Hines
"To Keep You in Your Seats"
  Company
Finale
  Entire Company

1921.33

THE LOVE LETTER

A Musical Play in Three Acts. Libretto by William LeBaron. Suggested by Franz [Ferenc] Molnár's story 'The Wolf.' (Adapted from the play 'The Phantom Rival' ['A farkas'] by Ferenc Molnár.) Music by Victor Jacobi. Entire production directed by Edward Royce. Scenery by Joseph Urban. Dresses designed by Lichtenstein Millinery Company (Act 1), Alice O'Neil (Act 2), Gilbert Clark, Inc. (Act 3). Orchestra under the direction of William Daly. Produced by Charles Dillingham. Opened 4 October 1921 at the Globe Theatre and closed 29 October 1921 after 31 performances.

CAST (in order of appearance): *Officers on Leave* (2): *Michael*: Townshend Ahern. *Julien*: Henry White. *Head Waiter*: Edgar Norton. *Eugene Bernard*: WILL WEST. *Countess Irma*: MARJORIE GATESON. *Miriam Charlot, engaged to Eugene*: CAROLYN THOMSON. *Madame Charlot, Miriam's mother*: Katharine Stewart. *Richard Kolnar*: FRED ASTAIRE. *Aline Moray*: ADELE ASTAIRE. *Philip Delmar*: JOHN CHARLES THOMAS. *Waiter*: Elliott Roth. *Bus-Boy*: Roger Davis. *Marie, Miriam's maid*: Alice Brady. *Gina*: Irma Irving. *Zena*: Dorothy Irving. *Betty Parker*: Jane Carroll. *Ambassador*: Tom Fitzpatrick.
Ladies of the Ensemble: Peggy Brady, Sophie Brenner, Gene Fleming, Kathleen Erroll, Lucille Darling, Betty Darling, Alma Drange, Hazel Donnelly, Marjorie Tooney, Jill Middleton, Dorothy Brown, Nancy Griffith, Mildred Morgan, Lorraine Sherwood, Muriel Cort, Margaret Morris, Marie Francis, Marguerite Draper, Gwendolyn Gordon, Lillian Kent, Marion Donnelly, Maida Harries, Pearl Eaton, Helen Halperin. *Gentlemen of the Ensemble*: Roger Davis, Lester Ostrander, Donald Rowan, William Murray, Joe McGurgan, Drake Smith, William Freeman, Elliott Roth, Eugene Elliott.

Act 1: The Restaurant.

Act 2, Scene 1: The Boudoir. *Scene 2*: The Dream Ball.

Act 3: Countess Irma's Party.

ACT 1
  "To the Girl You Dance With"
    T. Ahern, H. White, Ensemble
  "Any Girl"
    M. Gateson, Ensemble
  "I'll Say I Love You"
    F. Astaire, A. Astaire, Ensemble
  "I'll Return for You"
    J. C. Thomas, C. Thomson
  Finale

ACT 2
Scene 1
  "First Love"
    C. Thomson
Scene 2
  "The Only Girl" (There Is a Girl)
    J. C. Thomas, Ensemble
  "Scandal Town"
    M. Gateson, W. West
  "We Were in Love'
    J. C. Thomas, C. Thomson
  "Upside Down"
    F. Astaire, A. Astaire
  "Canzonetta"
    J. C. Thomas
  "Rainbow"
    J. Carroll
  Dance
    I. Irving, D. Irving, P. Eaton
ACT 3
  "You're Mine"
    J. Carroll, Ensemble

Dance
  I. Irving, D. Irving
"Man, Man, Man"
  M. Gateson, Male Ensemble
"Dreaming"
  F. Astaire, A. Astaire, Ensemble
"My Heart Beats for You"
  J. C. Thomas
"Twiddle Your Thumbs"
  W. West, Ensemble
  (*Music and Lyrics by* Will West.)
"Reminiscence"
  J. C. Thomas, C. Thomson
"Cotillion"
  J. C. Thomas, C. Thomson, F. Astaire, A. Astaire, M. Gateson, W. West, K. Stewart, Ensemble

1921.34

BOMBO

A Musical Extravaganza in Two Acts, 13 Scenes. Dialogue (book) and lyrics by Harold Atteridge. Music by Sigmund Romberg. Staged by J. C. Huffman. Dances staged by Allan K. Foster. Scenery designed by Watson Barratt. Costumes by Mode Costume Company. Orchestra under the direction of Alfred Goodman. Entire production under the personal supervision of J. J. Shubert. Produced by the Messrs. Lee and J. J. Shubert. Opened 6 October 1921 at Jolson's 59th Street Theatre and closed 8 April 1922 after 218 performances[71].

CAST (in order of appearance, 1921, 1492): *Paul Marcus, Alonzo*: Franklyn A. Batie. *Annabel Downing, Annabella*: Vera Bayles Cole. *Jenkins, Roderigo*: Frank Holmes. *Bud Wilson, Demendozo*: Russell Mack. *Hazel Downing, Hazella*: Mildred Keats. *Jack Christopher, Christopho Colombo*: FORREST HUFF. *Patricia Downing, Princess Isabella*: Gladys Caldwell. *Count Garibaldi, Prince Don*: Fred Hall. *Mrs. Downing, Queen Isabella*: FRITZI VON BUSING. *Inez, Lady Ynes de Cordoba*: Grace Keeshon. *Mona Tessa, A Soothsayer*: JANET ADAIR. *Red, King Ferdinand*: Harry Turpin. *Louis, The Courier*: Ernest Young. *Guiseppo, Guiseppo*: Jack Kearns. *Banditti, Indian Chiefs*: Ernest Miller, Dennis Murray, Walter White, Harry Sievers, Edward Pooley. *John and James*, (Butlers), *Sailors*: Thomas Ross, Theodore Hoffman. *Adele and Estelle, Pirates*: IRENE HART, BERNICE HART. *Lois, Luello*: Janette Dietrich. *Alfred, Alfredo*: Frank Bernard. *Charles Masterson*: Sam Critcherson. *Gus*: AL JOLSON. *Rosie*: VIVIENNE OAKLAND.
Ladies of the Ensemble: Dorothy Bruce, Charlotte Sprague, Charlotte Schuette, Diana, Jeane Voltaire, Loreene Pullinger, Bonnie Belle, Corynne Baker, Virginia Wilson, Thelma Turnbull, Edna Starck, Louise Darcy, Dixie O'Neil, Dorothy Wegman, Freddie Bond, Kitty Kane, Rose Gallagher, Dorothy Stone, Mary O'Shaugnessy, Alice Rohey, Evelyn Richmond, Lois Syrell, Helen O'Brien, Lebanon Hoffa, Mae Laroux, Gypsy Norman, Maud Satterfield, Belle Madulla, Orilla Smith, Edith Pierce, Ethel Bryant, Loralda Poppenay, Florence Wild, Pauline Dakla, Poppy Morton, Sidney Wilson, Marion Mooney, Alice Monroe, Billie Wagner, Marion Davis, Elsie Dunn, Lucille Mendez, Beatrice Jackson, Sonia Field, Florence Field, Dolores Russelle, Nan Phillips, Mary Brean, Lena Keefe, Florence Darling, Evelyn Mead, Kay Carlin, Bobby Boles, Beulah Rubens, Carroll Miller, Louise Starck.

Scene 1: The Grounds of Count Garibaldi's Castle, Genoa, 1921. *Scene 2*: On Board Jack Christopher's Yacht. *Scene 3*: In Old Spain. *Scene 4*: A Street in Cordova, Spain, 1492. *Scene 5*: At the Royal Palace. *Scene 6*: Throne Room in the Palace of the King Ferdinand and Queen Isabella. *Scene 7*: The Shop of Valero, the Money-Lender. *Scene 8*: The Port of Palos, Spain.

Scene 1: On the Deck of the *Santa Maria*. *Scene 2*: On the Island of San Salvador. *Scene 3*: On Board Jack Christopher's Yacht. *Scene 4*: In Gus' Kitchen. *Scene 5*: Count Garibaldi's Garden, Genoa, Italy. 1921.

ACT 1
  "Life Is a Gamble"[72]
    Guests, Teetotum Girls
  "In the Land Off There"
    J. Adair, M. Keats, F. Huff, S. Critcherson, F. von Busing

---

[71]Following a national tour, re-opened 14 May 1923 at the Winter Garden and closed 9 June 1923 after 32 additional performances. See program entry in 1922-23 season. Total: 250 performances.
[72]For subsequent tour, replaced by:
  "Neath Italian Skies"
    Guests, Teetotum Girls

"The Horse Trot"
    M. Keats
"Sleepy (Little) Village"[73]
    I. Hart, B. Hart
    (*Music and Lyrics by* Pete Wendling.)
"The Globe Trot"
    Globe Trotters, M. Keats, R. Dale, J. Dietrich, D. Duby, F. Bernard
Some Songs
    A. Jolson
"In Old Granada"
    F. A. Batie, Beauties of Spain
"Jazza-da-dada"
    Jazza-da-dada Girls, R. Dale, M. Keats
"No One Loves a Clown"
    V. B. Cole, F. Bernard, Some Clown Girls
"Rose of Spain"
    T. Huffman, V. B. Cole, Some Castilian Beauties
"I'm Glad I'm Spanish"
    J. Adair, a Group of Spanish Beauties
"In a Curio Shop"
    D. Duby, J. Dietrich, F. Bernard, Curio Girls
"Wait Until My Ship Comes In"
    F. A. Batie, Sailor Girls

ACT 2[74]
"A Girl Has a Sailor in Every Port"
    R. Dale, Sailor Girls
"Bylo Bay"
    I. Hart, B. Hart
"Wetona"
    T. Huffman, V. B. Cole, Rianna, Indian Boys and Girls
Songs[75]
    A. Jolson

---

[73]For subsequent tour, replaced by:
"How'd You Like to be a Kid"
    (*Music and Lyrics by* Jimmy McHugh, Bennett Sisters and Billy Colligan.)/
"Paradise Alley"
    Katherine and Gladys Bennett [Sisters]
[74]Added for subsequent tour to Act 2, following "Bylo Bay" and before "Wetona:"
"April Showers"
    A. Jolson
    (*Music by* Louis Silvers. *Lyrics by* Buddy G. DeSylva.)
Restored to Act 2 for tour after "The Daffodil:"
The Glide DeLuxe
    Mlle. Phebe
(Finale)
    A. Jolson, Company
[75]Jolson's Specialty Songs included:
"That Barber in Seville"
    (*Music by* Con Conrad. *Lyrics by* Harold Atteridge.
"Give Me My Mammy"
    (*Music by* Walter Donaldson. *Lyrics by* Buddy G. DeSylva.)
"Down South"
    (*Music by* Walter Donaldson. *Lyrics by* Buddy G. DeSylva.)
Later in the run and on tour:
"Toot, Toot, Tootsie! (Goodbye)"
    (*Music and Lyrics by* Ernie Erdman, Dan Russo and Gus Kahn.)
"Who Cares"
    (*Music by* Milton Ager. *Lyrics by* Jack Yellen.)
"Arcady"
    (*Music and Lyrics by* Al Jolson and Buddy G. DeSylva.)
"I'm Goin' South"
    (*Music and Lyrics by* Harry Woods and Abner Silver.)
"California, Here I Come"
    (*Music and Lyrics by* Al Jolson, Joseph Meyer and Buddy G.DeSylva.)
"Bebe" (added on tour in Washington D.C.)
    (*Music by* Abner Silver. *Lyrics by* Sam Coslow.)

"The Daffodil"
    R. Dale, M. Keats, Some Strutters
The Glide DeLuxe[76]
    Cortez and Peggy

1921.35 # LOVE DREAMS

A Melody Drama (Operetta) in Three Acts[77]. Book by Ann Nichols. Music by Werner Janssen. Lyrics by Oliver Morosco. Staged by Oliver Morosco and John McKee. Orchestra under the direction of Mario Agnolucci. Produced by Oliver Morosco. Opened 10 October 1921 at the Times Square Theatre, moved 17 October 1921 to the Apollo Theatre, and closed 12 November 1921 after 40 performances.

CAST (in order of appearance): *Larry Pell*: TOM POWERS. *Billy Parks*: Maurie Holland. *Dr. Duncan Pell*: ORRIN JOHNSON. *Cadillac Packard*: HARRY K. MORTON. *Renee d'Albret*: VERA MICHELENA. *Stage Manager*: Charles Yorkshire. *Hildegard*: Maude Eburne. *Cherry O'Moore*: Marie Carroll. *Premier Dancer*: Amelia Allen. *Pauline*: Pauline Maxwell. *Grace*: Grace Culvert. *Irene*: Irene Novotney. *Joan*: Joan Warner. *Ann*: Ann Pauley. *Grace*: Grace Elliott. *Maude*: Maude Lydiate. *Charmine*: Charmine Essley.

Act 1: Dr. Pell's New York Apartment.

Act 2: Green Room of Theatre where Renee d'Albret is appearing. Next day.

Act 3: Renee's Home in the Country. A few days later.

ACT 1
"Two's Company, Three's a Crowd"
    T. Powers, M. Holland, Girls
"Entre Nous"
    T. Powers, M. Holland, H. K. Morton, Girls
"Love Time"
    V. Michelena, T. Powers
ACT 2[78]
Specialty Dances
    P. Maxwell; A. Allen
"The Toddle Top Whirl"
    T. Powers, M. Holland, Girls

Other songs performed by Jolson in BOMBO per recordings, sheet music and other sources include:
"Ain't Love Grand"
    (*Music and Lyrics by* Walter Donaldson, Buddy G. DeSylva and Con Conrad.)
"Avalon"
    (*Music by* Vincent Rose. *Lyrics by* Al Jolson and Buddy G. DeSylva.)
"Carolina Mammy"
    (*Music and Lyrics by* Billy James.)
"Coo-Coo (Song)"
    (*Music and Lyrics by* Al Jolson and Buddy G. DeSylva.)
"Dirty Hands! Dirty Face!"
    (*Music by* Con Conrad. *Lyrics by* Harold Atteridge.)
"Don't Cry Swanee"
    (*Music and Lyrics by* Con Conrad, Buddy G. DeSylva and Al Jolson.)
"It's You"
    (*Music by* James Monaco. *Lyrics by* Grant Clarke, Edgar Leslie, Al Jolson)
"Last Night on the Back Porch (I Loved Her Best of All)"
    (*Music by* Carl Schaubstrader. *Lyrics by* Lew Brown.)
"Morning Will Come"
    (*Music and Lyrics by* Con Conrad, Al Jolson, Buddy G. DeSylva.)
"Old Fashioned Girl (in a Gingham Gown)"
    (*Music and Lyrics by* Al Jolson.)
"Tallahassee"
    (*Music by* C. Luckyeth Roberts. *Lyrics by* Buddy G.D eSylva.)
"Yoo-Hoo"
    (*Music by* Al Jolson. *Lyrics by* Buddy G. DeSylva.)
[76]Dropped during the run.
[77]Prior to New York, dances were credited to Carl Randall, and orchestrations by the composer.
[78]Added to Act 2 after "Here There and Everywhere:"
"Any Time Is Love Time"
    V. Michelena, T. Powers

"Here There and Everywhere"
    H. K. Morton, Girls
"The World Owes You This, My Dear"
    V. Michelena
"Reputation"
    M. Eburne, H. K. Morton
"Love Dreams"[79]
    V. Michelena
"(I'm Just Looking for a) Lonesome Boy"
    M. Carroll
ACT 3
Ensemble Dance
    Dancing Girls
Oriental Dance
    A. Allen
"Pity Me"
    M. Carroll, T. Powers
"My Dream of Love Is You"
    O. Johnson

1921.36   GOOD MORNING, DEARIE

A Musical Comedy in Two Acts, 6 Scenes. Book and lyrics by Anne Caldwell. Music by Jerome Kern. Staged by Edward Royce. Scenery designed by Frank Gates and Edward A. Morange. Costumes by Herman Patrick Teppe. Orchestra under the direction of Victor Baravalle. Orchestrations by Stephen Jones. Produced by Charles Dillingham. Opened 1 November 1921 at the Globe Theatre and closed 26 August 1922 after 347 performances.

CAST (in order of appearance): *Florrie*: Ruth Williamson. *Cherry*: Lilyan White. *Pat*: Patricia Clark. *Margie*: Pauline Hall. *George Mason*: JOHN PRICE JONES. *Ruby Manners*: PEGGY KURTON. *Madame Bompard*: ADA LEWIS. *Billy Van Cortlandt*: OSCAR SHAW. *Gimpy*: John J. Scannell. *Rose-Marie*: LOUISE GROODY. *Chesty Costello*: HARLAND DIXON. *Steve Simmons*: WILLIAM KENT. *Cutie*: Marie Callahan. *Kirby*: Raymond Moore. *Sing Lee*: Otis Harper. *Hoi Fat*: Irving Jackson. *Lim Ho*: Edouard LeFebvre. *Pierre*: Joseph Viau. *Gigi*: Daniel Sparks. *Mrs. Greyson Parks*: ROBERTA BEATTY. *Miss Hetherington*: Ingrid Zanders. *Pauline*: Hebe Halpin. *Dorothy*: Miriam Miller. *Muriel*: Muriel Harrison. *Winters*: Spaulding Hall. *Sylvia—Harriet*: Darling Twins. *Specialties*: Maurice with (Leonora) Hughes in their New Dance Creations. Leo Reisman's Band onstage.

Sixteen Sunshine Girls: Mary Read, Dorothy Sabin, Dolly Mosley, Isa Mosley, Chrissie Staller, Doris Smith, Josie Jones, Ida Berry, Sibyl Rowland, Elsie Hellewell, Phyllis Brown, Edith Harvey, Norine Callon, Florrie Stack, Alice Pitman, Muriel Curl. *Ladies of the Ensemble*: Helen Allan, Marie Berno, Evelyn Coombs, Lucille Cassidy, Lola Curtiss, Peggy Dana, Consuelo Flowerton, Margery Flynn, Gertrude Feeley, Carol Flowers, Jessie Howe, Ida Howe, Ona Hamilton, Hebe Halpin, Alice Hitchcock, Beatrice Hughes, Aileen Hamilton, Dorothy Harrigan, Doris Landy, Laura McClure, Lillian MacKenzie, Lydia Scott, Mildred Sinclair. *Gentlemen of the Ensemble* Sidney Ayres, Bill Bailey, Joseph Carey, Conway Dillon, Jack Hughes, Otis Harper, Edouard LeFebvre, Raymond Moore, Daniel Sparks, Francis Schultz, Joseph Viau, Irving Jackson.

Act 1: An Afternoon and Evening in Spring. *Scene 1*: Workroom of Madame Bompard's Shop. *Scene 2*: Exterior of the Dance Hall. *Scene 3*: Interior of Hell's Bells Dance Hall.

Act 2: An Afternoon and Evening One Week Later. *Scene 1*: Showroom of the Toddle Shop. *Scene 2*: Fragonard. *Scene 3*: Terrace of Mrs. Greyson Parks' Home.

ACT 1
Scene 1
"Every Girl"
    O. Shaw, J. P. Jones
"Way Down Town"
    L. Groody, H. Dixon
Musical Scena:
"Rose-Marie"
    L. Groody
"Didn't You Believe"
    O. Shaw
Finaletto
Scene 2
Coolie Dance
    16 Sunshine Girls

Scene 3
"The Teddy Toddle"
    Girls, Men
"Sing Song Girl"[80]
    W. Kent, 6 Fan-Tan Girls
Musical Scena:
Entrance of Sailors
"Blue Danube Blues"
    L. Groody, O. Shaw
Blue Danube Waltz[81]
    M. Hughes, L. Hughes
"Easy Pickins" (Trio)
    H. Dixon, W. Kent, J. J. Scannell
Finale
ACT 2[82]
Scene 1
"Melican Papa"[83]
    W. Kent, Darling Twins, Girls
"Niagara Falls"
    L. Groody, O. Shaw
Pas de Deux
    H. Dixon, M. Callahan
"Toddle Quartette"
    L. Groody, P. Kurton, W. Kent, J. P. Jones
Scene 2
Dance du Fragonard
    The Sunshine Girls
Scene 3
"Kailua" (Ka-Lu-A)
    O. Shaw, Girls
"Good Morning Dearie"
    L. Groody, Men
Dance
    H. Dixon, M. Callahan
Maurice, with Leonora Hughes (Dance Specialty)[84]
"Le Sport American"
    The Sunshine Girls
Reprise
    L. Groody, O. Shaw
Finale

1921.37   THE PERFECT FOOL

A Musical Concoction (Revue) in Two Acts, 18 Scenes. Book, music and lyrics by Ed Wynn. Production staged by Julian Mitchell. Costumes designed by Ada Fields, Cora MacGeachy, Albertine Randall Wheelan. Scenery by Triangle Scenic Studios. Lighting by Tony Greshoff. Orchestra under the direction of Antonio Bafunno. Orchestrations by Maurice DePackh. Produced by Abraham L. Erlanger under the direction of B. C. Whitney. Opened 7 November 1921 at the George M. Cohan Theatre and closed 1 July 1922 after 275 performances.

CAST: ED WYNN, JANET VELIE, FLO NEWTON, ALINE McGILL, TRUE RICE, ESTELLE PENNING, JOHN DALE, FRED ARDATH, GUY ROBERTSON, THE MEYAKOS (Florence, Esther, George), Kiku and Toma.
    Ladies of the Ensemble: Margaret Hoban, Anita Furman, Katharine Kay, Edna Terry, Irene Mayberry, Bobby Breslaw, Margie Ferguson, Dolla Harkins, Dade Winlack, Estelle Penning, Aline Gill, Johan Wittman, Madge McCarthy, Belle

---

[79]Dropped during the run.

[80]Dropped during the run.
[81]Dropped during the run.
[82]Added in the second month of the run to Act 2, Scene 3 after 'Ka-Lu-A:'
    Dance Eccentrique
        W. Kent
    Which was replaced late in the run by:
    Radium Dance
        Carol Flower, Lucille Cassidy
[83]Dropped during the run.
[84]Dropped during the run.

Gannon, Marion Rich, Kathryn Annis, Marjorie Grant, Peggy Ellis, Florence Brooks, Gladys Laird, Edna Hamel, Marion King, Rose Boulais, Grace Larue, Polly Bowman, Grace Russell, Harriette Keyes, Lorna Lincoln, Ivey Kirkwood, Helen Kerr.

ACT 1[85]

Scene 1

Something to Start
Himself: E. Wynn. *She*: F. Newton. *He*: T. Rice.

Scene 2

Something in Bronze
Jumping Jupiter: J. Dale. *Father Knick*: G. Robertson.
His Proteges (What We Fell in for in 1850):
Miss Bustle: M. Hoban. *Miss Sleeves*: A. Furman. *Miss Victorian*: K. Kay. *Miss Equestrian*: E. Terry. *Miss Shop Girl*: I. Mayberry. *Miss Bather*: B. Breslaw. *Miss Suburban*: M. Ferguson. *Miss Nightgown* (before lingerie was invented): D. Harkins.

Scene 3

"Girls, Pretty Girls"
Father Knick (E. Wynn)
Something in Hats (What We're Willing to Fall for Now)
Miss Wall Street: D. Winlack. *Miss Greenwich Village*: E. Penning. *Miss Central Park*: A. McGill. *Miss Gown*: J. Wittman. *Miss White Way*: M. McCarthy. *Miss Speed*: B. Gannon. *Miss Folly*: M. Rich. *The Misses Bandbox*: K. Annis, M. Grant, P. Ellis, F. Brooks, G. Laird, E. Hamel.

Scene 4

Something in Gold
Himself: E. Wynn. *Miss Central Park*: A. McGill. *Miss Greenwich Village*: E. Penning. And the Misses Bandbox.

Scene 5

Something in Lacquer[85a]
Kiku: F. Meyako. *Toma*: E. Meyako. *Yoichy*: G. Meyako.

Scene 6

"She Loves Me, She Loves Me Not"
J. Velie, G. Robertson
Scene: A Daisy Place.
Miss Petal: J. Velie. *Mr. Stem*: G. Robertson. *The Misses Daisy*: K. Kay, I. Mayberry, M. Ferguson, D. Winlack, J. Wittman, D. Harkins, M. McCarthy, M. Hoban. *The Misters Daisy*: M. King, R. Boulais, G. LaRue, P. Bowman, G. Russell, G. Laird, A. Furman, B. Breslaw.

Scene 7

Something in Green
Himself: E. Wynn.

Scene 8

"Visions That Pass in the Night"
J. Velie
Scene: Some Latin Quarters.
Himself: E. Wynn. *Andre*: G. Robertson. *Haigen Haig*: F. Ardath. *Polly*: M. Hoban. *Dolly*: D. Winlack. *Golly*: D. Harkins. *Miss Somnambulist*: J. Velie. *The Misses Tapestry*: A. McGill, E. Penning, M. Rich, B. Breslaw, M. McCarthy, E. Hamel, A. Furman, E. Terry, M. Ferguson, R. Boulais, B. Gannon.

Scene 9

Some Other Places
Himself: E. Wynn. *She*: F. Newton. *He*: T. Rice. *Miss Hap*: H. Keyes. *Miss Deed*: L. Lincoln. *Miss Fortune*: I. Kirkwood. *Miss Take*: H. Kerr.

Scene 10

"A Doll House"
G. Robertson, J. Velie
(*Lyrics by* Harry Richman, Lou Davis.)
Scene: A Lovely Place.
Miss Dolly: J. Velie. *Mr. Doll*: G. Robertson. *Kiku, Toma, Yoichy*: The Meyakos. *The Misses Lovely*: E. Penning, A. McGill. *Himself*: E. Wynn. *Welcomers*: Ensemble.

Scene 11

"Old Home Week (in Maine)"
J. Dale
Scene: Still Another Place.
Mr. Small Town: J. Dale. *The Misses Mainstreet*: G. Larue, G. Laird, P. Ellis, F. Brooks, M. Grant, E. Hamel. *The Misters Mainstreet*: M. King, A. Furman, G. Russell, M. Rich, P. Bowman, B. Gannon. *In and Out*: K. Mekayo, T. Meyako. *World's Worst Acrobats*: Messrs. Rice, Dale and Himself [E. Wynn]. *The Misses Village*: I. Mayberry, D. Winlack, K. Kay, D. Harkins, M. Hoban, M. Ferguson, J. Wittman, M. McCarthy, R. Boulais, B. Breslaw, K. Annis, E. Terry. *Miss Town*: E. Penning. *Miss Country*: A. McGill.

ACT 2

Scene 1

"My Garden of Perfumes"
J. Velie
Scene: Just a Place.
Miss Vendor: J. Velie.

Scene 2

A Place in Java: "The Ballet of Perfumes"
The Bride: Hasoutra. *The Imps*: G. Laird, K. Annis, E. Hamel, M. Grant. *The Perfumes (5)*: *Vanity*: G. Russell. *Coquetry*: M. Rich. *Envy*: B. Breslaw. *Hate*: A. Furman. *Love*: A. McGill. *Miss Vain*: M. McCarthy. *Miss Tempt*: F. Brooks.
A bridal custom of Javanese Royalty compels the future bride to submit to "The Test of Perfumes." As the Legend runs: the perfumes are made by the husband-to-be, from flowers of his selection. Five perfumes are made, each of which is supposed to cast a spell: one of Vanity, one of Coquetry, one of Envy, one of Hate, and one of Love. If the prospective bride possesses power enough to cast off the four temptations and succumbs to the Perfume of Love, she is considered worthy of becoming his consort.

Scene 3

Hall of Knowledge
Raja (Some Boy): E. Wynn. *The Assistant*: T. Rice.

Scene 4

"The Typewriter Song"
F. Newton, G. Robertson, Misses Keys
Scene: A Typing Place.
Miss Type: F. Newton. *Mr. Writer*: G. Robertson. *Miss Ink*: N. Breen. *The Misses Keys*: B. Gannon, M. Rich, A. Furman, M. Grant, E. Hamel, P. Bowman.

Scene 5

Something Light
Himself: E. Wynn.

Scene 6[86]

"Romantic Days" (Days of Romance)
G. Robertson
Scene: The Finishing Place.
Miss Knight: J. Velie. *Mam Zell*: N. Breen. *Mr. Knight*: G. Robertson. *Miss Foil*: E. Penning. *Miss Sword*: M. Grant. *The Rapier*: B. Gannon. *Miss Broadsword*: K. Annis. *Miss Cutlass*: G. Larue. *Miss Blade*: B. Breslaw. *Miss Hilt*: E. Hamel.

Finale
Entire Company

1921.38 SUZETTE

A Musical Comedy in Two Acts. Libretto by Roy Dixon. Music by Arthur H. Gutman. Book directed by Charles D. Pitt. Dances arranged by Larry Ceballos. Scenery by Golding Studios. Costumes by Brooks and Eaves. Orchestra under the direction of Arthur H. Gutman. Orchestrations by Arthur H. Gutman and Mr. Keifert. Produced by the Suzette Producing Company. Opened 24 November 1921 at the Princess Theatre and closed 26 November 1921 after 4 performances.

CAST (in order of appearance): *Armand*, a café proprietor: JOHN CHERRY. *Tony*, a waiter: FRANK LALOR. *Suzette*, a flower girl: MARIE ASTROVA. *Dora Dolores*, a prima donna: MARJORIE BOOTH. *Max Kalman*, an impressario: VICTOR MORLEY. *Paul Huntley*, a millionaire: JAMES R. MARSHALL. *Mme. Bimboula*, a modiste: Carola Parson.

---

[85]Added during the run to Act 1 as Scene 11, preceding Still Another Place, Act 1 closing scene:
A Musical Place
Himself: E. Wynn. *Miss Aspirant*: F. Newton. *Mr. Ten-or*: T. Rice. *Miss Hap*: H. Kayes. *Miss Deed*: L. Lincoln. *Miss Fortune*: I. Kirkwood. *Miss Take*: P. Babcock.

[85a]Specialty song interpolated as per published sheet music:
"Stealing"
Three Meyakos
(*Music and Lyrics by* Dan Sullivan.)

[86]After opening, the Finale was expanded into 2 scenes, and the following song addded:
"Sweetheart—(Will You) Answer Yes"
J. Velie
(*Music by* Rolf Piquet. *Lyrics by* James Brennan, and Al Wilson.)

Montmartre Models: Adele: Ann Roos. *Betty*: Bernice Ackerman. *Cheri*: Peggy Paulson. *Julie*: Beatrice Savage. *Liane*: Polly Mayer. *Mitzi*: Viola Fraas. *Peggy*: Genevieve Markham. *Sonya*: Carmen Johnston.

Artists: Andre: Tom Maynard. *Boris*: John Grieves. *Josef*: Austin Clark. *Marco*: Norman Jefferson.

Act 1: A Montmartre Café, Paris. Evening.

Act 2: A Garden Party, Deauville. Next evening.

ACT 1
Opening
J. Cherry, Ensemble
"No, No"
M. Astrova, J. Cherry
"Oh, Waiter"
V. Morley, M. Booth, F. Lalor
"Dreams of Tomorrow"
M. Astrova, J. R. Marshall
"A Modern Diplomat"
F. Lalor, Girls
"Suzette"
J. R. Marshall, Boys
"Gypsy Rose"
M. Astrova, Ensemble
Finale
Ensemble
ACT 2
Opening
Ensemble
"A Forest Legend"
V. Morley, M. Astrova, M. Booth
"Bagdad"
F. Lalor, Girls
"Honey-Love-Moon"
M. Astrova, J. R. Marshall, Ensemble
"Saturday Evening Post"
F. Lalor, C. Parson, V. Morley
"Sweetheart"
M. Astrova
Finale
Ensemble

THE WILD CAT

1921.39

A Spanish Music Drama in Three Acts, 5 Scenes[87]. (Original) Spanish music and libretto by Manuel Penella ('El Gato Montes'). English version by Marie B. Schrader. Staged by Manuel Penella. Scenery designed by Beaux Arts Studio (New York), V. Sanchiz Lazaro (Valencia). Costumes by Julio Perez (Madrid); bullfighters' costumes by Ripolles and Martin (Madrid/Seville). Andalusian girls' costumes designed by Senorita Matilde Lopez (Madrid). Orchestra under the direction of Manuel Penella. Produced by John Cort in association with Alex Aaronson [Aarons]. Opened 26 November 1921 at the Park Theatre and closed 28 January 1922 after 74 performances[88].

CAST (in order of appearance): *Soleá*: DOROTHY SOUTH. *Seña Frasquita*: VERA ROSS. *Loliya*: Grace Hamilton. *Father Anton*: W. H. Thompson. *Rafael*, the Macareno: SAM ASH. *Hormigon*, a Picador: Carlos Villarias. *Caireles*: Max Gonzales. *Gipsy*: Louise Barnolt. *Juanillo*, the "Wild Cat": MARION GREEN. *Gipsy Dancers*: CONCHITA PIQUER, Pilar Torralba. *A Shepherd*: Russell Ash. *A Flower Seller*: CONCHITA PIQUER. *El Pezuno*: Oliver T. McCormack. *Alguacil*: Fred Rogers.

Andalusian Peasant Girls, Gipsy Girls and Boys, Bullfighters, Picadores, Bandits, Rural Police, Bull Ring Attendants, Sand Throwers, Guards, Stable Boys, etc.: Ensemble.

Act 1: The Macareno's farmhouse near Seville. An afternoon in summer.

Act 2, Scene 1: Patio of the Macareno's House in Seville. The following Sunday. *Scene 2*: Interior of the Plaza des Toros in Seville. The same afternoon.

Act 3, Scene 1: The Macareno's farmhouse at Night. Two weeks later. *Scene 2*: A Cave in the Mountains. The Hiding Place of the "Wild Cat." The same evening.

THE CHOCOLATE SOLDIER

1921.40

A Revival of the Opera Bouffe in Three Acts[89]. Original Viennese book ('Der tapfere Soldat') and lyrics by Rudolph Bernauer and Leopold Jacks [Jacobson], based on George Bernard Shaw's play 'Arms and the Man.' English book and lyrics by Stanislaus Stangé. Music by Oscar Straus. Production and dances staged by Charles Sinclair. Costumes executed by Vanity Fair Costume Company. Musical director, Max Bendix. Revived by the Messrs. Lee and J.J. Shubert. Opened 12 December 1921 at the Century Theatre and closed 18 February 1922 after 83 performances[90].

CAST (in order of appearance): *Nadina Popoff*, Daughter of Colonel Popoff: TESSA KOSTA. *Aurelia Popoff*, Her Mother: MILDRED ROGERS. *Mascha*, Aurelia's Cousin: Virginia O'Brien. *Lieutenant Bumerli*, the "Chocolate Soldier," (a Swiss Mercenary in the employ of the Servian Army): DONALD BRIAN. *Captain Massakroff* of the Bulgarian Army: DETMAR POPPEN. *Colonel Casimir Popoff* of the Bulgarian Army: JOHN DUNSMURE. *Major Alexius Spiridoff* of the Bulgarian Army, betrothed to Nadina: John Humbird Duffey. *Volga*: Felicia Murelle. *Nicholas*: Victor Victoroff. *Popoff's Servants (2): Louka*: Beauton O'Quinn. *Stephen*: Jay Carlton McCormack.

Bulgarian Soldiers, Citizens, Citizenesses: Ladies of the Ensemble: Flo Clemons, Annette Carmichael, Vivian Kelley, Mary Manley, Marian Hoff, Lenore Darcy, Greta Drew, Isabelle Wilkes, Mary Rennie, Rose Maynard, Belle Mazelle, Maud Satterfield, Ruth Bannan, Grace Leon, Verna Shaff, Kay Swan, Myrtle Ashly, Estelle Murcier, Alice Burns, Betty Owen, Joy Ellis, Ethel Drury, Louise McGovern, Irene McGovern, Catherine Huth, Marion Weaver, Melba Lee, Elmira Lane, Beauton O'Quinn, Laura Grenville, Virginia Kirkland. *Gentlemen of the Ensemble*: Pat McCarty, Henri Cottave, William Foster, William Passman, Joe Werden, Harry Miller, Harold J. Varney, Elma Barhab, Harry Howell, Paul Herbert, Frank Markham, Garford Oliver, Allston Bent, Jay C. McCormack, Jack Bruns, Charles Hassing.

AIN'T IT THE TRUTH

1921.41

A Musical Revue in a Prologue and Two Acts. Sketches and lyrics by Jude Brayton. Music by Harry B. Olsen. Staged by Paul Blaufoix. Orchestra under the direction of Harry B. Olsen. Produced by the World War Veterans. Opened 19 December 1921 at the Manhattan Opera House and closed 24 December 1921 after 8 performances.

CAST: *Historian*: J. K. MURRAY. *Uncle Bill*: A. W. Goodell. *Mother*: Mary Chippendale. *Jane*: EDITH THAYER. *Captain Tracy*: A. Smithson. *First Man*: Bernard Martin. *Verdi*: Joe Merlino. *Corporal in U. S. Army*: ?? Demetrios. *Sailor Jim White*: Jim White. *Chief Petty Officer*: Herbert Lindholm. *First Red Cross Nurse*: Barbara Welty. *Head Nurse*: Elisabeth Freeman. *Eatsminet Keeper*: Royal Tracy. *Susette*: Katherine Ruvigny. *Captain Jack Allison*: GEORGE EVERETT. *Sergeant*: EDDIE WAKEFIELD. *Toney Stravetch*: CURTIS KARPE. *Jakey Moscovitz*: JOHN L. LYONS. *Pat Donohue*: EDDIE FETHERSTONE. *Les Sardeaux. A Doughboy*: A. Smith. *His Buddie*: Albert West. *John Arnold*: Charles Penman. *Employment Man*: J. K. Murray.

Prologue: Home.

Act 1: France, June 1918.

Act 2: Any Park, Christmas Morning, 1921.

MUSICAL NUMBERS[90a]
"Tally Ho"
G. Everett
"When You Come Back"
E. Thayer

HANKY PANKY LAND

1921.42

A Holiday Frolic in Three Acts. Book and lyrics by McElbert Moore. Music by J. Fred Coots. Produced by Emily Louise. Opened 26 December 1921 (afternoon) at the Century Roof and closed 31 December 1921 after 10 performances[91].

---

[87]The performance was through-sung without individual song titles.
[88]Musical numbers not listed in the program.

[89]First produced in New York 13 September 1909 at the Lyric Theatre for 296 performances. For Synopsis of Scenes and Musical Numbers, see original 1909 production. For this revival, the following were added:
"Then Shout Hurrah" (Opening Chorus Act 2)
(Ensemble)
(*Themes by* Max Bendix, arranged from Straus.)
Waltz (Act 2, following "The Chocolate Soldier")
V. O'Brien, D. Brian
(*Themes by* Max Bendix, arranged from Straus.)
[90]Settings uncredited.
[90a]No program available.
[91]No program available.

CAST: *Esther Time's Daughters*: Elsie Vokes, Miss Russell. *Father Time*: Mr. Horton. *Mary*: OLIVETTE. *The Fairy Queen*: Yvette Rolland. *Hanky Panky*: FRED HELDER. *Witches*: Misses Crompton, Davis, Goldstein. *Laddie*: Alfred Latte.
    Ensemble: Alice Brennan, Irene Taylor, Kathlene Small, Byron Russell, May Taylor, Charlotte Willis, Sadie Levine, Anita Goldstein, Muriel Mackay, E. Manzi.

1922.01   UP IN THE CLOUDS

An American Musical Play in Two Acts, 5 Scenes. Book and lyrics by Will B. Johnstone. Music by Tom Johnstone. Staged by Lawrence Marston. Dance numbers staged by Allan K. Foster, Max Scheck, Vaughn Godfrey. Scenery by H. Robert Law Studios. Costumes by Paul Arlington, Inc. and Anna Spencer, Inc. Orchestra under the direction of Hilding Anderson. Orchestrations by Hilding Anderson. Produced by Joseph M. Gaites. Opened 2 January 1922 at the Lyric Theatre, moved 23 January 1922 to the 44th Street Theatre, and closed 18 March 1922 after 89 performances.

CAST (in order of appearance): *Archie Dawson*, a young idealist: HAL VAN RENS-SELAER. *Curtis Dawson* Captain of Industry, Archie's Father: Walter Walker. *Betty Dawson*, Archie's sister: Florence Hedges. *Ferdie Simpson*, Heir to Millions: Mark Smith. *Jeffreys*, Dawson's Butler: Page Spencer. *Ruby Airedale*, a Faded Society Bud: Gertrude O'Connor. *Millicent Towne*, Archie's Fiancée: GLADYS COBURN. *Bud Usher*, Camera Man with the Movie Troupe: SKEET GALLAGHER. *Louise*, Dawson's Maid: June Roberts. *J. Herbert Blake*, a Movie Director: WILLIAM N. BAI-LEY. *Jean Jones*, a Movie Star in Disguise: GRACE MOORE. *Gypsy Venus*, a Movie Villainess: Dorothy Smoller. *Gerald*: Angelo Romeo. *Clerks in Simpson Bank* (3): *William Tuttle*: Van J. Melino. *Will Tuttle*: John J. Weis. *Willie Tuttle*: Roy Alexander. *Premiere Danseuse*: June Roberts. *Character Dancer*: Arthur Corey. *Classical Dancers*: Melissa Ten Eyck, Max Weily.
    Ladies of the Ensemble: Miss Ann Lemau, Mary Welsh, Elsie Young, Adrienne Hayes, Elsie Westcott, Tyra Babcock, Betty Soule, Inez Foster, Grace Hall, Phyllis Millar, Laura Gaynelle, Agnes Hall, Beverly Millar, Josephine Hurley, Thelma Holliday, Kathryn Valentine.

Act 1: Dawson Country mansion. Long Island. Late summer.

Act 2, Scene 1: Simpson Bank, New York City. Established 1830. *Scene 2*: The Six Months. *Scene 3*: Epilogue. Reception Room. Interior of Cinemopolis. Movie Palace on Opening Night of "Birth of America." *Scene 4*: Allegorical Vision of Archie's Dream.

ACT 1

"The Movie Lesson"
    F. Hedges, Society Girls, Dancers

Registering Love; Registering Laughter; Registering Jazz

"Look-a-Look"
    G. O'Connor, Society Girls

"Friends"
    H. Van Rensselaer, M. Smith, S. Gallagher

A Movie Incident
    The Director: W. N. Bailey. *The Cameraman*: S. Gallagher. *The Villain*: M. Smith. *The Villainess*: D. Smoller. *Gerald*: A. Romeo. *Dawson*: W. Walker.

"It's a Great Life If You Don't Weaken"
    D. Smoller, M. Smith

"Up in the Clouds"
    H. Van Rensselaer, G. Moore

"The Last Girl Is the Best Girl"
    S. Gallagher, J. Roberts, G. O'Connor, Girls

"At the Fountain" (A Posing Fantasy)
    M. Ten Eyck, M. Weily

"Jean"
    H. Van Rensselaer, S. Gallagher, G. Moore, M. Smith

Finale

ACT 2

Scene 1

Ballet of Wealth
    Elf of Riches: F. Hedges. *Dutch Ancestor*: M. Weily. *Indian Girl*: A. Lemau. *Colonial Ancestors*: P. Spencer, E. Westcott. *Private Ancestor*: B. Buchanan. *A Slave*: M. Ten Eyck. *Georgian Ancestors*: A. Romeo, M. Welsh. *Acquisition of Gold*: A. Corey. *Penny*: E. Young. *Nickel*: B. Soule. *Quarter*: A. Hayes. *Gold Eagle*: Y. Babcock. *Flight of Gold*: J. Roberts. *Silver Coins*: J. Hurley, A. Hall, T. Holliday, A. Hall, T. Holliday, K. Valentine. *Gold Coins*: G. Hall, B. Millar, L. Gaynelle, P. Millar.

"The Girl I Marry"
    H. Van Rensselaer, G. Moore

"Nobody Knows"
    M. Smith, M. Ten Eyck, G. O'Connor, Girls

"Betsy Ross"
    G. Moore, Girls

"Rum Tum Tiddle"
    V. J. Melino, J. J. Weis, R. Alexander, G. Hall, P. Millar, A. Hall

"Happiness"
    G. Moore

Scene 2

"Passing of Six Months"
    Spirits of the Months: J. Roberts, F. Hedges. *January*: E. Westcott. *February*: G. Hall. *March*: P. Miller. *April*: A. Hayes. *May*: B. Soule. *June*: E. Young.

Scene 3

"Birth of American Fantasy"
    M. Ten Eyck, M. Weily

Finale

1922.02   THE BLUE KITTEN

A Musical Comedy in Three Acts. Book and lyrics by Otto Harbach and William Cary Duncan. Based on the French farce 'Le Chasseur de Chez Maxim's' by Gustave Quinson and Yves Mirande. Music by Rudolf Friml. Staged by Edgar Selwyn, Leon Errol and Julian Mitchell. Scenery designed by Clifford Pember. Costume design by Shirley Barker, supervised by Anna Spencer. Orchestra under the direction of Herbert Stothart. Produced by Arthur Hammerstein. Opened 13 January 1922 at the Selwyn Theatre, moved 1 May 1922 to the Earl Carroll Theatre, and closed 13 May 1922 after 140 performances.

CAST (in order of appearance): *Louis*, a coat-room boy: Bill Hawkins. *Giglais*, a Parisian bon vivant: VICTOR MORLEY. *Theodore Vanderpop*, head-waiter and hall-porter at the 'Blue Kitten' restaurant: JOSEPH CAWTHORN. *Durand*, manager of the 'Blue Kitten': GEORGE LeSOIR. *Octave*, Theodore's nephew: ROBERT WOOLSEY. *Fifi*, a cloak-room girl: Betty Barlow. *Cri Cri* from the Follies Bergeres: MARION SUNSHINE. *Marcele* from the Follies Bergeres: Carola Parson. *Totoche*: LILLIAN LORRAINE. *Armand Duvelin*, a marquis: DOUGLAS STEVENSON. *Mme. Lucile Vanderpop*, Theodore's wife: JEAN NEWCOMBE. *Madelaine Vanderpop*, his daughter: LORRAINE MANVILLE. *Popinet*, Duvelin's tutor: Dallas Welford. *Dance of the Roses in Act 2 and Smoke Ring Dance in Act 3* by May Cory Kitchen. (*Specialties*: Ted Grant and Frances Wing.) *Habitues of the 'Blue Kitten,' Madeleine's friends in Fontainebleu, etc.*
    Girls: Eleanor Dell, Helen Lewis, Frisco DeVere, Evelyn Pluntadore, Frances Stone, Blanche Morton, Penny Rowland, Jeanne Osborne, Gladys Jordan, Grace LaRue, Bernice Ackerman, Peggy Stohl, Violet Lobelle, Dorothy Stokes, Ann Ross, Beatrice Savage, Helen McDonald. *Boys*: Chester Brown, Joseph Brennan, Boris Scott, Leo Howe, George Griffiths, William Mack, Robert Hurst, Lester New.

Act 1: The Foyer of 'The Blue Kitten' Restaurant in Paris. An evening in June 1921.

Act 2: At Vanderpop's Chateau at Fontainebleu. Two days later.

Act 3: 'The Blue Kitten' Café. Evening of the same day.

ACT 1

"Le Minuet Bleu" (The Blue Kitten)
    V. Morley, M. C. Kitchen, Men, Girls

"Tact"
    J. Cawthorn, R. Woolsey

"Cutie"
    L. Lorraine, J. Cawthorn

"A Bud Among the Roses"
    D. Stevenson, M. Sunshine, Chorus

Finale

ACT 2

"Her Love Is Always the Same"
    L. Manville, M. C. Kitchen, Ensemble

"Where the Honeymoon Alone Can See"
    L. Manville, D. Stevenson

"The Best I Ever Get Is the Worst of It"
    J. Cawthorn

"A Twelve O'Clock Girl in a Nine O'Clock Town"
    R. Woolsey, M. Sunshine

Finale

ACT 3[92]

"Smoke Rings"

V. Morley, T. Grant and F. Wing, Ensemble

"I Could Do a Lot for You"

R. Woolsey, Girls

"Sweet As You Can Be"

L. Manville, Boys

Reprise

M. Sunshine, D. Welford, Ensemble

"When I Waltz with You"

L. Lorraine, D. Stevenson

Finale

1922.03 ELSIE JANIS AND HER GANG

A New Attack[93] (Musical Revue) in Two Acts, 18 Scenes. (Sketches, music and lyrics) Written by Elsie Janis. (Staged by Elsie Janis.) Costumes designed by Charles LeMaire and Will R. Barnes. Scenery painted by Mark Lawson. Orchestra under the direction of John L. McManus. Orchestrations by Maurice DePackh. Produced by Elsie Janis. Opened 16 January 1922 at the Gaiety Theatre and closed 4 March 1922 after 56 performances.

CAST: ELSIE JANIS and THE GANG: JURIEN THAYER, GUS SHY, W. DORN-FOLD, CHARLIE LAWRENCE, BRADLEY KNOCHE, RED MURDOCK, MONK WATSON, HERBERT GOFF, LEWIS REID, DUANE NELSON, FRANK MILLER, DAN WALKER, LANE McLEOD, JAMES F. NASH, CHESTER GRADY, ELIZABETH MORGAN, MAUDE DRURY, INEZ BAUER, ELVA MAGNUS, MARGARET SOUSA.

The Eight Bobs: Misses Asta Valle, Patricia Mayer, Claire Daniels, Buddy Merriam, Eleanor Ladd, Florence Courtney, Adelaide de St. Clair, Paulette Winston.

ACT 1: Let's Go

Scene 1

Disclosing the Eight Bobs

Misses Valle, Mayer, Daniels, Merriam, Ladd, Courtney, de St. Clair, Winston

Scene 2

What you want and what you get are very different

Scene 3

"Discontent" (Song)

G. Shy, Company

(*Music by* Herman Finck.)

Scene: A Forest in the Kingdom of Discontent

King Constant Discontent: G. Shy. *Love,* His Pet Aversion: J. Thayer. *Pessimism,* His Prime Minister: B. Knoche. *Jealousy,* His Favorite Lady: I. Bauer. *Envy,* a Lady in Waiting: E. Magnus. *Spite,* a Lady in Waiting: E. Morgan. *Greed,* a Lady in Waiting: M. Drury. *Bolshevism,* His Henchman: W. Dornfeld. *Sarcasm,* His Court Jester: L. McLeod. *His Guards:* R. Murdock, J. F. Nash, L. Reid, C. Grady. *Content:* E. Janis.

Scene 4

"Goodbye Girls, I'm Through" (Song)(from CHIN-CHIN)

J. Thayer, Misses Magnus, Drury, Morgan, Courtney

(*Music by* Ivan Caryll. *Lyrics by* John L. Golden.)

"Love in the Springtime Is Not What It Used To Be" (Song)

H. Goff, Misses Magnus, Drury, Morgan, Courtney

(*Music by* George S. Hirst.)

Minuet

A. Valle, C. Grady

Jazz

P. Mayer, D. Walker

Scene: A Railway Station in England—because they are smaller there.

Porters: M. Watson, F. Miller. *News Agent* (Discontent): G. Shy. *Ticket Taker* (Bolshevism): W. Dornfeld. *Young Man,* in search of fiancée: D. Nelson. *Another Young Man:* B. Knoche. *The Hero* (Love): J. Thayer. *Still Another Young Man:* H. Goff.

Scene 5

Announcement

L. McLeod

Scene 6

"I've Been Waiting" ("I've Waited All My Life")(Duet)

E. Janis, J. Thayer

Scene: Honeymoon Cottage, a month later.

Bride (Content): E. Janis. *Groom* (Love): J. Thayer. *Gardener* (Discontent): G. Shy. *Maid* (Jealousy): I. Bauer.

Scene 7

"Property Man" (Song)

M. Watson

"Will You Remember?" (Song)

J. Thayer, G. Shy, Passengers

Scene: Crossing the Channel.

Passengers: J. Thayer, E. Magnus, G. Shy, M. Watson, E. Morgan, H. Goff, C. Daniels, J. F. Nash, E. Ladd, B. Knoche, M. Drury, C. Grady.

Scene 8

"Montmartre" (Song)

D. Nelson

"Mon Homme"[94] (Song)

E. Janis

(*Music by* Maurice Yvain. *French Lyrics by* Jacques Charles, Albert Willemetz.)

Scene: Montmartre, Paris.

The Singer: D. Nelson. *Mimi:* E. Janis. *American:* J. Thayer. *Pierre:* G. Shy. *Pierre Louis:* B. Knoche. *Rene:* W. Dornfeld. *Georges:* L. McLeod. *LaVache:* I. Bauer. *Chiquette:* A. de St. Clair. *The Dandy:* C. Grady. *Gendarmes:* H. Goff, R. Murdock. *Les Apaches:* E. Morgan, P. Mayer, D. Walker, J. F. Nash.

Scene 9

Painless Magic [Painless Dentistry]

W. Dornfeld

Scene 10

We Must Have a Ballet (*Ballet Music arranged by* Herman Finck.)

"Come, the Night Descends" (Ballet and Song)

J. Thayer

The Girl: E. Morgan. *The Dancer:* E. Janis. *The Singer:* J. Thayer. *The Rich Old Man:* G. Shy. And the Entire Gang.

ACT 2

Scene 1

"Broadway" (Song)

L. McLeod, B. Knoche

Uptown Dance [Jazz]

C. Daniels, P. Mayer, D. Walker

Dance

F. Miller, M. Watson

Downtown Dance [Bowery Dance]

G. Shy, A. de St. Clair

Scene: Broadway.

The Singer: L. McLeod. *Traffic Cop:* B. Knoche. *The One Steppers:* C. Daniels, P. Mayer, D. Walker. *The Downtown Couple:* G. Shy, A. de St. Clair. *The Cutie:* F. Miller. *The Clarinetter:* M. Watson. *Newsboy:* E. Janis.

Scene 2

"Memories" (Song)

J. Thayer

The Singer: J. Thayer. *Havana:* I. Bauer. *Montana:* A. Valle. *Peru:* A. de St. Clair. *Sweden:* M. Sousa. *Dollar Princess:* E. Ladd. *Holland:* M. Drury. *Quaker Girl:* E. Morgan. *Merry Widow:* E. Magnus.

Scene 3

"(The) Bonus Blues"

G. Shy, W. Dornfeld, Veterans

(*Music by* Carey Morgan, Arthur Swanstrom.)

Scene: Employment Agency.

Office Boy: G. Shy. *Heinrich Umplotz:* W. Dornfeld. *Eight Veterans of the Great War:* L. McLeod, C. Grady, H. Goff, D. Nelson, J. L. Reid, J. F. Nash, R. Murdock, and the One of Color: M. Watson.

Scene 4

---

[92]Added to Act 3 after opening, following "Smoke Rings." "I Could Do a Lot for You" moved back to Act 1 position:

"Meow"

M. Sunshine, R. Woolsey, Girls

[93]Billed as "Same Gang—New Show." A previous edition of ELSIE JANIS AND HER GANG appeared on Broadway 1 December 1919 for 55 performances.

---

[94]Previously performed by Fannie Brice on Broadway in English as "My Man" in ZIEGFELD FOLLIES OF 1921.

"All the World Is Wonderful" (Duet)
  E. Janis, J. Thayer
  (*Music by* Seymour Simons.)
    Scene: In the Park.
      Peg: E. Janis. *The Hero*: J. Thayer.

Scene 5

"Too Young to Love" (Song)
  C. Lawrence
    Scene: A Rehearsal.
      Stage Manager: B. Knoche. *Stage Carpenter*: R. Murdock. *Assistant Stage Manager*: F. Miller. *Miss Thompson*: I. Bauer. *The Understudy*: C. Lawrence.

Scene 6

Spanish March
  The Eight Bobs
The First Train (Dance)
  E. Morgan
"Why All This Fuss About Spain?" (Song)
  G. Shy, assisted by the Eight Spanish Onions

Scene 7

The Hero Brings Home What's Left of the Plot
"Nuthin'" (Song)
  E. Janis
  (*Music and Lyrics by* Seymour Simons.)
    Scene: Honeymoon Cottage.
      Bride: E. Janis. *Groom*: J. Thayer.

Scene 8

A Few Minutes with Elsie Janis
["I've Got the Red, White and Blues"]
Finale
  E. Janis, Company

1922.04 MARJOLAINE

A Musical Play in Three Acts. Book by Catherine Chisholm Cushing. Based on the comedy 'Pomander Walk' by Louis N. Parker. Music by Hugo Felix. Lyrics by Brian Hooker. Staged by Oscar Eagle. Dances and ensembles by Bert French. Scenery designed by Joseph Wickes. Costumes designed by William H. Matthews. Orchestra under the direction of Milan Roder. Produced by Russell Janney[95]. Opened 24 January 1922 at the Broadhurst Theatre and closed 20 May 1922 after 136 performances.

CAST (in order of appearance): *Admiral Sir Peter Antrobus*: ALBERT G. ANDREWS. *Jim*: Royal Cutter. *Mrs. Pamela Poskett*: Daisy Belmore. *The Reverend Jacob Sternroyd, D.D.*: COLIN CAMPBELL. *The Eyesore*: E. L. DeBrocq. *Punch and Judy Man*: Paul Warren. *Miss Barbara Sternroyd*: Mary Hay. *Mr. Basil Pringle*: Maurice Holland. *Jerome Brooke-Hoskyn, Esq.*: LENNOX PAWLE. *Jane*, Maid to Brooke-Hoskyn: Marle Stevens. *Madame Lucie Lachesnais*: NELLIE STRONG. *Nanette*, (Her Maid): Olga Treskoff. *Lieutenant The Honorable Jack Sayle*: IRVING BEEBE. *Tom*: Irving S. Finn. *Joe*: Addeson Youngs. *John Sayle*, Tenth Baron Otford: WORTHE FAULKNER. *Mlle. Marjolaine Lachesnais*: PEGGY WOOD.
  Seminary Girls: Eleanor Post, Joan Warner, Edith Slack, Grace Culbert, Pauline Maxwell, Madeline Dare, Grace Angelau, Elizabeth Page, Doris Green, Maida Harries, Florence Ashton, Bert Alden, Jane Raulette, Grace Elliott, Edna Coigne, Eunice Sizer. *Sailor Boys*: Addeson Youngs, Bland O'Connell, Irving S. Fine, Fred Grod, Malcolm Hicks, Robert Wells, Ted Wheeler, Conway Dillon, Horace Milleron.

The action takes place in Pomander Walk, 'out Chiswick Way,' in London, in the year 1806.

Act 1: Saturday afternoon, 25 May.

Act 2: Saturday morning, 1 June.

Act 3: The same, two hours later.

ACT 1[96]
  Prologue
    P. Wood

"Punch and Judy"
  P. Warren, A. G. Andrews, D. Belmore, Girls
"Song of a Sailor"
  I. Beebe, Sailor Boys
"If He Should Come"[97]
  P. Wood
"I Want You"
  M. Hay, M. Holland, Girls
  (*Music by* Hugo Felix. *Lyrics by* Anne Caldwell.)
"I'd Like You to Like Me a Little Bit More"
  I. Beebe
"Marjolaine"
  P. Wood, I. Beebe
Finale
  Ensemble

ACT 2
"Woman-Woman"
  L. Pawle, Girls
"Don't—Don't—Don't"
  P. Wood, M. Hay, Girls
"Ducks and Geese"[98]
  O. Treskoff, Boys
"Old Brown Coat" ("Cuddle Up Together")
  M. Hay, M. Holland, Ensemble
"Syringa Tree"
  W. Faulkner
"Oh, Dr. Sternroyd"
  P. Wood, C. Campbell, I. Beebe
Finale
  Ensemble

ACT 3
Nocturne[99]
  M. Holland
Barcarole ("Stars of Your Eyes")
  W. Faulkner, N. Strong
"In the Park"[100]
  L. Paule, Company
"Music Box"[101]
  P. Wood, E. Slack, P. Maxwell, J. Warner, G. Culbert, M. Dare, G. Angelau
Finale
  Ensemble

1922.05 PINS AND NEEDLES!

A Revue in Two Acts, 21 Scenes[102]. Book (sketches) by Albert de Courville, Wal Pink and Edgar Wallace. Music by James Hanley and Frederic Chappelle. Lyrics by Ballard Macdonald, Rupert Hazell and Irving Caesar. Staged by Albert deCourville, with the assistance of Julian Mitchell. Costumes by Bernard, Max Weldy, Leslie Roberts, Poole and Clarkson, Fisher and Berman, Evelyn Varon. Orchestra under the direction of Charles

---

[95]Subsequent tour produced by John Henry Mears.
[96]Added during the run after "Wonderland" and before "I Want You" to Act 1:
  "Dream Melody"
    W. Faulkner

[97]Replaced during the run by:
  "Wonderland"
    P. Wood
  Which was replaced for the subsequent tour by:
  "Nesting Place"
    P. Wood, Girls
[98]Dropped during the run.
[99]Dropped after the opening.
[100]Replaced for subsequent tour by:
  "On the Deep Blue Sea"
    A. G. Andrews, D. Belmore
[101]Replaced for subsequent tour by:
  "Blind Man's Bluff"
    P. Wood, A. G. Andrews, Ensemble
[102]Billed as "A Revue with Points from the Gaiety Theatre, London, with the Original Cast."

Previn. Produced by Albert deCourville. Opened 1 February 1922 at the Sam S. Shubert Theatre and closed 11 March 1922 after 46 performances[103].

<u>CAST:</u> HARRY PILCER, EDITH KELLY GOULD, JACK MORRISON, RUPERT HAZELL, EWART SCOTT, LILLIAN SMITH, AMY VERITY, JIMMY NERVO, TEDDY KNOX, MAISIE GAY, NAN C. HEARNE, TOMMY MOSTOL, ALICE POLLARD, JANE TAYLOR, Pamela Leroy, Phyllis Wolmer, Joan Morris, May Hern, Louise Wayne, Josephine Blythe, Elizabeth Coyle, Phyllis Bryan, Muriel Cort, Mary Philips, Florence McGuire, Lillian Smith, Tess Mayer, Frances Upton, Geneva Marlowe.

ACT 1[104]

Scene 1

The Night Before

"Love Spans the World"
E. Scott, Chorus

"Off We Go"
A. Verity, Chorus
The Manager: J. Morrison. *Stage Manager*: R. Hazell. *The Juvenile*: E. Scott. *First Girl*: P. Leroy. *Second Girl*: M. Verome. *Miss Treschand*: L. Smith. *The Understudy*: A. Verity. *The Dancers*: J. Nervo, G. Marlowe.

Scene 2

The World of Sport[105]
M. Gay
Assisted by J. Morrison, E. Scott, N. C. Hearne, R. Hazell, J. Nervo, T. Knox, Chorus.

Scene 3

The Rest Cure
The Doctor: E. Scott. *The First Nurse*: A. Pollard. *The Second Nurse*: M. Phillips. *The Cheerful Visitor*: R. Hazell. *The Undertaker*: T. Knox.

Scene 4

Song Souvenirs[106]
J. Taylor

Scene 5

Borrowing
The Friend: J. Morrison. *First Borrower*: E. Scott. *Second Borrower*: T. Knox. *Third Borrower*: R. Hazell. *The Victim*: T. Mostol.

Scene 6

"The Little Tin Soldier and the Little Rag Doll"
H. Pilcer, E. K. Gould
(*Music by* James F. Hanley. *Lyrics by* Darl MacBoyle.)
The Little Tin Soldier: H. Pilcer. *The Little Rag Doll*: E. K. Gould.

Scene 7

"Ah, Ah, Ah"
J. Morrison, Chorus
(*Music by* James F. Hanley. *Lyrics by* Ballard Macdonald.)

Scene 8

Mis' Arris
Jack Pinder: E. Scott. *Bobbie Prendergast*: J. Morrison. *Mis' Arris*: M. Gay. *Mabel Prinder*: A. Verity.

Scene 9

Monkey Dance
Chorus

"I'll Build a Home in the Jungle" (Jungle Bungalow)
E. K. Gould, H. Pilcer
(*Music by* James F. Hanley. *Lyrics by* Ballard Macdonald.)
Scene: A Tropical Fantasy.
The Explorer: T. Knox. *The Baboon*: J. Nervo. *The Marmosets*: H. Pilcer, E. K. Gould. And Full Chorus.

---

[103]Settings uncredited.
[104]Running order changed during the run. Added after opening to Act 1, before A Tropical Fantasy:
Caught
The Mistress: M. Gay. *The Butler*: J. Morrison. *The Detective*: R. Hazell. *The General*: E. Scott. *The Maid*: A. Verity.
[105]Dropped during the run.
[106]Dropped during the run and replaced by:
"All Pull Together"
M. Gay, J. Morrison

ACT 2

Scene 1

"South Sea Sweethearts"
J. Taylor, R. Hazell, Chorus
(*Music by* Maurice Yvain. *Lyrics by* Irving Caesar.)

"Melancholy Blues"
H. Pilcer, Full Chorus
Scene: At Deauville, France.
The Singer: J. Taylor. *The Phonofiddler*: R. Hazell. *Mr. Gigot*: J. Morrison. *Tommy*: E. Scott. *Nanette*: M. Gay.

Scene 2

The Village Blacksmith[107]
The Reciter: T. Mostol. *The Audience*: E. Scott, T. Knox, N. C. Hearne, A. Verity. *Baby Duncan*: M. Gay.

Scene 3

"The Vanity Box"
A. Pollard, Chorus
The Ostrich Feather Bag: J. Morris. *The Dorothy Bag*: M. Hern. *The Ivory Bag*: L. Wayne. *The Gold Mesh Bag*: P. Wolmer. *The Gold Lag Bag*: J. Blythe. *The White Moire Bag*: E. Coyle. *The Black Moire Bag*: P. Bryan. *The Lip Salve*: M. Cort. *The Eye Black*: M. Philips. *Rouge*: F. McGuire. *Perfume*: P. Leroy. *Lace Handkerchief*: L. Smith. *Looking Glass*: T. Mayer. *Powder Puff*: F. Upton. *The Rabbit Foot*: G. Marlowe.

Scene 4

"Slow Movies"
R. Hazell, T. Knox

Scene 5

"The Piccadilly Walk"
E. K. Gould, H. Pilcer, T. Motol, T. Knox, J. Nervo
(*Music by* Edward Horan. *Lyrics by* Arthur Francis [Ira Gershwin], Arthur Riscoe.)

Scene 6

"The Gipsy Warned Me"
M. Gay

Scene 7

I Will (A Dramatic Playlet)
The Helping Hand: T. Mostol. *The Heroine*: A. Pollard. *The Villain*: E. Scott. *The Hero*: R. Hazell.

Scene 8

Some Impersonations[108]
J. Morrison

Scene 9

A Winter Idyll
The Sunbeam: E. K. Gould. *The Snowman*: H. Pilcer. *The Little Girl*: A. Verity. *The Mistletoe*: P. Leroy. *The Holly*: L. Smith. *The Firtree*: P. Wolmer.

Scene 10

"Sunny Sunbeam"
A. Verity
(*Music by* James F. Hanley. *Lyrics by* Ballard Macdonald, Joe Goodwin.)
The Sunbum: J. Nervo. *The Snow-use*: T. Knox.

Scene 11

Sicilian Players in Dialect
Benedettino Crasho: T. Mostol. *Scaramaceia-Pipingallo*: M. Gay. *Antonio Manginbocca*: J. Nervo. *Mamma Mia*: N. C. Hearne.

Scene 12

"The Sincopated Minuet"
A. Pollard, J. Morrison, H. Pilcer, E. K. Gould
(*Music by* James F. Hanley. *Lyrics by* Ballard Macdonald.)

Dance
J. Nervo

"Hollow of My Hand" (Finale)
Full Company

1922.06 (BALIEFF'S) CHAUVE-SOURIS

A Russian Vaudeville Revue (Bat Theatre of Moscow) in Two Acts, 13 Scenes. Conceived by M. Nikita Balieff. Costumes and surroundings

---

[107]Dropped during the run.
[108]Dropped during the run.

(scenery) by Nicholas Remisoff, S. Soudeikine. Director and stage autocrat, Nikita Balieff. Artistic advisor, A. Koiransky. Chef d'orchestre, Elie Zlatin. Maitre de chorégraphie, Mr. Kotshetovsky. Presented by F. Ray Comstock and Morris Gest. Opened 4 February 1922 at the 49th Street Theatre, moved 5 June 1922 to the Century Roof, and closed 5 May 1923 after 544 performances. (Second edition opened 5 June 1922, Third edition opened 9 October 1922, Fourth edition opened 4 January 1923 all atop the Century Roof. Program detail for each edition follows below.)

CAST: Messrs. NIKITA BALIEFF, Wavitch, Gorodetsky, Birse, Boreo, Davidoff, Kochetovsky, Malakoff, Marievsky, Pons, Stoianovsky, Salama, Dalmatoff. Mmes. Birse, Ershova, Dianina, Karabanova, Deykarhanova, Fechner.

ACT 1
Scene 1

Porcelaine de Saxe (Music taken from an old French song "Sur le pont d'Avignon")
   Mmes. Dianina, Karabanova
   (*Music and Lyrics by* Frank Waller. *Costumes and surroundings by* Nicholas Remisoff.)
      In the hours of the night, when all the world is asleep, when dreams and old recollections rule, a mysterious life quickens the objects about us. Tender strains of olden melodies tell us of bygone days, of laughter, of tears, and in the haunting twilight, the little porcelain figures come to life and live over again in the romance of ancient days, reviving the echoes of the past. But the clock strikes . . . and they once again become just "porcelaines de Saxe," trifles of beauty created by the master hand of an artist.

Scene 2

Songs by (Mikhail) Glinka
   Mmes. Birse, Ershova; Messr. Gorodetsky
   (*Costumes and scenery by* S. Soudeikine.)

Scene 3

"The Parade of Wooden Soldiers"
   Messrs. Birse, Boreo, Davidoff, Kotchetovsky, Malakoff, Marievsky, Pons, Stoianovsky, Zotoff
   (*Music by* Leon Jessel. *Lyrics by* Ballard Macdonald.)
   (*Costumes and surrounding designed by* Nicholas Remisoff after Narbout.)

Scene 4

Souvenir of the Far East
   Mme. Deykarhanova; Messr. Gorodetsky
   (*Costumes and surroundings by* Nicholas Remisoff.)

Scene 5

A Quartette of Merry Artists
   Messrs. Wavitch, Birse, Stoianovsky, Zotoff
   (*Costumes by* Nicholas Remisoff.)

Scene 6

The Sudden Death of a Horse, or The Greatness of the Russian Soul
   Mme. Fechner, Messrs. Gorodetsky, Marievsky, Malakoff, Salama
      A young man elopes with the young wife of a Russian Count. The couple frantically urge the driver of the carriage bearing them away to hasten, as the offended husband is pursuing them, so much so, that the horse finally collapses and the husband catches up with the runaways. He offers the driver one hundred rubles to compensate him for the loss of his horse, but the latter in a grandiloquent manner refuses, saying he is quite happy if, owing to the sacrifice of his one horse, virtue triumphs. This sketch was written by the great Russian writer, Tchekoff [Chekhov], as a satire on the plays of his predecessor-dramatists so given to exaggerating the nobleness of the Russian peasant mind.
   (*Costumes and surroundings by* Nicholas Remisoff.)

Scene 7

"Katinka"
   Mmes. Dianina, Karabanova; Messr. Dalmatoff
   (*Music and Lyrics by* Alexei Archangelsky, Czaroulch.)
      An old Russian polka of the sixties. The setting is inspired by one of the wooden toy music boxes made by the Russian peasant artisans. Katinka is the too modern daughter of old-fashioned Russian merchants. To her parents' displeasure she has learned to dance the polka at boarding-school, and angers them furthermore by announcing her intention to marry an officer. They refuse to give their consent to such a marriage. Katinka then pretends to be dying, and the frightened parents yield to her wishes. She then expresses her happiness in an ecstatic dance.
   (*Costumes and surroundings by* S. Soudeikine.)

ACT 2
Scene 1

A Night at Yard's, Moscow, 1840
   Messr. Wavitch, Entire Company

The most striking feature of night life in Moscow were the gypsies. Their passionate songs evoked happiness, comforted the sad and distressed, awakened men to a new life and inspired love. The greater portion of Russian society life was spent outside their homes, in luxurious restaurants which were the abode of these gypsies. Yard's was one of the largest and most renowned of these restaurants. You see here a group of gypsies entertaining a young couple, spell-bound by the beauty of their weird melodies.
   (*Costumes and surroundings by* Nicholas Remisoff.)

Scene 2

The Tartar Dance (*Music by* [Alexsandr Afanasovich] Spendiaroff.)
   M. Kotchetovsky
      The Tartar tribes inhabiting the South of Russia are famed as musicians and dancers; and Spendiaroff, the talented Russian composer, collected the tunes to which the Tartar youths perform their open-air dances by way of serenading their sweethearts.

Scene 3

La Grande Opera Italiana
   Mme. Birse; Messrs. Wavitch, Birse, Stoianovsky, Zotoff
   (*Costumes and surroundings by* S. Soudeikine.)

Scene 4

"Chastoushki" (Russian workpeople's ditties)
   Mme. Fechner; Messrs. Davidoff, Salama
      Chastoushki are Russian ditties full of harsh humor, often improvised by the workpeople themselves. Accompanied by the accordion and dances, they brighten their hours of rest and leisure.
   (*Costumes and surroundings by* Nicholas Remisoff.)

Scene 5

Under the Eye of the Ancestors
   Mmes. Deykarhanova, Dianina, Karabanova; Messr. Malakoff
   (*Costumes and surroundings by* Nicholas Remisoff.)

Scene 6

"The Chorus of Zaitzeff Brothers"
   Leader: Messr. Wavitch. Supported by Messrs. Birse, Boreo, Dalmatoff, Gorodetsky, Marievsky, Stoianovsky, Salama.
   (*Designs and scenery by* Nicholas Remisoff.)

1922.06 (BALIEFF'S) CHAUVE-SOURIS

Second edition of the Russian Vaudeville Revue (Bat Theatre of Moscow) in Two Acts, 13 Scenes[109]. Conceived by M. Nikita Balieff. Composer, Alexei Archangelsky. Costumes and surroundings (scenery) by Nicholas Remisoff, S. Soudeikine. Director and stage autocrat, Nikita Balieff. Chef d'orchestre, Elie Zlatin. Maitre de choréographie, Mr. Kotchetovsky. Presented by F. Ray Comstock and Morris Gest. Second edition opened 5 June 1922 atop the Century Roof.

CAST: Messrs. NIKITA BALIEFF, Wavitch, Gorodetsky, Birse, Boreo, Davidoff, Kotchetovsky, Malakoff, Marievsky, Stoianovsky, Salama, Dalmatoff, Jourist, Zotoff, Doubinsky, Gontacharoff. Mmes. Birse, Ershova, Dianina, Karabanova, Deykarhanova, Fechner, Vassilkova, Komisarjevskaia, Lomakina, Kotchetovsky.

ACT 1
Scene 1

The Moscow Fiances
   Mmes. Deykarhanova, Dianina, Fechner; Messrs. Dalmatoff, Gorodetsky, Salama
      According to the old traditions, the homes of the Russian merchants were very difficult to penetrate. But when so great an attraction as beauty and wealth were hidden within its walls, means were always found to pass over all obstacles. Such is the case with a petulant hair-dresser and a gallant soldier, who manage to win the hearts of two girls, in spite of the desire of their matchmaker, whose chief aim is to get them married to people of their own station. The outdistanced candidate doesn't take it much to heart, and consoles himself with a heart drink of vodka, and 'all's well that ends well.'
   (*Costumes and scenery by* S. Soudeikine.)

Scene 2

"The Evening Bells"
   Mmes. Birse, Ershova; Messr. Doubinsky
   (*Music by* Gretchaninoff [Alexsandr Gretsjaninov]. *Orchestration and trio arranged by* Herman Hand.)

---

[109]First edition opened 4 February 1922 at the 49th Street Theatre for 137 performances. Third Edition opened 9 October 1922 at the Century Roof; Fourth edition opened 4 January 1923 at the Century Roof, closing after a cumulative total of 544 performances.

Scene 3

"The Parade of Wooden Soldiers"

Messrs. Birse, Boreo, Davidoff, Gorodetsky, Jourist, Kotchetovsky, Marievsky, Stoianovsky, Zotoff

(*Music by* Leon Jessel. *Lyrics by* Ballard Macdonald.)

(*Costumes and surrounding designed by* Nicholas Remisoff after Narbout.)

Scene 4

"The King Orders the Drums to Be Beaten" (An old French ballad)

Mmes. Deykarhanova, Dianina, Karabanova; Messrs. Doubinsky, Malakoff

The King orders the drums to be beaten. Their sound calls the dignitaries and ladies of the Court to an assembly. The beautiful wife of a Marquis suddenly awakens the flame of love in the King's heart. Accustomed to give way to his desires, the King urges the marquis to yield to his whim, and in reward promises to bestow upon him the highest dignities of his empire. The marquis, faithful to his oath, though heart-stricken, bows in obedience. But the repudiated queen presents the lady with a gorgeous bouquet of poisoned flowers and the latter, after inhaling their treacherous fragrance—falls dead.

(*Costumes and surrounding designed by* Nicholas Remisoff)

Scene 5

"The Nightingale" (Dear Nightingale)

Mmes. Birse, Vassilkova

(*Music by* Aliabeck [Aleksandr Aljabev]. *Lyrics by* Dailey Paskman.)

(*Costumes and surrounding designed by* Nicholas Remisoff.)

Scene 6

Quadro Caballeros Sevillanos

Messrs. Birse, Doubinsky, Jourist, Stoianovsky

(*Costumes and surrounding designed by* S. Soudeikine. *Orchestration by* Herman Hand.)

Scene 7

As in Front of Our Gates (Russian Folk Songs and Dances)

Mmes. Deykarhanova, Dianana, Ershova, Fechnere, Karabanova, Komisarejevskaia, Lomakina; Messrs. Kotchetovsky, Zotoff

(*Costumes and surrounding designed by* Nicholas Remisoff.)

ACT 2[110]

Scene 1

A Musical Snuff-Box

Mme. Karabanova; Messrs. Gorodetsky, Marievsky

(*Music by* Liadoff [Anatol Konstantinovich Lyadov]. *Costumes and surroundings by* S. Soudeikine.)

Scene 2

"(Songs of) The Black Hussar"[111]

Messr. Wavitch, supported by Messrs. Birse, Boreo, Gorodetsky, Gontcharoff, Dalmatoff, Doubinsky, Davidoff, Jourist, Marivesky, Malakoff, Stoianovsky, Zotoff

A group of characteristic songs of Russia.

(*Costumes and surroundings by* Nicholas Remisoff.)

Scene 3

Copenhagen Porcelaine (A dance designed by M. Remisoff.)

Mmes. Dianina, Karabanova; Messr. Kotchetovsky

Scene 4

"The Three Huntsmen" (Russian Popular Song)

---

[110]Act 2 running order revised after opening. Added to the Second Edition:

A Night at Yard's, Moscow, 1840 (Act 2 opening)

Messr. Wavitch, Entire Company

The most striking feature of night life in old Moscow were the gypsies. Their passionate songs evoked happiness, comforted the sad and distressed, awakened men to a new life and inspired love. The greater portion of Russian society life was spent outside their homes, in luxurious restaurants which were the abode of these gypsies. Yard's was one of the largest and most renowned of these restaurants. You see here a group of gypsies entertaining a young couple, spell-bound by the beauty of their weird melodies. (New songs)

(*Costumes and surroundings by* Nicholas Remisoff.)

Rhapsodie

Mme. Julia Bekeffi

(*Music by* Franz Liszt.)

Gypsy Song Intime

Mmes. Ershova, Birse; Messrs. Davidoff, Zotoff, Salama, Riadnoff, Jurist

The most striking feature of night life in old Moscow were the gypsies. Their passionate songs evoked happiness, comforted the sad and distressed, awakened men to a new life and inspired love.

[111]Dropped after opening.

Mmes. Fechner, Komisarjevskaia; Messrs. Boreo, Marivesky, Stoianovsky

(*Music [adapted] and Lyrics by* Dailey Paskman.)

A popular Russian song of the earlier part of last century. Three huntsmen meet a peasnt-girl collecting mushrooms in a forest. The each in turn attempt to court her. She spurns the attention of the first two and bestows her favors on the third. The happy lovers depart leaving the other two huntsmen with a mushroom as a consolation prize.

(*Costumes and surroundings by* S. Soudeikine.)

Scene 5

The Clown

Messr. Kotchetovsky

(*Music by* Frédéric Chopin. *Costumes by* Nicholas Remisoff.)

Scene 6

Soldiers' Songs before the Revolution

Whole Company

Soldiers' songs were very popular among the Russian troops during the first years of the Great War.

(*Costumes and surroundings by* S. Soudeikine.)

1922.06 (BALIEFF'S) CHAUVE-SOURIS

Third edition of the Russian Vaudeville Revue (Bat Theatre of Moscow) in Two Acts, 13 Scenes[112]. Conceived by M. Nikita Balieff. Composer, Alexei Archangelsky. Costumes and surroundings (scenery) by Nicholas Remisoff, S. Soudeikine. Director and stage autocrat, Nikita Balieff. Chef d'orchestre, Elie Zlatin. Maitre de choréographie, Mr. Kotshetovsky. Orchestrations by Herman Hand. Presented by F. Ray Comstock and Morris Gest. Third edition opened 9 October 1922 at the Century Roof Theatre.

CAST: Messrs. NIKITA BALIEFF, Wavitch, Gorodetsky, Birse, Davidoff, Kochetovsky, Malakoff, Marievsky, Jurist, Stoianovsky, Salama, Dalmatoff, Zotoff, Grobokoratal. Mmes. Birse, Dianina, Karabanova, Deykarhanova, Fechner, Lomakina, Vassilkova.

ACT 1[113]

Scene 1

The Fountain of Bakhchi-Sarai (A Dramatic Poem by Pushkin)

(*Music by* Alexei Archangelsky. *Costumes and Scenery by* S. Soudeikine.)

Zarema: Mme. Deykarhanova. Maria: Mme. Karabanova. Gerei Khan: Messr. Wavitch. The Eunuch: Messr. Marievsky. The Khan's Wives: Mmes. Birse, Davidova, Dianina, Ershova, Fechner, Komisarjevskaia, Lomakina, Vassilkova.

Alexander Pushkin, born in 1799 and killed in a duel by D'Anthès in 1837, was the greatest Russian poet. Under his influence, the whole of Russian literature was developed—from Gogol, Dostoievsky, Turgenieff and the two Tolstoys down to the poets, novelists and playwrights of our own generation.

In Bakhchi-Sarai, an ancient city of the Crimean Khans, a marble fountain still stands in the royal palace called "The Fountain of Tears." Pushkin wrote a legend about this fountain. It runs as follows:

Gerei Khan, chief of a Tartar tribe, lives in solitude among his wives at Bakhchi-Sarai. The tears of Zarema, whom he once loved, and the beauty of the Southern melodies no longer touch him. His heart yearns for Maria, a Polish princess, the last victim of his harem. The Khan sits among his wives, with Zarema at his feet, and the others sings songs of praise to her beauty. But Gerei Khan does not listen to them. Zarema watches him in despair. She speaks to him of their mutual love and implores him to return to her. The Khan, however, remains cold and immovable. Night approaches. Zarema resolves to speak with her rival, and with tears entreats Maria to restore the Khan's love to her. But the Polish princess does not understand her passionate words and longs only for one thing—to quit this world as soon as possible. Zarema then tries to draw a promise from her, namely, that she will not yield to the Khan's

---

[112]First edition opened 4 February 1922 at the 49th Street Theatre for 137 performances. Second edition opened 5 June 1922 at the Century Roof; Fourth edition opened 4 January 1923 at the Century, closing after a cumulative total of 544 performances.

[113]After the opening, the running order was repeatedly revised. In the last week of December 1922, the following new scenes were introduced:

The Moscow Fiancées (Act 1)

Mmes. Deykarbanova, Dianina, Fechner; Messrs. Dalmatoff, Gorodetsky, Salama

Songs by Glinka

Mmes. Birse, Ershova

The Dentist (by Anton Chekoff)(Act 1)

Messrs. Dalmatoff, Salama

love. Maria vouchsafes no answer, and Zarema kills her. The enraged Khan orders Zarema to be thrown into the sea, commands a marble fountain to be erected in memory of Maria, and in despair goes forth to war.

Scene 2

"Marlborough s'en va-t-en guerre" (Marlborough Goes to the Wars," an old French song)

Messr. Malaokff; Mmes. Birse, Dianina, Vassilkova, Lomakina
(*Music arranged by* Andrei Archangelsky.)
The famous song of Marlborough was doubtlessly composed after the battle of Malplaquet, in 1709, and not on the death of John Churchill, Duke of Marlborough, in 1722, as many historians assert.
(*Setting designed by* S. Soudeikine.)

Scene 3

Grief (An etude by Frédéric Chopin.)

Mme. Ershova, Messr. Doubinsky
(*Costumes and scenery by* Nicholas Remisoff.)

Scene 4

"The Chinese Billikens"

Mme. Fechner; Messrs. Birse, Jurist, Stoianovsky, Zotoff
(*Music by* Alexei Archangelsky. *Lyrics by* Dailey Paskman. *Costumes and surroundings by* S. Soudeikine.)

Scene 5

The Minuet (after a tale by de Maupassant)

Mme. Deykarhanova; Messr. Gorodetsky
(*Music by* Alexei Archangelsky.)
In the old park of Versailles an elderly couple meet and become acquainted. In the course of their conversation he tells her that during the reign of Louis XV, about forty years before, he was ballet master of the Royal Opera House, and that for his services, the King had presented him with a precious cane, which he shows to the old lady. It develops that she is the famous dancer Castri, the creator of the Minuet. Happy at this unexpected meeting, they recall olden times and to the strains of distant music dance the Minuet as they used to in their youth.
(*Costumes and scenery by* Nicholas Remisoff.)

Scene 6

Samurai (An exotic Japanese dance)

Messr. Kotchetovsky
(*Music by* Alexei Archangelsky.)
Samurai were Japanese warriors whose race was greatly privileged in Japan. Society was so keenly interested in them that they offered a constant subject for discussion in the Japanese theatres.
(*Costumes and surroundings by* Nicholas Remisoff.)

Scene 6

"Katinka's Unexpected Romance" (by Alexei Archangelsky)

Mmes. Gorodetsky and Karabanova; Messrs. Birse, Dalmatoff, Davidoff, Jurist, Marievsky, Stoianovsky, Zotoff
Katinka meets the commander of the Wooden Soldiers, who falls in love with her and begs permission to marry her. The parents protest, whereupon the commander summons his army. They attack Katinka's parents, who are compelled to give in, and all finishes up with the already well-known Polka—"Katinka."
(*Scenery by* S. Soudeikine.)

ACT 2

Scene 1

U Prikaznikh Vorot[114] (Scenes from the life of old Russia in the sixteenth century, after Count Alexei Tolstoy.)

The Company
(*Music by* Ilya Sats and Alexei Archangelsky. *Costumes and Scenery by* Nicholas Remisoff.)
Count Alexei Tolstoy , 1817-1875, cousin to Count Lyoff Tolstoy, was famous as a poet and more successful as a playwright than his noted relative. Richard Mansfield played his "Ivan the Terrible" many years ago; and the first of his great dramatic trilogy of Russian history "Tsar Fyodor Ivanovitch", the play with which the Moscow Art Theatre began its career a quarter of a century ago, will be in the New York repertory of that famous company in its forthcoming American engagement. Ilya Sats, now deceased, was a composer closely associated with the Moscow Art Theatre and the development of modern Russian music.
At the gates of judgement in ancient Moscow, a throng of people complain of their troubles to the "diak," the judge of the city. Some have not sufficient bread to eat, others are suffering from different maladies, and a third group is unable to sell their wares. But the "diak," who lives well and is abundantly paid by the State, accuses them of being liars and deceivers

and points out in a mocking way that, if he can live well on what he gets, the rest of them ought to be able to do the same.

Scene 2

"The Serenade of the Deceived Pierrot"

Mme. Birse
(*Costumes and scenery by* S. Soudeikine.)

Scene 3

"Le Joli Tambour" (Pretty Drummer, an old French song)

Mmes. Dianina, Fechner, Karabanova, Komisarjevskaia; Messr. Zotoff
(*Costumes and scenery by* Nicholas Remisoff.)

Scene 4

"The Night Idyl"

Mmes. Fechner, Lomakina, Vassilkova; Messrs. Salama, Stoianovsky, Zotoff
(*Music by* Alexei Archangelsky. *Costumes and surroundings by* Nicholas Remisoff.)

Scene 5

Trepak[115] (A Russian popular dance)

Messr. Kotchetovsky
(*Costume and Surroundings by* S. Soudeikine.)

Scene 6

Scenes from Life in Little Russia[116] (Fragments from Moussorgsky's music)

The Company
Modest Moussorgsky, 1835-1881, was the god-father of modern Russian music, master of Rimsky-Korsakoff and stimulus to Stravinsky and many others, besides greatly influencing the work of the great French composer, Claude Debussy. His opera, "Boris Godunoff" fitly identifies him to American audiences.
A woman already past the prime of life proves unfaithful to her old drunkard of a husband and turns her attentions to a young Ukrainian. A quarrel ensues in which the whole village participates. The women take the part of the wife; the men, that of the husband. Finally, however, everything turns out satisfactorily, owing to the appearance of a bucket of vodka, and all join in a merry dance, called the Gopak.
(*Costumes and Scenery by* S. Soudeikine.)

1922.06 ## (BALIEFF'S) CHAUVE-SOURIS

Fourth edition of the Russian Vaudeville Revue (Bat Theatre of Moscow) in Two Acts, 15 Scenes[117]. Conceived by M. Nikita Balieff. Composer, Alexei Archangelsky. Costumes and surroundings (scenery) by Nicholas Remisoff, S. Soudeikine. Director and stage autocrat, Nikita Balieff. Chef d'orchestre, Elie Zlatin. Maitre de choréographie, Mr. Kotshetovsky. Presented by F. Ray Comstock and Morris Gest. Opened 4 January 1923 at the Century Roof Theatre.

CAST: Messrs. NIKITA BALIEFF, Gorodetsky, Birse, Davidoff, Kochetovsky, Malakoff, Marievsky, Jurist, Stoianovsky, Salama, Dalmatoff, Zotoff, Doubinsky, Grobokopatel, Wavitch. Mmes. Birse, Dianina, Karabanova, Davidova, Ershova, Komisarjevskaya, Deykarhanova, Fechner, Lomakina, Vassilkova.

ACT 1[118]

Scene 1

Zaria-Zarianitsa (The Miracle of the Holy Virgin)(A Sacred Legend)

Mmes. Birse, Deykarhanova, Dianina, Davidova, Ershova, Komisarjevskaya, Lomakina, Vassilkova; Messr. Zotoff
(*Music by* N. Suvorovsky. *Words by* Fyodor Sologub.)
A group of young novices assemble at the door of a chapel to listen to an old pilgrim chanting a sacred legend of the Russian Church. The legened describes how once upon a time the Holy Mother came down upon earth adorned in the garb of a simple peasant woman bent on a pilgrimage to the

---

[114]Dropped shortly after opening.

[115]After one month, Messr. Kotchetovsky was joined in this number by Mmes. Deykarhanova, Dianina, Lomakina, Vassilkova; Messrs. Birse, Marievksy.

[116]Replaced after the opening by:
"The Chorus of the Zaitzeff Brothers"
Messr. Wavitch (Leader); supported by Messrs. Birse, Dalmatoff, Gorodetsky, Marievsky, Jurist, Grobokoratal, Dubinsky, Stoianovsky, Salama

[117]First edition opened 4 February 1922 at the 49th Street Theatre for 137 performances. Second edition opened 5 June 1922 at the Century Roof; Third edition opened 9 October 1922 at the Century Roof, production closed 5 May 1923 after a cumulative total of 544 performances.

[118]Running order revised four weeks after opening. Beginning 5 March 1923, a repertory program consisting of material from previous editions was reintroduced as the production neared the end of its run.

Holy Places. Passing through a certain village, she was refused alms and hospitality by the inhabitants. Saint Elijah, the Prophet, hearing of the treatment of the Holy Mother by the village, mounts his fiery chariot in order to chastise with lightning and thunder the hard-hearted peasants. But the Holy Virgin intervenes, telling Elijah that she has forgiven the defaulters for the sake of their children, and as the Saint is reluctant to yield to her appeal for mercy, she covers with her veil the entire village and saves the inhabitants from his wrath.

Scene 2

The See-Saw (Porcelaine de Meissen)[119]
Mmes. Dianina, Fechner, Karabanova, Komisarjevskaya
(*Music by* Alexei Archangelsky. *Surroundings by* Nicholas Remisoff.)

Scene 3

"The Parade of Wooden Soldiers"
Messrs. Gorodetsky, Davidoff, Jurist, Grobokopatel, Kotchetovsky, Malakoff, Marievsky, Stoianovsky, Zotoff
(*Music by* Leon Jessel. *Lyrics by* Ballard Macdonald.)
(*Costumes and surrounding designed by* Nicholas Remisoff.)

Scene 4

"Toi qui connais les Hussards de la garde" (An Old French Song)
Mmes. Deykarhanova, Dianina
(*Costumes and surrounding designed by* Nicholas Remisoff.)

Scene 5

The Tartar Dance
Messr. Kotchetovsky
(*Music by* Spendiaroff. *Costumes and surrounding designed by* Nicholas Remisoff.)

Scene 6

"Anushka" (Russian popular Song)
Mme. Deykarhanova; Messrs. Gorodetsky, Dalmatoff, Salama, Stoianovsky, Wavitch

Scene 7

"Marlborough s'en va-t-en guerre" (Marlborough Goes to the Wars," an old French song)
Messr. Malakoff; Mmes. Birse, Dianina, Lomakina, Vassilkova
(*Music arranged by* Andrei Archangelsky.)
The famous song of Marlborough was doubtlessly composed after the battle of Malplaquet, in 1709, and not on the death of John Churchill, Duke of Marlborough, in 1722, as many historians assert.
(*Setting designed by* S. Soudeikine.)

Scene 8

A Feast of the Hussars
Messr. Wavitch, supported by the Company

ACT 2

Scene 1

Une soirée intime[120]
Mmes. Birse, Ershova, Fechner, Karabanova
(*Music by* Veckerlain, arranged by Alexei Archangelsky.)
(*Surroundings by* Nicholas Remisoff.)

Scene 2

Napoleon's Love (A tragic episode of Napoleon's life before the battle of Waterloo)
Mme. Deykarhanova; Messrs. Birse, Gorodetsky, Jurist, Marievsky

Scene 3

"Ei Ukhnem" (The famous Volga Boat Song)
Men of the Company
(*Music arranged by* Alexei Archangelsky. *Scenery by* Nicholas Remisoff.)

Scene 4

The Sudden Death of a Horse, or The Greatness of the Russian Soul
Mme. Fechner, Messrs. Gorodetsky, Marievsky, Malakoff, Salama
A young man elopes with the young wife of a Russian Count. The couple frantically urge the driver of the carriage bearing them away to hasten, as the offended husband is pursuing them, so much so, that the horse finally collapses and the husband catches up with the runaways. He offers the driver one hundred rubles to compensate him for the loss of his horse, but the latter in a grandiloquent manner refuses, saying he is quite happy if, owing to the sacrifice of his one horse, virtue triumphs. This sketch was written by the great Russian writer, Tchekoff [Chekhov], as a satire on the plays of his predecessor-dramatists so given to exaggerating the nobleness of the Russian peasant mind.
(*Costumes and surroundings by* Nicholas Remisoff.)

Scene 5

"Il Barbiere di Siviglia"
Mmes. Birse, Ershova; Messrs. Birse, Doubinsky, Jurist, Riadnoff, Zotoff
(*Music by* Rossini, arranged by Alexei Archangelsky. *Surroundings by* S. Soudeikine.)

Scene 6

Alaverdi (Scenes from the life in the Caucasus)
Messrs. Birse, Davidoff, Doubinsky, Grobokopatel, Jurist, Riadnoff, Salama, Stoianovsky, Wavitch, Zotoff
(*Surroundings and costumes by* Nicholas Remisoff.)

Scene 7

"Kamarinskaya" (A popular Russian dance)
Messrs. Kotchetovsky
(*Music by* Rubinstein. *Surroundings by* S. Soudeikine.)

1922.07   # THE BLUSHING BRIDE

A Musical Comedy in Two Acts. Book and lyrics by Cyrus Wood. Based on a libretto by Edward Clark and the play 'The Third Party' by Brandon and Arthur adapted by Mark Swan. Music by Sigmund Romberg. Staged by Frank Smithson. Musical numbers arranged by Jack Mason. Scenes (designed) by Watson Barratt. Orchestra under the direction of George A. Nichols. Entire production under the personal direction of J. J. Shubert. Produced by Lee and J. J. Shubert. Opened 6 February 1922 at the Astor Theatre, moved 24 April 1922 to the 44th Street Theatre, and closed 10 June 1922 after 144 performances.

CAST: *Paul Kominski*: ROBERT O'CONNOR. *Flower Girl*: Violette Strathmore. *Cigarette Girl*: Kitty Flynn. *Francois*: Harold Gwynne. *Schwartz*: David Belbridge. *Cazazza*: George Craig. *Christopher Pottinger*: TOM LEWIS. *Alfred*: CLARENCE NORDSTROM. *Rose*: EDYTHE BAKER. *Justine*: Beatrice Swanson. *Lorraine*: Marcella Swanson. *Coley Collins*: CECIL LEAN. *Lulu Love*: CLEO MAYFIELD. *Judge Redwood*: HARRY CORSON CLARKE. *Doris Mayne*: JANE CARROLL. *Mrs. Pottinger*: GERTRUDE MUDGE. *Specialty Entertainers*: THE GLORIAS (Adelaide and Albert DiNovaloff.).
Ladies of the Ensemble: Alice Brady, Mabel Blake, Eva Cassanova, Clara Carroll, Virginia Calmer, Georgia Empey, Gene Gray, Clair Hooper, Anabelle Lewis, Margaret Morris, Rena Manning, Thelma Percy, Betty Ross, Louise Strong, Jean Woods. *Gentlemen of the Ensemble*: David Belbridge, Fred Blyler, George Luman, Charles Layton, John Muccia, John Barrott.

Act 1: The Cabaret of Paul Kominski.

Act 2: The Home of Mr. and Mrs. Pottinger.

ACT 1

Opening Dance
The Glorias
"Love's Highway"
C. Nordstrom, E. Baker
"I'll Bet on Anything But Girls"
C. Lean, Girls
"A Regular Girl"
C. Mayfield
"The Tick, Tick, Tick of the Ticker"
C. Nordstrom, R. O'Connor, B. Swanson, M. Swanson, The Glorias, Ensemble
"Good-bye"
C. Mayfield, C. Lean
"Cazazza"
C. Lean, R. O'Connor, Ensemble
"Mr. and Mrs."
C. Mayfield, C. Lean, Ensemble

ACT 2

Piano Specialty
E. Baker
"The Silver Wedding"
T. Lewis, G. Mudge, J. Carroll, E. Baker, C. Nordstrom, R. O'Connor, B. Swanson, M. Swanson, H. C. Clarke
Specialty Entertainers
The Glorias
"Bad Little Boy and Good Little Girl"
C. Mayfield, C. Lean

---

[119]Replaced during the run by:
Chirurgi (The Dentist)(*by* Anton Tchekhoff [Chekhov])
Messrs. Dalmatoff, Salama
[120]Dropped one month into the run.

"That's the Way It Goes"
  R. O'Connor, M. Swanson, B. Swanson, K. Flynn, V. Strathmore
"Rosy Posy"
  E. Baker, C. Nordstrom, The Glorias, Chorus
"Springtime"
  C. Lean, J. Carroll, C. Mayfield, R. O'Connor
"Patter"
  C. Lean
"Different Days"[121]
  C. Lean, C. Mayfield, T. Lewis, G. Mudge, H. C. Clarke, R. O'Connor
Finale
  Entire Company

1922.08 FRANK FAY'S FABLES

A Musical Revue in Two Acts, 7 Scenes. Book (sketches) by Frank Fay. Music by Clarence Gaskill. Lyrics by Frank Fay and Clarence Gaskill. Staged under the personal direction of Frank Fay. Ensembles and dances by Kuy Kendall. Scenery designed by P. Dodd Ackerman. Costumes designed by Ann Burrows, Helen A. Haas, William H. Matthews. Orchestra under the direction of Gus Salzer. Produced by Harry L. Cort. Opened 6 February 1922 at the Park Theatre and closed 4 March 1922 after 32 performances.

CAST: FRANK FAY, BERNARD GRANVILLE, FANIA MARINOFF, HERBERT CORTHELL, GEORGIANNA HEWITT, OLGA STECK, EDDIE CARR, THE FIFER TRIO (Albert, Ruth, Jean), HELEN GROODY, ROBERT CUMMINGS, LOUIS CASAVANT, OLIVETTE, DONALD LEE ROBERTS, CLARENCE GASKILL.
  The Six Red-Heads: Laura Lee MacLean, Helen Montagu, Ingrid Zanders, Celene Craven, Dorothy Lynch, Freckles Gordon. *Ladies of the Ensemble*: Cecil Boylan, Nellie Daley, Niobe Marwick, Venie Quincy, Elinor Matherson, Emily Russ, Greta Warburg, Thea Thompson, Marie Cattell, Kitty Leckie, June Martin, Florence Tilton, Marie Walsh, Elita Sinclair, Billie Shilling, Alice Gordon, Gertrude Lane. *Gentlemen of the Ensemble*: Leonard Moody, Walter Westley, Jack Swayne, Walter Radtke, Alfred Watson, Norman Earle, William McGuire, Arthur Budd.

ACT 1
Scene 1
  "It's Up to a Cop to Cop a Pretty Maid"
    Park Police, Maids
  "Swanee" (That Swanee River Melody)
    O. Steck, H. Groody, G. Hewitt, Entire Company
      Scene: Sheepfold in Central Park.
        Sheepfold Keeper: L. Cassavant. *Manager, "The Golden Pheasant" Company*: B. Granville. *The Prima Donna*: O. Steck. *The Soubrette*: G. Hewitt. *The Comedienne*: H. Groody. *First Comedian*: H. Corthell. *Second Comedian*: E. Carr. *Policemen, Nursemaids, Members of "the Golden Pheasant" Company*: Ensemble.
        Frank Fay—Himself
Scene 2
  "Columbus Wouldn't Know Columbus Circle as It Is To-day"
    B. Granville, Ensemble
  "The Merry Little Widows"
    H. Groody, the Six Red Heads
      Scene: An Episode in Columbus Circle.
        A Bachelor: H. Corthell. *A Girl*: O. Steck. *A Person*: E. Carr. *His Wife*: G. Hewitt. *Man About Town*: B. Granville. *Shoppers, Commuters, Policemen, Newsboys, etc.*: (Ensemble).
Scene 3
  The Double Cross
    Scene: A Cabin in the Klondike.
      Madge, a dance hall girl: F. Marinoff. *Get-It-Easy Pringle*, a gambler: F. Fay. *Joe*, the Indian: D. L. Roberts. *Tom Anderson*, a prospector: B. Granville.
  "Fables" (Don't Believe Their Fables)
    O. Steck, G. Hewitt, Ensemble
  Special Dance
    Olivette
  The Three Musical McGuickens
    H. Corthell, B. Granville, E. Carr

"Baby Moon"
  O. Steck
Scene 4
  Dance of the China Sea (Divertissement)
    A. Fifer, R. Fifer
  "Arms of the China Wall" (Song)
    B. Granville
      Scene: The China Wall.
        A Blind Beggar: B. Granville. *A Mandarin*: L. Cassavant. *A Tourist*: D. L. Roberts. *His Daughter*: H. Groody. *His Sons*: J. Fifer, L. Moody. *Chinese Fisherfolk and Maidens*: Ensemble.

ACT 2
Scene 1
  "My Land"
    B. Granville, assisted by O. Steck, Indian Ensemble
      Scene: Hudson River Heights opposite New York.
        Indian Chief: L. Cassavant. *Indian Runner*: B. Granville. *Indian Princess*: O. Steck.
  (Specialty)
    E. Garr, H. Corthell, F. Fay
  "Two Are One" (You Need Two Souls But One Thought)
    The Bride: G. Hewitt. *The Groom*: B. Granville. *The Minister*: L. Cassavant. *Brides, Bridegrooms, Bridesmaids, Ushers*: Ensemble.
  (Specialty)
    The Fifer Trio
Scene 2
  "Oh, What a Happy Day"
    B. Granville, H. Groody, Dancing Ensemble
      Scene: Ante Room of Dancing Academy.
  Frank Fay and Clarence Gaskill (Specialty)
Scene 3
  "A Popular Song" (It's a Pop, Pop, Popular Song)
    F. Fay, Entire Company
      Scene: In Music Land.
  Foxtrot
    G. Hewitt
  Gallop
    The Fifer Trio
  Waltz
    H. Groody, D. L. Roberts
  "Boosters" (Song)
    The Six Red Heads
  Operatic Version
    O. Steck, B. Granville, G. Hewitt
  Russian Version
    Olivette
  Finale
    Company

1922.09 THE FRENCH DOLL

A Comedy with a few songs in Three Acts. Play by A. E. Thomas, adapted from the French ('Jeunes filles de palaces') by Paul Armont and Marcel Gerbidon. Music by George Gershwin, Gus Edwards. Lyrics by Buddy G. DeSylva, Will D. Cobb. Staged by W. H. Gilmore. Scenery designed by Herbert Ward. Gowns by Milgrim, Joseph, Alice Bernard. Produced by E. Ray Goetz. Opened 20 February 1922 at the Lyceum Theatre and closed 3 June 1922 after 120 performances.

CAST (in order of appearance): *Baroness Mazulier*: ADRIENNE D'AMBRICOURT. *A Furniture Mover*: James Hunter. *Rene Mazulier*: EUGENE BORDEN. *Baron Mazulier*: EDOUARD DURAND. *Georgine Mazulier*: IRENE BORDONI. *Melanie*: Laura Lussier. *Jackson*: Will Deming. *T. Wellington Wick*: THURSTON HALL. *Emily Morrow*: Edna Hibbard. *Philip Stoughton*: DON BURROUGHS. *James Allen*: William Williams.

Act 1: Living Room in the Studio Apartment of the Mazuliers, West 59th Street, New York.

Act 2: Drawing Room in the Hotel Suite of the Mazuliers, Palm Beach, Florida. Four weeks later.

Act 3: Same as Act 2. The following morning.

---

[121]The satire on a New York cabaret was written and staged by Cecil Lean.

MUSICAL NUMBERS
"Do It Again"
  I. Bordoni
  (*Music by* George Gershwin. *Lyrics by* Buddy G. DeSylva.)
"When Eyes Meet Eyes (When Lips Meets Lips)"
  I. Bordoni
  (*Music by* Gus Edwards. *Lyrics by* Will D. Cobb.)

1922.10 FOR GOODNESS SAKE

A Musical Comedy in Two Acts[122]. Book by Fred Jackson. Music by
William Daly, Paul Lannin, (George Gershwin). Lyrics by Arthur Jackson,
(Arthur Francis [Ira Gershwin]). Staged by Priestly Morrison. Musical num-
bers staged by Allan K. Foster. Scenery designed by P. Dodd Ackerman.
Costumes designed by Paul Arlington. Orchestra under the direction of
William Daly. Produced by Alex A. Aarons. Opened 21 February 1922 at the
Lyric Theatre and closed 20 May 1922 after 103 performances.

CAST (in order of appearance): *Teddy Lawrence*, in love with Suzanne: FRED
ASTAIRE. *Suzanne Hayden*: ADELE ASTAIRE. *Joseph*, the Reynolds' butler: Harry R.
Allen. *Vivian Reynolds*, Perry's wife: MARJORIE GATESON. *Count Spinagio*:
CHARLES JUDELS. *Marjorie Leeds*: HELEN FORD. *Jefferson Dangerfield*, a lawyer:
VINTON FREEDLEY. *Perry Reynolds*: JOHN E. HAZZARD.
  Guests at the House Party: Violet Vale, Ann Poulson, Kitty Gray, Helen paine,
Lorraine Sherwood, Lenore Lukens, Doris Hyde, Phyllis Reynolds, Sylvia Jocelyn,
Muriel Lodge, Peggy Mitchell, Bebe LaVelle. Jack Goeirs, Fred Packard, Dana Mayo,
James Herold, Russell Swann, Roger Buckley.

Act 1: Veranda of the Reynolds' Place on Lake Content, New York.

Act 2: Drawing Room of the Reynolds' Place. The same night.

ACT 1
  Opening Chorus[123]
    Ensemble
  "All to Myself"
    F. Astaire, A. Astaire, Ensemble
  "Someone"
    H. Ford, V. Freedley, Ensemble
    (*Music by* George Gershwin. *Lyrics by* Arthur Francis. *Staged by* Julian
    Alfred.)
  "Tra-la-la"
    M. Gateson, J. E. Hazzard, C. Judels, Ensemble
    (*Music by* George Gershwin. *Lyrics by* Arthur Francis. *Staged by* Julian
    Alfred.)
  "When You're in Rome"
    F. Astaire, M. Gateson, C. Judels, Ensemble
  "Every Day"
    H. Ford, V. Freedley, Ensemble
    (*Music by* William Daly. *Staged by* Julian Alfred.)
  Finale
    Ensemble

ACT 2
  "Twilight" (Opening)
    Ensemble
  Dance: Waltz; Tango
    F. Astaire, A. Astaire
  "Greatest Team of All"
    H. Ford, V. Freedley, C. Judels, Ensemble
  "Oh, Gee, Oh Gosh"
    F. Astaire, A. Astaire
    (*Music by* William Daly. *Lyrics by* Arthur Francis.)
  "In the Days of Wild Romance"[124]
    J. E. Hazzard, V. Vale, H. Paine, B. LaVelle, P. Mitchell
  "When Somebody Cares"[125]
    V. Freedley, H. Ford

---

[122]Added after opening:
  "Hubby"
    (*Music by* William Daly. *Lyrics by* Arthur Francis.)
[123]Dropped after opening.
[124]Dropped after opening.
[125]Dropped after opening.

"The French Pastry Walk"
  C. Judels, F. Astaire, V. Freedley, Ensemble
  (*Music by* William Daly, Paul Lannin. *Lyrics by* Arthur Jackson, Arthur Francis)
"The Whichness of the Whatness"
  F. Astaire, A. Astaire
Finale
  Company

1922.11 THE ROSE OF STAMBOUL

An Operetta in Three Acts. Book and lyrics adapted by Harold Atteridge,
(from the Viennese 'Die Rose von Stamboul' with libretto by Julius Brammer
and Alfred Grünwald). Music by Leo Fall and Sigmund Romberg. Staged
by J. C. Huffman. Dances arranged by Allan K. Foster. Scenery designed by
Watson Barratt. Costumes designed by Charles Lemaire. Orchestra under
the direction of Alfred Goodman. Entire production under the personal
direction of J. J. Shubert. Produced by the Messrs. Lee and J.J. Shubert.
Opened 7 March 1922 at the Century Theatre and closed 10 June 1922
after 111 performances.

CAST: *Kemel Pasha*: HENRY WARWICK. *Kondja Gul*, his daughter: TESSA
KOSTA. *Achmed Bey*: MARION GREEN. *Howard Rodney Smith*: JACK McGOWAN.
Bob, his valet: JAMES BARTON. *Midili*, Kondja's dearest friend: MABEL WITHEE.
Desiree, Kondja's companion: Elizabeth Reynolds. *Abdul*, Guard of the Harem: Lon
Hascall. *Rodney Smith*, Howard's father: Rapley Holmes. *Bul-Bul*: Elmira Lane.
Saada: Ottilia Barton. *Maada*: Sibylla Bowhan. *Baada*: Emma Wilcox. *Guzela*:
Maude Satterfield. *Fatima*: Belle Mazelle. *Durlane*: Lillian Wagner. *Emire*: Marjorie
Wayne. *Haidee*: ZITA LOCKFORD. *Hassan*: NARO LOCKFORD. *Neidjal*: John
V. Lowe. *Desha*: Mlle. Desha. *Felicia*: Felicia Sorel. *Helen*: Helen Nelidova. *Jack*:
Jack Scott.
  Young Women of the Ensemble: Dorothy Addison, Violet Anderson, Irma Ansell,
Olive Brown, Betty Brown, Alice Burns, Bunny Castle, Marion Courtney, Alice
Curry, Jeanne Danjou, Leonore Darcy, Margot Dawson, Ann Delafield, Mary
Dunne, Katherine Duffy, Rae Fields, Hazel Frisbe, Jenee Gibson, Alice Harris,
Peggy Hofmann, Corinne Jackson, Thelma Johns, Kitty Kane, Margaret Kearns,
Monica Keefe, Mary Kissel, Fraun Koski, Alice Mack, Margaret Mackay, Katherine
Manion, Truda Marr, Kay MacCausland, Myrtle McCloud, Dalores Mendez, Alla
Nova, Helen O'Brien, Edna Richmond, Madeline Soisson, Renee Theorine, Jean
Thomas, Sally Wagner, Elizabeth Wash, Peggy White. *Men*: Irving Arnold, Sol
Feldman, William Brandt, Harry Howell, Oscar Martin, John O'Hanlon, Clifton
Randall, R. B. Marwick.

Act 1: The Harem of Kemel Pasha at Stamboul, Turkey.

Act 2: In the Palace of Achmed Bey, a few days later.

Act 3: On the Riviera.

ACT 1
  Opening
    Ensemble
  "The Ladies from the Cultured West"
    M. Withee, Ensemble
    (*Music by* Leo Fall.)
  "My Heart Is Calling"
    T. Kosta, Ensemble
    (*Music by* Sigmund Romberg.)
  "Lovey Dove"
    J. McGowan, M. Withee
    (*Music by* Sigmund Romberg.)
  "A Blue Book of Girls" (Little Blue Book)
    J. Barton, Ensemble
    (*Music by* Leo Fall.)
  "(The) Rose of Stamboul"
    M. Green, Male Octette
    (*Music by* Leo Fall.)
  Duet
    M. Green, T. Kosta

ACT 2
  Opening
    M. Withee, Ensemble
  "Ding-a-Ling" (Tingaling)(Quartette)
    J. Barton, J. McGowan, M. Withee, O. Barton
    (*Music by* Leo Fall and Sigmund Romberg.)
  Ballet Oriental
    Z. Lockford, N. Lockford, Ensemble

"The Wedding March"
M. Green, T. Kosta, Ensemble
"With Papers Duly Signed" (Duet)
M. Green, T. Kosta
"Why Do They Die at the End of a Classical Dance?"
J. Barton, Dancers
(*Music by* Jean Schwartz. *Lyrics by* William Jerome and Alex Gerber.)
Waltz—Duet
M. Green, T. Kosta

ACT 3[126]
"The Love Test"
Z. Lockford, N. Lockford, Ensemble
"Mazuma"
J. Barton, Girls
(*Music by* Sigmund Romberg.)
Waltz Song
M. Green, T. Kosta
Finale

THE HOTEL MOUSE

1922.12

A Play with Music in Three Acts. Book by Guy Bolton. Adapted from the French comedy ('Le Souris d'hôtel') by Marcel Gerbidon and Paul Armont. Music by Armand Vecsey and Ivan Caryll. Lyrics by Clifford Grey. Staged by John Harwood. Dancing numbers arranged by Max Scheck. Stage settings by Watson Barratt. Orchestra under the direction of Ira Jacobs. Produced by Messrs. Lee and J.J. Shubert. Opened 13 March 1922 at the Sam S. Shubert Theatre and closed 27 May 1922 after 88 performances.

CAST (in order of appearance): *Burroughs*: BARNETT PARKER. *Tiny*: Lois Wood. *Bob Biddle*: AL SEXTON. *Lola*: FAY MARBE. *Don Esteban*: STEWART BAIRD. *Wally Gordon*: TAYLOR HOLMES. *Caesar*: Richard Temple. *Mauricette*: FRANCES WHITE. *Detective*: Frank Green. *Victor*: Ted Stevens. *Marquis de Santa Bella*: Francis Lieb. *Albert*, dancer: Elliott Taylor. *Adele*, dancer: CYNTHEA PEROT. *Suzanne*: Violet Duval. *Marie*: Edna Duval. *Jeanne*: Marion Phillips. *Iote*: Amy Frank.

Guests at the Hotel: Edith Kessler, Kathleen Errol, Josephine McMahon, Nan Rainsford, Renee Hughes, Irene McGovern, Ruby Aguillar, Mary Van Pelt, Marie Kane, Teddy Piper, Helen Lockhart, Millie Dupree, Rose Nelson, Betty de Grasse, William McGurn, Louis Laub, Eugene Frazer, Armand King, Joe McGurgan, Harold Abbey, Louis Brown, Bob Gebhardt.

Act 1: Wally's Suite at the Hotel des Anglais. Night.

Act 2: Garden of the Hotel des Anglais. The next morning.

Act 3: Terrace of Don Esteban's Villa. A few days later.

ACT 1
Opening
C. Perot, Ensemble
(*Music by* Armand Vecsey.)
"Why Do the Girls"
A. Sexton, Girls
(*Music by* Ivan Caryll.)
"Nearly True to You" (Trio)
F. Marbe, S. Baird, A. Sexton
(*Music by* Ivan Caryll.)
Quintette
F. White, R. Temple, A. Sexton, C. Perot, F. Marbe, Ensemble
(*Music by* Armand Vecsey.)
"Romance" (Duet)
T. Holmes, F. Marbe
(*Music by* Armand Vecsey, Ivan Caryll.)
"I'll Dream of You"
T. Holmes, F. Marbe
(*Music by* Armand Vecsey.)
Finale
(*Music by* Armand Vecsey.)

ACT 2
"Oozey Woozey"
F. Marbe, L. Wood, A. Sexton, B. Parker, E. Taylor, C. Perot, Ensemble
(*Music by* Armand Vecsey.)
"Mauricette"
F. White, Men
(*Music by* Armand Vecsey.)
"One Touch of Loving"
F. White, T. Holmes, Ensemble
(*Music by* Armand Vecsey.)
"Rhyming" (Duet)
T. Holmes, B. Parker
(*Music by* Armand Vecsey.)
Finale
(*Music by* Armand Vecsey.)

ACT 3
"Where the Lanterns Gleam" (Opening)
S. Baird, Ensemble
(*Music by* Armand Vecsey.)
Dance
C. Perot, E. Taylor
"Little Mother" (Duet)
F. White, T. Holmes
(*Music by* Armand Vecsey and Ivan Caryll.)
"Everything I Do Goes Wrong" (Song)
F. White
(*Music by* Armand Vecsey.)
"Round on the End and High in the Middle" (Song)
F. White
(*Music by* Bert Hanlon. *Lyrics by* Alfred Bryan.)
Finale
(*Music by* Armand Vecsey.)

JUST BECAUSE

1922.13

A Melody Comedy in Two Acts, 4 Scenes. Book by Anna Wynne O'Ryan and Helen S. Woodruff. Music by Madelyn Sheppard. Lyrics by Helen S. Woodruff. Staged by Oscar Eagle. Dances and ensembles by Bert French. Scenery designed by H. Robert Law Studios. Costumes designed by Anna Spencer, Inc. Orchestra under the direction of Ivan Rudisill. Produced by Just Because, Inc. Opened 22 March 1922 at the Earl Carroll Theatre and closed 29 April 1922 after 46 performances.

CAST (in order of appearance): *Cherry Bartlett*, Matron: Priscilla Paul. *Bluebell*: RUTH WILLIAMSON. *Syringa*: QUEENIE SMITH. *Wisteria*: JEAN MERODE. *Mr. Cummings*: FRANK MOULAN. *Mrs. Bennett*: NELLIE GRAHAM-DENT. *Claude Wellington*: CHARLES TROWBRIDGE. *Mignonette*: JANE RICHARDSON. *Susan*, Awkward Orphan: Mary Hotchkiss. *Sarah*, Littlest Orphan: Ann Dale. *Foster Philips*: OLIN HOWLAND. *Leonard Wall*: Edgar Nelson. *Reverend Dr. Bombig*: Charles Froom.

The Cummings Girls: *Daisy*: Violet Mack. *Fuschia*: Betty Broughton. *Clematis*: Ethel Duffield. *Magnolia*, *Marigold*, Twins: Florence Kingsley, Gwendolyn Gordon.

The Orphans: *Ruth*: Lillian Hazel. *Elizabeth*: Blanche Terrell. *Sophia*: Claire Martin. *Martha*: Maud Lydiat. *Kate*: Jeanette Dix. *Nora*: Isabelle Bennett. *Ann*: Naomi Johnson. *Matilda*: Dawn Wolfe.

The Hikers: *Francis Savage*: H. M. Arden. *John Brown*: Jean Barney. *Peter Dale*: Gayle Mays. *Philip Duke*: William Wilson. *William Benton*: Charles Froom. *Joseph Crown*: John Daly. *Albert Stone*: Harold Wheeler.

Act 1: Adjoining Gardens of the Wellingtons' and Cummings'. Late afternoon.

Act 2, Scene 1: Knoll Overlooking the River. Next day. *Scene 2*: Garden Wall on Cummings' Estate. That evening. *Scene 3*: Parlor of the Cummings' Homestead. A week later.

ACT 1
Opening
Cummings' Girls, Orphans
"Oh Dad"
F. Moulan, Girls
"(Love—Just) Simply Love"
J. Richardson, Girls
"Chop Sticks"
J. Richardson, J. Merode, E. Nelson

---

[126]Added to Act 3 after "The Love Test" after opening:
Reprise
M. Withee, J. McGowan

"Orphans' Drill"
  Orphans, Hikers
"(Oh, Those) Jazzing Toes"
  Q. Smith, O. Howland
"Pep Up Your Step"
  Gils, Hikers
"Just Because"
  J. Richardson

ACT 2
Scene 1
  "The Line Is Busy"
    R. Williamson, J. Merode, Q. Smith, Girls
  "It's Hard To Be a Lady"
    Q. Smith, Hikers
  "I'll Name My Dolly for You"
    J. Richardson, Orphans
  "Widow's Blues"
    N. Graham-Dent, F. Moulan
  "Daisy Tell Me Truly"
    J. Richardson
  "Day Dream Bay"
    J. Richardson, Girls
Scene 2
  "Eloping"
    Q. Smith, O. Howland
Scene 3
  Music Scena
    Ensemble
  "Associated Press"
    O. Howland, Ensemble
  "Here's to the Bride"[127]
    J. Richardson, Girls, Boys
  Dance
    Q. Smith
  Finale

LETTY PEPPER
1922.14

A Musical Comedy Gem in Two Acts. Book by Oliver Morosco and George V. Hobart. Based on a story [the comedy 'Maggie Pepper'] by Charles Klein. Music by Werner Janssen. Lyrics by Leo Wood and Irving Bibo. Staged by George V. Hobart. Gowns by Frances, Joseph. Musical numbers and special dances arranged by Julian Alfred. Orchestra under the direction of Harry James. Orchestrations by Frank Barry. Produced by Oliver Morosco (Morosco Holding Company Inc.). Opened 10 April 1922 at the Vanderbilt Theatre and closed 6 May 1922 after 32 performances[128].

CAST (in order of appearance): *Hattie*: Jane King. *Abe Greenbaum, Jr.*: Paul Burns. *Imogene*: Mary King. *Mrs. Hatch*: JOSIE INTROPODI. *James Van Ness*: Thomas Walsh. *Hutchinson*: Hallam Bosworth. *Joseph Colby*: RAY RAYMOND. *Letty Pepper*: CHARLOTTE GREENWOOD. *Billy*: MASTER GABRIEL. *Caroline Van Ness*: Vera Halare. *Margery*: Frances Victory. *Tony Barrillobatso*: Stewart Wilson. *Mack*: William Balfour.

Ensemble: Emily Stead, Effie Shelley, Phyllis Hooper, Charline Essley, Lispa Taft, Claire Wegmen, Jean Wegmen, Lillian Hoffman, Margaret Leonia, Olive King, Delphine Deery, Virginia Taylor, May Mixon, Dorothy Clark, Florence Barry, Charlotte Starbuck, Beth Ormby, Myrtle Murray.

Act 1: Stock Room in Colby & Company's Store.

Act 2: Display Room in Colby & Company's Store. One year later.

ACT 1
  "Yes, Yes"
    Chorus
  "From the Bottom to the Top"
    R. Raymond, Chorus

---
[127]Dropped during the run.
[128]Settings uncredited.

"You Teach Me"
  C. Greenwood, M. Gabriel
  (*Music by* James F. Hanley. *Lyrics by* Ballard Macdonald.)
"Ray of Sunshine"
  C. Greenwood, R. Raymond
"Blue Bird Blues"
  C. Greenwood
"Every Little Miss"
  J. King, M. King, Chorus

ACT 2
  "I Love to Dance"
    M. Gabriel, J. King, Chorus
  "Dope Song"
    S. Wilson, V. Halare, Chorus
  "Coo-Ee-Doo"
    J. King, M. King
    (*Music by* James F. Hanley, Werner Janssen. *Lyrics by* Leo Wood.)
  "Lavender and Old Lace"
    C. Greenwood, R. Raymond
  "Paul Poiret Number"
    Ensemble
  "Sittin' Pretty"
    R. Raymond, Chorus
  "Long, Lean, Lanky Letty Pepper"
    C. Greenwood
  Finale
    Entire Company

MAKE IT SNAPPY
1922.15

A Musical Revue in Two Acts, 25 Scenes Sketches and lyrics by Harold Atteridge. Music by Jean Schwartz. Additional lyrics by Alfred Bryan. Staged by J. C. Huffman. Eddie Cantor's scenes by Harold Atteridge and Eddie Cantor. Dances by Allan K. Foster. Dances arranged by Allan K. Foster. Stage settings designed by Watson Barratt. Costumes designed by Cora MacGeachy. Orchestra under the direction of Louis Gress. Orchestrations by J. Dell Lampe. Entire production supervised by J. J. Shubert. Produced by the New York Winter Garden Company (Messrs. Shubert). Opened 13 April 1922 at the Winter Garden and closed 1 July 1922 after 96 performances.

CAST: EDDIE CANTOR, NAN HALPERIN, LEW HEARN, LILLIAN FITZGERALD, J. HAROLD MURRAY, MARGARET WILSON, JOE OPP, MURIEL DeFOREST, TEDDY WEBB, MARIE BURKE, GEORGIE HALE, TOT QUALTERS, JOHN BYAM, DOLLY HACKETT, ALICE WEAVER, CLEVELAND BRONNER, INGRID SOLFENG, NELL CARRINGTON, MARJORIE TOOMAY, CONCHITA PIQUER, CARLOS and INEZ, THE EIGHT BLUE DEVILS, M. T. Bohannon, Harry Cressey, Lew Browne, Alfred DeLoraine, Salayman Ali.

Ladies of the Ensemble: Betty Fitch, Evelyn Campbell, Sally Long, Mae Devereaux, Betty Marshall, Betty Palmer, Peggy Mermont, Grace Langdon, Alice Van Ryker, Mae Sullivan, Polly Lux, Cardinal Peaires, Vivien Nolty, Flo Evers, Vera Zimeleva, Charlotte Schuette, Madeline Levine, Mae O'Brien, Elsie May, Betty Dair, Gladys Montgomery, Elsa Peterson, Dorothy McCarthy, Margaret McCarthy, Portland Hoffa, Lebanon Hoffa, Helen Christie, Molly Christie, Eva Fuller, Lucille Pryor, Elsie Frank, Polly Mayer, Hermose Jose, Mildred Lee, Marian Joy, Margaret Toomey, Rose Devere, Bonna Odear, Nan Phillips, Vivien West, Evelyn Martin, Queene Queenen.

ACT 1[129]
Scene 1
  Prologue: Mr. and Mrs. Playgoer
    Usher: N. Carrington. *Mr. Playgoer*: T. Webb. *Mrs. Playgoer*: B. Fitch.

---
[129]Also performed, as per published sheet music:
"(The Wedding Ring Don't Mean a Thing) When You're Married"
(Wedding Blues)
  L. Fitzgerald
  (*Music and Lyrics by* Fred Fisher and Eddie Cantor.)
Added for subsequent tour:
March of the Centuries (Act 1)
  Ladies Ensemble

Scene 2

"Blossom Time"
M. Burke, J. Byam, Blossom Time Girls
(*Lyrics by* Alfred Bryan.)

"Goodbye Main Street"
T. Qualters, L. Hearn, M. Burke, J. Byam, Main Street Steppers
Jane: M. Burke. *Jack*: J. Byam. *Sue*: T. Qualters. *Cyrus*: L. Hearn.

Scene 3

Dance Town
A College Boy: G. Hale.

Scene 4

"When the Wedding Chimes Are Ringing"
J. H. Murray, D. Hackett, Bridesmaids

"Cheeky Kiki"
N. Halperin, Kiki Girls
(*Music and Lyrics by* William Friedlander.)

"To Make Them Beautiful Ladies"[130]
M. Wilson, Some Winter Garden Beauties
Scene: The Broadway Modiste Shop.
A *Bride*: D. Hackett. *The Groom*: J. H. Murray. *Fifine*: N. Carrington.
Cyrus: L. Hearn. *Margaret*: M. Wilson. *Ann Penny*: M. DeForrest. *Kiki*:
N. Halperin. *Jane*: M. Burke. *Sue*: T. Qualters.

Scene 5

The Stage Door
(Specialty)
(E. Cantor)
The Stage Doorman: J. Opp. *Eddie Cantor*: E. Cantor.

Scene 6

A Bouquet of Girls
"Bouquet of Girls"
J. Byam, Nosegays

Scene 7

A Bit of Kipling (adapted from Kipling's poem)
"I Learned About Women from Her"
J. H. Murray
The Widow: B. Fitch. *Burma Girl*: V. Zimeleva. *The She Devil*: H. Jose. *The Convent Girl*: M. Toomey.

Scene 8

In Front of the Police Station
The Little Cops: J. H. Christie, M. Christie, Mayer, DeVere, D. McCarthy,
Martin, Pryor, Frank.

Scene 9

The Police Station
The Doctor: J. Opp. *A Stenographer*: B. Roscoe. *The Applicant*: E. Cantor. *The Coppers*: M. T. Bohannon, H. Cressey, L. Browne, A. DeLoraine.

Scene 10

Eskimoland: The Hummerskimo's
"Humoresquimos"
T. Qualters, Carlos and Inez

Scene 11

Broadway Impressions:A Modern Lullaby; The Baby Flapper
"The Flapper"
N. Halperin

The Pierrotts and the Pierretts
Ladies Ensemble
The Vampire (Act 1)
The Man: W. Booth. *The Slave*: Alex. Salayman. *The Vampire*: L. Fitzgerald.
The Fool: E. Cantor. *The Husband*: J. Opp. *The Derelict*: T. Webb.
"Kiki Was a Good Girl"
L. Fitzgerald, J. Opp, L. Hearn, Girls
"20 After 1"
G. Hale, Girls
[130]Replaced for subsequent tour by:
"Beautiful Ladies"
M. Wilson, Girls

Scene 12

Joe's Blue Front
A Customer: M. T. Bohannon. A *Victim*: L. Hearn. *The Salesman*: J. Opp. *Moe the Tailor*: E. Cantor.

Scene 13

In Old Madrid
"My Castilian Girl"[131]
M. Burke, Spanish Beauties
"Won't You Buy a Flower?"
C. Piquer

Scene 14

Cafe DeGrande
"Hootch Rhythm"
T. Qualters, Inez and Carlos
(*Lyrics by* Alfred Bryan.)
Some Songs[132]
E. Cantor
"(Tell Me What's the Matter) Lovable Eyes"
J. H. Murray, D. Hackett, L. Hearn, C. Piquer, Lovable Girls
Miss Stepper: T. Qualters. *Dolly*: D. Hackett. *Hal*: J. H. Murray. *Garcon*: S.
Ali. *The Husband*: J. Opp. *The Bride*: N. Carrington. *Cyrus*: L. Hearn.
Conchita: C. Piquer. *Georgie*: G. Hale.

ACT 2[133]

Scene 1

"Princess Beautiful" (A Cleveland Bronner Ballet)

---

[131]Replaced for subsequent tour by:
"The Vermilion Girl" (My Vision in Vermilion)
M. Burke, E. Martin, Vermilion Girls
[132]Cantor's specialty songs also performed in Act 1, Scene 5, and Act 2,
Scene 14,
"The Sheik of Araby"
(*Music by* Ted Snyder. *Lyrics by* Harry B. Smith and Francis Wheeler.)
"Waikiki, I Hear You Calling Me"
(*Music by* Harry Ruby. *Lyrics by* Bert Kalmar.)
"The Wedding Ring Don't Mean a Thing When You're Married"
(*Music and Lyrics by* Fred Fisher and Eddie Cantor.)
"My Yiddisha Mammy"
(*Music and Lyrics by* Jean Schwartz, Eddie Cantor and Alex Gerber.)
"I'm Hungry for Beautiful Girls"
(*Music and Lyrics by* Fred Fisher.)
"Don't (Stop Loving Me Now)"
(*Music by* James F. Hanley. *Lyrics by* Joe Goodwin and Murray Roth.)
"I Love Her—She Loves Me"
(*Music by* Irving Caesar. *Lyrics by* Irving Caesar, Eddie Cantor.)
"Where the Bamboo Babies Grow"
(*Music by* Walter Donaldson. *Lyrics by* Lew Brown.)
"Lovin' Sam, the Sheik of Alabam'"
(*Music by* Milton Ager. *Lyrics by* Jack Yellen.)
"I Go So Far with Sophie"
(*Music and Lyrics by* Abner Silver.)
"I'll Be in My Dixie Home Again Tomorrow"
(*Music by* J. Russel Robinson. *Lyrics by* Roy Turk.)
"Little Rover (Don't Forget to Come Back Home)"
(*Music by* Walter Donaldson. *Lyrics by* Gus Kahn.)
Performed by Eddie Cantor during 1923 tour:
"Seven or Eleven (My Dixie Pair o' Dice)"
(*Music by* Walter Donaldson. *Lyrics by* Lew Brown.)
[133]Added to Act 2 for subsequent tour:
The Police Station
The Doctor: J. Opp. *A Stenographer*: B. Rosco. *The Applicant*: E. Cantor. *The Coppers*: J. Bruns, H. Cottave, W. Foster, P. Herbert.
The Restaurant Scene
"The Kingdom for Two"
J. Byam
A Waiter: H. Cottave. *The Husband*: J. Opp. *A Bride*: N. Carrington. *The Flirt*: L. Hearn.

(*Dances by* Alan K. Foster. *Music selected and arranged by* Louis Gress. *Scenery, costumes and effects designed by* C. Bronner.)

Cast (in order of appearance): *Imps of the Flames*: Misses Jose, Frank, Lee, Mayer, Martin, Pryor. *The Evil One*: C. Bronner. *Princess Beautiful*: I. Solfeng. *Her Maids*: Misses Langdon, Noltie, Peaires, Evers. *The Wind*: C. Bronner. *Spirits of the Wind*: Misses Hoffa, West, Phillips, Joy, Devere, Sullivan, Laverne, Queenen, Toomey, Fuller, Christia, Zimeleva. *Prince of the Golden Sword*: C. Bronner. *The Invisible Foe*: —. *Maids of Honor*: Misses O'Brien, Lux, Levene, Hoffa, Russell, Schuette.

> This is an imaginary story, based upon the ancient practice of offering human lives to the Gods of Fire. Princess Beautiful was chosen . It was considered a great honor, and we picture here what she dreamed would be her fate. The action begins just as she passes from this life. Imps of the flames dance with glee and wait for her soul to rise from the ashes. The Winds comes to play with her. They are attacked by the Imps. The Spirits of the Wind drive the Imps away. The Soul of Princess Beautiful is now caught in the spell of an invisible foe turned to crystal. She can be released only by one brave and strong enough to wield the magic sword of beaten gold. Her Prince accomplishes this. He beheads the Invisible Foe, releases Princess Beautiful and ac-companied by the Spirits of the Wind and Maids of Honor, leads her through the flames and into the heaven of which she has dreamed.

Scene 2

Step in My Taxi

A Taxi Driver: E. Cantor. *Cyrus*: L. Hearn. *The Officer*: J. Opp. *A Newsboy*: H. Cressey.

Scene 3

A Fragonard Picture

"My Beautiful Fragonard Girl"

M. Wilson, Fragonard Girls

(*Lyrics by* Alfred Bryan.)

The Fragonard Girl: M. Wilson. *The Boy*: J. Byam. *Miss Minuette*: A. Weaver.

Scene 4

The Price

The Man: T. Webb. *The Woman*: H. Carrington.

Scene 5

"He Was the Only Man I Ever Loved"

N. Halperin

(*Music and Lyrics by* William B. Friedlander.)

Scene 6

The Sheik

"Desert Rose"

J. H. Murray, Desert Roses

"The Sheik" (I'm a Sheik)

E. Cantor

Prince Kalif: J. H. Murray. *Arab*: J. Byam. *Slave Girl*: M. Burke. *Harun*: J. Opp. *Dr. Laideux*: T. Webb. *Sheik*: E. Cantor. *Arabs, Harem Girls, etc.*: Ensemble. The Eight Blue Devils.

Scene 7

Stepville

Miss Muriel: M. De Forrest.

Scene 8

"(Gay) Butterfly on the Wheel"

M. Burke, Girls

(*Lyrics by* Alfred Bryan.)

Scene 9

Some Songs[134]

E. Cantor

Scene 10

"Lamplight Land"

M. Wilson, J. H. Murray

Scene: In Lampland.

Scene 11

Finale

"The Little Cop Number"

The Coppers: Jose, H. Christie, M. Christie, Mayer, DeVere, D. McCarthy, Martin, Pryor, Frank.

[134]Cantor's specialty songs detailed in Act 1, Scene 14 footnote above.

SOME PARTY

A Revusical Entertainment (Musical Revue) in Two Acts, 9 Scenes. Sketches and lyrics by R. H. Burnside. Music by Silvio Hein, Raymond Hubbell, Percy Wenrich, Gustave Kerker. Arranged and staged by R. H. Burnside. Dances staged by Billy Grant. Orchestra under the direction of Anton Heindl. Produced by DeWolf Hopper. Opened 15 April 1922 at Jolson's 59th Street Theatre and closed 29 April 1922 after 17 performances[135].

CAST: DeWOLF HOPPER, JEFFERSON DeANGELIS, LEW DOCKSTADER, NANETTE FLACK, HERBERT WATEROUS, HARRY C. BROWNE, JOHN E. HENSHAW, SAM ASH, JED PROUTY, SCOTT WELSH, JOHN HENDRICKS, WILLIAM COURTLEIGH, WILLIAM B. MACK, LOUISE MACKINTOSH, PRIMROSE CARYLL, VIRGINIA FUTRELLE, JOHN ABBOTT, GEORGE AVER-ILL, BERT BOWLEN, WILLIAM GRANT, RUTH ADAIR, PERCY HASWELL, George Averill, Kathryn Yates, Clare Carroll, Rena Manning, Dorothy I. Harrigan, Dolly Byrnes, Alice McKenzie, Percy Haswell.

Dancers: Nelly Daily, Sylvia Ford, Marie Cattell, Asta Valle, Jose Riley, Jimmie Williams, Sid Williams, Murray Evans.

ACT 1

Scene 1

"Where Shall We Go Tonight?"

Mr. T. B. Mann: H. Waterous. *Mrs. T. B. Mann*: L Mackintosh. *John, the butler*: William Grant. *Julia, the maid*: R. Adair.

Behind the Scenes

Minstrelsy: H. C. Browne. *Comic Opera*: D. Hopper. *Grand Opera*: N. Flack. *Musical Comedy*: J. Prouty. *Tragedy*: W. Courtleigh. *Comedy*: S. Welsh. *Melo-drama*: W. B. Mack. *Vaudeville*: J. DeAngelis. *Movies*: V. Futrelle. *Revue*: P. Caryll. *A Good Friend*: S. Ash.

Scene 2

In the Dressing Room (*by* George V. Hobart)

Scene 3

Minstrel Days

Interlocutor: D. Hopper. *Tambourines*: L. Dockstader, H. C. Browne. *Bones*: J. DeAngelis, J. E. Heshaw. *Tenors*: S. Ash, J. Prouty, S. Welsh, B. Bowlen. *Bassos*: H. Waterous, J. Hendricks, J. Abbott, G. Averill. And Dancers.

Hits of the Season:

Opening Chorus

Entire Company

Marjolaine: K. Yates. *A Regular Girl*: C. Carroll. *Cutie*: R. Manning. *Margie*: D. L. Harrigan. *Sally*: D. Byrnes. *Sweet Lady*: A. McKenzie. *Dearie*: P. Caryll. *Music Box*: V. Futrelle.

"Keep on Building Castles in the Air"

S. Welsh

(*Music by* Percy Wenrich.)

"Minstrel Days"

J. E. Henshaw

(*Music by* Percy Wenrich.)

"Bells of the Sea"

H. Waterous

(*Music by* Albert Solman.)

"In Yama Yama Land"

J. DeAngelis

(*Music by* Turner Layton. *Lyrics by* Henry Creamer.)

"In Rose Time"

S. Ash

(*Music by* Mary Earl.)

Grand Finale (*Music arranged by* Raymond Hubbell.)

Scene 4

Harry C. Browne accompanied by His Banjo and the Dancing Dozen

Scene 5

"Uncle Tom's Saloon" (Up-to-date)

(*Syncopated by* R. H. Burnside. *Music by* Silvio Raymond and others.)

Uncle Tom: D. Hopper. *Little Eva*: S. Ash. *Topsy*: J. Prouty. *Simon Legree*: S. Welsh. *Lawyer Marks*: J. DeAngelis.

Scene : Uncle Tom's Saloon. *Time*: Present.

---

[135]Costumes and settings uncredited.

ACT 2

Scene 1

Among Thieves (*by* William Gillette. *Staged by* George Marion.)
Jim Conklin: W. B. Mack. *Ruth Conklin*: P. Haswell. *Billy Steele*: W. Courtleigh. *Scene*: Somewhere in Arizona.

Scene 2

"Rustic Ann" [Harmonized adaptation of "Cavalleria Rusticana"]
P. Caryll, K. Yates, A. McKensie, V. Futrelle, C. Caroll, R. Manning, S. Ash, H. C. Browne, S. Welsh, J. Hendricks, B. Bowlen, J. Prouty

Scene 3

Lew Dockstader [Telephone call to the White House sketch]

Scene 4

"Burning to Sing, or Singing to Burn" (Satire on Traditional Grand Opera Method)
(*Libretto by* R. H. Burnside. *Music by* Gustave Kerker. *Conducted by* the composer.)
Scene: An apartment on the fifth floor of the Accidental Hotel. *Place*: Any large city.
Madame Marguerita Trimoline: N. Flack. *Signer Edoarado Trimoline*, her husband: J. Hendricks. *Babette*, a maid: P. Caryll. *Thomasina*, a landlord of the Hotel: D. Hopper. *Billy*, a Bell Boy: J. Prouty. *Jim Higgins*: S. Welsh. *Tom Harris*: H. Waterous. *And Firemen, Maids, Guests of the Hotel*: Entire Company.

1922.17 GO EASY, MABEL

A Musical Comedy Different in Three Acts, 5 Scenes. Book, music and lyrics by Charles George. Staged by Bertram Harrison and Julian Alfred. Scenery designed by P. Dodd Ackerman. Gowns by Tappé, Bendel, Lucile Ltd., Milgrim, Mahieu, Bulger. Orchestra under the direction of Ross Mobley. Produced by the Hudson Productions Company, Inc. (Lou Morrison, Managing director). Opened 8 May 1922 at the Longacre Theatre and closed 20 May 1922 after 16 performances.

CAST: *Ted Sparks*: WILL J. DEMING. *Mabel Sparks*: ESTELLE WINWOOD. *Mabel Montmorency*: ETHEL LEVEY. *Edward Drenton*: JAMES C. MARLOWE. *Mrs. Edward Drenton*: MARGARET DUMONT. *Bruce Drenton*: RUSSELL MACK. *George Macdonald*: ARTHUR AYLESWORTH. *Tessie Claire*: EILEEN VAN BIENE

The Girls: Grace Duncan, Lucille Constante, Evelyn Gerald, Sonya Ivanoff, Sue Wilson, Beatrice Wilson, Victoria White, Virginia Roche, Eileen Adair.

Time: Now. *Place*: New York City.

Act 1, Scene 1: A Room in the Sparks' Home. Morning. *Scene 2*: A Lapse of Time. *Scene 3*: The Room in the Sparks Home. Next day.

Act 2: The Room in the Sparks Home, viewed from a different angle. Later in the afternoon.

Act 3: The Same. Evening.

ACT 1

"Love Is King"
E. Van Biene
"Girls, Girls, Girls"
W. Deming, Girls
"A Lapse of Time"
Girls
"I Want a Regular Man"
E. Levey, W. Deming, A. Aylesworth
"Go Easy, Mabel"
R. Mack, E. Levey, Girls

ACT 2

"Honey, I Love You"
E. Van Biene, Girls
"The Unveiling of a Broadway Girl"
R. Mack, Girls
"Oh, Papa"
E. Levey, J. C. Marlowe

ACT 3

"An Old-Fashioned Man Is Hard to Find"
E. Winwood, Girls

"When You Dance with the Girl You Love"
R. Mack, E. Levey
"Ethel Levey's Smile Song"
E. Levey
Finale
Ensemble

1922.18 RED PEPPER

A Musical Comedy in Two Acts, 8 Scenes[136]. Book by Edgar Smith and Emily M. Young. Music by Albert Gumble and Owen Murphy. Lyrics by Howard Rogers and Owen Murphy. Staged by Frank Smithson. Dancing numbers arranged by Allan K. Foster. Orchestra under the direction of Vernon Bestor. Orchestrations by J. Dell Lampe. Produced by the Messrs. Shubert. Opened 29 May 1922 at the Sam S. Shubert Theatre and closed 17 June 1922 after 24 performances[137].

CAST: *Juniper Berry*, Colored Gentleman of Misfortune: JAMES McINTYRE. *Jimpson Weed*, Get-Rich Quick Wallingford of the Colored Race: THOMAS HEATH. *Lilly Rose*, Colored Highbrow: MABEL ELAINE. *Nokomis*: VIVIAN HOLT. *Wah Letka*: LILLIAN ROSEDALE. *Colonel Shelby Bright*, Kentucky Colonel: DAN QUINLAN. *Sally*, His Daughter: FLORENCE RAYFIELD. *Richard Pitney*, Owner of Race Horses: BARRETT GREENWOOD. *Dolly Pitney*, His Sister, and Owner of Red Pepper: FERNE ROGERS. *Lord Gathe-Coyne*, English Lord and Owner of Sir Robert: CHARLES BROWN. *Scotty*, Race Track Tout: BOB NELSON. *Babe Stringer*, Stranded Chorus Girl: GLADYS FOOSHEE. *Billie Bull*, Her Pal: SYBIL FOOSHEE. *Jimmy Swift*, an American Jockey: DAN BRENNAN. *Tommy Dodd*, an English Jockey: HAL SANDS. *Lariat Ike*, Western Cowboy: Bee Ho Gray. *Nan*, a Western Cowgirl: Ada Summerville. *R. R. Attorney*: George Youngman. *Rembrandt*, a High-Toned Colored Gentleman: George Youngman. *Ramonda*, a Mexican: Escamillo.

Ladies of the Ensemble: Lottie Bell, Winifred Duffy, Grace Conrad, Loretta Duffy, Myrtle Stuart, Jean Weber, Norma Battle, Nell Pennington, May Barry, Lillian Dunning, Anna Maywood, Vivian Bartlett, Marie Dow, Marion Dowling, Sherry Demerest, Marie Frawley, Cele Murray, Caroline Warner, Estelle Raywood, Nan Henderson, Billie Lee. *Gentlemen of the Ensemble*: Eddie Scanlon, John Bauman, Gene Collins, Lovette Wilder, Fred McGregor, Armand Kane, Larry Mack, Tom Turner, Harry Brom, Charles Adams.

Act 1, Scene 1: Cafe of the Casino, Havana, Cuba. *Scene 2*: Grove of Palms and Poncianas in Havana, Cuba. *Scene 3*: Interior of Stables at Race Track, Havana, Cuba. *Scene 4*: Lawn in front of Clubhouse, Havana, Racetrack.

Act 2, Scene 1: Pitney's Ranch and Corral in Arizona. *Scene 2*: The Golf Links of the Dingeville Country Club. *Scene 3*: Gold Room in Colonel's Mansion. *Scene 4*: Mansion of Colonel Bright in Georgia.

ACT 1

Scene 1

Opening Chorus
H. Sands, J. Brennan, Ensemble
"Strong for Girls"
G. Fooshee, S. Fooshee, B. Nelson, Ensemble
"It Must Be You"
F. Rayfield, B. Greenwood, Ensemble
(*Music by* Albert Gumble. *Lyrics by* Howard E. Rogers.)
"Boys, Boys, Boys"
F. Rogers, Boys
"Butterfly"
F. Rogers, C. Brown
"Senora"
B. Nelson, Ensemble
"Strut Your Stuff"
M. Elaine, H. Sands, D. Brennan, Ensemble

Scene 2

Specialty
G. Fooshee, S. Fooshee

Scene 3

"Mississippi Cradle"
V. Holt, L. Rosedale

---

[136]Added for subsequent national tour:
"Land of Sky Blue Waters" (Act 1 Finale)
Calhoun Sisters
[137]Costumes, settings uncredited.

"Bugaboo"
    M. Elaine, H. Sands, D. Brennan, Ensemble
Scene 4
  "Ginger"
    S. Fooshee, G. Fooshee, H. Sands, D. Brennan, Ensemble
ACT 2
Scene 1
  "Hiawatha's Melody of Love"[138]
    V. Holt, L. Rosedale
    (*Music by* George W. Mayer. *Lyrics by* Alfred Bryan and Artie Mehlinger.)
  Lasso Queen
    S. Fooshee, G. Fooshee
  Specialty
    B. H. Gray, A. Summerville
  Dance
    H. Sands, D. Brennan
  "In the Starlight" (Duet)
    F. Rayfield, B. Greenwood

  "Game of Love" (Duet)
    F. Rogers, C. Brown
  "Chickens"
    B. Nelson, S. Fooshee, G. Fooshee, Ensemble
  "Levee Land"
    M. Elaine, Ensemble
Scene 2
  "Wedding Day"
    F. Rogers, F. Rayfield, C. Brown, B. Greenwood
    (*Music and orchestration by* Vernon E. Bestor.)
Scene 3
  Specialty
    B. Nelson
    At the piano: Herbert Hewson.
Scene 4
  "Wedding Bells"
    F. Rayfield, F. Rogers, B. Greenwood, C. Brown, Ensemble
Finale
    Entire Company

---

[138]Previously interpolated by Holt & Rosedale into HELLO, ALEXANDER AND CINDERELLA ON BROADWAY. Dropped during subsequent national tour.

Will Rogers (right) in ZIEGFELD FOLLIES OF 1922 (Photo: White Studio)
Billy Rose Theatre Collection, New York Public Library for the Performing Arts

1922–1923 SEASON

1922.19 ZIEGFELD FOLLIES OF 1922

A Musical Revue in Two A'rcts, 31 Scenes[1]. Book (sketches) by Ring Lardner, Ralph Spence. Music by Victor Herbert, Louis A. Hirsch and Dave Stamper. Lyrics by Gene Buck. Staged by Ned Wayburn. Scenes designed by Joseph Urban, (Ned Wayburn, H. Robert Law Studios, James Reynolds, Frank Gates and Edward A. Morange). (Costumes designed by Charles LeMaire, Evelyn Law, Ada Fields, James Reynolds, Cora MacGeachy.) 'Sicilian' and 'Frolicking Gods' Ballets arranged by Michel Fokine. Orchestra under the direction of Oscar Radin. Produced by Florenz Ziegfeld. Opened 5 June 1922 at the New Amsterdam Theatre and closed 23 June 1923 after 424 performances. (Revised Summer Edition[2] opened 25 June 1923 at the New Amsterdam Theatre and closed 15 September 1923 after 96 performances. Total: 520 performances.)

CAST: WILL ROGERS, AL SHEAN, ED GALLAGHER, GILDA GRAY, MARY EATON, LULU McCONNELL, ANDREW TOMBES, MARY LEWIS, JIMMY NERVO, TEDDY KNOX, MARTHA LORBER, THELMA CONNOR, VELMA CONNOR, VELMA CONNOR, MURIEL STRYKER, EVELYN LAW, ALEXANDER GRAY, SERGE PERNIKOFF, TILLER GIRLS, THE FOLLIES FOUR (Messrs. J. J. Shannon, Frank Tierney, Frank Lambert, George Truscott), Brandon Tynan, Rita Owin, Grant Simpson, Michel Barroy, John Scott, Al Ochs.

Ladies of the Ensemble: Marjorie Chapin, Helen Lee Worthing, Marie Shelton, Edna Wheaton, Mary McDonald, Marie Wallace, Beulah McFarland, Doris Lloyd, Olive Osborne, Avonne Taylor, Frances Reveaux, Fay West, Eva Brady, Gertrude Selden, Irene Marcellus, Jessie Reed, Helen Gates, Pauline Mason, Betty Dudley, Jean Arundel, Hazel Webb, Lillian Woods, Naomi Johnson, Marie Dahm, Clara Beresbach, Anastasia Reilly, Kathryn Mehaffey, Blanche Mehaffey, M. Wallace, Madeline Wales, Irene Wales, Hazel Donnelly, Frances Howden, Madge Merritt, Marcelle Earle, Alma Drange, Leonora Baron, Addie Rolf, Pansy Maness, Rita Royce, Dorothy Conroy, Hilda Moreno, Pearl Eaton, Nellie Davage, Beatrice Jackson, Kathryn Stoneburn, Hallie Manning, Vangie Valentine, Virginia King, Betty Rees, Ellen de Lerches, Nellie Savage, Jean Arundel, Betsy Rees, Albertina Vitak, Madelyn Morrissey, Polly Nally, Phoebe Lee, Marion Rich, Sonia Shand, Victoria Gale, Margery Chapin, Misses Mamay, Dana, Ray, Whittington, Ivanoff, Howell, Starhill. *English Ballet*: Irene Todd, Dolly Evans, Beatrice Singleton, Elsie Woodall, Babs Aitlen, Annie Patron, Jean Lloyd, Ada Hughes, Dolly Daggars, Audrey Darrell, Cora Neary, May Howard, Nellie Smith, Neta Hill, Betty Webb, Ivy Halstead.

ACT 1[3]

Scene 1

"Blunderland"

(*Sketch by* Ralph Spence. *Music by* Louis A. Hirsch. *Lyrics by* Gene Buck. *Painted by* Gates and Morange. *Costumes designed by* Charles LeMaire.) *Miss Take*: M. Lewis. *Youth*: A. Tombes. *Alice*: M. Eaton. *Ambassador Harvey*: B. Tynan. *Bootlegger*: T. Knox. *Capital*: E. Gallagher. *Retired Bankrupt*: A. Shean. *Labor*: J. J. Shannon. *Senator Sapp*: F. Lambert. *Movies*: M. Lorber. *Bonus Bill*: F. Tierney. *Flapper*: L. McConnell. *Peggy Hopkins*: H. L. Worthing. *Taxes*: G. Truscott. *Miss Calculate*: M. Chapin. *Miss Trial*: E. Wheaton. *Miss Fit*: M. McDonald. *Miss Treat*: B. McFarland. *Miss Trust*: I. Wales. *Miss Demeanor*: O. Osborne. *Miss Behave*: A. Taylor. *Miss Chief*: F. Reveaux. *Miss Fortune*: E. Brady. *Miss Government*: G. Selden. *Miss Hap*: I. Marcellus. *Miss Mate*: J. Reed.

"Hello! Hello! Hello!"

Ensemble

(*Music by* Dave Stamper.)

Finale[4]

Ensemble

Scene 2

45th Street and Broadway (*Painted by* Joseph Wickes)

"Flappers"

---

[1]The Sixteenth in the annual series of musical revues produced by Florenz Ziegfeld beginning in 1907.

[2]See complete program entry in 1923-1924 season.

[3]Added during the run, per published sheet music:

"If I Can't Get the Sweetie I Want (I Pity the Sweetie I Get)"

E. Law

(*Music by* Jean Schwartz. *Lyrics by* Joe Young and Sam. M. Lewis.)

[4]Replaced after opening by:

"My Melody"

Ensemble

J. Whiting, T. Connor, V. Connor, Flappers

(*Music by* Dave Stamper. *Lyrics by* Gene Buck. *Costumes designed by* Evelyn Law.)

Flappers: P. Mason, B. Dudley, J. Arundel, H. Webb, L. Woods, N. Johnson, M. Wales, C. Beresbach, A. Reilly, K. Stoneburn, L. Baron, V. Valentine, M. Earle, M. Merritt, A. Rolf, F. West.

Inebriated Dance[5]

J. Nervo

Scene 3

Rip Van Winkle (*by* Ring Lardner)(*Painted by* Joseph Wickes.)

Henry Wtz, a typographical error: B. Tynan. *Mrs. Wtz*, his wife: L. McConnell. *Gleason*, his servant: A. Shean. *Dr. Moore*: A. Tombes.

Scene 4

"I'm Satisfied"[6]

L. McConnell

Scene 5

"Rambler Rose"

A. Tombes

(*Music by* Dave Stamper, Louis A. Hirsch. *Lyrics by* Gene Buck. *Costumes designed by* Charles LeMaire.)

Dancing Partner: E. Law. *Roses*: Misses Wallace, Mamay, Gates, Moreno, Chapin, Beck, Howden, Starhill.

Scene 6

"(Listening on Some) Radio"

Messrs. Tierney, Shannon, Truscott, Lambert

(*Sketch by* Ralph Spence. *Music by* Dave Stamper. *Lyrics by* Gene Buck. *Scene painted by* H. Robert Law Studios.)

Scene 7

Speed and Action: Slow 'Movie' Novelty[7]

J. Nervo, T. Knox

Scene 8

Farm (*Painted by* Joseph Wickes)

"Throw Me a Kiss"

M. Eaton, Country Girls

(*Music by* Dave Stamper, Louis A. Hirsch. *Lyrics by* Gene Buck. *Costumes designed by* Ada Fields.)

Betty Sloan: M. Eaton. *Tom Parvis*: A. Gray. *Arnold Benhan of the New York Ledger*: G. Simpson. *Kathryn Martin*: F. West. *Country Girls*: F. West, A. Rolf, D. Conroy, H. Webb, M. Earle, L. Baron, M. Wales, B. Jackson, C. Beresbach, K. Stoneburn, B. Mehaffey, A. Drange, V. Valentine, L. Woods, P. Mason, M. Merritt.

Eccentric Dance

R. Owin

Scene 9

The Green-Eyed Monster[8] (*by arrangement with* Andre Charlot)

Joblin, the servant: J. Nervo. *George*, the husband: B. Tynan. *Jane*, the wife: L. McConnell. *Tripitt*, the visitor: A. Tombes.

(*Scene painted by* Joseph Wickes.)

Scene 10

"It's Getting Dark on Old Broadway"

G. Gray

(*Music by* Dave Stamper. *Lyrics by* Gene Buck. *Costumes designed by* Ada Fields.)

With Misses H. Webb, M. Wallace, L. Woods, L. Baron, A. Reilly, P. Maness, C. Beresbach, A. Drange, M. Wales, P. Eaton, P. Mason, F. West, M. Earle, D. Conroy, H. Manning, M. Merritt.

Scene 11

"The Sons of Jesse James"[9]

A. Tombes

Scene 12

Eccentric Dance (*Arranged by* John Tiller)

Tiller Girls

Scene 13

"South Sea Moon"

T. Spencer, Connor Twins, A. Gardner, Trio (M. Chapin, A. Reilly, I. Marcellus), The Follies Four

(*Music by* Dave Stamper and Louis A. Hirsch. *Lyrics by* Gene Buck. *Costumes designed by* Cora MacGeachy.)

---

[5]Dropped during run.

[6]Dropped during run.

[7]Dropped during run.

[8]Dropped during run.

[9]Dropped during run.

Ensemble: Misses West, M. Dahm, Rolf, Conroy, Dana, Maness, Ray, Webb, Woods, Whittington, Mason, Rees, Rich, Jackson, Stoneburn. *The Ukelele Players*: Misses Manning, Wallace, Valentine, Mehaffey, C. Beresbach, Chapin, Reilly, Marcellus, Merritt, Earle, Drange, Baron and Mamay.

Scene 14

Specialty (by, about and for themselves): ["Mr. Gallagher and Mr. Shean"]

E. Gallagher, A. Shean

(*Music and Lyrics by* Ed Gallagher, Al Shean and Ernest Ball.)

Scene 15

"Frolicking Gods" (*Ballet composed and produced by* Michel Fokine. *Music by* Pyotor Ilyich Tchaikowsky. *Scenery designed by* Joseph Urban. Costumes of Visitors in Museum *designed by* James Reynolds.)

The Girl: M. Lorber. *The Boy*: S. Pernikoff. *A Mother*: M. McDonald. *A Little Boy*: T. Connor. *A Little Girl*: V. Connor. *An Old Man*: M. Truscott. *His Jealous Wife*: H. Manning. *Girls*: J. Reed, H. L. Worthing, A. Brady, E. Wheaton. *Young Boys*: F. Reveaux, F. Howden. *Museum Attendant*: F. Lambert. *The Gendarme*: M. Barroy. *Apollo Belvedere*: J. Scott. *Venus of Milo* (restored): E. French. *The Amazone*: M. Stryker. *The Hercules*: A. Ochs. *The Three Graces*: N. Savage, H. Moreno. *The Satyr*: T. Knox. *A Basrelief: Two Bacchantes*: A. Vitak, B. Rees. *A Faun*: J. Nervo. *Caryatides*: C. Beresbach, A. Drange, L. Baron. *Two Hermes*: H. Webb, A. Reilly. *The Faun Girl*: P. Maness. *Menades*: M. Merritt, I. Wilson, V. Gale, R. Royce. *The Seven Muses*: E. deLerches, A. Rolf, H. Donnelly, M. Earle, N. Johnson, J. Arundel.

Note: Every time the marble Greek Gods remain alone in their museums, they start to enjoy themselves and to dance. However, a couple of lovers, who were unexpectedly locked in a Paris Museum of Art in 1851 have the chance to witness those divine actions. The Gendarme who hears the terrible noise in the museum finds the lovers undressed like ancient Greeks and takes them to the police.

Scene 16

Yankee Philosophy

W. Rogers

Scene 17

"Bring on the Girls"

T. Spencer

(*Music by* Dave Stamper. *Lyrics by* Gene Buck. *Marches by* Victor Herbert. *Setting devised by* Ned Wayburn. *Painted by* Joseph Urban.)

Ziegfeld Girls (*Costumes designed by* Charles LeMaire.): Misses Reed, Wheaton, Lee, Chapin, Selden, Marcellus, Reveaux, Brady, Nally, Osborne, McDonald, Worthing, Shelton, I. Wales, Taylor, McFarland. *Fencing Girls* (*Costumes designed by* Cora MacGeachy): Misses Webb, M. Dahm, Oakley, C. Beresford, Ivanoff, Miller, Reilly, Gates, Starhill, Rees, M. Dahm, Earle. *The Black Crook Amazons* (*Costumes designed by* Cora MacGeachy): Misses Valentine, Mehaffey, P. Eaton, Baron, F. Howden, Donnelly, Rousse, E. Beresbach, A. Drange, Whittington, Wallace. *Sure-Fire Dancers of Today*: Misses Moreno, Conroy, Howell, Stoneburn, Rich, Gale, Maness, Dana, Woods, Ray. *The English Pony Ballet*: I. Todd (Captain), D. Evans, B. Singleton, E. Woodall, B. Aitlen, A. Patron, J. Lloyd, A. Hughes, D. Daggars, A. Darrell, C. Neary, M. Howard, N. Smith, N. Hill, B. Webb, I. Halstead.

ACT 2[10]

Scene 1

"Farljandio" (*A Divertissement conceived and designed by* James Reynolds. *Music by* Victor Herbert. *Staged by* Michel Fokine.)

Scene: The Mountain Town of Accio, a haunt of the Sicilian Gypsies.

Arijo, a bride: M. Stryker. *Beppo*: J. Scott. *Gino*, a rival: S. Pernikoff. *Valcci*, father of the bride: M. Truscott. *Pancrazia*: H. L. Worthing. *Two Cronies*: I. Marcellus, M. McDonald. *A Jilted Lover*: F. Lambert. *Venucci*: J. Reed. *Sicetta*: G. Selden. *Annunziatta*: H. Gates. *Bici*: F. Reveaux. *Carolina*: A. Reilly. *Maggietta*: P. Nally. *Giulina*: E. Brady. *Carra*: M. Chapin. *Liseuzziza*: B. McFarland. *Palvicca*: P. Lee. *Monnavia*: S. Shand. *Razzi*: N. Savage, A. Vitak, H. Moreno, K. Stoneburn, C. Beresbach, B. Rees, L. Baron, M. Rich, A. Drange, L. Woods, M. Earle, M. Wallace. *Two Cartmen*: M. Barroy, J. Light.

Note: The "Dance of Allure" comes down from the tenth century and is still danced by the Gypsy Brides at their weddings.

Scene 2

Dance (*Arranged by* John Tiller.)

Tiller Girls

---

[10]Added after opening to Act 2:

The Filmless Movies (*by* Franklin P. Adams, Nate Salsbury and Emil Breitenfeld)

A. Tombes

"Suanee"(Sing a Swanee Song)(Act 2, later dropped)

T. Connor, V. Connor

(*Music by* Louis Breau. *Lyrics by* Nat Sanders.)

Scene 3

Disagreement Conference[11] (*by* Will Rogers and Ralph Spence)(*Painted by* Joseph Urban.)

Interpreter: E. Gallagher. *Sergeant-at-Arms*: A. Ochs. *Belgium*: M. Truscott. *Portugal*: F. Lambert. *Italy*: J. J. Shannon. *China*: A. Tombes. *Japan*: A. Shean. *France*: F. Tierney. *England*: B. Tynan. *Secretary of State*: W. Rogers.

Scene 4

Burlesk-Ballet[12] (Bally-Burlesk)

J. Nervo, T. Knox

Scene 5

Leg Dance

Tiller Girls

Scene 6

The Bull-Pen (*by* Ring Lardner. *Painted by* H. Robert Law Studios.)

Jim Carney, a regular pitcher: A. Ochs. *Cy Walters*, a busher: W. Rogers. *Joe Webb*, a busher: A. Tombes.

Scene 7

"Songs I Can't Forget"

T. Spencer, M. Lewis, Follies Four

(*Music by* Louis A. Hirsch. *Lyrics by* Gene Buck. *Costumes designed by* Charles LeMaire.)

Glow Worm: M. Chapin. *Alexander's Ragtime Band*: P. Eaton. *French*: A. Vitak. *Bedelia*: A. Reilly. *Robert E. Lee*: H. Webb. *La Paloma*: H. Moreno. *Annie Rooney*: H. Manning. *Hiawatha*: M. Stryker.

Scene 8

Uppers and Lowers (*by* Charles C. Mather amd Charles Sumner. *Painted by* Joseph Wickes.)

Stage Carpenter: G. Simpson. *Actor*: A. Tombes. *Porter*: J. Nervo. *Bride*: M. Lorber. *Bridegroom*: G. Simpson. *Masher*: A. Tombes.

"Dreams for Sale"[13]

M. Lewis, M. Dahm, M. Chapin, G. Selden

(*Music by* James F. Hanley. *Lyrics by* Herbert Reynolds.)

Scene 9

"Everybody's Making It Now"[14]

A. Tombes

(*Music and Lyrics by* Jimmie Duffy.)

Scene 10

Lace-Land: "Weaving (My Dreams)"

A. King

(*Music by* Victor Herbert. *Lyrics by* Gene Buck. *Lace Ballet devised and staged by* Ned Wayburn. *Scene by* Joseph Urban. *Costumes designed by* Charles LeMaire.)

The Lace-Maker: M. Lewis. *The Dutch Visions*: I. Marcellus, I. Wales, G. Selden, P. Nally. *The Trousseau (6): Lace Stockings*: A. Taylor. *The Parasol*: F. Reveaux. *The Handkerchief*: H. Worthing. *The Fan*: B. McFarland. *The Bridal Gown*: E. Brady. *The Veil*: J. Reed. *Butterfly*: M. McDonald. *Pages*: T. Connor, V. Connor. *Ballet of Motives*: Misses Stoneburn, Rich, Rees, Dana, Conroy, Manning, Merritt, Rolf, de Lerches, Earle, Arundel, A. Vitak.

Scene 11

"I Don't Want to Be in Dixie"[15]

L. McConnell

(*Music by* Louis A. Hirsch, Dave Stamper.)

Scene 12

Coconut Grove: "Sunny South"

M. Lewis

(*Music by* Louis A. Hirsch. *Lyrics by* Gene Buck.)

With Misses Reed, Lee, Wheaton, Brady, Taylor, Marcellus, Worthing, Chapin, F. Reveaux, Selden, I. Wales, Oakley, B. McFarland, Ivanoff, McDonald, Osborne, Nally, Gates, Starhill, Howden, Shelton, Beck, Miller, Mamay.

Dance

E. Law

Russian Dance

S. Karavaeff

"Come Along"

G. Gray

---

[11]Dropped during run.
[12]Dropped during run.
[13]Dropped during run.
[14]Dropped during run.
[15]Dropped during run.

(*Music by* Turner Layton. *Lyrics by* Henry Creamer. *Costumes designed by* Ada Fields.)

    With Misses Mahaffey, Woods, Howell, Dana, M. Dahm, Maness, Ray, Earle, C. Beresbach, A. Drange, M. Wales, Mason, F. West, Conroy, Manning, Merritt.

Some American Buck Dancing

    P. Eaton, H. Webb, M. Wallace, V. King, L. Baron, V. Valentine, B. Rees, A. Reilly

Scene 13

    Will Rogers, Andrew Tombes, (Ed) Gallagher, Al Shean

Scene 14

    Stage Door of the New Amsterdam Theatre (*Setting devised by* Ned Wayburn. *Painted by* H. Robert Law Studios.)

    Ensemble (Finale)

        Entire Company
        (*Music by* Dave Stamper, Louis A. Hirsch. *Lyrics by* Gene Buck.)

THE GRAND STREET FOLLIES (1922)

1922.20

A Low-Brow Show for High Grade Morons (a Musical Revue) in a Prologue, Two Acts, 6 Scenes and an Epilogue[16]. Book by Everybody. Music by Great Composers, mostly arranged by Lily M. Hyland. Lyrics, generally speaking, by Albert Carroll; but especially the music and words of "Personality." Costumes by Alice Beer and Polaire Weissmann. Dance numbers re-arranged by Albert Carroll. Produced by the Neighborhood Playhouse. Opened 13 June 1922 at the Neighborhood Playhouse and closed 25 June 1922 after 12 performances.

CAST: Albert Carroll, Whitford Kane, Aline MacMahon, Junius Mathews, Sol Friedman, Blanche Talmud, Anne Schmidt, Paula Trueman, Lily Lubell, Esther Mitchell, Eleanor Carroll, Helen Arthur, Agnes Morgan, John Roche, Polaire Weissmann, Irene Lewisohn, Dan Walker, Adrienne Morrison, Philip Mann, Michel Barroy.

    Piano: Lily M. Hyland. *Violin*: Mr. Ocko. *Saxophone*: Mr. Evans. *Drums*: Mr. Hagar.

PROLOGUE[17]

In the Beginning

    Scene: Home of the first dramatic critic, Adam Stale.
        Adam Stale: W. Kane. *Eve*, his wife: A. MacMahon. *Cain*, their son: J. Mathews. *The Rattle Snake*.

ACT 1: The Thing Happens

Scene 1

The Mattress House

    Constantine Madras: S. Friedman. *Siamese Wife*: B. Talmud. *Hindoo Wife*: A. Schmidt. *Chinese Wife*: P. Trueman. *African Wife*: L. Lubell. *Egyptian Wife*: E. Mitchell. *Japanese Wife*: E. Carroll. *Turkish Delight*, his favorite wife: H. Arthur. *Oriental Dream*, née Hattie Huxtable: A. Morgan. *Mr. Windowshame*, court costumer: J. Roche.

Scene 2

The Color Organ, based on Walt Whitman's poem, "Salut au Monde" or "I'll Tell the World"

    Walt Whitman: J. Roche. *Voices*: S. Friedman, P. Weissmann.

Scene 3

"The Royal Damn Fango" or "All Change Places"

    Torero: I. Lewisohn (who originally danced The Lady with the Fan). *Gypsy*: D. Walker (who originally danced the Prince). *Lady with the Fan*: A. Carroll (who originally danced the Torero). *Prince*: B. Talmud (who originally danced the Gypsy).

Scene 4

Making Light of Day

    Scene: New England School Room in Greenwich Village.
        Sally O'Monde, a teacher: A. Morgan. *Jimmy Grouchon*, her outside interest: J. Mathews. *The Kids*: S. Friedman, P. Trueman, L. Lubell.

Scene 5

The Green King, or The Vicious Circle

---

[16]The first in the annual series of satiric revues produced by the Neighborhood Playhouse for subscribers Off-Broadway; subsequent editions transferred to or originated on Broadway.

[17]Musical numbers, apart from "Personality" above, not listed individually in programs. Each sketch contained musical elements.

Sonia: E. Mitchell. *Chairman*: J. Roche. *Little Girls*: A. Morrison, A. MacMahon, P. Weissmann. *Little Boys*: W. Kane, I. Lewisohn, P. Mann, D. Walker.

ACT 2

As Far as Thought Can Reach: So Sorry

    Nikita Balieff: H. Arthur. *John Barrymore*: A. Carroll. *"Katinka"* (3): *Mother*: L. Lubell. *Father*: S. Friedman. *Katinka*: P. Trueman. *Roshanara*: B. Talmud. *Pavlova*: A. Carroll. *Elsie Janis*: D. Walker. *Anna Duncan*: A. Schmidt. *Irene Castle*: A. Carroll. *Chaliapin and Jeritza*: S. Friedman, M. Barroy.

EPILOGUE

The Tragedy of an Elderly Gentleman

    Scene: The Foyer of the neighborhood Playhouse at the close of the above performance. *Additional characters*: Joseph Prine (undertaker), Margot Asquith, David Belasco, Suzanne Lenglen, Mrs. Leslie Carter, Helen Westley and her Lion, Richard Bennett, Doris Keane, Laurette Taylor, Alla Nazimova, Margaret Wycherly.

(RAYMOND HITCHCOCK'S) PIN WHEEL

1922.21

A Kaleidoscopic Revel (Musical Revue) in Two Acts, 31 Scenes. Whirled (staged) by Michio Itow [Ito]. (Scenery designed by Zoltan Hecht, Walt Kuhn, Torosu.) Costumes designed by Lillian Greenfield, William Troy. Produced by Richard G. Herndon. Opened 15 June 1922 at the Earl Carroll Theatre and closed 8 July 1922 after 28 performances[18]. Second edition opened as MICHIO ITOW'S PIN WHEEL REVUE 31 July 1922 at the Little Theatre and closed 12 August 1922 after 16 performances (see separate entry below). Total: 44 performances.

CAST: RAYMOND HITCHCOCK, FRANK FAY[19], EVA CLARK, ISABEL VERNON, MARIA MONTERO, MICHIO ITOW [Ito], FELICIA SOREL, ZOLTAN HECHT, ROSALIND FULLER, SENIA GLUCK, YUJI ITOW, ANITA ENTERS, Florence McGuire, Victoria White, Louise Riley, Regina Devi, Margaret Petit, Dorothy Smoller, The Bennett Twins, Marguerite Agniel, Mercedes Guthrie, Josephine Head, Lon Denne, Lillian Greenfield, Phyllis Jackson, Marie Viscardi, Marian Williams, Hazel Wright, Yashushi Wuriu, Issye Boneck, Joe Burrows, John Burr, Hamilton Condon, Roger Dodge, Saret Lahiri, Maurice Lupue, Little Joe.

ACT 1[20]

Why I Bought the Show

    R. Hitchcock

Scene 1

Pastorale—

Little Shepherd (*Music by* Claude Debussy.)

    A. Enters

"Farmer's Son" (English Folk Song)

    R. Fuller, Y Itow, H. Condon

Pan (*Music by* Claude Debussy.)

    L. Riley

Masked Bacchante (*Music by* Dent Mowrey.)

    M. Petit

Argument

    (This composition is the Spanish Gypsy Dance from the musical setting to George Eliot's "Spanish Gypsy" which was presented at the University of Paris, 14 March 1914, and is now presented for the first time in New York.)

Scene 2

Ecclisastique[21] (*Music by* Pyotor Ilyich Tchaikovsky.)

    A. Enters, L. Greenfield, F. Sorel, M. Viscardi, H. Wright
    (*Setting by* Zoltan Hecht.)

---

[18]Musical director uncredited.

[19]Frank Fay appeared on opening night per reviews, but his name was omitted from the programs. His name is added to scenes in which he appeared, on the basis of the reviews and subsequent programs.

[20]The running order was revised after the opening; numerous revisions were made. Added after opening:

    "Tiddle de Winks" (dance)
        M. Petit
    Lilies of the Field (Act 1 Finale)
        I. Boneck, J. Burr, H. Condon, R. Dodge, M. Lupue
        (*Designed by* Walt Kuhn.)
    "A Heart That's Free" (Act 2)
        E. Clark

[21]Billed in the second week as Devotion.

Scene 3
Mr. Hitchcock and His Art Girls
Art Girls: B. Bruce, G. Kane, M. Warner, J. Piccard, V. Weller, K. Carlin.
Scene 4
Three Waltzes (*Music by* Johannes Brahms.)
J. Head, P. Jackson
Scene 5
Hindu Songs and Dances
R. Devi
Accompaniment: R. Devi (tambura), Sarat Lahiri (esraj), Nimbuker (tabla).
Scene 6
"My Lady of the Fan"
E. Clark
(*Music and Lyrics by* Earl Carroll.)
Scene 7
Faun and Nymph (dance)
F. Sorel, S. Gluck
(*Music by* Paul Paurel and Fritz Kreisler. *Choreography arranged by* Senia Gluck.)
Scene 8
The Explanation
R. Hitchcock
Scene 9
En Bateau[22]
L. Denne, M. Guthrie, J. Head, P. Jackson, M. Williams
(*Music by* Claude Debussy.)
Scene 10
"Silver Stars"
R. Hitchcock, F. Fay, Girls
(*Music, Lyrics and Patter by* Percy Wenrich.)
Girls: E. Clark, F. McGuire, V. White.
Scene 11
Rhythmic Setting—From the Clay[23]
Z. Hecht
A Psalm of Work, from a suite with Visualized Rhythms by Rosa Prindle Hecht.
Scene 12
Pipes[24] (*Music by* Claude Debussy.)
L. Riley
Scene 13
Feline[25] (*Music by* Claude Debussy.)
A. Enters
Scene 14
What's It All About? (*by* Frank Fay)
R. Hitchcock, F. Fay
Scene 15
Majolique (*Music by* Isaac Albéniz and Saraste.)
M. Montero, P. Gridier, M. Guthrie, M. Williams, H. Wright, J. Burr, H. Condon, M. Lupue, M. Fernandez
(*Setting by* Zoltan Hecht.)
Tsigane (*Music by* Paul Paurel and Alexander Glazunov.)
F. Sorel, S. Gluck

ACT 2
Scene 1
Spring (Japanese dance) (*Music by* Yamada and Sawada.)
A. Enters, Y. Wuriu, Y. Itow, L. Greenfield, P. Gridier, M. Guthrie, L. Riley, F. Sorel, M. Viscardi, M. Williams, H. Wright
Scene 2
Languor, Ecstasy and Languor[26]
I. Boneck, J. Burr, H. Condon, R. Dodge, M. Lupue
(*Designed by* Walt Kuhn.)
Scene 3
Song
R. Hitchcock

Scene 4
Rhythmic Setting—To the Sun[27]
Z. Hecht
(A dance in the spirit of primitive instruments by Rosa Prindle Hecht.)
Scene 5
Brigand
F. Sorel, S. Gluck
(*Music by* Alexander Borodin. *Choreography arranged by* Senia Gluck.)
Scene 6
The Shaving of the Hairy Ape (Burlesque on the play by Eugene O'Neill)
Scene a: Anywhere. *Scene b*: The Court of Jestus. *Scene c*: The Bastille.
a) *First Man*, *Second Man*: Callahan, Brothers.
b) *The Jedge*: R. Hitchcock. *District Attorney*: F. B. Manatt. *Bull Burke*, the Ape Man: F. Fay.
c) *First Attendant*, *Second Attendant*: Callahan Brothers.
Scene 7
"The Twa Sisters o' Binnorie" (Scotch Traditional Ballad)
R. Fuller, Y. Itow
Elder Sister: P. Jackson. *Younger Sister*: J. Head. *Knight*: H. Condon. *Harper*: J. Burr.
Scene 8
Repetition de Dance (after Degas)
M. Petit (Premiere danseuse)
(*Music by* Franz Schubert and Poldini. *Choreography arranged by* Margaret Petit.)
Ballet Girls of the French Opera: J. Bono, B. Snyder, M. Lane, L. Wagner.
Scene 9
"Oh Say, Oh Sue"
R. Hitchcock, F. Fay, Girls
(*Music by* Joseph Meyer. *Lyrics by* Irving Caesar.)
Scene 10
Jewish Moods[28]
E. Laska, Z. Hecht
Scene 11
I Forgot to Tell You[29]
R. Hitchcock
Scene 12
Arabesque[30] (*Music by* Robert Schumann. [*Dances*] *arranged by* Walt Kuhn.)
Pierrot: S. Gluck. *Waiter*: R. Dodge. *Tailor*: I. Boneck. *Banker*: M. Lupue. *Lady*: H. Wright.
Scene 13
Lion Dance[31]
Y. Wuriu, F. Sorel, M. Viscardi
(*Setting by* Yorosu.)
Scene 14
Character Dance—Pizzicato (*Music by* Léo Delibes.)
M. Itow
Scene 15
In Conclusion Let Me Say[32]
R. Hitchcock
Scene 16
A Quiet Evening at Home[33]
Entire Company

1922.21 MICHIO ITOW'S PIN WHEEL

A Midsummer Revel in Two Acts, 22 Scenes[34]. Whirled (staged) by Michio Itow. Costumes designed by Lillian Greenfield, William Troy. Musical

---

[22]Dropped after the opening.
[23]Dropped after the opening.
[24]Dropped after the opening.
[25]Dropped after the opening.
[26]Dropped after the opening.

[27]Dropped after the opening.
[28]Dropped after the opening.
[29]Dropped after the opening.
[30]Dropped after the opening.
[31]Dropped after the opening.
[32]Dropped after the opening.
[33]Performed on opening night at the finale per reviews:
Little Joe Taps (infant prodigy at the drums)
[34]Revised Version of the Dancing Revue which opened 15 June 1922 as RAYMOND HITCHCOCK'S PIN WHEEL at the Earl Carroll Theatre

director, Frederick Swarts. Produced by Richard G. Herndon. This edition opened 31 July 1922 at the Little Theatre and closed 12 August 1922 after 16 performances. Total for both editions: 44 performances.

CAST: MICHIO ITOW [Ito], FELICIA SOREL, SENIA GLUCK, MARGARET PETIT, ROSALIND FULLER, YUJI ITOW, ANITA ENTERS, FRANK CURRAN, HUNTER SAWYER, HAZEL WRIGHT, PHYLLIS JACKSON, JOSEPHINE HEAD, ISSYE BONECK, JOHN BURR, HAZEL M. ARCHIBALD, HELEN CUTTER.

ACT 1[35]

Scene 1

Pastoral (*Music by* Edvard Grieg. *Choreography by* Senia Gluck.)
M. Avery, V. Morgan, G. Robinson, L. Wagner, F. Sorel, B. Berkeley, J. Burr

Scene 2

"The Song of the Japanese Fisherman"
M. Itow
(*Music by* Komatsu.)

Scene 3

Ecclisastique (*Music by* Pyotor Ilyich Tchaikovsky.)
A. Enters, J. Head, P. Jackson, R. Wild, H. Wright
(*Costumes by* Willoughby Irons.)

Scene 4

Tiddle De Winks (*Music by* Léo Delibes. *Created by* Margaret Petit.)
Girl: G. Robinson. *Boy*: M. Avery.

Scene 5

Bird Fantasy
H. Cutter, M. Itow
(*Music by* Cyril Scott.)

Scene 6

"I've Lost My Job"
H. M. Archibald
"Honey, Honey, Honey"
H. M. Archibald
(*Music and Lyrics by* Hazel M. Archibald.)

Scene 7

Faun and Nymph (dance)
F. Sorel, S. Gluck
(*Music by* Paul Paurel and Fritz Kreisler. *Choreography arranged by* Senia Gluck. *Costumes by* William Troy.)

Scene 8

Jazz and Jazz (*Conceived and designed by* Walt Kuhn.)
M. Itow, M. Avery, P. Jackson, R. Wild, H. Wright, I. Bonek, F. Curran, J. Burr, R. M. Simson

Scene 9

Tribute to Gaugin (*Music by* Detts.)
A. Enters

Scene 10

"I'm Seventeen Come Sunday" (English Folk Song)
R. Fuller

Scene 11

Lilies of the Field (*Designed by* Walt Kuhn.)
B. Berkeley, I. Bonek, J. Burr, F. Curran, H. Sawyer, R. M. Simson

ACT 2[36]

Scene 1

La Repetition (after Degas)
M. Petit (Premiere danseuse)
(*Music by* Franz Schubert and Poldini. *Choreography arranged by* Margaret Petit. *Costumes by* Mrs. C. Petit.)
Ballet Girls of the French Opera (1870): M. Avery, V. Morgan, G. Robinson, L. Wagner. *Old Woman*: A. Enters. *Ballet Master*: A. Thorne.

---

for 28 performances. One third of the material was new, including 3 additional numbers for Michio Itow himself, and 2 additional numbers by Walt Kuhn.
[35]Added after opening to Act 1:
Japanese Sword Dance (Old Japanese War Song)
M. Itow
(*Chanted accompaniment by* K. Nanbu.)
Song (as sung by the Batsuto's of South Africa)
Sakabona Sonki
[36]Added after opening to Act 2:
Japanese Spring Dance
M. Itow, H. Cutter

Scene 2

Three Waltzes (*Music by* Johannes Brahms.)
J. Head, P. Jackson

Scene 3

An Adventure on a Staircase (Pantomime)
M. Itow, S. Gluck, F. Sorel

Scene 4

"I Could Be a DuBarry If"
H. M. Archibald
(*Music and Lyrics by* Hazel M. Archibald.)

Scene 5

Old Sea Shanties:
(Men)
"Blow the Man Down"
Company Ensemble
(b) "The Drunken Sailor"
F. Curran
(c) "A Roavin'"
H. Sawyer
(d) "He-Back, She-Back"
B. Berkeley
(e) "Sally Brown"
R. Simson
Assisted by I. Bonek, J. Burr, Y. Itow, A. Thorne.

Scene 6

Dragon du Chinois
R. Wild

Scene 7

Pizzicata (*Music by* Léo Delibes.)
M. Itow

Scene 8

"The Twa Sisters o' Binnorie" (Scotch Traditional Ballad)
R. Fuller, Y. Itow
Elder Sister: P. Jackson. *Younger Sister*: J. Head. *Knight*: A. Thorne. *Harper*: J. Burr.

Scene 9

The Masked Bacchante
M. Petit
(*Created by* Margaret Petit. *Music by* Dent Mowrey. *Costumes by* Mrs. C. Petit.)

Scene 10

"Twilight" (*Music by* Sawada.)
M. Itow

Scene 11

Tropical Night (*Designed by* Walt Kuhn.)
Company Ensemble

1922.22 STRUT, MISS LIZZIE

Glorifies the Creole Beauty (An All-Colored Revue) in Two Acts, 13 Scenes[37]. Music by Henry Creamer. Lyrics by Turner Layton. Staged by Henry Creamer. Scenery suggested and designed by Novelty Scenic Studio. Musical director, Joe Jordan. Produced by the Creole Producing Company (Minsky Brothers and Arthur Lyons). Opened 19 June 1922 at the Times Square Theatre, moved 10 July 1922 to the Earl Carroll Theatre under the auspices of the Strut Miss Lizzie Corporation (Arthur Lyons, K. Kendler, J. Cordon), and closed 26 August 1922 after 80 performances. (Total: 96 performances, including Off-Broadway run.)

CAST: HENRY CREAMER, TURNER LAYTON, ALICE BROWN, HAMTREE HARRINGTON, CORA GREEN, BREVARD BURNETT, GRACE RECTOR, GEORGE [Georgette] HARVE, JEAN ROUNDTREE, JAMES BARRETT, CHARLES FREDERICKS, IRIS HALL, EDDIE FIELDS, HENRY SAPARO, JIMMY [James] MOORE, (Joe) HENDERSON and (Bud) HALLIDAY, LAKE SISTERS.
Girls: Jennie Day, Beatrice Williams, Lena Dukes, Lottie Ames, Julia Aikman, Alberta Foster, Camille Barnes, Betty Page, Adelaide Jones, Minerva Lee, Carrie Edwards, Marry Goodwin, Helen Dunmore, Nona Burke, Daisy Fleming, Erma Ovington, Alberta Jones, Cornelia Richardson, Ethel Taylor, Blanche Thompson, Dorothy Bellis. *Boys*: Al Moore, Harry Watkins, John Gilliard, Bill Burke.

---

[37]Originally opened Off-Broadway 3-17 June 1922 at the National Winter Garden for 16 performances. Costumes uncredited.

ACT 1[38]
Scene 1
  Spirituals
    G. Harve, Entire Company
  Telephone Introduction
    H. Creamer, T. Layton
  "Dear Old Southland"
    G. Harve, Lake Sisters, J. Moore, Ensemble
  "Buzz Mirandy" (Mirandy Hear Them Buzz)
    C. Fredericks, Buzzing Creoles
Scene 2
  Vest Pocket Bert Williams
    H. Harrington
  Full House Poker Club
    A. Brown, H. Harrington
  "Darktown Poker Club"
    H. Harrington
  "Nobody's Gal"
    A. Brown, H. Harrington
Scene 3
  Creole Alley at the Ritz
    J. Henderson, B. Halliday and Girls
  "My Hometown"
    J. Henderson, B. Halliday
  "Creole Belles"
    J. Henderson, B. Halliday, Girls
  "Dixie"
    J. Henderson, B. Halliday
Scene 4
  Cafe D'Ella Lee
    a) Cafe Entertainers: "Lovesick Blues"[39]
      A. Brown, G. Rector
    b) "In Yama"
      C. Green, B. Williams, J. Moore, C. Chorus
    c) The Jazz Waiters: "Crooning;" "Wyoming Lullaby, "Down Yonder"
      J. Barrett, C. Fredericks
    d) Cafe Guests
      H. Harrington, B. Burnett, I. Hall, Girls, Men
  "Breakin' a Leg"
    J. Henderson, B. Halliday, A. Brown, D. Fleming, Leonard, Girls
    Head Waiter: H. Saparo.
Scene 5
  Just a Moment:
  "Brother-in-Law Dan"[40]
  "Lonesome Longing Blues"
    C. Green
Scene 6
  Spilling the Beans
    J. Moore, E. Fields
Scene 7
  All Aboard for New Orleans: "New Orleans"
    J. Roundtree, H. Saparo, Entire Company
    Spanish Dancers: J. Roundtree, H. Saparo, Lake Sisters, Entire Ensemble.
  Interval: Joe Jordan and His Velvet Band:
  "Ebony Rag" (Music by Joe Jordan.)
    Orchestra
  "Bernice" (Music by Joe Jordan.)
    Willie Tyler (Violin solo), J. Jordan (Piano)
  "At the Ball"
    W. Tyler, Orchestra
ACT 2[41]

---

[38]The running order of songs and sketches was revised during the run.
[39]Dropped during the run.
[40]During the run replaced by:
  "Some Sunny Day"
    C. Green
[41]Added during the run to Act 2:
  Foreign Songs
    G. Harve

Scene 1
  On a South Sea Isle: "Hoola, from Coney Isle"
    C. Green, C. Edwards, South Sea Islanders
Scene 2
  Comedy Nondescript
  Meet Miss Mandy
    G. Rector, E. Fields, Ensemble
  "Mandy"
    G. Rector, E. Fields, J. Henderson, B. Halliday, J. Barrett, C. Fredericks, Girls
Scene 3
  "I Wanna Dance"[42]
    Mr. Leonard
Scene 4
  "Fan Miss Fannie"
    J. Roundtree, H. Saparo, Fan Girls
    The Creole Fans: J. Roundtree, H. Saparo, A. Jones, C. Edwards, B. Williams, E. Taylor, Strutters.
Scene 5
  The Darktown Hod Carriers
    J. Green, B. Burnett
  "Il Trovatore"
    J. Green, B. Burnett
  "When You Look in the Eyes of a Mule"
    J. Green
  "Four Fo' Me"
    B. Burnett
  "Jazz Blues"
    J. Green, B. Burnett
  Miss Angelina: "Sweet Angeline"
    C. Green, J. Barrett, C. Fredericks, J. Henderson, B. Halliday, Creole Girls
  Creamer and Layton in Old and New Songs
Scene 6
  Grand Finale
    [Entire Company]

1922.23 # SPICE OF 1922

A Musical Revue in Two Acts, 32 Scenes. Sketches by Jack Lait. Music and lyrics by Everybody (Music by J. Fred Coots, Henry Creamer, James F. Hanley; lyrics by McElbert Moore, Jack Stanley, Turner Layton). Entire production staged by Allan K. Foster. Settings by H. Robert Law Studios; art director, Herbert Ward. Costumes designed by Ernest R. Schrapps. Orchestra under the direction of Alfred Goodman. Produced by Arman Kaliz[43]. Opened 6 July 1922 at the Winter Garden and closed 9 September 1922 after 85 performances.

CAST: ADELE ROWLAND, JIMMY HUSSEY, SAM HEARN, FLAVIA ARCARO, WILL OAKLAND, GEORGIE PRICE, REX STOREY, RATH BROTHERS (George, Dick), ARMAN KALIZ, VALESKA SURATT, JAMES WATTS, MIDGIE MILLER, GATTISON JONES, JAMES GAYLOR, (Cecile) D'ANDREA and (Harry) WALTERS, HELEN O'SHEA, JACK TRAINOR, Mlle. MARION, JAMES C. MORTON, FLORENCE BROWNE, HASOUTRA, JANE RICHARDSON, STANLEY BRENNAN, Lucille Ballantine, Marion Randall, Mart. Randall, E. H. Barlab, Nell Roy Buck, Charles Eaton.
  Spice Girls: Freckles Gordon, Virginia Shaar, Dorothy Gilbert, Helen Montague, Maris Chaney, Bobbie Boles, Isabella McLaughlin, Mae Fox, Sue Wilson, Lucille Constante, Jean Watson, Mary Dunne, Olga Borowska, Sunny Sanders, Nan Chapman, Gladys Parker, Marjorie Wall, Ann LeMeau, Dorothy Kendall, Pearl Betts, Frankie Feustal, Ann Poulson, Dorothy Frayser, Marion George, Gwyn Stratford, Emily DeVeaux, Yvette DuBois, Billie Jerome, Evelyn Gerald, Dorothea Jackson. Men: Leonard Mooney, Leonard Leeds, Dan Mayo, Roger Buckley, Stanley Brennan, Albert Bennett, John Daly, James Harold.

ACT 1[44]
Scene 1

  Spice of Park Avenue: Opening Chorus
    Ensemble

---

[42]Dropped during the run.
[43]Toured subsequently under the auspices of Edward L. Bloom.
[44]Added for the tour to Act 1:
  An Egyptian Frieze
    King Tut-Ankh-Amen: A. Corey.

(*Music by* J. Fred Coots. *Lyrics by* McElbert Moore.)
  Girls and Boys in Block Party: Misses Parker, Shaar, McCloud, Lemeau, Wall, Gilbert, Gordon, Montagu, Feustal, Poulson, Watson, Boles, Sanders, Fraser, Devoe, McLaughlin, Kendal. Messrs. Mayo, Barlab, Mooney, Bennett, Leeds, Daley, Buckley, Brennan.

Scene 2
  Interior of (Carnival) Tent
    "Society"
      M. Miller, Eight Pony Pepper Pots
      (*Music by* J. Fred Coots. *Lyrics by* McElbert Moore.)
        A Dancer: M. Marion. *The Policeman*: J. C. Morton. *A Censor*: S. Hearn. *The Manager*: A. Kaliz.

Scene 3
  The Green Room (Spilling the Spice)
    The Manager: A. Kaliz. *The Censor*: S. Hearn. *The Policeman*: J. C. Morton.

Scene 4
  The Tempter's Lair
    Voice of the Snake: F. Browne.

Scene 5
  The Garden of Eden (The Origin of Spice)(*Ballet by* Arman Kaliz.)
    Eve: C. D'Andrea. *Adam*: H. Walters. *Spirit of the Snake*: Hasoutra. *Spirit of Virtue*: H. O'Shea. *The Angel*: Mlle Marion.

Scene 6
  The Spice of Burlesque
    Adam: R. Storey. *Eve*: J. Watts.

Scene 7
  The Censor
    S. Hearn

Scene 8
  Lilies of the Field
    V. Suratt, Girls

Scene 9
  An Artist's Studio (Patent pending)
    "My Lady Silhouette"
      W. Oakland
      (*Music and Lyrics by* Owen Murphy.)
        The Artist: W. Oakland. *The Model*: L. Ballantine.

Scene 10
  A Dance Study[45]
    Marion Randall, Mart. Randall

Scene 11
  Je Vous Aime (The Spice of Honeymooning)
    "I'm in Love with You"
      A. Kaliz, J. Richardson
      (*Adapted by* Jack Lait *from the book by* William J. Hurlbut. *Music by* Kenneth Keith. *Lyrics by* Arman Kaliz.)
        The Newlyweds (2): *He*: A. Kaliz. *She*: J. Richardson. *Suki, the Butler*: J. Gaylor. *Marie, the Maid*: H. O'Shea. *Olga Valsov* (First Troublemaker): F. Browne. *Suzette* (Second Troublemaker): M. Miller. *Maud* (Third Troublemaker): F. Arcaro. *Chauffeur*: S. Brennan. *Officer*: J. C. Morton.

Scene 12
  A Prowler
    R. Storey

Scene 13
  A Javanese Temple
    A Woodcarver: W. Oakland. *A Javanese Idol*: Hasoutra. *A Girl in Jade*: E. DeVeaux. *A Fruit Seller*: G. Parker. *A Beggar*: S. Brennan. *A Girl in Gray*: S. Wilson. *Tourists*: Misses Wall, Feustal; E. H. Barlab. *A Girl in Black*: A. Lemeau.
    "Llamala"
      W. Oakland
      (*Music by* William J. Lewis. *Lyrics by* Guy Nankwill.)

Scene 14
  "The Swanee Sway"[46]
    A. Rowland
    (*Music by* James Hanley. *Lyrics by* Jack Stanley.)
      Scene: Before the Curtain.

Scene 15
  Cigars and Cigarettes
    A Cigarette Girl: M. Miller. *A Rounder*: G. Jones.
    "Egyptian Melange"
      M. Miller, G. Jones
      (*Music by* James F. Hanley. *Lyrics by* James F. Hanley, Jack Stanley.)

Scene 16
  The California Widow (Interstate Spice)
    The Widow: V. Suratt. *The Sheik*: A. Kaliz. *The Lover*: W. Oakland. *An Admirer*: J. C. Morton. *Attorney*: S. Hearn. *Judge*: J. Trainor. *A Butler*: J. Gaylor.

Scene 17
  Special Spice:
    G. Price
    ["Angel Child"
      (*Music by* Abner Silver. *Lyrics by* Benny Davis, Georgie Price.)
    "I'll Stand Beneath Your Window Tonight (and Whistle)"
      (*Music and Lyrics by* Jerry Benson, Jimmy McHugh, Georgie Price.)
    "Love Tunes"
      (*Music and Lyrics by* Georgie Price and Sam Hearn.)
    "Yankee Doodle Blues"
      (*Music by* George Gershwin. *Lyrics by* Buddy G. DeSylva, Irving Caesar.)
    "Lovin' Sam (The Sheik of Alabam)"
      (*Music by* Milton Ager. *Lyrics by* Jack Yellen.)]

Scene 18
  A Dutch Lane
    A Dutch Boy: A. Rowland. *A Dutch Girl*: J. Richardson.

Scene 19
  "Two Little Wooden Shoes"
    A. Rowland, J. Richardson, S. Hearn, Company
    (*Music by* James F. Hanley. *Lyrics by* Jack Stanley. *Conceived by* Allan K. Foster.)
      Peasant Girl: M. Miller. *A Peasant*: A. Leeming. *A Violinist*: S. Hearn. *Goodie Two Shoe*: N. R. Buck. *Goodie One Shoe*: Master C. Eaton. *Dutch Girls and Boys*: Misses Parker, Shaar, McCloud, Lemeau, Wall, Gilbert, Gordon, Montagu, Watson, Dunne, Sanders, Poulson, Betts, Feustal, DeVeaux, Boles, Chapman, Frzer, George, Stratford, McLaughlin, Dubois, Borowska, Fox, Gerald, Wilson, Chancy, Constante, Jerome, Jackson, Kendal. Messrs. Mayo, Money, Brennan, Daley, Bennett, Buckley, Barlab, Leeds.

ACT 2[47]
Scene 1
  Spice of the Red Lantern (Cafe)
    "Burglar Inn"
      H. O'Shea, G. Jones
      (*Music by* Seymour Furth. *Lyrics by* Ed Moran.)
        A Burglar Girl: G. Jones. *A Burglar Boy*: H. O'Shea.

Scene 2
  Gymnastic Spice
    Rath Brothers

Scene 3
  The Winsome Blondes[48]
    H. O'Shea

Scene 4
  "(In) My Little Red Book"
    J. Richardson, Boys
    (*Music by* J. Fred Coots. *Lyrics by* McElbert Moore.)
      A Country Girl: J. Richardson.

Which was later replaced by:
  "Had My Pitcher Tooken" and Wail of a Debutante
    N. Halperin
[47]Added for the tour to Act 2:
  The Vamp
    A Vamp: F. Browne. *The Censor*: S. Hearn. *The manager*: A. Kaliz.
  Lady of the Cameo
    Lady Grace: M. Throop. *The Prince*: A. Corey. *The Princess*: E. Wachta.
  "My Lady of the Cameo"
    M. Throop, Cameo Girls
  Casey at the Bat
    E. Brendel, Flo Bert
  A Bouquet of Songs
    F. Bert
[48]Dropped for subsequent tour.

---

[45]Dropped for subsequent tour.
[46]Replaced during the run by:
  Clothes and the Flapper
    Nan Halperin

Scene 5
  Two Fast Steppers
    D'Andrea and Walters
Scene 6
  Help (A Little Spice of Big Business)
    A Bookkeeper: J. Gaylor. *Charles Wilberforce Towne*: J. Trainor. *Charles Towne*, his son: G. Jones. *Kate*, Y.W.C.A. Habitué: V. Suratt. *Dollie Wheeler*: J. Watts. *Mary Gibbons*, a new face: M. Miller.
Scene 7
  Spice of Montmartre
  "A Little Side Street in Paree"
    A. Rowland
    (*Music by* James F. Hanley. *Lyrics by* Jack Stanley.)
    The Lady in Doorway: A. Rowland. *A Boy*: J. Watson. *Blue Devil*: L. Mooney. *His Father*: E. H. Barlab. *His Wife*: D. Kendal. *His Sister*: E. DeVeaux. *A Woman*: A. Lemeau. *A Man*: D. Mayo. *An Apache* S. Brennan.
Scene 8
  Himself[49] [includes 'The Sheik' skit]
    J. Hussey
Scene 9
  Spice of the Opera: 'Tosca'
    Madame He-Ritzed Her: J. Watts. *Signor Sloppy*: A. Kaliz.
Scene 10
  Out West (An Arizona Landscape)
  "A Girl from the Golden West"
    J. C. Morton, Eight Pony Pepper Pots
    (*Music by* J. Fred Coots. *Lyrics by* McElbert Moore.)
Scene 11
  Spice That's Nice (2 songs)
    A. Rowland
  ["Way Down Yonder in New Orleans" (from STRUT MISS LIZZIE)
    (*Music by* Turner Layton. *Lyrics by* Henry Creamer.)
  "Strut Miss Lizzie" (from ZIEGFELD FOLLIES OF 1921, STRUT MISS LIZZIE)
    (*Music by* Turner Layton. *Lyrics by* Henry Creamer.)]
      At the piano: Mildred Brown.
Scene 12
  All Night Long (A Satire) (Spice of the Triangle)
    The Husband: A. Kaliz. *The Wife*: V. Suratt. *The Lover*: J. Watts.
Scene 13
  Spice in Scarlet
  "An Old Fashioned Cakewalk"
    Entire Company
    (*Music by* James F. Hanley. *Lyrics by* Jack Stanley.)

1922.24 SUE, DEAR

A Musical Comedy in Two Acts. Book by Bide Dudley, Joseph Herbert and C. S. Montanye. Music by Frank H. Grey. Lyrics by Bide Dudley. Book staged by Joseph Herbert. Musical numbers staged by Jack Mason. Scenery by Beaux Arts Studios. Costumes by Paul Arlington, Inc. Orchestra under the direction of Frank H. Grey. Produced by Bide Dudley. Opened 10 July 1922 at the Times Square Theatre, moved 18 September 1922 to the Bijou Theatre, and closed 30 September 1922 after 96 performances.

CAST (in order of appearance): *Minerva West*: MAXINE BROWN. *Dave Craig*: MAURICE HOLLAND. *Aunt Mildred*: Madeline Grey. *Blithers*: Douglas Congrove. *Dolly*: Ruth Gray. *Polly*: Lucile Godard. *Molly*: Eileen Shannon. *Phillip West*: BRADFORD KIRKBRIDE. *Sue*: OLGA STECK. *Le Comte Emile Pouchez*: JOHN HENDRICKS. *Chick O'Brien*: BOBBY O'NEIL. *Zoe*: ALICE CAVANAUGH.
  Guests: *Mary*: Irma Coign. *Louise*: Edna Coign. *Fay*: Honor Tattersall. *Doris*: Emmey Tattersall. *Catherine*: Greta Warburg. *June*: Rose Courtney. *Nell*: Bobby Kane. *Gloria*: Mercedes Demordant. *Florence*: Kay Carlin. *Jack*: Paul Logan. *Billy*: Bobby Culbertson. *Lester*: Ted Wheeler. *George*: Norman Nicholson.

Act 1: Living-room of the West Home on Riverside Drive, New York.

Act 2: The Garden connected with the Apartment House in which the Wests live.

ACT 1[50]

Opening
  Principals, Ensemble
"Love's Corporation"
  M. Brown, M. Holland
"Lady Lingerie"
  M. Brown, Girls
"Smile and Forget"
  O. Steck
"That Samson and Delilah Melody"
  J. Hendricks, O. Steck, Ensemble
"Dance Me, Darling, Dance Me"
  B. O'Neil, A. Cavanaugh
"Lady of Dreams"
  B. Kirkbride
"Smile and Forget" (reprise)
  O. Steck
"My Little Full-Blown Rose"
  B. Kirkbride
ACT 2
Opening
  Principals, Ensemble
"Riverside Drive"
  B. O'Neil, Ensemble
"Key to My Heart"
  M. Brown, M. Holland
"Hiram Skinner's Comb"
  B. O'Neil, Girls
"Smile and Forget" (reprise)
  O. Steck, Ensemble
"Pidgie Widgie"
  A. Cavanaugh, B. O'Neil
"Foolishment"
  B. O'Neil, B. Kirkbride, J. Hendricks, M. Holland
"Smile and Forget" (reprise)
  O. Steck
"Lover's Lane with You"
  O. Steck, B. Kirkbride
Finale
  Entire Company

1922.25 PLANTATION REVUE

A Colored Musical Revue in Two Acts, (18 Scenes)[51]. Music and lyrics by J. Russel Robinson, Roy Turk, (Irving Berlin, Joe Young, Sam Lewis, George Meyer and Harry Akst). Settings designed by Lew Leslie. Costumes by Gertrude Johnson. Orchestra under the direction of Will Vodery. Entire production conceived and directed by Lew Leslie. Produced by Lew Leslie. Opened 17 July 1922 at the 48th Street Theatre and closed 12 August 1922 after 33 performances.

CAST: FLORENCE MILLS, SHELTON BROOKS, WILL VODERY'S PLANTATION ORCHESTRA, CHAPPY CHAPELLE, JUANITA STINETTE, JOHNNY DUNN, EDITH WILSON, ULYSSES S. [Lucky] THOMPSON, LEW KEANE, PLANTATION QUARTETTE, SIX DIXIE VAMPS[52].

ACT 1
Scene 1
  Master of Ceremonies: S. Brooks. *Ham from Birmingham*: U. S. Thompson. *Sam from Alabama*: L. Keane.
Scene 2
  Specialty
    Will Vodery and His Plantation Orchestra
Scene 3
  Specialty
    Plantation Quartette
Scene 4
  America's Popular Composer, Shelton Brooks:

---

[49]Dropped for subsequent tour.
[50]Added after opening:
  "Da, Da, Daddy Dear"

[51]Originally produced as a midnight revue for a 4-month run at the Plantation Club; subsequently played one week at the Lafayette Theatre in Harlem.
[52](Plantation Quartette and Six Dixie Vamps were unidentified in programs.

["The Darktown Strutters' Ball"
"Oh, Is She Dumb?"
"Unexpectedly"
"Marching Through Georgia"
    (*Music by* Henry Clay Work.)
"When You Speak of Vamps, Don't Leave Out Caroline"
    (*Music and Lyrics by* Shelton Brooks.)]

Scene 5
  Florence Mills and Her Six Dixie Vamps:
  ["That Kind of a Man"
  "Some Sunny Day"
    (*Music and Lyrics by* Irving Berlin.)]

Scene 6
  "Gypsy Blues" (from SHUFFLE ALONG)
    J. Stinette, C. Chappelle, F. Mills
    (*Music by* Eubie Blake. *Lyrics by* Noble Sissle.)

ACT 2
Prologue
  Scene and Place: Night Time in Dixieland.
  "Bugle Call Blues"
    J. Dunn (solo)
  "Old Black Joe"
    Plantation Quartette
  "A Southern Hobby"
    U. S. Thompson, L, Keane

Scene 1 (Revue)
  "Robert E. Lee"
    E. Wilson, Six Dixie Vamps

Scene 3
  "Swanee River"
    U. S. Thompson, L. Keane

Scene 4
  "(Dear Old) Southland"
    J. Stinette
    (*Music by* Turner Layton. *Lyrics by* Henry Creamer.)

Scene 5
  "Mandy"
    C. Chappelle, J. Stinette
    (*Music by* Turner Layton. *Lyrics by* Henry Creamer.)

Scene 6
  "Hawaiian Night in Dixieland"
    F. Mills, Six Dixie Vamps

Scene 7
  Specialty
    U. S. Thompson

Scene 8
  Specialty
    E. Wilson
  ["He May Be Your Man, But He Comes to See Me Sometimes"
    (*Music and Lyrics by* Perry Bradford.)
  "He Used to Be Your Man (But He's My Man Now)"
    (*Music and Lyrics by* Robert Kelly)]

Scene 9
  "I Want to Be Vamped in Georgia"
    C. Chappelle, Dixie Vamps

Scene 10
  Specialty
    F. Mills
  ["Sweet Man of Mine"
    (*Music by* Harry Akst. *Lyrics by* Roy Turk.)
  "I've Got What It Takes, But It Breaks My Heart to Give It Away"]

Scene 11
  "Minstrels on Parade"
    C. Chappelle, J. Stinette

Scene 12
  Finale
    Entire Company

1922.26

DAFFY DILL

A Musigirl (Musical) Comedy in Two Acts, 12 Scenes. Book by Guy Bolton and Oscar Hammerstein II. Music by Herbert Stothart. Lyrics by Oscar Hammerstein II. Staged by Julian Mitchell. Costumes designed by Charles LeMaire. Scenery designed by Clifford Pember. Orchestra under the direction of Herbert Stothart. Produced by Arthur Hammerstein. Opened 22 August 1922 at the Apollo Theatre and closed 21 October 1922 after 71 performances.

CAST: *Estelle*: MARION SUNSHINE. *Teacher*: Genevieve Markam. *Lucy Brown*: IRENE OLSEN. *School Inspector*: Ben Mulvey. *Frank Tinney*: FRANK TINNEY. *Dan Brown, Lucy's father*: Harry Mayo. *Kenneth Hobson*: GUY ROBERTSON. *Lucy's Grandma in 1867*: Jacquelyn Hunter. *Lucy's Grandpa in 1867*: Lynne Berry. *Lucy's Mother in 1899*: Imogene Wilson. *Harry Jones*: Rollin Grimes. *Gertie*: GEORGIA O'RAMEY. *Specialty Dancers*: Frances Grant and Ted Wing; Mary Haun and Galdino Sedano; Margaret and Elizabeth Keene; Frederick Renoff.

Ladies of the Ensemble: Jacqueline Hunter, Bernice Ackerman, Peggy Stohl, Grace LaRue, Fern Oakley, Violet Lobel, Imogene Wilson, Irene Anderson, Violet Andrews, Jessie Howe, Marjorie Clements, Grace Culbert, Marion Philips, Genevieve Markham, Yvette DuBoise, Beatrice O'Connor, Ethel Kinley, Joane Warner, Carolyn Maywood, Eleanor Dell. *Gentlemen of the Ensemble*: Lynne Berry, Charles Townshend, Harry Rocca, Harry Miller, Alfred Milaano, Victor Kenfield, Marius Rogate, Samuel Vean.

Act 1, Scene 1: The Old Swimmin' Hole. *Scene 2*: The Front Stoop of Lucy's House. *Scene 3*: Daniel Brown's Store, Down Town, New York. Ten years later. *Scene 4*: The Bungalow. *Scene 5*: Inside the Bungalow. *Scene 6*: A Rehearsal of 'The Coachman's Heart.' *Scene 7*: Kenneth Hobson's California Garden.

Act 2, Scene 1: Spanish Courtyard near the Burlingame Horseshow, California. *Scene 2*: At a Chinese Party. *Scene 3*: Screen Garden, Ken's Estate. *Scene 4*: A Musicale. *Scene 5*: The Jolly Roger, a Fashionable Inn.

ACT 1
Scene 1
  "Let's Play Hookey"/"Kindergarten Blues"
    M. Sunshine, Girls
  "Prince Charming"
    I. Olsen
  "Cinderella Meets the Prince" (Fantasy)
    I. Olsen, M. Keene, E. Keene

Scene 2
  "Two Little Ruby Rings"
    I. Olsen, G. Robertson, H. Mayo

Scene 3
  "My Boy Friend"
    M. Sunshine, Chorus
    Danced by F. Grant, T. Wing.
  "I'm Fresh from the Country"
    G. O'Ramey, Chorus
  "I'll Build a Bungalow"
    F. Tinney, G. O'Ramey, G. Robertson, I. Olsen

Scene 6
  "A Coachman's Heart" (Rehearsal Scene)
    F. Tinney, M. Sunshine

Scene 7
  Adagio
    M. Haun, G. Sedano
  "Fair Enough"
    G. Robertson, R. Grimes, H. Mayo, M. Keene, E. Keene, Chorus
  Finale

ACT 2
Scene 1
  "My Lucky Redskin"[53]
    M. Keene, E. Keene, F. Grant, Girls

Scene 2
  "Chinky Chink"
    M. Sunshine, M. Haun, M. Keene, E. Keene, B. Ackerman, G. Culbert, Y DuBoise

Scene 3
  "Doctor"
    G. O'Ramey, Chorus
    (*Lyrics by* Kenneth Keith.)

---

[53]Dropped for subsequent tour.

Fantasy—At the stroke of twelve, Cinderella runs away, leaving only a glass slipper
> I. Olsen, M. Keene, E. Keene, V. Lobel

Scene 4

"Pianologue"
> F. Tinney, J. Hunter, I. Wilson, F. Oakley, B. Ackerman, P. Stohl

Scene 5

Pirate Gold (Dance Pantomime)
> F. Grant, T. Wing, F. Renoff, E. Dell

"Captain Kidd's Kids"
> H. Mayo, M. Sunshine, M. Keene, E. Keene, Chorus

Finale

GEORGE WHITE'S
SCANDALS OF 1922

1922.27

A Musical Revue in Two Acts, 23 Scenes[54]. Book (sketches) by George White, W. C. Fields and Andy Rice. Music by George Gershwin. Lyrics by Buddy G. DeSylva and E. Ray Goetz, Arthur Francis. Staged by George White. Settings designed by Herbert Ward and John Wenger. Costumes designed by Erté. Orchestra under the direction of Max Steiner. Produced by George White. Opened 28 August 1922 at the Globe Theatre and closed 11 November 1922 after 89 performances.

CAST: GEORGE WHITE, PAUL WHITEMAN AND HIS ORCHESTRA, W. C. FIELDS, THE LIGHTNER SISTERS (Winnie, Thea) and (Newton) ALEXANDER, PEGGY DOLAN, ARTHUR BROOKS, PEARL REGAY, LESTER ALLEN, COLETTA RYAN, RICHARD BOLD, OLIVE VAUGHN, MARY REED, MYRA CULLEN, JACK WITTS, MARION COURTNEY, DIANA GORDON, SALLY LONG, ROGER LITTLE, KATHLYN ARDELLE, ALICE BURTON, MARY REED, ALBERT BARBER, MILDRED SHELLY, JACK McGOWAN, FRANKLYN ARDELL, THE TEMPLE QUARTETTE, THE ARGENTINAS, Charles Wilkens; (Original Piano Trio:) Edgar Fairchild, George Delworth, Herbert Clair.

Ladies of the Ensemble: Diana Gordon, Helen LaVonne, Sally Long, Catherine Chapman, Vera Colburn, Virginia Webb, Peggy Dolan, Dolores Costello, Sylvia Kingsley, Helen Miade, Anna Buckley, Peggy Jones, Misses Michell, Kimari, Jones, Lunney, Daniels, Paulson, Ringquist.

ACT 1

Scene 1

Garden of Eden
[Music of "'Neath the Shade of the Old Apple Tree"]
> *Eve*: P. Dolan. *Adam*: A. Barber. *Spirit of the Apple Tree*: A. Brooks.

Scene 2

The Modern Eves
> *First Eve*: O. Vaughn. *Second Eve*: M. Reed. *Third Eve*: M. Cullen. And Misses Burton, Lunney, Michell, Shelly, Paulson, Kimari, Dawn, Courtney, Smith, Marston, Jordon, Daniels.

Scene 3

> *A Flapper*: W. Lightner. *Her Admirer*: C. Wilkens.

Dance
> C. Wilkens

Scene 4

A Congested Corner in New York: Terrific Traffic (*by* W. C. Fields)
> *Mr. Bimbo*: W. C. Fields. *Mrs. Bimbo*: W. Lightner. *Baby Bimbo*: O. Vaughn. *Traffic Cop*: F. Ardelle. *Business Man*: J. Witts. *Neighbor*: H. LaVonne. *Another Neighbor*: P. Dolan. *Girl at the Window*: M. Courtney.

Scene 5

"Little Cinderelatives"[55]
> J. McGowan
> (*Lyrics by* Buddy G. DeSylva.)
> *Peg o' My Heart*: K. Ardelle. *Cinderella*: D. Costello. *Mary Ann*: A. Burton. *Irene*: M. Lunney. *Sally*: M. Reed. *Love Nest*: M. Courtney. *O'Brien Girl*: A. Buckley. *Good Morning Dearie*: M. Cullen.

Scene 6

"(Oh, See What) She Hangs Out in Our Alley"
> L. Allen
> *Girls on the Clothes Line*: Misses Burton, Jordan, Marston, Smith, Paulson, Ringquist.

Scene 7

Globe Theatre Stage Door
> *Doorman*: A. Brooks. With the Misses Long, Kingsley, Miade, Dolan, Webb, Chapman, Colburn, Costello, Jones. *Rufus Dodd*: F. Ardelle. *George White*: G. White. *A Good Fairy*: D. Gordon.

Scene 8

Three Different Homes with the Same Quarrel
> *The Poor Man*: L. Allen. *His Wife*: W. Lightner. *Well-to-Do Man*: N. Alexander. *His Wife*: F. Ardelle. *The Rich ManHis Wife*: T. Lightner.

Scene 9

The Seas: "My Heart Will Sail Across the Seas"
> C. Ryan
> *Girl in the Ship*: H. LaVonne. *The Tide*: R. Bold. *The Mediterranean Sea* (the Blue Sea), Pages: Misses Colburn, Miade, Webb, Courtney. *The Black Sea*, Pages: Misses Smith, Michell, Burton, Dawn. *The Red Sea*, Pages: Misses Kimari, Jones, Ardelle, Costello. *The White Sea*: Misses Lunney, Daniels, Jordan, Paulson. *The Ocean*: P. Regay. *The Waves*: M. Cullen, M. Reed.

Scene 10

Polo Grounds—The Big Leaguers (*by* W. C. Fields)
> *Umpire*: W. C. Fields. *Catcher*: F. Ardelle. *First Man Up*: A. Brooks. *Second Man Up*: A. Brooks. *Third Man Up*: N. Alexander. *Fourth Man Up*: C. Wilkens. *Spectators, etc.*

Scene 11

"I Found a Four Leaf Clover"
> C. Ryan, R. Bold
> (*Assisted by*) Miss LaVonne, Gordon, Long, Kingsley, Miade, Buckley, Dolan, Costello. *The Bunkem Twins*: L. Allen, C. Wilkens.

Scene 12

Paul Whiteman and His Palais Royal Orchestra

Scene 13

The Patent Leather Forest: "I'll Build a Stairway to Paradise"
> W. Lightner, P. Regay, C. Ryan, O. Vaughn, G. White, J. McGowan, R. Bold, N. Alexander, and a Rare Collection of New Beauties, (The Original Piano Trio, Paul Whiteman and His Orchestra)

ACT 2

Scene 1

"Blue Monday Blues"[56]
> *Prologue*: J. McGowan. *Mike*: A. Brooks. *Sam*: L. Allen. *Cokey*: R. Little. *Walter*: J. McGowan. *Vi*: C. Ryan. *Joe*: R. Bold. *Dancer*: G. White. And the Misses Cullen, Reed, Paulson, Michell. *Customers, etc.*

Scene 2

W. C. Fields

Scene 3

Specialty
> W. Lightner, T. Lightner, N. Alexander

Scene 4

"Argentina"
> J. McGowan

Dance
> The Argentinas (Dancers from Buenos Aires)

Scene 5

"I Can't Tell Where They're From When They Dance"
> G. White
> *The New York Dance*: M. Shelly. *Chicago Dance*: M. Reed. *Tennessee Dance*: M. Cullen.

Scene 6

"Just a Tiny Cup of Tea"
> P. Regay, R. Bold
> *English Tea Girls*: D. Gordon, H. LaVonne. *Attendants*: P. Dolan, D. Costello. *Russian Tea Girls*: S. Long, C. Chapman. *Attendants*: S. Kingsley, H. Miade. *Ceylon Tea Girls*: V. Colburn, V. Webb. *Attendants*: A. Buckley, P. Jones.

Scene 7

"Where Is the Man of My Dreams?"

Scene 8

The Original Piano Trio
> W. Lightner, Company, G. Delworth, E. Fairchild, H. Clair

---

[54]The fourth in the annual series of musical revues produced by George White beginning in 1919.
[55]Dropped after the opening.
[56]Dropped after the opening.

Scene 9

"You Can Tell Who We Are by the Things That We Have Done"
G. White, Entire Company

Exit Medley
Temple Quartette

1922.28 THE GINGHAM GIRL

A Musical Comedy in Three Acts, 4 Scenes. Book by Daniel Kusell. Music by Albert Von Tilzer. Lyrics by Neville Fleeson. Staged by Daniel Kusell and Edgar MacGregor. Dances and ensembles staged by Sammy Lee. Gowns by Lotty and Brice, Harry Collins; other costumes by Gilman and Bernstein, Anna Spencer, Inc., H. Mahieu & Company. Orchestra under the direction of Ivan Rudisill. Orchestrations by Stephen Jones and Maurice DePackh. Produced by Laurence Schwab and Daniel Kusell. Opened 28 August 1922 at the Earl Carroll Theatre, moved 30 April 1923 to the Central Theatre, and closed 2 June 1923 after 322 performances[57].

CAST (in order of appearance): *Gus:* Edgar Hamilton. *Conductor:* James T. Ford. *Silas O'Day:* Walter F. Jones. *Jack Hayden:* RUSSELL MACK. *Libby O'Day:* LOUISE ALLEN. *Mary Thompson:* HELEN FORD. *Harrison Bartlett:* Alan Edwards. *Mildred Ripley:* Eleanor Dawn. *John Cousins:* EDDIE BUZZELL. *Mazie Lelewer:* Dolly Lewis. *Sonya Maison:* BERTEE BEAUMONT. *Sophia Trask:* Amelia Summerville. *Waiter:* George Henry. *Mimi:* Helene Coyne. *Armand:* Henri French. *Pauline:* Valdene Smith. *Paulette:* Dorothy Faye Smith. *Butler:* Jack Mosser. *Rose:* Mildred Quinn. *Ann:* Maude Lydiate.

In the Village: She Who Runs the Pirates' Den: Elsie Lombard. *She Who Wears Batik:* Lillian Thomas. *She Who Loves Mythology:* Claire Martin. *She Who Wears a Derby:* Mildred Quinn. *She Who Throws Bombs:* Lucille Moore. *She Who Hails from Hobohemia:* Maude Lydiate. *She Who Kisses Fools:* Bernice Goesling. *She Who Makes Tamales:* Bobbie Breslaw. *She Who Provides the Puffs:* Betsy Walters. *He Who Paints:* Frank Daniels. *He Who Scribbles:* William Sholar. *He Who Loafs:* Alfred Opler.

Act 1: Centre Street, Crossville Corners, New Hampshire.

Act 2, Scene 1: A Café, New York City. *Scene 2:* A Studio down Greenwich Village Way.

Act 3: An Office, New York City.

ACT 1

"The Down East Flapper"
L. Allen, Girls

"The Twinkle in Your Eye"
H. Ford, L. Allen

"You Must Learn the Latest Dances"
E. Buzzell, R. Mack, Girls

Specialty
E. Lombard, B. Breslaw, B. Goesling

"As Long as I Have You"
H. Ford, E. Buzzell

Finale
All Concerned

ACT 2[58]

"Down Greenwich Village Way"
B. Beaumont, Girls

Specialty[59]
H. Coyne, H. French

"Tell Her While the Waltz Is Playing"
A. Edwards, Girls

"The Wonderful Thing We Call Love"
B. Beaumont, E. Buzzell

"A Gingham Girl"[60]
E. Buzzell, L. Allen

"The 42nd Street and Broadway Strut"[61]
V. Smith, D. F. Smith, Girls

Finale
All Concerned

ACT 3

"Sweet Cookie"
V. Smith, D. F. Smith, Girls

Specialty[62]
H. Coyne, H. French

"Newlyweds"
R. Mack, L. Allen

"Love and Kisses"
H. Ford, Girls

Finale
All Concerned

"Gingham Girl"
H. Ford, Girls

1922.29 MOLLY DARLING

A Musical Comedy in Two Acts, 9 Scenes. Book by Otto Harbach and William Cary Duncan. Music by Tom Johnstone. Lyrics by Phil Cook. Book directed by Walter Wilson. Staged by Julian Mitchell. Art director, Herbert Ward. Scenes painted by H. Robert Law Studios. Orchestra under the direction of Milton E. Schwarzwald. Orchestrations by Maurice DePackh. Produced by Menlo Moore and Macklin Megley. Opened 1 September 1922 at the Liberty Theatre, moved 13 November 1922 to the Globe Theatre, and closed 25 November 1922 after 101 performances.

CAST (in order of appearance): *Henri Ricardo,* a Violin Maker: Albert Roccardi. *'Chic' Jiggs,* a News Vendor: JACK DONAHUE. *Ted Miller,* a Vaudevillian: BILLY TAYLOR. *Trix Morton,* his Dancing Partner: BILLIE TAYLOR. *Molly Ricardo,* the Violin Maker's Daughter: MARY MILBURN. *Marivane,* Niece of Mrs. Redwing: CATHERINE MULQUEEN. *Oliver,* a Butler: Cecil Summers. *Mrs. Redwing,* a Wealthy Widow: EMMA JANVIER. *Jack Stanton,* a Club Attorney: CLARENCE NORDSTROM. *Chauncey Chesbro,* a Music Publisher: HAL FORDE. *'Spirit of Eve':* Nina Penn. *Archie Ames,* an Exponent of Victorious Thought: JAY GOULD. *Timmy,* a Bootblack: Ben Benny. *Tommy,* a Bootblack: Burke Wilson.

The Girls: Esther Morris, Marie Dolan, Betty Stewart, Liana Cloutier, Frances Lyndel, Lillian Mamet, Rhea Norton, Violet Follis, Mae Friend, Marion Rollins, Marie Pollitt, Yvette Reals, Lillian Downey, Myrtle Gilden, Dorothy Morris, Ida Miller. *The Boys:* Harold Bird, Bert McGuinnes, James Martin, Jack Stanley, William Warren, Charles LaValle, Norman Jefferson, Lester New.

Act 1, Scene 1: Ricardo's Workshop on East 31st Street, New York City. Early evening. *Scene 2:* Mrs. Redwing's Estate, Larchmont, New York. One hour later.

Act 2, Scene 1: Ricardo's Music Store. The following morning. *Scene 2:* Chic's New-Stand, near Ricardo's Store. *Scene 3:* Reception Room, Melody Hall. The same afternoon. *Scene 4:* Grand Salon, Melody Hall. The next afternoon. *Scene 5:* A Fantasy of the Orient. *Scene 6:* The Spirit of the Disc. *Scene 7:* A Radio Broadcasting Station. About 11 P.M.

ACT 1[63]

"You Know What to Do"
Billy Taylor, Billie Taylor, M. Milburn, J. Donahue
(*Music by* Milton Schwarwzald, Tom Johnstone.)

"There's an Eve in Ev'ry Garden"[64]
H. Forde, N. Penn, Girls

"Dear Little Gad-about"
C. Mulqueen, J. Gould, Boys

"They Love It"
H. Forde, J. Donahue, Billy Taylor, Billie Taylor

"Mellow Moon"
E. Janvier, C. Nordstrom, H. Forde, Girls

Chesbro's Entertainment for Mrs. Redwing's Guests:
(a) Eccentric Dance
J. Donahue

---

[57]Scenery uncredited.

[58]Act 2 was revised after the opening. Added shortly after the opening to Act 2, replacing the title song:
"Libby"
L. Allen, R. Mack, Company
Which was likewise replaced during the New York run by:
"Plunk, Plunk, Plunk"
L. Allen, R. Mack, Company

[59]Dropped during the New York run.

[60]Dropped during the New York run.

---

[61]For subsequent national tour, replaced by the title song, then later:
"When I Step with My Buddy" (When My Buddy Steps with Me)
M. Lydiate (Rose), B. Stanton (Ann), Girls

[62]Dropped during the New York run.

[63]The running order was revised for the tour.

[64]Dropped during subsequent national tour.

(b) Her Ballad
    M. Milburn
(c) "Stepping Some"
    Billy Taylor, Billie Taylor
"When Your Castles Come Tumbling Down"
    M. Milburn, C. Nordstrom, Ensemble
    (*Music by* Milton Schwarzwald. *Lyrics by* Arthur Francis.)
"Don't Tag Along"[65]
    J. Gould, Boys
Finale

ACT 2
"Syncopate"
    M. Milburn, J. Donahue, Billy Taylor, Billie Taylor, Ensemble
"Molly Darling"
    C. Nordstrom, M. Milburn, Boys
Boot Eccentrique[66]
    B. Benny, B. Wilson
"Contrary Mary"
    C. Mulqueen, J. Gould, N. Penn, Girls
An Oriental Episode[67]
    Billy Taylor, Billie Taylor
"Melody Dreams"
    M. Milburn, Ballet
Dance of the Disc
    N. Penn
"An Afterthought"
    J. Donahue, L. Cloutier
"Spirit of the Radio"
    Entire Company

1922.30   # BETTER TIMES

A Mammoth Musical Spectacle in Three Acts, 17 Scenes. Book and lyrics by R. H. Burnside. Music by Raymond Hubbell. Staged by R. H. Burnside. Scenery designed by Mark Lawson, Triangle Scenic Studio. Costumes designed by Will R. Barnes, Robert McQuinn, Gladys Monkhouse, William H. Matthews. Dances by William Holbrook and Mademoiselle Mantova. Musical director, A. J. Garing. Orchestrations by Charles Miller, Hilding Anderson, Frank Saddler. Produced by Charles Dillingham. Opened 2 September 1922 at the Hippodrome and closed 28 April 1923 after 405 performances.

CAST: MARCELINE, HAPPY LAMBERT, NANETTE FLACK, FRANK JOHN-SON, ROBERT McCLELLAN, FRED S. McPHERSON, LORNA LINCOLN, JOHN MURPHY, WILLIAM WILLIAMS, GLADYS COMERFORD, JOSEPH FRO-HOFF, VIRGINIA FUTRELLE, THOMAS JOYCE, HENRY STEVENS, RALPH BRAINARD, SARA EDWARDS, CLADIA IVANOVA, OLGA MIHAILOVAKAYA, THE ORLANDOS (Mlle. Othelia Orlando and their horses), THE GINNETT FAMI-LY (Poppy, Frank), JOHN F. BYRNE, ANDREW BYRNE, JAMES BYRNE, CHARLES RAVEL, ALBERT ALBERTO, DUANE NELSON, THE THREE BOBS, PATRICK and FRANCISCO, THE BELL BROTHERS, TORBAY, CLAUDIUS (Dane) and (Lillian) SCARLET, LONG TACK SAM (and His Troupe of [7] Chinese Jugglers and Acrobats)., GEORGE HERMAN, TOMY COLTON, (GEORGE) POW-ERS' DANCING ELEPHANTS, Tom Pender, Billy Smith, Archie Leach [Cary Grant], Jack Notman, Minna Hamm, Dorothy Gates, Edward Beck, Sid Williams, Murray Evans, Jimmy Brady, Amelia Rose, Beatrice Price, Alice Wilson, Nellie Melville, Lee Wilmott, Roland Gordon, Frank Ginnette, Jack Burley, Ellen Rose, John Murphy, Marven Morgan, Harry Tamaroff, Helen Ward, Lee Losch, Frances Blythe, Roy Binder, Mae Waldron, Betty Ross, Eddie Russell, Lillian Hauman, Gladys Cranston, Creco, Marie Mack, Billie Gilmore, Leo Post, Harry Ward, William Unangst, Colie Lorella, Jack Burley, Alexander Seabert, Hamadi Abdullah, Nick Provanzo, Joe Riley, Charles Ravel, Rae Stockdale, Marie DeYoung, Lorette Hauman, Dorothy Gates.
Principal Dancers of the Ballet: Ellen Rose, Winefride Verina, Maurice Lapue, George Kunowitch, Margaret Skaller, Ethel Downee, Sylvia Stone, William Holbrook, Lola Dalton, Nellie Daly, Sylvia Ford, Marie Cattell, Asta Valley, Ebba Sparre, Andre Lapue, Ruth Russell Matlock, Elna Hansen, Lolotta Armond, Gloria Meylan, Angela Sorrero, Dorothy Burke, Mary Anne Sawyer, Iran Tomaroff. *Members of the Ballet*:

Blanche Orteson, Grace McCrae, Lina Brandon, Agnes Hunter, Caroline Gunz, Marjorie Prentice, Marley, Therese, Marcelle Dulac, Thelma. *Ladies of the Ensemble*: Serrita Lorraine, Grace McCrea, Agnes Hunter, Lina Brandon, Marley, Betty Garson, Terry Bauer, Dorothy Lee, Thelma Bickford, Ruth Schrader, Blanche Orteson, Marjorie Prentice, Vivian Rose, Louise Allison, Olga Popova, Beatrice Houghton, Marjorie McKinnon, Jean Hamilton, Valeska Kawschara, Beatrice Bennet, Dorothy Collins, Guerrida Crawford, Muriel Gibson, Jean Schreiver, Millicent Bishop, Edna Koch, Anna Lambert, Bertha Herzog, Emma Warren, Tanaya Bader, Delamere, Vivian Arnold, Geneva Duker, Dorothy Wilson, Lillian Lane, Caroline Gunz, Belle Scholnick, Frances Sussman, Margaret Anderson, Louise Beautora, Ellen Mack, Trude Weisemaan, Elsie Ringle, Ethel Clark, Wally Warren, Lillian Quinn, Nellie Melville, Alice Marvin, Mary Sawyer, Dorothy Berke. *Some of the 100 High Divers*: Ruth Wood, Anna Fischer, Laura Murray, Ruth Loose, Victoria Wolfe, Lillian Hansen, the Berlo Sisters, Eva Miller, Adeline Claire, Louise Owens, Bertha E. Tomkins, May Dickson, Lillie Bolin, Mae O'Laughlin.

ACT 1[68]
Scene 1
    The Awakening of Spring (*Invented and arranged by* Max Teuber.)
        Scene a: The Arrival of the Birds. *Scene b*: An Approaching Storm. *Scene c*: Sunshine and the Growing Flowers. *Scene d*: At the Ocean Bed.
        Spring: E. Rose. *Summer*: L. Dalton. *Autumn*: Gracialita. *Winter*: G. Meylan.
Scene 2
    Powers' Dancing Elephants (Jennie, Lena, Roxie, Julia)
        Trained and introduced by George Powers, assisted by Marceline.
    At the Circus: At the Circus.
Scene 3
    "Peach Blossom Time"
        R. McClellan, Peaches
        Scene: Down on the Farm
        The Farmer: R. McClellan. *Polly*: E. Sparre. *Dolly*: S. Stone. *Some Peaches on the Farm*: Ensemble.
Scene 4
    Some Fun on a Hay-Wagon
        Patrick and Francisco
Scene 5
    The Marvelous Crow "Jacko" and His Pals, the Three Bobs
Scene 6
    The Stag Hunt[69] (*by* The Ginnett Family)
        The Wedding Party: The Master of Hounds: P. Ginnett. *A Farmer*: F. Ginnett. *The Squire*: J. F. Byrne. *The Parson*: A. Byrne. *The Doctor*: J. Byrne. *Innkeeper*: C. Ravel. *The Judge*: A. Alberto. *The Bride*: G. Comerford. *The Groom*: D. Nelson. *Waiters, Guests, Riders, etc.*
Scene 7
    "Blowing Bubbles All Day Long"
        F. McPherson, L. Lincoln
        Scene: In the Clouds.
        He: F. McPherson. *She*: L. Lincoln. *Bubble Boys, Balloon Girls, etc.*
Scene 8
    In a New York Cabaret: Vasco, the Mad Musician[70]
Scene 9
    The Land of Mystery (A Mystery in Black and White)
        Marceline: Himself. *Skeleton*: G. Herman. *The Cat*: T. Colton. *Pierrot*: H. Lambert. *The Gloomy Boys*: T. Pender, B. Smith. *The Joyful Girls*: A. Leach [Cary Grant], J. Notman. *Witches, Paper Dolls, Pajama Girls, Skeletons, Glooms, Joys, Marionettes, Pierrots, Pierrettes, Harlequins, Columbines*: Hippodrome Company.
    "Gloom and Joy"
        H. Lambert, Ensemble
    Finale: "Better Times"
        Entire Hippodrome Ensemble

---

[65]Dropped during subsequent national tour.
[66]Added for subsequent tour:
    "The Educated Whisk Brooms"
        B. Benny, B. Wilson
[67]Dropped during subsequent national tour.

[68]The running order was revised after the opening and throughout the run. Added after opening:
    Grand Entry Hippodrome Clowns (Act 2)
        Marceline, "La La" Herbert "Tiger" Alberto, "Kid" Ravel, "Happy" Ward, "Blinks" Becker, "Hoofer" Russell, "Stove" Byrne, "Side" Byrne, "Hoppie" Byrne, "Limey" Bleasdale, "Curly" Colton, "Rube" Rosaire, "One Round" Lorella, "Scotty" McKay, "Bad News" Stanley, " Twister" Pender, "Alibi" Leach, "Brakebeam" Smith, "Itchum" Post
[69]Replaced during the run by:
    Down on the Farm
        Pogo Girls, Jumping Rope Girls
[70]Dropped after opening.

ACT 2

Scene 1

Orlando and His Wonderful Horses
O. Orlando, Apollo (Her High School Horse)

Grand Entry of Hippodrome Clowns including Marceline and forty others.

Scene 2

Comic Studies in Black and White
Torbay

Scene 3

Long Tack Jams and His Troupe of Chinese Jugglers and Acrobats

Scene 4

"I Dreamt That I Went to the Grand Opera Ball"
H. Lambert, Company
Scene: At the Grand Opera Ball.
Pierrot: H. Lambert. *The Bohemian Girl*: N. Flack. *Scarpia*: R. Brainard. *Carmen*: Gracialita. *Lohengrin*: T. Joyce. *Aida*: M. Hamm. *Gilda*: D. Gates. *Toreador*: R. McClellan. *La Tosca*: S. Edwards. *Radames*: E. Beck. *Santuzza*: P. Rayfield. *Othello*: J. Frohoff. *Mimi*: C. Ivanova. *Mimi's Pals* (4): *Schaunard*: S. Williams. *Rudolph*: M. Evans. *Marcel*: J. Riley. *Colline*: J. Brady. *Madame Butterfly*: A. Rose. *The Child*: E. Downie. *Merry Wives of Windsor* (2): *Mrs. Page*: L. Beautora. *Mrs. Ford*: B. Price. *Mrs. Quickley*: A. Wilson. *Falstaff*: A. Alberto. *Tannhauser*: W. Williams. *Cleopatra*: N. Melville. *Meistersingers* (5): L. Wilmott, R. Gordon, F. Ginnette, A. Leach, J. Burley. *Hoffman*: B. Smith. *Julietta*: E. Rose. *Olympia*: L. Lincoln. *Lucia*: R. Stockdale. *Don Cesar de Bazan*: J. Murphy. *Salome*: M. Morgan. *Desdemona*: V. Futrelle. *Romeo*: F. Johnson. *Figaro*: H. Tamaroff. *The Flying Dutchman*: F. Herbert. *Marguerite*: E. Hansen. *Hamlet*: H. Stevens. *Thais*: H. Ward. *Prince Igor*: W. Holbrook. *Queen of Sheba*: G. Comerford. *Ernani*: A. Byrne. *William Tell*: J. Byrne. *Ophelia*: O. Mihailovhaya. *Martha*: D. Campbell. *Mignon*: M. Skaller. *Samson*: H. Ward. *Zaza*: L. Losch. *Nedda*: F. Blythe. *Tristan*: R. Binder. *Isolde*: M. Waldron. *Siegfried*: G. Kunowitch. *Girl from the Golden West*: B. Ross. *Faust*: F. C. McPherson. *Juliet*: W. Verina. *Don Giovanni*: G. Herman. *Friend of the Don*: T. Pender. *Mephistopheles*: D. Nelson. *Fra Diavolo*: C. Ravel. *Rigoletto*: R. Russell. *Fedora*: L. Hauman. *Natoma*: G. Cranston. *Manon*: R. Matlock. *Parsifal*: A. Lupue. *Don José*: M. Lupue. *Dinorah*: L. Armand. *John Philip Sousa*: T. Colton. *Gatti Gazazza*: J. Byrne. And Others. *The Ladies Jazz Band*: E. Claire, S. Claire, C. Claire, Y. Verlaine, M. Arnold, J. Arnold, B. Arnold.

Scene 5

Favorite Melodies of Bygone Days
Dane—Claudius & Scarlet—Lillian

Scene 6

The Story of a Fan: A Fantasy in Gold and Silver
"Just a Fan"
N. Flack, F. Johnson
(Costumes designed by Robert McQuinn and Cora McGeachy.)
The Lady: V. Futrelle. *The Officer*: F. McPherson. *Grecian Group*: E. Rose, L. Dalton, G. Meylan. *Egyptian Vases*: E. Sparre, S. Stone, Y. Verlaine, M. Skaller. *Golden Statues*: M. DeYoung, L. Hauman, D. Gates, P. Rayfield. *Pierrot*: G. Kunowitch. *Pierrettte*: W. Verina. *Harlequin*: W. Unangst. *Columbine*: R. Matlock. *Watteau Porcelain Group*: W. Holbrook, E. Hansen, N. Melville, M. Morgan, B. Price, R. Stockdale, M. Hamm. *Turkish Group*: M. Lapue, L. Armond. *Spanish Group*: Gracialita. *Russian Group*: A. Lapue, D. Berke. *Hungarian Group*: H. Tamaroff, Myrtle. *Japanese Group*: A. Sorriero, M. Sawyer. *Louis XIV Group*: R. Braianrd, S. Edwards, R. McClellan, G. Comerford, J. Murphy, C. Ivanova, F. Joyce, G. Cranston, H. Stevens, L. Lincoln, J. Frohoff, Gracialita, W. Williams, O. Mihailovakaya, D. Nelson. *Hippodrome Flying Ballet*: G. Schram, H. Barion, F. Baumler, W. Warren, E. Clark.

ACT 3

Scene 1

"Summertime"
R. McClellan, 24 Flappers
Scene: The Fat Man's Fair.
Canoe Girls: M. Mack, B. Gilmore. *The Fisherman*: Marceline. *Boatmen*: L. Post, H. Ward. *Police Inspector*: J. Byrne. *Policemen*: W. Unangst, A. Alberto, C. Lorella. *The Rubes*: J. Burley, A. Seabert, H. Abdullah, N. Provanzo. *Owners of Striking Machine*: J. Riley, C. Ravel. *Balloon Seller*: Creco. *Ma*: Mrs. Berlo. And the Hippodrome Diving Girls (where do they go?), The Bell Brothers.

Fancy Diving
The Berlo Sisters

Scene 2

Ballet of the Water Nymphs

Entrance of the Water Guards

"My Golden Dream Ship"
N. Flack

Grand Finale
Entire Hippodrome Ensemble
Scene: The Harbor of Prosperity.

1922.31 ## SALLY, IRENE AND MARY

A Musical Comedy in Two Acts, 9 Scenes. Book by Eddie Dowling and Cyrus Wood. Music by J. Fred Coots. Lyrics by Raymond Klages. Staged by Frank Smithson. Musical numbers staged by Allan K. Foster. Costumes by Vanity Fair Costume Company and Paul Arlington, Inc.; men's costumes by Ford Uniform Company. Scenery by the United Scenic Studios. Orchestra under the direction of Claude MacArthur. Entire production under the personal supervision of J. J. Shubert. Produced by the Messrs. Shubert. Opened 4 September 1922 at the Casino Theatre, moved 5 February 1923 to the 44th Street Theatre, moved 23 April 1923 to the Century Theatre, and closed 2 June 1923 after 313 performances.

CAST: *Jimmie Dugan*: EDDIE DOWLING. *Mrs. Dugan*, his mother: JOSIE INTROPODI. *Mary O'Brien*, his girl: EDNA MORN. *Mrs. O'Brien*, her mother: Maude Odell. *Sally*, friend of Mary: JEAN BROWN[71]. *Mrs. Clancy*, her mother: Clara Palmer. *Irene*, another friend of Mary: KITTY FLYNN. *Rodman Jones*, an aristocrat: Hal Van Rensselaer. *Mrs. Jones*, his mother: Winifred Harris. *Clarence Edwards*, a boy around town: ALFRED GERRARD. *Mr. Myers*, a theatrical manager: Joseph Clark. *Percy Fitzgerald*, friend of Clarence: BURFORD HAMPDEN. *Al Cleveland*, an author: Stanley Forde. *Sully*, stage door man: D. J. SULLIVAN. *Tony*: D. J. Sullivan. *Mr. Mulcahey*, of the neighborhood: Eddie O'Connor. *Dinty Moore*, pal of Jimmie: Gene Collins. *Frank*, night watchman: William Mason. *First Dresser to Girls*: Henrietta Byron. *Second Dresser to Girls*: Louise Arnold. *Detective of Hotel Astor*: Frank Binns. *Carriage Man*, Hotel Astor: Fred Packard. *Kitty Kelly*, East Side girl: Helen Heller. *Mabel Riley*, her friend: Mabel Kokin. *Tommy*, East Side boy: Bonna O'Dear. *Nellie Smith*, his girl: Mary Corday. *Mrs. Pomeroy Gilbert*: Bonna O'Dear. *Mrs. Kelly Pool*: Henrietta Byron. *Mrs. Fitzgibbons Conroy*: Louise Arnold. *Mrs. Carter Smith*: Helen Heller. *Mrs. de la Croix*: Mabel Kokin. *Mrs. Fitzroy*: Genise Corday.

Ladies of the Ensemble: Tiny Collins, Florence Field, Sonia Field, Milla Bay, Jean Danjou, Hazel Vernon, Gene Geberhart, Malvern Charles, Nora Francis, Alice Monroe, Guenevere Moore, Lillian Dunning, Sherry Gale, Kitty Leckie. *Gentlemen of the Ensemble*: Lovette Wilder, Richard Opler, Frank Binns, Ainsley Lambert, George Barnum, Fred Packard, James Miller.

Act 1, Scene 1: Tenement on the East Side, New York. *Scene 2*: Kitchen of the Dugan Home. Four years later. *Scene 3*: Stage Doors of the Knickerbocker, New Amsterdam and Vanderbilt Theatres. *Scene 4*: Mary's Dressing Room at the Knickerbocker Theatre. *Scene 5*: Dance of the ballet on the New Amsterdam Stage.

Act 2, Scene 1: Peacock Alley, Hotel Astor, New York. *Scene 2*: Charity Bazaar, Park Avenue. *Scene 3*: On the fire escape of the Dugan home. *Scene 4*: Wedding at Little Church Around the Corner.

ACT 1

Scene 1

"Kid Days" (Opening Chorus)
Ensemble

Song
E. Dowling, Dancing Girls

Dance[72]
M. Kokin

"Time Will Tell"
E. Dowling, E. Morn, Dancing Girls

Scene 2

"Pals"
E. Dowling

Scene 3

"Stage Door Johnnies"
B. Hampden, A. Gerrard, K. Flynn, 8 Dancing Girls, 8 Dancing Boys

"I Wonder Why"
E. Morn, Boys and Girls of Ensemble

"Do You Remember?"
D. J. Sullivan, W. Mason, H. Byron, L. Arnold, Ensemble

"How I've Missed You Mary"
E. Dowling, E. Morn

---

[71]Later billed as LOUISE BROWN.
[72]Dropped after opening.

Scene 4

"Right Boy Comes Along"
E. Morn, Eight Dancing Boys

"Our Home Sweet Home"[73]
E. Morn

Scene 5

Dance of the Ballet
J. Brown, 16 Ballet Girls

ACT 2

Scene 1

"Peacock Alley" (Opening Ensemble)
Ensemble

"Something in Here"[74]
B. Hampden, J. Brown

"Opportunity"
K. Flynn, A. Gerrard, Dancing Girls

"We Are Waiting"
D. J. Sullivan, Boys

Scene 2

"Clouds Roll By" (Dance)
J. Brown

"Until You Say Yes"[75]
H. Van Rensselaer, E. Morn

Scene 3

"Time Will Tell"
E. Dowling

Scene 4

"Wedding Time"
E. Dowling, E. Morn, B. Hampden, K. Flynn, A. Gerrard, J. Brown, Wedding Couples of Ensemble

Finale

Entire Company

THE GREENWICH VILLAGE FOLLIES (1922)

1922.32

A Musical Revusical Comedy (Revue) in Two Acts, 21 Scenes[76]. Book (sketches) by George V. Hobart. Music by Louis A. Hirsch. Lyrics by John Murray Anderson and Irving Caesar. Entire production devised and staged by John Murray Anderson. Ballets and incidental dances arranged by Carl Randall, Alexander Yakovleff. Costumes by Mrs. Ingeborg Hansell, Howard Greer, Erté, Earle Payne Franke, E. Amies, Georgianna Brown, Alice O'Neil, Brooks Uniform Company. Settings by Howard Greer, Mrs. Ingeborg Hansell, Cleon Throckmorton, Blanding Sloan, Alice O'Neil. Orchestra under the direction of Alfred Newman. Produced by The Bohemians, Inc. (A. L. Jones, Morris Green, managing directors) (Messrs. Shubert). Opened 12 September 1922 at the Sam S. Shubert Theatre and closed 10 March 1923 after 209 performances.

CAST: JOHN E. HAZZARD, LUCILLE CHALFANT, BERT SAVOY, JAY BRENNAN, FRANKIE HEATH, MARORIE PETERSON, CARL RANDALL, JULIA SILVERS, GEORGE RASELY, YVONNE GEORGE, JOHN SHEEHAN, HARRIETTE GIMBEL, ALEXANDER YAKOVLEFF, AZEADA, RUTH CONLEY, ULA SHARON, GRACE KAY WHITE, GEORGE CHRISTIE, JOSEPHINE MacNICOL, DINARZADE, GEORGE CLIFFORD, HELEN MacDONALD, PAUL K. HERBERT, DOROTHY ARNOLD, AMUND SJOVIK, Fortunello and Cirillano.

Ensemble: Eugenia Repelsky, Madge North, Della Vanna, Doris Green, Lucila Mendez, Alice Weaver, Virginia Roche, Cricket, Mollie Doherty, Edythe Nedd, Jeanne LaMonte, Linn Van Voorhees, Michel Sciapiro, Alice Weaver, Stella Wooten, Marguerite Young, Elsie Bartlett, Tarzanne, Louis and Frieda Berkoff.

ACT 1[77]

Scene 1

The Village Workshop

---

[73]Dropped for subsequent national tour.
[74]Replaced during subsequent tour by:
Tango Number
B. Hampden, Louise Brown [Mary]
[75]Dropped after opening.
[76]The fourth annual revue in the series which began in 1919.
[77]The running order was revised after the opening.

The Sculptor: G. Rasely. *The Wardrobe Mistress*: G. K. White. *The Property Man*: J. Sheehan. *A Lonely Romeo*: C. Randall. *A Village Milliner*: J. Silvers. *A Village Designer*: J. MacNicol. *The Village Model of 1922*: Dinarzade. *The Pearl Stringers*: Azeada, D. Green. *The Rose Girls*: L. Mendez, R. Conley. *The Girl with the Shoes*: E. Repelsky. *The Scene Painters and Magicians*: A. Weaver, V. Roche, Cricket, H. McDonald, M. Doherty, E. Nedd. *The Bohemians*: A. Sjovik, P. K. Herbert, O. Herbert, G. Clifford.

"Beautiful Girls"
C. Randall
(*Music by* Harry Ruby. *Lyrics by* Bert Kalmar.)
The Magic Cabinet Girls: Tarzanne, D. Vanna, D. Arnold, R. Hall, M. Palmer, E. Bartlett, L. Van Voorhees, M. Young, M. North. *A Lonely Juliet*: M. Peterson.

Scene 2

"The Nightingale and the Rose"
(*Adapted by* John Murray Anderson from the story of Oscar Wilde. *Music arranged by* Alfred Newman.)
The Singer: L. Chalfant. *The Story Teller*: G. Christie. *TheStudent*: A. Yakovleff. *The Coquette*: M. Peterson. *The Prince*: P. K. Herbert. *The Marchioness*: J. LaMonte. *The Hussar*: A. Sjovik. *The Countess*: D. Arnold. *The Duchess*: Dinarzade. *The Lady-in-Waiting*: E. Repelsky. *The Nightingale*: U. Sharon.

Scene 3

They Never Do (*by* George V. Hobart)
Scene: At Home.
The Wife: F. Heath. *The Husband*: J. E. Hazzard. *The Mother-in-Law*: G. K. Whhite. *The Brother*: G. Christie. *The Man Next Door*: J. Sheehan.

Scene 4

"Cinderella Blues"
C. Randall, Ensemble

Scene 5

The Village Siren (*by* William K. Wells)
The Siren: B. Savoy. *The Brother of One of Her Victims*: J. Brennan.

Scene 6

In Front of the Portal
F. Heath

Scene 7

The Rain-Beau: "You Are My Rain-Beau"
J. Silvers, G. Rasely
The North Wind: Azeada. *The West Wind*: R. Conley. *The East Wind*: L. Mendez. *The South Wind*: D. Green. *The Beaux*: A. Sjovik, P. K. Herbert, G. Clifford, O. Herbert. *The Sun*: J. MacNichol. *The Colors of the Rainbow*: H. MacDonald, A. Weaver, Cricket, E. Nedd, V. Roche, M. Doherty. *The Fair Weather Ladye*: E. Repelsky. *Her Rain-Beau*: M. Peterson.

Scene 8

"Antes de la Corrida Del Toro"
Danced by C. Randall. *The Singer at the Window*: M. North. *The Passers-By*: J. LaMonte, D. Arnold, L. Van Voorhees.

Scene 9

Futility[78] (*by* George V. Hobart, with humble apologies to Eugene O'Neil)
Winifred Fevversbeater: F. Heath. *Hector Fevversbeater*, her husband: J. Brennan. *Gramama Fevversbeater*: G. K. White. *Grandfather Fevversbeater*: P. E. Herbert. *The Undertaker*: J. E. Hazzard. *The Butler*: J. Sheehan. *The Cook*: B. Savoy.

Scene 10

"A Kiss from a Red-Headed Miss"
H. Gimbel
A Dancer: G. Clifford.

Scene 11

The Happy Hooligans
Fortunello and Cirillino

Scene 12

"Beethoven's Sonata" (posed after the well-known mezzo-tint)
The Singers: L. Chalfant, G. Rasely, O. Herbert, A. Sjovik, P. K. Herbert. *The Violinist*: M. Sciapiro. *The Pianist*: A. Newman.

Scene 13

"Sixty Seconds Ev'ry Minute (I Think of You)"
C. Randall, M. Peterson

---

[78]Replaced for subsequent national tour by:
Life Among the Advertisements (*by* George S. Kaufman)
The Father: J. E. Hazzard. *The Mother*: G. K. White. *Glastenbury*: G. Christie. *Edna*: F. Heath. *Mr. Warwick*: Roger Davis. *The Lover*: J. Sheehan.

Scene 14

The Village 'Box of Tricks'

(Incidental music arranged by Alfred Newman from the music of Rossini and others.)

The Old Shopkeeper: O. Herbert. *The Shopkeeper's Assistant*: C. Randall. *The Shopkeeper's Daughter*: M. Peterson. *The Knickerbocker Mother*: D. Arnold. *The Knickerbocker Father*: A. Sjovik. *The Knickerbocker Child*: E. Repelsky. *The Quaker Mother*: Dinarzade. *The Quaker Father*: P. K. Herbert. *The Quaker Child*: H. Gimbel. *The Sailor Doll*: G. Clifford. *The Spanish Doll*: L. Mendez. *The English Doll*: D. Green. *The Japanese Doll*: Azeada. *The French Doll*: R. Conley. *The Little Darkey Dolls*: A. Weaver, S. Wooten. *The Queen of Hearts*: D. Vanna. *The Queen of Diamonds*: J. LaMonte. *The Queen of Clubs*: E. Bartlett. *The Queen of Spades*: L. Van Voorhees. *The Russian Dolls*: L. Berkoff, F. Berkoff. *The Swedish Dolls*: G. K. White, M. Young, R. Hall, M. Palmer. *The Yarn Dolls*: V. Roche, M. Doherty, E. Nedd, H. MacDonald. *The Drummer*: "Traps." *Harlequin*: A. Yakovleff. *Columbine*: U. Sharon.

ACT 2[79]

Scene 1

a) "Batty" (A Chauve-Souris of Our Own)

F. Heath, Ensemble

(*Music and Lyrics by* Irving Caesar.)

The Director: A. Sjovik. *Katinka*: J. MacNicol.

b) Petroushka

Balieff: J. Sheehan. *The Peasant*: A. Yakovleff. *His Wife*: U. Sharon.

c) Yvonne George (Song Specialty)

Scene 2

Babes in the (A.H.) Woods

Himself: C. Randall. *His Wife*: H. MacDonald. *His Valet*: G. Clifford.

Scene 3

"Sweetheart Lane"

G. Rasely, J. Silvers

Scene: Washington Square.

The Girl at the Wishing Well: M. North. *The LittleGirl*: M. Peterson. *The Village Belle*: J. MacNicol. *The Sweethearts*: A. Sjovik, G. K. White, P. K. Herbert, D. Vanna, O. Herbert, E. Bartlett, G. Clifford, M. Young. *The Little Boy on the Fence*: H. Gimbel.

Scene 4

In Front of the Portal

B. Savoy, J. Brennan

Scene 5

The Animal Cage

The Trainer: A. Yakovleff. *And Corps de ballet.*

Scene 6

The Old Timers

a) When Songs Were Songs and Stars Were Really Stars

The Old Timer: J. Sheehan.

b) At Castle Garden

"Jenny Lind"

G. Rasely

(*Music by* Louis Hirsch. *Lyrics by* Irving Caesar.)

A Gentleman of the Period: G. Rasely. *Jenny Lind*: L. Chalfant.

c) The Hoffman House

The Widow Brown: B. Savoy. *The Sporty Widows*: D. Vanna, Tarzanne, D. Green, M. Young, G. K. White, Dinarzade, J. LaMonte, D. Arnold, M. Palmer, R. Hall, E. Bartlett, L. Van Voorhees.

d) The Bowery

A Dancer: C. Randall. *His Best Girl*: A. Weaver.

e) *Adeline Genée*: U. Sharon.

f) "Goodbye to Dear Old Alaska"

J. E. Hazzard

Scene 7

The Nights: "Greenwich Village Nights"

C. Randall

a) "Havana Nights"

J. Silvers

With D. Arnold, L. Van Voorhees, E. Bartlett, J. LaMonte.

b) "Vienna Nights"

L. Chalfant

With R. Conley, L. Mendez, H. MacDonald, Azeada.

c) "Manhattan Nights"

F. Heath

With A. Sjovik, O. Herbert, P. K. Herbert, G. Clifford.

d) "Parisian Nights"

Y. George

And *Erté Models (4)*: *The Peacock*: M. Palmer. *The Canary*: E. Bartlett. *The Riviera*: D. Vanna. *The Lover's Net*: Dinarzade. *The Greer Models (5)*: *The Caterpillar*: R. Hall. *The Silver Shadow*: G. K. White. *The Passion Flower*: Tarzanne. *The Cloak of Summer*: D. Green, M. Young. *The Spider's Web*: L. Van Voorhees. *Grisettes*: A. Weaver, Cricket, E. Nedd, M. Doherty, V. Roche, E. Repelsky.

e) "Greenwich Village Nights" (reprise)

B. Savoy, J. Brennan

Resume: The End

Romeo: J. E. Hazzard. *Juliet*: F. Heath. *Hamlet*: G. Christie. *Ophelia*: G. K. White. *Shylock*: J. Sheehan. *The Ghost*: R. Davis. *Shakespeare*: Charles Mantia.

1922.33 # ORANGE BLOSSOMS

A Comedy with Music in Three Acts. Book by Fred de Grésac[80]. based on the play 'La Passerelle.'[81] by Fred deGresac and François de Croisset. Music by Victor Herbert. Lyrics by Buddy G. DeSylva. Staged by Edward Royce. Scenery designed by Norman Bel Geddes. Ladies' costumes designed by Paul Poiret; gentlemen's costumes designed by Earl Benham. Orchestra under the direction of Gus Salzer. Produced by Edward Royce. Opened 19 September 1922 at the Fulton Theatre and closed 9 December 1922 after 95 performances.

CAST (in order of appearance): *Lawyer Brassac*: PAT SOMERSET. *Tillie*: QUEE-NIE SMITH. *Octave*: Maurice Darcy. *Baron Roger Belmont*: ROBERT MICHAELIS. *Kitty*: EDITH DAY. *Jimmy Flynn*: HAL SKELLEY. *Helene de Vasquez*: Phyllis LeGrand. *Auguste*: Robert Fischer. *Ninetta*: NANCY WELFORD.

Bressac's Clients: *Cecilia Malba*: Evelyn Darville. *Christiane de Mirandol*: Alta King. *Julie Bresil*: Dagmar Oakland. *Yolande DuPont*: Emily Drange. *Paulette de Trevors*: Fay Evelyn. *Simone Garrick*: Diana Stegman. *Regina Marnac*: Eden Gray. *Valentina Vendome*: Vera de Wolfe.

Gentlemen in the Case: Thomas Fitzpatrick, Abner Barnhart, Frank Curran, Jack Whiting, Oliver Stewart, Gayle Mays. Denny Murray, Clinton Merrill.

Dancers: QUEENIE SMITH, Elva Pomfret, NANCY WELFORD, Mary Lucas.

Act 1: Lawyer's Office, Paris.

Act 2: Kitty's Villa at Cannes.

Act 3: Garden of Kitty's Villa at Cannes.

ACT 1

Opening

P. Somerset, Ladies

"This Time It's Love"

R. Michaelis

"A Kiss in the Dark"

E. Day

"New York Is the Same Old Place"

H. Skelley, Q. Smith

"Then Comes the Dawning"[82]

R. Michaelis, P. LeGrand

"I Can't Argue with You"[83]

R. Michaelis, P. LeGrand, P. Somerset, E. Darville

"In Hennequeville"

E. Day

Finale: "A Kiss in the Dark" (reprise)

E. Day

ACT 2

"On the Riviera"

Ladies, Gentlemen (of the Ensemble)

"The Lonely Nest"

E. Day

"I Missed You"

E. Day, R. Michaelis, P. Somerset, N. Welford

---

[79]Added to Act 2 for subsequent national tour:

Juliet and Romeo, or The Hamlet of Venice (*by* Edith S. Isaacs and Anita Rice)

[80]Fréderique de Grésac was Mrs. Victor Maurel.

[81]Adapted into English by Cosmo Gordon-Lennox and produced in New York and London as 'The Marriage of Kitty.'

[82]Dropped late in the run.

[83]Dropped for subsequent tour.

"Just Like That"[84]
    H. Skelley, N. Welford
"Orange Blossoms"
    E. Day, Gentlemen
Finale
    Entire Company
ACT 3[85]
"Mosquito Ballet"
"Way Out West in Jersey"
    H. Skelley, Q. Smith
"Let's Not Get Married"
    Ladies, Gentlemen (of the Ensemble)
"This Time It's Love" (reprise)
    R. Michaelis
Finale
    Entire Company

1922.34   THE PASSING SHOW OF 1922

A Musical Revue in Two Acts, 26 Scenes[86]. Book (sketches) and lyrics by Harold Atteridge. Music by Alfred Goodman. Additional lyrics by Jack Stanley. Staged by J. C. Huffman. Musical numbers staged by Allan K. Foster. Art director, Watson Barratt. Settings designed by Watson Barratt, Rollo Wayne. Costumes designed by Ernest R. Schrapps, Erté. Orchestra under the direction of Alfred Goodman. Entire production supervised by J. J. Shubert. Produced by Messrs. Lee and J. J. Shubert. Opened 20 September 1922 at the Winter Garden and closed 2 December 1922 after 85 performances.

CAST: WILLIE HOWARD, EUGENE HOWARD, Mlle. ALCORN, GEORGE HASSELL, FRANCIS RENAULT, ETHEL SHUTTA, JANET ADAIR, SAM ASH, FOOSHEE SISTERS, FRED ALLEN, THE LOCKFORDS, NAT NAZARRO, JR., THE MACKWEYS, ARTHUR MARGETSON, GERTRUDE (Jessie) LANG, FRED WALTON, GEORGE ANDERSON, NELLIE BREEN, ALMA ADAIR, THE LOCKFORDS (Naro, Zita), MARY LAWLOR, M. T. Bohannon, William Brand, Jack Kearns, Alexander Frank, Wilbur DeRouge, Gilbert Barr, Joseph Riley, Emily Miles, Alfred Gilday, Dorothy Bruce.
Ladies of the Ensemble: Helen Fox, Louise Wayne, Elsie May, Phyllis Reynolds, Charlotte Schuette, Peggy Bond, Beatrice O'Brien, Edna Starck, Ethel Walker, Betty Fitch, Edith Pearce, Monica Boulais, Phyllis Miller, Nan Henderson, Gladys Hall, Helen Christie, Mary Breau, Portland Hoffa, Pauline Dakla, Beulah Reubens, Virginia Wilson, Florence Darling, Florence Summerville, Helen O'Brien, Madeline Smith, Dorothy Daniels, Dolores Edwards, Louise Starck, Grace Shea, Sidney Nelson, Marion Mooney, Belle McLaughlin, Orilla Smith, Rose Lee, Maxine Sickle, Jean Thomas, Olive Brown, Helen Rogers, Carol Miller, Beatrice Wilson, Sidney Shaar, Margie Himes, Mae Sullivan, Lousie Cross, Katherine Saxe, Rose Gallagher, Helen Herendeen, Helen Wright, Florence Wilde, Elsie Frank, Billie Wagner, Bobbie Boles, Agnes Hall, Mollie Christie, Bert Best, Maybell Olson, Grace Rossiter, Louise Winn.

ACT 1[87]

Scene 1[88]
    The International Circus
      Clown: S. Ash. *Lloyd George*: F. Walton. *India*: H. Herendeen. *Irish Free State*: N. Henderson. *Irish Republic*: O. Smith. *American Ambassador*: M. T. Bohannon. *Japan*: W. Brand. *Trotsky*: J. Kearns. *Germany*: A. Frank. *Servant*: W. DeRouge. *Prince of Wales*: N. Nazarro, Jr. *Uncle Sam*: G. Anderson.
      (*Setting designed by* Watson Barratt.)
    "The Passing Show"
      A. Adair
    "Circus Days"
      E. Shutta, N. Nazarro, Jr.
    The Mackweys
Scene 2
    Before the Curtain
      Announcer: F. Allen. *Horace*: W. DeRouge.
Scene 3
    The Sudden Death of a Horse[89]
      The Gentleman: S. Ash. *The Lady*: J. Adair. *The Husband*: G. Anderson. *The Driver*: G. Hassell. *The Horse*: G. Barr. *A Horse*: J. Riley.
Scene 4
    Futuristic: "A Study in Black and White"
      N. Breen, Futuristic Girls
Scene 5
    A Lesson in Etiquette
    "(My) Coal Black Mammy"[90] (from THE CO-OPTIMISTS)
      W. Howard, E. Howard
      (*Music by* Ivy St. Helieu. *Lyrics by* Laddie Cliff.)
      Scene: A Restaurant.
      Jean: E. Howard. *Sammy*: W. Howard. *A Lady*: E. Miles. *The Bride*: A. Adair. *Waiter*: W. DeRouge. *The Husband*: G. Anderson.
Scene 6
    Speaking of Kisses
    "I Came! I Saw! I Fell!"
      S. Ash, G. Lang, Kiss Girls
      The First Man: A. Margetson. *The Second Man*: S. Ash.
Scene 7
    "The Prince of Wales"
      N. Nazarro, Jr., Some Prince Girls
      Prince: N. Nazarro, Jr.
Scene 8
    The Mystery
      A Butler: A. Frank. *Bull Dog Drummond*: G. Anderson. *Sap*: G. Hassell. *The Man on the Telephone*: W. Brand. *The Lady of the Yellow Chrysanthemum*: J. Adair. *The Doctor*: F. Walton. *The Hindu*: A. Gilday. *A Guard*: W. DeRouge.
      (*Setting designed by* Rollo Wayne.)
Scene 9
    "Orphants of the Storm"[91] (Orphans of the Storm)
      Two Orphants: Fooshee Sisters.

---

[84]Replaced during the run by:
    "How Can I Win You Now?"
      H. Skelley, N. Welford
[85]Act 3 was wholly revised for the subsequent tour, whose running order was:
    Dance Mosquito
    "Why Do We Love Them?"
      N. Welford
    "Every Girl is Like a Weather Glass"
      R. Michaelis, Ladies, Gentlemen
    "Way Out West in Jersey"
      H. Skelley, Q. Smith
    Finale
      Entire Company
[86]The eleventh in the annual series of revues begun in 1894 and presented by the Messrs. Shubert since 1912.
[87]The running order was revised after the opening. Added for subsequent tour:
    Lightning: An Impression of Lightning Bill Jones (Act 1)
      W. Howard

[88]Willie and Eugene Howard changed their specialties during the run. According to published sheet music they also included:
    "Sonja" (Russian ballade)
      W. Howard, E. Howard
      (*Music by* Eugen Pártos. *Original Lyrics by* Beda. *Special Lyrics by* Al Wilson and James A. Brennan.)
    "Wanita (Wanna Eat? Wanna Eat?)"
      W. Howard, E. Howard
      (*Music and Lyrics by* Sam Coslow and Al Sherman.)
    "I Love Me (I'm Wild About Myself)"
      W. Howard, E. Howard
      (*Music by* Edwin J. Weber. *Lyrics by* Jack Hoins, Will Mahoney.)
    "Do You, Don't You, Will You, Won't You"
      W. Howard, E. Howard
      (*Music and Lyrics by* Willie Howard, Eugene Howard, George A. Little, Larry Schaetzlein.)
[89]Dropped for subsequent tour.
[90]Replaced for subsequent tour by:
    "Underneath the Palms"
      W. Howard, E. Howard
[91]Dropped for subsequent tour.

Scene 10

At Camps: "Camps Daily Dozen"
Winter Garden Athletic Girls
(*Setting designed by* Watson Barratt.)

Scene 11

Two Merchants[92]
David Warfield: W. Howard. *Barney Bernard*: E. Howard.

Scene 12

A Diamond Girl
"My Diamond Girls" (Diamond Girl)
F. Renault, S. Ash, Mlle. Alcorn
(*Setting designed by* Watson Barratt.)
The Singer: S. Ash. *The Kaffir*: F. Walton. *The Diamond Girl*: Mlle. Alcorn. *A Brilliant*: D. Bruce. *Another*: F. Renault.

Scene 13

The Old Joke Cemetery
F. Allen

Scene 14

The Hairy Ape (Burlesque)
"Eugene O'Neill's Hairy Ape"
E. Shutta, Some Winter Garden Dancers
Miss Don't Stop: E. Shutta.
(*Setting designed by* Rollo Wayne.)

Scene 15

In a Phonograph Shop: "Carolina (in the Morning)"
W. Howard, E. Howard
(*Music by* Walter Donaldson. *Lyrics by* Gus Kahn.)
Sammy: W. Howard. *Jean*: E. Howard. *A Lady Customer*: E. Miles. *Another Lady*: J. Adair.

Scene 16

Ballet Les Conquerants
"Love of Long Ago"
S. Ash, A. Adair
The Slave: F. Renault. *The Queen*: Mlle. Alcorn. *The Guard*: F. Walton. *The Minstrel*: S. Ash. *The Singer*: A. Adair. *Gladiators, Soldiers, Guards, Court Attendants*: (Company).
(*Setting designed by* Rollo Wayne.)

ACT 2

Scene 1

In Gold: "A Ballet of Siam"
The Lockfords

Scene 2

A Bit of the Orient
King Coriolanus: G. Anderson. *Fatima*: E. Miles. *Zobeide*: H. Fox. *Bul Bul*: B. Fitch. *Yossof*: A. Frank. *Tonsilitis*: W. Howard. *Abdullah*: E. Howard.
(*Setting designed by* Rollo Wayne.)

Scene 3

"Eleanor"
A. Adair, Winter Garden Beauties

Scene 4

"Pour J'en-Ai-Marre"
J. Adair
Scene: Railroad Tunnel on the Outskirts of Paris.
(*Setting designed by* Watson Barratt.)
Armand: A. Margetson. *Louis*: G. Hassell. *Mimi*: J. Adair. *The Watchman*: G. Anderson.

Scene 5

Fred Allen

Scene 6

The Radium Girl: "Radiance"
S. Ash, G. Lang, Radium Girls
(*Lyrics by* Jack Stanley.)
The Man: S. Ash. *The Maid*: G. Lang.
(*Setting designed by* Ernest R. Schrapps.)

Scene 7

Apache Dance
The Lockfords

Scene 8

In a Pullman Car
Mr. A: G. Anderson. *Mr. B*: G. Hassell. *The Girl in the Upper Berth*: L. Wayne. *A Lady*: H. Fox. *Porter*: W. DeRouge. *Mr. A*: J. Kearns. *Mr. B*: M. T. Bohannon. *Mr. X*: A. Frank. *Mr. Y*: F. Walton.

Scene 9

The Street Singers: "In Italy" (Burlesque Aria)
W. Howard, E. Howard
Sammy: W. Howard. *Jean*: E. Howard.

Scene 10

The Riviera: "American Jazz"
N. Nazarro, Jr., E. Shutta, American Jazzers
(*Setting designed by* Watson Barratt.)
Junior: N. Nazarro, Jr. *Ethel*: E. Shutta. *The Sisters*: Fooshee Sisters. *Mary*: M. Lawlor. *Nellie*: N. Breen. And Entire Ensemble.

1922.35   # THE YANKEE PRINCESS

A Musical Comedy in Three Acts. Book by William LeBaron, adapted from the Viennese operette 'Die Bajadere' by Julius Brammer and Alfred Grünwald. Music by Emmerich Kálmán. Lyrics by Buddy G. DeSylva. Staged by Fred G. Latham and Julian Mitchell. Scenery by Joseph Urban. Costume design by Wilhelm. Electrical effects by Tony Greshoff. Orchestra under the direction of William Daly. Produced by Abraham L. Erlanger. Opened 2 October 1922 at the Knickerbocker Theatre and closed 9 December 1922 after 80 performances.

CAST: *Prince Radjami of Lahore*: THORPE BATES. *Napoleon St. Cloche*: John T. Murray. *Phillipe La Tourette*: ROLAND BOTTOMLEY. *Manager Trebizonde*: Royal Tracy. *Pimprinette, Chief of Claque*: FRANK DOANE. *Colonel Parker*, British Resident at Lahore: George Grahame. *Dewa Singh*: Lionel Chalmers. *The Rajah of Punjab*: Mortimer White. *Reggie*: Colin Campbell. *Chief Usher*: Valentine Winter. *Odette Darimonde*: VIVIENNE SEGAL. *Marietta*, wife of Phillipe: VIVIAN OAKLAND. *Fifi*: Ruth Lee. *Marie*: Belle Miller. *Yvette*: Elsie Decker. *Princess Odys*: Jane Carrol. *Princess Rao*: Margaret Morris. *Princess Attha*: Violet Vale. *Princess Lydana*: Kathleen Errol. *Princess Ranja*: Evelyn Plumador. *Princess Sita*: Frisco DeVere. *Princess Rita*: Louise Joyce. *Indian Dancer*: PRINCESS WHITE DEER.

Ladies of the Ensemble: Charlotte Sprague, Carmen Larne, Ann Powers, Dolores Suarez, Elizabeth Coyle, Niada Kasanova, Marian Elliott, Alice Brady, Bert Alden, Dorothy Caldwell, Loretta Duffy, Winifred Duffy, Flo Clarke, Berta Savage, Agnes Allen, Sylvia Carrol, Ethelyn Earle, Nida Snow, Criss Joss, Helen Miller. *Gentlemen of the Ensemble*: Eugene Costello, Irving Finn, H. J. Wilson, Frank Hall, George Leroy, Phillip Wilcox, Russel Griswold, Paul Porter, Joseph Blair, George McCormick, Charles Frome.

Time: The Present.

Act 1: Foyer of the Chatelet Theatre, Paris.

Act 2: Palace of Prince Radjami, Paris. The same evening.

Act 3: The Directoire Club, Paris. Three months later.

ACT 1

"Lotus Flower" (Opening Chorus)
Misses Lee, Miller, Decker
"My Bajadere"
V. Segal, T. Bates, Ensemble
Entrance of Odette
Ensemble, F. Doane
"Stars of the Stage"
V. Segal
"Roses, Lovely Roses" (Duet)
V. Segal, T. Bates
"In the Starlight" (Duet and Ensemble)
V. Oakland, J. T. Murray, Ensemble
Finale

ACT 2

Opening
Ensemble
Dance
Misses Morris, Vale, Errol, Plumador, DeVere, Joyce
Dance[93]
Princess White Deer

----

[92]Dropped for subsequent tour.

[93]Dropped during the run.

"I'll Dance My Way into Your Heart" (Duet)
  V. Oakland, J. T. Murray
"I Still Can Dream" (Duet)
  V. Segal, T. Bates
"A Husband's Only a Husband" (Song)
  F. Diane, Ensemble
"Friendship" (Trio)
  V. Oakland, J. T. Murray, R. Bottomley
"Eyes So Dark and Luring" (Duet)
  V. Segal, T. Bates
Finale

ACT 3
Opening—Dance
  Princess White Deer
"Forbidden Fruit"[94] (Duet)
  V. Oakland, R. Bottomley
"Can It Be That I'm in Love"[95]
  V. Segal, Ensemble
"My Bajadere" (reprise)
  T. Bates
"Love the Wife of Your Neighbor" (Trio)
  V. Oakland, J. T. Murray, R. Bottomley
Finale

THE LADY IN ERMINE

1922.36

A Musical Play in Three Acts. Book by Frederick Lonsdale and Cyrus Wood. Adapted from the German operette ('Die Frau im Hermelin') by Rudolf Schanzer and Ernst Welisch. Music by Jean Gilbert and Alfred Goodman. Lyrics by Harry Graham and Cyrus Wood. Play staged by Charles Sinclair. Dances arranged by Jack Mason. Ballet by Allan K. Foster. Stage settings by Watson Barratt. Principal's gowns by Yvonne Routon. Orchestra under the direction of Oscar Bradley. Entire production under the personal direction of J. J. Shubert. Produced by the Messrs. Shubert. Opened 2 October 1922 at the Ambassador Theatre, moved 29 January 1923 to the Century Theatre, and closed 21 April 1923 after 238 performances.

CAST: *Colonel Belovar*: WALTER WOOLF. *Count Adrian Baltrami*: Henry Fender. *Baron Sprotti-Sprotti*: IGNACIO MARTINETTI. *Count Isolani*: Robert Calley. *Major Stogan*: Timothy Daley. *Dostal*: Detmar Poppen. *Count Busoni*: Neil Evans. *Mirko*, an orderly: Murray Minehart. *Suitangi*, a silhouette cutter: ROBERT WOOLSEY. *Sophia Lavalle*, a ballet dancer: Marie Burke. *Rosina*, maid to Mariana: HELEN SHIPMAN. *Angelina*, sweetheart of Adrian: Gladys Walton. *Mariana*, Adrian's sister: WILDA BENNETT. (*Dance Specialties*: Zita Lockford, [Isabelle] Rodriguez.)
  Ballet Girls: Wilma Ansell, Marjorie Lane, Marie Joyce, Virginia Ice, Estelle Mason, Alice Mack, Dorothy Lubow, Jeanne Jurad, June Stone, Anna Gordon, Ruby Poe, Sabina Loeb, Gladys Bryant, Emily Slater, Lola Fellegi, Irene Comer. *Show Girls*: Nan Rainsford, Paula Tully, Peggy Radford, Zella Lenney, Gladys Montgomery, Viola Ford, Louise Lancaster, Teddy Piper, Irene Vernon, Anita Miramer, Ruth Mills, Lenore D'Arcy, Elmira Lane, Barbara Walton, Margaret McKay, Virginia Calmer, Jean Gibson, Tara Fellegi. *Gentlemen*: Charles Hartvary, Frank DeNoble, Richard Kimball, Marty Jacobs, John Myrtle, George Elliott, Clair Hart, William Birdie, Arthur Budd, Larry Mack, George O'Donnell, Wayne Mattson, Leon Bartels, Murray Minehart, Donald Failes, William O'Neal.

Act 1: The Palm Court of the Castle Beltrami.

Act 2: Picture Gallery of the Castle Beltrami.

Act 3: Picture Gallery of the Castle Beltrami.

ACT 1[96]
"Little Boy" (Opening Duet)
  H. Fender, G. Walton

---

[94]Dropped during the run.
[95]Replaced during the run by:
  "The Waltz Was Made for Lovers"
    V. Segal, E. Costello
[96]For the start of the national tour, the following were added briefly, then dropped:
  "The Dove Song" (Act 1)
    Nancy Gibbs (Mariana)

"Lady in Ermine" (Trio)
  H. Fender, G. Walton, H. Shipman
  (*Music by* Alfred Goodman. *Lyrics by* Cyrus Wood.)
"Silhouette Duet" (My Silhouette)
  R. Woolsey, H. Shipman
  (*Music by* Jean Gilbert, Alfred Goodman. *Lyrics by* Harry Graham and Cyrus Wood.)
"Childhood's Days"[97]
  W. Bennett, H. Fender, R. Woolsey
"When Hearts Are Young" (Song)
  W. Bennett
  (*Music by* Sigmund Romberg. *Lyrics by* Cyrus Wood.)
"Farewell to Adrian"
  W. Bennett
  (*Music by* Sigmund Romberg, Alfred Goodman.)
Entrance
  M. Burke, I. Martinetti, R. Woolsey, Girls
"Land o' Mine" (Homeland)(Song)
  W. Woolf
  (*Music by* Alfred Goodman. *Lyrics by* Cyrus Wood.)
"How Fiercely You Dance" (Duet)
  W. Woolf, M. Burke
Finale
  Ensemble

ACT 2
Opening Chorus
Ballet
  Z. Lockford, Ballet
"Espagnole" (Solo Dance)
  I. Rodriguez
"Play With Fire"
  H. Shipman, Boys
  (*Music by* Sigmund Romberg, Alfred Goodman.)
Duet
  G. Walton, H. Fender
"Men Grow Older" (Trio)
  M. Burke, I. Martinetti, R. Woolsey
"Mariana" (Duet)
  W. Woolf, W. Bennett
  (*Music by* Jean Gilbert. *Lyrics by* Harry Graham.)

ACT 3
"Catch a Butterfly" (Song)
  W. Bennett, Ensemble
"Follow You All Over the World" (Quartette)(I'll Follow You to Zanzibar)
  H. Shipman, M. Burke, I. Martinetti, R. Woolsey
  (*Music by* Alfred Goodman. *Lyrics by* Cyrus Wood.)

REVUE RUSSE

1922.37

A Russian Vaudeville[98] in Two Acts, 15 Scenes. Directed by M. Boleslawski. Costumes and scenery designed by Leon Bakst, Sergei Soudeikine, Messr. Ousounoff. Orchestra under the direction of Eugene Plotnikoff. Ballets arranged by Anatole Bourman. Produced by Elizabeth Marbury in association with the Messrs. Shubert. Opened 5 October 1922 at the Booth Theatre and closed 21 October 1922 after 21 performances.

CAST: Messrs. BOLESLAWSKI (Conferencier), Dniestroff, Voljanin, Markoff, Bourman, Ratoff, Georges Posemkowski, Kouzoff, Aleneff. Mmes. MARIA KOUSNEZOFF, Leontowich, Miraeva, Platonoff, Xenia Morenschildt, Shishkina, Sanina, Smirnova, Mlle.Tanina.

"Bolero" (Song) (Act 2)
  N. Gibbs
"A Little Bit More" (Duet)(Act 3)
  Rollin Grimes (Adrian), G. Walton
[97]Dropped immediately after opening.
[98]Advertised as 'Direct from the Femina Theatre Paris; Imperial Theatre, Petrograd; Opera Theatre, Moscow; Opéra Comique, Paris.'

ACT 1
Scene 1
  Player's Parade
    Mme. Kousnezoff, supported by the Entire Company
    (*Costumes and scenery by* Sergei Soudeikine.)
Scene 2
  Russian Frolic
    Mlle. Tanina; Messrs. Dniestroff, Voljanin
    (*Scenery by* Messr. Ousounoff.)
Scene 3
  Grounka
    Mmes. Leontowich, Miraeva; Messr. Markoff
    (*Costumes and scenery by* Sergei Soudeikine.)

A Cossack regiment halts in a small village and the colonel enters a peasant's home asking for lodgings and a drink. He falls in love with Grounka, who is urged by her mother not to be shy. The colonel departs with his regiment, leaving Grounka a red rose as a souvenir, but Grounka is desperate and heartbroken.

Scene 4
  In the Parsonage
    Mme. Platonoff; Messrs. Bourman, Ratoff
    (*Costumes by* Leon Bakst.)

The assistant priest profits by his superior's absence to court the cook. Meeting encouragement and inspired by a little cupid, he becomes emboldened and soon the two lovers engage in a spirited dance.

Scene 5
  "Khootorok"
    Mme. X. Morenschildt; Messrs. G. Posemkowski, Markoff, Voljanin, Kouzoff
    (*Costumes and scenery by* Sergei Soudeikine.)

A little Russian romance portrayed after the fashion of a Punch and Judy show. The song tells of a young widow who entertains three rival suitors, a merchant, a fisherman and a young peasant. Jealousy brings about a tragic ending, and the little farmhouse where the widow lived becomes a lonely and abandoned place.

Scene 6
  "The Air of Violetta" ('A fors e lui' from LA TRAVIATA)
    M. Kousnezoff
    (*Music by* Giuseppe Verdi. *Costumes by* Leon Bakst.)
Scene 7
  The Swing
    Mmes. Platonova, Shishkina, Miraeva; Messrs. G. Posemkowski, Dniestroff, Voljanin
    (*Costumes and scenery by* Sergei Soudeikine.)
Scene 8
  The Caucasian Obezianna (Monkey impression)
Scene 9
  Old Spain
    Mmes. M. Kousnezoff, X. Morenschildt, Sanina, Shishkina, Smirnova; Messrs. Boleslawski, Bourman, Kouzoff, Ratoff
    (*Costumes by* Sergei Soudeikine and Diego Nestor.)

ACT 2
Scene 1
  Cowardice (A Mimodrama by Leon Bakst.)
    Mmes. Sanina, Smirnova; Messrs. Alenoff, Bourman, Kouzoff
    (*Music by* Nicholas Tcherepnin. *Costumes and Scenery by* Leon Bakst.)

A drama that takes place in 1916 in the "House of the People" at Petrograd. It is the trysting place of the working people of the suburbs, who look upon tragedy and romance with kindred emotions. To them life or death is but the hand of fate. Before this audience Bakst has portrayed a tragedy of untold anguish, wherein a young student is murdered at the instigation of the friend of the girl he loves. A little hunchback friend of the student comes upon the scene and drags away the body.

Scene 2
  "Serenade"
    G. Posemkowski
    (*Scenery by* Messr. Ousounoff.)
Scene 3
  The Squire's Romance
    Mlle. Tanina; Messrs. Aleneff, Dniestroff, Markoff
    (*Costumes by* Sergei Soudeikine.)

A story that tells of an old country squire who is on his way to the forest to hunt. He encounters a pretty maid, and startled by her beauty abandons the thought of hunting and engages in a dance that is meant to interpret the ecstasy of his love.

Scene 4
  Moscow
    Mmes. Leontowich, Miraeva, Platonova; Messrs. Voljanin, Ratoff
    (*Costumes and scenery by* Leon Bakst.)

An interpretation of the old Russian custom of arranging a wedding through the medium of a matchmaker. The matchmaker brings the prospective bridegroom to the house of a merchant who has a daughter to marry. During the discussion an argument arises which is soon settled by a generous serving of vodka. The contract is then celebrated by merriment and dance.

Scene 5
  "The Ukrainian Song"
    M. Kousnezoff
    (*Costume by* Leon Bakst.)
Scene 6
  The Russian Fair
    Mmes. Leontowich, Miraeva, Platonova, Sanina, Smirnova, Shishkina, Tanina; Messrs. Aneleff, Dniestroff, Bourman, Kouzoff, Ratoff, Voljanin, Markoff

A country fair in old Russia where the peddlers cry their wares and the merry crowd of buyers indulge in frolics, songs and dances.

1922.38   # QUEEN O' HEARTS

A Musical Comedy in Two Acts. Book by Frank Mandel and Oscar Hammerstein II. Music by Lewis Gensler and Dudley Wilkinson. Lyrics by Oscar Hammerstein II; extra lyrics by Sydney Mitchell. Staged by Ira Hards. Dances and ensembles arranged by David Bennett. Settings by Robert Law Studios, Herbert Ward, art director. Costumes by Cora MacGeachy, Schneider-Anderson. Orchestra under the direction of Gene Salzer. Produced by Max Spiegel. Opened 10 October 1922 at the George M. Cohan Theatre and closed 11 November 1922 after 40 performances.

CAST (in order of appearance): *Tom:* MAX HOFFMAN, JR. *Grace:* NORMA TERRISS. *Isabella Budd:* Florence Morrison. *Ferdinard Budd:* Franker Woods. *Miss Swanson:* Gladys Dore. *Alabama Smith* (Al): Georgie Brown. *Elizabeth Bennett:* NORA BAYES. *Henry Rivers:* HARRY RICHMAN. *Myra* (Mike): EDNA HIBBARD. *Dudley:* Dudley Wilkinson. *Alfred Armstrong:* LORIN RAKER. *William Armstrong:* ARTHUR UTTRY. *Policeman:* Sidney Brook. *Aunt Abigail:* Laura Alberta. *Georgia:* Eva Taylor. *Butler:* Thomas Bradley.
    Ladies of the Ensemble: Janet Megrew, Consuelo Flowerton, Elza Peterson, Cecille Ann Stevens, Lillian McKenzie, Muriel Harrison, Betty Hill, Loretta Morgan, Gladys Dore, Irene Enright. Violin obligatos by Cecille Ann Stevens, Consuelo Flowerton.

Act 1: Fifth Floor in a Building near Trinity Church, New York.

Act 2: Home of the Armstrong's, Fairfield, New Jersey.

ACT 1
  "Sizing Up the Girls"
    N. Terriss, M. Hoffman, Jr., Applicants
  "Dreaming Alone"
    A. Uttry
    (*Music by* Dudley Wilkinson.)
  "My Busy Day"
    N. Bayes, Office Force
  "Marriage C.O.D."
    L. Raker, E. Hibbard
  "You Need Someone, (Someone Needs You)"
    N. Bayes, A. Uttry
    (*Music by* Lewis Gensler.)
  "Topics of the Day"
    H. Richman, Girls
    (*Music and Lyrics by* Cliff Friend and Harry Richman.)
  "System"
    N. Bayes, Principals, Office Force
  Finale
    N. Bayes, A. Uttry

ACT 2
  "Dreaming Alone" (reprise)
    A. Uttry, Guests

"A Long Time Ago"
  E. Hibbard, L. Raker, M. Hoffman, Jr., N. Terriss
  (*Lyrics by* Morrie Ryskind.)
"That's That"
  N. Bayes, E. Hibbard, A. Uttry, L. Raker
  (*Music by* Dudley Wilkinson. *Lyrics by* Nora Bayes and Harry Richman.)
"Tom-Tom"
  H. Richman, Girls
  (*Music by* Lewis Gensler.)
"Dear Little Girlie"
  N. Bayes, E. Hibbard, Girls
  (*Music by* Dudley Wilkinson. *Lyrics by* Nora Bayes.)
"My Highbrow Fling"
  E. Taylor, G. Brown
Specialty[99]
  N. Bayes
["Mammy's Carbon Copy"
  (*Music and Lyrics by* Harry Richman, Bill Dugan and Lou Davis.)]
Finale
  Company

1922.39 MUSIC BOX REVUE (1922-23)

A Musical Revue in Two Acts, a Prologue and 22 Scenes[100]. (Sketches by Paul Gerard Smith, Frances Nordstrom, Walter Catlett, George V. Hobart.) Music and lyrics by Irving Berlin. All the numbers conceived by Irving Berlin. Staged by Hassard Short. Dances arranged by William Seabury; Porcelain Dance, Ballet and Crinoline dances arranged by Stowitts. Settings designed by Clark Robinson. Costumes designed by Ralph Mulligan, Adrian. Orchestra under the direction of Frank Tours. Orchestrations by Frank Tours, Steve Jones, Charles Grant, Alfred Dalby, Arthur Gutman, Will Vodery and Roy Webb, under the personal direction of Harry Akst. Produced by Sam H. Harris. Opened 23 October 1922 at the Music Box Theatre and closed 4 August 1923 after 330 performances.

CAST: GRACE LaRUE, JOHN STEEL, CHARLOTTE GREENWOOD, BOBBY CLARK, PAUL McCULLOUGH, MARGARET IRVING, WILLIAM GAXTON, THE McCARTHY SISTERS (Dorothy, Margaret), WILLIAM SEABURY, ROBINSON NEWBOLD, THE FAIRBANKS TWINS (Madeline, Marion), THE RATH BROTHERS (George, Dick), RUTH PAGE, STOWITTS, Mrs. ESTAR BANKS, AMELIA ALLEN, Trude Marr, Fraun Koski, Dorothy Brown, Hal Sherman, Hilda Ferguson, Helen Rich, Leila Ricard, Sherry Marshall, Rosemary, Margaret McKee, Olivette.
Ladies of the Ensemble: Jackie Hurlburt, Marie Russell, Polly Day, Viola Boles, Aphia Hurlburt, Sunshine Jarmann, Louise Dale, Lucille Constante, Margaret Redfield, Olga Borowski, Miriam Miller, Gladys Reith, Madeline Killeen, Nellie Roberts, Gloria Gale, Florence Barry, Margaret Stanley, Elaine Courtney, Cyrena Dahl, Viola Fraas, Eva Soble, Mary O'Brien, Misses Aphia, Dixie, Ange, Lynn, Claussen. *Men of the Ensemble*: John Walsh, Wynne Bullock, Herbert Goff, Joseph Marquis, Kendall Wood, Ward Tallman, T. Perry Higgins. *Satan's Lady Jazz Band*: Ruby Ernest, Elsie Wedda, Olga Serlis, Jean Miller, Estelle Hamiel, Dolly Bergere.

ACT 1[101]

Prologue
  Scene I: Boudoir on Park Avenue.
    Mrs. First Nighter: M. Irving. *Mr. First Nighter*: W. Gaxton.

---

[99]Reviewers did not identify the specialty songs apart from noting one was a love song, another a 'Southern mammy song,' and another 'a burlesque on Samson and Delilah,' and a medley of Broadway song hits in which she was joined by Arthur Uttry.
[100]The second of four in the annual series of musical revues conceived and written by Irving Berlin and produced by Sam H. Harris beginning in 1921.
[101]The running order was revised after the opening. Added were:
The Zoo (Act 1)
  The Husband: B. Clark. *The Wife*: C. Greenwood. *His Son*: E. Michales. *The Keeper*: P. McCullough.
Under the Chandelier (revised and shortened version of A Bit o' Ballet)(Act 2)
  (a) Fairbanks Twins, (b) A. Allen, (c) W. Seabury
The Bath Between (*by* Bobby Clark and Paul McCullough)(Act 2)
  Scene: A New York Hotel.
    Mrs. Al Ogelsbie: M. Irving. *Bell Boy*: E. Michales. *First Traveling Man*: W. Gaxton. *Second Traveling Man*: R. Newbold. *Bobby Tarkington*: B. Clark. *Paul Cunningham*: P. McCullough. *Al Ogelsbie*: I. Rose.

Scene II: Stage of the Music Box.
  The Dancer: Olivette. *The Musical Director*: J. Walsh. *The Chorus*: J. Hurlburt, M. Russell, P. Day, V. Boles, A. Hurlburt, S. Jarmann, L. Dale, L. Constante, M. Redfield, O. Borowski, M. Miller, G. Reith, M. Killeen, N. Roberts, G. Gale, F. Barry, M. Stanley. *The Dresser*: Mrs. E. Banks.
Scene 1
"Take a Little Wife"
  M. McCarthy, D. McCarthy
  Scene: The Curtains of the Music Box.
Scene 2
Up in the Air (*by* Frances Nordstrom)(*Directed by* Sam Forrest.)
  Scene: Aviaton Field.
  The Aviator: W. Gaxton. *His Bride*: C. Greenwood. *Philip Graves*: R. Newbold.
Scene 3
"Dance Your Troubles Away"[102]
  Two Little Girls in Blue: Fairbanks Twins. *The Boy*: W. Seabury. *Eight Music Box Dancers*: V. Fraas, F. Barry, G. Reith, M. Miller, L. Dale, O. Borowski, G. Gale, N. Roberts.
Scene 4
The Auction
  The Auctioneer: W. Gaxton. *Clerk*: T. P. Higgins.
Lot No. 1—Tapestry after Fragonard
  The Girl: H. Lyons. *The Boys*: E. Oliphant, H. Ferguson.
Lot No. 2—Jade
  The Idol of Jade: A. Allen.
Lot No. 3—The Harpsichord
  Chopin: J. Marquis. *The Man*: H. Goff. *The Old Lady*: Mrs. E. Banks. *The Girl on the Settee*: M. O'Brien. *The Girl Standing*: T. Marr. *Two Little Ghosts*: Fairbanks Twins.
Lot No. 4—The Wrestlers
  The Wrestlers: Rath Brothers.
Lot No. 5—Chinese Porcelain
"Porcelain Maid"
  The Boy: H. Rich. *The Girl*: E. Soble.
The Porcelain House
  The Dancers: *The Boy*: Stowitts. *The Girl*: R. Page. *Porcelain Figures*: Misses C. Dahl, Dixie, P. Day, M. Stanley, Aphia, A. Hurlburt, M. Redfield, V. Boles, M. Killeen, Ange, E. Courtney, J. Hurlburt, M. Russell, S. Jarmann.
Scene 5
The Interview
  Politicians: B. Clark, P. McCullough. *The Reporter*: M. Irving.
"Three Cheers for the Red, White and Blue"
  B. Clark, P. McCullough
Scene 6
The House Tops
  The Pierrot: J. Steel. *The Ladies of the Evening*: L. Ricard, S. Marshall, F. Koski, T. Marr, D. Durland, H. Lyons, C. Hooper, E. Oliphant, H. Gardner, M. Thoreau.
"Lady of the Evening"
  J. Steel
Scene 7
"(I'm Looking for a) Daddy Long Legs"
  C. Greenwood
Scene 8
"Crinoline Days"
  G. LaRue
  The Girl in the Crinoline: G. LaRue. *The Little Crinolines*: J. Hurlburt, M. Stanley, M. Killeen, C. Dahl, S. Jarmann, M. Russell, P. Day, V. Boles, M. Redfield, E. Courtney, A. Hurlburt. *The White Crinolines*: Fairbanks Twins. *The Boys*: J. Walsh, W. Bullock, H. Goff, J. Marquis, K. Wood, W. Tallman, T. P. Higgins.
Scene 9
"Dancing Honeymoon"
  The Bride: Olivette. *The Bridegroom*: W. Seabury. *The Spanish Honeymooners*: N. Roberts, O. Borowski. *The Russian Honeymooners*: G. Reith, F. Barry. *The Egyptian Honeymooners*: G. Gale, L. Dale. *The Hawaiian Honeymooners*: V. Fraas, M. Miller.
Scene 10
The Lady in Red (*by* George V. Hobart and Walter Catlett)(*Directed by* Sam Forrest.)

---

[102]Dropped after opening.

Note: This is what happened on the opening night of a melodrama as played by a stock company in Winniepasooga, Wisconsin.

    Scene: A room on the eighteenth floor of the house of Mahomed Mahoney, the arch-conspirator—being the fourth act of the drama.

        Hung Wai Low, a Chinaman: W. Gaxton. *Mahomed Mahoney*, an arch conspirator: B. Clark. *Beechowser*, his henchman: P. McCullough. *The Lady in Red*: G. LaRue. *Victor Fairhair*, her affianced: R. Newbold.

Scene 11

"Pack Up Your Sins and Go to the Devil"
    M. McCarthy, D. McCarthy, Entire Company
        Scene: On the way to "Satan's Palace."
            The Devil: C. Greenwood. *The Chancellor*: R. Newbold. *Don Juan*: Stowitts. *Catherine of Russia*: L. Ricard. *Salome*: T. Marr. *Madame DuBarry*: H. Lyons. *Cleopatra*: F. Koski. *The Announcer*: W. Gaxton. *Bee Palmer*: D. Brown. *Ted Lewis*: J. Walsh. *Gilda Gray*: H. Ferguson. *Frisco*: W. Seabury. *Satan's Lady Jazz Band*: Music Box Jazz Band.

ACT 2

Scene 1

a) The Story of "The Little Red Lacquer Cage"
    The Little Old Lady: Mrs. E. Banks. *The Canary*: H. Rich.

b) The Forest
    The Mocking Bird: M. McKee. *The Whipporwill*: Olivette. *The Love-Birds*: Fairbanks Twins. *The Bob-o-link*: M. Stanley. *The Nightingale*: Rosemary. *The Blue Bird*: V. Fraas. *The Calliste*: C. Hooper. *The Cockatoo*: D. Durland. *The Macaw*: F. Koski. *The Parrot*: T. Marr. *The Bird of Paradise*: L. Ricard.

Scene 2

Hal Sherman (Specialty)

Scene 3

This Suspense Is Terrible (*by Paul Gerard Smith*)(*Directed by* Sam Forrest.)
    Scene: The Mexican Wall.
        The General: B. Clark. *The Spy*: W. Gaxton. *The Army*: W. Bullock, H. Goff, J. Marquis, J. Walsh. *Insurance Agent*: R. Newbold. *The Golfer*: P. McCullough. *Newspaper Boy*: E. Michales.

Scene 4

"Will She Come from the East?"
    J. Steel
        Scene North South East West.
            East: H. Gardner. *North*: H. Lyons. *West*: E. Oliphant. *South*: M. O'Brien.

Scene 5

The Rath Brothers (Specialty)

Scene 6

The Diamond Horseshoe

"My Diamond Horseshoe of Girls"
    J. Steel
        Scene: The Metropolitan Opera House.
            The Ladies in the Boxes: Misses H. Lyons, M. Thoreau, D. Durland, Lynn, M. O'Brien, Claussen, C. Hooper, H. Gardner. *The Buglers*: D. Brown, H. Ferguson. *Carmen*: E. Oliphant. *Tosca*: S. Marshall. *Marguerite*: Rosemary. *Isolde*: L. Ricard. *Butterfly*: E. Soble. *Manon*: T. Marr. *Aida*: F. Koski. *Mimi*: H. Rich. *Thais*: G. LaRue.

Scene 7

"Too Many Boys"
    C. Greenwood, Music Box Boys

Scene 8

"Bring on the Pepper"
    M. McCarthy, D. McCarthy
        The Peppers: S. Jocelyn, Eight Music Box Dancers.
        (*Novelty Pepper costumes invented by* Sylvia Jocelyn.)

Scene 9

The Ballroom:

(a) Congo Dance[103] (*Designed, arranged and danced by* Stowitts.)
    The Idols: D. Durland, H. Gardner, M. Thoreau, E. Oliphant. *The Drummers*: Music Box Jazz Band.

(b) A Bit o' Ballet
    Music Box Girls, Olivette, Fairbanks Twins, A. Allen, W. Seabury, Eight Music Box Dancers

Scene 10

Grace LaRue (Specialty)

---

[103]Dropped after opening.

Scene 11

Finale
    C. Greenwood, G. LaRue, Entire Company

1922.40   # SPRINGTIME OF YOUTH

A Musical Play in Three Acts. (Original Viennese) Book ('Sterne, die wieder leuchtet') by Rudolf Bernhauser and Rudolph Schanzer[104]. Music by Walter Kollo and Sigmund Romberg. Lyrics by Harry B. Smith and Cyrus Wood. Staged by J. C. Huffman and John Harwood. Dances arranged by Allan K. Foster. Settings designed by Watson Barratt and Rollo Wayne. Costumes by Anna Spencer, Inc., Vanity Fair Costumes Inc.; men's costumes by Ford Uniform Co. Orchestra under the direction of J. Frank Cork. Orchestrations by Emil Gerstenberger. Produced by Messrs. Shubert. Opened 26 October 1922 at the Broadhurst Theatre and closed 23 December 1922 after 68 performances.

CAST (in order of appearance): *Mistress Prudence Stokes*: GRACE HAMILTON. *Nat Podmore*: Walter J. Preston. *Pepita*, proprietress of the Dolphin Tavern: ZELLA RUSSELL. *Hiram Baxter* of the Baxter Trading Company: Harry McKee. *Deacon Stokes*, Baxter's rival in business: HARRY KELLY. *Hopkins*, Stokes' clerk: Larry Wood. *Polly Baxter*: ELEANOR GRIFFITH. *Richard Stokes*: J. HAROLD MURRAY. *Timothy Gookin*: HARRY K. MORTON. *Keziah Hathaway*: Marie Pettes. *Priscilla Alden*, Roger Hathaway's ward: OLGA STECK. *Squire Hathaway*: Tom Williams. *Roger Hathaway*: GEORGE MacFARLANE. *The Mayor*: Ben Marion *Relatives of Roger Hathaway*: Myrtle Lawrence, Charles Peyton, Venie Atherton, Gertrude Hillman.
    Quaker Girls: Mildred Lee, Vivien Nulty, Polly Mayer, Eileen Adair, Julie Sabath, May O'Brien, Mabel Kern, Gladys Rogers, Loretta Koch, Gladys Struthers, Dorothy Ramesy, Lillian Wilck, Maude Rider, Mabel Griswold, Marjorie Elise, Patricia Gridier. *Navy Officers*: Edward Scofield, Alan Cochrane, Neil Courtney, Clement Taylor, Willard Fry, Robert Fisher, C. Burnett, Fred Slosson.

Act 1: A Wharf-side Street, Portsmouth, New Hampshire. 1812.

Act 2: The Living Room of Hiram Baxter's House.

Act 3: The Garden of Deacon Stokes' House.

ACT 1

"Love While You May" (Opening Chorus and Solo)
    G. Hamilton, Ensemble
    (*Music by* Sigmund Romberg.)

"Love Finds a Way"
    J. H. Murray
    (*Music by* Sigmund Romberg.)

"Pretty Polly"
    E. Griffith, W. J. Preston
    (*Music by* Sigmund Romberg.)

"I Knew 'Twould Be So"
    O. Steck
    (*Music by* Walter Kollo.)

"Best of Good Friends"
    O. Steck, J. H. Murray
    (*Music by* Walter Kollo.)

"A Sailor's Bride"
    Z. Russell, H. K. Morton
    (*Music by* Sigmund Romberg.)

"Starlight of Hope"
    O. Steck, G. MacFarlane
    (*Music by* Sigmund Romberg.)

Finaletto
    O. Steck, G. MacFarlane
    (*Music by* Sigmund Romberg.)

ACT 2

Opening Ensemble
    (*Music by* Walter Kollo.)

"Si, Si, Senorita"
    O. Steck, G. MacFarlane
    (*Music by* Sigmund Romberg.)

"Chorus of Welcome"
    Ensemble
    (*Music by* Walter Kollo.)

---

[104]American adaptation uncredited. Prior to New York the book was credited to Frank Dalton, most likely a pseudonym.

"Just Like a Doll"
E. Griffith, W. J. Preston
(*Music by* Sigmund Romberg.)
"But in Brazil"
Z. Russell, H. K. Morton
(*Music by* Sigmund Romberg.)
"Youth and Spring" (Duet)
O. Steck, J. H. Murray
(*Music by* Sigmund Romberg.)
Finale
G. MacFarlane, O. Steck, J. H. Murray
(*Music by* Sigmund Romberg.)

ACT 3
"Our Busy Needles Fly"
G. Hamilton, Quakeresses
(*Music by* Sigmund Romberg.)
"Won't You Take Me to Paris"
Z. Russell, H. Kelly
(*Music by* Sigmund Romberg.)
"Find the Right Girl"
O. Steck, E. Griffith, J. H. Murray, W. Preston
(*Music by* Sigmund Romberg.)
"Somewhere in Love's Garden"
G. MacFarlane, Chorus
(*Music by* Sigmund Romberg.)
Finale
Ensemble
(*Music by* Sigmund Romberg.)

1922.41 ## UP SHE GOES

A Musical Comedy in Three Acts, 5 Scenes[105]. Book by Frank Craven. (Based on the play 'Too Many Cooks' by Frank Craven.) Music by Harry Tierney. Lyrics by Joseph McCarthy. Staged by Frank Craven and Bert French. Dances arranged by Bert French. Gowns and hats by Milgrim; men's clothes by Copinger, Inc. Orchestra under the direction of Anton Heindl. Orchestrations by Frank Barry; additional orchestrations by Lake McCabe and Alfred Dalby. Produced by William A. Brady, Ltd. Opened 6 November 1922 at the Playhouse Theatre and closed 16 June 1923 after 256 performances.

CAST (in order of appearance): *Simpson*: Edward Dano. *Ella Mayer*: HELEN BOLTON. *Frank Andrews*: RICHARD [Skeet] GALLAGHER. *Albert Bennett*: DONALD BRIAN. *Alice Cook*: GLORIA FOY. *Mrs. Cook*: Lou Ripley. *Mr. Cook*: Martin Mann. *Aunt Louise*: Jennie Weathersbee. *Mary Cook*: Edith Slack. *Jerry Cook*: Conway Dillion. *Louis Cook*: Teddy McNamara. *Uncle Walter*: Richard Sullivan. *Bertha Cook*: Lucretia Craig. *Stella Cook*: Betty Allan. *Bus Driver*: George Williams. *Uncle Bob Bennett*: FREDERICK GRAHAM. *Minnie Spring*: Ann LeMeau.

Ladies of the Ensemble: Merle Stevens, Ruth Valerie, Virginia Sharr, Riza Royce, Katherine Hurst, Doris Greene, Ruth Hovey, Peggy Matthews, Joan Warner, Madeline Dare, Grace Culbert, Pauline Maxwell, Edna Coigne, Iris Meier, Mona Dale, Katherine Huth. *Gentlemen of the Ensemble*: Jack Grieves, Leo Howe, Louis Sears, Tom Chadwick, Alfred Oakley, Edward Lefebvre, Irving Jackson, Perry Davenport.

Act 1: (The) Foundation, Pleasantville.

Act 2, Scene 1: The Country Club. *Scene 2*: Cross Roads. *Scene 3*: Raising the Roof.

Act 3: Journey's End.

ACT 1
"The Visitors" (Opening)
H. Bolton, E. Dano, Ensemble
"Takes a Heap o' Love"
H. Bolton, R. Gallagher, Girls, Boys
"Journey's End"
G. Foy, D. Brian
"Let's Kiss and Make Up"
G. Foy, H. Bolton, D. Brian, R. Gallagher
"Nearing the Day"
G. Foy, D. Brian
Finale (The Mix-Up)
Entire Company

ACT 2
Opening (At the Club)
R. Gallagher, Ensemble
"Bob About a Bit"
F. Graham, Girls
"Tyup"
G. Foy, D. Brian, F. Graham, R. Gallagher, Ensemble
"Roof Tree"
Entire Company
"The Strike"
D. Brian, G. Foy
ACT 3
"Lady Luck Smile on Me"
D. Brian
"We'll Do the Riviera"[106]
H. Bolton, R. Gallagher
"Settle Down, Travel Around"
H. Bolton, R. Gallagher, Girls, Boys
"Journey's End" (reprise)
G. Foy
"Up With the Stars"
G. Foy, Company
"Up She Goes"
Entire Company

1922.42 ## THE '49ERS

A Modernistic Revue in Two Acts, 10 Scenes. Sketches by George S. Kaufman, Marc Connelly, Ring Lardner, Morrie Ryskind, Dorothy Parker, Howard Dietz, Robert Benchley. Music by Arthur Samuels and Lewis E. Gensler. Lyrics by Morrie Ryskind and Franklin Price Adams. General stage director, Howard Lindsay; directors, George S. Kaufman and Marc Connelly. Dances staged by Albert Carroll. Costumes by William H. Matthews. Settings designed by Sheldon K. Viele. Lighting by Anthony Greshoff. Conductor, Maurice Rumsey. Produced by George C. Tyler. Opened 6 November 1922 at the Punch and Judy Theatre and closed 18 November 1922 after 16 performances.

CAST: MAY IRWIN (Conferencier), ROLAND YOUNG, BERYL MERCER, SIDNEY TOLER, RUTH GILLMORE, DENMAN MALEY, DEVAH MOREL, ALLEN FAGAN, MARGOT MYERS, HOWARD LINDSAY, GLADYS BURGETTE, SOL FRIEDMAN, ANGELA WARDE, ALBERT CARROLL, CLYDE HUNNEWELL, WARD FOX, IRA UHR, EASTON YONGE, FRANK LYON.

Ladies of the Ensemble: Brenda Bond, Jeanne Chambers, Maida Harries, Louise Hunter, Monica Moore. *Gentlemen of the Ensemble*: Phillip Mann, Lewis Barrington, Paolo Grosso, Francis Elderon, James Bell.

ACT 1
The Trail Blazer
M. Connelly
Scene 1
The Allegorical Opening
"Allegorical Blues"
G. Burgette, B. Bond, J. Chambers, M. Harries, L. Hunter, M. Moore
(*Music by* Lewis Gensler. *Lyrics by* Morrie Ryskind.)
The Good Fairy: M. Myers. *Capital and Labor*: C. Hunnewell. *Beauty*: G. Burgette. *Youth*: A. Carroll. *Spirit of Public School No. 118*: D. Morel.
Scene 2
Life in the Back Pages (*by* George S. Kaufman)
Scene: An American Home.
The Father: D. Maley. *The Mother*: B. Mercer. *Oswald*: E. Yonge. *Edna*: R. Gillmore. *Mr. Warwick*: I. Uhr. *The Lover*: F. Lyon.
Scene 3
A Robe for the King (*by* Heywood Broun)
Scene: The Palace of a King.
The King: R. Young. *The Leading Republican*: H. Lindsay. *The Leading Democrat*: A. Fagan. *First Courtier*: C. Hunnewell. *Second Courtier*:

---

[105]During the run, Act 2 was reset in its entirety as one scene at the Country Club. Scenic design uncredited.

[106]Replaced after the opening by:
"Settle Down—We'll Travel"
H. Bolton, R. Gallagher

P. Mann. *An Imperial Footman*: L. Barrington. *A Tailor*: S. Friedman. A *Scullery Maid*: R. Gillmore.

Scene 4

American Folklore Series:

Chapters from 'American Economics' by Marc Connelly. *Music by* Lewis E. Gensler.

    a. "Autumn Dance of the Hat-Check Girls"
      A. Warde, G. Burgette, others
    b. "Spring Dance of the Small-Town Mayors"
      The Mayor of Braddock: A. Fagan. *The Mayor of East Liverpool*: I. Uhr. *The Mayor of New Castle*: E. Yonge. *The Mayor of McKeesport*: W. Fox.

Scene 5

Nero (A *Historical Drama by* Dorothy Parker and Robert C. Benchley)
    Scene: The Council Room of Robespierre.
    Robespierre: R. Young. *Richelieu*: S. Friedman. *Queen Victoria*: B. Mercer. *First Guard*: S. Toler. *Second Guard*: D. Maley. *Duc de Brinvilliers*: P. Mann. *Comtesse de Trusillac*: M. Myers. *General Grant*: L. Barrington. *General Lee*: W. Fox. *Mussolini*: P. Grosso.

ACT 2

Scene 1

Omit Flowers (*by* Montague Glass)
    Scene: Bonnie Dundee Funeral Parlors.
    George: R. Young. *Charles Williams*: D. Maley. *Sadie Williams*: M. Mercer. *Ed Hall*: C. Hunnewell. *Mamie Hall*: D. Morel. *Delos M. Randall*: A. Fagan. *The Widow*: A. Warde. *Henry Williams*: S. Toler. *A Colored Man*: F. Elderon.

Scene 2

The Music Ride (*Conceived and staged by* Walt Kuhn.)
    Ringmaster: I. Uhr. *Ladies*: S. Friedman, J. Bell, P. Mann. *Gentlemen*: W. Fox, L. Barrington, E. Yonge. *Attendants in the Ring*: M. Myers, B. Bond.

Scene 3

The Tridget of Greva (*by* Ring Lardner)
    Scene: A Fishing Box in Greva.
      Leonard Barhooter: S. Toler. *Desire Corby*: R. Young. *Oscar Laffler?*: D. Maley. *Perkins*: G. Burgette. *Messenger Boy*: E. Yonge.
      'Translator's note: Everybody in Greva has rheumatism.

Scene 4

The Love Girl [A burlesque of Viennese opera]

A Musical Comedy in Two Acts. Book and lyrics by Franklin P. Adams. Music by Arthur H. Samuels.

("Back, Back, Back to Akron" by Robert E. Sherwood.)

    Act 1
    "Can This Be Love?" (by Kelly and Grotto)
      Emily and Girls
    "You Never Can Tell About Love"
      Schmalz
    "Love, Love, Love" (Duetto)
      Emily and Prince
    "My Garden of Love"
      Sigmund Weservelt, Cloe and Jack
    "Oh Love Me Now"
      Emily, Pricne and Entire Company
    Act 2
    "The Love I Bear Thee"
      Wurzman and Annapolis Boys
    "Love Me Forever" (by Ernest Risse)
      Winifred, Edgar, Pierre and Flo-Flo
    "In Love With You" (reprise)
      Jimmy and Radio Girls
    "When Love Comes Trip, Trip, Tripping"
      Liederhof and Edgar
    "Just Love"
      Entire Thompson-Starrett Co.
    Act 1: Courtyard of The Golden Spider, Darmstadt.
    Act 2: Opposite the Palm Beach Inn, Palm Beach, Florida.
    Prince Robert of Darmstadt, son of the king and a chip of the old block: F. Lyon. *Princess Anastasia*, in love with Robert: D. Morel. *Count Herbert von Bayard*, classmate of Prince Robert's, and a good fellow: S. Friedman. *Countess von Ersatz*, in love with Herbert: M. Myers. *Hans Holstein*, proprietor of the Golden Spider, later owner of the Palm Beach Inn: S. Toler. *Schmickel*, a waiter in the Daytime, but a high flyer at night: L. Hunford. *Baron Friedrich*, Chancellor of Darmstadt: C. Hunnewell. *Beppo*, a Gypsy Chief: I. Uhr. *Gretchen, Pat Kerrigan*, two dancers from the Royal Opera: A. Warde, A. Fagan. *Irene Castle*: A. Carroll. *Villagers, Guests, Seminary Girls, Entertainers at the Golden Spider, Skaters, Gypsies, Hussars, Tourists, Life Guards, Friends of Bobby at Cuntry Club, Sunshine Girls*: G. Spelvin.

Scene 5

Finale: "Where Credit Is Due"
    Entire Company
    (*Music by* Lewis E. Gensler. *Lyrics by* Marc Connelly.)

1922.43   # LITTLE NELLIE KELLY

A New Song and Dance Show (Musical Comedy) with George M. Cohan's Comedians in Two Acts, 5 Scenes. Book, music and lyrics by George M. Cohan. Entire production staged under the supervision of George M. Cohan. Musical numbers staged by Julian Mitchell. Scenery designed by H. Robert Law Studios, Joseph Wickes Studio. Costumes designed by Charles LeMaire. Orchestra under the direction of Charles J. Gebest. Produced by George M. Cohan. Opened 13 November 1922 at the Liberty Theatre and closed 7 July 1923 after 276 performances.

CAST (in order of appearance): *Wellesley*, a butler: Harold Vizard. *Matilda*, a housekeeper: Edna Whistler. *Lloyd's chums* (2): Sidney Potter: Frank Otto. *Harold Westcott*: Joseph Niemeyer. *Jack Lloyd*, a young millionaire: Barrett Greenwood. *Francois DeVere*, proprietor of the shop: Robert Pitkin. *Jean*, a modiste: Dorothy Newell. *Nellie Kelly*, the girl: ELIZABETH HINES. *Mrs. Langford*, Lloyd's aunt: GEORGIA CAINE. *Marie*, her daughter: MARION SAKI. *Jerry Conroy*, from the Bronx: CHARLES KING. *Captain John Kelly*, of the New York Police Department: ARTHUR DEAGON. *Miss Spendington*, a costumer: Marjorie Lane. *Ambrose Swift*, a society detective: Mercer Templeton. *Shop Girls, Boys About Town, Policemen, Customers, etc.*

    Special Dances by Joseph Neimeyer, Aileen Hamilton, Lorraine Sisters, Cunningham and Clements, Carl Hemmer, James and Mercer Templeton, (Herbert Barnett).

Act 1, Scene 1: Reception Room of the Lloyd Mansion. (Law.) *Scene 2*: Exterior of the Conroy Home. (Law.)

Act 2, Scene 1: A Showroom in the Shop of DeVere. (Wickes.) *Scene 2*: Mystery Lane. (Wickes.) *Scene 3*: Exterior of the Langford Home on the Hudson. (Wickes.)

ACT 1

    "Over the Phone"
      B. Greenwood, Company
    "All in the Wearing"
      E. Hines, Company
    "Girls from DeVere's"
      R. Pitkin, Girls
    "Dancing My Worries Away"
      F. Otto, M. Saki
    "Nellie Kelly, I Love You"
      C. King, Company
    "When You Do the Hinky Dee"
      C. King, E. Hines, F. Otto, M. Saki, Company
    "Something's Got to Be Done"
      H. Vizard, E. Whistler, D. Newel, R. Pitkin
    "The Name of Kelly"
      A. Deagon, Company
    Ensemble
      Entire Company

ACT 2

    "The Busy Bees of DeVere's"[107]
      Boys, Girls
    "The Dancing Detective"
      M. Templeton, Girls
    "They're All My Boys"
      E. Hines, Boys, H. Barnett
    "The Flirting Salesmen" (Dance)
      J. Niemeyer, A. Hamilton
    "You Remind Me of My Mother"
      C. King, E. Hines
    "The Great New York Police"
      A. Deagon, Boys
    "The Mystery Play"
      M. Lane, Girls
    Mystery Dance
      J. Templeton, M. Templeton
    "Arrival of the Guests" (Medley)
      Ensemble

---

[107]On subsequent tour, renamed "The Boys and Girls of DeVere's."

Waltz
  E. Hines, C. Hammer
"The Voice in My Heart"
  E. Hines
"Till My Luck Comes Rolling Along"
  Company
Reprise
  C. King, E. Hines
Finale
  Entrie Company

1922.44   LIZA

A Musical Comedy in Two Acts, 10 Scenes[108]. Book by Irvin C. Miller. Music and lyrics by Maceo Pinkard. Special lyrics by Nat Vincent. Entire production staged by Walter Brooks. Costumes by Mme. Gilman. Scenery by Runnel-Amend, Inc. and Novelty Scenic Studios. Orchestra under the direction of J. Tim Brymn. Produced by Al Davis. Opened 27 November 1922 at Daly's Theatre, moved 12 March 1923 to the Nora Bayes Theatre, and closed 21 April after 172 performances.

CAST (in order of appearance): *Squire Norris*: Alonzo Fenderson. *Liza Norris*: MARGARET SIMMS. *Nora*: GERTRUDE SAUNDERS. *Uncle Pete*: William Simms. *Parson Jordan*: Packer Ramsey. *Judge Plummer*: Quintard Miller. *Ras Johnson*: R. EDDIE GREENLEE. *Dandy*: THADDIUS DRAYTON. *The Sheriff*: Will A. Cook. *Ice Cream Charlie*: IRVIN C. MILLER. *Bodiddly*: EMMETT ANTHONY. *Tom Liggett*: Billy Mills. *John Jones*: Doe Doe Green. *Mammy*: Elizabeth Terrill. *Mandy*: Maude Russell. *Harry Davis*: Snippy Mason. *Bill Jones*: Donald Fields.

Brown Skin Vamps: Bee Freeman, Doris Mignotte, Agnes Anthony, Thelma Greene, Zudora DeGaston, Gladys Robinson, Louise Dunbar, Elizabeth Welch. *Jimtown Flappers*: Blanche Thompson, Helen Dunmore, Lena Dukes, Edith Simms, Marion Jones, Ethel Taylor, May Green, Mary Fortune. *Dancing Girls*: Aurora Davis, Viola Branch, Clara Townsend, Millie Cooke, Angeline Hammond, Cornell Vigal, Gladys Scott, Helen Fenderson. *Struttin' Dandies*: Ruben Brown, St. Clair Dotson, Charles Lawrence, Lloyd Mitchell, Franklyn O'Cause, Cornelius Burton, John Gaelard, Paul Sullivan.

Time: Summer Time. *Place*: Jimtown, South Carolina.

Act 1, Scene 1: In front of Squire Norris' home. *Scene 2*: Town Jail. *Scene 3*: Sam Sykes' Barber Shop. *Scene 4*: A Street in Town. *Scene 5*: On the Levee.

Act 2, Scene 1: Jimtown Square. *Scene 2*: A Street in Jimtown. *Scene 3*: Jimtown Graveyard. *Scene 4*: Street to Jimtown. *Scene 5*: Corridor of Jimtown Ballroom. *Scene 6*: The Ball Room.

ACT 1[109]
Scene 1
  "Tag Day" (Opening Chorus)
    Ensemble
  "Pleasure" (Song)
    G. Saunders, Girls
  "I'm the Sheriff" (Song)
    W. Cook, Boys
  "Liza" (Song)
    T. Drayton, M. Simms, G. Saunders, Chorus
Scene 2
  Specialty (Memories)[110]
    A. Anthony, V. Branch, M. Green, G. Taylor, E. Taylor, A. Hammond
Scene 3
  "Just a Barber Shop Cord" (Song)
    The Gang

Scene 4
  "That Brownskin Flapper" (Song)
    G. Saunders, Flappers
Scene 5
  "On the Moonlit Swanee" (Ensemble)
    Town Folks
  "Essence" (Dance)
    R. E. Greenlee, T. Drayton, Boys
  "Forget Your Troubles" (Dance)
    Boys, Girls
  "My Old Man" (Song)
    E. Welch, E. Anthony, Quintette
    (*Lyrics by* Nat Vincent.)
  "(I've Got Those) Runnin' Wild Blues" (Song)
    G. Saunders, M. Simms, R. E. Greenlee, T. Drayton, Entire Company
ACT 2
Scene 1
  "The Charleston Dancy" (Song)
    M. Russell, Girls
    (*Lyrics by* Nat Vincent.)
  "Dandy" (Song)
    M. Simms, Dandies
  "My Creole Girl" (Song)
    R. E. Greenlee, Girls
Scene 2
  "Planning"[111] (Duet)
    M. Simms, T. Drayton
Scene 3
  The Ghost Dance
    S. C. Dotson. L. Mitchell
Scene 4
  "Love Me"
    G. Saunders
Scene 5
  Dance
    Four Steppers
  Jimtown Speedster
    J. Nit
  Specialty
    E. Anthony
  Specialty
    R. E. Greenlee, T. Drayton
  ["Lovin' Sam (The Sheik of Alabam'"
    (*Music by* Milton Ager. *Lyrics by* Jack Yellen.)]
  "Don't Be Blue" (Song)
    G. Saunders
Finale
  Entire Company

1922.45   THE BUNCH AND JUDY

A Musical Entertainment (Comedy) in Two Acts, 6 Scenes[112]. Book by Anne Caldwell and Hugh Ford. Music by Jerome Kern. Lyrics by Anne Caldwell. Staged by Fred G. Latham. Scenery designed by Frank Gates and Edward A. Morange. Costumes by Paul Poiret (Act 2, Scene 3), George Barbier (Act 1, Scene 2), 'Coin de Paris' of Wanamaker's (Act 1, Scene 3). Orchestra under the direction of Victor Baravalle. Orchestrations by Stephen Jones. Produced by Charles Dillingham. Opened 28 November 1922 at the Globe Theatre and closed 20 January 1923 after 63 performances.

CAST (in order of appearance): *Mrs. Shean*: Lydia Scott. *Kelly*: Eugene Revere. *Messenger*: Roger Davis. *Hazel Kirkwood*: Patrice Clark. *Marguerite de Belmont*: Lillian White. *Augustus de Forrest*: Augustus Minton. *Foxhall Davidson*: T. Wigney Percyval. *Lady Janet*: Roberta Beatty. *Lord Kinlock*: PHILIP TONGE. *Call Boy*: Al Watson, Jr.

---

[108]Although 11 Scenes were listed at the time of the opening, the corresponding song list listed only 10 Scenes. It appears likely from programs later in the run that Act 2, Scenes 4 and 5 were combined.
[109]The order and number of scenes was changed repeatedly during the run of the show. Added during the run (Act 1, Scene 2):
  "I'se Gwine to Talk"
    B. Mills
  "Jo-Jo Blues"
    Liza Trio (unidentified)
  Added for tour:
  "Reckless Baby"
    Madeline Belt (Mandy), Reckless Babies
[110]Dropped after opening, and replaced by "That Brown Skin Flapper."

[111]Moved to Act 1, Scene 4 after opening.
[112]Billed as the Annual Globe Show. Choreography uncredited, although Fred Astaire's autobiography suggests that Edward Royce may have contributed to the show's dances.

Otto Steger: JOHNNY DOOLEY. *Evie Dallas*: RAY DOOLEY. *Jack Jessop*: DELANO DELL. *Gerald Lane*: FRED ASTAIRE. *Judy Jordan*: ADELE ASTAIRE. *Georgia McNamara*: Helen Eby Rock. *Gladys Goldwin*: Elaine Palmer. *Estelle*: Ruth White. *Viola Esmond*: Carol Flower. *Mrs. Jordan*: Bertha Holley. *Robin*: George Tawde. *Earl of Torwood*: T. Wigney Percyval. *Pipers*: J. M. McKenzie, R. H. Wilder, W. McLellan. *Station Master*: R. H. Wilder. *Specialties in the Cabaret Scene*: GRACE HAYES, SIX BROWN BROTHERS.

Characters in the Operetta: *Caterina*, the Duke's Favorite: Patrice Clark. *Lizetta*, the Duke's Hand-Maiden: RAY DOOLEY. *Beppo*, a conspirator: Delano Dell. *The Duke di Monticuccoli*: Augustus Minton. *The Duke's Guests*[113] (2): *Tessa*: Mabel Claire. *Ninette*: Gladys Goldwin. *Paulina*, the Duke's Captive: Adele Astaire. *Antonio*, in love with Paulina: Fred Astaire. *Amelita*, a Venetian Lady: Helen Eby Rock. *Rocco*, the Inn Keeper: JOHNNY DOOLEY. *Courtiers, Gondoliers, Lackeys, Guests*.

Ensemble: Helen Allen, Marie Brady, Gertrude Feeley, Marjorie Flynn, Marie Francis, Doris Landy, Madeline Lombard, Louise Powell, Lydia Scott, Mildred Sinclair, Billie Wilcox, Ursula Dale, Betty Cline, Lola Curtis, Hazel Donnelly, Ona Hamilton, Eleanor Ladd, Edna Locke, Alida Middlecoat, Lee Patrick, Mary Pearce, Adelaide Robinson, Rita Royce, Jet Stanley, Kathleen Mullane. Roger Davis, Maurice Chapman, Louis Emery, Jack Hughes, Clifford Stone, Chester Grady, Edward Graham, George Wharton, Kenneth Munro, Charles Roberts, Clifford Daly, Alfred Watson, Jr.

Act 1, Scene 1: Before the Operetta ['Love Finds a Way' at the Grand Opera House]. *Scene 2*: The Operetta, (set in a Duke's Palazzo, Venice, mid-eighteenth century). *Scene 3*: After the performance.

Act 2, Scene 1: Torwood Castle, Scotland. *Scene 2*: Torwood Railroad Station. *Scene 3*: Paul Poiret's, London.

ACT 1: The Operetta
 Minuet
  Ensemble
 "Silenzio" (Duet)
  C. McBride, R. Dooley
 Entrance of Duke
  Ensemble
 "The Naughty Nobleman" (Song)
  A. Minton
 "Pale Venetian Moon" (Duettino)
  F. Astaire, A. Astaire
 Finaletto
  Ensemble
 "Hot Dog"[114] (Duet)
  H. E. Rock, D. Dell
 Dance Eccentrique[115]
  D. Dell
 "Morning Glory" (Song)
  A. Astaire, Ensemble
ACT 2
 "Lovely Lassie" (Scotch Pastoral)
  R. Beatty, Ensemble
 "Every Day in Every Way"[116] (Duet)
  A. Astaire, F. Astaire
 "Times Square" (Septette)
  A. Astaire, R. Dooley, P. Clark, J. Dooley, F. Astaire, C. McBride, A. Minton
 Clansman March and Fling
  A. Astaire, P. Tonge, Ensemble
 The Cabaret
 "Have You Forgotten Me"[117] (Blues)
  G. Hayes

---

[113]Neither Mabel Claire nor Gladys Goldwin appear in the ensemble or as character names elsewhere in the show.
[114]Replaced immediately after opening by:
 Song (later dropped)
  C. McBride
[115]Replaced immediately after opening by: "Peach Girl" (Duet)
  A. Astaire, F. Astaire
[116]Replaced after opening by (moved from later in Act 2):
 "How Do You Do, Katinka?"
  A. Astaire, F. Astaire
[117]Replaced during the run by:
 "Virginia"/
 "Belle of Avenue A"/
 "Loving Sam (The Sheik of Alabam')" (from MAKE IT SNAPPY)
  (*Music by* Milton Ager. *Lyrics by* Jack Yellen.)
  G. Hayes

"How Do You Do, Katinka?" (Duet)
 A. Astaire, F. Astaire
Specialty[118]
 Six Brown Brothers
"Peach Girl"[119] (Duet)
 A. Astaire, F. Astaire
Finale

1922.46

OUR NELL

A Musical 'Mellowdrayma' in Two Acts. Book and lyrics by A. E. Thomas and Brian Hooker. Music by George Gershwin and William Daly. Staged by W. H. Gilmore, Edgar MacGregor. Dances arranged by Julian Mitchell. Scenery by H. Robert Law Studios; Herbert Ward, director. Costumes by Bayer-Schumacher Company. Orchestra under the direction of Charles Sieger. Produced by Hayseed Productions, Inc. (Ed. Davidow and Rufus LeMaire, directors). Opened 4 December 1922 at the Nora Bayes Theatre and closed 6 January 1923 after 40 performances.

CAST (in order of appearance): *Malvina Holcombe*: MRS JIMMIE BARRY. *Mortimer Bayne*: JOHN MERKYL. *Pegleg Doolittle*: JIMMIE BARRY. *Joshua Holcombe*: FRANK MAYNE. *Frank Hart*: THOMAS CONKEY. *Deacon Calvin Sheldrake*: Guy Nichols. *Helen Ford*: EVA CLARKE. *Angeline Weems*: EMMA HAIG. *Chris Deming*: OLIN HOWLAND. *Mrs. Rogers*: LORA SONDERSON.

Rustic Maidens: Molly Murphy, Shirley Lewis, Alice Wood, Mary Maxwell, Lucille Darling, Elinore Tierney, Kathleen McLaughlin, Emme Tattersall, Honore Tattersall, Blanche Morton, Winthrop Wayne. *Farm Boys*: Ralph Bond, George Griffin, Don Gauthier, Ted Wheeler, John McCulloch, J. Donald Heebner.

Act 1: Joshua Holcombe's Farm in Old New England. Afternoon.

Act 2: Inside the Barn. The Wedding Night.

ACT 1
 Opening
 "Gol- Durn!"
  J. Barry, Boys
 "Innocent Ingenue Baby"
  J. Merkyl, Girls
 "Old New England Home"
  E. Clark, Boys
  (*Music by* William Daly.)
 "The Cooney County Fair"
  O. Howland, E. Haig, Chorus
  (*Music by* George Gershwin.)
 "Names I Love to Hear"
  O. Howland, E. Haig, J. Barry, Mrs. J. Barry, G. Nichols
 "By-and-By"
  T. Conkey, E. Clark
  (*Music by* George Gershwin.)
 Finale
ACT 2
 "Madrigal"
  Ensemble
 "We Go to Church on Sunday"
  (*Music by* George Gershwin.)
 "Walking Home with Angeline"
  O. Howland, E. Haig, Chorus
  (*Music by* George Gershwin.)
 "Oh, You Lady!"
  L. Sonderson, Boys
 "(All the) Little Villages" (Wedding Trip)
  J. Barry, Mrs. J. Barry
 Duet
  T. Conkey, E. Clark
 Barn Dance
  Ensemble
 Finale

---

[118]Dropped during the run.
[119]Dropped during the run and replaced by:
 Dance a la Russe
  R. Dooley, J. Dooley

1922.47
THE CLINGING VINE

A Comedy with Music in Three Acts, 4 Scenes. Book and lyrics by Zelda Sears. Music by Harold Levey. Staged by Ira Hards. Musical numbers staged by Julian Alfred. Costumes by Peggy Hoyt. Scenes designed by William Castle. Orchestrations by Russell Bennett. Orchestra under the direction of Harold Levey. Produced by Henry W. Savage. Opened 25 December 1922 at the Knickerbocker Theatre and closed 2 June 1923 after 188 performances.

CAST (in order of appearance): *Tessie*, Secretary to Miss Antoinette Allen: IRENE DUNNE. *Plummer*, her advertising manager: Nathaniel Wagner. *Billings*, head of her Art Department: Royal Hallee. *Titus M. Tutewiler*, her Eastern representative: CHARLES SCHOFIELD. *Bill*, her foreman: Christian Holtum. *Smith*, her accountant: Bradford Hunt. *Brown*, her shipping clerk: Roy Marvin. *Jones* of her Sales Department: William Rogers. *Antoinette Allen*, President of A. Allen, Inc.: PEGGY WOOD. *Mildred Mayo*, a step-niece of Antoinette's grandmother: JOSEPHINE ADAIR. *Janet Milton*, another step-niece of her grandmother: ELEANOR DAWN. *Francis Milton*, Janet's husband: James C. Marlowe. *Randolph Mayo*, Mildred's husband: RAYMOND C. CRANE.

Debutantes from the Country Club: Jane: Jane Arrol. *Jean*: Jean Ferguson. *Margery*: Margery Wall. *Rosa*: Rosa Vera. *Helen*: Helen Hipkins. *Louise*: Louise Scheerer.

Sub-Debutantes from the Country Club: Eleanor: Eleanor Livingston. *Virginia*: Virginia Clark. *Florence*: Florence McGuire. *Victoria*: Victoria White.

Mrs. Anthony Allen, Antoinette's grandmother: LOUISE GALLOWAY. *Vacarescou*, a steamship acquaintance of Mrs. Allen's: REGINALD PASCH. *Agnes*, a maid of Mrs. Allen's: Joyce White. *Bascom*, valet to Vacarescou: William C. Gordon. *Jimmy Manning*, a boyhood friend of Antoinette's: CHARLES DERICKSON. *Noel Graham*, a guest of Mrs. Allen's: Earl Gates.

Girls Sextet: Jane Arrol, Helen Hipkins, Margery Wall (sopranos); Jean Ferguson (lyric soprano); Rosa Vera, Louise Sheerer (contraltos). *Boys Sextet*: Nathaniel Wagner, Royal Hallee, Roy Marvin (tenors); William Rogers (baritone); Bradford Hunt, Christian Holtum (basses). *Dancing Quartet*: Eleanor Livingston, Virginia Clark, Florence McGuire, Victoria White.

Act 1, Scene 1: General Offices of A. Allen, Inc., Mixed Paints, Omaha, Nebraska. One morning in June. *Scene 2*: Living Room in the home of Mrs. Anthony Allen, Shippan Point, Stamford, Connecticut. Three days later.

Act 2: Living Room of Mrs. Anthony Allen. A week later.

Act 3: Mrs. Allen's Garden. Eight o'clock that night.

ACT 1
Scene 1
  "A Little Bit of Paint"
    P. Wood, I. Dunne, C. Schofield, Boys' Sextette
Scene 2
  "Grandma"
    L. Galloway, Boys' and Girls' Sextettes, Quartette
  "Roumania"
    R. Pasch, J. Adair, E. Dawn
  "Once Upon a Time"
    P. Wood
  "Lady Luck"
    E. Dawn, J. Adair, R. Crane, R. Pasch, C. Derickson, Girls' and Boys' Sextettes, Quartette

ACT 2
  "Spring Fever"
    J. White, W. C. Gordon, Girls' and Boys' Sextettes, Quartette
  "Age of Innocence"
    P. Wood, J. C. Marlowe, R. Crane
  "The Clinging Vine"
    P. Wood, C. Derickson
  "Cupid"
    R. Crane, Girls' Quartette, Boys' Sextette
  "Homemade Happiness"[120]
    P. Wood, C. Derickson, Girls' Sextette, Quartette

ACT 3
  "Serenade"
    Girls' and Boys' Sextettes, Quartette
  Reprise
    P. Wood
  "Song Without Words"
    R. Crane, Girls' Quartette, J. White, E. Gates

Finale
  Entire Company

1922.48
GLORY

A Musical Comedy in Two Acts, 7 Scenes. Book by James Montgomery. Music by Maurice DePackh and Harry Tierney. Lyrics by James Dyrenforth and Joseph McCarthy. Staged by Bert French. Scenery painted by Joseph Wickes Studio. Costumes by the Vanderbilt Producing Company Wardrobe Department. Orchestra under the direction of Max Hirschfeld. Produced by the Vanderbilt Producing Company (Carle Carleton). Opened 25 December 1922 at the Vanderbilt Theatre and closed 24 February 1923 after 74 performances.

CAST: *William Harriman*, a city chap, born in the town: WALTER REGAN. *Hiram Dexter*, the richest man: Jack Clifford. *Ansel Tollet* the singing constable: ROBERT HIGGINS. *Lem King*, Sarah's son: Raymond Hackett. *Sumner Holbrook*, the town's pride: JOHN CHERRY. *Deacon Eaton*, a pillar of the Church: ROBERT O'CONNOR. *Alonzo*, Harriman's valet: TED McNAMARA. *Abner Moore*, Glory's father: Peter Lang. *Glory Moore*, a country girl: PATTI HARROLD. *Glory's Friends (2): Lucy Ann Willing*: HELEN GROODY. *Myrtie Brown*: MABEL FERRY. *Sarah King*, the town trumpet: BERTHA CREIGHTON. *Amanda Dexter*, Dexter's daughter: BERNICE McCABE.

Ladies of the Ensemble: Frances Lynde, Constance Montague, Bessie Mulligan, Peggy Pidgin, Violet Bristow, Helen Pain, Edith McGovern, Constance Keating, Marjorie Harrold, Margaret Murray, Margaret Leona, Florence Kinsley, Elizabeth Page, Arden Benham, Irene Enright, Dorothy Whiteford. *Gentlemen of the Ensemble*: Thomas Weldon, Paul Winnell, David Brown, Bobby Culbert, Ainsley Lambert, Edward Smith, Edward Howell, Conway Dillon.

The action takes place in a small town in New England.

Act 1, Scene 1: The General Store. Afternoon. *Scene 2*: The Lawn in the rear of Hiram Dexter's House. *Scene 3*: The General Store. *Scene 4*: Dexter's Lawn. The Fair. The same evening.

Act 2, Scene 1: The General Store. Twilight. A short time later. *Scene 2*: Harriman's Home. The same evening. *Scene 3*: The General Store. A few moments later.

ACT 1
  The Opening
  Ensemble
    (*Music by* Harry Tierney. *Lyrics by* Joseph McCarthy.)
  "We've Got to Build"
    J. Cherry, Ensemble
    (*Music by* Harry Tierney. *Lyrics by* Joseph McCarthy.)
  "Glory"
    P. Harrold
    (*Music by* Maurice DePackh. *Lyrics by* James Dyrenforth.)
  "Buds and Blossoms"[121]
    Boys, Girls
    (*Music by* Harry Tierney. *Lyrics by* Joseph McCarthy.)
  "The Little White House with Green Blinds"
    P. Harrold
    (*Music by* Harry Tierney. *Lyrics by* Joseph McCarthy.)
  "The Moon That Was Good Enough for Dad and Mother"
    B. McCabe, Ensemble
    (*Music by* Maurice DePackh. *Lyrics by* James Dyrenforth.)
  "The Goodly Little Things We Do"
    B. Creighton, B. McCabe, R. Higgins, R. O'Connor
    (*Music by* Maurice DePackh. *Lyrics by* James Dyrenforth.)
  "When the Curfew Rings at Nine"
    H. Groody, M. Ferry, J. Cherry, T. McNamara
    (*Music and Lyrics by* Al W. Brown.)
  "Popularity"
    P. Harrold, Ensemble
    (*Music by* Harry Tierney. *Lyrics by* Joseph McCarthy.)

ACT 2
  The Opening
    W. Regan, Ensemble
    (*Music by* Harry Tierney. *Lyrics by* Joseph McCarthy.)
  "The Upper Crust"
    M. Ferry, T. McNamara, Ensemble
    (*Music by* Harry Tierney. *Lyrics by* Joseph McCarthy.)

---

[120]Dropped for subsequent tour.

[121]Dropped during the run.

"Mother's Wedding Dress"
P. Harrold Ensemble
(*Music by* Harry Tierney. *Lyrics by* Joseph McCarthy.)

"Saw Mill River Road" (The Same Old Story)
M. Ferry, H. Groody, J. Cherry, T. McNamara
(*Music by* Harry Tierney. *Lyrics by* Joseph McCarthy.)

"Post Office"
P. Harrold, Company
(*Music by* Harry Tierney. *Lyrics by* Joseph McCarthy.)

"(When) The Tenor Married the Soprano and the Alto Married the Bass"
F. Irwin, B. McCabe, R. Higgins, R. O'Connor
(*Music by* Maurice DePackh. *Lyrics by* James Dyrenforth.)

"(The) Same Old Story" (Saw Mill River Road)
P. Harrold
(*Music by* Harry Tierney. *Lyrics by* Joseph McCarthy.)

1923.01　LADY BUTTERFLY

A Musical Comedy in Two Acts, 5 Scenes. Book and lyrics by Clifford Grey. Based on the farce ("Somebody's Luggage") by Mark Swan and James T. Powers. Music by Werner Janssen. Staged by Ned Wayburn. Costumes designed by Shirley Barker. Art director (scenic design), Herbert Ward. Orchestra conducted by William Daly. Orchestrations by Oscar Radin[122]. Produced by Oliver Morosco (Morosco Holding Co., Inc.). Opened 22 January 1923 at the Globe Theatre, moved 19 March 1923 to the Astor Theatre, and closed 12 May 1923 after 128 performances.

CAST (in order of appearance): *Duval*, Steward on the Channel Boat: Vic Casmore. *Horatio Meak*, a Passenger: Lionel Pape. *Pansy*, his bride: Rona Wallace. *Jack Owen*, First Officer on the Channel Boat: Edward Lester. *Billy Browning*: ALLEN KEARNS. *Henry Crawford*, Heir to the Fairfax Estate: GEORGE TRABERT. *Fisher*: Frank Dobson. *Caroline*, a Stewardess on the Channel Boat: MAUDE EBURNE. *Mrs. Stockbridge*: Gertrude Maitland. *Mabel Stockbridge*: MABEL WITHEE. *Alfred Hopper*: FLORENZ AMES. *Enid Crawford*: MARJORIE GATESON. *Bobby*, Cabin Boy: Janet Stone. *Frances*, a Ladies' Man: Aline McGill. *Ruth*, another Stewardess: MARION HAMILTON. *Mr. Stockbridge*: Lionel Pape. *Briggs*, the Fairfax Butler: Edward Lester. *A Policeman*: Raymond Hunter.

Incidental Dancing Specialties: Janet Stone, Aline McGill, Marion Hamilton, Florentine Gasnova, Joe Donahue, Nick Long, Jr., Jack Lynch, Horton Spurr. *Butterfly Quartette*: Mark Youmans (first tenor), Vere Richards (second tenor), Raymond Hunter (baritone), Ray Coffey (second bass). *Ensemble*: Misses Muriel Lodge, Imogene Wilson, Carol Young, Rona Wallace, Florentine Gasnova, Ainslee Evans, Bernice Ackerman, Lillian MacKenzie, Diana Chase, Mary Carney, Margaret McKay, Leona Lukens, Virginia McGee, Anna Buckley, Rosemary Sill, Louis Carlton, Pearl Howell, Helen Fleming, Mildred Lunnay, Vilheda.

Act 1: Deck of a Channel Boat as she lies at the dock at Havre, France.

Act 2, Scene 1: The Tradesmen's Entrance. *Scene 2*: Reception Hall in the Fairfax Home, Hampshire, England. *Scene 3*: Outside the Garden. *Scene 4*: Reception Hall in the Fairfax Home.

ACT 1

"Soon We'll Be Upon the Sea"
Ensemble

"Girls I've Never Met"
A. Kearns, Ensemble

"Doll's House"[123]
M. Withee, A. Kearns

"Wonderful You"
G. Trabert, Chorus

Dance
A. McGill

"Waltz Time"
A. Kearns, J. Stone, M. Hamilton, Chorus

"Sailors Sail Away"
M. Withee, Sailors

Solo Dance
J. Donahue

"Beautiful Love"
F. Ames, M. Eburne

"Man Overboard"
Ensemble

ACT 2[124]

Scene 1

"By the Garden Wall"
Nurses and Bobbies

Eccentric Dance[125]
J. Lynch

Acrobatic Dance
J. Donahue, M. Hamilton

Scene 2

"The Bad Man Walk"
F. Dobson, Servants, Chorus

"My Cottage in Sunshine Lane"
M. Gateson, Chorus

"Lady Butterfly"
G. Trabert, M. Gateson

Dance
Butterfly: J. Stone. *Student*: N. Long, Jr. *Butterflies*: F. Gasnova, B. Ackerman, Vilhelda.

"Good Evening—Good Night"
M. Withee, A. Kearns

"Kiss Time"
G. Trabert, M. Gateson, Chorus

The First Kiss: *Boy*: A. Buckley. *Girl*: V. McGee.

The Kiss of Yore: *An Old-Fashioned Girl*: I. Wilson. *Her Suitor*: J. Lynch.

The Lingering Kiss: *A Vamp*: M. Lodge. *Her Victim*: R. Hunter.

The Mother's Kiss: *The Mother*: C. Young. *The Son*: N. Long, Jr.

Toe Dance
F. Gasnova, accompanied by M. Hamilton (harp)

Scene 3

"The Chase"
Ensemble

"The Booze of Auld Lang Syne"
F. Ames, F. Dobson, Butterfly Quartette

Reprise
M. Gateson, G. Trabert

"Sway With Me"
A. Kearns, Chorus

Tap Dance
N. Long, Jr.

Leg-Mania
A. McGill

Acrobatic Dance
H. Spurr

Finale
Ensemble

1923.02　THE DANCING GIRL

A Musical Play in Two Acts, 18 Scenes. Book and lyrics by Harold Atteridge. Music by Sigmund Romberg, (George Gershwin, A. J. Carey, Alfred Goodman). Staged by J. C. Huffman. Stage settings by Watson Barratt; smoking room and steerage settings by Rollo Wayne. Women's dresses by Milgrim, Joseph Hickson, Lucile, Gilbert Clark, Mme. Haverstick, Mme. Routon, Vanity Fair Company, Paul Arlington; men's clothes by Ford Uniform Company. Orchestra under the direction of Alfred Goodman. Entire production staged under the personal supervision of J. J. Shubert. Produced by Messrs. Shubert. Opened 24 January 1923 at the Winter Garden and closed 12 May 1923 after 142 performances.

CAST [in order of appearance]: *Mr. Jones*: Roy Remo. *Mr. Smith*: Henry Stremel. *Mr. Robinson*: Frank Greene. *Mr. Brown*: TED DONER. *Mr. Clark*: KITTY DONER. *The*

---

[122]Later in the run, Stephen Jones was added as co-orchestrator.
[123]Dropped during the run.

[124]The running order of songs in Act 2, Scenes 2 and 3 was revised during the run.
[125]Replaced during the run by:
"When the Wedding Bells Ring Out"
Alice Cavanaugh (Mabel), Maurice Holland (Billy)

Steward: Charles Mac. *Bruce Chattfield*: ARTHUR MARGETSON. *John Mercer*: CYRIL SCOTT. *Gloria Seabright*: Gilda Leary. *The Count*: Frank Byron. *Miss Grayson*: ROSE DONER. *Dellisho*: LLORA HOFFMAN. *A Russian Immigrant*: Michael Voljanin. *A Czechoslovak*: Michael Markoff. *The Violin Girl*: Marie Harcourt. *Eliza*: Sally Fields. *Anna*: TRINI. *Rudolpho*: TOM BURKE. *Chief Inspector*: Ben Bard. *His Assistant*: Jack Pearl. *First Inspector*: Frank Byron. *Second Inspector*: Henry Stremel. *First Lady*: Dorothy Bruce. *The Butler*: Charles Mac. *A Lady Passenger*: MARIE DRESSLER. *Another Victim*: Lou Holtz. *The Dope Fiend*: Ben Bard. *Jack*: Jack Pearl. *Lou*: Lou Holtz. *Mack*: TED DONER. *Mame*: KITTY. DONER. *Steve*: Charles Mac. *The Guide*: Frank Greene. *A Vamp Shop Girl*: ROSE DONER. *Pinkie*: KITTY DONER. *Amy*: Harriet Gustine. *Lilly*: Helen Fox. *Hope*: Hope Herendeen. *Francine*: Perle Germonde. *Camille*: Charlotte Sprague. *Geraldine*: Dorothy Bruce. *Clarice*: Marja Talwyn. *Melisande*: Virginia Calmer. *Helene*: Bobbie Muir. *Gustave*: Jack Pearl. *King Louis*: Frank Greene. *The Singer*: LLORA HOFFMAN. *The Dancer*: Martha Mason. *Joe*: Frank Byron. *Pete*: Ted Doner. *Doorman*: Henry Stremel. *Ben*: Ben Bard. *Benny Leonard*: Benny Leonard. *A Lady Patron*: MARIE DRESSLER. *A Gentleman*: Charles Mac. *The Referee*: Frank Greene. *Young Sullivan*: Allie Nack. *Mr. Campbell*: Jack Forrester. *Marie Dressler*: MARIE DRESSLER. *Mrs. Meyers*: LLORA HOFFMAN. *Water Girl*: Orilla Smith. *The Old Man*: TOM BURKE. *The Young Man*: ARTHUR MARGETSON. *The Minuet*: TED DONER, ROSE DONER. *The Singers*: LLORA HOFFMAN, Roy Remo. *The Dancer*: Trini. *Perry*: Frank Byron. *Pauo Pauo*: SALLY FIELDS. *First Stage Hand*: Charles Mac. *Second Stage Hand*: Jack Forrester. *Joe Horne*: Frank Greene. *The Doctor*: Frank Byron. *Mrs. Davidson*: Elsie May. *The Reverend Davidson*: Cyril Scott. *Sadie Thompson*: MARIE DRESSLER. *Sergeant O'Hara*: ARTHUR MARGETSON. *Father Time*: Jack Wesley. *Constable*: Henry Stremel. *Mrs. Sheldon*: LLORA HOFFMAN. (*Piano Specialty*: Edythe Baker.)

Ladies of the Ensemble: Mae Sullivan, Dolly Wegman, Louise Stark, Edna Stark, Florence Darling, Virginia Calmer, Bobby McCree, Lys Doree, Jeanne Travers, Lota Cheeck, Fay Reed, Jeanne Elise, Margaret Hansel, Dolores Edwards, Margaret Brill, Helen Rodgers, Billy Wagner, Jean Thomas, Sidney Nelson, Edith Pierce, Orilla Smith, Carol Miller, Elsie Frank, Kay Mahoney, Poppy Morton, Buela Rubens, Florence Wilde, Lucille Pryor, Marian Davis, Elsie May, Elsie Dunn, Renee Miller, Gladys Smith. *Gentlemen of the Ensemble*: William Neeley, Dona Mayo, Irvin Wesley, George Ellison, Jack Forrester, Rodger Buckley.

Act 1, Scene 1: The Card Room on an Atlantic Liner. *Scene 2*: The Steerage. *Scene 3*: At the Custom House. *Scene 4*: In Chinatown. *Scene 5*: At a Flower Stall. *Scene 6*: Monsieur Gustave's Models. *Scene 7*: A Musicale at the Biltmore. *Scene 8*: In Front. *Scene 9*: A Picture of Versailles. *Scene 10*: Training Quarters. *Scene 11*: The Boxing Contest.

Act 2, Scene 1: The Theatre Nightly. *Scene 2*: Romance. *Scene 3*: Cuddle Up. *Scene 4*: The Whip (*by* Harry Wagstaff Gribble). *Scene 5*: The School of Expression. *Part A*: Pianologue. *Part B*: In Spain. *Part C*: Rain. *Part D*: Pango Land. *Scene 6*: Bard and Pearl. *Scene 7*: Venetia at the Ball.

ACT 1[126]

"Lucky in Love"
Ensemble
"Any Little Girl Will Fall"
K. Doner, R. Doner
"Hail U.S.A."
L. Hoffman
"That American Boy of Mine"
S. Fields
(*Music by* George Gershwin. *Lyrics by* Irving Caesar.)
(Specialty)
Trini
"Why Am I (So) Sad"
T. Burke, Trini
(*Music by* George Gershwin.)
"What Have You to Declare"
R. Doner, T. Doner
"The Bowery of Today"
T. Doner, K. Doner
"My Love Bouquet"
Trini. A. Margetson

---

[126]During the run, the order of songs and scenes in Act 2 was revised. For subsequent tour, Act 2, Scenes 5 and 6 were dropped, and the order of scenes and songs revised. The following were added:
"The World Is Waiting for the Sunrise"/"Mattinata" (Act 1)
L. Hoffman
(*Music by* Ernest Seitz. *Lyrics by* Eugene Lockhart.)
"Innocent Eyes" (Act 2)
Vera Myers, J. Pearl
"The Strutter" (Act 2)
Jane Green

"I'm a Devil with the Ladies"
K. Doner
"I've Been Wanting You"
Trini, A. Margetson
(*Music by* A. J. Carey and Alfred Goodman.)
"Versailles"
L. Hoffman
"There Was the Punch"[127]
Ensemble
ACT 2
"That Romance of Mine"
T. Burke, L. Hoffman, A. Margetson, Trini
"Cuddle Up"
K. Doner, T. Doner, R. Doner
(*Music by* George Gershwin.)
"Play Me a Tune"[128]
E. Baker, T. Doner
"Pango Pango"
S. Fields
(*Music by* George Gershwin.)
Spanish Dance[129]
Trini
"Venetian"[130]
T. Burke, L. Hoffman, F. Greene, R. Remo

1923.03   CAROLINE

A Musical Romance (Comedy) in Three Acts. Book and lyrics by Harry B. Smith and Edward Delaney Dunn. Adapted from the German operette ("Der Vetter aus Dingsda") with libretto by Herman Haller and Edward Rideamus (based on a comedy by Max Kempner-Hochstädt). Music by Eduard Künneke and Edward Rideamaus, (Alfred Goodman). Staged by Fred G. Latham. Dances arranged by Frank M. Gillespie. Stage settings by Watson Barratt. Costumes for Miss Kosta and Miss Shipman by Mme. Routon; all other dresses by Vanity Fair Costume Company. Orchestra under the direction of Fred Hoff. Entire production under the personal direction of J. J. Shubert. Produced by Messrs. Shubert. Opened 31 January 1923 at the Ambassador Theatre and closed 9 June 1923 after 151 performances[131].

CAST: *Caroline Lee*, Ward of General Calhoun: TESSA KOSTA. *Helen*, the General's Daughter: HELEN SHIPMAN. *Brigadier General Randolph Calhoun*: HARRISON BROCKBANK. *Mrs. Calhoun*: Viola Gillette. *Digby Bretton*, Claim agent and intruder from the North: BARNETT PARKER. *Captain Robert Langdon* of the Third Louisiana Infantry: J. HAROLD MURRAY. *Roderick Gray*: JOHN ADAIR. *Amanda*, Cook in the Calhoun household: Mattie Keene. *Hannibal*, the General's Orderly: Ben Linn.

Friends of Helen and Caroline: Flora Wayne: Beatrice Wilson. *Isabel Marshall*: Edna Duval. *Edith Varden*: Jane Brown. *Gladys Carroll*: Kay Carlin. *Mabel Preston*: Viola Duval. *Joan Blythe*: Mabel Olson. *Josephine Hurley*: Vera Hoppe. *Irene Stone*: Vonnie James.

The action takes place from the evening of one day to the evening of the day following, just after the Civil War at the Old Calhoun Mansion near Richmond, Virginia.

Act 1: The Garden.

Act 2: The Veranda.

Act 3: The Veranda.

ACT 1[132]

---

[127]Dropped during the New York run.
[128]Dropped during the New York run.
[129]Dropped during the New York run.
[130]Dropped during the New York run.
[131]Despite the program credit, none of the published music credits any lyrics to Edward Delaney Dunn. During the show's tryout under the title VIRGINIA, Alfred Goodman was credited with revising Künneke's music and composing additional music; likewise Edward Rideamus is not credited as composer on any published music.
[132]Sigmund Romberg's biography "Deep in Your Heart" credits him as composer of "Man in the Moon," "Will-o-the Wisp," "Sweetheart" and "Shoulder Arms" which are all credited to Künneke in published sheet music.

"Telling Fortunes" (Your Fortune)(Opening Chorus)
  M. Keene, H. Shipman, Girls
  (*Music by* Eduard Künneke. *Lyrics by* Harry B. Smith.)

"When I Say It's So, It's So"
  H. Brockbank

"The Man in the Moon"
  T. Kosta
  (*Music by* Eduard Künneke. *Lyrics by* Harry B. Smith.)

"The Old Virginia Reel"
  M. Keene, B. Linn

"The Piper You Must Pay" (Pay the Piper)
  B. Parker, H. Shipman, Girls
  (*Music by* Eduard Künneke. *Lyrics by* Harry B. Smith.)

"Hello, Hello"
  J. H. Murray

"Land of Enchantment" (Land of Romance)
  T. Kosta, J. H. Murray
  (*Music by* Eduard Künneke and Alfred Goodman. *Lyrics by* Harry B. Smith.)

Finale

ACT 2

"Will O' the Wisp"
  T. Kosta, J. H. Murray, H. Brockbank, H. Shipman, V. Gillette
  (*Music by* Eduard Künneke. *Lyrics by* Harry B. Smith.)

"Sweetheart"
  T. Kosta, J. H. Murray
  (*Music by* Eduard Künneke. *Lyrics by* Harry B. Smith.)

"Shoulder Arms"
  B. Parker, H. Shipman, Girls
  (*Music by* Eduard Künneke. *Lyrics by* Harry B. Smith.)

"Argentine"
  Ensemble
  (*Music by* Eduard Künneke and Alfred Goodman. *Lyrics by* Harry B. Smith.)

"Love's Last Day"
  Ensemble

Finale

ACT 3

"Way Down South"
  H. Shipman, Girls
  (*Music by* Alfred Goodman. *Lyrics by* Harry B. Smith.)

"Who Cares for a Name"
  T. Kosta, J. H. Murray, J. Adair

1923.04 # SUN SHOWERS

A Musical Rainbow (Comedy) in Three Acts. Words (book, lyrics) and music by Harry Delf. Staged by Frederick Stanhope. Dances and ensembles by Seymour Felix; additional dances by Larry Ceballos. Costumes by Mabel Johnston. Scenery by Robert Law and Vitolo-Pearson Studios. Orchestra under the direction of Fred T. Fleming. Produced by Lew Cantor. Opened 5 February 1923 at the Astor Theatre and closed 17 March 1923 after 48 performances[133].

CAST (in order of appearance): *May Worthy*: Berta Donn. *Minnie Silver*: Harriette Lee. *Mrs. Thompson*: CLAIRE GRENVILLE. *Bobby Brown*: Douglas Stevenson. *Jerry Jackson*: HARRY DELF. *Alice Worthy*: ALLYN KING. *Tommy Dugan*: Tom Dingle. *Members of the Board of Education* (4): *Joseph Green*: Eddie Winthrop. *William Blue*: Mack Wells. *John Black*: William Schutt. *Ralph White*: Jack Kennedy. *Pierre, Maitre d'Hotel*: John Boswell. *Waiters* (3): *Francois*: Frank Anderson. *Louis*: Lee Houston. *Gaston*: George Berlow. *Specialty Dancers*: Tom Dingle, Patsey Delaney.
  Young Women of the Ensemble: Gene West, Ina Casidy, Helen Jackson, Grace Cassidy, Mae Reny Grady, Ethelyn Tillman, Sylvia Carol, Gerry Bachelor, Julia Warren, Betty Broughton, Beatrice O'Connor, Phyllis Reynolds.

The action takes place at the present time in New York City.

Act 1: Mrs. Thompson's Boarding House.

---

[133]Subsequently toured as HAPPY DAYS under the auspices of Jules Hurtig in association with Lew Cantor. Added for subsequent tour:
  "Fire and Mist" (Divertissement)
  Finale (Act 2)

Act 2: The Heliotrope Room—Savoy Hotel.

Act 3: Back Yard at Mrs. Thompson's.

ACT 1

"(Get Him) On a Moonlight Night"
  B. Donn, Girls

"He Loves Me"
  A. King, Girls

"How Do You Doodle?"
  B. Donn, H. Delf

"Sun Showers"
  A. King, B. Donn, D. Stevenson, H. Delf

"(I'm) a Greenwich Village Chambermaid"
  H. Lee, Girls

"Everyone Is Beautiful in Someone's Eyes"
  A. King, D. Stevenson

ACT 2

"Oh! Professor"
  Professors [Board of Education], Girls

Specialty Dance[134]
  M. Wells, E. Winthrop

"Worth While Waiting For"
  A. King, D. Stevenson

"In the Morning"
  B. Donn, H. Delf

"Each Little Jack (Is Some Girl's Little John)"
  D. Stevenson, Girls

"Speak Without Any Compunction" (You Can Speak Without Compunction)
  H. Lee, T. Dingle

Reprise

ACT 3

"Yours Truly"
  A. King, Girls

"Clip, Clip the Coupons"
  Waiters, C. Grenville

"Terpsichore, the Goddess of Dance"
  H. Delf

Dance
  T. Dingle

Finale

1923.05 # WILDFLOWER

A Musical Play in Three Acts. Book and lyrics by Otto Harbach and Oscar Hammerstein II. Music by Herbert Stothart and Vincent Youmans. Book staged by Oscar Eagle. Dances and ensembles by David Bennett. Gowns and costumes designed by Charles LeMaire. Settings by (Frank E.) Gates and (Edward A.) Morange. Orchestra under the direction of Herbert Stothart. (Orchestrations by Robert Russell Bennett.) Produced by Arthur Hammerstein. Opened 7 February 1923 at the Casino Theatre and closed 29 March 1924 after 477 performances.

CAST (in order of appearance): *Luigi*: Jerome Daley. *Gabrielle*: OLIN HOWLAND. *Gaston La Roche*: CHARLES JUDELS. *Bianca Benedetto*: EVELYN CAVANAUGH. *Count Alberto*: JAMES DOYLE. *Guido*: GUY ROBERTSON. *Nina Benedetto*: EDITH DAY. *Lucrezia La Roche*: ESTHER HOWARD. *Specialty Dancers*: Marion and Martinez Randall.
  Ladies of the Ensemble: Helen Lewis, Emmy Tattersall, Genevieve Markham, Marie Otto, Agnes Horter, Florence Ashton, Margarete Morris, Myrtle Miller, Ursula Mack, Elizabeth Coyle, Peggy Stohl, Viola Clarens, Sybil Steward, Verona Oakley, Marion Phillips, Marjorie Wood, Beverly Maude, Adele Hart, Muriel Harrison. *Gentlemen of the Ensemble*: Robert Hurst, Al Kinley, Paul Porter, Charles Froom, Louis Laub, Frank Grimel, William McGurn, Kenneth Smith.

Act 1: Luigi's Farm Yard near Casimo, a small village in Lombardy, Italy. Autumn.

Act 2: The Benedetto Villa on Lake Como, Spring.

Act 3: Luigi's Farm Yard. Next morning.

---

[134]Dropped for subsequent tour.

ACT 1

"Iloveyouiloveyou" (I Love You, I Love You, I Love You!)
O. Howland, Girls
(*Music by* Vincent Youmans.)

"Some Like to Hunt"
C. Judels, Girls
(*Music by* Herbert Stothart.)

"Wildflower"
G. Robertson
(*Music by* Vincent Youmans.)

"Bambalina"
E. Day, Ensemble
(*Music by* Vincent Youmans.)

"I'll Collaborate with You"
E. Howard, O. Howland
(*Music by* Herbert Stothart.)

"April Blossoms"
E. Day, G. Robertson
(*Music by* Herbert Stothart.)

Finale
Ensemble

ACT 2

"The Best Dance I've Had Tonight"
E. Cavanaugh, Chorus

"Course I Will"
E. Day, J. Doyle, O. Howland
(*Music by* Vincent Youmans.)

"(Girl from) Casimo"
G. Robertson, Chorus
(*Music by* Herbert Stothart.)

Dance
Marion and Martinez Randall

"If I Told You"[135]
E. Day, Boys
(*Music by* Vincent Youmans.)

"Good-Bye, Little Rosebud"
G. Robertson, Ensemble
(*Music by* Herbert Stothart.)

Finale
Ensemble

ACT 3

"Bambalina" (reprise)
E. Day, J. Doyle, Ensemble

"The World's Worst Women"
E. Howard, O. Howland
(*Music by* Herbert Stothart.)

"You Can Always Find Another Partner"
E. Day, Ensemble
(*Music by* Vincent Youmans.)

Finale
(Company)

1923.06   GO-GO

A Show (Musical Comedy) in Two Acts, 5 Scenes. Book by Harry L. Cort and George E. Stoddard. Music by C. Luckyeth Roberts. Lyrics by Alex Rogers. Staged by Walter Brooks. Costumes designed by Shirley Barker. Scenery designed by the Beaux Arts Studios. Orchestra under the direction of Hilding Anderson. Produced by John Cort. Opened 12 March 1923 at Daly's Theatre, moved 25 June 1923 to the Apollo Theatre, and closed 14 July 1923 after 138 performances.

CAST (in order of appearance): *Mrs. Parker*, the Mother: Kathi Murray. *Otis Hubbard*, the Wise Cracker: Paul Burns. *Isabel Parker*, the Country Girl: JOSEPHINE STEVENS. *Florabel Parker*, the City Twin Sister: JOSEPHINE STEVENS. *Margy*, the 'Phone Girl: Vangi Murray. *Mrs. Phyllis Full*, the Office Manager: MAY BOLEY. *Telma Finnish*, the Chief Stenog: LORA SONDERSON. *Senator Locksmith*, the Committee

of One: FRANK DOANE. *Oswald Piper*, the Agency Owner: DON BARCLAY. *Jack Locksmith*, the Senator's Son: BERNARD GRANVILLE. *Vernille*, the Dancer: Nitzi Vernille. *Briggs*, the Internal Revenue Man: D. L. Roberts. (*Dance Specialty*: Santley and Norton.) *Country Girls, Rubes, City Girls, Actresses, Actors, Guests.*

Dancers: Hilda Major, Agnes Allan, Helyn Miller, Ethel Loraine, Nellie Daly, May Whitney, Florence Gladstone, Bonnie Shaw, Paulette Winston, Marie Frawley, Jean Picard, Sophia Howard, Roslyn Roland, Adeline Brunner, Sadie Howard, Gladys Miller, Ceceilia Cullen, Marie Cattell, Jack McElroy, George Saule, Jack Kearney, George Schaffran, Henry Levey, Fred Harris, Mack Davis, Phil Newton.

Act 1, Scene 1: Rambler Rose Cottage, Honey Falls, New York. Morning. *Scene 2*: Office of the Oswald Theatrical Agency, New York. One week later. *Scene 3*: Street Scene in New York. That night. *Scene 4*: The Lounge at Cafe "The Pink Poodle." One hour later.

Act 2: The Summer Residence of Senator Locksmith at High Ball Point, Connecticut, on Long Island Sound. An Indian Summer Evening.

ACT 1
Scene 1

Descriptive Music

"New York Town" (Song)
P. Burns, Girls

"Whipperwill" (Song)
J. Stevens, Girls

"Good Bye, Honey Falls" (Ensemble)
J. Stevens, Girls

Scene 2

"Have You Any Little Thing?" (Ensemble)
Girls, Boys, V. Murray

"Any Old Time at All" (Song)
L. Sonderson, Chorus

"I'm Scared of You" (Duet)
B. Clifford, L. Sonderson

"Rosetime and You" (Song)
B. Granville, Chorus

Scene 3

"Happy"[136] (Song)
J. Stevens, P. Burns

Scene 4

"Strutting the Blues Away" (Opening)
J. Stevens, Others

Specialty[137]
Santley and Norton

"Honey" (Song)
M. Boley, D. Barclay

"Wonderful Dance" (Waltz)
B. Granville, Chorus

Dance
N. Vernille, B. Granville

Dance
B. Granville, A. Brunner

"Mo'lasses" (Ensemble)
J. Stevens, Company

ACT 2

"Indian Moon" (Opening)
L. Sonderson

Dance
N. Vernille

"Uno" (Song)
D. Barclay, Girls

"Isabel" (Song)
B. Granville

"Lolly-Papa" (Song)
M. Boley, Girls

---

[135]Replaced in March 1923 by:
"You Can't Blame a Girl for Dreaming"
E. Day, Boys
(*Music by* Vincent Youmans.)

---

[136]Replaced during the run by:
"The Mailman Must Be Mad at Me" (Song)
J. Stevens
[137]Replaced during the run by: Strutt.

"An Old Man's Darling" (Song)
  L. Sonderson, Boys
"Go-Go Bug" (Song)
  B. Granville, P. Burns
"Rosetime and You" (reprise)
  J. Stevens, B. Granville
"Pat Your Feet" (Song)
  P. Burns, Company

1923.07 JACK AND JILL

A Musical Comedy in Three Acts, a Prologue and 8 Scenes. Book by Frederick Isham and Otto Harbach. Based on the play ('The Cherry Tree') by Frederick Isham. Music by Augustus Barratt. Lyrics by John Murray Anderson, Otto Harbach and Augustus Barratt. Dialogue directed by John Harwood. Dances arranged by Larry Ceballos. Settings by Frederick Jones III. Costumes designed by Robert Locher, Gilbert Clark and Frederick Jones III. Orchestra under the direction of Charles Previn. Orchestrations by Maurice DePackh and Stephen Jones. Entire production devised and staged by John Murray Anderson. Produced by the Chelsea Producing Corporation (Hugh A. Anderson, Managing director). Opened 22 March 1923 at the Globe Theatre and closed 9 June 1923 after 92 performances.

CAST: *Prologue: A Descendant of Mary Ball*: Gladys Burgette.
  The Play: Jack Andrews: DONALD MacDONALD. *Donald Lee*: BROOKE JOHNS. *Marcia Manners*: Winifred Verina. *Phyllis Sisson*: BETH BERI. *Mrs. Malone*: GEORGIA O'RAMEY. *Duke of Dippington*: LENNOX PAWLE. *Jill Malone*: VIRGINIA O'BRIEN. *Jimmy Eustace*: CLIFTON WEBB. *Gloria Wynne*: ANN PENNINGTON. *Daniel Malone*: ROGER IMHOF. *The Maid*: LENA BASQUETTE. *The Footman*: Carlos Conte. *The Butler*: Russell Scott. *Mrs. Foote*: Eleanora Grover. *Mrs. DePeyster Fish*: America Chedister. *Mrs. Sylvester Jones*: Metta Louise Orr.
  Solo Dancers: Leon Barté, (Lena Basquette), Nyoka-Nyoka, Beatrice Collenette, Helene Blair, Gayle Mays, Ward Fox, Claudius Webster, Beth Beri. *Solo Singers*: Astrid Ohlson, Brenda Bond, Eileen Lawrie, Nathalie Malowan, Russell Scott, Jean Barney, Lester O'Keefe, Leslie Joy. *Ensemble*: Alden Gay, Eleanora Grover, Tarzanne, Cynthia Cambridge, Peggy Fish, Joan Clement, America Chedister, Anna Mae Clift, Violet Lobelle, Anne Buckley, Eleanor Labelle, Elizabeth North, Kathleen Ardelle, Edna Locke, Elsa Doris, Pauline Doria, Geraldine Markham, Barbara Cavello. *Corps de Ballet*: Geneva Price, Doris Vinton, "Cricket", "Kiki" Maxwell, Julia Parker.

Prologue: Beneath the Washington Family Tree.

Act 1, Scene 1: The Antique Galleries. *Scene 2*: Georgian-Colonial Episode. *Scene 3*: The Antique Galleries.

Act 2, Scene 1: The Crystal Ballroom in Mrs. Malone's New York Residence. *Scene 2*: A Corridor. *Scene 3*: Venetian Lace Episode. *Scene 4*: The Crystal Ballroom.

The Second Act covers a period of two days, namely the afternoon of the day before Jill's wedding, and her wedding day. The "Venetian Lace Episode" is a dream-incident which takes place during the intervening lapse of time.

Act 3: The Sunken-Gardens of the Eustace Estate.

ACT 1[138]

  Prologue ("Seated 'Neath My Family Tree")
    G. Burgette
  Scene 1
  "Antiques"
    D. MacDonald
  "Voodoo Man"
    B. Johns
    (*Music by* Alfred Newman. *Lyrics by* Otto Harbach.)

---

[138]The song order was revised during the run and subsequent tour. Added for tour:
  "How Did They Know I Was an American?" (Act 1, Scene 1)
    G. O'Ramey
  "Georgie" (Act 1, Scene 2)
    C. Webb, D. MacDonald, B. Beri, W. Verina
  "Back to Killarney" (Act 2, Scene 1)
    G. O'Ramey
  "I Love America" (Act 2, Scene 1)
    L. Pawle
  "I Love, Thou Lovest" (Act 2, Scene 1)
    D. MacDonald
  "Lace Maker's Song" (Act 2, Scene 2 after "Web of Dreams")
    A. Ohlson, G. Burgette

"Concentrate"
  A. Pennington, C. Webb
  (*Music by* Alfred Newman. *Lyrics by* Otto Harbach.)
"Girls Grow More Wonderful Day by Day"
  R. Imhof
Dances
  B. Beri, B. Collenette, H. Blair
"No Other Eyes"
  V. O'Brien
Scene 2
"The Keys of Heaven"[139] (traditional)
  A. Ohlson, L. O'Keefe, E. Lawrie, R. Scott, N. Malowan, L. Joy, V. O'Brien, D. MacDonald
Scene 3
"Hello! Good-Bye"
  C. Webb
  (*Music by* William Daly. *Lyrics by* Otto Harbach.)

ACT 2
Scene 1
"Married Life Blues"
  B. Johns
"(Snug as a) Bug in a Rug"
  V. O'Brien, C. Webb
"Pretty City Girl"[140]
  A. Pennington, B. Johns
  (*Music by* William Daly. *Lyrics by* Otto Harbach.)
    Pianist: Edna Baldwick.
Scene 2
"Web of Dreams"
  V. O'Brien
Scene 3
"Point Venice"[141] — A Ballad of the Bobbins (*Arranged by* Leon Barté.)
  (Ballet from a synopsis and design by Georgianna Brown Harbison)
    The Lacemaker: A. Ohlson. *The Story Teller*: G. Burgette. *The Lovers*: L. Basquette, L. Barté. *The Lace Pattern*: E. Lawrie, W. Fox, M. L. Orr, G. Mays. And the Corps de Ballet.
      In Venice, long ago, lived a lace maker who wove happiness into wedding bells for brides. One day while working on a pattern of dream lovers she fell asleep. The figures then came from their niches to dance new patterns and while they were playing blind man's bluff the lace maker awoke; the figures hastened to their niches, all but one lover who, blindfolded, could not find his way and so was left out of the pattern. Feeling sorry for his plight the lace maker rewove him into the lace design beside his lost sweetheart where they remained always together, an emblem of true love.
"(And) Her Mother Came Too!"[142]
  C. Webb
  (*Music and Lyrics by* Ivor Novello.)
Scene 4
"(Poor Little) Wall Flower"
  A. Pennington
  (*Music by* Muriel Pollock. *Lyrics by* Blanche Merrill.)

ACT 3
"Fleeting Honeymoon"
  R. Scott
Valse
  L. Basquette, L. Barté
"Dancing in the Dark"
  C. Webb, B. Beri
  (*Music by* Muriel Pollock. *Lyrics by* Oliver Deering.)
"Jack and Jill"
  V. O'Brien, D. MacDonald
Dance
  Nyoka-Nyoka

---

[139]Retitled for subsequent tour "The Keys of My Heart."
[140]Dropped for subsequent tour.
[141]Dropped for subsequent tour.
[142]First written for and performed in the London revue A TO Z; briefly interpolated into THE BUNCH AND JUDY during its tryout.

"Ophelia"
  G. O'Ramey, L. Pawle, C. Webb
"My Cherokee Rose"
  B. Johns and Ann Pennington

1923.08

ELSIE

A Musical Comedy in Three Acts. Book by Charles W. Bell. Music by Eubie Blake and Monte Carlo. Lyrics by Noble Sissle and Alma Sanders. Stage direction by Edgar MacGregor. Musical ensembles by Walter Brooks and Bert French. Costumes by Gilman Co., Brooks-Mahieu Co. Scenery by Rothe & Teichner. Orchestra under the direction of Eugene Salzer. Produced by John Jay Scholl. Opened 2 April 1923 at the Vanderbilt Theatre and closed 5 May 1923 after 40 performances.

CAST (in order of appearance). *Margery Hammond*: LUELLA GEAR. *Fred Blakely*: STANLEY RIDGES. *Anne Westford*: Ada Meade. *Alfie Westford*: John Arthur. *Mrs. Philip Hammond*: Maude Turner Gordon. *Philip Hammond*: Frederic Burt. *Elsie*: MARGUERITE ZENDER. *Irma*: Irma Marwick. *Harry Hammond*: VINTON FREEDLEY. *Parker*: WILLIAM CAMERON. *The Dancers from the "Fire Fly Co."* (4): *Julie*: Opal Hixson. *Vivienne*: Nell Ames. *Maureen*: Elyne Yselle. *Esme*: Helen Doty. *Specialty Dancers*: Layman and Kling.
  Elsie's Friends from the "Fire Fly Co.".: *Bunny*: Maida Harries. *Teddy*: Hilda Burt. *Babe*: Neida Snow. *Maisie*: Lucile Godard. *Toots*: Lucille Poirier. *Goldie*: Virginia Kelley. *Stella*: Helen Borden. *Floss*: Flo Clark. *Veda*: Helen Christian.

Act 1: Philip Hammond's Summer Residence at Idlewild. Late afternoon in early summer.

Act 2: Sun Parlor in the Same Home. Afternoon about three weeks later.

Act 3: Philip Hammond's Summer Residence at Idlewild. The same night.

ACT 1
  "A Regular Guy"
    W. Cameron, Girls
    (*Music by* Eubie Blake. *Lyrics by* Noble Sissle.)
  "One Day in May"
    Girls
    (*Music by* Alma Sanders. *Lyrics by* Monte Carlo.)
  "Hearts in Tune"
    V. Freedley, M. Zender
    (*Music by* Eubie Blake. *Lyrics by* Noble Sissle.)
  "Elsie"
    M. Zender
    (*Music by* Alma Sanders. *Lyrics by* Monte Carlo.)
  "My Crinoline Girl"
    V. Freedley, M. Zender, Girls, Four Crinoline Girl Dancers
    (*Music by* Eubie Blake. *Lyrics by* Noble Sissle.)
ACT 2
  "I'd Like to Walk with a Pal Like You"
    M. Zender, S. Ridges
    (*Music by* Eubie Blake. *Lyrics by* Noble Sissle.)
  "Two Lips Are Roses"
    S. Ridges, Girls, Four Crinoline Girl Dancers
    (*Music by* Alma Sanders. *Lyrics by* Monte Carlo.)
  "Baby Bunting"
    L. Gear, S. Ridges
    (*Music by* Eubie Blake. *Lyrics by* Noble Sissle.)
  "Honeymoon Home"
    V. Freedley, M. Zender, Girls
    (*Music by* Alma Sanders. *Lyrics by* Monte Carlo.)
  "Sand Flowers"
    M. Zender, Girls
    (*Music by* Eubie Blake. *Lyrics by* Noble Sissle.)
ACT 3
  "The Firefly"
    M. Zender, M. Harries, Girls
    (*Music by* Alma Sanders. *Lyrics by* Monte Carlo.)
  Miniature Ballet
    Four Sylphides
  Specialty Dance
    Layman and Kling

"Symphonic Poem"[143]
  J. Arthur
  (*Music by* Gene Salzer.)
"Everybody's Strutting Now"
  S. Ridges, L. Gear, Girls
  (*Music by* Eubie Blake. *Lyrics by* Noble Sissle.)
"Thunderstorm Jazz"[144]
  A. Meade, J. Arthur, L. Gear, S. Ridges, Girls, Four Goblins
  (*Music by* Eubie Blake. *Lyrics by* Noble Sissle.)
"Clouds of Love"[145]
  M. Zender
  (*Music by* Alma Sanders. *Lyrics by* Monte Carlo.)
Finale
  Company

1923.09

IRENE

A Revival of the Musical Comedy in Two Acts, 6 Scenes[146]. Book by James Montgomery. (Based on the play 'Irene O'Dare' by James Montgomery.) Music by Harry Tierney. Lyrics by Joseph McCarthy. Staged by Edward Royce. Produced by the Vanderbilt Producing Company (Carle Carleton). Opened 2 April 1923 at Jolson's Theatre and closed 14 April 1923 after 16 performances.

CAST: *Donald Marshall*: WALTER REGAN. *Robert Harrison*: James Young. *J. P. Bowden*: HENRY COOTE. *Lawrence Hadley*: John Keendon. *Clarkson*: George Mantell. *Irene O'Dare*: DALE WINTER. *Helen Cheston*: MARY MOORE. *Jane Gilmour*: Erica Mackay. *Mrs. Marshall*: DOROTHY LA MAR. *Eleanor Worth*: Bernadine Brady. *Mrs. O'Dare*: EMMA DeWEALE. *Mrs. Cheston*: Henrietta King. *Madame Lucy*: JERE DELANEY. *Ladies of the Ensemble*.

1923.10

CINDERS

A Comedy with Music in Two Acts, 6 Scenes. Book and lyrics by Edward Clark. Music by Rudolf Friml. Staged by Edward Royce. Settings designed by P. Dodd Ackerman. Gowns designed by Paul Poiret, Evelyn McHorter. Men's costumes by Earl Benham, Brooks-Mahieu. Orchestra under the direction of Victor Baravalle. Produced by Edward Royce. Opened 3 April 1923 at the Dresden Theatre (atop the New Amsterdam Theatre) and closed 28 April 1923 after 31 performances.

CAST (in order of appearance): *Tillie Olsen*, Cashier at Mme. Duval's: QUEENIE SMITH. *Slim Kelly*, Her Fiancée: FRED HILLEBRAND. *Cinders*, a Foundling: NANCY WELFORD. *John Winthrop*, Mrs. Winthrop's son: W. DOUGLAS STEVENSON. *Mrs. Horatio Winthrop*, a Society Leader: MARGARET DALE. *Major Drummond*: John H. Brewer. *Mrs. Delancey Hoyt*: Roberta Beatty. *Geraldine*, her daughter: Mary Lucas. *Butler at Mrs. Winthrop's*: Thomas Fitzpatrick. *Great Scott*, a Theatrical Magician: George Bancroft. *Miss Breckenridge*, a Southern Maiden Lady: Lillian Lee. *Mme. Duval*, Proprietress of Duval Modiste Shop: Edith Campbell-Walker. *A Sister Team in Vaudeville*: *Tottie*: Kitty Kelly. *Lottie*: Estelle Levelle.
  Ladies of the Ensemble: *Hortense*: Alta King. *Annabelle*: Diana Stegman. *Mathilde*: Dagmar Oakland. *Julie*: Evelyn Darville. *Yvette*: Elaine Gholson. *Ninette*: Eden Gray. *Cecelia*: Vera DeWolfe. *Simone*: Louise Bateman. *Dancers*: Gertrude McDonald, Elva Pomfret, Mildred Lunnay, Sydney Reynolds, Ralph Riggs, Katharine Witchie. *Gentlemen of the Ensemble*: *Bruce*: Jack Whiting. *Nat*: Nathaniel Gennes. *Frank*: Frank Curran. *Harry*: Harry Howell. *Cliff*: Abner Barnhart. *Denny*: Denny Murray. *Dewitt*: Dewitt Oakley. *Thomas*: Thomas Green. *Gene*: Eugene Jenkins.

Time: Present. Late Autumn.

Place: New York City.

Act 1, Scene 1: The Kitchen in Cinders' flat, East 39th Street. *Scene 2*: At Mrs. Winthrop's. The Conservatory adjoining the Ballroom. *Scene 3*: The Kitchen in Cinders' flat.

Act 2, Scene 1: The Showroom in Mme. Duval's modiste shop. The next morning. *Scene 2*: A bench in Central Park. That night. *Scene 3*: Drawing Room at Mrs. Winthrop's. The following afternoon.

---

[143]Dropped during the run.
[144]Dropped during the run.
[145]Dropped during the run.
[146]Originally produced in New York 18 November 1919 at the Vanderbilt Theatre for 675 performances. For Synopsis of Scenes and Musical Numbers, see original 1919 production.

ACT 1
"One Good Time"
N. Welford
"Get Together"
W. D. Stevenson, Ladies and Gentlemen
"You Got What Gets 'Em"
F. Hillebrand, Q. Smith
"I'm Simply Mad About the Boys"
N. Welford, Gentlemen
"You and I"
W. D. Stevenson, N. Welford, Ladies, Gentlemen
"The Argentine Arago"
F. Hillebrand, Q. Smith, Ladies and Gentlemen
Specialty Dance
R. Riggs, K. Witchie
"Finaletto"
Entire Company
"One Good Time"
N. Welford

ACT 2
"Hawaiian Shores"
A. King, Ladies
"You Remind Me of Someone"
W. D. Stevenson, N. Welford
"The Fashion Parade"
Ladies
"Three Thousand Years Ago"
V. DeWolfe
"Grandma's Day"
D. Oakland
"Flame of Love"
D. Stegman
"Modern Bride"
E. Darville
"La Favorite"
E. Gholson
"Moonlight on the Waters"
A. King
"Cinders"
N. Welford, Gentlemen
"The Belles of the Bronx"
K. Kelly, E. Levelle
Specialty Dance
R. Riggs, K. Witchie
"Rags Is Royal Raiments"
F. Hillebrand, Q. Smith
Finale
Entire Company

1923.11   HOW COME?

A Girly Musical Darkomedy in Two Acts, 10 Scenes. Book by Eddie Hunter. Score (Music and lyrics) by Ben Harris. Additional numbers by Henry Creamer and Will Vodery. Production staged by Sam H. Grisman. Dances arranged by Henry Creamer and Frank Montgomery. Scenery by Runnel-Amend Studio. Orchestrations by and orchestra under the direction of Will Vodery. Produced by Criterion Productions, Inc. Opened 16 April 1923 at the Apollo Theatre and closed 19 May 1923 after 40 performances[147].

CAST (in order of appearance): *Deacon Long Tack*: Andrew Fairchild. *Sarah Green*: Amanda Craig. *Brother Wire Nail*: LEROY BROOMFIELD. *Dolores Love*: NINA HUNTER. *Sister Doolittle*: Hilary Friend. *Ebeneezer Green*, President of the Mobile Chicken Trust Corporation: AMON DAVIS. *Brother Ham*, Financial Secretary of the M.C.T. Corporation: Alec Lovejoy. *A Smart*, Lawyer: CHAPPY CHAPPELLE. *Malinda Green*: JUANITA STINETTE. *Rufus Wise*, Buddy: GEORGE W. COOPER. *Rastus Skunkton Lime*: EDDIE HUNTER. *Dandy Dan*: George C. Lane. *Ophelia Snow*: ANDREW TRIBBLE. *Smiling Sam*: BILLY HIGGINS. *Brother Low Down*:

James Dingbat. *Sister Whale*: Octavia Sawyer. *Chief of Police*: Sidney Bechet. *First Policeman*: Harry Hunter. *Second Policeman*: Adrian Joyce. *Third Policeman*: Isaac Momen. *Miss Disappear*: Alice Brown.
Investors in the Mobile Chicken Trust Corporation: Sister Jones: NONA CHESTER. *Sister High*: Claire Campbell. *Sister Know All*: Rita Fairchild. *Sister Pull Back*: Olive Harrison. *Sister Brown*: Eunice Anderson. *Sister Ashes*: Violet Williams. *Sister Blue*: Catherine Jarvis. *Sister Scott*: Lottie Harris. *Brother Black*: Birch Williams. *Brother Samson*: George Haynes. *Brother Sharp*: Harry Watkins. *Brother Inkwell*: Charles Walker. *Brother Smoke*: Percy Wade.
Honorary Board of Directors M.C.T.C.: Sister Wright: Sadie Tapins. *Sister Wrong*: Mary Goodwin. *Sister Bridge*: Emma Maitland. *Brother Jenkins*: Alfred Chester. *Brother Coal*: Al Moore. *Brother Wood*: George Lynch.
Cathrine Peace: Helen Dunmore. *Lorabelle Wise*: Vivian Harris. *Millie Johnson*: Mabel Kemp. *Marie Fraine*: Dorothy Lewis. *Mobile Vamps (2): Ruth Johnson*: Elvetta Davis. *Hortense Carter*: Carrie Edwards. (*Specialties*: Donita Sisters, Johnny Nit.)

Act 1: Mobile, Alabama. *Scene 1*: Corporation Meeting. Lawn of Green's Home. *Scene 2*: A Rest Cure. *Scene 3*: A Back Yard. *Scene 4*: A Jail. *Scene 5*: A Railroad Station.

Act 2: Chicago, Illinois. *Scene 1*: A Drug Store. *Scene 2*: A Cafe. *Scene 3*: A Bootblack Parlor. *Scene 4*: Hall in Mansion of R. S. Lime, Esq. Six months later. *Scene 5*: Ball Room of Same.

ACT 1[148]
Opening Chorus
Ensemble
"Pretty Malindy"
L. Broomfield, N. Hunter, N. Chester, Company
"Certainly Is the Truth"
Ensemble
"Goodnight, Brother Green"
Ensemble
"Syncopated Strain"
A. Brown, N. Hunter, N. Chester, Company
"Bandanna Anna"
Dancing Girls
"Pickaninny Vamp"
C. Chappelle, J. Stinnette, Chorus
"Sweetheart, Farewell"
C. Chappelle, J. Stinnette, Company
"Dinah"
Ensemble

ACT 2
"Gingerena"
L. Broomfield, Company
"Charleston Swing" (The Cut-Out)
A. Brown, N. Hunter, N. Chester, Company
(*Music and Lyrics by Ben Harris, Henry Creamer and Will Vodery.*)
Specialty
S. Bechet
"In My Dixie Dreamland"
Donita Sisters, Company
"When I'm Blue"
J. Stinnette
"Love Will Bring You Happiness"
C. Chappelle, J. Stinnette
(*Music and Lyrics by Ben Harris.*)
"I Didn't Grieve Over Daniel"
A. Brown, A. Davis
"Keep the Man You've Got"
A. Brown
"Count Your Money"
A. Lovejoy, A. Fairchild
"E-Gypsy-Ann"
C. Chappelle, J. Stinnette, Company
(*Music and Lyrics by Ben Harris, Henry Creamer and Will Vodery.*)
Dance
Boys

[147]Costumes uncredited.

[148]Programs do not divide composer credits, which appear only in the published sheet music.

"Some More Dancing"
J. Nit

Charleston Finale
Entire Company

1923.12 BOMBO

A Return Engagement of the Musical Extravaganza in Two Acts, 14 Scenes[149]. Book and lyrics by Harold Atteridge. Music by Sigmund Romberg. Staged by J. C. Huffman. Dances staged by Allan. K. Foster. Scenery designed by Watson Barratt. Costumes by Mode Costume Company. Orchestra under the direction of Alfred Goodman. Entire production under the personal supervision of J. J. Shubert. Produced by the Messrs. Lee and J.J. Shubert. Opened 14 May 1923 at the Winter Garden and closed 9 June 1923 after 32 additional performances. Total, including first engagement: 250 performances.

CAST [in order of appearance]: *Paul Marcus*, Alonzo: FRANKLYN A. BATIE. *Annabelle Downing*, Annabella: Vera Bayles Cole. *Jenkins*, Roderigo: Frank Holmes. *Jack Christopher*, Christopho Columbo: FORREST HUFF. *Patricia Downing*, Princess Isabella: MILDRED KEATS. *Count Garibaldi*, Prince Don: Harold Crane. *Mrs. Downing*, Queen Isabella: Fritzi von Busing. *Inez*, Lady Inez de Cordoba: Mary Booth. *Mona Tessa*, a Soothsayer: Leah Norah. *Red*, King Ferdinand: Harry Turpin. *Louis*, the Courier: Albert Howson. *Guiseppo*: Harry Sievers. *Banditti*, Italian Chiefs: Edward Pooley, William Richards, Charles Fritsch, Walter White, Harry Sievers, George Ross. *Butlers*, Sailors (2): *John*: Larry Lawrence. *James*: Teddy Hoffman. *Pirates* (2): *Adele*: Katherine Bennett. *Estelle*: Gladys Bennett. *Lola*, Luello: Jeannette Dietrich. *Alfred*, Alfredo: FRANK BERNARD. *Flavia*: Phoebe Brown. *Charles Masterson*: Harold Crane. *Gus*: AL JOLSON. *The Ghost of Ferdinand*, King of Spain: Harry Turpin. *The Ghost of Christopho Columbo*: Albert Howson. *The Troubadour*: FRANKLYN A. BATIE. *Princess Boababella*: Ann Mason. *Bombo*: AL JOLSON. *The Court Singer*: Teddy Hoffmann. *Lady in Waiting* (to Princess Boababella): Mary Booth. *Valero*: Albert Howson. *Soothsayer*: Leah Norah. *Sailing Master*: Harry Turpin. *Servant*: Edward Pooley. *The Duke of Bombo*: AL JOLSON. *Pedro*: Albert Howson. *First Sailor*: Frank Holmes. *An Indian Princess*: Phoebe Brown. *The Indian Chief*: Harry Turpin.

---

[149]Originally produced in New York 6 October 1921 at Jolson's 59th Street Theatre for 218 performances. For Synopsis of Scenes and Musical Numbers, see original 1921 production. For this production Act 2, Scene 4 was reset 'On the Yacht.' The following song changes were also added:

"'Neath Italian Skies"
Guests, Teetotum Girls
(replacing "Life Is a Gamble," the opening to Act 1)

"How'd You Like to Be a Kid?"
K. Bennett, G. Bennett
(replacing "Sleepy (Little) Village," Act 1)
(*Music by* Jimmy McHugh. *Lyrics by* the Bennett Sisters, Billy Colligan.)

Specialty (Act 1, after "No One Loves a Clown")
F. Bernard

"Sweet One"
J. Adair, Girls

"The Glide de Luxe"
F. Bernard, P. Brown, Bennett Sisters

(Finale)
A. Jolson, Company

(Above three numbers replaced "The Daffodil" which closed Act 2)

In addition, the placement of Al Jolson's song specialties was revised in Act 2, appearing both before and after "Wetona." Jolson's specialties included:

"Arcady"
(*Music and Lyrics by* Buddy G. DeSylva and Al Jolson.)

"I'm Goin' South"
(*Music and Lyrics by* Abner Silver and Harry Woods.)

"California, Here I Come"
(*Music by* Joseph Meyer. *Lyrics by* Buddy G. DeSylva, Al Jolson.)

"Dirty Hands! Dirty Face!"
(*Music by* James Monaco. *Lyrics by* Grant Clarke, Edgar Leslie.)

"Morning Will Come"
(*Music and Lyrics by* Con Conrad, Buddy G. DeSylva, Al Jolson.)

"Don't Cry Swanee"
(*Music and Lyrics by* Con Conrad, Buddy G. DeSylva, Al Jolson.)

"Tell Me With Smiles"
(*Music and Lyrics by* Cliff Friend and Walter Hirsch.)

1923.13 DEW DROP INN

A Musical Comedy in Two Acts. Book by Walter DeLeon and Edward Delaney Dunn. Music by Alfred Goodman, (Rudolf Friml, J. Fred Coots, Jean Schwartz). Ensemble music by Sigmund Romberg. Lyrics by Cyrus Wood, (McElbert Moore). Staged by Fred C. Latham. Dance numbers by M. Francis Weldon. Settings by Watson Barratt. Costumes by Paul Arlington, Inc. and Vanity Fair Costume Co. Orchestra under the direction of Alfred Newman. Entire production under the supervision of J. J. Shubert. Produced by Messrs. Shubert. Opened 17 May 1923 at the Astor Theatre, closing 30 June 1923 after 52 performances; re-opened 30 July 1923 at the Astor Theatre and closed 25 August 1923 after 31 additional performances. Total: 83 performances.

CAST: *Jack Newton*: HARRY CLARK. *Madame Le Cordez*: Mary Robson. *J. P. Rocksly*: William Holden. *Grace Rocksly*: MARCELLA SWANSON. *Hope Rocksly*: BEATRICE SWANSON. *Ronald Curtis*: JACK SQUIRE. *Edith Tobber*: EVELYN CAVANAUGH. *Joseph Higgins*: Spencer Charters. *Bell Boy*: Danny Dare. *Maid*: Jean Carroll. *Nurse*: Sylvia Highton. *Violet Gray*: MABEL WITHEE. *Bobbie Smith*: ROBERT HALLIDAY. *Reggie Murray*: Frank Hill. *Ananias Washington*: JAMES BARTON. *M. Dupont*: RICHARD DORÉ. *Harry MacDonald*: Harry Ellsworth. *Grace MacDonald*: Grace Ellsworth. *Eleanor Jordan*: Margaret Morris. *Julia Kinsey*: Claire Hodgson. *Frances Moore*: Margaret Atherton. *Marion Stanley*: Alice Brady. *Bell Boy Number 2*: Lee Kelso. *Frank Maxwell*: Ben Jacklow. *Stephen Andrews*: Harry Rosedale. *Mooney*: In Person. *Guests, Maids, Bell Boys, etc.*

Ladies of the Ensemble: Helen O'Brien, Mary Kissel, Thelma Johns, Bobby Kane, Rena Miller, Gladys Davis, Billy Davis, Claire Hodgson, Juliet Strahl, Margaret Atherton, Helen Rogier, Millie Dupree, Sylvia Highton, Margaret Morris, Felicia Murelle, Alice Brady, Dorothy Deane, Katherine Manion. *Gentlemen of the Ensemble*: George Brown, Dale Grigsby, Ray Hall, Allan Stevens, Bernard Druce, Lee Kelso, Hal Peel, Lester Brown, Bob Gebhardt.

The action takes place at a hotel on the shore of a Southern California Seaside Resort.

Act 1: On the Terrace. Late afternoon.

Act 2: The Garden in the Moonlight.

ACT 1
 Opening Ensemble
  H. Clark, Ensemble
 "Pretty Ankle"
  M. Withee, Boys
 "We Two"
  R. Halliday, M. Withee
  (*Music by* Rudolf Friml.)
 "Porter! Porter!"
  J. Barton, Ensemble
 "Men"
  Ensemble
 "The Struttinest Strutter"
  J. Barton
 "A Girl May as Well Marry Well"
  E. Cavanaugh, J. Squire, Ensemble
 Finale
  R. Halliday, M. Withee, E. Cavanaugh, J. Barton, Ensemble

ACT 2
 "The Primrose Path"
  R. Halliday, E. Cavanaugh, J. Squire, G. Ellsworth
  B. Swanson, M. Robson, H. Clark, F. Hill, D. Dare, Ensemble
 "Goodbye Forever"
  R. Halliday, M. Withee
  (*Music by* Alfred Goodman and Rudolf Friml.)
 "Moonlight Waltz"
  E. Cavanaugh, R. Doré
 Travesty
  J. Barton
 "Lady"
  M. Withee, Boys
  (*Music by* J. Fred Coots, Jean Schwartz. *Lyrics by* McElbert Moore.)
 "You Can't Experiment on Me"[150]
  J. Barton

---

[150]Dropped during subsequent national tour.

"I'm a Flapper"
  E. Cavanaugh, J. Squire, H. Clark, B. Swanson, Bell Boys, Maids
  (*Music by* J. Fred Coots, Jean Schwartz. *Lyrics by* McElbert Moore.)
Finale

1923.14   BLOSSOM TIME

A Revival of the Operetta in Three Acts[151]. Book and lyrics by Dorothy Donnelly. Adapted from the Viennese original ('Das Dreimäderlhaus') by A. M. Willner and Heinz Reichert, based on a novel 'Schwammerl' by Rudolf H. Bartsch. Music adapted and augmented by Sigmund Romberg from the melodies of Franz Schubert selected and arranged by Heinrich Berté. Staged by J. C. Huffman. Dancing numbers arranged by F. M. Gillespie. Scenes by Watson Barratt. Costumes designed by the Mode Costume Co. Entire production under the personal direction of J. J. Shubert. Produced by the Messrs. Shubert. Opened 21 May 1923 at the Sam S. Shubert Theatre and closed 9 June 1923 after 24 performances.

CAST: *Mitzi*: GERTRUDE LANG. *Bellabruna*: Halina Bruzovna. *Fritzi*: Marian Abel. *Kitzi*: Sonya Leyton. *Mrs. Kranz*: AMY LESTER. *Greta*: DOROTHY SEEGAR. *Baron Franz Schober*: ROY CROPPER. *Franz Schubert*: HOLLIS DAVENNY. *Kranz*: Teddy Webb. *Vogl*: Eric Titus. *Kupelweiser*: Victor Henry. *Von Schwind*: Edmund Fitzpatrick. *Binder*: Elden Baker. *Erkman*: James Burroughs. *Count Sharntoff*: EDWIN TAYLOR. *Hansy*: L. Bietenkant. *Novotny*: OTIS SHERIDAN. *Rose*: Burtress Deitch. *Mrs. Coburg*: Julia Hurley. *Waiter*: David Resnick. *Dancer*: Burtress Deitch.

Ladies of the Ensemble: Ruth Miller, Anna Cutter, Verna Shaff, Jean Roberts, Edith Laurence, Shirley Stanley, Mae Chesterly, Ann Martin, Mary Granda, Monita Gray.

1923.15   BLOSSOM TIME

A Revival of the Operetta in Three Acts[152]. Book and lyrics by Dorothy Donnelly. Adapted from the Viennese original ('Das Dreimäderlhaus') by A. M. Willner and Heinz Reichert, based on a novel 'Schwammerl' by Rudolf H. Bartsch. Music adapted and augmented by Sigmund Romberg from the melodies of Franz Schubert selected and arranged by Heinrich Berté. Staged by J. C. Huffman. Dancing numbers arranged by F. M. Gillespie. Scenes by Watson Barratt. Costumes designed by the Mode Costume Co. Musical direction by Orivalle Maynard. Entire production under the personal direction of J. J. Shubert. Produced by the Messrs. Shubert. Opened 21 May 1923 at the 44th Street Theatre and closed 2 June 1923 after 16 performances.

CAST: *Mitzi*: LAUREL NEMETH. *Bellabruna*: Trina Varela. *Fritzi*: Jean Holt. *Kitzi*: (F.) DeVecmon Ramsey. *Mrs. Kranz*: ISABELLE VERNON. *Greta*: FERNE NEWELL. *Baron Franz Schober*: JOHN CLARKE. *Franz Schubert*: JOSEPH MENDELSOHN. *Kranz*: Dallas Welford. *Vogl*: Lucius Metz. *Kupelweiser*: Edward Orchard. *Von Schwind*: Perry Askin. *Binder*: James Curran. *Erkmann*: Frank E. Horn. *Count Sharntoff*: GREGORY RATOFF. *Hansy*: Frank Noyes. *Novotny*: DAVID ANDRADA. *Rose*: Peggy O'Donnell. *Mrs. Coburg*: Harriette Sheldon. *Waiter*: Henry Davis. *Dancer*: Tatiana Smirnovia.

Ladies of the Ensemble: Mae Watson, Olive Thornton, Engina Leonotowich, Emdokia Smirnovia, Peggy O'Donnell, Marjorie Harriman, Sibil Taube, Marion Greene, Ursula Murray, Grace Elliott.

1923.16   ADRIENNE

A Musical Comedy in Two Acts, 3 Scenes. Book and lyrics by A. Seymour Brown. Based on a story by Frances Bryant and William Stone. Music by Albert Von Tilzer. Staged by Edgar J. MacGregor. Dances and ensembles by David Bennett. Art director (scenic design), Herbert Ward. Costumes by Paul Arlington, Inc. Miss Tennyson's gowns by Frances. Men's clothes by

Brooks-Mahieu. Orchestra under the direction of Max Steiner. Produced by Louis F. Werba. Opened 28 May 1923 at the George M. Cohan Theatre and closed 15 December 1923 after 235 performances.

CAST (in order of appearance): *Sid Dazel, alias Nadir Sidarah*: CHARLES CAHILL WILSON. *Nora Malone, alias Nadja*: LAURA ARNOLD. *Prison Guard*: John Kearney. *First Prisoner*: William Creco. *Second Prisoner*: Mohammed Haussain. *Third Prisoner*: Robert Mazuz. *Bunk Allen, alias Ali Bunjke*: BILLY B. VAN. *Grace Clayton*: MABEL FERRY. *Thomas*: Robert Starr. *John Grey*: RICHARD CARLE. *Mrs. John Grey*: Jean Newcomb. *Bob Gordon*: DAN HEALY. *Adrienne Grey*: VIVIENNE SEGAL. *Stephen Hayes*: HARRY FENDER. *Shrine Attendant*: John Kearney.

Specialty Dancers: Carlos and Inez, May Cory Kitchen, The Keene Twins, Lou Lockett, Fridkin and Rhoda. *The Lyric Quartette*: Edith Holloway (lyric soprano), Pauline Miller (mezzo soprano), Jean Young (contralto), Angela Manilla (alto). *Ladies of the Ensemble*: Diana Chase, Muriel Wilson, Anita Monroe, Amy Atkinson, Louise Segal, Marjorie Clemens, Louise Joyce, Ruth Mills, Suzanne Conroy, Beatrice O'Connor, Jean Brown, Ethel Gibson, Phyllis Aves, Florence Courtney, Ursula Dale, Marguerite Ross, Ruby Poe, Lillian Dawn, The Hall Twins. *Gentlemen of the Ensemble*: Jerome Kirkland, Dan Rowan, Austin Clark, Sidney Ayres, Francis T. Schulze, Fred O'Brien, Roy Mason, Othello McCarver, Arthur Budd, Hugh Wilson.

Act 1, Scene 1: Outside Sing Sing Prison, Ossining, New York. February. *Scene 2*: The Terrace of John Grey's Home, near New York. July.

Act 2: At the Shrine of Ramah. Nearer New York.

ACT 1
  Opening Chorus
    Ensemble
  "Live While You're Here"
    M. Ferry, M. C. Kitchen, Rhoda, L. Lockett, Keene Twins, Ensemble
  "Sweetheart of Mystery"
    V. Segal
  "(The) Hindu Hop"
    D. Healy, M. Ferry, Keene Twins, Ensemble
  "Love Is All"
    V. Segal, H. Fender
  "As Long as the Wife Don't Know"
    L. Arnold, R. Carle
  "Cheer Up"
    H. Fender, D. Healy, L. Lockett, Ensemble
  Finale
    Entire Company

ACT 2
  "Oriental Divertissement"
    Fridkin and Rhoda, M. C. Kitchen, Keene Twins, L. Lockett, Carlos and Inez, Ensemble
  "Sing Sing"
    B. B. Van, C. C. Wilson, L. Arnold
  "(Just a) Pretty Little Home"
    V. Segal, M. Ferry, Lyric Quartette, Girls
  "King Solomon"
    R. Carle, Girls
  "Where the Ganges Flows"
    V. Segal, Lyric Quartette, Keene Twins, Ensemble
  "Dance With Me"
    D. Healy, M. Ferry, L. Lockett, M. C. Kitchen, Carlos and Inez, Ensemble
  "Love Is All" (reprise)
    H. Fender
  Finale
    Entire Company

---

[151] First presented in New York 29 September 1921 at the Ambassador Theatre for 516 performances. For Synopsis of Scenes and Musical Numbers, see original 1921 production. The Messrs. Shuberts promoted the novelty of two companies performing BLOSSOM TIME simultaneously across the street from one another for two weeks. Musical direction uncredited.
[152] First presented in New York 29 September 1921 at the Ambassador Theatre for 516 performances. For Synopsis of Scenes and Musical Numbers, see original 1921 production. The Shuberts promoted the novelty of two companies performing BLOSSOM TIME simultaneously across the street from one another for two weeks.

Elizabeth Welch (second from left) with the cast of RUNNIN' WILD (Photo: White Studio)
Billy Rose Theatre Collection, New York Public Library for the Performing Arts

1923–1924 SEASON

1923.17 THE PASSING SHOW OF 1923

A Musical Revue in Two Acts, 31 Scenes[1]. Sketches and lyrics by Harold Atteridge. Music by Sigmund Romberg and Jean Schwartz. Staged by J. C. Huffman. Dances arranged by Allan K. Foster. Settings designed by Watson Barratt. Costumes by Paul Arlington. Orchestra under the direction of Alfred Goodman. Entire production under the personal supervision of J. J. Shubert. Produced by the Messrs. Lee and J. J. Shubert. Opened 14 June 1923 at the Winter Garden and closed 15 September 1923 after 118 performances.

CAST: WALTER WOOLF, JOAN HAY, GEORGE HASSELL, GEORGE JESSEL, PHIL BAKER, HELEN SHIPMAN, JAMES WATTS, ROY CUMMINGS, BILLEE SHAW, JOSEPHINE DRAKE, BARNETT PARKER, BOB NELSON, NAT NAZARRO, JR., (Ed) FLANAGAN and (Alex) MORRISON, LOUISE DOSÉ, HAL VAN RENSSELAER, LIBBY and (Ida May) SPARROW, VERA ROSS, WILLIAM PRINGLE, JACK RICE, JEAN STEELE, FRANK BERNARD, ANDE JOCHIM, JAMES HAMILTON, THE TRADO TWINS (Pete, Frank), JEANETTE GILMORE, FRANCIS X. MAHONEY, BOB GILBERT, JACK HALL, ROY CUNNINGHAM, Joseph Wagstaff, James White, William Birdie, Neil Courtney, George Ford, Harriet Gustin, Ann Lowenworth, Tom Nip.

Show Girls: Dorothy Bruce, Perle Germonde, Mildred Soper, Helene Herendeen, Marja Talwyne, Bobbie McCree, Virginia Sullivan, Dolly Wegman, Lloyd Byron, Doris Downes, Betty Benton, Peggy Lockwood, Loretta Duffy, Christine Ecklund, Olive King, Muriel Seeley, Dorothy Vance, Martha Albert, Nancy Carroll, Therese Carroll, Alice Wheeler, Vera King, Dolores Edwards, Fay Reed. *Dancers:* Orilla Smith, Billee Wagner, Edith Pierce, Elsie Frank, Florence Wilde, Sidney Nelson, Belle McLaughlin, Rose Sarr, Alice Velour, Gladys Marston, Rose Mary Marston, Ruth Hamilton, Elsie May, Rose Lee, Cassie Godfrey, Ladas May, Viola Votruba, Norma Rossiter, Ethel Kenyon, Bobbie Lester, Paula Greenlee.

ACT 1[2]

Scene 1

"Prologue"
Messrs. Libby, J. Wagstaff, T. Nip, B. Gilbert, Trado Twinns; Misses O. Smith, E. Frank, E. Pierce, F. Wilde, S. Nelson, E. May

"Kissable Lips"
H. Shipman, H. Van Rensselaer, Kissable Girls
(*Music by* Jean Schwartz.)
Check Room of a Broadway Restaurant
Willie: J. Wagstaff. *Nellie:* H. Shipman. *Mr. Eatwell:* H. Van Rensselaer. *Mr. Burnson:* J. Hamilton.

Scene 2

"My Gaby Doll"
J. Steele, J. Gilmore, Gaby Girls
(*Music by* Jean Schwartz and Sigmund Romberg.)
The Doll Shop
Gaby Doll: J. Steele. *Toy Maker:* W. Birdie. *His Finished Doll:* J. Gilmore.

Scene 3

A Rehearsal

"Go Into Your Dance"
H. Shipman, T. Nip, J. Gilmore, Libby and Sparrow, N. Nazaaro, Jr., Girls
The Author: G. Jessel. *The Stage Director:* H. Van Rensselaer. *The Stage Manager:* J. Hall. *The Heroine:* H. Shipman. *The Lover:* B. Parker. *The*

---

[1]The eleventh in the series of annual revues presented by the Messrs. Shubert beginning in 1912.
[2]The running order of songs and sketches was revised during the run. Added during the run:

Song Titles' Drama (Act 2)
George: G. Hassell. *Kitty:* J. Watts. *Chauffeur:* J. Rice. *Freddy:* R. Cummings.

The Remuddled House (*by* Louise Bascom Barratt)(Act 2)
Mr. Jetter: W. Pringle. *Mrs. Jetter:* J. Hay. *Haskell Mayhappengood:* B. Parker. *Jane Wells:* J. Drake. *Henry:* J. Hall. *John:* B. Gilbert.

Foolish Husbands (Act 2)
added (c) The Mistake. At Mr. Jackson's.
Mr. Jackson: R. Cummings. *Mrs. Jackson:* J. Watts. *Mr. Green,* a teacher of jazz dancing: B. Gilbert. *A Servant:* J. Hall.

Fly Swatters Ballet (*by* Roger Dodge)(Act 2)
Fly: R. Cummings. *Miss Swatter:* J. Watts. *Ballet Ensemble:* Messrs. Libby, Trado Twins, Nip, Gilbert, Jochim, White, Hamilton, Mahoney, Hall, Rice.

Endurance Dancing at the Queen's Hall (Act 2)
Nat: N. Nazarro, Jr. *Helen:* H. Shipman. *Hal:* H. Van Rensselaer. *Bob:* B. Nelson.

Leading Man: G. Hassell. *An Actor:* J. Hamilton. *The Stage Carpenter:* W. Pringle. *The Property Man:* J. Rice. *An Actress:* V. Ross. *Another Actress:* L. Dosé. *Chorus Girls, Stage Hands, Dancers, etc..*

Scene 4

A Few Moments with Roy and Billee
Roy: R. Cummings. *Billee:* B. Shaw.

Scene 5

A Vase of Roses

"Rose of the Morning" (The Life of a Rose)
W. Woolf, I. M. Sparrow, Rose Girls
(*Music by* Sigmund Romberg. *Lyrics by* Cyrus Wood.)
Walter: W. Woolf. *Rose:* I. M. Sparrow.

Scene 6

Seeing Double
Mr. A: B. Nelson. *Mr. B:* B. Gilbert. *Bill:* G. Hassell. *Mrs. Brown:* J. Hay. A *Maid:* I. M. Sparrow. *Her Butler:* W. Pringle. *Mr. Brown:* J. Hamilton. *Butlers:* J. Hall, J. White. *Mr. Brown No. 2:* W. Birdie. *Mr. Brown No. 3:* N. Courtney. *Mrs. Brown No. 2:* V. Ross. *Mrs. Brown No. 3:* L. Byron. *Second Maid:* E. May. *Third Maid:* S. Nelson. *Fourth Maid:* F. Wilde. *Stage Manager:* A. Jochim. *Second Stage Manager:* J. Wagstaff. *Third Stage Manager:* F. X. Mahoney. *Fourth Stage Manager:* G. Ford. *Fifth Stage Manager:* B. Wilson.

Scene 7

The Twin Sixes: Specialty
Pete and Frank: Trado Twins.

Scene 8

8 of Our Best Sellers

"Beautiful and Damned"
B. Nelson, Vampires
Bob: B. Nelson. *Censor:* A. Jochim. *Black Oxen:* D. Vance. *Damned:* P. Germonde. *Panjola:* D. Bruce. *Beautiful and Damned:* N. Carroll. *Blood and Sand:* D. Edwards. *Simon Called Peter:* M. Soper. *Cytherea:* H. Herendeen. *If Winter Comes:* H. Gustin.

Scene 9

"Golfing Blues"
B. Nelson, Libby and Sparrow, Golf Girls
(*Music by* Jean Schwartz.)
Scene: On the Golf Course
An Elderly Golfer: W. Pringle. *Roy:* R. Cummings. *Bob:* B. Nelson.

Scene 10

A Lesson in Golf (*by* Ed Flanagan)

Specialty
E. Flanagan, A. Morrison
American Trick Golf Champion: A. Morrison. *Joan:* J. Hay. *Her Uncle:* J. Rice. *The Duffer:* E. Flanagan. *Golf Nuts, Tennis Sharks, Bridge Hounds, Croquet Friends, etc.*

Scene 11

It Happened in Dutchland

"My Dutch Lady"
N. Nazarro, Jr., H. Shipman, Dutch Cleanser Girls
(*Music by* Jean Schwartz.)
Hansel: N. Nazarro, Jr. *Gretel:* H. Shipman.

Scene 12

"A Royal Wedding"
Entire Company
Scene: Entrance to Westminster Abbey.
Lord Bottle a Bass: G. Hassell. *Lady Stout Guiness:* J. Drake. *Lady Bottle a Bass:* J. Watts. *Lord Crabtree:* B. Parker.

Scene 13

Scene: Interior Westminster Abbey
The King: A. Jochim. *The Queen:* M. Soper. *Prince of Wales:* N. Nazarro, Jr. *Duke of York:* J. Rice. *Lady Elizabeth,* the bride: D. Bruce. *Earl of Strathmore,* the bride's father: J. White. *Queen Elizabeth of Greece:* P. Germonde. *Princess Patricia:* M. Talwyne. *Princess Mary:* B. McCree. *Empress of Russia:* O. King. *Princess Victoria:* D. Vance. *Duchess of Fife:* H. Gustin. *Countess of Athol:* H. Herendeen. *Guests, Ambassadors, Royalty, etc.*

Scene 14

In an Upper Box at a French Comedy (*by* George Jessel)
George: G. Jessel. *Mamma:* A. Lowenworth. *The Maid:* R. Marston. *The Brother:* J. Hamilton. *The French Actress:* L. Dosé.

Scene 15

The Other Side of Every Woman
Hal: H. Van Rensselaer.

Scene 16

An Auction Shop

The Auctioneer: G. Hassell. *His Assistant*: B. Parker. *Second Assistant*: B. Gilbert. *A Lady Customer*: V. Ross. *First Gentleman*: J. Rice. *Second Gentleman*: F. X. Mahoney. *Third Gentleman*: J. Hall. *Fourth Gentleman*: A. Jochim. *A Deaf and Dumb Man*: J. Watts. *A Golfer*: J. Hamilton. *Customers, Assistats, Clerks, etc.*

Scene 17

"The Ball Begins"

J. Hay, Empire Girls

(*Music by* Sigmund Romberg.)

Scene: A Souper Dansant during the Second Empire in Paris

Center Chandelier: E. Pierce, F. Wilde, S. Nelson, M. Velour. *Right Chandelier*: E. May, L. Duffy, D. Downes. *Left Chandelier*: C. Ecklund, D. Edwards, L. Byron. *Fruit Basket*: R. Lee, N. Carroll, R. Sarro.

ACT 2

Scene 1

The Jewelled Curtain

"The Jewel Song"

L. Dosé

Scene 2

"My Little Lotus Flower" (Lotus Flower)

W. Woolf, J. Hay, L. Dosé, V. Ross, H. Shipman, Japanese Maidens

(*Music by* Sigmund Romberg. *Lyrics by* Cyrus Wood.)

Scene: Japanese Bridges

Yamadori: W. Woolf. *Miss Cherry Blossom*: J. Hay. *Miss Wistaria*: L. Dosé. *Miss Chrysanthemum*: V. Ross. *Snow Maiden*: H. Shipman.

Scene 3

Out Front (Specialty)

Piero, a Clown: F. Bernard.

Scene 4

Somewhere in Rye

Jack: G. Hassell. *Kitty*: J. Watts. *Chauffeur*: J. Rice. *Freddy*: R. Cummings.

Scene 5

The Mysterious Mirrors

"Mirror Mine"

L. Dosé, Mirror Girls

(*Music by* Jay Gorney.)

Miss Vanity: L. Dosé.

Scene 6

Necessary to Change a Scene (Some Songs)

Bob: B. Nelson.

Scene 7

"The Fatal Wedding"

R. Cummings, D. Cornwell

Roy: R. Cummings. *The Cornetist*: Dean Cornwell. *Alternating Cornetist*: Fred Sasse.

Scene 8

Foolish Husbands

(a) The Kiss. At Mr. Green's Home

Mr. Black: J. Hamilton. *Mr. Green*: J. Rice. *Mrs. Green*: J. Drake.

(b) Eyes. At Mr. Adam's House

Mr. Brown: W. Pringle. *Mrs. Adams*: J. Hay. *A Chauffeur*: H. Van Rensselaer. *Mr. Johnson*: A. Jochim. *Mr. Adams*: B. Nelson.

Scene 9

Beginning of French Revolution, 1789

"The French Revolution" (Aux Armes)

W. Woolf

Pierre, a young revolutionist: W. Woolf. *Helene*: L. Dosé. *Josephine*: V. Ross. *Andre*: W. Pringle. *Jacques*: J. Wagstaff.

Scene 10

Interlude

Phil: P. Baker.

Scene 11

It Happens in Every Musical Play

"My Rainbow (Girlie)" (Girl at the Rainbow's End)

H. Shipman, H. Van Rensselaer

The Girl: H. Shipman. *The Boy*: H. Van Rensselaer. *The Dancer*: N. Nazarro, Jr.

Scene 12

The Animated Curtain

"Birds of Plumage"

Ensemble

"Step On It"

Entire Company

GEORGE WHITE'S SCANDALS (1923)

1923.18

A Musical Revue in Two Acts, 25 Scenes[3]. Book (sketches) by George White and William K. Wells. Music by George Gershwin. Lyrics by Buddy G. DeSylva. Additional lyrics by E. Ray Goetz, Ballard Macdonald. Entire production staged by George White. Art director, Herbert Ward. Scenes by H. Robert Law Studios. Costumes designed by Cora MacGeachy. Additional costumes designed by Erté. Orchestra directed by Charles Drury. Produced by George White. Opened 18 June 1923 at the Globe Theatre, moved 5 November 1923 to the Fulton Theatre, and closed 10 November 1923 after 168 performances.

CAST: LESTER ALLEN, WINNIE LIGHTNER, TOM PATRICOLA, MARGA WALDRON, OLIVE VAUGHN, NEWTON ALEXANDER, JOHNNY DOOLEY, CHARLES DORNBERGER (and his orchestra), Thea Lightner, Beulah Berson, The Breen Brothers (F., D.), Delyle Alda, Richard Bold, Olivette, Helen Hudson, Tip Top Four, Mischa Vol Janin, Edna May Reed, James Miller, Lloyd Halicey, Harry Lang, Frank Webster.

London Palace Girls: Scandal Beauties: Mildred Klaw, Cleone Stamm, Myra Cullen, Vera Colburn, Hazel Donnelly, Marion Courtney, Dorothy Fenron, Peggy Jones, Anna Buckley, Hart, Vera Marsh, Bee Savage, Norma Cloos, Lerch, Alice Burton, Ringquist, Erickson, Madison, Alice White, Patricia Cross, Dorothy Smith, Crowell, Kent, Constance Meredith, Margaret Gollis, Brew, Belmont, Marie Nerval, Olivette, Margaret Breen.

ACT 1[4]

Curtain Pages

M. Klaw, C. Stamm

Scene 1

Self Explanatory (Made at the William Fox Studio. Courtesy of Mr. W. R. Sheehan.)

Scene 2

Movie Dance

London Palace Girls

Scene 3

"Little Scandal Dolls"

O. Vaughn

(*Assisted by*) Misses M. Cullen, V. Colburn, H. Donnelly, M. Courtney, D. Fenron, P. Jones, A. Buckley, Hart, V. Marsh, B. Savage, N. Cloos, G. Lerch.

Scene 4

Prologue

M. Vol Janin

Scene 5

Moscow Players

Butler: J. Miller. *Wayward Wife*: W. Lightner. *A Plumber*: L. Allen. *Silverman*: J. Dooley. *Bootlegger*: T. Patricola.

Scene 6

"You and I (in Old Versailles)"

B. Berson, Scandal Beauties

(*Music by* George Gershwin, Jack Green. *Lyrics by* Buddy G. DeSylva.)

Dance

M. Waldron

Scene 7

Back to California

Husband: J. Dooley. *Vamp*: M. Breen. *Wife*: T. Lightner. *Mrs. Newlyewed*: O. Vaughn. *Mr. Newlywed*: N. Alexander.

Scene 8

"Katinka"

L. Allen, London Palace Girls

Scene 9

"Lola Lo" (Lo-La-Lo)

---

[3]The fifth in the annual series of revues produced by George White beginning in 1919.

[4]Also performed in the show as a specialty, as per published sheet music, recordings and reviews:

"San" (Oriental Song Fox-Trot)

Charles Dornberger and His Orchestra

(*Music and Lyrics by* Lindsay McPhail and Walter Michels.)

Added for subsequent tour:

"Garden of Love"

H. Hudson, Tip Top Four

(*Lyrics by* Buddy G. DeSylva.)

R. Bold, O. Vaughn, T. Patricola
(*Lyrics by* Buddy G. DeSylva.)
(*Assisted by*) Misses M. Cullen, B. Savage, V. Marsh, C. Meredith, A.
Burton, Ringquist, Erickson, H. Donnelly, M. Courtney, N. Cloos, Madison,
G. Lerch, D. Smith, D. Fenron, A. White, P. Cross.

Scene 10

The Third Degree
Detective: N. Alexander. *Chief*: J. Dooley. *First Suspect*: M. Vol Janin. *Second
Suspect*: F. Webster. *Third Suspect*: J. Miller. *Fourth Suspect*: L. Allen.

Scene 11

"There Is Nothing Too Good for You"
R. Bold, H. Hudson, (Ensemble)
(*Lyrics by* Buddy G. DeSylva, E. Ray Goetz.)
Scene: Jewel Shop.
Salesman: L. Halicey. *Pages*: A. White, P. Cross. *Ring*: M. Klaw. *Earrings*:
D. Fenron, B. Savage. *Lavalier*: C. Stamm. *Bracelet*: N. Cloos, M. Nerval.
Tiara: M. Cullen, V. Marsh, C. Meredith. *Pearls*: Misses Burton, Brew, D.
Smith, Belmont, Fox, Crowell, Kent, Erickson, G. Lerch, Hart, Ringquist,
Madison. *Clasp*: H. Donnelly. *Ruby*: A. Buckley. *Sapphire*: P. Jones.
Amethyst: M. Courtney. *Emerald*: M. Gollis. *Diamond*: V. Colburn.

Scene 12

Winnie Lightner

Scene 13

A Fantasy in Four Scenes:
I. *Pages*: M. Cullen, O. Vaughn.
II. Manhattan Isle in the Seventeenth Century
Indian Chief: T. Patricola. *Peter Stuyvesant*: J. Dooley. *Interpreter*: H. Lang.
Indians: London Palace Girls, Scandal Beauties.
III. Year of 1923
Statue: J. Dooley. *Two New Yorkers*: R. Bold, H. Hudson.
IV. "Throw Her in High" (Throw 'Er in High!)[5]
W. Lightner
(*Lyrics by* Buddy G. DeSylva, E. Ray Goetz.)
Speaker for the Reds: W. Lightner. *Red Followers*: Misses O. Vaughn, Benson,
Breen, Olivette. *Speaker for the Blues*: L. Allen. *Blue Followers*: Messrs N.
Alexander, Vol Janin, F. Breen, D. Breen.

Scene 14

Folies Bergère Paris Curtain (*Designed by* Herbert Ward)
Curtain Girls: Misses N. Cloos, D. Fenron, D. Smith, A. Burton, M. Courtney,
V. Marsh.

ACT 2

Scene 1

Three Thousand Years Ago[6]
M. Waldron
(*Assisted by*) Misses Crowell, P. Cross, Madison, A. Buckley, Hart, Kent,
Erickson, C. Meredith, V. Colburn, M. Gollis, Brew, Belmont, M. Nerval,
Ringquist.

Scene 2

"Let's Be Lonesome Together"
R. Bold, B. Berson
(*Lyrics by* Buddy G. DeSylva, E. Ray Goetz.)

Scene 3

The Gall of the North

Scene 4

Songs:
W. Lightner
["Last Night on the Back Porch (I Loved Her Best of All)"
(*Music by* Carl Schraubstader. *Lyrics by* Lew Brown.)
"More" (A Modern Maiden's Prayer)
(*Music and Lyrics by* Abner Silver, Sidney D. Mitchell, Lew Pollack.)
"Stingo Stungo"
(*Music by* James F. Hanley. *Lyrics by* Lew Brown.)]

Scene 5

"The Life of a Rose"
R. Bold, M. Waldron
(*Lyrics by* Buddy G. DeSylva.)
Rose Girl: G. Lerch.

Scene 6

"Look in the Looking Glass"
H. Hudson, London Palace Girls

---

[5]Dropped for subsequent tour.
[6]Dropped for subsequent tour.

Scene 7

Juliet
Rummy: N. Alexander. *Juliet*: W. Lightner. *Archibald*: T. Patricola. *Baron Island*:
L. Allen.

Scene 8

Dance
The Breens

Scene 9

"Where Is She?"
Tip Top Four
(*Lyrics by* Buddy G. DeSylva.)
Scene: A Pullman Smoker.
Chicago: V. Marsh. *Boston*: H. Donnelly. *Philadelphia*: M. Courtney. *St.
Louis*: M. Cullen. *Washington*: D. Fenron. *New York*: N. Cloos.

Scene 10

The Three Musketeers
L. Allen, J. Dooley, T. Patricola, N. Alexander

Scene 11

"Laugh Your Cares Away"
Entire Company, Charles Dornberger's Orchestra
Scene: A New York Café.

1923.19 HELEN OF TROY, NEW YORK

Another Musical Comedy in Two Acts. Book by George S. Kaufman and
Marc Connelly. Music and lyrics by Bert Kalmar and Harry Ruby. Staged by
Bertram Harrison and Bert French. Scenery designed by Sheldon K. Viele
and Jimnolds. Costumes designed by Kiviette, Gilbert Clark, Inc., Milla
Davenport. Orchestra under the direction of Louis Silvers. Orchestrations
by Arthur Lange. Produced by Rufus LeMaire[7] and George Jessel (in associ-
ation with Wilmer and Vincent). Opened 19 June 1923 at the Selwyn
Theatre, moved 8 October 1923 to the Times Square Theatre, and closed 1
December 1923 after 191 performances.

CAST: *Elias Yarrow*: TOM LEWIS. *C. Warren Jennings*: ROY ATWELL. *Baron de
Cartier*: JOSEPH LERTORA. *Theodore Mince*: Charles Lawrence. *Harper Williams*:
Clyde Hunnewell. *David Williams*: PAUL FRAWLEY. *Helen McGuffey*: HELEN
FORD. *Maribel McGuffey*: QUEENIE SMITH. *Grace Yarrow*: Stella Hoban. *Mme.
Pasanova*: Joan Clement.
Specialty Dancers: Bobby Dale, Lovey Lee, Elise Bonwit, Neil Ames, Opal Hickson,
William Dunn, Marie Paynter. *The Trojan Women*: Madge McCarthy, Louise
Bateman, Helen Gladding, Anna Mae Dennehy, Mabel Stanford, Alice Akers, Madia
Harries, Madeline Soisson. *Smaller Ones*: Sybil Stokes, Kitty Malvern, Elsie Dunn,
Mildred Brown, Teddy Hudson, Heloise Sheppard, Virginia Birmingham, Virginia
Birmingham, Thelma Marshall, Helen Paine. *The Men*: Donald Heebner, Robert
Culbertson, Harold Raymond, Edward Price, Charles Townshend, Gene Collins,
Leon Bartels, William Leon.

Act 1: Directors' Room of the Yarrow Collar Factory, Troy, New York.

Act 2: Baron de Cartier's Studio, New York City. A week later.

ACT 1[8]

"Up on Our Toes"
R. Atwell, S. Hoban, Girls, Stenographers, Clerks, L. Lee, E. Bonwit, O.
Hickson, N. Ames, B. Dale, J. Collins
"Cry Baby"
H. Ford, Q. Smith
"I Like a Big Town"
C. Lawrence, S. Hoban, Girls, Boys
"Helen of Troy, New York"
H. Ford, Boys
"Happy Ending"
H. Ford, P. Frawley
"What the Girls Will Wear"
Q. Smith, Girls
"What Makes a Business Man Tired?"
T. Lewis, R. Atwell, C. Lawrence, J. Lertora

---

[7]During the run, Wilmer and Vincent joined George Jessel as co-produc-
ers; the production credits below were revised to read as follows: "Produced
under the direction of Rufus Lemaire."
[8]Running order of songs revised after opening. Interpolated as per published sheet music:
"Keep A-Goin'"
(*Music and Lyrics by* Byron Gay.)

Finale
  Entire Company
ACT 2
  "Advertising"
    J. Lertora, Girls
      Danced by Misses Stanford, Akers, Bateman, Gladding, Dennehy, Ames, Hickson, Marshall, Soisson, Malvern, Brown, Dunn, Hudson, Paine, Sheppard, Birmingham, L. Lee, E. Bonwit, Messrs. Dale and Collins.
  "If I Never See You Again"
    Q. Smith, C. Lawrence
  "Nijigo Novgo Glide"
    Q. Smith, J. Lertora, Boys, Girls
      (a) Q. Smith, B. Dale, (b) C. Adler, T. Hudson, (c) W. Dunn, M. Paynter, (d) Q. Smith, (e) L. Berkoff, S. Freda.
  "It Was Meant To Be"[9]
    H. Ford, P. Frawley
  "We'll Have a Model Factory"
    H. Ford, Q. Smith, P. Frawley, C. Lawrence
  "A Little Bit o' Jazz"
    H. Ford, Ensemble
  Finale
    Entire Company

ZIEGFELD FOLLIES
1923.20 (Summer Edition)

A Revised Version of the Musical Revue ZIEGFELD FOLLIES OF 1922 in Two Acts, 28 Scenes[10]. (Sketches by Ralph Spence, Eddie Cantor, others.) Music by Victor Herbert, Louis A. Hirsch and Dave Stamper. Lyrics by Gene Buck. Staged by Ned Wayburn. Scenes designed by Joseph Urban and others. Tableaus by Ben Ali Haggin. Orchestra under the direction of Oscar Radin. Produced by Florenz Ziegfeld. Summer Edition opened 25 June 1923 at the New Amsterdam Theatre and closed 15 September 1923 after 96 performances.

CAST: EDDIE CANTOR, AL SHEAN, ED GALLAGHER, GILDA GRAY, MARY EATON, ILSA MARVENGA, ANDREW TOMBES, MARY LEWIS, BRANDON TYNAN, ANN PENNINGTON, JIMMY NERVO, TEDDY KNOX, MARTHA LORBER, THELMA CONNOR, GRANT SIMPSON, VELMA CONNOR, MURIEL STRYKER, EVELYN LAW, ALEXANDER GRAY, SERGE PERNIKOFF, WILLY, WEST and McGINTY, Michael Barroy, Al Ochs, Jack Scott, TILLER GIRLS. THE FOLLIES FOUR (Messrs. J. J. Shannon, Frank Tierney, Frank Lambert, Mark Truscott).
  Ladies of the Ensemble: Sonia Ivanoff, Anastasia Reilly, Marie Wallace, Julia Kingsley, Clara Beresbach, Hilda Moreno, Hazel Jennings, Blossom Vreeland, Janet Megrew, Vivian Vernon, Shirley Vernon, Edna Wheaton, Marie Shelton, Sonia Ivanoff, Olive Osborne, Frances Reveaux, Polly Nally, Sonia Ivanoff, Gertrude Selden, Irene Marcellus, Jessie Reed, Hazel Webb, Constance McLaughlin, Pansy Maness, Vangie Valentine, Pearl Eaton, Pauline Mason, Fay West, Marcelle Earle, Mae Daw, Kitty Littlefield, Naomi Johnson, Leonora Baron, Eleanor Dana, Marie Wallace, Alma Drange, Helen Lee Worthing, Betty Williams, Beatrice Jackson, Helena D'Algy, Betty Carsdale, Dorothy Clarkson, Sylvia Kingsley, Miriam Vandergriff, Joan Gardner, Elsa Peterson, Victoria Gale, Madlyn Wells, Margie Whittington, Pearl Prosser, Hallie Manning, Erla Calame, Eleanor Dana, P. Eaton, Byron, Gale, Jackson, Kimari, King, Elaine Palmer, Rich, S. Vernon, Wales, Whittington, Wilde, Baron, McLaughlin.
  English Ballet: Irene Todd, Dolly Evans, Beatrice Singleton, Elsie Woodall, Babs Aitlen, Annie Patron, Jean Lloyd, Ada Hughes, Dolly Daggars, Audrey Darrell, Cora Neary, May Howard, Nellie Smith, Neta Hill, Betty Webb, Ivy Halstead.

ACT 1[11]

---

[9]"It Was Meant To Be," "We'll Have a Model Factory" and "A Little Bit o' Jazz" replaced for the national tour by:
  "Moonlight Lane"
    H. Ford, Hal van Rensselaer (David Williams)
    (*Music by* W. Frank Harling. *Lyrics by* Lorenz Hart.)
[10]This was the 17th Edition., revised from the 16th (presented 5 June 1922 at the New Amsterdam Theatre for 426 performances) in the annual series which began in 1907.
[11]The running order was revised after the opening. Added during the run:
  The Girl from the Golden West (Act 1)
    P. Salmon
      (Discovered by Heywood Broun, Bide Dudley and other sporting writers at Shelby, Montana while attending the Dempsey-Gibbons Fight)
  Added for subsequent tour:
  "Sweetie" (Act 2, Scene 8)
    E. Law

Scene 1
  "Blunderland"
    (*Sketch by* Ralph Spence. *Music by* Louis A. Hirsch. *Lyrics by* Gene Buck. *Painted by* Gates and Morange. *Costumes designed by* Charles LeMaire.)
      Miss Take: J. Megrew. *Youth*: A. Tombes. *Peggy Hopkins*: H. L. Worthing. *Movies*: M. Lorber. *Miss Calculate*: V. Vernon. *Miss Trial*: E. Wheaton. *Miss Fit*: M. Shelton. *Miss Treat*: S. Ivanoff. *Miss Trust*: B. McFarland. *Miss Demeanor*: O. Osborne. *Miss Behave*: S. Vernon. *Miss Chief*: F. Reveaux. *Miss Fortune*: P. Nally *Miss Government*: G. Selden. *Miss Hap*: I. Marcellus. *Miss Mate*: J. Reed.
  "Hello! Hello! Hello!"
    Blunders
    (*Music by* Dave Stamper.)
  "My Melody"
    Ensemble
Scene 2
  Follies Farm (*Painted by* Joseph Wickes.)
  "Throw Me a Kiss"
    I. Marvenga, Farm Girls
    (*Music by* Dave Stamper, Louis A. Hirsch. *Lyrics by* Gene Buck. *Costumes designed by* Ada Fields.)
      Farm Girls: Misses Byron, Calame, Dana, P. Eaton, Gale, Jackson, Kimari, King, Palmer, Rich, Mahoney, Vreeland, Wales, Webb, Whittington, Wilde.
  Rube Dance
    Kelo Brothers
Scene 3
  "Pep It Up"[12]
    B. Johns
    (*Music by* Dave Stamper. *Lyrics by* Gene Buck.)
      Assisted by Misses West, Beresbach, Littlefield, Daw, Reilly, Earle, Maness, Johnson, Drange, Mahoney, Stoneburn, Baron, Rolfe, McLaughlin, Valentine, Mason.
Scene 4
  "(Listening on Some) Radio"
    A. Gray, R. Urban
    (*Sketch by* Ralph Spence. *Music by* Dave Stamper. *Lyrics by* Gene Buck. *Scene painted by* H. Robert Law Studios.)
      With Messrs. Moore, Shannon, Truscott, Lambert.
Scene 5
  Eccentric Dance (*Arranged by* John Tiller)
    Tiller Girls
Scene 6
  "Rambler Rose"
    A. Tombes
    (*Music by* Dave Stamper, Louis A. Hirsch. *Lyrics by* Gene Buck. *Costumes designed by* Charles LeMaire.)
      Dancing Partner: E. Law. *Roses*: S. Vernon, A. Reilly, M. Wallace, J. Kingsley, C. Beresbach, E. Peterson, H. Jennings, B. Vreeland. *Soloist*: A. Gray.
Scene 7
  "A Kiss in the Dark"[13] (from ORANGE BLOSSOMS)
    I. Marvenga
    (*Music by* Victor Herbert. *Lyrics by* Buddy G. DeSylva. *Costumes designed by* Charles LeMaire.)
Scene 8
  The Kiss[14] (Pastel [Tableau] by Ben Ali Haggin.)
    A. Gray, M. Daw, J. Gardner, B. Carsdale, J. Megrew, H. D'Algy, J. Reed
Scene 9
  "It's Getting Dark on Old Broadway"
    G. Gray, the Follies Four
    (*Music by* Dave Stamper. *Lyrics by* Gene Buck. *Costumes designed by* Ada Fields. *Scene by* Herman Rosse.)
      With Misses H. Webb, C. McLaughlin, A. Reilly, P. Maness, V. Valentine, P. Eaton, P. Mason, F. West, M. Earle, M. Daw, K. Littlefield, N. Johnson, L. Baron, E. Dana, M. Wallace, A. Drange.

---

[12]Not in previous Ziegfeld Follies edition, but newly added for this Summer Edition.
[13]Not in previous Ziegfeld Follies edition, but newly added for this Summer Edition.
[14]Not in previous Ziegfeld Follies edition, but newly added for this Summer Edition.

Scene 10

Jerry & Co., the Builders: A New Light on the Housing Problem[15]
Willie, West and McGinty

Scene 11

"Some Sweet Days"[16]
B. Johns
(*Music by* Dave Stamper, Louis A. Hirsch. *Lyrics by* Gene Buck.)

Scene 12

Café de la Paix, Paris (*Painted by* Gates & Morange.)

Specialty (by, about and for themselves): ["Mr. Gallagher and Mr. Shean"]
E. Gallagher, A. Shean
(*Music and Lyrics by* Ed Gallagher, Al Shean and Ernest Ball.)
Introducing Misses. H. L. Worthing, J. Megrew, B. Williams, H. D'Algy, B. Carsdale, D. Clarkson, J. Gardner. Parisiennes, Waiters, Gendarmes, etc.

Scene 13

The Filmless Movies (*by* Franklin P. Adams, Nate Salsbury and Emil Breitenfeld)
A. Tombes

Scene 14

"Frolicking Gods" (*Ballet composed and produced by* Michel Fokine. *Music by* Pyotr Ilyich Tchaikowsky. *Scenery designed by* Joseph Urban. Costumes of Visitors in Museum *designed by* James Reynolds.)
The Girl: M. Lorber. *The Boy*: S. Pernikoff. *A Mother*: M. Shelton. *A Little Boy*: M. Merritt. *A Little Girl*: A. Rolfe. *An Old Man*: M. Truscott. *His Jealous Wife*: H. Manning. *Girls*: J. Reed, H. L. Worthing, J. Megrew, E. Wheaton. *Young Boys*: F. Reveaux, C. Beresbach. *Museum Attendant*: F. Lambert. *The Gendarme*: M. Barroy. *Apollo Belvedere*: S. Vernon. *Venus of Milo* (restored): E. Beresbach. *The Amazone*: K. Stoneburn. *The Hercules*: A. Ochs. *The Three Graces*: N. Savage, N. Byron. *The Satyr*: J. Scott. *A Basrelief: Two Bacchantes*: M. Rich, B. Rees. *A Faun*: S. Karavaeff. *Caryatides*: E. Peterson, P. Prosser, E. Dale, M. Wells. *Two Hermes*: L. Wild, V. Valentine. *The Faun Girl*: P. Maness. *Menades*: V. Gale, M. Rich. *The Seven Muses*: N. Johnson, S. Kingsley, E. Dana, B. Jackson, E. Calame, E. Palmer, A. Drange, C. McLaughlin.
Note: Every time the marble Greek Gods remain alone in their museums, they start to enjoy themselves and to dance. However, a couple of lovers, who were unexpectedly locked in a Paris Museum of Art in 1851 have the chance to witness those divine actions. The Gendarme who hears the terrible noise in the museum finds the lovers undressed like ancient Greeks and takes them to the police.

Scene 15

Eddie Cantor (Specialty)

["Eddie (Steady)"
(*Music and Lyrics by* Charles Tobias, Eddie Cantor.)
"Oh! Gee, Oh! Gosh, Oh! Golly I'm in Love"
(*Music by* Ernest Breuer. *Lyrics by* Chic Johnson, Ole Olsen.)
"If I Can't Get the Sweetie I Want (I Pity the Sweetie I Get)"
(*Music by* Jean Schwartz. *Lyrics by* Sam M. Lewis, Joe Young.)
"My Mammy" (from SINBAD)
(*Music by* Walter Donaldson. *Lyrics by* Sam M. Lewis, Joe Young.)
"My Girl Uses Mineralava (That's Why I'm Her Beau)"
(*Music and Lyrics by* Eddie Cantor.)]

Scene 16

"Bring on the Girls"
A. Gray
(*Music by* Dave Stamper. *Lyrics by* Gene Buck. *Marches by* Victor Herbert. *Painted by* Joseph Urban.)

Dance
E. Law
The Black Crook Amazons (*Costumes designed by* Cora MacGeachy): Misses Byron, A. Drange, Whittington, Jackson, Palmer, C. Beresbach, Dale, Rich, Calame, Kimari, Wilde. *Fencing Girls* (*Costumes designed by* Cora MacGeachy): Misses Vreeland, Earle, Gale, Jennings, Kingsley, Johnson, Rolfe, Merritt, McLaughlin, Mason, West, P. Maness. *The English Pony Ballet*: I. Todd (Captain), D. Evans, B. Singleton, E. Woodall, B. Aitlen, A. Patron, J. Lloyd, A. Hughes, D. Daggars, A. Darrell, C. Neary, M. Howard, N. Smith, N. Hill, B. Webb, I. Halstead. *Minstrel Misses*: Misses Webb, S.

Vernon, Daw, Reilly, King, Rees, Valentine, K. Littlefield, Baron, Dana, Wallace, Eaton. *Ziegfeld Girls* (*Costumes designed by* Charles LeMaire.): Misses Reed, Wheaton, Selden, Marcellus, Reveaux, Nally, Osborne, Worthing, Megrew, V. Vernon, McFarland, DeBussy.

Lunette[17] (A Tableau by Ben Ali Haggin)
M. Lorber
Assisted by B. Carsdale, M. Shelton, B. Williams, J. Gardner, H. D'Algy, M. Vandergriff.

ACT 2

Scene 1

Il Trionfo di Venere[18] (Cinque-cento)(A Tableau by Ben Ali Haggin.)
M. Lorber
With J. Reed, H. L. Worthing, J. Gardner, P. Nally, J. Megrew, D. Clarkson, B. Carsdale, H. D'Algy, A. Reilly, F. Reveaux, C. Berebach, E. Beresbach, M. Daw, M. Whittington, S. Vernon, P. Prosser, N. Savage.

Scene 2

Four Well Known Dames and a Guy[19]
(A Song Scene *by* Gene Buck. *Music by* Raymond Hubbell.)
The Guy (In Ermine): E. Gallagher. *Juliet*: B. Tynan. *Little Nellie Kelly*: A. Tombes. *Saidee Thompson* from 'Rain': A. Shean. *Florence Mills*: E. Cantor.

Scene 3

Dance (*Arranged by* John Tiller.)
Tiller Girls

Scene 4

Uppers and Lowers (by Charles C. Mather amd Charles Sumner. *Painted by* Joseph Wickes.)
Stage Carpenter: J. J. Shannon. *Actor*: A. Tombes. *Porter*: J. Scott. *Bride*: M. Lorber. *Bridegroom*: A. Gray. *Masher*: A. Tombes.

Scene 5

"South Sea Moon"
A. Gray

South Sea Dance
G. Gray
(*Music by* Dave Stamper and Louis A. Hirsch. *Lyrics by* Gene Buck. *Costumes designed by* Cora MacGeachy. *Scene painted by* Joseph Wickes.)
Ensemble: Misses Baron, Littlefield, Palmer, Manning, Gale, Johnson, Rolfe, Wilde, Dana, Daw, Jackson, Kimari, King, McLaughlin, Maness, Mason, Merritt, Rees, Rich, Stoneburn, Webb, Whittington, the "Follies Four." *The Ukelele Players*: Misses Valentine, Wales, Gale, Webb, Calame, Earle, Byron, A. Drange.

Scene 6

Getting a Ticket[20] (*by* Eddie Cantor)
E. Cantor
Motor Cycle Policeman: J. Opp. (Movie Scene taken by Fox Film Corporation.)

Scene 7

Lace-Land: "Weaving (My Dreams)"
I. Marvenga
(*Music by* Victor Herbert. *Lyrics by* Gene Buck. *Lace Ballet devised and staged by* Ned Wayburn. *Scene by* Joseph Urban. *Costumes designed by* Charles LeMaire.)
The Lace-Maker: I. Marvenga. *The Dutch Visions*: I. Marcellus, B. McFarland, G. Selden, P. Nally. *The Trousseau* (6): *Lace Stockings*: C. Beresbach. *The Parasol*: F. Reveaux. *The Handkerchief*: H. Worthing. *The Fan*: B. McFarland. *The Bridal Gown*: J. Megrew. *The Veil*: J. Reed. *Butterfly*: M. Shelton. *Pages*: M. Merritt, A. Rolfe. *Ballet of Motives*: Misses Stoneburn, Rich, Rees, Wilde, Littlefield, Earle, McLaughlin, Vernon, Vreeland, Valentine, P. Eaton, Calame. *The Inspiration*: H. O'Shea.

Scene 8

"Songs I Can't Forget"
A. Gray
(*Music by* Louis A. Hirsch. *Lyrics by* Gene Buck. *Costumes designed by* Charles LeMaire.)
Glow Worm: E. Petersen. *Bedelia*: A. Reilly. *La Paloma*: H. D'Algy. *School Days*: M. Daw. *Alexander's Ragtime Band*: P. Eaton. *Annie Rooney*: H. Manning. *Robert E. Lee*: H. Webb. *Hot Time in the Old Town Tonight*: S. Vernon. *In the Good Old Summer Time*: M. Lorber. *Sweet Adeline*: J. Reed.

---

[15]Not in previous Ziegfeld Follies edition, but newly added for this Summer Edition.

[16]Not in previous Ziegfeld Follies edition, but newly added for this Summer Edition.

[17]Not in previous Ziegfeld Follies edition, but newly added for this Summer Edition.

[18]Not in previous Ziegfeld Follies edition, but newly added for this Summer Edition.

[19]Dropped during the run.

[20]Not in previous Ziegfeld Follies edition, but newly added for this Summer Edition.

Scene 9

Ann Pennington, assisted by Brooke Johns

Scene 10

Coconut Grove (*Painted by* Gates & Morange.)

"Nobody But You"[21]

(*Music by* Louis A. Hirsch, Dave Stamper. *Lyrics by* Gene Buck.)
Visitors: Misses Reed, Wheaton, Marcellus, Peterson, Worthing, Reveaux, Selden, Osborne, Nally, Byron, Jackson, Howden, Shelton, Kingsley, Gardner, Clarkson, Carsdale, D'Algy, Williams, Moreno, Megrew, McFarland, V. Vernon, DeBussy, S. Vernon.

Dance

E. Law

Russian Dance

S. Karavaeff

"Come Along"

G. Gray

(*Music by* Turner Layton. *Lyrics by* Henry Creamer. *Costumes designed by* Ada Fields.)
With Misses Wales, Maness, Dana, Webb, Daw, Rees, Valentine, Baron, Eaton, Calame, Vreeland, Rolfe, McLaughglin, Reilly, King, Earle, A. Drange, Mason, West, Littlefield, Manning, Merritt, Johnson, Gale, Wilde.

Some American Buck Dancing

P. Eaton, H. Webb, V. King, L. Baron, V. Valentine, B. Rees, A. Reilly, M. Wallace

Stage Door of the New Amsterdam Theatre (*Setting devised by* Ned Wayburn. *Painted by* H. Robert Law Studios.)

Ensemble (Finale)

Entire Company
(*Music by* Dave Stamper, Louis A. Hirsch. *Lyrics by* Gene Buck.)

Scene 11

Eddie Cantor, Andrew Tombes, Ed Gallagher, Al Shean (Parody version of "Mister Gallagher and Mister Shean")

Scene 12

Stage Door of the New Amsterdam Theatre (*Setting devised by* Ned Wayburn. *Painted by* H. Robert Law Studios.)

Ensemble (Finale)

Entire Company
(*Music by* Dave Stamper, Louis A. Hirsch. *Lyrics by* Gene Buck.)

EARL CARROLL'S
VANITIES (1923)

1923.21

A Musical Revue in Two Acts, 32 Scenes[22]. Music and lyrics by Earl Carroll. Dialogue staged by William Collier. Dances by Sammy Lee. (Scenic) Designs by R. Reid Macguire. Dresses by Paul Arlington, Inc. Ballet by F. Renoff. Orchestra under the direction of William Daly. Orchestrations by Arthur Lange. Produced by Earl Carroll. Opened 5 July 1923 at the Earl Carroll Theatre and closed 29 December 1923 after 204 performances.

CAST: JOE COOK, PEGGY HOPKINS JOYCE, HARRY BURNS, IRENE RICARDO, JIMMY DUFFY, DOROTHY NEVILLE, MARGARET DAVIES, ROY GIUSTI, RENOFF and RENOVA, CHARLES SENNA, SAM HERMANN, CALLAHAN BOYS, CLAIRE ELGIN, CARLENA DIAMOND, J. FRANK LESLIE, JACK PATTON, LORETTA MARKS, REKOMA, DELMORE and LEE, AL THOMAS, GERTRUDE LEMMON, DOROTHY KNAPP, AMY FRANK, CHARLES ALEXANDER, Messrs. Wyatt and Lashly.

Peggy Joyce's Collegians: Abner Barnhart, Dennis Murray, Al Clair, Tracy Wood, Richard Oakley, Bennet Green, Alfred Oakley, William O'Rourke, Russell Markert, Harry Williams, Graham Brewer, Brooks Hall, Albert Coleman, Al Davis, Robert Spencer, Pat Quinten, Harry Howell, George McCormick, Carlos Hatvary, Alden Cooke, Alan Dale, Lester Ostrander, Dan Sparks, George West, Eddie Dowling. *Dancing Girls*: Billy Blythe, Margaret McKay, Rose Stone, Ethel Bryant, Betty Wright, Elsie Neal, Amy Rivere, Lucille Pryor, Amy Frank, Lucille Moore, Violet Bristow, Mary Carney, Olga Borowska, Sunny Saunders, Thelma Addison, Babette Mitchell, Flo Tempest, Poppy Morton, Emily Lorraine, Cardinal Piearo, Marjorie Miller, Myrtle Glenn, Marion Youron, Jean Watson. *Show Girls*: Vera Featherly, Edith Parker, Muriel Manners, Dolla Harkins, Ruth Hargraves, Helen Menette, Jean Caswell, Polly Lux, Hazel Wilder, Thelma DeLorez, Lota Cheeke, Betty Fitch. *Fur Models*: Frances Frost, Florence Gillingham, Charlotte Pleshette, Patricia Wright, Bernice Elen, Sarah Cavais, Jean Huntington, Flo White, Mae Mitchell, Gladys Jones, Lillian Sutherland, Florence Ames.

---

[21]Dropped during the run.
[22]The first in the annual series of lavish musical revues conceived by Earl Carroll.

ACT 1

Scene 1

"The Birth of a New Revue"

The Composer: R. Giusti. *The New-Born*: G. Lemmon. *The Cohan Revue*: P. Lux. *The Winter Garden*: T. DeLorez. *White's Scandals*: R. Hargraves. *Greenwich Village Follies*: D. Hawkins. *The Music Box*: E. Parker. *Ziegfeld Follies*: B. Fitch.

Scene 2

"Girls Were Made For Dancing"

M. Davies, L. Moore, A. Frank, some girls

Scene 3

Baritone Solo

J. F. Leslie

Scene 4

A Singing Lesson

I. Ricardo, H. Burns, C. Senna

Scene 5

"A Suggestion of 1851"[23]

D. Neville
Accompanied by C. Diamond.

Scene 6

Insanities of 1923[24]

J. Duffy

Scene 7

The Silver Gardens

Two Musicians: H. Burns, C. Senna.

"The Band Plays Home Sweet Home"

R. Giusti, D. Neville

"Pretty Peggy"

P. H. Joyce, Her Collegians

Scene 8

Travesty

J. Duffy, H. Burns, I. Ricardo, A. Thomas, Callahan Boys

Scene 9

Vocal Selections

J. F. Leslie

Scene 10

"(My) Cretonne Girl"

L. Marks, J. Patton, Girls

Scene 11

Joe Cook the Humorist (Presenting a portion of his "One Man Vaudeville Show")

Scene 12

Ballet Brute[25] (*Conceived and arranged by* Renoff.)

The Brute: Renoff. *The Girl*: Renova. *The Slaves*: Messrs. Wyatt, Lashly, Corps de Ballet.

Scene 13

Divertissement

M. Edwards

Scene 14

Finale of the Furs[26] (Mirror mosaic created by Alex Hall.)

---

[23]Replaced during the run by:
"The Soul of the Harp" (*Staged by* Senia Gluck.)
The Singer: Ruth Oswald. *The Harpist*: C. Diamond. *The Child*: Mildred Truece. *The Vision*: A. Frank, O. Borowska, Bonny Dalton, A. Rivere.
My string of pearls upon a harp belong
A golden harp of melody and song;
And as I play the string of pearls,
I see a girl, but who knows if what I behold
Is not the soul that dwells within my harp of gold?
[24]Scenes 6 and 7 replaced during the New York run by:
Lollies
J. Duffy
His Two Containers: Callahan Boys.
[25]Revised and renamed The Slave Mart immediately after opening.
[26]Added during the run to the Act 1 Finale:
"When the Snowflakes Fall"
B. Granville
Snow-Dears: M. Davies, C. Elgin.

INTERMISSION: Mr. Sol [Sam] Hermann at the Xylophone

ACT 2[27]

Scene 1

It Might Be a Beach—

"Get in a Bathing Suit"
C. Elgin, D. Knapp, Bathing Girls
A Balloon Vender: H. Burns. *Another Italian*: C. Senna.

Scene 2

"Spring Voices")
D. Neville

Scene 3

Baritone Solo
J. F. Leslie

Scene 4

Insanities of 1923
J. Duffy

Fur Fashions
J. Duffy, assisted by Callahan Boys, Debutantes

Scene 5

The Cloak (*by* Paul Frank)
Count Belini: H. Burns. *Countess Belini*: P. H. Joyce. *Wesley Brown*: J. Cook.

Scene 6

Eccentric Dance
A. Thomas

Scene 7

"(Chasing) Little Rainbows"
J. Patton, L. Marks, M. Davies, Rainbow Girls

Dance
G. Lemmon

Scene 8

Joe Cook meets the Senator and drifts back to his circus days.
The Senator: C. Alexander.

Scene 9

"Whoa Pagliacci"
I. Ricardo and Copettes

Scene 10

"A Girl Is Like Sunshine"
R. Giusti, Flower Girls
(*Music by* William Daly, J. Russel Robinson. *Lyrics by* Roy Turk.)

Adagio
Renoff and Renova

Dance of the Snowballs
Vanities Dancing Girls
Baby Lamb: C. Diamond. *Baby Lambs (from left to right)*: Misses Rapp, Cornish, S. Cavais, Golding. *Squirrel*: M. Edwards. *Squirrels (from left to right)*: Misses J. Huntington, Caswell, E. Parker, Davis. *Mole*: D. Knapp. *Moles (from left to right)*: Misses Hobbs, L. Cheeke, V. Featherly, P. Wright. *Seal*: C. Elgin. *Seals (from left to right)*: Misses Bell, H. Wilder, R. Hargraves, Lee. *Sable*: M. Davies. *Sables (from left to right)*: Misses F. Frost, T. DeLorez, M. Manners, F. Gillingham. *Ermine*: D. Neville. *Ermines (from left to right)*: Misses H. Mennette, D. Harkins, B. Fitch, P. Lux. *Chinchilla, Queen of All*: P. H. Joyce.]

[27]Added during the run:

The New Scene (later dropped)
The Hero: Don Barclay. *The Heroine*: M. Davies. *The Director*: H. Burns. *The Villain*: Charles Callahan.

Hotel Mills Society Orchestra (Act 2)
The Leader: H. Burns. *Xylophone Soloist*: J. Duffy, Callahan Boys. *Other Musicians*: J. F. Leslie, C. Alexander, C. Senna, A. Thomas, D. Cooke.

Added during last weeks of the New York run:

On the Midway (Act 2)
H. Burns, C. Senna
Oriental Dancers: J. Watson, O. Borowska, A. Rivere, M. McKay, A. Frank, E. Lorraine, V. Bristow., L. Pryor. *The Ballyhoo*: D. Barclay. *Madame Stupid*: C. Alexander.

Added to Act 2 for tour:

"The Gipsy Song"/"When Love Sings a Song in Your Heart"
Ruth Oswald, L. Barton Evans, Frank Blyler

Scene 11

Baritone Solo
J. F. Leslie

Scene 12

The Martines[28]—Lightning Club Jugglers and Droppers

Scene 13

The Alexanders, assisted and annoyed by Joe Cook

Scene 14

Vocal Selections
J. F. Leslie

Scene 15

"Fine Feathers"
D. Neville

Scene 16

"Jazzmania"
L. Marks, M. Davies, C. Elgin, A. Thomas, Ensemble

Scene 17

Specialty

Scene 18

"Mr. Wagner's Wedding March"
J. Patton, Entire Company

1923.22   **FASHIONS OF 1924**

An Authoritative Forecast of the Coming Season (Musical Revue) in Two Acts, a Prologue and 26 Scenes. (Sketches by Alexander Leftwich, Jimmy Hussey, John Kendrick Bangs, others.) Music by Ted Snyder. Lyrics by Harry B. Smith. Staged by Alexander Leftwich. Dances arranged by John V. Lowe. Costumes by Adrian, Travis Banton, Arnold Daly, Marie Nordstrom, Sophie Rosenberg. Orchestra under the direction of Milan Roder. Orchestrations by Arthur Lange and Milan Roder. Produced by Fashion Productions (Alexander Leftwich). Opened 18 July 1923 at the Lyceum Theatre and closed 28 July 1923 after 13 performances.

CAST: ARNOLD DALY, JIMMY HUSSEY, INA HAYWARD, DINARZADE, HELEN LaVONNE, JOHN V. LOWE, GENE DELMONT, EDITH TALIAFERRO, FLORENCE MORRISON, MARIE NORDSTROM, CARLOTTA MONTEREY, DE JARI, ALDEN GAY, (Harry) MASTERS and (Jack) KRAFT, EDDIE HICKEY, JOHN DAVENPORT SEYMOUR, JOSEPH KAYSER, ARNOLD DALY, EVELYN MARTIN.

Ensemble: Misses Tarazen, Smith, Louise Carlton, Elaine Field, Diana, Elsa Sterling, Silance, Maida Palmer, Teddie Gill, Marion Hamilton, Kingston, Brownie, Tillman, Mae Rena Grady, Cricket, Sallie Hurst, Ellsworth, Edythe Nedd, Vinton, Ethelyn Tillman, Muriel Kingston, Muriel Lodge. Messrs. Thomson, Seymour, Blakeley, John H. Roberts.

ACT 1

Prologue (*Conceived and designed by* Adrian.)
The Stage: C Monterey. *Comedy*: Silance. *Tragedy*: E. Field. *Music*: E. Sterling. *Dancing*: Diana. *Fashion*: Dinarzade.

Scene 1

Le Sacrifice (by H. R. Mallinson, executed by Pulliche. *Staged by* Sergei Pirnikoff.)
Lorné: J. V. Lowe. *Needle*: T. Gill. *Thread*: Brownie. *Eye*: M. R. Grady. *Hook*: E. Tillman. *Pincushion*: M. Hamilton. *Rose*: Cricket. *Headdress*: M. Kingston. *Silk*: D. Vinton. *The Golden Gown*: A. Gay.

Into the enchanted garden comes Lorné, a whimsical playfellow of prodigious imagination. His many fanciful moods are productive of all that is beautiful, his tiny existence is spent in a world of romance. With inspired grace he conjures forth the most precious Mysteries of Milady's gown, and that lovely woman may become even more lovely, our benefactor Lorné pleads for a universal sacrifice, and in the end gives his own life.

Scene 2

Any Time on Broadway (*by* Jimmy Hussey)
A Violet in Broadway's Garden: I. Hayward. *First Policeman*: E. Hickey. *Miss Vanderbilt*: Dinarzade. *Newsboy*: S. Hurst. *Bootblack*: E. Nedd. *Blind Man*: B. Thompson. *Miss Knickerbocker*: M. Palmer. *Miss Claridge*: M. Hamilton. *Mickey*: J. H. Roberts. *Gordon Ginn*: J. Kayser. *Officer Cohen*: J. Hussey. *Charles Bradstreet*: J. D. Seymour. *Monty Banks*: H. Masters. *"Hub" Hardy*: J. Kraft. *Liz*: M. Nordstrom.

---

[28]Dropped during the run.

Scene 3
"Bring on the Girls"
J. V. Lowe
Part 1: Forecasting Sportswear (Beaucraft, designed by William Bloom)
Misses Sterling, Field, Palmer, Gill, Diana, Silance, Lodge, Gay
Part 2: Forecasting Beachwear (Nusbaum)
Misses Carlton, Kingston, Brownie, Tillman, Grady, Vinton, Cricket, Nedd, Hurst, Ellsworth, Hamilton, Martin

Scene 4
"Passing Fancies"
DeJari
Forecasting Furs (H. Jaeckel & Sons)
Misses Dinarzade, LaVonne, Gay, Silance

Scene 5
"Underneath the Table"
Forecasting Footwear (I. Miller Shoes, Van Roalte Hosiery)
Milady's Slipper: D. Vinton. *The Waiter*: H. Masters. *The Girl*: M. Nordstrom. *The Young Lover*: J. V. Lowe. *The Gay Old Boy*: J. Kraft. And Misses Kingston, Carlton, Brownie, Tillman, Grady, Crciekt, Hurst, Ellsworth.

Scene 6
Sweethearts (by Alexander Leftwich)
Scene: The Apartment of Mario Palmeri.
Mario Palmeri: DeJari. *Bowling*: J. D. Seymour. *Louise Wainwright*: E. Taliaferro. *Helene Harvey*: C. Monterey.

Scene 7
"The Bride"
M. Nordstrom
(*Music by* Arthur Gutman. *Lyrics by* Frances Nordstrom.)

Scene 8
"Kitty Kat"
The Kitten: J. H. Roberts. *The Kid*: E. Taliferro. And Misses Vinton, Brownie, Cricket, Tillman, Grady, Nedd, Ellsworth, Hurst. *The Kid Grown Up*: Dinarzade.

Scene 9
Jimmy Hussey

Scene 10
"Stepping"
Masters and Kraft

Scene 11
When the Cat's Away (by Jimmy Hussey)
Scene: The Home of Sam and Sarah.
Minnie: H. Ellsworth. *Sarah*: M. Nordstrom. *Sam*: J. Hussey. *Nathan*: H. Masters. *Lew*: B. Thomson. *Jake*: J. D. Seymour. *Moe*: J. Kraft. *Isidor*: E. Hickey.

Scene 12
"(Just) a Little Bit of Love"
Mr. Younglove: DeJari. *Mrs. Younglove*: E. Taliaferro.

Scene 13
"The Tea Garden"
Forecasting Formal Wear (Franklin Simon & Co., Paris Importations)
The Misses Sterling, Field, Palmer, Diana, Silance, Carlton, Lodge, Gill, Kingston, Gay, Dinarzade, LaVonne. *Mrs. H. Van Harrington*: M. Nordstrom. *A Student of Law*: J. Hussey. *Maude Fitzgerald*: C. Monterey. *The Dancers*: M. Hamilton; E. Martin, J. V. Lowe. *The Moscow Art Playthings*: Masters and Kraft.
"In Days of Long Ago"
Dejari, E. Taliaferro, Company
The Debutantes: Misses Vinton, Brownie, Cricket, Tillman, Grady, Hurst, Nedd, Ellsworth.

Finale
Company

ACT 2

Scene 1
"Indu-Chi" (Corticelli)
Dancing Girl: E. Martin. *Hindu Prince*: J. Kayser. *Chinese Dancer*: J. V. Lowe. *Chinese Princess*: I. Hayward. *The American Girl*: H. LaVonne. *Hindu Girls*: Misses Dinarzade, Gill, Palmer. *Chinese Girls*: Misses Grady, Nedd.

Scene 2
The Triangle (A Drama of Yesterday, Today and Tomorrow *by* Alexander Leftwich)
Scene: The Library of the Anstruther's.
Mary Anstruther, the wife: C. Monterey. *Robert Anstruther*, the husband: A. Daly. *Harvey*, the butler: H. Masters. *Jack Henderson*, the friend: DeJari. *Blaney McGowan* of the 17th Precinct: B. Thompson. *Michael Thompson of*

Headquarters: J. Kayser. *John Kendall Travers*, the District Attorney: J. D. Seymour.

Scene 3
"Here Comes the Kid"
M. Nordstrom
(*Music by* Eric Nardo. *Lyrics by* Frances Nordstrom.)

Scene 4
Night and an Imaginative Man (*Conceived and designed by* Adrian.)
The Man: J. D. Seymour. *A Discordant Thought*: J. V. Lowe. *Grotesque Fancies*: Misses Sterling, Diana, Kingston, Palmer, Gill, Field, Silance, LaVonne.
A fantastic story of an imaginative man who, through continual puzzling over the mysteries of life, becomes insane. The ballet illustrates the bewildering fantasies that haunt him.

Scene 5
"Two Little Girls and a Boy"
M. Hamilton, H. Masters, E. Martin

Scene 6
The Real Thing (by John Kendrick Bangs)
Billy: J. Kraft. *"Doctor" St. Clair Evanston*: A. Daly. *Mrs. Horace Kent Browning*: A. Gay. *Mrs. Thaddeus Perkins*: E. Taliaferro. *Mrs. Van Henry Hawkins*: Dinarzade. *Mrs. Edmund Marlowe Kay, Jr.*: L. Carlton. *Mrs. H. H. Fox, Jr.*: M. Nordstrom. *Mrs. Delancey Pell*: C. Monterey. *Mrs. Olmstead Fenway, 3rd*: M. Palmer. *Mrs. Frances Xavia O'Hara*: F. Morrison.

Scene 7
"The Dancing Daily Dozen"
H. Masters, J. Kraft, and Misses Tillman, Grady, Brownie, Hurst, Vinton, Nedd, Ellsworth, Cricket

Scene 8
Dans le jardin de fashion (Bou Souers)
Robes pour l'apres-midi: Mireille, Cherulian, Bois Fleuri, Rose Pompon, Tolede, Collette, France, Ascot, Chaperon Rouge.
Costumes de bal: L'heure bleue, Pluie d'argent, Petit Saxe, Moonlight, La Rafalle, Versailles, Vestale, Pluie d'or, Mon Caprice.
"One Last Waltz"
I. Hayward
Interlude
Mlle. Martin, J. V. Lowe

Scene 9
"Oh, Joe!"
D. Vinton
And Misses Brownie, Cricket, Tillman, Nedd, Ellsworth, Hurst, Grady.
(*Lyrics by* Harry DeCosta.)

Scene 10
Jimmy Hussey

Scene 11
The Great Lover (as the pages of history are turned the chapters of woman's dress are written)
(Cheney Brothers)
"Love Through the Ages"
DeJari
1450: E. Sterling. *1588*: T. Gill. *1654*: Silance. *1756*: A. Gay. *1789*: M. Palmer. *1794*: M. Lodge. *1800*: Dinarzade. *1840*: Diana. *1924*: H. LaVonne.

Scene 12
"Miss Whoozis and Mr. Whatchaname"
Masters and Kraft

Scene 13
The Walker Law (by Jimmy Hussey)
The Referee: A. Daly. *"Memphis" Gene Delmont*: G. Delmont. *"Abe" Cohen*: J. Hussey. *A Friend of Cohen's*: E. Hickey. *Everybody's Friend*: J. Kraft. *Leonora Maitland*: C. Monterey. *Edith Carter*: M. Nordstrom. *Mademoiselle Caprice*: Dinarzade. *Marie Rogers*: I. Hayward. *The Kid*: E. Taliaferro .*Martha Harrison*: A. Gay. *Daisy Herself*: F. Morrison. *Joe*: J. V. Lowe. And Misses Tarazen, Smith, Carlton, Field, Diana, Sterling, Silance, Palmer, Gill, Martin, Hamilton, Kingston, Brownie, Tillman, Grady, Cricket, Hurst, Ellswirth, Nedd, Vinton; Messrs. Thomson, Seymour, Blakeley.

Finale
Entire Company

THE NEWCOMERS
1923.23 (WILL MORRISSEY'S NEWCOMERS)

A Musical Revue in Two Acts, 23 Scenes. Sketches by Joe Burrows and Will Morrissey. Music and lyrics by Will Morrissey. Staged by Will Morrissey.

Dances arranged by Paisley Noon. Scenery by Karl Amend Studio. Costumes by Renee, Brooks-Mahieu, and the Gilman Co. Orchestra under the direction of Florence Richardson. Produced by Will Morrissey. Opened 8 August 1923 at the Ambassador Theatre and closed 25 August 1923 after 21 performances.

CAST: WILLIAM MORRISSEY, AL FIELDS, PAISLEY NOON, LARRY BECK, FRANK GABY, JOE BURROWS, HENRY STREMEL, MASON and SHAW, FRANKIE JAMES, SOPHIE ROMM, FLORENCE STONE, GRACE MASTERS, ELSIE LAMONTE, GAIL BEVERLY, PEGGY HART, CONSTANCE EVANS, FRANK ROBB, CECIL and KAYE, HEER and MARTIN, JOHN IRVING FISHER (at the Piano).

Chorus: Dolly Casner, Arlene Andre, Anita B. Stewart, Billy Lyons, Carolyn James, Evelyn Crane, Kathryn MacDonald, Ruth Evers, Florence Ashton, Grace Cronin, Peggy Quinn, Irene Shay, Cecelia Verkooy, Alvild Ward, Julie Barnette, Silvia Shaw.

ACT 1

Scene 1

Any Morning Any Theatre Any Producer
Founder of the Newcomers: W. Morrissey. *The Oldtimer*: A Fields. *Johnnie Newcomers*: New Strutter: P. Hart. *New Cherry Sisters*: G. Masters, E. Lamonte. *New Dancer*: F. Robb. *New Trentini*: S. Romm. *New Broadway Comedian*: F. Gaby. *New Orville Harold*: H. Stremel. *New Blanche Ring*: F. James. *By Herself*: G. Beverly. And Chorus.

Scene 2

"When I Think of You"
Mason and Shaw

Dances
Red and Romeo; Masters and Lamonte; C. Evans

Scene 3

Acrobatic Diversion
F. Gaby, Heer and Martin

Scene 4

Rain Travesty: "Sun and Rain"
S. Romm
Sadie Thompson: F. Stone. *Reverend Davidson*: F. Gaby. *Handsome*: P. Noon. *Joe Horn*: L. Beck.

Scene 5

"(Down on) Pango, Pango Bay"
P. Noon, Ensemble

Scene 6

"(The Ultra) Peacock Strut"
F. James, Ensemble

Scene 7

Frank Gaby and Jerry

Scene 8

"Covered Wagon Days"
S. Romm, H. Stremel, Ensemble

Dance
Cecil and Kaye, Romeo

Scene 9

Specialty
Mason and Shaw

Scene 10

Florence Richardson and The Newcomers Orchestra
Solo Trumpeter: Abraham Small.

Scene 11

Finale
Entire Company

ACT 2

Scene 1

"California Sunshine"
P. Noon

Dance
Cecil and Kaye

Scene 2

Appeal for Funds (from THE '49ERS, revised)
W. Morrissey, F. Gaby, J. Burrows, H. Stremel, C. James, C. Verkooy

Scene 3

"Teach Me to Dance"
Mason and Shaw

Ballet Eccentrique
P. Hart, Cecil and Kaye, I. Crane, Red and Romeo, P. Noon

Scene 4

Dance Acrobatique
C. Evans, Masters and Lamonte

Scene 5

"Washington Square" — "Long Ago"
B. Shaw, Ensemble

Scene 6

"Time Wasted"
A. Fields, F. Gaby, Heer and Martin

Dance
Cecil and Kaye, P. Noon

Scene 7

"Take This Little Rosebud"
S. Romm

Scene 8

The Mystery Drama
Scene: A Room at the Laffingwells.
Spirit of Premonition: F. Stone. *First Butler*: A. Romeo. *Second Butler*: J. Burrows. *Detective*: J. Richardson. *Officer*: L. Beck. *Mr. Laffenwill*: P. Noon. *Sir Gilbert Nolan*: Mr. Heer. *Deader N. Head*: Mr. Martin. *Miss Steake*: G. Beverly. *The Spirit of Mystery*: F. Gaby.

Scene 9

John Irving Fisher (Piano Virtuoso)

Scene 10

Old Time Jokes
The Boys (Messrs. Fields, Noon, Morgan, Gaby)

Scene 11

Dance Orientale
Cecil and Kaye

Dance Dramatique
G. Beverly

Scene 12

"Mother Me and the Flag" (To my pal, George M.)

Finale ("Forgive Us")
Entire Company

1923.24   LITTLE JESSIE JAMES

A Musical Farce in Two Acts. Book and lyrics by Harlan Thompson. Music by Harry Archer. Staged by Walter Brooks. Costumes designed by Mabel E. Johnston. Setting by P. Dodd Ackerman. Orchestra ('The James Boys'), a Paul Whiteman Band, directed by Ernest Cutting. Produced by L. Lawrence Weber. Opened 15 August 1923 at the Longacre Theatre, moved 28 January 1924 to the Little Theatre, and closed 19 July 1924 after 385 performances.

CAST (in order of appearance): *Tommy Tinker*: ALLEN KEARNS. *Juliet*: MIRIAM HOPKINS. *Mrs. Flower*: Winifred Harris. *Geraldine Flower*: ANN SANDS. *Paul Revere*: JAY VELIE. *S. Block*: James B. Carson. *Mrs. Jamieson*: Clara Thropp. *Jessie Jamieson*: NAN HALPERIN. *William J. Pierce*: Roger Gray. *Clarence*: Carl Anderson. *Harold*: Herbert Bostwick. *Lucila*: Lucila Mendez. *Loretta*: Loretta Flushing. *Bobbie*: Bobbie Breslau. *Blanche*: Blanche O'Brien. *Frances*: Frances Upton. *Edna*: Edna Howard. *Emily*: Emily Stead. *Agnes*: Agnes Morrisey. *Bonnie*: Bonnie Shaw.

Act 1: Living Room of Paul's Apartment, Central Park West, New York City. Late afternoon.

Act 2: The same. That evening.

ACT 1

"(A) Quiet Afternoon"
M. Hopkins, A. Kearns

"Come On (Let's Step, Step Around)"
A. Kearns, Girls

"Suppose I Had Never Met You"
A. Sands, J. Velie

"I Love You"
A. Sands, J. Velie, Girls

"My Home Town in Kansas"
N. Halperin

"The Knocking Bookworms"
A. Kearns, Girls

"Little Jack Horner"
N. Halperin, J. Velie

Concerted Number
N. Halperin, A. Sands, J. Velie, A. Kearns, Girls

ACT 2

"The Bluebird"
R. Gray

"Little Jessie James"
A. Kearns, N. Halperin, Girls

"From Broadway to Main Street"
N. Halperin, Girls

"Talk It Over"[29]
C. Thropp, M. Hopkins, R. Gray, A. Kearns

"Such Is Life in a Love Song"
A. Sands, A. Kearns, Girls

Reprise
N. Halperin, J. Velie

Finale
Ensemble

1923.25 ARTISTS AND MODELS (1923)

A Novelty (Musical) Revue in Two Acts, 24 Scenes[30], designed, written and staged by the most famous artists of New York. Based on the revue staged by the Illustrators' Society of New York. (Sketches by Harry Wagstaff Gribble, James Montgomery Flagg, Harold Atteridge, George Rosener, Cyrus Wood, Watson Barratt.) Music by Jean Schwartz. Contributing artists, authors and composers: James Montgomery Flagg, Rube Goldberg, Watson Barratt, Billy deBeck, Jack Sheridan, Helena Smith Dayton, Eugene Lockhart, M. Francis Weldon, C. D. Williams, Adele Klaer, Edward Penfield, Clare Briggs, Fontaine Fox, H. T. Webster, David Robinson, Will Johnstone, Percy Waxman, Roger Dodge, George Herriman, Worth Colwell, Harold Atteridge, Winston McCoy, Harry Hershfield, Harry Wagstaff Gribble, Louise Bascom Barratt, Rea Irwin, Cyrus Wood, C. B. Falls, Dean Cornwell, Rollo Wayne. Art director, Watson Barratt. Staged by Harry Wagstaff Gribble and M. Francis Weldon. Orchestra under the direction of Alfred Goodman. Entire production under the personal supervision of J. J. Shubert. Produced by Messrs. Shubert. Opened 20 August 1923 at the Sam S. Shubert Theatre, moved 24 March 1924 to the Winter Garden billed as Second Edition[31], and closed 17 May 1924 after 312 performances.

CAST: FRANK FAY, HARRY KELLY, GEORGE ROSENER, ADELE KLAER, CHARLOTTE WOODRUFF, JOHN ADAIR, BOB NELSON, NIKOLA CUNNINGHAM, ROSE BOYLAN, ARTHUR BOYLAN, LEE MORSE, BUDDY DOYLE, ETTA PILLARD, GRACE HAMILTON, Veronica, Harriete Gimbel, Marie Pettes, Beth Elliott, Kyra, Fatelle Levelle, Annie Pritchard, Robert O'Connor, James R. Liddy, Nancy Gibbs.

Models: Misses Nikola Cunningham, Eleanor Stitt, Alice Kennedy, Hansel, Azeada Charkouie, Freddie Bond, Elsie Bambrick, Gloria Christie, Lorraine Weimer, Edna Starck, L. Starck, Shay, Rena Manning, Marian Mooney, Eileen Adair, LeVon, Rogers, Andrews, Mary Lash, Duval, Harland, Carlin, Leckie, Monroe, Kane, Rita Norton. *Male Ensemble*: Bartlett Simmons, Clare Thompson, Victor Bozart, Lester Dorr, John Adair, Rollo Wayne, Robert O'Connor.

ACT 1[32]

Scene 1: Prologue

The Artist's Studio (*by* Harry Wagstaff Gribble)
Arthur Poor, a Struggling Artist: J. Liddy. *Frank Famous*, a Successful One: F. Fay. *Mrs. Rich*, a Society Woman: G. Hamilton. *Grace*, Her Daughter: N. Gibbs. *Miss Hopper*: M. Pettes. *Johnnie*: H. Gimbel. *Dancers*: R. Boylan, A.

---

[29]Dropped after the opening.
[30]The first in the annual series of revues produced by the Messrs. Shubert. This production was inspired by THE ILLUSTRATORS SHOW, an annual revue, presented 11-12, 19 May 1923 at the Century Roof Theatre; several of its sketches were revised and reused in ARTISTS AND MODELS.
[31]Apart from the newly top-billed star, the noted Russian soprano Vera Lavrova (Baroness Michael Royce Garrett), the Second Edition was notable for minor cast changes and re-ordering of songs and sketches.
[32]The running order was revised after opening. Added for Second Edition:
First American appearance of Vera Lavrova (Baroness Michael Royce Garrett)(Act 1)
   (a) Hindu Song (from SADKO)
     (*Music by* Rimsky-Korsakoff.)
   (b) Waltz Song (from ROMEO AND JULIET)
     (*Music by* Gounod.)

Boylan, A. Pritchard. *Students*: C. Thompson, V. Bozart, L. Dorr, J. Adair, R. Wayne, B. O'Connor, L. Weimer, R. Norton. *Models*: Misses N. Cunningham, E. Stitt, A. Kennedy, Hansel, A. Charkouie, F. Bond, E. Bambrick, G. Christie, L. Weimer, Starck, Shay, R. Manning.

"Somehow" (Some How)
N. Gibbs, J. Liddy
(*Lyrics by* Cyrus D. Wood.)

"Johnnie"
H. Gimbel, Models

Scene 2: The Revue
(Specialty: Mostly Black and White)
B. Doyle

Scene 3

Popular Magazines (*by* James Montgomery Flagg)
A Traveller: B. Nelson. *Collier's*: E. Levelle. *Ladies Home Journal*: G. Hamilton. *Literary Digest*: H. Kelly. *Pictorial Review*: E. Pillard. *Adventure*: E. Bambrick. *Hearst's International*: A. Charkouie. *Saturday Evening Post*: J. Rogers. *Vanity Fair*: R. Wayne. *Cosmopolitan*: H. Gimbel. *Life*: G. Rosener. *Photoplay*: N. Cunningham. *International Studio*: M. Norton.

Scene 4

Echoes from Dixie
L. Morse

Scene 5

The Critic (*by* James Montgomery Flagg)
A Mother: G. Hamilton. *A Father*: R. O'Connor. *A Musician*: N. Gibbs. *A Critic*: G. Rosener. *An Actor*: J. Liddy. *An Artists*: J. Adair. *A Novelist*: L. Dorr.

Scene 6

Frank Fay

Scene 7

Men Who Make the Nation Laugh
The Cartoonist: A. J. Hadley. With Misses E. Bambrick, Mooney, G. Christie, L. Weimer, E. Starck, L. Starck, F. Bond, E. Adair.

Scene 8

If Ford Were President (*by* Harry Wagstaff Gribble and Harold Atteridge)
Secretary of Gas: C. Thompson. *Commissioner of Punctures*: R. Wayne. *Athletic Instructor to Muscle Shoales*: V. Bozart. *Flunkey*: L. Dorr. *Bore*: H. Kelly. *Henry Ford*: R. O'Connor. *Axel*, his son: F. Fay. *Thomas A. Edison*: J. Adair. *William Jennings Bryan*: G. Rosener. *Hattie*: M. Pettes.
(*Setting by* Rea Irvin.)

Scene 9

"Jackie Coogan"
E. Pillard, Ensemble
(*Lyrics by* Harold Atteridge.)

Scene 10

When Beauty Calls (*by* Watson Barratt)
C. Woodruff, Ensemble
The Artist: C. Thompson. *Beauty*: N. Cunningham. *Her Court*: Misses N. Cunningham, E. Stitt, E. Bambrick, L. Weimer, A. Kennedy, F. Bond, Shay, E. Adair, A. Charkouie, Mooney, G. Christie, E. Starck, L. Starck.

Scene 11

Bug House Fables (Coue Dreams)(by permission of Billy deBeck)
At Hotel Desk: L. Dorr, J. A. Liddy. *At Home*: A. Klaer, J. Adair. *At Full Speed*: F. Fay, B. Doyle. *At the Apartment*: H. Kelly, L. Dorr. *At the Insurance Office*: R. O'Connor, J. Adair. *At the Finish*: F. Fay, Company.

Scene 12

"Say It With a Ukulele"
B. Nelson, Ensemble
Dancer: Kyra.

Scene 13

Fashion Models of Yesterday (*by* Helena Smith Dayton)
1892 Model: G. Hamilton. *1923 Model*: A. Klaer. *Tennis Model*: E. Bambrick. *Bicycle Model*: L. Weimer. *Gibson Model*: N. Cunningham. *Worth Model*: F. Bond. *Bathing Model*: E. Starck. *Afternoon Model*: E. Adair. *Ball Model*: E. Stitt. *Casino Hits Model*: P. Hansel. *Bride Model*: R. Manning.

Scene 14

Memorial Day (*by* George Rosener and Harold Atteridge)
An Old Soldier: G. Rosener. *An Old Lady*: M. Pettes. *Three Doughboys*: Messrs. L. Dorr, Adair, R. Wayne.

Scene 15

Porcelain Statuettes (*Conceived by* Watson Barratt.)
Maytime: N. Gibbs, J. Liddy. *Blossom Time*: B. Simmons, N. Gibbs. *Lady in Ermine*: G. Hamilton, R. Wayne. *Caroline*: V. Bozart, E. Bambrick. *Sally*: M. Mooney. *Irene*: H. Gimbel. *Mary*: E. Levelle. *Jimmie*: B. Doyle.

"Music of Love"
C. Woodruff, L. Morse
(*Music by* Al Goodman[33]. *Lyrics by* Cyrus D. Wood.)
Dancers: R. Boylan, A. Boylan, Kyra, A. Pritchard, Veronica. *Chinese Center Group:* N. Cunningham, A. Kennedy, A. Charkouie, Shay, E. Stitt, G. Christie. *Burmese Right Group:* E. Adair, F. Bond, Worton, L. Weimar, R. Manning. *Javanese Left Group:* Hansel, LeVon, Rogers, Andrews, Lash. *Girls:* Duval, Harland, Duval, Carlin, Leckie, Monroe.

ACT 2
Scene 1

The Nymph (*by* Cyrus Wood. *Picture by* Watson Barratt.)
Daphne, a City Girl: A. Klaer. *Pan:* G. Rosener. *Two Wood Nymphs:* R. Boylan, A. Pritchard. *A Satyr:* A. Boylan. *The Nymph:* N. Gibbs. *The Artist:* J. Liddy.
"Flower of the Woodland"[34]
N. Gibbs, J. Liddy
Woodland Nymphs: Misses E. Stitt, N. Cunningham, L. Starck, Shay, E. Starck, G. Christie, F. Bond, A. Charkouie, E. Bambrick, R. Norton, R. Manning, A. Kennedy.

Scene 2

Your Kind Attention
F. Fay

Scene 3

Japanese Prints (*Conceived and designed by* Watson Barratt.)
Aermican Tourist: C. Woodruff. *A Seller of Prints:* J. Adair. *A Japanese Rickshaw Man:* R. Wayne.
Print 1: Cherry Blossom Time—Dance of Cherry Fate.
Print 2: Fujiyama—Dance of the Water and Wave.
Print 3: The Japanese Bridge—Dance of the Seasons.
Print 4: The Love Boat.
The Dancer: Kyra.

Scene 4

Keep Dancing (Stick to Your Dance)
R. Boylan, A. Boylan

Scene 5

All Wet (A burlesque on Somerset Maugham's "Rain" *by* Harold Atteridge and Harry Wagstaff Gribble)
First Native: R. Wayne. *Second Native:* G. Christie. *A Salesman:* J. Adair. *Joe Horne:* H. Kelly. *Mrs. Davidson:* M. Pettes. *Mrs. McPhell:* B. Elliott. *Dr. McPhell:* J. Liddy. *Reverend Davidson:* R. O'Connor. *Sadie Thompson:* G. Rosener. *Ameena:* E. Starck. *First Marine:* V. Bozart. *Second Marine:* L. Dorr.

Scene 6

"Samoa" (Take Me Back to Samoa Some More)
L. Morse, Dancers[35]
(*Lyrics by* Cyrus D. Wood.)

Scene 7

A Few Remarks
Senator Ford

Scene 8

The Living Curtain

Scene 9

The Epilogue: The Studio Frolic (Characters same as in the Prologue)
Songs
B. Nelson
"Carmencita"
B. Nelson
Spanish Girls: Misses A. Kennedy, E. Stitt, E. Starck, Shay, E. Bambrick, Hansel, F. Bond, Adair. *Dancers:* Misses Mooney, Monroe, Charles, Leckie, Harland, LeVon, Bay Sisters. *Specialty Dancers:* E. Pillard, R. Boylan, A. Boylan.
Finale
(Entire Company)

1923.26   LITTLE MISS BLUEBEARD

A Song-Play (Comedy with Music) in Three Acts. Play by Avery Hopwood. Adapted from the Hungarian play ('A kisasszony férje') by Gábor Drégely.

---

[33]Credited to Jean Schwartz in sheet music.
[34]Added after opening to Act 2, Scene 1:
Hurry Poem
A. Klaer
[35]After opening, this song was sung by B. Doyle, H. Gimbel, E. Lavelle, R. Boylan, A. Boylan.

(Music by E. Ray Goetz, José Padilla, Paul A. Rubens, George Gershwin. Lyrics by E. Ray Goetz, Buddy G. DeSylva, Ira Gershwin, Percy Graham Paul.) Staged by W. H. Gilmore. Settings designed by Herman Rosse. Miss Bordoni's costumes by Paul Poirte, Jean Patou, Chanel, Boué Soeurs, Travis Banton. Produced by Charles Frohman in association with E. Ray Goetz. Opened 28 August 1923 at the Lyceum Theatre and closed 26 January 1924 after 175 performances.

CAST (in order of appearance): *Larry Charters:* BRUCE McRAE. *Eva Winthrop:* Margaret Linden. *Smithers:* William Eville. *Sir John Barstow:* Arthur Barry. *The Honorable Bertie Bird:* ERIC BLORE. *Bob Talmadge:* STANLEY LOGAN. *Colette:* IRENE BORDONI. *Gloria Talmadge:* Jeannette Sherwin. *Lulu:* Eva Leonard-Boyne. *Paul Rondel:* Burton Brown.

Act 1: Larry Charters' Flat in London. An evening late in June. (Rosse.)

Act 2: Larry Charters' Flat in London. The following morning. (Rosse.)

Act 3: Reception Hall of the Talmadges' villa in Deauville. Two days later.

ACT 1

"So This Is Love"
I. Bordoni
(*Music and Lyrics by* E. Ray Goetz.)

ACT 2

"The Gondola and the Girl"
I. Bordoni
(*Music by* Paul A. Rubens. *Lyrics by* Percy Graham Paul and E. Ray Goetz.)

ACT 3

"Who'll Buy My Violets?" (La Violetera)
I. Bordoni
(*Music by* José Padilla. *English Lyrics by* E. Ray Goetz.)
"I Won't Say I Will (But I Won't Say I Won't)"
I. Bordoni
(*Music by* George Gershwin. *Lyrics by* Buddy G. DeSylva and Arthur Francis [Ira Gershwin].)

1923.27   POPPY

A Musical Comedy in Three Acts. Book and lyrics by Dorothy Donnelly. Music by Stephen Jones and Arthur Samuels, (John Egan). Staged by Dorothy Donnelly and Julian Alfred[36]. Musical numbers staged by Julian Alfred. Settings designed by Ralph Barton. Costumes designed by Charles LeMaire. Orchestra under the direction of Gus Salzer. Orchestrations by Stephen Jones. Produced by Philip Goodman. Opened 3 September 1923 at the Apollo Theatre and closed 28 June 1924 after 346 performances.

CAST: (in order of appearance): *Sarah Tucker:* Maude Ream Stover. *Amos Sniffen:* Jimmy Barry. *Mary Delafield:* LUELLA GEAR. *William Van Wyck:* Alan Edwards. *Princess Vronski Mameluke Pasha Tubbs:* EMMA JANVIER. *Mortimer Pottle:* ROBERT WOOLSEY. *Professor Eustace McGargle:* W. C. FIELDS. *Poppy McGargle:* MADGE KENNEDY. *Judge Delafield:* Hugh Chilvers. *Premiere Dancer:* Marion Chambers. *Special Dancers:* Hilda Burt, Lucretia White.
Girls of the Ensemble: Linelle Blackburn, Nancy Lay, Helen Evans, Evelyn Jerrell, Helen Miade, Virginia Kelley, Mildred Stevens, Dorothy Whiteford, Devah Worrell, Beatrice Wilson, Elizabeth Collins, Kathleen McLoughlin. *Boys of the Ensemble:* Ackland Powell, Thomas Monahan, Wally Myers, Gene Sinclair, Harry Blake, Al Watson, Norman Jefferson, Walter Wandell.

Act 1: Outside of the Fair Grounds, Greenmeadow, Connecticut. A September morning, 1874.

Act 2: The House on the Hill. That evening.

Act 3: At Mrs. Tucker's. A week later.

ACT 1

Opening Chorus
Boys and Girls
"Stepping Around"
L. Gear, J. Barry, Ensemble
"The Girl I've Never Met"
A. Edwards, V. White, V. Vale, H. Burt
"Hang Your Sorrows in the Sun"[37]
M. Kennedy
(*Music by* John Egan.)

---

[36]After the opening, the staging credit was revised to read, Staged by Dorothy Donnelly and Philip Goodman.
[37]Replaced for national tour by:
"Someone Will Make Me Cry" (Someone Will Make You Smile)
M. Kennedy
(*Music by* Rudolf Sieczynski. *Lyrics by* Irving Caesar.)

"Two Make a Home"
  M. Kennedy, A. Edwards
  (*Music by* Stephen Jones, Arthur Samuels.)
"Kadoola Kadoola Solo"
  W. C. Fields
"When Men Are Alone"
  R. Woolsey, H. Burt, L. Craig, V. Vale, V. White, Ensemble
"Fortune Telling"
  M. Kennedy, Boys

ACT 2[38]

"The Dancing Lesson" (Opening Number)
  M. Chambers, H. Burt, L. Craig, V. Vale, V. White, Ensemble
  (*Music by* John Egan.)
"Alibi Baby"
  L. Gear, Ensemble
  (*Music by* Arthur Samuels. *Lyrics by* Howard Dietz[39].)
"On Our Honeymoon"[40]
  M. Kennedy, A. Edwards
"Choose a Partner, Please"
  M. Kennedy, Ensemble
"Mary" (Whaddaye Do Sundays, Whaddaye Do Mondays, Mary?), or
(What Do You Do Sundays, Mary?)
  L. Gear, R. Woolsey, H. Burt, L. Craig, V. Vale, V. White, Ensemble
  (*Music by* Stephen Jones. *Lyrics by* Irving Caesar.)

ACT 3

"A Picnic Party with You"
  L. Gear, R. Woolsey, H. Burt, L. Craig, V. Vale, V. White, Ensemble
  (*Music by* John Egan.)
Finale
  Entire Company

1923.28 BALIEFF'S CHAUVE-SOURIS

A Return Engagement of the Russian Revue in Two Acts, 16 Scenes[41]. Conceived by M. Nikita Balieff. Music by Alexei Archangelsky. Costumes and surroundings (scenery) by Nicholas Remisoff, Sergei Soudeikine. Director and stage autocrat, Nikita Balieff. Artistic advisor, A. Koiransky. Chef d'orchestre, Elie Zlatin. Maitre de choréographie, Mr. Kotshetovsky. Presented by F. Ray Comstock and Morris Gest. Opened 3 September 1923 at Jolson's Theatre and closed 29 September 1923 after 32 performances.

CAST: Nikita Balieff (Conferencier), Mmes. Alekseyevtzeva, Anderson, Birse, Dianina, Ershova, Fechner, Karabanova, Komisarjevskaya, Koretzky, Nicolina. Messrs. Birse, Dalmatoff, Gorodetsky, Joukovitch, Loukin, Marievsky, Riadnoff, Salama, Semenoff, Stoianovsky, Tcherniavsky, Zotoff.

ACT 1

Scene 1
  U Prikazulka Vorot
    Scenes from the Life of Old Russia in the Sixteenth Century, after Count Alexei Tolstoy
      Entire Company
Scene 2
  The See Saw (Porcelaine de Meissen)
    Mmes. Dianina, Fechner, Karabanova, Komisarjevskaya
    (*Music by* Alexei Archangelsky.)
Scene 3
  "The Parade of the Wooden Soldiers"
    Messrs. Birse, Gorodetsky, Joukovitch, Marievsky, Riadnoff, Semenoff, Stoianovsky, Tscherniavsky, Zotoff
    (*Music and Lyrics by* Leon Jessel and Victor Olivier.)

Scene 4
  Songs of Sentiment
    Mmes. Birse, Ershova
    (*Costumes and Surroundings by* S. Soudeikine.)
Scene 5
  The Sudden Death of a Horse, or, The Greatness of the Russian Soul
    Mme. Fechner, Messrs. Gorodetsky, Marievsky, Salama, Tcherniavsky
Scene 6
  Duet from The Sleeping Beauty (Dance)
    Mme. Anderson, M. Semenoff
    (*Music by* Pyotor Ilyich Tchaikovsky.)
Scene 7
  La Grande Opera Italiana
    Mme. Birse; Messrs. Birse, Joukovitch, Stoianovsky, Zotoff
    (*Costumes and Surroundings by* S. Soudeikine.)
Scene 8
  The Minuet
    Mme. Deykarhanova; Messr. Gorodetsky
    (*Music by* Alexei Archangelsky.)
Scene 9
  "Katinka"
    Mmes. Dianina, Karabanova; Messrs. Dalamatoff
    (*Music by* Alexei Archangelsky. *Lyrics by* Fizchok Czarovich. *Costumes and Surroundings by* S. Soudeikine.)

ACT 2

Scene 1
  A Night at Yard's, Moscow, 1840 (Gypsy Songs)
    Entire Company
Scene 2
  A Musical Snufff-Box
    Mme. Karabanova; Messrs. Gorodetsky, Marievsky
    (*Music by* Liadoff. *Costumes and Surroundings by* S. Soudeikine.)
Scene 3
  The Night Idyll
    Mme. Fechner; Messrs. Salama
    (*Music by* Alexei Archangelsky. *Lyrics by* Dailey Paskman.)
Scene 4
  Thepak (from the ballet "The Nutcracker")
    Mme. Anderson; Messr. Semenoff;
      Mmes. Deykarhanova, Dianina, Ershova, Koretzky, Nicolina, Alekseyevtzeva
    (*Music by* Pyotor Ilyich Tchaikovsky. *Costumes and Surroundings by* S. Soudeikine.)
Scene 5
  El Ekhnem (The Famous Volga Boat Song)
    (*Music arranged by* Alexei Archangelsky. *Lyrics by* Dailey Paskman.)
Scene 6
  Chastoushki (Russian Workspeople's Ditties)
    Mme. Fechner; Messr. Marievsky
Scene 7
  The Chorus of the Brothers Zaitzeff
    Messrs. Birse, Dalmatoff, Gorodetsky, Joukovitch, Loukin, Marievsky, Riadnoff, Salama, Stoianovsky, Tcherniavsky, Zotoff

1923.29 THE MARIONETTE PLAYERS

The Famous Teatro dei Piccoli of Rome in a Marionette Revue in Two Acts, 12 Scenes. Orchestra under the direction of Peace Ottore. Produced under the direction of Cav. R. Fidora and Dr. Vittorio Podrecca. Presented by Charles Dillingham. Opened 10 September 1923 at the Frolic Theatre and closed 22 September 1923 after 16 performances.

CAST: [*Vocalists:*] Cissie Vaughan, Cyril Whittle, Nita Edwards, Heddle Nash, Tito Verger. *Marionette Operators:* The families of Gorno, Dell'Acqua and Corsi.

ACT 1

Scene 1
  Prologue
Scene 2
  Pierrots and Butterflies
Scene 3
  Miss Legnetti, Neapolitan Vocalist
    C. Vaughan

---

[38]Added for subsequent national tour:
  Minstrels on Parade (Act 2)
    W. C. Fields, George F. Moore (Mortimer Pottle), John Cherry (Amos Sniffen)
[39]Credited in sheet music to Dorothy Donnelly.
[40]Replaced after the opening by:
  "Poppy Dear"
    M. Kennedy, A. Edwards
  Which was later replaced by:
  Reprise Waltz
    M. Kennedy, A. Edwards
[41]Originally opened in New York 4 February 1922 at the 49th Street Theatre for 544 performances in four consecutive editions.

Scene 4
    Bil-Bal-Bul at Play (acrobat)
Scene 5
    "Crispino E Comare" (Duet)
       (*Music by* L. and F. Ricci. *Scenery by* Pierretto Blanco.)
        Annetta: C. Vaughan. *Crispino*: C. Whittle.
Scene 6
    Happy Hooligans in Pumpkin Land
Scene 7
    "Puss in Boots" (An Opera in Two Scenes, 4 Scenes, after Charles
    Perrault. *Music by* Cesar Cui. *Stage setting by* V. Grassi.)
        Puss: N. Edwards. *The Princess*: C. Vaughan. *Jack*: H. Nash. *The King*: C.
        Whittle. *The Ogre*: T. Verger.

ACT 2
Scene 1
    "Puss in Boots" [Part Two]
Scene 2
    Salome
Scene 3
    The Corporal with the Umbrella
Scene 4
    The Three Thieves in a Cage
Scene 5
    Tarantella (*Music by* Rossini.)
    H. Nash

SALLY

1923.30

A Return Engagement of the Musical Comedy in Three Acts, 5 Scenes[42]. Book by Guy Bolton. Music by Jerome Kern. Lyrics by Clifford Grey, (Anne Caldwell, P. G. Wodehouse, B. G. DeSylva). Butterfly Ballet Music by Victor Herbert. Production staged by Edward Royce. Settings designed by Joseph Urban. Costumes designed by Alice O'Neil. Orchestra under the direction of Gus Salzer. Produced by Florenz Ziegfeld, Jr. Opened 17 September 1923 at the New Amsterdam Theatre and closed 6 October 1923 after 24 performances.

CAST: *Pops*, Proprietor of the Alley Inn, New York: ALFRED P. JAMES. *Rosalind Rafferty*, a manicurist: KATHLENE MARTYN. *Madame Nookerova's Maid*: KATHLENE MARTYN. *Sascha*, Violinist at the Alley Inn: Jacques Rebiroff. *Otis Hooper*, a Theatrical Agent: WALTER CATLETT. *Mrs. Ten Broek*, a Settlement Worker: FELICE. *Sally* of the Alley, a Foundling: MARILYN MILLER. *Madame Nookerova*, a Wild Rose: MARILYN MILLER. *Premier Star of the Follies*: MARILYN MILLER. *Connie*, a Waiter at the Alley Inn: LEON ERROL. *Duke of Czechogovinia*: LEON ERROL. *Miss New York*, a Niece: Agatha Debussey. *Admiral Travers*, a gay one: Phil Ryley. *Blair Farquar*, an Only Son: PAUL FRAWLEY. *Jimmie Spelvin*: FLOYD ENGLISH. *Beatrice*: Mary McDonald. *Helen*: Joan Gardner. *Alta*: Vivian Vernon. *Agatha*: Agatha Debussey. *Winifred*: Betty Williams. *Virginia*: Virginia Ray. *Richard Farquar*: Frank Kingdon. *Foundlings (6)*: *Miss Rhinelander*: Bobby Deane. *Miss Vanderbilt*: Mae Daw. *Miss Worth*: Bernardine DeGraves. *Miss Bryant*: Ethel Kelly. *Miss Audubon*: Pauline Schaefer. *Miss Bowling Green*: Billie Stanfield. *Ensemble*.

THE GREENWICH VILLAGE FOLLIES (1923)

1923.31

A Musical Revue in Two Acts, 24 Scenes[43]. (Sketches by William K. Wells, Paul Gerard Smith, John Murray Anderson.) Music by Louis A. Hirsch and Con Conrad. Lyrics by Irving Caesar and John Murray Anderson. Sketches directed by Lew Fields. Scenery built under the direction of James Van Sickler. Costumes made by the Bohemians, Inc. under the supervision of Howard Greer; men's costumes by Brooks-Mahieu. Entire production devised and staged by John Murray Anderson. All modern dances staged by Larry Ceballos. East Indian dances by Michio Itow. Orchestra directed by Alfred Newman. Orchestrations by (Robert) Russell Bennett. Produced by The Bohemians, Inc. (A. L. Jones, Morris Green, managing directors) (Messrs Shubert). Opened 20 September 1923 at the Winter Garden and closed 12 January 1924 after 131 performances.

[42]Originally produced in New York 21 December 1920 at the New Amsterdam Theatre for 561 performances. For Synopsis of Scenes and Musical Numbers, see original 1920 production.
[43]The fifth in the annual series of revues which began in 1919.

CAST: MARION GREEN, JOE E. BROWN, AL SEXTON, TOM HOWARD, DENMAN MALEY, JOE LYONS, SAMMY WHITE, JOHANNES JOSEFsSON, DAPHNE POLLARD, EVA PUCK, RUTH URBAN, IRENE DELROY, JOSEPHINE ADAIR, MARTHA GRAHAM, GEORGE RASELY THE FOUR CANSINOS (Elisa, Eduardo, Paco, Angel), THE MANDELS (William, Joe), Astrid Ohlson, John Wells, Buster West, Ula Sharon, John Marshall, Chief O-Ke-Mun, Carlos Conte, The Two Briants, Gregory Safronic.
    Ensemble: June Elkin, Moretta Hale, Billye Weston, Lillian Morehouse, Marie Baudoux, Betty Hill, Gertrude Cahill, Anna Mae Clift, Grace Rivers, Elaine Arden, Betty Linn, Ruth Conley, Dolly Donnelly, Tommy Tremaine, Gertrude Walker, Mildred Lunnay, Margaret Mahou, Lisa Pavnova, Helen Richardson, America Chedister, Geneva Price, Geneva Duker, Bee Trevor, Grace Robinson, Madeline Killeen, Pauline Mason, Jean LaMarr, Marion Dabney, Muretta Hale.

ACT 1[44]

[44]The running order of songs and sketches was revised repeatedly during the run. Added to the show for national tour (or during Broadway run):
    On the Pier (Act 1)
        A Lady Teacher: H. Richardson. *Her Maid*: V. Wells. *A Sailor*: J. Wells. *A Cabin Boy*: B. West.
    An Impressionistic Plantation (Act 1)
        Florence Mills
    The Greenwich Village Circus (Act 1)
        Scene: The Midway.
        The Barker: J. Lyons. *The Baseball Pitcher*: W. Craig. *The Boob*: T. Howard.
    "Greenwich Village Circus Days"
        E. McElroy
    "Hota" (Dance)
        The Cansinos
        The Vella-Vella Mannequins: J. McMahon, L. Morehouse, H. Richardson, B. Hill, G. Lee, M. Boudoux, A. M. Clift, M. WIlson, J. Elkins, A. Chedister.
    "Shake a Little Hoof"
        I. Delroy, A. Sexton
        (*Accompanied by*) G. Duker, G. Price, R. Conley, B. Trevor, G. Robinson, N. Harkins, M. Killeen, D. Appleby, J. Kernan, M. Lunnay, G. Gordon, S. Mahon.
    Between the Scenes (*by* George Kelly)(Act 1)
        Miss Pine: J. Adair. *Miss Hickey*: D. Pollard. *The Stage Hands*: W. Mandell, J. Mandell.
    "Where Is My Boy?" (Act 1)
        I. Delroy, A. Sexton
        Scene: Before the Silver Fringe.
    The Dance of the Poison Kiss
        The Mandells
    The Eternal Triangle (Act 2)
        Barnyard Vamp: D. Pollard. *Barnyard Romeo*: S. White. *The Stranger*: J. E. Brown.
    The Dodger (Act 2)
        Scene: A Circus Tent.
        The Dodger: T. Howard. *A Harker*: J. Lyon.
    "(I Am) Thinking of You" (Act 2)
        A. Sexton, I. Delroy
        (*Music by* Louis Hirsch.)
    Petulant Petunias (*by* Walt Kuhn)(Act 2)
        E. Cansino, A. Cansino, J. Marshall, C. Conte, W. Craig, G. Safronic, F. Lyon
    Oh, Doctor! (*by* William K. Wells)(Act 2)
        Scene: In a Doctor's Building.
        A Chauffeur: J. E. Brown. *A Patient*: D. Pollard.
    "Spanish Love" (from BROADWAY BREVITIES OF 1920)
        G. Safronic
        (added to The Birthday of the Infanta Sequence, moved to Act 2)
        (*Music by* George Gershwin. *Lyrics by* Irving Caesar.)
    "Whiskers" (Act 2)
        S. White
        (*Music by* Lewis E. Gensler. *Lyrics by* Rube Goldberg.)
        Hezekiah Brown (First Growth): W. Craig. *Hezekiah Brown* (Second Growth): C. Conte. *Hezekiah Brown* (Third Growth): A. Cansino. *Hezekiah Brown* (Fourth Growth): Eduardo Cansino.
    Whiskers Ballet (*Written by* Rube Goldberg and Lewis E. Gensler.)
        The Storytellers: D. Maley. *King Ostermoor*: J. E. Brown. *The King's Barber*: T. Howard. *The King's Masseur*: J. Lyons. *The King's Dancers*: First Dancer: Eduardo Cansino. *Second Dancer*: A. Cansino. *Third Dancer*: W. Craig. *Fourth Dancer*: C. Conte. *The Slave Girl*: S. White. *Maa-han*: Himself.

Scene 1
The Paint Box
The Artist: A. Sexton.
The Colors in the Paint Box: *Yellow*: J. Elkin. *Blue*: M. Hale. *Scarlet*: B. Weston. *Rose*: L. Morehouse. *Fuschia*: M. Baudoux. *Purple*: B. Hill *Orange*: G. Cahill. *Violet*: A. M. Clift. *Orchid*: G. Rivers. *White*: E. Arden. *The Inspirations*: B. Linn, R. Conley, D. Donnelly, T. Tremaine, G. Walker, M. Lunnay, M. Mahon, F. Moore, H. Richardson, A. Chedister. *The Fallen Leaves*: G. Price, G. Duker, B. Trevor, G. Robinson, M. Killeen, P. Mason.
Scene 2
Sammy White and Eva Puck (Specialty)
Scene: The Outer Stage.
Scene 3
The Fatal Card[45] (*by* William K. Wells)
Scene: At Sea.
The Steward: J. E. Brown. *Purser*: T. Howard. *Captain*: J. Lyons. *Mate*: D. Maley.
Scene 4
"Lovey"
I. Delroy, A. Sexton
(*Music by* Con Conrad. *Conceived and designed by* Max Ree.)
Scene: The Outer Stage.
(*Accompanied by*) G. Walker, J. McMahon, T. Tremaine, F. Moore, R. Conley, M. Lunnay, M. Donnelly, B. Linn.
Scene 5
Everybody Welcome (*by* Paul Gerard Smith)
Scene: Pier 32.
An Immigrant: D. Pollard. *Harold*: E. McElroy. *Watchman*: W. Mandell. *Dr. Martin*: J. Lyons. *Dr. White*: W. Craig. *The Inspector*: D. Maley.
Scene 6
"Kama's Garden"
J. Adair
(*Music by* Louis A. Hirsch.)
Scene: The Garden of Kama.
"The Garden of Kama" (A Tragedy of India conceived and arranged by John Murray Anderson from the Indian love lyrics of Laurence Hope, set to the music of Amy Woodforde-Finden. *Costumes and settings designed by* Max Ree.)
The Story Tellers: M. Green, R. Urban.
In the Pantomime: *The Dancing Girl*: M. Graham. *A Toiler in the Garden*: G. Safronic. *The Maharajah*: J. Marshall. *The Maharanee*: B. Linn. *The White Peacock*: M. Dabney.
Scene 7
William and Joe Mandel
Scene: Back Stage.
Scene 8
"Bustle"
D. Pollard
Scene: The Outer Stage.
Scene 9
Three Cheers for the Red, Green and Yellow[46] (*by* Paul Gerard Smith)
Scene: A Dining Room in the Central Park West Apartment.
Mrs. West: E. Puck. *Mr. West*: D. Maley. *A Maid*: A. Chedister. *A Traffic Policeman*: J. Lyons.
Scene 10
Buster West and John Wells (Specialty)
Scene: The Outer Stage.
Scene 11
The Hold Up
Scene: A Street in Greenwich Village.
Zeke Silvers: T. Howard. *The Real Crook*: W. Craig. *The Victim*: D. Maley. *The Girl*: I. Delroy. *The Officer*: J. Lyons. *A Chinaman*: F. Lyon.
Scene 12
"Moonlight Kisses"
G. Rasely, I. Delroy, A. Sexton
(*Music by* Con Conrad.)
Scene: The Outer Stage.
The Movie Kisses[47]
The Douglas Fairbanks Kiss: A. M. Clift. *The Rudolf Valentino Kiss*: L. Morehouse. *The Ben Turpin Kiss*: G. Cahill. *The Jackie Coogan Kiss*: M.

Baudoux. *The Charlie Chaplin Kiss*: M. Hale. *The John Barrymore Kiss*: B. Hill. *The Harold Lloyd Kiss*: J. Elkin. *The William S. Hart Kiss*: G. Rivers.
"The Barcarole"[48]
G. Rasely, R. Urban
The Dancer: U. Sharon.
The Dream Lovers
Melisande: A. Ohlson. *Peleas*: W. Craig. *Beatrice*: H. Richardson. *Dante*: J. Marshall. *Mary Stuart*: B. Linn. *Rizzio*: C. Conte. *The Lady of Shallot*: M. Dabney. *The Black Knight*: G. Safronic. *Mme. de Pompadour*: A. Chedister. *Louis XV*: F. Lyon. *Camille*: B. Weston. *Armand*: F. Short. And G. Price, G. Duker, G. Robinson, B. Trevor, M. Killeen, P. Mason, E. McElroy.
Scene 1
Wanted—A Man
The Unwanted: D. Pollard. *A Policeman*: J. Lyons.
Scene 14
"The Birthday of the Infanta"
J. Adair
(*Music by* Louis Hirsch. *Lyrics by* Josephine Adair.)
Scene: A Spanish Fiesta.
The Infanta: M. Dabney, Ensemble.
"Conchita"
M. Green
(*Music by* Lewis E. Gensler.)
Spanish Dances:
Gypsy Dance and Bolero
The Cansinos
Hota
Elisa Cansino, Eduardo Cansino
Serenata Morisca
M. Graham
Torero[49]
The Cansinos
"Seeing Stars"
A. Sexton, Company
(*Music by* Con Conrad.)
ACT 2
Scene 1
"Cock-a-Doodle-Doo"
D. Pollard, J. E. Brown
(*Music by* Con Conrad. *Costumes designed by* Max Ree.)
Scene: A Greenwich Village Barnyard.
Scene 2
This Way Out
The Husband: J. Lyons. *The Wife*: E. Puck. *The Friend*: D. Maley.
Scene 3
"Annabelle Lee"[50]
G. Rasely
(*Music by* Louis Hirsch.)
Scene: Before the Violet Ray Curtain.
"The Raven"[51] (*Poem by* Edgar Allan Poe. *Music by* Lewis E. Gensler.)
Edgar Allan Poe: M. Green. *Lenore*: B. Linn.
Scene 4
Three Girls and a Fellow (*by* Paul Gerard Smith)
The Fellow: J. E. Brown. *The Girls*: E. Puck, I. Delroy, A. Chedister.
Scene 5
"The Golden Trail"
G. Rasely, A. Ohlson
(*Music by* Louis A. Hirsch.)
Scene: The Far West.
A Pioneer: M. Green. *The Driver of the Covered Wagon*: J. Josefsson. *An Indian Chief*: Chief Os-Ko-Mun. And Josefsson's Icelanders.
Scene 6
Daphne Pollard (Specialty)
Scene: The Outer Stage.
Scene 7
"Dancing Step Child"
B. West

---

[45]Sketch later known as 'The Raft.'
[46]Dropped during the run.
[47]Dropped during the run.

[48]Dropped during the run.
[49]Dropped during the run.
[50]Dropped during the run.
[51]Dropped during the run.

(*Music by* Con Conrad.)
  Scene: The Outer Stage.
Scene 8

  The Moving Man's Dream (A pantomime)
    The Two Briants
      Scene: In the Village.
Scene 9

  Eats
    T. Howard, J. E. Lyons
Scene 10

  "Raisin' the Roof"
    A. Sexton, Entire Company
    (*Music by* Con Conrad.)
  Finale

1923.32 MUSIC BOX REVUE (1923-24)

A Musical Revue in Two Acts, 27 Scenes[52]. (Sketches by George S. Kaufman, Robert Benchley, Edwin Burke, Bobby Clark, Paul McCullough, Stanley E. Rauh, Irving Strouse, Bertram Block.) Music and lyrics by Irving Berlin. Staged by Hassard Short. Dances arranged by Sammy Lee. Settings designed by Clark Robinson. Costumes designed by Ralph Mulligan, Charles LeMaire, Adrian. Orchestra under the direction of Frank Tours. Vocal harmony arrangements by Arthur Johnston. Orchestrations by Frank Tours, Maurice DePackh, Steve Jones, Charles Grant. Produced by Sam H. Harris. Opened 22 September 1923 at the Music Box Theatre and closed 17 May 1924 after 273 performances.

CAST: FRANK TINNEY, FLORENCE MOORE, JOSEPH SANTLEY, GRACE MOORE, JOHN STEEL, IVY SAWYER, ROBERT BENCHLEY, LORA SONDERSON, HUGH CAMERON, FLORENCE O'DENISHAWN, SOLLY WARD, Mme. DORA STROEVA, PHIL BAKER, THE BROX SISTERS (Kathlyn, Dagmar, Lorraine), Charles Columbus, Frances Mahan, Nelson Snow, Dorothy Dilley, Nellie King.
  Ladies of the Ensemble (Show Girls): Katherine Ardell, Virginia Crane, Billy Davis, Peggy Fish, Helene Gardner, Carol Goodner, Alice Harris, Frances Lee, Lillian MacKenzie, Helen Rich, Renee Theorin, Irene Wylie. *Music Box Girls*: Helen Lyons, Maida Palmer, Joan Clement, Adele McHatton, Teddy Gill, Diana Chase, Elaine Field, Diane Gordon. *Music Box Boys*: Peppo Albreu, Abner Barnhart, Elmer Brown, George Mays, Warren Crosby, Ralph Glover, Campbell Hicks, T. Perry Higgins, Gayle Mays, Richard Maxwell, Joseph Marquis, William J. Sholar. *Music Box Dancers*: Billie Blythe, Betty Block, Sherry Gale, Sunshine Jarmann, Pansy Maness, Thelma Van, Beulah Van, Buena Vista.

ACT 1[53]
Scene 1

  1923:

  The Calendar (Opening)
    The Months: Music Box Show Girls. *Music Box Revue-1923*: L. Sonderson.

---

[52]The third in the annual series of revues written by Irving Berlin, produced by Sam H. Harris, beginning in 1921.
[53]Running order revised after opening. Added after opening:
  Spirits of 1923 (*by* Bobby Clark and Paul McCullough)(Act 1)
    Scene: A Seance Parlor.
      Wife: F. Moore. *The Husband*: S. Ward. *The Rajah*: H. Cameron.
  Mme. Dora Stroeva (*by arrangement with* E. Ray Goetz)(Act 1)
    Accompanist: Serge Walter. *The Voyagers*: R. Glover, H. Lyons.
  Added for the tour:
  The Lucky Strike (*by* Bert Kalmar and Harry Ruby)(*Directed by* Joseph Santley.)(Act 1)
    Scene: A Room.
      Harry: Johnny Burke. *Grace*: F. Moore. *Billy Blakley*: J. Santley. *The Butler*: H. Cameron.
  The Wedding Ring (*by* Al Bosberg)(*Directed by* Joseph Santley.)(Act 1)
    I. Sawyer, J. Santley, H. Cameron
  Another Good Girl Gone Wrong (*by* Gilbert Clark)(Act 2)
    Scene: Water's Edge, Battery Edge.
      A Working Girl: F. Moore. *The Man*: J. Santley.
  The Motive (*by* Bert Kalmar and Harry Ruby)(*Directed by* Joseph Santley.)(Act 2)
    Scene: A Living Room.
      Maid: C. Goodner. *Inspector*: H. Cameron. *Assistant Inspector*: Elwood Gray. *Richard Carleton*: J. Santley. *Mrs. Carleton*: I. Sawyer. *Inspector's Wife*: R. Theorin.

Scene 2

  The Fraudway Ticket Office
    Gyp Brothers, Proprietors: S. Ward, P. Baker. *The Theatre Goers*: I. Sawyer, J. Santley.
Scene 3

  Before the Curtains
    The Music Box Girls and Boys
Scene 4

  The Music Box Garden of Girls
    Music Box Dancers
  "Dance" (song)
    L. Sonderson, Company
      The Dancers: F. Mahan.
Scene 5

  "When You Walked Out, Somebody Else Walked In"
    The Brox Sisters
Scene 6

  So This Is Marriage[54] (*by* Edwin Burke)(*Directed by* Sam Forrest.)
    Scene: A Room.
      The Husband: S. Ward. *A Wife*: L. Sonderson. *A Wife*: F. Moore.
Scene 7

  "Tell Me a Bedtime Story"
    G. Moore
      The Story Tellers: Music Box Boys. *The Nighties*: K. Ardell, C. Goodner, B. Blythe, B. Block, P. Maness, R. Noble.
Scene 8

  The Treasurer's Report[55] Will Be Read by
    R. Benchley
Scene 9[56]

  Hats[56]
    The Man's Hat: J. Santley. *The Girl's Hat*: I. Sawyer. *The Other Hats*: Girls and Boys of the Music Box.
  "Your Hat and My Hat"
    J. Santley, I. Sawyer
Scene 10

  "An Orange Grove in California"
    J. Steel, G. Moore
      The Boy: J. Steel. *The Girl*: G. Moore.
Scene 11

  Phil Baker
Scene 12

  Florence O'Denishawn
Scene 13

  The Maid of Mesh
    Scene: The Mesh Bag.
      The Maid: I. Sawyer. *The Boy*: J. Santley. *The Eight Girls*: M. Palmer, J. Clement, T. Gill, E. Field, A. McHatton, H. Rich, H. Gardner, P. Fish. *The Girl in the Mesh Bag*: F. O'Denishawn.
  "Maid of Mesh"[57]
    J. Santley, I. Sawyer
Scene 14

  "Climbing Up the Scale"
    F. Moore, Music Box Boys
    (*Assisted by*) *The Eight Notes*: B. Vista, K. Ardell, B. Blythe, T. Van, B. Van, B. Block, P. Maness, S. Jarmann.
Scene 15

  "Little Butterfly" (*Dances arranged by* Alexander Oumansky.)
    J. Steel
      The Man: J. Steel. *The Butterfly*: D. Dilley. *Two Admirers*: N. Snow, C. Columbus.
Scene 16

  Hunting Wild Game in Africa (*by* Stanley E. Rauh and Irving Strouse)
    The Professor: H. Cameron. *Mr. Zilch*: F. Tinney.
    (Motion picture directed by Clark Robinson.)

---

[54]Dropped for subsequent tour.
[55]Dropped for subsequent tour.
[56]Song and sketch dropped for subsequent tour.
[57]The mesh bags and dresses of gold and silver mesh were especially made for this scene by Whiting and Davis.

Scene 17

Strut: "Learn to Do the Strut"
The Brox Sisters, Entire Company

ACT 2

Scene 1

The Fisherman's Dream (Fisherman's Dream Ballet)
(*Music composed and orchestrated by* Frank Tours. *Dances arranged by* Alexander Oumansky.)
Scene: Under the Sea.
The Fisherman: C. Columbus. *The Fish*: H. Lyons, F. Lee, E. Field, V. Crane, A. McHatton, H. Rich, C. Goodner, R. Theorin, D. Gordon, J. Clement, H. Gardner, D. Chase. *The Moon Fish*: M. Palmer. *The Sun Fish*: T. Gill. *The Gold Fish*: D. Dilley, F. Mahan, S. Jarmann, B. Vista, B. Blythe. *The Star Fish*: F. O'Denishawn.

Scene 2

A Bit o' Grand Opera[58] ("Yes! We have No Bananas" Opera Burlesque Sextet)
F. Moore, G. Moore, L. Sonderson, F. Tinney, J. Steel, J. Santley

Scene 3

Mme. Dora Stroeva (by arrangement with E. Ray Goetz)
Accompanist: Monsieur S. Walter. *The Voyagers*: R. Glover, H. Lyons.

Scene 4

If Men Played Cards as Women Do (*by* George S. Kaufman)
Scene: Joe's Library.
Joseph: J. Santley. *Hugh*: H. Cameron. *Solly*: S. Ward. *Phil*: P. Baker. *The Cards*: K. Ardell, B. Block.

Scene 5

"One Girl"
J. Steel
The Man: J. Steel. *The Girl He Met in —Spain*: M. Palmer. *—Holland*: A. McHatton. *—Italy*: J. Clement. *—France*: T. Gill. *—Ireland*: K. Ardell. *One Girl*: H. Lyons.

Scene 6

Frank Tinney

Scene 7

"The Waltz of Long Ago"
G. Moore
Scene a: The Studio.
The Little Girl at the Party: D. Burgess. *The Boy With the Ukelele*: G. Mays. *The Host*: J. Santley. *The Hostess*: G. Moore.
Scene b: A Room in a House in Washington Square.
Her Grandfather: J. Santley. *Her Grandmother*: I. Sawyer.

Scene 8

The Silver Curtain[59]
Dancers: F. Mahan, C. Columbus, N. Snow.

Scene 9

She Must Be Kept Out of This[60] (A Mystery Melodrama *by* Bertram Block.)
(*Directed by* Sam Forrest and Joseph Santley.)
Scene: Chalmers' House, somewhere on Long Island.
Arnold Chalmers: F. Tinney. *Rose*, his wife: G. Moore. *Hassan*: J. Santley. *Mr. England*, a Wall Street victim of Chalmers: S. Ward. *Ruth*, his daughter: I. Sawyer. *Angelo*, an Italian organ-grinder: H. Cameron. *Katie*, a maid: F. Moore. *George*, a Detective: E. Brown. *The Woman*: L. Sonderson.

Scene 10

Finale
J. Santley, Entire Company

(BERNARD & COLLIER'S) NIFTIES OF 1923

1923.33

A Musical Revue 'Glorifying American Clean Humor' in Two Acts, 21 Scenes. Sketches by Sam Bernard and William Collier, (Edgar Smith.

Music by Bert Kalmar, Frank Crumit, Raymond Hubbell. Lyrics by Harry Ruby, Frank Crumit, Buddy G. DeSylva, Arthur Francis [Ira Gershwin].) Staged by R. H. Burnside and William Collier. Dances arranged by William Holbrook. Scenes designed by Herbert Ward and Ernest Gros. Costumes designed by Cora MacGeachy and Gilbert Adrian. Orchestra under the direction of Victor Baravalle Produced by Charles Dillingham. Opened 25 September 1923 at the Fulton Theatre and closed 3 November 1923 after 47 performances.

CAST: SAM BERNARD, WILLIAM COLLIER, HAZEL DAWN, RAY DOOLEY, FRANK CRUMIT, HELEN BRODERICK, LINA BASQUETTE, GUS VAN and JOE SCHENCK, HELYN EBY ROCK, JANE GREEN, FLORENZ AMES, WILLIAM HOLBROOK, CORTEZ and PEGGY, THE BREENS, Frederic Lyon, Harry Morrissey, Pearl Bennett, Gertrude McDonald, Helen McDonald, Fred Greene, Jack Scannell, Sidney Williams, Emil Nelson, Ona Hamilton, James F. Carty, Andre Lapue, Elm City Four, Geraldine Markham, James Brady.
Twelve Tiller Girls: (unidentified). *The Misses*: Markham, Hamilton, Murray, Robinson, Locke, Dare, Lobell, Miller, Belle. *Show Girls*: Flynn, Brady, Errol, Powers, Morris, Verina, Sterling, Lodge, Malowan.

ACT 1[61]

Scene 1

Tapestry (Dance)
L. Basquette, W. Holbrook
(A Gavotte in a Tapestry Room in Versailles. *Conceived by* P. L. Flers.)
Assisted by 12 Nifty Tiller Girls, Ensemble.

Scene 2

The Breens

Scene 3

The Cat's Canary (A Most Unusual Drama *by* William Collier.)
Scene: A Library in somebody's house.
John Martin: F. Ames. *Jim*: F. Crumit. *Joe*: H. Morrissey. *Messenger Boy*: F. Greene. *Harry the Hick*: J. Scannell. *Phil*: S. Williams. *Hokum*, a Slave: E. Nelson. *The Girl*: O. Hamilton. *Theda*: H. Dawn. *Will B. Heard*: J. F. Carty. *At the Piano*: H. E. Rock.
(The theme of this drama and character of Will B. Heard were stolen bodily from a sketch by George M. Cohan with his permission.) Next week: "East Lynne."

Scene 4

Old Pals ("Where Are the Old Pals of Yesterday?")
G. Van, J. Schenck
(*Music by* Gus Van. *Lyrics by* Joseph Schenk.)

Scene 5

Those Boys
S. Bernard, W. Collier

Scene 6

Mr. Butterfly
(*Conceived by* P. L. Flers. *Music by* Raymond Hubbell.)
Time: Morning; Night; the Next Morning.
Orchid: L. Basquette. *Butterfly*: W. Holbrook. *The Flame*: O. Hamilton. *Another Butterfly*: A. Lapue.
Unfaithful to Orchid, Butterfly is attracted to The Flame and is scorched, while Orchid flutters off with Another Butterfly.

Scene 7

"Opening Chorus" (Grinding Out a Revue)
(*Music by* Bert Kalmar. *Lyrics by* Harry Ruby. *Costumes designed by* Kiviette.)
Producer: F. Lyon. *Reporter*: H. Morrissey. *Angel*: P. Bennett. *Author*: G. McDonald. *Composer*: H. McDonald. *A Customer*: H. E. Rock. *The Misses*: Markham, Hamilton, Murray, Robinson, Locke, Dare, Lobell, Miller, Belle. *Show Girls*: Flynn, Brady, Errol, Powers, Morris, Verina, Sterling, Lodge, Malowan.

Scene 8

Sam Bernard
(*Music by* Harry Ruby. *Lyrics by* Bert Kalmar.)

Scene 9

Frank Crumit, assisted by the Elm City Four ("Little Brown Road")
(*Music and Lyrics by* Frank Crumit.)

Scene 10

Keep Off the Grass (*by* William Collier)
Otto Souerback, the husband: S. Bernard. *Al*, his brother-in-law: W. Collier. *Mrs. Tillie Souerback*, the wife: H. Broderick. *Pearl*, the daughter: R. Dooley.

---

[58]Irving Berlin adapted "Yes! We Have No Bananas" into a parody of arias from Aida, Lucia di Lammermoor, Rigoletto, Tales of Hoffman, Il Trovatore and The Messiah. Replaced for subsequent tour by:
Old Time Vaudeville Days (*Staged by* Joseph Santley.)
The Card Girls: C. Goodner, A. Harris. *The Pumpernickel Family*, Refined Acrobats: F. Moore, S. Ward, Johnny Burke, H. Cameron. *The Great LaTour and Brother*: J. Santley, P. Baker. *Mme. Lotta Pipes*. Soprano: F. Moore.
[59]Dropped for subsequent tour.
[60]Later known as 'You Must Be Kept Out of This.' Dropped for subsequent tour.

---

[61]Running order was revised after the opening. Added after the opening:
Vladimir Rasselloffsky (Professor of the Moscow Art College and Originator of the Living Curtain and Living Chandelier) will present some of his living tableaux. (Act 1).

Cicero, the son: F. Ames. *Joe Jackson*, motorcycle cop: F. Crumit. *Jack*, the tramp: G. Van. *Jill*, the other tramp: J. Schenck.

Scene 11

The Tramps

G. Van, J. Schenck

["Beside and Babbling Brook"

(*Music by* Harry Ruby. *Lyrics by* Bert Kalmar.)]

Scene 12

"Calico Days"[62]

J. Green, Entire Company

(*Music and Lyrics by* Ray Perkins, Eubie Blake, Noble Sissle.)

ACT 2

Scene 1

Snow (A Burlesque of Somerset Maugham's 'Rain' by Edgar Smith.)

Scene: The Island of Heliscuta.

Reverend Alfalfa Davidson: W. Collier. *Mrs. Davidson*: S. Bernard. *Sadie Thompson*: H. Dawn. *Doctor McKale*: F. Crumit. *Mrs. McKale*: H. E. Rock. *Joe Conn*: G. Van. *Nunmeena, his wife*: H. Broderick. *Sergeant O'Horror*: F. Ames. *Private Stockson*: J. Schenck. *Hanka Panki*: R. Dooley. *Haw Waya*: G. McDonald. *Huka Poka*: H. McDonald. *Hawaiian Police*: J. Brady, S. Williams.

"When It's Snowing in Hawaii"

R. Dooley

(*Music and Lyrics by* Frank Crumit.)

Scene 2

Frank Crumit and a Couple of His Songs

["Sweet Alice"

(*Music and Lyrics by* Gus Van and Joe Schenck.)]

Scene 3

"The Fabric of Dreams"

J. Schenck, H. Dawn

(*A Color Ballet conceived by* P. L. Flers.)

Assisted by Cortez and Peggy, Twelve Nifty Girls, Ensemble.

(*Music by* Raymond Hubbell. *Lyrics by* Buddy G. DeSylva and Arthur Francis [Ira Gershwin].)

Scene 4

The Nifty Four[63]

S. Bernard, R. Dooley, W. Collier, H. Broderick

Scene 5

Songs

J. Greene

Scene 6

"The Beast and the Beauties" (*Arranged by* John Tiller.)

12 Nifty Tiller Girls

Scene 7

Van and Schenck

["An Old Time Tune"

(*Music and Lyrics by* Gus Van and Joe Schenck.)]

"That Bran' New Gal o' Mine"

(*Music and Lyrics by* Gus Van and Joe Schenck, Benny Davis, Harry Akst.)]

Scene 8

A Striking Situation (*by* William Collier)

Scene: Conservatory in Schultzheimer's Country House. *Time*: Evening. *Place*: As usual—Long Island.

William Collier: W. Collier. *Leopold Schultzheimer*: S. Bernard. *Mrs. Schultzheimer*: H. Broderick. *Julia Marlowe*: H. Dawn. *E. H. Southern*: F. Greene. *Ethel Barrymore*: G. Markham. *John Barrymore*: J. Brady. *Lionel Barrymore*: H. Morrissey. *Butler*: F. Ames. *Members of the Servants' Union* (5): *First Footman*: J. F. Carty. *Second Footman*: A. Cardinal. *First Maid*: R. Dooley. *Second Maid*: H. E. Rock. *Third Maid*: O. Hamilton. *Mike Flanagan*, The Walking Delegate: J. Scannell.

Specialty (Dance)

Cortez and Peggy

Scene 9

Finale

S. Bernard, W. Collier, Entire Company

(*Music by* Bert Kalmar. *Lyrics by* Harry Ruby.)

1923.34

THE MAGIC RING

A Fantastic Comedy with Music in Three Acts and a Prologue. Book and lyrics by Zelda Sears. Music by Harold Levey. Staged by Ira Hards. Musical numbers staged by Dave Bennett. Costumes by Frances Inc. (Mitzi), Schneider-Anderson Co. Settings (prologue) designed by Adrian. Orchestra under the direction of Harold Levey. Produced by Henry W. Savage, Inc. Opened 1 October 1923 at the Liberty Theatre and closed 22 December 1923 after 96 performances.

CAST (in order of appearance): *Zobeide*: Madge North. *Vizier*: JOSEPH MACAULAY. *Abdullah*: Worth Faulkner. *Henry Brockway*: SYDNEY GREENSTREET. *Phoebe Brockway*: Janet Murdock. *Mrs. Bellamy*: Phoebe Crosby. *Iris Bellamy*: JEANETTE MacDONALD. *Tom Hammond*: Boyd Marshall. *Policemen*: Ed Wakefield, John Lyons. *Polly Church*: MITZI (HAJOS). *Minnie*: Wait Until You See Her [MITZI]. *Moe Bernheimer*: James B. Carson. *Stella*: Estelle Birney. *Specialty Dancers*: Carlos and Inez.

Singing Girls: Gladys Baxter, Jane Alden, Jo Duval, Hazel Gladstone, Edith Cooper, Arline Lloyd. *Dancing Girls*: Eleanor Livingston, Virginia Clark, Mildred Quinn, Flo Brooks. *Singing Boys*: Duane Nelson, Sverre Rasmussen, Curt Peterson, Roy Fernandez, Richard Ford, Valentine Nierle. *Dancing Boys*: Dan Sparks, Clifford Daly, Austin Clark, Eduard Lefebvre.

Prologue: A Room in the Seraglio of a Grand Vizier. Very, Very Long Ago.

Act 1: Henry Brockway's Antique Shop. The Present.

Act 2: Studio of Mrs. Bellamy's Home.

Act 3: Henry Brockway's Antique Shop. A few hours later.

PROLOGUE

Chant

M. North, Girls' Sextette

"The Love Song (of Yesterday)"

W. Faulkner, M. North

ACT 1

"Keepsakes"

J. MacDonald, S. Greenstreet, Ha. Gladstone, Ensemble

"Milaiya"

B. Marshall

"Education"

Mitzi, S. Greenstreet, B. Marshall, J. Lyons, E. Wakefield

"When the Organ Plays"

Mitzi, S. Greenstreet, Ensemble

ACT 2[64]

"Milaiya" (reprise)

P. Crosby, J. B. Carson, B. Marshall, J. MacDonald, Carlos and Inez, Ensemble

"Famous Falls"

Mitzi, Dancing Girls

"Imaginative Opera"

P. Crosby, J. B. Carson

"Broken Hearts"

J. MacDonald, B. Marshall, Carlos and Inez, Ensemble

"The Love Song (of Today)"

Mitzi, B. Marshall, E. Birney, Ensemble

"Deep in Someone's Heart"

J. MacDonald, J. Lyons, E. Wakefield, Boys

Finale

Mitzi, J. MacDonald, P. Crosby, E. Birney, Ensemble

ACT 3

"Abdullah's Farewell"

W. Faulkner

1923.35

HAMMERSTEIN'S 9 O'CLOCK REVUE

A Musical Revue in Two Acts, 20 Scenes, direct from the Little Theatre, London. Sketches by Harold Simpson and Morris Harvey. Music by Max Darewski, Muriel Lillie, M. D. Lyon, Harry Coleman, Jack Strachey, Kenneth Dutheld. Lyrics by Harold Simpson, Arthur Weigall, Dion Titheradge, Graham John. Directed by Geoffrey Wilmer. Dances and

---

[62]Dropped after the opening.
[63]Dropped after the opening.

[64]During the run, the running order of "Imaginative Opera" and "Broken Hearts" in Act 2 was reversed.

ensembles staged by Raymond Midgley. Produced by Arthur Hammerstein. Opened 4 October 1923 at the Century Roof Theatre and closed 13 October 1923 after 12 performances.

CAST: MORRIS HARVEY, CICELY DEBENHAM, WILLIAM VALENTINE, PHYLLIS JOYCE, WYN RICHMOND, IRENE OLSEN, FRANK HECTOR, ANN ROGERS, COLIN CAMPBELL, EVA BRICK.

ACT 1
Scene 1
  "Catching Up!"
    Entire Company
    (*Music by* Muriel Lillie. *Lyrics by* Harold Simpson.)
Scene 2
  "The Town Girl"
    W. Valentine, I. Olsen, W. Richmond, Girls
Scene 3
  The Play's the Thing
    Dixon: M. Harvey. *Henriette*: P. Joyce. *Ann*: A. Rogers. *Adrian*: W. Valentine. *The Mistress*: C. Debenham. *William Pinchley*: F. Hector. *The Master*: C. Campbell.
Scene 4
  "Shadow Man"
    I. Olsen, Girls
    (*Music by* Max Darewski.)
Scene 5
  The Gentleman
    Lorna: P. Joyce. *Paul*: W. Valentine. *George*: M. Harvey.
Scene 6
  "Susannah's Squeaking Shoes"
    C. Debenham, Girls
    (*Music by* Muriel Lillie. *Lyrics by* Arthur Weigall.)
Scene 7
  Backing a Winner
    Lord Clifford Petersham: M. Harvey. *Sir Harry Leventon*: F. Hector.
Scene 8
  "Simple Little Song"
    W. Richmond, Girls
Scene 9
  References
    The Mistress: P. Joyce. *The Maid*: C. Debenham. *The Caller*: A. Rogers.
Scene 10
  "Lucky Bargee"
    M. Harvey
Scene 11
  "(The) Girls of the Old Brigade"
    C. Debenham, Entire Company

ACT 2
Scene 1
  An Interrogation
    M. Harvey, F. Hector
Scene 2
  "Other Days"
    W. Valentine, Girls
Scene 3
  The Square Triangle
    Mabel: C. Debenham. *Charles*: M. Harvey. *Henry*: F. Hector. *Butler*: C. Campbell. *Fluff*: P. Joyce.
Scene 4
  "Glow Worm" (I Wonder Why the Glow Worm Winks His Eye at Me)
    C. Campbell, I. Olsen, Girls
    (*Music by* Herbert Stothart. *Lyrics by* Oscar Hammerstein II)
Scene 5
  Proverbs
    Mrs. Smith: C. Debenham. *Mr. Smith*: M. Harvey. *Dr. Brown*: C. Campbell. *Maid*: A. Rogers. *Coster*: J. Murtagh.
Scene
  Why a Man Lives In the Story??
    Lady Evelyn Velour: P. Joyce. *Sir Gay Clarering*: F. Hector. *Daphne*: E. Brick. *Maid*: A. Rogers. *Butler, A Hug*: C. Campbell. *Gentle Readers: A Larry, A Policeman*: J. Murtagh. *A Girl*: W. Richmond. *A Butcher's Boy*: C. Campbell. *A Clergyman*: W. Valentine. *A Servant*: A. Rogers. *Mannequins, Guests, etc.*

Scene 7
  "William the Conk"
    C. Debenham
    (*Music and Lyrics by* Alan Glen and H. Coleman.)
Scene 8
  "The Bed Time Follies"
    Entire Company
Scene 9
  "That's the Tune"
    C. Debenham, Entrie Company
    (*Music by* Max Darewski. *Lyrics by* Graham John, Nelson Keys.)

Note: CECIL LEAN and CLEO MAYFIELD joined the show on its second night. The program was revised as follows:

ACT 1
Scene 1
  "Catching Up!"
    Entire Company
Scene 2
  "The Town Girl"
    W. Valentine, I. Olsen, W. Richmond, Girls
Scene 3
  The Gentleman
    Lorna: P. Joyce. *Paul*: W. Valentine. *George*: M. Harvey.
Scene 4
  Cecil Lean and Cleo Mayfield
Scene 5
  "Shadow Man"
    I. Olsen, Girls
    (*Music by* Max Darewski.)
Scene 6
  Backing a Winner
    Lord Clifford Petersham: M. Harvey. *Sir Harry Leventon*: F. Hector.
Scene 7
  "Susannah's Squeaking Shoes"
    C. Debenham, Girls
    (*Music by* Muriel Lillie. *Lyrics by* Arthur Weigall.)
Scene 8
  Cecil Lean and Cleo Mayfield
Scene 9
  References
    The Mistress: P. Joyce. *The Maid*: C. Debenham. *The Caller*: A. Rogers.
Scene 10
  "Lucky Bargee"
    M. Harvey
Scene 11
  "(The) Girls of the Old Brigade"
    C. Debenham, Entire Company

ACT 2
Scene 1
  "Other Days"
    W. Valentine, Girls
Scene 2
  Cecil Lean and Cleo Mayfield
Scene 3
  The Square Triangle
    Mabel: C. Debenham. *Charles*: M. Harvey. *Henry*: F. Hector. *Butler*: C. Campbell. *Fluff*: P. Joyce.
Scene 4
  "I Wonder Why the Glow Worm Winks His Eye at Me" (Glow Worm)
    C. Campbell, I. Olsen, Girls
    (*Music by* Herbert Stothart. *Lyrics by* Oscar Hammerstein II.)
Scene 5
  Cecil Lean and Cleo Mayfield
Scene 6
  "The Bed Time Follies"
    Entire Company
Scene 7
  "That's the Tune"
    C. Debenham, Entrie Company
    (*Music by* Max Darewski. *Lyrics by* Graham John, Nelson Keys.)

1923.36 (MR.) BATTLING BUTTLER

A Musical (Comedy) Knock-out in Three Rounds (Acts)[65]. Book and lyrics by Ballard Macdonald, adapted from the English original of the same name[66]. Music by Walter L. Rosemont. Staged by Guy Bragdon. Dances arranged by Dave Bennett. Settings by William E. Castle Costumes by Kiviette. Orchestra under the direction of Paul Yartin. Produced by George Choos, by arrangement with Jack Buchanan and the Selwyns (Edgar, Arch). Opened 8 October 1923 at the Selwyn Theatre, moved 21 April 1924 to the Times Square Theatre, and closed 5 July 1924 after 313 performances.

CAST (in order of appearance): *Deacon Grafton*, who is always calling on the Buttler family to ask favors of Mrs. Buttler: EUGENE McGREGOR. *Mrs. Alfred Buttler*, whose two charming sisters arrive from a visit to Boston: HELEN ELEY. *Nancy*, the maid: Helen LaVonne. *Marigold*, Mrs. Buttler's older sister: Mildred Keats. *Edith*, the younger sister, more the flapper type but delightful: MARIE SAXON. *A Chauffeur*: George Sands. *Alfred Buttler*: CHARLES RUGGLES. *Frank Bryant*, a friend of the girls: JACK SQUIRE. *Ernest Hozier*, Frank's life-long buddy, familiarly known as 'Socks': WILLIAM KENT. *Sweeney*, Proprietor of a hotel with training quarters: Guy Voyer. *Spink*: Teddy McNamara. *Battling Buttler*: FRANK SINCLAIR. *Bertha Buttler*, his wife: FRANCIS HALLIDAY. *Featured Dancers*: Grant and Wing. *Eccentric Dancers*: George Sands, Mack Davis. *Exceptional Dancer*: GEORGE DOBBS. *Professional Boxers*: Tony Palmer, Willie Bradley.

Ensemble: *Ladies*: Claire Daniels, Julia Warren, Eva Knapp, Lucille Arden, Verdi Milli, Kay Karyll, Isobel Graham, Dotty Sheppard, Betty Campbell, Mildred Morgan, Liane Marmet, Zoe Knapp. *Men*: Fred Johnston, Hal Bird, Irving Mills, Henry Levoy, Ray Hall, Bob Williams, Edward P. Smith, Jack Siegler, Allen Stevens, Harry Gordon, Lester Elliott, Dale Grigsby. *Twelve English Rockets* (Specialty Dancers): Miss Bebe Barri (Captain), unidentified.

Act 1: The Home of Alfred Buttler, Silver Lake, New Hampshire.

Act 2: 'Sweeney's' at Malba, Long Island. Next day.

Act 3: The Four Hundred Athletic Club, New York City. One month later.

ACT 1
  Musical Opening
    E. McGregor, H. Eley, The Rockets, Ensemble
  "If Every Day Was Sunday"
    E. McGregor, Ensemble, Sands and Davis, The Rockets
    (*Music by* A. Dorian Otvos.)
  "You're So Sweet"[67]
    M. Keats, M. Saxon, Ensemble
    (*Music by* Joseph Meyer.)
  "Apples, Bananas and You"**
    C. Ruggles, H. Eley
  "Two Little Pals"
    J. Squire, W. Kent
  "Will You Marry Me?"
    M. Keats, G. Dobbs, Boys
  Finaletto
    Principals, Ensemble

ACT 2
  Musical Calisthenics (*Arranged by* Bebe Barri.)
    The Rockets
  "Tinkle Tune"
    T. McNamara, H. LaVonne, G. Dobbs, Ensemble, Grant and Wing
    (*Music by* A. Dorian Otvos and Louis Breau.)
  "Dancing Honeymoon"[68]
    J. Squire, M. Keats, G. Dobbs, M. Saxon, The Rockets, Ensemble
    (*Music by* Philip Braham. *Lyrics by* Douglas Furber.)
  Finaletto
    Principals, Ensemble

ACT 3
  Dancing Around
    Grant and Wing

---

[65]During the New York run, the show was renamed MR. BATTLING BUTTLER. For its Chicago tryout, the show was known as THE DANCING HONEYMOON.
[66]English book by Stanley Brightman and Austin Melford Music by Philip Braham. Lyrics by Douglas Furber. Additional numbers by Donovan Parsons, Melville Gideon and F. W. Thomas.
[67]Dropped during the New York run.
[68]Retained from the original London production.

"As We Leave the Years Behind"
  M. Keats, J. Squire, Anniversary Girls
  (*Music by* Joseph Meyer.)
"In the Spring"
  M. Saxon, W. Kent
  (*Music by* A. Dorian Otvos.)
Reprise (Finale)
  The Cast

1923.37 GINGER

A Galloping Musical Comedy in Two Acts, 4 Scenes. Book by Harold Orlob and H. I. Phillips. Music by Harold Orlob. Staged by Walter Brooks. Dances arranged by John Hughes. Settings designed by P. Dodd Ackerman. Costumes designed by Max Cohn. Orchestra under the direction of Leon Rosebrook. Produced by Harold Orlob. Opened 16 October 1923 at Daly's 63rd Street Theatre and closed 10 November 1923 after 30 performances.

CAST (in order of appearance): *Ruth Warewell*: NELLIE BREEN. *Mrs. Warewell*: OLIVE MAY. *Willie Fall*: JOE MACK. *Marjorie Frayne*: SIBYLLA BOWHAN. *A Buyer*: Virginia Andersen. *Dick Warewell*: WALTER DOUGLAS. *Clix Young*: NORMAN SWEETSER. *Virginia Warewell*, 'Ginger': LEETA CORDER. *Joe Bagley*: THOMAS F. SWIFT. *Joe Bagley*, Sr.: Charles J. Stine.

Ginger's Friends: Violet Larrus, Stella Bolton, Guerida Crawford, Mabelle Swor, Marie Gaylord, Marie White, Rhea Irving, Sophie Howard, Ona Vaughn, Paulette Winston, Katheryn O'Dell, Nerene Swinton, Florence Guenther, Ruth Waddell, Rose LeRoy. *Paramount Four Quartet*: Jack Gill, Jasper Stroup, Charles Lanlen, Arnold Ferrotta.

Act 1: Bazaar at Mrs. Warewell's Country House, Bronxville, New York. Late afternoon.

Act 2, Scene 1: Bagley's Camp, Catskill Mountains. Evening, next day. *Scene 2*: A Forest in the Catskills. *Scene 3*: Bagley's Camp. Next morning.

ACT 1
  "That Ought To Count for Something"
    N. Breen, W. Douglas, Girls
  "Ginger"
    L. Corder, Ensemble
  "Love's Art"
    L. Corder
  "Don't Judge a Girl By Her Name"
    S. Bowhan, T. F. Swift
  "Don't Forget"
    L. Corder, N. Sweetser, Quartette
  "Take a Chance"
    N. Breen, J. Mack, Girls
  "Quarrel Duet"
    L. Corder, N. Sweetser, Girls
  "Before You Take a Man"
    S. Bowhan, Girls
  Finale
    Ensemble

ACT 2
  Quartette
    Paramount Four
  "Mountain Moon"
    N. Sweetser, Quartette
  "Beware"
    S. Bowhan, J. Mack, N. Breen, W. Douglas
  "If Ever I Get Up My Irish"
    L. Corder, Girls
  "Pretty Girl"
    N. Breen, J. Mack, Bathing Girls
  "He Failed to Underwrite a Happy Home"
    S. Bowhan, W. Douglas
  "Teach Me How"
    T. F. Swift, Girls
  "Mating Time"[69]
    L. Corder, N. Sweetser, N. Breen, J. Mack, T. F. Swift, S. Bowhan
  Finale
    Entire Company

---

[69]Dropped late in the run.

1923.38 ## ZIEGFELD FOLLIES OF 1923

A Musical Revue in Two Acts, 33 Scenes[70]. (Sketches by Eddie Cantor, Gene Buck, etc.) Music by Victor Herbert, Rudolf Friml and Dave Stamper. Lyrics by Gene Buck. Staged by Ned Wayburn. Scenic investiture by Joseph Urban. Costumes designed by Erté, Alice O'Neil, Evelyn McHorter, James Reynolds. (Tableaux by Ben Ali Haggin.) Orchestra under the direction of Oscar Radin. Produced by Florenz Ziegfeld. Opened 20 October 1923 at the New Amsterdam Theatre and closed 10 May 1924 after 233 performances.

<u>CAST:</u> FANNIE BRICE, BROOKE JOHNS, WILLIAM ROSELLE, OLGA STECK, BERT WHEELER, PAULETTE DUVAL, HAP WARD, MARIE CALLA-HAN, LEW HEARN, BETTY WHEELER, ARTHUR WEST, HARLAND DIXON, PAUL WHITEMAN AND HIS ORCHESTRA, LINDA, EDNA LEEDOM, DAVE STAMPER, HARRY SHORT, HILDA FERGUSON, ROY CROPPER, ALEXAN-DER YAKOVLEFF, FLORENTINE GOSNOVA, MARIE DAHM, CATHERINE GALLIMORE, Helen Lee Worthing, Mme. Florianne, Billy Revel, Robert Quinault, Iris Rowe, Bob Karna and Daughter, Andre Dumont, Raymond O'Brien, Ruth Andrae.

The Empire Girls: Nelle Greasley, Doris Bennett, Millie Glossop, Hettie Cooper, Norah Jackson, Beatrice Thorburn, Gladys Ellison, Lilly Burgess, Winnie Keane, Marjorie Weaver, Dorothy Kelsall, Lily McWilliams, Jean Henderson, Phyllis Mawer, Maud Mansfield, Margaret Cummings. *Ziegfeld Girls*: Misses Emma Klige, Ruth Zoakay, Harriet Fowler, Ferral Dewees, Katherine Gallimore, Florence Kolinsky, Dorothy Van Alst, Mary Bancroft, Claire DeFitamiere, Charlotte Suddath, Margaret Langhorne, Alberta Faust, Dorothy Ellis, Alma Nash, Margaret Sloan, Elizabeth Kay, Lois Blackburn, S. Granzow, Marion Hamilton, Feon Vanmar, Mildred Billert, Linda, Goodie Montgomery, Hetty, Janet Megrew, Doris Wilson, Gladys Coburn, Dottie Wilson, May Daw, Helen D'Algy, Alice Knowlton, Moreno, Martha Pierre, Polly Nally, Vivian Vernon, Gertrude Selden, Addie Rolfe, Helen Henderson, Winton, Catherine Burke, Mary Julian, Betty Warrington, Virginia Beardsley, Bernice Ackerman, Imogene Wilson, Beryl Halley, Marie Dahm, Stella Wooten, Gladys Peterson, Marjorie Leet, Dorothy Van Alst, Dorothy Brown, Elsie Westcott, Louise Carlton, Wilma Ansell, Roberta Grant, Billie Tichenor, Helen Ellsworth, Irma McShane, Nondas Wayne, Joan Waddell, Harriet Marned, Lois Wilde, Peggy Shannon, Helen Dobbins, Hazel Vergess, Heloise Sheppard, Virginia Magee, Ethel Allis, Thelma Kay, Cynthia Cambridge, Dorothy Brown, Rita Moriarty, Violet Regal, Elsie Westcott, Flo Kennedy.

ACT 1[71]

Scene 1

"Glorifying the Girls"
Follies Girls
(*Music by* Dave Stamper. *Lyrics by* Gene Buck.)

Scene 2

"Webbing"
Misses E. Klige, Zacaky, Foller, Dewees, Gallimore, Kolinsky, D. Van Hest, Bancroft, C. DeFitamiere, Suddath, Langhorn, Faust, Ellis, Nash, Sloan, Kay, Blackburn, Granzow
(*Music by* Victor Herbert. *Dance arranged by* Gertrude Hoffman.)

Scene 3

"Kayo Tortoni"[72] (Song)
O. Steck

Introducing dances by
M. Hamilton, F. Vanmar, M. Billert, Linda

Scene 4

Fannie Brice

Scene 5

The Bridegroom[73] (*by* Frederic Lonsdale)
Willie James: W. Roselle. *William*: H. Ward. *Mary*: E. Leedom. *Ivette*: G. Coburn. *Marie*: H. L. Worthing. *Dorothy*: H. Ferguson.

Scene 6

"Take Those Lips Away"

---

[70]The 18th in the annual series of musical revues produced by Florenz Ziegfeld, beginning in 1907.
[71]Added after opening to Act 1:
The Sap (later, The Society Breakdown)(Limited Engagement)
Jack Norton, James J. Corbett
Scene: Near a Railroad Station in the Adirondack Montains.
"Just a Lullaby"
Julia Sanderson
(*Music by* Dave Stamper. *Lyrics by* Gene Buck.)
[72]Replaced after opening by:
Spanish Study
P. Duval
[73]Dropped after opening.

B. Johns
(*Music by* Harry Tierney. *Lyrics by* Joseph McCarthy.)
With Misses Allis, Fowler, Langhorn, Montgomery.

Scene 7

Old Fashioned Garden:[74]
(a) Mirror Dance
E. Klige
(b) "Old Fashioned Garden" (Song)
O. Steck
(*Music by* Victor Herbert. *Lyrics by* Gene Buck.)
(c) "Pretty Flowers from Me to You"
F. Brice

Scene 8

Spanish Studies[75]
(a) Dance
Mlle. P. Duval
(b) Burlesque Dance
Mlle. Florianne, B. Revel

Scene 9

Trying to Get into the Follies:
E. Leedom, D. Stamper
[(a) "I'm a Manicurist"
(*Music and Lyrics by* Blanche Merrill.)
(b) "What Thrills Can There Be"
(*Music by* Dave Stamper. *Lyrics by* Harry Ruskin.)]

Scene 10

A Russian Number
Danced by A. Yakovleff, Follies Chorus
(*Staged by* Ned Wayburn Studios; Alexander Yakovleff, Ballet Master.)

Scene 11

Russian Art Studies[76]
F. Brice

Scene 12

Shadowgraph (*Optical Illusion by* Laurens Hammond.)
This is the number where you use the Follies-Scope glasses which have been handed you with the program, the RED glass to cover the right eye. SOILING THE GLASSES IN ANY WAY WILL SPOIL THE EFFECT ENTIRELY.

Scene 13

Impromptu Dance Sketches by Follies Girls to set the next scene:
Original Dance[77] (*Devised, invented and executed by* H. Dixon.)
H. Dixon

Scene 14

"Broadway Indians" (Broadway Indians of Mine)
B. Johns
Indian Dance
H. Ferguson, Follies Chorus
March Dance
Empire Girls
(*Music by* Dave Stamper. *Lyrics by* Gene Buck.)

Scene 15

Snappy Stories of Broadway (*by* Eddie Cantor)
Girl: H. Ferguson. *Boy*: R. Cropper. *Pocohontas*: F. Brice. *Captain John Smith*: H. Short. *Servant*: B. Revel. *Queen Isabella*: F. Brice. (*Christopher Columbus*: W. Roselle.)

Scene 16

"Mammy"[78]
Bert and Betty Wheeler

Scene 17

"Shake Your Feet" (First Act Finale[79])
B. Johns, Follies Chorus
(*Music by* Dave Stamper. *Lyrics by* Gene Buck.)

ACT 2[80]

---

[74]Dropped after opening.
[75]Dropped after opening.
[76]Dropped after opening.
[77]Dropped after opening.
[78]Dropped after opening.
[79]Including a new dance invented by Ned Wayburn called The Charleston.
[80]Added to Act 2 after opening:
"Ex-Ray"
H. Ferguson, V. Halley, Winton, Burke, Ackerman, Kennedy, H. L. Worthing
Dance Specialty (Solo)

Scene 1

La Marquise (Picture and Pantomime by Ben Ali Haggin.)

"Lady Fair"

R. Cropper

(*Music by* Rudolf Friml. *Lyrics by* Gene Buck.)

"Maid of Gold"[81]

(*Music by* Rudolf Friml. *Lyrics by* Gene Buck. *Costumes by* Erté, Paris. *Staged by* Robert Quinault.)

The White Marquise: P. Duval. *The Marquise of the Bath*: B. Halley. *The Marquise of the Promenade*: Miss Megrew. *The Marquise of the Domino*: H. L. Worthing. *The Marquise Flirtacious*: I. Wilson. *Her Friend the Princess*: G. Coburn. *Her Lovers and Her Retinue*: Misses M. Daw, D'Algy, A. Knowlton, Moreno, M. Pierre, P. Nally, V. Vernon, G. Selden, A. Rolfe, H. Henderson, J. Winton, C. Burke, M. Julian, B. Warrington, V. Beardsley, B. Ackerman.

Scene 2

"Society Bud"[82]

F. Brice

(*Music by* Harry Ruby. *Lyrics by* Bert Kalmar.)

"Dancing Mad"[83]

F. Brice, B. Johns

(*Music by* Leo Edwards. *Lyrics by* Blanche Merrill.)

Scene 3

"Harlequin's Doll" (by arrangement with E. Ray Goetz)

(*Scenario by* Robert Quinault. *Music by* Gabriel Daray. *Devised and arranged by* Robert Quinault.)

The Harlequin: R. Quinault. *Harlequin's Doll*: I. Rowe.

Scene 4

"Little Old New York"[84]

E. Leedom

(*Music by* Victor Herbert. *Lyrics by* Gene Buck.)

Marion Davies Girls: B. Warrington, H. L. Worthing, A. Knowlton, G. Coburn, I. Wilson, B. Halley. *Marion Davies Boys*: M. Daw, M. Dahm, D. Wilson, M. Hamilton, D. Wilson, S. Wooten.

Scene 5

Jocko the Crow[85]

B. Karna and Daughter

Scene 6

"I'm Bugs Over You"[86]

H. Dixon, M. Callahan

(*Music by* Dave Stamper. *Lyrics by* Gene Buck.)

Scene: In the Slums.

Scene 7

"I'd Love to Waltz Through Life with You"[87]

O. Steck, R. Cropper

(*Music by* Victor Herbert. *Lyrics by* Gene Buck.)

Scene 8

Ballet

Danced by A. Yakovleff, F. Gosnova, C. Gallimore, Follies Corps de Ballet

Scene 9

Paul Whiteman and His Orchestra

["So This Is Venice"

(*Music by* Ambrose Thomas. *Lyrics by* Grant Clarke and Edgar Leslie.)]

Ann Pennington

Specialty

Frank Crumit

"Your Eyes Have Told Me"

J. Sanderson, Frank Crumit

(*Music by* Dave Stamper. *Lyrics by* Gene Buck.)

"Mary Rose" (A Song Scene by Gene Buck. *Music by* Maurice Yvain.)

Scene: A Side Street in New York.

A Policeman: W. Roselle. *Mary Rose*: M. Daw. *An Outcast*: F. Brice.

[81]After opening, moved to Act 1 Finale, then to Act 2 opening.

[82]Replaced after opening by:

The Covered Wagon

H. Ferguson, A. West

[83]Dropped after opening.

[84]Moved to Act 1 after opening.

[85]Dropped after opening.

[86]Dropped after opening.

[87]Dropped after opening.

Scene 10

"The Fool"[88]

F. Brice

Assisted by A. Yakovleff.

(*Music by* Lee David. *Lyrics by* Benton Ley.)

Scene 11

"Swanee River Blues"

B. Johns, O. Steck

(*Music by* Dave Stamper. *Lyrics by* Gene Buck.)

Dance (Solo)

Linda

Boys: Misses V. Beardsley, G. Peterson, M. Leet, K. Moore, D. Brown, E. Westcott, L. Carlton, W. Ansell, Doris Wilson, R. Grant, R. Grant, B. Tichnor, M. Billett, F. Vanmar, H. Ellsworth, I. McShane, N. Wayne. *Girls*: J. Waddell, E. Kay, L. Wilde, G. Montgomery, H. Marned, P. Shannon, M. Hamilton, H. Dobbins, M. Dahm, H. Vergess, H. Sheppard, V. Magee, M. Daw, Dottie Wilson, S. Wooten, E. Allis.

Scene 12

Fencing Number[89] (*Arranged by* Gertrude Hoffman.)

Misses M. Langhorne, R. Zoakey, F. Dewees, E. Kligge, H. Fowler, K. Gallimore, C. Suddath, S. Granzow, T. Kay, M. Sloan, F. Kolinsky, M. Bancroft, A. Faust, D. Van Hest, C. De Fitamiere, A. Nash, D. Ellis, L. Blackburne.

Scene 13

Dance

Empire Girls

(Direct from the Empire Theatre, London. Presented by Lawrence Tiller.)

Scene 14

"Legend of the Drums"

(*Music by* Victor Herbert. *Lyrics by* Gene Buck. *Designed by* James Reynolds.)

Men: A. Dumont, R. O'Brien. *Chinese Women*: H. Henderson, B. Warrington. *Chinese Princess*: M. Pierre. *Italian Women*: P. Nally, J. Megrew. *Italian Women with curtain*: C. Burke, F. Kennedy. *Juggler*: H. Dixon. *Drum-Major*: G. Selden. *Spanish Drummers*: R. Andre, H. Sheppard. *Infanta*: H. L. Worthing. *Moon Drums*: M. Leet, V. Beardsley. *Harvest Drums*: C. Cambridge, A. Knowlton, M. Julian, I. Wilson. *Tartar Women*: V. Vernon, B. Halley, J. Winton, H. Moreno, H. D'Algy, B. Ackerman. *Drummers*: E. Allis, D. Wilson, S. Wooten, A. Rolfe, N. Wayne, H. Vergess, M. Daw, H. Dobbins, M. Dahm, I. McShane, H. Ellsworth, M. Hamilton, M. Billett, B. Tichenor, H. Marned, L. Wilde, R. Grant, D. Wilson, J. Waddell, D. Van Alst, E. Westcott, L. Carlton, D. Brown, G. Peterson. *Nurse*: G. Coburn. *Child*: R. Moriarty.

Scene 15

Amateur Night at Miner's 8th Avenue Theatre 20 Years Ago[90] (*by* Gene Buck)

The Announcer: W. Roselle. *The Gallery God*: A. West. *Amachewers*: R. Cropper, Linda, B. Johns, F. Brice, H. Short, O. Steck, H. Dixon, E. Leedom, P. Whiteman, H. Ferguson, B. Wheeler, L. Hearn.

["On the Banks of the Wabash"

R. Cropper

"Won't you come over and tramp down the clover"

"When you know you're forgotten by the girl you can't forget"

F. Brice

"Cheer Up, Mary"

F. Brice

"Hearts and Flowers'

E. Leedom

"Won't You Come Home, Bill Bailey?"

B. Johns

If I Could Paint (recitation)

Little Egypt (dance)

H. Ferguson

"I Don't Care" (Eva Tanguay impression)

A. Pennington

Card trick, magic routine

B. Wheeler]

Scene 16

"Good Night Finale"[91]

Entire Company

(*Music by* Dave Stamper. *Lyrics by* Gene Buck.)

---

[88]Dropped after opening.

[89]Dropped after opening.

[90]Detail from sketch as published in Revue, A Book of Short Sketches, edited by Kenyon Nicholson, D. Appleton and Company, New York, 1926.

[91]Dropped after opening.

1923.39

RUNNIN' WILD

A Musical Comedy in Two Acts, 10 Scenes. Book by Flournoy E. Miller and Aubrey L. Lyles. Music by James P. Johnson. Lyrics by Cecil Mack. Dances arranged by Lyda Webb. Produced by George White. Opened 29 October 1923 at the Colonial Theatre and closed 3 May 1924 after 220 performances; returned with New Edition 23-28 June 1924 to the Colonial Theatre for an additional 8 performances. Total: 228 performances[92].

CAST (in order of appearance): *Uncle Mose*: C. Wesley Hill. *Uncle Amos*: ARTHUR D. PORTER. *Tom Sharper*: Lionel Montagas. *Ethel Hill*: REVELLA HUGHES. *Jack Penn*: George Stephens. *Detective Wise*: Paul C. Floyd. *Mrs. Silas Green*: Mattie Wilkes. *Mandy Little*: INA DUNCAN. *Adalaide*: ADALADE [Adelaide] HALL. *Steve Jenkins*: FLOURNOY E. MILLER. *Sam Peck*: AUBREY L. LYLES. *Willie Live*: Eddie Gray. *Chief Red Cap*: Tommy Woods. *Head Waiter*: CHARLES OLDEN. *Ruth Little*: ELIZABETH WELSH [Welch]. *Silas Green*: J. Wesley Jeffrey. *Boat Captain*: James H. Woodson. *Sam Slocum*: George Stamper. *Lacy Lanky*: Katherine Yarborough. *Ginger*: Bob Lee. *Lightning*: Ralph Bryson. *Angelina Brown*: GEORGETTE HARVEY.

Girls of the Chorus: Lyda Webb, Percy Wiggins, Amey Roden, Mildred Dixon, Marie DeVoe, Dorothy Rhodes, Hazel Anderson, Jessie Wallace, Leila Brogden, Therese West, Ela Thomas, Marguerite Howard, Beatrice Williams, Bessie Allison, Noma Davis, Dorothy Irving, Vivian Harris, Alice Allison, Adelaide Jones, Swendolyn Graham, Ruth Lambert, Leronya Bradley. *Boys of the Chorus*: Ralph Cooper, Charles Saltez, Arthur Mason, Joseph Wilson, Monte Hawley, Billy Foster.

Act 1, Scene 1: Market Place, Jimtown. *Scene 2*: Railroad Station. *Scene 3*: Four Corners, St. Paul, Minnesota. *Scene 4*: Rondo Street, St. Paul, Minnesota. *Scene 5*: Cabaret, St. Paul, Minnesota.

Act 2, Scene 1: Levee, Jimtown. *Scene 2*: Street, Jimtown. *Scene 3*: A Deserted Barn, Jimtown. *Scene 4*: Street, Jimtown. *Scene 5*: Country Club, Jimtown.

ACT 1[93]

Scene 1

Opening Chorus
  Company
"Open Your Heart"
  R. Hughes, G. Stephens
"Gingerbrown"
  A. Hall, B. Lee, Strutters

Scene 2

"Red Caps Cappers"
  T. Woods, Boys
"Old Fashioned Love"
  I. Duncan, A. Hall, A. D. Porter

Scene 3

"Keep Moving"[94]
  C. Olden, Chorus

Scene 4

Dance Specialties
  R. Bryson, G. Stamper

---

[92]Staging uncredited.
[93]Added during the run:
  Lazy Dance (Act 2, Scene 1, after Log Cabin Days)
    G. Stamper
  "Banjo-Land" (Act 2, Scene 1, after Log Cabin Days)
    (G. Stephens)
  "Set 'Em Sadie" (Act 1, Scene 1, after Opening Chorus, later moved to end of Scene)
    A. Hall, Miss Ward, Chorus
  Which was replaced for subsequent tour by:
  "Sun Kist Rose"
    R. Hughes, Chorus
  Added for subsequent tour:
  "Heart Breakin' Joe" (Act 1, Scene 4 opening)
    Jean Starr
  "Slow and Easy Goin' Man" (Act 2, Scene 4, before Fisticuffs)
    J. Starr
  "The Sheik of Alabam' Weds a Brown-Skin-Vamp"
    A. D. Porter, Chorus
[94]Replaced during the run by:
  "Snowtime"
    E. Welsh, Chorus

Scene 5

"Charleston"
  E. Welsh, Chorus
Finale
  Entire Company

ACT 2

Scene 1

"Roustabouts"
  Male Octette
"Log Cabin Days"
  G. Harvey, Octette
"Ghost Recitative"
  C. Olden
"Pay Day on Levee"
  A. D. Porter, Company

Scene 2

"Swanee River"
  R. Hughes
"Song Birds Quartette"
  R. Hughes, I. Duncan, E. Welsh, G. Harvey

Scene 3

"Ghost Ensemble"
  Ghost Association

Scene 4

"Love Bug"[95]
  A. Hall

Scene 5

"Juba Dance"
  Chorus
"Jazz Your Troubles Away"
  Entire Company

1923.40

STEPPING STONES

A Fantastic Musical Play in Two Acts, 13 Scenes. Book by Anne Caldwell and R. H. Burnside. (Suggested by the fairy tale of Little Red Riding Hood.) Music by Jerome Kern. Lyrics by Anne Caldwell. Staged by R. H. Burnside. Dances of the Sunshine Tiller Girls produced by Mary Read and John Tiller. Settings designed by Wilhelm of London, Robert McQuinn, P. Dodd Ackerman. Costumes designed by Wilhelm, Cora MacGeachy, Will R. Barnes, Robert McQuinn; men's costumes by Brooks-Mahieu Costume Company. Orchestra under the direction of Victor Baravelle. Orchestrations by (Robert) Russell Bennett. Produced by Charles Dillingham. Opened 6 November 1923 at the Globe Theatre and closed 31 May 1924 after 241 performances.

CAST (in order of appearance): *Peter Plug*: FRED STONE. *Prince Silvio*: ROY HOYER. *Otto DeWolfe*: OSCAR RAGLAND. *Remus*: JOHN LAMBERT. *Richard*: Harold West. *Captain Paul*: Jack Whiting. *Antoine*: Gerald Gilbert. *Gypsy Jan*: Bert Jordan. *Eddie*: Willie Torpey. *The Landlord*: George Herman. *Rougette Hood*: DOROTHY STONE. *Widow Hood*: ALLENE STONE. *Lupina*: EVELYN HERBERT. *Radiola*: Primrose Caryll. *Mary*: Lucille Elmore. *Nurse Marjorie*: Lydia Scott. *Charlotte*: Lilyan White. *Eclaire*: Ruth White. *Rose*: Hazel Glen.

Dance Specialty: (Cortez and Peggy, The Brightons). *Sunshine Tiller Girls*. *Globe Theatre Ensemble*. (*Puppet Specialty*: Tony Sarg's Marionettes)

Act 1, Scene 1: The Nursery. *Scene 2*: The Puppet Play, with Tony Sarg's Marionettes. *Scene 3*: The Corridor. *Scene 4*: The Sweet Shop. *Scene 5*: Cherryville Square. *Scene 6*: The Road to Broughton Woods. *Scene 7*: The Garden of Roses.

Act 2, Scene 1: The Haunted Inn. *Scene 2*: The Mystic Hussars. *Scene 3*: The Ghost of the Inn. *Scene 4*: The Dolls' Village. *Scene 5*: Outside the Inn. *Scene 6*: The Palace of Prince Silvio.

ACT 1

"The Nursery Clock" (Descriptive Music)
"Little Angel Cake" (Trio)
  P. Caryll, H. West, L. Elmore, Girls
Dance
  Tiller Sunshine Girls

---

[95]Replaced during the run by:
  Fisticuffs
    F. Miller, A. Lyles

"Because You Love the Singer" (Buffo Trio)
E. Herbert, O. Ragland, J. Lambert

"Little Red Riding Hood" (Ensemble and Song)
D. Stone, A. Stone, Girls

"Wonderful Dad" (Duet)
F. Stone, D. Stone

"Pie" (Trio)
F. Stone, O. Ragland, J. Lambert

"Babbling Babette" (Ensemble and Song)
E. Herbert, Ensemble

"In Love with Love" (Duettino)
D. Stone, R. Hoyer, Principals

"The Wood Nymphs" (Dance)
Tiller Sunshine Girls

"Our Lovely Rose" (Song)
E. Herbert

Rose Potpourri Finale
Entire Company

ACT 2

"Once in a Blue Moon" (Trio)
R. Hoyer, E. Herbert, J. Lambert, L. White, R. White, Girls

"The Mystic Hussars" (March)
Tiller Sunshine Girls

"The Skeleton Janitor" (Dance)
G. Hermann

The Rag Pickers[96]
The Brightons

"Raggedy Ann" (Song)
F. Stone, D. Stone, J. Lambert, Tiller Sunshine Girls, Globe Chorus, The Breens

"Dear Little Peter Pan" (Dance Duet)
F. Stone, D. Stone

Dances[97]
Cortez and Peggy

Palace Dance
Tiller Sunshine Girls

"Stepping Stones" (Coronation March)
E. Herbert, O. Ragland, J. Lambert, Ensemble

Finale
F. Stone, D. Stone, Entire Company

1923.41

TOPICS OF 1923

A Musical Revue in Two Acts, 20 Scenes. Sketches by Harold Atteridge and Harry Wagstaff Gribble. Music by Jean Schwartz and Alfred Goodman. Lyrics by Harold Atteridge. Staged by J. C. Huffman. Dances arranged by M. Francis Weldon. Costumes designed by Erté. Settings designed by Watson Barratt. Orchestra under the direction of Alfred Goodman. Entire production supervised by J. J. Shubert. Produced by the Messrs. Shubert. Opened 20 November 1923 at the Broadhurst Theatre, moved 14 January 1924 to the Winter Garden, and closed 22 March 1924 after 154 performances.

CAST: ALICE DELYSIA, HERBERT CORTHELL, JACK PEARL, HARRY McNAUGHTON, NAT NAZARRO, JR., JAY GOULD, FAY MARBE, LLORA HOFFMAN, ALLAN PRIOR, HELEN SHIPMAN, Barnett Parker, Billie Shaw, Ben Bard, Marie Stoddard, Frank Green, Roy Cummings, Paisley Noon, Dorothy Vance, Delano Dell, Flora Lea, Alexis Kosloff, Martin Burton, Helen Herendeen, W. Clay Inman, Anne Garrison, Cecil and Kaye, Henrietta O'Brien, Castleton and Mack, Gladys Marston.

Young Women of the Ensemble: Muriel Seeley, Dorothy Vance, Marjorie Talwyn, Harriet Gustine, Helen Herendeen, Dolores Edwards, Christine Eckland, Stella Shields, Marietta O'Brien, Dorothy Bruce, Elaine Sims, Dorothy Wegman, Cathleen Barrow, Mildred Gordon, Agnes Trask, Fay Reed, Julia Barker, Rae Hartley, Silance Leontevetch, Marie Gibson, Flo Lane, Yvette Reels, Jeannette Dawley, Billie Wagner, Elsie Frank, Norma Rossiter, Esta Mousey, Orilla Smith, Edith Pierce, Peggy O'Day, Eleanor Stack, Nellie Daly, Bevely Millar, Edith McGovern, Thelma Robinson, Ethel Fuller, Ann Garrison, Vera Trett, Juliet Strahl, Stella Hadden.

ACT 1

Scene 1

Opening Ensemble
H. McNaughton, M. Stoddard, F. Marbe, Cecil and Kaye, Ballet

"Oh, Alice"
A. Delysia

"When You Love"
A. Prior, A. Delysia (*Music by* Jean Schwartz)

"American Dancers"
A Group of All-American Girls

Dance
D. Dell
Scene: The Green Room of the Century Theatre
The Soubrette: F. Marbe. *Jennie:* M. Stoddard. *An Assistant Stage Manager:* H. McNaughton. *The Ingenue:* H. Shipman. *The General Understudy:* B. Parker. *The Theatre Manager:* F. Green. *The Leading Comedian:* H. Corthell. *Another Comedian:* D. Dell. *A Comic:* J. Gould. *The Leading Man:* A. Prior. *The Star:* A. Delysia. *The Call Boy:* R. Cummings. *Jack:* J. Pearl. *Ben:* B. Bard. *Fay:* F. Marbe. And the Famous Winter Garden Dancers, an All-American Set of Ponies, and Delano Dell. (Miss Delysia's Costumes designed by Travis Banton.)

Scene 2

The Revue Starts
Jack: J. Pearl. *Ben:* B. Bard. *Fay:* F. Marbe.

Scene 3

"(The) Flowers of Evil" (Garden of Evil)
A. Prior, Tulip Girls
Satan: A. Prior. *Youth:* M. Burton. *Tulip Girls:* D. Bruce, R. Hartley, H. Gustine, H. Herendeen, M. Talwyn, D. Edwards, D. Vance, M. Seeley, H. O'Brien, A. Trask.
(*Music by* Jean Schwartz)

Scene 4

A Bit of Fun
Roy: R. Cummings. *Billie:* B. Shaw.

Scene 5

"Queens of Long Ago"
L. Hoffman, Queens of Long Ago

"(Be) Good, Queen Bess"
A. Delysia
(*Music by* Bert Grant. *Lyrics by* Tot Seymour.)
Scene: A Room in the Palace.
Sir Francis Bacon: H. Corthell. *William Shakespeare:* F. Green. *Earl of Essex:* P. Noon. *Mary Fitton:* H. Shipman. *Queen Elizabeth:* A. Delysia. *Sir Walter Raleigh:* B. Parker. *Pages:* Misses Lane, O'Day.

Scene 6

A Jazz Appeal to 'Oedipus Rex' ("Oedipus Rex à la Jazz")
Ensemble
The Spirit of the Uplift Movement: R. Cummings. *The So-Called Human Race:* The Mob. *The Public:* The Tax Payers, etc.

Scene 7

In a Perfume Shop
Jack: J. Pearl. *Ben:* B. Bard. *Flora:* B. Shaw.

Scene 8

"(On) A Beautiful Evening"
H. Shipman, J. Gould
Scene: On the Boulevard
The Girl: H. Shipman. *The Boy:* J. Gould. *The Dancer:* N. Nazarro, Jr. *The Gendarmes:* H. McNaughton, D. Dell.

Scene 9

"Ran Tin Tin"
Castleton and Mack, F. Lea, Good Luck Girls

Scene 10

"The Minuette"
L. Hoffman, A. Prior, Minuette Girls
Marietta: L. Hoffman. *DuBarry:* A. Prior. *Antoinette:* A. Delysia. *Chamberlin:* H. Herendeen. *Minuette Girls:* R. Hartley, D. Bruce, H. Gustine, D. Edwards, D. Wegman, D. Vance, A. Trask, C. Barrow.

Scene 11

Her Wedding Day: "The Jazz Wedding"
H. Shipman, J. Gould, Brides
Scenes: East and West of Fifth Avenue.
Goodrich Eaton: P. Noon. *Mrs. Eaton:* D. Vance. *Philip Graves:* W. C. Inman. *Barney:* B. Parker. *Herb:* H. Corthell. *Margie:* F. Lane. *Jessie:* A. Garrison. *The Father:* D. Dell. *The Mother:* M. Stoddard. *The Bride:* H. Shipman. *The Bridegroom:* J. Gould. *The Maid:* O. Smith. *Milliner Girl:* F. Lea. *The Minister:* F. Green. *First Guest:* D. Bruce. *Second Guest:* R. Hartley. *Third Guest:* D. Vance.

---

[96]Dropped during the run.
[97]Dropped during the run.

Scene 12

"Diamond Finale" (Just Like a Diamond)
  L. Hoffman, Diamond Girls
    Radiant Diamonds: L. Hoffman, A. Prior, H. Shipman, J. Gould, F. Lea, Cecil and Kaye, P. Noon, N. Nazarro, Jr., The Diamond Beauties

ACT 2

Scene 1

Daughters of the West

"Lotus Flower"
  L. Hoffman
    Scene: A Chamber in the Palace of Men Sun Yang.
    Sing Low: L. Hoffman. *Pan Chi Yu*: D. Vance. *Daughter of the West*: A. Delysia. *The Figure Dancers*: Cecil and Kaye. *Chuang Tzu*: W. C. Inman. *Men Sun Yang*: F. Green. *Francois*: J. Gould. *Throne Girls*: Misses Lane, Rossiter, Dawley, O'Day. *Treasure Girls*: Misses Stackhouse, Gibson, Hall, Marston, Reels, Wagner. *Gift Bearers (4)*: *Jade*: D. Bruce. *Ivory*: D. Vance. *Silver*: R. Hartley. *Ebony*: H. Herendeen. *Guards*: Messrs. Mayo, White, Osteen, Kirby, Buckley, Burton, Berdie.

Scene 2

Out Front with Herbert Corthell and Alice Delysia

Scene 3

Three Bluffs
  (a) In the Home
    Wife: F. Marbe. *Husband*: D. Dell.
  (b) In the Bedroom
    Husband: H. McNaughton. *Wife*: M. Stoddard.
  (c) In the Lawyer's Office
    Mr. Reading: P. Noon. *Lawyer Black*: F. Green. *A Stranger*: H. Corthell.

Scene 4

"Doing the Apache"
  P. Noon, F. Marbe, Castleton and Mack, Apache Girls
    Scene: The Cave of Innocence
    Flower Girl: A. Delysia. *Cocotte*: D. Vance. *Jean*: H. O'Brien. *Pierre*: B. Bard. *Jacques*: J. Pearl. *Armand*: D. Dell. *Two Sailors*: Castleton and Mack.

Scene 5

A Few Fast Steppers
  R. Cummings, D. Dell, H. McNaughton, N. Nazarro, Jr., Castleton and Mack, E. Pierce, O. Smith, B. Miller, J. Strahl, S. Hadden, E. Frank

Scene 6

"The Legend of the Woodland"
  A. Delysia, A. Kosloff
    The Story Teller: L. Hoffman. *Hope*: E. Fuller. *Belief*: G. Marston. *The Princess*: A. Delysia. *Satyr*: A. Kosloff. *Nymph*: F. Lea. *Sprites*: Cecil and Kaye. *Ladies of the Court, Court Gallants*: D. Bruce, R. Hartley, D. Wegman, H. Gustine, H. Herendeen, H. O'Brien, D. Edwards, A. Trask.

Scene 7

A Few Minutes with (Ben) Bard and (Jack) Pearl

Scene 8

"Yankee Doodle Oo La La" (Finale)

1923.42

SHARLEE

A Musical Comedy in Two Acts, 4 Scenes. Book by Harry L. Cort and George E. Stoddard. Music by C. Luckyeth Roberts. Lyrics by Alex Rogers. Staged by Kuy Kendall. Costumes designed by Charles LeMaire. Scenery designed by Reid Maguire. Orchestra under the direction of Hilding Anderson. Produced by John Cort. Opened 22 November 1923 at Daly's 63rd Street Theatre and closed 22 December 1923 after 36 performances.

CAST (in order of appearance): *Mr. Watson Holmes*, the Mysterious Man: Winn Shaw. *Oscar Riley*, the Waiter: EDDIE NELSON. *I. Kahn*, the Business Man: Joe Morris. *Tom Mason*, the Fellow in the Case: SYDNEY GRANT. *Dolly Dare*, the Hostess: FRANCES ARMS. *Jack Vandeveer*, the Man About Town: JOSEPH R. DORNEY. *Sharlee Saunders*, the Girl: JULIETTE DAY. *Annabelle*, the Maid: Mitti Manley. *Jane Caldwell*, the Fiancée: Ottilie Corday. *Masenia*, the Dancer: Masenia. *May, June*, the Entertainers: Field Sisters. *Mrs. Vandeveer*, the Mother: Mrs. Mary Leroy. *Entertainers*: Nitza Vernille and Vernon. *Guests, Performers, Friends, Waiters.*

Act 1, Scene 1: Interior of Cabaret. Evening. *Scene 2*: Living Room of Sharlee's Apartment. One month later. *Scene 3*: Interior of Cabaret. (Next midnight.)

Act 2: Porch and Lawn of Jack Vandeveer's Summer Home. The next afternoon. Somewhere in Connecticut.

ACT 1

Scene 1

Ensemble
  Guests

"Loving Is a Habit"
  F. Arms, W. Shaw, Field Sisters, Chorus

"Sharlee"
  J. R. Dorney, Chorus

Ensemble Entrance
  J. Day

"Little Drops of Water"
  J. Day, S. Grant

"Princess Nicotine"
  W. Shaw, J. Morris

"Heart Beats"
  J. R. Dorney to J. Day

"Cry Baby"
  Field Sisters

Dance Specialty
  N. Vernille

Burlesque
  E. Nelson

"Love Today"
  J. Day, Ensemble

Scene 2

Reprises
  Orchestra

Scene 3

Ensemble Dance
  Guests

Dance
  Masenia

Specialty
  F. Arms

"Broadway Rose"
  J. R. Dorney, Chorus

"Toodle Oo"
  J. Day, Ensemble

Finale Act 1
  Orchestra Reprise

ACT 2

"Heart Beats" (reprise)
  J. R. Dorney to J. Day

"My Caveman — My Venus"
  M. Manley, E. Nelson

"My Sunshine"
  J. Day, J. R. Dorney, Ensemble

Dance Divertissement
  N. Vernille, Vernon

"Love Is the Bunk"
  F. Arms, W. Shaw, J. Morris, E. Nelson

"Honeymoon Row"
  O. Corday to J. R. Dorney, Ensemble

(Specialities)
  Field Sisters, Masenia, Riley's Crawl (E Nelson)

Finale: "Heart Beats" (reprise)
  Principals, Ensemble

1923.43

SANCHO PANZA

A Comedy (with Music) in Four Acts and a Prologue. Play (Sancho Panza Királysága) by Melchior Lengyel, (translated by Sidney Howard[98]). Based on certain episodes in Miguel y Cervantes' 'Don Quixote de La Mancha.' Music and songs by Hugo Felix. Directed by Richard Boleslawsky. Production (settings) and costumes designed by James Reynolds under the supervision of Emile Hapgood. Curtain designed by Reginald Marsh. Orchestra under the direction of Rupert Graves. Produced by Russell Janney. Opened 26 November 1923 at the Hudson Theatre and closed 29 December 1923 after 40 performances[99].

---

[98]Sidney Howard withdrew his name from the production because the producer took liberties with his text.

[99]No musical numbers listed in program. One was published:
  "When Her Lips Surrender"

CAST (in order of appearance): *Sancho Panza*: OTIS SKINNER. *Don Quixote*: ROBERT ROBSON. *Dapple*: ROBERT ROSAIRE. *A Scrivener*: Charles Halton. *Chamberlain*: Frederick Tiden. *Duke of Barataria*: Russ Whytal. *Father Hyacinth*: H. H. McCollum. *Donna Rodriguez*: Marion Barney. *Arvino*: Stewart Baird. *Hernando*: Richard Cramer. *Mayor of Barataria*: Harry Lewellyn. *Gralva*: Anthony Andre. *The Young Duchess*: MARGUERITE FORREST. *Gregory*: Herbert Delmore. *Ladies in Waiting (3)*: *Altisidora*: Grace Elliott. *Dolorida*: Kathleen George. *Isabella*: Marguerite Ingram. *The Page with the Mirror*: Olga Treskoff. *The Page with the Cape*: Roberta Renys. *The Page with the Crown*: Merle Stevens. *The Page with the Pin*: Elizabeth Page. *The Page with the Staff-of-Office*: Helen Grenelle. *The Page with the Insignia*: Eileen Grace. *The Court Physician*: Stewart Baird. *The Messenger from the King*: Stewart Baird. *A Tailor*: Charles Halton. *A Fruit Woman*: Olga Treskoff. *A Farmer*: Robert Robson. *A Dancer*: Helen Grenelle. *A Citizen*: William H. Browne. *An Old Man*: Royal Cutter. *A Young Thief*: Kirk Allen. *A Drab*: Ruby Trelease. *A Drover*: Meyer Berenson. *A Street Singer*: Malcolm Hicks. *Another Singer*: Harold Brown. *Another Singer*: Walker Moore. *The First Guard*: Michael Barroy. *The Second Guard*: William Venus. *The Third Guard*: Arthur C. Tennyson. *The Fourth Guard*: Richard Trott. *A Citizen*: Smiley W. Irwin. *Another Citizen*: Jack Cronin. *Another Citizen*: Fred Kotek.

The entire action of play takes place in Spain during the reign of Philip II.

Prologue: A Roadside in the Province of Andalusia. One summer night.

Act 1: The Pavilion of the Duke of Barataria. Afternoon of the day following.

Act 2: The Governor's Throne Room in Barataria. Evening of the same day.

Act 3: The Square Before the Cathedral. Evening of the same day.

Act 4: The Throne Room Again. The next morning.

1923.44 ONE KISS

A Comedy with Music in Two Acts. Book and lyrics by Clare Kummer, adapted from the French original 'Ta Bouche' by Yves Mirande (book) and Albert Willemetz (lyrics). Music by Maurice Yvain. Directed by Fred G. Latham. Musical numbers staged by Julian Alfred. Costumes designed by Jose de Zamora, Cora MacGeachy. Scenery by Ernest Gros. Orchestra under the direction of William Daly. Produced by Charles Dillingham. Opened 27 November 1923 at the Fulton Theatre and closed 16 February 1924 after 95 performances.

CAST: *Four Gossips*: *Marguerite*: Jane Carroll. *Margot*: Alden Gay. *Meg*: Dagmar Oakland. *Meregrette*: PAULINE HALL. *Madame Doremi, the Countess*: ADA LEWIS. *Eva, her daughter*: LOUISE GROODY. *General Pas-De-Vis*: JOHN E. HAZZARD. *Bastien, his son*: OSCAR SHAW. *Jean, Mme. Doremi's secretary*: JOHN PRICE JONES. *Mme. de Peyster, widow of a rich banker*: JOSEPHINE WHITTELL. *Georges, a waiter*: Fred Lennox. *Riquette*: Patrice Clark. *Bebe*: Janet Stone. *Babette*: Elaine Palmer. *Berte*: Irma Irving. *Beatrix*: Gertrude McDonald.

Act 1: Terrace of the Hotel at Morny-sur-Mer. A May morning.

Act 2: The same. A June afternoon. One year later.

ACT 1

Opening
    J. Carroll, A. Gay, D. Oakland, P. Hall

"Don't Ever Be a Poor Relation"
    J. P. Jones, Girls

"Your Lips"
    L. Groody, O. Shaw

"A Little Bit of Lace"
    J. E. Hazzard, Girls

"When We Are Married"
    L. Groody, O. Shaw

"A Little Love"
    O. Shaw, Girls

Finale

ACT 2

"Gentlemen"
    L. Groody, Girls

"There Are Some Things We Can Never Forget"[100]
    O. Shaw, Girls

"Is That So!"[101]
    L. Groody, O. Shaw

"In My Day"
    J. E. Hazzard, J. Whittell

"One Kiss"
    O. Shaw, Girls

---

[100]Sheet music published as "There Are Some Things You Never Forget."
[101]Dropped during the run.

"London Town"
    L. Groody, Girls

"Up There"
    L. Groody, O. Shaw

Finale

1923.45 MARY JANE McKANE

A Musical Play (Comedy) in Three Acts, a Scenic Overture (Prologue) and 11 Scenes. Book and lyrics by William Carey Duncan and Oscar Hammerstein II. Music by Herbert Stothart and Vincent Youmans. Book staged by Alonzo Price. Dances and ensembles by Sammy Lee. Gowns and costumes designed by Charles LeMaire. Settings by (Frank E.) Gates and (E. A.) Morange. Orchestra under the direction of Herbert Stothart. Entire production under the personal supervision of Arthur Hammerstein. Produced by Arthur Hammerstein. Opened 25 December 1923 at the Imperial Theatre and closed 3 May 1924 after 151 performances.

CAST (in order of appearance): *Joe McGillicuddy*: HAL SKELLEY. *Maggie Murphy*: KITTY KELLY. *Mary Jane McKane*: MARY HAY. *Cash and Carrie*: THE KEENE TWINS (Margaret, Elizabeth). *Martin Frost*: Dallas Welford. *Andrew Dunn, Jr. (Andy)*: STANLEY RIDGES. *Doris Dunn*: Laura deCardi. *Louise Dryer*: EVA CLARK. *George Sherwin*: Louis Morrell. *Andrew Dunn, Sr.*: JAMES HEENAN.

Ladies of the Ensemble: Muriel Harrison, Frances Lindell, Dorothy June, May Sullivan, Grace LaRue, Lillian Mitchell, Edna Miller, Dorothy Hollis, Ann Buckley, Bobby Pierce, Sunny Saunders, Peggy Quinn, May Fox, Theresa Carroll, Marietta Adams, Grace Culbert. *Gentlemen of the Ensemble*: Bert Crane, Lester New, Lionel Maclyn, Allan Grey, Eldred Murray, John Wainman, Joe Carey, Harry Howell.

The action takes place in New York City at the present time.

Scenic Overture: 1: Mary Jane leaves Slab City, Massachusetts. 2: Her First Sight of New York City. 3: View from Her Bedroom Window.

Act 1, Scene 1: In the Subway, on the Broadway Express. *Scene 2*: Private Office of Andrew Dunn, Jr. *Scene 3*: Mary Jane's Room—on the East Side. *Scene 4*: Private Office of Andrew Dunn, Jr.

Act 2: Office and Reception Room of the 'Dandy Dobbin Novelty Company.' Six weeks later.

Act 3, Scene 1: Garden of Andrew Dunn's Home. *Scene 2*: Mary Jane's Room—East Side. *Scene 3*: Central Park.

ACT 1[102]

Scene 1

"The Rumble of the Subway"
    Ensemble

Scene 2

"Speed"
    H. Skelley, Keene Twins

"Not in Business Hours"
    S. Ridges, E. Clark, Chorus

Scene 3

"Stick to Your Knitting"
    M. Hay, H. Skelley, Chorus
    (*Music by* Herbert Stothart.)

Scene 4

"My Boy and I"
    E. Clark, Chorus
    (*Music by* Vincent Youmans.)

"Toodle-oo"
    M. Hay, S. Ridges
    (*Music by* Vincent Youmans.)

"Down Where the Mortgages Grow"
    H. Skelley, K. Kelly, Chorus

ACT 2

"Time-Clock Slaves"
    Keene Twins, Chorus

"Laugh It Off"
    M. Hay, S. Ridges, K. Kelly

---

[102]Added during the run:
"You're Never Too Old to Love" (Act 1, Scene 3 after "My Boy and I")
    E. Clark, D. Welford, Chorus
"Just Look Around" (Act 2, after "Laugh It Off")
    M. Hay, S. Ridges, Chorus

"Stick To Your Knitting" (reprise)
   M. Hay, S. Ridges, Chorus
"The Flannel Petticoat Gal"
   H. Skelley, K. Kelly, Old Fashioned Girls, the Four Chums
   (*Music by* Vincent Youmans.)
ACT 3
Scene 1

"Thistledown"
   E. Clark, Specialty Dancer, Chorus
   (*Music by* Herbert Stothart.)
"Toodle-Oo" (reprise)
   S. Ridges, Girl, Keene Twins
Scene 2

"Mary Jane McKane"
   M. Hay, Boys
Scene 3

"Mary Jane McKane" (reprise)
   (Company)

1923.46   THE RISE OF ROSIE O'REILLY

George M. Cohan's Comedians in a New American Song and Dance Show[103] (Musical Comedy) in Two Acts, 6 Scenes. Words (Book, lyrics) and music by George M. Cohan. Musical numbers staged by Julian Mitchell. Book staged by John Meehan. Production supervised by George M. Cohan. Orchestrations by M. L. Lake. Scenery designed by Joseph Wickes Studio. Costumes designed by Cora MacGeachy and Ada B. Field, Brooks-Mahieu Company, Earl Benham. Orchestra under the direction of George A. Nichols, under the supervision of Charles J. Gebest. Produced by George M. Cohan. Opened 25 December 1923 at the Liberty Theatre and closed 15 March 1924 after 97 performances.

CAST (in order of appearance): *Jimmy Whitney,* Bob's Pal: BOBBY WATSON. *Bob Morgan,* Roscoe's Son: JACK McGOWAN. *Lillian Smith,* Kitty's Chum: MARJORIE LANE. *Kitty Jones,* Lillian's Chum: DOROTHY WHITMORE. *Casparoni,* Café Owner: ALBERT GLORIA. *Mrs. Casparoni,* His Wife: ADELAIDE GLORIA. *Buddie O'Reilly,* Rosie's Brother: Bobby O'Neill. *Johnson,* Plain Clothes Man: George Bancroft. *Rosie O'Reilly,* the Girl: VIRGINIA O'BRIEN. *Polly,* of the Waterfront: MARY LAWLOR. *Cutie Magee,* works for Rosie: Emma Haig. *Pete,* a Hanger-on: GEORGIE HALE. *Mrs. Montague Bradley,* a Wealthy Widow: MARGARET DUMONT *Steve,* a Brooklyn Hick: Johnny Muldoon. *Molly,* His Sweetheart: Pearl Franklin. *Hop Toy,* a Chinese Crook: Eddie Russell. *Fannie,* a Bridge Dancer: Betty Hale . *Annie,* another dancer: Bernice Speer. *Ethelburt,* a Butler: TOM DINGLE. *Gertrude,* a House-maid: Patsy Delany. *Roscoe Morgan,* Brooklyn Millionaire: Walter Edwin. *Flower Girls:* Woods Sisters. *Bootleggers, Policemen, Attendants, Social Cimbers,* and all sorts of peculiar persons sing and dance themselves into a musical comedy state of mind.

Act 1, Scene 1: Under the Brooklyn Bridge, Brooklyn Side. *Scene 2:* A Few Blocks Beyond. *Scene 3:* Reception Room in Mrs. Bradley's Brooklyn Home.

Act 2, Scene 1: Madame Regay's Florist Shop. *Scene 2:* In Front of the Draperies. *Scene 3:* Exterior of Morgan's Brooklyn Home.

ACT 1

"The Arrival of the Plot"
   B. Watson, J. McGowan, M. Lane, D. Whitmore, A. Gloria, Company
"Never Met a Girl Like You"
   J. McGowan, V. O'Brien
"Born and Bred in Brooklyn"
   B. Watson, M. Lawlor, Company
"My Gang"
   E. Haig, G. Hale, Company
"The Arrival of Society"
   Boys and Girls
"In the Slums of the Town"
   V. O'Brien
"Water Front Pastime" (Dance)
   J. Muldoon, P. Franklin
"The Whip" (characteristic dance)
   The Glorias
"Something's Happened to Rosie"
   Company

---

[103]Subtitled 'Poking Fun at Cinderella.'

"Poor Old World"
   B. O'Neill, Boys
"Stage Society"
   M. Lane, Girls
"All Night Long"
   D. Whitmore, Boys
"The Servants' Frolic" (characteristic dance)
   T. Dingle, P. Delaney
"Love Dreams"
   V. O'Brien, The Glorias, M. Lawlor
"Just Act Natural"
   B. Watson, B. O'Neill
"When June Comes Along with a Song"
   J. McGowan, V. O'Brien, B. Watson, Company
ACT 2
"At Madame Regay's"
   Boys and Girls
"On a Holiday"
   B. Watson, D. Whitmore, Boys, Girls
Dialogue in Verse
   J. McGowan, B. Watson, D. Whitmore, M. Lane
"Let's You and I Just Say Goodbye"
   J. McGowan, M. Lane
"A Ring to the Name of Rosie"
   V. O'Brien, Woods Sisters, Boys, Girls
"Keep A-Countin' Eight"
   B. O'Neill, E. Haig, Boys, Girls
Special Dances
   E. Haig, E. Russell, B. Hale, G. Hale, M. Lawlor, B. Speer, J. Muldoon, P. Franklyn, T. Dingle, P. Delany
Reprise
   V. O'Brien, Company
Characteristic Dance
   G. Hale
"Two Girls from the Chorus"
   Misses Frawley and King
Reprise Medley
   Company
"Nothing Like a Darned Good Cry"
   J. McGowan, V. O'Brien
"The Italian Whirlwind"
   The Glorias
"The Plot Again"
   G. Bancroft, Company
Gathering
   Principals
Finale
   Full Company

1923.47   KID BOOTS

A Musical Comedy of Palm Beach and Golf, in Two Acts, 8 Scenes. Book by William Anthony McGuire and Otto Harbach. Music by Harry Tierney. Lyrics by Joseph McCarthy. (Staged by Edgar Royce.) Scenery by Frank Gates and Edward A. Morange, Herman Rossi. Costumes by Evelyn McHorter, Henri Bendel, Alice O'Neil, Mme. Francis. Orchestra under the direction of Louis Gress. Orchestrations by Frank Barry. Produced by Florenz Ziegfeld. Opened 31 December 1923 at the Earl Carroll Theatre, moved 1 September 1924 to the Selwyn Theatre and closed 21 February 1925 after 479 performances.

CAST [in order of appearance]: *Peter Pillsbury,* a stern, grouchy manufacturer of sporting goods: HARRY SHORT. *Herbert Pendleton,* his foxy rival in business: PAUL EVERTON. *Harold Regan,* champion of Everglades Golf Club: JOHN RUTHERFORD. *Menlo Manville,* social observer: HARLAND DIXON.
   Society Buds: Miss Stymie: Avonne Taylor. *Miss Brassey:* Madelyn Morrisey. *Miss Putter:* Joan Gardner. *Miss Cleek:* Katharine Stuart. *Miss Driver:* Diana Stegman. *Miss Mashie:* Sonia Ivanoff. *Miss Fairway:* Sylvia Kingsley. *Miss Foursome:* Betty Grey. *Miss Hazard:* Perle Germond. *Miss Green:* Eunice Hall. *Miss Pinn:* Muriel Manners. *Miss Stroke:* Velma Ziegler.
   Tom Sterling, semi-pro of Everglades Golf Club: HARRY FENDER. *Polly Pendleton,* Herbert Pendleton's daughter: MARY EATON. *First Golfer:* Morton McConnachie. *Second Golfer:* Jack Andrews. *First Caddie:* Dick Ware. *Second Caddie:*

William Blett. *Third Caddie*: Frank Zolt. *Fourth Caddie*: Waldo Roberts. *Fifth Caddie*: Lloyd Keyes. *Kid Boots*, caddie master: EDDIE CANTOR. *Beth*: BETH BERI. *Carmen Mendoza*: ETHELIND TERRY. *Jane Martin*, in charge of ladies' lockers: MARIE CALLAHAN. *Dr. Josephine Fitch*, the hostess: JOBYNA HOWLAND. *Randolph Valentine*, champion of the Hudson River Golf Club: ROBERT BARRAT. *Federal Officer*: Victor Munroe. GEORGE OLSEN AND HIS ORCHESTRA.

Members of the Ensemble: Ladies: Rella Winn, Florence Ware, Blossom Vreeland, Carola Taylor, Carolyn Smith, Evelyn Sayers, Violet Regal, Elva Pomfret, Jessie Payne, Polly O'Claire, Edna Locke, Frances McHugh, Alma Mamay, Lily Kimari, Mareta George, Juanita Erickson, Eleanor Dell, Elizabeth Doughter, Doris Dixon, Eleanor Dell, Violet Browne, Eugenie Brew, Dove Atkinson, Jessie Madison, Gladys Keck. *Gentlemen*: Messrs. Jack Andrews, Rass, Ericksen, Thomas Green, Carlos Hatvary, Victor Munroe, William Maguire, Dennis Murray, Morton McConnachie, John Patterson, Ayers Tavitt, Frank Zolt, Robert Spencer.

Act 1, Scene 1: The Exterior of the Everglades Gold Club, Palm Beach, Florida. *Scene 2*: The Ladies' Locker Room. *Scene 3*: The Caddie Shop. *Scene 4*: Patio of the Everglades Club.

Act 2, Scene 1: The Trophy Room. *Scene 2*: The Eighteenth Hole. *Scene 3*: The Exterior of the Caddie House—The Nineteenth Hole. *Scene 4*: The Coconut Ball.

ACT 1: Going Out

First Hole

"A Day at the Club"
Ensemble

Second Hole

"Social Observer"
H. Dixon, Ensemble

Third Hole

"If Your Heart's in the Game" (A Twosome)
M. Eaton, H. Fender

Fourth Hole

"Keep Your Eye on the Ball"
E. Cantor, Caddies

Fifth Hole

"The Same Old Way" (A Twosome)
E. Terry, H. Fender

Sixth Hole

"Someone Loves You After All" (The Rain Song)
E. Cantor, M. Eaton, Ensemble

Seventh Hole

The Intruder Dance
M. Callahan, H. Dixon

Eighth Hole

"(We've) Got to Have More"
H. Spurr, Caddies

"Polly Put the Kettle On"
H. Fender, Ensemble

Ninth Hole

"Let's Do and Say We Didn't"[104] (Let's Don't and Say We Did)
E. Cantor, M. Callahan

Tenth Hole

"In the Swim"
First Stroke
E. Terry
Second Stroke
B. Beri
Third Stroke
Ensemble

Eleventh Hole

"(Along) The Old Lake Trail"
M. Eaton, Gentlemen

Twelfth Hole

"On With the Game"
All Members of This Club

ACT 2: Coming In[105]

Thirteenth Hole

[104]Dropped for national tour.
[105]Added for subsequent tour to Act 2:
"Skipping the Skips"
H. Dixon

"(Since Ma Is Playing) Mah Jong" (First Stroke)
(E. Cantor, Ensemble)
(*Music and Lyrics by* Con Conrad and Billy Rose.)
West Wind: L. Kimari. *East Wind*: A. Mamay. *North Wind*: F. Ware. *South Wind*: C. Taylor.

"Bet on the One You Fancy" (Second Stroke)
Ladies and Gentlemen

"I'm in My Glory" (Third Stroke)
H. Dixon, B. Beri

Fourteenth Hole

"A Play-Fair Man" (A Foursome)
M. Eaton, E. Terry, H. Fender, J. Rutherford

Fifteenth Hole

"Win for Me" (A Threesome)
E. Cantor, M. Eaton, E. Terry, Ensemble

Sixteenth Hole

"The Cake-Eaters' Ball"
M. Callahan, H. Dixon

Seventeenth Hole

"Down 'Round the 19th Hole" (First Stroke)
E. Cantor, J. Howland, H. Short, P. Everton, Caddies

"En Route"[106] (Second Stroke)

"The Coconut Ball"[107] (Third Stroke)
George Olsen and His Orchestra

"When the Coconuts Call"[108] (Fourth Stroke)
E. Terry, B. Beri, Ensemble

"In the Rough"[109] (Fifth Stroke)
E. Cantor of the Ziegfeld Follies

The Presentation of the Cup (Sixth Stroke)
M. Eaton

Eighteenth Hole

"That's All There Is" (Finish)
Company

ANDRÉ CHARLOT'S REVUE OF 1924

1924.01

A Musical Revue in Two Acts, 23 Scenes. (Sketches by Dion Titheradge, Jack Hulbert. Music by Philip Braham, Ivor Novello, Noël Coward, Eubie Blake, Bert Lee. Lyrics by Douglas Furber, Eric Blore, Ronald Jeans, Norah Blaney, Noël Coward, Noble Sissle, R. P. Weston, Collie Knox.) Conceived and directed by André Charlot. Dances and ensembles staged by David

[106]Dropped for national tour.
[107]Dropped for national tour. Specialty also included:
"Goin' Home Blues"
(*Music by* George Olsen and Edward Kilfeather. *Lyrics by* Willie Raskin.)
[108]Included specialty:
"He's the Hottest Man in Town"
(*Music by* Jay Gorney. *Lyrics by* Owen Murphy.)
"Hot Ziggity"
(*Music and Lyrics by* Eddie Cantor and Jerry Benson.)
[109]Cantor's Blackface Specialty slot, accompanied by George Olsen's orchestra, included:
"If You Do What You Do"
(*Music by* J. Russel Robinson. *Lyrics by* Eddie Cantor, Roy Turk.)
"Dinah"
(*Music by* Harry Akst. *Lyrics by* Sam M. Lewis, Joe Young.)
"Ma, He's Makin' Eyes at Me"
(*Music by* Con Conrad. *Lyrics by* Sidney Clare.)
"If You Knew Susie"
(*Music by* Joseph Meyer. *Lyrics by* Buddy G. DeSylva.)
"A Birdie"
"The Dumber They Come They Better I Like 'Em"
(*Music and Lyrics by* Fred E. Ahlert, Eddie Cantor and Harry DeCosta.)
"It's Just That Feeling for Home"
(*Music by* Fred E. Ahlert. *Lyrics by* Sam M. Lewis, Joe Young.)
"Let Me Introduce You to My Rosie"
(*Music and Lyrics by* Lew Brown, Eddie Cantor, Lew Santly.)

Bennett. Stage director, Douglas Furber. Scenery by Marc Henri and Laverdet. Costumes by G. K. Benda, Guy deGerald, Louise Boulanger, Lenief. Orchestra under the direction of Philip Braham. Produced by the Selwyns (Arch Selwyn, Edgar Selwyn). Opened 9 January 1924 at the Times Square Theatre, moved 21 April 1924 to the Selwyn Theatre, moved 1 September 1924 to the Times Square Theatre and closed 20 September 1924 after 298 performances.

CAST: BEATRICE LILLIE, GERTRUDE LAWRENCE, JACK BUCHANAN, HERBERT MUNDIN, FRED LESLIE, ROBERT HOBBS, DOROTHY DOLMAN, MARJORIE BROOKS, RONALD WARD, DOUGLAS FURBER, Milton Thomas, Edith Price, Guido Orlando, John Webster.
Show Girls: Ethel Barbour, June Kennedy, June Mackay, Ida Mowbray, Ruth Raymonde, Bobbie Storey. *Chorus*: Constance Carpenter, Wyn Clare, Marjorie Cogle, Lalla Collins, Gwen Egdell, Dore Hanbury, Elvira Henderson, Olive Lindfield, Jessie Matthews, Ida Parkinson, Barbara Roberts, Queenie Robertson, Jill Williams, Peggy Willoughby, Sybil Wilson, Eve Wynne.

ACT 1[110]

Scene 1

"How D'You Do" (Opening)
F. Leslie, M. Brooks, R. Hobbs, H. Mundin, D. Dolman, R. Ward, G. Lawrence, B. Lillie, J. Buchanan, Show Girls
(*Music by* Philip Braham. *Lyrics by* Ronald Jeans and Eric Blore.)

"Ready to Work" (from YES!, London)
F. Leslie, Chorus
(*Music by* Norah Blaney. *Lyrics by* Dion Titheradge.)

Scene 2

The Kiss[111] (*by* Ronald Jeans)(from A TO Z, London)
The Maid: G. Lawrence. *Dennis*: J. Buchanan. *Cynthia*: M. Brooks. *Edgar*: D. Furber.

Scene 3

"There Are Times" (from A TO Z, London)
B. Lillie, Chorus
(*Music by* Ivor Novello. *Lyrics by* Ronald Jeans.)

---

[110]Added during the run:
"Rough Stuff" (from A TO Z, London)(Act 2)
B. Lillie, H. Mundin
(*Music by* Ivor Novello. *Lyrics by* Ronald Jeans.)
"Sentiment" (from LONDON CALLING, London)(Act 2)(dropped for subsequent national tour)
J. Buchanan
(*Music and Lyrics by* Noël Coward.)
The Green-Eyed Monster (by Dion Titheradge)(from A TO Z, London)(Act 1)
Joblin: D. Furber. *George*: J. Buchanan. *Jane*: G. Lawrence. *Mr. Trippitt*: H. Mundin.
Telling Benny (by Dorota Flatau)(Act 1)
Ma: E. Price. *Pa*: H. Mundin. *Benny*: Nelson Keys.
Brigando (Act 1)
N. Keys, Irene Russell
A Change of Treatment (by George Elton)(Act 1)
I. Russell, R. Hobbs, N. Keys
"Nicholas" (Act 2)
N. Keys, Chorus
(*Music and Lyrics by* Arthur Wimperis and Herman Darewski.)
"I'm in Love with You" (Act 2)
N. Keys, I. Russell
Home At Last (Act 2)
The Husband: N. Keys. *The Wife*: I. Russell. *Mrs. Pip*: E. Price. *Girl*: D. Hanbury. *Milkman*: H. Mundin. *Major Pepper*: F. Leslie.
Courtship 1824—1924 (Act 2)
Beau: N. Keyes. *Belle*: I. Russell.
Jap Magic
Nelkon Sees and Miss Hashimoto
Jazz Impressions (Act 2)
N. Keys
Added for subsequent national tour:
"Last Thing On His Mind" (Act 2)
Sam. B. Hardy
(*Music and Lyrics by* Noël Coward.
[111]Dropped after opening.

Scene 4

Inaudibility (*by* Douglas Furber and Jack Hulbert)(from YES!, London)
Compere: R. Hobbs. *The Butler*: R. Ward. *The Daughter*: M. Brooks. *The Doctor*: J. Buchanan. *The Nurse*: D. Dolman. *The Patient*: H. Mundin.

Scene 5

"Parisian Pierrot" (from LONDON CALLING, London)
(*Music and Lyrics by* Noël Coward.)
Pierrot: G. Lawrence. *Harlequin*: B. Roberts. *Columbine*: J. Williams. *The Dolls*: Chorus.

Scene 6

The Company Will Recite (*by* Dion Titheradge)(from PUSS! PUSS!, London)
B. Lillie, H. Mundin, F. Leslie, D. Dolman

Scene 7

"I Was Meant for You" (from LONDON CALLING, London)
G. Lawrence, J. Buchanan
(*Music by* Eubie Blake. *Lyrics by* Noble Sissle.)

Scene 8

"Little Go Getter"[112]
Chorus
(*Music by* Philip Braham. *Lyrics by* Clifford Seyler.)

Scene 9

Tea Shop Tattle (*by* Dion Titheradge)(from CHARLOT'S REVUE, 1925, London)
Gwladys: B. Lillie. *Vera*: M. Brooks. *First Man*: D. Furber. *Second Man*: H. Mundin.

Scene 10

"I Don't Know" (from LONDON CALLING, London)
G. Lawrence
(*Music by* Philip Braham. *Lyrics by* Ronald Jeans.)

Scene 11

"Cigarette Land" (from POTLUCK, London)
(*Music by* Bert Lee. *Lyrics by* R. P. Weston.)
The Dreamer: J. Buchanan. *The Pages*: S. Wilson, M. Cogle. *Egyptian Cigarette*: M. Brooks. *Spanish Cigarette*: J. Williams. *Turkish Cigarette*: D. Dolman. *Russian Cigarette*: P. Willoughby. *Scented Cigarette*: B. Lillie. *French Cigarette*: G. Lawrence. *Cigar*: F. Leslie. *Snuff*: H. Mundin. *Smoking Tobacco*: R. Ward. *Chewing Tobacco*: R. Hobbs. *Tobacco Leaves*: Chorus. *Smoke*: B. Storey.

ACT 2

Scene 1

"There's Life in the Old Girl Yet" (from LONDON CALLING, London)
B. Lillie, Chorus
(*Music and Lyrics by* Noël Coward.)

Scene 2

"Limehouse Blues" (from A TO Z, London)
G. Lawrence, R. Hobbs, F. Leslie
(*Music by* Philip Braham. *Lyrics by* Ronald Jeans.)

Scene 3

Incredible Happenings (*by* Ronald Jeans)(from RATS, London)
J. Buchanan, Company

Mr. Charlot produced this sketch in London. Since then it has been staged by American producers without permission of Mr. Charlot.

Scene 4

"The Oldest Game (in the World)" or "Lovers of History"[113] (from A TO Z, London)
(*by* Ronald Jeans and Ivor Novello)
The Lovers: D. Dolman, R. Hibbs. *Cupid*: P. Willoughby. *Psyche*: L. Collins. *Sultan*: M. Thomas. *Sheherazade*: E. Barbour. *Dante*: O. Lindfield. *Beatrice*: G. Edgell. *Romeo*: J. Williams. *Juliet*: W. Clare. *Charles II of England*: E. Henderson. *Nell Gwynne*: C. Carpenter. *Louis XV of France*: E. Wynne. *La Pompadour*: I. Parkinson. *Bonnie Prince Charlie*: J. Mackay. *Flora Macdonald*: B. Storey. *Bonaparte*: G. Orlando. *Josephine*: M. Cogle. *Armand*: I. Mowbray. *Camille*: R. Raymonde. *George Washington*: J. Webster. *Martha Washington*: J. Kennedy. *Don Juan*: M. Brooks. *Donna Anna*: D. Hanbury.

---

[112]Dropped after opening.
[113]Dropped after opening.

Scene 5

The Indicator (*by* Dion Titheradge)

The Professor: D. Furber. *The Husband*: H. Mundin. *The Wife*: G. Lawrence.

Scene 6

"It's a Far, Far Better Thing"[114]

J. Buchanan, Chorus

(*Music by* Philip Braham. *Lyrics by* Ronald Jeans.)

Scene 7

"The Bolshie Quartet"[115]

D. Furber, H. Mundin, F. Leslie, B. Lillie

(*Music and Lyrics by* Ronald Jeans, Douglas Furber and Bob Alden.)

Scene 8

Peace and Quiet[116] (*by* Ronald Jeans)

(as The Ministering Angel, from LONDON CALLING, London)

The Doctor: D. Furber. *The Patient*: J. Buchanan. *The Wife*: D. Dolman. *The Maid*: E. Price. *The Lino Man*: H. Mundin.

Scene 9

"March With Me" (from LONDON CALLING, London)

B. Lillie, Chorus

(*Music by* Ivor Novello. *Lyrics by* Douglas Furber.)

Scene 10

"I Might" (from RATS, London)

(*Music by* Philip Braham. *Lyrics by* Ronald Jeans.)

Jenny: G. Lawrence. *George*: H. Mundin.

Scene 11

"I Did Feel a Dreadfully Ass"[117]

J. Buchanan

(*Music by* Philip Braham. *Lyrics by* Ronald Jeans.)

Scene 12

"Night May Have Its Sadness" (from A TO Z, London)

Entire Company

(*Music by* Ivor Novello. *Lyrics by* Collie Knox.)

1924.02

LOLLIPOP

A Dancing Musical Comedy in Three Acts. Book by Zelda Sears. Music by Vincent Youmans. Lyrics by Zelda Sears and Walter DeLeon. Book staged by Ira Hards. Dances arranged by Bert French. Tiller Girls' dances arranged by John Tiller and Mary Read. Settings designed by Sheldon K. Vielé, William Castle. Costumes by Schneider-Anderson, Bergdorf Goodman, Finchley. (Orchestra under the direction of Russell Tarbox. Orchestrations mostly by Robert Russell Bennett.) Produced by Henry W. Savage, Inc. Opened 21 January 1924 at the Knickerbocker Theatre and closed 31 May 1924 after 152 performances.

CAST (in order of appearance): *Mrs. Mason*: Adora Andrews. *Virginia*: GLORIA DAWN. *Tessie*: Aline McGill. *Don Carlos*: LEONARD CEILEY. *Omar K. Garrity*: NICK LONG, JR. *Petunia*: Virginia Smith. *Laura Lamb*: ADA-MAY (WEEKS). *Rufus*: A Dark Secret. *George Jones*: GUS SHY. *Bill Geohagen*: HARRY PUCK. *Mrs. Gerrity*: ZELDA SEARS. *Helene*: FLORENCE WEBBER. *Specialty Dancers*: Addison Fowler, Florenz Tamara. *Parkinson*: Mark Smith. *Lindsay*: Karl Stall. *Adrian*: Leonard St. Leo.

John Tiller's Dancing Lollipops: Muriel Marlowe, Ethel Helliwell, Connie Aldis, Florence McCabe, Vera Longren, Elsie Holt, Ethel Fraser, Pat Fraser, Alice Wright, Doris Carter, Veronica Preston, Edith Morgan. *Dancing Girls*: Evelyn Kindler, Guerida Crawford, Norene Swinton, Katherine Huth, Maude Troup, Carol Joyce, Ruth Tester, April Child, Lucille Constante, Mary Jayne, Eleanor Dana, Katherine Odell. *Dancing Boys*: Bobby Culbertson, George Rand, Walter Crisham, Harold Raymond, Charles Townshend, Carl Judd. *Special Singing Quartette*: Elsa Gray (soprano), Louise Scheerer (contralto), Royal Halée (tenor), Charles King (bass).

Act 1: Adoption Day at the Franco-American Orphanage. (Vielé)

Act 2: Mrs. Garrity's Summer Home. (Castle)

Act 3: Costume Party at Laura's Home. (Castle)

ACT 1[118]

Opening

A. Andrews, Tiller Girls, Ensemble

"Love in a Cottage"[119]

L. Ceiley, G. Dawn, Ensemble

"Honey-Bun"

Ada-May

"Time and a Half for Overtime"

H. Puck, G. Shy, Tiller Girls

"Take a Little One Step"

Ada-May, H. Puck, Ensemble

"Tie a String Around Your Finger"

Ada-May, H. Puck

Finale

ACT 2

Opening—Specialty Dance

A. Fowler, F. Tamara

"When We Are Married"

L. Ceiley, G. Dawn, V. Smith, N. Long, Jr.

"An Orphan Is the Girl for Me" (An Orphan Girl Is the Girl for Me)

Ada-May, M. Smith, Boys

"Bo Koo"

G. Shy, F. Webber

"Going Rowing"

H. Puck, Ada-May

Finale

ACT 3[120]

Opening-Specialty Dance

A. Fowler, F. Tamara

"Deep in My Heart"

L. Ceiley, G. Dawn

Ballet Moderne

Ada-May, Entire Company

1924.03

SWEET LITTLE DEVIL

The Gayest of Musical Comedies in Three Acts. Book by Frank Mandel and Laurence Schwab. Music by George Gershwin. Lyrics by Buddy G. DeSylva. Staged by Edgar MacGregor. Musical numbers staged by Sammy Lee. Miss Binney's Ballet arranged by Michel Fokine. Stage settings by Lee Simonson. Costumes by Kiviette. Orchestra under the direction of Ivan Rudisill. Produced by Laurence Schwab. Opened 21 January 1924 at the Astor Theatre, moved 25 February 1924 to the Central Theatre, and closed 3 May 1924 after 120 performances.

CAST (in order of appearance): *Rena*: RAE BOWDIN. *Joyce West*: MARJORIE GATESON. *May Rourke*: RUTH WARREN. *Sam Wilson*: FRANKLYN ARDELL. *Virginia Araminta Culpepper*: CONSTANCE BINNEY. *Tom Nesbitt*: IRVING BEEBE. *Fred Carrington*: WILLIAM WAYNE. *Jim Henry*: Charles Kennedy. *Susette*: Mildred Brown. *Joan Edwards*: Bobbie Breslaw. *Richard Brook*: William Holbrook. *Marian Townes*: Olivette.

The Young Ladies Who Sing: Evelyn Grieg, Lulu McGrath, Dorothy Hughes, Norma Forest, Betty Nevins, Margaret Morris, Florence Kingsley, Betty Wright. *The Young Ladies Who Dance*: Paulette Winston, Bobbie Breslaw, Sophie Howard, Ethel Bryant, Yvette DuBois, Penelope Rowland, Mae Rena Grady, Mildred Brown, Rose Sarro. *The Young Men*: Maurice Lapue, William Neely, Albert Burke, Frank Cullen, Fred Tozere, Edward Ross, Jack Stone, Lee Wentling, Alan Cook.

Act 1: Joyce West's Apartment on the Roof of a New York Apartment Building. August.

Act 2: The same place from another angle; two weeks later.

Act 3: Sierra Notre, Peru. Six weeks later.

ACT 1[121]

---

[114]Dropped for subsequent national tour

[115]Dropped after opening.

[116]Dropped after opening.

[117]Dropped after opening.

[118]Added after opening:

"Louis XIII Gavotte" (after 2, after "Bo Koo")

Tiller Girls

Novelty Dance (Act 3, after "Deep in My Heart")

Tiller Girls

---

[119]Replaced for subsequent tour by:

"Spanish Love"

L. Ceiley, Marie Stagg (Virginia), Ensemble

[120]Added for subsequent tour:

Finale (Act 3)

Ada-May, Entire Company

[121]Reinstated from tryout for subsequent tour:

"You're Mighty Lucky, (You Little Ducky)" (Lucky)

F. Ardell, M. Gateson, (Boys, Girls)

"Strike, Strike, Strike"
    M. Gateson, R. Bowdin, Boys, Girls
"Virginia, (Don't Go Too Far)"
    C. Binney, Boys, Girls
"Someone Who Believes in You"
    C. Binney, I. Beebe
"System"[122]
    C. Binney, M. Gateson, R. Warren
"The Jijibo"
    R. Warren, W. Wayne, Boys, Girls
Finale
    All Concerned

ACT 2
"Quite a Party" (Opening)
    Boys and Girls
Waltz
    B. Breslaw, W. Holbrook
"Under a One-Man Top"
    R. Warren, W. Wayne
Flirtation Ballet ("Virginia" reprise)
    C. Binney, Boys, Girls
"The Matrimonial Handicap"
    M. Gateson, I. Beebe, R. Warren, W. Wayne, Boys, Girls
"Supposing"
    C. Binney, I. Beebe
"Hey! Hey! (Let 'Er Go!)"
    W. Wayne, Boys, Girls
Party Dance
    Olivette
Finale
    All Concerned

ACT 3
Opening
    Boys and Girls
Special Dance
    W. Holbrook, Olivette
"The Same Old Story"[123]
    C. Binney, Boys, Girls
"Hooray for the U.S.A."
    F. Ardell, R. Warren, R. Bowdin
Finale
    Entire Company

1924.04

MOONLIGHT

A Musical Comedy Gem in Two Acts, 4 Scenes. Book By William LeBaron, (based on his play 'I Love You.') Music by Con Conrad. Lyrics by William B. Friedlander. Produced under the personal direction of (book staged by) William B. Friedlander. Dances and ensembles by Larry Ceballos. Scenery by Karl O. Amend Studios[124]. Costumes designed by Mabel Johnston. Orchestra under the direction of Hilding Anderson. Produced by L. Lawrence Weber. Opened 30 January 1924 at the Longacre Theatre and closed 28 June 1924 after 174 performances.

<u>CAST</u> (in order of appearance): *Jimmie Farnsworth*: LOUIS SIMON. *George Van Horne*: GLEN DALE. *Betty Duncan*: MAXINE BROWN. *Louise Endicott*: Allyn King. *Suzanne Franklin*: ELSA ERSI. *Brooks*: ROBINSON NEWBOLD. *Peter Darby*: ERNEST GLENDINNING. *Marie*: Helen O'Shea.
    Guests at Farnsworth's House Party: Misses Norah White, Irene Swor, Gertrude Livingstone, Agusta Orell, Helenya Koski, Bobbie Galvin, Sylvia Highton, Minerva Wilson, Elsie Schaeffer. Messrs. Ward Fox, Frank Kimball, Bob Sutherland, Jack Fraley, Burt McGuinnes, William Cooper, Alden Cook, Tom Maynard. *Special Dancers*: Lorraine Sisters.

Time: The present.

Added for subsequent tour:
    "Sweet Little Devil"
        C. Binney, W. Wayne, Boys and Girls
[122]Dropped for subsequent tour.
[123]Dropped for subsequent tour.
[124]A number of reviews referred to scenery designed by Joseph Urban, though he is nowhere credited.

Act 1: Lounge in Jimmie Farnsworth's Home on Long Island. Evening.

Act 2, Scene 1: Living Porch of Jimmie's Home. Evening, two days later. *Scene 2*: Exterior of Jimmie's Home. The passing of the night. *Scene 3*: Living Porch of Jimmie's Home. The next morning.

ACT 1[125]
"Fair Weather Friends"[126]
    L. Simon, Men
"The Daffydill"
    E. Ersi, Ensemble
"If I Were of the Hoi Polloi"
    M. Brown, R. Newbold
"Forever"
    G. Dale, Ensemble
"How Can a Lady Be Certain"[127]
    E. Ersi, Ensemble
"Aren't We All"
    E. Glendinning, Ensemble
"Say It Again"
    M. Brown, R. Newbold
Finale
    Ensemble

ACT 2
"On Such a Night"
    R. Newbold, G. Dale, E. Glendinning, L. Simon
    Japanese Girl: A. Orell. *East Indian Girl*: H. Koski. *South Sea Island Girl*: G. Livingstone. *Arabian Girl*: N. White.
"In a Bungalow"
    H. O'Shea, E. Glendinning
"Turn on the Popular Moon"[128]
    E. Ersi, Chorus
"How Do I Know He Loves Me?"[129]
    E. Ersi
Dance
    The Lorraine Sisters
Specialty
    R. Newbold
"The Passing of the Night"
    Instrumental
"Don't Put Me Out of Your Heart"[130]
    L. Simon, E. Ersi, Chorus
    (*Music and Lyrics by* William B. Friedlander.)
"Dancing"[131]
    M. Brown, Men
"Honeymoon Blues"
    E. Glendinning, H. O'Shea, Chorus
Finale
    Ensemble

1924.05

THE CHIFFON GIRL

A Romantic Musical Comedy in Three Acts. Book by George Murray. Music by Monte Carlo. Lyrics by Alma Sanders. Staged by Everett Butterfield. Dances and ensembles by Bert French. Gowns designed by Chez Routon and William Weaver. Scenery designed by Kahn & Bowman.

---

[125]Added during the New York run:
    "I Love Them All" (Act 1, after The Daffydill)
        M. Brown, Men
    Added for subsequent national tour:
    "I Cannot Live Without Love" (Act 2, after "In a Bungalow")
        E. Ersi, G. Dale, Chorus
    "Old Man in the Moon"(Act 2, following the above)
        M. Brown, R. Newbold
    (*Music and Lyrics by* William B. Friedlander.)
[126]Dropped during New York run.
[127]Dropped during New York run.
[128]Dropped for subsequent tour.
[129]Dropped during New York run.
[130]Dropped during New York run.
[131]Dropped for subsequent tour.

Orchestra under the direction of Fred Hoff. Orchestrations by Carl Kieffert. Produced by Charles Capehart. Opened 19 February 1924 at the Lyric Theatre, moved 3 March 1924 to Jolson's Theatre, moved 5 May 1924 to the Central Theatre, and closed 17 May 1924 after 103 performances.

CAST (in order of appearance): *The Spider*: Leah May. *Tough Boy*: William Green. *Mario Navarro*: GEORGE REIMHERR[132]. *Edward Lewis*: John Park. *Betty Lewis*: GLADYS MILLER. *Tonita Rovelli*: ELEANOR PAINTER. *Tim Delancy*: Shaun O'Farrell. *Woolsey*: Frank Doane. *Specialty Dancers*: Si Laymann, Helen Kling. *Lieutenant Dickie Stevens*: JAMES R. MARSHALL. *Mortimer Stevens*: James E. Sullivan. *Premier Danseuse*: Mlle. Pam. *Jeffrey*: Arthur E. Viall.

Ladies of the Ensemble: Amy Atkinson, Silvia Shawn, Hope Minor, Murray Canon, Emma Ramsey, Marion Vase, Helen Jackson, Anita Monroe, Ethel Guerard, Rose Adair, Rita Kirvit, Myrtle Gilden, Charlotte Davis, Ethel Moore, Marguerite Miller, Ellen Rose. *Gentlemen of the Ensemble*: Billy M. Green, Jack Scholl, Lehman Byck, Warren Bassette, George F. Brown, Frank Callahan, Louis Brown, J. C. Ames, Arthur Viall.

Act 1: 'Little Italy' in Lower New York.

Act 2: Edward Lewis' Home on Long Island.

Act 3: Café Boheme, New York City.

ACT 1
"New York Life"
    Ensemble
"My Tonita"
    G. Reimherr
"Mia Cara"
    E. Painter
"We're Sweethearts"
    E. Painter, G. Reimherr

ACT 2
"Dust Chasers"
    Ensemble
"When the Sun Goes Down"
    J. R. Marshall, G. Miller
"Just One Rose"
    E. Painter, Chorus
"Did You Come Back?"
    G. Reimherr
"Till the End of Time"
    E. Painter, G. Reimherr
"1908"
    J. E. Sullivan, F. Doane, J. Park, J. R. Marshall
"The Chiffon Girl"
    E. Painter, Ensemble

ACT 3
"Little Devils"
    Mlle. Pam, Ensemble
"The Café Boheme"
    G. Reimherr, E. Painter, Ensemble
"The Raindrop and the Rose"
    J. R. Marshall, G. Miller
"Bring Back Your Heart to Me"
    E. Painter
Specialty
    S. Layman, H. Kling
"Maybe Yes or No"
    E. Painter, Boys
"Cuddle Me Up"
    G. Miller, J. R. Marshall, S. Layman, H. Kling
Finale

1924.06

VOGUES OF 1924

A Musical Revue in Two Acts, 15 Scenes. Book (sketches) and lyrics by Fred Thompson and Clifford Grey. Music by Herbert Stothart. Staged by Frank Smithson and Alexander Leftwich. Dances and ensembles by David Bennett. Stage settings by Watson Barratt. All gowns designed by Charles LeMaire; men's furnishings by Nat Lewis Inc. Orchestra under the direction of Alfred Goodman. Produced by Messrs. Shubert in association with

George B. McLellan. Opened 27 March 1924 at the Sam S. Shubert Theatre; Second Edition[133] opened 25 June 1924 as VOGUES AND FROLICS and closed 12 July 1924 after 114 performances.

CAST: ODETTE MYRTIL, J. HAROLD MURRAY, MAY BOLEY, FRED ALLEN, IRENE DELROY, JIMMIE SAVO, ANNETTE BADE, GEORGE ANDERSON, BEATRICE SWANSON, MARCELLA SWANSON, BETTY COMPTON, HAL VAN RENSELLAER, James Alderman, Charles Brown, John V. Lowe, Joseph Toner, Joan Franza, Margery Thomas, Lucita Covera, Margaret Dailey, Alice Manning, Edward Scanlon, the Pasqualis.

Show Girls: Betty Carlstedt, Anna May Denehy, Marion Whitmore, Elsie Levy, Greta Warburg, Mary Carlson, Genevieve Tierney, Ivy Palmer, Sylvia Buckstein, Alice Keenan, Patricia Gerard, Flossie Tanney. *Dancers*: Darlene Van Gorder, Dinky Ozment, Virginia Serrar, Millie Dupree, Beatrice Reiss, Neida Snow, Marion Wilson, Consuelo Owens, May Adair, Polly Maxwell, Helen Sills, Mabel Baade, Lee Byrne, Nathalie Fish, Elene Rogier, Alice Monroe. *Special Singers*: Irma Bertrand, Lucille Arnold, Millie Shaw, Alice Huntington, Alma Barnes, Mary Rose Walsh. *Special Singing Men*: Coley Colson, Dean Newton, John Castle.

ACT 1
Scene 1
    The Bedroom of the Princess
        Marie: A. Bade. *Julie*: B. Compton. *Madame Collette*: M. Boley. *The Court Physicians*: C. Brown, J. V. Lowe, J. Alderman. *The Princess Katinka*: O. Myrtil. *The Speilman* of 'The Miracle': J. H. Murray. *Major Domo*: J. Toner.
    "Hush, Look Away"
        A. Bade, B. Compton, Maids
    "Medicos"
        J. V. Lowe, C. Brown, J. Alderman
    "Dressing"
        O. Myrtil, Maids
    "Katinka"
        O. Myrtil, Girls
    "The Speilman"
        J. H. Murray
    "When the Piper Plays"
        J. H. Murray, O. Myrtil
Scene 2
    Outside the Asylum
        F. Allen, J. Savo
Scene 3
    The Garden of the School of Dramatic Art
        Madame Callender, the principal: M. Boley. *Miss Luray*, a pupil: B. Swanson. *Miss Mannay*, a pupil: M. Swanson. *Miss Fannay*, a pupil: A. M. Denehy. *The Speilman*, of 'The Miracle': J. H. Murray. *The Princess Katinka*: O. Myrtil. *The Salesman*: G. Anderson. *The Victim*: J. Savo.
    "Three Little Maids"
        B. Swanson, M. Swanson, A. M. Denehy, Pupils
    "Pierrot"
        O. Myrtil
    "Rain"
        The Sadie Thompsons: B. Swanson, M. Swanson, A. Bade, M. Thomas, L. Covera, B. Compton. *The Reverend Davidsons*: J. V. Lowe, J. Alderman, J. Toner, G. Anderson, C. Brown, H. Van Rensellaer. *The Mrs. Davidsons*: M. Boley, A. M. Denehy, I. Palmer, G. Tierney, B. Carlstedt, F. Tanney.
    "The Belle of the Ball"
        J. H. Murray, I. Delroy, Girls
    "The Belle of Today"
        O. Myrtil, Girls
Scene 4
    In Front of the Curtains
        F. Allen, J. Savo
Scene 5
    The Land of Happiness
    "Eldorado"
        O. Myrtil, J. H. Murray
    "The Legend of the Shirt"
        J. H. Murray

---

[132]The New York Times reviewed Joseph Lertora in this role.

[133]Though no program could be found for VOGUES AND FROLICS, news items referred to two new scenes under the titles A Prehistoric Cabaret, and The Wedding Glide. Newcomer Tot Qualters joined Odette Myrtil, James Savo and Fred Allen in the cast. Additional music was provided by Robert Ayres.

Gypsy Kataka
  A. Manning
The Pasqualis
"Laugh and Play"
  J. Toner
"Star of Destiny"
  O. Myrtil, Ensemble

ACT 2

Scene 1

The Millionaire's Cafetaria
  Babette: A. Manning. *Miss Luray*: B. Swanson. *Miss Mannay*: M. Swanson. *Mr. Oswald Twissell*: J. Savo. *The Speilman*: J. H. Murray. *Miss Royal* (The Princess Incognito): O. Myrtil. *Madame Collette*: M. Boley. *Wilkins*: F. Allen. *Winnie*: M. Boley. *Walter*: G. Anderson.
W (*Sketch by* Basil Charlton)
  The Mohammedan Caucasians of the Legjine-Tartars under the Patronage of Prince and Princess Youssoupoff.
Dance Specialty
  A. Manning
  The Dancers are Prince Kadir-Sultan-Guercy, Captain Islam-Naterhoff and Lieutenant Kerefoff.
"It Does Feel Good to Go to the Bad"
  B. Swanson, M. Swanson, J. V. Lowe, Van Rensalear
"That's the Tune"
  O. Myrtil, B. Swanson, M. Swanson, A. Bade, B. Compton, M. Thomas, L. Covera, Girls

Scene 2

In Front of the Curtains
  F. Allen, J. Savo

Scene 3

"The Tea Kettle"
  I. Delroy, Old-Fashioned Girls

Scene 4

The Triangle (A Drama of Yesterday—Today—Tomorrow *by* Alexander Leftwich)
  Scene: The Library of the Anstruthers' during an evening early in December. *Mary Anstruther*, the wife: B. Swanson. *Robert Anstruther*, the husband: G. Anderson. *Harvey*, the butler: E. Scanlon. *Jack Henderson*, the friend: H. Van Rensellaer. *Michael Hennessey*, from Headquarters: J. Alderman. *Daniel McGinnis*, of the 17th Precinct: J. Toner. *William Kendall Travers*, the District Attorney: C. Brown.

Scene 5

"The Dancing Master" (*Arranged and produced by* Odette Myrtil)
  The Dancing Master: O. Myrtil. *The Pupils*: C. Owens, M. Adair, B. Reiss, D. Ozment. *The Daughter*: I. Delroy. *The Father*: J. Alderman.

Scene 6

Slow Motion
  Boy: J. Savo. *Girl*: J. Franza.

Scene 7

An Autumn Idyll (*Conceived and arranged by* Watson Barratt.)
  J. H. Murray

Scene 8

Disinfecting (*by* Fred Thompson)(With apologies to Frederick Lonsdale, author of "Spring Cleaning" now current at the Eltinge Theatre)
  Scene a: The Library of the Sones. *Scene b*: The Dining Room of the Sones. *Walters*, the butler: J. Alderman. *Richard Sones*: G. Anderson. *Margaret Sones*, his wife: B. Swanson. *Bobby*, her admirer: J. V. Lowe. *Ernest*, another admirer: H. Van Rensellaer. *Connie*, a member of the fast set: M. Swanson. *Fay*, a graduate of the fast set: A. Bade. *Archie*, a drunkard: C. Brown. *Lady Jane*, a dope-fiend: M. Thomas. *Irene*: L. Covera. *Mona*: M. Dailey.

Scene 9

Before the Curtains
  F. Allen, J. Savo

Scene 10

"The Love Cottage"
  O. Myrtil, J. H. Murray, I. Delroy, Entire Company

1924.07　　PARADISE ALLEY

A Musical Comedy in Two Acts, 6 Scenes. Book by Charles W. Bell and Edward Clark. Music by Carle Carlton, Harry Archer and A. Otvos. Lyrics by Howard Johnson. Book and entire prduction staged by Carle Carlton.

Ensemble numbers directed by Jack Mason. Costumes designed by William Weaver. Scenery by Frank Gates and Edward A. Morange. Orchestra under the direction of John L. McManus. Produced by Carle Carlton. Opened 1 April 1924 at the Casino Theatre, moved 10 May 1924 to the Vanderbilt Theatre, and closed 24 May 1924 after 64 performances.

CAST (in order of appearance): *Little Annie Rooney*: Hallie Manning. *Sweet Marie*: EVELYN MARTIN. *Mother O'Grady*, Boss of the Alley: Dorothy Walters. *Casey the Cop*: William Renaud. *Quinnie La Salle*: IDA MAY CHADWICK. *Bonnie Brown*: HELEN SHIPMAN. *Spike Muldoon*: ARTHUR WEST. *Jack Harriman*: CHARLES DERICKSON. *Rudolf Zatz*: GEORGE BICKEL. *Sylvia Van de Veer*: GLORIA DAWN. *Edward Harriman*: Edward Wonn. *Dusty*: BEN BENNY. *Benny*: BURKE WESTERN. *Four of the Finest and Reporters, Four Entertainers*: Lloyd Balliot, William Renaud, Frank Stanhope, Garfield Brown. *Alex Huxley*: Leslie Barrie. *Stage Door Keeper*: Arthur Atkinson.

Ladies of the Ensemble: Marian Gunn, Muriel Lodge, Juanita Wray, Louise Joyce, Adele Smith, Elizabeth Dougher, Billee Fennimore, Dolly Donnelly, Marilyn Evans, Kathryn Scott, Aileen Meehan, Jane Brew, Nina Byron, Virginia O'Brien, Marjorie O'Brien, Lucille King, Beatrice Coniff, Estelle Keeley, Jane Daniel, Marjorie Schweinert.

Act 1: Happiness: Paradise Alley, New York City.

Act 2: Success: Piccadilly Theatre, London. Two Years later. *Scene 1*: Foyer Scene. *Scene 2*: Stage Door during performance. *Scene 3*: Stars' Dressing Room. *Scene 4*: Stage Door after performance. *Scene 5*: The Garden Party.

ACT 1[134]

"Happiness"
  Principals, Company
"When I Made the Grade"
  D. Walters, W. Renaud
"Paradise Alley"
  H. Shipman
"As Long as They On Making 'Em"
  I. M. Chadwick
"Tell Me Truly"[135]
  H. Shipman, C. Derickson
"Promises"
  I. M. Chadwick, G. Bickel, A. West
"Friendship"
  G. Dawn, H. Shipman, C. Derickson
"Bob-haired Bandit"
  Four Entertainers, E. Martin, B. Benny, B. Western, Ensemble
"Musical Comedy"
  G. Bickel, H. Shipman, I. M. Chadwick, A. West, B. Benny, B. Western
"Your Way or My Way"
  H. Shipman, C. Derickson

ACT 2

"Success"
  G. Bickel, I. M. Chadwick, Ensemble
"The First Nighters"
  Double Sextette
"Rolland from Holland"
  I. M. Chadwick, Ensemble
"Reporters"
  Four Entertainers
"What the Future Holds"
  H. Shipman
"That's Why They Call Us Johns"
  Double Sextette
Garden Ballet
  E. Martin, Ensemble
"Put on the Ritz"
  H. Shipman, C. Derickson, B. Benny, B. Western, E. Martin, I. M. Chadwick, Company
Medley Finale
  Entire Company

---

[134]Added during the run:
  "Where Have the Old Timers Gone" (Act 2, after "Success")
    C. Derickson, A. West
[135]During the run replaced by:
  "If I Had You and You Had Me"
    H. Shipman, C. Derickson

1924.08

SITTING PRETTY

A Musical Comedy in Two Acts. Book and lyrics by Guy Bolton and P. G. Wodehosue. Music by Jerome Kern. Staged by Fred G. Latham and Julian Alfred. Settings designed by P. Dodd Ackerman. Costumes designed by Charles Lemaire (Act 1) and Alice V. O'Neill (Act 2). Orchestra under the direction of Max Steiner. Orchestrations by Robert Russell Bennett, Produced by F. Ray Comstock and Morris Gest. Opened 8 April 1924 at the Fulton Theatre, moved 9 June 1924 to the Imperial Theatre, and closed 28 June 1924 after 95 performances.

CAST (in order of appearance): *Mrs. Wagstaff*, a teacher: Marjorie Eggleston. *James*, a footman: Albert Wyart. *Roper*, a butler: Harry Lillford. *'Bill' Pennington*: RUDOLF CAMERON. *Judson Waters*, his friend: Eugene Revere. *Babe LaMarr*, a chorus girl: Myra Hampton. *May Tolliver*: GERTRUDE BRYAN. *Dixie*, her sister: QUEENIE SMITH. *The Pennington Relatives (4)*: *Jasper*: Edward Finley. *Wilhelmina*: Jayne Chesney. *Otis*: George Sylvester. *Wilhelmina*: Marian Dickson. *Mr. Pennington*, head of the Pennington family: GEORGE E. MACK. *Horace*: DWIGHT FRYE. *Joe*, his uncle: FRANK McINTYRE. *Professor Appleby*: George Spelvin. *Bolt*, a coachman: George O'Donnell. *Jane*, a housemaid: Terry Blaine.

   Characters at the Ball: *Jenny Lind*: Wynthrope Wayne. *Edgar Allen Poe*: George Sylvester. *Barbara Freitchie*: Marietta O'Brien. *Stonewall Jackson*: Edward Finley. *Rachel*: Marjorie Eggleston. *Harriet Beecher Stowe*: Frieda Fitzgerald. *Louisa M. Alcott*: May Clark. *George Sand*: Charlotte Wakefield. *Florence Nightingale*: Jayne Chesney. *Empress Eugénie*: Dorothy Janice. *Empress' Attendants*: Alice Akers, Dorothy West.

   Girls at the Pennington Charity School: Betty Campbell, Jean Castleton, Virginia Tracy Clark, Marian Dickson, Jean Emerson, Irene Griffith, Katherine Kohler, Harriet Marned, Marion Phillips, Phyllis Reynolds, Louise Segal Converse, Gertrude Waixel. *The Coaching Party*: Alice Akers, Mary Clark, Frieda Fitzgeald, Marietta O'Brien, Dorothy West, Doris Waldron, Wynthrope Wayne, Charlotte Wakefield, Edouard Lefebvre, Earl Marvin, Dana Mayo, George O'Donnell, William Powers, Charles Sabin, Roger Buckley, Albert White.

Act 1: Garden of Mr. Pennington's Summer Home at Far Hills, New Jersey.

Act 2: Patio of Mr. Pennington's Winter Home at Belle Air, Florida.

ACT 1[136]

   "The Charity Class"
      Charity Girls
   "Is This Not a Lovely Spot?" (Song Scena)
      G. E. Mack, R. Cameron, E. Revere, Coaching Party, Girls, Gardeners, etc.
   "Worries" (Trio)
      G. Bryan, Q. Smith, R. Cameron
   "Mr. and Mrs. Rorer" (Duet)
      Q. Smith, D. Frye, Cooking Class
   "Bongo on the Congo" (Trio)
      D. Frye, E. Revere, F. McIntyre
   "There Isn't One Girl" (Song Scene)
      R. Cameron, H. Lillford, G. Bryan
   "A Year from Today" (Duet)
      R. Cameron, G. Bryan
   "Shufflin' Sam" (Song)
      Q. Smith, Ensemble
   Finaletto
      Ensemble

ACT 2

   "The Polka Dot" (Chorus)
      Ensemble

---

[136]During the run, the song order was revised. The order of "Mr. and Mrs. Rorer" and "Bongo on the Congo" was reversed. The title song was dropped. A subsequent national tour was tailored to the talents of the Dolly Sisters the following season under the auspices of A. L. Jones and Morris Green. Added to Act 1 (following "Bongo" and replacing "Mr. and Mrs. Rorer") was:

   "Grab a Girl" (Duet)
      Jennie Dolly (Jennie), Fred Santle (Horace), Cooking Class
In Act 2, "A Desert Island" and "The Magic Train" were dropped and replaced by:
   "I'm Looking All Over for You" (Duet)
      F. Santle, J. Dolly
   "Dancing Time" (Duet)
      J. Dolly, Rosie Dolly (Rosie), Girls
The title song remained dropped.

Scene Music
   "Days Gone By" (Aria)
      D. Janice, Ensemble
   "All You Need Is a Girl" (Duettino)
      R. Cameron, G. Bryan
   "Dear Old Fashioned Prison of Mine" (Buffo Duo)
      D. Frye, F. McIntyre
   "A Desert Island" (Duet)
      G. Bryan, Q. Smith, Girls
   "The Magic Train" (Duet)
      R. Cameron, G. Bryan, Ensemble
   "Shadow of the Moon" (Song)
      Q. Smith, G. Bryan
   "Sitting Pretty"[137] (Duettino)
      D. Frye, Q. Smith, Ensemble
   Finale
      Ensemble

1924.09

PEG O' MY DREAMS

A Musical Comedy in Two Acts. Book by J. Hartley Manners. Based on his play 'Peg o' My Heart.' Music by Hugo Felix. Lyrics by Anne Caldwell. Production conceived and staged by Hassard Short. Dances arranged by Chester Hale. Book rehearsed under the direction of J. Hartley Manners. Costumes designed by Charles LeMaire. Settings designed by Clark Robinson. Orchestra under the direction of Gus Salzer. Orchestrations by Hugo Felix. Produced by Richard Herndon. Opened 5 May 1924 at Jolson's 59th Street Theatre, moved 19 May 1924 to the Imperial Theatre, and closed 31 May 1924 after 32 performances.

CAST: *Peg*: SUZANNE KEENER. *Jerry*: ROY ROYSTON. *Alaric*: G. P. HUNTLEY. *Ethel*: ROBERTA BEATTY. *Monica*: GILBERTA FAUST. *Arkady*: PAUL KLEEMAN. *Alexis*: CHESTER HALE. *Jarvis*: OSCAR FIGMAN. *Una*: ALBERTINA VITAK. *Blanche*: LOVEY LEE. *Banbury*: JOSEPH McCALLION. *Chris*: WILLIAM LADD. *Rita*: Henrietta Brewster. *Blossom*: Gladys Baxter. *Fay*: Jean Ferguson. *Muriel*: Helen Haines. *Joan*: Katherine Spencer. *Diana*: Julia Lane. *Bill*: Richard Ford. *Guy*: John R. Walsh. *Fred*: Charles Baum. *Michael*: Michael. *Pet*: Pet.

Act 1: Mrs. Chichester's House, Scarborough, England.

Act 2: The Garden of Mrs. Chichester's House. Evening; Night; Morning.

ACT 1

   "Hunt Ball Rehearsal"
      Ensemble
   "A Dainty Nosegay"
      R. Beatty, Ensemble
   "All Alone"
      C. Hale, A. Vitak, L. Lee, W. Ladd, J. McCallion
   "Rose in the Snow"
      R. Beatty, P. Kleeman
   "There's a Rainbow Waiting for You"
      R. Royston
   "Haven't We Met Before?"
      G. P. Huntley, Girls
   Dance
      A. Vitak, L. Lee, W. Ladd, J. McCallion
   "The Gap in the Hedge"
      S. Keener, O. Figman
   "Love's Young Dream"
      S. Keener, R. Royston
   "Lily Bell Polka"
      A. Vitak, L. Lee
   Finale
      Entire Company

ACT 2

   "Her Bright Shawl"
      R. Beatty, Ensemble
   Waltz
      C. Hale, A. Vitak

---

[137]Dropped during the run.

"Door Mats"
G. P. Huntley, R. Royston

"Shy Little Irish Smile"
S. Keener, H. Brewster, J. Ferguson, G. Baxter, H. Haines, K. Spencer, J. Lane

"Moscow Belles"*
P. Kleeman

Dance
L. Lee, W. Ladd, J. McCallion

"Love Is Like a Firefly"
S. Keener, R. Royston

"Peg o' My Dreams"
R. Royston

"L'Heure Bleu"[138] (Ballet)(The Passing of a Few Hours)
The Evening Star: A. Vitak. *The Man*: C. Hale. *The Night*: L. Lee. *The Heavens*: H. Brewster, J. Ferguson, G. Baxter, H. Haines, J. Lane, K. Spencer.

"Right-o"
A. Vitak, L. Lee, W. Ladd, J. McCallion, H. Brewster, J. Ferguson, G. Baxter, H. Haines, J. Lane, K. Spencer

1924.10

PLAIN JANE

A Musical Comedy in Two Acts, 8 Scenes. Book by Phil Cook and McElbert Moore. Music by Tom Johnstone. Lyrics by Phil Cook. Production staged by Walter Brooks. Scenes designed by Mabel Buell. Costumes by Evelyn McHorter, Brooks-Mahieu Costume Co., Vanity Fair Costumes, Inc. Orchestra under the direction of Ira Jacobs. Produced by Louis I. Isquith and Walter Brooks (Plain Jane, Inc.). Opened 12 May 1924 at the New Amsterdam Theatre, moved 23 June 1924 to the Sam H. Harris Theatre, moved 25 August 1924 to the Eltinge Theatre, and closed 4 October 1924 after 168 performances.

CAST (in order of appearance): *Jane Lee*: LORRAINE MANVILLE. *Nanny McGuire*: Elfin Finn. *Mrs. McGuire*: Alma Chester. *Kid McGuire*: JOE LAURIE, JR. *Rollins*: John M. Troughton. *Julian Kingsley*: RALPH LOCKE. *Countess Suzanne D'Arcy*: HELEN CARRINGTON. *Pierre*: Lew Christy. *Lord Gordon Hemmingsworth*: CHARLES MCNAUGHTON. *Ruth Kingsley*: MARION SAKI. *Buddy Smith*: LESTER O'KEEFE. *Dick Kingsley*: JAY GOULD. *Happy Williams*: DAN HEALY. *Little Miss Ritz*, Danseuse: MAY CORY KITCHEN. *Champ Kelly*: Allie Nack. *Kelly's Second*: Jay Gerrard. *Referee*: Jack Stanley. *Stenographer*: Pearl Howell. *Japanese Doll*: Edna Coigne. *Spanish Doll*: Liane Mamet. *Russian Doll*: Pearl Howell. *Hawaiian Doll*: Pauline Williams.

Ritz Dolls: Joey Benton, Edna Coigne, Liane Mamet, Pearl Howell. *Contestants*: Nesha Medwin, Honor Tattersall, Bianca Fernandez, Mabel Grete, Verdi Milli, Pauline Williams, Miriam Malloy, Frances Wilson. *Reporters*: Eugene Day, Russell King, Bernard Hazard, Jay Gerard, Charles LaValle, Fred Harris, George Bradley, Bud Penny.

Act 1, Scene 1: Jane Lee's Room in the Garret of the McGuire Home, Lower East Side, New York City. Late afternoon of a May day, present time. *Scene 2*: Corridor in the Kingsley Studio. *Scene 3*: The Kingsley Studio, Downtown, New York City. The following afternoon.

Act 2, Scene 1: Outside the Doll House—Cabaret Party in Greenwich Village. Evening, a week later. *Scene 2*: The Prize Ring in Madison Square Garden. Same evening. (An impression.) *Scene 3*: Outside the Doll House. *Scene 4*: Up in the Skies. *Scene 5*: In the Doll House. Morning, a few months later.

ACT 1

"Plain Jane"
L. Manville

"What's New?"
Reporters

"Winning the Prize"
C. McNaughton, H. Carrington, R. Locke, M. Saki, J. M. Troughton, Reporters, Girls

"If Flowers Could Speak"
M. Saki, L. O'Keefe, M. C. Kitchen, Ensemble

"Someone Like You"[139]
L. Manville, J. Gould

"When You Heart's in the Ring"
C. MacNaughton, Girls

"I Love a Fight"
J. Laurie, Jr., M. C. Kitchen, Girls

Reprise
L. Manville

"Along the Road to Love"
L. Manville, J. Gould, Ensemble

Finale
L. Manville, J. Laurie, Jr., J. Gould

ACT 2

"Puttin' on the Ritz"
D. Healy, M. C. Kitchen, Ensemble

"Proverbs"
C. McNaughton

"Don't Take Your Troubles to Bed"
H. Carrington, M. Saki, Ensemble

"Beneath the Stars"
M. Saki, L. O'Keefe, Ensemble

"A Playhouse Planned for You"[140]
L. Manville, J. Gould

"Come On, Feet, Let's Go"
D. Healy

"Tricks of the Trade"
M. Saki, L. O'Keefe, Girls

"When the Whistle Blows"
L. Manville, J. Gould, Ensemble

Specialties
F. Harris, P. Howell

"Follow Your Footsteps"[141]
J. Laurie, Jr., Ensemble

Finale
Entire Company

1924.11

I'LL SAY SHE IS

A Musical Comedy Revue in Two Acts, 24 Scenes. Book and lyrics by Will B. Johnstone. Music by Tom Johnstone. Book directed by Eugene Sanger. (Musical) Numbers staged by Vaughan Godfrey. Scenery by H. Robert Law Studio. Costumes by Brooks Mahieu. Orchestra under the direction of Ted Coleman. Entire production under the personal direction of James P. Beury. Produced by James P. Beury. Opened 19 May 1924 at the Casino Theatre and closed 7 February 1925 after 313 performances.

CAST (in order of appearance): *Theatrical Agent* (Richman): EDWARD METCALFE. *Office Girl*: Crissie Melvin. *Doctor*: HERBERT [Zeppo] MARX. *Poorman*: LEONARD [Chico] MARX. *Lawyer*: JULIUS H. [Groucho] MARX. *Beggarman*: ARTHUR [Harpo] MARX. *Chief*: LLOYD GARRETT. *Merchant*: PHILLIP DARBY. *Thief*: EDGAR GARDINER. *Chorus Girl*: Hazel Gaudreau. *Nanette*: Florence Arledge. *Social Secretary*: RUTH URBAN. *Beauty*: CARLOTTA [Lotta] MILES. *Pages*: Melvin Sisters (Mary, ??). *White Girl*: Cecile D'Andrea. *Hop Merchant*: Harry Walters. *Street Gamins*: Mildred Joy, Gertrude Cole. *Chinese Boy*: RUTH URBAN. *Bull and Bear*: Hazel Gaudreau, Edgar Gardiner. *Gold Man*: Ledru Stiffler. *Pierrots*: Jane Hurd, Florence Thorpe. *Hazel*: Hazel Gaudreau. *Marcella*: Marcella Hardie. *Specialty*: MARTHA PRYOR.

Ladies of the Ensemble: Gene Spencer, Bunny Parker, Florence Arledge, Jane Hurd, Alice McDonald, Marion Case, Gertrude Cole, Catherine Norris, Mary Carney, Helen Martin, Muriel Greel, Ethel Emery, Mildred Joy, Aileen Meehan, Jeane Green, Florence Thorpe, Vivian Spencer.

Act 1, Scene 1: Theatrical Agency. *Scene 2*: Art Curtain. *Scene 3*: Beauty's Reception Room. *Scene 4*: Art Curtain. *Scene 5*: Chinatown Street. *Scene 6*: The Opium Den. *Scene 7*: The Dream Ship. *Scene 8*: The Court Room. *Scene 9*: Art Curtain. *Scene 10*: Song "Rainy Day." *Scene 11*: Art Curtain. *Scene 12*: Wall Street. *Scene 13*: Industry: The Plaything of Wall Street.

Act 2, Scene 1: Art Curtain. *Scene 2*: The Inception of Drapery. *Scene 3*: Art Curtain. *Scene 4*: Hawaiian Scene. *Scene 5*: Art Curtain. *Scene 6*: The Marble Fountain. *Scene 7*: Art Curtain. *Scene 8*: The Hypnotist; Pierrot Dance. *Scene 9*: Napoleon's First Waterloo. *Scene 10*: Specialty. *Scene 11*: Beauty's Russian Garden.

---

[138]Costumes designed by Ralph Mulligan.
[139]During the run, replaced by:
"Hand in Hand"
L. Manville, J. Gould

---

[140]Dropped during the run.
[141]During the run, replaced by:
"Along the Road to Love"
J. Laurie, Jr., Ensemble

ACT 1

Scene 1

"Do It"
E. Metcalfe, Girls

"Pretty Girl"
Marx Brothers, E. Metcalfe, E. Gardiner, F. J. Corbett, P. Darby

Scene 2

"Give Me a Thrill"
R. Urban, E. Metcalfe, Marx Brothers, E. Gardiner, F. J. Corbett, 8 Maids

Scene 3

"Only You"
C. Miles

Scene 4

Descriptive
C. Miles, E. Metcalfe, Marx Brothers, P. Darby, L. Garrett

Scene 5

"When the Shadows Fall"
P. Darby

"Break Into Your Heart"
M. Hardie, E. Gardiner, Burglar Girls, M. Joy, G. Cole

Scene 6

Chinese Apache Dance
C. D'Andrea, H. Walters

"San Toy"
R. Urban

Scene 7

"San Toy"
M. Melvin

Scene 8

The Court Room
Marx Brothers, C. Miles, E. Metcalfe

Scene 9

Carlotta Miles and Frank J. Corbett

Scene 10

"Rainy Day"[142]
C. Miles, F. J. Corbett, Melvin Sisters, G. Cole, M. Joy

Scene 11

"Wall Street Blues"
M. Hardie, Melvin Sisters, H. Gaudreau, E. Gardiner, Ensemble

Scene 12

Wall Street
C. Miles, E. Metcalfe

The Tragedy of Gambling
The Fairy: M. Melvin. *The Gambler:* H. Walters. *Cards:* M. Bower. *Penny:* M. Joy. *Dice:* F. Bower. *Dime:* H. Bradley. *Racing:* A. Webb. *Dollar:* J. Hurd. *Roulette:* M. Shea. *Gold Coin:* G. Spencer. *The Greed of Gold:* L. Stiffler.

Silver Ballet
Misses Spencer, Perry, Laird, Joy, Bradley, G. Cole, E. Shea, Allen
The Lure of Gambling: C. D'Andrea, H. Walters.

Scene 13

The Plaything of Wall Street

ACT 2

Scene 1

Introduction
Melvin Sisters

Scene 2

The Inception of Drapery
Scarf Girls: C. Norris, Bradley, M. Shea, E. Shea. *Rose Petals:* Bower Sisters. *Pan:* C. Norris. *Beauty Dress:* C. Miles, P. Darby. *Japan:* B. Parker. *South Sea Isles:* M. Shea. *Zulu:* G. Cole. *Timbuctoo:* A. Webb. *Brittany:* F. Allen. *Russia:* J. Hurd. *Hindustan:* G. Spencer.

Scene 3

Cinderella Backwards
C. Miles, J. Marx

Scene 4

The 16 Yankee Girls: M. Hardie, Melvin Sisters, Bower Sisters, E. Shea, G.

Cole, M. Shea, J. Green, M. Joy, G. Laird, J. Hurd, A. Webb, B. Parker, H. Bradley, H. Gaudreau, C. Norris.

Scene 5

"Only You"
C. Miles, F. J. Corbett

Scene 6

The Marble Fountain
Misses G. Cole, M. Joy, E. Shea, M. Shea, C. Norris, V. Perry, J. Green, F. Allen

(a) Pygmalion and Galatea—The Awakening of Love
C. D'Andrea, H. Walters

The Death of Love
H. Marx, A. Marx, M. Riordan, L. Stiffler, E. Gardiner, J. Marx

Scene 7

Art Curtains
J. Hurd, A. Webb

Scene 8

Pierrot Dance

The Hypnotist
L. Marx, E. Metcalfe

Scene 9

Napoleon's First Waterloo

Court Reception at Versailles

"Glimpses of the Moon"
Court Singer: F. Hedges. *Court Violinist:* Albert Vigoli. *Court Pianist:* Herbert St. Clair. *Court Pages:* Melvin Sisters. *Josephine:* C. Miles. *Napoleon:* J. Marx. *Francois:* H. Marx. *Alphonse:* L. Marx. *Gaston:* A. Marx.

Scene 10

Specialty[143]
M. Pryor

Scene 11

"The Wonderful River"[144] (The Wonderful Nile)
F. Hedges, Ensemble

Specialty
H. Gaudreau

The Blue Tartar
L. Stiffler

Marcella Dance
M. Hardie

1924.12

BLOSSOM TIME

A Revival of the Operetta in Three Acts[145]. Book and lyrics by Dorothy Donnelly. Adapted from the original (Das Dreimäderlhaus) by A. M. Willner and Heinz Reichert, based on a novel "Schwammerl" by Rudolf H. Bartsch. Music adapted and augmented by Sigmund Romberg from the melodies of Franz Schubert selected and arranged by Heinrich Berté. Staged by J. C. Huffman. Dancing numbers arranged by F. M. Gillespie. Scenes [scenery] by Watson Barratt. Orchestra under the direction of Gabriel Hines. Produced by the Messrs. Shubert. Opened 19 May 1924 at Jolson's Theatre and closed 7 June 1924 after 24 performances.

---

[143]During the run, replaced by:

A Bit of Tango Jazz
H. Gaudreau, M. Greel, Nat Martin's Orchestra

Which was later replaced by:

A Bit of Melody
The King Sisters, Nat Martin's Orchestra

["There's Yes Yes in Your Eyes"
Nat Martin's Orchestra
(*Music by* Joseph H. Santle. *Lyrics by* Cliff Friend.)]

[144]Replaced for subsequent national tour by:

"I Dream of a Garden of Sunshine"
R. Urban, Ensemble

[145]First presented in New York 29 September 1921 at the Ambassador Theatre for 592 performances. For Synopsis of Scenes and Musical Numbers, see original 1921 production. Costumes uncredited.

---

[142]Replaced for subsequent national tour by:

"The Only, Only One Is You"
R. Urban

CAST: *Mitzi*: MARGARET MERLE. *Bellabruna*: Fenita de Soria. *Fritzi*: Alma Keller. *Kitzi*: Bee Brady. *Mrs. Kranz*: ISABELL VERNON. *Greta*: VERNA SHAFF. *Baron Franz Schober*: HOWARD MARSH. *Franz Schubert*: GREEK EVANS. *Kranz*: Robert Lee Allen. *Vogl*: Cliff Whitcomb. *Kupelweiser*: Edward Orchard. *Von Schwind*: William Lilling. *Binder*: Lee Bright. *Erkman*: Oliver T. McCormick. *Count Sharntoff*: GREGORY RATOFF. *A Violinist*: Ulysses Morell. *Novotny*: OTIS SHERIDAN. *Rose*: Ryth Randall. *Mrs. Coburg*: Elizabeth Hunt. *Waiter*: Harry F. Scott. *Dancer*: Ruth Remington.
Ladies of the Ensemble: Anna Bell, Ruth Ingalsbe, Leanora E. Scott, Shirley Stanley, Vergil Dodd, Florence Devoe, Virginia Serier, Marie Messier, May Clayton, Zana Gray.

1924.13

INNOCENT EYES

A Musical Revue in Two Acts, 16 Scenes. Book (sketches) by Harold Atteridge. Music by Sigmund Romberg and Jean Schwartz. Lyrics by Harold Atteridge and Tot Seymour. Staged by Frank Smithson. Dances arranged by Jack Mason and M. Francis Weldon. Orchestra under the direction of Alfred Goodman. Costumes designed by Charles Gesmar. Art decorations (settings) by Watson Barratt. Orchestrations by Alfred Goodman. Entire production supervised by J. J. Shubert. Produced by the Messrs. Lee and J. J. Shubert. Opened 20 May 1924 at the Winter Garden and closed 30 August 1924 after 126 performances.

CAST: MISTINGUETT, CECIL LEAN, CLEO MAYFIELD, LEW HEARN, EDYTHE BAKER, TED DONER, VANNESSI, EARL LESLIE, FRANCES WILLIAMS, FRANK DOBSON, MARJORY LEACH, CHARLES HOWARD, VERA LAVROVA, Maud Allen, Mabel Carruthers, Mildred Manley, Martin Mason, Gail Beverly, Franklyn Byron, Grace Bowman, James E. Phillips, Charles Mac, Harry A. White, Jack DeFay.
Dancers: Alice Boulden, Gladys Smith, Katherine Hill, Peggy Gillespie, Bella Heyman, Mae Cairns, Viola Watson, Norman Gould, Florence Courtney, Marie Warner, Dorothy Mantell, Leonora Hellekson, Billy Williams, Victoria Reigel, Ruth Hamilton, Myrtle Thompson, Ruby Lorraine, Violet Hayes, Lillian Dunning. *Show Girls*: Helene Dahlia, Peggy Lockwood, Irene Sharp, Loretta Sharpe, Lillian Stone, Peggy Neil, Flo Sheppard, Peggy Mermont, Violet Bache, Devera Anguillar, Suzanne Bennett, Carol Miller, Marjory Himes, Flo Summerville, Mlle. Tamara, Ann Dolores, Betty Castle. *Mistinguett Girls from the Casino de Paris*: Gaby Lorette, Nadjy Gallier, Zuzu Raymonne, Carmen Rosella, Jeanette Fleury, Bebe Cliquot, Ruby La Croix, Pepita Armadilla, Ninon Elysees, Pauline Pettibois, Babette Brigon, Olga Treskoff. *Moulin Rouge Boys*: Ralph Reader, Frank Wallace, William Brainard, Arthur Appel, Gordon Baker, Jack Oakie, Clinton Tustin, Josph Hughes.

Act 1, Scene 1: Conservatory of the Longuebois Villa in Paris. *Scene 2*: In front of the Moulin Rouge. *Scene 3*: Love Is Like a Pinwheel. *Scene 4*: The Gold Room in the Moulin Rouge. *Scene 5*: Organdy Days. *Scene 6*: The White Room.
Act 2, Scene 1: Stage of the Moulin Rouge. *Scene 2*: Inspiration. *Scene 3*: Damn Clever, These Chinese. *Scene 4*: A Creation of Mlle. Mistinguett. *Scene 5*: Out Front. *Scene 6*: The Main Cabaret. *Scene 7*: Venus Arising from the Sea. *Scene 8*: Milady's Fan. *Scene 9*: Pianologue. *Scene 10*: The Garden of the Longuebois Villa.

ACT 1
Scene 1
"I Loved Her Best of All"
  E. Baker, Ensemble
"Our Emblem Is the Lily"
  C. Lean, Puritans
"Garden of Love"
  T. Doner, E. Baker
  (*Music by* Jean Schwartz. *Lyrics by* Tot Seymour.)
"Let's Have a Good Time"
  F. Dobson, E. Leslie, E. Baker, M. Leach, M. Mason, E. Eaton
    Rose Longuebois: E. Baker. *Mme. Hortense Longuebois*: M. Allen. *Professor Honoré Longuebois*: C. Lean. *Esther*: M. Leach. *Aunt Dorothy*: M. Carruthers. *Georges Tremeres*: F. Dobson. *Jules Dubec*: T. Doner. *Phoebe*: M. Manley. *Amie*: M. Mason. *Harry*: E. Leslie. *Cyrus [later Pussyfoot] Stubbons*: L. Hearn.
Scene 2
"Dear Old Moulin Rouge"[146]
  C. Lean, Moulin Rouge Girls
Specialty Dance
  G. Beverly
    Ballet Girl: G. Beverly.
Scene 3
"Love Is Like a Pinwheel"
  F. Dobson, T. Doner, F. Williams, Vannessi
Scene 4
Ballet Dance
  M. Mason

[146]Dropped during the run.

"Day Dreams"[147]
  V. Lavrova
"Chiquette"
  Mistinguett, Spanish Girls
  (*Music by* J. Fred Coots, Jean Schwartz. *Lyrics by* McElbert Moore.)
"Su'l Boul'vard"
  Mistinguett
Spanish Dance
  Mistinguett, C. Howard
Dance de Volstead
  C. Mac
"Innocent Eyes"
  C. Mayfield, C. Lean, Serpentine Girls
  (*Music by* J. Fred Coots, Jean Schwartz. *Lyrics by* McElbert Moore.)
    Frances: F. Williams. *Lolita*: Vannessi. *Jules*: T. Doner. *Georges*: F. Dobson. *Miss Fleetfoot*: M. Mason. *Tortellini*: F. Byron. *La Truffe*: V. Lavrova. *Chiquette*: Mistinguett. *Dorothy*: D. Bruce. *Harry*: E. Leslie. *Esther*: M. Leach. *Fauvel*: J. E. Phillips. *Nanette*: M. Cairns. *Berlitz*: V. Reigel. *Fan Fan*: C. Mac. *First Model*: M. Cairns. *Second Model*: P. Neal. *Third Model*: C. Miller. *Gaston*: C. Howard. *Ninon*: C. Mayfield.
Scene 5
"Organdy Days"
  G. Bowman, Mistinguett, E. Leslie, Society Girls and Boys
  (*Music by* Jean Schwartz. *Lyrics by* Tot Seymour.)
    The Prima Donna: G. Bowman.
Scene 6
"Peacock Strut"
  Vannessi
"Yankee Jazz"
  F. Williams, F. Dobson, G. Beverly, T. Doner, Vannessi, E. Leslie, E. Eaton, H. White, Mistinguett, Entire Company
    Miss Rolls Royce: E. Eaton. *A Russian*: H. A. White.

ACT 2
Scene 1
"Africa"
  F. Williams, F. Dobson, G. Beverly, T. Doner
  (*Music by* James Hanley. *Lyrics by* Henry Creamer.)
African Specialty
  T. Doner, F. Williams, F. Dobson, G. Beverly, Radium Mask Girls
Hula Dance
  Vannessi
Scene 2
"Inspiration"
  V. Lavrova
Dance of Beauty
  M. Mason
    The Living Tableaux: M. Cairns, H. Dahlia, M. Himes, P. Mermont, C. Miller, L. Sharpe, P. Neal, L. Hellekson, F. Shepard.
Scene 3
"Damn Clever, These Chinese"
  C. Howard, M. Leach, L. Hearn
Scene 4
"En Douce"[148]
  Mistinguett
Apache Dance (created by Mistinguett)
  Mistinguett, J. DeFay, E. Leslie
    Zizi: Mistinguett. *Paul*: E. Leslie. *The Coalheaver*: J. DeFay. *The Mother*: M. Carruthers. *The Father*: F. Byron. *The Dog*: Alfred.
Scene 5
A Few Fast Steppers
  Winter Garden Girls
    A Few Fast Steppers: E. Eaton, M. Warner, A. Dawson, N. Gould, V. Watson, G. Smith, A. Boulden, D. Mantell, M. Thompson, F. Courtney, K. Hill, P. Gillespie, R. Hamilton, B. Williams, B. Heyman, H. White.
Scene 6
"Hula, Hula, Sailor Man"[149]
  F. Williams

[147]Dropped during the run.
[148]Dropped during the run.
[149]Replaced during the run by Three Songs

Perfume Waltz
  Vannessi, T. Doner
"Innocent Eyes" (reprise)
  Mistinguett, L. Hearn
"Spoony Croony Tune"[150]
  C. Lean, C. Mayfield
  (Society Gossip by Cecil Lean.)
    Commissionaire: J. E. Phillips. *Marie*: S. Bennett.

Scene 7
  "Surrounded by the Girls"
    E. Leslie, Dancing Girls
      Artist Model Tableaux: M. Cairns, C. Miller, H. Dahlia, M. Himes, P. Neal,
      L. Sharpe, P. Mermont, L. Stone.

Scene 8
  "(Behind) Milady's Fan"
    Mistinguett, G. Bowman, French Fan Girls

Scene 9
  Pianologue
    E. Baker, Society Girls

Scene 10
  Finale
    Entire Company

THE GRAND STREET FOLLIES (1924)

1924.14

A Musical Revue in Two Acts, 12 Scenes[151]. Book (sketches) and lyrics by Agnes Morgan. Music composed and arranged by Lily Hyland. Dances staged by Albert Carroll. Costumes and setting by Aline Bernstein. Staged under the technical direction of John F. Roche. Masks by Jo Davidson. Unicorn's head by Marjorie Content. Produced by The Neighborhood Playhouse (Helen Arthur, Business Manager). Opened 20 May 1924 at the Neighborhood Playhouse and closed 30 November 1924 after 172 performances.

CAST: Helen Arthur, Albert Carroll, Aline MacMahon, John F. Roche, Esther Mitchell, Dan Walker, Agnes Morgan, John Scott, Lily Lubell, George Bratt, Betty Prescott, Edmond Rickett, Joanna Roos, Edgar Kent, Florence Levine, Junius Matthews, Bertha Tuite, Adrienne Morrison, Martin Wolfson.
  Ensemble: Polaire Weissmann, Joanna Roos, Evan Mosher, Edla Frankau, Ann Schmidt, Sophie Hurwitz, Grace D. Hooper, William Stahl, Sophie Bernsohn, Paula Trueman, Edmond Kent, Hadra Spelvin, George Heller, Philip Mann, Sol Friedman, Ella Markowitz.

ACT 1[152]

Scene 1
  Opening Remarks
    President of the Super-Drama League: H. Arthur.

Scene 2
  Prologue
    Scene: On Board the *S. S. Algonquin*, outward bound for Three Mile Limit Bar.
    John, the Steward: J. F. Roche. *Percy*: E. Rickett. *Heywood*: G. Bratt. *Aleck*: J. Matthews. *Kenneth*: D. Walker. *Bob*: A. Carroll. *Ludwig*: E. Kent. *Stark*: E. Mosher. *First Page*: E. Frankau. *Last Page*: B. Tuite.

Scene 3
  The Shewing-Up of Jo Leblanco (A melodrama of wild frontier life among the cut-rates of New York-according to Gee B. Pshaw)

  F. Williams
  ["Tweet, Tweet"
  "Red-Hot Mama"
    (*Music and Lyrics by* Gilbert Wells, Bud Cooper, Fred Rose.)
  "Hard-Hearted Hannah"]
    (*Music by* Milton Ager, Robert Bigelow. *Lyrics by* Charles Bates, Jack Yellen.)]
[150]Dropped during the run.
[151]The second in the annual series of satirical revues which began at the Neighborhood Playhouse Off-Broadway in 1922.
[152]The running order was revised during the run. Added to Act 1 during the run:
  An Act from Vaudeville (Written and arranged by Dan Walker)
    The Ingenue: L. Lubell. *The Juvenile*: D. Walker.
      Time: Any day, twice a day. *Place*: Any vaudeville theatre, anywhere.

Scene: Basement of Black & White's Drug Store.
  B. Brady, the Sheriff: E. Kent. *Jo Leblanco*, a ticket speculator: P. Mann. *Cohenheimer*, for the P.M.A.: J. F. Roche. *Merton of the Movies*: A. Carroll. *Sadie Thompson*, of 'Rain': D. Walker. *Minnie*, of 'Expressing Willie': A. MacMahon. *Jurors (5)*: Tyson McBride, foreman: E. Mosher. *Cyrano de Bergerac*: G. Bratt. *Will Rogers*: W. Stahl. *Doug*: J. Scott. *Mary*: L. Lubell. A *Policeman*: J. Mathews. A *Scrub-Woman*: A. Morrison.

Scene 4
  Not So Long, Long Ago[153]
    The Lady: L. Lubell. *The Gentleman*: J. Scott.

Scene 5
  Sinfonica Domestica Triangula (Suite: Town and Country)
    Performed for the first time by the ensemble of The International Imposters Guild
      Conductor: E. Rickett. *Members of Ensemble*: P. Weissmann, E. Frankau, E. Mosher, J. Roos. *Soloist*: G. D. Hooper.

Scene 6
  "Play the Queen, or Old Irish Poker"
    A mediaeval musical comedy awarded the first Ignoble Prize as written by Poet Yeats and performed by Strolling Players in Ireland during the 14th century showing unmistakably that there is nothing new under the sun.
      Scene a: A street at dusk. *Scene b*: Throne Room of the Castle.
      First Wall Street Poet: G. Bratt. *Second Wall Street Poet*: P. Mann. *The Royal Attorney-General*: J. F. Roche. *Secretary of the Interior of the Castle*: M. Wolfson. *The Senators*: J. Mathews, E. Kent, W. Stahl, E. Mosher, G. D. Hooper. *The Maids-in-Waiting*: L. Lubell, A. Schmidt, F. Levine, J. Roos, B. Prescott, S. Hurwitz, S. Bernsohn. *The Real Queen*: P. Trueman. *The Unicorn*: J. Scott. *The False Queen*: A. MacMahon. *The Prince of Ails*: A. Carroll.

ACT 2

Scene 1
  A Business Conference
    Philip Cruller: E. Rickett. *Arthur Popkins*: H. Arthur.

Scene 2
  Who Killed the Ghost?
    The Greatest Mystery Story of the Ages with this dazzling cast:
      John Barrymore as Hamlet: A. Carroll. *Fanny Brice as Ophelia*: B. Prescott. *David Warfield as Shylock*: E. Kent. *Jane Cowl as Juliet*: A. Morrison. *Louise Closser Hale as Her Nurse*: P. Weissmann. *Claire Eames as Lady Macbeth*: F. Levine. *Ghost of Hamlet's Father*: E. Rickett. *Gallagher and Shean as the Grave-Diggers*: G. Bratt, J. Matthews. *Valentino as the Player King*: J. Scott. *Pola Negri as the Player Queen*: P. Trueman. (*Setting by* John Corbin.)

Scene 3
  "An English Favorite"
    (*Lyrics by* Ann MacDonald.)
      Gerty: A. MacMahon

Scene 4
  "The South Sea Islands According to Broadway"
    (*Lyrics by* Dan Walker.)
      The Sailor: M. Wolfson. *Gilded Gilda*: A. Schmidt.

Scene 5
  A Recital at Town Hall (*by* Dan Walker)
    Elsie Janis: D. Walker. *At the Piano*: E. Rickett.

Scene 6
  Epilogue: The Verdict
    Scene: Interior of Geddes Cathedral.
      Guests of Honor: *Mr. John T. King*, philanthropist: E. Rickett. *Emily Stevens*: A. Carroll. *Joan of Arc*: J. Roos. *Queen Victoria*: P. Weissmann. *Carpentier*: W. Stahl. *Beatrice Lillie*: A. Morrison. *Tondelayo*: L. Lubell. *Eva Le Gallienne*: A. Schmidt. *Miller & Lyles*: G. Bratt, D. Walker. *Two Angels*: F. Levine, S. Bernsohn.

Finale
  (*Music by* Max Ewing. *Lyrics by* Albert Carroll.)

ROUND THE TOWN

1924.15

A Musical Revue in Two Acts, 23 Scenes. Sketches by Herman Mankiewicz, S. Kay Kaufman, George S. Kaufman, Marc Connelly. Assembled and staged by Herman J. Mankiewicz and S. Jay Kaufman. Dances arranged by Lew Leslie. Scenery by Brunton Studios. Costumes designed by Gertrude Johnson. Orchestra under the direction of Oscar Radin. Orchestrations by Stephen Jones, Arthur H. Guttman, Will Vodery and E. Bial. Produced by

---

[153]Dropped during the run.

Herman J. Mankiewicz and S. Jay Kaufman. Opened 21 May 1924 at the Century Roof and closed 31 May 1924 after 15 performances.

CAST: HARRY FOX, HEYWOOD BROUN, ELISE BONWIT, IRENE DELROY, JULIUS TANNEN, JAY VELIE, JANET VELIE, GLORIA FOY, CHARLES CRAFTS, JACK HALEY, MABEL STANFORD, ROSE ROLANDO, TOM NIP, ROBERTA MEDRANO.

Girls of the Ensemble: Marcia Mack, Vera Trett, Zena Trett, Truly Jones, Francisca Carmen, Marguerite Carmen, Marion Grey, Blanche Field, Geneva Price, Clair Carroll, Geneva Duker, Alice Duker, Mildred Lunnay, Frances Ney, Dorothy Germaine, Dorothy Hardern, Betty Hill, Mae Reeves, Marie Bennett, Helen Gladding, Mabel Stanford, Cletas Edgar, Florence Ashton, Grace Cronin.

ACT 1
Scene 1

Mirrors of Manhattan (*by* S. Jay Kaufman)
J. Tannen, the Customers

Scene 2

War and Peace
J. Haley, C. Crafts, C. Hill, E. Bonwit, Company
(An Allegorical Ballet by Herman J. Mankiewicz.)
Argument—Sloth and Malice, Handmaidens of Idleness, are having a fine time picking wings off flies, when they are discovered by Ingenious and Ingenuous, the twin sisters. Things go on like this for some time, but eventually the dragon dies in a pool of his own blood and the faint dawn of Liberty is visible in the West.

Scene 3

"If One of Us Was You, Dear"
Janet Velie, Jay Velie
(*Music by* Jay Velie. *Lyrics by* George S. Kaufman.)
Scene: Just a Corner of Old Hyde Park, London, England.

Scene 4

She Ordered Lobster (*by* Herman J. Mankiewicz)
H. Fox

Scene 5

"Four Characters in Search of an Historian" (*by* Mortimer E. Freehof)
[Male quartet in burlesque]
Jay Velie, C. Crafts, J. Haley, C. Hill

Scene 6

"Wallflower"
G. Foy, Girls
(*Music by* Alfred Nathan. *Lyrics by* Ned Wever. *Screens designed by* John Wenger.)

Scene 7

It Seems to Me
H. Broun

Scene 8

"Romeo, Juliet, Johnny and Jane"
(*Conceived and Staged by* Joseph Santley. *Music by* Victor Herbert. *Lyrics by* Dorothy Parker.)
Romeo: Jay Velie. *Juliet*: Janet Velie. *Johnny*: J. Haley. *Jane*: G. Foy.

Scene 9

"It's Good for You to Exercise Your Mind"
H. Fox
(*Music by* Arthur H. Samuels. *Lyrics by* Dorothy Parker.)

Scene 10

"I've Never Been Kept Waiting"
I. Delroy, C. Crafts, M. Stanford, C. Hill

Scene 11

"Liza Jane"
J. Haley
(*Music by* Alfred Nathan. *Lyrics by* Ned Wever.)

Dance
J. Haley, E. Bonwit, T. Nip, G. Foy, Company

ACT 2
Scene 1

"Chiquita"
C. Crafts
(*Music and Lyrics by* Walter Donaldson.)

Dance
R. Rolanda, R. Medrano

Scene 2

A Word on Serious Drama
J. Tannen

Scene 3

Scene from 'Ghosts' (*by* Henrik Ibsen)[in the style of Mack Sennett]
(*Mrs. Alving*: Janet Velie. *Her Son*, a Painter: Jay Velie.)

Scene 4

"I Wonder Why That Glow-Worm Winks His Eye at Me"
I. Delroy, Girls
(*Music by* Herbert Stothart. *Lyrics by* Oscar Hammerstein II.)

Scene 5

An Evening at the Movies, Oh, So Long Ago
C. Crafts

Scene 6

Beggar Off Horseback (*by* George S. Kaufman and Marc Connelly)
[A burlesque of their own play 'Beggar on Horseback']
Neil McRae: H. Fox. *Albert*: J. Haley. *Cynthia*: G. Foy. *Gladys*: Janet Velie. *A Derelict*: Jay Velie. *A Dream Girl*: R. Rolando. *A Lot of Reporters*: E. Bonwit.

Scene 7

Before the Curtains
J. Tannen

Scene 8

Etcetera (*by* Robert E. Sherwood)
G. Foy

Scene 9

The Girl from WJZ (*by* Marc Connelly)
Regisseur: J. Tannen. *The Hero*: C. Crafts. *The Heroine*: R. Rolanda. *The Comedian*: J. Haley. *The Father of the Heroine*: Jay Velie. *Maiden Aunts*: Janet Velie, E. Bonwit. *Elsie*: G. Foy. And the Girls.

Scene 10

Raising the Old
H. Fox

Scene 11

"Save a Kiss for Rainy Weather" (Save a Kiss for a Rainy Day)
H. Fox, G. Foy
(*Music by* Will Ortmann, Richard A. Whiting. *Lyrics by* Raymond. B. Egan.)

Scene 12

Finale
Entire Company

KEEP KOOL

1924.16

A Singing—Dancing—Laughing (Musical) Revue in Two Acts, 23 Scenes. Book (sketches) and lyrics by Paul Gerard Smith. Music by Jack Frost. Dialogue directed by Harry Crawford. Dances and ensembles staged by Earl Lindsay. Entire production supervised by Edgar MacGregor. Art director, Walter Harvey. Scenery designed by H. Robert Law. Costumes designed by Kiviette. Orchestra under the direction of Oscar Loraine. Special orchestra arrangements by Albert Chiffarelli. Produced by E. K. Nadel. Opened 22 May 1924 at the Morosco Theatre, moved 7 July 1924 to the Globe Theatre, moved 1 September 1924 to the Earl Carroll Theatre, and closed 27 September 1924 after 148 performances.

CAST: HAZEL DAWN, CHARLES KING, JOHNNY DOOLEY, JESSIE MAKER, DICK KEENE, HAL PARKER, INA WILLIAMS, EDWARD TIERNEY, HELEN FABLES, LON HASCALL, ANN BUTLER, RITA HOWARD, DICK KEENE, JAMES DONNELLY, BELLE DeMONDE, WILLIAM REDFORD, JAMES KELSO, WALTER MORRISON, JACK WALDRON, WILLIAM HOWARD, VIOLA BLANEY.

Keep Kool Cuties: Dorothy Van Alst, Lillian Harnack, Mildred Stewart, Maerna Grady, Ethelyn Tillman, Dorothy Thattell, Dorothy Tiller, Ruth Laird, Helen Paine, Claire Miller, Ruby Stevens, Isabelle Mason, Val DeMar, Mimi Tattersall, Lucille Moore, Ethel Bryant.

ACT 1[154]

---

[154]The running order was revised during the run. Added during run:
Miscast (Act 2)
A Prima Donna Wife: B. DeMonde. *A Juggler Affinity*: J. Kelso. *An Acrobatic Husband*: J. Dooley. *A Maid from the Follies*: V. Blaney.
A New Twist (Act 2)
R. Howard
Nobody's Baby (translated from the French)(Act 2)
Toinette: H. Dawn. *Marcelle*: B. DeMonde. *Gaspard*: W. Redford. *Louis*: W. Howard. *Pierre*: H. Parker. *Mignonette*: V. Blaney.

Scene 1

"The Broadway Battle Cry"
Keep Kool Cuties

Scene 2

The Voice of the People
Scene: Times Square.
A Leader: H. Parker. *First Voice*: D. Keene. *Second Voice*: J. Donnelly. *Third Voice*: E. Tierney. *Fourth Voice*: J. Waldron. *A Girl*: H. Paine. *A Welcome Stranger*: L. Hascall.

Scene 3

Justifiable Homicide (in 8 Episodes)
Introduced by D. Keene. *Interpreted by* W. Howard, H. Parker, W. Redford, L. Hascall, J. Kelso, B. DeMonde, I. Williams.

Scene 4

"My Calicoquette" (Calicoquette)
E. Tierney, J. Donnelly
Assisted by H. Fables, R. Howard, Keep Kool Calicoquettes.

Scene 5

A Protest is registered by Miss Hazel Dawn
In a Taxicab
A Man About Town: C. King. *A Girl in a Hurry*: H. Dawn.

Scene 6

At the Stage Door
Good Time Charlie: C. King. *Straw Hat Johnny*: J. Dooley. *A Stage Manager*: H. Parker.

Scene 7

"Shall I Sing It Now"[155]
I. Williams, D. Keene

Scene 8

"Dandelion Time"
C. King, J. Maker
Assisted by D. Van Alst, R. Laird, Dandelionettes.

Scene 9

English As It Is Spoke
The Boy: J. Dooley. *The Girl*: I. Williams. *The Waiter*: W. Howard.

Scene 10

With Apologies To
Scene: A Corner in the Friars' Club.
George M. Cohan: C. King. *Avery Hopwood*: H. Parker. *Eugene O'Neill*: J. Donnelly. *William Squibbs*: W. Morrison.

A Kitchen Somewhere (Apologies to Eugene O'Neill)
Sloppy Jones: L. Hascall. *Mrs. Sloppy Jones*: A. Butler. *Mollie Rayne*: H. Dawn.

A Room Adjoining a Boudoir [later A Living Room] (Apologies to Avery Hopwood)
Mr. Jones: J. Kelso. *Mrs. Jones*: B. DeMonde. *A Collector*: J. Dooley. *A Business Man*: W. Redford. *A Maid*: C. Miller. *Dora*: D. Van Alst. *Agnes*: R. Stevens.

A Brooklyn Parlor (Apologies to George M. Cohan)
Nellie: J. Maker. *Jerry*: J. Waldron. *O'Shaughnessy*: W. Howard. *A Live Wire*: E. Tierney.

Scene 11

"Painted Rose"
A. Butler
An Old-Timer: L. Hascall. *Sightseers*: H. Parker, B. DeMonde.

Scene 12

The White Carnival: "How You Gonna Keep Kool?"
C. King, J. Maker

Finale
Entire Company

ACT 2

Scene 1

"Gypsy-Anna"
H. Dawn, C. King, Keep Kool Cuties
(*Special orchestra arrangements by* Albert Chiffarelli.)

Scene 2

Dancing Doubles
R. Howard, H. Fables

Scene 3

Beautiful But Dumb
A Model Evening Gown: B. DeMonde. *A Model Negligee*: D. Van Alst. *A Model Fur Coat*: C. Miller. *A Model Sport Suit*: J. Maker. *A Stroller*: J. Dooley.

"In They Go and Out They Come"
D. Keene, W. Howard, H. Parker, W. Redford, J. Kelso, E. Tierney, J. Waldron, J. Donnelly, The Poor Little Ritz Girls

"The Fifth Avenue Stride"
E. Tierney, J. Donnelly, D. Van Alst

Scene 4

The Yellow Peril
The Stage Manager: H. Parker. *The Author*: W. Morrison. *Ralph St. Clair*: J. Kelso. *Otokieuma*: J. Dooley. *Vera Van Vechtan*: H. Dawn.

Scene 5

"Nellie Kelly"
C. King

Scene 6

A Vision of India: "(By the) Shalimar"
W. Redford
Danced by H. Fables, the Maids of the Shalimar.
Burlesqued by E. Tierney, J. Donnelly.

Scene 7

"Fairy Tales"
J. Maker

Little Miss Muffet
Miss Muffet: A. Butler. *The Spider*: J. Waldron.

Red Riding Hood
The Wolf: E. Tierney. *Red Riding Hood*: R. Howard.

Scene 8

"Out Where the Pavement Ends"
C. King, H. Dawn, Keep Kool Cuties
Scene: The Bungalow.

Scene 9

The Daguerre Types[156]
I. Williams, D. Keene

Scene 10

"The Irish Sheik"
J. Dooley, Keep Kool Cuties

Scene 11

The Violin Nuttist[157]
O. Loraine

Scene 12

"Ring in the Joys"
Entire Company

Own Your Own Home (by arrangement with Minerva Courtney and Harry Irwin)(Act 2)

The Violent Ward (Act 2)
A Keeper: L. Hascall. *An Inmate*: J. Dooley. *His Friends*: H. Parker, J. Kelso, W. Morrison.

"Love in the Suburbs" (Act 2)
J. Kelso, B. DeMonde

[155]Replaced by:
"Beautiful Baby"
William Wayne, Ruth Warren

[156]Dropped after opening.
[157]Dropped after opening.

Bea Lillie in CHARLOT'S REVUE OF 1924 (Photo: White Studio)
Billy Rose Theatre Collection, New York Public Library for the Performing Arts

FLOSSIE

A Musical Comedy in Two Acts. Book and music by Armand Robi. Lyrics by Ralph Murphy. Staged by Armand Robi. Dances arranged by Jack Connors. Settings designed by Nicholas Yellenti. Costumes by Vanity Fair Costume Company. Lighting by Ben Leffler. Paul Specht's Lido Venice Orchestra conducted by Harold Lewis. Produced by Charles Mulligan. Opened 3 June 1924 at the Lyric Theatre and closed 28 June 1924 after 31 performances.

CAST (in order of appearance): *Marie*, a French maid: Jeanne Danjou. *Mr. Van Cortland*: HARRY McNAUGHTON. *Nellie*, a salesgirl: Mildred Kent. *Mildred*, a salesgirl: Viola Boles. *Ki Ki*, a salesgirl: Trix Taylor. *Sally*, a salesgirl: Jane McCurdy. *Irene*, a salesgirl: Paula Lee. *Adrienne*, a salesgirl: Betty Garson. *Poppy*, a salesgirl: Mildred Brown. *Mary*, a salesgirl: Helen Warren. *Liza*, a salesgirl: Mary O'Rourke. *Elsie*, a salesgirl: Nellie Roberts. *Jane*, a salesgirl: Carl Seidler. *Bessie*: ALICE CAVANAUGH. *Flossie*: DORIS DUNCAN. *Archie*: SYDNEY GRANT. *Senor Don Ribeiro*: ROBERT MAMELUCH. *Tommy*: JACK WALDRON. *Mrs. Van Cortland*: Rose Kessner. *Peggy*: Jane Van Rein. *Flick and Flock, Salesmen*: HANDERS and MILLIS. *Uncle Ezra*: SHEP CAMP. *Chummy*: EDWARD FETHERSTON.

Act 1: A Studio Apartment adjoining a Fifth Avenue Millinery Establishment. 9:30 P.M.

Act 2: Next morning, 8:30 A.M.

ACT 1[1]

"I Want to Be a Santa Claus"
  H. McNaughton, J. Danjou, M. Kent, Salesgirls
"Flossie"
  D. Duncan, A. Cavanaugh, M. Kent, J. Van Rein, Salesgirls
"I'm in Wonderland"
  D. Duncan, A. Cavanaugh
"Now Is the Time"
  D. Duncan, J. Waldron, Salesgirls
"That's in My Line"
  Handers and Millis
"Poogie-Woo"
  A. Cavanaugh, S. Grant
"Walla-Walla"
  S. Camp, E. Fetherston, Entire Company
"When Things Go Wrong"
  D. Duncan, S. Grant, Entrie Company
"Fraid Cat"[2]
  J. Waldron, Salesgirls
  (*Music by* Harold Lewis.
  Lyrics by Ralph Murphy.)

ACT 2

"Blind Man Buff"
  A. Cavanaugh, Handers and Millis
"The First Is (the) Last"
  D. Duncan, E. Fetherston, Salesgirls
"Just Another New Step"
  J. Waldron, Salesgirls
  (*Music by* Harold Lewis.
  Lyrics by Ralph Murphy.)
"The Battle Cry of Freedom"[3]
  S. Grant, S. Camp, E. Fetherston, H. McNaughton
"I'm in Wonderland" (reprise)
  S. Grant, A. Cavanaugh
Finale
  Entire Company

---

[1]Not in program but performed in the show per reviews: "From Under Your Hat"
[2]Dropped after opening.
[3]Dropped after opening.

ZIEGFELD FOLLIES OF 1924

A Musical Revue in Two Acts, 22 Scenes[4]. Dialogue (sketches) by William Anthony McGuire and Will Rogers. Music by Victor Herbert, Raymond Hubbell, Dave Stamper, Harry Tierney, James Hanley, Dr. Albert Szirmai [Sirmay]. Lyrics by Gene Buck, Joseph J. McCarthy. Staged by Julian Mitchell. Tableaux devised and staged by Ali Ben Haggin. Costume designs by Charles LeMaire. Scenery by Frank Gates and Edward A. Morange, Ludwig Kainer, John Wenger, H. Robert Law Studios. Orchestra under the direction of Victor Baravelle. Orchestrations by (Robert) Russell Bennett, Fred Barry, Harold Sanford, Steve Jones. Produced by Florenz Ziegfeld. Opened 24 June 1924 at the New Amsterdam Theatre, closing 29 October 1924 after 147 performances. Fall Edition (see separate listing below) opened 30 October 1924 and closed 7 March 1925 after 148 performances. Spring edition (billed as ZIEGFELD FOLLIES OF 1925, see separate listing below) opened 10 March 1925 and closed 4 July 1925 after 127 performances. Summer Edition (see separate listing below) opened 6 July 1925 and closed 19 September 1925 after 88 performances. Total of 510 performances.

CAST: WILL ROGERS, VIVIENNE SEGAL, ANN PENNINGTON, IRVING FISHER, EDNA LEEDOM, LUPINO LANE, TOM LEWIS, PHIL RYLEY, LINA BASQUETTE, EVELYN LAW, THE KELO BROTHERS, IMOGENE WILSON, GEORGE OLSEN'S BAND, MARTHA LORBER, BERNICE ACKERMAN, MAE DAW, GLORIA DAWN, BRANDON TYNAN, ALF JAMES, HILDA FERGUSON.
THE TILLER GIRLS: Empire Girls: Ziegfeld Girls: Misses Anastasia Reilly, Hurley, Nally, Francis, Doris Lloyd, Cynthia Cambridge, Andrea, Martha Pierre, McGee, Rasche, McDonald, Catherine Burke, Evelyn Goodwin, Sheldon, Calame, Brown, Marian Benda, Littlefield, Francis Reveaux, Constance McLaughlin, Cricket Wooten, Gladys Loftus, Ellsworth, Dorothy Leet, Wildo, Alma Drange, Johnson, Carlton, Byron, Julian, Martin, Boatwright, *Gentlemen of the Ensemble*: Messrs. Jack Shannon, Arthur Brown, Mark Truscott, Frank Lambert, Al Ochs, Serge Pernikoff.

ACT 1[5]
Scene 1
  The Plot (*by* Gene Buck) (*Music by* Raymond Hubbell.)
    Four Guys: Messrs. Shannon, Brown, Truscott, Lambert. *The Gal*: G. Dawn.
    The Hero: I. Fisher. *Miss Follies*: M. Daw.
    (*Follies curtain painted by* Ludwig Kainer of Vienna.)
Scene 2
  The Beauty Float (*Arranged by* Ali Ben Haggin. *Scene painted by* Ludwig Kainer.)
    M. Lorber, H. Ferguson, B. Compton, with Misses Daw, Reveaux, Cambridge, Francis, Halley, Benda, Ackerman, Goodwin, Rolfe, Wilson, Andrea, Lloyd
Scene 3
  "Adoring You"
    V. Segal, I. Fisher
    (*Music by* Harry Tierney. *Lyrics by* Joseph J. McCarthy.)
    Scene: Curtains.
Scene 4
  Bradbury Ranch, Oklahoma
    Stella: M. Lorber. *Jim Bradbury*: B. Tynan. *Percy*: L. Lane. *Jim Watts*: A. James.
    Sheriff: P. Ryley. *Tom*: T. Lewis. *Alfalfa Doolittle*: W. Rogers.
  "The Great Wide Open Spaces"
    E. Leedom
    (*Music by* Dave Stamper. *Lyrics by* Gene Buck. *Scene painted by* Ludwig Kainer.

---

[4]The Eighteenth Annual edition of the series of musical revues which began under Ziegfeld's auspices in 1907.
[5]The running order was revised during the run. Added during the run:
  Dance (added to Lonely Little Melody, Act 2)
    L. Basquette, Virginia King (violin)
  Shadowgraph (Shadow Pantomime) (Act 2)
    ("This is the number where you use the Follies-Scope glasses which have been handed you with program, the RED glass to cover the right eye. Soiling the glasses in any way will spoil the effect entirely. Optical Illusion by Laurens Hammond, U. S. Patent Number 1,481,006.")
Interpolated during the run, per published sheet music:
  "San" (also in GEORGE WHITE'S SCANDALS OF 1923)
    G. Olsen and His Music
    (*Music and Lyrics by* Lindsay McPhail and Walter Michels.)

"All Pepped Up"
    L. Lane
    (*Music by* Harry Tierney. *Lyrics by* Joseph J. McCarthy.)
Dance
    E. Law
"The Old Town Band"
    E. Leedom, L. Lane
    (*Music by* Harry Tierney. *Lyrics by* Joseph J. McCarthy.)
    Accompanied by George Olsen's Band.

Scene 5
"Dance Different"
    Kelo Brothers
    Scene: A Street.

Scene 6
A Couple of Senators (*by* Will Rogers)
    Scene: Washington, D.C.
    A Girl: M. Daw. *Senator Doolittle*: W. Rogers. *Senator Lodge*: B. Tynan.
    (*Scene painted by* Robert Law Studios.)

Scene 7
Edna Leedom[6]
    Scene: Curtains.

Scene 8
"Biminy"
    A. Pennington, Hooch Girls, George Olsen's Band
    (*Music by* Dave Stamper. *Lyrics by* Gene Buck. *Scene painted by* John Wenger.)

Scene 9
Chloride Gas Room Capitol: Investigating Investigations (*by* Will Rogers)
    Senator Doolittle: W. Rogers. *Senator Useless*: P. Ryley. *Senator Stall*: B. Tynan.
    Senator Chinchbug: T. Lewis. *One of the Help*: A. James.
    (*Scene painted by* Robert Law Studios.)

Scene 10
"The Beauty Contest"
    I. Fisher, M. Daw
    (*Music by* Victor Herbert and Harry Tierney. *Lyrics by* Joseph J. McCarthy.)
    Scene: A Garden.
    Eve: Miss Halley. *Brunhilde*: Miss Nally, Miss Reilly, Miss Francis.
    Cleopatra: Miss Lloyd, Miss Beardsley. *Gwenevieve*: Miss Cambridge, Miss Andrea. *Eloise*: Miss Pierce, Miss West, Miss Rasche. *Isabelle*: Miss McDonald, Miss Burke. *Gabrielle*: Miss Goodwin, Miss Sheldon. *Nell Gwynne*: Miss Ackerman, Miss Allis, Miss Brown. *DuBarry*: Miss Benda, Miss Littlefield. *Racamier*: Miss Reveaux, Miss McLaughlin. *Lady Hamilton*: Miss Carlton, Miss Wooten, Miss Byron. *Eugenie*: Miss Julian, Miss Martin. *The Merry Whirl*: L. Basquette. *Miss New York*: I. Wilson. *The Ziegfeld Girl*: E. Law. *Typical Girl of Today*: A. Pennington. And the Empire and Tiller Girls.
    (*Scene painted by* Ludwig Kainer. *Costumes designed by* Ben Ali Haggin.)

ACT 2
Scene 1
[Cane Dance]
    London Empire Girls
    (*Music by* Dave Stamper. [*Staged by* John Tiller.])

Scene 2
Pearl of the East
    (*by* Ben Ali Haggin. *Arrangement with special music by* Raymond Hubbell.)
    The Pearl: M. Lorber. *A Mountain Slave*: H. Ferguson. *A Dancer*: D. Lloyd. *Slaves*: B. Compton, L. Carlton, M. Wilson, C. Cambridge. *Dancers*: B. Halley, A. Rolfe, M. Pierre. *Musicians*: V. Beardsley, D. Leet, B. Ackerman. *A Tartar Prince*: S. Perkinoff. *His Warriors*: A. Ochs, F. Lambert, M. Truscott.

Scene 3
"A Night in June"
    L. Lane
    (*Music by* Raymond Hubbell. *Lyrics by* Gene Buck.)

Scene 4
Will Rogers[7]
    Scene: Curtains.

Scene 5
"Lonely Little Melody"
    I. Fisher, V. Segal, Jazz Girls
    (*Music by* Dave Stamper. *Lyrics by* Gene Buck.)
    Scene: Jazzland. (*Scene painted by* John Wenger.)

Scene 6
[Rope Dance]
    Tiller Girls
    (*Music by* Victor Herbert. [*Staged by* Lawrence Tiller.])
Belasco Sketch
    E. Leedom, L. Lane, B. Tynan, P. Ryley, A. James

Scene 7
"(I'd Like to Put You in a) Big Glass Case"[8]
    A. Pennington, L. Lane
    (*Music by* Harry Tierney. *Lyrics by* Joseph J. McCarthy.)

Scene 8
The Piano Next Door
    Clarence: L. Lane. *His Wife*: E. Leedom.
    His Landlady: G. Eller. *His Neighbor*: A. James.
    His Friend: P. Ryley. *His Baby*: Himself.

Scene 9
A Victor Herbert Fantasy (*Opening Poem by* Gene Buck.)
    An Old Musician: B. Tynan.
(a) "Gypsy Love Song" (from *THE FORTUNE TELLER*)
    I. Fisher, Gypsy Girls, Misses Carlton, Goodwin, Knowlton, McDonald, Nally, Wilson
    (*Music by* Victor Herbert. *Lyrics by* Harry B. Smith.)
(b) "I Can't Do That Sum" (from *BABES IN TOYLAND*)
    A. Pennington
    (*Music by* Victor Herbert. *Lyrics by* Glen MacDonough.)
    Red Riding Hood: Miss Daw. *Mary Mary*: Miss Ellsworth. *Miss Muffet*: Miss Valentine. *Bo Peep*:Miss Allis. *Jack*: Miss West. *Jill*: Miss Wilde. *Jack Horner*: Miss Wooten. And Miss Rolfe.
(c) "Absinthe Frappe" (from *IT HAPPENED IN NORDLAND*)
    (*Music by* Victor Herbert. *Lyrics by* Glen MacDonough.)
    Misses Reveaux, Halley, Lloyd, Ackerman, Pierre, Calame, Boatwright, Byron, McLaughlin, Drange, Sheldon, Littlefield
(d) "Kiss Me Again" (from *MLLE. MODISTE*)
    V. Segal
    (*Music by* Victor Herbert. *Lyrics by* Henry Blossom.)
(e) "Toyland" (from *BABES IN TOYLAND*)
    G. Dawn
    (*Music by* Victor Herbert. *Lyrics by* Glen MacDonough.)
(f) "March of the Toys" (from *BABES IN TOYLAND*)
    L. Lane, M. Daw, Tiller and Empire Girls
    (*Scene painted by* Ludwig Kainer.)

Scene 10
Out West
    W. Rogers

Scene 11
"Montmartre"
    I. Fisher, M. Lorber
    (*Music by* Raymond Hubbell. *Lyrics by* Gene Buck.)
Dances
    Kelo Brothers, E. Law, L. Lane, A. Pennington, H. Ferguson, Empire and Tiller Girls, Miss Reveaux, Ribbon Girls, Apache Boys and Girls, Hat Box Girls
    (*Scene painted by* John Wenger.)

Scene 12
"You're My Happy Ending"
    I. Fisher, V. Segal
    (*Music by* James Hanley. *Lyrics by* Gene Buck.)
Finale
    Ensemble

---

[6]Dropped during the run.

[7]Dropped during the run.
[8]Dropped during the run.

ZIEGFELD FOLLIES OF 1924
1924.18   (FALL EDITION)

A Revised Version of the Musical Revue in Two Acts, 21 Scenes[9]. Dialogue (sketches) by William Anthony McGuire and Will Rogers. Music by Victor Herbert, Raymond Hubbell, Dave Stamper, Harry Tierney. Lyrics by Gene Buck, Joseph J. McCarthy. Staged by Julian Mitchell. Tableaux devised and staged by Ali Ben Haggin. Costume designs by Charles LeMaire. Scenery by Frank Gates and Edward A. Morange, Ludwig Kainer, John Wenger, H. Robert Law Studios. Orchestra under the direction of Victor Baravelle. Orchestrations by (Robert) Russell Bennett, Fred Barry, Harold Sanford, Steve Jones. Produced by Florenz Ziegfeld. Fall Edition opened 30 October 1924 at the New Amsterdam Theatre and closed 7 March 1925 after 148 performances.

CAST: WILL ROGERS, VIVIENNE SEGAL, ANN PENNINGTON, IRVING FISHER, LUPINO LANE, MAE DAW, TOM LEWIS, EVELYN LAW, THE KELO BROTHERS, DOROTHY KNAPP, BERYL HALLEY, GEORGE OLSEN'S BAND, MARTHA LORBER, BERNICE ACKERMAN, HILDA FERGUSON, ARTHUR BROWN, BRANDON TYNAN, ALF JAMES, GIOLE ELLER, FRANK LAMBERT, MITTY and TILLIO (French dancers), RUSSIAN LILLIPUTIANS (under direction of A. Ratoucheff.)

THE TILLER GIRLS: Empire Girls: Ziegfeld Girls: Misses Anastasia Reilly, Hurley, Nally, Francis, Doris Lloyd, Cynthia Cambridge, Andrea, Martha Pierre, McGee, Rasche, McDonald, Catherine Burke, Evelyn Goodwin, Sheldon, Calame, Brown, Marian Benda, Littlefield, Francis Reveaux, Constance McLaughlin, Cricket Wooten, Gladys Loftus, Ellsworth, Marjorie Leet, Dorothy Leet, Wildo, Alma Drange, Johnson, Carlton, Byron, Julian, Martin, Boatwright, *Gentlemen of the Ensemble:* Messrs. Jack Shannon, Mark Truscott, Al Ochs, Serge Pernikoff.

ACT 1
Scene 1
   Bradbury Ranch, Oklahoma
     Stella: B. Ackerman. *Jim Bradbury:* B. Tynan. *Percy:* L. Lane. *Jim Watts:* A. James. *Sheriff:* J. Shannon. *Tom:* T. Lewis. *Alfalfa Doolittle:* W. Rogers. *The Target:* D. Knapp.
   "The Great Wide Open Spaces"
     A. Brown
     (*Music by* Dave Stamper. *Lyrics by* Gene Buck. *Scene painted by* Ludwig Kainer. *Bonfire effect created under patents of and by* Scene-in-action Co., Chicago.)
   "All Pepped Up"
     L. Lane, Ziegfeld, Empire and Tiller Girls
     (*Music by* Harry Tierney. *Lyrics by* Joseph J. McCarthy.)
   Dance
     E. Law
Scene 2
   "The Old Town Band"
     A. Brown, L. Lane
     (*Music by* Harry Tierney. *Lyrics by* Joseph J. McCarthy.)
     Accompanied by George Olsen's Band.
Scene 3
   The Piano Next Door
     Clarence: L. Lane. *His Wife:* M. Lorber. *His Landlady:* G. Eller. *His Neighbor:* A. James. *His Friend:* F. Lambert. *His Baby:* Himself.
Scene 4
   "Dance Different"
     Kelo Brothers
     Scene: A Street.
Scene 5
   "Ever-Loving Bee"
     V. Segal, I. Fisher
     (*Music by* Dave Stamper. *Lyrics by* Gene Buck.)
     The Bees: M. Daw, Tiller Girls, Follies Girls.
Scene 6
   Celebrated Russian Troupe of Lilliputians of Mr. A. Ratoucheff:
   "Story of the Paris Night" (Classical Ballet by Mr. A. Ratoucheff.)
     (*Music by* Russian and French composers.)
     Dolls: Acmolinsky. *Spanish:* A. Ratoucheff. *First Pierro:* Neigmane. *Second Pierro:* Lamschikua. *Arlekin:* Rishtu. *Marquise:* Rauranka. *Marquis:* Rozirenko. *Pasha:* Sandrak. *Servant:* Berezmo.

---

[9]Original edition opened 24 June 1924 at the New Amsterdam Theatre, closing 25 October 1924 after 147 performances.

Scene 7
   Pearl of the East: The Two Athenas
     (*by* Ben Ali Haggin. *Arrangement with special music by* Raymond Hubbell.)
     The Pearl: M. Lorber. *A Pink Slave:* B. Halley. *A Mountain Slave:* D. Knapp. *A Dancer:* D. Lloyd. *A Tartar Prince:* S. Perkinoff.
     The Athenas (The Two Strongest Artists in the World, direct from Europe, by arrangement with E. Ray Goetz.)
Scene 8
   A Couple of Senators (*by* Will Rogers)
     Scene: Washington, D.C.
     A Girl: M. Daw. *Senator Doolittle:* W. Rogers. *Senator Lodge:* B. Tynan.
Scene 9
   "Biminy"
     I. Fisher
     (*Music by* Dave Stamper. *Lyrics by* Gene Buck. *Scene painted by* John Wenger.)
   Dance
     A. Pennington, George Olsen's Band
Scene 10
   Investigating Investigations (*by* Will Rogers)
     Scene: Chloride Gas Room Capitol.
     Senator Doolittle: W. Rogers. *Senator Useless:* J. Shannon. *Senator Stall:* B. Tynan. *Senator Chinchbug:* T. Lewis. *One of the Help:* A. James.
     (*Scene painted by* Robert Law Studios.)
Scene 11
   "The Phantom Ship" (*Dance by* Jacques Charles)
     (*Music by* Fred Mels and Laurant Halet. *Staged by* Julian Mitchell.)
   Original Dances
     Mitty and Tillio

ACT 2
Scene 1
   The Chase (*by* Lupino Lane)
     Note: Patrons are requested to notice that the world's record is broken at every performance and if they wish to do so are invited to count and time same.
     67 Traps in ?? Minutes
     Mr. Lane is the only living person turning a complete Pierrot out of star trap with only a 22-inch opening.
Scene 2
   A Victor Herbert Fantasy (*Opening Poem by* Gene Buck.)
     An Old Musician: B. Tynan.
   (a) "Gypsy Love Song" (from *THE FORTUNE TELLER*)
     I. Fisher, Gypsy Girls,
     (*Music by* Victor Herbert. *Lyrics by* Harry B. Smith.)
   (b) "I Can't Do That Sum" (from *BABES IN TOYLAND*)
     A. Pennington
     (*Music by* Victor Herbert. *Lyrics by* Glen MacDonough.)
     Red Riding Hood: Miss McGee. *Mary Mary:* Miss Ellsworth. *Miss Muffet:* Miss Valentine. *Bo Peep:* Miss Allis. *Jack:* Miss Rasche. *Jill:* Miss Wilde. *Jack Horner:* Miss Wooten. And Miss Martyn.
   (c) "Kiss Me Again" (from *MLLE. MODISTE*)
     V. Segal
     (*Music by* Victor Herbert. *Lyrics by* Henry Blossom.)
   (d) "Toyland" (from *BABES IN TOYLAND*)
     B. Ackerman
     (*Music by* Victor Herbert. *Lyrics by* Glen MacDonough.)
   (e) "March of the Toys" (from *BABES IN TOYLAND*)
     L. Lane, M. Daw, Tiller Girls
     (*Music by* Victor Herbert. *Scene painted by* Ludwig Kainer.)
   (f) "Parade of the Wooden Soldiers" (from *CHAUVE-SOURIS*)
     Russian Lilliputians
     (*Music by* Leon Jessel. *Lyrics by* Ballard Macdonald. *Staged by* Mr. A. Ratoucheff.)
Scene 3
   "A Night in June"
     L. Lane
     (*Music by* Raymond Hubbell. *Lyrics by* Gene Buck.)
Scene 4
   "Lonely Little Melody"
     I. Fisher, V. Segal
     (*Music by* Dave Stamper. *Lyrics by* Gene Buck.)
     Scene: Jazzland. (*Scene painted by* John Wenger.)
   Dance
     M. Leet, Virginia King (violin)

Scene 5

Ann Pennington and George Olsen's Band

Scene 6

Rope Dance

(*Music by* Victor Herbert) Tiller Girls
(*Staged by* John Tiller.)

Scene 7

Shadowgraph (Shadow Pantomime)

("This is the number where you use the Follies-Scope glasses which have been handed you with program, the RED glass to cover the right eye. Soiling the glasses in any way will spoil the effect entirely. Optical Illusion by Laurens Hammond, U. S. Patent Number 1,481,006.")

Scene 8

The Mirage

(*Dance by* Jacques Charles)
(*Music by* Borel Clerc and Laurent Halet.)

Original Dance

Mitty and Tillio

Scene 9

Will Rogers

Scene 10

"The Beauty Contest"

I. Fisher, M. Daw
(*Music by* Victor Herbert and Harry Tierney. *Lyrics by* Joseph J. McCarthy.)
Scene: A Garden.
Pages: Misses Valentine, Orange. *Paris Crown*: Miss Kennedy.
Eve: Miss Hurley. *Brunhilde*: Miss Nally. *Cleopatra*: Miss Lloyd, Miss Fallows. *Gwenevieve*: Miss Cambridge, Miss Andrea. *Eloise*: Miss Pierre, Miss McGee, Miss Rasche. *Isabelle*: Miss McDonald, Miss Burke. *Gabrielle*: Miss Harten, Miss Sheldon. *Nell Gwynne*: Miss Ackerman, Miss Calame, Miss Ansell. *DuBarry*: Miss Benda, Miss Wild. *Racamier*: Miss Reveaux, Miss McLaughlin. *Lady Hamilton*: Miss Francis, Miss Byron, Miss Wooten. *Eugenie*: Miss Loftus, Miss Ellsworth. *Scheherazade*: B. Halley. *The Ziegfeld Girl*: E. Law.
Typical Girl of Today: A. Pennington. And the Tiller Girls, Mitty and Tillio.
(*Scene painted by* Ludwig Kainer. *Costumes designed by* Ben Ali Haggin.)

Scene 11

Finale

GEORGE WHITE'S SCANDALS (1924)

1924.19

A Musical Revue in Two Acts, 27 Scenes[10]. Book (sketches) by William K. Wells and George White. Music by George Gershwin. Lyrics by Buddy G. DeSylva and Ballard Macdonald. Additional music by James Hanley. Costumes and curtains by Erté. Scenes painted by William Oden-Waller. Finales designed by Siedle Studios. Additional costumes by Juliet. Art director, G. A. Weidhaas. Entire production staged by George White. Orchestrations by Maurice DePackh. Orchestra under the direction of William Daly. Produced by George White. Opened 30 June 1924 at the Apollo Theatre and closed 13 December 1924 after 196 performances.

CAST: LESTER ALLEN, WINNIE LIGHTNER, TOM PATRICOLA, OLIVE VAUGHN, RICHARD BOLD, HELEN HUDSON, WILL MAHONEY, ALICE WEAVER, TOM ROSS, NEWTON ALEXANDER, THEA LIGHTNER, FRED LYONS, SALLY STARR, THE ELM CITY FOUR (Jim Carty, Harry Morrissey, Tom Ross, James Miller), THE WILLIAMS SISTERS (Kitty, Hannah, Dorothy), THE DE MARCOS (Anthony, Nina).
Ladies of the Ensemble: Misses Alice Wilkie, Bee Savage, Norma Cloos, Peggy Dolan, Hazel Donnelly, Georgia Lerch, Louise Brooks, White, Lunnay, Dorothy Sebastian, LeCount, H. Costello, D. Costello, Jean Cullen, Clara Scott, Jean Scott, Edith Nash, Case, Mary Carlson, Gray, Grant, Grave, Fay Culmer, Kent, Ruth Wilcox, Violet Anderson, Katherine Chapman, O'Brien, Pru, Jean Darling, Florence O'Neill, Mildred Klaw, Dorothy Fenron, Viola Griffith, LaMont, Oken, Cavello, Culmer.

ACT 1

Scene 1

"Just Missed the Opening Chorus"

Williams Sisters

Scene 2

Don't Be Late[11]

First Episode

On Stage: H. Morrissey, J. Carty. *Passerby*: W. Mahoney.

Second Episode[12]

Gateman: J. Miller. *Traveler*: T. Ross. *Girl Pedestrian*: D. Fenron.

Third Episode

The Wife: O. Vaughn. *The Lover*: N. Alexander. *The Husband*: F. Lyons.

Fourth Episode

The Sap: T. Ross.

Fifth Episode

Mailman: J. Miller. *The Wife*: T. Lightner. *The Husband*: W. Mahoney.

Scene 3

Tillers

Misses Fenron, Wilkie, Savage, Cloos, Donnelly, Lerch, Brooks, White, Lunnay, Sebastian, LeCount, H. Costello, Starr, J. Cullen, C. Scott, J. Scott

Scene 4

Suicide

The Girl: W. Lightner. *The Man*: N. Alexander.

Scene 5

Southern Express

Gateman: J. Miller. *Passengers*: D. Sebastian, R. Wilcox, V. Anderson, S. Starr. *Another Passenger*: F. Lyons. *Another Passenger*: W. Mahoney.

"I'm Going Back"

W. Mahoney

Scene 6

Wild Irish Rose

Announced by O. Vaughn. *Abie*: L. Allen. *Rose*: W. Lightner. *The Baby*: P. Dolan. *The Stranger*: W. Mahoney.

Scene 7

"(I Need) a Garden"

H. Hudson, Elm City Four
(*Lyrics by* Buddy G. DeSylva.) *Danced by* A. Weaver.

Scene 8

Ups and Downs in Pogotown

Announced by O. Vaughn. *The Villain*: L. Allen. *The Heroine*: W. Lightner. *The Father*: W. Mahoney. *The Mother*: J. Miller. *The Parson*: N. Alexander. *Deserted Wife*: K. Williams. *The Baby*: T. Patricola.

Scene 9

"(Night Time in) Araby"

R. Bold
(*Lyrics by* Buddy G. DeSylva.)
Dances: The DeMarcos. *Musicians*: DeMarco Sheiks.

Scene 10

"Somebody Loves Me"

W. Lightner
(*Lyrics by* Buddy G. DeSylva and Ballard Macdonald.)
Romeo: T. Ross. *Anthony*: J. Carty. *Harold Lloyd*: F. Lyons. *Bill Hart*: H. Morrissey. *Jackie Coogan*: T. Patricola.

Scene 11

"Year After Year We're Together"

R. Bold, H. Hudson
(*Lyrics by* Buddy G. DeSylva.)
The Young Bride: O. Vaughn. *The Young Groom*: F. Lyons.
Lace Bride: V. Anderson. *Attendants*: N. Cloos, E. Nash. *Lace Curtain Girls*: Misses Dolan, Carlson, Gray, Case, Smith, Cant.
Silver Bride: P. Clark. *Attendants*: C. Scott, J. Scott. *Silver Curtain Girls*: Misses Kent, D. Costello, Pru, Savage, LeCount, Beryl.
Gold Bride: K. Chapman. *Attendants*: J. Darling, F. O'Neill. *Gold Curtain Girls*: Misses Lerch, Murray, Brooks, White, Lunnay, H. Costello. *Diamond Bride*: M. Klaw. *Attendants*: S. Starr, J. Cullen. *Diamond Curtain Girls*: Misses Fenron, Wilkie, Sebastian, Wilcox, Griffith, Donnelly.

---

[10]The Sixth in the annual series of musical revues produced by George White beginning in 1919.

[11]Added episode (third position) to "Don't Be Late" sketch during the run: *The Father*: J. Carty. *The Son*: J. Miller. *The Ranch Owner*: H. Morrissey.

[12]Dropped during the run.

Scene 12

Songs

W. Lightner

Scene 13

The Censors

Cornet: N. Alexander. *Obedient Beetlepup*: L. Allen. *Mrs. Beetlepup*: T. Lightner. *Uncle Beetlepup*: J. Miller. *Butch Boy*: T. Patricola. *Passerby*: V. Alexander. *Girl at Window*: W. Lightner. *Pedestrians, etc.*: (Ensemble).

Scene 14

Leave It to the Audience

"Tune in to (Station) J O Y"

W. Lightner

(*Lyrics by* Buddy G. DeSylva.)

Censors: L. Allen, T. Lightner, J. Miller.

First Incident: Arm Dance, Leg Dance, Art Censored

Girls

Second Incident: Art Uncensored

Girls

Third Incident: Drama Uncensored

The Lover: W. Mahoney. *The Girl*: H. Hudson. *The Waiter*: J. Carty.

Drama Censored:

Fourth Incident: Skirt Dance

S. Starr, Girls

Fifth Incident: Charleston Dance

Girls

Sixth Incident: Dance

S. Starr

Seventh Incident: Dance

T. Patricola

Eighth Incident: Dance

Girls

ACT 2[13]

Scene 1

Hot Chow[14]

Announced by: O. Vaughn. *First Brigand*: L. Allen. *Second Brigand*: N. Alexander. *Third Brigand*: J. Carty. *Heroine*: W. Lightner. *Hero*: W. Mahoney.

Scene 2

"Mah Jongg"

(*Lyrics by* Buddy G. DeSylva.)

The Mandarin: R. Bold. *The Kids*: Williams Sisters. *Chow*: T. Ross. *Fung*: A. DeMarco. *Mah Jongg*: N. DeMarco. *Bamboos*: Misses Cloos, Murray, H. Costello, Lunnay. *Characters*: Misses Dolan, Kent, Pru, Gray. *Circles*: Misses Wilcox, LeCount, Griffith, D. Costello. *Dragons*: Misses Case, Smith, LaMont. *Walls*: Misses Darling, White, O'Neill, Campbell, Oken, J. Scott, C. Scott, Cavello. *Flowers*: Misses Chapman, Klaw, Clark, Anderson. *Seasons: Spring*: A. Wilkie. *Summer*: D. Fenron. *Autumn*: G. Lurch. *Winter*: L. Brooks. *Winds: East Wind*: B. Savage. *South Wind*: H. Donnelly. *West Wind*: D. Sebastian. *North Wind*: M. Carlson.

Scene 3

"In My Pajamas"[15]

W. Mahoney

(*Music and Lyrics by* Sam Gould, Lew Pollack, Will Mahoney, Charlie Winston.)

Scene 4

The Thinkers[16]

Announced by O. Vaughn. *The Clerk*: T. Ross. *The Contractor*: F. Lyons. *The Housewife*: T. Lightner. *The Butcher*: W. Mahoney. *The Society Woman*: H. Hudson. *The Manufacturer*: H. Morrissey. *The Old Maid*: V. Alexander. *The Promoter*: J. Carty. *The Chorus Girl*: W. Lightner. *The Bookmaker*: N. Alexander. *The Flapper*: A. Weaver. *The Old Man*: A. DeMarco. *The Conductor*: J. Miller.

---

[13]Added during the run to Act 2:

"Lovers of Art"

Elm City Four, Bathing Girls

The stage effect used in this scene is invented and protected by A. Samoiloff of London and is presented by arrangement with E. Ray Goetz, the sole licensee for the Samoiloff Light Effects in the United States and Canada. The management wishes to acknowledge the kind assistance of Mr. Julian Wylie of the London Hippodrome in the staging of this number.

[14]Dropped during the run.

[15]Dropped during the run.

[16]Dropped during the run.

Scene 5

Ann Pennington: L. Allen. *Brooke Johns*: T. Patricola.

Scene 6

Black and White March

Some of the Girls

Scene 7

Colorature Poetry

Announced by W. Mahoney. *First Accompanist*: L. Allen. *Second Accompanist*: J. Miller. *Recitations by* W. Lightner. *Symphonic Gestures by* T. Patricola.

Scene 8

"Rose of Madrid"

R. Bold, H. Hudson

(*Lyrics by* Buddy G. DeSylva.)

Girls in the Shawl: Misses Chapman, Dolan, Klaw, Kent, Carlson, Griffith, Clark, Smith, Anderson, Gray, LaMont, Pru. *Girls in the Comb*: Misses Fenron, Wilkie, Savage, Cloos, Donnelly, Lerch, Brooks, Lunnay, Wilcox, Sebastian, O'Neill, H. Costello. *Behind the Fan*: DeMarcos, Sheik Orchestra.

Scene 9

"I Love You My Darling"

W. Mahoney

Scene 10

Without a Word[17]

The Wife: H. Hudson. *The Lover*: W. Mahoney. *The Husband*: N. Alexander. *The Cop*: J. Miller. *The Other Lover*: L. Allen.

Scene 11

In the Land of the Congo: ("Kongo Kate")

(*Lyrics by* Buddy G. DeSylva.)

Congo Kate: W. Lightner. *Congo Kids*: Girls. *A Congo Nutt*: T. Patricola. *Feather Curtain Girls*: Misses Culmer, Klaw, Gray, Carlson, Smith, Case, Wilcox, Sebastian, Anderson, Clark, Chapman, Kent, Dolan, D. Costello, Griffith, Beryl.

Scene 12

The Versatile Four

L. Allen, N. Alexander, H. Morrissey, J. Carty

Scene 13

Finale (in order of appearance)

W. Lightner, L. Allen, T. Patricola, W. Mahoney, H. Hudson, R. Bold, DeMarcos, N. Alexander, T. Alexander, Quartette, O. Vaughn, A. Weaver, S. Starr, J. Miller, Girls

SWEENEY TODD/ BOMBASTES FURIOSO

1924.20

A Double Bill of Revivals of the English Melodrama by George Dibdin Pitt, and the Burlesque Operetta by William Barnes Rhodes. Stage settings designed by Joseph Physioc. Musical director, Icilio Sadun. Produced by Wendell Phillips Dodge. Opened 16 July 1924 at the Frazee Theatre and closed 13 September 1924 after 67 performances.

SWEENEY TODD, The Barber of Fleet Street, or The String of Pearls A Revival of the English Melodrama[18] by George Dibdin Pitt in Two Acts, 8 Scenes.

CAST (by Her Majesty's Servants): *Colonel Jeffrey*, of the Indian Army: Percy Baverstock. *Jasper Oakley*, a Spectacle-maker: FRANK HUBERT. *Mark Ingestrie*, a Mariner: Charles Penman. *Sweeney Todd*, the Barber of Fleet Street: ROBERT VIVIAN. *Dr. Aminadab Lupin*, a Wolf in Sheep's Clothing: Elwyn Eaton. *Jarvis Williams*, a Lad with no small appetite: Edward Jephson. *Jonas Fogg*, the Keeper of a Mad-house: George Sydenham. *Attendants in Jonas Fogg's Mad-house*: Frank Hubert, Herbert Radus. *Jean Parmine*, a Lapidary: William A. Evans. *Tobias Ragg*, Sweeney Todd's Apprentice-boy: Jeanie Beggs. *Mrs. Oakley*, Jasper's Wife: Venie Atherton. *Johanna*, her Daughter: MERCEDES DESMORE. *Mrs. Lovett*, Sweeney Todd's Apprentice in Guilt: RAPHAELLA OTTIANO. *A Lamplighter*: Rina Cavalli. *Sir William Brandon*, a Judge: George Sydenham. *Clerk*: Frank Hubert. *Attendant*: Herbert Radus.

Act 1, Scene 1: Interior of Sweeney Todd's Barber Shop in Fleet Street. *Scene 2*: Parlour in the house of Jasper Oakley in Fore Street. *Scene 3*: Exterior of Mrs. Lovett's Pie-shop in Bell Yard, Temple Bar. *Scene 4*: Interior of the Bakehouse.

Act 2, Scene 1: Interior of Sweeney Todd's Barber Shop in Fleet Street. *Scene 2*: A Chamber in the Madhouse at Bedlam. *Scene 3*: Blackfriar's Bridge. *Scene 4*: A Court of Justice—Old Bailey.

---

[17]Sketch later known as 'Ah!'

[18]Originally produced in New York ?? 1866-67, 74.

MUSICAL NUMBERS

"My Heart Is Over the Sea, or Maggie's Secret" (by Claribel) [Charlotte Bernard]
M. Desmore

"Dick, Dick, the Lamplighter"
R. Cavalli

BOMBASTES FURIOSO

A Revival of the Burlesque Tragic Operetta[19] in One Act, 4 Scenes, by William Barnbes Rhodes.

CAST: *Artaaxominous*, King of Utopia: Elwyn Eaton. *Fusbos*, Minister of State: Charles Penman. *General Bombastes*: GEORGE SYDENHAM. *Court Jester*: Icilio Sadun. *Keeper of the Bowl*: William A. Evans. *Chamberlain*: Frank Hubert. *Attendants*: Percy Baverstock, Edward Jephson. *Soldiers*: Percy Baverstock, Edward Jephson, Frank Huber, Herbert Radus. *Pages*: Rina Cavalli, Jeanie Begg. *Ladies in Waiting*: Raphaella Ottiano, Venie Atherton. *Distaffina*: Mercedes Desmore.

Scene 1: Throne Room in the Palace. *Scene 2*: Another Throne Room in Palace. *Scene 3*: Inside of a Cottage. *Scene 4*: A Wood.

MUSICAL NUMBERS

"Joan to the Maypole" (Opening Chorus)

(Pills to Purge Melancholy, 1707-1719)

"Trio (*New Composition by* Iciclio Sadun.)
P. Baverstock, E. Eaton, F. Hubert

"The Happy Clown" (Occarina Solo)
I. Sadun

(The Dancing Master, 1718)

"Ladies of London" (Song)
R. Cavalli

(The Dancing Master, 1690)

Pipe Solo (Specialty)
(*New Composition by* Iciclio Sadun.) I. Sadun

"Come Jolly Bacchus, or Charles of Sweden" (Song)
G. Syndenham

(The Dancing Master, 1728)

"The Women All Tell Me" (Song)
E. Eaton

(Broadsides, with Music, 1740)

"The Humours of the Bath, or Spring's a Coming" (Song)
M. Desmore

(Watt's Musical Miscellaney, 1729)

"Here's a Health to His Majesty" (Trio)
M. Desmore, G. Sydenham, E. Eaton

(Playford's Musical Companion, 1667)

"Hope Told a Flattering Tale" (Song)
C. Penamn

(Composer unknown, 1795)

"The Derby Ram" (Duet)
C. Penman, G. Sydenham

(Derbyshire Country Song, 1784)

"Sweeney Todd, Oh Sweeney Todd" (Grand Finale)
Entire Company
(*Music by* Icilio Sadun. *Lyrics by* Wendell Phillips Dodge.)

1924.21

MARJORIE

A Musical Comedy in Three Acts. Book and lyrics by Fred Thompson, Clifford Grey and Harold Atteridge[20]. Music by Sigmund Romberg, Herbert Stothart, Philip Culkin and Stephen Jones. Dialogue directed by W. H. Gilmore. Dances and ensembles staged by David Bennett. Art director, scenery designed by Watson Barratt. Costumes designed by Charles LeMaire. Orchestra under the direction of Alfred Goodman. Entire production under the personal supervision of Rufus R. LeMaire. Produced by Rufus R. LeMaire and Richard W. Krakeur[21]. Opened

11 August 1924 at the Sam S. Shubert Theatre, moved 15 September 1924 to the 44th Street Theatre, and closed 13 December 1924 after 144 performances.

CAST (in order of appearance): *Luke Calvert*: Edwin Forsburg. *Howard Brindle*: Jack Squire. *Henry*: Donat Gauthier. *Eph Daw*: RICHARD (Skeets) GALLAGHER. *Marjorie Daw*: ELIZABETH HINES. *Brian Valcourt*, an Author-Manager: ROY ROYSTON. *Juliette Loti*, a Film Star: Nan Crawford. *Molly Daly* of Valcourt's Musical Comedy Company: ETHEL SHUTTA. *Garcia Pindora*, Valcourt's Publicity Manager: ANDREW TOMBES. *Hotel Clerk*: Joe Tinsley. *Biggs*, a Private Enquiry Agent: Cliff Heckinger. *Bell Boy*: EDWARD ALLEN.

Ladies of the Ensemble: Bobby Breslaw, Marguerite Dunne, Peggy Hart, Portland Hoffa, Edith Martin, Paulette Winston, Claire Wayne, Jena Wayne, Helen O'Brian, Naomi Harkins, Beth Milton, Rita Dunne, Mabel Baade, Consuelo Owens, Monica Boulaise, Rosemary Marston. *Gentlemen of the Ensemble*: Warren Crosby, Frank Cullen, Al Davis, Perry Higgins, Fred Packard, Dick Oakley, Dan Sparks, Frederic Tozere.

Act 1: Calvert's Estate—near Rockeepsie in the Catskills.

Act 2: The Tavern Inn at Southampton, Long Island.

Act 3: Roof Garden of Valcourt's Residence, Park Avenue, New York.

ACT 1

"Listening to the Radio"
Ensemble
(*Music by* Sigmund Romberg.)

Dance
Dunne Sisters, B. Breslaw

"Brindle's Farm"
H. Squire, Boys
(*Music by* Philip Culkin.)

"Song of Love"
E. Hines, Ensemble
(*Music by* Sigmund Romberg.)

"Popularity"
A. Tombes, R. Gallagher, E. Shutta, Girls
(*Music by* Stephen Jones.)

"Happy Ending"
E. Hines, R. Royston, Girls
(*Music by* Herbert Stothart.)

"Good Things and Bad Things"
R. Gallagher, E. Shutta
(*Music by* Sigmund Romberg.)

"Twilight Rose"
E. Hines, R. Royston
(*Music by* Sigmund Romberg.)

Finale
E. Hines, A. Tombes, R. Royston, E. Shutta
(*Music by* Sigmund Romberg.)

ACT 2

"Go Away, Girls, Go Away"
A. Tombes, Girls
(*Music by* Herbert Stothart.)

"Leading Man"
E. Hines, Gentlemen, A. Tombes
(*Music by* Stephen Jones.)

"Nature"
R. Gallagher, E. Shutta, Ensemble
(*Music by* Herbert Stothart.)

"Super-Sheik"
R. Gallagher, E. Shutta, Ensemble
(*Music by* Sigmund Romberg.)

"What Do You Say?"
E. Hines, R. Royston
(*Music by* Herbert Stothart.)

"Shuffle Your Troubles Away"
A. Tombes, R. Gallagher, E. Shutta, Ensemble
(*Music by* James Hanley. *Lyrics by* Henry Creamer.)

Dance
E. Allen

Finale
Ensemble
(*Music by* Sigmund Romberg.)

---

[19]Originally produced in New York 15 October 1816 at the Park Theatre.
[20]Published sheet music credits only Clifford Grey as lyricist.
[21]During the run, the producers' credit was revised to read "in association with Jack Nicholas."

ACT 3

"Forty-Second Street Moon"
R. Royston, Ensemble
(*Music by* Sigmund Romberg.)

"Marjorie Waltz"
E. Hines, R. Royston
(*Music by* Stephen Jones.)

"When I Show 'Em This"
E. Shutta, Ensemble, E Allen
(*Music by* Stephen Jones.)

Finale
Ensemble
(*Music by* Sigmund Romberg.)

1924.22   NO OTHER GIRL

A Charming Musical Comedy in Three Acts, 4 Scenes. Book by Aaron Hoffman. Music by Bert Kalmar. Lyrics by Harry Ruby. Staged by John Meehan. Dances by Larry Ceballos. Settings designed by Livingston Platt. Costumes designed by Erle Frank. Orchestra under the direction of Alfred Newman. Produced by A. L. Jones and Morris Green in association with A. H. Woods. Opened 13 August 1924 at the Morosco Theatre and closed 27 September 1924 after 56 performances.

CAST [in order of appearance]: *Joshua Franklin*: EARLE CRADDOCK. *Miss Smith*: Aileen Meehan. *Miss Jones*: Ruth Conley. *Amos Trott*: FRANCIS X. DONEGAN. *Obadiah Bingle*: JAMES FRANCIS-ROBERTSON. *Molly Lane*: DORIS EATON. *William Frawley*: WILLIAM SULLY. *Hope Franklin*: HELEN FORD. *Ananias Jones*: EDDIE BUZZELL. *Thomas Lord*: Henry Mortimer. *Mary Herrington*: Jane Carroll. *Bryan*: JOHN SHEEHAN. *Butler*: Eddie Gerard. *Mr. Van Etten*: FRANCIS X. DONEGAN.

Belles and Beaux of Quakertown: Dorothy Martin, Ruth Conley, Nonnie George, Vera Trett, Rose Stone, Billie Blythe, Helen Blair, Trix Taylor, Dorothy Kane, Aileen Meehan, Zita Mae, Sylvia Shawn, Helen Wilson, Jack Grieves, Fred Cowhick, William Hale, Frank Parker, David Brown, Richard Powell, Albert White.

Act 1: Quakertown, New Jersey. End of May.

Act 2, Scene 1: Ananias Jones' Office, New York City. Three months later. *Scene 2*: Thomas Lord's Home, Long Island, Same night.

Act 3: Quakertown, New Jersey. Nine months later.

ACT 1

"A Pleasant Greeting" (Quakertown Sextette)
J. Francis-Robertson, E. Craddock, Quaker Girls, Boys

"Molly"
D. Eaton, W. Sully

"The Best in the Trade"
H. Ford, F. X. Donegan, Quaker Boys

"After the Curfew Rings"
E. Buzzell, Quaker Girls

"No Other Girl"
H. Ford, E. Buzzell

"Doing the Town"
W. Sully, Quaker Girls, Seminary Girls

Reprise Finale
Company

ACT 2

"Keep the Party Going"
F. X. Donegan, 'Jenkins', H. Mortimer, Guests

Specialties
B. Blythe, D. Martin, R. Stone, H. Blair, E. Girard

"I Know That I Love You"
D. Eaton, W. Sully

"Honduras"
'LaSidelli', Guests

Specialty
F. X. Donegan, S. Shawn

"Corner of My Mind"
H. Ford, E. Buzzell

"It's the Dancer You Love"
D. Martin, W. Hale, B. Blythe, F. Cowhick, R. Stone, F. Parker, H. Blair, J. Grieves

"I Would Rather Dance a Waltz"
H. Ford, Dancers

Reprise
Company

ACT 3

"Look Out for Us Broadway"
J. Francis-Robertson, E. Craddock, F. X. Donegan, Ensemble

Reprise
H. Ford

"You Flew Away from the Nest"
E. Buzzell

"Day Dreams"
D. Eaton, W. Sully

Finale
Entrie Company

1924.23   THE DREAM GIRL

A Musical Play in Three Acts, 6 Scenes. Book by Rida Johnson Young and Harold Atteridge. Based on the play 'The Road to Yesterday' by Beulah Marie Dix and Evelyn Greenleaf Sutherland. Music by Victor Herbert[22]. Lyrics by Rida Johnson Young. Staged by J. C. Huffman and Laura Hope Crews. Dances and ensembles by David Bennett. Settings by Eleanor Abbott and Watson Barratt. Costumes by Milgrim, Franklin Simon & Co. Orchestra under the direction of Oscar Bradley. Produced by the Messrs. Lee and J.J. Shubert (by arrangement with William Harris, Jr.). Opened 20 August 1924 at the Ambassador Theatre and closed 29 November 1924 after 117 performances.

CAST: *Elspeth*: FAY BAINTER. *Malena*: VIVARA. *Dolly Follis*: WYN RICHMOND. *Wilson Addison*: GEORGE LEMAIRE. *Aunt Harriet*: MAUDE ODELL. *Jimmie Van Dyke*: BILLY B. VAN. *Elinor Levison*: Alice Moffat. *Nora*: Clara Palmer. *Jack Warren*: WALTER WOOLF. *Will Levison*: JOHN CLARKE. *Bobby Thompkins*: FRANK MASTERS. *Mr. Gillette*: William O'Neal. *Ken Paulton*: Edward Basse. *Antonio*: William O'Neal. *Cristoforo*: Edmund Fitzpatrick.

Specialty Dancers: Barbara Bennett, Evelyn Grieg, Virginia Shaar, Loretta Duffy, Elizabeth Mears. *American Girls*: Kathleen Barrow, Lebanon Hoffa, Rena Miller, Joan Kroy, May O'Brien, Virginia Allen, Aimee Salter, Victoria Reigel. *Artists' Models*: Jeanette Dawley, Lida May, Elizabeth Mears, Velma Joffre, Virginia Griffith, Ripples Covert, Sofia Jackson, Dorothy Cola. *Gentlemen of Ensemble*: Chandler Christie, Penn Thornton, Jack Parker, Dan Douglas, Maurice Kuhlman, Thomas Manahan, Frank Kimball, Fred Bush.

Act 1, Scene 1: Will Levison's Studio. Late afternoon in London, 1923. *Scene 2*: The Road to Long Ago.

Act 2, Scene 1: The Red Swan Inn. (An English Inn of the Fifteenth Century.) *Scene 2*: A Green before the Castle. (Fifteenth Century.) *Scene 3*: A Room in the Castle of Lord Strangevon. (Fifteenth Century.)

Act 3: Will Levison's Studio. After Midnight, 1923.

ACT 1

"Making a Venus"
F. Masters, Vivara, Models, Boys

"All Year Round"
W. Woolf, Chorus
(*Music by* Sigmund Romberg.)

"Dancing Round"
F. Bainter, Chorus

"(My) Dream Girl (I Loved You Long Ago)"
W. Woolf

"Old Songs"
Maidens, Quartette

Finale
F. Bainter, W. Woolf, Entire Company

ACT 2

"Maiden, Let Me In"
J. Clarke, Boys

"Gypsy Life"
Vivara, Chorus

---

[22]Produced posthumously after Victor Herbert's death.

"Stop, Look and Listen"
   F. Bainter, B. B. Van, F. Masters
"(The) Broad Highway"
   W. Woolf, Chorus
"My Hero"
   F. Bainter, W. Woolf
"I Want to Go Home"
   F. Bainter
   (*Music by* Sigmund Romberg. *Lyrics by* Harold Atteridge.)
ACT 3
"Bubbles"[23] (Bubble Song)
   W. Richmond, Chorus
"Make Love in the Morning"[24]
   B. B. Van, Specialty Dancers
"Saxophone Man"[25]
   F. Masters, W. Richmond, Chorus
Finale—"Dream Girl"
   F. Bainter, W. Woolf, Entire Company

1924.24

BYE, BYE, BARBARA

A Musical Comedy in Two Acts. Book by Sidney Toler and Alonzo Price. Music and lyrics by Monte Carlo and Alma Sanders. Staged by Alonzo Price. Settings designed by Walter Shaffner. Costumes designed by William Weaver. Orchestra under the direction of Antonio Bafunno. Orchestrations by William M. Redfield. Produced by Adolphe Mayer and Theodore Hammerstein, Inc. Opened 25 August 1924 at the National Theatre and closed 6 September 1924 after 16 performances.

CAST (in order of appearance): *Chin Lee*: Billy M. Greene. *Marjorie Palmer*: MILDRED KEATS. *John Palmer*: Albert Sackett. *Barbara Palmer*: JANET VELIE. *Stanley Howard*: ARTHUR BURCKLY. *Paulette*: LILLIAN FITZGERALD. *Fay*: FAY WEST. *Phillip Graham*: STANLEY RIDGES. *Captain Hal Cuttle*: Matt Hanley. *Tom Wiggins*: George Lynch. *The Great Karloff*: JOHN [Jack] E. HAZZARD. *Sheriff Bisbee*: Dan Marble. *George Frothingham*: COLIN CAMPBELL. *Sparks*: Charlotte Davis. *Phyllis*: PHYLLIS PEARCE. *Ann*: ANN NITA.

   Visitors and Guests at the Arlington Hotel, Santa Barbara: Agnes O'Laughlin, Jean Benton, Charlotte Davis, Marian Squire, Marian Dale, Neida Snow, Bernetice Hampshire, Mary Mellinger, Lucille Prior, Rita Adams, Madeline Dare, Ruth Jewell, Lillian Day, Hope Minor, Peggy Ellis, May Johnson, Charles Mantia, Louis Brown, Harold Spinelli, Jack Spinelly, William Jay Spencer, Joe Bernella.

The action takes place at the present time.

Act 1: The Grounds of the Arlington Hotel, Santa Barbara. Late afternoon.

Act 2: The Ball Room. Evening.

ACT 1
"China"
   J. Benton, C. Davis, Friends, B. M. Greene
   Chinese Girl: A. O'Loughlin.
"Live for Today"
   P. Pearce, A. Nita, Friends
"Curiosity"
   M. Keats, P. Pearce, A. Nita, Friends
"Kiss Invention"
   J. Velie, M. Keats, F. West
"Quaint Little House (Built for Two)"
   A. Burckly, J. Velie
"Gee, You Must Be in Love" (Gee, I Must Be in Love)
   S. Ridges, M. Keats
"Bo-Peep" (Waltz Song)
   J. Velie, A. Burckly, Shepherd Boys and Lambs
"Bye, Bye, Barbara"
ACT 2
"Harmony"
   A. Burckly, J. Velie, Friends

"Pas Seul"
   M. Keats
"Amusing Myself"
   L. Fitzgerald
"As Kipling Says (I Learned About Women from Her)"
   J. E. Hazzard
   (*Lyrics by* Benjamin Hapgood Burt.)
"Sittin' in Clover"
   S. Ridges, M. Keats, Ensemble
"Why Don't they Leave the Sheik Alone"
   J. E. Hazzard
"Pas Seul" (reprise)
   P. Pearce, Cigarette Girls
"Quaint Little House" (reprise)
   F. West, L. Fitzgerald
Finale

1924.25

TOP-HOLE

The Tip Top Musical Comedy in Three Acts, 4 Scenes. Book by Eugene Conrad and George Dill, revised by Gladys Unger. Music by Jay Gorney and Robert Braine. Lyrics by Owen Murphy and Eugene J. Conrad. Production staged by William Caryl. Dances arranged by David Bennett and Seymour Felix. Settings by Rollo Wayne. Costumes by Mme. Haverstick. Orchestra under the direction of Hilding Anderson. Produced by William Caryl. Opened 1 September 1924 at the Fulton Theatre, moved 10 October 1924 to the Knickerbocker Theatre, moved 3 November 1924 to the Liberty Theatre and closed 29 November 1924 after 104 performances[26].

CAST (in order of appearance): *Peggy Corcoran*: NINA PENN. *Dobson*: Richard Temple. *Marcia Willoughby*: CLARE STRATTON. *Mrs. John Corcoran*: Leah Winslow. *Mrs. Blunt*: Nellie Graham Dent. *Irving Naith*: Brandon Peters. *Judge John Corcoran*: Walter Walker. *Algernon Van Hooten*: Charles Brown. *Al Smith*: Earl Redding. *Robert Corcoran* (Bob): ERNEST GLENDINNING. *Aloysious Blunt*: John Daly Murphy. *Theodore Willoughby*: John Park. *A Caddy*: Billy Kelly. *Maureen*: ANN MILBURN.

   Friends of Peggy and Marcia: Madeline Calkins, Lillian Carmody, Sylvia Carol, Teddy Dauer, Frieda Dixon, Lila Dixon, Mary Grace, Eva Marie Gray, Mildred Morgan, Mabel Olsen, Jean Watson, Betty Wright.

Act 1: Living Room of Judge Corcoran's Home. Suburban New York. Morning.

Act 2, Scene 1: On the Top Hole Golf Course (Seventh Hole), California. One year later. *Scene 2*: Locker room of the Gold Club. One week later.

Act 3: Reception Hall of the Club. Same evening.

ACT 1
"We Ran Away from School"
   N. Penn, Girls
"Every Silken Lady Has a Touch of Calico"
   C. Stratton, Girls
"Dance Your Way to Paradise"
   N. Penn, Girls
"Come Over Eyes"('You Must Come Over' Eyes)
   E. Glendinning, Girls
   (*Music by* Jay Gorney. *Lyrics by* Owen Murphy.)
"(In) California"
   C. Stratton, Girls
   (*Music by* Jay Gorney. *Lyrics by* Owen Murphy.)
Finale
ACT 2
"Golf"
   Girls
   (*Music by* Robert Braine. *Lyrics by* Eugene Conrad.)
"Is It Any Wonder?"
   E. Glendinning, C. Stratton
   (*Music by* Jay Gorney. *Lyrics by* Owen Murphy.)
"The Girls"
   Girls
"Music of an Irish Song" (There is Music in an Irish Song)
   A. Milburn, E. Glendinning, Girls
   (*Music and Lyrics by* Jay Gorney and Owen Murphy.)

[23]Alternately credited to Sigmund Romberg, or Victor Herbert and Rida Johnson Young, per ASCAP.
[24]Dropped after the opening.
[25]Alternately credited to Sigmund Romnberg and Harold Atteridge, or Romberg, Schwartz and William Jerome, per ASCAP.

[26]Re-opened 22 December 1924 - 3 January 1925 at the Colonial Theatre for an additional 16 performances. Total: 120 performances.

"Love Is a Sandman"
E. Glendinning, C. Stratton
(*Music by* Robert Braine. *Lyrics by* Eugene Conrad.)

"When You're in Love"[27]
E. Glendinning, Girls
(*Music and Lyrics by* Jay Gorney, Harry Richman, Owen Murphy.)

Finale
E. Glendinning, C. Stratton, J. Park, Ensemble

ACT 3

"Wings of Love"
Girls
(*Music by* Robert Braine. *Lyrics by* Eugene Conrad.)

"Is It Any Wonder?" (reprise) (dance)
N. Penn

"When You're in Love" (reprise)
E. Glendinning, C. Stratton, A. Milburn, Girls

Finale

1924.26

STEPPING STONES

A Return Engagement of the Musical Play in Two Acts, 13 Scenes[28]. Book by Anne Caldwell and R. H. Burnside. Music by Jerome Kern. Lyrics by Anne Caldwell. Staged by R. H. Burnside. Costumes designed by Wilhelm of London, Cora MacGeachy, Will R. Barnes, Robert McQuinn. Men's costumes by Brooks-Mahieu Costume Company. Scenery designed by Wilhelm of London, Robert McQuinn, P. Dodd Ackerman. Orchestra under the direction of Roy Webb. Orchestrations by Robert Russell Bennett. Produced by Charles Dillingham. Opened 1 September 1924 at the Globe Theatre and closed 4 October 1924 after 40 performances. Total for both engagements: 281 performances.

CAST: *Peter Plug*: FRED STONE. *Prince Silvio*: ROY HOYER. *Otto DeWolfe*: OSCAR RAGLAND. *Remus*: John Lambert. *Richard*: Cynthia Foley. *Captain Paul*: Frederic Tozere. *Antoine*: William Murray. *Gypsy Jan*: Bert Jordan. *Eddie*: Willie Torpey. *The Landlord*: George Herman. *Rougette Hood*: DOROTHY STONE. *Widow Hood*: ALLENE STONE. *Lupina*: Hazel Glen. *Radiola*: Primrose Caryll. *Mary*: Lucille Elmore. *Nurse Marjorie*: Lydia Scott. *Charlotte*: Francetta Malloy. *Eclaire*: Jet Stanley.

Globe Theatre Ensemble: Lucille Darling, Ona Hamilton, Ruth Hurst, Sally Hurst, Maude Jerome, Doris Landy, Geraldine Markham, Mary Pearce, Louise Powell, Adelaide Robinson, Betty Roche, Helen Roche, Dolly Stanley, Betty Darling, Jean Webb, Hazelle Renaud, Dorothy Markey, Alice Akers, Dorothy Bate, Maidee Clewley, Lydia Campbell. *Tiller Sunshine Girls*: Ida Moseley, Dolly Moseley, Phyllis Brown, Doris Smith, Alice Pittman, Chrissie Spaller, Florence Stack, Edith Harvey, Dolly Maxted, Madge Read, Muriel Marlow, Doris Carter, Dorothy Sabin, Noreen Callow, Olga Sykes, Josie Elton.

1924.27

THE CHOCOLATE DANDIES

A Musical Comedy in Two Acts, 12 Scenes[29]. Book by Noble Sissle and Lew Payton. Music by Eubie Blake. Lyrics by Noble Sissle. Staged by Julian Mitchell. Costumes by John Newton Booth, Kiviette, Hugh Willoughby. Lighting by Tony Greshoff. Music director, Eubie Blake. Vocal arranger, Lorenzo Calduel. Orchestrations by Lorenzo Calduel. Entire production under the personal direction of Noble Sissle and Eubie Blake. Produced by B. C. Whitney. Opened 1 September 1924 at the Colonial Theatre and closed 22 November 1924 after 96 performances.[30]

CAST (in order of appearance): *At the Piano*: EUBIE BLAKE. *Mandy Green*, the Deacon's Wife: Amanda Randolph. *Sammy*, Mandy Green's Baby: Gwendolyn Feaster. *Black Joe, Jr.*: Addison Carey. *That Comedy Chorus Girl*: Josephine Baker. *Struttin' Drum Major and His Bamville Band*: J. Mardo Brown. *Bill Splivens*, Plantation Owner: W. A. HANN. *Mr. Hez Brown*, President of Bamville Fair: William Grundy. *Mrs. Hez Brown*, the Wife: Inez Clough. *Angeline Brown*, the daughter: LOTTIE GEE. *Jessie Johnson*: ELIZABETH WELSH [Welch]. *Manda*, Bill Spliven's Niece: VALADA [Valaida] SNOW. *Uncle Eph*, Trainer of Rarin' To-Go: Fred Jennings. *Dobby Hicks*, Race-Horse Tout: NOBLE SISSLE. *Dan Jackson*, Owner of Rarin' To-Go: IVAN H.

BROWNING. *Shorty*, Dumb Luck's Jockey: Ferdie Robinson. *Johnnie Wise* Village Rube: Russell Smith. *Mose Washington*, Owner of Dumb Luck: LEW PAYTON. *Joe Dolks* Owner of Jump Steady: JOHNNY HUDGINS. *Silas Green*, the Deacon: LEE. J. RANDALL. *Bookmaker*: GEORGE JONES, JR. *Snappy*, Rarin' To-Go's Jockey: CHARLIE DAVIS. *Sandy Scarecrow's Jockey*: Curtis Carpenter. *Jump Steady*: John Alexander, Chic Fisher.

In the Bank: *Bank Policeman*: Ferdie Robinson. *The Porter*: Fred Jennings. *Secretary*: VALADA [Valaida] SNOW. *Cashier*: Richard Cooper. *Bookkeeper*: Percy Colston. *Draft Clerk*: Claude Lawson. *Auditor*: Addison Carey. *Four Harmony Kings* (Quartet): Ivan H. Browning, W. H. Berry, George Jones, Jr., W. A. Hann.

At the Wedding: *Mischief*: Mildred Smallwood. *A Deserted Female*: Josephine Baker. *Her Bunco Attorney*: Lloyd Keyes. *Town Flappers, Bank Clerks, Barbers, Citizens, Clerks, etc.*

Bamville Opera House Band: Joe Smith (Director), J. M. Brown (Drum Major), E. C. Caldwell, J. W. Mobley, Ferdie Robinson, George Dosher, Horace Langhorne, L. J. Randall, R. Cooper, Willard Sinkford, Henry M. Batchelder. *Jazzy Jassmines*: Carmen Marshall, Aimee Bates, Rose Young, Anita Alexander, Virginia Wheeler, Violet Holland. *Bandannaland Girls*: Aimee Spencer, Bertha Wright, Ruby Barbee, Mae Cobb, Hilda Perlino, Marie Frane, Thelma Rhoten, Mae Fortune, Mildred Hudgins, Marion Gee, Lolita Hall, Viola Jackson, Dorothy Bellis, Gladys Bryant, Thelma McLaughlin, Helen Mitchell, Mabel Nichols, Catherine Parker, Jennie Salmon, Clara Titus, Lucille Smith, May Fanning, May Benjamin, Mildred Smallwood, Eleanor Greenwood, Marie Marsh, Annette Rody, Madge Roma, June Dodge, Peach Johns. *Bamville Vamps*: Doris Mignotte, Frankie Williams, Jaculine Williams, Hazel Cole, Dorothy Belis, Gladys Bryant. *Syncopated Sunflowers*: John Alexander, Chic Fisher, Howard Elmore, Alfred Chester, Willie Sheppard, Lloyd Keyes, Earl Crompton, Bournis Brown, Buster Miller.

Act 1: Last Day of the Bamville, Mississippi, Fair. *Scene 1*: South and Main Streets, Bamville. *Scene 2*: Jassamine Lane. *Scene 3*: Stables at the Fair Grounds. *Scene 4*: Betting Ring at the Fair Grounds. *Scene 5*: Paddock. *Scene 6*: Bamville Race Track in the stretch.

Act 2: Evening of the Same Day. *Scene 1*: Lawn Party, Bill Spliven's Plantation Home. *Scene 2*: Street in Bamville next morning. *Scene 3*: Bamville County Bank the following day. *Scene 4*: Moses' Awakening. (Only a dream.) *Scene 5*: Sissle and Blake's Studio. *Scene 6*: Wedding of Dan and Angeline on the Stage at the Bamville Opera House.

ACT 1[31]

"Mammy's Choc'late Cullud Chile"
A. Randolph

"Have a Good Time, Everybody"
Opening Chorus

"That Charleston Dance"[32]
E. Welsh

"The Slave of Love"
L. Gee, I. H. Browning

"I'll Find My Love in D-I-X-I-E"
N. Sissle, His Dixie Darlings

"Bandannaland"
L. T. Randall, R. Smith, Bandannaland Girls

"The Sons of Old Black Joe"
Syncopated Sunflowers
Old Black Joe: W. A. Hann

"Jassamine Lane"
L. Gee, I. H. Browning, Jassamine Chorus

"Dumb Luck"
L. Payton

"Jump Steady"
L. T. Randall

"Breakin' 'Em Down"[33]
V. Snow, Chorus
Introducing J. Smith (Jazz Cornetist), B. Miller.

"Jockey's Life for Mine"
C. Davis, Jockeys

ACT 2

"Dixie Moon"
G. Jones, Jr., Chorus

"Land of Dancing Pickaninnies"
C. Davis, Bamville Picks

---

[27]Later in the run billed as "Then (You Know) You're in Love."
[28]Originally produced 6 November 1923 at the Globe Theatre for 241 performances. For Synopsis of Scenes and Musical Numbers, see original 1923 production. For this engagement, The Rag Pickers (performed by the Brightons) and Dances (performed by Cortez and Peggy) in Act 2 were omitted.
[29]Played the Colonial Theatre, New York City the previous season on tour as IN BAMVILLE.
[30]Scenery uncredited.

---

[31]Added after the opening/for subsequent tour:
"You Ought to Know"
"Jazztime Baby" (Act 1)
V. Snow
[32]Dropped for subsequent tour.
[33]Dropped for subsequent tour.

"Thinking of Me"[34]
L. Gee, I. H. Browning
"All the Wrongs You've Done to Me"
L. Payton, J. Hudgins
(*Music and Lyrics by* Lew Payton, Chris Smith and Edgar Dowell.)
"Manda"
V. Snow, Syncopated Sunflowers
Selections
Four Harmony Kings
"Take Down Dis Letter"
L. Payton
In Their Studio, a Few Minutes with Sissle and Blake ("Shuffle Along" Medley)
"Chocolate Dandies"
N. Sissle, E. Blake, Their Struttin' Company
Joe Smith will syncopate you on your merry way.

1924.28 ROSE-MARIE

A Musical Play in Two Acts, 10 Scenes[35]. Book and lyrics by Otto Harbach and Oscar Hammerstein II. Music by Rudolf Friml and Herbert Stothart. Book staged by Paul Dickey. Dances arranged by Dave Bennett. Gowns and costumes designed by Charles LeMaire. Settings by (Frank E.) Gates and (E. A.) Morange. Orchestra under the direction of Herbert Stothart. Orchestrations by Robert Russell Bennett. Production under the personal supervision of Arthur Hammerstein. Produced by Arthur Hammerstein. Opened 2 September 1924 at the Imperial Theatre and closed 16 January 1926 after 557 performances.

CAST (in order of appearance): *Sergeant Malone*: ARTHUR DEAGON. *Lady Jane*: DOROTHY MACKAYE. *Black Eagle*: ARTHUR LUDWIG. *Edward Hawley*: FRANK GREENE. *Emile La Flemme*: EDWARD CIANELLI. *Wanda*, Black Eagle's Wife: PEARL REGAY. *Hard-Boiled Herman*: WILLIAM KENT. *Jim Kenyon*: DENNIS KING. *Rose-Marie La Flamme*: MARY ELLIS. *Ethel Brander*: LELA BLISS.

Ladies of the Ensemble: Almerita Voudry, Nadya Miller, Carol Joyce, Ann Wood, Mabel Martin, Peggy Sletner, Ruby Poe, Lee Byrne, Eve Wendt, Kathlyn McKinley, Violey McKinley, Lillian Burke, Nerene Swinton, Sylvia Stoll, Stella Bolton, Peggy Driscoll, Gladys LaResche, Janet Lord, Rosalee King, Alice Mitchell, Billie Fish, Marjorie Talcott, Mary Morrison, Connie Best, Ellen Rose, Alice Hanley, Virgil Dodd, Helen Bell, Ivia Perrine, Gloria Frank, Glada Gray, Billy Armstrong, Owen Gordon, Betty Carlstedt, Genevieve Tierney, Claire Rossi, Lillian White, Cynthia Whyte, Mary Walsh, Lenore Cornwall, Grace Carlisle. *Gentlemen of the Ensemble*: John Lambie, George Jimos, Patrick Tooney, Ellis Doyle, Edward Gargon, Joseph Ames, Morris Tepper, Norman Johnstone, Bill Struber, Jack Lerner, Leslie Ostander, Irwin Arnold, Bert Bowlen, Richard Neeley.

Act 1, Scene 1: Lady Jane's Hotel. Fond du Lac, Saskatchewan, Canada. *Scene 2*: A Campfire in the Hills. Later that night. *Scene 3*: A Pantomimic Vision of an Incident at Black Eagle's Cabin. Meanwhile. *Scene 4*: Campfire in the Hills. A half hour later. *Scene 5*: Totem Pole Lodge, near Kootenay Pass in the Canadian Rockies, a few weeks later.

Act 2, Scene 1: A Novelty Shop in Quebec. Eight months have passed. *Scene 2*: Grand Ballroom. Chateau Frontenac, Quebec. One month later. *Scene 3*: A Café on the River Front, Quebec. That night. *Scene 4*: The Cellar of the same building. *Scene 5*: The Castle. One month later.

ACT 1[36]
Scene 1
"Vive la Canadienne"
A. Deagon, Ensemble
(*Music by* Herbert Stothart.)
"Hard-Boiled Herman"
W. Kent, Ensemble
(*Music by* Herbert Stothart.)

"Rose-Marie"
D. King, A. Deagon
(*Music by* Rudolf Friml.)
"The Mounties"
A. Deagon, Ensemble
(*Music by* Rudolf Friml and Herbert Stothart.)
"Lak Jeem"
M. Ellis, Ensemble
(*Music by* Rudolf Friml.)
"Rose-Marie" (reprise)
M. Ellis, A. Deagon, F. Greene, E. Ciannelli, Ensemble
"Indian Love Call"
M. Ellis, D. King
(*Music by* Rudolf Friml.)
Scene 5
"Pretty Things"
M. Ellis, Ensemble
(*Music by* Rudolf Friml.)
Eccentric Dance
W. Kent, D. Mackaye, Ensemble
(*Music by* Herbert Stothart.)
"Why Shouldn't We?"
D. Mackaye, W. Kent
(*Music by* Herbert Stothart.)
"Totem Tom-Tom"
P. Regay, Ensemble
(*Music by* Rudolf Friml and Herbert Stothart.)
Finale Act 1
E. Ciannelli, M. Ellis, F. Greene, W. Kent, A. Deagon, Ensemble
(*Music by* Rudolf Friml and Herbert Stothart.)
ACT 2
Scene 1
"Pretty Things" (reprise)
L. Bliss, Girls
"Only a Kiss"
W. Kent, D. Mackaye, A. Deagon
(*Music by* Herbert Stothart.)
Finaletto ("I Love Him")
M. Ellis, D. King, F. Greene, E. Ciannelli, L. Bliss, P. Regay
(*Music by* Rudolf Friml.)
Scene 2
"The Minuet of the Minute"
M. Ellis, W. Kent
(*Music by* Herbert Stothart.)
"One Man Woman"
D. Mackaye, W. Kent, Ensemble
(*Music by* Herbert Stothart.)
"The Door of Her Dreams" (Door of My Dreams) (Bridal Procession)
Ensemble
(*Music by* Rudolf Friml.)
Bridal Finale
E. Ciannelli, P. Regay, M. Ellis, Ensemble
(*Music by* Herbert Stothart.)
Scene 5
Finale Ultimo
M. Ellis, D. King
(*Music by* Rudolf Friml.)

1924.29 THE PASSING SHOW OF 1924

A Musical Revue in Two Acts, a Prologue and 27 Scenes[37]. Book (sketches) and lyrics by Harold Atteridge. Additional lyrics by Alex Gerber. Music by Sigmund Romberg and Jean Schwartz. Staged by J. C. Huffman. Dances by Max Scheck and Seymour Felix. Ballets by Kotchetovsky. Stage settings by Watson Barratt. Costumes by Charles LeMaire and Ernest Schrapps. Orchestra under the direction of Alfred Goodman. Entire production under the personal supervision of J. J. Shubert. Produced by the Messrs. Lee and J. J. Shubert. Opened 3 September 1924 at the Winter Garden and closed 22 November 1924 after 106 performances.

---

[34]Dropped for subsequent tour.
[35]During the run and for the subsequent tour, Act 1, Scenes 2 and 4 were eliminated.
[36]Musical Numbers were not listed in the original program; list prepared from the libretto and Rodgers & Hammerstein Fact Book. The following note appeared in the original program: The musical numbers in this play are such an integral part of the action that we do not think we should list them as separate episodes. The songs which stand out, independent of their dramatic associations are "Rose-Marie," "Indian Love Call," "Totem Tom-Tom," "and "Why Shouldn't We?" in the first act and "The Door of My Dreams" in the second act.

[37]The twelfth and last in the annual series of musical revues which began in 1894, produced by the Messrs. Shubert since 1912.

CAST: JAMES BARTON, LULU McCONNELL, GEORGE HASSELL, OLGA COOK, ALLAN PRIOR, DOROTHY JANICE, JACK ROSE, ELEANOR WILLEMS, HARRY McNAUGHTON, JOYCE WHITE, MARIE SAXON, TRADO TWINS (Peter, Frank), The Lockfords, Barbette, Herbert Ashton, Harrington Sisters, Tracy and (Bessie) Hay, Robert Lee, William Simpson, Grant Simpson, Ben Franklin, James Steiger, Andrew Jochim, Helen Maria, Vi Patterson.

Young Women of the Ensemble: Dorothy Bruce, Carol Miller, Lucille LeSeuer, Julia Barker, Rose Velour, Madelon Smith, Harriet Gustine, Charlotte Sprague, Doris Downes, Alice McCormick, Nancy Corrigan, Doris Snibbe, Dolly Moray, Louise Carlworth, May Mulhearn, Bonna O'Dear, Jeanne Van Vliet, Gay Worrell, Ann Buckley, Betty St. Clair, Helen Claire, Adrienne Bono, Edith Pierce, Alice Perry, Virginia Banks, Helen Murray, Helen Seymore, Marcia Mack, Alice Blain, Fern LeRoy, Esther Tanney, Nathalie Lederer, Helen Doyle, Marie LeViness, Aime LaMar, Kay Sutton, Gypsy Mooney, Zena Trott, Alice Whalen, Dolly Casher, Rose Lee, Marion Davis, Mildred Schneider, Tania Smirnova, Jane Dobbin.

ACT 1

Prologue

Scene 1

"Joy and Gloom"
J. White, Tracy and Hay
Gloom: H. Ashton. *Blue Laws*: H. McNaughton. *Income Tax*: R. Lee. *The Gunman*: W. Simpson. *Second Gloom*: P. Trado. *Third Gloom*: F. Trado. *Miss Gaiety*: J. White.

Scene 2

The Average Citizen
The Citizen: G. Simpson. *Lecturer*: H. McNaughton. *Hotel Keeper*: B. Franklin.

Scene 3

Charles Jones' Home
Charles Jones: B. Franklin. *Wilbur*: P. Trado. *Mrs. Jones*: L. McConnell. *Julia*: C. Healy. *Joseph*: J. Steiger.

Scene 4

Some Club
The Son: W. Simpson. *The Father*: R. Lee. *The Grandfather*: H. Ashton. *The Great Grandfather*: G. Hassell. *The Waiter*: A. Jochim.

Scene 5

"Gold, Silver and Green"
D. Healy, the Lockwoods
Scene: The Money Bag.

Scene 6

An Asylum
The Radio Fiend: W. Simpson. *The Income Tax Fiend*: R. Lee. *The Automobile Fiend*: A. Jochim. *The Mah Jong Fiend*: H. Ashton. *The Telephone Fiend*: B. Franklin. *A Crazy Man*: J. Rose.

Scene 7

"The Beaded Bag"
(*Music by* Sigmund Romberg and Jean Schwartz. *Lyrics by* Alex Gerber.)
The Buyer: A. Prior. *The Saleslady*: O. Cook. *The Lady*: D. Janice. *The Dance*: E. Willems. *The Beaded Bag Girls*: D. Bruce, J. Barker, C. Sprague, L. LeSeuer, A. McCormick, R. Velour, D. Downes, H. Gustine, N. Corrigan, D. Snibbe, L. Carlworth.

Scene 8

The Telephone
Mr. Grey: H. Ashton. *Mr. Jones*: J. Barton. *Miss Innocence*: M. Saxon. *Mr. Fresh*: H. McNaughton. *First Man*: A. Jochim. *A Lady*: C. Healy. *Clerk*: P. Trado. *Mr. White*: A. Prior. *Second Man*: B. Franklin. *Third Man*: F. Trado. *The Husband*: R. Lee. *The Wife*: D. Janice.

Scene 9

"Society Blues"[38]
J. Barton

Scene 10

Two in One
The Manager: H. Ashton. *The Author*: A. Jochim. *The Maid*: C. Healy. *The Son*: D. Healy. *The Fiancee*: J. White. *The Curate*: H. McNaughton. *The Father*: G. Hassell. *The Mother*: L. McConnell.

Scene 11

"Everybody Dance"
E. Willems, Trado Twins

Scene 12

The Trado Twins

Scene 13

King Arthur's Round Table

Min: L. McConnell. *Jim*: J. Barton. *King Arthur*: H. Ashton. *Sir Gareth*: B. Franklin. *Sir Gawaine*: A. Prior. *Sir Galahad*: W. Simpson. *Sir Mordred*: R Lee. *Messenger*: A. Jochim.

"When Knighthood Was in Flower"
O. Cook, A. Prior
(*Music by* Sigmund Romberg and Jean Schwartz. *Lyrics by* Harold Atteridge.)
Queen Guinevere: O. Cook. *Lady*: C. Healy. *Sir Lancelot*: H. McNaughton. *Lady Morgan de Fay*: M. Saxon. *Page*: V. Patterson.

Scene 14

"Dublinola"
Harrington Sisters, Dan Healy, Trado Twins, Irish Colleens
(*Music by* Sigmund Romberg and Jean Schwartz. *Lyrics by* Harold Atteridge.)

Scene 15

Specialty
J. Rose

Scene 16

The Garden of the Tuilleries
Bonaparte: A. Prior. *Josephine*: O. Cook.

Scene 17

Crown Finale

ACT 2

Scene 1

"Nothing Naughty in a Nightie"
Harrington Sisters, M. Saxon, B. Hay

Scene 2

Flappers' Version of History
A Flapper: J. White. *The Professor*: A. Jochim. *General Garcia*: H. Ashton. *Messenger*: R. Lee. *Pharaoh's Daughter*: L. McConnell. *A Sage*: A. Prior. *A Woman*: C. Healy. *Paul Revere*: J. Barton.

Scene 3

"A Study in Porcelain"
A. Prior, D. Janice, Porcelain Girls
Porcelain Groups: Old Chelsea, Chinese, French, Wedgwood, Delft, Old Vienna, Dresden.

Scene 4

Outward Bound
A Delegate: G. Hassell. *The Steward*: W. Simpson. *Charles Bryan*: A. Jochim. *William Jennings Bryan*: H. Ashton. *John W. Davis*: A. Prior. *Dawes*: R. Lee. *Helen*: H. Maria. *Coolidge*: H. McNaughton. *La Follette*: B. Franklin. *Ma Ferguson*: L. McConnell.

Scene 5

Venetia
O. Cook, D. Janice

Scene 6

At Home
Scene: Floral Park, Long Island. 1 September .
The Wife: L. McConnell. *The Husband*: G. Simpson. *The Brother*: W. Simpson.

Scene 7

Some Court Room
The Judge: B. Franklin. *A Policeman*: R. Lee. *Attorney for the Defense*: D. Healy. *The State's Attorney*: H. Ashton. *George Washington Johnson*: J. Barton.

Scene 8

"Mooching Along"
J. Barton, Plantation Girls
(*Music by* Sigmund Romberg and Jean Schwartz. *Lyrics by* Alex Gerber.)

Scene 9

"The Holiday Number"
A. Prior, O. Cook, D. Janice, Holiday Girls
Holiday Girls: New Year's: H. Gustine. *St. Valentine's*: D. Bruce. *St. Patrick's*: C. Miller. *Easter*: D. Downes. *May Day*: N. Carroll. *Fourth of July*: C. Sprague. *Labor Day*: L. LeSuer. *Halloween*: M. Smith. *Thanksgiving*: B. O'Dear. *Christmas*: R. Velour.

Scene 10

The Winter Garden Girls
Harrington Sisters, Winter Garden Steppers

Finale

---

[38]Dropped for subsequent national tour.

1924.30

BE YOURSELF!

A Musical Comedy in Two Acts. Book and lyrics by George S. Kaufman and Marc Connelly. Music by Lewis Gensler and Milton Schwarzwald. Additional lyrics by Ira Gershwin. Play staged by William Collier. Dances and musical numbers staged by Vaughn Godfrey and Jack Mason[39]. Dresses designed by Mark Mooring. Scenery designed by the H. Robert Law Studios. Orchestra under the direction of Milton Schwarzwald. Orchestrations by Stephen Jones, Maurice DePackh. Produced by (Sidney) Wilmer and (Walter) Vincent. Opened September 3 1924 at the Sam H. Harris Theatre and closed 22 November 1924 after 93 performances.

CAST [in order of appearance]: *Marjorie Brennan*: DOROTHY WHITMORE. *Grandma Sarah Brennan*: GEORGIA CAINE. *Joseph Peabody Prescott*: G. P. Huntley. *David Robinson*: BARRETT GREENWOOD. *Matt McLean*: JACK DONAHUE. *Tony Robinson*: QUEENIE SMITH. *Eustace Brennan*: JACK KEARNEY. *Mordecai Brennan*: JAY WILSON. *Cyrus Brennan*: TED WELLER. *Hemp McLean*: JOHN KEARNEY. *Bull McLean*: RALPH BRAINARD. *Betty*: Teddy Hudson. *Adam McLean*: JAMES R. McCANN.

Marjorie's Girl Friends: Peggy Gillespie, Romona Kogan, Faith Cullen, Mabel Stanford, Ann Summers, Ruth Trott, Louise Wright, Edith Talbot, Christine Bernsman, Gladys Harris, Mollie Christie, Ray Smith, Helen Evans, Gladys Smith, Eleanor Dana, Florence Murphy, Peggy Anderson, Cleo Lombard, Mildred Brown.

Act 1: The Brennan Cottage in the Tennessee Mountains. A Summer Night.

Act 2: Outside the House. The following morning.

ACT 1[40]

Opening:

"Rain"

Girls

"High in the Hills"

D. Whitmore, Girls

"Life in Town"[41]

G. Caine, G. P. Huntley

"My Road"

D. Whitmore, B. Greenwood, Girls

(*Music by* Lewis Gensler. *Lyrics by* Marc Connelly and George S. Kaufman.)

"(A) Little Bit of This"

Q. Smith

(*Music by* Lewis Gensler. *Lyrics by* Marc Connelly and George S. Kaufman.)

"A Good Hand-Organ and a Sidewalk"

Q. Smith, J. Donahue, B. Greenwood, J. Kearney, Girls

"The Decent Thing to Do"

Q. Smith, J. Donahue

(*Music by* Lewis Gensler. *Lyrics by* Marc Connelly and George S. Kaufman.)

Finale

Company

ACT 2

Opening:

"Tennessee"[42] Mountaineers, Girls

Dance T. Hudson

"(Grandma's) a Flapper, Too"

G. Caine, Girls

"I Came Here"[43]

B. Greenwood, D. Whitmore, Girls

(*Music by* Lewis Gensler. *Lyrics by* George S. Kaufman, Marc Connelly, Ira Gershwin.)

"(The) Wrong Thing at the Right Time"

Q. Smith

(*Music by* Milton Schwarzwald. *Lyrics by* George S. Kaufman, Marc Connelly, Ira Gershwin.)

"Uh-Uh"

Q. Smith, J. Donahue

(*Music by* Milton Schwarzwald. *Lyrics by* George S. Kaufman, Marc Connelly, Ira Gershwin.)

"Money Doesn't Mean a Thing"[44]

Q. Smith, J. Donahue, B. Greenwood, D. Whitmore, Girls

(*Music by* Lewis Gensler. *Lyrics by* George S. Kaufman, Marc Connelly, Ira Gershwin.)

Dance Interlude

D. Whitmore, B. Greenwood, T. Hudson

Dance

Q. Smith

"Do It Now"

J. Donahue

Finale

Company

1924.31

EARL CARROLL'S VANITIES (1924)

A Musical Revue in Two Acts, 35 Scenes[45]. (Sketches by Earl Carroll, Ralph Spence.) Music and lyrics by Earl Carroll. Staged by Earl Carroll. Dances and ensembles staged by Sammy Lee. Art director, Max Ree. Technical director, Bernard Lohmuller. Orchestra under the direction of Ira Jacobs. Produced by Earl Carroll. Opened September 10 1924 at the Music Box Theatre, moved 10 November 1924 to the Earl Carroll Theatre, and closed 3 January 1925 after 133 performances.

CAST: JOE COOK, SOPHIE TUCKER, BERT ROME, DESIREE TAYLOR, HENRY DUNN, MARGARET DAVIES, JOHN MILLER, JAMES MACK, THELMA HARVEY, CHESTER FREDERICKS, AL K. HALL, BETTY FITCH, DAVE CHASIN [Chasen], JOEY BENTON, MARY CAREY, AGNES LEONARD, FRANK LESLIE, KATHRYN RAY, EDDIE LESLIE, ALBERT HAWTHORNE, JOHNNY COOKE, LEO CONWAY, BOB SIMMS, ALBERT DARE, WALTER WAHL.

Vanities Girls: Misses Leonard Oakley, Patterson, Corday, Keithley, DeLong, Vernon, F. McFadden, G. McFadden, Benit, Jones, Armes, Black, Rella Harrison, Josephine Libby, Lucille Osborne, Dorothy Harris, Betty Wilson, Lillian Derchin, Helen Mennette, Eleanor Meeker, Carol Cummings, Betty Vane, Frances Blythe, Janice Fair, Betty Blackburn, Bernice Rose, Virginia Beardsley, Jane Odette, Lillian Moorehouse, Kiddy Young, Norma Lea Forrest, Doria Tree, Anna Mae Dennehy, Catherine Ringquist, Amy Revere, Lorraine, Elsie Lombard, Roberts, Allen, Y. Dubois, Isham, Hutchinson, Pauline Blair, Howard, A. Banton, J. Benton, Baker, Hunt, F. Marchant, Amy Frank, McKay, Frances Stone, Malvern, Benton, Medwin, V. Marchant, Tremble, Betty Fitch, Karr, Keithley, Stout, Geneva Duker, Hunt, Gertrude Lemonn.

ACT 1[46]

Scene 1

The Spirit of Vanities

(a) The Broadcasting Station. (b) "Over the Radio"

The Announcer: B. Rome. *The Speaker*: H. Dunn. *Radio Girls*: Misses Leonard, Oakley, Patterson, Corday, Keithley, DeLong, Vernon, McFadden, Benit, Jones, Armes, Black. *Miss Boston*: R. Harrison. *Page*: J. Libby. *Miss Philadelphia*: L. Osborne. *Page*: D. Harris. *Miss Washington*: B. Wilson. *Page*: L. Derchin. *Miss Pittsburgh*: H. Mennette. *Page*: E. Meeker. *Miss Cleveland*: C. Cummings. *Page*: B. Vane. *Miss Detroit*: F. Blythe. *Page*: J. Fair. *Miss New Orleans*: B.

---

[39]Two months into the run, Dances and Musical Numbers were re-credited to Sammy Lee.

[40]Added two months into the run:

"Can't You See I'm in Love" (Act 2, after "Grandma's a Flapper")

J. P. Jones, N. Terris

(*Lyrics by* Owen Murphy.)

[41]Dropped during the run.

[42]Opening Number and Dance dropped during the run.

[43]Dropped during the run.

[44]Replaced during the run by:

"Bongo Boo"

John Paul Jones (David Robinson), Norma Terris (Marjorie Brennan), T. Hudson, J. Kearney, Girls

(*Music by* Milton Schwarzwald. *Lyrics by* Owen Murphy.)

[45]The second in the annual series of musical revues produced by Earl Carroll beginning in 1923.

[46]Added to Act 1 during the run:

The Motion Picture Studio

The Wife: T. Harvey. *The Husband*: E. Leslie. *The Hero*: J. Miller. *The Director*: B. Rome. *Camera Man*: A. Gamble. *The Hand*: E. Leslie.

Two Ambitious Youths

A. Dare, W. Wahl

Added to Act 1 for tour:

"Get Them All Over at Once" (Act 1)

C. Elgin

First Dance: Eight Little Ones. *Second Dance*: C. Elgin. *Third Dance*: I. Isham, N. Roberts. *Fourth Dance*: E. Lombard. *Fifth Dance*: F. Marchant.

The W. K. Baritone (Act 1)

E. Leslie

Blackburn. *Page*: B. Rose. *Miss St. Louis*: V. Beardsley. *Page*: J. Odette. *Miss Chicago*: L. Moorehouse. *Page*: K. Young. *Miss Los Angeles*: N. L. Forrest. *Page*: D. Tree. *Miss San Francisco*: A. M. Dennehy. *Page*: C. Ringquist. *Radio Dancers*: Misses Revere, Lorraine, Lombard, Roberts, Allen, Y. Dubois, Isham, Hutchinson, Blair, Howard, Banton, Baker, Hunt, F. Marchant. *Miss America*: K. Ray.

Scene 2

The Bouncing Bozoes
> J. Miller and J. Mack

The Bozette Octette
> Misses Frank, McKay, Stone, Malvern, Beuton, Medwin, V. Marchant, Tremble

Scene 3

The Mad Musicians[47]
> A. Hawthorne, J. Cook

Scene 4

"Shadowland" (Song)
> D. Tabor
> Posed by Misses Revere, Frank, Stone, Tremble, Malvern, F. Marchant, R. K. Odette, McKay, Medwin.
> (The projection of live gold fish and growing marine plants in this color-novelty is a secret process conceived by Max Teuber.)

Scene 5

The Polo Party:[48]

Fringe — Dance
> M. Davies

"I'm the One" (Song)
> And Misses Harrison, Osborn, Wilson, M. Young, Minnette, Cummings, Blythe, Blackburn, Armes, Moorehouse, Forrest, Dennehy.

The Syncopated Cocktail
> C. Fredericks
> *His 12 Flaskettes*: Misses Leonard, Oakley, Keithley, Vernon, MacFadden, G. Black, Corday, DeLong, Patterson, Benit, Beardsley, Jones. *The Hostess*: S. Tucker. *Men in Waiting*: J. Miller, J. Mack, A. Hawthorne, J. Cooke. "The Prince of Wales"

Scene 6

The Stage Door of the Earl Carroll Theatre, New York City.
> *The Sap*: A. K. Hall. *His Friend*: B. Rome. *Mary "Congenial"*: M. Davies. *Eleanor "Uncongenial"*: B. Fitch. *Lillian "Too Congenial"*: A. Leonard. *His Son*: C. Fredericks. Girls and More Girls.

Scene 7

The Electrical Laboratory
> *The Professor*: J. Cook. *A Committeeman*: C. Alexander. *Another Committeeman*: H. Dunn. *Third Committeeman*: D. Chasin. *Assistant*: J. Benton. *Elevator Boy*: G. Duker. *First Page*: J. Libby. *Second Page*: P. Blair.
> The electrical experiments made by Mr. Cook, while offered entirely as an amusement episode in the revue, are really of a serious nature, and anyone in the audience who is interested or skeptical is invited on the stage to act as a committee.

Scene 8

The Four Hawaiians

Scene 9

The Pile Driver of 1924
> *Superintendant*: J. Cook. *Foreman*: C. Alexander. *Oiler*: D. Chasin. *Engineer*: J Cooke.

Scene 10

"O Dry Those Tears"[49] (Baritone Duet)
> F. Leslie, E. Leslie

Scene 11

"Counting the Hours"
> *The Clockmaker*: L. Conway. *The Inspiration*: D. Tabor. *The Hour Glass*: G. Lemmon. *The Pendulum Girl*: K. Ray. *Twenty-Four Lovely Hours*: "Vanities Girls."

Scene 12

Dance
> C. Fredericks

Scene 13

Sophie Tucker

Scene 14

The Ten Iodine Brothers[50]
> J. Cook, C. Alexander, A. Hawthorne, J. Cooke, A. Dare, W. Wahl, J. Miller, J. Mack, D. Chasin, B. Simms

Scene 15

"Tiddlelee Tot" (Tiddle-lee-tot)
> B. Rome, H. Dunn

Scene 16

The Pyramid of Dance[51]
> *High Priestess of Pep*: S. Tucker.

(a) The Minuet (Solo)
> T. Harvey
> Assisted by Misses Blackburn, B. Wilson, Keithley, Cummings, Forrest, Armes.

(b) The Russian Solo (Solo)
> E. Lombard
> Assisted by Misses Marchant, V. Meeker, K. Young, Howard, Libby, Hunt.

(c) The Oriental (Solo)
> V. Beardsley
> Assisted by Misses Oakley, Ringquist, Mennette, Karr, Jones, Osborn.

(d) Acrobatic Solo
> M. Davies
> Assisted by Misses Derchin, F. Marchant, D. Harris, Fair, Lorraine, Allen.

(e) The Roman Sword (Solo)
> A. Revere
> Assisted by Misses Black, Leonard, DeLong, Vernon, Corday, A. DuBois.

(f) The Jazz Toe Ballet (Solo)"?[52]"
> Assisted by Misses Duker, Hutchinson, Y. DuBois, Blair, Isham, A. Banton.

(g) The Spanish (Solo)
> B. Fitch
> Assisted by Misses Patterson, S. Benit, M. Young, Moorehouse, Dennehy, Harrison.

(h) The Essence (Solo)
> A. Frank
> Assisted by Misses Rose, Ray, McKay, Odette, Tremble, Tree.

(i) The Charleston
> F. Stone
> Assisted by Misses McFadden, F. Malvern, Medwin, J. Benton, Vane, Roberts.

Scene 17

The Diamond Palm Grove
> C. Fredericks, 108 Vanities Girls

ACT 2[53]

Scene 1

Ballet of the Winds
> (*Staged by* Senia Gluck.)

---

[47]Dropped during the run.
[48]Dropped during the run.
[49]Dropped during the run.

[50]Dropped during the run.
[51]Dropped during the run.
[52]For the first month of the run unbilled, then later credited to Sophie Stutz.
[53]Added to Act 2 during the run:

The Broadcasting Station
> *Entertainers*: J. Cook, Messrs. Hall, Miller, Mack, Chasen, Alexander, Fredericks, The Leslies, Dare & Wahl.

Slo-Motion
> A. Dare, W. Wahl

Added to Act 2 for tour:

The Law of Truth
> (*by* Ralph Spence) (Act 2)
> *The Manager*: H. Dunn. *The Author*: A. Gamble. *Mr. Barefacts*: B. Rome. *Mrs. Barefacts*: D. Tabor. *Mrs. Yankers*: B. Fitch. *Mr. Yankers*: J. Miller. *Rankins*: J. Mack.

The Brick (Act 2)
> J. Miller, J. Mack

Professor Bunk, World's Greatest Calculator (Act 2)
> J. Cook

Song
  L. Conway
  The Spring Wind Misses: *The Spring Wind*: Misses Fair, Roberts, Lorraine, Hunt. *The Summer Wind*: Misses Dubois, Y. Libby, Duker, Isham. *The Autumn Wind*: Misses Hutchinson, F. McFadden, Lombard, Howard. *The Zephyr*: A. Revere, V. Beardsley.

Scene 2
  Laudlam[54]
  A. Hawthorne, J. Cooke

Scene 3
  Wanted[55]
  Head Clerk: J. Cooke. *His Assistant*: A. F. Hawthorne. *Miss Inquirer*: M. Davies. *Miss Informed*: S. Tucker.

Scene 4
  Dances
  A. K. Hall, C. Fredericks

Scene 5
  "You Got Me Wrong"
  S. Tucker
  Dance
  J. Miller, J. Mack
  Scene: Steamship Office.
  Ticket Agent: J. Cook. *Passenger*: S. Tucker. *Lovely Trip*: B. Fitch. *Traveler*: B. Rome. *Tourist*: H. Dunn.

Scene 6
  "In the South of France" (Song)
  B. Rome, H. Dunn

Scene 7
  "The Land of Lace"
  Silver Lace: Misses Mennette, Cummings, Harrison, Osborn, Blythe, Young, Moorehouse, Dennehy, Armes, Forrest, Wilson, Blackburn. *Magenta Lace*: Misses Leonard, DeLong, Corday, Benit, Karr, Vernon, Patterson, Keithley, Beardsley, Black, Jones. *Gold Lace*: Misses F. Marchant, J. Benton, McKay, Medwin, Lorraine, Tremble, Rivere, Ray, Malvern, Odette, Stout, Frank. *Black Lace*: Miss Duker, Hunt, Blair, Howard, Lombard, Hutchinson, Libby, F. McFadden, Y. Dubois, Roberts, Isham, A. Banton. *Orange Lace*: 60 Vanities Girls.

Scene 8
  Joe Cook

Scene 9
  Joe Cook will positively explain and possibly demonstrate 'Looping the Loop'

Scene 10
  Statuette[56]
  A. Dare, W. Wahl

Scene 11
  "Tondelayo"
  And 36 White Cargo Girls.
  Specialty Dance
  T. Harvey
  Scene: Congo Room, Alamac Hotel.
  Lucy Rolls: J. Miller. *A. Royce*: J. Mack. *Head Waiter*: D. Chasin. *Outoftowner*: H. Dunn. *Chinchilla*: B. Fitch. *Ordinary Waiter*: J. Cooke. *Maestro*: A. F. Hawthorne. *Alcohol*: A. K. Hall. *Bouncers*: A. Dare, W. Wahl. *Guests*: Misses Leonard, Oakley, DeLong, Keithley, Corday, Jones, Vernon, Beardsley, Patterson, Bennett, G. McFadden, Black. *White Cargo Girls*: (Ensemble).

Scene 12
  "Tondelayo"
  B. Rome

Scene 13
  "Tu-Lo-Zo-Lu"[57]
  A. K. Hall, A. Hawthorne, J. Cooke

Scene 14
  Battle of Color
  Solo
  L. Conway

Scene 15
  "Twelve Little Heels"
  C. Fredericks
  Assisted by Misses Lombard, Duker, Isham, Hunt, Hutchinson, Blair.

Scene 16
  "Silver Threads Among the Gold"[58]
  F. Leslie, E. Leslie

Scene 17
  "Frankie and Johnny"[59]
  J. Cook

Scene 18
  For the Sake of the Game[60]
  Captain: S. Tucker. *La Pinocle*: C. Alexander. *Fair Play*: J. Cooke. *Foul Ball*: J. Mack. *Sand Bunker*: A. F. Hawthorne. *T. Boxe*: J. Miller. *Motorcycle Policeman*: A. K. Hall.

Scene 19
  Nuit de Noel (Christmas Night)
  Scene: Roofs of Paris.
  Santa Claus: M. Davies. *Snow Flakes*: Misses Frank, Benton, Medwin, Stone, Tremble, Lombard, McKay, Malvern.
  Skating Specialty
  J. Miller
  Skaters: Misses Leonard, Black, Patterson, G. McFadden, Bennett, Vernon, Oakley, Jones.
  "Christmas Night"
  M. Carey, D. Tabor, B. Rome, H. Dunn

Scene 20
  Grand Finale: Temple of Flowers
  Entire Company

THE GREENWICH VILLAGE FOLLIES (1924)

1924.32

A Musical Revue in Two Acts, 26 Scenes[61]. (Sketches by Joe Hayman, J. Gordon Bostock, William K. Wells, Francis Nordstrom, John Murray Anderson, Arthur Caesar, Don Barclay.) Music by Cole Porter, (Jay Gorney, Owen Murphy, Phil Charig). Lyrics by Cole Porter, Irving Caesar, John Murray Anderson. Entire production devised and staged by John Murray Anderson. Comedy sketches directed by Lew Fields. Dances staged by Larry Ceballos. Settings executed under the direction Livingston Platt; some designs by James Reynolds. Costume designs by James Reynolds, others. Orchestra under the direction of Alfred Newman. Produced by The Bohemians, Inc. (A. L. Jones, Morris Green, Managing directors) (Messrs Shubert). Opened 16 September 1924 at the Sam S. Shubert Theatre, closing 22 November 1924 after 77 performances; New Mid-Winter Edition opened 24 November 1924 at the Winter Garden, and closed 3 January 1925 after 54 performances. Total for both editions: 131 performances.

CAST: THE DOLLY SISTERS (Jennie, Rosie), (George) MORAN & (Charles) MACK, GEORGIE HALE, DOROTHY NEVILLE, GEORGE RASELY, JULIA SILVERS, DON BARCLAY, BILLIE DE REX, GEORGE CHRISTIE, MAISIE CLIFTON, BOBBE ARNST, ROSHANARA, JAMES CLEMONS, (Anna) LUDMILLA, VEGA, James Naulty, Ethel Davis, John Sheehan, Robert Alton, Budd Williamson, Rosalie Claire, Gloria Pleasants, Mary Jane, Maida Palmer, Marjorie Alton, George Christie, Nitza Vernille, Charlotte LaTour, Jack Brooks, Donald Ross, VINCENT LOPEZ (and His Orchestra), Jud Brady's Collies.
  Showgirls: Catherine Janeway, Betty Hill, Ann Austin, America Chedister, Helen Gladding, Rachel Gould Chester, Josephine Karroll, Mildred Mann, Jean St. John, Catherine Crandell, Helene Dahlia. *Ladies of the Ensemble*: Marcelle Miller, Millie Shaw, Meeka Aldrick, Claire Hooper, Vivian Wyndham, Lucille Constante, Polly Williams, Josephine Payne, Mary Adams, Dorothy Gordon, Edith Shepard, Josephine Ehrlich, Grace Defendis, Ann Garrison, Betty Linn, Millie Shaw, Reata Hoyt, Renon. *Gentlemen of the Ensemble*: Budd Penny, Fred Harris, Gene Collins, Terrence Kennedy, Floyd English, Eugene Day.

---

[54]Dropped during the run.
[55]Dropped during the run.
[56]Dropped during the run.
[57]Dropped during the run.

---

[58]Dropped during the run.
[59]Dropped during the run.
[60]Dropped during the run.
[61]The sixth in the annual series of musical revues produced by The Bohemians beginning in 1919.

ACT 1[62]

---

[62]The show was radically revised during the run; all Cole Porter songs (except "Make Every Day a Holiday" which was retitled "Let Every Day be a Holiday") were dropped during the run and for subsequent tour. Added during the New York run (First Edition):

Information Please
  (*by* John Sheehan) (Act 1)
  Information Clerk: B. Williamson. *The Man*: J. Sheehan. *The Girl*: E. Davis.

"I'm in Love Again" (Act 1)
  Dolly Sisters
  (*Music and Lyrics by* Cole Porter.)
  Dancers: Ludmilla, R. Alton.

"Follow the Swallow" (also in ZIEGFELD FOLLIES OF 1924)
  J. Brooks, D. Ross
  (*Music by* Ray Henderson. *Lyrics by* Billy Rose and Mort Dixon.)

"On the Radio"
  G. Rasely
  (*Music and Lyrics by* Vincent Lopez and Owen Murphy.)
  (added to Christmas Eve in the Village, replacing "Broadcast à Jazz")

Added for Second (Mid-Winter) Edition:

"Do a Little This-Do a Little That" (Act 1)
  Keene Twins (Margaret, Elizabeth)
  (*Music by* Lee Davis. *Lyrics by* Benton Ley.)

Ain't Love Grand
  (*by* Philip Bartholomae) (Act 1)
  The Bride: Ethel Davis. *The Bridegroom*: J. Sheehan. *The Bell Boy*: M. Jane.

"Hobohemia" (Act 1)
  Edward Tierney, James Donnelly, Keene Twins, Ensemble
  Ballet Divertissement created and produced by Mikhail Mordkin (Act 1)
  The Court Jester has fallen hopelessly in love with his beautiful Queen, and he yearns above all else on earth to please her with his antics. If he can only win a smile of approval or recognition from her radiant Majesty, he is convinced he will be forever happy. So he strives to please her, but in vain; she turns indifferently towards her courtiers. The Jester is in an agony of despair. He rushes toward her supplicatingly, and kisses the hem of her royal robe, only to be thrown off by the page boys. At this rebuff the poor Jester gives up all hope, and pulling out a hidden dagger, he kills himself.

(a) Polichelle (The Jester)
  (*Music by* Rachmaninoff.)
  The Jester: M. Mordkin. *The Queen*: M. Aldrich. *The Chamberlain*: David K. Morris. *The Courtier*: R. Alton. *Ladies and Gentlemen in Waiting, Pages.*

(b) Minuet
  Bronislava Pozhitskaya, Mikhail Arshansky

(c) Bacchanale
  (*Music by* Glazounov.) M. Mordkin
  Supported by Lydia Semyonova, Ensemble of the Greenwich Village Follies.

"Bom-Bom-Beedle-Um-Bo" (Act 1 Finale)
  G. Rasely, Entire Company
  (*Music by* Jay Gorney. *Lyrics by* Irving Caesar, Owen Murphy.)

Quips That Pass in the Night
  (*by* A. Seymour Brown) (Act 2)
  Scene: On a Pullman.
  The Porter: G. Moran. *The Conductor*: D. D. Morris. *The Bride*: R. Claire. *The Groom*: Edward Tierney. *A Drummer*: J. Donnelly. *Another Drummer*: J. Naulty. *The Porter's Wife*: C. Mack. *The Man*: J. Sheehan. *The Beast*: Ernest D'Amato.

"Zulu Lou" (Act 2)
  Dottie Wilson, Rosalie Claire, Marjorie Alton
  (*Music by* Jay Gorney. *Lyrics by* Owen Murphy.)
  Danced by Fay Follies Girls.

Before the Portal (Act 2)
  The Girl: Toto (The Mechanical Doll). *The Man*: E. D'Amato.

"When Evening Shadows Fall" (Act 2)
  Dorothy Neville, Josephine Payne
  (*Music by* Jay Gorney. *Lyrics by* Owen Murphy.)
  Danced by Ludmilla, E. Tierney, J. Donnelly, Keene Twins.

"The Holidays" (Added to Act 2 Finale)
  G. Rasely

Added for subsequent tour:
"The Garden of Used To Be" (Act 1)
  D. South, G. Rasely
  (*Music by* Jay Gorney. *Lyrics by* Owen Murphy.)

Scene 1
  (a) The Washington Square Arch
    George Washington: D. Ross. *Lafayette*: J. Brooks. *Dana Gibson Models*: M. Miller, B. Hill, A. Austin, M. Shaw, R. G. Chester, M. Aldrick, J. Karroll, C. Hooper.
  (b) The Greenwich Village Barber Shop
    Manicurist: B. Arnst. *Manager*: G. Hale. *Mangeress*: J. Silvers. *Theatrical Manager*: J. Clemons. *Manicurists*: V. Wyndham, L. Constante, P. Williams, J. Payne, M. Adams, D. Gordon. *Bootblacks*: M. Mann, E. Shepard, J. St. John, J. Ehrlich, G. Defendis, A. Garrison. *Barbers*: B. Penny, F. Harris, G. Collins, T. Kennedy, F. English, E. Day.

Scene 2
  On the Beach[63]
    (*by* Joe Hayman and J. Gordon Bostock)
    The Thief: F. English. *The Dude*: J. Sheehan. *The Girl*: A. Chedister. *The Man*: B. Williamson.

Scene 3
  "Brittany"[64]
    G. Hale
    (*Music and Lyrics by* Cole Porter.)
    Scene: In Brittany.
    The Hackensack Girl: B. Arnst. *The Brittany Girl*: Ludmilla. And Ensemble.
    (Specialty)
      Vega

Scene 4
  The Kiss[65]
    (*by* William K. Wells)
    Scene a: Conservatory at the Country Club. *Scene b*: The Van Hoff home, the next afternoon. *Scene c*: The Van Hoff home, evening.
    Alva Van Hoff: E. Davis. *Ludwig Van Hoff*: J. Sheehan. *John Martin*: G. Christie. *Butler*: F. English.

Scene 5
  (a) "I Want Twins"[66]
    J. Clemons, J. Naulty
    Scene: In the Village.
    The Brunettes: P. Williams, V. Wyndham. *The Blondes*: D. Gordon, R. Hoyt. *The Chestnuts*: B. Linn, L. Constante. *The Titians*: M. Adams, J. Payne.
  (b) "The Dollys and Their Collies"[67]
    R. Dolly, J. Dolly
    With Jud Brady's Collies.

Scene 6
  Service
    (*by* Francis Nordstrom)
    Scene: New York City.
    Central: A. Chedister. *Western Union*: E. Davis. *The Man*: J. Sheehan. *The Girl*: R. Claire. *A Jewish Gentleman*: J. Clemons. *The Manager*: G. Moran.

Scene 7
  "The Happy Prince"[68]
    D. Neville, G. Rasely
    (*Adapted from the story by Oscar Wilde*, by John Murray Anderson. *Musical Setting from Chopin by* Alfred Newman. *Settings and costumes designed by* James Reynolds.) *The Story Teller*: G. Christie.
    Scene a: The Orangery at Sans Souci
    The Court Harpist: G. Pleasants. *The Little Marquise*: M. Jane. *The Comtesse*: R. G. Chester. *The Queen Mother*: A. Chedister. *The Duchesse*: M. Palmer. *The Princess Royale*: M. Alton. *The Happy Prince*: R. Alton. *Ladies of the Court*: L. Constante, P. Williams, B. Linn, M. Adams, D. Gordon, C. Crandell. *Courtiers*: B. Penny, E. Day, F. Harris, G. Collins, F. English, G. Cross.

"Normandy" (revised "Brittany Girl") (Act 1)
  The Normandy Girl: A. Ludmilla.
"Could You Get Along With Me?"
  Keene Twins
  (*Music by* Jay Gorney. *Lyrics by* Owen Murphy, Irving Caesar, John Murray Anderson.)
  Dancers: James Naulty, R. Alton.

[63]Dropped during the New York run and for tour.
[64]Dropped during the New York run and for tour.
[65]Dropped during the New York run and for tour.
[66]Dropped during the New York run and for tour.
[67]Dropped during the New York run and for tour.
[68]The published sheet music features music by Willy Engelberger, and lyrics by Irving Caesar and John Murray Anderson.

Scene b: A Public Square.
The Golden Statue of the Happy Prince: T. Kennedy. *The Disappointed Young Man*: F. English. *The Charity Children*: M. Mann, J. St. Jean, G. Defendis, E. Shepard, J. Ehrlich, A. Garrison. *The Poor Seamstress*: M. Aldrich. *Her Child*: M. Jane. *The Young Playwright*: B. Penny. *The Little Match Girl*: Renon. *The Mayor*: J. Sheehan. *The Town Councillor*: J. Clemons. *The Sister of Mercy*: Roshanara. *The Swallow*: Ludmilla.

Scene 8

The Yes Guy[69]

(*by* Arthur Caesar)

The Hired Boy[70]

(*by* Don Barclay)

Scene 9

"Happy Melody"[71]

B. Arnst

(*Music by* Phil Charig. *Lyrics by* Irving Caesar and John Murray Anderson.)
Scene: Before the Portals.

Dance

N. Vernille, M. Alton, R. Alton, J. Naulty, Ensemble

Scene 10

Destiny: "Toy of Destiny"[72] (Toys of Destiny)

J. Silvers

(*Settings and costumes designed by* James Reynolds.)
Scene a: Spring, in the Bois. Paris.
The Young Girl: R. Dolly. *The Governess*: M. Aldrich. *The Man*: G. Christie.
The Chocolate Soldier: R. G. Chester.
Scene b: Summer, the Star's Dressing Room. Paris.
The Star: J. Dolly. *The Maid*: H. Dahlia. *The Young Admirer*: F. English. *The Usher*: B. Penny. *The Man*: G. Christie.
Scene c: Autumn, The Café de Paris.
The Cocotte: R. Dolly. *The Man*: G. Christie. *The Lounge Lizard*: J. Naulty.
Scene d: Winter, in Montmartre. Paris.
The Street Walker: J. Dolly. *The Drunk*: J. Clemons. *The Barman*: B. Williamson. *The Man*: G. Christie. *The Young Girl*: R. Dolly. *The Governess*: M. Aldrich. *Apaches*: F. English, B. Penny, G. Collins, F. Harris.

Scene 11

James Clemons

Scene 12

Neighbors

(*by* William K. Wells)
Scene: A New York Apartment House.
Mr. Smith: D. Barclay. *Mrs. Smith*: R. Claire. *Mr. Brown*: J. Sheehan. *Mrs. Brown*: E. Davis.

Scene 13[73]

"Two Little Babes in the Wood"

J. Silvers, G. Hale

Scene: The Land of Make Believe.

Prologue

J. Silvers

First Tableau: In a Wood.
The Hans Christian Andersen Babes: Dolly Sisters. *The Roue*: J. Clemons. *His Chauffeur*: J. Naulty.

Interlude

G. Hale

Second Tableau: A New York Apartment.
The John Murray Anderson Babes: Dolly Sisters. *The Roue*: J. Clemons.

Scene 14

In Full Stage

Vincent Lopez and His Pennsylvania Orchestra

["Stars and Stripes Forever Waltz"

(*Music by* John Philip Sousa.

"Shadowland"

"It Had to Be You"

(*Music by* Isham Jones. *Lyrics by* Gus Kahn.)]

Scene 15

George Moran and Charles Mack

Scene 16

Christmas Eve in the Village

(*Costumes designed by* James Reynolds. *Setting by* Herman Rosse.)

"Bring Me a Radio"[74]

B. Arnst

The Postmen: J. Clemons, J. Naulty. *Christmas Tree*: J. Karroll, M. Aldrich, M. Shaw, H. Dahlia.

"Broadcast à Jazz"[75]

B. Arnst

ACT 2

Scene 1

"Wait for the Moon"[76]

J. Dolly, G. Rasely
Scene: Au Clair de Lune.
The Dancer: Ludmilla. And Ensemble.

Scene 2

Around the Corner: Chase and LaTour[77]

(*by* Paul Gerard Smith)
To the Right: Chimmy: B. Chase. *Aggie*: E. Davis.
To the Left: Gwendolyn: C. LaTour. *Monty*: G. Christie.

Scene 3

In the Village

M. Clifton, B. DeRex

Scene 4

Set in Black: "Liebestraum"

(An original interpretation of Franz Liszt's Nocturne by John Murray Anderson.)
The Dancers: Ludmilla, R. Alton. *The Statutory Group*: J. Payne, M. Alton, C. Crandell, Renon.

Scene 5

Lest We Forget[78]

(*by* Arthur Caesar)

At a Railroad Station[79]

(*by* Don Barclay)

Scene 6

"Syncopated Pipes of Pan"[80]

Dolly Sisters, G. Hale, Ensemble

Scene 7

The Board of Governors[81]

(*by* William K. Wells)
Scene: At a Board Meeting.
Chairman: G. Christie. *First Governor*: D. Ross. *Second Governor*: J. Sheehan. *Third Governor*: J. Brooks. *Fourth Governor*: J. Naulty. *Mulcahey*: B. Williamson.

Scene 8

America in the Eighteenth Century

(*Settings and costumes designed by* James Reynolds.)

"My Long, Long Ago Girl"[82]

G. Rasely

"Long, Long Ago"[83]

D. Neville

(*Music and Lyrics by* Thomas Haynes Bayly.)
The Harpist: G. Pleasants. *The Long Ago Girl*: J. Silvers. And Brooks and Ross, Ensemble.

Scene 9

George Moran and Charles Mack [Boxing Sketch]

Scene 10

"Make Every Day a Holiday"

J. Silvers

(*Music and Lyrics by* Cole Porter.)
Scene: The Hall of Mirrors.

---

[69]Dropped during the New York run and for tour.
[70]Dropped during the New York run and for tour.
[71]Dropped during the New York run and for tour. Published sheet music credits Ben Bernie as co-composer.
[72]Dropped during the New York run and for tour.
[73]Dropped during the New York run and for tour.

[74]Dropped during the New York run and for tour.
[75]Dropped during the New York run and for tour.
[76]Dropped during the New York run and for tour.
[77]Dropped during the New York run and for tour.
[78]Dropped during the New York run and for tour.
[79]Dropped during the New York run and for tour.
[80]Dropped during the New York run and for tour.
[81]Dropped during the New York run and for tour.
[82]Dropped during the New York run and for tour.
[83]Dropped during the New York run and for tour.

Trophy Bearers: B. Linn, J. Payne. *The Holidays: New Year's Day*: B. Hill. *Lincoln's Birthday*: C. Janeway. *St. Valentine's Day*: C. Crandell. *The Valentine*: M. Mann. *Washington's Birthday*: R. G. Chester. *St. Patrick's Day*: C. Hooper. *Micareme*: M. Shaw. *May Day*: A. Chedister. *May Pole Day*: V. Wyndham, L. Constante, R. Hoyt, D. Gordon. *Independence Day*: J. Karroll. *Columbus Day*: H. Gladding. *Hallowe'en*: H. Dahlia. *Hallowe'en Revellers*: Renon, E. Shepard, J. Ehrlich, A. Garrison. *Thanksgiving Day*: A. Austin. *Christmas Day*: M. Palmer. *Attendants*: G. Defendis, J. St. John. *The Follies Baby*: M. Jane.

(Finale)

Dolly Sisters, Entire Company

1924.33 HASSARD SHORT'S RITZ REVUE

A Musical Revue in Two Acts, 31 Scenes. (Sketches by Harold Atteridge, Roger Gray, Norma Mitchell, Ralph Bunker. Music by Roy Webb, Frank Tours, Raymond Hubbell, Werner Janssen, Jay Gorney, W. Franke Harling, Martin Broones, Tom Burke, H. M. Tennent. Lyrics by Kenneth Webb, Ann Caldwell, Roger Gray, Owen Murphy, W. Franke Harling, Harry Ruskin, May Tully, Eric Valentine, William Gaxton, Graham John.) Entire revue conceived and staged by Hassard Short. Sketches directed by Clyde North. Dances arranged by Seymour Felix. Settings designed by Clark Robinson. Costumes designed by Charles LeMaire. Ballets arranged by Chester Hale. Orchestra under the direction of Louis Silvers. Orchestrations by Frank Tours, Roy Webb, Russell Bennett, Oscar Radin, Charles Grant, W. Franke Harling, Hilding Anderson, Irving Schloss. Produced by Hassard Short. Opened 17 September 1924 at the Ritz Theatre and closed 20 December 1924 after 109 performances; reopened 2-7 February 1925 at the Winter Garden for 8 additional performances. Total: 117 performances.

CAST: RAYMOND HITCHCOCK, CHARLOTTE GREENWOOD, TOM BURKE, MYRTLE SCHAAF, HAL FORDE, MADELEINE FAIRBANKS, WILLIAM LADD, ALBERTINA VITAK, LEILA RICARD, STANLEY ROGERS, JAY BRENNAN, JACKIE HURLBURT, EDDIE CONRAD, DOROTHY BROWN, CHESTER HALE, WILLIAM SIMPSON, ELMER BROWN.

Ritz Girls: Ethel Allis, Alice Monroe, Sunshine Jarmann, Aphia Kirby, Goodee Montgomery, Jane Overton, Janet Winters, Adele McHatton, Winifred Soldan, Grace Robinson, Frances Lee, Katherine Spencer, Evelyn Oliphant, Ruth Hovey, Lulu McGrath, Helene Gardner, Jean Ferguson. *Ritz Boys*: Charles Baum, William J. Sholar, Campbell Hicks, Don Knobloch, Robert Williams, Marshall D. Sullivan.

ACT 1[84]

Scene 1

"From Cottage to Subway"

(*Music by* Roy Webb. *Lyrics by* Kenneth Webb.)
Time: 1725-1925.
Girl: M. Fairbanks. *Boy*: W. Ladd. *Gyp*: H. Forde.

Scene 2

"Broadway's Boudoir"

(*Music by* Frank Tours. *Lyrics by* Anne Caldwell.)
Miss Revue: L. Ricard. *Follies*: E. Allis. *Passing Show*: A. Monroe. *Greenwich Village Follies*: S. Jarmann. *Scandals*: A. Kirby. *Vanities*: G. Montgomery. *Grand Street Follies*: J. Overton. *Artists and Models*: J. Winters. *Music Box*: J. Hurlbert. *Ritz Revue*: M. Schaaf.

Scene 3

"The Little Black Cat"

M. Fairbanks, W. Ladd
(*Music by* Raymond Hubbell. *Lyrics by* Anne Caldwell. *Novelty costumes designed by* Max Ree.)
With H. Gardner, A. McHatton, F. Lee, K. Spencer, R. Hovey, E. Oliphant, C. Baum, C. Hicks, W. Tallman, W. J. Sholar, M. D. Sullivan, D. Knobloch.

Scene 4

Raymond Hitchcock

Scene 5

Crossed Wires

(*by* Harold Atteridge)
Operator: S. Rogers. *Jay*: J. Brennan. *Madeleine*: M. Fairbanks.

Scene 6

"Hello Girls"

(*Music by* Werner Janssen. *Book {sketch} and Lyrics by* Roger Gray.)
Miss Endicott: E. Allis. *Miss Bryant*: J. Overton. *Miss Yonkers*: S. Jarmann. *Miss Rector*: G. Montgomery. *Miss Flushing*: J. Hurlbert. *Miss Harlem*: W. Soldan.
Scene a: *Mr. Vandergraft*: H. Forde. *Mrs. Vandergraft*: L. Ricard.
Scene b: *Mr. Risenberg*: E. Conrad. *Mr. Rice*: E. Brown. And the Ritz Boys.

Scene 7

"Springtime"

M. Schaaf
(*Music by* Roy Webb. *Lyrics by* Kenneth Webb.)
Dancers: J. Hurlbert, J. Overton, E. Allis, S. Jarmann, A. Vitak. And *Maytime*: D. Brown. *Daytime*: K. Spencer. *Junetime*: F. Lee. *Moontime*: L. McGrath. *Suntime*: A. McHatton. *Funtime*: E. Oliphant. *Rosetime*: J. Ferguson. *Springtime*: H. Gardner.

Scene 8

"I Want to Belong"

C. Greenwood
(*Music by* Jay Gorney. *Lyrics by* Owen Murphy.)

Scene 9

The Predicament

(*by* Harold Atteridge) M. Fairbanks, A. McHatton, H. Forde

Scene 10

"Sun-Girl"

T. Burke
(*Music by* Frank Tours. *Lyrics by* Anne Caldwell.)
The Sun-Girl: L. Ricard. *Suns*: J. Ferguson, A. McHatton, F. Lee, K. Spencer, D. Brown, H. Gardner.

Scene 11

Raymond Hitchcock[85]

Scene 12

The Question[86]

(*by* Clyde North)
Scene: The Master's Study.
The Master: W. Simpson. *The Secretary*: E. Brown. *The Stranger*: H. Forde.

Scene 13

"Dancing Blues"

(*Music and Lyrics by* W. Franke Harling.) M. Fairbanks, J. Hurlbert, J. Overton, G. Montgomery, S. Jarmann, E. Allis, G. Robinson

Scene 14

Her Morning Bath

(*by* Norma Mitchell and Ralph Bunker)
Scene: Charlotte's Apartment.
Charlotte a Movie Star: C. Greenwood. *Leila*, Her Friend: L. Ricard. *Messenger Boy*: E. Brown.

Scene 15

"Uking the Uke"

J. Hurlbert, W. Ladd, Ritz Girls and Boys
(*Music and Lyrics by* W. Franke Harling.)

Scene 16

Two for the Ritz

(*by* Ralph Bunker)
Scene: A News Counter.
Herbie: J. Brennan. *May*: S. Rogers. *News Girl*: L. Ricard. *Hazel Dawn*: D. Brown. *Emily Stevens*: A. McHatton.

Scene 17

"(Our) Crystal Wedding Day"

T. Burke, M. Schaaf
(*Music by* Frank Tours. *Lyrics by* Anne Caldwell.)
Scene: The Crystal Room at the Ritz.
The Bride: M. Fairbanks. *The Groom*: W. Ladd. *Bridesmaids*: E. Allis, W. Soldan, A. Monroe, S. Jarmann.

ACT 2

Scene 1

"The Red Ladies"

(*Music by* Roy Webb. *Lyrics by* Kenneth Webb.)
The Man with the Mirror: T. Burke.

---

[84]The running order of the show, particularly Act 2, was revised after the opening. Added during the run:

Slow Motion (Act 1)

Boy: Jimmy Savo. *Girl*: J. Franza.

Jimmy Savo (Specialty)

The (Right) Type (*by* Ralph Bunker) (Act 2)

Scene: Manager's Office.
The Manager: H. Forde. *The Authoress*: J. Ferguson. *The Composer*: T. Burke. *The Actor*: E. Conrad. *The Dancing Master*: W. Ladd. *The Librettist*: E. Brown. *The Office Boy*: Charles Baum.

The Soul's Awakening (*by* Noel Scott) (Act 2)

Wife: C. Greenwood. *Husband*: J. Savo. *Stranger*: H. Forde.

---

[85]Dropped during the run.
[86]Dropped during the run.

Camille

    Camille: M. Fairbanks. *Armand*: W. Ladd. *The Croupier*: W. J. Sholar, Jr. *Two Lady Gamblers*: F. Lee, K. Spencer.

Macbeth

    Lady Macbeth: J. Ferguson.

Zaza

    Zaza: E. Oliphant. *Dufresne*: R. Williams. *Aza's Aunt*: A. McHatton.

Carmen

    Carmen: M. Schaaf. *The Toreador*: C. Hicks.

La Tosca

    Tosca: L. Ricard. *Scarpia*: D. Knobloch.

Salome

    Salome: A. Vitak.

Cleopatra

    Cleopatra: H. Gardner. *Antony*: C. Hale. *Slave*: M. D. Sullivan.

DuBarry

    DuBarry: R. Hovey. *Executioner*: E. Brown. *The Devil*: H. Forde.

Scene 2

Raymond Hitchcock[87]

Scene 3

"Beedle Um Bee"

    W. Ladd

    (*Music by* Martin Broones. *Lyrics by* Eric Valentine and William Gaxton.) *Dances by* C. Greenwood, W. Ladd, Ritz Girls, Boys.

Scene 4

Tom Burke, Eddie Conrad

"The Wanderer"

    T. Burke

    (*Music by* Jay Gorney and Tom Burke. *Lyrics by* Owen Murphy.)

Scene 5

Oh! Julie![88]

    (*by* Ralph Bunker and Norma Mitchell)
    Scene: Julie's Boudoir.
    Julie: C. Greenwood. *Hubert*: H. Forde. *Alphonse*: E. Conrad. *Nanette*: F. Lee.

Scene 6

"A Midsummer Night's Dream"

    M. Schaaf

    (*Music by* Frank Tours. *Lyrics by* Anne Caldwell. *Rainbow Dress designed by* Max Ree.)
    The Girl: A. Vitak. *The Boy*: C. Hale. *The Rainbow Roses*: R. Hovey, H. Gardner, F. Lee, K. Spencer, E. Oliphant, A. McHatton, J. Ferguson, L. McGrath. *The Sprites*: J. Overton, J. Hurlbert, E. Allis, G. Montgomery, S. Jarmann, W. Soldan.

Scene 7

Raymond Hitchcock[89]

Scene 8

Presence of Mind

    (*by* Harold Atteridge)
    A: L. Ricard, H. Forde. B: M. Fairbanks, A. McHatton. C: R. Hitchcock, J. Ferguson, E. Brown.

Scene 9

"Scandal and a Cup of Tea"

    C. Greenwood, Ritz Girls

    (*Music by* Roy Webb. *Lyrics by* Kenneth Webb.)

Scene 10

"What the Men Will Wear"

    Brennan and Rogers

    (*Music by* Roy Webb. *Lyrics by* Kenneth Webb.)
    Pajamas: K. Spencer. *Nightgown*: A. McHatton. *Negligee*: J. Ferguson. *Chemise*: E. Oliphant. *Corset*: H. Gardner. *Combination*: L. McGrath. *Pajamas*: E. Brown. *Nightshirt*: H. Forde. *Dressing Gown*: T. Burke. *B.V.D.*: R. Hitchcock. *Arrow Shirt and Paris Garter*: F. Jones. *Union Suit*: E. Conrad.

Scene 11

"When You and I Were Dancing" (Fox Trot)

    M. Fairbanks, W. Ladd

    (*Music by* H. M. Tennent. *Lyrics by* Graham John.)

Waltz

    Danced by C. Hale, A. Vitak

---

[87]Dropped during the run.
[88]Dropped during the run.
[89]Dropped during the run.

Dancing: J. Hurlburt, S. Jarmann, E. Allis, G. Montgomery, J. Overton, M. Fairbanks, W. Ladd, Ritz Boys.

Scene 12

"A Perfect Day"/"Too Tall"

    C. Greenwood

    (*Music by* Martin Broones. *Lyrics by* Harry Ruskin and May Tully.)

Scene 13

"Monsieur Beaucaire"

    M. Schaaf, T. Burke

    (*Music by* Frank Tours. *Lyrics by* Anne Caldwell. The costumes in this scene are the original costumes worn in the Famous Players Picture, "Monsieur Beaucaire" with Rudolph Valentino.)

Scene 14

Finale

    C. Greenwood, R. Hitchcock, Entire Company

1924.34

DEAR SIR

A Musical Comedy in Two Acts, 6 Scenes. Book by Edgar Selwyn. Music by Jerome Kern. Lyrics by Howard Dietz. Staged by David Burton. Dances and ensembles by David Bennett. Costumes designed by Kiviette and James Reynolds. Sets by Raymond Sovey. Orchestra under the direction of Gus Salzer. Orchestrations by Allan Foster. Produced by Philip Goodman. Opened 23 September 1924 at the Times Square Theatre and closed 4 October 1924 after 15 performances.

CAST (in order of appearance): *Oliver Russell*: GEORGE SWEET. *Louis*, Maitre d'Hotel at Sherry's: Arthur Lipson. *Laddie Munn*, man-about-Long Island: OSCAR SHAW. *Dorothy Fair*, a Southern girl: GENEVIEVE TOBIN. *Andrew Bloxom*, sometimes in vaudeville: WALTER CATLETT. *A Waiter*: Francis Murphy. *Sukie Sewell*, also in vaudeville: KATHLENE MARTYN. *Peters*, Laddie's butler: Joseph Allen. *Gladys Barclay*, a society girl: Helen Carrington. *Clair*: Clair Luce. (*Pierrot*: Ritchy Craig. *Specialty Dancer*: Lovey Lee.)

Ladies of the Ensemble: Ida Berry, Trudy Lake, Rita Royce, Geraldine Reavard, Julia Warren, Marion Donnelly, Beth Meakins, Devah Worrell, Clair Lipton, Madeleine Janis, Helen Orb, Dorothy Fitzgibbon, Betty Campbell, Janearl Johnson, Josephine Dunn, June Baldwin, Peggy Watts, Evelyn Plumadore, Dorothea Richmond, Victoire Dutel, Regina Daw, Margery Martyn, Katherine Kohler, Hazel Bunting. *Gentlemen of the Ensemble*: William Boren, Will Wilder, Francis Murphy, Ray Hall, Ainsley Lambert, Austin Clarke, Frank Schulze, Billy Wilson, John McCullough, Norman Jefferson, Cliff Daly, Allen Stevens.

Act 1, Scene 1: Sherry's. Park Avenue, New York. *Scene* 2: Entrance to Park Avenue Street Fair. *Scene* 3: Park Avenue Street Fair.

Act 2, Scene 1: Foyer of Laddie Munn's Long Island Residence. *Scene* : An Old Well on Laddie Munn's Estate. *Scene* 3: Garden of Laddie Munn's Residence on Long Island.

ACT 1

Scene 1

"Grab a Girl"

    G. Sweet, C. Luce, Boys, Girls

"What's the Use?"

    O. Shaw, Girls

"I Want to Be There"

    G. Tobin, Boys

"A Mormon Life"

    W. Catlett, Girls

"Dancing Time"

    G. Tobin, O. Shaw, Ensemble

Scene 2

"To the Fair"

    Ensemble

"My Houseboat on the Harlem"

    W. Catlett, K. Martyn

Scene 3

Opening Chorus

    Ensemble

Dance

    R. Craig

"All Lanes Must Reach a Turning"

    G. Tobin, O. Shaw

Finale

    Ensemble

ACT 2

Scene 1

Opening Chorus
Ensemble

"Seven Days"
G. Tobin, O. Shaw

"If You Think It's Love You're Right"
W. Catlett, K. Martyn, G. Sweet, H. Carrington, Ensemble

"Weeping Willow Tree"
O. Shaw, Ensemble

Finaletto[90]
Ensemble

Scene 2

Scene
G. Tobin, O. Shaw

Scene 3

Waltz
Ensemble

Dance
L. Lee

Finale
Company

1924.35 THE GRAB BAG

A Musical Revue in Two Acts, 15 Scenes[91]. Sketches, music and lyrics by Ed Wynn, others. Staged by Julian Mitchell. Costumes designed by Alice O'Neil, Charles LeMaire and Mabel Johnston. (Scenery painted by John Wenger.) Musical director, Max Steiner. Produced by Ed Wynn (Direction of Abraham L. Erlanger.) Opened 6 October 1924 at the Globe Theatre and closed 14 March 1925 after 184 performances.

CAST: ED WYNN ('The Perfect Fool'), JANET VELIE, JAY VELIE, (Ralph) RIGGS & (Katherine) WITCHIE, MARION FAIRBANKS, (Albert) SHAW & (Samuel) LEE, JANET ADAIR, AILEEN HAMILTON, (William) EARL & (Francis) BELL, ORMOND SISTERS (Mary, Jane, Daisy), THE LeGROHS (Pansy, Handy, Dandy), THE VOLGA BOYS (8), JOSEPH SCHRODE, Ed Fields, Tom Nip, Alfred Nathan, Jr., Ned Wever.
Dancers and Chorus Girls: Violet Vale, Phyllis Reynolds, Harriet Marned, Bee O'Quinn, Marge Ferguson, Gertrude Walker, Frieda Marr, Virginia Ray, Fraun Koski, Marion Meuller, Trixie Shevlin, Delphine Deery, Susanne Shard, Winthrop Wayne, Florence Parker, Bee Singer, Jean Castleton, Virginia Clark, Sybil Stuart, Virginia Kelly, Kay Annis, Gladys Pender, Mildred Sinclair, Betty Garson, Mae Rena Grady.

ACT 1

Scene 1

The Tent
(*Painted by* Triangle Scenic Studios.)
Himself: E. Wynn. *Manager*: Jay Velie.

Scene 2

The Birth of a Chorus Girl: ("A Chorus Girl's Song")
A Dancer: K. Witchie. *More Dancers*: V. Vale, P. Reynolds, H. Marned, B. O'Brien. *A Stork*: J. Schrode. *The Chorus Girl*: M. Fairbanks. *Atmospheric Maidens*: M. Ferguson, G. Walker, F. Marr, V. Ray, F. Koski, M. Meuller, T. Shevlin, D. Deery. *More Chorus Girls*: S. Shard, W. Wayne, F. Parker, B. Singer, J. Castleton, V. Clark, S. Stuart, V. Kelly, K. Annis, G. Pender, M. Sinclair, B. Garson, M. R. Grady.
(*Painted by* Triangle Scenic Studios.)

Scene 3

Himself: E. Wynn. *Sap*: A. Shaw. *Tap*: S. Lee. (Haircuts by 'The Barber of Seville.')
(*Curtain designed by* John Wenger.)

Scene 4

The Rose: ("The Heart of My Rose")
The Birds: P. Reynolds, H. Marned, V. Vale, B. O'Quinn. *The Dreamer*: Jay Velie. *The Dream Bride*: Janet Velie. *The Dream Petals*: F. Marr, V. Ray, F. Koski, T. Shevlin, S. Shard, M. Meuller, D. Deery, G. Walker, M. Ferguson, F. Parker, V. Clark, M. Sinclair, W. Wayne, M. R. Grady, J. Castelton, B. Garson. *The Green Tails*: G. Pender, V. Kelly, B. Singer, S. Stuart. *The Stem*: K. Annis.
(*Scenery designed by* John Wenger. *Lighting effect by* Daniel Casey.)

Scene 5

Himself: E. Wynn.

Scene 6

A Southern Girl: J. Adair.

Scene 7

The Apartment
Himself: E. Wynn. *The Female*: M. Fairbanks. *The Male*: Jay Velie. *The Powder Puffs*: V. Vale, B. O'Quinn, H. Marned, G. Pender. *The Surprise Girls*: B. Singer, G. Walker, V. Clark, F. Koski, F. Marr, K. Annis, B. Garson, F. Parker, P. Reynolds, D. Deery, V. Kelly, S. Stuart, M. Ferguson, J. Castleton, S. Shard, W. Wayne, M. Meuller, V. Ray, T. Shevlin, M. R. Grady.
(*Setting designed by* John Wenger.)

Scene 8

["Sing Sweet Juanita"
"The Pal That I Loved Stole the Gal That I Loved"
(*Music and Lyrics by* Harry Pease and Ed. G. Nelson.)
"Let It Rain! Let It Pour! (I'll Be in Virginia in the Morning)"
(*Music by* Walter Donaldson. *Lyrics by* Cliff Friend.)
"Doodle Doo Doo"
(*Music and Lyrics by* Art Kassel and Mel Stitzel.)]

Earl & Bell
Himself: E. Wynn. *First Senor*: W. Earl. *Second Senor*: F. Bell. *Senorita*: A. Hamilton.

Scene 9

The Scotch Fair
Himself: E. Wynn. *Sandy*: T. Nip. *Bandy*: R. Riggs. *Mary*: M. Ormond. *Jane*: J. Ormond. *Daisy*: D. Ormond. *Pansy*: P. LeGroh. *Handy*: H. LeGroh. *Dandy*: D. LeGroh. *Lassies*: Ladies of the Ensemble.

Scotch Folk Songs
Ormond Sisters

Some New Twists
Le Grohs

"Annie Laurie Rag" ("What Did Annie Laurie Promise?")
E. Wynn, A. Nathan, Jr., N. Wever
(*Music and Lyrics by* Ed Wynn, Ned Wever, Al Nathan.)

ACT 2

Scene 1

The Livery Stable
Himself: E. Wynn. *The Horse*: J. Schrode, E. Fields. *The Blacksmith*: W. Earl. *The Girl*: Janet Velie. *The Man*: Jay Velie. *The Other Man*: R. Riggs.

Scene 2

Abroad ("Volga Boat Song")
Himself: E. Wynn. And the Volga Boys.

Scene 3

The Woodland: "Ballet of the North Wind"
R. Riggs, K. Witchie
The Dancing Moth: A. Hamilton. *The Firefly*: Jay Velie. *The Flame Moth*: Janet Velie. *The Leaves*: V. Vale, P. Reynolds, O'Quinn, H. Marned, M. Sinclair, W. Wayne, M. R. Grady, G. Pender. *The Grass Hoppers*: F. Koski, F. Marr. *The Wasps*: T. Shevlin, G. Walker. *The Mantis*: V. Ray, M. Mueller. *The Lace Bugs*: M. Ferguson, D. Deery. *The Lady Bugs*: J. Castleton, S. Shard. *The Alley Rodels*: B. Singer, B. Garson. *The Beetles*: V. Clark, F. Parker. *The Buffalo Tree Hoppers*: V. Kelly, S. Stuart. *The Mosquitos*: V. Ray, K. Annis. *The Driad*: K. Witchie. *The North Wind*: R. Riggs.

"The Moth for My Flames"
Jay Velie, Janet Velie

Scene 4

Someplace
Himself: E. Wynn. *Sap*: A. Shaw. *Tap*: W. Lee.

Scene 5

The Grab Bag Review
Himself: E. Wynn. And Powder Puff Girls, Jay Velie, Janet Velie, The LeGrohs, A. Hamilton, Earl and Bell, M. Fairbanks, Riggs and Witchie, Shaw and Lee, Volga Boys, Ormond Sisters, J. Adair, Entire Company

"The Grab Bag"
J. Adair

Finale

1924.36 ARTISTS AND MODELS OF 1924

A Musical Revue in Two Acts, a Prologue and 21 Scenes[92]. (Sketches) Written, compiled and staged by Harry Wagstaff Gribble. Book by the

---

[90]Dropped from program during the run.
[91]The program announced 15 Scenes; Scene 13 was omitted.

[92]The second in the annual series of musical revues produced by the Messrs. Shubert beginning in 1923.

World's Most Famous Artists and Illustrators: Harry Herschfield, C. Willard Fairchild, Herb Roth, Lurelle Guild, Rube Goldberg, Flora Nash, Dean Cornwell, Charles Dana Gibson, Cliff Sterrett, David Robinson, C. Allen Gilbert, James Montgomery Flagg, Arthur William Brown, Helena Smith Dayton, Charles D. Williams, Will Johnstone, Watson Barratt, Louise Bascom Barratt, Fred Erving Dayton, Rollo Wayne. Music by Sigmund Romberg and J. Fred Coots. Lyrics by Clifford Grey and Sam Coslow. Additional music and lyrics by Jay Gorney and Owen Murphy. Dances by Seymour Felix. Art director, Watson Barratt. Orchestra under the direction of Alfred Goodman. Orchestrations by Emil Gerstenberger. Entire production staged and supervised by J. J. Shubert. Produced by the Messrs. Shubert. Opened 15 October 1924 at the Astor Theatre, moved 9 February 1925 to the Casino Theatre, and closed 23 May 1925 after 258 performances.

CAST: BARNETT PARKER, VALAIDA VESTOFF, [Senorita] TRINI, FRANK GABY, MABEL WITHEE, CHARLES MASSINGER, MARIE STODDARD, CHARLES CANNEFAX, NANCY GIBBS, JOSEPH SPREE, JOE MORRIS, FLO CAMPBELL, JACK HINES, LUCITA CORVERA, FLORA LEA, ALEXANDER FRANK, NED NORWORTH, VIOLET STRATHMORE, RALPH AUSTIN, PAULA TULLY.

Models: Kate Goldberg, Rena Manning, Mildred Soper, Ruth Shaw, Mary Kissel, Jean Gray, Gloria Christy, Stella Shields, Aileen Adair, Elsine Sims, Paula Tully, Jacques Sage, Nova Lynn, Leona Osborne, Elena Meade, Alma Traverse, Dolores Edwards, Ruth Hanson, Myrtle Thompson, Ruth Brady, Jean Caswell. *Dancers:* Betty Lyons, Josephine Mostler, Louise Stark, Eileen Murray, Beatrice Roma, Dorothy Vinton, Ewing Eaton, Marie Marcelain, Dorothy Addison, Thelma Addison, Eva Ball, Buddy Bush, Betty Bowman, Norma Nadine, Minerva Wilson, Evelyn Jacques, Virginia Moore, Marion Wilson, Aleneva Karola, Grace McKinnon. Francis X. Sinott, Billy Wilson, George Murray, Dana Mayo, Jack McElroy, Arthur Charmion, Frank Callahan, Alan Dale.

PROLOGUE
Wood Nymphs
(*Idea by* Louise Bascom Barratt and Helena Smith Dayton)[93]
Nymphs: Misses D. Vinton, E. Eaton, R. Manning, Marlowe, M. Wilson, B. Roma, Kingston, M. Marcelain, E. Ball, M. Ball, B. Bush, O'Day, Marston.

ACT 1[94]
Scene 1
"Artists and Models"
C. Massinger, C. Cannefax, Ensemble
"What a Village Girl Should Know"
M. Withee, Village Girls
"Tomorrow's Another Day"
C. Massinger, M. Withee
(*Music by* J. Fred Coots and Sigmund Romberg. *Lyrics by* Clifford Grey and Sam Coslow.)

---

[93]Dropped for subsequent national tour.
[94]The show was repeatedly revised and altered to suit the talents of the changing cast. Among the additions during the New York run were:
A Lesson in Golf (Act 2)
The Pro: Alex Morrison (American Trick Shot Champion). *Would-be Golfer:* B. Parker. *Caddy:* Frank Sinott.
Added for subsequent tour:
A Vision at Sunrise (Posed by Bee Lockwood.) (Act 1 Opening)
The Front Curtain: Songs (Act 1)
Grace Hayes
"Follow Your Star" (Act 1)
Nancy Gibbs, Twinkling Star Girls
"I Want to Dance" (Act 1)
Lillian Roth, Yellow Smock Girls
(*Music and Lyrics by* Alfred Goodman and Maurice Rubens.)
The Jazz Dancer: Ewing Eaton. *The Russian Dancer:* V. Vestoff. *The Buck Dancer:* Tommy Healy.
"Spanish Juanita" (Sing Sweet Juanita) (added to Act 1, Scene 15)
Fred Hillebrand
"Promenade Walk" (Act 2)
L. Roth
New Orleans Dancer: T. Healy. And 16 Charleston Strutters.
The Rose Ballet (Act 2)
Chiffon Dancer, Rose Sextette, Balloon Dancers
A Castilian Castle: "Titina" (Je cherche après Titina)
(also in PUZZLES OF 1925) (Act 2)
Dave Seed
(*Music by* Léo Daniderff. *Lyrics by* Bertal-Maubon and E. Ronn.)
Titina, the dancer: L. Corvera. With the Pink Lace Girls, The Senoritas.

"What a Beautiful Face Will Do"
F. Gaby, Models
Dance Specialty
V. Vestoff, Miss Eaton
"Off to Greenwich Village" (Finaletto)
C. Massinger, M. Withee, M. Stoddard, F. Lea, F. Gaby, Ensemble
Scene: A Wood in New Hampshire
Polly Prunes, a Country Girl: F. Lea. *Artie Apple,* a Country Boy: V. Vestoff. *Sally Gump,* President of Purity Leage: M. Stoddard. *Tony Comstock,* a Puritanical Mayor: A. Frank. *Hiram Stratton.* a Professional Reformer: J. Spree. *Seth Johnson,* Very Dry and All Well: J. Hines. *Jimmy Flag,* a Popular Artist: C. Massinger. *Arthur Brownie,* another Popular Artist: C. Cannefax. *Dean Cornflower,* an Illustrator: B. Parker. *Christy Candler,* a Designer: F. Gaby. *Phyllis Comstock,* a Girl who is not to blame for her father: M. Withee.

Scene 2
Call It What You Like
J. Morris, F. Campbell
Scene 3
A Model Laundress
(*Idea by* Lurelle Guild)
Scene: An Artist's Studio in the Village.
Lynn, a Stockholder: N. Norworth. *Lita,* a Model: F. Lea. *Marion,* Lynn's Wife: V. Strathmore.
Scene 4
"I Love to Dance When I Hear a March"
(*Music by* J. Fred Coots.)
Misses L. Corvera, E. Eaton, Marlowe, R. Manning, D. Vinton, B. Roma, Dancers
Scene 5
A New Indoor Sport (Alphabetical Alliteration)
First Club Member: F. Gaby. *Second Club Member:* B. Parker. *The Waiter:* J. Spree.
Scene 6
"Good Night"
N. Gibbs, C. Massinger
(*Music and Lyrics by* Leo Wood, Irving Bibo and Con Conrad.)
Scene: The porch of a Southern Home.
The Mother: M. Stoddard. *The Father:* J. Hines. *The Daughter:* N. Gibbs. *The Boy:* C. Massinger.
Scene 7
Past, Present, and Oh, What a Future—for the American Drama!
(*Idea by* C. Alan Gilbert)
Scene: Nina Ardayne's Home. (a) The Laura Jean Libby Period, 1884. (b) The Sam Shipman Period, 1924.
Introduced by: C. Cannefax. *George,* a Servant: J. Spree. *Nina Ardayne,* the Baker's Daughter: F. Campbell. *Della Norvell,* the Poor Dependent: M. Withee. *Mortimer Carruthers,* a Perfect Gentleman: J. Hines. *Maurice Van Auken,* the Villain: B. Parker.
Scene 8
The Unveiling
(*Idea by* Mitchell Rawson.)
"Pull Your Strings"
M. Withee, F. Campbell
Statue Girls: Models.
Scene 9
"Shoes"[95]
Misses D. Vinton, E. Eaton, R. Manning, ? Marlowe, B. Roma
(*Music by* Jay Gorney. *Lyrics by* Owen Murphy.)
Scene 10
Honesty
Scene: Around a Dining Table.
The Hostess: M. Stoddard. *Sally:* V. Strathmore. *Billy:* F. Gaby. *Fay:* F. Campbell. *Percy:* B. Parker. *Jimmy:* C. Cannefax. *A Servant:* J. Spree. *Guests:* Misses L. Corvera, Barclay, P. Tully. Messrs. F. X. Sinott, A. Dale, J. McElroy
Scene 11
"(The) Model Toddle"[96]
M. Withee
Dance Specialty: V. Vestoff, Toddle Girls, Model Girls, Model Toddle Boys.
Scene 12
The Lily Pool[97]
(*Idea conceived by* Watson Barratt.)

---

[95]Dropped for subsequent national tour.
[96]Dropped for subsequent national tour.
[97]Dropped for subsequent national tour.

"My Lily Maid"[98]
　　N. Gibbs, C. Massinger
　　The Girl: N. Gibbs. *The Troubadour*: C. Massinger. *The Reflections*: M. Thompson, G. Murray. *Lily Pool Girls*: R. Shaw, E. Sims, J. Sage, J. Gray.

Scene 13

Insanity
　　(*by* Harry Wagstaff Gribble)
　　Scene: Doctor's Office in an Insane Asylum.
　　The Doctor: J. Hines. *The Governor's Wife*: M. Stoddard. *An Inmate*: B. Parker.

Scene 14

"The Midnight Color Ball"
　　(*Idea Conceived by* Watson Barratt.)

Scene 15

(An Artist's Studio)
　　Scene: Jimmy Flag's Studio.
　　Jimmy Flag: C. Massinger. *Dean Conflower*: B. Parker. *Christy Candler*: F. Gaby. *Gold Ruberg*: N. Norworth. *Arthur Brownie*: C. Cannefax. *Vi*: V. Strathmore. *Flo*: F. Lea. *'Cita*: L. Corvera. *Head Waiter*: R. Austin. *Waiter*: D. Seed. *A Dancer*: Trini.

Scene 16

"Who's the Lucky Fellow?"
　　Trini, C. Cannefax, Boys
　　(*Music by* J. Fred Coots.)

Scene 17

The Color Tubes: "Dancing Colors"
　　M. Withee, F. Lea, V. Strathmore, C. Massinger, C. Cannnefax, J. Hines, Ensemble

Scene 18

The Living Palette
　　(*Idea by* Watson Barratt.)
　　Posed by Misses D. Edwards, S. Shields, G. Christy, L. Osborne, A. Adair, G. McKinnon, M. Kissel, B. Lyons, R. Manning, R. Brady, E. Meade, J. Gray.

ACT 2

Scene 1

"Jazz à la Russe"[99]
　　(*Composed and arranged by* Alfred Goodman.) N. Gibbs
　　Danced by H. White, A. Manning, Ensemble.

Scene 2

Frank Gaby, assisted by "Jimmy" and "Red"

Scene 3

There's Truth in China
　　(*by* Harry Wagstaff Gribble)
　　Scene: A Bed Room in a Very Old House.
　　Mr. Barratt, a Host: A. Frank. *Mr. Sullivan*, a Guest: B. Parker. *Mrs. Dayton*, a Guest: F. Lea.

Scene 4

"Mediterranean Nights"[100]
　　Trini, Ensemble

Scene 5

Everything the Same
　　Scene: Honeymoon Hall.
　　Richard Elderberry, the Husband: C. Massinger. *Emily*, His Wife: N. Gibbs. *Hobson*, a Butler: J. Spree. *Wedding Guests*: Misses B. Lyons, J. Caswell, A. Adair, P. Tully, D. Edwards, M. Thompson, Messrs. G. Murray, D. Mayo, A. Dale, F. Callahan, A. Charmion, J. McElroy.

Dance Specialty
　　L. Corvera, F. Lea

"Always the Same"
　　Gibbs, C. Massinger

Scene 6

"The Tiller Girls"[101]
　　(*Idea by* Will B. Johnstone.) F. Campbell

Scene 7

"(My) Riviera Rose"
　　(*Music by* Horatio Nicholls. *Lyrics by* Jean Frederick.)
　　A Flower: Trini. *A Gentleman*: C. Massinger. *A Dancer*: V. Vestoff. *Another Dancer*: L. Corvera.

Scene 8

Fata Morgana[102] (or the Mean Shoulder Blade)
　　(*by* Harry Wagstaff Gribble)
　　Scene: A Living Room in Hungary.
　　George: B. Parker. *Father*: A. Frank. *Mother*: M. Stoddard. *Rosalie*: V. Strathmore. *Francisca*: J. Caswell. *Mrs. Fay* from Buda Pest: F. Gaby. *The Sister*: P. Tully. *Mr. Fay*: N. Norworth.

Scene 9

"Behind My Lady's Fan"
　　N. Gibbs, C. Massinger

Minuet
　　L. Corvera, F. Lea, Ensemble

Scene 10

The Fan
　　(*Idea conceived by* Watson Barratt.)
　　Posed by Misses N. Lynn, P. Tully, G. Christy, S. Shiel, J. Gray, Barkley.

Finale

1924.37

DIXIE TO BROADWAY

A Musical Revue in Two Acts, 24 Scenes. Sketches by Walter De Leon, Tom Howard, Lew Leslie and Sidney Lazarus. Music by George W. Meyer and Arthur Johnston. Lyrics by Grant Clarke and Roy Turk. Entire production staged and conceived by Lew Leslie. Orchestra under the direction of Will Vodery. Orchestrations and arrangements by Will Vodery. Costumes by Brooks Costume Company. Produced by Lew Leslie[103]. Opened 29 October 1924 at the Broadhurst Theatre and closed 3 January 1925 after 77 performances[104].

CAST: FLORENCE MILLS, HAMTREE HARRINGTON, CORA GREEN, SHELTON BROOKS, MAUD RUSSELL, JUAN HARRISON, ALMA SMITH, DANNY SMALL, BILLY CAIN, ULYSSES S. THOMPSON, JOHNNY NIT, BYRON JONES, LEW KEENE, WILLIE COVAN, WALTER CRUMBLEY, WINIFRED and BROWN, E. Moses, L. Moses, William DeMott, Gwendolyn Graham, Anita Rivera, Jerry Clarke, Marian Tyler, Lillian Brown, Eva Metcalf, Aida Ward, Ralph Love, Charles Foster, Dick Whalen.

ACT 1

Scene 1

Prologue: Evolution of the Colored Race

Scene 2

"Put Your Old Bandana On"
　　D. Small, M. Russell, Plantation Chocolate Drops, Plantation Steppers

Scene 3

"Dixie Dreams"
　　F. Mills, Company

Scene 4

"A Few Steps in Front of the Curtain"
　　Plantation Steppers

Scene 5

Treasure Castle
　　(*by* Tom Howard)
　　Sam: H. Harrington. *Slim*: S. Brooks. *Charlie*: D. Small. *Svengali*: W. DeMott.

Scene 6

"He Only Comes To See Me Once in a While"
　　C. Green

Scene 7

"Jungle Nights in Dixieland"
　　F. Mills, Plantation Chocolate Drops

Scene 8

Prisoners Up-to-Date
　　J. Nit, B. Jones, L. Keene

Scene 9

The Right of Way
　　(*by* Walter DeLeon and Lew Leslie)
　　The Cop: W. Crumbley. *The Victim*: H. Harrington. *Mr. and Mrs.*: S. Brooks, M. Russell. *Miss High Hat*: C. Green.

---

[98]Dropped for subsequent national tour.
[99]Dropped for subsequent national tour.
[100]Dropped for subsequent national tour.
[101]Dropped for subsequent national tour.

[102]A burlesque of the successful play by James L.A. Burrell. Dropped for subsequent national tour.
[103]Though Lew Leslie is the producer of record in programs, A. H. Woods appears as producer in several New York opening night newspaper reviews, as well as on sheet music.
[104]Settings uncredited.

Scene 10

"Mandy Make Up Your Mind"

The Groom: F. Mills. *The Bride*: A. Smith. *Bridesmaids*: B. Cain, E. Moses, G. Graham, A. Rivera, J. Clarke, M. Tyler. *Four Maids of Honor*: M. Russell, L. Brown, E. Metcalf, A. Ward. *Four Best Men*: D. Small, J. Harrison, R. Love, C. Foster.

Scene 11

Hanging Around[105]

H. Harrington, C. Green

Scene 12

"Jazz Time Came from the South"

F. Mills, A. Smith, B. Cain

Scene 13

"Jazz Time Came from the South" (reprise)

Entire Company

ACT 2

Scene 1

"If My Dream Came True"

J. Harrison

Scene 2

If My Dream Came True:

First Episode:

Georgia Cohans

W. Covan, B. Jones, C. Walker

Second Episode:

Eva Tanguays

A. Smith, B. Cain, E. Moses, L. Moses, G. Graham, A. Rivera

Third Episode:

Gallagher & Shean

U. S. Thompson, L. Keene, D. Small, R. Love, Brown and W. DeMott

Fourth Episode:

Belasco's Kiki

M. Tyler, T. West, E. Meadows, J. Clarke, A. Rivera, A. Ward, E. Metcalf, N. Caldwell

Fifth Episode:

George Walker

J. Nit, D. Whalen

Sixth Episode:

Bert Williams

S. Brooks, S. Vanderhurst

Scene 3

Shelton Brooks[106] (Specialty included his own compositions)

["Marching Through Georgia"

(*Music and Lyrics by* Shelton Brooks.)]

Scene 4

"Darkest Russia"

Katinkas: D. Small, Plantation Chocolate Drops. *Wooden Soldiers*: F. Mills, Plantation Steppers.

Scene 5

The Sailor and the Chink

Winifred and Brown

Scene 6

"Dixie Wildflowers"

C. Green, Plantation Chocolate Drops

Scene 7

"I'm a Little Blackbird Looking for a Blue Bird"

F. Mills

Scene 8

A Nice Husband

(*by* Sidney F. Lazarus)

The Maid: M. Russell. *Georgette*: C. Green. *Freddy*: H. Harrington. *Jimmy*: S. Brooks.

Scene 9

Dance Specialty

U. S. Thompson, W. Covan

Scene 10

"Trottin' to the Land of Cotton Melodies"

D. Small, A. Smith, B. Cain, Entire Company

Scene 11

Finale

Entire Company

1924.38

ANNIE DEAR

A Musical Comedy in Three Acts, 4 Scenes. Book, music and lyrics by Clare Kummer. Based on her comedy 'Good Gracious, Annabelle.' All dance music and additional numbers by Sigmund Romberg; lyrics by Clifford Grey. Modern costumes designed by Mme. Frances. Scenic sketches for Acts 1 and 2 by Karl Koeck. Orchestra under the direction of Gus Salzer. Entire production staged by Edward Royce. Produced by Florenz Ziegfeld. Opened 4 November 1924 at the Times Square Theatre and closed 31 January 1925 after 103 performances.

CAST (in order of appearance): *Titcomb*, a clerk at the Hotel St. Swithin: John Byam. *Lottie*, one of Mr. Wimbledon's servants: MAY VOKES. (*A Flower Girl*: Florentine Gosnova.) *Wenceslaus Wickham*, a detective at the Hotel: Edward Allan. *George Wimbledon*, Owner of the Wimblemere: ERNEST TRUEX. *Twilly*, a costumer and interior decorator: BOBBY WATSON. *Annie Leigh*, who has a husband somewhere: BILLIE BURKE. *Alec*, a page at the Hotel: Spencer Bentley. *Ethel Deane*, Wilbur's fiancée, a poor artist: Phyllis Cleveland. *Gwen Morley*, Alfred's fiancée: MARY LAWLOR. *Alfred Weatherby*, whose father has lost millions: JACK WHITING. *Wilbur Jennings*, a poor poet: ALEXANDER GREY. *James Ludgate*, Mr. Wimbledon's butler: Spencer Charters. *Harry Murchison*, Annie's devoted friend: Gavin Gordon. *Mr. Gosling*, Annie's lawyer: Frank Kingdon. *John Rawson*, a wealthy Western mine owner: MARION GREEN. *Muriel Darling*, George Wimbledon's sweetheart: MARJORIE PETERSON. (*Dance Specialty*: Easter and Hazleton.)

The Brown Girls: *Lois Brown*: Anastasia Reilly. *Hazel Brown*: Gertrude McDonald. *Ruth Brown*: Dorothy Brown. *Gloria Brown*: Marguerite Boatwright. *Gladys Brown*: Pearl Eaton. *Helen Brown*: Catherine Littlefield. *The Jones Boys*: *Harry Jones*: Abner Barnhart. *Murray Jones*: Gayle Mays. *Edward Jones*: Norman Knox. *Thomas Jones*: Ned Hamlin. *Charles Jones*: Russell Smith. *Richard Jones*: William May. *The Twilly Girls*: *Dogwood*: Joan Clement. *Lipstick*: Katherine Sacker. *Shelmerdene*: Rona Lee. *Rendezvous*: Gladys Coburn. *Chinese Night*: Edna Johnson. *Clematis*: Peggy Steele. *Bonnie*: Virginia Crane. *Cherie*: Helen Barrow. *Deauville*: Helen Herendeen. *Anne*: Evelyn Grieg. *The Guests at Hotel*: Nyo Lee, Mary Almonti, Lelia McGuire, Charles Schenck, Harold Hennessey, George Ferguson, Barton Hepburn, Alfred Wyart, Lawrence Crowe. *The Page Boys at Hotel*: Jason Bauer, James Shelton, Fred Arnold.

Act 1: The Lounge and Palm Garden of the Hotel St. Swithin, New York City.

Act 2: Servants' Garden at Wimblemere, Long Island.

Act 3, Scene 1: Kitchen and Stove at Wimblemere, Long Island. *Scene 2*: Birch Gardens at Wimblemere, Long Island.

ACT 1

Opening

J. Byam, Guests of the Hotel, Pages, Brown Girls, Jones Boys

"Twilly of Fifth Avenue"

B. Watson, Twilly Girls

(*Music by* Sigmund Romberg. *Lyrics by* Clifford Grey.)

Dance

B. Watson, F. Gosnova, M. Eaton

"Come to My Party"[107]

B. Burke, M. Green

"The Only Girl"

M. Green, J. Whiting, A. Gray, Jones Boys, Gentlemen of the Ensemble

(*Music by* Sigmund Romberg. *Lyrics by* Clifford Grey.)

"Off to Wimblemere" (Finaletto)

Entire Company

ACT 2

"In Love Again" (Opening)

Brown Girls, Jones Boys

"Help, Help, Help"

M. Vokes, S. Charters, J. Whiting, P. Cleveland, M. Lawlor, A. Gray

---

[105]For subsequent national tour, replaced by:

Rain (burlesque)

H. Harrington, C. Green

[106]For subsequent national tour{Shelton Brooks had departed the cast}, replaced by:

Lillyn [Lillian] Brown (Specialty)

[107]Credited in sheet music and/or ACSAP listing to Sigmund Romberg.

Dance Eccentric[108]

(*Music by* Sigmund Romberg.) E. Allan

"Slither, (Slither)"

B. Burke, Jones Boys, Ensemble

"Etiquette"

B. Watson, Twilly Girls, Brown Girls

Dance

M. Lawlor

"One Man Is Like Another"

M. Peterson, Jones Boys

(*Music by* Sigmund Romberg. *Lyrics by* Clifford Grey.)

"I Want To Be Loved"[109]

B. Burke, M. Green

"Whisper to Me"[110]

M. Green

(*Music by* Sigmund Romberg. *Lyrics by* Clifford Grey.)

ACT 3

Scene 1

(*Written by* William Anthony McGuire and Florenz Ziegfeld.)

"Radio Voices"

M. Vokes, B. Watson

Annie Is Compelled to Cook

"Annie (Dear)"

B. Burke, assisted by E. Truex

Scene 2

Pajama Party: "Louwanna"[111]

A. Gray, P. Cleveland, M. Lawlor, Ensemble

(*Music by* Sigmund Romberg and Jean Schwartz. *Lyrics by* Clifford Grey.)

DanceF. Gosnova

"Gypsy Bride"

M. Vokes

"Bertie"

E. Truex, Brown Girls, Jones Boys, Ensemble

(*Music by* Sigmund Romberg. *Lyrics by* Clifford Grey.)

"A Comedy Fantasy"

(*Words and Music by* Clare Kummer.)

Scene I: The Lane. *Scene II*: The Bakery. *Scene III*: The Edge of the Woods. *Scene IV*: The Bird's Nest. *Scene V*: The Heart of the Woods. *Scene VI*: The Rainbow's End.

Head Chorister: Titcomb. *Four Choristers*: Four Guests of the Hotel. *Hedge*: Wilbur. *Stump*: Alfred. *Cloud*: A Twilly Girl. *Moon*: A Twilly Girl. *Sheep*: Pages of the Hotel. *Bo-Peep*: Muriel. *Cat*: Himself. *Boy Blue*: Annie. *Four School Children*: Brown Girls. *Baker*: Goslinbg. *Four All-Day SuckersThe Queen's Tarts*: The Twilly Girls. *Thunder*: The Jones' Boys. *Lightning*: Wickham. *WindRain*: The Twilly Girls. *Witch*: Twilly. *Timid (A Violet)*: Ethel. *Shrinking (A Violet)*: Gwen. *Golden Pheasants*: The Twilly Girls. *Gamekeeper*: Wimbledon. *Landlord Tree*: James. *Baby Birds*: Themselves. *Mother Bird*: Lottie. *Heart of the Woods*: A Twilly Girl. *Willow*: A Twilly Girl. *Miner*: Rawson. *Crock of Gold*: C. Littlefield.

The Dryad and the Faun (Duo Dance)

Easter and Hazleton

Finale: The Rainbow's End—Annie Dear

(Entire Company)

(*Music by* Sigmund Romberg.)

1924.39 ## MADAME POMPADOUR

A Play with Music in Two Acts. (Original German) Book and lyrics by Rudolph Schanzer and Ernst Welisch. Music by Leo Fall. (American) Adaptation by Clare Kummer. Produced under the direction of R. H. Burnside. Musical numbers staged by Julian Alfred. Costumes designed by Wilhelm. Scenery designed by Willy Pogany. Orchestra under the direction of Oscar Radin. Produced by Charles Dillingham and Martin Beck. Opened 11 November 1924 at the Martin Beck Theatre and closed 17 January 1925 after 80 performances.

<u>CAST</u>: *Madame la Marquise de Pompadour*: WILDA BENNETT. *Louis XV, The King of France*: FREDERICK LEWIS. *Rene, the Count D'Estrades*: JOHN QUINLAN. *Madeleine, a young wife*: EVA CLARK. *Belotte*, Madame Pompadour's maid: WANDA LYON. *Joseph Calicot*, a bibulous poet: FLORENZ AMES. *Maurepas*, Minister of Police: OSCAR FIGMAN. *Poulard*, his assistant: Louis Harrison. *Prunier*, Proprietor, "Stable of the Muses": Edgar Kent. *Collin*, Gentleman in Waiting to Madame Pompadour: Henry Vincent. *Boucher*, an artist: Raymond Cullen. *Tourelle*, an expert in porcelain: Curt Peterson. *The Austrian Ambassador*: Edgar Kent. *The Lieutenant*: Elliott Stewart.

Grisettes (6): *Pamela*: Pauline Miller. *Felice*: Margot Greville. *Caroline*: Janet Stone. *Leonie*: Elaine Palmer. *Valentine*: Irma Irving. *Amelie*: Dorothy Irving.

Artists, Bohemians, People of the Court, Soldiers: Betty Wilson, Leonora Darcy, Anne Makara, Rose Maynard, Marie Lambert, Mabel Knight, Ursula Dale, Mildred Mindell, Betty Lawrence, Joan Lindsey, Florence Fitzwalters, Berte Alden, Marjorie Flynn, Pauline Miller, Margot Greville, Beatrice Hughes, Pauline Hall, Eileen Seymour, Alice Brady, Margaret Morris, Loe Moran, Zachary Caulli, Fred Burke, DeWitt Matthews, Ivan Frank, Richard Allen, John Barney, Elliott Stewart, Raymond Cullen, Curt Peterson, Walter Costello, Herbert Pickett, John Fulco, Christian Holton, Rene Vanryha, Alexis Havrilla.

The action takes place in Paris and Versailles at the time of the reign of Louis XV.

Act 1: Cellar of the 'Stable of the Muses,' converted into a cabaret and frequented by Bohemian Paris. A night in spring.

Act 2: Boudoir of Madame la Marquise de Pompadour at Versailles. Late afternoon of the following day.

ACT 1

Introduction and Ensemble

"Oh! Pom-Pom-Pom-Pompadour"

F. Ames, Chorus

"Carnival Time"

J. Quinlan, Grisettes

"Magic Moments"

W. Bennett, W. Lyon

"By the Light of the Moon"

W. Bennett, J. Quinlan

"One Two and One Two Three"

W. Lyon, F. Ames

Finale

Company

ACT 2

Introduction and Ensemble

H. Vincent, Chorus

"I'll Be Your Soldier"

W. Bennett, J. Quinlan

"Tell Me What Your Eyes Were Made For"

W. Bennett, E. Clark, W. Lyon, Grisettes

"When the Cherry Blossoms Fall"[112]

F. Ames, W. Lyon

"Serenade, Madame Pompadour"

J. Quinlan, Male Chorus

"Oh! Joseph"

W. Bennett, F. Ames

"Reminiscence, Madame Pompadour"

W. Bennett, J. Quinlan

"Entrance of the King

Company

Finale

Company

1924.40 ## MY GIRL

A Musical Farce in Two Acts and an Interlude. Book and lyrics by Harlan Thompson. Music by Harry Archer. Staged by Walter Brooks. Settings designed by P. Dodd Ackerman. Costumes from designs by Travis Banton; Milgrim. Harry Archer Orchestra under the direction of Ernest Cutting. Produced by Lyle D. Andrews. Opened 24 November 1924 at the Vanderbilt Theatre and closed 1 August 1925 after 291 performances.

<u>CAST</u> (in order of appearance): *Mary White*: Jane Taylor. *Lily*: Gertrude Clemons. *Betty Brown*: MARIE SAXON. *Bob White*: RUSSELL MACK. *Oliver Green*: HARRY PUCK. *Cynthia Redding*: HELEN BOLTON. *Harold Gray*: EDWARD H. WEVER.

---

[108]Moved from Act 2 to Act 3 after the opening week.

[109]Credited in his biography to Sigmund Romberg.

[110]Moved from Act 2 to Act 3 after the opening week.

[111]Credited in sheet music and/or ACSAP listing to Sigmund Romberg.

---

[112]During the run, replaced by:

"Inspiration"

F. Ames, Grisettes, Maids

Nathaniel D. Green: Harry G. Keenan. *Mrs. Green*: Margaret Armstrong. *"Pinkie"*: Roger Gray. *Judge Black*: Patrick Rafferty. *Mrs. Brown*: Harriet Ross. *Cerise*: Lucilla Mendez. *Violet*: Frances Upton. *Coral*: Blanche O'Brien. *Rose*: Rose Adaire. *Heliotrope*: Liane Mamet. *Ruby*: Sybil Bursk. *Olive*: Peggy Watts. *Orchid*: Marie Shea. *Goldie*: Josephine Bryce.

Act 1: Living Room in the suburban home of the White's. Evening.

Interlude: Judge Black's Court Room and The Rainbow Club. Some months later. Afternoon.

Act 2: At the White's. That evening.

ACT 1
"A Little Place of Your Own"
J. Taylor, M. Saxon
"Rainbow of Jazz"
M. Saxon, H. Puck, Girls
"They Say" (Trio)
H. Bolton, H. Puck, J. Hartley
"You and I"
J. Taylor, R. Mack, Girls
"A Fellow Like Me"
M. Saxon, H. Puck
"Fifteen Minutes a Day"
R. Mack, R. Gray
"Desert Isle"
H. Bolton, E. H. Wever, Girls
"Before the Dawn"[113]
J. Taylor
Finale
Ensemble
ACT 2
"It Never Will Get You a Thing"
R. Mack
"There Was a Time"
M. Saxon, Girls
"(Women,) You Women!"
H. Puck, Girls
"A Solo on the Drum"
H. Bolton, R. Mack, Girls
"Love-Sick"
M. Saxon, H. Puck
Reprise and Finale
Ensemble

1924.41 THE MAGNOLIA LADY

A Musical Comedy in Two Acts, 5 Scenes. Book and lyrics by Anne Caldwell. Based on the comedy "Come Out of the Kitchen" by A. E. Thomas and Alice Duer Miller. Music by Harold Levey. Production staged by Hassard Short. (Musical) Numbers arranged by Chester Hale and Julian Alfred. Costumes designed by Charles LeMaire and William H. Matthews. Settings designed by William E. Castle. Orchestra under the direction of Harold Levey. Orchestrations by Robert Russell Bennett. Produced by Henry Miller. Opened 25 November 1924 at the Sam S. Shubert Theatre and closed 3 January 1925 after 47 performances.

CAST: *Lily-Lou Ravenel*: RUTH CHATTERTON. *Virginia Ravenel*: MURIEL STRYKER. *Betty Fane*: Berta Donn. *Mrs. Hallett*: Ethel Martin. *Liza*: Nellie Fillmore. *Stella Hallett*: LOVEY LEE. *Peter Ravenel*: RICHARD [Skeets] GALLAGHER. *Kenneth Craig*: RALPH FORBES. *Robert Ravenel*: MINOR WATSON. *Jefferson Page*: WORTHE FAULKNER. *Luther Hallett*: Frank Doane. *Wash Brimmage*: BILLY TAYLOR. *Cyril Brent*: BLAND O'CONNELL. (*Specialty*: Bob Young's Dixie Boys.)

Members of the Ensemble: Ladies: Virginia Beardsley, Bernice Furrow, Virginia Sharr, Harriet Chetwynd, Lucille Osborne, Mary Adams, Catherine Kohler, Halcyone Hargrove, Emma Wyche, Hazel Clayton, Sara Johnson, Julia Lane, Helen Haines. Gentlemen: Georgie O'Brien, Carl Rose, Louis Sears, Tom Chadwick, Tom Morrison, Edward McCullough, George Jefferson, John Munster, Ward Van Ness.

Act 1, Scene 1: The Living Hall of "The Magnolias," the Ravenel Mansion in Virginia. *Scene 2*: Road near the Station. *Scene 2*: The Terrace at "The Magnolias."

Act 2, Scene 1: The Kitchen. *Scene 2*: The Ballroom at "The Magnolias."
ACT 1
"On the Washington Train"
R. Stryker, W. Faulkner, M. Watson
"Three Little Girls"
W. Faulkner, M. Watson, R. Stryker, V. Beardsley, V. Sharr
"I Will Be Good"
R. Gallagher, B. Donn
"My Heart's in the Sunny South"
R. Chatterton
"When Whiteman Starts to Play"
B. Taylor, Girls
Songs
Bob Young's Dixie Boys
"The Magic Hour"
W. Faulkner
Dance
L. Lee
"Moon-Man"
R. Chatterton, R. Forbes
ACT 2
"Liza Jane"
R. Chatterton, R. Gallagher, M. Watson
"When the Bell Goes Ting-a-ling-ling"
R. Gallagher
"The Old Red Gate"
R. Chatterton, Ensemble
"A la Gastronome"
R. Gallagher, M. Watson, M. Stryker, B. Taylor, L. Lee
"The French Lesson"
R. Chatterton, R. Forbes
"Phantoms of the Ballroom"
W. Faulkner
Indians: M. Stryker, B. O'Connell.
Minuet
G. Jefferson, T. Morrison, H. Clayton, S. Johnson
Gavotte
E. McCullough, J. Munster, L. Osborne, M. Adams
Polka
L. Lee, B. O'Connell
Jazz
B. Taylor
"Tiger Lily-Lou"
R. Chatterton, B. O'Connell, Ensemble
Finale
R. Chatterton, Company

1924.42 PRINCESS APRIL

A Musical Comedy of Youth, Vitalizing the American Girl, in Three Acts. Book by William Cary Duncan and Lewis Allen Browne. Adapted from a story by Frank R. Adams. Music and lyrics by Monte Carlo and Alma Sanders. Book staged by Oscar Eagle. Dances arranged by Raymond Midgley. Costumes designed by D. Gilman, William Weaver. Settings designed by William Weaver. Orchestra under the direction of Louis Kroll. Orchestrations by Louis Kroll, William Redfield. Entire production under the personal supervision of Barry Townly. Produced by Barry Townly. Opened 1 December 1924 at the Ambassador Theatre and closed 20 December 1924 after 24 performances.

CAST (in order of appearance): *Flo*: LOUISE MELE. *Lisbeth*: SYDNEY REYNOLDS. *Sam Barry*: Stanley Forde. *A. Sharpe Quill*: HARRY CLARKE. *Roger Utley*: NATHANIEL WAGNER. *Patrick Daly*: HARRY ALLEN. *Kathryn Utley*: AUDREY MAPLE. *Mrs. Swifte*: MAY BOLEY. *Marjorie Hale*: Dorothy Appleby. *April Daly*: TESSA KOSTA. *Robert Ballou*: Alexis Luce. (*Dancer*: Sibylla Bowman.)

April Girls: Edith Shaw, Ardath DeSales, Dorothy Brown, Jane Sels, Blanche O'Donohue, Ann Langdon, Pauline Huss, Kitty Huss, Dorothy Hordern, Betty Myers, Marjorie Ross, Jane McCurdy.

Act 1: Floating Pier, Summer Resort. Saskanet, New Jersey.

Act 2: Living Room of Daly Suite in Hotel.

[113]During the run, "Before the Dawn" was moved to Act 2 (after "It Never Will Get You a Thing") as a duet for J. Taylor, J. Hartley.

Act 3: Foyer, Same Hotel.

ACT 1

"We're All in the Swim"
  Bathing Girls
"One Piece Blues"
  L. Mele, S. Reynolds, April Girls
"Dreamy Eyes"
  N. Wagner, April Girls
"Society"
  A. Maple, S. Bowman, April Girls
"Sweetheart of Mine"
  T. Kosta
"Dumbells May Be Foolish"
  H. Clarke, D. Appleby, April Girls
"Tantalizing Aprils"
  T. Kosta, N. Wagner
"Sweetheart of Mine" (reprise)
  T. Kosta

ACT 2

"Fantastic Dream Ballet"
Ballerino
  A. DeSales, J. Sels
"Tantalizing April"
  T. Kosta
"Scandal"
  H. Clarke, L. Mele, S. Reynolds, April Girls
"An Irish Rose for Me"
  H. Allen, L. Mele, S. Reynolds, April Girls
"Champagne"
  T. Kosta, Entire Ensemble

ACT 3

"Page a Man for Me"
  L. Mele, S. Reynolds, April Girls
"When Knights Were Bold"
  A. Maple, N. Wagner
"The Love Clock"
  T. Kosta, N. Wagner, April Girls
"String 'Em Along"
  H. Clarke, D. Appleby
Finale

LADY, BE GOOD!

1924.43

A Musical Comedy in Two Acts, 6 Scenes. Book by Guy Bolton and Fred Thompson. Music by George Gershwin. Lyrics by Ira Gershwin. Book staged by Felix Edwardes. Dances and ensembles staged by Sammy Lee. Settings designed by Norman Bel Geddes. Costumes by Kiviette, Jenkins, P. Leone. Orchestra under the direction of Paul Lannin. Orchestrations by Robert Russell Bennett, Charles N. Grant, Paul Lannin, Stephen Jones, Max Steiner, William Daly. Produced by Alex A. Aarons and Vinton Freedley. Opened 1 December 1924 at the Liberty Theatre and closed 12 September 1925 after 330 performances.

CAST (in order of appearance): *Dick Trevor*: FRED ASTAIRE. *Susie Trevor*: ADELE ASTAIRE. *Jack Robinson*: ALAN EDWARDS. *Josephine Vanderwater*: JAYNE AUBURN. *Daisy Parke*: Patricia Clark. *Bertie Bassett*: Gerald Oliver Smith. *J. Watterson Watkins*: WALTER CATLETT. *Shirley Vernon*: KATHLENE MARTYN. *Jeff*: CLIFF EDWARDS. *Manuel Estrada*: Bryan Lycan. *Flunkey*: Edward Jephson. *Victor Arden*: VICTOR ARDEN. *Phil Ohman*: PHIL OHMAN. *Rufus Parke*: James Bradbury.
Ladies of the Ensemble: Mary Hutchinson, Lillian Michell, Esther Morris, Tony Otto, Peggy Hart, Dorothy Hollis, Paulette Winston, Sylvia Shawn, Gertrude Livingstone, Jeanearl Johnson, Jessie Payne, Edna Farrell, Dorothy Hughes, Madeline Janis, Mildred Stevens, Dorothy Donovan, Frances Lindell, Peggy Pitou, Doris Waldron, Peggy Quinn, Ethel Lind, Elmira Lahmann, Irene Wiley, Grace Jones, Maxine Henry. *Gentlemen of the Ensemble*: Dan Sparks, Richard Devonshire, Alfred Hale, Jack Fraley, Harry Howell, Charles Bannister, Lionel Maclyn, Richard Renaud, Hal Crusins, Ward Arnold, Francis Murphy, Charles LaValle.

Act 1, Scene 1: Sidewalk in front of the old Trevor Homestead, Beacon Hill, Rhode Island. *Scene 2*: Entrance of the Vanderwater Estate. *Scene3*: The Vanderwater Garden Party.

Act 2, Scene 1: The Anchorage Hotel, Eastern Harbor, Connecticut. Three days later. *Scene 2*: Garden of the Hotel. *Scene 3*: The Eastern Harbor Yacht Club.

ACT 1

"Hang on to Me"
  F. Astaire, A. Astaire
"A Wonderful Party" (Numberette)
  Guests
"End of a String"
  Ensemble
"We're Here Because"
  P. Clarke, G. O. Smith, Guests
"Fascinating Rhythm"
  A. Astaire, F. Astaire, C. Edwards
"So Am I"
  A. Edwards, A. Astaire
"Oh, Lady Be Good"
  W. Catlett, Girls
Piano Specialty
  V. Arden, P. Ohman
Finale
  Ensemble, (A. Astaire, W. Catlett)

ACT 2

"Weatherman"/"Rainy Afternoon Girls"[114] (Opening)
  Ensemble
"The Half of It Dearie Blues"
  K. Martyn, F. Astaire
"Juanita"
  A. Astaire, Boys
"Leave It to Love"
  A. Astaire, A. Edwards, K. Martyn, F. Astaire
"Little Jazz Bird"[115]
  C. Edwards
["Insufficient Sweetie"
  C. Edwards
  (*Music and Lyrics by* Cliff Edwards and Gil Wells.)
"Who Takes Care of the Caretaker's Daughter (While the Caretaker's Taking Care)?"
  (*Music and Lyrics by* Chick Endor.)
"It's All the Same to Me"
  (*Music and Lyrics by* Chick Endor.)]
"Carnival Time"
  Ensemble
"Swiss Miss"
  A. Astaire, F. Astaire
  (*Lyrics by* Arthur Jackson and Ira Gershwin.)
Finale
  Entire Company

MUSIC BOX REVUE (1924-25)

1924.44

A Musical Revue in Two Acts, 30 Scenes[116]. (Sketches by Bert Kalmar, Harry Ruby, Bobby Clark, Paul McCullough, Ned Joyce Heaney, Gilbert Clarke.) Music and lyrics by Irving Berlin. Staged by John Murray Anderson. All of the numbers conceived by Irving Berlin and carried out under the supervision of John Murray Anderson. Sketches directed by Sam H. Harris. Dances arranged by Carl Randall and Madame Serova. Settings designed by Clark Robinson. Costumes by James Reynolds. Lighting by Frank Schneider. Orchestra under the direction of Frank Tours. Orchestrations by Maurice dePackh, Stephen Jones, Frank Tours. Vocal arrangements by Arthur Johnston. Produced by Sam H. Harris. Opened 1 December 1924 at the Music Box Theatre and closed 9 May 1925 after 184 performances.

---

[114]Replaced shortly after opening by:
  Opening (Linger in the Lobby)
    Ensemble
[115]Dropped during the run; in the last month of the run, replaced by:
  Specialty
    Barney Barnum, Bill Bailey
[116]The fourth and last in the annual series of musical revues written by Irving Berlin and produced by Sam Harris.

CAST: BOBBY CLARK, FANNIE [Fanny] BRICE, PAUL McCULLOUGH, GRACE MOORE, OSCAR SHAW, ULA SHARON, CARL RANDALL, CLAIR LUCE, JOSEPH MACAULAY, HELEN LYONS, IRVING ROSE, THE BROX SISTERS (Kathlyn, Dagmar, Lorraine), HAL SHERMAN, TAMIRIS, MARGARITA, Bud and Jack Pearson.

Ensemble: Phyllis Pearce, Pansy Maness, Marian Gunn, Deuel Sisters, Vivian Dovie, Peggy Fish, Wynne Bullock, Claire Hooper, Katherine Walsh, June Elkin, Frances Mann, Mary Ray, Dawn Allen, Viola Boles, Patty Parrish, Peggy Hastings, Kathleen Ardelle, Dorothy Durland, Evelyn Darville, Elizabeth North, Dorothy Fenton, Billie Blythe, Lehman Byck, F. T. Stevens, George Childs, George Clifford, Tom Roper, W. Cathcart, T. O'Brien, Joseph Weiner, Jules Leon, Henri Permane, Frank Allworth, Jerome Clifford, William Boren, Lawrence K. Downey, Wally Crisham.

ACT 1[117]

Scene 1

Opening

Scene: The Catskills

Rip Van Winkle: J. Macaulay. *Gnomes*: F. Mann, M. Kelly, D. Allen, I. Dane, M. Bay, P. Parrish, F. Harper, L. Lee. *A Mountain Climber*: O. Shaw.

Scene: Times Square

Miss Bronx: Margarita. *Miss Riverside Drive*: H. Lyons. *Miss Fifth Avenue*: P. Pearce. *Miss Tenth Avenue*: P. Maness. *Miss Broadway*: C. Luce. *Miss Greenwich Village*: Tamiris.

"Where Is My Little Old New York?"

J. Macaulay

Scene: Little Old New York

A Lady of Quality: M. Gunn. *A Colonial Sailor*: W. Crisham. *The Sailor's Sweethearts*: Deuel Sisters. *A Tavern Girl*: V. Doyle. *A Quaker Lady*: P. Fish. *A Quaker*: W. Bullock. *A Young Man*: L. K. Downey. *First Lady*: C. Hooper. *Second Lady*: K. Walsh. *Market Woman*: J. Elkin. *Inkeeper*: I. Rose. *Link Boys*: J. Clifford, W. Boren. *Children*: F. Mann, M. Bay.

Scene 2

"Sixteen, Sweet Sixteen"

C. Randall, Girls

Scene: In Front of the Curtains.

Scene 3

The Motive

(*by* Bert Kalmar and Harry Ruby)

· Scene: At Home.

The Maid: P. Maness. *The Inspector*: J. Macaulay. *Assistant Inspector*: P. McCullough. *Carlton*: O. Shaw. *Mrs. Carlton*: H. Lyons. *The Inspector's Wife*: K. Walsh.

Scene 4

"Rigoletto à la Danse" (Dance)

B. Pearson, J. Pearson

Scene: In front of the Curtains.

Scene 5

"Tokio Blues"

Brox Sisters

(*Originally conceived by* Hassard Short. *Costumes devised by* Adrian.)

Scene: In Tokio.

Dance

Tamiris, Margarita

The Kimono Girls: Deuel Sisters, P. Fish, M. Gunn, V. Doyle, J. Elkin, E. Field, D. Durland. *The Geisha Girls*: M. Kelly, M. Bay, I. Dane, L. Lee.

---

[117]The running order was revised after the opening. Added after opening:

The Honor System (by Bobby Clark, Paul McCullough, Wally Sharples.) (Act 1)

Chief of Police: F. Allworth. *Patrolman Murphy*: I. Rose. *Lead Pipe George*: B. Clark. *Sparks*: P. McCullough.

"Polly from Hollywood" (Act 2)

F. Brice

(*Music and Lyrics by* James Hanley and Buddy G. DeSylva.)

Scene: In front of the Curtain.

Added for subsequent tour:

"Don't Wait too Long " (Act 2)

G. Moore, O. Shaw

"All Alone" (Act 2)

G. Moore, O. Shaw

Shall She Invite Him?

(*by* Franklin P. Adams) (Act 2)

He: O. Shaw. *She*: G. Moore. *The Storyteller*: F. Allworth.

Scene 6

"A Couple of Senseless Censors"

B. Clark, P. McCullough

Scene: In Front of the Curtains.

Miss Inquisitive: H. Lyons. *The Bathing Beauty*: C. Luce.

Scene 7

The Immigrant: "Don't Send Me Back (to Petrograd)"

F. Brice

Scene: New York Harbor.

Scene 8

Ballet Dancers at Home

Mrs. Ballerina: U. Sharon. *Her Bally Husband*: C. Randall.

(*Setting designed by* James Reynolds.)

Scene 9

The Kid's First and Last Fight

(*by* Bobby Clark, Paul McCullough, Bard and Pearl)

Scene: The Garden Club.

Young Hamburger: B. Clark. *Hamburger's Friend*: P. McCullough. *A Fight Promoter*: F. Allworth. *A Trainer*: I. Rose. *Kid Taylor*: H. Permane. *Two Lightweights*: J. Weiner, J. Leon. *The Lightweight Seconds*: W. Cathcart, T. O'Brien. *Battling Bearcat*: T. Roper. *Bearcat's Second*: H. Sherman. *Referee*: J. Macaulay.

Scene 10

"Unlucky in Love"[118]

O. Shaw

Scene: In Front of the Curtains.

Scene 11

"Moving Picture Baby"[119]

F. Brice

(*Music and Lyrics by* Blanche Merrill and Leo Edwards.)

Scene: In Front of the Curtains.

Scene 12

"Tell Her in the Springtime"

G. Moore

Scene: Springtime.

The Dancer: U. Sharon.

Scene 14

"Who"[120]

Brox Sisters

Scene: In Front of the Curtains.

Scene 15

"Listening"

G. Moore, O. Shaw

Scene: At the Window.

Scene 16

The King's Gal

(*by* Ned Joyce Heaney)

Scene: A Salon of Louis Palace. *Time*: 1760.

La Pompadour: F. Brice. *Her Gentleman-in-Waiting*: J. Pearson. *Louis XV*: B. Clark.

Scene 17

Hal Sherman Dancing to Mr. Berlin's Old Songs

Scene 18

"The Call of the South"

O. Shaw, G. Moore, Deuel Sisters, J. Elkin, E. Darville, W. Bullock, J. Macaulay, L. Byck, L. Downey

Scene: In Front of the Tableau Curtains.

"Bandanna Ball"

F. Brice, Company

Scene: The Levee.

Intermission: Wynn's Panorama of Immortals

ACT 2

Scene 1

Alice in Wonderland

(*Costumes adapted by* James Reynolds from drawings by John Tenniel.)

"Come Along with Alice"

Brox Sisters

(a) Before the Looking Glass

Alice: U. Sharon.

---

[118]Dropped during the run.

[119]Dropped during the run.

[120]Dropped during the run.

(b) Behind the Looking Glass
  The Mad Hatter: C. Randall. *The Dormouse*: D. Allen. *The March Hare*:
  F. Mann. *The White Rabbit*: V. Boles. *The Walrus*: G. Clifford. *The Carpenter*:
  P. Maness. *Tweedledum and Tweedledee*: B. Pearson, J. Pearson. *The Coquette*:
  P. Parrish. *The Sailor*: G. Childs. *The Duchess*: D. Durland. *The Red Queen*:
  Margarita. *The White Queen*: H. Lyons. *The Queen of Hearts*: Tamiris. *The King
  of Hearts*: I. Rose. *Larkspurs*: M. Bay, L. Lee, I. Dane. *Tiger Lilies*: T. Taylor,
  F. Harper, M. Kelly. *Roses*: K. Ardelle, E. North. *Lobsters*: D. Esmonde, E. Day.
  Oysters: B. Block, M. Dennis. *Pawn Ladies*: J. Elkin, M. Gunn, Deuel Sisters.
  Pawns: M. Roosa, W. Crisham, L. K. Downey, W. Boren.

Scene 2
What'll I Do
  (*Sketch by* Bert Kalmar and Harry Ruby)
  Scene: A Living Room.
  The Butler: B. Clark. *First Caller*: H. Sherman. *Mr. Brown*: O. Shaw. *Second
  Caller*: I. Rose. *Mrs. Brown*: K. Walsh. *The Woman*: D. Durland. *The Cyclist*: P.
  McCullough.

Scene 3
"I Want to Be a Ballet Dancer"
  F. Brice, assisted by B. Clark, Corps de Ballete
  Scene: In Front of the Curtains.

Scene 4
"Rock-a-bye Baby" (A Lullaby)
  G. Moore
  At the age of four: P. Hastings.
  Schooldays
  The School Girl: P. Parrish. *Her Friends*: F. Mann, M. Bay, F. Harper, D. Allen.
  Her First Party
  The Debutante: K. Ardelle. *Her Guests*: L. Ridell, B. Blythe, E. Speaker. *The
  Boys*: L. K. Downey, G. Childs, L. Starbuck, M. Roosa.
  The Wedding
  The Bride: M. Gunn. *The Groom*: W. Crisham. *The Best Man*: G. Clifford.
  Bridesmaids: Misses Maness, Buckley, Miller, Blair, Davis, North. *The Young
  Mother*: E. Darville.
  (*Costumes designed by* Mabel Johnston.)

Scene 5
Fools Rush In
  (*by* Bobby Clark and Paul McCullough)
  Scene: At the Circus.
  Man Who Wants the Bear Trained: F. Allworth. *Man Who Wants to Train the
  Bear*: P. McCullough. *Man Who Does Train the Bear*: B. Clark. *The Bear That
  Should Have Been Trained*: I. Rose. *The Bear That Was Trained*: By Himself. *The
  Man Who Should Have Trained the Bear*: F. T. Stevens.

Scene 6
"Wild Cats"
  C. Randall
  Scene: In Front of the Curtains.
  Dance
  C. Luce, Ensemble
  (*Costumes designed by* Max Rée.)

Scene 7
Another Good Girl Gone Wrong
  (*by* Gilbert Clark)
  Scene: The Battery.
  The Girl: F. Brice. *The Man*: O. Shaw.

Scene 8
Brox Sisters[121]
  Scene: In Front of the Curtains.

Scene 9
"In the Shade of a Sheltering Tree"
  O. Shaw, G. Moore
  Scene: The Trees.
  The Palm: E. North. *Under the Palm*: H. Lyons, J. Macaulay. *The Pine*: K.
  Ardelle. *Under the Pine*: P. Pearce, L. Downey. *The Apple Tree*: D. Ferton.
  Under the Apple Tree: C. Luce, W. Bullock. *The Bamboo*: B. Blythe. *Under the
  Bamboo*: P. Parrish, L. Byck. *The Weeping Willow Tree*: Tamiris and Margarita,
  The Deuel Sisters, Misses Gunn, Durland, Doyle, Fish, Field, Elkin.
  (*Costumes designed by* Max Rée.)

Scene 10
Adam and Eve
  (*by* Bert Kalmar and Hary Ruby)

Scene: The Garden of Eden.
Eve: F. Brice. *Adam*: B. Clark. *Cain*: H. Boyd. *Abel*: J. Pearson.

Scene 11
The Runaway Four[122]

Scene 12
The Banquet
  The Guest of Honor: Rip Van Winkle [J. Macaulay]. *His Hosts and Hostesses*:
  Entire Music Box Company.
Finale

THE STUDENT PRINCE IN HEIDELBERG

1924.45

A Spectacular Operetta in a Prologue and Four Acts. Book and lyrics by Dorothy Donnelly. Music by Sigmund Romberg. (Based on the play 'Old Heidelberg' by Rudolf Bleichmann, adapted from 'Alt-Heidelberg' by Wilhelm Meyer-Förster.) Book and all ensembles staged by J. C. Huffman. Dances by Max Scheck. Settings by Watson Barratt. Costumes by Weldy of Paris, and Vanity Fair Costume Company. Orchestra under the direction of Oscar Bradley. Orchestrations by Emil Gerstenberger. Entire production under the personal supervision of J. J. Shubert. Produced by the Messrs. Shubert. Opened 2 December 1924 at Jolson's Theatre, moved 14 December 1925 to the Ambassador Theatre, moved 1 February 1926 to the Century Theatre, closing 29 March 1926; resumed 5 April 1926 at Jolson's Theatre and closed 26 May 1926 after 608 performances.

CAST [in order of their appearance]: *First Lackey*: Frank Kneeland. *Second Lackey*: William Nettum. *Third Lackey*: Lawrence Wells. *Fourth Lackey*: Harry Anderson. (*Prime Minister*) *von Mark*: FULLER MELLISH. *Dr. Engel*: GREEK EVANS. *Prince Karl Franz*: HOWARD MARSH. *Ruder*: W. H. White. *Gretchen*: VIOLET CARLSON. *Toni*: Adolph Link. *Detlef*: RAYMOND MARLOWE. *Lucas*: Frederic Wolff. *von Asterberg*: Paul Kleeman. *Nicolas*: Fred Wilson. *Kathie*: ILSE MARVENGA. *Lutz*: GEORGE HASSELL. *Hubert*: Charles Williams. *Grand Duchess Anastasia*: FLORENCE MORRISON. *Princess Margaret*: ROBERTA BEATTY *Captain Tarnitz*: JOHN COAST. *Countess Leyden*: DAGMAR OAKLAND. *Baron Arnheim*: Robert Calley. *Premier Dancer*: Martha Mason. *Rudolph Winter*: Lucius Metz. *Freshman*: Elmer Pichler. *Captain of the Guard*: C. Sparin.
  Flower Girls: Alice Bussy, Edith Alexander, Viola Green, Sylvia LaMarde, Cleo Lombard, Florence Turner, Gertrude Clifford, Rosemary Otter, Patricia O'Connell. *Waitresses*: Marion Barclay, Peggy Hansel, Miriam Stockton, Jane Waye, Olive Thornton, Isabelle Allen, Madeline Parker, Ann Webber, Phyliss Newkirk, Martha McDonald. *Ladies in Waiting*: Peggy Hansel, Isabelle Allen, Olive Thornton, Jane Waye, Phyliss Newkirk, Marion Barclay. *Maids*: Rosemary Otter, Edith Alexander, Alice Bussy, Martha McDonald. *Guests at the Palace*: Marion Barclay, Miriam Stockton, Cleo Lombard, Jane Waye, Rosemary Otter, Olive Thornton, Peggy Hansel, Patricia O'Connell, Isabelle Allen, Ann Webber, Madeline Parker, Edith Alexander, Florence Turner, Gertrude Clifford, Sylvia LaMarde, Phyliss Newkirk, Alice Bussy, Martha McDonald. *Waiters*: Cliff Whitcomb, James Bitman, Michael Kavanaugh. *Students at Heidelberg (Saxons)*: M.C. Scott, Jerry Merrick, Harry Anderson, William Galpen, George Elliott, Arthur Singer, James Currier, O. A. Olson, Charles Packer, Arthur King, Willard Fry, A. Gellert, J. Spira, Jack Jordan, Elmer Pichler, Chester Bennett. *Students at Heidelberg (Rheinishers)*: Donald Jackson, William Clark, William Rogers, Harvey Howard, William Ehlers, C. Sparin, Frank Miller, Tom Ryan, Eric Henning, John Merkle, John Helmken, Maurice Autier, F. Rasmussen, Clarence Scott, C. Pichler, Lawrence Wells, James Hallgreen. *Guests at the Palace*: Ambassadors, Officers, Soldiers, Gentlemen of the Court, Ladies of the Court, Ladies in Waiting, etc.

Prologue: Ante-chamber in the Palace at Karlsberg. Spring, 1860.

Act 1: Garden of the Inn of the Three Golden Apples. At the University of Heidelberg.

Act 2: Sitting Room of Prince Karl, at the Inn. Four months later.

Act 3: A Room of State in the Royal Palace at Karlsberg. Two years later.

Act 4: Garden of the Inn of the Three Golden Apples. The next day.

PROLOGUE
  "By Our Bearing So Sedate"
    Four Lackeys
  "Golden Days"
    H. Marsh, G. Evans

ACT 1
  "Garlands Bright"
    W. H. White, V. Carlson, Flower Girls, Waitresses
  "Drinking Song"
    R. Marlowe, Students

---

[121]Dropped during the run.
[122]Dropped during the run.

"To the Inn We're Marching"
R. Marlowe, P. Kleeman, F. Wolff, I. Marvenga, Students
"You're in Heidelberg"
H. Marsh, G. Evans
"Welcome to Prince"
I. Marvenga, W. H. White, V. Carlson, Girls
"Deep in My Heart Dear" (Duet)
H. Marsh, I. Marvenga
"Serenade" (Overhead the Moon Is Beaming)
H. Marsh, R. Marlowe, F. Wolff, P. Kleeman, Students
Finale, Act 1 (Come Sir, Will You Join Our Noble Saxon Corps)
H. Marsh, I. Marvenga, R. Marlowe, F. Wolff, P. Kleeman, W. H. White, G. Hassell, G. Evans, V. Carlson, C. Williams, Students, Girls

ACT 2
"Farmer Jacob (Lay a-Snoring)" (Opening)
R. Marlowe, Students
"Students' Life" (Student Life)
H. Marsh, I. Marvenga, G. Evans, V. Carlson, R. Marlowe, F. Wolff, P. Kleeman, Eight Students
"Farewell, Dear" (Duet)
H. Marsh, I. Marvenga
Finale, Act 2
H. Marsh, I. Marvenga, F. Mellish, G. Evans

ACT 3
"Waltz Ensemble" (Opening)
Ambassadors, Officers, D. Oakland, R. Calley, Ladies of the Court
Solo Ballet
M. Mason
"Just We Two"
R. Beatty, J. Coast, Officers
"Gavotte"
H. Marsh, R. Beatty, D. Oakland, R. Calley, J. Coast, Officers, Ambassadors, Ladies of the Court
"What Memories"
H. Marsh
Finale, Act 3
H. Marsh, I. Marvenga, G. Evans

ACT 4
"Sing a Little Song" (Opening)
Students, Girls
"To the Inn We're Marching" (reprise)
R. Marlowe, P. Kleeman, Students
"Serenade" (reprise)
R. Marlowe, Students
"Come Boys"
Students, R. Marlowe, P. Kleeman
Finale: "Deep in My Heart, Dear" (reprise)
H. Marsh, R. Beatty, I. Marvenga, L. Metz, V. Carlson, C. Williams, G. Hassell, F. Morrison, R. Marlowe, P. Kleeman, Students, Girls

1924.46

TOPSY AND EVA

A Musical Comedy in Three Acts. Book by Catherine Chisholm Cushing. Based on the novel 'Uncle Tom's Cabin' by Harriet Beecher Stowe. Music and lyrics by the Duncan Sisters (Rosetta, Vivian). Book staged under the direction of Oscar Eagle. Musical numbers staged by Jack Holland. Settings designed by Dickson Morgan. Costumes designed by Madam Keeler. Musical direction by Jerome Stewardson. Produced by Tom Wilkes. Opened 23 December 1924 at the Sam H. Harris Theatre and closed 9 May 1925 after 165 performances.

<u>CAST</u> (in order of appearance): *Chloe*: Aimee Torriani. *Harry*: Glory Minehart. *Uncle Tom*: BASIL RUYSDAEL. *George Shelby*: ROBERT HALLIDAY. *Mrs. Shelby*: HELEN CASE. *Friends of Mariette* (4): *Helen*: Renee Lowrie. *Ann*: Lea Swan. *Jane*: Edith Maybaun. *Bessie*: Antoinette Boots. *Austustine St. Clare*: Wilbur Cushman. *Henrique*: HARRIET HOCTOR. *Simon Legree*: FRANK K. WALLACE. *Gee Gee*: DAVIS GOODMAN. *Eliza*: FLORENCE MARTIN. *Mariette*: NYDIA D'ARNELL. *Erasmus Marks*: Ashley Cooper. *Ophelia St. Clare*: Myrtle Ferguson. *Topsy*: ROSETTA DUNCAN. *Eva St. Clare*: VIVIAN DUNCAN. *Danseuse Premiere*: HARRIET HOCTOR. *Rastus*: Ross Himes.
Plantation Quartette: Phillip Ryder, Harry Furney, Roy Collins, Floyd Carder. *Old-Fashioned Girls*: Ernay Goodleigh, Alice Averill, Dixie Harkins, Renee Lowrie, Lea

Swan, Antoinette Boots, Shirley Beauford, Jessie Pollard, Edith Maybaun, Natasha Verova, Lorraine Ray, Patricia Pattisson, Hazel Cushman. *Pickaninnies*, London Palace Theatre Dancers especially contracted for "Topsy and Eva": Billie Bart, Hettie Ward, Toresa McSpirit, Rosie Swettenham, Violet Little, Rosa Thompson, Ethel Swettenham, Minnie Shaw, Elsie Thompson, Kitty Dolan.

Act 1: Uncle Tom's Cabin, on the Shelby Plantation, Kentucky. An October afternoon in the 1850's.

Act 2: Courtyard of Augustine St. Clare's Home in New Orleans. An April evening.

Act 3: The Shelby Home in Kentucky. Early evening.

ACT 1[123]
Opening Selection—Plantation Melodies
B. Ruysdael, A. Torriani, G. Minehart, Darkies
Dance
R. Himes
Dance
H. Hoctor
Dance
F. Martin, D. Goodman
"Give Me Your Heart and Give Me Your Hand"[124]
N. d'Arnell, R. Halliday
"Um-Um-Da-Da"
R. Duncan, V. Duncan, Girls, Pickaninnies
"Moon Am Shinin'"
B. Ruysdael, A. Torriani, Pickaninnies
"Rememb'wring" (Rememb'ring)
N. d'Arnell, R. Halliday, H. Case
Finale
Principals, Ensemble

ACT 2
"The Land of Long Ago"
N. d'Arnell, Girls
"Do-Re-Mi" (The Music Lesson)
R. Duncan, V. Duncan, M. Ferguson
"In the Autumn"
R. Halliday, Girls, London Palace Dancers
"Give Me Your Heart"[125] (reprise)
N. d'Arnell
"Uncle Tom Cabin Blues"
B. Ruysdael, R. Duncan, V. Duncan
Bird Dance
H. Hoctor
"Rememb'ring" (reprise)
R. Duncan, V. Duncan

ACT 3
"Cotton Time"
Plantation Quartette
"Mariette" (Selection)
Southern Belles, Beaux, Pickaninnies
"Kiss Me"
N. d'Arnell, R. Halliday, Girls

---

[123]Songs added for subsequent national tour:
"Happy-Go-Lucky Days"
R. Duncan, V. Duncan
(*Music and Lyrics by* Al Wilson and J. A. Brennan.)
"Ukulele Lady" (Act 3)
R. Duncan, V. Duncan
(*Music by* Richard Whiting. *Lyrics by* Gus Kahn.)
"(In) Sweet Onion Time (in Bermuda)" (Act 3)
R. Duncan, V. Duncan
(*Music and Lyrics by* the Duncan Sisters and Sam Coslow.)
"Just For a Little While" (Act 2)
N. d'Arnell, R. Halliday, Beaux and Belles
"Heaven" (Act 2)
B. Ruysdael, R. Duncan, V. Duncan
[124]Dropped for subsequent national tour.
[125]Dropped for tour and replaced by:
"Smiling Through My Tears"
N. d'Arnell

Dance
    H. Hoctor
"Moon Am Shinin'" (reprise)
    B. Ruysdael
"Kiss Me" (reprise)
    D. Goodman, R. Himes, Pickaninnies
Dance
    F. Martin
Dance
    D. Goodman, R. Himes, F. Martin, Pickaninnies
"I Never Had a Mammy" (Topsy's Prayer)
    R. Duncan, V. Duncan
Dance
    R. Duncan, V. Duncan
Wedding Procession
    Principals, Ensemble
Finale
    Principals, Ensemble

1924.47   BETTY LEE

A Musical Comedy in Three Acts. Book by Otto Harbach. Based on the comedy 'Going Some' by Paul Armstrong and Rex Beach. Music by Louis Hirsch and Con Conrad. Lyrics by Irving Caesar and Otto Harbach. Dialogue directed by Bertram Harrison. (Play under the supervision of the author.) Dances and ensembles staged by David Bennett. Scenes designed by P. Dodd Ackerman. Costumes designed by Charles LeMaire. Musical director, John L. McManus. Produced by Rufus LeMaire. Opened 25 December 1924 at the 44th Street Theatre and closed 21 March 1925 after 98 performances.

CAST (in order of appearance): *Doc*: Jack Kearns. *Slim*: Ed Poole. *Hypo*: William Brandt. *Silent Pete*: Harry Sievers. *Stover*: Howard Boulden. *Willie Wolf*: James S. Barrett. *Carara*: Paisley Noon. *Mrs. Lila Keep*: Charlotte Woodruff. *Jeanne Chapin*: MADELINE CAMERON. *Berkley Fresno*: ALFRED GERRARD. *Betty Lee*: GLORIA FOY. *Muridetta*: DOROTHY BARBER. *Wallingford Speed*: HAL SKELLY. *Lawrence Glass*: JOE E. BROWN. *Buck*: Clifford J. O'Rourke. *Gabby Gallagher*: James Kearney. *Culver Covington*: George Sweet. *Skinner*: Anthony Hughes. *Whitey*: Carlo. *Conchita*: Kathryn O'Hanlon. *Chico*: Theo. Zambouni.
    The Betty Lee Girls: Dorothy E. Fitzgibbon, Grace M. Smith, Olive Lindsay, Edna Luce, Ada Winston, Helen Orb, Betty Colker, Madeleine Dare, Verdi Milli, Lucille Arden, Kay Karyll, Florence Courtney, Neida Snow, Isobel Graham, Yvonne Kent, Claire Daniels, Frieda Fitzgerald, Harriet Hasbrook, Nancy Lay, Marion Swords, Pearl Bennett, Jeanne West, Kathryn Brown, Penelope Rowland.

Act 1: Courtyard of the Chapin Spanish Villa, Southern California.

Act 2: Japanese Tea-house. Chapin Estate. One day later.

Act 3: Another view of Japanese Tea-house. Chapin Estate. One week later.

ACT 1
    "Along the Rio Grande"
        Quintette, D. Barber, P. Noon
    "Little Pony of Mine"
        M. Cameron, Girls
    "Betty Lee"
        H. Skelly, G. Foy, Cowboys, Ensemble
        (*Music by* Con Conrad[126].)
    "Sweet Cactus Rose"
        D. Barber, J. E. Brown
    "Athletic Boy"
        G. Foy, M. Cameron, A. Gerrard, Ensemble
    Finale
ACT 2
    "Monterey"
        C. Woodruff, Girls
    Dance
        Carlo, T. Zambouni
    "The Daily Dozen"
        G. Foy, H. Skelly, Ensemble

"They Always Run a Little Faster"
    J. E. Brown, Cowboys
"Sweet Arabian Dreams" (Arabian Dream)
    G. Foy, H. Skelly
    (*Music by* Louis Hirsch[127].)
Dance
    D. Barber
"Sweet Cactus Rose" (reprise)
    D. Barber, J. E. Brown
"Give Him Your Sympathy"
    C. Woodruff, H. Skelly, J. E. Brown, A. Gerrard, Ensemble
Specialties
    D. Barber, M. Finley, Carlo, Inez
"Baby, Be Good"
    M. Cameron, Ensemble
Finale
ACT 3
    Cowboy Songs (including "Pony Boy")
        Betty Lee Quintette
    "Apache Argentine"[128]
        K. O'Hanlon, T. Zambouni
    "I'm Going to Dance at Your Wedding"
        G. Foy, H. Skelly, A. Gerrard, Girls
        (*Music by* Con Conrad. *Lyrics by* Irving Caesar.)
    "Just Lean on Me"
        M. Cameron, G. Sweet
    "Cheer, Girls, Cheer"
        G. Foy, Ensemble
    Finale—Ultimo

1924.48   (YUSHNY'S) SEENIAYA PTITZA

Blue Bird Theater of Moscow and Berlin in a Russian Musical Revue in Two Acts. Conceived by Yasha Yushny. Chef d'Orchestra, Monsieur N. Gogotzky. Produced by Wendell Phillips Dodge. Opened 29 December 1924 in repertory season at the Frolic Theatre for 36 performances; Second Edition opened 29 January 1925 (see below) under the auspices of Sol Hurok, Inc. and closed 7 March 1925 after 44 performances. Total: 80 performances.

CAST: Mmes. V. Arenzwary, N. Sussanina, M. Mariewa, O. Valeri, L. Kosmowskaya, E. Porfiriewa, T. Taridina, E. Nienatshaiewa, L. Cosmowska, J. Sharol. Messrs. M. Dobrinine, P. Donskoy, E. Wachinoff, G. Nelidoff, Victor Chenkin, J. Riabinine, W. Svoboda, D. Libidins, K. Shein, P. Ukrainsky, YASCHA YUSHNY (Conférencier).

SCENES[129]
    Catherine the Great (Opening)
    Punch and Judy
        N. Sussanina; G. Nelidoff
    Chopin Nocturne (Dance)
        Mme. Yuriewa; W. Svoboda
    "The Volga Boat Song"
        Men's Chorus
    "The Barrel Organ"
        O. Valeri; D. Libidins
    "The Cossack Song"
    "The Rabbi and the Pupils"
    The King Causes the Drums to Be Beaten (Retablow)
    "The Travelling Circus"[130]

1924.48   (YUSHNY'S) THE BLUE BIRD

Second Edition of the Russian Musical Revue of Moscow and Berlin in Two Acts, 14 Scenes. Director and Conferencier, Yasha Yushny. Stage director, G. Nelidoff. Chef d'Orchestre, Mons. N. Gogotzky. Produced by Sol

---

[126]Published sheet music credits Louis Hirsch as co-composer.

[127]Published sheet music credits Con Conrad as co-composer.
[128]Dropped after opening.
[129]No program available.
[130]Dropped after opening.

Hurok, Inc. Opened 2 February 1925 at the Frolic Theatre and closed 7 March 1925 after 44 performances[131].

PROGRAMME

Scene 1

"La Dame Pique" (Tableau from the opera by Tchaikowsky)
Paulina: V. Arenzwari. *Liza*: N. Sussanina. *Participants*: Mmes. V. Arenzwari, N. Sussanina, J. Sharol, L. Kosmowskaya, E. Nienatshaiewa, E. Porfiriewa, O. Valeri, M. Mariewa, T. Taridina.

Scene 2

"Russian Inn" (Just a pretty little scene with some novel things in it)
V. Chenkin or J. Riabinine, Ensemble
(*Decorations by* P. Tshelishteff.)

Scene 3

"Old Dutch Porcelain" (Dance Duet)
Mmes. L. Cosmowska, E. Porfiriewa
(*Music by* W. Butzow. *Decorations by* P. Tshelishteff.)

Scene 4

"There Is Life Everywhere" (Russian Prison Songs)
(Idea inspired by an eighteenth century painting by Jaroschenko)
Mme. M. Mariewa; Messrs. V. Chenkin, N. Dobrinine, E. Wachinoff, J. Riabinine

Scene 5

"The Lady, the Coachman and Cupid"
Mmes. V. Arenzwari, O. Valeri; Messr. K. Shein
There once was a lady of state who secretly loved her coachman and she was wont to go riding and then leave the coach with her servant and go for a walk in the road. Embraces, kisses endearing terms that caused that little elf Cupid to step in and direct affairs. He took the reins and thereafter the lady and the coachman enjoyed their little affairs more than ever.
(*Decorations by* E. Stern. *Music by* W. Butzow.)

Scene 6

"Death of Swan" (Dance)
Mme. Yuriewa

Scene 7

"Warrior Dance"
V. Svoboda

Scene 8

"Russian Peasant Girls"
Mmes. V. Arenzwari, N. Sussanina, L. Kosmowskaya, E. Nienatschaiewa, E. Porfiriewa, M. Mariewa, J. Sharol, Messr. K. Shein
(*Costumes from the sketches of* A. Chudiakov. *Musical arrangement by* Messr. Popella Davidow. *Staged by* Yascha Yushny.)

Scene 9

"The Princess Who Never Smiled"
(A Fairy Tale by Agniwzeff.)
The King: V. Chenkin. *Anutka*: O. Valeri. *Vanka*: K. Shein. *The Princess*: M. Mariewa. Participants: T. Taridina, N. Sussanina, L. Kosmowskaya, E. Nienatschaiewa, E. Porfiriewa, J. Sharol; Messrs. G. Nelidoff, P. Donskoy, D. Libidins, P. Ukrainsky, E. Wadinoff, J. Riabinine, M. Dobrinine
(*Decorations by* G. Poshedajeff. *Music by* W. Wladimiroff. *Staging and General Direction by* Yascha Yushny.)

Scene 10

"Minuet Velasquez"
Mme. M. Yuriewa, Messr. V. Svoboda

Scene 11

"The Evening Bells" (Based on the poem by Thomas Moore)
Messr. Wachinoff

Scene 12

"Tchastushky" (Russian Factory Workers Song)
Mme. V. Arenzwari; Messrs. G. Nelidoff
(*Decorations by* P. Tshelisteff. *Accordeon*: P. Ukrainsky.)

Scene 13

"In the Merry Month of May"
Mme. N. Sussannina; Messr. V. Chenkin
(*Decorations by* Novikoff after the sketch of Mr. R. Smomow. *Staged by* Victor Chenkin.)

Scene 14

"The Loving Hairdresser"
Mme. E. Porfiriewa; Messrs. G. Nelidoff, P. Donskoy
(*Decorations by* A. Chudiakoff.)

---

[131]Cast same as for first edition.

1925.01

BIG BOY

A Musical Comedy in Two Acts, 12 Scenes. Book by Harold Atteridge. (Based on the play 'In Old Kentucky' by Charles T. Dazey.) Music by James F. Hanley and Joseph Meyer. Lyrics by Buddy G. DeSylva. Staged by J. C. Huffman. Dialog directed by Alexander Leftwich. Dances arranged by Larry Ceballos, Seymour Felix. Settings designed by Watson Barratt. Orchestra under the direction of Alfred Goodman. Orchestrations by Alfred Goodman[132] and Emil Gerstenberger. Entire production under the supervision of J. J. Shubert. Produced by the Messrs. Shubert. Opened 7 January 1925 at the Winter Garden, closing 24 January 1925 for a lay-off due to Jolson's illness, re-opening 9 February 1925 and closed 14 March 1925 after 56 performances.

CAST (in order of appearance): *Mrs. Bedford*: Maude Turner Gordon. *Phyllis Carter*: EDYTHE BAKER *Joe Warren*: HUGH BANKS. *Tessie Forbes*: FLO LEWIS. *Annabelle Bedford*: PATTI HARROLD. *Jack Bedford*: Frank Beaston. *"Coley" Reid*: Ralph Whitehead. *"Doc" Wilbur*: Leo Donnelly. *Jim Redding*: Franklyn Batie. *Judkins*: George Gilday. *Steve Leslie*: Colin Campbell. *Gus*: AL JOLSON. *Caroline Purdy*: Edith Scott. *"Bully" John Bagby*: William L. Thorne. *"Silent" Ransom*: George Spelvin. *Tucker*: Franklyn Batie. *Manager*: L. C. Sherman. *Wainwright*: William L. Thorne. *Legrande*: William Bonelli. *Danny*: Irving Carter. *Mr. Gray*: Charles Moran. *Dolly Graham*: Frankie James. *Tout*: Charles Moran. *Dancers*: Dorothy Rudac, George Andre.

Dancers: Peggy Bernier, Elsie Carroll, Lee Cutler, Jewel Dalores, Helen Doyle, Milie Dupree, Ethel Fuller, Peggy Gillespie, Janice Glenn, Mabel Grete, Alma Hookey, Naoe Kondo, Dottie Mae, Dinky Ormont, Thelma Robinson, Ruth Savoy, Rose Stone, Esther Tanney, Helen Wallace, Minnia White. *Show Girls*: Marion Andre, Wyn Ayres, May Birt, Freddie Bond, Nancy Carroll, Terry Carroll, Flo Evers, Rose Gallagher, Louise Hersey, Madge Lorraine, Mary Phillips, Madeline Smith, Dorothy Wegman. *Boys*: Adolphe Beck, Bobbie Brandeis, Irving Carter, Al Clair, Clifford Daly, Albert Ford, Harry Lake, Lewis Laub, Walter Lowery, Jack Ray, Ralph Reader, Walter Wandell. *Jubilee Singers*: William C. Elkins, Walter A. Gray, Wilbert B. Howard, George E. Jackson, Arthur H. Payne, Mose E. Ross, Arthur S. Shaw, Kelly Thompson, Casco Williams, Carl T. White.

Act 1, Scene 1: The Grounds of the Bedford Home, Kentucky. *Scene 2*: The Bedford Stables on the Estate. *Scene 3*: Portion of the Grounds. *Scene 4*: A Flashback of the Bedford Plantation in 1870. *Scene 5*: Portion of the Grounds. *Scene 6*: A Garden Fete.

Act 2, Scene 1: The Night before the Kentucky Derby at Brown's Cafe, Louisville. *Scene 2*: The Bedford Stables at Churchill Downs Race Track. *Scene 3*: Portion of the Grand Strand. *Scene 4*: The Kentucky Derby. *Scene 5*: Jockey's Locker Room. *Scene 6*: The Hunt Ball.

ACT 1

Scene 1

"Welcome Home"
Ensemble
"Born and Bred in Old Kentucky"
P. Harrold, Ensemble
"Lead 'Em On"
E. Baker, F. Lewis, H. Banks
"The Day I Rode Half Fare"
C. Campbell, Ensemble

Scene 2

Song
A. Jolson

Scene 3

"True Love"
P. Harrold, Girls

Scene 4

Negro Spirituals
A. Jolson, Jubilee Singers
Song
A. Jolson
"Tap the Toe"
P. Harrold, H. Banks, F. Beaston, Ensemble

Scene 6

"Come On and Play"
E. Baker, Boys
"The Dance from Down Yonder"
P. Harrold, E. Baker, F. Lewis, R. Whitehead, F. Beaston, H. Banks, Ensemble
Song
A. Jolson

---

[132]For Jolson's songs.

ACT 2

Scene 1

"Tamborina"
Ensemble

"Something for Nothing"
F. Lewis

"Lackawanna"
F. James

Song
A. Jolson

Scene 2

"Bookies and Cookies" (Cookies and Bookies)
Girls, Boys

Scene 4

"The Race Is Over"
Ensemble

Scene 5

By Himself (Specialty)[133]
A. Jolson

["Keep Smiling at Trouble" (Trouble's a Bubble)
(*Music by* Lewis Gensler. *Lyrics by* Buddy G. DeSylva and Al Jolson.)

"If You Knew Susie"
(*Music by* Joseph Meyer. *Lyrics by* Buddy G. DeSylva.)

"I'm Tellin' the Birds, Tellin' the Bees"
(*Music and Lyrics by* Cliff Friend and Lew Brown.)

"It All Depends on You" (1926)
(*Music by* Ray Henderson. *Lyrics by* Lew Brown and Buddy G. DeSylva.)

"Keep Smiling at Trouble"
(*Music by* Lewis Gensler. *Lyrics by* Al Jolson and Buddy G. DeSylva.)

"Miami"
(*Music and Lyrics by* Con Conrad, Al Jolson and Buddy G. DeSylva.)

"Nobody But Fanny" (1925)
(*Music and Lyrics by* Con Conrad, Al Jolson and Buddy G. DeSylva.)

"On the Z-R-3"
(*Music by* Walter Donaldson. *Lyrics by* Sam Lewis and Joe Young.)

"One O'Clock Baby" (1927)
(*Music by* Al Jolson. *Lyrics by* Lew Brown and Buddy G. DeSylva.)]

Scene 6

"The Hunt Ball" (Dance)
G. Andre, D. Rudac, Ensemble

Finale
Entire Company

1925.02 THE LOVE SONG

An Operetta of the Second Empire, based on Offenbach's Life and Music, in Three Acts. Original Hungarian libretto ('Offenbach') by Eugene [Jeno] Ferago, Michael [Mihály] Nador, and its German adaptation ('Meister von Montmartre,' 'Pariser Nächte') by James Klein and Carl Bretschneider. American adaptation and lyrics by Harry B. Smith. Music of Jacques Offenbach selected and arranged by, and original music by Edward [Eduard] Künneke. Staged by Fred G. Latham. Ballet by Alexis Kosloff. Dances and ensembles by Max Scheck. Settings designed by Watson Barratt. Costumes by Ernest R. Schrapps, Hubert of Paris. Orchestra under the direction of Alfred Goodman. Entire production under the personal direction of J. J. Shubert. Produced by the Messrs. Shubert. Opened 13 January 1925 at the Century Theatre and closed 6 June 1925 after 157 performances.

CAST (in order of appearance): *Pierre*: COOPER [William] LAWLEY. *Lizette*: ZELLA RUSSELL. *Herminie*: EVELYN HERBERT. *Petipas*: HARRY K. MORTON. *Hortense*: ODETTE MYRTIL. *Offenbach*: ALLAN PRIOR. *Bourbon*: WILLIAM ST. JAMES. *Colonel Bugeaud*: JOHN DUNSMURE. *Eugenie de Montijo*: DOROTHY FRANCIS. *Countess de Montijo*: Eda von Bulow. *Gypsy Girl*: Zola Talma. *Spanish Dancer*: Isabelle Rodriguez. *The Duke de Persigny*: John Moore. *Prosper Merimée*: Harry Glover. *Victorian Sardou*: J. Warren Hull. *The Emperor, Napoleon III*: HARRISON BROCKBANK. *Countess Castiglione*: Grace Carlyle. *Lackey*: Walter Kelly. *Duroc*: James Alderman. *Babette*: Edna Starck. *Margot*: Camille Robenette. *Mme. de Marsac*: Vivian Marlowe. *Mlle. Marceau*: Vera Hoppe. *Jacques d'Alcain*: Master Charles Walters. *Girls from the Bouffes Parisiennes* (2): *Franchette*: Adele

Howard. *Corinne*: Laura Hastings. *Lieutenant*: Donald Kinleyside. *First Officer*: Paul Keast. *Second Officer*: W. L. Robertson.

Peasants: Messrs. Stone, Moore, Gordon, Dettinger, Whited, Kelly, Moste. *Soldiers*: Messrs. Harold, Moran, Archer, Ismailov, Deits, Van Rhyn, Norman, Greenwood, Burns, Miller, Hull, Clifford, Evans, Klug, O'Neil, Robertson, Keast, Webb, Doctoroff, Willis, Vecsey, Glover, Caruso, Snyder, Black, Townsend, Beck, Jacobson, Conway, Rennie, Raymond, Kellar. *Ladies of Honor*: Bobby Muir, Fay Gilmore, Julia Strong, Evelyn Stone. *Ladies in Waiting*: Edna Starck, Margaret Draper, Eleanor Whitmore, Nancy Corrigan, Mary Arnoldi, Adele Howard, Jeanne Voltaire, Laura Hastings, Charlotte Sprague, Nikola Cunningham, Eleanor Wilson, Ethel Darcy. *Guests at the Court*: Vivian Marlowe, Berma Deane, Doris Stewart, Miriam Franklin, Alvina Zolle, Louise Farrar, Beatrice Durant, Lucita Arnold, Catherine Smith, Marie Lavelle, Mary Graham, Antoinette LaFarge, Nita Lamabrid, Vera Hoppe, Dorothy Harrington, Ila McCall, Virginia Allen, Camille Robinette, Inga Neilson, Florence Cazelle, Sophie Lubin, Helen Allerton, Shelton Bentley. *Girls from the Bouffes Parisiennes*: Misses Nancy Corrigan, Eleanor Whitmore, Louise Farrar, Berma Deane, Edna Starck, Lucita Arnold, Jeanne Voltaire, Laura Hastings, Mary Arnoldi, Julia Strong, Margaret Draper, Adele Howard.

Act 1: A Vineyard near Prades in the Pyrenees. (1840's) (Schrapps.)

Act 2: The Ballroom of the Tuilleries. (1860's) (Hubert.)

Act 3: Offenbach's Studio. (1870's) (Schrapps.)

ACT 1[134]

Opening Ensemble—Vintage Chorus
Peasant Girls, Boys

"When Your Life Seems a Rainy Day"[135] (Song)
C. Lawley

"Tell Me Not That You Are Forgetting" (Waltz Duet)
E. Herbert, C. Lawley

"All Aboard for Paris"
O. Myrtil, H. K. Morton, H. K. Morton

"Love Is Not For a Day"
A. Prior, Girls

"In Gardens Where Roses Bloom"[136]
A. Prior, E. Herbert

"The Hall of Fame Awaits for Me"[137]
O. Myrtil, A. Prior

"Follow the Flag We Love"[138] (Zouave Chorus)
Male Chorus

"When the Drum Beat Calls to Glory"[139] (Song)
J. Dunsmure, Soldiers

"Fair Land of Dreaming" (Song)
D. Francis
(*Music by* Eduard Künneke.)

Quartette ("He Writes a Song")
A. Prior, D. Francis, E. Herbert, O. Myrtil
(*Music by* Jacques Offenbach.)

"Remember Me" (The Love Song) (Duet)
D. Francis, A. Prior
(*Music by* Eduard Künneke.)

Finale
H. K. Morton, H. K. Morton, C. Lawley, W. St. James, J. Dunsmure, D. Francis, E. von Bulow, O. Myrtil, A. Prior, Soldiers, Peasants

Spanish Dance
I. Rodriguez

ACT 2

Opening Chorus
Officers

Entrance of the Emperor and Empress

---

[133]Songs performed by Jolson in his specialty spot or elsewhere in the show where the program indicated "Song," as per reviews and published sheet music.

[134]The show was much revised after the opening. After opening, added to Act 1, following Quartette:
"Take a Walk With Me" (Duet)
Z. Russell, H. K. Morton

[135]Dropped after the opening.

[136]After opening, replaced by:
"Love Will Find You Some Day" (Duet)
E. Herbert, A. Prior
(*Music by* Eduard Künneke.)

[137]Dropped after the opening.

[138]After opening, replaced by:
"Home from Algeria" (Zouave Chorus)
Male Chorus

[139]Dropped after the opening.

"Not For a Year, Not for a Day"[140] (Duet)
E. Herbert, C. Lawley
"A Farmer's Life" (Duet)
H. K. Morton, H. K. Morton
"When My Violin Is Calling"
A. Prior, Girls
"(I Know It Is) Only a Dream" (Duet)
D. Francis, A. Prior
(*Music by* Jacques Offenbach.)
"Military Men I Love" (Song)
O. Myrtil, Officers
"Make Up Your Mind"[141]
O. Myrtil, H. K. Morton
Scenes from 'La Belle Helene' Ballet
O. Myrtil, H. K. Morton, D. Francis, Ensemble, (Kosloff Ballet)
"The Love Song"[142] (You Will Forget) (Duet)
D. Francis, A. Prior
(*Music by* Eduard Künneke.)
Finale
O. Myrtil, J. Dunsmure, H. Brockbank, D. Francis, E. Herbert, A. Prior,
C. Lawley, G. Carlyle, J. Moore, W. St. James, Z. Russell, Officers, Guards,
Ambassadors, Ladies in Waiting, Court Guests
ACT 3[143]
"Violets" (Song)
A. Prior, Girls
Duet Reprise
E. Herbert, A. Prior, C. Lawley
"March On"[144]
J. Dunsmure, Members of the Jockey Club
Barcarolle
D. Francis, Ensemble
Finale
D. Francis, Ensemble

1925.03 (BALIEFF'S) CHAUVE-SOURIS

A New Edition of the Russian Revue (The Bat Theatre of Moscow) in Two
Acts, 13 Scenes[145]. All scenes conceived and devised by Nikita Balieff.
Production staged under the direction of Alexander Sanin. Dances directed
by Boris Romanoff. Scenery and costumes by Vassily Shoukhaeff, Nicholas
Benois, Sergei Soudeikine, Alexander Benois, Herman Rosse. Orchestra
under the direction of M. Zlatin. Produced by F. Ray Comstock and Morris
Gest. Opened 14 January 1925 at the 49th Street Theatre and closed 7
March 1925 after 69 performances.

CAST: Messrs. NIKITA BALIEFF, Amfimoff, Dalmatoff, Ermoloff, Mari-Touchnoff,
Wurzel, Zotoff, Davidoff, Gorodetsky, Marievsky, Stoianovsky, Okorotchenkoff,
Tcherniavsky, Sheftel, Touchnoff. Mmes. Deykarhanova, Tchoukleva, Karabanova,
Birse, Ershova, Fechner, Kommissarjevskaya, Sperantseva, Zlatina, Savina.

ACT 1[146]
Scene 1

"Stenka Razin" (A Famous Legend of the Volga)
(*Music by* Alexei Archangelsky. *Scenery and Costumes by* Vassily Shoukhaeff.)
Mmes. Deykarhanova, Tchoukleva; Messrs. Anfimoff, Dalmatoff, Ermoloff,
Marievsky, Okorotchenkoff, Sheftel, Stoianovsky, Touchnoff, Wurzel, Zotoff,
Davidoff
Stenka Razin was a legendary bandit who terrorized the regions bordering on the
River Volga toward the close of the seventeenth century. In the course of one of

his raids, Stenka has captured a Persian Princess of incomparable beauty and
carried her off with him. Her presence on the Chieftain's craft arouses discontent
among his whole crew and especially in the heart of his mistress, Alyona. Jealous
and vengeful, Alyona incites Stenka's comrades against their leader, and they
charge him with plotting to betray them for the beautiful eyes of the foreign
Princess. Stenka's warlike heart is roused by this reproach, he recovers from his
infatuation and hurls the Persian Princess into the Volga. His followers are deeply
impressed by this proof of his loyalty but, grieved at the tragic fate of the beautiful
Princess, they begin to chant a Requiem in her memory. Abruptly, Stenka halts
their sad chant, orders a gay song, and stands master over the orgy that follows.
Scene 2

"The Rendezvous of Love"
Mme. Karabanova, M. Gorodetsky
(An Old Polka based on the embroidered pattern of an old Russian cushion)
(*Scenery and Costumes by* Nicholas Benois.)
Scene 3

"A Winter Evening"
Mmes. Birse, Ershova
(A Musical Tableau arranged by Alexei Archangelsky.)
(*Scenery and Costumes by* Sergei Soudeikine.)
Scene 4

"Amour et Hierarchie" (Love in the Ranks) A Buffoonery of Ancient St.
Petersburg.
(*Music by* Alexei Archangelsky[147]. *American Lyrics by* Leo Wood. *Scenery and
Costumes by* Nicholas Benois.)
Mme. Fechner; Messrs. Dalmatoff, Gorodetsky, Ermoloff, Marievsky, Stoianovsky
The daughter of the regiment awaits her suitors. One by one they appear to
claim her favor—first the drummer boy, next the sergeant-major, next the lieu-
tenant, and then the colonel, each to rout his inferior and takes his
place in accordance with the established discipline of military seniority. Finally
the general arrives, puts them all in their place, reconciles them to their fate,
and struts off victor in this strange tournament.
Scene 5

An Ancient Cameo from Nikita Balieff's Collection left behind in Moscow
(*Music by* Weckerlin. Arranged by Alexei Archangelsky. *Scenery and Costumes
by* Nicholas Benois.)
Mmes. Birse, Ershova, Karabanova, Kommissarjevskaya, Sperantseva, Tchoukleva
Scene 6

"The Shepherdess Interlude" (from Tschaikovsky's opera "The Queen of
Spades")
Mmes. Birse, Ershova, Fechner, Karabanova, Kommissarjevskaya, Zlatina;
Messrs. Touchnoff, Gorodetsky
(*Scenery and Costumes by* Vassily Shoukhaeff.)
Scene 7

"The Zaporozhtsi" (The Dnieper Cossacks)
Based on the famous painting by Ilya Repin.
(*Music by* Alexei Archangelsky. *Scenery and Costumes by* Nicholas Benois.)
Messrs. Anfimoff, Dalmatoff, Gorodetsky, Marievsky, Okorotchenkoff,
Sheftel, Stoianovsky, Tcherniavsky, Touchnoff, Wurzel, Zotoff, Davidoff
The Zaporozhtsi, a branch of the Cossacks who lived along the River Dnieper
in Ukrainia, defended Central Russia and its capital, Moscow, in the seventeenth and eighteenth centuries, from the perpetual raids of the Turks. A people
of strange customs and dauntless bravery, the Zaporozhtsi inspired by their
deeds numerous Russian poets, novelists and painters. The first great Russian
novelist, Nicholas Gogol, took their wild life and courageous exploits for the
background of his story, "Taras Bulba." Likewise, the greatest of modern Russian
painters, Ilya Repin, has left us a famous painting which represents a humorous
episode in the bitter struggle between the Cossacks and the Sultan. This painting hangs in the Tretyakovsky Gallery, Moscow, the treasury of modern Russian
art. According to the version of Gogol, which Repin has spread on his canvas,
the Sultan sent a letter to the Zaporozhtsi demanding immediate payment of a
war levy. The Cossack council, the 'Rada,' considers the question of a fitting
reply. Full of indignation, tempered with grim humor, the Zaporozhtsi crowd
around their scribe, the only one of their number who can read and write. Each
one suggests to him a gibe or an insult to be incorporated in the message to the
Sultan. The most biting and the wittiest of phrases are smothered in bursts of
primitive and approving laughter.

ACT 2
Scene 1

The Arrival at Bethlehem (Taken from "The Golden Legends" of Yvette
Guilbert)
(*Scenery and Costumes by* Vassily Shoukhaeff.)
Mmes. Deykarhanova, Kommissarjevskaya, Karabanova; Messrs. Dalmatoff,
Okorotchenkoff, Wurzel

---

[140]Dropped after the opening.
[141]Dropped after the opening.
[142]After opening, replaced by:
"Yes or No" (Duet)
O. Myrtil, H. K. Morton
(*Music by* Jacques Offenbach and Eduard Künneke.)
[143]Added during the run to Act 3 (after "Violets"):
Violin Solo
O. Myrtil
[144]Dropped after the opening.
[145]Originally produced in New York 4 February 1922 at the 49th Street
Theatre for 544 performances.
[146]Reviewers remarked upon the return of two "old favorites" from previous
editions of CHAUVE-SOURIS which nonetheless do not appear in the programs during the run, "Katinka" and "The Parade of the Wooden Soldiers."

---

[147]Melody adapted from "General Boulanger's March" by Desornes.

Scene 2
 "Siciliana"
  Mme. Birse; Messrs. Anfimoff, Stoianovsky, Wurzel, Zotoff
  (*Music by* Alexei Archangelsky. *Scenery and Costumes by* Nicholas Benois.)
Scene 3
 "The King Orders the Drums to be Beaten" (An Old French Ballad)
  Mmes. Deykarhanova, Karabanova, Kommissarjevskaya; Messrs. Dalmatoff, Zotoff
  (*Scenery and Costumes by* Alexander Benois.)
Scene 4
 "The Four Corpses" (A Tragi-Comic Opera)
  (*Scenery and Costumes by* Nicholas Benois.)
  Mme. Zlatina, Messrs. Anfimoff, Stoianovsky, Zotoff
  In this terrific cloak and sword drama, two cavaliers, Edouard and Hidoubrand,
  are both in love with Cunegonde. She loves Edouard. Hidoubrand surprises
  them and challenges Edouard to a duel. They are both mortally wounded.
  Cunegonde herself gives Hidoubrand the death thrust and then, unwilling to
  survive her beloved Edouard, she takes poison. At sight of this horrifying tragedy,
  the mutual friend of all three, Schnouzi, also commits suicide.
Scene 5
 "The Quarrel of Two Dutchwomen" (An Old Time Dutch Dance)
  (*Music by* Edvard Grieg. *Scenery and Costumes by* Herman Rosse.)
  Mmes. Karabanova, Sperantseva; Messr. Gorodetsky
Scene 6
 "A Country Picnic in a Distant Province of Russia"
  (*Music by* Alexei Archangelsky. *Scenery and Costumes by* Vassily Shoukhaeff.)
  Mmes. Birse, Ershova, Savina, Tchoukleva, Zlatina,
  Messrs. Marievsky, Okorotchenkoff, Touchnoff, Sheftel, Wurzel, Zotoff

1925.04 ## CHINA ROSE

An Oriental Operetta in Two Acts, 3 Scenes. Book and lyrics by Harry L.
Cort and George E. Stoddard. Music by A. Baldwin Sloane. Staged by R. H.
Burnside. Scenery designed by Walter Schaffner. Costumes by Brooks
Company and Chinese-American Importing Co., Inc. Orchestra under the
direction of Hilding Anderson. Produced by John Cort. Opened 19 January
1925 at the Martin Beck Theatre, closing 14 February 1925; re-opened
23 February 1925 at Wallack's Theatre, moved 16 March 1925 to the
Knickerbocker Theatre and closed 9 May 1925 after 120 performances.

CAST (in order of appearance): *Bang Bang* The Soldier: ALFRED KAPPELER. *O
Mi,* The Governor: VIOLA GILLETTE. *Fli Wun,* The Flapper: MITI MANLEY. *Wi
Lee,* The Chancellor: GEORGE E. MACK. *Pa Pa Wu,* the Ruler: ROBINSON
NEWBOLD. *Sing Sing,* The Bandit's Aide: BILLY TAYLOR. *Lo,* The Other: HARRY
CLARKE. *Cha Ming,* The Bandit: J. HAROLD MURRAY. *Ro See,* The China Rose:
OLGA STECK, Nita Martan, alt. *Hi,* The Envoy: HARRY SHORT. *Wee Nee:* Alice
Bell. *Sis Ta,* The Dowager: Kathryn Miley. (*Specialties:* Princess Mikeladz, Joseph
Daniels, Margaret Daley.)
 Ladies: Misses Leona, Konegay, Seeley, George, Francis, Phillips, Abernathy, Gray,
Joy, Reed, Rider, Barry, Hardy, Mercer, Steiner, Price, Meyers, Lewis, Gallagher,
Merrill, Britton, LeVines, Hennessy, Douglas, Hawkes, Martin. *Gentlemen:* Logan,
Lessman, Martin, Kessler, Douglass, Monty, Byrnes, Johnston, Eastman, Cowley,
Sheldon, Werner, Niles, Whitney, Mario, Treggett, Carmin, Rice, Cross, Finn.

Act 1: Exterior of Pagoda of Pa-Pa Wu, Chinese Gardens. Morn.

Act 2, Scene 1: Slim Bamboo Forest. A Mountain Pass. Next Eve. *Scene 2:* Throne
Room Prince Cha Ming, Manchuria. Next day.

ACT 1
 "Sun Worship" (Opening)
  Natives
 "Soldiers True"
  Soldiers
 "Maiden Fair"
  A. Kappeler
 "Legend of the Rose" (Recitative)
  V. Gillette
 "Chinese Potentate" (Song)
  R. Newbold
 "(We'll Build a Brand New) Bamboo Bungalow" (Duet)
  M. Manley, B. Taylor
 "I'm Hi, I'm Lo" (Song)
  H. Short, H. Clarke
 "China Rose" (Song)
  J. H. Murray
 "I'm All Alone" (Song)
  O. Steck, Girls

 "Who Am I Thinking Of?" (Duet)
  A. Kappeler, O. Steck, Maids
 "I Like the Girls (Song)
  R. Newbold, Girls
 Finale Act 1
  Company
ACT 2
Scene 1
 "Through the Bamboo" (Opening)
  Girl in Moon
 "Chinese Lantern Man"
  Men
 "Home" (Male Chorus)
  J. H. Murray, Men
 "China Bogie Man" (Song)
  O. Steck, R. Newbold, G. E. Mack, V. Gillette, A. Kappeler, M. Manley
 "Just a Kiss" (Duet)
  J. H. Murray, O. Steck
Scene 2
 "Hail the Bridegroom" (Opening)
  Chorus
 Entertainers for the Royal Court
  P. Mikeladz, J. Daniels, M. Daley
 "Tomorrow" (Solo)
  J. H. Murray
 "Great White Way in China" (Song)
  M. Manley, B. Taylor
 "I'm No Butterfly" (Song)
  K. Miley, H. Clarke, H. Short
 "Calling You My Own" (Song)
  O. Steck, Others
 "Why Do They Make 'Em So Beautiful?" (Song)
  R. Newbold
 "Happy Bride" (Ensemble)
  Chorus
 Wedding Ceremony
 Finale
  Company

1925.05 ## PUZZLES OF 1925

A Musical Revue in Two Acts, 22 Scenes. Conceived by Elsie Janis (Her
Bird's Eye Revue). Staged by Elsie Janis. Musical numbers staged by Julian
Alfred. Costumes designed by James Reynolds, Mabel E. Johnston. Settings
painted by Bergman Studios. Orchestra under the direction of Raymond
Hubbell. Produced by Charles Dillingham. Opened February 2 1925 at the
Fulton Theatre and closed 2 May 1925 after 104 performances.

CAST: ELSIE JANIS, HELEN BRODERICK, JIMMY HUSSEY, DOROTHY
APPLEBY, WALTER PIDGEON, SHIRLEY VERNON, LESTER CRAWFORD,
HELEN McDONALD, CYRIL RITCHARD, IRMA IRVING, DOROTHY IRVING,
GEORGIE HALE, EILEEN SEYMOUR, BORRAH MINEVITCH, CORTEZ and
PEGGY, THE COMMANDERS BAND (under the direction of Irving Aaronson),
JANET STONE, WILLIAM HOLBROOK; (Charles H.) O'DONNELL, (Ethel)
BLAIR & CO.; (Carter) DeHAVEN and (Freddie) NICE.
 Ensemble: Misses Morris, Grady, Greville, Errol, Doree Leslie, Mollie Dodd, Yvette
DuBois, Lucille Moore, Bobby Breslau, Jeanette Dietrich, Peggy Doran, Viola Clarens,
Edward Hickey, Herman Hyde, Milton Bloom, Phil Saxe, Harold Saliers, C. Roscoe
Stanley, John D'Alessandro, Mack Walker, Stanley Johnston, Jimmy Taylor, Sal Cibell,
Thomas Neary, Charles Andrews, William Schesky.

ACT 1[148]

---

[148]The running order was revised after the opening. Added for subsequent
tour:
 "Sailor's Sweetheart" (Act 2)
  P. Saxe, C. R. Stanley
  (*Guitar accompaniment by* H. Hyde, J. D'Alessandro, H. Saliers, S. Johnston, J.
  Taylor.)
 "Uno" (Act 2)
  D. Appleby, W. Holbrooke
  (*Music by* C. Luckyeth Roberts. *Lyrics by* Alex Rogers.)
 Hula Maids: Lanoff Sisters. *Sailors—The Kids:* M. Dodd, A. Garrison, E.
 Franklin, S. Franklin, A. Volmer, D. Keelin, B. Morris, F. Darling, M. Donovan.

Scene 1
Opening
"We Beg to Announce"
C. Ritchard
(*Music and Lyrics by* Elsie Janis.)
Scene 2
"The Undecided Blues" (The Do I or Don't I Blues)
E. Janis, J. Hussey
(*Music and Lyrics by* Elsie Janis.)
Scene 3
It Served Her Right
(*by* Bert Kalmar and Harry Ruby)
The Stenographer: D. Appleby. *The Doctor*: L. Crawford. *The Social Worker*:
H. Broderick. *First Patient*: J. Hussey. *Second Patient*: E. Hickey. *Third Patient*:
H. Hyde. *Fourth Patient*: M. Bloom. *Fifth Patient*: P. Saxe. *Sixth Patient*:
H. Saliers. *Seventh Patient*: C. R. Stanley.
Scene 4
"Titina" (Je cherche après Titina)
C. Ritchard, I. Irving, D. Irving, S. Vernon
(*Music by* Léo Daniderff. *Lyrics by* Bertal-Maubon and E. Ronn.)
Scene 5
Apres Zuloaga
(*Settings and Costumes by* James Reynolds.)
Gitanas: H. McDonald, E. Seymour. *Las Hanadas*: Misses Morris, Brady, Greville,
Errol. *Pilar*: J. Stone. *Torero*: W. Holbrooke. *Ballerinas*: I. Irving, D. Irving.
Scene 6
Cortez and Peggy
Scene 7
The Sailors' Trundle
A Policeman: W. Pidgeon. *Liza*: E. Janis. *Anti-Prohibitionist*: G. Hale.
A Musician: B. Minevitch.
"Tra-la-la-la-la"
E. Janis
(*Music by* Vincent Scotto. *Lyrics by* Elsie Janis.)
Scene 8
"Just a Flower from an Old Bouquet"
W. Pidgeon
(*Music by* Lucien Denni. *Lyrics by* Gwynne Genni.)
A Modern Miss: D. Appleby. *Wild Rose*: J. Stone. *Cupid*: M. Dodd.
Scene 9
"Irish Jewish Jubilee"[149]
J. Hussey
(*Music and Lyrics by* Bert Kalmar and Harry Ruby.)
Scene 10
"You've Got to Dance"
C. Ritchard, I. Irving, D. Irving, Entire Company
(*Music and Lyrics by* Elsie Janis.)

ACT 2
Scene 1
The Commanders under the direction of Irving Aaronson:
John D'Alessandro (Banjo), Sal Cibelli (Violin), Herman S. Hyde, Phil Saxe,
Harold Saliers (Saxophones), Mack Walker (Tuba), C. Roscoe [Cliff 'Red']
Stanley, Jimmy Taylor, Milton [Mickey] Bloom (Brass), Stanley Johnston
(Drums), Irving Aaronson (Piano).
Scene 2
Helen McDonald and Eileen Seymour
Scene 3
DeHaven and Nice[150] (Comic dance)
Scene 4
Judge Nott
(*by* Bert Kalmar and Harry Ruby)
Judge Nott: J. Hussey. *Attorney for the Prosecution*: L. Crawford. *Attorney for the
Defense*: E. Hickey. *Prisoner*: H. Broderick. *Stenographer*: S. Vernon. *Attendants for
the Court*: H. Hyde, M. Bloom. *Jury*: J. D'Alessandro, M. Walker, S. Johnson, C. R.
Stanley, P. Saxe, H. Saliers, J. Taylor, S. Cibelli, T. Neary, C. Andrews, W. Schesky.
Scene 5
"When the Cat's Away"[151]
D. Appleby
(*Music and Lyrics by* Blanche Merrill.)

Scene 6
"Give the Little Kids a Chance"[152]
D. Leslie, M. Dodd, Y. DuBois, L. Moore, B. Breslau, J. Dietrich, P. Doran, V.
Clarens
(*Music by* Raymond Hubbell. *Scene and Costumes designed by* Max Ree.)
Scene 7
Helen Broderick meets Lester Crawford
"The Lady Osteopath"[153]
H. Broderick
(*Music and Lyrics by* Blanche Merrill.)
Scene 8
"Je Vous Aime" (I Love You)
E. Janis, W. Pidgeon
(*Music and Lyrics by* Arthur Beiner.)
Scene 9
"Old Established Firm"[154]
J. Hussey
(*Music and Lyrics by* Blanche Merrill.)
Scene 10
"We're Jumping into Something"[155]
J. Hussey, H. Broderick
(*Music and Lyrics by* Blanche Merrill.)
Scene 11
The Plasterers
O'Donnell, Blair & Co.
Scene 12
"(The) Doo-Dab"
D. Appleby, J. Stone, S. Vernon, C. Ritchard, G. Hale, W. Holbrooke
(*Music by* Bert Kalmar. *Lyrics by* Harry Ruby.)
Elsie Janis by Herself[156]
Finale
E. Janis, Entire Company

1925.06   NATJA

An Operetta in Three Acts. Book and lyrics by Harry B. Smith. Music by Karl
Hajós, adapted from melodies of [Pyotor Ilyich] Tschaikowsky. Staged by
Edgar MacGregor. Costumes by Mme. Freisinger. Scenery by Triangle Scenic
Studios, H. Robert Law Studios. Orchestra under the direction of Max
Hirschfeld. Produced by B. C. and F. C. Whitney. Opened 16 February 1925 at
the Knickerbocker Theatre and closed 14 March 1925 after 32 performances.

CAST: *Catherine II*, the Czarina: MARY MELLISH, Fanille Davies (alt.). *Prince
Potemkin*, Governor of the Crimea: GEORGE REIMHERR. *Count Panin*, a Courtier:
ALEXANDER CLARK. *Lieutenant Vladimir Strogonoff* of the Royal Guards:
WARREN PROCTOR. *Natja Narishkin*: MADELINE COLLINS, Ira Jeane (alt.).
Madame Mellin, Colonel of the Hussars: Claire Grenville. *Princess Lubina*, Major of
Artillery: Marguerite Austin. *Baron Wronsky*, Manager of the Imperial Opera: Matthew
Hanley. *Ali*, a Crimean Peasant: John Willard. *The Czarina's Maid*: Jamie Zucca. *A
Crimean Peasant*: Leon Kartavin. *A Peasant Girl*: Theresa Fellegi. *Pages*: Betty Archer,
Anne Tunney. *Ladies in Waiting*: Laura Saunders, Theola Vincent. *Court Ladies,
Courtiers, Pages, Officers, Cossacks, Men and Women of the Crimea*.

The action takes place during the reign of Catherine II of Russia. The visit of the
Czarina to the Crimea and the city built of scenery is founded on history.

Act 1: Reception Room in the Winter Palace in St. Petersburg. (Triangle.)

Act 2: In the Crimea. On the Banks of the Dnieper. (Law.)

Act 3: In the Crimea.

ACT 1
Opening
"Ups and Downs"
A. Clark, 4 Maids
"Honor and Glory"
G. Reimherr, Male Chorus
"Comrade, You Have a Chance Here"
M. Collins, W. Proctor

[149]Dropped for subsequent tour.
[150]Dropped during run and for subsequent tour.
[151]Dropped during run and for subsequent tour.

[152]Dropped for subsequent tour.
[153]Dropped during run and for subsequent tour.
[154]Dropped during run and for subsequent tour.
[155]Dropped for subsequent tour.
[156]Impressions of John Barrymore as Hamlet singing "Bananas;" Fannie
Brice as Peter Pan; Leonore Ulric as a singer; Bea Lillie song; Will Rogers
and rope trick.

"Love Calls Me" (I Hear Love Call Me)
M. Collins, G. Reimherr

Entrance and Song of Czarina ("For Queen and for Country")
M. Mellish, Ensemble

Finale ("In My Homeland"-Chanson Triste)
(M. Collins, Ensemble)

ACT 2

Opening Chorus and Dance
Chorus

"(Beside) The Star of Glory" (Song)
G. Reimherr

Entrance of Czarina
Chorus Ensemble

"You'll Have to Guess"
A. Clark, M. Hanley

"(The Magic of) Moonlight and Love"
M. Collins, M. Mellish

"Shall I Tell Him?" (Romance of Jealousy)
M. Collins

Finale
Ensemble

ACT 3

Reveille

"March On"
W. Proctor, Male Chorus

"Eyes That Haunt You" (Eyes That Haunt Me)
M. Collins, W. Proctor

"There Is a Garden in Loveland"
M. Mellish, Chorus

"Reminiscence"
M. Collins, G. Reimherr

Finale
Ensemble

1925.07   SKY HIGH

A Musical Play in Three Acts. Book and lyrics by Harold Atteridge and Captain Harry Graham. (Based on the English musical farce 'Whirled into Happiness' with book and lyrics by Harry Graham, adapted from the Viennese operette 'Der Tanz ins Glück' with book by Robert Bodanzky and Bruno Hardt-Warden, music by Robert Stolz.) Music by Robert Stolz, Alfred Goodman, Maurice Rubens, Carlton Kelsey. Additional lyrics by Clifford Grey. Staged by Fred G. Latham and Alexander Leftwich. Dances staged by Seymour Felix. Settings by Watson Barratt. Costumes designed by Paul Arlington, Inc, Vanity Fair Costume, Inc. Orchestra under the direction of Carlton Kelsey. Entire production supervised by J. J. Shubert. Produced by Messrs. Shubert in association with Eugene Howard. Opened 2 March 1925 at the Sam S. Shubert Theatre, moved 20 March 1925 to the Winter Garden, moved 15 June 1925 to the Casino Theatre, and closed 5 September 1925 after 217 performances.

CAST (in order of appearance): *Cloak Room Girl*: Dorothy McNulty. *Bar Maid*: Lily McNeil. *Florence Horridge*: JOYCE BARBOUR. *Helen*: Marcella Swanson. *Marian*: Emily Miles. *Attendant*: Walter Johnson. *Montague Lush*: Roland Hogue. *Patricia Devere*: Dorothy Hathaway. *Lord Brancaster*: Edward Douglas. *Aggie*: ANN MILBURN. *Sammy Myers*: WILLIE HOWARD. *Ratwell of Scotland Yard*: Bert Shadow. *Mr. Gray*: Thomas Whitely. *Delphine de Lavalliere*: VANNESSI. *Horace Deveridge*: JAMES R. LIDDY. *Alfred Horridge, Esq.*: FLORENZ AMES. *Dr. Carter*: Thomas Whitely. *Mrs. Horridge*: Violet Englefield. *Duke of Dulchester*: Roland Hogue. *Duchess of Dulchester*: Stella Shiel. *Lily, a manicurist*: Betty Pecan. *Philips*: Walter Johnson.

Ushers, Manicure Girls, Guests, Dancing Girls: Lucile Vinik, Elsie Frank, Norma Gould, Bella Heyman, Billie Smart, Billie Wagner, Carol Grey, Margy Lane, Ysabel Cayer, Gladys Smith, Mildred Morgan, Catherine Huth, Lorene Mumma, Betty Sheldon, Jeanne Tanny, Lucile Osborne, Emma Wyche, Margy Whitney, Emily Sherman, Emmy La Mar, Gene Philips, Ethel Guerard, Beatrice Reiss, Marie Warner, Marcia Mack, Betty Lee, Ruth Mayon, Peggy Brown, Helen Veronica, Hazel Beamer, Edith Pierce, Dorothy McNulty, Charlotte Ayres, Dorothy Hathaway. Johnnies, College Boys, Guests, Patrons: Wallace Milam, Allen Blair, Freddie Murray, Albert Royal, Joe Hughes, William Birdie, Arthur Appel, Jack Baker, John Creighton, William Brown, Hal Gibson, Charlie Dodge. Specialty Dancers: Margy Whitney, Emma Wyche, Peggy Brown, Freddie Murray. Six Little Dippers: Ruth Mayon, Dorothy Hathaway, Ysobel Cayer, Dorothy McNulty, Hazel Beamer, Charlotte Ayers, Marjorie Lane.

Act 1: Foyer of the Majestic Music Hall, London.

Act 2: The Horridge's House, 'The Pines' at Crouch End.

Act 3: Antoine's Beauty Shop in Bond Street.

ACT 1

Opening Chorus ["London Johnnies"]
Johnnies, Ushers
(*Music by* Carlton Kelsey, Maurice Rubens. *Lyrics by* Clifford Grey.)

"Hello, the Little Birds Have Flown"
J. Barbour, Girls
(*Music by* Robert Stolz. *Lyrics by* Harry Graham.)

"The Best Songs of All"
W. Howard, A. Milburn, Girls
(*Music by* Carlton Kelsey, Maurice Rubens. *Lyrics by* Clifford Grey.)

"Intermezzo"
J. Barbour, J. R. Liddy, Girls

"Give Your Heart in June"
J. Barbour, J. R. Liddy, Girls
(*Music by* Victor Herbert. *Lyrics by* Clifford Grey, Harold Atteridge.)

"There's Life in the Old Dog Yet"
Vannessi, F. Ames, Girls
(*Music by* Robert Stolz. *Lyrics by* Harry Graham.)

"Find a Good Time"
R. Hogue, Vannessi, F. Ames, Entire Company
(*Music by* Carlton Kelsey, Maurice Rubens. *Lyrics by* Clifford Grey.)

ACT 2

Opening Chorus ["Gossiping"]
V. Englefield, T. Whiteley, M. Swanson, E. Miles, Guests
(*Music by* Carlton Kelsey, Maurice Rubens. *Lyrics by* Clifford Grey.)

"Why Are They Following Me?"
W. Howard, Girls, A. Milburn, Boys
(*Music by* Carlton Kelsey, Maurice Rubens. *Lyrics by* Clifford Grey.)

"Somewhere in Lovers' Land"
J. Barbour, Girls
(*Music by* Robert Stolz.)

Ballet Specialties
Six Little Dippers

"The Letter Song"
J. Barbour, J. R. Liddy

"Man o' My Dreams"[157]
Vannessi, F. Ames

"Sky High"
J. Barbour, J. R. Liddy, Vannessi, F. Ames, A. Milburn

The Entertainment (Broadcasting)—

(a) Willie Howard

(b) Lancashire Lassies (Specialty by Marjorie Whitney)

(c) Ann Milburn

(d) Vannessi

(e) Willie Howard

["If You Knew Susie"
(*Music and Lyrics by* Buddy G. DeSylva.)

"Keep On Croonin' a Tune"
(*Music and Lyrics by* Sammy Fain, Irving Weill and Jimmy McHugh.)]

"Let It Rain"
W. Howard, J. R. Liddy
(*Music and Lyrics by* James Kendis and Hal Dyson.)

Finaletto
R. Hogue, S. Shiel, J. Barbour, J. R. Liddy, F. Ames, V. Englefield, Vannessi, A. Milburn, Chorus

"Let It Rain" (reprise)
W. Howard, J. R. Liddy, A. Milburn

ACT 3

Opening Chorus ["Manicuring"]
Manicure Girls, Patrons

Specialty
M. Whitney

"Trim Them All But the One You Love"
A. Milburn, Six Little Dippers
(*Music by* Carlton Kelsey, Maurice Rubens. *Lyrics by* Clifford Grey.)

"The Barbering Wop of Seville" (The Barber of Seville)
W. Howard
(*Music by* Carlton Kelsey, Maurice Rubens. *Lyrics by* Clifford Grey.)

---

[157]Dropped after the opening.

"We Make the Show"
    Six Little Dippers
"Whirled into Happiness"
    W. Howard, A. Milburn, R. Hogue, Vannessi, E. Douglas, Entire Company
    (*Music by* Robert Stolz. *Lyrics by* Harry Graham.)
Finale
    Entire Company

1925.08

LOUIE THE 14TH

A Musical Comedy in Two Acts, 6 Scenes. Book and lyrics by Arthur Wimperis, adapted from the German play ("Ludwig XIV") by (Paul) Frank and Julius Wilhelm. Music by Sigmund Romberg. Staged by Edward Royce. Scenes designed by Gretel Urban. Costumes designed by James Reynolds, Mme. Frances, Schneider-Anderson, Eaves Costume, Milgrims. Orchestra under the direction of Gus Salzer. Orchestrations by Emil Gerstenberger. Produced by Florenz Ziegfeld. Opened March 3 1925 at the Cosmopolitan Theatre and closed 5 December 1925 after 319 performances.

CAST (in order of appearance): *Major the Hon. Harold Byngham, D.S.C., M.C.:* HUGH WAKEFIELD. *The Village Cure:* Frederick Graham. *Captain Gallifet*, French Cavalry Officer: JOSEPH LERTORA. *Colette de Cassagnac*, a Village Fruitseller: DORIS PATSTON. *Doughboys (3): Bill:* Charles Mast. *Spud:* Al Baron. *Bob:* Al Havrilla. *Francois Pochard*, Landlord of the Little Blue Pig: Edouard Durand. *Captain William Brent, A.E.F.:* HARRY FENDER. *Sergeant, A.E.F.:* Charles Mast. *Louie Ketchup*, the Army Cook: LEON ERROL. *Gabrielle Trapmann:* ETHEL SHUTTA. *General Chanson:* Alfred James. *The Comptesse de Bellac*, a Parisienne: Judith Vosselli. *Marie Pochard:* Simone deBouvier. *Patricia Brent:* Pauline Mason. *Paul Trapmann*, newly rich oil magnate: J. W. DOYLE. *Madame Trapmann:* Catherine Calhoun Doucet. *Dominique Dindon*, a French oil magnate: Frederick Graham. *Aristide Brissac*, a French oil magnate: Alfred James. *Florentine:* FLORENTINE GOSNOVA. *Evelyn:* EVELYN LAW. *The Major Domo:* Louis Casavant. *American, British, French Officers, Continental Tourists, Doughboys, Tommies, Poiles, French Villagers, Market Women, Flower Girls, Gypsies, Waiters, Maids, etc.*
    Ziegfeld Cosmopolitan Girls: Virginia King, Marguerite Boatwright, Catherine Littlefield, Gertrude McDonald, Louise Brooks, Anastasia Reilly, Mabelle Swor, Maryland Jarboe, Consuelo Owens, Elsie Behrens, Mabel Baade, Ruth Fallows. *The Ladies:* Vera Colburn, Joan Clement, Anna May Denehy, Agatha DeBussy, Neel Francis, Helene Herendeen, Edna Johnson, Dorothy Lesley, Rona Lee, Nyo Lee, Betty Nevins, Teddy King, Fern Oakley, Dorothy Dickerson, Helen Haines, Therese Kelly, Marie Lambert, Lucy Monroe, Lelia McGuire, Elonora Ruggeri, Gertrude Selden, Claire Wayne, Gene Wayne, Lee Baron, Lorraine Webb, Helen Reinecke, Camille Griffith, Peggy Fears, Louise Scott, Pearl Sodders, Ida Barry, Jessie Madison, Julia Warren, Lilyan Dawn, Dorothy Dahm, Margaret Langhorne, Florence O'Neill, Ethel Kelly, Dorothy Brown. *The Gentlemen:* Billy Walsh, George Plank, Carmine DiGiovanni, Sam Guncharoff, Albert Kouiznetzoff, Robert Walker, John Fluco, Robert Moan, Moris Rubin, Al Small, Jack Rouger, Frank Vonne, Richard Powell, Norman Colvin, Murray Minehart, Haal Hennessy, Warren Crosby, Lawrence Chrow, Carl Rose, Morton Croswell, Owen Hervey, Leslie Kingdon, Jack Cronin, Al Wyatt, Ned Hamlin, Jack Leahy, William May, Al Stevens, Morris Wagman, Walter Costello, Al Havrilla, Al Baron. (*Specialty Dancers:* Messrs. Milek and Kindl.)

The action takes place in France in July, 1919, after the Armistice.

Act 1, Scene 1: The Market Place of Saint Ferien. *Scene 2:* A Country Lane near Saint Ferien. *Scene 3:* Exterior of 'The Little Blue Pig.'

Act 2, Scene 1: The Banquet Hall. *Scene 2:* An Arbor in the Garden. *Scene 3:* The Garden of the Chateau.

ACT 1[158]
Scene 1
"Market Day" (Opening)
    Entire Company
"Little Peach"
    D. Patston, Ladies, Gentlemen
"Homeland"
    H. Fender, Doughboys
"Wayside Flower"
    D. Patston, H. Fender

"Regimental Band"
    H. Wakefield, Ladies, Gentlemen
Finaletto
    H. Fender, L. Errol
Scene 2
"Taking a Wife"
    L. Errol, Cosmopolitan Girls
Scene 3
"The Little Blue Pig"
    Ladies, Gentlemen
"Schoe Plattler Tanz" (Dance)
    C. Littlefield, F. Gosnova, Messrs. Milek, Kindl
"Pep"
    P. Mason, Ladies
"True Hearts"[159]
    H. Fender, D. Patston
"Rin-tin-tin"
    E. Shutta, Cosmopolitan Girls, Ladies, Gentlemen
"Celebration of St. Joan the Good"
    (*Costumes designed by* James Reynolds.)
    Men-at-Arms, Haukers, Arches, Pickmen, Standard Bearers; Nuns, Choir Girls, Chateleains; Duchesses; Censer-bearers; Cardinal; Flower Girls and Boys; Primavera: (Ensemble). *Saint Joan of Arc:* D. Patston. *The Knight:* H. Fender.

ACT 2
Scene 1
"The Major-Domo" (Opening)
    L. Casavant, Gentlemen
Dance
    E. Law
"Follow the Rahjah"
    L. Errol, D. Patston, P. Mason, E. Shutta, C. C. Doucet, J. Clement, H. Herendeen, B. Nevins, H. Wakefield, H. Fender, J. W. Doyle, J. Lertora, F. Graham, A. James, Ladies, Gentlemen
Scene 2
"I'm Harold, I'm Harold"
    H. Wakefield, Six Cosmpolitan Girls
    (A. Reilly, V. King, C. Littlefield, M. Boatwright, L. Brooks, G. McDonald)
Finaletto
    D. Patston, J. Vosselli, H. Fender, J. Lertora
Scene 3
"Moon Flower"
    E. Ruggeri, Ladies, Gentlemen
Dance
    F. Gosnova
"(Don't Let Anybody) Vamp Your Man"[160]
    E. Shutta, Cosmopolitan Girls
Finale
    Entire Company

1925.09

PIERROT THE PRODIGAL

A Revival of the Pantomime (L'Enfant Prodigue) in Three Acts[161]. Libretto by Michel Carré, fils. Music by André Wormer, interpreted (at the piano) by George Copeland. Staged by Otokar Bartik. Settings under the supervision of Livingston Platt. Costumes from Miss Emma, Brooks Uniform Company. Produced by the Actors' Theatre. Opened 6 March 1925 at the 48th Street Theatre and closed 17 April 1925 after 14 performances[162].

CAST: *Young Pierrot:* LAURETTE TAYLOR. *Monsieur Pierrot:* Ivan Lazareff. *Madame Pierrot:* Michelette Burani. *Phrynette:* GALINA KOPERNAK. *The Baron:* CLARENCE DERWENT. *The Negro:* Jack Thornton.

---

[158]Added during the run to Act 2 (before Finaletto, Scene 3):
    "Give a Little, Get a Little Kiss"
        Elsa Ersi (as Countess Zichky)
        (*Lyrics by* Irving Caesar.)
        Countess Zichky was a new character replacing Judith Vosselli as Comptesse de Bellac.
Added late in the run:
    Specialty
        Norah Blaney, Gwen Farrar

[159]During the summer, replaced by:
    "Edelweiss"
        Glen Dale (Billy), D. Patston, Ladies, Gentlemen
        (*Lyrics by* Clifford Grey.)
[160]Dropped late in the run.
[161]First produced in New York 7 March 1891 at Daly's Theatre as THE PRODIGAL SON for 7 performances, and 21 August 1893 at Daly's Theatre as L'ENFANT PRODIGUE for 49 performances. For Synopsis of Scenes, see original 1891 production
[162]Matinees only, Tuesdays and Fridays.

1925.10 ZIEGFELD FOLLIES OF 1925

A Musical Revue in Two Acts, 22 Scenes[163]. Dialogue (sketches) by J. P. McEvoy, Will Rogers, W. C. Fields, Gus Weinberg. Music by Raymond Hubbell, Dave Stamper, Werner Janssen. Lyrics by Gene Buck. Staged by Julian Mitchell. Tableaux devised and staged by Ali Ben Haggin. Costume designs by John Held, Jr., Mabel Johnstone, John E. Stone. Scenery by Norman Bel Geddes, Robert Law Studios. Orchestra under the direction of Louis Gress. Orchestrations by (Robert) Russell Bennett, Fred Barry, Harold Sandford, Steve Jones. Produced by Florenz Ziegfeld. Opened 10 March 1925 at the New Amsterdam Theatre and closed 4 July 1925 after 127 performances. Revised Summer Edition (see entry in following season) opened 6 July 1925 and closed 19 September 1925 after 88 performances.

CAST: W. C. FIELDS, ANN PENNINGTON, WILL ROGERS, RAY DOOLEY, DOROTHY KNAPP, TOM LEWIS, MARTHA LORBER, CLARENCE NORDSTROM, VIVIENNE SEGAL, IRVING FISHER, BERYL HALLEY, AL OCHS, SERGE PERKINOFF, JACK SHANNON, BRANDON TYNAN, FRANK LAMBERT, ARTHUR BROWN, MARK TRUSCOTT, THE KELO BROTHERS, MARJORIE LEET, GEORGE OLSEN'S BAND, Vengie Valentine, Elise Cavanna.

Follies Girls: Misses Edith Babson, Katherine Burke, Frances Reveaux, Gladys Loftus, Evelyn Goodwin, Frances Harten, Flo Kennedy, Bernice Ackerman, Wayne, Alma Drange, Nally, Cambridge, Andrea, Pierre, Rasch, Virginia Magee, McDonald, Burke, Helen Sheldon, Calame, Ansell, Ellsworth, McLaughlin, Waddell, Naomi Johnson, Cricket Wooten, Marion Benda, Wild.

ACT 1[164]

Scene 1

"Everyone Knows What Jazz Is"
C. Nordstrom, Jazz Girls, Follies Girls, Tiller Girls
(*Music by* Werner Janssen. *Lyrics by* Gene Buck.)
Scene: A City Square.
Miss Mischief: M. Lorber.

Scene 2

"Someone, Someday, Somewhere"
I. Fisher, D. Knapp
(*Music by* Rudolf Friml. *Lyrics by* Gene Buck.)
Scene: The Curtains.

Scene 3

The Drug Store
(*by* J. P. McEvoy)
_____: C. Nordstrom. *Myrtle*: N. Johnson. *Pa*: W. C. Fields. *Phone Lady*: E. Cavanna. *Stamp Man*: T. Lewis. *Italian*: J. Shannon. *Gertie*: R. Dooley. *A Customer*: F. Lambert. *Nurse*: F. Reveaux. *An Officer*: B. Tynan.

Scene 4

Dance Different
Kelo Brothers

Scene 5

"Biminy"
I. Fisher
(*Music by* Dave Stamper. *Lyrics by* Gene Buck.)

Dance
A. Pennington, Hooch Girls, George Olsen's Band

Scene 6

A Senator
T. Lewis

Scene 7

A Back Porch
(*by* J. P. McEvoy)
Pa: W. C. Fields. *Milk Man*: J. Shannon *Newsboy*: A. Brown. *Rag Man*: F. Lambert. *Gertie*: R. Dooley. *Ma*: M. Lorber. *Myrtle*: A. Pennington. *Mrs. Favor*: E. Cavanna. *Mrs. Fuchwantz*: F. Reveaux. *Fruit Vendor*: G. Spelvin. *Scissor Grinder*: S. Perkinoff. *Ice Man*: M. Truscott.

---

[163]The nineteenth in the annual series of musical revues produced by Florenz Ziegfeld beginning in 1907.
[164]Added during the run:
George Olsen's Trumpeters (Act 1)
"Bertie" (Act 2) (added 23 March 1925)
C. Nordstrom, Pajama Girls
(*Music by* Sigmund Romberg. *Lyrics by* Clifford Grey.)
Song (Act 2)
I. Fisher, D. Knapp
Play Juror (Act 2)
W. Rogers, W. C. Fields, M. Lorber

"I'm Going to Wait Until the Right One Comes Along"
A. Pennington, Tray Girls, George Olsen's Band
(*Music by* Werner Janssen. *Lyrics by* Gene Buck.)

Scene 8

A City Park
(*by* J. P. McEvoy)
The Girl: V. Segal. *The Boy*: C. Nordstrom. *The Thug*: B. Tynan. *A Citizen*: S. Perkinoff. *A Cop*: T. Lewis. *Another Cop*: J. Shannon.

"Toddle Along"
V. Segal, C. Nordstrom, Follies Girls and Boys
(*Music by* Werner Janssen. *Lyrics by* Gene Buck.)

Scene 9

Out West
W. Rogers

Scene 10

"I'd Like to Corral a Gal"
I. Fisher, W. Rogers, George Olsen's Band, Follies Girls, Tiller Girls
(*Music by* Raymond Hubbell. *Lyrics by* Gene Buck.)
Scene: The Ranch.

ACT 2

Scene 1

"Ever-Loving Bee"
V. Segal, I. Fisher
(*Music by* Dave Stamper. *Lyrics by* Gene Buck.)
Scene: The Bee Hive.
The Bees: Tiller Girls, Follies Girls. *Queen Bee*: H. Sheldon.

Scene 2

Pearl of the East
(*by* Ben Ali Haggin. *Arrangement with special music by* Raymond Hubbell.)
The Pearl: M. Lorber. *A Pink Slave*: B. Halley. *A Mountain Slave*: D. Knapp. *A Dancer*: G. Loftus. *The Mongolian Giant*: A. Ochs. *Slaves*: M. Benda, B. Storey. *Dancers*: E. Babson, K. Burke, F. Reveaux, E. Goodwin, F. Harten. *Musicians*: M. Leet, F. Kennedy, B. Ackerman. *A Tartar Prince*: S. Perkinoff. *His Warriors*: F. Lambert, M. Truscott.

Scene 3

A Curtain

Scene 4

A Friend of Calvin's
(*by* Will Rogers)
Scene: A Country Store.
Lem: W. Rogers. *Hiram*: B. Tynan. *Zeke*: J. Shannon.

Scene 5

"Lonely Little Melody"
I. Fisher, V. Segal, Jazz Girls
(*Music by* Dave Stamper. *Lyrics by* Gene Buck.)

Dance
M. Leet, A. Pennington, George Olsen's Band
Scene: Jazzland. (*Scene painted by* John Wenger.)

"The Waltz of Love"
R. Dooley, W. C. Fields

Scene 6

Rope Dance
Tiller Girls
(*Staged by* John Tiller.)

Scene 7

"Titina" (Je cherche après Titine) (from *PUZZLES OF 1925*)
I. Fisher, D. Knapp, Follies Girls
(*Music by* Léo Daniderff. *Lyrics by* Gene Buck. *Original French Lyrics by* Bertal-Maubon and E. Ronn.)
Scene: The Beach.

Scene 8

A Road
(*by* W. C. Fields)
Pa: W. C. Fields. *Ma*: M. Lorber. *Gertie*: R. Dooley. *A Motor Cop*: T. Lewis.

Scene 9

The Picnic
(*by* J. P. McEvoy)

Scene 10

"The Beauty Contest"
I. Fisher, V. Valentine
(*Music by* Victor Herbert and Harry Tierney. *Lyrics by* Joseph J. McCarthy.)
Scene: A Garden.
Pages: Misses Wayne, Drange. *Paris Crown*: Miss Kennedy. *Eve*: Miss Hurley. *Brunhilde*: Miss Nally. *Cleopatra*: Miss Babson. *Gwenevieve*: Miss Cambridge,

Miss Andrea. *Eloise*: Miss Pierre, Miss Rasche, Miss McGee. *Isabelle*: Miss McDonald, Miss Burke. *Gabrielle*: Miss Harten, Miss Sheldon. *Nell Gwynne*: Miss Ackerman, Miss Calame, Miss Ansell. *Eugenie*: Miss Loftus, Miss Ellsworth. *Racamier*: Miss Reveaux, Miss McLaughlin. *Lady Hamilton*: Miss Waddell, Miss Johnson, Miss Wooten. *DuBarry*: Miss Benda, Miss Wild. *Scheherazade*: B. Halley. *The Ziegfeld Girl*: D. Knapp. *Typical Girl of Today*: A. Pennington. And the Tiller Girls.

(*Scene painted by Ludwig Kainer. Costumes designed by Ben Ali Haggin.*)

Finale

1925.11

SALLY, IRENE AND MARY

A Revival of the Musical Comedy in Two Acts, 9 Scenes[165]. Book by Eddie Dowling and Cyrus Wood. Music by J. Fred Coots. Lyrics by Raymond Klages. Staged by Frank Smithson. Musical numbers staged by Allan K. Foster. Costumes by Vanity Fair Costume Company and Paul Arlington, Inc. Scenery by the United Scenic Studios. Orchestra under the direction of Charles H. Drury. Entire production under the personal supervision of J. J. Shubert. Produced by Messrs. Shubert. Opened 23 March 1925 at the 44th Street Theatre and closed 4 April 1925 after 16 performances.

CAST: *Jimmie Dugan*: EDDIE DOWLING. *Mrs. Dugan, his mother*: JOSIE INTROPODI. *Mary O'Brien, his girl*: EDNA MORN. *Mrs. O'Brien, her mother*: Ida Fitzhugh. *Sally, friend of Mary*: LOUISE BROWN. *Mrs. Clancy, her mother*: GERTRUDE MUDGE. *Irene, another friend of Mary*: KATHLEEN MULQUEEN. *Rodman Jones, an Aristocrat*: GEORGE EISING. *Mrs. Jones, his mother*: GRACE STUDIFORD [Grace Van Studdiford]. *Clarence Edwards, a Boy around Town*: HERBERT HOEY. *Mr. Myers, a Theatrical Manager*: Patrick Henry. *Percy Fitzgerald, a friend to Clarence*: BURFORD HAMPDEN. *Al Cleveland, an Author*: Frank Connor. *Sully, Stage Door Man*: D. J. Sullivan. *Tony*: D. J. Sullivan. *Mr. Mulcahey, of the Neighborhood*: Eddie O'Connor. *Dinty Moore, pal of Jimmie*: FRED PACKARD. *Frank, Night Watchman*: William Mason. *First Dresser to Girls*: Lois Arnold. *Second Dresser to Girls*: Rebecca Ryeford. *Detective of Hotel Astor*: Fred Stanton. *Carraige Man, Hotel Astor*: Thomas Weldon. *Kitty Kelly, East Side Girl*: Monica Boulais. *Mabel Riley, her Friend*: Hazel Vernon. *Marguerite Hoban*: Grace DeViney. *Mrs. Pomeroy Gilbert*: Frances Dewey. *Mrs. Kelly Pool*: Rebecca Ryeford. *Mrs. Fitzgibbons Pomeroy*: Lois Arnold. *Mrs. Carter Smith*: Betty Dupre. *Mrs. De la Croix*: Hazel Vernon.

Ladies of the Ensemble: Grace DeViney, Beulah Merritt, Dorothy Cavanaugh, Isabel Brown, Margaret O'Connor, Anna Hooks, Lillian Bell, Olga O'Dell, Ray Lloyd, Monica Boulais. *Gentlemen of the Ensemble*: Thomas Weldon, James Ormonde, Walter Blair, Frank Binns, Joseph McGurgan.

1925.12

BRINGING UP FATHER

A Cartoon Musical Comedy in Two Acts, 5 Scenes. (A Travesty on breaking into society.) Book by Nat Leroy. Based on the comic strip cartoon of the same name by George McManus. Music by Seymour Furth. Lyrics by Richard F. Carroll. Staged by Richard F. Carroll. Dances and ensembles staged by William Koud. Scenery designed by William Weaver. Costumes by Benjamin O. Davis. Orchestra under the direction of Seymour Furth. Orchestrations by Charles H. Smith. Produced by Gus Hill. Opened 30 March 1925 at the Lyric Theatre and closed 18 April 1925 after 24 performances.

CAST: *Jiggs Mahoney, Himself in Person*: DANNY SIMMONS. *Maggie, His Better Than Half*: BEATRICE HARLOWE. *Kitty, a Chip Off the Old Block*: GERTRUDE LaVELLA. *Patsy Moore, Kitty's Sweetheart*: LEO HENNING. *Dinty Moore, Imprudent but Faithful*: JAMES COLLINS. *Eugenia Mendoza, a Lady of Title*: MARY MARLOWE. *Sandy McPherson, a Brawny Scot*: WILLIAM CAMERON. *Captain Steve McKenna*: Ollie Mack. *Commander of the Ship*: William Tomkins. *Captain of the Ship*: JAMES SULLIVAN. (*Specialty Dancers*: Dorothy Hale and Lloyd Mann.)

Ladies of the Ensemble: Iris Navarro, Kaye Renard, Ethel Jones, Gloria Sylvia, Yvonne Bacon, Ruth Rider, Lee Arnold, Eva Barborik, Margaret Gordon, Marion Meredith, Jayne Fillat, June Preston, Marion Currie, Margie Henley, Babe Joyce, Charlotte Koar, Carol Rogers.

Act 1: In the Emerald Isle.

Act 2, Scene 1: On Board the Yacht en route for Spain. *Scene 2*: In Poppyland. *Scene 3*: Royal Purple. *Scene 4*: Interior of Castle in Spain.

ACT 1

  Opening Chorus
    L. Henning, G. LaVella, Gossoons, Colleens

"When It Gets Dark"
  G. LaVella, L. Henning
  The Pajama Girls: Misses K. Renard, E. Jones, Y. Bacon, R. Rider, M. Gordon, J. Preston, M. Henley, G. Sylvia. *The Jazz Girls*: Misses I. Navarro, E. Barborik, Fillet, Meredith.

"They Hope to Make a Hit"
  J. Collins
  Toe Dancer: I. Navarro. *The Castinet Girl*: K. Renard. *The Russian Dancer*: E. Barborik. *The Girl with the Violin*: G. Sylvia. *The Singer*: C. Rogers. *The Acrobatic Girl*: L. Arnold.

"Play Me a Bagpipe Tune"
  W. Cameron, Scotch Lassies

Legmania Dance
  R. Hale

"When Dad Was Twenty-One"
  L. Henning
  On the Clock: The Minuet Girls: M. Currie, I. Navarro. *The Violin Girl*: G. Sylvia. *The Polka Girl*: J. Preston. *The Waltz Girl*: M. Gordon.

Dance of the Present
  L. Mann and D. Hale

"In Little Old New York"
  D. Simmons

"The Gainesboro Glide"
  M. Marlowe, Gainesboro Girls

A Few Moments with Miss Mary Marlowe

"The Merry Go Round"
  Company

Finale—"On the Way to Spain"
  Entire Company

ACT 2

Scene 1
  Opening
    Company
  "Moonlight" (Song)
    J. Sullivan
  "Jiggs"
    D. Simmons

Scene 2
  "Poppy the Dream Girl"
    (J. Sullivan, G. LaVella)
    The Princess: G. LaVella. *The Lover*: J. Sullivan.

Scene 3
  Maggie Makes Her Bow
    (B. Harlowe)

Scene 4
  "My Lady's Fan"
    M. Marlowe, Girls
    The Dancers: R. Hale, L. Mann.
  "Wedding Chimes"
    D. Simmons, B. Harlowe, G. LaVella, L. Henning, Flower Girls, Bridesmaids

Finale
  Entire Company

THE MIKADO,
1925.13 or, The Town of Titipu

A Revival of the Comic Opera in Two Acts[166]. Libretto by William S. Gilbert. Music by Arthur Sullivan. Staged by Milton Aborn. Art director, Watson Barratt. Settings by Rollo Wayne. Conductor, Alfred Goodman. Produced by the Messrs. Shubert. Opened 11 April 1925 at the 44th Street Theatre and closed 6 June 1925 after 65 performances.

CAST: *The Mikado of Japan*: WILLIAM DANFORTH. *Nanki-Poo, his son*: TOM BURKE. *Ko-Ko, Lord High Executioner of Titipu*: LUPINO LANE. *Pooh-Bah, Lord High Everything Else*: STANLEY FORDE. *Pish-Tush, a Noble Lord*: LEO de HIERAPOLIS. *A Noble*: John Willard. *Three Sisters, Wards of Ko-Ko*: Yum-Yum:

[165]Originally produced 4 September 1922 at the Casino Theatre for 312 performances. For Synopsis of Scenes and Musical Numbers, see original 1922 production. For this revival, "Our Home Sweet Home," "Something in Here" and "Until You Say Yes" were cut.

[166]First presented in New York 20 July, 10–29 August 1885 at the Union Square and People's Theatres for 22 performances. First authorized production presented 19 August 1885 at the Fifth Avenue Theatre by Richard D'Oyly Carte for 250 performances. For Synopsis of Scenes and Musical Numbers, see 19 August 1885 D'Oyly Carte production.

MARGUERITE NAMARA. *Pitti-Sing*: BARBARA MANUEL. *Peep-Bo*: ELSA PETERSON. *Katisha*: SARAH EDWARDS. *Attendants to Ko-Ko*: Messrs. Schumazuni, Kushiki. *Attendants to Yum-Yum*: Misses Yamardani, Miramuna.

Ladies of the Mikado's Suite: Evelyn Stone, Faye Gilmore, Florence Poyet, Kathleen Talbot, Jane Waye, Hedda Albrecht. *Ensemble of School Girls, Nobles, Guards and Coolies*: Lillian Clinton, Florence deBardi, Hedda Albrecht, Cathleen Strickland, Clarice Olsen, Caroline Canilou, Pola Sheva, G. Rossi, Marie Kebar, Mildred Windell, Zenada Nicolina, Evelyn Stone, Irma King, Travis Thames, Sioux Scarberry, Claudia Ivanova, Annette Hawley, Lillian Sanders, Adele Savoye, Phillis Laurelle, Eugenie Gregory, Faye Gilmore, Henrietta Merriman, Elizabeth Pierce, Colleen Craven, Martha Fiesell, Clarice Anderson, Rose Maynard, Antoinette LaFarge, Annette Lang, Florence Poyet, Katherine Thompson, Jane Weye, Freda Leary, Margaret Hoase, Jean Ackerman, Mignon Spence. B. Flack, G. L. Mortimer, P. McCarthy, Elton Calkins, H. P. Cooke, Francis Rosner, Frank Baker, Isolf Fiane, J. E. Hardin, H. Roberts, B. O. Wally, Arthur Curran, Eugene Ring, Lester Niles, John Williard, Louis Olari, Hans Haaman, Harry Lundquist, W. Dorman, Alex Bowman, Fred Burke, Imre Vecsey, Victor Rosales, I. Bogat, Byron Irving, William Baden, Louis Smelensky, Charles Mansfield, Leon Kartavin, George Foran, Marty Reese, S. A. Sabro, Sointri Syrjala, Joseph Wolf, Donald Murray.

TELL ME MORE!

1925.14

A Spring Musical Comedy in Two Acts, 6 Scenes. Book by Fred Thompson and William K. Wells. Music by George Gershwin. Lyrics by Buddy G. DeSylva and Ira Gershwin. Book staged by John Harwood. Dances and ensembles staged by Sammy Lee. Costumes designed by Charles LeMaire. Art director, Walter Harvey. Orchestra under the direction of Max Steiner. Produced by Alexander Aarons. Opened 13 April 1925 at the Gaiety Theatre and closed 11 July 1925 after 100 performances.

CAST: *Gertrude*: Ruth Raymonde. *Harry*: Eddie Dowling, Jr. *Kenneth Dennison*: ALEXANDER GRAY. *Peggy Van De Leur*: PHYLLIS CLEVELAND. *Billy Smith*, Peggy's brother: ANDREW TOMBES. *Bonnie Reeves*: EMMA HAIG. *Mannequins at Maison Elise (4)*: *Estelle*: Charlotte Esmone. *Lucy*: Nita Jacques. *Heather*: Marion Mueller. *Toots*: Dolla Harkins. *Edith*: Vivian Glenn. *Pages*: Mary Jane, Dotty Wilson. *Mrs. Pennyfeather*: Florence Auer. *Monty Sipkin*, Head Salesman at Maison Elise: LOU HOLTZ. *Jane Wallace*: ESTHER HOWARD. *Mrs. Wallace*, Jane's Mother: Maud Andrew. *George B. Wallace*, Jane's Father: Robert C. Ryles. *Monsieur Cerise*, Manager of The Balsams: Eugene Redding. *Cashier* of the B. & T. Restaurant: Cecil Bruner. *Waiters* at The Balsams: Willie Covan, Leonard Ruffin. *Doorman*: Morton McConnachie. *Specialty Dancers*: Vivian Glenn, Mary Jane, Dottie Wilson, (Willie) Covan and (Leonard) Ruffin.

Debutantes and Shop Girls: Sofia Howard, Mildred Brown, Maxine Marshall, Blossom Vreeland, Penelope Rowland, Gay Worrell, Jane Brew, Portland Hoffa, Betty Whitney, Margaret Lee, Ruth Mosley, Betty Waxton, Trudy Lake, Polly Luce, Virginia McCune, Betty Wright, Edna Locke. *Escorts*: Frank Cullen, Richard Oakley, Robert Gebhardt, Robert Samuels, Kenneth Smith, George Hughes, Daniel Oltash, Willie Scholer.

Act 1, Scene 1: The Three Arts Ball, Sutton Hall, New York City. *Scene 2*: A corridor, Sutton Hall. *Scene 3*: Maison Elise, Fifth Avenue.

Act 2: The Balsams, Viewport, New Hampshire. A week later. *Scene 2*: Lobby of the Hotel. *Scene 3*: Gardens of the Hotel.

ACT 1

Scene 1

"Tell Me More"
  P. Cleveland, A. Gray

Reprise
  P. Cleveland, A. Gray

Scene 3

Opening Ensemble (Shopgirls and Mannequins)
  Shop Girls, Debutantes, Escorts

"Mr. and Mrs. Sipkin"
  L. Holtz, Shop Girls

"When the Debbies Go By"[167]
  (E. Howard,) Debs, Boys

Reprise[168]
  P. Cleveland, A. Gray

"Three Times a Day"
  P. Cleveland, A. Gray

"Why Do I Love You?"
  E. Howard, L. Holtz, Pages, Boys, Girls

Duet ("How Can I Win You Now?")[169]
  E. Haig, A. Tombes

"Kickin' the Clouds Away" (Trio)
  E. Howard, L. Holtz, A. Tombes, Girls

Specialty Dance
  D. Wilson

Specialty Dance
  M. Jane

Finale
  Principals, Ensemble

ACT 2

Scene 1

"Love Is in the Air" (Opening)
  Girls, Boys

Specialty Dance
  M. Jane

"My Fair Lady"
  P. Cleveland, E. Howard, Boys

Specialty Dance
  V. Glenn

Reprise
  P. Cleveland, A. Gray

"In Sardinia"[170]
  L. Holtz, Girls

"Baby!"
  E. Haig, A. Tombes, Girls, Boys

Finaletto
  Principals, Ensemble

Scene 2

"The Poetry of Motion" (Dance)
  W. Covan, L. Ruffin

Scene 3

"Ukulele Lorelei"
  E. Haig, Girls

Specialty
  E. Haig

"Oh, So 'La' Mi"
  L. Holtz

Finale
  Principals, Ensemble

PRINCESS IDA,
or, Castle Adamant

1925.15

A Revival of the Comic Opera in Three Acts[171]. Libretto by William S. Gilbert. A Respectful Operatic per-version of Alfred Lord Tennyson's poem "The Princess—A Medley." Music by Arthur Sullivan. Scenery designed by John Wenger. Orchestra under the direction of Max Hirschfeld. Produced by Lawrence J. Anhalt. Opened 13 April 1925 at the Sam S. Shubert Theatre and closed 16 May 1925 after 40 performances.

CAST (in order of appearance): *Florian*: BERTRAM PEACOCK. *King Hildebrand*: DETMAR POPPEN. *Cyril*: SCOTT WELSH. *Hilarion*, King Hildebrand's Son: SUDWORTH FRASIER. *Sons of King Gama (3)*: *Arac*: Jerome Uhl. *Guron*: Jack Abbott. *Scynthius*: Karl Stall. *King Gama*: ROBINSON NEWBOLD. *Melissa*, Lady Blanche's Daughter: ROSAMONDE WHITESIDE. *Lady Psyche*, Professor of Humanities: VIRGINIA O'BRIEN. *Lady Blanche*, Professor of Abstract Science: BERNICE MERSHON. *Princess Ida*, Gama's Daughter: TESSA KOSTA. *Girl Graduates (3)*: *Sacharissa*: Ann Meyer. *Chloe*: Agusta Spette. *Ada*: Paula Ayers.

Vocal Ensemble: *Sopranos*: Anne Tunney, Anne Austin, Clare Lipton, Bessie Mulligan, Ethel Pastor, Mabel Zoeckler, Sue Lake, Lorraine Brooks, Betty Archer,

---

[167]Dropped late in the run.
[168]Dropped late in the run.

[169]Variously billed only as Duet, then Song and Dance. Replaced late in the run by:
  "Once"
    E. Haig, A. Tombes
    (*Music by* William Daly. *Lyrics by* Ira Gershwin.)
[170]Dropped during the run.
[171]Originally produced in New York 11 February 1884 at the Fifth Avenue Theatre for 48 performances. For Synopsis of Scenes and Musical Numbers, see original 1884 production. Costumes uncredited.

Marian Francis, Olga Bronnoff, Gertrude Toule, Fanille Davies, Maisie Thomas, Estelle Heller, Roberta Curry. *Contraltos*: Virginia Webb, Helen Evens, Gertrude Otto, Ethel Myers, Grace Strasburger, Theola Vincent, Sidonie Sutro, Evelyn Stockton, Alva McGill, Ruth Bieber. *Tenors*: Walter Dahl, Jay Carr, Walter Holmes, Bert Crane, B. Carman, John O'Daro, John Raye, Mortimer Lincoln, Ted Ambrose. *First Bass*: John Mealey, John Wainman, Francis Baldwin, Cliff Dailey. *Second Bass*: Armin Emnes, Carl Savage, Stanley Clark, Milton Karasol, Fred Frances, Sam Goodman, George Averill. *Soldiers, Courtiers, Girl Graduates*.

1925.16

MERCENARY MARY

A Musical Comedy in Two Acts, 3 Scenes. Book by William B. Friedlander and Isabel Leighton. Based on a farce ('What's Your Wife Doing?') by Herbert Hall Winslow and Emil Nyitray. Music and lyrics by William B. Friedlander and Con Conrad. Entire production staged by William B. Friedlander. Dances created by William Seabury. Costumes designed by Hugh Willoughby. Scenes designed by Karl O. Amend. Orchestra (The Ambassadors) conducted by Ira Jacobs. Orchestrations by Louis Katzman. Produced by L. Lawrence Weber. Opened 13 April 1925 at the Longacre Theatre and closed 8 August 1925 after 136 performances.

CAST: *Jerry*: ALLEN KEARNS. *Norah*: NELLIE BREEN. *Edith Somers*: MADELEINE FAIRBANKS. *Patrick O'Brien*: JERE DELANEY. *Lyman Webster*: JOHN BOLES. *Judge Somers*: Frank Kingdon. *June*: MARGARET IRVING. *Mary Skinner*: WINNIE BALDWIN. *Chris Skinner*: LOUIS SIMON. *Grandpa Skinner*: SAM HEARN. *Bellamy Shepard*: G. Davison Clark. *A Dancer*: Monya.

The Guests: Joyce Booth, Shirley Dahl, Sally Doran, Florence Forman, Mary Grace, Madelyn Killeen, Virginia Marchant, Frances Marchant, Elizabeth Mears, Louise Mele, Blanche O'Donahoe, Anita Pam, Dorothy Roy, Cecelia Romeo, Claire Stone, Joan Carter-Waddell.

Act 1, Scene 1: Outside the Gate of the Somers Estate. A summer afternoon. *Scene 2*: Inside the Gate. The same afternoon.

Act 2: Jerry's Apartment. An evening, several days later.

ACT 1
"Over a Garden Wall"
 A. Kearns, M. Fairbanks, Guests
"Just You and I and the Baby"
 J. Delaney, N. Breen
"Charleston Mad"
 M. Fairbanks, Guests
"Honey, I'm in Love (with You)"
 A. Kearns, M. Fairbanks
"They Still Look Good"
 S. Hearn, Guests
"Tomorrow" (Melody suggested by Chopin's Twelfth Nocturne)
 M. Irving, J. Boles
Dance
 N. Breen, J. Delaney
"Come On Along"
 L. Mele, Guests
"Mercenary Mary"
 W. Baldwin, Company
Finale
 Company

ACT 2
Dance
 N. Breen
"Beautiful Baby"
 J. Boles, Guests
"(I Want To Be a) Chaste Woman" (I've Got to be a Chaste Woman)
 W. Baldwin, A. Kearns
Dance[172]
 Monya
"Cherchez la Femme" (Get Your Woman)
 J. Delaney, N. Breen, Guests
"Everything's Going to Be All Right"
 J. Boles, M. Irving
Specialties
 J. Carter-Waddell, C. Romeo, A. Pam, L. Mele, F. Marchant, M. Killeen, F.

---

[172]Dropped during the run.

Forman, S. Dahl, C. Stone, D. Roy, B. O'Donahoe, E. Mears, V. Marchant, M. Grace, S. Doran, J. Booth
Finale
 Company

1925.17

THE GARRICK GAIETIES

A Musical Revue In Two Acts, 22 Scenes[173]. Staged by the Junior Members of the Theatre Guild. (Sketches by Benjamin M. Kaye, Arthur Sullivan, Morrie Ryskind, Louis Sorin, Sam Jaffe, Howard J. Green, Edith Meiser.) Music by Richard Rodgers. Lyrics by Lorenz Hart. Directed by Philip Loeb. Dances and musical numbers staged by Herbert Fields. Settings and costumes by Carolyn Hancock. Orchestra under the direction of Richard Rodgers. Choruses arranged by Eleanor Shaler. Produced by the Theatre Guild. Opened 17 May-5 June 1925 at the Garrick Theatre for a series of 7 special performances; opened an extended commercial run 8 June 1925 at the Garrick Theatre and closed 28 November 1925 after 211 performances.

CAST: Sterling Holloway, Romney Brent, Rosa Rolanda, June Cochrane, Philip Loeb, Edith Meiser, Starr Jones, Peggy Conway, Felix Jacoves, Dorothea Chard, James Norris, Mary Marsh, Willard Tobias, Louis Richardson, House Jamieson, Frances Hyde, Edward Hogan, Betty Starbuck, Paul Jones, Elizabeth [Libby] Holman, Sanford Meisner, Sally Bates, Alvah Bessie, John McGovern, Stanley Lindahl, Barbara Wilson, Hildegarde Halliday, Jack Quigley, Eleanor Shaler, Carolyn Hancock, Harold W. Conklin, Rose Rolanda, Henry Geiger, Lee Strasberg.

ACT 1[174]
Scene 1
 "Soliciting Subscriptions"
 S. Holloway, J. Norris, R. Brent, J. Cochrane
 In which we let you into one of the business secrets of an art theater.

---

[173]The first in a series of three musical revues produced by the Theatre Guild.
[174]Added for commercial run in June were:
 "(Romantic You and) Sentimental Me" (Act 1, Scene 3)
 J. Cochrane, J. Norris, E. Meiser, S. Holloway
 "And Thereby Hangs a Tail" (Act 2, Scene 1, dropped in August)
 (*Sketch by* Morrie Ryskind and Philip Loeb. *Music by* Richard Rodgers. *Lyrics by* Lorenz Hart.)
 Scene: An African Courthouse.
 Judge: L. Strasberg. *District Attorney*: E. Norris. *Defendant*: S. Holloway.
 Special Counsel (William Jennings Bryan): P. Loeb.
 "On With the Dance" (Act 2)
 J. Cochrane, Chorus
 Specialty Dance
 E. Shaler
Added during the run:
 Javanese Dance (Act 1)
 Stella Block
Added in October were:
 Subway Manners
 (*by* Benjamin M. Kaye) (Act 1)
 The Agent: H. Jamieson. *The Lady*: P. Conway. *First Passenger*: T. Brewster Board. *Second Passenger*: William Johnstone. *Other Passengers*: L. Strasberg, E. Hogan, A. Bessie, S. Mesiner, H. Halliday, J. Quigley, R. Brent, Patricia Barclay, E. Shaler. *Bootblack*: W. Tobias. *Announcer*: H. Geiger.
 One of the Finest
 (*by* Newman Levy) (Act 1)
 Chief of Police: P. Loeb. *A Lady*: E. Meiser. *Traffic Officer*: E. Hogan. *Sergeant*: R. Brent. *Four Policemen*: J. Norris, W. Johnstone, L. Strasberg, H. W. Conklin. *Civilians*: A. Bessie, T. B. Board, H. Geiger, J. Quigley, S. Meisner, W. Tobias. *Taxicabs*: P. Barclay, Gladys Laird, F. Hyde, Sylvia Shear, E. Shaler, Marjorie Warden.
 The Green Derby
 (A Travesty in 2 Scenes *by* Benjamin M. Kaye) (Act 1)
 Scene 1: Sutton Marle. *Scene 2*: A Hotel in Deauville.
 Iris March: E. Meiser. *Gerald March*: R. Brent. *Napier Harpenden*: S. Holloway. *Sir Maurice Harpenden*: E. Hogan. *Hilary*: H. Jamieson. *Boy Fenwick*: J. Norris. *Venice*: B. Starbuck. *Hotel Proprietor*: L. Strasberg. *Maid*: H. Halliday. *An Author*: P. Loeb. *A Producer*: W. Johnstone.
 Finale ("It's Quite Enough to Make Me Weep") (Act 2)
 Scene: Midnight at 10 Adelphi Terrace, N. W.
 George Bernard Shaw: P. Loeb. *Bluntchill*: J. Norris. *Raina*: E. Meiser. *St. Joan*: B. Starbuck. *Dick Dudgeon*: R. Brent. *Caesar*: S. Holloway. *Cleopatra*: J. Cochrane.

"Gilding the Guild"
B. Starbuck, Chorus
In which we introduce you to Betty Starbuck and the Guild Gaieties Chorus (the girls are all college and have undergone a course in the higher mathematics, which accounts for their keeping time so well).

Scene 2
The Guardsman[175]
(*Burlesque by* Benjamin M. Kaye)
With apologies to Franz Molnar, Alfred Lunt, Lynn Fontanne and Dudley Digges.
Alfred Lunt, the actor: R. Brent. *Lynn Fontanne*, the actress: E. Meiser. *Dudley Digges*, the critic: P. Loeb.

Scene 3
"Butcher, Baker, Candle-Stick Maker"
H. W. Conklin
Scientific exposition of a remarkable case of pre-natal influence.
(*Music by* Mana-Zucca. *Lyrics by* Benjamin M. Kaye. *Staged by* Edith Meiser.)
Marie: C. Hancock. *The Butcher*: S. Lindahl. *The Baker*: F. Jacoves. *The Candle-Maker*: J. Norris. *The Little Man*: W. Tobias.

Scene 4
The Theatre Guild Enters Heaven[176]
(*Written and Staged by* Edith Meiser.)
A highly improbable episode, written and staged by Edith Meiser in odd moments between listening through the key-hole of 'The Guardsman.'
St. Peter: R. Brent. *Jurors*: S. Mesiner, H. Geiger, A. Bessie, J. Quigley. *The Guardsman's Wife*: E. Meiser. *Amy*: P. Conway. *St. Joan*: M. Marsh. *Sadie Cohen*: H. Halliday. *Two Cherubs*: W. Tobias, L. Strasberg.

Scene 5
Comic Scarf Dance (Working with a Scarf)
E. Shaler

Scene 6
Sh! Shh!
(*by* Louis Sorin and Sam Jaffe)
Mabel: B. Wilson. *Her Husband*: H. Jamieson. *Jack*: E. Hogan. *Maid*: P. Conway.

Scene 7
"An Old-Fashioned Girl"
E. Meiser
(*Lyrics by* Edith Meiser.)
A song dealing with an extinct species, written by the Guild's antiquarian in feminalia.

Scene 8
"April Fool"
B. Starbuck, R. Brent, Chorus
One of those little things about spring which the children can't resist.

Scene 9
They Didn't Know What They Were Getting
(*by* Benjamin M. Kaye)
Awarded the Pulitzer Prize for debasing the morals of the community, with apologies to "They Knew What They Wanted," Sidney Howard, Mr. Richard Bennett, Miss Pauline Lord, Mr. Glenn Anders, Mr. Tazewell.
Tony: J. McGovern. *Amy*: P. Conway. *Joe*: E. Hogan. *The Doctor*: A. Bessie.

Scene 10
"Stage Managers' Chorus"[177]
W. Tobias, S. Holloway, R. Brent, E. Hogan, L. Strasberg, S. Lindahl, F. Hyde, S. Jones
(*Music by* Richard Rodgers. *Lyrics by* Dudley Digges and Lorenz Hart.)

Scene 11
Ruth Draper (maybe) (Impersonation)
H. Halliday

Scene 12
"The Joy Spreader"[178]
(An American Jazz Opera with Music by Richard Rodgers, Libretto by Lorenz Hart, Inspiration by Gilbert Seldes, who is primarily responsible for this outrage.)
Setting: The Main Floor of Price's Big Store. *Scene 1*: Closing Time. *Scene 2*: Opening Time.
Jeremiah Price, owner of Price's Big Store: E. Hogan. *Mary Brown*: B. Starbuck.

Tom Jones: R. Brent. *Stella Malloy*: J. Cochrane. *Doormen*: W. Tobias, L., Strasberg. *Floorwalkers*: S. Jones, F. Jacoves. *Mrs. Katz*, a customer: F. Hyde. *Employees, Shoppers.*

ACT 2
Scene 1
"Rancho Mexicano"
(*Music by* Tatanacho. *Settings and Costumes by* Miguel Covarrubias.)
Mexico is famous for its hot tamales, oil wells, revolutions, bandits and Covarrubias, who is now in New York engaged in putting Mexico on the map of Manhattan. In this sketch are two drunkards, indicating that the scene is not laid in the United States.
Two Drunkards: L. Strasberg, H. Jamieson. *Two Women Singing*: L. Richardson, F. Hyde. *Three Men Singing*: L. Strasberg, H. W. Conklin, E. Hogan. *A Policeman*: P. Jones. *Two Dancers*: R. Rolanda, S. Jones.

Scene 2
"Ladies of the Box Office"
B. Starbuck, E. Holman, J. Cochrane
In which we let you into more secrets of the American theater.

Scene 3
"Mr. and Mrs."
(*by* Arthur Sullivan and Morrie Ryskind)
With apologies to Briggs and other American institutions.
Mrs. Coolidge: E. Meiser. *President Coolidge*: J. McGovern.

Scene 4
"Manhattan"
J. Cochrane, S. Holloway
With acknowledgement to Major Hylan for the use of New York and to "The Subway Sun."

Scene 5
Where Credit Is Due
(*by* Howard J. Green [and Milton Hocky])
Julia: P. Conway. *Jim*: L. Strasberg. *Fred*: S. Jones. *Marie*, a Maid: S. Bates.

Scene 6
"The Three Musketeers"
R. Brent, S. Holloway, P. Loeb

Scene 7
"Do You Love Me (I Wonder)?"
L. Richardson
We have consulted all the classical authorities on the subject, and find that no revue is complete without some reference to the rapidly disappearing emotion known as love. We bow to the tradition.
Danced by R. Rolanda, Girl Chorus.

Scene 8
"Black and White"[179]
E. Holman, Chorus
This song is not intended to advertise a well-known commodity, now sold as pre-war quality at pre-posterous prices.
Danced by E. Shaler, W. Tobias.

Scene 9
Fate in the Morning
An example of the Buda-Pestiferous drama, inspired by 'Fata Morgana,' Miss Emily Stevens, Mr. Morgan Farley, and "The Dogs! The Dogs!"
Miss Emily Stevens (Mathilde): S. Holloway. *Mr Morgan Farley* (George): J. Norris. *The Dogs! The Dogs!*: R. Brent.

Scene 10
The Guild Gilded[180]
Six Directors, Company
Six Directors: P. Conway, E. Hogan, E. Meiser, J. Quigley, A. Bessie, L. Strasberg.

---

[175] Dropped in October.
[176] Dropped for commercial run in June.
[177] Dropped for commercial run in June.
[178] Dropped for commercial run in June.

[179] Dropped for commercial run in June.
[180] Dropped in October.

Queenie Smith in TIP-TOES (Photo: Debarron)
Billy Rose Theatre Collection, New York Public Library for the Performing Arts

1925–1926 SEASON

1925.18   LUCKY SAMBO

A Musical Mirthquake (Comedy) of Laughter in Two Shocks (Acts), 13 Shivers (Scenes)[1]. Book, music and lyrics by Porter Grainger and Freddie Johnson. Staged by Leigh Whipper and Freddie Johnson. Dances arranged by Freddie Johnson. Costumes by Mrs. A. E. Mathison. Scenery painted by Cirker and Robbins. Orchestra under the direction of Fred Tunstall. Produced by Harlem Productions, Inc. Opened 6 June 1925 at the Colonial Theatre and closed 13 June (matinee) 1925 after 7 performances.

CAST: *John Whitby*, owner of Whitby Hotel: Westley Hill. *Mrs. Whitby*, his wife: Gertie Moore. *June*, his daughter: MONETTE MOORE. *"Doc" August*, the town herb doctor: ARTHUR PORTER. *Rufus Johnson*, Whitby's yard man: JOE BYRD. *Sambo Jenkins*, his assistant: TIM MOORE. *Jack Stafford*, an oil promoter: Freddie Johnson. *Lena March*, the town vamp: LENA WILSON. *Edith Simpson*, the town gossip: "Happy" Williams. *John Law*, the police force: Billy Ewing. *Jim Nightengale*, owner of Nightengale Cabaret: CLARENCE ROBINSON. *Hitt Keys*, a song writer: PORTER GRAINGER. *Vera Blues*, a cabaret entertainer: JEAN STARR. *Nimble Foote*, the town dancer: AMELIA LOOMIS. *Minnie Tree*, the town vocalist: Mildred Brown. *Twilight Gadson*, Whitby's maid: Anna White. *Shoo Nuff*, a porter: JOHNNY HUDGINS. (*Dancers*: Louis Keene, Mae Barnes. *Singer*: Julia Mitchell.)

Ensemble: *Ladies*: Julie Sanchez, Roberta Lowery, Edith Oliver, Dorothy Wilson, Edna Young, Grace Michael, Anna Moore, Alice Samons, Creola Mays, Lottie Ames, Evelyn Keyes, Margaret Fiall, Elizabeth Still, Florence Laster, Jerry Wiley, Adelaide Jones. *Gentlemen*: James Gaines, James Harrison, Edward Shinault, Abdeen M. Ali, Charley Saltus, Herbert Walker, David Robinson, Brownie Campbell.

The action takes place in Boley, Oklahoma at the present time.

Act 1, Scene 1: Front of Whitby's Hotel. *Scene 2*: Strivers' Row. *Scene 3*: Aunt Jemima's Cabin on Magnolia Plantation. *Scene 4*: Front of Whitby's Hotel. *Scene 5*: Hokum Oil Wells. *Scene 6*: Oil Boulevard. *Scene 7*: Lawn of the Whitby Hotel.

Act 2, Scene 1: Lobby of Whitby Hotel. *Scene 2*: Oil Boulevard. *Scene 3*: The Jail at Boley. *Scene 4*: Running through Oklahoma. *Scene 5*: Lobby of Whitby Hotel. *Scene 6*: Nightengale Cabaret.

ACT 1

  "Happy" (Opening Ensemble)
    Town Folk
  "Stop"
    A. Loomis, Town Folk
  "June"
    M. Moore, F. Johnson
  "Don't Forget Bandana Days"
    A. Porter, Bandana Girls
  "Anybody's Man Will Be My Man"
    L. Wilson
  "Aunt Jemima (I'm Comin' Home)"
    M. Moore, Plantation Folk
  "Coal Oil"
    F. Johnson, Oil Prospectors
  "Charley from That Charleston Dancing School"
    M. Barnes, Stockholders
  "If You Can't Bring It You've Got to Send It"
    L. Wilson, J. Byrd
  "Strolling"
    A. Loomis, C. Robinson
  "Dreary, Dreary, Rainy Days"
    J. Mitchell, Town Folk
  "Take Him to Jail"
    Stockholders
  "Legomania"
    L. Keene

ACT 2

  "Always on the Job"
    Maids, Bellboys

  "Singing Nurses"
    Runnin' Wild Four
  "Dandy Dan"
    C. Robinson, Dandies
  "Porterology"
    J. Hudgins
  "Love Me While You're Gone"
    J. Starr, C. Robinson
  "Keep A-Diggin'"
    A. Porter
  "Runnin'"
    T. Moore, J. Byrd
  "Midnight Cabaret"
    Dancing Waiters
  "Havin' a Wonderful Time"
    J. Starr
  Selections by Two Composers
    P. Grainger, F. Johnson
  "Not So Long Ago"
    J. Starr
  "Alexander's Ragtime Wedding Day"
    A. Porter, Bridal Party
  "Keep A-Diggin'"
    Entire Company

1925.19   KOSHER KITTY KELLY

A Unique Comedy with Several Singable Songs in Three Acts, 5 Scenes. Book, music and lyrics by Leon DeCosta. Staged by A. H. Van Buren. Musical numbers staged by Ralph Riggs. Art director, Walter Harvey. Settings designed by H. Robert Law. Orchestra under the direction of George Hirst. Orchestrations by Hilding Anderson. Produced by Arch Productions, Inc.[2] Opened 15 June 1925 at the Times Square Theatre and closed 12 September 1925 after 105 performances; reopened 21 October 1925 at Daly's 63rd St and closed 12 December 1925 after 61 additional performances. Total: 166 performances.

CAST[3] (in order of appearance): *Kitty Kelly*: HELEN SHIPMAN, KATHLEEN MULQUEEN. *Morris Rosen*: BASIL LOUGHRANE. *Mrs. Mary Kelly*: DOROTHY WALTERS. *Wang Lee*: Paul Porter. *Mrs. Sarah Feinbaum*: Jennie Moscowitz. *Patrick O'Reilly*: FRED SANTLEY. *Rosie Feinbaum*: BEATRICE ALLEN. *Moses Ginsburg*: Robert Leonard. *Joe Barns*: Charles F. O'Connor. *Zella Barnes*: Dorothy Gay, Marjorie Rooney. *A Stranger*: William Brainard.

The action takes place on Hexter Street, New York City at the present time in summer.

Act 1, Scene 1: In front of Kitty Kelly's Home at 4 A.M. *Scene 2*: Kitty's Bedroom. Fifteen minutes later.

Act 2: Ginsburg's Kosher Delicatessen Store. Three months later, 10:15 P.M.

Act 3, Scene 1: Mrs. Kelly's Parlor. A few weeks later. *Scene 2*: In front of Kitty Kelly's home. Eight weeks later.

ACT 1

  "Dancing Time"
    H. Shipman, B. Loughrane
  "Kosher Kitty Kelly"
    F. Santley, H. Shipman

ACT 2

  Specialty[4]
    C. F. O'Connor, D. Gay
  "What's in Store For You"
    B. Allen, R. Leonard, B. Loughrane
  "I'll Cuddle Up to You"
    H. Shipman, F. Santley, B. Loughrane

---

[1]A revised version of this show played the Columbia Burlesque Theatre on Broadway in May of 1926.

[2]Costume design uncredited. Subsequent tour presented under the auspices of George M. Gatts.
[3]Cast replacements for return engagement follow the original artist; the role of the Stranger was dropped.
[4]Later in the run billed as "Why Should a Little Girl Be Lonely?"

ACT 3

Scene 1

"I Want to Dance with You"
   Company

Scene 2

"Where We Can Be in Love"
   H. Shipman, F. Santley

"Kosher Kitty Kelly" (reprise)
   Omnes (Entire Company)

THE GRAND STREET FOLLIES (1925)

1925.20

A Musical Revue in Three Acts, 10 Scenes[5]. Book (sketches) and lyrics by Agnes Morgan. Music by Lily Hyland. Settings by Russel Wright. Costumes by Russel Wright and Aline Bernstein. Dances staged by Albert Carroll. Produced by the Neighborhood Playhouse. Opened 18 June 1925 at the Neighborhood Playhouse and closed 29 November 1925 after 148 performances.

CAST: Helen Arthur, Albert Carroll, Irene Lewisohn, Ian Maclaren, Esther Mitchell, Edgar Kent, Lois Shore, Whitford Kane, Vera Allen, Otto Hulicius, Lily Lubell, Marc Loebell, Paula Trueman, Junius Matthews, Ann Schmidt, J. Blake Scott, Dorothy Sands, George Bratt, Sadie Sussman, George Hoag, Blanche Talmud, William Beyer, Michel Barroy, Allen Vincent, Philip Mann, Thomas Tilton, George Heller, Dan Walker, Polaire Weissman, Madeline Ross, Helen Mack, Mae Noble, George Bratt, Zita Johann, Harold Minjer, Edla Frankau, Lewis McMichael, George Hoag.

ACT 1[6]

Scene 1

A Committee Meeting
   A. Summer Winters: E. Kent. *Mrs. Longfellow Lowell*: I. Lewisohn. *Patrick McCall*: W. Kane. *Maisie Mahoney*: H. Arthur. *Mrs. Higgins*: E. Mitchell. *The Mothers of Ward 13, Borough of Manhattan*: P. Weissman, B. Talmud, M. Ross, H. Mack, M. Noble.

Scene 2

They Knew What They Wanted Under the Elms
   Walter Huston as Ephraim Cabot: O. Hulicius. *Mary Morris as Abbie*: V. Allen. *Ray Dooley as The Baby*: L. Shore. *The Gorilla (in person)*: G. Bratt. *Louis John Bartels as The Show-Off*: J. Matthews. *Vivienne Osborne as Aloma*: L. Lubell. *Helen Hayes as Cleopatra*: P. Trueman. *George Arliss as Old English*: J. B. Scott. *Lenore Ulric as Carla*: A. Schmidt. *Robert Armstrong as The Pugilist*: G. Hoag. *Pauline Lord as Amy*: D. Sands. *Holbrook Blinn as Don José*: M. Loebell. *Joseph Schildkraut as Benvenuto Cellini*: A. Carroll.

Scene 3

At Ciro's
   Clifton Webb: W. Beyer. *Mary Hay*: S. Sussman. *A Roshanara Indian*: B. Talmud. *Spanish Dancers*: A. Schmidt, B. Talmud.

Scene 4

Americana
   Gloria Swanson: L. Lubell. *The Marquis*: A. Vincent. *Lillian Gish*: P. Trueman. *George Jean*: P. Mann.

Scene 5

The Duncan Sisters: ("Broadway Mammy Blues")
   Topsy: L. Shore. *Eva*: D. Sands.

Scene 6

What Price Morning-Glories?
   The Captain: M. Loebell. *The Sergeant*: A. Carroll. *The Girl*: E. Mitchell.

ACT 2

Scene 1

Mr. and Mrs. Guardsman (illustrating the difficulties of keeping in the character when one is playing en famille)
   (*by* Albert Carroll)
   Lynn Fontanne as the Actress: A. Carroll. *Alfred Lunt as the Prince*: O. Hulicius. *Helen Westley as Mama*: I. Lewisohn.

Scene 2

Gala Performance of the Opera "L'Irlandesa Rosa Dell'Abie" (with an all-star cast in honor of the consolidation of The Irish Free State and Palestine)
   (*Words by* Marc Loebell.)
   Gigli as Abie: T. Tilton. *Jeritza as Rose*: M. Barroy. *Chaliapan as the Jewish Father*: J. Matthews. *Scotti as the Irish Father*: G. Bratt. *Galli-Curci as Mrs. Cohen*: L. Lubell. *Pavlova*: A. Carroll. *Mordkin*: J. B. Scott. *The Twins*: P. Trueman, G. Heller. *Corps de Ballet*: S. Sussman, P. Trueman, A. Schmidt, E. Frankau, B. Talmud, E. Mitchell. *Village Maidens*: P. Weissman, M. Ross, H. Mack, M. Noble, V. Allen, L. Shore, D. Sands. *Village Men*: H. Minjer, D. Walker, M. Loebell, G. Heller, W. Beyer, L. McMichael, G. Hoag.

ACT 3

The Midnight Show
   (*Words, Music and Dance Arrangement of* "Glory! Glory! Glory!" [I Want to be Glorified] *by* Dan Walker.)
   Scene: A Harlem cabaret.
   Othello: I. Maclaren. *Emperor Jones*: O. Hulicius. *A Charleston Stepper*: S. Sussman. *A Cabaret Clogger*: L. Lubell. *Al Jolson*: D. Walker. *Florence Mills*: A. Carroll. *Jazz Girls, Waiters, Guests*: (Company.)

ENGAGED

1925.21

A Burlesque in Three Acts. Play by W. S. Gilbert. Music and lyrics found by Brian Hooker[7]. Staged by Edward T. Goodman. Dances arranged by Caroll Weller. Settings by Robert E. Locher and Cleon Throckmorton. Costumes designed by Robert E. Locher. Produced by The Stagers[8]. Opened 18 June 1925 at the 52nd Street Theatre, moved 6 July 1925 to the 48th Street Theatre and closed 1 August 1925 after 44 performances.

CAST (in order of appearance): *Maggie Macfarlane*, a lowland lassie: MARJORIE VONNEGUT. *Angus Macfarlane*, a lowland peasant lad: ALBERT HECHT. *Mrs. Macfarlane*, a lowland widow: MARGARET LOVE. *Belvawney*, a gentleman from London: JAY FASSETT. *Belinda Treherne*, a lady in distress: ANTOINETTE PERRY. *Mr. Symperson*, a father: GEORGE RIDDELL. *Cheviot Hill*, a young man of property: J. M. KERRIGAN. *Major McGillicuddy*, an officer and a gentleman: PEAVEY WELLS. *Parker*, Minnie Symperson's maid: DOLLÉ GRAY. *Minnie*, Symperson's daughter: ROSAMOND WHITESIDE.

Time: 1877.

Act 1: Garden of a cottage near Gretna, on the border between England and Scotland.

Act 2: Drawing-room in Symperson's House in London. Three months later.

Act 3: The same. Three days later.

ACT 1

"Braes o' Ballachloe"
   M. Vonnegut, A. Hecht

"Love Is Enough" (Ballad)
   A. Perry, J. Fassett

"Love, I Will Love You Ever"
   J. M. Kerrigan

"All for Love" (Trio)
   M. Vonnegut, A. Hecht, J. M. Kerrigan

"What is This I See?" (Finale)
   A. Perry, M. Vonnegut, M. Love, J. M. Kerrigan, J. Fassett, A. Hecht, P. Wells

ACT 2

"I'm Going to Be Married Today"
   R. Whiteside, D. Gray, G. Riddell

"Unrequited"[9]
   A. Perry

"A Little Kiss" (Duet)
   D. Gray, J. M. Kerrigan

"Prince Charming"
   R. Whiteside, J. M. Kerrigan

---

[5]The third in the annual series of Off-Broadway revues originating with the Neighborhood Playhouse beginning in 1922, many of which transferred to or later originated on Broadway.

[6]Added during the run to Act 1:
   The Wild Duck of the 18th Century (as Ibsen would have treated the theme had he really been born before his time)
      Mr. Ekdal Scandal: H. Minjer. *Mrs. Gina Scandal*: A. Morgan. *Mr. Gregers Tattle*: I. Maclaren. *Ducky*: E. Mitchell.

---

[7]The music is taken from songs by (Arthur) Sullivan, James Lyman Molloy, Joseph Leopold Roeckel, Ciro Pinsuti and others of the period. A few numbers were composed for this production in the Victorian manner by Porter Steele. In some cases the original lyrics are used; other were written by Brian Hooker.

[8]The fourth production of their subscription season.

[9]Dropped during the run.

"The Story of a Sheep"
    J. Fassett, J. M. Kerrigan
"A Joyful Wedding Day" (Finale)
    R. Whiteside, A. Perry,
    M. Vonnegut, M. Love, D. Gray, J. M. Kerrigan, G. Riddell, A. Hecht
ACT 3
    "Sometimes" (Trio)
        R. Whiteside, A. Perry, J. Fassett
    "Dear, Dear Sisters" (Duet)
        A. Perry, R. Whiteside
    "A Jury of His Peers" (Quartet)
        R. Whiteside, A. Perry, J. M. Kerrigan, G. Riddell
    "Liberty"
        J. Fassett, J. M. Kerrigan
    Finale
        A. Perry, R. Whiteside, M. Vonnegut, M. Love, D. Gray, J. M. Kerrigan, J. Fassett, G. Riddell, A. Hecht

GEORGE WHITE'S SCANDALS (1925)

1925.22

A Musical Revue in Two Acts, 27 Scenes[10]. Book (sketches) by William K. Wells and George White. Music by Ray Henderson. Lyrics by Buddy G. DeSylva and Lew Brown. Entire production staged by George White. Albertina Rasch Girls' dances staged by Albertina Rasch. Costumes and curtains designed by Erté; additional costume sketches by Hugh Willoughby Art director, Gustave Weidhaus. Orchestrations by Maurice dePackh. Orchestra under the direction of William Daly. Produced by George White. Opened 22 June 1925 at the Apollo Theatre and closed 14 November 1925 after 169 performances.

CAST: HARRY FOX, HELEN MORGAN, TOM PATRICOLA, ALICE WEAVER, GORDON DOOLEY, HELEN HUDSON, NORMAN PHILLIPS, NORMAN PHILLIPS, JR., MRS. NORMAN PHILLIPS, MARTHA MORTON, ARTHUR BALL, HELEN WEHRLE, THE McCARTHY SISTERS (Dorothy, Margaret), VADA ALEXANDER, ELM CITY FOUR (Jim Carty, Fred Lyon, Harry Morrissey, Joe Sullivan).
    Chorus: Marjorie Shaw, Marion Courtney, Georgia Lerch, Dolly Donnelly, Kathryn Chapman, Helen Titus, Mildred Klaw, Alice Wilkie, Cris Crane, Myrtle Hammerstead, Muriel LeCount, Marjorie Murray, Mary Murray, Roberta Haynes, Clare Scott, Jean Scott, Adele Smith,
    ALBERTINA RASCH GIRLS: Solo Dancers: Jane Sels, Edna Bowman, Peggy Gallimore, Janet Flynn. *Dancers:* Mary Parsons, Mildred Turner, Marion Dickson, Kathleen Lambly, Viola Hage, Ethel Sager, Anita Gordon, Betty Dillon, Harriet Dillon, Mary Norris, Dorris Bryant, Alice Thalman, Laura Phillips, Emily Johns, Dorothy Ellfelt, Ruth Gordon.

ACT 1[11]
Scene 1
    Prologue
        N. Phillips, Jr.
Scene 2
    "Read What the Papers Say"
        The Boy: D. McCarthy. *The Girl:* N. Phillips.
Scene 3
    Drama Mixed with Revue
        Maxwell Zunzer: H. Fox. *Kathryn, his wife:* H. Morgan. *Irving Yates,* alias Borden: H. Morrissey. *Mrs. Brown:* Mrs. N. Phillips. *Dr. Brown:* T. Patricola. *Temptation:* C. Crane. *Gold:* M. Shaw. *Flaming Passion:* M. Murray. *Fruit:* A. Winston. *Cupid:* J. Miller.
Scene 4
    "The Whosis Whatsis"
        McCarthy Sisters, Scandal Beauties
    Dance
        H. Wehrle
Scene 5
    Home Coming (in Three Episodes)
        Announced by: A. Weaver.

First Episode
    The Boss: J. Carty. *First Workman:* G. Dooley. *Second Workman:* F. Lyon. *Workman's Wife:* Mrs. N. Phillips.
Second Episode
    Husband: H. Fox. *His Friend:* H. Morrissey.
Third Episode
    Mother: Mrs. N. Phillips. *Father:* N. Phillips. *Daughter:* M. Morton. *Money Lender:* J. Carty.
Scene 6
    "Rosetime"
        A. Ball
        The Girl Overhead: A. Weaver. *Sixty Rosebuds:* The Girls.
    Dance
        H. Wehrle
Scene 7
    "All Alone"
        (*Music and Lyrics by* Irving Berlin.)
        Announced by A. Weaver. *Irving Berlin:* G. Dooley.
Scene 8
    "I Want a Loveable Baby"
        H. Morgan
        Heavy Spending Baby: F. Lyon. *Fickle Fickle Baby:* J. Sullivan. *Prehistoric Baby:* J. Carty. *Old-Fashioned Baby:* H. Morrissey. *Lovable Baby:* T. Patricola.
Scene 9
    "Fly Butterfly"
        H. Hudson, Elm City Four
        (*Lyrics by* Buddy G. DeSylva.)
        Butterfly: A. Weaver.
    Dance
        Albertina Rasch Ballet
Scene 10
    "Even as You and I"
        H. Fox
        Astor: J. Miller. *Drake:* F. Lyon. *Statler:* J. Sullivan. *Ritz:* J. Carty. *Biltmore:* N. Phillips. *Mills:* G. Dooley.
Scene 11
    "Room Enough for Me"
        A. Ball
        A Girl: G. Lerch. *Clasp on Old-Fashioned Bag:* L. Williams. *Looking Glass:* M. Murray. *Clasp on New Bag:* C. Scott, J. Scott. And the Albertina Rasch Ballet
Scene 12
    The Last Shot
        Colonel Lord Baconfat: G. Dooley. *Mazda, his Wife:* M. Morton. *Captain Twinklepink:* F. Lyon. *Private:* N. Phillips. *Messenger:* J. Miller. *Sheik Ali Yup:* H. Morrissey.
Scene 13
    "Say It with a Sable"
        H. Hudson
        Salesman: F. Lyon. *Rabbit:* D. Donnelly. *Fox:* K. Chapman. *Panther:* M. Chandler. *Monkey:* H. Titus. *Sable:* M. Murray. *Seal:* M. Klaw. *Ermine:* M. Courtney. *Chinchilla:* Marjorie Murray, A. Wilkie, C. Crane, M. Hammersted, M. LeCount, Mary Murray, R. Haynes.
Scene 14
    A Sensible Conversation
        F. Miller, A. Lyles
Scene 15
    Dancing Teachers' Convention[12]
        Chairman: N. Phillips. *Delegate from Hoboken:* H. Wehrle. *Delegates from Paris:* Mlle. Mayonnaise: M. Morton. *Monsieur De Brie:* G. Dooley. *Delegates from the South:* T. Patricola.

---

[12]Added during the run to the Dancing Teachers' Convention scene:
    "We Want the Charleston" (Give Us the Charleston)
        McCarthy Sisters
        (*Lyrics by* Buddy G. DeSylva.)
    Dance
        T. Patricola
    Charleston Dance
        60 George White Girls

---

[10]The seventh in the annual series of revues presented by George White beginning in 1919.
[11]The running order was revised immediately after the opening.

ACT 2[13]

Scene 1

"The Girl of Tomorrow"

A. Ball, Albertina Rasch Girls

Scene 2

The Joneses

Mrs. Jones: H. Hudson. *Mr. Jones*: H. Fox.

Scene 3

"Lovely Lady"[14]

G. Dooley

Chorus Boys: H. Fox, N. Phillips, A. Ball, F. Lyon, J. Carty, J. Sullivan, H. Morrissey, T. Patricola, J. Miller.

Scene 4

Stock Company from Charleston, South Carolina

Announced by A. Weaver. *The Lover*: J. Carty. *The Daughter*: S. Starr. *The Father*: T. Patricola. *The Mother*: D. McCarthy.

Scene 5

"New Rhythm Ballet"

Albertina Rasch Ballet

Scene 6

"What a World This Would Be"

H. Fox, H. Morgan

First Episode: The New Cook

Cook: V. Alexander. *Madame*: Mrs. N. Phillips.

Second Episode: Magic Hair Restorer

Barber: T. Patricola. *Customer*: J. Miller.

Third Episode: The Pill of Youth

The Doctor: J. Carty. *The Patient*: N. Phillips, N. Phillips, Jr.

Fourth Episode: Too Good to be True

The Husband: G. Dooley. *The Wife*: M. Morton.

Scene 7

"Beware of the Girl with a Fan"

H. Hudson, Elm City Four

Scene 8

Chief of Police and His Honor, the Mayor

F. Miller, A. Lyles

Scene 9

Cheap Guy

T. Patricola, H. Fox, M. Morton, G. Dooley, H. Hudson, H. Morgan, McCarthy Sisters

Dance

T. Patricola

Scene 10

The Actors' Prayer

The Principals

Scene 11

The Girls' Prayer

60 George White Girls

Scene 12

Finale

Entire Company

ARTISTS AND MODELS

1925.23   (Paris Edition, 1925)

A Musical Revue in Two Acts, a Prologue and 33 Scenes[15]. Book (sketches) by Harold Atteridge, Harry Wagstaff Gribble. Music by Alfred Goodman, J.

---

[13]Added during the run to Act 2:

The New Director (later dropped)

The Director: N. Phillips, Jr. *The Wife*: Mrs. N. Phillips. *The Husband*: N. Phillips.

A Good Girl

Announced by A. Weaver.

Mother: Mrs. N. Phillips. *Father*: Mrs. N. Phillips. *Daughter*: M. Morton.

Money Lender: J. Carty.

[14]Dropped during the run.

[15]The third in the annual series of musical revues produced by the Messrs. Shubert beginning in 1923.

Fred Coots, Sigmund Romberg, Maurice Rubens. Lyrics by Clifford Grey. Dialogue arranged by Alexander Leftwich. Dances staged by Jack Haskell. All dances for the Gertrude Hoffmann Girls staged by Gertrude Hoffmann. Art direction (scenic design) by Watson Barratt. Costumes designed by Erté and Barbier of Paris. Orchestrations by Emil Gerstenberger. Orchestra under the direction of Oscar Bradley. Entire production staged and produced by J. J. Shubert. Presented by the Messrs. Shubert. Opened 24 June 1925 at the Winter Garden and closed 7 May 1926 after 416 performances.

CAST: PHIL BAKER, BILLY B. VAN, HERBERT CORTHELL, ALINE MacMAHON, WALTER WOOLF, LULU McCONNELL, FRANCES WILLEMS [Williams], SID SILVERS, LLORA HOFFMAN, LEON BARTÉ, JAY BRENNAN, JANE CARROLL, STANLEY ROGERS, BEATRICE SWANSON, ELEANOR WILLEMS, GEORGE ROSENOR, HERBERT ASHTON, SUNSHINE JARRMAN, THE CAITS BROTHERS (Joseph, Harry), MARGARET MERLE, TEDDY CLAIRE, ANDREW JOACHIM, THELMA CARLTON, ERIC TITUS, Gene Wallin, Carol Maybury, Miriam Fine, Shari Hockman, Betty Lawrence.

GERTRUDE HOFFMANN GIRLS: Louise Blackburne, Eileen Culshaw, Alberta Faust, Toots Gregory, Claire de Figaniere, Gladys Granzow, Ruth Zackey, Emma Kleigge, Harriet Fowler, Florence Kolinsky, Charlotte Suddaith, Dottie Ellis, Ferral Dewees, Dorothy Van Heft, Catherine Gallimore, Margaret Sloan, Sara Granzow, Thelma Kay. *Dancing Girls*: Florence Quinn, Peggy Timmons, June Wall, Marian Case, Minerva Wilson, May Alexander, Margaret McKay, Mildred Espy, Dorothy Weber, Helen Murray, Grace Cantrell, Mildred Douglas, Janice Glenn, Dorothea Hordern, Dorothy Burnell, Margie Hoffman, Marian Ross, May Judels, Pudgie Duker, Alice MacDonald, Florence Gunther. *Models*: Ada Landis, Patricia De Long, Margie Minor, Agatha Phillips, Marguerite Dalby, Dorothy Drumm, Evelyn Nelson, Morine Clark, Kathleen Karr, Yvonne Bacon, Katrina Trask, Jane Dobbins, Jean English, Helen Frederic, Mary Kissell, Jacquelin Surprise, Agnes Schroeder, Maxine Morton, Gloria Christy. *Boys*: Jack Oakie, Arthur Craig, John Kenny, Frank Phillips, Leon Bartels, Billy DeWolf, Billy McKay, Joe Higgins, Gene Owens, Neil Collins, Murray Browne, Al Allison, Penn Thornton, Lewis Walker.

ACT 1

Prologue

Prologue

P. Baker

Scene 1

"Maid of the Milky Way"

W. Woolf, D. Van Heft, Gertrude Hoffmann Girls

Scene 2

"Let Me Dance"

T. Claire, E. Willems, F. Willems, S. Jarmann, Ensemble of Girls and Boys

Scene 3

The Announcer

Scene: Broadcasting Room.

What Follows: E. Titus. *The Announcer*: B. B. Van. *His Assistant*: M. Brown. *Professor*: A. Jochim. *Man in the Moon*: T. Claire. *Mame*: B. Swanson. *Queen of the Air*: L. Hoffman. *Happiness Boys*: Caits Brothers. *The Talker*: P. Baker.

Scene 4

A Fast Stepper

T. Claire

Scene 5

"Charleston"

Gertrude Hoffmann Girls

Scene 6

What We Say and What We Really Think

Scene: A Drawing Room.

Announcer: A. Jochim. *A Hostess*: S. Rogers. *The Daughter*: A. MacMahon. *The Father*: H. Ashton. *The Son*: T. Claire. *The Mother*: L. Hoffman.

Scene 7

"Cellini's Dream"

W. Woolf

Jewel Girls: *In the Box*: M. Douglas, J. Dobbins, P. Duker. *Lavaliere*: Y. Bacon, G. Christie, J. Rogers. *Fountain*: M. Morton, M. Dalby, A. Fontaine. *Earrings*: A. Landis, A. Phillips. *Comb*: J. English, D. Drum, K. Karr, M. Kissel. And Famous Models.

Scene 8

The Dolls: "Take a Little Baby Home with You"

J. Caits, S. Jarmann, E. Willems, F. Willems, Girls and Boys

(*Music by* J. Fred Coots.)

Scene 9

Help Wanted

Scene: The Gray's Home.

The Cook: S. Rogers. *Mrs. Gray*: L. McConnell. *Mr. Gray*: G. Rosener. *Mr. Jones*: B. B. Van.

Scene 10
   "(The) Mothers of the World"
      L. Hoffman
      (*Music by* Sigmund Romberg. *Lyrics by* Clifford Grey.)
      Irish: M. Merle. *Japanese*: G. Wallin. *Russian*: C. Maybury.
      Hawaiian: M. Fine. *Jewish*: S. Hochman. *Negro*: B. Lawrence.
Scene 11
   A Few Minutes More with Margie
      Brennan and Rogers
Scene 12
   "Webbing"
      Gertrude Hoffmann Girls
Scene 13
   The Old New Yorker
      Scene: Christmas Eve in Madison Square.
      The Old New Yorker: G. Rosener. *The Young Fellow from the West*:
      T. Claire.
Scene 14
   Three Episodes of Life
   (a) A Mistake
      T. Claire, J. Carroll
   (b) Fear
      B. Swanson, A. McMahon
   (c) Nerve
      P. Baker, L. McConnell, S. Silvers
Scene 15
   The Star: "Follow Your Star"
      L. Hoffman, Entire Ensemble (*Music by* J. Fred Coots.)
   Dance
      T. Claire, T. Kay, S. Granzow
Scene 16
   The Gertrude Hoffmann Girls Specialties
   Buck Dance
      M. Sloan
   Flicker Dance
      R. Zackey
   Toe Jazz
      F. Dewees
   Ballet
      C. Gallimore
   Peacock's Mirror
      E. Kleigge
   Shimmy
      H. Fowler
   Leopard's Dance
      F. Kolinsky
Scene 17
   Phil Baker[16] (with the assistance of Ted Silvers)
Scene 18
   "The Magic Garden of Love"
      W. Woolf, B. Swanson, Ensemble, Models

ACT 2[17]
Scene 1

_____

[16]Replaced during the run by:
   A Bad Boy from a Good Family
      P. Baker
[17]Added during the run to Act 2, 20 March–24 April 1926:
   Al Jolson Specialty
   "Always"
      (*Music and Lyrics by* Irving Berlin.)
   "Keep Smiling at Trouble"
      (*Music and Lyrics by* Lewis Gensler, Al Jolson, Buddy G. DeSylva.)
   "I'm Sitting on Top of the World"
      (*Music by* Ray Henderson. *Lyrics by* Sam M. Lewis and Joe Young.)
   "Who Wants a Bad Little Boy?"
      (*Music and Lyrics by* Fred Fisher and Joe Burke.)

"Spring" (A Ballet Divertissement)
      E. Kleigge, L. Barte, Gertrude Hoffmann Girls
Scene 2
   The Reward of Crime[18]
      Scene: A Deportation Station on a South Sea Isle.
      Prisoner 642: B. B. Van. *Aloma*: J. Carroll. *Alova*: T. Carlton.
      Guard: A. Jochim. *The Governor*: H. Ashton. *Maids to Prisoner 642*:
      A. Landis, J. Barker, Y. Bacon.
   "Poi Ball"[19]
      Gertrude Hoffmann Girls
Scene 3
   Used by Every Author
      Scene: The Dramatist's Study.
      A Playwright: G. Rosener. *An Actor*: W. Woolf.
Scene 4
   "The Rôtisserie"
      T. Claire, E. Willems, S. Jarmann, Winter Garden Broilers
      Winter Garden Broilers: M. Espy, P. Duker, J. Dobbins,
      D. Weber.
Scene 5
   Out in Front
      A. MacMahon
Scene 6
   You Never Know
      Scene: A Drawing Room.
      The Father: H. Ashton. *Elise*, the maid: J. Carroll.
      The Mother: L. McConnell. *The Daughter*: B. Swanson.
      Percy: T. Claire.
Scene 7
   "The Pastels"
      L. Hoffman, L. Barte, Gertrude Hoffmann Girls
      (*Staged by* Gertrude Hoffmann.)
Scene 8
   What Wives May Look Forward to in the Near Future
      Scene: The Husband's Home.
      The Lover: W. Woolf. *The Wife*: A. MacMahon.
      The Husband: P. Baker.
Scene 9
   "The Promenade Walk at the Beach"
      F. Willems, Girls
Scene 10
   "Oriental Memories"
      W. Woolf, Gertrude Hoffmann Girls, Models
Scene 11
   The Caits Brothers (Dance Specialty)
Scene 12
   Sense of Censor[20]
      Scene: The Master's Studio.
      Hot Stuff: H. Ashton. *His Secretary*: A. Jochim.
      Pamela Bogwrat: J. Carroll. *Sol Vitals*: J. Brennan.
      Trixie DisGruntle: S. Rogers. *William Monday
      Brimstone*: G. Rosener. *Tom Peeper*: H. Corthell.
      Caroline Bluesox: L. Hoffman. *The Tired Businessman*:
      J. Caits. *A Critic*: H. Caits. *An Actor*: W. Woolf. *An Actress*:
      A. MacMahon.
Scene 13
   "Lucita"
      P. Baker, Gertrude Hoffmann Girls, Ensemble, Models
Scene 14
   What the Well Dressed Man Will Wear
      Scene: John's Home at Seven in the Morning.
      Alice: S. Rogers. *Fred*: J. Brennan. *John*: G. Rosener.
Scene 15
   "Fencing"
      Gertrude Hoffmann Girls
   Finale: "Flex-a-Tone" (Flexatone)
      T. Claire, Entire Company

_____

[18]Dropped during the run.
[19]Dropped during the run.
[20]Dropped during the run.

ZIEGFELD FOLLIES OF 1925

1925.24   (Summer Edition)

A Revised Edition of the Musical Revue in Two Acts, 22 Scenes[21]. Dialogue (sketches) by J. P. McEvoy, Will Rogers, W. C. Fields, Gus Weinberg. Music by Raymond Hubbell, Dave Stamper, Werner Janssen. Lyrics by Gene Buck. Staged by Julian Mitchell. Tableaux devised and staged by Ben Ali Haggin. Costume designs by John Held, Jr., Mabel Johnstone, John E. Stone. Scenery by Norman Bel Geddes, Robert Law Studios. Orchestra under the direction of Louis Gress. Orchestrations by (Robert) Russell Bennett, Fred Barry, Harold Sandford, Steve Jones. Produced by Florenz Ziegfeld. Summer Edition opened 6 July 1925 and closed 19 September 1925 after 88 performances.

CAST: WILL ROGERS, W. C FIELDS, ETHEL SHUTTA, RAY DOOLEY, CLARENCE NORDSTROM, EDNA LEEDOM, DAVE STAMPER, IRVING FISHER, VIVIENNE SEGAL, (Al) DARE and (Walter) WAHL, GEORGE OLSEN'S BAND, BERTHA BELMORE, THE KELO BROTHERS (Charles, Carralo), LINA BASQUETTE, BRANDON TYNAN, ADELAIDE SEAMAN, Beryl Halley, Dorothy Knapp, Vangie Valentine, Al Hardy, Tommy Mack, Frank Lambert, Bob Chase, Jack Shannon, Chaz Chase, Naomi Johnson, Elise Cavanna, Mark Truscott, Adelaide Seaman, Al Ochs.

Show Girls: Dorothy Van Alst, Peggy Fears, Louise Brooks, Barbara Newberry, Noel Francis, Helen MacFadden, Hilda Ferguson. *Ziegfeld Girls*: Bobby Storey, Cynthia Cambridge, Gladys Loftus, Norma Forrest, Frances Reveaux, Katherine Burke, Marion Hurley, Elsie Cavanna, Cricket Wooten, Mary Mulhern, Evelyn Goodwin, Harriet Chetwynd, Marion Benda, Doris Lloyd, Gertrude Michaels, Marjorie Leet, Flo Kennedy, Alma Drange, Helen Henderson, Virginia Magee. *Tiller Girls*.

ACT 1

Scene 1

"Home Again" (Opening Song)
D. Knapp, D. Van Alst, P. Fears, L. Brooks, B. Newberry, N. Francis
(*Music by* Raymond Hubbell. *Lyrics by* Gene Buck. *Scene designed by* Duke Murta and Jack Savage.)
Scene: A Transatlantic Pier at New York:
Emigrant Dance: Tiller Girls.

Scene 2

The Drug Store
(*by* J. P. McEvoy and W. C. Fields)
George: C. Nordstrom. *Myrtle*: N. Johnson. *Pa*: W. C. Fields. *Ma*: B. Belmore.
Phone Lady: E. Cavanna. *Stamp Man*: B. Tynan. *Russian*: J. Shannon. *Gertie*: R. Dooley. *A Customer*: F. Lambert. *Nurse*: F. Reveaux. *A Little Guy*: C. Chase.
(*Designed by* Norman Bel Geddes.)

Scene 3

"Syncopating Baby"
C. Nordstrom
(*Music by* Dave Stamper. *Lyrics by* Gene Buck.)
Scene: A Boudoir:
With H. Ferguson, L. Brooks, D. Van Alst, B. Newberry, H. McFadden, Ziegfeld Girls.

Scene 4

Rope Dance
Tiller Girls
(*Staged by* John Tiller.)

Scene 5

A Back Porch
(*by* J. P. McEvoy and W. C. Fields)
Pa: W. C. Fields. *Milk Man*: J. Shannon. *Newsboy*: A. Brown. *Rag Man*: F. Lambert. *The Baby*: R. Dooley. *Ma*: B. Belmore. *Myrtle*: C. Wooten. *Fruit Vendor*: J. Shannon. *Scissor Grinder*: T. Mack. *Ice Man*: M. Truscott.
(*Designed by* Norman Bel Geddes.)

Scene 6

Dance Different
Kelo Brothers
Scene: A Street.

Scene 7

A City Park
(*by* J. P. McEvoy)
The Girl: V. Segal. *The Boy*: C. Nordstrom. *The Thug*: J. Shannon. *A Citizen*: M. Truscott. *A Cop*: B. Tynan. *Another Cop*: A. Brown.

"Toddle Along"
V. Segal, C. Nordstrom, Follies Girls and Boys
(*Music by* Werner Janssen. *Lyrics by* Gene Buck.)

Scene 8

Songs
E. Leedom
At the Piano: D. Stamper.

Scene 9

Out West
W. Rogers

Scene 10

The Ranch (*Painted by* Ludwig Kainer.)
"In the Shade of the Alamo"
I. Fisher, V. Segal
(*Music by* Raymond Hubbell. *Lyrics by* Gene Buck.)
Dance
L. Basquette, Follies Girls, Tiller Girls
Rope Dance
W. Rogers, A. Seaman
Finale

ACT 2[22]

Scene 1

Pearl of the East
(*by* Ben Ali Haggin. *Arrangement with special music by* Raymond Hubbell.)
The Pearl: D. Knapp. *A Pink Slave*: M. Hurley. *A Dancer*: G. Loftus. *A Golden Slave*: E. Goodwin. *The Mongolian Giant*: A. Ochs. *Slaves*: M. Benda, B. Storey, D. Lloyd. *Dancers*: K. Burke, F. Reveaux, H. Chetwynd, M. Mulhern. *Musicians*: M. Leet, F. Kennedy, H. Henderson, V. Magee. *His Warriors*: F. Lambert, M. Truscott.

Scene 2

The Ziegfeld Living Curtain[23]

Scene 3

"Eddie, Be Good"
E. Shutta, George Olsen's Band, Follies Girls
(*Music by* Dave Stamper. *Lyrics by* Gene Buck.)
Scene: A Stage Door.

Scene 4

The Nagger
(*by* Gus Weinberg)
Scene: A Bedroom.
The Ball and Chain: E. Leedom. *Her Husband*: W. C. Fields.

Scene 5

The Curtains

Scene 6

"The Waltz of Love"[24]
R. Dooley, W. C. Fields, George Olsen's Band
Scene: A Ballroom. (*Painted by* Ludwig Kainer.)

Scene 7

"Titina" (Je cherche après Titine) (also in *PUZZLES OF 1925*)
I. Fisher, D. Knapp, B. Halley, Follies Girls
(*Music by* Leo Daniderff. *Lyrics by* Gene Buck.)
Scene: The Beach.

Scene 8

A Road—Joy Ride
(*by* J. P. McEvoy and W. C. Fields)
Pa: W. C. Fields. *Ma*: B. Belmore. *Gertie*: R. Dooley. *A Motor Cop*: B. Tynan.
(Scrambled Billboards courtesy of Leslie-Judge Company.)

Scene 9

"Bertie"[25]
C. Nordstrom, V. Valentine, Pajama Girls
(*Music by* Sigmund Romberg. *Lyrics by* Clifford Grey.)

---

[21]First Edition opened 10 March 1925 at the New Amsterdam Theatre and closed 4 July 1925 after 127 performances. The Twentieth in the annual series of revues which began in 1907.

[22]Added during the run to Act 2:
The Paris Girls
L. Brooks, D. Knapp, N. Francis, D. Van Alst, B. Newberry, P. Fears
[23]Dropped during the run.
[24]Dropped during the run.
[25]Dropped during the run.

Scene 10

The Picnic

(*by* J. P. McEvoy and W. C. Fields) (*Designed by* Norman Bel Geddes)
Pa: W. C. Fields. *Ma*: B. Belmore. *Gertie*: R. Dooley. *A Motor Cop*: B. Tynan.

Scene 11

Green Horns

A. Dare, W. Wahl

Scene 12

Fine Feathers Make Fine Birds

"I'd Like to Be a Gardener in a Garden of Girls"
I. Fisher
(*Music by* Raymond Hubbell. *Lyrics by* Gene Buck.)
Scene: A Garden. (*Painted by* Ludwig Kainer.)

Finale

1925.25 EARL CARROLL'S VANITIES (1925)

A Musical Revue in Two Acts, 48 Scenes[26]. Dialogue (sketches) by William A. Grew. Additional sketches and dialogue by Jimmy Duffy, Arthur 'Bugs' Baer, Blanche Merrill, Julius Tannen, Lester Allen, Owen Murphy, Jay Gorney, Ted Healy, Don Lindley and Harry Jentes. Music (and lyrics) by Clarence Gaskill. Sketches staged by William A. Grew. Dances and ensembles by David Bennett. Art and technical direction by Bernard Lohmuller. Decorations by Willy Pogany. Costumes designed by Charles LeMaire. Settings designed by Karle O. Amend. Special effects by Max Teuber. Music interpreted by Ross Gorman and his Earl Carroll orchestra under the direction of Donald Voorhees. Entire production staged under the personal direction of Earl Carroll. Produced by Earl Carroll. Opened 6 July 1925 at the Earl Carroll Theatre and closed 27 December 1925 after 199 performances.

CAST: JULIUS TANNEN, TED HEALY, WALLACE McCUTCHEON, MARJORIE PETERSON, M. DeJARI, FELICIA SOREL, PEARL EATON, JOSEPHINE SABEL, JESSICA DRAGONETTE, DAVE CHASEN, HAROLD YATES, VIVIAN HART, OSCAR LORRAINE, ADELE NEFF, VAN LOWE, M. SENIA GLUCK, BOBBY FOLSOM, BETTY HEALY, JACK NORTON, KATHRYN RAY, RAY HUGHES, THE WHIRLWINDS (Harry Avers, Frank Wisner, Buddy Carr), CELIA BRANZ, JEANETTE GILMORE, JULIA STEGER.

Ladies of the Ensemble: Rose Adaire, Anita Banton, Marjorie Bailey, Suzanne Bennett, Marjorie Bolton, Edith Cardell, Marion Cardell, Aileen Carmody, Vivian Carmody, Gertrude Crouch, Dane Daniels, Marion Dale, Teddy Dauer, Marion Dowling, Evelyn France, Olivette Florentine, Eva Marie Gray, Bobby Galvin, Dorothy Gordon, Helen Herms, Agnes Horter, Marjorie Kelly, Mildred Kelly, Jewel LaKota, Trudy Lake, Florence Lavalle, Polly Luce, Eva Lynn, Virginia Martin, Rita Mayer, Marcelle Miller, Marie Musselle, Margaret Miller, Lillian Morehouse, Ruth Mees, Frances Norton, Natalie Norton, Vera O'Brien, Blanche O'Brien, Agnes O'Laughlin, Gladys Pender, Nellie Roberts, Irene Swor, Esther Tanya, Lillian Thomas, Lucille Upton, Velma Valentine, Peggy Watts, Rose Wenzel, Marguerite Young. *Gentlemen of the Ensemble*: Dave Jones, Frank Wisner, Warren Hill, Basil Allis, Ross Hertz, Francis Thorne, Sid Daish, Herman Hoover, Pat Brown, Earl Taney, Kenneth Lackey, Richard Warren. *Ross Gorman and his Earl Carroll Orchestra*: Milton Suskind [Edgar Fairchild], Jack Harris, Saul Sharrow, Tony Colicchio, Jules Klein, Bernard Aquilino [Barney Acquilena], Nicholas Koupoukis, Al Evans, Harold Noble, William McGill, Red Nichols, Don Lindley, Jack Koza [James Kozak], Milford ("Miff") Mole, Dave Grupp.

ACT 1[27]

Scene 1

The Doors Open and We Meet the Hostesses

Hostesses

"This is a Night Club"
O. Lorraine
Hostesses: S. Bennett, H. Herms, M. Miller, Marie M. Musselle, R. Mees, M. Young, O. Florentine, L. Upton, O. Florentine, D. Gordon, L. Morehouse.
Usherettes: P. Eaton (Captain), P. Watts, M. Kelly, B. O'Brien, E. M. Gray, M. Bailey, G. Pender, V. Valentine, V. Carmody, A. O'Laughlin, R. Wenzel.

Scene 2

The Two Sisters

Scene 3

The Acrobats

Scene 4

A Bit of Spain

Scene 5

Twinkle Toes

"1-2-3-4"
H. Yates, You

Scene 6

Meeting the Waiters: "We Are the Waiters"
Waiters: K. Lackey, R. Warren, E. Taney, P. Brown, H. Hoover, S. Daish, F. Thorne, W. Hill, B. Allis.

"Hot Off the Oven"
J. Norton

Scene 7

Explaining the Idea

Scene 8

The Rôtisserie Song: "C-h-a-r-l-e-s-t-o-n"
V. Lowe, Chickens, Chefs
Chickens, Chefs: P. Luce, E. Tanya, D. Arden, P. Shannon, R. Mayer, M. Dowling, G. Crouch, A. Banton, A. Carmody, N. Roberta, V. O'Brien, M. Dale, F. Norton, L. Thomas, D. Wilson.

Scene 9

"The Coffee Pot"
M. Peterson

Pappy and Mammy
T. Healy, W. McCutcheon, A. Neff

Scene 10

"Venetian Nights"
M. Peterson, V. Lowe

Scene 11

Judgement Day

Scene 12

The Girl in the Back Alley
H. Hart

"Sentimental Sally"
V. Hart, M. deJari

Scene 13

All in White: "The Drill" (Ponies on Parade)
Visions of Vanities

Scene 14

All in Black: "The Drill" (Ponies on Parade)
Visions of Vanities

Scene 15

The "Yes" Girl and the "No" Girl: "Yes and No"
B. Folsom

Scene 16

One Night in a Bar-Room
W. McCutcheon, R. Hughes

Scene 17

The Birth of Light

Scene 18

The Tank Escape
T. Healy
The Storytellers: B. Healy, K. Hay. *The Singer*: A. Neff. *The Diver*: D. Chasen. *The Assistants*: S. Daish, R. Hertz, F. Thorne, R. Warren.

Scene 19

A Moonlit Garden: "A Kiss in the Moonlight"
V. Hart
Dancers: P. Eaton, B. Healy, V. Lowe.

Scene 20

Advertising Our Friends

Scene 21

In the Lamplight

"The Color Ballet"
M. Senia Gluck, F. Sorel, V. Lowe

Scene 22

Angles on the Triangles

---

[26]The third in the annual series of musical revues presented by Earl Carroll which began in 1923.
[27]The running order was revised immediately after the opening. Added for subsequent tour:

"Adorable"
(*Music and Lyrics by* Tom Ford, Ray Wynburn.)

(a) People Don't Do Such Things
B. Folsom, M. deJari, R. Hughes
(b) Waiting for a Taxi
T. Healy, K. Ray, W. McCutcheon
(c) The First Born
M. deJari, W. McCutcheon, R. Hughes
(d) I've Been Robbed
B. Folsom, R. Hughes
Scene 23
A Few Old Songs, But Good[28]
Scene 24
Le Ballet des Peintres
V. Lowe, R. Hughes, D. Chasen, H. Yates, S. Daish, B. Allis, R. Warren,
W. Hill, R. Hertz, E. Taney, H. Hoover, K. Lackey
Scene 25
The Inside of a Cow
T. Healy, J. Tannen
Scene 26
Finale, Act 1, And Why Not?
M. deJari, Girls
ACT 2[29]
Scene 1
At the Ampico (Piano Solo)
M. Suskind, the Chickering Ampico
Scene 2
Canada Dry Splits: "A Bottle of Canada Dry"
P. Eaton, Canada Dry Girls
Canada Dry Girls: P. Watts, M. Kelly, B. O'Brien, E. M. Gray, M. Bailey,
G. Pender, V. Valentine, V. Carmody, A. O'Laughlin, R. Wenzel.
Scene 3
The Gates to the South [Southland]
Introduction by J. Tannen, B. Folsom.
"Somebody's Crazy About You"
B. Folsom, J. Gilmore
(Music by Jay Gorney. Lyrics by Owen Murphy.)
Dance Divertissement
J. Gilmore
Scene 4
The Florida Land and Water Company[30]
Scene 5
Two Soldiers
The Duet Song: "Lonesome"
M. deJari, H. Yates
Scene 6
"Advancement Militaire"
M. deJari, accompanied by H. Yates
Characters in Pantomime: The Husband: R. Hughes. The Wife: K. Ray. The
Colonel: V. Lowe. The General: S. Daish. The King: W. McCutcheon.
Scene 7
The Three Ring Circus
The Dancer: B. Healy. The Pianist: H. Yates.
The Great Family Crisis
W. McCutcheon, B. Folsom, R. Hertz, S. Daish, A. Neff, V. Lowe
The Great Toe-to-Toe Act
T. Healy, D. Chasen, K. Lackey, R. Warren
Scene 8
The Mad Musician
Scene 9
Under the Trees: "The Bird Ballet"

---

[28]Dropped after the opening.
[29]Added during the run to Act 2:
"How Are the Boys?"
B. Folsom
"Rhythm of the Day"
M. Peterson, Visions of Vanities
(Music by Owen Murphy. Lyrics by Donald Lindley.)
[30]Dropped after the opening.

Scene 10
Down the Aisle with a Drum
Scene 11
In Pango-Pango Land: "Pango Pango Maid"
T. Healy, M. Peterson, F. Sorel
(Music by Irving Bibo. Lyrics by Fred Phillips.)
Marimba Band Accompaniment by R. Gorman,
D. Lindley, B. Aquilino, D. Grupp, M. Suskind, J. Klein,
W. McGill.
Scene 12
Dictated but Not Read
"Thinking of You"
M. deJari, C. Branz, J. Dragonette
Scene 13
The Hanging Gardens
Scene 14
Still Running in Freeport
Scene 15
A Bit of Drama
Scene 16
Hitting on All Sixteen: "Potpourri"
R. Gorman
Scene 17
Leon the 14th Butlers
Introduction by E. Tanya, R. Mayes, O. Borowska, T. Lake, M. Kelly,
J. Daniels.
("We Are the Leon Errol Butlers"
R. Hughes, Butlers)
Pick Up Your Hat
"I'm the Major Bozo"
J. Norton
Scene 18
The Stewdent Prince Boys
Introduction by B. Folsom, M. Dale, P. Watts, B. O'Brien, M. Bailey,
V. O'Brien, R. Adaire.
"He's a Stew" (I'm a Stew)
W. McCutcheon
Scene 19
The Rose Marie Mounted
Introduction by V. Valentine, I. Swor, F. Norton, N. Roberts,
E. M. Gray, N. Norton.
"The Northwest Mounted Police"
T. Healy, (the Royal Mounted)
Scene 20
The Whirlwinds
(H. Avers, F. Wisner, B. Carr)
Scene 21
Pick Up Your Hat: "Shake Yourself Out of Here"
Entire Company
Scene 22
The Grand Finale

1925.26   # JUNE DAYS

A Musical Comedy in Three Acts, 4 Scenes. Book by Cyrus Wood[31]. Based on the comedy 'The Charm School' by Alice Duer Miller and Robert Milton. Music by J. Fred Coots. Lyrics by Clifford Grey. Staged by J. C. Huffman. Dances and ensembles by Seymour Felix. Settings designed by Watson Barratt. Orchestra under the direction of John L. McManus. Entire production under the personal supervision of J. J. Shubert. Produced by Messrs. Shubert. Opened 6 August 1925 at the Astor Theatre, moved 7 September 1925 to the Central Theatre, and closed 17 October 1925 after 84 performances.

---

[31]Prior to New York, the book was jointly credited to Harry Wagstaff Gribble. Costumes uncredited in program.

CAST (in order of appearance): *Butler*: Ralph Reader. *Susie Rolles*: Gladys Walton. *Mrs. Rolles*: Winifred Harris. *Sally Boyd*: BERTA DONN. *George Boyd*: MAURICE HOLLAND. *Herman Van Zandt*: Lee Kohlmar. *David Stewart*: GEORGE DOBBS. *Austin Bevans*: ROY ROYSTON. *Miss Hayes*: Claire Grenville. *Miss Curtis*: MILLIE JAMES. *Elise Benedotti*: ELIZABETH HINES. *Johnson*: JAY C. FLIPPEN. *Helen*: Aileen Meehan. *Dorothy*: Bobbie Perkins. *Edna*: Sylvia Carol. *Muriel*: Bebe Stanton. *Renee*: Joan Lyons.

Pupils of the Bevans School: Winifred Beck, Isabelle Brown, Adelaide Candee, Sylvia Carol, Wilhemina DeBrauw, Dorothy Deeder, Helen Doyle, Frances Ebert, Ethel Fuller, Shirley Gulstin, Joan Lyons, Aileen Meehan, Mabel Olsen, Jacqueline Paige, Bobbie Perkins, Bebe Stanton, Flora Watson, Beatrice Wendell, June Zimmerman.

Act 1: The Drawing Room of the Rolles Suburban Home, near New York City.

Act 2: The Principal's Room at the Bevans School at Bevanstown, New York. Two weeks later.

Act 3, Scene 1: The Girls' Dormitory at the School. The following morning. *Scene 2*: The Principal's Room.

ACT 1

Opening
R. Reader, G. Walton, Girls

"Something Wrong with Me"
R. Royston, G. Dobbs, Girls

"Rememb'ring You"
G. Walton, R. Royston, Girls

"Lucky"
E. Hines, R. Royston
(*Music by* Alfred Goodman, Maurice Rubens.)

"June Days Waltz"
E. Hines, R. Royston, M. Holland

"A Busy Evening"
G. Dobbs, M. Holland, B. Donn, G. Walton, Girls

"Why Is Love"[32]
E. Hines, R. Royston

Finale
Ensemble

ACT 2

"Arithmetic Dancing Bee"
G. Dobbs, Girls

"You Can't Shush Katie"
J. C. Flippen

"Strike"
R. Royston, Girls

"Charming Women"
R. Royston, Girls

"Anytime, Anywhere, Anyhow"
E. Hines, R. Royston
(*Music by* Richard Rodgers. *Lyrics by* Lorenz Hart.)

"How Do You Doodle Do?"
E. Hines, R. Royston, B. Donn, G. Dobbs

"Naughty Little Step"
J. C. Flippen, Girls

Reprise

ACT 3

Scene 1

"Girls Dream of One Thing"
B. Donn, Girls

"Safety in Numbers"
R. Royston, B. Donn, Girls

Scene 2

"Please, Teacher"
Girls

"Take 'Em to the Door Blues"
J. C. Flippen

Finale
Entire Company

---

[32]Replaced during the run by:
"All I Want Is Love"
E. Hines, R. Royston
(*Music by* Hal Dyson. *Lyrics by* James Kendis.)

1925.27

GAY PAREE (1925)

A Continental (Musical) Revue in Two Acts, 34 Scenes[33]. Sketches by Harold Atteridge. Music by Alfred Goodman, Maurice Rubens, J. Fred Coots. Lyrics by Clifford Grey. Dialogue staged by Charles Judels. Dances staged by Earl Lindsy. Ballet by Alexis Kosloff. Settings by Watson Barratt. (Costume) Sketches by Ernest R. Schrapps. Orchestra under the direction of Alfred Goodman. Orchestrations by Emil Gerstenberger. Entire production staged and produced by J. J. Shubert. Presented by the Messrs. Shubert in conjunction with Rufus LeMaire. Opened 18 August 1925 at the Sam S. Shubert Theatre and closed 30 January 1926 after 181 performances.

CAST: CHARLES (Chic) SALE, WINNIE LIGHTNER, BILLY B. VAN, RICHARD BOLD, GEORGE LeMAIRE, ALICE BOULDEN, SALT and PEPPER [Frank Kurtz, Jack Culpepper], BARTLETT SIMMONS, MARGIE FINLEY, WILFRED SEAGRAM, MARGARET WILSON, JACK HALEY, RUTH GILLETTE, CLAUDIA DELL, BETH ELLIOTT, NEWTON ALEXANDER, VIOLA GRIFFITH, EDDIE CONRAD, FLORENCE [FAIR], LORRAINE WEIMAR, PAULINE BLAIR, (Harry) PROSPER and (John) MARET, DOROTHY RAE, DOROTHY BARBER, JOHNNIE DOVE, BYRDEATTA EVANS.

Ladies of the Ensemble: Ilsi Bott, Fern LeRoy, Bernadette Spencer, Florence Horne, Florence Golden, Viola Marshall, Lorraine Brooks, Isabel Dawn, Winifred Seale, Gertrude Lowe, Verdi Milli, Claire Daniels, Alice Hooke, Martha Linn, Rosemary Farmer, Lucille Arden, Edith Higgins, Viola Griffith, Edna Hopper, Betty Allen, Jeanette Simard, Claudia Dell, Clarice Durham, Dorothy Shepard, Betty Maurice, Frances Blythe, Thalie Hamilton, Jean Caswell, Carol Boyer, Katherine Janeway, Marie Price, Lillian Lane, Marie Simpson, Ruth Hamilton, Camille Renault, Nora Reed, Camille, Mabel Earle, Louise Dove, Louise Taylor, Helene Claire. *Boys*: Gus Hyland, William Brainard, William Baden, Art May, Frank Kimball, Chandler Christy, Walton Ford, Marty Kolinsky.

ACT 1

Scene 1

What Every Man Suffers
Mr. High Brow: R. Bold. *Mrs. High Brow*: M. Wilson. *High Brow's Maid*: W. Seale. *Mr. Middle Class*: B. Simmons. *Mrs. Middle Class*: B. Elliott. *Middle Class's Maid*: C. Dell. *Mr. Low Brow*: B. B. Van. *Mrs. Low Brow*: W. Lightner.

Scene 2

The Queen of Sheba
The Singer: R. Gillette. *Sheba*: F. Fair. *Pilgrim*: W. Seagram.

Scene 3

"A Study in Legs"
A. Boulden
Danced by D. Barber, a group of Athletic Girls.

Scene 4

The Puritan Hotel (*by* Harold Atteridge and C. E. Conrad)
Mr. Gulp: C. Sale. *Mrs. Gulp*: V. Griffith. *The Bell Boy*: J. Dove. *Moe Ginsberg*: E. Conrad. *Harold Blair*: J. Haley. *Clerk*: N. Alexander. *A Pippin*: B. Evans.

Scene 5

"Wide Pants Willie"
W. Lightner
(*Music by* James Hanley. *Lyrics by* Harold Atteridge, Henry Creamer.)
Danced by M. Finley, Some Wide Pants Willies.

Scene 6

Plastic Surgery
(*Cartoon drawings by* Rube Goldberg.)
Dr. Keencutter: G. LeMaire. *Cyrano de Bergerac*: B. B. Van. *Stenographer*: A. Boulden. *A Patient*: L. Weimar. *Another Patient*: K. Janeway. *Miss Jones*: B. Evans.

Scene 7

Some Spicy Ditties
Salt and Pepper
["Me Too (Ho-Ho! Ha-Ha!)"
(*Music and Lyrics by* Harry Woods, Charles Tobias and Al Sherman.)
"(That's Her—That's Her) What Did I Tell Ya?"
(*Music by* Walter Donaldson. *Lyrics by* Buddy G. DeSylva.]

Scene 8

"A Vision of Hassan"
R. Bold
Visions in the Perfume Bottles: *Caron*: F. Blythe. *Ma Mie Annette*: V. Griffith, C. Boyer, T. Hamilton, L. Lane. *Nuit de Noel*: L. Taylor. *Black Narcissus*:

---

[33]Messrs. Shubert also presented another edition of GAY PAREE 9 November 1926 at the Winter Garden Theatre for 175 performances.

H. Claire, M. Linn. *Powder Puff Girls*: N. Reed, K. Janeway,
R. Hamilton, M. Price. *Lotus*: B. Odear. *Fragrance*: A. Caldwell.
Pages: F. Leroy, F. Horne.

Scene 9
A Manicure Scene in Times Square[34]
(*by* Harry Wagstaff Gribble)
Tillie: W. Lightner. *Millie*: L. Weimar. *Elmer Fay*: C. Sale.
"Tillie of Longacre Square"[35]
(*Music by* James Hanley. *Lyrics by* Harold Atteridge, Ballard
Macdonald.)
Manicure Girls: B. Maurice, C. Dell, C. Durham, D. Shepard,
B. Spencer, B. Allen.

Scene 10
Where All Is Forgotten
A Boy in Blue: R. Bold. *A Boy in Gray*: B. Simmons.

Scene 11
Jealous Husband
The Husband: N. Alexander. *The Friend*: C. Christy.
Beds
The Salesman: J. Haley. *Old Maid*: L. Weimar.
Ten Pound Boy
The Father: B. B. Van. *George Fisher*: G. LeMaire.

Scene 12
"Every Girl Must Have a Little Bull"
A. Boulden, some Blue Ribbon Girls
(*Music by* Alfred Goodman, J. Fred Coots.)

Scene 13
It's Being Done[36]
(*by* Howard Emmet Rogers)
Jack Bryson: J. Haley. *Mrs. Montgomery*: F. Fair. *Mr. Montgomery*:
W. Seagram.

Scene 14
"My Sugar Plum"
W. Lightner, R. Bold, Salt and Pepper, J. Haley, E. Conrad
(*Music by* Joseph Meyer. *Lyrics by* Buddy G. DeSylva.)

Scene 15
"The Opera in 1860"
M. Wilson, B. Simmons, a Bouquet of Girls
The Dancer: P. Blair. *The Page*: D. Rae.
(*Staged by* Alexis Kosloff.)

Scene 16
The Country Church Choir (The Substitute Parson)
The Minister: C. Sale.

Scene 17
"Wonderful Girl"
J. Haley
(*Music by* Alfred Goodman, J. Fred Coots.)
The Dancer: D. Rae.

Scene 18
A Piano and Song Recital
W. Lightner, E. Conrad
"Give Me the Rain"
(*Music by* Maurice Rubens. *Lyrics by* Lester Allen, Henry Creamer.)

Scene 19
The Rookie
Police Captain: G. LeMaire. *The Rookie*: B. B. Van. *Miss Uptown*:
F. Fair.

Scene 20
"The Glory of the Morning Sunshine"
R. Bold, M. Wilson, B. Simmons, R. Gillette, Entire Ensemble

ACT 2
Scene 1
Venetian Nights: The Wedding of Venus to the Adriatic

"Venetian Wedding Moon"
R. Bold, M. Wilson
(*Music by* Alfred Goodman, J. Fred Coots, Maurice Rubens. *Lyrics by*
Clifford Grey.)
The Doge: W. Seagram. *Venus*: F. Blythe. *Thalie*: R. Gillette. *Matin*:
B. Simmons. *Flora*: K. Janeway. *The Dancer*: D. Barber. *Pages*: G. Lowe,
A. Hooke.

Scene 2
Riverside Drive at Any Time
Harry Brown, Jr.: J. Haley. *Miss Brodie*: W. Lightner. *Harry Brown, Sr.*:
N. Alexander.

Scene 3
The Athletes
H. Prosper, J. Maret

Scene 4
"Baby's Baby Grand"
A. Boulden, J. Haley, the Baby Grand Girls and Boys

Scene 5
Famous People:
The Speaker: W. Seagram.
A Bootlegger
The Warden: G. LeMaire. *The Bootlegger*: E. Conrad.
A Song Writer (*by* Harold Atteridge and Leonard Praskin)
A Song Writer: J. Haley. *His Mother*: F. Fair. *Claire*: B. Elliott.
A Memory School
Mr. Berlitzer: B. B. Van. *His Secretary*: L. Weimar.

Scene 6
"Wedgewood Maid"
R. Bold, M. Wilson
The Dancer: D. Barber.
The Wedgewood Curtain
Figures in the Curtain: *Left*: H. Claire, C. Boyer. *Center*: B. Odear, L. Taylor,
T. Hamilton. *Right*: M. Earle, M. Linn.

Scene 7
"Florida Mammy"
Salt and Pepper

Scene 8
Florida Land the Boob Company
Wilson Anderson: G. LeMaire. *Jimmie van Dyke*: B. B. Van.
Miss Studebaker: F. Fair. *A Native*: J. Haley. *Mr. Gillette*:
W. Seagram.
"Bamboo Babies
A. Boulden
(*Music by* James Hanley, Joseph Meyer. *Lyrics by* Ballard Macdonald.)
The Dancer: L. Taylor.

Scene 9
"Toddle Trot"
W. Lightner, some Toddle Trot Girls
The Dancers: D. Rae, Claudia Dell.

Scene 10
A Free Ride
Cy: C. Sale. *Conductor*: N. Alexander. *Passenger*: W. Seagram.

Scene 11
Quaint Old Lace
(*Staged by* Leon Barte.)
The Grandmother: F. Fair. *Young Bride*: M. Wilson.
The Bride Groom: B. Simmons. *The Marchioness*: D. Barber.
The Marquise: I. Bott.

Scene 12
Songs
W. Lightner
["Hocus Pocus"
(*Music by* James Hanley. *Lyrics by* Ballard Macdonald.)]

Scene 13
The Yogi
The Nurse: B. Elliott. *The Father*: N. Alexander. *The Yogi*: W. Seagram. *The
Doctor*: C. Christy. *The Iceman*: J. Dove.

Scene 14
Night Club in the Roaring Forties
Head Waiter: B. B. Van. *Cy Pettingell*: C. Sale. *Mrs. Pettingell*: L. Lane. *Check
Room Girl*: R. Gillette. *Cigarette Girl*: V. Griffith. *Texas Quinine*: L. Weimar.
The Entertainer: W. Lightner.

---

[34]Later revised as 'Seeing New York.
[35]Dropped during the run.
[36]Replaced during the run by:
At the County Fair
The Barker: G. LeMaire. *The Native*: C. Sale.

1925.28

BIG BOY

A Return Engagement of the Musical Comedy in Two Acts, 13 Scenes[37]. Book by Harold Atteridge. (Based on the play "In Old Kentucky" by Charles T. Dazey.) Music by James F. Hanley and Joseph Meyer. Lyrics by Buddy G. DeSylva. Staged by Alexander Leftwich. Dances and ensembles arranged by Seymour Felix. Settings designed by Watson Barratt. Orchestrations by Alfred Goodman and Emil Gerstenberger; Mr. Jolson's orchestrations by Alfred Goodman. Entire production under the personal supervision of J. J. Shubert. Produced by the Messrs. Shubert. Opened 24 August 1925 at the 44th Street Theatre and closed 5 December 1925 after 120 performances. Total, including first engagement: 176 performances.

CAST (in order of appearance): *Mrs. Bedford*: Maude Turner Gordon. *Phyllis Carter*: Edith Rose-Scott. *Joe Warren*: Hugh Banks. *Tessie Forbes*: Flo Lewis. *Annabelle Bedford*: EDYTHE BAKER. *Jack Bedford*: Ralph Glover. *"Doc" Wilbur*: Leo Donnelly. *"Coley" Reid*: Ralph Whitehead. *Jim Redding*: Franklyn Batie. *Judkins*: George Gilday. *Steve Leslie*: Colin Campbell. *Gus*: AL JOLSON. *"Bully" John Bagby*: William L. Thorne. *"Silent" Ransom*: George Spelvin. *Tucker*: Franklyn Batie. *Manager*: L. C. Sherman. *Wainwright*: William L. Thorne. *Legrande*: William Bonelli. *Mr. Gray*: Frank Holmes. *Dolly Graham*: Frankie James. *Tout*: Frank Holmes. *Dancers*: Dorothy Rudac, George Andre.

Dancers: Jewel Dalores, Elsie Carroll, Mabel Grete, Helen Wallace, Maxie White, Peggy Bernier, Thelma Robinson, Rose Stone, Millie Dupree, Elsie Frank, Edith Pierce, Eva Belmont, Geene Woodward, Elsie Marcus, LaVerne Donnan, Marin Murphy, Marie Marcelline, Ann Cluin, Peggy O'Day, Alma Hockey, Yvette Reals, Alyne Whalen. *Show Girls*: Marjorie Himes, Sidney Shaw, Louise Hersey, Madge Lorraine, Terry Carroll, Irene Warner, Grace Wiotte, Harriet Gustine, Naida Loeffler, Alice Harris, Flo Evers, Olive Lindsay. *Men*: Cliff Daly, Irving Jackson, Elmer Berl, Harry Lake, Jack Ray, Walter Lowery, Walter Wandell, Bobbie Brandeis, Jack Gordon, Arthur Schnitzer, Edward Mowen, Jack Hughes.

1925.29

CAPTAIN JINKS

A Romantic Musical Comedy in Two Acts, 3 Scenes. Book by Frank Mandel and Laurence Schwab. Based on the play 'Captain Jinks of the Horse Marines' by Clyde Fitch. Music by Lewis E. Gensler and Stephen Jones. Lyrics by Buddy G. DeSylva. Book staged by Edgar MacGregor. Musical numbers staged by Sammy Lee. Settings by Frederick Jones. Costume designs by Kiviette. Orchestra under the direction of Ivan Rudisill. Produced by Laurence Schwab and Frank Mandel. Opened 8 September 1925 at the Martin Beck Theatre and closed 30 January 1926 after 167 performances.

CAST: *Captain Robert Jinks, U.S. Marine Corps*: J. HAROLD MURRAY. *Lieutenant Charles Martin, U.S. Navy*: Max Hoffman, Jr. *Seaman Frederick Lane, U.S. Navy*: Arthur West. *Belliarti, Trentoni's Ballet Master*: Ferris Hartman. *Hap Jones*: JOE E. BROWN. *A Federal Inspector*: Sam Coit. *A Policeman*: O. J. Vanasse. *Mlle. Suzanne Trentoni*: LOUISE BROWN. *Honey Johnson*: MARION SUNSHINE. *Annie, Trentoni's Maid*: Nina Olivette. *Mrs. Hochpitz*: Bella Pogany. *Times Reporter*: Wally Crisham. *World Reporter*: Bill Brown. *Journal Reporter*: Frederick Murray. *News Reporter*: Jack Forrester. *Band Leader*: Jackie Taylor.

Ladies: Sophie Howard, Betty Vane, Irene Isham, Elsie Lombard, Joey Benton, Frances Stone, Katherine Malvern, Amy Frank, Helen Sills, Frankie De Voe, Lee Byrne, Isabelle Mason, Evelyn Farrell, Margaret Lee, Mary Meehan, Agnes Reilly, Blanche Morton, Penelope Rowland, Lillian Burke, Ann Lee, Ila Roy, Betty Whitney, Ginger Meehan, Beth Milton, Ruth Shaw, Idylle Shaw, Betty Richmond, Marie Bandoux, Lucille Osborne, Charlotte La Rose, Carol Cummings, Josephine Fontaine. *Gentlemen*: John Burns, Wayne Roberts, Charles Sabin, Al Downing, Frank Cullen, John Meehan, Alan Dale, Andreas Erwing, Marcel Dufan.

Act 1: A Dock of the French Line, New York City.

Act 2, Scene 1: Music Salon in Aronson's Town House. Late afternoon. *Scene 2*: The same. Midnight.

ACT 1
"So This Is the States" (Opening Ensemble)
   N. Olivette, Reporters, Visitors, Passengers
"Pals"
   J. H. Murray, A. West, M. Hoffman, Jr., Marines, Reporters, Sailor Band
"Kiki"
   L. Brown, Ensemble
"Ain't Love Wonderful"
   J. E. Brown, N. Olivette
"I Do"[38]
   L. Brown, J. H. Murray
"Sea Legs"
   A. West, M. Sunshine, Sailor Girls
Finale
   All Concerned

ACT 2[39]
"Strictly Business" (Opening Ensemble)
   N. Olivette, M. Hoffman, Jr., Reporters, Maids, Bouncers
"You Must Come Over Blues" (from *BE YOURSELF*)
   M. Sunshine, A. West
   (Music by Lewis E. Gensler. Lyrics by Buddy G. DeSylva, Ira Gershwin.)
"The Only One"
   J. H. Murray, Debutantes
"You Need a Man Suzanne"
   L. Brown, Men
"Oh! How I Hate Women"
   J. E. Brown
"Fond of You"
   M. Sunshine, M. Hoffman, Jr., A. West, Ensemble
Musical Scene[40]
   J. H. Murray, L. Brown
Dramatic Ballet
   L. Brown, Ensemble
"At the Party"
   J. Taylor, His Captain Jinks Band
Reprise
   J. H. Murray
"Kiki" (Reprise Dance)
   L. Brown, M. Hoffman, Jr.
"The New Game"
   J. E. Brown, M. Sunshine, N. Olivette
Finale
   All Concerned

---

[37]Originally produced in New York 7 January 1925 at the Winter Garden for 56 performances. For Synopsis of Scenes and Musical Numbers, see original 1925 production. One additional scene (Portion of the Grand Stand) was added to Act 2's order of scenes, with correlative changes in song order:
   Act 2, Scene 1: The Night before the Kentucky Derby at Brown's Cafe, Louisville. *Scene 2*: Portion of the Grand Stand. *Scene 3*: The Bedford Stables at Churchill Downs Race Track. *Scene 4*: The Kentucky Derby. *Scene 5*: Portion of the Grand Stand. *Scene 6*: Jockey's Locker Room. *Scene 7*: The Hunt Ball.
Al Jolson also performed the following in his specialty spot:
   "Miami"
     (Music by Con Conrad. Lyrics by Buddy G. DeSylva, Al Jolson.)
   "Nobody But Fanny [Fannie]"
     (Music by Con Conrad. Lyrics by Buddy G. DeSylva, Al Jolson.)
Later in the subsequent tour he performed the following specialties:
   "It All Depends on You"
     (Music by Ray Henderson. Lyrics by Lew Brown, Buddy G. DeSylva.)
   "One O'Clock Baby"

[38]Dropped and replaced by:
   "Fond of You"
     Ada-May (Suzanne), Louis Templeman (Jinks)
[39]For subsequent national tour, the song order in Act 2 was revised.
[40]Musical Scene, Dramatic Ballet, "At the Party" and "Kiki" reprise were dropped and replaced by:
   "Prast-Chi—Prast Chi"
     Ada-May, Ensemble
     (A gypsy folk-song brought from Russia and arranged for "Captain Jinks" by Ada-May.)

1925.30

NO, NO, NANETTE

A Musical Comedy in Three Acts. Book by Otto Harbach and Frank Mandel. (Based on the comedy 'His Lady Friends' by Frank Mandel and Emil Nyitray.) Music by Vincent Youmans. Lyrics by Irving Caesar and Otto

Harbach. Book staged by H. H. Frazee. Dances and ensembles arranged by Sammy Lee. Scenery by P. Dodd Ackerman. Costumes by Milgrims (Act 1), Schneider-Anderson (Act 2), Frances (Act 3), supervised by Corinne Barker. Orchestra under the direction of Nicholas Kempner. Produced by H. H. Frazee. Opened 16 September 1925 at the Globe Theatre and closed 19 June 1926 after 321 performances.

CAST (in order of appearance): *Pauline*, Cook at the Smiths': GEORGIA O'RAMEY. *Sue Smith*, Jimmy's Wife: ELEANOR DAWN. *Billy Early*, a Lawyer: WELLINGTON CROSS. *Lucille*, Billy's Wife: JOSEPHINE WHITTELL. *Nanette*, a Protégée of Sue: LOUISE GROODY. *Tom Trainor*, Lucille's Nephew: JACK BARKER. *Jimmy Smith*: CHARLES WINNINGER. *Betty* from Boston: Beatrice Lee. *Winnie* from Washington: Mary Lawlor. *Flora* from 'Frisco: Edna Whistler.

The Maids: *Helen*: Helen Keyes. *Ethel*: Ethel Gibson. *Beatrice*: Beatrice Wilson. *Eva*: Eva Vincent. *Beth*: Beth Milton. *Margery*: Margery Bailey. *Hazel*: Hazel Pando. *Ruth*: Ruth Kent. *Bonnie*: Bonnie Bland. *Lucille*: Lucille Moore.

The Marrieds, Friends of Lucille: *Mrs. Holmes-Gore*: Lillian MacKenzie. *Mrs. Smythe-Smith*: Veeda Burgett. *Mrs. Townley-Morgan*: Winefride Verina. *Mrs. Brown-Maddox*: Adele Ormiston. *Mrs. Ormesby-Willard*: Aline Martin. *Mrs. Webster-Wylie*: Ellen O'Brien. *Mrs. Parker-Lyne*: Peggy Johnstone. *Mrs. Codman-Russell*: Eleanor Rowe. *Mrs. Whitney-Cabot*: May Sullivan. *Mrs. Lane-Gardner*: Jane Hurd.

The Bachelors: *Edward*: Edward Nell, Jr. *Jerome*: Jerome Kirkland. *Alfred*: Alfred Milano. *William*: William Bailey. *Stanley*: Stanley Lipton. *Douglas*: Douglas Keaton. *Ray*: Ray Moore. *Frank*: Frank Parker. *Edouard*: Edouard Lefebvre. *Robert*: Robert Spencer.

Act 1: The Home of James Smith, New York.

Act 2: The Lawn at Chickadee Cottage, Atlantic City.

Act 3: The Living Room at Chickadee Cottage, Atlantic City.

ACT 1

Opening (Flappers Are We)
  G. O'Ramey, Maids, Marrieds, Bachelors
"The Call of the Sea"
  W. Cross, Maids, Bachelors
  (*Lyrics by* Otto Harbach.)
"Too Many Rings Around Rosie"
  J. Whittell, Maids, Marrieds, Bachelors
  (*Lyrics by* Irving Caesar.)
"I'm Waiting for You"
  L. Groody, J. Barker
  (*Lyrics by* Otto Harbach.)
"I Want To Be Happy"
  L. Groody, C. Winninger, Ensemble
  (*Lyrics by* Irving Caesar.)
  Dancers: B. Wilson, M. Bailey. *Ukelele Players*: B. Wilson, H. Keyes, P. Johnstone, V. Burgett.
"No, No, Nanette"
  L. Groody, Bachelors
  (*Lyrics by* Otto Harbach.)
Finale
  Entire Company

ACT 2

Opening "The Deep Blue Sea"
  L. Groody, Ensemble
"My Doctor"[41]
  G. O'Ramey
  (*Lyrics by* Otto Harbach.)
"Fight Over Me"
  C. Winninger, B. Lee, M. Lawlor, Maids
  (*Lyrics by* Otto Harbach.)
  Dance: M. Lawlor
"Tea for Two"
  L. Groody, J. Barker, Ensemble
  (*Lyrics by* Irving Caesar.)
"You Can Dance With Any Girl at All"
  J. Whittell, W. Cross, Ensemble
  (*Lyrics by* Irving Caesar.)
"I Want To Be Happy" (reprise)
  C. Winninger, W. Cross, E. Whistler, B. Lee, M. Lawlor
Finale
  Entire Company

---

[41]Dropped during the run.

ACT 3

"Hello, Hello, Telephone Girlie"
  W. Cross, B. Lee, M. Lawlor, E. Whistler, Ensemble
  (*Lyrics by* Otto Harbach.)
"Who's the Who?" (Where Has My Hubby Gone Blues)
  J. Whittell, Bachelors
  (*Lyrics by* Irving Caesar.)
"Pay Day Pauline"
  G. O'Ramey, C. Winninger, W. Cross
  (*Lyrics by* Otto Harbach.)
Finale
  Entire Company

1925.31   DEAREST ENEMY

An American Musical Comedy in Three Acts. Book by Herbert Fields. Music by Richard Rodgers. Lyrics by Lorenz Hart. Entire production staged by John Murray Anderson. Libretto directed by Charles Sinclair and Harry Ford. Dances and ensembles directed by Carl Hemmer. Settings designed by Clark Robinson. Costumes for Act 1 designed by Mark Mooring and Hubert Davis. Costumes for Acts 2 and 3 designed by James Reynolds. Orchestra under the direction of Richard Rodgers. Orchestrations by Emil Gerstenberger. Produced by George Ford. Opened 18 September 1925 at the Knickerbocker Theatre and closed 22 May 1926 after 286 performances.

CAST (in order of appearance): *Mrs. Robert Murray*: FLAVIA ARCARO. *Caroline*: Alden Gay. *Annabelle*: Marian Williams. *Peg*: Jane Overton. *Jane Murray*: HELEN SPRING. *Jimmy Burke*: Andrew Lawlor, Jr. *Captain Harry Tryon*: JOHN SEYMOUR. *General Henry Clinton*: William Evill. *Lieutenant Sudsby*: Arthur Brown. *General Sir William Howe*: HAROLD CRANE. *General John Tryon*: DETMAR POPPEN. *Captain Sir John Copeland*: CHARLES PURCELL. *Betsy Burke*: HELEN FORD. *General Israel Putnam*: Percy Woodley. *Major Aaron Burr*: James Cushman. *Morgan's Scouts (3)*: *Private Peters*: Jack Shannon. *Private Lindsay*: Mark Truscott. *Private Woods*: Percy French. *Envoy*: Frank Lambert. *General George Washington*: H. E. ELDRIDGE. (*Dance Specialties*: Jane Overton, Charles Bennington.)

Ladies of the Ensemble: Betty Linn, Rachel Chester, Marion Dabney, Roberta Curry, Mabel Zoeckler, Polly Williams, Josephine Payne, Peggy Bancroft, Elizabeth North, Marita Dennis, Joy Leitch, Devah Worrell, Gloria Faye, Geneva Price, Mildred Mann, Lucille Smyser, Eugenia Renon. *Gentlemen of the Ensemble*: George Harold, John Valentine, Burton McEvilly, Louis Gomez, Walter T. Burke, Edward Larkin, Conrad Gordon, James Cushman, Don Knobloch.

Act 1: The Murray Mansion, Murray Hill, New York City. 1776.

Act 2: The Drawing Room at the Murray Mansion. The same evening.

Act 3: The Murray Mansion. After the War.

ACT 1[42]

"Heigh-Ho, Lackaday!"
  F. Arcaro, Girls
"War Is War"
  F. Arcaro, Girls
"I Beg Your Pardon"
  H. Spring, J. Seymour
"Cheerio"
  C. Purcell, Officers
"Full Blown Roses"
  F. Arcaro, Officers, Girls
"The Hermits"
  F. Arcaro, D. Poppen
"Here in My Arms"
  H. Ford, C. Purcell
Finale (Tho' We've No Authentic Reason)
  Ensemble

ACT 2

"Gavotte"
  Officers, Girls
  (*Dance arranged by* John Murray Anderson.)

---

[42]The management acknowledges with gratitude the assistance of Anne Morrison and Madame Serova. During the run, the following credit was added in the program:

Specialty Dance (Act 2, after "Sweet Peter")
  Charles Bennington

"I'd Like To Hide It"
H. Ford, Girls

"Where the Hudson River Flows"
F. Arcaro, H. Crane, D. Poppen, Officers, Girls
Solo Dance: J. Overton

"Bye and Bye"
H. Ford, C. Purcell

"Old Enough to Love"
D. Poppen, Girls

"Sweet Peter"
H. Spring, J. Seymour, Officers, Girls

"Here's a Kiss"
H. Ford, C. Purcell

ACT 3 (EPILOGUE)

Opening
Ensemble

"Here in My Arms" (reprise)
H. Ford

(Finale)
(Company)

1925.32 THE VAGABOND KING

A Musical Play in Four Acts, 6 Scenes. Book and lyrics by Brian Hooker and W. H. Post. Based on Justin McCarthy's romance [play] 'If I Were King,' adapted from the novel by R. H. Russell. Music by Rudolf Friml. Staged by Max Figman. Musical numbers (staged) by Julian Alfred. Scenery and costumes designed by James Reynolds. Orchestra and singing under the direction of Anton Heindl. Entire production under the direction of Russell Janney and Richard Boleslawsky. Produced by Russell Janney. Opened 21 September 1925 at the Casino Theatre, moved 15 November 1926 to the Century Theatre, and closed 4 December 1926 after 511 performances.

CAST (in order of appearance): *René de Montigny*: Robert Craik. *Casin Cholet*: Leon Cunningham. *Margot*: Katherine Hayes. *Blanche*: Merle Stevens. *Isabeau*: Vivian Kelly. *Jehan Le Loup*: Marius Rogati. *Trois Échelles*: Joseph Miller. *Huguette du Hamel*: JANE CARROLL. *Jehanneton*: Mimi Hayes. *Guy Tabarie*: HERBERT CORTHELL. *Colin de Cayeul*: Carlton Neville. *Tristan L'Hermite*: H. H. McCullum. *Louis XI*: MAX FIGMAN. *François Villon*: DENNIS KING. *Katherine de Vaucelles*: CAROLYN THOMPSON. *Thibaut d'Aussigny*: Bryan Lycan. *Captain of Scotch Archers*: Charles Carver. *An Astrologer*: Leon Cunningham. *Lady Mary*: OLGA TRESKOFF. *Noel Le Jolys*: Herbert Delmore. *Oliver Le Dain*: Julian Winter. *First Court Lady*: Marian Alta. *Second Court Lady*: Ann Austin. *Toison d'Or, Burgundian Herald*: Earl Waldo. *The Queen*: Tamm Cortez. *The Dancer*: Helen Grenelle. *The Bishop*: G. L. Mortimer. *The Hangman*: William Johnson. *First Courtier*: Walter Cross. *Second Courtier*: John Mealey.

Tavern Girls: Eona Murilla, Mimi Hayes, Miriam Franken, Evelyn Stockton, Kathryne Richmond, Caroline Cantlion, Triny Broekman, Ethel Rea, Therese Hyle, Lucy Lawlor. *Scotch Archers*: Herbert Crane, Joseph Batistich, Michael Evans, Harry Clark, John Mealey, Francis Baldwin, Arthur P. Hoyt, Earl Clayton. *Tavern Men*: Arthur Kellar, Marius Rogati, George Mortimer, Walter Higgins, Edward Sheldon, E. H. Barlab, Joseph Miller, Ross Ericksen. *Court Ladies*: Margaret Grove, Ruth Gieber, Grace Angelau, Cynthia Farr, Theola Vincent, Beatrice Marsh, Helen Ely, Fern Adrian, Fanille Davies, Muriel Seaman, Florence DeBarde, Margaret LaMotte. *Courtiers*: Carlton Neville, Jack Roise, Louis Olary, Walter Cross, Edwin L. Rogers, John York, Alfred Cortez, Glenn Macauley. *Pages and Dancers*: Muriel Dawn, Florence Courtney, Madeline Dare, Estelle Mercier, Margot Miller, Dolores Frank, Mabel Lee, Nellie Paley, Betty Chapin, Virginia Kelley, Dorothy Fitzgibbon.

The action takes place in Paris at the time of Louis XI.

Act 1: The Tavern.

Act 2, Scene 1: The Court. That night. *Scene 2*: The Court. Next morning.

Act 3: The Masque.

Act 4: A Gate of Old Paris. *Scene 2*: The Gibbet.

ACT 1[43]

Opening Chorus
Ensemble

"Love For Sale"
J. Carroll, Chorus, Dance Ensemble

"Drinking Song" (A Flagon of Wine)
H. Corthell, Male Chorus

[43]The program included an incomplete song list; the list below was prepared from the production manuscript.

"Song of the Vagabonds"
D. King, Chorus

"Some Day"
C. Thomson

"Only a Rose"
C. Thomson, D King

Fight Music and Finaletto
Entire Company

ACT 2

"Hunting"
H. Delmore, Chorus
Ballet: Dance Ensemble

"Archers' Song"
C. Carver, Scotch Archers

"Tomorrow"
C. Thomson, D. King, Chorus

Finale
Entire Company

ACT 3

Nocturne
Ensemble

Tarantella
Dance Ensemble

"Serenade" (Trio)
J. Winter, H. Corthell, O. Treskoff

"Waltz Huguette" (Huguette Waltz)
J. Carroll

"Love Me Tonight"
C. Thomson, D. King

Finale
Entire Company

ACT 4

"Te Deum"
Ensemble

"Victory March" ("Song of the Vagabonds" reprise)
Ensemble

Finale Ultimo
Entire Company

1925.33 SUNNY

A Musical Comedy in Two Acts, 12 Scenes. Book and lyrics by Otto Harbach and Oscar Hammerstein II. Music by Jerome Kern. Staged by Hassard Short. Dances staged by Julian Mitchell and David Bennett. Miss Miller's Hunt Ball dance arranged by Alexis Kosloff. Eight Cocktail Dances staged by John Tiller. Miss Miller's dances with boys by Fred Astaire. Settings and costumes designed by James Reynolds. Musical director, Gus Salzer. Orchestrations by Robert Russell Bennett. Produced by Charles Dillingham. Opened 22 September 1925 at the New Amsterdam Theatre and closed 11 December 1926 after 517 performances.

CAST: *Mlle. Sadie*: Helene Gardner. *Bally Hoo*: Charles Angelo. *Tom Warren*: PAUL FRAWLEY. *Siegfried Peters*: JOSEPH CAWTHORN. *Harold Harcourt Wendell-Wendell*: CLIFTON WEBB. *Sue Warren*: Esther Howard. *Sam*: CLIFF EDWARDS. *'Sunny' Peters*: MARILYN MILLER. *Jim Deering*: JACK DONAHUE. *'Weenie' Winters*: MARY HAY. *Marcia Manners*: Dorothy Francis. *Magnolia*: PERT KELTON. *First Mate*: Louis Harrison. *First Ship's Officer*: Elmer Brown. *Second Ship's Officer*: Abner Barnhart. *Ship's Captain*: James Wilson. *Diana Miles*: Jeanne Fonda. *Millicent Smythe*: Joan Clement. *Groom*: Don Rowen. *Specialty Dancers*: Linda; (Marjorie) Moss and (Georges) Fontana. GEORGE OLSEN AND HIS ORCHESTRA.

Eight Marilyn Miller Cocktails: Peggy Soden, Lelia Riley, Grace Holt, Hilda Wynn Stanley, Doris Waterworth, May Cornes, Iris Smith, Nellie Douglas. *Show Girls*: Dorothy Durland, Trude Marr, Claire Hopper, Maida Palmer, Helene Gardner, Rita Glynde, Alice Brady, Pauline Hall, Anna May Dennehy, Tatiana. *Dancers*: Virginia Clark, Victoria Webster, Helen Shepard, Miriam Miller, Phyllis Reynolds, Helen MacDonald, Zelleta Johnson, Collette Francey, Jet Stanley, Betty McLaughlin, Beatrice de Shaw, Christine Conniff, Marie Maxwell, Betty Darling, Pearl Bennett, Rita Royce, Marion Swords, Adelaide Robinson, Louise Stark, Katheryn Frey, Elva Pomfret, Julia Lane, Lorna Sommerville, Margaret Kolloch, Vera Coburn, Laverne Lindsay, Lorraine Eason. *Boys*: Ward Tallman, Marshall D. Sullivan, William J. Sholar, Jr., Robert Williams, Maurice Lapue, Albert Birk, Marcos de Abreau, Minard Roosa, Irving Carter, Donald Oltrash, Bill O'Donnell, Walter Fairmont, Wensley Johnston, Ray Justus, Richard Renaud, Louis Yaeckel, Gordon Clark, Roy Moore, Lee

Moore, Russell Ash, Albert Royal, Bob Leroy, Eddie Graham, Don Rowen, Joe Billings, George Comtois, Fred Comtois, Ted Wenning.

Act 1, Scene 1: Outside a Circus Tent, Southampton, England. *Scene 2*: Back of the Circus. *Interlude*: A Street in Southampton. *Scene 3*: In Front of 'Weenie's' House. *Interlude*: The Gangplank. *Scene 4*: S. S. Triumphant. *Scene 5*: S. S. Triumphant. Noon, two days later. *Scene 6*: A Park in Southampton. Next day. *Interlude*: Jim's Cabin. Evening before landing. *Scene 7*: Grand Salon, S. S. Triumphant.

Act 2, Scene 1: Conservatory adjoining Jim's Gymnasium at a fashionable Southern resort. *Scene 2*: The Grove. That afternoon. *Scene 3*: A Poppy Field. *Scene 4*: The Woods. *Scene 5*: Ball Room of the Hotel.

ACT 1
Scene 1
Opening ("Here We Are Together Again")
    Ensemble
    (Dance) Marilyn Miller Cocktails
Scene 2
"Sunny"
    P. Frawley, Boys
"Who?"
    M. Miller, P. Frawley
Interlude
"So's Your Old Man"
    C. Webb, Marilyn Miller Cocktails
Scene 3
"Let's Say Good Night Till It's Morning"
    J. Donahue, M. Hay
Scene 4
"Do You Love Me?" (D'ye Love Me)
    M. Miller
    Dance: J. Donahue
"The Wedding Knell"
    M. Miller, Boys
Scene 6
"Two Little Blue Birds"
    C. Webb, M. Hay
Scene 7
Finale
    (Company)
ACT 2
Scene 1
Opening ("We're Gymnastic")
    Ensemble
"When We Get Our Divorce"
    M. Miller, J. Donahue
"Sunshine"
    D. Francis, Boys
    Dance: Linda
"Who?" (reprise)
    M. Miller, P. Frawley
    Dance: M. Miller, J. Donahue, C. Webb, M. Hay
    Dance: Ensemble
Scene 2
(Specialty[44]):
"Paddlin' Madelin' Home"
    C. Edwards
    (*Music and Lyrics by* Harry Woods.)

---

[44]Other songs interpolated by Cliff Edwards during the run:
    "I'll Say to You and You Say to Me"
        C. Edwards
        (*Music by* Eddie Ward. *Lyrics by* Chick Endor.)
    "I'm Moving Away"
        C. Edwards
        (*Music and Lyrics by* Cliff Edwards and Irving Caesar.)
When Borrah Minevitch replaced Cliff Edwards as Sam, his Specialty in Act 2, Scene 2:
    Harmoniconia
        B. Minevitch
When Borrah Minevitch departed the cast, the Act 2, Scene 2 Specialty was allotted to George Olsen and His Orchestra.

"Just a Little Thing Called Rhythm"
    C. Edwards
    (*Music by* Eddie Ward. *Lyrics by* Chick Endor.)
Scene 3
The Chase
    (Ensemble)
"Strolling, or What Have You?"
    C. Webb, M. Hay
Scene 4
"Magnolia in the Woods"
    P. Kelton
    (*Music and Lyrics by* Pert Kelton.)
Scene 5
The Hunt Dance
    M. Miller
Dance[45]
    M. Moss, G. Fontana
Finale
    M. Miller, Entire Company

1925.34   # MERRY, MERRY

A Musical Play in Two Acts, 6 Scenes. Book and lyrics by Harlan Thompson. Music by Harry Archer. Staged by Harlan Thompson. Dances arranged by Harry Puck. Settings designed by P. Dodd Ackerman. Costumes designed by Charles LeMaire. Orchestra under the direction of Ernest Cutting. Produced by Lyle D. Andrews. Opened 24 September 1925 at the Vanderbilt Theatre and closed 13 March 1926 after 197 performances.

CAST (in order of appearance): *Adam Winslow*: HARRY PUCK. *Eve Walters*: MARIE SAXON. *A Subway Passenger*: George Spelvin. *Sadi LaSalle*: SASCHA BEAUMONT. *Flossie Dell*: VIRGINIA SMITH. *Conchita Murphy*: LUCILLE MENDEZ. *J. Horatio Diggs*: WILLIAM FRAWLEY. *Stephen Brewster*: JOHN HUNDLEY. *Henry W. Penwell*: Robert Pitkin. *Mrs. Penwell*: Perqueta Courtney. *The Stage Manager*: Larry Beck.

Polly Schaefer: Polly Schaefer. *Molly Morey*: Molly Morey. *Ruth Conley*: Ruth Conley. *Vivian Marlowe*: Vivian Marlowe. *Gay Nelle*: Gay Nelle. *Ednor Fulling*: Ednor Fulling. *Frances Marchand*: Frances Marchand. *Gretchen Grant*: Gretchen Grant. *Ethel Emery*: Ethel Emery. *Ruth Farrar*: Ruth Farrar.

Act 1, Scene 1: A Subway Station. Not in the rush hour. *Scene 2*: Sadi LaSalle's Apartment, Riverside Drive. Early evening. *Scene 3*: A Street Corner Nearby. *Scene 4*: Sadi's Apartment.

Act 2, Scene 1: Sadi's Apartment. Next Day. *Scene 2*: The Stage of the Vanderbilt Theatre. Later.

ACT 1
"It Must Be Love"
    M. Saxon, H. Puck
"What a Life"
    S. Beaumont, V. Smith, L. Mendez, Girls
"Every Little Note"
    M. Saxon, Girls
"We Were a Wow"
    V. Smith, W. Frawley
"My Own"
    S. Beaumont, J. Hundley, Girls
Reprise
    Ensemble
"It Must Be Love" (reprise)
    M. Saxon
"Little Girl"
    M. Saxon, H. Puck
"I Was Blue—"
    H. Puck, Girls
ACT 2
"The Spanish Mick"
    L. Mendez, Girls
"Oh, Wasn't It Lovely?"
    P. Courtney, W. Frawley

---

[45]Dropped during the run.

"It Must Be Love" (reprise)
  M. Saxon, H. Puck
"Step, Step Sisters"
  V. Smith, L. Mendez, J. Hundley, Girls
"Poor Pierrot"/Valse Ballet
  M. Saxon, Girls

1925.35 WHEN YOU SMILE

A Musical Comedy in Three Acts, 5 Scenes. Book by Tom Johnstone and Jack Alicoate. (Based on the play 'Extra' by Jack Alicoate.) Music by Tom Johnstone. Lyrics by Phil Cook. Production staged by Oscar Eagle. Dances and ensembles staged by Raymond Midgley. Scenery by Pogany-Teichner Studios. Costumes by Arlington-Mahieu; Mme. Genevieve. Orchestra under the direction of F. Wheeler Wadsworth. Orchestral arrangements by Ronald Ross. Entire production under the personal direction of James P. Beury. Produced by James P. Beury. Opened 5 October 1925 at the National Theatre, moved 19 October 1925 to the Central Theatre, and closed 14 November 1925 after 49 performances.

CAST (in order of appearance): *Elaine LeMar*: NITA MARTAN. *Henderson*: HAROLD VIZARD. *Michael Malone*: Philip Lord. *John W. King*: JOHN MAURICE SULLIVAN. *Ann*: WYNNE GIBSON. *"Larry" Patton*: JACK WHITING. *Jack King*: John B. Gallaudet. *"Wally" King*: RAY RAYMOND. *June Willard*: CAROL JOYCE. *Jimmy Flynn*: Richard Saunders. *R. H. Osgood*: Thomas McKnight. *June*: June Justice. *Imogene*: Imogene Coca. *Florence*: Florence Arledge. *Myrtle*: Myrtle LeRoy. *Dorothy*: Dorothy Humphreys. *Babs*: Babs Grieg. *Woody*: Woody Lee Wilson. *Mildred*: Mildred Tolle. *Carol*: Carol Seidler. *Marjorie*: Marjorie Brooks. *Betty*: Betty Colet. *Edna*: Edna Pierce. *Margaret*: Margaret Miller.

Act 1: Home of John W. King, Los Angeles, California.

Act 2: Office of "The Movie News", Los Angeles.

Act 3, Scene 1: Home of John W. King. Two months later. *Scene 2*: "The Extra." *Scene 3*: Home of John W. King. Thirty minutes later.

ACT 1
  "Spanish Moon"
    N. Martan, Girls
  "Naughty Eyes"
    N. Martan
  "One Little Girl"
    J. Whiting, Girls
  "Let's Have a Good Time"
    R. Raymond, Girls
  "Gee, We Get Along"
    W. Gibson, J. Whiting
  "When You Smile"
    R. Raymond, C. Joyce

ACT 2
  "All Work and No Play"
    H. Vizard, Girls
  "Keep Them Guessing"
    N. Martan, Girls
  "Keep Building Your Castles"
    C. Joyce
  "Let's Dance and Make Up"
    W. Gibson, J. Whiting

ACT 3
  "Wonderful Rhythm"
    J. Whiting, J. P. Gallaudet
  "June"
    R. Raymond, the Four "Hoarse-Men"
  "Oh, What a Girl"
    W. Gibson, J. Whiting
  "Wonderful Yesterday"
    C. Joyce, R. Raymond
  "Buy an Extra"
    Girls
  "When You Smile" (reprise)
    C. Joyce, R. Raymond
  "She Loves Me"
    R. Raymond, C. Joyce, W. Gibson, J. Whiting

Finale
  C. Joyce, R. Raymond, Girls

1925.36 HOLKA POLKA

A Musical Comedy in Three Acts[46]. Book by Bert Kalmar and Harry Ruby from Derick Wulff's translation of the European success ('Frühling im Herbst')[Spring in Autumn] by Willi Walzer. Music by Will Ortmann. Lyrics by Gus Kahn and Raymond B. Eagan. Staged by Oscar Eagle. Dances arranged by Busby Berkeley. Entire production (settings) and costumes designed by Livingston Platt. Orchestra under the direction of Max Steiner. Produced by Carl Reed. Opened 14 October 1925 at the Lyric Theatre and closed 31 October 1925 after 21 performances.

CAST (in order of appearance): *Auctioneer*: Harry Anderson. *Adam Cook*: James C. Morton. *Marie Karin*: Francis H. Cherry. *Peter Novak*, known as "Nobody": ORVILLE HARROLD. *Gundel, Adam's Housekeeper*: MAY VOKES. *Peterle Novak*: PATTI HARROLD. *Ellen Novak*: Esther Lyon. *Max Munz*: HARRY HOLBROOK. *Karel Boleslav*: ROBERT HALLIDAY. *Baron von Bruck*: George E. Mack. *Coachman*: Charles Thompson. *Rudi Munz*: Thomas Burke, Jr. *Jan, Butler at Max Munz's*: Vincent Langan. *Henri Novothy*: John Sherlock. *Specialty Dancers*: Marion and Martinez Randall, (Lisa Parnova, Rosa de Cordoba, Edwin Strawbridge). *Country People, Artists, Guests.*

Ladies of the Ensemble: Jean Armstrong, Isabelle Benson, Aileen Booth, Phyllis Burkhardt, Ely DeMar, Lillian Clinton, Betty Creditor, Renee Lowrie, Ruth Elaine, Florence Crozier, Vera Dale, Barbara Dean, Adrienne DeSales, Josephine Doane, Willoa Fellows, Mary Huber, Beatrice King, Dorothy Johnson, Dorothy Wilson, Ray Lloyd, Sylvia LaMard, Milba LeVander, Ila McCall, Henrietta Merriman, Viola Wayne, Alice Mitchell, Olive Wanda, Patti Patterson, Frances Patton, Kaye Renard, Bess Ringwald, Clementine Regeau, Valerie Sargent, Christine Schyler, Mabel Williams, Edith Stich, May Speed, Lea Roy, Hilda Withers. *Gentlemen of the Ensemble*: Alec Bowman, Lloyd Briggs, Harry Ellston, Paul Elsoner, Ben Fleck, Nicholas Globatcheff, Buddy Carmin, Harry Heller, Russell King, Jack Lerner, Richard Lear, Maurice Martin, James Martin, Al Monty, Trope Reynolds, Fred Ortmann, F. D. Porterfield, Morris Ragalsky, Joe Rogers, Leon Kartavy, Albert Hurt, Reginald Thomas, Ben Trotman, Holmes Washburn, Val Sholar.

Act 1: A Village in Czecho-Slovakia. Spring.

Act 2: Home of Max Munz, near Prague. Three months later.

Act 3: A Village in Czecho-Slovakia. Autumn.

ACT 1
  "Mary to the Market Went" (Opening)
    Ensemble
  "I Want to Be a Bad Little Boy"
    P. Harrold
  "The Highway's Call"
    Art Students
  "Home of My Heart"
    O. Harrold
  "Spring in Autumn"
    O. Harrold, P. Harrold, H. Holbrook, F. H. Cherry, M. Vokes, Ensemble
  "In a Little While"
    P. Harrold, R. Halliday
  "Holka Polka"
    P. Harrold, R. Halliday, Ensemble
  Specialty Dance
    R. deCordoba, E. Strawbridge
  Finale

ACT 2
  "Fairy Tale"
    P. Harrold, T. Burke, Jr., Chorus
  Specialty Dance
    L. Parnova
  Dance Specialty
    Marion Randall, Martincz Randall
  "When Love Is Near"
    P. Harrold, O. Harrold
  "This Is My Dance"
    P. Harrold, R. Halliday, Ensemble

---

[46]Tried out under the titles SPRING IN AUTUMN and NOBODY'S GIRL.

419

Dance Specialty
Marion Randall, Martinez Randall
"Goodfellow Days"
H. Holbrook, Ensemble
Finale
ACT 3
"Chimes of the Chapel"
Ensemble
"Home of My Heart" (reprise)
O. Harrold, Ensemble
"Holka Polka" (reprise)
P. Harrold, R. Halliday, Ensemble
Finale

1925.37 ARABESQUE

A Musical Play in Two Acts, 10 Scenes. Play by Cloyd Head and Eunice Tietjens. Music by Ruth White Warfield[47]. Directed and designed by Norman Bel Geddes. Dances arranged by Michio Itow. Settings executed by Cleon Throckmorton. Produced by Norman Bel Geddes and Richard Herndon. Opened 20 October 1925 at the National Theatre and closed 7 November 1925 after 23 performances.

CAST (in order of appearance): *Cafe Proprietor, his name doesn't matter*: Ben Welden. *Waiter, he never had a name*: White Hawk. *Ali, a Young Chess Player*: VICTOR HAMMOND. *Baba Youssef, Old Chess Player*: CONRAD CANTZEN. *Maroc in the Doorway*: KAY McKAY. *A Kief Smoker*: Samuel Rosen. *The Ragged Old Beggar*: Logan Paul. *The Ever-Yawning Rug Merchant*: Mohammed Ben Ali. *Perfumer*: Hardwick Nevin. *Cloth Merchant*: Mohammed Basher. *Jeweler*: Herman O. Roberts. *The Dancing Girl in the cafe*: ANNA DUNCAN. *The Arab Woman*: Louise Mainland. *Porter who carries two citrons*: Edward Ray. *A Rich Jew*: Earle Caddock. *The Rich Jew's Son*: Larry Jason. *The Rich Jew's Wife*: Ruth Daniels. *The Rich Jew's Daughters*: Nancy Pethbridge, Marie Offerman. *Arab Children*: Geraldine Ballard, Robert Halloway, George Offerman, Merlin Ballard. *A Pilgrim on his way to Kirowan*: Hamad Attab. *Two Berber Women*: Gladys Green, Irene Joseph. *The Tailor who wears a long beard*: Clayton Braun. *Bearded Jew*: Charles Berkley. *Abs, the Water Carrier*: GEORGE THORNTON. *Porter who carries crates*: Ali Halel. *Grocer*: Bus Daniels. *Cobbler*: Roland Twombly. *Chief Bedouin, leader of a gang of thieves*: JACOB KINGSBURY. *Laila, a Bedouine from the Desert*: HORTENSE ALDEN. *A Tall Bedouin, to whom Laila belongs*: BOYD DAVIS. *Old Bedouin*: Philip Spector. *Ahmed Ben Tahar under the haystack*: CURTIS COOKSEY. *Abdullah, who carries the haystack off*: Sarat Lahiri. *The Sheik of Hammam, a Minor Official*: BELA LUGOSI. *Short Orderly, who carries umbrella*: M. Garboat. *M'na, The Pearl in a Bed of Oysters*: SARA SOTHERN. *Ma-bouba, the Mother of the Pearl*: OLIVE WEST. *Coppersmith*: Raphael Kadous. *The Herdsman who gets his hair cut*: Hamad Bisher. *The Barber who does the job*: Beine Makter. *The Money Changer*: Raise Lehassen. *Woodpeddler*: Ismut Hassen. *The Sheik's Mother, who would live in Tunis*: JULIA RALPH. *The Sheik's Sister*: NAOE KONDO. *The Sheik's Aunt*: Yetta Malamude. *Four Dancing Boys at the Wedding*: Mustapha Hantoot, Mactar Lehedder, Mohammed Houssian, Hamad B. Omar. *Three Arab Guests*: B. A. Fripp, Lackaye Grant, Claude Dougal. *Halima, the Professional Matchmaker*: HELEN JUDSON. *An Innocent Bedouin near the door*: John Brewster. *The Public Letter Writer*: Prince Singh. *A Negro Servant Woman*: Elsie Winslow. *Grain Vendor*: James Gaylor. *The Subcaid*: William Skavlan. *The Caid of Nadour, a superior offical*: ETIENNE GIRARDOT. *Four Bridesmaids*: Florence Brinton, Elsbeth Herbert, Helen Kim, Rona Fray. *The Muezzin*: Yuji Itow.

Act 1, Scene 1: The Moorish cafe in Hammam-el-Kedime, where Ahmed ben Tahar, late sergeant in the French Army, sees the face of the pearl M'na, and finds a talisman, and where the Sheik meets a Bedouine desert-cat, Laila. *Scene 2*: The House of Mabouba, where the Sheik's Mother, sent by her son, pays a visit of inspection to consider M'na—whom the Sheik had seen on the rooftops by Ma-bouba's design, and with whom he has fallen in love; and what happened at the interview. *Scene 3*: A navel of the desert, where the wandering Bedouins reveal that they are not only thieves but murderers and where they discover that they have lost a talisman taken from the dead man. Here the Sheik, thinking that they are only petty thieves, finds again the Bedouine and makes an unwritten bargain. *Scene 4*: The House of Ma-bouba, set for the wedding of her dead son to collect the money which according to custom was due him at his wedding. Here Ahmed learns that the Bedouins have murdered the Caid's nephew; and his wits sharpened by jealousy, baits the Sheik, whose traffic with the Bedouins he suspects. Also, Ma-bouba's own funeral, held to convince the Sheik's mother that Mabouba will be an unobtrusive mother-in-law, and how the scheme worked in spite of an unwelcome interruption.

Act 2, Scene 1: The House of Ma-bouba, where Ahmed commits the unpardonable sin, from a Mohammedan standpoint, of coming into a house and making love to a virgin. *Scene 2*: Before the Sheik's office, where Ahmed forces the Sheik to keep a tryst with the Bedouine and takes a long chance by telegraphing the Caid at Nadour to come to

Hammam, and of what Ahmed learned regarding the Sheik's suit for M'na. *Scene 3*: The House of Mabouba, where M'na under superior force changes her mind. *Scene 4*: Before a hermit shrine in the hills, where the Sheik keeps tryst with the bedouine while, at Mabouba's house M'na is dressed for the ceremony of engagement. *Scene 5*: On the roof-tops, the kingdom of the hidden Arab women, to which no man may come by inviolable custom. How Ahmed came to the ceremony of M'na's betrothal to the Sheik. *Scene 6*: The market-place, where Ma-bouba bewails what she has done to M'na. How the crowd attempts vengeance on Ahmed and how the Caid comes to the Hammam.

1925.38 THE CITY CHAP

A Comedy of Country Life with Musical Numbers, in Two Acts, 6 Scenes. Book by James Montgomery. Based on the play "The Fortune Hunter" by Winchell Smith. Music by Jerome Kern. Lyrics by Anne Caldwell. Book staged by R. H. Burnside. Dances staged by David Bennett. Costumes and settings designed by James Reynolds. Orchestra under the direction of Victor Baravalle. Orchestrations by Robert Russell Bennett. Produced by Charles Dillingham Opened 26 October 1925 at the Liberty Theatre and closed 26 December 1925 after 72 performances.

CAST (in order of appearance): *Robbins*: Fred Lennox. *Grace Bartlett*: IRENE DUNN [Dunne]. *Stephen Kellogg*: JOHN RUTHERFORD. *Nat Duncan*: RICHARD (Skeets) GALLAGHER. *Pete*: Robert O'Connor. *Wally*: EDDIE GIRARD. *Betty Graham*: PHYLLIS CLEVELAND. *Tracey Tanner*: Francis X. Donegan. *Angie*: MARY JANE. *Blinkey Lockwood*: Frank Doane. *Roland Barnett*: HANSFORD WILSON. *Sam Graham*: Charles Abbe. *George Spelvin*: George Raft. *Josie Lockwood*: INA WILLIAMS. *Miss Sperry*: Helyn Eby Rock. *Pearl*: Pearl Eaton. *Betty*: Betty Compton. *Specialty Dancers*: Marjorie Moss, Georges Fontana. GEORGE OLSEN AND HIS ORCHESTRA.

Ladies of the Ensemble: Beth Meakins, Blossom Vreeland, Constance Brown, Ona Hamilton, Danzie Goodell, Patricia Fitzpatrick, Bessie Mulligan, Gladys Lake, Frisco DeVere, Jerry Markham, Betty Winslow, Katherine Kohler, Nickie Pitell, Mildred Sinclair, Betty Block, Jane Lane, Peggy Dolan, Autumn Sims, Lucy Monroe, Katherine Burnside, Ursula Dale, Margaret Morris, Kathleen Errol, Beatrice Hughes, Joan Lindsay, Myrtle Cox, Rita Farrell, Mary Pierce, Jeanne Edwards, Hallie Manning, Bobbie Breslaw, Muriel Harrison, Edythe Flynn, Nell Kincaid.

Act 1, Scene 1: Stephen Kellogg's Apartment, New York City. *Scene 2*: On Train 106. *Scene 3*: Graham's Drug Store, Radford.

Act 2, Scene 1: Graham's Drug Store, Radford. *Scene 2*: Miss Bartlett's Private Car. *Scene 3*: The Ballroom in Miss Bartlett's House at Sarasota.

ACT 1[48]
"Like the Nymphs of Spring" (Chorus)
I. Dunn, Girls
"The Go-Getter" (Song)
J. Rutherford, I. Dunn, Girls
"Journey's End" (Song)
R. Gallagher
Finaletto
Ensemble
"Sympathetic Someone" (Duettino)
P. Cleveland, R. Gallagher
"The City Chap" (Quartette)
R. O'Connor, E. Girard, H. Wilson, I. Williams
"He Is the Type" (Song)
I. Williams, P. Cleveland, Girls
"Journey's End"[49] (Quartette)
R. Gallagher, P. Cleveland, I. Williams, M. Jane
"If You Are as Good as You Look" (Trio)
R. Gallagher, I. Williams, M. Jane
Finaletto
E. Girard, R. O'Connor, B. Compton, H. Wilson, Ensemble
ACT 2
"The Fountain of Youth" (Opening Chorus)
L. Monroe, H. E. Rock, M. Jane, D. Goodell, Mound City Blue Blowers
"A Pill a Day" (Duo)
H. Wilson, I. Williams

---

[47]No musical numbers listed in the program.

[48]The song order was revised during the run.
[49]Replaced after opening by:
"I'm Head and Heels in Love" (Song)
P. Cleveland, R. Gallagher
(*Music by* Leo Edwards. *Lyrics by* Irving Caesar)

"Walking Home with Josie" (Song)
  R. Gallagher, I. Williams, F. X. Donegan, M. Jane, C. Abbe, R. O'Connor, H. Wilson, P. Eaton, Boys, Girls
"Bubbles of Bliss"[50] (Chorus)
  Ensemble
  Dances: M. Jane, H. Wilson, G. Raft
"No One Knows"[51]
  P. Cleveland, J. Rutherford, R. Gallagher, I. Dunn
Dances
  M. Moss, G. Fontana, George Olsen and His Band
["I'm Knee Deep in Daisies;" "Journey's End"]
"When I Fell in Love"[52] (Quartet)
  J. Rutherford, P. Cleveland, R. Gallagher, I. Dunn
  Dance: H. Wilson
Finale
  Ensemble

1925.39 PRINCESS FLAVIA

An Operetta in Three Acts, 4 Scenes. Book and lyrics by Harry B. Smith. Based on Anthony Hope's novel and stage success 'The Prisoner of Zenda.' Music by Sigmund Romberg. Staged and produced [directed] by J. C. Huffman. Dances staged by Max Scheck. Settings by Watson Barratt. Costumes by Ernest R. Schrapps. Orchestra under the direction of Alfred Goodman. Orchestrations by Emil Gerstenberger. Entire production under the personal supervision of J. J. Shubert. Produced by the Messrs. Shubert. Opened 2 November 1925 at the Century Theatre, moved 1 February 1926 to the Sam S. Shubert Theatre, and closed 13 March 1926 after 152 performances.

CAST (in order of appearance): *Rudolf Rassendyl, and Rudolf, Crown Prince of Ruritania*: HARRY WELCHMAN. *General Sapt*: William Pringle. *Rupert of Hentzau*: JOHN CLARKE. *Franz Teppich*, Major Domo: WILLIAM DANFORTH. *Lieutenant Fritz von Tarlenheim*: James Marshall. *Gilbert Bertrand*, an artist: Alois Havrilla. *Michael, Duke of Strelsau*: Douglass R. Dumbrille. *Officers of Duke Michael's Bodyguard (9)*: *Detchard*: Joseph Toner. *De Gautet*: Earle Lee. *Bersonin*: Dudley Marwick. *Waldheim*: Phil Darby. *Sturm*: Edmund Ruffner. *Wurfner*: Joseph C. Spurin. *Lauba*: William Moore. *Nordstrom*: William H. Stamm. *Meller*: Donald Lee. *Princess Flavia*: EVELYN HERBERT. *Helga*: Margaret Breen. *Antoinette de Mauban*: Felicia Drenova. *Sophie, Frau Teppich*: Maude Odell. *Ladies in Waiting (11)*: *Charlotte*: Lucille Arnold. *Marta*: Miriam Lax. *Barbara*: Jessie Bradley. *Gella*: Sonia Veskova. *Teresa*: Ethel Louise Wright. *Minna*: Lilian Baker. *Marie*: Marjorie May. *Helene*: Helen Frederic. *Blanche*: Louise Fraer. *Rena*: Byrdeatta Evans. *Lamia*: Maria Laval. *Officers of General Sapt's Staff (3)*: *Lieutenant Blindenhoff*: George Harold. *Captain Strohman*: Herbert Goff. *Captain Fuerer*: Eugene Scudder. *Lackey*: Dudley Marwick. *Marshall Momsen*: Edmund Ruffner. *Senor Poncho*: Joseph C. Spurin. *Lord Topham*: Earle Lee. *Princess Edelstein*: Stella Shiel. *Innkeeper*: Dudley Marwick. *Josef*: Alois Havrilla. *Cardinal*: Donald Lee.

Ladies of the Ensemble: Edna Starck, Violet Gleason, Lola Taylor, Donna Dolores, Edna Coates, Ingrid Zanders, Jean Voltaire, Alys Schuman, Virginia Allen, Emily Wentz, Francine Marcella, Billie Perry, Octavia Bullard, Shirley Norton, Evelyn Grayson, Julia Strong, Xenia Lamakina, Edith Talbot, Doris Stewart, Florence O'Brien, Adele Savoye, Helen Gilligan, Florence Poyet, Clarice Olson, Helen Minto, Rosalie O'Reilly, Zena Mora, Jarvis Kerr, Ethel Aaron, Phyllis Marren, L. Sharpe, Irene Sharpe, Joan Kent, Lenora D'Arcy, Vivian Bell, Maida Marchand, Mary Barlow, Stella Shiel, Alva McGill, Zenaida Nicolina. *Gentlemen of the Ensemble*: J. Preston, Nat Broffman, J. M. Burger, Edwin F. Bennett, J. Becker, Jimmie Carroll, Charles H. Davis, Gerald Etchells, Lawrence Elwin, Paul Farber, Allen Gustaveson, Dan Harris, Henry Hanft, Verman Kimbrough, W. King, Peck Loyal, F. T. Miller, James Manning, Billy Murray, Charles McDonald, Jr., Joseph Moppert, William Provosky, Carl Park, Frank Pandoffi, Allen Reeves, Dan Richardson, William Russell, Robert Reitner, Bickley Reicher, Morris Siegel, Robert E. Smith, Lionel P. Spencer, Jack Spiegel, Theodore Schoof, Isaac Schrago, Deane Spaulding, Sam True, Roy Vitalis, John Schuyler Van Tuyle, Herman John Von Eck, Jerome H. Wallace, Jack Wilson, Francis J. Wroblewski, W. Elliott Zerkle, Warner Oakland, Richard Ellis, F. C. MacDan, John

Lieter, Philip Snyder, Frank York, John Maxwell, Larry Lawrence, G. Ribando, George Foxworth, Selig Norman, B. L. Williams, W. J. Lake, John Fredericks, J. Dillon.

Act 1: In the Forest of Zenda. Late afternoon.

Act 2: The Palace of Strelsau. The following day.

Act 3, Scene 1: The Armory of Zenda Castle. *Scene 2*: An Open Space in the Forest near Zenda.

ACT 1[53]
  Opening Ensemble
    A. Havrilla, L. Arnold, M. Lax, J. Bradley, Girls
  "Yes or No"
    J. Clarke, L. Arnold, M. Lax, Ensemble
  Chorus of Soldiers
    Men
  "On, Comrades"
    W. Pringle, J. Marshall, Men
  "Marionettes"
    M. Breen, J. Marshall
  "What Care I?"
    H. Welchman
  "Convent Bells Are Ringing"
    E. Herbert, Ladies
  "I Dare Not Love You"
    E. Herbert, H. Welchman
  Finale, Act 1
    E. Herbert, H. Welchman, W. Pringle, J. Marshall, Ensemble
  "By This Token"
    Ensemble

ACT 2
  "Dance With Me"
    J. Clarke, Ensemble
  "Twilight Voices"
    E. Herbert
  "Only One"
    M. Breen, J. Marshall, Men
  Coronation
    Ensemble
  Duet
    E. Herbert, H. Welchman
  Finale
    E. Herbert, H. Welchman, W. Pringle, J. Marshall, Ensemble

ACT 3
  "I Love Them All"
    J. Clarke, J. Toner, Men
  "In Ruritania"
    D. R. Dumbrille, Ensemble
  Kermesse Dance[54]
    Ensemble
  Duet (reprise)
    E. Herbert, H. Welchman
  Finale
    Ensemble

1925.40 FLORIDA GIRL

A Musical Comedy in Two Acts, 14 Scenes. Book and lyrics by Paul Porter, Benjamin Hapgood Burt and William A. Grew. Music by Milton Suskind [Edgar Fairchild]. Staged by Frederick Stanhope. Dances and ensembles by David Bennett. Art and technical direction by Bernard Lohmuller. Settings designed by Karl O. Amend, Will Pogany, Joseph Teichner. Costumes designed by John E. Stone. Orchestra under the direction of Donald Voorhees. Orchestrations by Will Vodery. Entire production under the personal direction of Earl Carroll. Produced by Earl Carroll. Opened 2

---

[50]Replaced after opening by: (Dance sequence remained)
  "Saratoga"
    H. Wilson, Ensemble
[51]Replaced after opening by:
  "Head Over Heels in Love" (reprise)
    P. Cleveland, R. Gallagher
[52]Replaced after opening by:
  "Head Over Heels in Love" (reprise/Trio)
    R. . Gallagher, I. Williams, H. Wilson

---

[53]Added for tour to Act 1, after "What Care I?":
  "Tell Me"
    E. Herbert
[54]Dropped for subsequent national tour.

November 1925 at the Lyric Theatre and closed 5 December after 40 performances.

<u>CAST</u> (in order of appearance): *Station Master*: Jack Fisher. *Train Man*: Thomas Herbert. *First Porter*: Kenneth Curry. *Second Porter*: Kenneth Haviland. *Horace Eagan*: JAMES S. BARRETT. *Mike*: PARKER FENNELLY. *Henry Elkins*: IRVING BEEBE. *Hop Morgan*, alias Edwards: William Foran. *Betty*: NELLIE BREEN. *Wilmer Bantam*: Jack Norton. *Madge Bantam*: ALLYN KING. *Sandy*: LESTER ALLEN. *Al Socrates, Jimmy Plato, Harry Aristotle*: THE RITZ BROTHERS. *Natalie*: Gertrude Lemmon. *Daphne*: VIVIENNE SEGAL. *Marcelle*: Jeannette Gilmore. *Wee Toy*: NINA PENN. *Marie*: HOPE VERNON. *Gregory*: CHESTER FREDERICKS. *Chocolate*: Arthur Bryson. *Vanilla*: Strappy Jones. *Ada*: Gracella. *Gio*: Theodor. *Satan*: Anally Pupp.

Show Girls: Miriam Avondale, Florence Allen, Barbara Carrington, Elvonne Hill, Dolla Harkins, Frances Joyce, Naan Lane, Nellie McCarthy, Grace Norman, Virginia Ray, Eleanor Rainke, Otis Schaefer. *Dancers*: Polly Blake, Emily Burton, Betty Campbell, Madeline Calkins, Margaret Callan, Geraldine Dryden, Hannah Dunner, Bessie DeBraw, Val DeMar, Marie Ellen, Renee Johnstone, Lowen Kildare, Kitty Leckie, Carlotta Marino, Mildred Marthain, Norrine Nash, Cheri Pelham, Lucille Pryor, Alice Raisen, Virginia Van, Justine Welsh, May Welsh, Claire White, Wren Wilson.

The action takes place in Florida amid the tropical beauty of Coral Gables, Miami Riviera.

Act 1, Scene 1: Railroad Station. *Scene 2*: A corridor. *Scene 3*: Mrs. Bantam's Villa. Afternoon. *Scene 4*: DeSota Plaza. *Scene 5*: The Boudoir. *Scene 6*: Outside again. *Scene 7*: Mrs. Bantam's Villa. Evening.

Act 2, Scene 1: The Living Room. *Scene 2*: The way upstairs. *Scene 3*: Wee Toy's Bedroom .*Scene 4*: The way downstairs. *Scene 5*: The Cellar. *Scene 6*: Outside the Casino. *Scene 7*: The Venetian Casino.

ACT 1
 "Travel, Travel, Travel"
  Ensemble
 Dance of the Porters
  A. Bryson, S. Jones
 "Oranges"
  L. Allen, Ensemble
 "The Collegians"
  Ritz Brothers
 "Lady of My Heart"
  I. Beebe, J. Gilmore, Ensemble
 "Skipper"
  C. Fredericks, N. Penn, Ensemble
 "Smile On"
  L. Allen, N. Breen
 "Into Society"·
  Ritz Brothers
 "Daphne"
  V. Segal, I. Beebe
 "Beautiful Sea"
  N. Breen, N. Penn, C. Fredericks
 "Oh You!"
  V. Segal, Ensemble
 Finaletto
  Entire Company

ACT 2
 Opening Reprise
  Principals and Ensemble
 "Trouble"
  J. Norton, Ensemble
 "Chinky China Charleston"
  N. Penn, Ritz Brothers
 "As a Troubador"
  H. Vernon
 Dance
  C. Fredericks
 "Venetian Skies"
  V. Segal
 Valse Ballet
  G. Lemmon
 Adagio
  Gracella and Theodor
 Finale
  Entire Company

1925.41 NAUGHTY CINDERELLA

A Romantic Song-Farce with Music in Three Acts. Play by Avery Hopwood adapted from the French (play 'Pouche') of René Peter and Henri Falk. Staged by W. H. Gilmore. Gowns and settings by Paul Poiret. Produced by Charles Frohman in association with E. Ray Goetz. Opened 9 November 1925 at the Lyceum Theatre and closed 20 February after 121 performances.

<u>CAST</u> (in order of appearance): *Gerald Gray*: HENRY KENDALL. *Jacques*: Marcel Rousseau. *Claire Fenton*: EVELYN GOSNELL. *Bunny West*: John Deverell. *Thomas Fenton*: ORLANDO DALY. *Germaine Leverrier*: IRENE BORDONI. *Chouchou Rouselle*: Adele Windsor. *K. O. Bill Smith*: Nat Pendleton. *An Italian Policeman*: Alfred Ilma.

Act 1: Gerald Gray's Apartment in Paris.

Act 2: An Apartment in a Hotel at the Lido, Venice. Two weeks later.

Act 3: The same. One hour later.

MUSICAL NUMBERS[55]
 "(Do I Love You When There's) Nothing But 'Yes' in My Eyes"
  I. Bordoni
  (*Music by* H. Christiné and E. Ray Goetz. *Lyrics by* E. Ray Goetz.)
 "J'ai deux amants" (from *L'AMOUR MASQUÉ*)
  I. Bordoni
  (*Music by* André Messager. *Lyrics by* Sacha Guitry.)
 "That Means Nothing to Me"
  I. Bordoni
  (*Music and Lyrics by* A. L. Keith, Lee Sterling.)
 "Mia Luna"
  I. Bordoni
  (*Music by* Giacomo Puccini. *Lyrics by* E. Ray Goetz.)

1925.42 THE CHARLOT REVUE OF 1926

A Musical Revue in Two Acts, 23 Scenes. Assembled by Andre Charlot. Dances and ensembles arranged by Jack Buchanan. Costumes designed by G. K. Benda. Orchestra director, Gene Salzer. Produced by Arch Selwyn. Opened 10 November 1925 at the Selwyn Theatre and closed 6 March 1926 after 138 performances.

<u>CAST</u>: BEATRICE LILLIE, JACK BUCHANAN, GERTRUDE LAWRENCE, HERBERT MUNDIN, DOUGLAS FURBER, BILLY STOCKFELD, FENNER IRVING, JILL WILLIAMS, ERIC FAWCETT, PHYLLIS AUSTEN, HUGH SINCLAIR, GEORGE PUGHE.

Showgirls: Betty Barbour, Violet Beck, Mollie Crafter, Velma Deane, Lola Mende, Pansy Wilde. *Chorus*: Effie Atherton, Gladys Barclay, Yvonne Bose, Vera Braund, Constance Carpenter, Wyn Clare, Billey Edis, Violet Hanbury, Aida Holland, Marianne Karelina, Ida Parkinson, Rhoda Sewell, Cavenda Stanislaw, Vivienne Vanetta, Hazel Wynne, Eve Wynne.

ACT 1[56]
Scene 1
 "How D'You Do?"
  F. Irving, B. Stockfield, E. Fawcett, J. Williams, H. Sinclair, H. Mundin, G. Lawrence, B. Lillie, J. Buchanan, Show Girls
  (*Music by* Philip Braham. *Lyrics by* Eric Blore and Dion Titheradge.)

---

[55]Not necessarily in performance order.
[56]Added after opening in third week of run to Act 1:
 Off the Lines (*by* Ronald Jeans)
  The Wife: G. Lawrence. *The Husband*: J. Buchanan.
Added in last week of December:
 All the World's a Stage (*by* Ronald Jeans)
  Dick: D. Furber. *Alfred*, his man-servant: G. Pughe. *Terry Kemble*, an actor: J. Buchanan. *Mrs. Cartwright*: P. Austen. *Phyllis cartwright*: B. Stockfield.
 Rough Stuff
  G. Lawrence, B. Lillie
 Inaudibility
Added for subsequent national tour to Act 1:
 Author, Actor and Victim (*by* Ronald Jeans)
  Author: D. Furber. *Actor*: H. Sinclair. *Victim*: J. Buchanan.
 "Snoops (the Lawyer)"
  B. Lillie
  (*Music by* Harry Ruby. *Lyrics by* Bert Kalmar.)

Scene 2
"Let's All Go Raving Mad"
G. Lawrence, Chorus
(*Music by* Philip Braham. *Lyrics by* Hugh E. Wright.)

Scene 3
Buying a Hat
(*by* Douglas Furber)
Jack: J. Buchanan. *John*: H. Mundin. *An Assistant*: H. Sinclair. *A Mannequin*: E. Fawcett. *A Lady*: J. Williams.

Scene 4
"Mouse! Mouse!"
B. Lillie
(*Music by* Muriel Lillie. *Lyrics by* Hilda Brighton.)

Scene 5
"The Mender of Broken Dreams"[57]
G. Lawrence, H. Mundin, Chorus
(*Music and Lyrics by* John W. Bratton.)

Scene 6
"The Fox Has Left His Lair"
J. Buchanan, Company
(*Music by* Peggy Connor. *Lyrics by* Douglas Furber.)

Scene 7
"Fallen Babies" (Baby Blues)
(*Music by* Ivor Novello. *Lyrics by* Ronald Jeans.)
First Nurse: P. Austen. *Second Nurse*: J. Williams. *Baby Boy*: B. Lillie. *Baby Girl*: G. Lawrence.

Scene 8
"Gigolette" (from *THE THREE GRACES*, London)
J. Buchanan
(*Music by* Franz Lehár. *Lyrics by* Irving Caesar and Dion Titheradge.)

Scene 9
"Susannah's Squeaking Shoes"
B. Lillie, Chorus
(*Music by* Muriel Lillie. *Lyrics by* Arthur Weigall.)

Scene 10
"Carrie!" (from *LONDON CALLING*, London)
G. Lawrence
(*Music and Lyrics by* Noël Coward.)

Scene 11
Fate
(*An Inevitable Drama by* Ronald Jeans.)
Aubrey: J. Buchanan. *Fabia*: G. Lawrence. *Claude Spender*, her lover: H. Mundin. *Selvidge*, a manservant: G. Pughe.

Scene 12
After Dinner Music:
[Beatrice Lillie as] Miss Fancy Robinson in selections from her repertoire:
"A Little Slut of Six"
Miss Robinson sings the works of Mr. Noël Coward.
At the Piano: Hugh Sinclair.

Scene 13
Wine—A Romantic Reverie
(*by* Douglas Furber)
J. Buchanan, Full Company

ACT 2[58]
Scene 1
"Take Them All Away"
J. Buchanan, Chorus

---

[57]Dropped after opening.
[58]Added after opening in third week of run to Act 2:
"March With Me"
B. Lillie, Chorus
(*Music by* Ivor Novello. *Lyrics by* Douglas Furber.)
The Tragedy of Jones (by Maurice Lane Norcott)
G. Lawrence
Added in last week of December:
Early Mourning (*by* Noël Coward)
Mistress: G. Lawrence. *Maid*: Effie Atherton.
"I Don't Know"
G. Lawrence
(*Music by* Philip Braham. *Lyrics by* Ronald Jeans.)

(*Music and Lyrics by* Jack Strachey.)

Scene 2
"Follow Mister Cook"[59]
B. Lillie, H. Mundin
(*Music by* Philip Braham. *Lyrics by* Douglas Furber.)

Scene 3
A Cup of Coffee
(*by* Ronald Jeans)
"A Cup of Coffee, a Sandwich and You"
J. Buchanan, G. Lawrence
(*Music by* Joseph Meyer. *Lyrics by* Al Dubin, Billy Rose, Irving Caesar.)

Scene 4
References
(*by* Harold Simpson and Morris Harvey)
The Maid: B. Lillie. *The Mistress*: P. Austen. *The Visitor*: B. Stockfield.

Scene 5
"Russian Blues"
G. Lawrence, Chorus
(*Music and Lyrics by* Noël Coward.)

Scene 6
Methods of Barberism
(*by* Arthur Wimperis)
The Barber: H. Mundin. *Mr. G*: E. Fawcett. *Mr. B*: J. Buchanan. *The Bolshie*: G. Pughe.

Scene 7
"Sealed Feet" (Burlesque on 'Les Sylphides')
(*Devised and Staged by* Quentin Tod. *Music by* Charles Prentice.)
Mesdames Bitova, Hangova, Halfseezova, Riteova, Cumova, Pastova, Pullova, Shottova, Turnova, Leanova, Beenova, Fallova, Wellova, Tideova, Thrownova, *and Madame Wanda Allova*: B. Lillie. *Supported by Monsieur Toldoff*: H. Wynne.

Scene 8
"Poor Little Rich Girl" (from *ON WITH THE DANCE*, London, by courtesy of Charles B. Cochran)
(*Music and Lyrics by* Noël Coward.)
Daisy: G. Lawrence. *Policeman*: G. Pughe. *George*: H. Sinclair. *Anne*: C. Carpenter.

Scene 9
"Oxford Bags"
J. Buchanan
(*Music by* Philip Braham. *Lyrics by* Arthur Wimperis.)

Scene 10
Finale
(Company)

MAYFLOWERS

1925.43

A Play with Music (Musical Comedy) in Two Acts, a Prologue and 4 Scenes[60]. Book and lyrics by Clifford Grey. (Based on the play 'Not So Long Ago' by Arthur Richman.) Music by Edward Künneke. Additional music by Frank E. Tours, (J. Fred Coots). Staged by William J. Wilson and Joseph Santley. Dances by Earl Lindsay. Settings by Watson Barratt. Costumes designed by Marian Frazee and Harriet Liebman. Orchestra under the direction of J. Frank Cork. Production under the personal supervision of J. J. Shubert. Produced by the Messrs. Shubert. Opened 24 November 1925 at the Forrest Theatre and closed 30 January 1926 after 81 performances.

CAST (in order of appearance): *A Gypsy*: WILLIAM O'NEAL. *His Daughter*: Josephine Duval. *Jane*: Nancy Carroll. *Alice*: Francetta Malloy. *Mary*: Virginia Lloyd. *Tom*: George C. Lehrain. *Harry*: Jules Cross. *Elsie Dover*: IVY SAWYER. *Sam*

Added for subsequent national tour to Act 2:
"There Are Times"
B. Lillie, Chorus
(*by* Philip Braham.)
Peace and Quiet (*by* Ronald Jeans)
The Husband: J. Buchanan. *The Wife*: J. Williams. *The Doctor*: D. Furber. *The Maid*: E. Atherton. *The Linoleum Man*: G. Pughe.
"There's Life in the Old Girl Yet" (from *CHARLOT REVUE OF 1924*)
B. Lillie
(*Music and Lyrics by* Noël Coward.)
[59]Dropped after opening.
[60]Title changed to MAY FLOWERS in December 1925 for balance of New York run and subsequent tour.

Robinson: ROBERT WOOLSEY. *Mr. Dover*: David Higgins. *Mrs. Ballard*: Ethel Morrison. *Ursula*: GAILE BEVERLY. *Miss Kaye*: Hazel Beamer. *Miss Watkins*: Charlotte Ayres. *Maid*: Lida Mae. *Cicero*: Norman Sweetser. *Rosamund Gill*: Nydia d'Arnell. *Billy Ballard*: JOSEPH SANTLEY. *Rupert Hancock*: William Valentine. *Sylvia*: Josephine Duval.

Personnel of the Chorus: Grace Candee, Kayo Tortoni, Peaches Tortoni, Sybil Stokes, Madeline Montelin, Marion Byrnes, Marie Jensen, Charlotte Fitzgibbons, Margaret Byrnes, Christine Ecklund, Theodora Loper, Betty Pascu, Sally Bronis, Ronnie Madison, Jean Duval, Kathryn Browne, Thelma Hoefle, Elaine Sims, June Leslie. Anthony King, Harry Pederson, George C. Deerking, George Lehrain, Jules Cross, Fred Burke, Will Gould, Nickolis Indiveri, Malcolm Duffield.

The action takes place in New York City, not so long ago.

Prologue: The Dover Home.

Act 1: The Ballard Home.

Act 2, Scene 1: The Park Gardens. Seven days later. *Scene 2*: The Dover Home. *Scene 3*: The Ballard Home. Seven days later.

PROLOGUE
  "Whoa, Emma!"
    J. Duval, V. Lloyd, F. Molloy, N. Carroll
  "(The) Road of Dreams"
    I. Sawyer, W. O'Neal
    (*Music by* J. Fred Coots, Maurice Rubens, Pat Thayer. *Lyrics by* Donovan Parsons, Clifford Grey.)
ACT 1
  "How Do You Do? How Do You Do?"
    Ensemble
  "The Grecian Bend"
    I. Sawyer, E. Morrison, N. d'Arnell, G. Beverly
  "Play Me a New Tune"
    W. Valentine, G. Beverly
    (*Music by* J. Fred Coots, Maurice Rubens.)
  "Foolish Wives"
    I. Sawyer, R. Woolsey
  "Take a Little Walk"
    N. d'Arnell, G. Beverly, J. Santley, W. Valentine
    (*Music by* J. Fred Coots, Maurice Rubens.)
  "Seven Days"
    I. Sawyer, J. Santley
  Finale
    I. Sawyer, J. Santley, Company
ACT 2
Scene 1
  Opening
    H. Beamer, C. Ayres, Ensemble
  "The Lancers"
    N. d'Arnell, G. Beverly, Morrison, R. Woolsey, W. Valentine
  "Oh! Sam"
    I. Sawyer, R. Woolsey, J. Duval, V. Lloyd, F. Molly, N. Carroll
    (*Music by* J. Fred Coots, Maurice Rubens.)
  "Mayflower, I Love You"
    I. Sawyer, J. Santley
    (*Music by* J. Fred Coots, Maurice Rubens, Pat Thayer.)
  The Regiment Loves the Girls"
    W. Valentine, C. Ayres, H. Beamer
  Finale
Scene 2
  "Good Night Ladies"
    Boys
  "Woman"
    J. Santley, R. Woolsey
  Reprise
    I. Sawyer, W. O'Neal
Scene 3
  "The Wedding Rehearsal"
    N. d'Arnell, G. Beverly, Girls
  "Put Your Troubles in a Candy Box"
    J. Santley, J. Duval, N. Carroll, F. Molloy, H. Beamer, C. Ayres, V. Lloyd
    (*Music by* J. Fred Coots.)
  "Down on a Country Farm"
    R. Woolsey

Finale
  I. Sawyer, J. Santley, Company

1925.44

OH! OH! NURSE!

A Musical Comedy in Two Acts. Book by George E. Stoddard. Music by (Alma) Sanders. Lyrics by (Monte) Carlo. Staged by Walter Brooks. Settings designed by Walter Schaffner. Orchestra under the direction of Hilding Anderson. Produced by Clark Ross. Opened 7 December 1925 at the Cosmopolitan Theatre and closed 2 January 1926 after 32 performances[61].

CAST (in order of appearance): *Jimmy Greet* the Office Assistant: Roy Sedley. *Marie, the Flapper Nurse*: Gladys Miller. *Otto Lift, the Office Mover*: Vincent Langan. *Dr. Sidney Killmore, the Physician*: JOHN PRICE JONES. *Marion Gay, the Head Nurse*: REBEKAH CAUBLE. *Monsieur Louis d'Bracz, the Great Lover*: Arthur Lipson. *Will Plant, the Town Undertaker*: Bill Adams. *James Fitzpatrick, the lawyer*: Leslie King. *I. Dye, the Victim*: DON BARCLAY. *Lily White, the Buter and Egg Babe*: GERTRUDE VANDERBILT. *Mrs. Rose d'Bracz, the Ex-wife*: MAY BOLEY. *Peggy, the Assistant Nurse*: Georgia Ingram. The Oh! Oh! Nurse Quartette.

Teachers, Nurses, Guests: Beryl Golden, Kitty Bird, Lucy Cawthorn, Bernetice Hampshire, Jean Watson, Ivanello Ladd, Alice McElroy, Helen Paige, Mercede Mordant, Winifred Bird, Gertrude Hartwick, Georgie Wilson, Bobby Schubert, Eve Wilson, Evelyn Van, Eva Barborik.

Act 1: Reception Room in Dr. Killmore's Sanitarium in the Catskill Mountains.

Act 2: Canary Lane, adjoining the Sanitarium. Three weeks later.

ACT 1
  Opening
  Descriptive
    R. Sedley
  "Show a Little Pep"
    R. Sedley, Nurses, Teachers
  "Love Will Keep Us Young" (Song)
    G. Miller, R. Sedley, Girls
  "You May Have Planted Many a Lily" (Duet)
    G. Vanderbilt, B. Adams
  "Way Out in Rainbowland" (Song)
    R. Cauble, J. P. Jones, Girls
  "Cleopatra" (Song)
    M. Boley, Girls
    Dance Oriental: G. Ingram
    Travesty: M. Boley, D. Barclay, B. Adams
  "Who Bites the Holes in Schweitzer Cheese?" (Trio)
    D. Barclay, B. Adams, A. Lipson
  "Keep a Kiss for Me" (Duet)
    G. Miller, R. Sedley
  "Pierre" (Song)
    A. Lipson, G. Vanderbilt, G. Ingram
  "Good Night, My Lady Love" (Finale Act 1)
    J. P. Jones, R. Cauble, Girls
ACT 2
  "I'll Give the World to You" (Opening—Waltz)
    J. P. Jones, Girls
  "No Hearts for Sale" (Song)
    G. Miller, R. Sedley
  "Is It Any Wonder?" (Song)
    R. Cauble, Girls
  "Butter and Egg Baby" (Song)
    G. Vanderbilt
  "Newlywed Express" (Song)
    J. P. Jones, R. Cauble, Girls
  "Under My Umbrella" (Song)
    G. Vanderbilt, B. Adams, Girls
  "No, I Won't" (Duet)
    D. Barclay, M. Boley
  Operatic Burlesque
    D. Barclay, M. Boley
  "Shooting Stars" (Song)
    R. Sedley, G. Miller, Girls

---

[61]Costumes uncredited.

"Rainbowland" (reprise/finale)
  Entire Company

1925.45   THE COCOANUTS

A Musical Comedy in Two Acts, 8 Scenes. Book by George S. Kaufman, [Morrie Ryskind]. Music and lyrics by Irving Berlin. Book directed by Oscar Eagle. Musical numbers staged by Sammy Lee. Settings designed by Woodman Thompson. Costumes designed by Charles LeMaire. Orchestra under the direction of Frank Tours. Orchestrations by Frank Tours, Maurice dePackh, Stephen Jones, Louis Katzman. Produced by Sam H. Harris. Opened 8 December 1925 at the Lyric Theatre and closed 7 August 1926 after 276 performances.

CAST (in order of appearance): *Jamison:* ZEPPO MARX. *Eddie:* Georgie Hale. *Mrs. Potter:* MARGARET DUMONT. *Harvey Yates:* HENRY WHITTEMORE. *Penelope Martyn:* JANET VELIE. *Polly Potter:* MABEL WITHEE. *Robert Adams:* JACK BARKER. *Henry W. Schlemmer:* GROUCHO MARX. *Willie the Wop:* CHICO MARX. *Silent Sam:* HARPO MARX. *Hennessy,* a Detective: BASIL RUYSDAEL. *Frances Williams:* FRANCES WILLIAMS. *Specialties:* The DeMarcos (Antonio, Nina), Breen Brothers, Bernice Speers, The De Marco Orchestra.

Ensemble: Dancing Girls: Grace Carroll, Mildred Kelly, Gladys Pender, Evelyn Kermin, Nesha Medwin, Maxine Marshall, Virginia McCune, Jessie Payne, Beatrice Coniff, Maude Lydiate, Sybil Stuart, Frances Mallory, Eleanor Meeker, Kitty Clay, Liane Mamet, Xela Edwards. *The Cocoanut Grove Girls:* Peggy Jones, Hazel Patterson, Billie Davis, Nancy Phillips, Roberta Haines, Helen Martin. *The Cocoanut Beach Octet:* Elsie Pedrick, Florence Regan, Hazel Stille, Madeline Janis, Maxine Robinson, Rella Harrison, Bonnie Murray, Billie Williams, Marjorie Murray, Adele McHatton, Beryle Williams. *Gentlemen:* Andre LaPue, Jerry White, Charles Knowlton, Ted Daniels, Mat Matus, Lionel Maclyn, Juan Marlow, Billy DeWolfe, Jr., Philip Mann, Eugene Day, Jerome Robertson, Lehman Byck.

Act 1, Scene 1: Lobby of 'The Cocoanuts,' Cocoanut Beach, Florida. *Scene 2:* Before the Palms. *Scene 3:* Two rooms in the Hotel. *Scene 4:* Before the Palms. *Scene 5:* Cocoanut Manor.

Act 2, Scene 1: The Lounge of the Hotel. *Scene 2:* Before the Palms. *Scene 3:* The Patio.

ACT 1

  Opening:
  "The Guests"
    Z. Marx, Cocoanut Grove Girls, Boys
  "The Bellhops"
    G. Hale, Sixteen Stepping Bell-hops
  "Family Reputation"[62]
    M. Withee, Cocoanut Grove Beauties
  "Lucky Boy"
    J. Barker, Boys
  "Why Am I a Hit with the Ladies?"[63]
    G. Marx, Girls
  "A Little Bungalow"[64]
    J. Barker, M. Withee, Cocoanut Grove Girls, Boys
  "Florida By the Sea"
    Z. Marx, Cocoanut Grove Girls, Boys
  "Monkey Doodle Doo"
    F. Williams, Breen Brothers, Ensemble
  Finale
    Entire Company

ACT 2

  Opening: Tea Dance
    Eight Tea Girls

---

[62]In June 1926, the musical score was substantially revised; this song was replaced by:
  "Why Do You Want to Know Why?"
    J. Barker, P. Cleveland, Ensemble
[63]In June 1926, the musical score was substantially revised; this song was replaced by:
  "Gentlemen Prefer Blondes"
    G. Marx, Girls
[64]In June 1926, the musical score was substantially revised; this song was replaced by:
  "Ting-a-Ling"
    J. Barker, P. Cleveland, Cocoanut Grove Girls, Boys

"Five O'Clock Tea"
  Cocoanut Grove Ensemble
  Specialty Dance: A. DeMarco, N. DeMarco
"They're Blaming the Charleston"[65]
  F. Williams, G. Hale, A. DeMarco, N. DeMarco, Charleston Girls
"We Should Care"[66]
  J. Barker, M. Withee, G. Hale, B. Speers, Ensemble
"Minstrel Days"
  J. Velie, Company
  Specialty: DeMarco Orchestra, A. DeMarco, N. DeMarco
"Tango Melody"
  J. Velie
  Specialty Dance: A. DeMarco, N. DeMarco
"The Tale of a Shirt"[67]
  B. Ruysdael, Company
Piano Specialty
  C. Marx
  Harp Specialty: H. Marx
Finale
  Entire Company

1925.46   LA PÉRICHOLE

A Revival of the Opéra-bouffe in Three Acts, 4 Scenes[68]. Performed by the Moscow Art Theater Musical Studio in Russian. Music by Jacques Offenbach. Russian text by Vladmir Nemirovitch Dantchenko and Mikhail Galperin. (French libretto by Ludovic Halévy and Henri Meilhac, based on 'La Carosse du Saint-Sacrement' by Prosper Mérimée.) Produced by F. Ray Comstock and Morris Gest. Opened 21 December 1925 at Jolson's Theatre and closed 9 January 1926 after 12 performances in repertory.

CAST: *La Périchole,* a Street Singer: OLGA BAKLANOVA. *Piquillo,* a Street Singer: IVAN YAGODKIN, Boris Belostotsky (alt.). *Don Andreas,* Count of Ribiera: VLADIMIR LOSSKY. *Don Miguel, Count Panatellas:* Semyon Rakhmanoff. *Don Pedro* of Hinojosa: Leonid Baratoff. *Kuzya:* Nina Polosova. *Ottala:* Nadiezhda Kemarskaya. *Suma:* Anna Sablukova. *Terrapot:* Sergei Obraztsoff. *The Duke of Acapulco:* Dmitry Kamernitsky. *Pablo:* Mikhail Skoboloff. *Carlos:* Nikolai Kursky.

Grandess and Ladies of the Court, Peruvians, Indians, Soldiers, Guards, Street Comedians, etc.: Members of the Moscow Art Theater Musical Studio .

1925.47   THE GREENWICH VILLAGE FOLLIES (1925)

America's Greatest (Musical) Revue in Two Acts, a Prologue and 27 Scenes[69]. Music by Harold Levey. Lyrics by Owen Murphy. Conceived and staged by Hassard Short. Dances and ensembles arranged by Larry Ceballos. Ballets by Alexander Gabrilov. Costumes designed by Charles LeMaire, Mark Mooring. Settings designed by Clark Robinson. Orchestra under the direction of Alfred Newman. Produced by The Bohemians, Inc. (A. L. Jones, Morris Green, Managing directors) (Messrs. Shubert). Opened 24 December 1925 at Chanin's 46th Street Theatre, closed 13 March 1926 after 92 performances; New Spring Edition (see separate entry immediately following) opened 15 March 1926 at the Sam S. Shubert Theatre, and closed 29 May 1926 after 88 performances. Total for both editions: 180 performances.

---

[65]In June 1926, the musical score was substantially revised; this song was replaced by:
  "Everyone In the World Is Doing the Charleston"
    The Brox Sisters (Kathlyn, Dagmar, Lorraine), Girls
[66]In June 1926, the musical score was substantially revised; this song was replaced by:
  "Why Do You Want to Know Why?" (reprise)
    J. Barker, P. Cleveland, The Brox Sisters, Ensemble
[67]A burlesque on The Toreador Song from Bizet's opera CARMEN; also known as "I Lost My Shirt."
[68]Original Two Act version performed in New York in French 4 January 1869 at Pike's Opera House for 44 performances; Three Act version in English 29 April 1895 at Abbey's Theatre for 24 performances. For Synopsis of Scenes and Musical Numbers, see original 1895 production. Settings and costumes uncredited.
[69]The seventh in the annual series of revues which began in 1919.

CAST: FRANK McINTYRE, FLORENCE MOORE, TOM HOWARD, IRENE DELROY, JANE GREEN, SAM HEARN, RENIE RIANO, JOE LYONS, WILLIAM LADD, IDA SYLVANIA, KENDALL CAPPS, HELENA MARSH, ROYAL HALEE, JEAN MYRIO, NATACHA NATTOVA, GAYLE MAYS, WARREN CROSBY, WILLIAM WALSH, DELLA VANNA, STERLING BARNEY, THE HEMSTREET SINGERS (Natalie Malonam, Olive Sibley, Letitia Bonta, Marion Adam), Grace Elbew, Dorothy Hathaway, Winifred Soldan, Marcella Donovan.

Ladies of the Ensemble: Show Girls: Elaine Fields, Teddy Gill, Irma Schubert, Fraun Koski, Olga Brounoff, Catherine Janeway, Ardath Leonhart, Gladys Glad, Lillian Morehouse. *Mediums:* Margaret Kolloch, Helen Shepard, Betty McLaughlin, Victoria Webster, Nina Lewis, Rita Dunne, Marguerite Dunne, Alice Harris, Emrita Monsch, Vivian Wyndham, Edith Sheperd, Gretchen Reinhart, Kitty Banks, Elaine Arden, Caroline Gerkin, Marjorie Himes, Mary Williams, Jean Williams, Betty Collet, Maria Hammans.

PROLOGUE (*by* Norman Mitchell and Russell Medcraft)

On the Road to the Greenwich Village Fair—1826
The Farmer: S. Hearn. *The Daughter*: I. Delroy.

The Greenwich Village Green
The Boy: W. Ladd. *The Girl*: I. Delroy. *The Lord Mayor*: R. Halee. *First Judge*: G. Mays. *Second Judge*: W. Crosby. *Third Judge*: W. Walsh.

The Latest Styles
Paris: B. McLaughlin. *Madrid*: E. Arden. *Stockholm*: E. Monsch. *Dublin*: N. Lewis. *St. Petersburg*: A. Harris. *Vienna*: V. Wyndham. *Constantinople*: H. Shepard. *New York*: G. Glad.

Four Weeks Before the Opening of the Greenwich Village Follies —1926
Irene Delroy: I. Delroy. *William Ladd*: W. Ladd. *The Managers*: W. Walsh, G. Mays, S. Barney.

The Inns
The Bird of Paradise: I. Schubert. *Red Pheasant*: T. Gill. *Lonely Deer*: L. Morehouse. *Green Monkey*: E. Fields. *Blue Cat*: O. Brounoff. *White Fox*: F. Koski. *Blind Tiger*: A. Leonhart. *Pink Bear*: C. Janeway.

ACT 1

Scene 1

Up in Mary's Room (*by* Bert Kalmar and Harry Ruby)
Mary: I. Delroy. *Burglar*: J. Lyons. *First Policeman*: F. McIntyre. *Second Policeman*: T. Howard.

Scene 2

"Whistle Away Your Blues"
J. Green
(*Music by* Richard Myers. *Lyrics by* Leo Robin.)
Danced by G. McCormack, B. Calvin.

Scene 3

Moving In
(*by* Norma Mitchell and Lewis Waller)
Mary: I. Delroy. *Fanny*: R. Riano. *Plumber*: F. McIntyre. *Paper Hanger*: W. Crosby. *Carpet Man*: T. Howard. *Curtain Man*: S. Hearn. *Electrician*: J. Lyons. *Iceman*: S. Barney.

Scene 4

"I Have You"
W. Ladd, I. Delroy

Scene 5

The Spy
(*by* Tom Howard and A. Dorian Otvos)
The Colonel: J. Lyons. *The Captain*: W. Crosby. *An Orderly*: W. Walsh. *A Soldier*: S. Barney. *The Spy*: T. Howard.

Scene 6

"The Lady of the Snow"
I. Sylvania, Hemstreet Singers
The White Chrysanthemum: R. R. Matlock. *Jack Frost*: G. McCormack. *The Snow Balls*: D. Hathaway, W. Soldan, M. Donovan, E. Shepard. *The Lady of the Snow*: D. Vanna. *Snow Ladies*: E. Fields, F. Koski, T. Gill, I. Schubert, L. Morehouse, A. Leonhart.

Scene 7

Before the Curtains
K. Capps

Scene 8

Then, Now and Sometime
(*by* Joseph E. Mitchell)
The Announcer: R. Halee.
"Then": The Girl: F. Moore. *The Lover*: J. Lyons.
"Now": The Girl: F. Moore. *The Lover*: T. Howard.
"Sometime": The Girl: F. Moore. *The Lover*: F. McIntyre.

Scene 9

"White Cargo" (Burlesque on play of the same name)
R. Halee, the Hemstreet Singers
Slave Girl: N. Nattova. *The Arab*: J. Myrie.

Scene 10

"The Window Cleaners"
F. McIntyre, S. Hearn
(*Music by* Harry Ruby. *Lyrics by* Bert Kalmar.)

Scene 11

"Go South"
J. Green, G. Elhew, D. Hathaway, W. Soldan, M. Donovan
(*Music by* Richard Myers. *Lyrics by* Harry Ruskin.)
Dance (A)
I. Delroy
Dance (B)
W. Ladd, Girls

Scene 12

"The Life of the Party"
R. Riano
(*Music by* Richard Myers. *Lyrics by* Harry Ruskin.)

Scene 13

Go Ahead, Sing
Violinist: S. Hearn. *Stage Door Man*: J. Lyons. *The Singer*: T. Howard.

Scene 14

"The Curse of Cinderella"
H. Marsh, I. Sylvania, The Hemstreet Singers, Ensemble

A. *Scene*: The Kitchen.
Cinderella: I. Delroy. *Stepsister*: F. Moore. *Stepsister*: R. Riano. *Stepmother*: F. McIntyre. *Messenger*: R. Halee. *Fairy Godmother*: D. Vanna.

B. *Scene*: The Road to the Palace.

C. *Scene*: The Palace Ballroom.
The Prince Charming: W. Ladd. *Lady Gavotte*: N. Nattova. *Lord Gavotte*: J. Myrie. *Sally*: M. Donovan. *Irene*: W. Soldan. *Mary*: D. Hathaway. *Peg o' My Heart*: G. Elhew. *Ladies and Gentlemen of the Court*: Ensemble.

ACT 2[70]

Scene 1

"Just a Card"
I. Sylvania, Hemstreet Singers
First Card: Easter Greetings.
The Lady: D. Vanna. *The Flower Girl*: N. Lewis. *The Easter Lily*: E. Fields.
Second Card: A Happy Birthday.
Little Lord Fauntleroy: E. Shepard. *His Grandma*: O. Brounoff. *The Surprise*: D. Hathaway.
Third Card: My Valentine.
First Suitor: M. Donovan. *Second Suitor*: W. Soldan. *The Sweetheart*: G. Elbew.
Fourth Card: Merry Christmas.
The Match Girl: I. Delroy. *The Newsboy*: W. Ladd. *The Snow Man*: K. Capps.

Scene 2

Before the Curtains
F. Moore

Scene 3

Furnished Rooms
(*by* Joseph Graham)
The Landlord: F. McIntyre. *The Landlord's Wife*: F. Koski. *The Landlord's Daughter*: I. Delroy. *The First Suspect*: R. Riano. *The Second Suspect*: J. Green. *The Third Suspect*: J. Lyons. *The Unsuspected*: S. Hearn, O. Brunoff.

Scene 4

"The Dancing Doctor"
I. Delroy, W. Ladd

Scene 5

The Closet Scene, 1926
(*by* Norma Mitchell and Russell Medcraft)
Hamlet: F. McIntyre. *Polonius*: S. Hearn. *Queen Mother*: F. Moore. *Ophelia*: R. Riano. *The Swede*: W. Ladd.

Scene 6

"Life Is Like a Toy Balloon"
H. Marsh, Four Hemstreet Singers
Blue Balloons: G. Elbew, D. Hathaway, W. Soldan, M. Donovan.

---

[70]The running order to Act 2 was revised immediately after the opening.

Scene 7

Before the Curtains

J. Green

Scene 8

Efficiency

(*by* A. Seymour Brown)

The Sergeant: T. Howard. *First Officer*: J. Lyons. *Second Officer*: W. Crosby. *Smelly, the Rat*: S. Hearn. *The Poisoner*: F. Koski. *The Lady in the Cloak*: G. McCormack. *The Man from Eighth Avenue*: R. Hallee.

Scene 9

The Moth and the Flame

The Moth: N. Nattova. *The Flame*: J. Myrio.

Scene 10

"I Want a Man Badly Blues"

J. Green

Scene 11

"An Horror-toria"

(A Village Choir Rehearsal *written and arranged by* Jack Waller.)

Scene 12

A Florida Estate[71]

Salesman: J. Lyons. *A Prospect*: T. Howard.

Scene 13

"See Yourselves in the Mirror"

Hemstreet Singers, F. Moore, Entire Company

THE GREENWICH VILLAGE FOLLIES

1925.47 (New Spring Edition)

A Revised Version of the Musical Revue in Two Acts, a Prologue and 25 Scenes[72]. Music by Harold Levey. Lyrics by Owen Murphy. Entire production conceived and staged by Hassard Short; revised and restaged by A. L. Jones and Morris Green. Dances and ensembles arranged by Larry Ceballos; additional dances arranged by Jack Heisler. Costumes designed by Charles LeMaire, Mark Mooring. Settings designed by Clark Robinson. Orchestra under the direction of Alfred Newman. Produced by The Bohemians, Inc. (A. L. Jones, Morris Green, Managing directors). New Spring Edition opened 15 March 1926 at the Sam S. Shubert Theatre, and closed 29 May 1926 after 88 performances. Total including both editions: 180 performances.

CAST: FLORENCE MOORE, TOM HOWARD, IRENE DELROY, SAM HEARN, RENIE RIANO, IDA SYLVANIA, KENDALL CAPPS, EDDIE SHUBERT, PHILIP CONVERS, HELENA MARSH, ROYAL HALEE, JEAN MYRIO, NATACHA NATTOVA, CLARENCE NORDSTROM, JOE LYONS, DELLA VANNA, BAILEY and BARNUM, WILLIAM V. POWERS, THE HEMSTREET SINGERS (Natalie Malonam, Olive Sibley, Letitia Bonta, Marion Adam), Grace Elbew, Dorothy Hathaway, Winifred Soldan, Marcella Donovan.

Ladies of the Ensemble: Show Girls: Teddy Gill, Fraun Koski, Olga Brounoff, Eleanor Ranke, Frances Thress, Gladys Glad, Maxine Wells. *Mediums*: Margaret Kolloch, Betty McLaughlin, Ruth Savoy, Rita Dunne, Marguerite Dunne, Carlotta Marino, Vivian Wyndham, Gretchen Reinhardt, Caroline Gerkin, Margie Himes, Betty Collette, Marte Hammans, Renie Johnson, Dorothy DeMerle, Agnes Riley, Frances DeFoe, Anita Pam.

PROLOGUE

"How Do You Do?"[73]

D. Hathaway, W. Soldan, M. Donovan, G. Elbew

"Follow Me"[74]

I. Delroy

ACT 1

Scene 1

"The Greenwich Village Green"[75]

C. Nordstrom

The Inns: The Bird of Paradise: M. Wells. *Red Pheasant*: T. Gill. *Lonely Deer*: E. Arden. *Green Monkey*: F. Koski. *Blue Cat*: O. Brounoff. *White Fox*: D. Vanna. *Blind Tiger*: E. Ranke. *Pink Bear*: F. Thress.

Scene 2

Suicide[76]

(*by* William K. Wells)

The Policeman: T. Howard. *The Clerk*: J. Lyons. *The Shop Girl*: L. Lane. *The Lawyer*: E. Shubert. *The Lawyer's Wife*: R. Riano. *The Rich Lady*: F. Moore.

Scene 3

"Whistle Away Your Blues"

Leota Lane, Lola Lane, Bailey and Barnum

(*Music by* Richard Myers. *Lyrics by* Leo Robin.)

Scene 4

Moving In

(*by* Norma Mitchell and Lewis Waller)

Mary: F. Moore. *Fanny*: R. Riano. *Plumber*: E. Shubert. *Paper Hanger*: W. V. Powers. *Carpet Man*: T. Howard. *Curtain Man*: S. Hearn. *Electrician*: J. Lyons. *Iceman*: P. Convers.

Scene 5

"Wouldn't You?"[77]

I. Delroy, K. Capps, S. Hearn, D. Hathaway, M. Donovan

Scene 6

The Spy

(*by* Tom Howard and A. Dorian Otvos)

The Colonel: J. Lyons. *The Captain*: P. Convers. *An Orderly*: W. V. Powers. *The Spy*: T. Howard.

Scene 7

"The Life of the Party"

R. Riano

(*Music by* Richard Myers. *Lyrics by* Harry Ruskin.)

Scene 8

"White Cargo"

C. Nordstrom, the Hemstreet Singers

Slave Girl: N. Nattova. *The Arab*: J. Myrie.

Scene 9

"The Window Cleaners"

E. Shubert, S. Hearn

(*Music by* Harry Ruby. *Lyrics by* Bert Kalmar.)

Scene 10

"Go South"

Bailey and Barnum

(*Music by* Richard Myers. *Lyrics by* Harry Ruskin.)

Dance

I. Delroy, G. Elbew, D. Hathaway, W. Soldan, M. Donovan

Scene 11

Before the Curtain

K. Capps

Scene 12

What's Wrong With This Picture?[78]

(*by* Herman J. Mankiewicz)

The Board of Censorship: T. Howard, R. Riano, J. Lyons.

Scene 13

"Faded Flowers"[79]

(*Music by* Sidney Clare. *Lyrics by* Lew Brown.)

Lily: E. Arden. *Violet*: G. Glad. *Rose*: R. Savoy. *Sunflower*: F. DeFoe. *Daisy*: B. Collett. *Seaweed*: D. DeMerle. *Pansy*: G. Reinhardt. *Tulip*: M. Himes. *Dandelion*: F. Moore.

Scene 14

Efficiency

(*by* A. Seymour Brown)

The Sergeant: T. Howard. *First Officer*: J. Lyons. *Second Officer*: P. Convers. *Smelly, the Rat*: S. Hearn. *The Poisoner*: F. Koski. *The Lady in the Cloak*: Leota Lane. *The Man from Eighth Avenue*: R. Halee.

Scene 15

"The Curse of Cinderella"

I. Sylvania, L. Bonta, The Hemstreet Singers, Ensemble

A. *Scene*: The Kitchen.

Cinderella: I. Delroy. *Stepsister*: F. Moore. *Stepsister*: R. Riano. *Stepmother*: F. Koski. *Messenger*: R. Halee. *Fairy Godmother*: D. Vanna.

---

[71] Dropped after opening.

[72] First Edition opened 24 December 1925 at Chanin's 46th Street Theatre for 92 performances.

[73] New Material for Second Edition, not in the First Edition.

[74] New Material for Second Edition, not in the First Edition.

[75] New Material for Second Edition, not in the First Edition.

---

[76] New Material for Second Edition, not in the First Edition.

[77] New Material for Second Edition, not in the First Edition.

[78] New Material for Second Edition, not in the First Edition.

[79] New Material for Second Edition, not in the First Edition.

B. Scene: The Palace Ballroom.
    The Prince Charming: C. Nordstrom. *Lady Gavotte*: N. Nattova. *Lord Gavotte*:
    J. Myrie. *Sally*: M. Donovan. *Irene*: W. Soldan. *Mary*: D. Hathaway. *Peg o' My
    Heart*: G. Elbew. *Ladies and Gentlemen of the Court*: Ensemble.

ACT 2
Scene 1
    "The Lady of the Snow"
        I. Sylvania, Hemstreet Singers
    The Lady of the Snow: D. Vanna. *Snow Ladies*: F. Koski, T. Gill, E. Ranke,
    M. Wells, O. Brounoff, F. Thress.
Scene 2
    Then . . . Now and Sometime
    (*by* Joseph E. Mitchell)
        The Announcer: R. Halee.
    "*Then*": *The Girl*: F. Moore. *The Lover*: J. Lyons.
    "*Now*": *The Girl*: F. Moore. *The Lover*: T. Howard.
    "*Sometime*": *The Girl*: F. Moore. *The Lover*: E. Shubert.
Scene 3
    "Those Knowing Nurses"[80]
        I. Delroy
    (*Music by* Sidney Clare. *Lyrics by* Lew Brown.)
    The Interne: K. Capps. *Special Nurses*: M. Donovan, G. Elbew, D. Hathaway,
    W. Soldan.
Scene 4
    Absent-Minded[81]
    (*by* Arthur Raphael)
    The Expositor: E. Shubert.
Scene 5
    Before the Curtain[82]
        Leota Lane, Lola Lane
Scene 6
    "The Sincerest Form of Flattery"
    (*Music by* Sidney Clare. *Lyrics by* Lew Brown.)
    The Optimists: F. Moore, E. Shubert, J. Lyons. *The Pessimist*: T. Howard. *Nora
    Bayes*: A. Riley. *Ethel Barrymore*: G. Elbew. *Fanny Brice*: O. Brounoff. *Marilyn
    Miller*: M. Donovan. *Jeanne Eagels*: W. Soldan. *Sophie Tucker*: D. Hathaway.
    Gloria Swanson: E. Arden. *Tetrazzini*: A. Pam. *Al Jolson*: R. Savoy. *Belle Baker*:
    M. Wells.
Scene 7
    Go Ahead, Sing
        Violinist: S. Hearn. *Stage Door Man*: J. Lyons. *The Singer*: T. Howard.
Scene 8
    Before the Curtains
        K. Capps
Scene 9
    The Moth and the Flame
        The Moth: N. Nattova. *The Flame*: J. Myrio.
Scene 10
    "An Horror-toria"
        A Village Choir Rehearsal *written and arranged by* Jack Waller.)
Scene 11
    Before the Curtains
        Bailey and Barnum
Scene 12
    "See Yourselves in the Mirror"
        Hemstreet Singers, F. Moore, Entire Company

EARL CARROLL'S
VANITIES (1926)

1925.48

An Utterly Unique and Different Form of Amusement (Musical Revue) in
Two Acts, 47 Scenes[83]. Sketches by William A. Grew. Additional sketches by

[80]New Material for Second Edition, not in the First Edition.
[81]New Material for Second Edition, not in the First Edition.
[82]New Material for Second Edition, not in the First Edition.
[83]Revised version of EARL CARROLL'S VANITIES OF 1925 which
played 6 July–27 December 1925 at the Earl Carroll Theatre for 199 performances. The Fourth in the annual series of musical revues which began
in 1923.

Jimmy Duffy, Arthur "Bugs" Baer, Blanche Merrill, Julius Tannen, Lester
Allen, Owen Murphy, Jay Gorney, James W. Cody, Don Lindley, Harry
Jentes. Music (and lyrics) by Clarence Gaskill. Sketches staged by William
A. Grew. Dances and ensembles by David Bennett. Art and technical direc-
tion by Bernard Lohmuller. Decorations designed by Willy Pogany. Cos-
tumes designed by Charles LeMaire. Settings designed by Karle O. Amend.
Special effects by Max Teuber. Orchestra under the direction of Donald
Voorhees. Staged by Earl Carroll. Produced by Earl Carroll. Opened 28
December 1925 at the Earl Carroll Theatre and closed 24 July 1926 after
230 performances. (Total for 1925 and 1926 editions played continuously:
429 performances.)

CAST: JULIUS TANNEN, JOE COOK, DOROTHY KNAPP, FRANK TINNEY,
SID DAISH, WALLACE McCUTCHEON, M. deJARI, VIVIAN HART, VAN
LOWE, FRANCES NORTON, MARIAN DOWLING, MICKEY SELDES,
MARIAN DALE, ISABEL DAWN, MADELYN KILLEEN, JANETTE GILMORE,
THEOL NELSON, VELMA VALENTINE, JACK WILSON, GRACELLA and
THEODORE, MAE PAIGE, CHARLES ORO, HAROLD YATES.

Hostesses: Lucille Upton, Ethel Dale, Marjorie Bolton, Margaret Dodds, Dorothy
Gordon, Lilian Thomas, Florence Darling, Bobby Meredith, Jewel LaKota, Olivette
Florentine, Peggy Neal, Bonna O'Dear, Dodge Plumer, Dorothy Stewart. *Usherettes*:
Madelyn Killeen (Captain), Marion Dale, Doreen Glover, Rose Wenzel, Laverne
Lambert, Agnes O'Loughlin, Polly Luce, Eva Marie Gray, Peggy Shannon, Muriel
Greer, Nina Sorel. *Waiters*: Edward Sallings, Ralph Hertz, Warren Hill, Sid Daish, Joe
Norton, Irwin Sherman, Hal Leonard.

The audience is cordially invited to join in the dancing on the forestage.

ACT 1[84]
Scene 1
    The Doors Open and We Meet the Hostesses
        Hostesses
Scene 2
    The Usherettes Escort Your to Your Seats
        Usherettes
Scene 3
    Meeting the Waiters: "We Are the Waiters"
        H. Yates, Waiters
Scene 4
    "Beautiful Ladies of the Night"
        H. Yates, Hostesses
Scene 5
    "This Is a Night Club"
        Usherettes
Scene 6
    Explaining the Idea
        J. Tannen
Scene 7
    Introducing the Chef
        V. Lowe
Scene 8
    The Culinary Department: "The Four Beautiful Birds" (One, Two,
    Three, Four)
        P. Luce, F. Norton, M. Dowling, M. Selden, D. Glover
Scene 9
    Make Them Hot Girls: ("Hot Off the Oven")
        M. Dale, I. Dawn, L. Lambert, A. O'Loughlin, E. M. Gray

[84]The show was revised immediately after the opening; added after the
opening:
    "I Thank You"
        M. de Jari
    The Medicine Man
        J. Cook
        Assisted by C. Alexander, C. Senna, R. Ellis.
    The Senator for the West
        J. Cook
        Assisted by C. Alexander, C. Senna, R. Ellis.
    Traps
        J. Cook
        Assisted by C. Alexander, C. Senna.
    Just a Little Chatter
        J. Tannen

Scene 10
  "The Chow Mein Girls"
    M. Killeen
  Dance Divertissements
    J. Gilmore, T. . Nelson, V. Valentine, A. O'Laughlin, D. Glover
Scene 11
  Back from Abroad
    F. Tinney, assisted by W. McCutcheon
Scene 12
  The Wrong Flat[85] (Drama)
    F. Tinney
  On the Telephone[86]
    W. McCutcheon, M. Killeen
Scene 13
  The Statue Scene:
  "Beautiful Girls"[87]
    H. Yates
    The Girl with the Shawl: F. Norton. *The Girl with the Fan*: L. Lambert.
    The Girl with the Pearls: P. Luce. *The Most Beautiful Girl in the World*:
    D. Knapp.
Scene 14
  The Great Shower Bath Mystery
    J. Cook
    Assisted by J. Wilson, C. Oro, P. Shannon, R. Wenzel.
Scene 15
  The Great Gate: "Somebody's Crazy About You"[88]
    E. Mura
  Dance Divertissement[89]
    J. Gilmore
Scene 16
  Introducing the Audience
    J. Tannen
Scene 17
  "Advancement Militaire"[90] (The French Soldier)
    M. deJari, H. Yates
    (*Pantomime Characters:*) *The Husband*: F. Tinney. *The Wife*:
    D. Knapp. *The Colonel*: V. Lowe. *The General*: S. Daish. *The King*:
    W. McCutcheon.
Scene 18
  Life's Mysteries in Four Episodes:
  (a) Christmas Morning
    The Husband: W. McCutcheon. *The Wife*: E. Dale. *The Child*: M. Dowling.
  (b) The House of Grief
    A Husband: J. Cook. *The Brother-in-Law*: M. deJari. *A Maid*: D. Knapp. *The Sister-in-Law*: J. LaKota.
  (c) The Three Sons
    Mother: E. Mura. *Father*: V. Lowe. *First Son*: E. Sallings. *Second Son*: J. Wilson. *Third Son*: H. Yates.
  (d) Big Shoes (Thermometer)
    The Beau: J. Cook. *The Girl*: D. Knapp. *Her Friend*: M. Killeen.
Scene 19
  Adagio[91]
    Gracella and Theodore
Scene 20
  "The Kinky Kids Parade"
    M. Killeen, Kinky Trombone Girls
    (*Music by* Walter Donaldson. *Lyrics by* Gus Kahn.)
Scene 21
  The Coachman
    F. Tinney
    Assisted by E. Mura, W. McCutcheon.

Scene 22
  "Thoughts of You"[92]
    V. Hart
Scene 23
  Specialty
    J. Cook
Scene 24
  In a Turkish Ballet[93]
    The Sultan: M. deJari. *Vizier*: H. Yates. *Favorite*: M. Killeen. *The Other Favorite*:
    P. Luce.
Scene 25
  In a Turkish Bath[94]
    The Insultan: J. Wilson. *A Buzzard*: C. Oro. *The Snake Seer*: V. Lowe.
Scene 26
  In a Turkish Towel[95]
    J. Tannen
Scene 27
  "Dorothy"
    M. deJari, (H. Yates)
    With D. Knapp, Visions of Venetian Vanities
Scene 28
  Finale, Act 1, And Why Not?

ACT 2[96]
Scene 1
  Informal Dance on the Forestage
Scene 2
  ("A Bottle of Canada Dry")
    Canada Dry Girls, Miltiades
Scene 3
  "The Hippity Hop"[97]
    M. Killeen, Girls
  Dance Divertissement
    J. Gilmore
Scene 4
  On a Florida Green: Coral Gables
    The Novice: F. Tinney. *The Pro*: J. Redmond. *The Caddy*: J. Wilson.
Scene 5
  A Song: "Duet"
    M. deJari, H. Yates
Scene 6
  "Yvonne"
    M. deJari, (H. Yates)

---

[92]Dropped shortly after the opening.
[93]Dropped shortly after the opening.
[94]Dropped shortly after the opening.
[95]Dropped shortly after the opening.
[96]The show was revised immediately after the opening; added after the opening:
  At the Ampico
    D. Voorhees, the Chickering Ampico
  The Gate of Roses: "At the Gate of Roses"
    M. Killeen
    A Lover: F. Tinney. *His Friend*: J. Tannen. And 'The Great Gate in Lovers' Lane.'
  "Rhythm of the Day"
    V. Lowe
    (*Music by* Owen Murphy. *Lyrics by* Donald Lindley.)
  "Thirty-One and Up"
    T. Nelson
  All Aboard: "Rhyme of the Sea"
    Vanities Skippers
  Once Upon a Time: A Story
    J. Cook
  The Match Makers)
    F. Tinney, W. McCutcheon, J. Redmond, R. Hertz
    Scene: Outside the Gym.
[97]Dropped shortly after the opening.

---

[85]Dropped shortly after the opening.
[86]Dropped shortly after the opening.
[87]Dropped shortly after the opening.
[88]Dropped shortly after the opening.
[89]Dropped shortly after the opening.
[90]Dropped shortly after the opening.
[91]Dropped shortly after the opening.

(a) The Studio
> *The Artist*: V. Lowe. *The Model*: D. Knapp.

(b) Somewhere in France
> *The Nurse*: D. Knapp. *The Captain*: V. Lowe. *Doughboys*: E. Sallings, S. Daish, W. Hill, R. Hertz, H. Leonard.

Scene 7

Specialty
> J. Cook

Scene 8

The Country Hotel
> *Scene*: Somewhere in the country late at night. *Time*: The Present.
> *The Daughter*: D. Knapp. *The Tourist*: W. McCutcheon. *The Father*: J. Wilson.

Scene 9

Silhouette
> (*Conceived and staged by Van Lowe.*) V. Lowe, F. Norton
> *Assisted by* M. Dale, L. Lambert, S. Daish, E. Sallings.

Adagio
> Gracella and Theodor

"Love in the Shadows"
> V. Hart, H. Yates

Scene 10

Introducing the Judge[98]
> J. Tannen

Scene 11

A Day in Court[99]
> *The Judge*; W. McCutcheon. *The Complainant*: J. Cook. *First Defendant*: M. deJari. *Second Defendant*: V. Lowe. *Third Defendant*: F. Tinney.

Scene 12

Neath Miami Skies: "Kiss in the Moonlight"
> V. Hart
> *Moonbeam Girls, Dancers*: J. Gilmore, R. Wenzel, V. Lowe. *The Lady of the Moon*: D. Knapp.

Scene 13

The Hammer of 1926
> J. Cook
> *Assisted by* C. Alexander, C. Senna, R. Ellis.

Scene 14

Specialty
> M. Killeen

Scene 15

"Ponies on Parade"

Scene 16

Outside the Gym
> F. Tinney, assisted by G. Romanoff, W. McCutcheon, R. Hertz

Scene 17

The Wrestling Match
> R. Wenzel, M. Paige, G. Romanoff, W. McCutcheon,

Scene 18

Pick Up Your Hat
> E. Mura

"Shake Yourself Out of Here"
> Entire Company

Scene 19

The Grand Finale: Hi-Ho

1925.49   TIP-TOES

A Musical Comedy in Two Acts, 5 Scenes. Book by Guy Bolton and Fred Thompson. Music by George Gershwin. Lyrics by Ira Gershwin. Book staged by John Harwood. Dances and ensembles staged by Sammy Lee. Additional dances staged by Earl Lindsay. Settings designed by John Wenger. Costumes designed by Kiviette. Orchestra under the direction of William Daly. Produced by Alex A. Aarons and Vinton Freedley. Opened 28 December 1925 at the Liberty Theatre and closed 12 June 1926 after 192 performances.

---

[98]Dropped shortly after the opening.
[99]Dropped shortly after the opening.

CAST (in order of appearance): *Sylvia Metcalf*: JEANNETTE MacDONALD. *Rollo Metcalf*: ROBERT HALLIDAY. *Peggy Schuyler*: AMY REVERE. *Al Kaye*: ANDREW TOMBES. *Hen Kaye*: HARRY WATSON, JR. *'Tip-Toes' Kaye*: QUEENIE SMITH. *Steve Burton*: ALLEN KEARNS. *Binnie Oakland*: GERTRUDE McDONALD. *Denise Marshall*: LOVEY LEE. *Steward*: Edwin Hodge. *Detective Kane*: Seldon Bennett. *Telephone Operator*: Lillian Michell. *At the pianos*: Victor Arden, Phil Ohman.

Ladies of the Ensemble: Edith Martin, Lillian Michell, Blanche O'Donohue, Peggy Quinn, Ethel Maye, Marie Otto, Alice O'Brien, Mildred Brower, Marcia Bell, Winifred Beck, Marjorie Bailey, Dorothy Cola, Betty Wright, Betty Waxton, Flora Watson, Marie Marcelline, Elsie Neal, Paulette Winston, Grace Jones, Alice Gordon, Diana Hunt, Peggy Hart, Lyn Dauer, Ann Exklund. *Gentlemen of the Ensemble*: Paul Dessey, Sam Fischer, Al Fisher, Bob Gebhardt, George Hughes, Thomas McLaughlin, Ted White, Barney Adams, Arthur Craig, George Rand, Jacques Stone, Harry Lake.

Act 1, Scene 1: Platform of the Palm Beach Station, Florida. *Scene 2*: The Gambling Casino.

Act 2, Scene 1: Deck of Steve's Houseboat. *Scene 2*: Lobby of the Everglades Inn. *Scene 3*: The Everglades Inn.

ACT 1

"Waiting for the Train" (Opening)
> Ensemble

"Nice Baby"
> J. MacDonald, R. Halliday, Ensemble

"Looking for a Boy"
> Q. Smith

"Lady Luck"
> Guests

"When Do We Dance?"
> A. Kearns, G. McDonald, L. Lee, Guests

"These Charming People"
> Q. Smith, A. Tombes, H. Watson, Jr.

"That Certain Feeling"
> Q. Smith, A. Kearns

"Sweet and Low Down"
> A. Tombes, L. Lee, G. McDonald, A. Revere, Guests

Finale
> Ensemble

ACT 2

"Our Little Captain"
> Q. Smith, Boys

"Looking for a Boy" (reprise)
> Q. Smith, A. Kearns

"It's a Great Little World"
> A. Kearns, J. MacDonald, A. Tombes, G. McDonald, L. Lee, Ensemble

"Nighty-Night"
> Q. Smith, A. Kearns

"Tip-Toes"
> Q. Smith, Ensemble

Finale
> Entire Company

1925.50   BY THE WAY

A Musical Revue (from the Apollo Theatre, London,) in Two Acts, 20 Scenes. (Sketches) Written by Ronald Jeans and Harold Simpson. Music by Vivian Ellis. Lyrics by Graham John. Arranged and constructed by Paul Murray and Jack Hulbert. Costumes designed by Guy de Gerald. Scenery painted by Delaney & Meynet. Musical director, Hilding Anderson. Produced [staged] by Jack Hulbert. Presented by Abraham L. Erlanger. Opened 28 December 1925 at the Gaiety Theatre, moved 12 April 1926 to the Central Theatre, and closed 29 May 1926 after 176 performances. (Second Edition opened 15 April 1926, see detail immediately following below.)

CAST: JACK HULBERT, CICELY COURTNEIDGE, HAROLD FRENCH, CELIA GLYNN, EDDIE CHILDS, DOROTHY HURST, PHYL ARNOLD, CHARLES COURTNEIDGE, BILLIE SHOTTER, LAWRENCE GREEN, MURIEL MONTROSE, JOSEPHINE QUEST, Doreen Lynch, April Harmon, A. Goodman.

ACT 1[100]

Scene 1

"By the Way"
 The Company

Scene 2

"Shall We Join the Ladies"
 M. Montrose, A. Harmon, J. Quest, B. Shotter
 D. Lynch, P. Arnold, Chorus, Charles Courtneidge, L. Green, E. Childs

Scene 3

So This Is Matrimony
 (*by* Ernest C. Ensor)
 Scene: Their Apartment.
 The Husband: J. Hulbert. *The Wife*: Cicely Courtneidge.

Scene 4

"What Can They See in Dancing?"
 C. Glynn, H. French

Scene 5

The Miracle
 (*by* Harold Simpson)
 Scene: A Room in a Nursing Home.
 John Manners: H. French. *Nurse Atkins*: P. Arnold. *Doctor Darlington*: Charles Courtneidge. *Nurse Tunnibell*: Cicely Courtneidge.

Scene 6

"My Castle in Spain" (from *TURNED UP*, London)
 D. Hurst, Chorus
 (*Music and Lyrics by* Isham Jones.)

Scene 7

Greek as She Is Taught
 (*by* Ronald Jeans)
 Scene: The Classroom.
 The Master: J. Hulbert. *The Boy*: Cicely Courtneidge.

Scene 8

"The Beauty of Bath"
 (*by* Graham John. *Music by* Vivian Ellis.)
 Scene: The Town of Bath about 1760.
 Captain Confident: Charles Courtneidge. *Captain Firebrace* of the Royal Navy: H. French. *The Beaty of Bath*: C. Glynn.

Scene 9

The Elopement
 (*by* Ronald Jeans)
 Scene: A Broadcasting Station.
 Prologue: *Mr. Brown*: Charles Courtneidge. *Mrs. Brown*: J. Quest.
 The Broadcast Drama: *Captain Slazenger*: H. French. *Lady B. Juniper*: Cicely Courtneidge. *Landlord*: A. Goodman. *Susan*: C. Glynn. *Lieutenant Carfax*: Charles Courtneidge. *The Property Man*: J. Hulbert.

Scene 10

Follies:
 Introduction: P. Arnold.
 "Gather Roses While You May"
  The Company
 "In the Same Way I Love You"
  D. Hurst, C. Glynn, Charles Courtneidge, H. French
  (*Music by* H. M. Tennant. *Lyrics by* Eric Little.)
 "I Know Someone Loves Me"
  J. Hulbert
 "High Street, Africa"
  Cicely Courtneidge
  (*Music and Lyrics by* Cumberland Clark, Huntley Trevor, Everett Lynton.)
  Dancers: E. Childs, J. Hulburt.

ACT 2[101]

Scene 1

"Hum a Little Tune"
 (*Music and Lyrics by* Vivian Ellis.)
 E. Childs, Dolls

Scene 2

All the World's a Link[102]
 (by Harold Simpson)
 Scene: A Suburban Sitting Room.
 Herbert: H. French. *Marjorie*: C. Glynn.

Scene 3

Clair de Lune
 (*Sketch by* Graham John)
 The Poet: Charles Courtneidge. *The Ordinary Man*: L. Green. *The Flappers*: A. Harmon, D. Lynch. *At the Piano*: D. Hurst. *Pierrot*: E. Childs. *Pierrette*: P. Arnold.

Scene 4

The Finishing Touch[103]
 (*by* Harold Simpson)
 Scene: The Osborne Apartment.
 Mrs. Osborne: J. Quest. *Mr. Osborne*: H. French. *The Maid*: B. Shotter. *Miss Longshaw*: Cicely Courtneidge.

Scene 5

Tasse de Thé[104]
 J. Hulbert, C. Glynn

Scene 6

"Nippy" (The London Tea Shop Waitress)
 H. French, Chorus

Scene 7

Honeymoon Hall
 Scene: A Sitting Room in a Seaside Boarding House.
 George Wassop: J. Hulbert. *Maria Wassop*: Cicely Courtneidge. *Mrs. Barking*: J. Quest. *James Porterhouse*: Charles Courtneidge. *A Maid*: M. Montrose.

Scene 8

"There's Nothing New Under the Sun"
 D. Hurst, H. French

Scene 9

The Trick Brothers
 Cicely Courtneidge, J. Hulbert

Scene 10

"Colour"
 Company

Finale

BY THE WAY

1925.50 (Second Edition)

A Second Edition of the Musical Revue from the Apollo Theatre, London, in Two Acts, 20 Scenes[105]. (Sketches) Written by Ronald Jeans and Harold Simpson. Music by Vivian Ellis. Lyrics by Graham John. Arranged and constructed by Paul Murray and Jack Hulbert. Costumes designed by Guy de Gerald. Scenery painted by Delaney & Meynet. Musical director, Hilding Anderson. Produced [staged] by Jack Hulbert. Presented by Abraham L. Erlanger. Second edition moved 12 April 1926 to the Central Theatre, opened 15 April 1926 and closed 29 May 1926 after 56 additional performances. Total for both editions: 176 performances.

CAST: JACK HULBERT, CICELY COURTNEIDGE, HAROLD FRENCH, CELIA GLYNN, EDDIE CHILDS, DOROTHY HURST, PHYL ARNOLD, CHARLES COURTNEIDGE, LAWRENCE GREEN, MURIEL MONTROSE, JOSEPHINE QUEST, Doreen Lynch, April Harmon, A. Goodman, Billie Dell, Herbert Darsey.

ACT 1[106]

---

[100]Added after opening to Act 1:
 The Cure (*by* Dion Titheradge)
  Mrs. Barker: Cicely Courtneidge. *John Barker*: J. Hulbert. *Mrs. Parrott*: C. Glynn. *Albert Parrott*: Charles Courtneidge.

[101]Added to Act 2 after opening:
 "Tea for Three (*by* Harold Simpson)[scene includes song below]
  Scene: Mr. Dennington's Apartment.
  Miss Carew: C. Glynn. *Mr. Dennington*: J. Hulbert. *Miss Lintop*: Cicely Courtneidge. *Butler*: Charles Courtneidge.
 "No One's Ever Kissed Me" (from *POT LUCK*, London)
  C. Glynn, J. Hulbert
  (*Music by* Philip Braham. *Lyrics by* Ronald Jeans.)

---

[102]Dropped after opening.
[103]Dropped after opening.
[104]Dropped after opening.
[105]First edition opened 28 December 1925 at the Gaiety Theatre for 120 performances
[106]Added to Second Edition, Act 1, during the run:
 Passing the Time (*by* Harry M. Vernon and Arthur Wimperis) (Act 1)
  Scene: Miss Endicott's Cottage in Devonshire.
  Mrs. Endicott: Cicely Courtneidge. *Rose*: J. Quest. *Laura Smith*: A. Harmon. *Herbert Smith*: J. Hulbert.

Scene 1
  "By the Way"
    The Company
Scene 2
  "Shall We Join the Ladies"
    M. Montrose, A. Harmon, J. Quest, B. Dell, D. Lynch, P. Arnold, Chorus, Charles Courtneidge, L. Green, E. Childs
Scene 3
  So This Is Matrimony
    (*by* Ernest C. Ensor, later Aubrey C. Ensor)
    Scene: Their Apartment.
    The Husband: J. Hulbert. *The Wife*: Cicely Courtneidge. *The Other Me*: Charles Courtneidge.
Scene 4
  "What Can They See in Dancing?"
    C. Glynn, H. French
Scene 5
  Seeing Is Believing
    (*by* Reginald Arkell)
    Scene: The Orderly Room.
    Colonel Arkwright: J. Hulbert. *Orderly Corporal*: H. Darsey. *Lieuteneant Mannering*: H. French. *Mrs. Arkwright*: A. Harmon.
Scene 6
  "My Castle in Spain" (from *TURNED UP*, London)
    D. Hurst, E. Childs, Chorus
    (*Music and Lyrics by* Isham Jones.)
Scene 7
  The Finishing Touch
    (*by* Harold Simpson)
    Scene: The Osborne Apartment.
    Mrs. Osborne: J. Quest. *Mr. Osborne*: H. French. *The Maid*: D. Lynch. *Miss Longshaw*: Cicely Courtneidge.
Scene 8
  "The Beauty of Bath"
    (*by* Graham John. *Music by* Vivian Ellis.)
    Scene: The Town of Bath about 1760.
    Captain Confident: Charles Courtneidge. *Captain Firebrace* of the Royal Navy: H. French. *The Beaty of Bath*: C. Glynn.
Scene 9
  Greek as She Is Taught
    (*by* Ronald Jeans and Jack Hulbert)
    Scene: The Classroom.
    The Master: J. Hulbert. *The Boy*: Cicely Courtneidge.
Scene 10
  Follies:
    Introduction: P. Arnold.
  "Gather Roses While You May"
    The Company
  "In the Same Way I Love You"
    D. Hurst, C. Glynn, Charles Courtneidge, H. French
    (*Music by* H. M. Tennant. *Lyrics by* Eric Little.)
  "I've Found the Bluebird"
    J. Hulbert
    (*Music by* Richard Myers. *Lyrics by* Leo Robin.)
  "Three Little Hairs"
    Cicely Courtneidge
    (*Music and Lyrics by* Trevor Butler.)

ACT 2
Scene 1
  "Hum a Little Tune"
    E. Childs, J. Quest, Dolls
    (*Music and Lyrics by* Vivian Ellis.)
Scene 2
  The Title Triangle
    (*by* Paul Murray and Jack Hulbert)
    Scene: The Home.
    The Wife: D. Hurst. *The Lover*: Charles Courtneidge. *The Maid*: P. Arnold. *The Husband*: H. French.
Scene 3
  Tea for Three
    (*by* Harold Simpson)

Scene: Mr. Dennington's Apartment.
Miss Carew: C. Glynn. *Mr. Dennington*: J. Hulbert. *Miss Lintop*: J. Quest. *Butler*: Charles Courtneidge.
  "I Was Meant for Someone"
    C. Glynn, J. Hulbert
    (*Music by* James Hanley. *Lyrics by* Ballard Macdonald.)
Scene 4
  Honour Among Thieves
    (*by* Harold Simpson)
    Scene: Lady Jim's Drawing Room.
    Lady Jim: Cicely Courtneidge. *Molly*: P. Arnold. *Cynthia*: A. Harmon. *Eric*: L. Green. *Jumbo*; Charles Courtneidge.
Scene 5
  The Elopement
    (*by* Ronald Jeans)
    Scene: A Broadcasting Station.
    Prologue: *Mr. Brown*: Charles Courtneidge. *Mrs. Brown*: D. Hurst.
    The Broadcast Drama: *Captain Slazenger*: H. French. *Lady B. Juniper*: Cicely Courtneidge. *Landlord*: A. Goodman. *Susan*: C. Glynn. *Lieutenant Carfax*: Charles Courtneidge. *The Property Man*: J. Hulbert.
Scene 6
  "You Modern Girls"
    H. French, Chorus
    (*Music and Lyrics by* Melville Gideon and Stanley West.)
Scene 7
  Which Taken at the Flood
    (*by* Harold Simpson)
    Scene: Mrs. Bossom's Parlour.
    Mrs. Bossom: Cicely Courtneidge. *Mr. Slocombe*: H. French. *The Maid*: M. Montrose. *Mr. Hopkins*: J. Hulbert.
Scene 8
  "There's Nothing New Under the Sun"
    D. Hurst, H. French
Scene 9
  The Trick Brothers[107]
    Cicely Courtneidge, J. Hulbert
Scene 10
  "Colour"
    Company
Scene 11
  Finale

THE DAUGHTER OF MADAME ANGOT

1925.51

A Revival of the Opéra-comique in Three Acts[108]. Performed by the Moscow Art Theater Musical Studio in Russian. Music by Charles Lecocq. Russian text by Vladmir Nemirovitch Dantchenko and Mikhail Galperin. (Original French libretto by Clairville, Paul Siraudin and Victor Koning.) Produced by F. Ray Comstock and Morris Gest. Opened 28 December 1925 at Jolson's Theatre and closed 2 January 1926 after 8 performances in repertory.

CAST: *Clairette Angot*: NADIEZHDA KEMARSKAYA, Galina Gorshuniova, Nadiezhda Krutova (alts.). *Lange*: OLGA BAKLANOVA, Lydia Belyskova (alt.). *Ange Pitou*: IVAN VELIKANOFF, Sergei Ostroumoff (alt.). *Larivaudière*: VLADIMIR LOSSKY. *Pomponnet*: BORIS BELOSTOTSKY, Ivan Yagodkin (alt.). *Louchard*: DMITRY KAMERNITSKY. *Amaranthe*: NINA DURASOVA, Yelizaveta Guadobina (alt.). *Trénitz*: SEMYON RAKIMANOFF, Mikhail Nemirovitch (alt.). *An Officer*: Joseph Tsitrinnik, Semyon Rakhmanoff (alt.).

---

[107]The Trick Brothers in Act 2 was revised to include:
  "Looking Around"
    (*Music by* Richard Myers. *Lyrics by* Leo Robin.)
  "All Day Long"
    (*Music and Lyrics by* R. P. Weston and Bert Lee.)
[108]Costumes, scenery and conductor uncredited. Originally performed in New York in French 25 August 1873 at the Broadway Theatre in repertory; in English 16 November 1874 at the Lyceum Theatre for 15 performances in repertory.) For Synopsis of Scenes and Musical Numbers, see original 1873 production.

1925.52

SONG OF THE FLAME

A Romantic Opera (Musical Play) in Two Acts, 9 Scenes, a Prologue and an Epilogue. Book and lyrics by Otto Harbach and Oscar Hammerstein II. Music by George Gershwin and Herbert Stothart. Book staged by Frank Reicher. Dances and ensemble pictures arranged by Jack Haskell. Scenery by Joseph Urban. Costumes designed by Mark Mooring. Orchestra under the direction of Herbert Stothart. Orchestrations by (Robert) Russell Bennett. Produced by Arthur Hammerstein. Opened 30 December 1925 at the 44th Street Theatre and closed 10 July 1926 after 219 performances.

CAST (in order of appearance): *Konstantin:* GREEK EVANS. *Aniuta, 'The Flame':* TESSA KOSTA. *Grusha:* Dorothy Mackaye. *Nicholas:* Hugh Cameron. *Count Boris:* Bernard Gorcey. *Nadya:* Ula Sharon. *Natasha:* Phoebe Brune. *Prince Volodya:* GUY ROBERTSON. *A Dancer:* Leonard St. Leo. *Olga:* Blanche Collins. *Alexis:* Paul Wilson. *An Avenger:* Louise Dalberg.
 Russian Art Singers directed by Alexander U. Fine: Konstantin Buketoff, Zina Ivanova, Anna Petrenko, Vasily Andrewsky (soloists). Mmes. Gorina, Chereko, Dubiago, Petrenko, Yestovitch, Schmidt, Michailova, Kustacheva, Ivaneva, Andriefskia, Tulchinova, Kucharskaia, Losieva, Chevdarova, Yzorova, Shaston, Grosheva, Trotzkaya, Steffan, Orolinskiawa, Grebenietzkaia. Mons. Trotski, Apolinoff, Prokofieff, Kiriliook, Andreefsky, Soostroeff, Troonin, Rutschkowsky, Dodoukin, Sr. Dodoukin, Jr., Petry, Davidenko, Klimnovitc, Ordinsky, Jackoleff, Ardatoff, Niejin, Pathamarenko, Yermeloff, Vinogradoff, Schillin, Pravdiook, Keberev, Krasik, Chardaroff, Torchinsky, Kottony, Davidoff, Bass, Goreinko, Dublenski, Ramonoff.
 American Ballet: Verdi, Milli, Lucille Osborne, Alice Ankers, Lotta Fanning, Louise Hersey, Marion Booth, Mary Green, Dorothy Booth, Eileen Wenzel, Frances Thress, Georgia Gwynne, Ann Constance, Miriam Avendale, Christine Moray, Audrey Sturges, Dorothy Thattell, Gene Hylan, Emily Sherman, Adelaide Permin, Terry Carroll, Elvinne Hall, Ruby Poe, Ruth Sato, Sylvia Pagano, Laurie Phillips, Elsie Marcus, Dorothy Lee, Carolyn Johnson, Margie Horton, Buddie Haines, Betty Credito, Helen Bowers, L. Ojala, Ima Berline, Adelaide Candee, Edith Higgens, Beth Hill, Lillyan Lyndon, Frances Nevins, Elsa Roelofsma, Jeannie St. John. *Gentlemen of the Ensemble:* Chester Bennett, Hal Bird, William Cooper, Paul Florence, James Herold, Bob LeRoy, Harry Long, Troupe Reynolds, Willard Tyson, Philip Titman, Donald Wells.

Prologue: A Street in Moscow, March, 1917.

Act 1, Scene 1: Near a Canal Tributary of the Volga. October 1917. *Scene 2:* The Western Gate of the Kazanov Palace. That night. *Scene 3:* Outside Aniuta's Lodgings. *Scene 4:* Art Salon of the Kazanov Palace.

Act 2, Scene 1: A Room in a Latin Quarter Pension, Paris. Two years later. *Scene 2:* Outside the Café des Caucasiens, Montmartre. *Scene 3:* Samovar Room of the Café des Caucasiens. *Scene 4:* Outside the Café des Caucasiens. *Scene 5:* Kazanov Estate in the Château District, France. Next morning.

Epilogue: Song of the Flame.

PROLOGUE
 Protest
 "Far Away"
  G. Evans, Russian Art Singers
  (*Music by* George Gershwin and Herbert Stothart. Refrain based on a folk song theme—the peasants' lament on a late spring.)
 "Song of the Flame" (Don't Forget Me)
  T. Kosta, G. Evans, Russian Art Singers
  (*Music by* George Gershwin and Herbert Stothart.)

ACT 1
Scene 1
 "Woman's Work Is Never Done"
  D. Mackaye, Ensemble
  (*Music by* George Gershwin.)
 "Great Big Bear"
  D. Mackaye, H. Cameron, Ensemble
  (*Music by* Herbert Stothart.)
 Dance Impromptu
  U. Sharon
Scene 2
 "The Signal"
  T. Kosta, G. Robertson, Octette
  (*Music by* George Gershwin.)
 "The Cossack Love Song"
  T. Kosta, G. Robertson, Ensemble
  (*Music by* George Gershwin and Herbert Stothart.)
 "Tartar"
  G. Evans, Russian Art Singers
  (*Music by* Herbert Stothart.)

Dance
 P. Brune, American Ballet
Scene 3
 "(You May) Wander Away"
  T. Kosta, G. Robertson
  (*Music by* Herbert Stothart.)
 Finaletto
  T. Kosta, G. Robertson, Ensemble
Scene 4
 "Vodka"
  D. Mackaye, Dance Ensemble, U. Sharon
  (*Music by* George Gershwin and Herbert Stothart.)
 Finale
  Company
  (*Music by* George Gershwin and Herbert Stothart.)

ACT 2
Scene 1
 "I Want Two Husbands"[109]
  D. Mackaye, B. Gorcey, H. Cameron
  (*Music by* Herbert Stothart.)
 "Midnight Bells"
  T. Kosta
  (*Music by* George Gershwin.)
 "The Cossack Love Song" (reprise)
  G. Robertson
Scene 3
 "The First Blossom Ballet"
  U. Sharon, American Ballet
  This ballet is symbolic of Russia's long winter of adversity and the arrival of the first blossom of victorious ideals. At first, the blossom is repulsed and chilled by the snows of bitterness, but the sunlight she brings with her melts the snows.
 A Capella[110]
  Russian Art Singers
  ("I Was There," "The Song of Gold," "Song of the Field, " "Village Pines," A Christmas Carol," "Down the Mother Volga")
 Finaletto
  Company
Scene 5
 "Going Home on New Year's Morning"
  Russian Art Singers

EPILOGUE
 Finale Ultimo
  Company

1926.01

A NIGHT IN PARIS

A Musical Revue in Two Acts, 33 Scenes. Sketches by Harold Atteridge. Music by J. Fred Coots and Maurice Rubens. Lyrics by Clifford Grey and McElbert Moore. Staged by J. C. Huffman. Dialogue directed by Alexander Leftwich. Dances staged by George Dobbs. Settings by Watson Barratt. Costumes by Joseph, Ernest R. Schrapps, Paul Caret, Erté. Ballets staged by Oyra. All numbers of the Gertrude Hoffmann Girls staged by Gertrude Hoffmann. Orchestra under the direction of Charles Drury. Entire production under the personal direction of J. J. Shubert. Produced by the Messrs. Shubert. Opened 5 January 1926 at the Casino de Paris (atop the Century Theatre), closing 10 July 1926 after 208 performances; Second Edition (see detail below, immediately following) opened 26 July 1926 at the 44th Street Theatre, moved 18 October 1926 to Jolson's Theatre, and closed 30 October 1926 after 113 performances. 321 performances total.

CAST: BARNETT PARKER, YVONNE GEORGE, JACK OSTERMAN, VANESSI, DAVID DROLLET, NORMA TERRIS, JACK PEARL, KATHRYN RAY, HARRY O'NEAL, MARIA KIEVA, GEORGE DOBBS, LOULOU HEGOBURU, OYRA, EMILY WOOLLEY, LEO BILL, RUTH-ANN WATSON, CARLOS CONTE, LORETTA RHODES, WILLIAM DAVIS, CATHERINE, Henri Garat, Vivienne

---

[109] "I Want Two Husbands" and "Midnight Bells" dropped after opening and replaced by:
 "Wander Away" (reprise)
  G. Evans
[110] List prepared from original cast recordings.

Purcell, Ralph Coram, Richard Lee, Aileen DeMeyer, Joan Lee, Olive McClure, Lucille Arnold, Miriam Lax, Frances Hart, Misses Gallier, Evanthea.

Gertrude Hoffmann Girls: Ann Rizzo, Lillian Weisberg, Edna Tobin, Helen Gay, Ann Sween, Annette Davies, Mary McGonigle, Margaret McGonigle, Marion Luzon, Madeline Luzon, Lillian Ford, Catherine Sheeran, Helen Franz, Myrtle Wagner, Margaret Marano, May Ferber, Betty Rappe, Ruth Rappe, Dorothy Chadwick. *Casino de Paris Girls:* Ruth Grace, Delmar Meyers, Metta Wooster, Bernice Gardner, Lola Cordoba, Jacqueline Brown, Rosemary Farmer, Katherine Johnson, Corinne Sylvae, Edna Webster, Olga Marye, Virginia Watts, Sunny Dale, Naoe Konda, Marietta O'Brien, Gladys Rennick, Carol Boyer.

ACT 1
Scene 1
> Prologue (Spoken)
>> Y. George, B. Parker
Scene 2
> "Poster Girl"
>> G. Dobbs, Gertrude Hoffmann Girls
>> (*Designed by* Duke Murta and Jack Savage.)
Scene 3
> "Sergeant's Dream"
>> E. Woolley, D. Drollet, Casino de Paris Girls
Scene 4
> "Step Sister"
>> Vannessi, G. Dobbs, Gertrude Hoffmann Girls
Scene 5
> The Doctor Calls
>> B. Parker, V. Purcell, E. Woolley, W. Davis
>> *Scene 1:* A Room at Mr. Brown's. *Scene 2:* A Room at Mr. Devere's.
Scene 6
> Impressions of Broadway Stars and 'Fascinating Lady'[111]
>> N. Terris
Scene 7
> The Girl Line
>> *Jack:* J. Osterman. *Harry:* H. O'Neal. And the Misses. Ray, Kieva, Evanthea, Dale, Purcell, Gallier, Marye.
Scene 8
> Zulu: ["Voodoo of the Zulu Isle"]
>> N. Terris, Oyra, Gertrude Hoffmann Girls
>> (*Music by* J. Fred Coots, Maurice Rubens. *Lyrics by* Clifford Grey, McElbert Moore. *Designed by* Duke Murta and Jack Savage.)
Scene 9
> Brazilian Nuts
>> J. Pearl, H. O'Neal
Scene 10
> The Miser
>> Vanessi, Oyra, Casino de Paris Girls
Scene 11
> A Box with the Green Hat [Burlesque of Michael Arlen's play 'The Green Hat']
>> *Scene:* At the Broadhurst Theatre.
>> *Mr. Manhattan:* B. Parker. *Jeannette:* K. Ray. *Her Aunt:* E. Woolley. *Iris March:* N. Terris. *Napier:* R. Coram.
Scene 12
> "The Newport Glide"
>> Vanessi, G. Dobbs, Gertrude Hoffmann Girls, Casino de Paris Girls
>> (*Music by* J. Fred Coots, Maurice Rubens. *Lyrics by* Clifford Grey.)
Scene 13
> "In Chinatown in Frisco"
>> R. Watson
>> (*Music by* Maurice Yvain. *Lyrics by* Clifford Grey, McElbert Moore.)
>> *Scene:* A Street in Chinatown.
>> *A Tourist:* H. Garat. *A Chinaman:* Oyra. *Mijama:* Catherine. *Chinamen, Chinese Street Children, etc.*
Scene 14
> A Young Boy Just Growing Up
>> J. Osterman
Scene 15
> Night Life
>> *Scene 1:* Midnight in a Parisian Café, in the Montmartre. *Scene 2:* A moment later, in the Bois.

---
[111]Dropped during the run.

The Proprietor: Oyra. *The Widow:* M. Kieva. *An Englishman:* R. Coram. *Jack:* J. Pearl. *Jones:* W. Davis. *"Kid" Popper:* H. O'Neal. *Neapolitan Singer:* D. Drollet. *An American:* R. Lee. *His Wife:* A. DeMeyer. *His Daughter:* R. Farmer. *Two Apache:* Loulou and Carlos. *A Spanish Dancer:* J. Lee. With the Gertrude Hoffmann Girls, Casino de Paris Girls. *Gendarmes, Vistors, Attendants.*

Scene 16
> Leo Bill (from Chez Fysher)
Scene 17
> The Friend
>> (*by* Howard Rogers)
>> *The Husband:* R. Lee. *His Friend:* B. Parker. *The Maid:* M. O'Brien. *The Butler:* W. Davis.
Scene 18
> "In the Gardens of the King"
>> R. Watson, L. Rhodes, Gertrude Hoffmann Girls
Scene 19
> "Powder Puff" (Finale)
>> Evanthea
>> (*Music by* J. Fred Coots, Maurice Rubens. *Lyrics by* Clifford Grey, McElbert Moore.)
>> *Caron's Face Powders: Narcisse Noir:* G. Webster. *N'Aimez Que Moi:* B. Gardner. *Infini:* M. Wooster. *Tabac Blond:* K. Ray. *Mes Jeunes Années:* E. Webster. And O. McClure, Catherine, F. Hart, Entire Ensemble.

ACT 2[112]
Scene 1
> "Sacrifice"
>> D. Drollet, Oyra, Catherine, Gertrude Hoffmann Girls, Casino de Paris Girls
Scene 2
> A Coward's Vortex [Burlesque of the play by Noël Coward 'The Vortex']
>> *Nicky:* B. Parker. *Florence, his mother:* N. Terris. *Tom:* R. Coram. *Bunty:* K. Ray.
Scene 3
> Yvonne George (from Parisiana)
>> [Impressions of Raquel, Mistinguette, Russian singers
>> "The Nile"
>> *Music and Lyrics by* Xavier Leroux.]
Scene 4
> "The Slave"
>> D. Drollet
>> *Danced by* O. McClure, Oyra, H. Garrat, Gertrude Hoffmann Girls.
Scene 5
> Bouquet (from Parisiana)
>> L. Hegoburu, C. Conte
Scene 6
> Promotion
>> *Scene:* Outside the home of Sergeant Smith.
>> *Sergeant Smith:* R. Lee. *Mary, his wife:* E. Woolley. *Officer Jones:* W. Davis. *Captain Thomas:* H. O'Neal.
Scene 7
> "Louisiana"
>> N. Terris, J. Lee, Gertrude Hoffmann Girls
>> (*Music by* J. Fred Coots, Maurice Rubens. *Lyrics by* McElbert Moore. *Designed by* Betty Duke.)
Scene 8
> Naughty?
>> *Scene:* The Boudoir of Madame.
>> *The Announcer:* H. O'Neal. *Jack:* J. Osterman. *The Wife:* M. Kieva. *The Maid:* E. Woolley. *The Husband:* W. Davis.
Scene 9
> "They Satisfy"
>> J. Osterman, K. Ray, Casino de Paris Girls
>> (*Designed by* Betty Duke.)

---
[112]Added during the run to Act 2:
> Insanity (*by* Harry Wagstaff Gribble)
>> *Scene:* Doctor's Office in an Insane Asylum.
>> *The Doctor:* R. Lee. *The Governor's Wife:* R. Watson. *An Inmate:* B. Parker.
> Specialty
>> Odette Myrtil
> Specialty
>> Lucienne Boyer

Scene 10
Lovers Are Misunderstood[113]
(by Thomas Jean)
The Husband: J. Pearl. His Wife: E. Woolley. His Best Friend: B. Parker.

Scene 11
"Dance Mad"
N. Terris, Vanessi, G. Dobbs, R. Coram, Gertrude Hoffmann Girls

Scene 12
Watch Your Step
The Gambler: H. O'Neal. The Visitor: J. Pearl. His Friend: W. Davis.

Scene 13
The Casino de Paris Quartette
D Drollett, L. Arnold, R. Watson, M. Lax
Announced by V. Purcell.

Scene 14
"Wedding Day"
K. Ray, J. Osterman, Entire Company
Finale

A NIGHT IN PARIS

1926.01   (Second Edition)

A Musical Revue in Two Acts, 29 Scenes[114]. Sketches by Harold Atteridge. Music by J. Fred Coots and Maurice Rubens. Lyrics by Clifford Grey and McElbert Moore. Staged by J. C. Huffman. Dialogue directed by Charles Judels. Dances staged by George Dobbs. Settings by Watson Barratt. Costumes by Ernest R. Schrapps, Erté. Ballets staged by Oyra. All numbers of the Gertrude Hoffmann Girls staged by Gertrude Hoffmann. Orchestra under the direction of Charles Drury. Entire production under the personal direction of J. J. Shubert. Produced by the Messrs. Shubert. Second Edition opened 26 July 1926 at the 44th Street Theatre, moved 18 October 1926 to Jolson's Theatre, and closed 30 October 1926 after 113 performances. Total, including First and Second Editions: 321 performances.

CAST: JACK PEARL, JACK OSTERMAN, KATHRYN RAY, HARRY O'NEAL, BARNETT PARKER, NORMA TERRIS, CATHERINE GALLIMORE, LUCIENNE MOINEAU, ANNIE PRITCHARD, OYRA, LUCIEN LaRIVIÈRE, GEORGE DOBBS, LORETTA RHODES, MISCHA FERENZO, RICHARD LEE, MARGIE FINLEY, OLIVE McCLURE, EMILY WOOLLEY, RALPH CORAM, RAY BOLGER, RUTH-ANN WATSON, ANTONIA FECHNER, WILLIAM DAVIS, MARIETTA O'BRIEN.

The Gertrude Hoffman Girls: Misses Painter, Gilberti, Tobin, Gay, Swan, Davies, May McGonigle, Marguerite McGonagle, Luzon, Ford, Shearan, Franz, Wagner, Margaret Marano, Betty Rappe, Ruth Rappe, Chadwick, Vernon. *The Maids Of Paris:* Corinne Sylvae, Edna Webster, Virginia Watts, Gladys Rennick, Ruth Brady, Ivy St. Clair, Patricia Caron, Rosemary Farmer, Naoe Kondo, Carol Boyer, Jacqueline Brown, Olga Marye, Isabelle Bennett, Mia Muselle, Frances Ebert, Nancy Phillips, June Wall, Eleneva Karola, Morine Clark, Jane Dobbins, Peggy Neil.

ACT 1

Scene 1
Prologue (Spoken)
L. LaRiviere, B. Parker

Scene 2
"Poster Girl"
G. Dobbs, Gertrude Hoffmann Girls
(Designed by Duke Murta and Jack Savage.)

Scene 3
"Sergeant's Dream"
L. Rhodes, M. Ferrenzo, Casino de Paris Girls

Scene 4
Twas the Night Before Christmas *
Husband: B. Parker. Wife: N. Terris. His Wife's Friend: R. Lee.

Scene 5
"Bob-Haired Baby"[115] (Staged by Seymour Felix.)
C. Gallimore
With G. Dobbs, M. Finley, Gertrude Hoffmann Girls.

Scene 6
Impressions of Hollywood[116]
The Movie Director: J. Osterman. The Girl: K. Ray.

Scene 7
Zulu: ["Voodoo of the Zulu Isle"]
N. Terris, Oyra, Gertrude Hoffmann Girls
(Music by J. Fred Coots, Maurice Rubens. Lyrics by Clifford Grey, McElbert Moore. Designed by Duke Murta and Jack Savage.)

Scene 8
The Interpreter[117]
Mr. Thompson: J. Pearl. Lawyer: H. O'Neal. Frenchman: L. LaRiviere.

Scene 9
The Miser
O. McClure, Oyra, Maids of Paris

Scene 10
A Box with a Green Hat [Burlesque of Michael Arlen's play 'The Green Hat']
Scene: At the Broadhurst Theatre.
Mr. Manhattan: B. Parker. Jeannette: K. Ray. Her Aunt: E. Woolley. Iris March: N. Terris. Napier: R. Coram.

Scene 11
"Daddy Long Legs"[118]
R. Bolger, Gertrude Hoffmann Girls
(Staged by Seymour Felix.)

Scene 12
"In Chinatown in Frisco"
R. Watson
(Music by Maurice Yvain. Lyrics by Clifford Grey, McElbert Moore.)
Scene: A Street in Chinatown.
A Tourist: L. LaRiviere A Chinaman: Oyra. Mijama: C. Gallimore. Chinamen, Chinese Street Children, etc.

Scene 13
A Young Boy Just Growing Up
J. Osterman

Scene 14
Night Life
Scene 1: Midnight in a Parisian Café, in the Montmartre. Scene 2: A moment later, in the Bois.
Cardo: M. Ferenzo. Lucien: L. LaRiviere. The Proprietor: Oyra. An Englishman: R. Coram. The Widow: A. Fechner. Mlle. Montmartre: L. Moineau. Jack: J. Pearl. Jones: W. Davis. "Kid" Popper: H. O'Neal. Violiniste: R. Rappe. An American: R. Lee. His Wife: C. Boyer. His Daughter: R. Farmer. A Spanish Dancer: A. Pritchard. With the Gertrude Hoffmann Girls, Maids of Paris. Gendarmes, Vistors, Attendants.

Scene 15
Norma Terris

Scene 16
The Search[119]
The Victim: B. Parker. Officer: W. Davis.

Scene 17
"Cleopatra's Barge"[120]
L. Rhodes, R. Watson, E. Woolley
Prologue
A. Pritchard, P. Caron
Procession led by C. Boyer.
Egyptian Slave Girl Dance
M. Marano, A Gertrude Hoffmann Girl, Misses Froggie, Gillberti, Gay, Luzon, McGonigle

Scene 18
Brazilian Nuts[121]
J. Pearl, H. O'Neal

---

[113]Dropped during the run.
[114]First edition opened 5 January 1926 at the Casino de Paris (atop the Century Theatre) for 208 performances.
[115]New material added for the Second Edition.

[116]New material added for the Second Edition.
[117]New material added for the Second Edition.
[118]New material added for the Second Edition.
[119]New material added for the Second Edition.
[120]New material added for the Second Edition.
[121]Dropped after opening.

Scene 19
"In the Gardens of the King"[122]
    R. Watson, L. Rhodes, Gertrude Hoffmann Girls
Scene 20
"Powder Puff" (Finale)
    A. Pritchard
    (*Music by* J. Fred Coots, Maurice Rubens. *Lyrics by* Clifford Grey, McElbert Moore.)
    With K. Ray. *Caron's Face Powders: Narcisse Noir*: C. Sylvae, G. Rennick. *N'Aimez Que Moi*: R. Brady, I. Bennett. *Infini*: I. St. Clair. *Mes Jeunes Années*: J. Brown. And C. Gallimore, Entire Ensemble.

ACT 2[123]
Scene 1
"Sacrifice"[124]
    M. Ferenzo, Oyra, C. Gallimore, Gertrude Hoffmann Girls, Maids of Paris
Scene 2
Kongo Dreams[125]
    John: B. Parker. *His Wife*: R. Watson. *The Butler*: W. Davis. *Little Min*: N. Kondo. *Mr. Kingsland*: R. Coram. *Craig*: W. O'Neal. *Annie*: N. Terris.
Scene 3
"The Slave"
    M. Ferenzo
    Danced by O. McClure, Oyra, Gertrude Hoffmann Girls.
Scene 4
"Lulu Belle"[126]
    N. Terris, Gertrude Hoffmann Girls, M. Finley
    (*Staged by* Seymour Felix.)
Scene 5
Exaggeration[127]
    Ferdinand: W. O'Neal. *His Secretary*: J. Pearl. *Mr. Hemmindinger*: R. Lee. *Mabel*: M. O'Brien. *Rose*: A. Pritchard. *First Maid*: V. Watts. *Second Maid*: P. Caron.
Scene 6
"Louisiana"
    N. Terris, A. Pritchard, Gertrude Hoffmann Girls
    (*Music by* J. Fred Coots, Maurice Rubens. *Lyrics by* McElbert Moore.)
    Designed by Betty Duke.)
Scene 7
Naughty
    Scene: The Boudoir of Madame.
    The Announcer: H. O'Neal. *Jack*: J. Osterman. *The Wife*: A. Fechner. *The Maid*: E. Woolley. *The Husband*: W. Davis.
Scene 8
"They Satisfy"
    J. Osterman, K. Ray, Maids of Paris
    (*Designed by* Betty Duke.)
Scene 9
The Friends
    (*by* Howard Rogers)
    The Husband: R. Lee. *His Friend*: B. Parker. *The Maid*: M. O'Brien. *The Butler*: W. Davis.
Scene 10
"Dance Fever"[128]
    (*Staged by* Seymour Felix.)
    N. Terris, R. Coram, G. Dobbs, Gertrude Hoffmann Girls
Scene 11
Watch Your Step
    The Gambler: H. O'Neal. *The Visitor*: J. Pearl. *His Friend*: W. Davis. *The Loser*: R. Lee. *His Wife*: M. O'Brien.

---

[122]Dropped after opening.
[123]Added late in the run:
    Damia (first American appearance of the famous French lyric tragedienne in a program of special songs).
[124]Dropped after opening.
[125]New material added for the Second Edition, then dropped after opening.
[126]New material added for the Second Edition.
[127]New material added for the Second Edition.
[128](Formerly billed as "Dance Mad."

Scene 12
The Quartet[129]
    M. Ferenzo, E. Woolley, R. Watson, L. Rhodes
    Announced by O. Marye.
Scene 13
"Wedding Day" (Finale)
    K. Ray, G. Dobbs, N. Terris, M. O'Brien, L. LaRiviere, Gertrude Hoffmann Girls, Maids of Paris

1926.02 **HELLO LOLA!**

A Musical Comedy in Three Acts, 5 Scenes. Book and lyrics by Dorothy Donnelly. Based on Booth Tarkington's novel 'Seventeen' and its stage adaptation by Hugh Stanislaus Stange and Stannard Mears. Music by William B. Kernell. Dances and ensembles staged by Seymour Felix. Costumes by Ernest R. Schrapps. Settings designed by Livingston Platt. Orchestra under the direction of Charles Sieger. Produced by the Messrs. Shubert. Opened 12 January 1926 at the Eltinge Theatre, moved 8 February 1926 to Maxine Elliott's Theatre, and closed 20 February 1926 after 47 performances[130].

CAST (in order of appearance): *Jane Baxter*: Marjorie White. *Bridget*: Kittye Casey. *Mr. Baxter*: Ben Hendricks. *Mrs. Baxter*: NANETTE FLACK. *Willie Baxter*: RICHARD KEENE. *May Parcher*: WYNN RICHMOND. *Johnnie Watson*: GEORGIE STONE. *Lola Pratt*: EDYTHE BAKER. *Joe Bullitt*: ELISHA COOK, JR. *Genesis*: JAY C. FLIPPEN. *Mr. Parcher*: Ben Franklin. *George Crooper*: Bert Gardner. *Miss Boke*: Margaret Sullivan. *Clematis, Genesis' Dog*: Clematis. *Flopit, Lola's Dog*: Flopit.
    May Parcher's Friends: Sylvia Carol, Frances Mildern, Emma Wyche, Dorothy Palmer, Cora Stephens, Avis Adair, Katherine Vercelle, Louise Vercelle. *Jane's Little Girl Friends*: Dorothy Casey, Constance Lahleet, Nancy Lea, Betty Noi, Virginia Ray, Beatrice Reiss, Diddie Read, Lillian Clerke. *Willie's Boy Friends*: Cullen Clewis, George Crouch, Don DeFrancis, Albert Miller, Larry Vale, Harry Wood, Howard Shea, Wally Stewart, Earl Atkinson.

Act 1: The Baxter Home. Afternoon.

Act 2: The Porch of the Parcher Home. Evening. A week later.

Act 3, Scene 1: The Baxter Garden. *Scene 2*: Going to the Baxter's. *Scene 3*: The Baxter Garden. Three hours later.

ACT 1
"Bread and Butter and Sugar"
    M. White, Little Girls
"The Summertime"
    W. Richmond, G. Stone, Girls
"Lullaby"
    N. Flack
"My Brother Willie"
    R. Keene, M. White
"My Baby Talk Lady"
    R. Keene
"Hello, Cousin Lola"
    E. Baker, W. Richmond, G. Stone, E. Cook, Jr., Boys, Girls
"Five-Foot-Two"
    J. C. Flippen
"My Baby-Talk Lady" (reprise)
    R. Keene

ACT 2
"Water, Water, Wildflowers"
    Little Girls
"Step on the Gasoline"
    G. Stone, W. Richmond
"Swinging on the Gate"
    R. Keene, E. Baker
    Ensemble
"That Certain Party"
    J. C. Flippen
Pianologue
    E. Baker

---

[129]Formerly Casino de Paris Quartette.
[130]Staging uncredited; out of town the staging was credited to J. J. Shubert.

"My Baby Talk Lady" (reprise)
    R. Keene, E. Baker
"In the Dark"
    R. Keene, G. Stone, J. C. Flippen, E. Cook, Jr., Boys, Girls

ACT 3
Scene 1
  "I Know Something"
    Ensemble
  "Little Boy Blue"
    R. Keene, W. Richmond, Girls
  "Grau Brae Nicht"
    M. White
Scene 2
  "Baxter's Party"
    Ensemble
Scene 3
  "Keep It Up"
    W. Richmond, G. Stone, E. Cook, Jr., Boys, Girls
  "Sophie"
    J. C. Flippen
  "Don't Stop"
    E. Baker, Boys
  "Good-By, Cousin Lola" (reprise)
    Entire Company
  "Lullaby" (reprise)
    N. Flack
  "My Baby Talk Lady" (reprise)
    Ensemble

1926.03   SWEETHEART TIME

A Musical Comedy in Two Acts, 6 Scenes. Book by Harry B. Smith. Based on the farce 'Never Say Die' by W. H. Post and William Collier. Music by Walter Donaldson, Joseph Meyer, (Jay Gorney). Lyrics by Ballard Macdonald, Irving Caesar, (Harry B. Smith). Book directed by William Collier. Dances by Larry Ceballos. Costumes designed by Charles Lemaire. Settings by Karl O. Amend and Nicholas Yellenti. Orchestrations by Stephen Jones, Maurice dePackh and Hans Spialek. Orchestra under the direction of John L. McManus. Produced by Rufus LeMaire[131]. Opened 19 January 1926 at the Imperial Theatre and closed 22 May 1926 after 143 performances.

CAST (in order of appearance): *Jeffries*: Starke Patterson. *Nina*: Laine Blaire. *Marian Stevenson*: MARION SAKI. *Roy Henderson*: AL SEXTON. *Mrs. Stevenson*: Marie Nordstrom. *Dr. Ralph Galesby*: GEORGE LeMAIRE. *Violet Stevenson*: MARY MILBURN. *Lord Hector Raybrook*: FRED LESLIE. *Griggs*: Wilmer Bentley. *Dion Woodbury*: EDDIE BUZZELL. *Detective James*: Harry Kelly. *Alphonse*: M. Marcel Rousseau. *Carita*: Rita Del Marga. *Waiter*: Bob Callahan. *Dorothy*: Dorothy Van Alst. *Alice*: Alice Wood. *Betty*: Betty Wright. *Bessie*: Bessie Kademova. *Dorothy*: Dorothy Brown. *Bobbie*: Bobbie Breslaw. (*Dance Specialty*): Bob Gordon, Harry King. *Specialty*: Nick Lucas, Dorothy McNulty [Penny Singleton].)
  Young Ladies of the Ensemble: Dorothy Van Alst, Alice Wood, Betty Wright, Bessie Kademova, Dorothy Brown, Bobbie Breslaw, Aida Winston, Dorothy Fitzgibbons, Ann Hardman, Neida Snow, Beverley Maude, Loretta Rehm, Adele Hart, Alice Monroe, Nellie McCarthy, Peggy Thayer, Millicent Olson.

Act 1, Scene 1: The Grounds of the Stevenson Estate. *Scene 2*: At the Church. *Scene 3*: The Grounds of the Stevenson Estate. Evening.

Act 2, Scene 1: Lord Raymond's reception in the Garden of the Piedmont Hotel. One year later. *Scene 2*: Corridor of Mr. Woodbury's Apartment. *Scene 3*: Mr. Woodbury's Apartment.

ACT 1[132]

Opening Chorus
    Ensemble
    (*Music by* Joseph Meyer. *Lyrics by* Harry B. Smith.)
"Marian"[133]
    M. Nordstrom, A. Sexton, M. Saki
    (*Music by* Walter Donaldson. *Lyrics by* Ballard Macdonald.)
"Step On It"
    F. Leslie, Girls
    (*Music by* Joseph Meyer. *Lyrics by* Irving Caesar.)
Dance
    D. Van Alst, A. Wood, B. Gordon, H. King
Dance
    S. Patterson, L. Blaire
"Sweetheart Time"[134]
    M. Milburn, Girls
    (*Music by* Joseph Meyer. *Lyrics by* Irving Caesar.)
"Two By Four"[135]
    A. Sexton, M. Saki
    (*Music by* Joseph Meyer. *Lyrics by* Irving Caesar.)
"Girl in Your Arms"
    M. Milburn, E. Buzzell
    (*Music by* Jay Gorney. *Lyrics by* Irving Caesar.)
"One Way Street"
    H. Kelly, Company
    (*Music by* Walter Donaldson. *Lyrics by* Ballard Macdonald.)
Finale
    Ensemble

ACT 2[136]
Scene 1
  "Tahiti (Sweetie)"[137]
    N. Lucas, Company
    (*Music by* Walter Donaldson. *Lyrics by* Ballard Macdonald.)
    Dancers: B. Wright, D. McNulty.
  Dance Specialty
    B. Gordon, H. King
  "Who Loves You as I Do?"[138]
    M. Milburn, A. Sexton
    (*Music by* Joseph Meyer. *Lyrics by* Irving Caesar.)
  "Who's Who?"
    A. Sexton, M. Saki, Girls
    (*Music by* Walter Donaldson. *Lyrics by* Ballard Macdonald.)
  "Rue de la Paix"
    E. Buzzell, Ensemble
    (*Music by* Walter Donaldson. *Lyrics by* Ballard Macdonald.)
  Dance
    D. Van Alst, B. Breslaw, D. McNulty
Scene 2
  Dance Specialty
    S. Patterson, L. Blaire
  "Cocktail Melody"
    F. Leslie, Girls
    (*Music by* Walter Donaldson. *Lyrics by* Ballard Macdonald.)

---

[131]James La Penner and Edward A. Miller took over as producers in February 1926.
[132]For subsequent tour, the show was radically revised, song order altered. The following songs were added:
  "Everybody Wants to Marry Me" (Act 1)
    Shirley Vernon (Violet Stevenson), Boys
  "Sympathy" (Act 1)
    S. Vernon, Stanley Ridges (Dion Woodbury), Male Quartette
  "Time for Love" (Act 2)
    S. Vernon, B. Gordon, H. King, Boys

---

[133]Dropped for subsequent national tour.
[134]Dropped for subsequent national tour.
[135]Dropped for subsequent national tour.
[136]Act 2, Scene 1 opening number replaced by:
  "At the Party"
    Entire Company
    (*Music by* Harry Ruby. *Lyrics by* Bert Kalmar.)
The song order was revised repeatedly during the run. Also added:
  "If Things Were Only Different" (Act 2, Scene 1) (later dropped)
    Irene Dunne (Violet Stevenson)
  Specialty (Act 2, Scene 2)
    E. Buzzell, M. Milburn, A. Sexton, M. Saki, H. Kelly, Girls
  "I Know That I Love You" (Act 2, Scene 3) (subsequently moved to Act 1)
    A. Sexton, Irma Marwick (Marian Stevenson), Girls
    (*Music by* Harry Ruby. *Lyrics by* Bert Kalmar.)
[137]Dropped after the opening.
[138]Dropped after the opening.

Scene 3
  Specialty[139]
    N. Lucas
  "On Such a Beautiful Night"
    A. Sexton, M. Saki, Girls
    (*Music by* Joseph Meyer. *Lyrics by* Irving Caesar.)
  Finale
    Entire Company

1926.04

THE MATINEE GIRL

A Musical Comedy in Two Acts, 6 Scenes. Book and lyrics by McElbert Moore and Bide Dudley. Music by Frank H. Grey. Staged by Oscar Eagle. Dances arranged by S. Lee Rose. Settings designed by Joseph Physioc. Costumes by Milgrim. Orchestra under the direction of Frank H. Grey. Produced by Edmund Rosenblum, Jr. for Edmund Enterprises, Inc. Opened 1 February 1926 at the Forrest Theatre and closed 20 February 1926 after 24 performances.

CAST (in order of appearance): *The Usherette*: Bernie Goe. *Bess Gordon*: Juliette Day. *"Bubbles" Peters*: OLGA STECK. *Jack Sterling*: JAMES HAMILTON. *Phil Taylor*: JACK SQUIRE. *Boggs*: Kevitt Manton. *Captain Mack*: John Kearney. *Archie de Witt*: GUS SHY. *Lill McCue*: Madeline Grey. *Ramon Mendez*: Rudolf Badeloni. *Philander Peters*: John Park. *Lucy Peters*: Helene Herman. *Maria Mendez*: Rose LaHarte.
  Usherettes: *Miss Sear Goe*: Bernie Goe. *Miss Cantbe Beat*: Ruth Farrar. *Miss Doer Die*: Hester Bailey. *Miss Proper Thyme*: Dorothy Proudlock. *Miss Nora Knowes*: Berta Claire Hall. *Miss Walker Home*: Ruth Penery. *Miss Rollser Owne*: Dorothy Charles. *Miss Lefter Wright*: Edith Shaw. *Miss Showser Style*: Emily Verdi. *Miss Sparklin Wyne*: Edna Hopper. *Miss Auter Fall*: Jerry Dryden. *Miss Maidter Order*: Helen Grey.
  The Matinee Steppers: Stanley Bailey, Joseph F. Brown, Lew Miller, Dick Gibbons, Frank McCormack, Harry Locke.

Act 1, Scene 1: A Stage Box of a New York Theatre. During a Matinee Performance. *Scene 2*: The Star's Dressing Room. Immediately afterwards. *Scene 3*: Aboard the Yacht 'Matinee Girl.' Afternoon of a June day. Two months later.
Act 2, Scene 1: Patio of Peters' Home, Cuba. Five days later. *Scene 2*: Under the Palms. *Scene 3*: Patio of Peters' Home. Evening.

ACT 1
  "At the Matinee"
    O. Steck, J. Hamilton
  "Mash Notes"
    J. Hamilton, Girls
    (*Music by* Frank Grey and McElbert Moore.)
  "Joy Ride"
    S. Bailey, J. F. Brown, Ensemble
  "The One You Love"
    O. Steck
  "When My Little Ship Comes In"
    O. Steck, J. Hamilton, Boys
  "Jumping Jack"
    O. Steck, G. Shy, Ensemble
  "Like-a-Me, Like-a-You"
    J. Day, J. Squire, Ensemble
    (*Music by* Frank Grey and McElbert Moore.)
  "Only One"
    J. Hamilton, Girls
    (*Music by* Frank Grey and McElbert Moore.)
  Finale
    Entire Company
ACT 2
  "His Spanish Guitar"
    R. LaHarte, Ensemble
  "Holding Hands"
    J. Day, J. Squire
  "Havanola Roll"
    O. Steck, Ensemble
  Specialty
    H. Bailey
  "What Difference Does It Make?"
    J. Day, O. Steck
    (*Music by* Constance Shepard.)

"Waiting All the Time for You"
  O. Steck, J. Hamilton
"A Little Bit of Spanish"
  G. Shy, B. Goe, Girls
"Only One" (reprise)
  J. Hamilton
Finaletto
  O. Steck
"The Biggest Thing in My Life"
  H. Herman, G. Shy
"Havanola Roll" (reprise)
  J. Brown, S. Bailey, Ensemble
Ballet
  R. Penery, G. Dryden, D. Charles, H. Bailey, B. C Hall, H. Grey
"Do I Dear, I Do"
  J. Day, J. Squire, H. Herman, G. Shy, Ensemble
  (*Music and Lyrics by* McElbert Moore.)
"The One You Love" (reprise)
  O. Steck
Finale
  Entire Company

1926.05

BLOSSOM TIME

A Revival of the Operetta in Three Acts[140]. Book and lyrics by Dorothy Donnelly. Adapted from the original ('Das Dreimäderlhaus') by A. M. Willner and Heinz Reichert, based on a novel "Schwammerl" by Rudolf H. Bartsch. Music adapted and augmented by Sigmund Romberg from the melodies of Franz Schubert selected and arranged by Heinrich Berté. Staged by J. C. Huffman. Scenes designed by Watson Barratt. Entire production under the personal direction of J. J. Shubert. Produced by the Messrs. Shubert. Opened 8 March 1926 at the Jolson Theatre and closed 20 March 1926 after 16 performances.

CAST: *Mitzi*: BEULAH BERSON. *Bellabruna*: Leeta Corder. *Fritzi*: Sioux Nedra. *Kitzi*: Genevieve Naegele. *Mrs. Kranz*: ALEXANDRA DAGMAR. *Greta*: MYRA LEE. *Baron von Schober*: WARREN FOSTER. *Franz Schubert*: KNIGHT MacGREGOR. *Kranz*: Robert Lee Allen. *Count Sharntoff*: JULES EPAILLY. *Vogl*: James Bardin. *Kupelweiser*: Norman Johnston. *von Schwind*: Harrison Wilson. *Binder*: Robert Tait. *Erkman*: Oliver T. McCormick. *Hanse*: Mack Ponch. *Novotny*: JOHN E. WHEELER. *A Dancer*: Louise Rothacker. *Mrs. Colburg*: Millie Freeman. *Domeyer*: Alex Drew.
  Dancers: Betty Walters, Lea Lake, Peggy Beck, Maria Verba, Dorothea Clegg, Paula Sherra. *Show Girls*: Mary McBirney, Margaret Walker, Bonnie Bonner, Cecilia Grayce, Dorothy Schamm, Estelle Hellers.

1926.06

RAINBOW ROSE

A Musical Play in Three Acts. Book by Walter De Leon. Based on the play 'A Lucky Break' by Zelda Sears. Music and lyrics by Harold Levey and Owen Murphy. Production staged by Walter Wilson. Dances staged by Ray Perez. Settings designed by William Castle. Costumes by Schneider-Anderson, Brooks Costume Company. Orchestra under the direction of Harold Levey. Produced by George MacFarlane Productions, Inc.[141] Opened 16 March 1926 at the Forrest Theatre and closed 1 May 1926 after 55 performances.

CAST (in order of appearance): *Martha*: Louise Galloway. *Hulda*: MARGARET WALKER. *Claudia Barrett*: BILLY TICHENOR. *Mrs. Barrett*: VIOLA GILLETTE. *David Martin*: Paisley Noon. *Benny Ketcham*: HANSFORD WILSON. *Abner Ketcham*: ALEXANDER CLARK. *Rose Haven*: SHIRLEY SHERMAN. *Tommy Lansing*: JACK WHITING. *John Bruce*: JACK SQUIRE. *The Expressman*: Fred Waldeck.
  The Charleston Charmers: Peggy Penn, Beauton O'Quinn, Evelyn Kindler, Shirley Guistin, Jean Unger, Jean Alden, Irene Shay, Katherine Roberts, Lois Annette, Isabelle Brown, Myrtle LeRoy, Woody Lee Wilson, Gertrude Kayser, Bernie Varden, Mary Norris, Guerida Crawford. *The Delirious Dancers*: Delbert Faust, Frank Marshall, Jack Wills, Clinton McLerr, Frank Sherlock, Jr., Jules Shear, Thomas Kerns, George

---

[139]Dropped after the opening.

[140]First presented in New York 29 September 1921 at the Ambassador Theatre for 592 performances. For Synopsis of Scenes and Musical Numbers, see original 1921 production.
[141]Production taken over by Earle Boothe in association with George MacFarlane 19 April 1926.

Carroll. *The Rainbow Rosebuds*: Evelyn Kindler, Peggy Penn, Beauton O'Quinn, Shirley Guistin.

Act 1: The Haven House, Mattasquan, Connecticut.

Act 2: Same. A few weeks later.

Act 3: The Garden of the Haven House. Evening.

ACT 1

"We Want Our Breakfast"
    L. Galloway, Girls

"Steppin' Baby"
    H. Wilson, M. Walker, Dancers

"You're All the World to Me"
    S. Sherman

"Jealous"
    S. Sherman, J. Whiting, B. Tichenor

"First, Last and Only"
    J. Squire, S. Sherman, Ensemble

Finale
    Tout Ensemble

ACT 2

Opening
    Ensemble

"Something Tells Me I'm in Love"
    J. Whiting, B. Tichenor, Dancers

"Going Over the Bumps"
    H. Wilson, M. Walker, Dancers

"If You Were Someone Else and Someone Else Were Only Here"
    J. Whiting, S. Sherman, Ensemble

"When the Hurdy Gurdy Plays"
    J. Squire, H. Wilson, M. Walker, Ensemble

Finale

ACT 3

"Dreams" (Opening)
    V. Gillette, Entire Company

Pas Seul
    B. Tichnor

Danse Eccentrique
    M. Walker

Specialty
    H. Wilson

"Let's Get Married"
    J. Whiting, B. Tichenor

"Rainbow"
    J. Squire, Girls

Finale

THE GIRL FRIEND

1926.07

A Musical Comedy in Two Acts, 6 Scenes. Book by Herbert Fields. Music by Richard Rodgers. Lyrics by Lorenz Hart. Book staged by John Harwood. Musical numbers and dances arranged and staged by Jack Haskell. Settings by P. Dodd Ackerman. Costumes designed by John N. Booth, Jr., Grace Carson, Hugh Willoughby. Orchestra under the direction of Ernest Cutting. Orchestrations by Maurice dePackh. Entire production under the supervision of Lew Fields. Produced by Lew Fields. Opened 17 March 1926 at the Vanderbilt Theatre and closed 4 December 1926 after 301 performances.

CAST (in order of appearance): *Fanny Silver*: Eva Condon. *Ellen*: Dorothy Barber. *Leonard Silver*: SAM WHITE. *Mollie Farrell*: EVA PUCK. *Thomas Larson*: John Hundley. *Arthur Spencer*: Frank Doane. *Wynn Spencer*: Evelyn Cavanaugh. *Irene Covel*: June Cochrane. *Donald Litt*: Francis X. Donegan. *Ann*: Silvia Shawn. *Mike*, a trainer: Jack Kogan. *Duffy*, another trainer: Walter Bigelow. *Jane Talbot*: Dorothy Barber. *Mme. Ruby DeLilly*: Jan Moore. *A Butler*: Ainsley Lambert. *Leon Rose's Band* (6): *Eddie*: Leon Rose. *Frank*: Joel Duroe. *Jim*: Paul Sabin. *Henry*: Herman Newman. *Walter*: William Marshall. *Bill*: Sanford Wolf.
    Girls: Gypsy Mooney, Olive Beebe, Eve Marie Gray, Helen Shepard, Dorothy Brown, Evelyn Ruth Urilda, Elizabeth Mears, Alice Kosta, Dorothy Roy, Virginia Otis, Carol Lynne, Gertrude Cole. *Boys*: Roy Clements, Eddie Leslie, Austin Clarke, Arthur C. Budd, K. Smith Stanley, A. Goodrich.

Act 1, Scene 1: Backyard of the Silver Dairy, Long Island. *Scene 2*: Railroad Station. Maple Villa, Long Island. *Scene 3*: Entrance Hall of the Blue Grass Inn, Long Island.

One week later. *Scene 4*: On the Road. *Scene 5*: Before the Spencer Estate at Ardsley-on-Hudson, New York. Next morning.

Act 2: Before the Spencer Estate, Ardsley-on-Hudson, New York. Two weeks later.

ACT 1

Scene 1

"Hey! Hey!"
    Ensemble

"The Simple Life"
    Ensemble

"The Girl Friend"
    E. Puck, S. White

Scene 2

"Goodbye, Lenny!"
    Ensemble

Scene 3

"The Blue Room"
    E. Puck, S. White

"Cabarets"
    Ensemble

"Why Do I?"
    J. Cochrane, F. X. Donegan, Ensemble

"The Damsel Who Done All the Dirt"
    E. Puck

"He's a Winner"
    F. Doane, Ensemble

Scene 5

"Town Hall Tonight"
    E. Puck, J. Cochrane, F. X. Donegan, S. White, Ensemble

Dance
    Urilda

"Good Fellow, Mine"
    E. Cavanaugh, J. Hundley, Ensemble

Reprise
    E. Puck

Finale
    Ensemble

ACT 2

"Creole Cooning Song"
    J. Hundley, Ensemble

Dance
    D. Barber

"I'd Like to Take You Home"
    J. Cochrane, F. X. Donegan

"What Is It?"
    F. Doane, Ensemble

Dance
    D. Barber

"Dance"
    S. White

Finale
    Entire Company

H.M.S. PINAFORE,
or, The Lass That Loved a Sailor

1926.08

A Revival of the Comic Opera in Two Acts[142]. Libretto by William S. Gilbert. Music by Arthur Sullivan. Entire production staged by Milton Aborn. Costumes by Ernest R. Schrapps. Setting by Rollo Wayne. Musical director, Max Hirschfeld. Produced by the Messrs. Shubert. Opened 6 April 1926 at the Century Theatre and closed 24 May 1926 after 56 performances.

CAST: *The Rt. Hon. Sir Joseph Porter, K.C.B.*, First Lord of the Admiralty: JOHN F. HAZZARD. *Captain Corcoran*, Commander of the *H.M.S. Pinafore*: MARION GREEN. *Ralph Rackstraw*, Able Seaman: TOM BURKE. *Dick Deadeye*, Able Seaman: WILLIAM DANFORTH. *Bill Bobstay*, Boatswain: Charles E. Galagher. *Bob*

---

[142]Originally presented in New York 15 January 1879 at the Standard Theatre for 175 performances. For Synopsis of Scenes and Musical Numbers, see original 1879 production.

Becket: Chester Bright. *Tom Tucker*: Master Durkin. *Sergeant of Marines*: Emmet Douglas. *Josephine*, the Captain's Daughter: MARGUERITE NAMARA. *Hebe*, Sir Joseph's First Cousin: Nydia d'Arnell. *Little Buttercup*, Mrs. Cripps, a Portsmouth bum-boat woman: FAY TEMPLETON.

First Lord's Sisters: Florence Poyet, Rene Zorelli. *His Aunts*: Marion Maria, Treva Stowell, Leonora D'Arcy. *His Cousins*: Irma King, Flo Georges, Cathleen Strickland, Mildred Windell, Sue Lake, Clarice Anderson, Viola Hailes, Charlotte Miles, Rose Maynard, Henrietta Merriman, Florence Poyet, Eleanor Swayne, Clementine Rigeau, Eileen Mayer, Mona Desmond, Annette Lang, Jean Lane, Gladys Maynard, Alice Schuman, Lucille Doreward, Mary Noonan, Caroline Euler, Evelyn Grayson, Nancy Corrigan, Florence Edwards, Joan Hope, Leona Pierce, Phyllis Paige, Leonora D'Arcy, Doris Coleman, Florence Burnham, Rene Zorelli, Mand Carlton, Adele Savoye, Therese Hyle, Marion Maria, Diana Bogart, Margaret Haase, Alan Moray, Isabel O'Niel, Vera Dale, Treva Stowell, Flo Mamson, Anne Chrystie, Margie Lowery, Olive Pearson, Freda Leary. *His Middies*: Clarice Anderson, Evelyn Grayson, Adele Savoye, Phyllis Paige, Caroline Euler, Clementine Rigeau, Margaret Haase, Annette Lang, Olive Pearson, Margie Lowery, Charlotte Miles, Isabel O'Niel. *Marine Band*: Arthur Williams, John Pruett, George Brown, Sydney Smith, Frederic Thompson, Bruce Adams, Jack Armstrong, Edwin Carrol, Frank Dixon, Albert Hernsen. *Marine Drum Corps*: Robert Burke, Geoffrey Erritt, Orlando DeSales, Jack Burger, Rene Bellinger, Aylward Martin. *Marine Guard*: Harry Watson, Benny Brush, Leiciate Furland, Emmit Douglas, Martin Sherdahl, Ernest Dolphy, Lawrence Arcuri, Serge Conchnoff. *Sailors*: Pat McCarthy, Ernest Henri, John W. Cooney, Emmit Douglas, William O'Brien, Mike Wagman, Benny Brush, James Ellenbecker, Benjamin Flack, Harry Young, Leiciate Furland, Ellis Doyle, Wallace Banfield, Frank Chapman, Harry Watson, Lloyd Still, Dudley Marwick, Jack Ray, Ralph Leigh, Jack Burger, Lawrence Arcuri, Robert Burke, Warren McGoldrick, Geoffrey Erritt, Ernest Dolphy, Orlando DeSales, Scott Allen, Granville Eagler, Chester Bright, Martin Sherdahl, Rene Bellinger, Glib Chandro, Aylward Martin, Fred Semore, Serge Conchnoff, William von Schlutter, Frank Dobert, Leo Nash, George Westwood, William Langon.

RAQUEL MELLER
1926.09

A One-Woman Revue of Spanish Songs. Symphonic Orchestra selected from the Philharmonic Society of New York under the direction of Victor Baravelle. Produced by E. Ray Goetz. Opened 14 April 1926 at the Empire Theatre and closed 15 May 1926 after 38 performances.

CAST: SEÑORITA RAQUEL MELLER.

MUSICAL PROGRAM

"El Relicario" (The Charm/My Toreador)

"Diguli Que Vengui" (Tell Him to Come/Hurry Mateo)

"El Peligro de las Rosas" (Beware of the Rose)

"Noi de la Marc" (The Lullaby)

"Ay! Cipriano" (Naughty Cipriano/That Waltz Espagnol)

"La Hija del Carcelero" (The Jailer's Daughter)

"La Tarde del Corpus" (The Procession)

"La Monteria" (Grandmother's Dress/At the Dance)

"Flor del Mal" (Flower of Sin/Poor Scentless Flower)

"Mimosa" (When Love Passes By)

"Gitanillo" (My Gypsy Sweetheart)

"La Violetera" (Who'll Buy My Violets/The Violet Girl)

Optional Numbers:

"Siempre Flor" (The Eternal Flower)

"Nena" (Your Wonderful Lips)

"La Farandulo Pasa" (Poor Pierrot)

IOLANTHE,
or, The Peer and the Peri
1926.10

A Revival of the Comic Opera in Two Acts[143]. Libretto by William S. Gilbert. Music by Arthur Sullivan. Staged by Winthrop Ames. Settings and costumes by Woodman Thompson. Dances by Louise Gifford. Conductor, Robert Hood Bowers. Produced by Winthrop Ames. Opened 19 April 1926 at the Plymouth Theatre and played a full 8-performance week schedule

[143]First presented in New York 25 November 1882 at the Standard Theatre for 105 performances. For Synopsis of Scenes and Musical Numbers, see original 1882 production.

until 27 November 1926; thereafter played twice weekly (Thursday matinees and evenings) in repertory with THE PIRATES OF PENZANCE before closing 24 March 1927 after 255 performances.

CAST: *The Lord Chancellor*: ERNEST LAWFORD. *Earl of Mountararat*: JOHN BARCLAY. *Earl of Tolloller*: J. HUMBIRD DUFFY. *Private Willis* of the Grenadier Guards: WILLIAM C. GORDON. *Strephon*, an Arcadian Shepherd: WILLIAM WILLIAMS. *The Train-Bearer*: Bert Prival. *Queen of the Fairies*: VERA ROSS. *Iolanthe*, a Fairy, Strephon's Mother: ADELE SANDERSON. *Celia*: Kathryn Reece. *Leila*: Sybil Sterling. *Fleta*: Paula Langlen. *Phyllis*, an Arcadian Shepherdess and Ward in Chancery: LOIS BENNETT.

Fairies: Phoebe Brand, Barbara Bronson, Carolyn Caldwell, Katherine Carrington, Dorothy Coulter, Dorothea Dale, Mildred Harrington, Irene Hubert, Judith Hutton, Sybil Kama, Agnes Ketcham, Milja Levander, Ruth Marion, Viola Thomas, Thea Zell. *Dukes, Marquises, Earls, Viscounts, Barons*: Joseph Ames, Frank Allison, A. L. Benson, Wesley Boynton, Hartwell DeMille, Franklin Foreman, Eduard Franz, Albert Hewitt, Thomas E. Knight, Benn K. Leavenworth, George C. Lehrian, Kirk Murray, Vidor Sparks, Deane Spaulding, Holmes Washburn, George Wharton.

BUNK OF 1926
1926.11

A Musical Revue in Two Acts, 35 Scenes[144]. Sketches and lyrics by Gene Lockhart and Percy Waxman. Music by Gene Lockhart. Additional music by Deems Taylor and Robert Armbruster. Staged by Gene Lockhart. Dances staged by Van Lowe. Costumes by Florence Froelich. Orchestra under the direction of Robert Armbruster. Orchestrations by Robert Armbruster and William Spielter. Produced by Wallace & Martins, Inc. Opened 22 April 1926 at the Broadhurst Theatre and closed 29 May 1926 after 44 performances; New summer edition (see detail below, immediately following) opened 31 May 1926, closing 5-8 June 1926 by action of Citizens Play Jury, reopened under injunction 9 June 1926 and closed 19 June 1926 after 14 performances. Total, including off-Broadway: 96 performances.

CAST: GENE LOCKHART, DOLLY STERLING, MARIE LAMBERT, JEANNE GREENE, PAULINE BLAIR, FLORENCE ARTHUR, HAZEL SHELLEY, JAY FASSETT, BOOTS McKENNA, JOSEPH McCALLIOM, JOHN MAXWELL.

Ensemble: Marie Ellen, Juliet De La Morcha, Bebe LaBelle, Marie Warner, Frances Ney, Ethelyn Tillman, Peggy Lee, Frances O'Brien, Renee Fenbow, Emily Slater, Ida Miller, Gerey Dean.

ACT 1
Scene 1
"You Never Hear a Single Word They're Singing" (Opening Chorus)
Company
(*Music by* Gene Lockhart. *Lyrics by* Percy Waxman.)
Scene 2
"Bunk"
G. Lockhart
(*Music and Lyrics by* Gene Lockhart.)
Scene 3
Those Indispensable Girls

[144]Settings uncredited. Originally produced Off-Broadway 16 February-20 March 1926 at the Heckscher Theatre for 38 performances. For original Off-Broadway run, Talbot Productions, Inc. was billed as producer of THE BUNK OF 1926. Dances were staged by Adrian S. Perrin. Settings by William A. Hanna. Costumes by Robert Stevenson. Orchestra under the direction of Robert Armbruster. Dropped from that Off-Broadway cast were: Carol Joyce, Ruth Tester, Milton Rieck. The production was vastly revised for its Broadway transfer. Material from that edition, but dropped for Broadway, included:

Just the Boys (Act 2)
Henry: G. Lockhart. *Ted*: J. Fassett. *Bill*: J. . Maxwell. *Jim*: M. Rieck. *Ethel*: F. Arthur.
"The Way to Your Heart" (Act 1)
J. Maxwell
(*Music and Lyrics by* Gene Lockhart.)
"Pan" (A Woodland Fantasy) (Act 2)
G. Lockhart
(*Music by* Gene Lockhart. *Lyrics by* Percy Waxman.)
Dance de Mystere (*Music by* Deems Taylor.) (Act 2)
"Love's Old Sweet Song" (Act 2)
J. Fassett
(*Music by* Gene Lockhart. *Lyrics by* Percy Waxman.)

Scene 4

"You Told Me That You Loved Me But You Never Told Me Why"

J. Fassett

(*Music by* Gene Lockhart. *Lyrics by* Percy Waxman.)

Scene 5

Second Thoughts (Demonstrating that the love-theme is the greatest of all educational forces)

Her Fiancé: G. Lockhart. *His Fiancée*: H. Shelley. *First Wife*: P. Blair. *First Husband*: J. McCallion. *Second Wife*: F. Arthur. *Second Husband*: B. McKenna. *Third Wife*: J. Greene. *Third Husband*: J. Fassett.

Scene 6

"Monte, the Model"

J. McCallion, Girls

(*Music by* Gene Lockhart. *Lyrics by* Percy Waxman.)

Scene 7

"Those Mammy Singers" (Those Mammy Boys)

D. Sterling

(*Music by* Gene Lockhart and Robert Armbruster. *Lyrics by* Percy Waxman.)

Scene 8

The Silk Hat

(*by* Phillip Kobbe)

The Woman: F. Arthur. *The Waiter*: G. Lockhart. *The Piano Tuner*: J. Fassett. *The Paper-Hanger*: B. McKenna. *The Silk Hat*: Dobbs and Company.

Scene 9

Taps

H. Shelley

Scene 10

A Geisha Legend: "The Geisha's Lament"

J. Maxwell, Girls

(*Music by* Gene Lockhart. *Lyrics by* Percy Waxman.)

Tableau

J. Greene, J. Fassett

Scene 11

"A Modest Little Thing"

J. Greene

(*Music and Lyrics by* Gene Lockhart.)

Scene 12

Good Old Smill, or Faithful to the End (This is one of those impossible things)

Scene: Tiddlesby Manor, Tiddleston-on-Tid, via Little Tid, Upper Tid, Bucks. *Lord Tiddlesby*, a taking old sport: J. Fassett. *Lady Tiddlesby*, in love with herself: F. Arthur. *Lord Marjoribanks*, pronounced Mush, and looking it: J. McCallion. *Smill*, a faithful old servitor: B. McKenna.

Scene 13

Danse Rhythmique

B. McKenna

Scene 14

The Amalgamated Rivetters Glee Club [The Amalgamated Rivetters' and Plume Knotters' Glee Club in a Harmonious Effort]

G. Lockhart, J. Maxwell, J. McCallion, J. Fassett

Scene 15

Specialty

D. Sterling

Scene 16

"Cuddle Up"

M. Lambert, J. McCallion, B. McKenna, Girls

(*Music by* Robert Armbruster. *Lyrics by* Percy Waxman.)

Scene 17

Vote for McGuff

G. Lockhart

Scene 18

A Movie Melodrama (*by* Gene Lockhart. *Music by* Deems Taylor.)

The Villain: G. Lockhart. *The Sheriff*: B. McKenna. *The Mother*: H. Shelley. *The Daughter*: F. Arthur. *The Father*: J. Fassett. *The Hero*: J. McCallion. *Props*: P. Blair, J. Greene.

Scene 19

Finale: "We're Going Away"

Company

ACT 2

Scene 1

"The Milky Way"

M. Lambert, Girls

(*Music by* Gene Lockhart. *Lyrics by* Percy Waxman.)

The Lady of the Moon: P. Blair.

Scene 2

Justice [Justice—Then and To Come]

The Judge: J. Fassett. *The Lawyer*: J. McCallion. *The Husband*: G. Lockhart. *The Wife*: F. Arthur. *The Maid*: P. Blair. *The Burglar*: J. McCallion.

Scene 3

Dance Specialty

B. McKenna

Scene 4

A Subway Son

A Man with Parcels: G. Lockhart. *A Ticket Seller*: J. Maxwell. *A Crook*: J. McCallion. *Another*: B. McKenna. *A Policeman*: J. Fassett. *A Girl*: J. Greene. *Another Girl*: F. Arthur.

Scene 5

"Chatter"

M. Lambert, Girls

(*Music and Lyrics by* Gene Lockhart.)

Scene 6

Aube—Un Ballet Fantastique (Dawn—A Fantastic Ballet)

Francesco: B. McKenna. *Roberto*: J. Maxwell. *Guglielmo*: G. Lockhart. *Giuseppe*: J. Fassett. *Pasquale*: J. McCallion.

Scene 7

Specialty

D. Sterling

Scene 8

"How Very Long Ago (It Seems)"

M. Lambert, J. McCallion

(*Music by* Gene Lockhart. *Lyrics by* Percy Waxman.)

Scene 9

Criminal Tendencies in Concert Artists

G. Lockhart

Scene 10

Situations

The Lady: F. Arthur. *The Lover*: J. McCallion. *The Husband*: J. Fassett. "One's position in life," as Emerson says, "depends more on one thing than another." Both are included in this drama.

Scene 11

"In Washington Square"

Company

(*Music by* Gene Lockhart. *Lyrics by* Percy Waxman.)

Scene 12

"Noces Españolas"

(*Music and Lyrics by* Gene Lockhart.)

Donna Maria Cobra Coloratura y Aguadiento: H. Shelley. *Don Jose Clare Maduro Optino y Monterey*: B. McKenna.

Scene 13

La Voce di Rosignuolo

Scene 14

Devil May Care

J. Fassett

Scene 15

"Do You Do the Charleston?"

M. Lambert, Girls

(*Music by* Gene Lockhart. *Lyrics by* Percy Waxman.)

Scene 16

Finale: "Bunk"

Company

1926.11   # BUNK OF 1926

New Summer Edition of the Revue in Two Acts, 28 Scenes[145]. Music and lyrics by James Bannister, James Dietrich and Wallace and Trent. Production

---

[145]Previous edition opened Off-Broadway 16 February–20 March 1926 at the Heckscher Theatre for 38 performances, before transferring 22 April 1926 at the Broadhurst Theatre for 44 performances. The material and running order changed frequently during the run.

directed and staged by Niles T. Granlund and Jack Wilson. Orchestra under the direction of Gus Klineke. Opened 31 May 1926 at the Broadhurst Theatre and closed (by Citizen's Play Jury) 5 June 1926; reopened under injunction 9 June 1926 at the Broadhurst Theatre and closed 19 June 1926 after 14 additional performances. Total for all engagements: 96 performances.

CAST: JACK WILSON, BERYL HALLEY, ERNEST LINNENKAMP, JOHN MAXWELL, RITCHIE CRAIG, JR., CHARLES FORSYTHE, BOOTS McKENNA, WILLIE WARD, (Jo) TRENT and ("Fats") WALLER, RUTH WHEELER, JANET STONE, PEGGY O'NEILL, CARLO and NORMA.

Chorus: The Van Lowe Specials: Bobby Breslaw, Bessie Kademova, Betty Wright, Maxine Demmler. *The Little Eves:* Bunny Hill, Jerry Dean, Dolores Giffin, Pearl de Orrell, Imogene Coca, Alice Lee, Gertrude Demmler, Georgie Decker, Rita Adams. *The Bunkies:* Alice Raisen, Peggy Timmons, Ann Hardman, Serene Swinton, Blanche O'Brien, Jerry Evans, Isabelle Mason, Bernie Varden, Peggy Dalson.

ACT 1
Scene 1
  Trumpeters
    B. Breslaw, B. Kademova
  Prolog
    B. Wright, M. Demmler
  Introduction
    C. Forsythe
Scene 2
  A Seeker of Thrills
    J. Wilson
Scene 3
  A Few Minutes on Tap
    P. O'Neill
Scene 4
  New York Any Night (A One-Act Drama of Modern Life)
    Husband: B. McKenna. *Wife:* B. Halley. *Lover:* J. Maxwell.
Scene 5
  A Few Minutes with Ritchie Craig, Jr.
Scene 6
  Those Indispensable Girls
    The Bunkies, The Eves
Scene 7
  Second Thoughts (A Play with a Moral)
    The Sweethearts: J. Maxwell, P. O'Neill. *First Husband and Wife:* J. Wilson, R. Wheeler. *Second Husband and Wife:* C. Forsythe, B. Breslaw. *Third Husband and Wife:* B. McKenna, J. Stone.
Scene 8
  Broadway's Modern Eve
    B. Halley, Little Eves
Scene 9
  A Bit of Nonsense
    J. Wilson, C. Forsythe, B. Breslaw
Scene 10
  Boots McKenna
Scene 11
  Bedtime Stories
    J. Wilson, J. Stone, assisted by the Van Lowe Specials
Scene 12
  A Slight Touch of Color
    Trent and Waller
Scene 13
  "Tickle Me"
    I. Coca, Girls
Scene 14
  Jack Wilson, Charles Forsythe, Ruth Wheeler
Scene 15
  "Stroll With Me"
    M. Brown, B. McKenna, Girls
  "At the Fountain" (Finale)
    B. Halley, Company

ACT 2
Scene 1
  The Rose Ballet
    J. Stone, Girls

Scene 2
  He's In Again
    R. Craig, Jr.
Scene 3
  Specialty
    J. Stone
Scene 4
  "The Very Latest Thing in Furs"
    C. Forsythe
    The Lady in Ermine: B. Halley. *Mannikins:* Girls.
Scene 5
  A Studio Party
    Place: Washington Square. *Time:* All the Time.
    With J. Wilson, C. Forsythe, B. McKenna, J. Maxwell, R. Craig, Jr., R. Wheeler, J. Stone, P. O'Neill, Carlo and Norma, Trent and Waller.
Scene 6
  Tap Charleston
    P. O'Neill
Scene 7
  New York Any Day (Another Drama of Real Life)
    J. Wilson, C. Forsythe, R. Wheeler
Scene 8
  "I Have a Letter for You"
    Janet Stone, Girls
Scene 9
  Boots McKenna (Step on It)
Scene 10
  An Important Way to Keep an Important Engagement
    J. Wilson, C. Forsythe, R. Wheeler
Scene 11
  The Persian Ballet
    B. Halley, Girls
Scene 12
  An Episode in Hollywood
    J. Wilson, C. Forsythe, R. Wheeler, W. Ward
Scene 13
  Finale: "In Zulu Land"
    (R. Wheeler, Entire Company)

1926.12   KITTY'S KISSES

A Musical Comedy in Two Acts, 7 Scenes. Book by Philip Bartholomae and Otto Harbach. Music by Con Conrad. Lyrics by Gus Kahn. Book staged by John Cromwell. Dances staged by Bobby Connolly. Sets designed by Livingston Platt. Costumes by Milgrim, Brooks Costume Co. Musical director, John McManus. Orchestrations by Maurice dePackh. Produced by William A. Brady. Opened 6 May 1926 at the Playhouse and closed 2 October 1926 after 170 performances.

CAST: *On a Train We Meet: Mrs. Burke:* Jane Corcoran. *Mr. Burke:* Frank Hatch. *A Country Girl:* Georgina Tilden. *Lulu:* Aileen Meehan. *Kittie Brown:* DOROTHY DILLEY. *Robert Mason:* JOHN BOLES. *A Track Walker:* Walter Bradbury. *Brakeman:* Mortimer Chadbourne. *Conductor:* Kenneth Shutts. *Pullman Conductor:* Leonard Scott. *Dining Car Steward:* Arthur Lang.

The Hotel Wendel Is Run By: The Day Clerk: WILLIAM WAYNE. *The Telephone Girl:* RUTH WARREN. *The Bell Boy:* Walter Bradbury. *The Maid:* Elizabeth Dunn. *The Night Clerk:* William Leith.

Stopping There We Find: Richard Dennison: MARK SMITH. *Mrs. Dennison:* FRANCES BURKE. *Philip Dennison:* NICK LONG, JR. *Miss Wendel,* whose father owns the hotel: MILDRED KEATS.

Rosemary Hall Girls: Mildred Anders, Pauline Bartlett, Polly Blake, Emily Burton, Billie Bostick, Irene Hamlin, Patty Hastings, Edna Hopper, Ruth Kelly, Ruth Laird, Aileen Meehan, Frances Nevins, Cherie Pelham. *Boys:* Warren Crosby, Lester Eldridge, Paul Florenze, Jack Gargin, Gene McVey, William Neely, George O'Brien, Joe Sargent.

Act 1, Scene 1: A Railway Siding. *Scene 2:* Lobby of the Hotel Wendel. *Scene 3:* Corridor of Hotel. *Scene 4:* The Bridal Suite.

Act 2, Scene 1: Bridal Suite. *Scene 2:* Corridor of Hotel. *Scene 3:* The Hotel Garden.

ACT 1
  "Walkin' the Track"
    A. Meehan, Boys

"Choo Choo Love"
  Train Crew
"Kitty's Kisses"
  D. Dilley, J. Boles
"I Love to Dance"
  M. Keats, N. Long, Jr.
"Thinking of You"
  R. Warren, W. Wayne
"Two Fellows and a Girl"
  D. Dilley, Boys
"I'm in Love"
  J. Boles, Boys
  (Lyrics by Gus Kahn and Otto Harbach.)
"Mr. and Mrs."[146]
  M. Keats, N. Long, Jr., Girls
"Promise Your Kisses"
  D. Dilley, M. Keats, Girls

ACT 2
"Early in the Morning"
  M. Smith, D. Dilley
"I Don't Want Him"
  D. Dilley, M. Smith, F. Bourke
"Needles"
  R. Warren, Girls, Boys
"Whenever I Dream"
  D. Dilley, J. Boles
"Bounce Me"
  M. Keats, N. Long, Jr., Girls, Boys
"Steppin on the Blues"
  W. Wayne, N. Long, Jr., Ensemble
  (Music by Con Conrad and Will Donaldson.)
Finale
  Entire Company

1926.13 THE GARRICK GAIETIES (1926)

A Musical Revue in Two Acts, 19 Scenes. (Sketches by Benjamin M. Kaye, Newman Levy, Herbert Fields, Chester D. Heywood, Marian Page Johnson, Edward Hope, Philip Lord.) Music by Richard Rodgers. Lyrics by Lorenz Hart. Production directed by Philip Loeb. Musical numbers (dances) arranged by Herbert Fields. Settings and costumes designed by Carolyn Hancock. Orchestra directed by Richard Rodgers (opening night), Roy Webb. Produced by the Theatre Guild. Opened 10 May 1926 at the Guild Theatre and closed 9 October 1926 after 174 performances.

CAST from the Theatre Guild Studio: Philip Loeb, Betty Starbuck, Blanche Fleming, Jack Edwards, Romney Brent, William M. Griffith, Edith Meiser, Sterling Holloway, Hardwick Nevin, Edward Hogan, John McGovern, Bobbie Perkins, George Frierson, Hildegarde Halliday, Ruth Morris, Eleanor Shaler, William Johnstone, Helen Ramsey, Tommy Law, Dorothy Jordan, Sylvia Shear, Gladys Rogers, Ann Moss, Gladys Laird, Jean Crittendon, Dorothea Chard, Mary Jordan, Marta Keyes, Philip Jones, Felix Jacoves, John Richards, Alex Tiers.

ACT 1[147]
Scene 1
  "Six Little Plays" (Opening) in which the Gaieties bury their parents

---

[146]Dropped during the run.
[147]The running order of songs and sketches was revised during the run. Added were:
  "Allez Up" (Act 1)
    B. Starbuck, B. Perkins, S. Holloway
  From the great American institution—the Three Ring Circus
  Washington and the Spy (by Newman Levy) (Act 1)
    George Washington: J. McGovern. General Grant: P. Loeb. Mary, Queen of Scots: E. Meiser. Napoleon: R. Brent. Guard: H. Nevin. Announcer: W. Griffith.
  Crossing the Avenue (by Sally Humason)
    Usher: K. Herold. Madge: E. Meiser. Tom: J. McGovern. Ethel: H. Halliday. Steward: W. Griffith. Sandwichman: J. Richards. Messenger Boy: J. Edwards. Bride: H. Woodruff. Bridegroom: E. Hogan. Girl: B. Fleming. Boy: W. Johnstone. Policeman: F. Jacoves.
For subsequent national tour, material from the 1925 edition was added.

with characteristic disrespect and make a prophecy as to the evening's outcome:
  Undertaker: P. Loeb. Arms and the Man: B. Starbuck. The Glass Slipper: B. Fleming. Merchants of Glory: J. Edwards. Androcles and the Lion: R. Brent. Goat Song: W. Griffith. The Chief Thing: E. Meiser. The Garrick Gaieties: S. Holloway, Company.
  ("We Can't Be as Good as Last Year")
  (S. Holloway, P. Loeb, Company)
Scene 2
  DeBock Song (A drama by Benjamin M. Kaye in which symbolism is solved and vagueness vindicated.)
    Student: R. Brent. Girl: B. Fleming. First Man: J. Edwards. Second Man: H. Nevin. Third Man: E. Hogan. High Priest: P. Loeb. Speaker: J. McGovern. Father: W. Griffith.
Scene 3
  "Mountain Greenery"
    B. Perkins, S. Holloway
    One of those little pastoral events inevitable to this time of year.
Scene 4
  Burglary à la Mode
    (by Newman Levy)
    The lengths to which society ladies will go in order to get into the papers nowadays.
    Miss Annabelle Van Blenkinsop: E. Meiser. Jevons, the butler: R. Brent. Schuyler Whiffle: P. Loeb. Mr. Van Blenkinsop: J. McGovern.
Scene 5
  "L'après-midi d'un papillon" (dance)
    E. Shaler
Scene 6
  "Keys to Heaven"
    B. Perkins, G. Frierson, B. Fleming, Company
    In which the lost cord is again found.
Scene 7
  Home Sweet Home
    (by Marian Page Johnson)
    Pa Hoskins: W. Griffith. Ma Hoskins: H. Halliday. Hector Hoskins: W. Johnstone. Clytemnestra Hoskins: R. Morris.
Scene 8
  "Sleepyhead"[148]
    S. Holloway
Scene 9
  "Rose of Arizona"
    (Book by Herbert Fields.)
    A hundred percent American musical comedy in the best traditional manner.
    Scene: The terrace of the Rosa Raisa Hotel on the border line of Mexico and Arizona.
    Rosabelle: E. Shaler. Gloria van Dyke: B. Fleming. Gustave van Dyke: P. Loeb. Allan Sterling: J. Edwards. Casaba Caramba: R. Brent. Pimento: E. Meiser. Mrs. van Dyke: R. Morris. Mcfadden: J. McGovern. Announcer: W. Griffith. Flowers (8): Bluebell: H. Ramsey. Lily: H. Halliday. Tulip: T. Law. Orchid: D. Jordan. Poppy: S. Shear. Violet: G. Rodgers. Chrysanthemum: A. Moss. Rose: G. Laird. Ensemble: J. Crittenden, D. Chard, L. Henry, H. Halliday, D. Jordan, T. Law, G. Laird, A. Moss, H. Ramsey, G. Rodgers, S. Shear, H. Woodruff. Soldiers: George Frierson, P. Jones, F. Jacoves, W. Johnstone, J. Richards, A. Tiers.
    ("Back to Nature")
    (Company)
    ("It May Rain")
    (B. Fleming, J. Edwards)
    ("David Crockett")
    (P. Loeb)
    ("American Beauty Rose")
    (E. Meiser)
    ("Mexico")
    (J. Edwards, Ensemble)

ACT 2
Scene 1
  "Viennese"
    (Music compiled by Ladislas Kun who also composed "So Sem" and plays the Cymbalom.)

---

[148]Dropped after opening.

Specialty Dance
  B. Starbuck, G. Frierson
  Flower Girl: B. Fleming. *Baron*: W. Griffith. *Proprietor*: E. Hogan. *Waltzers, Gipsy Girls, Men*: (Company.)

Scene 2
  "Tennis Champs"
  A Championship game in which love is often mentioned but seldom demonstrated.
  Helen Wills: R. Brent. *Bill Tilden*: E. Meiser. *Suzane Lenglen*: P. Loeb.

Scene 3
  Green Chartreuse
  (*by* Chester D. Heywood)
  Sir George Packenham: H. Nevin. *Brooke, his man servant*: J. McGovern. *The Man*: P. Loeb.

Scene 4
  "Four Little Songpluggers"/
  "Mountain Greenery" (reprise)
  D. Jordan, B. Starbuck, G. Laird, B. Perkins

Scene 5
  Addled, or The Psychopathic Ward
  (*by* Edward Hope)
  Being the awful effect of modern magazine advertising on an impressionistic young mind.
  Doctor: J. McGovern. *Interne*: H. Nevin. *Nurse*: R. Morris. *Patient*: R. Brent.

Scene 6
  "What's the Use of Talking?"
  B. Starbuck, S. Holloway, Company
  (The Dumb Belles Delight)

Scene 7
  "Idles of the King"
  A song of that obsolete affair immortalized by Mallory's 'Morte d'Arthur' but now superseded in literature by the 'Vie d'Algonquin.'
  King Arthur: R. Brent. *Sir Launcelot*: E. Hogan. *Sir Galahad*: P. Loeb.

Scene 8
  "Gigolo"
  B. Starbuck, Company
  The temptation and ultimate fall of a group of noble young men who (for a mere stipend) devote their lives to giving happiness to others.

Scene 9
  "Queen Elizabeth"
  E. Meiser
  A 300-year-old scandal revived.

Scene 10
  Finale ("I Call Upon You Gentlemen")
  In which the Garrick Gaieties come to a doubtful end.
  Judge: R. Brent. *Jury*: E. Hogan, H. Nevin, J. Edwards, P. Loeb. *Johann Straus*: E. Hogan. *Sir Arthur Sullivan*: H. Nevin. *W. S. Gilbert*: J. Edwards. *Irving Berlin*: P. Loeb. *The Garrick Gaieties*: S. Holloway.

1926.14   THE GREAT TEMPTATIONS

A Musical Revue in Two Acts, 34 Scenes. Sketches by Harold Atteridge. Music by Maurice Rubens. Lyrics by Clifford Grey. Staged by J. C. Huffmann. Dances and ensembles arranged by Earl Lindsay. Settings by Watson Barratt. Costumes by Max Weldy and Ernest R. Schrapps. Dances and ensembles by Earl Lindsay. Orchestra under the direction of Alfred Goodman. Entire production under the personal direction of J. J. Shubert. Produced by the Messrs. Shubert. Opened 18 May 1926 at the Winter Garden and closed 6 November 1926 after 223 performances.

CAST: HAZEL DAWN, WILFRED SEAGRAM, CHARLOTTE WOODRUFF, (Flournoy) MILLER and (Aubrey) LYLES, DOROTHY McNULTY, FLORENZ AMES, THE DEUEL SISTERS (Dorothy, Eleanor), JACK BENNY, THE GUY SISTERS, J. C. FLIPPEN, ARTHUR TREACHER, (Mlle.) ROSERAY and (M.) CAPPELLA, PAUL MAUL, MOLLY O'DOHERTY, PAT and TERRY KENDALL, GERTRUDE PURCELL, HALFRED YOUNG, RUTH MAYON, JACK WALDRON, NINA SUZOV, ARA GERALD, THE KELO BROTHERS (Charles, Carralo).

Sixteen Foster Girls: Erna, Helen, Gala, Frieda, Jo, Dottie, Winnie, Louise, Alex, Mary, Billie, Rose, Pat, Ruth, Beverley, Ernie. *Some of the Great Temptations*: Beatrice Anderson, Yvonne Bacon, Julia Barker, Gloria Chrystie, Charlotte Corday, Irene Cornell, Nikola Cunningham, Diana DeArle, Doris Dodge, Dorothy Drumm, Clarice Durham, Helen Frederic, Thalie Hamilton, Cecelia Healy, Phyllis Heron, Naan Lane, Neva Lynn, Margaret Mayer, Eleane Meade, Georgette Moore, Agatha Phillips, Dorothy Phillips, Leona Newell, Agnes Schroeder, Katrina Trask, Roslind Wichon.

Some of the Little Temptations: Sybil Bursk, Elsie Carroll, Cyrilla Casey, Lillian Clarke, Patsy Costello, Bobbie Decker, Mildred Douglass, Geneva Duker, Mildred Espy, Charlotte Fitzgibbons, Grace Fleming, Marge Harlan, Florence Horne, Betty Knox, Lottie Marcy, Margaret McKay, June Ray, Beatrice Vercelle, Dorothy Weber, Mazie White, Minerva Wilson, Billye Lambert, Bernadette Spencer, Florence Golden. *Some of the Koster & Bial Temptations of 1896*: Edna Thorp, Margie Webber, Lazelle Webber, Billy Bernard, Dorothy Griffith, Marie Holden, Betty Gordon, Lillian Newell, Jane Blair, Julia Ryan, Mazie Hunt, Pauline Bryceland.

ACT 1[149]

Scene 1
  "Art Has No Frontier"
  Scene: Mount Olympus.
  Charon: F. Ames. *Mercury*: A. Treacher. *Bacchus*: J. Waldron. *Jupiter*: W. Seagram. *Diana*: C. Woodruff. *A Reformer*: J. Dunn. *And Another One*: P. Mall. *Music*: M. Mayer. *Dance*: N. Lyon. *Gold*: N. Lane. *diamonds*: D. Drumm. *Wine*: A. Phillips. *Art*: E. Meade. *Opium*: P. Heron. *Chance*: D. DeArle. *Vice*: T. Hamilton. *Beauty*: N. Cunningham.

Scene 2
  "Never Say the World Was Made to Cry"
  C. Woodruff, Diana Girls

Scene 3
  "Any Step"
  J. Waldron, M. O'Doherty, Spanish Girls, E Gudrun, S. Galloway

Scene 4
  A Radio Entertainment
  Joseph: J. Dunn. *Arthur*: W. Seagram. *XYZ*: F. Ames. *WOR*: A. Treacher. *WHN*: G. Purcell. *KDA*: P. Mall. *KDKI*: A. Gerald.

Scene 5
  Paul Mall

Scene 6
  "The Spider's Web"
  D. Tabor, B. Allen, Foster Girls
  (*Music by* Milton Schwarzwald.)

Scene 7
  Miller and Lyles

Scene 8
  "The Sesqui Centennial Baby"
  P. Kendall, J. Waldron, Deuel Sisters, Sesqui Centennial Babies

Scene 9
  Questions
  The Wife: H. Dawn. *The Husband*: F. Ames. *The Maid*: R. Mayon.

Scene 10
  Jack Benny

Scene 11
  "A Pin Cushion"
  C. Woodruff
  (Dance)
  N. Susov, Foster Girls

Scene 12
  On the Veranda[150]
  Mr. Jones: B. B. Van. *Mr. Smith*: J. C. Flippen. *Mrs. Jones*: M. O'Doherty.

---

[149]The running order was revised during the run. Added after the opening to Act 1:
  The Friend
    Mr. Black: Billy B. Van. *Mr. Green*: W. Seagram.
  Parisian Jazz
    The Guy Sisters
    (from the Palace theatre, Paris. American debut.)
  The Pattern Wife
    The Wife: H. Dawn. *The Husband*: A. Treacher. *The Other Woman*: A. Gerald. *The Maid*: R. Mayon.
  Out of the Ether
    The Nurse: G. Purcell. *The Patient*: B. B. Van. *The Friend*: F. Ames. *The Doctor*: A. Treacher.
Added for subsequent tour to Act 1:
  Full Up
    The Clerk: F. Ames. *The Traveling Salesman*: B. B. Van. *The Girl*: Fodi Brown. *The Man*: Fred Irving Lewis.
[150]Dropped during the run.

Scene 13

"The Maid of Jade"

The Connoisseur: W. Seagram. *The Lady*: C. Woodruff. *The Chinese Mandarin*: H. Young. *The Maid*: Roseray. *The Boy*: Cappella.

Dance

Roseray, Cappella (from the Casino de Paris, Paris. American debut)
Each of the postures of the dance of Mlle. Roseray and M. Cappella is their conception in the living flesh of some famous statue in the great art galleries of the world such as the Louvre in Paris, the public collections of London, Vienna, Berlin and other world cities. In not a few cases they reproduce in the series of famous art works some well known paintings. Sculptors, painters and art students generally will readily recognize the works of art which Mlle. Roseray and M. Cappella combine in their dance.

Scene 14

"The Temptation Strut"

J. Waldron, D. McNulty, M. O'Doherty, Winter Garden Strutters
(*Music by* Earl Lindsay, Maurice Rubens.)

Scene 15

Three of a Kind[151]

First Man: B. B. Van. *Second Man*: J. C. Flippen. *Third Man*: J. Dunn. *Maid*: P. Kendall.

Scene 16

"The Guards of Fantasy"

H. Young, Foster Girls
a) The Crusaders. b) The Crusaders' Wives. c) The Girls of Koster & Bials of 1896

Scene 17

The Shanghai Mixture (A burlesque of "The Shanghai Gesture" by John Colton)

Scene: 7-11 Kaiou Road, Shanghai, China.
Daniel Reed: J. Waldron. *Miss Morris*: E. Deuel. *Chinese Dancers*: F. Ames, R. Mayon. *Hawkins*: A. Treacher. *Sir Guy Charteris*: W. Seagram. *Sir John Blessington*: T. Kendall. *Lady Blessington*: P. Kendall. *Mrs. Dudley Gregory*: D. Deuel. *Dudley Gregory*: B. B. Van. *Mother Goddam*: H. Dawn. *Mandarin*: Charles Kelo. *Poppy*: A. Gerald. *Prince Oshimay*: J. Dunn. *Nipau*: D. Weber.

Scene 18

"Love Birds"[152]

P. Kendall, T. Kendall, Deuel Sisters

Scene 19

Jack Benny and Dorothy NcNulty

Scene 20

"Querida"

H. Young, C. Woodruff, Spanish Boys?

Scene 21

"Valencia"

H. Dawn, H. Young, C. Woodruff, a Group of Spanish Beauties
(*Music by* José Padilla.)

ACT 2[153]

Scene 1

"A Garden of Memories"

H. Young, C. Woodruff, Guy Sisters, a Collection of Beauties from all over the world

Scene 2

The First Mirror

Scene: A Village near ancient Rome.
Marcus: J. Dunn. *Octavia*: H. Dawn. *Dolo Bella*: G. Purcell. *Julius*: F. Ames.

Scene 3

"Beauty Is Vanity"

C. Woodruff, Grecian Maidens
Scene: The Acropolis at Athens.

Scene 4

Miller and Lyles:

[13 Is 1/7 of 28, or Moneyless Debts]

Scene 5

"Dancing Town"

F. Ames, Deuel Sisters, J. Waldron, M. O'Doherty, D. McNulty, Girls from Harlem, Greenwich Village, The Bowery, Fifth Avenue, Foster Girls

Scene 6

Officer O'Fishent

(*by* Frank Conlan)
Officer O'Fishent: W. Seagram. *A Flapper*: G. Purcell. *An Old Lady*: A. Gerald. *Mr. Bunn*: B. B. Van. *A Girl*: N. Susov. *Mr. Jean*: A. Treacher.

Scene 7

"The Chevalier of the Highway"

N. Wagner, D. Tabor

Chevalier Dance

Roseray, Cappella

Scene 8

Hard Lives

The Artist: W. Seagram. *The Model*: N. Susov. *A Woman*: A. Gerald. *Another Woman*: E. Deuel.

Scene 9

Jay C. Flippen

Scene 10

"The Atlantic City Girl"

J. Waldron, a Group of International Bathing Beauties, 16 Foster Girls

Scene 11

The Kelo Brothers

Scene 12

A Harem Incident[154]

The Judge: F. Ames. *The Officer*: C. Kelo. *Mandy*: J. C. Flippen.

Scene 13

March of the Lanterns

---

[153]The running order was revised during the run. Added after the opening to Act 2:
  A Reflection of Greece (Act 2)
    R. Mayon, Greek Ballet
Added for subsequent tour:
  "Goodbye Charleston" (Act 2 Finale)
    R. Sedley, Deuel Sisters, D. McNulty, R. Mayon, Vercelle Sisters, Foster Girls, Bathing Beauties
[154]Dropped during the run.

---

[151]Dropped during the run.
[152]Dropped during the run.

1926–1927 SEASON

The Locust Sisters in HIT THE DECK (Photo: Debarron)
Billy Rose Theatre Collection, New York Public Library for the Performing Arts

1926–1927 SEASON

1926.15   ## THE MERRY WORLD

The International (Musical) Revue in Two Acts, 31 Scenes. Music by
Maurice Rubens, J. Fred Coots, Herman Hupfeld and Sam Timberg. Lyrics
by Clifford Grey. Staged by J. C. Huffman. Dialogue directed by Charles
Judels. Dances by Larry Ceballos. Settings by Watson Barratt. Costumes by
Max Weldy, Ernest R. Schrapps. Orchestra under the direction of Alfred
Goodman. Entire production under the personal direction of J. J. Shubert.
Produced by Messrs. Shubert in association with Albert de Courville.
Opened 8 June 1926 at the Imperial Theatre, moved 2 August 1926 to the
Sam S. Shubert Theatre as PASSIONS OF 1926, and closed 21 August 1926
after 87 performances[1].

<u>CAST:</u> MORRIS HARVEY, EVELYN HERBERT, DONALD CALTHROP, GRACE
GLOVER, DEZSO RETTER, GRACE HAYES, ALEXANDER GRAY, LOLA
RAINE, EMIL BOREO, LILY LONG, EDWIN LAWRENCE, DOROTHY
WHITMORE, NICHOLAS TRIPOLITOFF, MARGARET BREEN, SALT AND
PEPPER [Frank Culpepper], OLGA SMIRNOVA, SUDWORTH FRASIER, JANE
MOORE, STARKE PATTERSON, BERNARD DUDLEY, IRVING EDWARDS,
THOMAS WHITELEY, NICHOLAS GREY, LAINE BLAIRE, MABELLE SWOR,
LUCITA CORVERA, RAY BOLGER, FRED HARPER, (Elna) GUDRUN and
(Selby) GALLOWAY, FRANK JARVIS, MARYLAND COLLEGIANS.

Ladies of the Ensemble: Carmen Conley, Evan Southwell, Jaquelyn Marshall, Betty
DePascue, June Lovewell, Sylvia Neirick, Myrtle Thompson, Kao Tortoni, Peaches
Tortoni, Betty Pecan, Morhora Lloyd, Ruth Moore, Gale Moore, Helen Wallace,
Grace Connolly, Ritta Martin, Beatrice Bickel, Billy Blake, Ruth Simmons, Wilma
Crossman, Marian Boazo, Cookie Lane Lunsford, Dorothy Noble, Marian Mooney,
Lily Smart, Betty Sheldon, Bunnie Pedreau, Lillian Lorray, Helen Madigan, Ann
Burnes, Annie Rose, Leonie Spiro, Frances Lynn, Eva Lynn, Edith Davis, Mary
Dunckley, Rosalie Trego, Ann LaVerne, Virginia Whitmore, Yolanda Losee, Ada
Marcus, Maxine Morton, Frances Suzane, Louise Chowning. *Ladies of the Ballet*:
Frances Lynn, Edith Davis, Rosalie Trego, Ann LaVerne, Virginia Whitmore, Yolanda
Losee, Ada Marcus, Leonie Spiro, Mary Dunckley, Frances Suzane.

ACT 1[2]

Scene 1

A Conspiracy
First Attendant: B. Dudley. *Second Attendant*: T. Whiteley. *Comrade from
England*: M. Harvey. *Comrade from France*: E. Boreo. *Comrade from Russia*: N.
Grey. *Comrade from Scotland*: E. Lawrence. *Comrade from Hungary*: D. Retter.
Comrade from Germany: S. Patterson. *Comrade from Ireland*: D. Calthrop.
Comrade from America: A. Gray.

Scene 2

"Military Charleston"
M. Breen, L. Blaire, I. Edwards, Ensemble

Scene 3

"L'Enchaîneuse" (Enchanted)
G. Glover

Scene 4

Scotch to the Backbone
Maggie McDougal: L. Raine. *Sandy McPherson*: E. Lawrence. *Jock McDougal*:
B. Dudley.

Scene 5

"Don't Fall in Love (With Me)"
E. Boreo
(*Music and Lyrics by* Herman Hupfeld.)
Girl from France: M. Swor. *Girl from Spain*: L. Corvera. *Girl from Russia*: J.
Moore. And Ensemble.

---

[1]Sketches uncredited. Toured under the title THE PASSING SHOW OF
1926 with a revised running order.
[2]Added during the run:
  Laine Blaire and Starke Patterson (Specialty) (Act 1)
  Jack Osterman (Specialty) (Act 2, next to closing)
Performed in show at opening per reviews and sheet music, though not in
programs:
  "I Fell Head Over Heels in Love"
    (*Music by* Pat Thayer. *Lyrics by* Donovan Parsons.)

Scene 6

"Golden Gates (of Happiness)"
D. Whitmore, A. Gray, Golden Gate Girls
(*Music by* J. Fred Coots. *Lyrics by* Clifford Grey.)
Bridesmaid: G. Hayes.

Scene 7

Shoplifter
John Severly: M. Harvey. *Mrs. Severly*: L. Raine. *Mrs. Fitzallan*: L. Long.
Detective Smithers: B. Dudley.

Scene 8

Grace Hayes

Scene 9

"Tallahassee"
M. Breen, J. Moore, I. Edwards, Talahassee Girls

Scene 10

When Men Grow Old
Mr. Livingston: M. Harvey. *Young Mr. White*: A. Gray. *Maitre d'Hotel*:
D. Calthrop. *Pauline Cunningham*: M. Swor.

"Giroflé-Girofla"
E. Herbert, B. Dudley, Ensemble
(*Lillian Russell*: E. Herbert.)

Scene 11

"Silk Stockings"
D. Whitmore

Dances
I. Edwards, J. Moore, S. Galloway, E. Gudrun, Silk Stocking Girls

Scene 12

The Unexpected
Mrs. Gregory: L. Long. *John Goodman*, Butler: E. Lawrence. *Detective Snape*:
B. Dudley. *Flora Simpson*: M. Swor. *General Gregory*: M. Harvey.

Scene 13

"White Rose, Red Rose"
G. Hayes, A. Gray

Dance
O. Smirnova

Scene 14

An English Public House
Bar Maid: L. Raine. *'Enery 'Opkins*: M. Harvey. *'Erb Trott*: D. Calthrop. *'Alf
Muggins*: E. Lawrence.

Scene 15

Emil Boreo (Russian Comedian)

Scene 16

"Whispering Trees"
E. Herbert, A. Gray, Mysterious Forest Girls
(*Music by* J. Fred Coots, Maurice Rubens. *Lyrics by* Herbert Reynolds.)
Scene: The Enchanted Forest.

Scene 17

Twisted Hand
Margo: G. Hayes. *Peter*: D. Calthrop. *Leonie*: L. Raine. *The Russian*: B. Dudley.

Scene 18

La Potinière at Deauville: The Maryland Collegians
Two Uke Kings: Salt and Pepper. *Fast Step*: F. Harper. *Another*: R. Bolger. *Mr.
Wales*: M. Harvey. *Mrs. Wales*: L. Long. *Restaurant Manager*: E. Boreo. *Mr.
Scott*: E. Lawrence. *Mr. White*: T. Whiteley. *Mr. Jones*: D. Calthrop. *Mr. Green*:
B. Dudley. *A Souse*: D. Retter.

"(Come Over to) Deauville"
L. Blaire, S. Patterson, M. Breen, I. Edwards, E. Gudrun, S. Galloway, a Group
of Deauville Beauties
(*Music and Lyrics by* Herman Hupfeld.)

Scene 19

Just in Time—in Two Forms
Gwendolyn Frees: L. Raine. *Guy Armitage*. D. Calthrop. *Hildebeau Chatwyn*:
M. Harvey.

Scene 20

"Beauty Adorned"
E. Herbert
(*Music by* Maurice Rubens and J. Fred Coots.)
Sapphires: M. Lax, G. Moore, R. Martin, V. Whitmore, B. Sheldon. *Amethysts*:
D. Whitmore, E. Davis, H. Madigan, G. Connelly, R. Trego. *Emeralds*: M.

Breen, B. Wallace, L. Lorray, P. Tortoni, S. Neirick. *Topaz*: D. Noble, A. LaVerne, L. Chowning, J. Marshall. *Pearls*: G. Glover, A. Rose, M. Thompson, R. Moore, B. Bickel. *Ruby*: M. Swor, M. Mooney, R. Simmons, R. Moore, B. DePascue. *Diamonds*: G. Hayes, B. Lloyd, C. Conley, E. Southwell, M. Morton. *Aurora Borealis*: G. Hayes.

ACT 2

Scene 1

"The Fall of the Leaves"

D. Whitmore

(*Music by* Maurice Rubens and J. Fred Coots.)

Woodland Nymphs: L. Spiro, F. Lynn, E. Davis, M. Dunckley, R. Trego, A. LeVerne, V. Whitmore, Y. Losee, A. Marcus, F. Suzane. *The Première (Danseuse)*: M. Mason. *Autumn Leaves*: P. Tortoni, S. Netrick, B. Blake, B. Pedreau, L. Lorray, B. Wallace, A. Burnes, J. Lovewell, D. Noble, H. Madigan, L. Smart. *Golden Leaves*: M. Mooney, B. DePascue, K. Tortoni, B. Sheldon, J. Marshall, R. Moore, G. Moore, L. Chowning, A. Rose, R. Simmons, C. Conley, W. Crossman.

Scene 2

Suspicion

Maid: D. Whitmore. *Butler*: T. Whiteley. *Mrs. Trevlyn*: G. Hayes. *Sir Charles Trowbridge*: D. Calthrop. *George Trevlyn*: M. Harvey.

Scene 3

"Dangerous Devil"[3]

Salt and Pepper, L. Blaire

Dance

J. Moore, L. Blaire, S. Patterson, Some Dangerous Devils

Scene 4

A Wrestling Match

Not Hackenschmidt: D. Retter.

Scene 5

Salt and Pepper (Specialty):

["Wail of Their Sweeties"

"My Cutey's Due to Two-to-Two To-day"

(*Music by* Albert Von Tilzer. *Lyrics by* Leo Robin.)]

Scene 6

Silent Prompter

Evangeline: L. Raine. *Archibald*: D. Calthrop. *Prompter*: E. Lawrence. *His Assistant*: F. Jarvis.

Scene 7

Grace Hayes

Scene 8

Crusaders: "Ceinture de Chasteté"

First Man: D. Calthrop. *Second Man*: T. Whiteley. *Host*: M. Harvey. *First Lady*: D. Whitmore. *Second Lady*: L. Raine.

"Love's Call"

S. Frasier

(*Music by* J. Fred Coots, Maurice Rubens.)

Belles de Chastete: L. Smart, D. Noble, B. DePascu, B. Sheldon, K. Tortoni, R. Simmons, P. Tortoni, Y. Losee.

"Heroes of Yesterday"

E. Herbert

Crusaders: M. Thompson, G. Connolly, R. Moore, B. Lloyd, V. Whitmore, G. Moore, B. Bickel, L. Chowning, A. Rose, B. Wallace, C. Conley, W. Crossman, M. Mooney, R. Trego, E. Davis, J. Marshall, A. Burnes, H. Madigan, F. Lynn, A. Marcus, B. Pedreau, J. Lovewell, B. Blake, M. Dunckley, E. Southwell, R. Martin, M. Morton, L. Lorray.

Scene 9

Three Ways of Coming Home[4]

Lord Knightsbridge: D. Calthrop. *Lady Knightsbridge*: L. Raine. *Evelyn Knightsbridge*: M. Dunckley. *Ylma Gabbler*: L. Raine. *Torkman*: M. Harvey. *Bill*: E. Lawrence. *Lizzie*: L. Raine.

Scene 10

"Jabberwalky"[5] (Jabberwocky)

M. Breen

Dance

L. Blaire, S. Patterson, Jabberwalky Girls

---

[3]Dropped during the run.
[4]Dropped during the run.
[5]Dropped during the run.

Scene 11

You Can't Get Away from It[6]

The Woman: L. Raine. *The Man*: E. Lawrence.

Best to Know Beforehand

Mother: G. Hayes. *Father*: M. Harvey. *Daughter*: L. Raine. *Son-in-law*: A. Gray.

Scene 12

"Dancing Jim"

S. Galloway, M. Swor, M. Breen, Ensemble

(*Music by* Marc Anthony. *Lyrics by* Donovan Parsons.)

Dance

Moore Sisters (Jane, Ruth, Gayle)

Scene 13

Ping Ping[7]

Monsieur: M. Harvey. *Madame*: L. Raine. *Salesman*: E. Lawrence. *Young Man*: T. Whiteley. *Another Young Man*: E. Boreo. *Old Man*: D. Calthrop.

Scene 14

"Versailles"

E. Herbert

Minuette

L. Blaire, S. Patterson, Ensemble

Madame Pompadour: G. Hayes.

GEORGE WHITE'S SCANDALS (1926)

1926.16

A Musical Revue in Two Acts, 35 Scenes[8]. Book (sketches) by George White and William K. Wells. Music by Ray Henderson. Lyrics by Buddy G. DeSylva and Lew Brown. Costumes and curtains designed by Erté. Settings designed by Gustave Weidhaus and W. Oden Waller. Orchestrations by Maurice DePackh. Orchestra under the direction of William Daly. Entire production staged by George White. Produced by George White. Opened 14 June 1926 at the Apollo Theatre and closed 18 June 1927 after 432 performances.

CAST: ANN PENNINGTON, WILLIE HOWARD, FRANCES WILLIAMS, HARRY RICHMAN, THE McCARTHY SISTERS (Margaret, Dorothy), EUGENE HOWARD, THE FAIRBANKS TWINS (Marion, Madeline), LLOYD GARRETT, TOM PATRICOLA, FOWLER and TAMARA, BUSTER WEST, ROSE PERFECT, JAMES MILLER, JOHN WELLS, JANE SELS, JAMES CARTY, PEGGY GALLIMORE, JEAN KENIN, THE SCOTT SISTERS (Clare, Jean), THE HASTINGS SISTERS, FLO BROOKS, MURIEL LeCOUNT, LAVERTA McCORMACK, FRED LYON, MARGARET MANNERS, HARRY MORRISSEY, CATHERINE CHAPMAN, PATRICIA PURSLEY, ARTHUR CARDINAL, PEGGY MOSELEY, JAMES MILLER, MAY SLATTERY.

George White Ballet: Harriet Hastings, Doris Bryant, Ruth Wayne, Marge O'Shea, Ruth Gordon, Lillian Brushette, Etta Laughton, Edna Bowman, Janet Flynn, Dorothy Chilton, Marion Harcke. *Chorus*: Marjory Alford, Adrienne Alford, Evelyn Arden, Jessie Brown, Mildred Klaw, Georgia Lerch, Mae Chandler, Dolly Donnelly, Suzanne Conroy, Clare Douglass, Portland Hoffa, Marie Bowman, Odessa Morgan, Norma Cloos, Garnet Lane, Gene Cullen, Ruth Grey, Alice White, Peggy Wilcox, Nora Puntin, Peggy Penn, Etta Sparre, Alice Wilkie, Anna Wayne, Esta Lawton.

ACT 1

Scene 1

"Talent Is What the Public Wants"

Misses J. Kenin, F. Brooks, P. Gallimore, A. White, G. Cullen, M. LeCount, N. Cloos, E. Sparre, C. Scott, J. Scott, P. Penn, G. Lerch, O. Morgan, P. Moseley, A. Wilkie, P. Hoffa, M. Alford, A. Alford, S. Conroy, D. Donnelly

Scene 2

Announcement by The Hastings Twins

Scene 3

Dance[9]

Fairbanks Twins

Scene 4

"This Is My Lucky Day"

H. Richman

---

[6]Dropped during the run.
[7]Dropped during the run.
[8]The eighth in the annual series of revues which began in 1919.
[9]Dropped during the run.

Wishbone: P. Pursley. *Horseshoe*: L. McCormack. *Clover*: M. Slattery. *Star*: C. Chapman. *New Moon*: M. Manners. *Stack of Hay*: M. Klaw. *Lucky Dolls*: Misses D. Donnelly, P. Moseley, S. Conroy, C. Douglass, M. Chandler, G. Lerch.

Scene 5

6 O'Clock A.M.

Announcement: H. Richman. *Wife*: R. Perfect. *Husband*: H. Morrissey. *Intruder*: H. Richman.

Scene 6

Fifteen Years at the Winter Garden
(*by* B. G. DeSylva and Lew Brown)
W. Howard, E. Howard

Scene 7

The Orator
Orator: T. Patricola. *Workman*: J. Miller. *Jams Pierpont Morgan*: J. Carty. *Otto H. Kahn*: F. Lyon.

Scene 8

Phoney Talk
Husband: W. Howard. *His Wife*: R. Perfect. *Butterfly*: F. Williams. *Her Husband*: H. Morrissey.

Scene 9

"Tweet Tweet"
McCarthy Sisters
(*Staged by* Jane Sels under the direction of George White.)
Mother Bird: M. Manners. *Baby Birds*: Misses E. Bowman, P Gallimore, J. Kenin, J. Sels, George White Ballet.

Scene 10

Announcement
H. Richman

Scene 11

(A Western Union *by* Buddy G. DeSylva, Lew Brown and George White)
She: F. Williams. *He*: W. Howard. *Her Father*: E. Howard.

Scene 12

The Triumph of Woman:
"Lady Fair"
L. Garrett
Mme. St. Gene: M. Slattery. *Attendants*: P. Moseley, P. Hoffa. *Salome*: M. Klaw. *Attendants*: G. Lane, N. Cloos. *Mme. DuBarry*: M. Bowman. *Attendants*: G. Lerch, E. Arden. *Lucretia Borgia*: P. Pursley. *Attendants*: F. Brooks, O. Morgan. *Delilah*: L. McCormack. *Attendants*: G. Cullen, B. Hastings. *Cleopatra*: C. Chapman. *Attendants*: R. Gray, J. Brown. *Eve*: M. Manners. *Attendants*: C. Scott, J. Scott.
The Triumph of Woman (Tableau)
M. LeCount, P. Moseley

Scene 13

My
Wife: F. Williams. *Lover*: H. Richman. *Husband*: J. Carty. *Man*: J. Miller.

Scene 14

"Walking Dogs Around"
W. Howard, T. Patricola, H. Richman, E. Howard

Scene 15

Announcement
H. Richman

Scene 16

"The Black Bottom" (A New Dance)
A. Pennington
Followed by the McCarthy Sisters, A. Pennington, T. Patricola, George White Girls.

Scene 17

Buster West, John Wells, assisted by Margaret McCarthy

Scene 18

The Feud
(*by* Lew Brown, William K. Wells and George White)
Pincus: W. Howard. *Becky*: D. McCarthy. *Louis*: E. Howard. *Jake*: J. Carty. *Ignatz*: H. Morrissey. *Nathan*: F. Lyon. *McGuire*: J. Miller.

Scene 19

Frances Williams: Songs by DeSylva, Brown and Henderson
Accompanist: Leo Feiner.

Scene 20

"The Birth of the Blues"
H. Richman
(*Music by* Ray Henderson. *Lyrics by* Buddy G. DeSylva, Lew Brown.)
"Rhapsody in Blue"
(*Music by* George Gershwin. *Lyrics by* Buddy G. DeSylva and Lew Brown.)
Blue Singer: H. Richman. *The Classics*: W. Howard, E. Howard. *Memphis Blues*: M McCarthy. *St. Louis Blues*: D. McCarthy. *Traumerei*: Marion Fairbanks *Shubert's Melody*: Madeline Fairbanks. *Harps*: Misses H. Hastings, P. Gallimore, Brooks, A. White, R. Gray, G. Cullen, C. Scott, J. Scott. *Clouds*: P. Pursley, M. Manners, C. Douglass, L. McCormack. *Lightning*: M. Bowman. *Angel Harpists*: M. Klaw, C. Chapman. *Girl in Flower*: A. Pennington. *Principals*: R. Perfect, L. Garrett, J. Carthy, H. Morrissey, F. Lyon, A. Cardinal.

ACT 2

Scene 1

"Sevilla"
R. Perfect
Dances[10]
Fowler and Tamara, Girls

Scene 2

Lady Barber
Barber: F. Williams. *Customer*: W. Howard.

Scene 3

Announcement
H. Richman

Scene 4

"David and Lenore"
A. Pennington, T. Patricola

Scene 5

"The Girl Is You (The Boy Is Me)"
H. Richman, F. Williams
Pantomime
Hastings Twins, Scott Sisters

Scene 6

Announcement
H. Richman

Scene 7

Drama of Tomorrow
Duke: W. Howard. *Butler*: E. Howard. *Daughter*: A. Pennington. *Postman*: J. Miller. *Burglar*: J. Carty.

Scene 8

"My Jewels"
A. Pennington, T. Patricola
Tassel Girls in First Curtain: I. Gray, O. Morgan. *Tower Attendants*: P. Wilcox, E. Arden, L. Dixon, M. Alfred. *Emerald*: M. Slattery. *Sapphire*: L. McCormack. *Attendant*: S. Conroy. *Ruby*: M. Manners. *Attendants*: D. Donnelly, C. Chapman. *Diamond*: P. Pursley. *Attendants*: M. Klaw, M. Chandler. *Diamond Girls*: Misses Kenin, D. Bryant, N. Puntin, A. Wayne, L. Brushette, E. Bowman, J. Flynn, D. Chilton, M. Harcke, R. Gordon, M. O'Shea, E. Lawton, (George White Ballet). (*Staged by* Jane Sels under the direction of George White.)

Scene 9

"Twenty Years Ago"
A. Pennington, F. Williams, Fairbanks Twins, M. Alford, McCarthy Sisters

Scene 10

The Governor
Governor: T. Patricola. *Old Lady*: R. Perfect. *Old Man*: L. Garrett. *Little Girl*: B. Hastings. *Senator*: J. Carty. *Commissioner*: H. Morrissey.

Scene 11

The Good Old Days
Old Man: W. Howard. *Young Man*: L. Garrett. *Bewhiskered Man*: J. Miller. *Two Drunks*: F. Lyon, A. Cardinal. *Wife*: D. McCarthy. *Husband*: H. Morrissy.

Scene 12

Harry Richman, assisted by Flo Brooks

Scene 13

"Are You Satisfied?"
The Cast

---

[10]Dropped during the run.

Scene 14

Talent by the Girls

Scene 15

Adieu Curtain

Letter in Adieu Curtain: P. Pursley.

Finale

Entire Company

THE GRAND STREET FOLLIES (1926)

1926.17

A Musical Revue in Two Acts, 10 Scenes[11]. Book (sketches) and lyrics by Agnes Morgan. Music by Lily Hyland, Arthur Schwartz, Randall Thompson, (Robert A. Simon). Staged by Agnes Morgan. Dances directed by Irene Lewisohn, Albert Carroll and Blanche Talmud. Settings and costumes designed by Aline Bernstein. Lighting by Albert Hawkes. Music director, Howard Barlow. Orchestrations by Randall Thompson. Produced by the Neighborhood Playhouse. Opened 15 June 1926 at the Neighborhood Theatre and closed 8 August 1926 after 55 performances.

CAST: Albert Carroll, Helen Arthur, Otto Hulicius, Agnes Morgan, Ian Maclaren, Dorothy Sands, Marc Loebell, Blanche Talmud, Harold Minjer, Paula Trueman, John F. Roche, Vera Allen, Tom Morgan, Mae Noble, J. Blake Scott, Lois Shore, Jessica Dragonette, Lily Lubell, Juliette Gauthier (de la Verendrye), George Hoag, Lewis McMichael, George Heller, Grover Burgess, Edla Frankau, Frances Cowles, Wesley Boynton, George Knisely, Sadie Sussman, William Beyer.

ACT 1

Scene 1

In the Arctic Zone: Original Eskimo Chants:

J. Gauthier
The Seal Poke; Lullaby (old chant); Ghost Song; Weather incantation in healing the sick: Dance Song (Aton) (Very ancient); Dance Song, jazzed (Aboriginal) Replica by Marian Bauer.
Eskimo Mother: J. Gauthier. *Eskimo Father*: G. Hoag. *Eskimo Child*: L. Shore. *Other Eskimos*: B. Talmud, J. B. Scott, L. McMichael, G. Heller. *Will B. Sharp*, promoter: M. Loebell. *Toto, his assistant*: A. Carroll. *A Polar Bear*: G. Burgess.

Scene 2

Back in New York, six weeks later

Will B. Sharp, promoter: M. Loebell. *"Al" Smith*: H. Minjer. *Mrs. Feitelbaum*: M. Noble. *Lulu Belle Ulric*: L. Lubell. *Henry Hull*, Lulu's satellite: G, Hoag. *Mother Goshdarn*: D. Sands. *Craig's Wife*: V. Allen. *F.P.A.*: I. Maclaren. *Student Prince*: J. Matthews. *The Merry Widow*: E. Frankau. *The Great God Brown*: J. F. Roche. *Lorelei Lee*: P. Trueman. *Cicely Courtneidge*: F. Cowles. *Texas Guyem*: H. Arthur. *Irving Berlin*: G. Heller. *E. Z. Spender*: O. Hulicius. *The Vagabond King*: L. McMichael. *The Black Pirate*: J. B. Scott.

Scene 3

"Fixed for Life"

T. Morgan, G. Knisely, W. Boynton, G. Burgess
(*Music by* Randall Thompson.)

"Little Igloo for Two"

(*Music by* Arthur Schwartz.)
Everybody's Sweetheart: J. Dragonette. *The Snow Remover*: W. Boynton.

Scene 4

Back Again in the Arctic Zone the following summer: Civilization Follows the Flag

"Aurory Bory Alice"

(*Music by* Lily Hyland.)

"Taxi Drivers Lament"

(W. Boynton)
(*Music by* Randall Thompson.)

"The Discontented Bandits"

(*Music by* Lily Hyland.)

"My Icy Floe"

(*Music by* Randall Thompson.)

"Skating Ballet"

(*Music by* Lily Hyland.)

"Reindeer Dance"

(*Music by* Lily Hyland.)

With all your friends from Scenes 2 and 3, plus additional characters:
Eskimo Child: S. Sussman. *Miss Talley-Lewis*: P. Trueman. *An Ex Taxi Driver*: W. Boynton. *The Professor*: O. Hulicius. *The Discontented Bandits*: J. F. Roche, J. Matthews, G. Hoag, G. Heller, G. Burgess, G. Knisely. *Policeman*: J. B. Scott. *Skaters*: F. Cowles, B. Talmud, I. Lewisohn, G. Heller. *Ice Ballet*: L. McMichael, G. Hoag, O. Hulicius. *Reindeer*: L. Shore, S. Sussman, L. Lubell, P. Trueman. *The Ice Mazurka*: B. Talmud, J. B. Scott.
("Mrs. Feitelbaum Sees the Dybbuk" written especially for The Grand Street Follies by Milt Gross.)

ACT 2

Scene 1

At the Northern Lights Art Theatre: "Uncle Tom's Cabin" in a Constructivist Setting—An Example of the Sympathetic Elastic Theater.
(*Music by* Randall Thompson and Arthur Schwartz.)

"Ice Mazurka"

(*Music by* Randall Thompson.)
Little Eva: P. Trueman. *St. Clare*: I. Maclaren. *Emmeline*: L. Lubell. *Uncle Tom*: T. Morgan. *Topsy*: L. Shore. *Loker*: L. McMichael. *Marks*: J. Matthews. *Eliza*: I. Lewisohn. *The Blood Hound*: J. B. Scott. *Chorus of Slaves*: V. Allen, G. Burgess, F. Cowles, G. Heller, G. Hoag, G. Knisely, M. Noble, J. F. Roche, S. Sussman. *Chorus of Planters*: E. Frankau, B. Talmud, W. Beyer, O. Hulicius. *Chorus of Bloodhounds*: O. Hulicius, W. Beyer, B. Talmud, E. Frankau. *Three Angels*: J. Gauthier, W. Boynton, J. Dragonette.

Scene 2

At the Eskimo Neighborhood Playhouse

A. Morgan, H. Minjer

Beatrice Lillie at the North Pole

D. Sands

"Beatrice Lillie Ballad"

(*Music by* Randall Thompson.)

Scene 3

At the Gilt Theatre: A Symbolic Drama

(The Neighborhood Playhouse makes a suggestion to the Theatre Guild)
The Author: O. Hulicius. *The Stage Director*: I. Maclaren. *Jill*: E. Frankau. *Jack*: P. Trueman. *Katharine Cornell*: V. Allen. *Stage Hands*: G. Hoag, L. McMichael, G. Burgess.

Scene 4

At the Honeymoon Music Hall:

"If You Know What I Mean"

A. Carroll (with regards to Joseph Santley), (F. Cowles)
(*Music by* Arthur Schwartz. *Lyrics by* Theodore Goodwin and Albert Carroll.)
Prince Charming: A. Carroll. *The Dream Girl*: F. Cowles. *Raquel*: L. Lubell. *Peaches*: S. Sussman.

Scene 5

At the Ritz-Icicle

The Actor: H. Minjer. *The Actress*: I. Lewisohn. *The Reporter*: J. Matthews. *The Cartoonist*: G. Hoag.

Scene 6

The Arctic Night Club:

"The Polar Bear Strut"

(*Music and Lyrics by* Arthur Schwartz.)

"The Eskimo Blues"

(*Music by* Walter Haenschen. *Lyrics by* Robert Simon.)
Everybody Who Is Anybody in the Arctic Is Here Besides These Additional Characters: *Eskimo Jazz Band*: I. Lewisohn, O. Hulicius, M. Noble, G. Knisely, J. Matthews. *Eskimo Singer*: J. Gauthier. *Larry Tidbits*: T. Morgan. *Policeman*: I. Maclaren.

NO FOOLIN'

1926.18

A Musical Revue in Two Acts, 31 Scenes[12]. Comedy scenes (sketches) by J. P. McEvoy and James Barton. Music by Rudolf Friml. Additional tunes by James Hanley. Jokes, jingles and rhymes (lyrics) by Gene Buck, Irving Caesar, Ballard Macdonald. Staged by Edward Royce. Comedy scenes directed by Walter Willson. Tableaux by Ben Ali Haggin. Dances by John Boyle. Scenery by Joseph Urban and John Wenger. Costumes designed by John W. Harkrider. Orchestra under the direction of Alfred Goodman.

---

[11]The fourth in the annual series of satirical revues which began at the Neighborhood Playhouse Off-Broadway in 1922.

[12]The twentieth in the annual series of Ziegfeld revues which began in 1907. Retitled ZIEGFELD REVUE OF 1926 shortly after opening, then ZIEGFELD FOLLIES (1926) for subsequent national tour, which was restaged by Ned Wayburn.

Orchestrations by Charles Grant, Steve Jones, Will Vodery, Emil Gerstenberger. Special arrangements by Walter Haenschen. Produced by Florenz Ziegfeld. Opened 24 June 1926 at the Globe Theatre and closed 25 September 1926 after 108 performances.

CAST: JAMES BARTON, RAY DOOLEY, ANDREW TOMBES, LOUISE BROWN, CHARLES KING, EDNA LEEDOM, IRVING FISHER, BETH BERI, LEW CHRISTY, POLLY WALKER, ARTHUR (BUGS) BAER, PEGGY FEARS, (George) MORAN and (Charles) MACK, CLAIRE LUCE, YVONNE OCCENT and GENESKO, MARY JANE, EDNA COVEY, YACHT CLUB ENTERTAINERS (Chick Endor, George Walsh, Billy Mann, Tommy Purcell), GRETA NISSEN, GEORGE MOESER, KATHERINE PENMAN, HELEN O'SHEA, VICTOR MUNRO, BARBARA NEWBERRY, KAY ENGLISH, THE CONNOR TWINS (Thelma, Velma), Murray Minehart, George Baxter, Andrew Knox, Robert Shields, Noel Francis, Joseph Marievsky, Jack Cronin.

Show Girls: Gladys Glad, Myrna Darby, Shaw, Culmer, Krosby, Flo Kennedy, Bernice Ackerman, Norma Dyal, Mary Hopkins, Marian Benda. *Ziegfeld Girls*: Anastasia Reilly, Evelyn Greig, Lillian Adele Smith, Katherine Burke, Dorothy Wegman, Helene Herendeen, Mabel Baade, Elsie Behrens, Susan Fleming, Paulette Goddard, Mary Jane, Katherine Penman, Alys Fitzgerald, Kay English, Alice McKenzie, Mary Hopkins, Yvonne Grey, Alma Drange, Biddy Somerset, Ruth Grace, Norma Forrest, Dorothy Patterson, Hilda Olsen, Marjorie Leet, Mary Farrell, Marion Strasmick; Misses Ladd, Williams, Lane, LaMay, Dale, Wilson, Blackburne, Wayne, Mason, Ansell. *Gentlemen of the Ensemble*: Carmine DiGiovanni, William Murray, Edward Mowen, Clifford Daly, Croswell, Walter Costello, Leslie Ostrander, Owen Harvey, Bert McGuiness.

ACT 1[13]

Scene 1

"We're Cleaning Up Broadway"

(*Music by* Rudolf Friml. *Lyrics by* Irving Caesar.)
Scene: Broadway at Longacre Square.
Columbus: W. Power. *Mayor Jimmie Walker*: D. Murray. *George M. Cohan*: C. King. *Bobby Jones*: W. O'Rourke. *Gertrude Ederle*: D. Gilbert. *Bill Tilden*: M. Minehart. *Helen Wills*: M. Lunnay. *Jack Dempsey*: V. Munro. *Miss America 1925*: G. Glad.

Scene 2

The Wedding Night

(An arrangement by Ben Ali Haggin.)
The Bride: P. Goddard. *The Groom*: A. Reilly. *The Maid of Honor*: E. Greig. *The Best Man*: H. Herendeen. *The Page*: K. Burke. *Two Little Maids*: S. Fleming, M. Mulhern. *A Naughty Guest*: N. Francis. *The Guests*: M. Benda, B. Somerset, N. Forrest, D. Wegman, A. Smith, B. Ackerman, M. Darby.

Scene 3

"When the Shaker Plays a Cocktail Tune"[14]
P. Walker
(*Music by* James Hanley. *Lyrics by* Gene Buck.)

Dance

H. O'Shea
Cocktail Girls: Misses S. Fleming, Ladd, Williams, A. Fitzgerald, Lane, Y. Grey, K. English, P. Goddard, LaMay, Dale, A. McKenzie, Wilson, D. Patterson, M. Leet, E. Behrens, M. Baade, M. Farrell, A. Reilly, M. Strasmick, Blackburne, Wayne, Mason, A. Drange, N. Francis.

Scene 4

Dance

B. Newberry

Scene 5

"I Want a Girl to Call My Own"
I. Fisher
(*Music by* Rudolf Friml. *Lyrics by* Gene Buck. *Scene painted by* Joseph Urban.)
Scene: A Garden.

---

[13]The running order of songs and sketches was totally revised for the tour. Added for the tour:

"Minnie Haha"(Act 2)
  J. Barton
Double Crossing (*by* Paul Gerard Smith) (Act 2)
  Channel Cop: J. Barton. *Channel Crosser*: E. Leedom.
Touring (*by* Paul Gerard Smith) (Act 2)
  Tourists: J. Barton, C. King. *Salesmen*: V. Munro, D. Murray, W. Blett. *A Dealer in Remnants*: L. Christy. *A Buyer of Nick Nacks*: W. Power.
"Little Marie" (Act 1)
  C. King
  (*Music by* James Hanley. *Lyrics by* Gene Buck and Billy Rose.)

[14]Dropped for subsequent national tour.

St. Louis: Y. Grey. *Miami*: Miss Burke. *Philadelphia*: D. Wegman. *New Orleans*: N. Forrest. *Charleston*: N. Francis. *Boston*: H. Herendeen. *San Francisco*: E. Greig. *New York*: M. Benda. *Palm Beach*: A. Smith.

Scene 6

The Trial

(*by* J. P. McEvoy. *Scene painted by* Joseph Urban.)
The Judge: G. Baxter. *Mr. Kitch*: A. Tombes. *Mrs. Kitch*: E. Leedom. *Gertie*: R. Dooley. *Bessie*: C. Luce. *Michel, Jr.*: C. Mack. *The Cook*: E. Behrens.

Scene 7

"Honey, Be Mine"
C. King, H. O'Shea
(*Music by* James Hanley. *Lyrics by* Gene Buck.)

Dance

B. Newberry
Show Girls: Misses G. Glad, M. Darby, Shaw, Culmer, Krosby, F. Kennedy, B. Ackerman. *Boys*: Messrs. C. DiGiovanni, W. Murray, E. Mowen, C. Daly, Croswell, W. Costello, L. Ostrander, B. McGuinness. *Dancers*: A. Reilly, E. Behrens, M. Leet, M. Farrell, D. Patterson, A. McKenzie, A. Fitzgerald, H. Olsen, N. Francis, Ansell, Williams, M. Strasmick, The Connor Twins.

Scene 8

Indian Dance

C. Luce

Scene 9

The Pest

(*by* James Barton. *Scene painted by* John Wenger.)
Mickey, the Monster: J. Barton. *Mr. Charles McKnight*: L. Christy. *Mrs. Charles McKnight*: K. Penman. *Mr. Lockit*: V. Munro. *Louder*: B. McGuinness. *The Stranger*: O. Hervey. *The Guests*: W. Murray, W. Costello, R. Grace.

Scene 10

Arthur (Bugs) Baer[15]

Scene 11

"Poor Little Marie"

(A Song Scene by Gene Buck.)
(*Music by* James Hanley. *Lyrics by* Irving Caesar. *Scene painted by* Joseph Urban.)
Scene: A Little Cafe in Paris. *Time*: Armistice Night, 1925.
Little Marie: L. Brown. *His Ball and Chain*: E. Leedom. *A Boy from Broadway*: C. King. *A Boy of the Big Parade*: I. Fisher. *The Piano Player*: B. Beri. *The Second Fiddle*: K. English. *An Artist*: G. Baxter. *The Proprietor*: L. Christy. *The Absinthe Lady*: M. Mulhern. *Montmartre Rose*: B. Somerset. *Waiters, Soldiers, Dancers, etc.*

Dance

Y. Accent, Jenesko

Scene 12

Dance

H. O'Shea, Connor Twins

Scene 13

Day Coach

(*by* J. P. McEvoy. *Scene painted by* John Wenger.)
Mr. Kitch: A. Tombes. *Mrs. Kitch*: E. Leedom. *Gertie*: R. Dooley. *The Bride*: P. Walker. *The Groom*: C. King. *The Conductor*: J. Barton. *The Train Butcher*: V. Munro. *Bridesmaids*: Connor Twins. And Misses R. Grace, N. Dyal, B. Ackerman, Krosby, G. Glad, M. Benda, M. Hopkins. Messrs. B. McGuinness, C. Mack, J. Cronin, L. Ostrander.

Scene 14

Dance

M. Jane

Scene 15

"No Foolin'"

L. Brown, Boys
(*Music by* James Hanley. *Lyrics by* Gene Buck. *Staged by* Edward Royce. *Scene painted by* Joseph Urban.)

Scene 16

Yacht Club Entertainers

Scene 17

"Florida, the Moon and You"

I. Fisher, P. Fears
(*Music by* Rudolf Friml. *Lyrics by* Gene Buck. *Staged by* Ned Wayburn. *Scene painted by* Joseph Urban.)

---

[15]Dropped for subsequent national tour.

Scene 18

"Dans la Boule Lumineuse"—In the Luminous Ball
  C. Luce

The Goddess of Feathers

  (*Scene by* Joseph Urban.)
  The Goddess of the Feather: N. Forrest. *The Goddess of the White Paradise*: D. Wegman. *The Goddess of the White Peacock*: Y. Gray. *The Goddess of the White Cobra Bird*: B. Ackerman. *The Goddess of Plumes*: Miss Krosby. *The Goddess of the White Argas*: E. Greig. *The Goddess of the White Pheasant*: B. Somerset. *The Goddess of the White Eagle*: H. Herendeen. *The Goddess of the Ostrich*: G. Glad. *The Goddess of the White Robin*: M. Benda. *The Goddess of the White Nightingale*: A. Smith. *The Goddess of Feathers*: K. Burke.

Dance
  B. Beri

Finale

ACT 2

Scene 1

Treasures from the East (A Venetian Fantasy by Ben Ali Haggin)

  A Girl from Siam: K. Burke. *A Girl from China*: S. Fleming. *A Girl from Korea*: H. Herendeen. *A Girl from Greece*: E. Greig *A Girl from Burma*: M. Mulhern. *Venetian Ladies*: N. Forrest, M. Benda, B. Ackerman, M. Darby, D. Wegman. *The Captain*: J. Cronin. *Sailors*: Messrs. C. Mack, O. Harvey, Croswell.

Scene 2

"Every Little Thing You Do"
  P. Walker, Toodle OO Girls, Boys
  (*Music by* James Hanley. *Lyrics by* Gene Buck.)

Scene 3

"Whip Dance"
  (*Music by* Rudolf Friml.) J. Barton, R. Dooley

Scene 4

Spanish Dance[16]
  B. Beri

Scene 5

"Gentlemen Prefer Blondes"[17]
  E. Leedom
  (*Music by* Rudolf Friml. *Lyrics by* Irving Caesar.)

"Nize Baby"
  E. Leedom
  (*Sketch by* Ballard Macdonald. *Music by* James Hanley. *Lyrics by* Gene Buck.)

Dance
  M. Jane

Scene 6

Mlle. Bluebeard[18]
  (An Oriental pantomime by Greta Nissen.)
  Mlle. Bluebeard: G. Nissen. *Her Husband*: J. Marlevsky. *Her Friend*: G. Baxter.

Sabre Dance
  (*Arranged by* Michel Fokine.)
  (*Scene painted by* Joseph Urban. *Costumes created by* Greta and Agnes Nissen. Music adapted from themes of famous Russian composers by Ariel A. Rubstein.)

Scene 7

Moran and Mack[19]

Scene 8

"Wasn't It Nice?"
  C. King, P. Fears, Girls, Boys
  (*Music by* Rudolf Friml. *Lyrics by* Irving Caesar. *Staged by* Edward Royce.)

Scene 9

Rip's Birthday Party
  (*by* Gene Buck)
  Jack: A. Tombes. *Butler*: J. Cronin. *Lulu Belle*: C. Luce. *Mellie Dunham*: C. Daly. *N.T.G.*: M. Minehart. *Peggy Joyce*: E. Leedom. *Irving Berlin*: F. Zolt. *Ellen Mackay*: P. Walker. *Raquel Meller*: P. Fears. *'Peaches'*: P. Goddard. *'Cinderella' Browning*: R. Shields. *Countess of Cathcart*: R. Dooley. *Rip Van Winkle*: C. Mack.

---

[16]Dropped for subsequent national tour.
[17]Dropped for subsequent national tour.
[18]Dropped for subsequent national tour.
[19]Dropped for subsequent national tour.

Scene 10

"Spring"
  (*by* Ben Ali Haggin) Dance by L. Brown
  (*Dance arranged by* Ivan Tarasoff.)

Scene 11

The Dying Swan
  E. Covey

Scene 12

James Barton—Himself

Scene 13

The Patio: "Don't Do the Charleston"
  C. King
  (*Music by* James Hanley. *Lyrics by* Irving Caesar. *Scene painted by* John Wenger.)

Dances
  M. Jane, G. Moeser

Finale

1926.19   **MY MAGNOLIA**

An All-Colored Musical Comedy in Two Acts, 8 Scenes. Book by Alex C. Rogers and Eddie Hunter. Music by C. Luckeyth Roberts. Lyrics by Alex C. Rogers. Staged by Alex C. Rogers and Eddie Hunter. Dances arranged by Charles Davis. Settings by Frank Illo. Orchestra under the direction of C. Luckeyth Roberts at the piano. Entire production under the supervision of Walter Campbell. Produced by Walter Campbell. Opened 12 July 1926 at the Mansfield Theatre and closed 16 July 1926 after 6 performances.

CAST (in order of appearance): *Peggy*, Switchboard Operator: HILDA ROGERS. *Harvey*, Head Bellman: PAUL BASS. *Jodey*, Second Bellman: PERCY COLSTON. *Mr. Korkem*, Hotel Superintendant: Lionel Monagas. *Henry Upson*, Oof Dah, Elevator Boy: Dink Stewart. *Jasper Downson*, Elevator Boy: Barrington Carter, Henry "Gang" Jines. *Johnny*, Page Boy: George Randol. *Jenny*, Personal Maid: ADELAIDE HALL. *Chef*: Claude Lawson. *Dusty Snow*, Head Housemaid: Alberta Perkins. *Grenadine*, Housekeeper: Mabel Gant. *Sherman*, Head Porter: EDDIE HUNTER. *Lightfoot*: CHARLES DAVIS. *Detective*: George Randol. *Floor Manager*: PAUL BASS. *Doorman* (Oof Dah): Dink Stewart. *Jenny*: Estelle Floyd. *Messenger*: George Randol. *Outer Guard*: George Randol. *Expelled Member*: Lionel Monagas. *A Member of Dominoes*: George Nanton. *Two Winning Members*: Charles Davis, Clarence Peters. *Inner Guard*: Henry (Gang) Jines. *Chief Domino* (Oof Dah): Dink Stewart. *Train Announcer*: Claude Lawson. *Magnolia*, Uncle Fi's Foster Daughter: CATHERINE PARKER. *Widow Love*: LENA SANFORD ROBERTS. *Mr. Towles*: George Randol. *Mr. Hedlee*: Lionel Monagas. *Constable Sapp*: Barrington Carter. *Herman*: Charles Davis. *Snappy*: Snippy Mason. *Uncle Fi*: ALEX C. ROGERS.

Magnolia Blossoms: Fannie Henderson, Cornell Vigal, Sally Evans, Jackie Jackson, Rose Gilliard, Helen Dunmoore, Olive Harrison, Ermilie Brown, Elise Phillips, Edith Oliver, Frances Smith, Corinne Richards, Hilaris Friend, Marion Tyler, Gladys Phillips, Margaret Washington, Marie Warren, Janet White, Florence Tarby. *Feather Foot Dancers*: John Worthy, George Nanton, William McKelvey, Walter Gregory, Harry Hunter, Snippy Mason, Charles Saltez, Buddy Green, Clarence Peters.

Act 1, Scene 1: Hotel Strutt, (Help's Section), New York City. Noonday, 22 December. *Scene 2*: Street in Harlem, Shopping Section. Late afternoon, same day. *Scene 3*: Ballroom in Harlem. Mardi Gras Club's Ball. Evening, same day. *Scene 4*: Corner of Lenox Avenue and 135th Street, Harlem. Same evening. *Scene 5*: Street in Harlem Exterior of "Gallopin' Dominoes" Association and Professor Oof Dah's Office. Same evening. *Scene 6*: Interior of "Gallopin' Dominoes" Association. Same evening, a few minutes later. *Scene 7*: Railroad Station, Jersey City. Following morning, 23 December.

Act 2: Front yard of Uncle Fi's Home, outskirts of New Orleans. Christmas Day.

ACT 1

"At Your Service" (Opening Number)

"Dance of the Bellhops"

"Baby Mine"
  P. Colston, Chorus

"Shake Your Duster"
  A. Perkins, Girls

"Pay Day"
  H. Rogers, Chorus

"Magnolia"
  P. Bass, Chorus

"Hard Times"
  E. Hunter

"Spend It"
  A. Hall, C. Davis, Girls

"Jazz Land Ball"
   A. Hall, C. Davis, Chorus
"Laugh Your Blues Away"
   E. Floyd
"Gallopin' Dominoes"
   E. Hunter, Men
"Headin' South"
   H. Rogers, Company

ACT 2
   Opening:
      "Merry Christmas"
      "Magnolia" (reprise) (Tap Charleston)
   "Struttin' Time"
      C. Parker, Girls
   "Our Child"
      A. C. Rogers
   "Gee Chee"
      A. Hall, C. Davis, Girls, Boys
   "Magnolia" (reprise)
      P. Bass
   "Sundown Serenade"
      L. S. Roberts, Chorus
   "Baby Mine" (reprise)
      P. Colston
   "Parade of the Christmas Dinner"
      A. C. Rogers, L. S. Roberts, Ensemble
   "Baby Wants"
      A. Perkins, E. Hunter
   "The Oof Dah Man"
      D. Stewart, Girls
   "Sweet Popopper"
      E. Floyd
   Finale: "Baby Mine" (Finale)"
      Company

1926.20   THE BLONDE SINNER

A Smart Farce with Music in Three Acts. Book, music and lyrics by Leon DeCosta. Book staged by Edwin Vail. Musical numbers staged by Ralph Riggs. Scenery designed by Walter Sherwood. Hugo Frey's Troubadours (Orchestra) conducted by Irwin Abrams. Orchestrations by Hugo Frey. Produced by Musicomedies, Inc.(Ralph Payton, Manager). Opened 14 July 1926 at the Cort Theatre, moved 2 August 1926 to the Selwyn Theatre, moved 30 August 1926 to the Lyric Theatre, moved 20 September 1926 to the Frolic Theatre and closed 11 December 1926 after 179 performances.

CAST (in order of appearance): *George Hemmingworth*: RALPH BUNKER. *Betty Hemmingworth*: ENID MARKEY. *Flash Pinkney*: RUTH STEVENS. *Adonis Mulberry*: Clif Heckinger. *Jack Conelly*: Harold De Becker. *Alfred Bird*: Russell Morrison. *Ida*: MARJORIE GATESON. *Mike Reilly*: Matt Hanley. *Alexander Homer*: Frank Kingdon. *James Manton*: Howard St. John. *Charleston Maid*: Margy Lane.

Time: The Present. *Place*: The Living Room of a Summer Cottage in an exclusive manor on Long Island, New York.

Act 1: The Hemmingworth's Living Room at 9:30 P.M.

Act 2: The same at 9 P.M. the following evening

Act 3: The same at 10 A.M. the following morning.

ACT 1
   "Don't You Cheat"
      E. Markey, M. Gateson, R. Stevens, R. Bunker
   "Oh, What a Playmate You Could Make"
      M. Gateson, E. Markey, R. Bunker, M. Hanley, C. Heckinger, R. Stevens
   Reprise
      E. Markey, M. Hanley
   Finale—"Don't You Cheat" (reprise)
      Orchestra

ACT 2
   "If You Said What You Thought"
      E. Markey, M. Gateson, R. Stevens, R. Bunker

"Man Is a Mistake"
   M. Gateson
"The Whispering Song"
   R. Stevens, H. St. John
"Lips"
   M. Gateson, H. St. John
Finale—"Lips" (reprise)
   Orchestra

ACT 3
   "Byebye Babe"
      E. Markey, M. Gateson, R. Stevens
   Reprise
      H. DeBecker, E. Markey
   Reprise
      M. Gateson, H. DeBecker
   Finale
      Omnes [Entire Company]

1926.21   AMERICANA (1926)

A Musical Revue in Two Acts, 22 Scenes[20]. Sketches by J. P. McEvoy. Music by Con Conrad and Henry Souvaine. Special numbers by George Gershwin, Ira Gershwin, Philip Charig, Morrie Ryskind. Production staged by Allan Dinehart. Dances and ensembles by Larry Ceballos. Musical director, Gene Salzer. Orchestrations by Hans Spialek. Entire production (costumes, settings) designed by John Held, Jr. Produced by Richard Herndon. Opened 26 July 1926 at the Belmont Theatre and closed 5 February 1927 after 224 performances.

CAST: LEW BRICE, ROY ATWELL, BETTY COMPTON, MARIAN DALE, ROBERTA BELLINGER, TOM BURTON, BETTY COMPTON, CHARLES BUTTERWORTH, M. Charles Palazzi, Dorothy Deeder, Gay Nell [Nelle], Georgia Ingram, Arline Gardiner, Edgar Gardiner, Edna Fulling, Elizabeth Morgan, Helen Morgan, Evelyn Bennett, Arthur Lipson, Isabelle Mason, John Burton, Arthur Lipson, Fred Weeks, Tim O'Connor, Elizabeth Mason, Louis Lazarin, Lehman Byck, Victor Edmunds, Wayne Kohne, Lillian Ring. PAN-AMERICAN QUARTETTE: Charles H. Downz, Joe E. Loomis, John W. Turner, Walter Hilliard.

ACT 1[21]
Scene 1
   "American Revue Girls"
      (*Music by* Con Conrad. *Lyrics by* J. P. McEvoy.)
      Announcer: R. Atwell. *Tiller Girl*: D. Deeder. *Ziegfeld Girl*: I. Mason. *Junior League Girl*: E. Fulling. *Charleston Girl*: G. Nell. *Duncan Girl*: E. Morgan. *Anna Held Girl*: M. Dale. *Garrick Gaieties Girl*: E. Bennett. *Americana Girl*: B. Compton.
Scene 2
   Travelogue
   Announcement
      M. Dale
   a. Chicago
      Stranger: T. Burton. *Bandit*: E. Gardiner.
   b. Miami
      Salesman: R. Atwell. *Prospect*: C. Butterworth.
   c. New York
      Stranger: R. Atwell. *First New Yorker*: G. Nell. *Second New Yorker*: M. C. Palazzi. *Third New Yorker*: A. Lipson. *Policeman*: T. Burton.
Scene 3
   "Sunny Disposish"
      A. Gardiner, E. Gardiner
      (*Music by* Philip Charig. *Lyrics by* Ira Gershwin.)

---

[20]The first of three annual revues (1926, 1928, 1932) titled AMERICANA.
[21]Added during the run:
   The Unwritten Law (Act 1)
      Gunga Din: A. Lipson. *Perpetrator*: C. Butterworth.
   Tol'able David (Act 1)
      Mr. David Belasco: R. Atwell. *Miss Fannie Brice*: L. Brice. *Reporter*: E. Gardiner. *Secretary*: J. Booth. *First Assistant Secretary*: E. Fulling. *Second Assistant Secretary*: I. Mason.
   "Nobody Wants Me" (Act 2)
      H. Morgan
      (*Music by* Henry Souvaine. *Lyrics by* Morrie Ryskind.)

Scene 4

The Potters' Sunday Morning

Pa Potter: T. Burton. *Ma Potter*: R. Bellinger. *Bill Potter*: C. Butterworth.
Radio Announcer: M. C. Palazzi. *Gabrielle Gabrilowitch*: A. Lipson.
Reverend Francis X. Musseltoff: E. Gardiner. *Wham!*: F. Weeks. *Pow!*:
T. O'Connor.

Scene 5

Bricie's in Town[22]

L. Brice

Scene 6

"Lost Barber Shop Chord"

(*Music by* George Gershwin. *Lyrics by* Ira Gershwin.)
Bootblack: L. Lazarin. *Four Barbers*: Pan-American Quartette.

Scene 7

"Blowing the Blues Away"

L. Brice, B. Compton, H. Morgan, E. Bennett, G. Nell, E. Morgan
(*Music by* Philip Charig. *Lyrics by* Ira Gershwin.)

Scene 8

"Dreaming"[23]

H. Burke

(*Music by* Henry Souvaine. *Lyrics by* J. P. McEvoy.)

Dances

G. Ingram, W. Kohne

(*Ballet Music by* Henry Souvaine.)

Scene 9

After Dinner Speech

Mr. Buttercup: C. Butterworth. *Guests*: "Mesrrs. Winterbottom, Throckmorton,
Micks, Hautchin, Hooper, Fuss."

Scene 10

"Cavalier Americana" (An American Opera in Three Acts based on
authentic American Folk Tunes. *Music by* Henry Souvaine, with apologies. *Libretto by* J. P. McEvoy.)

French Peasant: L. Ring. *American Doughboy*: L. Byck. *American Mounted
Policeman*: L. Lazarin. *American Woman*, mother of doughboy: J. Booth.
Immigrant: G. Mead. *Cops*: T. Burton, A. Lipson. *Peddler*: A. Lipson.
Charleston Dancer: E. Fulling. *Prisoners*: C. H. Downz, J. E. Loomis, J. W.
Turner, W. Hilliard.

ACT 2

Scene 1

"Riverside Bus"

(*Music by* Con Conrad. *Lyrics by* J. P. McEvoy.)
Cowboy: T. Burton. *Traffic Cop*: G Nell. *Nurse*: D. Deeder. *Blind Man*: E.
Morgan. *Newsboy*: E. Bennett. *City Man*: E. Gardiner. *Bus Driver*: M. C.
Palazzi.

Scene 2

The Volga Boatman

L. Brice, Pan-American Quartette

Scene 3

"Tabloid Papers"

(*Music by* Con Conrad. *Lyrics by* J. P. McEvoy.)
Newsboy: E. Bennett.

Scene 4

Hollywood

Scene: Studio of the David Rex St. deMille.
David Rex St. deMille: R. Atwell. *Yes Man*: T. Burton. *Harold Strongface*:
C. Butterworth. *Camera Man*: A. Lipson. *Aspirants*: E. Morgan, M. Dale.
Artist: E. Gardiner.

Scene 5

The Life Guard[24]

Non-Union Life Guard: L. Brice. *Betty*: B. Compton. *Evelyn*: E. Bennett.
Walking Delegate: A. Lipson. *Distracted Mother*: R. Bellinger.

Scene 6

"Why D'ya Roll Those Eyes?"

E. Bennett, B. Compton, H. Morgan
(*Music by* Philip Charig. *Lyrics by* Morrie Ryskind.)

Scene 7

"Just Lovin'"[25]

A. Gardner, E. Gardner, L. Ring, L. Byck, G. Mead, L. Lazarin, J. Booth,
V. Edmunds
(*Music by* Henry Souvaine. *Lyrics by* J. P. McEvoy.)
Cops: W. Kohne, M. Dale, G. Nell, E. Fulling. *Nurses*: G. Ingram,
D. Deeder, E. Morgan, I. Mason.

Scene 8

Rollo and His Pa (A Salutary Lesson from McGuffey's
Third Reader)

Mother: R. Bellinger. *Father*: R. Atwell. *Rollo*: L. Brice.

Scene 9

"Scrubwomen's Ballet"

(*Music by* Henry Souvaine.)
Premiere Scrubeuse: G. Ingram. *Deuxieme Scrubeuse*:
E. Morgan. *Troisieme Scrubeuse*: M. Dale. *Quatrieme
Scrubeuse*: D. Deeder. *Concierge Americana*:
W. Kohne.

Scene 10

Collegiate

M. Dale, G. Nell, D. Deeder, E. Morgan, I. Mason,
E. Fulling, E. Bennett, E. Fulling, B. Compton, J. Booth,
A. Lee

Scene 11

"Thanks Awful"[26]

H. Morgan, L. Byck, Pan-American Quartette
(*Music by* Con Conrad. *Lyrics by* Joe Young and Sam Lewis.)

Scene 12

The Student Prince of Denmark

Announcement: M. Dale.
Scene 1: Office of J. J. Shubert.
Mr. J. J. Shubert: R. Atwell. *Theatre Guild Director*: E. Gardiner.
Scene 2: The Student Prince of Denmark.
Hamlet: L. Brice. *Ophelia*: B. Compton. *Horatio*: T. Burton. *King*: T. Burton.
Queen: R. Bellinger. *Laertes*: A. Lipson. *First Grave Digger*: T. O'Connor.
Second Grave Digger: F. Weeks. *First Girl*: M. Dale. *Second Girl*: E. Morgan.
Third Girl: G. Nell. *Fourth Girl*: I. Mason. *Fifth Girl*: D. Deeder. *Sixth Girl*:
E. Fulling.

1926.22   # NIC-NAX OF 1926

A Musical Revue in Two Acts, 26 Scenes. Words (sketches, lyrics) by Paul
W. Porter, Matt Kennedy, Roger Gray. Music by Gitz Rice, Werner Janssen.
Staged under the direction of Paul W. Porter. Dances and ensembles by Jack
Connors. Costumes by Esmonde. Scenery by John Dwyer. Musical director,
August Kleinecke. Set designer, John Dwyer. Orchestrations by Carl
Williams [Carl Williams orchestrated Gitz Rice's songs only.], Harold
Sanford, Werner Janssen. Produced by Knick Knacks, Inc. (Cooperative
venture under the management of George Mooser). Opened 2 August 1926
at the Cort Theatre and closed 14 August 1926 after 13 performances.

<u>CAST:</u> NANCY GIBBS, GITZ RICE, IRENE OLSEN, FREDERICK SANTLEY,
KATHERINE WITCHIE, ROGER GRAY, ESTELLE HUNT, RALPH RIGGS,
SUZANNE BENNETT, HARRY SHORT[27], LORRAINE SHERWOOD, SAM
SUMMERS, HELEN WEHRLE, NAT NAZARRO, JR., TOM COWAN, JOHN
CHERRY, GERTRUDE DEMMLER, LAURA PHILLIPS, MILTON C. HERMAN,
Dorothy E. Brown, Emily Verdi, Natalie Lorraine, Betty Lomax, Wanda Wood, Rose
Baye, Carolyn Gerken, Ann Summers, Dorothy Manners, Dorothy DeClue, Maxine
Demmler, Winnie Kerwin, Elena Loree, Bernice Walden.

---

[22]Replaced during run by:

"Kosher Kleagle"

L. Brice, V. Manuel, E. Fulling, A. Reilly, E. Mason
(*Music by* Philip Charig. *Lyrics by* J. P. McEvoy.)

[23]Later in the run, music credited to both Henry Souvaine and Con
Conrad.

[24]Dropped during the run.

---

[25]Dropped during the run.

[26]Replaced for National Tour by:

"Swanee River Melody"

Pan-American Quartette
(*Music by* Charles Weinberg. *Lyrics by* Al Wilson.)

[27]Though billed in the program, reviews indicate Harry Short did not
appear opening or thereafter.

ACT 1
Scene 1

Introducing "Nic-Nax"

(*Music by* Gitz Rice. *Lyrics by* Paul Porter.)
The Host: G. Rice. *Nic-Nax*: R. Riggs. *Beauty*: D. E. Brown, E. Verdi. *Grace*: N. Lorraine, B. Lomax. *Melody*: W. Wood, R. Baye. *Humor*: C. Gerken, A. Summers. *Ginger*: D. Manners, D. DeClue. *Spice*: M. Demmler, G. Demmler.

Scene 2

"Mortifying the American Man"

T. Cowan, J. Cherry, H. Short, N. Nazarro, Jr., R. Gray, F. Santley
(*Music by* Gitz Rice. *Lyrics by* Paul Porter.)

Scene 3

Love Pirates

(*by* Paul W. Porter)
Scene: Aboard the Good Ship Theatre.
Keg's Wife: E. Hunt. *Vera Ashcart*: S. Bennett. *Hera Well*: L. Sherwood. *A Stowaway*: K. Witchie. *May Westy*: I. Olsen. *Shady Thompson*: W. Wood. *Bride of the Slain*: L. Phillips. *Chowmein*: R. Baye. *Reste Under the Airs*: A. Summers. *Pearline*: D. E. Brown. *Settle*: B. Lomax. *Eyeris*: D. DeClue. *First Crib Nabber*: M. Demmler. *Second Crib Nabber*: G. Demmler. *One Guy's Dame*: C. Gerken. *Coggoleum*: B. Walden. *Mrs. Gosh Darn*: E. Verdi. *E. Z. Vertigo*: N. Lorraine. *Mrs. Cutex*: W. Kerwin. *Fairy Moron*: E. Loree. *Mammy Balaver*: D. Manners. *Lieutenant Gigg*: R. Riggs.

"Broads of Broadway"

(*Music by* Gitz Rice. *Lyrics by* Paul Porter.)

Scene 4

Valsette

H. Wehrle
(*Music by* Werner Janssen.)

Scene 5

Station GaRod Broadcasting

(*Conceived by* Joseph Santley. *Dialogue by* Paul W. Porter.)
Uncle Nic-Nax: H. Short. *The Hero*: F. Santley. *The Heroine*: N. Gibbs.

Scene 6

Advice

(*by* Matt Kennedy)
The Dumb Belle: E. Hunt. *The Smart Belle*: L. Sherwood. *The Drugstore Cowboy*: J. Cherry.

Scene 7

"Oh, Daddy"

I. Olsen, 16 Shebas
(*Music and Lyrics by* Gitz Rice.)

Scene 8

So I Hear (*by* Roger Gray)

Ronald Tippet: H. Short. *Harvey Tippet*: R. Gray. *Mrs. Tippet*: S. Bennett.

Scene 9

The Sun Kissed the Rose Good-Bye

(*Conceived by* Jack Connors.)
The Gardner: T. Cowan. *The Rose*: K. Witchie. *The Sun*: R. Riggs. *The Butterfly*: G. Demmler. *The Bee*: L. Phillips.

Song ("When the Sun Kissed the Rose Good-Night")

(*Music by* Gitz Rice. *Lyrics by* Tom Dodd.)

Flowers

(*Ballet by* Werner Janssen.)

Scene 10

The Fatal Question

(*by* Roger Gray and Werner Janssen)
Introduction: F. Santley. *Sweet Young Thing*: I. Olsen. *Nice Old Gentleman*: J. Cherry. *Cute Girl*: H. Wehrle. *Cute Man*: N. Nazarro, Jr. *Business Girl*: L. Sherwood. *A Nice Man*: F. Santley. *Eugenie Girl*: S. Bennett. *Eugenie Man*: R. Gray.

Scene 11

Frederic Santley and the Eight Little Nobodies

(*by* B. C. Hilliam and Gitz Rice)
Dance: D. DeClue. *Dinah*: E. Verdi. *Recitation*: D. E. Brown. *An Imitation*: C. Gerken. *Violin Solo*: N. Lorraine. *Topsy and Eva*: G. Demmler, M. Demmler. *'Frenchie'*: D. Manners.

Scene 12

The Remittance Man

(*by* Roger Gray)
Daisy LaMont: S. Bennett. *Lord Frothingham*: R. Gray. *Higgins*: H. Short. *Fifi*: L. Sherwood.

Scene 13

Nat Nazarro, Jr.

Scene 14

Conscience

(*by* Roger Gray)
(a) *A Crook*: N. Nazarro, Jr. *His Pal*: J. Cherry.
(b) *A Conductor*: R. Gray. *A Passenger*: H. Short.
(c) *A Bold She*: L. Sherwood. *A Timid He*: J. Cherry. *Conscience*: S. Bennett.

Scene 15

"Sesqui-Centennial"

(*Music by* Werner Janssen. *Lyrics by* Paul Porter.)

ACT 2
Scene 1

A Rangoon Wedding

(*Conceived by* Jack Connors.)
Burmese Priest: T. Cowan. *A Rangoon Princess*: N. Gibbs. *A Native Boy*: R. Riggs. *His Bride*: K. Witchie. *Spirit of Schwey Dragon*: H. Wehrle. *Slaves and Bridesmaids.*

"Burmah Moon"/"In Old Rangoon"

(*Music and Lyrics by* Gitz Rice.)

Scene 2

Wonder What a Bench Thinks About

(*by* Matt Kennedy and Roger Gray)
(a) *He*: S. Bennett. *She*: J. Cherry.
(b) *The Inquisitive Girl*: L. Sherwood. *Miss I-Told-You*: H. Wehrle. *The Husband*: R. Riggs. *The Up-to-Date Flapper*: E. Hunt. *Her Husband*: S. Summers.
(c) *Mr. Smith*: H. Short. *Hulda*: R. Gray.

Scene 3

"On a Wall"

(*Music by* Werner Janssen. *Lyrics by* Paul Porter.)
Humpty Dumpty: R. Riggs. *Contrary Mary*: K. Witchie. And Eight King's Ponies.

Scene 4

Giggles

(*by* Sam Summers)
He: S. Summers. *She*: E. Hunt.

Scene 5

The Enormous Procession

(*Conceived by* Paul W. Porter.)
Renee Adore: N. Gibbs. *John Gilbert*: F. Santley. *The Riveter*: H. Short. *The Bartender*: R. Gray. *A French Officer*: N. Nazarro, Jr. *Marie*: K. Witchie. *Morris Markowitz*: M. C. Herman. And Peasants.

"Almost"

(*Music by* Gitz Rice. *Lyrics by* Anna Fitziu.)

"For a Boy Like You" (For a Girl Like You)

(*Music by* Gitz Rice. *Lyrics by* Joe Goodwin.)

Scene 6

"High Yellow" (Everything Is High Yellow Now)

I. Olsen, Eight Somebodies
(*Music by* Gitz Rice. *Lyrics by* Paul Porter.)

Scene 7

Would You?

(*by* Matt Kennedy)
Scene: Brown's Apartment. Midnight.
Van Dyke Brown: F. Santley. *Bryant Parke*: J. Cherry. *A Visitor*: N. Gibbs.

Scene 8

The Vagabond Kings

(*by* Paul Lannin)
Divertissements En Route: *Trombone*: J. Cherry. *A Novelty*: H. Short. *Ballad*: T. Cowan. *Adagio*: R. Gray, R. Riggs. *A Mexican Revolution*: N. Nazarro, Jr.

Scene 9

"Syncopassion"

I. Olsen, N. Nazarro, Jr., Syncopassionists
(*Music by* Werner Janssen. *Lyrics by* Paul Porter.)

Scene 10

Gitz Rice

Scene 11

Good Night, Ladies and What's With You

EARL CARROLL'S VANITIES (1926)

1926.23

A Musical Revue in Two Acts, 39 Scenes[28]. Sketches by Stanley E. Rauh, William A. Grew, Harry Delf, Bert Kalmar, Harry Ruby, Charles Mack, Arthur Caesar. Music by Morris Hamilton, Ray Wynburn, Jesse Greer, Lou Alter, Jimmy Johnson, Berton Braley, M. deJari, Alex James. Lyrics by Grace Henry, Tom Ford, Ray Klages, Henry Creamer, Berton Braley, M. deJari and Alex James. Entire production staged under the personal direction of Earl Carroll. Sketches staged by William A. Grew. Dances and ensembles by David Bennett. Settings designed by August Vimnera. Art and technical direction by Bernard Lohmuller. Costumes by Booth-Willoughby, Brooks Costume Company, Kathryn Arlington, Vanity Fair Costumes, Schneider-Anderson, and Milgrim. Orchestra under the direction of Don Voorhees. Produced by Earl Carroll. Opened 24 August 1926 at the Earl Carroll Theatre and closed 1 January 1927 after 154 performances.

CAST: JULIUS TANNEN, YVETTE RUGEL, HARRY DELF, DOROTHY KNAPP, ROBERT RHODES, FLORENCE BRADY, (Charles) MACK and (George) MORAN, THELMA WHITE, (Joe) SMITH and (Charles) DALE, MAGDA deBRIES, BERNICE SPEER, BERNARD DUDLEY, HAZEL BOWMAN, M. deJARI, BEBE STANTON, NORMAN FRESCOTT, ISABEL MOHR, GILBERT WELLS, THE PATTERSON TWINS (Flora and Alice).

Twenty Foster Girls. Ensemble: Marie Ellen, Ednamay French, Ruth Martin, Margie Gilbert, Ann Whyte, Phyllis Loft, Bobby Meredith, Mildred Hiller, Laura Stephan, Polly Luce, Jean Murray, Flo Ward, Vivian Carmody, Nina Sorel, Frances Norton, Peggy Driscoll, Ruth Royce, Avis Adaire, Annette Lang, Bessie Green, Odeline Ogilvie, Helen Howe, Lee Byrne, Wanda Stephenson, Gladys Philbin, Jewel La Kota, Hazel Bailey, Irma Philbin, Myrtle Canddee, Marion Booth, Eileen Wenzel, Carmen Larn, Elisabeth Janeway, Helen Dean.

ACT 1[29]

Scene 1

Caballero Julius Tannen
The Gypsies: M. Ellen, E. French, R. Martin, M. Gilbert, A. Whyte, P. Loft, B. Meredith, M. Hiller, L. Stephan. *Flower Girls:* P. Luce, J. Murray, F. Ward, V. Carmody, N. Sorel, F. Norton, P. Driscoll, R. Royce. *Fortune Tellers:* A. Adaire, A. Lang, B. Green, O. Ogilvie, H. Howe, L. Byrne, M. Ellen, W. Stephenson.

Scene 2

Outside the Gates of Madrid: "(Open the) Gates of Madrid"
R. Rhodes
(*Music by* Morris Hamilton. *Lyrics by* Grace Henry.)
The Spirit of Spain: G. Philbin.

Scene 3

---

[28]Fourth in the annual series of revues which began in 1923.
[29]Added after the opening:
All Aboard (Act 2) (later a part of Railroading sketch, below)
  Miss Prim: B. Stanton. *Miss Slam:* I. Mohr. *Jack Looses:* H. Delf.
Feet Are Feet (Act 2)
  The Wife: B. Stanton. *Her Lover:* M. deJari. *The Husband:* H. Delf.
Railroading (Act 2)
(a) The Ticket Agent
  Just to Know: H. Delf. *The Agent:* G. Wells.
(b) Official Business
  The President: J. Smith. *A Switchman:* C. Dale.
(c) In the Pullman
  The Wife: B. Stanton. *Her Lover:* M. deJari. *The Husband:* H. Delf.
Stage Door of the Earl Carroll Theatre (Act 2)
  The Prima Donna: B. Stanton. *A Leading Lady:* I. Mohr. *Queen of the Ballet:* N. Sorel. *A. John:* J. Smith. *B. John:* C. Dale.
Imitations (Act 1)
  H. Delf
The Blackbirds (Act 2)
  G. Moran, C. Mack
Spades (*by* William A. Grew and Charles Mack) Act 1)
  G. Moran, C. Mack
In a Venetian Garden (Act 1)
  Romance: Y. Rugel. *Youth:* P. Loft. *Love:* Mildred Kelly. *Beauty:* F. Norton. *Life:* O. Ogilvie.
The Ballet of Hearts (Solo dance)
  Y. Rugel

"Cool 'Em Off"
  F. Brady
  (*Music by* Morris Hamilton. *Lyrics by* Grace Henry. *Costumes by* Booth Willoughby.)
  Servel Sweeties: Twenty Foster Girls.

Scene 4

Birth Control[30]
  (*by* Harry Delf) H. Delf, T. White, B. Speer

Scene 5

"We Are the Show Girls"
  J. LaKota, H. Bailey, I. Philbin, M. Candee, M. Booth, E. Wenzel, C. Larn, E. Janeway
  (*Music by* Morris Hamilton. *Lyrics by* Grace Henry. *Costumes by* Schneider Anderson.)

Scene 6

In the Fire House
  (*by* Bert Kalmar and Harry Ruby)
  Chief: C. Dale. *Assistant:* J. Smith. *Joe Burning:* H. Delf. *Al Afire:* B. Dudley.

Scene 7

"Natacha"
  M. deJari
  (*Music and Lyrics by* Berton Braley, M. deJari, Alex James)
  Russian Peasant Girls: Twenty Foster Girls.
  (*Costumes by* Booth Willoughby.)

Scene 8

Horses
  (*by* William A. Grew and Charles Mack)
  Darkey: G. Moran. *Darkey:* C. Mack. *Man:* N. Trescott. *His Wife:* I. Mohr.

Scene 9

Before the Billboard—Moscow
  The Girl: H. Bowman. *The Man:* M. deJari.

Scene 10

Stage of the Moscow Opera House
  Scene: A balcony in the Chinese quarter of San Francisco.
  Aria: Ah-Joy welcomes the coming of the dawn
  Y. Rugel

Scene 11

Terpsichore
  H. Delf

Scene 12

"Adorable"
  R. Rhodes, M. deJari
  (*Music by* Ray Wynburn. *Lyrics by* Tom Ford.)
  Dance
  B. Speer
  Introducing Dorothy Knapp, the most beautiful girl in the world
  (*Costumes designed by* Charles LeMaire.)

Scene 13

Toreador Julius Tannen

Scene 14

The Hospital
  (*by* Stanley E. Rauh)
  Nurse: D. Knapp. *Doctor:* N. Frescott. *Beckie:* F. Brady. *Father:* H. Delf. *Moe:* C. Dale. *Jake:* J. Smith. *Sarah:* B. Speer. *Mother:* I. Mohr.

Scene 15

"Climbing Up the Ladder of Love"
  T. White
  (*Music by* Jesse Greer. *Lyrics by* Raymond Klages.)
  Dance
  Vanities Girls, Patterson Twins, Foster Girls
  (*Costumes by* Schneider Anderson.)

Scene 16

Inside the Jail
  (*by* William A. Grew and Charles Mack)
  Jim: C. Mack. *Peter:* G. Moran. *Jailer:* G. Wells. *Big Tim Sullivan:* B. Dudley. *Plumber:* N. Frescott. *Prisoner:* R. Rhodes.

---

[30]Dropped after the opening.

Scene 17

El Capitan Julius Tannen and "Pete"

Scene 18

Adoration (Dance)
M. de Bries
Introduction: N. Frescott.

Scene 19

Lawyer's Office
(*by* Bert Kalmar and Harry Ruby)
Attorney: C. Dale. *Husband*: J. Smith. *Wife*: D. Knapp.
"The Lament of Shakespeare"
(*Music by* Morris Hamilton. *Lyrics by* Grace Henry.)
Shakespeare: H. Delf. *Iris Marsh*: T. White. *Ophelia*: J. LaKota. *Cleopatra*: E. Wenzel. *Craig's Wife*: B. Speer. *Katherine* the Shrew: C. Larn. *Cradle Snatchers*: F. Patterson. *Merry Wives of Windsor*: M. Candee. *Madam Goddam*: H. Bowman. *Lady Macbeth*: E. Janeway. *Abie's Irish Rose*: A. Patterson. *Juliet*: I. Philbin. *Maggie Shand*: B. Stanton. *Portia*: H. Bailey. *Desdemona*: M. Booth.

Scene 20

In the Mirror of Vanities
A. Lang, F. Ward, R. Royce, B. Meredith, E. French, J. Murray, P. Luce, A. Adaire, L. Byrne, H. Dean

Scene 21

The Glass Finale: "All Is Vanity" (Vanity)
74 Visions of Vanities, D. Knapp.
(*Music by* Morris Hamilton. *Lyrics by* Grace Henry. Entire scene is made of mosaic glass, executed by Alex Hall. *Costumes designed by* Charles LeMaire.)

ACT 2

Scene 1

Senor Julius Tannnen

Scene 2

"Twilight"
Y. Rugel
(*Music by* Morris Hamilton. *Lyrics by* Grace Henry.)

Scene 3

Bells of the Belfry
The Foster Girl
(*Costumes by* Booth Willoughby.)

Scene 4

(Gilbert) Wells and (Florence) Brady
(a) Jubilee Blues. (b) Sadie Green.

Scene 5

The Auction Block
(*by* Arthur Caesar)
Auctioneer: J. Smith. *First Trader*: C. Dale. *Second Trader*: N. Frescott. *Third Trader*: M. deJari. *Fourth Trader*: B. Dudley. *Slave*: G. Moran. *Heart's Desire*: B. Stanton. *Slaves, Traders, etc.*

Scene 6

"Hugs and Kisses"
T. White
(*Music by* Louis Alter. *Lyrics by* Raymond Klages. *Costumes by* Vanity Fair Costume Company.)

Scene 7

Hunting[31]
(*by* Stanley E. Rauh and Harry Delf)
Mr. Hunter: H. Delf. *Mrs. Hunter*: F. Brady.

Scene 8

"Excuse My Dust"[32]
G. Wells
(*Music by* A. Spencer. *Lyrics by* Gilbert Wells.)
Dance
B. Speer

Scene 9

"Pepita" (Dance)
Foster Girls
(*Costumes by* Madame Arlington.)

---

[31]Dropped after the opening.
[32]Dropped after the opening.

Scene 10

"The Chinese Idol"
M. deJari
(*Music and Lyrics by* Berton Braley, M. deJari and Alex James.)
(a) In Paris:
Model: D. Knapp. *Sculptor*: R. Rhodes.
(b) In Shanghai:
Chinamen: B. Dudley. *Sailor*: R. Rhodes. *Sing Song Girls*: F. Brady, M. deBries, B. Stanton, F. Patterson, A. Patterson.

Scene 11

Signs of the Zodiac
(*Conceived by* Norman Frescott.)
Sheepshead Bey: J. Tannen. *Professor Herrington*: N. Frescott. *Assisted by* C. Mack.
"The Hanging Gardens of Babylon"
H. Bowman
(*Music and Lyrics by* Monte Carlo and Alma Sanders. *Costumes by* Charles LeMaire.)
Babylonian Beauties: P. Luce, J. Murray, E. French, R. Royce, A. Adaire, A. Lang, L. Byrne, H. Howe, F. Norton, F. Ward, R. Martin, B. Meredith. *And*: D. Knapp.

Scene 12

Sweetheart Darling
(*by* Bert Kalmar and Harry Ruby)
Otto Rochman: J. Smith. *David Wolff*: C. Dale. *Mrs. Rochman*: D. Knapp. *Maid*: I. Mohr. *Louis Love*: R. Rhodes.

Scene 13

"Alabama Stomp"
F. Brady
(*Music by* James P. Johnson. *Lyrics by* Henry Creamer. *Costumes by* Madame Arlington.)
Dance
B. Speer, Patterson Twins, Rainbow Girls

Scene 14

Purgatory
(*by* Charles Mack and William A. Grew)
Mephistopheles: B. Dudley. *Henry*: C. Mack. *Assistant Devil*: G. Wells. A *Newcomer*: I. Mohr. *Al Tellem*: H. Delf. *Elevator Man*: N. Frescott.

Scene 15

Moran and Mack

Scene 16

Opera Salade
C. Dale, J. Smith, Y. Rugel, I. Mohr, M. deJari, R. Rhodes

Scene 17

Escalera Blanca: "Broadway to Madrid"
Entire Company
(*Music by* Morris Hamilton. *Lyrics by* Grace Henry.)

Scene 18

Grand Finale: Just a Crimson Rose

1926.24   CASTLES IN THE AIR

A Musical Comedy in Three Acts. Book and lyrics by Raymond W. Peck. Music by Percy Wenrich. Book staged by Frank S. Merlin. Ensembles by Julian Mitchell. Dances by John Boyle. Scenery designed by Hugh Willoughby, P. Dodd Ackerman. Costumes by Hugh Willoughby, John N. Booth, Jr. and Francis & Co. Music under the direction of Max Bendix. Orchestrations by Frank Barry. Entire production under the personal supervision of James W. Elliott. Produced by James W. Elliott. Opened 6 September 1926 at the Selwyn Theatre, moved 6 December 1926 to the Century Theatre, and closed 22 January 1927 after 160 performances.

CAST (in order of appearance): *Amos*: Robert Williamson. *Annie Moore*: Joyce White. *George Sedgewick*: Allen Waterous. *Philip Rodman*: STANLEY FORDE. *Mme. Joujou Durant*: Claire Madjette. *Evelyn Devine*: VIVIENNE SEGAL. *Count Draga*: Richard Farrell. *Monty Blair*: BERNARD GRANVILLE. *John Brown*: J. HAROLD MURRAY. *General Slodak*: Walter Edwin. *Kemlar*: William Hasson. *The Chancellor*: Gregory Ratoff. *Lieutenant*: Edward Gorman. *The Queen Regent*: THAIS LAWTON. *Ballet Dancer*: Mary Hutchinson.

The Boyle Double Dancing Sextet: Firlie Banks, Vera Trett, Mary Hutchinson, Beulah Baker, Edna Burford, Helen Warren, Tuxie Ondex, William Hale, Fred Cowhick, Jack Nellan, Don Donat, Tommie Mack. *Dancing Girls*: Mildred Morgan,

Lola Lavin, Jane Hurd, Doreen Roberts, Muriel Greel, Audrey Van Liew, Helene Bradley, Woody Lee Wilson, Virginia Beardsley, Betty Collett, Catherine Huth, Aili Radigan. *Singing Girls*: Bea King, Nina Piozet, Ruth Elaine, Rosalind Baker, Frances Philips, Ivia Perrine, Marie Dana, Lenore Cornwell, Sophie Hauser, Evelyn Grayson, Alice Mitchell, Clarice Anderson, Alva McGill, Sue Lake, Maude Carleton, Viola Hailes, Martha Ann, Cleona Quitt, Dale Leary, Carol Barbee. *Singing Boys*: William Warren, Werner Wennerstrand, Edgar Eastman, Jack James, Alfred Rusuznyak, Thomas Dendy, Stanley Simon, Val Sholar, John Lane, Walter Blair, Archie Rote, Edwin Young, Dwight Trucksess, Edward P. Smithe, George O'Donnell, Frank Rothwell, Edward Gorman, John Eagan, Miner Ellis, Hinsdale Latour.

Act 1: Evelyn's 21 Club, Westchester. June. (Willoughby.)

Act 2: The Castle. July. (Ackerman.)

Act 3: The Rodman Garden, Westchester. August. (Willoughby.)

ACT 1[33]

  Opening
    Ensemble

  "I Don't Blame 'Em"
    J. White, Boys

  "Love's Refrain"
    C. Madjette, Ensemble

  "Lantern of Love" (Lanterns of Love)
    V. Segal, Ensemble
    (*Lyrics by* R. Locke and Raymond W. Peck)

  "The Singer's Career, Ha! Ha!"
    C. Madjette, S. Forde

  "The Other Fellow's Girl"
    B. Granville, Sextette, Ensemble

  "If You Are in Love with a Girl"
    J. H. Murray, Ensemble

  "The Sweetheart of Your Dream"[34]
    V. Segal

  "I Would Like to Fondle You"
    J. White, B. Granville, Sextette, Ensemble

  "The Rainbow of Your Smile"[35]
    J. H. Murray

  Finale
    Ensemble

ACT 2

  Latavian Folk Dance
    Ensemble

  "Baby" (Fox Trot Lullaby)
    B. Granville, Ensemble

  "Latavia"
    J. H. Murray, Ensemble

  "Land of Romance"
    V. Segal

  "My Lips, My Love, My Soul!"
    J. H. Murray, V. Segal

  "The Latavian Chant"
    J. White, Ensemble

  Finale
    Entire Company

ACT 3

  The Ballet Dancer[36]
    M. Hutchinson

  "Girls and the Gimmies"
    B. Granville, Sextette, Ensemble

  "Love Rules the World"
    C. Madjette, J. H. Murray

  Finale
    Entire Company

---

[33]Added for subsequent tour to Act 1, after "The Singer's Career, Ha! Ha!":
  "Queen of Queens"
    Ray Raymond (Monty Blair), Dancers
[34]Replaced in the fourth month of the run by:
  "(The) First Kiss of Love"
    Era Briggs (Evelyn Devine)
[35]Dropped for subsequent tour.
[36]Dropped during the run.

1926.25

QUEEN HIGH

A Musical Comedy in Three Acts. Book by Laurence Schwab, Buddy G. DeSylva. Adapted from the play 'A Pair of Sixes' by Edward Peple. Music by Lewis E. Gensler. Lyrics by Buddy G. DeSylva. Book directed by Edgar McGregor. Musical numbers staged by Sammy Lee. Settings by Willy Pogany. Costumes designed by Jeanne Laurence. Orchestra under the direction of Ivan Rudisill. Orchestrations by (Robert) Russell Bennett. Produced by Laurence Schwab. Opened 8 September 1926 at the Ambassador Theatre and closed 23 July 1927 after 367 performances.

CAST: *T. Boggs Johns*, the Junior Partner: CHARLES RUGGLES. *George Nettleton*, the Senior Partner: FRANK McINTYRE. *Richard Johns*, Johns' nephew: CLARENCE NORDSTROM. *Jimmy*, the Office Assistant: Edwin Michaels. *Jerry Vanderholt*, the firm's lawyer: John Rutherford. *Polly Nettleton*, Nettleton's neice: MARY LAWLOR. *Mrs. Nellie Nettleton*: HELEN CARRINGTON. *Florence Cole*: LUELLA GEAR. *Coddles*, the Nettleton's maid: GAILE BEVERLY. *Patricia*, a Model: JUNE O'DEA. *Kitty*, a Model: BARBARA GRACE. *At the Pianos*: Edgar Fairchild and Ralph Rainger.

  Ladies: Margaret Lee, Lucille Moore, Elsie Lombard, Sophie Howard, Florence Blue, Katherine Ellis, Joey Benton, Lillian Burke, Peggy Hart, Barbara Carrington, Otis Schaefer, Betty Wright, Ann Lee, Mildred Stevens, Ethel Lawrence, Irene Warner, Carola Taylor. *Gentlemen*: Richard Oakley, Harold Hennessey, Daniel Sparks, Ward Arnold, Charles Bannister, Albert Hale, Al Downing, Jack Hughes, John McElroy.

Time: Now. Early summer.

Act 1: The Showroom of the Eureka Novelty Company.

Act 2: The Westchester Home of the Nettletons.

Act 3: The Westchester Home of the Nettletons.

ACT 1

  Opening
    E. Michaels, Boys, Girls

  "It Pays to Advertise"
    C. Nordstrom, J. O'Dea, B. Grace, Boys, Girls

  "Everything Will Happen for the Best"
    M. Lawlor, F. McIntyre, B. Grace, J. O'Dea, Boys, Girls

  "You'll Never Know"
    L. Gear, C. Ruggles

  "Don't Forget"
    M. Lawlor, C. Nordstrom, Boys, Girls
    (*Music by* James Hanley.)

  "Who? You!"
    F. McIntyre, C. Ruggles, Ensemble

  Finale
    Ensemble

ACT 2

  Opening
    H. Carrington, G. Beverly, Boys, Girls

  "The Weaker Sex"
    M. Lawlor, B. Grace, J. O'Dea, E. Michaels, Boys, Girls

  "Cross Your Heart"
    C. Nordstrom, M. Lawlor, Boys, Girls

  "Sez You! Sez I!"
    G. Beverly, C. Ruggles

  "Beautiful Baby"
    L. Gear, F. McIntyre, E. Michaels, J. O'Dea, B. Grace, Boys, Girls
    (*Music by* James Hanley.)

  Finale
    Ensemble

ACT 3

  "Who'll Mend a Broken Heart?"
    C. Nordstrom, B. Grace, J. O'Dea, Boys, Girls

  "Gentlemen Prefer Blondes"[37]
    L. Gear

---

[37]Later in the run, replaced by:
  "My Lady"
    June Cochrane (Florence), C. Nordstrom
    (*Music by* Ben Jerome. *Lyrics by* Frank Crumit.)
For subsequent national tour, it was replaced by:
  "You Must Come Over Blues"
    Winnie Baldwin (Florence), C. Ruggles

"Cross Your Heart" (reprise)[38]
    M. Lawlor, C. Nordstrom, C. Ruggles
"Springtime" (In the Spring)
    G. Beverly, Boys
Finale
    Entire Company

1926.26   NAUGHTY RIQUETTE

A Musical Play in Two Acts, 3 Scenes. Book and lyrics by Harry B. Smith. Adapted from the German original ('Riquette') by Rudolf Schanzer and Ernst Welisch. Music by Oscar Straus. Interpolations by Alfred Goodman, Maurice Rubens, (Kendall Burgess). (Book directed by Fred G. Latham. Dances by Seymour Felix. Settings by Watson Barratt.) Costumes by Kathryn Arlington and Brooks Costume Company. [Conductor uncredited at opening; later in the run, Ira Jacobs.] Entire production under the personal supervision of J. J. Shubert. Produced by the Messrs. Shubert. Opened 13 September 1926 at the Cosmopolitan Theatre and closed 27 November 1926 after 88 performances.

CAST (in order of appearance): *Faverolle*, Manager of Telephone Company: WALTER ARMIN. *Alphonse La Fleur*, Director of Telephone Company: GEORGE A. SCHILLER. *Clarisse (La Fleur)*, his wife: AUDREY MAPLE. *Gaston Rivière*: ALEXANDER GREY. *Telephone Girls (2)*: *Simone*: Connie Emerald. *Yvette*: Lenoria Spiro. *Théophile Michu*, an employee of the Telephone Company: STANLEY LUPINO. *Bardou*, an official of the Telephone Company: Joseph Spree. *Riquette Duval*, Operator of Telephone and Telegraph Company: MITZI (HAJOS). *Liane de Soucy*, of the Folies Bergère: MARY MARLOWE. *Officials of the Telephone and Telegraph Company (2)*: *Dupont*, Official of the Telephone and Telegraph Company: Oliver Hagan. *Maurel*, Official of the Telephone and Telegraph Company: Peter Hawley. *Abri-Dabri*, a heavyweight pugilist: Edward Basse. *Lord Billington*: Oliver Hagan. *Maître d'Hôtel* of the Hotel Sunbeam: Joseph Spree. *Professor DuBose*, Proprietor of the Hotel Sunbeam: WALTER ARMIN. *Dean*, Night Bell-boy: SYLVAN LEE. *Julie*, Maid, of the Hotel Sunbeam: JANE MOORE. *Cavalry Officers (2)*: *Colonel Latour*: Oliver Hagan. *Captain Duroc*: Peter Hawley.

Guests at the Sunbeam Hotel, Telephone Girls, Maids: Eva Lynn, Frances Suzanne, Dorothy DeMerle, Ethel Alderson, Virginia Whitmore, Norma Mason, Rosalie Trego, Yolanda Losee, Iris Novarro, Leonie Spiro, Vivian Fay, Evelyn Dehkers, Ada Marcus, Edith Davis, Ann LeVerne, Jane Moore, Frances Lynn, Caryl Bergman, Lillian Francis, Naomi Andrews, Dorothy Dawn, Lillian Lane, Bobby Lee, Thelma Lee, Ruth Norris, Ann Janeway, Evelyn Nelson, Rose Host, Marie Taylor, Stella Sheil, Anne Cornwell. *Employees of the Telephone Company, Guests, Waiters*: Harry Phelps, Gordon Phillips, Leo Neirle, Sid Russell, Clifford Smith, G. Douglas Evans, Leon Alton, George Mason, Wally Coyle, Milton Halpern.

Act 1: Central Telephone Exchange, Paris.

Act 2, Scene 1: The Lounge of the Hotel Sunbeam, near Monte Carlo. *Scene 2*: The same, the following morning.

ACT 1[39]
Opening Ensemble
    A. Maple, A. Gray, G. A. Schiller, W. Armin, Company
"Me"
    S. Lupino, Girls
"Somehow I'd Rather Be Good"
    Mitzi, S. Lupino
"You May Say 'Yes' Today"
    J. Moore, S. Lee, Ensemble
"Naughty Riquette"
    Mitzi, Boys
    (*Music by* Kendall Burgess, Maurice Rubens.)
"I May"
    Mitzi, A. Gray
    (*Music by* Kendall Burgess, Maurice Rubens.)
"In Armenia"
    M. Marlowe, S. Lupino, Ensemble
Finale
    Mitzi, Ensemble

ACT 2
Scene 1
Opening Ensemble
"Two Are Company"
    Mitzi, A. Maple, A. Gray
Toe Ballet
    Dancing Girls
"Make Believe"
    Mitzi, A. Gray
"What Great Men Cannot Do"
    S. Lupino
    (*Music by* R. P. Weston. *Lyrics by* Bert Lee.)
"Alcazar"
    Mitzi, Ensemble
"Someone"
    J. Moore, S. Lee
    (*Music by* Alfred Goodman, Maurice Rubens.)
Scene 2
"Someone" (Finale)
    Ensemble

1926.27   COUNTESS MARITZA

An Operetta in Three Acts and a Prologue. Book and lyrics by Harry B. Smith, adapted from the Viennese original ("Gräfin Mariza") by Julius Brammer and Alfred Grünwald. Music by Emmerich Kálmán. Additional dialogue by Isabel Leighton. Play and all ensembles staged by J. C. Huffman. Dances staged by Carl Randall and Jack Mason. Settings by Watson Barratt. Orchestra under the direction of Leon Leonardi. Entire production under the personal supervision of J. J. Shubert. Produced by the Messrs. Lee and J.J. Shubert. Opened 18 September 1926 at the Sam S. Shubert Theatre, moved 24 January 1927 to the 44th Street Theatre, moved 28 March 1927 to Jolson's Theatre, moved 16 May 1927 to the Sam S. Shubert Theatre, and closed 25 June 1927 after 321 performances[40].

CAST (in order of appearance): *Nepomuk*, a lawyer: Arthur Rogers. *Count Tassilo Endrody*: WALTER WOOLF. *Bela Torek*, an overseer: Louis E. Miller. *Tscheko*: Hugh Chilvers. *Lazlo*, a Gypsy Chief: Arthur Geary. *Manja*: ODETTE MYRTIL. *Stefan*: Nat Wagner. *Servant*: Frank Sinnott. *Zingo*: HARRY K. MORTON. *Countess Maritza*: YVONNE D'ARLE. *Lisa*: VIVIAN HART. *Prince Populescu*: GEORGE HASSELL. *First Officer*: Clarence H. Tolman. *Baron Koloman Szupan*: CARL RANDALL. *Freda*: Marjorie Peterson. *Princess Bozena Klopensheim*: Florence Edney. *Bela's Hungarian Gypsy Orchestra.*

Gypsy Girls: Louise Baer, Flo Cazelle, Maria Camerero, Marie Louise Cadwallader, Gloria Frank, Marian French, Dorothy Harrington, Claudia Ivanova, Sylvia LaMard, Alice Loftus, Ila McCall, Meliss Merriweather, Shirley Norton, Claire Rossi, Maryrose Walsh, Dorothy Wilson. *Peasants*: Merle Epton, Sylvia Francis, Malliela Farge, Patricia O'Connell, Katherine O'Neale, Mary L. Paterson, Elsie Reign, Kathryn Wilson. *Guests*: Marion Francis, Ann Gilbert, Marion Gillon, Ernistyne Jeanne, Helen Thompson, Eleanor Witmore, Edna Starck, Billy Perry. *Officers*: Sam Bunin, Jules Cross, Arthur Ekins, Nicolas Globatcheff, Charles Mansfield, Norman Colvin, Robert Boltner, Larry Roberts, Frederick Reinhard, Lex Sanderson, Clarence Tolman, Jules Waldeck, Milton Frome, George Butler, Cecil Jordan, Clarence Taylor.

Prologue: Grand Salon in the Château of Count Tassilo Endrody.

Act 1: Garden of Countess Maritza's Château in a Balkan State bordering on Hungary. Three months later.

Act 2: The Drawing Room of Countess Maritza's Château. The evening of the same day.

Act 3: The same. The next morning.

PROLOGUE
"Dear Home of Mine Goodbye"
    W. Woolf, A, Rogers
ACT 1
"Hola, Follow, Follow Me"
    A. Geary, Gypsies
"Come at the Call of Love"
    O. Myrtil, W. Woolf
"In the Days Gone By"
    W. Woolf, N. Wagner

---

[38]Late in the tour, "Cross Your Heart" and "Springtime" replaced by:
    "I Can't Stand the Spring"
        Georgette Armfield (Coddles)
[39]During the run, the song order was revised.

[40]Costumes uncredited.

"Make Up Your Mind"
  H. K. Morton, Gypsies

"The Music Thrills Me"
  Y. d'Arle, Gypsies, Peasants

"Golden Dreams"
  V. Hart, W. Woolf
  (*Music by* Harry K. Morton.)

"Flirtation Dance"
  V. Hart

"The One I'm Looking For"
  Y. d'Arle, C. Randall

"Play Gypsies"
  W. Woolf

Finale
  Y. d'Arle, W. Woolf, O. Myrtil, V. Hart, G. Hassell, C. Randall, M. Peterson, Gypsies, Peasants, Guests

ACT 2

Opening
  C. Randall, V. Hart, Guests

"Don't Tempt Me" (Violin duet)
  O. Myrtil, W. Woolf

"Love Has Found My Heart"
  Y. d'Arle
  (*Music by* Alfred Goodman.)

"I'll Keep on Dreaming"
  V. Hart, C. Randall

"Who Am I?"
  H. K. Morton, C. Randall

"Why Is the World So Changed Today?"
  Y. d'Arle, W. Woolf

Finale
  Y. d'Arle, W. Woolf, C. Randall, V. Hart, G. Hassell, H. K. Morton, Gypsies, Guests

ACT 3

"Brown Eyed Girl"
  O. Myrtil, H. K. Morton, C. Randall

Finale
  Y. d'Arle, W. Woolf, H. K. Morton, G. Hassell, V. Hart, F. Edney, Guests

THE RAMBLERS

1926.28

A Musical Comedy in Two Acts, 10 Scenes. Book by Guy Bolton, Bert Kalmar and Harry Ruby. Music and lyrics by Bert Kalmar and Harry Ruby. Book directed by John Harwood. Musical numbers arranged by Sammy Lee. Sets designed by Raymond Sovey. Costumes designed by Charles LeMaire. Orchestra under the direction of Alfred Newman. Entire production under the sole supervision of Philip Goodman. Produced by Philip Goodman. Opened 20 September 1926 at the Lyric Theatre and closed 28 May 1927 after 289 performances.

CAST [in order of appearance]: *Nettie Field*, who raffles things for charity: Norma Gallo. *Black Pedro*, a Mexican Bad Man: WILLIAM E. BROWNING. *Pancho*, his pal: Horton Spurr. *Joe Small*, cabaret proprietor: Lloyd Pedrick. *Anita*, a Tiajuana vamp: Eleanor Dawn. *Neil Farnham*, a movie director: WILLIAM SULLY. *Carter*, his assistant: Alfred Watson. *Dapper Dan*, a dancing demon: Richy Craig, Jr. *Jenny Wren*, Neil's fiancée: RUTH TESTER. *Hazel Knott*, who interrogates the Professor: Winefride Verina. *Lotta Moore*, who meets the Professor at the border line: Nita Jacques. *Professor Cunningham*, proficient in magic and spells: BOBBY CLARK. *Sparrow*, his associate: PAUL McCULLOUGH. *Ronald Roche*, a movie hero: Blaine Cordner. *Billy Shannon*, his double in perilous airplane stunts: JACK WHITING. *Ruth Chester*, who wants to get into movies: MARIE SAXON. *Fanny Furst*, who writes and produces her own scenarios: GEORGIA O'RAMEY. *The Old Father*: Henry Permane. *Lida Belmont*, who is lucky at the gambling machine: Marguerita Murray. *A Bootlegger*, merely one of a million: John Klendon. *Cissie O'Hearn*: Bonnie Murray.

Ladies of the Ensemble: Margarite Murray, Dolla Harkins, Elsie Pedrick, Winifred Verina, Bonnie Murray, Maxine Robinson, Elaine Lank, Nita Jacques, Marion Bownell, Ruth Kent, Nesha Medwin, Ida Berry, Holly Pembrooke, Edith Hayward, Alice Akers, Dorothy Fitzgibbon, Gertie Edwards, Patti Kenny, Madeline Janis, Dorothy Hackney, Beth Milton, Lucille Reece, Edith Joyce, Gertrude Lowe, Marie Marcelline, Val De Mar, Sybil Steward, Liane Mamet, Evelyn Kermyn, Cleo Cullen, Helene Sheldon, Mary Williams. *Gentlemen of the Ensemble*: Norman Jefferson, Martin Rheil, Floyd Marion, Edward Stone, Robert Hope [Bob Hope], Henry Lake, Dave Morton, Stanley Liton, Richard Tyle, Bill Bailey, Lew Parker, William Sahner, Jack Jordan.

Act 1, Scene 1: Joe Small's Dance Hall at Tiajuana. *Scene 2*: Clubhouse at Tiajuana Racetrack. *Scene 3*: Border Line at Tiajuana. *Scene 4*: Garden of Fanny Furst's Home at Beverly Hills, California.

Act 2, Scene 1: On the Lot at Fanny Furst's Movie Studio at Hollywood. *Scene 2*: Exterior of Black Pedro's House at Casa del Rey. *Scene 3*: Bedroom in Black Pedro's House at Casa del Rey. *Scene 4*: Exterior of Black Pedro's House. *Scene 5*: Corridor of Ballroom. *Scene 6*: Fanny Furst's Movie Ball.

ACT 1[41]

Opening Chorus
  Chorus

"Like You Do"
  R. Tester, W. Sully, Chorus

"(Oh! How We Love Our) Alma Mater"
  B. Clark, P. McCullough

"Just One Kiss"
  M. Saxon, Boys

"All Alone Monday"
  M. Saxon, J. Whiting, Chorus

"Any Little Tune"
  R. Tester, W. Sully, Chorus

"All Alone Monday" (reprise)
  M. Saxon, J. Whiting

"California Skies"
  Chorus

Dance Specialty
  N. Gallo

"You Smiled at Me"
  M. Saxon, J. Whiting, Chorus

ACT 2

Opening Ballet
  N. Gallo, Chorus

"All Alone Monday" (reprise)
  M. Saxon, J. Whiting, E. Dawn, B Cordner

"You Must—We Won't"
  M. Saxon, R. Tester, Chorus

"Good-Bye"
  Entire Company

"California Skies"[42] (reprise)
  E. Dawn

Dance Specialty
  H. Spurr

"You Smiled at Me" (reprise)
  J. Whiting

Dance Specialty[43]
  R. Craig, Jr.

"The Movie Ball"
  Chorus

Finale
  Entire Company

HONEYMOON LANE

1926.29

A Musical Comedy in Two Acts and a Prologue, 12 Scenes. Book and lyrics by Eddie Dowling Music by James Hanley. Staged by Edgar MacGregor. Dances by Bobby Connolly. Costumes designed by Ada Peacock, Schneider-Anderson Co. Settings designed by Triangle Scenic Co. Musical director, Arthur Lang. Orchestrations by Arthur Lang. Produced by Abraham L. Erlanger. Opened 20 September 1926 at the Knickerbocker Theatre and closed 23 July 1927 after 353 performances.

CAST (in order of appearance): *Mary Brown*: PAULINE MASON. *Ruth Adams*: Martha Morton. *Honey Duke*: JOHNNY MARVIN. *Tim Murphy*: EDDIE DOWLING. *John Brown*: George Pauncefort. *Ted Kleinz*: AL SEXTON. *Ethel Jackson*: Florentine

---

[41]Added after the opening:
  Specialty (Finale, Act 1)
    B. Clark, G. O'Ramey
[42]Dropped after opening.
[43]Dropped after opening.

Gosnova. *Matty Pathe*: Gordon Dooley. *Florence O'Denishawn*: FLORENCE O'DENISHAWN. *Dream Man*: Worthe Faulkner. *Station Master*: Jerre McAuliffe. *Conductor*: John McAvoy. *Tiny Little*: KATE SMITH. *Porter*: Dick Wheaton. *A Passenger*: Alyce Johnstone. *Mrs. Nelligan*: Josie Intropodi. *Addie*: Adelaide Seaman. *Marie Buck*: Helyn Eby-Rock. *Jessie*: Ivy Palmer. *Leo Scamp*: Leo Beers. *The Boss*: Bernard Randall. *Patrick Kelly*: D. J. Sullivan. *Elsie*: Ethel Allys. *Edith*: Edith Sheldon.

Bell Boys: Charles Davis, Dick Wheaton, Charles Walker, Louis Simons. *Dancers*: Helen Clare, Helen Ault, Ona Hamilton, Ginger Meehan, Kay Annis, Ethlyn Tillman, Patricia Parker, Lee Baron, Lorraine Weber, Mildred Pickard, Evelyn Farrell, Virginia Webb, Wilma Ansell, Mae Rena Grady, Isabel Dawn, Lucille Osborne. *Show Girls*: Janet Hale, Ivy Palmer, Margo Matson, Jean Casswell, Alyce Johnstone, Libby Hanley, Emerita Monsch, Beulah Van. *Boys*: John McAvoy, Charles Witzel, William Cooper, Arthur Craig, Patrick Flynn, Bud Penny, Andreas Erving, Thomas Weldon, Locques Lorraine, Carl Rose, Danny O'Brien, George O'Brien.

Prologue: Exterior of Mary Brown's Home, Canningville, Pennsylvania. Halloween Night.

Act 1, Scene 1: Packing and shipping room of the W. H. Kleinze Pickle Factory, Canningville, Pennsylvania. Present time. *Scene 2*: Exterior of Mary's home, same as Prologue. *Scene 3*: Halloween Night. *Scene 4*: Lehigh Valley Railroad Station, Canningville, Pennsylvania.

Act 2, Scene 1: Back Stage of a Theatre. Three weeks later. *Scene 2*: A dress rehearsal of the Riff Ballet in the theatre. *Scene 3*: Hotel Corridor. Atlantic City. *Scene 4*: A suite in the same hotel. *Scene 5*: In front of the Gold Curtain of the Theatre. *Scene 6*: In the Auditorium of the Theatre. *Scene 7*: Mary's Dressing Room. *Scene 8*: Exterior of Mary Brown's Home, Canningville, Pennsylvania. Halloween Night.

ACT 1

Opening Number
  M. Morton, Ensemble
"Little White House at the End of Honeymoon Lane"
  E. Dowling
"Dreams for Sale"
  W. Faulkner
"Dreams for Sale" (reprise)
  E. Dowling, P. Mason, W. Faulkner
  Kleinz Ensemble
"On to Hollywood"
  A. Sexton, M. Morton, P. Mason, Company
"Whad-d'ye say?"(Whad-d'ya say)
  A. Sexton, P. Mason, Boys, Girls
"Head Over Heels in Love"
  A. Sexton, F. O'Denishawn
"A Little Smile, a Little Sigh"
  G. Dooley, P. Mason, M. Morton, Ensemble
"The Stone Bridge at Eight"
  E. Dowling, M. Morton, Girls
"Little White House at the End of Honeymoon Lane" (reprise)
  E. Dowling, P. Mason
"Dreams for Sale"
  W. Faulkner
"Halloween"
  E. Dowling, M. Morton, Ensemble
"Half Moon"
  E. Dowling, Ensemble
  (*Lyrics by* Eddie Dowling and Herbert Reynolds.
"Halloween" (reprise)
  H. Ault
"Whad-d'ye say?" (reprise) (dance)
  Boys, Girls
"Half a Moon Is Better Than None"
  J. Marvin
Dance
  D. Wheaton, C. Walker
Finale

ACT 2

Opening Chorus
"Chorus Picking Time on Broadway"
  H. Eby-Rock, Ensemble
"Little Old New Hampshire"[44]
  E. Dowling, L. Beers

"The Ruffian Ballet"
  F. O'Denishawn, Ensemble
"Mary, Dear! I Miss You Most of All"
  E. Dowling
"Jersey Walk"
  Lulu and Her Lulubelles
Dance Specialty
  The Bell Boys
"Gee, But I'd Like to Be Bad"
  A. Sexton, P. Mason, Boys
Piano Specialty
  L. Beers
Specialty
  K. Smith
"Jersey Walk"[45] (reprise)
  K. Smith, J. Marvin, the Uke Girls
Dance Specialty
  F. Gosnova
"Mary, Dear! I Miss You Most of All" (reprise)
  K. Smith
"The Understudy Dance Specialty"
  P. Mason
"Dreams for Sale"
  E. Dowling, P. Mason, W. Faulkner
"Little White House at the End of Honeymoon Lane" (reprise)
Finale
  Company Ensemble

1926.30 # HAPPY GO LUCKY

A Musical Comedy in Three Acts. Book and lyrics by Helena Phillips Evans. Music by Lucien Denni. Production staged by Fred G. Latham. Dances and ensembles staged by Max Scheck. Settings designed by Gus Wimazal. Costumes designed by Ada Peacock, Clemons. Conductor, Lucien Denni. Produced by A. L. Erlanger. Opened 30 September 1926 at the Liberty Theatre and closed 13 November 1926 after 52 performances.

<u>CAST</u>: *Chester Chapin*: TAYLOR HOLMES. *Mildred Chapin*: Nydia D'Arnell. *Robert Chapin*: John Kane. *Lucy Manning*: Edith Shayne. *Courtney Thompson*: Jack Squires. *Mabel Holly*: Betty Gallagher. *Roy Hayden*: Ralph Whitehead. *Dawson*: Herbert Belmore. *Laura LaGuerre*: Madeline Cameron. *Elsie Dayly*: LINA ABARBANELL. *Kate*: Ethel Mulholland. *Clara*: Mary Bothwell. *Flora*: Zella Edwards. *Lora*: Belle Gannon. *Dora*: Geraldine Fitzgerald. *Dido*: Geraldine Downs. *Flo*: Natalie Loraine. *Betty*: Blanche Krebs. *Jessie*: Sherry Gale. (*Specialty Dancers*: William and Wilbur Williams.)

Ladies of the Ensemble: Catherine Roberts, Anna Riley, Ruth Collins, Florence Gunther, Alice Garvin, Anna Rex, Jessie Andrews, Eva Ball, Madeline Ball, Betty Sherman, Lydelle Bry, Beverley Maude. *Gentlemen of the Ensemble*: Jack Morton, Henry LeVoy, Walter Randall, George Murray, Al Siegel, Harry Ettus, Lester New, Jack Creighton, Walter Stewart, Harry Gordon, Louis Brown, Bob Kean.

Act 1: The Home of Chester Chapin. May.

Act 2: Reception Room—Floral Hall. A week later.

Act 3: The Home of Chester Chapin. The next morning.

ACT 1

Opening Chorus
  Ensemble
"Sing a Little Song"
  R. Whitehead, Ensemble
"Free, Free, Free"
  L. Abarbanell
"Love Thoughts"
  L. Abarbanell
"How Are You, Lady Love?"
  N. D'Arnell, J. Squires, Ensemble
"I Want a Million for You, Dear"
  N. D'Arnell, J. Squires, Ensemble

---

[44]Dropped for subsequent tour.

[45]On subsequent national tour, replaced by;
  "Headin' for Harlem" (from SIDEWALKS OF NEW YORK)
    K. Smith, Harry Robinson, Yuke Girls

Finale
N. D'Arnell, J. Squires, Ensemble

ACT 2[46]

Opening Chorus
Ensemble

"Happy Melody"
M. Cameron, Ensemble

"Choose Your Flowers"
N. D'Arnell, J. Squires, Ensemble

"It's In, It's Out"
B. Gallagher, R. Whitehead

"Zip"
L. Abarbanell, Ensemble

"It's Wonderful"
M. Cameron, Williams Brothers

"Happy Go Lucky"
T. Holmes, Ensemble

ACT 3

"In Vaudeville"
M. Cameron, R. Whitehead

"Sing a Little Song" (reprise)
T. Holmes, Ensemble

"Wall Street Zoo"[47]
J. Squires, Quartette

"You're the Fellow the Fortune Teller Told Me All About"
B. Gallagher, J. Kane

Finale
Ensemble

1926.31

DEEP RIVER

A Native Opera in Three Acts. Book and lyrics by Laurence Stallings. Music by Frank Harling. Staged by Arthur Hopkins. Settings and costumes designed by Woodman Thompson. Lighting by Geoge Schaff. Orchestra under the direction of Sepp Morscher. Produced by Arthur Hopkins. Opened 4 October 1926 at the Imperial Theatre and closed 30 October 1926 after 32 performances[48].

----

[46]Added during the run to Act 2 before "Zip":
"Love Thoughts"
L. Abarbanell
[47]Dropped during the run.
[48]Producers note—The New Orleans of 1835 offers a variety of themes for an American opera which no other field, setting or time in the history of our country presents. The Creoles were of mixed Spanish and French descent, a carefully preserved and sometimes regenerated aristocracy, brought bodily with all cultural and racial characteristics, into the new Latin world organized at the mouth of the Mississippi. They were never possessed of Negro strains, as is the general misconception. The Negro society with which they mingled, and by the aid of which they established a half-world of society unparalleled in American history, was founded upon a general series of liasons with quadroon women. These women were decorative, intelligent, beautiful and as a rule, faithful to their Creole protectors. They were chiefly of mixed blood, with a Negro strain imparted to them by refugees from the Negro states of the Caribbean. Many travelers have left their letters and diaries to attest the beauty and magnetism of these quadroon women, whose fortunes led them into liasons with Creole gentlemen. The quadroon woman, but never her father, mother or brother, was tolerated at the opera, the various cafés and haunts of the Creole gentlemen, in a special circle of sequestrated place. The quadroon balls were on a rating, for beauty and taste, of an equal importance with those of the high French-Spanish society of the time. At these balls matches were made. Chief among undercurrent forces in this society was the voodoo or gris-gris worship of the time. This worship was brought into New Orleans, as into no other part of the South, by the Negroes from Santo Domingo, Martinique and other Caribbean states. In "Deep River" the cabalistic chants and idioms used are taken authentically from notes by Lafcadio Hearn and other scholars who have endeavored to discover more of voodoo significance than ever they found. The choral influences in the second act are taken from Hearn and from accounts of the time left in newspapers.

CAST (in order of appearance): *Tizan:* JULIUS [Jules] BLEDSOE. *Octavie:* ROSE McCLENDON. *Sara:* Bessie Allison. *Julie:* Gladys White. *Henri:* Rollo Dix. *Paul:* Audre Dumont. *Jules:* David Sager. *Garçon:* Frederick McGuirk. *M. Brusard:* LUIS ALBERNI. *Hutchins:* Arthur Campbell. *Mugette:* LOTTICE HOWELL. *Colonel Streatfield:* FREDERICK BURTON. *Hazzard Streatfield:* ROBERTO ARDELLI. *Hercule:* ANTONIO SALERNO. *The Announcer:* Frank Harrison. *Mother of Mugette:* Louisa Ronstadt. *The (Voodoo) Queen:* Charlotte Murray. *Waiting Women:* Katherine Parker, Carrie Giles, Cora Gary, Alberta Dougal.

Ladies of the Ensemble: Ada Bary, Maria Bary, Lucia Bianco, Mignon Brezen, Nadine Corona, Helen Dmitrieff, Nadine Dubinsky, Helen Eastman, Anne Elliott, Galina Estravich, Merion Fritz, Helen Godsin, Muriel Harmon, Betty Harms, Danny B. Hayden, Helen Heed, Anne Honeycutt, Martha Jobson, Annette Kates, Marta Kurletski, Lonna Lea Hamlin, Rose Malowista, Erna Miro, Gladys Morgan, Anna Prinz, Norma Quinlan, Eva Rodriguez, Elizabeth Schaefer, Grace Morgan, Mignon Spence, Ida Von Lindon, Marion Lou Williams, Ruth Witmer. *Gentlemen of the Ensemble:* Wallace Banfield, Lee Borough, George Brown, Sidney Coryell, William Culloo, Gordon Davis, George Dorrence, V. Dubinsky, Robert L. Duenweg, James Garrett, Lynn Gearhart, George Gordon, Anton Hooft, Lionel Koslin, Effim Liversky, Aylward Martin, Charles V. Maynard, Francis G. Miller, William Montgomery, A. Mravin, Walter Owen, Walter Palm, Basil Prokopenia, Earle Sanborn, Leonard Saxon, Rosco Snyder, Maurice Staw.

Act 1: Café of the Theatre Orleans. New Orleans, 1835.

Act 2: The Place Congo. Showing a voodoo meeting.

Act 3: Patio at Mr. Hercule's Quadroon Ball.

ACT 1

Wherein it is learned that it is the day of the great quadroon ball of the spring. And, further, how M. Brusard has lost a mistress. And showing how plans are afoot by M. Jules to supply balm for M. Brusard's grievous wound. And how M. Jules bringeth the lovely quadroon, Mugette, to the cafe. And how all would have been well had not three Kentuckianes come down the great river to the quadroon ball.

ACT 2

Showing a voodoo meeting, and wherein the lovely Mugette defies her mother, who seeks a charm to catch the wealthy M. Brusard at the quadroon ball. And, further, showing how the lovely Mugette asks a charm for a Kentuckiane. And how the voodoo queen warns Mugette against pursuing her love for this Kentuckiane; how the lovely Mugette turns to God in prayer, which brings down the wrath of the voodoo worshippers of the devil.

ACT 3

How two Kentuckianes came to the quadroon ball; and wherein a pledge and a prophecy are fulfilled.

MUSICAL NUMBERS[49]

"Ashes and Fire"

"De Old Clay Road"

"Soft in de Moonlight" (Banjo Song)

"Dis is de Day" (A Gumbo Madrigal)
Ensemble

"Serenade Creole" (When your Creole eyes looked into mine)we
R. Ardelli

"Po' Lil' Black Chile"
C. Murray, Chorus

"Cherokee Rose"
L. Howell, L. Alberni, Ensemble

"Love Lasts a Day"
L. Howell, R. Ardelli

The "Heru mande" and "Ah tingonai ya" themes were set down by Hearn as an eyewitness at a voodoo ceremony. The songs of the voodoo queen are taken from newspaper accounts. The words are a bastard idiom of Congo, Spanish and French. The Creoles, until the advent of General Jackson as the hero of the battle of New Orleans, never tolerated the parity of other American breeds. Kentuckians, Tennesseans and others of Teutonic stocks filtering down into the city were always hostilely regarded as proponents of a democracy not to be countenanced in the Creole scheme. Only the War of Secession, when all strains of the South were confederated to defeat the oncoming of the democratic idea, brought an end to Creole glory. The abolition of slavery ended forever the quadroon half-world that French and Spanish society had created for the more favored quadroon women bearing strains of Negro blood.
[49]Individual musical were not listed in the program, as DEEP RIVER was performed as an opera. Song list was prepared from published piano vocal selections, not in performance order.

"Two Little Stars"
L. Howell, R. Ardelli

1926.32 CRISS CROSS

A Musical Comedy in Two Acts and a Prologue, 11 Scenes. Book and lyrics by Otto Harbach and Anne Caldwell. Music by Jerome Kern. Staged by R. H. Burnside. Dances by Dave Bennett. Sunshine Girls' Dances devised by Mary Read. Settings and costumes designed by James Reynolds. Orchestra under the direction of Victor Baravalle. Orchestrations by Maurice dePackh and Robert Russell Bennett. Produced by Charles Dillingham. Opened 12 October 1926 at the Globe Theatre and closed 9 April 1927 after 210 performances.

CAST (in the Prologue): *Fred Stone*: FRED STONE. *Cinderella*: DOROTHY STONE. *Abanazar*: OSCAR RAGLAND. *Sinbad*: JOHN LAMBERT. *Villanessa*: Lucy Monroe. *Fairy Godmother*: Primrose Caryll. *Widow Twanky*: Lydia Scott. *Skeleton*: George Herman. *Ali-Baba*: Auguste Aramini. *Puss-in-Boots*: Willie Torpey. *Queen of Hearts*: Kathryn Burnside. *Knave of Hearts*: Charles Baum. *Beauty*: Phyllis Pearce. *Indians*: Messrs. Shannon, Thomson. *Humpty Dumpty*: William Kerschell. *Footman*: Thomas Bell. *Coachman*: Joe Schrode. *Babbie*: Marietta Sullivan. *Bobby*: Cynthia Foley. *Cowboy*: Danzi Goodell. *Scarecrow*: Alice Donahue. *Indian*: Dorothy Bate. *Chinaman*: Pearl Eaton. *Raggedy Andy*: Virginia Franck. *Tony Chestnut*: Beth Neakins. *Jack Horner*: Marjorie Leet. *Rose Red*: Bobbie Breslaw. *Kings of Cards*: Messrs. Shannon, Lambert, Truscott, Thomson.
CAST (in the Play): *Countess de Pavazac*: ALLENE STONE. *Yasmini*: DOROTHY FRANCIS. *Renee*: Primrose Caryll. *Khadra*: Kathryn Burnside. *Lucie*: Lydia Scott. *Fifi*: Beth Meakins. *Badoura*: Phyllis Pearce. *Marie*: Lucy Monroe. *Arlette*: Pearl Eaton. *Babette*: Alice Donahue. *Suzette*: Virginia Franck. *Paulette*: Marjorie Leet. *Miquette*: Danzi Goodell. *Jeanne*: Bobby Breslau. *Goldie Digger*: Dorothy Bate. *Selima*: Lydia Scott. *Captain Carleton*: ROY HOYER. *Ilphrahim Benani*: OSCAR RAGLAND. *Professor Mazeroux*: JOHN LAMBERT. *Maestro Viaggiatore*: Auguste Aramini. *The Marabout of Oran*: Ralph Thomson. *An Argentine, a Soldier, a Juggler*: Charles Baum. *The Curé*: George Herman. *Cassim*: Mark Truscott. *Jadid*, a bazaar-keeper: Jack Shannon. *Nissim*, a beggar: Frank Lambert. *"Susie"*: Joseph Schrode, Thomas Bell. *Dolly Day*: DOROTHY STONE. *Christopher Cross*: FRED STONE.
CAST In the "Portrait Parade" in the Last Scene: *Philip of Spain* (Velasquez): FRED STONE. *The Infanta Eulalia* (Goya): DOROTHY STONE. *Marie Antoinette* (Vigee le Brun): ALLENE STONE. *Persian Princess* (from an illustrated missal): Dorothy Francis. *Principessa Oriana* (Veronse): Primrose Caryll. *Sir Walter Raleigh* (Zucchero): ROY HOYER. *Mme. Le Coudre* (Nattier): Lydia Scott. *Empress Josephine* (David): Phyllis Pearce. *Marquise de Lortanville* (Rouget): Lucy Monroe. *Princess Balladour* (from an illustrated missal): Kathryn Burnside. *The Children of Charles II* (Van Dyck): C. Foley, M. Sullivan. *Gainsborough Ladies*: Misses Eaton, Donahue, Meakins, Franck, Bate, Goodell, Leet, Breslau.
Ladies of the Ensemble: Elizabeth Childs, Goldie Flynn, Kathryn Hereford, Margaret Himes, Sally Hurst, Ruth Hurst, Margaret Kollock, Genevieve Kent, Jessie Madison, Emily Martin, Jane Lane, Gladys Pender, Florence Rice, Rhoda Sewell, Jane Stafford, Betty Roche, Helen Roche, Gwen Tremble, Peggy Timmons, Violet Hale, Lillian White, Alma Hookey, Star Woodman, Vera O'Brien. *Tiller Sunshine Girls*: Noreen Callow, Josie Elton, Doris Carter, Muriel Marlowe, Doris Smith, Phyllis Brown, Dolly Moseley, Mabel Sunderland, Florence Stack, Dorothy Sabin, Doris Yates, Phyllis Barnacle, Ethel Ramsden, Alice Wright, Elsie Burton, Violet Bryant. *Arabs*: A. Riffle, A. Hamid, M. Ambark, A. Mohamed, H. Mohamed, P. Motcelt. *Attendants*: Edward Mack, Walter Harris.

Prologue, Scene 1: Town Hollow in Fable-Land. *Scene 2*: Cinderella's Ride. *Scene 3*: 'On the Way to the Globe.'

Act 1, Scene 1: Outside a School in Southern France. *Scene 2*: Courtyard of the School.

Act 2, Scene 1: Benani's Home in Algiers. Three months later. *Scene 2*: The Street of the Yashmaks. *Scene 3*: The Bazaar of Jadid. *Scene 4*: The Jar of Ali Baba. *Scene 5*: Terrace in the Palace Garden. *Scene 6*: The Diamond Palace.

PROLOGUE
Opening:
a. "Indignation Meeting"/
b. "Hydrophobia Blues"P. Caryll, L. Scott, L. Monroe, C. Foley, M. Sullivan, O. Ragland, J. Lambert, G. Herman, J. Shannon, R. Thomson, W. Torpey, Ensemble
"Cinderella Girl"
D. Stone, Sunshine Girls, Ensemble
"Cinderella's Ride"[50]
D. Stone
"She's on Her Way"
J. Shannon, R. Thomson, J. Lambert, M. Truscott, Girls

ACT 1
"Flap-a-Doodle"
F. Stone, Misses Meakins, Eaton, Donahue, Franck, Goodell, Bate, Leet, Breslau
Dance of the Sunshine Girls
"Leaders of the Modern Regime" (Opening of School Scene)
P. Caryll, B. Meakins, Girls
"You Will—Won't You?"[51]
D. Stone, R. Hoyer, Girls
"In Araby With You"
D. Francis, Girls
Travelogue
F,. Stone, D. Stone, Sunshine Girls, C. Baum
Finale

ACT 2
Opening:
"Dear Algerian Land"/
"Dreaming of Allah"D. Francis, Ensemble
"The Dancers of the Cafe Kaboul"—
Dance of "The Rose of Delight"
D. Stone, R. Hoyer
Dance of "The Golden Sprite"
F. Stone, G. Herman
Dance of "The Camel Boys"
Sunshine Girls
"Rose of Delight" (Trio)
D. Francis, O. Ragland, J. Lambert
"I Love My Little Susie"
F. Stone, J. Schrode, T. Bell
"The Ali Baba Babies"
G. Herman, D. Bate, Girls
Dance of "The Four Leaf Clovers"
Sunshine Girls
The "Portrait Parade"
F. Stone, D. Stone, A. Stone, D. Francis, R. Hoyer, P. Caryll, L. Scott, P. Pearce, L. Monroe, K. Burnside, C. Foley, M. Sullivan
Finale
F. Stone, D. Stone, A. Stone, Company

1926.33 KATJA

An Operetta in Three Acts[52]. Book by Frederick Lonsdale (based on the original Viennese libretto ["Katja, die Tänzerin"] by Leopold Jacobson and Rudolf Österreicher). Music by Jean Gilbert. (English) Lyrics by Harry Graham. Additional scenes written and arranged by Isabel Leighton. Additional lyrics by Clifford Grey. Staged by J. C. Huffman. Dialogue staged by Lewis Morton. Dances by Max Scheck. Settings by Watson Barratt. Costumes by Weldy, Paris. Musical director, Oscar Radin. Entire production produced under the personal supervision of J. J. Shubert. Produced by the Messrs. Shubert. Opened 18 October 1926 at the 44th Street Theatre and closed 22 January 1927 after 112 performances.

CAST (in order of appearance): *Maud Sumerdahl*, Patricia's friend: Dorothy Whitmore. *Leander Billdorff*, Secretary to Count Orpitch: JACK SHEEHAN. *Count Orpitch*, Karujian Ambassador: BRUCE WINSTON. *Patricia*, Daughter of Count Orpitch: DORIS PATSTON. *Ivo*, Prince of Ogladin: DENNIS HOEY. *Katja Karina*, Princess Ilanoff: LILIAN DAVIES. *Edouard*, Major Domo to Count Orpitch: John Adair. *Carl*, Prince of Karuja: ALLAN PRIOR. *Simon*, Servant to the Prince: Oscar Figman. *André*, Lieutenant to Ivo: Frank Hemmingway. *Guests* (4): *Amilie*: Mary Buckley. *Hortense*: Betty Allen. *Louise*: Julia Strong. *Henri*: Tom Green. *Sergeant of Police*: Jack Walsh. *Boscart*, Chief of Police: Oscar Figman. *Inspector of Police*: Frank Walters. *Vladimir* of the Imperial Ballet: Valodia Vestoff. *Natasha* of the Imperial Ballet: Martha Mason. *Annette*: Kitty Coleman. *Guests, Police, Dancers, Conspirators, etc.*
Show Girls: Betty Allen, Sara Allen, Gloria Barrett, Mary Buckley, Shirley Carleton, Catherine Coleman, Georgie DuBrava, Sofia Grebow, Peggy Hansel, Ruth Kennedy,

---

[50]Dropped for subsequent tour.

[51]Replaced for subsequent tour by:
"That Little Something"
D. Stone, R. Hoyer, Girls
(*Lyrics by* Bert Kalmar and Harry Ruby.)
[52]Previously produced in London and in its American tryout under the title KATJA, THE DANCER.

Nailee Lindholm, Grace Norman, Sally Nye, Virginia Orth, Marie Brice, Sally Sayre, Irma Schubert, Julia Strong. *Dancers*: Lorraine Brooks, Ella Erne, Dorothy Chase, Gertrude Demmler, Millie Dupree, Peggy Ellis, Helen Elsworth, June Ferguson, Marion Kingston, Marcia Mack, Natalia, Claire Renaud, Margaret Seidel, Peggy South, Eleanor Sweet, Ethel Tatkewics, Peaches Tortoni, Zena Trett, Florence Turner. *Boys*: Reeder Boss, Bill Brainard, Lewis Downie, Malcolm Duffield, Thomas Glover, Thomas Green, Billie Hall, Murray Levin, Dan McGovern, Bob Morris, Robert Smith, Paul Wilcox.

The action of the play takes place in one night at Monte Carlo.

Act 1: The Reception Room, Villa of Count Orpitch. 9:30 P.M.

Act 2: A Room in Prince Carl's Villa. Midnight.

Act 3: The Office of the Chief of Police at Monte Carlo. 3 A.M.

ACT 1

"Love's in the Air"
D. Whitmore, Ensemble

"Cruel Chief"
D. Patston, J. Sheehan, B. Winston

"Balkan Dance"
V. Vestoff, M. Mason, Ensemble

"Euranian Anthem"
L. Davies, D. Hoey

"Dance with You"
L. Davies, D. Hoey

"All the World Loves a Lover"
A. Prior

"Just For a Night" (Just For Tonight)
L. Davies, A. Prior
(*Music by* Maurice Rubens, (Ralph Benatsky). *Lyrics by* Clifford Grey.)

"I Fell Head Over Heels in Love"
D. Patston, J. Sheehan

Ballet and Finale
V. Vestoff, M. Mason, L. Davies, A. Prior, D. Hoey, Ensemble

ACT 2

"Congratulations"
A. Prior, Ensemble

"If You Care"
D. Patston, A. Prior

"(Those) Eyes So Tender"
L. Davies, A. Prior

"Night Birds"
D. Whitmore, V. Vestoff, Ensemble

"Leander"
D. Patston, J. Sheehan

ACT 3

"In Jail"
D. Whitemore, Ensemble

Dance
V. Vestoff

"Oh, Woe Is Me"
D. Patston, J. Sheehan

Finale
Entire Company

1926.34

THE WILD ROSE

A Musical Play in Two Acts, 10 Scenes. Book and lyrics by Otto Harbach and Oscar Hammerstein II. Music by Rudolf Friml. Book staged by William J. Wilson. Dances by Busby Berkeley. Settings designed by Joseph Urban. Costumes designed by Mark Mooring. Orchestra under the direction of Herbert Stothart. Produced by Arthur Hammerstein. Opened 20 October 1926 at the Martin Beck Theatre and closed 11 December 1926 after 61 performances.

CAST (in order of appearance): *Baron Frederick*: JOSEPH MACAULAY. *General Hodenberg*: Len Mence. *"Monty" Travers*: JOSEPH SANTLEY. *"Buddy" Haines*: GUS SHY. *Luella Holtz*: INEZ COURTNEY. *Gideon Holtz*: WILLIAM COLLIER. *Countess Nita*: NANA BRYANT. *King Augustus III*: FULLER MELLISH. *Princess Elise*: DESIREE ELLINGER. *Carl*: Jerome Daley. *Peter*: Neil Stone. *Zeppo*: Dink Trout. *The Flower Vendor*: George Djimos. *Dancers*: The Randalls. *Street Entertainers*: Pasquali Brothers.

Ladies of the Ensemble: Jeanne LaMont, Marguerite Wyatt, Rachel Chester, Natalie Manning, Katherine Sacker, Anne Austin, Ann Constance, Lotta Fanning, Mary Paige, Lydia Shields, Mary Carney, Mary Harrison, Doris May, Elinore Heinemann, Mildred Brower, Polly Ray, Bobby Campbell, Sylvia Pagano, Ruth Sato, Helene McGlynn, May Boyle, Cora Andrews, Bella Graf, Eve Sinclair, Josephine Paretto, Bettye Holmes, Ethel Allen, Gene Hitch, Claire Davis, Frances Grace, Dorothy Forbes, Mabel Martin, Madeline Montelin, Patricia Ross, Mae Burke, Guerida Crawford. *Gentlemen of the Ensemble*: Frank Chapman, John Fredericks, Boris Milman, Arthur Nulens, Zachary Marr, Benn Carswell, Michael Afanasief, James Esipoff, Michael Miroshnik, John Krivokosenke, Leon Kartavy, Josef Zitrinik, George Fisher, Anatole Safanov, Eugene Gnotow, Morris Tepper, George Magis, Joseph Gary, Waevolod Anisimo, Jack Danziger, David Kladkoff, Philemon Zivaly, Orlando DeSalas, Dan Harris, Donald Robert, Clifford Stone, Charles Frye, Lawrence Arcuri, Richard Neely, Joseph Rogers.

Act 1, Scene 1: Outside of the Casino at Monte Carlo. Evening. *Scene 2*: Outside of the Tavern in Borovina. One month later. *Scene 3*: A Corner of the Tavern. *Scene 4*: Outside of the Tavern in Borovina. *Scene 5*: A Garden Wall. Next morning. *Scene 6*: Garden of the King's Palace.

Act 2, Scene 1: His Majesty's Study. *Scene 2*: Courtyard of the Palace. *Scene 3*: The Frontier. That night. *Scene 4*: Throne Room of the King's Palace.

ACT 1
Scene 1
Opening
"Riviera"
J. Macaulay, Ensemble
Dance
The Randalls
"Lovely Lady"
J. Santley, Chorus
Scene 3
"Her Eyes Are Brown" (Brown Eyes)
J. Santley, I. Courtney, G. Shy, Chorus
"Love Me, Don't You?"
N. Bryant, W. Collier, Girls
Scene 4
"It Was Fate"
D. Ellinger, Chorus
"Wild Rose"
D Ellinger, J. Macaulay, Male Chorus
"Lady of the Rose"
D. Ellinger, J. Macaulay, Male Chorus
Scene 5
"L'heure d'or" (One Golden Hour)
D. Ellinger, J. Santley
(*French lyrics by* J. B. Kantor.)
Finaletto—"One Golden Hour"
N. Bryant, J. Macaulay, J. Santley, Ensemble
Scene 6
"Lady of the Rose" (reprise)
Male Chorus
Finale
(Company)

ACT 2
Scene 1
Opening
F. Mellish, J. Daley, Male Chorus
"Our Little Kingdom" (We'll Have a Kingdom)
D. Ellinger, J. Santley
Scene 2
Revolution Festival (Dance)
Pasquali Brothers
Scene 3
Dramatico-Musical Scene
Finaletto
Scene 4
"Won't You Come Across?"
G. Shy, I. Courtney
"The Coronation"
D. Ellinger, J. Macaulay, Ensemble
Finale
Entire Company

1926.35
RAQUEL MELLER

A Return Engagement of the One-Woman Revue of Spanish Songs[53]. Symphonic Orchestra selected from the Philharmonic Society of New York under the direction of Victor Baravelle. Produced by E. Ray Goetz. Opened 25 October 1926 at the Henry Miller's Theatre and closed 6 November 1926 after 16 performances.

CAST: Señorita RAQUEL MELLER.

MUSICAL PROGRAM

"La Farandulo Pasa" (Poor Pierrot)

"Nena" (Your Wonderful Lips)

"Tus Ojus" (Your Eyes)

"Mariana"

"El Peligro de las Rosas" (Beware of the Rose)

"La Mujer d'en Manelic" (The Wife of Manelic)

"Noi de la Mare" (Joy and Pangs of Motherhood)

"El Relicario" (The Charm/My Toreador)

"Flor de Te" (Tea Blossom)

"Ay! Cipriano" (Naughty Cipriano/That Waltz Espagnol)

"Diguli Que Vengui" (Tell Him to Come/Hurry Mateo)

"La Virgen Roja" (The Red Virgin)

"La Tarde del Corpus" (The Procession)

"La Monteria" (Grandmother's Dress/At the Dance)

"Manola"

"La Hija del Carcelero" (The Jailer's Daughter)

"La Reina del Cortijo" (The Peasant Queen)

"Mimosa" (When Love Passes By)

"La Violetera" (Who'll Buy My Violets/The Violet Girl)

"Flor del Mal" (Flower of Sin/Poor Scentless Flower)

"Siempre Flor" (The Eternal Flower)

"Gitanillo" (My Gypsy Sweetheart)

"Mis Amores" (My Loves)

"El Pescadero" (The Fishmonger)

"Le Mujer del Torero" (The Wife of the Bullfighter)

"Como la Flor" (Like the Flower)

1926.36
OH, KAY!

A Musical Comedy in Two Acts, 5 Scenes Book by Guy Bolton and P. G. Wodehouse. (Based on the French comedy 'La Présidente' by Maurice Hennequin and Pierre Veber.) Music by George Gershwin. Lyrics by Ira Gershwin. Book staged by John Harwood. Dances and ensembles staged by Sammy Lee. Settings designed by John Wenger. Costumes designed by Hattie Carnegie, Brooks Costume Company. Orchestra under the direction of William Daly. Produced by Alex A. Aarons and Vinton Freedley in association with the Messrs. Shubert. Opened 8 November 1926 at the Imperial Theatre and closed 18 June 1927 after 256 performances.

CAST (in order of appearance): *Molly Morse*: BETTY COMPTON. *Peggy*: Janette Gilmore. *The Duke*: GERALD OLIVER SMITH. *Larry Potter*: HARLAND DIXON. *Phil (Phyllis) Ruxton*: MARION FAIRBANKS. *Dolly Ruxton*: MADELEINE FAIRBANKS. *'Shorty' McGee*: VICTOR MOORE. *Constance Appleton*: Sascha Beaumont. *Jimmy Winter*: OSCAR SHAW. *Kay*: GERTRUDE LAWRENCE. *Revenue Officer Jansen*: Harry T. Shannon. *Mae*: CONSTANCE CARPENTER. *Daisy*: Paulette Winston. *Judge Appleton*: Frank Gardiner. *At the Pianos*: Victor Arden, Phil Ohman.

Ladies of the Ensemble: Peggy Quinn, Marie Otto, Elsie Neal, Grace Jones, May Sullivan, Ann Ecklund, Marcia Bell, Betty Waxton, Anita Gordon, Blanche O'Donahue, Jean Carroll, Frances Stone, Jean Wayne, Maxine Marshall, Elsie Frank, Amy Frank, Dot Justin, Dorothy Saunders, Amy Weber, Kappie Fay, Bonnie Blackwood, Justine Welch, Sara Jane Heliker, Pansy Maness, Caroline Phillips, Peggy Johnstone, Polly Williams, Adrienne Armond, Gloria Murray, Grace Carroll, Claire Wayne, Betty Vane, Frances DeFoe. *Gentlemen of the Ensemble*: Al Fisher, Lionel Maclyn, Jacques Stone, Tom Martin, Melville Chapman, Alan Stevens, Ted White, Bob Gebhardt, Jack Fraley, Burton McEvilly, Dowell Brown, Ted Daniels, Eugene Day.

Act 1, Scene 1: Living Hall of Jimmy's House, Beachampton, Long Island. *Scene 2*: The same. Next morning.

Act 2, Scene 1: Terrace of Jimmy's House. *Scene 2*: The Cellar. *Scene 3*: Indian Inlet Inn.

ACT 1
Scene 1

   "The Woman's Touch"
      B. Compton, C. Carpenter, Ensemble

   "Don't Ask"
      H. Dixon, Marion Fairbanks, Madeleine Fairbanks

   "Dear Little Girl"
      O. Shaw, Girls

   "Maybe"
      G. Lawrence, O. Shaw

Scene 2

   "Clap Yo' Hands"
      H. Dixon, B. Compton, P. Winston, C. Carpenter, J. Gilmore, Ensemble

   "Do-Do-Do"
      G. Lawrence, O. Shaw

   Finale
      (Principals), Ensemble

ACT 2
Scene 1

   "Bride and Groom"
      S. Beaumont, O. Shaw, F. Gardiner, Guests

   "Someone to Watch Over Me"
      G. Lawrence

   "Fidgety Feet"
      H. Dixon, Marion Fairbanks, Ensemble

   "Heaven on Earth"
      O. Shaw, B. Compton, C. Carpenter, Ensemble

   Finaletto
      Ensemble

Scene 3

   Specialty Dance
      B. Compton, Marion Fairbanks, Marion Fairbanks, J. Gilmore

   "Oh, Kay"
      G. Lawrence, Boys

   Finale
      Entire Company

1926.37
GAY PAREE (1926)

A Musical Revue in Two Acts, 38 Scenes[54]. Dialogue (sketches) by Harold Atteridge. Music by Alberta Nichols, J. Fred Coots, Maurice Rubens. Lyrics by Mann Holiner, Clifford Grey, J. Fred Coots. Dialogue staged by Charles Judels. Entire production staged by J. C. Huffman. Ensembles and dances staged and conceived by Seymour Felix. Settings designed by Watson Barratt and Rollo Wayne. Costumes designed by Weldy of Paris, and Ernest Schrapps. Orchestra under the direction of Harry Nieman. Entire production under the personal direction of J. J. Shubert. Produced by the Messrs. Shubert. Opened 9 November 1926 at the Winter Garden and closed 9 April 1927 after 192 performances.

CAST: CHIC (Charles) SALE, WINNIE LIGHTNER, MAX HOFFMANN, JR., MARY MILBURN, RICHARD BOLD, HELEN WEHRLE, FRANK GABY, JANE [Jeanne] AUBERT, DOUGLASS LEAVITT, ALICE BOULDEN, NEWTON ALEXANDER, MARGIE FINLEY, CHESTER FREDERICKS, AZEADA CHARKOUIE, JACK HALEY, LORRAINE WEIMAR, BEN HOLMES, AL WOHLMAN, VERONA, LUCITA CAVARA, RATH BROTHERS (George, Dick), DOLLY THAIN.

Gay Paree Girls: Edith Humphreys, Ceceile Bodenham, Betty Leighton, Sylvia Carroll, Cavenda Stanislaw, Grace Candee, Adelaide Candee, Peggy Brown, Olive Pearson, Dorothy Palmer, Mary Phillips, Margaret Kennedy, Margaret Moore, Jean Caselton, Elizabeth Ryder, Mary Coyle, Jean Block, Emily Verdi, Gladys Nagle, Eva

---

[53]RAQUEL MELLER previously appeared in New York 14 April 1926 at the Empire Theatre for 38 performances.

[54]The second and last in an annual series of revues that began in 1925 produced by the Messrs. Shubert. Played 9 performances/week.

Belmont, Dorothy Kane, Margaret Hollis, Dotty Nadetta, Myrtle Allen, Raquel Rhu, Miriam Grace, Nydra Miller, Marjorie Thomas, Grace Wright, Babe Loris, Stephanie Peters, Betty Lawrence, Rosaline McCallion, Mae Russell, Mattie Kay, Beverly Booth, Loretta Flushing, Mabel Olsen, Shirley Guistin, Madeline Maier, Maxine Morton, Gloria Christie, Barbara Barondess, Frances Blythe, Azeada Charkouie, Lenora Wilder, Naan Lane, Neva Lynn, Leona Newell, Katrina Trask, Agatha Phillips, Thalie Hamilton, Julia Barker, Christine Ecklund, Dorothy Vance, Roslynd Wishon, Irene Schroeder, Elena Meade, Helene Fredricks, Muriel Seeley.

ACT 1

Scene 1

Prologue

Beau Broadway: A. Wohlman. *"Red" Grange*: M. Hoffmann, Jr. *Master of Ceremonies*: J. Haley. *Official Prologue*: B. Barondess. *Daring Prologue*: H. Wehrle. *Programme Girl*: A. Boulden. *Comedian*: F. Gaby. *Modern Flapper*: W. Lightner.

Scene 2

"College Days"

W. Lightner

Dance

M. Finley

"Red" Grange: M. Hoffmann, Jr. *Helen Craig*: M. Milburn. *Mrs. Craig*: L. Weimar. *Cash Grange*: D. Leavitt. *The Coach*: F. Gaby.

Eton Dance

Winter Garden Girls

Football Game and Flag Drill

Gay Paree Girls

Referee: M. Hoffman, Jr.

Scene 3

The Graduate of the I.C.S.

A. Wohlman

Scene 4

At the Movies

Usher: M. Hoffmann, Jr. *Dorothy*: W. Lightner. *Loreli*: A. Boulden. *McDonald*: B. Holmes. *Tough Boy*: F. Gaby. *Tough Girl*: A. Charkouie. *Wife*: L. Weimar. *Husband*: N. Alexander. *Jack*: J. Haley. *Jill*: F. Blythe. *Flirty Boy*: M. Hoffmann, Jr. *Ushers, Movie Fans.*

Scene 5

"No More Dancing"

Gay Paree Girls

Scene 6

"Fine Feathers"

M. Milburn, Winter Garden Beauties

Scene 7

Eagle Eyed Elmer

Elmer: C. Sale. *Judge*: N. Alexander. *Clerk of Court*: M. Hoffmann, Jr. *Attorney for Defense*: D. Leavitt. *Attorney for Plaintiff*: B. Holmes.

Scene 8

"Bad Little Boy With Dancing Legs"

C. Fredericks

Scene 9

Mother of Three

The Wife: W. Lightner. *The Husband*: N. Alexander.

Scene 10

"The More We Dance"

Gay Paree Girls

Scene 11

A Beautiful Fan

The Fan Salesman: R. Bold. *The Lady*: M. Milburn. *The Spanish Dancer*: L. Cavara. *Tango Dancers*: O. Pearson, R. McCallion. *Spanish Fan Girls*: D. Vance, M. Morton, T. Hamilton, E. Meade, N. Lynn, F. Fredricks, A. Charkouie, K. Traske. *The Japanese Dancer*: Verona. *Geisha Girls*: M. Olsen, M. Hollis. *Japanese Fan Girls*: A. Schroeder, L. Wilder, B. Barondess, S. Peters, R. Dhu, M. Seeley. *The French Dancer*: H. Wehrle. *Pompadour Girls*: V. Moore, G. Wright, G. Candee, L. Flushing. *Girls of the Diamond Fan*: C. Sylva, R. Wishon, G. Christie, A. Phillips, C. Ecklund, F. Blythe.

Scene 12

Mr. Craig Picks His Stenographer

Announcer: A. Wohlman. *Walter Craig*: D. Leavitt. *Percy*: F. Gaby. *Mrs. Craig*: L. Weimar. *Rosemary*: A. Boulden. *Mrs. Daisey*: H. Wehrle. *Miss Pearl*: M. Milburn.

Scene 13

"Broken Rhythm"

A. Boulden

Dance

Gay Paree Girls

Two Fast Steppers: C. Fredericks, M. Finley.

Scene 14

The Zither Club

C. Sale

Scene 15

"Kandahar Isle"

R. Bold

(*Music by* Alberta Nichols. *Lyrics by* Mann Holiner.)

Dance

A. Charkouie. Zulu Dancers, Gay Parree Girls

Scene 16

Now and Then

Announcer: F. Gaby. *The Mother*: M. Milburn. *The Grandmother*: L. Weimar. *The Daughter*: A. Boulden. *The Son-in-Law*: M. Hoffmann, Jr. *The Father*: D. Leavitt. *The Butler*: J. Haley.

Scene 17

Beau Geste

Beau Geste: R. Bold. *John*: J. Haley. *Digby*: B. Holmes. *Soldiers of the Legion*: W. Montgomery, C. Bree, W. Stamm.

Scene 18

"Morocco Drill"

Gay Paree Girls

Scene 19

Three Old Men

Tom: C. Sale. *Dick*: D. Leavitt. *Harry*: B. Holmes. *Percy*: M. Hoffmann, Jr. *Miss X*: L. Weimar.

Scene 20

Winnie Lightner

Scene 21

The Grape Vendor

R. Bold

Parade of the Grape Girls

Winter Garden Girls

Scene 22

"Bachanol"

O. Pierson, P. Brown, M. Coyle, S. Carol, M. Kennedy, E. Verdi, D. Nadette, J. Castleton, G. Nagle, D. Palmer, S. Peters, A. Candee, M. Moore, R. Dhu, E. Ryder, E. Belmont, B. Leighton, E. Humphries, M. Allen, R. McCallion *The Spirit of Wine*: D. Thain.

Scene 23

Vinter's Dream

ACT 2

Scene 1

"Oriental Nights"

R. Bold

Tableau

Gay Paree Girls

Scene 2

The Magician[55]

The Magician: F. Gaby. *The Princess*: G. Christie.

Scene 3

"Je t'aime (Means I Love You)"

J. Aubert

(*Music and Lyrics by* Powers Gouraud.)

Hotel Clerk: A. Wohlman. *Madeline*: J. Aubert. *Jimmy*: R. Bold. *George*: F. Gaby. *Bill*: D. Leavitt. *Husband*: M. Hoffmann, Jr.

Scene 4

The Doctor's Waiting Room

The Happy Patient: C. Sale. *The Nurse*: A. Boulden. *The Doctor*: N. Alexander. *First Patient*: B. Holmes. *Second Patient*: J. Haley. *Third Patient*: M. Hoffmann, Jr.

---

[55]Dropped during the run.

Scene 5

The Gold Plaque
The Dancer: H. Wehrle.

Scene 6

"The Prisoners' Song"
(*Music and Lyrics by* Guy Massey. *Conceived and designed by* Rollo Wayne.)
The Warden: D. Leavitt. *The Trusty*: B. Holmes. *Trusty Joe*: R. Bold.

Scene 7

"Shaking the Blues Away"
A. Boulden

Dance
Gay Paree Girls

Scene 8

He Knew Lincoln (Lincolniana)
[*by* Ida Tarbell]
A Reporter: B. Holmes. *An Old Soldier*: C. Sale.

Scene 9

Mlle. Jeanne Aubert ("La Violetera" Specialty)

Scene 10

Yukon Dance Hall
Parson's Son: J. Haley. *Bartender*: M. Hoffmann, Jr. *Prospector*: B. Holmes.
Klondike Jim: R. Bold.

Scene 11

Rath Brothers[56] (Acrobats)

Scene 12

"Paris Is a Paradise for Coons"
W. Lightner

Dance
Gay Paree Girls

Dance
C. Fredericks

Black Bottom (Dance)
A. Boulden, M. Hoffmann, Jr.

Scene 13

For Her Husband's Benefit
The Wife: W. Lightner. *The Husband*: F. Gaby. *The Girl Friend*: A. Boulden.

Scene 14

"There Never Was a Town Like Paris"
A. Wohlman, B. Holmes, D. Leavitt, J. Haley, F. Gaby, M. Hoffmann, Jr
(*Music by* Alberta Nichols. *Lyrics by* Mann Holiner.)

Scene 15

Grand Finale

1926.38 OLD BILL, M.P.

An Adventure in Three Trucks, Eight Loads and a Shovel Full. (A Comedy with Music in Three Acts, 9 Scenes.) Play by Bruce Bairnsfather[57]. Music by Abel Baer. Staged by Henry Herbert. Scenery designed by David Gaither from suggestions by Bruce Bairnsfather. Costumes by Charles Christie & Co., Beuville orchestra conducted by Ross Mobley. Entire Production under the personal supervision of Bruce Bairnsfather and Charles Coburn. (Produced by Charles Coburn.) Opened 10 November 1926 at the Biltmore Theatre and closed 27 November 1926 after 23 performances.

CAST (in order of appearance): *Maggie, Old Bill's Wife*: HELEN HANLON. *Kate, Old Bill's Niece*: HELEN TILDEN. *Three Pals*: *Bert*: CHARLES McNAUGHTON. *Alf*: CHARLES E. JORDAN. *Old Bill*: CHARLES COBURN. *Lady Barbara*: AUDREY RIDGEWELL. *Lord Hadenham*: LARENCE D'ORSAY. *A Constable*: N. St. Clair Hales. *Wells, Secretary to Lord Hadenham*: Leonard Ide. *Lord Bledlow, Lord Hadenham's Son*: C. T. Davis. *Mr. Clayton, Manger of the Long Tunnel Mine*: James Jolly. *Molly Parsons*: Evelyn Clayton. *Bessie Martin*: Lillian Spencer. *Suzannah Constance Saunderson*: Josephine Willis. *Raleigh*: Thomas P. Tracy. *Fenelli*: N. St. Clair Hales. *Maxwell, Foreman of the Long Tunnel Mine*: Herbert Ranson. *Mrs. Bardley*: Susannah Lawrence. *Bob Martin, an Under Foreman*: Roy Cochrane. *Miners (4)*: *Jim Bailey*: George Fitzgerald. *Tom Lloyd*: Lawrence Sterner. *Ed Brown*: Henry Carvil. *Steve Graddon*: Guido Alexander. *Frank Lewis, Cage Operator*: F. H. Day. *Ned Denton, a Lamp Boy*: Leighton Converse. *Jim Neil, a Pit Boy*: Allan Cromer. *John Bull.*

Mr. Montague, Lord Hadenham's Solicitor: Wallace Widdecombe. *Baxter, a Footman*: Herbert Belmore. *A Footman*: Guido Alexander. *Dave Long, the Singing Miner*: Colin Hunter. *Miners (3)*: *Joe Darvil*: Paul Dane. *Pete Saunders*: George V. Denny, Jr. *Jack Grey*: George Lamb. *A Woman*: Nancy DeSilva. *Clerk of the Court*: Thomas P. Tracy. *Mr. Ingram, a Justice of the Peace*: Roy Cochrane. *Inspector Ferguson of Scotland Yard*: Henry Carvil. *Mr. Morton, M. P. standing for Wolverbrun*: George Fitzgerald. *Mr. Chisel*: George Lamb. *A Postman*: Colin Hunter.

Miners, Miners Wives and Citizens of Wolverbrun: Maggie Weston, Josephine Neal, Catharine Campbell, Grace Anthony, Virginia Gordon, Geneva Willson, Lois Brown, Elisabeth Stevens, Mary Lucas. Bruce Scott, Smith Weller, Richard Bland, Wayne Witten, John McCambridge, Victor Katona, Charles Hamlin, Sol Padrone, F. Earl, Robert Mack, Henry Simon, A. Sayer, Fred. Steinway, John Kelly, G. Delouis, Ray Lenoue.

Time: The Present. *Place*: The Mining Town of Wolverbrun, England.

Truck 1, Load 1: Old Bill's Pub, "The Better 'Ole." Armistice Day. *Load 2*: The Pit Head of the Long Tunnel Mine. Three days later.

Truck 2, Load 1: Bledlow Hall. Evening of the same day. *Load 2*: "A mile deep." *Load 3*: "The Wetter 'Ole." *Load 4*: Outside the Gates. *Load 5*: "The Wetter 'Ole."

Truck 3, Load 1: The Board Room of the Long Tunnel Mine. Three days later. A *Shovel Full*: The Markey Square at Wolverbrun. The same evening.

MUSICAL NUMBERS

"Vi-o-lets"
(*Music by* Abel Baer. *Lyrics by* Bruce Bairnsfather.)

"So There You Are"
(*Music by* Abel Baer. *Lyrics by* Bruce Bairnsfather.)

"In the Used to Be"
(*Music by* Con Conrad, Harold Christy. *Lyrics by* Bruce Bairnsfather.)

"When We Are Spliced"
(*Music by* Ross Mobley. *Lyrics by* Charles McNaughton.)

1926.39 TWINKLE, TWINKLE

A Musical Comedy in Two Acts, 6 Scenes. Book and lyrics by Harlan Thompson. Music by Harry Archer. Additional scenes and (musical) numbers by Bert Kalmar and Harry Ruby. Book directed by Frank Craven. Musical numbers staged by Julian Alfred and Harry Puck. Costumes designed by Charles LeMaire. Settings designed by P. Dodd Ackerman. Orchestra under the direction of Max Steiner. Produced by Louis F. Werba. Opened 16 November 1926 at the Liberty Theatre and closed 9 April 1927 after 167 performances.

CAST (in order of appearance): *Jack Wyndham*: JOSEPH LERTORA. *Florence Devereaux*: PERQUETA COURTNEY. *Louise*: Elise Bonwit. *Dolores*: Dorothy Martin. *Suzette*: Anita Firman. *June*: Diana Day. *Gloria*: Ann Kelly. *Sam Gibson*: William J. McCarthy. *A Cutie*: Therese Kelly. *Alice James*: ONA MUNSON. *Jennie*: Patty Hastings. *Richard Grey*: ALAN EDWARDS. *Harry*: JOHN SHEEHAN. *Telegraph Operator*: John Gray. *P. T. (Peachy) Robinson*: JOE E. BROWN. *Bessie Smith*: FLO LEWIS. *Jane Robinson*: FRANCES UPTON.

The Six Sweet Sixteens: Elise Bonwit, Diana Day, Anita Firman, Patty Hastings, Ann Kelly, Dorothy Martin. *Ladies of the Ensemble*: Alice McDonald, Nerene Swinton, Helen Mirtel, Phyllis Hooper, Marion Nevins, Wanda Jarzy, Frances Nevins, Myrtle LeRoy, Hazel Vee, Dorothy Jordan, Diana White, Wanda Wood, Betty Sheldon, Allyn Loring, Anna Nito, Betty Veronica. *Gentlemen of the Ensemble*: Douglas Keaton, Ned McGarn, Frank Bryan, Henry Nelthrop, Buddy Jenkins, John O'Neil.

Act 1, Scene 1: Private Car of Alice James, somewhere in Kansas. Night. *Scene 2*: A Railroad Crossing. *Scene 3*: Railroad Eating House, Pleasantville, Kansas. Later that night. *Scene 4*: Outside Mrs. Green's Boarding House. The same evening. *Scene 5*: Back at the Railroad Eating House. Two weeks later.

Act 2: The Garden of Mrs. Green's Boarding House. Sunday Afternoon.

ACT 1

Opening
Ensemble

"You Know, I Know"
O. Munson, J. Lertora

"Get a Load of This"
P. Courtney, J. Lertora, Sextette, Chorus

Reprise
O. Munson

"We're on the Map"
Ensemble
(*Music by* Harry Ruby. *Lyrics by* Bert Kalmar.)

"Reuben"
J. E. Brown, F. Lewis, J. Robinson, Sextette, Chorus

---

[56]Dropped during the run.
[57]A sequel to the play with songs THE BETTER 'OLE.

"Twinkle, Twinkle"
O. Munson, A. Edwards
Finaletto
Ensemble
Reprise
O. Munson, A. Edwards
"Hustle, Bustle"
Ensemble
"Sweeter Than You"
O. Munson, A. Edwards, Chorus
(*Music by* Harry Ruby. *Lyrics by* Bert Kalmar.)
"Crime"
J. E. Brown
Finale
Ensemble
ACT 2
"Sunday Afternoon"
F. Upton, J. Sheehan, Sextette, Chorus
"Whistle"
O. Munson, Boys, Girls
(*Music by* Harry Ruby. *Lyrics by* Bert Kalmar.)
"I Hate to Talk About Myself"
J. Lertora, F. Upton, Sextette, Girls
"When We're Bride and Groom"[58]
J. E. Brown, F. Lewis, Girls, Boys
Finale
Ensemble

1926.40   GIROFLÉ-GIROFLA

A Revival of the Opéra-bouffe in Three Acts[59], performed alternately in French and English. Music by Charles Lecocq. French company directed by E. Thomas Salignac. American company directed by Max Bendix and Jefferson DeAngelis. French conductor, Julian Clemandl. English conductor, Max Bendix. Produced by the French-American Opera-Comique. Opened 22 November 1926 at Jolson's Theatre and closed 30 November 1926 after 10 performances.[60]

CAST (French Company): *The Twin Daughters of Bolero: Giroflé, Girofla*: MARCELLE EVRARD. *Don Boléro d'Alcazaras, Governor of a Spanish Province*: Mons. SERVATIUS. *Aurore: His Wife*: ANDREE MOREAU. *Marasquin, betrothed to Girofla*: GEORGES FOIS. *Mourzouk, Chief of the Moors*: M. Hirigaray. *Paquita, Attendant on Giroflé-Girofla*: Claire Briere. *Pedro, in love with Paquita*: Sonia Alny. *Pirate Chief*: M. Payen. *Fernando*: M. Spelvin. *Guzman*: Robert Cartier. *Four Boy Cousins of Giroflé and Girofla*: Persis Atwood, Henrietta Narcisse, Sally Conkley, Yvonna Gaby.

Pages, Bridesmaids, Pirates, Moors, Guests, etc.: Ladies of the Ensemble: Pages: Sally Coakley, Edna Kaier, Persis Atwood, Yvonne Gaby. *Bridesmaids*: Marjorie Devor, Lucille Dorward, Ottillie George, Olga Gray, Leonore Hubbard, Anna Hebert, Viola Hailes, Henrietta Narcisse, Florence Silverberg, Marianne Steichen, Alexandra Vaudarsky, Katherine Watts. *Guests*: Henrietta Blackwell, Maria Baykoff, Pauline Gorin, Margaret Hunt, Marie Thalbot, Marie Tavernier, Maryon Wade, Geraldine Samson.

Gentlemen of the Ensemble: Pirates, Moors and Guests: Robert Adams, Albert Cartier, Frank Dobert, Herman Navidvoritz, John Sindall, Victor Young, Walter Palm, Sidney Coryell, Jack Ehrenberg, Ernest Fairbarn, Olav Karstadt, Frank Luchetti, Robert Marco, Walter Owen, Robert Whinnery, Arthur Bourdon.

CAST (American Company): *The Twin Daughters of Bolero: Giroflé, Girofla*: IRENE WILLIAMS. *Don Boléro d'Alcazar, Governor of a Spanish Province*: JEFFERSON

---

[58]After opening, replaced by:
"Day Dreams"
J. E. Brown, F. Lewis, Girls, Boys
(*Music by* Harry Ruby. *Lyrics by* Bert Kalmar.)
[59]Originally produced in New York in French 4 February 1875 at the Park Theatre for 46 performances in repertory; in English 19 May 1875 at Robinson Hall for 61 performances. For Synopsis of Scenes and Musical Numbers, see original 1875 production. For this revival, performances were given in French Monday, Wednesday and Friday evenings, in English Tuesday, Thursday, Saturday matinee and evening, and Thanksgiving matinee. Settings and costumes uncredited.
[60]French libretto by Albert Vanloo and Eugène Leterrier; English libretto uncredited.

DE ANGELIS. *Aurore: His Wife*: ANNE YAGO. *Marasquin, betrothed to Girofla*: CHARLES HART. *Mourzouk, Chief of the Moors*: BERTRAM PEACOCK. *Paquita, Attendant on Giroflé-Girofla*: Nina Piozet. *Pedro, in love with Paquita*: Earl Weatherford. *Pirate Chief*: Francis Tyler. *Fernando*: Walter Owen. *Guzman*: Robert Cartier. *Four Boy Cousins of Giroflé and Girofla*: Persis Atwood, Henrietta Narcisse, Sally Conkley, Yvonna Gaby. *Pages, Bridesmaids, Pirates, Moors, Guests, etc.*: (Same as for the French Company above.)

1926.41   MOZART

A Comedy with Music in Three Acts and a Prologue[61]. (Original French) Book and lyrics by Sacha Guitry. English version by Ashley Dukes. Music by Reynaldo Hahn. Prologue by Brian Hooker. Staged by William H. Gilmore and Norman Loring. Interior decorations and furnishings selected from the collection and selected under the artistic direction of Edouard Jonas. Costumes by Pascaud (Paris), Brooks Uniform Co., Eaves Costume Co., H. Jaeckel & Sons, Inc. Musical direction by Victor Baravalle. Produced by E. Ray Goetz. Opened 22 November 1926 at the Music Box Theatre and closed 18 December 1926 after 32 performances.

CAST (in order of appearance): *Baron von Grimm*: FRANK CELLIER. *Madame d'Epinay*: LUCILLE WATSON. *Mlle. Marie-Anne de Saint-Pons*: Frieda Inescourt. *Grimaud*: Harold Heaton. *Louise*: Jeanne Greene. *Marquis de Chambreuil*: Stewart Baird. *La Guimard*: MARTHA LORBER. *Mozart*: IRENE BORDONI. *Monsieur Vestris*: J. Blake Scott. *At the harpsichord*: Lewis Richards.

Prologue: Library of Baron von Grimm in the year 1802.

Acts 1, 2 and 3: The Home of Madame d'Epinay in Paris in 1778.

1926.42   THE DESERT SONG

A Musical Play in Two Acts, 8 Scenes. Book by Otto Harbach, Oscar Hammerstein II and Frank Mandel. Music by Sigmund Romberg. Lyrics by Otto Harbach and Oscar Hammerstein II. Book directed by Arthur Hurley. Musical numbers staged by Robert Connolly. Orchestra under the direction of Oscar Bradley. Settings by Woodman Thompson. Costumes by Vyvyan Donner and Mark Mooring. Produced by Laurence Schwab and Frank Mandel. Opened 30 November 1926 at the Casino Theatre, moved 10 October 1927 to the Century Theatre, moved 2 November 1927 to the Imperial Theatre, and closed 7 January 1928 after 471 performances.

CAST [in order of appearance]: *Sid El Kar, the Red Shadow's Lieutenant*: WILLIAM O'NEAL. *Mindar*: O. J. Vanasse. *Hassi*: Earle Mitchell. *Benjamin Kidd, Society Correspondent of the Paris Herald*: EDDIE BUZZELL. *Captain Paul Fontaine*: GLEN DALE. *Azuri*: PEARL REGAY. *Sergeant La Vergne*: Albert Baron. *Sergeant DuBassac*: Charles Davis. *Margot Bonvalet*: VIVIENNE SEGAL. *General Birabeau, Governor of a French Moroccan Province*: EDMUND ELTON. *Pierre Birabeau, his son [Red Shadow]*: ROBERT HALLIDAY. *Susan, his ward*: NELLIE BREEN. *Ethel*: Elmira Lane. *Ali Ben Ali, Caid of a Riff Tribe*: LYLE EVANS. *Clementina, a Spanish 'Lady'*: Margaret Irving. *Neri*: Rachel May Clark. *Hadji*: Charles Morgan.

French Girls, Spanish Cabaret Girls: Maude Lydiate, Audree Van Lieu, Grace Fleming, Marion Case, Bobbe Decker, Winifred Seale, Blanche Granby, June Lovewell, Betty Lomax, Valeri Petrie, Bernice Walder, Gertrude Napp, Betty DeFest, Mildred Mann, Helen Shepard, Ethel Lorraine, Beatrice Fox, Gladys Lake, Edna Coates. *Soldiers' Wives, Ladies of the Brass Key*: Helen Bourne, Gertrude McKinley, Eileen Hargraves, Kathlyn Huss, Elmira Lane, Tatiana, Rowena Scott, Patricia O'Connell, Clementine Rigeau, Almajane Wilday, Florence Baker, Miriam Stockton, Hilda Steiner, Robey Lyle, Betty Holmes, Dorothy Lee. *Servants of Birabeau*: Victor Rosales, Benjamin Flack. *Soldiers of the French Legion, Members of the Red Shadow's Band*: Alan Green, Jack Kiernan, John Lister, B. Flack, Nathan Goodman, E. A. Harker, Peter Flomp, Raymond Winfield, John Stanley, Jack Edwards, Armond King, John Daly, Jack Spiegel, William D. Galpen, Charles Davis, John Hammond, William Ehlers, C. Pichler, Morton Croswell, Vance Elliott, Charles Mantia, Talbott Vaughn, George St. John, Z. Norman, Harold Westcott, Victor Rosales, Morris Siegel, Albert Coiner, Elmer Pichler, Nat Broffman, Phil Snyder. *Native Dancers*: Grace Fleming, Bobbe Decker, Winifred Seale, Blanche Granby, June Lovewell, Gertrude Napp, Mildred Mann. *Soldiers of Ali*: Jack Kiernan, E. A. Harker, Jack Spiegel, Charles Mantia, Phil Snyder.

Time: One year ago. *Place*: North Africa.

Act 1, Scene 1: Retreat of the Red Shadow in the Riff Mountains. Evening. *Scene 2*: Garden outside General Birabeau's Villa. That night. *Scene 3*: Drawing Room of General Birabeau's home. A few minutes later.

---

[61]No individual musical numbers billed in program. Lyrics for "Letter Song" at the end of Act 2 by E. Ray Goetz. For Musical Numbers in French, see subsequent production presented 27 December 1926 below.

Act 2, Scene 1: The Great Hall of Ali Ben Ali. Afternoon of the following day. *Scene 2*: A Corridor. A few minutes later *Scene 3*: The Room of the Silken Couch. *Scene 4*: The Edge of the Desert. The following morning a half hour before dawn. *Scene 5*: Courtyard of General Birabeau's home. Two days later.

ACT 1

Scene 1

Opening ("High on a Hill")
W. O'Neal, Riffs

"Ho!" (The Riff Song; Riding Song of the Riffs)
R. Halliday, W. O'Neal, Riffs

"Margot"
G. Dale, Soldiers

Scene 2

"I'll Be a Buoyant Girl"
N. Breen

Scene 3

Ensemble:

"Why Did We Marry Soldiers?"
Soldiers' Wives

"French Marching Song"
V. Segal, Ensemble

"Romance"
V. Segal, Soldiers' Wives

Trio:

"Then You Will Know"
R. Halliday, V. Segal

"I Want a Kiss"
G. Dale, V. Segal, R. Halliday, Ensemble

"It"
E. Buzzell, N. Breen, Girls

"The Desert Song"
R. Halliday, V. Segal

Finale
(Company)

ACT 2

Scene 1

("My Little Castagnette" Opening)
(M. Irving, Girls)

"Song of the Brass Key"
M. Irving, Girls

"One Good Man Gone Wrong"
E. Buzzell, M. Irving

"Eastern and Western Love"

"Let Love Go"
L. Evans, Men

"One Flower (Grows Alone) in Your Garden"
W. O'Neal, Men

"One Alone"
R. Halliday, Men

Scene 3

Opening
V. Segal, Girls

"The Saber Song"
V. Segal

Dramatic Finaletto
(R. Halliday, V. Segal, E. Elton)

Scene 4

"Farewell"
W. Cassel, Riffs

Scene 5

Opening ("All Hail to the General")
V. Segal, G. Dale, E. Elton, Girls

"Let's Have a Love Affair"[62]
E. Buzzell, N. Breen, Girls

---

[62]Replaced in January 1927 by:
"It" (reprise)
E. Buzzell, N. Breen, Girls

(Dance)
(Azuri)
(Finale)
(Company)

LA MASCOTTE

1926.43

A Revival of the Opéra-Comique in Three Acts[63], in French. Libretto by Henri Chivot and Alfred Duru. Music by Edmond Audran. Staged under the personal supervision of E. Thomas Salignac of the Opéra Comique of Paris. Conductor, Julian Clemandl. Presented by the French-American Opéra-Comique. Opened 1 December 1926 at Jolson's Theatre and closed 11 December 1926 after 14 performances.

CAST: *Bettina*, the Mascot: Mlle. JENNY SYRIL. *Fiametta*, Daughter of Lorenzo XVII: Mlle. SONIA ALNY. *Pippo*, a Shepherd: Mons. HIRIGARAY. *Lorenzo XVII*: Prince of Piombino: Mons. SERVATIUS. *Rocco*, a Farmer: Mons. DELAMARCIE. *Fritellini*: Prince of Pisa: Mons. GEORGES FOIX. *Parafanti*, Sergeant: Mons. Georges Grandais. *Matheo*, Innkeeper: Mons. Payen. *Pages (5)*: *Carlo*: Claire Briere. *Marco*: Henrietta Narcisse. *Angelo*: Marjorie Devoe. *Luigi*: Marianne Steichen. *Pappo*: Edna Kaier. *Peasant Girls (3)*: *Bacla*: Claire Briere. *Astonia*: Viola Hailes. *Francesca*: Alexandra Vaudarsky. *Ensemble*: (Same as in GIROFLÉ-GIROFLA above).

THE PIRATES OF PENZANCE,

1926.44 or The Slave of Duty

A Revival of the Comic Opera in Two Acts[64]. Libretto by William S. Gilbert. Music by Arthur Sullivan. Staged by Winthrop Ames. Settings and costumes by Woodman Thompson. Dances by Louise Gifford. Conductor, Sepp Morscher. Produced by the Gilbert and Sullivan Opera Company (Winthrop Ames). Opened 6 December 1926 at the Plymouth Theatre and closed 26 March 1927 after 110 performances (in repertory with IOLANTHE).

CAST: *Richard*, The Pirate King: JOHN BARCLAY. *Samuel*, His Lieutenant: J. HUMBIRD DUFFEY. *Frederic*, a Pirate Apprentice: WILLIAM WILLIAMS. *Major-General Stanley* of the British Army: ERNEST LAWFORD. *His Orderly*: Bert Prival. *Edward*, a Sergeant of Police: WILLIAM C. GORDON. *A Doctor of Divinity*: Bert Prival. *General Stanley's Daughters (4)*: *Mabel*: RUTH THOMAS. *Kate*: SYBIL STERLING. *Edith*: KATHRYN REECE. *Isabel*: Adele Sanderson. *Maud*: Paula Langlen. *Ruth*, a Piratical Maid of All Work: VERA ROSS.

General Stanley's Daughters: Phoebe Brand, Barbara Bronson, Elizabeth Carvel, Dorothy Coulter, Dorothea Dale, Mildred Gethins, Bettina Hall, Natalie Hall, Mildred Harrington, Ann Honeycutt, Irene Hubert, Sybil Kama, Milja Levander, Ruth Marion, Viola Thomas, Ethel Trethaway. *Pirates, Policemen*: Joseph Ames, A. L. Benson, Robert Caille, Hartwell deMille, Ellis Doyle, Franklin Foreman, Lynn Gearhart, Francis German, Thomas E. Knight, Benn. K. Leavenworth, George C. Lehrian, Lawrence L. Lewis, Ray Melton, Kirk Murray, Allyn Saurer, Henry M. Shope, Vidor Sparks, Holmes Washburn, George Wharton, Victor Wrenn.

1926.45 LES CLOCHES DE CORNEVILLE

A Revival of the Comic Opera in Three Acts, 4 Scenes[65], in French. (Libretto by Clairville and Charles Gabet.) Music by Robert Planquette. Staged by E. Thomas Salignac. Conductor, Julian Clemandl. Produced by the French-American Opera Comique. Opened 13 December 1926 at Jolson's Theatre and closed 18 December 1926 after 7 performances.

---

[63]Originally produced in New York 5 May 1881 at the Bijou Theatre for 200 performances in two engagements. For Synopsis of Scenes and Musical Numbers, see original 1881 production. Settings, costumes and musical direction uncredited.

[64]First presented in New York 31 December 1879 at the Fifth Avenue Theatre for 91 performances in two engagements. For Synopsis of Scenes and Musical Numbers, see original 1879 production. Settings and costumes uncredited.

[65]First presented in New York in English 22 October 1877 at the Fifth Avenue Theatre for 16 performances; in French 2 September 1879 at the Fifth Avenue and other theatres that season for 9 performances in repertory. For Synopsis of Scenes and Musical Numbers, see original 1879 production. Settings, costumes uncredited.

CAST: *Germaine*: Mlle. EVRARD. *Serpolette*: Mlle. JENNY SYRIL. *Gaspard*: Mons. SERVATIUS. *Le Marquis*: Mons. HIRIGARAY. *Grénicheux*: Mons. FOIX. *Le Bailli*: Mons. Delamarcie. *Le Tabellion*: Mons. Payen. *Griffardin*: Mons. Grandais. *Fouinard*: Mons. Dufac. *Manette*: Mlle. Briere. *Jeanne*: Mlle. Narcisse. *Gertrude*: Mlle. Kalet. *Suzanne*: Mlle. DeVoe. *Peasants, Servants, Coachmen, Sailors, Knights, Servant Girls*: (Ensemble same as in GIROFLÉ-GIROFLA above).

1926.46   OH, PLEASE!

A Farce (Musical) Revue in Two Acts, 4 Scenes. Book and lyrics by Otto Harbach and Anne Caldwell, based on a story [French farce 'La Présidente'] by Maurice Hennequin and Pierre Veber. Music by Vincent Youmans. Book staged by Hassard Short. Dances and ensembles arranged by David Bennett. Settings and costumes designed by James Reynolds. Orchestra under the direction of Gus Salzer. Orchestrations by Hans Spialek. Produced by Charles Dillingham. Opened 17 December 1926 at the Fulton Theatre and closed 26 February 1927 after 79 performances.

CAST [in order of appearance]: *Emma Bliss*: HELEN BRODERICK. *Miss Fall River*: Pearl Hight. *Miss South Bend*: Blanche Latell. *Miss Topeka*: Gertrude Clemens. *Miss Walla Walla*: Josephine Sabel. *Jane Jones*: Irma Irving. *Peter Perkins*: Nelson Snow. *Buddy Trescott*: Charles Columbus. *Jack Gates*: Nick Long, Jr. *Nicodemus Bliss*: CHARLES WINNINGER. *Fay Follette*: Kitty Kelly. *Thelma Tiffany*: Gertrude McDonald. *Ruth King*: Dolores Farris. *Clarice Cartier*: Cynthia MacVae. *Lily Valli*: BEATRICE LILLIE. *Robert Vandeleur*: CHARLES PURCELL. *Peter Perkins*: Robert Baldwin. *Dick Mason*: Floyd Carder. *Ted Foster*: James Garrett. *Sammy Sands*: Richard Bennett. *Billy Lan*: Charles Angle. *Joe Dillard*: Jack Wilson. *Chester Chase*: Leon Canova. *Marjorie Kenyon*: Dorothie Bigelow.

Ladies of the Ensemble: Ruth Goodwin, Flora Watson, Muriel Hayman, Anna Rex, Harriet Hamill, Antoinette Boots, Virginia Clark, Mary Elizabeth Kerr, Marianna Karelina, Geraldine Fitzgerald, Emily Burton, Betty Block, Mildred Sinclair, Cherie Pelham, Georgia Marne, Anne Varley, Chris Crane, Geraldine Downs.

Act 1: Bungalow of Nicodemus Bliss in Flower City, California.

Act 2: The Display Room of Vandeleur Perfume Company in New York. *Scene 2*: Outside the Bliss House, New Rochelle. *Scene 3*: Lawn Fête at Vandeleur's Estate, Westchester.

ACT 1

"Homely, But Clean"
    H. Broderick, J. Sabel, B. Latell, P. Hight, G.Clemens
"Snappy Show in Town"
    D. Farris, G. McDonald, C. MacVae, Ensemble
"Like She Loves Me"
    B. Lillie, Ensemble
"Nicodemus"
    B. Lillie, C. Winninger
"I'd Steal a Star"
    G. McDonald, N. Long, Jr., Ensemble
"I Know That You Know"
    B. Lillie, C. Purcell

ACT 2
Scene 1
Opening
    Ensemble
"Wonderful Girl"
    N. Long, Jr., N. Snow, C. Columbus, G. McDonald, C. MacVae, D. Farris, Ensemble
"Love and Kisses 'n' Everything"[66] (Duet)
    B. Lillie, C. Purcell
"Love Me"
    B. Lillie
    (*Music by* Phillip Braham. *Lyrics by* Reginald Arkell.)
"Nicodemus" (reprise)
    C. Winninger, Company
"I Can't Be Happy"
    B. Lillie
Scene 2
Charles Winninger and Helen Broderick

---

[66]Dropped after the opening.

Scene 3
Waltz[67]
    C. MacVae, C. Columbus
"The Girls of the Old Brigade"[68]
    B. Lillie
Finale
    B. Lillie, C. Winninger, Company

1926.47   LA FILLE DE MADAME ANGOT

A Revival of the Opéra-comique in Three Acts[69] (in French). Music by Charles Lecocq. (Libretto by Clairville, Paul Siraudin and Victor Koning.) Staged by Messrs. Servatius and Delamarcie. Conductor, Julian Clemandl. Produced by the French-American Opera Comique. Opened 20 December 1926 at Jolson's Theatre and closed 1 January 1927 after 7 performances (in repertory with LA PÉRICHOLE).

CAST: *Mlle. Lange*, Actress and Favorite of Barras: Mlle. SONIA ALNY. *Clairette Angot*, Betrothed to Pomponnet: Mlle. EVRARD. *Larivaudiere*, Friend of Barras and Conspiring against the Republic: Mons. SERVATIUS. *Pomponnet*, Barber of the Market and Hairdresser of Mlle. Lange: Mons. FOIX. *Ange Pitou*, a Poet in love with Clairette: Mons. HIRIGARAY. *Louchard*, Police Officer at the Orders of Larivaudiere: Mons. DELAMARCIE. *Amarante*, Market Woman: Mlle. MOREAU. *Hersilie*, Servant of Mlle. Lange: Mlle. Achart. *Trenitz*, Dandy of the Period, Officer of the Hussars: Mons. Maquaire. *Babet*, Clairette's Servant: Mlle. Briere. *De Launay*: Mlle. Narcisse. *Market Men (2)*: *Cadet*: Mons. Grandais. *Guillaume*: M. Payen. *Market Men, Women, Citizens, Ladies, Hussars, Soldiers, etc.* : (Ensemble same as Giroflé-Girofla above).

1926.48   LA PÉRICHOLE

A Revival of the Opéra-bouffe in Two Acts[70] in French. Music by Jacques Offenbach. (Libretto by Ludovic Halévy and Henri Meilhac, based on 'La Carosse du Saint-Scarament' by Prosper Mérimée.) Conductor, Julian Clemandl. Produced by the French-American Opéra Comique. Opened 27 December 1926 at Jolson's Theatre and closed 1 January 1927 after 8 performances (in repertory with LA FILLE DE MADAME ANGOT).[71]

CAST: *La Périchole*, a Street Singer: Mlle. JENNY SYRIL. *Three Cousins who keep a small inn*: *Guadalena*: Mlle. SONIA ALNY. *Berginella*: Mlle. Briere. *Mastrilla*: Mlle. Narcisse. *Piquillo*, a Street Singer: Mons. FOIX. *Don Andrès*, Viceroy of Peru: M. SERVATIUS. *Count Panatellas*, First Gentleman of Bedchamber: Mons. Delamarcie. *Don Pedro*, Governor of Lima: M. Payen. *Marquis of Tarapote*: Mons. Grandais. *First Notary*: Mons. Grandais. *Second Notary*: Mons. Dufac. *Courtiers, Guards, Notaries, Servants, Pages, the People, etc.*: (Ensemble same as in GIROFLÉ-GIROFLA above).

1926.49   MOZART

A Comedy with Music (Comédie musicale) in Three Acts[72] performed in French. Libretto by Sacha Guitry. Music by Reynaldo Hahn. Staged by Sacha Guitry. Preceded by the Second Act of DÉBURAU[73], a comedy in verse by Sacha Guitry, with music by André Messager. Interior furnishings selected from the collection and selected under the artistsic direction of Edouard Jonas. Costumes by Jean Lanvin and Callot, Paris. Conductor,

---

[67]Replaced during the run by:
    Opening
        Ensemble
[68]Interpolation not by Youmans.
[69]First produced in New York in French 25 August 1873 at the Broadway Theatre for 33 performances in repertory; in English 16 November 1874 at the Lyceum Theatre for 15 performances. For Synopsis of Scenes and Musical Numbers, see original 1873 production. Settings, costumes uncredited.
[70]Originally performed in New York in French 4 January 1869 at Abbey's Theatre for 44 performances; in English 29 April 1895 at Pike's Opera House for 24 performances. For Synopsis of Scenes and Musical Numbers, see original 1869 production.
[71]Direction, settings, costumes uncredited.
[72]Previously produced in English in New York 22 November 1926 at the Music Box Theatre for 32 performances.
[73]Previously produced in English translation by H. Granville Barker 27 December 1920 at the Belasco Theatre for 189 performances.

Raoul Labis. Produced by A. H. Woods. Opened 27 December 1926 at the 46th Street Theatre, closing 8 January 1927 (in repertory 10-22 January 1927 with 'L'Illusionniste'); resumed 25 January 1927 and closed 5 February 1927 after 32 performances.

CAST: *Deburau*: SACHA GUITRY. *Marie Duplessis*: YVONNE PRINTEMPS. *Mme. Rabsuis*: J. Leclerc. *A Servant*: A. Ritchy. *A Young Man*: DeGarcin.

Mozart: YVONNE PRINTEMPS. *Baron von Grimm*: SACHA GUITRY. *Madame d'Epinay*: Mme. GERMAINE GALLOIS. *Marie-Anne de Saint-Pons*: Mlle. J. Leclerc. *La Guimard*: Mlle. A. Ritchy. *Marquis de Chambreuil*: M. de Garcin. *Vestris*: M. Marionno. *A Lackey*: M. A. Chanot. *A Servant*: Renée Senac.

Mozart: The action takes place in the Home of Madame d'Epinay in Paris in 1778.

ACT 1[74]

"Je me suis longtemps souvenu"
S. Guitry

"Comme c'est facile"
Y. Printemps

"Etre adoré"
Y. Printemps

ACT 2

"Quand on pense"
Y. Printemps

"Madame n'est pas là?"
S. Guitry, R. Senac, Y. Printemps

"Comme elle danse"
Y. Printemps

"Depuis ton départ, mon amour" (Letter Song)
Y. Printemps

ACT 3

"Je t'y prendrais donc toujours"
A. Chanot, R. Senac

"La vérité"
G. Gallois

Melodrame
A. Chanot, Y. Printemps, A. Ritchy

"Alors, adieu donc . . . "
Y. Printemps

PEGGY-ANN

1926.50

A Musical Comedy in Two Acts, a Prologue and 6 Scenes. Book by Herbert Fields. (Suggested by the musical comedy 'Tillie's Nightmare' with book and lyrics by Edgar Smith, music by A. Baldwin Sloane.) Music by Richard Rodgers. Lyrics by Lorenz Hart. Book staged by Robert Milton. Musical numbers staged by Seymour Felix. Settings designed by Clark Robinson. Costumes designed by Mark Mooring. Orchestra under the direction of Roy Webb. Orchestrations by Roy Webb. Entire production under the personal supervision of Lew Fields. Produced by Lew Fields and Lyle D. Andrews. Opened 27 December 1926 at the Vanderbilt Theatre and closed 29 October 1927 after 333 performances.

CAST (in order of appearance): *Mrs. Frost*: LULU McCONNELL. *Mr. Frost*: Grant Simpson. *Dolores Barnes*: EDITH MEISER. *Alice Frost*: BETTY STARBUCK. *Guy Pendleton*: LESTER COLE. *Sally Day*: Dorothy Roy. *Peggy-Ann*: HELEN FORD. *Arnold Small*: Fuller Mellish, Jr. *Patricia Seymour*: MARGARET BREEN. *Freddie Shawn*: JACK THOMPSON. *A Policeman*: Patrick Rafferty. *Miss Flint*: Marion Trabue. *A Sailor*: Howard Eames. *Mr. Fish*: Harold Mellish.

Girls: Evelyn Ruh, Dorothy Roy, Leda Knapp, Louise Joyce, Velma Valentine, Enes Early, Margaret Miller, Sherry Gale, Grace Connelly, Maretta Kay, Beth Meredith. *Boys*: Barney Jackson, Gordon Phillips, Harold Lang, Wally Coyle, Jack Morton, G. Douglas Evans.

Time: The Present.

Prologue: In the Boarding House of Mrs. Barnes. Glens Falls, New York.

Act 1, Scene 1: Peggy dreams she sees Fifth Avenue. *Scene 2*: Peggy dreams of Guy Pendleton's Department Store.

Act 2, Scene 1: Peggy dreams she owns a yacht. *Scene 2*: The open sea. *Scene 3*: Peggy dreams she visits the races at Havana, Cuba. *Scene 4*: At Mrs. Barnes' Boarding House again.

---

[74]Musical numbers not listed in the program. Above list prepared from published text and recordings.

PROLOGUE

"Hello"
M. Breen, J. Thompson, Ensemble

"A Tree in the Park"
H. Ford, L. Cole

"Howdy Broadway" (Howdy to Broadway)
Ensemble

ACT 1

Scene 1

"A Little Birdie Told Me So"
H. Ford

Scene 2

"Charming, Charming"
Ensemble

"Where's That Rainbow?"
H. Ford, M. Breen, Ensemble

Finale (Wedding Procession)
Company

ACT 2

Scene 1

("We Pirates from Weehawken")[75]
(H. Ford, Ensemble)

"In His Arms"[76]
H. Ford

"Chuck It!"
J. Thompson, Girls

"I'm So Humble"[77]
H. Ford, L. Cole

Scene 3

"Havana"
M. Breen, J. Thompson, Ensemble

"Maybe It's Me"
H. Ford, L. Cole, E. Meiser, M. Breen, F. Mellish, Jr., B. Starbuck, J. Thompson, W. Coyle

"Give This Little Girl a Hand"
L. McConnell

"The Race" (Peggy, Peggy)
(H. Ford), Company

Scene 4

Finale
Company

BETSY

1926.51

A Musical Comedy in Two Acts, 9 Scenes. Dialogue (book) by Irving Caesar and David Freedman. Music by Richard Rodgers. Lyrics by Lorenz Hart. Staged and revised by William Anthony McGuire. (Dances) staged by Sammy Lee. Costumes designed by Charles LeMaire. Settings designed by Frank E. Gates, Edward A. Morange, Bergman Studios, Joseph Urban. Orchestra under the direction of Victor Baravelle. Entire production produced under the personal direction of Florenz Ziegfeld. Produced by Florenz Ziegfeld. Opened 28 December 1926 at the New Amsterdam Theatre and closed 29 January 1927 after 39 performances.

CAST: *Stonewall Moskowitz, a social luminary*: AL SHEAN. *Mama Kitzel*: PAULINE HOFFMAN. *Her Sons (3)*: *Louie, a tailor*: JIMMY HUSSEY. *Joseph, a barber*: RALPH WHITEHEAD. *Moe, a chef*: DAN HEALY. *Betsy*: BELLE BAKER. *Ruth*: BOBBY PERKINS. *Archie, a pigeon flyer*: ALLEN KEARNS. *Winnie Hill, rich, but Louie's sweetheart*: MADELINE CAMERON. *Flora Dale, rich, but Joe's sweetheart*: EVELYN LAW. *May Meadow, rich, but Moe's sweetheart*: BARBARA NEWBERRY. *Tom Maguire, a vaudeville agent*: Ed Hickey. *Dan Kelly*: Jack White.

---

[75]Performed but not listed in New York programs; listed for subsequent tour.
[76]Dropped in July 1927.
[77]Replaced shortly after opening by:
"Chuck It!" (reprise)
H. Ford, L. Cole

Tex Brown: Phil Ryley. *Mrs. Brown*: Vanita La Nier. BORRAH MINEVITCH'S HARMONICA SYMPHONY ORCHESTRA.

Show Girls: Jean Yoder, Blanche Satchel, Gertrude Walker, Gertrude McMahon, Claire Joyce, Molly Green, Gloria Begee, Ima Berline, Ethel Allen, Helene Gardner, Bella Harrison, Mixi, Doris Powell, Virginia Hawkins. *Dancers*: Lili Kimari, Aline Drange, Dorothy Patterson, Caryl Bergman, Jean Moore, Clara Blackath, Lillian Ojala, Katherine Wolf, May Carroll, Dorothy Day, Margaret Shea, Suzanne Conroy, Betty Gayl, Mickey Silden, Olga Royce, Ann Wood, Marjorie Bailey, Beatrice Wilson, Mary Irwin, Dorothy May, Viola Boles, Riffles Covert, Anita Banton, Irene Hamlin, Paulene Bartlett, Nellie Mayer. *Gentlemen of the Ensemble*: Harold Ettus, Milton Halpern, Frank Cullen, Lester New, Charles deBevers, Bernard Hassert, Jay Lagasse, Ross Burly, George Murray, Edward Mackey, Jack Talbott, Neil Collins.

Act 1, Scene 1: The Roof (of an East Side Tenement in New York City). *Scene 2*: The Fire Escape (outside the Kitzel flat). *Scene 3*: The Cleaners' Department of Vaudeville Circuit. *Scene 4*: Outside Louis Kitzel's Clothing Store. *Scene 5*: (Inside) The Clothing Store. *Scene 6*: The East Side Square.

Act 2, Scene 1: The Kitzel Concession, Coney Island. *Scene 2*: Outside of (Saskatchewan Country Club) Garden. *Scene 3*: The (Club) Gardens.

ACT 1
Scene 1

Opening:

Characteristic Dances
　Ensemble

"The Kitzel Engagement"
　A. Shean, Cameron, J. Hussey, E. Law, R. Whitehead, B. Newberry, D. Healy, Ensemble

"My Missus"
　E. Law, R. Whitehead, B. Newberry, D. Healy, Ensemble

"Stonewall Moscowitz March"
　A. Shean, Ensemble
　(*Lyrics by* Lorenz Hart and Irving Caesar.)

"One of Us Should Be Two"
　M. Cameron, E. Law, B. Perkins, B. Newberry

"Sing"
　B. Baker, A. Kearns, Ensemble

Scene 2
"In Our Parlor on the Third Floor Back"
　B. Perkins, A. Kearns

Scene 3
"This Funny World"
　B. Baker

Scene 5
"The Tales of Hoffman"[78]
　J. Hussey
　(*Music and Lyrics by* Irving Caesar and A. Segal.)

Scene 6
"Follow On"
　Daughters of the Belles of New York (Ensemble), M. Cameron, E. Law, B. Newberry
　Borrah Minevitch and His Harmonica Symphony Orchestra

National Dances
　Ensemble

"Push Around"
　B. Baker

"Bugle Blow"
　M. Cameron, Ensemble

Finale ("I Guess I Should Be Satisfied")
　Entire Company

ACT 2
Scene 1
"Cradle of the Deep"
　E. Law, Ensemble

"If I Were You"
　B. Perkins, A. Kearns

---

[78]Dropped during the run and replaced by:
"Don't Believe"
　J. Hussey
　(*Music and Lyrics by* Irving Caesar and M. Siegel.)

"Blue Skies"
　B. Baker, Ensemble
　(*Music and Lyrics by* Irving Berlin.)

"Leave It to Levy"
　J. Hussey, Ensemble
　(*Music and Lyrics by* Irving Caesar.)

Finaletto ("First We Throw Moe Out")
　Entire Company

Scene 2
Borrah Minevitch's Harmonica Symphony Orchestra

Scene 3
"Birds on High"
　A. Kearns, Ensemble

"Shuffle"
　M. Cameron, Ensemble

Dance Specialty
　E. Law

Song Specialty ("My Kid")
　B. Baker

Finale
　Entire Company

1927.01　THE NIGHTINGALE

A Musical Romance in Two Acts, 6 Scenes. Book by Guy Bolton based on the life of Jenny Lind. Music by Armand Vecsey. Lyrics by P. G. Wodehouse and Clifford Grey. Staged by Lewis Morton. Dances by Carl Hemmer. Settings designed by Watson Barratt. Costumes designed by Barbiere, Paris. Orchestra under the direction of Alfred Goodman. Entire production staged under the personal supervision of J. J. Shubert. Produced by the Messrs. Shubert. Opened 3 January 1927 at Jolson's Theatre and closed 26 March 1927 after 96 performances.

CAST (in order of appearance): *Major General Gurnee*: Lucius Henderson. *Mrs. Gurnee*: Sophie Everett. *Mr. Carp*: STANLEY LUPINO. *Colonel Wainwright*: John Gaines. *Mrs. Vischer Van Loo*: Clara Palmer. *Alice Wainwright*: Eileen Van Biene. *Captain Joe Archer*: Robert Hobbs. *Piper*: Thomas Whiteley. *Josephine*: Violet Carlson. *Cadet Officer*: Donald Black. *Jenny Lind*: ELEANOR PAINTER. *Whistler*: Harold Woodward. *Stephen Rutherford*: NICHOLAS JOY. *Captain Rex Gurnee*: RALPH ERROLLE. *P. T. Barnum*: TOM WISE. *Colonel Robert E. Lee*: VICTOR BOZARDT. *Dolly*, a maid: Eileen Carmody. *Susan*, a maid: Arline Melburn. *Otto Goldschmidt*: William Tucker. *Signor Belletti*: Ivan Dneproff. *Butler* at Rutherford's: John Gaines. *Footman* at Rutherford's: Neal Frank. *Usher* at Castle Garden: Robert Harper. *Cornelius Vanderbilt*: VICTOR BOZARDT.

Ladies of the Ensemble: Vira Galli, Ruth Johnston, Florence O'Brien, Ruth Ramsey, Viola Paulson, Marian Lynn, Ileen May, Madeline Biltmore, Mimi Hayes, Mabel Zoeckler, Dorothy Johnson, Virginia Schaar, Marie Chase, Catherine Janeway, Theo Loper. *Gentlemen of the Ensemble*: Harry Quinn, Gerald Goff, Neal Frank, Tom Denton, John Russell, Herbert Stanley, George Glasgow, Henry Riebeselle, Rober Harper, Walter Lunt, Jack Edmunds, Sonintu Syrjala, Edward Hoffman, George Brent, Albert Valnor, Jack Connett, Donald Black, Richard Bartlett, Sydnie Smith, Fred Barth, Bruce King, Lee Borough, John Muccio, John Gutscher, Luther Talbert, William Dillon, James McKay, Raymond Cullen, Byron Way, Leon Abrahamson, Robert W. Davis.

Act 1: The Terrace of the Old Hotel at West Point.

Act 2, Scene 1: Jenny Lind's Bedroom in a New York Hotel. A year later. *Scene 2*: Outside the Hotel. *Scene 3*: Steve Rutherford's House.

Act 3, Scene 1: The Lobby of Castle Garden. A year later. *Scene 2*: The Stage of Castle Garden.

ACT 1
Opening Chorus
　Girls

"Breakfast in Bed"
　S. Lupino, V. Carlson

March Song
　West Pointers

Waltz Song
　E. Painter

"Homeland"
　R. Errolle, Ensemble

"May Moon"
　E. Painter, R. Errolle

"Two Little Ships"
> E. Van Biene, R. Hobbs, Girls

"He Doesn't Know"
> S. Lupino

Finale

ACT 2

Scene 1

"Fairyland"
> E. Painter, M. Zoeckler, A. Melburn

Trio
> I. Dneproff, W. Tucker, V. Carlson

Scene 2

Spiritual Singers
> Men

Scene 3

Opening Chorus
> Ensemble

"Santa Claus"
> S. Lupino, T. Whiteley

"Josephine"
> S. Lupino, V. Carlson
> (*Lyrics by* Clifford Grey.)

Trio[79]
> E. Painter, W. Tucker, I. Dneproff

"Once in September"
> R. Errolle, E. Van Biene
> (*Lyrics by* Clifford Grey.)

Finale

ACT 3

Scene 1

Opening

"Breakfast in Bed" (reprise)
> S. Lupino, V. Carlson

Scene 2

"Comin' Thru the Rye"[80]
> E. Painter
> (*Music* traditional. *Lyrics by* Clifford Grey.)

Finale

1927.02 EARL CARROLL'S VANITIES (1927)
(International Edition)

A Revised Edition of the 1926 Musical Revue in Two Acts, 43 Scenes[81], featuring the New Charlot Show direct from the Prince of Wales Theatre, London. Sketches by Ronald Jeans. Music by Morris Hamilton. Lyrics by Grace Henry. Additional music by Noel Gay and Richard Addinsell. Additional lyrics by Ronald Jeans, Donovan Parsons and Rowland Leigh. (Additional songs by Ray Klages and Jesse Greer.) Dances and ensembles by Dave Bennett. (Charlot sketches staged by André Charlot.) Ballets arranged by Anton Dolin. Art and technical direction by Bernard Lohmuller. Interior and stage settings designed by August Vimnera, Paris. Costumes designed by Mabel Johnston, Cahrles LeMaire, Harriet Liebman, Hugh Willoughby and Dorothy Tennant. Entire production staged under the personal direction of Earl Carroll. Opened 4 January 1927 at the Earl Carroll Theatre and closed 14 May 1927 after 151 performances.

CAST: (George) MORAN and (Charles) MACK, JULIUS TANNEN, CHARLES KALEY, NORMAN FRESCOTT, BEBE STANTON, KAY SPANGLER, PHYLLIS LOFT, DOROTHY CROYLE, MARJORIE WHITNEY; MAX COOPER, JOHNNY DOOLEY, IRVING EDWARDS, HARRY WELCH, DOREEN GLOVER, ROY REDELLO, FRANCES NORTON, VIVIAN CARMODY, NINA SOREL, JILL WILLIAMS, FUZZY KNIGHT, PATRICK ADAIR, MARJORIE GILBERT, BERTHA CLAY, ODELINE OGILVIE.

---

[79]Dropped after the opening.
[80]Replaced by:
> "The Last Rose of Summer"
> > E. Painter
> > (*Music*, a traditional Irish air. *Lyrics by* Thomas Moore.)

[81]The fifth in the annual series of revues which began in 1923.

Charlot Revue: JESSIE MATTHEWS, HERBERT MUNDIN, HENRY LYTTON, JR., HAROLD WARRENDER, ALLAN MACBETH, HAZEL WYNNE, SUNDAY WILSHIN, GORDON SHERRY, MRS. MACBETH.

The Twenty-One Allan K. Foster Girls: Ingrid (Captain), Peggy, Betty No. 1, Dorothy, Rose, Esther, Ruth, May, Marion, Betty No. 2, Lillian, Linchen, Audrey, Sonya, Kiki, Eileen, Frances, Muriel, Hedda, Erna, Doreene. *Show Girls*: Jewel LaKota, Irma Philbin, Myrtle Candee, Eileen Wenzel, Dolores Gould, Vee Carroll, Gladys Philbin, Cleone Stamm. *Vanities Girls*: Ednamay French, Ruth Martin, Ann Whyte, Bobby Meredith, Mildred Hiller, Helen Stephan, Flo Ward, Peggy Driscoll, Ruth Royce, Gladys Redmond, Annette Lang, Mai Paige, Helen Howe, Lee Byrne, Wanda Stephenson, Marita Ellin, Jean Murray, Avis Adaire.

PROLOGUE

The theatre is decorated to represent a night in Spain and you are supposed to be at a Spanish Fiesta, a Garden Party.

ACT 1[82]

Scene 1

A Garden in Spain
> *The Gypsies*: E. French, R. Martin, M. Gilbert, A. Whyte, B. Meredith, M. Hiller, H. Stephan, F. Ward. *Program Girls*: F. Ward, N. Sorel, P. Driscoll, R. Royce, G. Redmond, V. Carmody. *Fortune Tellers*: A. Lang, M. Paige, O. Ogilvie, H. Howe, L. Byrne, W. Stevenson, M. Ellin.
> Caballero Julius Tannen Meets the Girls

Scene 2

Enter the Charlot Show, in which are introduced the Principals

Scene 3

"Pepita" (Dance)
> Foster Girls
> (*Costumes by* Katheryn Arlington, Inc.)

Scene 4

Six Little Maids
> D. Glover, M. Whitney, P. Loft, D. Croyle, K. Spangler, F. Norton

---

[82]Added during the New York run:
> Chicago (*by* Paul Gerard Smith) (Act 1)
> > *Introducing* I. Edwards. *Chick Slug*: J. Tannen. *Mike Wrap*: J. Dooley. *Quiver Leg*: G. O'Donnell. *A Taylor*: R. Redello. *The Inspector*: H. Welch. *Alfalfa Joe*: C. O'Rourke. *Miss Fit*: B. Stanton. *A Copper*: N. Frescott.
> Spades (Act 1) (added second week of run)
> > G. Moran, C. Mack
> A Recitation (Act 1)
> > H. Mundin, H. Wynne, H. Lytton, Jr., H. Warrender
> Living on Air (Act 1)
> > *Time*: 1945. *Place*: Up in the Air.
> > *The Groom*: J. Dooley. *The Bride*: D. Knapp.
> Signs of the Zodiac (*by* Norman Frescott) (Act 1) (added second week of run)
> > *Sheepshead Boy*: J. Tannen. *Professor Herrington*: N. Frescott. *Lem Simp*: C. Mack.
> Rhubarb (*by* Paul Gerard Smith) (Act 1)
> > *Introduction*: D. Croyle. *The Villain*: J. Dooley. *The Hero*: I. Edwards. *The Heroine*: D. Knapp. *The Handy Man*: H. Welch.
> On the Job (Act 2)
> > *The Boss Paperhanger*: J. Dooley. *The Assistant*: H. Welch. *Mrs. Storm*: B. Stanton.
> Fate (Act 2)
> > *The Wife*: S. Wilshin. *The Butler*: A. Macbeth. *The Husband*: H. Mundin. *Captain Spender*: H. Warrender.
> A Low-Down Dance (Act 2, accompanying The Charleston Outcasts)
> > C. Kaley
> Added for subsequent tour:
> "Open the Gates of Madrid" (Act 1)
> > William Taylor
> > (*Music by* Morris Hamilton. *Lyrics by* Grace Henry.)
> "Cool 'Em Off" (Act 1)
> > Bebe Stanton
> > (*Music by* Morris Hamilton. *Lyrics by* Grace Henry.)
> Better or Worse (Act 2)
> > *Joe Dokes*: J. Dooley. *Doctor Cuttem*: N. Frescott. *Interne Bitterpill*: Cliff Crane. *Interne Plaster*: Jerry Isaacs. *Nurse Shakewell*: Isabelle Mohr. *The Carpet-man*: Charles Stone. *A Blind Man*: W. Taylor.

Scene 5

"The One Woman in the World"[83]
Company

Scene 6

"We Are the Show Girls"[84]
Show Girls

Scene 7

Jessie Matthews Introduces[85]

Scene 8

Yours to Hand[86]
Lord Carbon: H. Warrender. *Honorable Corona Carbon*: S. Wilshin. *Parkins*, a footman: G. Sherry. *Lady Carbon*: Mrs. Macbeth. *Reginald Shorthand*: H. Mundin.

Scene 9

(Two Black Crows on) The Rock Pile
G. Moran, C. Mack, assisted by N. Frescott

Scene 10

Kay Spangler Introduces

Scene 11

Four to Six Thirty[87]
Mrs. Parbury: S. Wilshin. *Louise*, her maid: J. Matthews. *Captain Bisley*: H. Lytton, Jr. *Mr. Parbury*: H. Warrender.

Scene 12

The Charleston Outcasts
N. Sorel, D. Glover

Scene 13

"Alabama Stomp"
C. Kaley
(*Music by* Jimmy Johnson. *Lyrics by* Henry Creamer.)
Miss Alabama: D. Croyle.
Specialty
V. Carmody

Scene 14

The Brass Rail
J. Tannen

Scene 15

Dorothy Croyle introduces

Scene 16

The Price[88]
Jasper: H. Mundin. *Fleet*: G. Sherry. *Phyllis*: H. Wynne. *Jack*: H. Lytton, Jr.

Scene 17

Specialty[89]
J. Matthews
["The Good Little Girl and the Bad Little Girl"
(*Music by* Noel Gay. *Lyrics by* Ronald Jeans.)
"Journey's End"
(*Music by* Noel Gay. *Lyrics by* Donovan Parsons.)
"Friendly Ghosts"
(*Music by* Richard Addinsell. *Lyrics by* Rowland Leigh.)
"Silly Little Hill"
J. Matthews, H. Lytton, Jr.
(*Music by* Richard Addinsell. *Lyrics by* Rowland Leigh.)]

Scene 18

Hydroplaning[90]
G. Moran, C. Mack

Scene 19

"Who Do You Love?"
C. Kaley, J. Matthews
(*Music by* Hugo Frey, Max Rich. *Lyrics by* Raymond Klages.)

The Rain of Perfume and The Vanities Beauties.
(*Costumes by* Vanity Fair Costume Co.)

Scene 20

The Rain of Perfume

Scene 21

In the McAndrew's House[91]
James McAndrew: H. Mundin. *Maggie*, his wife: Mrs. Macbeth. *Jeannie*, their daughter: S. Wilshin.

Scene 22

A Gala Night at Galashiels[92]
Angus MacTowle, proprietor of Galashiels Frolics: A. Macbeth. *Bella*, his daughter: H. Wynne. *Weelum MacIntosh*, the band: G. Sherry. *Hamish MacGilliway*: H. Lytton, Jr. *Mrs. MacGilliway*: S. Wilshin. *Willie MacGilliway*: H. Warrender. *Jessie MacGilliway*: J. Williams. *Sandy Tosh*: C. Kaley. *Effie Tosh*: D. Croyle. *Mrs. Stevens*: B. Stanton. *Miss Stevens*: D. Whitney.

Scene 23

The Tree of Knowledge
Cecil: J. Tannen. *Papa*: N. Frescott.

Scene 24

"Mirrors of the Ages"
C. Kaley
Greece: J. LaKota. *Troy*: G. Philbin. *Carthage*: M. Candee, C. Stamm, D. Gould. *Babylon*: B. Klipp. *Rome*: E. Wenzel. *Pompeii*: I. Philbin.

Scene 25

In the Mirror of Vanities
A. Lang, F. Ward, R. Royce, B. Meredith, E. French, J. Murray, M. Hiller, A. Adaire, L. Byrne, R. Martin
(*Costumes by* Katherine Arlington, Inc.)

Scene 26

The Glass Finale: "All Is Vanity"
74 Visions of Vanities
(Entire scene is made of Mosaic Glass, executed by Alex Hall, conceived by Bernard Lohmuller. *Costumes by* Brooks Costume Co., from designs of Charles LeMaire.)

ACT 2

Scene 1

Bells in the Belfry
The Foster Girls
"In the Twilight" (Waltz)
(*Costumes by* Booth Willoughby.)

Scene 2

The Sculptor: J. Tannen. *The Model*: B. Clay.

Scene 3

The Last Cabby: "When the Hansom Cabs Was Lined Up on the Ranks"[93]
(*Music by* Noel Gay. *Lyrics by* Donovan Parsons.)
Sam: G. Sherry. *First Taximan*: C. Kaley. *Second Taximan*: H. Warrender. *Bill*: H. Lytton, Jr. *Blinkers*: H. Mundin.

Scene 4

"Hugs and Kisses"
H. Lytton, J. Matthews
(*Music by* Louis Alter. *Lyrics by* Raymond Klages.)
Specialty Dance
K. Spangler

Scene 5

Kay Spangler and Dorothy Croyle announce

Scene 6

"The Grand Guignol"
The Professor: A. Macbeth. *The Girl*: J. Matthews. *Godfrey*: H. Lytton, Jr. *A Police Inspector*: H. Mundin. *Policemen*: G. Sherry, C. Kaley, F. Knight.

Scene 7

Phyllis Loft, Kay Spangler, Frances Norton and Dorothy Croyle announce

---

[83]Dropped during the New York run.
[84]Dropped during the New York run.
[85]Dropped during the New York run.
[86]Dropped during the New York run.
[87]Dropped during the New York run.
[88]Dropped during the New York run.
[89]Dropped during the New York run.
[90]Dropped during the New York run.

---

[91]Dropped during the New York run.
[92]Dropped during the New York run.
[93]Dropped during the New York run.

Scene 8

"Lucia de Lammermoor"[94] [Burlesque of the opera by Gaetano Donizetti.]

In the Opera: J. Williams, H. Wynne, H. Lytton, Jr., G. Sherry, H. Warrender, P. Adair.

Scene 9

Marjorie Whitney, Dorothy Croyle, Kay Spangler, Phyllis Loft, Frances Norton, Marjorie Gilbert announce

Scene 10

The Ballet of the Lost Collar-Button[95]

Lord Seaworthy: H. Mundin. *Lady Seaworthy*: J. Matthews. *The Mother-in-Law*: Mrs. Macbeth. *The Father-in-Law*: G. Sherry. *The Housekeeper*: S. Wilshin. *Carter*, a manservant: C. Kaley. *A Taxi Driver*: H. Lytton, Jr. *The Parlormaid*: H. Wynne. *The Maids*: A. Ogelvie, N. Sorel. *First Footman*: H. Warrender. *Second Footman*: P. Adair.

Scene 11

Snowballs

20 Foster Girls

Scene 12

Locomotive No. 13 (Two Black Crows on the Locomotive)

G. Moran, C. Mack

Scene 13

"Climbing Up the Ladder of Love"

J. Matthews, assisted by C. Kaley and a Violin
(*Music by* Jesse Greer. *Lyrics by* Raymond Klages.)

Dance

Vanities Girls, M. Whitney, Foster Girls

Scene 14

Atmospherics

The Listener In: G. Sherry. *New York Announcing*: H. Warrender. *Dr. Porus Plaster*: H. Lytton, Jr. *Major Knapsack*: A. Macbeth. *Mr. Cable*: H. Mundin.

Scene 15

The Gates of Madrid

Scene 16

Escalera Blanca[96]

D. Knapp, C. Kaley, I. Edwards

Scene 17

Grand Finale

(Entire Company)

1927.03

LACE PETTICOAT

A Musical Comedy of Old New Orleans in Two Acts, 4 Scenes. Book by Stewart St. Clair. Music by Emil Gerstenberger and Carle Carlton. Lyrics by Howard Johnson. Staged by Carl Carlton. Dances by J. J. Hughes. Set design by Carle Carlton. Costumes designed by Raymond Tomlinson. Orchestra under the direction of Leon Rosebrook. Produced by Carle Carlton. Opened 4 January 1927 at the Forrest Theatre and closed 15 January 1927 after 15 performances.

CAST (in order of appearance): *Flower Girls (2)*: *Marie*: Erma Chase. *Lisette*: Ruth Matlock. *Raymond DeLaLange*, a Creole Don Juan: LUIS ALBERNI. *His Friends (2)*: *Jules*: Gerald Moore. *Louis*: Cullen Clewis. *Mammy Dinah*, of the Little Bayou Coffee House: Mercedes Gilbert. *Professor Bonalli*, a Fakir: JAMES C. MORTON. *Bozo*, His Assistant: Joseph Spree. *Leontine Pantard*, a Rich Creole Widow: STELLA MAYHEW. *Clarice*, Her Niece: Elcie Peck. *Dominic Deni Del aBouregard de Grand Pre*: Richard Powell. *Renita*, of the Little Bayou Coffee House: VIVIAN HART. *Paul Joscelyn*, an Ensign of the U.S. Navy: TOM BURKE. *Pere Modeste*, a Music Master: A. S. Byron.

Specialty Dancers: ADELAIDE and HUGHES. *Specialty Girls*: Veatrice Verle, Theresa Miller, Thelma Rankin, Gay LaSalle, Regina Beck, Erma Chase, Betty Dion, Marjorie Brown. *Dancing Girls*: Luva Stratton, Elizabeth Ussher, Mary Jane Smith, Gina Christie, Ruth Matlock, Charlotte Beverly, Rita Crane, Vacinia Ice. *Dancing Boys*: Murray Morrissey, John Pierce, Cullen Clewis, George Crouth, Don DeFrancis, Gerald Moore, Chuck Connors, Jr. *Singing Ensemble*: Betty Schafer, Elva Trede, Marie Rider, Marion Williams, Yukona Cameron, Aline Loeb, Nancy Trevelyn, Alice Francis. Don DeFrancis, George Couch, Murray Morrissey, John Pierce, Cullen Clewis, Gerald Moore, Chuck Connors, Jr., Carl Meldorf. *Bachelor Four*: Hal Clovis,

Stanley McCelland, Emil Coti, Fred Wilson. *Male Chorus*: John Fredericks, John Koroloff, Michael Miroshnik, Michael Vorobieff, Vsevolod Anissimo, Misail Speransky, Zacary Carr, Filemo Lavaly, John Krivkosenko, Lew Jatzine, Eugene Gnotow.

Act 1: The Flower Market, outside the Little Bayou Coffee House in Old New Orleans, in the French Creole Quarter.

Act 2, Scene 1: Exterior of the Old Cathedral. *Scene 2*: Interior of the Old Cathedral. *Scene 3*: Mardi Gras.

ACT 1

Opening Chorus

Entire Ensemble

"Watch the Birdies"

J. C. Morton

"Renita Reinette"

V. Hart

"Southwind Is Calling"

T. Burke, V. Hart

"Boy in the Blue Uniform"

V. Hart

"Engagement Ring"

V. Hart, T. Burke
(*Music by* Emil Gerstenberger.)

"Dear, Dear Departed"

S. Mayhew, R. Powell, J. C. Morton

"Creole Crawl"

Adelaide and Hughes, Ensemble

"(Little) Lace Petticoat"

V. Hart, Adelaide
(*Music by* Emil Gerstenberger. *Lyrics by* Carle Carlton.)

Finale

ACT 2

Scene 1

"Entre"

Ensemble

"Skeleton Ghost"

Ensemble

"Have You Forgotten?"

T. Burke

"Recitative" (trio)

V. Hart, T. Burke, L. Alberni

Scene 2

"The Rose Aria"

V. Hart, E. Peck, T. Burke, Ensemble

Scene 3

"Carnival of Roses"

Ensemble

Tango

Adelaide and Hughes

"The Heart Is Free"

V. Hart

Finale

1927.04

PIGGY

A Musical Comedy in Two Acts, 6 Scenes[97]. Book by Alfred Jackson and Daniel Kussel, based on the musical play "The Rich Mr. Hoggenheimer"[98] (with book and lyrics) by Harry B. Smith and (music by) Ludwig Engländer. Music by Cliff Friend. Lyrics by Lew Brown. Staged by William B. Friedlander. Dances staged by John Boyle. Settings by John Wenger. Costumes designed by Hugh Willoughby. Orchestra under the direction of Louis Gress. Produced by William B. Friedlander, Inc. Opened 11 January

---

[94]Dropped during the New York run.

[95]Dropped during the New York run.

[96]At first no performers were credited with this number. Eight weeks into the run the performance credits first appear.

---

[97]The show's title was changed to I TOLD YOU SO in the third week of the run.

[98]The popular character of Mr. Hoggenheimer originated with the English musical THE GIRL FROM KAY'S (2 November 1903, Herald Square); THE RICH MR. HOGGENHEIMER (22 October 1906, Wallack's Theatre) was an American sequel conceived as a vehicle for Sam Bernard.

1927 at the Royale Theatre, moved 7 February 1927 to Chanin's 46th Street Theatre and closed 19 March 1927 after 79 performances.

CAST (in order of appearance): *Butler*: James Jolley. *Mrs. Hoggenheimer*: LOTTA LINTHICUM. *Honorable Cecil Puffington*: Harry McNaughton. *Bobby Hunter*: BROOKE JOHNS. *Signor Chali-oppin*: Rodolpho Badaloni. *Monsieur Hohuho*: Eddie Conrad. *Suzanne Fair*: Wanda Lyon. *Piggy Hoggenheimer*: SAM BERNARD. *Lord Tyrone*: BERESFORD LOVETT. *Second Man*: Paul Winkopp. *Valet*: Dan Corbett. *Deck Steward*: John Crone. *Guy Hoggenheimer*: PAUL FRAWLEY. *Betty Marshall*: MARION MARSCHANTE. *Lady Mildred Vane*: GLADYS BAXTER. *Maid*: Rosalind Bernard. *Mr. Shapiro*: John Cronin. *Edna*: Joan Carter-Waddell. *Inspector*: James Jolley.

Brooke Johns' All-American Collegians: George Freeman, Frank Flynn, Jack Newlon, Jack Ford, Jack Mead, Norman Lanning. *American Girls*: Jerry Dryden, Clare Carroll, Sydelle Bry, Anita Pam, Edith Davis, Constance McKenzie, Billie Blake, Mabel Hill, Isabel O'Dell, Lillian Clark, Ruth Grant, Norine Bogan, Ruth Grady, Betty Wright, Jr., Hester Bailey, Louise Barrett. *English Girls*: Louise McCoy, Ruth Stickney, Elizabeth Anderson, Karin Keith, Bee Goldyn, Vera Braund, Wilma Novak, Dorothy Duncan, Natalia Lord, Wilma Roelofsma, Ethelyna Koski, Peggy Shannon, Helen Warner, Marcelle Miller, Guerida Crawford, Bobby Campbell, Polly Ray. *Gentlemen of the Ensemble*: Tom Riley, Jimmie Ormonde, Louis Bradley, George Frierson, William Stewart, Al Wilde, Willie Hale, John Meehan, Leon Alton.

Act 1, Scene 1: A Room in Hoggenheimer's London Home. *Scene 2*: A Quay at Southampton, England. *Scene 3*: Promenade Deck of an Ocean Liner. Mid-ocean. *Scene 4*: On another deck in sight of New York. *Scene 5*: A Dock in New York.

Act 2: The Garden of an Estate at Great Neck, Long Island.

ACT 1

"How D'You Do?" (Opening)
English Girls, Boys
"Follow Through"
B. Johns, Girls
"(I Wanna Go) Voom Voom Voo"
B. Johns, G. Montgomery, G. Clifford, Ensemble
"It's Easy to Say Hello"
Ensemble
"All Decked Out"
B. Johns, G. Montgomery, G. Clifford, Ensemble
"One of Those Windows"
B. Johns, Collegians
"Little Bit of Atmosphere"[99]
G. Baxter, B. Johns, Ensemble
"Didn't It Happen?"
S. Bernard
"(I'll Love You) Just the Same"
P. Frawley, M. Marschante
"Emigrants' Song"
Girls
Finale
Company

ACT 2

"Do It For Charity" (Opening)
Girls
Specialty
B. Johns, Collegians
"It Just Had to Happen"
P. Frawley, M. Marschante
"(Let's Stroll Along and Sing a) Song of Love"
B. Johns, M. Marschante
"Ding Dong Bell" (Ding Dong Dell)
P. Frawley, M. Marschante, Ensemble
Finale
Entire Company

1927.05   BYE BYE BONNIE

A Musical Bonbon (Comedy) in Two Acts, 4 Scenes. Book by Louis Simon and Bide Dudley. Music by Albert Von Tilzer. Lyrics by Neville Fleeson. Book directed by Edgar MacGregor. Dances and ensembles staged by Earl Lindsay. Settings by Karl O. Amend. Costumes designed by Robert

---

[99]Two songs were published with similar titles: "I Need a Little Bit, You Need a Little Bit" and "A Little Change of Atmosphere."

Stevenson. Orchestra under the direction of Milton Schwarzwald. Orchestrations by Maurice dePackh and Hilding Anderson. Produced by L. Lawrence Weber. Opened 13 January 1927 at the Ritz Theatre, moved 14 March 1927 to the Cosmopolitan Theatre and closed 30 April 1927 after 125 performances.

CAST (in order of appearance): *Flossie*: Laine Blaire. *Charles Phillips*: Georgie Hale. *Mrs. Noah Z. Shrivell*: Mabel Acker. *John Van Buren*: Douglas Wood. *Virginia Shrivell*: LOTTICE HOWELL. *Richard Van Buren*: JOHN BYAM. *Ted Williams*: RUDOLPH CAMERON. *Dottie*: DOROTHY VAN ALST. *Margie*: Margie Royce. *Babs*: Blanche Krebs. *Flo*: Florence Parker. (*Loring*: Dorothy Loring Humphreys.[100]) *Bonnie Quinlin*: DOROTHY BURGESS. *Noah Z. Shrivell*: LOUIS SIMON. *Bill Briggins*: Charles Henderson. *Alice*: Sue Saunders. *Jefferson Sparks*: Paul Huber. *Sanford Alden*: Cecil Owen. *"Butch" Hogan*: WILLIAM FRAWLEY. *Warden*: Cecil Owen. *Keeper*: Charles Henderson. *"Mugsie"*: Bernard Cavanaugh. *Ruby*: RUBY KEELER. *Simpson*: John Clemson. *At the Pianos*: Alan Moran, Walter Keldkamp.

Ladies of the Ensemble: Rose Adaire, Dorothy Brown, Sybil Bursk, Norma Butler, Mary Carlton, Elsie Carrol, Dorothy Chilton, Thelma Fenton, Helen McLaughlin, Ruth Penery, Evelyn Shea, Thelma Temple. *Gentlemen of the Ensemble*: Elmer Berl, Dan Berrigan, Arthur Budd, Walter Carson, Charles J. Dane, Arthur LaFrack, Dick Givens, Raymond Hall, Billy McKay, William Neely, Frank Sherlock, Jr., Charles Siler, Walter Wardell.

Act 1: The Outer Office of Shrivell Soft Soap Company, Shrivelton, New Jersey. An afternoon in June.

Act 2, Scene 1: The Warden's Office, Welfare Island,. Several days later. *Scene 2*: Exterior of Shrivell's Home. Thirty days later. *Scene 3*: Drawing Room of Shrivell's Home. Later that night.

ACT 1[101]

"Have You Used Soft Soap?"
G. Hale, Ensemble
"Promise Not to Stand Me Up Again"
L. Blaire, G. Hale
"Love Is Like a Blushing Rose"[102]
L. Howell, J. Byam
"Out of Town Buyers"
R. Cameron, D. Van Alst, M. Royce, F. Parker, B. Krebs, Ensemble
Specialty
M. Royce
"You and I Love You and Me"
D. Burgess, R. Cameron, The Bonnie Octette, Ensemble
"(Just) 'Cross the River from Queens"
R. Cameron, L. Simon, M. Acker, Ensemble
"Bye, Bye, Bonnie"
D. Burgess, Ensemble
Specialty
D. Van Alst, G. Hale
Finale
Company

ACT 2[103]

"I Like to Make It Cozy"
C. Owen, W. Frawley, Convicts

---

[100]Miss Humphreys' credit appears in the song list throughout the run, but appears to have been left out of the cast list at the start of the New York run.
[101]Revised as a vehicle for Fritzi Scheff for national tour the following season. Added to the show were new songs with *Lyrics by* A. Seymour Brown:
"There's a Woman Behind Every Man" (Act 1, after "Out of Town Buyers")
Fritzi Scheff (Mrs. Noah Z. Shrivell), Ensemble
"My Baby That' 'Ate Me" (Act 2, after "Lovin' Off My Mind")
Frances White (Bonnie)
"Anyone Who Do's That Can't Be So Dumb" (follows above)
F. White
(*Lyrics by* Seymour Brown.)
"(That) September Night" (follows above)
F. Scheff, Boys
(*Lyrics by* Seymour Brown.)
[102]Dropped after the opening.
[103]Added briefly during the run, then withdrawn:
"Every Day" (Act 2, after "Lovin' Off My Mind")
The Giersdorf Sisters

"Toodle-Oo"
R. Cameron, Ensemble
Specialty
L. Blaire
"When You Get to Congress'
J. Byam, L. Simon, Junior Voters
"In My Arms Again"[104]
L. Howell, J. Byam
"Lovin' Off My Mind"
G. Hale, L. Blaire, D. Humphreys, D. Van Alst, F. Parker, B. Krebs
Specialties
D. Humphreys, G. Hale
Tap Dance
R. Keeler
"Look in Your Engagement Book"
D. Burgess, Ensemble
Specialty
D. Van Alst, G. Hale
"Starlight"
L. Howell
"Tampico Tap"
L. Blaire, R. Keeler, Tampico Tappers
Specialty
R. Keeler
Finale
Company

1927.06

ROSE-MARIE

A Revival of the Musical Play in Two Acts[105]. Book and lyrics by Otto Harbach and Oscar Hammerstein II. Music by Rudolph Friml and Herbert Stothart. Staged by Paul Dickey. Supervised by Arthur Hammerstein. Produced by Arthur Hammerstein. Opened 24 January 1927 at the Century Theatre and closed 5 March 1927 after 48 performances.

CAST (in order of appearance): *Sergeant Malone*: CHARLES MEAKINS. *Lady Jane*: Peggy Pates. *Black Eagle*: NEIL MOORE. *Edward Hawley*: JAMES MOORE. *Emile La Flamme*: Frank Harrington. *Wandla*: GRACE WELLS. *Hardboiled Herman*: HOUSTON RICHARDS. *Jim Kenyon*: PAUL DONAH. *Rose-Marie La Flamme*: ETHEL LOUISE WRIGHT. *Ethel Brander*: Karyl Kunkel.

Gentlemen of the Ensemble: Arthur Barry, William Wilder, Clifford Wilson, Arnold Thompson, Russell Griswold, William Richards, Al Monty, Fred DeVeau, Jay C. McCormack, Thomas Rice, Ernest Ehler, Frank Grinnell, Leon Kartavey, Chester Bennett. *Ladies of the Ensemble*: Yvonne Destin, Patsey Watkins, Dorothea Phelan, Ellen Nivay, Betty Jordan, Tosca Querze, Hazel Warmsley, Lea Lake, Cherry Hodgson, Zana Gray, Marie Lelloz, Dorothea Clegg, Marie Verba, Bellie Delmar, Grace Gretchen Lynch, Eve Lynne, Edwina Collum, Lydia Langdon, True Grant, Pirrko Ahlquist, Lollie Madigan, Sue King, Jean Woods, Barbara Austin, Marjorie Talcott, Edna Costello, Marguerite Thompson, Helene McGlynn, Violet McKinley, Mary Carney, Maybel Martin, Dorothy Forbes, Ann Jurika, Marjorie Stewart, Edna Stewart, Nellie Gurney.

1927.07

YOURS TRULY

A Musical Play in Two Acts, 6 Scenes. Book by Clyde North. Music by Raymond Hubbell. Lyrics by Anne Caldwell. Book staged by Paul Dickey. Dances arranged by Ralph Reader. John Tiller Girls' Dances arranged by Mary Read. Scenery by Joseph Urban. Costumes designed by Mabel E. Johnston. Orchestra under the direction of Raymond Hubbell. Entire production staged under the personal direction of Gene Buck. Produced by Gene Buck. Opened 25 January 1927 at the Sam S. Shubert Theatre and closed 14 May 1927 after 127 performances.

---

[104]Dropped after the opening.
[105]Originally produced 2 September 1924 at the Imperial Theatre for 557 performances. For Synopsis of Scenes and Musical Numbers, see original 1924 production. Musical direction uncredited. Choreography, though uncredited, most likely recreated the original by David Bennett; settings, costumes, were also uncredited, but most likely were copies of the Broadway originals by Frank E. Gates, E. A. Morange (settings), Charles LeMaire (costumes).

CAST (in order of appearance): *Shuffling Bill*: JACK SQUIRES. *Joey Ling*, Chang's body servant: Jack Stanley. *Mac*, one of the 'Finest': John Kearney. *Phil*, the Guide: David Herblin. *Mike*, a taxi driver: Edgar Nelson. *Diana*: IRENE DUNNE. *J. P. Stillwell*, a Wall Street financier: THEODORE BABCOCK. *Helen*, a chum of Mary's: Eleanor Terry. *Truly*, from nowhere in particular: LEON ERROL. *Bonzolino*, transplanted from sunny Italy: Vic Casmore. *Ruth*, from uptown: Audrey Berry. *Scats*, from downtown: Ina Williams. *Mary Stillwell*: MARION HARRIS. *Bandit*, a 'stick-up' man: David Herblin. *Dinty Moore* of the 'Bowery': Harry Kelly. *Chang*, proprietor of the 'Open Door Night Club': GREEK EVANS. *Who's This*: Geneva Mitchell. *What Her Name*: Anastasia Reilly. *A Bowery Rose*: Hilda Ferguson. *Tillie Dupont*, a shop girl: Lotta Fanning. *Minnie Fletcher*: Joy Sutphen. *Old 'Pop'*: Earl Van Horn. *Cynthia Jones*, a country girl: Inez Van Horn. *Tom*, a waiter at Dinty Moore's: Harry Long. *Abe Levy*, a peddler: Ronald Wyse. *Wing Sing*, a laundryman: Charles Wheeler. *Paquita*, an Italian girl: Aida DeMaris. *Jimmie*, a newsboy: Jimmie McCallion. *Herbert*, another newsboy: Herbert Schwartz. *Chinese Girls*: Peggy Frawley, Eleanor Sweet, Dolly Pross.

Miss Longstreet: Bobby Story. *Miss Nembury*: Eunice Hall. *Miss Maywood*: Marge Lafayette. *Miss Stuyvesant*: Adele Smith. *Miss Rhinelander*: Ila Hopkins. *Miss Blydenburgh*: Beatrice Hughes. *Miss Glendening*: Muriel Manners. *Miss Wadsworth*: Olga Brounoff. *Miss Buckminster*: Lelia McGuire. *Miss Fairweather*: Katherien Sacker. *Miss Northcliffe*: Edith Maeborne. *Miss Matteson*: Joy Sutphen. *Miss Tillinghast*: Lotta Fanning. *Miss Southworth*: Evelyn Lawrence.

The John Tiller Girls: Rene Todd, Cora Neary, Alice Pitman, Marie Webster, Edna McCallum, Louis Gillette, Olive Hollingshead, Winnie Hollingshead, Frances Lunn, Marjory Griffiths, Edith Bennett, Connie Clements, Bella Pilling, Dolly Faulkner, Millie Cox, Sadie Hudson. *Dancing Girls*: Dorothy Brown, Agnes Frawley, Marta Keyes, Peggy Frawley, Emilie Marceau, Gladys Keck, Lily Smart, Juliet Morena, Georgie Moore, Peggy O'Connor, Elizabeth Oldfield, Eleanor Sweet, Mary Williams, Beverly Maude, Kay Stafford, Eve Sinclair, Aida DeMaris, Mary McGowan, Dolly Pross. *Gentlemen*: Ray Justice, Thomas Green, Charles Perry, Jack Rogers, Frank Callahna, Preston Lewis, Irving Jackson, Robert Rachford, Ronald Wyse, Donald Catlin, James Beattie, Edwin Young, Leo Williams, Charles Wheeler, Lawrence Arcuri, Paul Wilsox, Harry Long.

Act 1: Mission Square, New York City.

Act 2, Scene 1: A Garden on the Estate of J. P. Stillwell. *Scene 2*: Street Back of Dinty Moore's. *Scene 3*: Interior of The Mission. *Scene 4*: Underneath Dinty Moore's. *Scene 5*: Chang's 'Open Door Night Club.'

ACT 1
Opening
"Follow the Guide"
D. Herblin, Ensemble
"Mayfair"
I. Dunne, Showgirls
"Shufflin' Bill"
J. Squires, G. Mitchell, A. Reilly, Tiller Girls, Ensemble
"Look at the World and Smile"
M. Harris, J. McCallion, Ensemble
"Somebody Else"
M. Harris, J. Squires
"The Gunman"[106]
L. Errol
Entrance (of) Chinese Girls, Show Girls
"The Lotus Flower"
G. Evans, M. Harris
"Quit Kiddin'"
I. Williams, J. Kearney, G. Mitchell, A. Reilly, Tiller Girls, Ensemble
Finale
Principals, Ensemble
ACT 2
"Mary Has a Little Fair"
Ensemble
"Googly Gogly Goos" (Opening)
Tiller Girls
"Don't Shake My Tree"
L. Errol, I. Williams, G. Mitchell, A. Reilly, Ensemble
"I Want a Pal"
I. Dunne, Male Ensemble
"Yours Truly"
M. Harris, J. Squires, Ensemble
Specialty
Tiller Girls

---

[106]Dropped during the run.

"Jade"
G. Evans

"Open Door Club" (Opening)

"Four Aristocrats"[107] (Specialty)

Dance[108]
H. Ferguson

Skaters (Specialty)
I. Van Horn, E. Van Horn

"High Yaller" (Hoffin Number)
G. Mitchell, A. Reilly, Ensemble

"Dawn of Dreams"
G. Evans

Specialty
Tiller Girls

Finale
Company

1927.08   RIO RITA

A Musical Comedy in Two Acts, 6 Scenes. Book by Guy Bolton and Fred Thompson. Music by Harry Tierney. Lyrics by Joseph McCarthy. Book staged by John Harwood. Dances staged by Sammy Lee. Dances of Albertina Rasch Girls staged by Albertina Rasch. Settings designed by Joseph Urban. Costumes designed by John W. Harkrider. Musical director, Oscar Bradley. Orchestrations arranged by Frank Parry. Entire production staged under the personal direction of Florenz Ziegfeld. Produced by Florenz Ziegfeld. Opened 2 February 1927 at the Ziegfeld Theatre, moved 26 December 1927 to the Lyric Theatre, moved 12 March 1928 to the Majestic Theatre, and closed 7 April 1928 after 494 performances.

CAST (in order of appearance): *El Patron*: Juan Villasana. *Reporter*: Al Clair. *Roberto Ferguson*, Rita's brother: WALTER PETRIE. *Carmen*: HELEN C. CLIVE. *Ed Lovett*, a lawyer: ROBERT WOOLSEY. *Grim Gomez*, a bad man: Fred Dalton. *General Enrique Joselito Esteban*: VINCENT SERRANO. *His Friends (3)*: *Raquel*: Gladys Glad. *Conchita*: Marion Benda. *Juanita*: Dorothy Wegman. *Lolita*: Peggy Blake. *Margarita*: Myrna Darby. *Santiago*, a street musician: Kay English. *Rio Rita*: ETHELIND TERRY. *Chick Bean*: BERT WHEELER. *Dolly*, a cabaret girl: ADA-MAY. *Jim*: J. HAROLD MURRAY. *Sergeant McGinn* of the Texas Rangers: Harry Ratcliffe. *Sergeant Wilkins* of the Texas Rangers: Donald Douglas. *Davalos*, a bandit: ALF. P. JAMES. *Escamillo*, a dancer: Pedro Rubin. *Herminia*: Collette. *Katie Bean*, Chick's first wife: NOEL FRANCIS. *Montezuma's Daughter*: Katherine Burke. *At the Piano*: Constance Mering, Muriel Pollock.

The Gringitas—The Cabaret Girls: Naomi Johnson, Peggy Cornell, Elsie Behrens, Nondas Wayne, Virginia Biddle, Kay English, Marion Strasmick, Ivanelle Ladd. *Albertina Rasch Dancers*: Mollie Peck, Florence Miller, Portia Grafton, Rita Pischel, Naomi de Musie, Josephine Hayes, Helen Derby, Betty McHugh, Franciska Mueller, Vivian Morgan, Jennie Dolova, Margaret Godsworthy, Gladys Murphy, Elma Bayer, Janet Flynn, Harriet Hughes. *Ladies of the Ensemble*: Marion Benda, Myrna Darby, Agatha DeBussy, Elaine Field, Yvonne Hughes, Helene Gardner, Gladys Glad, Camille, Madeline Sheldon, Rosemary Wallace, Dorothy Wegmann, Amy West, Peggy Udell, Martha Ann, Malba Alter, Jean Crittenden, Dorothy Dickerson, Theresa Hyle, Mary Alter, Valerie Lennox, Louise Richardson, Maxine Wells, Philomena Yvsocka, Avis Adaire, Mabel Baade, Elsie Behrens, Virginia Biddle, Peggy Cornell, Audrey Dale, Kay English, Ann Hardman, Mignon Hawkes, Ivanelle Ladd, Lavergne Lambert, Mildred Lunnay, Cookie Lunsford, Naomi Johnson, Lottie Marcy, Marjorie May Martin, Frances Mildern, Alma Moore, Margaret Purple, Rosemary Ryder, Marion Strasmick, Lillian Shields, Norma Taylor, Florence Ware, Clarentine Wayne, Nondas Wayne, Marion Wilson, Jean Wayne, Bernice Varden, Dorothy Patterson, Pauline Bartlett, Ann Woods, Dorothy May, Margie Baily, Anita Banton, Suzanne Conroy, Carol Bergman. *Gentlemen of the Ensemble*: Earl Marvin, Lucien Farland, Jack Spinelly, Robert Mathews, Alfred Arnold, Charles A. McClelland, Joseph Rogers, Jack Phillips, Walter Palm, John Werner, Leo Nash, Morris Tepper, Charles Holly, Al Small, Edward Theopold, George Butler, M. Zaharia, Richard Vernon, Bill Otero, Raymond Toben, Rass Erickson, Douglas Steade, Frank Zolt, Jack Thomson, Owen Hervey, Henry Nelthropp, A. Safanow. *The Original Central American Marimba Band*: Señores Carlos Estrada, Francisco Torres, Jose Betancourt, Victor Bragamonte, Gabriel Herrera, Antonio Arreola, Vincente Murtado. *The South American Troubadours*: Señores Alcides Briseno, George Anez, Manuel Valdespino.

Act 1, Scene 1: The Mesa Francisca. *Scene 2*: A Mexican Rendezvous. *Scene 3*: General Esteban's Patio.

Act 2, Scene 1: A Floating Cabaret on the Rio Grande. *Scene 2*: On the Texas Side. *Scene 3*: A Triple Moonlight Wedding. Three weeks later.

---

[107]Dropped during the run.
[108]Dropped during the run.

ACT 1

Scene 1

"Siesta Time (in San Lucar)" (Opening)
(Chorus)

The Jingle Dance; The Tambourine Dance
P. Rubin, Albertina Rasch Girls

"The Best Little Lover in Town"
R. Woolsey

Eight Little Gringitas (Dance)
Gringitas

"Sweethearts"/

"River Song"
E. Terry, Ensemble

"Are You There?"
Ada-May, B. Wheeler

"Rio Rita"
J. H. Murray, E. Terry

"March of the Rangers" (The Rangers' Song)
J. H. Murray, H. Ratcliffe, D. Douglas, Rangers

Scene 3

"The Spanish Shawl"
H. Clive, Serenaders

"The Charra Dance"
P. Rubin, Albertina Rasch Dancers

"The Kinkajou"
Ada-May, Ensemble

"If You're in Love, You'll Waltz"
E. Terry, J. H. Murray

Moonlight Ballet
Albertina Rasch Dancers

"Out on the Loose"
B. Wheeler, Glorified Girls, Dancing Girls, Albertina Rasch Dancers

Finale
(Entire Company)

ACT 2

Scene 1

The Floating Cabaret:

The Pirates ("Yo Ho and a Bottle of Rum")
Ziegfeld Dancers

Dance
A. Clair

The Johnnies
Ziegfeld Dancers

Jazz Toe Dance
Collette

Topical Jingles
Ada-May

Black and White (Ballet)
Albertina Rasch Dancers

"Following the Sun Around"
J. H. Murray

"I Can Speak Español"
Ada-May, R. Woolsey

"Montezuma's Daughter" (Dance)
E. Terry, Albertina Rasch Dancers
Aztec Goddesses: *Palomita*: M. Benda. *Mariposita*: G. Glad. *Margarita*: M. Darby. *Manzanita*: D. Wegman. *Zinzontle*: A. West. *Esperanza*: H. Gardner. *Pepita*: Y. Hughes. *Marina*: A. DeBussey. *Montezuma's Daughter*: K. Burke.

"The Jumping Bean"
Ada-May, Ziegfeld Dancers, Albertina Rasch Dancers

Scene 2

"Moonshine"
B. Wheeler

Scene 3

The Triple Moonlight Wedding at Jim's Home (Finale)
N. Francis, R. Woolsey, Ada-May, B. Wheeler, E. Terry, J. H. Murray, Entire Company

1927.09 JUDY

A Musical Comedy in Two Acts, 6 Scenes. Book by Mark Swan, based on his play 'Judy Drops In.' Music by Charles Rosoff. Lyrics by Leo Robin. Book staged by John Hayden. Dances and ensembles staged by Bobby Connolly. Costumes designed by Hugh Willoughby. Scenery designed by P. Dodd Ackerman. Orchestra under the direction of Jay Gorney. Orchestrations by Maurice dePackh. Produced by John Henry Mears. Opened 7 February 1927 at the Royale Theatre and closed 30 April 1927 after 96 performances.

CAST (in order of appearance): *Tom Stanton*: GEORGE MEEKER. *Dick Wetherbee*: EDWARD ALLEN. *Harry Danforth*: FRANK BEASTON. *Anita*: Magda Bennett. *Babette*: Laura Hamilton. *Jack Lethbridge*: CHARLES PURCELL. *Mrs. Maguire*: LIDA KANE. *Lucy Lethbridge*: Alice Mackenzie. *Florence*: ELIZABETH MEARS. *Dorothy*: Mary Lucas. *Judy Drummond*: QUEENIE SMITH. *Nathan Gridley*: James Seeley. *Mathew Lethbridge*: John T. Dwyer.

Specialty Dancers: Helen Ellfelt, Magda Bennett, Mary Lucas, Dorothy Casey, Ethel Guerard, Madelyn Eubanks, Elizabeth Mears, Eleanor Meeker, Diana Hunt, Ann Loomis, Margaret Litz, Mildred Lorrain, Georgie Tapps, Frank Cornell.

Act 1, Scene 1: The Rookery in Greenwich Village. A night in June. *Scene 2*: Cinderella Lane. The same night. *Scene 3*: The Rookery. The next morning.

Act 2, Scene 1: The New Rookery. Three months later. Afternoon. *Scene 2*: Cinderella Lane. *Scene 3*: The New Rookery. The same evening.

ACT 1
"Hobohemia"
G. Meeker, E. Allen, F. Beaston, Girls
"Hard To Get Along With"
E. Mears, G. Meeker, E. Allen, F. Beaston, Girls
"Looking for a Thrill"[109]
A. Mackenzie, G. Meeker, E. Allen, F. Beaston, Girls
Dance
E. Allen, E. Mears
"(Poor) Cinderella"
Q. Smith
"Six Little Cinderellas"
E. Mears, D. Casey, M. Lucas, D. Hunt, M. Eubanks, E. Guerard
"Pretty Little Stranger"
C. Purcell, Q. Smith
"One Baby"
E. Mears, F. Beaston, Girls
Specialty
H. Ellfelt
"Wear Your Sunday Smile"
Q. Smith, C. Purcell, Girls
Dance[110]
G. Tapps, D. Casey
Finale
ACT 2[111]
"What a Whale of a Difference a Woman Can Make"
L. Kane, C. Purcell, E. Mears, Girls
Specialty
A. Loomis
"Judy"
Q. Smith, C. Purcell, G. Meeker, E. Allen, F. Beaston, Girls
Reprise
Q. Smith
"When Gentlemen Grew Whiskers and Ladies Grew Old"
E. Mears, C. Purcell, G. Meeker, E. Allen, F. Beaston, E. Mears, A. Loomis, M. Litz, F. Cornell
Reprise
Q. Smith
"Curfew Shall Not Ring To-night"
G. Meeker, E. Allen, F. Beaston, Girls

Specialty
M. Lucas, M. Bennett
"Six Little Cinderellas" (reprise)
"Start Stompin'"
E. Allen, Girls
Specialty
D. Hunt, E. Allen
Reprise
Q. Smith
Finale
Entire Company

1927.10 POLLY OF HOLLYWOOD

A Super-Feature Musical Comedy in Two Reels (Acts), a Prologue and 14 Scenes. Music, lyrics, scenario, titles and inserts by Will Morrissey and Edmund Joseph. Staged by Will Morrissey. Dances and ensembles staged by Walter Brooks. Costumes designed by Paul Aimes. Orchestra under the direction of Gus Salzer. Produced by Harry L. Cort. Opened 21 February 1927 at the George M. Cohan Theatre and closed 12 March 1927 after 24 performances[112].

CAST (in order of appearance): *Polly*: MIDGIE MILLER. *Roderick*: William Friend. *Gambler*: Edward Gargan. *Sheriff*: Jerome Daly. *Pablo*: Hugh Kidder. *Valencia*: Bertee Beaumont. *Tom Dix*: DAVE FERGUSON. *Chick*: FRANKER WOODS. *Nelse*: EARLE S. DEWEY. *Driver*: John Agee. *Roberta*: MARGUERITE ZENDER. *Assistant Director*: WILLARD HALL. *Camera Man*: Matty Fain. *Property Man*: R. Luketas. *Greener*: ROBERT G. PITKIN. *Julie*: Alice Wood. *Irene*: Lillian Jordan. *Abe Stein*: Barney Ward. *Moe Stein*: Hugh Herbert. *Hymie Cohen*: Jacob Prank. *Typist*: Anna Mycue. *Dancers*: DEENORA and BERINOFF.

Prologue
MAIN TITLE
REL ONE—OPENING SHOT—BAR X RANCH
CLOSE UP OF POLLY 15 YEARS AGO
ACT 1
Scene 1
FADE-OUT
FADE-IN
Polly: M. Miller. *Roderick*: W. Friend.
Scene 2
CLOSE UP OF POLLY TODAY
SUB-TITLE—TEXAS
SECOND SHOT—BAR X RANCH
CAST OF CHARACTERS—CLOSE UP
Scene 3
LONE SHOT—FADE IN—SUNRISE
Gambler: E. Gargan. *Sheriff*: J. Daly.
MEDIUM FOREGROUND—WIDE ANGLE
Pablo: H. Kidder. *Valencia*: B. Beaumont. *Roderick*: W. Friend.
INSPIRATION MUSIC
"Midnight Daddy"
Valencia and Roderick
ARRIVAL OF BAD MAN
Tom Dix: D. Ferguson.
"Polly of Hollywood" (Title Song)
Male Septet
Bryson and Jones
COMEDY RELIEF—SUPER-SPEED
Chick: F. Woods. *Nelse*: E. S. Dewey.
IRISED DOWN
LONE SHOT—FULL SET—3-INCH LENS
ARRIVAL OF STAGE COACH
Driver: J. Agee. *Roderick*: W. Friend. *Roberta*: M. Zender.

---

[109]Dropped after the opening.
[110]Dropped after the opening.
[111]Added after opening to Act 2, after title song, before its reprise:
"When the One You Care For"
C. Purcell

---

[112]Settings uncredited.

MEDIUM FOREGROUND
   Assistant Director: W. Hall. *Camera Man*: M. Fain. *Property Man*: R. Luketas.

CLOSE-UP—GAUZED
   Greener: R. G. Pitkin.

(A BRIEF SCRIPT)
   Julie: A. Wood. *Irene*: L. Jordan. Cowgirls, Cowboys, Mexicans

ARRIVAL OF THE MAIL—INTRODUCING

HARDWARE HARMONY—CHARLES GUGLIERI

CUT

LAP DISSOLVE—NATURAL COLOR
   Polly: M. Miller.
   "Texas Stomp"
      M. Miller, Quartet, Ensemble

LOVE INTEREST—MUSICAL INTERPOLATION
   "Wanting You"
      M. Zender, W. Hall

DISSOLVE

Scene 4

MEDIUM CLOSE UP—OFF-CENTRE
   "Exploitation Number"

PERSONAL APPEARANCE
   Tom Dix: D. Ferguson. *Julie*: A. Wood. *Irene*: L Jordan.

Scene 5

LONG SHOT—PANCHROMATIC

FIESTA—PABLO'S HACIENDA
   Tango
      Deenova, Berinoff
   Recitation (with Gestures)
      T. Dix
   Tambourine Dance
      Lenora Eight High Steppers
   "A Lot of Bull (Broadway)" (Musical and in the Flesh)
      M. Miller, Ensemble

SHADOWGRAPH—PANTOMIME

ATMOSPHERIC ACT—SHARPSHOOTING

JOHN AGEE—MIDGIE MILLER

VITAPHONE

GRAND ENSEMBLE—THE DEPARTURE

Scene 6

INTIMATE TOUCH

ALZENA PRESENTS POLLY WITH NECESSARY EQUIPMENT
   Finale

ACT 2

Scene 1

REEL TWO—FIRST SHOT—STUDIO IN HOLLYWOOD

Atmosphere . . . . .An Essential
   R. Pitkin, Extras

Scene 2

CASTING OFFICE
   Billy: W. Hall. *Julie*: A. Wood. *Irene*: L. Jordan. Types, Extras, Bathing Girls.
   Introducing "Two Gag Men"

STOP—MOTION

POLLY'S TEST
   "Doubles"
      M. Miller, F. Woods, E. S. Dewey
      (Exposing a Picture Secret to Music)

LAP DISSOLVE—INTERIOR—CLOSE

FOREGROUND

Scene 3

   Meet the Owners
      Abe Stein: B. Ward. *Moe Stein*: H. Herbert. *Billy*: W. Hall. *Abraham Lincoln*: E. Gargan. *Greener*: R. G. Pitkin. *Hymie Cohen*: J. Prank. *Typist*: A. Mycue.

QUICK FADE

DOUBLE CLOSE UP OFF CENTRE

FADE

Scene 4

DOUBLE EXPOSURE—SOFT FOCUS
   "Mr. DeMille"
      E. Gargan, D. Ferguson
      Four Pages: V. Hart, M. Mitchel, C. Hackett, A. Brunner. *Biblical*: O. Skriner. *Chinese*: P. Tueset. *Gainsboro*: I. Evans. *Egyptian*: H. Newton. *Champagne*: M. Shaw. *Black Beauty*: B. Tueset. *Elizabethan*: C. Durham. *Melody*: M. Wallace. *Springtime*: A. Wallace. *American Beauty*: K. Hunter. *Spider*: E. Wright.
   Ballet
      E. Smith, H. Cambridge, G. Fay, R. Ramsey, D. Baker, M. Bligh, J. Horton, S. Newton
   Adagio
      Deenova, Berinoff
      The Bride: A. Mycue.

SLOWLY DISSOLVE

Scene 5
   "Advice to Movie Mad Maidens" (with music)
      M. Miller

Scene 6
   Variety
      R. G. Pitkin

Scene 7

FOREIGN ELEMENTS—EUROPEAN TAKE

WHERE POLLY, CHICK, NELSE MEET
   The Flying Martins
   "Company Madness"[113]
      M. Zender, W. Hall

FADE OUT

Scene 8

FOREIGN NEGATIVE—UNCENSORED
   Beau Geste
      D. Ferguson, F. Woods, E. S. Dewey, H. Kidder, R. G. Pitkin
   Drill
      Ensemble

SCREEN'S GREATEST TRIUMPH "DON JUAN"

AS IT SHOULD HAVE BEEN DIRECTED
   Barrymore: D. Ferguson
   Waltz
      Deenova, Berinoff
   "(A) New Kind of Rhythm"
      M. Jinny

Bryson and Jones

The Ever Famous and Sometime Funny

'Good Night'

1927.11   THE NEW YORKERS

A Musical Revue in Two Acts, 26 Scenes. Sketches by Jo Swerling. Lyrics by Henry Myers. Music by Arthur Schwartz, Edgar Fairchild and Charles M. Schwab. Entire production under the personal supervision of Milton Bender. Costumes designed by Margaret Daye. Settings designed by Connors & Bennett; futuristic scenery by Mischa Solotaroff. Orchestra under the direction of Alex Magnes. Produced by Henry Myers and Associates[114]. Opened 10 March 1927 at the Edyth Totten Theatre and closed 23 April 1927 after 52 performances.

CAST: Chester Clute, Tamara Drasin, Rima Swan, Mona Sorel, Florence Faun, Elaine Lauren, Lilyan Lauren, Dorothy Hoffman, Isabel Zehner, Milton Lorance, Sue Baxter, Dorothy Daye, Milt Collins, Harry Benson, Benn Trivers, Roberta Gale, Gay LaSalle, Wes. L. Robertson, Genevieve Ames, Charles Bender, Elaine Gerard, Myrtle Miller.

---

[113]Sheet music published under the title "Company Manners."
[114]Management taken over by Jay and J. F. Liebman in April 1927.

ACT 1[115]

Scene 1

The Front Page
Pro Bono Publico: C. Clute.

Scene 2

Off to a Clean Start: "99% Pure"
(*Music by* Arthur Schwartz.)
Bathers: T. Drasin, R. Swan, M. Sorel, F. Faun, E. Lauren, L. Lauren, D. Hoffman, I. Zehner. *Attaché*: M. Lorance.

Scene 3

"Burn 'Em Up"
S. Baxter, D. Daye, L. Lauren, E. Lauren, R. Swan, F. Faun
(*Music by* Edgar Fairchild.)

Scene 4

Give This Little Scene a Name[116]
Balieff: H. Benson. *Girl*: T. Drasin. *Boy*: B. Trivers.

Scene 5

"Nothing Left But Dreams"
(*Music by* Edgar Fairchild.)
The Dreamer: C. Bender. *Wong*: H. Benson. *The Vision*: E. Lauren.

Scene 6

Caesar But Cleopatra[117]
Scene: Cleopatra's tent on Caesar's battlefield.
Caesar: M. Collins. *But Cleopatra*: R. Gale. *Roman Soldiers*: T. N. Wainwright, H. C. Macklin, O. Mapes, B. Gun, P. Stuyvesant, R. Nellis, C. Peabody, L. deP. Marlingate, P. Noakes, G. G. Geralds, B. Hammersley, V. Sims, V. R. Clemens, G. Spelvin.

Scene 7

Song
T. Drasin

Scene 8

"Here Comes the Prince of Wales"
(*Music by* Arthur Schwartz.)
Princesses (Reading from left to right): R. Gale, D. Daye, G. LaSalle. *Prince of Wales* (reading from top to bottom): M. Lorance, The Cuddly Cuties.

Scene 9

They Wanted What They Knew (*by* Al Posen)
Scene: 97th Street and Amsterdam Avenue, (New York City), or thereabouts.
Al: W. L. Robertson. *Cal*: B. Trivers. *Sal*: M. Miller. *A*: C. Clute. *B*: F. Faun. *C*: L. Lauren. (Note: With the unionization of actors proceeding apace, the time will come when piece-work may rule the theatre, and actors will charge by the word. When that time comes plays will be something like the above.)

Scene 10

"Old-Fashioned Ballet"
(*Music by* Edgar Fairchild.)
The Singer: G. Ames. *Premiere Ballerina*: D. Daye. And a Corps de Ballet composed of Cuddly Cuties.

Scene 11

"Triangle"
(*Music by* Charles M. Schwab.)
The Wife: R. Gale. *The Other Man*: W. L. Robertson. *The Husband*: M. Lorance.

Scene 12

"Slow River"
S. Baxter, H. Benson, M. Miller, Cuddly Cuties
(*Music by* Charles M. Schwab.)

Scene 13

"Self-Expression"
D. Daye
(*Music by* Arthur Schwartz.)

Scene 14

The Mystery of the Mysterious Mystery
Scene: The palatial Great Neck estate of Millionaire Clubman Harkins, the Wealthy Millionaire Clubman. *Time*: That night.
Characters (in order of their first appearance when they appear for the first time): *Millionaire Clubman Harkins*: M. Lorance. *Judkins*, a Butler: H. Benson. *"Get-your-man" Bly*, of Scotland Yard: R. Gale. *Georgie Arliss*: B. Trivers. *Adventuress*: G. LaSalle. *Mae Vokes*: G. Ames.

Scene 15

"He Who Gets Slapped"
(*Music by* Arthur Schwartz.)
The Clown: C. Bender. *The Circus Rider*: D. Daye. *The Young Fellow*: H. Benson.

Scene 16

Cafe Habima, with our own Unintelligible Habima Players in "Tapuach Lecho Eten" (A Kiss for Cinderella)
Entire Company

ACT 2

Scene 1

"Romany"
C. Bender, G. Ames, T. Drasin, F. Faun, Several Cuddly Cuties
(*Music by* Arthur Schwartz.)

Scene 2

"Pretty Little So-and-So" (You're My 'So and So')
(*Music by* Edgar Fairchild.)
So: R. Gale. *And So*: C. Clute.

Scene 3

Bernarr Hires a Stenographer
Scene: Office of the MacFadden Publications on National Build-Your-Chest-Expansion-Day.
Bernarr MacFadden: H. Benson. *Attaché*: M. Lorance. *First Applicant*: L. Lauren. *Second Applicant*: M. Sorel. *Third Applicant*: E. Gerard. *Fourth Applicant*: F. Faun.

Scene 4

"A Song About Love"
(*Music by* Arthur Schwartz.)
The Boy Friend: W. L. Robertson. *The Girl Friend*: G. LaSalle.

Scene 5

"A Side Street Off Broadway"
(*Music by* Edgar Fairchild.)
Scene 1: Broadway. *Scene* 2: One of the Side Streets. *Scene* 3: The Doll-Shop.
The New Yorker: C. Bender. *The Out-of-Towner*: W. L. Robertson. *Stilts*: B. Trivers. *The Soubrette*: G. Ames. *Schultz*, the Doll-Man: M. Collins. *The Doll Tina*: D. Daye. *The Sheik Doll*: M. Lorance.

Scene 6

"How to Welcome Home Your Hubby"[118]
R. Gale
(*Music by* Charles M. Schwab.)

Scene 7

"Floating Through the Air"
(*Music by* Arthur Schwartz.)
Scene: A roof-top on 117th Street, between Fifth and Madison Avenue.
Dorothy Daye: D. Daye. *Benn Trivers*: B. Trivers.

Scene 8

Invocation to the Thunder-Bird[119]
(A Choctaw legend conceived and staged by Wes L. Robertson): ("Indian Chant")
(*Music by* Arthur Schwartz.)
The Indian: W. L. Robertson.

Scene 9

"I Can't Get into the Quota"
(*Music by* Arthur Schwartz.)
The Immigrant: M. Collins.

---

[115]The running order was revised during the run. Added were:
Contraband (Act 1)
The Husband: C. Clute. *The Wife*: ?. *The Bootlegger*: W. L. Robertson.
The First Strike (Act 1)
King Solomon: M. Collins. *Eunuch*: C. Clute. *Messenger*: F. Faun. *First Wife*: G. LaSalle. *Second Wife*: E. Lauren. *Third Wife*: R. Gale. *La*: L. Lauren. *La La*: M. Sorel. *La La La*: D. Hoffman. *La La La La*: I. Zehner.
Preachment (Act 2)
Reverend Jean Southern
"Meat and Vegetables" (Act 2)
(*Music by* Arthur Schwartz.)
Meat: C. Clute. *Vegetables*: S. Baxter. *Waitress*: E. Lauren.
[116]Dropped during the run.
[117]Dropped during the run.

[118]Dropped during the run.
[119]Dropped during the run.

Scene 10

"Words and Music"
(*Music by* Charles M. Schwab.)
Composers: W. L. Robertson, C. Clute. *Lyricists*: B. Trivers, H. Benson. *Singers*: C. Bender, S. Baxter, G. Ames. *Dancers*: M. Miller, D. Daye. *Comediennes*: R. Gale, M. Lorance. *Sex Appeal*: G. LaSalle. *Shakespeare*: M. Collins. *Do*: T. Drasin. *Re*: E. Gerard. *Mi*: L. Lauren. *Fa*: F. Faun. *Sol*: M. Sorel. *La*: R. Swan. *Si*: D. Hoffman. *Do*: I. Zehner.

1927.12   LUCKY

A Musical Comedy in Two Acts, 9 Scenes. Book and lyrics by Otto Harbach. Music by Jerome Kern. Additional scenes and musical numbers by Bert Kalmar and Harry Ruby. Staged by Hassard Short. Dances and ensembles arranged by David Bennett. Ballets arranged by Albertina Rasch. Costumes designed by Mabel E. Johnston, others. Music under the direction of Gus Salzer. Orchestral arrangements by Robert Russell Bennett. Produced by Charles Dillingham. Opened 22 March 1927 at the New Amsterdam Theatre and closed 21 May 1927 after 71 performances[120].

CAST (in order of appearance): *Cyngie*, house boy: Kumara Singha. *Chuck Dugan*: Henry Mowbray. *A Pearl Thief*: Bert Gould. *Finch*, Government Inspector: Martin Berkeley. *Barlow*, the master mind of the pearl thieves: PAUL EVERTON. *Jack Mansfield*, a pearl buyer: JOSEPH SANTLEY. *Notoya*: Kathryn Hamill. *Teddy Travers*: RICHARD "SKEET" GALLAGHER. *First Tourist*: Joan Clement. *Second Tourist*: Jeanne Fonda. *Long Ling* of the Barlow Gang: Al Ochs. *Charlie Simpson*, a promoter: WALTER CATLETT. *Strawberry*: Princess White Deer. *Grace Mansfield*, Jack's sister: IVY SAWYER. *Mazie Maxwell*, her friend: RUBY KEELER. *Lucky*: MARY EATON. *Officer*: Hugh Francis Murphy. *The High Priest*: Charles Gibney. *Mendicant Monks*: Fred Wilson, Stanley McClelland, Hal Clovis, Emile Cote. *First Waiter*: Fred Lenox. *Second Waiter*: George Ferguson. *Third Waiter*: Al Wyart. *Page*: Charles Eaton. *Wilton*, U.S. Revenue Officer: Richard Farrell. *Shelbach*: Charles Mitchell. And PAUL WHITEMAN AND HIS ORCHESTRA. (*Specialties*: Keller Sisters and Al Lynch.)

Albertina Rasch Girls: Marian Dickson, Martha Wilbert, Eda Vittollo, Julia Barashkova, Lenore Shearer, Elvira Gomez, Betty Keen, Dorothy Belle, Dulce Bentley, Nita Rosso, Leonore Blair, Regina Tuahinska, Aili Halmenaa, Emily Slater, Katharine Lambly, Maxine Demmler. *Show Girls*: Kathleen Krosby, Olga Marye, Patricia Preston, Dorothy Phillips, Lillian Morehouse, Trude Marr, Kathryn Hamill, Pauline Hall. *Dancers*: Rosemary Farmer, Mary Brady, Virginia Clark, Peggy Cunningham, Alma Drange, Ethel Forrest, Lily Kimari, Myrtle Lane, Edna Locke, Josephine Mostler, Cherie Pelham, Nickie Pittell, Anna Rex, Phyllis Reynolds, Louise Starck, Peaches Tortoni, Teddy Ward, Dorothy Wyatt, Pearl Bradley, Eleanor Elden, Elizabeth Ryder, Betty Block. *Elida Webb Girls*: Elida Webb, Billie Cain, Rose Gaillaird, Hyacinth Curtis, Bessie Allison, Vivian Harris. *Gentlemen of the Ensemble*: Max Hugo, Alfred Arnold, Walter Arnold, Charles Bannister, Dick Bennett, Albert Birk, Charles Conkling, Jack de Lys, Milton Halpern, Jack Hughes, Ray Justus, Don Lee, Bob Maxwell, Bob Morris, Don Oltarsh, Hugh Sorenson, Jack Talbot, Ayres Tavitt, Archibald Thompson, George Vigouroux, Bill O'Donnell, Alfred Hall.

Act 1, Scene 1: Pearl Village, Ceylon. *Scene 2*: A Sacred Bo Tree. *Scene 3*: The Music Room of the *S. S. Washington*. *Scene 4*: A Street in Columbo, Ceylon. *Scene 5*: Exterior of a Buddhist Temple.

Act 2, Scene 1: The Green Room of Cabaret. *Scene 2*: A Doorway on East Twelfth Street, New York City. *Scene 3*: Paul Whiteman and His Orchestra. *Scene 4*: Dance Floor of Cabaret.

ACT 1

"The Treasure Hunt" (Opening)
Ensemble

"Cingalese Girls"
J. Santley, Albertina Rasch Girls, Ensemble
(*Music and Lyrics by* Otto Harbach, Bert Kalmar and Harry Ruby.)

"Without Thinking of You" (Quartette)
I. Sawyer, R. Keeler, W. Catlett, R. Gallagher

Entrance of Lucky
Ensemble

"Lucky"
M. Eaton, Ensemble
(*Lyrics by* Bert Kalmar and Harry Ruby.)

"That Little Something" (Duet)
M. Eaton, J. Santley
(*Music by* Jerome Kern. *Lyrics by* Bert Kalmar and Harry Ruby.)

Finaletto
Ensemble

---

[120]Settings designed by James Reynolds, uncredited in programs.

Coconut Dance
Albertina Rasch Girls

"When the Bo-Tree Blossoms (Again)" (Duettino)
M. Eaton, J. Santley
(*Music by* Jerome Kern. *Lyrics by* Bert Kalmar and Harry Ruby.)
Keller Sisters and Lynch

"Dancing the Devil Away"
M. Eaton, Ensemble
(*Music and Lyrics by* Bert Kalmar and Harry Ruby.)

The Elida Webb Girls

Finale
M. Eaton, Ensemble

ACT 2

Opening

"Pearl of Broadway"
R. Keeler, Ensemble
(*Music by* Jerome Kern. *Lyrics by* Bert Kalmar and Harry Ruby.)

"Spring Is Here"
M. Eaton, W. Catlett, R. Gallagher, Male Ensemble

"Same Old Moon"
I. Sawyer, J. Santley
(*Music and Lyrics by* Bert Kalmar and Harry Ruby.)

"If the Man in the Moon Was a Coon"
R. Keeler, Show Girls
(*Music and Lyrics by* Fred Fisher.)

"Shine On Harvest Moon" (from ZIEGFELD FOLLIES OF 1908)
Keller Sisters and Lynch
(*Music by* Nora Bayes and Jack Norworth. *Lyrics by* Jack Norworth.)

"By the Light of the Silvery Moon" (from ZIEGFELD FOLLIES OF 1909)
W. Catlett, R. Gallagher, Dancers
(*Music by* Gus Edwards. *Lyrics by* Edward Madden.)

"Once in a Blue Moon" (from STEPPING STONES)
M. Eaton, Albertina Rasch Girls
(*Lyrics by* Anne Caldwell.)

Paul Whiteman and His Orchestra:
Medley from "Lucky" and "Rhapsody in Blue"
(*Music by* George Gershwin.)

"The Pearl of Ceylon" (Ballet)
M. Eaton, Premiere, Albertina Rasch Girls

Finale
Ensemble

1927.13   RUFUS LeMAIRE'S AFFAIRS

A (Musical) Revue in Two Acts, 31 Scenes[121]. Book (sketches) and lyrics by Ballard Macdonald. Music by Martin Broones. Additional skits by Andy Rice. Dialogue directed by William Halligan. Dances arranged by Jack Haskell. Ballets staged by Albertina Rasch. Costumes designed by Charles LeMaire. Stage settings designed by Clark Robinson. Orchestra under the direction of John L. McManus. Musical arrangements and orchestrations by John L. McManus. Entire production under the supervision of Rufus LeMaire. Produced by Rufus LeMaire. Opened 28 March 1927 at the Majestic Theatre and closed 14 May 1927 after 56 performances.

CAST: CHARLOTTE GREENWOOD, TED LEWIS, LESTER ALLEN, BETH BERRI, JOHN PRICE JONES, LINA BASQUETTE, WILLIAM HALLIGAN, PEGGY FEARS, LON HASCALL, MARY LEWIS, JOHN HAMILTON, SALLY STARR, LESTER DORR, BOBBE ARNST, SUNNY DALE, MILTON FRAME, FRANK ROSS, PAULINE ALPERT, OLIVE BRADY, NELLIE FERNS, MITTY and TILLIO, MARTIN BROONES, WILLIAM MILLER, NAT PETERSON, ROY CROPPER, WALTER HUSTON PARKER, CARDELL TWINS.

Albertina Rasch Ballet: Mildred Turner, Rose Gale, Dorothy Ryan, Nona Otero, Mignon Dallette, Ida Lanvin, Marion Wellman, Vera Frederick, Eve Hellesness, Josephine Wolfe, Olga Chalmers, Doris Bryant, Marie Gale, Rita Glynde, Lucille O'Connor, Ruth Flatow. *Rufus LeMaire's Lovely Ladies*: Eileen Cullen, Helen Titus, Rita Whitney, Rella Harrison, Helen Herms, Claire Hooper, Ann Janeway, Elizabeth Janeway, Mixi, Bodil Lund, Pauline Sherman, Katherine Janeway, Betty Ewing, Helen

---

[121]Opening Night playbill reads RUFUS LEMAIRE'S AFFAIRS; subsequent playbills from Broadway, tour and tryouts used the shorter title LEMAIRE'S AFFAIRS. Sophie Tucker appeared in the Chicago tryout and not in the New York production.

Gant, Gloria Bujee, Jeanne Toner, Marcelle Miller. *Rufus LeMaire's Dancing Girls*: Flora Watson, Betty E. Karr, Dorothy Day, Mary Irwin, Fifi Dare, Doris Blaine, Minerva Wilson, Helen Madigan, Adeline Foley, Margaret Callan, Frances Woodward, Emily Burton, Jane Hamlin, Betty Cale, Jane Mayo, Margaret Shea, Ruth Grady, Claire Carroll, Betty Chapin, Evelyn Hannons, Jane Daniels, Roberta Greene, Vera Berg, Val Lester.

ACT 1[122]

1st Affair

The Beauty Parade
>*Announced by* W. Halligan. *Miss Davenport*: H. Titus. *Miss Muskegon*: Mixi. *Miss Information*: R. Harrison. *Miss Cornie Beef*: R. Whitney. *Miss Atlanta*: M. Wallace. *Miss Nicaragua*: .C. Hooper. *Miss Detroit*: A. Janeway. *Miss Mattewan*: E. Cullen. *Miss Chicago*: H. Herms.

2nd Affair

"Hot Steps" (dance)
>B. Arnst, S. Starr, Dancing Girls

3rd Affair

An Affair with Dangerous Dan Magrew (*by* Art Frank and Ballard Macdonald)
>*Announced by* W. Halligan. *Proprietor of the Malamut Saloon*: L. Hascall. *Dan Magrew*: J. Hamilton. *Card Players and Guests*: L. Dorr, N. Peterson, W. Miller. *At the Piano*: F. Ross.

4th Affair

Girls I Fell For (*by* Lester Allen)
>*School Girl*: O. Brady. *Bicycle Girl*: N. Ferns. *Antoinette*: S. Dale. *School Teacher*: S. Starr.

5th Affair

Absinthe Dance (from Casino de Paris, France)
>Mitty and Tillio

6th Affair

Specialty Dance
>Albertina Rasch Girls

7th Affair

"Wah-Wah"
>T. Lewis

Dance
>Dancing Girls

---

[122]The show's running order was revised repeatedly during the run; added during run:

Goodbye Sam (later known as: A Business Transaction) (Act 1)
>*Husband*: L. Allen. *Wife*: S. Dale. *Sweetheart*: J. Hamilton.

Specialty Dance (Act 2)
>Cardell Twins

Song Specialty (Act 2)
>Maxine Lewis

Specialty Dance (Act 2)
>B. Beri

For subsequent national tour with a different cast, the show was known as LEMAIRE'S AFFAIRS, Second Edition, a revised score was added:

"Since Henry Ford Apologized to Me"
>Jimmy Hussey
>(*Music by* Dave Stamper. *Lyrics by* Billy Rose and Ballard Macdonald.)

"Eenie Meenie Minie Mo" (When the Eenie-Meenies Do the Minie-Mo)
>Mimi Rollins
>(*Music by* Jesse Greer. *Lyrics by* Billy Rose.)

"Underneath the Wabash Moon"
>W. Lightner, H. Fox, Rialto Four
>(*Music by* Dave Stamper. *Lyrics by* Billy Rose.)

"Mississippi Show Boat"
>W. Lightner, 75 Banjoists

"You'll Find the End of the Rainbow (In Your Own Back Yard)"
>Harry Fox, Beatrice Curtis
>(*Music by* Jesse Greer. *Lyrics by* Billy Rose and Ballard Macdonald.)

"Nagasaki Butterfly"
>W. Lightner
>(*Music by* Jesse Greer. *Lyrics by* Billy Rose.)

"Love Baby"
>W. Lightner, H. Fox
>(*Music by* Jesse Greer. *Lyrics by* Billy Rose.)

8th Affair

Pre-War Scotch
>(*by* Robert Middlemas)
>*Announced by* S. Starr. *Two Traveling Men*: W. Halligan, L. Allen. *Bell-hop*: L. Dorr. *Hotel Proprietor*: L. Hascall.

9th Affair

Love Interest:
>"I Can't Get Over a Girl Like You Loving a Boy Like Me"
>J. P. Jones, B. Arnst
>(*Lyrics by* Harry Ruskin.)

10th Affair

Miss Charlotte Greenwood and Martin Broones
>Specialty (*Sketch by* Andy Rice. *Music by* Martin Broones. *Lyrics by* Earl Crooker.)

11th Affair

The Cameo Shop
>*Antique Dealer*: R. Cropper. *Customer*: J. P. Jones. *The Cameo Girl*: L. Basquette.

The Cameo Ballet
>Albertina Rasch Dancers
>*The Dancer*: L. Basquette.

12th Affair

A Busted Romance
>*Announced by* T. Lewis. *The Lady*: P. Fears. *A Friend*: J. Hamilton. *The Manager*: L. Dorr. *The Author*: W. Peterson. *A Box Party*: L. Hascall.

13th Affair

"Dancing by Moonlight"
>J. P. Jones, P. Fears, Dancing Girls

14th Affair

A Travesty on 'The Dove'
>(*by* Jack Lait)
>*Announced by* W. Halligan. *Mother*: N. Ferns. *Daughter*: S. Dale. *Senor Tostado*: L. Allen. *The Dove*: C. Greenwood. *Captain*: L. Dorr. *Soldiers*: W. Miller, N. Peterson. *Johnny Powell*: J. Hamilton.

15th Affair

"Wandering Through Dreamland" (Wandering in Dreamland)
>R. Cropper, P. Fears
>*Comet*: C. Hooper. *Eastern Star*: E. Cullen. *The Moon*: M. Wallace. *Northern Star*: J. Toner. *Morning Star*: Mixi. *Eclipse*: H. Herms. *Mars*: R. Whitney. *Aurora Borealis*: H. Titus. *Heavenly Twins*: A. Janeway, E. Janeway. *The Sun*: B. Beri.

Pleiades Ballet
>Albertina Rasch Girls

16th Affair

Specialty Dance
>Cardell Twins

17th Affair

The Bullet
>*Doctor*: J. Hamilton. *Nervous Patient*: C. Greenwood. *Nurse*: N. Ferns. *Excited Mother*: B. Arnst.

18th Affair

"Lights of Old Broadway"
>L. Allen

19th Affair

"Minstrel Days"
>J. P. Jones

a. Parade
>Male Principals

b. Minstrel, First Part

c. Charlotte Greenwood, Ted Lewis, Lester Allen, All Principals, Minstrel Maids
>("So Long Letty") (C. Greenwood)

ACT 2

20th Affair

"Mexico"
>J. P. Jones, B. Arnst, Mexican Girls and Sweethearts, Albertina Rasch Girls

21st Affair

Specialty Dance[123]
  Miller and Peterson
22nd Affair
  A Waste of Words
    (*by* A. Dorian Otvos, A. Seymour Brown and Andy Rice)
    Announced by S. Starr. *Mr. Brown*: L. Allen. *Mr. Smith*: W. Halligan. *Attorney*:
    J. P. Jones. *Mr. Gray*: L. Dorr. *Waiter*: L. Hascall.
23rd Affair
  "Land of Broken Dreams"
    T. Lewis
24th Affair
  "The Mirror Never Lies"[124]
    R. Cropper, P. Fears
  Dance Acrobatique
    O. Brady
    Lace: M. Wallace. *Large Bow*: R. Harrison. *Hat*: A. Janeway. *Chapeau*: R.
    Whitney. *Fringe*: Mixi. *Furs*: C. Hooper. *Veils*: M. Miller. *Feathers*: E. Cullen.
    La Valliere: E. Janeway. *Trimmings*: H. Herms.
25th Affair
  Movie Land
    Announced by S. Starr. *Mickey Phelan*: W. Halligan. *Assistant Director*:
    L. Hascall. *Camera Man*: W. Miller. *Yes Men*: L. Dorr, N. Peterson. *Author*:
    J. Hamilton. *Leading Lady*: C. Greenwood. *Leading Man*: L. Allen.
    Stenographer: O. Brady. *Gate Girl*: S. Starr. *Itchie, the Valet*: W. H. Parker.
26th Affair
  Ted Lewis, the High-Hatted Tragedian of Jazz, and His Merry Musical
  Clowns in a Symposium of Syncopated Melody and Song with Miss
  Bobbe Arnst:
  ["St Louis Blues"
    (*Music and Lyrics by* W. C. Handy.]
27th Affair
  "Travel-On"[125]
    M. Lewis, Dancing Girls
28th Affair
  The Golden Wedding
    L. Allen, J. Hamilton
29th Affair
  "Morning Glories" (Down Where the Morning Glories Twine)
    J. P. Jones, P. Fears, Dancing Girls
30th Affair
  Blondes Preferred (A Travesty on 'Gentlemen Prefer Blondes')
    Announced by S. Starr. *Lorelei*: C. Greenwood. *Dorothy*: B. Arnst. *Waiter*:
    J. Hamilton. *Millionaire*: L. Dorr. *His Friend*: L. Hascall.
31st Affair
  Finale
    Entire Company

1927.14   ## CHERRY BLOSSOMS

A Musical Play in Three Acts, 4 Scenes. Book by Harry B. Smith. Based on
the play "The Willow Tree" by J. H. Benrimo and Harrison Rhodes. Music
by Sigmund Romberg and William Ortman. Lyrics by Harry B. Smith and J.
Keirn Brennan. Staged by Lew Morton. Dances arranged by Ralph Reader.
Special dance arranged by Michio Ito. Costumes designed by Ernest R.
Schrapps. Settings designed by Watson Barratt. Orchestra under the direction of Alfred Goodman. Produced by Messrs. Shubert. Opened 28 March
1927 at the 44th Street Theatre, moved 2 May 1927 to the Cosmopolitan
Theatre, and closed 14 May 1927 after 56 performances.

CAST (in order of appearance): *Stella Maywood*: ANN MILBURN. *Jeffrey Fuller*:
JAMES MARSHALL. *George Washington Goto*: Bernard Gorcey. *Imaru*: Frederick
Kaufman. *Kamaru*: Fred Harper. *O-San Dam*: GOODIE GALLOWAY. *Yo-San*:
DESIRE ELLINGER, Helen Norde (alt.). *Ned Hamilton*: HOWARD MARSH.
First Shop Girl: Marie Laval. *Second Shop Girl*: Ronnie Madison. *Tomotado*:
William Pringle. *Shimamura*: Frank Greene. *The Bonze*: HAROLD KRAVITT. *Nogo*:
Frank Davenport. *Mary Temple*: GLADYS BAXTER. *First Officer*: El Thompson.

Second Officer: Dan Douglas. *Larry Fuller*: Walter Tenney. *O-Yuki-San*: DESIREE
ELLINGER, Helen Norde (alt.). *Kiku San*: Mario Keeler. *A Geisha Dancer*: Verona.
Mrs. Goto: Sylvia Peterson.
  Choral Boys: Jean Spiro, Efim Vitis, Ray Mace, Willard Fry, Coleman Ashe, Karl
Kreisel, Joseph Polasy, Charles V. Maynard, Frank Pandolfi. *Choral Girls*: Nadine
Rushanova, Helene Pandresco, Jennie Beach, Marjory Tell, Marion Macy, Adele
Arleon, Emily Wentz, Helen Dmitrieff, Alice Bussee. *Boys*: Rolland Carpenter, William
Brainard, John F. Roche, Jack Baker, Henry Clay, Howard Deighton, Dale Grigsby,
Arthur Schnitzer, Gerald Gehlert, Maurice Warner, Albert Fontaine, El Thompson,
Carlyle Lyndel, Dan Douglas, John Fredericks, Louis Sears. *Girls*: Margaret Speaks,
Marjorie Sutter, Helene Cunihan, Marie Laval, Florence Tyner, Sylvia Peterson, Naan
Lane, Elena Meade, Katrina Trask, Ethel Daniels, Lenora Wilder, Muriel Seeley,
Ronnie Madison, Diane D'Arle, Violet Code, Rosalind Rensing. *Dancing Girls*:
Evelyn Chambers, Bobby Bliss, Elsie Golden, Sally King, Ada Grae, Polly Shaw,
Camille Griffith, Yvette Reale, Peggy E. South, Helen Murray, Dorothy White.

Act 1: A Japanese Bazaar and Curio Shop.

Act 2, Scene 1: The Willow Garden of Hamilton's Home. *Scene 2*: The same, six
months later.

Act 3: A Tea House of the Yoshiwara. Seventeen years later.

ACT 1
  Choral Prelude
  Opening
    (a) Ensemble; (b) A. Milburn, Ensemble
  "I'll Peek-a-boo You"
    A. Milburn, J. Marshall
  "Legend Song"
    D. Ellinger, Girls
  Duet
    H. Marsh, D. Ellinger
  "If You Know What I Think"
    F. Harper, G. Galloway
  Finale
    H. Kravitt, Ensemble
  Choral Interlude

ACT 2
Scene 1
  "Feast of the Lanterns"
    Ensemble
  "Cigarette Song" (Tell Me Cigarette)
    H. Marsh
  "Happy Rickshaw Man" (Jinrikisha Song)
    A. Milburn, J. Marshall
  Finaletto
    H. Marsh, D. Ellinger
Scene 2
  "Japanese Serenade"
    F. Kravitt, Ensemble
  Reprise Duet
    H. Marsh, D. Ellinger
  "I Want to Be There"
    G. Baxter, Boys
  "Romance"
    D. Ellinger
  Finale
    G. Baxter, H. Marsh, D. Ellinger
  Choral Interlude

ACT 3
  Pit Solo[126]
    J. Beech
  Opening
    Ensemble
  "'Neath the Cherry Blossom Moon"
    D. Ellinger, W. Tenney, Ensemble
    (*Music by* William Ortmann. *Lyrics by* J. Keirn Brennan.)
  Finale
    Entire Company

---

[123]Dropped during the run.
[124]Dropped during the run.
[125]Dropped during the run.

[126]During the run, moved to precede the Act 1 finale.

1927.15

LADY DO

A Surprising Musical Comedy in Two Acts, a Prologue and 4 Scenes. Book by Jack McClellan and Albert Cowles. Music by Abel Baer. Lyrics by Sam M. Lewis and Joe Young. Production revised and staged by Edgar MacGregor. Dances and ensembles staged by Buzz [Busby] Berkeley. Costumes designed by Karyl Norman and Ellis Porter. Settings designed by Louis Kennel and Gus Wizamal. Orchestra under the direction of Frank Barry. Orchestrations by Frank E. Barry. Produced by Frank L. Teller[127]. Opened 18 April 1927 at the Liberty Theatre and closed 4 June 1927 after 56 performances.

CAST (in order of appearance): *Prologue: Dorothy*: NANCY WELFORD. *A Bricklayer*: James A. Waites. *Buddy*: KARYL NORMAN.

The Play: "Pop" Poulet: LUIS ALBERNI. *First Gendarme*: James A. Waites. *Second Gendarme*: Philip Duey. *Louis*: PAUL DARNELLE. *Fifi*: NINON NATALIE. *Mimi*: Marguerite Duane. *Henri*: Glenn McComas. *Marcel*: Henry M. Shope. *Georgette*: Ada Winston. *Marie*: Jean Watson. *Henriette*: Jane Swanson. *Georges*: Leonard Saxon. *Duke de Corsona*: JOSEPH LERTORA. *William Walthal*: A. S. BYRON. *Mrs. Withal*: Maude Odell. *Marion Hobart*: FRANCES UPTON. *Powers*: RALPH WHITEHEAD. *Dorothy Walthal*: NANCY WELFORD. *Valda de Corsona*: Harriett Lorraine (Baroness DeHollub). *Fleurette*: Rita Dunne. *The Paris Rose*: KARYL NORMAN. *Jacques*: Billy Skinner. *Buddy Rose*: KARYL NORMAN. *Pat Perkins*: LEW HEARN. *Jack*: Sylvan Lee. *Jill*: Jane Moore. *Rita*: Rita Howard. *Helen*: Helen Fables. *Rose Walthal*: KARYL NORMAN. *A Flunkey*: Julio Alvarez. *Another Flunkey*: Philip Duey. *The Nurse*: Juanita Zerbe.

Ladies of the Ensemble: Hesta Bailey, Cecil Boylan, Bobby Campbell, Rita Dunne, Marguerite Dunne, June Ferguson, Marion Herson, Elizabeth Huber, Helen Landis, Betty McMillan, Peggy Pidgin, Thelma Rankin, Edyth Ray, Polly Ray, Virginia Ray, Ruth Sato, Margaret Seidel, Frances Suzanne, Jane Swanson, Rosalie Trego, Johanna Unger, Jean Watson, Ada Winston, Juanita Zerbe. *Gentlemen of the Ensemble*: John McCoughlin, George Ganz, Glenn McComas, Edward Mackey, Buddy Niles, Billy Skinner, Oliver Wendell Twist, Lew Walker. *The Four Buddies*: Philip Duey, Leonard Saxon, Henry M. Shope, James A. Waites.

Prologue: Somewhere on Tenth Avenue, (New York City).

Act 1, Scene 1: "Pop" Poulet's Café, Paris! Five years later. Midnight! Montmartre! *Scene 2*: Somewhere on the Atlantic. Homeward Bound! A week later. *Scene 3*: The Lawn of the Walthal Estate, Roslyn, Long Island. The following afternoon.

Act 2: The Interior of the Walthal Home. From afternoon to midnight. One month later. The Plot Un-Plots.

PROLOGUE

"Buddy Rose"
N. Welford, K. Norman

ACT 1

"Live Today (—Love Today)"
J. Lertora, Ensemble

"Paris Taught Me Zis"
K. Norman

"Dreamy Montmartre"
K. Norman, Four Buddies, Ensemble

"(On) Double Fifth Avenue"
K. Norman, Four Buddies

"You Can't Eye a Shy Baby"
S. Lee, J. Moore, Ensemble

"O Sole Mio—Whose Soul Are You?"
J. Lertora, N. Welford

"Lady Do"
F. Upton, R. Whitehead, Ensemble

Specialty
N. Natalie, P. Darnelle

"Little Miss Small Town"
K. Norman, L. Hearn, Ensemble

Finale
Principals, Ensemble

ACT 2

"Snap Into It"
F. Upton, S. Lee, J. Moore, Maids, Butlers

"(Blah! But Not) Too Blue"
N. Welford

Reprisal! (Specialty)
S. Lee, J. Moore

"In the Long Run"
R. Whitehead, F. Upton, Ensemble

"(In) My Castle in Sorrento"
J. Lertora, K. Norman, N. Natalie, P. Darnelle

Burlesque Reprises
H. Lorraine, L. Hearn

"This Is My Wedding Day"
K. Norman, Boys

"Jiggle Your Feet"
F. Upton, Ensemble

Finale
Entire Company

1927.16

HIT THE DECK!

A Nautical Musical Comedy in Two Acts, 6 Scenes. Book by Herbert Fields. Based on the play "Shore Leave" by Hubert Osborne. Music by Vincent Youmans. Lyrics by Leo Robin and Clifford Grey. Book staged by Alexander Leftwich. Dances arranged by Seymour Felix. Costumes designed by Mark Mooring. Settings designed by Ward and Harvey. Orchestra under the direction of Paul Lannin. (Orchestrations by Stephen Jones and Paul Lannin.) Produced by Vincent Youmans and Lew Fields[128]. Opened 25 April 1927 at the Belasco Theatre and closed 25 February 1928 after 352 performances.

CAST (in order of appearance): *"Donkey"*: Brian Donlevy. *"Dinty"*: Arnold Brown. *Marine*: Jack Bruns. *"Battling" Smith*: Franker Woods. *Chick*: Ben Carswell. *Gus*: Cliff Whitcomb. *Bob*: Robert L. Duenweg. *Lavinia*: STELLA MAYHEW. *Loulou*: LOUISE GROODY. *Ensign Alan Clark*: JOHN McCAULEY. *Toddy Gaie*: Bobbie Perkins. *Charlotte Payne*: MADELINE CAMERON. *Mat*: ROGER GRAY. *"Bilge"*: CHARLES KING. *"Bunny"*: Edward Allan. *Captain Roberts*: Jerome Daley. *Ah Lung*: Anthony Knilling. *Mun Fang*: Billie Sibelle. *Rita*: Peggy Conway. *Coolie*: Ah Chong. *Chia Shun*: Nancy Corrigan. *Four Missionaries*: The Locust Sisters. *Four Mandarins*: Lyric Quartette.

Dancers: Celie Neska, Lila Anderson, Margie Collins, Florence Price, Olive Pierson, Mars Craft, Gladys Pender, Elsie Lawritson, Beatrice Wilson, Jane Hurd, Jeanne West, May Hunter, Fan Conway, William McGurn, Leo Nierle, Cecil Shires, Sid Salzberg, Jimmie Cushman, Murray Browne, Jack Mead, John Kneley, Dan Sparks. *Singers*: Ruth Witmer, Mary Carney, Jeanne Sutro, Billie Sibelle, Anne Austin, Harriet Britton, Nancy Corrigan, Rachel Chester, Kendall Northrup, Charles McClelland, Victor Young, John Perkins.

Act 1, Scene 1: Loulou's Coffee House on the Dock at Newport. *Scene 2*: The Dock. Six months later. *Scene 3*:The forward deck of the *U. S. S. "Nebraska."*Three days later.

Act 2, Scene 1: A Seaport Town in China. Four months later. *Scene 2*: Inside a Mandarin's Home. *Scene 3*: Outside Loulou's Coffee House. Later.

ACT 1

Scene 1

"Join the Navy"
L. Groody, Gobs, Girls

"What's a Kiss Among Friends?"
B. Perkins, M. Cameron, J. McCauley, Girls

"Harbor of My Heart"
L. Groody, C. King

Scene 2

"Shore Leave"
Girls, Boys

"Lucky Bird"
S. Mayhew

Scene 3

"Looloo"
L. Groody, Boys

"Why, Oh Why?"[129]
M. Cameron, Boys, Girls

"Sometimes I'm Happy"
L. Groody, C. King

---

[127]Management taken over by Karyl Norman and the cast on a cooperative basis in May 1927.

[128]Two days after the opening Vincent Youmans bought out his partner Lew Fields whose name was dropped from subsequent producing credits.
[129]In August 1927, the melody was given a new lyric "Nothing Could Be Sweeter."

Finale
Company
ACT 2
Scene 1
Opening
N. Corrigan, Ensemble
"Hallelujah!"
S. Mayhew, Boys, Girls
Finaletto
Ensemble
Scene 2
"Hallelujah!" (reprise)
S. Mayhew
Scene 3
"Looloo" (reprise)
L. Groody, Boys
"Utopia"[130]
L. Groody, E. Allen
Finale
Company

1927.17   THE CIRCUS PRINCESS

An Operetta in Three Acts, a Prologue and 7 Scenes. Book and lyrics by Harry B. Smith. Adapted from the Viennese original ('Die Zirkusprinzessin') by Julius Brammer and Alfred Grünwald. Music by Emmerich Kálmán. (Musical) Numbers staged by Allan K. Foster. Dialogue staged by M. H. Varnel. Settings designed by Watson Barratt. Costumes designed by Ernest R. Schrapps. Orchestra under the direction of Alfred Goodman. Play and all ensembles staged by J. C. Huffman. Produced by the Messrs. Lee and J. J. Shubert. Opened 25 April 1927 at the Winter Garden and closed 8 October 1927 after 192 performances.

CAST (in order of appearance): *Loris*: Roy Vitalis. *Nicholas*: Starr Jones. *Paul*: Herbert Lyle. *Constantine*: Harry Shackelford. *Ivan Panin*: Joseph Toner. *Prince Alexis Orloff*: GUY ROBERTSON. *Prince Palinsky*, Alexis' Uncle: ARTHUR BARRY. *Stanislavsky*, Circus Proprietor: Robert O'Connor. *Pinelli*, Ring Master: James C. Morton. *Baron Sakuskine*: Stanley Harrison. *Lieutenant Petrovitch*: Frank Horn. *Princess Fedora Palinska*: DESIRÉE TABOR. *Commissionaire*: Edmund Ruffner. *Grand Duke Sergius*: GEORGE HASSELL. *His Adjutant*: Starr Jones. *Toni Schlumberger*: TED DONER. *Mabel Gibson* (Fritzi Burgstaller): GLORIA FOY. *Barmaid*: Virginia Hassell. *Mr. X*: GUY ROBERTSON. *Bee Star*: Themselves. *6 Pachas*: Themselves. *Poodles Hanneford and Family*: Themselves. *An Old Clown*: Fred Derrick. *A Clown*: Oscar Lowande. *Footman*: Edouard Grobe. *First Cossack*: Poodles Hanneford. *Second Cossack*: James C. Morton. *Majordomo*: Edmund Ruffner. *An Officer*: Henry Lyle. *Archbishop*: John Henry. *Pelican*, Head Waiter: George Bickel. *First Waiter*: James C. Morton. *Bus Boy*: Poodles Hanneford. *Porter*: Billy Culloo. *Frau Schlumberger*: FLORENCE MORRISON. *16 Foster Girls*: (Guests, see below). *8 Liebling Singers*: (unidentified).

Hussars of the Palace Guard: Bill Arnold, Michael Brent, William Browne, Russell Bryant, Thomas Coppe, William Culloo, Edward Donohue, Tom Donohue, Herbert Eaddy, Frank Horn, Paul Jones, Starr Jones, Herbert Lyle, Gerald Moore, Donald McGill, Ray Moore, Alferd Russ, Bob Schutte, Harry Shackelford, Sam True, Roy Vitalis, Max Wolfe, John Zimmerman. *Circus Attendants*: William Culloo, Thomas Coppe, Edward Donohue, Gerald Moore, Alfred Russ, Max Wolfe. *Clowns*: Billy Arnold, Tom Donohue, Herbert Eaddy, Paul Jones, Donald McGill, Ray Moore, Sam True. *Equestrians*: Dorothy Chamber, Jessica Hagenah, Florence Kowalewska, Margaret Luerssen, Marie Minor, Stella Shields, Eleanor Witmar. *Guests*: Dorothy Chamber, Karin Colon, Rose Gordon, Virginia Hassell, Jessica Hagenah, Florence Kowalewska, Billy Luerssen, Wilma Miller, Marie Minor, Phyllis Newkirk, Katherine O'Neale, Mary Paterson, Lolita Savini, Katherine Scheerer, Stella Shields, Eleanor Witmar.

Prologue: The Cardroom in the Officers' Club in St. Petersburg. 1910.

Act 1, Scene 1: The Circus Posters. *Scene 2*: The Lobby of Circus Stanislavsky in St. Petersburg. 1912. *Scene 3*: The Circus Stanislavsky. *Scene 4*: The Lobby of the Circus Stanislavsky. *Scene 5*: The Circus Stanislavsky.

Act 2: The Ballroom in the Palace of the Grand Duke Sergius in St. Petersburg. One month later.

Act 3: The Lobby of the Archduke Charles Hotel in Vienna. Three months later.
PROLOGUE
"But Who Cares?"
G. Robertson, Officers
ACT 1
"Silhouette"
Foster Girls
"Bravo, Bravo"
R. O'Connor, J. C. Morton, Audience
"There's Something About You"
G. Foy, T. Doner
"Dear Eyes That Haunt Me"
G. Robertson
"Same Old Love Songs"
D. Tabor, Officers
"I Dare to Speak of Love to You"
D. Tabor, G. Robertson
"Girls, I Am True to All of You"
T. Doner, Foster Girls
Finale
D. Tabor, G. Foy, G. Robertson, G. Hassell, T. Doner, Company, P. Hanneford and Family, Foster Girls
ACT 2
"Joy Bells"
Guests
"The Hussars' Song"
G. Robertson, G. Hassell, Officers
"The Blue Eyes I Dream Of"
D. Tabor, G. Robertson
"I Like the Boys"
D. Foy, Officers, Foster Girls
"What Do You Say?" (What D'Ya Say?")
G. Foy, T. Doner
(*Music by* Jesse Greer. *Lyrics by* Raymond Klages.)
"Guarded"
T. Doner, P. Hanneford, J. C. Morton
Finale
D. Tabor, G. Hassell, R. O'Connor, Company, Foster Girls, Liebling Singers
ACT 3
"Waiters"
P. Hanneford, J. C. Morton, Foster Girls, Waiters
"Dear Eyes That Haunt Me" (reprise)
G. Robertson, Liebling Singers
"I'll Be Waiting"
G. Foy, T. Doner, Foster Girls
Finale
Entire Company

1927.18   THE SEVENTH HEART

An American Comedy with Music in Three Acts, 5 Scenes. Play by Sarah Ellis Hyman. Music and lyrics by Arthur Brander. Staged by Edward Elsner. Settings designed by R. N. Robbins. Dresses and gowns by Beau Mode Frocks; Rosenberg, Brilliant & O'Neil. Produced by Lionel Productions, Inc. Opened 2 May 1927 at the Mayfair Theatre and closed 7 May 1927 after 8 performances[131].

CAST: *Maybelle Wright*, Clara's Niece: Sylvia Beecher. *Clara Stewart*, Jack's wife: AILEEN POE. *Mrs. Thorne*: Mary Moore. *Mazie Kennedy*, Harold's sister: MILDRED KENT *Gloria Higgins*: Barbara Weeks. *Jane*, the maid: Helen Gray. *Harold Kennedy*, passing under the name of Colonel Barrie: ARTHUR BRANDER. *Jack Stewart*: Ralph Dunn. *Charlie Stewart*, Jack's brother: CHARLES GARLAND. *Robert Kennedy*, Harold's father: A. TREVOR BLAND. *Captain Dix*, Mrs. Thorne's brother: Robert Farrell. *Tommy Watkins*: Armand Lauret. *James Marshall*: Francis Felton, Jr.

Ladies in search of a husband: *Miranda Jones*: A Young Widow. *Julia*, the Romantic Lady: A Dancer. *Martha*: The Little School Teacher. *Pansy*: A Toe Dancer. *Daisy Cerina Brown*: An Old Maid. *Violet*: The Oriental Girl. *The Spanish Lady*: The Phantom Love. And other guests.

---

[130]Replaced shortly after opening by:
"If He'll Come Back to Me"
L. Groody, E. Allen

---

[131]Musical direction uncredited.

Act 1, Scene 1: The Stewart Villa, Palm Beach, Florida. Early evening. *Scene 2*: The same, one hour later.

Act 2, Scene 1: Stewart Villa, the following evening. *Scene 2*: Three days later at Mrs. Stewart's dinner and dance.

Act 3: Stewart Villa, later the same evening.

ACT 1

Scene 1

"I Wonder If Love Is a Dream"
M. Kent, C. Garland, A. Lauret

"Cinema Blues"
B. Weeks, A. Brander, M. Kent, C. Garland

ACT 2

Scene 2

"For I'm in Love"
M. Kent, C. Garland

ACT 3

"When My Eyes Meet Yours"
A. T. Bland, M. Kent, C. Garland

1927.19

A NIGHT IN SPAIN

An International (Musical) Revue in Two Acts, 34 Scenes. Book (sketches) by Harold Atteridge. Music by Jean Schwartz. Lyrics by Al Bryan. Dialogue staged by Charles Judels. Musical numbers (staged) by Ralph Reader and Gertrude Hoffmann. Costumes by Ernest Schrapps. Settings by Watson Barratt. Orchestra under the direction of Max Hoffman. Produced by the Messrs. Shubert. Opened 3 May 1927 at the 44th Street Theatre, moved 10 October 1927 to the Winter Garden, and closed 12 November 1927 after 174 performances.

<u>CAST:</u> PHIL BAKER, TED and BETTY HEALY, GEORGIE PRICE, (Jay) BRENNAN and (Stanley) ROGERS, NORMA TERRIS, GRACE HAYES, CORTEZ and PEGGY, MADAME (Emilia) VIDALI, LOLA RAINE, BARTLETT SIMMONS, GRACE BOWMAN, SID SILVERS, TITO CORAL, HELEN KANE, JIMMIE TRAINOR, GEORGE TRAINOR, BERT GARDNER, SHEMP HOWARD, HELBA HUARA, ANDREINI TRIO, J. Colvil Dunn, George Anderson, Sam Braun, Lou Warren, Xavier Cugat, Bobby Pinkus.

Gertrude Hoffmann Girls: Andrienne Brower, Aini Hendricks, Amanda Daisey, Barbara Vernon, Bert Haines, Betty Montgomery, Dollie Trucksess, Ellen Speeler, Evelyn Wright, Ethel Seiberling, Emily Sherman, Evangeline Raleigh, Florence Powell, Pearl Jentoft, Gladys Turner, Jeanette Wiate, Kay McHugh, Lillian Smith, Margaret Swanson, Ray Powell. *Allan K. Foster Girls*: Ann Sutherland, Bee Basil, Carla King, Charlotte Middlemore, Jean Henderson, Loretta Minogue, Mabel Pauley, Marie Caldwell, Olive Rector, Peggy Sickle, Peggy Burgess, Roslind Abbomonte, Victoria Winter, Helen Gesty, Dot Richman. *Show Girls*: Frances Blythe, Gloria Chrystie, Ann Cabot, Morine Clarke, Dorothy Drum, Mildred Douglas, Marion Fedro, Bernice Gardner, Thaile Hamilton, Agatha Phillips, Dollie Thain, Julia Barker.

Raccooner's Band: Jack Scherr, Harold Van Emberg, Ted Zapt, William MacMurray, Martin Tracy, Louis Horvath, Jack Russell, Ben Goldstein, Walker O'Neill, Jack Kotek.

ACT 1[132]

Scene 1

Tito Coral

Scene 2

Ted Healy

Scene 3

Valencia

"Argentine"
G. Bowman, Spanish Beauties (Hoffman Girls, Foster Girls)
Don Jose: T. Coral. *Innkeeper*: J. C. Dunn. *Conchita*: N. Terris. *Valencia*: G. Hayes. *Harry*: B. Simmons. *Mr. Smith*: G. Anderson. *Spanish Valencia*: S. Rogers. *The Boy Friend*: B. Gardner.

"International Vamp"
G. Hayes, S. Rogers, G. Anderson, B. Gardner

Scene 4

Barcelona Street
B. Gardner, T. Healy, B. Healy

Scene 5

"De Dum Dum"
H. Kane, Hoffman Girls, Foster Girls

Dance
Trainor Brothers, Dolly

Scene 6

Georgie Price[133]

Scene 7

County Fair and Circus, Barcelona
Mr. Barker: G. Anderson. *Second Barker*: T. Healy. *Mr. Chump*: S. Howard. *The Snake Charmer*: S. Rogers. *Mr. Barker's Son*: B. Gardner.

Scene 8

"The Sky Girl"
G. Bowman
On the Trapeze: Foster Girls. *Bee*: B. Healy. *Hank*: T. Healy. *Jim*: S. Howard. *Tom*: S. Braun. *Bill*: L. Warren.

Scene 9

Galloping Ponies
Foster Girls

Scene 10

Norma Terris: "C'est vous" (French Ballad)

Scene 11

Three Questions
Announcer: G. Anderson. *Tessie*: G. Hayes. *Lola*: L. Raine. *Van Tumbly*: G. Price. *Servant*: B. Gardner. *Taxi Driver*: S. Howard. *Wally Smith*: J. C. Dunn. *The Stranger*: B. Gardner.

Scene 12

"Promenade the Esplanade"
B. Simmons, Spanish Beauties

Scene 13

Brennan and Rogers[134] (Whoops Sisters)

Scene 14

"My Rose of Spain"
E. Vidali, B. Simmons

Dance
Cortez and Peggy

Scene 15

Grasshoppers
Foster Girls

Scene 16

Dressmaker's Drama
M. Moiret: G. Anderson. *Maire*: B. Gardner. *Camille*: G. Hayes. *Butler*: J. C. Dunn. *Armand*: B. Gardner. *Paul*: T. Healy. *Dodo*: P. Burgess.

Scene 17

A Spanish Cafe
Cortez and Peggy
The Manager: J. Brennan. *The Hostess*: S. Rogers. *Bert*: B. Gardner. *John*: J. C. Dunn. *The Bandits*: G. Anderson, J. Trainor. *The Detective*: T. Healy. *Lola*: L. Raine. *Jim*: S. Howard. *Bill*: L. Warren.

Moorish Dance
Hoffman Girls

The Dance of Fate
H. Huara

---

[132]Marion Harris succeeded Norma Terris beginning 5 September 1927. She brought her own specialties which are not specifically indicated in the program, Act 1, Scene 11, and Act 2, Scene 5, the latter marked only as A few moments with Phil Baker and Marion Harris. In this spot they performed:
"Did You Mean It"?
Her other interpolated specialties included:
"Nothin'"
(*Music by* Roy Turk and Lou Handman.)
Later in the tour Marion Harris was succeeded by Aileen Stanley. Added for subsequent tour:
"Simple Spanish Maid" (Act 1, Scene 3)
Barbara Vernon, Glen Dale

[133]Georgie Price billed in the show, but did not perform at the opening.
[134]Dropped shortly after opening.

In Spain
  T. Coral
  (*Music by* Andreini Brothers Band.)
Scene 18
Phil Baker (and Sid Silvers) Specialty[135]
["Rainy Day Pal"
  (*Music and Lyrics by* Phil Baker and Sid Silvers.)
  "Love and Kisses (from Baby to You)"
    (*Music and Lyrics by* Phil Baker and Sid Silvers.)]
Scene 19
Columbus at the Court of Queen Isabel:
("Columbus and Isabella")
  G. Bowman, B. Simmons
The March of the Invincibles
  Hoffman Girls, Foster Girls

ACT 2
Scene 1
"Hot, Hot Honey"
  H. Kane, Foster Girls, Hoffman Girls
Dance
  Jeanette, Lillian
Scene 2
Trainor Brothers (Acrobatic buck-and-wing dance)
Scene 3
Ted Healy and His Raccooners' Band
With Grace Healy, Norma Terris, Bobby Pinkus, Betty Healy
["Under the Clover Moon"
  (*Music and Lyrics by* Ted Healy.)]
Scene 4
"A Spanish Shawl"
  G. Hayes, T. Coral, Spanish Beauties
Scene 5
The Intelligence Test[136]
  The Announcer: L. Raine. *Dean*: J. C. Dunn. *Stenographer*: R. Powell. *The Student*: G. Price.
Scene 6
Dance of the Sports[137]
  G. Price, Hoffman Girls
Scene 7
"The Nocturn"
  G. Bowman, X. Cugat (violin)
Scene 8
A Few Moments with Phil Baker and Norma Terris
Scene 9
"The Curfew Walk"
  H. Kane, Hoffmann Girls, Foster Girls
Scene 10
The Photographer
  The Photographer: G. Anderson. *His Model*: B. Gardner. *His Assistant*: T. Healy. *Miss Pierce*: Ray (Powell). *Miss Backard*: Betty (Montgomery). *Mr. Shemp*: S. Howard. *Miss Pretty*: Lilly (Smith). *Miss Sweet*: Ethel (Seiberling). *Miss Picture*: L. Raine.
Scene 11
"Bambazoola"
  N. Terris, Hoffmann Girls, Foster Girls, B. Pinkus
Scene 12
The Practical Joker
  Harry: T. Healy. *Mrs. Filbert*: G. Hayes. *Maid*: B. Gardner. *Nan*: L. Raine.
Scene 13
"A Million Eyes"
  B. Simmons, some winsome and petite girlies
Scene 14
The Blue Bird Room

The Can Can
  Hoffmann Girls
The Radium Dance
  Foster Girls
Scene 15
Finale with Love and Kisses

1927.20

OH, ERNEST!

A Musical Comedy in Two Acts, 6 Scenes. Book and lyrics by Francis DeWitt. Based on the play "The Importance of Being Ernest" by Oscar Wilde. Music by Robert Hood Bowers. Production staged under the direction of William J. Wilson. Dances staged by Ralph Riggs. Settings designed by Walter Harvey. Costumes by the Nesor Costume Company. Orchestra under the direction of Robert Hood Bowers. Produced by P. T. Rossiter. Opened 9 May 1927 at the Royale Theatre, moved 6 June 1927 to the Earl Carroll Theatre, and closed 25 June 1927 after 56 performances.

CAST (in order of appearance): *Sir Percy Middowshire*: William Jordan. *James Lane*: Ralph Riggs. *Algernon Moncrieff*: HARRY McNAUGHTON. *Jessica Esmond*: Phyllis Austin. *Honorable John Worthing, J. P.*: HAL FORDE. *Lady Bracknell*: FLAVIA ARCARO. *Honorable Gwendolen Fairfax, Her Daughter*: MARJORIE GATESON. *Martha, Lane's Wife*: Katharine Witchie. *Jane*: VIVIAN MARLOWE. *Cecily Cardew*: DOROTHY DILLEY. *Miss Prism*: Sonia Winfield. *Reverend Canon Chasuble, D.D.*: Jethro Warner. *Pollyana Montague, an Actress*: BARBARA NEWBERRY. *Friends of Algy (4)*: Peggy Vernon: Patricia Wynne. *Anne Aubrey*: Edith Mae Wright. *Clarice Chitworth*: Dimples Riede. *Evelyn Stuart*: Dorothea Mabie. *Friends of Cecily*: Wilma Roelof, Florence Gunther, Anita Loring, Dorothy Dawn, Virginia Myers, Margo Miller, Erma Chase, Mae Bligh.

Act 1, Scene 1: Algernon Moncrieff's Rooms, London. *Scene 2*: At the Garden Wall. *Scene 3*: The Garden, Manor House, Woolton. Morning.

Act 2, Scene 1: The Garden. Afternoon. *Scene 2*: At the Garden Gate. *Scene 3*: Manor House Cloisters.

ACT 1
Scene 1
"On the Beach" (Duet)
  H. McNaughton, P. Austin, P. Wynne, E. M. Wright, D. Riede, D. Mabie
"Taken By Surprise" (Duet)
  M. Gateson, H. Forde
"Ancestry"[139] (Duet)
  H. Forde, F. Arcaro
"Cupid's College" (Trio)
  M. Gateson, H. McNaughton, H. Forde, P. Wynne, E. M. Wright, D. Riede, D. Mabie
"Didoes" (Ensemble)
  H. McNaughton, R. Riggs, P. Austin, K. Witchie, P. Wynne, E. M. Wright, D. Riede, D. Mabie
Scene 2
"Over the Garden Wall"
  V. Marlowe, Maids
Scene 3
"Cecily" (Duet)
  D. Dilley, S. Winfield
"Let's Pretend" (Duet)
  H. McNaughton, D. Dilley
Specialty Waltz
  R. Riggs, K. Witchie
"Pollyanna"
  B. Newberry, Girls
"Don't Scold" (Finale)
  Company
Interlude: Dastardly Attack on W. Epigram
  M. Gateson
  ("And he walked down Piccadilly with a poppy and a lily")

ACT 2
Scene 1

---

[135]As per reviews and published sheet music.
[136]Dropped shortly after opening.
[137]Dropped shortly after opening.

---

[139]Dropped immediately after opening.

Dance
Girls
"Give Me Someone"
D. Dilley, Girls
"Little Stranger"
B. Newberry, Girls
"Rose in Bloom"[140] (He Knows Where the Rose Is in Bloom) (Duet)
H. Forde, M. Gateson
"Tangles" (Finaletto)
Company
Scene 2
"There's a Muddle"[141]
H. Forde
Dance
R. Riggs, K. Witchie
Scene 3
"(Give Me) Someone"[142] (reprise)
D. Dilley, B. Newberry
"Never Trouble Trouble"[143] (Quartette)
M. Gateson, D. Diley, H. McNaughton, H. Forde, Girls
Finale

The show was radically rewritten after 3 weeks; Clifford Grey revised the book; new musical numbers (Music by Joe Meyer, Lyrics by Leo Robin) were interpolated, and new dance numbers were staged by Pearl Eaton; all of which remained uncredited in the programme. Act 2 was reset as one scene at the Garden, Manor House. The revised program (23 May 1927) reads:

ACT 1
Scene 1
"Tea" (Chorus)
Alan Allenworth (Percy), P. Austin, R. Riggs, Girls
"Mama" (Duet)
A. Allenworth, P. Austin, Girls
"On the Beach" (Duet)
H. McNaughton, P. Austin, Girls
Scene 2
"Over the Garden Wall"
Blanche Krebs (Jane), Maids
Scene 3
"Someone" (Song)
D. Dilley, Girls
"True to Two" (Trio)
H. McNaughton, D. Dilley, A. Allenworth
"Taken By Surprise" (Duet)
H. Forde, M. Gateson
Specialty Waltz
R. Riggs, K. Witchie
"Pollyanna"
B. Newberry, Girls
"Don't Scold" (Finale)
Company
ACT 2
"There's Trouble" (Song)
D. Dilley, Girls
"Cupid's College" (Duet)
H. Forde, H. McNaughton, Girls
"(Just a) Little Stranger" (Duet)
P. Austin, B. Newberry, Girls
"It's All Right with Me" (Duet)
H. Forde, M. Gateson
"Shake a Little Shoe" (Quartette)
H. Forde, H. McNaughton, D. Dilley, M. Gateson

---

[140]Replaced immediately after opening by:
"It's Alright with Me" (Duet)
H. Forde, M. Gateson
[141]Dropped immediately after opening.
[142]Dropped immediately after opening.
[143]Dropped immediately after opening.

Dance
R. Riggs, K. Witchie
"What Can a Girl Do?" (Song)
M. Gateson
Finale
Company

1927.21 ## THE COCOANUTS

A Return Engagement of the Musical Comedy in Two Acts, 8 Scenes[144]. Book by George S. Kaufman, [Morrie Ryskind]. Music and lyrics by Irving Berlin. Book directed by Oscar Eagle. Musical numbers staged by Sammy Lee. Settings designed by Woodman Thompson. Costumes designed by Charles LeMaire. Orchestra under the direction of George S. Hirst. Orchestrations by Frank Tours, Maurice dePackh, Stephen Jones, Louis Katzman. Vocal harmony arrangements, including The Brox Sisters' numbers, by Arthur Johnston. Produced by Sam H. Harris. Opened 16 May 1927 at the Century Theatre and closed 28 May 1927 after 16 performances. Total: 292 performances including first engagement.

CAST (in order of appearance): *Jamison:* ZEPPO MARX. *Eddie:* David Breen. *Mrs. Potter:* MARGARET DUMONT. *Harvey Yates:* HENRY WHITTEMORE. *Penelope Martyn:* JANET VELIE. *Polly Potter:* PHYLLIS CLEVELAND. *Robert Adams:* JACK BARKER. *Henry W. Schlemmer:* GROUCHO MARX. *Willie the Wop:* CHICO MARX. *Silent Sam:* HARPO MARX. *Hennessy,* a Detective: BASIL RUYSDAEL. *Frances Williams:* FRANCES WILLIAMS. *The Three Brox Sisters:* THREE BROX SISTERS. *Specialty Dancers:* The DeMarcos (Antonio, Nina).
Dancing Girls: Mildred Hamilton, Sybil Steward, Verdi Milli, Gertrude Cole, Hazel Vernon, Louise Thompson, Lucille Lee, Lotti Lee, Rita Carita, Dorothy Clarke, Frances Mallory, Mary Nesi, Essie Moore, Ethel Sweatman, Dorothy Knight, Muriel Buck. *The Cocoanut Girls:* Beverly Raynor, Mary Meys, Vivian Bartlett, Anna Bell, Emma Tuerfs, Crystal Moray, Lebanon Hoffa, Edna Caton. *The Cocoanut Beach Octette:* Rosita Kyle, Hazel Barnes, Marion Benda, Virginia Huff, Eleanor Hopkins, Dorothy Cadwell, Betty Frisby. *Gentlemen:* Jerome Robertson, Philip Porterfield, Philip Mann, Jerry Whyte, Warren Crosby, Joseph Riley, Mat Matus, Fred Greggor, Juan Marlow, Wilfred Shepard, Harold Abbey, Jerry Marlow.

1927.22 ## THE WHITE SISTER

A Musical Romance in Three Acts and a Prologue[145]. Libretto and music by Clement Giglio. Based on the novel of the same name by Marion Crawford. Staged by Clement Giglio. Musical director, Chavalier Lovreiglio. Produced by Arthur F. Warde. Opened 17 May 1927 at Wallack's Theatre and closed 21 May 1927 after 7 performances.

---

[144]Originally produced in New York 8 December 1925 at the Lyric Theatrefor 276 performances. For Synopsis of Scenes and Musical Numbers, see original 1925 production. For this engagement, the following changes were made:
"Why Do You Want to Know Why?" (replaced "Family Reputation")
"A Little Bungalow" (restored)
"Why Am I a Hit with the Ladies?," "Gentlemen Prefer Blondes" and "Ting-a-Ling" were dropped.
"Everyone in the World is Doing the Charleston" (restored)
"Why Do You Want to Know Why?" (reprise) replaced "We Should Care."
For this revival, credits for the specialty dances (uncredited during the original New York run) were added for "Everyone in the World Is Doing the Charleston" as follows:
Specialty Dance
A. DeMarco, N. DeMarco
English Charleston
D. Clark, H. Vernon, Lucille Lee, Lottie Lee
Spanish Charleston
B. Walker, F. Mallory, M. Buck, E. Moore
Lenox Avenue Charleston
G. Cole, R. Carita, L. Thompson, M. Hamilton
Russian Charleston
E. Sweetman, V. Milli, M. Nesi, D. Knight
[145]Produced with success the preceding season as an opera "Monaca Blanca" in Italian on 14th Street. Settings, costumes uncredited.

CAST (in order of appearance): *Sister Giovanna*: JOSIE JONES. *Countess Chiaramonte*: MARIA SPINELLI. *Captain Giovanni*: EUGENE SCUDDER. *Lieutenant Basile*: ENZO SARAFINI *Monsignor Seracinesca*: GEORGE PULITI. *Bresca*: Alexander Giglio. *Inspector*: S. Gridelli. *Doctor*: G. Magni. *Soldiers, Peasants, Nuns, etc.*

Prologue: The Cathedral.

Act 1: Courtyard of the Convent.

Act 2: A Room in the Observatory.

Act 3: Courtyard of the Convent.

THE GRAND STREET FOLLIES (1927)

1927.23

A Musical Revue in Two Acts, 19 Scenes[146]. Sketches and lyrics by Agnes Moran. Music by Max Ewing or from very familiar sources. Costumes and settings by Aline Bernstein. Music directed by Howard Barlow. Staged by the Neighborhood Playhouse. Produced by the Neighborhood Playhouse. Opened 19 May 1927 at the Neighborhood Theatre, moved 31 May 1927 to the Little Theatre, and closed 24 September 1927 after 148 performances.

CAST: Albert Carroll, Dorothy Sands, Marc Loebell, Agnes Morgan, Otto Hulicius, Aline Bernstein, John Francis Roche, Paula Trueman, Lois Shore, Junius Matthews, Lily Lubell, George Bratt, Blanche Talmud, Ralph Geddis, Sadie Sussman, J. Blake Scott, Mae Noble, George Hoag, Polaire Weissman, Bert Farjeon, Edna Frankau, Edmund Rickett, Ethel Frankau, George Heller, Odna Brandeis, William Challee, John Haggart, Estelle Helle.

ACT 1[147]

Scene 1

A Morning Lecture and Its Results
Professor Piffle: E. Ricket. *A Woman*: A. Morgan. *A Child*: L. Shore.

Scene 2

"Stars With Stripes"
(*Lyrics by* Dorothy Sands and Marc Loebell.)
Two Prisoners: D. Sands, M. Loebell. *Other Inmates*: Company.

Scene 3

Further Particulars
"La Prisonnière"
P. Trueman
(*Music by* Max Ewing. *Lyrics by* Albert Carroll.)
A Lady of Sex: M. Noble. *A 'Virgin Man'*: R. Geddis.

Scene 4

Salem Corners, or The Crime Wave Hits the Rural Districts[148]
(*by* Agnes Morgan)
Scene: A Country Store.
Rube Smith: O. Hulicius. *Hank Brown*: M. Loebell. *Si Simpkins*: G. Bratt. *Milly Snow*: P. Weissman. *Daisie Perkins*: E. Frankau. *Maisie Perkins*: M. Noble. *Village Men*: J. B. Scott, G. Hoag. *The Sheriff*: J. F. Roche.

Scene 5

Why Girls Leave Home
Professor Piffle: E. Rickett. *Violet*: L. Shore. *Jane Cowl*: D. Sands.

---

[146]The fifth in the annual series of satirical revues which began at the Neighborhood Playhouse Off-Broadway in 1922.
[147]Added to the show for its Broadway run:
A Hollywood Contest: "If You Haven't Got IT" ("It") (Act 1)
(*Music by* Max Ewing.)
Elinor Glyn: D. Sands. *John Gilbert*: M. Loebell. *Lillian Gish*: P. Trueman. *Harold Lloyd*: J. Blake Scott. *Clara Bow*: S. Sussman. *Rin-tin-tin*: W. Challee. *Jackie Coogan*: L. Shore. *John Barrymore*: A. Carroll. *Estelle Taylor*: L. Lubell. *Lya de Putti*: E. Frankau. *Mary Astor*: F. Cowles. *Eddie Cantor*: G. Heller. *Camera Men, Property Men and Movie Fans*: J. F. Roche, J. Matthews, O. Hulicius, G. Hoag, R. Geddis, J. Haggart, B. Farjeon, A. Hampel, B. Talmud, P. Weissman, M. Noble, J. Roos.
An Official Welcome (Act 2)
Mrs. Manhattan: M. Noble. *Mrs. Bronx*: P. Weissman. *Mrs. Kings*: J. Roos. *Mrs. Queens*: B. Talmud. *Mrs. Richmond*: F. Cowles. *His Honor, the Mayor*: A. Carroll.
"Unaccustomed As I Am"
(*Music by* Max Ewing. *Lyrics by* Albert Carroll.)
[148]Later retitled The Tabloids Reach Salem's Corners.

Scene 6

"Three Little Maids from Broadway Town"[149]
(*Music by* Max Ewing.)
Helen Ford: L. Lubell. *Mary Eaton*: P. Trueman. *Mary Hay*: S. Sussman.

Scene 7

A Fiord Joke
(*by* Albert Carroll)
Mrs. Fiske: A. Carroll. *Professor Woollcott*: J. Matthews.

Scene 8

Don't Ask Her Another: ("(Oh How) I Long to Be Simple")
(*Music by* Max Ewing.)
Professor Piffle: E. Rickett. *Violet*: L. Shore.

Scene 9

"Close Harmony at Detroit"[150] (A Minstrel Show)
Brudder Bones: G. Hoag. *Brudder Sambo*: O. Hulicius. *Interlocutor*: J. F. Roche. *Singer for the Workmen*: G. Heller. *Singer for the Farmers*: G. Bratt. *Other Workmen*: J. Haggart, R. Geddis, J. Matthews. *Their Wives*: P. Trueman, D. Sands, S. Sussman, E. Frankau. *Other Farmers*: M. Loebell, J. B. Scott, B. Farjeon. *Their Wives*: L. Lubell, B. Talmud, M. Noble, P. Weissman.

ACT 2

Scene 1

Miss Ethel Barrymore supported by an All-Star Cast in a revival of 'THE SCHOOL FOR SCANDAL'
in order of appearance the notable cast includes:
Mr. Holbrook Skinner as 'Sir Horace Huntwell': M. Loebell. *Miss Isabelle Irving Crosman as 'Lady Fanny Flounce'*: D. Sands. *Miss Francine Eagels as 'Flip'*: P. Trueman. *Mr. Wilton Drew as 'Sir Peter Flounce'*: E. Rickett. *Mrs. Helen Lowell Whiffen as 'Mistress Hazelnut'*: A. Morgan. *Moran and Mack as Two Men-Servants*: G. Heller, O. Hulicius. *Mr. Eddie Dowling Cohan as 'Percival Tripp'*: J. Matthews. *Miss Ethel Barrymore as 'Lydia Loose'*: A. Carroll.

Scene 2

Jazz Baby Learns Aesthetic Dancing
(*by* Blanche Talmud)
The Pupil: B. Talmud. *The Teacher*: S. Sussman.

Scene 3

A Criss-Cross Wordless Puzzle
(*by* J. Blake Scott and Lily Lubell)
Fred: J. B. Scott. *Dorothy*: L. Lubell.

Scene 4

"Hurray For Us!"
(A posthumous work of Gilbert and Sullivan, unearthed in the cellar of the White House during the recent excavations to install heating apparatus)
Scene: A Front Porch in Vermont.
'Cautious Cal,' President of the United Sewing Association: J. Matthews. *'Nervous Nelly,' Secretary of Home and Foreign Missions*: G. Bratt. *The Rah-Rah Boys*: J. F. Roche, G. Hoag, O. Hulicius, M. Loebell, G. Heller, J. Haggart, W. Challee, R. Geddis.

Scene 5

"A Bedtime Story"
(*Music by* Max Ewing.)
Laura Hope Crews as 'Mother': D. Sands. *Mother's Boy*: A. Carroll.

Scene 6

The Real Origin of the Black Bottom[152]
(*by* John Haggart and George Heller)
Mr. Drake: G. Heller. *Miss Ducky*: J. Haggart.

Scene 7

The Unknown Quantity: A Mystery Play
Scene: Dining Room of a Long Island Country House on a Summer's Evening.
Judge Farjeon: J. F. Roche. *Mr. Peck*: J. Matthews. *Mrs. Peck*: A. Morgan. *Doris*

---

[149]During the Broadway run, replaced by:
"Say It with Toes"
(*Music by* Edmond Rickett. *Dance by* J. B. Scott.)
Flossie Footlights: L. Lubell. *Tillie Trippit*: S. Sussman. *Kitty Kickum*: P. Trueman.
[150]Dropped during the run.
[152]During the Broadway run, replaced by:
A Society Benefit: "I'll Agree If You'll Agree"
(*Music by* Arthur Brander.)
Mrs. Stuyvesant Van Astor: A. Hampel. *Lady Phyllis Beresford*: E. Frankau. *Lord Cecil, her brother*: F. Cowles. *Master Emerson Lowell*: L. Shore. *Freddie Footloose*: G. Heller. *Trixie Trotter*: S. Sussman.

Seymour: P. Trueman. *Julia Riker*: E. Frankau. *Ralph Roche*: J. B. Scott. *John Geddes*: O. Hulicius. *Herbert*, a butler: M. Loebell.

Scene 8

"The Naughty Nineties"
  (*Music by* Max Ewing.)
  Florodora Fay: D. Sands.

Scene 9

The Reading of the Will[153]
  The Pages: J. Haggart, W. Challee. *John Barrymore*: A. Carroll.

Scene 10

Finale: ("The Banquet")
  (Company)
  (*Music by* Max Ewing. *Costumes designed by* Esther Peck, Donald Oenslager, Ernest de Weerth, Alice Bernstein.)
  Many Old Friends: Everybody.

RUDDIGORE,
1927.24 or The Witch's Curse

A Revival of the Comic Opera in Two Acts[154]. Libretto by William S. Gilbert. Music by Arthur Sullivan. Staged by Charles Jones. Entire production under the supervision of Lawrence J. Anholt. Sets designed by Rollo Wayne. Conductor, Max Hirschfeld. Choral director, Harry Gilbert. Produced by Lawrence J. Anholt. Opened 20 May 1927 at the Cosmopolitan Theatre and closed 4 June 1927 after 19 performances.

CAST: *Robin Oakapple*, a Young Farmer: ALEXANDER CLARK. *Richard Dauntless*, his Foster-Brother—A Man-o'-Wars Man: CRAIG CAMPBELL. *Sir Despard Murgatroyd of Ruddigore*, a Wicked Baronet: WILLIAM DANFORTH. *Old Adam Goodheart*, Robin's Faithful Servant: Harvey Howard. *Rose Maybud*, a Village Maiden: VIOLET CARLSON. *Mad Margaret*: SARAH M. EDWARDS. *Dame Hannah*, Rose's Aunt: DOROTHY PILZER. *Professional Bridesmaids (2)*: *Zorah*: RUTH RAMSEY. *Ruth*: JULIET BUELL.

Ghosts: *Sir Rupert Murgatroyd*, the First Baronet: Robert Willard. *Sir Jasper Murgatroyd*, the Third Baronet: John Russell. *Sir Lionel Murgatroyd*, the Sixth Baronet: Henry Riebeselle. *Sir Conrad Murgatroyd*, the Twelfth Baronet: Hugh Sorenson. *Sir Desmond Murgatroyd*, the Sixteenth Baronet: Noel Harland. *Sir Gilbert Murgatroyd*, the Eighteenth Baronet: Donald Black. *Sir Mervyn Murgatroyd*, the Twentieth Baronet: Paul Shorran. *Sir Roderic Murgatroyd*, the Twenty-First Baronet: HERBERT L. WATEROUS. *Chorus of Officers, Ancestors, Professional Bridesmaids, Bucks, Blades.*
Ladies: Dorothy Johnson, Vestol Christenberry, Madeline Biltmore, Rose Host, Helen Lehman, Hilda Withes, Alice Huntington, Mary Felder, Sue Lake, Juliet Buell, Ruth Ramsey, Alan Moray, Eva Syfert, Patricia Johnson, Beatrice Clark, Peggy Thomas, Cassandra Brown, Carolyn Ferree, Leona Mourton, Sally Coakley, Margaret Grove. *Gentlemen*: Paul Shorran, Herbert Rothwell, Lee Burroughs, Vernon Rudolph, Donald Black, Robert Bennett, John Russell, Basel Kirk, Henry Riebeselle, Hugh Sorenson, John Jendrick, Noel Harland, George Ganon, Walter Brennon, Edward Huffman, Robert Willard, Jack Edmunds, Andrew Burjoyne.

PATIENCE,
1927.25 or Bunthorne's Bride

A Revival of the Comic Opera in Two Acts[155]. Libretto by William S. Gilbert. Music by Arthur Sullivan. Staged by Robert Milton. Ensembles and incidental dances staged by Antoni Nelle. Costumes and settings designed by Clark Robinson. Orchestra directed by Perke Hamberg. Produced by Perke Hamberg Productions, Inc. Opened 23 May 1927 at the Masque Theatre and closed 4 June 1927 after 16 performances.

CAST: *Reginald Bunthorne*: JAMES WATTS. *Archibald Grosvenor*: JOSEPH MACAULAY. *Mr. Bunthorne's Solicitor*: Hartley Gregson. *Officers of the Dragoon Guards (3)*: *Colonel Calverley*: WILLIAM LANGAN. *Major Murgatroyd*: DUDLEY MARWICK. *Lieutenant, The Duke of Dunstable*: HAROLD HANSEN. *Rapturous Maidens (4)*: *The Lady Jane*: BERNICE MERSHON. *The Lady Saphir*: Elinor Edeson. *The Lady Angela*: BEATRICE KNEALE. *The Lady Ella*: MARGARET SCHILLING. *Patience*: VIVIAN HART.

Rapturous Maidens: Aida Conkey, Elsie Eyre, Pieter Dominick, Olga Myshkin, Dorothy Allen, Elizabeth Crandall, Keeta King, Mary Lang, Claire Lipton, Marjorie Melling, Mathilde Pasher, Edna May Hamilton, Pirrko Ahlquist, Wynn Ralph, Mildred Gethins, Nina Deane, Virginia Stevens. *Heavy Dragoons*: Vincent Curran, Cyril Joyce, Norman Murray, Lynn Root, Jack James, Edward DeLong, Daniel Wakeley, Theodore Kushell, George Macready, Sigmund Glukoff, Albert Valnor, Lester Niles, Carl Theman, Elliott Smith, David Sager, Sidney J. Smith.

TALES OF RIGO
1927.26

A Music Drama in Three Acts, 4 Scenes. Drama (book) by Maurice V. Samuels, based on a story by Hyman Adler. (Adapted from the play 'Drift' by the same authors.) Music and lyrics by Ben Schwartz, (Evelyn Adler.) Play and numbers staged by Clarence Derwent. Set design by August Vimnera. Costume design by Mahieu. Produced by Jacob Oppenheimer. Opened 30 May 1927 at the Lyric Theatre and closed 4 June 1927 after 8 performances[156].

CAST (in order of appearance): *Maria*: MILDRED HOLLAND. *Roberts*: Maurice M. Fein. *Bones*: Jay Fassett. *Jose*: Hugh Kidder. *Rigo*: HYMAN ADLER. *Zita*: MIRA NIRSKA. *Seton*: David Leonard. *Vivien Ranger*: Marguerite Borough. *Ralph Clark*: WARREN STERLING. *Mrs. Ranger*: MADELINE GREY. *Henry Clark*: George Stillwell. *C. Marsden*: Carl Reed. *Mrs. Marsden*: Gladys Wilson. *Gypsies (3)*: *Pablo*: Samuel Nusbam. *Kashi*: Walter Deloff. *Buzi*: Andrew Salama.

The action takes place in the summer in and around San Diego, California.

Act 1: Rigo's Camp of Gypsy Vagrants. Morning.

Act 2, Scene 1: Interior of Gypsy Tent. *Scene 2*: Drawing Room of Mrs. Ranger's Home.

Act 3: Rigo's Camp of Gypsy Vagrants. Night.

ACT 1

"I'll Tell You All Someday"
  H. Adler, M. Nirska

"In Romany"
  H. Adler, Gypsies

ACT 2

"What Care We?" (Song of Destiny)
  M. Nirska, Gypsies

"Little Princess"
  M. Nirska

"Zita"
  H. Adler, Gypsies

ACT 3

"Rigo's Last Lullaby"
  H. Adler, Gypsies
  (*Music and Lyrics by* Evelyn Adler.)

MERRY-GO-ROUND
1927.27

A Musical Revue in Two Acts, 24 Scenes. Book and lyrics by Morrie Ryskind and Howard Dietz. Music by Henry Souvaine and Jay Gorney. Entire production staged by Allan Dinehart. Ballets and pantomimes staged by Walt Kuhn. Dances and ensembles staged by Raymond Midgley. Settings designed by P. Dodd Ackerman Studios. Costumes designed by Walt Kuhn. Orchestra under the direction of Gene Salzer. Produced by Richard Herndon. Opened 31 May 1927 at the Klaw Theatre; Second Edition opened 4 July, 1927 moved 12 September 1927 to the Sam Harris Theatre, and closed 24 September 1927 after 135 performances.

CAST: WILLIAM COLLIER[157], MARIE CAHILL, PHILIP LOEB, EVELYN BENNETT, DON BARCLAY, LIBBY HOLMAN, TOM BURTON, FRANCIS PIERLOT, JAMES JOLLEY, Georgia Ingram, Arthur Lipson, John Picorri, Margaret Byers, Dorothy Deeder, Jack Edwards, Billy Murray, Leonard Sillman, Blanche Fleming, Clifford Walker, Louise Richardson, William Liebling, Joyce Booth, Etienne Girardot, Hal Murray, Jack Lenny, Al Wilde, Knox Herold, Victor Edmunds, Maurice Penfold, Dorothea Chard, Mary Stills, Daniel Higgins, Elsie Baird, George F. Fitzgerald, Burt Harger, Pan-American Quartet (Charles H. Downs, Joe E. Loomis, Walter Hilliard, James B. Brown), Frances Gershwin, Helen Howell, Marian Dale,

---

[153]Dropped during the run.

[154]First presented in New York 21 February 1887 at the Standard Theatre for 53 performances. For Synopsis of Scenes and Musical Numbers, see original 1887 production. Costumes uncredited.

[155]First presented in New York 22 September 1881 at the Standard Theatre for 177 performances. For Synopsis of Scenes and Musical Numbers, see original 1881 production.

[156]Musical direction uncredited.

[157]William Collier joined the show on short notice as its compere; though his name does not appear in the opening night programs, his performance was remarked upon in all opening night reviews. He departed the cast before the Second Edition.

Doris Vinton, Ysobel Mason, Myrtle Miller, Rose Wenzel, Blanche O'Donohue, Dorothy Humphreys, Dorothy Chilton, Devah Worrell, Woody Lee Wilson, Vida Manuel, Dorothy Justin, Winnie Kerwin, Madge Nutter, Reneee Wilde, Suzanne Bennett, Hilda Manners.

ACT 1[158]

Scene 1

Ellis Island:

(a) "Sea Chantey"[159]

Inspectors: H. Murray, J. Lenny, A. Wilde, J. Edwards, M. Penfold, K. Herold.

(b) The Invasion

Algerians, Moroccans, Australians, Peruvians, Veentians, Vesuvians, etc.: B. O'Donahue, R. Wenzel, D. Worrell, V. Manuel, D. Justin, F. Gershwin, W. Kerwin, D. Humphreys, D. Deeder, M. Miller, M. Nutter, R. Wilde.

(c) *Native Dancers*: M. Dale, D. Chilton, W. L. Wilson, Y. Mason.

(d) *The New Yorker*: E. Bennett.

(e) Examination Is Vexation

Chief Inspector: C. Walker. *Frenchman*: A. Lipson. *Englishman*: J. Jolley. *Countess*: M. Cahill. *Pat*: T. Burton. *Mike*: F. Pierlot.

Scene 2

"Mockowitz, Gogelich, Babblekroit & Svonk": The Four Lawyers

First Counselor: W. Liebling. *Second Counselor*: A. Lipson. *Third Counselor*: J. Picorri. *Fourth Counselor*: P. Loeb.

Scene 3

Happy Days

Pat: T. Burton. *Mike*: F. Pierlot. *Bartender*: J. Jolley.

Scene 4

"Park Avenue"

Park Avenue Girls: D. Humphreys, B. O'Donahue, D. Chilton, Y. Mason, M. Dale, D. Worrell. *Woolworth Girls*: F. Gershwin, D. Justin, R. Wenzel, W. L. Wilson, V. Manuel, M. Miller. *Chauffeurs*: K. Herold, H. Murray, A. Wilde, J. Lenny, M. Penfold, J. Edwards.

Scene 5

"Gabriel"

M. Cahill

Assisted by Pan American Quartette.

Scene 6

The Amalgamated Bus

---

[158]After opening, the running was revised. For the Second Edition (4 July 1927 premiere) the following were added:

America Through English Eyes (Act 1)

Sir John Dunn (Bart.)

Get the Point! (*by* Bradley Barker) (Act 1)

The Outcast: D. Barclay. *The Bartender*: F. Pierlot. *The Croupier*: J. Jolley.

Evolution (Act 1)

Wife: D. Worrell. *Nurse*: M. Stills. *Doctor*: W. Liebling.

The Beetle (Act 1) (Burlesque on "The Spider")

(*Conceived and staged by* Don Barclay.)

Chartreuse: D. Barclay. *Alexander the Great*: T. Burton.

"Swanee River Melody" (Blues) (Act 2)

Pan-American Quartette

The Master Builders (Act 2)

The Engineer: D. Barclay. *The Contractor*: Sir J. Dunn.

"Usher" (The Military Usher) (Act 2)

L. Sillman

(*Music by* Manning Sherwin. *Lyrics by* Edward Eliscu.)

Shave (*by* Newman Levy) (Act 2)

Customer: T. Burton. *Louis*: P. Loeb. *Bornsdorf*: J. Piccori. *Spitzenberg*: J. Jolley. *Miss Blintz*: R. Wenzel. *Lakington*: C. Walker.

Breakfast for Three

Topics of the Day (Act 2)

Sir J. Dunn (Bart.)

"Opera Ring" (Act 2)

Joe Humphrey: W. Liebling. *Honest John Kelly*: J. Piccori. *Kid Toscanelli*: V. Edmunds. *Tito Mascagni*: A. Lipson. *Toscanelli's Manager*: K. Herold. *Mascagni's Manager*: J. Lanny.

The Nickelodeon (Act 2)

(*Conceived and staged by* Don Barclay.)

[159]Dropped during the run.

The Starter: P. Loeb. *Mr. Ginsburg*: W. Liebling. *Father*: K. Herold. *Mother*: E. Baird. *Child*: M. Byers. *Pat*: T. Burton. *Mike*: F. Pierlot. *Bride*: D. Chard. *Groom*: M. Penfold. *Miss Dodge*: M. Stills. *Englishman*: C. Walker.

Scene 7

"Sentimental Silly"

B. Fleming, J. Edwards, L. Richardson, B. Murray, J. Booth, D. Higgins

Petulant Petunias: G. F. Fitzgerald, J. Lenny, H. Murray, W. Liebling, B. Harger, L. Sillman.

Scene 8

Grand Old College Game

First Graduate: C. Walker. *Second Graduate*: E. Girardot. *Red Mange*: P. Loeb. *Right & Left Tackle*: J. Jolley. *Quarter & Half Back*: V. Edmunds. *Three Quarters & Full Back*: V. Edmunds. *Right & Left End*: M. Penfold. *Forward & Backward Tackle*: W. Liebling. *Tackle*: A. Lipson.

Scene 9

"Let's Be Happy Now"

E. Bennett, L. Sillman, H. Murray, J. Lenny, A. Wilde

Scene 10

"If Love Should Come to Me"[160]

D. Higgins

Scene 11

"Bandannas on Broadway"[161]

L. Holman

(*With*) M. Dale, D. Chilton, B. O'Donahue, W. L. Wilson, R. Wenzel, Y. Mason, D. Worrell, V. Manuel, D. Justin, F. Gershwin, W. Kerwin, D. Humphreys, D. Deeder, L. Richardson, S. Bennett, J. Booth, H. Manners, B. Fleming, J. Lenny, B. Harger, J. Edwards, L. Sillman, A. Wilde, H. Murray, D. Higgins, B. Murray, Pan American Quartette.

ACT 2

Scene 1

The Son of Jack Dalton, or The Tenderfoot's Revenge

Hero: K. Herold. *Heroine*: J. Booth. *Villain*: M. Penfold. *Fiddler*: J. Jolley. *Father*: V. Edmunds. *Stage Coach Driver*: W. Liebling. *Dance Hill Girls*: E. Baird, V. Manuel, Y. Mason. *Cow-Boys*: J. Lenny, H. Murray. *Miner*: A. Wilde. *Indians*: D. Justin, D. Worrell, D. Chilton, W. L. Wilson, M. Miller, W. Kerwin, R. Wenzel, R. Wilde, F. Gershwin.

Scene 2

"Cinder Ella"

E. Bennett

Scene 3

"Bath Room Tenor"

P. Loeb

Scene 4

"Tampa"

L. Richardson

M. Dale, H. Howell, D. Humphreys, R. Wenzel, Y. Mason, V. Manuel, B. O'Donahue, D. Justin, W. L. Wilson, W. Kerwin, F. Gershwin, D. Worrell, H. Manners, D. Chilton, J. Booth, M. Miller, D. Higgins, B. Murray, J. Lenny, B. Harger, A. Wilde, H. Murray, J. Edwards.

Scene 5

"Spring Is in the Air"[162]

M. Stills, G. F. Fitzgerald

---

[160]Dropped during the run.

[161]Replaced during the run by:

"New York Town (Is Full of Strangers)"

L. Sillman

(*With*) M. Dale, D. Chilton, B. O'Donahue, W. L. Wilson, R. Wenzel, Y. Mason, D. Worrell, V. Manuel, D. Justin, F. Gershwin, W. Kerwin, D. Humphreys, B. Fleming, Patricia Bowman, J. Lenny, B. Harger, J. Edwards, Jimmy Orman, H. Murray, D. Higgins, Larry Kane, B. Murray, Pan American Quartette.

Added for subsequent tour:

The Gypsy Trail

Pepita: Lucielle Peterson. *Karo*: John Griffon. *Annette*: Helen Howell. *Batiste*: B. Harger. *Amelio*: T. Burton. *Chanis*: Jack Neilan. *Genita*: Marie Fanchonetti. *Carmen*: Frances Guinan. *Zita*: W. L. Wilson. *Coriana*: Dolores Arnold.

Because

First Cleaner: J. Griffon. *Second Cleaner*: T. Burton.

[162]Dropped during the run.

Scene 6

Sidewalks of New York[163]

Pat: T. Burton. *Mike*: F. Pierlot.

Scene 7

In the Park

Moonlight Dance

G. Ingram

"Moonbeams"

H. Howell, B. Harger

Scene 8

"Something Tells Me"[164]

M. Dale, J. Edwards, L. Richardson, B. Murray

Parasol Girls: B. O'Donohue, D. Chilton, D. Worrell, D. Humphreys.

Specialty Dance

D. Vinton

Scene 9

"Hogan's Alley"

(*Music by* Jay Gorney.)

The Singer: L. Holman. *Gangsters*: H. Murray, J. Lenny. *Blind Man*: B. Harger. *Child*: M. Byers. *Dope Fiend*: M. Penfold. *Italian*: J. Piccori. *Mother*: E. Baird. *Scarlet Women*: J. Booth, D. Deeder. *Derelict*: J. Jolley. *Policeman*: V. Edmunds. *Housewife*: B. Fleming. *Dancer*: D. Vinton. *Gang*: W. Liebling, L. Sillman, A. Lipson, K. Herold, H. Murray, J. Edwards, A. Wilde. *Girls*: D. Humphreys, D. Worell.

Scene 10

"What D'Ya Say"

M. Cahill

Scene 11

"(My) Yes Girl" (I've Got a 'Yes' Girl)

Boy: L. Sillman. *Yes Girls*: Y. Mason, M. Dale, M. Miller, R. Wenzel. *Dancer*: B. O'Donohue.

Scene 12

The Check Room[165]

Millionaire: P. Loeb. *Policeman*: T. Burton. *Flappers*: D. Chard, M. Miller, D. Humphreys. *Unsteady Gentleman*: G. F. Fitzgerald. *Father*: E. Girardot. *Brat*: M. Byers. *Englishman*: C. Walker.

Scene 13

Carnival: (Finale)

Street Vendors, Fakirs, Freaks, Acrobats, Ballet Dancers, Tight Rope Walkers, Harmonica Players, Barkers, etc.: Entire Company.

---

[163]Dropped during the run.
[164]Dropped during the run.

---

[165]Dropped during the run.

William Gaxton in A CONNECTICUT YANKEE (Photo: Vandamm Studio)
Billy Rose Theatre Collection, New York Public Library for the Performing Arts

1927–1928 SEASON

1927.28 ## NAMIKO-SAN

A Japanese Love Drama with Music in Two Acts. Translation by Leo Duran of a play of ancient Japan. Words and music by Aldo Franchetti. Ballet divertissements and Pantomime arranged and presented by Mme. Julia Hudak and Serge Sergieff. Japanese authenticity personally supervised by Sessue Hayakawa. Conductor, Aldo Franchetti. Stage and theatre decorations by Kosai Studios. Costumes designed by Tamaki Miura and Robert R. Van Deventer. Produced by Florence M.P. Van Kirk. Opened 6 June 1927 at the Selwyn Theatre and closed 18 June 1927 after 16 performances[1].

ACT 1

CAST: JULIA HUDAK, SERGE SERGIEFF, Louise Rothacker, Stella Rothacker, Celia Pekelner, Edna Kuhler.

DANCES AND PANTOMIMES

Mousme Dance
   Ensemble
   (*Music by* Edgar Stillman Kelly.)
A Flirtation
   J. Hudak, S. Sergieff
   (*Music by* Meyer Helmund.)
Cherry Blossoms
   Ensemble
   (*Music by* Strauss.)
A Mousme's Farewell to Her Forbidden Fisherman Sweetheart (Pantomime)
   J. Hudak, S. Sergieff
   (*Arranged by* Tamaki Miura.)
Broken Doll (Pantomime)
   Ensemble
   (*Music by* Tamaki Miura.)
Warrior Dance
   M. Sergieff
   (*Music by* Fosse.)
Variations
   J. Hudak
   (*Music by* Taliaferri.)
Wedding Dance
   J. Hudaj, M. Sergieff
   (*Music by* Michilos.)]
Fantasy Tzigane
   J. Hudak, M. Sergieff
   (*Music by* Bizet.)

ACT 2

CAST: *Namiko-San*: TAMIKO MIURA. *Jiro Vanyemon*, the Daymio: GRAHAM MAAR. *Yasui*, an Itinerant Monk: JULIAN OLIVER. *Sato*, an Old Gardener: Felice de Gergorio. *Kojiro*, an Assistant Gardener: Joseph Cavadore. *Towa-san*, a Widow: Hazel Cavadore. *An Ashigaru*, a Soldier: Fausto Bozza. *The Lovers*: Jolanda Rinaldi, Joseph Cavedore. *Spirits of the Woods*: Julia Hudak, Serge Sergieff, Louise Rothacker, Stella Rothacker, Celia Pekelner, Edna Kuhler. *Ashigaru, Samurai, Attendants of the Daymio.*

1927.29 ## TALK ABOUT GIRLS

A Musical Comedy in Two Acts, 3 Scenes. Book by William Carey Duncan and Daniel Kusell. Based on the play ('Like a King') by John Hunter Booth. Music by Harold Orlob and Stephen Jones. Lyrics by Irving Caesar. Book directed by Daniel Kusell. Dances and ensembles staged by Sammy Lee. Settings designed by Walter Harvey. Costumes designed by Gertrude Johnson. Orchestra under the direction of Louis Gress. Orchestrations and musical arrangements by Stephen Jones. Produced by Harry H. Oshrin and Sam H. Grisman. Opened 14 June 1927 at the Waldorf Theatre and closed 25 June 1927 after 15 performances.

CAST (in order of appearance): *Jane Riker*: Frances Upton. *Andrew Lowe*: William Cook. *Henry Quill*, Chief Constable: WILLIAM FRAWLEY. *General Weston*: Edwin

Forsberg. *Elsie*: Lillian Michel. *Calvin Lowe*, Andrew's father: Spencer Charters. *Abigail*: Madelyn Killeen. *Sue Weston*, Jane's cousin: JANE TAYLOR. *Charles Parsons*: Floyd Marion. *Mrs. Alden*: FLORENCE EARLE. *Philip Alden*, her son: RUSSELL MACK. *Dan Mason*: ANDREW TOMBES. *J. W. Savage*: Bernard McOwen. *Simmons*: John Meehan, Jr. *George V. Grubble*: Joseph Smiley. *May James*: Constance McKensie. *Ladies of the Ensemble*: Florence Murray, Marie Marceline, Alice Akers, Ellen O'Brien, Kathleen McLoughlin, Alice O'Brien, Madeline Janis, Edith Hayward, Betty Wright, Ida Berry, Gertrude Lowe, Lillian Michel, Gertrude Arthur, Edna Hopper, Liane Mamet, Cora Stephens, Beth Milton, Helene Sheldon. *Gentlemen of the Ensemble*: Harold Ettus, Bernard Hassert, Frank Phillips, William Sahner, William Bailey, Aaron Fischer, Floyd Marion, Richard Tyle, Kenneth Smith. .

Act 1, Scene 1: At Night in Central Park.

Scene 2: The Commons, Lower Falls, Massachusetts.

Act 2: Living Room at Mrs. Alden's.

ACT 1[2]
Scene 1
   "In Central Park"
      Ensemble
Scene 2
   "Come to Lower Falls" (Opening)
      Ensemble
   "The Only Boy"
      W. Cook, Ensemble
   "Oo, How I Love You"
      M. Killen, W. Frawley
   "Home Town"
      F. Earle, R. Mack
   "Talk About Girls"
      R. Mack, A. Tombes
   "A Lonely Girl"
      J. Taylor, R. Mack, Ensemble
   "Maybe I Will"
      F. Upton, A. Tombes, Ensemble
   Finale
      Principals, Ensemble
ACT 2
   "Heel and Toe" (Opening)
      M. Killen, Ensemble
      Specialty C. McKensie, J. Meehan, Jr.
   "In Twos"[3]
      J. Taylor, R. Mack
   "Sex Appeal"
      A. Tombes, Ensemble
   That's My Man"
      J. Taylor, F. Upton, M. Killeen
   "Nineteen Twenty-Seven"
      F. Upton, Ensemble
   Specialty
      C. McKensie, J. Meehan, Jr.
   "One Boy's Enough for Me"
      J. Taylor, Boys
   "Maybe I Will" (reprise)
      F. Upton, A. Tombes
   Finale
      Entire Company

1927.30 ## BOTTOMLAND

A Musical Comedy in Three Acts, 6 Scenes. Book, music and lyrics by Clarence Williams. Staged by Clarence Williams and Aaron Gates. Scenery by the Beaumont Studios. Orchestra under the direction of Clarence Williams. Produced by Clarence Williams, Inc. Opened 27 June 1927 at the Princess Theatre and closed 13 July 1927 after 19 performances[4].

---

[2]After opening, the text was revised, cast list order revised.
[3]"In Twos" and "Sex Appeal" were dropped after opening and replaced by:
   "Loving Time"
      J. Taylor, Ensemble
[4]Costumes uncredited.

---

[1]Musical numbers not listed individually.

CAST (in order of appearance): *May Mandy Lee*: EVA TAYLOR. *At the Piano*: CLARENCE WILLIAMS. *Mammy Lee*: SARA MARTIN. *Pappy Lee*: JAMES A. LIL-LIARD. *Jimmy*: Louis Cole. *Tough Tilly*: Katherine Henderson. *Joshua*: Slim Henderson. *The Dumb Waiter*: John Mason. *Henry Henpeck*: Charles Doyle. *Shiftless Sam*: "Nuggie" Johnson. *Skinny*: Raymond Campbell. *Rastus*: Edward Farrow. *Sally*: OLIVE OTIZ. *Mammy Chloe*: Willie Porter. *Kid Slick*: Emanuel Weston. *Policeman Doolittle*: Edwin Tonde. *Specialty*: Craddock and Shadney.

Chorus: Dot Campbell, Alice Carter, Gansea Otiz, Bertha Wright, Billie Yarbough, Dolly Langhorn, Portia Hands, Edith Dunbar, Mildred Pritchard, Walter Miller.

Act 1, Scene 1: Bottomland. *Scene 2*: A Country Road in Bottomland. *Scene 3*: A Barbecue Restaurant.

Act 2, Scene 1: A Street in New York. *Scene 2*: A Cabaret in Harlem.

Act 3: Bottomland.

MUSICAL NUMBERS[5]

"Steamboat Days"

"(I'm Going Back to) Bottomland"
  E. Taylor
  (*Lyrics by* Jo Trent.)

"Shoot Dat Pistol" (Shootin' the Pistol)(Finale Act 1)
  (*Lyrics by* Chris Smith.)

"You're the Only One That I Love"
  (*Lyrics by* Len Gray.)

"Come On Home"
  (*Music and Lyrics by* Donald Heywood.)

"Dancing Girl"
  (*Music and Lyrics by* Spencer Williams and Clarence Williams.)

"Any Time"
  (*Lyrics by* Joe Jordan.)

"When I March With April in May"
  (*Music and Lyrics by* Spencer Williams and Gerald Williams.)

"I'm Gonna Take My Bimbo Back to the Bamboo Isle"

Duet
  E. Taylor, L. Cole

1927.31 ## PADLOCKS OF 1927

A Summer Carnival (Musical Revue) in Two Acts, 26 Scenes. Sketches by Paul Gerard Smith and Ballard Macdonald. Music by Lee David, Jesse Greer, Henry H. Tobias. Lyrics by Billy Rose. Staged by William J. Wilson. Dances staged by John Boyle. Costumes designed by Robert Stevenson, Mahieu, Orry Kelly. Musical director, Carlton Kelsey. Musical arrangements by Joseph Nussbaum. Texas Guinan Strollers Orchestra under the direction of Anthony Giannitto. Produced by Duo Art Productions, Inc. (C. W. Morganstern, Anton F. Scibilia). (Messrs. Shubert) Opened 5 July 1927 at the Sam S. Shubert Theatre and closed 24 September 1927 after 95 performances.

CAST: TEXAS GUINAN, LILLIAN ROTH, HELEN SHIPMAN, DRINA BEACH, FLORENCE HEALY, VIRGINIA SMITH, LAURA WILKINSON, ROSEMARY RYDER, MARY TITUS, ELEANOR SMITH, MAE BURKE, HEDWIG LANGER, IRENE FAERY, SNOWBALL, HARRY JANS, HAROLD WHALEN, CARL D. FRANCIS, JAY C. FLIPPEN, A. S. BYRON, WALTER BURKE, DAVE MALLEN, DON FISER, GEORGE RAFT, OJEDA and INBERT, THE ROMANCERS QUARTET, THE PHELPS TWINS (Irene, Florine), RAYMOND MARLOW, HEDWIG LANGER, The Four Diamonds and the Little Tappers.

Dancing Ensemble: Carol Kingsbury, Jola Morena, Laurette Gilman, Helenya Koski, Doris Dellairs, Eileen Wenzel, Betty Clark, Edna Locke, Edna Burford, Gloria Glennon, Nora Cliff, Sugar O'Neill, Val Lester, Rurth Grady, Vee Carroll, Billee Blake, Jackie Cortez, Wilma Roelof, Bera Berg, Marcel Miller, Peggy Daubert, Rosalie Williams, Alice Outlaw, Edna French, Dolores Grant, Vivian Carmody, Catherine Ryder.

Texas Guinan and Her Gang in the Lobby

ACT 1[6]

Scene 1

  On the Way: "Texas"T. Guinan, Romancers Quartette and the Gang
    Scene: Times Square.

---

[5]Musical numbers not listed in the program, and are not in performance order. List prepared from reviews, published songs and recordings.
[6]The running order of songs and sketches was revised during the run. Added was:

  College Days (Act 2)
    H.Jans, H. Whalen

"Here I Am"
  T. Guinan
  (*Music by* Billy Rose. *Lyrics by* Billy Rose, Ballard Macdonald.)
Scene 2

"Texas, Barnum & Cohan"
  T. Guinan, A. S. Byron, D. Mallen
  (*Music by* Jesse Greer. *Lyrics by* Billy Rose, Ballard Macdonald.)
Scene 3

The Phelps Twins in Drapes (Dance)
Scene 4

"If I Had a Lover"
  H. Shipman, C. D. Francis, Dancing Girls
  (*Music by* Henry Tobias. *Lyrics by* Billy Rose, Ballard Macdonald.)
Scene 5

Blindsman's Buff (by Ballard Macdonald and Billy Rose)
  Wife: T. Guinan. *Lover*: W. Burke. *Maid*: D. Beach. *Husband*: A. S. Byron.
Scene 6

"Personality"/["Ain't He Sweet?"[7]
  L. Roth
  (*Music by* Milton Ager. *Lyrics by* Jack Yellen.)]
Scene 7

Ninety Days from Broadway
  J. C. Flippen, A. S. Byron, D. Mallen, V. Smith, L. Wilkinson, W. Burke
Scene 8

"(Tell Her in the) Summertime"
  The Phelps Twins
  (*Music by* Jesse Greer. *Lyrics by* Billy Rose, Ballard Macdonald.)
Dance
  D. Beach
Scene 9

Foolery
  H. Jans, H. Whalen
Scene 10

"The Tap Tap"
  L. Roth
  (*Music by* Jesse Greer. *Lyrics by* Billy Rose, Ballard Macdonald.)
Dance
  The Four Diamonds and the Little Tappers
Scene 11

Cut In (*by* Paul Gerard Smith)
  T. Guinan, C. D. Francis, D. Mallen, D. Fiser
  Announcement: F. Healy.
Scene 12

Flippenology
  J. C. Flippen, V. Smith
Scene 13

The Texas Guinan Club
  T. Guinan and Her Mob
"String Along with Texas"
  T. Guinan, Her Girls
Entertainment
  The Romancers Quartette, L. Wilkinson, R. Ryder, F. Healy, M. Titus, E. Smith, M. Burke, H. Langer, I. Faery, Snowball, G. Raft
Spanish Specialty
  Ojeda and Inbert
Texas Guinan Strollers
  Orchestra (Anthony Giannitto, Director)

ACT 2

Scene 1

"Hot Heels"
  H. Shipman, C. D. Francis, Dancing Girls
  (*Music by* Lee David. *Lyrics by* Billy Rose, Ballard Macdonald.)
Spanish Specialty
  Ojeda and Inbert

---

[7]Dropped during the run and replaced by:
  "Hotsy Totsy" (Act 1)
    Texas Guinan Strollers

Scene 2

"It's Tough to Be a Hostess"
T. Guinan, Brass Button Blues, assisted by the Romancers Quartette
(*Music by* Billy Rose. *Lyrics by* Billy Rose, Ballard Macdonald.)

Scene 3

Sing Sing
Newlyweds: H. Jans, V. Smith. *Charley:* H. Whalen. *Officer:* D. Fiser.

Scene 4

Jail Satire (by Ballard Macdonald and Billy Rose)
The Virgin Man: A. S. Byron. *Sex:* H. Shipman. *The Captive:* L. Roth. *The Drag:* D. Mallen.

Scene 5

"That Stupid Melody" (Stupid Melody)
H. Shipman, C. D. Francis
(*Music by* Billy Rose. *Lyrics by* Billy Rose, Ballard Macdonald.)

Scene 6

"Tom Tom (Days)"
R. Marlow, The Romancers Quartette
(*Music by* Jesse Greer. *Lyrics by* Billy Rose, Ballard Macdonald.)

Tiger Dance
D. Beach, Dancing Girls

Scene 7

Out of the Directory
Madame: H. Shipman. *Master:* C. D. Francis. *Villain:* D. Mallen.

Scene 8

"Rhinestones"[8]
Phelps Twins

Scene 9

Tiger Lily's Honkytonk (by Paul Gerard Smith)
Tiger Lily: T. Guinan. *The Kid:* D. Mallen. *Colorado:* C. D. Francis. *Goldie:* V. Smith. *Friend:* A. S. Byron. *Bartender:* D. Fiser. *Cowboys, Dance Hall Girls, Others.*

Scene 10

"Hoppin' the Buck"
The Four Diamonds, Dancing Girls

Scene 11

Preparedness
T. Guinan, H. Jans, H. Whalen, Guinan's Kids

Scene 12

Jay C. Flippen

Scene 13

On the Steps of the New Texas Guinan Club, Bigger and Better:
"Opened Up Again"
T. Guinan, Entire Company

1927.32 # AFRICANA

A Musical Revue in Two Acts, 12 Scenes. Music and lyrics by Donald Heywood. Conceived and staged by Earl Dancer. Dances and ensembles staged by Louis Douglas. Settings designed by Walter Lewis and James Tichenor. Costumes designed by Charles LeMaire. Orchestra under the direction of Allie Ross. Orchestrations by William [Grant] Still. Produced by Earl Dancer. Opened 11 July 1927 at Daly's Theatre, closing 16 August 1927; reopened 20 August 1927 at the National Theatre and closed 10 September 1927 after 72 performances[9].

CAST: ETHEL WATERS, BILLY MILLS, HENRY WINIFRED, MIKE RIELY, PAUL BASS, AL WILKINS, ED PUGH, MARGARET BECKETT, BABY and BOBBY GOINS, LOUIS DOUGLAS, EDNA BARR, THE TASKIANA FOUR, EDDIE and SONNY, "PICKANINNY" HILL, THE SOUTHLAND SYNCOPATORS (in the pit).

Ladies of the Ensemble: Margaret Beckett, Theresa Mason, Juanita Boyd, Bertye Byrd, Margaret Burns, Bernice Ackins, Laronia Bradley, Eva Bradley, Roberta Lowery, Adelaide Jones, Jenny Salmons, Lucille Smith, Claire Wilson, Rose Young.

---

[8]Dropped during the run and replaced by:
"Toy Soldier" (Dance)
Phelps Twins
[9]Sketches uncredited.

ACT 1[10]

Scene 1

"Black Cargo" (Entre)
Taskiana Four, African Girls

"Bugle Blues" (Dance)
E. Pugh

"Weary Feet"
E. Waters

Tap Drill by Aunt Hagar's Children
E. Waters, Girls

Scene 2

"A Step a Second" (Specialty)
M. Riely, A. Wilkins

Scene 3

The Chinese Revolution
H. Winifred, B. Mills

Scene 4

The Original Black Bottom Dance
E. Waters, Girls
[*Music by* Perry Bradford. *Lyrics by* Gus Horsley.]

Scene 5

Judgement Day
Scene: The Courtroom in Catch Air, Mississippi. *Time:* Any Monday Morning. *Defense Attorney:* M. Riely. *Prosecutor:* P. Bass. *Officer Allblack:* E. Pugh. *His Honor the Judge:* B. Mills. *One Lung:* H. Winifred. *Sadie Go About:* M. Beckett. *A Suspicious Character:* A. Wilkins.

Scene 6

Eccentric (Dance) Specialty
Baby Goins, Bobby Goins

Scene 7

The Minstrel Congress
"The Old-Fashioned Cakewalk"
E. Waters, Entire Company
(led by 'Pickaninny' Hill, champion cakewalker of the world)

Dance of the Tambourines
Africana Girls

A Little Minstrel and Spiritual Harmony
Taskiana Four

Finale: "The Cakewalk Strut"
Entire Company

ACT 2

Scene 1

The Mississippi
"Time Ain't Very Long" (Song)
Africana Octette

"Smile" (Song)
E. Waters

Scene 2

Specialty
L. Douglas

---

[10]The running order of songs and sketches was revised during the run. Added during the run of the show:

Tap Black Bottom Dance (Act 1, Scene 4)
Sonny and Eddie

"Here Comes the Showboat" (Act 1)
E. Waters
(*Music by* Maceo Pinkard. *Lyrics by* Billy Rose.)

At the Railroad Station (Act 2)
Clenn and Jenkins

"Shine 'Em Up!" (Act 2)
Snow Fischer, Robichaux, Johnson, Taylor, Johnson

Songs You Have Home on Your Records (Act 2)
E. Waters

Broom Dance (Act 2, Scene 5)
Glenn and Jenkins

"Chloe"
(*Music by* Neil Moret. *Lyrics by* Gus Kahn.)

Scene 3

A Romantic Interlude

"Clorinda"
P. Bass, E. Barr
The Boy: M. Beckett. *The Girl*: T. Mason. Clorinda Girls and Boys, The Taskiana Four, Baby and Bobby Goins.

Scene 4

"Argufyin'"
B. Mills

Scene 5

Harlem Transplanted to Paris
Scene: Chez Florence, a colored Parisian café.
Master of Ceremonies: P. Bass.
Specialty
African Jazzers directed by Allie Ross
'Banana Maidens' à la Josephine Baker
M. Beckett, Ten Little Bananas
Specialty
E. Waters
["My Special Friend Is in Town"
(*Music by* James C. Johnson. *Lyrics by* Andy Razaf.)
"Don't Mess Around with My Man"
"Shake That Thing"
(*Music and Lyrics by* Papa Charlie Jackson.)
"Take Your Black Bottom Out of Here"
(*Music by* Clarence Williams. *Lyrics by* ?.)
"I'm Comin' Virginia"
(*Music by* Donald Heywood. *Lyrics by* Will Marion Cook and Donald Heywood.)
"You Can't Do What My Last Man Did"
(*Music and Lyrics by* James C. Johnson.)

Scene 6

Eccentric (Dance) Specialty
Baby Goins, Bobby Goins

Scene 7

The Minstrel Congress
"The Old-Fashioned Cakewalk"
E. Waters, Entire Company
"Dinah"
(*Music by* Harry Akst. *Lyrics by* Sam M. Lewis, Joe Young.)]
Specialty
Baby and Bobby Goins
"Africana Stomp"
E. Waters, L. Douglas, Girls
Grand Finale
Entire Company

1927.33   # RANG TANG

A Musical Extravaganza (Revue) in Two Acts, 11 Scenes. Book by Kaj Gynt. Music by Ford Dabney. Lyrics by Jo Trent. Entire production staged by Flournoy E. Miller. Dances arranged by Charles Davis. Settings and costumes designed by Olle Nordmark. Masks, lantern heads and shields by H. Foster Anderson. Orchestra under the direction of Ford Dabney. Orchestrations and vocal arrangements by Russell Wooding. Produced by Messrs. Walker and Kavanaugh. Opened 12 July 1927 at the Royale Theatre, moved 12 September 1927 to the Majestic Theatre, and closed 22 October 1927 after 119 performances.

CAST: FLOURNOY E. MILLER, AUBREY LYLES, DANIEL L. HAYNES, ZAIDEE JACKSON, JOSEPHINE HALL, INEZ DRAW, GEORGE BATTLES, EVELYN PREER, JOSEPHINE JACKSON, LILLIAN WESTMORELAND, MAY BARNES, LAVINIA MACK, CRAWFORD JACKSON, BYRON JONES, JOE WILLIS.
Male Chorus: Daniel L. Haynes, Ambrose Allen, Howard Brown, C. H. Gordon, Gilbert Holland, Burkie Jackson, Snippy Mason, Llewellyn Ransom, James Strange, Joseph Willis, Clarence Todd, Edwin Alexander, George Battles, Edward Thompson.
Ladies of the Ensemble: Le'Etta Ravells, Pauline Jackson, Susie Baker, Gladyce Bronson, Doris Colbert, La Valla Cook, Inez Draw, Teddy Garnette, Alice Hoffman, Margie Hubbard, Frances Hubbard, Evelyn Keyes, Marie Mahood, Frankye Maxwell, Thelma McLaughlin, Hazel Miles, Thula Ortez, Thelma Rhoton, Gladys Schell,

Helen Smith, Norma Smith, Gomez Boyer, Mildred Coleman, Leonore Gadsden, Isabel Peterson, Ethelyn Boyd, Irma Miles, Marie Simmons, Anna Humphrey, Gertrude Williams.

Act 1, Scene 1: Public Square, Jimtown. *Scene 2*: Loafer's Lane, Jimtown. *Scene 3*: Adrift. *Scene 4*: The Shores of Africa. *Scene 5*: A Jungle Trail. *Scene 6*: The Bamboo Forest.

Act 2, Scene 1: A Dream. *Scene 2*: The Desert. *Scene 3*: The Native Village. *Scene 4*: A Jungle Trail. *Scene 5*: Harlem Cabaret.

ACT 1[11]

Scene 1

Daybreak
Mrs. Jenkins: L. Westmoreland. *Laborers, Washwomen, Cottonpickers.*
Barber Shop Business
Customer: J. Strange. *Villagers*: B. Jackson, A. Allen, E. Thompson.
"Everybody Shout"
Villagers, Jimtown Quartette
Jimtown Quartette: S. Mason, J. Willis, C. Todd, A. Allen.
Dance Specialty
B. Jones
"Sammy and Topsy"
I. Draw, M. Barnes
Magnolia: Z. Jackson. *Mrs. Jenkins*: L. Westmoreland.
"Brown"
Z. Jackson, Jimtown Dandies
Dance Specialty
C. Jackson
"Pay Me"
Jimtown Business Men
Steve Jenkins, a Barber: F. E. Miller. *Sam Peck*, another Barber: A. Lyles. *Sheriff*: E. Thompson. *Insurance Man*: E. Alexander.
"Sambo's Banjo"
Z. Jackson, Banjo Ensemble

Scene 2

Missing
L. Westmoreland, Alice, Villagers
"Some Day"
J. Hall, Jimtown Trio
Jimtown Trio: J. Willis, L. Revells, M. Simmons.
Spirituals
Jimtown Glee Club
(*Special arrangements* by Daniel L. Haynes.)

Scene 3

The (Lost) Aviators
F. E. Miller, A. Lyles

Scene 4

"Come to Africa"
J. Hall, Native Girls

Scene 5

Steve and Sam
F. E. Miller, A. Lyles

Scene 6

"Zulu Fifth Avenue"
E. Preer, Zulu Steppers
Jungle Love:
"Jungle Rose"
D. L. Haynes
Jungle Rose: E. Preer.
King of Madagascar: D. L. Haynes.
Monkey Business:
"Monkey Land"
F. E. Miller, A. Lyles
Simian: L. Ransom.
Apes, Monkey Band, Missing Links, Baboon Quartet, Chimpanzees, Monkeys.

ACT 2

Scene 1

---

[11]The running order of songs and sketches was revised during the run and for subsequent tour. Added to Act 2, Scene 3:

"Doctor Voodoo"
Maude Russell

498

A Dream
  The Queen of Africa: L. Westmoreland. Her Handmaiden: G. Williams.

Nymph Dance
  M. Mahood
  Jungle Rose: E. Preer. *The Queen of Sheba*: J. Hall. *A Courier*: F. Maxwell. Lantern Bearers, Handmaidens and Couriers.

"Sweet Evening Breeze"
  J. Hall

A Jungle Family
  Chief Bobo: J. Willis. *The Six Little Wives*: M. Hubbard, M. Mahood, E. Keyes, T. McLaughlin, H. Miles, F. Hubbard.

The Jungle School
  The Teachers: F. E. Miller, A. Lyles. *Native*: F. Maxwell. *Hunter*: J. Strange.

Voodoo"
  Voodoo Chief: G. Holland.

Voodoo Dance
  Natives

Scene 2

"Summer Nights"
  J. Hall

Dance
  M. Barnes, L. Mack, B. Jones

The Prospectors
  F. E. Miller, A. Lyles
  The Queen of Africa: L. Westmoreland.

The Mirage
  The Steppers

Scene 3

The Captive
  The Prisoner: F. E. Miller. *Stranger*: A. Lyles. *Chief*: G. Battles. *Guard*: E. Thompson.

Moon Dances

Scene 4

The Settlement
  Chief: G. Battles. *Steve and Sam*: F. E. Miller, A. Lyles.

Fisticuffs
  F. E. Miller, A. Lyles

Scene 5

"Harlem"
  E. Preer, Harlem Sextet, Harlemites

Dance Specialty
  M. Barnes, L. Mack
  Head Waiter: J. Willis. *Cigarette Girl*: M. Mahood. *Entertainer*: Z. Jackson. *Manager*: E. Thompson.

Dance Specialty
  B. Jones

A Couple of Live Ones
  F. E. Miller, A. Lyles
  A Beauty: L. Revells.

Dance Specialty
  Bryson and Jones

A New Dance: "Rang Tang"
  E. Preer, Entire Company

1927.34   KISS ME!

A Musical Comedy in Two Acts, 3 Scenes. Book by Derick Wulff, Max Simon. Based on an (unnamed) French farce adapted by a German playwright (Richard Kessler). Music by Winthrop Cortelyou. Lyrics by Derick Wulff. Staged by Edward Elsner. Dances arranged by M. Senia Gluck. Costumes designed by Robert Stevenson. Settings designed by August Vimnera. Orchestra under the direction of Alfred Newman. Produced by J. J. Levinson. Opened 21 July 1927 at the Lyric Theatre and closed 13 August 1927 after 28 performances.

<u>CAST</u> (in order of appearance): *Billings*, Paul's butler: William Sellery. *Denise*, a model: Marjorie Peterson. *Tom Warren*: RALPH WHITEHEAD. *Eugene Moreaux*: Charles Lawrence. *A Clerk in the Marriage License Office*: Eddie Russell, Jr. *Paul Travers*: FREDERIC SANTLEY. *Doris Durant Dodo*: DESIREE ELLINGER. *Prince Hussein Dschahangie Mirza*, Persian Prince: JOSEPH MACAULAY. *Gendarme*: Eddie Russell, Jr. *Talazada*, Favorite Wife of the Prince: Enid Romany.

Models and Harem Girls: Dorothy Dawn, Dorothy Dodd, Gladys Englander, Betty Andrews, Nettie Bennis, Crystal Moray, Dorothy Dixon, Mona Fay, Hazel Stanley, Helen Thompson, Olga Borowski, Alice Blaine, Myra Blaine, Rosalie Trego, Ursula Murray, Elvira Trego

Act 1: Reception Room in Travers' Studio in Paris.

Act 2, Scene 1: In the Shah's Harem. Two months later. *Scene 2*: Reception Room in Travers' Studio in Paris. Two weeks later.

ACT 1

Opening Ensemble
  Ladies of the Ensemble

"Kiss Me!"
  M. Peterson, R. Whitehead

"I Have Something Nice for You"
  C. Lawrence, Girls

"Sleeping Beauty's Dream"
  D. Ellinger

"Arab Maid with Midnight Eyes"
  M. Macauley, Girls

"You in Your Room; I in Mine"
  D. Ellinger, F. Santley

"Two Is Company"
  M. Peterson, R. Whitehead, C. Lawrence, Girls

Specialty
  E. Russell, Jr.

Finale
  D. Ellinger, F. Santley, R. Whitehead, C. Lawrence, W. Sellery, Girls

ACT 2

Scene 1

Dance
  Harem Girls

Dane of the Green Eyes
  E. Romany

"Rose of Iran"
  D. Ellinger, J. Macauley

Scene 2

"Welcome Home" (Opening Ensemble)
  M. Peterson, Girls

"If You'll Always Say Yes"
  D. Ellinger, F. Santley, Girls

"I Have Something Nice for You" (reprise)
  M. Peterson, R. Whitehead

"Rose of Iran" (reprise)
  D. Ellinger, J. Macauley

"Kiss Me!" (reprise)
  D. Ellinger, R. Whitehead, M. Peterson, Girls

SpecialtyGirls

"Dodo"
  D. Ellinger, J. Macauley, F. Santley, R. Whitehead, C. Lawrence

Specialty
  E. Russell, Jr.

"Pool of Love"
  D. Ellinger, F. Santley

"Always Another Girl"
  R. Whitehead, C. Lawrence, Girls

Finale
  D. Ellinger, F. Santley, Entire Company

1927.35   ALLEZ—OOP!

A Musical Revue in Two Acts, 27 Scenes. Sketches by J. P. McEvoy. Music by Philip Charig and Richard Myers. Lyrics by Leo Robin. Sketches directed by Andy Rice. Costumes designed by Mabel E. Johnston. Art and technical direction by Bernard Lohmuller. Block unit scenery created by George Damman. Other settings designed by Karl Amend. Musical director, Nicholas Kempner. Entire production staged under the personal direction of, and all numbers and dances originated by Carl Hemmer. Produced by Carl Hemmer. Opened 2 August 1927 at the Earl Carroll Theatre and closed 12 November 1927 after 119 performances.

CAST: VICTOR MOORE, CHARLES BUTTERWORTH, LON HASCALL, BOBBY WATSON, VALODIA VESTOFF, HERMAN and SEAMON, CLIFF O'ROURKE, EDGAR GARDINER, ALAN MORAN, ESTHER HOWARD, EVELYN BENNETT, MADELEINE FAIRBANKS, JOYCE BOOTH, THE GEORGE SISTERS (Doris, Phyllis), JOAN KARR, DRA LEA, GLADYS YATES, CATHERINE CRANDALL, DOUGLAS BERESFORD, KELLER SISTERS and LYNCH.

At the pianos: Alan Moran, Walter Feldkamp. *Ladies Ensemble:* Lillian Burke, Phyllis Cameron, Rita Crane, Mildred Collier, Aida Conkey, Dorothy Dean, Marita Ellin, Evelyn Ellsmore, Phyllis Emerson, Madge Evans, Loraine Frey, Sylvia Howard, Irene Kelly, Martha Mackey, Josephine Martinson, Virginia May, Mary Meehan, Marion O'Day, Sydney Reynolds, Wanda Valle, Marion Vaughn, Mary Wiley, Dorothy Wyatt, Isabel Zehner.

ACT 1[12]

Scene 1

"What Does It Mean?" (Opening)
E. Bennett, Ladies Ensemble

Scene 2

George Sisters

Scene 3

Announcement
C. Butterworth

Scene 4

The Traffic Cop
Scene 1: On the Job. *Scene 2:* At Home.
TThe Cop: L. Hascall. *The Foreigner:* E. Gardiner. *First Flapper:* W. Valle. *Second Flapper:* S. Reynolds. *Grandmother:* J. Booth. *Mrs. McCarthy:* E. Howard. *Molly McCarthy:* E. Bennett.

Scene 5

"How Time Flies"[13]
M. Fairbanks
The Hours: R. Crane (1), M. Vaughn (2), M. Evans (3), P. Emerson (4), A. Conkey (5), I. Kelly (6), M. Collier (7), M. O'Day (8), M. Ellin (9), L. Burke (10), W. Valle (11), S. Howard (12). *Minute Hand:* D. Dean, S. Reynolds, D. Wyatt. *Hour Hand:* J. Martinson, M. Meehan, I. Zehner.

Scene 6

Valodia Vestoff

Scene 7

The Shock[14]
The Warden: L. Hascall. *The Visitor:* E. Howard. *Dr. Butler:* B. Watson.

Scene 8

"(Where Have You Been) All My Life"
J. Karr, C. O'Rourke
Boys: P. Cameron, M. Evans, L. Frey, M. Mackey, M. O'Day, M. Wiley. *Girls:* M. Collier, D. Dean, M. Ellin, J. Martinson, W. Valle, I. Zehner.

Scene 9

Madeleine Fairbanks[15]

Scene 10

Announcement
E. Gardiner

Scene 11

---

[12]The show was substantially revised and recast during its run. Cecil Lean and Cleo Mayfield joined the cast as its only stars and were billed above the title; at this time Carl Hemmer's name disappears from all program credit. Added for them:

Hello, Everybody (Act 1)
C. Lean, C. Mayfield, L. Hascall

The Reading of the Scotsman's Will (by Cecil Lean)(Act 1)
The Barrister: C. Lean. *Widow Gawsey McSherry:* R. Crane. *Gregor McGregor:* C. Butterworth. *Ballard McSherry:* E. Gardiner. *Doctor Donaldson:* L. Hascall. *Clyde McSherry:* G. Yates. *Harry McSherry:* Edward P. Diamond. *Kitty McSherry:* Madge Evans.

Alley-Up 'Quartette'
C. Lean, L. Hascall, C. O'Rourke, C. Butterworth, E. Gardiner
[13]Dropped during the run.
[14] Rewritten during the run as follows:
The Wife: G. Yates. *The Youth:* E. Gardiner. *The It:* C. Butterworth. *The Officer:* L. Hascall. *The Mob:* V. Vestoff, F. Lynch, Herman and Seamon, E. P. Diamond.
[15]Dropped during the run.

Alone at Last
Scene: Bridal Suite of the Grand View Hotel, Niagara Falls. *Time:* June, 1890. *The Hotel Keeper:* L. Hascall. *The Bride:* E. Howard. *The Groom:* C. Butterworth. *The Maid:* J. Booth.

Scene 12

"A Kiss with a Kick"
E. Bennett
(*Assisted by*) L. Burke, R. Crane, A. Conkey, S. Howard, I. Kelly, M. Meehan, S. Reynolds, D. Wyatt.

Scene 13

Our Own Roxy and Our Own Gang
(a) Station WJZ
Announcer: E. Gardiner. *Mr. Roxy:* V. Moore.
(b) Overture
Symphony Orchestra of 249 Pieces
(c) The Presentation
Toe Dancers: P. Cameron, L. Frey, S. Howard, V. May, Dra Lea.
(d) Feature Film: 'Love Triumphant' with an all-star cast
(e) The Lady Gets a Seat Almost
A Lady Patron: E. Howard. *A Roxy Usher:* B. Watson.
(f) What-a-Phone Presentation

Scene 14

"Pull Yourself Together"
J. Karr
Dance
L. Burke, D. Dean, M. Ellin, S. Reynolds, W. Valle, M. Vaughn, D. Wyatt, I. Zehner, L. Frey, M. Collier, V. May, M. Meehan

Scene 15

The Champion Elocutionist of Perth Amboy[16]
V. Moore, assisted by L. Hascall

Scene 16

"Doin' the Gorilla"
M. Fairbanks, E. Gardiner
Warriors: D. George, L. Frey, M. Vaughn, P. George. *Jungle Girls:* L. Burke, P. Cameron, M. Collier, D. Dean, E. Ellsmore, P. Emerson, V. May, M. O'Day, S. Reynolds, D. Wyatt, I. Zehner. *A Jungle Inhabitant:* Dra Lea. *Another:* G. Yates. *Gorilla Girls:* R Crane, A. Conkey, M. Ellin, M. Evans, S. Howard, I. Kelly, M. Mackey, J. Martinson, M. Meehan, W. Valle, M. Wiley.

A Ballroom Version of "Doin' the Gorilla"
E. Bennett, V. Vestoff

ACT 2

Scene 1

"Star of Stars"
C. O'Rourke
Stars: Ladies Ensemble. *Pierrot:* V. Vestoff. *Columbine:* C. Crandall.

Scene 2

"What Did William Tell?"
B. Watson, E. Howard

Scene 3

Attorney for the Defense
The Defense: C. Butterworth.

Scene 4

"Blow Hot and Heavy"
E. Gardiner
Trombones: M. Ellin, D. Dean, L. Frey, E. Ellsmore, M. Evans, L. Burke. *Banjos:* A. Conkey, O'Day, M. Collier, M. Meehan, W. Valle, I. Kelly. *Saxophones:* P. Cameron, M. Wiley, V. May, D. Wyatt, M. Mackey, R. Crane. *Trumpets:* M. Vaughn, M. O'Day, S. Reynolds, J. Martinson, I. Zehner, S. Howard, P. Emerson.
Dance
G. Yates

Scene 5

The Spirit of Christmas
Mama Jones: E. Howard. *Gertie Jones:* E. Bennett. *Papa Jones:* V. Moore. *Santa Claus:* E. Gardiner.

Scene 6

"In the Heart of Spain"
C. O'Rourke, J. Karr
Tango

---

[16]Dropped during the run.

V. Vestoff, C. Crandall
Senoritas: Ladies Ensemble.

Scene 7

Herman and Seamon

Scene 8

The Rest Cure
Scene: Any Sanitarium.
First Intern: E. Gardiner. *Training Nurse:* J. Booth. *Mr. Fibbledipper:* V. Moore. *Graduate Nurse:* E. Howard. *Second Intern:* C. O'Rourke. *The Plumber:* L. Hascall. *The Sleepwalker:* M. Fairbanks. *Surgeon Goosenhopper:* C. Butterworth.

Scene 9

The Keller Sisters and Lynch[17]

Scene 10

"Hoof! Hoof!"
E. Gardiner, E. Bennett

Dance
M. Fairbanks, V. Vestoff, G. Yates, George Sisters, Girls

Scene 11

Finale
Company

1927.36   THE MANHATTERS

An Intimate Musical Revue in Two Acts, 23 Scenes. Sketches by Alene Erlanger, George S. Oppenheimer. Music by Alfred Nathan, Jr., (Morris Hamilton). Lyrics by George S. Oppenheimer, (Grace Henry, Alene Erlanger). Revue and musical numbers staged by Dave Bennett, assisted by Pearl Eaton. Book (sketches) staged by Elizabeth B. Grimball and Harlan Thompson. Settings and costumes designed by Henry Dreyfuss. Orchestra under the direction of Morris Goffin. Produced by The Manhatters Company (Arch Selwyn). Opened 3 August 1927 at the Selwyn Theatre, moved 19 September 1927 to the Ambassador Theatre, and closed 8 October 1927 after 77 performances[18].

CAST: EDWARD HALE, GEORGE FRANCIS BROWN, WILLIAM JOHNSTONE, RAYMOND KNIGHT, LEHMAN BYCK, ELEANOR SHALER, SALLY BATES, DORIS VINTON, DOROTHEA CHARD, KATHERINE RENWICK, MABEL ZOECKLER, MARY MARSH, AIDA WARD.
Ensemble: Betty Waisman, Betty Maloney, Gladys Law, Patsy Cullen, Irene Ransom, Ruth Justins, Olive LaMay, Katherine Glading, Dorothy Harris, Kathryn Downer, Virginia Bedford, Christine Crane, Lee Stockton, Ruth Simmons, Georgia Grey, Marjorie Rich, Gloria Murray.

ACT 1[19]

Scene 1

"Off to See New York"(Tourists, Sightseers)
Scene: The Cranks' Tourist Office.
Clerks: J. Norris, B. Boyce, E. Hale. *Tourists:* S. Bates, D. Vinton, K. Renwick, M. Zoeckler. *Sightseers:* Ensemble. *The Personal Guide:* D. Chard.

Scene 2

History in the Faking
Big Chief Black Bottom: G. F. Brown. *Little Chief Boylan:* W. Johnstone. *Peter Minuet:* B. Boyce. *Mrs. Peter Minuet:* E. Shaler.

Scene 3

"Up on High"
Scene: The Traffic Tower.
Officer Kelly: J. Norris. *The Missus:* D. Vinton.

Scene 4

"What We Pick Up"[20]
Scene: The Sidewalks of New York.
White Wings: E. Shaler, S. Bates, M. Marsh, K. Renwick. *The Refuse:* E. Hale, R. Knight, W. Johnstone, B. Boyce.

Scene 5

Taxi!
The Girl in the Boudoir: S. Bates. *The Man in the Garage:* W. Johnstone.

Scene 6

"The Great White Way"
Dave Bennett Girls

Scene 7

The Kiddies' Own Crime Wave[21]
Scene: Public Playgrounds.
The Spinster: E. Shaler. *The Criminals:* K. Renwick, W. Johnstone, J. Norris.

Scene 8

Dance of the Dragon[22] J. Cartier
Scene: Chinatown.

Scene 9

"Love's Old Sweet Song"/"I Don't Want a Song at Twilight"
M. Zoeckler
(Lyrics for latter song by Alene Erlanger.)
Scene: Grammercy Square, Old and New.
The Twilight Singers: M. Zoeckler, M. Marsh, E. Hale, B. Boyce. *The Highlight Singers:* S. Bates, J. Norris, K. Renwick.

Scene 10

Sad Songs of the Gay Nineties
E. Shaler
Scene: Tony Pastor's Music Hall.

Scene 11

Park Avenue
Her Social Secretary: K. Renwick. *Mrs. Van Rensselaer:* S. Bates.

Scene 12

"Close Your Eyes"
Scene: The Slums.
The Dreamers: M. Zoeckler, L. Byck.

Scene 13

"Down on the Delta"
S. Bates
Scene: The Delta Night Club.

Dances
D. Vinton, E. Shaler, S. Bates, G. Lee

Finale
Principals, Ensemble

ACT 2

Scene 1

("James, the Chauffeur")
(J. Norris)
Scene: The Sightseeing Bus.
The Chauffeur: J. Norris. *Decoy:* G. Lee. *The Girls:* Ensemble.

Scene 2

The Low-Down on Broadway[23]
G. F. Brown

Scene 3

"Too Bad"

---

[17]Departed the show during the run.
[18]Originally produced Off-Broadway 18-23 July 1927 at the Grove Street Theatre for 7 performances. For original Off-Broadway run, staging was credited to Alene Erlanger and Elizabeth B. Grimball; dances and ensembles staged by Jack Garn; settings and costumes by Jacqueline Knight; produced by Joseph Lawrence and Lawrence More.
[19]Song and sketch order was changed during the Broadway run. Added during the run:

"The Little Kleptomaniac" (Act 1)
S. Bates
(*Music by* Morris Hamilton. *Lyrics by* Grace Henry.)

Childs Restaurant (by Sam Jaffe and Louis Sorin)(Act 1)
The Epicurean: J. Malloy. *The Waiter:* J. Doyle.

Jungle Dance (Act 1)
J. Cartier

An American Indian (dance)(Act 2)
Harry Losee

Ben Bernie and His Orchestra (including George Raft)
Variety: Songs by Buddy Lee and Roy Bergere

---

[20]Dropped during the run.
[21]Dropped during the run.
[22]Dropped during the run.
[23]Dropped during the run.

Scene: The Subway.
The Bronx Straphanger: D. Vinton. *The Manhattan Straphanger*: L. Byck. And the Subway Crush.

Scene 4

"Every Animal Has Its Mate"
Scene: The Zoo.
First Mates: K. Renwick, B. Boyce. *Second Mates*: S. Bates, J. Norris. *Mismates*: E. Shaler, W. Johnstone.

Scene 5

The Majestic Roof
The Announcer: G. F. Brown. *The Entertainers*: W. Johnstone, K. Renwick, J. Norris, E. Shaler.

Scene 6

"Sailor Boy"
Scene: Central Park Lake.
The Sailor Man: L. Byck. *The Sailor's Sweetheart*: D. Vinton. *The Crew*: Ensemble

Scene 7

Trinity Churchyard: Dance
E. Shaler

Scene 8

Try and get in!
Scene: The Roxymont Theatre.
The Publix Usher: J. Norris. *The New Comers*: D. Vinton, B. Boyce. *The Old Timers*: S. Bates, W. Johnstone, K. Renwick, E. Hale. *The Veteran*: G. F. Brown.

Scene 9

"Nigger Heaven Blues"
A. Ward
Scene: Nigger Heaven.

Dance
E. Shaler, Ensemble
Jungle Dance
J. Cartier

Scene 10

"Mammy"
J. Norris
Scene: The Selwyn Theatre.
Sleeping Beauty: W. Johnstone. *The Cast*: The Cast.

1927.37 ZIEGFELD FOLLIES OF 1927

A Musical Revue in Two Acts, 23 Scenes[24]. Sketches by Harold Atteridge and Eddie Cantor. (Music and) Lyrics by Irving Berlin. Dances staged by Sammy Lee. Dialogue staged by Zeke Colvan. Ballets by Albertina Rasch. Scenes (designed) by Joseph Urban. Costumes designed by John W. Harkrider. Musical director, Frank Tours. Orchestrations by Ferde Grofé, Arthur Gutman, Louis Katzman, Paul Lannin, Frank Tours, Roy Webb. Produced by Abraham Erlanger and Florenz Ziegfeld. Opened 16 August 1927 at the New Amsterdam Theatre and closed 7 January 1928 after 167 performances.

CAST: EDDIE CANTOR, CLAIRE LUCE, ANDREW TOMBES, FRANCES UPTON, CLIFF EDWARDS (Ukelele Ike), PHIL H. RYLEY, RUTH ETTING, HARRY McNAUGHTON, LLORA FOSTER, LEO BILL, IRENE DELROY, FRANKLYN BAUR, THE BROX SISTERS (Kathlyn, Dagmar, Lorraine), DAN HEALY, JEAN AUDREE, WILLIAM H. POWER, MURREL FINLEY, PAUL GHEZZI, HELEN BROWN, ROSS HIMES, MYRIO and DESHA, (Edgar) FAIRCHILD and (Ralph) RAINGER, PEGGY CHAMBERLIN, Claudia Dell, Tommie Shannon.

Albertina Rasch Girls: Mignon Dallett, Rita Glynde, Ida Lanvin, Nona Otero, Frances Leighton, Rose Gale, Nildred Turner, Anita Avila, Olga Chalmers, Vera Fredericks, Marion Wellman, Lydia Krashinsky, Anna Dumar, Dorothy Ryan, Marie Gale, Dorothy Burr. *The Ingenues Orchestra*: Pauline Dove, Babe Colby, Velma Grimm, Billie Jenks, Mina Smith, Marguerite Lichti, Frances Gorton, Laura Standish, Blanche Olsen, Paula Jones, Dorothy Donahue, Mary Donahue, Marie Novak, Alice Pleis, Lucy Westgate, Gladys Young, Genevieve Browne, Virginia Roberts, Peggy O'Neil. *Show Girls*: Pirkko Ahlquist, Kathleen Krosby, Edith Hayward, Myrna Darby, Jean Ackerman, Bonnie Murray, Jean Audree, Gertrude Williams, Evelyn Graves, Antoinette (Tony) Boots, Kae Carroll, Blanche Satchell, Louise Powell, Lee Russell, Murrel Finley, Gloria Bujee, Eileen Cullen, Mixi, Margaret Mayer, Catherine Moylan, Gladys Rennick, Edna Bunte, Bunny Schum. *Ensemble*: Frank Phillips, Jack

Stevens, Frank Sherlock, Al Siegel, Bob Ingersoll, Lily Kimari, Alma Drange, Cora Stephens, Jessie Payne, Mary Irwin, Wanda Stevenson, Marjo Leet, Blossom Vreeland, Mina Sorel, Beth Milton, Wilma Ansell, Dorothy Bauman, Polly Luce, Mickie Seiden, Doreen Glover, Amy Frank, Bonnie Blackwood, Lillian Clark, Ripples Covert, Edna Hopper, Madeline Janis, Bettye Junod, Marie Marceline, Agnes O'Laughlin, Nickie Pitell, Anita Rice, Kathryn Ringquist, Olga Royce, Norma Taylor, Florence Ward, Frances Woodward, Grace Fleming, Bobbie Campbell, Helen Kaiser. .

ACT 1[25]

Scene 1

The Office of Florenz Ziegfeld
("We Want to be Glorified"
Female Ensemble)
A Group of Glorified Shop Girls: L. Kimari, A. Drange, C. Stephens, J. Payne, M. Irwin, W. Stevenson, M. Leet, B. Vreeland, M. Sorel, B. Milton, W. Ansell, D. Baumann, P. Luce, M. Seiden, D. Glover, A. Frank. *A Selected Set of Glorified Society Ladies*: P. Ahlquist, K. Krosby, E. Hayward, C. Dell, Mixi, M. Darby, J. Ackerman, B. Murray, J. Audree, G. Williams, E. Groves, A. Boots, K. Carroll, B. Satchell, L. Powell, L. Russell *Florenz Ziegfeld*: A. Tombes. *Ann Pennington*: L. Foster. *Fanny Brice*: M. Dallett. *Marilyn Miller*: H. Brown. *Dolores*: M. Finley.

Scene 2

The Star's Double
The Lover: E. Cantor. *The Wife*: C. Luce. *The Husband*: P. Ghezzi. *The Double*: F. Baur.

Scene 3

"Ribbons and Bows"
I. Delroy
Lingerie Ribbon: G. Williams. *Hair*: G. Rennick. *Sash*: P. Ahlquist. *Shoulder Knots*: C. Moylan. *Bonnet Bow*: J. Ackerman. *Reticule*: E. Hayward. *Parasol*: C. Dell. *Dolman*: J. Audree. *Love Knot*: M. Finley. *Blue Bows*: G. Fleming, L. Kimari, A. Drange, C. Stephens, W. Stevenson, M. Irwin, B. Vreeland, N. Sorel, A. O'Laughlin, M. Leet, B. Milton, D. Bauman, A. Frank, N. Pitell, J. Payne, M. Seiden.

Scene 4

The Trans-Atlantic Flight
President Bubble: P. H. Ryley. *Mr. Ashley*: D. Healy. *Major Brown*: W. H. Power. *Gregory*: E. Cantor.

Scene 5

"Shaking the Blues Away"
R. Etting, the Jazzbow Girls, Albertina Rasch Girls, Banjo Ingenues, D. Healy

Scene 6

The Doll Toto
Leo Bill: Himself. *Jeannette*: C. Dell.

Scene 7

Innovation—at Palm Beach
Host: A. Tombes. *Hostess*: F. Upton. *Mrs. Black*: J. Audree. *Frank Phillips*: D. Healy. *Miss Auburn*: E. Cullen. *Jack Hemingway*: W. H. Power. *Mrs. Gray*: P. Ahlquist. *Lawrence Stone*: P. Ryley. *Miss Diana*: M. Findlay. *Chauncey McCormack*: H. McNaughton.

Scene 8

"Ooh, Maybe It's You"
I. Delroy, F. Baur, Ziegfeld Dancing Girls, Brox Sisters

Scene 9

It Won't Be Long Now—A Taxi Ride
Josephine: F. Upton. *Eddie*: E. Cantor.

Scene 10

"Rainbow of Girls"
F. Baur

In the Clouds (Dance)
Albertina Rasch Girls
Premiere Danseuse: H. Brown. *Solo Dancers*: M. Dallett, R. Glynde, I. Lanvin, N. Otero, F. Leighton, R. Gae. *Dancers*: M. Turner, A. Avilla, O. Chalmers, V. Fredericks, M. Wellman, L. Krashinsky, A. Dumar, D. Ryan, M. Gale, D. Burr. *Aphrodite*, Goddess of Love: E. Groves. *Bubble Dance*: Desha. *Rainbow Girls*: M. Finley, G. Williams, P. Ahlquist, M. Darby, J. Ackerman, L. Russell, L. Powell, E. Cullen.

Scene 11

Eddie Cantor Himself:
["It All Belongs to Me"[26]
E. Cantor, (assisted by) L. Foster

[24]The twentieth in the annual series of musical revues produced by Florenz Ziegfeld starting in 1907.

[25]The order of songs and sketches were revised during the run.

"She Don't Wanna"
(Music by Milton Ager. *Lyrics by* Jack Yellen.)
"My Blue Heaven"
(Music by Walter Donaldson. *Lyrics by* George Whiting.)
"You Gotta Have 'IT'"[27]
(*Music and Lyrics by* Eddie Cantor and Irving Berlin.)]

Scene 12

"It's Up to the Band"
Brox Sisters, Male Ensemble
"Prisoner's Song" (If I Had the Wings of an Angel)
R. Etting
(*Music and Lyrics by* Guy Massey.)
"When My Baby Smiles at Me" (from GREENWICH FOLLIES OF 1919)
I. Delroy
(Music by Bill Munro. *Lyrics by* Andrew B. Sterling and Ted Lewis.)
"St. Louis Blues"
R. Etting
(*Music and Lyrics by* W. C. Handy.)

Finale:

Melody Land
The Ingenues, Fairchild and Rainger at the Pianos, 12 'Pianists'
'Pianists': A. Frank, M. Leet, L. Kimari, D. Bauman, A. Rice, F. Ward, G. Fleming, J. Payne, B. Campbell, W. Stevenson, H. Kaiser, M. Janis. A Group of Ziegfeld Beauties.
"Stars and Stripes"
Military Dancing Girls (Albertina Rasch Girls)

ACT 2

Scene 1

At the City Hall Steps:

"Jimmy"
R. Etting, the Ingenues
Mayor Jimmy Walker: E. Cantor. *His Secretary*: H. McNaughton. *Grover Whalen*: W. H. Power. *Gertrude Ederle*: L. Russell. *Helen Wills*: B. Murray. *Tommy Armour*: F. Phillips. *Bobby Jones*: J. Stevens. *Miss Rye*: E. Groves. *Miss Manhattan*: C. Moylan. *Miss Bronx*: G. Rennick. *Queen Marie*: M. Finley. *Princess Ida*: M. Mayer. *Commander Byrd*: F. Sherlock. *Lieutenant Noville*: A. Siegal. *Charles A. Lindbergh*: R. Himes. *Aviators, spectators, cameramen.*

The Spirit of Aviation (dance)
C. Luce

Scene 2

Getting a New Dress
Mr. Avery: D. Healy. *Mrs. Avery*: F. Upton. *Mrs. McPherson*: I. Delroy. *Mr. McPherson*: A. Tombes.

Scene 3

Near the Bridge
Jimmy: R. Himes. *Mame*: P. Chamberlin.

Scene 4

"Learn to Sing a Love Song"
F. Baur
Musicians: M. Lichti (harp), M. Smith, B. Colby V. Grimm (violins), L. Standish (cello).
Love Me and the World Is Mine
The Boy: J. Audree. *The Girl*: G. Williams.
Just a Little Love
The Girl: J. Ackerman. *The Boy*: E. Groves.
When You Were Sweet Sixteen
The Girl: M. Darby. *The Boy*: B. Murray.
Mame
The Girl: L. Foster. *The Boy*: P. Chamberlin.
Always
C. Dell

Scene 5

A Ballet Master's Idea of the Spoken Drama
Wife: I. Delroy. *Husband*: E. Cantor. *The Lover*: A. Tombes. *The Maid*: N.

Otero. *The Butler*: H. McNaughton. *Messenger Boy*: P. Ryley. *Milligan*: D. Healy. *Mulligan*: W. H. Power.

Scene 6

"Tickling the Ivories"
R. Etting, The Ingenues, F. Upton, L. Foster, Dancing Girls
At the Pianos: Fairchild and Rainger.

Scene 7

"The Jungle-Jingle"
Brox Sisters, Ostrich Dancers, Albertina Rasch Girls
Ostrich Dance
C. Luce
Gazelle: G. Williams. *Tigress*: M. Darby. *Giraffe*: E. Cullen. *Lion*: M. Finley. *Cobra*: K. Carroll. *Elephant*: L. Russell. *Flamingo*: G. Rennick. *Monkey*: L. Foster. *The Ostrich*: B. Ingersoll. *Black and White Apes*: Les Ghezzi. *The Keeper of the Sacred Ostrich*: T. Shannon.

Scene 8

"Now We Are Glorified"
Male Ensemble

Scene 9

The New York Dog Shop
Manager of Store: W. H. Power. *Mrs. Green*: I. Delroy. *Gertrude*: R. Etting. *Gladys*: F. Upton. *Algie De Von*: A. Tombes. *Eddie*: E. Cantor. *Grace*: L. Russell.

Scene 10

Cliff Edwards (Ukelele Ike) Specialty:[28]
["Everybody Loves My Girl"
(Music by Maurice Abrahams. *Lyrics by* Sam Lewis, Joe Young.)]

Scene 11

Finale
E. Cantor, F. Ziegfeld, summing up with the Entire Company

1927.38 # A LA CARTE

A Musical Revue in Two Acts, 24 Scenes. Sketches by George Kelly. Music and lyrics by Herman Hupfeld, Louis Alter, Norma Gregg, Paul Lanin, (Henry) Creamer and (James P.) Johnson. Sketches staged by George Kelly. Dances and ensembles staged by Sam Rose. Ballet staged by Theodore Bekefi. Settings designed by Livingston Platt. Costumes designed by Maria Willenz. Orchestra under the direction of Milton Schwarzwald. Orchestrations by Stephen Jones, Maurice dePackh, Louis Katzman, Hans Spialek, Hilding Anderson, Charles Grant. Giersdorf Sisters' vocal harmony arrangements by Arthur Johnston. Produced by Rosalie Stewart. Opened 17 August 1927 at the Martin Beck Theatre and closed 24 September 1927 after 45 performances.

CAST: HARRIET HOCTOR, CHARLES IRWIN, HELEN LOWELL, WILLIAM HOLBROOK, JAY VELIE, ROSE KING, LITTLE BILLY, BOBBE ARNST, CHICK YORK, MARIAN HAMILTON, BILLY BRADFORD, THE GIERSDORF SISTERS (Elvira, Irene, Rae), ROY FANT, VERNON WALLACE, MYRTLE HAYES, FRANK ROWAN, MAUDE POWERS, KOTCHETOVSKI, CYNTHIA FARR, FRED BISHOP, FRANCES STEIN, JOSEPH MACKENZIE, MARGARET SCHILLING, Maxine Lewis, Margery Mackay, HARRY SMITH, JACK STRONG, COLEY WORTH, SIMEON KARAVAEFF, Lorelei Kendler, Myrtle Allen, Shura Dante, Myrtle Hayes.
Girls: Sydele Bry, Una Daly, Berry Earle, Winnie Edwards, Kitty French, Ethel Guerard, Marian Herson, Catherine Huth, Dorothy Jarrett, May Kaydon, Margaret Litz, Ruth Marcus, Rosalie Milan, Miss Ojala, Gilda Paradise, Betty Rourke, Mae Russell, Johanna Unger, Grace Worth.

ACT 1

Scene 1

"Scene 1"
"Hors d'Oeuvres"
(Entire Company)
(*Music and Lyrics by* Herman Hupfeld.)
Toastmaster: C. Irwin.

Scene 2

"Give Trouble the Air"

---

[26]Replaced during the run by:
"(Here Am I) Broken-Hearted" (from ARTISTS AND MODELS 1927)
E. Cantor
(Music by Ray Henderson. *Lyrics by* Lew Brown, Buddy G. DeSylva.)
[27]Dropped early in the run, or perhaps prior to New York.

[28]When Edwards left the show, his spot was replaced by:
The Four Co-operatic Singers (Dieing to Sing)
E. Cantor, A. Tombes, F. Upton, H. McNaughton

W. Holbrook, F. Rowan, J. Velie, R. Giersdorf, M. Lewis, F. Stein, U. Daly
(*Music by* Louis Alter. *Lyrics by* Leo Robin.)

Scene 3

"(I'm) Stepping Out with Lulu"
B. Arnst, Girls
(*Music by* James P. Johnson. *Lyrics by* Henry Creamer.)

Specialty
M. Hayes

Scene 4

Charles Irwin

Scene 5

The Hotel Porch (*by* George Kelly)(*Staged by* George Kelly.)
Miss Shivers: I. Giersdorf. *Mr. Davenny:* F. Rowan. *Mr. Tweedle:* R. Fant. *Miss Whittaker:* H. Lowell. *Miss Rhodes:* E. Giersdorf. *Mrs. Potts:* M. Mackay. *Flapper:* R. Giersdorf. *Mr. Lutz:* V. Wallace. *Mrs. Lutz:* R. King. *Mrs. Harbison:* M. Powers. *Mr. Harbison:* C. York. *Mrs. DeGrant:* C. Farr. *Cafe Singer:* F. Stein. *Bathing Girls:* M. Allen, L Kendler, Miss Ojala, M. Lewis.

Scene 6

The Three Giersdorf Sisters[29]

Scene 7

"Italy"
J. Velie, M. Schilling, Girls
(*Music and Lyrics by* Herman Hupfeld and Paul Lanin.)
Luigi, a Street Vendor: H. Hoctor. *Neapolitan Dancers:* Bradford and Hamilton. *Violiniste:* I. Giersdorf. *Capri Fisherman:* C. York.

Scene 8

"Palm Beach Baby"
C. Irwin, F. Stein, M. Lewis, M. Mackay
(*Music and Lyrics by* Herman Hupfeld.)

Scene 9

Between Numbers (*Staged by* George Kelly.)
Miss Pine, a Prima Donna: R. King. *Annie, the maid:* H. Lowell.

Scene 10

"Baby's Blue"
B. Arnst, J. Velie, Girls, B. Bradford
(*Music and Lyrics by* Herman Hupfeld.)

Reprise
Three Giersdorf Sisters

Scene 11

Chick York and Rose King

Scene 12

"Never Again"
Little Billy, Girls
(*Music and Lyrics by* Norma Gregg.)

Scene 13

Charles Irwin and Marian Hamilton

Scene 14

The Bekefi Ballet presenting "The Fairy Doll"
(*Musical excerpts from the score by* Joseph Bayer. *Settings designed and painted by* A. Hudiakoff. *Staged by* Theodore Bekefi.)
Merchant: Kotchetovski. *Salesgirl:* M. Hayes. *Salesmen:* H. Smith, J. Strong. *Postman:* J. Velie. *Governess:* L. Kendler. *Farmer and Wife:* R. Fant, M. Mackay. *The English Family:* C. York, R. King, M. Allen, S. Dante, Little Billy. *Russian Boy and Girl:* S. Karavaeff, L. Kendler. *Harlequin:* B. Bradford. *Baby Doll:* G. Robinson. *Cowboy and Cowgirl:* C. Worth, G. Worth. *Pierrot:* W. Holbrook. *Pierrot:* Kothcetovski. *Dutch Doll:* K. French. *Porcelain Dolls:* M. Hayes, S. Dante, Miss Ojala, L. Kendler. *The General:* Little Billy. *Soldiers:* B. Earle, E. Guerard, C. Huth, M. Kaydon, R. Marcus, R. Milan, G. Paradise, B. Rourke. *The Fairy Doll:* H. Hoctor.

ACT 2

Scene 1

"Kangaroo"
F. Stein, Girls, B. Earle, Bradford and Hamilton
(*Music by* James P. Johnson. *Lyrics by* Henry Creamer.)

Scene 2

Daisies on the Green (*Staged by* George Kelly.)
Lotty: H. Lowell. *Eleanor:* M. Powers. *Ray:* M. Hamilton. *Marian:* C. Farr.

[29]Departed the show during the run.

First Caddy: F. Rowan. *Second Caddy:* Little Billy. *Third Caddy:* B. Bradford.

Scene 3

"Sort o' Lonesome"
B. Arnst, J. Velie
(*Music and Lyrics by* Herman Hupfeld.)

Scene 4

"Sunny Spain"
H. Hoctor, W. Holbrook, R. King, Girls
Toreadors: F. Bishop, J. Mackenzie.
(*Music and Lyrics by* Norma Gregg.)

Scene 5

Spirituals[30] (includes "Go Down, Moses")
M. Powers, V. Wallace

Scene 6

"The Calinda"
B. Arnst, M. Lewis, S. Karavaeff, Three Giersdorf Sisters
(*Music and Lyrics by* Herman Hupfeld.)

Scene 7

Charles Irwin

Scene 8

The Three Giersdorf Sisters[31]

Scene 9

Tin Types (*by* Chick York and Rose King)
Mommy: R. King. *Poppy:* C. York. *Elmer:* H. Smith. *Chubby:* J. Strong.

Scene 10

Patisserie

1927.39 FOOTLIGHTS

A Musical Comedy Novelty in Two Acts, 4 Scenes. Book by Roland Oliver [Henry White]. Music and lyrics by Harry Denny. Entire production staged by Bunny Weldon. Costumes by Mahieu Costume Company. Scenery by August Vimnera. Orchestra under the direction of Oscar Radin. Orchestrations by Otto Drescher. Produced by The Tom Cat, Inc. Opened 19 August 1927 at the Lyric Theatre, moved 19 September 1927 to Wallack's Theatre, and closed 24 September 1927 after 43 performances[32].

CAST (in order of appearance): *Oscar Jennings, the Stage Director:* LeROI OPERTI. *Roy Royal, the Straight Man:* JACK COYLE. *Jacob Perlstein, the Producer:* LOUIS SORIN. *Sam, Perlstein's Factotum:* JACK WILSON. *George Weston, the Backer:* J. Kent Thurber. *Meyer Schmidt, the Composer:* Harry Denny. *Violet Wilding, the Featured Girl:* RUTH WHEELER. *Elsie Quinn, the Second Woman:* LORRAINE SHERWOOD. *Hazel Deane, a Chorus Girl:* ELLALEE RUBY. *Billy Bamper, the Comic:* GEORGE SWEET. *Tom, the Boss Carpenter:* Edward Shaw. *Lola La Verne, the Wardrobe Mistress:* Francis Walker. *Fawn Rosey:* Lulu Thorne. *Cleo Patrick:* Nathalie Segal. *Rachel Murphy:* Vilma Walden. *Jeannie Grinkle:* Lenore Laurence. *Maisie Buckman:* Anne Page. *Patsie Cohen:* Rita Krivett. *Weenie De la Tour:* June Martin. *Marigold Murphy:* Tiah Devitt. *Estelle Flannigan:* Catherine Dixon. *Cutie Fischbaum:* Evelyn Warcoux. *Silvya Wimple:* Evelyn Eldridge. *Trilbie Jenkins:* Judy Gilmore. *Eileen Olsen:* Lily Burton. *Billie McIntyre:* Doris Babb. *Gloria Lyttle:* Mae Cathcart. *Mugsie Mulligan:* Dorothy Livingston. *Lucia Baccigaloupi:* Harriett Dixon.

Act 1: Stage of the Folly Theatre. An Early Rehearsal of the Show.

Act 2, Scene 1: Before the Dress Rehearsal, two weeks later. *Scene 2:* The Dress Rehearsal. *Scene 3:* Immediately after the First Performance, the following night.

ACT 1

"Love—O—Love"
E. Ruby

"Sure Sign You Really Love Me"
E. Ruby
(*Music and lyrics by* Harry Denny.)

"Champagne" (French song)
L. Operti, Company

"The Ducks Calls It Luck"

[30]Dropped during the run.
[31]Departed the show during the run.
[32]Title changed to BEYOND THE FOOTLIGHTS in late September 1927. Song list above taken from a Wallack's Theatre program; no song list included in programs during the Lyric engagement.

E. Ruby, G. Sweet, Ensemble

ACT 2

"College Pals"
J. Coyle, Company

"Just When I Thought I Had You All to Myself"
R. Wheeler
(*Music and lyrics by* Harry Denny and Joe Fletcher.)

"Footlight Walk"
R. Wheeler, Chorus
(*Music and lyrics by* Harry Denny.)

"You Can't Walk Home from an Aeroplane"
J. Wilson
(*Music and lyrics by* Irving Bibo and William B. Friedlander.)

"(Roam On, My Little) Gypsy Sweetheart"
J. Coyle, L. Sherwood, Chorus
(*Music by* TedSnyder. *Lyrics by* Francis Wheeler and Irving Kahal.)

"I Adore You"
G. Sweet, Chorus
(*Music by* Rene Mercier. *Lyrics by* Ballard Macdonald and Sam Coslow.)

"Sahara Moon"
R. Wheeler, E. Ruby, G. Sweet, Chorus
(*Music and lyrics by* Harry Denny and Dave Ringle.)

"Sure Sign You Really Love Me" (reprise)
E. Ruby

Finale
Entire Company

1927.40 THE BAND BOX FOLLIES

An Intimate Revue in Two Acts, 28 Scenes. Sketches by Menlo Mayfield and Ballard Macdonald. Music by John Milton Hagen. Lyrics by Marian Gillespie, Menlo Mayfield and John Milton Hagen. Additional numbers by Lillian R. Devine and Louis Katzman. Production, dances and ensembles staged by Jack Garn. Cosumes by Jacqueline Knight. Musical director, George Kruger. Produced by Maxwell Platt. Opened 5 September 1927 at Daly's Theatre and closed 10 September 1927 after 8 performances.[33]

CAST: Lucien LaRiviere, Wilda Ganeau, Garrit Kraber, Gordon Hawthorne, Mario Tosatti, James Eagen, Byron Tigges, Adele Hervey, Mary Margaret Hawes, Adrienne LaChamp, Jack Parsons, Ramon Savich, Mary Spoor, Sally Shaw, Nancy Jayne, Anita Case, Al Fox, Eugene Day, Reed McClelland, Margaret Speaks, Janey Hawes, Miriam Wimm.

Ladies Of The Ensemble: Chic Jayne, Miriam Wynn, Mary Margaret Hawes, Claire Du Pont, Sally Shaw, Janey Hawes, Cecile Sanger, Thea Phillips. *Gentlemen Of The Ensemble And Choir*: Tom Wilmot, Ramon Savich, Gordon Hawthorne, Bobby James, Gerrit Kraber, Mario Tasatti, Paul Lodson, S. Betish.

ACT 1

The Company Arrives
Cast

"Greenwich Village Violet"
Band Box Girls, L. LaRiviere, W. Ganeau

Scene 2

The Perfect Husband
The Husband: G. Kraber. *The Wife*: W. Ganeau.

Scene 3

"You Can't Stop the Sun from Shining"
M. Speaks, Band Box Girls

Scene 4

All in a Night's Work
The Clerk: G. Kraber. *Hotel Guests*: G. Hawthorne, M. Tosatti, J. Eagan.

Scene 5

"Girlie with a Bustle"
B. Tigges, A. Hervay, Band Box Girls, Boys

Scene 6

"Mimi"
M. M. Hawes, Band Box Girls

Scene 7

A Study in Hands—Study the Hands (A Mimo Drama)

As conceived and directed by Adrienne LaChamp at the Folies Bergère, Paris
A *Spirit*: A. LaChamp.*The Hands*: L. LaRiviere, J. Parsons, R. Savich, G. Hawthorne.

Scene 8

"The Romance in a Dance"
M. Spoor, J. Parsons, Band Box Girls
Interpretive Dance
S. Shaw, R. Savich

Scene 9

Half Shot at Sunrise
The Gentleman: G. Kraber. *The Burglar*: G. Hawthorne.

Scene 10

"Samoa Sam, Love Me Some Mo'"
L. LaRiviere, N. Jayne, A. Case, Band Box Girls, Band Box Choir

Scene 11

He Was Only a Plasterer's Daughter
B. Tigges, A. Hervay

Scene 12

"Sh! Sh! Shirley!"
N. Jayne, R. McClelland, J. Parsons, Band Box Girls

Scene 13

On Fifth Avenue
Any Girl: W. Ganeau. *Any Man*: J. Parsons. *The Protagonist*: A. Fox.

Scene 14

"Ola in Her Little Gondola"
M. M. Hawes, L. LaRiviere, A. Case, Band Box Girls

Scene 15

At the Nickelodeon (This Fox picture conceived, written and staged by Al Fox.)
Characters: A. Fox, Original Cast.

Scene 16

Evolution of the Bluestep: "Bluestep"
N. Jayne, R. McClelland, E. Day, B. Tigges, Band Box Girls, Boys

ACT 2

Scene 1

"I Follow the Ponies"
R. McClelland, Band Box Girls

Scene 2

Romeo and Juliet
Romeo: G. Kraber. *Juliet*: W. Ganeau. *Tabloid Reader*: A. Fox.

Scene 3

"The Moon and You and I"
M. Speaks, L. LaRiviere, N. Jayne (danseuse)

Scene 4

Loops, Dearie!
The Girl: J. Hawes. *The Gent*: B. Tigges.

Scene 5

Specialty
L. LaRiviere

Scene 6

"Eyes of Love"
M. Speaks, Band Box Girls

Scene 7

King Henry VIII
The King: G. Kraber. *The Woman*: J. Hawes. *The Page*: S. Shaw. *The Courtier*: M. Tosatti. *The Son of the King*: R. Savich.

Scene 8

"Rosemary"
M. Speaks, R. Savich

Scene 9

Specialty
M. Wynn

Scene 10

"Samoa Sam, Love Me Some Mo'" (reprise)
L. LaRiviere, N. Jayne, A. Case, Band Box Girls, Choir

Scene 11

Fear of the Unknown (A Mimo Drama)

---

[33]Settings uncredited.

505

Conceived, written and staged by Adrienne LaChamp
Spirit of Fear: A. L. Champ.

Scene 12

Give This Little Girl a Hand
An Evangelist: W. Ganeau. *Not an Evangelist*: B. Tigges. *Church Goers and Wild Oat Sowers*: band Box Girls and Boys.

Finale
Cast

MUSICAL NUMBERS[34]

"Bluestep"
"Eyes of Love"
"Girlie With a Bustle"
"Greenwich Village Violet"
"I Follow the Ponies"
"Mimi"
"The Moon and You and I"
"Ola in Her Little Gondola"
"The Romance in a Dance"
"Rosemary"
"Somoa Sam, 'Love Me Some Mo"
"Sh! Sh! Shirley!"
"You Can't Stop the Sun from Shining"

1927.41 ## GOOD NEWS

A Musical Comedy in Two Acts, 9 Scenes. Book by Laurence Schwab and Buddy G. DeSylva. Music by Ray Henderson. Lyrics by Buddy G. DeSylva, Lew Brown. Play directed by Edgar J. MacGregor. Musical numbers staged by Bobby Connolly. Settings designed by Donald Oenslager. Frocks (costumes) designed by Kiviette. George Olsen and His Music, Alfred Goodman, conductor. Advice in football technique by Knute Rockne. Produced by Laurence Schwab and Frank Mandel. Opened 6 September 1927 at the 46th Street Theatre and closed 5 January 1929 after 557 performances.

CAST: *Tom Marlowe*, Captain of the Tait Football Team: JOHN PRICE JONES. *"Beef" Saunders*, a Player: John Grant. *Bobby Randall*, a Substitute: GUS SHY. *"Big Bill" Johnson*, the Coach: Edwin Redding. *"Pooch" Kearney*, the Trainer: JOHN SHEEHAN. *Charles Kenyon*, Professor of Astronomy: Edward Emery. *Patricia Bingham*, the College Belle: SHIRLEY VERNON. *Constance Lane*, Patricia's Cousin: MARY LAWLOR. *Babe O'Day*, a Sophomore: INEZ COURTNEY. *Sylvester*, a Freshman: DON TOMKINS. *Windy*: Wally Coyle. *Slats*: Jack Kennedy. *Millie*: RUTH MAYON. *Flo*, a Freshie: ZELMA O'NEAL. *The Band Leader*: GEORGE OLSEN. *The College Band*: GEORGE OLSEN'S MUSIC. *The Glee Club Trio*: Bob Rice, Fran Frey, Bob Borger.

Boys and Girls of Tait College: Boys: Herbert Rothwell, Andreas Irving, Roy Nelson, Jack Kennedy, Frank Cullen, Joe Carey, William Pahlman, Arthur Appell, Charles Mayon, Phil Dewey, Gerald Gehlert, Jack Boggs, George Oliver, Dan Douglass, Richard Renaud, Larry Larkin, Mack Murray, John McAvoy, Irving Carter, Gilbert White. Girls: Ann Lee, Margaret Shea, Gwendolyn Vernon, Betty Gayle, Roberta Greene, Emily Burton, Zeda Mansfield, Bodil Lund, Claire Joyce, Christine Ecklund, Irene Hamlin, Minerva Wilson, Anita Pam, Dorothy Day, Carol Young, Clara Blackath, Sherry Pelham, Betty Garson, Ethel Lawrence, Mildred Stevens, Zilpha DeWitt, Valeda Duncan, Viola Goring, Irene Warner, Ruth Kelly, Elsie Lombard.

The action takes place at Tait College, a co-educational institution in a small town.

Time: The Fall of the Year.

Act 1, Scene 1: The Meeting Place. *Scene 2*: The Dormitory. *Scene 3*: The Campus.

Act 2, Scene 1: The Sorority House. *Scene 2*: The Gateway. *Scene 3*: The Locker Room. *Scene 4*: The Hole in the Fence. *Scene 5*: The End Run. *Scene 6*: The Boat House.

ACT 1

Scene 1

Opening Chorus
Ensemble

"A Ladies' Man"
Z. O'Neal, Boys, Girls

"Flaming Youth"
I. Courtney, R. Mayon, W. Coyle, Boys, Girls

"Just Imagine"
M. Lawlor, S. Vernon, R. Mayon, Girls

"The Best Things in Life Are Free"

---

[34]Not in performance order.

J. P. Jones, M. Lawlor

Scene 2

"On the Campus"
D. Tompkins, Z. O'Neal, W. Coyle, R. Mayon, Ensemble

Scene 3

"The Varsity Drag"
Z. O'Neal, R. Mayon, D. Tompkins, W. Coyle, Boys, Girls

"Baby! What?"
I. Courtney, G. Shy

"Lucky in Love"
M. Lawlor, J. P. Jones

Finale
Entire Company

ACT 2

Scene 1

Opening
S. Vernon, R. Mayon, Girls

"Girls of the Pi Beta Phi"
S. Vernon, Girls

Special Dance
R. Mayon

"In the Meantime"
G. Shy, I. Courtney

"Good News"
Z. O'Neal, Boys, Girls

Scene 6

Finale
Entire Company

1927.42 ## MY MARYLAND

A Musical Romance in Three Acts, 4 Scenes. Book and lyrics by Dorothy Donnelly. (Based on the play 'Barbara Freitchie' by Clyde Fitch.) Music by Sigmund Romberg. Book and ensembles staged by J. C. Huffman. Musical numbers arranged by Jack Mason. Settings by Watson Barratt. Costumes by Ernest R. Schrapps. Orchestra under the direction of Oscar Radin. Staged under the personal supervision of J. J. Shubert. Produced by the Messrs. Shubert. Opened 12 September 1927 at Jolson's Theatre, moved 30 April 1928 to the Casino Theatre, and closed 9 June 1928 after 312 performances.

CAST [in order of appearance]: *Sue Royce*: BERTA DONN. *Laura Royce*: MARGARET MERLE. *Mammy Lou*: Mattie Keene. *Edgar Strong*: ROLLIN GRIMES, JR. *Sally Negly*: JOAN RUTH. *Barbara Frietchie*: EVELYN HERBERT. *Jack Negly*: WARREN HULL. *Dr. Hal Boyd*: EDWIN DELBRIDGE. *Zeke Bramble*: GEORGE ROSENER. *Colonel Negly*: LOUIS CASAVANT. *Arthur Frietchie*: James Meighan. *Captain Trumbull*: NATHANIEL WAGNER. *Mr. Frietchie*: Fuller Mellish. *Sergeant Perkins*: George V. Dill. *Mrs. Hunter*: Marion Ballou. *Fred Gelwex*: Wallace Mattice. *Tim Green*: Arthur Cunningham. *General Stonewall Jackson*: JAMES ELLIS. *Young Southern Girls, Northern Soldiers, Southern Soldiers, Townspeople and Children.*

First Tenors: S. Simmons, A. Barratt, Robert Marco, Howard Schreiber, Walter Higgins, G. McGray, L. Provost, J. Cleary, R. Sabater, Leon Canova, Arthur Sherman, Edward Donahue, W. B. Brooks, Thomas Coppi, Leo Branson, Efim Knoff, Ernest McChesney, V. Rudolph, Joseph Johann, Lee Burroughs. *Second Tenors*: Walter Herbert, G. Simonelli, Donald Lee, E. B. Smythe, S. Rasmussen, Carl Linke, J. Berkley, L. Karcher. *Baritones*: Robert Smith, J. H. Halligan, J. H. Vantyle, L. Moran, C. Hallgren. *Bassos*: R. H. Thomas, M. Cavanuagh, Robert Moody, Al Green, L. R. Archer, Harrison Fuller, E. Sanborn, L. Wines, R. Schofield, E. Izmallov, C. Koster, Curt Combs, Herman Amend, Ivan Alexis, John Frederick, Leo Williams. *Sopranos*: Gladys Head, Frances Donovan, Viola Green, Marybeth Conoly, Isabel Blanca, Florence Herbert, Emily Smithson, Mildred Saunders, Florence Elmore. *Altos*; Norma Strouse, Marion Newman, Elsie Kornegay, Valerie Galanine, Vivian Bartlett, Lucie Belmont, Frances Wagner, Patty Patterson, Marian Sothern.

Act 1: A Street in Frederick, Maryland. Evening, 1862.

Act 2: The Minister's House in Hagerstown. The next morning.

Act 3, Scene 1: The Frietchie House in Frederick. Late afternoon, two days later. *Scene 2*: The Street in Frederick. Early the next morning.

ACT 1

"Strolling with the One I Love the Best" (Opening)
J. Ruth, M. Merle, R. Grimes, Jr., E. Delbridge, Chorus

"Mr. Cupid"
E. Herbert, J. Ruth, B. Donn, M. Merle

"Won't You Marry Me?"

E. Herbert, W. Hull

Schottische
E. Herbert, J. Ruth, B. Donn, M. Merle, E. Delbridge, R. Grimes, Jr.,
Boys, Girls

"Your Land and My Land"
N. Wagner, Men

"The Same Silver Moon"
N. Wagner, E. Herbert

"The Mocking Bird"
J. Ruth, B. Donn, M. Merle, E. Delbridge, R. Grimes, Jr., Boys, Girls

Finale
E. Herbert, N. Wagner, Male Chorus

ACT 2
"Strawberry Jam" (Opening)
M. Ballou, Girls

"Mexico"
G. Rosener, Girls

"Your Land and My Land" (reprise)
E. Herbert, N. Wagner

"Something Old, Something New"
E. Herbert, N. Wagner, M. Ballou, B. Donn

"The Same Silver Moon" (reprise)
E. Herbert, N. Wagner

"Old John Barleycorn"
E. Herbert, W. Mattice, A. Cunningham

Finale
E. Herbert

ACT 3
Scene 1
"Song of Victory"
J. Ruth, M. Merle, Girls

"Ker-Choo!"
B. Donn, M. Merle, J. Ruth

"Boys in Gray"
G. Rosner, R. Grimes, Jr., E. Delbridge, B. Donn, J. Ruth, Boys, Girls

Country Dance
G. Rosner, R. Grimes, Jr., E. Delbridge, B. Donn, J. Ruth, Boys, Girls

"Mother"
E. Herbert

"Won't You Marry Me?" (reprise)
E. Herbert, N. Wagner

Intermezzo
Orchestra

Scene 2
"Bonnie Blue Flag"
B. Donn, J. Ruth, M. Merle, Ensemble

"Hail Stonewall Jackson"
Entire Company

Finale
Entire Company

1927.43

HALF A WIDOW

A Musical Play of the World War in Three Acts, 5 Scenes. Book and lyrics by
Frank Dupree and Harry B. Smith. Music by Shep Camp. Production
staged by Lawrence Marston and Edwin T. Emery. Dances arranged by
Billy Pierce and Benny Rubin. Costumes by Orrin Kelly. Settings designed
by P. Dodd Ackerman. Orchestra under the direction of Henry C. Redfield.
Choral work directed by Geoffrey O'Hara. Entire production under the personal supervision of Wally Gluck. Produced by Wally Gluck. Opened 12
September 1927 at the Waldorf Theatre and closed 24 September 1927 after
16 performances.

CAST: *Babette*, Daughter of Pierre: GERTRUDE LANG. *Captain Bob Everett* of the
A.E.F.: HALFRED YOUNG. *Izzy Press*, formerly a Pants Presser, now a K.P.: BENNY
RUBIN. *Nita*, an Italian servant at Red Cross Hut: JULIA KELETY. *Captain Wagner*
of the A.E.F.: ROBERT C. CLOY. *Edith Proctor*, Red Cross Nurse: FRANCES
HALLIDAY. *Lieutenant Turner* of the A.E.F.: GEOFFREY O'HARA. *Jean Marie
Alphonse Bettincourt*, French Officer: Paul Doucet. *Pierre Lafarge*, Innkeeper: Albert
Froom. *The Three "Must Get-Theirs" of the A.E.F.: Gyp, the Dip*: Lew Christy. *Stubbs*:
Lewis Newman. *Brannigan*: Ralph D. Sanford. *June Love*, Red Cross Nurse: Beryl

Halley. *Antoinette*: Vivian Martin. *National Male Quartette, Hon. Comm. of Captain
Everett's Company, A.E.F.Murphy*: Harry Donaghy. *Tony*: Daniel DaSilva. *Red*: Henry
Jockin. *Scotty*: Edgar Welch. *Orderly*: George Rogers. *Special Entertainment (Act 3)*:
Carter-Waddell Dancers. *Novelty Toe Dancers*: Cochran Twins. *International Acrobatic
Dance*: Wantayo. *Dance de Luxe*: Joan Carter-Waddell.

Ensemble: Red Cross and Salvation Army Girls: Maud Allyn, Ruth Burr, Maria
Convere, Elizabeth Crandell, Fainille Davies, Pauline Grayce, Dorothy Lyons, Alan
Moray, Miriam Phillips, Ava Sand, Verna Scott, Beatrix Tinsley. *Peasant Girls*: Margot
Bazin, Louise Brooks, Bunny Brown, Blanche Bryer, Rose Fleming, Carolyn Gerken,
Hilda Hollis, Jesse James, Shirley Lyons, Bernice Plante, Genay Ramsey, Ilys Ravel,
Bernadette Spencer, Gertrude Waldon, Geraldine Wells, June Wells. *Boys of the
A.E.F.*: Harry Ardatoff, George Bratis, Andrew Burjoyne, Albert Carties, Gordon
Clarke, Alfred Cortez, William Dunn, Roman Von Sternberg Elsky, Benno Juerling, Al
Josephs, Cyril Joyce, Zachary Karr, John Krivokosenko, Benjamin Lewis, Leon
Mandas, Harry Miller, Abraham Mitchell, Bernard Mitchell, Arthur Nulens Gregory
Pravduk, George Sawyer, Marshall Scott, Norman Stengel, Charles Salton, Benjamin
Tilberg, Walter Timoff, Serge Vinogradoff, Efin Vitis, Peter Zengel.

Act 1: Refreshment Garden of the Maison Lafarge adjoining the Red Cross Canteen at
Lucy-le-Bocage.

Act 2, Scene 1: Interior, Red Cross Canteen. *Scene 2*: Communication Trench near the
Front. *Scene 3*: Front Line Trench at Château-Thierry.

Act 3: Refreshment Garden of the Maison Lafarge. One year later.

ACT 1
Opening Chorus
Ensemble

"Let's Laugh and Be Merry"
G. O'Hara, R. C. Cloy, Male Choir

"Under the Midsummer Moon"
F. Halliday, R. C. Cloy
(*Lyrics by* Harry B. Smith.)

"It's Great to Be a Doughboy"
G. Lang, Male Choir
(*Lyrics by* Frank Dupree.)

"Longing for You"
G. Lang, H. Young
(*Lyrics by* Frank Dupree.)

"I Wonder If She Will Remember"
H. Young, National Quartette

"Song and Dance"
J. Kelety, B. Rubin, Girls

"AMERICA"
H. Young, Entire Company

ACT 2
Scene 1
"Step, Step, Step"
B. Rubin, B. Halley, V. Martin, Girls
(*Music and Lyrics by* Jack Murray and Joe Brandfon.)

"Tell Me Again"
G. Lang, H. Young
(*Lyrics by* Frank Dupree.)

"A Thousand Times"
J. Kelety, B. Rubin

"Soldier Boy"
G. Lang, H. Young

Scene 2
"I Don't Want To Be a Soldier"
B. Rubin

Specialty
National Male Quartette

ACT 3
"Babette's Wedding Day"
Ensemble

"Babette's Military Dance"
V. Martin, B. Rubin, Girls

"You're a Wonderful Girl"
F. Halliday, R. C Cloy

"I'm Thru with War"
R. Sanford, L. Christy, L. Newman

"Spanish Love"
J. Kelety, Girls

"France Will Not Forget"

R. C. Cloy, Male Choir
(*Music and Lyrics by* Geoffrey O'Hara and Gordon Johnstone.)
Grand Finale
Entire Company

THE MIKADO,

1927.44 or, The Town of Titipu

A Revival of the Comic Opera in Two Acts[35]. Libretto by William S. Gilbert. Music by Arthur Sullivan. Staged by Winthrop Ames. Dances by Michio Ito. Settings and costumes by Raymond Sovey. Conductor, Sepp Morscher. Produced by Winthrop Ames' Gilbert and Sullivan Company. Opened 17 September 1927 at the Royale and closed 7 January 1928 after 110 performances in repertory.

CAST: *The Mikado of Japan*: JOHN BARCLAY. *Nanki-Poo, his son*: WILLIAM WILLIAMS. *Ko-Ko, Lord High Executioner of Titipu*: FRED WRIGHT. *Pooh-Bah, Lord High Everything Else*: WILLIAM C. GORDON. *Pish-Tush, a Noble Lord*: J. HUMBIRD DUFFY. *Three Sisters, Wards of Ko-Ko*: *Yum-Yum*: LOIS BENNETT. *Pitti-Sing*: S. SUISSABELL STERLING. *Peep-Bo*: BETTINA HALL. *Katisha, an Elderly Lady in love with Naki-Poo*: VERA ROSS. *The Mikado's Umbrella-Bearer*: George C. Lehrian. *The Mikado's Sword-Bearer*: Paula Langlen.

School Girls: Florence Barbiers, Barbara Bronson, Dorothy Coulter, Nina Deane, Virginia Fox, Mildred Harrington, Ann Honeycutt, Sybil Kama, Edna D. Lambert, Milja Levander, May MacFarlane, Hilga Rorlund, Louise Smith, Mollie Stockard. *Nobles and Attendants*: Joseph Ames, Adolph L. Benson, Robert Caille, Hartwell DeMille, Melvin Hemphill, Harry Lauder, Palmer Laughlin, Benn K. Leavenworth, Lawrence L. Lewis, Ray Melton, Walter Owens, John Pendergrast, Allyn C. Saurer, J. Gordon Selwood, John Sindall, Miller Sparks, George Wharton, Victor S. Wrenn.

ENCHANTED ISLE

1927.45

A Musical Romance in Three Acts. Book, music and lyrics by Ida Hoyt Chamberlain. Staged by Oscar Eagle. Dances arranged by Jack Connors. Solo dance staged by Porta Povitch. Settings designed by Ida Hoyt Chamberlain. Costumes by St. Germain. Orchestra under the direction of Charles Berton. Orchestrations by Charles Berton. Produced by American Allied Arts, Inc. (J. Osborne Clemson, Manager). Opened 19 September 1927 at the Lyric Theatre and closed 15 October 1927 after 32 performances.

CAST [in order of appearance]: *Mrs. Stewart Haverhill-Smith*: MADELINE GREY. *Count Romeo de Spagino*: GEORGE E. MACK. *Stewart Haverhill-Smith*: BASIL RUYSDAEL. *Bill Capps*: HANSFORD WILSON. *Maria (Whozis)*: MARGA WALDRON. *Enoch*: HARRY HERMSEN. *Yen Sing*: MARTIN WOLFSON. *Bob Sherill*: GREEK EVANS. *Julianne Sanderleigh*: KATHRYN REECE. *Angela*: Thera Dawn. *Bella*: Lucile Reece. *Captain Yacht*: Philip Snyder. *John P. Stone*: Paul Callan.

Ensemble: Lucille Dreher, Florence Fontain, Harriet Carling, Helen Bradley, Estelle Dean, Vivian Patterson, Ellen Starr, Marie Dana, Florence Spink, Rhea Leddy, Lea Roy, Ione Miller, Gertrude Hartwick, Lucia Lucine, Hope Bartel, Ruth Collins, Dorothy Bond, Maurine McNeil, Dorothy Moore, Mildred Kirk, Hugh Sorenson, Tommy Tucker, Gordon Davis, William Kuehn, Ronald Bell, Jack Murray, Norman Murray, Elia Bey, Raimond Jones, Stanley Howard, Mark J. Christie, John C. Panter, Philip Harvey, Lewis Downie, Robert W. Davis, Eugene Sayer.

Act 1: 'Hacienda Garden,' Bob Sherill's Ranch-house in Southern California, near the Mexican Border.

Act 2: 'Enchanted Isle,' Living Room, Bob Sherill's Summer Home, Santa Catalina Island. Six months later.

Act 3: 'Dream Boat,' Deck of Haverhill-Smith's Yacht, *Pandora*. Same night.

ACT 1[36]

"Hacienda Garden" (Opening)
Ensemble
"Enchanted Castle"
G. Evans, K. Reece
"Jazz"
H. Hermsen, M. Wolfson, Ensemble

"Business Is Business"
B. Ruysdael, G. E. Mack
"Whoa Gal"
H. Wilson, M. Waldron
"Julianne"
Ensemble
"Close in Your Arms"
K. Reece, G. Evans, Ensemble
"Harmonica Dance"
H. Wilson
"California"
M. Waldron, Ensemble
"Dream Girl" (Finale)
G. Evans, K. Reece

ACT 2
"Enchanted Isle" (Opening)
Ensemble
"Abandon"
K. Reece
"Cowboy Potentate"
H. Wilson, T. Dawn, L. Reece
"Love Thought Garden"
(*Music by* Macheu.)
K. Reece, Girls
"Spanish Dance"
M. Waldron
"What a Jamboree"
K. Reece, B. Ruysdael, G. E. Mack, M. Grey
"Voice of the High Sierras" (Finale)
G. Evans

ACT 3
"Dream Boat" (Opening)
Ensemble
"Roulette"
P. Snyder, H. Sorenson
Roulette Ball Dance (*Arranged by* Porta-Povitch.)
M. Waldron
"Down to the Sea"
B. Ruysdael, Boys
"Could I Forget"
K. Reece, G. Evans
"Melody Medley" (Finale)
Ensemble

MANHATTAN MARY

1927.46

A Musical Comedy 'Clean from Beginning to End' in Two Acts, 17 Scenes. Book by George White and William K. Wells. Music by Ray Henderson. Lyrics by Buddy G. DeSylva and Lew Brown. Curtains and costumes by Max Wendy from designs by Erté. Additional curtains and draperies from designs by Emil Friedlander. Additional costumes from designs by Mabel Johnston. Scenery by William Oden-Waller. Musical conductor, orchestrations by Maurice dePackh. Entire production staged by George White. Produced by George White. Opened 26 September 1927 at the Apollo Theatre and closed 12 May 1928 after 264 performances.

CAST (in order of appearance): *Sam Katz, a Bond Salesman*: LOU HOLTZ. *Policeman*: Jimmy Scott. *R.C. (Arcy) Blair, a Bond Broker*: Paul Stanton. *Helen King, Premiere Danseuse of 'Scandals'*: Amy Revere. *A Society Bud*: Suzanne Fleming. *Police Sergeant*: Harry Oldridge. *Mary Brennan*: ONA MUNSON. *"Ma" Brennan*: DOROTHY WALTERS. *Jimmy Moore, Mary's sweetheart*: PAUL FRAWLEY. *Al, Assistant Stage Manager of 'Scandals'*: Sam Ledner. *Bob Sterling, Stage Manager of 'Scandals'*: HARLAND DIXON. *Diana Day*: Mary Farley. *Tiny Forsythe*: SUZANNE FLEMING. *Fritzie DeVere*: DOREE LESLIE. *Viola Fay*: Mae Clark. *Show Girl*: Adele Smith. *A Dramatic Actress*: Vada Alexander. *Embassy Boys*: Messrs. Goff, Kerr, (Fred) Barth. *McCarthy Sisters*: McCARTHY SISTERS (Dorothy, Margaret). *Crickets*: ED (The Perfect Fool) WYNN. *Micky, a Hudson Duster*: Victor Munro. *"Two-Gun" Terry*: James Scott. *George White*: GEORGE WHITE. *Ruth Beverly, an understudy*: Suzanne Fleming. *M. Max Duval of the Folies Bergere, Paris*: Marcel Rousseau. *Scott Sisters*:

---

[35]First presented in New York 20 July, 10–29 August 1885 at the Union Square and People's Theatres for 22 performances. First authorized production presented 19 August 1885 at the Fifth Avenue Theatre by Richard D'Oyly Carte for 250 performances. For Synopsis of Scenes and Musical Numbers, see 19 August 1885 D'Oyly Carte production. During the run, Iolanthe and The Pirates of Penzance joined The Mikado in alternating repertory.

[36]The order of songs throughout was revised immediately after the opening.

SCOTT SISTERS. *Newsboy*: Ray Hunt. *His Honor, the Mayor of New York City*: HARRY OLDRIDGE.

George White Ballet, Hudson Dusters (24), George White Beauties (100).

Act 1, Scene 1: Broadway. *Scene 2*: Barrow Street, Greenwich Village. *Scene 3*: Stage Manager's Office. *Scene 4*: Stage of the Apollo Theatre. *Scene 5*: Five-Step Curtain. *Scene 6*: Mother Brennan's Lunch Room. *Scene 7*: A Tree in the Park. *Scene 8*: "400" Club. *Scene 9*: A Secluded Spot. *Scene 10*: Memories. *Scene 11*: "Scandals" Dress Rehearsal, Apollo Theatre.

Act 2, Scene 1: Barrow Street, Greenwich Village. *Scene 2*: A News Stand, New York City. *Scene 3*: Folies Bergère, Paris, France. *Scene 4*: Huber's Museum. *Scene 5*: The Meeting Place. *Scene 6*: Roof Garden.

ACT 1[37]

Scene 1
"Pedestrian Song"
Ensemble
"Broadway" (The Heart of the World)
L. Holtz, Embassy Boys

Scene 2
"Hudson Duster"
O. Munson, Hudson Dusters
"Manhattan Memory"
O. Munson, P. Frawley

Scene 3
Stage Manager's Office, H. Dixon, Company

Scene 4
"Five-Step"
McCarthy Sisters
Five-Step Dance
H. Dixon, Ensemble

Scene 5
Double Dance
H. Dixon, M. Clarke
Buck Five-Step[38]
D. Leslie

Scene 6
Mother Brennan's Lunch Room
E. Wynn

Scene 7
"Nothing But Love"
O. Munson, P. Frawley

Scene 8
"Broadway" (reprise)
Embassy Boys
"It Won't Be Long Now"
McCarthy Sisters
Dance
M. Clarke, S. Fleming, H. Dixon
Dance
H. Dixon
"Manhattan Mary" (reprise)
P. Frawley

Scene 9
A Secluded Spot
E. Wynn

Scene 10
"Memories"
F. Barth
Ballet Dance
George White Ballet

Scene 11
"Five-Step" (reprise)
G. White

ACT 2

Scene 1
"Manhattan Mary" (reprise)
Ensemble
"My Blue Bird's Home Again"
O. Munson, McCarthy Sisters, S. Fleming, M. Clarke, H. Dixon, Ensemble
"Hudson Duster" (reprise)
E. Wynn, Hudson Dusters
"Nothing But Love" (reprise)
O. Munson

Scene 3
"Dawn"
Embassy Boys
Dance
O. Munson
Ballet Dance
George White Ballet

Scene 4
Huber's Museum
E. Wynn

Scene 5
"It Won't Be Long Now"[39] (reprise)
McCarthy Sisters, H. Dixon, Ensemble

Scene 6
"It Won't Be Long Now"[40] (reprise)
Ensemble
Dance
D. Leslie
Song
L. Holtz
Dance
E. Wynn, H. Dixon
"Manhattan Mary" (reprise)
Ensemble
"Nothing But Love" (reprise)
P. Frawley
Finale
Entire Company

THE MERRY MALONES

1927.47

George M. Cohan's Comedians in His Newest Song and Dance Show (A Musical Comedy) in Two Acts, 10 Scenes. Book, music and lyrics by George M. Cohan. Entire production staged by Edward Royce. Book staged by Sam Forrest. Foot Work (dances arranged) by Jack Mason. Settings by Joseph Wickes. Costumes designed by E. J. Heuett, Mabel Johnston, Cora MacGeachy. Orchestra under the direction of Charles J. Gebest. (Orchestrations by Mike Lake). Produced by George M. Cohan. Opened 26 September 1927 at Erlanger's Theatre and closed 10 March 1928 after 192 performances; reopened 9 April 1928 at Erlanger's Theatre and closed 28 April 1928 after 24 additional performances. Total: 216 performances.

CAST (in order of appearance): *Announceress*: Jane Manners. *Martin*: LEO HENNING. *Carlysle*: DAVID LONDON. *Mrs. Van Buren*: INA HAYWARD. *Annabelle*: MARJORIE LANE. *Mr. Westcott*: ROBINSON NEWBOLD. *Gloria Westcott*: MARY JANE. *Joe Thompson*: ALAN EDWARDS. *Joe Westcott*: ALAN EDWARDS. *Molly Malone*: POLLY WALKER. *Tony Howard*: FRANK OTTO. *Kennedy*: FRANK MASTERS. *Captain of Police*: MERCER TEMPLETON. *Captain of Police*: JAMES TEMPLETON. *Delia Malone*: DOROTHY WHITMORE. *John Malone*: GEORGE M. COHAN. *Helen Malone*: SARAH EDWARDS. *Annie*: Patsy Ball. *Charlie Malone*: CHARLES FININ. *Tom*: Richard Barry. *Jenkins*: Harry Rose. *Mr. Rosinsky*: Nat S. Jerome. *Mrs. Rosinsky*: Angela Jacobs. (*Specialties*: Adler and Bradford, Andre and Rudac, Feon Van Marr, Cleo Pergain.)

Show Girls: Orchid Wess, Ellen Gordon, Marie Baudoux, Alice Donahue, Theresa

---

[37]Added after opening:
Fan Dance (Act 1, Scene 10, after Ballet Dance)
D. Leslie
[38]Dropped after the opening.

[39]Replaced by:
"My Blue Bird's Home Again" (reprise)
McCarthy Sisters, H. Dixon, Ensemble
[40]Dropped after the opening.

Donahue, Mildred Gethins, Katharine Bourne, Jeanette Clyde, Crystal Moray, Margie Blanchard, Libby Pearl, Dolores Muray, Florence O'Brien, Anne Glass, Gloria Gray, Veatrice Verle. *Ballet Dancers:* Kitty O'Dare, Gwenn Bennett, Mildred Hamilton, Dorothy Dion, Elinor Meeker, Ethelyn Allen, Catheryn Koehler, Lina Belis, Elinore Heineman, Mary Elizabeth Kerr, Virla Buley, Hazel Vee, June Wall, Hazel McGuire, Marguerite Dunne, Madge Meryl. *Acrobatic Dancers:* Ann Loomis, Terry Kent, Gladys Holt, Clare Blessington, Erna Kunzin, Grace Palma, Betty DeMattia, Betty Meryl. *George Smith's Violin Girls:* Francis Flanigan, Zosia Spierer, Catherine Meryl, Rita Mario, Mary Toher, Miriam Carni, Lillian Fields, Lois Grant. *Gentlemen of the Ensemble:* Ray Dowley, Donald Joy, Larry Clark, Jimmy Babbits, Jack MacElroy, Ernest Petty, Harry DuBall, Lou Lesser. *The Dancers:* Ande Fay, Ande Vacari, Gaby Estaire, Jack Bennett, Frank Lillis, Lester Dan, John Pierce, Sam Sheppard. *The Diplomat's Vocal Quartette:* Ande Hamilton (first tenor), Hal Saliers (lead), Johnny Ferrara (first baritone), Leonard Nelson (second baritone). *Mike Lake's Yankee Doodle Band:* Frank Carmen (drum major), Charles Harris, Arthur Danner, Maurice Hamilton, Victor Welte, Al Kelty, Al Pinard, James Brearton, Arthur Walker, Charlie Vassette, Fred Hillthaler, Louis Mehling.

Act 1, Scene 1: Westcott Home. Reception Room. *Scene 2*: A Drug Store in the Bronx. *Scene 3*: John Malone's Home. The Living Room. *Scene 4*: The Bronx Express. *Scene 5*: The Stage Door. *Scene 6*: The Ball Room of the Van Buren Home.

Act 2, Scene 1: A Street in the Bronx. *Scene 2*: Westcott's Office. *Scene 3*: The Pathway to the "Rose Garden." *Scene 4*: The "Rose Garden" of the Westcott Home.

MUSICAL NUMBERS[41]

"Talk About a Busy Little Household"
Ensemble

"Like a Wandering Minstrel"
M. Lane, D. London, Violin Girls

Flirtation Waltz
Andre and Rudac

"The Plot"
I. Hayward, M. Jane, R. Newbold, L. Henning, Ensemble

Dance
M. Jane, L. Henning

"(Like a) Wandering Minstrel" (reprise)
A. Edwards

"Son of a Billionaire"
M. Templeton, J. Templeton, Ensemble

"Molly Malone"
D. Whitmore, S. Edwards, G. M. Cohan

"Honor of the Family"
P. Walker, D. Whitmore, C. Finan

"A Feeling in Your Heart" (You'll See a Great Big Beautiful Smile)
P. Walker, G. M. Cohan

"The Bronx Express"
P. Walker, A. Edwards, Ensemble, Diplomats Quartette

Trio Dance
F. Van Marr, F. Masters, L. Henning

"A Night of Masquerade"
Ensemble

"Behind the Mask"
I. Hayward

"We've Had a Grand Old Time"
R. Newbold

Dance (eccentric)
M. Jane

Dance (adagio)
F. Adler, T. Bradford

"Charming"
P. Walker, Male Ensemble

"We've Got Him"
Company

"A Busy Little Center"

Characteristic Dance
Burnoff and Josephine

"Our Own Way of Going Along" (If You Like Coffee and I Like Tea)
D. Whitmore, P. Ball, F. Otto, C. Finan

"Easter Parade"

P. Walker, Ensemble

Danse Comique
(a) M. Templeton, J. Templeton; (b) F. Van Marr

"Opera-Bouffe Cohanesque"
I. Hayward, M. Jane, M. Lane, R. Newbold, L. Henning, D. London, F. Masters, Ensemble

"Roses Understand"
M. Lane, D. London, Ensemble

Dance Cyclonic
C. Pergain

"God's Good to the Irish"
G. M. Cohan

"Blue Skies, Gray Skies"
D. Whitmore

"Like a Little Ladylike Lady Like You"
A. Edwards

Reprise

1927.48 ## SIDEWALKS OF NEW YORK

A Musical Comedy in Two Acts, 9 Scenes. Book, music and lyrics by Eddie Dowling and James Hanley. Book staged by Edgar MacGregor. Dances staged by Earl Lindsay. Settings by Sheldon K. Viele. Costumes by Maybelle Manning, Robert Stevenson, Francillon, Inc. Orchestra under the direction of Arthur Lange. Produced by Charles Dillingham. Opened 3 October 1927 at the Knickerbocker Theatre and closed 7 January 1928 after 112 performances.

CAST (in order of appearance): *August Brewster,* Philanthropist: FRANK KINGDON. *Dorothy Brewster,* Settlement Worker: LINDA. *Mrs. Brewster,* Social Climber: WINIFRED HARRIS. *Honorable Percival Short:* CARL FRANCIS. *Perkins,* the Brewster Butler: T. F. Thomas. *Sergeant Daley:* FISKE O'HARA. *Mrs. O'Brien:* ELIZABETH MURRAY. *Mickey O'Brien:* DICK KEENE. *East Side Gangsters (5): Whitey:* Charles Gale. *Izzy:* Alex Calm. *Monk:* Lester Hope [Bob Hope]. *Fingers:* George Byrne. *Goofy:* Will Ahern. *Muggsy:* Henry Dowling. *Settlement Workers (2): Miss Brown:* Carolyn Nolte. *Miss Smith:* Woodey Lee Wilson. *Gertie,* an Orphan: RAY DOOLEY. *Parker,* Superintendent of Orphanage: CECIL OWEN. *The Governor:* Harry Short. *Children of Orphanage (3): Mamie:* RUBY KEELER. *Gladys:* Gladys Ahern. *Willie:* WILLIAM AHEARN. *Buckley,* Manager of a Garage: Sam Morton. *Proprietors of Coney Island Buses (2): Abe Cohen, Moe Zimmermann:* (Charles) DALE & (Joe) SMITH. *A Policeman:* Emile Cote. *Three Old Timers:* JIM THORNTON, JOSEPHINE SABEL, BARNEY FAGAN. *Ruby:* RUBY KEELER. *Carrie:* Carolyn Nolte. *Dolly:* Woodey Lee Wilson. *Organ Grinder:* Edward Maurelli.

Dancing Girls: Gene West, Phyllis Reynolds, Elva Pomfret, Adeline Foley, Peggy Timmons, Louise Stark, Wanda Woods, Sybil Bursk, Virginia Webb, Lorraine Webb, Jeanne Edwards, Helen MacDonald, Kathryn Hereford, Dolly Gilbert, Virginia Clark, Betty Wright, Marjorie Gilbert, Pearl Bradley, Anna May Rex, Woodey Lee Wilson, Evelyn Farrell. *Dancing Boys:* Bob Maxwell, George Murray, Billy O'Rorke, Jack Gargin, Ward Tallman, Georgie Rand, Dick Bennett, Hal Hennessey, Walter Carson, Francis X. Sinott, Melvin Halpern, George Rand, Don Lee. *Charles Davis' Harlem Red-Hots:* Charles Davis, Billy Shepperd, John Alexander, Pete Nugent, Irving Beaman, Joe Wilson, Bobby Shields, Edward Shanault. *New York Bluecoats Octette:* Fred Wilson, Hall Clovis, Stanley McClelland, Emile Cotie Ross Wright, Paul A. Weber, Edward Marshall, Vance Elliott.

Act 1, Scene 1: Brewster's Home on Fifth Avenue, New York City. *Scene 2*: Outside of an Orphanage. Somewhere on the East Side, New York. A few months later. *Scene 3*: The Orphanage Yard. Same day. *Scene 4*: Outside of the Orphanage. Same day. *Scene 5*: Outside of Brewster's Home. Some time later. *Scene 6*: Reception Room of Brewster's Home. That night.

Act 2, Scene 1: Laundry on the East Side. Two years later. *Scene 2*: Corridor in New Playground in the Sky. The next night. *Scene 3*: Roof of one of the Tenements of the Playground in the Sky. The same night.

ACT 1[42]

Scene 1

"The Younger Set"
Chorus

Dance
Reprise

Specialty
Linda

Scene 2

---

[41]Added to the show during the run (after Dance Cyclonic):
"Gip-Gip"
S. Edwards

[42]Note: The scene breaks in the song listing (Act 1) are undoubtedly incorrect; without more thorough documentation from a production manuscript, it appears above as in the original program.

"Way Down Town"
 R. Keeler, C Gale, A. Calm

"Confirmation"
 Orphans

"Wherever You Are"
 D. Keene, R. Dooley

"Nothing Can Ever Happen in New York"
 F. O'Hara, Bluecoats

"Sidewalks of New York"
 Orphan Boys and Girls
 (*Music by* C. B. Lawlor. *Lyrics by* J. W. Blake.)

"Oh, For the Life of a Cowboy"
 W. Ahearn, Orphans

"Sidewalks of New York (reprise for Governor's entrance)
 Orphans

"Playhouse in the Sky"
 R. Dooley, D. Keene, Orphans

"Wherever You Are" (reprise)
 C. Francis, Linda

"Little Bum"
 F. O'Hara, Boys

"Springtime of Long Ago"
 J. Thornton, J. Sabel, B. Fagan

(introducing some of the most popular songs of thirty years ago by the same artists who wrote and performed them. e.g. "When You Were Sweet Sixteen," "My Sweetheart's the Man in the Moon," "She May Have Seen Better Days," "Irish Jubilee," "There'll Be a Hot Time in the Old Town Tonight," "My Girl's a Highborn Lady")

"Headin' for Harlem"
 E. Murray, Ensemble

Dance Specialty
 R. Keeler

Finale
 Entire Company

ACT 2
Scene 1
 "We're the Girls You Can't Forget"
 Laundry Boys and Girls

 "Way Down Town" (reprise)
 R. Keeler, W. Ahearn, Laundry Boys and Girls

Scene 2
 "Headin for Harlem" (reprise)

 Specialty
 Harlem Red Hots

 "Just a Little Smile"
 Linda, C. Francis

Scene 3
 "Goldfish Glide"
 R. Keeler, Chorus

 Specialty Dance
 R. Keeler

 Burlesque Dance
 R. Dooley, D. Keene

 Finale
 Entire Company

1927.49   YES, YES, YVETTE

A Musical Comedy in Three Acts. Book by James Montgomery and William Cary Duncan. Based on a story (and the play "Nothing But the Truth") by Frederick S. Isham. Music by Philip Charig and Ben Jerome. Lyrics by Irving Caesar. Staged by H. H. Frazee. Dances and ensembles staged by Sammy Lee. Settings by P. Dodd Ackerman. Costumes by Milgrim. Orchestra under the direction of Ben Jerome. Produced by H. H. Frazee. Opened 3 October 1927 at the Sam H. Harris Theatre and closed 5 November 1927 after 40 performances.

<u>CAST</u> (in order of appearance): *Ethel Clark*, a Debutante: Brenda Bond. *Dick Donnelly* of Ralston's Sunnyland: Roland Woodruff. *Mr. Van Dusen*, a Speculator: Joseph Herbert. *S. M. Ralston*, Owner of Sunnyland: CHARLES WINNINGER. *Mrs.*

Ralston, His Wife: Virginia Howell. *Yvette Ralston*, Their Daughter: JEANETTE MacDONALD. *Bishop Doran*: Arnold Lucy. *Robert Bennett* of Ralston's Sunnyland: JACK WHITING. *Vaudeville Artistes (2): Mabel Terry*: Helene Lynd. *Sabel Terry*: Dorothy Waterman. *J. P. Clark*, Leader of the Winter Colony: Frederick B. Manatt.

Ladies of the Ensemble: Joey Benton, Edith Martin, Cleo Cullen, Frances Stone, Mary Phillips, Florence Blue, Nesha Medwin, Irene Isham, Edith Humphrey, Rita Marks, Dorothy Hackney, Ida Berry, Kathleen McLoughlin, Patricia Ferguson, Wilma Novak, Peggy Hart, Patricia Campbell, Parthenia Mason, Charlotte Otis, Carola Taylor. *Gentlemen of the Ensemble*: Alfred Milano, Jerome Kirkland, Floyd English, Louis Elmer, Thomas McLoughlin, Jack Closson, Wallace Jackson, Don Gallagher, Bernard Hassett, William Bailey.

The action takes place on Washington's Birthday in Palm Beach, Florida.

Act 1: Drawing-Room of Ralston's Winter Home. 6 P.M.

Act 2: On Board Ralston's Yacht, Lake Worth. 9:20 P.M.

Act 3: Garden of Ralston's Home, Palm Beach. 10:20 P.M.

ACT 1
 Opening Chorus
 Ensemble

 "What Kind of a Boy?"
 B. Bond, R. Woodruff, Ensemble

 "Pack Up Your Blues (and Smile)"
 H. Lynd, D. Waterman, Ensemble
 (*Music by* Peter DeRose, Albert Von Tilzer. *Lyrics by* Jo Trent.)

 "You're So Nice to Me"C. Winninger, H. Lynd

 "My Lady" (from QUEEN HIGH)
 J. MacDonald, J. Whiting
 (*Music by* Frank Crumit. *Lyrics by* Ben Jerome.)

 Finale

:ACT 2[43]
 Opening
 Ensemble

 Dance
 D. Waterman

 "My Lady" (reprise)
 J. MacDonald, J. Whiting

 "Yes, Yes, Yvette"
 J. MacDonald, Boys
 (*Music by* Phil Charig.)

 "Maybe I Will"
 C. Winninger, H. Lynd, Ensemble

 Finale

ACT 3
 Opening
 Ensemble

 "How'd You Like To?"
 J. MacDonald, J. Whiting, Ensemble
 (*Music by* Stephen Jones.)

 "Woe Is Me"[44]
 C. Winninger

 Finale
 Company

1927.50   MY PRINCESS

A Modern Operetta in Two Acts, 6 Scenes. Book and lyrics by Dorothy Donnelly, based on the play 'Princess Zin-Zin' by Edward Sheldon and Dorothy Donnelly. Music by Sigmund Romberg. Dialogue staged by Sam Forrest. Dances and ensembles staged by Dave Bennett. Rasch Ballet dances arranged by Albertina Rasch. Costumes designed by Charles LeMaire. Settings designed by P. Dodd Ackerman. Orchestra under the direction of Charles A. Prince. Orchestrations by Emil Gerstenberger. Produced by Alfred E. Aarons. Opened 6 October 1927 at the Sam S. Shubert Theatre and closed 22 October 1927 after 20 performances.

<u>CAST:</u> (in order of appearance): *Faxon*: Leo Stark. *Mrs. Johnson*: Marie Stoddard. *Darwin P. Johnson*: Donald Meek. *Augustus Tonks*: Robert Woolsey. *Minnie Johnson, Mimosa*: HOPE HAMPTON. *Maud Satterlee*: Evelyn Darville. *Polly Carter*: Miriam

---

[43] Song order in Act 2 revised during the run.

[44] Dropped during the run.

Wooton. *Guiseppe Ciccolini*, Chick: LEONARD CEELEY. *Mrs. Cruger Ten Eyck*: AUDREY MAPLE. *Lord Barchester*: VERNON KELSO. *Peter Loomis*: ROBERT F. FORD. *Mitchell*: Granville Bates. *The Ambassador*: Luis Alberni. *Palchi*: James Moore. *Mamma Pompilia*: Phyllis Newkirk. *Richotto*: John Emerson Haynes. *Street Singer*: Frank Pandolphi. *Tango Dancers*: Amerique and Neville.

Albertina Rasch Dancers: *Solo Dancers*: Geraldine Spencer, Alvera Gomez, Frances Michele, Florence Wall, Marion Dickson, Eda Vitolo. *Dancers*: Dorothy Campbell, Jeanette Creagan, Martha Wilbert, Regina Tushinska, Beatrice Squire, Florence Mahoney.

Ensemble: *Maids*: Elizabeth Kelly, Nadja Dubinsky, Betty Garon, Madeleine Ward, Helen Johnston, Betty Chay. *Flunkeys*: Vladimir Dubinsky, George Koenig, Gregory Frisch, Eugene Demady, Boris Millman, Jean Spiro, Clinton Corwin, Clifford Patterson. *Society Girls*: Patricia O'Connell, Lillian White, Ruth Brady, Dorothy Blese, Helen Bourne, Wilma Miller, Dorothy Button, Olga Marie, Jane Alden. *Specialty Dancers*: Betty Veronica, Anita Furman, Etna Ross, Peggy Gallimore, Anita Gordon, Paulette Winston, Zayda Lord, Margaret Kelly. *Society Boys*: Charles Gomez, Jack Douglass, Henry Levey, Murray Morrissey, Carl Deis, Robert Gray, William Douglas, Gordon Clark. *Dancing Girls*: Rita Carita, Lee Byrne, Peggy Driscoll, Madeleine Eubanks, Gladys Redmond, Cris Bernsman, Mae Selden. *Male Singers*: Anton Teero, Buddy Carmin, George Fisher, Melvin Redden, Robert Millikin, Huey Mack, Theo Schoof, Frank Paudolfi, George Clidd, Richard Lynn, Jack Irwin, Henry Schween. *Girl Singers*: Fleurette Andre, Olivia Martin, Elizabeth Wilson, Hela Brandes, Dulcie Bond, Virginia Bennett, Mary Landon.

Time: The present.

Act 1, Scene 1: Garden of the Johnson Country Home, Long Island. *Scene 2*: A Room in the Johnson Residence, New York. Four weeks later. *Scene 3*: Reception Hall at the Johnson Residence. Same day.

Act 2, Scene 1: A Block Party, Cherry Street, New York. The same night. *Scene 2*: Chick's Room in a Tenement. A half hour later. *Scene 3*: The Consul General's Residence, Washington Square, New York. Midnight.

ACT 1[45]

Opening:
The Steppe Sisters P. Gallimore, P. Winston
The Moulin Rouge Girls

"The Glorious Chase"
R. Ford, Boys

The Hunting Dance
Albertina Rasch Girls

"Gigolo"
R. Woolsey, Society Girls, Specialty Girls, Dancing Girls, Albertina Rasch Girls

"I Wonder Why?"
H. Hampton

"Follow the Sun to the South"
L. Ceeley, H. Hampton

Finale
Entire Company

Opening Ensemble
A. Maple, Society Girls, Wedding Ushers, Footmen

"When I Was a Girl Like You"
A. Maple, Society Girls, Albertina Rasch Girls

"Here's How"

"Dear Girls, Good Bye"
L. Ceeley, V. Kelso, R. Ford, Guests, Footmen

Wedding Ensemble

Finale
Entire Company

ACT 2

Scene 1

Opening
Ensemble

"Tympany Dance"
Ensemble, Albertina Rasch Girls

(Devised and staged by Dave Bennett.)

Finalette

Scene 2

"I Wonder Why?" (reprise)

H. Hampton

"Eviva"
J. Moore, P. Newkirk, Ensemble

"Our Bridal Night"
H. Hampton, L. Ceeley

Finalette

Scene 3

"My Passion Flower"
E. Darville, M. Wootton, R. Ford, V. Kelso, Ensemble

Tango
Amerique and Neville

Specialty
Albertina Rasch Ballet

Finale

1927.51 (BALIEFF'S) CHAUVE-SOURIS

A New Edition of the Russian Entertainment (The Bat Theatre of Moscow) in Two Acts, 20 Scenes[46]. Numbers invented and devised by Nikita Balieff. Music arranged by Alexei Archangelsky. Chef d'Orchestra, S. Koran. Presented by F. Ray Comstock and Morris Gest. Opened 10 October 1927 at the Cosmopolitan Theatre and closed 17 December 1927 after 80 performances.

CAST: Messrs. Dedovitch, Goukovsky, Kondratieff, Shevtchenko, Terestchenko, Zotoff, Gorodetsky, Tamiroff, Tcherniavsky, Lepoukhin. Mmes. Birse, Ershova, Gramnotina, Kandaky, Komisarshevskaya, Karabanova, Vladmirskaya, Deykarhanova, Efimovskaya, Willi Mir, Tamara Geva.

ACT 1[47]

Scene 1

Russian Matrimonial Rites
Mmes. Birse, Ershova, Gramnotina, Kandaky; Messrs. Dedovitch, Goukovsky, Kondratieff, Shevtchenko, Terestchenko, Zotoff
(*Music by* Mikhail Ivanovitch Glinka. *Scenery and costumes by* Dmitry Semyonovitch Stelletsky.)

A fragment from Glinka's opera, "Rusland and Liudmila." The picture represents a certain part of a wedding ceremony in old Russia at the time of the Boyars, and is painted by the celebrated Russian artist in the style of an ancient Russian ikon.

Scene 2

The Pastrycook's Wife (*A Poem* by Gustave Nadaud.)
Mme. Komisarzhevskaya; Messrs. Gorodetsky, Dalmatoff, Tamiroff, Tcherniavksy
(*Music by* Alexei Archangelsky. *Scenery and costumes* by Mstislaff Valerianovitch Dobuzhinsky.)

The pastrycook's wife is courted by three dandies, who compare her with different tasty delicacies in her husband's shop. The dozing pastrycook wakes up and, angered by the courting of his wife, explains to the dandies that, while to them his wife is a tasty morsel, to him she is his daily household bread.

Scene 3

A Russian Barcarolle
Mmes. Birse, Ershova; Messrs. Dedovitch or Goukovsky, Shevtchenko
(*Music by* Varlamoff. *Scenery and costumes by* Sergei Sudeykin.)

Scene 4

"Returning from the War" (An Old French Song)
Mmes. Karabanova, Komisarzheevskaya, Vladmirskaya, Will amd M. Tamiroff

Three toy soldiers, returning from the war, offer their hands and hearts to a toy shepherdess. One offers her his riches, the second his titles, and the third—his heart. But the toy shepherdess merely toys with them, for she loves her toy shepherd.

Scene 5

The Cavalry[48]

---

[45]Shortly after the opening, an intermission was added after the first Finale in Act 1, dividing the show into three acts.

[46]First produced in New York 1 February 1922 at the 49th Street Theatre for 544 performances.
[47] The running order of scenes was revised after opening.

Mmes. Birse, Ershova, Gramotina, Kandaky; Messrs. Dedovitch, Goukovsky, Konstratieff, Shevtchenko, Zotoff
(*Music by Alexei Archangelsky.*)

Scene 6

The Abduction from the Seraglio (An Oriental Pantomime)
Mmes. Deykarhanova,Komisarzhevskaya, Will; Messrs. Gorodestky, Lopoukhin, Tamiroff, Tcherniavsky
(*Music by V. Bernardi and Alexei Archangelsky. Scenery and costumes by R. Dobuzhinsky.*)

This pantomime is taken from the renowned German humorist, Busch, who not only wrote but illustrated his own works. The scene represents a wealthy Sultan, diverted by odalisques and his principal wife. The wife has a lover. The Sultan, suspecting her of infidelity, calls for his chief eunuch, who locks her up and mounts guard over her prison. The lover makes the eunuch drunk and serenades the captive. Obtaining a ladder, he climbs to the window, and they fall into each other's arms. During their meeting the Sultan awakens and hastens with his whole court to the prison. But the happy lovers, taking advantage of the confusion, have time to enter a boat and escape. The Sultan and his court are left in despair.

Scene 7

The Nightingale
Mmes. Efimovskaya, Ershova
(*Music by Aliabieff.*)

Scene 8

The Passing Band
Mmes. Birse, Deykarhanova, Gramotina, Karabanova, Komisarzhevskaya, Kandaky, Vladimirskaya, Will; Messrs. Dalmatoff, Dedovitch, Gorodetsky, Goukovsky, Konstraieff, Lopoukhin, Shevtchenko, Tamiroff, Tcherniavsky, Terestchenko, Zotoff
(*Scenery and costumes by Mstislaff Valerianovitch Dobuzhinsky.*)

An episode in the life of a small town where old and young, hearing the strains of a military band, leave their work to greet the passing regiment.

Scene 9

Romanesque (A Dance)
T. Geva
(*Music by Alexander Constantinovitch Glazunoff. Scenery by Perez Sucre.*)

Scene 10

Love Waxes . . . and Wanes
Mme. Deykharhanova, Messrs. Gorodetsky, Tamiroff
(*Sketch by Bastia. Translated by Nichols.*)

Scene 11

La Traviata (A Burlesue Parody of Verdi's Opera)
Mmes. Birse, Karabanova, Gramotina, Kandaky; Messrs. Dedovitch, Kondtraieff, Shevtchensko, Terestchenko, Zotoff
(*Scenery and costumes by Mstislaff Valerianovitch Dobuzhinsky.*)

Certain American business men have complained that Verdi's famous opera, in its original form, is too long and too depressing. To meet this criticism, the Chauve-Souris version retains only the most important sections of the opera. This condensed form will be found far less melancholy than the original.

ACT 2

Scene 1

The Shooting Gallery (Pictures of a French Fair)
(*Music by Alexei Archangelsky.*)
1. The Thermometer of LoveMme. Karabanova, M. Gorodetsky
2. The ConvictMessrs. Dedovitch, Kondratieff, Teretshenki, Shevtchenko
3. The Mother-in-Law Has ComeMme. Komisarzhevskaya, Messrs. Loupoukin, Tcherniaavsky
4. A Night in Spain Mme. Deykarhanova, M. Tamiroff
5. An African IdyllMmes. Will, Vladimirskaya

Scene 2

Grotesque Espagnol (A Dance)
T. Geva
(*Music by Albenitz.*)

Scene 3

An Eighteenth Century Fan (from Nikita Balieff's Collection left in

Russia)
Mmes. Birse, Deykarhanova, Ershova, Karabanova, Vladimirskaya, Will
(*Scenery and costumes by A. Zinovieff.*)

Scene 4

Love in the Ranks (A Buffoonery of Old St. Petersburg)
Mme. Komisarzhevskaya; Messrs. Gorodetsky, Dalmatoff, Tamiroff, Tcherniavsky, Zotoff
(*Music by Alexei Archangelsky. Scenery and costumes by Nikolai Benois.*)

A charming young woman is sitting outside the barracks. A drummer boy, a sergeant-major, a lieutenant and a colonel arrive. Each in turn obliges his inferior to yield him place, in accordance with the established discipline of military rank. Finally a general appears, reconciles them all and emerges victorious with the lady on his arm.

Scene 5

Russian Folk Songs
Mmes. Birse, Ershova, Efimovskaya, Gramotina, Kandaky
(*Scenery and costumes by Geoge Pozhedaieff.*)

Scene 6

The Chinese Theatre in a Russian Market Place
A *Chinese Woman*: Mme. Karabanova. A *Chinese*:M. Terestchenko. A *Cossack Woman*: Mme. Vladimirskaya. A *Cossack*: M. Lopoukhin. A *Puppet*: Mme. Will.

Scene 7

"Where Is Our Meyer, Where's Himalaya?" (A Song in the American Manner)
Messrs. Dalmatoff, Dedovitch, Gorodetsky, Goukovsky, Kondratieff, Lopoukhin, Shevtchenko, Tamiroff, Tcherniavsky, Zotoff

Scene 8

Sarcasm (A Dance)
T. Geva

Scene 9

Round the Hay-Wain (Vocal Scenes from Little Russia)
Mmes. Birse, Ershova, Efimovskaya, Karabnova, Gramtina, Vladimirskaya, Kandaky, Will; Messrs. Dedovitch, Kondratieff, Shevtchenko, Tcherniavsky, Terestchenko, Zotoff
(*Scenery and costumes by Sergei Sudeikine.*)

1927.52   # THE 5 O'CLOCK GIRL

A Musical Comedy (A Fairy Tale in Modern Clothes) in Two Acts, 10 Scenes. Book by Guy Bolton and Fred Thompson. Music and lyrics by Bert Kalmar and Harry Ruby. Book staged by John Harwood. Dances staged by Jack Haskell. Additional principal dances assisted by Danny Dare. Scenes designed by Norman Bel Geddes. Costumes designed by Charles LeMaire. Orchestra under the direction of Gus Salzer. Entire production under the personal supervision of Philip Goodman. Produced by Philip Goodman. Opened 10 October 1927 at the 44th Street Theatre, moved 16 April 1928 to the Sam S. Shubert Theatre, and closed 2 June 1928 after 280 performances.

CAST: (in order of appearance): *Madame Rosalie*: VEHRAH VERBA. *Elsie*: Vera Trett. *Jane*: Brownie Walsh. *Maisie*: BIDDY Wilkenson. *Ronnie Webb*: DANNY DARE. *Dorothy*: Lola deLille. *Ethel*: Gloria Gilbert. *Marie*: Frances Thress. *Roy*: AL SHAW. *Oswald*: SAM LEE. *Policeman*: Carl Judd. *Susan Snow*: PERT KELTON. *Hudgins*, Gerry's valet: LOUIS JOHN BARTELS. *Patricia Brown*: MARY EATON. *Photographer*: Jack Hughes. *Gerald Brooks*: OSCAR SHAW. *Mollie*, Gerry's maidservant: Marian Bonnell. *Eugene*: Mary Phillips. *Priscilla*: Marjorie Phillips. *Cora Wainright*: ALLYS DWYER. *Jasper Cobb*: FRANK McNELLIS. *Jules*, headwaiter at Kit Kat Klub: Michael Barroy. *Billy*: Billy Walsh. *Footman*: Chester Bennett.

Ladies of the Ensemble: Marian Booth, Dorothy Brown, Myrtle Cox, Mary Carlton, Daye Dawne, Helen Deane, Lola deLille, Dorothy Fitzgibbon, Gloria Gilbert, Buddie Haines, Evelyn Hannons, Virginia Hassell, Elizabeth Janeway, Ethel Kelly, Myrtle Lane, Jane Lauderdale, Jessie Madison, Helen Madigan, Pauline Maxwell, Verdi Milli, Virginia Moore, Virginia Mortimer, Helen Mirtel, Alice O'Brien, Gwen Orlando, June Paget, Ruby Poe, Marjorie Phillips, Mary Phillips, June Ray, Alice Raisen, Helen Sanderson, Rosemari Sill, Audrey Sturgis, Elizabeth Surran, Frances Thress, Vera Tertt, Elsa Varga, Brownie Walsh, Mary Williams, Biddle Wilkinson, Betty Waxton. *Gentlemen of the Ensemble*: Russell Ash, Albert Birk, Arthur Budd, Charles Bennett, Charles Conklin, Ray Hall, Leo Howe, Jack Hughes, Arthur May, Fred May, Bobby Morris, Lowell Stray, Jack Kay, Ted Schultz, Philip Tiltman, Billy Walsh, Ted White.

Act 1, Scene 1: A Block Party near Beekman Place, New York. *Scene 2*: On the Telephone. *Scene 3*: A Room near Gerry's Roof Garden Apartment. *Scene 4*: The Snow Flake Cleaner's Shop. *Scene 5*: The Kit Kat Club.

---

[48]Dropped shortly after the opening.

Act 2, Scene 1: Outside the Field and Stream Hotel, Southampton, Long Island. *Scene 2*: The Snow Flake Cleaner's Shop. *Scene 3*: Ronnie's Roof Garden Apartment. *Scene 4*: Eavesdropping on the Telephone. *Scene 5*: Outside the Church.

ACT 1

   Opening
      Ensemble

   "I'm One Little Party"
      D. Dare, Girls

   "We Want You"
      A. Shaw, S. Lee, P. Kelton

   "Thinking of You"
      M. Eaton, O. Shaw

   "Happy Go Lucky"
      O. Shaw, Girls

   "Up in the Clouds"
      M. Eaton, O. Shaw, Ensemble

   "Any Little Thing"
      L. J. Bartels, P. Kelton

   "Following in Father's Footsteps"
      A. Shaw, S. Lee

   "Lonesome Romeos"
      M. Eaton, Boys

   "Tea Time Tap" (dance)
      M. Eaton, P. Kelton, D. Dare

   "Thinking of You" (reprise)
      M. Eaton, O. Shaw

ACT 2

   Opening
      Ensemble

   "Who Did?"
      M. Eaton, O. Shaw

   "Society Ladder"
      P. Kelton, A. Shaw, S. Lee

   "Tell the World I'm Through"
      O. Shaw, Boys

   "Up in the Clouds" (reprise)
      M. Eaton, O. Shaw

   "Who Did?" (reprise)
      M. Eaton, O. Shaw

   Finaletto
      Entire Company

   Specialty
      A. Shaw, S. Lee

   Dance
      D. Dare

   Specialty
      P. Kelton

   Dance
      M. Eaton

   Finale
      Entire Company

1927.53   WHITE LIGHTS

A Unique Musical Comedy of Broadway in Two Acts, 6 Scenes. Book by Paul Gerard Smith and Leo Donnelly. Music by J. Fred Coots, (James Steiger). Lyrics by Al Dubin, Dolf Singer. Dances arranged by Walter Brooks and Ray Perez. Settings designed by Walter Harvey. Costumes by Brooks Costume Company. Orchestrations by Louis Katzman. Orchestra under the direction of T. L. Jones. Produced by James La Penna. Opened 11 October 1927 at the Ritz Theatre and closed 5 November 1927 after 31 performances[49].

CAST: (in order of appearance): *Flossie Finch*: ROSALIE CLAIRE. *Danny Miles*: SAM ASH. *Jimmy*: James Steiger. *Polly Paige*: MARIAN MARSCHANTE. *Syd Burke*: LEO DONNELLY. *Toodles*: Florence Parker. *Teddy Harlow*: Tammany Young. *Billy Winslow*: Robert Lynn. *Head Waiter*: James Barbour. *Mercedes*: Dorothy Deeder. *Mazie*: MOLLY O'DOHERTY. *William Parson*: James S. Barrett. *Mr. Higgins*: J. Harry

---

[49]Staging uncredited; prior to New York, staging credited to Ira Hards.

Jenkins. *A Maid*: Edna Skodak. *"The Villain"*: Frank Leslie. *Johnny*: Leonard Scott. *George, the "Country Lover"*: JAMES HOWKINS. *Gordon & King*: GORDON and KING.
   Specialty Girls: Ada Winston, Edna Skodak, Bessie Kademova, Doris Delanti, FLorence Parker, Vera Clarke, Diana White, Mildred Morrow, Evelyn Shea, Mildred Lorrain. *Guests, Waiters, Dancers, Musicians, Chorus Girls, Stage Hands, Electricians, etc.*

Act 1, Scene 1: A Dressing Room at "The Monastery." *Scene 2*: "The Monastery."

Act 2, Scene 1: The Stage of a Broadway Theatre. *Scene 2*: Polly's Dressing Room. *Scene 3*: Opening Night at a Broadway Theatre. *Scene 4*: The Stage of a Broadway Theatre.

ACT 1

Scene 2

   "Romany Rover"
      Girls of the Cabaret

   "Some Other Day"
      S. Ash

   "Tappin' the Toe"
      M. O'Doherty, Cabaret Girls

   Specialty
      A. Winston

   Specialty
      B. Kademova

   "Deceiving Blue Bird"
      M. Marschante, Quartette

   Specialty
      J. Alvarez

   Specialty
      F. Parker

   "Don't Throw Me Down"
      R. Claire
      "White Lights"
      M. O'Doherty, Entire Company
      D. Deeder

   Specialty
      Gordon & King

   "Dreaming of You"
      S. Ash

ACT 2[50]

Scene 3

   "Eyeful of You"
      M. O'Doherty, J. Howkins, Girls

   Specialty
      Gordon & King, M. O'Doherty

Scene 4

   "We Are the Girls in the Chorus"
      Specialty Girls

   "Sitting in the Sun"
      M. O'Doherty, Gordon & King

   "Dreaming of You"
      Sylvia[51], Girls

   "Better Times"
      Entire Company

1927.54   JUST FANCY!

An American Musical Romance in Two Acts, a Prologue and Epilogue and 9 Scenes. Book by Joseph Santley and Gertrude Purcell. Based on the play ('Just Suppose') by A. E. Thomas. Music by Joseph Meyer and Philip Charig. Lyrics by Leo Robin. Staged by Joseph Santley. Dances arranged by Johnny Ford. Chester Hale Girls' dances arranged by Chester Hale. Settings designed by P. Dodd Ackerman. Costumes designed by Emery J. Herrett. Orchestrations by Maurice dePackh. Orchestra under the direction of Milton Schwarzwald. Produced by Joseph Santley. Opened 11 October 1927 at the

---

[50]For the duration of the New York run, Act 2's musical numbers were inaccurately assigned to Scenes 1 and 2, corrected above.
[51]No character named Sylvia appears in the cast list. Prior to New York, the song was sung by Polly (Marion Marschante) and Girls.

Casino Theatre and closed 17 December 1927 after 79 performances.

CAST (in order of appearance): Now: *Griggs:* George Harcourt. *Jimmy:* Archie Thomson. *Helen:* Peggy O'Neill. *Jill:* Thelma Edwards. *Bobby Vanderpool:* Charles Baron. *Harold:* Jack Bauer. *Jonsey:* Frank Sills. *Gloria:* Frances Nevins. *Aunt Linda Lee:* MRS. THOMAS WHIFFEN. *His Royal Highness:* JOSEPH SANTLEY. *Harvey Warren:* Harry Kendall.

Then: *Flora,* a charming neighbor: Peggy O'Neill. *Jane Stafford,* elder daughter of Mrs. Stafford: BERENICE ACKERMAN. *Kay,* another neighbor: Thelma Edwards. *Geraldine de Peyster,* a society belle: Kathryne Burnside. *Linda Lee Stafford,* younger daughter of Mrs. Stafford: IVY SAWYER. *Mrs. Kingley Stafford,* mother of Linda Lee and Jane: Peggy Whiffen. *Hannibal,* a faithful retainer: Edward Cutler. *Sir Calverton Shipley,* aide to His Royal Highness the Prince: ERIC BLORE. *Jack Warren,* in love with Jane: JOHN HUNDLEY. *Edward Chester,* a visitor: JOSEPH SANTLEY. *Honorable Philander J. Wood,* Mayor of the City of New York: George Harcourt. *First Alderman:* George Spelvin. *Second Alderman:* Willard Charles Fry. *Third Alderman:* Allan Greene. *Charlie Van Bibber,* Chairman of the Mayor's Entertainment Committee: RAYMOND HITCHCOCK. *Lola,* a ballet dancer: Gertrude Lemmon. *Chiquita,* a temperamental star: Mlle. MARGUERITE. *A Gentlemanly Highwayman:* Willard Charles Frey. *The Marquis of Karnaby,* a diplomat: H. REEVES-SMITH. *Musicians at Niblo's Garden (4): Carlo, Jose, Ramon, Rafael:* The Sevilla Four. *Chester Hale Girls:* Pavla Pavlicek, Jean Kroll, Mary Hiscox, Agnes Hall, Clara Fay, Evelyn Chilla [Schiela], Etta Moore, Lenore Allan, Erma Chase, Gertrude Westling. *Show Girls:* Dorothy Durland, Doris Dodge, Rachel Chester, Kaye deFranza, Fraun Koski, Helene LeSoir, Trude Marr, Clare Hooper. *Medium Dancers:* Ruby Nevins, Ellen O'Brien, Alice Akers, Kathryn Lambly, Mildred Hiller, Val Lester, Melba Lee, Lillie Short, Dolores Nito, Jean Watson, Dorothy Martin. *Boys:* Archie Thomson, Jack Bauer, Ernest Preach, Lester Niles, Charles LaValle, Frank Sills, George Ford, Ted Bradshaw, Robert Easton, William O'Donnell.

Prologue: Home of Harvey Warren, Sands Point, Long Island, 1927.

Act 1, Scene 1: The Path to Yesterday. 1860. *Scene 2:* The Stafford Home on the Hudson. *Scene 3:* Banquet Room at the old Astor House. *Scene 4:* A Reception Room at the old Academy of Music.

Act 2, Scene 1: Auditorium of Niblo's Garden. *Scene 2:* Back Stage at Niblo's Garden. *Scene 3:* A Toll House on the road to Harlem. *Scene 4:* The Stafford Home. *Scene 5:* The Stafford Garden. (Ten days later.)

Epilogue: Home of Harvey Warren, Sand Point, Long Island, 1927.

PROLOGUE and ACT 1[52]

"Ain't Love Grand?"
  F. Nevins, P. O'Neill, T. Edwards, C. Baron
"Shake, Brother!"
  J. Santley, P. O'Neill, T. Edwards, Chester Hale Girls, Ensemble
"Memories"
  Show Girls
"Sunday Beau"
  I. Sawyer, P. O'Neill, T. Edwards, Girls
"Two Loving Arms"
  I. Sawyer, J. Santley
Schottische
  Chester Hale Girls
"Humpty-Dumpty"
  B. Ackerman, J. Hundley, Ensemble
Ballet
  G. Lemmon, Chester Hale Girls
"Naughty Boy"
  R. Hitchcock, Mlle. Marguerite

---

[52]During the New York run, the following changes were made: "Ain't Love Grand?" dropped. Act 2, Scene 1 and "Love Conquers All" finale were dropped. "Mi Chiquita" was replaced by:
  "La Sandunga"
    Bobbie Tremaine (Chiquita)
  "Youth Will Have Its Fling" (added after "La Sandunga")
    Mlle. Marguerite, Ensemble
For the subsequent national tour, the show title's exclamation was dropped and the show was billed as a Merry Musical Comedy. The changes above were retained, and the following changes were made:
  "Meeting Royalty" (Opening, replacing "Ain't Love Grand")
    Ensemble
  "The Path to Yesterday" (Transition, after "Shake, Brother!")
    Show Girls, Medium Dancers
  "Mister You and Missus Me" (replaced "Humpty-Dumpty" reprise)
    B. Ackerman, J. Hundley, Ensemble

Finale
ACT 2 and EPILOGUE
  Finale of 'Love Conquers All'
    Niblo's Garden Company
  "Mi Chiquita"
    Mlle. Marguerite, F. Gill
  "Humpty-Dumpty" (reprise)
    B. Ackerman, J. Hundley, Ensemble
  "You Came Along"
    I. Sawyer, J. Santley
  Dance
    Chester Hale Girls
  "You Came Along" (reprise)
    B. Ackerme, J. Hundley
  "Two Loving Arms" (reprise)

1927.55 THE LOVE CALL

A Musical Play in Three Acts, 4 Scenes. Book by Edward Locke and Harry B. Smith. (Based on Augustus Thomas' play "Arizona.") Music by Sigmund Romberg[53]. Lyrics by Harry B. Smith. Staged by J. C. Huffman. Book staged by Lew Morton. Musical numbers staged by Earl Lindsay. Art director, Watson Barratt. Costumes designed by Ernest Schrapps (Act1 1, 2), Charles LeMaire (Act 3). Orchestra under the direction of Max Steiner. Orchestrations by Emil Gerstenberger. Produced by the Messrs. Shubert in association with L. Lawrence Weber. Opened 24 October 1927 at the Majestic Theatre and closed 7 January 1928 after 88 performances.

CAST (in order of appearance): *Sam Wong:* Carlos Mejia. *Joe:* Frank Erwin. *Tim:* John L. King. *Mike:* Bradley F. Lane. *Slim Carter:* Shep Camp. *Lena Keller:* JANE EGBERT. *Tony Mustano:* JOSEPH MACAULAY. *Estrella-Canby-Bonham:* ROBERTA BEATTY. *Colonel Bonham:* William T. Carleton. *Henry Canby:* W. L. Thorne. *Reginald Pargester:* BARRY LUPINO. *Doctor Fenlon:* Charles Lawrence. *Miss McCullagh:* VIOLET CARLSON. *Mrs. Canby:* Alice Fischer. *Bonita Canby:* BERNA DEANE. *White Horse:* William Balfour. *Captain Hodgman:* JOHN RUTHERFORD. *Sergeant Keller:* Richard Lee. *Lieutenant Denton:* JOHN BARKER. *Red Crow:* Frederick Kaufman. *Black Hawk:* Stanley Jessup. *Fiesta Dancers:* Veloz and Yolanda. *Manuel,* a Peon: Frank King.

Singers: Jeanette O'Connor, Katherine Richmond, Marion Dollbeare, Violet Code, Katherine Harvey, Claudia Papineau, Florence Tynor, Vera Deane, Emily Wentz, Helen Detrich, Annette Taylor, Peggy Hansel, Guinevere Sandy, Jean Haven, Clare Toy, Ann Gilbert, Kitty Coleman, Margaret Clark. *Dancers:* Margaret Szabo, Ellen Sparks, Vivian McGill, Katherine Mausier, Ruby Udell, Peggy South, Dorothy DeLukas, Princess Wynneman, Elina DuVal, Elsie Merer, Margaret Alexander, Nadine Prescott, Lucille Poirier, Nina Romanos, Peggy O'Connor, Kathlyn Kerrigan, Gerry Dean, Carmen DeBois, Agatha Dowd. *First Tenors:* Jack Ribaude, Lee Roltman, John Muccio, Henry Corsell, Harry Erwin. *Second Tenors:* Louis Rottman, Robert Kienast, William Magill, Lawrence Watts, Jack Jendrek, Isadore Gladstone, Frank Quigley, John Weeple, John L. King. *Baritones:* Richard Ellis, Nick Krissuk, Eddy Green, Bart Shilling, William Jennings, Ed Drake, Charles McGrath, Dick Doober, Emil Stetz, Frank Lane. *Bassos, Al Fontain's Octette:* Al Fontain, Leonard Berry, Emil Stetz, Bradley Lane, Evan Doctoroff, Frank Erwin, John Weeple, John L. King.

Act 1: The Canby Ranch, Aravaipa Valley, Arizona. 1869.

Act 2: Colonel Bonham's Quarters at Fort Apache, Arizona. One week later.

Act 3, Scene 1: The Del Ario Rancho. A month later. Evening. *Scene 2:* The Del Ario Rancho. Before daybreak, the next morning.

ACT 1
  Opening Number
    L. Berry, E. Drake, C. McGrath, J. Ribaudo, Cowboys
  "Tony, Tony, Tony"
    J. Egbert, J. Maacaulay, Guests
  "'Tis Love"
    R. Beatty, Male Chorus
  "When I Take You All to London"
    B. Lupino, L. Berry, E. Drake, C. McGrath, W. Magill
  "Bonita"
    B. Deane, Ensemble
  "Eyes That Love"
    B. Deane, J. Barker

---

[53]The Indian music in the score is based on authentic Chippewa themes.

"If That's What You Want"
B. Lupino, V. Carlson

"The Rangers' Song"
J. Barker, Cowboys

Finale, Act 1
Entire Company

ACT 2

"'Tis Love" (Opening)
Entire Company

"The Lark"
B. Deane, R. Beatty, Ensemble

"Good Pals"
J. Barker, Entire Company

"Poker Game"
B. Lupino, W. P. Carleton, J. Rutherford, W. L. Thorne, C. Lawrence

"I Am Captured"
J. Rutherford, J. Barker, B. Deane, R. Beatty

"Hear the Trumpet Call"
J. Rutherford, J. Barker, B. Deane, R. Beatty, Entire Ensemble

"I Live I Die for You"
J. Macauley, J. Egbert

"You Appeal to Me"
V. Carlson, B. Lupino, C. Lawrence

Finale, Act 2
J. Barker, R. Beatty, W. P. Carleton, J. Rutherford, B. Deane

ACT 3

"Fiesta" (Opening)
J. Rutherford, Entire Ensemble

Spanish Dance
Veloz and Yolanda

"I Live I Die for You"
J. Macauley, J. Egbert, Ensemble

"Spanish Love"
B. Lupino, V. Carlson

Finaletto, Scene 1

Finale Ultimo

1927.56   A CONNECTICUT YANKEE

A Musical Comedy in Two Acts, 5 Scenes, a Prologue and an Epilogue. Book by Herbert Fields. Based on Mark Twain's novel "A Connecticut Yankee in King Arthur's Court." Music by Richard Rodgers. Lyrics by Lorenz Hart. Staged by Alexander Leftwich. Dances by Busby Berkeley. Settings and costumes designed by John F. Hawkins, Jr. Art director, Herbert Ward. Musical director, Roy Webb. Orchestrations by Roy Webb. Produced by Lew Fields and Lyle D. Andrews. Opened 3 November 1927 at the Vanderbilt Theatre and closed 27 October 1928 after 421 performances.

CAST (in order of appearance): *In the Prologue: Albert Kay:* Gordon Burby. *Gerald Lake:* JACK THOMPSON. *Merlin:* William Norris. *Martin:* WILLIAM GAXTON. *Arthur Pendragos:* Paul Everton. *Fay Morgan:* NANA BRYANT. *Alice Carter:* CONSTANCE CARPENTER. *Lawrence Lake:* William Roselle.
In the Play: Sir Kay, the Seneschal: Gordon Burby. *The Yankee:* WILLIAM GAXTON. *The Demoiselle Alisande La Carteloise:* CONSTANCE CARPENTER. *King Arthur of Britain:* PAUL EVERTON. *Sir Launcelot of the Lake:* WILLIAM ROSELLE. *Sir Galahad, His Son:* JACK THOMPSON. *Merlin, a Mighty Magician:* WILLIAM NORRIS. *Maid Angela,* Lady-in-Waiting to Morgan le Fay: Dorothy Roy. *Mistress Evelyn La Belle-Ans:* JUNE COCHRANE. *Queen Morgan Le Fay:* NANA BRYANT. *Queen Guinevere:* Celeste Deuth. *Sir Bors:* G. Douglas Evans. *Sir Sagramore:* John Morton. *Sir Tristan:* Chester Bree. *Mistress Phoebe Sauce de Pommes:* Regina Diamond.
Slaves, Knights, Ladies of the Court, Factory Hands: Olive Bertram, Grace Connelly, Ednor Fulling, Enes Early, Harriet Hamell, Leoda Knapp, Mareta Mackay, Margaret Miller, Dorothy Rubino, Kaye Renard, Evelyn Ruh, Valma Valentine. G. Douglas Evans, Chester Bree, Martin Denis, John Creighton, Don Donaldson, George Magis, Jack Morton, Ward Arnold, Vernon Downing, Frank Norton, Jack Baker, Leslie Cooley, Richardson Brown, Frank Bocchetta, Philip Kobe, Lew Douglas.

Prologue: Grand Ball Room of a Hotel in Hartford, Connecticut. 1927.

Act 1, Scene 1: On the Road to Camelot. In the year 528, A.D. *Scene 2:* Courtyard of the Castle of King Arthur.

Act 2, Scene 1: A Corridor of the Royal Factory. Three months later. *Scene 2:* On the Road from Camelot. *Scene 3:* The Palace of Queen Morgan Le Fay.

Epilogue: The Gardens of the Hotel in Hartford. Ten minutes later than the Prologue.

PROLOGUE

"A Ladies' Home Companion"
N. Bryant, Principals, Ensemble

"My Heart Stood Still"[54]
W. Gaxton, C. Carpenter, Ensemble

ACT 1

Scene 1

"Thou Swell"
W. Gaxton, C. Carpenter

Scene 2

"At the Round Table"
P. Everton, W. Norris, W. Roselle, J. Thompson, Knights, Ladies

"On a Desert Isle {Island} with Thee"
J. Thompson, J. Cochrane, Knights, Ladies

"My Heart Stood Still" (reprise)
W. Gaxton, C. Carpenter

Finale (Ibbidi Bibbidi Sibbidi Sab)
Company

ACT 2

Scene 1

Opening
Ensemble

"Nothing's Wrong"
C. Carpenter

"I Feel at Home with You"
J. Thompson, J. Cochrane, Ensemble

Dance
C. Carpenter, J. Thompson

Scene 2

"The Sandwich Men"
Knights

Scene 3

"Evelyn, What Do You Say?"
J. Cochrane, Knights

EPILOGUE

Finale

Company

IOLANTHE,
1927.57   or, The Peer and the Peri

A Return Engagement of the Comic Opera in Two Acts[55]. Libretto by William S. Gilbert. Music by Arthur Sullivan. Entire production staged by Wintrop Ames. Dances by Louise Gifford. Settings and costumes designed by Woodman Thompson. Conductor, Sepp Moracher. Produced by Wintrop Ames. Opened 14 November 1927 at the Royale Theatre (joining "The Mikado" and "The Pirates of Penzance" in repertory) and closed 7 January 1928 after 12 performances.

CAST *The Lord Chancellor:* FRED WRIGHT. *Earl of Mountararat:* JOHN BARCLAY. *Earl of Tolloller:* J. HUMBIRD DUFFY. *Private Willis:* WILLIAM C. GORDON. *Strephon:* WILLIAM WILLIAMS. *The Train-Bearer:* George C. Lehrain. *Queen of the Fairies:* VERA ROSS. *Iolanthe:* BETTINA HALL. *Celia:* Virginia Fox. *Leila:* Suissabell Sterling. *Fleta:* Paula Langlen. *Phyllis:* LOIS BENNETT. *Chorus of Fairies, Dukes, Marquises, Earls, Viscounts, Lords, Barons, Peers.*[56]

---

[54]Previously introduced in the revue ONE DAM THING AFTER ANOTHER, London.

[55]First presented in New York 25 November 1882 at the Standard Theatre for 105 performances; this revival first presented in New York 19 April 1926 at the Plymouth Theatre for 255 performances. For Synopsis of Scenes and Musical Numbers, see original 1882 production.

[56]Same as in THE MIKADO revival 17 September 1927.

1927.58 ARTISTS AND MODELS (1927)

A Musical Revue in Two Acts, 26 Scenes[57]. Music by Harry Akst and Maurice Rubens. Lyrics by Benny Davis, J. Keirn Brennan additional lyrics by Jack Osterman, (Ted Lewis). Staged by J. C. Huffman. Dialogue staged by Charles Judels. Dances by Ralph Reader and Earl Lindsey. Ensembles of ballets by Jan Oyra. Settings by Watson Barratt. Costumes designed by Ernest Schrapps. Orchestra under the direction of Max Meth. Produced by the Messrs. Shubert. Opened 15 November 1927 at the Winter Garden and closed 24 March 1928 after 151 performances[58].

CAST: TED LEWIS and HIS MUSICAL CLOWNS, FLORENCE MOORE, JACK PEARL, JACK OSTERMAN, JACK SQUIRES, JAN OYRA, KING and KING, MANILLA POWERS, NAYAN PEARCE, GLADYS WHEATON, MARIETTA O'BRIEN, JOHN McDOWELL, EDDIE CHESTER, HARRY O'NEAL, CATHERINE GALLIMORE, WALTER JOHNSON, MARGIE EVANS, CHAUNCEY PARSONS, LUCILLE ARNOLD, JSCHEREY and HULLY, ELEANORE BROOKS, VELOZ and YOLANDA, KAY SIMMONS.

Dancing Girls: Tennylis Allyn, Adelaide Candee, Cyrilla Casey, Ethel Daniels, Molly Davis, Wilhelmina DeBrauw, Peggy Deighton, Helen Doyle, Mildred Espy, Mary Ellis, Ethel Fuller, Lillian Ford, Margaret Hollyn, Marion Luzon, Madeline Luzon, Peggy LeMay, Betty LeMay, Margaret Moore, Dorothy Palmer, Roslyn Rensing, Katherine Sheeran, Jo Storace, Josephine White, Mazie White, Dorothy Webber, Mary Hillyer. *Winter Garden Girls:* Bee Bickel, Annette Davies, Louise Chowing, Mary Chandler, Doris Downs, Doris Delairs, Helen Farez, Beth Hill, Barbara Lloyd, Maybell Leather, Henrietta Livingston, Elena Meade, Imogene Phillips, Madeleine Russell, Mozel Stapp, Pat Paterson, Bee Walz, Marjorie Younger, Amy von Hansa, Katrina Trask, Mirtle Wagner, Peggy Neil, Iris Morse, Muriel Seeley, Marie Lovette, Ruth Grace, Dolly Thain, Neva Lynn, Thalia Hamilton, Julia Barker, Agatha Phillips, Marjorie Vernelli. *Winter Garden Boys:* Howard Deighton, Jack Dayton, Dan Berrigan, Allan Blair, William Neely, Phillip Ott, Buddy Carpenter, Jack White, Herman Grossman, William Baden, George Leland, Arthur Schnitzer, Jack Norris, Dana Mayo, Walter Gilfoyle, Gene Roberts, Charles Collins.

ACT 1

Scene 1

A Disagreement
Stage Manager: J. Squires. *Manager:* H. O'Neal. *Jack Pearl:* J. Pearl. *Jack Osterman:* J. Osterman. *Florence Moore:* F. Moore. *Ted Lewis:* T. Lewis.

"I'll Be Your Artist and You Be My Model"
J. Osterman, assisted by N. Pearce

Scene 2

The Artists Dancing Models

Scene 3

Point of View
The Artist: J. Squires. *Police Sergeant:* W. Johnson. *Policeman:* C. Parsons.

Scene 4

Five Hundred Dollars
The Man: J. Osterman. *The Wife:* M. O'Brien. *The Husband:* H. O'Neal. *The Maid:* A. Candee.

Scene 5

"Oh, Lady"
N. Pearce, Dancing Boys

Scene 6

The Cynic
The Clerk: W. Johnson. *The Bell Boy:* C. Collins. *Herman Pfeiffer:* J. Pearl. *Wolff:* H. O'Neal. *The First Lady:* K. Simmons. *The Second Lady:* L. Arnold. *The Third Lady:* M. Stapp. *The Fourth Lady:* M. O'Brien. *Hotel Guests:* (Ensemble.)

Scene 7

"Bangaway Isle"
E. Chester, E. Brooks, J. Storace

Specialty Dance
Jscherey and Hully, Bangaway Dancers

Scene 8

Vive la France
Madame Sangene: F. Moore. *Jack:* J. Osterman. *Ted:* T. Lewis.

Scene 9

"The Chair Bottom Dance"
Dancing Girls, Boys

Scene 10

Tenth Avenue
Mrs. Brown: F. Moore. *Billy Brown:* H. O'Neal. *Aggy:* M. Evans. *Amy:* M. O'Brien. *Smith:* E. Chester. *Jones:* W. Johnson.

Scene 11

The Voice of the World
Music: J. Squires. *The Cantor:* C. Parsons. *Egyptians:* C. Gallimore, J. McDowell, G. Roberts. *Taj Mahal:* [G. Wheaton (singer)], N. Pearce (dancer)
"The Rheims Cathedral"
M. O'Brien, M. Powers, L. Arnold, G. Wheaton, Chorus

Scene 12

A Gentleman's Boudoir
The Chauffeur: A. Blair. *The Man:* J. Osterman. *The Lady:* M. O'Brien.

Scene 13

Jack Osterman
["Baby Feet Go Pitter Patter"
(*Music and Lyrics by* Gus Kahn.)]

Scene 14

The Lady Killer
The Waiter: W. Johnson. *Baron Pfeiffer:* J. Pearl. *Wolff:* H. O'Neal. *The Lady:* M. O'Brien. *The Flirt:* M. Evans. *Head Waiter:* J. Oyra. *Night Club Guests:* (Ensemble.)

"What Women and Men Will Wear"
F. Moore, Fashion Parade

Scene 15

"Start the Band"
E. Brooks, (Ted Lewis and His Orchestra)

Specialties
Dancing Girls, King and King, J. Storace,

Dancing Boys, C. Gallimore, Veloz and Yolanda, Ensemble

ACT 2[59]

Scene 1

The Tree of Love
The Man: C. Parsons. *The Girl:* M. Powers. *The Pages:* LeMaye Sisters
With the Winter Garden Girls in the Tree of Love.

Scene 2

Florence Moore

Scene 3

Bad News
The Coach: H. O'Neal. *The Doctor:* W. Johnson. *The Fullback:* A. Blair. *The Sophomore:* J. Pearl.

Scene 4

Parasols[60] (Dance)
Dancing Girls

Scene 5

"The Love Boat"
The Singer: L. Arnold. *Lantern Bearers:* LeMaye Sisters. *Owner of Boat:* E. Chester. *The Servant:* W. Johnson. *The Doorkeeper:* G. Leland. *Slave Girls:* M. Vernelli, M. Younger, H. Livingston, E. Meade, B. Walz, M. Stapp. *The Father:* G. Roberts. *The Daughter:* C. Gallimore. *The Mandarin:* J. Oyra. *The Guards:* P. Ott, J. Dayton. *The Lover:* J. McDowell.

Scene 6

Oh, Nurse
The Doctor: H. O'Neal. *The Nurse:* F. Moore. *The Patient:* J. Osterman.

Scene 7

"Bracelets"
J. Squires

Dance
N. Pearce, Winter Garden Girls

---

[57]The fourth in the annual series of musical revues presented by Messrs. Shubert beginning in 1923.
[58]Sketches uncredited.

---

[59]Added after opening:
"You Dear" (Act 2)
J. Squires
Dance
Dancing Girls
[60]Dropped after opening.

Scene 8
King and King
Scene 9
Honey Land
The Playmaker: H. O'Neal. *The First Victim*: J. Osterman. *The Second Victim*: J. Pearl. *The Little Bees*: N. Pearce, M. O'Brien, K. Simmons, J. Storace.
Scene 10
Ted Lewis and His Musical Clowns, assisted by Eddie Chester and Eleanore Brooks
["The Call of Broadway"
(Music by Maurice Rubens. *Lyrics by* Ted Lewis, Jack Osterman.)
"Do That Thing"
"(Here Am I) Broken-Hearted"
(Music by Ray Henderson. *Lyrics by* Buddy G. DeSylva, Lew Brown.)
"Oh, Peggy"
(Music by Harry Akst. *Lyrics by* Benny Davis.)
"The Only One for Me"
(Music by Harry Akst. *Lyrics by* Benny Davis.)
"Snap Out of It"]
(Music by Harry Akst. *Lyrics by* Benny Davis.)]
Scene 11
"Is Everybody Happy (Now)?"
T. Lewis, J. Pearl, F. Moore, J. Osterman, Dancing Girls, Boys
(Music by Maurice Rubens. *Lyrics by* Ted Lewis, Jack Osterman.)

1927.59 FUNNY FACE

A Musical Comedy in Two Acts, 7 Scenes. Book by Fred Thompson and Paul Gerard Smith. Music by George Gershwin. Lyrics by Ira Gershwin. Staged by Edgar MacGregor. Dances and ensembles by Bobby Connolly. Settings designed by John Wenger. Costumes designed by Kiviette. Orchestra under the direction of Alfred Newman. Produced by Alex A. Aarons and Vinton Freedley. Opened 22 November 1927 at the Alvin Theatre and closed 23 June 1928 after 250 performances.

CAST (in order of appearance): *Dora*: BETTY COMPTON. *June*: GERTRUDE McDONALD. *"Frankie"*: ADELE ASTAIRE. *Jimmy Reeve, their guardian*: FRED ASTAIRE. *"Dugsie" Gibbs*: WILLIAM KENT. *Chester*: Earl Hampton. *Herbert*: VICTOR MOORE. *Peter Thurston*: ALLEN KEARNS. *Sergeant of Police*: Ted MacLean. *Hotel Clerk*: Edwin Hodge. *Porter*: Walter Munroe. *Bell Hop*: Dorothy Jordon. *Ritz Quartette*: ?. *At the Pianos*: Victor Arden, Phil Ohman.
Ladies of the Ensemble: Kay Annis, Mildred Brower, Marcia Bell, Vera Berg, Helen Clare, Jean Carroll, Peggy Daubert, Dorothy Dawn, Ann Ecklund, Adelyn Endore, Elsie Frank, Sherry Gale, Gloria Glennon, Alma Hookey, Ona Hamilton, Dorothy Jordan, Helen Leslie, Adrienne Lampel, Lillian Michell, Estelle Mercier, Maxine Marshall, Ethel Maye, Frances Markey, Pauline Mason, Jo Navarro, Marie Otto, Ruth Penery, Boo Phelps, Peggy Quinn, Rita Romero, Ruth Sato, Marjorie Seltzer, Bobby Shutta, Marion Tierney, Billee Walker, Polly Williams, Winifred Beck. *Gentlemen of the Ensemble*: Edwin Bidwell, Dowell Brown, Austin Clark, William Cooper, Arthur Craig, Eugene Day, Norman Curtis, Jack Fraley, Bob Gebhardt, Thomas Hodges, W. L. Mack, Gordon Merrick, Lionel Maclyn, Tom Martin, Richard Neely, Edwin Preble, Fritz Reinhard, Walter Wandell, Paul Jansen, Richard Keith, Walter Munroe, Sam Simpson, Marshall Scott, Ray Stilley.

Act 1, Scene 1: Living Room of Jimmy Reeve's House. *Scene 2*: Outside Peter Thurston's House. *Scene 3*: Living Room of Jimmy Reeve's House.

Act 2, Scene 1: The Canoe Inn, Lake Wapatog, New Jersey. *Scene 2*: A Suite at the Paymore, Atlantic City. *Scene 3*: The Ward Room *Scene 4*: The Two Million Dollar Pier.

ACT 1
"Birthday Party"
B. Compton, G. McDonald, Guests
"Once"
W. Kent, B. Compton, Ensemble
"Funny Face"
A. Astaire, F. Astaire
"High Hat"
F. Astaire, Boys
"'S Wonderful"
A. Astaire, A. Kearns
"Let's Kiss and Make Up"
A. Astaire, F. Astaire, Ensemble

Finale (Come Along, Let's Gamble)
Entire Company
ACT 2
"In the Swim" (Opening)
Girls
"He Loves and She Loves"
A. Astaire, A. Kearns
"Tell the Doc"
W. Kent, Girls
"What Am I Going to Do?" (Funny Face)
F. Astaire, G. McDonald, B. Compton, Girls
"Sing a Little Song" (reprises)
Arden & Ohman, Ritz Quartette, Boys
"What Am I Going to Do" (reprise)
B. Compton, G. McDonald, Chorus
"The Babbitt and the Bromide"
A. Astaire, F. Astaire
Finale
Entire Company

1927.60 TAKE THE AIR

A Musical Comedy of Aviation in Two Acts, a Prologue and 7 Scenes. Book and lyrics by Anne Caldwell and Gene Buck. Airs (music) by Dave Stamper. Staged by Alexander Leftwich. (Additional numbers by James Hanley, J. Russel Robinson, Willard Robison, Al Dubin, Con Conrad and Abner Silver.) Dances staged by Ralph Reader. Settings by William Oden Waller. Costumes designed by Charles LeMaire, Cora McGeachy, Evelyn McHorter. Orchestra under the direction of Charles Drury. Entire production under the personal direction of Gene Buck. Produced by Gene Buck. Opened 22 November 1927 at the Waldorf Theatre, moved 16 April 1928 to the Earl Carroll Theatre, and closed 19 May 1928 after 206 performances.

CAST (in order of appearance): *"Mink"*: Al Ochs. *"Monte"*: Hugh Bennett. *Gloria*: Geneva Mitchell. *Marguerite*: Audrey Berry. *"Happy" Hokum*: WILL MAHONEY. *"Goldie"*: ROSE KING. *Lieutenant Sullivan*: BUD PEARSON. *Lieutenant Berg*: JACK PEARSON. *Sergeant Mooney*: CHICK YORK. *Broncho Liz*: KITTY O'CONNOR. *Lieutenant Dale*: Walter Scott Kolk. *Captain Halliday*: GREEK EVANS. *"Red", the Mule Skinner*: William F. Donohue. *The Mule*: George Spelvin. *Lillian ("Baby") Bond*: DOROTHY DILLEY. *Señor José*: Maurice Lapue. *Señorita Carmela Cortez*: TRINI. *Wing*: Simeon Karavaeff. *Sing Song*: Gladys Keck. *Nagasaki*: Kikobi Murai. (*Specialty*: Charlotte Ayres.) And MAX FISHER AND HIS CALIFORNIA ORCHESTRA
Show Girls: Frederica Finley, Helen Hermes, Nellie King, Muriel Manners, Marcel Miller, Marie Muselle, Agnes White, Mabel Williams, Carol Kingsbury, Loretta McCarver. *Dancers*: Bobby Bliss, Muriel Buck, Violet Casey, Edris Diamond, Diana Day, Helga Farringmore, Gene Fontaine, Beryl Golden, Frances Guinan, Irene Griffith, Ethel Handler, Eleanor Hunt, Loretta Jefferson, Rosabelle Kay, Gladys Keck, Florence Kinney, Carol Lynn, Lee Manners, Helen Murray, Adelaide Permin, Marjorie Spahn, Blanche Victoria, Dorothy Waller, Bobby Weeks. *Boys*: Andrew Burgoyne, Vincent Curran, Edward Conant, Norman Donald, Joseph Gorrien, Paul Jones, Starr Jones, Julio Martel, Herman Maier, Hazard Newbury, Herbert Pickett, Basil Rallis, Charles Rainsford, John Roach, Donald Wells, Leo Williams.

Prologue: A Railroad Station Platform Somewhere on the Texas-Mexican Border.

Act 1, Scene 1: The Kennels. *Scene 2*: Rickenbacker Field, U. S. Army Aviation Border Patrol. *Scene 3*: Office at Headquarters, Rickenbacker Field. *Scene 4*: Inside a Hangar, that evening.

Act 2, Scene 1: A Ranch House Courtyard, the next evening. *Scene 2*: A Road in the Texas Desert. *Scene 3*: A Fête on the Estate of Oliver Bond, Sands Point, Long Island.

ACT 1[61]
"All Aboard for Times Square"
G. Mitchell, A. Berry, Girls

---

[61]Interpolated during the run, according to published sheet music:
"You're the First Thing I Think of In the Morning—(and the Last Thing I Think of at Night)
C. York, R. King
(Music by Jack Stanley. Lyrics by Billy Tracey.)

"Silver Wings"
G. Evans, Aviators

"The Wild and Woolly West"
D. Dilley, Cowboys, Girls

"Carmela"
Trini, Ensemble

"Carmen Has Nothing on Me"
R. King, Girls

"Maybe"
D. Dilley, W. Mahoney

"We'll Have a New Home in the Morning"
K. O'Connor, Cowboys, Girls
(*Music by* Willard Robison. *Lyrics by* J. Russel Robinson, Gene Buck.)

"Take the Air"
Trini, Aviators

Dance
B. Pearson, J. Pearson, C. Ayres, S. Karavaeff

ACT 2

"Aviation Ballet"
D. Dilley, Girls

"Tango Espagnol"
Trini, M. Lapue

"(On) A Pony for Two"
D. Dilley, W. Mahoney, C. York, R. King, Girls
(*Music by* James Hanley.)

Dance
B. Pearson, J. Pearson

"Lullaby"
K. O'Connor

"We'd Rather Dance Than Eat"
Gene Buck Dancers

"Japanese Moon"
D. Dilley, Guests

Butterfly Dance[62]
C. Ayres

"Ham and Eggs"
Trini, W. Mahoney
(*Music by* Con Conrad and Abner Silver. *Lyrics by* Al Dubin.)

Finale
Entire Company

THE PIRATES OF PENZANCE,
or, The Slave of Duty

1927.61

A Return Engagement of the Comic Opera in Two Acts[63]. Libretto by William S. Gilbert. Music by Arthur Sullivan. Entire production staged by Winthrop Ames. Settings and costumes designed by Woodman Thompson. Dances directed by Louise Clifford. Produced by Winthrop Ames. Opened 24 November 1927 at the Royale Theatre (joining 'The Mikado' and 'Iolanthe' in repertory) and closed 7 January 1928 after 9 performances.

CAST: *Richard*, The Pirate King: JOHN BARCLAY. *Samuel*, His Lieutenant: J. HUMBIRD DUFFEY. *Frederic*, a Pirate Apprentice: WILLIAM WILLIAMS. *Major-General Stanley* of the British Army: FRED WRIGHT. *His Orderly*: George C. Lehrian. *Edward*, a Sergeant of Police: WILLIAM C. GORDON. *Doctor of Divinity*: George C. Lehrian. *General Stanley's Daughters (4)*: Mabel: LOIS BENNETT. *Kate*: SUISSABELL STERLING. *Edith*: VIRGINIA FOX. *Isabel*: Bettina Hall. *Maud*: Paula Langlen. *Ruth*, a Piratical Maid of All Work: VERA ROSS. *Chorus of General Stanley's Daughters and Pirates, Policemen.*[64]

1927.62 ## HARRY DELMAR'S REVELS

A Musical Revue in Two Acts, 24 Exhibits (scenes). Sketches by William K. Wells. Music by Jimmy Monaco, Jesse Greer and Lester Lee. Lyrics by Billy Rose and Ballard Macdonald. (Staged by Harry Delmar.) Dances by Harry Delmar and Sam Rose. Ballets by Chester Hale. Costumes designed by Jeanne Hackett. Settings and lighting by Clarke Robinson. Music director, John L. McManus. Produced by Samuel Baerwitz and Harry Delmar. Opened 28 November 1927 at the Sam S. Shubert Theatre and closed 3 March 1928 after 112 performances.

CAST: WINNIE LIGHTNER, FRANK FAY, BERT LAHR, HUGH CAMERON, JEANNE HACKETT, CARL SHAW, DICK LANCASTER, GLEN DALE, BILLY [William Gaxton], ARTIE LEEMING, TRADO TWINS (Frank, Peter), IVAN TRIESAULT, HELEN EBY ROCK, PATSY KELLY, DOROTHEA JAMES, LEW MANN, E. MERCEDES, CAROLYN NOLTE, PATTERSON TWINS (Flora, Alice), JEAN CARROLL, IRMA MOORE, JOE SARGENT, JOHN BARNEY, STUART ROSS, TEDDY WALTERS and ROY ELLIS.
Ensemble: Helene Bradley, Jane Daniel, Margit Dybfest, Dorothy Harris, Gertrude Green, Truly Jones, Ione Miller, Jola Morena, Gloria Murray, Sugar O'Neill, Janette Patrick, Irene Ransom, Marjorie Rich, Thelma Temple, Gertrude Young, Mary Young, Marjorie Graham, Dorothy Stewart, Mae Selden, Kae Clements. *Showgirls*: Florence Allan, Billie Bennett, Gene Brady, Vee Carroll, Winifred Carter, Peggy Davis, Ann Janeway, Patrice Oliver, Eileen Wenzel, Tania Tanovska, Alla Pedrova, Lenore Leonard. *Chester Hale Dancers*: Hilda Peterson, Inez St. Claire, Beatrice Lorraine, Mary Wynn, Ester Whelton, Ann Shannon, Getrude Kornblum, Florence May, Phyllis Jordan, Rolande Poucel, Winona Sweet, Violet Lundberg, Gladys Glorita, Lillian Messmer, Sylvia Greene, Jewel T'Gens.

ACT 1[65]

Scene 1
Exterior of Court House

Scene 2
Interior of Courtroom

Exhibit A
Chester Hale Dancers

Exhibit B
Zoo-Logic[66]
Wife: I. Moore. *Lover*: D. Lancaster. *Husband*: F. Fay. *Announcement by* P. Kelly.

Exhibit C
"I Love a Man in a Uniform"
W. Lightner, Her Eight Cadets
(Music by James V. Monaco.)

Exhibit D
"Limbs of the Law"
Singer: E. Mercedes. *Frenchman*: G. Dale. *Woman Scorned*: C. Nolte. *Sergeant*: D. Lancaster. *Policeman*: B. Lahr.

Exhibit E
"My Rainbow"
F. Fay, Rainbow Girls
(Music by Lester Lee. Lyrics by Jeanne Hackett.)
Chartreuse: L. Leonard. *Blue*: W. Carter. *Green*: A. Pedrova. *Violet*: B. Benentt, G. Brady. *Orchid*: E. Wenzel. *Magenta*: A. Janeway. *Coral*: P. Davis. *White*: F. Allan, T. Tanovska, P. Olivier. *A Rainbow*: V. Carroll.

Dance
Chester Hale Girls
Jeanne Hackett, P. Kelly.

---

[62]Dropped during the run.
[63]First presented in New York 31 December 1879 at the Fifth Avenue Theatre for 91 performances in two engagements; this revival presented 6 December 1926 at the Plymouth Theatre for 128 performances. For Synopsis of Scenes and Musical Numbers, see original 1879 production.
[64]Same as in THE MIKADO revival, 17 September 1927.

[65]Added after the opening:
Bed Time Stories (Act 1)
F. Fay
Announcer: P. Kelly.

Mixed Drinks (Act 1)
Butler: I. Triesault. First Guest: E. Mercedes. Second Guest: G. Dale. Third Guest: C. Nolte. Fourth Guest: D. Lancaster. Hostess: H. E. Rock. The Friend: B. Lahr. The Husband: F. Fay.

Lillian Roth (Songs)(Act 1)

"I Can't Give You Anything But Love"(Act 1, added late January)
L. Mann
(*Music by* Jimmy McHugh. *Lyrics by* Dorothy Fields.)
[66]Dropped after the opening.

Exhibit F

Reincarnation[67]

Exhibit G

Carl Shaw[68]

Exhibit H

In a Persian Garden
The Maids: F. Patterson, A. Patterson. *The Favorite Wife*: J. Hackett. *The Lover*: I. Triesault. *The Husband*: W. Gaston.

Exhibit I

A Helping Hand
First Girl: H. E. Rock. *Second Girl*: K. Clements. *The Sailor*: J. Barney. *The Sap*: B. Lahr.

Exhibit J

"Say It with a Solitaire"
G. Dale
(Music by James V. Monaco.)
Bar Pins: B. Bennett, G. Brady. *Fleur de Lys*: A. Pedrova, T. Tanovska. *Star Buckles*: P. Oliver, F. Allan. *Diamond Wreaths*: L. Leonard, P. Davis. *Baguettes*: V. Carroll, W. Carter. *Solitaires*: A. Janeway, E. Wenzel.

Exhibit K

The Straganota Players
Lover: W. Gaston. *Husband*: L. Mann. *Wife*: H. E. Rock. *Maid*: I. Moore. *Announcer*: F. Fay.

Exhibit L

Winnie Lightner

Exhibit M

"The Jigaboo Jig"
Trado Twins, P. Kelly, L. Mann, C. Shaw, Entire Ensembel
(Music by Lester Lee.)

ACT 2

Exhibit N

Undersea Ballet (Under the Sea Ballet)
Jelly Fish: Chester Hale Girls. *Pearl Divers*: R. Ellis, I. Triesault. *Sea Nymph*: T. Walters.

Dance
T. Walters, R. Ellis.
Octopus: A. Sorreiro. *Undersea Plants, Fish, etc.*: Misses W. Carter, L. Leonard, P. Davis, A. Pedrova, G. Brady, B. Benentt, A. Janeway.

Exhibit O

Four Famous Horsemen
Don Quixote: A. Leeming. *Paul Revere*: H. Cameron. *Ben Hur*: W. Gaston. *Jesse James*: B. Lahr.

Exhibit P

The Peacemaker
Mrs. A: W. Lightner. *Mrs. B*: C. Nolte. *Mrs. C*: I. Moore. *Mr. A*: F. Fay. *Mr. B*: D. Lancaster. *Mr. C*: G. Dale. *The Peacemaker*: A. Leeming.

Exhibit Q

Milady's Boudoir
"Golden Memories of Perfume"
C. Nolte
La Lys: P. Davis. *Deja La Printemps*: L. Leonard. *Amber*: A. Janeway. *Maskee*: G. Brady. *Nuit de Chine*: A. Pedrova. *Emeraud*: P. Oliver. *Pavots D'Argent*: V. Carroll. *Dans La Nuit*: B. Bennett. *Orchidee Blue*: W. Carter. *Nuit de Noel*: T. Tanovska. *L'Heure Blue*: F. Allan. *"Ybry Femme de Paris"*: E. Wenzel. *Ybry Powder Puffs*: Chester Hale Girls. (Ybry Femme de Paris Perfume used.)

Exhibit R

Trado Twins

Exhibit S

Efficiency
President: B. Gaston. *Superintendent*: D. Lancaster. *Secretary*: F. Trado. *Stenographer*: I. Moore. *"Nutley"*: H. Cameron.

Exhibit T

"Naga Saki"
W. Lightner
(Music by Harry Warren. *Lyrics by* Mort Dixon.)

Exhibit U

Tea Time
F. Fay, P. Kelly, L. Mann

Exhibit V

"Laff 'Em Away" (If You Have Troubles, Laugh Them Away)
Trado Twins, D. James, Ensemble
(*Music and Lyrics by* Lester Lee.)

Exhibit W

Crossed Wires
Boy: D. Lancaster. *Girl*: E. Mercedes. *Wife*: H. E. Rock. *Husband*: B. Lahr.

Exhibit X

Frank Fay (Specialty)
["Four Walls"
(*Music and Lyrics by* Al Jolson, Billy Rose, Dave Dreyer.)]

Exhibit Y

The Verdict Is in Your Hands

Finale
Entire Company

1927.63   # GOLDEN DAWN

A Musical Play in Two Acts, 11 Scenes. Book and lyrics by Otto Harbach and Oscar Hammerstein II. Music by Emmerich Kálmán and Herbert Stothart. Book staged by Reginald Bennett. Dances and ensembles staged by Dave Bennett. Settings by Joseph Urban. Costume research and design by Mark Mooring. Orchestra under the direction of Herbert Stothart. Associate musical director, Mario Agnolucci. Produced by Arthur Hammerstein. Opened 30 November 1927 at Hammerstein's Theatre and closed 5 May 1928 after 184 performances.

CAST (in order of appearance): *Dago*: Carlo Benetti. *Anzac*: Archie Leach [Cary Grant]. *Pigeon*: Len Mence. *Mooda*: Marguerita Sylva. *Hasmali*: Kumar Goshal. *Captain Eric*: Reginald Pasch. *Sister Hedwig*: Paula Ayers. *Shep Keyes*: ROBERT CHISHOLM. *Steve Allen*: PAUL GREGORY. *Blink Jones*: GIL SQUIRES. *Sir Alfred Hammersley*: OLIN HOWLAND. *Dawn*: LOUISE HUNTER. *Johanna*: NYDIA D'ARNELL. *Colonel Judson*: W. Messenger Bellis. *Ann Milford*: BARBARA NEWBERRY. *Dr. Milford*: Henry Pemberton. *An Old Man of Africa*: Robert Paton Gibbs. *A Witch Doctor*: Jacques Cartier. *A Dancing Girl*: (Princess) Kohana. *Mombassa Moll*: HAZEL DRURY. *An Ensemble of English, French and Italian Prisoners, German Soldiers and Askari Guards, Native Men and Women, Women of Mombassa, Nurses and Sisters.*

Ladies of the Ensemble: Wilma Roelof, Lucy Lawler, Irene Carroll, Peggy Messinger, Vivian Russell, Barbara Carrington, Hellene Counihan, Norine Bogen, Mimi Jordan, Bunny Schumm, Sorena Mumma, Frances Denny, Frances Dumas, Janet Hale, Leona Riggs, Jean Hitch, Leola Buelow, Grace LaRue, Mabel Olsen, LeVergne Evans, Alice Busee, Maud Carlton, Alva McGill, Norma France, Karol Kayne, Ann Anderson, Louise Baer, Marie Foster, Geraldine Gooding, Rosena Weston, Inez Clough, Geneva Grant, Julia F. Mitchell, Alma Reynolds, Maud White, Christine David, Mary Mason, Beneventa Washington, Ruth Matson, Louise Turner, Elizabeth Holloway, Zina Ivanova, Klara Grosheva, Magda Trauber, All Kisselava, Saloma Bartolm, Dora Grebenetsky, Maria Grushko, Valia Valentinova, Lida Ordynsky, Ann Ouzoroff, Helene Chaudaroff, Emilia Andrievska, Xenia Dalsky.

Gentlemen of the Ensemble: Tom Chadwick, Joseph Vitale, Milton Rae, Arnold Basil, Frank Dobert, Raymond Otto, Edward Watkins, Tom Rider, Irving Andrievsky, Valdimir Danieloff, Miki Dalsky, Joseph Davidenko, Konstantine Smith, Alexander Ouzoroff, Leonard Gorlenko, Peter Ordunsky, Vsevolad Andrenoff, Peter Kosloff, Vladimir Chavdaroff, George Brant, Toni Klimovitch, F. J. Accoll, James Earl, William Walker, Harold DesVerney, Adolph Henderson, McKinley Reeves, William McFarland, H. Webster Elkins, W. Service Beel, Amos Guerrant, Earl Wilson, James Grey, Robert Jackson, Henry Brown. Alexander U. Fine's Russian Art Choir.

Act 1, Scene 1: Mooda's Canteen near a Prison Camp in German East Africa. 1917. *Scene 2*: The Temple Cave. Immediately after. *Scene 3*: The Jungle. The Passing of the Night. The Next Morning. *Scene 4*: The Prisoners' Stockade. *Scene 5*: The Tree of Mulunghu.

Act 2, Scene 1: The Canteen. 1919. *Scene 2*: The Old Stockade. That night. *Scene 3*: Geng Lee's Joint in Mombassa. Two months later. *Scene 4*: The Temple Cave. Two months later. *Scene 5*: The Gate to the Mission. Immediately after. *Scene 6*: The Golden Dawn.

MUSICAL NUMBERS[69]
"When I Crack My Whip" (The Whip)
R. Chisholm

---

[67]Dropped after the opening.
[68]Dropped after the opening.

[69]A complete list of musical numbers not provided in the program; above list includes principal melodies, in the word of the show's management.

"We Two"
    O. Howland, N. d'Arnell
"Here in the Dark"
    L. Hunter, P. Gregory, R. Chisholm
"My Bwanna"
    L. Hunter, (Chorus)
"Consolation"
    G. Squires, B. Newberry
"Africa"
    R. Pasch, Ensemble
"Dawn"
    L. Hunter, P. Gregory
    (*Music by* Robert Stolz and Herbert Stothart.)
"Jungle Shadows"
    H. Drury
"Mulunghu Thabu"
    K. Ghoshal, Chorus
"It's Always the Way"

1927.64
HAPPY

A Musical Comedy in Three Acts, 6 Scenes. Book by Vincent Lawrence and McElbert Moore. Music by Frank Grey. Lyrics by Earle Crooker and McElbert Moore. Book and dances staged by Walter Brooks. Additional dances staged by Jack Heisler. Costumes by Mme. Josette. Orchestra under the direction of Carleton Kelsey. Produced by Murray Phillips. Opened 5 December 1927 at the Earl Carroll Theatre and closed 21 January 1928 after 56 performances; re-opened under the auspices of Happy Productions, Inc. 6 February 1928 at Daly's Theatre and closed 25 February 1928 after 24 additional performances[70]. Total: 80 performances.

CAST (in order of appearance): *Bill Wentworth*: JOHN KANE. *Teddy*: GENE COLLINS. *Tommy*: BILL BROWN. *Marion Brooker*: VIRGINIA SMITH. *Siggy Sigler*: PERCY HELTON. *Jack Gaynor*: FRED SANTLEY. *Edith Dale*: SHIRLEY SHERMAN. *Lorelei Lynn*: MADELEINE FAIRBANKS. *Grace*: Lucille Reece. *Milly*: Rosa Lee. *President Dale*: Joseph Clayton. *Lewis Pollock*: Donald Campbell. *Harry*: Bob Nelson. *Mr. Bennett*: Willard Dashiell. *Marjorie*: Alice Cochran. *Helen*: Ann Cochran. *Blanche*: Betty Rourke. *Butler*: George Fredericks.
    Hadley College Students: Girls: Lois Alexander, Harriett Dixon, Daisie Bay, Alice Cochran, Ann Cochran, Katherien Glading, Vasso Pan, Rosa Lee, Clay Long, Mabel Martin, Anna Marie McKenney, Paula Sidman, Nanie Possiel, Lucile Reece, Ruth Simmons, Hatty White, Edith Mae Wright. *Boys*: Don Cortez, Edwin Gaillard, Richard Sumner, Donald Rand, Bob Nelson, Hugh Saunders, Hermes Pan, Bill Eckhardt.

Act 1: Living Room in a College Rooming House just off the Campus of Hadley College, Hadley, Massachusetts. Late afternoon of Commencement Day, June. Present time.

Act 2, Scene 1: A Corner in a Railroad Station. *Scene 2*: Outside Sigler's Home at South Hampton, Long Island. The next afternoon. *Scene 3*: A Corner in a Railroad Station. *Scene 4*: Sigler's Home A few hours later.

Act 3: Sigler's Home. Evening. A week later.

ACT 1
"Plastic Surgery"
    G. Collins, B. Brown, Students
"Check Your Troubles"
    V. Smith, Students
"Through the Night"
    S. Sherman, F. Santley
"Sunnyside of You"
    V. Smith, M. Fairbanks, P. Helton, J. Kane
"Lorelei"
    M. Fairbanks, F. Santley, Students
"If You'll Put Up With Me"
    V. Smith, P. Helton
"The Serpentine"
    G. Collins, B. Brown, M. Fairbanks, Students

---

[70]Return engagement principal cast changes: *Bill Wentworth*: JOE McCALLON. *Marion Brooker*: PERQUETA COURTNEY. *Siggy Sigler*: CHARLES WILLIAMS. *Jack Gaynor*: TRUMAN STANLEY. *Mr. Bennett*: Henry Crosby. *Helen*: Vasso Pan.

Finale
    Entire Party
ACT 2
Opening:
"Lorelei" (reprise)
    F. Santley
"The Younger Generation"
    M. Fairbanks, V. Smith, P. Helton, J. Kane, Guests
"Here's to You, Jack"
    Guests
"Happy"
    F. Santley, M. Fairbanks, Guests
"Lorelei" (reprise)
    F. Santley
One Good Friend"
    S. Sherman, F. Santley
"Hitting on High"
    V. Smith, G. Collins, B. Brown, Guests
"Blacksheep"
    M. Fairbanks, J. Kane, Ann Cochran, Alice Cochran, Guests
"Which Shall It Be?"
    S. Sherman
    (*Music and Lyrics by* Ethelberta Hasbrook and Frank Grey.)
"Through the Night" (reprise)
    S.S herman, Boys
Finale
    Entire Party
ACT 3
Opening:
"What a Lovely Night"
    S. Sherman, Friends
Dance Specialty
    The Cochran Twins
"Mad About You"
    M. Fairbanks, J. Kane, G. Collins, B. Brown, Guests
"If You'll Put Up With Me" (reprise)
    M. Fairbanks, P. Helton
Grand Finale
    Entire Party

1927.65
THE WHITE EAGLE

A Musical Play in Three Acts and a Prologue. Book and lyrics by Brian Hooker and W. H. Post. Based on the play 'The Squaw Man' by Edwin Milton Royle. Music by Rudolf Friml. Staged by Richard Boleslavsky. Dances by Busby Berkeley. Scenes and costumes by James Reynolds. Lighting by Ray Barnet. Music and orchestra under the direction of Anton Heindl. Orchestrations by Joseph Majer. Entire production under the personal direction of Olga Treskoff and Russell Janney. Produced by Russell Janney. Opened 26 December 1927 at the Casino Theatre and closed 4 February 1928 after 48 performances.

CAST (in order of appearance): *The Sun Watcher*: Ralph Moana. *The Medicine Man of the Utes*: John Mealey. *Tabywana*, Great Chief of the Utes: Charles E. Galagher. *Silverwing*, his daughter: MARION KEELER. *The Indian Dancer*: Aysa Kaz. *The English Dancers (2): Shepherd Boy*: Paula Lind. *Goddess*: Helen Grenelle. *Lady Mabel*: Blanche Fleming. *Lady Mary*: Roberta Curry. *Lieutenant Henry George*: Carlton Neville. *Lieutenant Alex. McGrath*: Arthur Kellar. *Captain James Wynnegate*, later Jim Carson: ALLAN PRIOR. *Captain Leslie*: Jock McGraw. *Sir John Applegate*: Lawrence D'Orsay. *The Dowager Lady Kerhill*: Isabelle O'Madigan. *Countess of Kerhill*: Hazel Glen. *Earl of Kerhill*: FRED TILDEN. *Mr. Chiswick*, his secretary: Ernest Ehler. *Malcolm Petrie*, his solicitor: Horace Pollock. *Bates*, his butler: Walter Cross. *Sadie* of the Longhorn Saloon: Kay Hawley. *Lily*: Paula Lind. *Nick*, the barkeeper: George Shields. *Bud Hardy*, the Sheriff: Charles Henderson. *Big Bill*: Mark Smith. *Happy*: Jay Fassett. *Gloomy*: Earl Mayne. *Andy*, the Parson: Royal Cutter. *Thunder Face*: Michael Evans. *Pete*: Leon Cunningham. *Punk*: Marius Rogati. *Cash Hawkins*, Rustler and Bad Man: Forrest Huff. *Little Hal*: Master Albert Shaw. *Officers of the 16th Lancers, English Girls, Cow Punchers, Honky Tonk Girls, Indians of Tabywana's Tribe, etc.*
    The Twelve Chiefs: Wallace Banfield, Nat Christensen, Jack Rose, Paul Winnell, Thomas Mengert, Lamar Hessenberg, Alex Shishman, Armin Mueller, Earl Kardux, Edward Sheldon, Michael Evans, Serge Vino. *Indians*: Randall Freyer, John Fredericks, Harry James, William Hagen, Simeon Sabro, William Wally, Raymond

Toben, Richard Rowley, Charles Trott, Barton Hall. *Squaws*: Vida Hanna, Laura Novea, Beatrice Marsh, Alice Huntington, Rae Ring, Mabel Purdy, Rene Berteau, Alice Harper, Helena Koffler, Helen Berger, Harriet Standon, Mary Quinn, Jewel Welter, Mae Robinson, Muriel Dawn, Elizabeth Kelley. *Dancers*: Lucille Constant, June Day, Grace Cantrell, Alice Olsen, Edna Kulker, Florence Gunther, Grace DeViney, Florence Turner, Mary Morris, Helen Landis, Caroline Phillips, Theresa Miller, Peggy Horan, Billie Lanctot, Lucille Arden, Virginia Nachant. *Officers of the 16th Lancers*: Charles Froom, Earl Kardux, Eldon Edwards, Richard Rowley, Efim Vitis, Randall Freyer, John Fredericks, Harry James, Barton Hall, Arthur Young, Raymond Toben, Simeon Sabro, Carlos Fessler, William Hagen, George Leach, William MacDargh, George Kingsley, Ross Ericson, Harold Currier, Edward Sheldon, Elmer Barlab. *English Ladies*: Joan Marren, Roberta Curry, Olyvve Bakke, Ruth Norris, Constance Durand, Margaret Grove, Dorothy Forsyth, Edith Gwen, Helen Ely, Dorothy Davis, Pauline Hall, Evelyn Stockton, Shirley Carlton, Elizabeth Kelley, Madeline Clancy, Mildred Gordon, Catherine Van Brunt, Bessie Masters, Rowena Baker, Sue Lake. *Butlers*: Fred Rogers, Charles Trott, William Venus. .

Prologue: The Great Rock. Somewhere in Western America.

Act 1: Maudsley Towers. Somewhere in England.

Act 2: The Long Horn Saloon. Somewhere in Western America.

Act 3: The Green River Ranch. Somewhere in Western America.

MUSICAL NUMBERS[71]
  "Alone" (My Lover)
  "Thunder Dance"
  "Regimental Song"
  "Gather the Rose"
  "Smile, Darn You, Smile!"
  "Give Me One Hour"
  "Follow On"
  "Silverwing"
  "Black Eagles"
  "Winona"
  "Bad Man Number"
  "A Home for You"
  "Dance, Dance, Dance"
  "Indian Lullaby"
  "My Heaven with You"

1927.66   EXCESS BAGGAGE

A Comedy (with Songs) in Three Acts, 6 Scenes. Play by Jack McGowan. Staged by Melville Burke. Dances staged by John Boyle. Settings designed by P. Dodd Ackerman. Miss Hopkins' Gowns by Jenkins; other gowns by Maison Simone. Uniforms and vaudeville costumes by Mahieu Costumers, Inc. Technical director, Edward Clark Lilley. Musical director, Morris Zentner. Entire play under the personal supervision of Paul Dickey. Produced by Barbour, Crimmins & Bryant. Opened 26 December 1927 at the Ritz Theatre and closed 30 June 1928 after 216 performances.

CAST (in order of appearance): *Jimmy Dunn*: FRANK McHUGH. *Sarah Benton*: Maud Blair. *Jack Merrill*: Nace Bonville. *Four Buddies Quartette*: *Bob*: Vladimir Dubinsky. *Charlie*: Charles Dalton. *Bill*: Merald Tollefsen. *Frank Arnold*: John H. Dilson. *Mabel Ford*: SUZANNE WILLA. *Marvin*: Lawrence O'Sullivan. *Eddie Kane*: ERIC DRESSLER. *Betty Ford*: DORIS EATON. *Elsa McCoy*: MIRIAM HOPKINS. *Herbert Chammon*: Boyd Marshall. *Val D'Errico*: Herbert Clark. *Al Kent*: Frank Horton. *Joe DeLeon*: William Boulia. *George McCarthy*: MORTON DOWNEY. *Harry Hart*: Denton Vane. *Rita Rydell*: FRANCES GOODRICH. *Dad*: Howard Morgan. *Band*: The Admirals Band, directed by Bruce Healy.

Act 1: The basement under the stage of a small time vaudeville theatre in Los Angeles.

Act 2, Scene 1: The National Vaudeville Artists Club, New York City. One year later. *Scene 2*: Elsa's Apartment on Park Avenue. A half hour later.

Act 3, Scene 1: Eddie Kane's Dressing Room in the Palace Theatre, New York. *Scene 2*: The Stage of the Palace Theatre. A few minutes later. *Scene 3*: Eddie Kane's Dressing Room in the Palace Theatre. A few minutes later.

ACT 1

  "For Old Times' Sake"
    M. Downey
    (*Music by* Ray Henderson. *Lyrics by* Lew Brown and Buddy G. DeSylva.)

---

[71]A complete list of musical numbers was not provided in the program; above list includes "outstanding" melodies, in the words of the show's management.

ACT 2

  Gene Buck Song
    M. Downey

ACT 3

  Jimmy Dunn and the Ford Sisters: "Those Two Girls and That Boy"
    Eddie Kane: Sensational Juggler and Rope Walker

1927.67   SHOWBOAT

An American Musical Play in Two Acts, 17 Scenes. Book and lyrics by Oscar Hammerstein II. Based on the novel of the same name by Edna Ferber. Music by Jerome Kern. Staged by Zeke Colvan, (Oscar Hammerstein II). Choreography by Sammy Lee. Settings by Joseph Urban. Costumes by John Harkrider. Musical director, Victor Baravalle. Orchestrations by Robert Russell Bennett. Choral director, William Vodery. Produced by Florenz Ziegfeld. Opened 27 December 1927 at the Ziegfeld Theatre and closed 4 May 1929 after 572 performances.

CAST (in order of their appearance): *Windy (McClain)*: Allan Campbell. *Steve (Baker)*: Charles Ellis. *Pete (Gavin)*: Bert Chapman. *Queenie*: AUNT JEMIMA [Tess Gardella]. *Parthy Ann Hawkes*: EDNA MAY OLIVER. *Cap'n Andy (Hawkes)*: CHARLES WINNINGER. *Ellie (May Chipley)*: EVA PUCK. *Frank (Schultz)*: SAMMY WHITE. *Rubber Face*: Francis X. Mahoney. *Julie (Laverne)*: HELEN MORGAN. *Gaylord Ravenal*: HOWARD MARSH. *(Sheriff Ike) Vallon*: Thomas Gunn. *Magnolia (Hawks Ravenal)*: NORMA TERRIS. *Joe*: JULES BLEDSOE. *Faro Dealer*: Jack Wynn. *Gambler*: Phil Sheridan. *Backwoodsman*: Jack Daley. *Jeb*: Jack Wynn. *La Belle Fatima*: Dorothy Denese. *Old Sport*: Bert Chapman. *Landlady*: Annie Hart. *Ethel*: Estelle Floyd. *Sister*: Annette Harding. *Mother Superior*: Mildred Schwenke. *Kim (as a child)*: Eleanor Shaw. *Kim (as a young woman)*: NORMA TERRIS. *Jake*, a piano player: Robert Faricy. *Jim*: Ted Daniels. *Man With Guitar*: Ted Daniels. *Charlie*, Doorman at the Trocadero: J. Lewis Johnson. *Lottie*: Tana Kamp. *Dolly*: Dagmar Oakland. *Old Lady on Levee*: Laura Clairon. (*Specialty*: Sidell Sisters.)

Ladies of the Ensemble: Constance McKenzie, Mary Farrell, Sophie Howard, Nancy Kaye, Adrienne Armand, Lillian Clark, Betty Collette, Betty Junod, Una Val, Pansy Maness, Nellie Mayer, Essie Moore, Clementine Rigeau, Kathryn Ringquist, Rosalyn Smith, Eleanor Tierney, Frances Hope, Maurine Holmes, Dinorah Castillo, Peggy Green, Peggy Udell, Ethel Allen, Rose Gallagher, Hazel Jennings, Helen Chandler, Martha Marr, Tana Kemp, Ethel O'Dell, Annette Harding, Modette Hunt, Dorothy Foster, Mildred Schwenke. *Gentlemen of the Ensemble*: John Daly, Ted Daniels, William Ehlers, Dell Fradenburg, William Galpen, Ed Hale, Rees Jenkins, Ralph Knight, Ray Mace, Pat Mann, William Bailey, Joseph Minitello, Earl Sanborn, Phil Sheridan, Jack Wynn, William Lawless. *Jubilee Singers*: Blanche Thompson, Henrietta Lovelace, Estelle Floyd, Bertha Wright, Mamie Cartier, Josephine Gray, Lolo Waters, Maine Briggs, Gertrude Harris, Bertha Des Verney, Gladys Greenwood, R. Jamison, Maude Simmons, Angeline Lawson, Charlotte Junius, Julienne Barbour. George Nixon, James A. Lillard, J. Mardo Brown, Willis Bradley, John Warner, L. Pinard, William Waithe, J. Lewis Johnson, E. D. Killingsworth, George Myrick, Richard Cooper, J. W. Moberly, H. George Iuano, Edgar Hall, Llewellyn Ransom. *Dahomey Jubilee Dancers*: Elida Webb, Jessie Crawford, Alma Smith, Billie Caine, Ethel Sheppard, Rose Gillard, Theresa Jentry, Catherine Pearce, Dorothy Bellis, Betty Allison, Selma Myrick.

Act 1, Scene 1: The Levee at Natchez on the Mississippi, in the late 1880s. *Scene 2*: Kitchen Pantry of the "Cotton Blossom." A half hour later. *Scene 3*: Outside a Waterfront Saloon. Simultaneous with Scene 2. *Scene 4*: Auditorium and Stage of the "Cotton Blossom." One hour later. *Scene 5*: Box Office on the Foredeck. Three weeks later. *Scene 6*: Auditorium and Stage of the "Cotton Blossom" during Third Act of "The Parson's Bride." That evening. *Scene 7*: Upper Deck of the "Cottton Blossom." Later that night. *Scene 8*: The Levee. Next morning.

Act 2, Scene 1: The Midway Plaisance at the Chicago World's Fair, 1893. *Scene 2*: A Room in Onatrio Street in Chicago, 1904. *Scene 3*: Rehearsal Room of the Trocadero Music Hall. About 5 P.M. *Scene 4*: St. Agatha's Convent. Meanwhile. *Scene 5*: Corner of the Lobby of the Sherman Hotel, Chicago. 8 P.M., New Year's Eve. *Scene 6*: Trocadero Music Hall, New Year's Eve. 11:30, 1904. *Scene 7*: In front of the Office of the "Natchez Evening Democrat," 1927. *Scene 8*: Top Deck of the New "Cotton Blossom." 1927. *Scene 9*: The Levee at Natchez. The next night.

ACT 1

Scene 1

  Opening:
  "Cotton Blossom"
    Stevedores, Townspeople
  Parade and Ballyhoo
    C. Winninger, Show Boat Troupe, Townspeople
  "Where's the Mate for Me?"
    H. Marsh
  "(Only) Make Believe"
    H. Marsh, N. Terris

"Ol' Man River"
J. Bledsoe, Jubilee Singers

Scene 2

"Can't Help Lovin' Dat Man"
H. Morgan, T. Gardella, N. Terris, J. Bledsoe, A. Campbell

Scene 3

"Life Upon the Wicked Stage"
E. Puck, Girls

"Till Good Luck Comes My Way"
H. Marsh, Men

Scene 4

"Misery" (theme)
Jubilee Singers

Scene 5

"I Might Fall Back on You"
E. Puck, S. White, Girls

"C'mon Folks" (Queenie's Ballyhoo)
T. Gardella, Jubilee Singers

Scene 7

"You Are Love"
H. Marsh, N. Terris

Scene 8

Finale
Ensemble

ACT 2

Scene 1

Opening:

"At the Fair"
Sightseers, Barkers, Dandies

Adagio dance
Sidell Sisters

"Dandies on Parade"
Sightseers, Barkers, Dandies

"Why Do I Love You?"
N. Terris, H. Marsh, C. Winninger, E. M. Oliver, Chorus

"In Dahomey"
Jubilee Singers, Dahomey Dancers

Scene 3

"Bill" H. Morgan
(*Lyrics by* P. G. Wodehouse and Oscar Hammerstein II.)

"Can't Help Lovin' Dat Man" (reprise)
N. Terris

Scene 4

Service and Scene Music

Scene 6

Apache Dance
Sidell Sisters

"Goodbye, My Lady Love"
S. White, E. Puck
(*Music and Lyrics by* Joseph E. Howard.)

(Magnolia's Debut at the Trocadero:)

After the Ball" (from A TRIP TO CHINATOWN)
N. Terris
(*Music and Lyrics by* Charles K. Harris.)

Scene 7

"Ol' Man River" (reprise)
J. Bledsoe

"Hey, Feller"
T. Gardella, Jubilee Singers

Scene 8

"You Are Love" (reprise)
H. Marsh

Scene 9

"Why Do I Love You?" (reprise)
N. Terris, Flappers

Eccentric Dance

Imitation of her mother and stars of the 1920s
N. Terris

Tap Dance
U. Val

Finale
Company

1927.68   # LOVELY LADY

A Musical Comedy in Two Acts, 3 Scenes. Book by Gladys Unger and Cyrus Wood, based on the French play 'Déjeuner de Soleil' by André Birabeau. Music by Dave Stamper and Harold Levey. Lyrics by Cyrus Wood. Production staged by J. C. Huffman. Dances by Dave Bennett. Chester Hale Girl Dances arranged by Chester Hale[72]. Settings by Watson Barratt. Orchestra under the direction of Harold Levey; Eddie Ward's Barbecue Band. Costumes designed by Charles LeMaire and Ernest R. Schrapps. Produced by the Messrs. Shubert. Opened 29 December 1927 at the Sam H. Harris Theatre and closed 19 May 1928 after 164 performances.

CAST (in order of appearance): Jacques, Manager of 'Royale Hotel': Adrian Rosley. François, Head Waiter: Jules Epailly. A Decoy: Franklin J. Dix. A Decoy: Maryan Lynn. Lord Islington: Frank Greene. Toe Dancer: Mary Dunckley. Paul deMorlaix: GUY ROBERTSON. Max: Wesley Pierce. Aline Beaumont: Doris Patston. Louis Farrell: Jack Sheehan. Monsieur Watteau: William Holden. Folly Watteau: EDNA LEEDOM. Parthenia: Eloise Bennett. Page: Mae Russell. Lisette: Hazel Harris. Yvonne: Dorothy Jarrett. Yvette: Margaret Liste. Claudette: Miriam Crosby. Desiree: Louise Barrett. Celeste: Ruth Gordon. Marcelle: Mary Dunckley. Gendarme: Anthony Sterling. Eddie Ward's Barbecue Band. At the Pianos: Eddie Ward, Gene LePique.

Chester Hale Girls: Erma Chase, Gertrude Westling, Irene Isham, Etta Moore, Clara Fay, Mary Hiscox, Pavla Pavlicek, Agnes Hall, Lenore Allen, Evelyn Schiela, Jeanne Kroll, Alice Lorraine. *Dave Bennett's Dancing Girls*: Pat Carroll, Helen Liste, Nadya Miller, Eve Lynne, Mildred Tolle, Louise Hunt, Alice Monroe, Catherine Ryder, Mary Elizabeth Ryder, Mae Russell, Mattie Kay, Margaret Bragaw, Ann Cluin, Grace Carroll, Peaches Tortoni, Evelyn French, Dottie Jolson, Greta Granda, Marian Phillips, Mildred Kelly, Peggy Driscoll, Grace Grey, Dorothy Keith, Cleo Brown. *Show Girls*: Maryan Lynn, Dorothy Maurice, Joanna Parker, Sydna Morgan, Elizabeth Darling, Billie Perry, Ann Gilbert, Regina Daw. *Boys*: Stewart Steppler, Hal Bird, Franklin J. Dix, Fred Reynolds, Dick Kennedy, Ralph Stark, Jack Coleman, John Wolf, Barton Smith, Ted Wrynn, Anthony Sterling.

Act 1: The Room Rendezvous of the 'Royale Hotel' on the Island of Caprice, off the Coast of France.

Act 2, Scene 1: Boudoir, Suite 210. *Scene 2*: The Screen Room of the 'Royale Hotel'.

ACT 1

Opening Chorus
M. Crosby, M. Dunckley, R. Goodwin, L. Barrett, H. Harris, W. Pierce

"Decoys"
F. Greene, J. Epailly, C. LaTorre, M. Dunckley, 8 Show Girls

"Bad Luck, I'll Laugh at You"[73]
G. Robertson, Chester Hale Dancers, Boys

"The Lost Step"
D. Patston, J. Sheehan, M. Crosby, L. Barrett, R. Goodwin, M. Dunckley, Dave Bennett's Dancers, Chester Hale Girls

"Make Believe You're Happy"
D. Jarrett, M. Liste, H. Harris, W. Pierce, M. Crosby, L. Barrett, R. Goodwin, M. Dunckley, Dave Bennett's Dancers, Chester Hale Girls

"Lovely Lady"
E. Leedom, G. Robertson
(*Lyrics by* Harry A. Steinberg, Eddie Ward.)

Waltz
H. Harris, W. Pierce

Finale
Entire Company

ACT 2

Scene 1

"Breakfast in Bed"
E. Leedom, G. Robertson

"Lingerie"
D. Jarrett, M. Liste, Dave Bennett's Dancing Girls, Chester Hale Girls

---

[72]For national tour, the Albertina Rasch Dancers replaced the Chester Hale Girls.

[73]Dropped for national tour.

"Lovely Lady" (reprise)
G. Robertson

Piano Specialty
E. Ward, G. LePique

Scene 2

Ballet
Chester Hale Girls, H. Harris, W. Pierce

"At the Barbecue"[74]
M. Elaine, M. Crosby, L. Barrett, R. Goodwin, M. Dunckley, Dave Bennett's Dancers
(*Lyrics by* Harry A. Steinberg, Eddie Ward.)

Finale
Entire Company

1928.01

OH, KAY!

A Return Engagement of the Musical Comedy in Two Acts, 5 Scenes[75]. Book by Guy Bolton and P. G. Wodehouse. Music by George Gershwin. Lyrics by Ira Gershwin. Book staged by Harry Howell. Dances created by Sammy Lee. Settings designed by John Wenger. Costumes designed by Brooks Costume Company. Orchestra under the direction of Earl Busby. Produced by Alex A. Aarons and Vinton Freedley in association with the Messrs. Shubert. Opened 2 January 1928 at the Century Theatre and closed 14 January 1928 after 16 performances.

CAST (in order of appearance): *Phyllis Ruxton*: Edith Cardell. *Dolly Ruxton*: Marion Cardell. *The Duke*: CHARLES BROWN. *Larry Potter*: FRED HARPER. *Tom Powers*: Allen McKenzie. *Shorty McGee*: JOHN E. YOUNG. *Constance Appleton*: Beatrice Swanson. *Jimmie Winter*: FRANK CRUMIT. *Kay*: JULIA SANDERSON. *Revenue Officer Jansen*: Shep Camp. *Molly Morse*: NORMA BRYNE. *Mae*: HELEN ARDEN. *Peggy*: May Wynn. *Judge Appleton*: Frank Gardiner.

Ladies of the Ensemble: Eva Ball, Marie O'Donnell, Bessie DeBraus, Rose Malvin, Marion Harvey, Beverly Miller, Dorothy Dow, Viola Clerans, Norma Byrne, Kathryne Frobosh, Rita Martin, Rita Rosso, Helen Bowers, Mary Valerin, Rose Miller, Dorothy Blaine, Flora Lee, Gloria Lee, Helen Mahoney, Wanda Joyce, Mary Lane, Lynn Black, Angela Cummings, Marjorie Ross, Deena Drew, Maggie Henely, Doris Coleman, Martha Wallace, Ann Wallace, Mickey Dugan, Hazel Wandova. *Gentlemen of the Ensemble*: Harry Quinn, Barton Myers, Lew Ritter, Wallace Furie, Charlie Phillips, Tommy Schmidt, Charles Thurman, Cullen Clewis, Eddie Murry, Eddie Pierce, Billy Burnett, Robert Silva.

1928.02

SHE'S MY BABY

A Musical Farce Comedy in Two Acts, 5 Scenes. Book by Guy Bolton, Bert Kalmar and Harry Ruby. Music by Richard Rodgers. Lyrics by Lorenz Hart. Staged by Edward Royce. John Tiller Dances staged by Mary Read. Settings by Raymond Sovey. Costumes by Raymond Sovey and Francillon, Inc. Orchestra under the direction of Gene Salzer. Produced by Charles Dillingham. Opened 3 January 1928 at the Globe Theatre and closed 3 March 1928 after 71 performances.

CAST (in order of appearance): *Pearl*: Pearl Eaton. *Phyllis*: Phyllis Rae. *The Dance Director*: NICK LONG, JR. *The Stage Manager*: William McCarthy. *Joan*: Joan Clement. *Meadows*: William Frawley. *The Nightingale Quartette*: Evelyn Sayers, Loretta Sayers, Jessie Payne, Doreen Glover. *Josie*: ULA SHARON. *Polly*: IRENE DUNNE. *Bob Martin*: JACK WHITING. *Tilly*: BEATRICE LILLIE. *Clyde Parker*: CLIFTON WEBB. *Mr. Hemingway*: FRANK DOANE.

John Tiller's Lillie Cocktails: Peggy Sowden, Lily Reilly, Grace Holt, Hilda Winstanley, Doris Waterworth, May Cornes, Iris Smith, Elsie Holt. *Ladies of the Ensemble*: Cleo Cullen, Peggy Cunningham, Evelyn Dehkers, Teddy Denton, Evelyn Ellsmore, Geraldine Fitzgerald, Violet Hansbury, Muriel Hayman, Catharine Navarro, Blanche O'Donahue, Charlotte Otis, Anna Riley, Georgia Sewell, Pearl Sodders, Florence Ware, Hazel Webb, Vivian Wilson, Dorothy Wyatt, Peti Reed, Topsy Humphries, Mary Louise.

Act 1, Scene 1: The Stage. *Scene 2*: Bob's Home in Greenwich.

---

[74]Replaced for national tour by:
"One Step to Heaven"
Janet Murdock, Dorothy Llewellyn, Mabel Harding, D. Harding, M. Russell, Dancers
(*Music by* Jesse Greer. *Lyrics by* Raymond Klages.)

[75]Originally produced in New York 8 November 1926 at the Imperial Theatre for 256 performances. Total for both engagements: 272 performances. For Synopsis of Scenes and Musical Numbers, see original 1926 production.

Act 2, Scene 1: Bob's Home in Greenwich. *Scene 2*: Alley adjoining Stage Door. *Scene 3*: Sutton Place.

ACT 1[76]

Scene 1

"This Goes Up"
N. Long, Jr., P. Eaton, P. Rae, Ensemble

"My Lucky Star"
(from ONE DAM THING AFTER ANOTHER, London)

Nightingale Quartette,
Ensemble

"You're What I Need"
I. Dunne, J. Whiting, Nightingale Quartette, Ensemble

"Here She Comes"
Ensemble

"The Swallows"
B. Lillie

"When I Go on the Stage"
B. Lillie, Ensemble

"Try Again Tomorrow"
C. Webb, U. Sharon

"You're What I Need" (reprise)
I. Dunne, J. Whiting

Scene 2

Dance
John Tiller's Lillie Cocktails

"You're What I Need" (reprise)
I. Dunne, J. Whiting

"Camera Shoot"
B. Lillie, C. Webb, J. Whiting

Finale ("When I Saw Him Last")(C. Webb, F. Doane),
Company

ACT 2

Scene 1

"Where Can the Baby Be?"
F. Doane, P. Eaton, J. Clement, P. Rae, Ensemble

"I Need Some Cooling Off"(from ONE DAM THING AFTER ANOTHER, London)
N. Long, Jr., P. Eaton, P. Rae, Ensemble

"A Little House in Soho"[77]
C. Webb, U. Sharon, Ensemble

"A Baby's Best Friend"
B. Lillie

"You're What I Need" (reprise)
I. Dunne, J. Whiting, P. Rae, Nightingale Quartette

"Whoopsie"[78]
B. Lillie, C. Webb, Ensemble

Scene 2

Dance
John Tiller's Lillie Cocktails

Scene 3

Trio
C. Webb, J. Whiting, N. Long, Jr.

Dance
John Tiller's Lillie Cocktails

---

[76]Added after opening:"If I Were You" (from BETSY)
I. Dunne, J. Whiting

Dance
P. Rae

"Smart People" (added before opening per Kimball?)
Ensemble

Dance
C. Webb, P. Rae

"March With Me"
B. Lillie
(*Music by* Ivor Novello. *Lyrics by* Douglas Furber.)

[77]Revised version of "A Little Flat in Soho Square" from LIDO LADY, London.

[78]Dropped after opening.

"Wasn't It Great?"[79]

    J. Whiting, N. Long, Jr., W. McCarthy, J. Clement, P. Eaton, P. Rae, Ensemble

Finale

    Company

1928.03 ROSALIE

A Musical Comedy in Two Acts, 11 Scenes. Book by William Anthony McGuire and Guy Bolton. Music by George Gershwin and Sigmund Romberg. Lyrics by P. G. Wodehouse and Ira Gershwin. Scenes (designed) by Joseph Urban. Costumes designed by John W. Harkrider. Dances by Seymour Felix. Dialogue staged by William Anthony McGuire. Orchestrations by Emil Gerstenberger, William Daly, Maurice DePackh, (Hans Spialek, Max Steiner, Hilding Anderson). Vocal arrangements by Arthur Johnston. Produced by Florenz Ziegfeld. Opened 10 January 1928 at the New Amsterdam Theatre and closed 27 October 1928 after 335 performances.

CAST (in order of appearance): *Captain Carl Rabisco*: Halford Young. *Michael O'Brien*: Clarence Oliver. *Mary O'Brien*: BOBBE ARNST. *Prince Rabisco*, Chancellor of Romanza: A P. KAYE. *His Royal Highness King Cyril*: FRANK MORGAN. *Her Royal Highness Queen*: MARGARET DALE. *Ladies in Waiting (5)*: *Rosita*: Claudia Dell. *Marcia*: Gladys Glad. *Alla*: Jeanne Audree. *Xenia*: Hazel Forbes. *Maritza*: Yvonne Grey. *Sister Angelica*: Katherine Burke. *Bill Delroy*, of the West Point Corps: JACK DONAHUE. *Lieutenant Richard Fay, U.S.A.*: OLIVER McLENNAN. *Princess Rosalie*: MARILYN MILLER. *Marinna*: Antonina Lalaew. *Steward*, on the S.S. *Isle de France*: CHARLES GOTTHOLD. *Corps Lieutenant*: Jack Bruns. *Superintendent of West Point*: Charles Gotthold. *Captain Banner*: CLAY CLEMENT. *The Ex-King of Portugal*: Charles Davis. *The Ex-King of Bulgaria*: Clarence De Silva. *The Ex-King of Prussia*: Henri Jackin. *The Ex-King of Greece*: Mark Shull. *The Ex-King of Bavaria*: Harry Donaghy. *The Ex-Sultan of Turkey*: Edgar Welch. *Eight Estelle Liebling Singers.*

    Lyric Quartette: Benn Carswell, Robert Duenweg, Cliff Whitcomb, Jack Bruns. *Ladies of the Ensemble*: Ethel Raye, Gladys Redmond, Addie Rolf, Rose Shaw, Beatrice Smith, Leslie Storey, Ruth Tara, Gladys Turner, Diana White, Paulette Winston, Mabel Baade, Star Woodman, Marion Young, Joan Adaire, Colette Ayers, Elsie Behrens, Joey Benton, Caryl Bergman, Marion Brinkley, Sydelle Bry, Dorothy Campbell, Jeanette Creagan, Anne Fallon, Mary Gassman, Dolores Grant, Sylvia Howard, Ethel Kriston, Phyllis Loft, Martha Mackay, Virginia Magee, Edith Martin, Doris Maye, Wilma Novak, Patsy O'Day, Lucille Osborne, Lillian Ostrom. *Gentlemen of the Ensemble*: Frank Atwell, Jack Bauer, Jack Blair, Berkman Bauer, Gordon Clark, Lewis Dower, George Elsing, Walter Fairmont, Carlos Gomez, Bernard Hazzert, James Howkins, David Labris, Preston Lewis, Leon Lashay, Fred May, Jack Mulder, Gene McVey, John McCahill, Howard Phillips, Fielden Reed, Mark Shull, Frank Subers, Romulo Santos, Charles Davis.

Act 1, Scene 1: The Palace Square, Romanza. *Scene 2*: Street in Romanza. *Scene 3*: On Board the S. S. Ile de France. *Scene 4*: Lovers Lane, West Point. *Scene 5*: The Terrace at West Point.

Act 2, Scene 1: The Ball Room at West Point. *Scene 2*: Inspiration Point. *Scene 3*: Bill Delroy's Quarters. *Scene 4*: Exterior Building, West Point. *Scene 5*: Foyer of Ex-Kings' Club. *Scene 6*: Ball Room of Ex-Kings' Club.

ACT 1

Scene 1

  "Here They Are"

    (Opening Chorus)Ensemble

    (*Music by* Sigmund Romberg. *Lyrics by* P. G. Wodehouse.)

  "Show Me the Town"

    B. Arnst, Ensemble

    (*Music by* George Gershwin. *Lyrics by* Ira Gershwin.)

  "Entrance of Hussars"

    Lyric Quartette, Hussars (Ensemble)

    (*Music by* Sigmund Romberg. *Lyrics by* P. G. Wodehouse.)

  "Hussar March"

    M. Miller, Hussars

    (*Music by* Sigmund Romberg. *Lyrics by* P. G. Wodehouse, Ira Gershwin.)

  "Say So!" (Duet)

    M. Miller, O. McLennan

    (*Music by* George Gershwin. *Lyrics by* Ira Gershwin, P. G. Wodehouse.)

  Finalette

    M. Miller, O. McLennan, Ensemble

Scene 3

  "Let Me Be a Friend to You"

    M. Miller, J. Donahue

    (*Music by* George Gershwin. *Lyrics by* Ira Gershwin.)

Scene 4

  "West Point Bugle"

    O. McLennan, Boys

    (*Music by* Sigmund Romberg. *Lyrics by* P. G. Wodehouse.)

Scene 5

  "West Point March"

    Ensemble

    (*Music by* Sigmund Romberg. *Lyrics by* P. G. Wodehouse.)

  "Oh Gee—Oh Joy" (Oh Gee! Oh Joy!)(Duet)

    M. Miller, O. McLennan

    (*Music by* George Gershwin. *Lyrics by* Ira Gershwin, P. G. Wodehouse.)

  "Say So" (reprise)

    J. Donahue

  "Kingdom of Dreams"M. Miller

    (*Music by* Sigmund Romberg. *Lyrics by* P. G. Wodehouse.)

  Finale (Act 1)

    Ensemble

ACT 2

Scene 1

  Opening Valse

    Ensemble

  "New York Serenade"

    B. Arnst, Ensemble

    (*Music by* George Gershwin. *Lyrics by* Ira Gershwin.)

    Dancers: M. Baade, J. Benton, C. Ayers, J. Adaire, G. Turner, P. O'Day, P. Loft, D. Grant, E. Behrens, C. Bergman, L. Ostrom, E. Martin, W. Novak, L. Osborne, E. Raye, S. Woodman.

  "The King Can Do No Wrong"[80]

    F. Morgan, Show Girls

    (*Music by* Sigmund Romberg. *Lyrics by* P. G. Wodehouse.)

  "Follow the Drums"

    M. Miller, Ensemble

    (*Music by* George Gershwin. *Lyrics by* Ira Gershwin.)

Scene 2

  "How Long Has This Been Going On"

    B. Arnst

    (*Music by* George Gershwin. *Lyrics by* Ira Gershwin.)

Scene 3

  "Setting-up Exercises"

    M. Miller, J. Donahue

    (*Music by* Sigmund Romberg. *Lyrics by* P. G. Wodehouse.)

Scene 4

  "Oh Gee—Oh Joy" (reprise)

    Lyric Quartette

  Dance

    J. Donahue

Scene 5

  "(At) The Ex-Kings' (Club)"

    A. P. Kaye, Flunkeys (Gentlemen of the Ensemble)

    (*Music by* George Gershwin. *Lyrics by* Ira Gershwin.)

Scene 6

  "The Goddesses of Crystal"

    The Goddess of Ancient Crystal: K. Burke. *The Goddess of Crystal Flowers*: C. Dell. *The Goddess of Crystal Jewels*: G. Glad. *The Goddess of Crystal Mirrors*: H. Forbes. *The Goddess of Crystal Braid*: P. Nally. *The Goddess of Crystal Stained Crystal*: Y. Grey. *The Goddess of Crystal Fringe*: J. Audree. *The Goddess of Crystal Wings*: F. Mierse. *The Goddess of Crystal Mosaics*: A. Landis.

  "The Ballet of the Flowers" (Arranged by Michel Fokine.)

    M. Miller, Ensemble

  Finale (Abdication)

---

[79]Dropped after opening.

---

[80]Added after opening, after "The King Can Do No Wrong:"

  "Everybody Knows (I Love Somebody)"

    B. Arnst, J. Donahue

    (*Music by* George Gershwin. *Lyrics by* Ira Gershwin.)

THE OPTIMISTS

1928.04

A Musical Novelty (Revue) in Two Acts, 25 Scenes[81]. Sketches and lyrics by Clifford Grey, Greatrex Newman and Austin Melford. Music by Melville Gideon. Staged by Melville Gideon. Dances and ensembles staged by Jack Haskell. Settings designed by Watson Barratt. Pierrot Costumes by Vanity Fair; Miss Gear's evening gown by Joseph. Orchestra conducted by Harold Stern. Produced by Melville Gideon. Opened 30 January 1928 at the Casino de Paris and closed 18 February 1928 after 24 performances.

CAST: MELVILLE GIDEON, LUELLA GEAR, GEORGE HASSELL, SALLY STARR, BOBBY WATSON, FLORA LeBRETON, FRED HILLEBRAND, EVELYN DE LA TOUR, RICHARD BOLD, ELEANOR POWELL.

ACT 1

Scene 1

"Bow-Wow" (The Opening)
(Entire Company)

In which the Optimists introduce themselves

Scene 2

George Hassell starts something

Scene 3

"Rolling Stone"
R. Bold

Scene 4

"I Made Them Step"
S. Starr
Assisted by the usual male chorus.

Scene 5

"Amapu"
M. Gideon
(*Lyrics by* Edward Knoblock.)
Note: This is a stupendous production number.

Scene 6

"Dreamy Days"
F. LeBreton

Scene 7

"(I Promise I'll Be) Practically True to You"
L. Gear, B. Watson
(*Lyrics by* Clifford Grey.)

Scene 8

(The Last Shot, or a Story of the Indian Mutiny)
L. Gear

Scene 9

Optimistic Golf ("Golfing Love")(song and sketch)
Male Members (of the cast)

Scene 10

Our Little Flat (A Domestic Drama by Installments)
S. Starr, F. Hillebrand

Scene 11

"Love's Agony" (A Rural Romance in Ruthless Rhythms)

Scene 12

Finale: "Russianata"

(Being Russian Realism and 'Slavish' Splendour in Three Furious Fragments)
a. "The Song of the (Very) Vulgar Boatmen"
b. The Swan (Ballet)(Olga Petrovitski)
(*The Swan* – at enormous expense: G. Hassell.
c. Ballet à la Russe (Tremendous-Spectacular-Corybantic)
In which will be seen the combined Artistes of Petrograd, Vienna and Paris, Texas.

ACT 2

Scene 1 .

"To the Races"
(Company)

The Optimists revert to Chorus days.

Scene 2

"Neuftette" "Three Little School-Girls"
Featuring School Girls, Eton Boys and London Policemen

Scene 3

"London Town"
R. Bold

"If I Gave You a Rose"
R. Bold
(*Music and Lyrics by* Granville English.)

Scene 4

The Marriage Go-Round (A Fistic Solution of the Eternal Problem)
Contestants: L. Gear vs. F. Hillebrand. *Seconds*: E. De Latour, S. Starr. *Referee*: G. Hassell.

Scene 5

"(Little) Lacquer Lady"
Imagined by M. Gideon
(*Lyrics by* Clifford Seyler.)
With aid from E. Powell, G. Hassell, R. Bold.

Scene 6

Fred Hillebrand (Tout Seul)

Scene 7

Eleanor Powell dances (A Chinese Fantasy)

Scene 7a

Bobby Watson as The Vamp.
Sex Appeal Plus. Interference by F. Hillebrand.

Scene 8

Luella Gear fails to Get Her Man: ("Isn't There a Man for Me?")

Scene 9

A Whitechapel Episode
Bill 'Awkins: G. Hassell. *Liz 'Awkins*: F. LeBreton. *Policeman*: R. Bold.

Scene 10

A Phantom Phantasy (sketch and dance)
B. Watson, F. Hillebrand

Scene 11

Melville Gideon on his own

Scene 12

"We All Play the Grand Piano"
L. Gear, Ensemble

SIR HARRY LAUDER

1928.05

A Vaudeville Entertainment in Two Acts. Orchestra under the direction of Charles Frank. Produced by William Morris. Opened 30 January 1928 at the Knickerbocker Theatre and closed 10 March 1928 after 55 performances.

CAST: SIR HARRY LAUDER, Novello Brothers, Kharum, Bert Darrell, Nellie and Sara Kouns, Sybil Sanderson Fagan.

ACT 1[82]

Novello Brothers (Musical Clowns)

Kharum (The Persian Pianist, the Sensation of London, Paris and Berlin)

Bert Darrell (Unusual Dancer)

Nellie and Sara Kouns (World-Renowned Vocalists)

ACT 2

Sybil Sanderson Fagan (America's Mocking Bird)

Sir Harry Lauder will sing selections from the following new and old songs in character:

"Tobermory"

"Just Off the Chain"

"Saftest o' th' Family"

"Roamin' in the Gloamin'"

"I Love a Lassie"

"Doughie the Baker"

---

[81]Based on THE CO-OPTIMISTS, entertainments from London; its contents were a composite of songs and sketches from various editions of THE CO-OPTIMISTS. Also included in performance: "Spare a Little Love."

[82]Advertised change of program every week for the opening acts; Kouns Sisters stayed for the first month.

"When I Was Twenty-One"

"There Is Somebody Waiting for Me"

"She's Ma Daisy"

"O'er th' Hills tae Ardentinny"

"When I Meet MacKaye"

"End of the Road"

"Susie McLean"

"It's Nice to Get Up in th' Morning"

"I Think I'll Get Wed in th' Summer"

"How I Weary"

"Th' Waggle o' th' Kilt"

"I Know a Lassie Out in O-H-I-O"

"Nanny"

"Wedding o' Sandy McNab"

"Wee Deoch-an-Doris"

"January O"

"Singing Is the Thing to Make Ye Cheery"

"I Love to Be a Sailor"

"Flower o' th' Heather"

"Queen Amang th' Heather"

"Parted on the Shore"

1928.06 THE MADCAP

A Comedy with Music in Three Acts. Book by Gertrude Purcell and Gladys Unger. Based on the French farce 'Chibi' by Regis Gignoux and Jacques Thery. Music by Maurice Rubens. Lyrics by Clifford Grey. Book staged by Duane Nelson. Dances staged by Harry Puck. Musical director, Bernard Smith. Produced by the Messrs. Shubert. Opened 31 January 1928 at the Royale Theatre, moved 20 February 1928 to the Casino Theatre, and closed 28 April 1928 after 103 performances[83].

CAST (in order of appearance): *Petunia*, Madame Valmont's maid: Marie Dayne. *Helene*, Claire's friend: Lillian Lane. *Claire Valmont*: ETHEL INTROPIDI. *Lord Clarence Steeple*: SYDNEY GREENSTREET. *Lady Mary Steeple*: ETHEL MORRISON. *Honorable Harry Steeple*, Lord Steeple's nephew: HARRY PUCK. *Chibi*: MITZI (HAJOS). *Emmeline Hawley*: MARCELLA SWANSON. *Cuthbert Custard*: CHARLEY SYLBER. *James*, Lord Steeple's butler: Pat Clayton. *Sir Bertram Hawley*: ARTHUR TREACHER. *Footman*: Clifford Smith.

Deauville Girls: Madeline Morley, Theresa Sadowska, Maria Paris, Sally Saunders, Peggy de la Plant, Virginia Sharon, Genevieve Brown, Eleanor DeViane, Edna Paris, Helen Newton, Olga Grannis, Bert Winnek, Madeline Parker, Betty Barclay, Constance Ford, Agnes Kiley, Marian Grozan, Gene McGee, Marie Price, Moravia. *Deauville Boys*: William Bartly, Thomas Graham, George Mason, Harry Phelps, D. Edwards, Clifford Smith.

Act 1: Claire Valmont's Villa on the Outskirts of Deauville.

Act 2: Lord Steeple's House in Deauville.

Act 3: Claire Valmont's Garden. Three hours later.

ACT 1

"Buy Your Way"
    S. Greenstreet, The Little Collectors

"Old Enough to Marry"
    S. Greenstreet, E. Morrison, H. Puck, Chorus

"I Want to Tell You a Story" (Duet)
    Mitzi, H. Puck

"What Has Made the Movies?"
    C. Williams

Finale
    Mitzi, E. Intrpodi, S. Greenstreet, E. Morrison, H. Puck, M., Swanson, M. Dayne, Chorus

ACT 2

"Honeymooning Blues"
    E. Intropidi, S. Greenstreet, H. Puck, M. Swanson, Chorus

"Stop-Go"
    Mitzi, A. Treacher, "Stop-Go" Prancers
    (*Music by* Maurice Rubens, J. Fred Coots.)

"Why Can't It Happen to Me?"
    M. Dayne, P. Clayton

"Odle De O Do 'I Do'" (Duet)
    Mitzi, H. Puck

"Me, the Moonlight and Me"
    M. Swanson, C. Sylber

"Birdies"
    Mitzi

"My Best Pal"
    H. Puck, Boys

ACT 3

"Step to Paris Blues"
    Mitzi, Chorus

Finale
    Entire Company

1928.07 SUNNY DAYS

A Musical Comedy in Three Acts. Book and lyrics by Clifford Grey and William Cary Duncan. Adapted from the French farce ('Le Monsieur de Cinq Heures' [A Kiss in a Taxi]) by (Maurice) Hennequin and (Pierre) Veber. Music by Jean Schwartz. Additional musical numbers by Helen Dunsmuir. Staged by Hassard Short. Dances staged by Ralph Reader. Settings designed by Watson Barratt. Orchestra under the direction of John L. McManus. Produced by Hassard Short. Opened 8 February 1928 at the Imperial Theatre and closed 5 May 1928 after 101 performances.

CAST (in order of appearance): *Victor Duval*, Owner of Duval's Florist Shop: Maurice Holland. *Nanine*: Marjorie Finley. *Babette*: Peggy Cornell. *Georgette*: Evangeline Raleigh. *Lulu*: Maxine Carson. *Robert*: Sid Hawkins. *Angele Larue*: ROSALIE CLAIRE. *Rudolph Max*, Head Cashier of Dorsay et Cie., Bankers: BILLY B. VAN. *Ginette Bertin*: JEANETTE MacDONALD. *Maurice Vane*: LYNNE OVERMAN. *Leon Dorsay*, President of Dorsay et Cie., Bankers: FRANK McINTYRE. *Paul Morel*: CARL RANDALL. *A Thief*: Harry Gordon. *Bergeot*, Police Inspector: Bob Lively. *Countess D'Exmore*: Claire Hooper. *Premier Dancer*: Charlotte Ayres. *Madame d'Orsay*: AUDREY MAPLE.

Flower Shop Girls: Aida Conkey, Doris deLanti, Lillian Dixon, Jacqueline Feeley, Sophia Grebow, Ruth Hartman, Irene Kelly, Esther Lloyd, Liane Memet, Vida Manuel, Isobel Mason, Virginia Otis, Jane Patrick, Alli Raddigan, Ada C. Winston, Virginia May. *Guests*: Claire Hooper, Verenetta Hoots, Charlotte Joyce, Fraun Koski, Trude Marr, Helen Rich, Edna Starck. *Customers*: George Clidd, Sidney Kane, Robert Lee, Reed McClelland, Fred Mayon, Leonard Reid, William Tasek.

Act 1: Shop of Victor Duval et Cie., Florist, Rue de la Paix, Paris.

Act 2: The Gardens of Leon Dorsay's Château, Fontainebleau. The same evening.

Act 3: Reception Room in Leon Dorsay's Château. One week later.

ACT 1

"A Belle, a Beau and a Boutonniere"
    M. Finley, P. Cornell, E. Raliegh, M. Carson, S. Hawkins, Ensemble

"One Sunny Day"
    R. Claire, M. Holland, M. Finley, P. Cornell, E. Raleigh, M. Carson, Ensemble

"Ginette"
    J. MacDonald, Boys

I'll Be Smiling"
    C. Randall, P. Cornell, Ensemble

"Really and Truly"
    J. MacDonald, L. Overman

Finale
    J. MacDonald, L. Overman, M. Holland, Ensemble

ACT 2

Waltz
    C. Ayres, C. Randall

"I've Got to Be Good"
    F. McIntyre, Guests

"Hang Your Hat on the Moon"
    R. Claire, B. B. Van, C. Randall, Ensemble

"So Do I"
    J. MacDonald, L. Overman

[83]Costumes, sets uncredited.

"Girls' Brigade"
 C. Randall, Ensemble
Finale
 Entire Company

ACT 3

"Orange Blossoms"
 M. Holland, Ensemble
"Trample Your Troubles"
 J. MacDonald, C. Randall, Ensemble
Finale
 Entire Company

1928.08   RAIN OR SHINE

A Musical Play in Two Acts, 12 Scenes. Book by James Gleason and Maurice Marks. Music by Milton Ager and Owen Murphy. Lyrics by Jack Yellen. Staged by Alexander Leftwich. Dances directed by Russell E. Markert and Tom Nip. Dance ensembles by Russell E. Markert. Art director (scenic design), Clark Robinson. Costumes designed by Charles LeMaire. Orchestra under the direction of Don Voorhees. Orchestrations by William (Grant) Still and Arthur Schutt. Produced by A. L. Jones and Morris Green. Opened 9 February 1928 at the George M. Cohan Theatre and closed 15 December 1928 after 356 performances.

CAST [in order of appearance]: *Amos K. Shrewsberry*: TOM HOWARD. *Katie*: ETHEL NORRIS. *Harry*: EDGAR GARDNER. *Frankie Schultz*, The Princess de Chimay: HELEN LYND. *Zelda*, Oriental Dancer: Rita Garcia. *Jesse Dalton*: JOE LYONS. *Mary Wheeler*: NANCY WELFORD. *Jack Wayne*: WARREN HULL. *Rosie*: ROSIE MORAN. *"Smiley" Johnson*: JOE COOK. *The Policeman*: Walter Pharr. *The Mother*: Dimples Riede. *The Child*: Marian Herson. *The Ticket Seller*: James Gregory. *Smiley's Protegé*: Dave Chasen. *Grocko, the Clown*: Vernon Jacobson. *The Head Waiter*: DAVE CHASEN. *The Barker*: Joe Lyons. *Folte, the Lion Tamer*: William V. Powers. *The Acrobat*: Paul Brack. *Mrs. Patricia Conway*: JANET VELIE. *Grace Forsythe*: Devah Worrell. *Lord Gwinnie Llandridrodd Wells, R.A.F.*: Ernest Lambert. *The New Yorkers*: Vance Elliott, Ben Cutler, Alex McKee, Walter Bremer. DON VOORHEES and His 'Rain or Shine' Band. *Siamese Twins, Bearded Lady, Three-Legged Girl, the Tattooed Lady, Midgets, Acrobats, Trapeze Walkers, Bareback Riders, Roustabouts, etc.*

Members of the Junior League: Maxine Wells, Dimples Reide, Dolla Harkins, Olga Brounoff, Kae Carroll, Helen Wilson, Helen Fowbie, Georgia English. *Young Ladies from Higginstown, Rhode Island*: Daphne Windsor, Rita Stone, Nina Sorel, Beth Milton, May Page, Rita Garcia, Frances de Foe, Mary Phillips. *School Girls of Higginstown, Rhode Island*: Claire Stone, Amy Weber, Peggy Sickle, Marion Herson, Virginia Ray, Eleanor Martin, Ruth Marcus, Doris Baker, Sarah Newton, Marion Lane, Gladys Englander, Dorothy Brown, Alice Dera, Lilian Field, Marie Hensley, Nettie Pollinger. *The Boys of Higginstown, Rhode Island*: Sam Wiser, Steve LaMarr, Jack Lomas, Joseph Cowan, William Moyer, Richard Girens, Dan Harrington, Fred Nay, Jules Schwartz, Paul Santo, Lou Atlas, Bob Easton, William Hale, Bill Benton, Frank Sherlock. *Russell E. Markert's Sixteen American Rockets*: Misses Alyse, Maxine, Kathleen, Marion, Mildred, Pearl, Virginia, Audrey, Estelle, Rosalie, Irene, Dorothy, Irma, Anna, Irene, Virginia, Amy Frank (Captain).

Act 1, Scene 1: The Public Square in Higginstown, Rhode Island. *Scene 2*: Outside the Circus Grounds. *Scene 3*: The Freak Tent. *Scene 4*: Main Entrance to the Big Show. *Scene 5*: The Pad Room, just off the Big Top. *Scene 6*: Near the Entrance. *Scene 7*: The Big Top.

Act 2, Scene 1: On the Terrace of a Fashionable Hotel, near Higginstown. *Scene 2*: Near the show cars. *Scene 3*: The Elephants. *Scene 4*: The Clown Dolls. *Scene 5*: On the Lot.

ACT 1

"Circus Days" (Opening)
 Members of the Junior League, Young Ladies, School Girls, Boys, The American Rockets
"Glad Tidings"[84]
 N. Welford, W. Hull, Bachelor Quartette, the New Yorkers, Ensemble
The Parade
 The John T. Wheeler Show
"Circus Days" (reprise)
 Girls, Boys
"So Would I"
 J. Cook, Village Kids

"Add a Little Wiggle"
 H. Lynd
Dances
 Nip Dancers, The American Rockets
"Rain or Shine"
 N. Welford, W. Hull, Bachelor Quartette, the New Yorkers, Ensemble
"Laugh, Clown, Laugh"[85]
 V. Jacobson
 (*Music by* Ted FioRito. *Lyrics by* Sam M. Lewis, Joe Young.)
Recitation[86]
 W. Hull
 Ballet: *The Pierrots*: Nip Dancers. *The Pierrettes*: The Rockets. *The Clown*: R. Moran.
"Oh, Baby"
 E. Norris, E. Gardner, Ensemble
 (*Music and Lyrics by* Owen Murphy.)
"Roustabout Song" (We Follow the Trail)
 W. Hull, the New Yorkers, Men's Ensemble
"Hey Rube"
 V. Jacobson, Company

ACT 2

"Falling Star" (Opening)
 J. Velie, the New Yorkers, Ensemble
"Feelin' Good"
 H. Lynd, Ensemble
 (*Music by* Owen Murphy.)
"Forever and Ever"
 W. Hull, F. Shelley, the New Yorkers, Ensemble
"Who's Gonna Get You?"
 N. Welford, Boys
Acrobatic Dance
 Nip Girls
Stair Dance[87]
 R. Moran, Boys
Dance
 E. Norris, Bachelor Quartette
Hand Drill
 The American Rockets
Elephant Trainers
 The American Rockets
The Clown Dance
 The Nip Girls
Finale
 Entire Company

1928.09   PARISIANA

A Continental Cocktail (Musical Revue) in Two Acts, 41 Scenes. Sketches, music and lyrics by Vincent Valentini. Staged by Vincent Valentini. Dances and ensembles by Jack Heisler. Costumes by Marguerite and Strauss, Esmonde Costume Studios, Brooks Costume Company. Settings designed by Charles Teichner Studios. Orchestra under the direction of Paul Specht. Orchestrations by Lorenzo Calduel and Billy Baker. Produced by the Associated Artists, Inc. by arrangement with Valentini. Opened 9 February 1928 at the Edythe Totten Theatre and closed 3 March 1928 after 28 performances.

CAST: NEIL FLETCHER, OLIVE MAY, MELVIN STOKES, KATHLEEN TERRY, BILLY BANN, MILDRED SKINNER, HORACE KOLA, PEGGY HEAVENS, GEORGE LAIRD, BETH MILLER, CAROL LYNNE, MARIA RAYCELLE, ILYA RAYCELLE, THE THOMAS SISTERS.
Parisiana Steppers: Dorothy Morrison, Carol Lynne, Nellie Brenner, Ethel Douglas, Joan Morgan, Billie Coretz, Urilda Ulivera, Mae Burke, Marjory T. Thomas, Alice Hutchinson, Madelain Main, Violet Grey.

---

[84]For subsequent tour, replaced by:
 "I Must Be in Love"
 Nell Roy (Mary), W. Hull, E. Norris, James Howkins (Harry), Ensemble

[85]Two months into the run, replaced by:
 "Pierrot and Pierrette"
 Frances Shelley (Mary), the New Yorkers
[86]Dropped during the run.
[87]Dropped during the run.

ACT 1

Scene 1

Opening

The Man in the Moon: N. Fletcher. *Venus*: O. May.

Scene 2

A Producer's Dilemma

The Producer: M. Stokes. *First Lady Friend*: K. Terry. *Second Lady Friend*: M. Skinner. *The Seminary Girls*: Ensemble, and who ask to "Help the Girlies Along."

Scene 3

What Made Lohen Grin

The Preacher: B. Bann. *The Bride*: K. Terry. *The Groom*: N. Fletcher.

Scene 4

"Keep On Dancing"

P. Heavens, Parisiana Steppers

Scene 5

The Radio Phone

First Business Man: B. Bann. *Second Business Man*: M. Stokes. *The Sweetheart*: P. Heavens. *The Wife*: M. Skinner. *The Sister*: K. Terry.

Scene 6

"Maybe"

O. May, N. Fletcher
One of the Steppers: M. Burke.

Scene 7

The Seer

First Girl: K. Terry. *Second Girl*: P. Heavens. *The Seer*: B. Bann.

Scene 8

"When You Say No to Love"

O. May, M. Stokes
Atmosphere: H. Kola, I. Raycelle. *At the Piano*: M. Raycelle.

Scene 9

Piano Solo

M. Raycelle
The Living Skeletons: Parisiana Steppers.

Scene 10

"Levee Lou"

The Thomas Sisters

Scene 11

The Great American Home

The Wife: B. Miller. *First Daughter*: K. Terry. *Second Daughter*: M. Skinner. *The Husband*: M. Stokes. *The Son*: D. Morrison.

Scene 12

"Keep It Under Your Hat"

D. Morrison, G. Laird, Parisiana Steppers
Solo Dance
H. Kola

Scene 13

"Who Wouldn't"

K. Terry, P. Heavens

Scene 14

The Vulgar Boatmen

Scene 15

The Waif of the Street

Scene 16

"Since Nora Brought Her Angora Around"

Parisiana Steppers

Scene 17

"Parisiana Roses" (Song and sketch)

The Girl: C. Lynne. *The Man*: M. Stokes.

First Episode

Marie Antoinette: M. Skinner. *Court Ladies*: Thomas Sisters. *The Jester*: B. Bann. *Court Dancers*: H. Kola, I. Raycelle.

Second Episode

Joan of Arc: K. Terry. *Halberdier*: G. Laird.

Third Episode

The Poilu: N. Fletcher. *The Nurse*: B. Miller.

Fourth Episode

The Martyr: P. Heavens. And Grand Ensemble.

Scene 18

Solo Dance

C. Lynne

Scene 19

The Trial of Mary Looney

Chief Inspector: B. Bann. *Lieutenant*: N. Fletcher. *The Woman*: M. Skinner. *The Husband*: M. Stokes.

Scene 20

"What's Become of the Bowery?"

Newsboy: O. May. *Atmosphere*: Thomas Sisters, Entire Company.

Scene 21

Her First Affair

M. Stokes, B. Bann

Scene 22

"The Ghost of Old Black Joe"

Mammy: B. Miller. *The Pickanninies*: Parisiana Steppers. *Old Black Joe*: M. Stokes.
Grand Reprise—Finale
Entire Company

ACT 2

Scene 1

"Paris Green"

The Two Americans: N. Fletcher, G. Laird. *The Drunken Waiter*: B. Bann. *Two Midinettes*: K. Terry, P. Heavens. And the Parisiana Steppers.

Scene 2

Solo Dance

A. Hutchinson

Scene 3

Hell on Earth

The Angel: B. Miller. *The Victim*: B. Bann. *The Beauty*: P. Heavens.

Scene 4

"In a Gondola With You"

O. May

Scene 5

So This Is Venice

First Fisherman: B. Bann. *Second Fisherman*: G. Laird. *The Warden*: M. Stokes. *The Loved One*: M. Skinner. *The Girl*: B. Miller.

Scene 6

"Golliwog"

Thomas Sisters, Parisiana Steppers
Solo
G. Laird

Scene 7

In the Wild and Wooly West

Wild Nell: B. Miller. *The Gambler*: N. Fletcher. *The Cowboys*: G. Laird, H. Kola. *The Bad Man*: B. Bann.

Scene 8

"Silk"

The Slave Girl: O. May. *Mandarin*: M. Stokes. *The Soothsayer*: N. Fletcher. *The Joss Girls*: Thomas Sisters. *The Cocoons*: Parisiana Steppers.
Slave Dance
H. Kola, I. Raycelle

Scene 9

The Suicide Club

B. Bann, M. Stokes, N. Fletcher, G. Laird, H. Kola, V. Gray, M. Main

Scene 10

"What's It Coming To?"

B. Bann, M. Stokes, N. Fletcher, G. Laird, H. Kola

Scene 11

Chicago After Dark

Scene 12

"Unfortunate Rosie"

G. Laird, N. Fletcher, P. Heavens, Parisiana Steppers

Scene 13

The Thomas Sisters

Scene 14

Biskhra

The Soldier: M. Stokes. *The Nautch Girl*: P. Heavens.

Scene 15

"They're Hot Now Up in Iceland"
B. Miller, Parisiana Steppers

Scene 16

"Peepin' Tommy"
Thomas Sisters

Scene 17

Beth Miller

Scene 18

Gettin' Gertie's Gumdrop
M. Stokes, B. Bann

Scene 19

"Paree Has the Fever Now" (Grand Finale)
Entire Company

1928.10 KEEP SHUFFLIN'

A Musical Comedy in Two Acts, 8 Scenes[88]. Book by Flournoy Miller and Aubrey Lyles. Music by James P. Johnson, [Thomas] Fats Waller, Clarence Todd. Lyrics by Henry Creamer and Andy Razaf. Staged by Con Conrad. Dances and ensembles staged by Clarence Robinson. Costumes by H. Mahieu Costumes Inc. Settings designed by Karl O. Amend. Music director, James P. Johnson. Orchestrations by Will Vodery. Produced by Con Conrad, Inc. Opened 27 February 1928 at Daly's Theatre, moved 23 April 1928 to the Eltinge Theatre and closed 26 May 1928 after 104 performances.

CAST (in order of appearance): *Boss*: Jerry Mills. *Henry*: George Batttles. *Brother Jones*: John Gregg. *Mose*: JOHN VIGAL. *Walter*: CLARENCE ROBINSON. *Scrappy*: BYRON JONES. *Evelyn*: EVELYN KEYES. *Honey*: Honey Brown. *Alice*: JEAN STARR. *Mrs. Jenkins*: Margaret Lee. *Steve Jenkins*: FLOURNOY MILLER. *Sam Peck*: AUBREY LYLES. *Ruth*: JOSEPHINE HALL. *Maude*: MAUDE RUSSELL. *Yarbo*: Billie Yarbough. *Hazel*: Hazel Sheppard. *Grit*: Gretta Anderson. *Marie*: Marie Dove. *Bill*: Gilbert Holland. *Joseph*: Herbert Listerino.

Orchestra: On the White Keys: FATS WALLER. On the Black Keys: JIMMY JOHNSON. Behind the Bugle: JABBO SMITH.

Ladies of the Ensemble: Gussie Williams, Hazel Sheppard, Ethel Moses, Marie Buschell, Marion L. Tyler, Vivienne G. Brooks, Lila Brogdan, Evelyn Irving, Gladyce Bronson, Hazel Coles, Gertrude Gaines, Violet Speedy, Marie Dove, Mineola Phillips, Shirley Abbey, Jean Kane, Edna Ellington, Peggy Burnett, Pauline MacDowell, Billie Rickmon, Marion Ford, Madeline Odlum, Olive Harrison, Byrdie Wallace, Clarice Egbert, Ruth Cherry, Ruth Lambert. *Jubilee Singers and Dancers*: Charles Lawrence, Herman Listerino, Lloyd Mitchell, Howard Browne, George Battles, Joseph A. Willis, Burkie Jackson, Chris Gordon, Edwin Alexander, Sandy Brown, Kenneth Harris.

Act 1, Scene 1: Exterior of Industrial School, Jimtown. *Scene 2*: Street in Jimtown. *Scene 3*: Front yard of Steve Jenkins' home.

Act 2, Scene 1: Town Hall. *Scene 2*: Main Street, Jimtown. *Scene 3*: Interior of Steve Jenkins' home. *Scene 4*: Outskirts of Jimtown. *Scene 5*: Back in the Front Yard of Steve Jenkins' home.

ACT 1[89]

Opening Chorus
Ensemble
(*Music by* Will Vodery. *Lyrics by* Henry Creamer.)

---

[88]A sequel by the same librettists to SHUFFLE ALONG which opened 23 May 1921 at the 63rd Street Theatre for 484 performances.
[89]Added after opening:
"Buck Up to Me" (Act 1, after Opening Chorus)
J. Vigal, G. Anderson, Company
This was subsequently replaced by:
"Teasing Mama"
J. Vigal, G. Anderson, Company
(*Music by* James P. Johnson. *Lyrics by* Henry Creamer.)
For subsequent tour, character names were changed, song order revised, and the following songs added (authorship uncredited):
"Teasin' Baby" (revised version of "Teasin' Mama")
G. Anderson, Compton White
"Brothers"
Male Octette
"Where Jazz Was Born" (revised version of "How Jazz Was Born")
Joyce Robinson, Rookie Davis
"Don't Wake 'Em Up"
Hilda Perlino, Chorus

"Cho'late Bar"
E. Keyes, B. Jones
(*Music by* Fats Waller. *Lyrics by* Andy Razaf.)

"Labor Day Parade"
C. Robinson, Company
(*Music by* Clarence Todd. *Lyrics by* Andy Razaf.)

"Give Me the Sunshine"
J. Starr, J. Vigal, C. Robinson
(*Music by* James P. Johnson, Con Conrad. *Lyrics by* Henry Creamer.)

"Pining"[90]
J. Hall, C. Robinson
(*Music by* Clarence Todd. *Lyrics by* Henry Creamer.)

"Leg It"
M. Russell, Company
(*Music by* Clarence Todd, Con Conrad. *Lyrics by* Henry Creamer.)
"Washboard Ballet"[91] (*Music by* Fats Waller.)
H. Brown

"Exhortation"[92]
G. Battles, Jubilee Glee Club
(*Music by* Con Conrad. *Lyrics by* Henry Creamer.)

"'Sippi"
M. Russell
(*Music by* James P. Johnson, Con Conrad. *Lyrics by* Henry Creamer.)

"How Jazz Was Born"
J. Starr, Company
(*Music by* Fats Waller. *Lyrics by* Andy Razaf.)

Finale
Entire Company

ACT 2

"Keep Shufflin'"
J. Vigal, Company
(*Music by* Fats Waller. *Lyrics by* Andy Razaf.)

"Everybody's Happy in Jimtown"
Male Octette
(*Music by* Fats Waller. *Lyrics by* Andy Razaf.)

"Give Me the Sunshine" (reprise)
F. Miller, A. Lyles

"Dusky Love"
J. Hall, C. Robinson, Company
(*Music by* Will Vodery. *Lyrics by* Henry Creamer.)

"Charlie, My Back Door Man"
J. Starr, Strut Men
(*Music by* Clarence Todd. *Lyrics by* Henry Creamer.)

"On the Levee"
M. Russell, Girls
(*Music by* James P. Johnson. *Lyrics by* Henry Creamer.)

"Harlem Rose"[93]
M. Russell
(*Music by* Con Conrad. *Lyrics by* Gladys Rogers.)

"Whoopem Up"
J. Robinson, Chorus

"Bugle Blues"
R. Davis

"Deep Blue Sea"
Arthur Porter

"My Old Banjo"
A. Porter

"Pretty Soft, Pretty Sweet"
J. Robinson

"Let's Go to Town"
E. Keyes, H. Perlino, Byron Jones, Louis Keen

"You May Be a Whale in Georgia"
J. Robinson, R. Davis

[90]Dropped after opening.
[91]Dropped after opening.
[92]Dropped during the run and replaced by:
""Exhortation Theme from Yamekraw Negro Rhapsody"
J. Vigal, Jubilee Glee Club
(*Music by* James P. Johnson. *Lyrics by* Henry Creamer.)
[93]Dropped after opening.

Finale[94]
Entire Company

1928.11

YOURS TRULY

A Return Engagement of the Musical Play in Two Acts, 6 Scenes[95]. Book by Clyde North. Music by Raymond Hubbell. Lyrics by Anne Caldwell. Book staged by Paul Dickey. Dances arranged by Ralph Reader. The John Tiller Girls' Dances arranged by Mary Read. Scenery by Joseph Urban. Costumes designed by Mabel E. Johnston. Men's costumes by Eaves Costume Company. Orchestra under the direction of Paul Yartin. Entire production under the personal supervision of Gene Buck. Produced by Gene Buck. Opened 12 March 1928 at the Century Theatre and closed 31 March 1928 after 24 performances.

CAST (in order of appearance): *Shuffling Bill*: IRVING FISHER. *Joey Ling*, Chang's body servant: Jack Stanley. *Mac*, one of the "Finest": John Kearney. *Phil*, the Guide: Jean Kirkland. *Diana*: ELIZABETH DURAY. *J. P. Stillwell*, a Wall Street financier: THEODORE BABCOCK. *Truly*, from nowhere in particular: LEON ERROL. *Bonzolino*, transplanted from Sunny Italy: VIC CASMORE. *Ruth*, from uptown: Lotta Fanning. *Scats*, from downtown: VERA MYERS. *Mary Stillwell*: EVELYN HOEY. *Bandit*, "stick-up" man: Jean Kirkland. *Dinty Moore*, of the "Bowery": TOM WATERS. *Chang*, proprietor of the "Open Door Night Club": FORREST YARNALL. *A Bowery Rose*: Eunice Hall. *Tillie Dupont*, a shop girl: Valerie Raemere. *Minnie Fletcher*, a shop girl: Eve Johnston. *Cynthia Jones*, a country girl: Inez Van Horn. *Abe Levy*, a peddler: Earl Van Horn. *Pacquita*, an Italian girl: Marguerite Marano. *Jimmie*, a newsboy: JIMMIE McCALLION. *Chinese Girls*: Peggy Frawley, Dolly Pross. *Flower Girl*: Gladys Lake. *Victor*, head waiter at Chang's "Open Door Night Club": Jean Kirkland.

Miss Longstreet: Diane Du Verne. *Miss Newbury*: Eunice Hall. *Miss Stuyvesant*: Edith Babson. *Miss Hemingway*: Virginia Hawkins. *Miss Glendening*: Gladys Lake. *Miss Butterfield*: Eve Johnston. *Miss Buckminster*: Queenie French. *Miss Fairweather*: Valerie Raemere. *Miss Northcliffe*: Betty MacDonald. *Miss Matteson*: Lucille Rich. *Miss Tillinghast*: Lotta Fanning. *Miss Southworth*: Olive Manlet. *The John Tiller Girls*: Gladys Holt, Cora Neary, Babs Aitken, Marie Webster, Edna McCallum, Louis Gillette, Olive Hollingshead, Winnie Hollingshead, Frances Lunn, Marjorie Griffiths, Edith Bennett, Connie Clements, Bella Pilling, Sybil Chester, Sadie Hudson, Hilda Simmonette. *Dancing Girls*: Jeanette Spaulding, Janice Glenn, Dolly Pross, Marguerite Marano, Petra Oleson, Rosalie McCallion, Florence Madison, Rose Knight, Nina Wolffe, Thelma Kay, Anna Brickman, Evelyn Bligh, Pauline Abbott. *Gentlemen*: Jack Rogers, Irving Jackson, Bob Rachford, Dale Grisby, Louis Sears, Louis Brown, Lenord Mooney, Frank Callahan, Charles Perry, Kenneth Smith. .

1928.12

THE THREE MUSKETEERS

A Musical Play in Two Acts, 12 Scenes. Book by William Anthony McGuire. Based on the novel of the same name ("Les Trois Mousquetaires") by Alexandre Dumas. Music by Rudolf Friml. Lyrics by P. G. Wodehouse and Clifford Grey. Book staged by William Anthony McGuire. Ballets and dances staged by Albertina Rasch. Ensembles staged by Richard Boleshavsky. Scenes (settings designed) by Joseph Urban. Costumes designed by John Harkrider. Duels arranged by Louis Hector. Musical director, Gus Salzer. Produced by Florenz Ziegfeld. Opened 13 March 1928 at the Lyric Theatre and closed 15 December 1928 after 318 performances.

CAST (in order of appearance): *Sergeant Jussac*: Robert D. Burns. *Comte de la Rochefort*: LOUIS HECTOR. *Innkeeper*: HARRISON BROCKBANK. *Zoe*: Naomi Johnson. *Lady deWinter*: VIVIENNE OSBORNE. *Porthos*: DETMAR POPPEN. *Athos*: DOUGLASS R. DUMBRILLE. *Aramis*: JOSEPH MACAULAY. *Constance Bonacieux*: VIVIENNE SEGAL. *Planchet*: LESTER ALLEN. *D'Artagnan*: DENNIS KING. *The Duke of Buckingham*: JOHN CLARKE. *Anne, Queen of France*: YVONNE D'ARLE. *M. de Treville*: John Kline. *Cardinal Richelieu*: REGINALD OWEN. *Louis XIII*: CLARENCE DERWENT. *Brother Joseph*: William Kershaw. *Premiere Danseuse of the Court*: HARRIET HOCTOR. *Aubergiste*: Catherine Hayes. *The Bo'sun*: Richard Thornton. *Patrick*, Valet to Buckingham: Raymond O'Brien. *Cardinal's Guards*: Andy Jochim, Randolph Leyman. *Ladies in Waiting*: Evelyn Groves, Lee Russell, Gertrude Williams, Mary McDonald, Pirkko Ahlquist, Marion Dodge, Edna Bunte. *King's Attendant*: Gerald Moore.

---

[94]During the run, the finale was rebilled as follows:
Finale—"Skiddle de Scow" (from MESSIN' AROUND)
(Music by James P. Johnson. Lyrics by Perry Bradford.)
[95]Originally produced in New York 25 January 1927 at the Sam S. Shubert Theatre for 129 performances. Total for both engagements: 153 performances. For Synopsis of Scenes and Musical Numbers, see original 1927 production. In addition to those songs cut during the run of the original production ("The Gunman," Dance-Hilda Ferguson, "Four Aristocrats"-Specialty), "High Yaller" was also omitted for this return engagement.

Albertina Rasch Dancers: Virginia Beardsley, Dona Desne Curry, Rose Gale, Eva Hellesnes, Marguerite Eisele, Nora Puntin, Louise Raymond, Yvonne Beaupre, Regina Tushinsky, Nona Otero, Lydia Krushinsky, Lucille O'Connor, Wilma Kaye, Helen Derby, Jeanette Bradley, Mildred Turner. *Ladies of the Ensemble*: Nancy Corrigan, Lillian White, Pauline Hall, Vida Hanna, Eleanor Buffington, Marie Merrifield, Julia Lane, Esther Peters, Sylvia Derby, Margaret Clarke, Byrdetta Evans, Eleanor Little, Emily Hadley, Libby Hanley, Ivy Palmer, Marye Bern, Frances Kelley, Lotta Marcy, Ann Moss, Helen Withers, Elaine Lank, Katherine Cavelli, Audrey Davis, Sally Hadley, Ellen Moray, Joan Marren, Hilda Steiner, Elsie Reign, Dorothy Greenley, Miriam Stockton, Dorothy Sutton, Margaret Valient. *Gentlemen of the Ensemble*: Martin Sheppard, A. Muzzi, Glen McCauley, John Zak, Ernest Ehler, Harry James, William Dillon, A. Van Mueller, William Hagen, Robert Shields, Norman Ives, Stanley Howard, Charles Kirby, L. Dumbadse, Ivan Ismailov, Serge Vino.

Act 1, Scene 1: Inn of the Jolly Miller. *Scene 2*: Lane leading to Rue du Colombier. *Scene 3*: Courtyard in Rue du Colombier outside the Convent of Carmier. *Scene 4*: Cardinal Richelieu's Chambers in the Palace of the King. *Scene 5*: The Garden of the Tuilleries.

Act 2, Scene 1: An Inn at the Port of Calais. *Scene 2*: Duke of Buckingham's Palace, England. *Scene 3*: The Shrine. *Scene 4*: Before the Inn of the Jolly Miller. *Scene 5*: Milady's Bedchamber. *Scene 6*: Cabinet of the Queen. *Scene 7*: The Ballroom of the Hotel de Ville.

ACT 1[96]
Scene 1
"Summer Time" (Opening)
  Villagers
"All for One and One for All"
  J. Macaulay, D. R. Dumbrille, D. Poppen
"The 'He' for Me"
  V. Segal, Girls, J. Macaulay, D. R. Dumbrille, D. Poppen
Sabot Dance
  Albertina Rasch Dancers
"My Sword"[97]
  D. King, Company
"Heart of Mine"
  D. King, V. Segal
Finalette ("My Sword and I")
  D. King, Villagers
Scene 3
"Vesper Bell"
  The Pensionaires
"(My) Dreams"
  Y. D'Arle
"Te Deum"[98]
  D. King, Nuns
"(March of the) Musketeers"
  D. King, D. R. Dumbrille, D. Poppen, J. Macaulay, Musketeers
Scene 4
"Colonel and Major"
  L. Allen, Girls
Scene 5
Ballet Romantique
  H. Hoctor, Albertina Rasch Dancers
"Love Is the Sun"
  Y. D'arle, V. Segal, J. Clarke
"Heart of Mine"[99]
  V. Segal, D. King
"Welcome to the Queen"
  Ladies and Courtiers

---

[96]Added after opening:
"My Sword (and I)" (reprise)(Act 2, Scene 1 Finale)
  D. King, Company
"Every Little While" (Act 2, Scene 4 before "Gossips")
  V. Segal, L. Allen
[97]Dropped after opening and replaced by:
"Gascony"
  D. King, Company
[98]Dropped after opening.
[99]Dropped after opening and replaced by:
"Your Eyes"
  V. Segal, D. King

Finale
Entire Company

ACT 2
Scene 1

"With Red Wine"
D. Poppen, Company

Danse Bohemian
H. Hoctor

"Ma Belle"
J. Macaulay

"Kiss Before I Go" (One Kiss)
V. Segal, D. King

Scene 2

"Pages" (Dance)
Albertina Rasch Dancers

Scene 3

"Queen of My Heart"
J. Clarke

Scene 4

"Gossips"
L. Allen, Ladies

Scene 6

"Until We Say Goodbye"[100]
V. Segal

Scene

Ballet of the King
H. Hoctor, Albertina Rasch Dancers

Finale
Entire Company

1928.13   THE BEGGAR'S OPERA

A Revival of the Comic Opera (Ballad Opera) in Three Acts, 6 Scenes[101]. Libretto by John Gay. (Original music score selected and arranged by Johann Christoph Pepusch.) New settings of the airs and additional music by Frederic Austin. Costumes designed by Claud Lovat Fraser. Musical director, Sebastian Unglada. Produced by James C. Duff, in association with A. L. Jones and Morris Green. Opened 28 March 1928 at the 48th Street Theatre and closed 28 April 1928 after 36 performances[102].

CAST: *Peachum*: CHARLES MAGRATH. *Lockit*: Norman Williams. *Macheath*: GEORGE BAKER. *Filch*: Alfred Heather. *Drawer, The Beggar*: George Gregson. *Mrs. Peachum*: LENA MAITLAND. *Polly Peachum*: SYLVIA NELIS. *Lucy Lockit*: CELIA TURRILL. *Diana Trapes*: Julie Meo.
   The Ladies of the Town: Mrs. Coaxer: Marjorie Chard. *Dolly Trull*: Beatrice Morson. *Mrs. Vixen*: Vera Hurst. *Betty Doxy*: Julie Meo. *Jenny Diver*: ALLISON RAMSAY. *Mrs. Slammekin*: Audrey Mildmay. *Molly Brazen*: Zaidee White. *Suky Tawdry*: Julie Cornelius. *Members of Macheath's Gang*: Boris Milman, Leon Mandas, Raimonde Aubrey, Harry Taylor, Norman Stengel, James MacGregor.

Act 1: Peachum's House.

Act 2, Scene 1: A Tavern near Newgate. *Scene 2*: Newgate.

Act 3, Scene 1: A Gaming House. *Scene 2*: Newgate. *Scene 3*: The Condemn'd Hold.

ACT 1[103]

Thro' all the employments of life
'Tis woman that seduces all mankind
If any wench Venus's girdle wear
If love the virgin's heart invade
A maid is like the golden ore
Virgins are like the fair flower

Our Polly is a sad slut (Duet)
Can love be controlled by advice?
O Polly, you might have toyed and kissed (Duet)
I, like a ship in storms, was tossed
A fox may steal your hens, sir
O ponder well!
The turtle thus with plaintive crying
Pretty Polly, say (Duet)
My heart was so free
Were I laid on Greenland's coast (Duet)
O what pain it is to part (Duet)

ACT 2
Scene 1

Fill every glass (Solo and Chorus)
Let us take the Road (Solo and Chorus)
If the heart of a man
Youth's the season (Chorus and Dance)
Before the barn-door crowing (Solo and Chorus)
At the tree I shall suffer with pleasure

Scene 2

Man may escape from rope and gun
Thus when a good housewife sees a rat
How cruel are the traitors
The first time at the looking-glass
When you censure the age
Is then his fate decreed, Sir?
You'll think ere many days ensue
Thus when the Swallow, seeking prey
How happy could I be with either
I'm bubbled
Cease your funning
Why how now, Madam Flirt
No power on earth can e'er divide

ACT 3
Scene 1

Thus gamesters united in friendship are found

Scene 2

The modes of the Court so common are grown
In the days of my youth
I'm like a skiff on the ocean tossed
A curse attends that woman's love
Come, sweet lass
Hither, dear husband
Which way shall I turn me?
The charge is prepared

Scene 3

O cruel, cruel, cruel case
Of all the friends in time of grief
But valour the stronger grows
But can I leave my pretty hussies
Their eyes, their lips, their busses
Would I might be hanged
Thus I stand like the Turk

1928.14   GREENWICH VILLAGE FOLLIES (1928)

A Musical Revue in Two Acts, 27 Scenes[104]. Sketches by Harold Atteridge. Music by Ray Perkins and Maurie Rubens. Lyrics by Max and Nathaniel Lief. Staged by J. C. Huffman. Dances staged by Ralph Reader. All dances by Chester Hale Girls staged by Mr. Hale. Costumes designed by Ernest Schrapps. Settings by Watson Barratt. Orchestra under the direction of Max Meth. Produced by The Bohemians, Inc. (Messrs. Shubert). Opened 9 April 1928 at the Winter Garden and closed 28 July 1928 after 128 performances.

---

[100]Dropped after opening.
[101]Originally produced in New York 3 December 1750; this adaptation first presented 29 December 1920 Off-Broadway at the Greenwich Village Theatre for 37 performances.
[102]Staging by Nigel Playfair recreated, uncredited. Settings uncredited.
[103]The program does not contain any song list; the above was prepared from the published text (Gowans & Grey, Ltd., 1923) which notes Frederick Austin's revisions to the original.

[104]The eighth and final in the annual series of revues which began in 1919.

CAST: DOCTOR (George) ROCKWELL, GRACE LaRUE, HAROLD WHALEN, FLORENCE MISGEN, HARRY JANS, EVELYN LAW, BOBBY WATSON, GRACE BRINKLEY, BENNY FIELDS, LAURA LEE, EDDIE SHUBERT, BLOSSOM SEELEY, WALTER ARMIN, LOLA RAINE, BILLY McLEOD, SHEILA BARRETT, CARLOS and VALERIA, ANNIE PRITCHARD, ARNOLD JOHNSON'S ORCHESTRA. Marie Kosco, Hoyt Meredith, Jack Stanford, Ben Dova, Max Alexander, Ross Twins, John Donahue, James Grant, Jack Kelly, Sylvia Carol.

Graham Dancers: Betty MacDonald, Evelyn Sabin, Rosina Savelli. *SIXTEEN CHESTER HALE GIRLS*: Mary Wynn, Violet Lundberg, Beatrice Rupp, Inez Goetz, Ester Wheaton, Phillis Jordan, Hilda Paterson, Rolanda Poucel, Lillian Messmer, Jewel Tidgens, Winona Sweet, Bonnibelle Beard, Sylvia Green, Gladys Glorita, Gertrude Cornbloom, May Sigler. *Greenwich Village Follies Dancing Girls*: Florence Arganza, Dorothy Casey, Jean Gordon, Marie Regan, Violet Renault, Ethel Ross, Maude Ross, Midge Sydney, Sally Argo, Adrienne Brower, Kay Burnell, Helene Cambridge, Phyllis DeCastro, Annette Davies, Mickey Ellis, Patsy Hickey, Marie Kosco, Adelaide Loraine, Zayda Lord, Yolanda Losee, Peggy McDonald, Georgia Moore, Josephine Mostler, Viola Paulsen, Evelyn Sintae, Irene Stephens, Emmy Petri, Lillian Thomas, Myrtle Wagner, Dorothy Winters. *RALPH READER GREENWICH VILLAGE GIRLS*: Francine Blythe, Azeada Charkouie, Maurine Clark, Dorothy Drum, Irene French, Marian Gillon, Joan Kent, Ngaio Lee, Renie Luers, Leona Newell, Imogene Phillips.

ACT 1[105]

Scene 1

Bus to Greenwich Village
Tom: H. Jans. *Dick*: H. Whalen. *Mrs. Green*: S. Barrett. *Conductor*: B. McLeod. *Richard*: B. Watson. *Mrs. Hemingway*: L. Raine. *Grace*: G. Brinkley.

Scene 2

The Jungle Café in Greenwich Village: "Down at the Village"
A. Pritchard, M. Kosco, H. Meredith
(*Music by* Maurice Rubens.)
Proprietor: W. Armin. *Waiter*: J. Stanford. *Angela*: L. Raine. *Tom*: H. Jans. *Dick*: H. Whalen. *Headwaiter*: B. McLeod. *Chicago Benny*: B. Fields. *Grace*: G. Brinkley. *Daddy Stevens*: E. Shubert. *Dr. Rockwell*: G. Rockwell.

"Padlock Your Blues"
L. Lee, Girls
(*Music by* Maurice Rubens.)

Radio Specialty
Arnold Johnson's Orchestra
Roxie: B. Seeley.

"Golden Gate"
B. Seeley, B. Fields, Chester Hale Girls, Ralph Reader Girls
(*Music by* Maurice Rubens.)

Scene 3

Dr. Rockwell announces

Scene 4

Grace LaRue (Specialty)

Scene 5

The Violent House (The Violet House)
Grace: G. Brinkley. *Daddy Stevens*: E. Shubert. *Harold*: H. Whalen. *Harry*: H. Jans. *Ah Fong*: B. Dova. *Dr. Chang Fu*: W. Armin. *Deaf Servant*: M. Alexander. *First Lady Sleep Walker*: L. Raine. *Second Lady Sleep Walker*: L. Lee. *Third Lady Sleep Walker* (Roxie Hart): B. Seeley. *Policeman*: B. McLeod. *Man from the Gas Company*: G. Rockwell.

"What's the Reason?"
H. Jans, G. Brinkley, H. Whalen, L. Lee, B. Seeley, B. Fields
(*Music by* Maurice Rubens. *Lyrics by* Harold Atteridge.)

Scene 6

Dance
E. Law

Scene 7

Lecture on Health
Dr. Rockwell

Scene 8

Dr. Rockwell announces

Scene 9

The Trials and Tribulations of Mary Dugan
Judge: E. Shubert. *Prosecuting Attorney*: B. Fields. *Doctor*: G. Rockwell.

Dagmar: L. Lee. *Mary*: B. Seeley. *Defense Lawyer*: H. Whalen. *Clerk*: W. Armin. *Mrs. Rice*: L. Raine. *Jimmy*: H. Jans. *Chief*: B. McLeod.

Scene 10

"Calypso Isle"
F. Misgen
(*Music by* Ray Perkins.)
Calypso: Valeria. *Ulysses*: Carlos. *Pages*: Ross Twins. *Ballet*: Chester Hale Girls, Ensemble.

Scene 11

Jans and Whalen (Specialty)

Scene 12

Broadway: "Get Your Man"
L. Lee, Ralph Reader Girls
(*Music by* Ray Perkins.)

Dance
B. Dova
Cabby: E. Shubert. *Rounder*: B. Fields. *Aristophanes*: J. Donahue, J. Grant. *Cruiser*: H. Meredith. *Beggar*: J. Kelly. *Actor Bill*: B. McLeod. *Matinee Idol*: M. Alexander. *Star*: N. Lee. *Gold Diggers*: I. French, D. Drum, F. Blythe, M. Clark, A. Charkouie. *Dope Fiend*: J. Kent. *Rube*: J. Kelly.

"Slaves of Broadway"
B. Fields
(*Music by* Maurice Rubens.)
Chorus Girl: L. Newell. *Flirt*: M. Gillon. *Big Time Ben*: W. Armin. *Old-Time Singer*: R. Luers. *Pedestrians, Newsboys, etc.*: Ensemble.

Scene 13

Jack Stanford (Specialty)

Scene 14

Social Escort Office
Dick: H. Whalen. *Laura*: L. Lee. *Tom*: H. Jans.

Scene 15

"High, High Up in the Clouds"
G. Brinkley, B. Watson, Chester Hale Girls, Ensemble
(*Music by* Maurice Rubens.)
Finale

ACT 2

Scene 1

"Mauruf Ballet" (Song)
F. Misgen
Love: Carlos. *Rich Pasha*: W. Armin. *Sultan's Daughter*: Valeria. And Ralph Reader Girls, Chester Hale Girls, Nautch Dancers, Guards, etc.

Scene 2

Blossom Seeley and Benny Fields (Specialty)

Scene 3

Dr. Rockwell announces

Scene 4

School Room
Teacher: Dr. Rockwell. *Annie*: A. Pritchard. *Laura*: L. Lee. *Sylvia*: S. Carol. and D. Casey, J. Gordon, Ross Twins.

Scene 5

Frieze[106]
The Graham Dancers

Scene 6

"Dirty Dig"[107]
L. Lee, J. Stanford, Ralph Reader Girls

Scene 7

Psycho-analysis[108]
H. Jans, H. Whalen, S. Barrett

Scene 8

Grace Larue
At the Piano: Lou Alter.

---

[105]Added after opening:
Symphony in Color (Act 2)
Chester Hale Girls
"Little Boy's Blue" (Act 2)
G. Brinkley, Ralph Reader Girls, Chester Hale Girls
(*Music by* Maurice Rubens.)
Ballerina: A. Pritchard

---

[106]Dropped after opening.
[107]Dropped after opening.
[108]Replaced during the national tour by:
Sing Sing
H. Jans, H. Whalen, S. Barrett, M. Alexander

Scene 9

The Merediths and Dr. Rockwell

Scene 10

Dr. Rockwell announces

Scene 11

The Demand to Love (The Demand of Love)

Count Villiers: M. Alexander. *French Ambassador*: W. Armin. *Lackey*: H. Meredith. *Gaston Marquis du Saint Lac*: B. Watson. *Secretary A*: E. Shubert. *Secretary B*: B. Fields. *Secretary C*: B. McLeod. *Secretary D*: J. Donahue. *Wife of the Prime Minister of England*: L. Raine. *Wife of the Spanish Ambassador*: B. Seeley. *Wife of the Austria-Hungary Minister*: G. Brinkley.

Specialty

B. Seeley, B. Fields

Scene 12

"Cinderella"

G. Brinkley, B. Watson, Ensemble
(Music by Ray Perkins.)

Dance

Chester Hale Girls, Ensemble

Dance

E. Law

Finale

1928.15 COUNTESS MARITZA

A Return Engagement of the Operetta in Three Acts and a Prologue[109]. Book and lyrics by Harry B. Smith. Adapted from the Viennese original ('Gräfin Mariza') by Julius Brammer and Alfred Grünwald. Music by Emmerich Kálmán. Book and all ensembles staged by J. C. Huffman. Dances staged by Carl Randall and Jack Mason. Settings designed by Watson Barratt. Entire production under the personal supervision of J. J. Shubert. Produced by the Messrs. Lee and J. J. Shubert. Opened 9 April 1928 at the Century Theatre and closed 21 April 1928 after 16 performances.[110]

CAST (in order of appearance): *Bela Torek*: Louis E. Miller. *Nepomuk*: Robert Rotner. *Count Tassilo Endrody*: LEONARD CEELEY. *Tscheko*: Hugh Chilvers. *Lazlo*: Arthur Geary. *Manja*: ODETTE MYRTIL. *Stefan*: Clarence Tolman. *Servant*: Jules Waldeck. *Zingo*: JAMES C. MORTON. *Countess Maritza*: GLADYS BAXTER. *Lisa*: MARJORIE PETERSON. *Prince Populescu*: ROBERT GREIG. *First Officer*: Robert Roltner. *Baron Koloman Szupan*: GEORGE DOBBS. *Freda*: Mitzi Kish. *Princess Bozena Klopensheim*: Alexandra Dagmar.

Gypsy Girls: Katherine Allen, Anna Balton, Frances De Lessio, Belle Glass, Mae Golding, Leatrice Sherman, Mitzi Kish, Sybil Larayne, Billie Lee, Vera Reynolds, Nell Rutter, Marjorie Brooks, Dorothy Vinton. *Peasants*: Jeanne Geddes, Jackie Lee, Dorothy Mellor, Terry Vine, Jeanne Wells, Rita Monteray, Alycia Dupont, Maybelle Deane. *Guests*: Mary Clifford, Viola Lagergren, Betty Murrow, Goldie Reeves, Helen Paige, June Elvida, Doris Kingston, Carmen Cortez. *Officers*: John Collins, Ray Larkin, Harold Nash, Louis Rusoff, Larry Roberts, Frank Weiner, Jules Waldeck, James Russell, Palmer Johnson, Parker Colby, Allen Schaefer, Douglas Alexander, Joseph Ferguson, George Shierloh, Frank Gibbons, William Boylan. .

1928.16 PRESENT ARMS

A Musical Comedy in Two Acts, 9 Scenes. Book by Herbert Fields. Music by Richard Rodgers. Lyrics by Lorenz Hart. Staged by Alexander Leftwich. Musical numbers staged by Busby Berkeley. Art director, (settings by) Herbert Ward. Costumes by Milgrim. Orchestra directed by Roy Webb. Entire production under the personal supervision of Lew Fields. Produced by Lew Fields. Opened 26 April 1928 at the Mansfield Theatre and closed 1 September 1928 after 155 performances.

CAST (in order of appearance): *McKabe, a Top Sergeant*: Jock McGraw. *Frank Derryberry, a Buck Private*: FRANKER WOODS. *Chick Evans, Another*: CHARLES KING. *McKenna, Another*: FULLER MELLISH, JR. *Gadget, Another*: Robert Spencer. *Douglas Atwell, Sergeant*: BUSBY BERKELEY. *Captain Wiggins, Captain of the Outfit*: Richard Lane. *Edna Stevens, a Tourist*: JOYCE BARBOUR. *Fay, Another*: Rachel Chester. *Lady Delphine*: FLORA LE BRETON. *Luana, a Native Girl*: Alma Ross. *Lord Oliver Witherspoon, Lady Delphine's Father*: Sydney Smith. *Herr Ludwig von Richter*: Anthony Knilling. *Maria*: Florence Hunter. *Hortense Mossback*: GAILE

---

[109]Originally produced in New York 18 September 1926 at the Sam S. Shubert Theatre for 318 performances. Total for both engagements: 334 performances. For Synopsis of Scenes and Musical Numbers, see original 1926 production.
[110]Musical Direction uncredited.

BEVERLEY. Daisy: DEMARIS DORÉ. *Minerva, a Maid*: Aline Green. *Karl*: Alexander Lewis. *Elsa*: Frances Hess. *Moulika, a Native Fortune Teller*: Alma Ross.

Ladies of the Ensemble: Dorothy Brown, Elva Adams, Wilda Barnum, Evelyn Crowell, Rachel Chester, Irene Evans, Aline Green, Sherry Gale, Kay Hunt, Geneva Jensen, Rita Jarson, Louise Joyce, Henrietta Kay, Gladys Kelley, Charlotte LaRosse, Beth Meredith, Ann Mycue, Dorothy McKeon, Christine Nolan, Loraine Power, Polly Ray, Patricia Ross, Ruth Stickney, Genevieve Street, Greta Swanson, Helen Shepard, Gertrude Sheffield, Marion Stuart, Jean Sutro, Jessica Worth, Barbara Lee, Wanda Wood. *Gentlemen of the Ensemble*: Thomas Arnold, Russell Bryant, Milton Brodus, James Beattie, William Burdee, Norman Clifton, William Cullo, Jack Douglas, Louis Delgado, Frank Gagen, Edward Gaillard, Albert Jordan, Frank Kimball, Frank Losee, Edwin Larkin, Dury Lane, Henry Ladd, Jerome Maxwell, David North, Bernard Mitchell, Julio Martell, Glenn McComas, Joe McCafferty, Ned McGurn, William Creston, Walter Pharr, Wilburn Riviere, Thomas Sternfield, Louis Talbott, Joe Vitale.

Time: The present, spring.

Act 1, Scene 1: The Barracks of the Marine Base at Pearl Harbor, Hawaii. *Scene 2*: Within the Quarters. *Scene 3*: Sir Oliver's Home, Honolulu.

Act 2, Scene 1: Promenade Deck of Edna's Yacht. *Scene 2*: A Raft at Sea. *Scene 3*: A Deserted Island off Maui. *Scene 4*: Delphine's Room in Honolulu. *Scene 5*: Aboard the Transport St. Mihiel bound for Kohala. *Scene 6*: The Dock at Kohala.

ACT 1

Scene 1

"Tell It to the Marines"

C. King, F. Woods, F. Mellish, Jr., B. Berkeley, Marines

"You Took Advantage of Me"

J. Barbour, B. Berkeley, Ensemble

"Do I Hear You (Saying "I Love You")?"

F. LeBreton, C. King

Scene 2

"A Kiss For Cinderella"

B. Berkeley, F. Mellish, Jr., F. Woods, C. King

Scene 3

"Is It the Uniform?"

F. LeBreton, Ensemble

Reprise ("Do I Hear You")

C. King, F. LeBreton

"Crazy Elbows"

D. Doré, Ensemble

Finale

Company

ACT 2

Scene 1

"Down By the Sea"

C. King, Company

"I'm a Fool for You" ("I'm a Fool, Little One")

J. Barbour, B. Berkeley, F. Woods, G. Beverley

Scene 3

Reprise

J. Barbour, B. Berkeley

Finaletto

Ensemble

Scene 5

"Blue Ocean Blues"

C. King, Marines

Scene 6

"Hawaii"

Natives

"Kohala, Welcome"

Natives, Marines

Finale

Company

1928.17 HERE'S HOWE

A Spring Musical Comedy in Two Acts, 8 Scenes. Book by Fred Thompson and Paul Gerard Smith. Music by Roger Wolfe Kahn and Joseph Meyer. Lyrics by Irving Caesar. Dances and ensembles by Sammy Lee. Costumes by Kiviette. Settings designed by John Wenger. (Ben Bernie's) Orchestra under the direction of Paul J. Lannin. Produced by Alex A. Aarons and Vinton Freedley. Opened 1 May 1928 at the Broadhurst Theatre and closed 30 June 1928 after 71 performances.

CAST [in order of appearance]: *Cora Bibby*: PEGGY CHAMBERLAIN. *Mr. Petrie*: ROSS HIMES. *Edwin Treadwell*: ARTHUR HARTLEY. *Toni Treadwell*: Helen Carrington. *Sir Basil Carraway*: ERIC BLORE. *Joyce Baxter*: IRENE DELROY. *Billy Howe*: ALLEN KEARNS. *Dan Dabney*: BEN BERNIE. *Toplis*: William Frawley. *Mary*: JUNE O'DEA. *Pelham*: "FUZZY" KNIGHT. *Claudette Pernier*: Colette D'Arville. *Wilbur*: Dillon Ober.

Ladies of the Ensemble: Florence Allan, Nitza Andre, Billie Blake, Marion Bonnell, Gene Brady, Betty Clark, Elsie Connor, Evelyn Ellsmore, Peggy Hart, Edith Hayward, Madeline Janis, Evelyn Kirmin, Polly Luce, Nesha Medwin, Elsie Neal, Adeline Ogilvie, Gladys Pender, Sylvia Shawn, Helen Sheldon, Kay Smythe, Cora Stephens, Lee Stockton, Beryl Wallace, Florence Ward, Ingrid Aakesson. *Gentlemen of the Ensemble*: Douglas Carter, Ralph Chaterdon, Alan Crane, Alan Hale, Ray Hall, Jack Miller, Charles McClelland, Kendall Northrop, Charles Scott, Al Siegel, Jack Stevens, Jacques Stone, Howard Stuart. .

Act 1, Scene 1: Rest Room of the Community Hall of the Treadwell Motors Co., Inc. *Scene 2*: The Barber Shop. *Scene 3*: Outside Edwin Treadwell's Gardens. *Scene 4*: The Gardens of Edwin Treadwell's House.

Act 2, Scene 1: Lounge Room of the Track Club, Havana. Six months later. *Scene 2*: Gardens of the Club. *Scene 3*: Private Suite at the Sevilla-Biltmore Hotel. *Scene 4*: Boston Post Road. Two months later.

ACT 1

Specialty (a)("He's My Man")
B. Bernie, Orchestra

Dance (b)(Apache burlesque)
P. Chamberlain, R. Himes

Dance (c)
I. Delroy

"Dismissal Whistle"
P. Chamberlain, Employees

Specialty (a)("He's My Man")
B. Bernie, Orchestra

Dance (b)(Apache burlesque)
P. Chamberlain, R. Himes

Dance (c)
I. Delroy

"Beauty in the Movies"
A. Hartley, J. O'Dea, Girls

Specialty (a)("He's My Man")
B. Bernie, Orchestra

Dance (b)(Apache burlesque)
P. Chamberlain, R. Himes

Dance (c)
I. Delroy

"Life as a Twosome"
I. Delroy, A. Kearns, Ensemble

Specialty (a)("He's My Man")
B. Bernie, Orchestra

Dance (b)(Apache burlesque)
P. Chamberlain, R. Himes

Dance (c)
I. Delroy

"Crazy Rhythm"
B. Bernie, P. Chamberlain, J. O'Dea, Ensemble

"Imagination"
I. Delroy, A. Kearns

Specialty (a)("He's My Man")
B. Bernie, Orchestra

Dance (b)(Apache burlesque)
P. Chamberlain, R. Himes

Dance (c)
I. Delroy

Finale

ACT 2

Opening
Ensemble

"I'd Rather Dance Here Than Hereafter"
P. Chamberlain, R. Himes

"Here's Howe"
A. Kearns, Girls

"A New Love"
I. Delroy, Girls

Finaletto

Specialty (pianolog)
F. Knight

"Boston Post Road"
A. Kearns, Helpers

Finale
Entire Company

(LEW LESLIE'S) BLACKBIRDS OF 1928

1928.18

A Distinctive and Unique Entertainment (Musical Revue) in Two Acts and a Prologue, 19 Scenes. Entire production staged and conceived by Lew Leslie. Music by Jimmy McHugh. Lyrics by Dorothy Fields. Costumes designed by Kiviette. Scenery by Premier Scenic Studios. Conductor, Allie Ross. Orchestral arrangements, Will Vodery, Ken MacComber, Arthur Goodman. Produced by Lew Leslie. Opened 9 May 1928 at the Liberty Theatre, moved 15 October 1928 to the Eltinge Theatre, and closed 15 June 1929 after 518 performances[111].

CAST: ADELAIDE HALL, BILL ROBINSON, AIDA WARD, TIM MOORE, Ruth Johnson, Crawford Jackson, Marjorie Hubbard, Blue McAllister, Eloise Uggams, Lloyd Mitchell, Billie Cortez, George W. Cooper, Mamie Savoy, Mantan Moreland, Elizabeth Welsh [Welch], Harry "Shorty" Lucas, Baby Banks, Willard McLean, Phillip Patterson, Earl "Snake Hips" Tucker, Milton Crawley (clarinet).

(Chorus:) Mabelle Staples, Burkie Jackson, Margaret Rhodes, Rosie White, Thelma Salmonds, Irma Miles, Dorothy Irving, Asalyn Lynch, Bernice Smith, Dorothy Dobson, Julia Noisette, Lydia Burke, Alice Hoffman, Blanche Howell, Margaret Cherot, Dorothy Williams. Joseph Attles, James Strange, Clement Hall. Hall Johnson's Blackbird Choir.

PROLOGUE[112]

Way Down South
Scene and Place: Dixie.

"The Call of the South"
Hall Johnson's Blackbird Choir

"Shuffle Your Feet"
R. Johnson, M. Hubbard

"Dixie"
A. Ward, Entire Company

ACT 1

Scene 1

Aunt Jemima Stroll
C. Jackson, B. McAllister, L. Mitchell

Scene 2

Scene in Jungleland: "Diga, Diga, Do"
A. Hall, Her Blackbird Chorus

---

[111]Sketches uncredited. After 31 December 1928, the show was titled simply Blackbirds, dropping the year 1928.
[112]During the run the song order was altered substantially. Added were:

We Must Have 'It' (Act 2, after "Doin the New Low Down;" later moved to Act 1)
(A colored version based on Eleanor Glyn's novel by Salem Tutt Whitney)
Ham: T. Moore. Sudds: M. Moreland. Sam: G. W. Cooper. Miss Mandy: E. Welsh. Miss Wilson: Rose Poindexter. Miss Moore: Mina Mae McKinney.

Just Pals (Act 2)
Beebee Joyner, Clarence Foster

Johnny Hudgins: The Man Who Talks Too Much (Act 1)
Sherman Robinson in his impression of the World Famous Johnny Hudgins—

The Man Who Talks Too Much (Act 2)

Who's on the Phone? (Act 2)
Husband: J. Hudgins. *Wife*: E. Welsh.

A Happy Business Man (Act 2)
Husband: Hamtree Harrington. *Wife*: Fannia Laine. *Lover*: C. Foster.

"I Can't Give You Anything But Love" (Operatic version)(Act 2)
(Staged, Conceived and Written by Lew Leslie. Musical Arrangement by Russell Wooding.)
Scene: Musical Studio, New York.
Inspiration: A. Hall. *The Composer*: A. Ward. *Metropolitan Chorus*: Cecil Mack's Blackbird Choir. *Metropolitan Orchestra*: Plantation Orchestra.

Winfred and Mills in China (Act 2)

Scene 3

Bear Cat Jones' Last Fight

Scene: Mrs. Jasmine Wilson's Lawn.

Bill Green, A Fight Promoter: G. W. Cooper. *Jack Sterling*, Time Keeper: L. Mitchell. *Eberneezer Doozenbury*, a Bully: T. Moore. *Sam Skinner*, His Buddie: M. Moreland. *Beat Car Jones*, Champion: B. McAllister. *Big Boy*, Bear Cat's Second: H. Lucas. *Mrs. Jasmine Wilson*: E. Uggams.

Scene 4

"I Can't Give You Anything But Love"

A. Ward, W. McLean

Trio Reprise

A. Hall, A. Ward, W. McLean

Scene 5

What a Night

Slippery Jim: L. Mitchell. *The Sheriff*: P. Patterson. *Billy the Dope*: M. Moreland. *The Woman*: A. Hall.

Scene 6

"Bandana Babies"

A. Hall, R. Johnson, C. Jackson, Blackbird Chorus

Scene 7

Playing According to Hoyle

Scene: A Gin Mill Somewhere in Harlem.

Spike Jones: B. McAllister. *Jim Jackson*: T. Moore. *Billy Henry*: M. Moreland. *Smithie*: G. W. Cooper. *Bar Tender*: L. Mitchell. *Policeman*: P. Patterson.

Scene 8

Milton Crawley accompanied by his low-down clarinet

Scene 9

"Magnolia's Wedding Day"

Bridesmaids: R. Johnson, T. Salmonds, I. Miles, D. Irving, M. Hubbard, A. Lynch, B. Smith, D. Dobson, J. Noisette, L. Burke, A. Hoffman, B. Howell, M. Cherot, D. Williams. *Aunts*: E. Uggams, B. Cortez, E. Welsh, M. Staples. *Uncles*: P. Patterson, W. McLean, J. Strange, C. Hall, J. Attles. *Preacher*: T. Moore. *Intruder*: A. Ward. *Bride*: B. McAllister. *Groom*: M. Moreland.

Scene 10

Finale

Entire Company

ACT 2

Scene 1

"Porgy" (with apologies to the Theatre Guild and Dorothy and DuBose Heyward)

A. Ward, Hall Johnson's Blackbird Choir. Including J. Attles, B. Cortez, G. W. Cooper, P. Patterson, W. McLean, J. Strange, C. Hall, E. Welsh, M. Staples, E. Uggams, B. Jackson, M. Rhodes, R. White.

Scene 2

Three Bad Men from Harlem

B. McAllister, M. Moreland, L. Mitchell

Scene 3

Picking a Plot

Undertaker: G. W. Cooper. *Ross Jones*: T. Moore. *Do Little Jackson*: M. Moreland. *Grave Digger*: J. Strange. *A Departed Brother*: W. McLean. *Little Bits*: H. Lucas. *Another Departed Brother*: P. Patterson. *A Friend of the Departed*: M. Savoy.

Scene 4

"Doin' the New Low Down"

B. Robinson, Blackbird Chorus

Scene 5

"I Must Have That Man"

A. Hall

Scene 6

Getting Married in Harlem

Scene: Reverend Green's Apartment on 135th Street.

Maid: R. White. *Ross*: T. Moore. *Pandora*: E. Welsh. *Do Little*: M. Moreland. *Lizzie*: B. Cortez. *Atta Boy*: B. McAllister. *Minnie*: E. Uggams. *Sister Low Down*: B. Banks. *Big Boy*: H. Lucas. *Reverend Green*: G. W. Cooper.

Scene 7

Earl (Snake Hips) Tucker giving his exception of the Low Down [Snake Hip] Dance

Scene 8

"Here Comes My Blackbird"

A. Hall, B. McAllister, C. Jackson, Blackbird Chorus

A Memory of 1927

Impersonated by A. Ward

Scene 9

Finale

Entire Company

THE GRAND STREET FOLLIES (1928)

1928.19

A Topical Revue of the Season in Two Acts, 19 Scenes[113]. Book (sketches) and lyrics by Agnes Morgan, unless otherwise indicated. Music by Max Ewing, Lily Hyland, Serge Walter. Settings and costumes by Aline Bernstein. Entire production directed by Agnes Morgan. Dances by James Cagney. Music directed by Fred Fleming. Produced by the Actor-Managers, Inc. Opened 28 May 1928 at the Booth Theatre and closed 29 September 1928 after 144 performances.

CAST: Albert Carroll, Dorothy Sands, Marc Loebell, Vera Allen, James Cagney, Paula Trueman, Otto Hulett, Joanna Roos, Harold Minjir, Lily Lubell, George Bratt, Mae Noble, Hal Brogan, Mary Williams, George Hoag, Frances Cowles, Richard Ford, Edla Frankau, Blake Scott, Laura Emond, George Heller, Jean Crittenden, Milton LeRoy, Ruth McConkie, Michael McCormack, John Rynee, Harold Hecht, Sophia Delza, Robert White, Robert Gorham, Gene and Sven von Hallberg.

ACT 1[114]

Scene 1

An Old Traveller in a New World

Trader Horn: G. Bratt. *Mrs. Beekman-Sutton*: V. Allen.

Scene 2

"My Southern Belle"

---

[113]The sixth and last in the annual series of satirical revues which began at the Neighborhood Playhouse Off-Broadway in 1922.

[114]For subsequent national tour billed as The New Gala Edition, the following scenes were added:

Opening Remarks (Act 1)

President of the Super Drama League: June de Roche.

South of the Rio Grande (Act 1)

(a) Then and Now: A Cafe Pantomime

(*Music by Lily Hyland.*)

The Singer: Michael Barroy. *The Senorita*: Sophia Delza. *Her Lover*: Hal Brogan. *His Rival*: George Heller. *A Modern Miss*: Lily Lubell.

(b) From Tango to Taps

(*Music by Serge Walter.*)

Dancers: S. Delza, Bill Brown.

What Price, Morning Glories? (Act 1)

The Captain: M. Loebell. *The Sergeant*: A. Carroll. *The Girl*: P. Trueman.

Civilization Hits the Antarctic (Act 1)

(*Music of "Little Igloo for Two" by Arthur Schwartz. Numbers arranged by George Heller.*)

An Eskimo Boy: G. Heller. *An Eskimo Girl*: K. Gauthier.

"Sinfonica Domestica Triangular" (Act 1)

Suite: Town and Country. First performance by any orchestra.

(*Music by Lily Hyland.*)

Conductor: John Rynee. *Soloist*: Frances Cowles. *Members of the Orchestra*: O. Hulett, Wallace Furie, Milton LeRoy, John McNeeley, Hal Brogan, Mae Noble, Bill Brown, Michael McCormack, Gita Zucker.

"His Honor, the Mayor"

(*Music by Max Ewing. Lyrics by Albert Carroll.*) *James J. Walker*: A. Carroll.

The Mysterious Bedroom (A Super Mystery Play)

Scene: Dining Room of a Long Island Country Home on a Summer's Evening. *Professor Heintz*: Michael Barroy. *Mr. Peck*: John Rynne. *Mrs. Peck*: J. De Roche. *Doris Seymour*: P. Trueman. *Julia Riker*: Julia Frankau. *Ralph Roach*: H. Minjir. *John Geddes*: O. Hulett. *Herbert*, a butler: M. Loebell.

Gala Performance of the Opera "L'Irlandesa Rosa Dell' Abie"

The Letter Scene from the Merry Wives of Windsor

Mrs. Fiske as Mistress Page: One Side of A. Carroll. *Miss Ethel Barrymore as Mistress Ford*: Other Side of A. Carroll.

Jazz Baby Learns Aesthetic Dancing

The Teacher: F. Cowles. *The Pupil*: P. Trueman.

(Numbers arranged by Blanche Talmud.)

The Wild Duck of the Eighteenth Century

Miss Haidee Wright in "The Royal Family"

A. Carroll

"The Stepping Stones"

(*Music by Serge Walter. Arranged by Lily Lubell and J. Blake Scott.*) *Fred*: Bill Brown. *Dorothy*: L. Lubell.

Qualifications for the A.B. Degree (1928 Model)

Senior Passing Final Exams: Bill Brown.

Professor George White's Class in Playwriting makes a musical comedy out of "Coquette" with this result. Dr. Sigmund Speath's Class in Musical Research collaborates, with this stupendous array of very original song hits.
(*Book and Lyrics by* Marc Loebell. Music arranged by Lily Hyland.)
Coquette: P. Trueman. *Michael*: M. Loebell. *Stanley*: H. Brogan. *Jimmie*: J. Cagney. *Betty Lee*: L. Lubell. *The Colonel*: O. Hulett. *Mammy Julia*: M. Noble. *Southern Belles (8): Ethel*: S. Delza. *Pearl*: M. Williams. *Eloise*: J. Roos. *Ruby*: L. Emond. *Rose*: R. McConkie. *Violet*: J. Crittenden. *Pansy*: F. Cowles. *Myrtle*: E. Frankau. *Collegiate Boys (8): Percy*: H. Minjir. *Claude*: G. Heller. *Reginald*: G. Hoag. *Bertie*: H. Hecht. *Jasper*: R. White. *Lionel*: R. Gorham. *Archie*: M. McCormack. *Willie*: M. LeRoy.

Scene 3

"Command to Love"
(*Music by* Serge Walter.) *Mary Nash*: A. Carroll.

Scene 4

A Dinner Date
Ina Claire: D. Sands.

Scene 5

"From Tango to Taps"
R. Ford
(*Music of tango "Tu Sais" by* Serge Walter.)
The Gypsy Dancers: S. Delza, B. Scott. *The Tango Dancers*: L. Lubell, R. Gorham, R. White. *The Tap Dancers*: J. Cagney, S. Delza.

Scene 6

A Conference to End Mystery Plays
Scene: The Library of McAuliffe's Country Home—'Cock-Robin Roost:'
Ho-Fang (from "The Silent House"): A. Carroll. *McAuliffe* (from "Cock-Robin"): H. Minjir. *Count Dracula* (from "Dracula"): M. Loebell. *Detective Garrity* (from "Sh! The Octopus"): O. Hulett. *A Butler* (from any play): G. Hoag. *A Maid* (Helen Chandler): P. Trueman.

Scene 7

"Just a Little Love Song"
(*Music and Lyrics by* Max Ewing.)
1928 Couple: J. Cganey, L. Lubell. *1830 Couple*: R. Ford, M. Williams. *Other Gentlemen*: G. Heller, R. Gorham, M. McCormack, R. White. *Other Ladies*: J. Crittenden, S. Delza, L. Emond, R. McConkie. *The Dancers*: L. Lubell, B. Scott.

Scene 8

Don Juan's Busy Day (or What Happened to a Screen Comedy on the day its Fightamoan accompaniment went wrong)
Scene: A Living Room in Bob Banks' Duplex Apartment on Park Avenue, New York City.
Bob Banks: H. Minjir. *Ethel*, his sister: F. Cowles. *Valerie*, his fiancee: E. Frankau. *Fifi*, his guest: J. Roos. *Mrs. Snookums*, a charwoman: M. Noble. *Fightamoan Voices*: R. White, D. Sands, V. Allen.

Scene 9

"Someone to Admire, Someone to Adore"
(*Music by* Serge Walter.)
The Ingenue: D. Sands. *The Vamp*: L. Lubell. *The Old Maid*: P. Trueman. *The Mother*: L. Emond. *The Washerwoman*: J. Crittenden. *The Sport*: F. Cowles. *The Flapper*: R. McConkie. *The Reporter*: S. Delza. *The Debutante*: M. Williams. *The East-Sider*: M. Noble.

Scene 10

"Marked Millions"
(*Music by* Lily Hyland.) Lifted from "The Grand Street Follies of 1924" and brought up to date; showing that in politics the old order changeth not. Dedicated admiringly to Senator Walsh.
Scene 1: A Street in the Far East. Scene 2: Throne Room of the Palace.
Trader Sinclair: O. Hulett. *Trader Fall*: G. Heller. *G.O.P., a Poet*: M. Lobell. (Court Censor) *Willie Hays, Postmaster General*: R. Ford. (General Repnatcom) *The Queen*: P. Trueman. *Mayor Walker, U.S.A.*: A. Carroll. *Members of the Queen's Cabinet*: G. Hoag, H. Minjir, M. McCormack, R. Gorham, H. Brogan, R. White, H. Hecht, M. LeRoy. *Maids-in Waiting*: L. Lubell, E. Frankau, J. Crittenden, F. Cowles, S. Delza, J. Roos, M. Williams, R. McCockie. *Court Ladies*: V. Allen, M. Noble, L. Emond.

ACT 2[115]

Scene 1

A Party on the S.S. Ile de France in Port
(*Music of "The Briny Blues" by* Serge Walter.)

The Captain: M. Loebell. *Billie Burke*: J. Roos. *Lionel Atwill*: R. Ford. *Eva Le Galliennne*: P. Trueman. *Beatrice Lillie*: E. Frankau. *Colonel Lindbergh*: M. LeRoy. *Dolores Costello*: M. Williams. *A Spanish Singer*: L. Emond. *The Announcer*: R. McConkie.

Scene 2

The Ship's Entertainment:
(a) *Mrs. Fiske as Mistress Page, Mis Ethel Barrymore as Mistress Ford, in* 'The Merry Wives of Windsor': A. Carroll.
(b) *Miss Haidee Wright as Lady Macbeth*: D. Sands.
(c) South Sea Islands Dance
B. Scott
(Music from original sources, arranged by Gene and Sven von Hallberg, and played in this number by Sven von Hallberg. *Dance arranged by* Michel Fokine.)

Scene 3

The Strange Inner Feud
Lynn Fontanne as Columbia: V. Allen. *Calvin*: J. Rynne. *Al*: H. Minjir. *Herbert*: M. McCormack.

Scene 4

Jes' Shufflin' Along
Sam Snow: O. Hulett. *Rufus Green*: G. Heller.

Scene 5

The Porgy Players present "Camille Causes a Doctor's Dilemma"
(*Music and Lyrics* of the Spiritual by Max Ewing.)
Camille: P. Trueman. *Armand*: H. Hecht. *Doctor Snow*: O. Hulett. *Doctor Tucker*: J. Rynne. *Doctor Greene*: G. Heller. *Doctor Jones*: M. Loebell. *The Neighbors*: G. Hoag, R. White, H. Brogan, M. LeRoy, R. Gorham, M. McCormack; J. Roos, E. Frankau, J. Crittenden, M. Noble, S. Delza, R. McConkie, M. Williams, L. Emond, F. Cowles.

Scene 6[116]

"Husky, Dusky Annabelle"
(*Music by* Max Ewing.)
Trader Horn: G. Bratt. *A Little Cannibal*: F. Cowles.

Scene 7

The Duchess Entertains[117]
Constance Collier: V. Allen. *The Belle-Hop*: R. McConkie. *Laurette Taylor in* 'The Furious Interlude': A. Carroll.

Scene 8

On the Honeymoon Deck, bound for Africa[118]
(a) *The Elopers*: G. Heller, L. Lubell.
(b) *The Blue Singers*: J. Cagney, J. Crittenden. (*Music of "The Briny Blues" by* Serge Walter.)
(c) *The Missionary*: H. Minjir.

Scene 9

'Romeo and Juliet' according to Max Reinhardt
(Music arranged by Lily Hyland.)
"Hey, Nonny, Hey!"
(*Music by* Max Ewing.)
In gathering an American cast to support Moissi as Romeo, Professor Reinhardt has chosen the following superlative company—each member selected for his or her special suitability.
Scene: The Steps of the New York Public Library, Fifth Avenue, New York City. *Moissi as Romeo*: A. Carroll. *Mae West as Juliet*: D. Sands. *Helen Westley as the Nurse*: V. Allen. *Hal Skelley as Friar Laurence*: O. Hulett. *Dennis King as Mercutio*: B. Scott. *Harland Dixon as Tybalt*: J. Cagney. *Corse Payton as Capulet*: M. Loebell. *Julia Hoyt as Lady Capulet*: E. Frankau. *Stuart Walker as Montague*: R. Ford. *Stella Mayhew as Lady Montague*: M. Noble. *Capulet's Stock Company*: H. Hecht, G. Heller, G. Hoag, White, M. Williams, P. Trueman, R. McConkie, L. Emond. *Montague's Stock Company*: R. Gorham, H. Brogan, M. LeRoy, O. Hulett, L. Lubell, J. Roos, J. Crittenden, S. Delza.

---

[115]Added during the run:
Finale: "Hey, Nonny, Nonny" (Act 2)
Entire Company

---

[116]During the run, Act 2, Scene 6 was revised and appeared as follows:
Broadcasting from Station W.H.Y.
(a) Announcing the Safety Clutch Suspenders HourJ. Cagney
(b) Laurette Taylor in "the Furies"A. Carroll
(Written by Albert Carroll with a bow to Zoe Atkins.)
(c) An African Jungle Lullaby
(Music of "Husky, Dusky Annabelle" by Max Ewing.)
Trader Horn: G. Bratt. Annabelle: F. Cowles.
(d) Reverend Percy Snowflake has an IdeaH. Minjir
[117]Dropped during the run.
[118]Dropped during the run.

1928–1929 SEASON

Irene Bordoni in PARIS (Photo: Adepa)
Billy Rose Theatre Collection, New York Public Library for the Performing Arts

1928–1929 SEASON

PATIENCE,
1928.20
or, Bunthorne's Bride

A Revival of the Comic Opera in Two Acts[1]. Libretto by William S. Gilbert. Music by Arthur Sullivan. Staged by T. M. Cushing. Costumes by Elizabeth Alters and Nancy Arnold. Settings designed by Isaac Benesch. Produced by The Play-Arts Guild, Inc. Opened 25 June 1928 at the Masque Theatre and closed 14 July 1928 after 24 performances.

CAST: *Patience*: MARY BOKEE. *Reginald Bunthorne*: DONALD KIRKLEY. *Archibald Grosvenor*: EDMUND LEONARD. *Rapturous Maidens (5)*: *The Lady Jane*: GERTRUDE M. GOSSMAN. *The Lady Saphir*: Wilma Lanyon. *The Lady Angela*: NANCY ARNOLD. *The Lady Ella*: EUNICE SCHRAMM. *The Lady Celia*: Margaret Gilner. *Officers of the Dragoon Guards (3)*: *Colonel Calverley*: BURT B. ROYCE, JR. *Major Murgatroyd*: CARROLL ROBINSON. *Lieutenant, The Duke of Dunstable*: WILLIAM LESTER. *An Ecstatic Dancing Maiden*: Estelle Dennis. *Mr. Bunthorne's Solicitor*: Earl Jordan.

Rapturous Maidens: Emma Baum, Margaret Brinkley, Eleanor Etheridge, Betty Marriss, Lillian Moore, Dorothy Miller, Carolyn Parker, Gertrude Schanze, Marjorie Springer, Lonah Straw, Beatrice Wilson, Betty Woodall. *Dragoon Guards*: Joseph Arnold, Graye Boone, Ellis Farber, John Head, Ralph Hoyt, Arthur Lawder, Stanley Mitten, Henry Miller, Lynn Perkins, Norton Smith, William Randolph, William Wambold.

SAY WHEN
1928.21

An Intimate Musical Comedy in Two Acts. Book by Calvin Brown[2]. Based on the play 'Love in a Mist' by Amelie Rives and Gilbert Emery. (Music by Ray Perkins, Kay Warburg [Swift], W. Franke Harling, Jesse Greer, Daisy deSegonzac, Irma Hopper. Lyrics by Max and Nathaniel Lief, Paul James, W. Franke Harling, James J. Walker, Raymond Klages, Irma Hopper.). Book staged by Bertram Harrison. Dances staged by Max Scheck. Production (settings designed) by Livingston Platt. Costumes by Lord & Taylor. Orchestra conducted by Ernest Cutting. Produced by Elisabeth Marbury and Carl Reed. Opened 26 June 1928 at the Morosco Theatre and closed 7 July 1928 after 15 performances.

CAST (in order of appearance): *Michael Graham*: RAYMOND GUION. *Cora*: CORA LA REDD. *Toody Hubbard*: DORIS VINTON. *Sydney Farnham*: Jane Alden. *Diana Wynne*: DOROTHY FITSGIBBONS. *Gregory Farnham*: BARTLETT SIMMONS. *Comtessa Scaracchi*: Alison Skipworth. *Colin*: Duquesne Miller. *Count Scippio Varelli*: JOSEPH LERTORA. *Joe Turner*: Roger Gray. *Assistant Radio Announcer*: J. Gibbs Penrose. *The Four Recorders*: William J. Cleary, Donald Wells, Robert Moody, Alan Ray. HENRY BUSSE AND HIS ORCHESTRA.

Miss Jefferson: Mildred Quigley. *Miss Lee*: Sally Anderson. *Miss Jackson*: Anne Freshman. *Miss Thomas*: Patricia McGrath. *Miss Gordon*: Kathryn Hamill. *Miss Brady*: Ruth Fallows. *Miss Davis*: Peggy Fish. *Miss Randall*: Ruth Altman. *Miss Carter*: Joyce Arling. *Miss Stuart*: Josephine Adair. *Miss Stean*: Dorothy Jones. *Miss Scott*: Helen Kaiser. *Miss Udall*: Genevieve Kent. *Miss Hewitt*: Katherine Herriford. *Miss Custis*: Mabel Martin. *Miss Monroe*: Anna Rex. *Miss Warrenton*: Beverly Maude. *Mr. Grant*: Archie Thompson. *Mr. Meade*: Warren Crosby. *Mr. McClellan*: Harold Williams. *Mr. Lincoln*: Bradley Cass. *Mr. Chase*: Harry Kirk.

ACT 1: Drawing Room in the Wynne Homestead, Wynnefield, Virginia.

ACT 2: The Garden at Wynnefield, a few weeks later.

ACT 1
Opening Chorus
 Ensemble
 (*Music by* Daisy deSegonzac. *Lyrics by* Max and Nathaniel Lief.)
"Who's the Boy?"
 D. Vinton, R. Guion, Girls, Boys
 (*Music by* Ray Perkins. *Lyrics by* Max and Nathaniel Lief.)
"Little White Lies"[3]
 D. Vinton, J. Alden, D. Fitsgibbons, Girls

Specialty Dance
 K. Hereford
 (*Music by* Arthur Sheekman. *Lyrics by* Helen Wallace.)
"My One Girl"
 B. Simmons, D. Fitsgibbons
 (*Music and Lyrics by* W. Franke Harling.)
"How About It?"
 D. Vinton, R. Guion, Ensemble
 (*Music by* Jesse Greer. *Lyrics by* Raymond Klages.)
"No Room in My Heart for You"
 D. Fitsgibbons, Boys
 (*Music by* Ray Perkins. *Lyrics by* Max and Nathaniel Lief.)
"Cheerio"
 J. Lertora, Girls
 (*Music by* Jesse Greer. *Lyrics by* Mayor James J. Walker.)
"One Step to Heaven"
 C. LaRedd, H. Busse, Ensemble
Specialty Dance
 C. LaRedd, D. Miller
 (*Music by* Jesse Greer. *Lyrics by* Raymond Klages.)
Finale
 Ensemble

ACT 2
In My) Love Boat"
 J. Adair, R. Altman, Girls
 (*Music by* Ray Perkins. . *Lyrics by* Max and Nathaniel Lief.)
"Say When"
 D. Vinton, Ensemble
 (*Music by* Jesse Greer. *Lyrics by* Raymond Klages.)
"Give Me a Night"
 J. Alden, J. Lertora, Four Recorders
Specialty Dance
 J. Alden, J. Lertora
 (*Music and Lyrics by* W. Franke Harling.)
Finale
 Company

GEORGE WHITE'S
1928.22
SCANDALS (1928)

A Musical Revue in Two Acts, 27 Scenes[4]. Assembled by George White. Book (sketches) by William K. Wells and George White. Music by Ray Henderson. Lyrics by Buddy DeSylva, Lew Brown. Entire production staged by George White. Dances staged by Russell Markert and George White. Art director, G. A. Weidhaas; assistant art director, William Oden-Waller. Costumes and curtains designed by Erté, Charles LeMaire. Orchestra under the direction of William Daly. Produced by George White. Opened 2 July 1928 at the Apollo Theatre and closed 19 January 1929 after 240 performances.

CAST: ANN PENNINGTON, HARRY RICHMAN, WILLIE HOWARD, EUGENE HOWARD, TOM PATRICOLA, FRANCES WILLIAMS, ROSE PERFECT, Bernice and Emily, William O'Neal, Arthur Page, Ruth Goodwin, Belle Osborne, Elm City Four, Lois Eckhart, Isabel Mohr, June MacCloy, Mabel Hill, Dolly Gilbert, Hastings Twins, Peggy Moseley, Margaret Manners, James Carty, Harry Morrissey, William Blanche, Arthur Cardinal, Georgia Lerch, June MacCloy, LaVerta McCormick, Arnold Johnson and His Orchestra.

George White Girls: Marjorie Barley, Elsie Duffy, Marjorie Gilbert, Ann Hardman, Renee Johnson, Wynne Larke, Marion Martin, Mae Slattery, Pearl Bradley, Alvina Carson, Violet Carson, Marion Cutler, Jean Cutler, Marion Dickson, Jacqueline Feeley, Elise Gerndon, Ivena Hall, Muriel LeCount, Jo NaVarro, Catherine NaVarro, Margie O'Shea, Sally Parsons, Florence Robinson, Catherine Reynolds, Selma Freeman, Marie Cole, Mitzi Hayes, Helen Howe, Alice Lorraine, Frances Lyle, Boots Mallory, Gloria O'Neil, Edna Rabbe, Gertrude Smith, Lilyan Sabolis. RUSSELL MARKERT DANCERS: Dorothy Dawn, Ivy Cayner, Cloria Murray, Dorothy Stewart, Mildred Ott, Ednamay French, Beryl Collinson, Barbara Bright, Elsie St. Clare, Gladys Astor, Mary Brown, Katherine Cathcart, Geraldine Wright, Louise Newman, Marie Keve, Rae Davis.

---

[1]First presented in New York 22 September 1881 at the Standard Theatre for 177 performances. For Synopsis of Scenes and Musical Numbers, see original 1881 production. Musical director uncredited.
[2]A likely pseudonym. Prior to Broadway, book was credited to Marc Connelly.
[3] Prior to Broadway, this song was credited as follows:
 Music by Kay Warburg [Swift], *Lyrics by* Paul James.

[4]The ninth in the annual series of musical revues presented by George White beginning in 1919.

ACT 1
Scene 1
  "Not as Good As Last Year"
    J. Feeley, D. Gilbert, M. Cutler, E. Duffy, G. Lerch,
    L Eckhart, P. Moseley, C. Reynolds, M. Cole, R. Johnson, M. LeCount,
    M. Dixon, J. Cutler, A. Carson, V. Carson
  Dance
    Russell Markert Dancers
Scene 2
  "Second Childhood"
    W. Howard, E. Howard
Scene 3
  "On the Crest of a Wave"
    H. Richman
      Pacific: M. Manners. *Atlantic*: L. McCormick. *Red*: F. Lyle. *Dead*: H. Howe.
      Adriatic: M. Martin. *Arctic*: L. Eckhart. *Bathing Girl*: E. Gernon.
Scene 4
  Credits
    Announcement: H. Richman. *Mr. A*: J. Carty. *Mrs. A*: F. Williams. *Mr. X*: H.
    Richman.
Scene 5
  The Pride of Italy
    T. Patricola
Scene 6
  "An Old Fashioned Girl"
    H. Richman
      Young Man: H. Richman. *Old Man*: W. Howard.
    Girls of 1948
      Chauffeur: B. Mallory. *Judge*: M. Martin. *Iceman*: F. Lyle. *Salesman*: H. Howe.
    Girls of 1928
      Flapper, short dress: E. Gernon. *Flapper*, sweet: P. Moseley. *Flapper*, cigarette:
      L. Eckhart. *Flapper*, night club: D. Gilbert.
    Girls of 1848
      Charming: M. Manners. *Real Endeavor*: S. Freeman. *Sweetheart*: L.
      McCormick. *Mother*: E. Rabbe.
    Girls in the Crinoline
      M. Slattery, L. Sabalis, G. Lerch, A. Lorraine, M. Cutler, J. Feeley, M. Gilb ert,
      M. O'Shea, P. Bradley
Scene 7
  Ann Pennington, assisted by Arnold Johnson and His Orchestra
Scene 8
  A Strange Interlude
    Announcement: H. Richman. *Husband*: J. Carty. *Friend*: H. Richman. *Wife*: F.
    Williams.
Scene 9
  Fathers of the World
    W. Howard, E. Howard, T. Patricola, A. Page
Scene 10
  "Pickin' Cotton"
    F. Williams
      Announcement: H. Richman.
    Dance
      White Girls, A. Pennington, T. Patricola
Scene 11
  Vocafilm[5]
    H. Richman, W. Howard, G. White
      Announcement: H. Richman. (Motion picture and sound synchronization
      apparatus furnished by the Vocafilm Corporation of America.)
Scene 12
  The Ambulance Chaser
    Announcement: Hastings Twins. *The Patient*: W. Howard. *The Nurse*: F.
    Williams. *The Lawyer*: E. Howard.
Scene 13
  Bernice and Emily
    Announcement: H. Richman.
Scene 14
  "A Real American Tune"
    H. Richman

---
[5]Dropped for subsequent tour.

Hall of Fame: *American*: H. Richman. *Foreigner*: W. Howard. *Ave Maria
Tableau*: W. O'Neal. *Gypsy Love Song Tableau*: E. Howard. *Evening Star
Tableau*: W. O'Neal. *Kiss Me Again Tableau*: R. Perfect. *March of the Toys
Tableau*: (Company).
    (Victor Herbert Music courtesy of M. Witmark & Sons.)
ACT 2
Scene 1
  "Where You Carved Your Name"
    R. Perfect, W. O'Neal
    (*Assisted by*) L. Eckhart, E. Gernon, G. Lerch, M. , L. McCormick, H. Howe,
    M. Martin, B. Mallory.Slattery
  Dance
    Russell Markert Dancers
Scene 2
  Frances Williams
  ["What a Night for Spooning"
    (*Music and Lyrics by* Ballard Macdonald and Dave Dreyer.)]
Scene 3
  Chicago
    Announcement: Hastings Twins. *The Salesman*: W. Howard. *The Merchant*: E.
    Howard. *The Policeman*: H. Morrissey. *The Nurse*: J. MacCloy. *The Baby*: W.
    Blanche. *First Gunman*: A. Cardinal. *Second Gunman*: J. Carty. *Third Gunman*:
    A. Page.
Scene 4
  "What D'Ya Say?"
    F. Williams, H. Richman
Scene 5
  Willie Howard
Scene 6
  Home Brew
    Mrs. Smiler: F. Williams. *Mr. Smiler*: A. Page. *Mr. Tippler*: H. Richman. *Mrs.
    Tippler*: R. Perfect.
Scene 7
  "Origin of the Tap Dance"
    F. Williams
      Announcement: H. Richman. *Monkey*: G. Lerch. *Cave Girl*: H. Howe.
      Indian: L. Eckhart. *Southern*: M. Martin. *Newsboy*: P. Moseley. *Modern*: L.
      McCormick.
        (a) A. Pennington, T. Patricola. (b) Russell Markert Dancers. (c) Bernice
        and Emily. (d) Ann Pennington, George White Girls.
Scene 8
  "Bums"
    H. Richman, W. Howard, E. Howard, A. Page
Scene 9
  Scandals of 1968
    T. Patricola
Scene 10
  Ransom
    Pedro: J. Carty. *The Girl*: F. Williams. *The Wolf*: H. Richman.
Scene 11
  Welsh Trio
    W. Howard, E. Howard, B. Osborne
    Announcement: Hastings Twins.
Scene 12
  Harry Richman:
  ["King for a Day"
    (*Music by* Ted FioRito. *Lyrics by* Sam M. Lewis and Joe Young.)
  "That's My Mammy"
    (*Music by* Abel Baer. *Lyrics by* Ed. G. Nelson and Harry Pease.)
  "Moonlight Madness"
    (*Music by* J. Fred Coots. *Lyrics by* Lou Davis.)
  "You're the Cream in My Coffee" (from HOLD EVERYTHING)
    (*Music by* Ray Henderson. *Lyrics by* Lew Brown and Buddy G.
    DeSylva.)
  "She's Funny That Way"
    (*Music by* Neil Moret. *Lyrics by* Richard Whiting.)]
Scene 13
  "Stars, Stars, Shining Bright (You May See Future Stars To-night)"
    A. Pennington, F. Williams, R. Perfect, Bernice and Emily, H. Richman,
    T. Patricola, W. O'Neal, Elm City Four, A. Page, All Star Cast, All
    Star Chorus

EARL CARROLL'S VANITIES (1928)

1928.23

A Musical Revue in Two Acts, 47 Scenes[6]. Assembled by Earl Carroll. Sketches by W. C. Fields, Paul Gerard Smith, Joe Frisco, Robert T. Tarrant, Herman Meyer. Music by Morris Hamilton; additional music by George Bagby, G. Romilli, (Michael Cleary, George Whiting, Lou Alter, Mario Savino, Jesse Greer, Ernie Golden, Abner Silver). Lyrics by Grace Henry; (additional lyrics by Paul Jones, Ned Washington, Joe Burke, Ray Klages, Ernie Golden, Jack Le Soir, Roy Doll). Entire production directed by Earl Carroll. Musical numbers staged by Busby Berkeley. Machinery Ballet created and staged by the Marmein Sisters. Dialogue staged by Edgar J. MacGregor. Art and technical direction by Bernard Lohmuller. Settings designed by Hugh Willoughby. Costumes designed by Mabel E. Johnston, William H. Matthews. Musical director, Ray Kavanaugh. Orchestral arrangements by Lang, Anderson and [Kenn] Sisson. Produced by Earl Carroll. Opened 6 August 1928 at the Earl Carroll Theatre and closed 2 February 1929 after 200 performances.

CAST: W. C. FIELDS, RAY DOOLEY, JOE FRISCO, DOROTHY KNAPP, GORDON DOOLEY, MARTHA MORTON, VINCENT LOPEZ AND HIS BAND, Ernest Charles, Beryl Halley, Brian MacDonald, Lillian Roth, Edward Graham, Dorothy Lull, Maurice LaPue, the Vercell Sisters (Katherine, Louise), Joey Ray, Jean Tennyson, (Dewey) Barto and (George) Mann, Naomi Johnson, Ted Bradford, Fay Adler, Richard Bold.

Vanities Girls: Vivian Wilson, Louise Brooks[7], Nelda Kincaid, Marion Harke, Lillian Bond, Florence Ward, Polly Luce, Jean Murray, Violet Arnold, Lillian Bond, Florence Ward, Polly Luce, Jean Murray, Violet Arnold, Edyth Hansen, Dorothea Frank, Bonnie Blackwood, Frances Delacy, Rose Wenzel, Wanda Stevenson, Eileen Wenzel, Peggy Blake, Frances Joyce, Bobbie Storey, Hazel Bailey, Ruth K. Patterson, Peggy Andre, Ruth Kent, Elizabeth Suran, Rita Jason, Peggy Purcell, Elsie Connor, Catherine Clark, Faith Bacon, Dana Merrill, Alyce Johnson, Angeline Hassell, Diana White, Blanche Satchel, Marion O'Day, Dorothy Britton, Marion Carewe.

ACT 1[8]

Scene 1

Opening Chorus[9]

    Vincent Lopez and His Band
    (*Music by* Morris Hamilton. *Lyrics by* Grace Henry.)

Scene 2

"Say It With Girls"

    16 Vanities Girls
    V. Wilson (Miss Lansing), L. Brooks (Miss Boston), M. Mackay, M. Harcke, J. Schally (Miss Paris), L. Bond (Miss England), F. Ward, B. Blackwood (Miss Oklahoma), N. Kincaid (Miss Birmingham), V. Arnold (Miss New Jersey), E. Britton, D. Frank, M. O'Day (Miss Irvington), F. DeLacey (Miss Queens), R. Wenzel, W. Stevenson (Miss Washington).
    (*Music by* Morris Hamilton. *Lyrics by* Grace Henry.)
      Introducing Vanities Votaphonevitotone Movies (Effect created by Max Teuber.)
      With glorious enlargements of E. Wenzel, A. Hassell, F. Joyce, K. Krosby, D. Britton, R. K. Patterson.

Scene 3

"Pretty Girl"

    N. Golden

---

[6]The sixth in the annual series of musical revues presented by Earl Carroll beginning in 1923.

[7]Not the well-known film star of the same name.

[8]Added for subsequent national tour:

  Fish Story (Act 1)
    A Love Child: Al Bennett. *His Friend:* Ben Blue.
  The Checker Player (Act 1)
    First Player: Joe Bennett. *Second Player:* John Bennett. *A Kibitzer:* W. C. Fields.
  Minuet" (Act 1)
    Pat Henry, B. Blue, Bennett Boys, Dorothy Barton, Vivian Wilson, Elsie Connor, Rita Kerwin
    (*Lyric by* Edward P. Diamond.)
  A Whisper Low (Act 2)
    First Drunk: A. Bennett. *Second Drunk:* John Bennett. *Third Drunk:* Joe Bennett. *A Barkeep:* B. Blue.
  It Happens Everyplace (Act 2)
    Mr. Kokomo: B. Blue. *An Officer:* J. Raye. *The Peanut Vendor:* W. C. Fields.
  On the Links (Act 2)
    The Golfer: W. C. Fields. *The Caddy:* A. Bennett. *The Lady:* D. Britton.

[9]Dropped for subsequent tour.

    (*Music by* Morris Hamilton. *Lyrics by* Grace Henry.)
    Yellow Roses: Evelyn Crowell (Miss Orange, New Jersey), Peggy Andre, Vanita Carol (Miss Denmark), Elizabeth Suran, Peggy Purcell, Elsie Connor (Miss Cleveland), Catherine Clark (Miss Bronx), Faith Bacon, Dana Merrill (Miss Deauville), Alyce Johnstone (Miss Long Beach), Angeline Hassell (Miss Pittsburgh), Jean Murray (Miss Toronto), Dorothy Britton (Miss Universe).

Scene 4

"Garden of Beautiful Girls"

    (*Entire scene, {music, lyrics} written by* George Bagby and G. Romilli.)
    First Rose: B. Satchel (Miss Australia). *Second Rose:* E. Wenzel (Miss St. Louis).

"Tell Me Truly"

    C. Hanneford
    Third Rose: M. Carewe. *Fourth Rose:* F. Joyce (Miss San Francisco).

"The Dryad"

    N. Golden
    Fifth Rose: D. White (Miss Louisiana). *Sixth Rose:* K. Krosby (Miss Alaska).

"Forever Mine"

    F. Zimmock

"Pretty Girl" (reprise)

    B. McDonald

Scene 5

The Pillar of Fame

"Rose of the World"

    B. McDonald
    (*Music by* Morris Hamilton. *Lyrics by* Grace Henry.)
    The White Rose (Miss New York Prize Winner Atlantic City Beauty Pageant): R. K. Patterson. *The Form Divine:* B. Halley.

Scene 6

The Dance Marathon

    Scene: Madison Square Garden.
    Promoter: E. Graham. *Couple 77:* M. Morton, G. Dooley. *Couple 45:* L. Vercell, J. Ray. *Couple 41:* F. Adler, T. Bradford. *Couple 63:* D. Lull, D. Barto. *Couple 94:* N. Johnson, M. LaPue. *Couple 26:* K. Vercell, R. Bold.

Scene 7

"Vaniteaser"

    L. Roth
    (*Music by* Michael H. Cleary. *Lyrics by* Paul Jones.)
    Introducing The 32 Vaniteaser Dancers.

Scene 8

"Getting (the) Beautiful Girls"

    J. Frisco
    (*Music by* Michael H. Cleary. *Lyrics by* Ned Washington.)
    Assisted by America's Star Beauties: B. Satchel, E. Wenzel, K. Krosby, F. Joyce, R. K. Patterson, D. Britton.

Scene 9

Stolen Bonds (*by* W. C. Fields)

    Scene: The Snavely Cabin on a cold night.
    Chief Big Spear: E. Graham. *Little Small Blanket:* R. Bold. *Snavely:* W. C. Fields. *Mrs. Snavely:* R. Dooley. *Chester:* J. Ray.

Scene 10

Specialty[10]

    Barto and Mann

Scene 11

"Raquel"

    B. McDonald
    (*Music by* Joseph Burke. *Lyrics by* George Whiting.)
    Chiquita: N. Johnson.
      Introducing Dorothy Knapp, the Most Beautiful Girl in the World

"Raquel Tango"

    D. Knapp, M. LaPue
    (*Music by* Morris Hamilton. *Lyrics by* Grace Henry.)
    The Jeweled Curtain of Raquel

Scene 12

Dance

    Vercell Sisters

"Tell Me Truly" (reprise)

    (*Music and Lyrics by* G. Romilli.)

---

[10]Dropped for subsequent tour.

Scene 13

Mrs. Hubbard's Cupboard

Mrs. Hubbard: M. Morton. *Mr. Hubbard*: W. C. Fields. *Baby Hubbard*: R. Dooley. *Mr. Whoopee*: G. Dooley.

Scene 14

Red and Silver: "My Arms Are Open"[11]

J. Ray

(*Music by* Michael H. Cleary. *Lyrics by* Ned Washington.)

Scene 15

The Tassel Curtain, introducing the Double Dozen Tassellettes

Scene 16

Turquoise and Silver: Slow Control Dance

D. Lull

Introducing the New Venetian Waltz

"Gliding Gondola"

(*Music and Lyrics by* George Bagby.)

Scene 17

Long Distance (*by* Joe Frisco)

Scene: Carlton Hotel, Washington.

Percentage Sam Collins: J. Frisco. *Joey Blake*: J. Ray. *Tillie*: R. Dooley.

Scene 18

The Caledonian Express (*by* W. C. Fields)

Lord Derby: G. Dooley. *Porter*: E. Graham. *Breeze*: J. Frisco. *The Guard*: W. C. Fields. *The Conductor*: W. C. Fields. *The Station Master*: W. C. Fields. *The Policeman*: W. C. Fields.

Scene 19

"Flutterby Baby"

L. Roth

(*Music by* Morris Hamilton. *Lyrics by* Grace Henry.)

Scene 20

The Butterfly and the Spider[12] (Introducing F. Adler and T. Bradford)

The Butterfly: F. Adler. *The Faun*: T. Bradford. *The Spider*: M. LaPue.

Scene 21

The Female Impersonator: Helen Morgan[13]J. Frisco

Announcement: B. McDonald.

Scene 22

The Casual Meeting[14] (*by* Thomas R. Tarrant)

Interpolator: J. Frisco.

1878: *Elsie Dinsmore*: D. Knapp. *Bella Della*: N. Johnson.

1928: *Margie*: L. Roth. *Babe*: B. Halley.

Scene 23

All Aboard (*by* Thomas R. Tarrant)

Scene: Cabin on the *S. S. Paris*.

George: W. C. Fields. *Josephine*: D. Knapp.

Scene 24

"Blue Shadows"

J. Ray

(*Music by* Lou Alter. *Lyrics by* Ray Klages.)

A Shade of Blue: B. Halley. *Mythology*: N. Johnson.

Scene 25

The Portals of Mythology

Song

L. Roth

(*Music and Lyrics by* Lou Alter, Mario Savino, Grace Henry.)

Goddesses in Blue

Introductions: J. Ray. *Fiora*: D. White. *Psyche*: D. Britton. *The Muses: Fortuna*: E. Crowell. *Irene*: J. Murray. Misses E. Suran, D. Merrill, A. Johnstone, A. Hassell, E. Connor, P. Andre, P. Purcell, M. Carewe, C. Clarke.

Scene 26

The Curtain of Gold

Scene 27

The Temple of Mythology

Introductions: B. McDonald. *Iris*: B. Satchel. *Vesta*: F. Joyce. *Aurora*: R. K. Patterson. *Minerva*: E. Wenzel. *Diana*: K. Krosby. *Juno*: F. Bacon. *Venus*: D. Knapp. *Grecian Dancers*: W. Stevenson, F. Ward, B. Blackwood, F. DeLacy, D. Frank, L. Bond, M. Harke, M. O'Day, V. Arnold, L. Brooks, V. Carol, R. Wenzel, N. Kincaid, G. Schoener, M. Mackay, J. Schally, E. Britton, V. WIlson.

Scene 28

The Flaming Deity

B. Halley

(*Effect created by* George Hanlon.)

Scene 29

Finale:

"Blue Shadows" (reprise)

(*German Silver Scenery created by* Hugh Willoughby.)

ACT 2

Scene 1

The Gates of the Foundry:

"Wheels"J. Ray, N. Johnson

(*Music by* Morris Hamilton. *Lyrics by* Grace Henry.)

Scene 2

Machinery Ballet

D. Lull, E. Graham, F. Adler and T. Bradford, Vanities Girls

(*Created and staged by* The Marmeins.)

This scene was inspired by a visit to a large automobile plant, and is the first serious attempt to present a modernistic ballet in a revue.

Scene 3

Specialty:

L. Roth

"Oh How That Man Can Love"

(*Music and Lyrics by* Lillian Roth and Herb Magidson.)

"Watch My Baby Walk"

(*Music by* Peter DeRose. *Lyrics by* Jo Trent.)

Scene 4

School Belles[15]

F. Joyce, B. Satchel, K. Krosby, E. Wenzel, R. K. Patterson

Scene 5

School Days[16] (*by* W. C. Fields)

Scene: The School Room.

Teacher: M. Morton. *First Reader*: J. Ray. *Second Reader*: G. Dooley. *Third Reader*: W. C. Fields.

Scene 6

"Once in a Lifetime"

B. McDonald

(*Music by* Jesse Greer. *Lyrics by* Raymond Klages.)

His Little Sister: N. Johnson.

Introducing the Feather and Diamond Girls, and Dorothy Knapp

Valse Blondes-Brunette: Vercell Sisters, M. LaPue.

"Gliding Gondola" (reprise)

Scene 7

The Curtain of Brilliants and Plumes

Scene 8

Specialty[17]

J. Frisco

Scene 9

The Mormon's Prayer (*by* Herman Meyer)

Brigham Young: W. C. Fields. *Wives*: B. Halley, Vercell Sisters, B. Satchel, A. Hassell, Murray, V. Wilson. *Brides*: R. K. Patterson, F. Joyce, E. Wenzel, K. Krosby, M. Carewe, D. Britton.

Scene 10

"Painting a Vanities Girl"[18]

R. Bold, M. LaPue, J. Ray, E. Graham, T. Bradford, B. McDonald

(*Music and Lyrics by* Ernie Golden and Grace Henry.)

---

[11]For subsequent tour, replaced by:

"Fascinating You" (simultaneously used in EARL CARROLL'S SKETCHBOOK-1929)

J. Ray

(*Music and Lyrics by* Charles Tobias, Harry Tobias and Vincent Rose.)

[12]Dropped for subsequent tour.

[13]Dropped for subsequent tour.

[14]Dropped for subsequent tour.

[15]Dropped for subsequent tour.

[16]Dropped for subsequent tour.

[17]Dropped for subsequent tour.

[18]Dropped for subsequent tour.

Scene 11

Marilyn Eaton[19]

R. Dooley

Scene 12

"I'm Flyin' High"

L. Roth

(*Music and Lyrics by* Abner Silver, Jack LeSoir and Ray Doll.)

Specialty

D. Lull

Scene 13

On the Orchestralift[20]

Vincent Lopez and His Band

["Blue Shadows," "Once in a Lifetime"]

Scene 14

Specialty[21]

Barto and Mann

Scene 15

An Episode at the Dentist's (*by* W. C. Fields)

Scene: Dr. Pain's Office.

Dr. Pain: W. C. Fields. *Gene Farrell*: B. McDonald. *Nurse*: M. Morton. *Mr. Benford*: E. Graham. *Mr. Foliage*: G. Dooley. *Miss Minkey*: R. Dooley. *Miss Doodab*: D. Knapp.

Scene 16

"The Collegiate Vaniteaser"

L. Roth, J. Ray

(*Music by* Michael H. Cleary. *Lyrics by* Paul Jones.)

Scene 17

The Curtain of Plumes

Scene 18

Grand Finale

Entire Company

1928.24

THE SONG WRITER

A Play in Three Acts, 4 Scenes. Play by Crane Wilbur. Music and lyrics by Phil Baker, Sid Silvers, Abner Silver and Georgie Price. Settings by (William) Oden Waller. Staged by Alexander Leftwich. Produced by Alexander Yokel. Opened 13 August 1928 at the 48th Street Theatre and closed 29 September 1928 after 56 performances.

CAST (in order of speaking): *Ruth Sabath*: BEATRICE BLINN. *Joe*, a Porter: F. A. Walton. *Fanny Kaye*: Ethel Wilson. *Andy Little*: Neil Pratt. *David Bernard*: GEORGIE PRICE. *Patricia Thayer*: MAYO METHOT. *Willie Abrams*: Irving Hirsch. *Belle Ryan*: Marian Winston. *Dolly Ryan*: Bea Thrift. *Benny Hart*: Robert Sinclair. *Mrs. Bernard*: JENNIE MOSCOWITZ. *J. Rodman Peck*: HUGH HUNTLEY.

ACT 1, *Scene 1*: The Star Rehearsal Room of the Bernstein Music Publishing Company. New York City, June. *Scene 2*: The same. Next day.

ACT 2: J. Rodman Peck's Apartment in the Hotel Berwyck. August.

ACT 3: The Bernard Apartment. The following June.

ACT 1

"You Are My Heaven"

G. Price

(*Music by* Georgie Price. *Lyrics by* Herb Magidson.)

"(Sing Me a) Song of the South"

G. Price

(*Music by* Georgie Price. *Lyrics by* Abner Silver.)

ACT 2

"You're Gone"

G. Price

(*Music by* Georgie Price. *Lyrics by* Phil Baker and Sid Silvers.)

1928.25

GOOD BOY

A Musical Play in Two Acts, 32 Scenes. Book by Otto Harbach, Oscar Hammerstein II and Henry Myers. Music and lyrics by Herbert Stothart, Bert Kalmar and Harry Ruby. Book staged by Reginald Hammerstein. Dances staged by Busby Berkeley. Stage settings designed by John Wenger. Mechanical and treadmill effects by Peter Clark, Inc. and Edward Dolan. Costumes designed by Mark Mooring. Orchestra under the direction of Herbert Stothart. Produced by Arthur Hammerstein. Opened 5 September 1928 at the Hammerstein Theatre and closed 13 April 1929 after 253 performances.

CAST: *Pa Meakin*: SAM HEARN. *Ma Meakin*: EFFIE SHANNON. *Elvira Hobbs*: EVELYN BENNETT. *Cicero Meakin*: CHARLES BUTTERWORTH. *Walter Meakin*: EDDIE BUZZELL. *Pansy McManus*: HELEN KANE. *A. A. Stone*: Lester Bernard. *"New York"*: Ariel Millars. *Manhattan*: Milton Douglass. *Betty Summers*: BARBARA NEWBERRY. *Bobby D'Arnell*: DAN HEALY. *Jimmie*: BORRAH MINEVITCH. *Policeman*: Dick Neely. *Brakeman*: Stan Rock. *Ticket Speculator*: Joseph Ames. *Movie Doorman*: Neil Stone. *Old Lady*: Elsie Percival. *A Grafter*: Gus Quinlan. *Miss Badger*: Virginia Case. *Hotel Clerk*: Jack O'Hare. *First Bellboy*: Tom Martin. *Second Bellboy*: Arthur Sullivan. *Elevator Boy*: Gordon Merrit. *Trevor*: Austin Clark. *Pawnbroker*: Morris Tepper. *Justice of the Peace*: Joseph Ames. *License Clerk*: Bob Abbott. *Landlady*: Muriel Greel. *Theatre Doorman*: Neil Stone. *Theatre Treasurer*: William Meek. *Theatregoer*: Phil Daly. *His Girl Friend*: Louise Blakeley. *Street Cleaner*: Howard Raymond. *Gob*: Henry Corsell. *A Frail*: Jean Unger. *Dago*: Will Withe.

Members of the Chorus: Louise Allen, Alice Akers, Mary Bay, Louise Blakeley, Lillian Burke, Margaret Callan, Irene Carroll, Virginia Case, Georgette Caryl, Billie Cortez, Sylvia Collinson, Betty Croke, Ruth Cunliffe, Peggy Driscoll, Madeliene Eubanks, Jeanne Fayal, Rosemary Farmer, Loretta Flushing, Muriel Greel, Beryl Golden, Bobby Gorman, Muriel Griswold, Buddy Haines, Dorothy Jocelyn, Aida Conkey, Olive Kenyon, Grace LaRue[22], Mildred Lorain, Ruth Mason, Lucille Mercier, Delores Nito, Mabel Olsen, Alice Raisen, Helen McGlyn, Boo Phelps, Bunny Schumm, Jean Unger, Betty Wright, Flo Whyte, Kay Wolf, Dorothy Ward, Robert Abbott, Henry Corsell, Austin Clark, Arthur Craig, Edwin Gaillard, Jack Irwin, Ned Lynn, Gordon Merrick, Tom Martin, Dick Neely, Gus Quinlan, Howard Raymond, Neil Stone, Morris Tepper.

ACT 1, *Scene 1*: Outside the Meakin Farmhouse, Butlersville, Arkansas. *Scene 2*: Section 10 of "The Arkansas Flyer." *Scene 3*: The Bow of the New Jersey-New York Ferry. *Scene 4*: The Skyline of New York. *Scene 5*: Broadway, (a) 23rd Street, (b) 28th Street, (c) 31st Street, (d) 34th Street, (e) 39th Street, (f) 43rd Street, (g) 48th Street, (h) 53rd Street, (i) 66th Street, (j) Outside the Paramount Theatre. *Scene 6*: Upper Broadway. *Scene 7*: Outside of a Boardinghouse. *Scene 8*: On the Street. *Scene 9*: On the Street. *Scene 10*: Interior of Meakin Home in Butlerville. *Scene 11*: The Stage of a Theatre. *Scene 12*: A Taxicab. *Scene 13*: A Hotel Entrance. *Scene 14*: Corridor of the Hotel. *Scene 15*: A Hotel Suite. *Scene 16*: A Balcony.

ACT 2, *Scene 1*: The Meakin Home. *Scene 2*: Wally's Wedding (as Ma Imagines It). *Scene 3*: A Country Road. *Scene 4*: A Pawn Shop. *Scene 5*: License Bureau. *Scene 6*: A Justice of the Peace. *Scene 7*: Betty's Room. *Scene 8*: Telephone Pay Station. *Scene 9*: A Street. *Scene 10*: A Theatre Lobby. *Scene 11*: The Stage. *Scene 12*: Cellar of the Boys' Club. *Scene 13*: Peacock Alley. *Scene 14*: Hotel Lobby. *Scene 15*: A Hotel Bedroom. *Scene 16*: Fantasia.

ACT 1[23]

Scene 1

Opening ("Down in Arkansas")

S. Hearn, Girls

"What Makes You So Wonderful?"

E. Bennett, C. Butterworth

"Good Boy"

E. Shannon, E. Buzzell

Finaletto

Ensemble

Scene 5

"Voice of the City"

A. Millars, M. Douglass, Gyps that Pass in the Night (Chorus)

Scene 6

"Manhattan Walk"

D. Healy, B. Newberry

Scene 8

"Some Sweet Someone"

E. Buzzell, B. Newberry

---

[19]Burlesque on Marilyn Miller and Mary Eaton. Dropped for subsequent tour.

[20]Dropped for subsequent tour.

[21]Dropped for subsequent tour.

[22]Not the famous musical star of the 1910s.

[23]Added in March 1929:

"Oh Promise Me" (Act 2, before Wedding March)

George Djimos (Choir Singer)

Scene 10

"I Have My Moments"

S. Hearn, E. Bennett, C. Butterworth

Scene 11

"I Wanna Be Loved By You"

H. Kane, D. Healy

Scene 13

"Some Sweet Someone" (reprise)

E. Buzzell, B. Newberry

Scene 14

"The Three Bears"[24]

H. Kane, B. Minevitch

Scene 15

"Oh, What a Man"[25]

Danced by D. Healy

Scene 16

Finale

E. Buzzell, B. Newberry

ACT 2

Scene 1

"Voice of the City" (reprise)

M. Douglass

Scene 2

"Good Boy Wedding March"

Ensemble

Scene 7

"Nina"

B. Newberry, Girls

Scene 11

Specialty

B. Minevitch and His Gang

Scene 14

"I Wanna Be Loved By You" (reprise)

H. Kane, D. Healy, S. Hearn, E. Shannon, E. Bennett

Scene 16

Fantasia

E. Buzzell, B. Newberry, Ensemble

1928.26

WHITE LILACS

A Romance with Music (Operetta) in Three Acts. (Original German) Book ('Chopin') by Sigurd Johannsen[26], based on the life of Frédéric Chopin. Music by Karl Hajos [Károly Hájos] from melodies by Frédéric Chopin. (English) Book and lyrics by Harry B. Smith. (Book) Staged by George Marion. Ensembles staged by Vaughn Godfrey. Settings by Rollo Wayne. Costumes designed by Barbier and Ernest Schrapps. Maurice dePackh Symphony Orchestra under the direction of Pierre deReeder. Entire production under the personal supervision of J. J. Shubert. Produced by the Messrs. Shubert. Opened 10 September 1928 at the Sam S. Shubert Theatre, moved 8 October 1928 to Jolson's Theatre, and closed 12 January 1929 after 136 performances.

<u>CAST</u> (in order of appearance): *Countess D'Agoult*: CHARLOTTE WOODRUFF. *Prince Obelenski*: Frank Horn. *Delphine Potocka*: GRACE BRINKLEY. *Gaston de Flavigny*: MAURICE HOLLAND. *Heinrich Heine*: ERNEST LAWFORD. *Giacomo Meyerbeer*: Charles Croker-King. *Dubusson*: DeWOLF HOPPER. *Madame George Sand*: ODETTE MYRTIL. *Frédéric Chopin*: GUY ROBERTSON. *Luselle*: ALLAN

[24]In November, replaced by:

"Don't Be Like That"

H. Kane

(*Music and Lyrics* by Archie Gottler, Maceo Pinkard and Charles Tobias.)

[25]In November, replaced by:

"Let's Give a Cheer"

[26]In his Encyclopedia of The Musical Theatre (Blackwell, 1994), Kurt Gänzl credits the Hungarian musical play ('Chopin') by Jenö Faragó and István Bertha as this production's source.

ROGERS. *Balzac*: Franklin Van Horn. *Mademoiselle Taglioni*: EVA MASCAGNO. *Louison*: Melba Alter. *Franz Liszt*: Vernon Rudolph. *Catherine*: Louise Beaudet. *Marquise de Nemours*: Phyllis Newkirk. *Juanita*: Juanita. *Paco*: Paco. *Trio*: Charlotte Woodruff, Melba Alter, Phyllis Newkirk.

Ladies of the Ensemble: Helen Page, Louise Randolph, Vivian Lynn, Dora Zommerowna, Edna Stark, Dorothy Forsythe, Diana Doering, Helen Bishop, Mae Golding, Eliz Ferguson, Catherine Allen, Madeline Clancy. *Gentlemen of the Ensemble*: Phil Reep, Douglas Vincent, John Campbell, Frank Weiner, Wallace Magill, Steven McNulty, William Hall, Edwin Drake, William Demorest, Frank Horn, Vernon Rudolph.

The action takes place in France in 1840.

ACT 1: The Fragonard Room in the Countess D'Agoult's House, Paris.

ACT 2: The Gardens at George Sand's Villa, on the Island of Majorca. A month later.

ACT 3: Chopin's Studio in Paris.

ACT 1

"The Music Call" (Opening)

C. Woodruff, Guests

"Adorable You"

G. Brinkley, M. Holland

(*Music by* Maurie Rubens. *Lyrics by* David Goldberg.)

"Words, Music, Cash"

D. Hopper, E. Lawford, C. Croker-King

"I Love Love"

O. Myrtil, Ensemble

"White Lilacs"

G. Robertson, G. Brinkley

(*Lyrics by* J. Keirn Brennan.)

"Far Away and Long Ago"

O. Myrtil, G. Robertson

"Inspiration"[27] (Quartette)

G. Robertson, Trio

"Star in the Twilight"

A. Rogers, Quartette

Ballet[28]

E. Mascagno

Finale

Entire Company

ACT 2

Opening:

"Harvest Moon," "Dance of Majorca,"[29] "Tarantella"[30]

Juanita, Paco, Ensemble

"Melodies Within My Heart"[31]

O. Myrtil, G. Robertson

"Know When to Smile"

O. Myrtil, Girls

"(Our) Castle of Love"

G. Brinkley, M. Holland

(*Music by* Sammy Timberg.)

"I Love You, I Adore You"

A. Rogers, O. Myrtil

Finale

ACT 3

Chopin's "A-Flat Polonaise"

G. Robertson, Ensemble

"White Lilacs" (reprise)

G. Robertson

"Be Happy in Your Dreams"

G. Robertson, O. Myrtil

Nocturnes (with Violin Solo)

O. Myrtil

Finale

[27]Dropped for subsequent national tour.

[28]Dropped for subsequent national tour.

[29]Dropped for subsequent national tour.

[30]Dropped for subsequent national tour.

[31]Dropped for subsequent national tour.

LUCKEE GIRL

1928.27

A Musical Comedy in Three Acts and a Prologue. Book by Gertrude Purcell, based on the French operette "Un Bon Garçon" by André Barde. Music by Maurice Yvain. Lyrics by Max Lief and Nathaniel Lief. Staged by Lew Morton. Dances and ensembles by Harry Puck. Dances by Kelley Dancers arranged by Marie Kelley. Settings designed by Watson Barratt. Costumes designed by Ernest Schrapps. Orchestra under the direction of Earl Busby. Produced by the Messrs. Shubert. Opened 15 September 1928 at the Casino Theatre, moved 29 October 1928 to the Sam H. Harris Theatre, and closed 24 November 1928 after 81 performances.

CAST (in order of appearance): *Arlette*, a Midinette: IRENE DUNNE. *Colette*, a Model: Flo Perry. *Man*: Clifford Smith. *Lucien deGravere*, a Young Law Student: IRVING FISHER. *Tampon*, an Artist: LOU POWERS. *Lulu*, Dancer at Coco's: GERTRUDE McGUSHION. *Lili*, Dancer at Coco's: DOROTHY McGUSHION. *Celina*, a Cashier at Coco's: DOROTHY BARBER. *Pontavès*, a Lawyer: FRANK LALOR. *Hercules*, a Waiter at Coco's: BILLY HOUSE. *Camille*, Mme. Falloux's Daughter: DORIS VINTON. *Madame Falloux*, a Provincial Widow: JOSEPHINE DRAKE. *Jean*, Mme. Falloux's Servant: Clifford Smith. *Paul Pechard*, Nephew of Pontavès: HARRY PUCK. *Madame Pontavès*, Pontavès' Wife: Lorraine Weimar. *deGravere*, Lucien's Father: Harold Vizard. *Four Diplomats*: Andy Hamilton, Lenny Nelson, Johnny Ferrara, Hal Saliers. (*Specialty*: Ayres, Malinoff and Rasche.)

Kelley Dancers: Dorothy Kirtley, Lucille Leverich, Georgia O'Brien, Thelma Dye, Evelyn Carpenter, Elizabeth Whitehead, Albertina Rexroth, Carmen Morales, Helen Hackbarth, Frances Stevens, Mildred Lyons, Virginia Cartlich. *Showgirls*: Neva Lynn, Elena Meade, Viola Paulson, Jinny Evans, Roberta Parnell, Betty Montgomery, Julia Barker, Kay Simmons, Malease Bisland. *Boys*: Harry Phelps, Dan Berrigan, Ted Clarke, Larry Rockwell, Edward Brown, Billy Skinner, Don Cortez, Charles Baker.

Time: The Present.

Prologue: Rue Pigalle, Montmartre, outside Coco's, Paris.

ACT 1: Private Room at Coco's. Six months later.

ACT 2: Drawing Room in Madame Falloux's house in the Provinces. Afternoon of next day.

ACT 3: Garden outside Madame Falloux's. Afternoon a week later.

PROLOGUE
"A Flat in Montmartre"
    I. Dunne, I. Fisher

ACT 1
"If You'd Be Happy, Don't Fall in Love" (Opening)
    L. Powers, F. Perry, 4 Diplomats, Kelley Dancers, Boys, Girls
"When I'm in Paree"
    F. Lalor, G. McGushion, D. McGushion, 4 Diplomats, Kelley Dancers, Boys, Girls
"I Love You So"
    I. Dunne, I. Fisher
"Hold Your Man"D. Barber, G. McGushion, D. McGushion, Kelley Dancers, Boys, Girls
"A Good Old Egg"
    B. House, 4 Diplomats, Kelley Dancers, Boys, Girls
"A Flat in Montmartre"[32] (reprise)
    I. Dunne, I. Fisher
"I Love You So" (reprise)
    I. Dunne
"I'll Take You to the Country" (Finale)
    B. House, G. McGushion, D. McGushion, F. Perry, L. Powers, I. Dunne, Kelley Dancers, Boys, Girls

ACT 2
"Facts of Life" (Opening)
    D. Vinton, Kelley Dancers, Girls
"Wild About Music"
    H. Puck, Kelley Dancers, Boys, Girls
"Chiffon"
    I. Dunne, D. Vinton
"I Hate You"[33]
    I. Dunne, I. Fisher

"Come on Let's Make Whoopee"[34]
    B. House, Kelley Dancers, Boys, Girls
    (*Music by* Werner Janssen. *Lyrics by* Mann Holiner.)
"Magic Melody"
    I. Dunne, H. Puck, 4 Diplomats, Kelley Dancers, Boys, Girls
Finale
    L. Powers, I. Fisher, B. House, I. Dunne, J. Drake, B. House, L. Weimar, F. Lalor, D. Barber, Kelley Dancers, Boys, Girls

ACT 3
Opening—Ballet
    Kelley Dancers
(Specialty)
    Ayres, Malinoff and Rasche
"Friends and Lovers"
    H. Puck, I. Dunne, 4 Diplomats, Kelley Dancers, Boys, Girls
"Bad Girl"
    D. Vinton
"Come On Let's Make Whoopee"[35] (reprise)
    B. House
Finale
    Entire Company

CROSS MY HEART

1928.28

A Musical Comedy in Two Acts, 10 Scenes. Book by Daniel Kusell. Music by Harry Tierney. Lyrics by Joseph McCarthy. Book staged by John Harwood. Dances staged by Sammy Lee. Settings by P. Dodd Ackerman. Costumes designed by Mabel E. Johnston. Orchestra under the direction of Louis Gress. Orchestrations by Maurice dePackh. Entire production staged under the personal direction of Sammy Lee. Produced by Sammy Lee. Opened 17 September 1928 at the Knickerbocker Theatre and closed 10 November 1928 after 64 performances.

CAST (in order of appearance): *Charles Graham*: BOBBY WATSON. *Mrs. T. Montgomery Gobble*: LULU McCONNELL. *Elsie Gobble*, Her Daughter: DORIS EATON. *Sally Blake*, a Niece: MARY LAWLOR. *The Maharajah of Mah-ha*: EDDY CONRAD. *Maxie Squeeze*, the Rajah's Attendant: HARRY EVANS. *Richard Todd*: CLARENCE NORDSTROM. *Irene, Elvira, Rae*: The Three Giersdorf Sisters (Irene, Elvira, Rae). *Tommy Fitzgerald*: Franklyn Ardell. *Marie*, a Maid: Arvil Avery. *Beatrice Van Ness*, Richard's Sister: Amy Atkinson. *Cigarette Girl*: Edith Martin. *A Guest Artiste*: CHARLES PETERS. *Bennett*, a Detective: Martin LeRoy. *Finnie*, Maxie's Girl Friend: Dorothy Bow. *Specialty Dancers*: Bob Gilbert, Arvil Avery. Edgar Fairchild and Ralph Rainger and Their Brunswick Recording Orchestra.

The Ten Little Tappers: Geneva Duker, Topsy Humphrey, Cora Stephens, Ann Brown, Bobbe Campbell, Anna Rex, Frances Stone, Dorothy Patterson, Dorothy Bow, Joey Benton. *The Slave Girls*: Marie Marceline, Ona Hamilton, Ruth Savoy Miller, Billie Drews, Genevieve Kent, Gracie Fleming, Nesha Medwin, Beth Holt, Muriel Moore, Madeleine Janis. *Those from Park Avenue*: Florence Murray, Peggy Udell, Antoinette Boots, Lillian Lamonte, Wynn Terry, Harriet Ingersoll, Helene Gardner, Ann Ayres, Elsie Pedrick, Helen Hermes, Dan Sparks, Warren Crosby, Jerry White, Charles McClelland, Bill Antonius, Dowell Brown, Hal Clyne, Wilburne Riviere, Bernard Hassert, Stanley Lewis.

The Action takes place during the afternoon and evening of a day in the early autumn.

:ACT 1,*Scene 1*: The Living Room in Mrs. T. Montgomery Gobble's Home. *Scene 2*: Gramercy Park, New York. *Scene 3*: The Living Room. Sally Forgets to Cross Her Heart. *Scene 4*: Gramercy Park, New York. *Scene 5*: Elsie's Boudoir. *Scene 6*: Entrance to the Slave Ship Café, Greenwich Village. *Scene 7*: The Slave Ship Café.

ACT 2: The Next Evening. *Scene 1*: The Gardens of Mrs. T. Montgomery Gobble's Estate. *Scene 2*: A Corner in the Gardens. *Scene 3*: The Gardens of the Estate.

ACT 1[36]

---

[32]Dropped after opening.
[33]Dropped after opening.

[34]Dropped for subsequent tour and replaced by:
"Slow Down"
    B. House, Kelley Dancers
    (*Music and Lyrics by* Billy House.)
[35]Dropped for subsequent tour and replaced by:
"Laugh the Clouds Away"
    B. House
    (*Music and Lyrics by* Billy House.)
[36]Added during run to Act 1, Scene 3 (after Reception):
"Hot Sands"
    L. McConnell, E. Conrad, B. Gilbert, Ensemble

Scene 1

Opening—

Arrival of Guests
Ensemble

"Step Up and Pep Up the Party"
B. Watson, Ensemble

"Sold"
D. Eaton, B. Watson, Ensemble

"Dream Sweetheart"
M. Lawlor, Her Boy Friends

"Salaaming the Rajah"
L. McConnell, B. Watson, Ensemble

Scene 2

"Right Out of Heaven Into My Arms"
M. Lawlor, C. Nordstrom

Scene 3

Reception
Ensemble

Finaletto
Entire Company

Scene 4

"Right Out of Heaven" (reprise)
M. Lawlor, C. Nordstrom

Scene 5

"Dream Sweetheart" (reprise)
M. Lawlor, D. Eaton

Scene 7

Opening—

"Step Up and Pep Up" (reprise)
Slave Girls

Specialty[37]
The Three Giersdorf Sisters

Specialty
Ten Little Tappers
Whirlwind Dance
B. Gilbert, A. Avery

Finale
Entire Company

ACT 2

Scene 1

Reception to the Maharajah—

Scheherazade Serenade
C. Peters

"In the Garden of Noor-Ed-Deen"
C. Peters, Ensemble

At the Pianos[38]
E. Fairchild, R. Rainger

Adagio
B. Gilbert, A. Avery

"Right Out of Heaven" (reprise)
M. Lawlor, Ensemble

"Come Along, Sunshine"
M. Lawlor, D. Eaton, C. Nordstrom, B. Watson, H. Evans, Ensemble

"Such Is Fame"[39]
L. McConnell, E. Conrad, B. Watson, F. Ardell, H. Evans

"Lady Whipporwill"
C. Nordstrom, M. Lawlor, Ensemble

"Good Days and Bad Days"[40]
L. McConnell, F. Ardell, B. Gilbert, D. Eaton, Ensemble

Scene 3

"Come Along, Sunshine" (reprise)
Entire Company

[37]Dropped after the opening.
[38]Dropped after the opening.
[39]Dropped after the opening.
[40]Dropped after the opening.

"Thanks for a Darn Nice Time" (Finale)
Everybody

1928.29 THE NEW MOON

A Romantic Musical Comedy (Musical Romance) in Two Acts, 12 Scenes. Book and lyrics by Oscar Hammerstein II, Frank Mandel and Laurence Schwab[41]. Music by Sigmund Romberg. Musical numbers staged by Bobby Connolly. Settings by Donald Oenslager. Costumes designed by Charles LeMaire. Orchestrations by Emil Gerstenberger, Alfred Goodman. Orchestra under the direction of Alfred Goodman. Produced by Laurence Schwab and Frank Mandel. Opened 19 September 1928 at the Imperial Theatre, moved 18 November 1929 to the Casino Theatre and closed 14 December 1929 after 509 performances.

CAST {in order of appearance}: *Julie, Marianne's Maid:* MARIE CALLAHAN. *Monsieur Beaunoir, a Ship Owner of New Orleans.* PACIE RIPPLE. *Captain Paul Duval, Commander of "The New Moon":* EDWARD NELL, JR. *Vicomte Ribaud:* MAX FIGMAN. *Robert (Misson), a Bondservant of Beaunoir:* ROBERT HALLIDAY. *Alexander, another Bondservant:* GUS SHY. *Besac, Boatswain of "The New Moon":* LYLE EVANS. *Jacques, a Ship's Carpenter:* Earle Mitchell. *Marianne, Beaunoir's Daughter:* EVELYN HERBERT. *Philippe, a Friend of Robert:* WILLIAM O'NEAL. *Clotilde Lombaste, of the Bride Ship:* ESTHER HOWARD. *Proprietor of the Tavern:* Daniel Barnes. *Flower Girl:* Olga Albani. *A Spaniard:* Herman Belmonte. *A Dancer:* Edith Sheldon. *Fouchette:* Thomas Dale. *The Dancers:* Rosita and Ramon. *The Musicians:* Hernandez Brothers Trio. *Captain Dejean:* Lester Dorr.

Courtiers, Ladies, Pirates, Servants, Sailors, Pirates, etc.: Ensemble: *Ladies:* Elizabeth Taylor, Sylvia LaMarde, Marion Frances, Phyllis Marren, Dulcie Bond, Elmira Lane, Dorothy Verlaine, Barbara Dare, Kay Burnell, Dorothy Christy, Dean Wheeler, Marjorie Sneller, Sylvia Roberts, Beulah Baker, Doddy Donnelly, Constance King, Frances Mildern, Olga Grannis, Rosalie Brumm, Ida Berry, Ruth Grady, Rae Powell, Rosalie Trego, Novella Fromm, Tina Jensen, Helen Casey, Dorothy Higgins, Carola Taylor, Rita Marks, Dorothy Grady, Gloria Lee, Ruth Jennings, Marnie Sawyer, Cecilia Caskey, Christine Morey, Dorice Covert, Gloria Glennon. *Gentlemen:* R. E. Garcia, Edward Smythe, Frank Dowling, Herman Belmonte, Leon Kairoff, Charles Muhs, Lazlo Aliga, Sol Leimas, David DeGrave, Leon Sabater, A. Keller, Basil Prock, Cornell Pilcher, Irving Weinstein, Frank Dobert, Al Monty, Howard Schreiber, Bart Shilling, Arthur Verbowvans, Joe Rogers, Vance Campbell, John Cardini, James Davis, Wallace McLeod, W. M. Rytter, John Gutcher, Ernest McChesney, Sigmund Glukoff, Thomas Coppe, William Prevost, Patrick Henry, George Kirk, Jack Murray, Charles Maynard, Frank Grinnel, T. W. Kendall, Carl Linke, Sverre Rasmussen, Ned Byers, Carl Streib, Frank Vaughn.

ACT 1, *Scene 1*: Grand Salon of Monsieur Beaunoir's Mansion near New Orleans. *Scene 2*: Entrance to Chez Creole. *Scene 3*: Interior of Chez Creole. *Scene 4*: Entrance to Chez Creole. *Scene 5*: Grand Salon of Monsieur Beaunoir's Mansion. Evening, 1788.

ACT 2, *Scene 1*: The Deck of *"The New Moon."* Late afternoon, three days later. *Scene 2*: The Road from the Beach, two days later. *Scene 3*: The Stockade, one year later. *Scene 4*: The Road from the Beach, that evening. *Scene 5*: Marianne's Cabin, that night. *Scene 6*: The Road from the Beach. Midnight. *Scene 7*: The Stockade. Daylight, next morning.

ACT 1

Scene 1

Opening ("Dainty Wisp of a Thistledown")
Ensemble

"Marianne"
R. Halliday

"The Girl on the Prow"
E. Herbert, Ensemble

"Gorgeous Alexander"
M. Callahan, G. Shy, Girls

"An Interrupted Love Song"
E. Nell, E. Herbert, R. Halliday

Scene 3

"Tavern Song" (Red Wine)
O. Albani, E. Sheldon, Ensemble

"Softly, as in a Morning Sunrise"vW. O'Neal, Ensemble

"Stouthearted Men" (Liberty Song)
R. Halliday, W. O'Neal, Men

[41]Uncredited staging by authors Oscar Hammerstein II, Laurence Schwab, Frank Mandel. Program note: The authors wish to state that the basic story of the play is founded on the life of Robert Misson, a French aristocrat whose autobiography was written in the late eighteenth century.

Scene 5

Tango ("Fair Rosita")

(Girls), *Danced by* Rosita, Ramon

"One Kiss"

E. Herbert, Ensemble

"Ladies of the Jury" (The Trial)

G. Shy, M. Callahan, E. Howard, Girls

"Wanting You"

E. Herbert, R. Halliday

Finale

Ensemble

ACT 2

Scene 1

Opening ("A Chanty")

L. Evans, Men

"Funny Little Sailor Man"

E. Howard, L. Evans, Ensemble

"Lover, Come Back to Me"

E. Herbert

Finaletto

E. Herbert, R. Halliday, W. O'Neal, Men

Scene 2

"Love Is Quite a Simple Thing"

E. Howard, L. Evans, G. Shy, M. Callahan

Scene 3

"Try Her Out at Dancing"

G. Shy, M. Callahan, Girls

Scene 4

"Softly, as in a Morning Sunrise"

W. O'Neal, Men

Scene 5

"Never (for You)"

E. Herbert

"Lover, Come Back to Me" (reprise)

R. Halliday, Men

Finaletto

E. Herbert, R. Halliday

Scene 7

Finale

Company

1928.30 ## CHEE-CHEE

A Musical Narrative (Comedy) in Two Acts, 7 Scenes. Book by Herbert Fields. Based on the novel "The Son of the Grand Eunuch" by Charles Pettit. Music by Richard Rodgers. Lyrics by Lorenz Hart. Book staged by Alexander Leftwich. Dances and ensembles staged by Jack Haskell. Settings designed by John F. Hawkins, Jr. Costumes designed by John Booth. Miss Ford's costumes designed by James Reynolds. Orchestrations by Roy Webb. Orchestra under the direction of Roy Webb. Entire production under the personal supervision of Lew Fields. Produced by Lew Fields. Opened 25 September 1928 at the Mansfield Theatre and closed 20 October 1928 after 31 performances.

CAST (in order of appearance): *A Eunuch*: Ralph Glover. *Another*: Alan Lowe. *Prince Tao-Tee*, Son of His Majesty, the Holy Emperor, Son of Heaven: STARK PATTERSON. *Li-Li-Wee*, Daughter of His Excellency the Grand Eunuch: BETTY STARBUCK. *Li-Pi Siao*, the Most Noble and August Grand Eunuch: GEORGE HASSELL. *Miss Smile of a Rose at the Dawning of Spring*: Dorothy Roye. *Li-Pi Tchou*, Son of the Grand Eunuch: WILLIAM WILLIAMS. *Chee-Chee*, His Dutiful Wife: HELEN FORD. *San Toy*: George Ali. *A Very Narrow Minded Owl*: William Griffith. *Innkeeper*: PHILIP LOEB. *The Tartar Chief*: GEORGE HOUSTON. *Leader of Khonghouses*: Marshall Bradford. *Radiance and Felicity*, a Bonze: William Griffith. *Profundity and Meditation*, the Grand Prior: PHILIP LOEB. *Holy Emperor*: Ralph Glover. *Dancing Idols*: Masa Sanami, Violetta Aoki.

Eunuchs, Concubines, Tartars, Khonghouses, Peasants, etc.: *Girls of the Ensemble*: Gloria Rymar, Biddy Boyd, Helen Mirtel, Jean Casewell, Catherine Huth, Ann Mycue, Velma Valentine, Eugenia Reno, Betty Glass, Betty Shirley, Grace Shipp, Marie Felday, Ruby Poe, Evelyn Hannons, Evelyn Kane, Bunny Moore, Urilda Smith, Pauline Hartman, Helen Sheppard. *Gentlemen of the Ensemble*: Gene Byrom, Charles Townsend, Frank White, Robert Davis, Al Birk, Ted White, Jay Lindsey, Paul Jensen,

James Dale, Bob Matthews, Buddy Penny, R. P. Hall, Richardson Brown, George Lehrian, Ted Shultz, Eddie Larkin.

ACT 1, *Scene 1*: A Corridor in the Palace of the Holy Emperor, Son of Heaven, in the Violet Town of Peking. *Scene 2*: The Road to the Future. *Scene 3*: A Wayside Tavern.

ACT 2, *Scene 1*: A Forest. *Scene 2*: Visiting Day at the Monastery of Celestial Clouds. *Scene 3*: The Gallery of Torments. *Scene 4*: The Palace.

ACT 1[42]

"We're Men of Brains"

Eunuchs (Men's Ensemble)

"I Am a Prince"

S. Patterson

"In a Great Big Way"

B. Starbuck

"The Most Majestic of Domestic Officials"

(Entrance of the Grand Eunuch)Ensemble

"Holy of Holies"

G. Hassell, B. Starbuck

"Her Hair Is Black as Licorice" (Food Solo)

G. Hassell

"Dear, Oh Dear"

H. Ford, W. Williams

"Await Your Love" (Concubines' Song)

G. Hassell, D. Raye, Ensemble

"Joy Is Mine"[43]

W. Williams

"I Wake at Morning"

W. Williams

"I Grovel to Earth" (Chee-Chee's First Entrance)

H. Ford

"Just a Little Thing"

W. Williams, H. Ford

"You Are Both Agreed" (Finaletto Scene 1)

G. Hassell, W. Williams, H. Ford

"I Must Love You"

H. Ford, W. Williams

"Owl Song" (Song of the Owl)

W. Griffith

"I Must Love You" (reprise)

"I Bow a Glad Good Day" (Tavern Opening)

P. Loeb, G. Hassell, Ensemble

"Better Be Good to Me"

B. Starbuck, S. Patterson

"The Tartar Song"

G. Houston, Ensemble

Chee-Chee's Second Entrance

(H. Ford)

Finale (Act 1)

ACT 2

"Khonghouse Song"

W. Williams, Ensemble

"Sleep, Weary Head"

H. Ford

"Singing a Love Song"

G. Houston, Ensemble

Monastery Opening

Chinese Dance

"Living Buddha" (Impassive Buddha)

P. Loeb

"Moon of My Delight"

B. Starbuck, S. Patterson

---

[42]No song list appears in the program. Complete song list prepared from "The Complete Lyrics of Lorenz Hart," ed. by Dorothy Hart and Robert Kimball. (Knopf, New York, 1986). Those few which appeared in the program were "Dear, Oh Dear," "I Must Love You," "Better Be Good to Me," "The Tartar Song."

[43]May have been dropped prior to New York opening.

"I Grovel to Your Cloth" (Chee-Chee Third Entrance)
    H. Ford
The Bonze Entrance
    "I Must Love You" (reprise)
"We Are the Horrors of Deadliest Woe"
    Ensemble
"Oh, Gala Day, Red-Letter Day" (Palace Opening)
    Principals, Ensemble
"Farewell, O Life" (Finale Act 2)
    W. Williams, Ensemble

1928.31   BILLIE

An American Musical Play in Two Acts, 7 Scenes. Book, music and lyrics by George M. Cohan, based on his farce "Broadway Jones." Entire production staged by Edward Royce and Sam Forrest. Settings by Joseph Wickes. Costumes designed by Don Frist and Babette DuGuary. Tapestry curtain designed by Ted Weidhaas. Orchestra under the direction of Charles J. Gebest. Orchestral arrangements by Mike Lake. Produced by George M. Cohan. Opened 1 October 1928 at the Erlanger's Theatre and closed 5 January 1929 after 112 performances.

CAST (in order of appearance): *Maid:* JUNE O'DEA. *Rankin:* JOE ROSS. *Bob Wallace:* ROBINSON NEWBOLD. *Jackson Jones:* JOSEPH WAGSTAFF. *Winnie Sheldon:* MARJORIE LANE. *Mrs. Ambrose Gerard:* INA HAYWARD. *Peter Pembroke:* CARL FRANCIS. *Billie:* POLLY WALKER. *Wilbur Cheatington:* ERNIE STANTON. *Sir Alfred Huntington:* VAL STANTON. *Harry Thompson:* DAVID LONDON. *Higgins:* Richard Barry. *Judge Spotswood:* Joseph Kennedy. *Page:* Ethel Allen. *Will:* Billy Bradford. *Marion:* Marion Hamilton. *Charles:* Charles Sabin. *Sheriff:* Larry L. Wood. *Grover Sheldon:* Albert Froom.
    Ladies of the Ensemble: Nancy Trevelyan, Rose Collins, Alice Everling, Juliette Jones, Aura Orleans, Dorothy McKeon, Valerie Galantine, Margie Nugent, Sue Lake, Ilus de Pongo, Mildred Gethins, Helen E. Held, Florence O'Brien, Martha Ann, Dorothy Dion, Geraldine Wells, Marguerite Dunn, Evelyn Laurie, Carolyn James, Ann Loomis, Valerie Dolaro, Kathryn Koehler, Helen Kelly, Erna Kunzin, Bobby Heather, Mildred Hamilton, Micky MacKillop, June Wall, Bernadette Fox, Hazel Maguire, Mae Burke, June Wells, Elinore Heinemann, Dorothy Stratton. *Gentlemen of the Ensemble:* Emmett O'Brien, Robert Vreeland, Leonardo J. Reid, Jack Lazariff, Henry Simon, Murrray, Minehart, Ray Dowley, Harry DuBall, Terrence McIlwine, Walter Blair, Jack Bedford, Basil Hambury, Donald Joy, Jack McElroy, Kendall Northrup, Roland Carpenter. *Ballet Specialty Dancers:* Anita Avila, Gertrude Stanton, Marie Grimaldi, Eddee Belmont, Elvira Gomez, Ruth Love, Mildred Glasson, Martha Galston.

Time: The present.

ACT 1, Scene 1: The New York Home of Jackson Jones. *Scene 2:* Curtains. *Scene 3* The Business Office of the Jones Chewing Gum Plant. *Scene 4:* Exterior of the Plant.

ACT 2, Scene 1: The Gardens of the Jones' Home in Havenford, Connecticut. *Scene 2:* Wilbur Cheatingham's Law Office. *Scene 3:* The New York Home of Jackson Jones.

ACT 1
"New York"
    R. Newbold, J. O'Dea, J. Ross, Ensemble
"Come to St. Thomas's"
    I. Hayward, J. Wagstaff, M. Lane, R. Newbold, Ensemble
"Happy"
    J. Wagstaff, Ensemble
"Billie"
    P. Walker
"Go Home Ev'ry Once in a While"
    P. Walker, Ensemble
"Friends"
    V. Stanton, E. Stanton
"The Cause of the Situation"
    D. London, P. Walker, Ensemble
"Ev'ry Boy in Town's My Sweetheart"
    P. Walker, Male Ensemble
"They Fall in Love"
    M. Lane, D. London, Ensemble
Finaletto
    P. Walker, J. Wagstaff, R. Newbold, C. Francis, I. Hayward, M. Lane, D. London, Ensemble
Dance
    B. Bradford, E. Martin
"Where Were You? (Where Was I?)"
    J. Wagstaff, P. Walker, Ballet

Finale
    P. Walker, J. Wagstaff, R. Newbold, D. London, V. Stanton, E. Stanton, C. Francis, I. Hayward, Ensemble
ACT 2[44]
"The Jones' Family Friends"
    Ensemble
Dance
    J. O'Dea, J. Ross
"One Girl Man"
    J. Wagstaff, M. Lane, R. Newbold, D. London, Ensemble
"Personality"
    P. Walker, Ensemble
Waltz
    P. Walker, C. Sabin
Finaletto
    Entire Company
Dance
    J. Ross
Dance
    Ballet Dancers
Dance[45]
    B. Bradford, M. Hamilton
"Where Were You?" (reprise)
    P. Walker, J. Wagstaff, Ensemble
"Bluff"
    R. Newbold, C. Francis, V. Stanton, E. Stanton, J. O'Dea, J. Wagstaff, D. London, M. Lane, P. Walker, I. Hayward, J. Ross, A. Froom
"The Two of Us"
    M. Lane, D. London, P. Walker, J. Wagstaff
Finale
    Entire Company

1928.32   SUNNY DAYS

A Return Engagement of the Musical Comedy in Three Acts[46]. Book and lyrics by Cliffford Grey and William Cary Duncan. Adapted from the French farce ('A Kiss in a Taxi') by (Maurice) Hennequin and (Pierre) Veber. Music by Jean Schwartz. Additional numbers by Eleanor Dunsmuir. Dances staged by Ralph Reader. Settings designed by Watson Barratt. Orchestra under the direction of Leon Rosebrok. Produced by Montmartre Productions, Inc. Opened 1 October 1928 at the Century Theatre and closed 27 October 1928 after 32 performances.

CAST (in order of appearance): *Victor Duval,* Owner of Duval's Florist Shop: Bob Lively. *Nanine:* Elyse La Deaux. *Babette:* Elsie Elliott. *Georgette:* Phoebe Wallace. *Angele Larue:* Ruth Lockwood. *Ginette Bertin:* MILDRED KEATS. *Maurice Vane:* JACK SHEEHAN. *Leon Dorsay,* President of Dorsay et Cie., Bankers: DOUGLAS LEAVITT. *Paul Morel:* GATTISON JONES. *A Thief:* Harry Gordon. *Bergeot,* Police Inspector: George Clidd. *Countess d'Exmore:* Verenetta Hoots. *Madame Dorsay:* Audrey Maple. *Rudolph Max,* Head Cashier of Dorsay et Cie., Bankers: BILLY B. VAN. *Butler:* Edward Cobham.
    Flower Shop Girls: Renee Crandall, Rose Doheny, Jewell Dolores, Lea Sherman, Masie Yorke, Katherine Deighton, Bee Walz, Dorothy Chadwick, Virginia Otis, Adelaide Candee, Helen Daas, Mary Downs, Marie Clyde, Minka Devoe, Rita Miles, Ritta Pitts. *Guests:* Louise Baldwin, Gladys Brown, Helen Rowland, Jane Mussey, Terry Vine, Virginia Hanser, Myrtle Candee, Dolly Burke. *Customers:* Henry Moriarty, Herbert Carnegie, William Tasek, Phil Thomas, Jack Deighton, Bob Lee, Eddie Pierce, Billy Carpenter.

---

[44]Added during the run to Act 2 (after the Waltz, before the Finaletto):
    "I'm a Millionaire"
        C. Francis
[45]Dropped during the run.
[46]Originally produced 8 February 1928 at the Imperial Theatre for 101 performances. For Synopsis of Scenes and Musical Numbers, see original 1928 production. Costumes were uncredited. For this engagement, the Solo Dance in Act 3 was dropped, and the Ballet which opened Act 2 was replaced by:
    Waltz
        E. Elliott, G. Jones

1928.33

PARIS

A Musicomedy (Comedy with Music) in Three Acts. Book by Martin Brown. Songs (music and lyrics) by Cole Porter, E. Ray Goetz. Staged by William H. Gilmore. Setting by William Castle. Miss Bordoni's Costumes by Jeanne Lanvin, Martial and Armand, Cyber, Max Weldy, Lenief, Louise Boulanger. Produced by Gilbert Miller in association with E. Ray Goetz. Opened 8 October 1928 at the Music Box Theatre and closed 23 March 1929 after 195 performances.

CAST (in order of appearance): *Andrew Sabot*: ERIC KALKHURST. *Harriet*: Florence Edney. *Valet*: Reed Hamilton. *Brenda Kaley*: Elizabeth Chester. *Cora Sabot*: LOUISE CLOSSER HALE. *Guy Pennel*: ARTHUR MARGETSON. *Vivienne Rolland*: IRENE BORDONI. *Marcel Prince*: Theodore St. John. IRVING AARONSON'S 'THE COMMANDERS,' featuring PHIL SAXE, "RED" STANLEY.

ACT 1: Vivienne Rolland's Hotel Apartment in Paris.

ACT 2: One month later.

ACT 3: That evening.

ACT 1

    "The Land of Going To Be"
        I. Bordoni, A. Margetson
        (*Music by* Walter Kollo. *Lyrics by* E. Ray Goetz.)

ACT 2

    "Paris" (Medley)
        I. Bordoni
        (*Music by* Louis Alter. *Lyrics by* E. Ray Goetz.)

    "Babes in the Wood"
        I. Bordoni
        (*Music and Lyrics by* Cole Porter.)

    "Don't Look at Me That Way"
        I. Bordoni
        (*Music and Lyrics by* Cole Porter.)

    "(Let's Do It) Let's Fall in Love"
        I. Bordoni, A. Margetson
        (*Music and Lyrics by* Cole Porter.)

    "The Land of Going To Be" (reprise)
        I. Bordoni
        Accompaniment and Specialties by Irving Aaronson and "The Commanders" introducing "Vivienne" and "Heaven Hop" by Cole Porter. "Heaven Hop" dance created and staged by "Red Stanley."

[Additional Aaronson Specialties:

    "An' Furthermore"
        (*Music by* Harry Warren. *Lyrics by* Bud Green.)

    "(Oh You) Sweet Old Whatcha-May-Call-It"
        (*Music by* Fred Ahlert. *Lyrics by* Roy Turk.)]

ACT 3

    "The Land of Going To Be" (reprise)
        I. Bordoni

1928.34

JUST A MINUTE

A Timely Musical Play in Two Acts, 14 Scenes. Book by Harry C. Greene. Music by Harry Archer. Lyrics by Walter O'Keefe. Book staged by Harry C. Greene. Dances and ensembles staged by Russell Markert. Settings designed by P. Dodd Ackerman. Costumes by Mahieu. Orchestra under the direction of Count Berni [Bernard] Vici. Orchestrations by Claude MacArthur and William Moore. Produced by Phil Morris and Harry C. Greene. Opened 8 October 1928 at the Ambassador Theatre, moved 19 November 1928 to the Century Theatre, and closed 15 December 1928 after 80 performances.

CAST (in order of appearance): COUNT BERNI VICI and His Symphonic Girls (in the Orchestra Pit). *Mandy*: Billie Yarbo. *Mrs. Callahan*: Madeline Grey. *Helen*: GYPSY BYRNE. *Carlson*: HARRY HOLBROOK. *Patricia Callahan*: HELEN PATTERSON. *Mr. O'Brien*: Tommy Havel. *Miss Reynolds*: Helen Lockhart. *Louis Schultz*: Sam Sidman. *Joe Winston*: ARTHUR HAVEL. *Charlie Winston*: MORTON HAVEL. *The Three Recorders, Nifty Three*: *Tom*: Dale Jones. *May*: Helen Lockhart. *Dick*: Harold Madsen. *Jerry Conklin*: JOHN HUNDLEY. *Policeman*: Dave Bender. *Bev Johnson*: VIRGINIA SMITH. *Kay Bolton*: BRENDA BOND. *Spike*: George Leonard. *Boxers at Madison Square Garden (3)*: *Kid Gans*: Frankie Stevens. *Battling Brown*: Al Mario. *Eddie Frisco*: Eddie Frisco. *Kid Williams*: ARTHUR HAVEL. *Announcer*: Dave Bender. *Referee*: FLAVIO THEODORE. *Stage Director*: BURT HARGER. *Pickings Club Orchestra*: Peek-a-Boo Jimmie and His Band. *Soubrette*: Maude Russell. *Waiter*:

Walter Brogsdale. *Specialty Dancers*: Walker and Thompson, Helen Howell, Messrs. Harger and Theodore.

    Russell Markert Dancers: Hanna Dunner, Emily Ryan, Amanda Daisy, Dorothy Martin, Mickey LeRoy, Lottie Hentschel, Pauline Nesson, Irene Griffith, Helene Bradley, Diana Anitra, Myra Burton, Blanche Granby, Gene Doughty, Florence Sorel, Bert Haines, Lily Smart (Captain). *Count Berni Vici and His Symphonic Girls*: Peggy Riat, Digna Ebbley (pianists), Grace Fisher, Helen Patten, Helen Tracey, Lillian Wood (violins), Marie Carpentier, Sylvia McFarland, Ethel Seidel, Ruth Volmer (saxophones, flutes), Marvelle Armand, Margaret Rivers (cello, bass), Peggy Oneal (banjo), Darby Brown, Jean Miller, Mabelle Harvey, Irene Hartel (trumpets, trombone), Ruth Rams (drums). *Ebony Steppers*: Billie Yarbo, Mae Fanning, Mae Fortune, Millie Cooke, Tillie Meadows, Lucille Smith, Dorothy Young, Margaret Cherat, Jennie Salmons.

The entire action of the play occurs in New York City.

ACT 1, *Scene 1*: Living Room of Mrs. Callahan's Boarding House. Upper West Side. 5 P.M., late August. *Scene 2*: In front of Mrs. Callahan's Boarding House, a half hour later. *Scene 3*: Outside of Madison Square Garden. 8 P.M., the same day. *Scene 4*: Interior of Madison Square Garden. 9:30 P.M. the same day. *Scene 5*: In front of Madison Square Garden. *Scene 6*: In front of Mrs. Callahan's Boarding House. Midnight.

ACT 1, *Scene 1*: Backstage at Carlson's Theatre. Next afternoon. *Scene 2*: Entrance to Pickings Club. 10 P.M., the same day. *Scene 3*: Interior of Pickings Club. A little later. *Scene 4*: In front of Mrs. Callahan's Boarding House. *Scene 5*: Stage Entrance, Carlson's Theatre on Opening Night. *Scene 6*: Interior of Carlson's Theatre on Opening Night (showing last half hour of Carlson's Revue). *Scene 7*: Stage Entrance, Carlson's Theatre. Immediately after. *Scene 8*: Living Room of Mrs. Callahan's Boarding House. Midnight.

ACT 1

    "You'll Kill 'Em!"
        G. Byrne, Girls

    "Doggone"
        Three Recorders

    "We'll Just Be Two Commuters"
        A. Havel, M. Havel, V. Smith, B. Bond

    "You'll Kill 'Em!" (reprise)
        G. Byrne, Girls

    "Anything Your Heart Desires"
        J. Hundley, H. Patterson

    Specialty
        Markert Girls

    "Coming Out of the Garden"
        H. Lockhart, Girls

    "Anything Your Heart Desires" (reprise)
        J. Hundley, A. Havel, M. Havel

ACT 2

    Specialty Dance (Opening)
        Markert Girls

    "I Got a Cookie Jar But No Cookies"
        M. Russell, Ebony Steppers

    Specialty Dance[47]
        Walker and Thompson

    "The Break-Me-Down"
        M. Russell, Ebony Steppers

    Hundley, Three Recorders

    "I'm Ninety-Eight Pounds of Sweetness"
        H. Patterson, Girls

    "Heigh-ho Cheerio"
        G. Byrne, Three Recorders

    Specialty
        H. Howell, Harger and Theodore

    Specialty[48]
        Russell Markert Girls

    "Just a Minute"
        Entire Company

1928.35

UPS-A-DAISY

A Musical Comedy in Two Acts, 4 Scenes. Book and lyrics by Clifford Grey and Robert A. Simon. Based on the play 'Der Hochtourist' by Curt Kraatz.

---

[47]Dropped after opening.

Music by Lewis E. Gensler. Book staged by Edgar J. MacGregor. Dances staged by Earl Lindsay. Settings by John Wenger. Costumes by Kiviette. Orchestra under the direction of Gene Salzer. Orchestrations by Frank Black. Produced by Lewis E. Gensler. Opened 8 October 1928 at the Sam S. Shubert Theatre and closed 1 December 1928 after 64 performances.

CAST: *Polly Mallory*: MARIE SAXON. *Ethel Billings*, Polly's married sister: LUELLA GEAR. *Roy Lindbrooke*: ROY ROYSTON. *Jimmy Ridgeway*: RUSS BROWN. *Madge Mallory*: JOAN CARTER WADDELL. *Lurline*: NELL KELLY. *"Pinky" Parks*: BUSTER WEST. *Montmorency Billings*: WILLIAM KENT. *Fletcher*, Pinky's tutor: JOHN WEST. *Mountain Guides (2)*: *Oskar*: JOSEPH CAITS. *Sepp*: LOUIS CAITS. *Ambrose Wattle*, President of the Alpine Society: George Paunceforte. *Screeves*, a butler: Bob Hope. *Scrams*, a footman: Alan Fox. *Marigold*: Georgia Moore. *Irene*: Mildred Tolle. *Mary*: Jocelyn Lyle. *Gertrude*: Rita Crane. *Freddie*: Fred Maye. *Walter*: Billy Neely. *A Page*: Alan Crane. *At the Pianos*: Muriel Pollock, Constance Mering.

Guests, Peasants, Members of the Alpine Society, etc.: Sybil Bursk, Teddy Cameron, Rita Crane, Virginia Crowe, May Delaney, Margaret Dybfest, Adeline Foley, Ruth Gaudens, Carlyn Gerken, Ruth Hartman, Mitzi Hayes, Florence Healy, Muriel Hoey, Lebanon Hoffa, Amalia Ideal, Irene Kelly, Myrtle Lambert, Lorry LeNoie, Marilyn Mack, Jocelyn Lyle, Dolly Martinez, Virginia Maye, Marjorie Miller, Georgia Moore, Lucille Moore, Odessa Morgan, Petra Olsen, Charlotte Otis, Patricia Pitcher, Mildred Pitchler, Blanche Reeves, Ruth Timmons, Wanda Wood, Betty Wright, Grace Wright, Dorothy Wyatt. Al Berl, Harry Blake, Sam Bradley, John Coughlin, Alan Crane, Alan Fox, Bob Hope, Sydney Kane, Arthur LaFrack, Jimmy Lee, Walter Lowery, Herbert Lund, Fred Maye, John McCahill, Billy Neely, George Smith, Francis X. Sinnott.

ACT 1: Drawing Room at Billings' Home in Surrey.

ACT 2, Scene 1: An Inn in the Alps. *Scene 2*: A Mountain Road. *Scene 3*: Garden of the Billings' Home in Surrey.

ACT 1

Opening Chorus
"Ups-a-Daisy"
  J. C. Waddell, R. Brown
"Great Little Guy"
  W. Kent, L. Gear, N. Kelly, R. Brown
"Oh, How Happy We'll Be"
  M. Saxon, R. Royston, Ensemble
"I've Got a Baby"
  B. West, Ensemble
"Tell Me Who You Are"
  N. Kelly, R. Brown
"Will You Remember? (Will You Forget?)"
  M. Saxon, R. Royston, Ensemble
Finale

ACT 2

Opening
  Ensemble
"Desire Under the Alps"
  Caits Brothers
"Specialty
  Caits Brothers
"Oh, How Happy We'll Be" (reprise)
  L. Gear, W. Kent
"Sweet One"
  M. Saxon, R. Royston
"Sweetest of the Roses"
  M. Saxon, Boys
"Oh, How I Miss You Blues"
  L. Gear, Boys
Finaletto
Specialty
  B. West, J. West
"Will You Remember?"[49] (reprise)
  M. Saxon, R. Royston
"Ups-a-Daisy" (reprise)
  Ensemble
"Hot"
  N. Kelly, Ensemble
Finale

---

[49]Replaced during run by:
  Ups-A-Daisy Quartet (Specialty)

HOLD EVERYTHING

A Musical Comedy in Two Acts, 9 Scenes. Book by Buddy G. DeSylva and John McGowan. Music and lyrics by Buddy G. DeSylva, Lew Brown and Ray Henderson. Dances and ensembles staged by Jack Haskell and Sam Rose. Costumes by Kiviette. Settings designed by Henry Dreyfuss. Orchestra under the direction of Oscar Radin. Produced by Alex A. Aarons and Vinton Freedley. Opened 10 October 1928 at the Broadhurst Theatre and closed 5 October 1929 after 409 performances.

CAST (in order of appearance): *Marty*: BUDDY HARAK. *Mack*: HARRY LOCKE. *"Murf" Levy*: Harry Shannon. *"Pop" O'Keefe*: Edmund Elton. *Norine Lloyd*: BETTY COMPTON. *Betty Dunn*: ALICE BOULDEN. *Gink Shiner*: BERT LAHR. *Sue Burke*: ONA MUNSON. *"Toots" Breen*: NINA OLIVETTE. *"Sonny Jim" Brooks*: JACK WHITING. *Dan Larkin*: Frank Allworth. *"Nosey" Bartlett*: VICTOR MOORE. *Bob Morgan*: Robert O'Brien. *"The Kicker"*: Phil Sheridan. *Gladys Martin*: Anna Locke.

Ladies of the Ensemble: Edna Burford, Katheryn Black, Gene Brady, Mildred Clark, Rose Doll, Helen Doyle, Dorothy Deane, Adele Fitzgerald, May Rena Grady, Dorothy Graham, Emily Losen, Dian La Shay, Melba Lee, Betty Morton, Jolo Marino, Georgianna Orr, Sugar O'Neill, Lylian Ojala, Pollie Rose, Ruth Sato, Gene Scott, Clare Scott, Betty Wheeler, Elinor Wheeler, Frances Woodward. *Gentlemen of the Ensemble*: Jimmy Babbitts, Raymond Gray, Wallie Gardner, Raymond Hunt, Harry King, Joe Mann, Andrew Marinko, Sol Perla, Gus Schilling, Robert Silva, Jack Raymond, Jerry Rogers, Herbert Sampson.

ACT 1, Scene 1: "Pop" O'Keefe's Training Camp, Long Island. *Scene 2*: The Gymnasium. *Scene 3*: A Street. *Scene 4*: Terrace Garden at Home of Norine Lloyd, Westbury, Long Island.

ACT 2, Scene 1: Lounge Room in the Hotel Wood, New York City. *Scene 2*: A Dressing Room, Madison Square Garden. *Scene 3*: A Corridor. *Scene 4*: The Ring. *Scene 5*: Atop the Hotel Wood.

ACT 1

"We're Calling on Mr. Brooks"
  B. Harak, H. Locke, Visitors
"An Outdoor Man for My Indoor Sports"
  B. Compton, Boys
"Footwork"
  J. Whiting, Ensemble
"You're the Cream in My Coffee"
  O. Munson, J. Whiting
"When I Love, I Love"
  B. Lahr, N. Olivette
"Too Good to Be True"
  J. Whiting, Ensemble
"To Know You Is To Love You"
  J. Whiting, O. Munson, Girls
"Don't Hold Everything"
  A. Boulden, B. Harak, H. Locke, A. Locke, Ensemble
Finale
  Entire Company
ACT 2[50]
"For Sweet Charity's Sake"
  B. Compton, Girls, Boys
"Genealogy"
  V. Moore, B. Harak, H. Locke
"Oh, Gosh"
  N. Olivette, B. Lahr
"It's All Over But the Shoutin'"
  O. Munson, N. Olivette, B. Compton, Ensemble
Reprise
  A. Boulden, Girls
Finale
  Entire Company

THREE CHEERS

A Musical Entertainment (Comedy) in Two Acts, 12 Scenes. Book by Anne Caldwell and R. H. Burnside. Music by Raymond Hubbell. Lyrics by Anne Caldwell. Additional music and lyrics by Buddy G. DeSylva, Lew Brown, Ray Henderson. Produced (book staged) by R. H. Burnside. Dances staged

---

[50]During the run, a Specialty for Betty Compton was added before the Act 2 Finale following the reprise.

by Dave Bennett. Tiller Girls' dances arranged by Mary Read. Settings designed by Sheldon K. Viele and Raymond Sovey. Costumes designed by Charles LeMaire. Orchestra under the direction of George Hirst. Presented by Charles Dillingham. Opened 15 October 1928 at the Globe Theatre and closed 13 April 1929 after 210 performances.

CAST: *George Mullins*: ANDREW TOMBES. *Barry Vance*: ALAN EDWARDS. *Spike*: EDWARD ALLAN. *Prince Josef*: William Valentine. *The Duke*: OSCAR RAGLAND. *Malotte*: John Lambert. *The Mayor*: William Torpey. *Daphne de Lorne*: Janet Velie. *Queen Ysobel*: Maude Eburne. *Bobbie Bird*: PATSY KELLY. *Audrey Nugent*: Evangeline Raleigh. *Floria Farleigh*: Thea Dore. *Ermyntrude*: Cynthia Foley. *Letty*: Florine Phelps. *Betty*: Irene Phelps. *Zazia*: Phyllis Rae. *Mike*: Kathryn Hereford. *Wellington Westland*: Ralph Thomson. *Cameraman*: (Charles Mast). *Inn Keeper*: William Kerschell. *Captain Meurice*: James Murray. *Princess Sylvia*: DOROTHY STONE. *King Pompanola*: WILL ROGERS (pinch hitting for Fred Stone[51]).

Ladies in Waiting to Princess Sylvia: Sally Anderson, Anna May Dennehy, Tanya Dumova, Evelyn Nelson, Dorothy Phillips, Florence Rice, Frances Thress, Winthrop Wayne, Mimi Jordan. *Dancers*: Jean Castleton, Ruth Farrar, Helen Kaiser, Maxine Lorenz, Nickie Pitell, Jane Stafford, Phyllis Reynolds, Blanche O'Donohue, Regina Burke, Peggy Cunningham, Jeanne Edwards, Helene Franz, Geraldine Fitzgerald[52], Ottille George, Evelyn Greer, Geraldine Markham, Helen MacDonald, Leona Pennington, Gladys Pender, Anna Riley, Mozelle Ransome, Jet Stanley, Peggy Timmons, Vera O'Brien, Emily Marth. *Guardsmen*: Bub Baldwin, Charles Conkling, Floyd English, Richard Ellis, Irving Jackson, Dick Kennedy, Tom McLaughlin, Wilbur Reviere. *The Dorothy Stone Tiller Girls*: Doris Carter, Noreen Callow, Clara Gillette, Louise Gillette, Marjorie Griffiths, Mabel Hall, Sadie Hudson, Queenie James, Cora Meary, Muriel Marlowe, Dolly Mosely, Bella Pilling, Dorothy Sabin, Florence Stack, Alice Wright, Doris Yates.

ACT 1, *Scene 1*: The Palace Square in Itza. *Scene 2*: Curtain. *Scene 3*: The Kitchen. *Scene 4*: In the Palace. *Scene 5*: The Dock.

ACT 2, *Scene 1*: A Modest Bungalow in Hollywood. *Scene 2*: A Corridor. *Scene 3*: The Silver Screen. *Scene 4*: Polka Dot Studio. *Scene 5*: Curtain. *Scene 6*: Outside a Railroad Station in Itza. *Scene 7*: Throne Room of the King's Palace in Itza.

ACT 1

"The Americans Are Here" (Opening)
J. Velie, P. Kelly, E. Raleigh, T. Dore, A. Tombes, J. Lambert, R. Thomson, Ensemble

"(My) Orange Blossom Home"[53]
A. Tombes, Phelps Twins

"Lady Luck"
D. Stone, Ensemble

The Tiller Sunshine Girls

"Maybe This Is Love"
D. Stone, A. Edwards
(*Music by* Ray Henderson. *Lyrics by* Buddy DeSylva, Lew Brown.)

"It's an Old Spanish Custom"
W. Rogers

"Pompanola"
D. Stone, A. Edwards, Phelps Twins, P. Rae, C. Foley, Ensemble (*Music by* Ray Henderson. *Lyrics by* Buddy DeSylva, Lew Brown.)

The Tiller Sunshine Girls

"Because You're Beautiful"
A. Tombes, P. Kelly, C. Foley, T. Dore, K. Hereford, Ensemble

"Bobby and Me"
D. Stone, Tiller Sunshine Girls

The Tiller Sunshine Girls

Finale

ACT 2[54]

"The Silver Tree" (My Silver Tree)
J. Velie, E. Raleigh, T. Dore, P. Rae, Ensemble

"Gee, But It's Great to Be Alive"
D. Stone, E. Allan

"Look Pleasant"[55]
A. Tombes, P. Kelly, E. Allan

"Two Boys"
D. Stone, A. Edwards, W. Valentine

---

[51]Stone was unable to open the show due to illness, so Rogers opened the show until Stone was able to return.
[52]Not the famed dramatic actress of the 1950–1970s.
[53]Dropped after opening.
[54]The song order in Act 2 was revised after the opening.
[55]Dropped after opening.

"Let's All Sing the Lard Song" (Courtesy of Jerome Kern)
W. Rogers, A. Tombes
(*Music by* Leslie Sarony. *Lyrics by* Anne Caldwell.)

"Putting on the Ritz"
D. Stone, E. Allan, Tiller Sunshine Girls, Ensemble

"Happy Hoboes"
D. Rogers, W. Rogers

The Tiller Sunshine Girls (*Dance arranged by* Gamby-Hale.)

"Bride Bells"
J. Velie, O. Ragland, J. Lambert

Finale

1928.38 ANIMAL CRACKERS

A Musical Comedy in Two Acts, 6 Scenes. Book by George S. Kaufman and Morrie Ryskind. Music and lyrics by Bert Kalmar and Harry Ruby. Play directed by Oscar Eagle. Dances arranged by Russell E. Markert. Settings designed by Raymond E. Sovey. Costumes designed by Mabel Johnston. Men's costumes by Eaves Costume Company. Orchestra under the direction of Gus Salzer. Produced by Sam H. Harris. Opened 23 October 1928 at the 44th Street Theatre and closed 6 April 1929 after 191 performances.

CAST: *Hives*: Robert Greig. *Mrs. Rittenhouse*: MARGARET DUMONT. *M. Doucet*: Arthur Lipson. *Arabella Rittenhouse*: ALICE WOOD. *Mrs. Whitehead*: Margaret Irving. *Grace Carpenter*: BOBBY PERKINS. *Wally Winston*: Bert Mathews. *John Parker*: MILTON WATSON. *Roscoe W. Chandler*: Louis Sorin. *Mary Stewart*: BERNICE ACKERMAN. *Jamison*: ZEPPO MARX. *Captain Spalding*: GROUCHO MARX. *Emanuel Ravelli*: CHICO MARX. *The Professor*: HARPO MARX.

Showgirls: Helen Fowble, Patricia Pursley, Aileen Shaw, Virginia Stone, Annette Davies, Jessica Worth, Jewell La Kota, Marie Muselle, Marcelle Miller. *Dancing Girls*: Helen Cambridge, Virginia Meyers, Lucille Milam, Cleo Brown, Genevieve Kent, Helene Sheldon, Maxine Marshall, Gypsy Hollis, Kay Donegan, Gerry Hoffman, Billie Blake, Dorothy Knowlton, Gertrude Cole, Patsy O'Keefe, Hazel Bofinger, Muriel Buck, Mary O'Rourke. *Sixteen Markert Dancers*: Janice Glenn, Irma Nicholas, Audrey Volmer, Thelma Witzig, Mildred Burkhardt, Ivena Baker, Florine Meyers, Serrita Lorraine, Louise Mills, Alpha Wellemkotter, Eleanor McCabe, Mildred Hatfield, Frances Wise, Erma Shy, Dorothy Marmon, Alyse Green, Florence Wall (Captain). *Gentlemen*: Edward Young, Jack Buaer, Preston Lewis, John Elliott, Walton Ford, Harry Pederson, Allan Blair, William Bradley, Hermes Pan, Albert D'Amato, George K. Wallace, Marty Rhiel.

ACT 1, *Scene 1*: The Long Island Home of Mrs. Rittenhouse. Afternoon. *Scene 2*: On the Grounds. *Scene 3*: The Drawing Room. Same evening.

ACT 2, *Scene 1*: The Breakfast Room. The next morning. *Scene 2*: On the Grounds. *Scene 3*: The Garden. That night.

ACT 1

Opening Chorus
Hives and Butlers
The MaidsSixteen Markert Dancers
The GuestsEnsemble

"News"
B. Mathews, Sixteen Markert Dancers

"Hooray for Captain Spalding"
R. Grieg, Z. Marx, M. Dumont, G. Marx, Ensemble

"Who's Been Listening to My Heart?"
B Ackerman, M. Watson

"The Long Island Low-Down"
B. Mathews, B. Perkins

"Go Places and Do Things"
Ensemble
The Carsons

"Watching the Clouds Roll By"
B. Ackerman, M. Watson

Piano Specialty
C. Marx

Finale
Company

ACT 2

"When Things Are Bright and Rosy"
B. Mathews, A. Wood

Reprise
B. Ackerman, M. Watson

"Cool Off"
B. Perkins, Ensemble

The Royal Filipino Band
The Court of Louis the 57th
Harp Specialty
 H. Marx
"Musketeers"
 Marx Brothers
Finale
 Company

1928.39   ## BLACK SCANDALS

A Musical Novelty in Two Acts, 4 Scenes. Conceived, directed and produced by George Smithfield. Opened 26 October 1928 at the Edyth Totten Theatre and closed 27 October 1928 after 3 performances.[56]

CAST: *Pirika*: Bee Wells. *Princess Malachrino*: Waldine Williams. *Rastus*: STEWART HAMPTON. *Henry*: CLARENCE NANCE. *King Bobo*: Frank Lloyd. *Lieutenant*: Robert Johnson. *Arab*: Henry Richardson. *Slave Girls*: Eva Wingo, Bee Wells.

Scene: The Land of Azuwere.

1928.40   ## AMERICANA (1928)

A Musical Revue in Two Acts, 27 Scenes[57]. Book by J. P. McEvoy. Music by Roger Wolfe Kahn. Lyrics by J. P. McEvoy and Irving Caesar. Sketches directed by Edward Goodman. Dances (for Americana Girls) staged by Russell E. Markert, Max Scheck and (for Harlem Girls) by George Stamper. Singing directed by Edward Ziman and for spirituals by J. Rosamond Johnson. Settings designed by Herman Rosse. Costumes designed by John Held, Jr., and Herman Rosse. Masks by William Stahl. Roger Wolfe Kahn Orchestra under the direction of Don Voorhees. Orchestrations by William [Grant] Still and Arthur Schutt. Entire production under the personal supervision of J. P. McEvoy. Produced by J. P. McEvoy. Opened 30 October 1928 at Lew Fields' Theatre and closed 3 November 1928 after 7 performances[58].

CAST: DOUGLAS BURLEY, WANDA VALLE, MARY STAUBER, BRADLEY CASS, THOMAS BURTON, STANLEY CABLE, J. ROSAMOND JOHNSON, FRANCES GERSHWIN, STELLA SEAGER, JOE DONAHUE, DORIS CARSON, GEORGE TAPPS, BABY BANKS, GEORGE STAMPER, OLIVE McCLURE, JOHN HAMILTON, WILLIAMS SISTERS (Hannah, Dorothea), DUKE MILLER, MURRAY GITLITZ, MARVIN SCHECTOR.
 Americana Octet: Martha Peterson, Alice Swanson, Dorothy Johnson, Cathryn Woods, Dorothy Coulter, Elizabeth Holmes, Dorothy Bacon, Arta Revelle.
 Americana Girls: Florence Graham, Dorothy Chilton, Edith May Wright, Greta Lewis, Betty O'Rourke, Hazel Landers, Gearl Jentoft, Nadya Miller, Helen Fried, Liane Mamet, Gladys Travers, Betty Travers.
 Bachelor Octet: A. G. Bowes, E. J. Rauth, T. F. Adler, Ben Davies, Al Reeves, Julius Behrandt, Fred Goodwin, Henry Mershon.
 J. Rosamond Johnson Quartet: Taylor Gordon, Penman Lovingood, J. D. Brown, J. Rosamond Johnson.
 Four Wanderers: Maceo Johnson, Herman Hughes, George Chiles, George Clinkscale.
 Harlem Girls: Margaret Fenner, Jessie Easton, Althea Legare, Anita Bogarte, Edith Randolph, Anita Wharton, Lenora Simmons, Pearl Howell, Bobby Johns.
ACT 1
Scene 1
 Tabloid Murder
 Husband: D. Burley. *Sweetie*: W. Valle. *Wife*: M. Stauber. *Reporter*: B. Cass. *Photographer*: T. Burton.
Scene 2
 "Goodbye Forever"
 Good News Chorus: Americana Girls. *Hombre*: S. Cable. *Helen Morgan* (What Again?): F. Gershwin. *Rose Marie* (Remember?): S. Seager. *Connecticut Yankee*: J. Donahue. *Three Musketeers*: The Four Wanderers. *Seven Heroes* (Assorted): Bachelor Octette. *Eight Sopranos*: Eight Sopranos.

Scene 3
 Subscription Drive
 M. Stauber
Scene 4
 Train Announcer
Scene 5
 Travel Broadens the Mind
 Husband: D. Burley. *Wife*: M. Stauber. *Porter*: J. R. Johnson.
Scene 6
 "Life as a Twosome"
 F. Gershwin, J. Donahue, D. Carson, G. Tapps, B. Banks, G. Stamper,
 Bachelor Octette, Americana Dancers, Harlem Dancers and Singers
 (*Music by* Roger Wolfe Kahn. *Lyrics by* Irving Caesar.)
Scene 7
 Will Hays
Scene 8
 Americanaphone
 Scene: A Kentucky Mountain Home.
 Ma: W. Valle. *Gertie*: F. Gershwin. *Pappy*: D. Burley. *Doctor*: T. Burton.
Scene 9
 Williams Sisters
Scene 10
 Chain Gang (*[Musical] Arrangements by* J. Rosamond Johnson.)
 J. R. Johnson, T. Gordon, M. Johnson, P. Lovingood, H. Hughes, G. Chiles, G. Clinkscale, J. D. Brown
Scene 11
 Shackle Dance
 O. McClure
Scene 12
 Strange Interlude[59]
 Marsden: J. Hamilton. *Professor Leeds*: T. Burton. *Nina*: S. Seager. *Sammy Evans*: B. Cass. *Mrs. Evans*: M. Stauber. *Dr. Darrell*: J. Donahue.
Scene 13
 "The Ameri-Can-Can"
 Williams Sisters, D. Carson, J. Donahue, W. . Valle, G. Tapps, Americana and Harlem Dancers
 (*Music by* Roger Wolfe Kahn. *Lyrics by* Irving Caesar.)
Scene 14
 "He's Mine"
 S. Seager
 (*Music by* Roger Wolfe Kahn. *Lyrics by* Irving Caesar.)
Scene 15
 "Rubber Heels"
 (*Music by* J. Rosamond Johnson. *Lyrics by* J. P. McEvoy.)
 Mr. Swatch: J. Hamilton. *Sales Convention*: Entire Company.
ACT 2
Scene 1
 We, the Peepul
 (a) The B.M.T.
 Mr.: T. Burton. *Mrs.*: D. Johnson. *Frankie*: S. Seager. *Johnny*: B. Cass.
 (b) Roxy's
 Customer: G. Tapps. *Ushers*: Americana Girls. *Loud Speaker*
Scene 2
 Taylor Gordon, J. Rosamond Johnson and Double Quartette
Scene 3
 Chicago School
 Teacher: W. Valle. *Cop*: D. Burley. *Muggsy*: B. Cass. *Mike*: J. Hamilton. *Gunmen*: Bachelor Octette. *Children*: Americana Girls.
Scene 4
 "Young Black Joe"
 D. Miller, B. Banks, G. Stamper, Four Wanderers, Harlem Girls
 (*Music by* Roger Wolfe Kahn. *Lyrics by* Irving Caesar.)
Scene 5
 "Home"
 S. Seager, B. Cass, W. Valle, G. Tapps, Americana Girls
 (*Music by* Roger Wolfe Kahn. *Lyrics by* Irving Caesar.)

---

[56]No program available. The musical score, according to reviewers, consisted mostly of interpolations.
[57]The second of three musical revues presented by J. P. McEvoy beginning in 1926.
[58]After its closing, this production was radically revised and recast; it reopened 29 November 1928 as "New Americana" at the Liberty Theatre; see separate entry below.

---

[59]A burlesque of Eugene O'Neill's drama of the same name.

Scene 6

"Remember the Face of Your Driver"

(*Music by* Roger Wolfe Kahn. *Lyrics by* J. P. McEvoy.)
Taxi Drivers: Bachelor Octette. *Girl*: W. Valle. *Sunday Driver*: S. Cable. *Traffic Cop*: B. Cass.

Scene 7

George Bernard Shaw

Scene 8

The Manly Art

(a) The Coney Island Club (1900 A.D.)
First Fighter: M. Gitlitz. *Second Fighter*: M. Schector. *Referee*: J. Hamilton. *Radio Announcer*: J. Behrandt.
(b) Madison Square Garden (1928 A.D.)
Champion: J. Donahue. *Challenger*: D. Burley. *Referee*: B. Cass. *Radio Announcers*: J. Hamilton, T. Burton.

Scene 9

"Woman's Work is Never Done"

US Girls: S. Seager, M. Stauber, O. McClure, F. Gershwin. *Operators*: William Sisters, W. Valle, D. Carson. *Boys*: J. Donahue, B. Cass, J. Behrandt, A. Reeves.

Scene 10

Texas Guinan

Scene 11

The Black Bottle

Lecturer: M. Stauber.

Scene 12

"Hot Pants"

(*Music by* Roger Wolfe Kahn. *Lyrics by* I. Caesar.)
(a) Joe Donahue, (b) George Tapps, (c) Williams Sisters, (d) Frances Gershwin, Doris Carson, George Tapps, J. Held's Girls of the Future, (e) Baby Banks, and Harlem Girls of the Future.

1928.41 · HELLO YOURSELF!!!!

A Rah! Rah! Musical Comedy in Two Acts, 9 Scenes. Book by Walter DeLeon. Music by Richard Myers. Lyrics by Leo Robin. Book staged by Clarke Silvernail. Dances arranged by Dave Gould. Settings by P. Dodd Ackerman. Costumes designed by Charles LeMaire. Men's costumes by Jack L. Lipshutz. Orchestra under the direction of Paul Martin. Orchestral arrangements by Maurice dePackh; orchestral arrangements for Waring's Pennsylvanians by Fred C. Buck, Jr., Paul Mertz, Frank Hower. Entire production under the personal supervision of George Choos. Produced by George Choos. Opened 30 October 1928 at the Casino Theatre and closed 12 January 1929 after 87 performances.

CAST (in order of appearance): *"Speed" Warren*, a Student at Westley, who is haranguing a group of students: Blaine Cordner. *Polly*, a Co-Ed: Evelyn Nair. *Nell*, a Co-Ed: Betty Reddick. *"Scotty"*, a Freshman: "Scotty" Bates. *Sue Swift*, just another Co-Ed: DOROTHY LEE. *Isabel Manning*, still another Co-Ed: PEGGY HOOVER. *Professor Sutton*, President of Westley: William Robertson. *Chet*, son of Professor Sutton: Joseph Fay. *Bobby Short*, Westley's Student Leader: AL SEXTON. *Mrs. MacLauren*, youngest sister of Professor Sutton: LUCY MONROE. *Kate Stevens*, a Co-Ed: Edythe Maye. *"Big" Bertha*, a healthy Co-Ed: HELEN GOODHUE. *Cicero*, a diminutive student: GEORGE HAGGERTY. *"Tub" Washburn*, an overstuffed student: Al Nord. *Fred*: FRED WARING. *Dale Hartley*, from New York, niece of Professor Sutton: RUTH SENNOTT. *Duke*, cheer leader: WALTER REDDICK. *Nimble Wesleyans*: Jimmy Ray, The Reddicks.
Fred Waring's Fraternity Brothers: "Poley" McClintock, "Freddie" Buck, "Art" Horn, "Jimmy" Gilliland, "Nelse" Keller, "Curly" Cockerell, "Bill" Townsend, "Eddie" Radel, "Georgie" Culley, "Willie" Morgan, "Fred" Campbell, "Fred" Culley, "Francy" Foster, "Scotty" Bates, "Poll" Mertz, "Wade" Schlegel, "Eclair" Hanlon, "Frankie" Hower. *Sorority Members*: Patsy O'Day, Lolly Taschetta, Alice Hutchinson, Iris Wayne, Lillian Sullivan, Flora Sahagin, Vera Berg, Henrietta Jean Adams, Evelyn Dehkes, Louisa Wilson, Dulcy Dowd, Eleanor LaFleur, Sue Hardy, Margaret Knight, Willa De Brauw, Esther Wright, Doris St. Clare, Ruth Collins, Sunny Young, Norma Daly, Marion Obert, Nita Rosso, Estelle Jensen, Bonney Winslow. *Fraternity Members*: Jack Fraley, Ernest Petty, Fred Mayon, Charles Raymond, Barton Smith, Jack Coleman, Laurence Smith, Bill Eckhard, Jack Starr, George LeLand, Wallace Royce, Burdett Soule.

Place: Westley University. *Time*: Today.

ACT 1, *Scene 1*: The Old Oak. *Scene 2*: The Library. *Scene 3*: The Gymnasium.

ACT 2, *Scene 1*: Bobby's Fraternity House. *Scene 2*: The Campus Walk. *Scene 3*: The Dream Chapel. *Scene 4*: The Campus Walk. *Scene 5*: Section of the Bowl. *Scene 6*: The Sunken Garden.

ACT 1

"We Might Play Tiddle De Winks"

D. Lee, Co-Eds, Students

"Hello Yourself"

A. Sexton, E. Nair, B. Reddick, Co-Eds, Students

"You've Got a Way With You"

P. Hoover, F. Waring, Waring's Pennsylvanians

"He Man"

H. Goodhue, Co-Eds, Students

(Dance)

W. Reddick, I. Luttman, J. Ray

"Say That You Love Me"

R. Sennott, A. Sexton, L. Monroe, Co-Eds, Students

"True Blue"

F. Waring, Students, Waring's Pennsylvanians

"Daily Dozen"

H. Goodhue, Co-Eds

(Dance)

W. Reddick

Finale

The Whole University (Entire Company)

ACT 2

"Tired of It All"

G. Haggerty, Co-Eds

"I Want the World to Know"

D. Lee, Co-Eds, Students

Reprise

D Lee, E. Nair, The Reddicks, J. Ray

"Bobby's Nightmare"

P. Hoover

(Dance)

D. St. Clare, E. Dehkes, N. Rosso, L. Sullivan

Reprise

D. Lee, W. Reddick, Students, Co-Eds

The Concert

Fred Waring and His Pennsylvanians

["Jericho"

(*Music by* Richard Myers. *Lyrics by* Leo Robin.)]

Finale

1928.42 · THIS YEAR OF GRACE

A Musical Revue in Two Acts, 20 Scenes. Sketches, music and lyrics by Noël Coward. Staged by Frank Collins. Dances and ensembles by Max Rivers, except where specified by Tilly Losch. Costumes by Oliver Messel, Gladys E. Calthrop, Doris Zinkeisen, Gaston Zanel, Norman Hartnell, Idare et Cie. Settings by Marc Henri & Laverdet, Oliver Messel, Gladys E. Calthrop. Orchestra under the direction of Frank Tours. Entire production under the personal supervision of Charles B. Cochran. Produced by Arch Selwyn. Opened 7 November 1928 at the Selwyn Theatre and closed 23 March 1929 after 157 performances.

CAST: BEATRICE LILLIE, NOËL COWARD, Dick Francis, Madeline Gibson, Tommy Hayes, Queenie Leonard, Sonny Ray, Rita Mackay, Georges Fontanna, Marjorie Moss, Tom Devine, Phyllis Harding, G. P. Huntley, Jr., Albertina Vitak, Philip Wade, Florence Desmond, Mervyn Pearce, Muriel Montrose, James Cameron, Mimi Hayes, Nelson Welch, Audrey Pointing, James Hepburn, Oriel Ross, William Harn, Nan C. Hearne, Billy Milton, Sheila Rawle.
Ensemble: Richard Lang, Eddie Orpwood, Jim Sadler, Noel Clifford, Bill Rolston, Peter Crawford. *Mr. Cochran's Young Ladies*: Rita Mackay, Billie Tevlin, Elsie Hazlitt, Joan Elkins, Mai Orton, Lily Birchall, Wyn Clare, Peggy Kendall, Felicity Seddon, Hilary Charles, Joan O'Neil, Carolyn Sammon, Jimmy McCallion, Robinson Powell, Timothy Dobson, Verena Shaxon, Greta Foster, Adeline Philson, Pat Charles, Ann Barberova, Jill Armytage, Yvonne Bose, Sybil Davidson.

ACT 1

Scene 1

A Tube Station (Underground) in London

"Waiting in a Queue"

S. Ray

Fred, a Bookstall Attendant: D. Francis. *Female Passengers*: S. Davidson, Y. Rose, G. Foster, B. Tevlin, M. Orton, L. Birchall, W. Clare, A. Pointing, A. Barberova, J. Elkins, P. Kendall, A. Philson, F. Seddon, J. Armytage, V.

Shaxon, S. Rawle, P. Charles, E. Hazlitt. *An Office Boy*: T. Hayes. *Male Passengers*: J. Cameron, R. Lang, E. Orpwood, J. Sadler, N. Clifford, N. Welch, J. Hepburn, B. Rolston, P. Crawford, W. Harn. *A Bank Clerk*: S. Ray. *A Lift Man*: T. Devine. *Lady Gwendolyn Verney*: Q. Leonard. *The Honorable Millicent Bloodworthy*: O. Ross. *Harry, a Booking Clerk*: P. Wade. *Charles*: M. Pearce. *Mary*: M. Gibson. *First Girl*: M. Montrose. *Second Girl*: F. Desmond. (*Madeline Gibson's and female passengers' dresses and hats by* Idare et Cie. *Queenie Leonard's, Oriel Ross' Murile Montrose's Florence Desmond's dresses by* Norman Hartnell, *and hats by* Chaumet, Ltd. *Mervyn Pearce's clothes by* Johns & Bonham, Ltd. *Scene by* Marc Henri & Laverdet.)

Scene 2

"Mary Make Believe"

M. Gibson, Mr. Cochran's Young Ladies
(*Dresses and hats by* Idare et Cie.)

Scene 3

The Theatre Guide[60]

Announcer: N. Coward. *Sign Bearer*: M. Hayes.
   (a) The Trial of Mary Dugan
      The Judge: P. Wade. *Mary Dugan*: P. Harding. *Mrs. Rice*: O. Ross. *District Attorney*: D. Francis. *Mary's Brother*: T. Devine. *Two Policemen*: N. Welch, J. Hepburn. *A Luncher*: J. Cameron.
   (b) The Silver Cord
      A Young Man: J. Hepburn. *A Woman*: N. C. Hearne.
   (c) Young Woodley
      Two School Boys: P. Wade, W. Harn.
   (d) Any Civic Repertory Play
      The Woman: A. Pointing.

Scene 4

"Try to Learn to Love"

Q. Leonard, B. Milton, Mr. Cochran's Young Ladies
(*Queenie Leonard's dress by* Norman Hartnell. *Mr. Cochran's Young Ladies' dresses by* Idare et Cie.)

Scene 5

The Bus Rush

The People: B. Lillie, P. Harding, T. Hayes, G. P. Huntley, N. C. Hearne, M. Montrose, A. Pointing, W. Clare, O. Ross, N. Welch, P. Crawford.

Scene 6

"Lorelei"

R. Mackay, Q. Leonard
Lorelei: A. Vitak. *Sailor*: T. Devine.
   (*Dress by* Christabel Russell, Ltd. *Albertina Vitak's and Tom Devine's designed by* Oliver Messel. *Queenie Leonard's dress by* Idare et Cie. *Scene designed by* Oliver Messel.)

Scene 7

"Lilac Time"

B. Lillie, N. Coward
(*Dresses and scene designed by* G. E. Calthrop.)

Scene 8

Ignorance is Bliss
   (a) 1890
      Mrs. Blake, Proprietress of Private Hotel: N. C. Hearne. *Husband*: W. Harn. *Wife*: M. Montrose. *Annie, a Servant*: P. Harding.
   (b) 1928
      Reception Clerk: M. Pearce. *Husband*: B. Milton. *Wife*: O. Ross. *Page*: T. Hayes.
      (*Dresses in 1890 designed by* G. E. Calthrop. *Oriel Ross' dress by* Norman Hartnell. *Scenes designed by* G. E. Calthrop.)

Scene 9

"A Room With a View"

M. Gibson, N. Coward, Mr. Cochran's Young Ladies
(*Madeline Gibson's dress by* Christabel Russell, Ltd. *Mr. Cochran's Young Ladies' dresses designed by* G. E. Calthrop. *Scene designed by* G. E. Calthrop.)

Scene 10

"I Can't Think" (With apologies to Gertrude Lawrence)

---

[60]During the run, The Trial of May Dugan, The Silver Cord and Young Woodley were dropped and replaced by:
   (a) Front Page
      The Company
   (b) Jealousy
      He: D. Francis. *She*: W. Clare.
   (c) Congai
      The Girl: F. Desmond. *The Lover*: P. Wade.

B. Lillie
(*Beatrice Lillie's dress by* Norman Hartnell.)

Scene 11

"Teach Me to Dance Like Grandma"

M. Gibson, Mr. Cochran's Young Ladies

The following dance numbers arranged by Tilly Losch:

Mazurka

B. Lillie, N. Coward

Polka Children

B. Tevlin, E. Hazlitt, J. Elkins, Y. Bose, M. Orton, L. Birchall, W. Clare, P. Kendall
   Young Ladies: F. Seddon, H. Charles, V. Shaxon, G. Foster, A. Philson, P. Charles, A. Barberova, J. Armytage. *Young Gentlemen*: N. Welch, N. Clifford, B. Rolston, J. Cameron, T. Devine, J. Sadler, E. Orpwood, J. Hepburn.

The Three Graces

Grisi: S. Rawle. *Ellsler*: A. Pointing. *Paglioni*: A. Vitak.

Waltz

M. Moss, G. Fontana

Finale

Entire Company
(*Dress for "Teach Me to Dance Like Grandma" by* Idare et Cie. *Polka, Mazurka and Waltz dresses designed by* Doris Zinkeisen. *Ladies' and little boys' costumes by* Gaston Zanel. *Polka Gentlemen's by* L. and H. Nathan. *Waltz by* Morris Angel & Son, Ltd.)

ACT 2

Scene 1

The Lido Beach

The Contessa: O. Ross. *Lady Fenchurch*: M. Hayes. *Lady Saltwood*: P. Harding. *Lady Verlap*: H. Charles. *Sir John Verlap*: G. P. Huntley, Jr. *Sir Frederick Saltwood*: P. Wade. *The Conte*: D. Francis. *Sir Charles Fenchurch*: B. Milton. *Violet*: M. Gibson. *Jane*: F. Desmond. *Ivy*: M. Montrose. *Ruth*: Q. Leonard.

Opening Chorus ("The Lido")

"Little Women" (Quartette)

M. Gibson, Q. Leonard, F. Desmond, M. Montrose
(*Bathing dresses, pyjamas and hats by* Idare et Cie., Mayfair Lingerie Co., Chaumet Ltd. *Men's dressing gowns by* A. Sulka & Co., Ltd. *Philip Wade's suit by* Johns & Bonham, Ltd. *Scene designed by* G. E. Calthrop.)

Scene 2

The English Lido Beach

Opening Chorus ("English Lido")

"Mothers' Complaint"

N. C. Hearne, W. Clare, F. Desmond, P. Harding

"Britannia Rules the Waves"

B. Lillie, Company
   Announcer: B. Milton. *Mr. Freeman*: D. Francis. *Mrs. Freeman*: N. C. Hearne. *Alice*: M. Montrose. *Frankie*: T. Hayes. *Official*: P. Wade. *Madge*: A. Pointing. *Doris*: Q. Leonard. *Mr. Harris*: N. Coward. *Mrs. Harris*: W. Clare. *Vi*: J. O'Neil. *George*: J. McCallion. *Mrs. Clark*: F. Desmond. *Phyllis*: C. Sammon. *Mrs. Jones*: P. Harding. *Daisy Kipshaw*: B. Lillie.
   (*Scenes designed by* G. E. Calthrop.)

Scene 3

"The Legend of the Lily of the Valley" (Ballet)

Announcer: N. Coward. *Flanelette*: A. Vitak. *Bergamot*: F. Desmond. *Fairies*: S. Davidson, S. Rawle, M. Orton, B. Tevlin, E. Hazlitt, J. Elkins. *Female Courtiers*: F. Seddon, H. Charles, V. Shaxon, P. Charles, J. Armytage, A. Barberova. *Male Courtiers*: R. Lang, J. Cameron, E. Orpwood, J. Sadler, N. Clifford, N. Welch. *Marquis de Poopinac*: S. Ray.
(*Dresses designed by* G. E. Calthrop. *Scene designed by* G. E. Calthrop. *Choreography by* Noël Coward.)

Scene 4

"World Weary"

B. Lillie

Scene 5

Rules of Three

Announcer: O. Ross.
   (a) (James) Barrie
      The Wife: F. Desmond. *The Lover*: P. Wade. *The Husband*: D. Francis.
   (b) (Frederick) Lonsdale
      The Wife: O. Ross. *The Lover*: N. Coward. *The Butler*: M. Pearce. *The Husband*: B. Milton.
   (c) Adaptation from the French

The Wife: M. Montrose. *The Lover*: G. P. Huntley, Jr. *The Maid*: W. Clare. *The Husband*: W. Harn.

Scene 6

"Dance Little Lady"
  N. Coward
    The Little Lady: F. Desmond. *Dancers*: J. Elkins, A. Philson, G. Foster, B. Tevlin, L. Birchall, M. Orton, A. Barberova, V. Shaxon, P. Kendall, E. Hazlitt, J. Cameron, N. Clifford, P. Crawford, R. Long, E. Orpwood, B. Rolston, J. Sadler, N. Welch, J. Helpburn, T. Devine.
    (*Masks and dresses designed by* Oliver Messel.)

Scene 7

"Chauve Souris"[61]
  B. Lillie, D. Francis, P. Wade, M. Pearce, G. P. Huntley, Jr.
  (*Dresses designed by* Doris Zinkeisen.)

Scene 8

"Love, Life and Laughter" (song and sketch)
    Scene: Paris 1890.
      Herbert: D. Francis. *Rupert*: N. Coward. *A Woman*: P. Harding. *Madame Crapotte*: N. C. Hearne. *Customers of 'La Chatte Vierge'*: W. Clare, A. Pointing, A. Philson, M. Pearce, T. Devine, W. Harn. *Waiter*: P. Wade. *La Flamme*: B. Lillie.
      (*Scenes and dresses designed by* G. E. Calthrop

Scene 9

"Velasquez"[62]
  R. Mackay
    Two Pages: R. Powell, T. Dobson. *Dancers*: M. Moss, G. Fontana.
    (*Arranged by* Tilly Losch. *Scene and dresses designed by* Doris Zinkeisen.)

Scene 10

Finale
  Entire Company
  ("The Sun, the Moon and You" {Burlesque of American Musical})
  ("Playing the Game")
    (*Scene designed by* G. E. Calthrop. *Beatrice Lillie's and Mr. Cochran's Young Ladies' dresses by* Christabel Russell, Ltd. *Evening gowns by* Idare et Cie.)

1928.43 TREASURE GIRL

A Musical Comedy in Two Acts, 6 Scenes. Book by Fred Thompson and Vincent Lawrence. Music by George Gershwin. Lyrics by Ira Gershwin. Book staged by Bertram Harrison. Dances and ensembles by Bobby Connolly. Costumes designed by Kiviette. Settings by Joseph Urban. Orchestra under the direction of Alfred Newman. Produced by Alex A. Aarons and Vinton Freedley. Opened 8 November 1928 at the Alvin Theatre and closed 5 January 1929 after 68 performances.

CAST (in order of appearance): *Betty*: Dorothy Jordan. *Madge*: Virginia Franck. *Kitty*: Peggy O'Neill. *"Nat" McNally*: CLIFTON WEBB. *Polly Tees*: MARY HAY. *Mary Grimes*: Gertrude McDonald. *Jack Wrigley*: Charles Baron. *Footman*: Frank G. Bond. *Larry Hopkins*: WALTER CATLETT. *Ann Wainwright*: GERTRUDE LAWRENCE. *Neil Forrester*: PAUL FRAWLEY. *Mortimer Grimes*: FERRIS HARTMAN. *Bunce*: Norman Curtis. *"Slug" Bullard*: John Dunsmure. *First Mate*: Stephen Francis. *Postman*: Edwin Preble. *At the pianos*: VICTOR ARDEN, PHIL OHMAN.

Ladies of the Ensemble: Florence Allan, Nitza Andre, Marcia Bell, Claire Carroll, Jean Carroll, Betty Clark, Peggy Conklin, Cleo Cullen, Constance Cummings, Dotte DeSylva, Kathleen Edwardes, Evelyn Farrell, Sherry Gale, Alma Hookey, Joy Johnson, Adrienne Lampel, Anabel McMann, Maureen McNeil, Helen Mann, Vida Manuel, Frances Markey, Mabel Martin, Pauline Mason, Ysobel Mason, Ethel Maye, Lillian Michel, Elsie Neal, Wilma Novak, Tony Otto, Ruth Penery, Peggy Quinn, Aili Raddigan, Marvyne Ray, Wilma Roelof, Helen Sills, Kay Smythe, Florence Spink, Betty Vine, Gwen Vernon, Beryl Wallace, Betty Wright. *Gentlemen of the Ensemble*: Sidney Ayres, Edwin Bidwell, Norman Curtis, Eugene Day, E. M. Gall, Regis Geary, Bob Gebhardt, Thomas Hodges, Edward Humbert, Richard Keith, John McAvoy, Billy McCarver, William L. Mack, Lionel Maclyn, Jack Morton, Alfonso Mullarkey, Daniel O'Brien, Edwin Preble, Fritz Reinhardt, W. Kenneth Shepard, Sam Simpson, Jack Stevens, Jacques Stone, Sims Walker, Walter Wandell.

ACT 1, *Scene 1*: The Pirate Party. *Scene 2*: The Drive. *Scene 3*: The Garden.

ACT 2, *Scene 1*: The Island. *Scene 2*: The Drive. *Scene 3*: The Ballroom.

---

[61]A burlesque of the popular English-Russian revue of 1921 and subsequent editions.

[62]Dropped after opening and replaced by:Caballero (Dance)
  Moss and Fontana

ACT 1

"Skull and Bones"
  Ensemble
"(I've Got a) Crush on You"
  M. Hay, C. Webb, Ensemble
"Oh, So Nice"
  G. Lawrence, P. Frawley
"According to Mr. Grimes"
  F. Hartman, Ensemble
"Place in the Country"
  P. Frawley, N. Curtis, Girls
"K-ra-zy for You"
  C. Webb, M. Hay, Girls
"I Don't Think I'll Fall in Love Today"
  G. Lawrence, P. Frawley
"I've Got a Rainbow"
  W. Catlett, C. Baron, G. McDonald, D. Jordan, V. Franck, P. O'Neill, Girls
"Feeling I'm Falling"
  G. Lawrence, P. Frawley
Finale
  (W. Catlett, G. Lawrence, C. Webb, P. Frawley, Ensemble)

ACT 2

Opening (Treasure Island)
  Ensemble
"What Causes That?"
  M. Hay, C. Webb, Girls
"What Are We Here For?"
  G. Lawrence, C. Webb, Girls
"Got a Rainbow"[63] (reprise)
  Girls
"Where's the Boy? (Here's the Girl!)"
  G. Lawrence, Boys
Piano Specialty
  V. Arden, P. Ohman
Finale
  Entire Company

1928.44 RAINBOW

A Romantic Musical Play of California in the days of '49, in Two Acts, 8 Scenes. Story (book) by Laurence Stallings and Oscar Hammerstein II. Music by Vincent Youmans. Lyrics by Oscar Hammerstein II. Book staged by Oscar Hammerstein II. Musical numbers staged by Busby Berkeley. Costumes designed by Charles LeMaire. Settings by Frank Gates and Edward A. Morange. Research and technical director, Leighton K. Brill. Orchestra under the direction of Max Steiner. Orchestrations by Max Steiner. Entire production under the personal supervision of Philip Goodman. Produced by Philip Goodman. Opened 21 November 1928 at the Gallo Theatre and closed 15 December 1928 after 29 performances.

CAST (in order of appearance): *Major Davolo*: RUPERT LUCAS. *Lotta*: LIBBY HOLMAN. *Mess Sergeant*: Ned McGurn. *Sergeant Major*: HARLAND DIXON. *Penny*: Helen Lynd. *Colonel Brown*: Henry Pemberton. *"Nasty" Howell*: CHARLES RUGGLES. *Captain Robert Singleton*: Brian Donlevy. *Virginia Brown*: LOUISE BROWN. *Fanny*: Herself. *Harry Stanton*: ALLAN PRIOR. *Corporal*: Leo Mack. *First Private*: Stewart Edwards. *Second Private*: Leo Dugan. *Third Private*: Ward Arnold. *Rookie*: Randall Fryer. *Bartender*: Frank King. *Senora Mendoza*: Mary Carney. *Peon*: Leo Nash. *Servant*: Charles Ralph. *Spanish Girl*: Valia Valentinova. *Snow Ball*: May Barnes. *Frenchie*: George Magis. *Mr. Jackson*: Chester Bree. *Egg*: Edward Nemo. *Tough*: Ralph Walker. *Kitty*: Kitty Coleman.

Show Girls: Ann Austin, Harriette Brinton, Mary Carney, Kitty Coleman, Ann Constance, Chistine Gallagher, Margaret Grove, Dorothy Pensel, Rowena Scott, Valia Valentinova, Emily Wentz, Elinor Witmar. *Dancers (Girls)*: Margaret Alexander, Phyllis Buck, Virla Buley, Lee Byrne, Bobbie Campbell, Christine Crane, Dorothy Dodd, Irene Evans, LaVergne Evans, Grace Fleming, Evelyn Kermin, Helen Madigan, Edith Martin, Ruth Martin, Pauline Maxwell, Betty McNulty, Mildred Morgan, Beth Meredith, Ruby Nevins, Margaret Pidgin, Helen Rauth, Betty Sherman, Margaret Todd, Jean Watson, Betty Waxston, Claire White. *Dancers (Boys)*: Ward Arnold, Milton Brodus, Frank Gagen, Frank Kimball, Harry Lake, Larry Larkin, Glenn McComas,

---

[63]Dropped during the run.

Clinton McLeer, Ned McGurn, Lewis Parker, John Perkins, Thomas Sternfield, Paul Taft. *Men Singers*: James H. Beattie, Chester Bree, Vladimir Chavdaroff, Vincent Curran, Thomas Dendy, Vincent Funaro, Christopher Gerard, Don Heebner, Ludovic Huot, Cyril Joyce, Charles Mack, George Magis, Leo Nash, Raymond Otto, Efin Vitis, Victor Young, Randall Fryer, Lu Talbot, Ralph Walker.

ACT 1, Scene 1: Fort Independence, Missouri. A Spring Evening at the time of the California Gold Rush. 1849. *Scene 2*: The Guard Room at the Fort. The next morning. *Scene 3*: The Wagon Train on the Plains. A few weeks later. *Scene 4*: In the Mountains. *Scene 5*: Red Dog, California, a Mining Town. A week later.

ACT 2, Scene 1: The Gambling Room of the Silver Dollar Saloon in Sacramento. A year later. *Scene 2*: Outside the Silver Dollar Saloon. Six months later. *Scene 3*: The Presidio of San Francisco. A year later.

ACT 1

Scene 1

"On the Golden Trail" (Opening)
Ensemble

"My Mother Told Me Not to Trust a Soldier"
H. Dixon, H. Lynd

"Virginia"
L. Brown, B. Donlevy, Boys

"I Want a Man"
L. Holman

Scene 2

"Soliloquy"
A. Prior

Scene 3

"I Like You As You Are"
A. Prior, L. Brown

Finaletto
L. Holman

Scene 4

Dance
L. Brown

"The One Girl"
A. Prior, Men

Finaletto, "Let Me Give All My Love to Thee" (Hymn)
L. Brown, L. Holman, A. Prior, Ensemble

Scene 5

"Diamond in the Rough"
C. Ruggles, H. Lynd

"Who Wants to Love Spanish Ladies?"
Ensemble

Dance
H. Dixon

"I Like You Are You Are" (reprise)
A. Prior, L. Brown

Finale
(Company)

ACT 2

Scene 1

Opening
Ensemble

"Hay! Straw!"
L. Brown, H. Dixon

"I Want a Man" (reprise)
L. Holman

Finaletto
A. Prior, L. Brown, L. Holman, B. Donlevy, Men

Scene 2

"The Bride Was Dressed in White"
C. Ruggles, H. Lynd

Scene 3

"On the Golden Trail" (reprise)
(Ensemble)

Finale
(Company)

1928.45

NEW AMERICANA

A Revised Version of the Musical Revue AMERICANA in Two Acts, 28 Scenes[64]. Sketches by J. P. McEvoy and Arthur (Bugs) Baer. Music by Roger Wolfe Kahn. Lyrics by Irving Caesar. Sketches directed by A. Seymour Brown. Dances and ensembles arranged by Russell E. Markert. Settings designed by Herman Rosse. Costumes designed by John Held, Jr., and Herman Rosse. Orchestra under the direction of Don Voorhees. Entire production under the personal supervision of J. P. McEvoy. Produced by Americana, Inc. (Roger Wolfe Kahn). Opened 29 November 1928 at the Liberty Theatre and closed 8 December 1929 after 12 performances.

CAST: JULIUS TANNEN, ULA SHARON, CARL RANDALL, TOMMY (Bozo) SNYDER, FRANCES SHELLEY, VIRGINIA WATSON, WILLIAMS SISTERS (Hannah, Dorothea), DUGLAS BURLEY, MARY STAUBER, HENRY MERSHON, JAMES LORNER, TOM BURTON, GORDON BENNETT, JAMES HARRIS, HENRY GENNERT, SAM GREEN, TOM ADLER, A. G. Bowes, Fred Goodwin, Ben Davies, E. J. Rauth, Allen Reeves, Julius Behrendt, Dorothy Johnson, Alice Swanson, Martha Peterson, Kay Wood, Dorothy Coulter, Arta Revelle, Betty Holmes, Dorothy Bacon.
Russell Markert Dancers: Hanna Dunner, Emily Ryan, Amanda Daisy, Dorothy Martin, Micky LeRoy, Lottie Hentschel, Pauline Nesson, Irene Griffith, Helene Bradley, Diana Anitra, Myra Burton, Blanche Granby, Gene Doughty, Florence Sorel, Bert Haines, Lily Smart (Captain).

ACT 1

Scene 1

Opening (or Finale, What Have You?)
The Husband: D. Burley. *The Sweetheart*: V. Watson. *The Wife*: M. Stauber. *Cameraman*: H. Mershon. *Hombre*: J. Lorner. *Connecticut Yankee*: C. Randall. *Helen Morgan*: F. Shelley. *The Three Musketeers*: T. Burton, G. Bennett, H. Gennert. *The Heroes*: A. Bowes, F. Goodwin, B. Davies, E. Rauth, A. Reeves, J. Behrendt. *The Heroines*: D. Johnson, A. Swanson, M. Peterson, K. Wood, D. Coulter, A. Ravelle, B. Holmes, D. Bacon. And The Russell Markert Dancers.

Scene 2

Julius Tannen

Scene 3

Any Night in a Pullman Car
The Conductor: T. Burton. *The Passengers*: M. Stauber, D. Johnson, D. Burley, J. Behrendt.

Scene 4

"Life As a Twosome"
U. Sharon, C. Randall
Assisted by V. Watson, G. Bennett, J. Lorner, Floradora Girls, Men, Boys and Girls of Today.

Scene 5

Announcement
J. Tannen

Scene 6

Talking Movies
The Father: D. Burley. *The Mother*: M. Stauber. *The Doctor*: T. Burton. *The Daughter*: F. Shelley.

Scene 7

The Williams Sisters

Scene 8

"Rainbow's End"
U. Sharon, assisted by J. Lorner, G. Bennett
(*Conceived by* Don Lee. *Staged by* Harry Krivit.)

Scene 9

The Paperhangers
T. Snyder, S. Green

Scene 10

The Russell Markert Dancers

Scene 11

Strange Interlude
Marsden: J. Lorner. *Sam Evans*: G. Bennett. *Nina*: V. Watson. *Mrs. Evans*: M. Stauber. *The Professor*: T. Burton. *Dr. Darrell*: C. Randall.

---

[64]Originally produced 30 October 1928 at the Mansfield Theatre for 7 performances. Retained from earlier version were "Life as a Twosome," Strange Interlude, "He's Mine," "Hot Pants."

Scene 12

"He's Mine"
Cigarette Girl: F. Shelley. *Cabaret Girls*: Russell Markert Dancers.

Scene 13

Julius Tannen

Scene 14

"(The) Ameri-Can-Can"
Williams Sisters, C. Randall, V. Watson, Russell Markert Dancers

ACT 2

Scene 1

"Taking the Subway to Roxy"
The Boy: J. Lorner. *The Girl*: V. Watson. *The Patron*: C. Randall. *Passengers, Guards, Roxy Ushers*: (Ensemble).

Scene 2

The Piano Movers[65]
T. Snyder, S. Green

Scene 3

"Wild Oat Joe"
H. Williams, Russell Markert Dancers

Scene 4

Cane Dance[66]
C. Randall

Scene 5

Julius Tannen

Scene 6

"A Tartar Legend" (*Conceived by* Don Lee. *Staged by* Harry Krivit.)
U. Sharon, assisted by G. Bennett, J. Lorner.

Scene 7

Frances Shelley

Scene 8

The Storm
The Husband: T. Burton. *The Wife*: D. Johnson. *Two Travelers*: T. Snyder, S. Green.

Scene 9

Home
V. Watson, C. Randall

Scene 10

Chicago
The Teacher: M. Stauber. *The Gang Leader*: T. Adler. *The Policeman*: D. Burley. *Gangsters and School Children*: (Ensemble).

Scene 11

Julius Tannen

Scene 12

The Taxi Drivers
The Girl: U. Sharon. *The Sunday Driver*: D. Burley. *The Policeman*: T. Burton. *Taxi Drivers*: (Ensemble).

Scene 13

"Hot Pants"
Williams Sisters, Russell Markert Dancers

Scene 14

Finale
Entire Company

1928.46 ANGELA

A Comedy with Music in Three Acts, 4 Scenes. Book by Fanny Todd Mitchell, based on the play 'A Royal Family' by Captain Robert Marshall. Music by Alberta Nichols. Lyrics by Mann Holiner. Staged by George Marion. Dances staged by Chester Hale. Settings designed by Watson

Barratt. Costumes designed by Barbier of Paris and Ernest Schrapps. Orchestra conducted by Joseph Benavente. Orchestrations by Emil Gerstenberger. Entire production under the personal supervision of J. J. Shubert. Produced by the Messrs. Shubert. Opened 3 December 1928 at the Ambassador Theatre, moved 24 December 1928 to the Century Theatre and closed 5 January 1929 after 40 performances.

CAST (in order of appearance): *Duke of Berascon*, Comptroller of the Royal Household: GATTISON JONES. *Louis VII*, King of Arcacia: ERIC BLORE. *Margaret*, Queen Consort of Arcacia: AUDREY MAPLE. *Queen Ferdinande*, Mother of Louis VII: Alison Skipworth. *Countess Carini*: Meeka Aldrich. *Baron von Holdenson*: Oscar Figman. *Grand Duke Hubert*, Uncle of King Louis: FLORENZ AMES. *Princess Alestine Victorine Angela*, only daughter of King Louis: JEANETTE MacDONALD. *Bijou*, Danseuse: PEGGY CORNELL. *Servant*: James Ray. *Count Bernadine*: ROY HOYER. *Phileon Button*: Gus Alexander. *Mr. Sneckkenberger*: Arthur Cole. *The Girl from London*: Jane Manners. *At the Pianos*: Ralph Rainger, Adam Carroll. (*Specialty*: Reed McClelland.)

Ladies in Waiting: Meeka Aldrich, June Cavendish, Billie Fanning, Ann Glass, Claire Hooper, Charlotte Joyce, Louise Joyce, Jane Manners. *Ladies of the Court*: Nina Bennett, Blanche Bryer, Eleanor Ross, Hildreth Judkins, Ursula Mack, Beth Mann, May Meredith, Jo Moor, Helen Newton, Marion Sayres, Kathleen Odette, Beatrice Walters. *Aides de Camps*: Del Holleran, Ernest Seldon, Segurd Larsen, Milton Jefferies, Bob Morton, Marin Hennifly, James Roy, Rex Boyd. *Chester Hale Girls*: Pavla Pavlicek, Mary Hiscox, Adeline Bornheim, Jeanne Kroll, Gertrude Westling, Dorothy Pierce, Lillian Bennett, Karen Taft, Agnes Hickey, Gladys Glorita, Evelyn Ford, Jane Tennant.

Time: The Present.

ACT 1: The Ante-Room of the Royal Palace at Caron, Capital of Arcacia. Early spring.

ACT 2: The Palace Garden at Cassantra. About ten days later.

ACT 3, Scene 1: A Room in the Palace. The following evening. *Scene 2*: The Throne Room of the Royal Palace at Carron. The same evening.

ACT 1

Opening
Ensemble

"The Weaker Sex"
F. Ames, Girls, Chester Hale Girls

"Love Is Like That"
J. MacDonald, Chester Hale Girls

"Don't Forget Your Etiquette"
G. Jones, P. Cornell, Girls, Boys

"The Baron, the Duchess and the Count"
J. MacDonald, R. Hoyer, Chester Hale Girls, Boys

"The Regal Romp"
F. Ames, P. Cornell, G. Jones, Entire Company

ACT 2

Opening
R. McClelland, Chester Hale Girls, Boys, Girls

"Tally-Ho"
G. Jones, P. Cornell, Chester Hale Girls, Girls, Boys

"I Can't Believe It's True"
J. MacDonald, R. Hoyer

"Bundle of Love"
P. Cornell, G. Jones, Chester Hale Girls, Girls

"Maybe So"
J. MacDonald

"You've Got Me Up a Tree"
J. MacDonald, R. Hoyer, Chester Hale Girls, Girls

Finale
Entire Company

ACT 3

"Bearing the Silver Platters"
Boys

"Oui, Oui!!"
P. Cornell, G. Jones

Reprise
F. Ames, Girls

Scene Dansant
Chester Hale Girls

Finale
Entire Company

---

[65]Dropped after opening.
[66]Dropped after opening.

1928.47

WHOOPEE

A Musical Comedy in Two Acts, 11 Scenes. Book by William Anthony McGuire. Based on the play 'The Nervous Wreck' by Owen Davis, (adapted from a story 'The Wreck' by E. J. Rath). Music by Walter Donaldson. Lyrics by Gus Kahn. Dialogue staged by William Anthony McGuire. Dances and ensembles staged by Seymour Felix. Modernistic Ballet staged by Tamara Geva. Settings by Joseph Urban. Costumes designed by John W. Harkrider. Musical director, Gus Salzer. Produced by Florenz Ziegfeld. Opened 4 December 1928 at the New Amsterdam Theatre, closing for vacation 13 July 1929 after 255 performances; re-opened 5 August 1929 at the New Amsterdam Theatre and closed 23 November 1929 after 157 additional performances. Total: 407 performances.

CAST (in order of appearance): *Leslie Daw:* RUTH ETTING. *Pearl:* Olive Brady. *Betty:* Gladys Glad. *Mable:* Josephine Adaire. *Estelle:* Jean Ackerman. *Alice:* Adele Smith. *Irene:* Katherine Burke. *Virginia:* Myrna Darby. *Lucille:* Muriel Finley. *Vivian:* Freda Mierse. *Judson Morgan:* Louis Morrell. *The Padre:* Frank Colleti. *Jim Carson:* Jack Shaw. *Pete:* Fran Frey. *Joe:* Bob Rice. *Jack:* Jack Gifford. *Mary Custer:* ETHEL SHUTTA. *Sheriff Bob Wells:* JOHN RUTHERFORD. *Sally Morgan:* FRANCES UPTON. "*Brand Iron*" *Edwards:* James P. Houston. *Henry Williams:* EDDIE CANTOR. *Wanenis:* PAUL GREGORY. *Black Eagle:* CHIEF CAUPOLICAN. *Jerome Underwood:* Spencer Charters. *Chester Underwood:* ALBERT HACKETT. *Timothy Sloane:* Jack Shaw. *Harriet Underwood:* Mary Jane. *Andy Nab:* Will H. Philbrick. *Morton:* Bob Rice. *Ma-Ta-Pe:* Sylvia Adam. *Comulo:* James P. Houston. *An Indian:* Edourd Grobe. *Tejou:* Jack Shaw. *Yolandi:* TAMARA GEVA. *Eleanor:* Olive Brady. And GEORGE OLSEN AND HIS MUSIC. *4 Cowboys:* Fran Frey, Bob Rice, Bob Berger, Jack Gifford.

Stetson Boy Dancers: Harry Ettus, Bill Erickson, Charles Mayon, Gil White, Tom Hughes, Joseph Minitello, Buddy Ebsen, Jack Lewis. *Modernistic Ballet in Black:* Madeline Dunbar, Dorothy Flood, Eleanor Hunt, Olga Loft, Agnes O'Laughlin, Marion Roberts, Lillian Ostrum, Dorothy Brown. *Gypsy Joe Dancers:* Agnes Ayres, Mabel Baade, Elsie Behrens, Dorothy Brown, Mary Coyle, Madeline Dunbar, Dorothy Flood, Muriel Gray, Eleanor Hunt, Louise Joyce, Olga Loft, Wynne Larke, Gwendolyn Milne, Elaine Mann, Patsy O'Day, Connie Owens, Agnes O'Laughlin, Dorothy Patterson, Rita Riecker, Marion Roberts, Bobby Weeks, Marie Conway, Lillian Ostrum, Ann Brown. *Ziegfeld Glorified Girls:* Gladys Glad, Jean Ackerman, Myrna Darby, Hazel Forbes, Muriel Finley, Catherine Moylan, Adele Smith, Josephine Adair, Peggy Bancoft, Betty Dumbris, Meredith Howard, Yvonne Hughes, Frieda Mierse, Valerie Raemer, Betty Gray, Jerry Rogers, Helen Walsh, Ruth Downey, Lillian Knight, Colette Ayers, Mabel Baade, Elsie Behrens, Dorothy Brown, Mary Coyle, Madeline Dunbar, Dorothy Flood, Muriel Gray, Eleanor Hunt, Louise Joyce, Olga Loft, Wynne O'Day, Gwendolyn Milne, Elaine Mann, Patsy O'Day, Connie Owens, Agnes O'Laughlin, Dorothy Patterson, Vera Rieckler, Marion Roberts, Bobbie Wellsley, Marie Conway, Vivian Hall, Frances Guinan, Helen Lehigh, Pauline Ray, Lillian Ostrum, Ann Brown. *Gentlemen of the Ensemble:* Harry Ettus, Frank Ericson, Charles Mayon, Gil White, Tom Hughes, Joseph Minitello, Buddy Ebsen, Jack Lewis, Bob Forte, Edward Nadeau, George Huntington, Jack James, Irving Ross, Tom Leventhal, David Labris, Matt Webster, Don Hudson, Sam Bunin, Charles Pettinger, Waldo Roberts.

ACT 1, *Scene 1*: Mission Rest, California. *Scene 2*: Black Top Canyon, a mountain road. *Scene 3*: The Gas Station. *Scene 4*: Kitchen of Bar M Ranch. *Scene 5*: The Corral. *Scene 6*: Bar M Ranch.

ACT 2, *Scene 1*: The Reservation of the Mojave Tribe. *Scene 2*: Poppy Field. *Scene 3*: Interior of the Ranch House, Bar M Ranch. *Scene 4*: Indian Retreat. *Scene 5*: "Halloween."

ACT 1

"It's a Beautiful Day Today"
> Ensemble

Dance
> O. Brady

"Here's to the Girl of My Heart"
> P. Gregory, Cow Boys

"(I'm Bringing a) Red, Red Rose"
> F. Upton, P. Gregory

"Gypsy Joe"
> R. Etting, Gypsy Joe Dancers

"Makin' Whoopee"
> E. Cantor
> *Assisted by* M. Finley, G. Glad, J. Ackerman, A. Smith, H. Forbes, M. Dunbar

"Go Get 'Im" (Finaletto)
> J. Rutherford, Ensemble

"Until You Get Somebody Else"
> E. Cantor, F. Upton

"Taps"M. Jane

"Come West, Little Girl, Come West"
> E. Shutta, 4 Cow Boys

"The Movietone of the Gypsy Song"—

"Where the Sunset Meets the Sea"R. Etting, Miss Conway (Violinist), Gypsies

Gypsy DanceT. Geva, Ensemble

"Stetson"
> E. Shutta, F. Frey, B. Rice, B. Borcia, J. Griffith

Dance
> Cow Boy-Girl Dancers

The Singing Waiter:
> E. Cantor

["Hungry Women"
> (*Music by* Milton Ager. *Lyrics by* Jack Yellen.)

"My Blackbirds Are Bluebirds Now"
> (*Music by* Cliff Friend. *Lyrics by* Irving Caesar.)

"I'm Wild About Horns on Automobiles That Go 'Ta-Ta-Ta Ta'" (Eddie Cantor's Automobile Horn Song)
> (*Music and Lyrics by* Clarence Gaskill.)

"I Faw Down an' Go Boom"
> (*Music and Lyrics by* James Brockman, Leonard Stevens, B. B. Donaldson.)

"Big Hearted Baby"
> (*Music by* Phil Philips. *Lyrics by* Raymond B. Egan.)

"If I Give Up the Saxophone (Will You Come Back to Me?)
> (*Music and Lyrics by* Sammy Fain, Irving Kahal and Willie Raskin.)]

Finale
> Entire Company

ACT 2

"The Song of the Setting Sun"
> C. Caupolican, His Tribe

"Love Is the Mountain" (Trio; Paraphrase of "The Song of the Setting Sun")
> C. Caupolican, P. Gregory, S. Adam

"Red Mama"
> M. Jane

"We'll Keep on Caring"[67]
> F. Upton, P. Gregory

Mohave War Dance

Invocation to the Mountain God
> C. Caupolican, His Tribe
> (a) The Prayer, (b) The Dance, (c) The Offering of Beauty.

"Hallowe'en Tonight"[68]
> George Olsen and His Music

"Love Me or Leave Me"
> R. Etting

Modernistic Ballet in Black (*Staged by* Tamara Geva.)
> T. Geva, Ballet Company

"Hallowe'en Whoopee Ball"
> E. Shutta, Boys, O. Brady, Ensemble

Finale
> G. Olsen and His Band, Entire Company

WHOOPEE!!!

1928.48

THE RED ROBE

A Romantic Play with Music in Three Acts, 5 Scenes. Based on a novel ('Under the Red Robe') by Stanley Weyman. Book by Harry B. Smith and Edward Delaney Dunn. Music by Jean Gilbert. Lyrics by Harry B. Smith. Production staged by Stanley Logan. Revised and restaged by José Ruben. Dances and ensembles staged by Raymond Midgley; dances by Hale Girls by Chester Hale. Settings designed by Watson Barratt. Costumes designed by Barbier of Paris and Ernest Schrapps. Musical director, John L. McManus. Produced by the Messrs. Shubert. Opened 25 December 1928 at the Sam S. Shubert Theatre, moved 13 May 1929 to Jolson's Theatre and closed 18 May 1929 after 167 performances.

CAST (in order of appearance): *Nanette:* MARJORIE PETERSON. *Lieutenant Roland de Brissac:* GEORGE DOBBS. *Servant at Café Zaton:* Walter Brennan. *Captain La Rolle:* Barnett Parker. *Hercule:* BARRY LUPINO. *Jacques:* Ivan Arbuckle.

---

[67]Dropped after opening.
[68]Dropped after opening.

A Lady: Peggy Dolan. *Marquis de Pombal*: ROY GORDON. *de Fargis*: Gerald Gehlert. *Gil de Berault*, a Soldier of Fortune: WALTER WOOLF. *Marie*, Nanette's sister: VIOLET CARLSON. *Renée de Cocheforet*: HELEN GILLILAND. *Sir John Blunt*: John H. Goldsworthy. A *Conspirator*: Edward Marshall. *His Eminence, Cardinal Richelieu*: José Ruben. *Friar Joseph*, Richelieu's confidante: Lee Beggs. *Sergeant Corbeau*: Edward Orchard. *Maids in Café Zaton*: Alice Harper, Alice Kennedy, Nell Moran, Grace Driggs. *Elaine, Countess de Cocheforet*: MANILA POWERS. *Henri*, Count de Cocheforet: S. Herbert Braggiotti. *Lieutenant Manet*: Charles Carver. *François*, Servant at de Cocheforet's: Hugh Chilvers. *Sergeant Malpus*: Fred von Golisch. *An Abbe*: Charles Froom. A *Courtier*: Ernest Goodhart. *The King's Chamberlain*: Ivan Arbuckle. *Louis XIII*: Edward Marshall.

Chester Hale Girls: Charlotte Beverly, Theo Van Tassel, Martha Eaton, Paula Bassaner, Josephine Roberts, Beatrice Rupp, Jean Devlyn, Veva Burns, Winona Sweet, Nina Dalenge, Evelyn Grant, Gohanna Fredhoven, Mara Rosoff, Catheryn Laughlin, Margaret Stone, Georgene Stokes. *Ladies of the Ensemble*: Dorothy Cartier, Ruth Elaine, Alice Kennedy, Grace Driggs, Mary Clifford, Mabel McCarthy, Berta Gitel, Alice Harper, Kathryn Richmond, Peggy Dolan, Alfreda Oakes, Betty Murrow, Nell Moran, Edith Artley, Laura Novea, Sally Coakley, Adeline Bradley, Lillian Lane, Esther Oyen, Helene Gardner, Helen Hermes, Elaine Arden, Peggy Udell, Sara Granzor, Aini Hendricks, Nancy Corrigan, Elaine Reign, Rowena Scott, Madge McAnally, Frances Spencer, Roberta Kent, Genevieve Semashko, Julia Barker, Gladys Granzor. *Gentlemen of the Ensemble*: Jack Lister, Charles Froom, Alphonse Iglesias, Alexander Creighton, Alfred Deste, Harrison Fuller, Bernard Mills, Clarence Wheeler, Ernest Goodhart, J. L. McCarthy, John Mangum, Donald Catlin, Fred von Golisch, Nino Nonomo, John Cameran, Theo. Bayer, Edward Marshall, Earl Vincent, George Rolland, Parker Colby, Walter Cross, Richard Scharff, John Walsh, Waldemar Asmus, Gregory Pavlovsky, Peter Prihodsky, W. J. Brennan, Paul Moran, Evon Alexis, Frank Ryan, Thomas Glover, Efin Vitis, Glenn McAully, Jack Bauer, John Early, Marc Christie.

Time: 1630.

ACT 1: Café Zaton in Paris.

ACT 2, *Scene 1*: A Room in the Chateau de Cocheforet in Provence. *Scene 2*: The Park of the Chateau. *Scene 3*: The Garden of the Chateau.

ACT 3: A Salon in the Palais de Richelieu.

ACT 1

Opening
M. Peterson, Ensemble

"Roll of the Drum"
G. Dobbs, M. Peterson, Ensemble

"I'll Love Them All to Death"
M. Peterson, G. Dobbs, Hale Girls, Boys

"King of the Sword"
W. Woolf
(*Music by* Robert Stolz and Maurice Rubens. *Lyrics by* J. Keirn Brennan.)

"Only a Smile"
W. Woolf, H. Gilliland

"Whatever It Is, I've Got It" (I've Got It)
B. Lupino, V. Carlson
(*Music by* Alberta Nichols. *Lyrics by* Mann Holiner.)

"Joy or Strife"
W. Woolf, Boys

"Only a Smile" (reprise)
W. Woolf, H. Gilliland

Finale
H. Gilliland, W. Woolf, G. Dobbs, R. Gordon, G. Gehlert, Ensemble, Chester Hale Girls

ACT 2

"A Plaintive"
M. Powers

"Home o' Mine"
H. Gilliland, M. Powers

"Where Love Grows" (Duet)
H. Gilliland, W. Woolf

"Soldiers Like You and Me"[69]
M. Peterson, G. Dobbs, Chester Hale Girls

"The Thrill of a Kiss" (Burlesque Duet)
V. Carlson, B. Lupino

"Cavalier"[70]
W. Woolf, Boys
(*Music and Lyrics by* Harden Church.)

[69]Dropped after opening.
[70]Replaced during the run by:
"Joy or Strife"
W. Woolf, Boys

Ballet
Chester Hale Girls

"(Oh,) How the Girls Adore Me"
B. Parker, B. Lupino, Ladies

"The Gallop"
Chester Hale Girls

Finale
. Woolf, H. Gilliland, M. Powers, Ensemble

ACT 3

Opening
Chester Hale Girls, Ensemble

"Whatever It Is, I've Got It" (reprise)
V. Carlson, B. Lupino

"I Plead, Dear Heart" (Solo)
H. Gilliland

Finale
W. Woolf, H. Gilliland, Ensemble

THE HOUSEBOAT ON THE STYX

1928.49

A Smart Musical Version with Songs in Two Acts, 7 Scenes. Book by Kenneth Webb and John E. Hazzard. Adapted from the satire of the same name by John Kendrick Bangs. Music and lyrics by (Monte) Carlo and (Alma) Sanders. Play directed by Oscar Eagle. Dances and ensembles arranged by Ray Perez and supervised by Chester Hale. Settings designed by Willy Pogany. Costumes designed by John Booth. Musical director, Hilding Anderson. Orchestrations by Stephen P. Jones, Hans Spialek, Charles Miller, Hilding Anderson. Entire production under the personal supervision of Ned Jakobs. Produced by The Houseboat on the Styx, Inc. (Ned Jakobs). Opened 25 December 1928 at the Liberty Theatre and closed 23 March 1929 after 103 performances.

CAST (in order of speaking): *Charon*, Ferryman of the River Styx: BERTRAM PEACOCK. *Ponce de Leon*: SAM ASH. *Queen Elizabeth*: BLANCHE RING. *Salome*: Virginia Watts. *Mrs. Noah*: Jessie Graham. *Sappho*: Millicent Bancroft. *Lucretia Borgia*: Mary McDonald. *Queen of Sheba*: PAULINE DEE. *Delilah*: Helene Arden. *Helen of Troy*: Georgia Gwynne. *Josephine*: Marion Stuart. *Madame DuBarry*: Dorothy Acker. *Sir Walter Raleigh*: HAL FORDE. *The Six Wives of Henry VIII: Catherine of Aragon*: Dorothy Humphreys. *Anne Boleyn*: Edith Britton. *Jane Seymour*: Grace Cantrelle. *Anne of Cleves*: Gloria Clare. *Katherine Howard*: Myrtle Arnette. *Katherine Parr*: Katharine Porter. *Henry VIII*: WILLIAM DANFORTH. *A Servant*: Richard MacAleese. *Captain William Kidd*: JOHN E. HAZZARD. *Cleopatra*: ALICE MacKENZIE. *Adam, Eva*: Maurine and Norva. *George Washington*: Cliff Heckinger. *Napoleon*: Johnny Fields. *P. T. Barnum*: Harry Bates. *Nero*: Harry Hermsen. *Shakespeare*: John Osborne Clemson. *Morgan*: Richard MacAleese. *A Pirate, a Slave*: Maurine and Norva. *Captain of Police*: DOROTHY HUMPHREYS. *Columbus*: Johnny Fields. *Noah*: Cliff Heckinger. *Sherlock Holmes*: Charles Gibney. *Specialty Dancers*: Al Jordan, Vera Clarke, Petra Olsen, Dorothy Humphreys.

Famous Ladies of History: Rita Jason, Kay Apgar, Vera Villon, Joan Collier, Peggy Wilson, Joanna Allen. *Club Members and Pirates*: Robert Spencer, A. William Packer, Alfred Parrot, Herman Amend, Tom Maynard, N. Clifton, Victor Esker, Tom Denton, Raleigh Orbit, Warren Pittinger, Richard Lynn, Maurice Warner, Jules Oshim, John Coraldo. *The Little Hellions*: Mildred Rye, Marjorie Rich, Ethel Guerrard, Vera Clarke, Margaret Randolph, Gene Fontaine, Myrna Dale, Nadia Gary, Dorothy Waller, Vasso Pan, Renee Crandall, Petra Olsen, Florence Madison, Sydney Reynolds, Sydna Morgan, Bobby Bliss.

ACT 1, *Scene 1*: Charon's Ferry on the River Styx. *Scene 2*: Grand Hall in Henry VIII's Castle. *Scene 3*: Snuggery of the Houseboat. *Scene 4*: The Houseboat at the Dock.

ACT 2, *Scene 1*: The Deck of the Houseboat. *Scene 2*: A Street in Hades. *Scene 3*: The Deck of the Houseboat.

ACT 1

Scene 1

"Ode to the Styx"
B. Peacock

Scene 2

Opening:
Arrival of Guests Ensemble
"Queen Elizabeth's Tea" B. Ring, Ensemble

"The Houseboat on the Styx"
H. Forde, B. Ring, Ensemble

"The Roll Call in the Morning"
W. Danforth, D. Humphreys, E. Britton, G. Cantrelle, G. Clare, M. Arnette, K. Porter

"Cleopatra, We're Fond of You"
A. MacKenzie, Boys
"The Fountain of Youth"
A. MacKenzie, S. Ash, B. Ring, H. Forde
"My Heaven"
S. Ash, A. MacKenzie, Ensemble
Scene 3
Dance of the Apple[71]
Maurine, Norva
Scene 4
"Club Song"
Club Members
"Back in the Days of Long Ago"
B. Peacock, Club Members
Scene 5
"An Irate Pirate Am I"
J. E. Hazzard, Pirates
Finale
J. E. Hazzard, B. Peacock, S. Ash, A. MacKenzie, B. Ring, Ensemble
ACT 2[72]
Scene 1
"Pirate Dance"
Pirate, Slave
"Red River"
P. Dee, Ensemble
"Soul Mates"
S. Ash, A. MacKenzie
Finaletto
J. E. Hazzard, A. MacKenzie, S. Ash, B. Peacock, Ensemble
Scene 2
"Hell's Finest"
D. Humphreys, Police Imps
"Men of Hades"
H. Forde, B. Peacock, W. Danforth, S. Ash, Club Members
Scene 3
Specialty Dance[73]
Three Little Sailors
Scene 4
"My Heaven"[74] (reprise)
S. Ash, A. MacKenzie
Scene 7
"You've Got to Know How to Make Love"
B. Ring
"Someone Like You"
H. Forde, M. McDonald, Ensemble
Finale
Entire Company

1928.50

HELLO DADDY

A Musical Comedy in Two Acts, 4 Scenes. Book by Herbert Fields. Based on a farce ('The High Cost of Loving') adapted from the German by Frank Mandel. Music by Jimmy McHugh. Lyrics by Dorothy Fields. Book staged by Alexander Leftwich. Musical numbers staged by Busby Berkeley. Costumes designed by Charles LeMaire. Settings designed by Herman Rosse. Orchestrations by Maurice dePackh, Stephen Jones, Fod Livingston, Hans Spialek. Musical numbers played by Ben Bernie and his Central Park Hotel Orchestra, William Moore, conductor. Musical arrangements of the Giersdorf Sisters' songs by Arthur Johnston. Entire production under the

supervision of John Murray Anderson. Produced by Lew Fields. Opened 26 December 1928 at the Mansfield Theatre, moved 21 January 1929 to the George M. Cohan Theatre, moved 6 May 1929 to Erlanger's Theatre and closed 15 June 1929 after 198 performances.

CAST (in order of appearance): *Miss Prichard, Principal at Cedarhurst*: Florence Earle. *Students at Cedarhurst* (6): *Betty Hauser*: BETTY STARBUCK. *Grace*: MARJORIE MAY MARTYN. *Dot*: DOROTHY ROY. *Eloise*: Ethel Allen. *Ellen*: Elizabeth Crandall. *Edna*: Dorothy Croyle. *Anthony Bennett*: WILFRED CLARK. *Lawrence Tucker*: ALLEN KEARNS. *Mary Block*: MARY LAWLOR. *Henry Block*: LEW FIELDS. *Emma Block*: ALICE FISCHER. *Helen*: WANDA GOLL. *Noel Burnham*: BILLY TAYLOR. *Edward Hauser*: GEORGE HASSELL. *Mathilde Burnham*: Madeline Grey. *Godfrey Burnham*: Carroll Glucas. *Helen, Gertrude, Marguerite*: THE GIERSDORF SISTERS (Irene, Elvira, Rae).
Girls of the Chorus: Annette Atherton, Bobby Brodsley, Harriet Carling, Jean Egan, Helen Fried, Doris Jay, Henrietta Kay, Betty Lockwood, Frances Norton, Valerie Petri, Emmy Lou Petri, Paula Sands, Inez Tremble, Peggy Tebbs, Jae Voll, Jane Sherman. *Boys of the Chorus*: David Morton, Jerome Maxwell, James Bradleigh, Donald Brown, Larry Regan, Jack Waldron, Charles Scott, Edward Hackett. *Singers*: Mae Muth, Shirley Buford, Elizabeth Crandall, Patricia Ross, Bob Burk, Albert Hewitt, George C. Lehrian, Donn Carney.

ACT 1, Scene 1: Before the Cedarhurst School for Girls. Graduation Day. Scene 2: The Club Car of a local train. Scene 3: The Reception Room at Block's.

ACT 2: The Sun Parlor at Block's. Next morning.

ACT 1[75]
Scene 1
"Three Little Maids from School"
B. Starbuck, D. Roy, M. M. Martyn, Ensemble
"I Want Plenty of You"
M. Lawlor, A. Kearns
"Futuristic Rhythm"
W. Goll, Ensemble
Scene 2
"Let's Sit and Talk About You"
A. Kearns, M. Lawlor
Reprise
Giersdorf Sisters
Scene 3
"My Lady's Fan"[76] (*Arranged by* Madame Lenora.)
Ensemble
"Your Disposition Is Mine"
M. Lawlor, A. Kearns, Ensemble
"In a Great Big Way"
B. Starbuck, B. Taylor, Ensemble
Finale
Ensemble
ACT 2
"Maybe Means Yes"
W. Goll, Chorus
"As Long as We're in Love"
M. Lawlor, A. Kearns, Giersdorf Sisters
"Out Where the Blues Begin"
B. Taylor, Chorus
"Maybe Means Yes"
M. Lawlor, A. Kearns, B. Starbuck, B. Taylor
Finale
Company

1929.01

DEEP HARLEM

A Musical Comedy in Two Acts, 15 Scenes. Book by (Salem) Whitney and (J. Homer) Tutt. Music by Joe Jordan. Lyrics by Homer Tutt and Henry Creamer. Entire production staged by Henry Creamer. Costumes by Brooks Costume Company. Settings by Mallard H. Frane's Sons. Orchestrations by, and orchestra under the direction of Joe Jordan. Produced by Samuel

---

[71]Dropped after opening.
[72]Act 2 revised during the run, song order rearranged. Added during run:
"Men" (Opening of Act 2)
Ensemble
Irate Pirate Dance (Act 2, following "Pirate Dance")
J. E. Hazzard, V. Pan [Kiddy}
[73]Dropped after opening.
[74]Dropped after opening.

[75]Act 2 song order revised during the run. Added to Act 1, Scene 2 (end):
"Let's Sit and Talk About You" (reprise)
A. Kearns, M. Lawlor
[76]During the run, replaced by: "Party Line"
Ensemble

Grisman. Opened 7 January 1929 at the Hudson Theatre and closed 12 January 1929 after 8 performances.

CAST [in order of appearance]: *An Author*: Andrew Bishop. *King*: SALEM WHITNEY. *Queen*: Rosa White. *Crown Prince*: J. HOMER TUTT. *Princess Lulu*: JUANITA STINNETTE. *Princess Ola*: Mabel Ridley. *Princess of Bataboula*: CHAPPIE CHAPPELLE. *Temptress*: NEEKA SHAW. *Prophet*: JIMMY BASKETT. *Jethro, Jester*: JOHN MASON. *Nebo, Jester*: COLUMBUS JACKSON. *Slave Traders*: Andrew Bishop, Sterling Grant. *Belgian Slave Traders*: William Edmonson, Billy Andrews. *African Native*: August Golden. *Congo-Lulu*: Rookie Davis. *Africana*: NEEKA SHAW. *Elder Toots*: SALEM WHITNEY. *Bridesmaids*: H. Wallace, J. Wallace, W. Walker, D. Walker. *Auctioneer*: Andrew Bishop. *Colored Picnickers*: Marietta Warren, Lucy Yarborough. *Dancing Dan*: Howard Elmore. *Dancing Ivy*: Ivy Black. *Soft-Steppers*: Gertrude Gardeen, Virginia Branum. *Mrs. Jenkins*: LENA WILSON. *Glory*: Gertrude Gardeen. *Hally*: Alice Sampson. *Lulia*: Virginia Branum. *Billy*: Billy Andrews. *Jen*: Pearl McCormack. *Miranda, Jethro's Wife*: JUANITA STINNETTE. *High Yaller*: Mabel Ridley. *Crow Jane*: Harriet Williams. *Officer*: William Edmundson. *Quartette*: Birmingham Four. *Jelly Bean*: HOMER TUTT. *Red*: Sterling Grant. *Pearl*: Pearl McCormack. *Officer*: JIMMY BASKETT. *Citizen*: Billy Andrews. *Ticket Girl*: Mabel Ridley. *Detective*: William Edmonson. *The Creeper*: HOMER TUTT. *His Gal*: Alice Gorgas. *It*: Howard Elmore. *That*: Rosa White. *The Orator*: SALEM WHITNEY. *Salvation Girls*: The Creole Four. *Officer*: Charles Ridley. *The Porter*: George Whittington. *Entertainer*: LENA WILSON. *Pianist*: Mabel Ridley. *Sailors*: Cutout and Leonard. *Boss*: Columbus Jackson. *The Real Boss*: John Mason. *The Dancer*: NEEKA SHAW. *Her Friend*: Billy Andrews. *Haly*: Gertrude Gardeen. *Her Boy Friend*: Sterling Grant.

(*Dance Specialties*: Cutout and Leonard, Ivy Black, Virginia Branum, Marietta Warren, Mary Welch, Louise Williams, Mary King, Charles Ridley, Alice Gorgas, Thomas R. Hall, George Whittington.) *Female Singers*: The Creole Four: Helen Wallace, Jean Wallace, Winifred Walker, Dorothy Walker. And Marietta Warren, Inez Glover, Carrie Huff, Lucy Yarborough, Harriet Williams. *Male Singers*: August Golden, Thomas R. Hall, A. G. Edwards. *The Birmingham Four*: Messrs. Keys, Gaytzera, Ausbrook, Bridges. *The Northern Brothers*: Joe, Felix, Ralph, Robert. Joe Robinson, Cherokee Thornton. *Dancing Misses*: Louise Williams, Rose Anderson, Alice Sampson, Gertrude Gardeen, Virginia Branum, Bobby Johns, Anita Wharton, Elmira Britt, Mary Welch, Ivy Black, Emily Malloy, Thula Oryiz, Rebecca Braxton, Mary King, Claudia Heyward, Palm Roberts, Marie Fraine, May King, Ruby Meyers, Frances Johnson.

ACT 1, Scene 1: Banquet Hall, Castle of the Cushites. *Scene 2*: Desert in Africa. *Scene 3*: The Slave Ship. *Scene 4*: Jungle in Africa. *Scene 5*: Southern Slave Mart. *Scene 6*: Southern Lane. *Scene 7*: The Plantation Jubilee.

ACT 2, Scene 1: Outskirts of Savannah, Georgia. *Scene 2*: Street of Savannah. *Scene 3*: Outskirts of Savannah, Georgia. *Scene 4*: 135th Street and Lenox Avenue, New York City. *Scene 5*: Outside Variety Theatre, 131st Street and Seventh Avenue, New York City. *Scene 6*: The Black Puppy Cabaret in Harlem. *Scene 7*: 139th Street, between Seventh and Eighth Avenues in New York City. *Scene 8*: Rockefeller Apartments, 150th Street and Seventh Avenue, New York City.

ACT 1

Scene 1

"Cushite Dance"
    Ensemble
"I Shall Love You" (Duet)
    C. Chappelle, J. Stinnette
"Dance of the Temptress"
    N. Shaw
Comic Dance
    J. Mason, C. Jackson
"I Shall Love You" (reprise)
    C. Chappelle, J. Stinnette

Scene 2

"Deliver"
    Slave Ensemble

Scene 3

"Slave Ship"
    Slave Ensemble

Scene 4

"Africana"
    R. Davis, N. Shaw, Africanas

Scene 6

"Tappin' to the Picnic"
    H. Elmore, Dancing Girls, I. Black, G. Gardeen, V. Branum, Cutout and Leonard
"Kentucky"/"Mexican Blues"
    C. Chappelle, J. Stinnette

Scene 7

"Old Plantation"
    L. Wilson, Company
"Virginia Reel"
    Company
"I'm Loving" (Song)
    B. Andrews, G. Gardeen, Entire Company

ACT 2

Scene 1

"Possum Trot"
    R. Davis, Girls, L. Wilson, G. Gardeen, V. Branum, A. Sampson, Cutout and Leonard, N. Shaw
"Real High Yaller and Sealskin Brown"
    J. Mason, C. Jackson

Scene 4

"Deep Harlem" J. Baskett

Scene 5

"Rags and Tatters"
    G. Whittington
"Deep Harlem" (reprise)
    J. Baskett

Scene 6

Floor Dance
    Company
Sailors Dance
    Cutout and Leonard
Song
    L. Wilson
"Y Como Le Va"
    N. Shaw
Floor Dance
    Company

Scene 7

"Why?" (Duet)
    C. Chappelle, J. Stinnette

Scene 8

"I Shall Love You" (reprise)
    C. Chappelle, J. Stinnette
"Deep Harlem" (reprise)
    Company

1929.02 POLLY

A Musical Comedy in Two Acts, 6 Scenes. Book by Guy Bolton, George Middleton and Isabel Leighton. Based on the play 'Polly With a Past' by David Belasco. Music by Herbert Stothart, Philip Charig. Lyrics by Irving Caesar. Book staged by John Harwood. Dances and ensembles staged by Jack Haskell. Scenery by Joseph Urban. Costumes designed by Mark Mooring. Orchestra under the direction of Herbert Stothart. Produced by Arthur Hammerstein. Opened 8 January 1929 at the Lyric Theatre and closed 19 January 1929 after 15 performances.

CAST (in order of appearance): *Clay Cullen*: Leonard Sillman[77]. *Sue*: Marion Saki. *Betty*: Inez Courtney. *Harry Richards*: HARRY K. MORTON. *Polly Shannon*: JUNE. *Addie Stiles*, Reporter on The Sag Harbor Bee: FRED ALLEN. *Bill Collector*: Alonzo Price. *Bill Collector*: Alonzo Price. *Rex Van Zile*: JOHN HUNDLEY. *Myrtle Grant*: LUCY MONROE. *Mrs. Van Zile*, Rex's Mother: ISABEL O'MADIGAN. *Prentice Van Zile*: Charles Esdale. *Arturo*: Tudor Penrose.

Waiters, Cigarette Girl, Hat Check Girl, etc. Specialty Dancers: Thalia Zanou, Asya Kaz, Gus and Will, George Andre. *Dancers*: Louise Allen, Norine Bogan, Dorothy Brown, Billie Cortez, Hellene Counihan, Martha Carroll, Anita Gordon, Buddy Haines, Evelyn Hannons, Dorothy Hiller, Sandra LaMar, Jessie Madison, Peggy Messinger, Dolly Mannon, Ruby Poe, Lucille Reece, Marcella Rio, Bunny Schumm, Audrey Sturgess, Greta Swanson, Edna May Wright, Grace Wright, Paulette Winston, Rosalie Wynn. *Boys*: William Tasek, Louis Delgado, William Preston, Hal Bird, Howard Rand, Jimmy Lee, Robert Matthews, Charles Townsend, Robert Hall, William Penney, Howard Bradford, Geoffrey Luck. *The Manhatters Quartet*: Joseph Anderson, Don Buchanan, Jack Norman, Walter Bunker. *The Happy Go-Lucky Trio*: Hubert Hilton, Cliff Daly, Edward Mowan.

---

[77]Opening night programs and Variety credit Leonard Sillman in this role; other reviews credit William Seabury.

Time: The Present.

ACT 1, *Scene 1*: The Abadaba Night Club. *Scene 2*: Editorial Room, Hampton Bee. *Scene 3*: The Southampton Golf Club.

ACT 2, *Scene 1*: Garden of Mrs. Van Zile's Home in Southampton. *Scene 2*: The Railroad Station. *Scene 3*: The Spanish Inn.

ACT 1

"The Abadaba Club" (Opening)
Ensemble

"When a Fellow Meets a Flapper (on Broadway)"
L. Sillman, M. Saki
(*Music by* Phil Charig.)

"Be the Secret of My Life"
H. K. Morton, I. Courtney

"Polly"
June, H. K. Morton, L. Sillman, Ensemble
(*Music by* Phil Charig.)

"Sing a Song in the Rain"
June, J. Hundley
(*Music by* Harry Rosenthal. *Lyrics by* Douglas Furber and Irving Caesar.)

Song
Happy-Go-Lucky Trio

"Lover Come Back to Me"
L. Monroe, Boys

Dance
Gus and Will

"Comme Si, Comme Ça"
June, Ensemble
(*Music by* Phil Charig.)

"Nobody Wants Me"
H. K. Morton, I. Courtney

Finale
Entire Company

ACT 2

"Little Bo-Peep" (Opening)
June, Ensemble

"Heel and Toe"
I. Courtney, Ensemble
(*Music by* Phil Charig.)

"Sweet Liar"
June, J. Hundley\
(*Music by* Herbert Stothart.)

Reprise
June

"Life Is Love"
T. Penrose, Ensemble

Danse Espagnol
Zanou and Kaz

Spanish Dance
H. K. Morton, I. Courtney

Ballet de Bagdad
June, assisted by G. Andre

Finale
Entire Company

1929.03

FOLLOW THRU

A Musical Slice of Country Club Life (Musical Comedy) in Two Acts, 12 Scenes. Book by Laurence Schwab and Buddy G. DeSylva. Music by Ray Henderson. Lyrics by Buddy G. DeSylva and Lew Brown. Book directed by Edgar MacGregor. Dances staged by Bobby Connolly. Settings by Donald Oenslager. Frocks (costumes) by Kiviette. Orchestra under the direction of Alfred Goodman. Produced by Laurence Schwab and Frank Mandel. Opened 9 January 1929 at the 46th Street Theatre and closed 21 December 1929 after 401 performances.

CAST: *"Mac" Moore*, a Golf Professional: ARTHUR AYLESWORTH. *Thomas Darcy "Dinty" Moore*, his 16-year old son: DON TOMKINS. *Lora Moore*, his daughter: IRENE DELROY. *Angie Howard*, her girl-friend: ZELMA O'NEAL. *Martin Bascomb*, President of the Bound Brook Country Club: Frank Kingdon. *Babs Bascomb*, his 15-year old daughter: MARGARET LEE. *J. C. Effingham*, a New

Member: JOHN SHEEHAN. *Jerry Downs*, a Young Golf Champion: JOHN BARKER. *Jack Martin*: JACK HALEY. *Ruth Van Horn*, an Amateur Golf Champion: MADELINE CAMERON. *Mrs. Bascomb*, the President's Wife: EDITH CAMPBELL. *Mr. Manning*: Al Downing. *Molly*: Eleanor Powell. *Steve*: Paul Howard. *Olive*: Dorothy Christy. *Glenna*: Yvonne Grey. *Virginia*: Constance Lane. *Cynthia*: Sherry Pelham.

The Country Club Boys: Carrick Douglas, Jack Lawrence, W. E. Critzer, Oscar Ellinger, John Hammond, Fred Kuhnly, Arthur Bryan, Maurice Siegel. *Boys, Girls, Caddies, etc.*: *Ladies*: Ruth Kent, Zilpha DeWitt, Claire Joyce, Ethel Lawrence, Christine Ecklund, Mildred Stevens, Katherine Cornell[78], Elaine Lank, Bodil Lund, Jane Brown, Margaret Banks, Minerva Wilson, Irene Hamlin, Ann Lomax, Sherry Pelham, Renee Vilon, Mildred Webb, Drucilla Strain, Dorothea Dunn, Arlyne White, Irene Warner, Dorothy Day, Hilda Burkhart, Dody Donnelly, Anita Pam, Marguerite Kennedy, Jocelyn Lyle. *Gentlemen*: Herbert Rothwell, Phil King, Samuel Quinn, Harry Moore, Mortimer O'Brien, John McCahill, Gordon Merrick, Richard Neely, Joe Evans, William Sahner, Arthur Craig, Ned Lynn, Fred Murray, Phil Farley, Richard Renaud, Jerry White, Paul Mann.

The Action takes place at the Bound Brook Country Club in early July.

ACT 1, *Scene 1*: The Bound Brook Country Club in Gay 1908. *Scene 2*: On the Golf Course. 20 Years Later. *Scene 3*: The Sun Porch. A few hours later. *Scene 4*: Behind the First Tee. That night. *Scene 5*: In Front of the Clubhouse. The following day.

ACT 2, *Scene 1*: In front of the Clubhouse, the next day. *Scene 2*: Near the Clubhouse. *Scene 3*: The Ladies' Dressing Room. *Scene 4*: At the 14th Hole. *Scene 5*: On the 18th Green. *Scene 6*: Behind the First Tee. *Scene 7*: At the Gate.

ACT 1

"The Daring Gibson Girl"
The Gibson Girls

"The 1908 Life"
Ensemble

"It's a Great Sport"
M. Lee, I. Delroy, M. Cameron, Ensemble

"My Lucky Star"
J. Barker, Girls, Country Club Boys

"Button Up Your Overcoat"
Z. O'Neal, J. Haley

"You Wouldn't Fool Me, Would Ya'?"
J. Barker, I. Delroy, Ensemble

Special Dance[79]
P. Howard

"He's a Man's Man"
M. Cameron, Boys

Reprise
I. Delroy, J. Barker

"Then I'll Have Time for You"
M. Lee, D. Tomkins

"I Want To Be Bad"
A. O'Neal, Ensemble

Finale
Entire Company

ACT 2

"Married Men and Single Men"
D. Tomkins, M. Lee, Ensemble

"If There Were No More You"
J. Barker, I. Delroy, Country Club Boys

"I Could Give Up Anything But You"
J. Haley, Z. O'Neal

"Follow Thru"
M. Cameron, Ensemble

Special Dance
E. Powell

Finaletto
Entire Company

Reprise
J. Haley, Z. O'Neal

Finale
Entire Company

---

[78]Not the well-known dramatic actress of the 1930s and 1940s.
[79]Dropped during the run.

1929.04 NED WAYBURN'S GAMBOLS

A Musical Revue in Two Acts, 28 Scenes. (Sketches by Eddie Welch, Lew Hearn, Morrie Ryskind, Roger Gray, George Haight, Jr.) Music by Walter G. Samuels; additional melodies by Arthur Schwartz, Lew Kessler. Lyrics by Morrie Ryskind; some (additional) lyrics by Clifford Grey. Staged by Ned Wayburn. Costumes designed by Charles LeMaire. Settings designed by William Weaver and Ted Weidhaus. Musical director, George McKay. Produced by Ned Wayburn. Opened 15 January 1929 at the Knickerbocker Theatre and closed 9 February 1929 after 31 performances.

CAST: LEW HEARN, ROGER GRAY, LIBBY HOLMAN, OLIVE McCLURE, CHARLES IRWIN, WILLIAM HOLBROOK, GRACE BOWMAN, JOHN BYAM, ANN PRITCHARD, FUZZY KNIGHT, SHIRLEY RICHARDS, CHARLES ELBEY, CAPERTON, (Earl) BIDDLE and (Jack) RANDALL, Virginia Alexander, (Ann) Butler and (Hal) Parker, Patricia McGrath, Frances Cole, Eileen Healy, Priscilla Gurney, Frank May.

Senior Promenaders: Charlotte Earle, Marietta Murphy, Dorothy Koster, Helen Koster, Onyte Burke, Claire Waska, Ann Lawrence, Patricia McGrath, Margaret O'Berg, Heather Haldern, Betty Welton, Azilee Phillips, Luonora Davis. *Junior Promenaders*: Frances Cole, Virginia MacNaughton, Margaret Reynolds, Grace Welsh, Eleanor Rumrill, Garnet O'Brien, Edyth Walton, Virginia Roundey, Romayne Campbell, Florence Marrener, Alyce Swanson, Rojean Reynolds, Eileen Healy.

ACT 1[80]
> *The Author*: C. Irwin.

Scene 1
Harem Life
"Crescent Moon"
> G. Bowman, Promenaders
> *The Sultan*: J. Randall. *Fatima*: V. Alexander. *Oriental Dancer*: O. McClure.

Scene 2
"I Bring My Boys Along"
> A. Pritchard
> (*Lyrics by* Clifford Grey.)
> *Assisted by* F. Knight, W. Holbrook, J. Randall, J. Byam, E. Biddle, F. May.
"I Bring My Girls Along"
> C. Elbey
> *Assisted by* V. Alexander, B. Welton, P. Gurney, L. Davis, H. Koster, M. Murphy.

Scene 3
Broadway (*by* Eddie Welch)
> *Traffic Cop*: R. Gray.

Scene 4
Eccentric Dance
> C. Elbey

Scene 5
Grandmother's Garden
"In Days Gone By"
> W. Holbrook
> *Assisted by* the Senior Promenaders.
"Last Rose of Summer"
> V. Alexander
> *Tea Rose*: A. Pritchard. *Sweetest Little Fellow*: W. Holbrook. *Pages*: R. Reynolds, V. Roundey.
Toe Ballet
> *Headed by* A. Pritchard
> *Assisted by* the Junior Promenaders.

Scene 6
The General
> C. Irwin

Scene 7
"The Church Around the Corner"
> J. Walsh, to P. Gurney

Scene 8
Gentlemen of the Evening (*by* Lew Hearn)
> *An Actress*: L. Holman. *Charlie*: L. Hearn. *O'Malley*: R. Gray.

Scene 9
"Sweet Old-Fashioned Waltz"
> J. Byam
> *Pink Lady*: S. Richards. *Sympathy*: P. McGrath. *Blue Danube*: D. Koster. *Kiss in the Dark*: C. Earle. *Merry Widow*: L. Davis. *Sweetheart*: O. Burke. *Kiss in the Dark*: G. Bowman. *Three O'Clock in the Morning*: C. Waska.

Scene 10
Nite Life
Eccentric Toe Dance
> F. Cole
"(There Ain't No Sweet Man Worth the) Salt of My Tears"
> L. Holman
> (*Music and Lyrics by* Fred Fisher.)
Acrobatic Fox Trot
> O. McClure
Exhibition Waltz
> W. Holbrook, A. Pritchard
The Little Red Piano and Fuzzy Knight.
> *The Host*: C. Irwin. *The Snooper*: L. Hearn. *Setting designed by* T. Weidhaas.

Scene 11
"Savannah Stomp"
> J. Byam, to S. Richards
> *Danced by* the Senior Promenaders.

Scene 12
A Triple-Time Tap Dance
> S. Richards

Scene 13
War Is Swell[81] (*by* Morrie Ryskind)
> *The General*: C. Irwin. *A Private*: R. Gray. *Another*: F. Knight. *Still Another*: L. Hearn.

Scene 14
"Mothers O'Men"[82]
> L. Holman
Tableau[83]
> *Gold Mother*: A. Pritchard. *Daughter*: E. Healy. *Red Cross Nurse*: P. Gurney. *Shell-Shocked Private*: F. Knight. *In the Trenches*: L. Hearn, F. May. *Another Nurse*: Miss Vereaux. *Doctor*: C. Irwin. *Stretcher Bearer*: E. Biddle. *The Unknown Soldier*: C. Elbey.
Finale: The Drawbridge of Dreams
> *Mars*: R. Gray. *Setting designed by* T. Weidhaas.
> Introducing the Promenaders, headed by S. Richards, executing a manual of arms while performing a Triple-time military tap dance. *Setting designed by* T. Weidhaas.

ACT 2
Scene 1
Ballet Noir
> *Statue*: A. Pritchard. *The Grim Reaper*: F. May. *Pierrots*: M. O'Berg, A. Lawrence. *Danced by* G. Walsh, R. Reynolds, R. Campbell, F. Marrener, P. McGrath, Burke, E. Rumrill, V. MacNaughton, V. Roundey, C. Waska, A. Phillips, D. Koster.
A Few Remarks by Charles Irwin

Scene 2
At Home: "The Sun Will Shine"
> G. Bowman, J. Byam
> (*Music by* Arthur Schwartz.)
> *Danced by* the Promenaders, S. Richards, O. McClure, P. Gurney.

Scene 3
So I Hear (*by* Roger Gray)
> *Ronald, who is deaf*: L. Hearn. *Harvey, who is likewise*: R. Gray. *Harvey's Wife*: L. Holman.

Scene 4
"Indian Prayer"
> J. Byam
> *Indian Priestess*: P. Gurney. *Indians*: Senior Promenaders.
"Ride 'Em Cowboys"
> A. Pritchard
> (*Sketch by* Roger Gray. *Music by* Arthur Schwartz. *Lyrics by* Clifford Grey.)
> *Cowboys*: Junior Promenaders.

---

[80]Order of songs and sketches revised after opening. Added after opening:
The Memory Course (Act 2)
> A. Butler, H. Parker

[81]Dropped after opening.
[82]Dropped after opening.
[83]Dropped after opening.

Scene 5

"What Is the Good?"[84]
J. Walsh, G. Bowman
(*Music by* Lew Kessler. *Lyrics by* Clifford Grey.)

Scene 6

The Price of Fame (*by* George Haight)
Scene: An Apartment in the Fifities, New York.
The Actress: G. Bowman. *The Maid*: P. Gurney. *First Man*: F. Knight. *Second Man*: C. Elbey.

Scene 7

"Montmartre"
L. Holman

Scene 8

Florida, the Moon and You: "The Palm Beach Walk"
J. Byam, to S. Richards
Assisted by the Senior Promenaders. Finishing with a high kicking dance by S. Richards, introducing the 'Control Kick.'

Scene 9

The Last Straw (*by* Gus Weinberg and Emmet Crozier, played by permission of Jack Norworth)
Scene: Their Apartment.
Peg: L. Holman. *Jack*: C. Irwin.

Scene 10

In a Gypsy Camp:

Victor Herbert's Serenade
V. Alexander

"Gypsy Days"
G. Bowman
(*Music by* Arthur Schwartz.)

"Shackle Dance"
O. McClure

Tambourine Dance
The Promenaders

"March Gypsies"
J. Byam

Scene 12

Classical Adagio Trio
Caperton, Biddle and Randall

Scene 13

Gotham Gossip
A. Butler, H. Parker

Scene 14

The Stage Door
Modern Stage Door Tender: C. Elbey. *Old Stage Door Tender*: L. Hearn. *Lew Dockstader*: F. Knight. *George Primrose*: W. Holbrook.

Scene 15

Finale: "The Shades of Minstrelsy"
Company

"The Lancashire Clog"
The Promenaders
(*Setting designed by* T. Weidhaas.)

1928.05 (BALIEFF'S) CHAUVE-SOURIS

A New Edition of the Musical Revue "The Bat Theatre of Moscow" in Two Acts, 19 Scenes[85]. Scenes invented and devised by Nikita Balieff. Maître de choréographie, G. Bulanchin [George Balanchine]. Music arranged by Alexei Archangelsky. Chef d'orchestre, S. Kogan. Director and stage autocrat, Nikita Balieff. Staged by Nikita Balieff. Produced by Morris Gest. Opened 22 January 1929 at Jolson's Theatre and closed 2 March 1929 after 47 performances.

CAST: Mmes. Alexandrova, Guerman, Karabanova, Tarassova, Birse, Ershova, Safonova, Valina, Deykarhanova, Komisarjevska, Selinskaya, Gelikhovsky, Voronoff. Messrs. NIKITA BALIEFF, Avrey, Dalmatoff, Gelikhovsky, Gorodetsky, Grebenetsky, Mostovoy, Tcherkassky, Tcherniavsky, Voronoff, Zotoff, Gairabetoff, Dedovitch, Romoff, Tavetaieff, Tsvetaleff.

---

[84]Dropped after opening.
[85]Originally produced in New York in 4 consecutive editions 1 February 1922 at the 49th Street Theatre and Century Roof for 544 performances.

ACT 1

Scene 1

Musical Introduction
Orchestra directed by S. Kogan

Scene 2

The Blind Street Musicians
Messrs. Dedovitch, Vornoff, Grebenetsky, Zotoff, Tcherkassky
(*Music by* Andrei Archangelsky. *Scenery and costumes by* S. Tchekhonin.)
There is an old legend in Russia that the blind musicians of the street prayed to Christ for help. He offered to give them a mountain of gold, but the Apostle John said: "Give them no gold, but give them your name; and with that they can live without worrying."

Scene 3

The Romance of the Toys
Mmes. Alexandrova, Guerman, Karabanova, Tarassova, Messrs. Gorodetsky, Tcherniavsky
(*Music by* Charles Laurent. *Scenery and costumes by* S. Sudeykin.)
At midnight the toys come to life and drama appears in their ranks. The shepherdess is in love with the soldier, but the latter becomes enamored of the modern doll with her fine clothes. Suddenly a bear appears and menaces the soldier. Through the power of her love the little shepherdess is able to kill the bear. When the soldier sees this, he returns to his shepherdess, and all the dolls dance in honor of true love.

Scene 4

Russian Folk Songs
Mmes. Birse, Ershova, Safonova, Valina
(*Music by* Alexei Archangelsky. *Scenery and costumes by* M. Dobuzhinsky.)

Scene 5

"The Billeting of the Hussars"
Mmes. Birse, Deykarhanova, Karabanova Komisarjevska, Safonova, Messrs. Avrey, Dalmatoff,
Gorodetsky, Mostovoy, Tcherkassky, Zotoff
(*Scenery and costumes by* M. Dobuzhinsky.)
The hussars come to a little town where, instead of sleeping, they make merry all night with the inhabitants of the house in which they are quartered. In the morning when the bugle sounds for the departure, the maidens all dissolve in despair. One poor hussar is late in getting started, and the maidens seize him and refuse to let him go. This ballad by (Vassily) Zhukovsky, famous Russian poet and the preceptor of (Alexander) Pushkin, sung for a hundred years in Russia to music by (Mikhail) Glinka, is known in America only through the voice of Fyodor Chaliapin. In dramatizing it for the first time, Mr. Balieff has enlisted the ardent imagination of Napoleon's compatriot, the celebrated modernist, Paul Colin.

Scene 6

Russian Folk Rhymes
Mme. Selinskaya; Messrs. Gelikhovsky, Voronoff
(*Scenery and costumes by* V. Remizoff.)

Scene 7

The Midnight Review
Mmes. Birse, Ershova, Safonova, Valina; Messrs. Dedovitch, Gairabetoff, Grebenetsky, Tcherkassky, Tsvetaeff, Voronoff, Zotoff
(*Scenery and costumes by* Mstislav Dobuzhinsky.)
Napoleon and his marshals review a ghostly array of the troops of all his great battles. Napoleon gives the watchword of his career—"France," and the password—"St. Helena."

Scene 8

"The Knife Grinder"
Mme. Komisarjevska; Messrs. Dalmatoff, Gorodetsky, Mostovoy, Tcherniavsky, Zotoff
(*Scenery and costumes by* Mme. Vera Shoukhaieff.)
The knife grinder reviews in succession all the suitors for his daughter's hand. The refrain of this popular song is sung all over France.

Scene 9

"In a Little French Café"
Mme. Birse
(*Music by* Sammy Fain. *Lyrics by* Mitchell Parish.)

Scene 10

"Boublitchki"

Mmes. Alexandrova, Birse, Deykarhanova, Ershova, Guerman, Karabanova, Komisarjevska, Safonova, Selinskaya, Tarassova, Valina; Messrs. Gairabetoff, Gelikhvsky, Gorodetsky, Grebenetsky, Dedovitch, Mostovoy, Romoff, Tcherkassky, Tcherniavsky, Tsvetaieff, Voronoff, Zotoff

A scene from Soviet life, reviewing the character types to be met on the streets of Moscow today—members of the Tcheka, ice cream sellers, doughnut sellers, flappers, orphans, policemen, Red Army soldiers, sailors from the Red Fleet, Nepmen, aristocrats down at the heels, peasants and peddlers.

ACT 2

Scene 1

The Talking Pictures of 1929

Scenario by Will Rogers, Ring Lardner, Marc Connelly and Irving Caesar. Designed and painted by Carl Link. Portrait caricatures by Ralph Barton and Carl Link. Staged by Morris Gest. Released through United Artists Corporation.)

CAST: F. P. Adams, Frances Alda, John Anderson, J. Brooks Atkinson, Fay Bainter, Phil Baker, Nikita Balieff, Vilma Banky, Ralph Barton, Ethel Barrymore, John Barrymore, David Belasco, Robert C. Benchley, Irving Berlin, Anthony Biddle Jr., Paul Block, Arthur Bodansky, Lucrezia Bori, Herbert Brenon, Christian Brinton, Arthur Brisbane, Heywood Broun, Billie Burke, Nicholas Murray Butler, Irving Caesar, Eddie Cantor, Walter Catlett, Charles Spencer Chaplin, Fyodor Chaliapin, Edna Woolman Chase, Ina Claire, George M. Cohan, Ronald Coleman, Robert Bruce Coleman, F. Ray Comstock, Marc Connelly, Katharine Cornell, Jane Cowl, Frank Crowninshield, Walter Damrosch, Gerhard M. Dahl, Nemirovich-Dantchenko, Dolores Del Rio, Ruth Draper, Bide Dudley, Leon Errol, St. John Ervine, Dougals Fairbanks, Geraldine Farrar, Lynn Fontanne, Gilbert W. Gabriel, Giulio Gatti-Casazza, Robert Garland, Mary Garden, Norman Bel Beddes, George Gershwin, Morris Gest, Reina Belasco Gest, Charles Dana Gibson, Benjamino Gigli, Lillian Gish, David W. Griffith, William Guard, Percy Hammond, Jed Harris, Jascha Heifetz, Norman Hapgood, Raymond Hitchcock, Josef Hoffmann, Herbert Hoover, Fannie Hurst, Mrs. William Randolph Hearst, William Randolph Hearst, Elsie Janis, Maria Jeritza, Robert Edmond Jones, Al Jolson, Otto H. Kahn, George S. Kaufman, Karl K. Kitchen, Ring Lardner, Jesse L. Lasky, Ludwig Lewisohn, Robert Littell, Carl Link, Richard Lockridge, Ray Long, Anita Loos, Pauline Lord, Alfred Lunt, John McCormack, O.O. McIntyre, Neysa McMein, Lady Diana Manners, Burns Mantle, Elisabeth Marbury, Lester Markel, Don Marquis, Leo Marsh, Quinn Martin, Giovanni Martinelli, Willem Mengelberg, Paul Meyer, Marilyn Miller, Grace Moore, George Jean Nathan, Condé Nast, Adolph S. Ochs, Eugene O'Neill, E. W. Osborn, Mary Pickford, Rosamond Pinchot, Arthur Pollock, Ralph Pulitzer, Sergei Rachmaninoff, Stephen Rathbun, Max Reinhardt, Harry Richman, Will Rogers, Theodore Roosevelt, Harold Ross, Samuel Rothfael, John Rumsey, Oliver M. Sayler, Joseph Schenck, Nicholas Schenck, Antonio Scotti, Edgar Selwyn, Robert E. Sherwood, J. J. Shubert, Lee Shubert, Constantin Stanislavsky, Leopold Stokowski, Fred Stone, Gloria Swanson, Herbert Bayard Swope, Constance Talmadge, Norma Talmadge, Charles Hanson Towne, Lenore Ulric, Louis Untermeyer, Joseph Urban, Mrs. W. K. Vanderbilt, Carl Van Vechten, Armand Veczsy, Lupe Velez, Mayor James J. Walker, Grover Whalen, George White, Walter Winchell, Mrs. Harry Payne Whitney, Alexander Woolcott, Ed Wynn, Florenz Ziegfeld, Edward Ziegler, Adolph Zukor.

Scene 2

The Celebrated Popoff's Porcelains

Mmes. Alexandrova, Guerman, Karabanova; Messrs. Romoff, Tcherniavsky (*Music by* Pyotor Ilyich Tchaikovsky. *Scenery and costumes by* S. Tchekhonin.)

Scene 3

"The Doorman at Maxim's"

M. Dalmatoff (*Music by* Mischa Spoliansky. *Lyrics by* Mme. Guillome. *Scenery and costumes by* R. Dobujinsky.)

Scene 4

"Les Amours de Jean-Pierre"

Mmes. Alexandrova, Birse, Deykarhanova, Ershova, Karabanova, Komisarjevska, Safonova, Selinskaya, Tarassova, Valina, Messrs. Avrey, Dalmatoff, Gelikhovsky, Gorodetsky, Grebenetsky, Mostovoy, Tcherkassky, Tcherniavsky, Voronoff, Zotoff (*Music by* M. Betove. *Scenery and costumes by* Mlle. Genny Carre.)

This is a parody of an operatic production given sixty years ago at the Gaîté Lyrique in Paris, with an exact copy of the setting and the costumes. At a celebration of the countryside, Jean-Pierre is absent because, to his despair, the local farmer insists upon giving his daughter to the Duke instead of to him. The daughter herself is in love with Jean-Pierre, and the latter's mother puts a curse on everybody because of the slight to her son. But a messenger announces the death of the Duke and all ends happily for all.

Scene 5

Fragment of an Etruscan Vase (A Dance Tableau)

Mmes. Alexandrova, Guerman; Messrs. Romoff, Tcherniavsky (*Music by* Claude Debussy. *Scenery and costumes by* G. Annyenkoff.)

Scene 6

In the Square (Scene from Russian Provincial Life)

Mmes. Deykarhanova, Selinskaya; Messrs. Avrey, Gairabetoff, Gelikhvsky, Gorodetsky, Mostovoy, Tcherniavsky, Tsvetaeff (*Scenery and costumes by* V. Krivoutz.)

Scene 7

The Russian Cossacks (An Old Russian Print)

Mmes. Birse, Ershova, Safonova, Valina; Messrs. Dedovitch, Gairabetoff, Grebenetsky, Romoff, Tcherkassky, Tsvetaeff, Voronoff, Zotoff (*Scenery and costumes by* M. Dobuzhinsky.)

Scene 8

The Organ Grinder

Mme. Selinskaya; Messrs. Gelikhovsky, Gorodetsky (*Scenery by* V. Popoff.)

Scene 9

"You Ought to Hear Olaf Laugh" (A Dutch Song by Two American Writers)

Mmes. Alexandrova, Birse, Deykarhanova, Ershova, Karabanova, Komisarjevska, Safonova, Tarassova, Valina; Messrs. Avrey, Dalmatoff, Gorodetsky, Tcherkassky, Tcherniavsky, Zotoff (*Music and Lyrics by* L. Wolfe Gilbert and Abel Baer. *Scenery by* A. Ross. *Costumes by* Mlle. Genny Carre.)

1929.06   # BOOM-BOOM

A Musical Comedy in Two Acts, a Prologue and 4 Scenes. Book by Fanny Todd Mitchell adapted from the French play 'Mademoiselle Ma Mere' by Louis Verneuil. Music by Werner Janssen. Lyrics by Mann Holiner and J. Keirn Brennan. Book staged by George Marion. Dances arranged by John Boyle. Settings designed by Watson Barratt. Costumes designed by Barbier of Paris, Joseph's of New York, and Orry Kelly. Orchestrations by Werner Jannsen. Orchestra under the direction of Tom Jones. Produced by the Messrs. Shubert. Opened 28 January 1929 at the Casino Theatre and closed 30 March 1929 after 72 performances.

CAST (in order of appearance): *Jean:* JEANETTE MacDONALD. *Tony Smith:* STANLEY RIDGES. *Skippy Carr:* KENDALL CAPPS. *Texas:* Eddie Nelson. *Gussie:* LAURETTE ADAMS. *Tilly McGuire:* NELL KELLY. *Worthington Smith:* FRANK McINTYRE. *Sigmund Squnk:* Richard Lee. *Reggie Phipps:* ARCHIE LEACH [Cary Grant]. *Maybella La Tour:* Marcella Swanson. *Head Waiter:* Harry Welsh. *Cortez:* Cortez. *Peggy:* Peggy. *Four Nightingales:* Evelyn Sayres, Loretta Sayres, Doreen Glover, Jessie Payne. *Friend of Tilly McGuire:* Jackie Hurlbut.

Jack Donahue and John Boyle Girls: Doreen Roberts, Alice Edrique, Jackie Hurlbut, Maybel Van, Virgie Vane, Tina DeBrauw, Ann Loomis, Pat Hunter, Evelyn Shay, Kathryn Dayton, Dorothy Palmer, Bobby Shutta. *John Boyle Eight Lightning Dancers:* Katherine Hoevel, Margaret Gilligan, Virginia Martin, Jean Russell, Willie Hale, Frank Sherlock, Charles Roth, Jack Edwards. *Show Girls:* Bee Walz, Elva Adams, Rosalind Rensing, Tennylis Allyn, Evelyn Sintae, Azeada, Lucille Mercier, Frances Stevens. *Boys:* Harry Kirby, Clement Cancid, George Oliver, Ray Cirake, Jimmy Ardelle, Sam Wasserman, Bob Richards, George Leland.

Prologue: On Deck of the S.S. Argentine.

ACT 1, Scene 1: Roof Garden of Worthington Smith's Penthouse. Six months later. *Scene 2*: Worthington Smith's Living Room. Four months later.

ACT 2, Scene 1: Frolic Farms, on the Albany Post Road. Same evening. *Scene 2*: Sun Parlor, Worthington Smith's Apartment. The following morning.

PROLOGUE

"What Could I Do?"

J. MacDonald, S. Ridges

ACT 1

"On Top"

K. Capps, Lightning Dancers, Chorus

"Be That Way"

N. Kelly, Lightning Dancers, Donahue-Boyle Girls, Chorus

Reprise

J. MacDonald, S. Ridges

"Shake High, Shake Low"
  L. Adams, K. Capps, Four Nightingales, Lightning Dancers, Donahue-Boyle Girls, Chorus
"Nina"
  J. MacDonald, A. Leach, Cortez and Peggy, Lightning Dancers, Donahue-Boyle Girls, Chorus
"What a Girl"
  N. Kelly, K. Capps, Lightning Dancers, Donahue-Boyle Girls, Chorus
"Just a Big-Hearted Man"
  F. McIntyre, Show Girls
"He's Just My Ideal"
  N Kelly, Donahue-Boyle Girls, Lightning Dancers, Chorus
ACT 2
"Pick 'Em Up and Lay 'Em Down"
  K. Capps, Donahue-Boyle Girls, Chorus
Dance Specialty
  V. Martin
"Messin' Round"
  L. Adams, Donahue-Boyle Girls, Lightning Dancers, Chorus
Specialty
  Cortez and Peggy
Reprise
  J. MacDonald, S. Ridges
"We're Going to Make Boom-Boom"
  N. Kelly, K. Capps, Donahue-Boyle Girls, Lightning Dancers, Chorus
"Blow Those Blues Away"
  E. Nelson, K. Capps, Lightning Dancers, Donahue-Boyle Girls, Chorus
Finale
  Entire Company

1929.07

LADY FINGERS

A Musical Comedy in Two Acts, 7 Scenes. Book by Eddie Buzzell, adapted from the comedy "Easy Come, Easy Go" by Owen Davis. Music by Joseph Meyer. Lyrics by Edward Eliscu. Production staged by Edgar J. MacGregor. Dances and ensembles staged by Sammy Lee. Settings by Ward and Harvey Studios. Frocks (costumes) by Kiviette. Orchestrations by Hans Spialek, Roy Webb. Orchestra under the direction of Roy Webb. General supervision, Lew Levenson. Produced by Lyle D. Andrews. Opened 31 January 1929 at the Vanderbilt Theatre, moved 1 April 1929 to the Liberty Theatre and closed 25 May 1929 after 132 performances.

CAST (in order of appearance): *Mortimer Quayle*: HERBERT WATEROUS. *Horace Winfield*: Al Sexton. *Hope Quayle*: LOUISE BROWN. *Ruth*, a Newsgirl: Ruth Gordon. *Red*, a Newsboy: Red Harnden. *Jim Bailey*: EDDIE BUZZELL. *Dick Tain*: JOHN PRICE JONES. *Policeman*: Jack Dugan. *Policeman*: James Curran. *A Porter*: John Bragg. *Nash*: Edwin Walter. *Masters*: Robert Fleming. *Molly Maloney*: Marjorie White. *Shadow Martin*: Jim Diamond. *Dr. Jasper*: WILLIAM GRIFFITH. *Barbara Stanford*: Gertrude MacDonald. *Margie*: Dorothy McCarthy. *Betty*: Margaret McCarthy. *Mrs. Wright*: Esther Muir. (*Specialty*: Charles Troy.)
  Girls: Lucille Moore, Joey Benton, Cleo Cullen, Anna May Rex, Marcia Bell, Mildred Espy, Charlotte Otis, Violet Dell, Valma Valentine, Ann Mycue, Aline Green, Enes Early, Louise Garnett, Ruth Gordon, Frances Nevins, Grace Connelly, Margaret Miller. Boys: Alan Crane, Al Berl, Degnan Harnden, Sidney Kane, Billy Neely, Lew Walker, Martin Dennis, Harry Lake, Jack Morton.

ACT 1, *Scene 1*: Pennsylvania Station, New York. *Scene 2*: The Lower Level. *Scene 3*: En Route. *Scene 4*: At Dr. Jasper's Health Farm.

ACT 2, *Scene 1*: The Glorified Gymnasium. *Scene 2*: A Room. *Scene 3*: The Garden.

ACT 1
"There's Something in That"[86]
  A. Sexton, L. Brown, Ensemble
"All Aboard"
  Ensemble
Specialty
  Pullman Sextette

---

[86]Replaced by:
  "I Want You All to Myself"
    A. Sexton, L. Brown, Ensemble

"You're Perfect"[87]
  L. Brown, J. P. Jones
"The Life of a Nurse"
  M. White, R. Fleming, Ensemble
"An Open Book"
  A. Sexton, G. MacDonald, Ensemble
"I Love You More Than Yesterday"[88]
  L. Brown, J. P. Jones, Ensemble
  (*Music by* Richard Rodgers. *Lyrics by* Lorenz Hart.)
"Sing Boom"[89]
  M. McCarthy, D. McCarthy, Ensemble, C. Troy
Finale
  Company
ACT 2
"Follow Master"
  W. Griffith, J. Diamond, Ensemble
"Ga-Ga"
  E. Buzzell, M. White
"My Wedding"
  . Brown, Ensemble
Reprise
  L. Brown, J. P. Jones
"Shah! Raise the Dust!"
  M. White, G. MacDonald, Ensemble
Specialty[90]
  D. McCarthy, M. McCarthy
Reprise
  E. Buzzell, M. White
Ballet (*Arranged by* Ivan Tarasoff)
  L. Brown
Finale
  Company

1929.08

FIORETTA

A Romantic Venetian Musical Comedy in Two Acts, 17 Scenes. Book by Earl Carroll, adapted by Charlton Andrews. Music and lyrics by George Bagby and G. Romilli. Additional lyrics by Grace Henry, Jo Trent, Billy Rose. Book staged by Clifford Brooke and Edgar J. MacGregor. Dance ensembles by LeRoy Prinz. Art direction (settings) by Clark Robinson. Costumes designed by William H. Matthews and Charles LeMaire. Orchestral score by Domenic Savino. Orchestra under the direction of Hans Fredhoven. Entire production under the personal direction of Earl Carroll. Produced by Earl Carroll. Opened 5 February 1929 at the Earl Carroll Theatre and closed 11 May 1929 after 111 performances.

CAST [in order of appearance]: *Duke of Venice*: THEO KARLE. *Duchess of Venice*: ETHEL JUNE WALKER. *Jester*: Clement Taylor. *Sergeant*: Martin Sheppard. *Count Matteo Di Brozzo*, Minister of State: LIONEL ATWILL. *Ugo*, a Mute, His Attendant: Leo Pardello. *Spanish Ambassador's Daughter*: Blanche Satchel. *Lady from Rome*: Carol Kingsbury. *Lady from Milan*: Margaret Manners. *Lady from Pisa*: Elsie Pedrick. *Lady from Naples*: Irma Philbin. *Dancer from Paris*: Evelyn Crowell. *Captain of the Guard*: G. Davison Clark. *Guiseppa*: Rita Crane. *Julio Pepoli*: LEON ERROL. *A Herald*: Alphonso Mullarkey. *Pietro*: Leonard Trion. *Enrico*: Frank Fiore. *Giacomo*: Frank Cullen. *Fioretta Pepoli*, Julio's Daughter: DOROTHY KNAPP. *Roberto*: August Lindauer. *Rosamanda*: Lillian Bond. *Silvia*: Vivian Wilson. *Lucetta*: LOUISE BROOKS. *Beatrice*: Elsie Connor. *Orsino*, Count di Rovani: GEORGE HOUSTON. *Tito*: Harry Goldberg. *Luigi*, a Gondolier: Giovanni Guererri. *Marco*, a Gondolier:

---

[87]Replaced by:
  "I Kiss Your Hand, Madame"
    L. Brown, J. P. Jones
    (*Music by* Ralph Erwin. *Lyrics by* Sam M. Lewis and Joe Young.)
[88]Replaced by:
  "Something to Live For"
    L. Brown, J. P. Jones, Ensemble
[89]Replaced by:
  "Sing" (from BETSY)
    D. McCarthy, M. McCarthy
    (*Music by* Richard Rodgers. *Lyrics by* Lorenz Hart.)
[90]Dropped after opening.

Sidney Schlesser. *Marchesa Vera Di Livio*: FANNIE BRICE. *Caponetti*, Her Cicisbeo: JAY BRENNAN. *Marquis Filippo Di Livio*, Her Husband: Charles Howard. *Harlequin*: Nelson Snow. *Harlequin*: Charles Columbus. *Soldier*: Vic Banks. *Corporal*: Stuart N. Farrington. *Rosa*: Peggy Taylor. *Bishop*: Gean Greenwald. *Bishop*: Wallace Magill. *Turnkey*: Jackson Fairchild. *Paulo*: David Gerry. *Geranium*: Himself.

Ladies: Dorothy Britton, Elsie Pedrick, Carol Kingsbury, Ruth K. Patterson, Blanche Satchel, Margaret Manners, Irma Philbin, Evelyn Crowell; *Misses* Faith Bacon, Catherine Clark, Angeline Hassell, Elsie Connor, Rita Stone, Rae Powell, Sylvia Derby, Betty Goodwin, Autumn Simms, Margaret Joyce, Rita Crane, Vivian Wilson, Marion Harcke, Nelda Kincaid, Frances DeLacy, Lillian Bond, Odessa Morgan, Ida Michael, Doris Maye, Rosa Shaw, Dorothy Corrigan, Virginia Hawkins, Dorice Covert, Louise Brooks, Violet Arnold, Dorothea Frank. *Gentlemen*: Leo Bronson, Costanza Venturella, Harry Goldberg, Martin Sheppard, Ordoni Muzzi, Albert Sanchez, Ernest Tello, Wallace Magill, Frank Cullen, Alfonso Mullarkey, Armin Muller, Louis Ruff, Jackson Fairchild, Dow Walling, Stanley Howard, Clement Taylor, Benjamin Tilberg, Sidney Schlesser, Leon Dumbadse, Charles Naylor, J. Allen Ware, Jack Boggs, John Zimmerman, Gean Greenwald, John Roland, Russell McLelland, Leonard Ross, Bob Lee, Roy Hansen, William Billinghurst, John Marlowe, Hugh Saunders, Jack Leps, Paul Banker, David Gerry, Martin LeeRoy.

ACT 1, *Scene 1*: The Carnival Square. *Scene 2*: The Garret of Julio. *Scene 3*: The Proclamation. *Scene 4*: The Coronation. *Scene 5*: The Prison Corridor. *Scene 6*: The Silver Gondola. *Scene 7*: The Bridge of Sighs. *Scene 8*: The Royal Park. *Scene 9*: The Wine Cellar of the Castle. *Scene 10*: The Wedding Procession. *Scene 11*: The Great Hall Above.

ACT 2, *Scene 1*: The Great Cave Below. *Scene 2*: Aboard the Marchesa's Barge. *Scene 3*: Cicisbeo's Dancing Studio. *Scene 4*: The Road to Orvieto. *Scene 5*: The Grand Canal. *Scene 6*: The Ducal Palace.

ACT 1[91]

"Pierrot and Pierrette" (dance)

"Blade of Mine"
> G. Houston
> (*Music by* George Bagby. *Lyrics by* Grace Henry and Jo Trent.)

"Carnival of Venice" (dance)
> Messrs. Snow, Columbus

"Coronation of the Queen"
> Ensemble

"Dream Boat"
> G. Houston, D. Knapp
> (*Music by* George Bagby. *Lyrics by* Grace Henry and Jo Trent.)

"Roses of Red"
> (*Music and Lyrics by* G. Romilli.)

"Wicked Old Village of Venice"
> F. Brice, J. Brennan, C. Howard

"Carissima"
> G. Houston
> (*Music by* G. Romilli. *Lyrics by* Grace Henry.)

"Wedding of Fioretta"
> Ensemble

Dance
> D. Knapp

ACT 2

"Chant of the Monks"
> Monks

"Little Flower"

"In My Gondola"

"My Heart Belongs to You"
> E. J. Walker
> (*Music by* George Bagby, G. Romilli. *Lyrics by* Grace Henry, Jo Trent.)

"Soliloquy of the Minister"
> L. Atwill

Dance
> Three Demons (V. Banks, S. Barrington, P. Taylor)

"Alone With You"
> E. J. Walker, L. Atwill
> (*Music and Lyrics by* G. Romilli.)

The Theme Waltz

---

[91]A complete song list was not included in the program, but only the excerpted list which appears above. Vocals were assigned based on their attributions in the Washington D.C. tryout. Not in performance order.

"Fioretta"
> (*Music and Lyrics by* G. Romilli.)

1929.09

PLEASURE BOUND

A Musical Revue in Two Acts, 12 Scenes. Book by Harold Atteridge. Music by Muriel Pollock. Lyrics by Max and Nathaniel Lief, Harold Atteridge. (Additional music and lyrics by Phil Baker and Maurice Rubens.) Book staged by Lew Morton. Dances arranged by Busby Berkeley. The Jack Donahue-John Boyle Girls' Specialty Dances arranged by John Boyle. Settings by Watson Barratt. Costumes designed by Ernest Schrapps. Orchestra under the direction of Harold Stern. Orchestrations arranged by Emil Gerstenberger and Archie Bleyer. Produced by the Messrs. Shubert. Opened 18 February 1929 at the Majestic Theatre and closed 15 June 1929 after 136 performances.

CAST (in order of appearance): *Mazie*: VIRGINIA BARRETT. *Betty*: GRACE BRINKLEY. *Herman Pfeiffer*: JACK PEARL. *Rudolph Fisher*: JACK PEARL. *Sheriff*: William Bonnelli. *Bob Stewart*: FRED HILLEBRAND. *Paisley*, First Process Server: AL SHAW. *Packy*, Second Process Server: SAM LEE. *Phil Baker*: PHIL BAKER. *Tom Westover*: ROY HOYER. *Lola Hopkins*: AILEEN STANLEY. *Marcella Standish*: BETTY BOWMAN. *Eddie*: Chester Herman. *Detective* of Maison Coralie: George Gilday. *Mr. Westover, Sr.*: Harold Crane. *Jans*: Dorothy Drum. *Dolly*: Rosalind Wishon. *First Revenue Officer*: James Thompson. *Second Revenue Officer*: John Slattery. *Chief of the Revenue Officers*: Roland Hudson. *Mr. Zill*: Thomas MacMillan. *Homely Girl*: Allie Smith. *Pretty Girl*: Henrietta Livingston. *Pullman Porter*: Frank Jones. *First Girl*: Betty Dair. *Second Girl*: Mary Chandler. *Third Girl*: Agatha Phillips. *Fourth Girl*: Sheila Burke. *Tito*: Tito Carol. *Dancers*: (Frank) VELOZ and YOLANDA (Casazza). *Pepita*: ROSITA MORENO. *Senor Alvarez*: Paco Moreno. (*Specialty*: John Humphrey Muldowney.)

The Jack Donahue-John Boyle Girls: Lucille Osborn, Irene Peck, Mae Selden, Ruth Parker, Vivian Morgan, Lenore Blair, Betty Borden, Evelyn Monte, Lillian Darville, Emily Sherman, Isabelle Marsh, Mary Gibson. *Dancers*: Irene Brown, Georgette Lampsi, Marilyn Mack, Gene DeViney, Lee Manners, Rosa Kay, Virginia May, Margot Nelson, Jannie Adams, Beth Meredith, Rennie Evans, Evaline Engers, Elsie Lauritsen, Marion Phillips, Adelaine Candee, Cicely Dodenham. *Show Girls*: Sheila Burke, Kay Simmons, Neva Lynn, Margaret DeCoursey, Betty Van Allen, Eleanor Gordon, Mary Chandler, Rosalind Wishon, Betty Dair, Dolly Thain, Sherry Frayne, Henrietta Livingston, Jane Manners, Dorothy Drum, Adrienne DeSayles, Bobbie Storey, Claire Hooper, Agatha Phillips. *Boys*: Preston Coombs, Richard Lowell, Harry Gordon, George Clidd, Jack Dayton, Hazzard Newberry, Tommy Schmidt, Eddie Murray.

ACT 1, *Scene 1*: Studio of Designer, The Maison Coralie, New York City. *Scene 2*: Broadcasting Station in the Maison Coralie. *Scene 3*: Sales Room in the Maison Coralie. *Scene 4*: Corridor of the Maison Coralie. *Scene 5*: Fashion Promenade, The Maison Coralie.

ACT 1, *Scene 1*: Garden Entrance, Piccolo Farms, Westemere, Long Island, New York. Three weeks later. *Scene 2*: Corridor of Roadhouse. *Scene 3*: Cabaret in Roadhouse. *Scene 4*: Entrance of Piccolo Farms. *Scene 5*: Interior of Pullman on the Florida Flyer. *Scene 6*: Front of the Flamingo Hotel, Florida. *Scene 7*: Lawn of the Flamingo Hotel, Florida.

ACT 1

Scene 1

"We Love to Go to Work" (Opening)
> Dancers, Show Girls, Boys, Jack Donahue-John Boyle Girls

"Just Suppose"
> G. Brinkley, R. Hoyer
> (*Music by* Phil Baker and Maurice Rubens. *Lyrics by* Sid Silvers and Moe Jaffe.)

"We'll Get Along"
> F. Hillebrand, B. Bowman, Jack Donahue-John Boyle Girls, Boys, Girls

Scene 2

"Cross Word Puzzles"
> A. Shaw, S. Lee

Phil Baker and His Gang—
> (a) Shaw and Lee
> (b) Phil Baker and Paco Moreno

Songs (*At the piano*, Bob Butternuth)
> A. Stanley

Scene 3

"Park Avenue Strut"
> G. Brinkley, R. Hoyer, R. Moreno, F. Hillebrand, Dancers, Boys
> (*Music by* Phil Baker and Maurice Rubens. *Lyrics by* Moe Jaffe and Harold Atteridge.)

Scene 4
  Phil Baker
  Band Box Dance
    R. Moreno, Show Girls, Dancers
  Parisian Fashion Parade

    Models
Scene 5
  "(Sweet Little) Mannikin Dolls"
    J. H. Muldowney, Dancers, Jack Donahue-John Boyle Girls
    (*Music by* Phil Baker and Maurice Rubens.)
ACT 2
Scene 1
  "Spanish Fado"
    T. Coral, R. Moreno, F. Veloz, Yolanda, Models
Scene 2
  Shaw and Lee
Scene 3
  Dance Number, Cabaret
    Dancers, Girls, Boys
  Spanish Dance
    F. Veloz, Yolanda
  Aileen Stanley
  Sand Paper Number
    Jack Donahue-John Boyle Girls
Scene 4
  Phil Baker and Aileen Stanley
  ["My Melody Man"
    (*Music by* Peter DeRose. *Lyrics by* Charles Tobias and Sidney Clare.)
  "(You Can't Take Away) The Things That Were Made for Love"
    (*Music by* Peter DeRose. *Lyrics by* Charles Tobias and Irving Kahal.)
  "Why Do You Tease Me?"
    (*Music by* Muriel Pollock. *Lyrics by* Max and Nathaniel Lief.)]
Scene 6
  Doll Dance
    Jack Donahue-John Boyle Girls
Scene 7
  "Glory of Spring" (Waltz)
    Veloz, Yolanda, assisted by Tito, MacQuarrie Harp Ensemble
  Finale
    Entire Company

1929.10   TROIS JEUNES FILLES NUES

A Musical Comedy in Three Acts, in French (Three Young Maids from the Folies Bergère). Book and lyrics by Yves Mirande and Albert Willemetz. Music by Raoul Moretti. Play directed by Pazzi-Preval. Settings by Bertin, Paris. Costumes by Weldy, Paris. Orchestra under the direction of J. Clemande. Produced by J. A. Gauvin. Opened 4 March 1929 at Jolson's Theatre and closed 6 April 1929 after 8 performances in repertory.

CAST: *Hégésippe*, Tutor to Lotte and her sisters: [HANS] SERVATIUS. *Patara*, a Sailor: ANDRÉ FADEUILHE. *Jacques:* GEORGES FOIX. *The Commander:* M. PAZZI-PREVAL. *Marcel:* GASTON GARCHERY. *The Director:* José Daufy. *Maurice:* M. Laurenzo. *The Author:* M. Decart. *Lord Cresson:* M. José. *The Compere:* M. Luguet. *The Gardener:* M. Darcey. *The Mailman:* M. Jules. *The Delivery Man:* M. Gardet. *First Sailor:* M. Henri. *Second Sailor:* M. Georges. *Lotte:* SONIA ALNY. *Lilette*, Lotte's sister: GINIA BARTY. *Mrs. Ducos* [*Mme. Ducros*]: JANE dePOUMEYRAC. *Tapsy:* Marion Gaillard. *Lola*. Lotte's sister: Yvette Herbaux. *Lulu*, Lotte's sister: Alice Penven. *The Lobster Woman:* Mado Thys. *The Opener:* Luce Lucior. *A Girl:* Henriette. *Girls from the Folies Bergere:* The Terry Girls.

ACT 1: Mme. Ducros' Villa at Garches.

ACT 2: Backstage of the Folies Bergère.

ACT 3: On Board the *S. S. Espadon.*

ACT 1[92]

---

[92]Musical numbers not listed in program. This list was prepared from the published French piano vocal score (F. Salabert, Paris, 1926).

H. Servatius"Je suis dans les branches"
  S. Alny, Messrs. Gardet, Jules, Darcey
"Le bureau de Tabac"
  J. dePoumayrac
"Quatuor des jeunes filles" (Ah j'aimerais tant. .)
"On n'fait pas ça"
  H. Servatius
"Quant on ne dit rien"
  S. Alny
"A qui le dites-vous"
  H. Servatius
"Elles sont Jolies" (Quatuor)
  H. Servatius, les 3 officiers
"Si ce n'était qu'une amusette"
  G. Barty
Finale
  J. dePoumayrac, H. Servatius, les jeunes filles, les 3 officiers
ACT 2
"Les Crevettes" (Les Girls)
"Raymonde"
  M. Gaillard
"Quand on n'en a pas"
  A. Fadeuilhe
Entré d'Hégésippe et des jeunes filles
"Les Crevettes"
"Pour trouver un mari"
  G. Barty, M. Laurenzo
"Est-ce que je te demande?"
  H. Servatius
Entrée de Lotte
New Charleston (Ballet)
Reprise du Charleston
"C'est pas gentil"
  S. Alny
"J'n'ai pas connu"
  H. Servatius
Finale
  Tutti
ACT 3
Musique de scène
Chanson des Matelots
  A. Fadeuilhe
"On a d'la peine"
  J. dePoumayrac, les 4 jeunes filles
"Ils ont une allure charmante"
  G. Barty
"Je suis malade"
  H. Servatius
"Chez les Zoulous"
  S. Alny
"On s'en passe"
  Tutti

1929.11   PASSIONNÉMENT!

A Musical Comedy in Three Acts, in French [Passionately]. Book and lyrics by Maurice Hennequin and Albert Willemetz. Music by André Messager. Play directed by Pazzi-Preval. Settings by Bertin, Paris. Costumes by Weldy, Paris. Orchestra under the direction J. Clemandh. Produced by J. A. Gauvin. Opened 7 March 1929 at Jolson's Theatre and closed 6 April 1929 after 8 performances in repertory.

CAST: *Kitty (Stevenson):* SONIA ALNY. *Julia:* GINIA BARTY. *Hélène (Le Barrois):* JANE dePOUMEYRAC. *John:* Mado Thys. *Robert Perceval:* GEORGES FOIX. *Le Barrois:* [HANS] SERVATIUS. *(William) Stevenson:* JOSÉ DAUFY. *(Captain) Harris:* ANDRÉ FADEUILHE. *Auguste:* Mr. Lorenzo.

:ACT 1: On board Stevenson's yacht, *the Arabella.*

ACT 2: The Villa des Roses.

ACT 3: The Villa des Roses.

ACT 1[93]

"Terre, terre, droit devant nous! (Introduction)
    J. Daufy, S. Alny, G. Barty, A. Fadeuilhe

"Quand l'Éternel, au Paradis" (Legend)
    S. Alny

"On ne faut pas croire aux serments de femmes"
    S. Alny, J. Daufy

"Si l'Amérique est le plus grand pays du monde"
    J. Daufy

"L'amour est un oiseau rebelle"
    G. Barty

"Pour sortir en toute saison"
    J. dePoumeyrac

"Dès que l'âge"
    S. Alny, J. dePoumeyrac, G. Foix

"Allons, soyez raisonnable" (Finale)
    S. Alny, G. Foix

ACT 2

"Tout cela pour les hommes"
    J. Daufy, G. Foix, S. Alny

"Ah Madame"
    J. dePoumeyrac

"Je lui ai dit"
    S. Alny, G. Foix

"Chanson du petit bateau"
    G. Barty, A. Fadeuilhe, S. Alny, G. Foix, J. Daufy

"Moi tout la vie"
    G. Barty

"C'est une affaire extraordinaire"
    J. Daufy, G. Foix

" . . . Passionément"
    G. Foix

"Non, nous, vous, n'irez pas" (Finale)
    G. Foix, S. Alny, G. Barty, A. Fadeuilhe

ACT 3

"J'ai lu dans les saintes écritures"
    G. Barty

"Partis avant qu'on en profite!"
    S. Alny

"Cette nuit, la chose est trop forte"
    G. Foix, G. Barty, A. Fadeuilhe

"N'imaginez pas (qu'il me coûte)"
    J. dePoumeyrac

"Julia, jusqu'à cette heure"
    J. Daufy

"Le bon et le doux vin de France" (Finale)
    S. Alny, G. Foix, J. Daufy

1929.12   SPRING IS HERE

A Musical Comedy in Two Acts, 6 Scenes. Book by Owen Davis (based on his play 'Shot-Gun Wedding'). Music by Richard Rodgers. Lyrics by Lorenz Hart. Play staged by Alexander Leftwich. Dances staged by Bobby Connolly. Settings designed by John Wenger. Costumes designed by Kiviette. Orchestra under the direction of Alfred Newman. Produced by Alex A. Aarons and Vinton Freedley. Opened 11 March 1929 at the Alvin Theatre and closed 8 June 1929 after 104 performances.

CAST (in order of appearance): *Emily Braley*: MAIDEL TURNER. *Maude Osgood*: THELMA WHITE. *Mary June*: INEZ COURTNEY. *Steve Alden*: DICK KEENE. *Willie Slade*: GIL SQUIRES. *Peter Braley*: CHARLES RUGGLES. *Betty Braley*: LILLIAN TAIZ. *Stacy Haydon*: JOHN HUNDLEY. *Terry Clayton*: GLENN HUNTER. *Rita Conway*: JOYCE BARBOUR. *Ebens*: Cy Landry. *Jennings*: Lewis Parker. *Policeman*: Frank Gagen. *At the pianos*: Victor Arden, Phil Ohman.

---

[93]Musical numbers not listed in program. This list was prepared from the production typescript, the published French piano vocal score (F. Salabert, Paris, 1926).

Ladies of the Ensemble: Florence Allen, Louise Allen, Emily Burton, Dorothy Brown, Louise Blakeley, Marjorie Bailey, Mary Carlton, Billie Cortez, Marion Dixon, Ann Ecklund, Edith Martin, Madeleine Janis, Gladys Kelly, Beth Milton, Vida Manuel, Lillian Michel, Elsie Neal, Ruby Nevins, Adeline Ogilvie, Wilma Roelof, Kay Stewart, Gladys Travers, Wanda Wood, Beryl Wallace. *Gentlemen of the Ensemble*: Ward Arnold, William Cooper, Billy Carver, Frank Gagen, Edwin Gall, Bob Gebhardt, Fred May, Daniel O'Brien, Billy O'Rourke, Victor Pullman, Thomas Sternfield, Jack Stevens.

The Action takes place at the Braley's Home on Long Island.

ACT 1, Scene 1: The Garden. Morning. *Scene 2*: The Garden Wall. *Scene 3*: The Garden. That evening.

ACT 2, Scene 1: Maude Osgood's Barn Dance. *Scene 2*: Betty's Bed Room. *Scene 3*: Morning Room at Maude Braley's.

ACT 1

Scene 1

Opening
    Guests

"Spring Is Here"
    D. Keene, I. Courtney, Ensemble

"Yours Sincerely"
    G. Hunter, L. Taiz, Ensemble

FinalettoG. Hunter, J. Barbour, I. Courtney, G. Squires, L. Taiz, T. White, Ensemble

Scene 2

"You Never Say Yes"
    J. Barbour, G. Squires, Ensemble

"(With a) Song in My Heart"
    L. Taiz, J. Hundley

Scene 3

"Baby's Awake Now"
    I. Courtney, T. White, Girls

Finale
    Company

ACT 2

Scene 1

Opening
    Ensemble

"Red Hot Trumpet"
    T. White, G. Squires, Girls

"What a Girl"
    G. Hunter

"Rich Man! Poor Man"
    I. Courtney, D. Keene, Ensemble

Specialty Dance
    C. Landry

Scene 2

"Why Can't I?"
    L. Taiz, I. Courtney

Scene 3

"(With a) Song in My Heart" (reprise)
    J. Hundley, L. Taiz

Finale
    Company

1929.13   COMTE OBLIGADO

A Musical Comedy (Opérette) in Three Acts, in French [Count Obligado]. Book and lyrics by André Barde. Music by Raoul Moretti. Play directed by Pazzi-Preval. Settings by Bertin, Paris. Costumes by Weldy, Paris. Orchestra under the direction of C. Clemandh. Produced by J. A. Gauvin. Opened 11 March 1929 at Jolson's Theatre and closed 6 April 1929 after 4 performances in repertory.

CAST: *Antoine, Comte Obligado*: [Hans] SERVATIUS. *Robert du Moustier*: GEORGES FOIX. *Cristobal*: José Daufy. *Amandine*: GASTON GARCHERY. *Poligny*: André Fadeuilhe. *Gustave*: Mr. DeCart. *Mitaine*: GINIA BARTY. *Madame Xavière de Miranda*: SONIA ALNY. *Martine*: Yvette Herbeaux. *Jane Sibat*: Jane dePoumeyrac. *Monique*: Marion Gaillard. *Simone*: Alice Penven. *Luce*: Mado Thys.

ACT 1: The Reception Room in Amandine and Victor's, Paris Dressmakers.

ACT 2: A Room in Mme. de Miranda's Home, Paris.

ACT 3: The Bar-room at the Auteuil Racetrack.

Act 1[94]

    Choeur d'entrée

        M. Thys, A. Penven, M. Gaillard, J. dePoumeyrac, A. Fadeuilhe, Y. Herbeaux, G. Garchery

    "Mon pauvre amour"

        S. Alny

    "Ça fait passer un moment"

        G. Barty, G. Foix

    "C'est un char"

        H. Servatius

    "Le petit oiseau des îles"

        J. Daufy

    "Si maman le veut"

        H. Servatius

    Trio

        J. Daufy, S. Alny, G. Foix

    "La caravane, ou La fille de Bédouin"

        H. Servatius

    Final

        Tous

ACT 2

    Choeur d'entrée

    "Je n'sais pas me refuser"

        H. Servatius

    "Un petit bout de femme"

        G. Barty, G. Foix

    "Mio Padre"

        J. Daufy

    "Un amoureux" (Trio)

        H. Servatius, S. Alny, G. Foix

    "You-oo ma Caroline"

        S. Alny

    "Les artichauts"

        H. Servatius

    "Ca monte et ça descend" (Quintette)

        H. Servatius, J. Daufy, G. Foix, G. Garchery, A Fadeuilhe

    Final

        Tous

ACT 3

    Choeur d'entrée

        M. Thys, A. Penven, G. Garchery, M. Gaillard, J. dePoumeyrac, A. Fadeuilhe, Y. Herbeaux, G. Barty, Mr. DeCart

    "Quand ton heure sonnera"

        S. Alny

    "Qu'est-ce que les femmes ont cette année"

        J. Daufy

    Que vous dites " (Duet)

        H. Servatius, G. Foix

    "La Rose tendre"

        G. Barty, G. Foix

    Musique de Scène

    Final

        Tous

TA BOUCHE

1929.14

A Musical Comedy (Opérette) in Three Acts, in French [Your Lips]. Book by Yves Mirande. Music by Maurice Yvain. Lyrics by Albert Willemetz. Play directed by Pazzi-Preval. Settings by Bertin, Paris. Costumes by Weldy, Paris. Orchestra under the direction of C. Clemandh. Produced by J. A. Gauvin. Opened 14 March 1929 at Jolson's Theatre and closed 6 April 1929 after 12 performances in repertory.

---

[94]Musical numbers not listed in program. List prepared from published French piano vocal score (F. Salabert, Paris, 1927).

CAST: *Du Pas de Vis:* [Hans] SERVATIUS. *Bastien,* His Son: GEORGES FOIX. *Jean (Leduc),* valet de chambre: ANDRÉ FADEUILHE. *Eva:* SONIA ALNY. *The Countess,* Bastien's mother: JANE dePOUMEYRAC. *Mélanie,* chambermaid: GINIA BARTY. *Marguerite:* Yvette Herbaux. *Margot:* Marion Gaillard. *Mag:* Alice Penven.

@ACT 1: Truc-sur-Mer, a Watering Resort.

ACT 2: Pouic-sur-Mer, Another Resort, a Year later.

ACT 3: Eric-les-Bains, Another Resort, a Year later.

ACT 1[95]

    "Trio des Cancans"

        V. Herbaux, M. Gaillard, A. Penven

    "Ta bouche" (Valse)

        S. Alny, G. Foix

    "Voilà comment est Jean"

        J. dePoumeyrac, H. Servatius

    "Le petit amant"

        S. Alny

    "Des terres et des coupons" (Duet)

        J. dePoumeyrac, H. Servatius

    "Si tu savais Maman" (Duet)

        S. Alny, J. dePoumeyrac

    "Quand on veut plaire" (Couplets)

        H. Servatius

    Finale (Le temps devient frisquet . . .)

        Entire Company

ACT 2

    Musique de scène

    "Non, non jamais les hommes"

        S. Alny, Chorus

    "De mon temps"

        J. dePoumayrac

    "Ça c'est une chose"

        G. Foix

    "Machinalement"

        G. Foix

    "Puisqu'un heureux hasard" (Quartette)

        J. de Poumeyrac, G. Barty, H. Servatius, A. Fadeuilhe

    "La seconde étreinte" (Duet Waltz)

        S. Alny, G. Foix

    Finale (C'est i nou i comme il fait chaud)

        Y. Herbaux, A. Penven, M. Gaillard, G. Foix, S. Alny, H. Servatius, J. Poumeyrac

ACT 3

    "Duet des Domestiques"

        G. Barty, A. Fadeuilhe

    Duet (Ce brav' monsieur Jean est assez changeant)

        Y. Herbaux, A. Penven

    "Quand on a du sens"

        H. Servatius, J. dePoumeyrac

    "Pour toi"

        S. Alny

    Duet (Au milieu d'notre entretien)

        G. Barty, A. Fadeuilhe

    Quartette (Comment pourrions nous fair' pour reconnaître)

        J. Poumeyrac, G. Barty, H. Servatius, A. Fadeuilhe

    Finale (Notre bonheur va être immense)

        Entire Company

UN BON GARÇON

1929.15

A Musical Comedy (Opérette) in Three Acts, in French [A Good Boy]. Book and lyrics by André Barde. Music by Maurice Yvain. Play directed by Pazzi-Preval. Settings by Bertin, Paris. Costumes by Weldy, Paris. Orchestra under the direction J. Clemandh. Produced by J. A. Gauvin. Opened 18

---

[95]Musical numbers not listed in program. List was prepared from the published French piano vocal score (F. Salabert, Paris, 1922).

March 1929 at Jolson's Theatre and closed 6 April 1929 after 4 performances in repertory.

CAST: *Arlette Méryl*: SONIA ALNY. *Camille*: GINIA BARTY. *Mme. Bouillon Falloux*: JANE dePOUMEYRAC. *Célina*: Yvette Hervaux. *Madame Pontavès*: Luce Lucyor. *Lili*: Marion Gaillard. *Lulu*: Alice Penven. *Colette*: Mado Thys. *Achille*: (HANS) SERVATIUS. *Savinien Pechard*: Georges Foix. *Pontavès*: JOSÉ DAUFY. *Lucien de Gravère*: GASTON GARCHERY. *(Abbé) Colignac*: Mr. PAZZI-PREVAL. *Monsieur de Gravère*: Mr. LAURENZO. *Deodat*: André Fadeuilhe. *Loupot*: Mr. Decart.

ACT 1: Lucien's Home in Paris.

ACT 2: Mme. Bouillon's Home in Bourges.

ACT 3: The same.

ACT 1[96]

  Choeur d'entrée
    S. Alny, G. Garchery, A. Penven, M. Gaillard, M. Thys, H. Servatius, Y. Hervaux

  "Quand on veut être heureux"
    J. Daufy

  "Nous sommes un ménage à la page" (Duetto)
    S. Alny, G. Garchery

  "Je n'ai jamais compris"
    G. Garchery

  "La Musique grisante"
    S. Alny

  "Je suis un bon garçon"
    H. Servatius

  "J'aime d'amour" (Duo-valse)
    S. Alny, J. Daufy

  "Je t'emmène à la campagne"
    H. Servatius

  Finale
    Tous

ACT 2

  "Ah m les soirées de province"
    (Petit choeur)

  "Ce n'était pourtant pas bien difficile"
    G. Barty

  "Pour danser le Charleston"
    H. Servatius

  "Chiffons légers" (Duo)

  "Quand une femme a tort" (Duetto de la dispute)
    G. Garchery, S. Alny

  "Je fais tout à contretemps"
    J. Daufy

  "Pour te faire plaisir"
    H. Servatius

  Sextuor et final

ACT 3

  "Dites oui!"
    H. Servatius, J. dePoumeyrac

  "Je dis toujours le mot qu'il faut pas dire"
    Camille

  "En camarades"
    S. Alny, G. Foix

  "Avec ma voix"
    A. Fadeuilhe

  "Toujours y love you"
    J. Daufy

  Couplet final

1929.16   ## PAS SUR LA BOUCHE

A Musical Comedy (Opérette) in Three Acts, in French [Not on the Lips]. Words (book) and lyrics by André Barde. Music by Maurice Yvain. Play directed by Pazzi-Preval. Settings by Bertin, Paris. Costumes by Weldy, Paris.

Orchestra under the direction J. Clemandh. Produced by J. A. Gauvin. Opened 25 March 1929 at Jolson's Theatre and closed 6 April 1929 after 4 performances in repertory.

CAST: *Gilberte Valandray*: SONIA ALNY. *Mlle. Poumaillac, Gilberte's aunt*: JANE dePOUMEYRAC. *Huguette Verberie*: GINIA BARTY. *Mme. Fouin, the concierge*: LUCE LUCYOR. *Georges Valandray, Gilberte's present husband*: GEORGES FOIX. *Eric Thomson, Gilberte's first husband*: JOSÉ DAUFY. *Charley*: GASTON GARCHERY. *Faradel*: ANDRÉ FADEUILHE. *Juliette*: Yvette Herbaux. *Suzanne*: Marion Gaillard. *Yvonne*: Alice Perven. *Colette*: Mado Thys.

ACT 1: The Apartment of Gilberte Valandray, in Paris.

ACT 2: The same.

ACT 3: Faradel's Bachelor Apartment, Paris.

ACT 1[97]

  Opening Chorus
    Invited Guests, A. Fadeuilhe

  "Je l'aime mieux autrement" (Duet)
    G. Barty, A. Fadeuilhe

  "Ce qu'on dit et ce qu'on pense"
    J. dePoumeyrac

  "Comme j'aimerais mon mari"
    S. Alny

  "Je suis venu (simplement) te dire bonjour"
    G. Foix

  "C'est de la réclame"
    S. Alny, J. dePoumeyrac, G. Garchery

  "Pic et pic et colegram"
    G. Barty, G. Garchery

  "Couplets-Valse et la Péruvienne"
    S. Alny, G. Foix

  Finale
    Entire Company

ACT 2

  "La bouquet"
    A. Fadeuilhe

  "Je me suis laissé embouteiller"
    G. Foix

  "Quand on n'a pas ce que l'on aime"
    J. dePoumeyrac

  "Soirs de Mexique"
    S. Alny

  "Ça c'est gentil (ça c'est pas mal)"
    G. Barty, G. Garchery

  "Il suffit d'un rien"
    S. Alny, G. Foix

  "Pas sur la bouche"
    J. Daufy

  Quartette
    S. Alny, J. dePoumeyrac, G. Foix, J. Daufy

  Finale (Sur le quai Malaquais)
    Entire Company

ACT 3

  "Mon Bon!"
    G. Foix

  "Est-ce bien ça?"
    G. Barty

  "Par le trou (de la serrure)"
    L. Lucyor

  "Bonjour, Bonsoir"
    S. Alny, G. Garchery

  "O Sam!"
    J. dePoumeyrac, J. Daufy

  Finale
    Entire Company

---

[96]Musical numbers not listed in program. List was prepared from the published French piano vocal score (F. Salabert, Paris, 1926).

[97]Musical numbers not listed in program. This list was prepared from the published French piano vocal score (F. Salabert, Paris, 1925).

1929.17

MUSIC IN MAY

A Musical Play (Operetta) in Three Acts, 5 Scenes. Book by Fanny Todd Mitchell, adapted from the Viennese original ("Musik in Mai") by Heinz Merley and Kurt Breuer. Music by Emile Berté and Maurice Rubens. Lyrics by J. Keirn Brennan. Staged by Lew Morton and Stanley Logan. Dances arranged by Chester Hale. Settings designed by Watson Barratt. Costumes designed by Ernest Schrapps and Orry Kelly. Orchestra under the direction of Ivan Rudisill. Orchestrations by Emil Gerstenberger. Produced by the Messrs. Shubert. Opened 1 April 1929 at the Casino Theatre and closed 8 June 1929 after 80 performances.

CAST (in order of appearance): *Hans*, Vita's Student Sweetheart: JOSEPH TONER. *Vita*, Belle of the University Town: GERTRUDE LANG. *Karl von Dorn*, Professor of Music and Composer: GREEK EVANS. *Popkin*, Member of the Quartette: Charles Lawrence. *Zenzi*, Vita's Sister: Marjorie Leach. *Rausenbach*, Purveyor of Umbrellas and Sunshades to the Emperor: SOLLY WARD. *Baron Metternich*: JOSEPH LERTO-RA. *Prince Stephan*, Attaché at the German Embassy: BARTLETT SIMMONS. *Comtesse Olga*, Stephan's Discarded Sweetheart: GLADYS BAXTER. *Pupils of Professor von Dorn (4)*: *Lisa*: Edith Scott. *Alois*: George Offerman, Jr. *Kranz*: Charles Chesney. *Loibner*: Francis Lyman. *Student Leaders (2)*: *Kuhmeier*: James Norris. *Prinz*: Peter Petraitis. *Butler*: Earl T. Plummer. *Courier*: Francis Lyman. *Officers, Aides to Prince Stephan*: Charles Chesney, Francis Lyman, James Norris, Peter Petraitis. *Officer, Aide to Prince Metternich*: Frazer McMahon. *Lintchy*, a Barmaid: Julia Lane. *Footmen at the Prince's Palace*: E. T. Plummer, J. Spiro, H. Hertel, G. St. John.

Eight Special Singers: Zola M. Gray, Eileen O'Malley, Norma Leyland, Dorothy Beckloff, Lorena L. Walcott, Marice Christie, Violette M. Code, Julia Lane. *George Smith's Ensemble*: Rita Mario; Evelyn Klein (violin solo), Nan Berr (violin), Emily Eldridge (violin), Florence Fisher (violin), Fern Saunders (violin), Loret Fillion (violin), Catherine Merrill (violin), Frances Flanigan (viola), Frances Wright (viola), Helen Ward (cello), Emily Hagstrom (cello), Josephine Rice (cello), Anne Bruyn (cello), Leona Burgess (harp), Edith Sinclair (harp). *Chester Hale Dancing Specialists*: Erma Chase, Comfort Collins, Margaret Gibson, Norma Schutt, Sylvia O'Neal, Jeanette Balder, Sally Ritz, Rolande Poucel, Eleanor Gilbert, Luba Dubiago, Dorothy Blair, Sylvia Blythe. *Students*: Milton Gallagher, Earl T. Plummer, John Fredericks, Arthur Singer, Joseph Barlow, Leon Mandas, Herman Hertel, Fred Kruger, El Thompson, Louis Elmer, Frazer McMahon, Robert Dudley, Jack Jendrek, Earl Wisong, Helmut Wessels, Isadore Gladstone, Michael Kavanaugh, Eddie Bird, Gerald Moore, Jack Wilhelm, Robert Stevens, George St. John, Frank Staley, Alfred Russ, Jean Spiro, Robert Davis, Joseph Posner, Joseph Rose, Frank Ryan.

The action takes place in Vienna in 1820.

ACT 1: A Garden in Rausenbach's House.

ACT 2: A Drinking Place, "The Hofbrau" of the Students. *Scene 2*: A Salon in the Embassy.

ACT 3, Scene 1: A Garden at the Embassy. *Scene 2*: The Studio of Professor von Dorn.

ACT 1

"Open Your Window" (Opening)
  G. Lang, J. Toner, Ensemble

"Finnan Haddie"[98]
  C. Lawrence, M. Leach

"(The) Glory of Spring" (Song)
  G. Evans

"Sweetheart of Our Student Corps"
  G. Lang, Boys

"Open and Shut Idea"
  S. Ward, Chester Hale Girls

"I Found a Friend" (Duet)
  . Lang, G. Evans

"Unto Your Heart" (Duet)
  G. Lang, B. Simmons
  (*Music by* Emile Berté. *Lyrics by* Heinz Merley, Kurt Breuer.)

Intermezzo
  String Ensemble

Finale
  Company

ACT 2

Scene 1

"Seidels" (Opening)
  Students, Ensemble

"High, High, High"
  J. Toner, Male Ensemble

Scene 2

Gavotte
  Chester Hale Girls

"There's Love in the Heart I Hold" (Song)
  G. Baxter, Eight Singers

"I'd Like to Love Them All"
  S. Ward, Chester Hale Girls
  (*Music by* Maurice Rubens and Phil Svigals.)

"I'm in Love" (Duet)
  G. Lang, B. Simmons

"No Other Love Was Meant for Me"
  G. Baxter, Ambassadors

"For the Papa"
  S. Ward, M. Leach, C. Lawrence

Finale
  Entire Company

ACT 3

"Metternich"
  J. Lertora, Male Ensemble

"Lips That Laugh at Love" (Trio)
  G. Baxter, B. Simmons, J. Lertora

Intermezzo
  Symphony Ensemble

"It's the Cooks, Not the Looks"[99] (Duet)
  M. Leach, C. Lawrence, Chester Hale Girls

"Unto Your Heart" (reprise)

Finale
  Company

1929.18

MESSIN' AROUND

An (All-Colored) Modern Musical Novelty (Revue) in Two Acts, a Prologue and 12 Scenes. (Sketches by Louis Isquith.) Music by Jimmy [James P.] Johnson. Lyrics by Perry Bradford. Entire production conceived and staged by Louis Isquith. Dances staged by Eddie Rector. Costumes designed by Marguerite and Strauss, Inc. Settings by Lou Wertheim. Orchestra under the direction of Jimmy Johnson. Produced by Louis Isquith. Opened 22 April 1929 at the Hudson Theatre and closed 20 May 1929 after 33 performances.

CAST: STERLING GRANT, PAUL FLOYD, CORA LaREDD, BILLY McLAURIN, JIMMIE JOHNSON, JAMES (Slim) THOMPSON, WALTER BROGSDALE, SAM CROSS, FRANK DAVIS, HILDA PERLENO, SUSIE WROTEN, FRANK LLOYD, EMMA MAITLAND, WILLIAM McKELVEY, AURELIA WHEELDIN, THREE HARMONY SISTERS (Olive, Pearl, Gladys).

"Messin' Around" Choir: Charlee Downz, Inez Glover, Oliver Ball, Pearl Johnson, Gladys Wells, Lena Shadney, Audrey Thomas, Monette Moore, Arthur Porter, James Thomas, Sam Cross, Louis Craddock, Joseph Willis, James Shank, Bamboo McCarver, Fred A. Wheeldin, James K. Love. *Our Gang Kids: Dancing Waiters*: William Tyus, Quentin Gregory, Charles Johnson, James Dyer, "Pimples." *Maids*: Pearl McCarver, Anna Brown, Joyce Richardson, Rachel Beech, Enid Morgan, Vincent Boyce, Bebe Lynn, Vernet Christie. *Chorus*: Freda Jackson, Queenie Price, Catherine Upshur, Pearl McCarver, Bebe Lynn, Pearl McLaurin, Emily Malloy, Enid Morgan, Edith Randolph, Vincent Boyce, Anna Brown, Vernet Christie, Joyce Richardson, Gladys Webster, Rachel Beech, Evelyn Dickerson.

PROLOGUE

On to Harlem
  P. Floyd

ACT 1

Scene 1

Harlem Street Scene
  Scene: Lenox Avenue and 135th Street, New York City.

"Harlem Town"
  Choir

I'm the Law
  P. Floyd

Makin' Time
  Maids

---

[98]Dropped after opening.

[99]Dropped after opening.

Papers
  Our Gang Kids
Blues
  M. Moore
"Harlem Town"
  Entire Company
On Parade
  P. Floyd, F. Jackson, M. Moore, A Porter, C. LaRedd
"Your Love Is All I Crave" (Your Love I Crave)
  H. Perleno, S. Grant, Chorus
Where?[100]
  B. McLaurin, J. Thompson, P. Floyd
"Get Away from My Window" (Get Away from That Window)
  A. Thomas, B. McLaurin, J. Thompson
"Shout On"
  W. Brogsale, A. Porter, P. Floyd, Choir
Predictions
  W. Brogsdale, P. Floyd, F. Jackson, Q. Price, Our Gang Kids and Entire Company
"Sciddle-De-Scow" (Skiddle-De-Skow)
  C. LaRedd, Our Gang Kids, J. Dyer, Company
Scene 2
"I Need You"[101]
  L. Shadney, L. Craddock
Scene 3
Specialty
  W. McKelvey
Scene 4
Telling Fortunes
  Scene: A Gypsy Camp Fire.
  Fortune Teller: O. Ball. *He*: S. Grant. *She*: H. Perleno. *A Fortune Teller*: B. McLaurin. *His Friend*: J. Thompson.
Scene 5
"I Don't Love Nobody (but You)"
  Thomas, S. Cross, E. Dickerson, R. Beech, Q. Price,P. McLaurin, B. Lynn, W. Tyus, Q. Gregory, J. Dyer, W. McKelvey, "Pimples"
Scene 6
Dynamite
  Crook: P. Floyd. *Guardian*: J. Thompson. *Dummy*: B. McLaurin.
Scene 7
Mississippi:
"Roustabouts"
  Choir, B. Lynn, "Pimples," R. Beech, E. Dickerson, Chorus
"Mississippi Moan"
  W. Brogsdale, Entire Company
"Mississippi"
  W. Brogsdale, Entire Company
ACT 2[102]
Scene 1
At the Carnival
  Scene: Outside the Entrance of Main Tent.
  Tapso, the Dancing Skater: B. McCarver. *La Ballerina*: S. Wroten. *Ajax, the Strong Man*: F. Lloyd.
"Circus Time"[103]
  P. Floyd, Chorus
Hiring Help
  Barker: P. Floyd. *Applicant*: B. McLaurin. *Second Applicant*: J. Thompson. *Rolo*: J. K. Love. *Jolo*: J. Skank.
Scene 2
Battle for World's Female Championship
  World's Female Junior Lightweight Champion: E. Maitland. *World's Female Bantamweight Champion*: A. Wheeldin. *Miss Maitland's Second*: B. McLaurin.

Miss Wheeldin's Second: F. Thompson. *Referee*: F. A. Wheeldin. (*Spectators*: Entire Company.) (Note: Miss Maitland and Miss Wheeldin are the only two licensed female boxers in America.)
Scene 3
Spirituals
  Three Harmony Sisters
Scene 4
Paying Off
  Scene: Outside the Entrance of Main Tent.
  Carnival Barker: P. Floyd. *First Second*: B. McLaurin. *Second Second*: J. Thompson.
Scene 5
Harlem's Midnight Frolic:
"Sorry"
  H. Perleno, S. Grant
Waltz Clog[104] (Specialty)
  C. LaRedd, C. Johnson
Russian Specialty
  F. Davis
Hopping the Buck
  W. McKelvey
"Tapcopation"
  C. La Redd, Dancing Waiters
"Put Your Mind Right On It"
  M. Moore, J. Willis, Guests, Choir, Dancing Waiters, C. LaRedd, Chorus
"Yamekraw" (Piano Symphony)
  J. Johnson
Whirlwind
  Ebony Trio (A. Thomas, J. Thomas, S. Cross)
"Messin' Around"
  M. Moore
Finale
  Entire Company
  Master of Ceremonies: S. Grant. *First Guest*: B. McLaurin. *Second Guest*: J. Thompson.

1929.19 # THE LITTLE SHOW

A Musical Revue in Two Acts, 27 Scenes[105]. (Sketches by Howard Dietz, Newman Levy, George S. Kaufman, Marya Mannes and Fred Allen.) Music by Arthur Schwartz, (Frank Gray, Henry Sullivan, Morris Hamilton, Kay Swift, Herman Hupfeld, Charlotte Kent, Ralph Rainger.) Lyrics by Howard Dietz, (Earle Crooker, Grace Henry, Paul James, Lew Levenson, Henry Myers, Herman Hupfeld, Charlotte Kent, Harry Ruskin.) (Sketches staged by Dwight Deere Wiman.) Dances conceived and staged by Danny Dare. Settings designed by Jo Mielziner. Costumes designed by Ruth Brenner. Orchestra under the direction of Gus Salzer. Entire production under the supervision of Dwight Deere Wiman and Alexander Leftwich. Produced by William A. Brady, Jr. and Dwight Deere Wiman, in association with Tom Weatherley. Opened 30 April 1929 at the Music Box Theatre and closed 1 February 1930 after 321 performances.

CAST: CLIFTON WEBB, FRED ALLEN, LIBBY HOLMAN, ROMNEY BRENT, HELEN LYND, PEGGY CONKLIN, JOHN McCAULEY, KAY LAZELL, ERNEST SHARPE, BETTINA HALL, HAROLD MOFFET, JOAN CARTER-WADDELL, PAUL BISSINGER, ADAM CARROLL, PORTLAND HOFFA, RALPH RAINGER, ADAM CARROLL, AL WYART.
  The Little Show Girls: Dorothy Humphreys, Jean Kenin, Collette Francey, Constance Cummings, Marie Skorat, Peggy Conklin, Thelma Temple, Mary Bay, Kay Lazell, Estelle Phillips, Paulette Winston, Catherine Porter, Virginia May, Florence Healey.

ACT 1
Scene 1
Prologue
  E. Sharpe

---
[100]Dropped after opening.
[101]Dropped after opening
[102]Act 2 song and sketch order revised after opening.
[103]Whole scene revised after opening. "Circus Time" retitled "Circus Days."

---
[104]Dropped after opening.
[105]The first in the series of three annual intimate musical revues produced by Dwight Deere Wiman.

Scene 2

"Man About Town"
   J. McCauley, Chorus
   (*Music by* Arthur Schwartz. *Lyrics by* Howard Dietz.)

Scene 3

"Six Little Sinners"
   (*Music by* Frank Gray. *Lyrics by* Earle Crooker.)
   Gigolo: C. Webb. *Demi-Mondaine*: L. Holman. *Man About Town*: J. McCauley. *Society Matron*: B. Hall. *Chauffeur*: E. Sharpe. *Cook*: H. Lynd.

Scene 4

The Tiller Girls at Home (*by* Howard Dietz)
   Announcement: P. Conklin. *Tiller Girls*: K. Lazell, J. Kenin, P. Winston, M. Bay.

Scene 5

The Man Who Reads the Ads (*by* Newman Levy)
   Waiter: H. Moffet. *First Diner*: B. Hall. *Second Diner*: E. Sharpe. *Third Diner*: J. Carter-Waddell. *Fourth Diner*: C. Webb. *The Stranger*: F. Allen.

Scene 6

"Get Up on a New Routine"
   D. Humphreys, Chorus
   (*Music by* Arthur Schwartz. *Lyrics by* Howard Dietz.)

Scene 7

Embarrassing Moments
   Announcement: F. Allen.

Scene 8

"Caught in the Rain
   J. McCauley, J. Carter-Waddell
   (*Music by* Henry Sullivan. *Lyrics by* Howard Dietz.)

Scene 9

The Still Alarm (*by* George S. Kaufman)
   Ed Jamison: R. Brent. *Mr. Barclay*: C. Webb. *Bellboy*: P. Bissinger. *First Fireman*: F. Allen. *Second Fireman*: H. Moffet.

Scene 10

"Or What Have You?"
   B. Hall, J. McCauley
Dance
   C. Webb, J. Carter-Waddell
   (*Music by* Morris Hamilton. *Lyrics by* Grace Henry.)
   At the Pianos: R. Rainger, A. Carroll.

Scene 11

Fred Allen, with Portland Hoffa and Harold Moffet

Scene 12

"I've Made a Habit of You"
   H. Lynd, J. McCauley, Chorus
   (*Music by* Arthur Schwartz. *Lyrics by* Howard Dietz.)

Scene 13

"Can't We Be Friends?"
   L. Holman
   (*Music by* Kay Swift. *Lyrics by* Paul James.)

Scene 14

Napoleon (*by* Marya Mannes, with apologies to Robert E. Sherwood, John Erskine, and other debunkers.)
   A Carthaginian Soldier: C. Webb. *First Guard*: R. Brent. *Second Guard*: E. Sharpe. *The Queen*: H. Lynd.

Scene 15

Finale: "Little Old New York"
   B. Hall, C. Webb, Chorus
   (*Music by* Arthur Schwartz. *Lyrics by* Howard Dietz.)

ACT 2

Scene 1

"Song of the Riveter"
   E. Sharpe
   (*Music by* Arthur Schwartz. *Lyrics by* Lew Levenson.)

Scene 2

"What Every Little Girl Should Know"
   H. Lynd, R. Brent, Chorus
Dance
   J. Carter-Waddell
   (*Music by* Arthur Schwartz. *Lyrics by* Henry Myers.)

Scene 3

"The Theme Song"
   (*Music by* Arthur Schwartz. *Lyrics by* Howard Dietz.)
   Milton Lifshin, a Popular Song Writer: R. Brent. *Big Business Man*: H. Moffet. *Secretary*: D. Humphreys. *First Efficiency Expert*: A. Wyart. *Second Efficiency Expert*: R. Rainger. *Third Efficiency Expert*: A. Carroll.

Scene 4

"Hut in Hoboken"
   J. McCauley, B. Hall, Chorus
Dance
   K. Lazell
   (*Music and Lyrics by* Herman Hupfeld.)

Scene 5

"Stick to Your Dancing, Mabel"
   C. Webb, H. Lynd
   (*Music and Lyrics by* Charlotte Kent.)
   At the Piano: R. Rainger.

Scene 6

The Prize Winners (*by* Fred Allen)
   The Interpreter: F. Allen. *Mrs. Lime*: L. Holman. *Mr. Lime*: E. Sharpe. *Chow Chow*: V. May. *Grandfather Gherkin*: J. McCauley.

Scene 7

"I Guess I'll Have to Change My Plan"
   C. Webb
   (*Music by* Arthur Schwartz. *Lyrics by* Howard Dietz.)

Scene 8

"High Finance"
   (*Music by* Arthur Schwartz. *Lyrics by* Harry Ruskin.)
   First Financier: J. McCauley. *Second Financier*: R. Brent. *Street Cleaner*: H. Moffet. *Policeman*: P. Bissinger.

Scene 9

"Work Alike"
   Chorus (The Little Show Girls)
   (*Music by* Frank Gray. *Lyrics by* Earle Crooker.)

Scene 10

Fred Allen, with Portland Hoffa and Harold Moffet

Scene 11

"Moanin' Low"
   C. Webb, L. Holman
   (*Music by* Ralph Rainger. *Lyrics by* Howard Dietz. *Conceived and Directed by* Clifton Webb.)

Scene 12

Finale
   Entire Company

THE GRAND STREET FOLLIES OF 1929

1929.20

A Topical Revue in Two Acts, 19 Scenes[106]. Book (sketches) and lyrics by Agnes Morgan. Music by Arthur Schwartz, Max Ewing. Additional music by William Irwin and Serge Walter. (Additional lyrics by Max Ewing, Dave Goldberg, Howard Dietz, Max and Nathaniel Lief, Albert Carroll.) Entire production directed by Agnes Moran. Dances arranged by Dave Gould. Settings and costumes by Aline Bernstein. Music directed by Fred Fleming. Produced by The Actor-Managers, Inc. in association with Paul Moss. Opened 1 May 1929 at the Booth Theatre and closed 13 July 1929 after 85 performances.

CAST: Albert Carroll, Dorothy Sands, Otto Hulett, Paula Trueman, Marc Loebell, Edla Frankau, James Cagney, Mary Williams, Junius Matthews, Mae Noble, Hal Brogan, Kathleen Kidd, Blaine Cordner, Katherine Gauthier, George Heller, Ben K. Leavenworth, John Rynne, George Heller, Robert White, Walter Owens, Wallace Furle, Marion Harwick, Christine Burton, Merle Harrold, Wilma Lanyon, Una Hawthorne, Vernon Dowling, George Magis, Paul Jensen, George Raymond, Maurice Warner.

---

[106]The seventh and last in the annual series of revues which began in 1923.

ACT 1
Scene 1

The Garden of Eden: Things Get Started
(*Incidental Music by* Will Irwin.)
"The Amoeba's Lament"
(M. Williams)
(*Music by* Arthur Schwartz.)
A Benevolent Old Gentleman: O. Hulett. *Adam*: J. Cagney. *Eve*: E. Frankau. *The Serpent*: P. Trueman. *Lucifer*: A. Carroll. *An Amoeba*: M. Williams.

Scene 2

The Flood: As Handled by Herbert Hoover
"The Double Standard"
(*Music by* Arthur Schwartz.)
"The Vineyards of Manhattan"
(*Music by* Arthur Schwartz.)
Press Agent for Each Production: H. Brogan. *Noah*: O. Hulett. *Mrs. Noah*: M. Noble. *Their Three Sons: Shem*: B. K. Leavenworth. *Ham*: J. Rynne. *Japheth*: G. Heller.

Scene 3

The Siege of Troy: As Produced by David Belasco
"Priam's Little Congai"
(*Music by* William Irwin.)
Dances
(*Music by* William Irwin.)
"I've Got You on My Mind"
(*Music and Lyrics by* Max Ewing.)
Ulysses: J. Matthews. *Menelaus*: B. Cordner. *Leonore Ulric as Helen*: D, Sands. *Eunice, Her Maiden*: E. Frakau. *Helen Menken as Priam's Congai*: P. Trueman. *Paris*: M. Loebell. *A Trojan Maiden*: K. Kidd. *Two Trojan Warriors*: R. White, W. Owens. *A Greek Warrior*: W. Furie. *Two Children*: M. Harwick, C. Burton. *Five Maidens*: K. Gauthier, M. Williams, M. Harrold, W. Lanyon, U. Hawthorne. *Two Youths*: J. Cagney, G. Heller.

Scene 4

Caesar's Invasion of Britain: As Set to Music by Noël Coward
"British Maidens"
(*Music by* Max Ewing.)
"A Room With a Bath"
(*Music by* Max Ewing.)
"Force and Montana Waltz"
(*Music by* Max Ewing.)
"The Girl I Might Have Been"
(*Music and Lyrics by* Max Ewing.)
Caesar: O. Hulett. *An Early British Ingenue*: K. Kidd. *Force and Montana, Two Dancing Pixies*: M. Noble, J. Cagney. *Beatrice Lillie as Encyclopedia Brittanica*: A. Carroll. *Primitive English Virgins*: K. Gauthier, C. Burton, M. Harrold, M. Williams, U. Hawthorne, W. Lanyon, M. Harwick, E. Frankau. *Roman Soldiers*: B. K. Leavenworth, V. Downing, W. Owens, G. Magis, P. Jensen, G. Raymond, W. Furie, R. White, J. Rynne, M. Warner.

Scene 5

Nero's Policy: As Issued by the Aetna Fire Insurance Co.
"Rome Is Burning"
(*Music by* Arthur Schwartz.)
Nero: G. Heller. *Slave Girls*: M. Harwick, C. Burton.

Scene 6

The Jolly Troubadours: As Run by the Associated Press
(*Music by* Arthur Schwartz.)
Troubadours: B. K. Leavenworth, W. Owens, G. Magis, M. Warner, R. White, W. Furie, P. Jensen, G. Raymond, V. Downing. *Two Medieval Steppers*: K. Gauthier, C. Burton.

Scene 7

Serena Blandish at the Court of Louis XV: As Staged by Messrs. Banton & Sumner
Ruth Gordon as Serena: P. Trueman. *Constance Collier as Mme. Pompadour*: A. Carroll. *The Marquise de Pistache*: J. Matthews. *The Comte de Chocolate*: B. Cordner. *The Duc Creme de la Creme*: O. Hulett. *Louis XV*: M. Loebell.

Scene 8

"I Need You So": A Commedia dell' Arte Production
(*Music by* Arthur Schwartz. *Lyrics by* Dave Goldberg and Howard Dietz.)
An Italian Page: J. Rynne. *Pierrot*: B. Cordner. *Pierrette*: K. Kidd. *Harlequin*: J. Cagney. *Columbine*: K. Gauthier.

Scene 9

In the Reign of Queen Elizabeth—A Beaux Arts Ball: As Staged by Arthur Hopkins
"Don't Do It"
(*Music by* Arthur Schwartz.)
"I Love You But I Like You Even More"
(*Music by* Arthur Schwartz. *Lyrics by* Max and Nathaniel Lief.)
Queen Elizabeth: A. Carroll. *Sir Walter Raleigh*: M. Loebell. *The Herald*: J. Rynne. *Essex as Master of Ceremonies*: J. Matthews. *Irene Bordoni as Juliet*: D. Sands. *Eddie Cantor as Romeo*: G. Heller. *Bert Lahr as Marc Antony*: O. Hulett. *Hope Williams as Cleopatra*: P. Trueman. *Elizabethan Ladies*: E. Frankau, M. Noble, M. Harrold, M. Williams, C. Burton, W. Lanyon, U. Hawthorne, M. Harwick. *Elizabethan Courtiers*: B. K. Leavenworth, V. Downing, W. Owens, G. Magis, P. Jensen, M. Warner, G. Raymond, W. Furie, R. White.

ACT 2
Scene 1

The Landing of the Pilgrim Fathers: As Done by the Four Marx Brothers
"The Pilgrim Fathers"
(*Music by* Serge Walter.)
Groucho: M. Loebell. *Chico*: G. Heller. *Zeppo*: B. Cordner. *Harpo*: A. Carroll. *Fighting Rooster, an Indian Chief*: R. White. *Setting Hen, His Squaw*: M. Noble. *Cute Chicken, His Daughter*: E. Frankau. *Battling Bantam, an Indian Brave*: W. Furie.

Scene 2

Paul Revere's Ride: As Produced by Jed Harris
Reporters from "the Front Page": O'Brien: J. Rynne. *Sweeney*: J. Matthews. *Limburger*: O. Hulett. *Hellett Loose*: J. Cagney.

Scene 3

Washington and the Cherry Tree: As Dramatized by the Child Study Group
The Boy Washington: P. Trueman. *His Father*: B. Cordner. *The Psychoanalyst*: M. Lobell.

Scene 4

Washington Crossing the Delaware: As Staged by Earl Carroll
"The Textile Troops"
(*Music by* Max Ewing.)
"When George Crossed the Delaware"
(*Music by* Arthur Schwartz.)
Fannie Brice: A. Carroll. *Leon Errol*: J. Matthews. *The Textile Troops*: V. Downing, B. K. Leavenworth, G. Magis, W. Owens, M. Warner, P. Jensen, G. Raymond, W. Furie, R. White. K. Kidd, M. Williams, K. Gauthier, C. Burton, M. Harrold, U. Hawthorne, W. Lanyon, M. Harwick, M. Noble.

Scene 5

A Victorian Victim: Produced by the Civic Repertory Theatre
Alla Nazimova: D. Sands. *A Dominant Male*: J. Cagney.

Scene 6

"The Age of Innocence" (Masculine): As Hitherto concealed by Mrs. Wharton
(*Music by* Arthur Schwartz. *Dance originated by* Paula Trueman.)
His Love: P. Trueman.

Scene 7

The A.B.C. of Traffic: As Listed by Commissioner Whalen
Grover: M. Loebell. *Five of the Finest*: V. Downing, G. Raymond, W. Owens, B. K. Leavenworth, G. Magis. *The Dancing Cop*: J. Cagney.

Scene 8

Fashions in Love (1929) or What Have You?—Typical Love Scenes from:
(a) A Whimsical Milne Comedy: As Presented by Alexander Woolcott
Goo-Goo: D. Sands. *Coo-Coo*: J. Matthews.
(b) A Lonsdale Drama of English Society: As Imported by Gilbert Miller
Lady Cecily: E. Frankau. *Sir Harry*: M. Loebell.
(c) The Latest Eugene O'Neill Opus: A Theatre Guild Production
"My Dynamo"
(*Music by* Arthur Schwartz.)
Glenn Anders in 'Dynamo': O. Hulett.

Scene 9

England Sends U.S. Interest on the Debt: As Arranged by Messrs. Morgan and Young
"I'll Never Forget"
(*Music by* Max Ewing. *Lyrics by* Albert Carroll.)

Gertrude Lawrence: A. Carroll. *Her Boys*: P. Jensen, R. White, W. Furie, M. Warner.

Scene 10

Ghosts at the Waldorf: As Revived by George Tyler

The Dowager: M. Noble. *The Debutante*: W. Lanyon. *Her Fiance*: V. Downing. *Her Father*: G. Raymond. *Mrs. Martin*: U. Hawthorne. *Mr. Martin*: P. Jensen. *Edouard de Reszke*: B. K. Leavenworth. *Pol Plancon*: W. Owen. *Kubelik*: G. Magis. *Major-Domo*: M. Warner. *Ward McAllister*: B. Cordner. *Maude Adams*: P. Trueman. *Li Hung Chang*: J. Matthews. *Anna Held*: E. Frankau. *John Philip Sousa*: M. Loebell. *Colonel Roosevelt*: O. Hulett. *Lillian Russell*: D. Sands. *Modern Jazzers*: K. Gauthier, K. Kidd, C. Burton, M. Harwick, G. Heller, J. Cagney, W. Furie, R. White, J. Rynne. *Gertrude Lawrence*: A. Carroll.

1929.21   PANSY

An All-Colored Novelty (Musical Comedy) in Two Acts, 10 Scenes. Book by Alex Belledna. Music and lyrics by Maceo Pinkard. Book staged by Frank Rye. Ensembles staged by Nat Cash. Settings by Theatrical Art Studios. Orchestra: George Francis and His Society Entertainers. Produced by Maceo Pinkard. Opened 14 May 1929 at the Belmont Theatre and closed 16 May 1929 after 3 performances.

CAST (in order of appearance): *Dean Liggett*: Ralph Harris. *James*: AL FRISCO. *Campus "Cut Ups"*: COLE BROTHERS (Tom, Austin). *Miss Wright*: IDA ANDERSON. *Bill*, Proposition Kid: ALFRED CHESTER. *Miss Merritt*: Elizabeth Taylor. *Pansy*: PEARL McCORMACK. *Ulysses Grant Green*, father of Pansy: SPEEDY WILSON. *Mrs. Green*: Amon Davis. *Bob*: Billy Andrews. *Sadie*: JACKIE YOUNG. *Penn Comedy Four*: Walter Crumbley, Lee J. Randall, H. Mattingly, D. Davis. *Bessie Smith*: BESSIE SMITH.

Ladies of the Ensemble: Lenore Gadsden, Mildred Hart, Gypsy Bonte, Dorothy Boyd, Isabel Peterson, Alice Sampson, Rosita Williams, Julia Hassan, Eloise Thompson, Lucile Lind, Libby Robinson, Aubrey Clark, Beatrice Summerville, Judy Bonte, Virginia Branum.

ACT 1, *Scene 1*: Commencement Day at a Southern University. Interior of an Administration Building. *Scene 2*: Exterior of "I Ate a Pie" Sorority House. *Scene 3*: A Room in Jones' Cottage. *Scene 4*: On the University Campus. *Scene 5*: Party on Deke Johnson's Farm. (Impressionistic)

ACT 2, *Scene 1*: The Lower Level of Prenn Station. (Just an impression.) *Scene 2*: The Front of a Downtown Skyscraper. *Scene 3*: A Stranger Interlude. *Scene 4*: A Surprise. *Scene 5*: A Bouquet of Fond Memories.

ACT 1

Scene 1

"It's Commencement Day"
    Ensemble
"Break'n th' Rhythm"
    Cole Brothers, Campus Cuties
"Pansy"
    B. Andrews, P. McCormack, Ensemble

Scene 2

"Campus Walk"
    Campus Steppers

Scene 3

"I'd Be Happy"
    J. Young, A. Chester

Scene 4

"Gettin' Together"
    A. Frisco, Cole Brothers

Scene 5

"Shake a Leg"
    J. Young, Steppers, Company

Finale
    Entire Company

ACT 2

Scene 1

"If the Blues Don't Get You"
    B. Smith
Specialty
    Penn Comedy Four

Scene 2

Specialty
    Cole Brothers

Scene 3

"A Stranger Interlude"
    I. Anderson, Others

Scene 4

A Surprise

Scene 5

"A Bouquet of Fond Memories"
    Entire Company

Finale

1929.22   A NIGHT IN VENICE

A Musical Extravaganza (Revue) in Two Acts, 25 Scenes. Music by Lee David and Maurie Rubens. Lyrics by J. Keirn Brennan and Moe Jaffe. Book (sketches) staged by Lew Morton and Thomas A. Hart. Staged by Busby Berkeley. Dances and ensembles by Busby Berkeley. Chester Hale Dances by Chester Hale. Settings designed by Watson Barratt. Costumes designed by Erté, Barbier and Ernest Schrapp. Orchestra under the direction of Max Meth. Produced by the Messrs. Shubert. Opened 21 May 1929 at the Sam S. Shubert Theatre, moved 16 September 1929 to the Majestic Theatre and closed 19 October 1929 after 175 performances[107].

CAST: *Harry DeCosta*: JOHN BYAM. *Jack Graham*: MORTON HAVEL. *Josephine Gray*: LAURA LEE. *Bud O'Neill*: ARTHUR HAVEL. *May Gray*: JACKIE PAIGE. *Ernest Fairworth*: WALTER ARMIN. *Ted*: TED HEALY. *Shemp*: SHEMP HOWARD. *Moe*: HARRY HOWARD. *Larry*: LARRY FINE. *Freddy*: FRED SANBORN. *Ambrose Trainer*: DUDLEY CLEMENTS. *Count Muzzini*: WALTER ARMIN. *Maria Livia*: ANITA CASE. *Beppo*: ENJIO BADII. *Mussolini*: DAVID TULI. *Gondoliers*: GEORGE TERECHENKO, E. RIADNOFF. *Irene Trainer*: ANN SEYMOUR. THE DODGE SISTERS (Beth, Betty), BETSY REES, JOE MICHON, PETER MICHON, HALFRED YOUNG, SARAH GRANZOW, STANLEY ROGERS, FLORENCE POWELL, JOHN BYAMS, FODI BROWN, FERRAL and PAUL, THE JOHNSONS, SHADURSKAYA and KUDEROFF, THE STEVENS BROTHERS and BEAR, PAUL DeWEES.

CHESTER HALE GIRLS: Mary Hiscox, Jeanne Kroll, Agnes Hickey, Gertrude Westling, Adeline Bornheim, Lillian Bennett, Dorothy Pierce, Gladys Glorita, Evelyn Ford, Erma Echt, La Vonne Gundry, Hazel Landers, Evelyn Shields, Frances Johnson, Dorothy Davies, Blanche de Clerc. *ALLEN FOSTER GIRLS*: Lee Nutter, Polly McCann, Peggy DeRoy, Adele Jay, Betty Mayfair, Doris Smith, Jerry Pole, Edna Tobin, Gladys Miller, Bobby Carswell, Bobbie Baker, Ruth Martin, Judy Garey.

Dancing Girls: Olive Hollingshead, Dorothy Chadwick, Gladus Granzow, Jeannette Waite, Jackie Paige, Evelyn Dehkers, Betty Allen, Sara Granzow. *Show Girls*: Marion Gillon, Emmita Casonova, Mozel Stapp, Kay Norwood, Evelyn Wetherbee, Ireen King, Edna Lynn, Marvelle Dawn, Myrtle Candee, Louise Chowning, Marion Crozan, Florence Powell, Julia Barker, Billie Fanning, Peggy Udell. *Boys*: Jack Ray, James Lee, Tommy Kerns, Ed Stanbridge, Allen Blair, James Maxwell, Hal Gibson, Eddie Hackett, Charles McClelland, James H. Beattie.

ACT 1[108]

Scene 1

Opening Chorus
    J. Byam, Ensemble
"Sliding Down a Silver Cloud"
    M. Havel, A. Havel, J. Paige, L. Lee
    Scene: Roosevelt Aviation Field.

Scene 2

A Hangar on the Aviation Field

Scene 3

Chester Hale Girls

Scene 4

The Cockpit of the Aeroplane

---

[107]Sketches uncredited. Prior to Broadway, book credited to Harold Atteridge. The third and final in the annual series of "A Night in...." revues produced by the Messrs. Shubert.
[108]Added to show during run:
"Loose Ankles" (Act 2, Scene 3)
    Mlles. Beth and Betty Dodge
    (*Music and Lyrics by* Maurice Rubens, Powers Gouraud, Clay Boland, Moe Jaffee.)
Added to show for subsequent tour:
"Right or Wrong" (Act 2, Scene 3)
    Ann Seymour
    (*Music and Lyrics by* Ted Healy and George Goodwin.)

Scene 5

"The Lure of the Night with the *Ile de France* on the Horizon"
H. Young
Accompanied by a Group of Venetian Beauties on the Ice Flow.

Scene 6

Arthur and Morton Havel

Scene 7

"One Night of Love"
E. Badii, A. Case, H. Young, Venetian Quartette, Entire Ensemble

Scene 8

Ann Seymour

Scene 9

Mlles. Beth and Betty Dodge

Scene 10

Corridor of the Excelsior Hotel

Scene 11

"Cellini's Plate"
H. Young, A. Case, J. Byam, Venetian Quartette

Scene 12

Ted Healy and his Gang
The Stevens Brothers and Their Bear

Scene 13

"Fans"
J. Byam
Danced by Mlles. Beth and Betty Dodge, Dancing Girls, a Group of Venetian Show Girls.

Scene 14

Joe and Pete Pichon
Scene: In the Locker Room of the *S. S. Paris*.

Scene 15

"The One Girl" (from RAINBOW)
J. Byam, A. Case, H. Young, L. Lee, J. Paige, Entire Ensemble
(*Music by* Vincent Youmans. *Lyrics by* Oscar Hammerstein II. *Orchestrated by* Vincent Youmans.)

Scene 16

The Grand Staircase
Mlles. Beth and Betty Dodge
Assisted by B. Rees on her toes, Xylophone Ensemble by Albert and James Johnson, All K. Foster Girls.

ACT 2

Scene 1

"Lido Shores"
J. Byam, Entire Ensemble

Scene 2

"The Stork Don't Come Around Anymore"
A. Havel, M. Havel, J. Byam,
D. Clements, W. Armin, S. Howard, H. Howard, H Young, Venetian Show Girls

Scene 3

Ted Healy and His Band
With A. Seymour, B. Rees, P. Dewees, L. Lee, The Gang, S. Granzow, Dancing Girls.

Scene 4

"The Legend of Leda"
A. Case, J. Byam

Dance
Mlles. Beth and Betty Dodge

Ballet
Chester Hale Girls (Swans)
On the Silver Fountain: Venetian Beauties.

Scene 5

"Little Old Dreamy New York"[109]
J. Byam, A. Case, H. Young, Venetian Ensemble
Scene: A Street Scene on any Side Street of New York.
Mr. Buchanan: J. Byam. *Mrs. Jones*: S. Howard. *Vincent Jones*: F. Sanborn. *Mae Jones*: Beth Dodge. *Frank Moran*: D. Clements. *Anna Moran*: A. case. *Rose Moran*: A. Seymour. *Sam Kaplan*: H. Howard. *Harry Easter*: M. Havel. *Dick*: A. Havel. *Mrs Fiorentino*: F. Brown. *Felippo Fiorentino*: W. Armin. *Mrs. Buchanan*: M. Candee. *Mrs. Smith*: L. Chowning. *Sankey*: H. Young. *Policeman*: C. McClellan. *Passerby*: J. Beattie. *Milk Driver*: A. Havel. *Letter Carrier*: A. Gibson. *Newsgirl*: J. Paige. *Peddler*: T. Kerns.

Scene 6

"Tondelayo"
H. Young
Danced by F. Powell.

Scene 7

The Jungle (Dance)
Ensemble
(The Medicine Man and Witch Dances by Mr. Kuderoff and Mme. Shadurksaya are authentic African Jungle Dances.)

Scene 8

A Lesson in French
T. Healy, Mlles. Beth and Betty Dodge

Scene 9

Carnival Time
(Entire Company)
Scene: St. Mark's Square.

---

[109] Burlesque of Elmer Rice's drama 'Street Scene.'

1929–1930 SEASON

Kate Smith as Pansy Sparks in George White's FLYING HIGH (Photo: Vandamm Studio)
Billy Rose Theatre Collection, New York Public Library for the Performing Arts

1929-1930 SEASON

(CONNIE'S)
HOT CHOCOLATES

1929.23

A New Tanskin Revel (Musical Revue) in Two Acts, a Prologue and 23 Scenes. Comedy sketches by Eddie Green. Music by Thomas [Fats] Waller and Harry Brooks. Lyrics by Andy Razaf. Staged by Leonard Harper. Musical arrangements by Russell Wooding; additional musical arrangements by Ken Macomber. Settings designed by Gene Lankas, P. Dodd Ackerman. Costumes designed by Gene and Jeanne. Men's wardrobe by Steiner Costume Company. Orchestra conducted by LeRoy Smith. Entire production supervised by George Immerman. Produced by Connie Immerman. Opened 20 June 1929 at the Hudson Theatre and closed 14 December 1929 after 219 performances.

CAST: BABY COX, EDITH WILSON, JIMMIE BASKETTE, MARGARET SIMMS, PAUL BASS, EDDIE GREEN, BILLY MAXEY, 'JAZZLIPS' (AMANZIE) RICHARDSON, LOUISE HIGGINS, BILLY HIGGINS, LOUISE ('JOTA') COOK, MADALINE BELT, (Louis Armstrong).
RUSSELL WOODING'S JUBILEE SINGERS: Ina Duncan, Elice Todd, Mary Pervall, Natalie Long, Anita Reed, Louise Williams, Gladys Jordan, Dick Campbell, A. A. Haston, Thomas R. Hall, J. W. Leguen, Jesse Wilson, Clarence Todd, J. E. Lightfoot, Toussaint Duers, William McKelvey, Paul Meeres, Thelma Meeres, George Staton, Ernest Taylor. *Ensemble: THE SIXTEEN HOT CHOCOLATE DROPS*: Billie Bow, Dolly McCormick, Billie Campbell, Loraine Harris, Frances Hubbard, Pearl Baines, Lucille Smith, Amy Spencer, Marion Egbert, Virginia Wheeler, Ruth Cherry, Arline Cisco, Marion Davis, Dorothy Young, Bernice Miles, Eva Bradley. *The Bon-Bon Buddies*: George Norton, James K. Love, Llewelyn Crawford, Lloyd Mitchell, Freddie Heron, Bobby Johnson, Julius Howard, John Perry.

ACT 1[1]

Prologue

At Connie's Inn
Head Waiter: J. E. Lightfoot. *Doorman*: C. Todd. *First Waiter*: J. Wilson. *Second Waiter*: J. W. Leguen. *Attendant*: T. R. Hall. *Master of Ceremonies*: J. Baskette. Guests, Orchestra and Entertainers.

Waltz Divine
P. Meeres, T. Meeres

The Club Revue: "Pickaninny Land"
G. Staton, E. Taylor, W. McKelvey, The Hot Chocolate Drops, the Bob Bon Buddies

Scene 1

"Song of the Cotton Fields"
Jubilee Singers

"Sweet Savannah Sue"
M. Simms, P. Bass, The Hot Chocolate Drops, the Bon Bon Singers

Scene 2

The Unloaded Gun
E. Green, B. Maxey, J. Baskette

Scene 3

"Say It With Your Feet"
D. McCormick, the Hot Chocolate Drops, the Bob Bon Buddies, with Taffy-Tootsie Timoney

Scene 4

"Ain't Misbehavin'"
M. Simms, P. Bass, Sextette

---

[1]Added shortly after opening:
Somewhere in Harlem (Act 2)
E. Green, E. Wilson, B. Higgins, J. Baskette, L. Williams
"Redskinland" (Act 2)
J. Baskette
Second Couple: J. Richardson, E. Wilson.
"My Man Is Good For Nothin' But Love" (Act 2)(dropped after July 1929)
E. Wilson, L. Armstrong, Thomas (Fats)Waller
The Six Crackerjacks (Acrobatic Dance Specialty) (Act 2)

Scene 5

Big Business
Kid Licorice: J. Richardson. *Manager*: E. Green. *Promoter*: B. Higgins. A *Reporter*: B. Maxey. *Gamblers*: J. Wilson, D. Campbell, J. W. Lightfoot. *Referee*: T. R. Hall. *Moving Picture Magnate*: A. A. Haston.

Scene 6

"Goddess of Rain"
J. Baskette

Dance
L. Cook, Ensemble

Scene 7

"Dixie Cinderella"
B. Cox, B. Maxey

Scene 8

Southland Medley[2] (including "Old Black Joe")
Jubilee Singers

Scene 9

Somewhere in Harlem
E. Wilson, B. Higgins, E. Green, J. Baskette, L. Williams

Scene 10

"Jungle Jamboree"[3]
B. Cox, Hot Chocolate Drops

Scene 11

Specialty[4]
J. Richardson

Scene 12

"That Rhythm Man"
J. Baskette, Entire Company

ACT 2
(Entr'acte: Trumpet Solo)
(Louis Armstrong)

Scene 1

The Wedding of the Rabbit and the Bear
Hostess: E. Wilson. *Bunnies*: Hot Chocolate Drops. *Bear*: B. Cox. *Rabbit*: M. Belt. *Fox*: P. Bass. *Monkeys*: M. Prevall, L. Williams, N. Long. *Pussy-Cat*: M. Simms. *Snakes*: J. Richardson, L. Cook, E. Taylor. *Jackass*: B. Maxey. *Zebras*: Bob Bon Buddies. *Birds*: Jubilee Singers.

Scene 2

In a Telegraph Office (Sending a Wire)
Clerk: J. Baskette. *Hallow*: E. Green.

Scene 3

"Black and Blue"
E. Wilson

Scene 4

Traffic in Harlem
The Chaufeurettes: Hot Chocolate Drops. *Motorcycle Cops*: Bob Bon Buddies. *The Sergeant*: B. Maxey. *Lieutenant*: J. Richardson. *Captain*: B. Higgins. *The Buick*: M. Belt. *The Rolls-Royce*: M. Simms. *The Diana*: D. Campbell. *The Ford*: E. Wilson. *An Entertainer*: B. Cox. *Cabaret Girls*: Hot Chocolate Drops.

'Snake Hips' Dance
B. Cox, Girls

Specialty Dance
P. Meeres, T. Meeres

Scene 5

Harlem Street Scene
B. Maxey, D. Campbell, F. Hubbard, P. Baines

Scene 6

"Can't We Get Together?"
D. McCormick, M. Belt

Scene 7

Hello Hollywood[5]
Camera Man: B. Maxey. *Director*: P. Bass, Ensemble.

---

[2]Later in run, identified as Negro Spirituals.
[3]Dropped after opening.
[4]Dropped after opening.
[5]Dropped after opening.

Scene 8

"Pool Room Papa"[6]
B. Maxey, E. Wilson

Scene 9

"Off-Time"
M. Simms, E. Taylor, W. McKelvey, Boys

Scene 10

SpecialtyThree Midnight Steppers

Scene 11

Finale
Entire Company

1929.24 KEEP IT CLEAN

An Intimate Musical Revue in Two Acts, 38 Scenes. Sketches by Jimmy Duffy and Will Morrissey. Music and lyrics by Lester Lee, Jimmy Duffy, Harry Archer, Benny Ryan, James Hanley, Clarence Gaskill, Violinsky, Charles Tobias, Harry Converse, American Society of Composers. Dances staged by Russell E. Markert. Principals' costumes by Faye. Ensemble costumes by Reine, Inc. Orchestra under the direction of Jimmy Carr. Produced by William Duffy and John Hickey, Jr. Opened 24 June 1929 at the Selwyn Theatre and closed 6 July 1929 after 16 performances[7].

CAST: WILL MORRISSEY, MIDGIE MILLER, JIMMY DUFFY, EDITH MURRAY, TED MARCEL, PAULINE GASKINS, JIM HARKINS, ROSEMARY RYDER, JIMMY O'BRIEN, MLLE. AMERIQUE & NEVILLE, DOUGLAS STANSBURY, KAROL KANE, FRANK FARNUM, HELEN GLEASON, DON KENNELLY, (Mammy) MAE DAILEY, SIDNEY HAWKINS, JACK INGLIS, MADAME REINE, JACOB FRANK, TOM MCNAMARA, FRANK LYNCH, GENE OLIVER, THE MOROSCO BROTHERS, SID ASHERMAN, ORVILLE KNAPP, JIMMY CARR'S ORCHESTRA.

The Sixteen Markert Dancers: Diana Anitra, Helene Bradley, Amanda Daisy, Gene Doughty, Hanna Dunner, Anitra Furman, Blanche Granby, Irene Griffith, Bert Haines, Jean Hassemer, Lottie Hentschel, Loretta Jefferson, Dorothy Martin, Beth Mann, Elsie McLeod, Emily Ryan, Irma Wurster.

ACT 1

Scene 1

A Left Over from the Charlot Revue
T. Marcel

Scene 2

Jimmy Carr, the Doctor of Melody and His Orchestra

Scene 3

Exposures
The Head Man: W. Morrissey. *The Bank Roll Man*: J. Frank. *The Critic*: D. Kennelly. *The Costumer*: M. Reine. The Russell Markert Dancers. *Stagehands*: J. Harkins, T. McNamara. *Stagedoor Man*: J. O'Brien. *The District Attorney of the Head Man's Home*: M. Miller.

Scene 4

An Interruption
(a) Sweeney from HeadquartersG. Oliver
(b) Keep It Clean SketchM. Miller, T. Marcel
(c) The Other SketchH. Gleason, T. Marcel, J. Harkins

Scene 5

Followed by the Jones Law DanceMorosco Brothers

Scene 6

"I See You But What Do You See in Me?"
K. Kane, S. Hawkins
(*Music and Lyrics by* Lester Lee.)
Dance
P. Gaskins, Markert Dancers

Scene 7

Jimmy Duffy

Scene 8

Tango Blues
Amerique and Neville

Scene 9

"Someone to Love You"
E. Murray
(*Music by* Harry Archer. *Lyrics by* Charles Tobias.)

Scene 10

English Actors at Home (*by* Will Morrissey)
M. Miller, H. Gleason, T. Marcel, J. Harkins

Scene 11

"Broadway Mammy"
M. Dailey, D. Stanbury
(*Music and Lyrics by* Clarence Gaskill and Jimmy Duffy.)

Scene 12

Intelligencia
First Street Cleaner: J. Duffy. *Second Street Cleaner*: J. Harkins. *First Gentleman*: T. Marcel. *Second Gentleman*: J. O'Brien.

Scene 13

"(Doin the) Hot-Cha-Cha"
E. Murray
(*Music and Lyrics by* Lester Lee.)
DanceM. Miller, Markert Dancers

Scene 14

Frank Farnum

Scene 15

Dog Tales
J. Duffy, H. Gleason

Scene 16

A Few Moments at the Silver Slipper
Jimmy Carr and Orchestra
(a) Whoopee Hat BrigadeS. Asherman, the Boys
(b) The Hit of the Block PartyJ. O'Brien
(c) Some Sweet DayJ. Carr
(d) The Saxophone StepperO. Knapp
(e) A Few Hot NotesE. Murray
(f) Marching HomeD. Stanbury
(g) Boots as Kipling Did Not Write ItJ. Carr

Scene 17

Finale
Entire Company
Introducing R. Ryder, the Lucky Strike Spin Girl.

ACT 2

Scene 1

The Explainer
J. Harkins

Scene 2

Ballet Divertissement
(*Music by* Clarence Gaskill.)
Dancers: G. Doughty, E. Ryan, L. Hentschel, B. Granby. *The Swan*: Mlle. Amerique.

Scene 3

Prosperity—Revolution of the Middle Classes
J. Duffy, Ensemble

Scene 4

Dance Specialty
P. Gaskins

Scene 5

Dance Fantastique
F. Farnum

Scene 6

On the 18th of April in '75
J. Inglis, Patriot's Wives

Scene 7

SpecialtyD. Kennelly

Scene 8

A Few Minutes with Midgie and Will

Scene 9

"Just a Little Blue for You"
K. Kane, S. Hawkins
(*Music and Lyrics by* James Hanley.)

---

[6]Dropped after opening.
[7]Staged by Will Morrissey, uncredited. Settings uncredited.

Scene 10

Mommy Mae Dailey

Scene 11

"H-O-K-U-M"

M. Miller, J. Duffy, J. Harkins, T. Marcel, J. O'Brien, F. Farnum
(*Music by* James Hanley. *Lyrics by* Jimmy Duffy.)

Scene 12

"See No Evil"

D. Stanbury
(*Music and Lyrics by* Clarence Gaskill and Jimmy Duffy.)

Scene 13

Will Morrissey Meets an Old Friend from Hollywood

W. Morrissey, J. Frank, G. Oliver

Scene 14

A Good Skate

T. Marcel

Scene 15

Doll Dance

Markert Dancers

Scene 16

Sitting in a Booth

J. Duffy

Scene 17

"Upstairs over a Speakeasy"

M. Miller, D. Kennelly
(*Music and Lyrics by* Harry Converse.)

Scene 18

Ensemble Tap Dance

Markert Dancers

Scene 19

The Russian Sympathy Orchestra

J. Duffy and His Band

Scene 20

Will Morrissey

Scene 21

Finale

Entire Company

1929.25   BOMBOOLA

A Unique Afro-American Musical Comedy in Two Acts, 6 Scenes. Book by D. Frank Marcus. (Based on the suggestion of a theme by Jimmie Cooper.) Music and lyrics by D. Frank Marcus and Bernard Maltin. Dances and ensembles staged by Sam Rose. Chorus directed by Allie Ross. Settings by Theatrical Art Studio and Beaumont Studios. Costumes designed by Lili. Musical arrangements by Ken Macomber, Arthur Gutman, Hal Brown and Carl F. Williams. Singing arrangements by Arthur Johnston. Electrical effects by Display Stage Lighting Company. Produced by Irving Cooper. Opened 26 June 1929 at the Royale Theatre and closed 18 July 1929 after 27 performances.

CAST (in order of appearance): *The Harmonizers (4)*: *Eb*: Robert Ecton. *Jeb*: Oliver Foster. *Ned*: Charles Lawrence. *Fred*: Claude Lawson. *Rhodendra Frost*: MERCEDES GILBERT. *'Lije Frost*: MONTE HAWLEY. *Sheila Nesbit*: Hilda Perleno. *Samson Frost*: PERCY WINTERS. *Ludlow Bassom*: GEORGE RANDOL. *Anna Frost*: ISABELL WASHINGTON. *Deputy Sheriff*: Ray Giles. *Sambo*: John Mason. *"Dusty"*: DUSTY FLETCHER. *Stage Doorman*: Cora Merano. *First Pedestrian*: Cora Merano. *Second Pedestrian*: Ruth Krygar. *J. Quentin Creech, the Star*: BILLY ANDREWS. *Myrtle Wyms, the Soubrette*: BILLIE CORTEZ. *Tom Gin, The Chief Comedian*: BREVARD BURNETT. *"The Song Bird"*: REVELLA HUGHES. *Anna's Maid*: Cora Merano. *The Preacher*: Ray Giles. Cecil Mack's Southland Singers.

Ensemble: *Dusky Damsels*: Alice Bowen, Fannie Cotton, Violet Fisher, Estella Finley, Clara Howard, Pearl Howell, Mabel Hopkins, Ruth Krygar, Carmen Lopez, Adelaide Marshall, Josephine McClain, Ernestine McClain, Jenny Salmons, Ollie Schoonmaker, Edna Scarez, Georgina Spelvina, Marian Tyler, Catherine Upshur. *Boys (Bomboola Steppers)*: Charles Banks, Johnnie Bragg, Ernest Creanshaw, Frank Davis, Kenneth Harris, Dominick Mendez, Arthur Oliver, (Thomas Schriner, Timoney Gladstone, "Derby.") *Quartet*: Robert Ecton, Oliver Foster, Charles Lawrence, Claude Lawson.

Act 1, Scene 1: Front Yard of the Frost home on the outskirts of Savannah, Georgia. Late afternoon, September. *Scene 2*: Stage Entrance of the Jackson Theatre, New York.

Four weeks later. *Scene 3*: The stage of the Jackson Theatre during rehearsal. Immediately following.

Act 2, Scene 1: The Stage of the Jackson Theatre on the Opening Night of "Bamboola." *Scene 2*: Anna's Dressing Room, immediately following. *Scene 3*: The Wedding Procession. The following night. *Scene 4*: The Stage of the Jackson Theatre. Immediately following.

ACT 1

Scene 1

"Evenin'" Cecil Mack's Southland Singers, Swanee Four

"Ace of Spades"

H. Perleno, P. Winters, Ensemble

"Dixie Vagabond"

G. Randol, Ensemble

"Rub-a-Dub Your Rabbit's Foot"

I. Washington

Dance

J. Bragg, Ensemble

Scene 2

"The Way to Do Bomboola"

B. Cortez, P. Winters, Ensemble

"Somebody Like Me"

I. Washington, G. Randol, R. Hughes, H. Perleno, J. Mason, D. Fletcher, B. Burnett

Finale

Ensemble

ACT 2

Scene 1

"Tailor Made Babies"

B. Cortez, J. Bragg, Ensemble

"African Whoopee"

I. Washington, Her Wild Animals

"Tampico Tune"

H. Perleno, R. Hughes, B. Andrews, 'Derby,' Girls

"Song of Harlem"

I. Washington, Swanee Four

"Shoutin' Sinners"

B. Cortez, H. Perleno, B. Burnett, D. Fletcher, Southland Singers, Swanee Four

"Anna"

I. Washington, B. Andrews, Ensemble

Specialty 'Derby'

Brevard Burnett's One Man Crap Game

Mason & Fletcher's 'Strange Inter-Feud' (with due apologies to the Theatre Guild)

The Hot Dog Man: J. Mason. *The Soft Shell Crab Man*: D. Fletcher. *First Customer*: R. Krygar. *Second Customer*: B. Cortez. *Cop*: C. Lawrence.

The Other Side of Harlem (More or Less a travesty on the play 'Harlem')

The Lady Killer: B. Andrews. *The Host*: B. Burnett. *The Sweet Mama*: H. Perleno. *The Host's Lady Friend*: B. Cortez. *Three Card Monte*: J. Mason. *The Shill*: D. Fletcher. *The Interrupter*: I. Washington. *Detective*: M. Hawley. *Cop*: T. Schriner. Cecil Mack's Southland Singers, Swanee Four, Ensemble.

Two in One

(a) Clothes Make the Woman

The Wife: H. Perleno. *The Friend*: G. Spelvina. *The Husband*: M. Hawley.

(b) 'Suicide'

Sambo: J. Mason. *'Dusty'*: D. Fletcher. *The Woman in the Case*: B. Cortez.

The Wall Between

The Husband: D. Fletcher. *The Wife*: H. Perleno. *The House Man*: B. Burnett. *First Poker Player*: J. Mason. *Second Poker Player*: R. Giles. *Third Poker Player*: C. Lawrence.

Additional Specialties:

The Boy with the Shufty Shoes ('Derby' Himself)

Percy Winters, Cora Merano

Johnnie Bragg

Timoney Gladstone

Swanee Four

Cecil Mack's Southland Singers

The Bamboola Steppers

Scene 2
> Reprise
>> :G. Randol, Quartette

Scene 3
> "Wedding Procession"
>> Ensemble

Scene 4
> "Hot Patootie Wedding Night"
>> I. Washington, Company
> Finale
>> Entire Company

EARL CARROLL'S
1929.26   SKETCH BOOK (1929)

A Musical Revue in Two Acts, 54 Scenes[8], by Eddie Cantor. (Conceived by Earl Carroll. Sketches by Eddie Cantor, Sidney Skolsky; additional dialogue by Eddie Welch.) Music and lyrics by Jay Gorney and E. Y. Harburg, (Billy Rose, Harry Tobias, Charles Tobias, Benny Davis, Ted Snyder, Vincent Rose, Renee Russell, Charles L. Sansone, Irving Kahal, Arnold Johnson, Jean Hubert, Irving Actman, Abner Silver). Book staged by Edgar J. MacGregor. Dance ensembles by LeRoy Prinz. Art and technical direction by Bernard Lohmuller. Settings designed by Joseph Teichner Studio and Hugh Willoughby. Costumes designed by Florence Weber. Orchestrations by Domenico Savino. Orchestra conducted by Ray Kavanaugh. Entire production under the supervision of Earl Carroll. Produced by Earl Carroll. Opened 1 July 1929 at the Earl Carroll Theatre, moved 30 September 1929 to the 44th Street Theatre, moved 10 March 1930 to the 46th Street Theatre, and closed 7 June 1930 after 392 performances.

CAST: WILL MAHONEY, WILLIAM DEMAREST, THE THREE SAILORS (Bert Jason, Bob Robson, Harry Blue), DOROTHY CARROLL, DOROTHY BRITTON, DON HOWARD, PATSY KELLY, COLY [Coley] WORTH, GRACE WORTH, GEORGE GIVOT, THE PHELPS TWINS (Irene, Florine), FAITH BACON, CARLTON EMMY, SAMMY DUNCAN, EILEEN HEALY, ESTELLE FRATUS, DOROTHY CARROLL, OMAR, BOB GERAGHTY, SLIM CAVANAUGH, GRACE DuFAYE.

America's Premier Show Girls: Collette Francis, Ann Faye, Winifred Starr, Frances Joyce, Evelyn Crowell, Eileen Wenzel, Irma Philbin, Marion Carewe. *(Ensemble):* Vera Milton, Frances De Lacey, Flo Ward, Odessa Morgan, Beryl Wallace, Marion Harcke, Eleanor Ahren, Nelda Kincaid, Dorothea Frank, Catherine O'Neill, Marion O'Day, Louise Garnett, Margaret Joyce, Mary Masher, Blanche Reeves, Maryjo Engers, Diana White, Henrietta Kay, Etna Ross, Peggy Purcell, Vivian Wilson, Angeline Hassen, Catherine Clark, Rita Stone, Renee Johnson, Violet Arnold, Janet Currie, Elsie Connor, Nancy Decker.

ACT 1[9]

Scene 1
> Sketch Book Photophone[10] (in which Earl Carroll explains to you the idea that Eddie Cantor explained to him.)
> "Legs, Legs, Legs"[11]
>> E. Cantor (recorded by the RCA Photophone System)
>> (*Music by* Jay Gorney. *Lyrics by* E. Y. Harburg.)

Scene 2

Scene 3
> The Old Fashioned Girls of Today

---

[8]The first of Earl Carroll's two sketchbook revues, and the seventh in the annual series of revues (Vanities, Sketchbooks) presented under his auspices beginning in 1923.

[9]Order of songs and sketches revised after opening. Added after opening:
> The Want Add (Act 1)
>> *Peggy:* G. Worth. *Kitty:* D. Carroll.
> Once a Week (Act 1)
>> *Husband:* B. Robson. *Wife:* D. Britton. *Doctor:* B. Geraghty.
> In 71 (Act 2)
>> *The Golfer:* W. Demarest. *His Admirer:* C. Worth.
> A Fatal Mistake (Act 2)
>> *The Druggist:* R. Robson. *His Pal:* H. Blue. *Customer:* B. Jason.

[10]Dropped after opening.

[11]Replaced for subsequent national tour by:
> "Sketch Book"
>> D. Howard

"Song of Symbols"
> *Misinterpreted by* D. Howard
>> *First Group:* V. Milton, F. DeLacey, F. Ward, O. Morgan, B. Wallace, M. Harcke, E. Ahren, N. Kincaid, D. Frank, E. O'Connor. *Second Group:* C. O'Neill, M. O'Day, L. Garnett, M. Joyce, M. Masher, B. Reeves, M. Engers, D. White, M. Carewe, H. Kay. *Third Group:* E. Ross, P. Purcell, I. Philbin, V. Wilson, A. Hassell, C. Clarke, R. Stone, R. Johnson, V. Arnold, J. Currie.

Scene 4
> On a Green Hillside: "For Someone I Love"
>> The Phelps Twins
>> (*Music by* Ted Snyder. *Lyrics by* Benny Davis.)
>> *Cires*, the Goddess of the Earth: F. Beacon.

Scene 5
> QuickiesD. Britton

Scene 6
> An Artist's Studio
>> *The Model:* E. Wenzel. *The Man:* C. Emmy.

Scene 7
> "Honolulu"[12]
>> *Guitarist:* C. Worth. *Hula Hula:* G. Worth.

Scene 8
> Long Beach
>> *Father:* S. Duncan. *Daughter:* E. Healy. *Life Guard:* H. Blue.

Scene 9
> Philanthropist
>> *Eccentric Millionaire:* W. Demarest. *And America's Premier Show Girls: Collette:* C. Francis. *Ann:* A. Faye. *Winnie:* W. Starr. *Frances:* F. Joyce. *Evelyn:* E. Crowell. *Eileen:* E. Wenzel.

Scene 10
> Herr Mahoney und hunds[13]

Scene 11
> Writing the Hit Song: "Song of the Moonbeams"
>> D. Howard
>> (*Music by* Vincent Rose. *Lyrics by* Charles Tobias, Harry Tobias.)

Scene 12
> In a Grecian Garden
>> *Grecian Maidens:* E. Crowell, F. Joyce, C. Francis, E. Wenzel, D. White, W. Starr, M. Carewe, A. Faye.

Scene 13
> Crescent Moonbeams
>> 36 Moon Dreams

Scene 14
> Uniforms[14]
>> *Faithful Husband:* G. Givot. *Faithful Wife:* D. Britton. *Her Sailor Friend:* B. Robson.

Scene 15
> Lifesavers
>> C. Worth, G. Worth

Scene 16
> Two in One
>> *Bell Boy:* P. Kelly. *First Guest:* W. Mahoney. *Second Guest:* W. Demarest. *Wife:* D. Britton. *Husband:* C. Emmy.

Scene 17
> "Kinda Cute"
>> G. Givot
>> (*Music by* Jay Gorney. *Lyrics by* E. Y. Harburg.)
>> *Assisted by* E. Fratus, Phelps Twins, G. Worth, D. Carroll.

Scene 18
> Infinite Black
>> (a) Cerise DanceLed by D. Carroll
>> (b) Turquoise DanceLed by E. Fratus
>> (c) Orchid DanceD. Frank, L. Garnett, E. Ross, M. Masher
>> (d) Chartreuse DanceLed by G. Worth
>> (e) Amber DanceLed by Omar

---

[12]Dropped after opening.

[13]Dropped after opening.

[14]Later retitled A Pleasant Surprise.

Scene 19

Every Thursday[15]
Husband: W. Demarest. *Wife*: D. Britton. *Doctor*: C. Emmy.

Scene 20

Three O'Clock in the Morning
Husband: W. Mahoney. *Wife*: P. Kelly.

Scene 21

Journey's End[16]
Nat: B. Robson. *Matt*: B. Jason.

Scene 22

"Fascinating You"[17]
P. Kelly, W. Demarest
(*Music and Lyrics by* Benee Russell, Charles Tobias, Harry Tobias, Vincent Rose.)

Scene 23

The Broadway Ltd. (Impression of a Train created by the Marmeins)

Scene 24

When the Fleet Is In (Scene on Riverside Drive)

Scene 25

(On a Furlough): "Like Me Less—Love Me More"
(*Music by* Jay Gorney. *Lyrics by* E. Y. Harburg.)
A Singing Gob: D. Howard. *His Girl Friends*: Phelps Twins. *An Able Seaman*: S. Duncan. *His Friend*: D. Carroll. *Another Gob*: Omar. *S.P.*: G. Givot. *A Loving Gob*: C. Worth. *His Lady Friend*: E. Fratus. *A Factory Flapper*: P. Kelly. *A Riverside Gold Digger*: G. Worth. *Two Park Avenue Debs*: *Francine*: F. Joyce. *Winifred*: W. Starr. *A Sailor's Admirer*: D. Britton. *A Gob*: B. Geraghty. *A Lieutenant*: W. Demarest. *Three Sailors, AWOL*: B. Jason, B. Robson, H. Blue. *Shorty*: S. Cavanaugh.

Scene 26

An Easy Living
W. Mahoney

Scene 27

The Golden Gates: "Crashing the Golden Gates"
D. Carroll
(*Music by* Jay Gorney. *Lyrics by* E. Y. Harburg.)

Scene 28

The All-Seeing Eye

Scene 29

A Radium Paradise
Entire Company

ACT 2

Scene 1

Tambourines (*by* Charles L. Sansone)
The Tambourine Girls
Introducing E. Healy. *On the Comb*: F. Joyce.

Scene 2

Not So Quickies
D. Britton

Scene 3

Surprised Party[18]
Diddy: D. Howard. *Daddy*: G. Givot. *Dody*: E. Crowell.

Scene 4

Cry Baby[19]
Baby: G. Worth. *Man*: W. Demarest.

Scene 5

Their First Ocean Trip
Papa: W. Mahoney. *Mama*: P. Kelly. *Willie*: E. Fratus.

Scene 6

Dance
Omar

Scene 7

For Napoleon and France
Josephine: D. Britton. *Ladies in Waiting (6)*: *First*: E. Wenzel. *Second*: F. Joyce. *Third*: E. Crowell. *Fourth*: C. Francis. *Fifth*: A. Faye. *Sixth*: W. Starr. *Chamberlin*: C Emmy. *Dr. Flore*: G. Givot. (*Demare*: W. Demarest.)

Scene 8

Out of the Sea: "Rhythm of the Waves"
D. Carroll, Phelps Twins
(*Music by* Vincent Rose. *Lyrics by* Charles Tobias, Harry Tobias.)

Scene 9

On the Surf Boards: "You Beautiful So and So"
(*Music by* Ted Snyder. *Lyrics by* Billy Rose.)

Scene 10

(Acrobatic) Dance
The Three Sailors

Scene 11

Party of the Second Part[20]
George: G. Givot. *Elsie*: D. Britton. *Dr. Proctor*: W. Demarest. *Jimmie*: W. Mahoney. *Assistant*: C. Worth.

Scene 12

The Glittering Tree: "Don't Hang Your Dreams on a Rainbow"
D. Howard
(*Music by* Arnold Johnson. *Lyrics by* Irving Kahal.)
The Rainbow Curtain
Red: E. Wenzel. *Orange*: F. Joyce. *Green*: A. Faye. *Lavender*: M. Carewe. *Yellow*: E. Crowell. *Blue*: C. Francis. *Goddess*: F. Bacon.

Scene 13

The Rainbow Curtain[21]
Red: E. Wenzel. *Orange*: F. Joyce. *Green*: A. Faye. *Lavender*: W. Starr. *Yellow*: E. Crowell. *Blue*: C. Francis.

Scene 14

At the End of the Rainbow
Introducing Grace DuFaye, America's Most Sensational Control Dancer

Scene 15

A Morning at Cranes
Wife: P. Kelly. *Husband*: W. Mahoney. *The Plumber*: W. Demarest. *The Police Officer*: B. Robson.

Scene 16

"Tip-Toe Tip-Tap"
Phelps Twins
(*Music by* Irving Actman. *Lyrics by* Jean Hubert.)
Toe Dancer: E. Healy. *Tap Dancer*: E. Fratus.

Scene 17

A Noble Experiment (*by* Eddie Cantor and Sidney Skolsky)
Mark Winchell: W. Mahoney. *Gus, a Bar Tender*: G. Givot. *Waiter*: Omar. *Business Man*: C. Emmy. *Show Girl*: F. Joyce. *Model*: W. Starr. *Cigarette Girl*: Mystery Girl. *Cowboy*: S. Cavanaugh. *Flapper*: G. Worth.

Scene 18

Thrown Out: Outside the Speakeasy
The Three Sailors

Scene 19

In Arizona: "Papa Likes a Hot Papoose"
G. Givot
(*Music by* Jay Gorney. *Lyrics by* E. Y. Harburg.)
(a) Pow-Wow:
Chief Big Bear: G. Givot. *First Chief*: C. Worth. *Second Chief*: Omar. *Third Chief*: B. Jason. *Fourth Chief*: B. Robson. *Fifth Chief*: H. Blue. *Sixth Chief*: S. Cavanaugh. *Seventh Chief*: C. Emmy. *Eighth Chief*: D. Howard. *Indian Runner*: W. Mahoney.
(b) Grounds for Divorce
Chief Big Bear: G. Givot. *Judge of Travelling Court*: C. Emmy. *Clerk of Traveling Court*: Omar. *His Squaw*: P. Kelly.

Scene 20

Into the Dusk[22]
Indian Maids: F. Bacon, E. Connor, N. Kincaid, F. Ward

[15]Dropped after opening.
[16]Dropped after opening.
[17]Replaced for subsequent national tour by:
"You Beautiful So and So"
G. Worth, W. Demarest
[18]Later retitled Caught in the Act.
[19]Dropped after opening.

[20]Later rewritten with different character names.
[21]Dropped after opening.
[22]Dropped for national tour.

Scene 21

    Willie and Lillie[23]

        Willie: W. Mahoney. *Lillie*: P. Kelly.

    "Lillie"[24]W. Mahoney

Scene 22

    Southern Plantation: "My Sunny South"[25]

        W. Mahoney

        (*Music and Lyrics by* Abner Silver.)

Scene 23

    Sketch Book Exchange

Scene 24

    The Stock Ticker: Clicking the Stock Ticker

        D. Britton, N. Decker, Phelps Twins, D. Carroll, Mystery Girl, F. Bacon

Scene 25

    Grand Finale

        (Entire Company)

SHOW GIRL

1929.27

A Musical Comedy in Two Acts, 14 Scenes. Book by William Anthony McGuire, based on the novel of the same name by J. P. McEvoy. Music by George Gershwin. Lyrics by Gus Kahn and Ira Gershwin. Book staged by William Anthony Maguire. Dances staged by Bobby Connelly. Ballets by Albertina Rasch. Scenes by Joseph Urban. Costumes designed by John W. Harkrider. Entire production under the personal supervision of Florenz Ziegfeld. Orchestra under the direction of William Daly. Produced by Florenz Ziegfeld. Opened 2 July 1929 at the Ziegfeld Theatre and closed 5 October 1929 after 111 performances.

CAST (in order of appearance): *In 'Magnolia'*: *Sombre Eyes*: JIMMIE DURANTE. *Colonel Witherby*: Calvin Thomas. *Aunt Jennie*: Althea Heinly. *Virginia Witherby*: BARBARA NEWBERRY. *Captain Robert Adams*: Matthew Smith. *Steve*: Blaien Cordner.

    Back Stage: *Frank*: Andy Jochim. *Sunshine*: BARBARA NEWBERRY. *Estelle*: Althea Heinly. *Roy Collins, Stage Manager*: Calvin Thomas. *Bessie*: Wanda Stevenson. *Peggy Ritz*: Noel Francis. *Gypsy, Carpenter*: LOU CLAYTON. *Deacon, Electrician*: EDDIE JACKSON. *Snozzle, Property Man*: JIMMIE DURANTE. *Alvarez Romano*: JOSEPH MACAULAY. *Raquel, His Partner*: DORIS CARSON. *Jimmy Doyle*: Frank McHugh. *Matt Brown, Stage-Door Man*: Howard Morgan. *Dixie Dugan*: RUBY KEELER (JOLSON). *Anna*: Caryl Bergman. *Denny Kerrigan*: EDDIE FOY, JR. *Bobby*: Kathryn Hereford. *Mr. Wright*: Andy Jochim. *Rudy*: NICK LUCAS. *John Milton*: Austin Fairman. *Sylvia*: Caryl Bergman. *Mrs. Dugan*: Sadie Duff. *Tony Morato*: EDDIE JACKSON. And DUKE ELLINGTON'S ORCHESTRA.

    Albertina Rasch Dancers: Mildred Turner, Vera Frederick, Virginia Whitmore, Lucille O'Connor, Agatha Johann, Virginia Allen, Ruth Hayden, Dorothy Morgan, Evelyn Nichols, Dona Dene Curry, Sunny Van, Ruth Love, Viola Hage, Eddie Belmont, Dorothy Ryan, Louise Raymond. *Show Girls*: Althea Heinly, Blanche Satchel, Gertrude Dahl, Mary MacDonald, Ada Landis, Edna Bunte, Betty Bassett, Mildred Swunke, Moreen Holmes, Dorothy Carrigan, Dolores De Fina, Doris Downes, Caja Eric, Georgia Payne, Camilla Lanier, Mildred Klaw, Leonia Pennington. *Dancers*: Pat Okeef, Virginia Frank, Cleo Cullen, Bobby Brodsley, Jean Althan, Selma Althan, Jane Barry, Peggy Carthew, Beatrice Powers, Dolores Grant, Pamela Bryant, Janet Gibbard, Dorothy Bow, Lois Peck, Vivian Porter, Florence Allen, Virginia Case, Katherine Downer, Juliette Jones, Doris May, Patricia McGrath, Orine Bryne, Rena Landeau, Claire Wayne, Jean Wayne, Alma Drange, Mildred Defina, Lottie Marcy, Dolores Ray, Hazel Bofinger, Kae English, Marcia Bell, Emily Burton, Billie Cortez, Wanda Stevenson, Violet Dell, Dore Nodine.

Act 1, Scene 1: Last Scene of Ziegfeld's production 'Magnolias,' Colonel Witherby's Estate, Virginia, 1863. *Scene 2*: Back stage, Ziegfeld Theatre. *Scene 3*: Western Union Desk, Stacy Trent Hotel, Trenton, New Jersey. *Scene 4*: Pent House Apartment of John Milton, New York. *Scene 5*: Foyer of the Pent House. *Scene 6*: 412 and 414 Flatbush Avenue, Brooklyn. *Scene 7*: Club Caprice, New York.

Act 2, Scene 1: Opening Night of the Ziegfeld Follies at The Ziegfeld Theatre. First Appearance of Dixie Dugan. *Scene 2*: An American in Paris. *Scene 3*: Stage Door of the Ziegfeld Theatre (shortly before the preceding scene ends). *Scene 4*: "The Minstrel Scene" from the Ziegfeld Follies. *Scene 5*: Dixie Dugan's Dressing Room (after the performance). *Scene 6*: On the Stage of the Ziegfeld Theatre. *Scene 7*: Stage Door of the Ziegfeld Theatre after the Show Finale.

---

[23]Dropped after opening.
[24]Dropped after opening.
[25]Dropped for national tour.

ACT 1

    Opening

    "Happy Birthday"

        Girls

    "My Sunday Fella"

        B. Newberry, Girls

    Albertina Rasch Dancers[26] (Specialty)

    "How Could I Forget?"[27] (Finaletto)

        Entire 'Magnolias' Company

    "Can Broadway Do Without Me?"J. Durante, L. Clayton, E. Jackson

        (*Music and Lyrics by* Jimmie Durante.)

    "Lolita, (My Love)"[28]

        J. Macaulay

    "Do What You Do"

        R. Keeler, F. McHugh

    "Spain"[29]J. Durante, L. Clayton, E. Jackson

    "One Man"

        B. Newberry, Girls

    "So Are You"

        E. Foy, Jr., K. Hereford, Girls

    "I Must Be Home By Twelve O'Clock"

        R. Keller, Girls

    Songs[30]:

        N. Lucas

    "Because They All Love You"

        (*Music by* J. Little. *Lyrics by* Thomas Malie.)

    "Who Will be With You When I Am Far Away?"

        (*Music and Lyrics by* W. H. Farrell.)

    "Black and White"

        Dancers

    African Daisies

        Albertina Rasch Girls

    "Jimmie, the Well-Dressed Man"

        J. Durante, L. Clayton, E. Jackson

        (*Music and Lyrics by* Jimmie Durante.)

    "Harlem Serenade"

        R. Keeler, Girls

ACT 2

    "(An) American in Paris" (Blues Ballet)

        H. Hoctor, Albertina Rasch Dancers

    "Home Blues"

        J. Macaulay

    "Broadway, My Street"

        J. Durante, L. Clayton, E. Jackson

        (*Music by* Jimmie Durante. *Lyrics by* Sidney Skolsky.)

    "(So) I Ups to Him"

        J. Durante

        (*Music and Lyrics by* Jimmie Durante.)

    "Follow the Minstrel Band"[31]

        E. Jackson, (Duke Ellington's) Band

    "Liza (All the Clouds'll Roll Away)"[32]

        N. Lucas, R. Keeler, Girls

    Finale

        Entire Company

---

[26]Dropped after the opening.
[27]Replaced by:
    "Mississippi Dry"
        Jubilee Singers, (Duke Ellington's Band)
        (*Music by* Vincent Youmans. *Lyrics by* J. Russel Robinson.)
[28]Dropped after the opening.
[29]Dropped after the opening.
[30]Dropped 3 weeks after the opening.
[31]Dropped after the opening.
[32]Al Jolson is widely credited with popularizing this song by singing it to his bride, Ruby Keeeler, from the audience on opening night. Nick Lucas departed the show after 3 weeks, and the song was reassigned to others in the cast.

1929.28

BROADWAY NIGHTS

A Musical Revue in Two Acts, 26 Scenes. Book (sketches) by Edgar Smith. Music by Sam Timberg, Lee David, Maury Rubens. Lyrics by Moe Jaffe. Book staged by Stanley Logan. Dances and ensembles staged by Busby Berkeley. Chester Hale dances by Chester Hale. Settings designed by Watson Barratt. Costumes designed by Barbier, Ernest Schrapps. Orchestra under the direction of John McManus. Produced by the Messrs. Shubert. Opened 15 July 1929 at the 44th Street Theatre and closed 17 August 1929 after 40 performances.

CAST: *Stage Manager*: Ray King. *Mr. Cain*: FRANK GABY. *Flo DeForrest*: LAURA LEE. *Boots McAllister*: RUTH GORMLEY. *Joe White*: JOE PHILLIPS. *Mr. Finkbinder*: Harry Welsh. *Duckey Stevens*: GEORGE DOBBS. *Marian Lavarre*: ODETTE MYRTIL. *Wilbur Scrump*: HARRY J. CONLEY. *Doris Williams*: Ethel Dunton. *The Author*: Eddie Shubert. *The Composer*: Hoyt Meredith. *Dr. Rockwell*: DR. ROCKWELL. *Three Baggage Men*: King, King and King. *Two Porters*: The Martin Brothers. *The Gambler*: Archie Foulk. *The Girl Friend*: LILLIAN LANE. *Singer*: MARGARET MERLE. *Singer*: HARRY STOCKWELL. *The Book Seller*: Ray King. *Mrs. Wentworth*: Mary Manson. *The Sultan's Dancers*: Dolores, Eddy and Douglas. *Kay*: Kay Simmons. *Leonie*: Sheila Barrett. *Elvira Snodgrass*: Madeline Meredith.

Chester Hale Girls: Bonnibal Beard, Esther Whetton, Gertrude Mazza, Gertrude Kornblum, Hilda Peterson, Inez Goetz, Jeanne Walton, Julie Tiedgens, Karen Kaaber, Lillian Messner, Marian Paitson, Mary Wynn, Phyllis Jordan, Ruth Gormly, Sylvia Greene, Violet Lundberg, Verta Kunkel. *The Alan K. Foster London Palladium Girls*: Alice Rogers, Doris Beridge, Dolly Waring, Edna Cowley, Emily Cowley, Hilda Long, Frances Duran, Hazel Frazer, Hetty Hayes, Iris Worthington, Larry Hodgson, Marie Day, Margie Harlan, May Squires, Moya Beridge, Olive Crane, Winnie Channon, Vena Hollingworth. *Show Girls*: Florence Davidson, Mary Ferguson, Grace Grey, Vivian Hunter, Greta Kuhnrich, Eva Lewis, Lillian Lane, Gloria Lebow, Betty Montgomery, Ray Powell, Margaret Samson, Loris Taylor, Dorothy Darley, Ann Davis, Flo Sterling, Edwina Skorat, Peggy Davis. *Boys*: George E. Burke, Bob Derdin, Louis S. Delgado, Harry Griffin, Harry Hylander, Tom Jordan, Jay Tully, Clinton McLeer, Julio Martell, Alfred Parrot, Kenneth Pulsifer, Murray Swanson.

ACT 1

Scene 1

Opening Chorus
H. Stockwell, Ensemble
"Why Don't We?"
L. Lee, J. Phillips
(*Music by* Maury Rubens and Sammy Timberg.)
Scene: The Stage of the Greenburg Opera House.

Scene 2

The Alan K. Foster Girls

Scene 3

"Stranded in a One-Horse Town
J. Phillips, L. Lee
"Hotsy Totsy Hats"
G. Dobbs, R. Gormly, E. Dunton, Ensemble
Scene: The Hotel Lobby, Greenburg.

Scene 4

Dr. Rockwell

Scene 5

Dance
King, King and King
"The Right Man"
H. Conley, O. Myrtil
(*Music by* Maury Rubens and Sammy Timberg.)
"White Lights Were Coming"
G. Dobbs, R. Gormly, J. Phillips, L. Lee, Ensemble
Scene: Railroad Station of Greenburg.

Scene 6

Train Effect

Scene 7

The Author: E. Shubert. *The Composer*: H. Meredith. *Mr. Cain*: F. Gaby. *Dr. Rockwell*: Dr. Rockwell.
Scene: Mr. Cain's Office.

Scene 8

"Mile's End Road"
Alan K. Foster's Palladium Girls

Scene 9

Seven Bucks
J. Phillips, A. Foulk, L. Lane, V. Hunter

Scene 10

"Johann Strauss, Who Made the World Dance" (The Strauss Fantasy)
O. Myrtl, M. Merle, J. Coles, Hale Girls, Models

Scene 11

Just Twenty-One
H. J. Conley
Scene A: The Bookshop. *Scene B*: The Boudoir.

Scene 12

"Heart of a Rose" (from GAY PAREE, 1926)
M. Merle, Ensemble
(*Music by* J. Fred Coots and Maury Rubens. *Lyrics by* Clifford Grey.)
Dance
J. Coles

Scene 13

Dr. Rockwell

Scene 14

Outside the Sultan's Tent in Persia.

Scene 15

"Arabian Nights"
H. Stockwell, M. Merle, Slave Girls, Attendants, Sultan's Dancers
Scene: Inside the Tent.

ACT 2

Scene 1

Toe Dance
Hale Girls
"I Kiss Your Hand, Madame"[33]
O. Myrtil
(*Music by* Ralph Erwin. *Lyrics by* Sam M. Lewis and Joe Young.)
"Lobster Crawl"
L. Lee, Chester Hale Troupe, Alan K. Foster Girls
Chain Dance
King, King and King
Scene: The Golden Slipper Restaurant.

Scene 2

Lobby of a New York Theatre, after the First Act

Scene 3

"Bracelet Number"
L. Lee
Dance J. Coles

Scene 4

Car Knocker
H. Conley, A. Foulk, Others

Scene 5

"Baby's Doll" (Baby Doll Dance) M. Meredith, G. Dobbs, Hale Girls
(*Music by* Maury Rubens and Phil Svigals. *Lyrics by* J. Keirn Brennan and Moe Jaffe.)

Scene 6

King, King and King

Scene 7

"The Orchid"
O. Myrtil, G. Dobbs, E. Shubert, M. Meredith, Ensemble

Scene 8

The Bullet
H. J. Conley

Scene 9

"Come Hit Your Baby"
L. Lee, R. Gormly, M. Meredith, E. Dunton, B. Montgomery, Ensemble

Scene 10

An Artists's Handicap
Dr. Rockwell, O. Myrtil
Artist: E. Shubert. *Butler*: H. Meredith.

Scene 11

"Broadway Nights from the Roof Garden"
L. Lee, Entire Company

---

[33]An interpolation, previously used in LADY FINGERS.

MURRAY ANDERSON'S ALMANAC (1880–1930)

1929.29

A Revusical Comedy of Yesterday—Today—Tomorrow (Musical Revue) in Two Acts, an Opening and 29 Pages (scenes). Comedy (sketches) by Rube Goldberg, Noël Coward, Ronald Jeans, Paul Gerard Smith, Harry Ruskin, John McGowan, Peter Arno and Wynn, (Trixie Friganza). Music by Milton Ager and Henry Sullivan. Lyrics by Jack Yellen, (Edward Eliscu, Clifford Orr, Harry Ruskin, John Murray Anderson, Neville Fleeson, Henry Myers). Entire production staged by John Murray Anderson. Dances staged by William Holbrook. Comedy scenes staged by Harry Ruskin. Scenic illustrations by Clark Robinson, (Peter Arno, Reginald Marsh, Rube Goldberg, Wynn and Ted Weidhaas). Costume illustrations by Charles LeMaire, Robert E. Locher, Peter Arno, Wynn, Jacques Darcy, (Louis M. Pinkey). Combined orchestras of Red Nichols and His Five Pennies and the Maurice DePackh Ensemble under the direction of Gene Salzer. Produced by The Almanack Theatrical Corporation (John Murray Anderson, Gil Boag, directors). Opened 14 August 1929 at Erlanger's Theatre and closed 12 October 1929 after 69 performances.

CAST: JIMMIE SAVO, TRIXIE FRIGANZA, ROY ATWELL, ELEANOR SHALER, WALLY COYLE, HENRIETTA, RITA GLYNDE, HELEN THOMPSON, FRANCES MANN, FREDERICK CARPENTER, HELEN ROYAL, CHARLES ROYAL, BILLIE GERBER, FRANC LASSITER, WARREN LASSITER, ELEANOR TERRY, GEORGE CHRISTIE, CHARLES BARNES, MATT DUFFIN, JESSIE DRAPER, WILLIAM M. GRIFFITH, JACK POWELL, CHARLOTTE AYRES, JEAN MYRIO, HARVEY KARELS, WILLIAM RASCHE, ANITA, ROY RICE, MARY WERNER, JERRY COE, JOHN MAXWELL, FRED KEATING, STELLA POWER, RED NICHOLS AND HIS FIVE PENNIES.

Ladies of the Ensemble: Norma Maxine, Dolores Lavin, Dorothy Koster, Evan Southwell, Helen Brownell, Naida, Josephine Karroll, Mary Pearson, Elizabeth Janeway, Helen Koster, Barbara Bright, Paula Sands, Helen Fried, Jean Castleton, Patricia Parsons, Svea Tingdale, Ethel Sager, Claire Stenz, Doris Jay, Carol Renwick, Ethel Kriston, Helene Franz, Jean Egan, Nondas North, Ruth Spevack, Elinor Millard, Lola DeLille, Delmar Meyer. *Gentlemen of the Ensemble*: H. Donald Knobloch, Dowell Brown, M. McNear, Hermes Pan, Reeder Boss, Edward J. Denny, Jack Wilhelm, T. R. Pahl, Jack Bauer, Paul Foltz.

ACT 1
Opening
"The Almanac Covers"
(*Music by* Henry Sullivan. *Lyrics by* Edward Eliscu.)
Introduced by N. Maxine, D. Lavin, D. Koster, E. Southwell, H. Brownell, Naida, J. Karroll, M. Pearson, E. Janeway, H. Koster.
a. The Eighteenth Century Cover
Singer: S. Power.
b. The Nineteenth Century Cover
Singer: E. Shaler.
c. The Twentieth Century Cover
Singers: W. Coyle, Henrietta.
Murray Anderson's Almanac
Introduced by F. Keating
Scene 1 (Page One)
"The Polka Dot"
R. Glynde
(*Music by* Henry Sullivan. *Lyrics by* Clifford Orr.)
And B. Bright, P. Sands, H. Fried, J. Castleton, P. Parsons, S. Tingdale, E. Sager, C. Stenz, D. Jay, C. Renwick, E. Kriston, H. Franz, J. Egan, N. North, R. Spevack, E. Millard, J. Maxwell.
Scene 2 (Page Two)
Lost Souls (*by* Ronald Jeans)
The Author: G. Christie. *Marigold*: E. Terry. *The Maid*: E. Shaler. *M. Chateau la Fite*: W. Griffith. *The Husband*: R. Atwell.
Scene 3 (Page Three)
"Tinkle-Tinkle" (An Episode in White and Porcelain)
H. Thompson
(*Music by* Milton Ager. *Lyrics by* Jack Yellen. *Ballet arranged by* Rita Glynde.)
The Girl: F. Mann. *The Boy*: F. Carpenter. *The Busybody*: Anita. *The Two Figures Under Glass*: H. Royal, C. Royal.
Scene 4 (Page Four)
"In the Village by the Sea"
J. Savo
(*Background by* Reginald Marsh.)
Scene 5 (Page Five)
"I Can't Remember the Words"
B. Gerber
(*Music by* Milton Ager. *Lyrics by* Jack Yellen.)

With the Helen Morgan Girls: H. Franz, B. Bright, C. Stenz, D. Jay, E. Millard, H. Fried, N. North, J. Egan, P. Sands, C. Renwick. *The Pianists*: Gentlemen of the Ensemble. And Henrietta.
Scene 6 (Page Six)
Gossip
T. Friganza
Scene 7 (Page Seven)
"Schrafft's University"
F. Lassiter, W. Lassiter.
(*Music by* Henry Sullivan. *Lyrics by* Edward Eliscu. *Settings and Costumes designed by* Wynn.)
And *Schrafft's Collegiates*: Gentlemen of the Ensemble.
Scene 8 (Page Eight)
The Age in Which We Live (*by* John McGowan)
He: R. Atwell. *Her*: E. Terry. *Him*: G. Christie.
Scene 9 (Page Nine)
"The Song of the Nightingale"
S. Power
(*Music by* Milton Ager. *Lyrics by* Jack Yellen.)
Celeste Soloist: Henrietta.
Scene 10 (Page Ten)
Tabloids (*by* William Griffith)
The Editor: T. Friganza. *The Reporter*: R. Glynde. *Second Reporter*: F. Mann. *Third Reporter*: B. Gerber. *Fouth Reporter*: M. Werner.
Scene 11 (Page Eleven)
"Golden Rod" (Traditional)
E. Shaler
The Voice in the Box: R.Boss. *The Amazons*: L. DeLille, N. Maxine, D. Lavin, D. Koster, E. Southwell, H. Brownell, Naida, J. Karroll, M. Pearson, E. Janeway, H. Koster, D. Meyer.
Scene 12 (Page Twelve)
"I May May Be Wrong (But I Think You're Wonderful)"
T. Friganza, J. Savo
(*Music by* Henry Sullivan. *Lyrics by* Harry Ruskin.)
Scene 13 (Page Thirteen)
"(Wait for) The Happy Ending"
The Boy: C. Barnes. *The Girl*: H. Thompson. (*Setting designed by* Rube Goldberg.)
Scene 14 (Page Fourteen)
The Big Eye-Dea 'Knock Wood' (*by* Harry Ruskin)
The Father: R. Atwell. *The Prospective Son-in-Law*: J. Savo.
Scene 15 (Page Fifteen)
Matt Duffin and Jessie Draper
(*Music by* Henry Sullivan. *Costumes designed by* Wynn)
Scene 16 (Page Sixteen)
Homework (*by* Paul Gerard Smith)
Mrs. Albeit: E. Shaler. *Hariette*: T. Friganza. *Robert*: R. Atwell. *Humphrey*: W. Griffith. *William*: W. Lassiter.
Scene 17 (Page Seventeen)
"Jazz in a Kitchenette"[34]
(J. Powell)
(*Music by* Jack Powell.)
Scene 18 (Page Eighteen)
Metropolis (*Music by* Henry Sullivan.)
The Rivet: Charlotte. *First Riveter*: J. Myrio. *Second Riveter*: H. Karels. *Third Riveter*: W. Rasche.
Scene 19 (Page Nineteen)
"The New Yorker" (The New Yorkers)
(*Music by* Milton Ager. *Lyrics by* Jack Yellen. *Sky Scraper Screens invented by* Wynn.)
Introduced by W. Coyle. *The High Hat Aristocrat*: B. Gerber. *Patrons of Automats*: D. Brown, J. Bauer, M. McNear, H. D. Knobloch, T. R. Pahl, H. Pan, R. Boss, E. J. Denny, J. Wilhelm, P. Foltz. *Greenwich Elite*: N. Maxine, D. Lavin, D. Koster, E. Southwell, H. Brownell, Naida, J. Karroll, M. Pearson, E. Janeway, H. Koster. *Delancey Street*: M. Duffin, J. Draper. *Harlem Browns*: Henrietta, P. Sands, J. Egan, B. Bright, H. Fried, C. Stenz, H. Franz, E. Millard, D. Jay. *Buyers from Western Towns*: F. Lassiter, W. Lassiter. *College Grads*: C. Barnes, F. Carpenter. *The Bosses' Daughters*: F. Mann, H. Thompson. *Stenogs*: Anita, J. Castleton, E. Kriston, R. Spevack,

---

[34]Virtuoso drum and percussion specialty

N. North, S. Tingdale, E. Sager, C. Renwick, P. Parsons. *The Bootlegger*: J. Savo. *The New Yorker*: T. Friganza.

ACT 2

Entr'acte Divertissement
Red Nichols and His Five Pennies, M. DePackh Ensemble

Scene 1 (Page 1)

"Same Old Moon"
H. Thompson, C. Barnes, B. Gerber
(*Music by* Henry Sullivan. *Lyrics by* John Murray Anderson and Clifford Orr.)

Scene 2 (Page Two)

On the Scaffold
Sam: R. Rice. *Magnolia*: M. Werner.

Scene 3 (Page Three)

"Educate Your Feet"
W. Coyle, Henrietta
(*Music by* Milton Ager. *Lyrics by* Jack Yellen. *Costumes and Setting designed by* Wynn.)
Dance by J. Coe.

Scene 4 (Page Four)

Whoops (*by* Noël Coward)
Grace Hubbard: R. Atwell. *Violet Banks*: W. Griffith. *Charlie French*: F. Lassiter. *Stephen Harris*: G. Christie.
(*Setting and Costumes designed by* Peter Arno.)

Scene 5 (Page Five)

"Getting into the Talkies"
T. Friganza
(*Music and Lyrics by* Neville Fleeson. *Curtain designed by* Wynn.)

Scene 6 (Page Six)

The Young King (Pantomime)
(*Adapted from the story of* Oscar Wilde *by* John Murray Anderson. *Music by* Henry Sullivan. *Masks designed by* W. T. Benda.)
The Story Teller: G. Christie. *The Young King*: F. Carpenter. *His Pages*: E. Sager, R. Spevack. *A Weaver*: R. Glynde. *The Galley Master*: W. Rasche. *The Shark Charmer*: W. Lassiter. *The Pearl Diver*: M. Duffin. *Death*: D. Meyer. *Avarice*: Naida. *Fever*: J. Karroll. *Plague*: M. Pearson. *A Pilgrim*: P. Foltz. *Ruby Miners*: J. Myrio, H. Karels, F. Lassiter, C. Barnes. *Noblewomen*: L. de Lille, E. Southwell, N. Maxine, D. Lavin, E. Janeway, H. Brownell, D. Koster, H. Koster. *Noblemen*: J. Bauer, N. McNear, H. Pan, R. Boss. *The Chamberlain*: H. D. Knobloch. *The Counsellor*: D. Brown. *Soldiers*: T. R. Pahl, J. Wilhelm. *The Bishop*: E. J. Denny. *A Saint*: E. Kriston. *The Madonna*: S. Power.

Scene 7 (Page Seven)

"Tiller, Foster, Hoffman, Hale and Albertina Rasch"
(*Music by* Henry Sullivan. *Lyrics by* Henry Myers.)
The Tiller Girl: Henrietta. *The Alan K. Foster Girl*: F. Mann. *The Gertrude Hoffman Girl*: N. Maxine. *The Chester Hale Girl*: R. Glynde. *The Albertina Rasch Girl*: Anita.

Scene 8 (Page Eight)

Mother (with apologies to Whistler)
The Mother: T. Friganza. *The Son*: F. Lassiter.

Scene 9 (Page Nine)

Jimmie Savo

Scene 10 (Last Page of the Alamanc)

"Builders of Dreams"
(*Music by* Henry Sullivan. *Lyrics by* John Murray Anderson.)
Harlequin: C. Barnes. *Columbine*: H. Thompson.

The Waltz
F. Mann, F. Carpenter

Reprise
Entire Company

1929.30   A NOBLE ROGUE

An Musical Melodrama in Two Acts. Book, music and lyrics by Kenyon Scott. Book staged by Paul Gilmore. Dances and ensembles by Adrian S. Perrin and J. R. O'Neil. Settings by Joseph Allen Physioc. Orchestra under the direction of Jack Press. Entire production under the supervision of Adrian S. Perrin. Produced by Adrian S. Perrin. Opened 19 August 1929 at the Gansevoort Theatre and closed 26 August 1929 after 9 performances.

CAST (in order of appearance): *Jules Le Blanc*; R. A. Rose. *Celeste Beauregard*: Cecil Carol. *Colonel Mulford*: Frank Howson. *Señorita Velasquez*: Melba Marcelle. *Grambo*:

Esteban Cerdan. *Madame Le Blanc*: Nanette Flack. *Major Villere*: Robert Hobbs. *Captain Lockyer*: Gordon Richards. *Virginia Mulford*: MARGUERITE ZENDER. *Evalina*: Helen Heed. *Jean Lafitte*: ROBERT RHODES. *Captain Dominique You*: Wiliam Balfour. *Captain O'Shaughnessy*: Alfred Heather. *Alphonse*: Jimmie Carr. *François*: Andre Borice. *Rina*: Marie La Verni. *Louise*: Irma Friend. *Señor Antonio*: Barry Devine. *Rancher*: Lionel Sainer. *Guests, Entertainers, Members of Jean Lafitte's Crew, 'Cajans, Flower Girls, Fisher Maidens*.

Members of the Ensemble: Claudia Tyce, Julie La Chane, Evelyn Hamilton, Kay Harkins, Betty Howson, Irma Friend, Florence Fields, Viola Pye, Elsie Melvin, Beulah Yorkin, Madeline Levey, Hortense Hector, Lucy Barbaro, Margaret Collins, Harry Shapiro, Billy Nation, Jack Greenburg, John Arcelo, Jay Altman, Carmelo Amora, Fred Armerson, Billy Gallagher, Emmett Anderson.

The action takes place during the War of 1812.

Act 1: Patio of the Café Mespero, New Orleans, near Jackson Square, French Quarter, New Orleans. September 1814.

Act 2: The Camp of Jean Lafitte and His Followers at the Island of Grand Terre, Baratarian Bay, Louisiana. A month later.

1929.31   SWEET ADELINE

A Musical Romance of the Gay Nineties in Two Acts, 15 Scenes. Book and lyrics by Oscar Hammerstein II. Music by Jerome Kern. Book staged by Reginald Hammerstein. Dances and ensembles staged by Danny Dare. Costumes by Charles LeMaire. Sets by Frank E. Gates and E. A. Morange. Orchestrations by Robert Russell Bennett. Orchestra under the direction of Gus Salzer. Produced by Arthur Hammerstein. Opened 3 September 1929 at Hammerstein's Theatre and closed 22 March 1930 after 234 performances.

CAST (in order of appearance): *Sergeant Malone*: Thomas Chadwick. *August*, a Student: George Raymond. *Lena*: Pauline Gorim. *Dot*, a Piccolo Player: VIOLET CARSON. *Emil Schmidt*: ROBERT C. FISCHER. *Addie*, His Older Daughter: HELEN MORGAN. *Nellie*, His Younger Daughter: CARYL BERGMAN. *Lulu Ward*, an Actress: IRENE FRANKLIN. *Dan Ward*, a Theatrical Advance Agent: ROBERT EMMETT KEANE. *Tom Martin*, First Mate, S.S. St. Paul: MAX HOFFMAN, JR. *Ruppert Day*: CHARLES BUTTERWORTH. *Doctor*: Jack Gray. *Orderly*: Tom Thompson. *Colonel*: Martin Shepard. *James Day*: ROBERT CHISHOLM. *Gus*: Gus. *Will*: Will. *Sam Herzig*, a Theatrical Manager: LEN MENCE. *Eddie*, Man of All-Work around theatre: Wally Crisham. *Sid Barnett*, a Composer and Orchestra Leader: JOHN D.SEYMOUR. *The Sultan*: THOMAS CHADWICK. *The Jester*: George Djimos. *Maizie O'Rourke*: Helen Ault. *Head Carpenter*: William Sheppard. *Props*: Joe Reilly. *Gus*, First Violin: Gus Salzer. *George*: Borra Levinson. *Young Blood*: Jackson Fairchild. *Gabe Case*, Proprietor, McGowan's Pass Tavern: Ben Wells. *A Cabby*: Tom Rider. *Old Sport*: Harry Esmond. *Doc*: George Magis. *Jim Thornton*: JIM THORNTON. *Mr. Gilhooley*: JERRY JARNAGIN. *Hester Van Doren Day*: SALLY BATES. *Willie Day*: Peter Bender.

George Smith's All Girl Band: Frances Flanigan, Polly Fisher, Josephine Rice, Mabel Thilbault, Gertrude Clave, Laura Mutch. *Girls of the Gay Nineties*: Helen Ault, Louise Bernhardt, Harriet Britton, Mary Carney, Dorothy Brown, Lillian Burke, Kaye Carroll, Louise Chowning, Nora Clifft, Aida Conkey, Myrtle Cox, Betty Croke, Nonie Dale, Fanilla Davies, Christine Gallagher, La Vergne Evans, Helene Gardner, Mildred Getkins, Pauline Gorin, Evelyn Hannons, Muriel Harrison, Dorothy Hiller, Cyrilla Juitt, Helen Kelly, Grace LaRue, Evelyn Laurie, Madge MacAnally, Helen McDonald, Marion Martin, Peggy Messinger, Gladys Nelson, Ruby Nevins, Ruth Penery, Robertina Robertson, Madgio Schmylee, Bertha Mae Swan, Elenore Tierney, Emily Van Hoven, Genevieve Van Hoven, Marion Young, Lorena Walcott, Gloria LeBow, Baum Sturtz. *Gentlemen of the Ensemble*: John Campbell, Don Carter, Joseph Davidenko, Frank Dobert, Lynn Eldridge, Jackson Fairchild, Andy Lieb, George Magis, Paul Moran, George Raymond, Tom Rider, Len Sasion, Martin Shepard, Bob Shutta, Alexis Sokoloff, Morris Tepper, Tom Tompson, Efim Vitis, Robert Vernon.

Act 1, Scene 1: Schmidt's Beer Garden, Hoboken, New Jersey, 1898. *Scene 2*: A Hospital Tent near San Juan Hill, Cuba. Two months later. *Scene 3*: Kitchen Entrance to the Schmidt Home. One month later. *Scene 4*: Under the Stage of the Olympia Burlesque Theatre, the Bowery. Same night. *Scene 5*: Stage and Auditorium. Immediately following.

Act 2, Scene 1: Corridor in front of the Parterre Boxes, a Broadway Theatre. Eighteen months later. *Scene 2*: McGowan's Pass Tavern. Next morning. *Scene 3*: Summer. (a) A Horse Car going down Avenue A. (b) A Hansom going up Broadway, at the same time. *Scene 4*: Hoffman House Bar. A week later. *Scene 5*: Jim's Sloop. The following Sunday evening. *Scene 6*: Madison Square Garden. Next night. *Scene 7*: The Stage of Madison Square Garden Roof. Lulu does her act. *Scene 8*: On Fort George Hill. One month later. *Scene 9*: Alongside the *City of Paris*., an hour later *Scene 10*: A Broadway Theatre. Next month.

"Fin de Siècle" (Based by Jerome Kern on melodies of the period)

ACT 1

Scene 1

"Let Us Play a Polka Dot" (Song and Dance)
V. Carson, Boys, Girls

"'Twas No So Long Ago" (Folk Song)
H. Morgan, Ensemble

"My Husband's First Wife" (Song)
I. Franklin
(*Lyrics by* Irene Franklin.)

Scene 3

"Here Am I" (Air and Scene)
H. Morgan, V. Carson

"First Mate Martin" (Entrance and Chorus)
M. Hoffman, Jr., C. Butterworth, Ensemble

"Spring Is Here" (Buffo Duo)
V. Carson, C. Butterworth, Girls

Scene 4

"Out of the Blue" (March Ballad)
R. Chisholm, M. Hoffman, Jr., Boys

"Out of the Blue" (Reprise)
V. Carson, C. Begman, Girls

"Out of the Blue" (Drill)
Gus, Will

"Naughty Boy" (Song)
I. Franklin, C. Butterworth, Girls

Scene 5

Rehearsal:
"Oriental Moon"T. Chadwick, G. Djimos, Ensemble
"Mollie O'Donahue"H. Ault, Girls

"Why Was I Born?" (Air)
H. Morgan

Finale
Ensemble

ACT 2

Scene 1

"'Twas Not So Long Ago" (Scene, Music and Reprise)
R. Fischer

Scene 2

"Winter in Central Park" (Scene, Music and Ensemble)
Ensemble

"The Sun About to Rise" (Waltz Ballad)
J. D. Seymour, H. Morgan

Scene 4

"Some Girl Is on Your Mind" (Song and Chorus)
R. Chisholm, M. Hoffman, Jr., J. D. Seymour, J. Thornton, Male Ensemble

Scene 5

"Don't Ever Leave Me" (Duet)
H. Morgan, R. Chisholm

"Here Am I" (Reprise)
V. Carson

FinalettoH. Morgan

Scene 7

"Indestructible Kate" (Miss Lulu Ward's Specialty)
I. Franklin
(*Music by* Jerry Jarnagin. *Lyrics by* Irene Franklin.)

Scene 8

"Take Me for a Honeymoon Ride" (Duettino and Dance)
V. Carson, C. Butterworth, Gus, Will, Bicycle Girls

Harbor Scena

Scene 9

Scene
H. Morgan, J. D. Seymour, R. Chisholm

Scene 10

"'Twas Not So Long Ago" (Reprise)
Chorus

Finale
Ensemble

1929.32   THE STREET SINGER

A Musical Comedy of Americans Abroad, in Two Acts, 4 Scenes. Book by Cyrus Wood and Edgar Smith. Music by Nicholas Kempner, Sam Timberg,

Richard Meyers. Lyrics by Graham John and Edward Eliscu. Entire production staged and directed by Busby Berkeley. Settings by Watson Barratt. Costumes by Orry Kelley and Barbier. Orchestra under the direction of Pierre de Reeder. Produced by Busby Berkeley. Opened 17 September 1929 at the Sam S. Shubert Theatre, moved 17 February 1930 to the Royale Theatre, and closed 7 March 1930 after 191 performances.

CAST (in order of appearance): *Mabel Brown*: Jane Alden. *Ronnie*: Nick Long, Jr. *Claire*: Ruth Shields. *Manager of the Cafe Royal*: Philip Reep. *Colonel Brown*: Edward Garvie. *Muriel*: Peggy Cornell. *Waiter*: Jack Kelley. *Annette*: Nell Kelly. *Louis*: Harry K. Morton. *Picot*: ANDREW TOMBES. *Doorman*: Walter Johnson. *First Tourist*: Don Cortez. *Second Tourist*: Frank Gagen. *A Lady*: Kay Ross. *John*: Cesar Romero. *Suzette*: QUEENIE SMITH. *George*: GUY ROBERTSON. *Prefect of Police*: Frank Lalor. *First Agent of Police*: Bentley Stone. *Second Agent of Police*: Larry Hogan. *The Baron*: Jimmy Lyman. *Erminie, Wife of the Prefect of Police*: Audrey Maple. *Jean Baptiste*: Philip Reep. *Manager of the Folies Bergère*: Walter Johnson. *Theatre Attendant*: Walter Johnson. *Louise, Picot's Secretary*: Marian Palmer.

Dancing Girls: Edith Blaire, Virla Burley, Ruth Cunliff, Maxine Darrell, Rita Hogan, Catherine Huth, Elsie Lauristen, Barbara Lee, Jane Love, Isabelle McLaughlin, Hazel Maguire, Mildred Morgan, Betty O'Day, Dorothy Snowden, Jean Swanson, Peggy Tebbs, Jean Watson. *Show Girls*: Anne Austin, May Meeris, Helen Hall, Dorothy Joy, Agnes Kielty, Dora Lee, Kathryn Ross, Grace Stogner, Wynn Terry, Marjorie Younger, Mary Ferber, Shirley Parshall. *Boys*: Don Cortez, Clark Eggleston, Frank Gagen, Larry Hogan, George Saylor, Arthur Shnitzer, Bentley Stone, Milton Brodus.

Act 1: Foyer of the Café Royal in Paris.

Act 2, Scene 1: Reception Room in George's Summer Place, three months later. *Scene 2*: Foyer of the Folies Bergère in Paris. *Scene 3*: Green Room of the Folies Bergère.

ACT 1[35]

OpeningJ. Alden, N. Long, Jr., Ensemble

"You Never Can Tell"
J. Alden, N. Lucas, Jr., P. Cornell, Ensemble

"I Am"
N. Kelly, H. K. Morton

"When Everything Is Hunky-Dory
Q. Smith, G. Robertson

"The Girl That I'll Adore"
G. Robertson, Ensemble

"You've Made Me Happy Today"
Q. Smith, G. Robertson

"Somebody Quite Like You"[36]
P. Cornell, N. Long, Jr., Ensemble

Finale
Entire Company

ACT 2

Opening
R. Shields, Ensemble

"Statues"
N. Kelly, H. K. Morton, Girls

"Oh Theobald, Oh Elmer"
A. Tombes, F. Lalor

"From Now On"
Q. Smith, G. Robertson
(*Music by* Richard Meyers. *Lyrics by* Edward Eliscu.)

"Knocking on Wood"[37]
N. Long, Jr., Ensemble

---

[35]The production was revised during the run and also for subsequent national tour.

[36]Replaced during the run by:
"My Little Piano Man"
P. Cornell, N. Long, Jr., Ensemble
For subsequent tour, this was replaced by:
"I May Be Wrong" (from MURRAY ANDERSON'S ALMANAC OF 1929)
Mildred Green (Muriel), N. Long, Jr., Ensemble
(*Music by* Henry Sullivan. *Lyrics by* Harry Ruskin.)

[37]Replaced during the run by:
"Jumping Jimminy"
N. Long, Jr., Ensemble
For subsequent tour, this was preceded by:
"So Beats My Heart For You"
Q. Smith, Archie Leach (George), Ensemble
(*Music and Lyrics by* Pat Ballard, Charles Henderson, Tom Waring.)

Finaletto
Entire Company
Reprise
N. Kelly, H. K. Morton
Ballet
Q. Smith, Ensemble
Finale
Entire Company

1929.33 CAPE COD FOLLIES

A Musical Revue in Two Acts, 28 Scenes. Book (sketches) and lyrics by Stewart Baird. Music by Alexander Fogarty, (Kenneth Burton. Additional lyrics by Walter Craig). Arranged and staged by Stewart Baird. Dances arranged by John Lonergan. Orchestrations by Hans Spialek. Orchestra under the direction of Martin Fried. Produced by the Cape Playhouse, (Messrs. Shubert). Opened 18 September 1929 at the Bijou Theatre, moved to the Casino Theatre 30 September 1929, and closed 12 October 1929 after 29 performances.

CAST: L'Estrange Millman, Ellen Love, Corbet Morris, Dorothy Llewellyn, David London, Doris Glaenzer, Marion Glaenzer, Peter Joray, Cecil Clovelly, Vera Hurst, William Watson, Betty Barr, Bobby Fulton, Mary Rose Walsh, Peggy Ellis, Kenneth Burton, Norma Mason, Justine De Paul, Lloyd Nolan, Carmen Larranaga, Eliot Leonard, (Joe. Byrd, Jr.).

The Six Cape Cod Belles: Luonora Davis, Mildred Babcock, Grace Nealy, Lucia Bennett, Ray Riley, Kathryn Hayman. The King's Highway Four: Douglas Beddingfield, Dean Goodsell, George Ford, Thornton Boatwright. The Cape Cod Twins: Dorothy and Elvira Jones.

ACT 1[38]

Those Who Draw the Curtains
E. Jones, D. Jones
Scene 1
"Cape Cod Chanty"
Scene: Craigville Beach a Hundred Years Ago.
The Old Salt: L. Millman. The Singing Fisherman: D. London. And the King's Highway Four.
Scene 2
"In the Swim"
Scene: Craigville Beach Fifty Years Ago.
The Jolly Bather: E. Love, Cape Cod Belles.
Scene 3
"Out of the Swim"
Scene: Craigville Beach Now.
The Jazzy Bather: D. Llewellyn, Cape Cod Belles, King's Highway Four.
Scene 4
Goin' O'Neill
C. Morris, D. Glaenzer, L. Millman
Scene 5
"Clutching at Shadows"
D. London, D. Llewellyn
The Dancing Shadow: K. Hayman.
Scene 6
Ambitious Ella
E. Love
Scene 7
The Provincetown Art Association
C. Morris, C. Clovelly, Nutty Art Students
Scene 8
"That's Why We Misbehave" (Stepping on the Cape)
D. Llewellyn, Cape Cod Belles
Scene 9
Dramatic Moments in the Life of a Big City
V. Hurst, D. Glaenzer, B. Barr, D. Llewellyn, L. Millman, C. Morris, W. Watson

Scene 10
"That Old Hooked Rug"[39]
M. R. Walsh, Cape Cod Ladies' Quartette
Scene 11
Puppet Land
B. Fulton
Assisted by B. Barr, D. Jones, E. Jones, Saki
Scene 12
"Tales on Ivories"
P. Ellis
The Antique Collector: B. Barr. The Boy and Girl That Drop In: D. Beddingfield, D. Llewellyn.
Scene 13
The Ladies Aid Society Dips into French History
a. The Natives K. Burton, E. Jones
b. Versailles of Long Ago V. Hurst, D. London, (J. Byrd)
c. Pas de Deux G. Nealy, D. Goodsell
d. Story on My Fan M. R. Walsh
e. Any Old Revolution C. Morris, D. Llewellyn, Cape Cod Belles
Scene 14
Finaletto
Entire Company
ACT 2
Scene 1
"The Lure of the Cape"
V. Hurst
Scene 2
"Mary, Mary, Quite Contrary"
D. Llewellyn, King's Highway Four
Scene: In a Cape Cod Garden.
Scene 3
"Oh, Those Puritans!" (Dance)
B. Barr
Scene 4
"Cranberry Pickin'"
K. Burton
The Farmer Boy: T. Boatwright. The Cranberries: Cape Cod Belles.
Scene 5
The Toy Sailor Windmill[40]
E. Leonard
Scene 6
"Wondering Who"
M. R. Walsh, D. London, Cape Cod Belles
Scene 7
"Boxing at Shadows"
L. Nolan, Cape Cod Belles
Scene 8
"Looking a Life Through a Rainbow"
M. R. Walsh, V. Hurst, E. Love, D. Llewellyn, B. Barr, D. Glaenzer, E. Jones, N. Mason, J. DePaul, L. Millman, C. Morris, K. Burton, D. London, D. Beddingfield, M. Glaenzer
(Music by Kenneth Burton. Lyrics by Walter Craig.)
Scene 9
"Wonderful Cafe Girls"
P. Ellis, L. Nolan, Cape Cod Belles
Scene 10
Intimate Moments with Her Majesty Queen Victoria
P. Joray
Scene 11
"What Well Dressed Humanity Will Wear"
D. Gleanzer, K. Burton, Mannikins
Scene 12
"That's the Time When I Miss You"
E. Love, D. London, Cape Cod Belles, King's Highway Four
Ship Models: C. Clovelly, L. Millman, C. Morris, L. Nolan, D. London, D. Glaenzer, E. Love.

---

[38]Added during the run:
Collette Sisters (Specialty)
The Daros (Specialty)
The Kelo Brothers (Specialty)

---

[39]Dropped during the run.
[40]Dropped during the run.

Scene 13

Aboard the Cape Cod Pirate Ship

  a. Prologue: Provincetown PlaywritingD. Glaenzer, L. Millman, C. Morris

  b. Moonlight on the Carribees with apologies to Eugene O'Neill

  c. "Cape Cod Chanty" (reprise)K. Burton, D. London, G. Ford, l. Nolan, V. Hurst, W. Watson

  d. Every Show Must Have a CabaretL. Nolan

  e. Dancing PiratesD. Beddingfield, K. Riley, L. Davis, M. Babcock, L. Bennett

  f. Very Grand OperaE. Leonard

  g. "Wonderful Cape Cod Girl"V. Hurst, B. Barr, K. Burton, Cape Cod Belles

Scene 14

Finale

  Entire Company

SWEETHEARTS
1929.34

A Revival of the Comic Opera (Operetta) in Two Acts[41]. Book by Harry B. Smith and Fred de Grésac. Music by Victor Herbert. Lyrics by Robert B. Smith. Entire production staged by Milton Aborn. Costumes by Tams. Orchestra under the direction of Louis Kroll. Produced by the Jolson's Theatre Musical Comedy Company (Messrs. Shubert, Milton Aborn). Opened 21 September 1929 at Jolson's Theatre and closed 5 October 1929 after 17 performances.

CAST: *Sylvia*, Princess of Zilania: GLADYS BAXTER. *Prince Franz*, Heir Presumptive to the Throne: CHARLES MASSINGER. *Liane*, a Milliner of Bruges: GENEVIEVE NAEGELE. *Mikel (Mikelovicz)*, a Diplomat of Zilania: RICHARD POWELL. *Paula*, Proprietress of the Laundry of the White Geese: FLAVIA ARCARO. *Lieutenant Karl*, betrothed to Sylvia: PAUL DAVIN. *Honorable Percival Slingsby*: William J. McCarthy. *Petrus Van Tromp*: Detmar Poppen. *Aristede Caniche*: Lee Daly. *Daughters of Dame Paula* (6): *Jeanette*: Wee Griffin. *Clairette*: Mary Thurman. *Babette*: Edith Artley. *Lisette*: Lisette Braddock. *Toinette*: Florence Cazelle. *Nanette*: Ethel Lynne. *Captain Louvent*: Roland Tudor. *First Footman*: Donald Catlin. *Second Footman*: Bronek Wrobleski. *Coquette*: Lucyle Keeling. *Disdainful Girl*: Frances Baviello. *Village Belle*: Sally Galbreath. *Military Girl*: Frances Moore. *Heralds*: Cecilia Stockdale, Lucyle Keeling. *Laundresses, the Military, Wedding Guests and Servants.*
Pages: Mary Leavitt, Elizabeth Flannigan, Lillian Wallace, Dorothy Wadleigh. *Ladies of the Ensemble*: Helen Held, Florence Lamaere, Meredith Young, Marian Blau, Maud Carleton, Nell McCormick, Ione Anne Haals, Peggy Guilbert, Evelyn Brown, Florine LaCluyze, Cecilia Stockdale, Eileen McGann, Ida Goodrich, Blanche Shock, Ruth Sharpe, Emma Curtis, Anna Koons, Pearl Saunders, Adeline White, Eleanor Meyer, Helen Petrie, Theresa Masters, Grace Alden, Marjorie Booth, Betty Hines, Helen Smythe, Dolly Pierce, Jane Walters, Gertrude Noble, Agnes Holt. *Gentlemen of the Ensemble*: Bernie Sager, Harry Knabenshue, Louis Diamond, George Koenig, James Carlin, William Burbank, Hobson Young, Francesco Yannelli, Edward Taylor, Bert Melrose, William Ellis, Milton Gallagher, Roy Miller, Frank Alexander, Homer Wright, Alexander Stock.

GEORGE WHITE'S SCANDALS (1929)
1929.35

A Musical Revue in Two Acts, 25 Scenes[42]. Sketches by William K. Wells, George White. Music by Cliff Friend, George White. Lyrics by Cliff Friend, George White, Irving Caesar. Entire production devised and staged by George White. Abbott dancers' routines by Merriel Abbott. Art director, G. A. Weidhaas. Assistant art director, William Oden-Waller. Parisian costumes and curtains by Max Weldy from designs by Erté. American costumes by Schneider-Anderson from designs by Cora MacGeachy, Orry Kelly and Charles LeMaire. Men's costumes by Brooks Costume Company. Orchestra under the direction of William Daly. Orchestrations by Maurice DePackh. Produced by George White. Opened 23 September 1929 at the Apollo Theatre and closed 8 February 1930 after 161 performances.

CAST:GEORGE WHITE, WILLIE HOWARD, EVELYN WILSON, EUGENE HOWARD, FRANCES WILLIAMS, (Frank) MITCHELL and (Jack) DURANT, MARIETTA, CAROLYN NOLTE, ERNEST CHARLES, JIM CARTY, JACK WHITE, VADA ALEXANDER, HARRY MORRISSEY, FRED LYON, THE ELM CITY FOUR, SALLY AND TED, ARTHUR CARDINAL, SCOTT SISTERS.
Ladies of the Ensemble: Claire Scott, Anna May Rex, Kathleen Reichner, Etta

---

[41]Originally produced in New York 8 September 1913 at the New Amsterdam Theatre for 136 performances. For Synopsis of Scenes and Musical Numbers, see original 1913 production. Settings uncredited.
[42]The tenth in the annual series of musical revues produced by George White beginning in 1919.

Sparre, Nitza Andre, Stella Bayliss, Ethel Britton, Pauline Brooks, Marion Dickson, Inez du Plessis, Mildred Green, Joanna Allen, Kay Apgar, Pearl Bradley, Elsie Duffy, Sue Elliott, Renee Johnson, Peggy Moseley, Ida Michael, Gertrude Lowe, Edwina Skorat, Mae Slattery, Jeanne Scott, Dolly Gilbert, Billie Hart, Theo Hollie, Beatrice Jay, Julia Gorman, Alice Kerwin, Mildred Klaw, Gladys Law, Marilyn Mack, Leslynn Miller, Margie O'Shea, Margaret Manners, Patsy O'Day, Edith Pragen, Elise Gernon, Elizabeth Rapieff, Lenore Petitt, Leslie Storey, Marion Sweet, Elizabeth Scott, Peggy Schaber, Youda Wood, Elizabeth Sundmark. *THE ABBOTT DANCERS*: Florence Wilson, Pauline Bensinger, Marion Ford, Alice Fogg, Eleanor Gillespie, May Hass, Jessie Kassel, Amy McKay, Pearl McKnight, Myrtle Messer, Mabel Rickert, Rose Turman.

ACT 1

Scene 1

Tenth Birthday of George White's Scandals

  First Baby ("Shaking the Shimmy"): L. Storey. *Second Baby* ("Stairway to Paradise"): A. Kerwin. *Third Baby* ("Somebody Loves Me"): J. Allen. *Fourth Baby* ("The Charleston"): P. Moseley. *Fifth Baby* ("This Is My Lucky Day"): P. Schaber. *Twins* [Sixth] ("Birth of the Blues" and "Rhapsody in Blue"): S. Elliott, M. Manners. *Seventh Baby* ("Black Bottom"): C. Scott. *Eighth Baby* ("Crest of Wave"): M. Klaw. *Ninth Baby* ("Pickin' Cotton"): D. Gilbert. *The New Baby* ("Bigger and Better Than Ever"): F. Robinson.
  Hostesses: M. Green, B. Scott, G. Law, J. Scott, J. Gorman, R. Johnson, M. Dixon, P. Bradley, Rex, M. Sweet, N. Andre, T. Hollie, L. Miller, Reichner, B. Hart, P. Brooks, Britton, Michaels, I. du Plessis, B. Sundmark.

Scene 2

Dance

  Abbott Specialty Dancers

Scene 3

What the Well-Dressed Man Will Wear

  W. Howard, E. Howard

Scene 4

"Bigger and Better Than Ever"

  F. Williams

  (*Music and Lyrics by* Cliff Friend and George White.)

    Page 1: M. O'Shea, B. Scott. *Page 2*: I. du Plessis. *Page 3*: E. Duffy. *Page 4*: G. Law. *Page 5*: E. Pragen. *Page 6*: A. Kerwin. *Page 7*: J. Allen. *Page 8*: P. Schaber.

Scene 5

George White

Scene 6

It Could Happen (*by* Ben F. Holzman and William K. Wells)

  The Woman: E. Wilson. *The Man*: J. Carty. *The Visitor*: W. Howard.

Scene 7

Beauty and the Beast (Dance)

  Marietta

Scene 8

"Sitting in the Sun (Just Wearing a Smile)"

  W. Howard

  (*Music and Lyrics by* Cliff Friend and George White.)

    Sun Tan Girls: M. Klaw, A. Kerwin, J. Allen, P. Moseley. *Hoop Skirt*: S. Elliott. *Big Hat*: E. Skorat. *Bustle*: M. Manners. *Mannish*: K. Apgar. *The Girl in the Sun*: I. du Plessis. *Girls on the Beach*: M. Dixon, P. Bradley, B. Scott, B. Hart, M. O'Shea, Rex, Reichner, L. Miller, P. Brooks, M. Sweet, Michaels, Bayliss, Lowe, Holley, E. Sundmark, Wood, N. Andre, O'Day, M. Green, Jay, Slattery, L. Storey, Britton, Duffy, J. Gorman, Mack, R. Johnson, E. Sparre, E. Pragen, G. Law. *Life Guards*: Elm City Four.

Scene 9

Stocks

  Announcers: Scott Sisters. *The Broker*: J. White. *The Butler*: H. Morrissey. *The Girl*: F. Williams. *First Detective*: W. Howard. *Second Detective*: E. Howard. *Messenger Boy*: F. Mitchell.

Scene 10

"Bottoms Up"

  F. Williams, G. White, F. Robinson, Girls of the Ensemble

  (*Music and Lyrics by* Cliff Friend and George White.)

Scene 11

The Lost Flyers (*by* Lew Brown, George White and William K. Wells)

  The Captain: W. Howard. *The Doctor*: E. Howard. *The Pilot*: J. White. *The Mechanic*: J. Carty. *The Radio Announcer*: J. Durant. *Pincus*: H. Morrissey.

Scene 12

Abbott Specialty Dancers

Scene 13

Evelyn Wilson

Scene 14

We Americans

Scotland: E. Howard. *Germany*: H. Morrissey. *Russia*: J. Carty. *Spain*: J. White. *Italy*: F. Lyon. *France*: W. Howard.
Girls of the Ensemble: *The Indian*: M. Klaw. *Germany*: E. Skorat. *Spain*: I. du Plessis. *Russia*: J. Allen. *Scotland*: Y. Wood. *England*: A. Kerwin. *France*: P. Schaber. *Italy*: M. Manners. *China*: S. Elliott. *Java*: L. Storey. *South Seas*: P. Bradley. *Japan*: B. Jay. *Egypt*: E. Britton. *Holland*: E. Duffy. *Czecho-Slovakia*: G. Law. *Persia*: E. Pragen. *Ireland*: D. Gilbert. *Turkey*: P. Moseley. *India*: M. Slattery. *Germany*: R. Johnson. *Balkan*: M. O'Shea. *Holland*: S. Bayliss. *Japan*: B. Scott. *Scandinavia*: M. Sweet. *Venetian*: K. Apgar. *Miss Liberty*: B. Sundmark.

ACT 2

Scene 1

"You Are My Day Dream"

. Nolte, E. Charles, Elm City Four
(*Music by* Cliff Friend. *Lyrics by* Irving Caesar.)
Turban: S. Elliott. *Turban*: P. Schaber. *Feather*: J. Allen. *Hat Pin*: M. Sweet. *Necklace*: B. Jay. *Necklace*: G. Law. *Necklace Bearer*: B. Scott. *Necklace Bearer*: B. Sundmark. *Earring*: E. Storey. *Artist*: P. Moseley. *Artist*: S. Bayliss.

Dance

Abbott Specialty Dancers

Scene 2

Frances Williams

Scene 3

The False Friend

Mr. Podnick: W. Howard. *Mrs. Podnick*: V. Alexander. *Mr. Goldfarb*: E. Howard. *The Maid*: C. Nolte.

Scene 4

"Drop Your Kerchief"

F. Williams
(*Lyrics by* Irving Caesar.)
First Old-Fashioned Girl: E. Skorat. *First Old-Fashioned Beau*: H. Morrissey. *Second Old-Fashioned Girl*: M. Manners. *Second Old-Fashioned Beau*: F. Lyon.
Girls in Curtain: J. Allen, B. Scott, M. Klaw, A. Kerwin, G. Law, I. duPlessis.

Flirtation Dance

Ted and Sally

Scene 5

The Man of the Hour (*by* Irving Caesar, Lew Brown and Buddy G. DeSylva)

Announcement: F. Robinson. *Rodriquez Alvarez* (El Presidente): W. Howard. *Senora Alvarez, His Wife*: F. Williams. *Comrado Obispo, His Friend*: J. Carty. *Emil Valverde*, Radio Announcer: J. White.

Scene 6

"Love Birds"

E. Wilson
(*Music and Lyrics by* Cliff Friend and Irving Caesar.)
Two Love Birds: J. Scott, C. Scott. *Attendants*: M. Manners, S. Elliott. And the Abbott Specialty Dancers.
(Note: This is the first and only dancing unit to execute a tap dance on toes.)

Scene 7

Willie Howard

Scene 8

"18 Days Ago"

F. Williams, E. Wilson, V. Alexander, Y. Wood, L. Storey, M. Manners
(*Music by* Ray Henderson. *Lyrics by* Lew Brown and Buddy G. DeSylva.)

Scene 9

Phoneyfibs

Announcer: D. Gilbert. *The Husband*: W. Howard. *The Girl Friend*: E. Wilson. *The Wife*: F. Williams. *The Boy Friend*: F. Lyon. *Second Boy Friend*: A. Cardinal. *Second Girl Friend*: M. Mack.

Scene 10

Mitchell and Durant

Scene 11

George White and Party at the Café Lido, Paris

Entire Company

1929.36

MLLE. MODISTE

A Revival of the Comic Opera in Two Acts, 3 Scenes[43]. Book and lyrics by Henry Blossom. Music by Victor Herbert. Entire production staged by Milton Aborn. Ballet staged by Albertina Rasch. Costumes by Tams; Miss Scheff's modern gowns by Rose Mandel. Orchestra under the direction of Louis Kroll. Produced by the Jolson's Theatre Musical Comedy Company (Messrs. Shubert, Milton Aborn). Opened 7 October 1929 at Jolson's Theatre, moved 21 October 1929 to the Casino Theatre, and closed 16 November 1929 after 48 performances.

CAST: *Henry de Bouvray*, Comte de St. Mar: DETMAR POPPEN. *Captain Étienne de Bouvray*, his nephew: ROBERT RHODES. *Hiram Bent*, an American Millionaire: RICHARD POWELL. *Gaston*, an Artist, Mme. Cécelie's Son: ARTHUR BURCKLEY. *General Le Marquis de Villefranche*: William J. McCarthy. *Lieutenant Rene Le Motte*, engaged to Marie Louise: Roland Tudor. *François, Porter at Mme. Cécelie's*: Lee Daly. *Mme. Cécelie*, Proprietress of a Parisian hat-shop: FLAVIA ARCARO. *Her Daughters* (2): *Fanchette*: Edith Artley. *Nanette*: Florence Cazelle. *Marie Louise*, Étienne's Sister: Lucyle Keeling. *Bebe*, Dancer at the Folies Bergère: Frances Baviello. *Mrs. Hiram Bent*: Bernice Mershon. *Fifi*: FRITZI SCHEFF. *Milliners, Guests, Dancers, Soldiers, Flower Girls, Footmen*. (Premier Danseuse: Marie Grimaldi.)

Errand Boys: Wee Griffin, Ethel Lynne. *Footmen*: Harry Knabenshue, Bert Melrose, Edward Taylor, Hobson Yound, Francesco Yannelli, Bronek Wrobleski. *Ladies of the Ensemble*: Edith Artley, Sally Galbreaith, Florence Lamorer'e, Helen Held, Meredith Young, Marian Blau, Maude Carlton, Nell McCormick, Ione (Anne) Haals, Peggy Guilbert, Evelyn Brown, Florine LaCluyze, Cecelia Stockdale, Eileen McGann, Ida Goodrich, Blanche Schock, Ruth Sharpe, Emma Curtis, Anna Koons, Pearl Saunders, Adeline White, Eleanor Meyer, Helen Petrie, Theresa Masters, Grace Alden, Marjorie Booth, Betty Hines, Helen Smythe, Dolly Pierce, Jane Walters, Gertrude Noble, Amy Alexander, Mary Leavitt, Elizabeth Flannigan, Lillian Wallace, Dorothy Wadleigh. *Gentlemen of the Ensemble*: Bernie Sager, Harry Knabenshue, Louis Diamond, George Koenig, James Carlin, William Burbank, Hobson Yound, Francesco Yannelli, Edward Taylor, Bert Melrose, William Ellis, Milton Gallagher, Roy Miller, Frank Alexander, Homer Wright, Alexander Stock, Bronek Wrobleski, Ralph Hoyt.

1929.37

GREAT DAY

A Musical Comedy in Two Acts, 7 Scenes. Book by William Cary Duncan and John Wells. Music by Vincent Youmans. Lyrics by William Rose, Edward Eliscu. Dialogue (book) staged by R. H. Burnside, Frank M. Gillespie. Dances staged by LeRoy J. Prinz. Settings by (Frank E.) Gates and (E.A.) Morange. Costumes designed by Mabel Johnston. Orchestra under the direction of Paul Lannin, Nicklas [Nicholas] Kempner. Produced by Vincent Youmans. Opened 17 October 1929 at the Cosmopolitan Theatre and closed 16 November 1929 after 36 performances[44].

CAST: *Pete*: Frank Daley. *Tom*: Ken Pulsifer. *Richard*: Bob Burton. *Ida May*: Letha Burson. *Kitty*: Blanche Le Clair. *Carolyn*: Kitty Coleman. *Phil Randolph*: Billy Taylor. *Susie Totheridge*: ETHEL NORRIS. *Emmy Lou Randolph*: MAYO METHOT. *Henry White, Babe Jackson*: (Flournoy) MILLER and (Aubrey) LYLES. *Pepita Padilla*: VANESSI. *Carlos Zarega*: JOHN HAYNES. *Jim Brent*: ALLAN PRIOR. *Judge Totheridge*: WALTER C. KELLY. *Mazie Brown*: MAUDE EBURNE. *Charlie*: Vincent Simonin. *Lantern Man*: Hugh Chilvers. *Lijah*: Lois Deppe.

Show Girls: Georgia English, Roberta Kent, Diane Doering, Emily Martin, Marjorie Porter, Doris Delairs, Loise Gay. *Dancing Girls*: *Mediums*: Margaret Miller, Beth Meredith, Irene Evans, Vera Villon, Grace Connelly, Dixie Lester, Frances Stevens, Josephine Mostler, Peggy Deighton, Helen Newton. *Ponies*: Jackie Cortez, Adelaide Kaiser, Jean Warren, Billy Toy, Buddy Lavon, Jean Joyce, Rita Garcia, May Brenton, Paulyne Wynter, Olga Fox, Mildred Schroder. *Singing and Dancing Boys*: Bob Burton, Herman Hylander, Kenneth Pulsifer, Vincent Simonin, Alfred Milano, Frank Daley, Frank Larsen, William Ehlers. *JUBILEE SINGERS*: Assorta Marshall, Mildred Dawson, Kay Mason, Olive Wanamaker, Helen Wallace, Margie Woods, Elizabeth Carroll, Harriett Williams, Christine Davis, Carrie Huff, Gladys Wells, Olive Hopkins, Josephine Gray, Estell Richardson, Mary Mason, Gertrude Fayde, Alma Reynolds, Essie Queen, Ismay Andrews, Lillian Howard, Olive Ball, Pearl Johnson, Millie Holmes, Mayme Briggs, Jewell Fisher, Louise Reynolds, Harold Des Verney, Snippy Mason, Halle Howard, Ralph Northern, J. DeWitt Spencer, George Battle, Edward Cartier, Larry Lorear, Herbert Skinner, Hamilton McLean, S. H. Gray, Lackey Grant, Jean Donnald, James Downes.

---

[43]Originally produced 25 December 1905 at the Knickerbocker Theatre for 202 performances. For Synopsis of Scenes and Musical Numbers, see original 1905 production. Settings uncredited. "Hats Make the Woman" dropped for this production.

[44]Orchestrations for "Great Day" and "Without a Song" by Frank Skinner. Additional orchestrations by Stephen Jones. Scene numbers in song list have been corrected to follow scene list.

Act 1, Scene 1: The Randolph Plantation. Near New Orleans, Louisiana. *Scene 2*: The Levee. A week later. *Scene 3*: The Spanish Casino. Next night.

Act 2, Scene 1: The Levee. *Scene 2*: On the Mississippi. *Scene 3*: The Cornfield, Randolph Plantation. *Scene 4*: The Randolph Homestead.

ACT 1

Scene 1

Opening
B. Taylor, Ensemble

"Does It Pay to Be a Lady?"
E. Norris, Ensemble

"I Like What You Like"
B. Taylor, M. Methot, Girls

"Happy Because I'm in Love"
M. Methot, A. Prior, Ensemble

"Great Day"
L. Deppe, Jubilee Singers

"One Love"[45]
A. Prior

Scene 3

"Si, Si, Senor"
Ensemble

Spanish Dance
Vanessi

"Open Up Your Heart"
B. Taylor, E. Norris

"Wedding Bells Ring On"[46]
M. Eburne, W. C Kelly, B. Taylor, E. Norris

"More Than You Know"
M. Methot

"Play the Game"
A. Prior, Ensemble

"Happy Because I'm in Love"
M. Methot

Finale

ACT 2

Scene 1

Levee Scene and Hymn
Jubilee Ensemble

Scene 3

"Sweet As Sugar Cane"
Ensemble

Specialty
Trainor Brothers

"Without a Song"
L. Deppe, Jubilee Ensemble

"Happy Because I'm in Love" (reprise)
A. Prior, M. Methot

"Scarecrows"
E. Norris, B. Taylor, Dancers

Scene 4

Dance
Negro Ensemble

Finale
Entire Company

1929.38 ## NAUGHTY MARIETTA

A Revival of the Comic Opera (Musical Comedy) in Two Acts, 3 Scenes[47]. Book and lyrics by Rida Johnson Young. Music by Victor Herbert. Entire

---

[45]Replaced after opening by:
  "Happy Because I'm in Love" (reprise)
    A. Prior
[46]Dropped after the opening.
[47]Originally produced in New York 7 November 1910 at the New York Theatre for 136 performances. For Synopsis of Scenes and Musical Numbers, see original 1910 production. Settings uncredited. For this revival, the following changes were made:

production staged by Milton Aborn. Costumes by Tams. Musical director, Louis Kroll. Produced by the Jolson's Theatre Musical Comedy Company (Messrs. Shubert, Milton Aborn). Opened 21 October 1929 at Jolson's Theatre and closed 2 November 1929 after 16 performances.

CAST: *Captain Richard Warrington*, an American known as Captain Dick: ROY CROPPER. *Lieutenant Governor Grandet*: HERBERT L. WATROUS. *Étienne Grandet, His Son*: LOUIS TEMPLEMAN. *Sir Harry Blake*, an Irish Adventurer: Wesley McCloud. *Silas Slick*, Captain Dick's Servant: RICHARD POWELL. *Rudolfo*, Keeper of the Marionette Theatre: James S. Murray. *Florenze*, Secretary to Lieutenant Governor: William J. McCarthy. *Marietta D'Alténa*: ILSE MARVENGA. *Lizette*, a Casquette Girl: Eulalie Young. *Adah*, a Quadroon Slave: LYDIA VAN GILDER. *Fanchon*: Wee Griffin. *Felice*: Frances Baviello. *Graziella*: Ruth Sharpe. *Indian*: Edward Taylor. *East Indian*: Hobson Yound. *Knife Grinder*: Bernie Sager. *Quadroon Belles, Spanish Girls, French Girls, Captain Dick's Followers, Italians, etc.*
  Ladies of the Ensemble: Sally Galbreaith, Florence Lamorer'e, Lizette Braddock, Helen Held, Meredith Young, Marian Blau, Maude Carleton, Nell McCormick, Ione Anne Haals, Peggy Guilbert, Mary Thurman, Evelyn Brown, Florine LaCluyze, Cecilia Stockdale, Eileen McGann, Ida Goodrich, Blanche Burtt, Emma Curtis, Anna Koons, Pearl Saunders, Adeline White, Eleanor Meyer, Helen Petrie, Theresa Masters, Grace Alden, Marjorie Booth, Betty Hines, Helen Smythe, Dolly Pierce, Jane Walters, Gertrude Noble, Amy Alexander, Mary Leavitt, Elizabeth Flannigan, Lillian Wallace, Dorothy Wadleigh, Adele Savoy, Frances Moore. *Gentlemen of the Ensemble*: Harry Knabenshue, Louis Diamond, George Koenig, James Gardner, William Barry, Francesco Yannelli, Bert Melrose, William Ellis, Milton Gallagher, Roy Miller, Frank Alexander, Homer Wright, Alexander Stock, Bronek Wrobleski.

1929.39 ## A WONDERFUL NIGHT

An Operetta in Three Acts, 14 Scenes. Book adapted by Fanny Todd Mitchell, following the story of "Le Réveillon" (by Henri Meilhac and Ludovic Halévy) from which "Die Fledermaus" was adapted. Music by Johann Strauss. Staged by José Ruben. Dances directed by Chester Hale. Settings designed by Watson Barratt. Costumes designed by Orry Kelley, Ernest Schrapps. Orchestra under the direction of Robert A. Goetzl. Produced by the Messrs. Shubert. Opened 31 October 1929 at the Majestic Theatre and closed 15 February 1930 after 125 performances.

CAST (in order of appearance): *Latzo Garbo*: BARTLETT SIMMONS. *Footman at Grunewald's*: Robert Irving. *Mme. Agout*: Sarah Brown. *Kathie*, Maid to the Grunewalds: MARY McCOY. *Mathilda Grunewald*: GLADYS BAXTER. *Leo*, Adjutant to Prince Koslofsky: Charles Chesney. *Max Grunewald*: ARCHIE LEACH [Cary Grant]. *Doctor von Lubke*: JOSEPH LERTORA. *Bochmeister*, Warden of the Jail: HAL FORDE. *Frieda*, Kathie's Sister: Dorothy Kane. *Prince Koslofsky*: ALLAN ROGERS. *Frau Hickenlooper*: Sallie Stembler. *Countess Malakoff*: Peggy Udell. *Baroness von Pogenhardt*: Julia Barker. *Marquise de Montmarte*: Gretchen Wilson. *Countess Vichy*: Thalie Hamilton. *Countess Perrier*: Anna May Denehy. *Lady Buttonshire*: Marian Alden. *Madame de Chaumont*: Rosalind Wishon. *Baroness Metelier*: Georgia Gwynne. *Madame de Esplanade*: Mabel Ellis. *Duchess de Montparnasse*: Marion Gillon. *Princess Fleur de Lys*: Virginia Bethel. *Alfred*: M. Varrele. *First Flunkey*: Robert Smith. *Second Flunkey*: Ray Wright. *Third Flunkey*: Truman Gaige. *Fourth Flunkey*: Charles Townshend. *Richard Lowen*: Robert Burke. *Blatz*, the Jailer: SOLLY WARD. *A Keeper*: Arthur Wood. *Messenger*: George Smith.
  Sopranos: Florence Starr, Marnella Ney, Irene Day, Frances Ellington, Marie Valdez, Meekie Ruth, Alice Everling. *Altos*: Madeline Clancy, Evelyn Lowman, Jean Kriston, Kathryn Krech, Ann Scarborough. *Tenors*: Chester J. Williams, Ramy Varnell, Valtine Sholar, Eddie Bird, Evert Woodsma, Ernest Pavano, John Fredericks, Robert Burk. *Second Tenors*: Lawrence Elwin, James Santry, Donald Gale, Ray Wright, Armand Vallerie, Ken J. Butler. *Baritones*: Charles Townshend, Truman Gaige, Robert Smith, William Spencer, Robert Turner. *Bassos*: Robert Irving, Zachary Karr, Jack London, Gwillym Williams, Glib Chandro. *Chester Hale Girls*: Norma Schutt, Sally Ritz, Dolores Distasio, Catherine Gray, Florence Mallee, Charlotte Joslin, Chula Morrow, Lula Dubagio, Evangeline Edwards, Betty Stratton, Garda Norheim, Alma Wertley. *Dancers*: Harold Haskine, Constant Nickoll, Jashe Crandall, Reed McClelland, Roland Guerard, Edward Browne. *Show Girls*: Virginia Bethel, Georgia Gwynne, Gretchen Wilson, Mabel Ellis, Marian Alden, Marion Gillon, Peggy Udell, Bobbie Hamilton, Rosalind Wishon, Julia Barker, Anna May Denehy, Dorothy Gilbert.

Act 1, Scene 1: The Prater Café. *Scene 2*: Hallway att Grunewald's. *Scene 3*: Salon at Grunewald's.

"Marry a Marionette" was dropped.

"Dream Melody" moved to precede "New Orleans Jeunesse Dorée;"

"It's Pretty Soft for Simon" changed to "It's Pretty Soft for Silas" pursuant to the character's change of name.

Added to the production to open Act 2, Scene 2:
  "Gambling"
    Male Ensemble

Act 2, Scene 1: Entrance to Prince Koslofsky's Villa. *Scene 2*: Foyer of Prince Koslofsky's Villa. *Scene 3*: Buffet Room at Prince Koslofsky's. *Scene 4*: Roulette Room at Prince Koslofsky's. *Scene 5*: Conservatory at Prince Koslofsky's. *Scene 6*: An Anteroom at Prince Koslofsky's. *Scene 7*: Ball Room at Prince Koslofsky's.

Act 3, Scene 1: Corridor of the Jail. *Scene 2*: Office of the Warden. *Scene 3*: A Narrow Street in Vienna. *Scene 4*: The Prater Café.

ACT 1

Opening

Serenade ("Two in Love")
B. Simmons

"Letter Song"
M. McCoy

Duet
A. Leach, J. Lertora

Trio
A. Leach, M. McCoy, G. Baxter

Duet
G. Baxter, B. Simmons

Trio
G. Baxter, B. Simmons, H. Forde

ACT 2

Opening
Ensemble, Chester Hale Girls

"Chacun à son goût"
A. Rogers

Song
M. McCoy, Ensemble

Czardas
G. Baxter, Ensemble

Finale
Entire Company

ACT 3

Song
S. Ward

Duet
G. Baxter, B. Simmons

"Girls Must Live"[48]
Eight Ladies of Vienna

Finale
Entire Company

THE FORTUNE TELLER
1929.40

A Revival of the Comic Opera in Three Acts[49]. Book (libretto) by Harry B. Smith. Music by Victor Herbert. Entire production staged by Milton Aborn. Costumes by Tams. Orchestra under the direction of Louis Kroll. Produced by the Jolson's Theater Musical Comedy Company (Messrs. Shubert, Milton Aborn). Opened 4 November 1929 at Jolson's Theatre and closed 16 November 1929 after 16 performances.

CAST: *Musette, Irma, Lieutenant Fedor*: TESSA KOSTA. *Fresco*: Detmar Poppen. *Count Berezowski*: WILLIAM J. McCARTHY. *Sandor*: CHARLES E. GALLAGHER. *Ladislas*: ROY CROPPER. *Boris*: Harry Hermsden. *Pompom*: CHARLOTTE WOODRUFF. *Vaninka*: Dene Dickens. *Rafael, Wakdemar, Prompter*: Bernie Sager. *General Korbay*: Leslie McLeod. *First Detective*: Francesco Yanelli. *Second Detective*: Edward Taylor. *Gardener*: James Carwin. *Lieutenant*: Hobson Young. *Ballet Girls, Hussars, Transpeople, Vivandiers.*

Drum Corps: Adele Savage, Nell McCormack, Florence Flanigen, Mary Levitt, Sally Galbreath, Ione Anne Haals, Lillian Wallace, Evelyn Brown, Frances Moore, Dorothy Wadleigh, Helen Etheridge. *Ladies of the Ensemble*: Wee Griffin, Lizette Braddock, Ethel Lynne, Mary Thurman, Helen Rae, Frances Baviello, Florine La Cluyze, Meredith Young, Eleanor Gilmore, Adele Savage, Nell McCormack, Florence E. Lamorer'e, Elizabeth Flanigen, Mary Levitt, Sally Galbreath, Ione Anne Haals, Lillian Wallace, Evelyn Brown, Frances Moore, Dorothy Wadleigh, Helen Etheridge. *Gentlemen of the Ensemble*: William Burbank, Donald Catlin, Louis Diamond, George Koenig, Harry Knabenshue, Bert Melrose, Bernie Sager, Edward Taylor, Bronek Wrobleski, Hobson Young, Francesco Yanelli, George Plummer.

[48]After opening, moved to Act 1, following "Serenade."
[49]First produced in New York 26 September 1898 at Wallack's Theatre for 40 performances. For Synopsis of Scenes and Musical Numbers, see original 1898 production. Settings uncredited.

BITTER SWEET
1929.41

An Operette in Three Acts, 6 Scenes. Book, music and Lyrics by Noël Coward. Settings and costumes designed by Gladys E. Calthrop, Professor Stern. Entire production staged by Noël Coward. Orchestra under the direction of Frank Tours. Produced by Florence Ziegfeld in association with Arch Selwyn. A Charles B. Cochran production. Opened 5 November 1929 at the Ziegfeld Theater, moved 17 February 1930 to the Sam S. Shubert Theatre, and closed 22 March 1930 after 159 performances.

CAST (in order of appearance): *Act 1, Scene 1*: *Parker*: Trevor Glyn. *Dolly Chamberlain*: Audrey Pointing. *Lord Henry*: Patrick Ludlow. *Vincent Howard*: Max Kirby. *The Marchioness of Shayne*: EVELYN LAYE. *Nita*: Joan Stanbrough. *Helen*: Constance Perrin. *Jackie*: Cecile Maule-Cole.

Guests: Leah Warne, Gladys Hay-Dillon, Mildred Allen-Letts, Eva Scott-Thompson, Kathleen Holt, Pauline Desmond, Sybil Davidson, Peggy Lovat, Vera Caprice, Edna Earle, Vicky Lynn, Cecile Maule-Cole, Iris White, Marjorie Simpson, George Woof, Alfred Fairhurst, Mervyn Pearce, Anthony Neville, Reginald Allen, Noel Clifford, Herbert Garry, Claude Brittin-Eldred, Richard Thorpe, Paul Spender-Clay, Bruce Anderson, Hugh Cuenod, Roy Arcourt, William Dawson.
Scene 2: *Sarah Millick*: EVELYN LAYE. *Carl Linden*: GERALD NODIN. *Mrs. Millick*: Isabel Ohmead. *The Honorable Hugh Devon*: Tracy Holmes.
Scene 3: *Carl Linden*: GERALD NODIN. *Lady Devon*: Kathleen Lambelet. *Mrs. Millick*: Isabel Ohmead. *The Honorable Hugh Devon*: Tracy Holmes. *Sir Arthur Fenchurch*: Charles Mortimer. *Sarah Millick*: EVELYN LAYE. *The Marquis of Steere*: Donald Gordon. *Lord Edgar James*: Richard Thorpe. *Lord Sorrel*: Hooper Russell. *Mr. Vale*: Leslie Bannister. *Mr. Bethel*: Anthony Neville. *Mr. Proutie*: Douglas Graeme-Brooke. *Victoria*: Marjorie Raymond. *Harriet*: Audrey Pointing. *Gloria*: Nancy Brown. *Honor*: Isla Bevan. *Jane*: Winifred Talbot. *Effie*: Vesta Sylva. *Footmen*: Graham Yarborough, Trevor Glynn, John W. Thompson, Albert Chapman.

Guests: Elsie Hulme, Iris White, Isabel Marden, Kathleen Holt, Peggy Lovat, Jane Moore, Sybil Davidson, Myfany Jenkins, Cecile Maule-Cole, Mildred Allen-Letts, Vera Caprice, Mary David, Roma Presano, Joan Stanbrough, Doris Colston, Leonora Hilton, Pauline Desmond, Gwladys Hay-Dillon, Joyce Fletcher, Eva Scott-Thompson, Cunningham Glen, George Woof, Alfred Fairhurst, Noel Clifford, Herbert Garry, William Herbert, Claude Brittin-Eldred, James Reid, Mervyn Pearce, Roy Hall, Anthony Neville, James Prescott, Paul Spender-Clay, Reginald Allen, Bruce Anderson, Hugh Cuenod, Louis Miller. *Musicians*: Sydney Perlstone, Kenneth Burston, Arthur Woolf, Edmond Ford, Vernon Rudolf.
Act 2, Scene 1: *Waiters*: Paul Spender-Clay, Claude Brittin-Eldred, James Reid, Bruce Anderson, Anthony Neville, William McGuigan. *Cleaners*: Roma Presano, Isabel Marden, Leonta Proctor, Gwladys Hay-Dillon, Enid Settle, Iris Hulme. *Piccolo*: Peter Donald. *Lotte*: Zoe Gordon. *Hansi*: Dorothy Debenham. *Gussie*: Sylvia Leslie. *Carl Linden*: GERALD NODIN. *Manon, La Crevette*: MIREILLE. *Captain August Lutte*: DESMOND JEANS. *Herr Schlick*: CHARLES MORTIMER. *Sari Linden*: EVELYN LAYE. *Musicians*: Sydney Perlstone, Kenneth Burston, Edmond Ford, Eddie Lisbona, Vernon Rudolf.
Scene 2: *Sari Linden*: EVELYN LAYE. *Lotte*: Zoe Gordon. *Captain Lutte*: Desmond Jeans. *Gussie*: Sylvia Leslie. *Lieutenant Tranisch*: Louis Miller. *Hansi*: Dorothy Debenham. *Freda*: Nancy Barnett. *Herr Schlick*: Charles Mortimer. *The Prater Girls*: Sybil Davidson, Cecile Maule-Cole, Vicky Lynn. *Boys*: Leah Warne, Edna Earle, Peggy Blake. *Manon, La Crevette*: MIREILLE.

Officers, Guests, Waiters, Musicians: Hooper Russell, Leslie Bannister, Donald Gordon, Roy Hall, Gordon Brand, Douglas Graeme-Brooke, Hugh Cuenod, John W. Thompson, Trevor Glynn, Herbert Garry, Graham Yarborough, Gustav Wallenberg, Paul Spender-Clay, Claude Brittin-Eldred, James Reid, Bruce Anderson, Anthony Neville, William McGuigan, Kathleen Lambelet, Isabel Ohmead, Isabel Marden, Iris Hulme, Constance David, Leonora Hilton, Enid Settle, Gladys Hay-Dillon, Doris Colston, Joan Stanbrough, Pauline Desmond, Joyce Fletcher, Myfany Jenkins, Peggy Lovat, Jane Moore, Kathleen Holt, Vera Caprice, Leonta Proctor, Mildred Allen-Letts, Eva Scott Thompson, Leah Russell, Marcel Turner, Patruck Ludlow, James Cameron, William Dawson, Reginald Allen, Albert Chapman, Richard Thorpe, George Woof, James Prescott, Tracy Holmes, Alfred Fairhurst, Mervyn Pearce, Cunningham Glen, Noel Clifford, William Herbert.
Act 3, Scene 1: *Burley*, a Butler: Albert Chapman. *The Marquis of Shayne*: JOHN EVELYN. *Mrs. Bethel* (Effie): Vesta Sylva. *Mr. Bethel*: Anthony Neville. *Mrs. Vale* (Jane): Winifred Talbot. *Mr. Vale*: Leslie Bannister. *Mrs. Proutie* (Gloria): Nancy Brown. *Mr. Proutie*: Douglas Graeme-Brooke. *The Duchess of Tenterton* (Victoria): Marjorie Raymond. *The Duke of Tenterton*: Donald Gordon. *Lady Sorrel* (Honor): Isla Bevan. *Lord Sorrel*: Hooper Russell. *Lord Edgar James* (Harriet): Audrey Pointing. *Lord Edgar James*: Richard Thorpe. *Sir Hugh Devon*: Tracy Holmes. *Lady Devon*: Jane Moore. *Madame Sari Linden*: EVELYN LAYE. *Vernon Craft*: Cunningham Glen. *Cedric Ballantyne*: Paul Spender-Clay. *Bertram Sellick*: Hugh Cuenod. *Lord Henry Jade*: George Woof. *Accompanist* (to Madame Linden): Eddie Lisbona.

Guests: Constance Perrin, Leah Warne, Cecile Maule-Cole, Joyce Fletcher, Leah Russell, Myfany Jenkins, Iris White, Joan Stanbrough, Kathleen Holt, Vera Caprice, Roma Presano, Elsie Hulme, Gwladys Hay-Dillon, Peggy Lovat, Pauline Desmond, Doris Colston, Enid Settle, Mildred Allen-Letts, Leonora Hilton, Isabel Marden, Eva Scott-Thompson, Sybil Davidson, Leonta Proctor, John W. Thompson, James Prescott, James Reid, William Herbert, Graham Yarborough, Trevor Glynn, Claude Brittin-Eldred, Alfred Fairhurst, Roy Hall, Anthony Neville, Reginald Allen, Herbert Garry, Bruce Anderson, William Dawson, William McGuigan, Gustav Wallenberg, Mervyn Pearce, Noel Clifford.

Act 1, Scene 1: Lady Shayne's House in Grosvenor Square, 1929. *Scene 2*: The Millicks' House in Belgrave Square, 1875. *Scene 3*: The Ballroom of the Millicks' House in Belgrave Square, 1875.

Act 2, Scene 1: Herr Schlick's Café in Vienna, 1880, 12 Noon. *Scene 2*: Herr Schlick's Café, about 2 A.M.

Act 3, Scene 1: Lord Shayne's House in London, 1895. *Scene 2*: Lady Shayne's House in Grosvenor Square, 1929.

ACT 1

Scene 1

("That Wonderful Melody")
  (Singer, Dancing Chorus)
The Call of Life"
  . Laye, Chorus

Scene 2

"If You Could Only Come With Me"
  G. Nodin
"I'll See You Again"
  E. Laye, G. Nodin

Scene 3

"Tell Me What Is Love"
  E. Laye, Chorus
"The Last Dance"
  D. Gordon, R. Thorpe, H. Russell, L. Bannister, A. Neville, D. Graeme-Brooke, M. Raymond, A. Pointing, N. Brown, I. Bevan, W. Talbot, V. Sylva
Finale

ACT 2

Scene 1

Opening Chorus ("Life in the Morning")
  Waiters, Cleaners
"Ladies of the Town"
  Z. Gordon, N. Barnett, D. Debenham, S. Leslie
"If Love Were All"
  Mireille
"Evermore and a Day"
  E. Laye
"(Dear) Little Café"
  E. Laye, G. Nodin

Scene 2

Officers' Chorus
  Officers, Chorus
"Tokay"
  G. Nodin, Officers, Chorus
"Bonne Nuit, Merci"
  Mireille
"Kiss Me"
  Mireille, Chorus

ACT 3

"Ta Ra Ra Boom De Ay"
  A. Neville, L. Bannister, D. Graeme-Brooke, D. Gordon, H. Russell, R. Thorpe, M. Raymond, A. Pointing, N. Brown, I. Bevan W. Talbot, V. Sylva
  (*Music and Lyrics by* Henry J. Sayers.)
"Alas, the Time Is Past"
  M. Raymond, A. Pointing, N. Brown, I. Bevan, W. Talbot, V. Sylva
"Green Carnations"
  H. Cuenod, G. Woof, C. Glen, P. Spender-Clay
"Zigeuner"
  E. Laye

1929.42   HEADS UP!

A Musical Comedy in Two Acts, 9 Scenes. Book by John McGowan and Paul Gerard Smith. Music by Richard Rodgers. Lyrics by Lorenz Hart. (Direction,) Dances and ensembles by George Hale. Settings designed by Donald Oenslager. Costumes designed by Kiviette. Orchestra under the direction of Alfred Newman. Orchestra arrangements, Robert Russell Bennett. Pianist, Phil Ohman. Produced by Alex A. Aarons and Vinton Freedley. Opened 11 November 1929 at the Alvin Theatre and closed 15 March 1930 after 144 performances.

CAST (in order of appearance): *Martha Trumbell*: JANET VELIE. *Peggy Pratt*: ALICE BOULDEN. *Rex Cutting*: JOHN HUNDLEY. *Larry White*: JOHN HAMILTON. *Betty Boyd*: BETTY STARBUCK. *Georgie*: RAY BOLGER. *"Skippy" Dugan*: VICTOR MOORE. *Captain Denny*: ROBERT GLECKLER. *Mary Trumbell*: BARBARA NEWBERRY. *Jack Mason*: JACK WHITING. *James Clarke*: Lewis Parker. *Bob, Harry*: Atlas and LaMar. *Carson*: Louis Delgado. *Dillon*: Richard Macaleese. *Hanson*: Chester Bree. *Gladys, Helene*: The Reynolds Sisters. *At the Piano*: Phil Ohman.

Ladies of the Ensemble: Gene Brady, Margery Bailey, Margot Bazin, Helen Collins, Catherine Cathcart, Violet Carson, Alvina Carson, Helen Doyle, Ann Ecklund, Eleanor Etheridge, Fay Greene, Ruth Gordon[50], Gypsy Hollis, Eva Hart, Pat Hamill, Rita Jason, Clara Larinova, Muriel Lawlor, Helen Lee, Jane Lane, Betty Morton, Elsie Neal, Clarita Nash, Lylie Olive, Helen Reinecke, Ruth Sato, Amy Weber, Wanda Wood, Paulette Winston, Grace Wright, Geraldine Pratt, Mary Elizabeth Kerr. *Gentlemen of the Ensemble*: Jerry Cushman, Hal Clyne, Louis Delgado, Bob Derden, Jack Fago, Harry Griffin, Bob Gebhardt, Tommy Jordan, Al Jordan, Lewis Parker, Jack Ross, George Rand, Bob Spencer, Edoard Gates, Charles McGrath, William Cooper, Fran Heyser, Chester Bree, Gordon Clark, Bud Tipton, Ben White, Richard Macaleese, LeRoy Kent, Paul Jensen, George Meyer.

Act 1, Scene 1: The Garden of Mrs. Trumbell's Home at New London. *Scene 2*: The Dock. *Scene 3*: "Skippy's" Galley Aboard the *Silver Lady*. *Scene 4*: The Yacht Club.

Act 2, Scene 1: The Water Front. *Scene 2*: Headquarters Office, U. S. Coast Guard, New London. *Scene 3*: Aboard the *Silver Lady*. *Scene 4*: An Island. *Scene 5*: Mrs. Trumbell's Home.

ACT 1

Scene 1

"You've Got to Surrender"
  Ensemble
"Play Boy"
  R. Bolger, Ensemble

Scene 2

"Mother Grows Younger"
  J. Velie, B. Newberry, Cadets
"Why Do You Suppose?"
  B. Newberry, J. Whiting, Girls

Scene 3

"Me for You"
  B. Starbuck, R. Bolger
"Why Do You Suppose?" (reprise)
  B. Newberry, J. Whiting

Scene 4

"Ongsay and Anceday"
  The Reynolds Sisters, Irlsgay
"It Must Be Heaven"
  B. Newberry, J. Whiting
"My Man Is on the Make"
  A. Boulden, Chorus
Specialty Dance
  Atlas, LaMar
Finale

ACT 2

Scene 1

"The Lass Who Loved a Sailor"
  B. Starbuck, Gobs (Sailors)
"A Ship Without a Sail"
  J. Whiting, Sailors

Scene 3

"Why Do You Suppose?" (reprise)
  B. Newberry
"Knees"
  A. Boulden, R. Bolger, Girls
"My Man Is on the Make" (reprise)
  A. Boulden, Girls

Scene 5

Specialty
  Atlas, LaMar, Reynolds Sisters
Finale
  Entire Company

---

[50]Not the famed dramatic actress of the 1920-1960s.

1929.43

ROBIN HOOD

A Revival of the Romantic Operetta (Comic Opera) in Three Acts[51]. Book and lyrics by Harry B. Smith. Music by Reginald De Koven. Entire production staged by Milton Aborn. Costumes by Tams. Produced by the Jolson's Theatre Musical Comedy Company (Messrs. Shubert, Milton Aborn). Opened 18 November 1929 at Jolson's Theatre and closed 30 November 1929 after 16 performances; re-opened 23 December 1929 at the Casino Theatre, and closed 4 January 1930 after 15 additional performances. Total: 31 performances.

CAST: *Robert of Huntington*, afterwards Robin Hood: ROY CROPPER. *Sheriff of Nottingham*: WILLIAM DANFORTH. *Sir Guy of Gisborne*: JOHN CHERRY. *Little John*: GREEK EVANS. *Will Scarlet*: CHARLES E. GALAGHER. *Friar Tuck*: WILLIAM J. McCARTHY. *Alan-a-Dale*: LORNA DOONE JACKSON. *Lady Marian Fitzwater*: OLGA STECK. *Dame Durden*: IDA BROOKS HUNT. *Annabel*: DOROTHY SEEGAR.

Ladies of the Ensemble: Wee Griffin, Lisette Braddock, Mary Thurman, Helen Rae, Frances Baviello, Ethel Lynne, Eleanor Gilmore, Adele Savage, Nell McCormick, Florence Lamorer'e, Elizabeth Flannigan, Sally Galbreaith, Lillian Wallace, Evelyn Brown, Frances Moore, Dorothy Wadleigh, Helen Etheridge, Catherine Kent, Fritzi Bullard, Faye Joffee, Betty Wald, Dene Dickens. *Gentlemen of the Ensemble*: William Burbank, Donald Catlin, Louis Diamond, George Koenig, Harry Knabenshue, Bernie Sager, Bronek Wrobleski, Francesco Yannelli, George Plummer, Jack Willard, Daniel Medwin, Alfred Deste.

ACT 1[52]

  "Halo—Halo—Halo" (Opening Chorus)
    Ensemble
  "Come the Bowmen in Lincoln Green"
    C E. Galagher, L. D. Jackson, G. Evans, Chorus
  Morris Dance
    D. Seegar, C. E. Galagher, G. Evans, L. D. Jackson
  "The Milk Maids"
    L. D. Jackson, D. Seegar, Milkmaids
  "Hey for the Merry Greenwood"
    R. Cropper, Ensemble
  "I Come as a Cavalier"
    O. Steck, Ensemble
  "Come Dreams So Bright"
    O. Steck, R. Cropper
  "(I Am the) Sheriff of Nottingham"W. Danforth, J. Cherry, Chorus
  "Churning, Churning"
    O. Steck, W. Danforth, J. Cherry
  Finale
    Principals, Chorus

ACT 2

  Opening Chorus
    L. D. Jackson, G. Evans, C. E. Galagher, Chorus
  "Jet Black Crow"
    G. Evans, Chorus
  "(Song of) Brown October Ale"
    G. Evans, Chorus
  "Oh, Promise Me"
    L. D. Jackson
    (*Lyrics by* Clement Scott.)
  "Dance of the Nymphs and Satyrs"
    Albertina Rasch Ballet
    (*Music by* Louis Kroll.)
  "(The) Tinkers' Song"
    W. Danforth, J. Cherry, Tinkers

"See the Little Lambkins Play"
    G. Evans, W. J. McCarthy, C. E. Galagher, W. Danforth, J. Cherry, R. Cropper
"(The) Forest Song"
    O. Steck
"Serenade"
    R. Cropper, Quartette
Finale
    Entire Company

ACT 3

  "The Armorer's Song"
    C. E. Galagher
  "When a Maiden Weds"
    O. Steck
  "The Bells of St. Swithins"[53]
    L. D. Jackson, Chorus
  Finale
    Entire Company

1929.44

SONS O' GUNS

A Musical Comedy in Two Acts, 15 Scenes. Book by Fred Thompson and Jack Donahue. Music by J. Fred Coots. Lyrics by Arthur Swanstrom, Benny Davis. Entire production staged by Bobby Connelly. Military direction by Harry Holbrook, U.S.M.C. Ballets by Albertina Rasch. Scenery designed by Joseph Urban. Costumes designed by Charles LeMaire. Musical director, Max Steiner. Produced by Bobby Connolly and Arthur Swanstrom. Opened 26 November 1929 at the Imperial Theatre and closed 9 August 1930 after 295 performances.

CAST: *Jimmy Canfield*: JACK DONAHUE. *Mary Harper*, his fiancée: SHIRLEY VERNON. *Hobson*, his personal valet: WILLIAM FRAWLEY. *Arthur Travers*, his friend: MILTON WATSON. *Carl Schreiber*, his enemy: Barry Walsh. *Bernice Pearce*, his "indiscretion": MARY HORAN. *General Harper*, his fiancée's father: Richard Temple. *Billswater*, his first valet: Eddie Hodge. *Parker*, his second valet: Robert Dohn. *Oswald*, his third valet: Alfred Bardelang. *Marie*, a French girl: Ann Karyle. *Jeanette*: Gwendolyn Milne. *Joan*: Marion Chambers. *Colette*: Frances Markey. *Irene*: Isobel Zehner. *Major Archibald Ponsonby-Falcke*, of the British R.F.A.: DAVID HUTCHESON. *Pierre*, a spy: Raoul de Tisne. *A British Officer*: Charles E. Bird. *A British Tommy*: Joseph Spree. *Captain, U.S.A.*: Harry Holbrook. *Bugler, U.S.A.*: Charles Dodson. *A German Prisoner*: Robert Dohn. *A German Prisoner*: Alfred Bardelang. *Yvonne*: LILY DAMITA.

Albertina Rasch Girls: Jeanette Bradley, Wilma Kaye, Josephine Wolfe, Virginia Allen, Nora Pontin, Lillian Jordan, Virginia Whitmore, Frances Wise, Ethel Greene, Ruth Hayden, June English, Evelyn Nichols. *Ladies*: Ann Constance, Nora Kildare, Millicent Bancroft, Marcella Miller, Della Harkins, Edna Bunte, Marion Santre, Sylvia Roberts, Anne Goddard, Clare Hooper, Wanda Stevenson, Billie Cortez, Muriel Hoey, Iola Sparks, Enda Burford, Mae Rena Grady, Adel Story, Gloria Clare, Adrienne Lampel, Muriel Hayman, Ruth Grady, Topsy Humphrey, Firlie Banks, Ida Berry. *Gentlemen*: Ray Stully, Ward A. Tallman, Herbert Warren, M. J. Forbes, Preston Lewis, Dan Sparks, Robert Milton, Russell Duncan, Tuxie Ondek, Wallace Banfield, Albert Henkel, Chris Gerard, Del Daven, Byron Earle, Tom Weldon, Leo Branson, Gladstone Waldrip, George Lamb, William Dunn, Frank Strang, Roy Santor, Cliff Whitcomb, Joe Carey, Ray Prescott, Roderick Murray, Paul Bristbois, Henry Mirshon, Efim Konoff, Merrill Oslin, James Garrett, Guy Daly, Robert Saidler, Stanley Howard, Fred Kruger, Russell Ash, Bill Mack, Jack Little, John M. Malone, Ben K. Leavenworth, George Rolland, Carl Rose, Richard F. Ellis, George K. Wallace, Michael Cavanaugh, Earle Sanford, Victor Young, Lawrence Waite, Jack Spiegel, John Heming, Gordon Davis.

The action takes place in 1918–1919.

Act 1, Scene 1: Jimmy Canfield's Private Golf Course at Newport, Rhode Island. *Scene 2*: A Troop Ship. *Scene 3*: Courtyard of the Inn at Pontrisson, France. *Scene 4*: A Bedroom in the Inn. *Scene 5*: The Bedroom, the next morning.

Act 2, Scene 1: The Public Room of the Inn. *Scene 2*: Guardroom. *Scene 3*: Outside of the Guardroom. *Scene 4*: A Café in Montmartre. *Scene 5*: No Man's Land. *Scene 6*: Le Arc de Triomphe. *Scene 7*: Hotel Crillon. *Scene 8*: A Room at the Hotel Crillon. *Scene 9*: Another Room. *Scene 10*: The Victory Ball.

ACT 1

  "The Younger Set" (Opening)
    American Girls

---

[51]Originally presented in New York 28 September 1891 at the Standard Theatre for 77 performances in two separate engagements. Settings uncredited. For Synopsis of Scenes, see original 1891 production. For the return engagement, changes in the principal roles were as follows: *Friar Tuck*: WILLIAM H. WHITE. *Dame Durden*: SARA CAMP.
[52]For this revival, the following songs were dropped from the original production: "Auctioneer's Song," Duet (Love, now we nevermore will part), Quintette (When life seems made of pains and pangs), Country Dance. Added for this revival were: Morris Dance, "Hey for the Merry Greenwood," "Jet Black Crow," "Dance of the Nymphs and Satyrs" (composed by Louis Kroll for this production).

[53]In original production, this song was known as "The Legend of the Chimes."

"May I Say that I Love You?"
  M. Watson, S. Vernon
"I'm That Way Over You"
  J. Donahue
"We'll Be There"
  M. Watson, Doughboys
"The Can-canola"
  Albertina Rasch Girls, French Peasants
"Why?"
  L. Damita, J. Donahue
"Cross Your Fingers"
  M. Watson, S. Vernon
"Red Hot and Blue Rhythm"
  M. Horan, American Entertainers
"Over Here"
  W. Frawley, Doughboys
"It's You I Love" ("C'est vous que j'aime")
  L. Damita
ACT 2
Opening French Officers, Girls
"Let's Merge"
  . Hutcheson, M. Horan
Reprise
  L. Damita
"Sentimental Melody"
  Albertina Rasch Girls
"There's a Rainbow on the Way"
  M. Horan, Guests
The Victory Parade
  Ensemble
A Dance
  J. Donahue
Grand Finale
  Entire Company

1929.45   FIFTY MILLION FRENCHMEN

A Musical Comedy Tour of Paris in Two Acts, a Prologue and 10 Scenes. Book by Herbert Fields. Music and lyrics by Cole Porter. Book staged by Edgar M. [Monty] Woolley. Musical numbers by Larry Ceballos. Scenery designed by Norman Bel Geddes. Costumes by Brooks Costume Company, supervised by James Reynolds. Orchestra directed by Gene Salzer. Entire production under the personal direction of E. Ray Goetz. Produced by E. Ray Goetz. Opened 27 November 1929 at the Lyric Theatre and closed 5 July 1930 after 254 performances.

CAST (in order of appearance): *Michael Cummins*: JACK THOMPSON. *Billy Baxter*: Lester Crawford. *Marcelle Fouchard*: Dorothy Day. *Louis*, a Bookmaker: Ignatio Martinetti. *Joyce Wheeler*: BETTY COMPTON. *Emmitt Carroll*, of Terre Haute, Indiana: Thurston Hall. *Gladys Carroll*, His Wife: Bernice Mershon. *Peter Forbes*, of "The Street": WILLIAM GAXTON. *Looloo Carroll*: GENEVIEVE TOBIN. *Sylvia*, a Tourist: Fifi Laimbeer. *May De Vere*, a Cabaret Artist: EVELYN HOOEY. *Mrs. De Vere*, Her 'Ma': Gertrude Mudge. *Mr. Ira Rosen*, of Battle Creek, Michigan: Robert Leonard. *Mrs. Rosen*: Annette Hoffman. *Junior*, Their Son: Larry Jason. *Violet Hildegarde*: HELEN BRODERICK. *Boule de Neige*, Oscar, a Stable Boy: LOU DUTHERS. *Monsieur Pernasse*, Manager at the Claridge: Mario Villani. *Le Sahib Roussin*, a Fakir: Jean Del Val. *The Grand Duke Ivan Ivanovitch of Russia*: Manart Kippen. *Joe Zelli*: Jean Del Val. *Maitre d'Hotel at the Chateau Madrid*: Oscar Magis. (*Specialty*: California Collegians.)

Ceballos' Hollywood Dancers: Doris Toddings, Billie Cline, Lu Ann Meredith, Peggee Standlee, Blanche Poston, Helen Splane, Lucille Lester, Julia Blake, Melva Cornell, Josephine Barnhardt, Valeda Duncan, Marie Valli, Billie Smith, Teddy Lura, Adelaide Kaye, Marusa Roberti, Frankie Silvers, Frances Grant, Lorraine Platt, Helen Fairweather, Eileen Gorlet, Sue Rainey, Grace Davies, Betty Bowen. *Dancing Girls*: Anna (May) Rex, Marion Thompson, Mildred Espy, Patsy O'Keefe, Jeanette Marion, Pansy Maness, Pearl Shepard, Nancy Dolan, Florine Meyers, Mary Dunckley. *Showgirls*: Tanya Dumova, Theresa Donahue, Edna Storey, Marie Sorel, Marjorie Phillips, Marjorie Arnold, Meta Klinke, Josephine Carroll, Betty Knight, Ethel Odell, Carol Kingsbury. *French Singers*: Belle Olska, Charlotte Geraud, Marguerite Denys, Nanette Deaustro, Frances Newbaker, Catherine Palmer. *Dancing Boys*: Ernest Rayburn, Bob Gordon, Jack Tucker, Bill Douglas, Sid Salzer, Jack Bauer, Billy O'Rourke, Nor Norcross, Henry Ladd, William Broder, Charles Conkling, Beau Tilden, Bob Morgan, Regis Geary, Jack Barrett, Jack Fraley. *Singing Boys*: Frank Bochetta, William [Billy] Culloo, Sam Suchman, David Tulin, Syuleen Krasnoff, John Matsin, George O'Brien, Arthur Ver Bownes.

The action takes place this summer.
Prologue: The Foyer, Cocktail Room and Bar at the Ritz, Paris. 4 June.
Act 1, Scene 1: The American Express Company, Rue Scribe. *Scene 2*: A Bookstall on the Left Bank. *Scene 3*: The Café de la Paix, Place de L'Opera. *Scene 4*: On the Boulevard. *Scene 5*: The Racetrack at Longchamps.
Act 2, Scene 1: The Lounge of the Hotel Claridge. *Scene 2*: The Corridor at the Claridge. *Scene 3*: Zelli's. *Scene 4*: Les Halles. *Scene 5*: The Chateau Madrid. 4 July.
ACT 1[54]
"A Toast to Volstead"[55] (Opening)
  California Collegians, Men's Ensemble
"You Do Something to Me"
  W. Gaxton, G. Tobin
"The American Express"
  Ensemble
"You've Got That Thing"
  J. Thompson, B. Compton
"Find Me a Primitive Man"
  E. Hoey, B. Reed, L. Duthers, Ensemble
"Where Would You Get Your Coat?"
  H. Broderick
"Do You Want to See Paris?"
  W. Gaxton, California Collegians, Tourists
"At Longchamps Today"
  Ensemble
("Yankee Doodle")
  (Ensemble)
"The (Happy) Heaven of Harlem"
  B. Reed, L. Duthers, Chorus
"Why Shouldn't I Have You?"
  B. Compton, J. Thompson, Chorus
Finale
  G. Tobin, W. Gaxton
ACT 2
("Somebody's Going to Throw a Big Party")
  (Ensemble)
"It Isn't Done"
  Ensemble
"I'm in Love"
  G. Tobin, Ensemble, F. Graham, Ceballos' Hollywood Dancers
"The Tale of an Oyster"[56]
  H. Broderick
Specialty W. Gaxton, California Collegians
"Paree, What Did You Do to Me?" B. Compton, J. Thompson
"You Don't Know Paree"
  W. Gaxton
"I'm Unlucky at Gambling"
  E. Hoey, Ceballos' Hollywood Dancers

1929.46   THE SILVER SWAN

A Viennese Musical Romance in Two Acts, 3 Scenes. Book by William S. Brady and Alonzo Price. Music by H. Maurice Jacquet. Lyrics by William S. Brady. Staged by Alonzo Price. Dances and ensembles staged by Leroy J. Prinz. Settings designed by Ward and Harvey Studios, Inc. Costumes designed by William H. Matthews, John Booth. Orchestra under the direction of Augustus Barratt. Produced by Herman Gantvoort. Opened 27 November 1929 at the Martin Beck Theatre and closed 14 December 1929 after 21 performances.

CAST (in order of speaking): *Lieutenant Berthold*: Robert Roltner. *Adolf*: David D. Morris. *Lieutenant Walther*: Alexander Leftwich, Jr. *Lieutenant Erich*: Walter Munroe.

_____

[54] Added to Act 2 during the run:
  "The Boy Friend Back Home" (before "The Tale of an Oyster")
    E. Hoey
Which was later replaced by:
  "Stepping Out" (Let's Step Out)
    E. Hoey, B. Compton, B. Reed, L. Duthers
[55] Dropped after opening.
[56] Dropped one month after opening.

Seppel: Harry Miller. *Denise*: LAINE BLAIRE. *Hortense Zorma*: ALICE MACKENZIE. *Gurlitt*: Robert G. Pitkin. *Alexandrine*: Ninon Bunyea. *Captain Richard Von Orten*: EDWARD NELL, JR. *Tiger*: Paul Joyce. *Princess Von Auen*: LINA ABARBANELL. *Gabrielle*: VIVIAN HART. *General von Auen*: FLORENZ AMES. *Marie*: Lucille Constant. *Theresa*: Jill Northrup. *Lieutenant Karl*: William Dillon. *The Dancers*: Fawn and Jordon.

Singers of the Gurlitt Opera Company: Azita Cortez, Dorothy Coulter, Constance Durand, Marie Endicott, Margaret Grove, Edith Gwen, Mildred Harrington, Mary Hennessy, Irene Lee, Phyllis Lee, Beatrice Marsh, Jean Mawar, Mildred Newman, Marvel Ober, Elsa Paul, Peggy O'Riley, Grace Starr, Elizabeth Thomas. *Dancers of the Gurlitt Opera Company*: Lucille Constant, Marcia de Baum, Gene Fontaine, Arlene Holmes, Gwendolyne MacMurray, Jill Northup, Florentine Sherman, Virginia Toland. *Officers of the Emperor's Guard*: George Ammonn, Leslie Coullard, Antonia Diaz, Thomas Follis, Walter Higgins, Eugene Hoffman, Luther G. Hoobyar, William H. Jenkins, Nicholas Krasink, August Loring, Antonio Mali, Leon Mandas, Walter E. Munroe, Hawkins Nelson, Irving Parker, Charles Shumaker, Ottanio Valentino, Patrick Walters.

Act 1: The Garden of The Silver Swan. An Afternoon in September.

Act 2, Scene 1: A Room in The Silver Swan. A week later. *Scene 2*: The Same. After the performance. (During Act 2, curtain will be lowered to denote the passing of six hours.)

ACT 1

"The Only Game I Would Play"
  R. Roltner, Officers, Girls

"Á La Viennese"
  A. Mackenzie, R. G. Pitkin, Ensemble

"I Like the Military Man"
  L. Blaire, H. Miller

"Trial Song"
  V. Hart, Ensemble

"The Brave Deserve the Fair"
  F. Ames, Girls

"Till I Met You"
  V. Hart, E. Nell, Jr.

Finale

ACT 2

Scene 1

"Graceful and Fair"
  Girls, Ballet

Ballet

Polka
  Fawn and Jordon

"Cigarette"
  E. Nell, Jr., Officers

Till I Met You" (reprise)
  Ensemble

"Love Letters"
  A. Mackenzie, F. Ames

"Shoe-Clap-Platter"
  L. Blaire, H. Miller

"I Love You"
  V. Hart, E. Nell, Jr.

Finaletto

Scene 2

"Serenade" (Chorus a Cappela)
  Officers, Ladies

Divertissement
  Fawn and Jardon

"Till I Met You" (reprise)
  V. Hart

"Merry-Go-Round"
  A. Mackenzie, Ensemble

Finale

1929.47   THE MERRY WIDOW

A Revival of the Operetta in Three Acts[57]. (Original Viennese) Book ("Die Lustige Witwe") by Victor Léon and Leo Stein after "L'Attaché d'Ambas-

sade" by Henri Meilhac. Music by Franz Lehár. Staged by Milton Aborn. Costumes by Brooks. Music director, Louis Kroll. Revived by the Jolson's Theatre Musical Comedy Company (Messrs. Shubert, Milton Aborn). Opened 2 December 1929 at Jolson's Theatre and closed 14 December 1929 after 16 performances.

CAST: *Sonia*, a young widow: BEPPIE DE VRIES. *Vicomte Camille de Jolidon*: ROY CROPPER. *Marquis de Cascada*: Francesco Yanelli. *M. de St. Brioche*: Donald Catlin. *General Novakovich*, Military Attaché: William H. White. *M. Khadja*, Counselor of Legation: Clarence Harvey. *Nisch*, Messenger to the Legation: W. J. McCarthy. *Prince Danilo*, Secretary of Legation: EVAN THOMAS. *Baron Popoff*, Marsovian Ambassador: RICHARD POWELL. *Natalie*, his wife: Mary Patterson. *Olga*, wife of Novakovich: Dene Dickens.

Girls at Maxim's: *Lo-Lo*: Wee Griffin. *Fi-Fi*: Lisette Braddock. *Do-Do*: Amy Alexander. *Zo-Zo*: Ethel Lynne. *Jou-Jou*: Frances Baviello. *Frou-Frou*: Eleanor Gilmore. *Clo-Clo*: Helen Etheridge. *Margot*: Mary Thurman.*Willie*: Bernie Sager. *Head Waiter*: Leslie McLeod. *Ladies of the Ensemble*: Wee Griffin, Lisette Braddock, Mary Thurman, Ethel Lynne, Helen Rae, Frances Baviello, Eleanor Gilmore, Adele Savage, Nell McCormick, Florence Lamorer'e, Elizabeth Flannigan, Sally Galbreaith, Lillian Wallace, Evelyn Brown, Frances Moore, Dorothy Wadleigh, Helen Etheridge, Catherine Kent. *Gentlemen of the Ensemble*: William Burbank, Louis Diamond, George Koenig, Harry Knabenshue, Bernie Sager, Bronek Wroblewski, George Plummer, Jack Willard, Daniel Medwin, Alfred Deste.

1929.48   BABES IN TOYLAND

A Revival of the Musical Comedy in Three Acts, a Prologue and 9 Scenes[58]. Libretto by Glen MacDonough. Music by Victor Herbert. Staged by Milton Aborn. Ballet by Virginie Mauret. Settings by Rollo Wayne. Costumes by Tams. Musical director, Louis Kroll. Produced by the Jolson's Musical Theatre Company (Messrs. Shubert, Milton Aborn). Opened 23 December 1929 at Jolson's Theatre and closed 11 January 1930 after 32 performances.

CAST (in order of appearance): *Uncle Barnaby*, a rich miser in love with Contrary Mary: WILLIAM BALFOUR. *Frances*: Frances Moore. *Adele*: Adele Savoye. *Tom Tom*, eldest son of the Widow Piper: MARCELLA SWANSON. *Hilda*, maid of all work in the Piper household: Mona Moray. *Gonzorgo*, a hard-hearted ruffian: BARRY LUPINO. *Roderigo*, his sentimental partner: RUPERT DARRELL. *The Widow Piper*, a lonely widow with 14 children: JAYNE WATEROUS. *Bo Peep*, who is a careless shepherd: Margaret Byers. *Jill*, who does chores: Helene Rae. *Bobby Shaftoe*, who wants to be a sailor: Barry Lupino, Jr. *Jack*, who helps Jill: Mary Thurman. *Sallie Waters*, who wants to get married: Eleanor Gilmore. *Curly Locks*, who wants to wed a title: Martha Gale. *Tommy Tucker*, who sings for his supper and everything else: Evelyn Brown. *Simple Simon*, who is fond of fairs: Frances Baviello. *Little Red Riding Hood*, who is devoted to her grandmother: Ethel Lynne. *Miss Muffett*, who is afraid of spiders: Helen Etheridge. *Boy Blue*, who wants to be a farmer: Dene Dickens. *Jane*, niece of Barnaby: BETTY BYRON. *Alan*, nephew of Barnaby: FRANK GALLAGHER. *First Dandy*: Frank (Francesco) Yanelli. *Second Dandy*: Don Catlin. *Contrary Mary*, the Widow Piper's eldest daughter: LEOTABEL LANE. *Inspector Marmaduke*, of the Toyland Police: W. J. McCARTHY. *Master Toymaker*, who designs the toys of the world: DEAN RAYMOND. *Grumio*, apprentice at the Master Toymaker's workshop: CHESTER HERMAN. *Max*: Frank Yanelli. *The Brown Bear*: Bernie Sager. *The Baby Bear*: Barry Lupino, Jr. *The Giant Spider*: JOSEPH SCHRODE. *A Fairy*: Dene Dickens. *Santa Claus*: Louis Diamond.

Toyland Midgets: The Hoy Sisters (Helen, Elizabeth, Marguerite), Prince Ludwig, Adolf Piccolo, Addie Frank, Freddie Goodrow, Thomas Keenan. *Toyland Tots*: June Meier, Anita Stewart, Anna Marie Fink, Shirley Gordon, Alice Farley, Barry Lupino, Jr., Toni Lupino, Doreen McShane. *Girls of the Ensemble*: Wee Griffin, Mary Thurman, Ethel Lynne, Helene Rae, Frances Baviello, Eleanor Gilmore, Adele Savoye, Nell McCormack, Florence Lamorer'e, Elizabeth Flanigan, Sally Galbreaith, Lillian Wallace, Evelyn Brown, Frances Moore, Dorothy Wadleigh, Helen Etheridge, Dene Dickens, Martha Gale, Valema Lois Sutton, Nettie Smith, Martha Joiner, Maxine Inman, Thelma Goodwyn, Anne Balthy, Beth Renard, Catherine Cale, Adele Lacey, Ada Lubin, Clarice Carr. *Boys of the Ensemble*: William Burbank, Louis Diamond, George Koenig, Harry Knabenshue, Bernie Sager, Bronek Wrobleski, George Plummer, Jack Willard, Daniel Meduri, Alfred Deste, Frank Yanelli, Don Catlin. *Virginie Mauret Ballet*: Helen Selva, Judith Gorney, Mildred Reeves, Sally Merrill, Mildred Harris, Anna Fair, Betty Knox, Betty Howson, Sunny Risk, Thaisa Gotkova, Shura Dante, Catherine LuEyles.

Prologue: Electrical storm at sea and wreck of the "Galleon."

---

[57]Originally presented in New York 21 October 1907 at the New Amsterdam Theatre for 416 performances. For Synopsis of Scenes and Musical Numbers, see original 1907 production. English libretto uncredited. Settings uncredited.

[58]First presented in New York 13 October 1903 at the Majestic Theatre for 192 performances. This revival eliminated Prologue, Scene 1; and Act 1, Scene 4; and restructured Act 3 into 3 scenes. Dropped from the original production were: "The Legend of the Castle," "My Rag Doll Girl," "An Old-Fashioned Rose," "Jane," "Maybe the Moon Will Help You Out." Added for this revival were: "Beatrice Barefacts," "The Jolly Tars," "Doll Dance." Played a holiday schedule with additional matinees.

Act 1, Scene 1: Country fête in Contrary Mary's garden. *Scene 2*: Garden wall back of the garden. *Scene 3*: The Spider's Forest.

Act 2, Scene 1: The Christmas Tree Grove in Toyland. *Scene 2*: A Street in Toyland. *Scene 3*: March of the Toys.

Act 3, Scene 1: The Master Toymaker's Workshop. *Scene 2*: A Street in Toyland. *Scene 3*: The Temple of the Toyland Palace of Justice.

ACT 1

Prologue; Country Fête

"Never Mind, Bo-Peep, We Will Find Your Sheep"
M. Byers, M. Swanson, J. Waterous, Widow Piper's Children

"Floretta"
F. Gallagher, Ensemble

"Mary Mary" (Entrance of Contrary Mary)
Ensemble

"Barney O'Flynn"
L. Lane, Ensemble

"I Can't Do That Sum"
B. Byron, J. Meier, J. Waterous

In the Forest

"Go to Sleep, Slumber Deep"
B. Byron, F. Gallagher, D. Dickens, Ensemble

The Spider's Den

"The Birth of the Butterfly" (Finale)
Virginie Mauret Ballet

ACT 2

"Hail to Christmas"[59] (Opening Chorus)
Ensemble

"Song of the Poet" (Rock-a-Bye Baby)
F. Gallagher, Ensemble

"Beatrice Barefacts" (from IT HAPPENED IN NORDLAND)
L. Lane, W. J. McCarthy

"March of the Toys"

"The Jolly Tars"
B. Lupino, R. Darrell

In the Toymakers Workshop

"Toyland"
M. Swanson, Male Ensemble

Doll Dance
B. Lupino, C. Herman

Finale

ACT 3

"Before and After"
L. Lane, F. Gallagher

Dance
M. Moray, C. Herman

Finale
Ensemble

1929.49 TOP SPEED

A Musical Comedy in Two Acts, 7 Scenes. Book, music and lyrics by Guy Bolton, Bert Kalmar and Harry Ruby[60]. Book staged by John Harwood. (Musical) Numbers staged by John Boyle, LeRoy Prinz. Scenery designed by Raymond J. Sovey. Costumes designed by Kiviette. Orchestra under the direction of Ivan Rudisill. Produced by Bolton, Kalmar & Ruby, Ltd. Opened 25 December 1929 at the 46th Street Theatre, moved 10 March 1930 to the Royale Theatre, and closed 22 March 1930 after 104 performances.

CAST in order of appearance): *Tad Jordan*, of Jordan's Hot Water Bottles: Harland Dixon. *Daisy Parker*, Social Directress of Onawanda Lodge: Sunny Dale. *Bellows*, a Servant of the Lodge: Lloyd Pedrick. *Of the Great Army of Workers (2)*: Elmer Peters: LESTER ALLEN. *Gerry Brooks*: PAUL FRAWLEY. *Molly*, a Guest at the Lodge: Elaine Blaire. *Pete Schoonmaker*, Sheriff and Game Warden: Lon Hascall. *Virginia*

Rollins: IRENE DELROY. *Babs Green*, a Young Millionairess: GINGER ROGERS. *Chauffeur*: Ken Williams. *Shirley*, a Flapper: Shirley Richards. *Mr. Rollins*, Virginia's Father: Theodore Babcock. *Vincent Colgate*, in love with Virginia: Sam Critcherson. *Spencer Colgate*, Vincent's Uncle: John T. Dwyer. *Waiter at the Yacht Club*: George del Drigo. *Souvenir Storekeeper*: William Hale.

Showgirls: Frances Thress, Hilda Knight, Lorraine Power, Ray Apgar. *Special Dancing Girls*: Marie Keve, Martha Carroll, Nondas Wayne, Mildred Franke, Paula Sands, Olga Fox, Beth Meredith, Charlotte Silton. *Dancing Girls*: Billie Blake, Elinor Walent, Mildred Hosee, Dodo Wyatt, Helen Rauth, Peggy Driscoll, Irene Carroll, Adele Dickson, Louise Francis, Valerie Dolaro, Carolyn James, Flo Allen, Enes Early, Mildred Rye, Dixie Lester, Norine Bogan, Kay Reilly. *Male Chorus*: Kendall Northrop, Daniel Wyler, Jerry Kirkland, Arthur May, Fred Furman, Willis Lawrence, George del Drigo, Hermes Pan. *Eight Top Speed Boys*: Hal Morton, Ken Williams, Irving Lesser, Tom Barrett, Alan DeSylva, Gene Johnson, John Quinn, George King.

Act 1, Scene 1: The Terrace of the Onawanda Lodge, after dinner. *Scene 2*: A Bench near the Lodge at Dawn. *Scene 3*: The Main Lounge, Onawanda Lodge.

Act 2, Scene 1: The Border Line Yacht Club. *Scene 2*: In the Woods. *Scene 3*: A Bedroom in Onawanda Lodge. *Scene 4*: The Regatta Ball.

ACT 1

Opening: "In the Summer"
Ensemble

"The Papers"
H. Dixon, Ensemble

"Try Dancing"
H. Dixon, S. Dale, Ensemble

"I'd Like to Be Liked"
I. Delroy, P. Frawley

"Keep Your Undershirt On"
L. Allen, G. Rogers, Ensemble

"We Want You"
I. Delroy, Boys

"What Would I Care"
I. Delroy, P. Frawley, Girls

"Dizzy Feet"
H. Dixon, Ensemble

Finale

ACT 2[61]

"On the Border Line" (Opening)
State Troopers, Girls

"Hot and Bothered" (Trio)
G. Rogers, Ensemble

"Sweeter Than You"
I. Delroy, P. Frawley

"You Couldn't Blame Me for That"
L. Allen, G. Rogers

Finaletto

"Fireworks"
H. Dixon, E. Blaire, Ensemble

Finale

1929.50 WOOF, WOOF

A Romantic Musical Comedy in Two Acts, 9 Scenes. Book by Estelle Hunt, Sam Summers, Cyrus Wood. Additional dialogue by Eugene Conrad. Music by Edward Pola. Lyrics by Eddie Brandt. Play directed and staged by William Caryl. Musical numbers staged by Dan Healy. Ballet of Dreams, Act 1, staged by Leonide Massine. Settings designed by Clark Robinson. Costumes designed by Mabel Johnson. Orchestra under the direction of Ernest Cutting. Music on stage by the Hollywood Collegians. Musical arrangements by Ken Macomber. Produced by Demarest & Lohmuller, Inc. (William Demarest, Bernard Lohmuller). Opened 25 December 1929 at the Royale Theater and closed 1 February 1930 after 46 performances.

CAST (in order of appearance): *Stage Manager*: William Plunkett. *Babe Birdy*: HELEN GOODHUE. *Monte Fleming*: AL SEXTON. *Tommy Clair*: JACK SQUIRES. *Elmer Green*: "SUNKIST" EDDIE NELSON. *Chosty*: OLIVE FAY. *Susie Yates*: LOUISE BROWN. *Henry*: George Haggerty. *Mrs. Clair*: MADELINE GREY.

---

[59]Titled "Christmas Fair Waltz" in the original 1903, presumably the same song.
[60]Contrary to the collaborative program credit, Bolton is usually regarded as the librettist, Harry Ruby the composer, and Bert Kalmar the lyricist. Kalmar and Ruby undoubtedly helped with the book.

[61]Added during the run (after Act 2 Opening):
Dance Specialty
S. Richards

Colonel Penny: Louis Casavant. *Virginia Lee Penny*: GLADYCE DEERING. *Harv McDaniel*: ANDREW MACK. *Al Stafford*: Edwin Walter. *Sugar Betty Ann*: Martha Copeland. *Dude*: Arthur Bryson. *Sluefoot*: U. S. Thompson. *Soapy Blake*: John Kennedy. (*Dance Specialty*: Wesley Pierce, Hazel Harris.)

Hollywood Collegians: "Cal" Earl, "Slim" Gorstenkorn, "Ken" Howell, "Bud" Carlton, "Hal" Gustafson, "Bill" Griffin, "Russ" Erickson. (*Specialty*: Billy and Elsie Newell.) *Girls*: Rosalind Schneider, Kathelene Reichner, Teddy Dauer, Alyce Swanson, Elinore Whitney, Pauline Nesson, Ida Walker, Gertrude Byrnell, Dolores Nadine, Virginia Welch, Carol Renwick, Ida Michael, Dorothy Leslie, Nondas North, Evelyn Anderson, Alice Laurie, Jae Voll, Viola Hart, Peggy Timmons, Roslyn Smith, Betty Wright, Mickey MacKillop, Agnes Young, Dorothea Frank, Dorothy Morgan. *Dancing Show Girls*: Evan Southwell, Helen Koster, Dorothy Koster, Elizabeth Janeway, Dolores Lavin, Norma Maxine. *Boys*: Jack Waldron, Bob Long, Eddie Clifford, Phil Shaw, Jack Star, George Ford, Al Dillon, Bob Easton, Sam Weiser, Eddie Judge, Fred Nay, Alvin Ray.

Act 1: New York and New Jersey in the Summer. *Scene 1*: Back Stage. In the Wings. *Scene 2*: Dressing Room Corridor after performance. *Scene 3*: Tommy Clair's Home in New Jersey. The following day. *Scene 4*: Tree Top Inn. Evening.

Act 2: In and Near Mobile, Alabama. *Scene 1*: Auto Camp on the Outskirts of Mobile. Evening. *Scene 2*: Corridor of a Hotel in Mobile. The following day. *Scene 3*: The Training Camp near Mobile. The same day. *Scene 4*: Pari Mutuel Betting Booths at the Track in Mobile. Several weeks later. *Scene 5*: On the Course. The Home Stretch!

ACT 1

Opening Chorus
Girls

"I Like It"
O. Fay, Girls

"I'll Take Care of You"
L. Brown, A. Sexton

"That Certain Thing"
G. Deering, J. Squires

"I Mean What I Say"
L. Brown, A. Sexton

Dance
Show Girls

"Tree Top Toddle"[62]
Ensemble of Girls

"You're All the World to Me"
G. Deering, J. Squires

Dance
W. Pierce, H. Harris

"Satanic Strut"
O. Fay, Little Devils

"Trip Around the World"
Hollywood Collegians

"A Girl Like You"
L. Brown, Boys

Finale

ACT 2

"Fair Weather"
Ensemble

Specialties
Show Girls

Specialty O. Fay, E. Nelson

"Shh!"
Bell Hops, Phone Girls (Ensemble)

Dance
U. S. Thompson, A. Bryson

"Topple Down"
O. Fay, Ensemble

"Won't I Do"
A. Sexton, L. Brown, Ensemble

Ballet of Dreams
L. Brown, Girls

"Lay Your Bets"
Girls, Boys

Finale

[62]Program note: Rehearsal for Tree Top Inn and Interpolated Number in Tree Top Inn enacted by Billy and Elsie Newell.

1929.51

WAKE UP AND DREAM

A Musical Revue in Two Acts, 26 Scenes. Book (sketches) by John Hastings Turner. Music and lyrics by Cole Porter. Staged by Frank Collins. Dances and ensembles by Tilly Losch, Jack Buchanan, Max Rivers. Costumes designed by Oliver Messel, Ada Peacock, Idare et Cie., Norman Wilkinson. Settings designed by Oliver Messel, Paul Colin, Marc Henri and Laverdet, Norman Wilkinson, Rex Whistler, Doris Zinkeisen. Orchestra under the direction of Charles Prentice. Produced by Arch Selwyn under the personal direction of C. B. Cochran. Opened 30 December 1929 at the Selwyn Theatre and closed 26 April 1930 after 136 performances.

CAST: JACK BUCHANAN, JESSIE MATTHEWS, TILLY LOSCH, TONI BIRKMAYER, TINA MELLER, DAVE FITZGIBBON, WILLIAM STEPHENS, JEAN BARRY, LANCE LISTER, MARJORIE BROOKS, WYN CLAIRE, FRANCES SHELLEY, A. B. IMESON, GRETA WOOD, DOUGLAS PHILLIPS, THE GOMEZ TRIO (Antonio, Esperanza, Luis), MARY TOMLINSON, THE PAVILION QUARTETTE, ANTONIO RODRIGUEZ, THE GRIFFITHS BROTHERS, MISS LUTIE, Claude Newman, Ann Barberova, Roy Mitchell, William Tinkler, William Rolston.

Ladies Of the Ensemble: Marjorie Robertson, Eve Shotter, Florita Fey, Margaret Braithwaite, Sheila Watson, Maisie Green, Marion Morgan, Peggy de Reske, Pearl Rivers, Marie Masters, Mina Hillman, Glenore Pointing, Roma Darrell, Lalla Collins, Gloria Beaumont, Bunty Pain, Eileen Clifton, Marion Cripps. *Gentlemen Of the Ensemble*: Ronald Dalmayne, H. E. Ferguson, Victor Etheridge, Robert Lindsay, Eddie Orpwood, Albert Lorimore.

ACT 1[63]

Scene 1

The Wrong Room in the Wrong House
The Man of Money: W. Stephens. *His Wife*: G. Wood. *His Sense of Humour*: L. Lister. *The Spirit of All Good Things*: J. Matthews.
(*Scenery and Costumes designed by* Oliver Messel.)

Scene 2

"Wake Up and Dream"
J. Matthews
(*Scenery and Costumes designed by* Oliver Messel.)

Scene 3

The Dream (*Ballet Choreography by* Tilly Losch. *Scenery and Costumes designed by* Oliver Messel.)
The Blue Bird's Attendants: M. Robertson, E. Shotter, F. Fey, M. Braithwaite, S. Watson, M. Green, M. Morgan, P. de Reske. *The Spirit of Magic*: T. Birkmayer. *Columbine*: P. Rivers. *Egyptian*: M. Masters. *Venus*: B. Pain. *Goblins*: R. Dalmayne, W. Tinkler. *The Dancers*: J. Barry, D. Fitzgibbon. *The Eighteenth Century Lady*: M. Brooks. *Niggers*: R. Mitchell, H. E. Ferguson. *Mediæval Page*: A. Barberova. *Earl of Essex*: V. Etheridge. *Queen Elizabeth*: E. Clifton. *Pelias*: R. Lindsay. *Melisande*: M. Cripps. *Love*: M. Hillman. *Music*: G. Pointing. *Art*: E. Orpwood. *Poetry*: W. Rolston. *Carmen*: T. Meller. *Spanish Gypsies*: Gomez Trio. *Lady of the Moon*: R. Darrell. *Marionette Boy*: C. Newman. *Marionette Girl*: L. Collins. *The Blue Bird*: T. Losch.

Scene 4

"More Incredible Happenings"
J. Buchanan, Company
(*Music and Lyrics by* Ronald Jeans.)

Scene 5

"I Loved Him (but He Didn't Love Me)"[64]
J. Matthews

Scene 6

"Coppelia"[65] (Ballet) (*Music by* Léo Delibes.)
Scene: At the Empire (Theatre), Leicester Square, London, 1910.

[63]The song order was revised during the run, and songs reassigned. Added after opening:
"(I Dream of) A Girl in a Shawl" (*Dance arranged by* Tilly Losch.) (Act 2)
(W. Stephens)
A Coolie: W. Stephens. *A Manchu Marchioness*: T. Losch.
(*Scene and Costumes designed by* Oliver Messel.)
The Audition (*by* Mindret Lord) (Act 2)
Sam Sheridan: J. Buchanan. *His Secretary*: L. Collins. *Miss De Vere*: W. Clare. *The Tumbling Ginsbergs*: L. Lister, C. Newman. *Mrs. Sherman*: M. Brooks.
"Looking at You" (Act 2)
J. Matthews, D. Fitzgibbon, Mr. Cochran's Young Ladies
(*Jessie Matthews' and Mr. Cochran's Young Ladies' Costumes by* Idare et Cie.)
[64]Dropped immediately after the opening.
[65]Dropped immediately after the opening.

(a) Outside the Empire Theatre.
Sign-Bearer: M. Brooks.
(b) Overture
The Flunkeys: R. Mitchell, H. E. Ferguson.
(c) The Ballet from the Wings (*Choreography by* Tilly Losch.)
Coppelius, a toy maker: C. Newman. *Swanhilda*, The Doll: T. Losch. *Franz*, her lover: T. Birkmayer. *Her Friends*: B. Pain, M. Robertson, F. Fey, R. Darrell, M. Braithwaite, P. Rivers. *Peasants*: R. Lindsay, W. Tinkler, W. Rolston, V. Etheridge, M. Masters, M. Green, P. deReske, M. Cripps. *An Undressed Doll*: M. Morgan. *A Toy Soldier*: R. Dalmayne. A *Chinaman*: E. Orpwood. *A Marionette*: A. Lorimore. *The Manager of the Empire*: A. B. Imeson. *A Patron of the Empire*: D. Philips.
(*Scenery designed by* Marc Henri and Laverdet, C. R. W. Nevinson. *Costumes by* Doris Zinkeison, ballet costumes after original designs for 1910 production.)

Scene 7

"Operatic Pills"

(J. Buchanan, Ensemble)
Sir Thomas Beecham: J. Buchanan. *The Barber of Seville*: A. B. Imeson. *Louise*: M. Hillman. *The Toreador*: D. Phillips. *Madame Butterfly*: W. Clare. *Elsa*: M. Brooks. *Lohengrin*: H. E. Ferguson.
(*Scene designed by* Rex Whistler.) Note: Sir Thomas Beecham is at present fighting an intensive battle for Grand Opera in England. His father, Sir Joseph Beecham, was, too, the father of the world-famous pills. Musically, therefore, and medicinally, their countrymen are greatly in their debt.

Scene 8

"Why Wouldn't I Do?"[66]

J. Matthews, T. Birkmayer, Mr. Cochran's Young Ladies
(*Music and Lyrics by* Desmond Carter and Ivor Novello. *Costumes by* Idare et Cie.)

Scene 9

The Griffiths Brothers and Miss Lutie Present Their Famous Performing Horse, "Pogo."

Scene 10

The Decline of Sin
a. *The Lover*: J. Buchanan. *His Friend*: L. Lister.
b. *The Lady*: J. Matthews. *The Lover*: J. Buchanan. *The Husband*: D. Phillips.
(*Scene designed by* Marc Henri and Laverdet. *Jessie Mathews' Dress by* Idare et Cie.)

Scene 11

Arabesque (Dance of the Hands)
T. Losch
(*Music by* Maurice Ravel, from "Ma mere l'oye.")

Scene 12

"She's Such a Comfort to Me"
J. Buchanan
(*Music by* Arthur Schwartz. *Lyrics by* Douglas Furber, Donovan Parsons.)

Scene 13

Adapted from the French (*by* Douglas Furber)
a. English version
Henrietta, the maid: W. Clare. *Charles*: L. Lister. *Mary*, his wife: M. Brooks. *Henry*, their son: J. Buchanan.
b. French version
Henriette, the maid: W. Clare. *Charles*: L. Lister. *Marie*, his wife: M. Brooks. *Henri*, their son: J. Buchanan.

Scene 14

"The Banjo That Man Joe Plays"
W. Stephens
Dance of the Crinoline Ladies (*Arranged by* Tilly Losch.)
T. Losch
Scene: San Francisco, The Gold Rush, 1849.
Crinoline Ladies: A. Barberova, B. Pain, P. Rivers, M. Hillman, E. Shotter, G. Beaumont, M. Green, E. Clifton.
Flirtation Dance
T. Losch, T. Birkmayer
A Flower Girl: S. Watson. *Ladies of the Town*: G. Wood, W. Clare, F. Shelley. *Gentleman of the Town*: A. Lorimore.
Old Fashioned Buck and Wing Dance
J. Matthews
Ragamuffins: M. Masters, F. Fey, R., Darrell, M. Braithwaite, M Morgan, G. Pointing, M. Cripps, M. Robertson. *Two Gamblers*: W. Rolston, H. E. Ferguson. *A Dance Hall Girl*: L. Collins. *A Waitress*: P. de Reske.

"Entrance of Emigrants"
(Ensemble)
Emigrants: A. Barberova, B. Pain, P. Rivers, M. Hillman, E. Shotter, G. Beaumont, M. Green, E. Clifton, R. Lindsay, C. Newman, V. Etheridge, R. Mitchell, W. Tinkler.
Dance: "Farruca" (Traditional Spanish Air)
T. Meller
Guitarist: A. Rodriguez.
Dances: "Saragossa Jota"
Gomez Trio
Finale (*Arranged by* Tilly Losch.)
Entire Company
Banjoists: Pavilion Quartette.
(*Scene designed by* Marc Henri and Laverdet. *Costumes designed by* Ada Peacock.)

ACT 2

Scene 1

Opening
a. Mr. Cochran's Young Ladies (*Arranged by* Max Rivers.)
b. Tango "Negresco" (*by* Orlando)J. Barry, D. Fitzgibbon
(*Costumes designed by* Ada Peacock.)

Scene 2

Bed-Time Stories
Announcer: J. Buchanan.
a. 1740
The Husband: L. Lister. *His Friends*: W. Stephens, A. B. Imeson. *His Wife*: M. Brooks. A *Gentleman in an Unfortunate Position*: W. Tinkler. "1930" *Girls*: M. Robertson, E. Clifton, B. Pain, G. Pointing. *The Girl*: J. Matthews. *The Man*: J. Buchanan.
(*Costumes and Decor designed by* Norman Wilkinson. "1930" *Girls' Costumes designed by* Ada Peacock.)

Scene 3

"What Is This Thing Called Love?"
F. Shelley
(*Dance arranged by* Tilly Losch.)
The Statue: T. Birkmayer. *The Girl*: T. Losch.
(*Costumes and Setting by* Oliver Messel.)

Scene 4

The Big Brother (*by* Douglas Furber)
Jim: W. Stephens. *The Butler*: R. Mitchell. *Dick*: J. Buchanan. *Fifi DuBarri*: J. Matthews.
"Fancy Our Meeting" (Duet)
J. Matthews, J. Buchanan
(*Music by* Joseph Meyer and Philip Charig. *Lyrics by* Douglas Furber.)

Scene 5

"Gothic"[67] (*Dance created by* Tilly Losch)
T. Losch, A. Barberova
(*Music by* Johan Sebastian Bach. *Scene and Costumes designed by* Oliver Messel.)
Violin soloist: Alcot Vail.

Scene 6

"An Old English Folk Song"[68]
J. Buchanan, M. Tomlinson, W. Stephens
(*Music and Lyrics by* Douglas Furber, Jack Buchanan and Charles Prentice.)

Scene 7

Dance: "Romba" ("Ay Mama Tuey" *by* Elisco Grenet.)
T. Meller
Scene: A Seville Dance Hall. (*Scene designed by* Norman Wilkinson.)

Scene 8

"(After All, I'm) Only a Schoolgirl"
J. Matthews, Mr. Cochran's Young Ladies
A Young Lady: J. Matthews. *A Porter*: A. B. Imeson. *A Man*: W. Stephens. *A Woman*: W. Clare. *Winifred*: M. Brooks.
(*Jessie Matthews' and Mr. Cochran's Young Ladies Dresses designed by* Ada Peacock. *Wyn Clare's and Marjorie Brooks' Dresses designed by* Idare et Cie. *Scene designed by* Paul Colin.)

Scene 9

The Man with the Red Tie[69] (Adapted from the French of Rip)
Bill: L. Lister. *Charlie*: J. Buchanan.
(*Scene designed by* Marc Henri and Laverdet.)

---

[66]Dropped immediately after the opening.

[67]Dropped immediately after the opening.
[68]Dropped immediately after the opening.
[69]Dropped immediately after the opening.

Scene 10

At a Night Club

The Man: J. Buchanan. *The Girl*: J. Matthews. *Waiters*: W. Tinker, C. Newman.

"Which Is the Right Life?"

J. Matthews

"I'm a Gigolo"

J. Buchanan

Scene 11

A Butterfly at the Wheel (*by* Ronald Jeans)

A Policeman: H. E. Ferguson. *Richard Grayson*: J. Buchanan. *"A.A." Lawyer*: L. Lister. *Prosecuting Lawyer*: W. Rolston. *Magistrate*: A. B. Imeson. *Clerk of the Court*: R. Mitchell. *Miss Iris Carstairs*: W. Clare. *Sergeant Buffy*: D. Phillips.

Scene 12

Finale (*Arranged by* Jack Buchanan.)

Entire Company

(*Scene designed by* Doris Zinkeisen. *All Dresses by* Idare et Cie.)

GINGER SNAPS

1929.52

An All-Colored Dance Revue in Two Acts, 18 Scenes. Book (sketches) and lyrics by J. Homer Tutt, Donald Heywood and George Morris. Music by Donald Heywood. Entire production staged by the authors. Dances arranged by George Stamper. Settings by Ben Glick. Costumes designed by Hilda Farnum. (Produced by George Morris.) Opened 31 December 1929 at the Belmont Theatre and closed 4 January 1930 after 7 performances.

CAST: ROSCOE ('Red') SIMMONS, BOOTS SWAN, JOHN LEE, J. HOMER TUTT, VIVIAN BABER, BOBBY DeLEON, BARRINGTON GUY, SELMA SMITH, JAMES MONDAY, MAUDE DeFOREST, GEORGE STAMPER, FRANK (Pimples) DAVIS.
Southland Choir: Anthony Gaytzera, LARRY SEYMOUR, Walter Hilliard, WALTER MEADOWS, Joseph Loomis, J. Grace Walton, Thelma Rhoten, Mary Mason, BERTHA WRIGHT, Margaret Watson. *Snapperetttes*: Mabel Garey, Ethel Moses, Marion Fleming, Estello De Polanco, Marie Robinson, Gladyce Bronson, Frankie Scott, Elvire Sanchez, Marie Aken, Enid Morgan, Margaret Jackson, Ruth Curtiss.

FIRST CARTOM (ACT 1)

Snap 1

"Birth of Dixie"

R. Simmons

Scene: A Plantation set on the stage of the Harlem Theatre.

A Fowl Deed

Boots: B. Swan. *John*: J. Lee. *The Sheriff*: H. Tutt. *Lindy*: V. Baber.

Snap 2

"Crazy Walk" (A new dance creation)

B. DeLeon, Snappperettes

Snap 3

The Same Old Clown

B. Guy

Snap 4

Sweet Lips

E. Mores, R. Simmons, B. DeLeon, S. Smith

Snap 5

"Let's Make Hey, Hey (While the Sun Is Shinin')"

Hot Shots, Snapperettes

Dance Specialty

The Five Hot Shots

Snap 6

In Agan and Out Agan

Mr. Inagan: B. Swan. *Mr. Outagan*: J. Lee. *The Warden*: J. H. Tutt.

Snap 7

(a) Sambo's in the Movies

Location: Hollywood.

The Director: R. Simmons. *The Cameraman*: J. Monday. *Aunt Jemima*: B. Wright. *Armour's Chef*: W. Meadows. *The Gold Dust Twins*: B. deLeon, S. Smith.

(b) Travesty on "Hallelujia"

Daniel Haynes: H. Tutt. *Nina Mae McKinney*: V. Baber. *Victoria Spivey*: M. DeForest. *The Preacher*: B. Guy. And the Southland Choir.

SECOND CARTON (ACT 2)

Snap 1

"My Jungle Home"

Tar Zan: B. Guy. *Boola*: V. Baber. And the Jungle Maids, Tom-tom Beaters.

Snap 2

Hot StuffB. Swan, J. Lee

Snap 3

"Change My Luck"

The Janitor: J. H. Tutt. *The Scrubwoman*: M. DeForest.

Snap 4

"Spread Your Knees"

V. Baber, Snapperettes

Snap 5

"Big Boy, I Gotta Belong to You"

B. DeLeon, S. Smith

Snap 6

See the Point

The Stranger: G. Stamper. *The Croupier*: J. Monday. *The Proprietor*: J. H. Tutt.

Snap 7

Some Stepping

Five Hot Shots

'Low' Stepping

F. Davis

Snap 8

He Always Gets His Man! (A Drama of the Canadian Wilds)

Time: The Present.

Scene A: Somewhere in the Saskatchewan. *Scene B*: Interior of Cabin.

Cast (in order of appearance): *Jean Baptiste*, a trapper: G. Stamper. *Marcel Corot*, a sled driver: J. H. Tutt. *Gitchie*, a halfbreed: L. Seymour. *Rastus*, a cook: B. Swan. *"Stranger" Crane*, a fugitive from justice: B. Guy. *Benchley* of the Canadian Royal Northwestern Mounted Police: R. Simmons.

Snap 9

"Let's Make Hey, Hey" (Specialty/reprise)

B. deLeon

Snap 10

"I'll Do Anything for Love" (A Lenox Avenue Incident)

B. Swan, J. Lee, B. Guy, V. Baber, M. DeForest, R. Simmons

Snap 11

Finale:"You're Something to Write Home About" (Meaning You Our Dear Audience)

B. deLeon, S. Smith, Entire Company

THE PRINCE OF PILSEN

1930.01

A Revival of the Musical Comedy in Two Acts, 6 Scenes[70]. Book and lyrics by Frank Pixley. Music by Gustav Luders. Staged by Milton Aborn. Musical director, Louis Kroll. Produced by the Jolson Theatre Musical Comedy Company (Messrs. Shubert, Milton Aborn). Opened 13 January 1930 at Jolson's Theatre and closed 25 January 1930 after 16 performances.[71]

CAST (in order of appearance): *François*: Robert O'Connor. *Edith Adams*: ALICE WELLMAN. *Cook's Courier*: Melvin Redden. *Jimmy*: Wee Griffin. *Arthur St. John Wilberforce, Lord Somerset*: DENNIS GURNEY. *Mrs. Madison Crocker*: INDIA COX. *Hans Wagner*: AL SHEAN. *Nellie Wagner*: VIVIAN HART. *Lieutenant Tom Wagner*: JOSEPH TONER. *Carl Otto, the Prince of Pilsen*: ROY CROPPER. *Sidonie*: Marjorie Seltzer. *Sergeant Brie*: Carl Dews. *Dene*: Dene Dickens. *Frances*: Frances Baviello. *Premiere Danseuse*: MONA MORAY. *American Girls (5)*: *Boston*: Dene Dickens. *Baltimore*: Mona Moray. *New Orleans*: Frances Baviello. *Chicago*: Clara Martens. *New York*: Leonore Brody.
Ladies of the Ensemble: Dene Dickens, Frances Baviello, Adele Savoye, Velma Lois Sutton, Sylvia Gillis, Leonore Brody, Sylvia Caplan, Eleanor Richmond, Helen Choat, Eleanor Jenkins, Billie Dogin, Genevieve Jagger, Elizabeth Crandall, Helene Hewitt, Mabel Thompson, Edith Sears, Clara Martens, Rita Stonefield, Ida Korost, Gertrude Waldon, Helen Cowan, Mary Stuart, Susan Hopkins, Margaret Urrntiea, Tybelle Kane, Gertrude Lindross. *Gentlemen of the Ensemble*: Joel Berloe, Melville Redden, Carl Dews, Harold Bomgardner, Donald Gale, Barton Frazier, John Mangum, Angelo Boschediti, Sol Trell, Earl Plummer, Cosmo D'Almada, Emile Stetz.

---

[70]Originally produced 17 March 1903 at the Broadway Theatre for 143 performances. For Synopsis of Scenes and Musical Numbers, see original 1903 production. The libretto has been revised and updated. Added for this production:

"The Song of the Nightingale" (from WOODLAND)(Act 2)

V. Hart

[71]Settings, costumes uncredited.

STRIKE UP THE BAND
1931.02

A Musical Comedy in Two Acts, 8 Scenes. Book by Morrie Ryskind, based on a libretto by George S. Kaufman. Music by George Gershwin. Lyrics by Ira Gershwin. Staged by Alexander Leftwich. Dances staged by George Hale. Settings by Raymond Sovey. Costumes designed by Charles LeMaire. Music director, Hilding Anderson. Produced by Edgar Selwyn. Opened 14 January 1930 at the Times Square Theatre and closed 28 June 1930 after 191 performances.

CAST [in order of appearance]: *In the Story: Timothy Harper:* GORDON SMITH. *Richard K. Sloane:* Robert Bentley. *Horace J. Fletcher:* DUDLEY CLEMENTS. *Myra Meade:* Ethel Kenyon. *Mrs. Grace Draper:* BLANCHE RING. *Anne Draper:* DORIS CARSON. *Joan Fletcher:* MARGARET SCHILLING. *Jim Townshend:* JERRY GOFF. *Two Men About Town:* BOBBY CLARK, PAUL McCULLOUGH. *Doctor:* Maurice Lapue.

In the Dream: Horace J. Fletcher: DUDLEY CLEMENTS. *Richard K. Sloane:* Robert Bentley. *Colonel Holmes:* BOBBY CLARK. *Gideon:* PAUL McCULLOUGH. *Mrs. Grace Draper:* BLANCHE RING. *Joan Fletcher:* MARGARET SCHILLING. *Jim Townshend:* JERRY GOFF. *Timothy Harper:* GORDON SMITH. *Anne Draper:* DORIS CARSON. *Myra Meade:* Ethel Kenyon. *Doris Dumme:* Marion Miller. *Herr Konrad:* Maurice Lapue. *Suzette:* Ethel Britton. *Soisette:* Virginia Barnes. *Sergeant:* Walter Fairmont. *Premiere Danseuse:* Joyce Coles. And RED NICHOLS AND HIS ORCHESTRA [includes Benny Goodman, Gene Krupa, Glenn Miller, Jimmy Dorsey, Jack Teagarden]. *Dancing Girls:* Virginia Barnes, May Brenton, Ethel Britton, Sybil Bursk, Norma Cloos, Katherine Downer, Marion Phillips, Betty Etcove, Amy Frank, Libby Holliday, Doris Jay, Ethel Kriston, Gertrude Lindle, Martha Louise Maggard, Vera Perry, Jean Egan, Vivian Porter, Polly Ray, Kay Stewart, Inez Trimble, Dorothy Talbot, Patricia Whitney, Jean Warren, Irene Kelly. *Singing Girls:* Peggy Greene, Lorraine Johnson, Tana Kamp, Joan Kent, Marion Miller, Kathryn Hamill, Ruth Valentine, Clare Waring. *Dancers:* Beekman Bauer, Arthur Craig, Ray Clark, Norman Clifton, Frank Lavin, Fred May, Jerome Maxwell, Buddy Penny, Frank Sherlock, Jack Douglas, Jack Bond, Larry Regan. *Singers:* Kenneth Atkins, Vincent Curran, Walter Fairmont, Norman Curtis, Donald Knoblock, Tully Millet, Dick Neeley, John Sciortino, Murray Swanson, Fred Vengelisch, Harold Ten-Brook, Vincent Vernon.

Act 1, Scene 1: In front of the Horace J. Fletcher Chocolate Works. *Scene 2:* The Main Office. *The Dream: Scene 3:* The Main Office. *Scene 4:* The Private Office. *Scene 5:* Gardens of Mr. Fletcher's Home.

Act 2, Scene 1: Switzerland. *We Then Resume the Story: Scene 2:* Mr. Fletcher's Private Office. *Scene 3:* The Reception Hall.

Act 1

"Fletcher's American Chocolate Choral Society" (Opening)
   G. Smith, R. Bentley, D. Clements
"I Mean To Say"
   G. Smith, D. Carson
"Typical Self-Made American"
   D. Clements, J. Goff, Yes-Men
"Soon"
   M. Schilling, J. Goff
"A Man of High Degree" (Entrance of Colonel Holmes)
   Entire Company (B. Clark, D. Clements, P. McCullough, Ensemble)
"The Unoffical Spokesman"
   B. Clark, Company
"Three Cheers for the Union" (Patriotic Rally)
   Company
"This Could Go On For Years"
   Company
"If I Became President"
   B. Clark, B. Ring
"Soon" (reprise)
   M. Schilling, J. Goff
"(What's the Use of) Hanging Around with You?"
   G. Smith, D. Carson
"He Knows Milk" (Finaletto)
   J. Goff, M. Schilling, R. Bentley, D. Clements, Ensemble
"Strike Up the Band"
   J. Goff, Entire Company, Red Nichols and His Band

Act 2

"In the Rattle of the Battle" (Opening)
   Company
"Military Dancing Drill"
   Company
"Mademoiselle from New Rochelle"
   B. Clark, P. McCullough, Swiss Girls

"I've Got a Crush on You"
   G. Smith, D. Carson
"(How About a Boy) Like Me?"
   B. Ring, B. Clark, P. McCullough, D.Clements
Unofficial March of General Holmes
"Official Resumé"
   Ensemble
"Ring a Ding a Ding Dong Bell" (Ding Dong)
   Bridesmaids, Company
Finale
   Entire Company

THE CHOCOLATE SOLDIER
1930.03

A Revival of the Operetta in Three Acts[72]. Original Viennese book ("Der tapfere Soldat") and lyrics by Rudolph Bernauer and Leopold Jacks [Jacobson], based on George Bernard Shaw's play "Arms and the Man." American book and lyrics by Stanislaus Stange. Music by Oscar Straus. Entire production staged by Milton Aborn. Settings by Rollo Wayne. Costumes by Tams. Musical director, Louis Kroll. Revived by the Jolson's Theatre Musical Comedy Company (Milton Aborn, Messrs. Shubert). Opened 27 January 1930 at Jolson's Theatre and closed 15 February 1930 after 25 performances.

CAST: *Nadina Popoff,* Daughter of Colonel Popoff: ALICE MACKENZIE. *Aurelia Popoff,* Her Mother: VERA ROSS. *Mascha,* Aurelia's Cousin: Vivian Hart. *Lieutenant Bumerli,* the "Chocolate Soldier," a Swiss Mercenary in the employ of the Serbian Army: CHARLES PURCELL. *Captain Massakroff* of the Bulgarian Army: William C. Gordon. *Popoff's Servants (2): Louka:* Frances Baviello. *Stephan:* Wee Griffin. *Colonel Casimir Popoff* of the Bulgarian Army: JOHN DUNSMURE. *Major Alexius Spiridoff* of the Bulgarian Army, betrothed to Nadina: Roy Cropper.

Bulgarian Soldiers, Citizens, Citizenesses: Ladies of the Ensemble: Leonore Brody, Frances Baviello, Elizabeth Crandall, Susan Hopkins, Eleanor Jenkins, Genevieve Jagger, Ida Korost, Tybelle Kane, Gertrude Lindross, Clara Martens, Eleanor Richmond, Velma Sutton, Rita Stonefield, Mary Stuart, Mabel Thompson, Gertrude Waldon, Emily Harris, Marvel Ober, Helen Cowan, Corine Jessop, Golda Orleans, Thelma Goodwyn. *Gentlemen of the Ensemble:* Joel Berloe, Harold Bomgardner, Angelo Boschediti, Carl Dews, Cosmo D'Almada, Barton Frazier, Donald Gale, John Mangum, Earl Plummer, Sol Trell, Melvin Redden, Hobson Young.

SARI
1930.04

A Revival of the Operetta in Two Acts[73]. Original (Viennese) libretto ("Der Zigeunerprimás") by Julius Wilhelm and Fritz Greenbaum [Grünbaum]. English adaptation by C. S. Cushing and E. P. Heath. Music by Emmerich Kálmán. Book staged by Mitzi (Hajós). Dances and ensembles staged by Albertina Rasch. Settings and costumes designed by Willy Pogany. Symphony orchestra under the direction of Paul Yartin. Produced by Eugene Endrey. Opened 28 January 1930 at the Liberty Theatre and closed 8 February 1930 after 15 performances.

CAST (in order of appearance): *Pali Rácz,* the Gypsy Leader: BOYD MARSHALL. *His Children (3): Laczi Rácz:* J. HUMBIRD DUFFY. *Sári Rácz:* MITZI (HAJÓS). *Klari Racz:* Gloria Frey. *Joska Fekete,* his Friend: David D. Morris[74]. *Juliska Fekete,* his

---

[72]First produced in New York 13 September 1909 at the Lyric Theatre for 296 performances. For Synopsis of Scenes and Musical Numbers, see original 1909 production. For this revival, "Thank the Lord the War Is Over" does not appear in programs, but was most likely performed as part of "Alexius, the Heroic." Act 2 included a specialty dance by Mona Moray. To Act 3 was added a Scene and Melodrama for Bumerli between the "Letter Song" and the "Letter Duet."

[73]Originally produced in New York 13 January 1914 at the Liberty Theatre for 151 performances. For Synopsis of Scenes and Musical Numbers, see original 1914 production. For this revival the following changes were made in the score: "Triumphant Youth" and "Love Live the King" were dropped. Added were:

   Ballet (Added to Act 2 after "Follow Me")
      Albertina Rasch Dancers
   "Sinple Little Village Maid" (replaced "There's No Place Like Home for You")
      M. Hajós, Dancers

[74]All reviewers but two (including Billboard) saw Morris in the role; others cite Duane Nelson.

Daughter: MARJORIE SWEET. *Gaston*, Count Irini: JACK SQUIRES. *Cadeaux*, his Shadow: Bernard Jukes. *Count Estragon*, H. R. H. King of Massilia: Eduardo Ciannelli. *Pierre*: Pat Clayton. *Other children of Rácz, Villagers, Guests of Count Irini*: (Ensemble).

Albertina Rasch Dancing Girls: Geraldine Spencer, Anita Avila, Claire Deerfield, Margareta Eiselle, Ida Lanvin, Jean Densmore, Drusilla Harrington, Lee Nugent, Babs Little, Dorothy Burr, Nona Otero, Marjorie McLaughlin. *Solo Dancers*: Geraldine Spencer, Anita Avila, Ida Lanvin, Claire Deerfield, Nona Otero. *Ladies of the Ensemble*: Doris Coleman, Corris DeBrauw, Flora Sahagian, Mary Cole, Janet Gibson, Janice Ewing, Dorothy Rose, Eleanor La Fleur, Stella Maison, Margaret Szabo, Laurette Madison, Florence Madison, Georgia Budde, Doris Ekert, Elizabeth Morton, Edna Lee, Rhea Sampson, Anna Delphine, Ilonka Villon, Ruth Collins, Lily Brunner. *Gentlemen of the Ensemble*: Harry Phelps, George Hunt, Leslie Coullard, Richard Lynn, Leonard Mooney, Charles Perry, Jimmie Carr, Charles Fromm, Donald Gallagher. *Original Gypsy Band*: Karoly Bencze (Leader), Edmund Berki, Lajos Barna, Bela Horvath, Lajos Francko, Simon Nyolcas.

1030.05   RIPPLES

A Musical Extravaganza (Comedy) in Two Acts, 11 Scenes. Book by William Anthony McGuire. Music by Oscar Levant and Albert Sirmay. Lyrics by Irving Caesar and Graham John. Book staged by William Anthony McGuire. Dances and ensembles by William Holbrook; Tiller dances by Mary Read. Settings designed by Joseph Urban. Costumes designed by Charles LeMaire and James Reynolds. Orchestra under the direction of Gus Salzer. Produced by Charles Dillingham. Opened 11 February 1930 at the New Amsterdam Theatre and closed 29 March 1930 after 55 performances.

CAST [in order of appearance]: *Herman Dutcher*: Arthur Cunningham. *Honus*: William Kerschell. *Malcolm Fairman*: Edward Allen. *Ripples*: DOROTHY STONE. *Richard Willoughby*: CHARLES COLLINS. *Mrs. Willoughby*: MRS. FRED STONE. *Rip (Van Winkle)*: FRED STONE. *Mary Willoughby*: PAULA STONE. *John Pillsbury*: ANDREW TOMBES. *Jane Martin*: KATHRYN HEREFORD. *Mrs. John Pillsbury*: Althea Heinly. *Corporal Jack Sterling*: EDDIE FOY, JR. *State Troopers* (4): J. Marshall Smith, Dwight Synder, Ray Johnson, Del Porter. *Sergeant Banner*: Charles Mast. *Mrs. Sterling*: Pearl Hight. *Millicent*: Peggy Bancroft. *Little Billie Sheer*: Paul Paulus. *Lollipop*: Colonel Casper.

Guests of Mrs. Willoughby: Dorothy Bond, Helen Cant, Peggy Bancroft, Dimple Reide, Margaret Porter, Gaby France, Anna May Dennehy, Helene Haskin. *Dancers*: Sally Anderson, Wilma Roelof, Ethel Raye, Margaret Purple, Marjorie Purple, Beth Milton, Rosalie Trego, Claire Wayne, Jean Wayne, Nina Valero, Evelyn Greer, Florence Rice, Ann Horace, Lillian Lorray, Nickie Pitell, Myrtle Arnette, Ruth Farrar, Helene Franz, Roslyn Smith, Alma Walker, Mary Grace Vannoy, Kathleen Vannoy, Collette Francey, Mildred Clark. *Mary Read Tiller Girls*: Grace Holt, Gladys Holt, Elsie Holt, Iris Smith, May Corness, Kathleen Gue, Winnie Hollingshead, Hilda Winstanley, Doris Waterworth, Lily Riley, Peggy Sowden, Ann East. *State Troopers*: Floyd English, Ned Lynn, Richard Renaud, Robert G. Vreeland, Robert Milton, Carl Duart, Joe Carroll, Raymond Hunt. *Little Folk*: Elizabeth Hoy, Helen Hoy, Marguerite Hoy, Charles Hoy, Prince Ludwig, Adolph Piccolo, Frank Packerd, Major Doyle, Herbert Rice, Paul Paulus.

Act 1, Scene 1: The Van Winkle Inn in the Catskills. *Scene 2*: Outside of the Inn. *Scene 3*: The Cottages of Rip and the Sterlings. *Scene 4*: The Catskills at Sunrise. *Scene 5*: Exterior of the Headquarters of the State Troopers. *Scene 6*: Colonial Room in Mrs. Willoughby's Country House.

Act 2, Scene 1: A Woodland on the Willoughby Estate. *Scene 2*: A Tree in Sleepy Hollow. *Scene 3*: Interior of the Headquarters of State Troopers. *Scene 4*: A Moment with Rip. *Scene 5*: Ballroom of the Willoughby Residence.

Act 1

OpeningCollege Girls, A. Cunningham
"Gentlemen of the Press"
   E. Allen, Show Girls, Boys, The Foursome
"Barefoot Girl"
   D. Stone, Mary Read Tiller Girls
"Is It Love"[75]
   C. Collins, D. Stone
   (*Music by* Oscar Levant. *Lyrics by* Irving Caesar.)
"We Never Sleep"[76]
   A. Tombes, The Foursome, The State Troopers
"I Take After Rip"
   F. Stone, D. Stone, P. Stone

Finaletto
"Gentlemen of the Press" (reprise)
   E. Allen, A. Heinly, P. Bancroft
"Babykins"[77]
   D. Stone, A. Tombes
   (*Music by* Oscar Levant. *Lyrics by* Irving Caesar and Graham John.)
The Sunrise Dance
   Mary Read Tiller Girls
"I'm Afraid"[78]
   F. Stone
   (*Music by* Albert Sirmay. *Lyrics by* Irving Caesar and Graham John.)
The Little Folk
"We Never Sleep"[79]
   A. Tombes, State Troopers
"There's Nothing Wrong in a Kiss"
   A. Tombes, P. Stone
   (*Music by* Oscar Levant. *Lyrics by* Irving Caesar and Graham John.)
Dance
   Mary Read Tiller Girls
"Girls of Long Ago"
   Ensemble
"Is It Love" (reprise)
   D. Stone, C. Collins, The Foursome, Ensemble
Cane Dance
   F. Stone, D. Stone, P. Stone
Finale

Act 2
"Hunting Days"
   Ensemble
"Babykins"[80] (reprise)
   D. Stone, A. Tombes
"Talk With My Heel and Toe"
   D. Stone, P. Stone, A. Tombes, C. Collins, Ensemble
   (*Music by* Oscar Levant. *Lyrics by* Irving Caesar.)
Autumn Ballet
   Mary Read Tiller Girls
"I'm a Little Bit Fonder of You" (from MERCENARY MARY-London production)
   (*Music and Lyrics by* Irving Caesar.) A. Heinly, K. Hereford
Rip
   (F. Stone)
Heel and Toe Dance
   Mary Read Tiller Girls
Finale

1930.06   (RUTH SELWYN'S) NINE FIFTEEN REVUE

A Musical Revue in Two Acts, 35 Scenes. Sketches by Ring Lardner, Paul Gerard Smith, Eddie Cantor, Anita Loos and John Emerson, Geoffrey Kerr, H. W. Hanemann, Robert Riskin, Adorian Otvos. Music by Victor Herbert, George Gershwin, Rudolf Friml, Vincent Youmans, Roger Wolfe Kahn, Kay Swift, Philip Broughton, Harold Arlen, Ralph Rainger, Richard Myers, Ned Lehak, Manning Sherwin. Lyrics by Ted Koehler, Edward Eliscu, Paul James, Ira Gershwin, Irving Caesar. Sketches staged by the authors. Musical numbers staged by Busby Berkeley. Ballet numbers directed by Leon Leonidoff. Settings designed by Clarke Robinson. Costumes designed by Kiviette. Produced by Ruth Selwyn. Orchestra under the direction of Don Voorhees. Opened 11 February 1930 at the George M. Cohan Theatre and closed 15 February 1930 after 7 performances.

[75]Dropped after opening and replaced by:
   "You Can Never Tell About Love"
      D. Stone, C. Collins, Ensemble
      (*Music by* J. Fred Coots. *Lyrics by* Benny Davis.)
[76]Dropped after opening.

[77]Dropped after opening and replaced by:
   "Big Brother to Me"
      D. Stone, A. Tombes
      (*Music by* Arthur Schwartz. *Lyrics by* Howard Dietz.)
[78]Dropped after opening.
[79]Dropped after opening.
[80]Dropped after opening.

CAST: RUTH ETTING, FRED KEATING, FRANCES SHELLY, HARRY McNAUGHTON, JOE and PETE MICHON, PAUL KELLY, CHARLES LAWRENCE, HELEN GRAY, LYNNE DORE, MARY MURRAY, THE LOVEY GIRLS (Erma, Lucille), GRACELLA and THEODORE, DIANE ELLIS, MICHAEL TRIPP, WALLY CRISHAM, OSCAR RAGLAND, NAN BLAKSTONE, EARL OXFORD, JAMES HOWKINS, PEPPI LEDERER, LOUISE BARRETT, MARGARETE MERLE, DON VOORHEES and HIS ORCHESTRA.

Ruth Selwyn's Specialty Girls: Carmen Mathews[81], Dorothy Donnelly[82], Lillian Ostrom, Jane Sherman, Mary Sawyer, Ruth Gormly, Teddy Walters, Ginger Meehan, Thelma Temple, Pat Hastings. *Ensemble:* Stella Bayliss, Dorothy Davis, Catherine Devery, Alyce Fields, Doris Grant, Beatrice Jay, Nancy Kaye, Sharon Lloyd, Carol MacKay, Marie Marceline, Ginger Meehan, Ann Moss, Josephine Mostler, Charlotte Otis, Mary Sadler, Kathleen Sullivan, Margie Taylor, Mary Deiden, Ethel Hampton.

ACT 1

Scene 1

Times Square at Night

Fred Keating arrives to introduce the sketches and musical numbers as they appear.

Scene 2

Ruth Selwyn's Specialty Girls in Their Dressing Room
L. Ostrom, J. Sherman, M. Sawyer, R. Gormley, T. Walters, P. Hastings, T. Temple, G. Meehan

Scene 3

(Fred) Keating

Scene 4

Have One on Me (*by* W. H. Hanemann)
Lucrezia Borgia: L. Dore. *Caesar Borgia:* P. Kelly. *Matteo:* H. McNaughton

Scene 5

"Up Among the Chimney Pots"
(*Music by* Kay Swift. *Lyrics by* Paul James.)
The Girl: R. Etting. *The Artist:* W. Crisham. *The Chimney Sweep:* M. Tripp.

Scene 6

What Has Happened to Tragedy? (*by* Anita Loos and John Emerson)
Eugene O'Neill: O. Ragland. *Philip Moeller:* P. Kelly. *Lady Isabel:* M. Murray. *Richard Carlyle:* C. Lawrence. *Sir Francis Levinson:* H. McNaughton. *Butler:* J. Michon.

Scene 7

"Toddlin' Along"
N. Blakstone, Ensemble
(*Music by* George Gershwin. *Lyrics by* Ira Gershwin.)

Scene 8

(Fred) Keating

Scene 9

Meet the Wife (*by* Paul Gerard Smith)
The Girl: F. Malloy. *The Wife:* R. Etting. *Jim Carroll:* P. Kelly. *Maid:* N. Blakstone.

Scene 10

"World of Dreams"
M. Merle
(*Music by* Victor Herbert. *Lyrics by* Edward Eliscu. *Ballet directed by* Leon Leonidoff.)
Ballet Dance
Gracella & Theodore

Scene 11

"Ta Ta, Ol' Bean"
H. Gray, H. McNaughton
(*Music by* Manning Sherwin. *Lyrics by* Edward Eliscu.)
Specialty Dancers: C. Mathews, R. Gormley, P. Hastings, D. Donnelly, L. Ostrom, M. Sawyer, J. Sherman, T. Walters.

Scene 12

(Fred) Keating

Scene 13

The Gunman at Home (*by* Paul Gerard Smith)
The Gunman: H. McNaughton. *The Wife:* L. Dore. *The Son:* C. Lawrence. *The Daughter:* L. Lovey. *Grandma:* D. Ellis. *The Butcher:* J. Michon.

[81]Not the Broadway musical actress of the 1950-1970s.
[82]Not the lyricist for THE STUDENT PRINCE and MY MARYLAND, etc.

Scene 14

Dance Specialty
W. Crisham

Scene 15

"Knock on Wood"
Lovey Girls, Girls of the Ensemble
(*Music by* Richard Myers. *Lyrics by* Edward Eliscu.)

Scene 16

(Fred) Keating
The Three Bears
The Reader: O. Ragland. *The Big Girl:* C. Mathews. *The Medium Girl:* J. Baron. *The Tiny Girl:* R. Gormley.
"Get Happy"
R. Etting, Entire Company
(*Music by* Harold Arlen. *Lyrics by* Ted Koehler. *Electrical effect invented by* J. W. Simmons.)

ACT 2

Scene 1

Reve de Marquise: "Winter and Spring"
M. Merle
(*Music by* Rudolf Friml. *Lyrics by* Edward Eliscu. *Ballet by* Kay Swift.)
The Marquise: Gracella. *The Marquis:* C. Lawrence. *First Revolutionist:* Theodore. *Second Revolutionist:* Normand.

Scene 2

(Fred) Keating will introduce a Group of Half Minute Dramas

Scene 3

The Plumber (*by* Eddie Cantor)
The Woman: L. Dore. *The Plumber:* C. Lawrence.

Scene 4

Love Is Like That (*by* A. Dorian Otvos)
First Stiff: P. Kelly. *Second Stiff:* E. Oxford. *Third Stiff:* O. Ragland.

Scene 5

There Are No Children (*by* Ruth Wilcox)
A Boy: J. Michon. *Another Boy:* P. Michon. *A Lady:* D. Ellis.

Scene 6

Spanish Dancer (*by* Ruth Wilcox)
The Lady: P. Lederer. *The Man:* O. Ragland.

Scene 7

Naturalism (*by* Robert Riskin)
The Director: H. McNaughton. *The Thief:* C. Lawrence. *The Commissioner:* P. Kelly. *A Detective:* W. Crisham.

Scene 8

Dance Specialty
M. Tripp

Scene 9

"Boudoir Dolls"
(*Music by* Ned Lehak. *Lyrics by* Edward Eliscu.)
The Lady: F. Shelley. *The Dolls:* Lovey Girls.

Scene 10

"Breakfast Dance"
N. Blakstone
(*Music by* Ralph Rainger. *Lyrics by* Edward Eliscu.)

Scene 11

Round One (*by* Ring Lardner)
The Broadcaster: P. Kelly. *Joe Lipski,* a Fighter: H. McNaughton. *Moe Stein,* a Fighter: C. Lawrence. *Young Pearson,* a former champ: E. Bush. *Jack Gallagher,* Referee: O. Ragland. *The Haymaker:* M. Tripp. *Second for Lipski:* J. Michon. *Second for Stein:* P. Michon.

Scene 12

"How Would a City Girl Know"
R. Etting, F. Shelly, H. Gray
(*Music by* Kay Swift. *Lyrics by* Paul James.)

Scene 13

"A Purty Little Thing"
Ruth Selwyn's Eight Specialty Girls
(*Music by* Philip Broughton. *Lyrics by* Will B. Johnstone.)

Scene 14

(Fred) Keating

Scene 15

Talkies (*by* Geoffrey Kerr)

The Director: H. McNaughton. *The Star*: D. Ellis. *The Leading Man*: P. Kelly. *First Voice*: C. Lawrence. *Second Voice*: H. Gray. *Third Voice*: E. Oxford. *Property Man*: O. Ragland. *Electrician*: W. Crisham. *Camera Man*: Alexander. *The Maid*: D. James.

Scene 16

"Gotta Find a Way To Do It"
L. Dore, Girls of Ensemble
(*Music by* Roger Wolfe Kahn. *Lyrics by* Paul James.)

Scene 17

"You Will Never Know"
R. Etting
(*Music by* Vincent Youmans. *Lyrics by* Paul James.)

"Gee, I'm So Good It's Too Bad"
R. Etting
(*Music by* Harold Arlen. *Lyrics by* Ted Koehler.)

Scene 18

The Michon Brothers

Scene 19

Finale

1930.07 THE COUNT OF LUXEMBOURG

A Revival of the Operetta in Two Acts[83]. (Original Viennese) Book ("Der Graf von Luxemburg") by A. M. Willner and Robert Bodansky (based on Willner and Bernard Buchbinder's libretto "Die Göttin der Vernunft"). American adaptation by Glen MacDonough. Music by Franz Lehár. Lyrics by Basil Hood, Adrian Ross. Staged by Milton Aborn. Settings by Rollo Wayne. Musical direction by Louis Kroll. Produced by the Jolson's Theatre Musical Comedy Company (Milton Aborn, Messrs. Shubert). Opened 17 February 1930 at Jolson's Theatre and closed 1 March 1930 after 16 performances.

CAST (in order of appearance): *Pierre*: Hobson Young. *Juliette*: Trudy Mallina. *Raymonde*: Carl Dews. *Anatole Brissard*: J. CHARLES GILBERT. *Foyot*: Clif Heckinger. *Nicolai*: Maurice Holland. *Coralie*: Helen Cowan. *Sidonie*: Alice O'Donnell. *Count of Luxembourg* (René): ROY CROPPER. *Mentschikoff*: Ralph Brainard. *Pelegrin*: Ivan Arbuckle. *Paulovitch*: Charles Carver. *Grand Duke Rutzinoff*: FLORENZ AMES. *Angèle Didier*: MANILA POWERS. *Registrar*: Hobson Young. *Fanchot*: Frances Baviello. *Mimi*: Wee Griffin. *Princess Kokozeff*: Elizabeth Crandall.

Ladies of the Ensemble: Frances Baviello, Elizabeth Crandall, Helen Cowan, Anne Chrystie, Emily Harris, Genevieve Jagger, Corinne Jessop, Ida Korost, Tybelle Kane, Gertrude Lindross, Clara Martens, Eleanor Richmond, Velma Lois Sutton, Rita Stonefield, Mabel Thompson, Gertrude Waldon, Golda Orleans, Martha Gale, Eleanor Jenkins, Wee Griffin. *Gentlemen of the Ensemble*: Joel Berloe, Harold Bomgardner, Angelo Boschediti, Carl Dews, Cosmo D'Almada, Barton Frazier, Donald Gale, John Mangum, Earl T. Plummer, Sol Trell, Melvin Redden, Hobson Young.

1930.08 SIMPLE SIMON

A Musical Comedy in Two Acts, 13 Scenes. Book by Ed Wynn and Guy Bolton. Music by Richard Rodgers. Lyrics by Lorenz Hart. Dialogue staged by Zeke Colvan. Ensembles and dances directed by Seymour Felix. Settings by Joseph Urban. Artistic director, (costumes by) John Harkrider. Music director, Oscar Bradley. Produced by Florenz Ziegfeld. Opened 18 February 1930 at the Ziegfeld Theatre and closed 14 June 1930 after 135 performances[84].

CAST (in order of appearance): *Bert Blue*, Bluebeard: Paul Stanton. *Fingy*, Bluebeard's Henchman: Alfred P. James. *Jack Horner* (Jack): WILL AHERN. *Gilly Flower* (Jill): BOBBE ARNST. *Simon*, Keeper of Information and Newspaper Shop: ED WYNN. *Policeman*: Anthony Hughes. *Elaine King*, Cinderella: DOREE LESLIE. *Olee King*, King Cole: LENNOX PAWLE. *Otto Prince*: Hugh Cameron. *Jonah*, Genii: Master George Offermann. *Popper*: Gil White. *Tony Prince*, Prince Charming: ALAN EDWARDS. *Telescope Operator*: Benn Carswell. *Sal*: RUTH ETTING. *Jewel Pearce*: Helen Walsh. *Gladys Dove*: HAZEL FORBES. *Captain in Dullna Army*: Douglas

Stanbury. *The Horse*: Joseph Schrode, Pete La Della. *The Giant Head*: Frank DeWitt. *The Frog*: William J. Ferry. *Premiere Danseuse*: HARRIET HOCTOR. *Little Boy Blue*: Mary Coyle. *Red Riding Hood*: Helen Walsh. *Wolff*: Clementine Rigeau, Elaine Mann. *Goldylocks*: Agnes Franey, Virginia McNaughton. *Puss in Boots*: Patsy O'Day. *Hansel*: Elsie Behrens. *Gretel*: Mabel Baade. *Jazz*: BOBBE ARNST. *Cat and the Fiddle*: Marie Conway. *Cow*: Gladys Pender. *Dog*: Dorothy Patterson. *Dish*: Lois Peck. *Spoon*: Neva Lynn. *Bo-Peep*: Dolores Grant. *Old Lady in the Shoe*: Frieda Mierse. *Miss Muffet*: Georgia Payne, Caja Eric. *The Fairy Goddesses*: Blanche Satchel, Marion Dodge. *Snow Queen*: Pirkko Alquist. *Rapunzel*: HAZEL FORBES. *Snow White*: HARRIET HOCTOR.

Ladies of the Ensemble: Caja Eric, Georgia Payne, Vili Milli, Marion Dodge, Helen Walsh, Pirkko Alquist, Frieda Mierse, Blanche Satchell, Neva Lynn, Mildred Ivotry, Dolores Grant, Marie Conway, Mary Coyle, Elsie Behrens, Patsy O'Day, Elaine Mann, Mabel Baade, Gladys Pender, Dorothy Patterson, Cleo Cullen, Clementine Rigeau, Agnes Franey, Virginia McNaughton, Lois Peck, Hazel Forbes. *Gentlemen of the Ensemble*: Messrs. Roberts, (Alan) Edwards, Fowler, Siegel, Uray, Sager, Doctoroff, Mandes, Butterworth, Lewis, Hervey, Costello, Simmons, Hall, Carswell, (Gil) White, Barry.

Act 1, Scene 1: Coney Island. *Scene 2*: Ferrymen Alley. *Scene 3*: The Boundary Line between Dullna and Gayleria. *Scene 4*: The Hunting Room in King Cole's Palace. *Scene 5*: The Forest at Christmas. *Scene 6*: Fairyland. In the Woods. *Scene 7*: In the Clouds.

Act 2, Scene 1: The Corner Drug Store in Dullville (Chief Village of Dullna). *Scene 2*: Outside the Walled City. *Scene 3*: The Kissing Forest. *Scene 4*: Inside the Citadel of King Otto's Palace. *Scene 5*: Ferryman Alley. *Scene 6*: The Magic Hall.

ACT 1[85]

Scene 1

"Coney Island" (Opening)
Girls, Boys, Barkers, Dancers

"Don't Tell Your Folks"
W. Ahern, B. Arnst

Scene 2

"Magic Music"
B. Arnst, Magic Girls

"I Still Believe in You"[86]
R. Etting

"Send for Me"
D. Leslie, A. Edwards, Girls

Scene 3

"Dull and Gay"
D. Stansbury

Scene 4

"Sweetenheart"
W. Ahern, B. Arnst

"Hunting the Fox"
Leader of the Hunt, Hunters

Hunting Ballet
H. Hoctor, Toe Dancers, Show Girls

Scene 5

"Mocking Bird"
E. Wynn

Finaletto
Entire Company

Scene 6

"Fairyland" (I Love the Woods)
Girls, (H. Hoctor)

ACT 2

Scene 1

"On With the Dance"
Drug Store Girls

---

[83]Originally produced in New York 16 September 1912 at the New Amsterdam Theatre for 120 performances. For Synopsis of Scenes and Musical Numbers, see original 1912 production. Costumes uncredited.
[84]Played a return engagement 13 March 1931 at the Majestic Theatre for 16 performances; see separate entry for revised cast and song list in 1930-31 season. Total including return: 151 performances.

---

[85]Added for subsequent tour and return engagement:
"I'm Yours" (replacing "Happy Days, Lonely Nights")
Sal (Wini Shaw), E. Wynn
(*Music by* Johnny Green. *Lyrics by* E. Y. Harburg.)
"Bluebeard's Beard"
G. Stanton (Blue Beard)
"Peter Pan"
Renee Rivir (Peter Pan)
[86]Dropped from show in April 1930.

Scene 2

"I Could Do Wonders With You"[87]
D. Leslie, A. Edwards

"Ten Cents a Dance"[88]
R. Etting

"In Your Chapeau"[89]
E. Wynn

"Roping"E. Wynn, W. Ahern

Scene 3

Kissing Forest Ballet
H. Hoctor, Dancers

Scene 4

"The Trojan Horse"[90]
King Otto's Soldiers

Scene 5

"Rags and Tatters"
Vagabond, Boys

Scene 6

Finale—Magic ("Cottage in the Country")
Entire Company

(LEW LESLIE'S)
1930.09 ## INTERNATIONAL REVUE

A Musical Revue in Two Acts, 32 Scenes. Sketches by Nat N. Dorfman and Lew Leslie. Music by Jimmy McHugh. Lyrics by Dorothy Fields. Entire production staged and conceived by Lew Leslie. Sketches directed Edward Clark Lilley. Special dance arrangements staged by Busby Berkeley; incidental dances staged by Harry Crosley. Sketches staged by Harry Levant. Scenery designed by Anthony W. Street. Costumes designed by Dolly Tree. Orchestra directed by Harry Levant. Produced by Lew Leslie. Opened 25 February 1930 at the Majestic Theatre and closed 17 May 1930 after 95 performances.

<u>CAST</u>: GERTRUDE LAWRENCE, HARRY RICHMAN, FLORENCE MOORE, JACK PEARL, ARGENTINITA, ANTON DOLIN, (Marjorie) MOSS and (Georges) FONTANA, (Harry) JANS and (Harold) WHALEN, BERNICE and EMILY, RADAELLI, LIVIA MARRACCI, BERINOFF and EULALIE, ROSEMARY DEERING, 3 McCANN SISTERS, RICHARD RYAN, BABS LaVALLE, VIOLA DOBOS, RICHARD GORDON, ROBERT CONCHE, ESTHER MUIR, ROBERT HOBBS, Ralph Cook, Eileen Culshaw, Lillian Gordon, Joseph Herbert, Leon Kairoff, Harry Pohl.
Chester Hale's International Girls: Bonnibelle Beard, Dorothy Goodman, Inez Goetz, Sylvia Greene, Agnes Gruno, Dorothy Hess, Phyllis Jordon, Karen Kaaber, Gertrude Kornblum, Verta Kunkel, Violette Lundberg, Georgia MacTaggert, Gertrude Mazza, Hilda Peterson, May Sigler, Jewel Tiedgens, Jeanne Walton, Ester Whetton, Mary Wynn, Marjorie Hartoin. *Show Girls*: Evelyn Groves, Josephine Larkin, Valerie Ramiere, Vera King, LaVerta McCormack, Margaret Trevor, Dorothy Dodge, Dawn Darley, Yvonne Hughes, Peggy Fish, Dorothy Drum.

ACT 1[91]

Scene 1

"Make Up Your Mind"
Chester Hale's International Girls

---

[87]Dropped from show in April 1930, and replaced by:
"I Want That Man"
B. Arnst, Girls
[88]In April 1930 "Ten Cents a Dance" was moved to Act 1, and replaced by:
"Happy Days and Lonely Nights"
R. Etting
(*Music by* Fred Fisher. *Lyrics by* Billy Rose.)
"Love Me or Leave Me" (from WHOOPEE)(followed "Happy Days. .")
R. Etting
(*Music by* Walter Donaldson. *Lyrics by* Gus Kahn.)
[89]Dropped from show in April 1930.
[90]Dropped from show in April 1930.
[91]The running order and cast of songs and sketches was radically revised after the opening. Added:
You Can't Beat It! (Act 1)
Fred: H. Jans. *Bill*: H. Whalen. *Jim*: H. Richman.

Scene 2

Such Is Life[92]
Wife: E. Groves. *Broker*: H. Jans. *Husband*: H. Whalen.

Scene 3

"Big Papoose Is On the Lose"
E. Muir
Chester Hale's International Girls, Show Girls.

Scene 4

Gertrude Lawrence

Scene 5

Catherine the Great
Gregory: L. Kairoff. *Count*: R. Gordon. *Simonovitch*: R. Hobbs. *Ratofsky*: R. Ryan. *Alexis*: J. Pearl. *Catherine the Great*: F. Moore. *Pages*: V. Kunkel, I. Goetz.

Scene 6

"On the Sunny Side of the Street"
H. Richman
Assisted by McCann Sisters, Chester Hale's International Girls, Show Girls.

Scene 7

On Her Hands and Feet[93]
B. LaValle

Scene 8

The Matinee Idol
Time: The Present. *Place*: Paris.
Yvonne: G. Lawrence. *Marie*: E. Culshaw. *Paul Renaud, the Matinee Idol*: H. Richman. *Pierre*: R. Hobbs. *Albert Muller*: J. Pearl. *Gordon Selfridge*: R. Ryan.

Scene 9

"Keys to Your Heart"
R. Hobbs

Dance
R. Deering, Chester Hale's International Girls
Floating Around: M. Moss, G. Fontana.

Scene 10

Peerage (*by* Stanley Rauh)
Herman Fifer: J. Pearl. *Sandy McTavish*: R. Gordon. *Harold Thompson*: R. Hobbs. *Benjamin Poppoffsky*: H. Whalen. *Samuel Ginsberg*: H. Jans.

Experience
J. Pearl, H. Whalen

Scene 11

"Exactly Like You"
G. Lawrence, H. Richman

Scene 12

"Here Comes the Bride"[94]
F. Moore
(*Music by* Alberta Nichols. *Lyrics by* Mann Holiner.)

Scene 13

"The Rout" with Anton Dolin
Scene: Montmartre.
Pet of the Montmartre: A. Dolin. *His Sweetheart*: Eulalie. *A Rival Apache*: Berinoff. *Flower Girl*: L. Gordon. *Society Girl*: V. Ramiere. *Drug Addict*: E. Culshaw. *Doorkeeper*: R. Ryan. *The Drunk*: R. Cook. *His Companion*: Y. Hughes. *Midnight Rounder*: R. Hobbs. *Blind Beggar*: R. Gordon. *Beggar Girl*: D. Goodman. *Organ Grinder*: H. Pohl. *Girls with Doc*: Bernice, Emily. *Knife Grinder*: J. Herbert. *The Wandering Jew*: L Kairoff. *In the Mob*—Gendarmes, Soldiers, People of All Nations, Apache, Italians, Russians, Belgians, Germans, Swedes, Slavs, Hungarians, Japanese, Chinese and Algerians.
(*Staged and conceived by* Lew Leslie and Anton Dolin. *Special music arranged by* Lew Leslie.)

Scene 14

Experience[95]
J. Pearl, H. Whalen

Scene 15

"The Margineers"
J. Pearl

---

[92]Dropped after opening.
[93]Dropped after opening.
[94]Dropped after opening.
[95]Dropped after opening.

Scene 16

"International Rhythm"

H. Richman

Reprise

G. Lawrence

Miss France: D. Drum. *Miss Japan*: J. Larkin. *Miss Siam*: M. Trevor. *Miss Checko-Slovakia*: D. Dodge. *Miss Egypt*: P. Fish. *Miss Mexico*: V. King. *Miss Sweden*: D. Darley. *Miss Germany*: Y. Hughes. *Miss America*: V. Ramiere. And Chester Hale's International Girls.

ACT 2

Before rise of the second act curtain, Robert Conche, young musical genius from the Empire, Paris, will entertain.[96]

Scene 1

"Gypsy Love"

L. Marracci

Hungarian Dance

V. Dobos, Chester Hale's International Girls

Scene 2

Upside Down

Bernice and Emily

Scene 3

A Few Moments with Jans and Whalen

Scene 4

Under Venetian Skies: "Exactly Like You" (reprise)

L. Maracci, Showgirls

Scene 5

Radaelli (Star of La Scala Opera Company, Milan, Italy)

Scene 6

A Modern Version of 'Oliver Twist'[97]

Oliver: E. Culshaw. *Nancy*: F. Moore. *Fagan*: R. Ryan. *Bill Sykes*: R. Gordon. *The Dodger*: R. Hobbs.

Scene 7

"Cinderella Brown"

G. Lawrence

Assisted by McCann Sisters, Chester Hale's International Girls.

Soft Shoe Dance

G. Lawrence, H. Whalen

Scene 8

The Peddlers

Krausmeyer: J. Pearl. *Mandelbaum*: H. Richman.

Scene 9

Argentinita (The Idol of Spain in her Dance Specialty)

"Spain" (Tango)

M. Moss, G. Fontana

With Chester Hale's International Girls, Show Girls

Scene 10

"Boop-Boop-Poop-a-Doop"[98]

F. Moore

(*Music by* Alberta Nichols. *Lyrics by* Mann Holiner.)

Scene 11

"Classical Blues"[99]

(*Music by* Raie DaCosta.)

Scene 12

Anton Dolin[100]

Scene 13

Women[101]

Tom: H. Jans. *Bill*: H. Whalen. *The Woman*: E. Muir.

Scene 14

Harry Richman

---

[96]Dropped after opening.
[97]Dropped after opening.
[98]Dropped after opening.
[99]Dropped after opening.
[100]Dropped after opening.
[101]Dropped after opening.

Scene 15

"That's Why We're Dancing"

E. Muir

In the Air: Berinoff and Eulalie. And Chester Hale's International Girls.

Scene 16

Finale

Entire Company

1930.10   # THE GREEN PASTURES

A Fable (with Music) in Two Acts, 18 Scenes. Play by Marc Connelly. Suggested by Roark Bradford's Southern Sketches "Ol' Man Adam an' His Chillun." Production (settings, costumes, lighting) by Robert Edmund Jones. Directed by Marc Connelly. Music under the direction of Hall Johnson. All choral arrangements used have been written especially for "The Green Pastures" by Hall Johnson. Produced by Lawrence Rivers, Inc. Opened 26 February 1930 at the Mansfield Theatre and closed 29 August 1931 after 640 performances.

CAST (in order of appearance):*Mr. Deshee*: CHARLES H. MOORE. *Myrtle*: Alicia Escamilla. *First Boy*: Jazzlips Richardson, Jr. *Second Boy*: Howard Washington. *Third Boy*: Reginald Blythwood. *Randolph*: Joe Byrd. *A Cook*: Frances Smith. *Custard Maker*: HOMER TUTT. *First Mammy Angel*: ANNA MAE FRITZ. *A Stout Angel*: JOSEPHINE BYRD. *A Slender Angel*: EDNA THROWER. *Archangel*: J. A. SHIPP. *Gabriel*: WESLEY HILL. *The Lord*: RICHARD B. HARRISON. *Choir Leader*: McKinley Reeves. *Adam*: DANIEL L. HAYNES. *Eve*: INEZ RICHARDSON WILSON. *Cain*: LOU VERNON. *Cain's Girl*: Dorothy Randolph. *Zeba*: EDNA M. HARRIS. *Cain the Sixth*: JAMES FULLER. *Boy Gambler*: Louis Kelsey. *First Gambler*: Collington Hayes. *Second Gambler*: Ivan Sharp. *Voice in Shanty*: JOSEPHINE BYRD. *Noah*: (Salem) TUTT WHITNEY. *Noah's Wife*: Susie Sutton. *First Woman*: DINKS THOMAS. *Second Woman*: ANNA MAE FRITZ. *Third Woman*: Geneva Blythwood. *First Man*: EMORY S. RICHARDSON. *Flatfoot*: FREDDIE ARCHIBALD. *Ham*: J. HOMER TUTT. *Japheth*: STANLEIGH MORRELL. *First Cleaner*: JOSEPHINE BYRD. *Second Cleaner*: FLORENCE FIELDS. *Abraham*: J. A. SHIPP. *Isaac*: Charles H. Moore. *Jacob*: EDGAR BURKS. *Moses*: ALONZO FENDERSON. *Zipporah*: MERCEDES GILBERT. *Aaron*: McKinley Reeves. *A Candidate Magician*: Reginald Fenderson. *Pharoah*: GEORGE RANDOL. *The General*: Walt McClane. *First Wizard*: Emory S. Richardson. *Head Magician*: ARTHUR PORTER. *Joshua*: STANLEIGH MORRELL. *First Scout*: Ivan Sharp. *Master of Ceremonies*: BILLY CUMBY. *King of Babylon*: JAY MONDAYE. *Prophet*: Ivan Sharp. *High Preist*: J. HOMER TUTT. *The King's Favorites*: Leonore Winkler, Florence Lee, Constance Van Dyke, Mary Ella Hart, Inez Persand. *Officer*: Emory Richardson. *Hezdrel*: DANIEL L. HAYNES. *Another Officer*: Stanleigh Morrell.

The Children: Philistine Bumgardner, Margery Bumgardner, Freda Longshaw, Wilbur Cohen, Jr., Verdon Perdue, Ruby Davis, Willmay Davis, Margerette Thrower, Viola Lewis. *Angels and Townspeople*: Amy Escamilla, Elsie Byrd, Benveneta Washington, Thula Ortiz, Ruth Carl, Geneva Blythwood. *Babylonian Band*: Carl Shorter, Earl Bowie, Thomas Russell, Richard Henderson. *The Choir: Sopranos*: Bertha Wright, Geraldine Gooding, Marie Warren, Mattie Harris, Elsie Thompson, Massie Patterson, Marguerite Avery. *Altos*: Evelyn Burwell, Ruthena Matson, Leona Avery, Mrs. Willie Mays, Viola Mickens, Charlotte Junius. *Tenors*: John Warner, Joe Loomis, Walter Hilliard, Harold Foster, Adolph Henderson, William McFarland, McKinley Reeves, Arthur Porter. *Baritones*: Marc D'Albert, Jerome Addison, Walter Whitfield, D. K. Williams. *Basses*: Lester Holland, Cecil McNair, Tom Lee, Walter Meadows, Frank Horace.

Act 1, Scene 1: The Sunday School. *Scene 2*: A Fish Fry. *Scene 3*: A Garden. *Scene 4*: Outside the Garden. *Scenes 5*: A Roadside. *Scene 6*: A Private Office. *Scene 7*: Another Roadside. *Scene 8*: A House. *Scene 9*: A Hillside. *Scene 10*: A Mountain Top.

Act 2, Scene 1: The Private Office. *Scene 2*: The Mouth of a Cave. *Scene 3*: A Throne Room. *Scene 4*: The Foot of a Mountain. *Scene 5*: A Cabaret. *Scene 6*: The Private Office. *Scene 7*: Outside a Temple. *Scene 8*: Another Fish Fry.

ACT 1

"Oh, Rise and Shine"

"When the Saints Come Marchin' In"

"Cert'n'y, Lord"

"My God Is So High (You Can't Get Over It)"

"Hallelujah!"

"In Bright Mansions Above"

"Don't You Let Nobody Turn You Roun'"

"Run, Sinner, Run"

"You Better Min'"

"Dere's No Hidin' Place Down Dere"

"Some o' Dese Days"

"I Want To Be Ready"

"De Ole Ark's a-Moverin"
"My Soul Is a Witness"
"City Called Heaven" (Entr'acte)

ACT 2
"My Lord's a-Writin' All de Time"
"Go Down, Moses" (*Bass Solo by* Cecil T. McNair.)
"Oh, Mary, Don't You Weep"
"Lord, I Don't Feel Noways Tired"
"Joshua Fit de Battle of Jericho"
"I Can't Stay Away"
"Hail de King of Babylon!" (*Composed by* Hall Johnson.)
"Death's Gointer Lay His Cold, Icy Hands on Me"
"De Blin' Man Stood on de Road an' Cried"
"March On!"
"Oh, Rise and Shine" (reprise)
"Hallelujah, King Jesus!" (*Composed by* Hall Johnson.)

FLYING HIGH

1930.11

A Musical Comedy in Two Acts, 14 Scenes. Book by Buddy G. DeSylva, Lew Brown and John McGowan. Music by Ray Henderson. Lyrics by Buddy G. DeSylva, Lew Brown. Book directed by Edward Clark Lilley. Dances directed by Bobby Connolly. Settings by Joseph Urban. Costumes designed by Charles LeMaire. Orchestra under the direction of Al Goodman. Entire production staged under the direction of George White. Produced by George White. Opened 3 March 1930 at the Apollo Theatre and closed 3 January 1931 after 355 performances.

CAST (in order of appearance): *Eileen Cassidy*: GRACE BRINKLEY. *Bunny McHugh*: PEARL OSGOOD. *Tod Addison*: OSCAR SHAW. *Gordon Turner*: HENRY WHITTEMORE. *Tim*: Bob Lively. *Judy Trent*: Dorothy Hall. *'Sport' Wardell*: RUSS BROWN. *Pansy Parks*: KATE SMITH. *'Rusty' Krause*: BERT LAHR. *Major Watts, M.D.*: Fred Manatt. *Mr. Henry*: Len Shaw. *Mr. Charles*: Jack Bruns. THE GALE QUADRUPLETS: Jane, Jean, Joan, June.

Aviatrixes, Aviators, Mechanics, Witnesses, Visitors, etc.: Ladies of the Ensemble: Joanna Allen, Jane Brown, Hazel Boffinger, Bobbie Campbell, Virginia Case, Doddy Donnelly, Lois Eckhart, Peggy Gallimore, Rita Horgan, Barbara Lee, Dorothy Morgan, Florence Marriner, Vivian Mathison, Maurine McNeil, Peggy Moseley, Edith Martin, Helene B. Miller, Carroll Miller, Beth Holt, Gladys Page, Cornelia Rogers, Jane Stafford, Flora Taylor, Betty Travers, Mildred Webb, Renee Johnson, Carolyn Sickle, Diana Seaby, Al Vickers, Peggy Ring. *Gentlemen of the Ensemble*: Jack Bedford, Don Hudson, Elmer Hertel, Jesse James, Phil King, John McCahill, James Notarro, William Murray, Gus Schilling, Herbert Sampson, Robert Silva, Benjamin R. Tilberg, George Ford, Andy Anderson, Walter Blair, Warren Crosby, Charles B. Davis, Bernie Dossitt, James Howard, Robert Lewis, Clarence Meyers, Charles Rose, Micky Ray, Daniel Wakeley.

Time: The Present.

Act 1, Scene 1: Roof of an Apartment House in Manhattan. July. *Scene 2*: In front of the Apartment House. A moment later. *Scene 3*: Canteen at Newark Airport. Two weeks later. *Scene 4*: Medical Examiner's Office. The same day. *Scene 5*: The Flying Field. Next day. *Scene 6*: In front of the Canteen. Same day.

Act 2, Scene 1: The Waiting Room at the Newark Airport. 38 hours later. *Scene 2*: Outside the Waiting Room. Same day. *Scene 3*: An Anteroom. Same day. *Scene 4*: In front of Major Watts' office. Next day. *Scene 5*: The Flying Field at Midnight. Next night. *Scene 6*: The Flight. Same night. *Scene 7*: In front of the Reception Hall. *Scene 8*: Reception Hall at the Flying Field. 36 hours later.

ACT 1
"I'll Know Him"
    G. Brinkley
"Wasn't It Beautiful While It Lasted"
    O. Shaw, G. Brinkley
"I'll Know Him" (reprise)
    P. Osgood, G. Brinkley
"Air Minded"
    Ensemble
"The First Time for Me"
    B. Lahr, K. Smith
"Flying High"
    P. Osgood, The Gale Quadruplets, Ensemble
"Thank Your Father"
    O. Shaw, G. Brinkley, Ensemble

"Happy Landing"
    O. Shaw, Men
"Good For You—Bad for Me"
    R. Brown, P. Osgood
"Red Hot Chicago"
    K. Smith, The Gale Quadruplets, Ensemble
Finale
    Entire Company

ACT 2
"Rusty's Up in the Air" (Opening Chorus)
    Ensemble
"Without Love"
    G. Brinkley, Boys, Girls
"Mrs. Krause's Blue-Eyed Baby Boy"
    B. Lahr, H. Miller, D. Seaby, J. Allen, P. Moseley, L. Eckhart, H. Boffinger
"Without Love" (reprise)
    O. Shaw
"I'll Get My Man"
    K. Smith, Ensemble
Specialty Dance
    The Gale Quadruplets
"Wasn't It Beautiful" (reprise)
    G. Brinkley
"Without Love" (reprise)
    K. Smith
Specialty Dance
    P. Osgood
Finale
    Entire Company

THE SERENADE

1930.12

A Revival of the Operetta (Comic Opera) in Three Acts[102]. Book and lyrics by Harry B. Smith. Music by Victor Herbert. Directed by Milton Aborn. Settings by Rollo Wayne. Musical director, Louis Kroll. Produced by Jolson's Theatre Musical Comedy Company (Messrs. Shubert, Milton Aborn). Opened 4 March 1930 at Jolson's Theatre and closed 15 March 1930 after 15 performances.

CAST (in order of appearance): *The Duke of Santa Cruz*, a Spanish Grandee: FORREST HUFF. *Dolores*, the Duke's ward, in love with Alvarado: LORNA DOONE JACKSON. *Alvarado*, baritone of the Madrid Opera: GREEK EVANS. *Romero*, an outlaw chief: Charles E. Galagher. *Lopez*, one of Romero's Band: ROY CROPPER. *Colombo*, formerly a Grand Opera tenor: JOHN CHERRY. *Inez*, his daughter, Première Danseuse of the Madrid Opera: OLGA STECK. *Gomez*, a Tailor: William White. *The Colonel*: Hobson Young. *Captain Anselmo*: Carl Dews. *Senora Valdez*, head of a girls' school: Elizabeth Crandall. *School Girls (2)*: *Isabella*: Wee Griffin. *Juana*: Frances Baviello.

Servants, Soldiers, Outlaws, Peasants, School Girls: Ladies of the Ensemble: Frances Baviello, Elizabeth Crandall, Helen Cowan, Anne Chrystie, Emily Harris, Genevieve Jagger, Corinne Jessop, Ida Korost, Tybelle Kane, Gertrude Lindross, Clara Martens, Eleanor Richmond, Velma Lois Sutton, Mabel Thompson, Gertrude Waldon, Eleanor Jenkins, Wee Griffin, Vera Stanley, Joan Lee, Betty Shirley, Florence Fields. *Gentlemen of the Ensemble*: Harold Bomgardner, Angelo Boschediti, Carl Dews, Cosmo D'Almada, Barton Frazier, Donald Gale, Melvin Redden, Hobson Young, John Weeple, E. E. Glassey, Irving Murray, Michael O'Halloran.

Act 1: The Duke's Castle in the Mountainous Region of Spain.

Act 2: Senora Valdez School for Girls and Barracks of Spanish Dragoons.

Act 3: Same as Act 1.

ACT 1
Opening Chorus
    Ensemble
"The Song of the Carbine"
    C. E. Galagher, Ensemble
"Peering Right and Left"
    Ensemble

---

[102]Originally produced 16 March 1897 at the Knickerbocker Theatre for 79 performances. For Synopsis of Scenes and Musical Numbers, see original 1897 production. The libretto, particularly Act 2, was substantially revised by Harry B. Smith. Costumes uncredited.

"For I'm a Jolly Postillon"
G. Evans, Ensemble

Duke's Entrance
F. Huff, Ensemble

"The Funny Side of That"
F. Huff, Ensemble

"I Love Thee, I Adore Thee" (Duet)
L. D. Jackson, G. Evans

EntranceO. Steck, J. Cherry, W. White

"The Singing Lesson" (Trio)
O. Steck, J. Cherry, W. White

"Gaze on This Face So Noble" (Duet)
O. Steck, R. Cropper

Finale

ACT 2

Introduction and Opening Chorus

"In Fair Andalusia"
O. Steck, Ensemble

"Charity"C. E. Galagher, Male Chorus

"Who Can This Be"
F. Huff, L. D. Jackson, Ensemble

"Woman, Lovely Woman"
F. Huff, Ensemble

"The Angelus"
L. D. Jackson, Ensemble

"Cupid and I"
O. Steck

Scene and Quartette
O. Steck, G. Evans, L. D. Jackson, C. E. Galagher

"The Serenade" (reprise)
Male Chorus

Finale

ACT 3

Opening Chorus
Ensemble

"Don José of Sevilla"
L. D. Jackson, G. Evans, Ensemble

"I Envy the Bird" (Romance)
R. Cropper

"Dreaming, Dreaming" (Trio)
F. Huff, O. Steck, W. White

Finale

AN EVENING WITH
MAURICE CHEVALIER

1930.13

A Musical Revue in Two Acts. Produced by Charles Dillingham. Opened 30 March 1930 at the Fulton Theatre and closed 12 April 1930 after 16 performances.

CAST: MAURICE CHEVALIER, ELEANOR POWELL, DUKE ELLINGTON AND HIS COTTON CLUB ORCHESTRA, Henry Wetzel and Ananias Berry (Harlem dance specialties).

ACT 1

DUKE ELLINGTON AND HIS COTTON CLUB ORCHESTRA[103] introducing Henry Wetzel and Ananias Berry in their Harlem dance specialties

"Awful Sad"
(*Music by* Duke Ellington.)

"Mississippi Dry" (from SHOW GIRL)
(*Music by* Vincent Youmans.)

"St. Louis Blues"
(*Music and Lyrics by* W. C. Handy.)

"Black Beauty"
(*Music by* Duke Ellington.)

"When You're Smiling (the Whole World Smiles with You)"
(*Music and Lyrics by* Mark Fisher, Joe Goodwin, Larry Shay.)

"Dear Old Southland"
(*Music by* Turner Layton. *Lyrics by* Henry Creamer.)

"Sweet Jazz o' Mine" [Jas O'Mine]

"The Mooche"
(*Music by* Duke Ellington.)

"Swampy River"
(*Music by* Duke Ellington.)

"East St. Louis Toodle-Oo"
(*Music by* Duke Ellington and Bubber Miley.)

"Come Along, My Mandy" (from THE JOLLY BACHELORS)
(*Music and Lyrics by* Tom Mellor, Harry Gifford. *Lyrics by* Nora Bayes, Jack Norworth.)

"Liza" (from SHOW GIRL)
(*Music by* George Gershwin. *Lyrics by* Gus Kahn and Ira Gershwin.)

Act 2

Maurice Chevalier[104]

French Repertoire

"Dites moi ma mère" (interpolated into INNOCENTS OF PARIS and PLAYBOY OF PARIS, films)
(*Music by* Maurice Yvain. *Lyrics by* Albert Willemetz.)

"En plus grand"

"Je n'peux pas vivre sans amour"
(*Music by* Gaston Gabaroche. *Lyrics by* Fred Pearly.)

"Mon p'tit Tom" (Amour d'Éléphants)
(*Music by* Charles Pothier. *Lyrics by* Albert Willemetz.)

"Ma regulière"
(*Music and Lyrics by* Borel-Clerc, Albert Willemetz, Saint-Granier, Jean Le Seyeux.)

"(Ah,) Si vous saviez"

"Valentine" (interpolated into INNOCENTS OF PARIS, film)
(*Music by* Henri Christiné. *Lyrics by* Albert Willemetz.)

"Si fatigue"

"Pas pour moi"

"Oui or non"

English Repertoire

"All I Want Is Just One Girl" (from PARAMOUNT ON PARADE, film)
(*Music by* Richard A. Whiting. *Lyrics by* Leo Robin.)

"(Up on Top of a Rainbow) Sweepin' the Clouds Away" (from PARAMOUNT ON PARADE, film)
(*Music and Lyrics by* Sam Coslow.)

"It's a Habit of Mine" (from INNOCENTS OF PARIS, film)
(*Music by* Richard A. Whiting. *Lyrics by* Leo Robin.)

"Louise" (from INNOCENTS OF PARIS, film)
(*Music by* Richard A. Whiting. *Lyrics by* Leo Robin.)

"Les Ananas" (from INNOCENTS OF PARIS, film)
(*Music and Lyrics by* Fred Pearly and ? Eddy.)

"Livin' in the Sunlight, (Lovin' in the Moonlight)" (from THE BIG POND, film)
(*Music by* Al Sherman. *Lyrics by* Al Lewis.)

"You Brought a New Kind of Love to Me" (from THE BIG POND, film)
(*Music by* Sammy Fain and Pierre Norman. *Lyrics by* Irving Kahal.)

"My Love Parade" from THE LOVE PARADE, film)
(*Music by* Victor Schertzinger. *Lyrics by* Clifford Grey.)

"Nobody's Using It Now" (from THE LOVE PARADE, film)
(*Music by* Victor Schertzinger. *Lyrics by* Clifford Grey, Victor Schertzinger.)

"Paris, Stay the Same" (Paris, je t'aime d'amour)(from THE LOVE PARADE, film)
(*Music by* Victor Schertzinger. *Lyrics by* Clifford Grey.)

---

[103]Mr. Ellington will play a program of selections (from the listed numbers) in impromptu rotation.

[104]Maurice Chevalier's repertoire not listed in programs; representative list prepared from his 1930 December repertoire as presented in London at the Dominion Theatre.

1930.14

JONICA

A Musical Comedy in Two Acts, 6 Scenes. Book by Dorothy Heyward and Moss Hart (based on an unproduced play "Have a Good Time, Jonica" by Dorothy Heyward). Music by Joseph Meyer. Lyrics by William Moll. Production staged by William B. Friedlander. Dances and ensembles arranged by Pal'mere Brandeaux. Settings designed by William Hawley. Costumes by Faye Graham, Martha Norden, H. Mahieu, Inc. Orchestra under the direction of Carl C. Gray. Produced by William B. Friedlander. Opened 7 April 1930 at the Craig Theatre and closed 10 May 1930 after 40 performances.

CAST (in order of appearance): *A Nun*: Julia Baron. *The Abbess*: Mabel Gore. *Jonica*: NELL ROY. *A Woman*: Clara Thropp. *Millie*: Dorothy Murray. *Benjamin Flood*: BERT MATTHEWS. *A Pullman Porter*: Charles Doyle. *Barney Morton*: EARLE S. DEWEY. *Fanny*: JOYCE BARBOUR. *Mr. Burdick*: George S. Schiller. *Don Milan*: JERRY NORRIS. *Officer Quinn*: HARRY T. SHANNON. *Mary Alice*: JUNE O'DEA. *Mrs. Emma Ross-Benton*: Madeline Gray. *A Butler*: Larry Beck. *Betty*: Priscilla Gurney. *Peggy*: Ruth Goodwin. *Mabel*: IRENE SWOR. *Peter*: Jack Stillman. *Orchestra Leader*: Ralph Hertz. *Wilma and Earlyne Wallace*: The Wallace Sisters (Wilma, Earlyne).

Showgirls, Town Boys, Artists, Bridemaids, Ushers, etc.: *Debutantes*: Mildred Bart, Viola Breit, Gertrude Byrnell, Jean Crittenden, Gertrude Engel, Audrey Gay, Thelma Hackert, Marian Herson, Tina Marie Jensen, Madelyn May, Ida Michael, Rosalie Milan, Vivian McNamara, Georgianna Orr, Estelle Phillips, Elinor Walent, Eleanor Whitney. *Guests*: Leon Alton, Jimmy Ardell, Allan Blair, Bob Burton, Billy Carver, Jack Douglass, Robert Grey, Wallace Jackson, Bob Lamarre, Hazzard Newberry, Chet O'Brien, Gus Quinlan.

Act 1, Scene 1: A Room in a Convent near Buffalo, New York. Nine o'clock at night. *Scene 2*: A Railroad Station, Buffalo, New York. Twenty minutes earlier. *Scene 3*: Interior of a Sleeping Car. Ten minutes later. *Scene 4*: The Plaza of the Berkeley Apartments, New York. The following night. *Scene 5*: Barney Morton's Apartment at the Berkeley. Ten minutes later.

Act 2: The Sun Parlor of Mrs. Ross-Benton's Home in Connecticut.

ACT 1[105]

"The Night It Happened"
  N. Roy, Girls
"Au Revoir"
  Ensemble
Dance
  B. Matthews, I. Swor
"Tonight or Never"
  E. S. Dewey, J. Barbour
"One Step Nearer the Moon"
  J. Barbour, Ensemble
Dance
  Wallace Sisters, P. Gurney
"Specially Made for You"
  B. Matthews, J. O'Dea
"Tie Your Cares to a Melody"
  J. Norris, J. Barbour, B. Matthews, Ensemble
Dance
  R. Goodwin, J. Stillman
"I Want Someone"
  N. Roy, J. Norris
"Beautiful Girls"
  J. Norris, Ensemble
Finale
  Entire Company

ACT 2
"March of the Rice and Old Shoes"
  Ensemble
Dance
  J. Stillman, I. Swor, Wallace Sisters
"A Million Good Reasons"
  J. O'Dea, B. Matthews, Ensemble
"I Want Someone" (reprise)
  N. Roy, J. Norris
"Gotta Do My Duty"[106]
  E. S. Dewey, Girls

Dance
  P. Gurney
"The Apple and the Bough"
  J. Norris, N. Roy, Ensemble
"My Story Ends That Way"[107]
  J. Barbour
"The Wedding Parade"
  Ensemble
Finale
  Entire Company

1930.15

THREE LITTLE GIRLS

A Musical Romance in Three Acts, a Prologue and 16 Scenes. (Original German) Book ("Drei arme kleine Mädels") by Herman Feiner and Bruno Hardt-Warden, adapted by Marie Armstrong Hecht and Gertrude Purcell. Music by Walter Kollo. Lyrics by Harry B. Smith. Staged by J. J. Shubert. Settings designed by Ernest Schrapps. Costumes designed by Ernest Schrapps. Musical director, Louis Kroll. Produced by the Messrs. Shubert. Opened 14 April 1930 at the Sam S. Shubert Theatre, laid-off 30 June–6 July 1930, and closed 19 July 1930 after 104 performances.

CAST (in order of appearance): *Prologue*: *Wendolin*: Charles Brown. *Attendant at the Opera*: Tom Houston. *Baron von Rankenau*: Edward Lester. *Beate-Marie, his daughter*: NATALIE HALL. *Baron von Biebitz-Biebitz*: RAYMOND WALBURN. *Count von Rambow*: JOHN GOLDSWORTHY. *Hendrik Norgard*: CHARLES HEDLEY.

Act 1: *Mrs. Munke, a Landlady*: LORRAINE WEIMAR. *Kunz, a Cobbler*: Stephen Mills. *Otto Kunz, his Nephew*: HARRY PUCK. *Wendolin, who is now Count von Rambow's servant*: Charles Brown. *Count von Rambow, who has lost his fortune*: JOHN GOLDSWORTHY. *Baron von Biebitz-Biebitz, also impoverished*: RAYMOND WALBURN. *Daughters of Count von Rambow (3)*: *Beate*: NATALIE HALL. *Marie*: BETTINA HALL. *Annette*: MARTHA LORBER. *Karl Norgard, son of Hendrik Norgard*: CHARLES HEDLEY. *Fritz von Tormann*: Rollin Grimes. *Franz Walden*: George Dobbs.

Act 2: *von Hoffenstein, Chamberlain to H.S.H. Prince von Hochberg*: Raymond O'Brien. *H.S.R. Prince von Hochberg*: Tom Houston.

Act 3: *Charlotte Forelady in the Doll Shop*: Thelma Goodwin. *Little Marie, Beate's Child, 8 years old*: Frances Hess. *Mme. Beate, owner of the Doll Shop*: NATALIE HALL. *Little Hans Norgard, Karl's son*: Buddy Proctor. *Mademoiselle, his Governess*: Mary Bell. *Marie, Mme. Beate's daughter, now 18*: Margaret Adams. *Elsa, Mme. Beate's assistant in the Doll Shop*: Lillian Lane. *Hans von Kursten, in love with Marie*: John Edwards. *Madame Morrosini, a famous diva*: Bettina Hall. *Escamillo, the Toreador in "Carmen"*: Francis Riley.

Ensemble: *Sopranos*: Margaret Stevenson, Peggy Rose, Isabel Henderson, Diane Doering, Lillian Lane, Thelma Goodwin, Mary Bell. *Altos*: Mary Bowman, Alice Douglas, Dorothy Wyndham, Ruth Adele, Patricia Allen. *First Tenors*: Eric Birlenbach, Ralph Jameson, Jerry Cummings, Maurice Dobell. *Second Tenors*: Charles McClelland, Lu Talbott, George D'Andria. *Baritones*: Tom Houston, Harry Kornbluth. *Bassos*: Caven Jones, Simeon Jurist, Sam Bunin. *Dancers*: Elaine Melchior, Frances Stevens, Norma Perrin, Rosalind Rensing, Artemis Faque, Helen Turner, Marion Mayon, Mary Ray.

Prologue: Court Theatre in Vienna, 1846. The Foyer, during a performance of the opera, "The Prophet," by Giacomo Meyerbeer.

Act 1, Scene 1: The Courtyard of von Rambow's Lodgings—a middle-class district in Vienna—25 years later. *Scene 2*: The Cobbler's Shop. *Scene 3*: The Garden. *Scene 4*: The Courtyard.

Act 2, Scene 1: Chateau Mon Bijou, Home of Count von Rambow. The Boudoir, a month later. *Scene 2*: Small Library. *Scene 3*: Drawing Room. *Scene 4*: In the Garden at the Sun Dial. *Scene 5*: Yellow Salon. *Scene 6*: Small Reception Room. *Scene 7*: The Ballroom.

Act 3, Scene 1: Interior of Beate's Doll Shop in Vienna—10 years later. *Scene 2*: A Room in Beate's Home, adjoining the Doll Shop—10 years later. *Scene 3*: Grand Tier of Boxes, Court Theatre, Vienna, during a performance of "Carmen." *Scene 4*: Antechamber of a Box in the Court Theatre, the same evening. *Scene 5*: Madame Morrosini's Suite at the Hotel—later that evening.

PROLOGUE
"Love's Happy Dream"
  N. Hall, B. Hall, C. Hedley
Finaletto ("Letter Song")
  C. Hedley

ACT 1
Opening Chorus
  Ensemble

---

[105]The song order was revised during the run.
[106]Dropped after opening.

[107]Dropped after opening.

"Whistle While You Work, Boys"
    H. Puck, Boys
    (*Music by* Maurice Rubens.)
"Dream On, (Little Sister)"
    N. Hall, B. Hall
    (*Music by* Maurice Rubens.)
Sextette
    N. Hall, B. Hall, M. Lorber, C. Hedley, R. Grimes, G. Dobbs
"Letter Song"
    N. Hall, C. Hedley
"Annette"
    H. Puck, M. Lorber, G. Dobbs
Finale
    Entire Company
ACT 2
"I'll Tell You"
    B. Hall, Girls
    (*Music by* Maurice Rubens.)
"Habanera" from 'Carmen'[108]
    (*Music by* Georges Bizet.)
    B. Hall
"Lesson in Letter Writing"
    N. Hall, B. Hall, M. Lorber, R. Walburn
Waltz Reprise
    N. Hall, C. Hedley
"Cottage in the Country"[109]
    H. Puck, M. Lorber
Finale
    Entire Company
ACT 3[110]
"Doll Song" (Toy Number)
    T. Goodwin, Girls
"Waltz With Me"
    H. Puck, M. Lorber, Boys, Girls
"Letter Song" (reprise)
    N. Hall
"Love Comes Once in a Lifetime"
    N. Hall, M. Adams
    (*Music by* Harold Stern. *Lyrics by* Stella Unger.) ·
"Love's Happy Dream"
    N. Hall, C. Hedley

KILPATRICK'S
OLD-TIME MINSTRELS

1930.16

A Minstrel Show in Two Acts, an Olio and an Afterpiece. Material selected and edited by Henry Meyers. Staged by J. A. Shipp. Musical numbers staged by Donald Heywood. Technical direction by Walter F. Scott. Produced by Thomas Kilpatrick. Opened 19 April 1930 at the Royale Theatre and closed 26 April 1930 after 9 performances.

<u>CAST</u>: *Bones*: Tom Bethel, Harrison Blackburn, Stanford McKissick, Dan C. Michaels. *Tambourine*: Amon Davis, Sidney Easton, J. Lewis Johnson, John La Rue. *Interlocutor*: HENRY TROY. *Tenors*: John W. Cooper, Louis Craddock, William Hart, Bert Howell, George W. Nixon. *Baritones*: George Battle, Thomas H. Brandon, Rudolph Dawson, Billy Demont. *Basses*: J. W. Mobley, George Myrick, Donald Hayes, James K. Love, R. C. Raines. *Soprano*: Jarahal. *Drum Major*: J. Mardo Brown. (*Ventriloquist*: uncredited.) *Dancers*: William ("Porkchop") Cornish, Rudolph Dawson, etc.

MUSICAL NUMBERS[111]
"We'll Raise the Roof Tonight"
"White Wings, They Never Gow Weary"
    G. W. Nixon
    (*Music and Lyrics by* Banks Winter.)

"Li'l Gal"
    G. Battle
"(There'll Be a) Hot Time in the Old Town Tonight"
    (*Music and Lyrics by* Thedore Metz.)
"Good Morning, Carrie"
    (*Music and Lyrics by* R. C. McPherson, Elmer Bowman, Chris Smith.)
"In the Good Old Summertime"
    (*Music by* George Evans. *Lyrics by* Ren Shields.)
"When the Sunset Turns the Ocean's Blue to Gold"
    L. Craddock
"Trans-Mag-Ni-Fi-Can-Bam-Dam-U-Ality"
"When the Bell in the Lighthouse Rings, Ding Dong"
    R. C. Rains
"My Castle on the (River) Nile"
    (*Music by* James Weldon Johnson. *Lyrics by* Bob Cole.)
"My Babe from Boston Town"
"What You Gonna Tell Massa Peter When You Meet Him at the Gate"
"Bleeding Moon"
    Jarahal
"Down South" (traditional)
Levee Levities (Finale)

1930.17 ## SIR HARRY LAUDER

A Return Engagement of the Vaudeville Entertainment in Two Acts[112]. Produced under the direction of William Morris. Opened 21 April 1930 at the Jolson Theatre and closed 26 April 1930 after 9 performances.

<u>CAST</u>: SIR HARRY LAUDER (Scotch comedy and song), Uyeno Troupe, Fitzgerald and Hoag, Stella Powers, Arnaut Brothers, Don Julian.
ACT 1
Uyeno Troupe (Japanese jugglers)
Fitzgerald & Hoag (The Hollywood Horse)
Stella Powers (prima donna)
Arnaut Brothers ("Two Loving Birds")
Don Julian (continental cartoonist)
ACT 2
Sir Harry Lauder's repertoire will include:
"Flower of the Heather"
"I Love a Lassie"
"When I Get Tae Scotland"
"Roaming in the Gloaming"
"Ta! Ta! Ma Bonnie Maggie Darlin'"
"Waggle o' the Kilt"
"Safest o' th' Family"
"The End of the Road"
"She's Ma Dasiy"
"Nice t' Get Up in th' Morning"
"Hame o' Mine"
"When I Meet McKaye"
"Just Got Off th' Chain"
"Somebody's Waiting for Me"
"Doughie the Baker"
"Cronies o' Mine"

---

[108]Replaced by the Jewel Song from "Faust" (*Music by* Charles Gounod.) for subsequent tour.
[109]Dropped for subsequent national tour.
[110]A Finale to Act 3 appears in programs for subsequent tour, sung by the Entire Company.
[111]Not in performance order.

[112]Sir Harry Lauder previously appeared on Broadway 30 January 1928 at the Knickerbocker Theatre for 55 performances.

1930–1931 SEASON

Fred and Adele Astaire in SMILES (Photo: White Studio)
Billy Rose Theatre Collection, New York Public Library for the Performing Arts

1930–1931 SEASON

1930.18 THE GARRICK GAIETIES (1930)

A Musical Revue in Two Acts, 27 Scenes[1]. Sketches by Carroll Carroll, Leo Poldine (Leopoldine Damrosch), Gretchen Damrosch Finletter, Benjamin M. Kaye, Newman Levy, Sterling Holloway, Louis Simon, Sally Humason, Landon Herrick. Music by Richard Myers, Charles Schwab, Willard Robison, Everett Miller, Vernon Duke, Kay Swift, Marc Blitzstein, Ned Lehak [Lehac], Peter Nolan, Harold Goldman. Lyrics by Edward Eliscu, Henry Myers, Johnny Mercer, Ira Gershwin, E. Y. Harburg, Thomas McKnight, Newman Levy, Paul James [James P. Warburg], Ronald Jeans, Allen Boretz, Joshua Titzell, Marc Blitzstein. Staged by Philip Loeb. Dances by Olin Howland, assisted by Stella Bloch. Settings by Kate Drain Lawson, Costumes by Kate Drain Lawson, Louis Simon, (Henri Peine du Bois.) Music Director, Tom Jones. Produced by the Theatre Guild Inc. Opened 4 June 1930 at the Guild Theatre and closed 8 October 1930 after 158 performances; re-opened a return engagement (see separate entry below) prior to tour in revised form 16 October 1930 at the Guild Theatre and closed 25 October 1930 after 12 performances. Total performances: 170.

CAST: ALBERT CARROLL, EDITH MEISER, PHILIP LOEB, STERLING HOLLOWAY, NAN BLACKSTONE, RUTH SHORPENNING, HILDEGARDE HALLIDAY, JAMES NORRIS, OTTO HULETT, CYNTHIA ROGERS, IMOGENE COCA, VELMA VAVRA, DONALD STEWART, RAY HEATHERTON, THEODORE [Ted] FETTER, WILLIAM TANNEN, EDWIN GILCHER, EDITH SHELDON, THELMA TIPSON, KATE DRAIN LAWSON, Micky Burton, Ginger Meehan, Jo Meyers, Polly Rose, Florentine Sherman, Jane Sherman, Midge Sidney, Ruth Montague, Evelyn LaTour.

ACT 1
Scene 1

Opening Number
Principals, Chorus
A modernistic impression of the Gaieties of 1930 in which the principal members of the cast and chorus appear.

Scene 2

How to Write for the Movies (*by Sally Humason*)
Secretary: I. Coca. *Author*: S. Holloway. *Great Talkie Magnate*: P. Loeb.
The Garrick Gaieties lets you into the secret of how to make money easily and honestly.

Scene 3

"Ankle Up to the Altar"
W. Tannen, T. Tipson
(*Music by* Richard Myers. *Lyrics by* Eddie [Edward] Eliscu.)
Stimulated by Walter Winchell's courageous campaign in the *Daily Mirror* , for the personal privacy of our public citizens. William Tannen and Thelma Tipson represents two 'celebs' who are Adam-and-Lilithing.

Scene 4

The Woman Pays to Advertise (*by Leo Poldine*)
Mr. Hayfoot: A. Carroll. *Mrs. Schuyler Thornton*: R. Chorpenning. *Mrs. Gloria Sanderhoff*: H. Halliday. *Duchesse de Barbizon*: E. Meiser. *Marjorie Boyle*: T. Tipson.
The Junior Members of the Senior League contribute to Dr. Watson's bad-behavioristic theories of advertising.

Scene 5

"You Lost Your Opportunity"
J. Norris, E. Sheldon, I. Coca, Chorus
(*Music by* Charles M. Schwab. *Lyrics by* Henry Myers.)
We are told that the Lost Opportunity never returns. James Norris is the Opportunity, Edith Sheldon is the young girl who loses the Opportunity. The girl who takes the Opportunity is Imogene Coca. The chorus is also given an opportunity.

Scene 6

The Soda Fountain (*by Carroll Carroll*)
A. Carroll, J. Norris, Chorus
The effect of our newer Soda Counter concoctions upon the tender sensibilities of a very tender and sensitive young man portrayed by Albert Carroll, with James Norris and everyone else rendering the first aid.

[1] The third and final musical revue in the annual Theatre Guild series which began in 1925.

Scene 7

"Do Tell"
(*Music by* Charles M. Schwab. *Lyrics by* Henry Myers.)
The Chatelaine: H. Halliday. *The Demi-Chatelaine*: R. Chorpenning. *The Demi-Semi-Chatelaine*: K. D. Lawson.
The dear old gossips get together in one of the more exclusive Catskill resorts.

Scene 8

"Lazy Levee Loungers"
N. Blackstone, Chorus
(*Music and Lyrics by* Willard Robison.)
The labor problems of the South are here ventilated for the first time. Nan Blackstone is the labor agitator or anything else you please; it makes no difference to this song. The chorus portrays a group of Southern radicals.

Scene 9

Mei Lan-Fang (*by* Benjamin M. Kaye. *Music by* Vernon Duke.)
Interpreter: H. Halliday. *Tony*: W. Tannen. *Judge*: J. Norris. *Opera Singer*: D. Stewart. *Boy from Orange, N.J.*: T. Fetter. *Muriel*: A. Carroll. *Property Man*: E. Gilcher.
The inimitable Albert Carroll imitates the inimitable Mei Lan-Fang in "Strictly Honorable,"[2] a play translated from the American.

Scene 10

"Out of Breath (and Scared to Death of You)"
S. Holloway, C. Rogers
(*Music by* Everett Miller. *Lyrics by* Johnny Mercer.)
Two 'Fraidy-cats' at work.

Scene 11

A Famous Lawyer at Home (*by* Newman Levy)
The Great Trial Lawyer: P. Loeb. *His Wife*: E. Meiser. *The Maid*: I. Coca.
The audience (is) requested to act as the jury and to decide who is to win this case.

Scene 12

"I Am Only Human After All"
(*Music by* Vernon Duke. *Lyrics by* E. Y. Harburg and Ira Gershwin. *Orchestration by* Johnny Green.)
The Boy: J. Norris. *The Girl*: V. Vavra. *The Broker*: P. Loeb. *The Girl Friend*: I. Coca. *The Tough*: N. Blackstone. *Her Victim*: S. Holloway.
We feel there should be a solemn moment in our revue. In the midst of our ecstatic flights of fancy, we remind you that we, too, are human.

Scene 13

"Just a Sister"
E. Meiser
(*Music and Lyrics by* Thomas McKnight.)
Edith Meiser does a sister-act with herself.

Scene 14

They Always Come Back (*by* Newman Levy)
"I'm Grover"
(*Music by* Vernon Duke. *Lyrics by* Newman Levy.)
"Johnny Wanamaker"
(*Music by* Kay Swift. *Lyrics by* Paul James.)
Traffic Saleslady: R. Chorpenning. *Body Guard*: K. D. Lawson. *Grover*: P. Loeb. *Floorwalkers*: D. Stewart, W. Tannen, R. Heatherton, T. Fetter. *First Customer*: C. Rogers. *Second Customer*: O. Hulett. *His Wife*: H. Halliday. *His Daughter*: M. Sidney. *Beautiful Customer*: T. Tipson.
As our audiences probably know, Wanamaker's is one of the oldest and best conducted stores in New York, but some members of our audiences may not know that Mr. Whalen was loaned by Wanamaker's to the New York Police Department for one year, and has since resumed his old position. The following phantasy is offered as a possibility of what might have happened (but did not happen) had Mr. Whalen decided to apply the methods which he learned in the Police Department in running this famous department store.

ACT 2[3]

[2] A burlesque of Preston Sturges' play 'Strictly Dishonorable.'
[3] Added during run to Act 2:
"George and Mary"
E. Meiser, A. Carroll
(*Music by* Charles M. Schwab. *Lyrics by* Thomas McKnight.)
A visit to Buckingham Palace with Edith Meiser and Albert Carroll.
Shoo (*by* Hi Alexander)
The Clerk: A. Carroll. *The Customer*: P. Loeb.
Going to the Play (*by* Gretchen Damrosch Finletter)

Scene 1

"Triple Sec"

(*Book by* Ronald Jeans. *Music by* Marc Blitzstein.)
Hostess: R. Montague. *Perkins I*: J. Sherman. *Hopkins I*: J. Norris. *Lord Silverside I*: R. Heatherton. *Stranger I*: R. Chorpenning. *Lady Betty I*: E. LaTour. *Hopkins II*: D. Stewart. *Stranger II*: V. Vavra. *Lord Silverside II*: T. Fetter. *Lady Betty II*: T. Tipson. *Lady Betty III*: I. Coca. *Perkins 2, 3, 4, 5, 6, 7, 8*: Ensemble.
A modernistic operetta which is not to be taken too seriously.

Scene 2

"Beauty"[4]
E. Meiser
(*Music by* Ned Lehak. *Lyrics by* Allen Boretz.)
Edith Meiser tells us in her own manner just what beauty is, just what clothes are, how to get along with them, and how to get along without them.

Scene 3

"Love Is Like That"
S. Holloway, I. Coca, Chorus
(*Music by* Ned Lehak. *Lyrics by* Allen Boretz.)
Sterling Holloway and Imogene Coca in a metaphysical discourse on the nature, origins, causes and effects of love, assisted with demonstration by the chorus.

Scene 4

Uncle Sea Gull (*by* Landon Herrick)
Masha: E. Meiser. *Pasha*: T. Tipson. *Vasha*: H. Halliday. *Lasha*: C. Rogers. *Chasha*: R. Chorpenning. *Sasha*: W. Tannen. *Golosha*: E. Gilcher.
(The alternative title is 'Ten Years in the Country.') One of those cheerful little things from the Russian, produced under the influence of the Moscow Art Theatre.

Scene 5

"Four Infant Prodigies"
(*Music by* Ned Lehak. *Lyrics by* Allen Boretz.)
Child Poet: E. Meiser. *Child Violinist*: P. Loeb. *Child Evangelist*: R. Chorpenning. *Child Movie Actor*: S. Holloway.
All by the permission of the Society for the Prevention of Cruelty to Children.

Scene 6

"Put It Away Till Spring"
(*Music by* Peter Nolan. *Lyrics by* Josiah Titzell.)
The Unenterprising Boy: W. Tannen. *The Girl*: I. Coca. And Chorus.
In which the younger generation fails to take advantage of an obvious method of warming up during the cold weather. The chorus symbolizes the Weather Bureau pushing the season ahead.

Scene 7

Life in Hollywood (*by* Benjamin M. Kaye)
Ginnigan, the great movie director: O. Hulett. *The Great Super-Great Movie Star*: C. Rogers. *The Greater Super-Greater Star*: T. Tipson. *The Great Super-Super-Great Crowd of Authors, Actors, Directors, etc.*: Cast.
The function of a formal afternoon tea as observed in ultra-conservative Hollywood circles.

Scene 8

"Got It Again"
N. Blackstone
(*Music by* Ned Lehak. *Lyrics by* Allen Boretz.)
A lady laments her inability to control her emotions.

Scene 9

"Scheherezade"
(*Music and Lyrics by* Harold Goldman.)
The Serious-Minded Young Travelling Kibbitzer: P. Loeb. *The Sultan*: S. Holloway. *Scheherezade*: E. Meiser. *The Sultan's Favorite (pro tem)*: K. D. Lawson. *The Entourage*: Chorus.
The important question of what goes on in the common or garden harem.

Scene 10

Three Little Time Killers[5]
M. Sidney, J. Sherman, P. Rose

Scene 11

The Last Mile (*by* Louis M. Simon and Sterling Holloway)

The Man in the Box Office: A. Carroll. *The Ticket Buyers*: J. Norris, T. Fetter. *The Would-Be Theatre Patron*: R. Chorpenning.
Theatre ticket shopping before the opening of the New York Theatre Ticket League.

[4]Dropped during run.
[5]Dropped during run.

Stout Lady: R. Chorpenning. *Little Boy*: T. Fetter. *His Mother*: E. Meiser. *Old Man*: A. Carroll. *Young Man*: S. Holloway. *Well Dressed Man*: J. Norris. *Motorman*: O. Hulett. *Negro*: D. Stewart. *Old Lady*: H. Halliday.
This is inspired directly by the recent prison breaks, combined with a trip on a cross-town street car.

Scene 12

"Shavian Shivers"
(*Music by* Vernon Duke. *Lyrics by* E. Y. Harburg.)
Hostess: C. Rogers. *Hope Williams*: T. Tipson. *Bill Robinson*: E. LaTour. *Helen Kane*: J. Meyers. *Chevalier*: W. Tannen. *Mrs. Fiske*: A. Carroll. *Ann Pennington*: E. Sheldon. *Ann Pennington II*: I. Coca. And Chorus.
A song about Shaw which is expected to make Shakespeare turn in his grave with envy.

Scene 13

"When the Sun Meets the Moon in Finale-Land"
D. Stewart
(*Music by* Charles M. Schwab. *Lyrics by* Henry Myers.)
The Sun: R. Heatherton. *The Moon*: E. Meiser. *The Eclipse*: E. Gilcher. *The Stars*: Chorus. *The Signs of the Zodiac*: Principals. *The Three Graces*: P. Loeb, K. D. Lawson, T. Fetter.
An exaggeration of the usual thing, based on the new astronomy of Albert Einstein. The action is somewhat complicated, so we will explain it in detail. The Sun meets the Moon, thereby causing the Eclipse. The stars followed by the Signs of the Zodiac and the Three Graces come in for no particular reason and create a general disturbance of the Universe.

1930.19 # CHANGE YOUR LUCK

A Negro Musical Comedy in Two Acts, 9 Scenes. Book by Garland Howard. Music and lyrics by J. C. Johnson. Directed by Cleon Throckmorton. Dances by Lawrence Deas, Speedy Smith. Settings by Cleon Throckmorton. Costumes designed by Hilda Farnham. Musical director, Stanley Bennett. Produced by Cleon Throckmorton. Opened 6 June 1930 at the George M. Cohan Theatre and closed 19 June 1930 after 16 performances.

CAST: *Big Bill*: Alex Lovejoy. *Cateye*: Jimmy [James] Thomas. *Hot Stuff Jackson*: GARLAND HOWARD. *Malindy*: ALBERTA PERKINS. *Profit Jones*: SAM CROSS. *Skybo Snowball*: SPEEDY SMITH. *Bandana Babe Peppers*: CORA LA REDD. *Romeo Green*: STERLING GRANT. *Josephine Peppers*: NEEKA SHAW. *Mary Jane*: ALBERTA HUNTER. *Diamond Joe*: Chick McKenney. *Ebeneezer Smart*: HAMTREE HARRINGTON. *Mathilda*: Mabel Gant. *Evergreen Peppers*: LEIGH WHIPPER. *Passionate Sadie*: Millie Holmes. *Rat Row Sadie*: Emma Maitland. *Tack Annie*: Aurelia Wheeldin. *Sisters of Mercy (3)*: *Dottie*: Dorothy Embry. *Mary*: Mary Mason. *Lil*: Lillian Cowan. *Hot Pepper Henry*: Henry Davis. *Hot Pepper Jimmy*: James Davis. *Hot Pepper Van*: Van Jackson. *Ansy*: Bertha Roe. *Percolatin Gertie*: Gertie Chambers. *Short Dog*, the Hoofer: Yank Bronson. *Charleston Sam*, the Hoofer: SAMMY VAN. *Shake a Hip*, a Bellboy: Louis Simms. *Shake a Leg*, a Bellboy: Buster Bowie. *Captain Jones*: J. Lewis Johnson. *The Four Flash Devils*: S. W. Warren, Charles Gill, Billy Cole, C. P. Wade. *Dancing Girls, Levee Maids, Rat Row Randies, Roustabouts, Stevedores, High Yellows and Seal Skin Browns, Church Folks, Citizens of Sundown.*

Members of the Uplift Leage: Pauline Jackson, Fred McCoy, Charles H. Downz, Mae Haywood, Alice Cannon, DeWitt Davis, Harry Watkins, Millie Holmes, Luther Henderson, J. W. Mobley, Angeline Lawson, J. Lewis Johnson, James McPeters, Sally Goldman, Frederick Wheeldin, Sylvia Collins, Emma Thomas, Ida Dewey, Chester Jones, Ida Rowley, Cy Williams.

Act 1, Scene 1: The Levee, Sundown, Mississippi. *Scene 2*: Street in Sundown. *Scene 3*: Sunflower Lane. *Scene 4*: Interior of Evergreen Pepper's Funeral Parlor. *Scene 5*: Street in Sundown. *Scene 6*: Lobby of Sundown Hotel.

Act 2, Scene 1: Rat Row. Across the River. *Scene 2*: Street in Rat Row. *Scene 3*: Lawn Fete at Evergreen Pepper's Home.

ACT 1[6]

Opening Chorus ("Roll Dem Bales Along")
Ensemble
"Sweet Little Baby o' Mine"
N. Shaw, G. Howard, L. Simms, B. Bowie, Ensemble
"Can't Be Bothered Now"
C. La Redd, Four Hot Peppers, Sisters of Mercy
"Ain't Puttin' Out Nothin'"
A. Lovejoy, A. Perkins
"Religion in My Feet"
Sundown Trio, Four Flash Devils, S. Van, Ensemble

---

[6]Added during run:
"Rat Row Drag"
"Boxing Bout"

"You Should Know"
    N. Shaw, S. Grant, Ensemble
"Wasting Away"
    A. Hunter, C. McKenney
"Walk Together, Children"
    S. Cross, Uplift League
"Honesty"[7]
    S. Grant, N. Shaw, Sundown Trio, Dance Sextet
"Mr. Mammy Man"
    N. Shaw, G. Howard, Girls
Dance Specialty
    L. Simms, B. Bowie
"My Regular Man"
    C. La Redd, S. Van, Ensemble
"I'm Honest"
    S. Grant, Sundown Trio
"Reprisal"[8]
    Entire Company

ACT 2
"We're Here"
    A. Perkins, Ensemble
"Low Down Dance"[9]
    C. McKenney, S. Van, Girls
"Open That Door"[10]
    S. Smith, M. Holmes
"Change Your Luck"
    H. Harrington, A. Hunter
"Percolatin'"
    C. La Redd, Girls
Dance Specialty
    G. Chambers
"Travellin'"
    S. Cross, A. Hunter, Ensemble
"St. Louis Blues"[11]
    Four Hot Peppers
    (*Music and Lyrics by* W. C. Handy.)
"What Have I Done?"[12]
    N. Shaw, S. Grant
Dance
    S. Grant, G. Howard, N. Shaw
"Rhythm Feet"[13]
    L. Simms, B. Bowie
Finale
    Entire Company

1930.20 ARTISTS AND MODELS (1930)

A Musical Revue (Paris-Riviera Edition) in Two Acts, 18 Scenes[14]. (New) Music and lyrics by Harold Stern and Ernie Golden.[15] Dialogue staged by Frank Smithson. Dances by Pal'mere Brandeaux. Settings by Watson Barratt. Costumes by Ernest Schrapps. Music director, Max Meth. Produced by the Messrs. Shubert. Opened 10 June 1930 at the Majestic Theatre and closed 26 July 1930 after 55 performances.

CAST (in order of appearance): *Pierre*: HALFRED YOUNG. *Bournet*: George Del Drego. *Maurice*: GEORGE HASSELL. *Mr. Harris*: STANLEY HARRISON. *Waiter*: Harry Welsh. *Naomi*: Naomi Johnson. *Girl*: Dorothy Drum. *Paul*: WESLEY PIERCE.

[7]Dropped during run.
[8]Dropped during run.
[9]Dropped during run.
[10]Dropped during run.
[11]Dropped during run.
[12]Dropped during run.
[13]Dropped during run.
[14]The fifth in the annual series of musical revues produced by the Messrs. Shubert beginning in 1923.
[15]Book and lyrics uncredited; based on the English musical "Dear Love," book by Dion Titheradge, Lauri Wylie, Herbert Clayton. Music by Haydn Wood, Joseph Tunbridge, Jack Waller. Lyrics by Dion Titheradge.

Jeanette: VERA PEARCE. *Mrs. Maurice*: AILEEN STANLEY. *Marie*: DOLORES DE MONDE. *Suzanne*: MARY ADAMS. *Butler*: Archie Roberts. *Nanette*: HAZEL HARRIS. *Denise*: Kay Simmons. *Kay*: KAY MCKAY. *Policewoman*: Dimple Reide. *Blonde*: Jane Manners. *Brunette*: Elaine Orlove. *Attendant*: Kay Simmons. *Swimming Instructor*: Violet Carson. *First Girl*: Vivian Hall. *Second Girl*: Dorothy Drum. *Specialties*: PHIL BAKER, MISS FLORENCE (Eileen Speeler, Vivian Hall), HAVANA CUBANOLA RUMBA BAND, Terry Horne, Naomi Johnson, Rath Brothers, Rosemary Deering.

Show Girls: Marian Alden, Emmita Casanova, Dolores Bara, Theresa Meredith, Jeannett Mundel, Vasilka Petrova, Georgia MacKinnon, Mary Clark, Alice Wood, Billy Hill, Dimple Riede, Alicia Parnahay, Sylks Fontaine, Dorothy Drum, Helen Worth, Peggy Fish, Vivian Hall, Bobby Hamilton, Elaine Orlove, Jane Manners, Gloria Christy, Patricia Marquise, Jose Larkin. *Dancers*: Violet Carson, Lillian Carson, Alvina Carson, Peggy Thomas, Ruth Bannon, Inez Goetz, Jeanne Walton, Esther Whetton, Georgia MacTaggart, Verta Kunkel, Dorothy Goodman, Jane Love, Margot Nelson, Rosalie Milan, Maxine Darrell, Peggy O'Day, Evelyn Ford, Sally Ritz, Eleanor Whitney, Jackie Marquise, Ethel Dunton. *Gentlemen of the Ensemble*: Jimmie Carr, Jack Fago, Al Bloom, Frazier McMahon, Ed Murray, Gus Quinlan, Fred Packard, Jack Ross, George Del Drego, Kaji Hansen, John Perkins, William Burdee.

Act 1, Scene 1: Cafe Parisienne, overlooking the Mediterranean. 11 P.M. *Scene 2*: Parade of Show Girls. *Scene 3*: Jeanette's Boudoir. A few minutes later. *Scene 4*: Artists and Models Ballet. *Scene 5*: Salon of Maurice's Villa. A few minutes later. *Scene 6*: Phil Baker. *Scene 7*: Banquet Scene in Cafe Parisienne.

Act 2, Scene 1: Exterior of the School of Art. *Scene 2*: Wesley Pierce and Hazel Harris. *Scene 3*: "The Tree." *Scene 4*: Front of Solarium. *Scene 5*: Interior of Solarium. *Scene 6*: Phil Baker, Naomi Johnson and Boys. *Scene 7*: Pierre's Studio. *Scene 8*: Aileen Stanley. *Scene 9*: "Nargileh." *Scene 10*: "Sex Appeal." *Scene 11*: Terrace of the Hotel DeMaxim, on the Riviera.

ACT 1[16]
Scene 1
    "Perfect Models"
        Dancers
        (*Music and Lyrics by* H. Wood, J. Tunbridge, J. Waller, D. Titheradge.)
    "Ups and Downs"
        W. Pierce, Ensemble
    "Budapest"
        V. Pearce, Ensemble
        (*Music and Lyrics by* H. Wood, J. Tunbridge, J. Waller, D. Titheradge.)
Scene 3
    "My Real Ideal"
        M. Adams, D. De Monde
        (*Music by* Burton Lane. *Lyrics by* Samuel Lerner.)
Scene 5
    Ballet
        R. Deering, Ballet Ensemble
    "Ro-Ro-Rollin' Along"
        A. Stanley
    "Jimmie and Me"
        A. Stanley
    "Old Lady in the Shoe"
        A. Stanley
    "Two Perfect Lovers"
        M. Adams, H. Young
        (*Music and Lyrics by* H. Wood, J. Tunbridge, J. Waller, D. Titheradge.[17])
    "Parisian Tango"
        W. Pierce, H. Harris
Scene 7
    "Perfect Models" (reprise)
        H. Young
    Specialty
        E. Speeler, V. Hall
    "In Old Havana Town"
        P. Baker, Girls
    "The Rumba"
        Entire Company, acc. by Havana Cubanola Rumba Band

[16]Added during run to Act 1:
    Specialty
        Shaw & Lee
    "Sirens of Ceylon" Undersea Ballet
        (Ballet Ensemble)
[17]Elsewhere credited to Burton Lane and Samuel Lerner.

ACT 2

Scene 1

"Dance, Dance, Dance"
    Ensemble
"Without a Shadow of a Doubt"
    M. Adams, H. Young
    (*Music and Lyrics by* Ord Hamilton.)
"L-O-V-E"
    D. De Monde, W. Pierce, Ensemble
    (*Music and Lyrics by* H. Wood, J. Tunbridge, J. Waller, D. Titheradge.)
"I Want You to Love Me"
    G. Hassell, V. Pearce
    (*Music and Lyrics by* H. Wood, J. Tunbridge, J. Waller, D. Titheradge.)

Scene 2

Dance
    W. Pierce, H. Harris

Scene 3

"The Tree"
    H. Young
    Danced by R. Deering.

Scene 8

"Where You Are"
    A. Stanley

Scene 9

"Nargileh"
    E. Speeler, V. Hall

Scene 10

"Sex Appeal"[18]
    K. McKay, Little Models

Scene 11

Finale
    Entire Company

MYSTERY MOON

1930.21

A Novelty Musical Comedy in Two Acts. Book by Fred [Frederick] Herendeen. Music and lyrics by Monte Carlo and Alma Sanders. Staged by Victor Morley. Dances and ensembles by Bunny Weldon. Settings by Theatrical Art Studios. Costumes by Brooks. Music director, Ernie Valle. Orchestrations, Hilding Anderson, Maurice DePackh, Hans Spillach [Spialek], Joe Weiss. Juliana's routines devised and staged by Bert Angeles. Entire production under the supervision of Paul M. Trebitsch. Produced by James M. Graf, in association with Paul M. Trebitsch. Opened and closed 23 June 1930 at the Royale Theatre after 1 performance.

CAST: *Lee Foo*, a Chinaman: Curtis Karpe. *"Flash" Darrell*, Manager: Arthur Uttry. *Mildred Middleton*, Soubret: KITTY KELLY. *Queenie North*, ex-Tiller Girl: Winifred Barry. *Smith Banks*, Comedian: Harry Short. *Don Bradley*, Juvenile: ARTHUR CAMPBELL. *Lola Harriott*, Specialty Singer: FRANCES SHELLEY. *May Delight*, Leading Lady: Maude Brooks. *Goldie Del Monte*, Prima Donna: PAULINE DEE. *Premiere Danseuse*: JULIANA. *Orchestra Leader*: Ernie Valle. *James Boyd*, Specialty Dancer: Frank J. Marshall, Jr. *Gladys St. James*, a Chorus Girl: Virginia Watts. *Pearl Lindy*, a Chorus Girl: Marjorie Gaines. *Bessie Van Neer*, a Chorus Girl: Virginia Dawe. *Sam Martin*, Property Boy: CHARLES LAWRENCE. *Joe Hendricks*, Janitor, etc.: Frank Shannon. *Ben Flint*: Proprietor of the Theatre: Harrison Brookbank. *Doris Flint*, His Granddaughter: JANE TAYLOR. *Constable Smedley Baker*, also M.D.: Larry Woods. *Specialty*: Nat Lazarro, Jr.

Chorus Girls: Dorothy Waller, Helen Swift, Doris Delante, Ellen Sparks, Vivian Roscoe, Louise Baldwin, Faith Hope, Leonra Theodra, Vera Clark, Ruth Hatch, Gene Fontaine, Bee Walz, Dorothy Dawn, Rosalie Trego, Kay Apgar, Lenore Simone, Elsie Thorne.

Acts 1 and 2: The Stage and Interior of the Portal Palace Theatre, Portal, North Dakota.

ACT 1

"Pepper and Salt"
    M. Gaines, Chorus
"Mechanical Man"
    K. Kelly, C. Lawrence, Chorus

---

[18]Replaced during the run with:
"Feminine Rhythm"
    N. Johnson, D. De Monde, J. Muldowney

Solo
    F. J. Marshall, Jr.
"You Always Talk of Friendship"
    F. Shelley
"One Night in the Rain"
    P. Dee, Chorus
"What Could I Do, But Fall in Love With You?"
    K. Kelly, C. Lawrence
"It's All O.K."
    A. Campbell, J. Taylor, Chorus
Solo Dance
    Juliana
Finale

ACT 2

"Mystery Moon"
    J. Taylor, A. Campbell, P. Dee
Interpretive Solo
    Juliana, Ballet
"Why Couldn't We Incorporate?"
    K. Kelly, C. Lawrence
"Milkmaids of Broadway"
    M. Gaines, Chorus
"It's All O.K." (reprise)
    A. Campbell, J. Taylor
"Clean Out the Corner"
    F. Shelley, M. Gaines, Chorus
Specialty
    N. Nazarro, Jr.
Naval Conference
    Napoleon: H. Brookbank. *Prince Karl*: A. Campbell. *Mussolini*: A. Uttry. *Lady Astor*: W. Barry. *Empress Josephine*: P. Dee. *Queen Marie of Rumania*: K. Kelly. *Hon. Al. Smith*: H. Short. *"Hardboiled" Smith, U.S.N.*: C. Lawrence. *News Reporter*: V. Dawe. *Major Domo*: C. Karpe. *Ladies of the Court, Pages, Reporters*.
Finale
    Entire Company

EARL CARROLL VANITIES (1930)

1930.22

A Musical Revue in Two Acts, 67 Scenes[19]. Assembled by Earl Carroll. Dialogue (sketches) by Eddie Welch, Eugene Conrad. Music by Harold Arlen, Jay Gorney. Lyrics by Ted Koehler, E. Y. Harburg. Staged by Earl Carroll, Priestley Morrison. Dances by LeRoy J. Prinz. Settings by Hugh Willoughby. Costumes by Charles LeMaire, Vincente Minnelli. Music director, Ray Kavanaugh. Orchestrations by Domenico Savino. Produced by Earl Carroll. Opened 1 July 1930 at the New Amsterdam Theatre and closed 3 January 1931 after 215 performances.

CAST: JIMMIE [Jimmy] SAVO, DOROTHY BRITTON, IRENE AHLBERG, HERB WILLIAMS, JACK BENNY, PATSY KELLY, COLETTE SISTERS (Mildred, Ruth), JOHN HALE, BETTY VERONICA, HARRY STOCKWELL, FRANK and HARRY CONDOS, THELMA WHITE, FAITH BACON, Ronald Fielder, Claiborne Bryson, Naomi Ray, Edward Harrison, Louis Harrison, Billy Rolls, Murray Bernie, Maurice, Vivian Fay.

Ensemble: Eileen Wenzel, Frances Joyce, Marion Carewe, Kae Carroll, Constance Trevor, Marion O'Day, June Brewster, Nelda Kincaid, Beryl Wallace, Alice Kerwin, Elizabeth Sundmark, Rose Shaw, Renee Havel, Helen Arlan, Geraldine Pratt, Julia Jenner, Martha Devine, Renee Bonnie, Edith Pragan, Rosa Fronson, Paula Sands, Ida Michael, Vera Milton, Mary Pleasants, Genie Fursa, Nondas Metcalf, Mabel Nordman, Dorothy Lamb, Rita Kerwin, Myrtle Allen, Sunny Trowbridge, Pearl Shepherd, Diane Cullen, Betty Bassett, Angeline Hassel, Harriet Hagman, Violet Arnold, Blanche Reeves.

ACT 1[20]

---

[19]The eighth in the annual series of musical revues (Vanities, Sketchbook) produced in Earl Carroll beginning in 1923.
[20]Added for tour:
"Nevertheless"
    Collette Sisters
"Goodnight, Sweetheart"
    V. Fay, H. Stockwell
    (*Music by* Ray Noble. *Lyrics by* James Campbell, Reg Connelly.)

Scene 1

The Unseen Host
E. Carroll

Scene 2

The Most Beautiful Girls in the World
M. O'Day (Miss Irvington, N.J.), J. Brewster, N. Kincaid (Miss Alabama), B. Wallace (Miss Brooklyn), A. Kerwin, B. Sundmark (Miss Philadelphia), R. Shaw, R. Havel, H. Arlan, G. Pratt, J. Jenner, M. Devine (Miss Boston), R. Bonnie (Miss California), E. Pragan, R. Fronson, P. Sands, I. Michael, V. Milton (Miss England), B. Reeves, M. Carewe, G. Fursa (Miss Bronx), N. Metcalf (Miss New Orleans), M. Nordman (Miss Westchester), D. Lamb, R. Kerwin, M. Allen (Miss Cleveland), D. Cullen, S. Trowbridge (Miss Medford), P. Shepherd, B. Bassett (Miss New York), A. Hassel (Miss Pittsburgh), H. Hagman (Miss Finland), V. Arnold (Miss New Jersey).

Scene 3

"Kneedeep in June"
T. White, Collette Sisters
(*Music by* Jay Gorney. *Lyrics by* E. Y. Harburg.)

Scene 4

A Field of Daisies
"One Love"
J. Hale
(*Music by* Harold Arlen. *Lyrics by* Ted Koehler.)
Fan Dance; Heart of the Daisies
F. Bacon

Scene 5

Revolving Flowers (Effect by Max Teuber)

Scene 6

Announcement
Miss New York: B. Bassett. *Miss America*: I. Ahlberg. *Miss Universe*: D. Britton.

Scene 7

Apartment Hunting
Gentleman: R. Fielder. *Lady*: E. Wenzel. *Janitor*: M. Bernie.

Scene 8

The Ballroom
He: J. Hale. *She*: B. Veronica.

Scene 9

Nautical Justice
Captain: H. Williams. *First Officer*: H. Stockwell. *Surgeon*: R. Fielder. *Stewardess*: N. Ray. *Stowaway*: J. Savo. *Boy*: E. Harrison. *A Passenger*: P. Kelly. *Sailors*: F. Condos, H. Condos, M. Bernie, B. Rolls.

Scene 10

Midinette Lane
Collette Sisters

Scene 11

Modes—A Window at Merls
The Girl in Pink: I. Ahlberg (Miss America). *The Girl in Chartreuse*: C. Trevor. *The Girl in Eggshell*: E. Wenzel (Miss St. Louis). *The Girl in White*: F. Joyce (Miss San Francisco). *The Girl in Maize*: K. Carroll. *Mme. Franco*: N. Ray. *Window Trimmer*: H. Stockwell. *Gustave*: J. Savo. *Late Customer*: B. Veronica.

Scene 12

After the Ball
He: H. Williams. *She*: P. Kelly. *Musical Director*: R. Fielder.

Scene 13

Cellar of the Giants

Scene 14

Bottles: "Hittin' the Bottle"
B. Veronica
(*Music by* Harold Arlen. *Lyrics by* Ted Koehler.)

Scene 15

Three Gentlemen
F. Condos, H. Condos, M. Bernie

Scene 16

Just Kids
First Child: B. Veronica. *Second Child*: T. White. *Passerby*: C. Bryson.

Scene 17

Voice With a Smile

Scene 18

A Grimm Tale
Guard: J. Savo. *Passerby*: E. Harrison.

Scene 19

Brown Pastures (*by* Billy Hughes)
Mother: N. Ray. *Milkmaid*: D. Britton. *Salesman*: J. Benny. *The Cow*: Gabriella.

Scene 20

Flirtation Dance
T. White, M. Bernie

Scene 21

A Curtain from Nanking
Chinese Tassels: M. Allan, N. Kincaid, A. Hassel, V. Arnold, E. Pragan, M. O'Day.

Scene 22

The Noted Chinese Actor, Satsunmon (featured in every movie marquee in the country)
Mee Got Yen: H. Williams. *Property Man*: J. Savo. *Mee Hot*: P. Kelly. *Keeper*: C. Bryson. *Servant*: E. Harrison. *Imperial Manchu Melodists*: J. Benny, B. Rolls, R. Fielder, H. Rogers.

Scene 23

Dance
B. Rolls

Scene 24

Planet X: "The March of Time"
(*Music by* Harold Arlen. *Lyrics by* Ted Koehler.)
Pluto: H. Stockwell. *Time*: J. Hale.

Scene 25

Strange Inhabitants of the Skies
(*Costumes designed by* C. Boehm, Berlin.)

Scene 26

The Mysterious Stars
R. Havel, M. Nordman, H. Hagman, I. Michael, J. Jenner, G. Pratt, R. Shaw, H. Arlan
Celestial Bodies: *Mars*: M. Carewe. *Venus*: K. Carroll. *Mercury*: I. Ahlberg. *Neptune*: E. Wenzel. *Uranus*: C. Trevor. *Jupiter*: F. Joyce. *Saturn*: F. Bacon. And 24 Satellites. (*Costumes designed by* Florence Weber.)

Scene 27

The Diamond Studded Sky

Scene 28

The Sling Shot
J. Savo

Scene 29

Where There's a Will (*Suggested by* Ray Mayer)
Lawyer: J. Benny. *Ruthie Ruth*: B. Veronica. *Dimples O'Shaughnessy*: T. White. *Ike Watercress*: H. Stockwell. *Agatha*: D. Britton. *Cynthia*: P. Kelly. *Meadows*: R. Fielder. *Mrs. Lucy Watercress*: N. Ray. *Aloysius Watercress, II*: B. Rolls. *Aloysius Watercress, III*: E. Harrison. *Yvonne*: F. Bacon. *Buttercup*: F. Joyce. *Chrysanthemum*: C. Trevor. *Begonia*: E. Wenzel. *Daffodil*: K. Carroll. *Callalily*: I. Ahlberg. *Aloysius Watercress*: H. Williams.

Scene 30

Let Freedom Ring

Scene 31

Drummers of Discontent
F. Condos, H. Condos, M. Bernie

Scene 32

Voices of the People
J. Hale, H. Stockwell, C. Bryson

Scene 33

The Spun Glass Curtain

Scene 34

Independence Hall, 1776
A Patriot: J. Benny.

Scene 35

On Parade
The Blue Grenadiers

Scene 36

Gettysburg, 1863.
The Words of Lincoln: J. Benny.

Scene 37

   Is This the Law?

      The White Grenadiers

Scene 38

   Over There, 1917

Scene 39

   Ring Out the Blues

      The Red Grenadiers

Scene 40

   House of Representatives, 1930

      Congressman: J. Benny.

Scene 41

   Capitol, 1935

Scene 42

   Finale

ACT 2

Scene 1

   The Subterranean Gardens

Scene 2

   Tableau—From Out of the Sea

      Neptune's Daughter: F. Bacon. *Mermaids*: M. Devine, E. Pragan, M. Allan,
      H. Hagman, B. Bassett, A. Kerwin, B. Reeves, J. Brewster.

Scene 3

   The Sunken Submarine

      "Love Boats"

      J. Hale, H. Stockwell

      (*Music by* Jay Gorney. *Lyrics by* E. Y. Harburg.)

      Goldfish: K. Carroll. *Seaweed*: C. Trevor. *Jellyfish*: E. Wenzel. *Siren*: I. Ahlberg.
      Sturgeon: F. Joyce. *Little Neck*: I. Michael. *Cherry Stone*: V. Milton. *Sardine*:
      B. Wallace.

Scene 4

   In the Bed of the Ocean: Water Ballet

      Mildred and Maurice

Scene 5

   Explaining the Fight[21]

      J. Benny

Scene 6

   The Havana Casino: "La Rumba"

      C. Bryson, Collette Sisters

      (*Music by* James P. Johnson. *Lyrics by* Della [Stella] Unger.)

Scene 7

   Moonlit Palms

      The Royal Rumba Orchestra, 40 Rumba Girls

Scene 8

   Lobby of the St. Moritz (*Scene suggested by* Ken Kling)

      Bell Boy: E. Harrison. *Clerk*: B. Rolls. *Bride*: P. Kelly. *Groom*: J. Savo.
      Man: J. Benny. *Girl*: T. White.

Scene 9

   Corridor of the Hotel

      Man in 25-A: H. Williams. *The Maid of Honor*: D. Britton.
      Bridesmaids: I. Ahlberg, F. Joyce, C. Trevor, E. Wenzel.

      Specialty Dance

      E. Harrison

Scene 10

   Virtue's Bed

      The Lost Lady: K. Carroll. *Chambermaid*: N. Ray. *First House
      Detective*: M. Bernie. *Second House Detective*: C. Bryson. *Miss Irving*:
      B. Veronica. *Miss Gold*: M. Collette.

Scene 11

   The Gold Curtain: Dance

      T. White

---

[21]Replaced during run with:
  Pardon the Interruptions
    J. Benny

Scene 12

   Announcement

      E. Carroll

Scene 13

   A New Star in the East

      V. Fay

Scene 14

   The Curtain of Splendor

      Curtain of Vanity: V. Fay. *Curtain of Luxury*: V. Arnold, B. Sundmark,
      N. Kincaid. *Curtain of Wealth*: B. Wallace, G. Fursa. *Curtain of Riches*:
      J. Brewster, M. Allan, A. Kerwin. *Curtain of Glamor*: V. Milton, R. Havel,
      H. Hagman, M. O'Day, R. Shaw, H. Arlan, I. Michael. *Curtain of Beauty*:
      R. Kerwin, E. Pragan, B. Reeves.
      (*Curtains and Costumes designed by* Vincente Minnelli.)

Scene 15

   Filigree and Diamonds

      Rose and Feather Girls

      The Goddesses of Inspiration: K. Carroll, I. Ahlberg, C. Trevor, E. Wenzel,
      F. Joyce, M. Carewe, D. Britton. (*Costumes by* Vincente Minnelli.)

   "I Came to Life"

      J. Hale, H. Stockwell

      (*Music by* Jay Gorney. *Lyrics by* E. Y. Harburg.)

Scene 16

   Tights and Tarlatan

      Premier Danseuse: N. Ray. *Albert Rasch*: E. Harrison.

Scene 17

   All Quiet (*by* Philip Kobbe)

      Mr. Stewart: H. Williams. *Salesman*: J. Benny. *Steamfitter*: J. Savo. *Secretary*: D.
      Britton. *Foreman*: B. Rolls. *Carpenter*: H. Stockwell. *Apprentice*: M. Bernie.
      Mimeotypist: F. Bacon. *Typists*: K. Carroll, E. Wenzel, I. Ahlberg, C. Trevor, F.
      Joyce.

Scene 18

   "Out of a Clear Blue Sky"

      Collette Sisters

      (*Music by* Harold Arlen. *Lyrics by* Ted Koehler.)

Scene 19

   The Terrace of Color

      56 Dancing Prisms

      (This is the first introduction on any stage of the famous Colorama as created by
      Fernando Cadenas in the experimental laboratories of the General Electric
      Company, Schenectady.)

Scene 20

   Stepping High

      L. Harrison

Scene 21

   Condos Brothers

Scene 22

   Station YRU

      Announcer: J. Benny. *First Violinist*: M. Bernie. *Don Juan*: J. Savo. *Miss
      Lummock*: N. Ray. *Her Secretary*: H. Stockwell. *General Verismutty*: H.
      Williams. *His Interpreter*: R. Fielder. *Mme. Doreme*: P. Kelly. *Station Assistants*:
      M. Bernie, F. Condos. *Trickster*: B. Rolls.

Scene 23

   Aboard the Graf Zeppelin: "Going Up"

      B. Veronica, H. Stockwell, M. Collette, C. Bryson, R. Collette, J. Hale.
      (*Music by* Jay Gorney. *Lyrics by* E. Y. Harburg.)

Scene 24

   In the Bag

Scene 25

   Grand Finale

      Entire Company

1930.23   # WHO CARES?

A Musical Revue in Two Acts, 31 Scenes.[22] Sketches by Edward Clarke
Lilley, Bertrand Robinson, Kenneth Webb, John Cantwell. Music by Percy
Wenrich. Lyrics by Harry Clarke. Staged by George Vivian and Edward

---

[22]Revue material assembled from the Lambs' Club Gambols.

Clarke Lilley. Dances and ensembles by William Holbrook. Settings by Cirker & Robbins. Costumes by Brooks. Music director, Irving Schloss. Orchestrations by Irving Schloss, Frank Barry and John McManus. Produced by The Satirists, Inc.[23] Opened 8 July 1930 at the 46th Street Theatre and closed 2 August 1930 after 32 performances.

CAST: ARTHUR HARTLEY, WILLIAM HOLBROOK, PEGGY O'NEILL, PERCY HELTON, OLIVA MAY, GRANT MILLS, SIBYLLA BOWHAN, ROBERT G. PITKIN, JOHN CHERRY, MARGARET DALE, RALPH RIGGS, TEMPLETON BROTHERS (James, Mercer), OLIVE OLSEN, DON LANNING, MARJORIE SELTZER, FLORENZ AMES, Mignon Laird, Frank Allworth, Dorothy Martin, Mary Ridgley, Bobby Edwards, Jane Bowers, Ann Cochran, Ruth Cross, Jeane Deane, Edna Eustace, Aune Hanson, Tina Marie Jensen, Leone Richter, Leonard Lord, James Marshall, Charles Williams, (George Sweet).

ACT 1
Scene 1

Opening Number
Entire Company
Manager: F. Ames. *Man With Songs*: G. Sweet. *Girl With Sketches*: D. Martin. *Man With Black Outs*: F. Allworth. *Girl With Joke Book*: S. Bowhan. *Man With Costumes*: P. Helton. *Girl With Taps*: M. Ridgley. *Chef*: D. Lanning.

Scene 2

"Believe It or Not"
M. Seltzer, A. Hartley
(*Blackouts by* Edward Clarke Lilley.)

Scene 3

The End of That
Man: G. Mills. *Woman*: S. Bowhan. *Husband*: F. Allworth.

Scene 4

The First Parting
Wife: P. O'Neill. *Man*: D. Lanning.

Scene 5

Action
Director: R. Pitkin. *Leading Lady*: M. Laird. *Cameraman*: J. Cherry. *Leading Man*: L. Lord.

Scene 6

"Tennis"
S. Bowhan, W. Holbrook

Scene 7

What's Wrong With the Theatre (*by* Edward Clarke Lilley)
Scene 1: Box Office of Motion Picture Theatre.
Scene 2: Lobby of Motion Picture Theatre.
Doorman: L. Lord. *Box Office Girl*: M. Dale. *Customer*: G. Sweet. *First Maid*: R. Cross. *Second Maid*: J. Bowers. *First Usher*: Alice Cochran. *Second Usher*: Ann Cochran. *Cadets*: G. Mills, M. Templeton, J. Templeton.
Scene 3: Box Office of Legitimate Theatre.
Scene 4: Interior of Legitimate Theatre.
Treasurer: F. Allworth. *Customer*: G. Sweet. *Speculators*: F. Ames, C. Williams. *Candy Boy*: J. Cherry. *Coat Boy*: P. Helton. *Usher*: P. O'Neill. *Manager*: R. Pitkin.

Scene 8

The Templeton Brothers

Scene 9

A Quiet Night in Chicago (*by* Harry Clarke)
Scene: A Room in Any Hotel—Who Cares?
Mr. Evans: F. Ames. *Mrs. Evans*: S. Bowhan. *Junior*: P. Helton. *Bell Boy*: J. Cherry. *Edna*: M. Seltzer. *Joe*: G. Mills. *Liquor Man*: L. Lord. *Two Barrel Men*: A. Hartley, R. Pitkin. *Stranger*: J. Marshall.

Scene 10

Bobby Edwards

Scene 11

"Dance of the Fan"
O. May
With Ann and Alice Cochran, O. Olsen. *The Lenora Girls*: E. Eustace, M. Dale, A. Hanson, R. Cross, J. Bowers, T. M. Jensen, J. Deane, D. Martin.
Harpist: M. Laird.

Scene 12

Olive Olsen

Scene 13

"Who Cares?"
D. Lanning, P. O'Neill, Lenora Girls

Scene 14

Tin Whistle[24] (*by* Bertrand Robinson)
Scene: A Shell hole.
Kelly: G. Mills. *Captain*: R. Pitkin. *Red*: L. Lord. *Hayes*: F. Allworth. *The Kid*: P. Helton.

Scene 15

"The Heldites"
Boys: A. Hartley, J. Marshall, R. Riggs, G. Sweet, J. Templeton, M. Templeton. *Girls*: D. Martin, L. Richter, E. Eustace, M. Dale, R. Cross, J. Deane.

The Cheering Section (*by* Edward Clarke Lilley)
Entire Cast
Cheer Leader: P. Helton.

Scene 16

William Holbrook

Scene 17

"Broadway"
Spirit of Broadway: R. Pitkin. *Chorus Girls*: M. Dale, D. Martin, L. Richter, J. Deane. *Policemen*: J. Templeton, M. Templeton. *Lady of Broadway*: S. Bowhan. *Chorus Boys*: L. Lord, G. Mills. *Brokers*: A. Hartley, J. Marshall. *Dames*: M. Seltzer, P. O'Neill. *Dope*: F. Ames. *Crooks*: J. Cherry, R. Riggs. *Song Writers*: P. Helton, G. Sweet. *Actors*: F. Allworth, D. Lanning. *Ad Man*: C. Williams. *Salvation Nell*: Ann Cochran. *News Boy*: E. Eustace. *Sailor*: T. M. Jensen. *Broadwayites*: Alice Cochran, O. May, R. Cross, A. Hanson, J. Bowers, M. Ridgley, B. Edwards.

ACT 2
Scene 1

"Sun Up"
A. Hartley, M. Seltzer, Entire Company

Scene 2

Templeton Brothers

Scene 3

An Expensive Night
Scene: Office of a Country Hotel.
Father: J. Cherry. *Son*: G. Sweet. *Man*: J. Marshall. *Wife*: J. Deane.

Scene 4

Peggy O'Neill

Scene 5

Olive Olsen and Leonard Lord

Scene 6

Thisishota (*by* Edward Clarke Lilley. Different from the 'Lysistrata' of Aristophanes.)
First Greek Mama: R. Pitkin. *Second Greek Mama*: A. Hartley. *Third Greek Mama*: J. Marshall. *Fourth Greek Mama*: J. Templeton. *Old Mama*: J. Cherry. *First Greek Papa*: D. Lanning. *Second Greek Papa*: M. Templeton. *Third Greek Papa*: R. Riggs. *Fourth Greek Papa*: F. Allworth. *Old Papa*: F. Ames. *Greek Boy*: C. Williams. *Flappers*: L. Richter, M. Laird, Ann Cochran, Alice Cochran.

Scene 7

Sibylla Bowhan

Scene 8

So This Is Television (*by* Kenneth Webb)
Old Lady: G. Mills. *Her Son*: G. Sweet. *Announcer*: J. Cherry. *Grace, a Wife*: M. Seltzer. *Marie, a Maid*: Alice Cochran. *Paul, a Lover*: L. Lord. *Arthur, a Husband*: D. Lanning.

Scene 9

Olive Olsen

Scene 10

"(I Make My Bed Down in) Dixieland"
D. Lanning, Lenora Girls, Leonie, M. Ridgley, B. Edwards

Scene 11

A Big Surprise (*by* John Cantwell)
Sister: O. Olsen. *Wife*: S. Bowhan. *Daughter*: M. Laird.

---

[23]A collaborative of otherwise unidentified Lambs' Club members.

[24]Dropped during run.

Scene 12

"The Hunt"
> M. Seltzer, O. May, S. Bowhan

Scene 13

The Hunting Ballet[25] (Without the permission of Florenz Ziegfeld. With acknowledgements to Seymour Felix. Kindest Regards to Harriet Hoctor.)
> *Danced by* F. 'Angot' Ames, J. 'Cecille' Cherry, A. 'Hortense' Hartley, P. 'Hattie' Helton, D. 'Lucy' Lanning, J. 'Marcella' Marshall, R. 'Pansy' Pitkin, R. 'Ruby' Riggs, G. 'Susie' Sweet, J. 'Tilley' Templeton, M. 'Theresa' Templeton, C. 'Wiseria' Williams. *Premiere Danseuse*: W. 'Harriet' Hoctor.

Scene 14

Finale

HOT RHYTHM

1930.24

'A Sepia Tinted Little Show' (A Musical Revue) in Two Acts, 25 Scenes. Scenes (sketches) by Ballard Macdonald, Will Morrissey, Edward Hurley; contributed to by Johnny Lee Long, Dewey "Pigmeat" Markham. Music by Porter Grainger. Lyrics by Donald Heywood. Additional songs by Irving Actman, Jean Herbert, Harry Canter, Will Morrissey. Staged by Will Morrissey. Dances and ensembles by Nat Cash. Additional dances by Midgie Miller, Eddie Rector. Settings by Wertheim Studios. Costumes by Reine Costume Co. Music director, Maurice Coffin. Produced under the personal supervision of Will Morrissey. Produced by Max Rudnick. Opened 21 August 1930 at the Times Square Theatre, moved 29 September 1930 to the Waldorf Theatre, and closed 18 October 1930 after 68 performances.

<u>CAST</u> (in order of appearance): JOHNNY HUDGINS, EDDIE RECTOR (Master of Ceremonies), ARTHUR BRYSON, JOHNNY LEE LONG, EDITH WILSON, MAE BARNES, JAHARAL, DEWEY "PIGMEAT" MARKHAM, REVELLA HUGHES, AL VIGAL, HILDA PERLENO, MADELINE BELT, INEZ SEELEY, Doris Rheubottom, Laura Duncan, Ina Duncan, Hazel Van Vlerah, Sam Paige, Slaps Wallace, Lois Simms, Buster Bowie, George Wiltshire, Amon Davis, Willie Taylor, Billy Sheppard, Hendricks Mattingly, King Washington, Joseph Brown, Llewelyn Ransom, Toussaint Duers, Roland Smith, (Baby Goins).

Ladies of the Ensemble: Isabelle Peterson, Lenora Gadson, Evelyn Ortez, Erlise Thompson, Doris Alexander, Juanita Boyd, Dorothy Seeton, Hazel Miles, Julia Noissette, Regina James, Helen Robinson, Eda Bell, Alberta Puggsley, Dolores Watson, Mabel Gary, Elverta Brown, Blanch Farrow, Madge Fox, Ethel Carr, Dorothy Saunders. *Singers*: St. Claire Dodson, Natalie Long, Mal Dumas, Larrie Lawlor, Freddie Waithe, Lou Rasom.

ACT 1[26]

Scene 1

Tree of Hope
> Believe it or not Ripley will vouch for the actors' wishing tree in Harlem. This is the spot where all the colored artists not working can be found at all times.

Songs
> A. Vigal, M. Dumas, Ensemble

Scene 2

Nora Green
> I. Seeley, L. Simms, B. Bowie, S. Dodson, W. Taylor

Scene 3

A Harlem Rent Party[27]
> J. Long, D. Markham, G. Wiltshire, E. Wilson, H. Van Vlerah, D. Rheubottom

"Mama's Gotta Get Her Rent"
> E. Wilson

---

[25]A burlesque of Ziegfeld's Rodgers and Hart musical 'Simple Simon.'

[26]Added during run:

I Thought It Was You (What Did He Get?)
> E. Wilson, D. Markham, A. Vigal

"Big Boy" (Act 1, Scene 14)
> M. Belt

Rector's Waltz

Also featured as per published sheet music:

"Will You Be Hating Me To-morrow (For Loving You To-night)"
> (*Music by* Irving Actman. *Lyrics by* Jean Herbert and Al Koppell.)

[27]Program note: Numbers is a Harlem gambling system.

Scene 4

"Say the Word That Will Make You Mine"
> M. Barnes
> (who Boop-Boop-a-Dooped a Lotta Boops Long Before Helen Kane Ever Heard of Boop)

Scene 5

A Harlem Spelling Bee (He graduated from High School at eight-in the evening.)
> D. Rheubottom, G. Wiltshire, And a No Good Brat

Scene 6

"Loving You the Way I Do"
> R. Hughes, A. Vigal, M. Barnes, A. Bryson, Ensemble
> (*Music by* Eubie Blake. *Lyrics by* Jack Scholl, Will Morrissey.)

Scene 7

"Rector Rhythm" (1000% Fahrenheit)
> M. Belt, E. Rector, Ensemble

Scene 8

"The Penalty of Love"
> T. Duers, Ensemble
> (*Music by* Donald Heywood. *Lyrics by* Donald Heywood and Heba Jannath.)
> With I. Seeley, A. Davis, W. Taylor, G. Wiltshire, M. Dumas, B. Sheppard, J. Long, D. Markham. *Condemned Man*: T. Marcel. *Broadcaster*: J. Hudgins.

Scene 9

"Since You Went Away"[28]
> H. Perleno, A. Vigal
> *Danced by* L. Simms, B. Bowie.

Scene 10

A Certain Lady on Trial
> M. Barnes, J. Long, D. Markham, A. Davis, G. Wiltshire, S. Dodson, E. Rector

Scene 11

Sepia Melodies[29] (Revella Hughes Arrangements)
> Revella. Hughes Trio (R. Hughes, I. Duncan, L. Duncan)

Scene 12

"Florodora Sextette (à la Harlem)"
> Ensemble Post-Graduates, J. Hudgins

Scene 13

A Gangster Incident
> Jaharal

Scene 14

The Cave (A hot spot in hot Harlem)
> Rector Girls

"Alabamy"
> M. Belt

A Harlem Skate
> J. McGarver

Tumbling Around
> B. Goins

The Tornado
> A. Bryson
> Finale: Sepia Vanities (Beautifying Harlem)

ACT 2

Scene 1

"Up in the Sky"
> I. Seeley, A. Vigal

Afro-Fresh Air, Inc.
> J. Long, D. Markham

Scene 2

In the Air
> L. Simms, B. Bowie

Scene 3

Anywhere in Africa: "Tropical Moon"
> R. Hughes, Ensemble

Dramatic Interlude
> B. Sheppard

---

[28]Dropped during run.
[29]Dropped during run.

Scene 4
Perhaps
S. Paige, S. Wallace
Scene 5
"Hungry For Love"
H. Perleno
Cupid's Hospital
Nurses: R. Hughes, L. Duncan, I. Duncan. *Dr. Smith*: G. Wiltshire.
Scene 6
Episodes of a Broadway Producer
E. Wilson, H. Van Vlerah, G. Wiltshire, A. Vigal, D. Markham,
E. Rector, etc.
Scene 7
"Hot Rhythm"
M. Barnes, Girls
Scene 8
Edith Wilson struts her stuff with E. Rector, M. Belt
Scene 9
Othello—Put on the Spot
M. Barnes, J. Long, D. Markham, A. Davis
Another Strange Interlude: Johnnie Hudgins on the Old Sole Hour
Scene 10
"Steppin' On It"[30]
E. Rector, M. Belt
Arthur Bryson shakes a foot.
Scene 11
Finale
Entire Company

1930.25 THE SECOND LITTLE SHOW

A Musical Revue in Two Acts, 26 Scenes[31]. Assembled by Dwight Deere Wiman. Sketches by Norman Clark, Marc Connelly, William B. Miles, Donald Blackwell, James Coghlan, Bert Hanlon. Music by Arthur Schwartz, (Herman Hupfeld, William M. (Morgan) Lewis, Jr., Will Irwin). Lyrics by Howard Dietz, (Herman Hupfeld, Ted Fetter). Musical numbers staged by Dwight Deere Wiman. Sketches staged by Monty Woolley. Dances by Dave Gould. Settings by Jo Mielziner. Costumes by Raymond Sovey, Helen Pons. Music director, Gus Salzer. Produced by Dwight Deere Wiman and William A. Brady, Jr. in association with Tom Weatherley. Opened 2 September 1930 at the Royale Theatre, moved 20 October 1930 to the Sam S. Shubert Theatre, and closed 25 October 1930 after 63 performances.

CAST: AL TRAHAN, YUKONA CAMERON, RUTH TESTER, JAY C. FLIPPEN, GLORIA GRAFTON, TASHAMIRA, JOEY RAY, NED WEVER, HELEN GRAY, DAVEY JONES, KAY HAMILL, GUS HYLAND.
The Little Show Girls: Kay Arnold, Jayne Barrett, Fay Brady, Gertrude Blake, Ruth Gordon[32], Arline Judge, Kay Lazelle, Betty Lewis, Eleanor Moffett, Mickey MacKillop, Frances Nevins, Carol Renwick, Albertina Rexroth, Lenore Simone, Dorothy Waller, Buddy York. *The Little Show Boys*: Charles Conkling, Frank Edmunds, George King, Jack Mason, Jack Montgomery, Stewart Steppler, Bentley Stone.

ACT 1[33]
Scene 1
"New New York"
A Window in City Hall. *Speaker*: N. Wever.
The Anthem of New New York
Girls, Boys

The Wall of New New York
The Company
Scene 2
"Swing Your Tails"
Boys
Scene 3
Sleepless Nights (*by* Norman Clark)
Husband: G. Hyland. *Wife*: G. Grafton. *Doctor*: N. Wever.
Scene 4
"Foolish Face"
R. Tester, D. Jones, Girls, Boys
Scene 5
Husbands, Wives and Lovers
N. Wever, J. Ray, G. Grafton, K. Hamill, H. Gray, J. C. Flippen, G. Hyland,
A. Trahan
Announcement: J. C. Flippen.
Scene 6
"My Heart Begins to Thump! Thump!"
R. Tester, Girls
(*Music by* William M. [Morgan] Lewis. *Lyrics by* Ted Fetter.)
Scene 7
"You're the Sunrise"
G. Grafton, J. Ray
Dance: H. Gray, K. Hamill, Boys.
Scene 8
The Critics (*by* Bert Hanlon)
First Critic: N. Wever. *Second Critic*: D. Jones. *Third Critic*: G. Hyland. *Waiter*:
J. C. Flippen.
Scene 9
Davey Jones
Introduced by K. Lazelle, M. MacKillop, E. Moffett, F. Nevins, C. Renwick,
D. Waller.
Scene 10
The Guest (*by* Marc Connelly)
Mr. Mercer: A. Trahan. *Bellboy*: J. Mason. *Assistant Manager*: D. Jones.
Headwaiter: G. Hyland. *Mr. Pitcairn*: N. Wever. *Electricians, Waiters, Busboys, etc.*: Boys.
Scene 11
"Tired of Love"[34]
G. Grafton
(*Music by* Del Cleveland. *Lyrics by* Ted Fetter.)
Scene 12
"What a Case I've Got on You"
H. Gray, D. Jones, Girls, Boys
Specialty Dance
E. Moffett
Scene 13
Al Trahan, Yukona Cameron
Scene 14
"Good Clean Sport"
J. Ray, Boys, Company

ACT 2
Scene 1
"Lucky Seven"
J. Ray, Company
Scene 2
"My Intuition"
G. Grafton, A. Trahan
Scene 3
"Lonely Hearts' Ball"[35]
D. Waller, Boys, Girls
Scene 4
Tashamira (Specialty)
(*Music by* Will Irwin.)

---

[30]Dropped during run.
[31]The second in the annual series of revues produced by Dwight Deere Wiman beginning in 1929.
[32]Not the famed dramatic actress of the same name.
[33]Added to the show for Marion Harris during run:
"Mannequin"
M. Harris
(*Music by* Johnny Green. *Lyrics by* Edward Heyman.)

---

[34]Dropped during the run.
[35]Dropped during the run.

Scene 5

Jay C. Flippen, annoyed by Fay Brady. (*Annoyances by* Bert Hanlon.)

"I Like Her and She Speaks Well of Me"
 J. C. Flippen
 (*Music by* Del Cleveland. *Lyrics by* Ted Fetter.)

Scene 6

"I Started on a Shoestring"
 A Business Man: J. Ray. *The Stenographer*: A. Rexroth. *Reporters*:
 K. Arnold, F. Brady, A. Judge, M. MacKillop, F. Nevins, B. York,
 Girls, Boys.
 Specialty Dance
 K. Lazelle

Scene 7

X = A + B (*by* William Miles and Donald Blackwell)
 Announcement: K. Hamill. *Irene Alexandrovna Mussorsky*:
 H. Gray. *Masha*: Tashamira. *Dmitri Alexeivitch Vishnevski*:
 N. Wever.

Scene 8

"Sing Something Simple"
 R. Tester, F. Brady, A. Judge, Boys
 (*Music and Lyrics by* Herman Hupfeld.)

Scene 9

The Handy Man (*by* James J. Coghlan.)
 Elmer: J. C. Flippen. *Mrs. Elmer*: K. Hamill. *Benny Glink*: A. Trahan.

Scene 10

The Little Show Girls and Boys

Scene 11

Al Trahan with Yukona Cameron

Scene 12

(Finale)
 The Company

1930.26   LUANA

A Musical Romance (Play) of the South Seas in Two Acts, 8 Scenes. Book by Howard Emmett Rogers, adapted from the play "The Bird of Paradise" by Richard Walton Tully. Music by Rudolph Friml. Lyrics by J. Keirn Brennan. Book staged by Howard Emmett Rogers. Dances and ensembles by Earl Lindsey. Settings by Cirker & Robbins. Costumes by Charles LeMaire. Music director, Ivan Rudisill. Orchestrations by Joseph Mayer [Meyer]. Entire production under the supervision of Arthur Hammerstein. Produced by Arthur Hammerstein. Opened 17 September 1930 at Hammerstein's Theatre and closed 4 October 1930 after 21 performances.

CAST (in order of appearance): *Keipia*: George Djimos. *Mahuna*: MARGUERITA [Marguerite] SYLVA. *Hewanena*: William Pringle. *Neikia*: LILLIAN BOND. *Hoheno*: DONALD NOVIS. *Luana*: RUTH ALTMAN. *Paul Wilson*: JOSEPH MACAULEY. *Captain Hatch*: George Nash. *Sergeant Cavanaugh*: William Gordon. *"Sure-Fire Thompson"*: HARRY JANS. *Jimmy Smith*: HAROLD WHALEN. *Mr. Sawyer*: Harry C. Bradley. *Diana Larned*: Diana Chase. *Robert Dean*: ROBERT CHRISHOLM. *Polly Hatch*: DORIS CARSON. *Major Andrews*: Harold Ten Brook. *Lemuele*: Raymond O'Brien. *Hula Dancer*: Swani-Lani. *Hawaiian Children*: Joseph Rayia, John Rayia, Michael Rayia.

Girls: Alvina Carson, Eda Vitale, Grace Larue, Evelyn Laurie, Ruby Nevins, Josephine Depree, Charlett Silton, Madeliene Eubanks, Connie Madison, Loretta Madison, Ruth Morgan, Frances Gordon, Diana Le Shay, Olga Fox, Ruby Poe, Bunny Moore, Adelaide Candee, Evelyn Hannons, Sally Rand, Polly Kirke, Marjorie Baglin, Lillian Burke, Hellene Trevor, Margaret Miller, Maxine Darrell, Ann Constance, Mary Anderson, Diana Deering, Alice Harper, Dora Zemerowna, Mae Joy, Helen Goodrich, Leola Buelow, Joan Kent, Millicent Bancroft, Marion Stockton, Lillian Honiver, Dorothy Wyndham, Dorothy Johnson, Mabel Lee, Jean Brown, Delores Delmer, Louise Chowning, Ming Carters, June Cavendish. *Boys*: Wallace Jackson, Jack Stone, Robert Gray, Francis Conway, Al Berl, Jack Raymond, Jules Martin, Walter Gardiner, Tom Brynn, R. P. Hall, Harry Murray, Bob Matthews, Efim Vitis, Edward O'Brien, Harold Baumgartner, John Fredericks, Henry Phillips, Berton Hall, Don Cortez, Ferris Martin, Harold Ten Brook, Ed Barry, Lynn Eldridge, Morris Tepper, Arnold Rand.

Act 1, Scene 1: Outside of Luana's House, Puna, (Hawaii). *Afternoon. Scene 2*: A Road near Dean's Shack. A few hours later. *Scene 3*: The Bathing pool. Dusk.

Act 2, Scene 1: Interior of Luana's House. Two years later. *Scene 2*: A Road in Puna. Same day. *Scene 3*: Exterior of Moana Hotel, Waikiki Beach, Honolulu. Two weeks later. *Scene 4*: At the Base of Pelée. Three days later. *Scene 5*: The Volcano. A half hour later.

ACT 1

Opening—"Hoku Loa"
 Ensemble

"Luana"
 D. Novis, Natives

"Aloha"
 R. Altman, Ensemble

"Hawaii's Shore"
 L. Bond, Hula Girls

"My Bird of Paradise"
 J. Macaulay, R. Altman

"Shore Leave"
 H. Jans, H. Whalen, L. Bond, Ensemble

"A Son of the Sun"
 R. Chisholm, Natives

"By Welawela"
 R. Altman

"Yankyula"
 H. Jans, H. Whalen, L. Bond, D. Carson

"Where You Lead"
 R. Chisholm, D. Chase

"Magic Spell of Love"
 R. Altman, J. Macaulay

Finale

ACT 2

Opening
 R. Altman, Girls

Finaletto
 R. Altman, J. Macaulay, M. Sylva, W. Pringle, Girls

"Drums of Kane"
 Ensemble

"In the Clouds"
 R. Chisholm, Male Chorus

"Wanapoo Bay"
 L. Bond, D. Carson, H. Jans, H. Whalen, Ensemble

Finale
 R. Altman, D. Novis, M. Sylva, W. Pringle, Ensemble

1930.27   NINA ROSA

A Musical Play (Comedy) in Two Acts, 8 Scenes. Book by Otto Harbach. Music by Sigmund Romberg. Lyrics by Irving Caesar. Production under the personal direction of J. J. Shubert. Dialogue staged by J. C. Huffman. Settings by Watson Barratt. Costumes by Orry Kelly. Music director, Max Meth. Orchestrations by Hans Spialek. Produced by the Messrs. Shubert. Opened 20 September 1930 at the Majestic Theatre and closed 17 January 1931 after 137 performances.

CAST (in order of appearance): *Tom*: Frank Horn. *Dick*: George Kirk. *Harry*: Zachary Cauly. *Chinaman*: Richard Koch. *Yana*: Belle Sylvia. *Corinna*: ARMIDA. *Bob Wilson*: George Anderson. *Silvers*: DON BARCLAY. *Jimmy Blakely*: JACK SHEEHAN. *Don Fernando*: Clay Clements. *Pablo*: LEONARD CEELEY. *Jack Haines*: GUY ROBERTSON. *Nina Rosa Stradella*: ETHELIND TERRY. *John Craig*: Stanley Jessup. *Elinor Haines*: MARION MARCHANTE. *Cholo*: Katherine Skidmore. *Chico*: Victor Casmore. *Gaucho Dancer*: STEPHEN CORTEZ. *Chiquita*: PEGGY. *Dolores*: Evelyn Klein. *Mona*: Mona Soltis. *Ramido*: John Tomney. *High Priestesses (3)*: *Maca*: Judy Lane. *Enta*: Sybil Comer. *Paca*: Norma Leyland. *Spirit Dancers*: YO-HAY-TONG, KALIL-OGLY. *Gauchos*: Arthur Singer, Walter Palm, Roy Vitalis, Edwin Drake. *Peddler*: Alfred Russ. *Indians Girls, Senoritas, Gauchos, Mining Engineers, Indians, etc.*

Singing Girls: *Sopranos*: Judy Lane, Esther Orr, Katherine Skidmore, Marynia Apel, Betty Dair, Zola Gray, Georgia Gwynne. *Altos*: Norma Leyland, Sybil Comer, Betty Davis, E. McIntyre, Eleanore Standish. *Show Girls*: Julia Barker, Margaret Samson, Frances Blythe, Muriel Seeley, Emmita Casanova, Billy Fanning, Azeada Charkouie, Henrietta Livingstone. *Dancers*: Joan Neilan, Mae Muth, Lillian Duncan, Mona Soltis, Frances Stevens, Louise Taylor, Rae Powell, Florence Powell, Elaine Melchiore, Dorothy Snowden, Sunny Wright, Elaine Shepard, Margaret Deane, Ruth Bannon, Henrietta Keller, Kate Blacker. *First Tenors*: Walter Tarone, Alphonse Inglesias, Alfred Russ, A. Leadman, Carol Godwin, Charles Kinsella, Earl Hoppe, Earl Mason. *Second Tenors*: Nino Bonomo, Roy Vitalis, Richard Koch, Peter Dadoukin, Norman Broderick. *Baritones*: George Ebert, James Morgan, Arthur Singer, James McClymont, Richard Drake, Charles Coleman, George Hempleman. *Bassos*: Walter Palm, Ivan Izmailov, Giovanni Petroucci, Serge Vino, Vido Guido, James Duffus, Wilbur Demarest.

Act 1, Scene 1: Yana's Piqueno. Near Cuzco, Peru, South America. Present. *Scene 2*: A street in Cuzco. Two days later. *Scene 3*: The Cafe de los Gauchos.

Act 2, Scene 1: A Don Fernando's Hacienda. 2 A.M. the same night. *Scene 2*: In a tunnel of the Nina Rosa mine. The same night. *Scene 3*: In the Cave of the Incas. Later. *Scene 4*: A street in Cuzco. The following afternoon. *Scene 5*: At Don Fernando's Hacienda. The following afternoon.

ACT 1
Scene 1

Opening
F. Horn, G. Kirk, Z. Caully

"Pay Day"
Armida, Dancing Girls

"Pablo"
L. Ceeley

"Nina Rosa"
G. Robertson, F. Horn, G. Kirk, Z. Caully, Male Chorus

"With the Dawn"
E. Terry

"Payador"
E. Terry, Ensemble

"The Secret in My Life"
J. Sheehan, Dancing Girls

"Your Smiles, Your Tears"
E. Terry, G. Robertson

"Serenade of Love"
L. Ceeley, E. Terry, Armida, Ensemble

Scene 2

"Pizarro Was a Very Narrow Man"
J. Sheehan, M. Marchante

Scene 3

"A Kiss I Must Refuse You"
Armida, Ensemble

"Latigo"
S. Cortez, Peggy

"The Only One For Me"
J. Sheehan, Dancers

"A Gaucho Love Song"
L. Ceeley, Ensemble

Finale Act 1
G. Robertson, E. Terry, L. Ceeley, Armida, C. Clements, M. Marchante, Ensemble

ACT 2
Scene 1

Arrival of Guests
L. Ceeley, Ensemble

Tango
S. Cortez, Peggy

"My First Love, My Last Love"
E. Terry, G. Robertson
(*Lyrics by* Irving Caesar and Otto Harbach.)

Finaletto
L. Ceeley, G. Robertson, E. Terry, Armida, C. Clements, Ensemble

Scene 3

Religious Ceremony
B. Sylvia, Y. Tong, K. Ogly, Ensemble

Dramatic Interlude
E. Terry, G. Robertson, Armida, L. Ceeley, Gauchos

Scene 5

Opening Ensemble

Finale Ultimo
Entire Company

1930.28 # FINE AND DANDY

A Musical Comedy in Two Acts, 10 Scenes. Book by Donald Ogden Stewart. Music by Kay Swift. Lyrics by Paul James [James P. Warburg]. Directed by Morris Green. Dialogue directed by Frank McCoy. Dances by Dave Gould, Tom Nip. Dance for Mechanical Ballet arranged by Eugene Van Grona. Routines of Abbott Dancers arranged by Merriel Abbott.

Settings by Henry Dreyfuss. Costumes by Charles LeMaire. Music director, Gene Salzer. Orchestrations by Hans Spialek. Produced by Morris Green and Lewis E. Gensler. Opened 23 September 1930 at Erlanger's Theatre and closed 2 May 1931 after 255 performances.

CAST: *Joe Squibb*: JOE COOK. *Wiffington*: DAVE CHASEN. *Mrs. Fordyce*: DORA MAUGHAN. *Maribelle Fordyce*: NELL O'DAY. *Nancy Ellis*: ALICE BOULDEN. *George Ellis*: JOE WAGSTAFF. *Mr. Ellis*: GEORGE A. SCHILLER. *Edgar Little*: JOHN W. EHRLE. *Miss Hunter*: ELEANOR POWELL. *Aunt Lucy*: Laura Clairon. *Office Boy*: Jimmy Hadreas. *Clergyman*: Jack Burley. *Hugo Giersdorf*: Herman Ergotti. *Johann Giersdorf*: Paul Brack. *A. Giersdorf*: Frank Naldi. *P. Giersdorf*: Frank Innis. *A Clerk*: Joe Clayton. *The Old Man*: GEORGE NEVILLE. *Insurance Agent*: Joe Lyons. *Ukelele Mike*: Jack McClusky. *Harmonica Player*: Joe Clayton. *First Workman*: John R. Hall. *Second Workman*: Dick Erskine. *Third Workman*: Joe Riley. *Fourth Workman*: J. Rousseaux. *Fifth Workman*: Frank Naldi. *Sixth Workman*: Ben Bernard. *Seventh Workman*: Billy Randall. *Eighth Workman*: Scott Jensen. *J. Newton Wheer*: Pat Walshe. *Foreman*: DAVID D. MORRIS. *Miss Hargrave*: Eleanor Etheridge. *R. V. Wilkins*: Walter Fehl. *The Four Horsemen*: Murray Evans, Jack Flaherty, Joe Reilly, Jack Burley. *The Colt*: Herman Ergotti, Pat Walshe. Tommy Atkins Sextet.

Merriel Abbott Specialty Dancers: Florence Wilson, Genvieve Irwin, Nette Solomon, May Hass, Rose Kirsner, Peaches Dahl, Fritzie Deuss, Pearl McKnight. *Young Ladies of the Fordyce Drop Forge and Tool Factory*: Amy Weber, Elene Ross, Alda Deery, Cara Gould, Marion Herson, Carmen Morales, Claribel Skinner, Violet Casey, Marjorie Bailey, Wanda Wood, Frances DeFoe, Adele Goulding, Patsy Schenck, Peggy Timmons, Muriel Lawlor, Gypsy Hollis, Odette Swan, Bonnie Blackwood, Eva Lewis, Eleanor Etheridge, Joan Burgess, Flo Ward, Edna Abbey, Kathleen VanNoy, Mary Grace Van Noy, Phyllis Cameron, Teddy West, Jeanne Adams, Margaret Dixon, Rheta Stone, Catherine Reynolds, Mildred Schroder. *Boys of the Fordyce Drop Forge and Tool Factory*: Fred Nay, Bob Long, Chet O'Brien, Victor Pullman, Jimmy Babbitt, Jimmy Mahr, Hal Clyne, Dick Kirby, Jack Ross, Gus Quinlan, Glen Meyers, Jack Richardson, Frank Gagen, Bert Doughty, Tom Denton, Mortimer O'Brien.

Act 1, Scene 1: The Machine Room of the Fordyce Drop Forge and Tool Factory. *Scene 2*: The Caddy House of the Country Club. *Scene 3*: A Sand Trap in a Golf Course. *Scene 4*: Joe's Office. *Scene 5*: In front of Squibb's Finance Chart. *Scene 6*: On the Way to the Graduation. *Scene 7*: Garden of the Fordyce Night School.

Act 2, Scene 1: Employees' Picnic Grounds. *Scene 2*: Interior of a Bank. *Scene 3*: Mrs. Fordyce's Garden.

ACT 1

Chant
Entire Ensemble

"Rich or Poor"
N. O'Day, J. Wagstaff, Ensemble

"Fine and Dandy"
J. Cook, A. Boulden

"Wheels of Steel"
J. Ehrle

"Mechanical Ballet"
Tommy Atkins Sextet, Jack Hanlen, Ensemble

"Starting at the Bottom"
J. Wagstaff, Ensemble

"Can This Be Love"
A. Boulden

"I'll Hit a New High"
E. Powell, Tommy Atkins Sextet, Ensemble

"Fine and Dandy" (reprise)
N. O'Day, Tommy Atkins Sextet, Ensemble

"Giddyup Back"
J. Cook, Horses

"Fordyce"
Ensemble

Finaletto
Entire Company

"Let's Go Eat Worms in the Garden"
A. Boulden, J. Wagstaff, Betsy Rees, Uninternational Four, Ensemble

ACT 2

Opening
Ensemble, Specialty Dancers

"Jig Hop"
E. Powell, Ensemble

Specialties
H. Ergotti, P. Brack, F. Naldi, F. Innis

"That Thing I Can't Seem to Forget"
D. Maughan

"Starting at the Bottom" (reprise)
Specialty Dancers, Boys, J. Hadreas
"Can This Be Love" (reprise)
J. Ehrle, N. O'Day, J. Wagstaff
"Wedding Bells"
Ensemble
Waltz Ballet
Betsy Rees, Specialty Dancers
Finale
Entire Company

1930.29 ## BROWN BUDDIES

A Musical Comedy in Two Acts, 8 Scenes. Book by Carl Rickman. Music by Joe Jordan. Lyrics by Millard Thomas. Additional music and lyrics by Shelton Brooks, Ned Reed, Porter Grainger, James C. Johnson, J. Rosamund Johnson, George A. Little, Arthur Sizemore, Edward G. Nelson. Staged by Ralph Rose. Dances staged by Addison Carey, Charles Davis. Settings by Theodore Kahn, Edward Sundquist Studios. Costumes by Brooks, Inc., Ida Bell. Music director, Charles L. Cooke. Orchestrations by Charles L. Cooke, Joe Jordan. (Produced by Padrae Inc., Marty Forkins.) Opened 7 October 1930 at the Liberty Theatre and closed 10 January 1931 after 111 performances.

CAST (in order of speaking): *Spider Bruce*: John Mason. *Mathews*: Thomas Moseley. *Hamfat*: "Little Ferdie" Lewis. *Mammy Johnson*: ADA BROWN. *Jessie Watkins*: ALMA SMITH. *George Brown*: Andrew Tribble. *Ukelele Kid*: Putney Dandridge. *Bill Jones*: Walter Brogsdale. *Pete Jackson*: Maurice Ellis. *Deacon Siccomore*: SHELTON BROOKS. *Mabel*: Ethel Jackson. *A Woman*: Nancy Sharpe. *Sam Wilson*: BILL ROBINSON. *Betty Lou Johnson*: ADELAIDE HALL. *A Policeman*: Sam Jones. *A Trumpeter*: Hank Smith. *Lieutenant Pugh*: WILLIAM E. FOUNTAINE. *Houstin Charlie*: Joseph Willis. *Captain Andrews*: JAMES A. LILLARD. *Medical Officer*: Carroll Tate. *Orderly*: Pete Thompson. *A Guard*: Edgar Brown. *Privates Red and Struggy*: Red and Struggy. *Y.M.C.A. Man*: Thomas Wye. *A Corporal*: Archie Toms. PIKE DAVIS and His Brown Buddies Orchestra. *Soldiers, Sailors, Dixie Dancing Girls and Male Chorus.*

Act 1, Scene 1: A Street in the Mud Flats of East St. Louis. Late summer, 1917. *Scene 2*: Outside the Barracks. One month later. *Scene 3*: Aboard a Transport. Early spring, 1918.

Act 2, Scene 1: Y.M.C.A. Entertainment Hut. Somewhere in France. *Scene 2*: A Road to the Front. *Scene 3*: A Forest Trail. *Scene 4*: A Street in East St. Louis. July 1, 1920. *Scene 5*: Home of Captain Andrews in East St. Louis. July, 1920.

ACT 1
"Gettin' Off"
P. Dandridge, A. Smith
"Happy"
B. Robinson, A. Hall
(*Music by* Nat Reed. *Lyrics by* Bob Joffe.)
"Brown Buddies"
B. Robinson, Boys
"When a Black Man's Blue"
A. Brown, Boys
(*Music by* Ed G. Nelson, Art Sizemore. *Lyrics by* Ed G. Nelson, George A. Little.)
Specialty
B. Robinson
"Sugar Cane"
P. Dandridge, A. Smith
"My Blue Melody" (I Hate Myself for Falling in Love with You)
A. Hall
(*Music by* Abner Silver. *Lyrics by* Dave Oppenheim.)
Finale — "Carry On"
J. A. Lillard, Entire Company

ACT 2
Opening Chorus
"Dance Away Your Sins" (Dancin' 'Way Your Sin)
A. Brown, Ensemble
(*Music and Lyrics by* James C. Johnson.)
"I Lost Everything Losing You"[36]
W. E. Fountaine

---

[36]Dropped during run.

"Sweetie Mine"
Dixie Dancing Girls
Specialty
Red and Struggy
"Give Me a Man Like That"
A. Hall
(*Music by* Art Sizemore. *Lyrics by* George A. Little.)
Specialty
P. Dandridge, Boys
"Betty Lou"
A. Brown
(*Music by* Joe Jordan. *Lyrics by* J. Rosamund Johnson.)
"In Missouria" (Missouri)
P. Dandridge, Boys
(*Music and Lyrics by* Nat Reed.)
"Taps"
B. Robinson, Girls
Finale
Entire Company

1930.30 ## PRINCESS CHARMING

A Musical Romance (Operetta) in Two Acts, 7 Scenes. Book by Jack Donahue. Adapted from the Hungarian operetta "Alexandra" by Franz [Ferenc] Martos, and its English adaptation "Princess Charming" by Arthur Wimperis and Lauri Wylie. Music by Albert Sirmay and Arthur Schwartz. Lyrics by Arthur Swanstrom. Book directed by Edward Clarke Lilley. Entire production staged under the direction of Bobby Connolly. Ballets by Albertina Rasch. Military direction by Harry Holbrook, U.S.M.C. Settings by Joseph Urban. Costumes by Charles LeMaire. Music director, Alfred Goodman. Produced by Bobby Connolly and Arthur Swanstrom. Opened 13 October 1930 at the Imperial Theatre and closed 29 November 1930 after 56 performances.

CAST: *Baron Sigman*: Roy Gordon. *Lieutenant of the Elyria*:: John Kane. *Second Lieutenant*: Ernest McChesney. *Marie, stenographer at the Embassy*: Betty Gallagher. *Wanda Navarro, who assumed the title of Countess*: JEANNE AUBERT. *Irving Huff, Continental Manager for the Indispensable Insurance Co.*: VICTOR MOORE. *Princess Elaine of Novia*: EVELYN HERBERT. *Captain Torrelli of the Cruiser Elyria*:: ROBERT HALLIDAY. *Ivanoff, leader of the revolutionists*: Douglas Dumbrille. *Christian II of Elyria*: GEORGE GROSSMITH. *Aide de Camp to the King*: Howard St. John. *Atttorney General*: Paul Huber. *Lord Chamberlain to the King*: Raoul de Tisne. *Lulu, maid at the Embassy*: Dorothea James. *Page*: Duke McHale. *Veronique*: Yvonne Grey. *Colette*: Irene Bostick. *Anastasia*: Frances Markey. *Marguerite*: Wilma Roeloff.

Officers of the Guard of Honor from the Cruiser Elyria: Ray Covert, John Fulco, Thomas Bourke, William Ruppel, Leslie Ostrander, Jack Stevens, Edouard Grobe. *Albertina Rasch Ballet*: *Premiere Danseuse*: Portia Grafton. *Solo Dancers*: Louise Hansen, Jeannette Bradley, Ruth Cook, Ruth Hayden, Virginia Allen, Frances Wise. *Ballet Dancers*: Mildred Turner, Wilma Kaye, June English, Marie Grimaldi, Nona O'Tero, Josephine Wolfe, Agatha Johann, Stella Kehr, Lee Nugent, Elsie Kain, Adeline Bendon, Regina Kovale, Martha Wilbert, Tessie Pearson, Margaret Slattery, Beatrice Lauri, Ruth Sproule.
Dancers: Patti Hastings, Ann Hardman, Peggy Sickle, Patricia Whitney, Dorothy Nodine, Louise Allen, Carola Taylor, Evelyn Monte, Billy Sallier. *Show Girls and Singers*: Edna Bunte, Marian Santry, Anne Goddard, Pam Sweeney, Ilus de Pongo, Peggy Dolan, Kay Burnell, Mabel Potter, Norma Nash, Wynne Ralph, Evelyn Dallas. *Sailors, Revolutionaries, Hussars, etc.*: Merritt Moore, William Prevost, Howard Johnson, Pat Quinton, Joseph Carey, Jack Lister, Fred Barry, Lewis Moore, William Leon, Albert Leroy, Donald Gordon, Bart Schilling, William Hagen, Edward Young, Brian Davis, Robert Saidler, John Walsh, Serge Ury, Leon Dunar, William Ritter, Fred Brook, Arduino Muzzi, Donald Plover, John Mangum, Walter Asmus, Israfel Weinstein, Roberto Marco, Basil Rallis, James Dowling, Jack Var, Andor Keller, Erle Danley, Walter Wandell, Leo Tatzin, Tom Kelly, Leon Nash, Maurice Siegel, John Krikoff, Jack James.

Act 1, Scene 1: The Crystal Room in the Palace of the Elyrian Embassy in Novia. *Scene 2*: Outside the Embassy on the way to the Cruiser Elyria . *Scene 3*: On the Deck of the Cruiser *Elyria*. . Ten days later.

Act 2, Scene 1: In the Throne Room, Royal Palace, Elyria. *Scene 2*: Exterior of Baron Sigman's Castle. *Scene 3*: Bedroom of the Countess Wanda Navarro at Baron Sigman's Castle. The same night. *Scene 4*: In the Garden of the Sigman Castle adjoining the Royal Palace. The next morning.

ACT 1
Opening
Ensemble

"Take a Letter to the King"
    R. Gordon, B. Gallagher, Girls

"Palace of Dreams"
    E. Herbert, Officers, Girls

"The Panic's On"
    D. James, Girls

"I'll Be There"
    J. Aubert, V. Moore, Rasch Ballet

"Trailing a Shooting Star"
    E. Herbert, R. Halliday

"Here Is a Sword"
    R. Halliday, Sailors

"I'll Be There" (reprise)
    J. Aubert, D. Dumbrille

"One for All"
    D. Dumbrille, Revolutionists

"I Love Love"[37]
    J. Aubert, Officers, Girls
    (*Music by* Robert (Emmett) Dolan. *Lyrics by* Walter O'Keefe.)

"You"
    E. Herbert, R. Halliday

Finale
    Ensemble

ACT 2
Opening
"A Wonderful Thing for the King"[38]
    G. Grossmith, D. James, Girls

"I'll Be There" (reprise)
    J. Aubert, G. Grossmith

Reception of the Court
    E. Herbert, R. Halliday, G. Grossmith, Ensemble

"I'll Never Leave You"
    E. Herbert, R. Halliday

"You" (reprise)
    E. Herbert

"I'll Never Leave You" (reprise)
    E. Herbert, R. Halliday

"Wings of the Morning"
    Rasch Ballet

First Sunbeam
    P. Grafton

Finale
    Ensemble

1930.31

GIRL CRAZY

A Musical Comedy in Two Acts, 8 Scenes. Book by Guy Bolton and John McGowan. Music by George Gershwin. Lyrics by Ira Gershwin. Staged by Alexander Leftwich. Dances and ensembles by George Hale. Settings by Donald Oenslager. Costumes by Kiviette. Music director, Earl Busby. Orchestrations by (Robert) Russell Bennett. Produced by Alex A. Aarons and Vinton Freedley. Opened 14 October 1930 at the Alvin Theatre and closed 6 June 1931 after 272 performances.

CAST (in order of appearance): *Danny Churchill:* ALLEN KEARNS. *Molly Gray:* GINGER ROGERS. *Pete:* Clyde Veaux. *Lank Sanders:* Carlton Macy. *Gieber Goldfarb:* WILLIE HOWARD. *Flora James:* EUNICE HEALEY. *Patsy West:* Peggy O'Connor. *Kate Fothergill:* ETHEL MERMAN. *Slick Fothergill:* WILLIAM KENT. *Sam Mason:* Donald Foster. *Tess Parker:* Olive Brady. *Jake Howell:* LEW PARKER. *Eagle Rock:* Chief Rivers. *Hotel Proprietor:* Jack Classon. *Lariat Joe:* Starr Jones. THE FOURSOME: Marshall Smith, Ray Johnson, Del Porter, Dwight Snyder. Antonio and Renée DeMarco, "Red" Nichols and His Orchestra.

Ladies of the Ensemble: Lillian Ostrom, Kay Downer, Gertrude Lowe, Norma Butler, Gloria Beaumont, Kathryn Cathcart, Julia Pirie, Vivian Porter, Drucilla Strain, Mary Mascher, Virginia Kay, Marion Harcke, Muriel LaCount, Lillian Lorray, Elsie Neal, Faye Greene, Nondas Wayne, Ruth Timmons, LaVern Evans, Betty Morton, Margie O'Shea, Vivian Keefer, Dorothy Donnelly[39], Jane Lane, Gene Brady, Lillian

Carson, Marvyn Ray, Thomasine Haye, Dorothy Gordon, Lelia Laney, Jackie Feeley, Rena Landeau, Kathy Schauer. *Gentlemen of the Ensemble:* Bob Gebhardt, Bob Derden, Hazard Newberry, Bob Burton, Harry Griffin, Jack Fago, James Notono, Starr Jones, Norman Curtiss, John Sciortino, Jack Closson, Kendall Northrop, Mickie Forbs, Jack Barrett, Arthur Craig, Dick Nealy.

Act 1, Scene 1: Exterior of the Custer House, Custerville, Arizona. *Scene 2:* The Dude Ranch. *Scene 3:* Gieber's Election Headquarters. *Scene 4:* Outside the Custerville Post Office. *Scene 5:* Barroom at the Dude Ranch.

Act 2, Scene 1: Hotel Los Palmos, San Luz, Mexico. *Scene 2:* The Railroad Station, San Luz. *Scene 3:* Outside the Dude Ranch.

ACT 1
"Bidin' My Time"
    M. Smith, R. Johnson, D. Porter, D. Snyder

"The Lonesome Cowboy"
    Cow Punchers (Men's Ensemble)

"Could You Use Me"
    G. Rogers, A. Kearns

"Bronco Busters"
    Dudeens, Cowboys (Ensemble)

"Barbary Coast"
    G. Rogers, O. Brady, E. Healy, Chorus

"Embraceable You"
    G. Rogers, A. Kearns

Finaletto ("Goldfarb, That's I'm!")
    W. Howard, W. Kent, Ensemble

"Embraceable You" (reprise)
    G. Rogers, A. Kearns

"Sam and Delilah"
    E. Merman

"I Got Rhythm"
    E. Merman, Chorus

Specialty Dance
    A. DeMarco, R. DeMarco

Finale
    (D. Foster, G. Rogers, A. Kearns, E. Merman, Ensemble)

ACT 2
"Land of the Gay Caballero"
    Ensemble

Specialty
    A. DeMarco, R. DeMarco

"But Not for Me"
    G. Rogers, W. Howard

"Treat Me Rough"
    W. Kent, Chorus

"Boy! What Love Has Done to Me"
    E. Merman

"(When It's) Cactus Time in Arizona"
    G. Rogers, Chorus

Finale
    Entire Company

1930.32

THREE'S A CROWD

A Musical Revue in Two Acts, 25 Scenes. Conceived and compiled by Howard Dietz. (Sketches by Howard Dietz, Groucho Marx, Arthur Sheekman, William B. Miles, Donald Blackwell, Laurence Schwab, Fred Allen, Corey Ford, Hazel Flynn.) Music by Arthur Schwartz, (Vernon Duke, Burton Lane, Alec Wilder, Johnny Green, Philip Charig, Richard Myers). Lyrics by Howard Dietz, (Edward Brandt, Edward Heyman, Robert Sour, Charles Schwab). Staged and lighted by Hassard Short. Dances by Albertina Rasch. Settings by Albert R. Johnson. Costumes by Kiviette. Music director, Nicholas Kempner. Produced by Max Gordon. Opened 15 October 1930 at the Selwyn Theatre and closed 6 June 1931 after 271 performances.

CAST: CIFTON WEBB, FRED ALLEN, LIBBY HOLMAN, TAMARA GEVA, EARL OXFORD, Portland Hoffa, Margaret Lee, Amy Revere, Marybeth Conoly, Wally Coyle, Harold Moffett, Joan Clement, The California Collegians (Fred MacMurray, Rene DuPlessis, Lou Wood, Percy Launders, Alan Jones, Herb Montei, Ray Adams).

Albertina Rasch Specialty Dancers: Dorissa Nelova, Rose Gale, Helene Carson, Marguerite Eisele. *Girls:* Nonie Dale, Pat Hamill, Gladys Page, Aida Conkey, Enes

---

[37]Dropped after opening.
[38]Dropped after opening.
[39]Not the actress turned Broadway librettist Dorothy Donnelly, remembered for THE STUDENT PRINCE.

Early, Josephine Roberts, Amelie Ideal, Georgiana Orr, Greta Lewis, Betty Travers, Lorraine Power, Dorothy Graham, Genevieve Tighe.

ACT 1
Scene 1
Bedroom Scene (*by* Howard Dietz)
The Wife: M. Conoly. *The Husband*: H. Moffett. *The Lover*: L. Wood.
Scene 2
Meet the Girls
Specialty Dancers, Girls
Scene 3
In Marbled Halls (*by* William Miles and Donald Blackwell)
He: C. Webb. *She*: T. Geva.
Scene 4
"Practising Up on You"
M. Lee, W. Coyle, H. Montei, A. Jones, R. DuPlessis, Girls
(*Music by* Philip Charig. *Lyrics by* Howard Dietz.)
Scene 5
"Something to Remember You By"
L. Holman
(*Music by* Arthur Schwartz. *Lyrics by* Howard Dietz.)
Scene 6
The Curse of Versatility
F. Allen, P. Hoffa
Scene 7
"Out in the Open Air"
C. Webb, M. Lee, other babes in the wood
(*Music by* Burton Lane. *Lyrics by* Howard Dietz.)
Scene 8
The Event (*by* Groucho Marx and Arthur Sheekman)
Introduced by P. Hoffa.
The Age of Innocence
W. Coyle, M. Conoly, H. Moffett
The Age of Innocence
L. Wood, J. Clement
This Age of Ours
L. Holman, F. MacMurray
Scene 9
"Je T'Aime"
C. Webb, M. Lee, California Collegians
(*Music by* Arthur Schwartz. *Lyrics by* Howard Dietz.)
Scene 10
"Talkative Toes"
T. Geva, Girls
(*Music by* Vernon Duke. *Lyrics by* Howard Dietz.)
Scene 11
The Private Life of a Roxy Usher (*by* Arthur Sheekman and Hazel Flynn.)
Scene: The Miggles at Home.
Private Ethelbert Miggie: C. Webb. *Mrs. Miggle*, his wife: J. Clement.
The Lover: F. MacMurray.
Scene 12
"All the King's Horses"
M. Lee, Girls
(*Music and Lyrics by* Alec Wilder, Eddie Brandt and Howard Dietz.)
Scene 13
"Body and Soul"
L. Holman
(*Music by* Johnny Green. *Lyrics by* Edward Heyman, Robert Sour, Frank Eyton. *Vocal and Orchestral Arrangement by* Ralph Rainger.)
Scene 14
On the Wire (*by* Laurence Schwab)
F. Allen, M. Conoly, H. Moffett
Scene 15
"The Moment I Saw You"
C. Webb, A. Revere, Ensemble
(*Music by* Arthur Schwartz. *Lyrics by* Howard Dietz.)

ACT 2
Scene 1
Rear Admiral Allen
"Welcome Home"
Ensemble
"My Gallant Boys"
Dr. Winterbottom: H. Moffett. *Malcolm Weir*: A. Jones. *Mr. Blue*: P. Launders. *Mr. Forsythe*: F. MacMurray.
Scene 2
Body and Soul Dance
C. Webb, T. Geva.
Musical Accompaniment
L. Holman, California Collegians
Scene 3
"Forget All Your Books"
M. Lee, W. Coyle, Girls
(*Music by* Burton Lane. *Lyrics by* Howard Dietz.)
Scene 4
Among the Magazines (*by* Corey Ford and Howard Dietz)
Office of *College Humor*
L. Wood, H. Montei, A. Jones, W. Coyle
Office of *True Confessions*
F. Allen, R. DuPlessis, T. Geva
Office of *Ladies' Home Journal*
J. Clement, P. Hoffa, C. Webb
Scene 5
"Yaller"
L. Holman, Ensemble
(*Music by* Charles M. Schwab. *Lyrics by* Henry Myers.)
Scene 6
In a Nutshell
F. Allen
Scene 7
"Night After Night"
C. Webb, Ensemble
(*Music by* Arthur Schwartz. *Lyrics by* Howard Dietz. *Ballet Music by* Will Irwin. *Masks designed by* Constance Ripley.)
Scene 8
The California Collegians
F. MacMurray, R. DuPlessis, L. Wood, P. Launders, A. Jones, H. Montei, R. Adams
(*Music by* Arthur Schwartz. *Lyrics by* Howard Dietz.)
Scene 9
"Right at the Start of It"
C. Webb, F. Allen, L. Holman
(*Music by* Arthur Schwartz. *Lyrics by* Howard Dietz.)
Scene 10
"Right at the End of It" (Finale)
Entire Company

THE GARRICK GAIETIES

1930.33 (3RD EDITION)

A Return Engagement of the Musical Revue in Two Acts, 24 Scenes[40]. (Sketches by Sally Humason, Carroll Carroll, Hi Alexander, Newman Levy, Edward Hope, Albert Carroll, Benjamin M. Kaye, Dorothy Fletcher.) Music mostly by Vernon Duke. (Additional music by Richard Rodgers, Ned Lehak, Manna-Zucca, Charles M. Schwab, Kay Swift, Willard Robison, Jay Gorney, Everett Miller.) Lyrics mostly by E. Y. Harburg. (Additional lyrics by Allen Boretz, Benjamin M. Kaye, Ira Gershwin, Thomas McKnight, Newman Levy, Paul James [James P. Warburg], Lorenz Hart, Howard Dietz, Johnny Mercer.) Staged by Philip Loeb. Settings by Kate Drain Lawson, Costumes by Kate Drain Lawson, Louis Simon, (Henri Peine du Bois). Music director, Tom Jones. Dances arranged by John E.

[40]A revised version of the revue originally produced in New York 4 June 1930 at the Guild Theatre for 158 performances.

Lonergan. Orchestra directed by Hilding Anderson. Produced by the Theatre Guild Inc. Opened 16 October 1930 at the Guild Theatre and closed 25 October 1930 after 12 performances.

CAST[41]: PHILIP LOEB, ALBERT CARROLL, DORIS VINTON, STERLING HOLLOWAY, KATHERINE CARRINGTON, NEAL CALDWELL, OTTO HULETT, EDGAR STEHLI, WILLIAM HOLBROOK, NEILA GOODELLE, DONALD BURR, IMOGENE COCA, JAMES NORRIS, ROSALIND RUSSELL, BOBBY ROBERTS, RUTH CHORPENNING, Roger Stearns, Edwin Gilcher, Ginger Meehan, Anna Marie Cotter, Anna Delphine, Viola Wilson, Kathleen Whitcomb, Emily Thompson, Alice Bankert, Irene Carroll, Dot Stemme, Bonny Brenner, Sylvia Miller, Mildred Muller, Mary Brown.

ACT 1

Scene 1

"Opening Number"[42]
(*Music by* Richard Rodgers. *Lyrics by* E. Y. Harburg.)
Nina Guild: R. Russell. *George Bernard Shaw*: S. Holloway. *Ferenc Molnar*: J. Norris. *Eugene O'Neill*: N. Caldwell. *Gordon Gaieties*: R. Stearns.
The Strange Interlude that gave birth to the Garrick Gaieties.

Scene 2

"Shavian Shivers"
S. Holloway, Chorus
(*Music by* Vernon Duke. *Lyrics by* E. Y. Harburg.)
Which proves that Shaw will not leave the stage once he gets it.

Scene 3

How to Write for the Movies (*by* Sally Humason)
Secretary: I. Coca. *Author*: A. Carroll. *Great Talkie Magnate*: P. Loeb.
The Garrick Gaieties lets you into the secret of how to make money easily and honestly.

Scene 4

"Four Infant Prodigies"
(*Music by* Ned Lehak. *Lyrics by* Allen Boretz.)
Child Poetess: R. Russell. *Child Violinist*: O. Hulett. *Child Evangelist*: R. Chorpenning. *Child Movie Actor*: S. Holloway.
All by the permission of the Society for the Prevention of Cruelty to Children.

Scene 5

The Soda Fountain (*by* Carroll Carroll)
A. Carroll, J. Norris, Chorus
The effect of our newer Soda Counter concoctions upon the tender sensibilities of a very tender and sensitive young man portrayed by Albert Carroll, with James Norris and everyone else rendering the first aid.

Scene 6

"Butcher, Baker and Candlestickmaker"
(*Music by* Manna-Zucca. *Lyrics by* Benjamin M. Kaye.)
Singer: D. Burr. *Butcher*: O. Hulett. *Baker*: R. Stearns. *Candlestickmaker*: J. Norris. *Marie*: I. Coca. *Little Bald Man*: E. Stehli.
A scientific exposition of a remarkable case of pre-natal influence.

Scene 7

Shoo (*by* Hi Alexander)
The Clerk: A. Carroll. *The Customer*: P. Loeb.
Our clerks should extend the utmost in courtesy to our customers . . . an entente cordiale should be established quickly.

Scene 8

"A Little Privacy"[43]
(*Music by* Vernon Duke. *Lyrics by* E. Y. Harburg.)
Boy: W. Holbrook. *Girl*: D. Vinton. *Riveter*: B. Roberts. *Heywood Broun*: O. Hulett. *Champion*: S. Holloway. *Four Tammany Leaders*: J. Norris, B. Roberts, E. Stehli, D. Burr. *Photographer*: R. Stearns.
A new campaign issue for the attention of voters.

Scene 9

Washington and the Spy[44] (*by* Newman Levy)
Announcement: I. Coca. *Washington*: N. Caldwell. *Orderly*: E. Gilcher. *Grant*: P. Loeb. *Mary*: R. Chorpenning. *The Spy*: A. Carroll.
Or, as you might call it, scrambled history. It only goes to prove that there is a kinship between the great of all ages.

Scene 10

"There Ain't No Love"[45]
R. Russell, D. Vinton, I. Coca, N. Goodelle, K. Carrington
(*Music by* Vernon Duke. *Lyrics by* E. Y. Harburg.)
Boys: J. Norris, R. Stearns, D. Burr, B. Roberts, W. Holbrook. *Maids*: G. Meehan, A. M. Cotter, A. Delphin, V. Wilson, K. Whitcomb.

Scene 11

A Famous Lawyer at Home (*by* Newman Levy)
Introduction: N. Caldwell. *The Great Trial Lawyer*: P. Loeb. *His Wife*: R. Russell. *The Maid*: I. Coca.
The audience (is) requested to act as the jury and to decide who is to win this case.

Scene 12

"I Am Only Human After All"
(*Music by* Vernon Duke. *Lyrics by* E. Y. Harburg, (Ira Gershwin).)
The Boy: D. Burr. *The Girl*: K. Carrington. *The Broker*: O. Hulett. *The Girl Friend*: I. Coca. *The Tough*: R. Russell. *Her Victim*: S. Holloway.
We feel there should be a solemn moment in our revue. In the midst of our ecstatic flights of fancy, we remind you that we, too, are human.

Scene 13

Addled, or the Psychopathic Ward[46] (*by* Edward Hope)
The Doctor: E. Stehli. *The Patient*: N. Caldwell. *The Interne*: O. Hulett. *The Nurse*: E. Thompson.
Being the awful effect of modern advertising on an impressionable young mind.

Scene 14

"George and Mary"
R. Russell, A. Carroll
(*Music by* Charles M. Schwab. *Lyrics by* Thomas McKnight.)
A visit to Buckingham Palace with Rosalind Russell and Albert Carroll.

Scene 15

They Always Come Back (*by* Newman Levy)
"I'm Grover"
(*Music by* Vernon Duke. *Lyrics by* Newman Levy.)
"Johnny Wanamaker"
(*Music by* Kay Swift. *Lyrics by* Paul James.)
Traffic Saleslady: R. Chorpenning. *First Customer*: D. Vinton. *Second Customer*: E. Stehli. *His Wife*: S. Miller. *His Daughter*: I. Coca. *Special Messenger*: E. Gilcher. *Body Guard*: K. Carrington. *Floorwalkers*: J. Norris, D. Burr, N. Caldwell, B. Roberts. *Grover*: P. Loeb. *Beautiful Customer*: R. Russell.
As our audiences probably know, Wanamaker's is one of the oldest and best con-ducted stores in New York, but some members of our audiences may not know that Mr. Whalen was loaned by Wanamaker's to the New York Police Department for one year, and has since resumed his old position. The following phantasy is offered as a possibility of what might have happened (but did not happen) had Mr. Whalen decided to apply the methods which he learned in the Police Department in running this famous department store.

ACT 2

Scene 1

"Lazy Levee Loungers"
N. Goodelle, R. Stearns, N. Caldwell, D. Burr, J. Norris
(*Music and Lyrics by* Willard Robison.)

Scene 2

"Three Musketeers" (from *THE GARRICK GAIETIES*, 1926)
P. Loeb, S. Holloway, N. Caldwell
(*Music by* Richard Rodgers. *Lyrics by* Lorenz Hart.)
In which the equality phase of Liberty, Fraternity and Equality is applied to a division of feminine spoils.

---

[41]Doris Vinton, Katherine Carrington, Neal Caldwell, Edgar Stehli, William Holbrook, Neila Goodelle, Donald Burr, Rosalind Russell, Bobby Roberts, Roger Stearns, Anna Marie Cotter, Anna Delphine, Viola Wilson, Kathleen Whitcomb, Emily Thompson, Alice Bankert Irene Carroll, Dot Stemme, Bonny Brenner, Sylvia Miller, Mildred Muller, Mary Brown were newly added for return engagement and subsequent tour.
[42]Music previously used in "Six Little Plays" in GARRICK GAIETIES OF 1926. New lyrics for this edition of GARRICK GAIETIES; not in previous June 1930 edition; added for this edition and subsequent tour.
[43]Not in previous June 1930 edition; added for this edition and subsequent tour.

[44]Not in previous June 1930 edition; added for this edition and subsequent tour.
[45]Not in previous June 1930 edition; added for this edition and subsequent tour.
[46]Not in previous June 1930 edition; added for this edition and subsequent tour.

Scene 3

The Lunts Revive 'The Guardsman'[47] (by Albert Carroll)
Lynn Fontanne, as the Actress: A. Carroll. *Alfred Lunt*, as the Guardsman: O. Hulett. *Helen Westley*, as Mama: R. Chorpenning.
And he might have mentioned Helen Westley, too.

Scene 4

"In the Bathroom"[48]
P. Loeb
(*Music by* Jay Gorney. *Lyrics by* Howard Dietz.)
Or, the urge to sing brought about by the reflection of the morning sun on white tile.

Scene 5

Life in Hollywood (by Benjamin M. Kaye)
Introduction: N. Caldwell. *Ginnigan, the great movie director*: O. Hulett. *The Great Super-Great Movie Star*: I. Coca. *The Greater Super-Greater Star*: D. Vinton. *The Great Super-Super-Great Crowd of Authors, Actors, Directors, etc.*: Cast.
The function of a formal afternoon tea as observed in ultra-conservative Hollywood circles.

Scene 6

"Out of Breath (and Scared to Death of You)"
S. Holloway, D. Vinton
(*Music by* Everett Miller. *Lyrics by* Johnny Mercer.)
Two 'Fraidy-cats' at work.

Scene 7

Panic's End (by Dorothy Fletcher)
Sanford: N. Caldwell. *Baldwin*: E. Stehli. *Pawley*: A. Carroll. *Williams*: W. Holbrook. *Stock Clerk*: E. Gilcher.
The spirit of "Journey's End" applied to the recent catastrophe in Wall Street.

Scene 8

"Unaccustomed As I Am"[49]
N. Goodelle, S. Holloway
(*Music by* Vernon Duke. *Lyrics by* E. Y. Harburg.)
Reprise
D. Vinton, P. Loeb
Quartette: E. Stehli, W. Holbrook, O. Hulett, N. Caldwell.

Scene 9

"The Rose of Arizona" (from *THE GARRICK GAIETIES*, 1926)
(*Music by* Richard Rodgers. *Lyrics by* Lorenz Hart.)
Rosabelle: R. Chorpenning. *Gloria*: K. Carrington. *Van Dyke*: P. Loeb. *Allan*: J. Norris. *Mrs. Van Dyke*: D. Vinton. *Caramba*: S. Holloway. *Pimento*: R. Russell. *Macfadden*: B. Roberts. *Soldiers*: O. Hulett, A. Carroll, D. Burr, N. Caldwell, W. Holbrook, E. Stehli, R. Stearns, E. Gilcher.

1930.34

BLACKBIRDS OF 1930

A Musical Revue in Two Acts, 18 Scenes[50]. Sketches by Flourney [Flournoy] Miller. Music by Eubie Blake. Lyrics by Andy Razaf. Entire production conceived and staged by Lew Leslie. Dances by Al Richards. Settings by Ward & Harvey. Costumes by Vincente Minnelli. Music director, Eubie Blake. Orchestrations by Ken Macomber. Vocal arrangements by (J.) Rosamund Johnson. Produced by Lew Leslie. Opened 22 October 1930 at the Royale Theatre and closed 13 December 1930 after 62 performances.

CAST: ETHEL WATERS, [John W.] BUCK & BUBBLES [Ford L. Washington], FLOURNEY MILLER, BERRY BROTHERS (Ananias, Warren and James), MANTAN MORELAND, NEEKA SHAW, MERCIA MARQUISE [Marquiz], JIMMY BASKETTE, BROADWAY JONES, MINTO CATO, BLUE MCALLISTER, CRAWFORD JACKSON, CECIL MACK'S CHOIR, (Jazzlips Richardson).
Chorus: Ulma Banks, Blanche Dunn, Mary Bethune, Estelle Bernier, Emma Jones, Dorothy Kennedy, Ionya Hayes, Dolores Blaine, Marmetta Newton, Marie Robinson, Louise Uggams, Howard Johnson, Al Richards, Bill Bailey, Roy Atkins, J. Lewis Johnson.

ACT 1[51]

Scene 1

The Levee on the Mississippi
Cotton Pickers and Levee Workers: Cecil Mack's Blackbird Choir. *Deacon Brown*: J. H. Johnson. *River Jordan*: B. Jones. *Sunshine Susie*: N. Shaw. *Mammy Jones*: M. Cato. *Mississippi Steppers*: Chorus. *Mississippi Beauties*: U. Banks, B. Dunn, M. Bethune, E. Bernier, E. Jones, D. Kennedy, I. Hayes, D. Blaine. *Amos and Andys*: A. Richards, C. Jackson, B. Bailey, R. Atkins.
"Roll, Jordan"
B. Jones, Cecil Mack's Choir
"Cabin Door"
N. Shaw, Chorus, Entire Company
"Memories of You"
M. Cato, Entire Company

Scene 2

A Charleston Honeymoon
Train Announcer: J. L. Johnson. *Steve*: F. Miller. *Caesar*: M. Moreland. *Hannah*: E. Waters. *Diploma*: M. Newton. *Liza*: M. Robinson. *A Stranger*: E. Bernier. *Ticket Agent*: J. Baskette.

Scene 3

"Mozambique"
M. Marquise
Scene: An African Jungle.

Scene 4

Shadow Dance
Berry Brothers

Scene 5

A Dark Triangle
Hannah: E. Waters. *Caesar*: M. Moreland. *Steve*: F. Miller. *Mandy*: L. Uggams. *Her Husband*: B. McAllister.

Scene 6

"Take a Trip to Harlem"
M. Marquise, R. Atkins, C. Jackson, Chorus
Specialty
B. Bailey, C. Jackson

Scene 7

My Best Gal[52]
Two Pals: Bucks & Bubbles. *Melinda*: N. Shaw.
"Lucky to Me"
N. Shaw, J. Bubbles
"Lucky to Me" (reprise)
E. Waters

Scene 8

The Last Smile (With apologies to the author of 'The Last Mile')
Steve: F. Miller. *Caesar*: M. Moreland. *River Jordan*: B. Jones. *Napoleon*: J. Baskette. *Butch*: J. L. Johnson. *Hoofer*: B. Bailey. *Bride*: E. Bernier.

Scene 9

"We're the Berries"
Berry Brothers

Scene 10

"Green Pastures"—A travesty based on the famous book and play, with apologies to Marc Connelly and Roland Stebbins.
(*Lyrics by* Will Morrissey and Andy Razaf.)

---

[47]Not in previous June 1930 edition; added for this edition and subsequent tour.
[48]Not in previous June 1930 edition; added for this edition and subsequent tour.
[49]Not in previous June 1930 edition; added for this edition and subsequent tour.
[50]The second in the American series of black musical revues conceived by Lew Leslie beginning in 1928.

[51]Added for subsequent tour:
"Blackbirds Are Blue"
Geneva Washington, Entire Company
"(That) Lindy Hop"
Berry Brothers, Billy Yarbo, Chorus
"Wakin' Up the Folks Downstairs"
Helena Justa, Chorus
"Porgy" (Travesty on the play)
E. Waters, Cecil Mack's Choir
"St Louis Blues"
E. Waters
"Harlem"
Valaida Snow, Chorus
[52]Dropped during run.

Scene 1: Heaven. *Scene 2*: Earth. *Scene 3*: Hades.
The Lord: B. Jones. *An Angel*: E. Waters. *Satan*: J. Baskette. *A Harlem Midnight Rounder*: J. Bubbles. *She Devils*: Southern Beauties. *Harlem Steppers*: Chorus. *Angels in Heaven*: Cecil Mack's Blackbird Choir.

ACT 2

Scene 1

In Slumberland
N. Shaw

Scene 2

Aunt Jemima's Divorce Case
Aunt Jemima: B. McAllister. *Cream of Wheat*, her husband: M. Moreland. *The Ham What Am*, the Judge: J. L. Johnson. *Sambo*, the Lawyer: F. Miller. *The Jury*: Blackbird Ginger Browns. *The Gold Dust Twins*, Aunt Jemima's Children: Chorus. *Aunt Jemima's Relatives*: Female Choir. *Sambo's Officers of Law*: Cecil Mack's Choir.

Scene 3

"Baby Mine"[53]
E. Waters, J. Baskette, Chorus

Scene 4

A Few Minutes of Jazzlips Richardson[54]

Scene 5

All Quiet on the Darkest Front[55] (with apologies to the noted author of the novel)
Steve: F. Miller. *Caesar*: M. Moreland. *Blue*: B. McAllister. *Buck*: Himself. *Bubbles*: Himself.

Scene 6

"Blackbirds on Parade"
J. Baskette, J. Bubbles, A. Richards, C. Jackson, B. Bailey, R. Atkins, B. McAllister, Cecil Mack's Choir, Chorus

Scene 7

Specialty
E. Waters
["Dinah"[56]
(*Music by* Harry Akst. *Lyrics by* Sam M. Lewis and Joe Young.)]

Scene 8

Always Broke
Steve: F. Miller. *Caesar*, his pal: M. Moreland. *Janitress*: L. Uggams. *Insurance Agent*: J. Baskette. *Nurse*: M. Cato. *Doctor*: B. Jones. *Manicurist*: E. Jones.

Scene 9

A Few Minutes with Buck and Bubbles

Scene 10

1930 Minstrel Episode
Entire Company
Interlocutor: E. Waters. *Mr. Ham*: F. Miller. *Mr. Bones*: M. Moreland. *And a Happy Group of Minstrel Artists*: Entire Company.
"Dianna Lee"
E. Waters, Entire Company
Minstrel Strut
Chorus
Tambourines a la Harlem
Entire Company

Scene 11

Finale
Entire Company

1930.35 THE VANDERBILT REVUE

A Musical Revue in Two Acts, 29 Scenes. Assembled by Lew Fields. Sketches by Kenyon Nicholson, Ellis O. Jones, Sig Herzig, E. North, (Edwin Gilbert, Arthur Birn, James J. Coghlan). Music by Jacques Fray, Mario Braggiotti, (Jimmy McHugh, Cole Porter, Ben Black, Edward Horan, Michael H. Cleary). Lyrics by E. Y. Harburg, (Dorothy Fields, Cole Porter, Edward Eliscu, Ben Black, David Sidney, Herb Magidson, Ned Washington). Dialogue directed by Theodore J. Hammerstein. Dances by John E. Lonergan, Jack Haskell. Settings by (Herbert) Ward & Harvey Studios. Costumes by Robert Stevenson. Music director, Gus Salzer. Entire production directed by Lew Fields. Produced by Lew Fields and Lyle D. Andrews. Opened 5 November 1930 at the Vanderbilt Theatre and closed 15 November 1930 after 13 performances.

CAST: LULU NCCONNELL, JOE PENNER, EVELYN HOEY, RICHARD LANE, OLGA MARKOFF, FRANKER WOODS, JACQUES FRAY, MARIO BRAGGIOTTI, FRANCESCA BRAGGIOTTI, TEDDY WALTERS, TONIA INGRE, CHARLES BARNES, DOROTHY DIXON, JEAN CARPENTER, Paul Everton, Eileen Poe, Richard Ryan, Billy Stephens, Francetta Malloy, Dorothy Humphries, Adeline Seaman, Jimmy Ray, Charlotte Ayres, Harry Dixon, Joe Lennon, Wallace Sisters, Rene de Rouche, Julianna, Gus Schilling, Carlos Lopez, Victor Etheridge, Jean Carpenter, Stella Royal, Carlos Roca, M. Dalsky's Russian Choir.

ACT 1

Scene 1

Stage Door
Police Captain: R. Ryan. *Officer Woods*: F. Woods. *An Actress*: L. McConnell.

Scene 2

Courtroom
Judge: P. Everton. *An Actress*: L. McConnell. *District Attorney*: R. Lane. *An Attorney*: C. Barnes. *Police Captain*: R. Ryan. *Court Attendants, Glorified Beauties, the Jury*.

Scene 3

"Button Up Your Heart"
E. Hoey, C. Barnes
(*Music by* Jimmy McHugh. *Lyrics by* Dorothy Fields.)

Scene 4

Open and Above Board (*by* Kenyon Nicholson)
Hazel Dewey: L. McConnell. *Bert Dewey*: J. Penner. *Dolly Winterbottom*: E. Poe.

Scene 5

M. Dalsky's Russian Choir

Scene 6

West Point Cut In: "Cut In"
T. Walters, Ensemble
(*Music by* Jimmy McHugh. *Lyrics by* Dorothy Fields.)

Scene 7

Mid Ocean
Johnson: R. Lane. *Smithson*: J. Penner. *Commander*: R. Ryan.

Scene 8

Dock: "Blue Again"
E. Hoey
(*Music by* Jimmy McHugh. *Lyrics by* Dorothy Fields.)
Nothing to Declare (*by* Sig Herzig)
Inspector Donovan: P. Everton. *Mrs. Carney*: L. McConnell. *Mme. Flore*: F. Braggiotti.

Scene 9

Dance
J. Ray

Scene 10

Lady of Manhattan (*by* Edwin Gilbert and Arthur Birn)
Proprietress of Gigolo Agency: F. Malloy. *Secretary*: D. Humphries. *Mrs. Woodruff*: L. McConnell. *First Gigolo*: B. Stephens. *Second Gigolo*: C. Barnes. *Third Gigolo*: R. Lane. *Fourth Gigolo*: C. Roca. *Mr. Nine*: J. Penner.

Scene 11

"Ex-Gigolo"
B. Stephens
(*Music by* Mario Braggiotti. *Lyrics by* E. Y. Harburg.)

Scene 12

Mickey, the Mouse
The Hero: H. Dixon. *The Heroine*: D. Dixon. *Father Mouse*: J. Lennon. *The Villain*: J. Ray. *The Minister*: G. Schilling. *The Villain's Child*: S. Royal. *Cats and Mice*: Boys, Girls.

Scene 13

Wanna Buy a Duck?
J. Penner

---

[53]Dropped during run.
[54]Dropped during run.
[55]Dropped during run.
[56]Introduced by Ethel Waters at the Plantation Club revue in 1925, then in AFRICANA on Broadway in 1927.

"Then Came the War"
J. Penner
(*Music and Lyrics by* Ben Black.)

Scene 14

Finale—Spanish Patio
Dance
Wallace Sisters

"I'm From Granada"
T. Ingre
(*Music by* Mario Braggiotti. *Lyrics by* David Sidney.)

Dance Tarantella
F. Braggiotti

Dance
A. Seaman

Tango
C. Ayers, R. de Rouche, C. Roca, C. Lopez, O. Markoff

Finale
T. Ingre, Dalsky's Russian Choir, Entire Ensemble

ACT 2

Scene 1

The Jackdaw of Rheims—A Tom Inglesby Legend
(*Musical Setting by* Edward Horan.)
The Cardinal: P. Everton. *The Jackdaw:* S. Royal. *The Virger:* V. Etheridge. *Monks:* Dalsky's Russian Choir.
The above scene is a monastery at Rheims, France, and unfolds a Tom Inglesby Legend. Carefree Monks are discovered at the festive board; they are interrupted by a dancing Jackdaw. The Cardinal enters. Before dipping his hands in water he removes his ring, placing it on a cushion held by an altar boy. The Jackdaw steals the ring. Upon discovering the theft, consternation seizes the Monks and the Cardinal; the latter delivers a denunciation. Night passes and the Jackdaw, repentant, returns the ring. The cardinal grants his forgiveness, and all ends in a paean of glory and thanks.

Scene 2

Specialty Dance
H. Dixon, D. Dixon

Scene 3

"What's My Man Gonna Be Like?"
E. Hoey
(*Music and Lyrics by* Cole Porter.)
At the pianos: J. Fray, M. Braggiotti.

Scene 4

A Quiet Game of Bridge (*by* Ellis O. Jones)
Mrs. Hyman: F. Malloy. *Mr. Hyman:* R. Lane. *Mrs. Simpson:* L. McConnell. *Mr. Simpson:* F. Woods.

Scene 5

"Better Not Try It"
J. Penner, T. Walters
(*Music by* Michael H. Cleary. *Lyrics by* Herb Magidson and Ned Washington.)

Scene 6

Over the Radio
Kenneth Thompson: R. Lane. *Mrs. Thompson:* F. Malloy. *The Rajah:* F. Woods.

Scene 7

"I Give Myself Away"
C. Barnes, E. Hoey
(*Music by* Jacques Fray. *Lyrics by* Edward Eliscu.)

Scene 8

Nice Girl (*by* James J. Coghlan)
Rose: F. Malloy. *Harry:* B. Stephens. *Henry:* P. Everton. *The Detective:* R. Ryan.

Scene 9

In Distress (*by* Edwin Gilbert and Arthur Brin)
Husband: J. Penner. *Wife:* D. Humphries.

Scene 10

"You're the Better Half of Me"
J. Carpenter
(*Music by* Jimmy McHugh. *Lyrics by* Dorothy Fields.)

Scene 11

Birthday Party
E. Hoey, F. Woods, B. Stephens, T. Walters, L. McConnell, J. Penner, R. Ryan, R. Lane, S. Royal, A. Seaman

Scene 12

Dance
J. Ray

Scene 13

"Half Way to Heaven"
C. Barnes, J. Carpenter
(*Music by* Mario Braggiotti. *Lyrics by* David Sidney.)

Scene 14

"Lady of the Fan"
T. Ingre
(*Music and Lyrics by* Mario Braggiotti, Jacques Fray.)

Scene 15

Grand Finale
Entire Company

1930.36 THE WELL OF ROMANCE

A Comic Operetta in Two Acts. Libretto by Preston Sturges. Music by H. Maurice Jacquet. Staged by J. H. Benrimo. Dances by Florence Rogge. Settings by Gates & Morange. Costumes by Eaves, Schneider & Blythe. Chorus directed by Jacques Pintel. Music director, H. Maurice Jacquet. Produced by G. W. McGregor. Opened 7 November 1930 at the Craig Theatre and closed 12 November 1930 after 8 performances.

CAST (in order of appearance): *Ann Schlitzl:* LAINE BLAIRE. *Wenzel:* TOMMY MONROE. *Frau Schlitzl:* LINA ABARBANELL. *Gertrude:* Elsa Paul. *Mildred:* Mildred Newman. *Louise:* Louise Joyce. *His Excellency, the Grand Chancellor:* LOUIS SORIN. *Her Serene Altesse*, the Princess: NORMA TERRIS. *Poet:* HOWARD MARSH. *Lieutenant Schpitzelberger:* Louis Rupp. *Second Lieutenant:* Syuleen Krasnoff. *Third Lieutenant:* Eugene Racine. *General Otto*, Baron Von Sprudelwasser: MAX FIGMAN. *Butterfly*, the Cow: Lo Iven (front), Ruth Flynn (rear). *A Gypsy:* Edis Phillips. *Joseph:* Joseph Roeder. *A Waiter:* Pat Walters. *First Guardsman:* Rowan Tudor. *Second Guardsman:* James Libby. *Specialty Dancers:* Nicholas Daks, Dorothy Kamdin, Etna Ross, Betty Nylander, Grayce Heath.
Beauty Chorus: Nina Allen, Lauretta Brislin, Anne Bryan, Valerie Galanine, Alice Harper, Louise Joyce, Charlotte LaRose, Jeanne LaVal, Deborah Ledger, Kathryn Mayfield, Mildred Newman, Edis Phillips, Elsa Paul, Eleanor Pierce, Mary Stager, Velma Lois Sutton, Vanda Talma, Dean Wheeler, Helene Wylie. *Officers of His Majesty's Guard:* George Magis, Efim Vitis, Morris White, Earl Wysong, Edward O'Brien, Gustave Godwin, Paul Warde, Albert Martinek, Eugene Racine, Richard Lynn, James Libby, Patrick Walters, Martin Daniel, Louis Rupp, Gene Huffman, Clark Butler, Syuleen Krasnoff, Henry Dean, Rowan Tudor. *The (Leon) Leonidoff Ballet:* Lorraine Allen, Evangeline Edwards, Ruth Haidt, Irene McBride, Hilda Eclar, Lo Iven, Ruth Flynn, Loila Porter, Hene Fried, Mary Martin[57], Katherine Nolan, Alice Morse, Alice Wright.

Act 1: Exterior of an Inn. The Distant Kingdom of Magnesia. Afternoon in Spring of 1849.

Act 2: Covered Courtyard of the Inn. Same night.

ACT 1

"At Lovetime"
Beauty Chorus, L. Blaire

"The Well of Romance"
L. Blaire, T. Monroe, Ensemble, Dancers

"Be Oh So Careful, Ann"
L. Abarbanell

"Hail the King"
Male Chorus, N. Terris

"Dream of Dreams"
N. Terris, H. Marsh

"Since You're Alone"
H. Marsh

"Cow's Divertissement"
L. Sorin, L. Iven, R. Flynn

"How Can You Tell?"
L. Blaire, T. Monroe, Dancers

"I'll Never Complain"
N. Terris

[57]Not the same Mary Martin who later appeared in *LEAVE IT TO ME, ONE TOUCH OF VENUS, SOUTH PACIFIC,* etc.

"Mazourka"
  Ensemble, Dancers, N. Terris, H. Marsh
"Fare Thee Well"
  N. Terris, H. Marsh

ACT 2
  "Hail the King" (reprise)
    Ensemble
  "The Moon's Shining Cool" (Roumanian Gypsy Song)
    N. Terris, Ensemble, Dancers
  "One Night"
    L. Abarbanell
  "Dream of Dreams" (reprise)
    N. Terris, Chorus, Dancers
  "Fare Thee Well" (reprise)
    Ensemble
  German Country Dance (Pantomime)
    L. Abarbanell, M. Figman
  "Rhapsody of Love"
    H. Marsh, Ensemble
  "For You and For Me"
    L. Blaire, T. Monroe, Dancers
  "Serenade"
    Ensemble
  "Dream of Dreams" (reprise)
    N. Terris, H. Marsh
  "Hail the King" (reprise)
    Entire Cast

1930.37

HELLO, PARIS

A Musical Comedy in Two Acts, 13 Scenes. Book by Edgar Smith, based on the novel "They Had to See Paris" by Homer Croy. Music by Russell Tarbox, Maury Rubens. Lyrics by Charles O. Locke, Frank Bannister. Staged by Ben Holmes. Dances by Pal'mere Brandeaux. Settings by Watson Barratt. Costumes by Bonwit Teller & Co., Eaves, Schneider & Blythe, Marguerite & Strauss. Music director, Tom Jones. Produced by the Messrs. Shubert. Opened 15 November 1930 at the Sam S. Shubert Theatre and closed 13 December 1930 after 33 performances.

CAST (in order of appearance): *Opal Peters, Ide's Daughter:* POLL WALKER. *Clark McGurley, Opal's Steady:* CHARLES COLUMBUS. *Ide Peters, Pike's Daughter-in-Law:* ETHEL WILSON. *Lady Wolvertress,* formerly Maude Crow: CLAIRE HOOPER. *Aunt Minnie, engaged to Eggars:* STELLA MAYHEW. *Ed Eggars,* with an open mind: NAT C. HAINES. *Ross Peters, Opal's Brother:* JACK GOOD. *Lem Putt, The Specialist:* CHARLES ("Chic") SALE. *Gracie Jones, Ross' sweetheart:* MARY ADAMS. *Pike Peters, proprietor of the Pawnee Garage:* CHARLES ("Chic") SALE. *Wheel Wilson, Leader of the Clearwater Band:* Roy Peck. *A Tourist, looking for information:* J. Clifford Rice. *Captain, the gang foreman:* Lois Deppe. *Tony, an Italian friend of Pike and Ed:* LOUIS LA GRANNA. *The Bartender, in the Speakeasy:* Fred Packard. *The Wife:* MISS AMERIQUE. *The Lover:* NEVILLE GODDARD. *The Husband:* J. CLIFFORD RICE. *The Donation Collector:* Marie Starner. *The Chemist:* Charles Garland. *Fleurie Capel:* GEORGIE HAYES. *Captain S.S. Île de France:* Roy Peck. *Marquis de Coudray:* MAURICE LA PUE. *Deck Steward:* Jester Hairston. *A Passenger:* Helen Thompson. *Another Passenger:* Jimmy Ardell. *A Devoted Husband:* Charles Garland. *His Sick Wife:* Iris Hald. *Ship Officer:* J. CLIFFORD RICE. *Anita:* Olga Markoff. *Lulu:* Riva Reyes. *Major Domo:* Roy Peck. *Monsieur Ville:* Ray Honheimer. *Antoine, of the Lapin Agile Cafe:* J. CLIFFORD RICE. *Miss Banker:* Alicia Parnahay. *Miss Clark:* Iris Hald. *Specialty:* LOIS DEPPE AND HIS JUBILEE SINGERS. *Guests, Oil Drillers, Tourists, Models, Students, Entertainers, etc.*

Dancers: Elsie Barter, Noreen Bogen, Mary Caralon, Cecilia Carl, Charlotte Fauvre, Agatha Hoff, Mildred Hosee, Gladys Granzow, Frances Lopez, Sharon Lloyd, Vi Mansfield, Jean McGee, Vivian Matheson, Lucille LaMar, Jackie Paige, Rosalie Trego. *Girls:* Onyte Burke, Wynn Terry, Iris Hald, Alicia Parnahay, Dorothy Sande, Helen Thompson, Ethel Thorsen, Edie Bly. *Boys:* James Ardell, Charles Garland, Eddie Hackett, Joe Kay, David Morton, Freddie Packard, Harry Sangar, George Oliver. *Jubilee Singers:* Snippy Mason, Clement Hall, Halle Howard, Teddy Wood, Hamilton McLean, George McLean, Harold Thompson, Carl Taylor, Ralph Northern, S. E. Bell, Jester Hairston, DeWitt Spencer, Larri N. Lorear, F. Barclay Trigg.

Act 1, Scene 1: The old Judge Crow Mansion in the suburbs of Clearwater, Oklahoma. *Scene 2:* Pawnee Garage. *Scene 3:* The Oil Field. *Scene 4:* Auditorium of Clearwater Hotel. *Scene 5:* A Speakeasy, in the Roaring Forties. *Scene 6:* The Pier in New York. *Scene 7:* Promenade Deck of the *Île de France*. *Scene 8:* The Drapes. *Scene 9:* Salon of the *Île de France*.

Act 2, Scene 1: Conservatory of the Peters' Chateau, near Paris. *Scene 2:* A Cottage in the Country, near Paris. *Scene 3:* The Foyer of the Cafe Lapin Agile. *Scene 4:* Cafe Lapin Agile.

ACT 1
Scene 1
  "Unacccustomed As I Am"[58]
    P. Walker, C. Columbus
  "Dance Your Troubles Away"
    M. Adams, J. Good
Scene 2
  "I Stumbled Over You"
    P. Walker, C. Columbus
    (*Music by* Maury Rubens. *Lyrics by* Henry Dagand.)
Scene 3
  "Deep Paradise"
    L. Deppe and Jubilee Singers
    (*Music by* Russell Tarbox. *Lyrics by* Charles O. Locke.)
Scene 4
  Specialty
    C. Sale
Scene 5
  "You Made a Hit With Me"
    M. Adams, J. Good, P. Walker, C. Columbus
Scene 6
  "Pack Your Suitcase With Love"
    P. Walker, C. Columbus, M. Adams, J. Good, Boys, Dancers, D. Morrell
Scene 7
  "Every Bit of You"
    C. Columbus, P. Walker
    (*Music and Lyrics by* Kenneth Friede, Adrian Samish and Harold Stern.)
Scene 8
  "Deep Sea Roll"
    P. Walker, Boys, Dancers
Scene 9
  Dance
    M. Starner
  Tango
    Amerique, N. Goddard
  "On to Paris"
    G. Hayes, P. Walker, J. Good
  Finale
    Ensemble

ACT 2
Scene 1
  Waltz
    Amerique, N. Goddard
  Reprise[59]
    P. Walker, C. Columbus
  "Got to Have Hips Now"
    S. Mayhew
    (*Music by* Russell Tarbox. *Lyrics by* Charles O. Locke.)
  "Heavenly Days"
    J. Good, Ensemble
Scene 2
  Specialty
    G. Hayes, Boys
Scene 3
  "Rosie Road"
    L. Deppe and Jubilee Singers
  "Give It"[60]
    M. Adams, Boys, Dancers
  Finale
    Entire Company

---

[58]Dropped during run.
[59]Dropped during run.
[60]Dropped during run.

1930.38

SWEET AND LOW

A Musical Revue in Two Acts, 25 Scenes. Sketches by David Freedman. Songs by Mr. (Billy) Rose and his friends. (Music by Harry Archer, Charlotte Kent, Will Irwin, Harry Warren, Ned Lehak, Vivian Ellis, Mischa Spoliansky, Dana Suesse, Duke Ellington, Bubber Miley, Louis Alter, Phil Charig, Joseph Meyer. Lyrics by Edward Eliscu, Charlotte Kent, Mort Dixon, Ira Gershwin, Malcolm McComb, Allen Boretz, Ballard Macdonald.) Staged by Alexander Leftwich. Dances by Danny Dare, Busby Berkeley. Settings by Jo Mielziner. Costumes by James Reynolds. Orchestra directed by Charles Drury. Produced by Billy Rose. Opened 17 November 1930 at the 46th Street Theatre, moved 19 January 1931 to the 44th Street Theatre, and closed 25 April 1931 after 184 performances.[61]

CAST: JAMES BARTON, FANNY BRICE, GEORGE JESSEL, BORRAH MINEVITCH (and His Musical Rascals), MOSS and FONTANA, Hannah Williams, Paula Trueman, Arthur Treacher, Hal Thompson, Jerry Norris, Roger Pryor Dodge, Roger Davis, Shirley Richards, Peggy Andre, Lucille Osborne, Cy Landry, Sam Krevoff, Arthur Mahoney, Jack Nile.
Ladies: Betty Croke, Ethel Brice, Polly Rose, Gladys Aster, Marion Bonnell, Viola Paulson, Nancy Dolan, Lucille Osborne, Kathleen Ayres, Ruth Sato, Peggy Andre, Dorothy Van Hess, Emily Van Hoven, Ruth Dana, Mildred Tully, Charlotte Stoll, Emily Burton, Loretta Flushing, Pauline Schaefer, Muriel Markert, Kitty Brady, Rita Jason, Ray Stuart, Arline Baber, Baun Sturtz, Ethel Kriston. *Gentlemen:* Harry Edwards, James Lee, Jack Ray, Charles Millang, Daniel C. Wyler, Joe Barry, Edwin Murray, Jack Bauer.

ACT 1[62]

Scene 1

"Outside Looking In"
Ladies
(*Music by* Harry Archer. *Lyrics by* Edward Eliscu.)

Scene 2

Poor Mr. Jessel
Mr. Jessel: G. Jessel. *Pipkins:* R. Davis. *Author:* A. Treacher.
"Mr. Jessel"
G. Jessel, Ladies
(*Music and Lyrics by* Charlotte Kent.)

Scene 3

"Dancing With Tears in Their Eyes"
J. Barton, F. Brice, G. Jessel
(*Music by* Will Irwin. *Lyrics by* Billy Rose and Mort Dixon.)

Scene 4

"Cheerful Little Earful"
H. Williams, J. Norris
(*Music by* Harry Warren. *Lyrics by* Ira Gershwin and Billy Rose.)

Scene 5

The Mad Dog
J. Barton alone

Scene 6

"Ten Minutes in Bed"
P. Trueman
(*Music by* Ned Lehak. *Lyrics by* Allen Boretz.)

Scene 7

"When a Pansy Was a Flower"
G. Jessel
(*Music by* Will Irwin. *Lyrics by* Billy Rose and Malcolm McComb.)

Scene 8

Venetian Reprise
Moss and Fontana

Scene 9

In a Venetian Box
Ladies
(*Music by* Vivian Ellis, courtesy of C. B. Cochran.)

Scene 10

Swan Song—and Dance[63]
F. Brice

Scene 11

Stereopticon Slides
G. Jessel

Scene 12

"Would You Like to Take a Walk"
H. Williams, H. Thompson, Ladies
(*Music by* Harry Warren. *Lyrics by* Mort Dixon and Billy Rose.)

Scene 13

Shirley Richards and Sam Krevoff

Scene 14

Stocks and Blondes: "Revival Day"
H. Williams
(*Music by* Will Irwin. *Lyrics by* Malcolm McComb.)

Scene 15

Mr. Barton Still Alone

Scene 16

Strictly Unbearable[64]
Isabel Paisley, a Southern Girl: F. Brice. *Count Gus de Raviola,* of Italy: G. Jessel

ACT 2

Scene 1

Customary Spanish Number:
"For I'm in Love Again"[65]
J. Norris, Ladies
(*Music by* Mischa Spoliansky. *Lyrics by* Billy Rose and Mort Dixon.)
Dance
Moss and Fontana
"I Knew Him Before He Was Spanish"
F. Brice
(*Music by* Dana Suesse. *Lyrics by* Billy Rose and Ballard Macdonald.)

Scene 2

"East St. Louis Toodle-O"
R. P. Dodge, A. Mahoney, J. Nile
(*Music by* Duke Ellington, Bubber Miley.)

Scene 3

"Overnight"
F. Brice
(*Music by* Louis Alter. *Lyrics by* Billy Rose and Charlotte Kent.)

Scene 4

Overnight (sketch)
Lady: F. Brice. *Gentleman:* G. Jessel.

Scene 5

"You Sweet So and So"
H. Williams, J. Norris, Ladies
(*Music by* Phil Charig and Joseph Meyer. *Lyrics by* Ira Gershwin.)
Scene: A Solarium.

Scene 6

George Jessel

Scene 7

Chinese White
Lize: F. Brice. *Chang:* J. Barton.

---

[61]A revised version of SWEET AND LOW entitled BILLY ROSES'S CRAZY QUILT opened 19 May 1931 at the 44th Street Theatre for 67 performances. See complete entry below.
[62]Added during run:
"I Wonder Who's Keeping Him Now" (Act 1)
F. Brice
(*Music by* Lou Alter. *Lyrics by* Billy Rose and Charlotte Kent.)
"You Can Buy Kisses But You Can't Buy Love" (Act 1)
F. Brice
(*Music and Lyrics by* Billy Rose and Fred Fisher.)
The Spirit of Labor (Act 2)
Eugene Von Grona
"The King's Horses" (Act 2) (from FOLLY TO BE WISE, London revue)
J. Barton, Boys
(*Music and Lyrics by* Noel Gay and Harry Graham.)
Shooting of Dan McGrew (Act 2)
J. Barton

---

[63]Dropped during run.
[64]A burlesque of Preston Sturges' play "Strictly Dishonorable."
[65]Dropped during run.

Scene 8

Borrah Minevitch and His Musical Rascals

Scene 9

Finale—Rose's Rendezvous

J. Barton, F. Brice, G. Jessel, Company

1930.39

SMILES

A Musical Comedy in Two Acts, a Prologue and 9 Scenes. Book by William Anthony McGuire. Music by Vincent Youmans. Lyrics by Clifford Grey, Harold Adamson; additional lyrics by Ring Lardner. Dialogue staged by William Anthony McGuire. (Dances) Staged by Ned Wayburn. Scenes (settings) by Joseph Urban. Artistic director (costumes) by John Harkrider. Music director, Frank Tours. (Orchestrations by Paul Lannin.) Produced by Florenz Ziegfeld. Opened 18 November 1930 at the Ziegfeld Theatre and closed 10 January 1931 after 63 performances.

CAST (in order of appearance): *Holy Joe*: TOM HOWARD. *Pierre*: Edward Raquello. *Tony*: Adrian Rosley. *Dick*: PAUL GREGORY. *Madelon*: Lorraine Jaillet. *First Sailor*: Gilbert White. *Slim*: Frank Coletti. *Izzy Cohen*: Pat Mann. *Arline*: Arline Aber. *Charline*: Charline Aber. *Doughface*: Bernard Jukes. *Bob Hastings*: FRED ASTAIRE. *Larry*: Larry Adler. *Mackin*: Joe Lyons. *Mother Jones*: Mary Collins. *Smiles*: MARILYN MILLER. *Dot Hastings*: ADELE ASTAIRE. *Lillian*: Jean Ackerman. *Clara*: Clare Dodd. *Mrs. Hastings*: Georgia Caine. *Gilbert Stone*: EDDIE FOY, JR. *Officer Dennis O'Brien*: Harry Tighe. *Sankee*: Charles Sager. *Pat*: Kathryn Hereford. *Chang Lang Foo*: C. Sager Czaja. *Miss Parker, a Society Reporter*: Ruth Morgan. *Kiki*: Hilda Moreno. *Betty*: Ruth K. Patterson. *Ann*: Katherine Burke. *Mrs. Brown*: Jean Ackerman. *Mr. Brown*: Gilbert White. *Mr. Green*: Louis Delgado.

Dancing Girls: Pamela Bryant, Mabel Baade, Elsie Behrens, Dorothy Bow, Joey Benton, Bobby Broadsley, Betty Collette, Madeline Dunbar, Louise Estes, Agnes Franey, Maxine Gross, Jacky Hurlbut, Juliet Jordan, Doris May, Nellie Mayer, Olive McLay, Constance McKenzie, Patsy O'Day, Agnes O'Laughlin, Dorothy Patterson, Anna May Rex, Olga Royce, Norma Taylor, Ruth Tara, Jean Warren, Dolores Ray, Virginia Biddle, Martha Louise Maggard. *Boys*: Gordon Clark, Louis Delgado, Bob Hope, Burnie Halloway, Roy Mace, Ken Huntington, David Johns, Pat Mann, Joseph Minitello, Gilbert White, Phil Sheridan, Michael Stark, Jack Spinello, Ward A. Tallman, Walter Costello, Lee Timmins, Preston Lewis, Irving Carter. *A Group of Glorified Girls*: Pirko Alquist, Virginia Bruce, Betty Dumbris, Marion Dodge, Caja Eric, Georgia Ellis, Marcel Edwards, Dorothy Flood, Maurine Holmes, Meredith Howard, Neva Lynn, Marjorie LaVoe, Rose Mariella, Christine Maple, Peggy Peacock, Blanche Satchel, Helen Walsh, Gertrude Dahl.

Prologue: The Outskirts of a Deserted Village in France, 1918.

Act 1, Scene 1: East Side, New York City. Twelve years later. *Scene 2*: Interior of the Salvation Army Mission. *Scene 3*: A Bar in the Hastings' Residence at Southampton. The next day. *Scene 4*: A Garden on the Hastings' Estate.

Act 2, Scene 1: The Café Le Berry, Paris. Anniversary of Armistice Night. *Scene 2*: A Street in Montmartre. *Scene 3*: A Bedroom in the Hotel Crillon. *Scene 4*: Steamship Dock, New York. Arrival of *The Bremen*. *Scene 5*: The Roof Garden of the Hastings' City Home, New York.

ACT 1

"The Bowery"

A. Aber, C. Aber, Entire Company

"Say Young Man of Manhattan"

F. Astaire, Boys

"Rally 'Round Me"[66]

M. Miller, Salvation Army Lassies

(*Lyrics by* Ring Lardner.)

"Hotcha Ma Chotch"[67]

A. Astaire, E. Foy, Jr., Girls

"Time on My Hands"

M. Miller, P. Gregory

---

[66]During December 1930, replaced by:

"Carry On, Keep Smiling"

M. Miller, Salvation Army Lasses

(*Lyrics by* Ring Lardner.)

Which was subsequently replaced by:

"Keep Smiling and Carry On"

M. Miller, Salvation Army Lasses

(*Music and Lyrics by* Walter Donaldson.)

[67]During December 1930, replaced by:

"You're Driving Me Crazy"

A. Astaire, E. Foy, Jr., Girls

(*Music and Lyrics by* Walter Donaldson.)

Refrain: "What Can I Say?"

M. Miller

(*Lyrics by* Ring Lardner.)

"Time on My Hands" (reprise)

Girls, Boys

"Be Good to Me"

F. Astaire, A. Astaire

(*Lyrics by* Ring Lardner.)

The Chinese Party

The Lantern Girls

Chinese Jade

The Jade Girls

The Crystal Lady (*Staged by* Theodore Kosloff.)

M. Miller

"Clever, These Chinese"

K. Hereford, E. Foy, Jr., Chinese Girls and Boys

"Anyway, We've Had Fun"

M. Miller, F. Astaire, A. Astaire

(*Lyrics by* Ring Lardner.)

"Something to Sing About"

Girls of the Ensemble

Finale

Entire Company

ACT 2

"Here's a Day to Be Happy"

P. Gregory, Company

"If I Were You, Love"

F. Astaire, A. Astaire

(*Lyrics by* Ring Lardner.)

"I'm Glad I Waited"

M. Miller, F. Astaire

"La Marseilles"[68] (dance)

M. Miller, Boys

"Why Ain't I Home?"

E. Foy, Jr. Girls

(*Lyrics by* Ring Lardner.)

"Dancing Wedding"

Entire Company

Finale

1930.40

THE NEW YORKERS

A Sociological Musical Satire in Two Acts, a Prologue, 11 Scenes and an Epilogue. Book by Herbert Fields from a story by E. Ray Goetz and Peter Arno. Music and lyrics by Cole Porter. Book directed by Monty Woolley. Entire production staged under the supervision of E. Ray Goetz. Dances and ensembles directed by George Hale. Settings by Dale Stetson from sketches by Peter Arno. Costumes by Peter Arno, Charles LeMaire. Lighting by Clark Robinson. Special numbers staged and directed by Fred Waring. Music director, Al Goodman. Orchestrations by Hans Spialek. Produced by E. Ray Goetz. Opened 8 December 1930 at the Broadway Theatre and closed 2 May 1931 after 168 performances.

CAST (in order of appearance): *A Nurse*: Marjorie Arnold. *Assistant Nurse*: Hilda Knight. *Dr. Cortlandt Jenks*: Paul Huber. *Alice Wentworth*: HOPE WILLIAMS. *Felix, Captain at the Club Toro*: Charles Angelo. *Dr. Windham Wentworth*: RICHARD CARLE. *Lola McGee*: ANN PENNINGTON. *Gloria Wentworth*: MARIE CAHILL. *Alfredo Gomez*: Maurice La Pue. *James Livingston*: Barrie Oliver. *Mona Low, a hostess at the Toro*: FRANCES WILLIAMS. *Al Spanish*: CHARLES KING. *Jimmie Deegan*: JIMMY DURANTE. *Cyril Gregory*: LOU CLAYTON. *Ronald Monahan*: EDDIE JACKSON. *Butch McGeehan*: Tammany Young. *Burns, Waiter in Reuben's*: Ralph Glover. *Dopey, a Henchman*: Billy Culloo. *May*: Kathryn Crawford. *Attendant at Sing Sing*: Donald McGinnis. *Plague*: Oscar Ragland. *Mildew*: Stanley Harrison. *An Interne*: Owen Coll. *Debutantes, Matrons, Waiters, Newsboys, Gentlemen of Leisure, Ladies of the Evening, etc.*

Waring's Pennsylvanians: Scott F. Bates, Fred C. Buck, Jr., Donald Bryan, Elton C. Cockerill, Stuart Churchill, George A. Culley, Fred C. Campbell, Francis F. Foster, James J. Gilliland, Arthur P. Horn, Frank W. Hower, Nelson A. Keller, James N. Mullen, James R. McClintock, D. Wade Schlegel, Paul Sterrett, Will I. Townsend, Will Morgan, Charles E. Henderson, Clare Hanlon. *Three Girl Friends*: June Shafer,

---

[68]Dropped late in the run.

Ida Pearson, Stella Friend. *Clayton, Jackson and Durante Orchestra*: Harry Donnelly, Jack Roth, Irving Sherman, Larry Hart, Al Atkins, Bill Drewes, Norman Moran, Herman Drewes, Nat London. *Dancing Girls*: Bobbie Hall, Iris Adrian, Evelyn Saether, Lu Ann Meredith, Elinore Tierney, Pansy Maness, Martha Carroll, Betty Bowen, Adele Kay, Eileen Gorlet, Harriet Fink, Alvina Carson, Lillian Burke, Mildred Espy, Janet Marion, Pearl Harris, Barbara Smith, Muriel Reed, Grace Fleming, Blanche Poston, Mickey MacKillop, Marjorie O'Shea, Melva Cornell, Buddy York, Mary Carroll, Eileen Allen, Billie Doyle, Jackie Feeley, Aline Green, Adrienne Lampel, Helen Sheppard, Olive Bertram, Barbara Bright. *Show Girls*: Marion Nevins, Ethel Lawrence, Inez du Plessis, Hilda Knight, Helene Cambridge, Wilma Roelo, Marcelle Miller, Alberta Woods, Tinetta Walker, Josephine Carroll, Meta Klinke, Delmar Meyers, Peggy Fish, Virgil Dodd, Florence Sterling, Marjorie Arnold, Drucilla Strain. *Boys*: Ward Arnold, Charles Conkling, Don Knobloch, Frank Ericson, Larry Larkin, James Libby, Joe Rogers, Vincent Curran.

Prologue: The Consulting Office of Dr. Cortlandt Jenks, New York. These days.

Act 1, Scene 1: The Club Toro, New York. *Scene 2*: A Cellar. *Scene 3*: The Amendment Import Company. *Scene 4*: In Front of Reuben's. *Scene 5*: Reuben's, That All! *Scene 6*: Entrance to St. Pierre Plaza Roof. *Scene 7*: The St. Pierre Plaza Roof.

Act 2, Scene 1: The Lounge at Sing Sing. *Scene 2*: A Hospital Ward. *Scene 3*: A Street in New York. *Scene 4*: The Lawn of Al's Home in Miami.

Epilogue: The Consulting Office of Dr. Cortland Jenks, New York.

ACT 1[69]

"Go Into Your Dance"
F. Williams, A. Pennington, Toro Girls

"The Hot Patata"
J. Durante, E. Jackson, L. Clayton
(*Music and Lyrics by* Jimmy Durante.)

"Where Have You Been?"
C. King, H. Williams

"Say It With Gin"
Ensemble, Trainor Brothers

"Venice"
F. Williams, E. Jackson, J. Durante, L. Clayton

"I'm Getting Myself Ready for You"
F. Williams, B. Oliver, A. Pennington, M. Lapue

"Drinking Song"
Waring's Pennsylvanians
(*Music by* Fred Waring. *Lyrics by* Charles Henderson.)

"Love For Sale"
K. Crawford, J. Shafer, I. Pearson, S. Friend

"The Great Indoors"
F. Williams, Girls

"Money!"
J. Durante, E. Jackson, L. Clayton
(*Music and Lyrics by* Jimmy Durante.)

"Wood"/Finale
J. Durante, E. Jackson, L. Clayton, Company
(*Music and Lyrics by* Jimmy Durante.)

ACT 2

"Sing Sing for Sing Sing"
C. King, Convicts

Reprise
F. Williams

"Data"
J. Durante, E. Jackson, L. Clayton, Waring's Pennsylvanians
(*Music and Lyrics by* Jimmy Durante.)

"Take Me Back to Manhattan"
F. Williams

"Let's Fly Away"
C. King, H. Williams

Reprise
F. Williams, Company

Finale
(Entire Company)

ACT 2

Song
J. Shafer, I. Pearson, S. Friend

Song
F. Williams

"Sheikin Fool"
J. Durante, E. Jackson, L. Clayton
(*Music and Lyrics by* Jimmy Durante.)

"Let's Fly Away"
B. Oliver, H. Williams, Ensemble

"I Happen to Like New York"
O. Ragland

"Let's Fly Away" (reprise)
B. Oliver, H. Williams, Ensemble

"Sing Sing for Sing Sing"
C. King, Waring's Pennsylvanians

"Sing Sing for Sing Sing" (reprise)
F. Williams, J. Shafer, I. Pearson, S. Friend, Waring's Pennsylvanians

"Data"
J. Durante, E. Jackson, L. Clayton, Waring's Pennsylvanians
(*Music and Lyrics by* Jimmy Durante.)

"Sing Sing for Sing Sing" (reprise)
Waring's Pennsylvanians

"Take Me Back to Manhattan"
C. King, A. Pennington, F. Williams, B. Oliver, Ensemble

Finale
Entire Company

1930.41

BABES IN TOYLAND

A Revival of the Musical Comedy in Three Acts, 9 Scenes[70]. Book and lyrics by Glen McDonough. Music by Victor Herbert. Staged by Milton Aborn. Ballet by Virginie Mauret. Settings by Rollo Wayne. Musical director, Max Hirschfeld. (Produced by the Messrs. Shubert.) Opened 20 December 1930 (matinee) at the Imperial Theatre and closed 10 January 1931 after 33 performances.[71]

CAST (in order of appearance): *Uncle Barnaby*, a rich miser in love with Contrary Mary: WILLIAM BALFOUR. *Frances*: Frances Moore. *Betty*: Betty Flanigen. *Tom Tom*, eldest son of the Widow Piper: RUTH GILLETTE. *Hilda*, maid of all work in the Piper household: Mary Wilson. *Gonzorgo*, a hard-hearted ruffian: Jack Cameron. *Roderigo*, his sentimental partner: Robert Darrell. *The Widow Piper*, a lonely widow with 14 children: Jayne Waterous. *Bo Peep*, who is a careless shepherd: Margaret Byers. *Jill*, who does chores: Ethel Lynne. *Peter*, who has a passion for pumpkin pie: Florence Little. *Bobby Shaftoe*, who wants to be a sailor: Mabel Thompson. *Jack*, who helps Jill: Betty Hayden. *Sallie Waters*, who wants to get married: Eleanor Gilmore. *Curly Locks*, who wants to wed a title: Dorothy May. *Tommy Tucker*, who sings for his supper and everything else: Lydia Lucke. *Simple Simon*, who is fond of fairs: Frances Baviello. *Little Red Riding Hood*, who is devoted to her grandmother: Gertrude Waldon. *Miss Muffett*, who is afraid of spiders: Lillian Morris. *Boy Blue*, who wants to be a farmer: Billie Williams. *Jane*, niece of Barnaby: BETTY BYRON. *Alan*, nephew of Barnaby: CHARLES BARNES. *First Dandy*: Frank (Francesco) Yannelli. *Contrary Mary*, the Widow Piper's eldest daughter: DOROTHY KANE. *Inspector Marmaduke*, of the Toyland Police: BERT MATTHEWS. *Master Toymaker*, who designs the toys of the world: Leslie Stowe. *Grumio*, apprentice at the Master Toymaker's workshop: Joseph Knight. *Max*: Frank Yannelli. *The Brown Bear*: Harry Knabenshue. *The Giant Spider*: Bernie Sager. *A Fairy*: Dene Dickens. *Santa Claus*: Edward Bird.

Toyland Tots: June Meier, Anita Stewart, Alice Farley, Ann Middleton, Rhoda Lax, Leona Serkes, Alexander Lewis. *Girls of the Ensemble*: Edith Artley, Frances Baviello, Margaret Bicket, Flo Cazelle, Eleanor Gilmore, Maxine Inman, Dene Dickens, Betty Flanigen, Ione Haals, Betty Hayden, Peggy Hollomon, Florence Little, Ethel Lynne, Lydia Lucke, Dorothy May, Catherine Mayfield, Frances Moore, Lillian Morris, Helen Nedo, Caroline Rickman, Olga Schumacher, Louise Sellergren, Rosalind Shaw,

---

[69]Three weeks into the run, Act 2 was substantially revised as follows: *Scene 1*: Salon at the Wentworth House. *Scene 2*: Corridor at the Wentworth Home. *Scene 3*: The Lounge at Sing Sing. *Scene 4*: Before the Walls of Sing Sing. *Scene 5*: A Hospital Ward. *Scene 6*: Hall of the Hospital, (Later revised to Before Al's Home in Miami). *Scene 7*: Al's Home in Miami. "I'm Getting Myself Ready" and "Drinking Song" moved briefly to Act 2; song order changed frequently. Revised song list:

---

[70]First presented in New York 13 October 1903 at the Majestic Theatre for 192 performances. For Synopsis of Scenes and Musical Numbers, see original 1903 production.

[71]Costumes uncredited. Ralph Benatzky's credit in programs and sheet music as English language lyricist is highly suspect; Gribble and the Messrs. Shubert more likely assigned and supervised work for hire.

Mabel Thompson, May Valle, Gertrude Waldon, Marie Wagner, Margaret Walker, Madeleine Walsh, Billie Williams. *Boys of the Ensemble*: Edward Bird, Jerry Cummins, Harry Knabenshue, Walter Franklyn, Maurice Warner, Lynn Eldridge, Pedro Giovanni, Henry Dean, C. Raviol, Owen Pauline, Frank Yannelli. *Singer's Midgets*.

1930.42

BALLYHOO

A Musical Comedy in Two Acts, 18 Scenes. Book and lyrics by Harry Ruskin and Leighton K. Brill. Music by Louis Alter. Supervision of (and additional lyrics by) Oscar Hammerstein II. Book staged by Reginald Hammerstein. Dances and ensembles by Earl Lindsay. Settings by Cirker & Robbins. Costumes by Charles LeMaire. Music director, Oscar Bradley. Produced by Arthur Hammerstein[72]. Opened 22 December 1930 at Hammerstein's Theatre and 21 February 1931 after 68 performances.

CAST (in order of appearance): *Sam*: DON TOMKINS. *Ruth*: JEANIE LANG. *Manager*: Neil Moore. *Harry*: Al Downing. *Flora Fay*: GRACE HAYES. *Whitey Duke*: ANDY RICE, JR. *Goldie La Marr*: JANET READE. *Runners (3): Brown, Smith, Jones*: Three Slate Brothers (Henry, Jack, Syd). *Larry*: JACK COLBY. *Betty*: Patricia Murphy. *A Gourmand*: CHAZ CHASE. *Vera*: FLORIA VESTOFF. *Drum Major*: J. Mardo Brown. *Q. Q. Quale*: W.C. FIELDS. *Shorty*: William Blanche. *Landlord*: Neil Moore. *Cowboys*: Slate Brothers, Al Downing. *Bill Collector*: James Cushman. *Reporter*: Harvey Murray. *Mr. Miner*: Arthur Cardinal. *Mr. Pidgeon*: Gus Wicke. *Photographer*: Herbert Weber. *Camera Man*: Craig Kershaw. *Sound Man*: Herb Lund. *Bank President*: Anthony O'Dea. *Junior*: MAX HOFFMAN, JR. *The King*: Richard Lambert. *Jim*: Douglas Alene. *Sam*: Charles Evans. (*Specialty*: Val Vestoff.)

Ted Black's Band: Al Giroux, Samuel Kahn, Sherman Brande, Bill Doerflinger, James Bander, Fred Barber, Sam De Bonis, Walter Jewhurst. *The Cheer Leaders*: Raymond Clark, Charlie Fowler, Herb Hall, Fred Shawhan. *Girls*: Betty Lewis, Anita Pam, Sara Jane, Kay Arnold, Marjorie Baglin, Madeleine Eubanks, Maxine Darrell, Josephine Dupree, Frances Guinan, Rose Armand, Florence Winkle, Blanche Percy, Adelaide Raleigh, Betty Lee, Stella Bailey, Gloria Ray, Theo Phane, Albertina Rexroth, Dorothy Graves, Betty Greenwood, Grace Bradley, Sue Austin, Inez Purdy, Winnie Torney, Dorothy Humphries. *Boys*: George Cowan, Chester Toomer, George Burkholder, Harry Murray, James Cushman, Frank Daley, Walter Dolan, Robert Spencer, Earl McCutcheon, Francis Kummer, Morton Kingsland, Eugene Aldrich.

Act 1, Scene 1: A Street in New York. *Scene 2*: A Dance Hall in New York. *Scene 3*: Street in Shamokin, Ohio. 23rd Day of the Race. *Scene 4*: Public Square, Shamokin. Same day. *Scene 5*: Room in Commercial Hotel, El Toro, New Mexico. 42nd Day of the Race. *Scene 6*: Corridor, same hotel. *Scene 7*: A Street in El Toro. *Scene 8*: Corridor, Commercial Hotel. *Scene 9*: Patio of Hotel, Butte, Arizona. 65th Day of the Race.

Act 2, Scene 1: Back Stage, Opera House, Salome, Arizona. Next afternoon. *Scene 2*: Railroad Station, Salome, Arizona. That night. *Scene 3*: The Stage, Opera House, Salome, Arizona. *Scene 4*: First Trust Bank, Hollywood. *Scene 5*: Sound Stage, Colossal Studios. *Scene 6*: Another part of Sound Stage. *Scene 7*: A Café, Hollywood. *Scene 8*: Quayle's Pharmacy, Beverly Hills. *Scene 9*: Ruth's Beverly Hills Home. That night.

ACT 1

Opening

"How Could I Go For You"
J. Lang, D. Tomkins, Ensemble

"That Tired Feeling"
J. Reade, A. Rice, Slate Brothers, Ensemble
(*Music by* Rudolf Friml. *Lyrics by* Oscar Hammerstein II and Otto Harbach.)

"No Wonder I'm Blue"
G. Hayes
(*Lyrics by* Oscar Hammerstein II.)

Finaletto
J. Lang, G. Hayes, Ensemble

"Throw It Out the Window"
D. Tomkins, J. Lang, Ensemble

Dance
J. Colby, P. Murphy

"Blow Hot, Blow Cold"
G. Hayes, F. Vestoff, Ensemble

Finale

ACT 2

Opening

"If I Were You"
J. Lang, D. Tomkins, Ensemble

"No Wonder I'm Blue" (reprise)
J. Lang, Cheer Leaders

"I'm One of God's Children"
J. Reade, Ensemble
(*Lyrics by* Oscar Hammerstein II and Harry Ruskin.)

"I'm One of God's Children (reprise)
J. Reade, Ted Black's Band, Ensemble

"Good Girls Love Bad Men"[73]
G. Hayes, A. Rice, D. Tompkins, J. Reade, F. Vestoff, Slate Brothers, Ensemble

Finale

1930.43

MEET MY SISTER

A Musical Comedy in Two Acts, a Prologue and Epilogue. Book by Harry Wagstaff Gribble. Adapted from the German musical comedy "Meine Schwester und Ich" by Robert Blum, based on a French play ("Ma soeur et moi") by (Georges) Berr and (Louis) Verneuil. Music and lyrics by Ralph Benatzky. Staged by William Mollison. Dances by John Pierce. Settings by Watson Barratt. Music director, Irving Schloss. Produced by the Messrs. Shubert. Opened 30 December 1930 at the Sam S. Shubert Theatre, moved 6 April 1931 to the Imperial Theatre, and closed 21 May 1931 after 167 performances[74].

CAST (in order of appearance): *President of the Divorce Court*: Donald Campbell. *Assessor to the Court*: Niska Stefanini. *Clerk of the Court*: Graham Velsey. *Eric Molinar*, a Professor of Psychology: WALTER SLEZAK. *Dolly Molinar*: BETTINA HALL. *Her Maid*: KAY MCKAY. *Her Butler*: BOYD DAVIS. *Her Footman*: George Spelvin. *Charles*, a butler: BOYD DAVIS. *Henriette*, a maid: KAY MCKAY. *Dolly*, the Countess (Ste.) La Verne: BETTINA HALL. *Marquis de Chatelard*: GEORGE GROSSMITH. *Irma*, Finkel's assistant: OLIVE OLSEN. *Otto H. Finkel*, a shoe store proprietor: HARRY WELSH. *A Waiter*: Julius Campo.

Prologue: A Divorce Court in Paris.

Act 1: The Countess La Verne's Library in her Chateau, near Paris. Late afternoon.

Act 2: Finkel's Shoe Store at Nancy. Next morning.

Epilogue: The Divorce Court in Paris.

PROLOGUE

"Love Has Faded Away"
B. Hall, W. Slezak

ACT 1

"Five Thousand Francs"
W. Slezak, K. McKay

"Tell Me, What This Can Be"
B. Hall, W. Slezak

"Always in My Heart"
B. Hall

"Always in My Heart" (reprise)
B. Hall

"Radziwill"
B. Hall, W. Slezak

"Look and Love Is Here"
B. Hall, W. Slezak

"The Devil May Care"
W. Slezak

"The Devil May Care" (reprise)
W. Slezak

ACT 2

"I Gotta Have My Moments"
O. Olsen

"It's Money—It's Fame—It's Love"
O. Olsen, H. Welsh, B. Hall

"I Like You"
O. Olsen, G. Grossmith

"Friendship"
B. Hall

---

[72]Arthur Hammerstein withdrew as producer in January 1931; the show continued to operate as a cooperative venture.

---

[73]During run, replaced by:
Specialties
J. Colby, P. Murphy, V. Vestoff

[74]Costumes uncredited.

"My Ideal"
W. Slezak
"Birds in the Spring"
B. Hall, H. Welsh, O. Olsen
"My Ideal" (reprise)
B. Hall, W. Slezak

1931.01 YOU SAID IT

A Musical Comedy in Two Acts, 13 Scenes. Book by Jack Yellen and Sid Silvers. Music by Harold Arlen. Lyrics by Jack Yellen. Staged by John Harwood. Dances by Danny Dare. Settings by Donald Oenslager, Dale Stetson. Costumes by Kiviette, Ben Rocke. Music director, Louis Gress. Orchestrations by Howard Jackson. Special music effects, Fred Waring. Vocal arrangements, Charles Henderson. Produced by Jack Yellen and Lou Holtz. Opened 19 January 1931 at the 46th Street Theatre and closed 4 July 1931 after 192 performances.

CAST (in order of appearance): *Hal Foster '30:* HENRY SLATE. *Fuzzy Shawowsky '32:* Benny Baker. *Eddie Brown '30:* Oscar Grogan. *Frank Pennell '31:* SYD SLATE. *Douglas Richardson '31:* Allan D'Sylva. *Frank Murphy '30:* JACK SLATE. *Kewpie Andrews '32:* HUGHIE CLARKE. *Loren Brooks '31:* Kendall Capps. *Tommy '33:* Tommy Miller. *Grace Carroll '31:* BILLIE LEONARD. *Florence Hart '30:* Betty Sundmark. *Hattie Hudson '32:* PEGGY BERNIER. *Helen Holloway '30:* MARY LAWLOR. *Walter Prescott '30:* Walter Petrie. *Bob Smith '30:* STANLEY SMITH. *"Pinkie" Pincus:* LOU HOLTZ. *Fanny:* LYDA ROBERTI. *Willoughby Pinkham '33:* GEORGE HAGGERTY. *Gladys Dorsey:* Paula Sands. *Nicholas Holloway,* Dean of Kenton: John T. Dwyer. *Hemingway Potts:* Victor Etheridge. *Scotty,* a taxi driver: Vic Munro. *Squires,* of the town police force: J. Francis Robertson. *Dr. Fairbairn:* John Walsh. *Prof. Healy:* Brian Davis. *The Nurse:* Betty Nylander. Six John Boyle Dancers. *Merry-Makers Quartette:* Jack Harcourt, Ed Ellington, Al Stafford, Clark Bremmer. *The Campus Four:* Archie Ford, Robert Shafer, Yorke Coplen, Ralph Erwin.
   Coeds: Alyce Chapelle, Patsy Clair, Dorcas Cochran, Leslie Cornell, Marjorie Fisher, Joan Harley, Rita Horgan, Agatha Johann, Florence Johnson, Eileen Leahy, Dixie Lester, Gertrude Lindle, Mary Joan Martin, Betty Nylander, Peggy O'Day, Virginia Rennaud, Mildred Rye, Paula Sands, Betty Sundmark, Kay Smythe, Dorothy Stewart, Helene Traver, Rene Vilon, Jae Voll, Patricia Whitney, Betty McNulty. *Freshmen and Sophomores:* Jack Barns, William Broeder, Ray Clarke, Brian Davis, Martin Dennis, Alan D'Sylva, John Elliott, Vic Etheridge, Vernon Hammer, Harry Moore, Emmett O'Brien, Stewart Steppler, Jules Shearer, John Walsh.

Act 1, Scene 1: Railroad Station at Kenton. *Scene 2:* Campus Walk, Kenton College. *Scene 3:* On the Campus. Nine months later. *Scene 4:* Hollow Oak Lane. *Scene 5:* The Hollow Oak. *Scene 6:* Campus Walk. *Scene 7:* Alpha Chi Fraternity House.

Act 2, Scene 1: On the Campus. *Scene 2:* Campus Walk. *Scene 3:* In Front of the Dean's Office. *Scene 4:* A Room in the Medical Laboratory. *Scene 5:* On the Way to the Glen. *Scene 6:* The Glen, on Cap-Burning Night.

ACT 1
   "Wha'd You Come to College For?"
      H. Clarke, O. Sands, T. Miller, Ensemble
   "You Said It"
      M. Lawlor, S. Smith
   "They Learn About Women From Me"
      P, Bernier, Ensemble
   Specialty Dance
      K. Capps
   "While You Are Young"
      W. Petrie, Kenton Glee Club
   "It's Different With Me"
      L. Holtz, L. Roberti
   Specialty Dance
      Slate Brothers
   "You Said It" (reprise)
      M. Lawlor, S. Smith, Ensemble
   "Learn to Croon"
      S. Smith, Merry-Makers Quartette, Ensemble
   "Sweet and Hot"
      P. Bernier, H. Clarke, L. Roberti, Ensemble
   Specialty Dance
      Slate Brothers
ACT 2
   Opening Chorus
      Coeds, Students

"If He Really Loves Me"
   M. Lawlor, S. Smith
"What Do We Care?"
   H. Clarke, Ensemble
"You'll Do"
   P. Bernier, G. Haggerty, Ensemble
College Medley
   Kenton Glee Club

1931.02 GREEN GROW THE LILACS

A Folk Play (with Cowboy Songs) in Two Acts, 6 Scenes. Play by Lynn Riggs. Production directed by Herbert J. Biberman. Settings by Raymond Sovey. Produced by the Theatre Guild, Inc. Opened 26 January 1931 at the Guild Theatre and closed 21 March 1931 after 64 performances.

CAST (in order of appearance): *Curly McClain:* FRANCHOT TONE. *Aunt Eller Murphy:* HELEN WESTLEY. *Laurey Williams:* JUNE WALKER. *Jeeter Fry:* RICHARD HALE. *Ado Annie Carnes:* RUTH CHORPENNING. *A Peddler:* LEE STRASBERG. *Old Man Peck:* TEX COOPER. *A Cowboy:* WOODWARD [TEX] RITTER. *Another Cowboy:* Paul Ravell. *An Old Farmer:* William T. Hayes. *A Young Farmer:* A. L. Bartolot. *Marthy:* Jane Alden. *Fiddler:* William Chosnyk. *Banjo Player:* Everett Cheetham. *Other Farmers:* Carl Beasley, Joe Wilson, Roy Ketcham, Gordon Bryant, Everett Cheetham, Elmo Carr, Tommy Pladgett. *Cowboys:* Slim Cavanaugh, Chick Hannan, Norton Worden, Jack Miller, Pete Schwartz, J. B. Hubbard. *Girls:* Jean Wood, Lois Lindon, Orlanda Lee, Alice Frost, Faith Hope, Eleanor Powers, Peggy Hannan.

The action takes place in Indian Territory in 1900. Oklahoma, which was admitted to the Union as a state in 1907, was formed by combining Indian and Oklahoma Territories.

Act 1, Scene 1: The Williams' farm houses. A June morning. *Scene 2:* The same, showing Laurey's bedroom. *Scene 3:* The same, showing the smoke house.

Act 2, Scene 1: The Porch of Old Man Peck's house. *Scene 2:* The hayfield back of Williams' house, a month later. *Scene 3:* The living room of the Williams' house, three nights later.

ACT 1[75]
Scene 1
   "Whoopee Ti Yi Yo" (Git Along, Little Dogies)
      F. Tone
   "Goodbye Old Paint"
      F. Tone
   "Green Grow the Lilacs"
      F. Tone
Scene 2
   "Miner Boy"
      J. Walker
   ("Sing Down, Hidery Down"/"Wo, Larry, Wo")
      H. Westley
Scene 3
   "Sam Hall"
      F. Tone

ACT 2
Scene 1
   "The Little Brass Wagon"
      Entire Company
   "Custer's Last Charge"
      T. Cooper
   "And Yet I Love Her Till I Die"
      F. Tone
   "My Lover's Gone Off on a Train"
      R. Chorpenning

---

[75]Musical numbers not listed in program. List prepared from production type-script and acting edition (Samuel French, New York, 1931). Also performed: "The Next Bigga River I'm Bound to Cross," "I Wish I Was Single Again," "Home on the Range" (recorded), "Way Out in Idyho," "Old Chisholm Trail" (recorded), "Strawberry Roan," "Blood on the Saddle" (recorded), "Goodbye Old Paint" (recorded), "Oh Bury Me Not on the Lone Prairie" (recorded), "Rye Whiskey" (recorded).

"Skip to My Lou"
Crowd
Scene 3
"Green Grow the Lilacs" (reprise)
F. Tone

THE STUDENT PRINCE IN HEIDELBERG

1931.03

A Revival of the Operetta in Four Acts and a Prologue[76]. Book and lyrics by Dorothy Donnelly. (Based on the play "Old Heidelberg" by Rudolf Bleichmann, adapted from "Alt-Heidelberg" by Wilhelm Meyer-Förster.) Music by Sigmund Romberg. Costumes by Weldy of Paris, Vanity Fair Costume Co. Staged by Edward Scanlon. Musical direction, Pierre de Reeder. Produced by the Messrs. Shubert. Opened 29 January 1931 at the Majestic Theatre and closed 7 March 1931 after 45 performances.

CAST (in order of their appearance): *First Lackey*: Zachary Caully. *Second Lackey*: Frazer McMahon. *Third Lackey*: Irving Green. *Fourth Lackey*: Lynn Eldredge. (*Prime Minister*) *von Mark*: WILLIAM PRINGLE. *Dr. Engel*: HOLLIS DAVENNY. *Prince Karl Franz*: EDWARD NELL, JR. *Ruder*: Lee Beggs. *Gretchen*: MARION WEEKS. *Toni*: Adolph Link. *Detlef*: Charles Chesney. *von Asterberg*: Charles Angle. *Lucas*: H. C. Howard. *Kathie*: ELIZ GERGELY. *Lutz*: GEORGE HASSELL. *Hubert*: Gus Alexander. *Grand Duchess Anastasia*: MARIE STODDARD. *Princess Margaret*: MARGARET ADAMS. *Captain Tarnitz*: ALEXANDER CALLAM. *Countess Leyden*: Gustava Malstrom. *Baron Arnheim*: Jerry Maxwell. *Rudolph Winter*: Kaji Hansen. *Freshman*: Harold E. Bomgardner. *Captain of the Guard*: Dave Morton.

Girls of Heidelberg: Justine De Paul, Roberta Blake, Pauline Hall, Dolores Lacy, Frances Kaywood, Cornelia Chason, Melba Marcel, Golda Orleans, Edna Roebling, Gustava Malstrom, Mona Medlin, Lois Landis, Hannah Brandt, Frances Wade, Katherine Curl. *Students (Saxons)*: Gene Spiro, Donald Smith, Ed Caulley, Herman Belmonte, Irving Greene, Jerry Moore, Walter Franklin, Harold Bomgarder, Larry Odell, R. E. Garcia, Sigmund Gluckoff, Frazer McMahon, Lynn Eldridge, Dave Morton, Jerry Maxwell. *Students (Rheinishers)*: Theo Bayer, Arthur Verbouwens, William Dunn, Jack Spiegel, Ed Young, Kaji Hansen, Hal Murphy, Leo Nash, Paul Jensen, Warren Pittinger, Frank King, Owen Pauline, John Eaton, Buck Williams. *Waiters*: George Nash, Frank King. *Ladies in Waiting*: Pauline Hall, Gustava Malstrom, Dolores Lacy. *Maids in Attendance*: Mona Medlin, Edna Roebling, Frances Wade, Roberta Blake.

AMERICA'S SWEETHEART

1931.04

A Musical Comedy in Two Acts, 11 Scenes. Book by Herbert Fields. Music by Richard Rodgers. Lyrics by Lorenz Hart. Book directed by Monty Woolley. (Dances by and) Entire production under the supervision of Bobby Connolly. Settings by Donald Oenslager. Costumes by Charles LeMaire. Music director, Alfred Goodman. Orchestrations, (Robert) Russell Bennett. Produced by Laurence Schwab and Frank Mandel. Opened 10 February 1931 at the Broadhurst Theatre and closed 6 June 1931 after 135 performances.

CAST (in order of appearance): *S. A. Dolan*, General Manager of Premier Pictures: JOHN SHEEHAN. *Larry Pitkin*, of the Comedy Films: GUS SHY. *Madge Farrell*, His Partner: INEZ COURTNEY. *Michael Perry*, from St. Paul: JACK WHITING. *Geraldine March*, also from St. Paul: HARRIETTE LAKE[Ann Sothern]. *Denise Torel*, an Imported Star: JEANNE AUBERT. *Movie Actresses (2): Paula*: VERA MARSH. *Dorith*: DOROTHY DARE. *Lottie*, a Waitress: Sue Moore. *Miss Mulligan*, a Secretary: VIRGINIA BRUCE. *Telephone Operator*: Alice Burrage. *Dolores*: Francetta Malloy. *A Stenographer*: Terry Carroll. *Studio Executives (5): Mr. Corrigan*: Jay Ford. *Mr. Clark*: Fred Shawhan. *Mr. Goulding*: Herbert Hall. *Mr. Butler*: Budd Clark. *Mr. McCarey*: Charles Fowler. *A Booking Agent*: Al Downing. *Georgia, Georgiana and Georgette*: Hilda, Louise and Maxine Forman. *Radio Announcer*: Raoul DeTisne. *A Policeman*: O. J. Vanasse. *Actors, Tourists, etc.*

Girls: Mildred Webb, Jean Fursa, Flo Spink, Dorothy Day, Carola Taylor, Dorothy Van Hest, Patti Hastings, Ann Hardman, Wilma Novak, Billie Sallier, Jerry Downes, Sherry Pelham, Margaret Carolan, Frances Markey, Anita Pam, Evelyn Monte, Pamela Sweeney, Vida Manuel, Lorraine Webb, Virginia Webb, Adele Story, Rosalie Trego, Kay Stewart, Lucille Osborne, Sara Jane, Pamela Bryant. *Boys*: Jack Donohue, Frank Hulser, Jack Hubert, Don Lannon, William Cooper, Hy Mohon, Jack Ross, Gene Sherrin, Jack Ray, Al Bloom, Robert Penny, William Meader.

---

[76]First presented in New York 2 December 1924 at the Jolson Theatre for 608 performances. For Synopsis of Scenes and Musical Numbers, see original 1924 production. For this production, the Solo Ballet in Act 3 was dropped. Scenery design uncredited.

Act 1, Scene 1: The Cafeteria on the Lot of Premier Pictures, Inc. (Hollywood.) *Scene 2*: Corridor of Main Executive Building. *Scene 3*: A Private Conference Room. *Scene 4*: A Cabin in the Tennessee Mountains. *Scene 5*: Before the Casino at Agua Caliente. *Scene 6*: The Back Porch of Madge's Bungalow. *Scene 7*: The Reception Room at the Beverly-Wilshire Hotel.

Act 2, Scene 1: The Casting Office at Premier Pictures, Inc. *Scene 2*: The Silver Screen, Hollywood Theatre. *Scene 3*: Roof Garden at the Embassy Club. *Scene 4*: The Bungalow Again. *Scene 5*: Grauman's Chinese Theatre, Hollywood.

ACT 1
Scene 1
"Mr. Dolan Is Passing Through"
J. Sheehan, Executives, Ensemble
"In Califor-n-i-a"
D. Dare, V. Marsh, Movie Actresses
Scene 2
"My Sweet"
I. Courtney, G. Shy
Scene 3
"I've Got Five Dollars"
H. Lake, J. Whiting
"I've Got Five Dollars" (reprise)
H. Lake, J. Whiting
Scene 4
"Sweet Geraldine"
Forman Sisters
Scene 5
"There So Much More"
J. Aubert, G. Shy
"We'll Be the Same"
H. Lake, J. Whiting, Ensemble
"We'll Be the Same" (reprise)
J. Whiting, G. Shy
Scene 6
"How About It"
I. Courtney, J. Whiting
Scene 7
"Innocent Chorus Girls of Yesterday"
Movie Stars
"A Lady Must Live"
J. Aubert

ACT 2
Scene 1
Opening
J. Sheehan, Directors
Scene 3
"You Ain't Got No Savoir Faire"
I. Courtney, G. Shy
"Two Unfortunate Orphans"
V. Marsh, D. Dare, Ensemble
"I Want a Man"
J. Aubert
Scene 5
"Tennessee Dan"
Forman Sisters
"How About It" (reprise)
J. Aubert, J. Whiting, G. Shy, Ensemble
Finale
H. Lake, J. Whiting

THE GANG'S ALL HERE

1931.05

A Musical Comedy Revue in Two Acts, 13 Scenes. Book compiled by Russel Crouse, under the direction of Oscar Hammerstein II and Morrie Ryskind. Music by Lewis E. Gensler. Lyrics by Owen Murphy and Robert A. Simon. Dialogue directed by Frank McCoy. Staged by Oscar Hammerstein II. Dances and ensembles staged by Dave Gould, assisted by Boots McKenna. Ballet staged by Tilly Losch. Settings by Henry Dreyfuss. Costumes by

Russell Patterson. Music director, Gene Salzer. Orchestrations by Hans Spialek. Produced by Morris Green and Lewis E. Gensler. Opened 18 February 1931 at the Imperial Theatre and closed 9 March 1931 after 23 performances.

CAST: *Mr. Horace Winterbottom*: TOM HOWARD. *Julie Winterbotttom*: GINA MALO. *A Man*: Jack Bruns. *A Woman*: Anita Avila. *A Girl*: Phyllis Cameron. *A Young Man*: Hal Morton. *Another Woman*: Elsie Duffy. *Another Man*: Harry Anderson. *His Wife*: Ethel Britton. *"Baby Face" Martini*: JACK MCCAULEY. *Andy Lennox*: JACK BARKER. *Hal Le Roy*: HAL LEROY. *Professor Cavanaugh*: Eddie Moran. *Doctor Indian Ike Kelly*: TED HEALY. *Stooges*: Paul Garner Jack Wall, Dick Hackins. *Big Casino*: Ben Wise. *Little Casino*: Joe McKeon. *Le Jongleur de Notre Dame*: Monsieur DuPont. *Swiss Bell Ringer*: Dr. Faust. *Two on the Aisle*: Johnnie Dale, Rheta Stone. *Dr. T. Slocum Swink*: Thomas F. Tracy. *Longfellow, Whittier*: (Al) SHAW, (Sam) LEE. *Peggy*: RUTH TESTER. *Hotel Manager*: Jack Bruns. *"Willy" Wilson*: ZELMA O'NEILL. *Hector Winterbottom*: JOHN GALLAUDET. *Dancers*: GOMEZ & WINONA. *Chief of Police*: Earl Gilbert. *Street Vendor*: Joe Verdi. *A Sailor*: Bert Fay. *Hotel Proprietor*: Albert F. Hawthorne. *Ballet Soloist*: Gertrude Stanton. *Lyric Quartet*: Robert Duenweg, Jack Bruns, Harry Anderson, Joseph Vitale. *Tilly Losch Ballet*: Joan English, Senta Stephany, Marie Grimaldi, Catherine Laughlin, Jeanie Lavera, Katherine Gallimore, Anita Avila, Alice Kellerman.

Dancers: Lois Maye, Phyllis Saule, Getrude McPherson, Arline Ingram, Bunny Moore, Evelyn Hannon, Dorothy Foster, Bonnie Alvin, Estelle Phillips, Ruth Raidt, Ruth Martin, Dorothy Waller, Julia Gorman, Carrol Renwick, Mary Alice Rice, Agnes Reilly, Gene Carpenter, Elsie Lauritsen. *Ladies of the Ensemble*: Wynn Terry, Irma Philbin, Helen Edwards, Irene King, Madgio Smylie, Ethel Britton, Elsie Duffy, Louise Joyce, Loretta Goss, Jeanne Adams, Phyllis Cameron, Margaret Dixon, Rheta Stone, Beth Holt, Gloray Pierre. *Gentlemen of the Ensemble*: Joseph Lennon, Hal Morton, Frank Reynolds, Jack Montgomery, Beau Tilden, Tom Jordan, Jack Kay, Jack Voeth, Kenneth Williams, Frank Edmonds, Gus Hyland, Jack Raymond, Russel Duncan, Henry King, Jimmy Ryan, George Weeden.

Act 1, Scene 1: On the Boardwalk at Atlantic City. *Scene 2*: Peacock Alley, Ritz Carlton Hotel, Atlantic City. *Scene 3*: The Winterbottom Suite. *Scene 4*: Doctor Kelly's Office. *Scene 5*: Approach to a Private Boathouse. *Scene 6*: The Boathouse.

Act 2, Scene 1: A Square in Nantucket. *Scene 2*: The Square in Nantucket. *Scene 3*: The Lobby of the Wilson Hotel. *Scene 4*: Wing of Hotel .*Scene 5*: A Dock. *Scene 6*: The Deck of a Revenue Cutter. *Scene 6*: A Street. *Scene 7*: A Night Club.

ACT 1
Scene 1
Opening
Ensemble
"What Have You Done to Me?"
G. Malo, J. Barker, Ensemble
Dance
H. LeRoy
"The Gang's All Here"
J. McCauley, Lyric Quartet, Racketeers, Ensemble
Scene 2
"Dumb Girl"
R. Tester, J. McCauley
Scene 3
Dance
Butlers, Maids
"Gypsy Rose"
J. Gallaudet
"Baby Wanna Go Bye-Bye With You"
Z. O'Neal, J. Gallaudet
Scene 4
"Adorable Julie"
T. Healy, G. Malo, Ensemble
Scene 5
"Husband, Lover and Wife"
Z. O'Neal, A. Shaw, S. Lee
Scene 6
"Speaking of You"
J.Barker, G. Malo, Gomez and Winona, Ensemble
"By Special Permission of the Copyright Owners, I Love You"
R. Tester, J. McCauley
Finale
Company

ACT 2
Scene 1
"The Moon, the Wind and the Sea"
G. Malo, Lyric Quartette, Tilly Losch Ballet, Ensemble
"By Special Permission of the Copyright Owners, I Love You" (reprise)
R. Tester, J. McCauley, Ensemble
Dance
H. LeRoy
Scene 3
"It Always Takes Two"
Z. O'Neal, J. Gallaudet
Scene 5
"How Can I Get Rid of Those Blues?"
J. Barker, Tilly Losch Ballet
Scene 7
"What Have You Done to Me?" (reprise)
Ensemble
Scene 8
"Speak Easy"
F. Swanee, Ensemble
Dance
Gomez and Winona
Finale
Company

THE VENETIAN GLASS NEPHEW

1931.06

A Little Opera (Operetta) in Two Acts, a Prologue and 6 Scenes. Dramatized (book) by Ruth Hale. Based on the novel of the same name by Elinor Wylie. Music and lyrics by Eugene Bonner. Staged by Walter Greenough. Settings by Edgar Bohlman. Costumes by Brooks. Conductor, Leon Barzin. Produced by Walter Greenough. Opened 23 February 1931 at the Vanderbilt Theatre and closed 28 February 1931 after 8 performances.

CAST: *Peter Innocent, Cardinal Bon*: DOD MEHAN. *Rosalba Bernis*: MARY SILVEIRA. *Chevalier de Chastelneuf, alias Giacomo Casanova*: GEORGE HOUSTON. *Virginio*: LOUIS YAECKEL. *Alvise Luna*: EDGAR STEHLI. *Angelo Querini*: RAYMOND HUNTLEY. *Count Carlo Gozzi*: GAGE CLARKE. *Maria Loredan*: LEE BURGESS. *Bianca Contarini*: Joan Carter-Waddell.

Six Masquers (Sextette): *Columbina Pisani*: Dorothy Johnson. *Isabella Moncenigo*: Gretchen Haller. *Zerbinetta Tron*: Adele Sanderson. *Pedrolino Zorzi*: Florence Rand. *Arlechino Bembo*: Roy Mace. *Scaramuccia Balbi*: Norman Oberg.

Act 1, Scene 1: Palazzo Querini, Venice. Late Eighteenth Century. *Scene 2*: House of Alvise Luna, Venice. *Scene 3*: Palazzo Querini.

Act 2, Scene 1: Garden of Querini's Villa, Altichiere. *Scene 2*: Workroom of the Brothers Dubois, near Versailles. *Scene 3*: House of Virginio and Rosalba, Venice.

Prologue
Sextette

ACT 1[77]
Scene 1 (Peter Innocent)
Opening
D. Mehan
"You Are a Rose"
G. Houston
Finale Scene 1
G. Houston, M. Silveira
Scene 2 (Virginio)
"These to Me Are Beautiful People"
D. Mehan
"Conjuration"
G. Houston
"Boy, I Give You Now"
G. Houston

[77]No song titles appear in the program. List prepared from holograph of production score.

Finale Scene 2
  L. Yaeckel, M. Silveira
Scene 3 (Rosalba)
  Entr'acte
    Sextette
  "Rosalba's Minuet"
    L. Yaeckel, M. Silveira
ACT 2
Scene 1 (Spiderweb Tangle)
  "Ballade des Dames du Temps Perdu"
    (*Words by* François Villon.)
  "It Is My Thoughts"
    M. Silveira
  "My Love, You Know That I Have Never Used"
    G. Houston
  Duet
    M. Silveira, G. Houston
  Finale Scene 1
    M. Silveira, G. Houston, D. Johnson
Scene 2 (Ordeal By Fire)
  "The Icicles"
    M. Silveira
  "For This She Starred Her Eyes With Salt"
    Sextette
  Finale Scene 2
    L. Yaeckel, M. Silveira, D. Mehan, G. Houston, Sextette
Scene 3 (Interior by Longhi)
  Finale Scene 3 (It Has Been Said . . .)
    G. Houston, Sextette

1931.07

BLOSSOM TIME

A Revival of the Operetta in Three Acts[78]. Book and lyrics by Dorothy Donnelly. Adapted from the Viennese original ("Das Dreimäderlhaus") by A. M. Willner and Heinz Reichert, based on a novel "Schwammerl" by Rudolf H. Bartsch. Music adapted and augmented by Sigmund Romberg from the melodies of Franz Schubert selected and arranged by Heinrich Berté. Staged by Edward Scanlon. Produced by the Messrs. Shubert. Opened 4 March 1931 at the Ambasssador Theatre and closed 28 March 1931 after 29 performances.[79]

CAST: *Kupelweiser*: Harry Rabke. *Vogl*: Joseph Wilkins. *Von Schwind*: Joseph Toner. *Binder*: Maurice Tyler. *Erkman*: Truman Gaige. *Domeyer*: Walter Wahl. *Greta*: MARICE CHRISTIE. *Bella Bruna*: Gladys Baxter. *Count Sharntoff*: JOSEPH LERTORA. *Mitzi*: GRETA ALPETER. *Kitzi*: Marie Starner. *Fritzi*: Mary Wilkins. *Franz Schubert*: JOHN CHARLES GILBERT. *Kranz*: Robert Lee Allen. *Baron Von Schober*: CLIFFORD NEWDAHL. *Violinist*: Howard Samples. *Mrs. Kranz*: EVELYN REIDE. *Novotny*: ROBERT O'CONNOR. *Mrs. Colburg*: Millie Freeman.

Dancers: Gerry Dean, Stella Doyle, Georgia MacTaggert, Herta Rittell, Inez Goetz, Peggy Baldwin. *Show Girls*: Peggy Scevioure, Dorothy Drum, Agatha Phillips, Marie Craigin, Ann Johnson, Eleanor Lewis.

1931.08

SIMPLE SIMON

A Return Engagement of the Musical Comedy in Two Acts, 13 Scenes[80]. Book by Ed Wynn and Guy Bolton. Music by Richard Rodgers. Lyrics by Lorenz Hart. Dialogue staged by Zeke Colvan. Ensembles and dances directed by Seymour Felix. Settings by Joseph Urban. Artistic director, (costumes design by) John Harkrider. Music director, Emil Newman. Produced by Florenz Ziegfeld. Opened 9 March 1931 at the Majestic Theatre and closed 21 March 1931 after 16 performances. Total including first engagement: 151 performances.

CAST (in order of appearance): *Fingy*, Bluebeard's Henchman: Albert Baron. *Bert Blue*, Bluebeard: GIL SQUIRES. *Olee King*, King Cole: WILLIAM H. WHITE. *Gilly Flower* (Jill): LAINE BLAIRE. *Jack Horner* (Jack): DAVID BREEM. *Policeman*: Paul Butterworth. *Simon*, Keeper of Information and Newspaper Shop: ED WYNN. *Gladys Dove*: FRIEDA MIERSE. *Jonah*, Genii: Master George Offermann. *Popper*: James McKay. *Elaine King*, Cinderella: MARGARET BREEN. *Tony Prince*, Prince Charming: JACK SQUIRES. *Otto Prince*: Harry Shannon. *Sal*: WINI SHAW. *The Horse*: Joseph Schrode, Pete LaDella. *Premiere Danseuse*: HARRIET HOCTOR. *The Giant Head*: Frank DeWitt. *The Frog*: William Ferry. *Peter Pan*: Renee Rivir. *Little Boy Blue*: Ruth Simmons. *Red Riding Hood*: Mimi Sherman. *Wolf*: Irma Montague. *Goldylocks*: Frances Williams. *Puss in Boots*: Virginia MacNaughton. *Three Bears*: Muriel DeLova, Peggy Driscoll, Betty Blake. *Hansel*: Flora Taylor. *Gretel*: Muriel Harrison. *Jazz*: LAINE BLAIRE. *Dog*: Jerrie Craigin. *Dish*: Patricia Palmer. *Bo-Peep*: Marie Shea. *Fairy Goddesses*: Billie Seward, Buff Bullard, Barbara Hamilton, Jerry Rogers, Adele Smith, Lulu Gray. *Snow Queen*: Villi Milli. *Rapunzel*: FRIEDA MIERSE.

Ladies of the Ensemble: Marie Shea, Flora Taylor, Eva Lynn, Elinor James, Betty Blake, Marjorie Hassard, Mimi Sherman, Renee Rivir, Jerrie Cragin, Shula Morrow, Sue Brighton, Muriel L. Harrison, Virginia MacNaughton, Patricia Palmer, Frances Krane, Dorothy Campbell, Edna R. Eccles, Ruth Simmons, Frances Lynn, Ruth Hurley, Arlyne Taylor, Irma Montague, Peggy Driscoll, Mildred S. Clark, Lulu Gray, Hope Western, Villa Milli, Billie Seward, Buff Bullard, Jerry Rogers, Barbara Hamilton, Adele Smith. *Gentlemen of the Ensemble*: James McKay, Paul Butterworth, Messrs. Myers, Sedlock, Mackey, Leslie, Bennett, Connolly, Roemer, Read, Walters, Dodge.

ACT 1
  "Coney Island" (Opening)
    Girls, Boys, Barkers, Dancers
  "Don't Tell Your Folks"
    D. Breem, L. Blaire
  "Send for Me"
    M. Breen, J. Squires
  "Magic Music"
    L. Blaire, Magic Girls
  "Ten Cents a Dance"
    W. Shaw
  "Send for Me" (reprise)
    M. Breen, J. Squires
  "Dull and Gay"
    W. H. White, H. Shannon, Ensemble
  "Bluebeard's Beard"[81]
    G. Squires
  "Hunting the Fox"
    J. Squires, Hunters
  Hunting Ballet
    H. Hoctor, Toe Dancers, Show Girls
  "Mocking Bird"
    E. Wynn
  Finaletto
    Entire Company
  "Peter Pan"[82]
    R. Rivir
  "Fairyland" ("I Love the Woods")
    Girls
  Jazz
    L. Blaire
  The Ballet Blue
    H. Hoctor
  In the Clouds
ACT 2
  "Drug Store Girls"
    A. Baron, Girls
  "Sweetheart"[83]
    D. Breem, L. Blaire
  "I'm Yours"[84] (from *LEAVE IT TO LESTER* film)
    W. Shaw, E. Wynn
    (*Music by* Johnny Green. *Lyrics by* E. Y. Harburg.)

---

[78]First presented in New York 29 September 1921 at the Ambassador Theatre for 592 performances. For Synopsis of Scenes and Musical Numbers, see original 1921 production.
[79]Settings, costumes uncredited.
[80]Originally opened in New York 18 February 1930 at the Ziegfeld Theatre for 135 performances.

---

[81]Added for this return engagement and national tour.
[82]Added for this return engagement and national tour.
[83]Previously titled "Sweetenheart."
[84]Added for this return engagement and national tour.

"On With the Dance"
   Drug Store Girls
"Love Me or Leave Me"[85] (from *WHOOPEE!*)
   W. Shaw
   (*Music by* Walter Donaldson. *Lyrics by* Gus Kahn.)
"Roping"
   E. Wynn, B. Breem
Kissing Forest Ballet
   H. Hoctor, Dancers
"Rags and Tatters"
   J. Squires, Vagabond Girls and Boys
Finale—"Cottage in the Country"
   W. Shaw, Entire Company

1931.09 THE WONDER BAR

A Continental Novelty of European Night Life in Two Acts. Book by Irving Caesar and Aben Kandel, adapted from the (Viennese) original ("Die Wunder-Bar") by Geza Herczeg and Karl Farkas. Music by Robert Katscher. Lyrics by Irving Caesar. Staged by William Mollison. Dances by Albertina Rasch, John Pierce. Settings by Watson Barratt. Costumes by Charles LeMaire, others. Music director, Louis Silver. Produced by Morris Gest in association with the Messrs. Shubert. Opened 17 March 1931 at the Nora Bayes Theatre and closed 29 May 1931 after 76 performances.

CAST (in order of appearance): *Richard*, Headwaiter at The Wonder Bar: Gustav Rolland. *Marcel*, Porter: Auguste Armini. *Cocottes (4)*, Habituées of The Wonder Bar: *Sonya*: Antonina Fechner. *Billie*: Dagmar Oakland. *Rosette*: Adriana Dori. *Martha*: Elvira Trabert. *Prince Nikolas Engalitcheff*: Prince Nikolas Engalitcheff. *Helen Brown*, American Guest: Laura Pierpont. *Mary Evans*, American Guest: Jean Newcombe. *Elmer Evans*, Her Husband: C. Jay Williams. *Edgar Banks*, American Guest: Henry Crosby. *Monsieur Al*, Proprietor of The Wonder Bar: AL JOLSON. *Inez*, Professional Dancer: TRINI. *Ramon Colmano*: REX O'MALLEY. *Lord Cauldwell*: ARTHUR TREACHER. *Francois Vale*: Stuart Casey. *Oscar Wayne*: Clarence Harvey. *Liane Duval*, Guest: WANDA LYON. *Pierre Duval*, Her Husband: VERNON STEELE. A *Gendarme*: Roman Arnoldoff. *Monsieur Simon*, Vaudeville Agent: Adrian Rosley. *Electra Pivonka*, Entertainer: PATSY KELLY. *Charlie*, Her Brother: AL SEGAL. A *Rajah*: Mohammid Ibrahim. *Count Rugtoffsky*: Michael Dalmatoff. *Signorina Medea Colombara*: Signora Medea Colombara. *Benno Bondy*, Commercial Traveler: Hugo Brucken. *Mrs. Soloman*, American Guest: Bertha Walden. *Sam Soloman*, Her Husband: Leo Hoyt. *Baroness Rosseau*: Marie Hunt.

Guests of The Wonder Bar: Marjorie Ezequelle, Kay Dooley, Grenna Sloane, Florence Wessels, Edna Frecker, Gladys Sugden, Therese Menjou, Elsa Stadt, Anna Hitler, Rosa Timponi, Chistine Nolander, Odine Odeon, Alma Wainwright, Belle Osmond, Phyllis Collier, Robert Aubert, Donald Gordon, Jan Flentke, Niska Stefanini, Charles Garland, Ted Tenbrook, Ivan Petroff, Herbert Hemeter, Christian Holmes, Delano Griggsby, Philip Lane, Chester Hadden, Lindsley Keresky, Hubert Von Der Fehr. *Barmen*: Thomas Connors, Waldo McDonald, Robert Uhl, Harry Driscoll, Knute Robertson. *Waiters*: Robert Rech, Marshall Rech, Albert Cheriff, Herman Smithson, Hamp Leipsig. *Coat Boys*: Buddy Schubert, Charles Powers. *Cigarette Girl*: Lully Yuen.

Entertainers: *Audrey Depew Four*: Salvatore Giano, George Severin, Ernest Joresco, Audrey Depew. DORIS GRODAY. *Albertina Rasch Girls*: Claire Deerfield, Margaret Jacobson, Jeanette Bradley, Clayton Estes. CAROL CHILTON, MACEO THOMAS. Martin Freed, Jack Stein, Henry Hartman, Steve Kirkpatrick, Don Moore, Harry Tardio, Harold Sturr, Earl Richards, Lee Conna, Ernest Nagel, Nicholas Garragusi, Irving Finkstein, Sol Deutsch, Philip Bernalfo.

Act 1: The Wonder Bar, a Parisian Night Club. About 1929.

Act 2: The Wonder Bar, one year later.

ACT 1[86]

---

[85]Added for this return engagement and national tour.
[86]Program note: There is dancing on the stage before the action of the play begins and members of the audience are cordially invited to take part. The adaptors gratefully tender their thanks to Mr. George Jessel for his helpful suggestions.Other songs performed or interpolated:
   "Trav'lin All Alone"
      A. Jolson
      (*Music and Lyrics by* J. C. Johnson.)
   "Something Seems to Tell Me"
      A. Jolson
      (*Music by* Robert Katscher. *Lyrics by* Irving Caesar.)
   "Lenox Avenue"
      A. Jolson
      (*Music and Lyrics by* Al Jolson, Irving Caesar-Joseph E. Meyers.)

"Good Evening, Friends"
   A. Jolson
Song
   A. Jolson
Specialty
   Trini
Specialty
   Audrey Depew Four
"Valse Amoureuse"
   Inez, R. O'Malley
   (*Dance arranged by* John Pierce.)
"The Dance We Do For Al"
   D. Groday, Albertina Rasch Girls
   (*Dance arranged by* Albertina Rasch.)
"I'm Falling in Love"
   R. O'Malley, A. Jolson
"(Oh,) Donna Clara"
   A. Jolson
   (*Music by* J. Petersburski. *Original Lyrics by* Fritz Löhner-Beda. *English Lyrics by* Irving Caesar.)
ACT 2
"The Dying Flamingo"[87]
   P. Kelly
Specialty
   A. Segal
"Estrellita"
   M. Colombara
   (*Music and Lyrics by* Manuel M. Ponce.)
"Valse Amoreuse" (reprise)
   W. Lyon, R. O'Malley
   (*Dance arranged by* John Pierce.)
"Elizabeth" (My Queen!)
   P. Kelly, Company
   (*Dance arranged by* Albertina Rasch.)
(Yiddish) Folk Song ("The Cantor"-Ohf Shabbes)
   A. Jolson
Specialty
   C. Chilton, M. Thomas
Reprise

THE MIKADO,
1931.10 or The Town of Titipu

A Revival of the Comic Opera in Two Acts[88]. Libretto by William S. Gilbert. Music by Arthur Sullivan. Staged by Milton Aborn. Costumes by Eaves. Musical director, Louis Kroll. Produced by the Civic Light Opera Company (Milton Aborn, director). Opened 4 May 1931 at Erlanger's Theatre and closed 16 May 1931 after 16 performances.[89]

CAST: *The Mikado of Japan*: WILLAIM DANFORTH. *Nanki-Poo*, his son: HOWARD MARSH. *Ko-Ko*, Lord High Executioner of Titipu: FRANK MOULAN. *Pooh-Bah*, Lord High Everything Else: HERBERT L. WATEROUS. *Pish-Tush*, a Noble Lord: WILLIAM C. GORDON. *Three Sisters, Wards of Ko-Ko*: *Yum-Yum*: HIZI KOYKE. *Pitti-Sing*: ETHEL CLARKE. *Peep-Bo*: MARGARET BICKEL. *Katisha*: VERA ROSS.

   "Ma Mere"
      A. Jolson
      (*Music and Lyrics by* Al Jolson, IrvingCaesar, HarryWarren.)
   "Ev'ry Day Can't Be a Sunday"
      A. Jolson
      (*Music and Lyrics by* Al Jolson.)
[87]Dropped for subsequent tour.
[88]First presented in New York 20 July, 10-29 August 1885 at the Union Square and People's Theatres for 22 performances. First authorized production presented 19 August 1885 at the Fifth Avenue Theatre by Richard D'Oyly Carte for 250 performances. For Synopsis of Scenes and Musical Numbers, see 19 August 1885 D'Oyly Carte production.
[89]Settings uncredited.

Ladies of the Mikado's Suite: Frances Moore, Olga Schumacher, Rosalyn Shaw, Patricia Clark, Florence Little, Edith Artley. *The Mikado's Bodyguard*: Charles Froom, Edward Taylor, Bert Melrose, Hobson Young, Charles Maduro, Edward Lambert. *Chorus of School Girls, Nobles, Guards and Coolies*: Eleanor Gilmore, Patricia Clark, Gertrude Waldon, Frances Baviello, Florence Little, Margaret Bickel, Olga Schumacher, Mabel Thompson, Rosalyn Shaw, Flora Bell, Helen Hosp, Isabel Norwood, Belle Flower, Rosa Rubenstein, Mary Joe Matthews, Edith Artley, Frances Moore, Georgina Dieter, Marie Pittman, Harrison, Charles Froom, Bert Melrose, Edward Taylor, Hobson Young, Felix Noonan, Allen Ware, Frank Murray, Martin Lilienfeld, Frank Dowling.

1931.11 RHAPSODY IN BLACK

A "Symphony of Blue Notes and Black Rhythm" (A Musical Revue) in Two Acts, a Prologue and 18 Scenes. Music by Alberta Nichols. Lyrics by Mann Holiner. (Additional music and lyrics by George Gershwin, Dorothy Fields, Jimmy McHugh, Ken Macomber, Pat Carroll, J. Rosamund Johnson, Cecil Mack, W. C. Handy.) Staged by Lew Leslie. Music director, Pike Davis. Costumes designed by Charles LeMaire. Produced by Blackbirds Productions, Inc. (Lew Leslie). Opened 4 May 1931 at the Sam H. Harris Theatre and closed 11 July 1931 after 80 performances[90].

CAST: ETHEL WATERS, VALAIDA, CECIL MACK'S CHOIR, BERRY BROTHERS (Ananias, Warren and James), AL MOORE, EDDIE RECTOR, BLUE MCALLISTER.

Cecil Mack's Choir: Eloise Uggams, Avis Andrews, Louise Howard, Mayme Richardson, Selika Pettiford, Geneva Washington, Olive Ball, Maude Simmons, Ernest Boyd, Robert Ecton, Leon Diggs, Frank Jackson, Samuel Gray, Ernest Allen, Harold Thompson, James Skelton, Rolland Smith.

PROLOGUE[91]
Harlem Interlude (*by* Nat Dorfman)
Scene: A Gin Mill in Harlem.
Liza: E. Waters. *George Washington Aaron Burr Brown*: S. Gray. *Patrons, Hangers-on, Visitors, etc.*: Cecil Mack's Choir.

ACT 1
Scene 1
"Rhapsody in Black"
Valaida
(*Music by* Ken Macomber and Pat Carroll.)
A musical transition of the Negro from Africa to Harlem.
Scene 2
"Wash Tub Rub-sody"
E. Waters
(*Music by* Alberta Nichols. *Lyrics by* Mann Holiner.)
Accompanist: Pearl Wright.
Scene 3
"Gettin' Up Mornin'"
R. Ecton, Cecil Mack's Choir
"Heard Nobody Pray"
E. Uggams, Cecil Mack's Choir
Scene 4
"Till the Real Thing Comes Along"
Valaida
(*Music by* Alberta Nichols. *Lyrics by* Mann Holiner.)
Reprise
Berry Brothers
Scene 5
"Dance Hall Hostess"
E. Waters
(*Music by* Alberta Nichols. *Lyrics by* Mann Holiner.)
Accompanist: Pearl Wright.

Scene 6
"Exhortation"
R. Smith, Cecil Mack's Choir
"Chloe"[92]
G. Washington, Cecil Mack's Choir
(*Music by* Neil Moret. *Lyrics by* Gus Kahn.)
Scene 7
"Harlem Rhumbola"
Valaida, A. Moore
(*Music by* Jimmy McHugh. *Lyrics by* Dorothy Fields.)
Scene 8
"Where's My Prince Charming?" (What's Keeping My Prince Charming?)
E. Waters, B. McAllister
(*Music by* Alberta Nichols. *Lyrics by* Mann Holiner.)
Scene 9
"Rhapsody in Blue"
Valaida, Cecil Mack's Choir, A. Berry, A. Moore
(*Music by* George Gershwin. *At the piano*: Joseph Steel.)

ACT 2
Scene 1
Soul of a Trumpet[93]
A Siren of the Jungle: Valaida. *Her Prey*: A. Moore. *Trumpet Player*: Demus Dean.
Scene 2
"Pullman Porter's Lament"
E. Waters
Scene 3
"Eili, Eili"
A. Andrews, E. Uggams, Cecil Mack's Choir
"The Three Guitars"[94]
Valaida, Cecil Mack's Choir
Scene 4
Rhapsody in Taps
E. Rector
Scene 5
"I'm Feeling Blue"
E. Waters
(*Music by* Jimmy McHugh. *Lyrics by* Dorothy Fields.)
Scene 6
"Ain't Gonna Rain"
E. Boyd, R. Ecton, L. Diggs, F. Jackson, S. Gray, E. Allen, H. Thompson, J. Skelton, R. Smith
Scene 7
"Dream of the Chocolate Soldier"
Valaida, E. Rector
(*Music by* Victor Herbert. *Special Arrangement by* Ken Macomber.)
Scene 8
Specialty ("You Can't Stop Me from Loving You")
E. Waters
Scene 9
Lew Leslie's version of "St. Louis Blues"
Cecil Mack's Choir
(*Music and Lyrics by* W. C. Handy.)
Soloists: R. Ecton, G. Washington.

[90]Settings uncredited.
[91]Added for tour:
Rhythm in Rhapsody
Earl (Snakehips) Tucker, Bessie Dudley
"Papa Di-Da-Da"
Berry Brothers
(*Music and Lyrics by* Spencer Williams, Clarence Williams, Clarence Todd.)

[92]Previously introduced by Ethel Waters in AFRICANA, 1927.
[93]Replaced on subsequent tour by:
"St. James Infirmary"
Valaida, Cecil Mack's Choir
(*Music and Lyrics by* Joe Primrose. *Choral Arrangement by* Russell Wooding. *Special Music and Lyrics* for choir by Valaida.)
[94]Replaced on subsequent tour by:
"Dark Eyes" (Russian folk song)
Valaida, Cecil Mack's Choir
(*Music and Lyrics by* A. Salama.)

H.M.S. PINAFORE,
1931.12 or The Lass That Loved a Sailor

A Revival of the Comic Opera in Two Acts[95]. Libretto by William S. Gilbert. Music by Arthur Sullivan. Staged by Milton Aborn. Costumes by Eaves. Musical director, Louis Kroll. Produced by the Civic Light Opera Company (Milton Aborn, director). Opened 18 May 1931 at Erlanger's Theatre and closed 30 May 1931 after 17 performances[96].

CAST: *The Rt. Hon. Sir Joseph Porter, K.C.B.,* First Lord of the Admiralty: FRANK MOULAN. *Captain Corcoran,* Commander of the *H.M.S. Pinafore:* JOSEPH MACAULEY. *Ralph Rackstraw,* Able Seaman: HOWARD MARSH. *Dick Deadeye,* Able Seaman: WILLIAM DANFORTH. *Bill Bobstay,* Boatswain: William C. Gordon. *Josephine,* the Captain's Daughter: RUTH ALTMAN. *Little Buttercup,* Mrs. Cripps, a Portsmouth bum-boat woman: FAY TEMPLETON. *Hebe,* Sir Joseph's First Cousin: Ethel Clark. *Mid-Ship Mite:* Joseph Ruggiero.

Sailors, First Lord's Sisters, His Cousins, His Aunts: Charles Froom, Edward Taylor, Bert Mclrose, Hobson Young, Charles Maduro, Felix Noonan, Allan Ware, Frank Murray, Martin Lilienfield, Frank Dowling, Harrison Fuller. Frances Moore, Olga Schumacher, Rosalyn Shaw, Patricia Clark, Florence Little, Edith Artley, Eleanor Gilmore, Gertrude Waldon, Frances Baviello, Mabel Thompson, Flora Bell, Helen Hosp, Isabel Norwood, Belle Flower, Rosa Rubenstein, Mary Joe Matthews, Georgina Dieter, Marie Pittman.

BILLY ROSE'S CRAZY QUILT
1931.13

A Musical Revue in Two Acts, 25 Scenes[97]. Assembled by Billy Rose. Sketches by David Freeman. Additional dialogue by Herman Timberg. Songs by Billy Rose and his friends. (Music by Harry Warren, Richard Rodgers, Rowland Wilson, Manning Sherwin, Carroll Gibbons. Lyrics by Mort Dixon, Bud Green, Ira Gershwin, Lorenz Hart, James Dyrenforth, Ned Wever.) Staged by Billy Rose. Musical numbers staged by Sammy Lee. Scenery painted by R. W. Bergman and Triangle Studios. Costumes by Fannie Brice. Lighting by Clark Robinson. Music director, Charles Drury. Produced by Billy Rose. Opened 19 May 1931 at the 44th Street Theatre and closed 25 July 1931 after 67 performances.

CAST: FANNIE BRICE, PHIL BAKER, TED HEALEY, GOMEZ & WINONA, LEW BRICE, ETHEL NORRIS, TAMARA [DRASIN], Vale & Stewart, Tom Monroe, Rodger Davis, Marion Bonnell.

Crazy Quilt Sextet (also Ladies of the Evening): Edythe Paige, Florence Moore, Helene Hughes, Helen Edwards, Billie Hill, Patricia Dolan. *Ladies:* Viola Paulson, Rita Jason, Arline Baber, Emily Von Hoven, Baun Sturtz, Muriel Markert, Marion Bonnell, Grace Berry, Adeline Ogilvie, Mary Wayne, Gertrude Sheffield, Maryan Malmuth, Jacqueline Feeley, Margaret Dawn, Patricia Palmer, Lula Gray, Helen Becker, Sara Grand, Gladys Grand, Betty Byrne, Betty Barrett, Alda Deery, Geraldine Worthing, Joan English, Violet Casey. *Gentlemen:* Joe Barry, Russell Duncan, Brian Davis, Tom Reilly, Ray Dawley, Sam Fisher.

ACT 1[98]

---

[95]Originally presented in New York 15 January 1879 at the Standard Theatre for 175 performances. For Synopsis of Scenes and Musical Numbers, see original 1879 production. Returned 27 July 1931 under Civic Light Opera Company auspices on a double-bill with TRIAL BY JURY (see entry in following season).
[96]Settings uncredited.
[97]This was a revised version of SWEET AND LOW presented 17 November 1930 at the 46th Street Theatre for 184 performances.

    Finale
[98]Added during run:
    "Rest Room Rose"
      F. Brice
      (*Music by* Richard Rodgers. *Lyrics by* Lorenz Hart.)
    "It's in the Air"
      T. Healy
      (*Music by* Louis Alter. *Lyrics by* Billy Rose and E. Y. Harburg.)
    "Overnight"
      F. Brice
      (*Music by* Louis Alter. *Lyrics by* Billy Rose and Charlotte Kent.)
    "Doorstep Baby"
      M. Bonnell, Ladies
      (*Music by* Michael Cleary. *Lyrics by* Max and Nathaniel Lief. *Staged by* John Boyle.)

Scene 1
  Mr. Healy Produces
Scene 2
  "Sing a Little Jingle"
    E. Norris, T. Monroe, Vale & Stewart, Ensemble
    (*Music by* Harry Warren. *Lyrics by* Mort Dixon.)
Scene 3
  Phil Baker and His Men
    Ted Healy Without His Men
Scene 4
  "I Found a Million Dollar Baby in a Five and Ten Cent Store"
    T. Healy, P. Baker, F. Brice, L. Brice, Ensemble
    (*Music by* Harry Warren. *Lyrics by* Billy Rose and Mort Dixon.)
Scene 5
  Customary Waltz
    Gomez and Winona
Scene 6
  "The Crazy Quilt Sextette"
    (*Music and Lyrics by* Billy Rose and E. Y. Harburg.)
Scene 7
  Mill's Grand Hotel (*by* David Freedman)
    F. Brice, P. Baker, T. Healy, L. Brice, M. Bonnell
Scene 8
  "I Want To Do a Number With the Boys"[99]
    F. Brice, T. Healy, R. Davis, L. Brice, Mr. Healy's Men
    (*Music by* Rowland Wilson. *Lyrics by* Ned Wever.)
Scene 9
  "Under the Clock at the Astor"
    P. Baker
    (*Music by* Manning Sherwin. *Lyrics by* Ned Wever.)
Scene 10
  In a Museum with Mr. Healy (*by* Herman Timberg)
    (T. Healy)
Scene 11
  Mr. Healy Explains
Scene 12
  "In the Merry Month of Maybe"
    E. Norris, T. Monroe, Gomez & Winona, Ensemble
    (*Music by* Harry Warren. *Lyrics by* Ira Gershwin and Billy Rose.)
Scene 13
  "Kept in Suspense"
    P. Baker, Four Little Ladies
    (*Music by* Carroll Gibbons. *Lyrics by* Billy Rose and James Dyrenforth.)
Scene 14
  "Crazy Quilt"
    M. Bonnell, L. Brice, Vale & Stewart, Ensemble
    (*Music by* Harry Warren. *Lyrics by* Bud Green.)
ACT 2
Scene 1
  "Would You Like to Take a Walk?"
    E. Norris, T. Monroe, Ensemble
    (*Music by* Harry Warren. *Lyrics by* Billy Rose and Mort Dixon.)
Scene 2
  Mr. Baker and Tamara
Scene 3
  "Peter Pan"
    F. Brice
    (*Music by* Carroll Gibbons. *Lyrics by* Billy Rose and James Dyrenforth.)
Scene 4
  The "Crazy Quilt" Sextette Again
Scene 5
  Gomez & Winona — Mr. Baker at the Accordion

---

[99]Dropped during the run.

Scene 6

"I Found a Million Dollar Baby in a Five and Ten Cent Store"
(reprise)
Mr. Healy's Men

Scene 7

Strictly Unbearable (*by* David Freedman)
Isabel Paisley, a Southern Girl: F. Brice. *Count Gus de Raviola*, of Italy:
T. Healy.

Scene 8

And Again

Scene 9

Phil Baker, Ted Healy, and Fannie Brice's Brothers

Scene 10

Mr. Healy's Dressing Room (*by* James Dyrenforth and Herman
Timberg.)
T. Healy, P. Baker, B. Davis

Scene 11

1931–1932 SEASON

Tilly Losch in THE BAND WAGON (Photo: Vandamm Studio)
Billy Rose Theatre Collection, New York Public Library for the Performing Arts

1931–1932 SEASON

1931.14 ## THE THIRD LITTLE SHOW

A Musical Revue in Two Acts, 29 Scenes. (Sketches by Noël Coward, S. J. Perelman, Harry Wall, Peter Spencer, Edward Eliscu, Marc Connelly. Lyrics by Max and Nathaniel Lief, Harold Adamson, Earle Crooker, Edward Eliscu, Grace Henry, Noël Coward, Herman Hupfeld, Ted Fetter, Dave Oppenheim, Carl Randall. Music by Michael H. Cleary, Burton Lane, Noël Coward, Henry Sullivan, Ned Lehac [Lehak], Morris Hamilton, Herman Hupfeld, Will Irwin, William (Morgan) Lewis, Jr.) Editing by Edward Eliscu. Staged by Alexander Leftwich. Dances conceived and staged by Dave Gould. Settings by Jo Mielziner. Costumes by Raymond Sovey. Al Goodman Orchestra under the direction of Max Meth. Orchestrations by Howard Jackson. Produced by Dwight Deere Wiman in association with Tom Weatherly. Opened 1 June 1931 at the Music Box Theatre and closed 26 September 1931 after 136 performances.

<u>CAST:</u> BEATRICE LILLIE, ERNEST TRUEX, CONSTANCE CARPENTER, CARL RANDALL, EDWARD ARNOLD, JERRY NORRIS, WALTER O'KEEFE, GERTRUDE MCDONALD, SANDRA GALE, WILLIAM M. GRIFFITH, DOROTHY FITZGIBBON, Jack Riano.

Girls: Louise Allen, Jane Barrett, Gertrude Blake, Maxine Darrell, Kay Devery, Lonita Foster, Frances Gordon, Ruth Gormly, Sara Jane, Julie Jenner, Betty Lee, Martha Maggard, Elaine Mann, Doris Maye, Polly Porter, Kay Riley, Rose Shaw, Dorothy Waller. *Boys*: Milton Brodus, Frank Edmunds, Dick Kirby, Marvin Lawlor, Bob Long, Mickey Ray, Beau Tilden, Jack Voeth, George Weedon.

ACT 1
Scene 1

Meet the Principals

Scene 2

"I'll Putcha Pitcha in the Papers"
Girls, Boys
(*Music by* Michael H. Cleary. *Lyrics by* Max and Nathaniel Lief.)

Scene 3

Cat's Cradle (*by* Noël Coward)
Miss Tassell: B. Lillie. *Mr. Maudsley*: E. Truex.

Scene 4

"Say the Word"
D. Fitzgibbon, J. Norris, Girls, Boys
(*Music by* Burton Lane. *Lyrics by* Harold Adamson.)

Scene 5

Walter O'Keefe

Scene 6

"Mad Dogs and Englishmen"
B. Lillie, Girls, Boys
(*Music and Lyrics by* Noël Coward.)

Scene 7

His Wedding Night[1] (*by* S. J. Perelman)
Announcement: C. Carpenter. *Grimes*: W. O'Keefe. *Maid*: D. Fitzgibbon. *Lord Philbert*: E. Truex. *The Rt. Hon. Harry Bellairs*: J. Norris. *Lady Kitty*: S. Gale. *Lord Melton*: W. M. Griffith.

Scene 8

"Falling in Love"
C. Carpenter, J. Norris
(*Music by* Henry Sullivan. *Lyrics by* Earle Crooker.)

Scene 9

Carl Randall

Scene 10

Sang-froid (*by* Harry Wall)
Miss Hammond: B. Lillie. *Miss Harvey*: C. Carpenter. *La Patronne*: S. Gale. *Un Apache*: C. Randall. *Gigolo*: J. Norris. *Gendarme*: E. Arnold. *Les Autres*: W. M. Griffith, D. Fitzgibbon.

---
[1]Moved to Act 2 during run and replaced by:
The Guest (*by* Marc Connelly)
Mr. Mercer: E. Truex. *Bellboy*: M. Ray. *Assistant Manager*: W. O'Keefe. *Headwaiter*: W. Griffith. *Mr. Pitcairn*: E. Arnold. *Electricians, Waiters, Busboys, etc.*: Boys.

Scene 11

"Going, Going, Gone!"
E. Truex
(*Music by* Henry Sullivan. *Lyrics by* Edward Eliscu.)

Scene 12

"You Forgot Your Gloves"
C. Carpenter, J. Norris, Ensemble
(*Music by* Ned Lehak. *Lyrics by* Edward Eliscu.)

Scene 13

The Late Comer (*by* Peter Spencer)
B. Lillie
Announcement: E. Truex. *Assisted by* W. M. Griffith, D. Fitzgibbon, E. Arnold, J. Norris, G. McDonald, D. Waller, Girls, Boys.

Scene 14

"I've Lost My Heart"
G. McDonald, C. Randall, Boys
(*Music by* Morris Hamilton. *Lyrics by* Grace Henry.)

Scene 15

"When Yuba Plays the Tuba" ("When Yuba Plays the Rhumba on His Tuba")
(*Music and Lyrics by* Herman Hupfeld.) W. O'Keefe

Scene 16

"Sevilla"
B. Lillie
(*Music by* Ned Lehak. *Lyrics by* Edward Eliscu.)

ACT 2
Scene 1

"African Shrieks"
(*Music by* Ned Lehak. *Lyrics by* Edward Eliscu.)
The Director: E. Arnold. *The Hunter*: B. Long. *Bango*: E. Truex. *Fango*: S. Gale. *Chango*: W. O'Keefe. *Rango*: C. Carpenter. *Mango*: J. Riano. *Monkey Specialty*: J. Riano. And the Girls.

Scene 2

Beatrice Lillie (Specialty):
["There Are Fairies at the Bottom of My Garden"
(*Music and Lyrics by* Rose Fyleman and Liza Lehmann.)]

Scene 3

Catchelor-the-Bachelor (*by* Edward Eliscu)
Mother: C. Carpenter. *Child*: E. Truex. *Catchelor-the-Bachelor*: C. Randall. *Maxie-the-Taxi*: W. M. Griffith. *Norman-the-Doorman*: J. Norris. *Ratcheck-the-Hatcheck*: G. McDonald. *Traitor-the-Waiter*: W. O'Keefe. *Toastess-the-Hostess*: S. Gale. *Dorine-the-Chorine*: D. Fitzgibbon.

Scene 4

Walter O'Keefe
["The Man on the Flying Trapeze"
(*Music and Lyrics by* Walter O'Keefe, adapted from the English music hall song by George Leybourne and Alfred Lee.)]

Scene 5

The Traveler (*by* Marc Connelly)
Morton: W. M. Griffith. *Mr. Mercer*: E. Truex. *Mr. Barclay*: E. Arnold.

Scene 6

"You Might As Well Pretend"
J. Norris, C. Carpenter, Girls
(*Music by* William M. Lewis, Jr. *Lyrics by* Edward Eliscu and Ted Fetter.)

Scene 7

"Little Geezer"
(*Music by* Michael H. Cleary. *Lyrics by* Max and Nathaniel Lief, Dave Oppenheim.)
Big Shot: E. Arnold. *Secretary*: D. Fitzgibbon. *Frankie*: W. O'Keefe. *Ida May Tong*: S. Gale. And the Boys.

Scene 8

On the Western Plains (with apologies to Ruth Draper)
B. Lillie

Scene 9

"Le Five O'Clock"
(*Music by* Will Irwin. *Lyrics and Choreography by* Carl Randall.)
He: C. Randall. *She*: G. McDonald. *The Chorus*: Show Girls.

Scene 10

The "Little Show" Boys

Scene 11

"Cinema Lorelei"[2]
B. Lillie, Girls
(*Music by* Ned Lehak. *Lyrics by* Edward Eliscu.)

Scene 12

Walter O'Keefe

Scene 13

Finale
The Company

THE GONDOLIERS,
1931.15   or, The King of Barataria

A Revival of the Comic Opera in Two Acts[3]. Libretto by William S. Gilbert. Music by Arthur Sullivan. Staged by Milton Aborn. Art director, John C. Baatz. Costumes by Eaves. Musical director, Louis Kroll. Produced by the Civic Light Opera Company. Opened 1 June 1931 at Erlanger's Theatre and closed 13 June 1931 after 16 performances; re-opened 11 January 1932 at Erlanger's Theatre and closed 16 January 1932 after 8 performances. Total this season: 24 performances.

<u>CAST:</u> *The Duke of Plaza-Toro*, a Grandee of Spain: FRANK MOULAN. *Luiz*, His Attendant: DUDSWORTH FRASER. *Don Alhambra Del Bolero*, the Grand Inquisitor: WILLIAM DANFORTH. *Four Venetian Gondoliers: Marco Palmieri:* HOWARD MARSH. *Giuseppe Palmieri:* JOSEPH MACAULEY. *Antonio:* BOBBY FULLER. *Francesco:* Sano Marco. *The Duchess of Plaza-Toro:* VERA ROSS. *Casilda,* Her Daughter: RUTH ALTMAN. *Five Contadine: Gianetta:* DOROTHY SEEGAR. *Tessa:* CECILIA BRANZ. *Fiametta:* Frances Moore. *Vittoria:* Mabel Thompson. *Giulia:* Rosalind Shaw. *Inez,* the King's Foster Mother: Belle Flower.
Chorus of Gondoliers, Contadine, etc.: Frances Moore, Olga Schumacher, Rosalyn Shaw, Patricia Clark, Florence Little, Edith Artley, Eleanor Gilmore, Gertrude Waldon, Frances Baviello, Margaret Bickel, Mabel Thompson, Flora Bell, Helen Hosp, Isabel Norwood, Belle Flower, Rosa Rubenstein, Mary Joe Matthews, Georgina Dieter, Marie Pittman. Charles Froom, Edward Taylor, Bert Melrose, Hobson Young, Charles Maduro, Edward Lambert, Felix Noonan, Allan Ware, Frank Murray, Martin Lilienfield, Frank Dowling, Harrison Fuller.

THE BAND WAGON
1931.16

A Musical Revue in Two Acts, 23 Scenes. Sketches by George S. Kaufman and Howard Dietz. Lyrics by Howard Dietz. Music by Arthur Schwartz. Staged by Hassard Short. Dances by Albertina Rasch. Settings by Albert R. Johnson. Costumes by Kiviette, Constance Ripley. Music director, Al Goodman. Orchestrations by (Robert) Russell Bennett. Production supervised by Howard Dietz. Produced by Max Gordon in asssociation with Erlanger Productions, Inc.. Opened 3 June 1931 at the New Amsterdam Theatre and closed 16 January 1932 after 260 performances.

<u>CAST:</u> FRED ASTAIRE, ADELE ASTAIRE, FRANK MORGAN, HELEN BRODERICK, TILLY LOSCH, PHILIP LOEB, JOHN BARKER, ROBERTA ROBINSON, FRANCES PIERLOT, JAY WILSON, PETER CHAMBERS, HELEN CARRINGTON, Ed Jerome.
Girls: Joey Benton, Topsy Humphries, Marcia Sweet, Nona Otero, Carol Renwick, Ruth Sproule, Evelyn Nichols, Alice Kellerman, Lillian Duncan, Virginia Allen, Florence Chumbecas, Catherine Laughlin, Phyllis Cameron, Dorothy Dodd, Virginia Whitmore, Gracea Fleming, Marjorie Baglin, Wilma Roelof, Helene Shepard, Marcelle Edwards. *Boys:* Ward A. Tallman, James Lee, Albert Amato, Buddy Irwin, Roy Santos, Leon Alton, Jack Douglas, Gilbert White, Vernon Hammer, James Cushman, Harold Voeth.

ACT 1

Scene 1

As Others See Us: "It Better Be Good"
(Entire Company)

Scene 2

"Sweet Music"
F. Astaire, A. Astaire

Scene 3

"High and Low"
R. Robinson, J. Barker, Girls

---

[2]Dropped during the run.
[3]Originally presented in New York 7 January 1890 at Park Theatre for 103 performances. For Synopsis of Scenes and Musical Numbers, see original 1890 production.

Scene 4

When the Rain Goes Pitter Patter
F. Morgan, H. Broderick

Scene 5

"The Flag" (Dance)
T. Losch

Scene 6

For Good Old Nectar
A. Astaire, R. Robinson, F. Morgan, J. Wilson, P. Loeb, F. Pierlot, F. Astaire, J. Barker, others

Scene 7

"A Nice Place to Visit"
H. Broderick

Scene 8

"Hoops"
F. Astaire, A. Astaire

Scene 9

"Confession"
Girls, Boys

Scene 10

The Pride of the Claghornes
Scene: The living room in the home of the Claghornes, in Virginia.
Jasper: P. Loeb. *Col. Jefferson Claghorne:* F. Morgan. *Sarah,* his wife: H. Broderick. *Breeze,* their daughter: A. Astaire. *Simpson Carter:* F. Astaire. *Ely Carter:* F. Pierlot. *Martin Carter:* J. Wilson.

Scene 11

"New Sun in the Sky"
F. Astaire

Scene 12

"(What's the Use of Being) Miserable With You"
A. Astaire, F. Morgan
(Miserable With You monologue)
(F. Morgan)

Scene 13

"I Love Louisa"
F. Astaire, A. Astaire, Company

ACT 2

Scene 1

Again!
P. Loeb, J. Wilson, P. Chambers

Scene 2

"Dancing in the Dark"
J. Barker
Danced by T. Losch, Girls.

Scene 3

"Nanette"
F. Morgan, P. Loeb, F. Pierlot, P. Chambers

Scene 4

The Great Warburton Mystery
Scene: Library in the home of Hugh Warburton.
Ivy Meredith: A. Astaire. *Inspector Cartwright:* F. Morgan. *Mrs. Boule:* H. Carrington. *Mr. Boule:* E. Jerome. *Miss Hutton:* R. Robinson. *Mr. Dodd:* P. Chambers. *Mr. Wallace:* J. Barker. *Walker:* P. Loeb. *First Policeman:* J. Wilson. *Second Policeman:* L. Alton. *The Murdered Man* (Warburton): F. Pierlot.

Scene 5

"Where Can He Be?"
H. Broderick, Boys

Scene 6

"The Beggar Waltz" (Dance)
T. Losch, F. Astaire, Ensemble

Scene 7

P.S.
F. Morgan

Scene 8

"White Heat"
F. Astaire, A. Astaire, Ensemble

Scene 9

Pour Le Bain

Scene: The Showroom of the Eclipse Tile and Marble Company.
Mr. Prescott: H. Broderick. *Mr. Knipper*: J. Barker. *Mr. Cadwallader*: F. Pierlot.
An Attendant: E. Jerome. *The Demonstrator*: F. Astaire. *Mr. Leftwich*: P. Loeb.

Scene 10

Five Star Finale

(Entire Company)

PATIENCE,
or Bunthorne's Bride

1931.17

A Revival of the Comic Opera in Two Acts[4]. Libretto by William S. Gilbert. Music by Arthur Sullivan. Staged by Milton Aborn. Art director, John C. Baatz. Costumes by Eaves. Musical director, Louis Kroll. Produced by the Civic Light Opera Company. Opened 15 June 1931 at Erlanger's Theatre and closed 27 June 1931 after 16 performances.

CAST: *Colonel Calverley*: WILLIAM DANFORTH. *Major Murgatroyd*: WILLIAM C. GORDON. *Lieut. The Duke of Dunstable*: HOWARD MARSH. *Reginald Bunthorne*: FRANK MOULAN. *Archibald Grosvenor*: JOSEPH MACAULEY. *The Lady Agatha*: DENE DICKENS. *The Lady Saphir*: Frances Moore. *The Lady Ella*: SARAH BAIR. *The Lady Jane*: ANNE YAGO. *Patience*: VIVIAN HART.

Chorus of Rapturous Maidens and Dragoons: Olga Schumacher, Rosalyn Shaw, Patricia Clark, Florence Little, Edith Artley, Eleanor Gilmore, Gertrude Waldon, Frances Baviello, Margaret Bickel, Mabel Thompson, Flora Bell, Helen Hosp, Isabel Norwood, Belle Flower, Rosa Rubenstein, Mary Joe Matthews, Georgina Dieter, Marie Pittman, Marynia Apel, Julia Reid, Adele Story, Charlotte LaRose. Charles Froom, Edward Taylor, Bert Melrose, Hobson Young, Charles Maduro, Edward Lambert, Felix Noonan, Allan Ware, Frank Murray, Martin Lilienfield, Frank Dowling, Harrison Fuller, Alphonso Iglesias, Francis Clark, Ramon Recalde, John Cardini, Bernard Lane, Lee Talbot.

THE PIRATES OF PENZANCE,
or The Slave of Duty

1931.18

A Revival of the Comic Opera in Two Acts[5]. Libretto by William S. Gilbert. Music by Arthur Sullivan. Staged by Milton Aborn. Art director, John C. Baatz. Costumes by Eaves. Musical director, Louis Kroll. Produced by the Civic Light Opera Company. Opened 29 June 1931 at Erlanger's Theatre and closed 11 July 1931 after 16 performances; re-opened 19 October 1931 at Erlanger's Theatre and closed 24 October 1931 after 8 performances. Total this season: 24 performances.

CAST: *Richard*, The Pirate King: HERBERT L. WATEROUS. *Samuel*, His Lieutenant: SANO MARCO. *Frederic*, a Pirate Apprentice: HOWARD MARSH. *Major-General Stanley* of the British Army: FRANK MOULAN. *Edward*, a Sergeant of Police: WILLIAM DANFORTH. *General Stanley's Daughters (4)*: *Mabel*: VIVIAN HART. *Edith*: FRANCES MOORE. *Kate*: GEORGINA DIETER. *Isabel*: Frances Baviello. *Ruth*, a Piratical Maid of All Work: ANNE YAGO.

Chorus of General Stanley's Daughters and Pirates, Policemen: Olga Schumacher, Rosalyn Shaw, Patricia Clark, Edith Artley, Eleanor Gilmore, Gertrude Waldon, Mabel Thompson, Helen Hosp, Isabel Norwood, Rosa Rubenstein, Mary Joe Matthews, Marie Pittman, Marynia Apel, Julia Reid, Adele Story, Charlotte LaRose. Edward Taylor, Bert Melrose, Hobson Young, Felix Noonan, Allan Ware, Frank Murray, Martin Lilienfield, Frank Dowling, Harrison Fuller, Francis Clark, Ramon Recalde, John Cardini, Bernard Lane, Lee Talbot.

ZIEGFELD FOLLIES OF 1931

1931.19

A Musical Revue in Two Acts, 22 Scenes[6]. Assembled by Florenz Ziegfeld. Sketches by Mark Hellinger, J. P. Murray, Gene Buck. Lyrics by Gene Buck, Joseph McCarthy, Charles Farrell, Mack Gordon, J. P. Murray, Barry Trivers, E. Y. Harburg, Jack Norworth, Noël Coward. Music by Harry Revel,

Ben Oakland, Dave Stamper, Dimitri Tiomkin, Noël Coward, Nora Bayes, James Monaco, Chick Endor, Walter Donaldson, Jay Gorney, Hugo Riesenfeld. (Staged by Florenz Ziegfeld, Gene Buck.) Dialogue staged by Edward Clarke Lilley. Dances staged by Bobby Connolly, Albertina Rasch. Settings by Joseph Urban. Costumes by John Harkrider. Music director, Oscar Bradley. Orchestrations by Maurice DePackh, Will Vodery, Howard Jackson, Joe Jordan. Produced by Florenz Ziegfeld. Opened 1 July 1931 at the Ziegfeld Theatre and closed 21 November 1931 after 165 performances.

CAST: HARRY RICHMAN, HELEN MORGAN, RUTH ETTING, JACK PEARL, HAL LE ROY, MITZI MAYFAIR, ALBERT CARROLL, FAITH BACON, CLIFF HALL, Gladys Glad, Frank and Milt Britton and Their Gang, Pearl Osgood, (Ford) Buck and (John) Bubbles, Arthur Campbell, Dorothy Dell, Leonard Stokes, Milton Le Roy, Earl Oxford, The Collette Sisters (Ruth And Mildred), Ethel Borden, John Daly Murphy, Reri, Netta Deuschateau, Anne Lee Patterson, Lena Thomas, Kay English, Dorothy Dell, George Lamar, Gene Gory.

Girls: Marjorie Levoe, Dorothy Dodge, Georgia Ellis, Grace Moore, Yvonne Grey, Ruth K. Patterson, Christine Maple, Joan Burgess, Betty Dumbris, Blanche Satchel, Dorothy Flood, Frieda Mierse, Eileen Wenzel, Barbara Smith, Pearl Harris, Virginia Biddle, Betty Real, Cassie Hanley, Vera Milton, Mildred Borst, Olive McLay, Bernice Roberts, Sunny Trowbridge, Iris Adrian, Billie Cortez, Jean Audree, Caja Eric, Lorelle McCarver, Alice Burrage, Catherine Clark, Emmita Casanova, Eunice Holmes, Helen Walsh, Billie Seward, Marie Stevens, Jean Howard, Katherine Burke, Boots Mallory, Mary Alice Rice, Vivian Porter, Patsy O'Day, Helen Hannan, Rosa Fronson. *Boys*: Jack Bruns, John Gurney, George Lamar, Ernest McChesney, William Royal, Conrad Sparin, Joseph Toner, Russell Johns, Thomas Arace, Jack Arthur, David Drollet, Tom Kendall, Frank Lang, Herschel Martin, Robert Walker, Dennis McCurtin, Billy Hughes, Jim Moore, Robert White, Paul Gursdorf, Gordon Carper, Robert Baldwin, Frank McCormack. *Albertina Rasch Dancers*: Dorissa Nelova, Rose Gale, Marguerite Eisele, Helen Carson, Clayton Estes, Marguerite Durand, Virginia Bethel, Marjorie McLaughlin.

ACT 1[7]

Scene 1

Opening—The Spirit of the Follies

F. Bacon

"Bring on the Follies Girls"

(*Music by* Dave Stamper. *Lyrics by* Gene Buck.)
The Follies Girl of 1931: G. Glad.

"Help Yourself to Happiness"

H. Richman
(*Music by* Harry Revel. *Lyrics by* Mack Gordon.)

Scene 2

Grand Hotel[8] (*by* Mark Hellinger)

Doctor Crechsen in the lobby for years: D. Murphy. *Beigle*, a dying youth: L. Stokes. *Polly Adlervitch*, Queen of the Russian Ballet: H. Morgan. *Alphonso Smith*, late King of Gibraltar: M. LeRoy. *Baron Al Capone*, from Chicago: H. Richman. *Cecil B. Goldwarner* of Hollywood: J. Pearl. *Morosco*, Secretary to Alphonso: E. Oxford. *Hotel Room Clerk*: C. Hall. *Doorman*: C. Sparin. *Elevator Attendant*: J. Gurney. *Capone's Men*: J. Bruns, F. Lang, W. Royal, R. Johns. *Bellhops*: T. Arace, A. Samish. *'Stooge' Bellhop*: H. Martin. *Guests*.

Scene 3

"Sunny Southern Smile"

E. Oxford, Girls, Boys
(*Music by* Harry Revel. *Lyrics by* Mack Gordon.)
Danced by H. LeRoy, Collette Sisters.

Scene 4

Frank and Milt Britton and Their 'Gang,' with G. Gory and Tito.

Scene 5

Impressions by Albert Carroll

Scene 6

"Fandango—Bolero" (Dance)

Albertina Rasch Dancers
(*Music by* Dmitri Tiomkin.)

---

[4]First presented in New York 22 September 1881 at the Standard Theatre for 177 performances. For Synopsis of Scenes and Musical Numbers, see original 1881 production.

[5]First presented in New York 31 December 1879 at the Fifth Avenue Theatre for 91 performances in two engagements. For Synopsis of Scenes and Musical Numbers, see original 1879 production

[6]The 21st in the annual series of musical revues produced by Florenz Ziegfeld, and the last produced under his personal supervision; the series began in 1907.

---

[7]Added to Act 1 during run:

The Stork

H. Richman, G. Glad, C. Hall, R. Collette
Interpolated specialty during the run:

"I'm Good For Nothing But Love"

R. Etting
(*Music by* Bernard Maltin. *Lyrics by* Pat Ballard.)

[8]Burlesque of the Broadway play by Vicki Baum.

Scene 7

Singapore Song: "Half-Caste Woman"[9]
H. Morgan
(*Music and Lyrics by* Noël Coward.)

Scene 8

Broadway Reverie(*by* Gene Buck and Mark Hellinger)
A. *Scene One*: A Penthouse.
Reception to Hostess: E. Borden. *Miss Universe*: N. Deuschateau
(of Belgium). *Miss U.S.*: A. L. Patterson. *Miss Memphis*: L. Thomas.
Winners of First, Second and Third Prize at Galveston Beauty Contest,
June 14, 1931.
Frank Jordon: H. Richman. *Hal Jackson*: H. LeRoy. *Jack Williams*:
L. Stokes.
"Broadway Reverie"
H. Richman
(*Music by* Dave Stamper. *Lyrics by* Gene Buck.)
B. *Scene Two*: 'Rectors' before Prohibition.
Sam Bernard: J. Pearl. *Diamond Jim Brady*: D. Drollet. *Lillian
Russell*: F. Mierse. *'Brinkley Girl'*: E. Wenzel. *Nora Bayes*: R. Etting.
Jack Norworth: E. Oxford. *Hazel Dawn*: K. English. *Al Jolson*:
H. Richman. *Guests*: M. Levoe, D. Dodge, G. Ellis, G. Moore, Y. Grey,
R. Patterson, C. Maple, J. Burgess, B. Dumbris, B. Satchell, D. Flood,
F. McCormack, R. Johns, J. Gurney, J. Arthur, T. Arace, J. Toner, E.
McChesney. *Head Waiter*: C. Hall. *First Waiter*: J. Bruns. *Second
Waiter*: H. Martin.
"Pink Lady" Waltz (Violin Solo) (from *THE PINK LADY*)
K. English
(*Music by* Ivan Caryll.)
"(Shine On) Harvest Moon" (from *ZIEGFELD FOLLIES OF 1908*)
R. Etting
(*Music by* Jack Norworth and Nora Bayes. *Lyrics by* Jack Norworth.)
"(Who Paid the Rent for Mrs.) Rip Van Winkle"[10]
(*Music by* Alfred Bryan. *Lyrics by* Fred Fisher.) J. Pearl (as Sam Bernard)
"You Made Me Love You"[11]
H. Richman
(*Music by* James V. Monaco. *Lyrics by* Joseph McCarthy.)
C. *Scene Three*: Leonard Stokes and Hal LeRoy.
D. *Scene Four*: In the Club Piccadilly during Prohibition.
Cigarette Girl: R. Etting. *Jackie Jean*: A. Carroll. *Miss Universe*:
D. Dell. *'Heckler'*: A. Campbell. *Hal Jackson*: H. LeRoy. *Jack Williams*:
L. Stokes. *A Drunk*: J. D. Murphy. *First Gangster Leader*: C. Hall.
Second Gangster Leader: J. Toner. *Gangsters*: W. Royal, C. Sparin,
J. Bruns, R. Walker, D. McCurtin. *Butch*: B. Hughes. *Head Captain*:
J. Moore. *Captain*: G. Lamar. *Dancers*: B. Smith, P. Harris, V. Biddle,
B. Real, C. Hanley, V. Milton, M. Borst, O. McLay, B. Roberts,
S. Trowbridge, I. Adrian, B. Cortez. *Guests*: C. Eric, E. Wenzel, L. McCarver,
A. Burrage, C. Clark, E, Casanova, E. Holmes, H. Walsh, B. Steward,
M. Stevens, J. Howard, R. Johns, E. McChesney, R. Walker, T. Arace,
H. Martin, M. LeRoy, G. Gory. *Waiters*: F. Lang, T. Kendall, B. White,
P. Gursdorff, G. Carper, R. Baldwin.
Dance
(*Music by* Harry Revel and Mack Gordon.)
Collette Sisters
"Was I (Drunk)"
D. Dell
(*Music by* Chick Endor. *Lyrics by* Charles Farrell.)
Dance
M. Mayfair
"Cigarettes, Cigars"
R. Etting
(*Music by* Harry Revel. *Lyrics by* Mack Gordon.)

Scene 9

"I'm With You"
H. Morgan, H. Richman
(*Music and Lyrics by* Walter Donaldson.)

Scene 10

In Dutch
J. Pearl, C. Hall

Scene 11

Finale: "Doing the New York"
H. Richman
(*Music by* Ben Oakland. *Lyrics by* J. P. Murray, Barry Trivers.)
Scene: Streets of New York, Empire (State) Building.

ACT 2

Scene 1

"Legend of the Islands"
T. Arace, J. Arthur, J. Bruns, D. Drollett, J. Gurney, R. Johns, T. Kendall, F.
Lang, G. Lamar, M. LeRoy, H. Martin, E. McChesney, E. Oxford, W. Royal,
C. Sparin, L. Stokes, J. Toner, R. Wacker
(*Music and Lyrics by* Powell and Stevens.)
Tom Tom Dance (*Music by* Dmitri Tiomkin.)
Albertina Rasch Dancers
Scene: The Jungle.
The Queen: G. Glad. With M. Levoe, D. Flood, G. Moore, E. Wenzel,
F. Bacon, K. Burke, B. Mallory, V. Biddle.

Scene 2

"Clinching the Sale"
H. Richman
(*Music by* Ben Oakland. *Lyrics by* J. P. Murray and Barry Trivers.)
The Customer: D. Dell. *Whisk Broom*: F. Bacon. *Floor Broom*: K. Burke.
Finger Brush: G. Moore. *Bath Brush*: B. Mallory. *Scrubbing Brush*: M. Levoe.
Floor Mop: B. Seward. *Dusters*: V. Milton, B. Smith, B. Real, M. A. Rice,
V. Porter, P. O'Day, H. Hannan, R. Fromson. *Boys*: L. Stokes, R. Johns,
E. McChesney.

Scene 3

"Dance Away the Night" (Dance)
M. Mayfair
(*Music by* Dave Stamper.)

Scene 4

The Africans Had a Word For It (*by* Mark Hellinger)
Scene: In Africa.
Judge Crater Horn: J. Pearl. *Rumba, a Servant*: J. Bubbles. *Ravioli, Son of Horn's
Oldest Friend*: H. Richman. *Beautiful White Goddess*: G. Glad.

Scene 5

The Picture Bride (*by* Gene Buck)
(*Music by* Dave Stamper and Dr. Hugo Reisenfeld.)
Scene: At the Pier. *Lena*: R. Etting. *Amiel Spiegal*: J. Pearl.

Scene 6

"Mailu"[12]
A. Campbell
(*Music by* Jay Gorney. *Lyrics by* E. Y. Harburg.)
Scene: South Sea Islands.

Scene 7

"Changing of the Guards"
J. Bruns, J. Gurney, G. Lamar, E. McChesney, E. Oxford, W. Royal,
C. Sparin, L. Stokes, J. Toner, R. Walker
(*Music by* Ben Oakland. *Lyrics by* J. P. Murray, Barry Trivers.)
Scene: Buckingham Palace. *Danced by* H. LeRoy, M. Mayfair,
The Follies Girls.

Scene 8

"Victim of the Talkies"
(*Music by* Ben Oakland. *Lyrics by* J. P. Murray and Barry Trivers.)
Romney Renaldo: G. Lamar. *Louella, his wife*: H. Morgan.
Julius McQuiff, the director: J. Pearl. *Joe Eppes, his assistant*: G. Gory.
Maid: H. Hannon.

Scene 9

"Illusion in White" (Dance)
Albertina Rasch Dancers
(*Music by* Dmitri Tiomkin.)

Scene 10

In Harlem
Buck and Bubbles

Scene 11

Finale: "Help Yourself to Happiness" (reprise)
Entire Company
Scene: Near Central Park.

---

[9]Dropped during run.
[10]Though first interpolated by Al Jolson into THE HONEYMOON
EXPRESS (1913), Jack Pearl's impression was of Sam Bernard's rendition
of the song in THE BELLE OF BOND STREET (1914).
[11]A staple of Al Jolson's repertory.

---

[12]Dropped during run.

IOLANTHE,
1931.20
or The Peer and the Peri

A Revival of the Comic Opera in Two Acts[13]. Libretto by William S. Gilbert. Music by Arthur Sullivan. Staged by Milton Aborn. Sets from the Winthrop Ames revival of 1926. Art director, John C. Baatz. Costumes by Eaves. Musical director, Louis Kroll. Produced by the Civic Light Opera Company. Opened 13 July 1931 at Erlanger's Theatre and closed 25 July 1931 after 16 performances; re-opened 4 January 1932 at Erlanger's Theatre and closed 9 January 1932 after 8 performances. Total this season: 24 performances.

CAST: *The Lord Chancellor*: FRANK MOULAN. *Earl of Mountararat*: FREDRICK PERSSON. *Earl of Tolloler*: HOWARD MARSH. *Private Willis*: HERBERT L. WATEROUS. *Strephon*: JOSEPH MACAULEY. *Queen of the Fairies*: VERA ROSS. *Iolanthe*: DENE DICKENS. *Celia*: Georgina Dieter. *Leila*: Gertrude Waldon. *Fleta*: Eleanor Gilmore. *Phyllis*: VIVIAN HART.

Chorus of Fairies, Dukes, Marquises, Earls, Viscounts, Lords, Barons, Peers: Olga Schumacher, Rosalyn Shaw, Patricia Clark, Edith Artley, Eleanor Gilmore, Gertrude Waldon, Frances Baviello, Mabel Thompson, Helen Hosp, Isabel Norwood, Rosa Rubenstein, Mary Joe Matthews, Marie Pittman, Marynia Apel, Julia Reid, Adele Story, Charlotte LaRose, Bert Melrose, Hobson Young, Felix Noonan, Allen Ware, Frank Murray, Martin Lilienfield, Frank Dowling, Harrison Fuller, Francis Clark, John Cardini, Bernard Lane, Harold Raymond, Caroll Godwin, Patrick Quinton.

SHOOT THE WORKS!
1931.21

A Musical Revue in Two Acts, 33 Scenes. (Assembled by Heywood Broun and Milton Raison.) Dialogue mainly by Nunnally Johnson. Sketches by Heywood Broun, Nunnally Johnson, Peter Arno, E. B. White, Sig Herzig, Milton Lazarus, Jack Hazzard, Edward J. MacNamara, (H. I. Phillips, Dorothy Parker). Music by Irving Berlin, Michael H. Cleary, Jimmy McHugh, Ann Ronell, Robert Stolz, Jay Gorney, Vernon Duke, Philip Charig, Joseph Meyer. Lyrics by Nathaniel and Max Lief, Dorothy Fields, E. Y. Harburg, Leo Robin, Ira Gershwin, Irving Berlin, Walter Reisch, Armin Robinson. Dialogue directed by Ted [Theodore] Hammerstein. Dances by Johnny Boyle. Settings and lighting by Henry Dreyfuss. Costumes by Charles LeMaire, Kiviette. Music director, Harry Archer. Orchestrations by Frank Barry, King Ross. Produced by Heywood Broun in association with Milton Raison. Opened 21 July 1931 at the George M. Cohan Theatre and closed 3 October 1931 after 87 performances.

CAST: HEYWOOD BROUN, GEORGE MURPHY, WILLIAM O'NEAL, JACK HAZZARD, JOHNNY BOYLE, IMOGENE COCA, FRANCES DEWEY, AL GOLD, BOBBY GILLETTE, LEE BRODY, JULIE JOHNSON, TAYLOR GORDON, FRANCES NEVINS, Margot Riley, Edward J. MacNamara, Virginia Smith, Percy Helton, Lela Manor, Lila Manor, Edgar Nelson.

Girls: Rose Armand, Alice Bankert, Evelyn Carpenter, Margaret Doncaster, Jerry Downes, Madelyn Eubanks, Mae Rena Grady, Frances Guinan, Irene Kelly, Constance Madison, Lela and Lila Manor, Vida Manuel, Dolly Martinez, Nellie Mayer, Leslyn Miller, Frances Nevins, Nora Puntin, Inez Purdy, Dorothy Snowden, Marjorie Sohmer, Winnie Turner, Helen Tuttle, Florence Winkel. *Boys*: Frank Ericson, Mickey Forbes, J. Gonzales, Frank Hauser, Jack Irwin, Albert Jordan, Tom Jordan, Joe Kay, Don Lannon, James Libby, John McAvoy, Edward Murray, James Notarro, Jack Ray, Jerry Reardon. *Singers*: Cornelia Chason, Fanille Davies, John Muccio, Dick Neely, Lester Ostrander, Anne Stanley, Morris Tepper.

ACT 1

Scene 1

Opening
J. Boyle, H. Broun, Ensemble

Scene 2

Selecting the Songs (*by* Nunnally Johnson)
G. Murphy, H. Broun, J. Hazzard, J. Boyle, I. Coca
At the pianos: M. H. Cleary, R. O'Brien.
"In the Stars" and "Taken for a Ride"
(*Music by* Michael H. Cleary. *Lyrics by* Max and Nathaniel Lief.)

Scene 3

"How's Your Uncle?"
A. Gold, F. Dewey, Boys, Girls
(*Music by* Jimmy McHugh. *Lyrics by* Dorothy Fields.)

Scene 4

In the Dressing Room
H. Broun, E. J. MacNamara

Scene 5

"Shoulders"
T. Gordon
(*Music and Lyrics by* Alexander Williams and Herbert Goode.)

Scene 6

Turtle Bay Drovers' and Breeders' Social Club[14]
Proprietor: J. Hazzard. *Man About Town*: H. Broun. *Cornelius Swaggerbilt*: P. Helton. *A Girl About Town*: L. Brody. *A Customer*: E. Nelson. *Slit-throat McGillicuddy*: G. Murphy.
"Back in Circulation Again"
(*Music by* Michael H. Cleary. *Lyrics by* Max and Nathaniel Lief.)

Scene 7

"I Want to Chisel in on Your Heart"
G. Murphy, J. Johnson
(*Music by* Michael H. Cleary. *Lyrics by* Max and Nathaniel Lief.)

Scene 8

Lo, the Poor Doctor (*by* E. B. White and Sig Herzig)
Mrs. Coe: M. Riley. *Mr. Coe*: P. Helton. *Miss Straight*: L. Brody. *Dr. Fenway*: W. O'Neal. *Dr. Campbell*: E. Nelson.

Scene 9

"(I'm Just a) Doorstep Baby"
F. Dewey, Girls, Boys
(*Music by* Michael H. Cleary. *Lyrics by* Max and Nathaniel Lief.)

Scene 10

Heywood Broun

Scene 11

"(Let's Go) Out in the Open Air"
B. Gillette (Banjo), I. Coca
(*Music and Lyrics by* Ann Ronell and Muriel Pollock.)

Scene 12

The Radiomaniac
Otto K. Attelbury: J. Hazzard. *His Daughters*: L. Brody, M. Riley.

Scene 13

"Das Lied ist aus" (from German film of the same name)
(Don't Ask Me Why)
W. O'Neal, Ensemble
(*Music by* Robert Stolz. *(German) Lyrics by* Walter Reisch and Armin Robinson. *English lyrics by* Joe Young.)

Scene 14

Johnny Boyle, introduced by Heywood Broun

Scene 15

Finale: "Pie in the Sky"
Entire Company
(*Music by* Michael H. Cleary. *Lyrics by* Max and Nathaniel Lief.)

ACT 2

Scene 1

"Muchacha"
F. Nevins, Girls, Boys
(*Music by* Jay Gorney and Vernon Duke. *Lyrics by* E. Y. Harburg.)

Scene 2

You Were Perfectly Fine[15] (*by* Dorothy Parker)
A. Gold, V. Smith

Scene 3

"The First Lady of the Land"
L. Brody
(*Music by* Michael H. Cleary. *Lyrics by* Max and Nathaniel Lief.)

Scene 4

Heywood Broun Again

Scene 5

Johnny Boyle

---

[13]First presented in New York 25 November 1882 at the Standard Theatre for 105 performances. For Synopsis of Scenes and Musical Numbers, see original 1882 production.

---

[14]Dropped during run.
[15]Dropped during run.

Scene 6

"Hot Moonlight"
W. O'Neal, Ensemble
(*Music by* Jay Gorney. *Lyrics by* E. Y. Harburg.)

Scene 7

"I Want to Chisel in on Your Heart" (reprise)
H. Broun, Lela and Lila Manor, J. Downs, M. Sohmer

Scene 8

Another Triangle
The Man: P. Helton. *The Wife*: L. Brody. *The Lover*: J. Hazzard. *The Waiter*: A. Bloom.

Scene 9

"(Just) Begging for Love"
G. Murphy, J. Johnson
(*Music and Lyrics by* Irving Berlin.)

Scene 10

Death Says It Isn't So[16] (*by* Heywood Broun)
The Patient: P. Helton. *The Nurse*: M. Riley. *The Doctor*: E. Nelson. *The Visitor*: E. J. MacNamara.

Scene 11

"My Heart's a Banjo"
B. Gillette, I. Coca, Girls
(*Music by* Jay Gorney. *Lyrics by* E. Y. Harburg.)

Scene 12

Believe It or Not (*by* Milton Lazarus and Sig Herzig)
P. Helton, F. Dewey, B. Gillette

Scene 13

"Do As You Like" (Do What You Like)
G. Murphy, J. Johnson, Boys, Girls
(*Music by* Philip Charig. *Lyrics by* Leo Robin.)

Scene 14

Still More Broun

Scene 15

The Light-Ups[17] (*Suggested by* Sig Herzig and Peter Arno)

Scene 16

Park Avenue[18] (*by* H. I. Phillips)
Fifi: V. Smith. *Herman*: E. Nelson.

Scene 17

"Chirp Chirp"
A. Gold, F. Dewey, Ensemble
(*Music by* Philip Charig and Joseph Meyer. *Lyrics by* Ira Gershwin.)

Scene 18

Finale
Entire Company

TRIAL BY JURY

1931.22

A Revival of the Comic Opera in One Act[19]. Libretto by William S. Gilbert. Music by Arthur Sullivan. Staged by Milton Aborn. Art director, John C. Baatz. Costumes by Eaves. Musical director, Louis Kroll. Revived by the Civic Light Opera Company. Opened 27 July 1931 at Erlanger's Theatre and closed 8 August 1931 after 16 performances.

CAST: *The Learned Judge*: FRANK MOULAN. *Foreman of the Jury*: FREDERICK PERSSON. *The Defendant*: HOWARD MARSH. *Counsel*: JOSEPH MACAULEY. *Usher*: WILLIAM DANFORTH. *Plaintiff*: THEO PENNINGTON.
Chorus of Jurymen, Bridesmaids and Public: Bert Melrose, Hobson Young, Felix Noonan, Allan Ware, Frank Murray, Martin Lilienfield, Frank Dowling, Harrison Fuller, Francis Clark, John Cardini, Bernard Lane, Patrick Quinton. Frances Moore, Olga Schumacher, Rosalyn Shaw, Patricia Clark, Gertrude Waldon, Frances Baviello, Mabel Thompson, Isabel Norwood, Rosa Rubenstein, Mary Joe Matthews, Marynia Apel, Adele Story, Harriet Gottlieb, Marie Kelley, Lillian Koniver, Katherine Calle, Mary Harper. followed by

---

[16]Dropped during run.
[17]Dropped during run.
[18]Dropped during run.
[19]First presented in New York 15 November 1875 at the Eagle Theatre for 8 performances. For Synopsis of Scenes and Musical Numbers, see original 1875 production.

H.M.S. PINAFORE,
1931.23   or The Lass That Loved a Sailor

A Revival of the Comic Opera in Two Acts[20]. Libretto by William S. Gilbert. Music by Arthur Sullivan. Staged by Milton Aborn. Art director, John C. Baatz. Costumes by Eaves. Musical director, Louis Kroll. Revived by the Civic Light Opera Company. Opened 27 July 1931 at Erlanger's Theatre and closed 8 August 1931 after 16 performances.

CAST: *The Rt. Hon. Sir Joseph Porter, K.C.B.*, First Lord of the Admiralty: FRANK MOULAN. *Captain Corcoran*, Commander of the *H.M.S. Pinafore*: JOSEPH MACAULEY. *Ralph Rackstraw*, Able Seaman: HOWARD MARSH. *Dick Deadeye*, Able Seaman: WILLIAM DANFORTH. *Bill Bobstay*, Boatswain: Frederick Persson. *Josephine*, the Captain's Daughter: THEO PENNINGTON. *Little Buttercup*, Mrs. Cripps, a Portsmouth bum-boat woman: FAY TEMPLETON. *Hebe*, Sir Joseph's First Cousin: Ethel Clark. *Mid-Ship Mite*: Joseph Ruggiero.
Sailors, First Lord's Sisters, His Cousins, His Aunts: Bert Melrose, Hobson Young, Felix Noonan, Allan Ware, Frank Murray, Martin Lilienfield, Frank Dowling, Harrison Fuller, Francis Clark, John Cardini, Bernard Lane, Patrick Quinton. Frances Moore, Olga Schumacher, Rosalyn Shaw, Patricia Clark, Gertrude Waldon, Frances Baviello, Mabel Thompson, Isabel Norwood, Rosa Rubenstein, Mary Joe Matthews, Marynia Apel, Adele Story, Harriet Gottlieb, Marie Kelley, Lillian Koniver, Katherine Calle, Mary Harper.

RUDDIGORE,
1931.24   or The Witch's Curse

A Revival of the Comic Opera in Two Acts[21]. Libretto by William S. Gilbert. Music by Arthur Sullivan. Staged by Milton Aborn. Art director, John C. Baatz. Costumes by Eaves. Musical director, Louis Kroll. Revived by the Civic Light Opera Company. Opened 10 August 1931 at Erlanger's Theatre and closed 22 August 1931 after 16 performances.

CAST: *Robin Oakapple*: FRANK MOULAN. *Richard Dauntless*: CRAIG CAMPBELL. *Sir Despard Murgatroyd*: WILLIAM DANFORTH. *Old Adam Goodheart*: Sano Marco. *Rose Maybud*: ETHEL CLARK. *Mad Margaret*: ANN CAREY. *Dame Hannah*: SARAH EDWARDS. *Zorah*: FRANCES MOORE. *Ruth*: FRANCES BAVIELLO.
Ghosts: Sir Rupert Murgatroyd: Hobson Young. *Sir Joseph Murgatroyd*: Allan Ware. *Sir Lionel Murgatroyd*: Felix Noonan. *Sir Conrad Murgatroyd*: Harrison Fuller. *Sir Desmond Murgatroyd*: Frank Dowling. *Sir Gilbert Murgatroyd*: Francis Clark. *Sir Mervyn Murgatroyd*: Patrick Quinton. *Sir Roderic Murgatroyd*: HERBERT L. WATEROUS.
Chorus of Officers, Ancestors, Professional Bridesmaids, Bucks, Blades: Bert Melrose, Hobson Young, Felix Noonan, Allan Ware, Frank Murray, Martin Lilienfield, Frank Dowling, Harrison Fuller, Francis Clark, John Cardini, Bernard Lane, Patrick Quinton. Olga Schumacher, Rosalyn Shaw, Patricia Clark, Gertrude Waldon, Mabel Thompson, Isabel Norwood, Rosa Rubenstein, Mary Joe Matthews, Marynia Apel, Adele Story, Harriet Gottlieb, Marie Kelley, Lillian Koniver, Katherine Calle, Mary Harper.

THE MIKADO,
1931.25   or The Town of Titipu

A Revival of the Comic Opera in Two Acts[22]. Libretto by William S. Gilbert. Music by Arthur Sullivan. Staged by Milton Aborn. Art director, John C. Baatz. Costumes by Eaves. Musical director, Louis Kroll. Produced by the Civic Light Opera Company. Opened 24 August 1931 at Erlanger's Theatre, closing 5 September 1931 after 16 performances; reopened 26-31 October 1931 for an additional 8 performances, and 25 December 1931-2 January 1932 for 12 additional performances. Total this season: 36 performances.

CAST: *The Mikado of Japan*: WILLIAM DANFORTH. *Nanki-Poo*, his son: HOWARD MARSH. *Ko-Ko*, Lord High Executioner of Titipu: FRANK MOULAN. *Pooh-Bah*, Lord High Everything Else: HERBERT L. WATEROUS. *Pish-Tush*, a

---

[20]Originally presented in New York 15 January 1879 at the Standard Theatre for 175 performances. For Synopsis of Scenes and Musical Numbers, see original 1879 production.
[21]First presented in New York 21 February 1887 at the Standard Theatre for 53 performances. For Synopsis of Scenes and Musical Numbers, see original 1887 production.
[22]First presented in New York 20 July, 10-29 August 1885 at the Union Square and People's Theatres for 22 performances. First authorized production presented 19 August 1885 at the Fifth Avenue Theatre by Richard D'Oyly Carte for 250 performances. For Synopsis of Scenes and Musical Numbers, see 19 August 1885 D'Oyly Carte production.

Noble Lord: ALLEN WATEROUS. *Three Sisters, Wards of Ko-Ko*: *Yum-Yum*: HIZI KOYKE. *Pitti-Sing*: ETHEL CLARKE. *Peep-Bo*: ELEANOR GILMORE. *Katisha*: VERA ROSS.

Ladies of the Mikado's Suite: Frances Moore, Harriet Gottlieb, Marie Kelley, Isabel Norwood, Marynia Apel, Katherine Calle. *The Mikado's Bodyguard*: Felix Noonan, Allan Ware, Frank Murray, Richard Scharff. *Chorus of School Girls, Nobles, Guards and Coolies*: Mabel Thompson, Isabel Norwood, Rosa Rubenstein, Harriet Gottlieb, Marie Kelley, Lillian Koniver, Katherine Calle, Mary Harper, Olga Schumacher, Frances Moore, Marynia Apel, Gertrude Waldon, Rosalyn Shaw, Frances Baviello, Patricia Clark, Adele Story. Felix Noonan, Allan Ware, Frank Murray, Richard Scharff, Harrison Fuller, Francis Clark, John Cardini, Bernard Lane, Patrick Quinton.

1931.26 EARL CARROLL VANITIES (1931)

A Musical Revue in Two Acts, 57 Scenes[23]. (Conceived and assembled by Earl Carroll.) Dialogue (sketches) by Ralph Spence, Eddie Welch. Music by Burton Lane. Lyrics by Harold Adamson. Directed by Earl Carroll. Dialogue revised and staged by Edgar MacGregor. Dances and ensembles staged by George Hale. Ballets by Gluck Sandor. Settings by Vincente Minnelli, Hugh Willoughby. Costumes by Vincente Minnelli, Charles LeMaire. Music director, Ray Kavanaugh. Orchestrations by Domenico Savino. Illusions and optical effects by Professor Tax Teuber. Produced by Earl Carroll. Opened 27 August 1931 at the Earl Carroll Theatre, moved 29 February 1932 to the 44th Street Theatre, and closed 9 April 1932 after 300 performances.

CAST: WILL MAHONEY, LILLIAN ROTH, WILLIAM DEMAREST, FRANK MITCHELL, JACK DURANT, MILTON WATSON, LUCILLE PAGE, WOODS MILLER, THE SLATE BROTHERS (Jack, Henry, Syd), OLIVE OLSEN, HELEN LYND, DAN CARTHE, BERYL WALLACE, IRENE AHLBERG, Frank Miller, Al Norman, Doris Andress, Rooney Ensemble, Enrique de los Ruelos, Alie Sellier, Frank Schegar, Theremin Ensemble.

Girls: Claire Carter, Marion Harcke, Nelda Kincaid, Marcelle Edwards, Mickey Devine, Betty Dell, Helen Oakes, Dolores Grant, Genie Fursa, Louise Allen, Ida Michael, Audrey Arlington, Sunny Kest, Jane Moxen, Doris Andrese, Betty Schleindl, Lucille Adair, Helen Arlan, Dorothy Knowlton, Vivian Keefer, Lydia Resh, Florence Ward, Violet Arnold, Alice Kerwin, Betty Sundmark, Edythe Paige, Lois Maye, Renee Bonnie, Rosemary Murphy, Theresa Meredith, Harriet Hagman, Martha Mackay, Irma Philbin, Gay Orlova, Agatha Hoff, Lorna Rodionoff, Ferne McAllister, Maryjo Engers, Eileen Wenzel, Marion Carewe, Collette Francis, Jacqueline Swift, Julia Mooney, Louise Porach, Shirley Parshall, Villi Milli. *Boys*: Raymond Young, Norman C. Rucker, Charles Benjamin, Jasper Thomas, Peter Clark, Samuel Brown, William Hart, William Barton, Ernest Brown, Edgar Hughes, Herbert Ellis, Glenfield Knight, John George, Irving Carter, Albert Harris, Howard Garvin, William Dyas, Charles Maynard, George Turner, Fred Byer, Julius Corsack, Arthur Berry, John Hilliman, James Tamm, Irving Mangott, Brooks Berkwich, Phil Thomas, Paul H. Phillips, George Bailey, Anderson Lewis.

ACT 1[24]

Scene 1

The New Stage Entrance

---

[23]The Ninth in the annual series of revues produced by Earl Carroll which began in 1923.

[24]Order of numbers in Act 2 revised after opening. Added during run:

A Domestic Discussion
Announcement: L. Dawson. *Husband*: W. Demarest. *His Friend*: M. Watson. *His Wife*: I. Ahlberg. *Her Friend*: B. Wallace. *Her Mother*: H. Lynd. *The Deacon*: W. Mahoney.

"Sandy Mahatma Gandhi"
W. Mahoney
(*Music and Lyrics by* Will Mahoney and Bob Geraghty.)

Western Girls
V. Keefer, S. Kest, B. Sundmark, A. Kerwin, M. Devine, G. Fursa

"I Go Haywire"
W. Mahoney
(*Music and Lyrics by* Will Mahoney and Bob Geraghty.)

"Good Night Sweetheart"
M. Watson, W. Miller
(*Music by* Ray Noble. *Lyrics by* Jimmy Campbell and Reg Connelly.)
Danced by I. Ahlberg, B. Wallace.

Which was replaced for subsequent tour by:
"Masquerade"
(*Music and Lyrics by* Paul Francis Webster and John Jacob Loeb.)

Scene 2

The Most Beautiful Girls in the World

Scene 3

"It's Great To Be in Love"
M. Watson, H. Lynd
(*Music and Lyrics by* Cliff Friend.)

Scene 4

The Magic Blackboard

Scene 5

Flashing Feet
36 Vanities Dancers
Dance by George Hale. *Costumes by* Charles LeMaire.)

Scene 6

Holmes' Sweet Homes (*by* John J. McNally, Jr.)
Mr. Holmes: W. Mahoney. *Mr. Smiths*: W. Demarest. *Mr. Browns*: F. Mitchell. *Mrs. Browns*: H. Lynd. *Mrs. Smiths*: O. Olsen. *June*: I. Ahlberg. *Mary*: H. Arlan. *Alice*: D. Andrese.

Scene 7

Dixie College

Scene 8

Graduation Day
The Dean: J. Durant. *The Graduates*: M. Edwards, S. Kest, M. Carewe, J. Mooney, L. Porach, E. Wenzel, S. Parshall, C. Frances, J. Swift, V. Milli, C. Carter, M. Engers, N. Kincaid, L. Resh, A. Kerwin, D. Grant.

Scene 9

"Have a Heart"
L. Roth, W. Miller
(*Music by* Burton Lane. *Lyrics by* Harold Adamson.)
Scene: The Greenhouse.

Scene 10

The Tree of Life[25]

Scene 11

Dance
A. Norman

Scene 12

Reno-vated (*by* Beth Wendell)
Judge: F. Mitchell. *The Bride*: I. Ahlberg. *The Groom*: W. Mahoney. *The Bridesmaid*: H. Lynd. *The Best Man*: W. Demarest.

Scene 13

"Going to Town With Me"
O. Olsen, Girls
(*Music by* Burton Lane. *Lyrics by* Harold Adamson.)
(*Dance by* George Hale. *Costumes by* Charles LeMaire.)

Scene 14

The Girl in the Sky[26] (*Effect by* Max Teuber.)
L. Roth

Scene 15

Bedlam (*Suggested by* Eddie Cantor.)
Proprietor: M. Watson. *Glendenning*: W. Demarest. *Chick, the Greek*: F. Miller. *His Wife*: B. Wallace. *The Lady Customer*: L. Roth. *Her Husband*: W. Mahoney. *Second Lady Customer*: O. Olsen. *Her Husband*: J. Durant. *Third Lady Customer*: H. Lynd. *Salesman*: W. Miller.

Scene 16

Dance
The Slate Brothers

Scene 17

"Tonight or Never"[27]
L. Roth, M. Watson
(*Music and Lyrics by* Raymond Klages, Jack Meskill and Vincent Rose.)
Scene: Atop the Empire State. (*Costumes and tableau suggested by* Vincente Minnelli.)

---

[25]Dropped during the run.
[26]Dropped during the run.
[27]For subsequent tour, replaced by:
"My Darling"
(*Music by* Richard Myers. *Lyrics by* Edward Heyman.)

Scene 18

Chromium (*Modern Ballet Created and Staged by* Gluck Sandor)

Scene 19

Ladies of the Veil

Scene 20

Frieze of Metal

Scene 21

Pajama Dance

L. Page

Scene 22

Reelism (*by* Jack Henley)

Mr. Fineman: W. Demarest. *Miss Bromo*: L. Roth. *Jackson*: W. Miller. *Watkins*: M. Watson. *Miss Gettem*: O.Olsen. *Boy*: A. Norman. *Chester*: F. Mitchell. *Script Girl*: B. Wallace. *Lester*: J. Durant.

Scene 23

The Beauty Pageant (*by* Jacques Kopfstein and Melvin Stanley Cahn)

Radio Announcer: W. Miller. *Prize Winning Beauties*: H. Hagman, M. Edwards, S. Kest, H. Lynd, V. Keefer, L. Resh, A. Kerwin, B. Sundmark, D. Grant, G. Fursa, B. Dell, M. Carewe, J. Mooney, E. Joslyn, L. Porach, E. Wenzel, S. Parshall, C. Frances, J. Swift, V. Milli.

Scene 24

"The Mahoneyphone"

W. Mahoney

(*Music by* Burton Lane. *Lyrics by* Harold Adamson.)

Scene 25

"Bolero" (*Music by* Maurice Ravel.)

Danced by D. Carthe

Scene 26

The White Figure

I. Ahlberg

Drummers: Boys.

Scene 27

Ivory Tympanes

B. Wallace, I. Michael

Scene 28

Golden Pheasants

M. Carewe, J. Mooney, L. Porach, E. Wenzel, S. Parshall, C. Frances, J. Swift, V. Milli

Scene 29

Glass Scimitars

Scene 30

Finale

(*Dance staged by* George Hale. *Settings and Costumes by* Vincent Minnelli.)

ACT 2

Scene 1

"Masks and Hands"

(*Dance Created and Staged by* Gluck Sandor.)

Scene 2

The Frenzy of Hands

The Figure: I. Ahlberg.

Scene 3

In the Subway

Guard: S. Slate. *Passenger*: A. Norman.

Scene 4

That Smith Baby (*by* Nathaniel Lief)

Mrs. Sprague: L. Roth. *Mr. Sprague*: W. Demarest. *Mrs. Smith*: O. Olsen. *Mr. Smith*: W. Mahoney.

Scene 5

On the Street

First Man: M. Watson. *Second Man*: W. Miller.

Scene 6

Modern Music[28]

Ensemble of Theremins

(This is the first presentation on any stage of Professor Leon Theremin's marvelous invention of producing musical sounds from the air.)

"Love Came into My Heart"[29]

M. Watson, W. Miller

(*Music by* Burton Lane. *Lyrics by* Harold Adamson.)

Scene 7

Prehistoric Curtain

(a) Primordial, (b) Dawn, (c) Awakening, (d) Fetish, (e) Flesh, (f) Passion, (g) Monster, (h) Peace. (*Costumes and Curtain by* Vincente Minnelli.)

Scene 8

Two Hundred Million Years Ago

"Dance of the Dinosaur"

L. Page

(*Music by* Hyman Grossman. Dinosaur created by Gustave Weidhaas under the guidance of Charles J. Lang of the Museum of Natural History.)

Scene 9

Thirty-Third Street (*by* Harry Ruskin)

Prisoner: F. Mitchell. *Detective*: J. Durant.

Scene 10

The Bread Line[30]

Grandma: W. Mahoney. *Mother*: H. Lynd. *Daughter*: O. Olsen.

Scene 11

Central Park Casino (*by* Harry Hershfield)

Phyllis: L. Roth. *Girl*: B. Wallace. *Man*: W. Demarest. *Jack*: M. Watson. *Guests*: E. Wenzel, Slate Brothers. *Head Waiter*: E. de los Ruelos. *Waiter*: A. Sellier.

"I'm Back in Circulation"[31]

L. Roth

(*Music by* Michael H. Cleary. *Lyrics by* Nathaniel and Max Lief.)

Scene 12

"Parasols on Parade"

W. Miller

(*Music by* Larry Besson. *Lyrics by* Clifford Adams.)

Scene 13

Parasols Eugénie

Scene 14

Parasols Créole

Scene 15

Parasols Sans-gêne

Scene 16

Parasols Rose et Noir

Scene 17

Parasols Dolly Varden

Scene 18

Parasols DuBarry

Scene 19

Parasols Pistachio (*Setting and Costumes by* Vincent Minnelli.)

Scene 20

"Oh My Yes"[32]

H. Lynd, O. Olsen, F. Mitchell, J. Durant

(*Music by* Burton Lane. *Lyrics by* Harold Adamson.)

Scene 21

Musique[33]

Le Maestro: W. Demarest. *Le Grand Danseur*: W. Mahoney. *La Petite Danseuse*: Y. Magna.

Scene 22

Dance

The Slate Brothers

Scene 23

Somewhere in Paree (*by* Beth Wendell)

Miss Duval: L. Roth. *Photographer*: W. Demarest. *Maid*: B. Wallace. *Collette*: H. Lynd. *Mitzi*: O. Olsen. *Sara*: I. Ahlberg. *Fifi*: E. Wenzel. And V. Milli, L. Porach, S. Parshall, C. Frances, J. Swift, J. Mooney.

---

[28]Dropped during the run.

[29]Dropped during the run.
[30]Dropped during the run.
[31]Dropped during the run.
[32]Dropped during the run.
[33]Dropped during the run.

Scene 24

"(I've Got)Ants in My Pants"[34] (Bugology)
W. Mahoney
(*Music and Lyrics by* Cliff Friend.)

Scene 25

Brown Bartenders: "Heigh Ho the Gang's All Here"
Rooney Ensemble
(*Music by* Burton Lane. *Lyrics by* Harold Adamson.)

Scene 26

The Bar of Gold

Scene 27

Grand Finale (*Dance staged by* George Hale.)

THE MERRY WIDOW

1931.27

A Revival of the Operetta in Three Acts[35]. (Original German) Book ("Die lustige witwe") by Victor Léon and Leo Stein (after "L'Attaché d'Ambassade" by Henri Meilhac). Music by Franz Lehár. Staged by Milton Aborn. Art director, Charles Baatz. Music director, Louis Kroll. Costumes by Brooks. Revived by the Civic Light Opera Company. Opened 7 September 1931 at Erlanger's Theatre and closed 19 October 1931 after 16 performances; re-opened 22 February 1932 at Erlanger's Theatre and closed 5 March 1932 after 16 performances. Total this season: 32 performances.

CAST: *Popoff*, Marsovian Ambassador: HAL FORDE. *Natalie*, his wife: RUTH ALTMAN. *Prince Danilo*, Embassy attaché: DONALD BRIAN. *Sonia*, a young widow: MANILLA POWERS. *Camille deJolidon*: ROY CROPPER. *Marquis Cascada*: Sano Marco. *Raoul De St. Brioche*: Milton Tully. *Khadja*: Edward Orchard. *Nova Kovich* of the Embassy: William White. *Olga*, his wife: Dene Dickens. *Nish*, messenger of the Embassy: Will Philbrick. *Head Waiter*: Walter Franklyn. *Zo-Zo*: Frances Baviello. *Fifi*: Theo Van Tassell. *Lo-Lo*: Olga Schumacher. *Frou-Frou*: Dorothy Duncan. *Clo-Clo*: Therese Hyle. *Margot*: Mary Moss. *Zu-Zu*: Dhenise Delehante. *Sapho*: Frances Moore.

Guests, Servants, Marsovian Dancing Men, Marsovian Troubadours: Frances Baldwin, Sylvia Gans, Mary Rysz, Kathryn Curl, Dorothy Watson, Vera Muller, Irene Hubert, Marie Dolan, Cryilla Tuite, Theo Van Tassell, Dhenise Delehante, Frances Moore, Mary Adeline Moss, Frances Baviello, Dorothy Duncan, Therese Hyle, Olga Schumacher, June Yorkin, Walter Franklyn, Lloyd Ericsson, Rudy Glaisek, Siegfried Langer, August Loring, Sigmund Glukoff, Serge Ury, Mario Pichler, Otis Holwerk, Thomas Green.

FREE FOR ALL

1931.28

A Musical Comedy in Two Acts, 8 Scenes. Book by Oscar Hammerstein II and Laurence Schwab. Music by Richard A. Whiting. Lyrics by Oscar Hammerstein II. Staged by Oscar Hammerstein II. Dances by Bobby Connolly. Settings by Donald Oenslager. Costumes by Kiviette. Music director, John McManus. Produced by Laurence Schwab and Frank Mandel. Opened 8 September 1931 at the Manhattan Theatre and closed 19 September after 15 performances.

CAST: *Tom*, a Butler at Mr. Potter's Home: Peter Lang. *Stephen Potter, Sr.*, a Captain of Industry: Edward Emery. *Joe Butler*, Perpetual Student at Leland Stanford: DAVID HUTCHESON. *Gracie Maynard*: THELMA TIPSON. *Anita Allen*: VERA MARSH. *Michael Byrne*, a Radical Poet: PETER HIGGINS. *Marishka Tarasov*: TAMARA [DRASIN]. *Andy Bradford*: DON TOMKINS. *Joan Summer*, Youngest of the Gang: DORIS GRODAY. *Steve Potter, Jr.*, Son of Stephen Sr.: JACK HALEY. *Marie Sinnot*, Editor of 'Free for All': Lillian Bond. *Miss Gibbs*, the Secretary at Dr. Allen's Office: Dorothy Knapp. *Dr. Raymond Allen*, a Psychoanalyst, Anita's Father: Philip Lord. *Mr. Vergil Murgatroyd*, a Patient: Charles Althoff. *Mrs. Ida Jones*, Another Patient: Jeanette Loff. *Pete Weber*, a Nevada Sheriff: Seth Arnold. *Miners*: Gus Howard, Clair Kramer, John Donahue. *Terence Canavan*, a Mine Foreman: G. Pat Collins. *Jim Allison*, a Metallurgist: Harry Shannon. *Silver Dollar Kate*: GRACE JOHNSTON. *Divorcees*: Dorothea James, Olive Bayes, Julia Chandler. *Digger Watkins*: Robert Randall. *A Reporter*: Al Downing. *A Nurse*: Rae Powell. *Mr. Preston*: E. Saulpaugh. *A Judge*: Edward Walters. (Benny Goodman's Band, including Glenn Miller.)

Act 1, Scene 1: Dining Room of Stephen Potter's Home in Palo Alto, California. *Scene*

2: Office of Dr. Raymond Allen, Psychoanalyst, in Sacramento. *Scene 3*: The Rambler Copper Mine in Nevada. Top of the Shaft. *Scene 4*: The 'Free for All' Community Houses. Near the Mine.

Act 2, Scene 1: 'Silver Dollar Kate's,' a Speakeasy near New Leaf Corners, Nevada. *Scene 2*: Top of the Shaft Again. *Scene 3*: Down in the Mine. *Scene 4*: The Square in New Leaf Corners.

ACT 1

Scene 1

"I Love Him, the Rat"
V. Marsh, D. Hutcheson

"Free for All"
P. Higgins, the Gang

Scene 2

"The Girl Next Door"
V. Marsh, J. Haley

Scene 3

"Living in Sin"
T. Tipson, D. Groday, D. Hutcheson, D. Tomkins

Scene 4

"Just Eighteen"
D. Groday, D. Tomkins

"Not That I Care"
V. Marsh, J. Haley

"Slumber Song" (Goodnight)
Tamara, P. Higgins

Finale
Principals

ACT 2

Scene 1

Dance
D. Groday, D. Tomkins

Reprise
P. Higgins, Tamara, O. Bayes, D. James, J. Chandler

Scene 2

"When Your Boy Becomes a Man"
G. Johnston, V. Marsh

Scene 3

"Tonight"
Tamara, P. Higgins

Scene 4

"Nevada Moonlight"
D. Hutcheson, T. Tipson, Ensemble

Finale
Company

THE SINGING RABBI

1931.29

An Operetta in Three Acts. Book by Bores and Harry Thomashefsky. Music by J. Rumshinsky, Harry Lubin. Lyrics by L. Wolfe Gilbert. Staged by William E. Morris. Dances and ensembles arranged by Florenz Ames. Settings by Orestes Rainieri. Costumes by David Spero, M. Teitelbaum, Meth & Gropper. Lighting by Louis Marmorstein. Music director, Harry Lubin. Produced by Harry Thomashefsky. Opened 10 September 1931 at the Selwyn Theatre and closed 12 September 1931 after 3 performances.

CAST (in order of apperance): *Rifka*: WINIFRED WEE GRIFFIN. *Miriam*: Edna Archer Crawford. *Yankele*: FLORENZ AMES. *Jacob*: Will Claire. *The Widow Sheindel*: REGINA ZUCKERBERG. *Shloima*: PHILIP RYDER. *Nuchem*: SAM ASH. *Regina*: FLORA LEBRETON. *Gidalia*: BORES THOMASHEFSKY. *Padula*: Tino Valenti. *Bianca*: Francez Dumas. *Baron Koch*: Adolph Lyons. *Madame Dodee*: Gertrude Mudge. *Bettie*: Donna Fairchild. *Jean*: Robert Rhodes. *The Captain*: Harry Pierson. *First Mate*: Russell Harvey. *Miss Van Buren*: Betty Keyes. *Miss Du Peyster*: Jacqualine Alderman.

Act 1: Home of the Widow Sheindel in Galicia.

Act 2: Aboard Steamer en route to New York.

Act 3: The Widow Sheindel's Home in New York. Fourteen Months Later.

ACT 1

"One Galician Miss"
W. W. Griffin
(*Music by* J. Rumshinsky.)

---

[34]Dropped during the run.
[35]Originally presented in New York 21 October 1907 at the New Amsterdam Theatre for 416 performances. For Synopsis of Scenes and Musical Numbers, see original 1907 production. English libretto uncredited.

"Yankele and Refkele"
F. Ames, W. W. Griffin
(*Music by* Harry Lubin.)
"Kaddish" (Hebrew Prayer)
R. Zuckerberg
(*Music by* J. Rumshinsky.)
"The Fifth Commandment"
R. Zuckerberg, W. Claire
(*Music by* J. Rumshinsky and Harry Lubin)
"The Fifth Commandment" (reprise)
R. Zuckerberg, W. Claire, P. Ryder
"Back Home"
S. Ash
(*Music by* J. Rumshinsky.)
"The Fifth Commandment" (reprise)
R. Zuckerberg, W. Claire, P. Ryder, S. Ash
"Playing the Harpsichord"
F. LeBreton
(*Music by* Harry Lubin.)
"Only Your Heart Can Tell"
F. LeBreton, S. Ash
(*Music by* Harry Lubin.)
Finale—"Sholem Aleichem"
Entire Company
(*Music by* J. Rumshinsky.)

ACT 2

"In a Life Boat"
W. W. Griffin, F. Ames
(*Music by* Harry Lubin.)
"In Napoli"
F. Dumas, T. Valenti
(*Music by* Harry Lubin.)
"Just Answer With a Kiss"
F. LeBreton, R. Rhodes
(*Music by* Harry Lubin.)
"I'm Wide Awake When I Dream"
S. Ash
(*Music by* Harry Lubin.)
"A Vision of the Future"
B. Thomashefsky, S. Ash, W. Claire, R. Zuckerberg, P. Ryder, F. LeBreton
(*Music by* J. Rumshinsky.)
Finale—"Port of the World"
Entire Company
(*Music by* Harry Lubin.)

ACT 3

"What's in a Name?"
W. W. Griffin, F. Ames, T. Valenti, F. Dumas
(*Music by* Harry Lubin.)
"Hear, O Israel!"
S. Ash
(*Music by* J. Rumshinsky.)
Finale
Entire Company

GEORGE WHITE'S SCANDALS (1931)

1931.30

A Musical Revue in Two Acts, 25 Scenes[36]. Assembled by George White. Sketches by George White, Lew Brown, Irving Caesar, (Harry Conn). Music by Ray Henderson. Lyrics by Lew Brown. Staged by George White. Settings by Joseph Urban. Costumes by Charles LeMaire. Music director, Al Goodman. Orchestrations by Howard Jackson. Produced by George White. Opened 14 September 1931 at the Apollo Theatre and closed 5 March 1932 after 202 performances.

CAST: RUDY VALLEE, ETHEL MERMAN, WILLIE and EUGENE HOWARD, EVERETT MARSHALL, RAY BOLGER, GALE QUADRUPLETS (Jane, Jean, Joan, June), Ethel Barrymore Colt, the Loomis Sisters (Maxine, Virginia), Barbara Blair,

Ross MacLean, Jane Alden, Joan Abbott, Dorothy and Harry Dixon, Fred Manatt, Alice Frohman, Danny Tannen, Joseph Vitale, Helen Lee, Sidney Limb.
Girls: Hazel Boffinger, Pearl Bradley, Lois Eckhart, Joanna Allen, Peggy Moseley, Renee Johnson, Cornelia Rogers, Mae Slattery, Jacqueline Feeley, Inez DuPlessis, Anne Morgan, Peggy Ring, Julia Gorman, Mary Ann Carr, Patricia Hayward, Margaret Haller, Hazel Nevin, Alice Faye, Marion Thompson, Adelaide Raleigh, Ethel Lawrence, Joan English, Myra Gerald, Beth Foth, Betty Allen, Dorothy Daly, Patsy Clarke, Gay Delis, Rose Collins, Dorothy Keene, Gloria Mossman, Hilda Knight, Gloria Pierre, Florence Johnson, Gay Hill.

ACT 1[37]

Scene 1

The Marvelous Empire State
Show Girls
Ex-Governor Al Smith: R. Bolger.

Scene 2

The Interview (*by* Harry W. Conn)
The Interviewed: W. Howard, E. Howard. *Female Reporter*: E. B. Colt.

Scene 3

"Life Is Just a Bowl of Cherries"
E. Merman
Musician: E. Howard. *Prize Beauty Winner*: B. Blair. *Plumber*: W. Howard. *Danced by* Show Girls.

Scene 4

Dance
Gale Quadruplets

Scene 5

It Happened in Venice
W. Howard, J. Alden, E. Howard

Scene 6

"Beginning of Love"
Loomis Sisters
Adam: R. Bolger. *Eve*: B. Blair. And the Show Girls.

Scene 7

The Gale Quadruplets Tell You All About the Fleischmann Hour
Graham McNamee: R. Bolger. *Doctor Bolgareen*: W. Howard. *Rudy Vallee*: R. Vallee.

Scene 8

"The Thrill Is Gone"
E. Marshall, R. Vallee, R. MacLean
Danced by D. Dixon, H. Dixon.

Scene 9

The Duel
General: W. Howard. *The Spy*: J. Alden. *First Orderly*: D. Tannen. *Second Orderly*: J. Vitale.

Scene 10

"This Is the Missus"
R. Vallee, P. Moseley, Show Girls

Scene 11

Pay the Two Dollars [*by* Billy K. Wells]
Sam Pincus: W. Howard. *Abe Steiner*: E. Howard. *Special Officer*: D. Wakely. *Judge*: R. MacLean. *Presiding Judge*: F. Manatt. *Warden*: J. Vitale.

Scene 12

"Ladies and Gentlemen, That's Love"
E. Merman

Scene 13

Ray Bolger (Eccentric Dance Specialty)

Scene 14

"That's Why Darkies Were Born"
E. Marshall

ACT 2

Scene 1

Peanuts
Marie: J. Alden. *Husband*: E. Howard. *Spanish Lover*: R. Vallee. *Hebrew Lover*: W. Howard.

---

[36]The 11th in the annual series of musical revues produced by George White beginning in 1919.

[37]Interpolated during the run, according to published sheet music:
"Hummin' to Myself" (I've Got the Words—I've Got the Tune)
J. Abbott
(*Music by* Sammy Fain. *Lyrics by* Herb Magidson and Monty Siegel.)

Scene 2

"Song of the Foreign Legion"
E. Marshall

Scene 3

The Pedestrian
Commissioner of Licenses: F. Manatt. *Applicant*: W. Howard. *Assistants*:
J. Vitale, D. Tannen, R. MacLean, D. Wakely.

Scene 4

"Here It Is"
J. Abbott
Danced by the Gale Quadruplets, R. Bolger, Show Girls.

Scene 5

"My Song"
R. Vallee, E. Merman
'*Sweet Sixteen*': R. MacLean, G. Delis. '*Song of Love*': E. Marshall,
G. Mossman.

Scene 6

The Daily Reflector
Walter Windshield: R. Bolger. *Cobbler*: W. Howard. *City Editor*: E. Howard.
Rewrite Man: D. Tannen. *Reporter*: D. Wakely. *Gorilla*: J. Vitale. *Typesetter*:
R. MacLean.

Scene 7

"Back From Hollywood"
B. Blair, J. Gorman, H. Knight, B. Allen

Scene 8

The Gale Quadruplets Tell You All About the Chinese Drama
Chinese Housewife: H. Lee. *Laundryman*: S. Limb. *Housewife*: A. Frohman.
Janitor: R. Bolger.

Scene 9

"The Good Old Days"
R. Vallee, W. Howard
Old-Fashioned Honeymoon: E. Lawrence, R. MacLean. *Modern Honeymoon*:
H. Boffinger, D. Wakely. *Girl in Modern Bathroom*: L. Eckhart.

Scene 10

Ethel Merman[38]

Scene 11

The Wonder Bar
Entire Company

1931.31   FAST AND FURIOUS

A Musical Revue in Two Acts, 36 Scenes. Sketches by Forbes Randolph and
John Wells, Zora Neale Thurston, Lottie Meaney, Tim Moore, Clinton
'Dusty' Fletcher, Jackie 'Moms' Mabley, Leighton K. Brill, Sigmund Herzig.
Lyrics mostly by Mack Gordon. Music mostly by Harry Revel. Additional
music and lyrics by J. Rosamond Johnson, Porter Grainger, Joe Jordan and
Allie Wrubel, (John Dallavo, Harold Adamson). Production staged under
the personal supervision of Forbes Randolph. Dialogue staged by Howard
Smith. Dances by Al Richard, Jack Donohue. Settings by Cirker and
Robbins. Costumes by Eaves, Schneider and Blythe. Music director, Joe
Jordan. Produced by Forbes Randolph. Opened 15 September 1931 at the
New Yorker Theatre and closed 19 September 1931 after 7 performances.

CAST: TIM MOORE, CLINTON (Dusty) FLETCHER, JUANO HERNANDEZ,
JACKIE (Moms) MABLEY, NEEKA SHAW, RUSSELL SHAW, MAURICE ELLIS,
LEE (Boots) MARSHALL, ANTONIO MACHIN, ETTA MOTEN, RUBY ELZY,
RUBY GREENE, LOIS DEPPE, EDNA GUY, CLARENCE TODD, LLOYD
MITCHELL, LILY YUEN, ZORA (NEALE) THURSTON, Baby Goins, Grace
Smith, Melva Boden, Helmsley Winfield, Emma Maitland, Al Richards, Gilbert
Holland, Earl Shanks, Midgie Lane, J. Rosamond Johnson Quartet.
Forbes Randolph Choir: Girls: Ruby Greene, Sibol Cain, Ruby Elzy, Gladys
Freeland, Marion Hairston, Rosina Lefroy, Emma Maitland, Julia F. Mitchell, Aurelia
Wheeldin, Billy Wallace. *Boys*: Cecii Burrows, Jean Donnell, Maurice Ellis, Clement
D. Hall, Larri N. Lorear, Penman Lovingood, Alexander O. Moody, Carl H. Taylor,
Fred A. Wheeldin, L. Chappelle Glenn. *Dancing Girls*: Doris Alexander, Juanita

---

[38]Merman's autobiography (Merman, with George Eells, Simon &
Schuster, New York, 1978) and *Merman: An Auto-Bibliography*, By George
B. Bryan (Greenwood Press, Westport, 1992) both suggest that Merman
also performed "The Good Old Days" but offer no indication of what her
specialty, Act 2, Scene 10, was.

Boisseau, Bertie Boyd, Thelma Brunder, Mary Goodwin, Marion Green, Virginia
Groves, Chickita Martin, Inez Persaud, Carolyne Rich, Edna Richardson, Evelyn
Sheppard, Catherine Upshur, Wilhelmina Wade, Pearl White, Grace Hall, Cleopatra
Ward. *Dancing Boys*: Edward Jones, Thomas Smith, Frank Walker, Maurice Young.

ACT 1

Scene 1

Parody of "The Band Wagon"

Scene 2

"Fast and Furious"
G. Smith
(*Music and Lyrics by* Mack Gordon and Harry Revel.)
Danced by 4 Dancing Boys, Chorus.

Scene 3

Ham What Am (*by* Leighton K. Brill and Sigmund Herzig)
Tim: T. Moore. *Dusty*: C. Fletcher. *Jackie*: J. Mabley. *Policeman*: J. Hernandez.

Scene 4

Baby Goins

Scene 5

Gift of Gab (*by* Leighton K. Brill and Sigmund Herzig)
Husband: R. Lee. *Doctor*: M. Ellis. *Wife*: J. Mabley.

Scene 6

"Walking on Air"
N. Shaw, L. Marshall
(*Music and Lyrics by* Mack Gordon and Harry Revel.)
Danced by N. Shaw, L. Marshall, C. Martin, W. Wade, Chorus.

Scene 7

Al Richard

Scene 8

The Courtroom (*by* Zora Neale Thurston)
(The traditional courtroom scene without which a Negro revue is
incomplete.)
Judge: T. Moore. *Clerk of Court*: M. Ellis. *Prosecuting Attorney*: C. Todd.
Lawyer: L. Mitchell. *Officer Simpson*: M. Boden. *John Barnes*: J. Hernandez.
Cliff Mullins: R. Lee. *Mrs. Mullins*: J. Mabley. *Jessie Smith*: E. Maitland. *A
Lawyer*: L. Mitchell. *Eva*: E. Moten.

Scene 9

"Rumbatism"
J. Mabley
(*Music and Lyrics by* Mack Gordon and Harry Revel.)

Scene 10

"So Lonesome"
R. Greene, R. Elzy, G. Freeland
(*Music and Lyrics by* Joe Jordan and J. Rosamond Johnson.)

Scene 11

Raid on Jake's (*by* Tim Moore)
Jake: T. Moore. *Dizzy*: M. Boden. *A Guest*: E. Moten. *Another Guest*: E.
Shanks. *Two Detectives*: J. Hernandez, J. Willis. *Other Guests*: M. Ellis, B.
Wallace, L. Mitchell, A. Wheeldin.

Scene 12

"Frowns"
L. Deppe
(*Music and Lyrics by* Mack Gordon and Harry Revel.)

Scene 13

Gymnasium: "Doing the Dumb-bell"
N. Shaw
(*Music and Lyrics by* Mack Gordon and Harry Revel.)
Dances by N. Shaw, J. Mabley, Chorus. *World's Female Junior Lightweight
Champion*: E. Maitland. *World's Female Bantamweight Champion*: A.
Wheeldin. (Misses Maitland and Wheeldin are the only two licensed female
boxers in America.)

Scene 14

Madrassi Nautch (East Indian Street Dance)
E. Guy
(Through the courtesy of Miss Ruth St. Denis.)

Scene 15

Clinton 'Dusty' Fletcher (Specialty)

Scene 16

At Home in Georgia: "East Coast Blues"
S. Cain
(One of the oldest 'blue' songs, it originated on the east coast of Florida.)

"John Henry"

E. Shanks, Fast and Furious Quartet, J. Rosamond Johnson Quartet
(The hero-classic of Negro work songs, it is one of the oldest, if not the oldest, of the southern work camp folk-songs. Many versions of this song exist in the south today, from Carolina to Texas, but the rendition offered here is, as far as it can be traced, the oldest.)

Scene 17

The Last Word (*by* Tim Moore)

The Husband: T. Moore. *The Wife*: B. Goins.

Scene 18

"Modernistic"

L. Yuen
(*Music and Lyrics by* Porter Grainger and John Dallavo.)
Danced by L. Yuen, Chorus.

Scene 19

"Shadows on the Wall"

E. Moten
(*Music and Lyrics by* Mack Gordon and Harry Revel.)

Scene 20

Rhumba Band: "The Peanut Vendor's Song" (El Manisero)

A. Machin
(*Music by* Moisés Simons. *English lyrics by* Marion Sunshine and L. Wolfe Gilbert.)
(Sr. Machin introduced this song to the United States.)
Rhumba Dance by O. Diaz.

Scene 21

"Jacob's Ladder" (*Conceived and Written by* Allie Wrubel and J. Rosamond Johnson.)

Elder Simmons: L. Deppe. *Cigarette Girl*: N. Shaw. *Rhythm Girl*: M. Hairston. *Cabaret Dancer*: M. Lane. *Singing Waiters*: C. Todd, J. Willis, L. Mitchell, E. Skanks. *Number King*: G. Holland. *Cabaret Entertainer*: E. Moten. *Danny*: H. Winfield. *Sisters and Brothers of the Church*: Forbes Randolph's Choir. *Guests at the Cabaret.*

ACT 2
Scene 1

Football Game (*by* Zora Neale Thurston)

Capt. of Howard's Team: T. Moore. *Capt. of Lincoln's Team*: C. Fletcher. *Referee*: L. Deppe. *Cheerleaders*: J. Mabley, Z. N. Thurston. *Lincoln's Wrestler*: G. Holland. *Howard's Wrestler*: J. Hernandez. Teams, Bands, Chorus and Choir.

Scene 2

"Where's My Happy Ending?"

R. Elzy
(*Music and Lyrics by* Mack Gordon and Harry Revel.)

Scene 3

"Dance of the Moods"

Danced by H. Winfield
(*Music by* Porter Grainger.)

Scene 4

"Hot, Hot, Mama"

M. Moore
(*Music and Lyrics by* Porter Grainger.)

Scene 5

The Silent Bootlegger (*by* Clinton 'Dusty' Fletcher)

The Bootleger: C. Fletcher. *First Customer*: G. Smith. *Second Customer*: L. Yuen. *Detective*: C. Todd.

Scene 6

"Boomerang"

M. Lane
(*Music and Lyrics by* J. Rosamond Johnson and Joe Jordan.)
Danced by H. Winfield, M. Lane, Chorus.

Scene 7

Fast and Furious Quartet

Scene 8

Pansies (*by* Lottie Meaney)

Young Man: H. Winfield. *Business Man*: R. Lee. *Gardener*: L. Marshall. *The Flowers (9)*: *Orchid*: M. Boden. *Violet*: J. Donnell. *Forget-Me-Not*: A. Moody. *Lily*: L. Lorear. *Daffydill*: P. Lovingood. *Dancing Pansies*: T. Smith, E. Jones, F. Walker, M. Young.

"Pansies on Parade"

L. Marshall
(*Music and Lyrics by* Porter Grainger.)

Scene 9

"Hot Feet"

N. Shaw
(*Music and Lyrics by* Mack Gordon and Harry Revel.)
Danced by A. Richard, M. Lane, Chorus.

Scene 10

Baby Goins

Scene 11

Macbeth (*by* John Wells and William Shakespeare)

The Doctor: M. Boden. *A Gentlewoman*: E. Moten. *Lady Macbeth*: J. Mabley. *A Servant*: E. Shanks. *Seyton*: J. Hernandez. *Macbeth*: T. Moore. *A Messenger*: J. Willis. *Young Siward*: M. Ellis. *MacDuff*: C. Fletcher. *King of Scotland*: R. Lee. *Prompter*: C. Todd.

Scene 12

Four Dancing Boys

Scene 13

Hell

The Devil: G. Smith. *The Angel*: E. Guy. Imps and Sojourners in Hell.

"Let's Raise Hell"

G. Smith
(*Music and Lyrics by* Porter Grainger.)

Scene 14

"Road to Heaven"

Fast and Furious Quartet, Choir

Scene 15

Heaven: The Lord, Michael, Gabriel, and Angels

Entire Ensemble

1931.32   SINGIN' THE BLUES

A Colored Musical Drama in Three Acts, 11 Scenes. Play by John McGowan. Songs by Jimmy McHugh and Dorothy Fields, Harold Adamson and Burton Lane. Staged by Bertram Harrison. Dances staged by Sammy Lee. Settings designed by Donald Oenslager. Costumes designed by Kiviette. Orchestrations by (Robert) Russell Bennett. Produced by Alex Aarons and Vinton Freedley. Opened 16 September 1931 at the Liberty Theatre and closed 24 October 1931 after 45 performances.

CAST (in order of appearance): *"Potato-Eyes" Johnson*: ASHLEY COOPER. *"Knuckles" Lincoln*: MANTAN MORELAND. *Jim Williams*: FRANK WILSON. *"Bad Alley" Joe*: John Sims. *Dooley*: James Young. *Colored Policeman*: Joe Byrd. *Rocky*: Johnny Reid. *Eddie*: Shirley Jordon. *Mazie*: Jennie Sammons. *Jay*: S. W. Warren. *Dave Crocker*: JACK CARTER. *Edith*: Estelle Bernier. *Sam Mason*: Ralph Theodore. *"Whitey" Henderson*: Millard F. Mitchell. *Tod*: C. C. Gill. *Sid*: Percy Wade. *Susan Blake*: ISABELL WASHINGTON. *Elise Joyce*: Fredi Washington. *Jack Wilson*: Percy Verwayne. *"Sizzles" Brown*: Maud Russell. *Officer Frank*: James Stark. *A Singer*: Susaye Brown. *The Lindy Hoppers*: Shorty and Esalene, Jordon and Jordon, George and Betty. The Four Flash Devils. Bruce Johnson's Washboard Serenaders; Wen Talbert's Choir; Eubie Blake and His Orchestra.

Chorus at the Magnolia Club: Jeannie Sammons, Amy Bates, Ethel Duke, Irma Miles, Elida Webb, Dora White, Hyacinth Curtis, Lucia Moses, Reta Walker, Selma Sales, Susan Whaley, Delores Watson, Estelle Bernier, Theresa Jentry, Ruby Kennedy, Ethel Moses, Selma Sammons.

Act 1, Scene 1: Johnson's Pool Room, Chicago. *Scene 2*: A Chicago Street. *Scene 3*: Crocker's Place, Harlem. New York City. A month later.

Act 2, Scene 1: Susan's Room. Two weeks later. *Scene 2*: The Magnolia Club. The same evening.

Act 3, Scene 1: A Dressing Room at the Magnolia Club. *Scene 2*: Stage of the Magnolia Club. *Scene 3*: The Dressing Room. *Scene 4*: The Stage. *Scene 5*: The Harlem Police Station. *Scene 6*: Crocker's Office.

MUSICAL NUMBERS[39]

"(It's) The Darndest Thing"
(*Music by* Jimmy McHugh. *Lyrics by* Dorothy Fields.)

"Singin' the Blues"
(*Music by* Jimmy McHugh. *Lyrics by* Dorothy Fields.)

"Crazy Strut"
(*Music by* Burton Lane. *Lyrics by* Harold Adamson.)

---

[39]Musical numbers not listed in programs; not necessarily in performance order.

1931.33

THE CHOCOLATE SOLDIER

A Revival of the Operetta in Three Acts[40]. Original German book ("Der tapfere Soldat") and lyrics by Rudolph Bernauer and Leopold Jacobson, based on George Bernard Shaw's play "Arms and the Man." Music by Oscar Straus. American book and lyrics by Stanislaus Stange. Staged by Milton Aborn. Art director, Charles Baatz. Costumes by Brooks. Musical director, Louis Kroll. Produced by the Civic Light Opera Company. Opened 21 September 1931 at Erlanger's Theatre and closed 3 October 1931 after 16 performances.

CAST: *Nadina*, Daughter of Colonel Popoff: VIVIENNE SEGAL. *Aurelia*, Wife of Colonel Popoff: Ann Carey. *Mascha*, Aurelia's Cousin: Vivian Hart. *Bummerli*, a Swiss Mercenary in the employ of the Servian Army: CHARLES PURCELL. *Captain Massakroff*, Captain in the Bulgarian Army: DETMAR POPPEN. *Colonel Casimir Popoff* of the Bulgarian Army: Hal Forde. *Major Alexis Sparidoff* of the Bulgarian Army: ROY CROPPER. *A Dancer*: Theo Van Tassell. *Bulgarian Soldiers, Citizens, Citizenesses.*

1931.34

NIKKI

A Musical Comedy in Two Acts, 15 Scenes. Book by James Monk Saunders. Based on his short stories, "Nikki and Her War Birds," the novel "A Single Lady," and the film "The Last Flight." Music by Philip Charig. Lyrics by James Dyrenforth. Staged by William B. Friedlander. Dances by Pal'mere Brandeaux. Settings by P. Dodd Ackerman, James Morcom, Karle O. Amend. Costumes by Bergdorf Goodman, Samuel Lorber, Stein & Blaine, Faye Graham, Edith Faggen. Music director, Jules Lenzberg. Orchestrations by Louis Katzman. Produced by Harrison Hall. Opened 29 September 1931 at the Longacre Theatre, moved 19 October 1931 to the George M. Cohan Theatre, and closed 31 October 1931 after 39 performances.

CAST: *Shepard (Shep) Lambert*: DOUGLASS MONTGOMERY. *Nikki*: FAY WRAY. *Francis*, The Washout: JOHN BROOKE. *William (Bill) Talbot*: NATHANIEL WAGNER. *Cary Lockwood*: ARCHIE LEACH [Cary Grant]. *Willard (Wiffie) Crouch*: LOUIS JEAN HEYDT. *Kiss-me-Quick*: BOBBIE TREMAINE. *Benj*: RUDOLFO BADALONI.

Specialties and Bits: Marcel Rousseau, Albert Fontaine, Lois Sterner, Modesca and Michael, Bobbie Tremaine, Ali Sellier, Page Inness, Frank Chapman, Julia Barron. *Chorus*: Maxine Bennett, Gertrude Byrnell, Ruth Cunliffe, Adele Dixon, Sandra Laxer, Sharon Lloyd, Jean Love, Rosalie McCallion, Harriett Murray, Bobbie Sheehan, Toni Soral, Helen Tschirgi. *Show Girls*: Agnes Marshall, Peggy Stebbins, Alva Vaughn, Marjorie Younger. *Ensemble*: Alexandra Alexander, Elizabeth Brown, Cora Burlar, Anna Criena, Jean DeKoven, Natalie Dunhan, Mimi Elsasser, Eugenie Erganow, Marjorie Fenton, Lillian Okun, Lidia Ordinsky, Anna Ouzonoff, Mimi Ruskin, Fania Tulin, Charles Bath, Manuel Duarte, Hunter Kaufman, Martin Muriel, John Stellato, George Wald.

Act 1, Scene 1: Claridge's Bar. Paris, France. After the Armistice. *Scene 2*: Sidewalk Cafe. One year later. *Scene 3*: Bal Tabarin. *Scene 4*: Nikki's Sitting Room, Carleton Hotel. *Scene 5*: The same. *Scene 6*: Sidewalk Cafe near Père Lachaise; Père Lachaise Cemetery. *Scene 7*: Nikki's Sitting Room.

Act 2, Scene 1: Plaza Outside Bull Ring. Lisbon, Portugal. *Scene 2*: Informary. *Scene 3*: Corridor. *Scene 4*: Nikki's Room. Avenida Palace Hotel. *Scene 5*: Avenida Palace Bar. *Scene 6*: Amusement Park. *Scene 7*: Street in Lisbon. *Scene 8*: Nikki's Sitting Room, Carleton Hotel, Paris.

ACT 1

Scene 3

Bal Tabarin
  Master of Ceremonies: M. Rousseau. *Head Waiter*: A. Fontaine.
Dance
  L. Sterner
Dance
  Modesca, Michael
"Screwy Little Tune"[41]
  B. Tremaine

Scene 4

"Taking Off"
  D. Montgomery, N. Wagner, J. Brooke, A. Leach

Scene 5

"Wonder Why"
  F. Wray
"Now I Know"[42]
  P. Inness, F. Chapman

Scene 7

"Taking Off" (reprise)
  N. Wagner, Ensemble

ACT 2

Scene 1

Fiesta
  Ensemble
"My Heart Is Calling"
  J. Barron, F. Chapman

Scene 6

"The Ghost of Little Egypt"[43]
  B. Tremaine

1931.35

THE GEISHA

A Revival of the Musical Comedy (Japanese Musical Play) in Two Acts[44]. Book by Owen Hall. Music by Sidney Jones. Lyrics by Henry Greenbank. Staged by Milton Aborn. Art director, Charles Baatz. Costumes by Brooks. Musical director, Louis Kroll. Produced by the Civic Light Opera Company. Opened 5 October 1931 at Erlanger's Theatre and closed 17 October 1931 after 16 performances.

CAST (in order of appearance): *O Mimosa San*: HIZI KOYKE. *Juliette Diamant*: Ethel Clark. *Nami (Wave of the Sea)*: Theo. Van Tassell. *Geishas (4)*: O Kiku San *(Chrysanthemum)*: Dhoris Delehante. A Hana San *(Blossom)*: Margaret Walker. O Kinkoto San *(Golden Harp)*: Olga Schumacher. *Komurasaki (Little Violet)*: Mary Moss. *Lady Constance Wynne*: ANN CAREY. *English Ladies (4), Guests of Lady Constance*: *Miss Marie Worthington*: Cyrilla Tuite. *Miss Ethel Hurst*: Irene Hubert. *Miss Mabel Grant*: Kathryn Curl. *Louie Plumpton*: Mary Rysz. *Miss Molly Seamore*: RELLA WINN. *Reginald Fairfax*: ROY CROPPER. *Officers of H.M.S. The Turtle (5)*: *Dick Cunningham*: SANO MARCO. *Arthur Cuddy*: Otis Holwerk. *George Grimson*: August Loring. *Lieutenant Charles Baker*: Siegfried Langer. *Lieutenant Vernon Johnson*: Sigmund Glukoff. *Captain Katana*: MILTON TULLY. *Takemine*: Edward Orchard. *Wun Hi*: JAMES T. POWERS. *The Marquis Imari*: DETMAR POPPEN.

Coolies, Attendants, Guards, etc.: Frances Baldwin, Sylvia Gans, Mary Rysz, Kathryn Curl, Dorothy Watson, Vera Miller, Irene Hubert, Marie Dolan, Cyrilla Tuite, Dhenise Delehante, Frances Moore, Mary Adeline Moss, Frances Baviello, Dorothy Duncan, Theresa Hyle, Olga Schumacher, June Yorkin, Walter Franklyn, Lloyd Ericsson, Rudy Glaisek, Siegfried Langer, August Loring, Sigmund Glukoff, Serge Ury, Mario Pichler, Otis Holwerk, Thomas Green.

1931.36

EVERYBODY'S WELCOME

A Musical Comedy in Two Acts, a Prologue and 8 Scenes. Book by Lambert Carroll[45]. Based on the play "Up Pops the Devil" by Frances Goodrich and Albert Hackett. Lyrics by Irving Kahal, (Herman Hupfeld, Mack Gordon, Edward Eliscu, Arthur Lippmann, Milton Pascal). Music by Sammy Fain, (Harry Revel, Herman Hupfeld, Manning Sherwin). Directed by William Mollison. Dances staged by William Holbrook, under the supervision of Albertina Rasch. Settings by Watson Barratt. Wardrobe (costumes) designed by Ernest Schrapps, Alison McLellan Hunter. Music director, Tom Jones. Produced by the Messrs. Shubert. Opened 13 October 1931 at the Sam S. Shubert Theatre and closed 13 February 1932 after 139 performances.

CAST (in order of appearance): *Buddy Hill*: Andrew Carr. *"Biny" Hatfield*: JACK SHEEHAN. *Polly Bascom*: FRANCES WILLIAMS. *Ann Cathway*: HARRIETTE LAKE [Ann Sothern]. *Gilbert Morrell*: Roy Roberts. *Steve Merrick*: OSCAR SHAW. A *Drunk*: Thomas Harty. *George Kent*: CECIL LEAN. *Mrs. George Kent*: Jean

---

[40]First produced in New York 13 September 1909 at the Lyric Theatre for 296 performances. For Synopsis of Scenes and Musical Numbers, see original 1909 production.
[41]Dropped during the run.

[42]Replaced during the run by:
  "On Account of I Love You"
    F. Wray, D. Montgomery, N. Wagner, A. Leach
[43]Dropped during the run.
[44]First presented in New York 9 September 1896 at Daly's Theatre for 161 performances. For Synopsis of Scenes and Musical Numbers, see original 1896 production.
[45]Very likely a pseudonym for bookwriter Harold Atteridge who was credited prior to New York.

Newcombe. *Louella May Carroll*: ANN PENNINGTON. *Laundryman*: Spencer Barnes. *Kelly*: Jack Ross. *Mr. Platt*: Charles Garland. *Mrs. Platt*: Lucille Osborne. *Grace*: Bernice Lee. *Betty*: Phoebe Wallace. *Jane*: Elsie Duffy. *Helen*: Edna Hedin. *Dora*: Mary Brooks. *Trixie*: Naida Pahl. *Premier Danseuse*: Louise Hansen. *Specialty Dancers*: Andrew Carr, Louise Carr. DORSEY BROTHERS ORCHESTRA.

Albertina Rasch Girls: Louise Hansen, Beatrice Lauri, Ruth Cook, Una Ralph, Tesha Pearson. *Ladies of the Ensemble*: Edna Hedin, Elsie Duffy, Evan Ritter, Mary Brooks, Helen Hawkins, Naida Pahl, Dorothy Koster, Sally Lynne, Virginia Davis, Gladys Carter, Etna Ross. *Gentlemen of the Ensemble*: Charles Garland, Don Gordon, Jack Barratt, Hazzard Newberry, Carl Duart, Charles McClelland, Edwin Murray, Clark Leston, Jack Moore, Jack Ross, Edwin Murray.

Prologue: Rehearsal Hall in "Biny" Hatfield's Dancing Academy, New York.

Act 1: Studio Apartment of the Merricks' in Greenwich Village. One year later.

Act 2, Scene 1: Kitchen of the Merricks' Apartment. Several months later. *Scene 2*: The screen of Proxy's Theatre. *Scene 3*: Dressing Room Corridor. Backstage of Proxy's Theatre. *Scene 4*: Stage of Proxy's Theatre. Nocturne. *Scene 5*: Stage of Proxy's Theatre. *Scene 6*: Stage of Proxy's Theatre. *Scene 7*. The Merricks' Apartment.

PROLOGUE

Dance Exercise. 'Pas de Deux'
A. Carr, Girls, Boys

"One in a Million"
O. Shaw, Girls

Specialty
A. Carr, L. Carr

ACT 1

"All Wrapped Up in You"
O. Shaw, H. Lake
(*Music by* Harry Revel. *Lyrics by* Mack Gordon, Harold Adamson.)

"Pie Eyed Piper"
F. Williams, Girls, Boys

"Ta, Ta, Old Bean"
O. Shaw, H. Lake, F. Williams, J. Sheehan
(*Music by* Manning Sherwin. *Lyrics by* Edward Eliscu.)

"As Time Goes By"
F. Williams
(*Music and Lyrics by* Herman Hupfeld.)

"Even As You and I"
O. Shaw, H. Lake

"Even As You and I" (reprise)
O. Shaw, H. Lake

ACT 2

Scene 1

"Feather in a Breeze"
A. Pennington, Girls, Boys

"Lease in My Heart"
O. Shaw, H. Lake

"Lease in My Heart" (reprise)
O. Shaw, A. Pennington, T. Harty, Boys, Girls

"Nature Played a Dirty Trick on You"
F. Williams, J. Sheehan
(*Music by* Manning Sherwin. *Lyrics by* Arthur Lippmann, Milton Pascal.)

Scene 3

"As Time Goes By" (reprise)
F. Williams, J. Sheehan

"Even As You and I" (reprise)
O. Shaw, H. Lake

Scene 4

Nocturne
Albertina Rasch Girls, Ensemble

Scene 5

"I Shot the Works"[46]
F. Williams
(*Music by* Manning Sherwin. *Lyrics by* Arthur Lippmann and Milton Pascal.)

---

[46]For subsequent tour, replaced with:
"Under the Statler Clock"
F. Williams
(*Music by* Manning Sherwin. *Lyrics by* Arthur Lippmann.)

Scene 6

"Four Grecians"
J. Sheehan, C. Lean, T. Harty, A. Carr

Scene 7

"Is Rhythm Necessary?"
F. Williams, A. Pennington, Girls, Boys

Finale
Entire Company

1931.37   THE CAT AND THE FIDDLE

A Musical Love Story in Two Acts, 14 Scenes. Book and lyrics by Otto Harbach. Music by Jerome Kern. Staged by José Ruben. Ensemble dances staged by Albertina Rasch. Settings by Henry Dreyfuss. Costumes by Constance Ripley; Kiviette. Music director, Victor Baravalle. Orchestrations by Jerome Kern, Robert Russell Bennett. Produced by Max Gordon. Opened 15 October 1931 at the Globe Theatre, moved 24 May 1932 to the George M. Cohan Theatre, and closed 24 September 1932 after 395 performances.

CAST (in order of appearance): *Book Vendor*: George Kirk. *Mme. Abajoue*: LUCETTE VALSY. *Alexander Sheridan*: EDDIE FOY, JR. *Shirley Sheridan*: BETTINA HALL. *Pompineau*: GEORGE MEADER. *Victor Florescu*: GEORGES METAXA. *Angie Sheridan*: DORIS CARSON. *A Waiter*: George Magis. *Odette*: ODETTE MYRTIL. *Constance Carrington*: Margaret Adams. *Chester Biddlesby*: Fred Walton. *Major Sir George Wilfred Chatterly*: LAWRENCE GROSSMITH. *Clement Daudet*: JOSÉ RUBEN. *Maizie Gripps*: FLORA LE BRETON. *Jean Colbert*: PETER CHAMBERS. *Claudine*: LUCETTE VALSY. *Pedestrians, Grisettes, Soldiers, Stage Hands, etc.*.

Act 1, Scene 1: A Quay in Brussels. A Night in July. *Scene 2*: Entrance to 'La Petite Maison.' Four weeks later. An August morning. *Scene 3*: Victor's Rooms. Two days later. *Scene 4*: Entrance to 'La Petite Maison.' A Night one week later. *Scene 5*: Shirley's Apartment. Afternoon of next day. *Scene 6*: A Limousine. Five weeks later. September. *Scene 7*: (a) Prologue before the curtain of a theatre in Louvain. One hour later. (b) Finale of Victor's play, 'The Passionate Pilgrim' [Le Pèlerin Passionné]. Immediately after. (c) On the stage. Immediately after.

Act 2, Scene 1: Daudet's Apartment in Brussels. Four hours later. *Scene 2*: The Street under Daudet's Window. Immediately after. *Scene 3*: Victor's Rooms. Next morning. *Scene 4*: A Phantasy. *Scene 5*: Dressing room in theatre. Brussels. Two weeks later, October. *Scene 6*: Exterior of 'La Petite Maison.' Immediately after. *Scene 7*: Al Fresco Café of 'La Petite Maison.'

ACT 1

"The Night Was Made for Love"
G. Meader

"The Breeze Kissed Your Hair"
G. Metaxa

"The Love Parade"
G. Meader, F. LeBreton

"Try to Forget"
B. Hall, E. Foy Jr., D. Carson

"Poor Pierrot"
P. Chambers, L. Valsy

Episode in Victor's Play, "The Passionate Pilgrim"
O. Myrtil, L. Valsy, M. Adams, P. Chambers

Finaletto
(B. Hall, G. Metaxa, J. Ruben)

ACT 2

"She Didn't Say 'Yes'"
B. Hall

"A New Love Is Old"
G. Metaxa

"One Moment Alone"
B. Hall, G. Metaxa

"Hh! Cha! Cha!"
B. Hall, others

Cafe Scene
G. Meader, G. Metaxa, B. Hall

Finale ("She Didn't Say Yes" reprise)
(G. Meader, G. Metaxa, B. Hall)

(Nikita Balieff's)
1931.38 NEW CHAUVE-SOURIS

A New Edition of the Russian Language Musical Revue (Letuchaya Muish) in Three Acts[47]. Assembled by Nikita Balieff. Musical director, Alexei Archangelsky. Choreography, Boris Romanoff. Scenery and costumes by Natalia Gontcharova, Yury Annyenkof. Produced by Morris Gest. Opened 21 October 1931 at the Ambassador Theatre and closed 14 November 1931 after 29 performances.

CAST: M. NIKITA BALIEFF, Mlle. Diakonova, Mlle. (Alice) Nikitina, Mlle. (Tatiana) Riabouchinska, Boris Romanoff [Romanov], M. Dolinoff, Mme. (Yelena) Poliakova, Mlle. Komisarjevskaya, M. Vetchor, Mme. Cortis, M. Zotoff, George Hayes, K. Moyseenko, Norman Duggan, Gordon Weld, Irina Hicks Anatarova, Alexei Tcherkassky, Nicholas Moyseenko, William Whitehead, William Home, Geoffrey King, Helen Kingstead, Mary Ault, Messrs. Sergieff, Stark, Bologovskoy.

ACT 1

"A Romantic Adventure of an Italian Ballerina and a Marquis"
    Ballet Gallant by Boris Romanoff. Music from Mozart ('Petits Riens'). Costumes and scenery by Natalia Gontcharova. Produced (directed) by Boris Romanoff.

CAST: Prologue: The Lady in Black: Mlle. Diakonova. The Lady in Red: Mlle. A. Nikitina. Ballet: Carlotta Chesi, a Ballerina in the Royal Opera: Mlle. T. Riabouchinska. The Marquis of Boseral: B. Romanoff. Angelo Piranesi, Chief of the Bandits: M. Dolinoff. Dolores del Castillo, his accomplice: Mlle. Y. Poliakova. Aldeana, a peasant girl: Mlle. Komisarjevskaya. Saniboldo del Cofone, a gunman: K. Moyseenko. Robbers and Bandits of the Piranesi Band: I. H. Antarova, Mlle. Diakonova, Mlle. A. Nikitina, Messrs. Sergieff, Stark, Bologovskoy.

The action represents a Court Performance in the Halls of San Souci in the Epoch of Frederick the great.

ACT 2

"The Queen of Spades"
    A fantastic story in 11 Tableaux after the story by Alexander Pushkin. Music by Alexei Archangelsky. Scenery and costumes by Yury Annyenkoff. Produced (directed) by Theodore Komisarjevsky and Nikita Balieff.

CAST (in order of appearance): Herman: G. HAYES. First Madman: N. Duggan. Second Madman: G. Weld. The Young Countess: I. H. ANTAROVA. The Duke of Orleans: A. Tcherkassky. The Italian Count Cagliostro: N. Moyseenko. Officers of the Guard (2): Sourin: W. Whitehead. Naroumoff: W. HOME. Tomsky: G. King. First Officer: G. Weld. Second Officer: N. Duggan. Lisa: H. Kingstead. The Old Countess: M. AULT. Tchekalinsky: A. TSCHERKASSKY.

Prologue: In a Madhouse. 1830. Scene 1: At Versailles. About 1775. Scene 2: At Naroumoff's in St. Petersburg. 1830. Scene 3: Outside the Countess' House. Scene 4: Outside the Spanish Embassy. Scene 5: The Countess' Room. Scene 6: A Passage Outside the Countess' Room. Scene 7: The Countess' Funeral. Scene 8: Hermann's Room. Scene 9: Tchekalinsky's Gaming House. Epilogue: The Madhouse.

ACT 3

"1860, or, An Interrupted Festival"
    A Musical Buffonade inspired by airs of Jacques Offenbach and Charles Lecocq. Scenery and Costumes by Natalia Gontcharova. Produced (directed) by Boris Romanoff and Nikita Balieff.

CAST: General Pepinster: N. BALIEFF. Blanche, his daughter: Mlle. VETCHOR. Viscount Nestor d'Armagnac, her fiancé: A. TSCHERKASSKY. Cora des Entournures, a Courtesan: Mme. Cortis. Marquis of Topinambour, disguised as a Major-domo: M. Zotoff. The Chief of Police: K. Moyseenko. Four Policemen: Messrs. Stark, Dolinoff, Sergieff, Bologovskoy. Dancers of the Moulin Rouge: Mlle. T. RIABOUCHINSKA, M. ROMANOFF. Guests at the Ball: Mlles. Toropva, Ivannikova, Boborikina, Nikitina, Poliakova, Diakonova, Anatrova. Messrs. Aplitcheyeff, Loukin, Rekonenko, Dolinoff, Stark, Sergieff, Bologovskoy.

EAST WIND
1931.39

A Musical Play in Two Acts, 12 Scenes. Book by Oscar Hammerstein II and Frank Mandel. Music by Sigmund Romberg. Lyrics by Oscar Hammerstein II. Play staged by Oscar Hammerstein II. Dances staged by Bobby Connolly. Settings by Donald Oenslager. Costumes by Charles LeMaire. Music director, Oscar Bradley. Orchestrations by Hans Spialek. Produced by Laurence Schwab and Frank Mandel. Opened 27 October 1931 at the Manhattan Theatre and closed 14 November 1931 after 23 performances.

CAST (in order of appearance): Monsieur Granier: GREEK EVANS. Jacques: Vance Elliott. Gabrielle: Betty Junod. Julie: Francis Markey. Claudette Fortier: CHARLOTTE LANSING. René Beauvais: WILLIAM WILLIAMS. Claire: Rose Mullen. Mimi: Sherry Pelham. Lorraine Fortier: DENNIE MOORE. Marie Martel: VERA MARSH. Capt. Paul Beauvais: J. HAROLD MURRAY. Capt. Dejan: Thomas Chadwick. Taxi Driver: I. Anchong. A Tourist: Gus Howard. Pierre Fortier: Jules Epailly. Victor Cliquot: JOE PENNER. Tsoi Tsing: AHI. King of Luang-Prabang: Ivan Izmailov. His Interpreter: Y. Y. Hsu. King of Cambodia: Frank Dobert. His Interpreter: S. Wong. Hop Sing: J. C. Donsu. Capt. Gervais: Gladstone Waldrip. Papa Gouli: Raymond Bramley. Pianist: Bobby [Robert Emmett] Dolan. A Maid: Marjorie Dille. The Stage Manager: O. J. Vanasse. The Compére: Emile Ladoux. The McNulty Sisters: Lorraine Pearl, Leatrice Pearl. King in Ballet: Alexander Yakovleff. Prince in Ballet: Aron Tomaroff. Dr. Duval: George Chapell.

Sopranos and Contraltos: Anna Mae Colburn, Sylvia Nelson, Mildred Gethins, Olga Leigh, Sylvie Roberts, Norma Nash, Helen Haynes, Peggy Strickland, Marie DeJardin. Tenors, Baritones and Bassos: Jackson Stuart, Harry Pickering, James Renard, Bert LeRoy, Edward Martin, Alfonso Inglasia, Eugene King, Alfred Russ, John Fredericks, Walter Leven, Herman Belmonte, Paul Aines, Andrew Keller, William Warren, Frank Vaughn, Bart Shilling, Cornelius Pichler, Basil Prock, Nat Broffman, Tom Chadwick, Charles Glazer, Gladstone Waldrip, Ivan Sokoloff, Ivan Izmailov, Vance Elliott, Frank Dobert.

Dancers: Sherry Pelham, Kay Stewart, Carola Taylor, Anita Pam, Ruth Green, Katherine Cameron, Amy Weber, Frances Markey, Clara Blackath, Dorothy Van Hest, Rita Marks, Rosalie Trego, Ruth Gordon[48], Betty Junod, Gypsy Hollis, Jocelyn Lyle, Adrienne Lampel. The International Gypsies: Alada Sio, Fred Orbowski, Harry Sacher, Bennie Ladner, Milton Stecker.

Act 1, Scene 1: A Country Fair, near Marseilles. The time is the present. Scene 2: On Board Ship. Scene 3: Pierre Fortier's Casino, Saigon, Indo-China. Scene 4: Vic's Elephant Enclosure. Scene 5: Pierre Fortier's Home. Scene 6: Vic's Elephant Enclosure. Scene 7: Along the River Front, Saigon.

Act 2, Scene 1: Restaurant "Aux Belles Poules," Paris. Scene 2: Papa Gouli's Apartment. Scene 3: Stage of a Music Hall in Paris. Scene 4: Monsieur Granier's Study. Scene 5: Lorraine's Wine Shop, Marseilles.

ACT 1

Scene 1

    Opening
        Ensemble
    "It's a Wonderful World"
        C. Lansing, G. Evans, Ensemble
    Musical Interlude
        C. Lansing, W. Williams, V. Marsh, D. Moore

Scene 2

    "East Wind"
        J. H. Murray, Ensemble
    "I Saw Your Eyes"
        C. Lansing, J. H. Murray, W. Williams, Officers

Scene 3

    "These Tropics"
        V. Marsh, J. Penner, Dancers
    "Congai"
        Ahi, W. Williams, Ensemble

Scene 5

    Wedding Scene
        C. Lansing, W. Williams, J. H. Murray, Ensemble
    "Are You Love?"
        C. Lansing, W. Williams, J. H. Murray
    "You Are My Woman"
        J. H. Murray

Scene 6

    "Minnie"
        J. Penner

Scene 7

    "Embrace Me"
        W. Williams, Mullen Sisters

ACT 2

Scene 1

    "The Americans Are Coming"
        V. Marsh, Ensemble

---

[47]The original CHAUVE SOURIS was first produced in 4 consecutive editions in New York 1 February 1922 at the 49th Street Theatre for 544 performances.

[48]Not the dramatic actress of the same name.

"I'd Be a Fool"
C. Lansing
Finaletto
J. H. Murray, G. Evans
Scene 3
"Regardez-Moi"
Lorraine and Leatrice Pearl
Indo-Chinese Ballet
Ahi, A. Yakovieff, A. Tomaroff, Dancers
Scene 4
"When You Are Young"
J. H. Murray, G. Evans
Scene 5
Finale
Entire Company

1931.40 THE LAUGH PARADE

A Musical Revue in Two Acts, 19 Scenes. Dialogue (sketches) by Ed Wynn and Ed Preble. Music by Harry Warren. Lyrics by Mort Dixon and Joe Young. Staged and ideas by Ed Wynn. Dances and ensembles staged by Albertina Rasch. Settings and costumes by Weld. Lighting by Clark Robinson. Music director, John McManus. Orchestrations by (Robert) Russell Bennett, Hans Spialek, Henry Sallinger. Produced by Ed Wynn. Opened 2 November 1931 at the Imperial Theatre and closed 21 May 1932 after 231 performances.

CAST: ED WYNN, JEANNE AUBERT, LAWRENCE GRAY, BARTLETT SIMMONS, EUNICE HEALY, JACK POWELL, ED CHENEY, Sara Jane, Albert Baron, Frieda Mierse, Adam and Amelia DiGatano, Wilbur Hall, Levenoria Sabalis, Frank and Harry Seaman, George Prentice, William Crowley.
The Wynnsome Dancing Girls: Roxey Fay Green, Margery Bailey, Virginia Case, Jane Dunlap, Margaret Dawn, Dorothea Frank, Vivian Hall, Renee Havel, Juliette Jordan, Mary Aster, Frances Krane, Lillian Ostrom, Evelyn Paulson, Mary Phillips, Sunny Reddy, Billie Reynolds, Mimi Sherman, Arlene Taylor, Sara Jane, Flora Taylor, Elizabeth Turner, Betty Wright, Francis Woodward, Janice Williams, Jacqueline Paige, Viola Paulson. *Keep Kissable Girls:* Levenoria Sabalis, Kathleen Bryan, Diana Curzon, Jerry Rogers, Virgil Dodd, Madeline Dunbar, Joyce Whitney, Madge Smylee. *Albertina Rasch Dancers:* Florence Nelson, Mabel Barry, Mary Wilkinson.

ACT 1
Scene 1
The Starting Place
Ed Wynn: Himself. *A Modern Girl:* S. Jane. *A Chorus Boy:* A. Baron.
A Beautiful Wife: F. Mierse. *A Housewife:* Amelia DiGatano. *An Iceman:*
H. Seaman.
Scene 2
In the Second Place
Actresses, Actors, Singers, Dancers, Acrobats, Musicians, Dancing Girls, Show Girls, Company: (The Rest of the Company).
Scene 3
An Odd Place: "Punch and Judy Man"
E. Healy
Punch and Judy Man: E. Wynn. With Wynnsome Dancing Girls, Keep Kissable Girls.
Scene 4
A Dandy Place
Johnnie: A. Baron. *An Actress:* K. Bryan. *Johnnie:* J. Powell. *Chorus Girls:* S. Jane, L. Sabalis, M. Dunbar. *Johnny:* E. Wynn. *Johnnie:* B. Simmons. *Chorus Girls:* V. Dodd, D. Curzon. *Jerry:* J. Rogers. *An Actress:* F. Mierse. *Alf.:* E. Cheney. *Muss.:* Adam DiGatano. *Eins.:* F. Seaman. *Shaw:* A. Baron. *Cal.:* W. Crowley. *A Star:* J. Aubert.
Scene 5
A Corking Place
Frieda: F. Mierse. *Sara:* S. Jane. *Bart:* B. Simmons. *Jerry:* J. Rogers. *Maddy:* M. Dunbar. *Kate:* K. Bryan. *Noria:* L. Sabalis. *Diana:* D. Curzon. *Virge:* V. Dodd. *Joyce:* J. Whitney. *Madge:* M. Smylie. *Al:* A. Baron. *Wilbur:* W. Hall. *The Dancers:* The DiGatanos. *The Drunk:* G. Prentice.
"Got to Go to Town"
E. Cheney, Wynnsome Dancing Girls
Scene 6
A Familiar Place
A Johnnie: H. Seaman. *An Acrobat:* E. Wynn. *Another Acrobat:* F. Seaman.

Scene 7
A Nice Place
Bench Sitter: E. Wynn. *Jeanne:* J. Aubert. *Lawrence:* L. Gray. *Sara:* S. Jane.
"Ooh! That Kiss"
J. Aubert, L. Gray
With Albertina Rasch Dancers, Wynnsome Dancing Girls, Keep Kissable Girls.
Scene 8
Himself: E. Wynn. *Street Cleaner:* J. Powell. *Policeman:* A. Baron. *Delivery Boy:* W. Hall.
Scene 9
A Commanding Place
"The Laugh Parade"
B. Simmons
The Captain: F. Mierse. With Wynnsome Dancing Girls, Keep Kissable Girls.
ACT 2
Scene 1
A Hot Place
"The Torch Song"
B. Simmons
With Wynnsome Dancing Girls, Keep Kissable Girls, Albertina Rasch Dancers.
Scene 2
A New Place
Ed Wynn: Himself. *Wilbur:* W. Hall. *Marline:* K. Bryan. *Bicycler:* S. Jane.
Scene 3
A Mysterious Place
The Actor: E. Wynn.
Scene 4
A Tapping Place
"Excuse for Song and Dance"
E. Healy, E. Cheney
Scene 5
A Musical Place
A Boy: E. Wynn. *Proprietor:* A. Baron. *Musician:* W. Hall. *Customer:* B. Simmons. *A Tourist:* F. Mierse. *Customers:* S. Jane, E. Healy.
Scene 6
A Meeting Place
The Producer: E. Wynn. *Lawrence:* L. Gray. *Jeanne:* J. Aubert.
"You're My Everything"
J. Aubert, L. Gray
Scene 7
A Movie Place
Picture Patron: E. Wynn.
Scene 8
A Lovely Place: "Love Me Forever"
He Who Sings: B. Simmons. *She Who Dances:* E. Healy. With Albertina Rasch Dancers, Wynnsome Dancing Girls, Keep Kissable Girls.
Scene 9
A Foolish Place
The Cameleer: E. Wynn. *The Policeman:* A. Baron. *Jeanne:* J. Aubert.
Scene 10
The Finishing Place: Finale
Entire Company
Thank You All
Good Night

1931.41 THE CHIMES OF NORMANDY

A Revival of the Comic Opera in Three Acts, 5 Scenes[49]. (Original French libretto "Les Cloches de Corneville" by Clairville and Charles Gabet.) Music by Robert Planquette. Staged by Milton Aborn. Art director, Charles Baatz. Costumes by Brooks. Musical director, Louis Kroll. Produced by the Civic Light Opera Company. Opened 2 November 1931 at Erlanger's Theatre and closed 14 November 1931 after 16 performances.

[49]First presented in New York in English 22 October 1877 at the Fifth Avenue Theatre for 16 performances. For Synopsis of Scenes and Musical Numbers, see original 1877 production.

CAST: *Serpolette*, the Good-for-Nothing: VIVIAN HART. *Germaine*, the Lost Marchioness: VERA MYERS. *Village Maidens (4): Gertrude*: Ann Johnson. *Jeanne*: Dhenise Delehante. *Nanette*: Theo. Van Tassel. *Suzanne*: Georgina Dieter. *Henri, Marquis de Corneville*: EDWARD NELL, JR. *Jean Grénicheux*, a Fisherman: ROY CROPPER. *Gaspard*, a Miser: HERBERT GOULD. *The Bailiff*: DETMAR POPPEN. *Notary*: Robert Capron.

Villagers, Attendants of the Marquis: Mary Hennessy, Keitha Gillette, Dhenise Delehante, Georgina Dieter, Ann Abbott, Mary St. John, Mitzi Eder, June B. Clarke, Winefred McClary, Doris Colman, Vera Mueller, Lauretta Brislin, Olga Schumacher, Maria Julian, Theo. Van Tassell, Cyrilla Tuitt, Gertrude Rittenhouse, Lloyd Ericsson, Alexander Black, Rudy Glaisek, Hudson James, Otis Holwerk, Siegfried Langer, August Loring, Paul Graham, George Koenig, Buck Williams, Robert Dawson.

1931.42   HERE GOES THE BRIDE

A Musical Comedy in Two Acts, 11 Scenes. Book by Peter Arno; additional dialogue by Roger Pryor. Lyrics by Edward Heyman. Music by John W. Green; additional music by Richard Myers. Staged by Edward Clarke Lilley. Dances and ensembles by Russell Markert. Scenery sketched by Peter Arno, designed by Dale Stetson. Costumes by Kiviette. Music director, Adolph Deutsch. Orchestrations by Conrad Salinger. Produced by Peter Arno. Opened 3 November 1931 at the 46th Street Theatre and closed 7 November 1931 after 7 performances.

CAST (in order of appearance): *Roddy Trotwood*: ERIC BLORE. *Tarkington*: Joseph Spree. *Etta Fish*: COLLETTA RYAN. *Diddles Stuyvesant*: DOROTHY DARE. *Bubbles Stuyvesant*: Pauline Gaskins. *Doddles Stuyvesant*: Ann Roth. *Toodles Stuyvesant*: Roberta Robinson. *Roger Loring*: JOHN GALLAUDET. *Betty Fish*: GRACE BRINKLEY. *Tony Doyle*: PAUL FRAWLEY. *June Doyle*: VICTORIA [Vicki] CUMMINGS. *Hives*: BOBBY CLARK. *Blodgett*: PAUL MCCULLOUGH. *June's Maid*: Norma Taylor. *Eloise Bell*, a Reporter: Mary Pettis. *Judge Humphrey*: DUDLEY CLEMENTS. *Taxi Drivers*: Al and Ray Samuels. *Hotel Clerk*: Bruce Carrington. *Flossie*, a Cow: Chick & Andy. *Baroness Von Ga Ga*: Charlotte Homann. *Rose*: FRANCES LANGFORD. *Sparker*, a Gambler: Harry Holbrook. *House Detective*: Philip Lord. *Clerk of the Court*: Gordon Clark. *June's Attorney*: Harry Holbrook.

Dancers: Norma Perrin, Anna Rex, Mildred Espy, Muriel LeCount, Terry Lawlor, Mary Mascher, Madeline Lynch, Anna Rita Lynch, Margot Bazin, Muriel Markert, Meda Cordova, Vida Manuel, Lilian Ward, Gertrude O'Donnell, Ann Hastings, Ethel Hampton, Gene Doughty. *Show Girls*: Charlotte Homann, La Verne Barker, Loretta Goss, Doris De Lairs, Dorothy Talbot, Vera King, Marion Glass, Helen Thompson. *Singers*: Frank King, Edwin Drake, Bruce Carrington, Gordon Clark, Dick Neeley, Gus Hyland, Fred Barry, George Lamb, George O'Brien.

Act 1, Scene 1: Scandal Sheet. *Scene 2*: Trotwood's Penthouse. *Scene 3*: Reno Station. *Scene 4*: Hotel Riverview Lobby. *Scene 5*: Hotel Promenade. *Scene 6*: Ross Alley.

Act 2, Scene 1: Corridor in the Hotel. *Scene 2*: Two Bedrooms. *Scene 3*: The Hotel Garden. *Scene 4*: The Divorce Court. *Scene 5*: Cal-Neva Lodge.

ACT 1
  "The Inside Story"
    The Girls
  "Remarkable People We"
    C. Ryan, E. Blore, The Girls
    (*Music by* Richard Myers.)
  "My Sweetheart 'Tis of Thee"
    G. Brinkley, P. Frawley, The Girls
  "Shake Well Before Using"[50]
    D. Dare, The Girls
  "My Sweetheart 'Tis of Thee" (reprise)
    G. Brinkley
  "We Know Reno"
    Ensemble
  Dance
    A. Samuels, R. Samuels
  "Well, You See"
    C. Ryan, B. Clark
  "What's the Difference"
    D. Dare, Ensemble
  "One Second of Sex"
    V. Cummings, J. Gallaudet
    (*Music by* Richard Myers.)
  "Hello, My Lover, Goodbye"
    F. Langford, Ensemble

ACT 2
  "It's My Nature"
    D. Dare, J. Gallaudet, The Girls
  "It Means So Little to You"
    P. Frawley, G. Brinkley
  "Music in My Fingers"
    F. Langford, Ensemble
    (*Music by* Richard Myers.)
  Dance
    A. Samuels, R. Samuels
  Finale
    Entire Company

1931.43   NAUGHTY MARIETTA

A Revival of the Musical Comedy in Two Acts, 3 Scenes[51]. Music by Victor Herbert. Book and lyrics by Rida Johnson Young. Staged by Alonzo B. Price. Art director, Charles Baatz. Costumes by Brooks. Marionettes by Tony Sarg. Musical director, Louis Kroll. Produced by the Civic Light Opera Company (Milton Aborn, director). Opened 16 November 1931 at Erlanger's Theatre and closed 28 November 1931 after 16 performances; re-opened 7-12 December 1931 at Erlanger's Theatre for an additional 8 performances. Total: 24 performances.

CAST: *Captain Richard Warrington*: ROY CROPPER. *Lieutenant Governor Grandet*: DETMAR POPPEN. *Etienne Grandet*, Son of Lieutenant Governor: LOUIS TEMPLEMAN. *Sir Harry Blake*, an Irish Adventurer: LESLIE MCCLOUD. *Rudolfo*, Keeper of Marionette Theatre: James Murray. *Florenze*, Secretary to Lieutenant Governor: Tom Collins. *Lizette*, a Casket Girl: Eulalie Young. *Adah*, a Quadroon: ANN CAREY. *Silas Slick*, Captain Dick's Servant: ROBERT CAPRON. *Nanette*: THEO. VAN TASSELL. *Felice*: Ann Johnson. *Fanchon*: Dhoris Delehante. *Night Watchman*: Buck Williams. *Pirate*: Paul Graham. *Indian*: Paul Graham. *East Indian*: Siegfried Langer. *Marietta D'Altena*: ILSE MARVENGA.

Ensemble: Mary Hennessy, Dhoris Delehente, Georgina Deiter, Mitzi Eder, Winifred McClary, Doris Colman, Vera Mueller, Lauretta Brislin, Olga Schumacher, Maria Julian, Theo. Van Tassel, Gertrude Rittenhouse, Ethel Sheridan, Muriel Day, Elsie Frank, Deborah Ledger, Bella Girard. Lloyd Ericsson, Alexander Black, Rudy Glaisek, Hudson James, Otis Holwerk, Siegfried Langer, August Loring, Paul Graham, George Koenig, Buck Williams, Lowell Handshaw.

1931.44   BOCCACCIO

A Revival of the Operette in Three Acts[52]. (Original German libretto by F. Zell and Richard Genée, based on a play by Bayard, de Leuwen and de Beauplan.) Music by Franz von Suppé. New musical and English version by Bonnell Bennett. Staged by Horace Sinclair. Dances arranged by Thomas Cannon. Costumes by Eaves, Blythe and Schneider. Musical director, Ethel Leginska. Produced by Charles L. Wagner. Opened 17 November 1931 at the New Yorker Theatre and closed 5 December 1931 after 21 performances.[53]

CAST: *Checco*, a Beggar: FREDERIC JENKS. *Beggars (6): Giocometto*: Hunter Sawyer. *Anselmo*: Paul Farber. *Toto*: Roland Lash. *Gianno*: William Schuster. *Ercole*: Henry Richardson. *Pepi*: Frank Barron. *Leonetto*, a friend of Boccaccio: Floyd Townsley. *Fresco*, Lotteringhi's Apprentice: BRUCE NORMAN. *Lotteringhi's Apprentices (7): Alberto*: Walter McCord. *Guidotto*: Martin Remneck. *Fedoro*: Paul Farber. *Angelo*: Hunter Sawyer. *Gerbino*: Walter Ross. *Riccardo*: Kenneth Brown. *Rostogio*: Henry Faust. *Mistress Jancifiore*: Alice Morello. *Elise*, her niece: Germaine Roland. *Marietta*, a young girl: Edis Phillips. *Mistress Nona Pulchi*: Marie Roberts. *Her Daughters (3): Augustina*: Edith Audrey Mann. *Elena*: May Kynock. *Angelica*: Rose Gardner. *Lambertuccio's Maids (3): Filippa*: Marjorie Sumner. *Oretta*: Patricia Parsons. *Violanta*: Ruth Valentine. *Townspeople*: Huntington Rice, Jean Spiro, Agnes Traynor, Leone Neumann, Rosel Benda, Florence Novic, Lavinia Knight, Leonore Brown, Jessie Griggs, Nita Vaudry. *Students and Boccaccio's Friends (8): Tofano*:

---

[50]"Shake Well Before Using" and all incidental music arranged by John W. Green.

[51]Originally produced in New York 7 November 1910 at the New York Theatre for 136 performances. For Synopsis of Scenes and Musical Numbers, see original 1910 production. For this production, an Opening Chorus to Act 2 was added. "Marionette Song" became Dance of the Marionettes for Richard and Marietta; the Dream Melody in Act 2 was moved to follow the Dance of the Marionettes.

[52]First presented in English 17 May 1880 at the Union Square Theatre for 28 performances; previously presented in German 23 April 1880 at the Thalia.

[53]Scenery uncredited. No individual song titles listed for this production.

Charles Coleman. *Chichibio*: Murray Kendrick. *Guido*: Hugh Sweeney. *Cisti*: Claire Booher. *Federico*: Charles Stone. *Renieri*: Ralph McDowell. *Giotto*: Alvan Sternlund. *Lanto*: Harold Steinberg. *Fratelli*, a Bookseller: Hubert Raidich. *Lotteringhi*, a Cooper: WLLIAM HEUGHAN. *Lambertuccio*, a Grocer: MICHAEL RAGGINI. *Scalza*, a Barber: GEORGE MORGAN. *Beatrice*, Scalza's Wife: ANNA HAMLIN. *Giovanni Boccaccio*, Novelist and Poet: ALLAN JONES. *Peronella*, Lambertuccio's Wife: MAY BARRON. *Fiametta*, Adopted Daughter of Lambertuccio: CARLOTTA KING. *Pietro*, Prince of Palermo: EDWARD LAY. *Isabella*, Lotteringhi's Wife: LAURA ROBERTSON. *The Unknown, Butler of the Duke of Tuscany*: FREDERICK JENCKS. *The Dancing Master*: Thomas Cannon.

Characters in the Commedia Dell'Arte: *Columbine*: Frances Mann. *Archelino*: Thomas Cannon. *Brighella*: Reba Campbell. *Pulchinello*: Roland L. Lash. *Pantaleone*: William Schuster. *Scarpino*, Columbine's Lover: Bruce Norman. *Narcissino*, Columbine's Wooer: Charles Stone. *Premier Danseur*: Thomas Cannon. *Premiere Danseuse*: Frances Mann.

Act 1: A Public Square in Florence Italy. June 24, 1331. The Feast of St. John.

Act 2: The Houses and Gardens of Lambertuccio and Lotteringhi. The next morning.

Act 3: The Ducal Palace, Florence. One week later.

1931.45

THE FIREFLY

A Revival of the Operetta in Three Acts[54]. Book and lyrics by Otto Harbach. Music by Rudolf Friml. Staged by Milton Aborn. Art director, Charles Baatz. Costumes by Brooks. Musical director, Louis Kroll. Produced by the Civic Light Opera Company (Milton Aborn, director). Opened 30 November 1931 at Erlanger's Theatre and closed 5 December 1931 after 8 performances.

CAST: *Sybil Vandare*: AMY ATKINSON. *Suzette*: EULALIE YOUNG. *Pietro*: LESLIE MCCLOUD. *Geraldine Vandare*: ANNA MAE COLBURN. *Jack Travers*: ROY CROPPER. *John Thurston*: Louis Templeman. *Mrs. Oglesby Vandare*: Mrs. HERBERT L. WATEROUS. *Jenkins*: Robert Capron. *Herr Franz*: DETMAR POPPEN. *Nina*: ILSE MARVENGA. *Antonio Columbo*: Georgina Dieter. *Correlli*: SIEGFRIED LANGER.

Ensemble: Mary Hennessy, Dhoris Delehante, Georgina Dieter, Mitzi Eder, Winefred McClary, Doris Colman, Vera Mueller, Lauretta Brislin, Olga Schumacher, Maria Julian, Theo. Van Tassell, Gertrude Rittenhouse, Ethel Sheridan, Muriel Day, Elsie Frank, Deborah Ledger, Bella Girard. Lloyd Ericsson, Alexander Black, Rudy Glaisek, Hudson James, Otis Holwerk, Siegfried Langer, August Loring, Paul Graham, George Koenig, Buck Williams, Lowell Handshaw.

1931.46

JACK AND THE BEANSTALK

A Fairy Opera for the Childlike in Three Acts, 13 Scenes[55]. Libretto by John Erskine. Music by Louis Gruenberg. Musical director, Albert Stoessel. Stage director, Alfredo Valenti. Settings by Margaret Linley. Produced by George Bye (The Juilliard School of Music Production). Opened 21 December 1931 at the 44th Street Theatre and closed 2 January 1933 after 18 performances.

CAST: *Jack*: MARY KATHERINE AKINS, ALMA MILSTEAD. *Mother*: BEATRICE HEGT, MARION SELEE. *Princess* [previously the Old Woman]: PEARL BESUNER. RUBY MERCER. *Cow*: RODERIC CROSS, GEORGE NEWTON. *Giant*: RAYMOND MIDDLETON, JULIUS HUEHN. *Locksmith*: Willard Young. *Butcher*: Roy Nichols, Mordecai Bauman. *Tanner*: John Barr. *Barker*: Roland Partridge. *Magic Harp Soli*: Apolyna Stoskus, John Barr, Janice Kraushaar.

Ensemble: Misses. Antoine, Chapelle, Couchman, Dorff, Gilman, Huddle, Kraushaar, Leshure, Lockwood, Lapidus, Malolie, Marshall, O'Connell, Olson, Schwan, Stoskus, Waltenberg, Wisecup, Wooten, Strickler. Messrs. Bauman, Haywood, Hill, Marsh, Nichols, Partridge, Pratt, Worthington, Young, Audenci, Kaminet, Bogges, Weisecup.

Act 1, Scene 1: Outside Jack's House. *Scene 2*: On the Road to Market. *Scene 3*: The Country Market. *Scene 4*: On the Road Home. *Scene 5*: Outside Jack's House.

Act 2, Scene 1: Country near Giant's Castle. *Scene 2*: Kitchen in Giant's Castle. *Scene 3*: Country near Giant's Castle. *Scene 4*: Kitchen in Giant's Castle. *Scene 5* Country near Giant's Castle. *Scene 6*: Kitchen in Giant's Castle. *Scene 7*: Country near Giant's Castle.

Act 3: Outside Jack's House.

---

[54]First presented in New York 2 December 1912 at the Lyric Theatre for 120 performances. For Synopsis of Scenes and Musical Numbers, see original 1912 production.

[55]First produced in New York 19-21 November 1931 at the Juilliard School. No individual musical numbers listed. Costumes uncredited.

ACT 1[56]

Scene 1

No meat, no bread, no milk
M. K. Akins, B. Hegt

When I had youth I had beauty
B. Hegt

Mother, your tears are silly
M. K. Akins

What should I do
R. Cross

Scene 2

Come on, won't you
M. K. Akins, R. Cross

Scene 3

This way, ladies and gentlemen
R. Partridge

Will you marry me, Princess? (Country Dance)
Ensemble

Who'll buy my cow?
M. K. Akins, R. Nichols, J. Barr, W. Young, Ensemble

We ought not to have come
M. K. Akins, R. Cross

Scene 4

Young man, young man (Scene)
P. Besuner, R. Cross, M. K. Akins

Scene 5

He is long coming
B. Hegt

Yes, she's sold
M. K. Akins, B. Hegt

ACT 2

Scene 1

Love is a magic lifted
P. Besuner

I left you at the market
M. K. Akins, P. Besuner

Scene 2

Most of all blessings
R. Middleton

Scene 3

Love is a magic lifted (reprise)
P. Besuner [Old Woman]

Be quick! He is after me!
M. K. Akins, P. Besuner

Did he come this way?
R. Middleton, P. Besuner

Scene 4

He will steal you too, will he?
R. Middleton

Scene 5

Be quick now, he's after us! (reprise)
M. K. Akins, P. Besuner [Princess]

Scene 6

And who may you be (Scene)
R. Middleton, M. K. Akins

Grasshopper, sing me a tune I can shimmy to
A. Stoskus

It has a fine voice too (Scene)
M. K. Akins, R. Middleton

Scene 7

My true love has a way with him
P. Besuner

I've got it! Let's go!
M. K. Akins, P. Besuner

---

[56]Musical numbers not listed in program. List prepared from published libretto (Bobbs-Merrill, Indianapolis, 1931).

ACT 3

What is keeping him? (Solo)
B. Hegt

Who's ringing that bell (Scene)
B. Hegt, M. K. Akins

Mother, this is my love (Scene)
M. K. Akins, P. Besuner, B. Hegt, R. Cross

Of hours not mine (Love Song)
M. K. Akins, B. Hegt, P. Besuner

Time is a magical snare
A. Stoskus, Ensemble

Now to his love (Bridal Chorus)
A. Stoskus, Ensemble

I don't care for weddings
R. Cross

Time is a magical snare (Finale)
Entire Company

SUGAR HILL

1931.47

An Epoch of Negro Life in Harlem (A Musical Comedy) in Two Acts. Book by Charles Tazewell. Music by Jimmy [James P.] Johnson. Lyrics by Jo Trent. Settings by Theodore Kahn. Costumes by Mahieu. Produced by the Moveing Day Company, Inc. Opened 25 December 1931 at the Forrest Theatre and closed 2 January 1932 after 11 performances.[57]

CAST: *Sister Huff*: CARRIE HUFF. *Matilda Small*: Margerite Lee. *Steve Jenkins*: FLOURNEY [Flournoy] MILLER. *Sam Peck*: AUBREY LYLES. *Loucinda*: JUANITA STINNETTE. *Jasper*: CHAPPY CHAPPELLE. *Gyp Penrose*: BROADWAY JONES. *Joe*: Albert Chester. *Mitzie*: Kay Mason. *Cleo*: EDNA MOTEN. *Tress*: TRESSA MITCHELL. *Uncle Henry*: Harrison Blackburn. *Officer Brown*: ANDREW COPELAND. *Cleo's Mother*: INA DUNCAN. *Parson Johnson*: J. Lewis Johnson.

Girls: Lela Brogden, Laura Duncan, Jennie Day, Edna Ellington, Aurora Edwards, Thelma Green, Inez Gray, May Haygood, Josephine Heathman, Alberta Lowery, Catherine Noizette, Gussie Williams, Boby Smith, Charle Downs, Norma Alderonte.
Boys: Joe Loomis, Maurice Ellis, Pedro Turner, Hallie Howard, E. A. Midleton, Adolph Henderson, George Mason, James Moses, Richard Shopsire, DeWitt Davis, Alfred Anderson, Pagasusth-Mule, Himself.

Act 1: Sugar Hill. A twenty-four hour day.

Act 2: Sugar Hill. Next day.

ACT 1

"Noisy Neighbors"
M. Lee, C. Huff, Ensemble

"I Love You, Honey"
C. Chappelle, J. Stinnette, Ensemble

"Hanging Around Yo Dore"
E. Moten, B. Jones, Dancing Boys

"Hot Harlem"
B. Jones, Ensemble

"Boston"
K. Mason, Drucila[58], Meers, Chester, Norton & Ford

"What Have I Done?"
I. Duncan, Ensemble

ACT 2

"Hot Rhythm"
T. Mitchell, K. Mason, McCormack, Norton & Ford

"Fooling Around With Love"
E. Moten, T. Woods, Miss Wallace

"Rumbola"
T. Mitchell, Miss Meers, Miss Lawson, Girls

"Something's Going to Happen to You"
C. Chappelle, J. Stinette

"Moving Day"
C. Huff, Entire Company

---

[57]Director, musical director (presumably James P. Johnson) uncredited.
[58]Character name; no actor named in this role.

OF THEE I SING

1931.48

A Musical Comedy in Two Acts, 11 Scenes. Book by George S. Kaufman and Morrie Ryskind. Music by George Gershwin. Lyrics by Ira Gershwin. Staged by George S. Kaufman. Dances by George Hale. Settings by Jo Mielziner. Costumes by Charles LeMaire. Music director, Charles Previn. Orchestrations by (Robert) Russell Bennett, William Daly. Produced by Sam H. Harris. Opened 26 December 1931 at the Music Box Theatre, moved 10 October 1932 to the 46th Street Theatre, and closed 14 January 1933 after 441 performances.

CAST [in order of appearance]: *Louis Lippman*: SAM MANN. *Francis X. Gilhooley*: HAROLD MOFFET. *Maid*: Vivian Barry. *Matthew Arnold Fulton*: DUDLEY CLEMENTS. *Senator Robert E. Lyons*: GEORGE E. MACK. *Senator Carver Jones*: EDWARD H. ROBBINS. *Alexander Throttlebottom*: VICTOR MOORE. *John P. Wintergreen*: WILLIAM GAXTON. *Sam Jenkins*: GEORGE MURPHY. *Diana Devereaux*: GRACE BRINKLEY. *Mary Turner*: LOIS MORAN. *Miss Benson*: JUNE O'DEA. *Vladimir Vidovitch*: Tom Draak. *Yussef Yussevitch*: Sulo Hevonpaa. *The Chief Justice*: RALPH RIGGS. *Nora*: Leslie Bingham. *The French Ambassador*: FLORENZ AMES. *Senate Clerk*: Martin Leroy. *Guide*: Ralph Riggs.

Photographers, Policemen, Supreme Court Justices, Secretaries, Sight-seers, Newspapermen, Senators, Flunkeys, Guests, etc.: Ruth Adams, Olgene Foster, Peggy Greene, Yvonne Gray, Billie Seward, Grenna Sloan, Adele Smith, Jessica Worth, Kathleen Ayres, Bobbie Brodsley, Martha Carroll, Mary Carroll, Dorothy Donnelly, Ann Ecklund, Virginia Franck, Dorothy Graves, Georgette Lampsi, Terry Lawlor, Lillian Lorray, Martha Maggard, Mary Mascher, Anita Pam, Barbara Smith, Baun Sturtz, Peggy Thomas, Patricia Whitney. Robert Burton, Ray Clark, Charles Conklin, Frank Erickson, Jack Fago, Frank Gagen, Hazzard Newberry, Jack Ray, Bruce Barclay, Tom Curley, Leon Dunar, Michael Forbes, David Lawrence, Charles McClelland, Richard Neely, John McCahill.

The Jack Linton Band: Jack Linton, Dave Allman, Charles Bennett, Walter Hinger, Milton Hollander, Frank Miller, Pete Shance, Jake Vander Meulen.

Act 1, Scene 1: Main Street. *Scene 2*: A Hotel Room. *Scene 3*: Atlantic City. *Scene 4*: Madison Square Garden. *Scene 5*: Election Night. *Scene 6*: Washington.

Act 2, Scene 1: The White House. *Scene 2*: The Capitol. *Scene 3*: The Senate. *Scene 4*: Again the White House. *Scene 5*: The Yellow Room.

ACT 1
Scene 1
"Wintergreen for President"
Ensemble

Scene 3
"Who Is the Lucky Girl To Be?"
G. Brinkley, Ensemble

"The Dimple on My Knee"
G. Brinkley, G. Murphy, Ensemble

"Because, Because"
G. Brinkley, G. Murphy, Ensemble

Finaletto:
("As the Chairman of the Committee")
(D. Clements, Company)

("How Beautiful")
(Company)

"Never Was There a Girl So Fair"
Company

"Some Girls Can Bake a Pie"
W. Gaxton, Company

Scene 4
"Love Is Sweeping the Country"
G. Murphy, J. O'Dea, Ensemble

"Of Thee I Sing"
W. Gaxton, L. Moran, Company

Scene 6
Finale:
Entrance of Supreme Court Justices
(Supreme Court Justices)

"(Here's) a Kiss for Cinderella"
W. Gaxton, Ensemble

"I Was the Most Beautiful Blossom"
G. Brinkley

("Some Girls Can Bake a Pie")
(reprise)
(W. Gaxton, G. Brinkley, Judges, Ensemble)

ACT 2
Scene 1

"Hello, Good Morning"
G. Murphy, J. O'Dea, Secretaries

"Who Cares?"
W. Gaxton, L. Moran, Reporters

Finaletto:

"Garçon, S'il vous plaît"
French Soldiers

Entrance of French Ambassador
(F. Ames, Ensemble)

"The Illegitimate Daughter"
F. Ames, (Ensemble)

("Because, Because") (reprise)
(G. Brinkley, Ensemble)

("We'll Impeach Him")
(G. E. Mack, H. Moffet, Ensemble)

("Who Cares?") (reprise)
(W. Gaxton, L. Moran)

Scene 3

"The (Senatorial) Roll Call"
V. Moore, (Ensemble)

Finaletto:

(Impeachment Proceeding)
(V. Moore, D. Clements, S. Mann, H. Moffet, G. E. Mack, E. H. Robins, M. Leroy, Ensemble)

("Garçon, S'il Vous Plaît") (reprise)
(F. Ames, French Soldiers)

("The Illegitimate Daughter") (reprise)
(F. Ames, French Soldiers)

"Jilted"
G. Brinkley, Company

"Who Could Ask For Anything More?" ("I'm About to Be a Mother")
L. Moran, Company

"Posterity (Is Just Around the Corner)"
W. Gaxton, Company

Scene 5

"Trumpeter, Blow Your (Golden) Horn"
(Ensemble)

Finale ("On That Matter No One Budges")
(Entire Company)

1932.01 A LITTLE RACKETEER

A Musical Comedy in Two Acts, 9 Scenes. Book by Harry Clarke (adapted from a German play by K. Kalbfuss and R. Wilde). Music by Haskell Brown. (Additional music by Dmitri Tiomkin.) Lyrics by Edward Eliscu. Staged by William Caryl. Dances by Jack Donohue under the supervision of Albertina Rasch. Settings by Watson Barratt. Costumes by Ernest Schrapps, Alison McLellan Hunter. Music director, Maury [Maurie] Rubens. Produced by the Messrs. Shubert. Opened 18 January 1932 at the Sam S. Shubert Theatre and closed 27 February 1932 after 48 performances.

CAST (in order of appearance): *Donnie Parker*: CARL RANDALL. *Mr. Knoblock*: John Perkins. *Frank Leave*: GEORGE MARSHALL. *Alberta Lawrence*: BARBARA NEWBERRY. *Ethel Pierson*: GRACE HAYES. *Dick Barrison*: JOHN GARRICK. *Head Waiter*: George Del Rigo. *Flossie*: Kay Simmons. *May*: Evelyn Reide. *Donovan*: Daniel J. Sullivan. *Jay Slump*: WILLIAM KENT. *Dixie*: QUEENIE SMITH. *Mrs. Alameda Snook*: LORRAINE WEIMAR. *Henry*: HAMTREE HARRINGTON. *Grayson*: Walter Johnson. *The Ghost Priest*: Khalil Oglou Mazini. *Yo Hay Tong*: Princess Yo Hay Tong.
Show Girls: Leone Sousa, Julia Barker, Eleanor Arden, Jerry Rogers, Dorothy Drum, Bobby Hamilton, Marion Gillon, Agatha Phillips. Dancers: Marjorie Crane, Madeline Eubanks, Elsie St. Clair, Billy Joy, Martha Pacini, Colleen Ward, Snookie Gordon, Inez Goetz, Joan Abbey, Gertrude Medwin. Gentlemen: John Perkins, George Del Rigo, Harold Offer, Kai Hansen, Al. Berl, Marty Rhiel, Steve Mikol, Ned Lynn, Jimmie Corke, Stanley Ledman, George Marshall. Specialty Dancers: Tom and Betty Wonder.

Act 1, Scene 1: Main Room of the (Central Park) Casino. 1 A.M. The present. *Scene 2*: Parking space in front of the Casino. *Scene 3*: Dick's Apartment. The living room—later that night. *Scene 4*: Exterior of a restaurant. 2 A.M. *Scene 5*: Dixie's Room in the West Sixties. Next morning. *Scene 6*: Library of Dick's Apartment. Later the same night.

Act 2, Scene 1: The Living-room of Dick's Apartment. The next day. *Scene 2*: Parking space in front of the Casino. *Scene 3*: Main room of the Casino. Same evening.

ACT 1
Scene 1

Opening Chorus: "Night Club Nights"
Entire Ensemble

"Thanks to You"
C. Randall, B. Newberry
(*Music by* Berenece Kazounoff. *Lyrics by* Earl Crooker.)

"Dou Dou"[59]
J. Garrick, G. Marshall, C. Ward

"Blow, Gabriel"
G. Hayes, Ensemble

Specialty
T. Wonder, B. Wonder

Scene 2

"Mr. Moon"
J. Garrick, G. Hayes
(*Music by* Lee Wainer. *Lyrics by* Lupin Fein and Moe Jaffe.)

"When That Band Plays"
Q. Smith, Albertina Rasch Dancers
("Southern Belles" *Ballet Music by* Dmitri Tiomkin.)

Reprise
Q. Smith

"Throwing a Party"
W. Kent, Girls

Scene 3

"You and I Could Be Just Like That"
Q. Smith, J. Garrick

Finaletto
Q. Smith, J. Garrick

"Ballyhoo"
C. Randall, B. Newberry, Albertina Rasch Dancers, Ensemble
(*Music by* Dmitri Tiomkin.)

Scene 4

Specialty
Albertina Rasch Dancers

Specialty
T. Wonder

Scene 5

"Danger If I Love You"
Q. Smith, J. Garrick

Songs
G. Hayes

Scene 6

"I Have a Run in My Stocking"[60]
Q. Smith, Albertina Rasch Dancers

Finale
Entire Company

ACT 2
Scene 1

"You've Got to Sell Yourself"
C. Randall, Entire Ensemble

Rio de Janeiro Dance (*Music by* Dmitri Tiomkin.)
Albertina Rasch Dancers

Tango
B. Newberry, C. Randall

Gitana
Albertina Rasch Dancers

Brazilian Dance
B. Newberry, C. Randall

"Spring Tra La"
W. Kent, L. Weimar
(*Music by* Lee Wainer. *Lyrics by* Lupin Fein and Moe Jaffee.)

---

[59]Dropped after opening.
[60]Dropped after opening.

Reprise
    Q. Smith, J. Garrick
"What Great Big Eyes You Have"
    G. Marshall, I. Goetz, Dancing Girls, Boys
Scene 2
"Starry Sky"
    J. Garrick, Albertina Rasch Dancers
    (*Music by* Dmitri Tiomkin.)
Dance Reprise
    C. Randall, B. Newberry
Scene 3
"Srimpi"—Javanese Sacred Dance
    Y. H. Tong, K. O. Mazini
    (*Choreography and Costumes arranged and designed by* Khalil Oglou Mazini.)
Specialty
    T. Wonder, B. Wonder
Finale
    Entire Company

ROBIN HOOD

1932.02

A Revival of the Comic Opera in Three Acts[61]. Book and lyrics by Harry B. Smith. Music by Reginald DeKoven. Staged by Milton Aborn. Costumes by Brooks. Settings by Civic Light Opera Co. Studios. Musical director, Louis Kroll. Produced by the Civic Light Opera Company (Milton Aborn, director). Opened 27 January 1932 at Erlanger's Theatre and closed 20 February 1932 after 29 performances.

<u>CAST</u>: *Alan-a-Dale*: ELEANORE LA MANCE. *Little John*: ALLEN WATEROUS. *Will Scarlet*: FRED PATTON. *Annabel*: VIVIAN HART. *Friar Tuck*: FRANK LALOR. *Dame Durden*: HELEN BERTRAM. *Robert of Huntington*, afterwards Robin Hood: HOWARD MARSH. *Lady Marian Fitzwater*: CHARLOTTE LANSING. *Sheriff of Nottingham*: WILLIAM DANFORTH. *Sir Guy Gisborne*: JOHN CHERRY. *Herald*: JOHN EATON. *Jailer*: Pat Quinton. *Sexton*: Frank Clark.
    Children (courtesy of Mrs. J. E. Wilcox Professional School): Norma Edwards, Evelyn Messer, Harriet Irwin, Mary Combs, Alice Farley, June Wilcox, Donna Leonard, Mary McQuade. *Milkmaids*: Gertrude Waldon, Frances Baviello, Georgina Dieter, Patricia Clark, Isabel Norwood, Mary Harper. *Sheriff's Guard*: Bernard Lane, John Eaton, John Cardini, Richard Scharff, Frank Dowling, Felix Noonan. *Tinkers*: Harrison Fuller, Bert Melrose, Patrick Quinton, Harold Raymond, Hobson Young, Thomas Seabrooke, Francis Clark, Frank Murray. *Lady Marian Fitzwalter's Mounted Escorts*: Adele Story, Frances Moore, Isabel Norwood, Mary Hennessy, Rosa Rubenstein, Marynia Apel. *Male Horseback Riders*: John Eaton, Frank Dowling, Bernard Lane, Felix Noonan, Richard Scharff, John Cardini. *Choir Boys*: Lillian Koniver, Adele Story, Ann Johnson, Mabel Thompson, Mary Hennessy, Jean Adams, Debora Ledger, Rosa Rubenstein. *Bridesmaids*: Gertrude Waldon, Frances Baviello, Isabel Norwood, Eleanor Gilmore, Rosalyn Shaw, Georgina Dieter, Patricia Clark, Mary Harper. *Pages*: Frances Moore, Katherine Calle, Harriet Gottlieb, Marynia Apel, Marie Kelly, Paula Reades, Julia Reed, Anna May Coburn.

THROUGH THE YEARS

1932.03

A Romantic Musical Play in Three Acts, 5 Scenes. Book by Brian Hooker, based on the play "Smilin' Through" by Allan Langdon Martin and Jane Cowl. Music by Vincent Youmans. Lyrics by Edward Heyman. Staged by Edward MacGregor. Dances by Jack Haskell and Max Scheck. Scenery designed by Ward and Harvey Studios, Inc. Costumes designed by John Booth. Musical direction, William Daly. Produced by Vincent Youmans. Opened 28 January 1932 at the Manhattan Theatre and closed 13 February 1932 after 20 performances.

CAST (in order of appearance): *Kathleen*: NATALIE HALL. *Kenneth*: MICHAEL BARTLETT. *Ellen*: Marion Ballou. *Dr. Owen Harding*: CHARLES WINNINGER. *John Carteret*: REGINALD OWEN. *Willie Ainley*: NICK LONG, JR. *Penelope*: Caryl Bergman. *Betty Fallow*: MARTHA MASON. *Captain Moreau*: GREGORY GAYE. *Lucy*: Leone Neumann. *Mary Clare*: Audrey Davis. *Jeremiah Wayne*: MICHAEL BARTLETT. *Moonyeen*: NATALIE HALL. *Arabella*: MARTHA MASON. *Roger*: NICK LONG, JR. *Mrs. Ainley*: Lelane Rivera.
    Singing Girls: Kay Adams, Dee Collins, Adline Forbes, Mildred Gethins, Estelle Malin, Marie Valot, Anna Worth, Leone Neumann. *Dancing Girls*: Peggy Andre, Gloria Beaumont, Emilie Burton, Evelyn Hannons, Ann Hardman, Gertrude Lowe,

Dolly Martinez, Evelyn Monte, Sonny Nelson, Peggy Schenck, Winnie Torney, Paulette Winston, Patricia Francis. *Boys*: Frank Barron, John Frederick, Ray Thomas, Ivan Sokoloff, Jack Lawrence, Anton Luksor, Irving Pichler, Norman Van Emburgh.

Act 1: The Carteret Garden, in 1914.

Act 2, Scene 1: The Carteret Garden, 40 Years before Act 1. *Scene 2*: The Carteret Garden, again in 1914.

Act 3, Scene 1: The Hedge Corner on the Ainley Estate, in 1919. *Scene 2*: The Carteret Garden, same evening.

ACT 1
"Kathleen Mine"
    N. Hall, M. Bartlett
"An Invitation"
    C. Winninger, R. Owen, N. Long, Jr., Ensemble
"Kinda Like You"
    M. Mason, N. Long, Jr.
"I'll Come Back to You"
    N. Hall, M. Bartlett
Finale

ACT 2
"How Happy Is the Bride"
    L. Neumann, M. Mason, Ensemble
"Through the Years"
    N. Hall, Ensemble
"It's Every Girl's Ambition"
    M. Mason, Girls
"The Trumpeteer and The Lover"
    C. Winninger, N. Long, Jr., M. Mason
"You're Everywhere"
    N. Hall, M. Bartlett
Finaletto
"Through the Years" (reprise)
    N. Hall

ACT 3
"The Road to Home"
    N. Long, Jr.
"Drums in My Heart"
    G. Gaye, Ensemble
"Kinda Like You" (reprise)
    M. Mason, N. Long, Jr., Girls
Finale

MAURICE CHEVALIER

1932.04

An Intimate Song Recital in Two Acts, 6 Scenes. Piano accompanists, Jacques Fray and Mario Braggiotti. Produced by Charles Dillingham. Opened 9 February 1932 at the Fulton Theatre and closed 22 February 1932 after 17 performances.

ACT 1
Scene 1

Jacques Fray, Mario Braggiotti play a Medley of popular Maurice Chevalier songs.

Scene 2

Maurice Chevalier recites a Prologue.

Scene 3

Fray and Braggiotti play "Dark Eyes" (*Music by* A. Salama; Impression of a Russian Orchestra with Cymbalum), "Gershwiana," and "Bolero" (*Music by* Maurice Ravel.).

Scene 4

Maurice Chevalier sings:
"Little Hunka Love"
"C'était Moi" (That Was Me)
"Oh! That Mitzi" (from *ONE HOUR WITH YOU* film)
    (*Music by* Oscar Straus. *Lyrics by* Leo Robin.)
"Mon Petit Tom" (Love Story of Mr. and Mrs. Elephant)
    (*Music by* Charles Pothier. *Lyrics by* Albert Willemetz.)

---

[61]First presented in New York 28 September 1891 at the Standard Theatre for two engagements of 35 and 42 performances. For Synopsis of Scenes and Musical Numbers, see original 1891 production.

Inpersonation of Dorville, Boucot, Mayol, famous French comedians, singing "You Brought a New Kind of Love to Me," "Hello, Beautiful," "Oh! That Mitzi."

ACT 2

Scene 1

Fray and Braggiotti play a medley of popular Chevalier songs, Fantasy on "Dancing in the Dark," "Yankee Doodle" variations (1) à la Chopin, (2) à la Gershwin.

Scene 2

Maurice Chevalier sings:

"Ma regulière" (My Regular Girl)
(*Music and Lyrics* by Charles Borel-Clerc.)

"What Would You Do?" (from film *ONE HOUR WITH YOU*)
(*Music* by Richard A. Whiting. *Lyrics* by Leo Robin.)

"Dites-moi ma mère" (Tell Me Mother)
(*Music and Lyrics* by MauriceYvain, Hermann Haller, Marcellus Schiffer.)

Imitations of Rudy Vallee and Willie Howard imitating him in "All I Want Is Just One" and "Sweeping the Clouds Away"

"Valentine" (from films *INNOCENTS OF PARIS* and *FOLLIES BERGERE*)
(*Music* by Henri Christiné. *Lyrics* by Albert Willemetz.)

"Louise" (from film *INNOCENTS OF PARIS*)
(*Music* by Richard A. Whiting. *Lyrics* by Leo Robin.)

1932.05   FACE THE MUSIC

A Musical Comedy Revue in Two Acts, 20 Scenes. Book by Moss Hart. Music and lyrics by Irving Berlin. Staged by Hassard Short. Book directed by George S. Kaufman. Dances by Albertina Rasch. Settings by Albert R. Johnson. Costumes by Kiviette, Weld. Music director, Frank Tours. Orchestrations by (Robert) Russell Bennett, Frank Tours, Maurice DePach [DePackh]. Produced by Sam H. Harris. Opened 17 February 1932 at the New Amsterdam Theatre and closed 9 July 1932 after 165 performances.

CAST (in order of appearance): *Hal Reisman*: ANDREW TOMBES. *Kit Baker*: KATHERINE CARRINGTON. *Pat Mason, Jr.*: J. HAROLD MURRAY. *Mrs. Meshbesher*: MARY BOLAND. *Her Footman*: Peter Sargent. *Miss Eisenheimer*: Helen Lyons. *Martin Van Buren Meshbesher*: HUGH O'CONNELL. *Mr. O'Rourke*: EDWARD GARGAN. *A Sister Team*: Aida Conkey, Dorothy Waller. *Pickles*: MARGARET LEE. *Joe*: JACK GOOD. *Louis*: DAVE [David] BURNS. *Mme. Elise*: Frances Halliday. *Her Assistant*: Elizabeth Houston. *A Lady of the Evening*: Jean Sargent. *Postman*: Ward Arnold. *May*: Dorothy Claire. *Rodney St. Clair*: JOSEPH MACAULEY. *Rivington*: OSCAR POLK. *Sheriff*: Clyde Filmore. *Mr. Delaney*: Martin Shepard. *Stage Doorman*: Charles Burrows. *Detective*: Thomas Arace. *Clerk of the Court*: Charles Coleman. *Prosecuting Attorney*: JOSEPH MACAULEY. *Judge Furioso*: Vernon Jayson. *Specialty*: Blue & White Marimba Band (Alfred Jamesworth, Director).

Albertina Rasch Dancers: Dorissa Nelova, Vida McLain, Valerie Huff, Alice Kellerman, Kathleen Vannoy, Mary Vannoy, Virginia Bethel. *Girls*: Mary Brooks, Aida Conkey, Leslie Cornell, Maxine Darrell, Elsie Duffy, Nancy Dolan, Mary Kennedy, Irene Kelly, Jeanette Lea, Betty Lee, Dorothy Lamb, Ruth Martin, Patsy O'Keefe, Etna Ross, Wilma Roeloff, Helen Thompson, Teddy West, Dorothy Waller, Rita Horgan, Evelyn Nielson, Peggy Dell. *Boys*: Chester O'Brien, Mortimer O'Brien, Eddie Crosswell, Jack Barnes, Martin Dennis, Guy Daly, Bert Doughty, George Ford, Phil King, Clark Leston, Bob Long, Jay Hunter, Harry Murray, Howard Morgan, Fred Nay, Jimmy Ryan, Jack Ross, Stuart Steppler, Dan Wyler, Jack Wolfe, Emmett O'Brien.

Act 1, Scene 1: Outside the Automat. (New York City). *Scene 2*: Inside the Automat. *Scene 3*: Fifth Avenue. *Scene 4*: Meshbesher's Office. *Scene 5*: Along Broadway. *Scene 6*: In front of the Palace Theatre. *Scene 7*: Meshbesher's Penthouse. *Scene 8*: The Stage of Reisman's Theatre. *Scene 9*: Ante Room of the Casino. *Scene 10*: The Ballroom. *Scene 11*: The Mirrors.

Act 2, Scene 1: Outside the Theatre. *Scene 2*: The Speakeasy. *Scene 3*: The Theatre Boxes. *Scene 4*: Inside the Theatre. *Scene 5*: The Station House. *Scene 6*: Mrs. Meshbesher's Boudoir. *Scene 7*: Times Square. *Scene 8*: A Hotel. *Scene 9*: City Hall.

ACT 1

Scene 1

"Lunching at the Automat"
Ensemble

Scene 2

"Let's Have Another Cup of Coffee"
J. H. Murray, K. Carrington

Scene 5

"Torch Song"
J. Sargent

Scene 6

"You Must be Born With It"
M. Lee, J. Good

Scene 7

"(On) A Roof in Manhattan"
J. H. Murray, K. Carrington
Danced by the Albertina Rasch Dancers.

Scene 8

"My Beautiful Rhinestone Girl"
J. Macaulay

Scene 10

"Soft Lights and Sweet Music"
J. H. Murray, K. Carrington

ACT 2

Scene 1

Opening
Ensemble

"I Say It's Spinach"
J. H. Murray, K. Carrington

Scene 2

"Drinking Song"
J. Macaulay, Boys

Scene 4

"Dear Old Crinoline Days"
K. Carrington
Danced by Boys, Albertina Rasch Dancers.

Scene 5

"I Don't Want To Be Married"
M. Lee, J. Good

Scene 7

"Manhattan Madness"
J. H. Murray

Scene 9

(Finale)
A. Tombes, Entire Company

1932.06   MARCHING BY

A Musical Play in Two Acts, a Prologue and 3 Scenes. Book by Harry B. Smith and Harry Clarke, adapted from the original German operetta "Hotel Stadt-Lemberg" by Ernst Neubach (and the novel by Lajos Biró). Music by Jean Gilbert. Lyrics by Harry B. Smith. Additional music and lyrics by Harry Revel and Mack Gordon. Play and ensembles staged by J. C. Huffman. Dances by Allan K. Foster. Settings by Watson Barratt. Costumes by Ernest Schrapps. Music director, George Hirst. Produced by the Messrs. Shubert. Opened 3 March 1932 at the 46th Street Theatre and closed 12 March 1932 after 12 performances.

CAST: *Prologue: Elsa*: Cornelia Chason. *Lieutenant Muller*: Jack Lee. *Butler*: Herbert Weber. *Hans Von Arnheim*: Jack Leslie. *Lieutenant Franz Almasy*: GUY ROBERTSON. *Countess Anna Von Hatfield*: DESIREE TABOR. *Edda Von Goetzen*: Betty Davis. *Captain Goerlich*: Walter Palm. *Sergeant*: Kenneth Paige. *Lieutenant Hauser*: Ralph Slear. *Colonel Popen*: Philip Lord. *Eva*: Betty Dair. *Officers, Soldiers, Guests*.

The Play: Captain Von Zedlitz: John J. Walsh. *Lieutenant Kaufman*: Walter Meek. *Lieutenant Donnheim*: Walter Nagle. *Captain Bauer*: Charles Christie. *Lieut Dorch*: Roy Vitalis. *Lieutenant Schantz*: Victor Young. *Sergeant*: Kenneth Paige. *A Cossack*: Herbert Weber. *Colonel Popen*: Philip Lord. *Ilsa*: KATHERINE EDWARDES. *Mitzi*: Katherine Skidmore. *First Girl*: Joan Dudley. *Second Girl*: Betty Dair. *Third Girl*: Marie Valday. *Anton Androssy*: VICTOR CASMORE. *Elias Butterman*: SOLLY WARD. *Anna*: DESIREE TABOR. *Ilma Sachalow*: ETHEL NORRIS. *Lieutenant Franz Almasy*: GUY ROBERTSON. *Sergeant Karloff*: John Walsh. *Sacha Sachalow*: DONALD BURR. *Colonel Petroff*: LEONARD CEELEY. *Ivan Tarnoff*: HUGH MILLER. *Major Orloff*: ARTHUR GEARY. *Orderly*: Gerald Moore. *Nicoli*: Samuel Krevoff.

Ladies and Maids: Marie Valday, Sonia De Calva, Cornelia Chason, Margaret Miller, Carol Laski, Betty Dair, Eleanor Standish, Elizabeth Taylor, Evelyn Muller, Marie Costello, Betty Davis, Eva Sawyer, Mary McDonald, Joan Dudley. *Officers and Soldiers*: Earl Mason, Donald Smith, Charles Kingsley, Charles Christie, Jerry Moore,

Larry Lawrence, Jack Lee, Jack Leslie, Arthur Singer, Claude Goehring, Herbert Weber, James Sheri, Earl Marvin, Owen Pauline, Frederick Grieve, Ralph Slear, Giles McIntyre, Roy Vitalis, Robert Grant, Walter Nagle, William Hubert, Wilbur Demarest, Kenneth Paige, Sam Bunin, Joseph Conley, Victor Young, Walter Palm, Fred Stamm.

Prologue: Chateau of the Countess Von Hatfeld near Lemberg, Austria. August, 1914.

Act 1: The Lobby and Lounge of the Hotel Imperial, 1915.

Act 2, Scene 1: The same. Evening of the same day. *Scene 2*: The next morning. After the bombardment.

PROLOGUE

"On Thru the Night"
    Officers, Ladies
    (*Music by* Harry Revel. *Lyrics by* Mack Gordon.)
"Here We Are in Love"
    D. Tabor, G. Robertson

ACT 1

"Marching By"
    G. Robertson, Ensemble
    (*Music by* Gus Edwards. *Lyrics by* Harry Clarke, Guy Robertson.)
"Here We Are in Love" (reprise)
    D. Tabor
"It Might Have Been You"
    E. Norris, D. Burr
    (*Music by* Gus Arnheim, Neil Moret. *Lyrics by* George Waggoner.)
"We're on Our Way to Hell"
    Officers, Soldiers
    (*Music by* Harry Revel. *Lyrics by* Mack Gordon.)
"All's Fair in Love and War"
    L. Ceeley, Ensemble
"Let Fate Decide"
    D. Tabor, L. Ceeley
    (*Music by* Maurie Rubens. *Lyrics by* Harry B. Smith.)
"I Gotta Keep My Eye on You"
    E. Norris, D. Burr
    (*Music by* Harry Revel. *Lyrics by* Mack Gordon.)
"Finery"
    D. Tabor, L. Ceeley
Finale
    D. Tabor, G. Robertson, L. Ceeley

ACT 2

Opening—"Light Up"
    L. Ceeley, Officers
"Forward March into My Arms"
    E. Norris, D. Burr
"I Love You (My Darling)"
    D. Tabor, G. Robertson
    (*Music by* Jean Gilbert. *Lyrics by* Edward Eliscu, George Hirst.)
"All's Fair in Love and War" (reprise)
    L. Ceeley, Officers, Soldiers, Maids
Finale
    Entire Company

HOT-CHA!
Laid in Mexico

1932.07

A Musical Comedy in Two Acts, 11 Scenes. Book by Lew Brown, Ray Henderson, Mark Hellinger, H. S. Kraft. (Based on the story "An Old Spanish Custom" by H. S. Kraft.) Music by Ray Henderson. Lyrics by Lew Brown. Dialogue staged by Edgar MacGregor, Edward Clarke Lilley. Dances staged by Bobby Connolly. Settings by Joseph Urban. Technical director, T. B. McDonald. Costumes by Charles LeMaire. Music director, Al Goodman. Orchestrations by (Robert) Russell Bennett. Produced by Florenz Ziegfeld. Opened 8 March 1932 at the Ziegfeld Theatre and closed 18 June 1932 after 119 performances.

CAST (in order of appearance): *Jack Whitney*: BUDDY ROGERS. *Hoffman*: Arthur Page. *Revenue Man*: Roy Sedley. *José Diaz*: Robert Gleckler. *Mae Devlin*: JUNE MacCLOY. *Toodles Smith*: MARJORIE WHITE. *Dorothy Maxwell*: JUNE KNIGHT. *Alky Schmidt*: BERT LAHR. *Bus Boy*: Nick Basil. *Conductor*: Jack Daley. *Brakeman*: Louis Delgardo. *Girl in Compartment*: Rose Louise [Gypsy Rose Lee]. *Ramon La Grande*: TITO CORAL. *Hap Wilson*: LYNNE OVERMAN. *Conchita*: LUPE

VELEZ. *Store Keeper*: Jules Epailly. *Three Troubadours*: Hernandez Brothers. *Gendarme*: John Fulco. *Servant*: Alma Ross. *Lopez*: Vic Munro. *Doctor*: Charles La Torre. *Ramona*: Miriam Batista. *Manuel*: Jules Epailly. *Specialties*: ANTONIO and RENEE DeMARCO (The DeMarcos), VELOZ and YOLANDA, ELEANOR POWELL.

Ladies of the Ensemble: Pauline Moore, Dorothy Flood, Neva Lynn, Lilyan Picard, Lorelle McCarver, Joan Burgess, Marion Santre, Alice Burrage, Mina Ruskin, Georgia Ellis, Diana Walker, Ethel O'Dell, Grace Moore, Jean Howard, Frances Kruger, Dorothy Kal, Marjorie Fisher, Kay Stewart, Louise Allen, Theo Phane, Pearl Harris, Polly Ray, Mary Alice Rice, Molly Wakefield, Prudence Edgar, Lorraine Webb, Theo Holley, Sherry Pelham, Mary Ann, Dorothy Day, Mercedes Hughes, Florence Healy, Gloria Kelly, Dody Donnelly, Gertrude Sheffield, Lou Ann Meredith, Frances Markey, Evelyn Lowrie, Jane Lane, Harriet Fink, Patty Hastings, Catherine O'Neill, Rosalie Milan, Iris Adrian, Marion Volk, Virginia Biddle, Carol Renwick, Marion Dixon, Mildred Webb, Mary Joan Martin, Mary Coyle, Marie Stevens, Betty Dumbris.
Gentlemen of the Ensemble: Alan DeSylva, Herman Belmonte, Lester Ostrander, Wilburn Riviere, Louis Delgardo, John Fulco, Basil Prock, Alfonso Iglesias, Thomas Thompson, Stanley Howard, George O'Brien, Efir Vitis, Tom Kelly, Leonard Berry, Edwin Marsh, William Ruppel.

Act 1, Scene 1: The Golden Fleece Club, New York City. 1:30 A.M. *Scene 2*: En route to Mexico. At the Station, At Manhattan Transfer, Before a Compartment. 72 hours later. *Scene 3*: A Public Square in Mexico City. Ten days later. *Scene 4*: Living Quarters over José's Café. *Scene 5*: The Training Camp for Matadors. *Scene 6*: The Fiesta.

Act 2, Scene 1: The Governor's Party. *Scene 2*: A Street in Mexico City. *Scene 3*: Outside the Arena. *Scene 4*: Matador's Entrance to the Bull Ring. *Scene 5*: Outside the Arena (later revised to José's Cafe).

ACT 1[62]

Scene 1

Opening Chorus
    R. Milan, T. Phane, L. A. Meredith, I. Adrian, M. Webb, C. O'Neill, J. Lane, A. Rice, L. Allen, P. Hastings, C. Renwick, P. Harris, M. Coyle, P. Edgar
"You Can Make My Life a Bed of Roses"
    J. Knight, B. Rogers
"You Can Make My Life a Bed of Roses" (reprise)
    Ensemble

Scene 3

"So This Is Mexico"
    American Girls
"Conchita"
    L. Velez, Ensemble
"I Want Another Portion of That"
    M. White, B. Lahr
"Say What I Wanna Hear You Say"
    L. Velez, B. Rogers, Ensemble

Scene 4

"Little Old New York"[63]
    J. MacCloy
"José, Can't You See!"
    M. White, R. Gleckler, Ensemble

Scene 6

"Fiesta"
    T. Coral, Male Ensemble
Shawl Dance
    Entire Ensemble, Veloz and Yolanda, The De Marcos
"It's Great To Be Alive"[64]
    J. Knight, Ensemble
"Say What I Wanna Hear You Say" (reprise)
    L. Velez, B. Rogers
"I Make Up For That in Other Ways"
    B. Lahr, M. Ann, M. Lavoe, D. Flood, C. O'Neill, A. Rice, D Donnelly, P. Hastings, J. Lane

ACT 2

Scene 1

Opening Chorus
    Entire Ensemble

---

[62]Added during the run:
    "They All Need a Little Hot-Cha"
    L. Velez
[63]Dropped during run.
[64]Dropped during run.

"There I Go Dreaming Again"
  J. Knight, Ensemble
"There's Nothing the Matter With Me"
  M. White, Ensemble
Scene 3
"You Can Make My Life a Bed of Roses" (reprise)
  J. Knight, B. Rogers
The Procession the Day of the Bull Fight
  Entire Company
"Song of the Matadors"
  T. Coral, Ensemble
Scene 5
Finale
  Entire Company

BLACKBERRIES OF 1932

1932.08

A Sepia Musical Revue in Two Acts, 26 Scenes. Book (sketches) by Eddie Green. Music and lyrics by Donald Heywood and Tom Peluso. Staged by Ben Bernard. Dances by Sidney Sprague, Lew Crawford. Settings by Myer Kanin, Buell Scenic Studios. Gowns by Gladys Douglas. Music director, Sam Wooding. Produced by Max Rudnick and Ben Bernard. Opened 4 April 1932 at the Liberty Theatre and closed 23 April 1932 after 24 performances.

CAST: EDDIE GREEN, TIM MOORE, SUSAYE BROWN, MANTAN (MORELAND), DEWEY ("PIGMEAT") MARKHAM, JACKIE ('Moms') MABLEY, GERTRUDE SAUNDERS, SAMMY PAIGE, JOHNNY LEE LONG, HAROLD NORTON, THELMA NEERS, JOHN DICKENS, ALICE HARRIS, Monte Hawley, Robert Raines, Helen Powell, Martin and Boisseau, Charles Ray, The Three Yorkers, The Three Bubbles, Amon Davis, The Bon Bons (Georgette Harvey, Kay Parker, Musa Williams, Natalie Long), Baby Goins, Drake and Morton, the Burma/Zulu Maids, Bill Shepard.

ACT 1
Scene 1
"On the Levee"
  G. Harvey, R. Raines, Ensemble
"Blackberries"
  Martin and Boisseau, the Brown Madcaps
Scene 2
In Steps and Taps
  The Three Bubbles
Scene 3
Harlem Rotisserie (*by* Pigmeat Markham and Johnny Lee Long)
  The Waiter: D. Markham. *A Customer*: K. Parker. *Clarence*: C. Ray. *Rudolph*: J. L. Long.
Scene 4
"Brown Sugar"
  S. Brown, the Brown Madcaps
Scene 5
Bucking the Traffic
  E. Green, M. Hawley, A. Davis
Scene 6
A Few Moments with Sammy Paige
Scene 7
"Love Me More (Love Me Less)" (The Harmonious Heart of the Blackberries)
  (*Music by* Tom Peluso. *Lyrics by* Ben Bernard.)
  The Sweethearts: C. Ray, A. Harris. *The Harmony*: The Bon Bons. *Bliss*: B. Goins. *The Presents*: The Madcaps.
Scene 8
Pay Me My Dime (*by* Mantan Moreland and Tim Moore)
  T. Moore, M. Moreland
Scene 9
Rhythm
  Drake and Morton
Scene 10
"Burma Lou"
  J. Dicksn, A. Harris, the Burma Maids
Dance of the Soudan
  T, Meers, H. Norton

Scene 11
Dance Specialty
  The Three Yorkers
Scene 12
The Bon Bons
Scene 13
Big Doings in the Big House (*by* Pigmeat Markham and Johnny Lee Long)
  A Prisoner: J. L. Long. *Another Prisoner*: D. Markham. *Condemned*: B. Shepard. *A Gun Moll*: J. Mabley. *Guards, Prisoners, Others*.
Scene 14
The Georgia Camp Meeting (*by* Tim Moore and Mantan Moreland)
  The Wayward Boy: T. Moore. *The Deacon*: Mantan. *The Sisters*: The Bon Bons.
Scene 15
A Real Ripe Blackberry
  G. Saunders
  (*Musical Numbers by* Eddie Green and Hughie Walke.)
Scene 16
The Dice Game
  E. Green, M. Hawley
Scene 17
Making the Picture
  The Extra: E. Green. *The Director*: M. Hawley.
Scene 18
On the Old Washboard
  At the Board: G. Harvey.
"Washing Your Blues Away"
  Entire Company
ACT 2
Scene 1
Drums of Africa
  The Chief: R. Raines. *The Girl*: H. Powell. *The Rival*: M. Hawley. And Zula Maids.
Scene 2
Midnite Steppers (They will actually burn your tongue)
Scene 3
A Harlem "Speak"
  The Bartender: D. Markham. *The Detective*: J. L. Long. *Customers*: S. Paige, A. Davis. *The Owner*: M. Hawley. *Hot Mama*: G. Saunders.
  (Song
  G. Saunders)
Scene 4
"Harlemania" (*Conceived by* Lee Posner)
  S. Brown, The Brown Madcaps, Martin and Boisseau
Scene 5
Dial It
  Trying to Dial It: E. Green. *Dialing It With Ease*: N. Long.
Scene 6
Jackie Mabley (Harlem's Queen of Comedy)
Scene 7
"Ye Olde Hock Shop" (*by* Tim Moore and Mantan Moreland)
  The Boss: T. Moore. *His Partner*: Mantan. *Trying to Borrow*: G. Harvey. *On the Stuff*: M. Hawley.
Scene 8
"Those Good Old Minstrel Days"
  C. Ray, Company
Finale

THE BLUE BIRD

1932.09

A Revival of the Russian Language (Musical) Revue in Two Acts, 16 Scenes[65]. Staged by Yascha Yushny. Conductor, incidental music and musical arrangements by N. Gogotzky. Stage director, G. Sjusin. Produced by

---

[65]Originally produced in New York as SEENIAYA PTITZA 28 December 1924 at the Frolic Theatre for 80 performances.

Sol Hurok. Opened 21 April 1932 at the Cort Theatre and closed 8 May 1932 after 20 performances.[66]

CAST: Messrs. YASCHA YUSHNY, A. Damansky, N. Dobrinin, J. Jaroff, K. Javorsky, D. Libidins, L. Resnik, J. Spivak, G. Sjusin, E. Wadimoff, Ivan Orlik. Mmes. M. Chenkina, P. Kosmowskaja, L. Kosmowskaja, E. Porfiriewa, A. Arenzwari-Yushny, Elena Lelik, E. Runich, M. Marewa, ISA KREMER.

ACT 1

Scene 1

St. Petersburg (1825)

Mmes. M. Chenkina, P. Kosmowskaja; Messrs. A. Damansky, N. Dobrinin, J. Jaroff, K. Javorsky, D. Libidins, L. Resnik, J. Spivak, G. Sjusin, E. Wadinoff
A hundred years ago, in Catharine Square of the city that is now Leningrad. The bronze monument of the famed Empress, flanked by the statues of her old favorites—Derjavin, the court poet; Potemkin, the social lion, and the noted general, Souvoroff. A night watchman reminisces sadly and moistly. Three maudlin cab drivers sing of the old days. At the stroke of the chimes the statues come to life and sing of old, dead glories.

Scene 2

The Bottle Stoppers

Mmes. L. Kosmowskaja, E. Porfiriewa; Messrs. A. Damansky, K. Javorsky, J. Jaroff, D. Libidins, L. Resnik

Scene 3

"Yugoslavian Washerwomen"

Mmes. V. Arenzwari-Yushny, E. Lelik, P. Kosmowskaja, M. Chenkina, E. Runich, M. Marewa
While playing in the city of Zagreb, in Yugoslavia, Mr. Yushny was greatly amused at the picture presented by the peasant women of the town on the way to the river banks to do their laundering. So dresses, baskets and red umbrellas were procured from the original and only store; music was composed, and "The Yugoslavian Washerwomen" was presented.

Scene 4

"The Volga Boatmen's Song"

Messrs. A. Damansky, N. Dobrinin, K. Javorsky, J. Jaroff, D. Libidins, L. Resnik, J. Spivak
This familiar melody of the Volga River bargemen, who sing while pulling the heavy-laden craft, has been used in Russia for more than 250 years.

Scene 5

"At the School-Gate"

Mmes. E. Runich, M. Marewa, E. Porfiriewa, E. Lelik, L. Kosmowskaja. Messr. N. Dobrinin
(After a painting by Bogdanoff-Belsky) Formerly education was not compulsory in Russia, consequently schools remained closed, and children from the neighboring villages often walked miles in hope of being admitted to the one that stayed open, only to have the door closed to them. This picture shows the Russian lad, eager to attend school, at the closed gate.

Scene 6

Dance of the Boyars

Mme. E. Lelik, Messr. I. Orlik

Scene 7

The Little Huntsman: ("The Huntsman's Song of Love;" Das Lied vom Jägerlein)

Mmes. L. Kosmowskaja, M. Marewa, E. Porfiriewa; Messr. N. Dobrinin
(Words and Music by N. Gogotsky. German words by Friedrich Jàrossy. English version by Leo Robin.)

Scene 8

Souvenir of Switzerland

Mmes. M. Marewa, E. Porfiriewa, Messrs. K. Javorsky, N. Dobrinin, L. Resnik, J. Spivak
(Music by Modest Moussorgsky.)
This Swiss mechanical toy-box shows how dolls and toys can be made to live when properly wound up; also, how human beings can become mechanical when their springs become slack.

Scene 9

With the Gypsies: (A picture of Moscow in 1860)

"A Friendly Chat"

D. Libidins

"The Gypsies Were Coming"

P. Kosmowskaja

"Flow, My Wine"

E. Wadimoff

"Sparkle, My Star"

I. Kremer

"It Will Storm, It Will Rain"

E. Runich

Dance

I. Orlik, E. Lelik
Merchant: N. Dobrinin. *An Old Crony*: K. Javorsky.

ACT 2

Scene 1

Alkmaar (A Cheese Market in Holland)

Blue Bird Ensemble
Mr. Yushny was so impressed with the types of costumes of the cheese workers that he later reproduced the same in the theatre where he was then playing. The success of this number was immediate, and upon the following evening the foremost Aklmaar cheese dealers replaced the "prop" cheese used on the stage with hundreds of the real article.

Scene 2

Folk Songs and Ballad

I. Kremer

Scene 3

Yushny's Cossack Chorus

Conductors: M. Marewa, Y. Yushny.

Scene 4

The Evening Bells (A *Poem by* Thomas Moore.)

J. Jaroff, Ensemble

Scene 5

Gossips 'Round the Samovar

Mmes. V. Arenzwari-Yushny, L. Kosmowskaja, M. Chenkina, M. Marewa, E. Porfiriewa, E. Runich

Scene 6

The Russian Market-Women

Mmes. V. Arenzwari-Yushny, L. Kosmowskaja, M. Marewa, E. Porfiriewa
This picture is an interpretation of a composition by the noted Russian composer (Modest) Moussorgsky.

Scene 7

Easter-Time in Russia (A province in 1890)

I. Kremer, Entire Company
Easter in Russia, in pre-revolution times, was a holiday when vendors, traders and even Punch and Judy shows took advantage of the assembled throngs and sold their wares to the village people who came out in masses on the public square to sing and dance.

THERE YOU ARE

1932.10

A Musical Play in Two Acts. Book by Carl Bartfield. Music by William Heagney. Lyrics by William Heagney and Tom Connell. Staged by Horace Sinclair. Dances by Vaughn Godfrey. Settings by Carlo Studios. Costumes by Eaves, Bertha Beres. Music director, Fred Hoff. Orchestrations, Irving Schloss, Roy Webb. Entire production supervised by Hyman Adler. Produced by Hyman Adler. Opened 16 May 1932 at the George M. Cohan Theatre and closed 21 May 1932 after 8 performances.

CAST: *Chita*, A seller of love potions: Melba Marcel. *Pasquale Costeo*, Proprietor of "The Blue Dove": ADRIAN ROSLEY. *Captain Louis Fidelio*, A.D.C. to Governor Gomez: Bruce Norman. *Don Jose Gomez*, Governor of the District: JOSEPH LERTORA. *Hidalgo Fernandez Bravo Herrara*: Walter Armin. *Dick Longwood*, 'Klondike': Robert Capron. *Pedro*, Waiter at "The Blue Dove": Arthur Marlowe. *Julia Danville*, "Snooky": BERTA DONN. *Carolita Rodriguez*: ILSE MARVENGA. *Peggy Hastings*, Carolita's Chaperon and Teacher: PEGGY O'CONNOR. *Pancho*, Diablo's Lieutenant: Andrew Kellar. *Señor Cambro*: HYMAN ADLER. *Lloyd Emerson*: ROY CROPPER. *Friar Francesco*: Louis Salvo. *La Mariposa*, a Dancer: GERTRUDE STANTON.

Hostesses at "The Blue Dove": Wee Griffin, Roberta Blake, Mona Medlin, Georgina Dieter. *Dancers at "the Blue Dove"*: Mary Downes, Marjorie Rich, Eleanor Martin, Dorothy Richmond, Helen Newton, Marjorie Sohmer, Rosalind Rensing, Virginia May. *Villagers*: Eddis Phillips, Dorothy Turry, Ruth Kramer, Theresa Hyle. *Aviators*: David Johns, Jack Malone, Arthur Van Haelst, Cornelius Pilcher. *Peasants*: Armundi Muzzi, William Dunn, David Tulin, Gwilym William. *Peons*: Marvin Briggs, Edwardo Salvo, George Zorini. *Musicians*: Louis Napolis, Leon Sabater. *Waiters at "The Blue Dove"*: Arthur Marlowe, Andrew Keller. *Diablo's Followers*: Andrew Keller, Tom Green, Jose Spiro, Louis Carrera. *Friars*: Juan Perez, Antonio Gonzalez, Julian Morales.

Act 1: The Patio of the Inn of "The Blue Dove," Satero, Mexico. An afternoon in August. Time is the present.

---

[66]Settings, costumes uncredited.

Act 2: The same, that evening.

ACT 1

Opening Ensemble
  M. Marcel, A. Rosley, Ensemble

"Haunting Refrain"
  J. Lertora, Hostesses, Ensemble

"There You Are"
  R. Capron, Hostesses, Ensemble

"Lover's Holiday"
  I. Marvenga, Ensemble

"They All Love Me"
  A. Rosley, Cabaret Girls

"Aces Up"
  R. Cropper, Aviators

"Safe in Your Arms"
  I. Marvenga, R. Cropper

"Love Lives On"
  H. Adler, Ensemble

Finaletto
  I. Marvenga, H. Adler, J. Lertora, P. O'Connor, B. Donn, R. Capron, B. Norman, Ensemble

ACT 2

Opening Scene
  A. Rosley, Ensemble

"More and More"
  I. Marvenga

"The Sound of the Drum"
  B. Norman, Dancers

"Wings of the Morning"
  R. Cropper

"The Love Potion"
  I. Marvenga, B. Donn, P. O'Connor

"Just a Little Pent-house and You"
  P. O'Connor, R. Capron

"Carolita"
  J. Lertora, Ensemble

Tamborine Dance
  Dancers

"La Zarzuelm" (Dance Solo) (*Music by* P. Lacome.)
  G. Stanton

"Senorita"
  B. Donn, R. Capron

"Legend of the Mission Bells"
  H. Adler, Ensemble

Finale
  Entire Company

1932.11

SHOWBOAT

A Revival of the Musical Comedy (Play) in Two Acts, 17 Scenes[67]. Book and lyrics by Oscar Hammerstein II. Based on the novel of the same name by Edna Ferber. Music by Jerome Kern. Scenery by Joseph Urban. Costumes by John Harkrider. Musical director, Oscar Bradley. Produced by Florenz Ziegfeld. Opened 19 May 1932 at the Casino Theatre and closed 22 October 1932 after 180 performances.[68]

CAST (in order of their appearance): *Windy*: Allan Campbell. *Steve*: Charles Ellis. *Pete*: James Swift. *Queenie*: TESS GARDELLA[Aunt Jemima]. *Parthy Ann Hawkes*: EDNA MAY OLIVER. *Cap'n Andy*: CHARLES WINNINGER. *Elly*: EVA PUCK. *Frank*: SAMMY WHITE. *Rubber Face*: Francis X. Mahoney. *Julie*: HELEN MORGAN. *Gaylord Ravenal*: DENNIS KING. *Vallon*: Thomas Gunn. *Magnolia*: NORMA TERRIS. *Joe*: PAUL ROBESON. *Backwoodsman*: Jack Daley. *Jeb*: Gladstone Waldrup. *La Belle Fatima*: Dorothy Denese. *Old Sport*: James Swift. *Landlady*: Annie

---

[67]Originally presented in New York 27 December 1927 at the Ziegfeld Theatre for 572 performances. For Synopsis of Scenes and Musical Numbers, see original 1927 production.

[68]Direction by Oscar Hammerstein II, choreography by Sammy Lee; vocal direction by William Vodery, uncredited in programs.

Hart. *Ethel*: Estelle Floyd. *Sister*: V. Ann Kaye. *Mother Superior*: Mildred Schwenke. *Kim* (child): Evelyn Eaton. *Mary* (another child): Mari Helgren. *Kim* (as a young woman): NORMA TERRIS. *Jake*, Piano Player: Robert Faricy. *Jim*: Jack Daley. *Man With Guitar*: Pat Mann. *Charlie*, Doorman at Trocadero: J. Lewis Johnson. *Lottie*: Gertrude Walker. *Dolly*: Tana Kamp. *Old Lady on Levee*: Laura Clairon. *Ensemble.*

1932.12

YEAH MAN

An All Negro Revue of Song, Dance and Laughter in Two Acts, a Prologue and 23 Scenes. Dialogue (sketches) by Leigh Whipper and Billy Mills. Music and lyrics by Al Wilson, Charles Weinberg, Ken Macomber, (Porter Grainger). Staged by Walter Campbell. Dances by Marcus Slayter. Scenery by the Fredericks Studios. Costumes by Brooks. Music director, Billy Butler. Orchestrations, Charles L. Cooke, Lorenzo Caldwell, Billy Butler. Produced by Walter Campbell and Jesse Wank. Opened 26 May 1932 at the Park Lane Theatre and closed 27 May 1932 after 2 performances.

CAST: MANTAN MORELAND, BILLY MILLS, LEIGH WHIPPER, MARCUS SLAYTOR, EDDIE RECTOR, THE MELODEE FOUR, ROSE HENDERSON, LILY YUEN, HILDA PERLENO, ROY and RASTUS, Peggy Phillips, Walter Brogsdale, Russell Graves, Adele Hargraves, Harry Fiddler, Jarahal, Eloise Bennett and Stepping Quintette, The Lindy Hoppers (Pansey Peryment, Ralph Henry, Edith Austin, Rabbit Taylor, Esselene Hinton, Shorty Snowden), Yeah Man Singers, Billy Butler's "Yeah Men", Marcus Slayter's Sixteen Brownskin Hurricanes.
  Millie Holmes, Jack Hutchins, Annie Davis, Larri Lorear, Harry Priolieu, Bernice Gray, Ernest Coleman, Helen Heartwell.

ACT 1

Prologue
  R. Henderson, B. Mills

Scene 1

"Mississippi Joys"
  Ensemble

"Gotta Get De Boat Loaded"
  Stevedores

"Dancing Fool"
  L. Yuen, Chorus

Miniature—Fighting Sin
  Captain: B. Mills. *Brother Lowdown*: S. Snowden. *Sister Newcomer*: P. Peryment. *Brother Hightower*: W. Brogsdale. *Sister Broadcast*: R. Henderson. *Brother Soblack*: M. Moreland. *Brother Newcomer*: H. Fiddler. *Sister Beenyer*: M. Holmes.

"That's Religion"
  B. Mills, Singing Syncopaters
  (*Music and Lyrics by* Porter Grainger.)
  Scene: Mississippi Levee.

Scene 2

"At the Barbecue"
  E. Bennett, Stepping Quintette

Scene 3

Boy Wanted
  The Boy: M. Moreland. *The Boss*: W. Brogsdale. *A Friend*: J. Hutchins. *Million Dollar Baby*: A. Hargraves. *Razor Jim*: L. Whipper.

Scene 4

Specialty
  Roy & Rastus

Scene 5

"I'm Always Happy When I'm in Your Arms"
  H. Perleno, M. Slayter, E. Rector

Scene 6

Racketeers
  Beer Paraders: M. Moreland, B. Mills. *On the Spot*: R. Graves. *Racketeers*: L. Whipper, W. Brogsdale.

Scene 7

"I've Got What It Takes"
  E. Bennett, Girls, assisted by E. Coleman

Scene 8

The Village Thief

"Lonely Pickaninny"
  Jarahal
  Thief: Jarahal. *Sheriff*: W. Brogsdale. *First Woman*: M. Holmes. *Second Woman*: A. Davis.

Scene 9

Dr. Jasper

Patient: M. Moreland. *Doctor*: W. Brogsdale. *Nurse*: E. Bennett. *First Girl Friend*: H. Heartwell. *Second Girl Friend*: A. Davis. *Third Girl Friend*: M. Holmes. *Boy Friend*: B. Mills.

Scene 10

"Crazy Idea of Love"

A. Hargraves, Girls

Scene 11

"Qualifications"

R. Henderson, B. Mills

(*Music and Lyrics by* Porter Grainger.)

Scene 12

Specialty

E. Rector

Finale—"It's Modernistic"

L. Yuen, Lindy Hoppers, Entire Company

ACT 2

Scene 1

"Come to Harlem"

B. Mills, Harlemites

Harlem Kid: S. Snowden. *Hot Mamma*: P. Peryment. *A Piece of Harlem Driftwood*: R. Henderson.

"The Spell of Those Harlem Nights"

R. Henderson, E. Rector, M. Moreland

Scene: Seventh Avenue at 131st Street.

Scene 2

"Baby, I Could Do It for You"

L. Yuen, R. Graves, Girls

Scene 3

Sightseeing in China

B. Mills, H. Fiddler

Scene 4

"Shady Dan"

E. Bennett, Stepping Quintette

Scene 5

"Give Me Your Love"

H. Perleno, E. Rector

Scene 6

"The Town of It"

Autoist: B. Mills. *Brother Hightower*: W. Brogsdale. *Sister Beenyer*: M. Holmes. *Lowdown*: M. Moreland.

Scene 7

A Harmonious Interlude

The Melodee Four

Scene 8

"Shake Your Bamboo"

A. Hargraves, Girls

Scene: Bamboo Land. *Tourists*: B. Mills, W. Brogsdale.

Native Dance

L. Lorear

Scene 9

Railroading—Place, Deepo, Lefhere, Mississippi

Tarin Caller: H. Priolieu. *Ticket Agent*: L. Whipper. *Porter*: M. Moreland. *Brother Soblack*: B. Mills. *Minnie Redd*: L. Yuen. *Sally Green*: E. Bennett. *Bessie White*: H. Perleno. *Mammy*: R. Henderson. *Magnolia*: B. Gray.

Scene 10

Specialty

Roy & Rastus

Scene 11

Finale

E. Rector, Entire Company

Paul McCullough and Bobby Clark in WALK A LITTLE FASTER (Photo: White Studio)
Billy Rose Theatre Collection, New York Public Library for the Performing Arts

1932–1933 SEASON

1932.13   HEY NONNY NONNY!

A Musical Revue in Two Acts, 27 Scenes. (Sketches by Frank Sullivan, Florence Calkins, E. B. White, Ogden Nash, Richy Craig, Jr., Harry Ruskin.) Lyrics mostly by Max and Nathaniel Lief, (Will Irwin, Herman Hupfeld). Music mostly by Michael H. Cleary, (Herman Hupfeld). Staged by Alexander Leftwich. Dances conceived and staged by Dave Gould. Settings designed by Raymond Sovey, Jo Mielziner. Costumes by Helene Pons, Mme. Berthe. Orchestra under the direction of Sherry Magee. Produced by Forrest C. Haring and John H. Del Bondio. Opened 6 June 1932 at the Sam S. Shubert Theatre and closed 2 July 1932 after 32 performances.

CAST: FRANK MORGAN, ANN SEYMOUR, RICHY CRAIG, JR., DOROTHY MCNULTY [Penny Singleton], JACK MCCAULEY, JOAN CARTER-WADDELL, JERRY NORRIS, ERNEST SHARPE, RALPH SANFORD, Wilma Cox, Mildred Tolle.

The Hey Nonny Nonny Girls: Gertrude Blake, Billie Burns, Edna Eustace, Mitzi Garner, Ruth Gordon[1], Gypsy Hollis, Tina Marie Jensen, Joann Larkin, Bunny Moore, Jean O'Neill, Estelle Phillips, Rita Reese, Virginia Renaud, Charlotte Stoll, Bee Sullivan, Peggy Walsh, Deniston Wilson.

ACT 1[2]

Scene 1

Televison (*by* Florence Calkins)
> F. Morgan, Company

Scene 2

"Personally Yours"
> The Hey Nonny Nonny Girls
> (*Music by* Michael H. Cleary. *Lyrics by* Max and Nathaniel Lief.)

Scene 3

"Tell Me Something About Yourself"
> D. McNulty, J. McCauley
> (*Music by* Michael H. Cleary. *Lyrics by* Max and Nathaniel Lief.)

Scene 4

Permanent Passion (*by* E. B. White)
> *Louisa*: A. Seymour. *Mr. Blauvelt*: J. Norris. *Mrs. Blauvelt*: J. Carter-Waddell. *Dr. Ludwig*: E. Sharpe. *Mrs. Ludwig*: W. Cox.

Scene 5

Richy Craig, Jr.

Scene 6

"Hey Nonny Nonny"
> The Principals
> (*Music by* Will Irwin. *Lyrics by* Ogden Nash.)

Scene 7

Easily Amused (*by* Ogden Nash)
> F. Morgan

Scene 8

"This Is Different, Dear"
> The Hey Nonny Nonny Girls
> (*Music by* Michael H. Cleary. *Lyrics by* Max and Nathaniel Lief.)

Scene 9

"Manhattan Lullaby"
> A. Seymour
> (*Music by* Michael H. Cleary. *Lyrics by* Max and Nathaniel Lief.)

Scene 10

"Three Little Columnists"
> J. McCauley, J. Norris, E. Sharpe
> (*Music by* Michael H. Cleary. *Lyrics by* Max and Nathaniel Lief.)

---

[1]Not the famous dramatic actress of the same name.
[2]Added to Act 1 during the run:
> "For Better or Worse"
> J. McCauley, J. Carter-Waddell, Hey Nonny Nonny Girls
> (*Music by* Michael H. Cleary. *Lyrics by* Max and Nathaniel Lief.)

Scene 11

"Be a Little Lackadaisical"
> D. McNulty, The Hey Nonny Nonny Girls
> (*Music and Lyrics by* Herman Hupfeld.)

Scene 12

Life Is Just a Bowl of Eugene O'Neill's (*by* Frank Sullivan)
> *Gene*: F. Morgan. *Earl*: J. McCauley. *Alice*: J. Carter-Waddell. *Alla*: A. Seymour. *General Baddum*: E. Sharpe. *Norn*: M. Tolle.

Scene 13

Richy Craig, Jr. assisted by Mildred Tolle.

Scene 14

"Lady in Waiting"
> A. Seymour
> (*Music by* Alberta Nichols. *Lyrics by* Mann Holiner.)

Scene 15

Majestic Hotel[3] (*by* Richy Craig, Jr., Jerry Norris, Ernest Sharpe, Ralph Sanford, Mildred Tolle)
> *The Editor*: R. Craig, Jr. *The Reporter*: F. Morgan. *The Others*: J. McCauley, E. Sharpe, J. Norris, D. McNulty, W. Cox, R. Sanford, A. Loftus, A. Leftwich, Jr.

Scene 16

"On My Nude Ranch With You"
> D. McNulty, J. McCauley, The Company
> (*Music by* Michael H. Cleary. *Lyrics by* Max and Nathaniel Lief.)

ACT 2

Scene 1

"I Didn't Know That It Was Loaded"
> M. Tolle, E. Sharpe, The Hey Nonny Nonny Girls
> (*Music by* Michael H. Cleary. *Lyrics by* Max and Nathaniel Lief.)

Scene 2

"Orientale Moderne" (dance)
> J. Carter-Waddell
> (*Music by* Will Irwin.)

Scene 3

"Minsky's Metropolitan Grand Opera"
> (*Music by* Michael H. Cleary. *Lyrics by* Max and Nathaniel Lief.)
> *First Director*: J. Norris. *Second Director*: E. Sharpe. *Tillie Bons*: A. Seymour. *Otto Kahn*: J. McCauley. *Minsky*: R. Craig, Jr. *Miss America*: J. O'Neill. *Candy Butcher*: R. Sanford. *Minsky's Maidens*: The Hey Nonny Nonny Girls. *Carmen*: D. McNulty. *First Comic*: R. Sanford. *Second Comic*: A. Loftus. *The Juvenile*: E. Sharpe. *Cokey Joe*: A. Loftus. *The Cop*: E. Sharpe.

Scene 4

"I'm Really Not That Way"
> F. Morgan
> (*Music by* Will Irwin. *Lyrics by* Malcolm McComb.)

Scene 5

"Wouldn't That Be Wonderful"
> D. McNulty, J. Norris
> (*Music and Lyrics by* Herman Hupfeld.)

Scene 6

Richy Craig, Jr. assisted by Mildred Tolle

Scene 7

"In Those Good Old Horsecar Days"
> E. Sharpe, J. McCauley, J. Norris
> (*Music by* Will Irwin. *Lyrics by* Malcolm McComb.)

Scene 8

Hollywood (*by* Harry Ruskin)
> F. Morgan, J. Carter-Waddell

Scene 9

"Let's Go Lovin'"
> D. McNulty, J. Norris, R. Sanford, J. McCauley, The Hey Nonny Nonny Girls
> (*Music and Lyrics by* Herman Hupfeld.)

Scene 10

"The Season Ended"
> J. Carter-Waddell, J. Norris
> (*Music by* Michael Cleary. *Lyrics by* Max and Nathaniel Lief.)

---

[3]A Burlesque of Vicki Baum's "Grand Hotel."

Scene 11

Finale (*Conceived by* Florence Calkins.)
The Company

CHAMBERLAIN BROWN'S SCRAP BOOK

1932.14

21 Acts of Ace Vaudeville (A Vaudeville Revue in Two Acts, 21 Scenes.) Assembled by Chamberlain Brown. Sketches by Chamberlain Brown. Staged by Charles Schofield and Robert Lively. Orchestra conducted by Smith Ballew. Produced by Chamberlain Brown. Opened 1 August 1932 at the Ambassador Theatre and closed 8 August 1932 after 10 performances[4].

CAST: INA HEYWARD, FRANK HUYLER, ALMIRA SESSIONS, CARL CARMEN, CHARLES SCHOFIELD, HAROLD KENNEDY, VINTON HAWORTH, RAY HEDGE, TERRY CARROLL, LEDA LOMBARD, FLORENCE AUER, BARRE HILL, STELLA DEMETTE, CHARLES HEDLEY, PRISCILLA KNOWLES, CECILE SHERMAN, MAE DIX, DOROTHY MacDONALD, KATE WOODS FISKE, RITZ QUARTETTE (Chester Bree, Neil Evans, James Ryan, William H. Stamm), SMITH BALLEW and His Orchestra, Herbert Warren, Leslie Urbach, Terry Carroll, Louis Tanno, Ernest Whitman, 3 Flashes of Lightning, William L. Andrews, Percy Verwaynen, Lillian Ridley, Helen Bertram, Frazer Coleman, Nancy McCord, Pierre Watkin, Jonathan Hole, Peter Smallwood, Valerie Valaire, John Patrick, Dwight Butcher, Salvatore LoCurto, John Armstrong, Ruth Conley, Robert Gordon, Barbara Blair, Ethel Norris, Betty Hanna, Edwin MacKenna, Marjorie Hoffman, Francis Lyman, Valerie Bergere, Robert Williamson, Edwin Wilson, Autumn Simms, Laurette Adams, Paul Jacchia, Paul Taubman, David Morris, Danny Simmons.

Entire action takes place inside a vaudeville theatre during a vaudeville show.

ACT 1

Scene 1

Overture
Smith Ballew's Orchestra

Scenes 2, 3 and 4

The Birth of the Vaudeville Bill:

"If It Ain't Love"
I. Hayward
(*Music and Lyrics by* Andy Razaf, Don Redman, Thomas "Fats" Waller.)
Mistress of Ceremonies: I. Hayward. *The Man in the Box*: F. Huyler. *Mrs. Knickerbocker*: A. Sessions. *The Usher*: C. Carmen. *Mr. Knickerbocker*: C. Schofield. *A Patron*: H. Kennedy.

Myrt and Marge (radio sketch)
V. Haworth, R. Hedge

Scene 5

Moving Pictures
The Casting Director: H. Warren. *Office Boy*: L. Urbach. *Terry Carroll*: Herself. *The Director*: L. Tanno.

Scene 6

Harlemade:

"My Mom"
E Whitman
(*Music and Lyrics by* Walter Donaldson.)

Specialty
3 Flashes of Lightning

The Penitent
Monte: W. L. Andrews. *Williams*: P. Verwaynen. *Freddi*: L. Ridley. *Ashley*: E. Whitman.

Scene 7

The Torch Singer:

"Another Love Affair"
L. Lombard

Scene 8

Operetta — The Mode 'Costume Room'
Helen Bertram: Herself. *Toni Cummings*: F. Coleman. *Mable Stork*: N. McCord.

Medley
Ritz Quartette

---

[4]Settings, costumes uncredited.

"Song of the Vagabonds" (from *THE VAGABOND KING*)
C. Hedley, Chorus
(*Music by* Rudolf Friml. *Lyrics by* Brian Hooker.)

Scene 9

Shakespeare: 'King John'
Constance: F. Auer. *The Cardinal*: P. Watkin.

Scene 10

In a Radio Station:
Ray: R. Hedge. *Ina*: I. Hayward. *Station Announcer*: J. Hole. *The Noises*: P. Smallwood. *The Pilot*: V. Haworth. *Edna Wallace Hopper*: V. Valaire. *Tony Wons*: F. Coleman. *The Mills Brothers*: Ritz Quartette.

Scene 11

Grand Opera:

Prologue from 'I Pagliacci' (*Music by* Ruggero Leoncavallo.)
B Hill

End of Act IV from 'Carmen' (*Music by* Charles Bizet.)
Carmen: S. De Mette. *Don José*: C. Hedley. *Escamillo*: B. Hill. *Claque*: F. Huyler, J. Patrick, C. Carmen, D. Butcher, S. Lo Curto, J. Armstrong.

Scene 12

East Lynne
Spirit of Dramatic Stock: P. Smallwood. *Lady Isabel*: P. Knowles. *Joyce*: V. Valaire. *Barbara Hare*: R. Conley. *Sir Francis Leveson*: P. Watkin. *Archibald Carlyle*: R. Gordon.

Scene 13

Musical Comedy: 'That New Gang of Mine'
Scene: A Speakeasy in East 63rd Street.

"Skit Skat"
B. Blair, Ritz Quartette
Francis Cameron: J. Hole. *Drina, his wife*: E. Norris. *Wanda*: B. Hanna. *Pierre Roy*: E. MacKenna. *Larsen Todsen*: L. Tanno. *Therese*: M. Hoffman. *Phil*: F. Lyman.

"Foreward March" (dance)
E. Norris, F. Lyman
Bartender: R. Williamson. *The Lieutenant*: L. Urbach. *The Gang*: Ritz Quartette. *Martin Wentworth Rutledge, the butler*: E. Wilson. *Isadore, the maid*: A. Simms. *Cynthia Cameron*: V. Valaire.

Dance
E. MacKenna

"(Lovin You) The Way I Do" (from *HOT RHYTHM*)
E. Norris
(*Music by* Eubie Blake. *Lyrics by* Will Morrissey and Jack Scholl.)

"Die Walküre" (Entrance of Todsen)
L. Tanno
(*Music by* Richard Wagner.)

"My Hideaway"
F. Coleman

"Oceans of Love"
V. Valaire, Company

ACT 2

Scene 1

Songs
Smith Ballew's Orchestra

Scene 2

The Community Players: Picking a Play
Kitty De Wolfe: V. Bergere. *Enid*: L. Adams. *Grace*: A. Simms. *Helene Gillette*: B. Hanna. *Kenneth*: P. Jacchia. *Cab*: L. Urbach. *John De Wolpe*: H. Warren. *Mr. Volpi*: L. Tanno.

Scene 3

Concert:

"Come to the Fair"
C. Hedley
(*Music and Lyrics by* Easthope Martin and Helen Taylor.)

Piano Concert — Stuck Op. 79 — Weber
P. Taubman

'Il Travatore'
C. Sherman, C. Hedley
(*Music by* Giuseppe Verdi.)

Scene 4

Burlesque
The Woman: M Dix. *The Man*: H. Kennedy.

Scene 5

Strip Dance: "You're My Everything" (from *THE LAUGH PARADE*, film)

(*Music by* Harry Warren. *Lyrics by* Mort Dixon and Joe Young.)
D. MacDonald

Scene 6

Drama: 'Taken from Life'

Mother: F. Auer. *Father*: P. Watkin. *Older Son*: C. Hedley. *His Wife*: R. Conley. *His Brother*: D. Morris.

Scene 7

Vaudeville:

"My Silent Love"

I. Hayward
(*Music by* Dana Suesse. *Lyrics by* Edward Heyman.)

"Lullaby of the Leaves"

I. Hayward
(*Music by* Bernice Petkere. *Lyrics by* Joe Young.)

"Sleep Baby Sleep"

K. W. Fiske
(*Music and Lyrics by* Johnny Tucker and Joe Schuster.)

"The Irish Rag"

D. Simmons

Scene 8

Finale—"O.K. America"

Entire Company

1932.15

SMILING FACES

A Musical Comedy in Two Acts, 6 Scenes. Book by Harry Clarke. Music by Harry Revel. Lyrics by Mack Gordon. Staged by R. H. Burnside. Dances by Merriel Abbott. Settings by Watson Barratt. Costumes by Ernest Schrapps. (Produced by the Messrs. Shubert.) Opened 30 August 1932 at the Sam S. Shubert Theatre and closed 24 September 1932 after 31 performances.[5]

CAST (in order of appearance): *Helen Sydney*: Barbara Williams. *George Black*: Bradford Hatton. *Robert Bowington*: ROY ROYSTON. *Perkins, his butler*: Boyd Davis. *Arthur Lawrence*: CHARLES COLLINS. *Amy Edwards*: HOPE EMERSON. *First Assistant*: RAY ROMAIN. *Second Assistant*: TOM ROMAIN. *Peggy Post*: DOROTHY STONE. *Monument Spleen*: FRED STONE. *Sybilla Richter*: ISABEL O'MADIGAN. *Cordonia Potts*: ADORA ANDREWS. *Horatio Dalrymple*: ALI YOUSSOF. *Edward Richter*: EDDIE GARVIE. *Mildred McKay*: DORIS PATSTON. *A Waiter*: Bradford Hatton. *A Bellhop*: Harold Offer. *A Minster*: Rex Coover. *A Bishop*: Carl Duart.

Merriel Abbott Dancers: Peaches Dahl, May Haas, Rose Kirsner, Fritzi Deuss, Eileen Moss, Lorraine Santchi, La Norma Bourgeois, Genevieve Irwin, Dorothy Bell, Merle Smith, Evelyn Pearce, Josephine Buckley, Pauline Bensinger, Peggy Marshall, Mildred Ocen, Florence Wilson. *Show Girls*: Leone Krans, Myrtle Candee, Jeanne Ellyn, Helene Cambridge, Rena McAfee, Janice Winter, Eleanor Fairley, Agatha Phillips. *Boys*: Thomas Sternfield, Joe Kaye, Harold Offer, John Perkins, Frank Kimball, Clark Leston, Carl Duart, Rex Coover.

Act 1, Scene 1: Lawn of Bowington's estate, Southampton, Long Island. Present Day. *Scene 2*: Corridor of Bowington house. *Scene 3*: Ballroom of Country Club.

Act 2, Scene 1: Terrace of Grand Hotel, Havana, Cuba. *Scene 2*: Outside of Hotel and Annex. *Scene 3*: Ballroom of Hotel.

ACT 1

"Sport Is Sport" (Opening)

B. Williams, T. Romain, R. Romain, Dancers, Chorus

"I've Fallen Out of Love"

D. Stone, Show Girls, Boys

"Sweet Little Stranger"

D. Stone, C Collins, Dancers

"Shakin' the Shakespeare"

B. Williams, Ensemble

"Thank You, Don't Mention It"

D. Stone, C Collins, R. Royston

"Smart Set"

Four Abbotters, Ensemble

"Poor Little, Shy Little, Demure Little Me"

H. Emerson, Boys

"Landlord at My Door!"

F. Stone, Show Girls

"There Will Be a Girl"

D. Stone, C. Collins

Finale

Entire Company

ACT 2

"In Havana"

B. Williams, Ensemble, Dancers

"Think of My Reputation"

D. Stone, R. Royston

"Quick Henry, the Flit"

R. Royston

"Can't Get Rid of Me"

F. Stone, H. Emerson

"Little Stucco in the Sticks"

D. Patston, R. Royston, Dancers

"(I) Stumbled Over You"

D. Patston, C. Collins

"Falling Out of Love"

D. Stone, Boys

Acrobatic Dance

D. Bell, Dancers

Specialty

F. Stone

"There Will Be a Girl" (reprise)

D. Stone, R. Royston
Dance by T. Romain, R. Romain.

"(Just an) Old Spanish Custom"

H. Emerson

Finale

Entire Company

1932.16

BALLYHOO OF 1932

A Musical Revue in Two Acts, 25 Scenes. Book (sketches) by Norman Anthony. Additional dialogue by Sig Herzig. Lyrics by E. Y. Harburg. Music by Lewis Gensler. Directed by Norman Anthony, Lewis Gensler, Bobby Connolly, Russell Patterson. Book directed by Gus Shy. Dances by Bobby Connolly. Settings and costumes by Russell Patterson. Music director, Max Meth. Orchestrations by Hans Spialek. Produced by Ballyhoo Productions Inc. (Bobby Connolly, Lewis Gensler, Norman Anthony, Russell Patterson.) Opened 6 September 1932 at the 44th Street Theatre and closed 26 November 1932 after 95 performances.

CAST: WILLIE HOWARD, EUGENE HOWARD, JEANNE AUBERT, LULU MCCONNELL, BOBHOPE, VERA MARSHE [Marsh], HUGH CAMERON, GLORIA GILBERT, TOM HARTY, DONALD STEWART, RALPH SANFORD, PAUL HARTMAN, GRACE HARTMAN, SUNNY O'DEA, Nina Mae McKinney, Lucille [Clay] Osborne, Florence Earle, Edna Pence, Alice Carleton, Ray Halberg, Billy Marvil, Al Bloom, Milton LeRoy, John Peters, Paul Murdock.

ALBERTINA RASCH SPECIALTY DANCERS: DORISSA NELOVA, Helene Carson, Vida McLain, Margaret Durande, Ruth Fischer, Josephine Robert, Inga Anderson, Mary Brooks, Marguerite Slattery. *Dancers*: Marjorie Baglin, Firley Banks, Mildred Borst, Lucille Brodin, Marion Forbes, Barbara Coswell, Dorothy Day, Gigi Gilpin, Gloria Glennon, Rosalind Golden, Irene Hamlin, Helen Hannan, Ann Hardman, Pearl Harris, Jane Lane, Constance Madison, Evelyn March, Sonny Nelson, Catherine Reynolds, Bernice Roberts, Rita Stone, Ruth Tara, Dorothy Van Hest, Amy Weber, Flo Spink. *Show Girls*: Julia Barker, Patricia Brooks, Ethel Britton, Phyllis Carrol, Theresa Cordova, Pat Dolan, Irene Stevens, Ruth Reiter, Olivia Scevioure, Frances Sinclair, Drucilla Strain. *Gentlemen of the Ensemble*: Leon Alton, Al Bloom, Jack Coogan[6], Ray Dawley, Jack Douglas, Buddy Hertelle, Dock Kennedy, Bill Meader, Gordon Merrick, John Peters, Jack Ross, Sid Salzer, Dan Weyler, Joe Carey. *Singers*: Nixon Gro, Todd Clarence, Simmons Gro, Felix Douglas, Joe Willis, Maurice Willis, Lloyd Mitchell, Paul Johnson, Frederick Whieldin, E. N. Broadnox, Juane Hernandez, John Ricks.

ACT 1

Ballyhoo Complaint Department

B. Hope

Scene 1

---

[5]Musical director uncredited in New York; prior to New York credited to Oscar Bradley.

[6]Not the famous child film star Jackie Coogan.

Times Square

Newsboy: A. Bloom. Delivery Man: B. Hertelle. Miss Park Avenue: F. Earle. Minister: P. Hartman. Nurse: F. Banks. Baby: R. Golden. D.A.R.: L. C. Osborne, D. Van Hest, G. Glennon, R. Reiter. Sandwich Men: S. Salzer, J. Douglas, J. Ros, J. Cary, Ensemble.

Scene 2

"Falling Off the Wagon"
T. Harty, V. Marshe, Girls, Boys

Scene 3

Penthouse
Mr. Goldman: W. Howard. Mr. Goldman: E. Howard. Shanahan: R. Sanford.

Scene 4

"Thrill Me"
She: J. Aubert. He: M. LeRoy. Street Singer: D. Stewart.

Scene 5

Bob Hope

Scene 6

Street Car
First Passenger: W. Howard. First Lady: L. McConnell. Second Lady: L. C. Osborne. Conductor: R. Sanford. Drunk: P. Hartman.

Scene 7

"Old Fashioned Wedding"
B. Hope, V. Marshe, Girls, Boys
Specialty by Albertina Rasch Dancers.

Scene 8

Columbus Circle (Comes the Revolution)
Orator: W. Howard. Radicals: (Ensemble.)

Scene 9

"How Do You Do It?"
D. Stewart, Ladies Ensemble
Dance
J. Stillman, P. Gurney

Scene 10

A Hollywood Training Camp
Doorman: R. Sanford. Margreta Garbitch: J. Aubert. Manager: P. Murdock. Entourage: L. C. Osborne, P. Brookes, P. Gurney, G. Hartman. Ronald Gable: J. Peters. Clark Montgomery: P. Hartman. Whattaman Jones: T. Harty. Fiddler: B. Marvil. Reporters, Spectators, Ushers.

Scene 11

Hillbillies
W. Howard, E. Howard, R. Halberg, B. Marvil

Scene 12

Big Business
First Operator: V. Marshe. Second Operator: L. C. Osborne. Mr. Throckmorton: H. Cameron. Mr. McGillicuddy: R. Sanford.

Scene 13

"Man About Yonkers"
W. Howard, V. Marshe, L. C. Osborne, Girls

Scene 14

Talker Backer
B. Hope

Scene 15

Finale: "Ballyhujah"
W. Howard
President: E. Howard. Senator from Maine: P. Hartman. Senator from Kentucky: T. Harty. Senator from Texas: H. Cameron. Senator from California: R. Sanford. Porter: W. Howard. Politician: R. Sanford. Minsky: B. Hope. Recruiting Officer: P. Murdock. Newsboy: T. Harty. Realtor: J. Stillman. Auctioneer: A. Bloom. Medicine Man: D. Stewart. Movie Barker: L. Elton. Senators, Pages, Ladies of the Ensemble, Choir.

ACT 2[7]

---

[7]Added to Act 2 after opening:
Reunion in the 60's
Miss Finnegan: J. Aubert. Mr. Throckmorton: B. Hope. Mr. Goofus: T. Harty. Mr. Glutz: P. Murdock. Mr. Butterfield: P. Hartman. Fire Chief: R. Sanford.

Scene 1

"Love, Nuts and Noodles"
N. M. McKinney
Dance by Girls.

Scene 2

A Pullman Smoker
First Traveller: E. Howard. Second Traveller: B. Hope. Third Traveller: W. Howard. Conductor: R. Sanford.

Scene 3

"How Do You Do It?" (reprise)
Albertina Rasch Specialty Dancers

Scene 4

An Evening at Home
Mr. Pincus: W. Howard. Mrs. Pincus: L. McConnell.

Scene 5

Roulette Wheel: "Riddle Me This"
D. Stewart
Dance by G. Gilbert, S. O'Dea, Girls, Boys.

Scene 6

Bob Hope

Scene 7

"What Have You Got to Have?"
J. Aubert, W. Howard, Girls

Scene 8

An Old-Fashioned Garden
Dick: B. Hope. Bill: D. Stewart. Betty: V. Marshe. Mrs. Colfay: F. Earle. Meadows: H. Cameron. Yvonne: B. Roberts.

Scene 9

Rigoletto (Burlesque sketch)
Soprano: E. Pence. Tenor: E. Howard. Contralto: A. Carleton. Baritone: W. Howard.

Scene 10

Finale
Entire Company

1932.17 FLYING COLORS

A Musical Revue in Two Acts, 26 Scenes. (Sketches by Howard Dietz. Additional dialogue by Charles Sherman, George S. Kaufman, Corey Ford.) Music by Arthur Schwartz. Lyrics by Howard Dietz. Staged by Howard Dietz. Dances and ensembles staged by Albertina Rasch. Production (settings) designed and lighting by Norman Bel Geddes. Costumes by Constance Ripley. Music director, Al Goodman. Orchestrations by (Robert) Russell Bennett, Hans Spialek, Edward Powell, Arthur Schutt. Vocal arrangements by Andre Kostelanetz, Bobby [Robert Emmett] Dolan. Produced by Max Gordon. Opened 15 September 1932 at the Imperial Theatre and closed 25 February 1933 after 188 performances.

CAST: CLIFTON WEBB, CHARLES BUTTERWORTH, TAMARA GEVA, PATSY KELLY, PHILIP LOEB, VILMA EBSEN, BUDDY EBSEN, LARRY ADLER, IMOGENE COCA, JEAN SARGENT, MONETTE MOORE, Jay Wilson, George Kirk, June Blossom, Albertina Vitak, Helen Carrington.
Albertina Rasch Dancers: Dorothy Dodd, Aida Conkey, Carol Renwick, Rosalie Trego, Catherine Laughlin, Teddy West, Florence Chumbecos, Katherine Mullowny, Irene McBride, Lillian Duncan, Virginia Whitmore, Wilma Roelof, Phyllis Cameron, Enes Early, Evelyn Monte, Ruth Gormley, Frances Nevins, Nancy Dolin, Maxine Darrow, Janet Carver.
Ensemble: Girls: Bobby Johns, Consuelo Harris, Jackie Godfrey, Mildred Davenport, Lucille Wilson, Leonore Cox, Winnie Johnson, Muriel Cook, Dolores Townshend, Elsie Burrows, Myrtle Quinland, Billie Yarbo, Wilhelmina Gray, Vera Bracken, Alfreda Allman, Lucille Cole, Dora White, Elida Webb. Boys: David Johns, George Magis, George Raymond, William Miley, Maurice Siegel, Lloyd Ericson, John Walsh.

ACT 1

Scene 1

"Celebration"
The Company

Scene 2

Lost in a Crowd (by Howard Dietz and Charles Sherman)
C. Butterworth, others

Scene 3

"Two-Faced Woman"
T. Geva, Girls

Scene 4

"A Rainy Day"
C. Webb

Scene 5

Just Around the Corner
J. Wilson, G. Kirk, P. Loeb

Scene 6

"Mother Told Me So"
Albertina Rasch Dancers

Scene 7

On the American Plan (*by* Howard Dietz and George S. Kaufman)
C. Webb, P. Kelly, others

Scene 8

"A Shine on Your Shoes"
B. Ebsen, V. Ebsen, M. Moore, L. Adler

Scene 9

A Christmas Card
G. Kirk, D. Johns, G. Magis, G. Raymond, W. Miley, M. Siegel, L. Ericson, J. Walsh

Scene 10

Sister Act
C. Webb, C. Butterworth, P. Loeb

Scene 11

Bon Voyage (*by* Howard Dietz and Corey Ford)
Scene: The S..S. *Paresis* Sailing Pier.
Lessie Bevis: P. Kelly. *Uncle Norman:* P. Loeb. *Papa:* J. Wilson. *Mama:* H. Carrington. *Cousin Carrie:* J. Blossom. *Mr. Oliver:* G. Kirk. *Mrs. Oliver:* V. Ebsen. *Junior:* L. Adler. *Jo-Jo:* I. Coca. *Passengers, Steward, Porter, etc.:* (Ensemble).

Scene 12

"Alone Together"
J. Sargent
(*Danced by*) C. Webb, T. Geva.

Scene 13

The Harvey Woofter Five Point Plan
C. Butterworth

Scene 14

"Louisiana Hayride"
C. Webb, T. Geva, M. Moore, Ensemble

ACT 2
Scene 1

Reprise
Ensemble

Scene 2

"Fatal Fascination"
C. Butterworth, P. Kelly

Scene 3

"Mein kleine Akrobat"
C. Webb, Girls

Scene 4

Service (*by* George S. Kaufman and Marc Connelly)
C. Butterworth, P. Loeb

Scene 5

Valse Finaletto — "My Heart Is Part of You"
C. Webb, A. Vitak

Scene 6

"It Was Never Like This"
B. Ebsen, V. Ebsen, I. Coca, L. Adler

Scene 7

The Surgeon's Debut
Scene: An Operating Room.
Dr. Eric Trevelyan: C. Webb. *Harold Jasper,* the patient: C. Butterworth. *Miss Maris,* the nurse: I. Coca. *Dr. Kaufman,* the interne: P. Loeb. *Mrs. Balfour-Chatfield:* H. Carrington. *Katherine:* J. Blossom. *Fanny:* J. Sargent. *Photographer, Attendant, Musicians, etc.:* (Ensemble).

Scene 8

Now That the Party Is Over
T. Geva

Scene 9

The Salesman (*by* Howard Dietz and Corey Ford)
Scene: The Living Room of Mrs. McVitty's House.
Mr. Tillinghast: C. Butterworth. *Mrs. McVitty:* P. Kelly.

Scene 10

"Smokin' Reefers"[8]
J. Sargent, Ensemble

Scene 11

"Day After Day"
C. Webb

Scene 12

"All's Well"
C. Webb, C. Butterworth, T. Geva, P. Kelly, Company

EARL CARROLL'S VANITIES (1932)

1932.18

A Musical Revue in Two Acts, 61 Scenes[9]. Dialogue (sketches) by Jack McGowan. (Additional dialogue by Eugene Conrad.) Lyrics by Ted Koehler, (Edward Heyman, Haven Gillespie, Charles Tobias, Sidney Clare). Music by Harold Arlen, (Richard Myers, Henry Tobias, André Renaud, Peter Tinturin). Dialogue staged by Edgar MacGregor. Entire production conceived by Earl Carroll. Dances by Ned McGurn. Ballets by Gluck Sandor. Settings and costumes by Vincente Minnelli. Music director, Ray Kavanaugh. Orchestrations by Edward B. Powell. Produced by Earl Carroll. Opened 27 September 1932 at the Broadway Theatre and closed 10 December 1932 after 87 performances.

CAST: WILL FYFFE, ANDRE RANDALL, EDWIN STYLES, MILTON BERLE, HELEN BRODERICK, HARRIET HOCTOR, LILLIAN SHADE, JOSEPHINE HUSTON [Houston], MAX WALL, BARYL WALLACE, MARCELLE EDWARDS, KEITH CLARK, ANDRE RENAUD, JOHN HALE, Lester Crawford, Earle Christie, Keith Clark, Ted Wilson, Andy Costello, Bruno Sarti, Martin Roses, Ubaldo Russo, Euna Sinnott.
THE HELEN JACKSON GIRLS: Marjorie, Lilly Lee, Cecelia, May, Peggy, Molly, Jacqueline, Elsie, Doris, Eileen, Babs, Marie, Chilli, Gladys, Ethel, Lenore, Sheila.
Chorus: The Tall Ones: Nelda Kincaid, Vivian Keefer, Flo Ward, Flo Johnson, Dolores Grant, Agatha Hoff, Betty Sundmark, Lorna Rodionoff, Ida Michaels, Gay Orlova, Lydia Resh, Betty Dell, Clare Carter, Evelyn Crowell, Evelyn Kelly, Anna Taranda, Ann Howard, Helen Callahan, Martha Mackay, Evelyn Goslyn, Marion Volk, Audrey Arlington, Louise Estes, Hazel Nevin, Rosalie Fromson, Fay Lytell, Olive McLay, Helen Marano, Barbara Rand, Ruth Mann, Billy Joyce. *The Small Ones:* Elizabeth Deignan, Patricia Roe, Sybil Elaine Krinney, Hilda Regal, Katheryn Becker, Sylvia P. Brown, Kathaleen Gaughran, Cora Joyce Melnick, Betty Ann Pulis, Jacqueline Mousette, Peggy Hunter, Renee Goldberg, Phyllis Ann Slattery, Elinor Keenan, Ruth Snyder, Mazie Gibson, Hazel Brandt.

ACT 1
Scene 1

Cafe de la Paix, Paris

Scene 2

"My Darling"
J. Hale, J. Huston
(*Music by* Richard Myers. *Lyrics by* Edward Heyman.)

Scene 3

The Celebrated Helen Jackson Girls
(Conceded to be the world's most famous group of precision dancers. They have been the reigning success of London, Paris and Berlin. This is their first appearance in America.)

Scene 4

French Line Pier, New York

---

[8]Program note: A 'reefer' is a narcotic cigarette, made from the marihuana weed, frequently smoked in the tropics and recently made popular in Harlem.
[9]Billed as the tenth edition in the annual series of musical revues (Vanities, Sketchbooks) produced by Earl Carroll beginning in 1923.

Scene 5

The Docking of the Champlain; Introduction of Lillian Shade (the most promising of the young singers of modern American music); Introduction of André Randall.

Scene 6

Song
A. Randall
(This charming star of Paris, London, Havana, Buenos Aires and Mexico City makes his first bow to American audiences.)

Introduction of Edwin Styles.
(The sophisticated star of many London successes is a distinct novelty to the American theatregoer. His personality and charm have won him a high place on the English stage.)

Introduction of Helen Broderick.
(This beloved comedienne needs no introduction, but there are pleasant recollections of her many superb performances.)

Introduction of Milton Berle.
(The rising young American comedian, who has been the outstanding discovery of the present season, and makes his first bow to the legitimate theatregoers.)

Introduction of Will Fyffe.
(Three command performances before the King and Queen of England have stamped this artiste as Scotland's greatest character comedian.)

Scene 7

Through These Portals Pass—"The Most Beautiful Girls in the World"
(Music by Harold Arlen. Lyrics by Ted Koehler.) Chorus

Scene 8

"Along Came Love"
J. Huston
(Music by Henry Tobias. Lyrics by Charles Tobias and Haven Gillespie.)

Scene 9

A Swing of Gardenias (Mechanical Effects by Peter Clark.)

Scene 10

The Luminous Maypole (Effect by Stewart C. Whitman.)
(This is the first use of cold light on the stage.)

Scene 11

Introduction of Max Wall.
(The first appearance in New York of London's most popular dancing pantomimist.)

Scene 12

Mourning Becomes Impossible[10]
Mortimer: M. Berle. Millie: J. Huston. Sidney: W. Fyffe. Emma: H. Broderick. Girl: B. Wallace. George: L. Crawford. Pennant Man: E. Christie. Sara: L. Shade. Chuck: J. Hale.

Scene 13

Introduction of Keith Clark
(A Parisian of rare ability, who, by dexterous manipulation of lighted cigarettes, has made himself an outstanding novelty in the European Music Halls.)

Scene 14

Introduction of André Renaud
(The most popular pianist of France. The only artist who has mastered the playing of two pianos at one time. Sohmer pianos used.)

Scene 15

Introduction of Harriet Hoctor
(America's Premier Danseuse.)
"Love Is My Inspiration" (Love You Are My Inspiration)
J. Hale
(Music by André Renaud. Lyrics by Ted Koehler.)

Scene 16

What Price Jokes
Joe Miller, Jr.: M. Berle. Mrs. Joe Miller, Jr.: L. Shade. John Madison ,Sr.: E. Styles.

Scene 17

The Hospital
The Nurse: E. Crowell. First Girl: M. Edwards. Second Girl: B. Wallace. Third Girl: J. Huston. Fourth Girl: H. Broderick. The Doctor: A. Randall.

Scene 18

"I've Got a Right to Sing the Blues"
L. Shade
(Music by Harold Arlen. Lyrics by Ted Koehler.)

Scene 19

"The Golden Pillars of Justice" (Blues Ballet)
B. Wallace, M. Edwards
(Judgement of Modern Music)

Scene 20

Announcement
A. Randall

Scene 21

The Problem
Bo: M. Berle. Hank: L. Crawford.

Scene 22

"The Centenarian"
Minister: E. Styles. John: W. Fyffe.

Scene 23

The Oriental Express
The Helen Jackson Girls

Scene 24

The Telegram
Mrs. Bragg: H. Broderick.

Scene 25

The Inebriate
W. Fyffe
["I Belong to Glasgow"
(Music and Lyrics by Will Fyffe.)
"He's Been on the Bottle Since a Baby"
(Music and Lyrics by Will Fyffe and ? Bell.)]

Scene 26

The Cabinet of Doctor X (Electrical Effect by Stewart C. Whitman.)
Mimi: J. Huston. Albert: A. Randall. Dr. X. Lummox: E. Styles. Miss Scrib: H. Broderick. John: M. Wall. Paul: M. Berle.

Scene 27

A Street in Vienna
The Viennese Publisher: T. Wilson. His Daughter: B. Wallace. Lady: M. Edwards. Gentleman: A. Costello. Johann Strauss: J. Hale.

Scene 28

Vision of Lovely Girls

Scene 29

The Source of the Danube

Scene 30

The Soul of the Danube (Ballet)
H. Hoctor

Scene 31

Finale—The Blue Danube (Plastic Setting by Weidhas. Music by Johann Strauss.)

Scene 32

Finale

ACT 2

Scene 1

Through a Mirror—"Take Me Away"
J. Huston, B. Sundmark, J. Hale
(Music by Peter Tinturin. Lyrics by Sidney Clare and Charles Tobias.)

Scene 2

The Cherry Orchard

Scene 3

A Tree of Mystic Beauty

Scene 4

Love in Five Languages
A. Randall

Scene 5

English Girl: J. Huston. Englishman: A. Randall.

Scene 6

French Girl: H. Callahan. Frenchman: A. Randall.

[10]A burlesque of Eugene O'Neill's drama "Mourning Becomes Electra."

Scene 7
> *German Girl*: M. Edwards. *German*: A. Randall.

Scene 8
> *Spanish Girl*: B. Wallace. *Spaniard*: A. Randall.

Scene 9
> *Russian Girl*: G. Orlova. *Russian*: A. Randall.

Scene 10
> *Russian*: B. Sarti. *Spaniard*: M. Wall. *German*: M. Roses. *Frenchman*: U. Russo. *Englishman*: E. Styles.

Scene 11

Studio W. M. C. A.
> *Announcer*: M. Berle. *Singer*: L. Shade.

Scene 12

Tela-vision
> 56 Vanities Girls

Scene 13

W(h)ater Mess
> *The Aviator*: A. Randall. *The Aviatrix*: H. Broderick.

Scene 14

"Forsaken"
> J. Huston
> (*Music by* Richard Myers. *Lyrics by* Edward Heyman.)

Scene 15

The Raven
> H. Hoctor

Scene 16

Gossip
> *Clare*: C. Carter. *Vivian*: V. Keefer. *Evelyn*: E. Crowell. *Nelda*: N. Kincaid. *Marcelle*: M. Edwards. *Beryl*: B. Wallace.

Scene 17

"The Engineer"
> W. Fyffe
> (*Music and Lyrics by* Will Fyffe.)

Scene 18

Strictly Professional (*by* Ethel Shannon Jackson)
> *Lil*: H. Broderick. *Mazie*: J. Huston. *Bill*: J. Hale. *Pedestrian*: L. Crawford. *Santa Claus*: M. Berle.

Scene 19

"Rockin' in Rhythm"
> L. Shade
> (*Music by* Harold Arlen. *Lyrics by* Ted Koehler.)

Scene 20

On the Side of the Building

Scene 21

The Mysterious Red Light
> (Effect of a Hundred Hands, copyrighted by Stewart C. Whitman.)

Scene 22

The Sinking City (Fire Illusion by Prof. Max Tauber.)

Scene 23

The Apache

Scene 24

Trial By Jury (*by* Raymond Peck)
> *The Judge*: W. Fyffe. *Clerk of the Court*: E. Jones. *Foreman of the Jury*: T. Wilson. *Defendant*: M. Berle. *Attorney for Defense*: E. Styles. *Prosecutor*: L. Crawford. *Blind Justice*: E. Sinott.

Scene 25

The Midshipmen
> The Helen Jackson Girls

Scene 26

The Bar Relief
> *McPherson*: W. Fyffe. *Helen*: H. Broderick. *Barman*: M. Roses. *Andre*: A. Randall. *Milton*: M. Berle. *Teddy*: E. Styles.

Scene 27

The International Four[11]

Scene 28

The Spiral Curtain

Scene 29

Grand Finale
> (Entire Company)

BELMONT VARIETIES

1932.19

A Vaudeville Revue in Two Acts, 41 Scenes. Sketches by Helen and Nolan Leary, Sam Bernard II. Music and lyrics by Serge Walter, Sam Bernard II, Alvin Kaufman, Charles Kenny, Henry Lloyd, Mildred Kaufman, Robert Burk. Staged by Max Schenck (Chief engineer), Sam Bernard II (First Officer). Musical arrangements by Bernabe Roxas Solis. Produced by (Captain) Richard G. Herndon. Opened 28 September 1932 at the Belmont Theatre and closed 1 October 1932 after 6 performances[12]. Reopened as MANHATTAN VARIETIES 21 October 1932 at the Cosmopolitan Theatre for 11 performances. (See detail immediately following)

<u>CAST</u>: MONSIEUR MAURICE, MARYON DALE, ROY BENSON, MARION YOUNG, LEO HENNING, MARJORIE ENTERS, LUCIEN LARIVIERE, JANE DUDLEY, PHILIPPE BORGIA, MAURICETTE DUCRET, GUSTAVO CARRASCO, LILYAN ASTAIRE, MURA DEHN, CHARLES KENNY, SHAWNI LANI.

James Kelly, Bert Prival, Diane Andre, Robert Burk, Lita Lope, Baroness Erzi, Blanche Collins, Carol Holmes, Margie Barrett, Virginia Mortimer, William Sunderman, Harriette Wesley, Josette Tapie, Edith Reinhardt, Martha Merrill, Roslyn Harvey, Ted Allen, Eleanore Wood, Jeanette Leland, Eddie Leslie, Ray Lee, Pierce O'Hearn, Gordon Clarke, Grace Sherman. *Steward of the Keyboards*: Henry Lloyd, Louis Polansky.

ACT 1

Scene 1

Pier 57 (*by* Helen and Nolan Leary)
> *Inspector*: J. Kelly. *Valet*: B. Prival. *Impressario*: M. Maurice. *Valet*: D. Andre. *Photographer*: G. Carrasco. *Reporter*: R. Burk. *Maurice Chevalier*: L. Astaire. *Passengers Arriving*: R. Benson, M. Young, L. Lope, L. LaRiviere, M. Dehn, L. Henning, B. Erzi, M. Dale, B. Collins, S. Lani, C. Holmes, M. Barrett, V. Mortimer, M. Enters, P. Borgia, C. Kenny, W. Sunderman, H. Wesley, M. Ducret, J. Tapie, E. Reinhardt, M. Merrill, R. Harvey, T. Allen, E. Wood, J. Leland, J. Dudley, E. Leslie, R. Lee, P. O'Hearn, G. Clark.

Scene 2

Monsieur Maurice

Scene 3

"Hitting the New High"
> M. Dale, L. Henning
> (*Music by* Henry Lloyd. *Lyrics by* Sam Bernard II and Robert Burk.)

Scene 4

What Time Bulova?
> E. Leslie

Scene 5

"Sparkling Champagne"
> B. Ezri
> (*Music by* Victor Jacobi.)

Scene 6

Canadian Trappers
> *Batiste*: W. Sunderman. *Chanine*: C. Kenny.

Scene 7

"Lontananza"
> G. Carrasco
> (*Music by* Angelo Bettinelli.)

Scene 8

"Back Seat of a Taxi"
> M. Enters, L. LaRiviere
> (*Music by* Serge Walter. *Lyrics by* Charles Kenny. *Dialogue by* Helene and Nolan Leary.)
> *Dance by* M. Enters, P. Borgia.

Scene 9

Charming Interlude (*by* Roslyn Harvey)
> R. Harvey

---

[11]Most likely Messrs. Fyffe, Wall, Renaud, Styles.

[12]Sets, costumes uncredited.

Scene 10

Another Language
B. Collins

Scene 11

Skit-Bits (*by* Sam Bernard II and Nolan Leary)
Say It With Flowers; On the Wrong Track; It Pays to Advertise.

Scene 12

Oahu
Dancer: S. Lani. *Player*: T. Allen.

Scene 13

"I Paused, I Looked, I Fell"
E. Reinhardt, L. Henning
(*Music by* Henry Lloyd. *Lyrics by* Sam Bernard II and Robert Burk.)
Dance *by* B. Prival.

Scene 14

A Nice Young Man (With a Magic Personality)
R. Benson, assisted by D. Andre

Scene 15

Left Bank:
"Blind Alleys"
(*Music by* Serge Walter. *Lyrics by* Charles Kenny.)
"Lament"
(*Music by* Henry Lloyd. *Lyrics by* Robert Burk, Sam Bernard II.)
"Mauricette"
(*Music by* Henry Lloyd. *Lyrics by* Robert Burk, Sam Bernard II.)
M. Ducret, J. Tapie, W. Sunderman, C. Kenny, R. Lee, P. O'Hearn, G. Clark

Scene 16

"The Primitive Ebony"
M. Dehn
(*Music by* Anna Bacon Dodge.)

Scene 17

"Something New and It's You"
M. Dale, L. Henning
(*Music by* Alvin Kaufman. *Lyrics by* Mildred Kaufman.)

Scene 18

"Park Ave."
W. Sunderman, C. Kenny
(*Music by* Serge Walter. *Lyrics by* Charles Kenny.)

Scene 19

A Lady of the Jury
L. Astaire
(*Dialogue and Continuity by* Sam Bernard II, Henry Lloyd, Robert Burk.)

Scene 20

Dance ("His Invitation to Love")
L. Lope, L. LaRiviere, G. Carrasco, M. Enters, P. Borgia, E. Wood
(*Music by* Alvin Kaufman. *Lyrics by* Mildred Kaufman.)

ACT 2

Scene 1

"Degas Ballet"
V. Mortimer, D. Andre, C. Holmes, R. Harvey, M. Young, J. Tapie, B. Prival
(*Music by* Charles Godard. *Staged by* Constantin Kobeleff.)

Scene 2

Echoes of Seville: L. Lope, with explanation by R. Benson
"Clavelitos"
(*Words and Music by* [Joaquín] Quirito Valverde.)
"Capullito de Aleli"
(*Words and Music by* Hernandez.)

Scene 3

A Good Reason (*by* Sam Bernard II and Nolan Leary)
Detective: J. Kelly. *Inspector*: W. Sunderland. *Bride*: J. Leland.

Scene 4

The Swan
M. Dehn

Scene 5

"That's You"
M. Ducret, W. Sunderman
(*Music by* Serge Walter. *Lyrics by* Charles Kenny.)

Scene 6

"No Thank You"
M. Ducret
(*Music by* Alvin Kaufman. *Lyrics by* Mildred Kaufman.)

Scene 7

"You Took My Breath Away"
M. Young, L. LaRiviere
(*Music by* Henry Lloyd. *Lyrics by* Sam Bernard II and Robert Burk.)

Scene 8

Hungarian Chanson (*Music by* Hubas.)
B. Erzi

Scene 9

"The River Will Sweep You Away"
(*Music by* Henry Lloyd. *Lyrics by* Sam Bernard II and Robert Burk.)
Courier: W. Sunderman.

Scene 10

"Autograph of You"
M. Dale, R. Lee, P. O'Hearn, G. Clark
(*Music by* Alvin Kaufman. *Lyrics by* Mildred Kaufman.)

Scene 11

"Goona'Goona" (A Balonese Idyll)
E. Wood, S. Lani
(*Music by* Serge Walter. *Lyrics by* Charles Kenny.)

Scene 12

"Automotivation"
M. Dale, E. Reinhardt
(*Music by* Henry Lloyd. *Lyrics by* Sam Bernard II and Robert Burk.)

Scene 13

Tango Eschuchame (Solo Dance)
M. Enters

Scene 14

"Bonbonera"
L. Lope
(*Music by* Serge Walter. *Lyrics by* Charles Kenny.)

Scene 15

"Tu Sais"
M. Ducret
(*Music by* Serge Walter. *Lyrics by* Charles Kenny.)

Scene 16

"When Greek Meets Greek" or Lizi-Strata
M. Dehn, J. Dudley
(*Music by* Charles Posnak.)

Scene 17

"Love, Where Are You Now?"
G. Carrasco, M. Enters, P. Borgia, H. Wesley
(*Music by* Serge Walter.)

Scene 18

High Yellow
B. Collins

Scene 19

"Yes and No"
L. LaRiviere
(*Music by* Non Egen. *Lyrics by* Lucien LaRiviere.)

Scene 20

"Etiquette"
L. Astaire, L. LaRiviere
(*Music by* Henry Lloyd. *Lyrics by* Sam Bernard II and Robert Burk. *Dialogue by* Helen and Nolan Leary.)

Scene 21

Bon Voyage (Finale)
(Company)

1932.20   MANHATTAN VARIETIES

A Musical Revue in Two Acts, 39 Scenes. [All credits the same as BELMONT VARIETIES above.] Opened 21 October 1932 at the Cosmopolitan Theatre and closed 29 October 1932 after 11 performances.

<u>CAST:</u> LILYAN ASTAIRE, MARYON DALE, VALODIA VESTOFF, DOROTHY DARE, LUCIEN LARIVIERE, SHAWNI LANI, EDDIE LESLIE, ROY BENSON,

T.F.S., DON DELEO, ROSLYN HARVEY, GRACE CORNELL, RENEE GRAFF, GUSTAVO CARRASCO, MURA DEHN, JANE DUDLEY, MARTHA MERRILL, BERT PRIVAL, LITA LOPE, FLORENCE HERBERT, RAY LEE, WILLIAM SUNDERMAN, CHARLES KENNY, PHIL ARNOLD.

James Kelly, Diane Andre, Robert Burk, Carol Holmes, Margie Barrett, Virginia Mortimer, Marjorie Enters, Philippe Borgia, Harriette Wesley, Mauricette Ducret, Josette Tapie, Edith Reinhardt, Tad Allen, Elenore Wood, Jeanette Leland, Pierce O'Hearn, Gordon Clark, Louise Baer, Phil Arnold, Alexis Rothov, Jeanne Walton, J. F. Kelly, Herbert Bien, Violet Dell, Violet Paulson.

ACT 1[13]

Scene 1

Pier 57 (*by* Helen and Nolan Leary)

Inspector: J. Kelly. *Valet*: B. Prival. *Impressario*: T. F. S. *Valet*: D. Andre. *Photographer*: G. Carrasco. *Reporter*: R. Burk. *And*: L. Astaire. *Passengers Arriving*: R. Benson, G. Cornell, L. Lope, L. LaRiviere, M. Dehn, R. Graff, M. Dale, S. Lani, C. Holmes, M. Barrett, V. Mortimer, M. Enters, P. Borgia, C. Kenny, W. Sunderman, H. Wesley, M. Ducret, J. Tapie, E. Reinhardt, M. Merrill, R. Harvey, T. Allen, E. Wood, J. Leland, J. Dudley, E. Leslie, R. Lee, P. O'Hearn, G. Clark, F. Herber, D. Dare, V. Vestoff, L. Baer, P. Arnold, A. Rothov, J. Walton.

Scene 2

The Master

T. F. S.

With R. Harvey, J. Leland, J. F. Kelly, R. Burk, H. Bien.

Scene 3

"Something New and It's You"

M. Dale, V. Vestoff

Scene 4

What Time Bulova?

E. Leslie

Scene 5

"Back Seat of a Taxi"

D. Dare, L. LaRiviere

Dances by M. Enters, P. Borgia, V. Dell.

Scene 6

T. F. S.

Scene 7

"Oahu"

S. Lani

Scene 8

What Time Bulova?

E. Leslie

Scene 9

A Nice Young Man (With a Magic Personality)

R. Benson, assisted by D. Andre

Scene 10

Left Bank

J. Leland, L. LaRiviere, H. Wesley, M. Ducret, J. Tapie, W. Sunderman, C. Kenny, R. Lee, P. O'Hearn, G. Clark, V. Mortimer, V. Paulson, G. Carrasco, B. Prival, H. Bien, A. Rothov

Scene 11

T. F. S.

Scene 12

"Do the Swank"

D. DeLeo

Scene 13

Roslyn Harvey

Scene 14

"Romance"

G. Cornell, R. Graff

Scene 15

Modernistic Rhythm

V. Vestoff

Scene 16

"Vurria" (*by* M. Sandoual)

G. Carrasco

Scene 17

"When Greek Meets Greek" or Lizi-Strata

M. Dehn, J. Dudley

Scene 18

"A Lady of the Jury"

L. Astaire

Scene 19

"An Invitation to Love" (Dance)

L. Lope, L. LaRiviere, G. Carrasco, M. Enters, P. Borgia, F. Herbert, L. Baer, M. Ducret, R. Lee, P. O'Hearn, G. Clark

ACT 2

Scene 1

"A Degas Ballet" (*Staged by* Constantin Kobeleff.)

M. Merrill, B. Prival

With V. Mortimer, D. Andre, C. Holmes, R. Harvey, J. Watson, J. Tapie.

Scene 2

"Automotivation"

E. Reinhardt, M. Dale

Scene 3

"Bonbonera"

L. Lope

Scene 4

T. F. S.

Scene 5

"I Paused, I Looked, I Fell"

D. Dare, L. LaRiviere

Dance by. B. Prival.

Scene 6

"Lover, Where Are You Now?"

F. Herbert, R. Lee

Dance by M. Enters, P. Borgia.

Scene 7

"Park Ave."

W. Sunderman, C. Kenny

Scene 8

Echos of Seville

L. Lope, with explanations by R. Benson

"Clavelitos"

(*Words and Music by* [Joaquín] Quirito Valverde.)

"Capullito de Aleli"

(*Words and Music by* Hernandez.)

The Toreador: A. Rothov.

Scene 9

T. F. S.

Scene 10

"The Phantom President"

L. Astaire

Scene 11

"Dance of Death"

G. Cornell, R. Graff

Scene 12

"Yes and No"

L. LaRiviere

Scene 13

"River's Gonna Sweep You Away"

W. Sunderman

Scene 14

"Autograph of You"

M. Dale, V. Vestoff

With R. Lee, P. O'Hearn, G. Clark.

Scene 15

Phil Arnold

Scene 16

T. F. S.

Scene 17

"Radio"

---

[13]Songs uncredited, see BELMONT VARIETIES above.

Scene 18

 "Dance Africana"
   M. Dehn, J. Dudley
Scene 19

 "Mysteries of Life"
   T. F. S., R. Benson
Scene 20

 Aboard the *S.S. Ile de France* : "Bon Voyage"
   Entire Company

(J. P. McEVOY'S)
NEW AMERICANA

1932.21

A Musical Revue in Two Acts, 22 Scenes[14]. Book (sketches) by J. P. McEvoy. Lyrics by E. Y. Harburg, (Johnny Mercer). Music by Jay Gorney, Harold Arlen, Richard Myers, (Burton Lane, Vernon Duke, Henry Souvaine, Herman Hupfeld). Book staged by Harold Johnsrud. Dances staged by John Boyle, Charles Weidman. Production (settings) designed and lighted by Albert R. Johnson. Costumes by Constance Ripley. Music director, Jay Gorney. Orchestrations, Conrad Salinger. Vocal arrangements, Mabel Pearl. Production supervised by Peter Davis. Produced by Lee Shubert. Opened 5 October 1932 at the Sam S. Shubert Theatre and closed 10 December 1932 after 77 performances.

CAST: GEORGE GIVOT, ALBERT CARROLL, DON BARCLAY, GORDON SMITH, REX WEBER, RALPH LOCKE, LILLIAN FITZGERALD, FRANCETTA MALLOY, PEGGY CARTWRIGHT, LLYOD NOLAN, GEORGIE TAPPS, ALLAN MANN, DORIS HUMPHREY DANCE GROUP, Alfredo Rode and His Royal Tzigane Orchestra, Sue Hastings' Marionettes (Sue Hastings, Myrtil Turner, Frank Sullivan, Yvonne Magna), The Musketeers, Gene Hirsch, John Perkins, Carl Hoppe, Kathryn O'Neill, Pauline Laurence, Paul Davin, Rennie McEvoy, Paul Davin.

 CHARLES WEIDMAN AND DANCERS: José Limón, Letitia Ide, Cleo Atheneos, Sylvia Manning, William Matons. (Doris Humphrey Dance Group, "Americana" Girls, Ensemble.)

ACT 1

Scene 1

 Dedication
   Mr. Bustlebumper: G. Givot. *Mr. Button:* R. Locke. *Cynthia Block-Bullock:* P. Cartwright. *"Nails" Malarky:* L. Nolan. *Mr. Blott:* R. Weber. *The Forgotten Man:* D. Barclay.
 "Uncle Sam Needs a Man Who Can Take It"
   D. Barclay, Ensemble
Scene 2

 "Get That Sun into You"
   F. Malloy, Girls
   (*Music by* Richard Myers. *Lyrics by* E. Y. Harburg.)
   Dance: G. Tapps.
Scene 3

 Seance
   Medium: A. Carroll. *Little Arbutus:* L. Fitzgerald. *Mr. Button:* R. Locke. *Mr. Bustlebumper:* G. Givot. *Mr. Blott:* R. Weber. *The Forgotten Man:* D. Barclay.
Scene 4

 "Whistling for a Kiss"
   P. Davin, Musketeers, L. Fitzgerald, R. Weber, Ensemble
   (*Music by* Richard Myers. *Lyrics by* E. Y. Harburg and Johnny Mercer.)
Scene 5

 Speakeasy
   'Nails' Malarky: L. Nolan. *Malarky's Moll:* F. Malloy. *Customer:* R. Weber. *Buddy:* G. Smith. *Cynthia:* P. Cartwright.
 Dance Fantastique
   A. Mann
 "Satan's Little Lamb"
   F. Malloy, Musketeers
   (*Music by* Harold Arlen. *Lyrics by* E. Y. Harburg and Johnny Mercer.)
   Danced by Charles Weidman Dancers, Doris Humphrey Dance Group, 'Americana' Girls.

Scene 6

 Doom Over Kansas
   Alfalfa: D. Barclay. *Neuristhenia,* his wife: L. Fitzgerald. *Anemia,* their daughter: P. Laurence. *Mope,* the hired hand: R. Weber. *Bunke:* R. Locke.
Scene 7

 "You're Not Pretty, But You're Mine"
   P. Cartwright, G. Smith, Girls
   (*Music by* Burton Lane. *Lyrics by* E. Y. Harburg.)
Scene 8

 Breadline
   'Nails' Malarky: L. Nolan. *Butch,* his bodyguard: A. Carroll. *Mr. Bustlebumper:* G. Givot. *Mrs. Warren Block-Bullock:* L. Fitzgerald. *Cynthia,* her daughter: P. Cartwright. *Breadline:* R. Weber, R. McEvoy, J. Limón, W. Matons, G. Hirsch, G. Tapps, A. Mann, Musketeers, Men.
 "Brother, Can You Spare a Dime?"
   R. Weber, Musketeers, Men
   (*Music by* Jay Gorney. *Lyrics by* E. Y. Harburg.)
 Dance—"The Forgotten Man"
   P. Cartwright, G. Tapps, A. Mann
Scene 9

 "Let Me Match My Private Life With Yours"
   A. Carroll, Girls
   (*Music by* Vernon Duke. *Lyrics by* E. Y. Harburg.)
   Dance by G. Tapps.
Scene 10

 Ringside—Madison Square Garden (*Music by* Winthrop Sargent.)
   Referee: C. Weidman. *Boxers:* J. Limón, W. Matons.
Scene 11

 Reunion in Receivership
   Stage Doorman: D. Barclay. *Mr. Button:* R. Locke. *Harry Richman:* G. Givot. *Lynn Fontanne:* A. Carroll. *Jack Pearl:* R. Weber.
Scene 12

 "Five Minutes of Spring"
   (*Music by* Jay Gorney. *Lyrics by* E. Y. Harburg.)
 Finale
   (*Staged by* Charles Weidman.)

ACT 2

Scene 1

 Alfredo Rode and His Royal Tzigane Orchestra[15]
Scene 2

 North Woods Romance
   D. Barclay
Scene 3

 "Wouldja for a Big Red Apple?"
   P. Cartwright, G. Smith, Girls
   (*Music by* Henry Souvaine and Everett Miller. *Lyrics by* Johnny Mercer.)
Scene 4

 Dividend to You[16] (*by* Sig Herzig)
Scene 5

 "Amour à la Militaire"
   (*Danced by*) C. Weidman, C. Atheneos, J. Limón, S. Manning
   (*Music by* Bernard Herrmann.)
Scene 6

 Vox Pop
   Sol Nebbick: R. Locke. *Jitters:* R. McEvoy. *Mr. Button:* L. Nolan.
Scene 7

 "The Shakers"
   (*Danced by*) Doris Humphrey Dance Group
   (*Accompaniment by* Pauline Laurence and Bernard Hermann.)
   Note: The Shakers believed they could live forever by dancing and shaking their bodies free from sin and by maintaining a rigid separation of the sexes. In their meeting house men and women danced opposite each other—never together. This religious sect flourished in New England during the nineteenth century.

---

[14]Previous editions of the Americana revues were presented 30 October 1928 at the Mansfield/Liberty Theatres for 127 performances, and 7 July 1926 at the Belmont for 224 performances.

---

[15]Dropped during the run.
[16]Dropped during the run.

Scene 8

Pooh-Pooh-Pourri

Sue Hastings' Marionettes
Introducing Al Smith, John D. Rockefeller, Herbert Hoover, Ella Wendell Muffins, Little Toby. (Marionette masks by William Stahl.)
Puppeteers: S. Hastings, M. Turner, F. Sullivan. *Announcement:* Y. Magna.

Scene 9

The Dictator

Scene: Malarky's Office, Malarky's Senate.
'Nails' Malarky: L. Nolan. *Mr. Bustlebumper:* G. Givot. *Mr. Bottom:* R. Locke. *Page:* K. O'Neill. *Herbert Blott:* R. Weber. *The Forgotten Man:* D. Barclay.

Scene 10

Finale—Senatorial Broadcast

Entire Company

1932.22 TELL HER THE TRUTH

A Musical Farce in Three Acts. Adaptation (book) and Lyrics by R. P. Weston and Bert Lee. Based on the play "Nothing But the Truth" by James Montgomery from the novel by Frederick Isham. Music by Jack Waller and Joseph Tunbridge. Staged by Morris Green and Henry Thomas. Settings by Joseph Tiechner Studios. Costumes by Jay-Thorpe. Music director, Gene Salzer. (Produced by Morris Green for Mrs. Tillie Leblang.) Opened 28 October 1932 at the Cort Theatre and closed 5 November 1932 after 11 performances.

CAST: *Dick:* Raymond Walburn. *Office Boy:* Lou Parker. *Maclean:* HOBART CAVANAUGH. *Mr. Ralston:* ANDREW TOMBES. *Mr. Parkin:* WILLIAM FRAWLEY. *Bobbie:* JOHN SHEEHAN, JR. *Polly:* THELMA WHITE. *Helen:* Edith Davis. *Mrs. Raslton:* MARGARET DUMONT. *Gwen:* LILLIAN EMERSON. *Ethel:* Louise Kirtland. *Martha:* Berta Donn. Special Vocalizations by May Muth, Muriel Muth, Dorothy Essig.

Act 1: A Real Estate Office in Shingle Haven.

Acts 2 and 3: Interior of the Ralston Home.

ACT 1

"Hoch Caroline"

T. White, E. Davis, J. Sheehan, A. Tombes, R. Walburn

"Happy the Day"

J. Sheehan, L. Emerson

ACT 2

"Won't You Tell Me Why?"

L. Kirtland

"Sing, Brothers"

W. Frawley, Company

"That's Fine"

J. Sheehan, L. Emerson

"Tell Her the Truth"

T. White, E. Davis, J. Sheehan, R. Walburn

ACT 3

"Horrortorio"

J. Sheehan, A. Tombes, R. Walburn, W. Frawley, H. Cavanaugh

1932.23 MUSIC IN THE AIR

A Musical Adventure (Comedy) in Two Acts, 11 Scenes. Book and lyrics by Oscar Hammerstein II. Music by Jerome Kern. Staged by Oscar Hammerstein II and Jerome Kern. Scenery by Joseph Urban. Costumes designed by John W. Harkrider. Modern clothes by Howard Shoup. Music director, Victor Baravalle. Orchestrations by (Robert) Russell Bennett. Produced by Peggy Fears, (A. C. Blumenthal). Opened 8 November 1932 at the Alvin Theatre, closing 13 March 1933 after 146 performances; reopened 31 March 1933 at the 44th Street Theatre, and closed 16 September 1933 after an additional 196 performances. Total: 342 performances

CAST (in order of speaking): *Karl Reder,* the Schoolmaster: WALTER SLEZAK. *Frau Pflugfelder:* Gabrielle Guelpli. *Pflugfelder,* the Hotel Proprietor: Robert Williamson. *Dr. Walther Lessing,* the Music Teacher: AL SHEAN. *Herman:* Charles Belin. *Tila:* Mary McQuade. *Sieglinde Lessing,* Walther's daughter: KATHERINE CARRINGTON. *Burgomaster:* Marty Semon. *Town Crier:* Robert Rhodes. *Heinrich,* the Postman: Cliff Heckinger. *Father Joch,* the Priest: Paul Donah. *The Apothecary:* George Bell. *Widow Schreimann:* Lydia Van Gilder. *Hans,* the Goatherd: Edward Hayes. *Cornelius,* a Bird Breeder: REINALD WERRENRATH. *Ernst Weber,* the Music Publisher: Nicholas Joy. *Uppmann,* the Orchestra Leader: Harry Mestayer.

Marthe, Secretary to Ernst: Dorothy Johnston. *Frieda Hatzfeld,* the Star: NATALIE HALL. *Bruno Mahler,* the Playwright: TULLIO CARMINATI. *Hulde,* a Bubble Dancer: Desha. *Stout Mother:* Carrie Weller. *Stout Father:* Earl Edem. *Stout Boy:* George Dieter. *Waiter:* George Ludwig. *Zoo Attendant:* Alfred Russ. *The Bear:* Laura. *Bear Trainer:* H. Pallenberg. *Herr Direktor Kirschner:* Alexis Obolensky. *Frau Direktor Kirschner:* IVY SCOTT. *Sophie,* Sieglinde's Dresser: Kathleen Edwards. *Assistant Stage Manager:* Frank Dobert. *Anna,* Frieda's Maid: Marjorie Main. *Baum,* the Lawyer: Carl Spiegel. *Gusterl,* His Clerk: William Torpey. *The Tobacconist:* George Gerhardi. *The Doctor:* Paul Janvert.

Members of the Edendorf Choral Society: Sopranos: Leone Newman, Kathleen Edwards, Finette Walker, Claire Cole. *Mezzos:* Marion Stuart, Sally Hadley, Gertrude Houk. *Contraltos:* June Elkins, Vivian Vance, Rose Collins, Frances Marion. *Tenors:* Eugene King, Alfred Russ. *Second Tenors:* George Gerhardi, Alexander McKee, Robert Rhodes. *Baritones:* Norman Gray, Paul Donah, Paul Janvert. *Bassos:* Anton Lieb, Frank Dobert, John Brook. *Members of the Edendorf Walking Club: Sopranos:* Rita Marks, Beatrice Berenson, Marie Cartwright, Leone Newman, Ann Moss, Theo Bayles, Finette Walker, Grace Panvini, Kathleen Edwards, Carol Gay. *Mezzos:* Katherine Spector, Nomy Bencid, Marguerite Morano, Peggy Burgess, Helen Taylor, Virginia Ray, Marion Stuart. *Contraltos:* Peggy Frazier, Elise Joyce, Rosalind Shaw, Mary Alice Rice, Georgina Dieter, Betty Howson, Beatrice Hannen, Tamara Zoya, Vivian Vance, Frances Marion, Messrs. Alexander McKee, Robert Rhodes, Norman Gray, John Brook. *Edendorf Girls:* Joan Kent, Marcelle Miller, Rene McAfee, Noel Gordon, Diana Walker, Frances Kruger, Mary Lange, Stella Bailey, Jane Manners.

Act 1, Scene 1: Leit Motif. Dr. Walter Lessing's Home, Edendorf, Bavaria. The Present. *Scene 2: Etude.* Karl Reder's Classroom—two weeks later. *Scene 3: Pastoral.* Stony Brook … on the Road to Munich—that afternoon. *Scene 4: Impromptu.* Ernst Weber's Office, Munich—three days later.

Act 2, Scene 1: Sonata. The Zoo—later that day. *Scene 2: Nocturne.* Frieda's Suite, Four Seasons Hotel, Munich—that night. *Scene 3: Caprice.* Sieglinde's Room in her hotel—later that night. *Scene 4: Rhapsody.* A Star Dressing-Room—four weeks later. *Scene 5: Intermezzo.* A Stage and Orchestra Pit—a few hours later. *Scene 6: Humoresque.* The Star Dressing-Room—one hour later. *Scene 7: Rondo.* Edendorf—three weeks later.

ACT 1

Scene 2

Dr. Lessing's Chorale:

"Melodies of May"[17]

Edendorf Choral Society

"I've Told Ev'ry Little Star"

W. Slezak

"Prayer"

W. Slezak, K. Carrington, Ensemble

"There's a Hill Beyond a Hill"

E. Hayes, Edendorf Walking Club

Scene 3

"And Love Was Born"

R. Werrenrath

Scene 4

(Bubble) Dance

Desha

"I've Told Ev'ry Little Star" (reprise)

W. Slezak, K. Carrington

Scena from Bruno's play 'Tingle Tangle':

"I'm Coming Home" (Letter Song)

T. Carminati

"I'm Alone" (Aria)

N. Hall

"I Am So Eager" (Duo)

T. Carminati, N. Hall, Ensemble

Finaletto

D. Johnson, N. Joy, A. Shean

ACT 2

Scene 1

"One More Dance"

T. Carminati

"Night Flies By"

N. Hall

("I've Told Ev'ry Little Star") (reprise)

(K. Carrington)

[17]Based on the second movement of Beethoven's Piano Sonata No. 3 in C, Opus 2. Vocal arrangement by Jerome Kern.

Scene 2

(I'm Alone") (reprise)
(N. Hall)

Scene 3

"When the Spring Is in the Air"
K. Carrington, Ensemble

"(In) Egern on the Tegern See"
I. Scott

Scene 4

"The Song Is You"
T. Carminati

Scene 5

Excerpts from 'Tingle Tangle'
Orchestra

Scene 6

"I'm Alone" (reprise)
N. Hall

"The Song Is You" (reprise)
N. Hall, T. Carminati

Scene 7

"We Belong Together"
W. Slezak, K. Carrington, R. Werrenrath, Company

Finale

1932.24 THE DUBARRY

An Operetta in Two Acts, 15 Scenes. English adaptation (book) by Rowland Leigh and Desmond Carter. Adapted from the German operette "Die Dubarry" by Paul Knepler and Ignaz. M. Willeminsky, based on "Gräfin Dubarry" by F. Zell and Richard Genée. Lyrics by Rowland Leigh. Music by Karl Millöcker, arranged by Theo Mackeben. Staged by Morris Green. Book directed by Rowland Leigh. Settings and costumes by Vincente Minnelli. Ballet and dances staged by Dorothea Berke. Music director, Gustave Salzer. Produced by Morris Green (and Tillie Leblang) by arrangement with Crescendo Theatreverlag, Berlin (Management, Bernard Klawans). Opened 22 November 1932 at the George M. Cohan Theatre and closed 4 February 1933 after 87 performances.

CAST{in order of appearance}: *Margot*: PERT KELTON. *Madame Labille*: Lolita Robertson. *Gwen May*: Iris Newton. *Marquis De La Marche*: ROBINSON NEWBOLD. *Comte DuBarry*: PERCY WARAM. *Elise*: Melba Forsythe. *Jeanne*: GRACE MOORE. *Rene Lavallery*: WILLIAM HAIN. *Hubert Oronais*: Alexis Sandersen. *La Jeune Moreau*: Len Saxon. *Landlady*: Mildred Gethins. *Comte Bordenau*: HAROLD CRANE. *Prince de Soubise*: Fenton Barrett. *Baron Chamard*: Charles Angelo. *Comte Fragonard*: James Philips. *Therese*: Roberta Pierre. *Didine*: Helen Withers. *Madame Sauterelle*: HELEN RAYMOND. *Sophie*: Vivian Vernon. *Ninon*: Patricia Clarke. *Josephine*: Marion Santre. *Violet*: Mildred Manning. *Maitre Cascal*: Craig Williams. *Maid to Madame DuBarry*: Ethel Britton. *Duc de Choiseul*: MAX FIGMAN. *La Camargo*: Joyce Coles. *Maréchal de Luxembourg*: NAN BRYANT. *Comte Lammond*: John Clarke. *Louis XV*: MARION GREEN.

Ladies of the Ensemble: Madaline DeSauter, Mildred Gethers, Eleanor Manning, Marjory Miller, Jean Audree, Patricia Clarke, Iris Newton, Patricia Parsons, Roberta Pierre, Melba Forsythe, Helen Withers, Vivian Vernon, Paula Maysak, Ethel Britton, Marion Santre, Ruth Hale. *Dorothea Berke Ballet*: Georgine Stokes, Esther Whetton, Jeanne Kroll, Jerry Williams, Verta Kunkel, May Sigler, Lo Iven, Clare Gould, Marjory Marlow, Ruth Haidt, Rolande Poucel, Marie Rio. *Gentlemen of the Ensemble*: Stanley Lipton, Leslie Ostrander, J. Horn, Tully Millet, Carl Rose, Henry Devitt, Herman Belmonte, L. Davis, M. Remneck, Jack Lee, Arthur Roland, Paul Owen.

Act 1, Scene 1: Workroom in Madame Labille's Hat Shop. *Scene 2*: Near Port Maillot. Same evening. *Scene 3*: Rene's Garret. Six months later. *Scene 4*: In Front of DuBarry's House. Six months later. *Scene 5*: DuBarry's Dining-Room. Immediately following. *Scene 6*: In Front of DuBarry's House. Immediately following. *Scene 7*: The Salon of Madame Sauterelle. Same evening.

Act 2, Scene 1: Jeanne's Boudoir in DuBarry's House. One year later. *Scene 2*: Rene's Study. Simultaneously. *Scene 3*: The House of la Maréchale de Luxembourg. Same evening. *Scene 4*: Near the House of la Maréchale. Immediately following. *Scene 5*: On the Road to Versailles. Immediately following. *Scene 6*: Louis XV's Salon in the Palace of Versailles. Immediately following. *Scene 7*: A Corner of a Garden. One year later. *Scene 8*: The Gardens of the Palace Luciennes. Same evening.

ACT 1

Opening Chorus
P. Kelton, Girls

"Today" (Song)
G. Moore, Girls

Finaletto
G. Moore

"On the Stage" (Duet)
P. Kelton, R. Newbold

"Without Your Love" (Duet)
G. Moore, W. Hain

"If I Am Dreaming" (Song)
W. Hain

"Happy Little Jeanne" (Song)
G. Moore

"Pantalettes" (Sextette)
C. Angelo, H. Crane, R. Newbold, P. Waram, F. Barrett, J. Philips

"Pantalettes" (reprise)

"Dance for the Gentlemen" (Song)
H. Raymond, Girls

"I Give My Heart" (Song)
G. Moore

Finale—"I Give My Heart" (reprise)
G. Moore

ACT 2

Minuet
J. Rees, M. Rio, Berke Ballet

"Beauty" (Song)
G. Moore, Chorus

"The Road to Happiness" (Duet)
G. Moore, W. Hain

Finaletto
G. Moore, W. Hain

"If I Am Dreaming" (reprise)
W. Hain, Chorus

"Ga-Ga" (Duet)
P. Kelton, R. Newbold

Ballet
J. Coles, Berke Ballet

"The Dubarry" (Song)
G. Moore, Chorus

Finale
G. Moore, Company

1932.25 GEORGE WHITE'S MUSIC HALL VARIETIES

A Musical Revue in Two Acts, 27 Scenes. Sketches by William K. Wells, George White. Lyrics by Irving Caesar, Herb Magidson, Herman Hupfeld, Ted Koehler. Music by Irving Caesar, Carmen Lombardo, Sam H. Stept, Harold Arlen, Herman Hupfeld. Staged by George White. Dances staged by Russell Markert. Settings by Dazian. Costumes designed by Charles LeMaire, Kiviette. Music director, Al Goodman. Orchestrations by Maurice DePackh. Produced by George White. First edition opened 22 November 1932 at the Casino Theatre, closing 31 December 1932 after 47 performances; Second edition opened 2 January 1933 at the Casino Theatre and closed 21 January 1933 after 24 performances. Total: 71 performances.

First Edition CAST: HARRY RICHMAN, LILY DAMITA, BERT LAHR, ELEANOR POWELL, VIVIAN FAY, BARRE HILL, JOSEPH DONATELLA, THOMAS PHILLIPS, THE LOOMIS SISTERS (Maxine, Virginia), THE FOUR MULLEN SISTERS (Kathleen, Imelda, Mary, Monica), HELEN GORDON, JOSEPH VITALE, BETTY KEAN, HERR AL GORDON, HELEN ARNOLD, JAMES HOWARD.

George White's Dancing Beauties: Peggy Moseley, Hilda Knight, Ethel Lawrence, Hazel Boffinger, Joanna Allen, Vivian Porter, Peggy Ring, Betty Allen, Alma Saunders, Gay Delys, Barbara Pepper, Nancy Nelson, Edwina Steel, Maria Steel, Marjorie Baglin, Sunny Kest, Lila Manors, Lela Manors, Evelyn Nichols, Ruth Doran, Betty Collette, Pam McAvoy, Evelyn Neilson, Zynaida Spencer, Alice Jordan, Paula Sands, Helen Dongan, Connie Alderson, Lenora McDermott, Gwyn Tremble, Renee Landeau, Peggy Van Oden, Marie Garham, Peggy Seal, Madeline Lawson, Joy Marsh, Edna Eustace, Rita Mackin.

ACT 1

Scene 1

"Il Prologo"
H. Richman

Scene 2

George White's Dancing Beauties

Scene 3

Dance
E. Powell

Scene 4

Third Degree
A Suspect: B. Lahr. *A Detective*: T. Phillips. *Chief*: H. Richman. *A Second Suspect*: A. Gordon. *A Third Suspect*: B. Hill. *A Fourth Suspect*: J. Howard.

Scene 5

"Birds of a Feather"
The Loomis Sisters
(*Music by* Carmen Lombardo. *Lyrics by* Irving Caesar.)
Dance by V. Fay.

Scene M

"(And) So I Married the Girl"
H. Richman, L. Damita
(*Music by* Sam H. Stept. *Lyrics by* Herb Magidson.)

Scene 7

"The Waltz That Brought You Back to Me"
B. Hill, H. Arnold, Dancing Beauties
(*Music by* Carmen Lombardo. *Lyrics by* Irving Caesar.)

Scene 8

All's Wet That Ends Wet
Mr. Smyler: B. Lahr. *Mrs. Smyler*: B. Kean. *Mr. Tipler*: H. Richman. *Mrs. Tipler*: H. Gordon. *Policeman*: T. Phillips. *Announcement*: N. Nelson.

Scene 9

Song Specialty
The Four Mullen Sisters
(*Arrangements by* David Ringle.)

Scene 10

The Wolf
The Girl: L. Damita. *Pedro*: T. Phillips. *The Wolf*: H. Richman.

Scene 11

Herr Gordon's Dogs
Announcement: H. Knight.

Scene 12

"Sweet Liar"
H. Richman, L. Damita
(*Music and Lyrics by* Irving Caesar.)

Scene 13

"Cabin in the Cotton"
B. Lahr, Dancing Beauties
(*Music by* Harold Arlen. *Lyrics by* Irving Caesar.)

Scene 14

Dance
E. Powell

Scene 15

"Two Feet in Two-Four Time"
The Loomis Sisters, Dancing Beauties, H. Richman, L. Damita, B. Lahr
(*Music by* Harold Arlen. *Lyrics by* Irving Caesar.)

ACT 2

Scene 1

"Rah, Rah, Rah!"
Dancing Beauties
(*Music by* Sam H. Stept. *Lyrics by* Irving Caesar and Herb Magidson.)

Scene 2

A Close Shave
Barber's Daughter: H. Gordon. *Customer*: B. Lahr.

Scene 3

Beauty And the Beast
Dance by V. Fay

Scene 4

"Oh, Lady!"
H. Richman, L. Damita
(*Music by* Sam H. Stept. *Lyrics by* Herb Magidson.)

Scene 5

Song Specialty
The Loomis Sisters

Scene 6

My
The Wife: L. Damita. *The Friend*: H. Richman. *The Husband*: T. Phillips. *The Other Fellow*: B. Lahr.

Scene 7

"Hold Me Closer"
B. Hill, H. Arnold, Dancing Beauties
(*Music and Lyrics by* Max Rich, Frank Littau, Jack Scholl.)

Scene 8

"A Bottle and a Bird"
B. Lahr
(*Music and Lyrics by* Irving Caesar.)

Scene 9

Dance
J. Donatello

Scene 10

Song Specialty
H. Richman

Scene 11

The Date
A Fellow: B. Lahr. *Another Fellow*: H. Richman. *The Girl*: L. Damita.

Scene 12

"(Let's) Turn Out the Lights and Go to Bed"
H. Richman, L. Damita, Bert Lahr, Dancing Beauties
(*Music and Lyrics by* Herman Hupfeld.)

GEORGE WHITE'S
1932.25 MUSIC HALL VARIETIES
(Second Edition)

A Musical Revue in Two Acts, 28 Scenes. [Same credits as above.] Second edition opened 2 January 1933 at the Casino Theatre and closed 21 January 1933 after 24 performances.

Second edition CAST: HARRY RICHMAN, BERT LAHR, WILLIE HOWARD, EUGENE HOWARD, TOM PATRICOLA, ELEANOR POWELL, THE LOOMIS SISTERS (Maxine, Virginia), MELISSA MASSON, ROGER GRAY, Herr AL GORDON, JOSEPH VITALE, JAMES HOWARD, HELEN GORDON, LUCILLE OSBORNE, THOMAS PHILLIPS, Edna Pence, Alice Carleton.
George White's Dancing Beauties: Barbara Pepper, Florence Healy, Betty Allen, Marjorie Baglin, Lila Manor, Lela Manor, Marion O'Day, Beverly Gordon, Kay Michels, Pearl Bradley, Myra Gerald, Rita Mackin, Helen Dell, Nancy Nelson, Betty Sundmark, Dorothy Daly, Pearl Harris, Amy Weber, Jewell Morse, Julia Gorman, Zynaida Spencer, Marie Graham, Leonore McDermott, Joan Marsh, Chic Jordan, Eleanor Witt, Peggy Seal, Madeline Lawson, Connie Alderson, Gwen Tremble, Edna Eustace, Dorothy Phillips.

ACT 1

Scene 1

George White's Dancing Beauties

Scene 2

Tom Patricola

Scene 3

"There Never Was a Girl Like You"
H. Richman, B. Pepper, M. O'Day, D. Phillips, B. Sundmark, B. Allen, N. Nelson
(*Music by* Cliff Friend. *Lyrics by* Herb Magidson.)

Scene 4

A Close Shave
Barber's Daughter: H. Gordon. *Customer*: B. Lahr.

Scene 5

"A Hundred Years Ago"
The Loomis Sisters, Dancing Beauties

Scene 6

Pay the Two Dollars
Sam Pincus: W. Howard. *Abe Steiner*: E. Howard. *Special Officer*: J. Howard. *Judge*: R. Gray. *Warden*: J. Vitale.

Scene 7

Close to You

Dancing Beauties

Scene 8

Bert Lahr

Scene 9

Dance

M. Mason

Scene 10

"Two Feet in Two-Four Time"

Dancing Beauties

(*Music by* Harold Arlen. *Lyrics by* Irving Caesar.)

Scene 11

Dance

F. Powell

Scene 12

The Feud

W. Howard, E. Howard, V. Loomis, T. Phillips, J. Vitale, J. Howard, R. Gray

Scene 13

"Cabin in the Cotton"

B. Lahr

(*Music by* Harold Arlen. *Lyrics by* Irving Caesar.)

Scene 14

Harry Richman

Scene 15

"Rhapsody in Blue"

H. Richman, W. Howard, E. Howard, Dancing Beauties

(*Music by* George Gershwin.)

ACT 2

Scene 1

"A Hundred Years Ago" (reprise)

Dancing Beauties

Scene 2

Bums

H. Richman, W. Howard, E. Howard

Scene 3

"A Bottle and a Bird"

B. Lahr

(*Music and Lyrics by* George White and Irving Caesar.)

Scene 4

The Duel

The General: W. Howard. *Aide*: J. Vitale. *The Spy*: H. Gordon.

Scene 5

(Song Specialty)

The Loomis Sisters

Scene 6

"The Waltz That Brought You Back to Me"

Dancing Beauties

(*Music by* Carmen Lombardo. *Lyrics by* Irving Caesar.)

Scene 7

Herr Gordon's Dogs

Scene 8

The Governor

T. Patricola

Scene 9

"So I Married the Girl"

H. Richman, E. Powell

(*Music by* Sam H. Stept. *Lyrics by* Herb Magidson.)

Scene 10

Quartet from "Rigoletto"[18]

W. Howard, E. Howard, E. Pence, A. Carleton

Scene 11

The Date

A Fellow: B. Lahr. *Another Fellow*: H. Richman. *The Girl*: V. Loomis.

[18]Burlesque of Giuseppe Verdi's opera.

Scene 12

Dance

E. Powell

Scene 13

Club Richman

1932.26 # TAKE A CHANCE

A Musical Comedy in Two Acts, 10 Scenes. Book by Buddy G. DeSylva, Laurence Schwab. Additional dialogue by Sid Silvers. Lyrics by Buddy G. DeSylva. Music by Richard A. Whiting, Herb Brown Nacio [Nacio Herb Brown]. Additional songs by Vincent Youmans. Book directed by Edgar MacGregor. Musical numbers staged by Bobby Connolly. Settings by Cleon Throckmorton. Frocks (costumes) by Kiviette, Charles LeMaire. Music director, Max Meth. Orchestrations by Stephen Jones, Edward Powell, (Robert) Russell Bennett, William Daly[19]. Produced by Laurence Schwab and B. G. DeSylva. Opened 26 November 1932 at the Apollo Theatre and closed 1 July 1933 after 243 performances.

CAST: *Duke Stanley*: JACK HALEY. *Louie Webb*: SID SILVERS. *Toni Ray*: JUNE KNIGHTS. *Wanda Brill*: ETHEL MERMAN. *Kenneth Raleigh*: JACK WHITING. *Andrew Raleigh, His Father*: Douglas Wood. *Consuelo Raleigh, His Sister*: MITZI MAYFAIR. *Mike Caruso*, Owner of Mike's Place: Robert Gleckler. *Thelma Green*: Josephine Dunn. *Butler*: George Pauncefort.

Actors and Actresses in Kenneth Raleigh's Revue "Humpty Dumpty": Oscar Ragland, Sara Jane, John Grant, Louise Seidel, Lee Beggs, Al Downing, Andrew Carr, Louise Carr. *Dancers*: Louise Allen, Gerry Billings, Lucille Brodin, Flo Brooks, Jean Carson, Marian Dixon, Helen Fairweather, Emily Fitzpatrick, Arline Garfield, Frances Gordon, Ethel Green, Marian Herson, Julie Jenner, Dorothy Kal, Gloria Kelly, Paula King, Jane Lane, Evelyn Laurie, Florence Mallee, Anna Marie McKenney, Frances McHugh, Dorothy Morgan, Julia Pirie, Blanche Poston, Adelaide Raleigh, Mildred Webb, James Ardell, Henry King, Clark Leston, Edward Shane. *Ritz Quartette*: William H. Stamm, Edward Delridge, Neil Evans, Chet Bree. *The Admirals*: Tommy Ladd, Jack Armstrong, Budd Kehlner, Paul Pegue.

Act 1, Scene 1: Mike's Place. *Scene 2*: A Bedroom in a Hotel. *Scene 3*: Stage of Embassy Theatre. Rehearsal. *Scene 4*: The Raleigh Town House.

Act 2, Scene 1: Outside of Stage Door, Embassy Theatre. *Scene 2*: Opening Night of the Revue, 'Humpty Dumpty.' *Scene 3*: Dressing Room Corridor, backstage, during performance of 'Humpty Dumpty.' *Scene 4*: In front of Revue Curtain. *Scene 5*: Behind the Scenes. An Emergency Rehearsal, Revue Scene—'Daniel Boone's Defense.' *Scene 6*: Outside the Stage Door after the performance of 'Humpty Dumpty.'

ACT 1

"The Life of the Party"

Night Club Girls, Guests

"Should I Be Sweet"

J. Knight

(*Music by* Vincent Youmans.)

"So Do I"

J. Whiting, J. Knight, Guests

(*Music by* Vincent Youmans.)

"I Got Religion"

E. Merman

(*Music by* Vincent Youmans.)

Specialty

A. Carr, L. Carr

Revue Sketch: Blackmail

Ronald: J. Whiting. *Maid*: J. Jenner. *Mrs. Krankel*: J. Dunn. *Jeeves*: O. Ragland. *Connolly*: J. Grant. *Lora*: E. Merman. *Mr. Krankel*: L. Beggs.

"She's Nuts About Me"

J. Haley

"Tickled Pink"

J. Whiting, Girls

"Turn Out the Light"

S. Silvers, J. Haley, J. Knight, J. Whiting, Girls

"Charity"

Guests

Waltz

M. Mayfair

[19]Musical sequence for "Eadie Was a Lady" and Miss Merman's vocal arrangements by Roger Edens.

"(Oh, How) I Long to Belong to You"
  J. Whiting, J. Knight
  (*Music by* Vincent Youmans.)
"Rise and Shine"
  E. Merman, Ensemble
  (*Music by* Vincent Youmans.)
ACT 2
"Tonight Is Opening Night"
  Ensemble
"(You're an Old) Smoothie"
  J. Haley, E. Merman
Specialty
  A. Carr, L. Carr
"Eadie Was a Lady"
  E. Merman, Ensemble
"Should I Be Sweet" (Revue version)
  J. Knight
  (*Music by* Vincent Youmans.)
Revue Scene: Daniel Boone's Defense
  Preacher: O. Ragland. *Boone's Wife*: J. Knight. *Trapper*: S. Silvers. *Daniel Boone*: J. Whiting. *Indian Girl*: M. Mayfair. *General Duquesne*: J. Haley.
Specialty
  M. Mayfair
Finale
  Ensemble

1932.27 GAY DIVORCE

A Musical Comedy in Two Acts, 5 Scenes. Book by Dwight Taylor, adapted by Kenneth Webb and Samuel Hoffenstein from an unproduced play ("An Adorable Adventure") by J. Hartley Manners. Music and lyrics by Cole Porter. Directed by Howard Lindsay. Dances by Carl Randall, Barbara Newberry. Settings by Jo Mielziner. Costumes by Raymond Sovey. Music director, Gene Salzer. Orchestrations by Hans Spialek and (Robert) Russell Bennett. Produced by Dwight Deere Wiman and Tom Weatherly. Opened 29 November 1932 at the Ethel Barrymore Theatre, moved 16 January 1933 to the Sam S. Shubert Theatre, and closed 1 July 1933 after 248 performances.

CAST (in order of appearance): *Robert*: Taylor Gordon. *Teddy*: G. P. HUNTLEY, JR. *Guy*: FRED ASTAIRE. *Gladys*: Jean Frontai. *Vivian*: Helen Allen. *Doris*: Mary Jo Mathews. *Barbara*: BETTY STARBUCK. *Phyllis*: Eleanor Etheridge. *Joan*: Joan Burgess. *Joyce*: Dorothy Waller. *Waiter*: ERIC BLORE. *Ann*: Billie Green. *Hortense*: LUELLA GEAR. *Mimi*: CLAIRE LUCE. *Porter*: Martin Cravath. *Tonetti*: ERIK RHODES. *Pat*: Pat Palmer. *Diana*: Mitzie Garner. *Claire*: Edna Abbey. *Elaine*: Jacquie Simmons. *Edith*: Ethel Hampton. *Evelyn*: Grace Moore[20]. *Beatrice*: Bobby Sheehan. *Elizabeth*: Hulda Hedvig. *Mr. Pratt*: ROLAND BOTTOMLEY.

Act 1, Scene 1: Guy's London Flat. A June afternoon. *Scene 2*: A Seaside Hotel. The next day.

Act 2, Scene 1: Mimi's Suite. The same evening. *Scene 2*: A Hotel Corridor. Later. *Scene 3*: Mimi's Suite. The next morning.

ACT 1
Scene 1
  "After You, Who?"
    F. Astaire
Scene 2
  "Why Marry Them?"
    B. Starbuck, Girls
  "Salt Air"
    G. P. Huntley, B. Starbuck, Girls
  "I Still Love the Red, White and Blue"
    L. Gear
  "After You, Who?" (reprise)
    F. Astaire
  "Night and Day"
    F. Astaire, C. Luce
  "How's Your Romance?"
    E. Rhodes, Girls

ACT 2
Scene 1
  "What Will Become of Our England?"
    E. Blore, Girls
  "I've Got You on My Mind"
    F. Astaire, C. Luce
Scene 2
  "Mr. and Mrs. Fitch"
    L. Gear
Scene 3
  "You're in Love"
    F. Astaire, C. Luce, E. Rhodes

1932.28 WALK A LITTLE FASTER

A Musical Revue in Two Acts, 24 Scenes. (Sketches by S. J. Perelman, Robert MacGunigle.) Music by Vernon Duke, (Henry Sullivan, William Walter). Lyrics by E. Y. Harburg, (Earl Crooker, Rowland Leigh). Staged by Albertina Rasch and Monty Woolley. Dances and ensembles by Albertina Rasch. Production (settings) conceived and designed by Boris Aronson. Costumes by Kiviette. Music director, Nick Kempner. Orchestrations by (Robert) Russell Bennett and Conrad Salinger. Produced by Courtney Burr. Opened 7 December 1932 at the St. James Theatre, moved 20 February 1933 to the Selwyn Theatre, and closed 18 March 1933 after 119 performances.

CAST: BEATRICE LILLIE, BOBBY CLARK, PAUL McCULLOUGH, JOHN HUNDLEY, DONALD BURR, BERNICE LEE, EVELYN HOEY, DAVE FITZGIBBON, DOROTHY FITZGIBBON, JERRY NORRIS, DOROTHY McNULTY [Penny Singleton], Sue Hicks, Douglas Gerard, Jerome Andrews, Owen Coll, Katherine Hall, Lloyd Harris, Bernice Lee, Patricia Dorn, Albertina Vitak, Stephen Irving, Leslie McLeod, William Culloo, Serge Krasnoff. *At the Steinways*: EDGAR FAIRCHILD and ROBERT LINDHOLM.
Specialty Dancers: Melva Cornell, Virginia Allen, Margarette Slattery, Barbara Williams, Kathleen Van Noy, Mary Grace Van Noy, Kay Lazelle, Rose Tyrrel, Nona O'Tera, Molly Peck. *Ladies of the Ensemble*: La Vonne Gundry, Alyce Downey, Joan English, Ruth Cunliffe, Amalie Ideal, Greta Lewis, Ruth Porter, Charlotte Stoll, Sunny Reddy, Wanda Wood, Denny Wilson, Bee Sullivan, Tina Marie Jensen, Polly Porter, Georgia MacTaggart.

ACT 1
Scene 1
  Opening—"Can Can"—"That's Life"
    B. Clark, P. McCullough
Scene 2
  "Unaccustomed As I Am"
    B. Lee, D. Burr, Girls
    Dance by D. Fitzgibbon.
Scene 3
  Scamp of the Campus (*by* S. J. Perelman)
    Scene: A dormitory room at Voorhees College, 1906.
    "Babs" Huneker: R. Tyrrel. *"Boots" Kaplan*: P. Dorn. *Alice Bread*: D. Fitzgibbon. *Penelope Goldfarb*: B. Lillie. *Sport Cardini*: B. Clark. *Stacy Updegraff*: J. Hundley. *Policemen*: D. Gerard, L. Harris.
Scene 4
  "Off Again, On Again"
    P. Dorn, K. Hall, B. Lee
Scene 5
  "Marionettes"
    Dancing Ensemble
Scene 6
  Quel Bijou (*by* R. MacGunigle)
    B. Lillie
Scene 7
  "April in Paris"
    E. Hoey
    Dance by A. Vitak, J. Andrews.
Scene 8
  Beatrice Lillie
Scene 9
  Moscow Merry-Go-Round (*by* S. J. Perelman)
    Scene: Council Chamber of the Dictator of the U.S.S.R.

---

[20]Not the same Grace Moore who appeared this season in The Dubarry.

The Dictator: B. Clark. *Boris*, his secretary: P. McCullough. *Commissars*: L. Harris, D. Gerard, S. Irving, L. McLeod. *Commissar from the Volga*: D. Burr. *Red Guards*: W. Culloo, S. Krasnoff. *The Bearded Stranger*: O. Coll.

Scene 10

Specialty

Scene 11

"Where Have We Met Before?"
J. Hundley, S. Hicks, D. Burr, P. Dorn

Scene 12

"A Penny for Your Thoughts"
J. Norris, D. McNulty
Dance by Girls, K. Lazelle.

Scene 13

"Frisco Fanny"
(*Music by* Henry Sullivan. *Lyrics by* Earl Crooker.)
Scene: A Saloon in the Yukon.
Frisco Fanny: B. Lillie. *Sourdough*, a Miner: B. Clark. *A Bartender*: P. McCullough. *Miners*: L. Harris, D. Gerard, S. Irving, L. McLeod, W. Culloo, S. Krasnoff.

Scene 14

"Saturday Night" Finale
E. Hoey
Dances by A. Vitak, J. Andrews, Dave Fitzgibbons, Dorothy Fitzgibbons, Girls.

ACT 2

Scene 1

Opening—"Pomp and Circumstance"

Scene 2

The Girl Friend (*by* R. MacGunigle)
Scene: A star's dressing room.
Nancy Fixit: B. Lillie. *An Actress*: K. Hall. *A Maid*: D. Fitzgibbons.

Scene 3

"Nonchalant"
E. Hoey
Dance by Girls, Dave Fitzgibbons, Dorothy Fitzgibbons.

Scene 4

The Professor Himself (*by* R. MacGunigle)
Scene: The Van Rensellaer Library—Sutton Place.
Prof. Peter Peckham, a criminologist: B. Clark. *Mr. Amos Van Rensellaer*: J. Hundley. *Mrs. Amos Van Rensellaer*: K. Hall. *Inspector Barry*: O. Coll. *Renfrew*, a butler: P. McCullough. *Murphy*, a policeman: L. Harris.

Scene 5

Beatrice Lillie (with apologies): ["I Apologize" (parody)
(*Music and Lyrics by* Al Hoffman, Al Goodhart and Ed Nelson.)]

Scene 6

"Time and Tide" (with a bow to Herr Offenbach)
J. Handley, Girls

Scene 7

"End of a Perfect Night"
B. Lillie, B. Clark

Scene 8

"Speaking of Love"
D. Burr, Dave Fitzgibbon, Dorothy Fitzgibbon, Girls

Scene 9

"Mayfair"
(*Music by* William Waliter. *Lyrics by* Rowland Leigh.)
Scene: A drawing room in Mayfair, London.
Mrs. George Buckingham: B. Lillie. *Mr. George Buckingham*: J. Hundley. *A Maid*: E. Hoey. *Lord Slosh*: O. Coll. *Lady Slosh*: K. Hall. *Butler*: L. McLeod.

Scene 10

Finale
Entire Company

ALICE IN WONDERLAND and
1932.29 THROUGH THE LOOKING GLASS

A Play with Music in Two Acts. Adapted by Eva Le Gallienne and Florida Freibus from 'Alice in Wonderland' and 'Through the Looking Glass' by Lewis Carroll. Music by Richard Addinsell. Devised and directed by Eva Le Gallienne. Scenery and costumes, after Sir John Tenniel's drawings, by

Irene Sharaff. Choreography by Ruth Wilton. Animal heads, masks and marionettes by Remo Bufano. Orchestra under the direction of Sig Sanders. Produced by the Civic Repertory Theatre. Opened 12 December 1932 at the Civic Repertory Theatre, moved 30 January 1933 to the New Amsterdam Theatre, and closed 6 May 1933 after 127 performances.

CAST(in order of speaking): *Part 1*: *Alice*: JOSEPHINE HUTCHINSON. *White Rabbit*: RICHARD WARING, Freddy Rendulic, Doris Sawyer. *Mouse*: Nelson Welch. *Dodo*: Joseph Kramm. *Lory*: Walter Beck. *Eaglet*: Robert H. Gordon. *Crab*: Landon Herrick. *Duck*: Burgess Meredith. *Caterpillar*: Sayre Crawley. *Fish Footman*: Tonio Selwart. *Frog Footman*: Robert F. Ross. *Duchess*: Charles Ellis. *Cheshire Cat*: FLORIDA FREIBUS. *March Hare*: DONALD CAMERON. *Mad Hatter*: LANDON HERRICK. *Dormouse*: Burgess Meredith. *Two of Spades*: David Marks. *Five of Spades*: Arthur Swenson. *Seven of Spades*: Whitner [Whit] Bissell. *Queen of Hearts*: JOSEPH SCHILDKRAUT. *King of Hearts*: Harold Moulton. *Gryphon*: Nelson Welch. *Mock Turtle*: Lester Scharff. *Cook*: Howard da Silva. *Knave of Hearts*: David Turk. *Clubs*: Jacobsen, Lloyd, Green, Dwenger. *Hearts*: Tittoni, Ballantyne, Cotsworth, Pollock, Fox, Scourby, Milne, Marsden, Leonard.

Part 2: *Red Chess Queen*: Leona Roberts. *Train Guard*: Robert H. Gordon. *Gentleman Dressed in White Paper*: Robert F. Ross. *Goat*: Richard Waring. *Beetle*: FLORIDA FREIBUS. *Hoarse Voice*: David Turk. *Gnat*: May Sarton. *Gentle Voice*: Agnes McCarthy. *Tweedledum*: Landon Herrick. *Tweedledee*: Burgess Meredith. *White Chess Queen*: EVA LE GALLIENNE. *Sheep*: Margaret Love. *Humpty Dumpty*: Walter Beck. *White Knight*: Howard da Silva. *Horse*: *Front Legs*: Robert F. Ross. *Back Legs*: William S. Phillips. *Old Frog*: Sayre Crawley. *Shrill Voice*: Adelaide Finch. *Singers*: Ruth Wilton, Adelaide Finch. *Marionettes worked by* English, Beck, Snaylor, Nurenburg, Hill, Tittoni, Marsden, Bauer, Pollock, *under the direction of* A. Spolidoro.

ACT 1

Alice at Home
The Looking Glass House
White Rabbit
Pool of Tears
Caucus Race
Caterpillar
Duchess
Cheshire Cat
Mad Tea Party
Queen's Croquet Ground
By the Sea
The Trial

ACT 2

Red Chess Queen
Railway Carriage
Tweedledum and Tweedledee
White Chess Queen
Wool and Water
Humpty Dumpty
White Knight
Alice Crowned
Alice With the Two Queens
The Banquet
Alice at Home Again

THE PICCOLI
1932.30 OF VITTORIO PODRECCA

A Musical Marionette Revue in Three Acts, 14 Scenes[21]. (Conceived and directed by Vittorio Podrecca.) Orchestra and singers under the direction of Emilio Cardellini. Settings designed by Bruno Angoletta. Costumes designed by Caramba. Produced by Sol Hurok. Opened 22 December 1932 at the Lyric Theatre, moved 6 February 1933 to the George M. Cohan Theatre, and closed 5 March 1933 after 141 performances.

Principal Singers: Emilio Cabello (baritone), Lia Podrecca (light soprano), Thea Carugati (soprano), Mario Serangeli (baritone), Giuseppe Costa (tenor), Dario Zani

---

[21]Vittorio Podrecca's Marionette Revue previously appeared on Broadway as THE MARIONETTE PLAYERS under the auspices of Charles Dillingham 10 September 1923 at the Frolic Theatre for 16 performances.

(baritone), Augusto Galli (basso), Irma Zappata (soprano), Carlo Pessina (tenor), Rosina Zotti (soprano). (Cissie Rossi.)

Manipulators and Operators: The families of Gorno, Dell' Acqua, Possidoni, Forgioli, Borgogni, Donati, Braga, Rosagni, Venaelli, Gabutti. *Technical direction*: L. and M. Gorno.

ACT 1

Mme. Blondinette, Equilibrist

In the Manner of Mistinguett

Bil-Bal-Bul, a Little Acrobat

Clowns

Redemtor's "Night in Venice"

Divertissement de Ballet

La Corrida—The Bullfight

Patio, *sung by* I. Zappata; Arena.

ACT 2 (evenings)

THE GEISHA—Short selection of Sidney Jones' Japanese operetta.
Mimosa San: L. Podrecca. *Wun-Hi*, chinaman: M. Serangeli. *Katana*, Mimosa's Sweetheart: C. Pessina. *Marquis Imari*, governor: A. Galli. *Molly*: R. Zotti.

Little Tropical Revue
Singing in Rain

Tim-Tom-Tam

In the Manner of Josephine Baker (*sung by* L. Podrecca)

Salome, Equatorial dancer

Sisters

Finale

ACT 2 (matinees)

The Sleeping Beauty (Three Acts, 7 Scenes)
by Gian Bistolfi, with music by Ottorino Respighi specially written for the Teatro dei Piccoli.

CAST: *The King*: E. Cabello. *The Queen*: R. Zotti. *The Princess*: I. Zappata. *Prince Charming*: C. Pessina. *The Blue Fairy*: L. Podrecca. *The Green Fairy*: C. Rosi. *The Old Spinner*: G. Palazzo. *The Jester*: N. Calli. *The Ambassador*: D. Zani. *Nightingale, Cuckoo, Good Fairies, The Roses, Torches, Spiders, Dignitaries and Ladies of the Court*.

Act 1: Nocturne; Invitation to the Fairies; Baptism of the Princess; Vengeance of the Green Fairy; The Blessing of the Stars. 1620.

Act 2: The Old Spinner; The Enchantment. 1640.

Act 3: Three hundred years afterward.

ACT 3

Chinese Ladder Act

Miss Legnetti, songs

Three Thieves in a Cage

The Learned Donkey

Concert Party

1932.31 SHUFFLE ALONG OF 1933

A Musical Comedy in Two Acts, 8 Scenes[22]. Book by Flournoy E. Miller. Music by Eubie Blake. Lyrics by Noble Sissle. Staged by Walter Brooks. Dances directed by (Charlie) Davis and (Addison) Carey. Settings designed by Karl O. Amend. Costumes designed by Robert Stevenson. Music director, Eubie Blake. Choral arrangements and orchestrations by Will Vodery. Noble Sissle's Park Central Hotel Orchestra under the direction of Eubie Blake. Produced by Mawin Productions Inc. (George E. Wintz, Mansfield Theatre). Opened 26 December 1932 at the Mansfield Theatre and closed 7 January 1933 after 17 performances.

CAST (in order of appearance): *Edith Wilkes*: LAVAIDA CARTER. *Taxi Ben*: Marshall Rodgers. *Mrs. Jones*: EDITH WILSON. *Caesar Jones*: MANTAN MORELAND. *A Customer*: Louise Williams. *Jim Williams*: George Jones, Jr. *Sylvia Williams*: Fay Conty. *Tom Sharp*: NOBLE SISSLE. *Steve Jenkins*: FLOURNOY MILLER. *Dave Coffey*: GEORGE McCLENNON. *Harry Walton*: Clarence Robinson. *Alice Walker*: VIVIAN BABER. *Sam*: Howard Hill. *Farmer Taps*: TAPS MILLER. *Sheriff*: Joe Willis. *Summons Server*: James Arnold. *Stenographer*: Catherine

[22]Previous editions of SHUFFLE ALONG were presented on Broadway in 1921 and 1930

Brooks. *Office Boy*: Herman Reed. *Telephone Girl*: Ida Brown. *Shipping Clerk*: Romaine Johns. *Waiter*: Adolph Henderson. *At the Piano*: EUBIE BLAKE. *Lodge Members, Civil War Veterans, Factory Men, Cooks, Waiters, Farmers, etc.*

Singing Ensemble: Louise Williams, Ida Brown, Catherine Brooks, Aurora Edwards, Annis Davis, Roy Holland, Adolph Henderson, Douglass Felix, Rudolph Scott, Herman Reed, Bernie Brown, Larry Seymour, Joe Willis, Romaine Johns, James Arnold, Tony Gaytzera, James Anderson, David Collins. *Dancing Girls*: Julia Moses, Roberta Lowery, Dorothy Williams, Eloise Thompson, Grayce Browne, Carolyn Rich, Claudette Heyward, Nannine Joyce, Thelma Salmons, Iris Parker, Peggy Wharton, Mildred Roberts, Virginia Brannum, Lyle Smith, Edna Mae Holly. *Dancing Boys*: Willie Avant, Roy Carter, Arthur Daily, Taps Miller, Bill Bailey, Derby Wilson, Henry Williams. *Dance Specialty*: Four Flash Devils.

Act 1, Scene 1: City Square, Jimtown, Mississippi. *Scene 2*: The Jones Cabin. *Scene 3*: U-Eat-Em Molasses Factory.

Act 2, Scene 1: City Square, Jimtown, Mississippi. Six weeks later. *Scene 2*: A Sugar Cane Field. *Scene 3*: Office of U-Eat-Em Molasses Factory. *Scene 4*: Ben's Taxi Stand. *Scene 5*: Roof of U-Eat-Em Molasses Factory.

ACT 1

Scene 1

"Labor Day Parade"
Ensemble

"Sing and Dance Your Troubles Away"
L. Carter, Ensemble

"Chickens Come Home to Roost"
G. Jones, Jr., L. Carter, F. Conty

"Bandana Ways"
E. Wilson, Four Flash Devils, T. Miller, P. Wharton, Ensemble

"Breakin' 'Em In"
T. Miller, D. Wilson, B. Bailey

"In the Land of Sunny Sunflowers"
C. Robinson, F. Canty, Ensemble

Scene 2

"Sugar Babe"
N. Sissle, L. Carter, V. Baber

Scene 3

"Joshua Fit de Battle"
E. Wilson, Male Ensemble

Dance Specialty
R. Carter, A. Daily

"Sore Foot Blues"
G. McClennon

"Glory"
N. Sissle, Company

ACT 2

Scene 1

"Saturday Afternoon"
Store Clerks, Ensemble

"Here 'Tis"
L. Carter, M. Mooreland, N. Joyce, J. Willis, Ensemble, A. Davis, L. Williams

Scene 2

"Falling in Love"
F. Canty, C. Robinson

Scene 3

"Dusting Around"
G. McClennon

Scene 4

"If It's Any News to You"
E. Wilson, M. Mooreland

Scene 5

Reminiscing
N. Sissle, E. Blake

"Harlem Moon"
L. Carter

"You Got to Have Koo Wah"
N. Sissle

Finale
Entire Company

1933.01

PARDON MY ENGLISH

A Musical Comedy in Two Acts, 10 Scenes. Book by Herbert Fields. Music by George Gershwin. Lyrics by Ira Gershwin. Book directed by Jack McGowan. Production staged by Vinton Freedley. Musical numbers staged by Georgie Hale. Settings by John Wenger. Costumes by Robert Ten Eyck Stevenson. Music director, Earl Busby. Orchestrations by (Robert) Russell Bennett, William Daly, Adolph Deutsch. Produced by Alex A. Aarons and Vinton Freedley. Opened 20 January 1933 at the Majestic Theatre and closed 25 February 1933 after 43 performances.

CAST (in order of appearance): *Mr. Preston*: Tony Blair. *Mrs. Preston*: Eleanor Shaler. *Robin*: Jack Davis. *College Student*: Robert Spencer. *Another College Student*: William Lilling. *Schultz*: CLIFF HALL[23]. *Girl*: Betty Hamilton. *Johnny Stewart*: CARL RANDALL. *Gerry Martin*: BARBARA NEWBERRY. *McCarthy*: HARRY T. SHANNON. *Gita*: LYDA ROBERTI. *Michael Bramleigh*: GEORGE GIVOT. *Commissioner Bauer*: JACK PEARL. *Dr. Richard Carter*: GERALD OLIVER SMITH. *Ilse Bauer*: JOSEPHINE HUSTON. *Magda*: Ruth Urban. *Anna*: Wilma Roeloff. *Inn-Keeper*: George Shields. *Karl*: John Cortez. *Heinrich*: Jack Carver.

Ladies of the Ensemble: Gene Brady, Lauretta Bruns, Maxine Darrell, Eva Farrell, Dorothea Frank, Betty Hamilton, Virginia Howard, Peggy Bancroft, Meredith Howard, Marion Harcke, Irene Kelly, Ruth Marshal, Marion Nevins, Elsie Neal, Jacqueline Paige, Clare Carter, Edith Nelson, Helen Hannan, Gloria Pierre, Myrtle Patterson, Wilma Roeloff, Cynthia Thompson, Meta Korbett, Irene Kimmel, Rosil Benda, Marion Newberry, Billie Seward, Marie Clyde, Mildred Fenton, Barbara Smith. *Gentlemen of the Ensemble*: Harry Griffin, Tom Lannon, Jack Barrett, Albert Amato, Eddie Ryan, Raymond Hitchcock, Kenneth Rogers, Eugene Ashley, Kal Hansen, Jimmy Thompson, Joe Kaye, Beau Tilden, Gordon Cross, Thomas Burke, Efin Vitis, Don Cortez, Vance Elliott, Harold Sternberg, Norman Curtis, William Lilling, Irving Green, John Perkins. *Schuhpladlers*: Joe Gerhei, Hans Kiendl, Mack Gassl, Alex Atzenbeck, Joe Wagner, Max Seidl.

Act 1, Scene 1: A Beer Garden in Dresden. *Scene 2*: A Street. *Scene 3*: Living-Room in the Home of Commissioner Bauer. *Scene 4*: The Police Station. *Scene 5*: Garden of Bauer's Home.

Act 2, Scene 1: An Inn at Schandau. *Scene 2*: Front of Bauer's House. *Scene 3*: The American Bar. *Scene 4*: The Den. *Scene 5*: Garden of Bauer's Home.

ACT 1

"In Three Quarter Time"
  J. Cortez, R. Urban, Ensemble
"The Lorelei"
  C. Randall, B. Newberry, Ensemble
"Pardon My English"
  L. Roberti, G. Givot
"Dancing in the Streets"
  Ensemble
"So What?"
  J. Pearl, J. Huston, Ensemble
"Isn't It a Pity?"
  G. Givot, J. Huston
"My Cousin in Milwaukee"
  L. Roberti, Ensemble
"Hail the Happy Couple"
  C. Randall, B, Newberry, Ensemble
"The Dresden Northwest Mounted"
  J. Pearl, Ensemble
"Luckiest Man in the World"
  G. Givot, Ensemble
"What Sort of Wedding Is This?" (Finale Act 1)
  J. Pearl, R. Urban, Ensemble

ACT 2

"Tonight"
  G. Givot, J. Huston
"Where You Go, I Go"
  L. Roberti, J. Pearl
"I've Got To Be There"
  C. Randall, B. Newberry, Girls
Finaletto
  Principals, Ensemble
"The Dresden Northwest Mounted" (reprise)
  J. Pearl, Ensemble

"He's Not Himself" (Finale Act 2)
  Principals, Ensemble

1933.02

FACE THE MUSIC

A Return Engagement of the Musical Comedy Revue in Two Acts, 20 Scenes[24]. Book by Moss Hart. Music and lyrics by Irving Berlin. Staged by Hassard Short. Book directed by George S. Kaufman. Dances by Albertina Rasch. Settings by Albert R. Johnson. Costumes by Kiviette, Weld. Music director, Emil Newman. Orchestrations by (Robert) Russell Bennett, Frank Tours, Maurice DePackh. Produced by Producing Associates, Inc. by arrangement with Sam H. Harris. Opened 31 January 1933 at the 44th Street Theatre and closed 25 February 1933 after 31 performances.

CAST (in order of appearance): *Hal Reisman*: ROBERT EMMETT KEANE. *Kit Baker*: NANCY MCCORD. *Pat Mason, Jr.*: JOHN BARKER. *Mrs. Meshbesher*: MARY BOLAND. *Her Footman*: Peter Sargent. *Miss Eisenheimer*: Margot Adams. *Martin Van Buren Meshbesher*: CHARLES LAWRENCE. *Mr. O'Rourke*: GEORGE ANDERSON. *A Sister Team*: Inez Goetz, Colleen Ward. *Pickles*: MARGARET LEE. *Joe*: JACK GOOD. *Louis*: DON COSTELLO. *Mme. Elise*: Dorothy Drum. *Her Assistant*: Martha Tibbetts. *Postman*: Daniel Sullivan. *May*: Pat O'Keefe. *Rodney St. Clair*: JOHN EHRLE. *Rivington*: OSCAR POLK. *Sheriff*: Frank Dobson. *Mr. O'Ryan*: Don Costello. *Stage Doorman*: George Marshall. *Detective*: Thomas Arace. *Bartender*: Bob Baldwin. *Prosecuting Attorney*: JOHN EARLE. *Judge Furioso*: Thomas Reynolds.

Albertina Rasch Dancers: Betty Eisner (leading dancer), Vera Fredericks (captain), Janet Carver, Peggy Dell, Martha Merrill. *Girls*: Pat O'Keefe, Dolly Widell, Alice Brent, Martha Tibbetts, Marie Gale, Margot Adams, Virginia Mandracia, Vivian Roscoe, Louise Taylor, Inez Goetz, Colleen Ward, Kay Apgar, Margaret Fitzpatrick, Carol Clyde, Janet Biesantz, Joan Abbey. *Boys*: Bob Long, Howard Morgan, Fred Nay, Guy Daly, Martrin Dennis, Bert Doughty, Jack Wolfe, Ed. Crosswell, Ray Santos, James Babbitt, Bob Grey, Frank Conway, Ed. Murray, Jack Richards, Marty Rhiele, E. D. Howell.

1933.03

MELODY

A Musical Romance in Two Acts, 13 Scenes. Book by Edward Childs Carpenter. Lyrics by Irving Caesar. Music by Sigmund Romberg. Directed by George White. Musical numbers staged by Bobby Connolly. Settings by Joseph Urban. Costumes by Charles LeMaire. Music director, Al Goodman. Produced by George White. Opened 14 February 1933 at the Casino Theatre and closed 22 April 1933 after 79 performances.

CAST (in order of appearance): *Act 1: Jean Blanchon*, a concierge: Harrison Brockbank. *Mariette*, his wife: MILDRED PARISETTE. *Leon Tabar*, a law student: MILTON DOUGLAS. *Henri Fanchery*, a medical student: Carl Rose. *Lizette*: Marjorie Dille. *Tristan Robillard*, a composer: EVERETT MARSHALL. *François Trapadoux*: HAL SKELLY. *Jacqueline Grimaud*, first secretary: VIVIAN FAY. *Sergeant Perecin*: Neil Moore. *Andree de Nemours*: EVELYN HERBERT. *Lise*, nurse to Andree: Valerie Bergere. *Compte Gustave de Nemours*, Andree's father: VICTOR MORLEY. *Pierre, Vicomte de Laurier*: GEORGE HOUSTON. *Antoine*, Major-domo to Compte Gustave: Jerome Daley. *Camille*, François' second secretary: Peggy Moseley. *Claire Lolive*, Pierre's mistress: ROSE LOUISE[Gypsy Rose Lee]. *Bridesmaids*: Hope Dare, Alma Saunders, Georgia Ellis, Lois Eckhart, Hazel Boffinger, Hilda Knight, Peggy Moseley, Johanna Allen, Toni Chase. *Lazare*, Sergeant-at-Arms: Frederick B. Manatt.

Act 2: Max de Laurier, Andree's son: Milton LeRoy. *Designer*: David Morton. *Dress Models*: Hazel Boffinger (No. 1—Pour Le Sport), Georgia Ellis (No. 2—Pour Le Voyage), Lois Eckhart (No. 3—Pour Le Matin), Hilda Knight (No. 4—Pour Midi), Hope Dare (No. 5—Pour Déjeuner), Peggy Moseley (No. 6—Pour L'Après Midi), Joanna Allen (No. 7—Pour Diner), Toni Chase (No. 8—Pour L'Opéra). *Butler*: Glenn Graham. *Angelique Normand*, François' secretary: Venita Varden. *Eugénie Revelle*: JEANNE AUBERT. *Ninon Revelle*, her stepdaughter: LOUISE KIRTLAND.

Act 3: A Clerk: Neil Moore. *Phoebe Jones*: INA RAY (HUTTON). *Anstruther*, butler to Trapadoux: Harrison Brockbank. *George Richards*, Francois' grand-nephew: WALTER WOOLF. *Sabine Pataille*, a working girl: MILDRED PARISETTE. *Vivienne Grandet*, another working girl: Marjorie Dille. *Paula de Laurier*, Andree's grand-daughter, known as Mlle. DeChatelain: EVELYN HERBERT. *Toby*, a friend of George's: MILTON DOUGLAS. *Bob*, another friend of George's: CHARLES FOWLER. *Marie*: Consuelo Flowerton. *Boris*, proprietor of Café de la Cote d'Or: Michael Dalmatoff. *Waiter*: Jack Saltzman. *Shabby Man*: Lyle Evans. *Louis Le Beau*: Carlos Roca.

Ladies of the Ensemble: Toni Chase, Johanna Allen, Peggy Moseley, Hilda Knight, Hazel Boffinger, Lois Eckhart, Georgia Ellis, Alma Saunders, Hope Dare, Ruth Doran, Betty Collette, Drucila Strain, Pam McAvoy, Billy Cortez, Jane Moxon, Paula Sands,

---

[23]Well known comic for 'Vas you dere, Sharlie?', which was a provisional title for the show.

[24]Originally produced in New York 17 February 1932 at the New Amsterdam Theatre for 165 performances. For Synopsis of Scenes and Musical Numbers, see original 1932 production. For this engagement, "Torch Song" was dropped.

Evelyn Neilson, Evelyn March, Winnie Torney, Peggy Ring, Edwinna Steele, Maria Steele, Anne Collins, Gay Delys, Mildred Borst, Evelyn Nichols, Gloria Mossman, May Muth, Jeanne Kriston, Marjorie Dille, Sylvia Roberts, Olga Leigh, Consuelo Flowerton, Madge Symile. *Gentlemen of the Ensemble*: Edward Martin, Barry Hyams, David Leigh, Carroll Godwin, John Fredericks, Walter Taron, Arthur Craig, David Norton, George Collins, Al Bennett, Carl Rose, Carl Weber, Carlos Roca, Ralph Moran, Richard Black, Glenn Graham.

Act 1, Scene 1: The Quarters of the Concierge in the Mansion of Compte Gustave de Nemours, Paris. Six o'clock in the evening. Paris, 1881. *Scene 2*: Compte Gustave's Library. An hour later. *Scene 3*: The Grand Salon in the Mansion of Compte Gustave. 8:15 P.M. *Scene 4*: The Faubourg St. Honoré in front of Compte Gustave's Mansion. A few minutes later. *Scene 5*: The Quarters of the Concierge as before. 8:30 P.M.

Act 2: Terrace of Compte Gustave's Château, Loos, France. 1906.

Act 3, Scene 1: Corridor, Tenth Floor, Universal Radio Building, New York. 1933. *Scene 2*: Penthouse Apartment of François Trapadoux, atop the Universal Radio Building. A few minutes later. *Scene 3*: A Street near the Étoile, Paris. A week later, night. *Scene 4*: L'Auberge du Coq d'Or in the Bois, Paris. The same night. *Scene 5*: Same as Scene 4, three hours later. *Scene 6*: Sidewalk Café, Paris. Afternoon, a few days later. *Scene 7*: L'Auberge du Coq d'Or. Night of the same day.

ACT 1

Scene 1

Opening
M. Douglas, M. Parisette, Ensemble

"Our Little Lady Upstairs"
E. Marshall, Ensemble

"Melody"
E. Herbert

"I'd Write a Song"
E. Marshall

Scene 3

Ballet
V. Fay, Girls

"Good Friends Surround Me"[25]
G. Houston, E. Herbert, Ensemble

Scene 4

"On to Africa"
H. Skelly, F. B. Manatt, Conscripts

Scene 5

Reprise
E. Marshall

"I Am the Singer, You Are the Song"
E. Herbert, E. Marshall

Finale, Act 1
E. Herbert, E. Marshall

ACT 2

Musical Interlude
M. LeRoy, G. Houston, V. Morley

"In My Garden"
E. Herbert

"Rendezvous"
J. Aubert, G. Houston, V. Morley

"Pompadour"
J. Aubert, H. Skelly

Finaletto
L. Kirtland, E. Herbert, M. LeRoy

ACT 3

Scene 1

"Never Had an Education"
I. Ray, Girls

Scene 2

Musical Interlude
W. Woolf, I. Ray, H. Skelly

Scene 3

"The Whole World Loves"
W. Woolf, M. Douglas, C. Fowler, M. Parisette, Ensemble

Scene 4

"Give Me a Roll on a Drum"
E. Herbert

"Tonight May Never Come Again"
E. Herbert, W. Woolf

Scene 7

Finale Ultimo
E. Herbert, W. Woolf, H. Skelly, Entire Ensemble

1933.04   RUN, LITTLE CHILLUN!

A Negro Folk Drama with Music in Two Acts, 4 Scenes. Play by Hall Johnson. Incidental music composed and arranged by the author. Choral direction by Hall Johnson. Settings designed by Cleon Throckmorton. Costumes designed by Helene Pons. Dances arranged by Doris Humphrey. Directed by Frank Merlin. Produced by Robert Rockmore. Opened 1 March 1933 at the Lyric Theatre and closed 17 June 1933 after 126 performances[26].

CAST (in order of appearance): *Ella*: Edna Thomas. *Children (7)*: *Organist*: Esther Hall. *Bessiola Hicks*: Marietta Canty. *Jeems Jackson*: Jimmie Waters. *Other Children*: Henri Wood, Bennie Tattnall, Nell Taylor, Edna Commodore. *The Rev. Sister Luella Strong*: Olive Ball. *Sister Mattie Fullilove*: Mattie Shaw. *Sister Flossie Lou Little*: BERTHA POWELL. *Brother Bartholomew Little*: Ray Yeates. *Brother Esau Redd*, Chairman of Deacon Board of Hope, Baptist Church: Walter Price. *Sister Mahalie Ockletree*: Rosalie King. *Sister Judy Ann Hicks*: Pauline Rivers. *Sister Lulu Jane Hunt*: Lulu Hunt. *Sister Susie May Hunt*: Carolyn Hughes. *Brother George W. Jenkins*: Edward Broadnax. *Brother Jeremiah Johnson*: Milton Lacey. *Brother Goliath Simpson*: Gus Simons. *Rev. Jones*, Pastor of the Hope Baptist Church: Harry Bolden. *Jim*, Rev. Jones' Son: Alston Burleigh. *Sulumai*: FREDI WASHINGTON. *Brother Lu-Te*, Chief Singer of the New Day Pilgrims: JAMES BOXWILL. *Brother Jo-Ba*, Herald of Joy: Milton Martin. *Sister Mata*, Priestess: Ethel Purnello. *Reba*, Daughter of Kanda: Waldine Williams. *Mother Kanda*, Daughter of Tongola: Olga Burgoyne. *Brother Moses*, Young Priest: Jack Carr. *Elder Tongola*, Prophet of the New Day Pilgrims: Harold Sneed. *Belle* of Toomer's Bottom: Bessie Guy. *Mame* of Toomer's Bottom: Mabel Diggs. *Mag*, Sulamai's Mother: Cecil Scott. *Sue Scott* of Toomer's Bottom: Lulu King. *The Rev. Ebeneezer Allen*, Local Preacher: ANDREW TAYLOR. *Townspeople, Members of Hope Baptist Church, etc.*

Pilgrim Choir: Sopranos: Jean Cutler, Effie McDowell, Bessie Guy, Irma Allen, Katherine Ahnor, Lucille Dickson, Blanche Eckles. Altos: Lavetta Albright, Marietta Canty, Amy Goodwin, Dorothy Perry, Rosalie King. Tenors: Arthur Walker, George White, Carrington Lewis, Jimmie Waters, Charlie Frye, Milton Martin, Perrin Knight. Baritones: Service Bell, George Clark, Ernest Shaw, Milton Lacey. Bases: Ernest Baskett, Oliver Hartwell, Edward Broadnax, Ernest Brown. *Pilgrims*: Eneida Hamlett, Ray Polite, Alma Reynolds, Rosina Weston, Paul Smellie, Assotta Marshall. *Pilgrim Orchestra*: C. Harris, L. DePaure, A. Izanaga, G. Allen, R. Brown, T. Moody, A. Stokes, C. Lewis. *Novitiates*: E. Davis, Alice Grant, Eva Evelyn, Jack Meredith, Emma Sealy, Annie Jennings, H. J. Williams, Mayme Davis. *Tansadi Tongole* (Tongola's Dancers): Esther Hall, Irene Ellington, Nell Taylor, Alice Magee, Dorothy Boxwill, Maggie Carter, Odelle Ricks, Larri Laurier, Clarence Yates, Bruce Nugent, O. Portier, E. Wilson, R. Alday, E. Adderly, I. Baker, A. Ferguson, A. Adderly, L. Stirrup, J. Nealy, W. Polhamus, O. Gordon, A. McCullough, R. Branch, J. Gordon, M. Sands, E. Caesar, C. Gibson, R. Brathwaite.

Act 1, Scene 1: The Parsonage in a small Southern town. An August Evening. *Scene 2*: The Meeting Place of the New Day Pilgrims. Later the same night.

Act 2, Scene 1: Toomer's Bottom. Three days later. *Scene 2*: Hope Baptist Church. The same night.

1933.05   STRIKE ME PINK

A Musical Revue in Two Acts, 29 Scenes. Sketches by Lew Brown, Ray Henderson; Additional dialogue by Mack Gordon, (Jack McGowan). Lyrics by Lew Brown. Music by Ray Henderson. Entire production supervised by Ray Henderson and Lew Brown. Sketches directed by Jack McGowan. Dances and ensembles staged by Seymour Felix. Settings by Henry Dreyfuss. Costumes by Kiviette, Charles LeMaire. Music director, Al Goodman. Orchestrations by Edward Powell. Produced by Lew Brown, Ray Henderson, (Waxey Gordon). Opened 4 March 1933 at the Majestic Theatre and closed 10 June 1933 after 122 performances.

CAST: LUPE VELEZ, JIMMY (Schnozzle) DURANTE, HOPE WILLIAMS, HAL LEROY, ROY ATWELL, EDDIE GARR, GEORGE DEWEY WASHINGTON, RUTH HARRISON, ALEX FISHER, JOHNNY DOWNS, GRACIE BARRIE, ABER

---

[25]Musical paraphrase of well-known continental drinking song of the period.

[26]Musical Numbers not listed in program. For detail of song list, see 1943 revival.

TWINS, MILTON WATSON, DOROTHY DARE, CAROLYN NOLTE, WILMA COX, BARBARA MacDONALD, FRANK CONLAN, M. VODNOY.

Show Girls: Claiborne Arms, Marguerite DeCoursey, Ruth Dod, Dorothy Dodge, Geraldine Dvorak, Mabel Ellis, Peggy Fish, Ricky Newell, Leonore Pettit, Louise Sheldon. *Dancers*: Mary Ann, Vicky Belling, Emmy Bock, Helane Brown, Norma Butler, Barbara Caswell, Elsie Duffy, Louise Estes, Peggy Gallimore, Eleanor Garden, Ruth Grady, Lula Gray, Pearl Harris, Diana Lynn, Charlotte Joslin, Leoda Knapp, Betty Lee, Mary Joan Martin, Leslie Laurence, Jewel Morse, Rosalie McCallion, June McNulty, Lillian Pertka, Jean Ryan, Phyllis Lynd, Jackie Sherman, Davenie Watson, Marguerite Wiley. *Boys*: Hal Clyne, Bill Douglas, Clark Leston, Jack Moore, George Murray, Jack Ross, Jimmy Ryan, Ted Schultz, George Weeden, Gil White. *WILL VODERY SINGERS*: James Brown, George Duke, Daniel Johnson, Charles Lawrence. *Concert Singers*: Mary Chappelle, Mary Moore, Madeline Southworth, Roberta West, David Johns, Jack Harcourt, Earl Mason, Olaf Olson.

ACT 1

Scene 1

"An Old Hollywood Custom"
L. Velez, J. Durante, H. Williams, R. Atwell, E. Garr, Entire Company

Scene 2

Our Dancers

Scene 3

Speed—Roy Atwell Explains
Mr. Duncan: J. Durante. *Mrs. Duncan*: C. Nolte. *Their Son*: J. Downs. *His Wife*: D. Dare. *A Friend*: M. Watson. *Nurse*: W. Cox. *Butler*: F. Conlan.

Scene 4

"It's Great To Be Alive"
G. Barrie, Ensemble

Scene 5

Ultra Modern (*by* Richard Jerome)
Husband: R. Atwell. *Wife*: H. Williams. *Pat*: J. Downs. *Bobby*: H. LeRoy. *Jerry*: L. Velez.

Scene 6

"Strike Me Pink"
J. Downs, D. Dare, N. Butler, M. J. Martin, P. Gallimore, J. Morse, Entire Company
Dance by H. LeRoy, B. MacDonald.

Scene 7

A Bit of Temperament
L. Velez, J. Durante

Scene 8

"Home to Harlem"
G. D. Washington, Singing Ensemble

Scene 9

Dinner at Ten
L. Velez, J. Durante, H. Williams

Scene 10

Techno-Crazy
Professor: J. Durante. *His Secretary*: W. Cox. *Board of Directors and Their Secretaries*: (Ensemble.)

Scene 11

Eddie Garr

Scene 12

Design For Loving[27] (*by* John McGowan)
Butler: J. Brown. *Ernest*: R. Atwell. *Gilda*: H. Williams. *Leo*: E. Garr. *Otto*: J. Durante. *Baldo*: F. Conlan.

Scene 13

"Love and Rhythm"
L. Velez, Ensemble

Scene 14

Buy American!
Orator: F. Conlan. *Hawker*: E. Garr.

Scene 15

"Let's Call It a Day"
C. Nolte, M. Watson

Scene 16

Jimmy Durante and Hope Williams

Scene 17

Hal LeRoy

Scene 18

A Smoking Car
Man: E. Garr. *Woman*: L. Velez. *Conductor*: M. Watson.

Scene 19

Jimmy (Schnozzle) Durante

Scene 20

"Restless"
C. Nolte, Ensemble

ACT 2

Scene 1

Memories
Entire Company

Scene 2

"Ooh, I'm Thinking"
L. Velez, J. Durante

Scene 3

The Trip (*by* John McGowan)
Mrs. Laura Thomas: H. Williams. *Butler*: R. Atwell. *Maid*: W. Cox. *Mrs. Thomas*: M. Watson.

Scene 4

A Modernistic Interpretation of "Restless" (dance)
R. Harrison, A. Fisher

Scene 5

External Triangle
Wife: L. Velez. *Lover*: M. Watson. *Husband*: J. Durante. *Pest*: F. Conlan.

Scene 6

"I Hate To Think That You'll Grow Old, Baby"
D. Dare, J. Downs
Dance by H. LeRoy, Aber Twins, Ensemble.

Scene 7

"Hollywood, Park Avenue and Broadway"
L. Velez, J. Durante, H. Williams

Scene 8

"On Any Street"
J. Durante

Scene 9

Finale
Entire Company

HUMMIN' SAM

1933.06

A Sepia Musical Comedy in Two Gallops, 4 Scenes. Story (book) by Eileen Nutter. Based on the play "In Old Kentucky" by Charles T. Dazey. Music and lyrics by Alexander Hill. Dances and ensembles staged by Carey and Davis. Costumes by Brooks. Music director, Jimmie Davis. Orchestrations by Arthur Knowlton. Produced by Allan K. Foster. Opened and closed 8 April 1933 at the New Yorker Theatre after 1 performance[28].

CAST {in order of appearance}: *Hummin' Sam*: GERTRUDE "BABY" COX. *Uncle Ned*: SPEEDY SMITH. *Totem*: Alonzo Bozan. *Hot Cakes*: Bunny Allen. *First Jockey, Second Jockey*: The Two Chesterfields. *Harlem Dan*: ROBERT UNDERWOOD. *Louise Lovelle*: LOUISE LOVELLE. *Three Sepia Songbirds*: *Esmaraldae*: Dorothy Embry. *Emmaraldae*: Catherine Brooks. *Mamaraldae*: Mary Mason. *Yellow George*: Lionel Monogas. *Edward Holton*: Lorenzo Tucker. *Mr. Conners*: John Lee. *Mike*: Sandy. *Madge Carter*: MADELINE BELT. *Caesar, Cicero*: JONES & ALLAN. *Mr. Carter*: Al Watts. *Mae Carter*: FLO BROWN. *Freddie Marlowe*: CECIL RIVERS. *Nina May*: EDITH WILSON. *Clara*: Hannah Sylvester. *Drum Major*: J. Mardo Brown. *Miss Jitters*: Louise Cook. *Specialty*: THREE MILLER BROTHERS. *Trainers, Jockeys, Exercise Boys, Waiters and Patrons of 'Boogoo Inn'*.

Ladies of the Ensemble: Georgie Greene, Lola Montenegro, Connie Thompson,. Mae Brennan, Charlotte Cheek, Laurabelle Jones, Juanita Cole, Baby Fischer, Lolita Hall, Goldie Cisco, Doris Scott, Madeline Odlum, Elizabeth Brown, Marion Akins, Frankie Scott, Dorothy Moppins, Alberta Martrin, Jean Martin, Catherine Upshaw. *Showgirls*: Aurora Edwards, Doris Francis, Ethel Boyd, Elizabeth Simon.

Act 1, Scene 1: The stables at a well-known race track in Kentucky. *Scene 2*: The exterior of the race track. *Scene 3*: The home stretch.

---

[27]Burlesque of the play DESIGN FOR LIVING by Noël Coward.

[28]Director uncredited, Allan K. Foster (producer) supervised the staging.

Act 2: The Bogoo Inn, Kentucky. The evening after the race.

ACT 1

Scene 1

"Steppin' Along"
  H. Sylvester, Girls, Boys, Ensemble

"Harlem Dan"
  R. Underwood, Girls, Ensemble

"How the First Song Was Born"
  L. Lovelle

"They're Off"
  G. Cox, Girls

"Pinching Myself"
  G. Cox, M. Belt

"Change Your Mind About Me"
  F. Brown, C. Rivers, Two Chesterfields, Ensemble

Scene 2

"If I Didn't Have You"
  D. Embry, C. Brooks, M. Mason

Dancing Specialty
  Three Brown Buddies

Scene 3

"In the Stretch" (Finale)

ACT 2

"Jubilee"
  Girl Ensemble

"A Little Bit of Quicksilver"
  Daly & Carter

"Answer My Heart"
  L. Lovelle

"Stompin Em Down"
  H. Sylvester, J. Mardo Brown, Two Chesterfields, Girls

"I'll Be True—But I'll Be Blue"
  D. Embry, C. Brooks, M. Mason

"Jitters"
  L. Cook, Girls

"Fifteen Minutes a Day"
  E. Wilson

"Aintcha Glad You Got Music"
  G. Cox

"Dancing, and I Mean Dancing"
  Three Miller Brothers

Finale—"Aintcha Glad You Got Music"

1933.07 THE THREE-PENNY OPERA

An Operetta (The Threepenny Opera) in Three Acts, Prologue and 7 Scenes. (Original German libretto by Bertolt Brecht.) Adapted into English by Gifford Cochran and Jerrold Krimsky from the German "Die Dreigroschenoper" by (Elisabeth Hauptmann), Bertolt Brecht, based on "The Beggar's Opera" by John Gay. Music by Kurt Weill. Staged by Francesco von Mendelssohn. Settings by Cleon Throckmorton, after designs by Caspar Neher. Music director, Macklin Marrow. Orchestrations by Kurt Weill. Produced by Gifford Cochran and Jerrold Krimsky. Opened 13 April 1933 at the Empire Theatre and closed 22 April 1933 after 12 performances.

CAST{in order of appearance}: *Legend Singer*: GEORGE HELLER. *Jonathan Peachum*: REX WEBER. *Mrs. Peachum*: EVELYN BERESFORD. *Polly Peachum*: STEFFI DUNA. *Captain Macheath*, alias Mackie Messer: ROBERT CHISHOLM. *Jenny Diver*: MARJORIE DILLE. *Filch*: HERBERT RUDLEY. *Matthew*: Anthony Blair. *Crooked Finger Jack*: BURGESS MEREDITH. *Walter*: HARRY BELLAVER. *Robert*: GEORGE HELLER. *Jimmy*: Francis Kennelly. *Wing*: H. L. Donsu. *Reverend Campbell*: John Connolly. *Sheriff Brown*: REX EVANS. *Beggar*: Harry Hornick. *Vixen*: Mary Heberden. *Trull*: Eugenie Reed. *Madame*: Lotta Burnell. *Tawd*: Hilda Kosta. *Dolly*: Ruth Thomas. *Betty*: Lilian Okun. *Molly Brazen*: Jean De Koven. *Smith*: Gerald Hamer. *Constable*: Arthur Brady. *Lucy Brown*: JOSEPHINE HUSTON.

Constables: Clyde Turner, Larry Larkin, James Harvey. *Beggars*: Tom Morgan, Harold Imber, Gus Alexander, Thomas Murphy, Richard Bengali, Morton Ulman, Louis Halperin, Jack Carstairs, Geraldine Lunby, Lillian Ardell, Barbara Winchester, Ellen Love, Corine Anderson.

Prologue: Fair in Soho.

Act 1, Scene 1: A Stable in Soho. *Scene 2*: Mr. Peachum's Beggars' Establishment.

Act 2, Scene 1: A Stable in Soho. *Scene 2*: In Turnbridge Alley. Thursday evening. *Scene 3*: The Old Bailey Gaol.

Act 3, Scene 1: Mr. Peachum's Beggars' Establishment. Three o'clock Friday morning. *Scene 2*: The Old Bailey Gaol. Friday morning.

PROLOGUE

"The Legend of Mackie Messer"
  G. Heller

ACT 1

Scene 1

"Wedding Song"
  The Gang

"The Pirate Jenny"
  S. Duna

"The Soldiers' Song"
  R. Chisholm, R. Evans

"Love Duet"
  S. Duna, R. Chisholm

Scene 2

First Finale
  R. Weber, E. Beresford, S. Duna

ACT 2

Scene 1

"Farewell Song"
  S. Duna, R. Chisholm

Scene 2

"Tango Ballad"
  M. Dille, R. Chisholm

Scene 3

"Lucy Song"
  J. Huston

"Ballad of the Easy Life"
  R. Chisholm

"Jealousy Duet"
  J. Huston, S. Duna

Second Finale
  M. Dille, R. Chisholm, Chorus

ACT 3

Scene 1

"Song of the Aimlessness of Life"
  R. Weber

Scene 2

"Cry from the Dungeon"
  R. Chisholm

"Testament"
  R. Chisholm

Third Finale
  R. Evans, R. Chisholm, S. Duna, M. Dille, J. Huston, E. Beresford, R. Weber, Chorus

THE MIKADO,
1933.08   or The Town of Titipu

A Revival of the Comic Opera in Two Acts[29]. Libretto by William S. Gilbert. Music by Arthur Sullivan. Staged by Milton Aborn. Produced by the Civic Light Opera Company. Opened 17 April 1933 at the St. James Theatre and closed 29 April 1933 after 16 performances.[30]

CAST: *The Mikado of Japan*: WILLIAM DANFORTH. *Nanki-Poo*: ROY CROPPER. *Ko-Ko*: FRANK MOULAN. *Pooh Bah*: HERBERT L. WATEROUS. *Pish Tush*:

---

[29]First presented in New York 20 July, 10-29 August 1885 at the Union Square and People's Theatres for 22 performances. First authorized production presented 19 August 1885 at the Fifth Avenue Theatre by Richard D'Oyly Carte for 250 performances. For Synopsis of Scenes and Musical Numbers, see 19 August 1885 D'Oyly Carte production.
[30]Settings, costumes, musical director uncredited.

ALLEN WATEROUS *Three Sisters, Wards of Ko-Ko: Yum-Yum*: HIZI KOYKE. *Pitti-Sing*: ETHEL CLARKE. *Peep-Bo*: MABEL THOMPSON. *Katisha*: VERA ROSS.

Ladies of the Mikado's Suite: Martha Wallace, Leone Krauss, Frances Sinclair, Mildred Cory, Helen Ryan, Ruth Dawson, Mildred Guthins, Pearle Wible. *The Mikado's Bodyguard*: Thomas Green, Donald Smith, Frederick Grieve, John Willard. *Ensemble of School Girls, Nobles, Guards and Coolies*: Frances Baviello, Frances Moore, Gertrude Waldon, Paula Rodes, Victoria Menou, Mary Hennessey, Olga Schumacher, Adele Story, Patty Gray, Pearl Olmstead, Vera Muller, Catherine Cale, Marjorie DeVoe, Geraldine Olive, Rebecca Wilkison, Adel De Syova, Harrison Fuller, Frank Clarke, Gus Loring, Thomas Green, Donald Smith, Frederick Grieve, Bert Melrose, Basil Prock, Hobson Young, John Willard, John Cardini, Norman Van Emburgh, Rudolph Glaisek, Leo Nash. *Kiddies*: Donna Leon Ard, Iris Posner.

THE YEOMEN OF THE GUARD,
1933.09   or The Merryman and His Maid

A Revival of the Comic Opera in Two Acts[31]. Libretto by William S. Gilbert. Music by Arthur Sullivan. Staged by Milton Aborn. Produced by the Civic Light Opera Company. Opened 1 May 1933 at the St. James Theatre and closed 6 May 1933 after 8 performances.[32]

CAST: *Sir Richard Cholmondeley*: FREDERIC PERSSON. *Colonel Fairfax*: ROY CROPPER. *Sergeant Meryll*: HERBERT L. WATEROUS. *Leonard Meryll*: ALLEN WATEROUS. *Jack Point*: FRANK MOULAN. *Wilfred Shadbolt*: WILLIAM DANFORTH. *Elsie Maynard*: VIVIAN HART. *Phoebe Meryll*: LAURA FERGUSON. *Dame Carruthers*: VERA ROSS. *Kate*: FRANCES MOORE. *First Yeoman*: Hobson Young. *Second Yeoman*: Frederick Grieve. *First Citizen*: Harrison Fuller. *Headsman*: Norman Van Emburgh.

Chorus of Yeomen of the Guard, Gentlemen, Citizens, etc.: Frances Baviello, Frances Moore, Gertrude Waldon, Paula Rodes, Victoria Menou, Mary Hennessey, Olga Schumacher, Adele Story, Patty Gray, Pearl Olmstead, Vera Muller, Catherine Cale, Marjorie DeVoe, Geraldine Olive, Rebecca Wilkison, Adel De Syova, Harrison Fuller, Frank Clarke, Gus Loring, Thomas Green, Donald Smith, Frederick Grieve, Bert Melrose, Basil Prock, Hobson Young, John Willard, John Cardini, Norman Van Emburgh, Rudolph Glaisek, Leo Nash.

TRIAL BY JURY
1933.10

A Revival of the Comic Opera in One Act[33]. Libretto by William S. Gilbert. Music by Arthur Sullivan. Staged by Milton Aborn. Produced by the Civic Light Opera Company. Opened 8 May 1933 at the St. James Theatre and closed 20 May 1933 after 16 performances.[34]

CAST: *The Learned Judge*: FRANK MOULAN. *Foreman of the Jury*: FREDERICK MOULAN. *The Defendant*: ROY CROPPER. *Counsel*: ALLEN WATEROUS. *Usher*: WILLIAM DANFORTH. *Plaintiff*: RUTH ALTMAN.

Jurors: Harrison Fuller, Frank Clarke, Gus Loring, Thomas Green, Donald Smith, Frederick Grieve, Bert Melrose, Basil Prock, Hobson Young, John Willard, John Cardini, Norman Van Emburgh, Rudolph Glaisek, Leo Nash. *Bridesmaids*: Frances Baviello, Frances Moore, Gertrude Waldon, Paula Rodes, Victoria Menou, Mary Hennessey, Olga Schumacher, Adele Story, Pearl Olmstead, Vera Muller, Catherine Cale, Marjorie DeVoe, Geraldine Olive, Rebecca Wilkison, Adel De Syova.
followed by:

H.M.S. PINAFORE,
1933.11   or The Lass That Loved a Sailor

A Revival of the Comic Opera in Two Acts[35]. Libretto by William S. Gilbert. Music by Arthur Sullivan. Staged by Milton Aborn. Produced by the Civic Light Opera Company. Opened 8 May 1933 at the St. James Theatre and closed 20 May 1933 after 16 performances.[36]

CAST: *The Rt. Hon. Sir Joseph Porter, K.C.B., First Lord of the Admiralty*: FRANK MOULAN. *Captain Corcoran, Commander of the H.M.S. Pinafore*: ALLEN WATEROUS. *Ralph Rackstraw, Able Seaman*: ROY CROPPER. *Dick Deadeye, Able Seaman*: WILLAIM DANFORTH. *Bill Bobstay, Boatswain*: Frederick Persson. *Josephine, the Captain's Daughter*: RUTH ALTMAN. *Little Buttercup, Mrs. Cripps, a Portsmouth bum-boat woman*: VERA ROSS. *Hebe, Sir Joseph's First Cousin*: Marjorie Eyre.

First Lord's Sisters, His Cousins, His Aunts: Frances Baviello, Frances Moore, Gertrude Waldon, Paula Rodes, Victoria Menou, Mary Hennessey, Olga Schumacher, Adele Story, Pearl Olmstead, Vera Muller, Catherine Cale, Marjorie DeVoe, Geraldine Olive, Rebecca Wilkison, Adel De Syova. *Sailors*: Harrison Fuller, Frank Clarke, Gus Loring, Thomas Green, Donald Smith, Frederick Grieve, Bert Melrose, Basil Prock, Hobson Young, John Willard, John Cardini, Norman Van Emburgh, Rudolph Glaisek, Leo Nash.

CANDIDE
1933.12

A Dance Drama in Two Acts, 4 Scenes and an Interlude. Arranged and adapted by Charles Weidman from the story of the same name by Voltaire. Music arranged and composed by Genevieve Pitot, John Coleman. Narrative by Ian Wolfe. Costumes by Pauline Lawrence. Music instrumented by Vivian Fine. Mask of Voltaire designed and executed by Anita Weschler. Entire production conceived and directed by Charles Weidman. Produced by Michael Myerberg. Opened 15 May 1933 at the Booth Theatre and closed 20 May 1933 after 8 performances.

CAST (in order of appearance): ACT 1: *Scene 1: Master of Ceremonies*: JOSÉ LIMÓN. *Baron Thunder*: Gene Martel. *Baroness*: Katharine Manning. *Cunegonde*: Eleanor King. *Candide*: CHARLES WEIDMAN. *Dr. Pangloss*: John Glenn. *Paquette*: Cleo Atheneos. *Martin*: William Matons. *Scene 2: Priest*: JOSÉ LIMÓN. *Candide*: CHARLES WEIDMAN. *Pangloss*: John Glenn. *Jew*: William Matons. *Interlude. Dr. Pangloss*: John Glenn. *Materialistic Hag*: Katharine Manning. *Martin*: William Matons. ACT 2: *Scene 1: Cunegonde*: Eleanor King. *Candide*: CHARLES WEIDMAN. *Don Fernando and Judge*: JOSÉ LIMÓN. *Martin*: William Matons. *Scene 2: Candide*: CHARLES WEIDMAN. *Martin*: William Matons. *Fate*: JOSÉ LIMÓN. *Cunegonde*: Eleanor King. *Demi-Mondaine*: Cleo Atheneos.

Voice (of Voltaire): Richard Abbott. *Narrator (Mime)*: JOSÉ LIMÓN.[37]

Members of Doris Humphrey's Concert Group: Cleo Atheneos, Ernestine Henorh, Letitia Ide, Eleanor King, Katherine Manning, Gail Savery, Helen Stromloff. *From Academy of Allied Arts, Members of Charles Weidman's Group*: Marcus Bleckman, Kenneth Bostock, John Glenn, Jack Hazzard, Benny Jacobs, JOSÉ LIMÓN, Irving Lansky, Gene Martel, William Matons, Max Morris, Gabriel Zuckerman.

ACT 1
Scene 1

Vision: Conflict between Pessimism and Optimism
Pantomime: A day's routine in Castle Westphalia
Dance of Pangloss and Paquette
Dance of Candide's awakening
Gambol: Cunegonde and Candide
Pursuit and Candide's banishment
Military Dance of Bulgarian Soldiers, and orgy of plunder and rape
Fugue: D. Pangloss expounds

Scene 2

Vision: (The Church) Praise and Supplication
Dance of Love and Wrath
Frenzy of the Inquisition
Pantomime: Cunegonde, Candide, Inquisitor and Semite
Fugue: Candide has solved a situation

INTERLUDE
ACT 2
Scene 1

Vision : Travel and Promenade
Pantomime : Don Fernando craves new fields to conquer
Dance of Pursuit
Molto Dolce: Utopian Dream
Wrangle: Disintegration
Fugue: Martin expounds

---

[31]First presented in New York 17 October 1888 at the Casino Theatre for 100 performances. For Synopsis of Scenes and Musical Numbers, see original 1888 production.

[32]Settings, costumes, musical director uncredited.

[33]First presented in New York 15 November 1875 at the Eagle Theatre for 8 performances. For Synopsis of Scenes and Musical Numbers, see original 1875 production.

[34]Settings, costumes, musical director uncredited.

[35]Originally presented in New York 15 January 1879 at the Standard Theatre for 175 performances. For Synopsis of Scenes and Musical Numbers, see original 1879 production.

[36]Settings, costumes, musical director uncredited.

[37]Program Note: As in the Oriental theatre, the narrator Mime (Mr. Limón) appears in many characters symbolizing Power and Dominance, in order to unify the action.

Scene 2

> Vision: Fate intervenes
> Pantomime and Dance: Parisian mannerisms
> Soliloquy after Candide's disillusionment
> Fugue: Cunegondes, Martins, Pangloyses, and Paquettes

1933.13

OF THEE I SING

A Return Engagement of the Musical Comedy in Two Acts, 11 Scenes[38]. Book by George S. Kaufman and Morrie Ryskind. Music by George Gershwin. Lyrics by Ira Gershwin. Book staged by George S. Kaufman. Singing and dancing ensembles staged by George Hale. Settings by Jo Mielziner. Costumes by Charles LeMaire. Music director, Eugene Fuerst. Orchestrations, (Robert) Russell Bennett, William Daly. Produced by Sam H. Harris. Opened 15 May 1933 at the Imperial Theatre and closed 10 June 1933 after 32 performances.

CAST {in order of appearance}: *Louis Lippman*: ABE REYNOLDS. *Francis X. Gilhooley*: HAROLD MOFFET. *Maid*: Vivian Barry. *Matthew Arnold Fulton*: DUDLEY CLEMENTS. *Senator Robert E. Lyons*: GEORGE E. MACK. *Senator Carver Jones*: EDWARD H. ROBINS. *Alexander Throttlebottom*: VICTOR MOORE. *John P. Wintergreen*: WILLIAM GAXTON. *Sam Jenkins*: GEORGE MURPHY. *Diana Devereaux*: BETTY ALLEN. *Mary Turner*: HARRIETTE LAKE[Ann Sothern]. *Miss Benson*: JUNE O'DEA. *Vladimir Vidovitch*: Tom Draak. *Yussef Yussevitch*: Sulo Hevonpaa. *The Chief Justice*: RALPH RIGGS. *Nora*: Leslie Bingham. *The French Ambassador*: FLORENZ AMES. *Senate Clerk*: Martin Leroy. *Guide*: Ralph Riggs.

Photographers, Policemen, Supreme Court Justices, Secretaries, Sight-seers, Newspapermen, Senators, Flunkeys, Guests, etc.: Helen Erickson, Olgene Foster, Peggy Greene, Yvonne Gray, Jessica Worth, Barbara Hamilton, Kathleen Ayres, Bobbie Brodsley, Terry Lawlor, Ann Ecklund, Virginia Franck, Lillian Lorray, Martha Maggard, Mary Mascher, Lilyan O'Jela, Baun Sturtz, Peggy Thomas, Patricia Whitney, Irma Philbin, Lillian Burke, Tana Kamp, Florence Fouchia, Alma LeBlanc, Doris May, Nancy Dolan. Robert Burton, Ray Clarke, Gus Cooper, Frank Ericson, Jack Fago, Frank Gagen, Hazzard Newberry, Jack Ray, Bruce Barclay, Tom Curley, Leon Dunar, Michael Forbes, David Lawrence, Richard Neely, John McCahill, John Creighton.

The Dave Allman Band: Dave Allman, Ronald Perry, Walter Hinger, Milton Hollander, Frank Miller, Pete Chance, Jake Vander Meuelen, Sidney Tropp.

PATIENCE,
1933.14
or Bunthorne's Bride

A Revival of the Comic Opera in Two Acts[39]. Libretto by William S. Gilbert. Music by Arthur Sullivan. Staged by Milton Aborn. Produced by the Civic Light Opera Company. Opened 22 May 1933 at the St. James Theatre and closed 27 May 1933 after 8 performances.[40]

CAST: *Colonel Calverley*: WILLIAM DANFORTH. *Major Murgatroyd*: FREDERICK PERSSON. *Lieut. The Duke of Dunstable*: ROY CROPPER. *Reginald Bunthorne*: FRANK MOULAN. *Archibald Grosvenor*: ALLEN WATEROUS. *Mr. Bunthorne's Solicitor*: Bert Melrose. *The Lady Agatha*: DEANE DICKENS. *The Lady Saphir*: Frances Moore. *The Lady Ella*: MARY RODES. *The Lady Jane*: VERA ROSS. *Patience*: VIVIAN HART.

Chorus of Rapturous Maidens and Officers of the Dragoon Guards: Harrison Fuller, Frank Clarke, Gus Loring, Thomas Green, Donald Smith, Frederick Grieve, Bert Melrose, Basil Prock, Hobson Young, John Willard, John Cardini, Norman Van Emburgh, Rudolph Glaisek, Leo Nash. Frances Baviello, Frances Moore, Gertrude Waldon, Paula Rodes, Victoria Menou, Mary Hennessey, Olga Schumacher, Adele Story, Pearl Olmstead, Vera Muller, Catherine Cale, Marjorie DeVoe, Geraldine Olive, Rebecca Wilkison, Adel DeSyova.

---

[38]Originally produced in New York 26 December 1931 at the Music Box Theatre for 441 performances. For Synopsis of Scenes and Musical Numbers, see original 1931 production.

[39]First presented in New York 22 September 1881 at the Standard Theatre for 177 performances. For Synopsis of Scenes and Musical Numbers, see original 1881 production.
[40]Settings, costumes, musical director uncredited.

Willie Howard and Fannie Brice in the ZIEGFELD FOLLIES OF 1934 (Photo: White Studio)
Billy Rose Theatre Collection, New York Public Library for the Performing Arts

1933-1934 SEASON

1933.15 ## TATTLE TALES

A Musical Revue in Two Acts, 29 Scenes. Sketches by Frank Fay and Nick Copeland. (Lyrics by George Waggoner, Leo Robin, Edward Eliscu, William Walsh, Frank Fay, Willard Robison. Music by Edward Ward, Ralph Rainger, Willard Robison, Howard Jackson, Eddie Byrnbriar.) Entire production under the personal supervision of Frank Fay. Musical numbers staged by John Lonergan, Danny Dare, Leroy Prinz. Scenery by Martin. Costumes by Elizabeth Zook. Musical director, Arnold Johnson. Orchestrations by Howard Jackson, Edward Ward. Produced by Frank Fay. Opened 1 June 1933 at the Broadhurst Theatre and closed 24 June 1933 after 28 performances.

CAST: FRANK FAY, BARBARA STANWYCK, NICK COPELAND, WILLIAM HARGRAVE, RAY MAYER, DOROTHY DELL, EDYTH EVANS, DON CUMMING, LILLIAN REYNOLDS, MARY BARNETT, LES. CLARK, James Mack, John Dyer, (Jack) Beuvell and Miss Tova, Jane Morgan, Betty Doree, Betty Nylander, Eddie Byrnbriar.

The Misses "Tattle Tales" (Ensemble): Helen Eades, Evelyn Page, Lois Ackerman, Jane Hayes, Sylvia Schiller, Beverly Royde, Charlotte Neste, Betty Norton, Barbara Near, Collece Legget, Ione Collombe, Elsa Walbridge, Jerry Archer, Wilma Flannigan, Wilma Wray, Lucille Matthews.

ACT [1]

Scene 1

"The Court of Louis XIV"
Entire Company
(*Music by* Howard Johnson.)

Scene 2

Frank Fay and Don Cumming (Meet Our Hero and Heavy)

Scene 3

"Percy With Perseverance"
L. Reynolds
(*Music by* Edward Ward. *Lyrics by* George Waggoner.)

Scene 4

The Crash [2] (by Nick Copeland)
Sir Herbert Martin: J. Mack. *Hon. Wilbur Peabody*: J. Dyer. *Nathan Jackson*: N. Copeland.

Scene 5

Don Cumming

Scene 6

The Official Mr. "Eh "Eh"
R. Mayer

Scene 7

"I'll Take an Option on You" [3]
F. Fay, B. Doree
(*Music and Lyrics by* Ralph Rainger and Leo Robin.)

Scene 8

"Hasta Mañana" (So This Is Havana)
W. Hargrave, (J.) Beuvell, Miss Tova
(*Music and Lyrics by* Howard Jackson.)

---

[1]Added during the run to Act 1, Scene 13:
"Everyone Made Happy"
B. Doree, D. Cumming
(*Music and Lyrics by* Frank Fay.)

[2]Replaced during run by another sketch:
The Power of Suggestion (by Nick Copeland)
Husband: J. Dyer. Wife: J. Archer. Neighbor: E. Evans.

[3]Moved elsewhere in Act I during run, and the following song added:
"Here We Are Together"
F. Fay, B. Stanwyck
(*Music by* Edward Ward. *Lyrics by* Frank Fay, William Walsh.)

Scene 9

The Nervous Waltz [4]
F. Fay, E. Page

Scene 10

"Harlem Lullaby"
E. Evans
(*Music and Lyrics by* Willard Robison.)

Scene 11

The Mind Readers (*by* Frank Fay)
J. Dyer, J. Archer

Scene 12

"Breaking Up a Rhythm"
D. Dell, L. Reynolds, Ensemble
(*Music by* Edward Ward. *Lyrics by* George Waggoner.)

Scene 13

Still the Nervous Waltz
(F. Fay, E. Page)

Scene 14

"You Gotta Do Better Than That"
M. Barnett, L. Clark, Ensemble

Scene 15

"The Interview" (*by* Frank Fay)
Scene 1: A Living Room.
Barbara Stanwyck: Herself. *Maid*: H. Eades. *First Interviewer*: J. Dyer. *Second Interviewer*: W. Hargrave.
Scene 2: Kay and Dot's Apartment (from the motion picture "Ladies of Leisure," courtesy of Columbia Pictures Corporation).
Kay Arnold: B. Stanwyck. *Dot LaMar*: E. Evans. *Mrs. Strong*: J. Morgan.
Scene 3: Same as Scene 1.
Scene 4: From the motion picture "The Miracle Woman," courtesy of Columbia Pictures Corporation.

Scene 16

"Hang Up Your Hat on Broadway"
F. Fay, Company
(*Music by* Edward Ward. *Lyrics by* George Waggoner, Bernie Grossman and Dave Silverstein.)

ACT 2

Scene 1

"The First Spring Day"
W. Hargrave
(*Music by* Howard Jackson. *Lyrics by* Edward Eliscu.)
Polka by M. Barnett, L. Clark.

Scene 2

Not to Be Trusted (*by* Frank Fay)
The Sneak: D. Cumming. *The Abused*: F. Fay.

Scene 3

Hook & Eye No. 1: N. Copeland. *Engine Co. No. 2*: J. Mack.

Scene 4

Mr. Eh-Eh Gets a Letter

Scene 5

Valse Modernistsic
(J.) Beuvell and Miss Tova

Scene 6

Parafox Studio
"Extra Man"
F. Fay
Casting Director: J. Dyer. *Actors, Extras*: Ensemble.

Scene 7

Frank (Fay) and Barbara (Stanwyck)

Scene 8

"Jig Saw Jamboree"
L. Reynolds, M. Barnett, L. Clark, Ensemble
(*Music by* Eddie Byrnbriar. *Lyrics by* William Walsh.)

---

[4]Dropped during the run.

Scene 9

Betty Doree[5] (Specialty)

Scene 10

Grand Centre Terminal[6] (*by* Frank Fay)
Information: N. Copeland. *Baggage Supervisor*: J. Mack.
Col. Tapeapeek, Peekskill bound: F. Fay. *Madamme YO YO*:
J. Morgan. *Jenny Grab*: E. Evans. *Officer Take*: R. Mayer.
Announcer: J. Dyer. *The Wife*: B. Nylander. *Retitred
Time Table Folder*: D. Cumming. *A Son of New Rochelle*:
E. Byrnbriar. *Mr.-Mrs. Lady*: Miss Tova. *Inspector of Transients*:
J. Beuvell. *Atmosphere, Transients, Autograph Seekers*

Scene 11

"Sing American Tunes"
D. Dell, M. Barnett, L. Clark, Ensemble
(*Music by* Edward Ward. *Lyrics by* Frank Fay, William
Walsh.)

Scene 12

Frank Fay

Scene 13

Finale
(Entire Company)

SHADY LADY

1933.16

A Musical Comedy in Two Acts, 3 Scenes. Book by Estelle Morando[7].
Lyrics by Bud Green, Stanley Adams. Music by Sam H. Stept, Jesse Greer.
Staged by Theodore J. Hammerstein. Dances and ensembles by Jack
Donohue. Settings by Tom Adrian Cracraft. Costumes by Brooks, Billi
Livingston. Music director, Max Hoffmann, Sr. Orchestrations by Charles
L. Cooke, Henry Redfield. Produced by Harry Meyer. Opened 5 July
1933 at the Sam S. Shubert Theatre and closed 29 July 1933 after 30
performances.

CAST (in order of appearance): *Richard Brandt*: CHARLES PURCELL. *Tracy*:
Harold Webster. *Geoffrey Benson*: MAX HOFFMANN, JR. *Francine*: Audrey Christie.
Clarisse: Phyllis Cameron. *Sonia*: Vivian Vernon. *Al Darcy*: LESTER ALLEN. *Peggy
Stetson*: LOUISE KIRTLAND. *Millie Mack*: HELEN KANE. *Lulu Stetson*: HELEN
RAYMOND. *Taxi Driver*: William Meader. (*Specialty Dancer*: Jack Donohue.)
Ladies of the Ensemble: Kay Cameron, Lauretta Brislin, Joan Connor, Marie
Felique, Rita Jason, Gladys Keating, Jeanette Lea, Jean Lawrence, Beth Reynolds,
Janice Winter, Dorothy Van Hest. *Gentlemen of the Ensemble*: Maurice Ash, Dick
Langdon, Tully Millet, Ed Murray, Emmet O'Brien, Bruce Riley.

Act 1: The Studio of Richard Brandt's Summer Home on Long Island. An afternoon in
August.

Act 2, Scene 1: The same, several days later—evening. *Scene 2*: The next morning.

ACT

"You're Not the One"
M. Hoffmann, C. Purcell, Girls, Boys
(*Music by* Jesse Greer. *Lyrics by* Stanley Adams.)

"Live, Laugh and Love"
M. Hoffmann, A. Christie, Girls
(*Music by* Sam H. Stept. *Lyrics by* Bud Green.)

"Isn't It Swell to Dream"
C. Purcell, L. Kirtland

"I'll Betcha That I Getcha"
H. Kane, L. Allen
(*Music by* Jesse Greer. *Lyrics by* Stanley Adams.)

"Swingy Little Thingy"
M. Hoffmann, A. Christie, L. Allen, Boys, Girls
(*Music by* Sam H. Stept. *Lyrics by* Bud Green.)

"Everything But My Man"
H. Kane
(*Music and Lyrics by* Serge Walter.)

Finaletto

ACT

Scene 1

"Isn't It Remarkable"
M. Hoffmann, Girls
(*Music by* Jesse Greer. *Lyrics by* Stanley Adams.)

"Any Way the Wind Blows"
M. Hoffmann, A. Christie, Boys, Girls
(*Music by* Sam H. Stept. *Lyrics by* Bud Green.)

"Your Type Is Coming Back"
H. Raymond, L. Allen, Girls, Boys
(*Music by* Sam H. Stept. *Lyrics by* Bud Green.)

"Isn't It Swell to Dream" (reprise)
C. Purcell, L. Kirtland

"One Heart"
C. Purcell, Girls
(*Music by* Sam H. Stept. *Lyrics by* Bud Green.)

Scene 2

"Hiya Sucker"
H. Raymond
(*Music by* Jesse Greer. *Lyrics by* Stanley Adams.)

"Get Hot Foot"
A. Christie, Girls
(*Music by* Sam H. Stept. *Lyrics by* Bud Green.)

"Parisian Lover" (Specialty)
L. Allen

Specialty
J. Donohue

"Where, Oh Where Can I Find Love?"
H. Kane
(*Music by* Jesse Greer. *Lyrics by* Stanley Adams.)

Finale
Company

THE BOHEMIAN GIRL

1933.17

A Revival of the Comic Opera in Three Acts, 7 Scenes[8]. Libretto by Alfred
Bunn. Music by Michael William Balfe. Staged by Milton Aborn. Dances
by Albertina Rasch. Produced by the Aborn Opera Company. Opened
27 July 1933 at the Majestic Theatre and closed 5 August 1933 after 11
performances.[9]

CAST: *Count Arnheim*: ALLAN WATEROUS. *Little Arline*: Patricia Roe. *Florestein*:
MAURICE LAVIGNE. *Buda*: Frances Baviello. *Thaddeus*: ROY CROPPER.
Devilshoof: DETMAR POPPEN. *Captain of the Guard*: Norman Van Emburgh.
Queen of the Gypsies: MARIE BARD. *Arline*: RUTH ALTMAN. *A Gypsy*: Hobson
Young. *Major Domo*: John Willard. *Nobles, Soldiers, Gypsies, Retainers, Peasants*.

Act 1: Chateau of Count Arnheim, in Austria.

Act 2, Scene 1: On the road to the Gypsies' Encampment. (Twelve years later.) *Scene 2*:
The Encampment. *Scene 3*: Road to the Fair. *Scene 4*: A Square in Pressburg. *Scene 5*:
The Hall of Justice.

Act 3: Reception Room in the Château of Count Arnheim.

THE PIRATES OF PENZANCE,
1933.18 or The Slave of Duty

A Revival of the Comic Opera in Two Acts[10]. Libretto by William S. Gilbert.
Music by Arthur Sullivan. Staged by Milton Aborn. Costumes by Brooks.
Produced by Milton Aborn. Opened 7 August 1933 at the Majestic Theatre
and closed 12 August 1933 after 8 performances.[11]

---

[5]Dropped during the run.
[6]Dropped during the run.
[7]Uncredited revisions by Irving Caesar.

[8]First presented in New York 25 November 1844 at the Park Theatre
for 17 performances in repertory. For Musical Numbers, see original 1844
production.
[9]Settings, costumes, musical director uncredited.
[10]First presented in New York 31 December 1879 at the Fifth Avenue
Theatre for 91 performances in two engagements. For Synopsis of Scenes
and Musical Numbers, see original 1879 production.
[11]Settings, musical director uncredited.

CAST: *Richard*, a Pirate King: HERBERT L. WATEROUS. *Samuel*, his Lieutenant: ALLEN WATEROUS. *Frederic*, a Pirate Apprentice: ROY CROPPER. *Major-General Stanley*, of the British Army: FRANK MOULAN. *Edward*, a Sergeant of Police: WILLIAM DANFORTH. *General Stanley's Daughters* (4): *Mabel*: RUTH ALTMAN. *Edith*: FRANCES MOORE. *Kate*: MABEL THOMPSON. *Isabel*: Frances Baviello. *Ruth*, a Piratical Maid of All Work: VERA ROSS.

General Stanley's Daughters, Pirates, Policemen, etc.: Frances Baviello, Frances Moore, Gertrude Waldon, Mary Hennessy, Olga Schumacher, Adele Story, Margaret Walker, Eleanor Manning, Celia Schiffrin, Charlotte La Rose, Angela Marsh, Madeleine de Souter, Mabel Thompson, Geraldine Olive, Vera Muller, Gertrude Rittenhouse, Kaye Janice, Harrison Fuller, Frank Clarke, Gus Loring, Norman Van Emburgh, Donald Walter, Thomas Green, Frederick Grieve, Rudolph Glaisek, Basil Prock, Bert Melrose, Hobson Young, John WIllard, John Cardini, Kenneth Brown.

THE YEOMEN OF THE GUARD,
1933.19   or The Merryman and His Maid

A Return Engagement of the Revival of the Comic Opera in Two Acts[12]. Libretto by William S. Gilbert. Music by Arthur Sullivan. Staged by Milton Aborn. Produced by the Civic Light Opera Company. Opened 14 August 1933 at the Majestic Theatre and closed 19 August 1933 after 8 performances.[13]

CAST: *Sir Richard Cholmondeley*: FREDERIC PERSSON. *Colonel Fairfax*: ROY CROPPER. *Sergeant Meryll*: HERBERT L. WATEROUS. *Leonard Meryll*: ALLEN WATEROUS. *Jack Point*: FRANK MOULAN. *Wilfred Shadbolt*: WILLIAM DANFORTH. *Elsie Maynard*: RUTH ALTMAN. *Phoebe Meryll*: LAURA FERGUSON. *Dame Carruthers*: VERA ROSS. *Kate*: FRANCES MOORE. *First Yeoman*: Hobson Young. *Second Yeoman*: Frederick Grieve. *First Citizen*: Harrison Fuller. *Headsman*: Norman Van Emburgh. *Chorus of Yeomen of the Guard, Gentlemen, Citizens, etc.*[14]

1933.20   MURDER AT THE VANITIES

A Dramatic (Musical) Mystery Comedy in Two Acts, 30 Scenes. Book by Earl Carroll and Rufus King; additional dialogue by Eugene Conrad. Lyrics by Edward Heyman, (Ned Washington, Paul Francis Webster, Herman Hupfeld). Music by Richard Myers, (Victor Young, John Jacob Loeb, Herman Hupfeld, Johnny Green). Entire production directed by Earl Carroll. Dialogue staged by Burk Symon. Dances by Chester Hale; additional dance arrangements by Ned McGurn. Scenery projections by Max Teuber. Costumes by Brymer. Music director, Ray Kavanaugh. Orchestrations by Edward Powell, Hans Spialek. Produced by Earl Carroll. Opened 12 September 1933 at the New Amsterdam Theatre, moved 6 November 1933 to the Majestic Theatre, and closed 10 March 1934 after 207 performances.

CAST (in order of appearance): *Charles*, the Stage Manager: Charles Ashley. *Liane Ware*, a Vanities Girl: PAULINE MOORE. *Mr. Martin*, the General Manger: Frank Kingdon. *Mr. Kerrick*, Assistant District Attorney: Lew Eckles. *Inspector Ellery*, Homicide Squad: JAMES RENNIE. *Miss Jones*, Police Department: NAOMI RAY. *Cornish*, Police Chauffeur: Amby Costello. *Manger*, Homicide Squad: Al Webster. *Officer Johnson*: Walker Thornton. *Walter Buck*, Assistant Stage Manager: BILLY HOUSE. *Hope Carol*, a Vanities Girl: BERYL WALLACE. *Madame Tanqueray*, Wardrobe Mistress: JEAN ADAIR. *Biggers*, Day Doorman: William Fay. *Jack Purdy*, Carpenter: Robert Cummings. *Noomhouse*, Night Watchman: William Balfour. *Sonya Sonya*: OLGA BACLANOVA. *Hulda*, Her Maid: LISA GILBERT. *Siebenkase*: BELA LUGOSI. *Scrubwoman*: Barbara Winchester. *Billy Slade*: Ben Lackland. *Mrs. Foreman*, Assistant Wardobe Mistress: Martha Pryor. *Fred Bernie*, the Electrician: James Coughlin. *Doris*, a Dancer: Mickey Braatz. *Vila*, a Vanities Girl: Villi Milli. *Elsie*, a Vanities Girl: Elsie Rossi. *Greeves*, an Ambulance Man: Charles G. Johnson. *Scrubwoman*: Helena Rapport. *Moore*, Property Man: Edwin Vickery. *Tom*, Assistant Property Man: F. X. Mahoney. *Fred*, a Police Officer: Wiley Adams. *Scrubwoman*: Eileen Burns. *Winchester*, an Actor: Phil Sheridan. *Mack*, a Police Officer: Ben Lewis. *Williams*, a Police Officer: F. Raymond. *A Bostonian*: Al Lee. *Another Bostonian*: Samuel Shaw. *Woods Miller*: WOODS MILLER. *Una Vilon*: UNA VILON. *The Blottos*: Mackie & Lavallie. *The Dancers*: Lewis & Van. *The Skater*: Paul Gerrish.

The Most Beautiful Girls in the World: Alice Kerwin, June Raymond, Dolores Grant,

Flo Harris, Gay Orlova, Anya Taranda, Evelyn Kelly, Ferne Ward, Martha Murray, Hazel Nevin, Lorna Rode, Helen Madison, Anita Patterson, Ruth Mann, Joyce Johnson, Evelyn Knapp, Dorothy Plant, Alma Saunders, Dorothy Dawes, Sybil Aarons, Joan Webster, Marion Callahan, Patricia Hayward, Janet Abbott, Muriel Evans, Irene Kelly, Constance Jordan, Nancey Dolan, Ruth Miller, Betty French, June Mahr, Evelyn Witt, Ernestine Anderson, Ednamay Adair, Renee Armour, Alice Nelson, Kay Murphy, Laurie Shevlin, Francine Sinclaire, Marion Semler, Silvia Curry, Patsy Drew, Adeline Martin, Ruth Hillard, Leone Sedalle, Emily Von Hoven, Eunice Coleman, Ann Rothey, DeDon Blunier, Elise Joyce, Marie Warren, Sari Leone, Marie Kahrkahn, Villi Milli, Elsie Rossi, Caja Eric.

Act 1, Scene 1: The (Earl Carroll) Vanities, 11th edition. *Scene 2*: Song. *Scene 3*: Fountain of Flames. *Scene 4*: The Blottos. *Scene 5*: Shaw & Lee. *Scene 6*: Una Vilon. *Scene 7*: The Step-Children. *Scene 8*: On the Stage. The Investigation. 45 minutes later. 6 P.M. *Scene 9*: Backstage, and in the Auditorium of the theatre before the evening performance. 45 minutes later, 6:45 P.M. *Scene 10*: The Vanities, 3 hours later, middle of first act. 9:45 P.M. *Scene 11*: Lewis & Van. *Scene 12*: Song. *Scene 13*: "Fans." *Scene 14*: Skater Specialty. *Scene 15*: Backstage. Dressing Room Corridor. *Scene 16*: Backstage before Act 1 Finale. *Scene 17*: Curtain of Light. *Scene 18*: First Act Finale.

Act 2, Scene 1: Song. *Scene 2*: Backstage—Dressing Room Hallway. 10:30 P.M. *Scene 3*: Musicians' Room. *Scene 4*: Quick Change Room of the Chorus. *Scene 5*: The Wardrobe Room. *Scene 6*: Under the Stage. *Scene 7*: The Vanities during Act 2. *Scene 8*: Song. *Scene 9*: Shaw & Lee. *Scene 10*: Backstage, Corridor of Dressing Rooms. 11 P.M. *Scene 11*: Backstage. Wardrobe Room. *Scene 12*: The Wedding Party, sometime later.

Note: The entire action of the play takes place between the finale of the Saturday matinee and the finale of the Saturday evening performance.

ACT 1[15]
Scene 1
   "We're Going to Be Dramatic"
      Girls
Scene 2
   "Sweet Madness"
      W. Miller
      (*Music by* Victor Young. *Lyrics by* Ned Washington.)
Scene 3
   Fountain of Flames
Scene 4
   Street in Paris
      Mackie & Lavallie
Scene 5
   Cafe de la Paix
      A. Lee, S. Shaw
Scene 6
   Song
      U. Vilon
Scene 7
   The Hand Drill
      The Step-Children
Scene 9
   "Virgins Wrapped in Cellophane"
      (Girls)
      (*Music by* John J. Loeb. *Lyrics by* Paul Francis Webster.)
Scene 10
   Song[16]
      U. Vilon
      Introduced by B. Wallace.
Scene 11
   (Dance) Specialty
      Lewis & Van

---

[12]First presented in New York 17 October 1888 at the Casino Theatre for 100 performances; this revival previously presented 1 May 1933 at the St. James Theatre for 8 performances. For Synopsis of Scenes and Musical Numbers, see original 1888 production.
[13]Settings, costumes, musical director uncredited.
[14]Chorus same as THE PIRATES OF PENZANCE above.

[15]Added during the first month of run:
   "Dust in Your Eyes"
      (*Music and Lyrics by* Irving and Lionel Newman.)
[16]Moved from Act 1, Scene 10 to Scene 14 during the run:
   "Weep No More My Baby"
      B. House, U. Vilon
      (*Music by* John W. Green. *Lyrics by* Edward Heyman.)

Scene 12

"You Love Me"
O. Baclanova
(*Music and Lyrics by* Herman Hupfeld.)

Scene 13

"Fans"
(Girls)
Principal Figure: G. Orlova

Scene 14

(Skating) Specialty
P. Gerrish

Scene 16

"Me For You Forever"
W. Miller
(*Music by* Richard Myers. *Lyrics by* Edward Heyman.)

Scene 17

Curtain of Light

Scene 18

Act 1 Finale

ACT 2

Scene 1

"Who Committed the Murder"
B. Wallace, Girls
Dance Specialty: M. Braatz.

Scene 8

"Savage Serenade"
U. Vilon, Girls
(*Music and Lyrics by* Herman Hupfeld.)

Scene 9

(Drunk) Specialty
S. Shaw & A. Lee, L. Eckles

Scene 12

Grand Finale
(Entire Company)

1933.21   HOLD YOUR HORSES

A Musical Runaway (Comedy) in Two Acts, 19 Scenes. Book by Russel Crouse and Corey Ford. Based on their story written with Charles Beahan. And with many nonsensical moments (additional dialogue) by Joe Cook. Music and lyrics by (Robert) Russell Bennett, Owen Murphy, Robert A. Simon. Louis Alter, Arthur Swanstrom, Ben Oakland. Staged by R. H. Burnside. (Produced under the supervision of John Shubert.) Dances by Robert Alton. Ballets by Harriet Hoctor. Scenery and costumes by Russell Patterson. Music director, Gene Salzer. Orchestrations by (Robert) Russell Bennett. (Produced by the Messrs. Shubert and Joe Cook.) Opened 25 September 1933 at the Winter Garden and closed 9 December 1933 after 88 performances.

CAST {in order of appearance}: *Bill, Doorman at Rector's*: REX WEBER. *Charles Rector*: Walter Armin. *Flash Ricardo*: Douglas Gilmore. *Dolly Montague*: FRANCES UPTON. *Diamond Jim Brady*: Jack Howard. *Anna Held*: Frances Ford. *Lillian Russell*: Phyllis Carroll. *Gwen Fordyce*: INEZ COURTNEY. *Kid Hogan*: TOM PATRICOLA. *John L. Sullivan*: Edwin Guhl. *Boss Donovan*: Edward J. McNamara. *Alan Donovan*: Stanley Smith. *Spike Ahearn*: W. K. Brady. *Dan Guiness*: Jack Morrissey. *Big Bill Haenckle*: C. E. Smith. *Nervy Nat*: Jimmy Fox. *Hold-Up Man*: Robert J. Mulligan. *Broadway Joe*: JOE COOK. *Marjory Ellis*: ONA MUNSON. *Magnolia, the Horse*: Jack Burleigh, Ernest Recco. *Felix*: Joey McKeon. *Frothingham*: DAVE CHASEN. *Peanut Vendor*: Charles Senna. *Luigi*: Jack Anthony. *Guiseppe* Harry Rogers. *Bartender at Nigger Mike's*: Walter Palm. *Irving*: Lehman Byck. *Patron at Nigger Mike's*: Clarence Harvey. *Steve Brody*: Eugene Winchester. *Ambrose McGillicuddy*: George Schiller. *First Chorus Girl*: Margie Finley. *Second Chorus Girl*: Emeeta Casanova. *Third Chorus Girl*: Hene D'Amur. *Fourth Chorus Girl*: Dorothy Drum. *First Croupier*: Jack Byrne. *Dick Canfield*: Jack Howard. *Dowager*: Maurine Holmes. *Three-Card Monte Man*: Eugene Winchester. *Al Smith*: Dick Wallace. *Kid Hogan's Second*: Olaf Olsen. *Mr. Milquetoast*: Jimmy Fox. *Stenographer*: Margie Finley. *G. A. R. Veteran*: Clarence Harvey. *Committeeman*: Donnell O'Brian.

Dancing Girls: Alayne Blair, Barbara Coswell, Mary Connor, Helen Day, Helene Ecklund, Marion Farrish, Peggy Gallimore, Ruth Gormley, Jeryl Joyce, Adelaide Kaye, Josephine Kaye, Marguerite Kennedy, Lila Manor, Lola Manor, Connie Madison,

Rosalie McCallion, Eileen O'Connor, Pat Palmer, Tesha Pierson, Polly Rose, Jean Ryan, Myra Scott, Edna Strong, Tanya Tschergi, Sunny Wright.
Showgirls: Julia Barker, Phyllis Carroll, Emeeta Casanova, Cecile Clancy, Colleen Cooper, Carmen Cuyler, Helen Folson, Francis Ford, Maurine Holmes, Meredith Howard, Virginia Howard, Jayne Manners, Ethel O'Dell, Evelyn Page, Lovee Sabalis, Frances Stutz. *Boys*: Jimmy Babbitt, Andre Charise, Jay Conley, John Glenn, Tully Millett, Gene Martel, Emmett O'Brien, Jack Wolf, Dan Wyler.

Act 1, Scene 1: New York City at the turn of the century. Exterior, Rector's. *Scene 2*: Interior, Rector's. *Scene 3*: Private Dining Room at Rector's. *Scene 4*: Exterior, Rector's. *Scene 5*: Central Park outside the Lion House. *Scene 6*: Nigger Mike's in the Bowery. *Scene 7*: Backstage at the Casino Theatre. *Scene 8*: Stage, Casino Theatre. *Scene 9*: Canfield's Gambling House. *Scene 10*: On Broadway. *Scene 11*: Ballroom in Waldorf-Astoria Hotel.

Act 2, Scene 1: Coney Island. *Scene 2*: Outside the Flea Circus, Coney Island. *Scene 3*: At the Flea Circus. *Scene 4*: Central Park. *Scene 5*: The Mayor's Office. *Scene 6*: The Chase Up Broadway. *Scene 7*: On Broadway. *Scene 8*: The Subway.

ACT 1

Opening
R. Weber, Ensemble

"Good Evening, Mr. Man in the Moon"
F. Upton

"Galloping Through the Park"
Cabbies

"Hold Your Horses"
J. Cook, O. Munson

"Peanuts and Kisses"
O. Munson, C. Smith

Opening of Nigger Mike's—Old Time Songs

"High Shoes"
I. Courtney, T. Patricola

"Singing to You"
O. Munson, C. Smith
(*Music by* Ben Oakland, Margot Millham. *Lyrics by* Robert A. Simon, Margot Millham.)

Sextette ("Tell Me, Pretty Maiden") (from FLORODORA)
(*Music by* Leslie Stuart. *Lyrics by* Owen Hall.)
I. Courtney, O. Munson, F. Upton, M. Finley, C. Cooper, P. Rose, Boys

"If I Love Again"
R. Weber
(*Music by* Ben Oakland. *Lyrics by* J. P. Murray.)

Ballet at the Casino Theatre
H. Hoctor, Ballet Girls

"I Guess I Love You"
I. Courtney, T. Patricola

Cotillion at the Waldorf-Astoria
Ensemble

Finale
J. Fox, C. Senna, C. Smith, Entire Company

ACT 2

"Happy Little Week-end"
F. Upton, Ensemble

The Fuller Construction Company's Latest Model Recording Orchestra

"Singing to You" (reprise)[17]
R. Weber

Flea Circus Ballet
H. Hoctor, Ballet Girls

"Singing to You" (reprise)
F. Upton, C. Smith

---

[17]During run replaced by:
"Take Me in Your Arms"
R. Weber
Later replaced with:
"Stay Out of the Moonlight"
F. Upton

"Old Man Subway"
  F. Upton, Ensemble
Finale
  J. Cook, Entire Company

1933.22 AS THOUSANDS CHEER

A Musical Revue in Two Acts, a Prologue and 21 Scenes. Sketches by Moss Hart. Music and lyrics by Irving Berlin. Staged by Hassard Short. Dances by Charles Weidman. Settings by Albert Johnson. Costumes by Irene Sharaff, Varady. Music director, Frank Tours. Orchestrations by Adolph Deutsch, Frank Tours, Eddie Powell, Russell Wooding, Helmy Kresa. Produced by Sam H. Harris. Opened 30 September 1933 at the Music Box Theatre and closed 8 September 1934 after 400 performances.

CAST: MARILYN MILLER, CLIFTON WEBB, HELEN BRODERICK, ETHEL WATERS, Leslie Adams, Hal Forde, Jerome Cowan, Harry Stockwell, Thomas Hamilton, Hamtree Harrington, Peggy Cornell, Harold Murray.
  Charles Weidman Dancers: Letitia Ide, José Limón (lead dancers), Helen Bache, Debby Coleman, Paula Yasgour, Robert Gorham, Harry Joyce, William Matons.
  The Girls: Jeanette Bradley, Dorothy Dodd, Elsie Duffy, Helen Ericson, Katherine Litz, Irene McBride, Katherine Mulowney, Jeanette Mundell, Margaret Sande, Toni Sorel, Elsa Walbridge, Teddy West, Lucille Taylor. *The Boys:* Jack Barnes, Robert Castaine, Arthur Craig, Jay Hunter, Fred Mayon, Chester O'Brien, Mortimer O'Brien, John Perkins, Paul Pierce, Ward Tallmon, Harold Voeth, Jack Voeth.

PROLOGUE
Scene 1
  Dining Room in Park Avenue
    Langley, a Butler: H. Forde. *Mr. Andrews:* L. Adams. *Mrs. Andrews:* H. Broderick.
Scene 2
  Editor's Office
    Editor: J. Cowan. *Reporter:* H. Stockwell.
Scene 3
  Columbus Circle
    Boys, Girls

ACT 1
Scene 1
  Franklin D. Roosevelt Inaugurated Tomorrow
    Mr. Hoover: L. Adams. *Mrs. Hoover:* H. Broderick. *Charlie:* H. Harrington.
Scene 2
  Woolworth Declares Regular Dividend
  Barbara Hutton to Wed Prince Mdivani
    The Lackey: H. Voeth. *Prince Hohenstein:* C. O'Brien. *Prince Donatelli:* J. Hunter. *Prince Austerliebe:* P. Pierce. *Prince DeLuneville:* H. Murray.
  "How's Chances?"
    M. Miller, C. Webb
Scene 3
  Heat Wave Hits New York
  "Heat Wave"
    E. Waters
    The Dancers: L. Ide, J. Limón, Weidman Dancers.
Scene 4
  Joan Crawford to Divorce Douglas Fairbanks, Jr.
    Joan Crawford: M. Miller. *Douglas Fairbanks, Jr.:* C. Webb. *Will Hays:* L. Adams. *First Reporter:* H. Murray. *Second Reporter:* J. Cowan. *Third Reporter:* W. Tallmon. *Fourth Reporter:* J. Perkins.
Scene 5
  "Majestic Sails at Midnight"
    L. Adams, H. Forde, H. Stockwell, J. Cowan, H. Broderick
Scene 6
  Lonely Heart Column
  "Lonely Heart"
    H. Stockwell
    Danced by L. Ide, J. Limón, Ensemble.

Scene 7
  World's Wealthiest Man Celebrates 94th Birthday
    John D. Rockefeller, Sr.: C. Webb. *John D. Rockefeller, Jr.:* L. Adams. *Mrs. John D. Rockefeller, Jr.:* H. Broderick. *John D. Rockefeller, Jr.'s Children:* P. Cornell, J. Cowan, H. Murray, T. Hamilton. *Reporter and Cameraman:* H. Forde, W. Tallmon.
Scene 8
  "The Funnies"
    M. Miller, Ensemble
Scene 9
  Green Pastures Starts Third Road Season
    Man: H. Harrington. *Woman:* E. Waters.
  "To Be or Not To Be"
    E. Waters
Scene 10
  Rotogravure Section
Scene 11
  Easter Parade on Fifth Avenue—1883.
  "Her Easter Bonnet" ("Easter Parade")
    M. Miller, C. Webb

ACT 2
Scene 1
  Metropolitan Opera Opens in Old Time Splendor
    Radio Announcer: J. Cowan. *Mons. Peppiton:* C. Webb. *Mr. Williams:* L. Adams. *Mrs. Williams:* H. Broderick. *Her Daughter:* M. Miller.
Scene 2
  Unknown Negro Lynched by Frenzied Mob
  "Supper Time"
    E. Waters
Scene 3
  Gandhi Goes on New Hunger Strike
    Mahatma Gandhi: C. Webb. *Aimee Semple MacPherson:* H. Broderick. *Counterman:* H. Forde. *Cameramen:* H. Murray, J. Hunter. *Reporter:* J. Cowan. *Native Messenger:* W. Tallmon.
Scene 4
  Revolt in Cuba
    The Dancers: L. Ide, J. Limón.
Scene 5
  Noël Coward, Noted Playwright, Returns to England
    First Bellboy: W. Tallmon. *Second Bellboy:* H. Murray. *Mrs. Fisher,* housekeeper: H. Broderick. *Ella,* a scrubwoman: E. Waters. *Aggie,* a chambermaid: M. Miller. *Henry Perlmutter,* a Waiter: C. Webb. *Window Cleaner:* L. Adams.
Scene 6
  Society Wedding of the Season: Outside St. Thomas'
    Bridesmaids: H. Ericson, T. West, L. Taylor, D. Dodd, I. McBride, J. Bradley, E. Walbridge, J. Mundell, T. Sorel, E. Duffy. *Ushers:* C. O'Brien, M. O'Brien, J. Voeth, J. Barnes, J. Hunter, F. Mayon, W. Tallmon, A. Craig, J. Perkins, R. Clark.
  "Our Wedding Day"
    M. Miller, C. Webb
Scene 7
  Josephine Baker Still the Rage of Paris
    Josephine Baker: E. Waters. *Her Secretary:* J. Cowan. *Maitre d'Hotel:* J. Cowan.
  "I've Got Harlem on My Mind"
    E. Waters
Scene 8
  Prince of Wales Rumored Engaged
    The King: L. Adams. *The Queen:* H. Broderick. *The Prince:* T. Hamilton. *The Prime Minister:* H. Forde.
Scene 9
  Broadway Gossip Column: "Through a Key Hole"[18]
    C. Webb

[18]Dropped after opening.

Scene 10

Supreme Court Hands Down Important Decision
Editors' Office: *Editor*: J. Cowan. *Reporter*: H. Stockwell.

"Not For All the Rice in China"
M. Miller, C. Webb, Entire Company

CHAMPAGNE, SEC
1933.23

An Operetta in Three Acts, 5 Scenes. Book by Alan Child [Lawrence Langner]. Adapted from the Viennese operetta "Die Fledermaus" by Karl Haffner and Richard Genée, based on the French play "Le Réveillon" by Henri Meilhac and Ludovic Halévy, (from a German story "Das Gefängnis" by Roderich Benedix). Music by Johann Strauss, Jr. Lyrics by Robert A. Simon. Staged by Monty Woolley. Settings by Jo Mielziner. Costumes by Brooks. Music director, Rudolph Thomas. Produced by Dwight Deere Wiman[19] in association with the Westport Country Playhouse (Lawrence Langner) by arrangement with the producers of "One Wonderful Night." Opened 14 October 1933 at the Morosco Theatre, moved 30 October 1933 to the Sam S. Shubert Theatre, moved 30 November 1933 to the 44th Street Theatre and closed 20 January 1934 after 113 performances.

CAST {in order of appearance}: *Alfred*: GEORGE TRABERT. *Adele*: HELEN FORD. *Rosalinde*: PEGGY WOOD. *von Eisenstein*: GEORGE MEADER. *Dr. Blind*: William J. McCarthy. *Falke*: JOSEPH MACAULAY. *Frank*: John Barclay. *Ida*: Olive Jones. *Prince Orlofsky*: KITTY CARLISLE. *Frosh*: JOHN E. HAZZARD. *A Dancer*: PAUL HAAKON. *Second Dancer*: ELEANOR TENNIS.

Footmen, Guests, Ladies of the Ballet: Claire Miller, Carol Chandler, Pierce Hearn, David Rogers, Bruce Norman, Gudrun Ekelund, Nina Dean, Nellilew Winger, Betty Quay, Glenn Darwin, Don English, Samuel Mendel, Alan M. MacCracken, Wilfried Klamroth, Ronald Jones, John Thomas.

Act 1, Scene 1: Von Eisenstein's Garden, Vienna. *Scene 2*: Interlude. *Scene 3*: Rosalinde's Boudoir.

Act 2: The Grand Salon in the Palace of Prince Orlofsky.

Act 3: A Jail.

ACT 1[20]

Scene 1

"Just a Little Chambermaid"
H. Ford

"Little Bird"
G. Trabert

"Just a Little Chambermaid" (reprise)
H. Ford, P. Wood

"It Would Be Best If You Would Go Now" (Trio)
G. Meader, P. Wood, W. J. McCarthy

"Come Along to the Ball" (Duet)
J. Macaulay, G. Meader

"Oh Dear! It's Not Right!" (Trio)
P. Wood, G. Meader, H. Ford

Scene 2

Interlude
H. Ford, P. Wood

Scene 3

"So Drink a Cup of Cheer" (Duet)
G. Trabert, P. Wood

"So Drink a Cup of Cheer" (reprise)
G. Trabert, J. Barclay

Act 1 Finale (Trio)
P. Wood, G. Trabert, J. Barclay

ACT 2

Scene 1

"What a Night"
Chorus

---

[19]Mr. Wiman acknowledges his indebtedness for the assistance of Madam Lina Abarbanell.
[20]Musical Numbers not listed in program; this list prepared from production manuscript and score.

"Chacun à son gout"
K. Carlisle

Finale Act 2 Scene 1 (A Very Ludicrous Mistake)
K. Carlisle, J. Macaulay, H. Ford, G. Meader, Ensemble

Scene 2

Duet
G. Meader, H. Ford

"Voices of My Homeland"
P. Wood

"Champagne the First"
K. Carlisle, G. Meader, H. Ford, J. Barclay, J. Macaulay, Chorus
"We'll Dance the Polka"
Chorus

ACT 3

"I Ought To Be on the Stage"
H. Ford

"Vengeance" (Trio)
P. Wood, G. Trabert, G. Meader

Finale
Entire Company

THE SCHOOL FOR HUSBANDS
1933.24

A Comedy with Music in Two Acts and a Ballet Interlude. Adapted in rhyme from the original play ("L'École des maris") by Molière by Arthur Guiterman and Lawrence Langner. Music composed and arranged by Edmond W. Rickett. Lyrics by Arthur Guiterman. Directed by Lawrence Langner. Settings and costumes by Lee Simonson. Ballet interlude choreography by Doris Humphrey and Charles Weidman. Music director, Edmond W. Rickett. Produced by the Theatre Guild. Opened 16 October 1933 at the Empire Theatre and closed 20 January 1934 after 116 performances.

CAST (in order of appearance): *Sganarelle*: OSGOOD PERKINS. *Ergaste*: JAMES JOLLEY. *Street Vendor*: PARKER STEWARD. *Lisette*: FLORA LE BRETON. *Ariste*: STUART CASEY. *Valere*: MICHAEL BARTLETT. *Leonor*: JOAN CARR. *Isabelle*: JUNE WALKER. *Lysander*: GEORGE MACREADY. *Sylvester*: Lewis Martin. *First Lackey*: Francis Tyler. *Second Dancers*: DORIS HUMPHREY, CHARLES WEIDMAN. *Bear*: Marcus Blechman. *First Girl*: Janice Joyce. *Second Girl*: Dorothea Petgen. *Third Girl*: Lee Whitney. *Fourth Girl*: Virginia Marvin. *Pierrot*: PARKER STEWARD. *Columbine*: DORIS HUMPHREY. *Harlequin*: CHARLES WEIDMAN. *Magician*: Robert Reinhardt. *Third Lackey*: John Cherry. *First Bravo*: George Macready. *Second Bravo*: Lewis Martin. *Magistrate*: Stanley Harrison. *Notary*: Horace Sinclair. *Link Boy*: Kenneth Bostock.

Ballet Interlude: *Sganarelle*: OSGOOD PERKINS. *Athenée*: Janice Joyce. *Shepherdess*: DORIS HUMPHREY. *Solomon*: Lewis Martin. *Socrates*: Horace Sinclair. *First Egyptian*: Ada Korvin. *Second Egyptian*: Eleanor King. *Dancing Master*: CHARLES WEIDMAN. *Tircis*: Stuart Casey. *Olympians*: Ernestine Henock, Ada Korvin, Katherine Manning, Hyla Rubin, Marcus Blechman, Kenneth Bostock, Jack Cole.

Act 1: A Square in Paris. Morning.

Act 2: The same. Evening of the same day.

ACT 1

Street-vendor's Song
P. Steward
(The refrain is an authentic Parisian street-cry, as recorded by Clement Jannequin. Sixteenth century.)

"So My Dashing Roving Blade"
F. Le Breton
(Based upon "La Bergère que je sers." Brunette. The refrain is original.)

"Life, unbar the door"
(J. Walker, J. Carr, F. Le Breton)
(From "La Guirlande," Ballet by J. Ph. Rameau, 1751.)

"As one brother to another"
(O. Perkins, S. Casey, J. Carr, F. Le Breton)
(Based upon "En revenant à Versailles." "Chanson à danser." Seventeenth century.)

"Yes, Mama" (original)
G. Macready, L. Martin

("The world is dark and lonely")
M. Bartlett
("La Fontaine," of unknown origin, long known both in France and England.)

"When I say, My darling"
F. Le Breton, J. Jolley
(Based on folk-song of the Franche-Comté.)

"One must be extremely careful"
O. Perkins
(Based on "Gardez-vous d'être sévère."—Brunette.)

"I love you"
M. Bartlett
("Bergère legère" from J. B. Wekerlin's Collection of old Bergerettes.)

Dance
D. Humphrey, C. Weidman
("Tambourin" by Rameau from the ballet "Les Fêtes d'Hébé.")

Finale, Act 1
(M. Bartlett, S. Casey, J. Walker, J. Jolley, O. Perkins, Chorus)
(Based upon the Lorraine folk-song "en passant par la Lorraine.")

INTERLUDE

"The Dream of Sganarelle"
Adapted from the ballet "Le Mariage forcé," originally danced by His Majesty Louis XIV and his court, 29 January 1664.
Overture, based on Sganarelle's song in Act 1.

"Love Is Always Young" (Song)
(J. Joyce)
The Egyptians. Adapted from "La Gemissante." Air by Dandrieu.

Gavotte by Lully. (1633-1687)

Menuet d'Exaudet.

Gavotte by Rameau from the ballet "Les Fêtes d'Hébé."

Wedding Procession. Pavane of the fifteenth century.

A "Musette" and a "Contredanse" from "Les Fêtes d'Hébé."

ACT 2

"Ignorance is bliss"
(J. Jolley, M. Bartlett, F. Tyler, W. Miley, P. Steward)
("Ah! vous dirai-je, maman," eighteenth century.)

"Lovers two have sought my hand"
(J. Walker, O. Perkins, M. Bartlett)
(Original, with a slight nod of recognition in the direction of "Le beau Séjour," Brunette.)

"Au clair de la lune" (by Lully)
(P. Steward)

Dance
(D. Humphrey, C. Weidman)
("Musette" from "Les Fêtes d'Hébé.")

"The Moon is above"
M. Bartlett
("Plaisir d'amour," by Padre Martini.)

Final dance
(Entire Company)
("A Parthenay." A folk-tune of Touraine.)

1933.25   LET 'EM EAT CAKE

A Musical Comedy in Three Acts, Two Acts, 12 Scenes[21]. Book by George S. Kaufman and Morrie Ryskind. Lyrics by Ira Gershwin. Music by George Gershwin. Book staged by George S. Kaufman. Dances and ensembles staged by Eugene Van Grona, Ned McGurn. Settings by Albert R. Johnson. Costumes by Kiviette, John Booth. Music director, William Daly. Orchestrations by Edward Powell. Produced by Sam H. Harris. Opened 21 October 1933 at the Imperial Theatre and closed 6 January 1934 after 90 performances.

CAST {in order of appearance}: *General Adam Snookfield, U.S.A.*: FLORENZ AMES. *Trixie Flynn*: GRACE WORTH. *A. Flunkey*: David Lawrence. *Francis X. Gilhooley*: HAROLD MOFFAT. *Mrs. Gilhooley*: Alice Burrage. *Louis Lippman*: Abe Reynolds. *Mrs. Lippman*: Grenna Sloane. *Senator Carver Jones*: EDWARD H. ROBINS. *Mrs. Jones*: Vivian Barry. *Senator Robert E. Lyons*: GEORGE E. MACK. *Mrs. Lyons*: CONSUELO FLOWERTON. *Matthew Arnold Fulton*: DUDLEY CLEMENTS. *Mrs. Fulton*: Mary Jo Matthews. *Mary Wintergreen*: LOIS MORAN.

John P. Wintergreen: WILLIAM GAXTON. *Chief Justice of the Supreme Court*: RALPH RIGGS. *Alexander Throttlebottom*: VICTOR MOORE. *Kruger*: PHILIP LOEB. *President of the Union League Club*: RALPH RIGGS. *Uncle William*: J. Francis Robertson. *Lieutenant*: George Kirk. *John P. Tweedledee*: Richard Temple. *Secretary*: Charles Conklin. *Flunkey*: David Lawrence. *Policeman*: Don Hudson. *Customers*: Terry Lawlor, Pat Hastings. *Snodgrass*: Charles Fowler. *Passersby*: Michael Forbes, Leon Dunar. *Dignitaries*: Robert Burton, Robert Lewis, Martin Leroy. *Secretary*: Charles Conklin. *Nurse*: Evelyn Hannons. *Photographers*: David Lawrence, Charles Fowler. *Vendor*: Martin Leroy. *Russian*: Morris Tepper. *Prison Guards*: Vance Elliott, Bruce Barclay.

Ladies Ensemble: Kay Adams, Ruth Adams, Peggy Bancroft, Gail Darling, Olgene Foster, Yvonne Gray, Peggy Green, Viola Hunter, Jessica Worth, Kathleen Ayres, Alyce Downey, Enes Early, Louise Estes, Dorothy Graves, Ethel Hampton, Pat Hastings, Evelyn Hannons, Amalie Ideal, Kay Lazell, Betty Lee, Terry Lawlor, Ruth Porter, Baun Sturtz, Martha Tibbetts, Wanda Wood, Nonie Dale, Elinor Witte. *Men's Ensemble*: Bruce Barclay, Robert Burton, Paul Brachard, Tom Curley, Gordon Clark, Leon Dunar, Bryan Davis, Vance Elliott, Michael Forbes, Charles Flower, David Gross, Don Hudson, Tom Harris, David Lawrence, Martin Leroy, Robert Lewis, Ed Loud, Al LeFebevre, Richard Neely, Martin Sheppard, Harold Sternberg, Morris Tepper, Norman Van Emburgh, John Walsh, Ray Clarke, Charles Conklin, Frank Gagen, Phil King, Hazzard Newberry, Fred Nay, Victor Pullman, Steward Steppler.

Act 1, Scene 1: Main Street. *Scene 2*: The White House. *Scene 3*: Union Square. *Scene 4*: The New Store. *Scene 5*: The Union League Club. *Scene 6*: On to Washington. *Scene 7*: Outside the White House.

Act 2, Scene 1: The Blue House. *Scene 2*: The Ball Park. *Scene 3*: The Tribunal. *Scene 4*: A Jail. *Scene 5*: The Guillotine.

ACT 1

Scene 1

"Wintergreen for President"
Ensemble

"Tweedledee for President"
Ensemble

Scene 3

"Union Square"
Ensemble

"Down With Everyone Who's Up"
P. Loeb, Agitators

Scene 4

"Shirts by Millions"
Wives, Ensemble

"Comes the Revolution"
V. Moore, Ensemble

"Mine"
W. Gaxton, L. Moran, Ensemble

"Climb Up the Social Ladder"[22]
L. Moran, Wives, Ensemble

Scene 5

"Cloistered from the Noisy City" (The Union League)
R. Riggs, Club Members

Scene 6

"On and On and On"
W. Gaxton, L. Moran, Company

Scene 7

Finale, Act 1:
("I've Brushed My Teeth")
F. Ames, R. Burton, R. Lewis, M. Leroy

Double Dummy Drill (Dance)

("On and On and On") (reprise)
Blue Shirts

("The General's Gone to a Party")
R. Temple, W. Gaxton, G. Kirk, Men

("All the Mothers of the Nation")
L. Moran, Wives, Girls

("Yes, He's a Bachelor")
W. Gaxton, Blue Shirts, G. Kirk

("There's Something We're Worried About")
G. Kirk, Army, Women, R. Temple, P. Loeb

---

[21]Conceived as a sequel by the same authors whose OF THEE I SING opened 26 December 1931 at the Music Box Theatre for 441 performances.

[22]Dropped from show after opening.

("What's the Proletariat?")
L. Moran, Wives, Committee, Army, All

"Let 'Em Eat Cake"
W. Gaxton, Company

ACT 2

Scene 1

"Blue, Blue, Blue"
Wives, Ensemble

"Who's the Greatest?"
W. Gaxton, Ensemble

Finaletto: League of Nations

"No Comprenez, No Capish"
League of Nations, W. Gaxton, L. Moran, Ensemble

("Who's the Greatest?") (reprise)
W. Gaxton, Ensemble

Scene 2

("Play Ball")
Girls

"When the Judges Doff the Ermine"
R. Riggs, Blue Shirts
(includes "Nine Supreme Ball Players," No Better Way to Start a Case,"
"The Whole Truth,") "Up and At 'Em"

Scene 3

The Trial of Throttlebottom

"That's What He Did"
V. Moore, P. Loeb, Ensemble

"I Know a Foul Ball"
V. Moore

"Throttle Throttlebottom"
P. Loeb, Ensemble

(The Trial of Wintergreen)

"A Hell of a Hole" ("A Hell of a Fix")
W. Gaxton, P. Loeb, Soldiers

("Down With Everyone Who's Up") (reprise)
P. Loeb, Ensemble
("It Isn't What You Did")
W. Gaxton, Ensemble
("Mine") (reprise)
W. Gaxton, L. Moran, Ensemble
"Let 'Em Eat Caviar"
P. Loeb, Ensemble

Scene 5

"Hanging Throttlebottom in the Morning"
(G. Kirk,) Ensemble

1933.26 ROBERTA

A Musical Comedy in Two Acts, a Prologue and 9 Scenes. Book and lyrics by Otto Harbach. Based on the novel "Gowns by Roberta" by Alice Duer Miller. Music by Jerome Kern. (Directed and lighted by Hassard Short.) Dances by José Limón of the Charles Weidman Group. Settings by Clark Robinson. Costumes by Kiviette. Music director, Victor Baravalle. Orchestrations by Robert Russell Bennett. Produced by Max Gordon. Opened 18 November 1933 at the New Amsterdam Theatre and closed 21 July 1934 after 295 performances.

CAST (in order of speaking): *Billy Boyden*, the Hoofer: GEORGE MURPHY. *John Kent*, the Fullback: RAYMOND MIDDLETON. *Sophie Teale*, the Debutante: Helen Gray. *Huckleberry Haines' Orchestra*: CALIFORNIA COLLEGIANS (Lou Wood, Herb Montei, Ray Adams, Alan Jones, Neil Wood, Rene Du Plessis, Fred MacMurray.) *Huckleberry Haines*, the Crooner: BOB HOPE. *Mrs. Teale*, the Mother: Roberta Beatty. *Aunt Minnie* (Trade name, Roberta), the Modiste: FAY TEMPLETON. *Stephanie*, the Manager at Roberta's: TAMARA [DRASIN]. *Angele*, the Assistant: Bobette Christine. *Lord Henry Delves*, the Friend of Roberta: SYDNEY GREENSTREET. *Mme. Nunez*, Clementina Scharwenka, the Star Customer: LYDA ROBERTI. *Ladislaw*, the Doorman: WILLIAM HAIN. *Mme. Grandet*, the Fitter: Marion Ross. *Luella*, the Model: NAYAN PEARCE. *Marie*, the Stylist: Mavis Walsh. *M. Leroux*, the Solicitor: Ed Jerome. *Sidonie*, the Presser: Berenice Alaire. *The Buyer*: Gretchen Sherman. *The Flower Girl*: Virginia Whitmore. *The Bartender*: William Torpey. *The Singer at Café Russe*: George Djimos. *The Proprietor of Café Russe*: Stanislaw Sarmatoff.

Debutantes at Alpha Beta Pi Fraternity House: Carol Renwick, Dorothy Lane, Aida Conkey, Norma Butler, Ruth Shaw, Rosalie Trego, Barbara Williams, Evelyn Monte, Elsie Behrens, Bunny Hallow. *Members of Alpha Beta Pi*: Bert Doughty, Vernon Hammer, Buddy Hertelle, Jack Douglas, John Muccio, Michael Alvarez, Bob Gray, John Peters, Jimmy Ryan, Leon Alton, Bob Barrett. *Mannequins at Roberta's*: Edna Johnson Florence Chumbecos, Lillian Lamonte, Phyllis Cameron, Catherine Laughlin, Dorothy Atkins, Barbara Child, Tania Sanina, Rose Gale, Barbara Adams, Virginia Whitmore, Ruth Hamilton, Josephine Roberts, Sally Bynum, Lola DeLille, Clara Waring, Sandra Walters.

Prologue: Fraternity House at Haverhill College, U.S.A. May.

Act 1, Scene 1: Roberta's Paris Office. June. *Scene 2*: The Fitting Room at Roberta's. July. *Scene 3*: A Corridor at Roberta's. August. *Scene 4*: The Show Room at Roberta's. The same time.

Act 2, Scene 1: Roberta's Private Office. September. *Scene 2*: Willie's American Bar in Paris. The next evening. *Scene 3*: Roberta's Employees' Entertainment. That night. *Scene 4*: Wardrobe at Roberta's. Later that night. *Scene 5*: Café Russe, Paris. After midnight.

PROLOGUE

"Let's Begin" (Scene Music)
G. Murphy, Ensemble

"Alpha, Beta, Pi" (Fraternity Song)
B. Hope, G. Murphy, R. Middleton, Ensemble

"You're Devastating" (Scene)
B. Hope

"Let's Begin" (Trio) (reprise)
G. Murphy, R. Middleton, B. Hope, Male Ensemble

ACT 1

"You're Devastating" (Reminiscence) (Reprise)
Tamara

"Yesterdays" (Air)
F. Templeton

"Something's Got to Happen" (Trio)
L. Roberti, B. Hope, R. Middleton

Prose Recital
B. Hope

"The Touch of Your Hand" (Duettino)
Tamara, W. Hain

Scene and Pas de Seul
B. Alaire, M. Walsh, M. Ross, N. Pearce

The Showing at Roberta's
Sales No. 27 "On the Beach: B. Williams. "*Sales No. 28* "On the Avenue: S. Bynum. "*Sales No. 29* "Radiant"(Suitable for Easter): P. Fish. *Sales No. 30* "The Kick-Off" (Cocktail Dress): C. Waring. *Sales No. 31* "A Day in the Country": J. Roberts. *Sales No. 33* "Innocence Abroad: S. Walters. "*Sales No. 34* "Chartreuse Green": E. Johnson. *Sales No. 35* "Glamour": D. Atkins. *Sales No. 36* "And So To Bed": L. Lamonte. *Sales No. 37* "Seventh Heaven": T. Sanina. *Sales No. 38* "Devastating": N. Pearce. *Sales No. 39* Group "Shadows of Silver": F. Chumbecos, P. Cameron, C. Laughlin, R. Fisher, B. Adams, R. Gale, J. Roberts. *Preview* "The Bride's Soliloquy": *The Bride*: L. Roberti. *The Bridesmaids*: C. Renwick, D. Lane, A. Conkey, N. Butler, R. Trego, E. Monte, E. Behrens, V. Whitmore. *The Pages*: R. Shaw, B. Hallow.

"I'll Be Hard to Handle"
L. Roberti
(*Lyrics by* Bernard Dougall.)

Finaletto

ACT 2

"Hot Spot" (Scena)
L. Roberti, G. Murphy, M. Walsh, B. Christine, N. Pearce

"Smoke Gets in Your Eyes" (Proverb)
Tamara

"Let's Begin" (Reminiscence) (reprise)
B. Hope, Tamara

Dance Finaletto
G. Murphy, H. Gray

"Something's Got to Happen" (Duettino) (reprise)
L. Roberti, R. Middleton

"Let's Begin" (Scena) (reprise)
B. Hope, R. Middleton, L. Roberti, S. Greenstreet

Roberta Employees' Entertainment:

Sewing Department Dance
Girls, Boys

"Don't Ask Me Not to Sing" (Travesty)
 B. Hope, California Collegians
 Bing Crosby: N. Wood. *Ruth Etting*: H. Montei. *Ethel Merman*: L. Wood. *Rudy Vallee*: F. MacMurray. *Morton Downey*: A. Jones. *Arthur Tracy, the Street Singer*: R. Adams. *Helen Morgan*: R. Du Plessis.

"The Touch of Your hand" (Scene and Duet) (reprise)
 Natcha, the Peasant Girl: Tamara. *Volodya*, the Officer: W. Hain.

Finaletto
 Dressing Stephanie (Scena)
 Tamara, N. Pearce, M. Ross, M. Walsh

Scene Music
 G. Djimos

Entrance of Clementina Schwarenka
 "I'll Be Hard to Handle" (Impromptu)
 (L. Roberti)

Entrance of Stephanie

Finale
 (Entire Company)

LEW LESLIE'S BLACKBIRDS

1933.27 (1933-1934 EDITION)

A Musical Revue in Two Acts, 22 Scenes[23]. Book (sketches) by Nat N. Dorfman, Mann Holiner, Lew Leslie. Lyrics by Mann Holiner, Ned Washington, Joe Young. Music by Alberta Nichols, Victor Young. Entire show conceived and staged by Lew Leslie. Dances by Al Richard. Settings by Mabel A. Buell. Costumes by Charles LeMaire. Music director, Ken Macomber. Orchestrations, Ken Macomber, Ferde Grofé, Will Vodery, Joseph Jordan. Produced by Sepia Guild Players, Inc. Opened 2 December 1933 at the Apollo Theatre, closing 16-24 December 1933 for revisions[24], re-opened 25 December 1933 and closed 30 December 1933 after 25 performances.

CAST: BILL ROBINSON, JOHN MASON, EDITH WILSON, EDDIE HUNTER, (John) WORTHY & (Eddie) THOMPSON, KATHRYN PERRY, SPEEDY SMITH, SLAPPY WALLACE, BRADY JACKSON, BLUE McALLISTER, JAMES THOMAS BOXWILL, LIONEL MONAGAS, HENRY WILLIAMS, MARY MATHEWS, CECIL MACK'S CHOIR, PIKE DAVIS' CONTINENTAL ORCHESTRA, Gretchen Branche, Louise Madison, Phil Scott, Al Richard, Eloise Uggams, Toni Ellis, Martha Thomas, James Skelton, Musa Williams, Duncan Sisters[25] (Ina, Laura).

Blackbirds Beauties: Toni Ellis, Baby Simmons, Evelyn Sheppard, Gertrude Williams, Louise Patterson, Deanie Gordon, Emma Smith, Inez Persaud, Thelma Williams, Muriel Cook, Maudine Simmons, Clarice Cook, Ronetta Hutchens, Lillian Roberts, Dorothy Saunders, Kathryn Evans. *Show Girls*: Inez Gray, Josephine Grier, Judy Sunshine, Cynthia Richardson, Viola Paradees, Alberta Castor. *Cecil Mack's Choir*: Frank Jackson, Alonzo Bosan, James Skelton, W. E. Allen, Abner Dorsay, David Collins, Earl L. Sydnor, James Armstrong, Clarence Lenton, David Bethe, Eloise Uggams, Jessie Zachary, Anna Bell Ross, Ina Duncan, Laura Duncan, Musa Williams, Waldine Williams, Edythe Sewell.

ACT 1

Scene 1

 "Prologue"
 (*Music by* Alberta Nichols. *Lyrics by* Mann Holiner.)

 First Episode: A Street in Harlem.
 Policeman: J. Skelton. *Man*: L. Monagas.

 Second Episode: A Harlem Flat.
 Woman: E. Wilson. *Man*: E. Hunter.

 Third Episode: Another Harlem Flat.
 Woman: M. Williams. *Man*: J. Mason. *Child*: M. Thomas.

 Fourth Episode: An Audition Back Stage.
 Stage Director: L. Monagas. *Dancers*: Worthy & Thompson.
 Comics: J. Mason, S. Smith. *Singers*: K. Perry, G. Branche.
 Cecil Mack's Choir, Chorus.

Scene 2

 "Great Gettin' Up Mornin'"
 J. T. Boxwill, Cecil Mack's Choir

Scene 3

 "I'm Walkin' the Chalk Line"
 H. Williams, M. Mathews, Chorus, B. Jackson
 (*Music by* Alberta Nichols. *Lyrics by* Mann Holiner.)

Scene 4

 What Price Accident?[26] (*by* Charles Sherman)
 Jasper: S. Smith. *Luther*: J. Mason. *Doctor*: E. Hunter. *Nurse*: M. Mathews.
 Attendants: J. Skelton, E. Sydnor. *Patients*: W. E. Allen, A. Dorsay, A. Bosan.

Scene 5

 "I Just Couldn't Take It, Baby"
 G. Branche, P. Scott
 (*Music by* Alberta Nichols. *Lyrics by* Mann Holiner.)

 Reprise
 K. Perry, Duncan Sisters, E. Uggams

Scene 6

 Harlem Bridge (*by* Nat N. Dorfman)
 Jasper: J. Mason. *Romeo*: S. Smith. *Alabama*: E. Hunter. *Rufus*: L. Monagas.
 Bill: B. McAllister.

Scene 7

 "Your Mother's Son-in-Law"
 J. Mason, E. Wilson, T. Ellis, M. Thomas, Chorus, Worthy & Thompson
 (*Music by* Alberta Nichols. *Lyrics by* Mann Holiner.)

Scene 8

 Design for Harlem[27] (*by* Nat N. Dorfman with apologies to Noël Coward)
 Hannah: E. Wilson. *Steve*: J. Mason. *Caesar*: E. Hunter. *Henry*: S. Smith.

Scene 9

 "Tappin' the Barrel"
 M. Mathews
 (*Music by* Victor Young. *Lyrics by* Joseph Young and Ned Washington.)

 Reprise
 Chorus, L. Madison, Worthy & Thompson

Scene 10

 Emperor Bones[28] (*Musical Score arranged by* Ferde Grofé.)
 (*Prologue by* Mann Holiner with apologies to Eugene O'Neill.)
 Casper: E. Hunter. *Luke*: L. Monagas. *Sam*: J. Skelton. *Emperor Bones*: J. Mason. *Voodoo Sorceress*: E. Wilson. *Witch Doctor*: H. Williams.

 "Victim of the Voodoo Drums"
 E. Wilson, Cecil Mack's Choir, Chorus, H. Williams
 (*Music by* Victor Young. *Lyrics by* Joseph Young and Ned Washington.)

 "Voodoo Pageant"
 Entire Company
 (*Music by* Victor Young.)

ACT 2[29]

Scene 1

 "Mikado in Harlem" (With apologies to Gilbert & Sullivan)
 (*Adaptation by* Mann Holiner and Alberta Nichols. *Musical score arranged by* Will Vodery.)
 Nanki Poo: H. Williams. *Pish Tush*: L. Monagas. *Ko Ko*: E. Hunter. *Pooh Bah*: S. Smith. *Yum Yum*: K. Perry. *Pitti Sing*: G. Branche. *Peep Bo*: E. Uggams. *Katisha*: M. Williams. *The Mikado*: J. Mason. *Gentlemen and Ladies of Japan, Maids from School, Noblemen and Noblewomen*: (Chorus, Choir.)

 "Gentlemen of Japan"
 Cecil Mack's Male Choir

 "Minstrel Man"
 H. Williams, Cecil Mack's Male Octette

 "Three Little Maids from School"
 K. Perry, G. Branche, E. Uggams, Cecil Mack's Female Choir

 "Ensemble"
 Entire Company

---

[23]The third (on Broadway) in the series of black musical revues presented by Lew Leslie beginning in 1928.
[24]Revisions: New Act 2 Finale, 2 new sketches, Bill Robinson departed cast.
[25]Not to be confused with the Duncan Sisters (Rosetta, Vivian).

---

[26]Dropped after opening.
[27]Burlesque of 'Design for Living' by Noël Coward.
[28]Burlesque of 'The Emperor Jones' by Eugene O'Neill.
[29]Added during run to Act 2:
 "St. James Infirmary"
 K. Perry, Cecil Mack Choir
 (*Music and Lyrics by* Joe Primrose.)

Scene 2

"Doin' the Shim Sham"
B. Robinson, M. Thomas, Chorus
(*Music by* Alberta Nichols. *Lyrics by* Mann Holiner.)

Scene 3

On the Spot (*by* Nat. N. Dorfman)
Steve: S. Smith. *Rastus*: E. Hunter. *Jones*: L. Monagas. *One-Up*: J. Worthy. *Jack*: J. Skelton. *Girls*: I. Gray, J. Grier. *Jim Bradley*: Too Sweet.

Scene 4

"A Hundred Years From Today"
K. Perry
(*Music by* Victor Young. *Lyrics by* Joseph Young and Ned Washington.)

Scene 5

Maedchen Without Uniform (*by* Nat N. Dorfman)
Teacher: E. Wilson. *Olivia*: D. Gordon. *Eliza*: I. Persaud. *Pupils*: Chorus.

Scene 6

"Pullman Porters on Parade" (Dance)
S. Wallace, E. Thompson, J. Worthy

Scene 7

"Let Me Be Born Again"
J. T. Boxwill, Cecil Mack's Choir
(*Music by* Victor Young. *Lyrics by* Joseph Young and Ned Washington.)

Scene 8

"Concentrate a Little on Love"
E. Wilson, B. McAlister
(*Music by* Alberta Nichols. *Lyrics by* Mann Holiner.)

Scene 9

Bill Robinson and His Shadow

Scene 10

"What—No Dixie?"
K. Perry, Cecil Mack's Choir, Chorus
(*Music by* Victor Young. *Lyrics by* Joseph Young and Ned Washington.)

Scene 11

No Dinner at Eight[30] (*by* Nat N. Dorfman with apologies to Metro-Goldwyn-Mayer)
Mrs. Peabody: M. Williams. *Rufus Peabody*: S. Smith. *Eliza Brown*: E. Wilson. *Pete Jackson*: J. Mason. *Cynthia Jackson*: T. Ellis. *Dr. Johnson*: L. Monagas. *Mark Fable*: E. Hunter. *Edith Peabody*: M. Mathews. *Mose Pearce*: P. Scott.

Scene 12

Finale
Entire Company

ZIEGFELD FOLLIES
OF 1933-1934

1934.01

A Musical Revue in Two Acts, 29 Scenes[31]. (Sketches by H. I. Phillips, Fred Allen, Harry Turgend, David Freedman.) Lyrics by E. Y. Harburg, (Ballard Macdonald, Billy Rose, Billy Hill, Edward Heyman.) Music by Vernon Duke, Samuel Pokrass, (Joseph Meyer, Richard Myers, Dana Suesse, Peter DeRose, Billy Hill, James F. Hanley.) Staged by Bobby Connolly. Production lighted and additional numbers staged by John Murray Anderson. Dialogue staged by Edward Clarke Lilley. Additional dances staged by Robert Alton. Settings by Watson Barratt, Albert Johnson. Costumes by Russell Patterson, Raoul (Pène) du Bois, Charles LeMaire, Kiviette. Music director, John McManus. Produced by Mrs. Florence Ziegfeld [Billie Burke] (and the Messrs. Shubert). Opened 4 January 1934 at the Winter Garden and closed 9 June 1934 after 182 performances.

CAST: FANNIE BRICE, WILLIE HOWARD, EUGENE HOWARD, EVERETT MARSHALL, JANE FROMAN, VILMA EBSEN, BUDDY EBSEN, PATRICIA BOWMAN, DON ROSS, Oliver Wakefield, Cherry Preisser, June Preisser, Vivian Janis, Eve Arden, Betzi Beaton, Victor Morley, Brice Hutchins [Robert Cummings], Judith Barron, Ina Ray (Hutton), Loretta Dennison, John Adair, Jacques Cartier, The Vikings, Fred Mannat, James Kitson.

The "Follies" Girls: Dorothy Buckley, Hope Dare, Edith Roark, Marian Santre, Marie Stevens, Gladine Sweetser, Ethel Thorsen, Florence Mallee, Ruth Reiter, (Betty Worth). *Model Guild Girls*: Carolyn Ryan, Louene Ambrosius, Helen Frederic, Charlotte Mann, Leone Susa, Bobbie Miller. *Dancers*: Joanne Allen, Virginia Allen, Peggy Ann, Marjorie Baglin, Mary Bay, Helen Bennett, Hazel Bofinger, Mildred Borst, Mary Ellen Brown, Joanne Cannon, Jean Carson, Maxine Darrell, Dorothy Daly, Lonita Foster, Marjorie Gayle, Gloria Glennon, Julia Gorman, Helen Hannon, Pearl Harris, Irene Hamlin, Juliet Jenner, Glyse Keating, Evelyn Laurie, Pamela McAvoy, Frances McHugh, Jane Moxin, Evelyn Nielson, Evelyn Nichols, Thora Roberts, Edwina Steele, Maria Steele, Jean Stuart, Mildred Webb, Gloria Cook. *Gentlemen*: Herman Belmonte, Al Bloom, Joseph Carey, Jack Coogan, Frank Ericson, Clark Leston, Dinty Moore, Jack Ross, Sid Salzer, Gil White. *Sara Mildred Strauss Dancers*: Marguerite White, Susanne Remos, Anna Bell Green, Ruth Saks, Dorothy MacKinnon, Lucile Stuart, Eva Desca, Rose Lipton, Lillian Mann, Naomi Leaf, Sara Mazo, Vicki Michak, Camilla Masters, Mary Bolles, Sunya Shurman, Adlynn Swan.

ACT 1[32]

Scene 1

Opening: "That's Where We Come In"
J. Barron, Ensemble
(*Music by* Samuel Pokrass. *Lyrics by* E. Y. Harburg.)

Reprise
B. Beaton, H. Dare, M. Santre, M. Stevens, H. Frederic, C. Mann, L. Sousa, L. Ambrosius, C. Ryan, B. Miller, E. Thorsen

Scene 2

All Quiet in Havana (*by* H. I. Phillips)
Gonzales Machado: W. Howard. *Night Club Hostess*: E. Arden. *An Entertainer*: J. Barron. *President's Courier*: J. Adair. *A Guest*: R. Reiter. *Another Guest*: L. Dennison. *Revolutionist*: F. Mannat. *The Bridge Players*: V. Morley, E. Arden, J. Kitson, G. Sweetser. *Two Tourists*: B. Worth, E. Roark.

Scene 3

"Soul Saving Sadie"
F. Brice
(*Music by* Joseph Meyer. *Lyrics by* Billy Rose and Ballard Macdonald.)

Scene 4

"Water Under the Bridge"
E. Marshall
(*Music by* Vernon Duke. *Lyrics by* E. Y. Harburg.)
Danced by P. Bowman, Sara Mildred Strauss Dancers.

Scene 5

"I Like the Likes of You"
B. Hutchins, J. Barron
(*Music by* Vernon Duke. *Lyrics by* E. Y. Harburg.)
Danced by V. Ebsen, B. Ebsen, Ensemble.

Scene 6

Barnyard Theatre, Inc. (*by* Fred Allen and Hary Tugend)
Manager: W. Howard. *Constable*: B. Ebsen. *Phoebe Colt*: E. Arden. *A Gentleman*: J. Adair. *A Lady*: L. Dennison. *Meyer Lonsdale*: V. Morley. *Rennie*: O. Wakefield. *Julia*: F. Brice. Ladies and Gentlemen of the Audience.

Scene 7

"Ivory and Old Gold" (Dance)
C. Preisser, J. Preisser

Scene 8

"Suddenly"
J. Froman, E. Marshall
(*Music by* Vernon Duke. *Lyrics by* E. Y. Harburg and Billy Rose.)
The Little Women: J. Froman, P. Bowman, I. Ray, J. Barron. *The Suitors*: B. Hutchins, D. Ross. *The Chaperone*: B. Beaton. *The Beaux*: The Vikings.

---

[30]Burlesque of George S. Kaufman and Edna Ferber's 'Dinner at Eight' and its film adaptation.
[31]The twenty-second in the series of annual musical revues beginning in 1907; this was the first edition produced after Ziegfeld's death (1933).

[32]Added during run:
"You Oughta Be in Pictures" (from the film *New York Town*)
J. Froman
(*Music by* Dana Suesse. *Lyrics by* Edward Heyman.)
"The House Is Haunted"
Josephine Houston
(*Music and Lyrics by* Billy Rose and Basil Adlam.)
Added for tour:
"Why Am I Blue?"
Neila Goodelle
(*Music and Lyrics by* Billy Hill and Peter DeRose.)

Scene 9

Mr. Oliver Wakefield

Scene 10

"The Follies Choral Ensemble"
(*Music by* Samuel Pokrass. *Lyrics by* E. Y. Harburg.)
Soloists: W. Howard, E. Howard.

Scene 11

Fifth Avenue: "A Sidewalk in Paris"
B. Hutchins, J. Barron
(*Music by* Samuel Pokrass. *Lyrics by* E. Y. Harburg.)
Bus Conductor: F. Mannat.

(a) Greenwich Village
The Painter: J. Cartier. *Art Critics, Poets, Communists, The Short-Haired Women, The Long-Haired Men, The Figures Within the Frame:* Sara Mildred Strauss Dancers.

(b) Forty-Second Street
The Traffic Cop: J. Coogan. *The Stenographers:* C. Preisser, J. Preisser.

(c) Fifth-Ninth Street
The Dowagers: R. Reiter, D. Buckley, F. Malley. *Elizabeth Arden:* M. Santre. *Dorothy Grey:* L. Dennison. *Helena Rubinstein:* M. Stevens. *The Debutante:* P. Bowman. *The Man About Town:* J. Cartier.

(d) Harlem
V. Ebsen, B. Ebsen, I. Ray.

Scene 12

"Before the Black Cire Curtain"
B. Beaton, Follies Girls

Scene 13

Baby Snooks (*by* David Freedman)
Father: V. Morley. *Mother:* E. Arden. *Baby Snooks:* F. Brice.

Scene 14

"Moon About Town"
J. Froman
(*Music by* Dana Suesse. *Lyrics by* E. Y. Harburg.)

Scene 15

Reviewing Stand (*by* H. I. Phillips)
The Mayor: W. Howard. *A Military Man:* V. Morley. *The Secretary:* E. Howard. *A Politician:* J. Carey.

Scene 16

"Countess Dubinsky"
F. Brice
(*Music by* Joseph Meyer. *Lyrics by* Billy Rose and Ballard Macdonald.)

Scene 17

"To the Beat of the Heart"
E. Marshall
(*Music by* Samuel Pokrass. *Lyrics by* E. Y. Harburg.)
Standard Bearer: J. Cartier. Sara Mildred Strauss Dancers, Entire Ensemble.

ACT 2

Scene 1

Street Scene: "What Is There to Say?"
(*Music by* Vernon Duke. *Lyrics by* E. Y. Harburg.)
The Bride: J. Froman. *The Groom:* E. Marshall. *Ushers:* The Vikings.

Scene 2

"The Last Round-Up"
D. Ross
(*Music and Lyrics by* Billy Hill.)
The Hill Billies: W. Howard, E. Howard, J. Kitson.

Scene 3

"Careful With My Heart"[33]
E. Marshall
(*Music by* Samuel Pokrass. *Lyrics by* E. Y. Harburg.)
The Ballerina: P. Bowman. Sara Mildred Straus Dancers.
(*Ballet Music by* Samuel Pokrass.)

Scene 4

Beatzi Beaton and the Follies Girls

Scene 5

Sailor, Behave![34] (*by* David Freedman)
Rosie: V. Janis. *Annie:* F. Brice. *Moe:* W. Howard.

Scene 6

"Green Eyes"
J. Froman
(*Music by* Robert (Emmett) Dolan. *Lyrics by* E. Y. Harburg.)

Scene 7

The Maxixe (Dance)
V. Ebsen, B. Ebsen

Scene 8

"Wagon Wheels"
E. Marshall
(*Music by* Peter De Rose. *Lyrics by* Billy Hill.)

Scene 9

The Man Who Came Back (*by* David Freedman)
Rubinoff: W. Howard. *The Wife:* E. Arden. *First Son:* C. Leston. *Second Son:* J. Kitson. *Third Son:* B. Hutchins. *Fourth Son:* B. Ebsen. *Natasha:* B. Worth.

Scene 10

"This Is Not a Song"
V. Janis
(*Music and Lyrics by* Vernon Duke, E. Hartman and E. Y. Harburg.)
Danced by I. Ray, V. Ebsen, B. Ebsen.

Scene 11

"Sarah, the Sunshine Girl"
F. Brice
(*Music by* Joseph Meyer. *Lyrics by* Billy Rose and Ballard Macdonald.)

Scene 12

Finale: "Time Is a Gypsy"[35]
E. Marshall, Entire Company
(*Music by* Richard Meyers. *Lyrics by* E. Y. Harburg.)

THE PICCOLI OF VITTORIO PODRECCA

1934.02

A Return Engagement of the Marionette Revue in Three Acts[36]. (Conceived and directed by Vittorio Podrecca.) Orchestra and singers under the direction of Angelo Canarutto. Settings designed by Bruno Angoletta. Costumes designed by Caramba. Opened 8 January 1934 at the Hudson Theatre, moved 22 January 1934 to the Ambassador Theatre, and closed 4 February 1934 after 45 performances.[37]

CAST: *Principal Singers:* Thea Carugati (soprano), Lia Podrecca (light soprano), Giuseppe Costa (tenor), Mario Serangeli (baritone), Augusto Galli (basso), Dario Zani (baritone), Wilfred Smith (tenor), Rosina Zotti (soprano). (Cissie Rosi, Gina Palazzo, Nino Galli, Nino Smith.)
Manipulators and Operators: The families of Gorno, Dell' Acqua, Possidoni, Forgioli, Borgogni, Donati, Braga. *Pianist:* Aron Pressman.

ACT 1

Prologue:
V. Podrecca.

Scene 1

Seraphine—Equilibrist on the Ball

Scene 2

Little Tropical Revue
(a) In the Manner of Josephine Baker (*sung by* L. Podrecca)
(b) Sisters
(c) Finale

---

[33]Dropped during run.

[34]Burlesque of the play 'Sailor, Beware!' by Kenyon Nicholson and Charles Robinson.
[35]Dropped during run.
[36]First presented 22 December 1932 at the Lyric Theatre for 141 performances. An earlier edition was presented on Broadway as THE MARIONETTE PLAYERS, 10 September 1923 at the Fulton Theatre for 16 performances.
[37]No producer credited.

Scene 3

The Man on the Flying Trapeze

Scene 4

Fantasy

Scene 5

Marta—Aria of tenor music by Flotow

Scene 6

Divertissement de Ballet

Scene 7

La Corrida—The Bullfight
(a) Patio, *sung by* I. Zappata.
(b) Arena.

ACT 2 (evenings)

Selection of the Opera "Don Juan" (Don Giovanni)
Libretto by L. La Ponte. *Music by* W. A. Mozart.
Don Giovanni: D. Zani. *Leporello*: M. Serangeli. *Don Ottavio*: G. Costa. *Don Pedro*: A. Galli. *Donna Anna*: R. Zotti. *Donna Elvira*: T. Carugati. *Zerlina*: L. Podrecca. *Masetto*: N. Smith. Peasants, Servants, etc.
The Opera is laid in Spain in the middle of the seventeenth century.
Scene 1: A Duel. *Scene 2*: The Fete of Masetto and Zerlina. *Scene 3*: Minuette. *Scene 4*: A Serenade. *Scene 5*: The Statue of the Commander. *Scene 6*: The Invited Statue. *Scene 7*: The Punishment.

ACT 2 (matinees)

The Sleeping Beauty (Three Acts, 7 Scenes)
by Gian Bistolfi, with music by Ottorino Respighi specially written for the Teatro dei Piccoli.

CAST: *The King*: M. Serangeli. *The Queen*: R. Zotti. *The Princess*: T. Carugati. *Prince Charming*: G. Costa. *The Blue Fairy*: L. Podrecca. *The Green Fairy*: C. Rosi. *The Old Spinner*: G. Palazzo. *The Jester*: N. Galli. *The Ambassador*: D. Zani. *Nightingale, Cuckoo, Good Fairies, The Roses, Torches, Spiders, Dignitaries and Ladies of the Court.*

Act1: Nocturne; Invitation to the Fairies; Baptism of the Princess; Vengeance of the Green Fairy; The Blessing of the Stars. 1620.

Act 2: The Old Spinner; The Enchantment. 1640.

Act 3: Three hundred years afterward.

ACT 3

Scene 1

Old Vienna:
(a) Beer and Wine.
(b) Song of Spring.
(c) Waltz.

Scene 2

Miss Legnetti, songs

Scene 3

Betty Boop and the Big Bad Wolf

Scene 4

Bil Bal Bul, the Little Acrobat

Scene 5

The Learned Donkey

Scene 6

Concert Party

1934.03   COME OF AGE

A Play in Music and Words in Three Acts, 6 Scenes. Play (and lyrics) by Clemence Dane. Music by Richard Addinsell. Staged by Clemence Dane. Settings by James Reynolds. Musical director, Macklin Marrow. Produced by Delos Chappell. Opened 12 January 1934 at the Maxine Elliott Theatre and closed 10 February 1934 after 35 performances.

CAST (in order of appearance): *A Boy*: STEPHEN HAGGARD. *A Shadow of Death*: FREDERICK G. LEWIS. *A Woman*: JUDITH ANDERSON. *Man*: JOHN W. AUSTIN. *Friends of the Woman*: Edna James, Clara Palmer, Dorothy Johnson, Mabel Gore, Virginia Volland, Katherine Tracey, Helen Wills, Alice Swanson, Malcolm Soltan, Jeremy Bowman, Judd Carrel, Harold Webster, Wheeler Dryden, Ralph

Stuart. *Singer for the Woman*: Dorothy Johnson. *River Music*: Helen Wills. *Singer for the Boy*: Ralph Stuart. *An Entertainer*: Muriel Rahn. *Pianists*: Morton Gould, Bert Shefter.

Act 1, Scene 1: A summer evening, 1770. London. *Scene 2*: A summer evening, the present day.

Act 2, Scene 1: A summer morning, a few days later. *Scene 2*: The same evening before sunset.

Act 3, Scene 1: The same evening at sunset. *Scene 2*: The same evening after sunset.

ACT 1[38]

Scene 1

"The River Song"
S. Haggard, H. Wills

Scene 2

"The River Song" (reprise)
H. Wills

"I Come Out of a Dream"
S. Haggard

"I Cam to Your Room"
D. Johnson

"The Golden Peri-banou"
S. Haggard

ACT 2

Scene 1

"I Come Out of a Dream" (reprise)
S. Haggard

Scene 2

"Too Much Work"
M. Rahn

"I'm Afraid of the Dark"
M. Rahn

ACT 3

Scene 1

"I'm Afraid of the Dark" (reprise)
Recorded Voice

"The River Song" (reprise)
H. Wills

Scene 2

"The River Song" (reprise)
H. Wills

1934.04   ALL THE KING'S HORSES

A Romantic Musical in Two Acts, 7 Scenes. Book and lyrics by Frederick Herendeen. Based on the play "Carlo Rocco" by Lawrence Clarke and Max Giersberg. Music by Edward A. Horan. Staged by José Ruben. Dances by Theodor Adolphus. Settings by Herbert Ward & Harvey. Costumes by John Booth, Jr. Music director, Oscar Bradley. Orchestrations by (Robert) Russell Bennett, Hans Spialek. Produced by Harry L. Cort and Charles Abramson by arrangement with E. Steuart-Tavant. Opened 30 January 1934 at the Sam S. Shubert Theatre, moved 19 February 1934 to the Imperial Theatre, and closed 12 May 1934 after 120 performances.

CAST (in order of appearance): *Kessel, the Royal Barber*: Robert O'Connor. *Albert, His Assistant*: Arthur F. Otto. *A Patron*: Manart Kippen. *Loli, Another Assistant*: Frances Thress. *Baron Koritz*: FRANK GREENE. *King Rudolph of Langenstein*: JACK EDWARDS. *Con Conley*: ANDREW TOMBES. *Donald McArthur*: GUY ROBERTSON. *Sherry Shannon*: DORIS PATSTON. *Joseph*: Louis Morrell. *Count Ergard Regitard Betthy*: RUSSELL HICKS. *Countess Putkammer*: BETTY STARBUCK. *Queen Erna of Langenstein*: NANCY McCORD. *A Mother*: Edna West. *A Father*: Howard Morgan. *A Spinster*: Blanche Lytell.
Ladies in Waiting: Doris Anderson, Helen Ryan, Virginia Davies, Etna Ross, Getrude Hogan, June Tempest, Joan Orner, Frances Thress, Naida Pahl, Mora

---

[38]Musical Numbers do not appear in the program, but are taken from the published playscript.

Vordkin, Winnie Duncan, Dorothy Koster. *Peasants from the Southern Province*: Frank Augustyn, Einar Holt, Leonard Rogall, Harold Freeman.

Act 1, Scene 1: Andre Kessel's Barber Shop in the little European kingdom of Langenstein. *Scene 2*: In front of the Palace. *Scene 3*: A Room in the King's Quarters. Several days later. *Scene 4*: The Royal Bed Chamber.

Act 2, Scene 1: The Morning Room in the Palace. Next morning. *Scene 2*: In front of the Palace. *Scene 3*: The Royal Gardens.

ACT 1

"Fame Is a Phoney"[39]
G. Robertson, A. Tombes

"Tamboree"
D. Patston, G. Robertson, A. Tombes, Girls

"The Hair of the Heir"
F. Thress, Girls

"You're Asking Me"[40]
D. Patston, F. Greene

"Evening Star"
N. McCord

"I Found a Song"
G. Robertson, N. McCord

"I Found a Song" (reprise)
G. Robertson, N. McCord

ACT 2[41]

"Langenstein in the Spring"
Girls

"Charming"
G. Robertson, N. McCord

"Nuts Over You"
A. Tombes, B. Starbuck

"I Found a Song" (reprise)[42]
G. Robertson, N. McCord

"Mamazelle Papazelle"
A. Tombes, B. Starbuck

Ballet
Girls

"Romance Is Calling"
G. Robertson, N. McCord

1934.05 **4 SAINTS IN 3 ACTS**

An Opera in Four Acts and a Prelude. Words by Gertrude Stein. Music by Virgil Thomson. Scenario by Maurice Grosser. Production (directed) by John Houseman. Choreography by Frederick Ashton. Settings and costumes designed by Florine Stettheimer and Kate Drain Lawson. Lighting by (Abe) Feder. Music director, Alexander Smallens. Choral director, Eva Jessye. Produced by Harry Moses (in association with the Friends and Enemies of Modern Music). Opened 20 February 1934 at the 44th Street Theatre, closing 17 March 1934 after 32 performances; re-opened 2 April 1934 at the Empire Theatre, and closed 14 April 1934 after an additional 16 performances. Total: 48 performances[43].

CAST: *St. Ignatius*: EDWARD MATTHEWS. *St. Theresa I*: BEATRICE ROBINSON WAYNE. *St. Theresa II*: BRUCE HOWARD. *Commere*: ALTONELL HINES. *Compere*: ABNER DORSEY. *St. Chavez*: Leonard Franklyn. *St. Settlement*: Bertha Fitzhugh Baker. *St. Plan*: Randolph Robinson. *St. Stephen*: David Bethe. *St. Cecilia*: Kitty Mason. *St. Giuseppe*: Thomas Anderson. *St. Anselmo*: Charles Spinnard. *St. Sara*: Marguerite Perry. *St. Bernadine*: Flossie Roberts. *St. Absalom*: Edward Batten. *St. Answers*: Florence Hester. *St. Eustace*: George Timber.

Male Saints: William Holland, Cecil Murray, William O'Neill, Paul Smellie,

---

[39]Dropped during run.
[40]Dropped during run.
[41]Added to Act 2 during the run:
"Ouch"
A. Tombes, B. Starbuck
[42]Dropped during run.
[43]Performed as an opera with no individual musical numbers listed.

Andrew Taylor, Lee Jenkins, Harold Slappy, Thomas Bolden, Albert Moss, Benjamin Parks. *Female Saints*: Charlotte Alford, Dorothy Bronson, Josephine Gray, Lena Halsey, Sadie McGill, Assotta Marshall, Olga Maillard, Cordelia Patterson, Jessie Swan, Eva Vaughn, Alma Dickson, Helen Dorody Moore. *Dancers*: Card Lynn Baker, Elizabeth Dickerson, Mable Hart, Floyd Miller, Maxwell Baird, Billie Smith.

Prelude: A Narrative of Prepare for Saints

Act 1: Avila: St. Theresa half indoors and half out of doors

Act 2: Might It be Mountains if it were not Barcelona

Act 3: Barcelona: St. Igantius and One of Two Literally

Act 4: The Saints and Sinners reassembled and reenacting why they went away to stay.

1934.06 **NEW FACES (OF 1934)**

A Musical Revue in Two Acts, 41 Scenes[44]. Conceived by Leonard Sillman. Sketches by Viola Brothers Shore, Nancy Hamilton, (Newman Levy, John Goodwin, William Griffith, Mindret Lord, Jeannie MacPherson, Carl Randall, Beth Wendel). Lyrics by Nancy Hamilton, June Sillman [June Carroll], (Everett Marcy, Viola Brothers Shore, J.J. Robbins, E. Y. Harburg, Robert Sour, John Goodwin, George Hickman, Harold Goodman, James Shelton, Haven Johnson). Music by Warburton Guilbert, Donald Honrath, Martha Caples, James Shelton, Morgan Lewis, (Haven Johnson, Sandro Corona, George Grande, Cliff Allen, George Hickman, Charles Schwab, Walter Feldkamp). Directed by Leonard Sillman. Production supervised by Elsie Janis. Settings and costumes by Sergei Soudeikine. Music director, Gene Salzer. Orchestrations by Hans Spialek. Produced by Charles B. Dillingham. Opened 15 March 1934 at the Fulton Theatre and closed 21 July 1934 after 149 performances.

CAST: LEONARD SILLMAN, IMOGENE COCA, NANCY HAMILTON, LOUISE [Teddy] LYNCH, HILDEGARDE HALLIDAY, DOROTHY KENNEDY FOX, FRANCES DEWEY, BILLIE HAYWOOD, CLIFF ALLEN, CHARLES WALTER, JAMES SHELTON, ROGER STEARNS, O.Z. WHITEHEAD, HENRY FONDA, EDITH SHERIDAN, MILDRED TODD, ALLEN HANDLEY, GORDON ORME, MELVIN PARKS, DOLORES HART, HELEN O'HARA, GUSTAVE [Gus] SCHIRMER, Kenneth Bates, Jean Briggs, Peggy Hovenden, Edward Potter, Marvin Lawler, Jeanne Palmer, Harry Peterson, Reeder Boss, Reed McClelland, Beverly Phalon, Sandra Gould, Grace Gray, June McNulty, Moyne Rice.

ACT 1[45]

Scene 1

"New Faces"
J. Shelton, R. Stearns, Company
(*Music by* Martha Caples. *Lyrics by* Nancy Hamilton.)

Scene 2

Embarassing Moment
O.Z. Whitehead, H. O'Hara, G. Orme, H. Fonda

Scene 3

"Something You Lack"
(*Dialogue by* Viola Brothers Shore. *Music by* Warburton Guilbert. *Lyrics by* Nancy Hamilton and June Sillman.)
A Girl: I. Coca. A Sailor: C. Walter. A Tired Girl: H. Halliday. A Tired Boy: K. Bates.

Scene 4

Katharine Hepburn Gets in the Mood for "Little Women" (*by* Nancy Hamilton)
Katharine Hepburn: N. Hamilton. *Director*: K. Bates. *Cameraman*: G. Orme. *Stage Hands*: J. Shelton, R. Stearns, E. Potter. *Props*: H. O'Hara, J. McNulty, F. Dewey.

---

[44]The first in the series of revues (1934-1968) conceived by Leonard Sillman to introduce unknown talent.
[45]Added during NY run and for subsequent tour:
"Wedding Song"
T. Lynch
(*Music and Lyrics by* James Shelton.)
Lady With Hay Fever (by Hildegarde Halliday)
H. Halliday
Poetically Speaking (by O. Z. Whitehead and Viola Brothers Shore)
O. Z. Whitehead

Scene 5

Strange Interlude

H. Fonda, I. Coca, M. Lawler, A. Handley

Scene 6

"Visitors Ashore"

L. Lynch, M. Todd, G. Orme

(*Music by* Warburton Guilbert. *Lyrics by* Everett Marcy and Nancy Hamilton.)

Scene 7

Ferry Tale (*by* Newman Levy and Viola Brothers Shore)

Dockhand: H. Peterson. *A Girl*: F. Dewey. *Captain*: A. Handley. *Mate*: K. Bates. *Stewards*: E. Potter, C. Walter. *Cabin Boy*: G. Schirmer. *Detective*: R. Boss. *Passengers*: H. Halliday, E. Sheridan, S. Gould, R. Stearns, M. lawler, J. Shelton, M. Rice, B. Haywood, H. O'Hara, B. Phalon, J. McNulty.

Scene 8

"Lamplight"

J. Shelton

(*Music and Lyrics by* James Shelton.)

Illustrated by I. Coca, H. Fonda.

Scene 9

"The Byrd Influence"

(*Music by* Warburton Guilbert. *Lyrics by* June Sillman and Nancy Hamilton.)

Penguins: F. Dewey, R. McClelland, Ensemble.

Scene 10

An Afternoon with the English Juvenile Players (*by* Nancy Hamilton)

Introduced by K. Bates. *Aubrey*: N. Hamilton. *Cecily*: P. Hovenden. *Bertie*: E. Potter. *Cholmondley*: R. Stearns. *Butler*: A. Handley.

Scene 11

"Frustration"

(*Music by* Morgan Lewis. *Choreography by* Dorothy Kennedy Fox.)

Danced by D. K. Fox. *Introduced by* S. Gould, B. Phalon, G. Gray, I. Coca.

Scene 12

Laughter on the Air (*by* Viola Brothers Shore)

Mr. Arbuckle: L. Sillman. *Miss Chick and Mr. Dick*: F. Dewey, H. Fonda. *Mr. Sims*: R. Stearns. *Miss Pertwhistle*: M. Todd. *Radio Artists*: The Company.

Scene 13

"The Gangster Influence"

(*Music by* Warburton Guilbert. *Lyrics by* Viola Brothers Shore and June Sillman.)

The Girl: I. Coca. *The Boy*: C. Walter.

Scene 14

"Music in My Heart"

(*Music by* Warburton Guilbert. *Lyrics by* June Sillman.)

A Girl: E. Sheridan. *A Boy*: G. Orme. *Cupid and Psyche*: J. Shelton, P. Hovenden.

Scene 15

Important Question (*by* Nancy Hamilton)

N. Hamilton, O. Z. Whitehead

Scene 16

Brief Moment

H. Fonda, I. Coca, M. Lawler, A. Handley

Scene 17

"My Last Affair"

B. Haywood, C. Allen

(*Music and Lyrics by* Haven Johnson.)

Scene 18

We Also Recognize Russia

a. Double Bed (*by* John Goodwin and Viola Brothers Shore)

Played by P. Hovenden, E. Potter.

b. "The Village Gossip"

J. Palmer

(*Music by* Sandro Corona. *Lyrics by* J. J. Robins.)

Danced by L. Lynch, N. Hamilton, E. Sheridan, J. Shelton, K. Bates, A. Handley.

c. Mouse Trap (*by* William Griffith)

Ermingarde: H. Halliday. *Pythias*: O. Z. Whitehead. *Guard*: H. Fonda.

Scene 19

We Also Recognize Harlem

a. "Emperor Jones"

(*Music by* Donald Honrath and George Grande. *Lyrics by* June Sillman.)

Taxi Starter: L. Sillman.

b. The Coal Bin: "Smoky Rhythm"

L. Lynch, B. Haywood, Company

(*Music and Lyrics by* George Hickman.)

ACT 2

Scene 1

"Service With a Smile"

(*Music by* Warburton Guilbert. *Lyrics by* Viola Brothers Shore and June Sillman.)

Bartenders: A. Handley, H. Fonda, G. Orme, K. Bates, R. Stearns, H. Peterson, E. Potter. *Busboy*: M. Lawler.

Scene 2

"The Gutter Song"

J. Shelton

(*Music and Lyrics by* James Shelton.)

Scene 3

"You're My Relaxation"

(*Music by* Charles Schwab. *Lyrics by* Robert Sour.)

Girl and Boy: F. Dewey, G. Orme. *A Woman*: H. Halliday. *Her Relaxation*: A. Handley. *Quartette*: J. McNulty, G. Gray, R. Boss, M. Lawler.

Scene 4

Six Managers in Search of an Actress—As They Never Are

(*by* Nancy Hamilton. *Suggested by* Leonard Sillman.)

Miss Smith's Secretary: M. Todd. *Guthrie McClintic*: E. Potter. *Theatre Guild*: K. Bates. *Max Gordon*: H. Fonda. *Daniel Frohman*: R. Stearns. *Jed Harris*: L. Sillman. *Noël Coward*: J. Shelton. *Gertrude Lawrence*: I. Coca. *A Producer*: R. McClelland.

Scene 5

"Modern Madrigal"

E. Sheridan

(*Music by* Warburton Guilbert. *Lyrics by* Viola Brothers Shore and June Sillman.)

Troubadors: L. Lynch, J. Briggs, G. Orme, A. Handley.

Scene 6

Position in Life (*by* Mindret Lord)

Played by N. Hamilton, R. Stearns.

Scene 7

Bird in Hand

H. Fonda, I. Coca, M. Lawler, A. Handley

Scene 8

The Petroushka Influence: "Harlequinade"

(*Story by* Jeannie MacPherson. *Music by* Donald Honrath.)

Harlequin: L. Sillman. *Columbine*: B. Phalon. *Puppeteers*: K. Bates, H. Fonda.

Scene 9

The Disney Influence (*by* Nancy Hamilton)

Ermingarde: H. Halliday. *Pythias*: O. Z. Whitehead.

a. The Green Bay Tree

Julian: H. Fonda. *Dulcimer*: E. Potter. *Trump*: R. Stearns. *Leonora*: P. Hovenden.

b. Ah. Wilderness

Boy: G. Schirmer. *Girl*: F. Dewey.

c. Tobacco Road

Dude: J. Shelton. *Jeeter*: C. Walter. *Ellymae*: M. Rice. *Grandma*: H. O'Hara.

Scene 10

"Gloomy Heaven"

L. Lynch

(*Music by* Walter Feldkamp. *Lyrics by* Harold Goldman.)

Scene 11

"'Cause You Won't Play House"
I. Coca, C. Walter
(*Music by* Morgan Lewis. *Lyrics by* E. Y. Harburg and Nancy Hamilton.)
(*Dance staged by* Morgan Lewis.)

Scene 12

Chez De L'Eclair (*by* Beth Wendel and Viola Brothers Shore)
Customer: S. Gould. *Princess*: P. Hovenden. *Mrs. Finklebaum*:
E. Sheridan. *Madame de L'Eclaire*: J. Briggs. *Renee*: M. Todd. *Models*:
M. Rice, B. Phalon, L. Lynch.

Scene 13

Vaudeville Turn (*by* Carl Randall)
H. Halliday

Scene 14

"So Low"
L. Lynch, E. Sheridan, J. Briggs, Company
(*Music by* Donald Honrath. *Lyrics by* Nancy Hamilton and
June Sillman.)
Dancers: C. Walter, I. Coca, L. Sillman, D. K. Fox, J. Shelton,
R. Stearns.

Scene 15

Little Accident
H. Fonda

Scene 16

"People of Taste"
(*Dialogue and Lyrics by* Nancy Hamilton. *Music by* Martha Caples.)
a. 277 Park Avenue
R. Stearns
b. 45 E. 52nd
L. Lynch, J. Briggs
c. 253 W. 25th
E. Potter
d. 422 1/2 E. 30th
P. Hovenden, M. Rice
e. At Elsa Maxwell's
Company
Remarks by J. Briggs.

Scene 17

Three's a Crowd
I. Coca, H. Fonda, M. Lawler, A. Handley

Scene 18

"He Loves Me"
B. Haywood, Ensemble
(*Music by* Cliff Allen. *Lyrics by* Nancy Hamilton.)

Scene 19

Swing Song (*by* Viola Brothers Shore)
Collette: H. O'Hara. *Andre*: J. Shelton. *Raoul*: L. Sillman. *Louis*: R. Stearns.
Pierre: E. Potter. *Dr. Eisenblot*: H. Fonda.

Scene 20

"Spring Song"[46]
E. Sheridan
(*Music by* Warburton Guilbert. *Lyrics by* Viola Brothers Shore and
June Sillman.)

Scene 21

"On the Other Hand"
N. Hamilton
(*Music by* Martha Caples. *Lyrics by* Nancy Hamilton.)

Scene 22

"Look at Me, Please"[47]
R. Stearns, Company
(*Music and Lyrics by* James Shelton.)

---

[46]Later in the run credits were revised to read: *Music by* Martha Caples.
Lyrics by Nancy Hamilton.
[47]During run replaced by a reprise of "New Faces"
The Company

THE MIKADO,
1934.07   or The Town of Titipu

A Revival of the Comic Opera in Two Acts[48]. Libretto by William S. Gilbert.
Music by Arthur Sullivan. Staged by Lee Daly. Settings by Franklyn
Ambrose. Costumes by Eaves. Musical director, J. Albert Hurley. Produced
by S. M. Chartok. Opened 2 April 1933 at the Majestic Theatre and closed 7
April 1933 after 8 performances; re-opened 23-28 April 1934 at the Majestic
Theatre for 8 additional performances; re-opened 21-26 May 1934 at
the Majestic Theatre for 8 additional performances. Total this season: 24
performances.

CAST: *The Mikado of Japan*: WILLIAM DANFORTH. *Nanki-Poo*: ROY CROPPER.
Ko-Ko: JOHN CHERRY[49]. *Pooh-Bah*: HERBERT L. WATEROUS. *Pish-Tush*:
ALLEN WATEROUS. *Three Sisters, Wards of Ko-Ko*: *Yum-Yum*: HIZI KOYKE. *Pitti-
Sing*: VIVIAN HART. *Peep-Bo*: LAURA FERGUSON. *Katisha*: VERA ROSS.
Ladies of the Mikado's Suite: Caroline Cantlin, Doris Snyder, Charlotte LaRose,
Elizabeth Kerr, Olga Schumacher, Geraldine Olive. *The Mikado's Bodyguard*: John
Willard, Allen Ware, Lloyd Ericson, Thomas Greene. *Ensemble of School Girls,
Nobles, Guards and Coolies*: Frances Baviello, Margaret Walker, Olga Schumacher,
Celia Schiffrin, Elinore Gilmore, Barbara Martsin, Charlotte LaRose, Beatrice Pons,
Caroline Cantlin, Doris Reed, Jean Chase, Doris Snyder, Geraldine Olive, Margaret
Henzel, Lauretta Brislin, Elizabeth Kerr. Harrison Fuller, Francis Clarke, John
Cardini, Siegfried Langer, John Willard, Lloyd Ericson, Hobson Young, Sidney
Dunay, Thomas Green, John Best, Allen Ware, Frank Murray, Walter Bartholomew,
John Eaton.

THE PIRATES OF PENZANCE,
1934.08   or The Slave of Duty

A Revival of the Comic Opera in Two Acts[50]. Libretto by William S. Gilbert.
Music by Arthur Sullivan. Staged by Lee Daly. Musical director, J. Albert
Hurley. Settings by Franklyn Ambrose. Costumes by Eaves. Settings built by
Edward Golding. Produced by S. M. Chartok. Opened 9 April 1934 at the
Majestic Theatre and closed 14 April 1934 after 8 performances; re-opened
7-12 May at the Majestic Theatre for 8 additional performances. Total: 16
performances.

CAST: *Richard*, a Pirate Chief: HERBERT L. WATEROUS. *Samuel*, His Lieutenant:
ALLEN WATEROUS. *Frederic*, a Pirate Apprentice: ROY CROPPER. *Major-General
Stanley* of the British Empire: JOHN CHERRY. *Edward*, a Sergeant of Police:
WILLIAM DANFORTH. *General Stanley's Daughters (4)*: *Mabel*: VIVIAN HART.
Kate: FRANCES BAVIELLO. *Edith*: LAURA FERGUSON. *Isabel*: Olga
Schumacher. *Ruth*, a Piratical Maid of All Work: VERA ROSS.
Chorus of Pirates, Police and General Stanley's Daughters: Caroline Cantlin, Doris
Snyder, Charlotte LaRose, Elizabeth Kerr, Geraldine Olive, Margaret Walker, Celia
Schiffrin, Elinore Gilmore, Barbara Martsin, Beatrice Pons, Doris Reed, Jean Chase,
Margaret Henzel, Lauretta Brislin. Harrison Fuller, Francis Clarke, John Cardini,
Siegfried Langer, John Willard, Lloyd Ericson, Hobson Young, Sidney Dunay,
Thomas Green, John Best, Allen Ware, Frank Murray, Walter Bartholomew, John
Eaton, Frank Benedict.

1934.09   ## TRIAL BY JURY

A Revival of the Comic Opera in One Act[51]. Libretto by William S. Gilbert.
Music by Arthur Sullivan. Staged by Lee Daly. Costumes by Eaves. Settings

---

[48]First presented in New York 20 July, 10-29 August 1885 at the
Union Square and People's Theatres for 22 performances. First
authorized production presented 19 August 1885 at the Fifth Avenue
Theatre by Richard D'Oyly Carte for 250 performances. For Synopsis
of Scenes and Musical Numbers, see 19 August 1885 D'Oyly Carte
production.
[49]Return engagement cast change: FRANK MOULAN.
[50]First presented in New York 31 December 1879 at the Fifth Avenue
Theatre for 91 performances in two engagements. For Synopsis of Scenes
and Musical Numbers, see original 1879 production.
[51]First presented in New York 15 November 1875 at the Eagle Theatre
for 8 performances. For Synopsis of Scenes and Musical Numbers, see
original 1875 production.

built by Edward Golding. Musical director, J. Albert Hurley. Produced by S. M. Chartok. Opened 16-21 April 1934 at the Majestic Theatre and closed 21 April 1934 after 8 performances; re-opened 14-19 May 1934 at the Majestic Theatre for 8 additional performances. Total: 16 performances.

CAST: *The Learned Judge*: JOHN CHERRY. *Foreman of the Jury*: HERBERT L. WATEROUS. *The Defendant*: ROY CROPPER. *Counsel*: ALLEN WATEROUS. *Usher*: WILLIAM DANFORTH. *Plaintiff*: VIVIAN HART.

Jurors: Harrison Fuller, Francis Clarke, John Cardini, Siegfried Langer, John Willard, Lloyd Erickson, Hobson Young, Sidney Dunay, Thomas Green, John Bast, Allen Ware, Frank Murray, Walter Bartholomew, John Eaton, Frank Benedict. *Bridesmaids*: Caroline Cantlin, Doris Snyder, Charlotte LaRose, Elizabeth Kerr, Geraldine Olive, Margaret Walker, Celia Schiffren, Frances Baviello, Olga Schumacher, Eleanor Gilmore, Barbara Martsin, Beatrice Pons, Doris Reed, Jean Chase, Margaret Henzel, Lauretta Brislin.

followed by

H.M.S. PINAFORE,
1934.10   or The Lass That Loved a Sailor

A Revival of the Comic Opera in Two Acts[52]. Libretto by William S. Gilbert. Music by Arthur Sullivan. Staged by Lee Daly. Musical director, J. Albert Hurley. Costumes by Eaves. Settings built by Edward Golding. Produced by S. M. Chartok. Opened 16-21 April 1934 at the Majestic Theatre and closed 21 April 1934 after 8 performances; re-opened 14-19 May 1934 at the Majestic Theatre for 8 additional performances. Total: 16 performances.

CAST: *The Rt. Hon. Sir Joseph Porter, K.C.B., First Lord of the Admiralty*: JOHN CHERRY. *Captain Corcoran, Commander of the H.M.S. Pinafore*: ALLEN WATEROUS. *Ralph Rackstraw, Able Seaman*: ROY CROPPER. *Dick Deadeye, Able Seaman*: WILLIAM DANFORTH. *Bill Bobstay, Boatswain*: Herbert L. Waterous. *Josephine, the Captain's Daughter*: VIVIAN HART. *Little Buttercup, Mrs. Cripps, a Portsmouth bum-boat woman*: VERA ROSS. *Hebe, Sir Joseph's First Cousin*: Laura Ferguson.

Sailors: Harrison Fuller, Francis Clarke, John Cardini, Siegfried Langer, John Willard, Lloyd Erickson, Hobson Young, Sidney Dunay, Thomas Green, John Bast, Allen Ware, Walter Bartholomew, John Eaton, Frank Benedict. *First Lord's Sisters, His Cousins, His Aunts*: Caroline Cantlin, Doris Snyder, Charlotte LaRose, Elizabeth Kerr, Geraldine Olive, Margaret Walker, Celia Schiffren, Frances Baviello, Olga Schumacher, Eleanor Gilmore, Barbara Martsin, Beatrice Pons, Doris Reed, Jean Chase, Margaret Henzel, Lauretta Brislin.

IOLANTHE,
1934.11   or The Peer and the Peri

A Revival of the Comic Opera in Two Acts[53]. Libretto by William S. Gilbert. Music by Arthur Sullivan. Staged by Lee Daly. Costumes by Eaves. Settings built by Edward Golding. Music director, J. Albert Hurley. Produced by S. M. Chartok. Opened 30 April 1934 at the Majestic Theatre and closed 5 May 1934 after 8 performances.

CAST: *The Lord Chancellor*: WILLIAM DANFORTH. *Earl of Mountararat*: FREDERICK PERSSON. *Earl Tolloler*: ROY CROPPER. *Private Willis*: HERBERT WATEROUS. *Strephon*: ALLEN WATEROUS. *Queen of the Fairies*: VERA ROSS. *Iolanthe*: DEAN DICKENS. *Celia*: Frances Baviello. *Leila*: Eleanor Gilmore. *Fleta*: Olga Schumacher. *Phyllis*: VIVIAN HART.

Chorus of Fairies, Dukes, Marquises, Earls, Viscounts, Barons and Peers: Margaret Walker, Celia Schiffren, Frances Baviello, Olga Schumacher, Eleanor Gilmore, Barbara Martsin, Beatrice Pons, Doris Reed, Jean Chase, Margaret Henzel, Lauretta Brislin, Caroline Cantlin, Doris Snyder, Charlotte LaRose, Elizabeth Kerr, Geraldine Olive. Harrison Fuller, Francis Clarke, John Cardini, Siegfried Langer, John Willard, Lloyd Erickson, Hobson Young, Sidney Dunay, Thomas Green, John Bast, Allen Ware, Walter Bartholomew, John Eaton, Frank Benedict.

THE CHOCOLATE SOLDIER
1934.12

A Revival of the Operetta in Three Acts[54]. Original German libretto ('Der tapfere Soldat') by Rudolph Bernauer and Leopold Jacobson, based on George Bernard Shaw's "Arms and the Man." Music by Oscar Straus. American book and lyrics by Stanislaus Stange. Staged by Alonzo Price. Costumes by Tams. Produced by Charles Purcell and Donald Brian. Opened 2 May 1934 at the St. James Theatre and closed 12 May 1934 after 13 performances.[55]

CAST: *Nadina*: BERNICE CLAIRE. *Aurelia*: Olivia Martin. *Mascha*: Lauretta Brislin. *Lieutenant Bummerli*: CHARLES PURCELL, DONALD BRIAN. *Capt. Massakroff*: Detmar Poppen. *Colonel Casimir Popoff*: John Dunsmure. *Major Alexius Spiridoff*: Parker Steward. *Lucca*: Theo Van Tassle. *Stephan*: Frank Worden.

Bulgarian Soldiers, Citizens, Citizenesses: Girls: Audrey Mott, Aida Conkey, Theo Bayles, Betty Hawsin, Bernice Hampshire, Anita Duncan, Verd Twiford, Hazel Andrews, Leah Baliver, Alberta Doone, Ruth Clayton, Helen Sada, Sheila Gibbs, Cora Wallace, Lillian Gast, Tamara Charle, Suzanne Black, Leona Neumann. *Boys*: John Albert, Paul Largay, Frank Clark, Ernest Pavano, Dick Kneely, Joseph Napalis, Frank Manda, John Rowan, Paul Owen, Frank Worden, Jack Bruns, Morris Tepper, Chris Gerard, Albert R. Miller.

BITTER SWEET
1934.13

A Revival of the Operetta in Three Acts, 7 Scenes[56]. Book, music and lyrics by Noël Coward. Staged by Edward J. Scanlon. Settings by Watson Barratt. Costumes by Ernest R. Schrapps. Music director, Pierre Dereeder. Produced by the Messrs. Shubert. Opened 7 May 1934 at the 44th Street Theatre and closed 19 May 1934 after 16 performances.

CAST (in order of appearance): *The Marchioness of Shayne*: EVELYN HERBERT. *Dolly Chamberlain*: Mary Wrick. *Lord Henry Jekyll*: Herbert Weber. *Vincent Howard*: Cameron York. *Sarah Millick*: EVELYN HERBERT. *Carl Linden*: ALLAN JONES. *Mrs. Millick*: Elizabeth Crandall. *Hugh Devon*: HENRY RABKE. *Lady Devon*: Ethel Morrison. *Sir Arthur Fenchurch*: Victor Casmore. *Victoria*: Martha Boyer. *Harriet*: Marion Carlisle. *Gloria*: Beatrice Berenson. *Honor*: Ruth Adams. *Jane*: Anna Werth. *Effie*: Beulah Blake. *The Marquis of Steere*: Jay Conley. *Lord Edgar James*: Samuel Thomas. *Lord Sorel*: Brian Davis. *Mr. Vale*: Jack Richards. *Mr. Bethel*: Harold Abbey. *Mr. Proutie*: Trueman [Truman] Gaige. *Four Footmen*: Earl Mason, Leon Sabater, Martin Shepherd, Don Drew. *The Butler*: Jack Fago. *Sari Linden*: EVELYN HERBERT. *Manon (La Crevette)*: HANNAH TOBACK. *Lotte*: Carol Boyer. *Freda*: Beatrice Berenson. *Hansi*: Marion Carlisle. *Gussie*: Kay Simmons. *Captain August Lutte*: Leonard Ceeley. *Herr Schlick*: Victor Casmore. *The Marquis of Shayne*: Clyde Kelly. *Lady James*: Marion Carlisle. *Mrs. Proutie*: Beatrice Berenson. *Mrs. Bethel*: Beulah Blake. *Lady Sorel*: Ruth Adams. *Mrs. Vale*: Anna Werth. *The Duchess of Tenterton*: Martha Boyer. *The Duke of Tenterton*: Frank Grinnell. *Mrs. Devon*: Frances Marion Comstock. *Vernon Craft*: Don Drew. *Cedric Ballantyne*: Brian Davis. *Bertram Sellick*: Frank Grinnell. *Lord Henry Jade*: Jack Richards. *Accompanist*: Theodore Schnyder.

Singing Girls: Carol Boyer, Dorothy Forsythe, Katherine Sheridan, Ruth Adams, Marion Carlisle, Florence Witt, Carol Chandler, Suzanne Gaye, Sherry Lee, Martha Boyer, Beulah Blake, Carol Laski, Anne Werth, Beatrice Berenson. *Boys*: Harold Abbey, Leon Sabater, Brian Davis, Frank Grinnell, Gerald Moore, Martin Shepard, Jack Fago, Jack Richards, Earl Mason, Sam Thomas, Don Drew, John Moore. *Dancing Girls*: Johanne Fredhoven, Muriel Brown, Sonya Davies, Leila Laney, Pavla Pavlicek, Catherine Grey, Charlotte Beverly, Zylpha Jane, Leonora Jumps, Cheri Medbury.

THE ONLY GIRL
1934.14

A Revival of the Musical Comedy in Three Acts[57]. Book and lyrics by Henry Blossom. Based on the comedy "Our Wives" by Frank Mandel (and Helen

---

[52]Originally presented in New York 15 January 1879 at the Standard Theatre for 175 performances. For Synopsis of Scenes and Musical Numbers, see original 1879 production.
[53]First presented in New York 25 November 1882 at the Standard Theatre for 105 performances. For Synopsis of Scenes and Musical Numbers, see original 1882 production.

[54]First produced in New York 13 September 1909 at the Lyric Theatre for 296 performances. For Synopsis of Scenes and Musical Numbers, see original 1909 production.
[55]Settings, musical director uncredited.
[56]Originally presented in New York 5 November 1929 at the Ziegfeld Theatre for 159 performances. For Synopsis of Scenes and Musical Numbers, see original 1929 production.
[57]Originally presented in New York 2 November 1914 at the 39th Street Theatre for 240 performances. For Synopsis of Scenes and Musical Numbers, see original 1914 production.

Craft, adapted from "Jugendfreude" by Ludwig Fulda). Music by Victor Herbert. Gowns by Ernest Schrapps. Musical director, Robert Hood Bowers. Staged by R. H. Burnside. Produced by the Messrs. Shubert. Opened 21 May 1934 at the 44th Street Theatre and closed 2 June 1934 after 16 performances.[58]

CAST: *Alan Kimbrough*, Kim, a Librettist: ROBERT HALLIDAY. *Sylvester Martin*, Corksey, a Broker: BILLY TAYLOR. *John Ayer*, Fresh, a Lawyer: RICHARD KEENE.

Andrew McMurray, Bunkie, a Painter: ROBERT EMMETT KEANE. *Ruth Wilson*, a Composer: BETTINA HALL. *Saunders*, Kimbrough's valet: GEORGE MEADER. *Birdie Martin*, Corksey's Wife: BETZI BEATON. *Margaret Ayer* Fresh's Wife: DOROTHY DARE. *Jane McMurray*, Bunkie's Wife: LOUISE KIRTLAND. *Patricia La Montrose*, Patsy, a Soubrette: NEILA GOODELLE.

All Friends of Patsy: *Ruby*: Frances Foley. *Violet*: Evelyn Bonefine. *Viola*: Louise Joyce. *Paula*: Antoinette Bartlett. *Pearle*: Louise Ryan. *Renee*: Grena Sloan. *Diana*: Sylvia Roberts. *Aimee*: Ulita Torgerson.

---

[58]Settings uncredited. Dropped from this production were "Antoinette" and "Equal Rights." Interpolated into Act 2:

"I Always Go to Parties Alone" (after "Connubial Bliss")
B. Beaton
(*Music and Lyrics by* James Shelton.)

"I Paused, I Looked, I Fell" (Act 2 Finale) (previously in Belmon Varieties)
B. Taylor, D. Dare
(*Music by* Henry Lloyd. *Lyrics by* Sam Bernard, Jr., Bobby Burk.)

1934–1935 SEASON

Bert Lahr and Luella Gear in LIFE BEGINS AT 8:40 (Photo: White Studio)
Billy Rose Theatre Collection, New York Public Library for the Performing Arts

1934–1935 SEASON

CAVIAR

A Musical Romance in Two Acts, 6 Scenes. Book by Leo Randole. Lyrics by Edward Heyman. Music by Harden Church. Staged by Clifford Brooke. Dances by John Lonergan. Settings and costumes by Steele Savage. Music director, Ivan Rudisill. Orchestrations by Hans Spialek, Edward Powell, Don Walker. Produced by Patrick A. Leonard. Opened 7 June 1934 at the Forrest Theatre and closed 23 June 1934 after 20 performances.

CAST (in order of appearance): *Jeannine:* VIOLET CARLSON. *Messenger:* George Gordon. *A Manicurist:* Mitzi Garner. *Another Manicurist:* Amelie Ideal. *A Massesuse:* Gene Ashley. *Another Masseuse:* Tully Millet. *A Pedicure:* Kai Hansen. *A Hairdresser:* Nonie Dale. *Facialist:* Mary Mascher. *Another Facialist:* George Hunter. *Midinette:* Drina Hill. *Elena:* NANETTE GUILFORD. *Jack,* an Author: DON CONNOLLY. *Helen,* a Composer: BILLIE LEONARD. *Count Chipolita:* WALTER ARMIN. *Wallace,* Elena's Manager: HUGH CAMERON. *Carol:* FRANKLYN FOX. *Maid:* Alice Dudley. *Sailor:* Jack Cole. *Organ Grinder:* Walter Armin. *Tesore Mio:* Herself. *Carabinieri:* Joseph Olney. *Dimitri:* GEORGE HOUSTON. *Pavel:* DUDLEY CLEMENTS. *Wassili:* John J. Walsh. *A Reporter:* Frank Coletti. *An English Sailor:* Tully Millet. *A French Sailor:* George Hunter. *An American Sailor:* Gene Ashley. *A Turkish Detective:* Ed Loud. *Moofty:* Joseph Long. *Lenotcha,* a Princess: Drina Hill. *Ray:* Ray Miller.

Girls: Maxine Carter, Nonie Dale, Paula Denning, Mitzi Garner, Rita Horgan, Amelie Ideal, Betty Lyon, Mary Mascher. *Boys:* Gene Ashley, George Gordon, Kai Hansen, George Hunter, Richard Langdon, Ed Loud, Tully Millet, Joseph Olney, Edward Murray.

Time: The present.

Act 1, Scene 1: Elena's Boudoir, Venice. *Scene 2:* Curtains. *Scene 3:* Venice.

Act 2, Scene 1: A Suite in a Hotel, Constantinople. *Scene 2:* A Street in Constantinople. *Scene 3:* A Russian Cabaret.

ACT 1

Scene 1

Opening
V. Carlson, Beauticians

"One in a Million"
D. Connolly, B. Leonard, Beauticians

"Dream Kingdom"
N. Guilford

"Here's To You"
N. Guilford, F. Fox, W. Armin, H. Cameron

"Dream Kingdom" (reprise)
N. Guilford

Scene 2

"My Heart's an Open Book"
D. Connolly, B. Leonard, Girls

Scene 3

"Silver Sails"
G. Houston

"Nightwind"
G. Houston

Carnival
Ensemble

Finale
N. Guilford, G. Houston

ACT 2

Scene 1

"Tarts and Flowers"
N. Guilford, Ensemble

Dance
N. Guilford, R. Miller

"Prince Charming"
N. Guilford

"Gypsy"
N. Guilford

"I Feel Sorta—"
N. Guilford, D. Clements

"Your Prince Was Not So Charming"
N. Guilford

Scene 2

"Haywire"
D. Connolly, B. Leonard
(*Music by* Edward Heyman.)

Scene 3

"Cavachok"
Ensemble

"Apassionette"
J. Cole, A. Dudley

Finale
G. Houston, N. Guilford,
Ensemble

KYKUNKOR

A Native African Opera (The Witch Woman) in Three Acts[1]. Written by Asadata Dafora. Entire production including music, songs, choreography and costumes by Asadata Dafora. Musical director, Margaret Upshur Kennedy. Produced by Asadata Dafora. Opened 10 June 1934 at the Little Theatre and closed 4 August 1934 after 65 performances.

CAST: *Bridegroom:* ASADATA DAFORA (Horton). *Bride:* MUSU ESAMI. *Witch Doctor:* ABDUL ESSEN. *Witch Woman:* MIRAMMU. *Otobone:* RIMERU SHIKERU. *Aguga Dancer:* Matta. *Chief Burah:* TUGUESE. *Mother:* Yama Koro. *Eboe:* Alala. *Matrons, Maidens, Warriors, Specialty Dancers.*
Drummers: Abrodun Salako, Uno Eno, Sakor Jar, Ezebro Ejiho.

Scene: An African Maiden Village.

ACT 1

The Mendi Tribe maidens undergo training in the "maiden village" (or finishing school) in the bush for six months or a year, to learn their domestic duties, and tribal rites, and secrets known only to the women. They are beating rice under the direction of a chaperon, the Otobone, as the curtain rises. Bokari, from the nearby Temini tribe, comes to pick a bride. The Otobone, overjoyed, hurries the maidens into their hut to prepare themselves, and the matrons clear the ground for the dancing. The maidens dance the Bonda, or maidens' dance, and Bokari selects his bride from among them. He then sings his love to his bride, and together they dance the Susu, or engagement dance. Bokari summons his followers to prepare a feast. They carry on their kill, a wild cow. For the bride's tribe this is a bad omen. She and her attendants kneel and sing to drive out any evil spirits. The trousseau is then prepared. Meanwhile, the Burah, the groom's father, and chief of the Temini tribe, arrives with gifts. In his honor, the Fugule, the dance of welcome, is given, and then the Aguga, a dance depicting the strength of man.

ACT 2

The groom sings the wedding song, telling his father of his love, and of the gifts the bride will bring the chief. The slave girls dance for the chief and are accepted by him. The marriage service begins. The bride is called, and the Otobone sings of her love for the girl who is leaving her care. A song of thanks follows, and the groom dances. Then he and the bride dance the Apomba, or wedding dance. Kykunkor, the witch woman, appears, sent by a jealous rival. She casts a spell over the groom, who falls stricken. A devil dancer is called to cast out the evil spirit, and dances the Oummoie. She fails, and the Witch Doctor is then brought in. With prayer and magic, he saves the groom from death.

ACT 3

The festival starts in real earnest. There is first the Agunda, the dance of joy; then the Eboe, the jester, dances. The Battoo, or dance of challenge follows, then the war-dance, and then the Jabawa or festival dance.

---

[1]First produced in New York Off-Broadway by the Unity Theatre Group for 13 performances at East 23rd Street, 4 performances at City College, 15 performances at the Chanin Auditorium.

1934.17

GYPSY BLONDE

A Musical Comedy in Three Acts. Based on the opera "The Bohemian Girl," libretto by Alfred Bunn[2]. Music by Michael Balfe. Book by Kenneth Johns. Lyrics by Frank Gabrielson. Staged by Dmitri Ostrov. Dances by Vaughn Godfrey. Settings by Karl Amend. Costumes by Eaves. Musical director, Fred Hoff. Produced by Dmitri Ostrov. Opened 25 June 1934 at the Lyric Theatre and closed 14 July 1934 after 24 performances.

CAST: *Arline*: ISABEL HENDERSON. *Philip Arnheim*: JOHN HENDRICKS. *Florrie*: ARTHUR PAGE. *Devilshoof*: JOHN DUNSMURE. *Trusty*: GEORGES TRABERT. *Baba*: HELENE ARDEN. *A Dancer*: BELLE DIDJAH. *A Butler*: Simeon Greer.

Dancers: Helen Ecklund, Betty Blake, Myra Scott, Madeline MacDonald, Zabelle Thall, Diane Demler, Suzanne Cort, Grace Gillern, Mildred Hamilton. *Singers*: Neil Gebest, Vera Beaumont, Marie Falica, Maudeline Smith, Beulah Blake, Marla Forbes, Virginia Vallance, Helen Barricklow, Betty Gravier, Elizabeth Kerr, Evelyn Wycoff, Lotti Tilsen. *Men*: Dan Meduri, Leon Sabater, Carl Robertson, Earl Mason, Elvin Howland, Zachary Carr, Frank Grinnell, Bernard Warren.

Act 1: Westchester Estate of Philip Arnheim. The Present.

Act 2: The Gypsy Camp near State Fair—Four weeks later.

Act 3: The Gypsy Camp—Several hours later.

ACT 1

Introductory Chorus
Ensemble

Air
J. Hendricks

Dance
Chorus

"In the Gypsy's Life"
I. Henderson

"'Tis Sad to Leave" (Aria)
G. Trabert

"The Broad Highway" (from *THE DREAM GIRL*)
J. Dunsmure
(*Music by* Victor Herbert. *Lyrics by* Rida Johnson Young.)

"Comrade Your Hand" (Duet)
G. Trabert, J. Dunsmure, Chorus

Concerted Number
C. Roberts, J. Dunsmure, H. Arden, Chorus

"You'll Remember Me" (Aria)
G. Trabert

"Ombo" (Interpolated Song)
I. Henderson

Gypsy Chorus Dance Specialty (interpolated)
Dancers

"Is No Succor Near" (Aria)
C. Roberts

Finale
G. Trabert, J. Dunsmure, J. Hendricks, Ensemble

ACT 2

Opening—"Malagueña"
Ensemble
(*Music by* Ernesto Lecuona.)

"Silence"
J. Dunsmure, Chorus

"Dance, Gypsy"
B. Didjah
(*Music by* Paul J. Girlando.)

"I Dreamt I Dwelt in Marble Halls"
I. Henderson

Duet
I. Henderson, G. Trabert

Recitative and Chorus
I. Henderson, H. Arden, J. Dunsmure, Chorus

[2]Based on the ballet "The Gypsy" by Jules Henri Vernoy de St. Georges.

"Come With the Gypsy Bride"
I. Henderson

"Bliss Forever Past" (Lament)
H. Arden

ACT 3

"Is No Succor Near" (reprise)
C. Roberts

Opening—Hunters' Dance
Dancers, Ensemble

"The Heart Bow'd Down"
J. Hendricks

Quartette and Fair Scene
I. Henderson, H. Arden, J. Dunsmure, J. Hendricks

Dance (at the Fair)
B. Didjah

Quintette and Chorus
I. Henderson, H. Arden, G. Trabert, J. Hendricks, C. Roberts

Scene
I. Henderson, G. Trabert, J. Hendricks

Aria
G. Trabert

"I'm a Gypsy Blonde"
I. Henderson, Chorus

1934.18

KEEP MOVING

A Musical Revue in Two Acts, 31 Scenes. (Sketches by Newman Levy, Jack Scholl, George Rosener, Tom Howard.) Music by Max Rich. Lyrics by Jack Scholl. Dialogue staged by George Rosener. Dances staged by Harry Losee. Scenery designed by Clark Robinson. Costumes designed by Robert Stevenson and Raoul (Pene) du Bois. Music director, Dell Lampe. Entire production supervised by Theodore H. Wing, Jr. Produced by White Horse Tavern Productions, Inc. [Walter Latendorf]. Opened 23 August 1934 at the Forrest Theatre and closed 8 September 1934 after 20 performances.

CAST: TOM HOWARD, HARRIET HUTCHINS, KAY PICTURE, META CARLYLE, THE DELMAR TWINS (Frank, John), ERNEST LAMBART, NAYAN PEARCE, DAN CARTHAY, WILLIAM REDFORD, JOHN ADAIR, BILLY TAYLOR, WOODS MILLER, CLYDE HAGER, GEORGE SHELTON, CLIFF CRANE, JOAN ABBOTT, SALLY GOODING, Fritz Tarabula, Freddie Retter, Fini Balluch, Michael Balluch, Karl Florian, Sonia Kasten, Charles Becker, Nita, SINGER'S MIDGETS.

Ladies of the Dancing Ensemble: Virginia Case, Mary Dailey, Helen Hampton, Yvonne Harte, Florence Hayes, Hazel Hayes, Charlotte Lorraine, Viola Paulson, Carol Pillard, Jerry Rogers. *THE METROPOLITAN OCTETTE*: Muriel Lake, Petrea Murray, Joy Sweet, Elinor Walden, Alexander Ancharoff, John Panter, George Meyer, Anatole Gresheff.

ACT 1

Scene 1

Murder in a Fishbowl (*by* Jack Scholl)
Gertrude Stein: H. Hutchins. *Girl With Wedding Cake*: K. Picture. *Four Girls in Waiting (But What For)*: Y. Hart, V. Case, C. Pillard, C. Lorraine. *Lights and Shadows*: M. Carlyle. *The Other Four, and Two More*: F. Hayes, J. Rogers, H. Hampton, V. Paulson, M. Dailey, H. Hayes. *Two Other People*: Delmar Twins. *Jeeves*: E. Lambart. *Terpsichorines*: N. Pearce, D. Carthay. *Golf Scientist*: W. Redford. *Manhattan Knights*: J. Adair, B. Taylor. *Chicago*: H. Hutchins. *The Singer*: W. Miller.

Scene 2

"The Play Is the Bunk"
W. Miller

Scene 3

"A Page from Jonathan Swift"
W. Miller
(*Music by* Henry Sullivan. *Staged by* John Murray Anderson.)

Scene 4

The Singer's Midgets, The Delmar Twins, and the Ensemble

Scene 5

"A Bit of Optimism"
H. Hutchins

Scene 6

Two Strangers
    C. Hager, W. Redford

Scene 7

Tom Howard, assisted by George Shelton

Scene 8

"Lovely, Lovely Day"
    B. Taylor, M. Carlyle, Ensemble
    (*Music by* Max Rich and Billy Taylor.)

Scene 9

"Cartoonist's Dream"
    Cast: W. Redford, K. Florian, F. Tarabula, J. Adair, Singer's Midgets.

Scene 10

Interlude
    John Adair "Karchie"

Scene 11

Dance
    C. Crane

Scene 12

"Command to Love"
    W. Miller
    (*Music by* Henry Sullivan. *Staged by* John Murray Anderson. *Dance staged by* Robert Alton.)
    Dancers: M. Carlyle, The Delmar Twins, Nita, Ensemble.

Scene 13

"Mother Eve"
    J. Abbott

Scene 14

When Knighthood Flowered (*by* George Rosener)
    Cast: T. Howard, F. Tarabula, N. Pearce, W. Redford, F. Retter.

Scene 15

Broadway Episode
    C. Hager

Scene 16

"Midtown"
    W. Miller, S. Gooding, the Metropolitan Octette
    Danced by N. Pearce, D. Carthay, The Delmar Twins, M. Carlyle, K. Picture, Ensemble.

ACT 2

Scene 1

Midway (*by* George Rosener and Tom Howard)
    Barker: C. Hager. *Our Girls*: The Ensemble. *Hula Dancer*: S. Kasten.
    Bystanders: T. Howard, W. Redford.

Scene 2

"Hotcha Chiquita"
    J. Abbott
    Assisted by The Delmar Twins, K. Picture, M. Carlyle, Ensemble, Singer's Midgets.

Scene 3

The Customary Blackouts (*by* Messrs. Scholl, Rosener, Adair, Redford, Gould)

Before the Curtain
    J. Adair, W. Miller, C. Becker

Street Scene
    J. Adair, B. Taylor, B. Redford

Matrimonial Interlude
    W. Miller, E. Lambart, N. Pearce

Scene 4

"Superstition"
    S. Gooding
    Dance by Ensemble.

Scene 5

Clyde Hager

Scene 6

"Springtime and a Love Song"
    W. Miller
    Interpreted by Margie and Freddie.

Scene 7

Tom Howard, assisted by George Shelton

Scene 8

"(Wake Up,) Sleepy Moon"
    B. Taylor, K. Picture, J. Delmar, W. Miller, J. Abbott

Scene 9

"The Torch Singer"
    H. Hutchins

Scene 10

The Candy Store
    Cast: T. Howard, F. Balluch, F. Retter, M. Balluch.

Scene 11

"Isn't It a Funny Thing"
    B. Taylor, K. Picture, Ensemble

Scene 12

Cocktails (*by* Jack Scholl)

Scene 13

"Come to the Aid of the Party"
    N. Pearce, D. Carthay

Scene 14

Cocktail Orchestra
    Singer's Midgets

Scene 15

Finale—"Keep Moving"
    Entire Company

1934.19 # LIFE BEGINS AT 8:40

A Musical Revue in Two Acts, 28 Scenes. (Sketches by David Freedman, H. I. Phillips, Allan Baxter, Henry Clapp Smith, Ira Gershwin and E. Y. Harburg, Frank Gabrielson.) Music by Harold Arlen. Lyrics by Ira Gershwin and E. Y. Harburg. Staged by John Murray Anderson. Sketches directed by Philip Loeb. Dances by Robert Alton. The Weidman Group Dances by Charles Weidman. Settings by Albert Johnson. Costumes by Kiviette, James Reynolds, Raoul (Pene) du Bois, Billi Livingston, Wynn, Pauline Lawrence, Irene Scharoff [Sharaff]. Music director, Al Goodman. Orchestrations by Hans Spialek. Additional orchestrations by (Robert) Russell Bennett and Don Walker. Produced by the Messrs. Shubert. Opened 27 August 1934 at the Winter Garden and closed 16 March 1935 after 237 performances.

CAST: BERT LAHR, RAY BOLGER, LUELLA GEAR, FRANCES WILLIAMS, BRIAN DONLEVY, EARL OXFORD, DIXIE DUNBAR, Bartlett Simmons, Ofelia & Pimento, Esther Junger, Jack Starr, James MacColl, Josephine Houston, Walter Dare Wahl, Emmett Oldfield, Adrienne Matzenauer, Charles Fowler, Winifred Harris, Frances Comstock, Robert Wildhack.
    Weidman Dancers: Regina Beck, Geri Chopin, Aline Davis, Darley Fuller, Ilse Gronau, Mary Howard, Ethel Medsker, Betty Schlaffer, Josephine Schwarz, George Bockman, Tom Draper, Willem Gerard, Michael Logan. *Singers*: Sally Gibbs, Grena Sloan, Ethel Thorsen, Anya Toranda. *Show Girls*: Sally Bynum, Hope Dare, Marjory Ezequelle, Jane Moxon, Jessica Pepper, Gloria Pierre. *Dancers*: Mary Bay, Vicki Belling, Helen Bennett, Hazel Boffinger, Mary Ann Carr, Noreen Carr, Jean Carson, Aida Conkey, Maxine Darrell, Helen Ecklund, Peggy Gallimore, Pearl Harris, Julie Jenner, Jane Lane, Sherry Stuart, Peggy Thomas, Mildred Webb. *Boys*: Eugene Ashley, Jack Barrett, Edward Browne, Billy Ehlers, Kai Hansen, Arthur Manning, Sid Salzer, Eddie Wells.

ACT 1[3]

---

[3]Added during run:

New Deal Ladies' Circle (*by* David Freedman)
    Teresa Tittlebat: F. WIlliams. *Winnie Whittlebone*: L. Gear. *Lydia Gooseberry*: W. Harris. *Gwendolyn Pinchfaucet*: J. Houston. *Hallibut*: J. MacColl.

Scene 1

"Life Begins" (At Exactly 8:40 Or Thereabouts)
The Juvenile: E. Oxford. *The Young Ladies*: Singers, Show Girls.
The Sister Act: M. Howard, B. Schaffer, I. Gronau. *The Crooner*: C. Fowler.
The Hoofer: T. Draper. *The Husband, Lover and Wife*: W. Gerard, M. Logan,
A. Davis. *The Ingenue*: G. Chopin. *The Comedian*: G. Bockman. *The Torch Singer*: J. Schwartz. And Ensemble.

Scene 2

The Radio Announcer's Bride (8:44 O.T.) (*by* H. I. Phillips)
The Announcer: B. Donlevy. *The Bride*: L. Gear. *The Clergyman*: J. MacColl.

Scene 3

"Spring Fever" (8:47 O.T.)
F. Williams
Danced by the Weidman Dancers, Ensemble.

Scene 4

The Samaritan (8:50 O.T.) (*by* Allan Baxter)
The Barker: B., Donlevy. *The Picket*: C. Fowler. *The Samaritan*: B. Lahr.

Scene 5

"You're a Builder-Upper" (8:56 O.T.)
R. Bolger, D. Dunbar, Ensemble

Scene 6

"My Paramount-Publix-Roxy-Rose" (9:03 O.T.)
The Juvenile: E. Oxford. *The Rose*: L. Gear.

Scene 7

She Loves Me (9:07 O.T.) (*by* David Freedman)
Paul Naughton: B. Lahr. *Curly Flagg*: F. Williams. *The Intruder*: B. Donlevy.

Scene 8

"Shoein' the Mare" (9:13 O.T.)
A. Metzenauer
Danced by E. Junger, The Weidman Dancers, Ofelia and Pimento,
Ensemble.

Scene 9

"Quartet Erotica" (9:20 O.T.)
Rabelais: J. MacColl. *Boccaccio*: R. Bolger. *De Maupassant*: B. Donlevy.
Balzac: B. Lahr.

Scene 10

The Window Dresser Goes to Bed (9:23 O.T.) (*by* Henry Clapp Smith)
The Window Dresser: R. Bolger. *The Window Dresser's Wife*: L. Gear.

Scene 11

"Fun To Be Fooled" (9:31 O.T.)
F. Williams
Danced by E. Junger, The Weidman Dancers.

Scene 12

Ray Bolger (9:37 O.T.)

Scene 13

Chin Up (9:44 O.T.) (*by* Allan Baxter)
Richard: B. Lahr. *Agatha*: L. Gear. *The Father*: J. MacColl. *The Mother*: W.
Harris. *The Butler*: C. Fowler.

Scene 14

"C'est la vie" (9:48 O.T.) (*Sketch by* Ira Gershwin and E. Y. Harburg.)
Prologue: A. Metzenauer, E. Oxford, F. Comstock. *Pierre*: R. Bolger. *Jacques*: B.
Lahr. *Frou-Frou*: L. Gear.

Scene 15

"What Can You Say in a Love Song (That Hasn't Been Said Before)?"
(9:54 O.T.)
J. Houston, B. Simmons

1780: 'A Theatre by Candlelight'
The Lovers: M. Howard, M. Logan. *The Chorus*: A. Conkey, H. Boffinger, H.
Benntt, M. Darrell, J. Lane, P. Thomas. *The Lady in the Box*: F. Comstock. *The
Gentleman in the Box*: E. Oxford.

1880: 'A Theatre by Gaslight'
The Lovers: R. Beck, G. Bockman. *The Chorus*: M. Bay, J. Jenner, M. Webb, J.
Carson, V. Belling, P. Harris. *The Lady in the Box*: A. Metzenauer. *The
Gentleman in the Box*: C. Fowler.
1934: *The Lovers*: A. Davis, T. Draper. *The Chorus*: G. Chopin, E. Medsker, D.
Fuller, B. Schlaffer, K. Schwarz, I. Gronau.

ACT 2

Scene 1

"Let's Take a Walk Around the Block" (10:11 O.T.)
E. Oxford, D. Dunbar, Ensemble

Scene 2

Sound Phenomena (10:17 O.T.) (*by* Robert Wildhack)
R. Wildhack

Scene 3

O'Neill Without End (10:24 O.T.) (*by* Frank Gabrielson)
John: J. MacColl. *His Second Self*: B. Donlevy. *His Third Self*: R. Bolger.
Lucy: J. Huston. *Her Second Self*: G. Sloan. *Her Third Self*: L. Gear.

Scene 4

"Things" (10:29 O.T.)
B. Lahr

Scene 5

"(All) The Elks and the Masons" (10:34 O.T.)
R. Bolger, D. Dunbar, Ensemble

Scene 6

"I Couldn't Hold My Man" (10:39 O.T.)
L. Gear

Scene 7

"A Weekend Cruise" (Will You Love Me Monday Morning as You Did
on Friday Night?) (10:43 O.T.)
F. Williams, E. Oxford
A Passenger: B. Lahr.

Scene 8

Jack Starr (10:48 O.T.)

Scene 9

"It Was Long Ago" (10:50 O.T.)
J. Huston, A. Metzenauer, G. Sloan, S. Gibbs, F. Comstock, E. Thorsen,
A. Taranda

A Quiet Evening at Home (*Pantomime by* Lewis Shayon)
The Grandmother: E. Junger. *The Grandfather*: M. Logan. *The Sons*: W. D.
Wahl, E. Oldfield, G. Bockmann, W. Gerard. *The Granddaughter*: D. Dunbar.

Scene 10

Walter Dare Wahl and Emmett Oldfield (10:54 O.T.)

Scene 11

"I'm Not Myself" (11:00 O.T.)
R. Bolger, Ensemble
(*Arranged by* R. Bolger)

Scene 12

A Day at the Brokers (11:03 O.T.) (*by* David Freedman)
The Broker: B. Donlevy. *Bill Leonard*: B. Lahr.

Scene 13

"Life Begins at City Hall" (Beautifying the City) (11:14 O.T.)
(*Sketch by* Ira Gershwin and E. Y. Harburg.)
Il Duce: J. MacColl. And G. Whalen, E. Ashley, J. Barrett, E. Wells, K. Hansen.
The Dictator: B. Lahr. *The First Lady*: L. Gear. *The Stowaways*: F. Williams,
R. Bolger. And Entire Company.

1934.20 # SALUTA

A Musical Comedy in Satire in Two Acts, 11 Scenes. Book by Will Morrissey,
revised by Eugene Conrad and Maurice Marks. Music by Frank D'Armond.
Lyrics by Will Morrissey, Milton Berle. Book staged by Edwin Saulpaugh,
(William Morrissey). Dances by Boots McKenna. Production (settings)
designed by Hugh Willoughby. Costumes by John Booth, Jr. Music director,
John McManus. Entire production under the direction of Frank Merlin.
Produced by R. A. Reppil [Arthur Lipper, Jr.]. Opened 28 August 1934 at the
Imperial Theatre and closed 29 September 1934 after 39 performances.

CAST (in order of appearance): *Pete Fondana*: William Edmunds. *Tony Carello*:
MILTON WATSON. *Moe Ginsburg*: EDWARD J. LAMBERT. *Nicholo Lorenzo*:
CHAZ CHASE. *Guard*: Cliff Whitcomb. *Two Patrons*: Fritz and Jean Hubert. *"Windy"
Walker*: MILTON BERLE. *George Palalis*: Ralph Sanford. *Henry Bradley*: DUDLEY
CLEMENTS. *Eleanor Bradley*: ANN BARRIE. *Betty Baxter*: THELMA WHITE.
Captain Sardi: L. C. Phillips. *Chief Officer*: William Hargrave. *Felicia Sorel, Demetrios*

Vilan: Themselves. *Stephano Milano*: Daniel Makarenko. *Priest*: William Hargrave. *Monk*: George Ortell. *The Dictator*: Frank Marino. *Guard*: Edwin Delbridge. *Cafe Entertainers, Ship Officers, Passengers, Sailors, Stagehands.*

Dancing Ensemble: Elene Ross, Marion Herson, Gladys Glancy, Edna Flynn, Gertrude McPherson, Mary Kennedy, Althea Elder, Ruth Carlin, Irma Philbin, Tina Marie Jensen, Marion Allen, Carnie Ellis, Doris Farmer, Mary Mascher, Julia Gorman, Eleanor Ethridge, Patricia Haywood, Page Manning, Amelie Ideal, Peggy Morrison. *Singing Ensemble*: Virginia Vallance, Nora Anderson, Betty Gravier, Florence Manners, Anne Buhr, Dorothy Bradshaw, Peggy Love, Marcelle Diecel, Dave Bell, Otto Simanek, Edwin Delbridge, Albert Wellington, Cliff Whitcomb, Don English, Don Catlin, George Ortell.

Act 1, Scene 1: The Jail. *Scene 2*: The Black Horse Tavern. *Scene 3*: S.S. *"Rex." Scene 4*: The Deck. *Scene 5*: The Ship's Concert.

Act 2, Scene 1: The Italian Street. *Scene 2*: The Opera House. *Scene 3*: The Rehearsal. *Scene 4*: The Deck. *Scene 5*: The Opera. *Scene 6*: Finale.

ACT 1

"Black Horse Tavern"
D. Catlin

"Just Say the Word"
M. Watson

"Walking the Deck"
Ensemble

"I'll Produce for You"
M. Berle, T. White

"Night"
A. Barrie, M. Watson

Ballet Moderno
Created and Danced by F. Sorel, D. Vilan

"Help the Seamen"
W. Hargrave, Men

"You Have My Heart"
A. Barrie, M. Watson

ACT 2

"Tarantella Rhythm"
T. White, Ensemble

"Mi! Mi!"
Choral Ensemble

"We Incorporated"
A. Barrie, M. Watson

"La vita"
M. Berle, A. Barrie, M. Watson, P. Love, M. Ricalde

Opera

(a) "Religioso"
W. Hargrave, Choral Ensemble

(b) "Ma perche"
M. Watson

(c) "Ritorna a me"
A. Barrie

"There's a Chill in the Air"
T. White

"The Great Dictator and Me"
M. Berle

Finale
Entire Company

THE GONDOLIERS,
or The King of Barataria

1934.21

A Revival of the Comic Opera in Two Acts[4]. Libretto by William S. Gilbert. Music by Arthur Sullivan. Directed by James McRobbie Gordon. Scenery and costumes designed by Charles Ricketts. Orchestra directed by Isidore Godfrey. Produced by the D'Oyly Carte Opera Company. Opened 3 September 1934 at the Martin Beck Theatre and closed 5 September 1934

---

[4]Originally presented in New York 7 January 1890 at Park Theatre for 103 performances. For Synopsis of Scenes and Musical Numbers, see original 1890 production.

after 4 performances; re-opened 1-8 October 1934 for 8 performances, re-opened 22-24 November 1934 for 4 performances, re-opened 14-15 December for 3 performances, and closed 15 December 1934 after 19 performances total in repertory.

CAST: *The Duke of Plaza-Toro*: MARTYN GREEN. *Luiz*: JOHN DEAN. *Don Alhambra Del Bolero*: SYDNEY GRANVILLE. *Marco Palmieri*: DEREK OLDHAM. *Giuseppe Palmieri*: LESLIE RANDS. *Antonio*: Richard Walker. *Francesco*: Robert Wilson. *Giorgio*: Radley Flynn. *Annibale*: Frank Steward. *The Duchess of Plaza-Toro*: DOROTHY GILL. *Casilda*: EILEEN MOODY. *Gianetta*: MURIEL DICKSON. *Tessa*: MARJORIE EYRE. *Fiametta*: Doreen Denny. *Vittoria*: Elizabeth Nickell-Lean. *Giulia*: Margaret O'Brien. *Inez*: Josephine Curtis. *Chorus of Gondoliers, Contadine, Men-at-Arms, Heralds and Pages.*

COX AND BOX,
or The Long Lost Brothers

1934.22

A Revival of the Triumviretta in One Act[5]. Libretto by F. C. Burnand, based on J. Maddison Morton's farce "Box and Cox." Music by Arthur Sullivan. Directed by James McRobbie Gordon. Scenery and costumes designed by William Nicholson. Orchestra directed by Isidore Godfrey. Produced by the D'Oyly Carte Opera Company. Opened 6 September 1934 at the Martin Beck Theatre and closed 8 September 1934 after 4 performances, re-opened 8-10 October 1934 for 4 performances, re-opened 10-11 December 1934 for 2 performances, for a total 10 performances (accompanied by "The Pirates of Penzance") in repertory. Also performed 15-17 November 1934 for 4 performances (accompanied by "H.M.S. Pinafore"). Total: 14 performances in repertory.

CAST: *Cox, a Journeyman Hatter*: MARTYN GREEN. *Box, a Journeyman Printer*: JOHN DEAN. *Bouncer, their Landlord*: DARRELL FANCOURT.

followed by

THE PIRATES OF PENZANCE,
or The Slave of Duty

1934.23

A Revival of the Comic Opera in Two Acts[6]. Libretto by William S. Gilbert. Music by Arthur Sullivan. Directed by James McRobbie Gordon. Costumes designed by George Sheringham. Orchestra directed by Isidore Godfrey. Produced by the D'Oyly Carte Opera Company. Opened 6 September 1934 at the Martin Beck Theatre and closed 8 September 1934 after 4 performances, re-opened 8-10 October 1934 for 4 performances, re-opened 10-11 December 1934 for 2 performances, and closed 11 December 1934 after 10 performances (accompanied by "Cox And Box") in repertory. Re-opened 8-10 November 1934 for 4 performances (accompanied by "Trial By Jury"). Total: 14 performances in repertory.

CAST: *Major-General Stanley*: MARTYN GREEN. *The Pirate King*: DARRELL FANCOURT. *Samuel*: RICHARD WALKER. *Frederic*: DEREK OLDHAM. *Sergeant of Police*: SYDNEY GRANVILLE. *General Stanley's Daughters (4)*: *Mabel*: KATHLEEN FRANCES. *Edith*: MARJORIE EYRE. *Kate*: MAISIE BAXTER. *Isabel*: Elizabeth Nickell-Lean. *Ruth*: DOROTHY GILL. *Chorus of Pirates, Police and General Stanley's Daughters.*

IOLANTHE,
or The Peer and the Peri

1934.24

A Revival of the Comic Opera in Two Acts[7]. Libretto by William S. Gilbert. Music by Arthur Sullivan. Directed by James McRobbie Gordon. Costumes for "Phyllis," "Strephon" and the Fairies designed by Charles Ricketts. Orchestra directed by Isidore Godfrey. Produced by the D'Oyly Carte Opera

---

[5]First presented in New York 14 August 1879 at the Standard Theatre for 48 performances. For Synopsis of Scenes and Musical Numbers, see original 1879 production.
[6]First presented in New York 31 December 1879 at the Fifth Avenue Theatre for 91 performances in two engagments. For Synopsis of Scenes and Musical Numbers, see original 1879 production. Settings uncredited.
[7]First presented in New York 25 November 1882 at the Standard Theatre for 105 performances. For Synopsis of Scenes and Musical Numbers, see original 1882 production. Settings uncredited.

Company. Opened 10 September 1934 at the Martin Beck Theatre and closed 12 September 1934 after 4 performances; re-opened 25-27 October 1934 for 4 performances, re-opened 10-21 November for 4 performances, re-opened 12-15 December 1934 for 3 performances, and closed 15 December 1934 after 15 performances total in repertory.

CAST: *The Lord Chancellor*: MARTYN GREEN. *Earl of Mountararat*: DARRELL FANCOURT. *Earl Tolloller*: DEREK OLDHAM. *Private Willis*: SYDNEY GRANVILLE. *Strephon*: LESLIE RANDS. *Queen of the Fairies*: DOROTHY GILL. *Iolanthe*: ELIZABETH NICKELL-LEAN. *Celia*: Kathleen Frances. *Leila*: Maisie Baxter. *Fleta*: Margaret O'Brien. *Phyllis*: MURIEL DICKSON. *Chorus of Dukes, Marquises, Earls, Viscounts, Barons and Fairies.*

TRIAL BY JURY

1934.25

A Revival of the Comic Opera in One Act[8]. Libretto by William S. Gilbert. Music by Arthur Sullivan. Directed by James McRobbie Gordon. Scenery and costumes designed by Charles Ricketts. Orchestra directed by Isidore Godfrey. Produced by the D'Oyly Carte Opera Company. Opened 13 September 1934 at the Martin Beck Theatre and closed 15 September 1934 after 4 performances, re-opened 22-24 October 1934 for 4 performances, re-opened 28-29 November 1934 for 3 performances. Re-opened 8-10 November 1934 (accompanied by "The Pirates of Penzance") for 4 performances; closed 29 November 1934 after 15 performances total in repertory.

CAST: *The Learned Judge*: SYDNEY GRANVILLE. *Counsel for the Plaintiff*: LESLIE RANDS. *The Defendant*: ROBERT WILSON. *Foreman of the Jury*: FRANK STEWARD. *Usher*: RICHARD WALKER. *Associate*: C. William Morgan. *The Plaintiff*: DOREEN DENNY. *First Bridesmaid*: Kathleen Frances. *Chorus of Jurymen, Bridesmaids and Public.*

followed by

H.M.S. PINAFORE,

1934.26 or The Lass That Loved a Sailor

A Revival of the Comic Opera in Two Acts[9]. Libretto by William S. Gilbert. Music by Arthur Sullivan. Directed by James McRobbie Gordon. Scenery and costumes designed by Charles Ricketts. Orchestra directed by Isidore Godfrey. Produced by the D'Oyly Carte Opera Company. Opened 13 September 1934 at the Martin Beck Theatre and closed 15 September 1934 after 4 performances, re-opened 22-24 October 1934 for 4 performances, re-opened 28-29 November 1934 for 3 performances; also performed 15-17 November 1934 (accompanied by "Cox And Box") for 4 performances; closed 29 November 1934 after 15 performances total in repertory.

CAST: *The Rt. Hon. Sir Joseph Porter, K.C.B., First Lord of the Admiralty*: MARTYN GREEN. *Captain Corcoran, Commander of the H.M.S. Pinafore*: LESLIE RANDS. *Ralph Rackstraw, Able Seaman*: DEREK OLDHAM. *Dick Deadeye, Able Seaman*: DARRELL FANCOURT. *Bill Bobstay, Boatswain*: Richard Walker. *Bob Becket*: Radley Flynn. *Josephine, the Captain's Daughter*: MURIEL DICKSON. *Hebe, Sir Joseph's First Cousin*: Marjorie Eyre. *Little Buttercup*, Mrs. Cripps, a Portsmouth bum-boat woman: DOROTHY GILL. *First Lord's Sisters, His Cousins, His Aunts, Sailors, Marines, etc.*

THE MIKADO,

1934.27 or The Town of Titipu

A Revival of the Comic Opera in Two Acts[10]. Libretto by William S. Gilbert. Music by Arthur Sullivan. Directed by James McRobbie Gordon. Scenery and costumes designed by Charles Ricketts. Orchestra directed by Isidore Godfrey. Produced by the D'Oyly Carte Opera Company. Opened 17

September 1934 at the Martin Beck Theatre and closed 19 September 1934 after 4 performances, re-opened 15-20 October for 8 performances, re-opened 12-14 November 1934 for 4 performances, re-opened 5-7 December 1934 for 4 performances, closing 7 December 1934 after 20 performances total in repertory.

CAST: *The Mikado of Japan*: DARRELL FANCOURT. *Nanki-Poo*: DEREK OLDHAM. *Ko-Ko*: MARTYN GREEN. *Pooh-Bah*: SYDNEY GRANVILLE. *Noble Lords* (2): *Pish-Tush*: LESLIE RANDS. *Go-To*: Radley Flynn. *Three Sisters, Wards of Ko-Ko: Yum-Yum*: KATHLEEN FRANCES. *Pitti-Sing*: MARJORIE EYRE. *Peep-Bo*: ELIZABETH NICKELL-LEAN. *Katisha*: DOROTHY GILL. *Chorus of School Girls, Nobles, Guards and Coolies.*

THE YEOMEN OF THE GUARD,

1934.28 or The Merryman and His Maid

A Revival of the Comic Opera in Two Acts[11]. Libretto by William S. Gilbert. Music by Arthur Sullivan. Directed by James McRobbie Gordon. Costumes designed by Percy Anderson. Orchestra directed by Isidore Godfrey. Produced by the D'Oyly Carte Opera Company. Opened 20 September 1934 at the Martin Beck Theatre and closed 22 September 1934 after 4 performances, re-opened 29-31 October 1934 for 4 performances, re-opened 30 November 1-December 1934 for 3 performances, and closed 1 December 1934 after 11 performances total in repertory.

CAST: *Sir Richard Cholmondeley*: LESLIE RANDS. *Colonel Fairfax*: DEREK OLDHAM. *Sergeant Meryll*: DARRELL FANCOURT. *Leonard Meryll*: JOHN DEAN. *Jack Point*: MARTYN GREEN. *Wilfred Shadbolt*: SYDNEY GRANVILLE. *First Yeoman*: Robert Wilson. *Second Yeoman*: Samuel Mooney. *First Citizen*: C. William Morgan. *Second Citizen*: Frank Steward. *Elsie Maynard*: MURIEL DICKSON. *Phoebe Meryll*: MARJORIE EYRE. *Dame Carruthers*: DOROTHY GILL. *Kate*: KATHLEEN FRANCES. *Chorus of Yeomen of the Guard, Gentlemen, Citizens, etc.*

THE GREAT WALTZ

1934.29

A Musical Play in Two Acts, 11 Scenes. Book by Moss Hart. Adapted from the Viennese operetta ("Walzer aus Wien") by Dr. A.M. Willner, Heinz Reichert and Ernst Marischka, and its English adaptation by Caswell Garth and Desmond Carter. Music by Johann Strauss, Sr. and Johann Strauss, Jr. Lyrics by Desmond Carter. Production conceived and directed by Hassard Short. Dances by Albertina Rasch. Settings by Albert Johnson. Costumes by Doris Zinkeisen, Irene Sharaff. Lighting, staging, scenic and mechanical effects created by Hassard Short. Music director, Frank Tours. Orchestrations by Erich Wolfgang Korngold, Julius Bittner, G. A. Clutsam, Herbert Griffith, Frank Tours, (Robert) Russell Bennett. Produced by Max Gordon. Opened 22 September 1934 at the Center Theatre and closed 8 June 1935 after 298 performances; re-opened 5 August 1935 at the Center Theatre and closed 16 September 1935 after additional 49 performances. Total: 347 performances.

CAST: *Greta*: JESSIE BUSLEY. *Ebeseder*: ERNEST COSSART. *Leopold*, Poldi, Greta's nephew: DENNIS NOBLE. *Therese*, Resi, Ebeseder's daughter: MARION CLAIRE[12]. *Johann Strauss, Jr., Schani*: GUY ROBERTSON. *The Brides* (2): *Augustina*: Ruby Asquith. *Lottie*: Josephine McKendrick. *The Bridegrooms* (2): *Paul Heinrich*: Lew Christiansen. *Hans Heinrich*: Harold Christiansen. *Countess Olga Baranskaja*: MARIE BURKE. *Wilhelm*, Footman to the Countess: Richard Lambart. *Friends of the Countess* (8): *Lili*: Frances Hayes. *Franzi*: Tanya Sanina. *Tini*: Diana Walker. *Mali*: Sandra Walters. *Sini*: Rosalynd Hutner. *Mitzi*: Nina Dean. *Nini*: Ruth Clayton. *Betti*: Dorothy Forsyth. *Karl Hirsch*: Ambrose Manning. *Johann Strauss, Sr.*: H. REEVES-SMITH. *Kathi Lanner*: ALEXANDRA DANILOVA. *Dommayer*: SOLLY WARD. *Captain Boris Androff*: Ralph Magelssen. *Dreschler*: Robert C. Fischer. *Hartkopf*: Richie Ling. *Franz Ludwig*: Charles Romano. *Gretchen Ludwig*: Aphie James. *Lieutenant Carl Boch*: Ralph Glover. *Captain Hal Fredrich*: Charles Brokaw. *Lieutenant Ferdinand Holmann*: Edgar Allan.

Corps de Ballet: Leading Dancers: Frances Wise, Florence Chumbecos, Claire Manners, Mary Manners, Kathryn Mullowney, Jane Overton, Rabana, Marioe Rio, Wiora Stoney. *Ballet*: Virginia Allen, Ruby Asquith, Marion Bancroft, Martha Coy, Alita Duncan, Viola Einarsen, Patti Heaton, Thekla Horn, Adrienne Kann, Jeanne Kroll, Sharon Lewis, Thalia Mara, Josephine McKendrick, Florence Miller, Nona Otero, Billie Partridge, Virginia Peck, Nora Puntin, Marjorie Shaw, Geraldine Spencer, Claire Stone, Virginia Watkins, Mary Wilkinson. *Girls in the Ensemble*: Alice Banks, Beulah Blake, Carol Chandler, Ruth Clayton, Clarice Cole, Nina Dean,

---

[8]First presented in New York 15 November 1875 at the Eagle Theatre for 8 performances. For Synopsis of Scenes and Musical Numbers, see original 1875 production.

[9]Originally presented in New York 15 January 1879 at the Standard Theatre for 175 performances. For Synopsis of Scenes and Musical Numbers, see original 1879 production.

[10]First presented in New York 20 July, 10-29 August 1885 at the Union Square and People's Theatres for 22 performances. First authorized production presented 19 August 1885 at the Fifth Avenue Theatre by Richard D'Oyly Carte for 250 performances. For Synopsis of Scenes and Musical Numbers, see 19 August 1885 D'Oyly Carte production.

[11]First presented in New York 17 October 1888 at the Casino Theatre for 100 performances. For Synopsis of Scenes and Musical Numbers, see original 1888 production. Settings uncredited.

[12]For return engagement, played by LEE WHITNEY.

Shirley Dorman, Mary Francis, Dorothy Forsyth, Vera Gorska, Sally Hadley, June Hauger, Gladys Haverty, Frances Hayes, Ingar Hill, Fay Hope, Florence Hurst, Rosalynd Hutner, Constance MacDonald, Emily Marsh, Sue Mason, Ruth Mather, Meg Mundy, May Muth, Rosalie Norman, Zoe Parenteau, Mary Rodes, Helen Sada, Tanya Sanina, Madgieo Smylle, Eleanora Standish, Doris Swanstrom, Virda Twiford, Theo Van Tassel, Nina Verde, Diana Walker, Sandra Walters, Marion Winchester. *Boys in the Ensemble*: Albert Amato. Bruce Barclay, Freeman Bloodgood, Roger Carr, Neil Collins, John Crayton, Tom Curley, Glenn Darwin, Roderick Deane, Martin Dennis, Eugene DePrussing, Jack Donaldson, Bert Doughty, William Douglas, Frank Floyd, Michael J. Forbes, John Fredrick, Herbert Goff, George Gordon, Al Kacher, David King, Leslie Kingdon, Donald Lee, Frank Leonard, Robert Lewis, Philip Man, Frank Moffa, Jerry Moore, Fred Nay, Pat O'Brien, Joseph Olney, Jimmy Ryan, Dave Sachs, Morrie Siegel, Ward Tallman, Harold Voeth, Gilbert White, Castle Williams, Roger Williams.

Act 1, Scene 1: Outside Ebeseder's Pastry Shop, Vienna. *Scene 2*: The Little Garden. *Scene 3*: The Big Garden. *Scene 4*: The Little Garden. *Scene 5*: The Big Garden. *Scene 6*: The Sitting Room.

Act 2, Scene 1: Dommayer's Gardens. The Ballet. *Scene 2*: The Pavilion. *Scene 3*: The Gardens. *Scene 4*: Another Part of the Gardens. *Scene 5*: The Ballroom.

ACT 1

"Radetsky March"
The Brass Band

"Morning"
M. Claire

"Look Before You Leap"[13]
M. Claire, D. Noble

"You Are My Songs"
M. Claire, G. Robertson, Ensemble

"Love Will Find You"
M. Claire, G. Robertson

"On Love Alone"
Ensemble, Ballet

"Like a Star in the Sky"
M. Burke, G. Robertson

"With All My Heart"
M. Claire

ACT 2

"Night"
Ensemble

Ballet
V. Fay, Corps de Ballet

"Love's Never Lost"
M. Burke, D. Noble, R. Magelssen

"We Love You Still"
M. Burke

"While You Love Me"
M. Claire, G. Robertson

"Love and War"
D. Noble, Ensemble

Quadrille
Ensemble

"The Blue Danube" (Danube So Blue)
M. Claire, Entire Company

RUDDIGORE,
1934.30   or The Witch's Curse

A Revival of the Comic Opera in Two Acts[14]. Libretto by William S. Gilbert. Music by Arthur Sullivan. Directed by James McRobbie Gordon. Costumes designed by Percy Anderson. Orchestra directed by Isidore Godfrey. Produced by the D'Oyly Carte Opera Company. Opened 24 September 1934 at the Martin Beck Theatre and closed 26 September after 4 performances, re-opened 26-27 November 1934 for 2 additional performances. Total: 6 performances in repertory.

CAST: *Sir Ruthven Murgatroyd*: MARTYN GREEN. *Richard Dauntless*: JOHN DEAN. *Sir Despard Murgatroyd*: SYDNEY GRANVILLE. *Old Adam Goodheart*: Radley Flynn. *Sir Roderic Murgatroyd*: DARRELL FANCOURT. *Rose Maybud*: EILEEN MOODY. *Mad Margaret*: MARJORIE EYRE. *Dame Hannah*: DOROTHY GILL. *Zorah*: Kathleen Frances. *Ruth*: Elizabeth Nickell-Lean. *Chorus of Officers, Ancestors, Professional Bridesmaids, etc.*

PRINCESS IDA,
1934.31   or Castle Adamant

A Revival of the Comic Opera in Three Acts[15]. Libretto by William S. Gilbert. Music by Arthur Sullivan. Directed by James McRobbie Gordon. Costumes designed by Percy Anderson. Orchestra directed by Isidore Godfrey. Produced by the D'Oyly Carte Opera Company. Opened 27 September 1934 at the Martin Beck Theatre and closed 29 September 1934 after 4 performances; re-opened 1-3 November 1934 for 4 additional performances, re-opened and closed 8 December 1934 for 2 additional performances. Total: 10 performances in repertory.

CAST: *King Hildebrand*: SYDNEY GRANVILLE. *Hilarion*: DEREK OLDHAM. *Hilarion's Two Friends*: Cyril: JOHN DEAN. *Florian*: LESLIE RANDS. *King Gama*: MARTYN GREEN. *His Sons*: Arac: DARRELL FANCOURT. *Guron*: RICHARD WALKER. *Scythius*: Radley Flynn. *Princess Ida, Gama's Daughter*: MURIEL DICKSON. *Lady Blanche, Professor of Abstract Science*: DOROTHY GILL. *Lady Psyche, Professor of Humanities*: DOREEN DENNY. *Melissa, Lady Blanche's Daughter*: MARJORIE EYRE. *Sacharissa*: KATHLEEN FRANCES. *Chloe*: Maisie Baxter. *Ada*: Elizabeth Nickell-Lean. *Soldiers, Courtiers, Girl Graduates, Daughters of the Plough, etc.*

CONTINENTAL VARIETIES
1934.32

An International Vaudeville Revue in Two Acts, 14 Scenes. Mr. Balieff's vocabulary by Irving Caesar. Produced by Arch Selwyn and Harold B. Franklin. First edition opened 3 October 1934 at the Little Theatre and closed 13 November 1934 after 44 performances. Second edition opened 14 November 1934 at the Little Theatre and closed 9 December 1934 after 33 performances. Total: 77 performances.

CAST: LUCIENNE BOYER, VICENTE ESCUDERO and his SACRE MONTE GYPSIES, CARMITA, RAPHAEL, (GEORGES) DE ROZE, LYDIA CHALIAPINE, EMMA RUNITCH, NIKITA BALIEFF.
Iza Volpin (Orchestra conductor for Mlle. Boyer), Boris Kogan (Pianist for Raphael, Lydia Chaliapine and Escudero), Jean Delettre (Pianist and composer for Mlle. Boyer).

ACT 1

Scene 1

Caprice Viennois (*by* Fritz Kreisler)

La Guitana[16] (*by* Fritz Kreisler)

Valse No. 6 (*by* Frédéric Chopin)
Raphael

Scene 2

"Two Guitars"
L. Chaliapine

Scene 3

"Berry-Pickers"

"It Will Rain"
L. Chaliapine, E. Runitch, Raphael

Scene 4

Cordoba (by Isaac Albéniz)
V. Escudero, Carmita

Scene 5

El Camino del Sacro Monte (Sacred Mountain Road) (ballet)
V. Escudero, Sacre Mont Gypsies, Carmita

Baile de la Boda (Marriage Dance)

Por Tanguiyo (Tango)

La Farruca de la Nina (Farruca of the Little One)

---

[13]Dropped during the run.
[14]First presented in New York 21 February 1887 at the Standard Theatre for 53 performances. For Synopsis of Scenes and Musical Numbers, see original 1887 production. Settings uncredited.

---

[15]Originally presented in New York 11 February 1884 at the Fifth Avenue Theatre for 48 performances. For Synopsis of Scenes and Musical Numbers, see original 1884 production. Settings uncredited.
[16]Replaced during the run by "Doyna" (Roumanian Folk Song).

La Mosca (The Fly)

Garrotin del Camino[17] (Garrotin of the Sacre Mont)

Bulerias: Los Cuatro Muleros (The Four Muleteers)
Opening on this road, on the cliff above Grenada, are the gypsy caves. In the decor on the stage are pictured the actual caves where the gypsies of Senor Escudero's company live, also the tavern, 'La Mosca' (The Fly) which they frequent. The dances and songs here given are authentic to Sacre Mont, rarely performed there for outsiders, unknown even to the rest of Spain, for this is the first time the Sacre Mont Gypsies have left Grenada. (*Decor and Costumes by* Angel Carretero.)

Scene 6

Nikita Balieff in a new role

Scene 7

Farruca (A Dance of the Possessed)
V. Escudero

Scene 8

"Les Gueues" (The Street Walkers)
(*Music and Lyrics by* Vincent Scotto.)

"Attends!" (Wait!)
(*Music by* Jean Lenoir. *Lyrics by* Jacques-Charles.)

"Viens danser quand-même" (Dancing with My Darling, or Come Dance Anyway)
(*Music by* Jean Delettre. *Lyrics by* Jamblan.)

"Moi, j'crache dans l'eau" (I Spit in the Water)
(*Music and Lyrics by* Jean Tranchant.)

"Parlez-moi d'amour" (Speak to Me of Love)
(*Music and Lyrics by* Jean Lenoir.) L. Boyer

ACT 2[18]

Scene 1

"La Feria" (The Fair) (Romero)
V. Escudero, Carmita, La Jardin

Scene 2

Fandango del Alabaicin
Sacre Mont Gypsies

Scene 3

Bolero
Carmita

Scene 4

Rhythms (without music)
V. Escudero

Scene 5

The Wonder Barman
De Roze

Scene 6

"D'amour en amour"[19] (From Love to Love)
(*Music by* Jean Delettre. *Lyrics by* Leo Delievre.)

"Je ne savais pas" (I Did Not Know)
(*Music by* Jean Delettre. *Lyrics by* Maurice Aubret.)

"Si petite" (So Small)
(*Music by* Gaston Claret. *Lyrics by* Pierre Bayle.)

"Parlez-moi d'autre chose" (Speak to Me of Something Else)
(*Music and Lyrics by* Jean Delettre.)

"Prenez mes roses" (Buy Me Roses)
(*Music by* Fugaro[20]. *Lyrics by* Chamfleury.) L. Boyer

---

[17]Dropped after opening.
[18]Added to Act 2 after opening: 3 Russian Folk Songs:
An Old Waltz; Play, My Daughter; Soldatskaya
L. Chaliapine, E. Runitch, Raphael
[19]Replaced during the run by:
"Hands Across the Table"
(*Music by* Jean Delettre. *Lyrics by* Mitchell Parish.)
[20]CAP identifies the composer as Roberto Santiago Fugazot and the lyricist (presumably English translation) as Milton Pascal and Eugene J. Gohin.

CONTINENTAL VARIETIES

1934.32   (Second Edition)

An International Vaudeville Revue in Two Acts, 9 Scenes. Mlle. Boyer's gowns by Jeanne Lanvin, Marcel Rochas. Mlle. Chaliapine and Mme. Runitch's costumes designed by Lydia Chaliapine. Senor Escudero's costumes for the ballet of Sacre Mont by Angel Carretero. Second edition opened 14 November 1934 at the Little Theatre and closed 9 December 1934 after 33 performances.[21]

CAST: LUCIENNE BOYER, LYDIA CHALIAPINE, EMMA RUNITCH, CARMITA, VICENTE ESCUDERO, RAPHAEL, GEORGES DE ROZE, NIKITA BALIEFF, SACRE MONTE GYPSIES, IZA VOLPIN ORCHESTRA, DESLYS & CLARK, GALI-GALI.

ACT 1

Scene 1

Bulerias (Teresa Maya)

Tango del Cerro (Maria La Hardin)

La Zambra (Ensemble)
Original Sacre Mont Gypsies

Scene 2

Little Conversation (Ocki-Albi)

Fantaisie Faust (*by* Pablo Sarasate)
Raphael
Piano: Boris Kogan.

Scene 3

Three Russian Folk Songs
E. Runitch, Raphael

Scene 4

Sophisticated Songs
Deslys & Clark

Scene 5

Asturianas (Carmita)

Rhythms (V. Escudero)
V. Escudero, Carmita
Piano: Boris Kogan.

Scene 6

Fragments of "L'Amour Sorcier" Ballet (*Music by* Manuel de Falla.);

Fire Dance; The Game of Love
V. Escudero, Sacre Mont Gypsies, Carmita

ACT 2

Scene 1

A "Touch of Magic" from Cleopatra's Land on the Banks of the Nile
Gali-Gali

Scene 2

Lucienne Boyer will sing selections according to her mood from the following songs of her répertoire:

"Désir"

"Parlez-moi d'amour" (Speak to Me of Love)
(*Music and Lyrics by* Jean Lenoir.)

"Ne dis pas toujours" (Do Not Say Always)
(*Music and Lyrics by* Jean Lenoir.)

"Nuits blanches"
(*Music by* Annet P. E. Badel. *Lyrics by* Michel B. Rosenstein.)

"Le train du rêve"
(*Music by* Jean Lenoir. *Lyrics by* Maurice Aubret.)

"Sans toi" (Without You)
(*Music and Lyrics by* Vincent Scotto.)

"Beaucoup"
(*Music and Lyrics by* H. Fax and Michel Emer.)

---

[21]All other credits same as in First Edition.

"Des mots nouveaux" (I Need New Words)
(*Music by* Jean Delettre. *Lyrics by* Maurice Aubret. *English lyrics by* E. Y. Harburg.)

"Comme une femme"

"Reste"

"Le plus joli rêve"
(*Music and Lyrics by* X. and d'Arezzo.)

"Landerirette"

"Viens dans mes bras"
(*Music and Lyrics by* Marguerite Monnot and Victor Hambert.)

"Dans la fumée" (In the Smoke)
(*Music and Lyrics by* Jean Bos.)

"Les filles qui, la nuit . . . "

"C'est pas la peine"

"L'hôtel des amours faciles"
(*Music by* Raoul Moretti. *Lyrics by* Maurice Aubret.)

"La barque d'Yves"
(*Music and Lyrics by* Jean Tranchant.)

"Je ne savais pas" (I Did Not Know)
(*Music by* Jean Delettre. *Lyrics by* Maurice Aubret.)

"Pourquoi rêver?" (Why Dream?)
(*Music by* Jean Delettre. *Lyrics by* Ted Grouya and Mauprey.)

"Si petite" (So Small)
(*Music by* Gaston Claret. *Lyrics by* Pierre Bayle. *English Lyrics by* Mitchell Parish.)

"Ballade"

"Prenez mes roses" (Buy Me Roses)
(*Music by* Fugaro. *Lyrics by* Chamfleury.)

"La roussotte"

"La voyageuse"
(*Music by* Jean Delettre. *Lyrics by* Maurice Aubret.)

"Les Gueuses" (The Street Walkers)
(*Music and Lyrics by* Vincent Scotto.)

"Moi, j'crache dans l'eau" (I Spit in the Water)
(*Music and Lyrics by* Jean Tranchant.)

"Viens danser quand-même" (Come Dance Anyway, or Dancing with My Darling)
(*Music by* Jean Delettre. *Lyrics by* Jamblan.)

"Attends!" (Wait!)
(*Music by* Jean Lenoir. *Lyrics by* Jacques-Charles.)

"Is it the Singer or is it the Song?"
(*Music and Lyrics by* Annette Mills.)

"Hands Across the Table"
(*Music by* Jean Delettre. *Lyrics by* Mitchell Parish.)
(*Orchestra Conductor:* Iza Volpin. *Pianist and Composer:* Jean Delettre.)

Scene 3

The Wonder Barman
De Roze

PATIENCE,
or Bunthorne's Bride

1934.33

A Revival of the Comic Opera in Two Acts[22]. Libretto by William S. Gilbert. Music by Arthur Sullivan. Directed by James McRobbie Gordon. Orchestra directed by Isidore Godfrey. Produced by the D'Oyly Carte Opera Company. Opened 11 October 1934 at the Martin Beck Theatre and closed 13 October 1934 after 4 performances, re-opened 5-7 November 1934 for 4 performances, re-opened 3-4 December 1934 for 2 performances, and closed 4 December 1934, after 10 total performances in repertory.

CAST: *Colonel Calverley:* DARRELL FANCOURT. *Major Murgatroyd:* FRANK STEWARD. *Lieut. The Duke of Dunstable:* JOHN DEAN. *Reginald Bunthorne:*

---

[22]First presented in New York 22 September 1881 at the Standard Theatre for 177 performances. For Synopsis of Scenes and Musical Numbers, see original 1881 production. Settings and costumes uncredited.

MARTYN GREEN. *Archibald Grosvenor:* LESLIE RANDS. *Mr. Bunthorne's Solicitor:* W. F. Hodgkins. *The Lady Angela:* MARJORIE EYRE. *The Lady Saphir:* Maisie Baxter. *The Lady Ella:* KATHLEEN FRANCES. *The Lady Jane:* DOROTHY GILL. *Patience:* MURIEL DICKSON. *Chorus of Rapturous Maidens and Officers of the Dragoon Guards.*

1934.34

CONVERSATION PIECE

A Romantic Comedy with Music in Three Acts, 15 Scenes. Book, music and lyrics by Noël Coward. Directed by Noël Coward. Settings and costumes by Gladys E. Calthrop. Miss Printemps' costumes by Lanvin, Paris. Music director, Victor Baravalle. Orchestrations by Charles Prentice. Produced by Arch Selwyn and Harold B. Franklin, in association with Charles B. Cochran. Opened 23 October 1934 at the 44th Street Theatre and closed 8 December 1934 after 55 performances.

CAST (in order of appearance): *Sophie Otford:* SYLVIA LESLIE. *Martha James:* MOYA NUGENT. *Mrs. Dragon:* BETTY SHALE. *Paul, Duc de Chaucigny-Varennes:* PIERRE FRESNAY. *Rose:* Maidie Andrews. *Mélanie:* YVONNE PRINTEMPS. *The Marquis of Sheere:* Carl Harbord. *The Earl of Harringford:* George Sanders. *Regency Rakes (3): Lord Braceworth:* Pat Worsley. *Lord Doyning:* Antony Brian. *Mr. Hailsham:* Sidney Grammer. *The Duchess of Beneden:* Winifred Davis. *The Duke of Beneden:* ATHOLE STEWART. *Lady Julia Charteris:* IRENE BROWNE. *Hannah,* her maid: Jill Anthony. *A Tiger:* Leonard Goodman. *Miss Goslett:* Phyllis Harding. *Miss Mention:* Dorothy Drover. *Lord Kenyon:* Penryn Bannerman. *Lord St. Marys:* George Sanders. *Fishermen:* Reginald Thurgood, William McGuigan, Evan Jones, Roy Hall. *Countess Harringford:* Sheila Patrick. *Lady Braceworth:* Eileen Clifton. *Mrs. Hailsham:* Winifred Campbell. *Hon. Julian Kane:* St. John Lauri. *Lord Mosscrock:* Edwin Underhill. *Mr. Amos:* Alex Robertson. *Butler:* Claude Farrow. *Mr. Jones:* Leonard Michel. *Courtesan:* Brenda Clether.

Soldiers, Guests: Albert Dudley, Ronald Pope, Geoffrey Brighton, Esmond Wilding. *Milliners, Ladies of the Town, Visitors:* Maysie Anderson, Jean Beckwith, Grace Gorrod, Joan Grundy, Vivienne Lambelet, Enid Settle, June Spencer-Dyke, Winifred Talbot, Peggy Davannah, Lucy Feord, Yvonne O'Dell. *Children:* Harriet Irwin, Agnes Heller, Evelyn Smith, Doris Markey, Donna Leonard, Dean Jenks, Richard Brummer, Joe Benny.

Acts 1,Scene 1: Prologue. Painted Curtains which depict Regency Brighton, England, 1811. *Scene 2:* Part of the Parade. About 11:00 on a sunny spring morning. *Scene 3:* The Living-room of Melanie's House. *Scene 4:* Part of the Parade. *Scene 5:* The Living-room of Melanie's House. *Scene 6:* Painted Curtains which depict Regency Brighton. *Scene 7:* The Public Gardens. Evening.

Act 2, Scene 1: Painted Curtains which depict Regency Brighton. *Scene 2:* The Living-room of Melanie's House. Early afternoon. *Scene 3:* Painted Curtains which depict Regency Brighton. *Scene 4:* A Large Room on the Ground Floor of Melanie's House.

Act 3, Scene 1: The Steyne. About noon. *Scene 2:* Melanie's Room. *Scene 3:* The Public Gardens. Evening. *Scene 4:* Melanie's Room. Night.

ACT 1

Scene 2

The Parade

Scene 3

"I'll Follow My Secret Heart"
Y. Printemps

Scene 4

"Regency Rakes"
S. Grammer, A. Brian, P. Worsley

Scene 5

"Charming, Charming"
Y. Printemps, M. Andrews, S. Leslie, M. Nugent

"Dear Little Soldiers'
Y. Printemps, M. Andrews, S. Leslie, M. Nugent

Scene 6

"There's Always Something Fishy About the French"
S. Leslie, M. Nugent

ACT 2

Scene 1

"Regency Rakes" (reprise)
S. Grammer, A. Brian, P. Worsley

Scene 2

"English Lesson"
Y. Printemps

"I'll Follow My Secret Heart" (reprise)
Y. Printemps

Scene 3

"There Was Once a Little Village By the Sea"
Fishermen

Scene 4

Finale (Act 2)
Y. Printemps, Ensemble

ACT 3

Scene 2

"Nevermore"
Y. Printemps

1934.35   SAY WHEN

A Musical Comedy in Two Acts, 10 Scenes. Book by Jack McGowan. Music by Ray Henderson. Lyrics by Ted Koehler. (Directed by Bertram Harrison.) Musical numbers staged by Russell Markert. Settings by Clark Robinson. Costumes by Charles LeMaire. Music director, Max Meth. Orchestrations by Conrad Salinger and (Robert) Russell Bennett. Produced by Jack McGowan and Ray Henderson. Opened 8 November 1934 at the Imperial Theatre and closed 12 January 1935 after 76 performances.

CAST (in order of appearance): *Alice*: Helen Buck. *Freddie*: J. Elliott Leonard. *Betty*: Betty Dell. *Jane*: LINDA WATKINS. *Ellen*: LILLIAN EMERSON. *Jimmy Blake*: BOB HOPE. *Bob Breese*: HARRY RICHMAN. *Deck Steward*: John Albert. *Reginald Pratt*: NICK LONG, JR. *An Inspector*: Martin Sheppard. *Carter Holmes*: CHARLES COLLINS. *Murphy*: Frederick Manatt. *Aimee Bates*: DENNIE MOORE. *Charles Palmer*: TAYLOR HOLMES. *Tompkins*: J. P. WILSON. *Myra Palmer*: CORA WITHERSPOON. *Prince Michael*: MICHAEL ROMANOFF. *Pete*, the Punk: Clyde Veaux. *Junior*: Donald Brown. *Bank Guard*: Jack Richards. *Bank Guard*: Joe Carroll. *Bishop*: Fred Lyon.

Ladies of the Ensemble: Joanna Allen, Ronnie Beck, Phyllis Cameron, Gloria Cook, Helene Cambridge, Lois Eckhart, Frances Foley, Marjorie Gayle, Joan Igou, Lorraine Jannee, Arlene Leahy, Charlotte Lorraine, Viola Paulson, Gedda Petry, Etna Ross, Edwina Steele, Martha Tibbetts, Aimee La Rue, Sylvia Stone. *Gentlemen of the Ensemble*: John Albert, Joe Carroll, Don Drew, George B. Herman, Dick Langdon, Mickey Moore, Ed Murray, M. O'Brien, Jack Richards, Martin Sheppard, John Walsh, Frank Worden.

Act 1, Scene 1: Deck of a Transatlantic Liner. *Scene 2*: Pier 57, New York City. *Scene 3*: Living Room, Palmer Home, Southampton. *Scene 4*: Upstairs Corridor, Palmer Home. *Scene 5*: The Veranda.

Act 2, Scene 1: Outside of Waldorf-Astoria. *Scene 2*: Garden of Palmer Home. *Scene 3*: Living Room of Aimee Bates' Apartment. *Scene 4*: Vaults of the Palmer Trust Company. *Scene 5*: Living Room, Palmer House.

ACT 1

"When Love Comes Swinging Along"
H. Richman, L. Emerson

"Declaration Day"
Girls and Boys

"It Must Have Been the Night"
C. Collins, N. Long, L. Emerson

"Say When"
H. Richman

"Don't Tell Me It's Bad"
L. Watkins, B. Hope

"Sunday Morning"
M. Romanoff, Ensemble

"Isn't It June?"
L. Emerson, Girls

"Put Your Heart in a Song"
H. Richman, Ensemble

"Say When" (reprise)
H. Richman

ACT 2

"So Long for Ever So Long"
C. Collins, Boys

Bridesmaids' Ballet
L. Emerson, Girls

Palmer Hour
H. Richman, B. Hope

"When Love Comes Swinging Along" (reprise)
H. Richman

"Torch Parade"
H. Richman

"Let's Take Advantage of Now"
N. Long, L. Watkins

Finale
Entire Company

1934.36   ANYTHING GOES

A Musical Comedy in Two Acts, 9 Scenes. Book by Guy Bolton, P. G. Wodehouse, (revised by) Howard Lindsay and Russel Crouse. Music and lyrics by Cole Porter. Staged by Howard Lindsay. Dances by Robert Alton. Settings by Donald Oenslager. Costumes and gowns by Jenkins. Music director, Earl Busby. Orchestrations by (Robert) Russell Bennett and Hans Spialek. Choral arrangements by Ray Johnson. Produced by Vinton Freedley, Inc. Opened 21 November 1934 at the Alvin Theatre, moved 30 September 1935 to the 46th Street Theatre, and closed 16 November 1935 after 420 performances.

CAST (in order of appearance): *Bartender*: George E. Mack. *Elisha J. Whitney*: PAUL EVERTON. *Billy Crocker*: WILLIAM GAXTON. *Bell Boy*: Irvin Pincus. *Reno Sweeney*: ETHEL MERMAN. *Reporter*: Edwin Delbridge. *First Cameraman*: Chet Bree. *Second Cameraman*: Neal Evans. *Sir Evelyn Oakleigh*: LESLIE BARRIE. *Hope Harcourt*: BETTINA HALL. *Mrs. Wadsworth T. Harcourt*: HELEN RAYMOND. *Bishop Dodson*: Pacie Ripple. *Ching*: Richard Wang. *Ling*: Charlie Fang. *Snooks*: Drucilla Strain. *Steward*: William Stamm. *Assistant Purser*: Val Vestoff. *First Federal Man*: Harry Wilson. *Second Federal Man*: Arthur Imperato. *Mrs. Wentworth*: May Abbey. *Mrs. Frick*: Florence Earle. *Reverend Dr. Moon*: VICTOR MOORE. *Bonnie Letour*: VERA DUNN. *Chief Officer*: Houston Richards. *Ship's Drunk*: William Barry. *Mr. Swift*: Maurice Elliott. *Little Boy*: Billy Curtis. *Captain*: John C. King. *Babe*: Vivian Vance.

The Foursome: Marshall Smith, Ray Johnson, Dwight Snyder, Dee Porter. *The Ritz Quartette*: Chet Bree, Bill Stamm, Neal Evans, Edwin Delbridge. *The Alvin Quartette*: Arthur Imperato, David Glidden, Richard Nealy, Stuart Fraser. *Ship's Orchestra*: The Stylists. *Reno's Angels*: Ruth Bond, Norma Butler, Enes Early, Marjorie Fisher, Ruth Gomley, Irene Hamlin, Renee Johnson, Irene Kelly, Leoda Knapp, Doris Maye, Lillian Ostrom, Jackie Paige, Mary Philips, Cornelia Rogers, Frances Stewart, Ruth Shaw, Eleanore Sheridan. *Passengers*: Kay Adams, Lola Dexter, Maurine Holmes, Helen Folsom, Marquita Nicholai, Ethel Sommerville, Finette Walker, Evelyn Kelly.

Act 1, Scene 1: The Weylin Caprice Bar. *Scene 2*: The Afterdeck. Midnight Sailing. *Scene 3*: Mr. Whitney's and Dr. Moon's Cabins. The next morning. *Scene 4*: The Afterdeck. Same morning. *Scene 5*: Sir Evelyn's Cabin. *Scene 6*: The Deck.

Act 2, Scene 1: The Lounge. That evening. *Scene 2*: The Brig. Five days later. *Scene 3*: Conservatory of Sir Evelyn's Home in England.

ACT 1

"I Get a Kick Out of You"
E. Merman, W. Gaxton

"Bon Voyage" (There's No Cure Like Travel)
Ensemble

"All Throught the Night"
B. Hall, W. Gaxton

"Sailors' Chanty" (There'll Always Be a Lady Fair)
The Foursome

"Where Are the Men?"
V. Dunn, H. Richards, Girls

"You're the Top"
E. Merman, W. Gaxton

"Anything Goes"
E. Merman, The Foursome, Ensemble

ACT 2

"Public Enemy Number One"
Passengers

"Blow, Gabriel, Blow"
E. Merman, Ensemble

"Be Like the Bluebird"
V. Moore

"All Through the Night" (reprise)
B. Hall, W. Gaxton

"Buddie Beware"[23]
E. Merman

"The Gypsy in Me"
B. Hall, Girls

Finale
Entire Company

1934.37

AFRICANA

An Operetta in Two Acts, 16 Scenes. Book, music and lyrics by Donald Heywood. Additional lyrics by Abe Tuvim. Staged by Peter Morell. Settings by Anthony Continer. Music director, Donald Heywood. Orchestrations by Philip Ellis, Fredda Feranda. Choral director, Philomena Perry. Produced by John Mason. Opened 26 November 1934 at the Venice Theatre and closed 28 November 1934 after 3 performances[24].

CAST: *Banjo*, Witch Woman: Ismay Andrews. *Princess Yasogi*: HESHLA TAMAYANA. *King Yafouba*: JACK CARR. *Prince Sayonga*: WALTER RICHARDSON. *Colonel Henri Petain*: HOWARD GOULD. *Mme. Adrienne Petain*: NITA GALE. *Witch Doctors* (4): *Bastaboo*: Richard Webb. *Luka*: Leonard Sturrup. *Rahmo*: E. W. Barber. *Poungla*: Earl Carter. *Rufus*: JOSEPH BYRD. *Rastus*: Dan C. Michaels. *Sonny*: Leo Bailey. *Tanganya*, Ritual Dancer: Ethel Williams. *Officers of the Foreign Legion* (6): *Francois*: Barrington Guy. *Jean*: John Hastings. *Petion*: Sy Altman. *Alvarez*: Charles Ware. *Leoni*: Jerry Sylvon. *Kini*: Douglas Martin. *Congi*: Olivette Miller. *Wamba*: GRETCHEN BRANCH. *Janoba*: Alice Ramsay. *Sanja*: Margaret Clinton. *African Jumpers* (8): *Darna*: Ruby Cole. *Siloka*: Rooney Branch. *Jubo*: Leonard Sturrup. *Moca*: Isaac Baker. *Zebo*: Ernest Adderly. *Puka*: John Dawson. *Bayla*: Joseph Nealy. *Nuba*: Alexander Adderly. *Corima*: Sally Ellis. *Trema*: Emma Moorehead. *Court Guards*: James Cooper, C. M. Davis. *Court Crier*: Ivan Lewis. *Roko*: Walter Roper. *Lemo*: E. A. Jackson. *Kunka*: Mulford Lee.

Dancing Girls, Ju-Ju Dancers, Spirit Worshippers, Natives, Spearmen, Legionnaires, Merchants: Girls' Singing Ensemble: Hannah Lance, Virginia Robinson, Ethel Owen, Millie Holmes, Mary Alice Stripling, Lillian Howard, Ora Hines, Dora Bacote, Edna Brevard, Mary Brown. Mens' Singing Ensemble: E. A. Jackson, William Waters, Jo Stripling, Thomas Bolden, Arnold Nelson, Cashious Hall, Gordon Osborne, Mulforo Lee, Andrew Harding, Walter Roper, Roy De Lapina, Ernest Brown, Leon Threadgill, Fred Lane, Robert Price, Lee David, Ed Perkins, Charles Ford, Murray Jackson. Ju-Ju Stompers: Ena Brown, Margaret Clinton, Emily Malloy, Victoria Hunt, Marie Clinton, Emma Moorehead, Florence Gould, Ruby Cole, Geneva Reed, Nancy Hunt, Wilhelmina Bridgewater, Elmina Padgett, Mildred Kelly, Helen Taylor, Viola Gibson, Augustine Joseph, Ernestine Robinson, Capitola Taylor, Beatrice Lewis, Evelyn Brevard, Lillian Pryor, Mary Lewis.

Act 1, Scene 1: An African Trail. *Scene 2*: Lawn of Palace of King Yafouba. *Scene 3*: Barracks of French Foreign Legion. *Scene 4*: Street. *Scene 5*: Exterior of Palace Wall. *Scene 6*: Office of King Yafouba. *Scene 7*: Street. *Scene 8*: Carnival in the Jungle.

Act 2, Scene 1: Colonel Petain's Home; Legion Outpost; Parade of Legion; Drums Tableaux. . *Scene 2*: Shrine of Ishnoo. *Scene 3*: Market Place. *Scene 4*: Shrine, Tribal Dance, God's. *Scene 5*: Street Scene. *Scene 6*: Lawn of Palace. *Scene 7*: Canteen. *Scene 8*: Altar of Sacrifice.

MUSICAL NUMBERS[25]

"Just a Promise"

"No Peace in My Soul"
(*Lyrics by* Abe Tuvim.)

"Stop Beating Those Drums"

"Yamaboo"

"Africana"

"Love Me"

1934.38

REVENGE WITH MUSIC

A Musical Play in Two Acts, 17 Scenes. Book and lyrics by Howard Dietz. Based on the Spanish novel "El Sombrero de Tres" (The Three-Cornered Hat) by Pedro de Alarcon, adapted from a folk tale. Music by Arthur Schwartz. Staged by Komisarjevsky, (Worthington Miner, Howard Dietz, Marc Connolly). Dance ensembles by Michael Mordkin. Music direction, Victor Baravalle. Settings by Albert Johnson. Costumes by Constance

---

Ripley. Orchestrations by (Robert) Russell Bennett. Produced by Arch Selwyn and Harold B. Franklin. Opened 28 November 1934 at the New Amsterdam Theatre, closed 15 December 1934 after 22 performances; re-opened 24 December 1934 and closed 27 April 1935 after 136 additional performances, for a total of 158 performances[26].

CAST (in order of appearance): *Manuelo*, Proprietor of the Tavern: Jay Wilson. *Miguel Rodriguez*, the Mayor: DETMAR POPPEN. *Pablo*: REX O'MALLEY. *Alonzo*, Doorman at the Official Residence: JOSEPH MACAULAY. *Dona Isabella*, Wife of Don Emilio: ILKA CHASE. *Don Emilio*, Gobernador of the Province: CHARLES WINNINGER. *Maria*: LIBBY HOLMAN. *Margarita*, Carlos' Cousin: MARGARET LEE. *Eduardo*, a Soldier, Maria's Cousin: George Kirk. *Carlos*, the Miller: GEORGES METAXA. *Consuela*: IVY SCOTT. *Constantina*: Natali Danesi. *Salvador*, a Bailiff: Walter Armin. *Josefa*: Helen Arden. *Mule Driver*: George Thornton. *Rosalia, Juanita*, Dona Isabella's Maids: Beatrice Berens, Berta Donn. *Guitarists*: Hernandez Brothers. *Dancing Soloists*: Rosita Ortega, Nunez de Polanco, Omero Valencia, Frances Farnsworth, Tamara Doriva.

Guests, Attendants, Townspeople, Pedestrians, etc.: Vocal Ensemble: Beatrice Berens, Gertrude Berggren, Geraldine Bork, Margaret Daum, Frank Davenport, Earle MacVeigh, Charles Scanlon, Madeline de Souter, Rowan Tudor, Eleanor Waldon, Cliff Whitcomb. Dance Ensemble: Margaret de Anguera, Marcus Bleakman, Andre Charise, William Elliott, Raoul Fernandez, David Friedkin, Ernestone Henock, Eleanor King, Ada Korvin, Marion Lawrence, Tom Long, Gene Martel, Paul Mathis, Harry Pick, Frances Reid, Hyla Roberts, Bianca Volland, Herman Weiner, Paula Yasgour.

Act 1, Scene 1: Manuelo's Tavern. A township in Andalusia, Spain. Approximately 1800. *Scene 2*: The Arbor. *Scene 3*: The Road. *Scene 4*: Outside the Tavern. *Scene 5*: Dona Isabella's Room. *Scene 6*: The Arbor. *Scene 7*: Don Emilio's Office. *Scene 8*: The Mill Kitchen. *Scene 9*: The Millrace.

Act 2, Scene 1: A Corner at Manuelo's. *Scene 2*: The Millrace. *Scene 3*: The Mill Kitchen. *Scene 4*: The Courtyard. *Scene 5*: The Door. *Scene 6*: Dona Isabella's Room. *Scene 7*: The Door. *Scene 8*: The Ballroom.

ACT 1

"Flamenco" (dance)
N. de Polanco, F. Farnsworth, T. Doriva

"When You Love Only One"
L. Holman

"Never Marry a Dancer"
M. Lee

"If There Is Someone Lovelier Than You"
G. Metaxa

"In the Noonday Sun"
I. Scott, Ensemble

"That Fellow Manuelo"
J. Macaulay, O. Valencia, R. Ortega, Hernandez Brothers Trio, Ensemble

"In the Noonday Sun" (reprise)
G. Metaxa, Company

"Think It Over"
C. Winninger

"Maria"
G. Metaxa, L. Holman, Ensemble

"My Father Said"
G. Kirk, M. Lee, Ensemble

"You and the Night and the Music"
G. Metaxa, L. Holman

ACT 2

Dance
R. Ortega

"Once-in-a-While"
M. Lee, D. Poppen, Ensemble

"That Fellow Manuelo" (reprise)
G. Metaxa, Ensemble

"In the Middle of the Night"
J. Macaulay, Ensemble

"Wad'ring Heart"
L. Holman

Moorish Dance and Finale
Entire Company

---

[23]Replaced early in the run by "I Get a Kick Out of You" (reprise) sung by E. Merman.

[24]Costumes uncredited.

[25]No program available. Musical numbers incomplete and not in perfo

[26]Program note: The management makes acknowledgement to Worthington Miner for assistance during the engagement prior to New York.

1934.39 CALLING ALL STARS

A Musical Revue in Two Acts, 23 Scenes. Sketches by Lew Brown, A. Dorian Otvos, Alan Baxter, (Homer Fickett, William K. Wells, H. I. Philips). Music by Harry Akst. Lyrics by Lew Brown. Dialogue and sketches directed by Lew Brown and Thomas Mitchell. Dances and ensembles directed by Maurice L. Kussel. Strauss dances directed by Sara Mildred Strauss. Settings by Nat Karson. Costumes by Billi Livingston. Lighting by Abe Feder. Music director, Al Goodman. Orchestrations by Hans Spialek, Conrad Salinger. Entire production supervised by Lew Brown. Produced by Lew Brown. Opened 13 December 1934 at the Hollywood Theatre and closed 12 January 1935 after 36 performances.

CAST: LOU HOLTZ, PHIL BAKER, EVERETT MARSHALL, GERTRUDE NIESEN, MITZI MAYFAIR, JACK WHITING, PATRICIA BOWMAN, JUDY CANOVA, MARTHA RAYE, AL BERNIE, PATSY FLICK, Harry (Bottle) McNaughton, Ella Logan, Peggy Taylor and Her Kitchen Pirates, Pete Canova, Zeke Canova, Anne Canova, Estelle Jayne, Anthony Blair, Arthur Auerbach. *At the pianos:* Edgar Fairchild, Robert Lindholm.
  Showgirls: Enda Abbey, Ann Budnik, Catherine Clark, Marguerite DeCoursey, Marion Heemsath, Revalie Haber, Viola Lenn, Eleanore Low, Helen Mack, Joan Manners, Ann Metzger, June Murphy, Rose Palmer, Ellen Patti, Frances Sinclair, Lorraine Teatom, Joan Whitney, Irene Coleman. *Dancing Girls:* Alice Anderson, Alice Anthon, Alice Bankert, Alice Blair, Olga Burke, Gloria Claire, Marie Cole, Gladys Glancy, Roxy Green, Orchid Henson, Iris Kingsley, Ruth Morgan, June McNulty, Polly Sturgeon, June Tempest, Bobby Theiss, Cynthia Thompson, Emily Von Hoven. *Sara Mildred Strauss Dancers:* Eunice Altea, Babette Bissinger, Mary Bolles, George Brady, Emma Burke, Dolores Campbell, Nathalie Crandall, Rena Dell, Anita Ferne, Sel Jos, Janet Abbott, Ned Masiel, Camille Masters, Gloria Mausier, Sara Mazo, June McGrail, Gertrude Michaels, Elsie Mindell, Grace Pearce, Grace Patterson, Grace Rochester, Jean Rauley, Munice Sich, Marguerite White. *Boys:* George Gordon, George Hunter, Bill Hale, Eddie Johnson, Clark Leston, William Meader, Harry Patterson, Jack Tally.

ACT 1

Scene 1

  "Calling All Stars"
    P. Baker, L. Holtz, H. McNaughton, E. Jayne, E. Logan, Show Girls

Scene 2

  "Thinking Out Loud"
    J. Whiting, M. Mayfair, Ensemble

Scene 3

  Streamline (*by* Homer Fickett)
    Bride: E. Jayne. *Groom:* P. Baker. *Porter:* P. Canova.

Scene 4

  "I've Nothing to Offer"
    E. Marshall
    Dance by P. Bowman, Sara Mildred Strauss Dancers.

Scene 5

  Lethargy (*by* Alan Baxter)
    Mrs. Tuxedo Fitzhugh-Tigthleigh: D. Raymond. *Mr. Tuxedo Fitzhugh-Tigthleigh:* L. Holtz. *Mrs. Atwater Wimbledon-Fuynals:* E. Jayne. *Yardsmore, the Butler:* H. McNaughton. *Pasty Young Man:* J. Talley.

Scene 6

  "If It's Love"
    J. Whiting, E. Logan, M. Ray, J. Canova, Boys, Girls

Scene 7

  Absent-Minded Doctor
    Doctor: P. Baker. *Nurse:* E. Jayne. *Patient:* H. McNaughton.

Scene 8

  Specialty Dance
    M. Mayfair

Scene 9

  So This Is Hollywood (*by* Lew Brown and A. Dorian Otvos)
    George Gershwin: P. Baker. *Bill Jones,* his friend: A. Blair. *Harry Horowitz,* Playboy: L. Holtz. *Flossie,* his wife: E. Jayne. *A Baby Wampus:* M. Ray. *Another Baby Wampus:* E. Logan. *Officer:* Z. Canova.

Scene 10

  "I Don't Want to Be President (If It Means Losing You)"
    J. Whiting, M. Mayfair, Ensemble

Scene 11

  Lou Holtz and Phil Baker, assisted by Harry ("Bottle") McNaughton

Scene 12

  Finale: "Straw Hat in the Rain"
    E. Marshall, Entire Company

ACT 2

Scene 1

  Opening
    L. Holtz

Scene 2

  "I'd Like to Dunk You in My Coffee"
    J. Whiting, M. Mayfair, Ensemble

Scene 3

  Last of the Hill Billies (*by* Lew Brown and H. I. Phillips)
    Pappy: P. Flick. *Clem:* P. Canova. *Eppie:* Z. Canova. *Mammy:* A. Canova. *Abbey:* J. Canova. *Neighbor:* A. Auerbach. *Grandmammie:* D. Raymond.

Scene 4

  "I'm Stepping Out of the Picture"
    G. Niesen
    Dance by the Sara Mildred Strauss Dancers.

Scene 5

  The Hiker (*by* Alan Baxter)
    The Scout: L. Holtz. *Mrs. Jenkins:* D. Raymond. *Wife:* E. Jayne. *Scoutmaster:* P. Baker.

Scene 6

  "He Just Beats a Tom Tom"
    M. Ray
    Dance by the Sara Mildred Strauss Dancers. *Jungle Interlude by* P. Taylor and Her Kitchen Pirates.

Scene 7

  The Stein-Way (*by* William K. Wells)
    Announcement by D. Raymond. *The Betrayer:* L. Holtz. *The Woman Scorned:* E. Jayne.

Scene 8

  "My Old Hoss"
    E. Marshall

Scene 9

  When Are Ya Comin' To See Me
    L. Holtz, P. Baker, J. Canova

Scene 10

  "Just Mention Joe"
    G. Niesen
    Dance by P. Bowman, Sara Mildred Strauss Dancers, Entire Ensemble.

Scene 11

  Finale
    Entire Company

1934.40 FOOLS RUSH IN

A Musical Revue in Two Acts, 43 Scenes. Sketches by Norman Zeno, Viola Brothers Shore, Richard Whorf. Lyrics by Norman Zeno. Music by Will Irwin. Additional music and lyrics by June Sillman, Richard Lewine, (Richard Jones, John Rox, Bud Harris). (Additional sketches by Jaro Fabray, Leonard Sillman, Barnett Warren, June Sillman, O. Z. Whitehead, Julian Chein, Patrick Goldrick, Vandy Cape.) Entire production conceived and directed by Leonard Sillman, assisted by Chester O'Brien. Dances staged by Chester O'Brien, Edwin Strawbridge, (Arthur Bradley). Settings and costumes by Russell Patterson and Eugene Dunkel. Music director, Max Meth. Orchestrations by Conrad Salinger, Hans Spialek, (Robert) Russell Bennett. Produced by William A. Brady, (Marilyn Miller). Opened 25 December 1934 at the Playhouse and closed 4 January 1935 after 14 performances.

CAST: IMOGENE COCA, RICHARD WHORF, LEONARD SILLMAN, BETZI BEATON, BILLY MILTON, O. Z. WHITEHEAD, Miriam Battista, Cyrena Smith, Robert Quigley, Ellen Howard, Teddy Lynch, Vandy Cape, Charles Walter, Mildred Todd, Lee Brody, Peggy Hovenden, Albert Whitley, Dorothy Kennedy-Fox, Robert Burton, Olga Vernon, Cliff Allen, Billie Haywood, Edward Potter, Virginia Campbell, Karl Swenson, Elinor Flynn, Roger Stearns, Janet Fox, Mortimer O'Brien, Joan Larkin, Harry Smith, June Nicholson, Ana Estasen, Bertram Thorn, Roger Stearns, Frank

Gagen, Jack McCann, Eve Bailey, Fred Nay, Waverlyn Lambert. *The Edwin Strawbridge Dancers:* Valeska Hubbard, Mischa Pompianov, Eva Desca, Lili Mann, Susanne Remos, Bert Linden.

ACT 1[27]

Scene 1

The Playhouse Presents
The Company

Scene 2

Puritanically Speaking
O. Z. Whitehead

Scene 3

"Building Up to a Let-Down"
T. Lynch, R. Burton, Ensemble
(*Lyrics by* Lee Brody and Norman Zeno.)

Scene 4

"I Want to Dance"
C. Walter
Danced by I. Coca, C. Walter. (*Choreography by* Chester O'Brien and Ward Fox.)

Scene 5

Ode to the Unemployed
R. Quigley, R. Whorf

Scene 6

"Napoleon"
L. Sillman

Scene 7

Surprise, Surprise (*by* Leonard Sillman)
Indulged in by B. Beaton, R. Burton.

Scene 8

The Distaff Side (*by* Norman Zeno)
Chairwoman: M. Todd. *Mrs. Roosevelt:* J. Fox. *Mrs. Hoover:* P. Hovenden. *Guard of the Troop:* L. Brody. *Girl Scouts:* C. Smith, J. Nicholson, E. Howard, A. Estasen.

Scene 9

"Jim Dandy"
R. Quigley, Ensemble

Scene 10

"Sitting Over There"
B. Beaton, R. Burton

Scene 11

Gala Concert (*by* Barnett Warren)
Pastorelli: L. Sillman. *Young Man:* H. Smith.

Scene 12

"Love, Come Take Me"
O. Vernon
Danced by the Strawbridge Dancers.

Scene 13

A-Hunting the Grouse (*by* Richard Whorf)
Lady Agatha: I. Coca. *Sir Twarmley:* R. Whorf. *Carstairs:* B. Thorn.

Scene 14

"Shoes"
B. Haywood, C. Allen
Danced by C. Walter.

Scene 15

Five Star Final (*by* June Sillman and Viola Brothers Shore)
Mr. Dionne: K. Swenson. *Mrs. Dionne:* M. Battista. *Mrs. William Randolph Hearst:* C. Smith. *Agent:* A. Whitley. *Nurses:* E. Flynn, J. Nicholson, A. Estasen, M. Todd. *Mounties:* B. Linden, F. Gagen, J. McCann, H. Smith. *Guard:* R. Burton. *Cameraman:* R. Quigley.

----

[27]Added during run:

In Collaboration (*by* Norman Zeno)
Announcer: E. Potter. *Amanda:* B. Beaton. *Alfred:* B. Milton. *Lord Fellows:* R. Stearns. *Butler:* K. Swenson.

Scene 16

"New Sensation"
B. Milton
Danced by the Strawbridge Dancers.

Scene 17

Practically Nothing
I. Coca, R. Whorf

Scene 18

Ladies of Wealth
Doris Duke: B. Beaton. *Gloria Baker:* C. Smith. *Barbara Hutton Mdivini:* M. Todd.

Scene 19

"Rhythm in My Hair":

a. Cubanacan
T. Lynch, Ensemble

b. Park Avenue
O. Vernon, Ensemble

c. Harlem
B. Haywood, Ensemble
(*Choreography by* Arthur Bradley.)

d. Forty-Second Street
D. Kennedy-Fox, C. Walter
(*Choreography by* D. Kennedy-Fox, C. Walter.)

Scene 20

Busman's Holiday (*by* Viola Brothers Shore)
Marian: M. Todd. *Herman:* B. Milton.

Scene 21

Calling All Sinners
Sister Leader: I. Coca. *Sister Koor:* C. Smith. *Sister Grace:* P. Hovenden. *Drummer:* R. Quigley. *Cymbalist:* O. Z. Whitehead. *Organist:* R. Burton. *Lieutenant:* A. Whitley.

Scene 22

"Life of Sin"
L. Sillman

Scene 23

"Ça, C'est Sixth Avenue"
(*Dialogue, Music and Lyrics by* Lee Brody and Richard Jones.)
Announcer: E. Potter. *Mrs. Cohen:* L. Brody. *Mrs. Goldstein:* M. Battista. *A Musician:* B. Thorn. *He:* K. Swewnson. *She:* V. Campbell. *Phoebe:* P. Hovenden. *Hester:* M. Todd. *Miss Within Gates:* B. Beaton. *A Woman:* J. Fox. *A Waiter:* C. Allen. *Willie:* C. Walter. *A Boy:* A. Whitley. *A Girl:* E. Flynn. *Mrs. Zwawitz:* E. Bailey. *Mrs. Brody:* T. Lynch. *First Man:* R. Quigley. *Second Man:* H. Smith. *A Drunk:* R. Burton. *A Mother:* V. Cape. *A Child:* E. Howard. *A Gangster:* M. O'Brien. *Old Clothes Man:* F. Nay. *Policeman:* F. Gagen. *First Street Cleaner:* R. Stearns. *Second Street Cleaner:* B. Milton. *Stroller:* W. Lambert.

ACT 2

Scene 1

"Willie's Little Whistle"
R. Burton, I. Coca, V. Cape
Willie: R. Whorf. *Mourners:* The Company.

Scene 2

Politically Speaking (*by* O. Z. Whitehead)
O. Z. Whitehead

Scene 3

Man in the Moon (from a suggestion by Jeannie MacPherson)
Boy: E. Potter. *Girl:* I. Coca. *Man in the Moon:* L. Sillman.

Scene 4

Britishtics (*by* Julian Chein and Patrick Goldrick)
Cavendish: B. Milton. *Bottomley:* R. Whorf.

Scene 5

"The Story of Buster"
B. Beaton, R. Burton

Scene 6

"Two Get Together"
B. Milton, T. Lynch, Ensemble

Scene 7

The Opera Opens (*by* Norman Zeno)
Julie: E. Bailey. *John*: E. Potter. *Mabel*: M. Battista. *Mrs. Vanderloop*: P. Hovenden. *Parker*: A. Whitley. *Duchess*: V. Cape.

Scene 8

"I'm So in Love"
T. Lynch, B. Milton.
Co-Ed: A. Estasen. *Old Maid*: J. Fox. *Bachelor*: O. Z. Whitehead. *Scrubwoman*: C. Smith. *Feet*: R. Burton, R. Quigley, A. Whitley, C. Swenson.

Scene 9

Blubber or Bust (*by* Richard Whorf)
Abbie: I. Coca. *Captain*: R. Whorf.

Scene 10

"Ghost Town"
O. Vernon
Romeo: B. Linden. *Juliet*: V. Hubbard. *Assisted by* the Edwin Strawbridge Dancers, Ensemble.

Scene 11

Her First Radio Broadcast (*by* Vandy Cape)
Announcer: R. Quigley. *Accompanist*: R. Stearns. *Mme. Pupette de la Chose de la Republique*: V. Cape.

Scene 12

"Wicked, Unwholesome, Expensive"
(*Music and Lyrics by* John Rox.)
Wicked: C. Smith, R. Stearns. *Unwholesome*: M. Todd, R. Burton. *Expensive*: P. Hovenden, B. Milton.

Scene 13

"Sixty Second Romance"
B. Haywood, C. Allen
(*Music by* Bud Harris. *Lyrics by* Lawrence Harris.)

Scene 14

Love All
B. Beaton, R. Burton

Scene 15

Body by Fuller (*by* Norman Zeno)
Dr. Ludehoun: L. Sillman. *Lady Ludehoun*: I. Coca. *A. J. Digby*: R. Whorf. *Parker*: R. Stearns. *Lutgoff*: B. Thorn.

Scene 16

Two People in Three-Four (*Choreography by* Dorothy Kennedy-Fox.)
Danced by D. Kennedy-Fox, C. Walter.

Scene 17

"Let's Hold Hands"
E. Flynn, B. Milton, B. Thorn, Ensemble
(*Music by* Richard Lewine. *Lyrics by* June Sillman.)

Scene 18

"Personal Appearance"
L. Sillman
The Star: I. Coca. Assisted by the Company.

Scene 19

"Rhythm in My Hair" (reprise)
Danced by the Edwin Strawbridge Dancers
Sailor: M. Pompianov. *Dowager*: E. Desca. *Society Woman*: L. Mann. *Streetwalker*: V. Hubbard. *Chinese Girl*: S. Remos.

Scene 20

"The Party's Over"
The Company

1934.41   THE O'FLYNN

An Operetta in Four Acts, 8 Scenes. Book and lyrics by Brian Hooker and Russell Janney. Based on Justin Huntly McCarthy's play of the same name. Music by Franklin Hauser. Staged by Robert Milton. Dances by Louis Chalif. Settings and costumes by James Reynolds. Music director, Giuseppe Bamboschek. Produced by Russell Janney. Opened 27 December 1934 at the Broadway Theatre and closed 4 January 1935 after 11 performances.

CAST: *Hendrigg*, a Spy in the Service of King William: WILLIAM BALFOUR. *The Captain of the Soleil d'Or*: Hugo Baldi. *The Lady Benedetta Mount-Michael*: LUCY MONROE. *The Cook*: Jules Epailly. *Jacques*, Servant to O'Flynn: WILL H. PHILBRICK. *Captain Flynn O'Flynn (The O'Flynn)*: GEORGE HOUSTON. *The Landlord* on the Dock at Cork: WALTER MUNROE. *Conacher O'Rourke*, Servant to O'Flynn: COLIN CAMPBELL. *Bailiffs (2)*: *Gosling*: Thomas Williams. *Coin*: James Ross. *Principal Members of His Majesty's Players (7)*: *Burden*: H. H. McCollum. *Beggles*: Raymond O'Brien. *Conamur*: Lee Randall. *Fancy Free*: Anna Trockowna. *Mrs. Old Mixon*: Jean Newcombe. *The Drummer Boy*: Wilson Angel. *The Dancer*: Helen Grenelle. *Strolling Platers (4)*: *The Ham*: Charles Homer. *The Fat Player*: Eugene W. King. *Comedian*: Don Valentine. *Tall Player*: John Zak. *The Landlord* of the Isle of Cyprus: George Shields. *The Landlord's Daughter*: Merle Stevens. *Lord Sedgemouth*, Commander-in-Chief of the King James Forces in Ireland: FRANK FENTON. *His Majesty King James II*: H. COOPER CLIFFE. *Sir George Mayhew*: Henry Vincent. *Lord Fawley*: Edward Martyn. *General Van Dronk*, in Command of Knockmore: Charles E. Galagher. *Lieutenant Trusham*: John Mealey. *The Duchess of Tyrconnel*: Doris Rich. *The Bishop*: WALTER MUNROE. *A Tailor*: John Cardini. *A Colleen*: Paula Lind. *Sailors of the Soleil D'Or, Irish Peasants, Colleens, Soldiers in O'Flynn's Own, English Soldiers, Ladies of the Court, Ballet Dancers, etc.*

Girls: Ruth Adams, Florence De Barde, Pauline Chandler, Magnheld Fjeldheim, Helene Hampton, Anna Heindl, Elizabeth Kerr, Amanda King, Vera Kingsley, Rose Kearney, Leone Krauss, Vera Lix, Ona Leonovitz, Paula Lind, Maria Lama, Sylvia La Mard, Edith Maison, Adrienne Munkeberg, Madge Parker, Marion Ross, Marie Russel, Mariam Stockton, Rosalind Shaw, Lillian Sullivan, Sophie Stern. *Dancing Girls*: Misses Charlotte Beverley, Emmy Bock, Barbara Blair, Lis Braemer, Virginia Brown, Lucille Constant, Virginia Collins, Mitzie Garner, Marcia Grey, Lucille Gottlieb, Beverly Hosier, Amelie Ideal, Nancy Knott, Eleanor Keenan, Lelia Laney, Sallee Merrill, Madeline MacDonald, Genevieve Svesson. *Boys*: David Bell, John Cardini, Burr Crandall, Richard Cody, N. Cardosia, Vance Elliott, Walter Franklyn, John Fulco, Joel Hamilton, Elwin Howland, Herman Holt, Eugene W. King, Earl Mason, George Monteer, Raymond O'Toole, Basil Prock, Orville Race, Basil Rallis, Albert Soback, Joseph Scandur, Charles Tress, Roy J. Williams, Buck Williams, John Zak.

The entire action takes place a certain summer, during the days when James II had been driven from the English throne by William of Orange.

Act 1, Scene 1: The Boat. *Scene 2*: The Dock. *Scene 3*: Castle Famine.

Act 2: The Tavern.

Act 3, Scene 1: The Camp. *Scene 2*: The Knockmore Tower.

Act 4, Scene 1: The Great Hall of Tapestries, Knockmore. *Scene 2*: Castle Famine.

MUSICAL NUMBERS[28]

"A Lovely Lady"
(*Lyrics by* Russell Janney.)

"Child of Erin"
(*Lyrics by* Russell Janney.)

"Song of My Heart"
(*Lyrics by* Brian Hooker.)

"The Man I Love Is Here"
(*Lyrics by* Brian Hooker.)

"So You Will Walk With Me"

1934.42   THUMBS UP!

A Musical Revue in Two Acts, 26 Scenes. Comedy scenes (sketches) by H. I. Phillips, Harold Atteridge, Alan Baxter, (Ronald Jeans, Ballard Macdonald, Charles Sherman). Lyrics by Ballard Macdonald, Earle Crooker, (John Murray Anderson, Irving Caesar, Jean Herbert, Karl Stark, Vernon Duke, James F. Hanley). Music by James F. Hanley, Henry Sullivan, (Gerald Marks, Vernon Duke). Entire production devised and staged by John Murray Anderson. Comedy scenes directed by Edward Clarke Lilley. Dances by Robert Alton. Production (settings) designed by Ted Weidhaas. Additional settings designed by James Reynolds and Raoul Pene du Bois. Costumes by James Reynolds, Raoul Pene du Bois, Thomas Becher, James Morcom. Music director, Gene Salzer. Orchestrations by Hans Spialek, Conrad Salinger, David Raksin. Trio harmony arrangements by Jane Pickens. Produced by Eddie Dowling. Opened 27 December 1934 at the St. James Theatre and closed 11 May 1935 after 156 performances.

CAST: EDDIE DOWLING, BOBBY CLARK & PAUL McCULLOUGH, HAL LeROY, J. HAROLD MURRAY, EDDIE GARR, RAY DOOLEY, THE PICKENS SISTERS (Helen, Jane, Patti), PAUL DRAPER, ROSE KING, SHEILA BARRETT, MARGRET ADAMS, EUNICE HEALEY, JACK COLE, ALICE DUDLEY, AL SEXTON, HUGH CAMERON, BARNETT PARKER, IRENE McBRIDE, RUBEN

---

[28]No individual musical numbers listed in the program. Incomplete list, prepared from published music and reviews, is not in performance order.

GARCIA, JOHN and FRANK DELMAR, THE FALLA SISTERS (Holly, Dolly), the Demnati Troupe.

Three Young Ladies (Showgirls): Helen Bent, Joan Nelson, Louene Ambrosius. *Dancers*: Agnes Franey, Frances Nevins, Ruth Nicholson, Dionne Farrel, Vida Manuel, Billie Worth, Althea Elder, Beth Roland, Sandra Gould, Dawn Greenwood, Lucy Mann, Marion Vannemann, Yvonne Marchand, Frances Rand, Phyllis Lind. *Boys*: Henry Dick, Phil Shaw, Robert Alan, Adrian Anthony, John Fearnley, Emerson Frone, George Church, Stanley Rash, William Chandler, Marty Rhiel, Don Knobloch, Howard Morgan, Prescott Brown.

ACT 1

Scene 1

"Beautiful Night" (Jogging Through the Park)
Pickens Sisters, A. Sexton, M. Adams
Skating in Central Park by Ensemble.
(*Music by* James Hanley. *Lyrics by* Ballard Macdonald and Karl Stark. *Setting by* Raoul Pene du Bois after Currier and Ives.)

Scene 2

The Sleigh Ride
The Gentleman: B. Clark. *The Lady*: R. King.

Scene 3

"Zing! Went the Strings of My Heart"
H. LeRoy, E. Healey, Ensemble
(*Music and Lyrics by* James Hanley.) (Mr. LeRoy's dance arranged by himself.)

Scene 4

Domination[29] (*by* Alan Baxter)
Mr. Sledgehammer: E. Dowling. *Miss Treacle*: R. King. *Herman*: H. LeRoy. *Goodhue*: H. Cameron. *Mr. Bucket*: B. Clark. *Clerks*: B. Parker, H. Bent, J. Nelson, L. Ambrosius.

Scene 5

"Words Without Music"
(*Danced by*) P. Draper
(*Music by* Vernon Duke. *Lyrics by* Ira Gershwin.)
The Girl: I. McBride.

Scene 6

"Lily Belle May June"
R. Dooley, H. LeRoy
(*Music by* Henry Sullivan. *Lyrics by* Earle Crooker.)
Danced by Ensemble.

Scene 7

The Endorsement Family (*by* H. I. Phillips)
Mrs. Vandergould: S. Barrett. *Chidsy Vandergould*: B. Clark. *Gloria Vandergould*: M. Adams. *Grandma Vandergould*: R. Dooley. *First Cameraman*: S. Liebert. *Second Cameraman*: H. LeRoy. *Man With Mattress*: B. Parker. *The Butler*: H. Cameron.

Scene 8

"Flamenco"
A. Sexton
(*Music by* Henry Sullivan. *Lyrics by* Earle Crooker.)
The Flamenco Dancer: R. Garcia. *Flamenco*: I. McBride. *The Three Women in Black*: H. Bent, L. Ambrosius, J. Nelson. *The Two Dancers in White*: J. Cole, A. Dudley. And Ensemble.

Scene 9

Eddie Garr (impersonations)

Scene 10

"Eileen Avourneen"[30]
(*Music by* Henry Sullivan. *Lyrics by* John Murray Anderson)
The Man: J. H. Murray. *The Ladies wth White Killarney Roses*: J. Nelson, H. Bent, L. Ambrosius, I. McBride. *The Gentlemen*: H. Morgan, D. Knobloch, W. Chandler, R. Garcia. *The Young Ladies*: H. Falla, D. Falla. *The Young Gentlemen*: F. Delmar, J. Delmar. *Eileen Avourneen*: M. Adams.

Synopsis:

"Come to me in the Silence of the Night;

Come in the Speaking Silence of a Dream."
     —Christina Rossetti

On Midsummer's Eve in Ireland a man is sitting alone in a faded room. The rising moon steals through the open window and restores the old room to its former beauty, while down the path of moonlight come the beautiful women he has known. Each one leaves with him a white Killarney rose. Finally, there comes to him—for a fleeting moment—his long-lost love—Eileen Avourneen.

Scene 11

"The Torch Singer" (What Do You Think My Heart Is Made Of?)
S. Barrett
(*Music by* Henry Sullivan. *Lyrics by* Earle Crooker.)

Scene 12

Aired in Court (*by* H. I. Phillips)
Mr. Busby: H. Cameron. *Mr. Horne*: J. H. Murray. *Mr. Abernathy*: E. Garr. *Court Clerk*: B. Parker. *Court Officer*: P. McCulloch. *Foreman of the Jury*: S. Liebert. *The Prisoner*: S. Barrett. *Policeman*: G. Church. *The Judge*: B. Clark. *A Sponsor*: H. LeRoy.

Scene 13

"My Arab Complex"
R. Dooley, the Demnati Troupe
(*Music by* James Hanley. *Lyrics by* Ballard Macdonald.)

Scene 14

"Soldier of Love"
(*Dialogue by* Arthur Swanstrom. *Music by* Gerald Marks. *Lyrics by* Irving Caesar.)
Bob Sweetapple: J. H. Murray. *Seidlitz*: E. Dowling. *Pianist*: H. LeRoy. *Senator Screwy Short*: B. Clark. *Congressman Standin Doolittle*: P. McCulloch. *Speaker of the House*: H. Cameron. *Member from California*: B. Parker. *Member from Rhode Island*: A. Sexton. *Mademoiselle from Armentieres*: S. Barrett. *Captain of the Roxyettes*: E. Healey. *Her Lieutenants*: H. Falla, D. Falla, J. Delmar, F. Delmar. *Newsboy*: R. Garcia. *The Announcer*: E. Garr. *The Statue*: P. Draper. *The Ladies Who Unveil It*: R. King, R. Dooley. And Entire Company.

ACT 2[31]

Scene 1

"Color Blind"
A. Sexton
(*Music by* Henry Sullivan. *Lyrics by* Earle Crooker.)
Danced by E. Healey, Ensemble.

Scene 2

A Scottish Wedding (*by* Ronald Jeans)
The Bride: R. Dooley. *The Bride's Father*: H. Cameron. *The Bridesmaid*: S. Gould. *The Mother*: R. King. *The Brother*: H. LeRoy. *The Organist*: B. Clark. *The Minister*: J. H. Murray. *The Bridegroom*: E. Dowling.

Scene 3

"Tango Rhythms"
Danced by P. Draper
(*Music by* Steve Child.)

Scene 4

"Continental Honeymoon"
Pickens Sisters, Ensemble
(*Music by* James Hanley. *Lyrics by* Ballard Macdonald and James Hanley. *Setting designed by* Raoul Pene du Bois.)

Scene 5

"A Ship's Concert in the Eighties" (A Taste of the Sea)
R. King
(*Music by* Henry Sullivan. *Lyrics by* Earle Crooker.)
The Accompanist: E. Frome.

Scene 6

"Catherine the Great" (*by* Ballard Macdonald)
S. Barrett, the Imperial Guard
(*Musical Setting by* Henry Sullivan)

Scene 7

"Rehearsal Hall"
(*Music by* Henry Sullivan.)
The Tap Dancer: H. Dick. *The Acrobatic Dancers*: H. Falla, D. Falla. *The Ballerina*: E. Healey.

_____

[29]Dropped during the run of the show.
[30]Dropped during the run of the show.

[31]Added during the run of the show to Act 2, as Scene 2:
Tourist Camp (*by* Harold Atteridge)
Amos: H. Cameron. *Jennie*: R. King. *Snakey*: A. Sexton. *Blackey*: Sam Liebert. *Globetrotter*: B. Clark. *Blodget*: P. McCullough. *Sleepwalker*: E. Healey. *Husband*: J. Fearnley. *Warden*: George Houston. *Policeman*: G. Church.

Scene 8

Eddie Garr (impersonations)

Scene 9

"Merrily We Waltz Along"
(*Music by* Henry Sullivan. *Lyrics by* Earle Crooker. *Setting and Costumes designed by* James Reynolds.)
Sonia: R. Dooley. *Danilo*: B. Clark. *The Singer*: M. Adams. And Ensemble.

Scene 10

"I've Gotta See a Man About His Daughter"[32]
H. LeRoy
(*Music by* James Hanley. *Lyrics by* Jean Herbert, Karl Stark.)

Scene 11

The Dance (*by* Charles Sherman)
Pascha: E. Dowling. *Sascha*: S. Liebert. *The Customer*: B. Clark.

Scene 12

"Autumn in New York"
J. H. Murray, Entire Company
(*Music and Lyrics by* Vernon Duke. *Setting designed by* Raoul Pene du Bois.)

1934.43 MUSIC HATH CHARMS

A Play with Music in Two Acts, 13 Scenes. Book and lyrics by Rowland Leigh, George Rosener, John Shubert. Music by Rudolf Friml. Book directed by George Rosener. Dances and ballet by Alex Yakovleff. Settings by Watson Barratt. Costumes by Ernest Schrapps. Orchestra under the direction of Al Goodman. Produced by the Messrs. Shubert. Opened 29 December 1934 at the Majestic Theatre and closed 19 January 1935 after 25 performances.

<u>CAST</u> (in order of appearance): *Period 1934*: *Spokesman*: Robert Long. *Theophilus Roberts*, a guide for tourists: ANDREW TOMBES. *Charles Parker*: ROBERT HALLIDAY. *Maria, Marchese Del Monte Nee Di Orsano*: NATALIE HALL. *Giovanni, Duke of Orsano*: HARRY MESTAYER. *Two Venetian Hooligans*: PAUL HAAKON, NINA WHITNEY. *A Honeymoon Couple (2)*: *Lovey*: BILLY REY. *Dovey*: GRACIE WORTH. *Rudolfo, Marchese Di Orsano*, Maria's father: JOHN CLARKE. *Isabella*, Maria's mother: ELIZABETH CRANDELL. *Giaconda*, Maria's sister: CONSTANCE CARPENTER. *Duke of Umbria*, suitor for Maria's hand: CYRIL CHADWICK. *A Footman* in the Palazzo Orsano: TRUMAN GAIGE. *Dancers in the Interlude between 1934 and 1770*: PAUL HAAKON, NINA WHITNEY, Ensemble.

Period 1770: *A Villager*: Robert Long. *Angela*: Betti Davis. *Maria Sovrani*, Venetian fishermaid: NATALIE HALL. *Vittorio Sovrani*, Maria's father: JOHN CLARKE. *Petronella*, Maria's mother: ELZABETH CRANDALL. *Pappio*, Chamberlain to the Duke of Orsano: ANDREW TOMBES. *Marella*, Maria's sister: CONSTANCE CARPENTER. *Venetian Politicians (3)*: *Senator Bellanqua*: Robert Lee Allen. *Senator Nocio*: Stanley Harrison. *Senator Burranto*: Paul Burns. *Emilio*: George Schiller. *Pidgy*: BILLY REY. *Widgy*: GRACIE WORTH. *Signora Barbara Bellanqua*: Sheila Harling. *Spokesman*: Robert Long. *Fillipo*, attendant to the Duke of Orsano: TRUMAN GAIGE. *Duke of Orsano*, a famous beau of the period: ROBERT HALLIDAY. *Luigi*, Signora Barbara's lover: William Lilling. *Old Duke*, uncle to the Duke of Orsano: HARRY MESTAYER. *Senators' Wives (6)*: *Cornelia*: Vonda Norin. *Signora Nocio*: Jane Mackenzie. *Nella*: Ruth Reiter. *Laspera*: Salley Warren. *Leonora*: Isa Lane. *Signora Burranto*: Marie Wilson.

Period 1934: *Bishop*: Robert Long. *Bridesmaids*: CONSTANCE CARPENTER, Frances Wallace.

Girls: Geraldine Botkin, Eleanor Ries, Charlotte Lockwood, Betti Davis, Ruth Reiter, Jane Mackenzie, Sally Warren, Kathleen Edwards, Josephine Hall, Sue Franklin, Edith Lane, Lois Stylle, Gudron Ekeland, Yvonne Cyr, Marie Ferguson, Jayne Manners, Renee Gordon, Frances Stutz, Lucille Osborne. *Dancing Girls*: Valerie Huff, Sonja Karlow, Frances Wallace, Helen Lane, Evelyn Bonefine, Miriam Curtis, Vida Barnell, Mary Van Noy, Una Val, Elsie St. Clare, Wilma Kaye, Bobbie Howell, Isabelle Kempel, Marial Mosher, Evan Ritter, Dorothy Denton, Barbara Williams. *Boys*: *First Tenors*: Fred Hoffman, Jack Lester, Ross Lockwood, Alfred Russ, Zach Caully. *Second Tenors*: Frank Dirth, William Hubert, Harry Edwards. *Baritones*: Ralph Hunsecker, Stanley Howard, William Langley, Louis Delgado. *Bases*: Guy Hamilton, Bradley Lane, Jack Cannon, Kenneth Page, Fred Small.

Act 1, Scene 1: By the Grand Canal, Venice, 1934. *Scene 2*: A Street, 1934. *Scene 3*: The Palazzo Orsano House, 1934. *Scene 4*: Dance of Years. *Scene 5*: Fishing Village, 1770. *Scene 6*: A Square in Venice, 1770.

Act 2, Scene 1: The Palazzo Orsano, 1770. *Scene 2*: A Corridor, 1770. *Scene 3*: The Private Room of the Duke, 1770. *Scene 4* A Corridor, 1770. *Scene 5*: Ballroom, 1770. *Scene 6*: By the Grand Canal, 1770. *Scene 7*: Outside of St. Mark's Cathedral, 1934.

---

[32]Dropped during the run of the show.

ACT 1

Opening—"Gondolier Song"
Ensemble

"Maria"
R. Halliday, Male Ensemble

Dance Characteristique
Dancers, Corps de Ballet

Specialty
P. Haakon, N. Whitney

"Lovey-Dovey"
B. Rey, G. Worth, Dancers

"It's Three O'Clock"
H. Mestayer, E. Crandall, J. Clarke, C. Carpenter

"Romance"
N. Hall

"Love Is Only What You Make, Love" (Duet)
N. Hall, R. Halliday

Dance of Times

Moderne
P. Haakon, N. Whitney

Polka
D. Denton, E. Ritter, U. Val, M. Curtis

Gavotte
V. McLain, S. Karlow, V. Huff, M. Van Noy, J. Sobers, E. Williams

Tarantella
8 Dancers

Specialty
P. Haakon

"Frutti di Mare"
N. Hall, Entire Ensemble

"Let Me Be Free"
N. Hall, Fishermen

"Sweet Fool"
C. Carpenter, A. Tombes, P. Haakon, N. Whitney, Dancers

"Cavalier"
B. Rey, G. Worth, The Cavaliers

"Ladies, Beware"
R. Halliday, Dancers, Entire Ensemble

"Exquisite Moment"
R. Halliday, N. Hall

Finale, Act 1
Entire Company

ACT 2

Minuet
Corps de Ballet

Dance Divertissement
P. Haakon, N. Whitney

"Palace of Dreams"
N. Hall

"Midnight Flirtation"
N. Hall, R. Halliday, Ensemble

"It Happened"
B. Rey, G. Worth

Ballet—"Carnival"
Corps de Ballet, P. Haakon, N. Whitney

"A Smile, a Kiss"
C. Carpenter, A. Tombes

"It's You I Want to Love Tonight"
N. Hall

"My Heart Is Yours" (Duet)
R. Halliday, N. Hall

Finaletto
N. Hall, R. Halliday, Entire Ensemble

"Scandal Number"
R. L. Allen, S. Harrison, P. Burns

"Processional"
Entire Company

Grand Finale
Entire Company

1935.01 **THE GREEN PASTURES**

A Revival of the Fable Play (with Music) in Two Acts, 18 Scenes[33]. Play by Marc Connelly, suggested by Roark Bradford's Southern sketches "Ol' Man Adam an' His Chillun." Staged by Marc Connelly. Production (settings, costumes, lights) designed by Robert Edmund Jones. Choir directed by Evelyn Burwell and Oliver Foster. All choral arrangements used have been written especially for "The Green Pastures" by Hall Johnson. Produced by Laurence Rivers Inc. Opened 26 February 1935 at the 44th Street Theatre and closed 27 April 1935 after 71 performances.

CAST (in order of appearance): *Mr. Deshee*: Charles H. Moore. *Myrtle*: Nonie Simmons. *Carlyle*: Charles Hill. *Second Boy*: Wilbur Cohen, Jr. *Third Boy*: Roland Jones. *Randolph*: Lloyd Warren. *A Cook*: Irene Watts. *Custard Maker*: Randall Watts. *First Mammy Angel*: Anna Mae Fritz. *A Stout Angel*: Laura Anderson. *A Slender Angel*: Leonore Winkler. *Archangel*: Allen Charles. *Gabriel*: Oscar Polk. *The Lawd*: RICHARD B. HARRISON. *Choir Leader*: Roy McKinley. *Adam*: Daniel L. Haynes. *Eve*: Geraldine Gooding. *Cain*: Thomas Russell. *Cain's Girl*: Benveneta Washington. *Zeba*: Edna M. Harris. *Cain the Sixth*: James Fuller. *Boy Gambler*: Jazzlips Richardson, Jr. *First Gambler*: Richard Emory. *Second Gambler*: Harold Hines. *Voice in Shanty*: Mary Francis. *Noah*: Morris McKinney. *Noah's Wife*: Susie Sutton. *Shem*: Milton J. Williams. *First Woman*: Harriet Hoyt. *Second Woman*: Janet Stevens. *Third Woman*: Alice Geneva. *Fourth Woman*: Mildred Allison. *First Man*: Henry Blake. *Flatfoot*: Freddy Archibald. *Ham*: J. Homer Tutt. *Japheth*: Harry Thompson. *First Cleaner*: Florence Fields. *Second Cleaner*: Frances Smith. *Abraham*: Charles Winter Wood. *Isaac*: John Charles. *Jacob*: William McFarland. *Moses*: Frank Wilson. *Zipporah*: Mercedes Gilbert. *Aaron*: McKinley Reeves. *A Candidate Magician*: Reginald Fenderson. *Pharoah*: George Randol. *The General*: Charles Winter. *The Admiral*: James Lindsay. *First Wizard*: George Milton. *Second Wizard*: Carl Shorter. *Head Magician*: Arthur Porter. *Outer Guard*: George Brown. *Joshua*: D. Jay Sidney. *First Scout*: Charles Ivan. *Master of Ceremonies*: Billy Cumby. *King of Babylon*: William Fenton. *Prophet*: Ivan Sharp. *High Priest*: J. Homer. *The King's Favorites*: Leonora Winkler, Nonie Simmons, Viola Mickens, Florence Lee, Constance Van Dyke. *Officer*: Emory Richardson. *Hezdrel*: Daniel L. Haynes. *Another Officer*: James Morrison.

The Children: Marie Benton, Beatrice Davis, Ruby Davis, Alice Cottingham, Theon Lewis, Alice Snyder, Lloyd Warren, Rudolph Williams, Ashley Webb, Roland Jones, Charles Hill, George Carroll, Booker T. Washington, Jr., Wilbur Cohen, Jr. *Angels and Townspeople*: Ruth Carl, Willis Norton, Franklyn Brown, Anna Washington, Earl Gough. *Baylonian Band*: Carl Shorter, Richard Henderson, Thomas Russell, Edgar Yancey. *The Choir*: Sopranos: Bertha Wright, Geraldine Gooding, Almalillie Hubbard, Neil Hunter, Mattie Harris, Gertrude De Verney, Marie Warren, Mabel Ridley, Massie Patterson. *Altos*: Olive Ball, Willie Mays, Viola Mickens, Benveneta Washington, Myrtle Anderson. *Tenors*: Robert P. Ecton, Arthur Porter, James Taylor, Jr., McKinley Reeves, William McFarland, Augustus Simons, Carrington Lewis. *Baritones*: T. Lloyd Hickman, Jerome Addison, Dow K. Williams, Benjamin Ragsdale, Walter Whitfield. *Bassos*: Walter Meadows, Frank Horace, J. E. Lightfoot.

1935.02 **THE LAND OF BELLS**

A Musical Romance (Il Paese Dei Campanelli) in Three Acts, in Italian. Book (and lyrics) by Carlo Lombardo. Music by Virgilio Ranzato. Directed by Edison Rice. Orchestra under the direction of Cesare Sodero. Artistic advisor, Alfredo Gandolfi. Guest director from Italy, Mario Mattoli. Dances arranged by Alex Yakovleff. Chorus mistress, Beatrice Plummer. Produced by the Permanent Italian Theatre. Opened 9 May 1935 at the Majestic Theatre and closed 12 May 1935 after 5 performances[34].

CAST (in order of appearance): *Tarquinio*: Amadeo Varney. *Attanasio*: Giovanni Fulco. *Basilio*: Aldo Varis. *Nela*: ALBA NOVELLA. *Pomerania*: MARIA GARUFFI. *Bombon*: WANDA MORELLI. *Hans*: MARIO PALERMO. *Legaffe*: CARLO GARUFFI. *Tony*: Aldo D'Alessandro. *Jack*: Vincenzo Mattina. *Ethel*: FRANCESCA MARINARO. *Prima Ballerina*: JOYCE COLES. *Primo Ballerino*: LEON FOKINE.

Soloists: Grace Walsh, Bea Lyn, George Kiddon, Vladimir Gueral. *Ensemble*: *Ladies*: Helen Benson, Anna Blitzer, Muriel Block, Anita Bruehl, Kathryn Curl, Nancy Dodd, Caroline Finni, Helen Hampton, Joanna Keelon, Vyra Kingsley, Phyllis

Marren, Edith Nason, Dorothy Steinmetz, Alma Tollefson, Frances Wade. *Gentlemen*: Alexius Alexander, Aldo Bertini, Frank Day, Lipman Duckat, Dino Galli, Fred Guiliano, Harold Green, Russel Heustis, Earl Liften, Daniel Meduri, Lucien Paris, Giovanni Petrucci, Cornelius Piller, Leon Sabater, Phil Triestman, Bob Malone. *Corps de Ballet*: Madeline Lewisk, Gedda Petri [Petry], Nora Koreff [Kaye], Didi Skoug, Margaret Gay, Marjorie Michamer, Hild Wagner, Babbie Howell.

Act 1: The Town Square on the Seacoast of a Legendary Country—The Land of the Bells.

Act 2: The Next Morning. Late Afternoon. Spring.

Act 3: That Afternoon.

ACT 1
Opening Chorus
"Milkmaid's Song"
A. Novella, Ensemble
"Flower Song"
W. Morelli, Ballet Ensemble
Arrival of the Officers; Sailor Dance
M. Palermo, Ensemble
"Legend of the Bells"
W. Morelli, Ensemble
Love Duet
A. Novella, M. Palermo
Japanese Number
W. Morelli, C. Garuffi
Waltz Ballet
J. Coles, Ballet
Concertato
A. Novella, M. Palermo, Entire Ensemble
Finale—Legend of the Bells
Company

ACT 2
Opening Chorus and Pantomime
Entire Ensemble
Duet
A. Novella, M. Palermo, Ensemble
"La Giava"
W. Morelli, C. Garuffi, Ballet, Ensemble
Duet
A. Novella, M. Palermo
Luna, Tu
F. Marinaro, Ballet
Finale
Company

ACT 3
Duet
A. Novella, M. Palermo
Pantomime
J. Cole, L. Fokine, Ensemble
Finae
Company

1935.03 **PARADE**

A Satirical Revue in Two Acts, 30 Scenes. Sketches by Paul Peters, George Sklar, Frank Gabrielson, David Lesan, (Kyle Crichton, Michael Blankfort, Alan Baxter, Harold Johnsrud, Turner Bullock). Lyrics by Paul Peters, George Sklar, Kyle Crichton. Music by Jerome Moross. Dialogue staged by Philip Loeb. Musical and dance numbers supervised and staged by Robert Alton. Settings by Lee Simonson. Costumes by Constance Ripley, Irene Sharaff, Billi Livingston, Lee Simonson. Orchestra under the direction of Max Meth. Orchestrations by Conrad Salinger, (Robert) Russell Bennett, David Raksin, Jerome Moross. Produced by the Theatre Guild. Opened 20 May 1935 at the Guild Theatre and closed 22 June 1935 after 40 performances.

CAST: JIMMY SAVO, CHARLES D. BROWN, VERA MARSHE, EARL OXFORD, ESTHER JUNGER, EVE ARDEN, RALPH RIGGS, JEAN TRAVERS, DOROTHY FOX, CHARLES WALTERS, LEON JANNEY, EVELYN DALL, AVIS ANDREWS,

---

[33]Originally presented in New York 2 February 1930 at the Mansfield Theatre for 640 performances. For Synopsis of Scenes and Musical Numbers, see original 1930 production.
[34]Settings and costumes uncredited.

Ezra Stone, Edgar Allen, David Lesan, David Lawrence, Lois Leng, Irwin Shurack, J. Elliott Leonard, George Ali.

Parade Girls: Wanda Allen, Stella Clausen, Miriam Curtis, Mary Katherine Dougherty, Beverly Hosier, Eunice Thawl, Grace Kaye, Evelyn Monte, Doris Newcombe, Polly Rose, Lillian Moore, Marguerite White. *Modern Dance Group*: Doris Ostroff, Stella Sanders, Ethel Selwyn, Ethel Axel, Ida Bildner, Lulu Morris, Ruth Ross, Susanne Remos. *Parade Octet*: Norman Lind, John Weidler, William Houston, Geoffrey Errett, Melton Moore, Bradley Roberts, Ernest Taylor, Norman Van Emburgh. *Gentlemen*: Jack Ross, Andre Charise, Jerome Thor, Robert Gray, Robert Long, Joseph Lennon, Roger Logan, Harry Smith, Clyde Walters, Yisrol Libman.

ACT 1[35]

Scene 1

The Police Station (*by* Paul Peters and George Sklar)
The Sergeant: R. Riggs. *The Desk Officer*: D. Lesan. *A Man*: J. E. Leonard. *A Girl*: E. Dall. *Commissioner O'Brien*: C. D. Brown. *Policemen*: Parade Octette.

Scene 2

"On Parade"
E. Allen
(*Lyrics by* Paul Peters and George Sklar.)

Scene 3

The Last Jackass (*by* Paul Peters and George Sklar)
The Jackass: G. Ali. *Farmer Brown*: R. Riggs. *Mrs. Brown*: E. Arden. *Baby Brown*: L. Leng. *Mr. Butterspread*: C. D. Brown. *Manfred*: D. Lawrence. *Ethelbert*: D. Lesan. *Ronald*: L. Janney.

Scene 4

"I'm Telling You, Louie!"
V. Marshe, E. Oxford
(*Lyrics by* Paul Peters and George Sklar.)

Scene 5

Specialty Dance
C. Fox, D. Walters

Scene 6

The Crisis (*by* Frank Gabrielson, David Lesan, Michael Blankfort)
The Pickets: Parade Octette. *The Radio Announcer*: E. Oxford. *Lester M. Puffle*: J. Savo.

Scene 7

"Selling Sex"[36]
E. Dall
(*Lyrics by* Kyle Crichton.)

Scene 8

The Dead Cow (*by* Alan Baxter and Harold Johnsrud)
Paw: C. D. Brown. *Maw*: E. Arden. *Johnny*: L. Janney. *Mary*: L. Leng. *The Official*: J. E. Leonard.

Scene 9

"Decadence" (Smart Set)
Danced by C. Fox, D. Walters
(*Music by* Will Irwin.)

Scene 10

"Life Could Be So Beautiful"
J. Travers, D. Lawrence
(*Lyrics by* Paul Peters and George Sklar.)
Solo Dance by E. Junger.

Scene 11

"Send for the Militia"
E. Arden
(*Music and Lyrics by* Marc Blitzstein.)

Scene 12

College Daze[37] *by* Frank Gabrielson and David Lesan)
The Secretary: V. Marshe. *The Freshman*: J. Savo.
The Dean: C. D. Brown.

Scene 13

"You Ain't So Hot"
A. Andrews
(*Lyrics by* Paul Peters and George Sklar.)

Scene 14

Sugar Cane (Dance)
Leader of the Revolt: E. Junger. *Workers*: Modern Dance Group. *The Overseer*: I. Shurack.

Scene 15

Hot Dog (*by* Paul Peters and George Sklar)
The Wayfarer: J. Savo. *The Chestnut Vendor*: R. Riggs. *The Hot Dog Vendor*: J. E. Leonard. *The Hot Dog Customer*: L. Janney. *Policemen*: Parade Octette.

Scene 16

Our Store (*by* Turner Bullock)
Mr. Fisher: C. D. Brown. *Miss Jessup*: J. Travers. *Miss Howard*: E. Arden. *Dr. Carrthers*: R. Riggs. *Miss Mason*: L. Leng.

Scene 17

The Tabloid Reds (*by* Paul Peters and George Sklar)
Leader of the Bomb Throwers: E. Junger. *The Bomb Throwers*: Y. Libman, A. Charise. *The Girl Communists*: Modern Dance Group. *The Policeman*: R. Long. *The Communist Leader*: J. Travers. *The Communist Newsy*: L. Janney. *The Communist Baby*: P. Rose. *Comrade No. 1*: E. Oxford. *Comrade No. 2*: J. E. Leonard. *Comrade No. 3*: D. Lawrence. *Mr. Capitalist*: R. Logan. *Mrs. Capitalist*: E. Monte. *Junior Capitalist*: E. Stone.

ACT 2

Scene 1

"Fear in My Heart"
E. Oxford, J. Travers
(*Lyrics by* Paul Peters and George Sklar.)
Specialty Dance by D. Fox, C. Walters.

Scene 2

"My Feet Are Firmly Planted on the Ground"
J. Savo
(*Lyrics by* Emanuel Eisenberg.)

Scene 3

The Happy Family (*by* Frank Gabrielson and David Lesan)
Mother: E. Arden. *Father*: C. D. Stone. *Willie*: E. Stone. *Egbert*: L. Janney. *Big Brother*: J. E. Leonard. *Sister*: L. Leng.

Scene 4

"Marry the Family"
V. Marshe, E. Oxford
(*Lyrics by* Michael Blankfort.)
The Family: *Grandma*: S. Remos. *Grandpa*: Y. Ribman. *Papa*: M. Moore. *Mama*: S. Sanders. *Sister*: P. Rose. *Brother*: L. Janney. *Three Aunts*: R. Ross, E. Axel, I. Bildner. *Three Uncles*: J. Thor, N. Van Emburgh, W. Houston.

Scene 5

Home of the Brave (*by* Frank Gabrielson and David Lesan)
The Announcer: E. Oxford. *Mr. John Smith*: C. D. Brown. *Mrs. John Smith*: E. Arden. *Joe*: J. Savo. *The Inspector*: R. Riggs.

Scene 6

"I'm an International Orphan"
E. Dall
(*Lyrics by* Paul Peters and George Sklar.)

Scene 7

The Free Clinic (*by* Frank Gabrielson and David Lesan)
The Nurse: V. Marshe. *First Man*: C. D. Brown. *Second Man*: J. Savo. *Dr. Lewis*: D. Lesan. *Dr. Jenkins*: E. Oxford. *Dr. Broadley*: D. Lawrence.

Scene 8

"Letter to the President"
A. Andrews
(*Lyrics by* Paul Peters and George Sklar.)

Scene 9

The Plague[38] (*by* Frank Gabrielson and David Lesan)
Mr. Brown: C. D. Brown. *Mrs. Brown*: E. Arden. *The Visitor*: R. Riggs.

---

[35]Added during run to Act 1, prior to "The Tabloid Reds":
"Boys in Blue"
J. Savo
(*Lyrics by* Paul Peters and George Sklar.)
[36]Dropped during run.
[37]Dropped during run.

---

[38]Dropped during run.

Scene 10

Bourgeois Processional

The Laborers: H. Smith, J. Thor, C. Walters. *The Dowagers*: S. Remos, E. Axel, R. Ross. *The Salvation Army Girl*: D. Newcombe. *The Politicians*: J. Lennon, J. Ross, R. Gray, R. Logan. *The Ballerina*; E. Thawl. *The Debutantes*: L. Moore, B. Hosier, M. White. *The Minister*: J. E. Leonard. *The Street Walker*: L. Morris. *The Boy Scout*: L. Janney. *The Cheerleader*: Y. Libman. *The Collegians*: S. Sanders, D. Ostroff, E. Selwyn, I. Bildner. *The Chorus Girls*: S. Claussen, G. Kaye, K. Dougherty, P. Rose, W. Allen, M. Curtis. *The Banker*: A. Charise. *The Professor*: R. Long. *The Widow*: E. Monte. *Leading Politician*: R. Riggs.

Scene 11

Flight from the Soviet (*by* Paul Peters, George Sklar, Kyle Crichton)

The Announcer: R. Riggs. *The Lecturer*: E. Arden.

Scene 12

"Bon Voyage"

(*Lyrics by* Kyle Crichton.)

The Reporter: D. Lawrence. *The Soldier*: C. D. Brown. *The Cleric*: R. Riggs. *The Statesman*: J. Savo.

Scene 13

Finale—"Parade"[39]

E. Allen, Entire Company

(*Lyrics by* Paul Peters and George Sklar.)

---

[39]Replaced during the run by:

"Join Our Ranks"

E. Allan, Entire Company

(*Lyrics by* Paul Peters and George Sklar.)

Jimmy Durante and Rosie in JUMBO (Photo: Vandamm Studio)
Billy Rose Theatre Collection, New York Public Library for the Performing Arts

1935–1936 SEASON

EARL CARROLL'S
SKETCH BOOK (1935)

1935.04

A Hysterical Historical (Musical) Revue in Two Acts, 50 Scenes[1]. Being a History of These United States as Seen Through the Eyes of a Chorus Girl. Sketches by Eugene Conrad, Charles Sherman, Royal Foster. Music and lyrics by Charles Tobias, Murray Mencher, Charles Newman, (Norman Zeno, Will Irwin, Sam Lewis, Henry Tobias, Ray Egan, Gerald Marks). Production conceived and directed by Earl Carroll. Dialogue staged by Edward Clarke Lilley. Dances by Boots McKenna. Settings by Clark Robinson. Gowns by Samuel Lang. Costumes by John N. Booth, Billi Livingston, Wynn, Bob Stevenson, Giles Borbridge. Musical director, Ray Kavanagh. Orchestrations by Robert Russell Bennett, Donald J. Walker, David Raksin. Opened 4 June 1935 at the Winter Garden, moved 4 September 1935 to the Majestic Theatre, and closed 30 November 1935 after 207 performances.

<u>CAST:</u> KEN MURRAY, PETER HIGGINS, LILLIAN CARMEN, ARTHUR GRIFFIN, BERT LYNN, MILTON CHARLESTON, BILLY RAYES, BERYL WALLACE, SIBYL BOWAN. GEORGE LESSEY, ROBERT WILLIAMS and RED DUST, BILLY REVEL and JANE MOORE, (Matt) DUFFIN & (Jessie) DRAPER, THREE CRACKERJACKS, THREE JAYS, (Charlotte) ARREN and (Johnny) BRODERICK, ELAINE ARDEN, SUNNIE O'DEA, THE HUDSON WONDERS (Ray and Sunshine Hudson), BRENTON BEATTIE, JULIA MOONEY, ALLEN LEE, MLLE. NIRSKA, SASSAFRAS, A. LABRIOLA, GEORGE R. TAYLOR, (MIRA NIRSKA).

Show Girls: Faith Harding, Mary Louise Harper, Louise Illington, Lillian Martin, Frances March, Dolly Miller, Julia Mooney, Mary Alice Moore, Leila Stepp, Carol Sterling. *Chorus Girls:* Nora Anderson, Libby Bennett, Dorothy Buck, Marion Callahan, Lois Carlile, Connie Crandall, Nancy Dolan, Janet Davis, Joan Evans, Althea Elder, Marie Farley, Irene Frank, Peggy Gill, Ruth Greeley, Rose Heitner, Bernice Hanlon, Agatha Hoff, Amelie Ideal, Grace Jackson, Carol Karson, Lillian Keyes, Nancy Lee, Dionis Little, Fay Lytell, Ruth Mann, Helen Marano, Patricia Martin, Joan Mears, Ann Metzger, Barbara Nelson, Alice Oland, Pat Palmer, Ellen Patti, Sandra Roy, Caroline Russ, Alice Sampers, Marion Semler, Thelma Shearon, Ann Simms, Marlyn Stewart, Paula Surelle, Helen Terris, Lucille Turner, Lorraine Teatom, Marion Volk, Davenie Watson.

ACT 1
Scene 1

"Through These Portals Pass the Most Beautiful Girls in the World"
P. Higgins
(*Music by* Murray Mencher. *Lyrics by* Charles Tobias, Charles Newman.)

Scene 2

Entrepreneurs
Show Girls

Scene 3

A Blue Paradise
The Lovely Ones (Chorus Girls)

Scene 4

The Glass Trees—"Let's Swing It"
L. Carmen
(*Music by* Murray Mencher. *Lyrics by* Charles Tobias, Charles Newman. Tree Design by Bob Stevenson.)

Scene 5

Covering the Saturday Evening Post. *Time:* 1776.
Benjamin Franklin: A. Griffin. *Printer's Devil:* B. Lynn.

Scene 6

"The Spirit of '76"
(*Music by* Murray Mencher. *Lyrics by* Charles Tobias, Charles Newman.)
The Grandfather: M. Charleston. *The Father:* B. Rayes. *The Grandson:* B. Revel.

Scene 7

The President Is On the Air
B. Wallace

Scene 8

Washington, D.C. and A.C. *Time:* 1789.
George Washington: G. Lessey. *Martha Washington:* S. Bowan. *Steven Fentriss:* K. Murray. *The Flunkey:* R. Williams.

Scene 9

The Louisiana Purchase. *Time:* 1803.
"Anna Louise of Louisiana"
D. Drew
(*Music by* Will Irwin. *Lyrics by* Norman Zeno, Jr.)
Ladies of the Court: Show Girls.

Scene 10

A Garden in France.
Napoleon: B. Revel. *Anna Louise:* J. Draper. *American Ambassador:* M. Duffin.

Scene 11

Dance
M. Duffin, J. Draper

Scene 12

Webster Had a Word For It. *Time:* 1828.
Daniel Noah Webster: K. Murray.

Scene 13

Nomenclature. *Time:* 1829.
First Woman: C. Arren. *Second Woman:* J. Moore.

Scene 14

Nocturnal. *Time:* 1831.
The Girl: L. Carmen. *The Lover:* B. Rayes.

Scene 15

Ambiguity. *Time:* 1833.
Judge: A. Griffin. *Plaintiff:* B. Wallace.

Scene 16

Superfluity. *Time:* 1835.
Doctor: G. Lessey. *Patient:* E. Arden.

Scene 17

The Covered Wagon. *Time:* 1836.
"At Last"
(*Music by* Henry Tobias. *Lyrics by* Sam Lewis, Charles Tobias.)
The Girl: S. O'Dea. *The Man:* P. Higgins.

Scene 18

The Indian Uprising. *Time:* 1838.
Dance
The Girls, The Hudson Wonders

Scene 19

Tableau
Heap Big White Feathers

Scene 20

"Historical Histrionics"
(*Music by* Murray Mencher. *Lyrics by* Charles Tobias, Charles Newman.)
School Mistress: S. Bowan.

Scene 21

The Indian Giver. *Time:* 1840.
The Squaker: E. Arden. *Her Squaw:* B. Wallace. *The Squaw Man:* B. Rayes.

Scene 22

The Eastern Pioneer. *Time:* 1842.
The Farmer: K. Murray. *His Wife:* C. Arren. *The Pioneer:* M. Charleston.

Scene 23

Silver Gulch Saloon. *Time:* 1844.
Singer: C. Arren. *Juanita:* E. Arden. *Piano Player:* J. Broderick. *Pedro:* B. Rayes. *Custer:* B. Beattie. *Young Bill Cody:* K. Murray. *Honest Jim Brody:* M. Charleston. *The Dancers:* J. Moore, B. Revel.

Scene 24

Annapolis (in the East). *Time:* 1845.
Announcement: B. Wallace. *A Midshipman:* R. Williams. *A Sweetheart:* J. Mooney. *Red Dust:* Himself.

Scene 25

That Mexican Trouble. *Time:* 1846.
"Gringola"
L. Carmen
(*Music by* Murray Mencher. *Lyrics by* Charles Tobias, Charles Newman.)
Dance: S. O'Dea. *Gringolettes:* The Girls.

---

[1]The second in a series of musical revues, apart from Earl Carroll's Vanities, produced by Earl Carroll. Previous edition presented in 1929.

Scene 26

The First Revival of Uncle Tom's Cabin. *Time*: 1863.
Harriet Beecher Stowe: E. Arden. *Nephew*: B. Rayes. *Niece*: A. Elder.

Scene 27

"The Gates of Heaven"
The Keeper: K. Murray. *A Man*: B. Revel. *Mrs. Smith*: B. Wallace. *Gen. Grant*: B. Beattie. *A Lady*: S. Bowan. *Joe Miller*: M. Charleston. *The Heavenly Bodies*: Show Girls.

Scene 28

Along the Potomac. *Time*: 1865.
"There's Music in a Kiss"
(*Music and Lyrics by* Al Lewis, Al Sherman and Abner Silver.)
The Girl: B. Wallace. *Ben Johnson*: P. Higgins.

Scene 29

Abraham Lincoln
A. Lee

Scene 30

Finale (Ballet)
Entire Ensemble
Premiere Danseuse: Mlle. (M.) Nirska.
(Radium Effect produced by the Empire Radiolite Company. Butterfly idea conceived and originated by Mlle. Nirska.)
Entr'Acte
R. Kavanagh's Sketch Book Band, Three Jays, Three Crackerjacks

ACT 2[2]

Scene 1

Opening Chorus — "Young Ideas"
The Girls
(*Music by* Murray Mencher. *Lyrics by* Charles Tobias, Charles Newman.)

Scene 2

We Had With Us Tonight — A Juggling Resume
B. Rayes

Scene 3

Announcement
B. Wallace

Scene 4

The Girl Who Missed the Mayflower. *Time*: 1870.
S. Bowan
(with affectionate apologies to dear Bea Lillie)

Scene 5

The Ringmistresses
Show Girls

Scene 6

There's One Born Every Minute. *Time*: 1875.
P. T. Barnum's Press Agent: K. Murray. *Mrs. Bayonne*: E. Arden. *Mr. Bayonne*: Sassafras. *Nurses*: N. Dolan, A. Hoff, R. Mann, P. Martin, P. Palmer, A. Metzger.

Scene 7

Castle Garden.
Jennie Lind: C. Arren. *Pianist*: J. Broderick. *Musicians*: Sassafras, R. Williams, M. Duffin.

Scene 8

Thru the Ages: Guns
"Let the Man Who Makes the Gun"
L. Carmen
(*Music by* Gerald Marks. *Lyrics by* Raymond B. Egan.)
1812 British Soldier: B. Rayes. *British Girl*: S. O'Dea. *1846 Mexican Soldier*: B. Revel. *Mexican Girl*: E. Arden. *1861 Southern Soldier*: M. Charleston. *Southern Girl*: M. Semler. *1898 American Soldier*: T. Barry. *American Girl*: B. Wallace. *1917 German Soldier*: M. Duffin. *German Girl*: J. Moore.

Scene 9

Yowzar — The Gay Nineties. *Time*: 1890.
"Rustle of Your Bustle"
L. Carmen

_____

[2]Added during run to Act 2:
"The Doll Dance" *Time*: 1910.
M. Duffin, J. Draper
(*Music by* Murray Mencher. *Lyrics by* Charles Tobias, Charles Newman.)

(*Music by* Will Irwin. *Lyrics by* Norman Zeno, Jr.)
Dance: Girls. *Deacon*: A. Labriola.

Scene 10

For Utah. *Time*: 1890 1/2
Simeon: K. Murray. *Maria*: E. Arden. *Cynthia*: C. Arren. *Effie*: S. Bowan.

Scene 11

Extra! Extra! Extra![3]
Newsette: S. O'Dea.
1902—The Wright Brothers invent the airplane. 1906—San Francisco has an earthquake again. 1907—North Pole is discovered by Admiral Perry. The world Moves On! Hurry! Hurry!

Scene 12

The Oval Room. *Time*: 1900.
President McKinley: A. Griffin. *Attendant*: R. Williams. *Hawaiian Representative*: P. Higgins.

Scene 13

"Silhouettes Under the Stars"
(*Music by* Murray Mencher. *Lyrics by* Charles Tobias, Charles Newman.)

Scene 14

Moonlight and Mirrors
The Girls
Dance: B. Wallace. *Vibrolyn*: B. Lynn. (A new musical instrument introduced for the first time.)

Scene 15

"Mardi Gras Day in New Orleans"[4]
The Crackerjacks
(*Music by* Will Irwin. *Lyrics by* Norman Zeno, Jr.)
Danced by M. Duffin, J. Draper.

Scene 16

Theodore Roosevelt. *Time*: 1919.
B. Beattie

Scene 17

Many Happy Returns. *Time*: 1934
(*Sketch by* Kenneth Webb.)
The Assistant Manger: B. Rayes. *Herbert*: G. R. Taylor. *Alfred*: K. Murray.

Scene 18

"Sunday Night in New York" *Time*: 1935.
(*Music by* Murray Mencher. *Lyrics by* Charles Tobias, Charles Newman.)

Scene 19

Foyer of the Someday Theatre

Scene 20

Grand Finale
Entire Company

THE MIKADO, or, The Town of Titipu

1935.05

A Revival of the Comic Opera in Two Acts[5]. Libretto by William S. Gilbert. Music by Arthur Sullivan. Staged by R. H. Burnside. Settings by Eugene Dunkel. Costumes designed by Brooks Costume Company, from sketches by Billie Livingston. Musical conductor, Louis Kroll. Produced by Lodewick Vroom. Opened 15 July 1935 at the Adelphi Theatre, closing 20 July 1935 after 8 performances; re-opened 19-21 August for 4 additional performances, and 5-7 September 1935 for 4 additional performances, closing 7 September 1935 after 16 performances total in repertory.

CAST: *The Mikado of Japan*: WILLIAM DANFORTH. *Nanki-Poo*: HOWARD MARSH. *Ko-Ko*: FRANK MOULAN. *Pooh-Bah*: HERBERT L. WATEROUS. *Go-To*: John Cosby. *Pish-Tush*: BERTRAM PEACOCK. *Yum-Yum*: MARGARET DAUM. *Pitti-Sing*: VIVIAN HART. *Peep-Bo*: NINA DEAN. *Katisha*: VERA ROSS.
Ladies of the Mikado's Suite: Joan Boekholtz, Jane Rondthaler, Edith Gibson, Marion Ross, Jean Matus, Helene Bush. *The Mikado's Bodyguards*: Roger Ingham,

_____

[3]Dropped during the run.
[4]Dropped during the run.
[5]First presented in New York 20 July, 10-29 August 1885 at the Union Square and People's Theatres for 22 performances. First authorized production presented 19 August 1885 at the Fifth Avenue Theatre by Richard D'Oyly Carte for 250 performances. For Synopsis of Scenes and Musical Numbers, see 19 August 1885 D'Oyly Carte production.

John Cosby, Solon West, Serg Ury. *Ensemble of School Girls, Nobles, Guards and Coolies*: Emily Marsh, Margaret Walker, Marion Castleray, Marie Valez, Eleanor Gilmore, Frances Baviello, Ione Haals, Madeline de Souter, Gertrude Waldon, Mildred Burke, Alma Tollefsen, Grace Garnett, Elfrida Andabel, Jean Talcott, Vera Muller, Marion Ross, Mildred Mercer, Ruth Manners, Jane Rondthaler, Helene Bush, Jean Matus, Edith Gibson, Joann Boekholtz, Adele Drury. Frederick Rudin, William Venturo, Rudolph Wagner, George Ebert, John Muccio, Roger Ingham, Don Becker, Alfred Drake, Solon West, Serge Ury, John Cosby, Robert Irving, George Rogers, Jay Amiss, John Albert, Siegfried Langer.

THE PIRATES OF PENZANCE,
1935.06   or, The Slave of Duty

A Revival of the Comic Opera in Two Acts[6]. Libretto by William S. Gilbert. Music by Arthur Sullivan. Staged by R. H. Burnside. Settings by Eugene Dunkel. Costumes designed by Brooks Costume Company, from sketches by Billie Livingston. Musical conductor, Louis Kroll. Produced by Lodewick Vroom. Opened 22 July 1935 at the Adelphi Theatre and closed 27 July 1935 after 8 performances; re-opened 22-24 August 1935 for 4 additional performances, closing 24 August 1935 after 12 performances total in repertory.

CAST: *Richard, a Pirate King*: HERBERT L. WATEROUS. *Samuel*: Bertram Peacock. *Frederic*: HOWARD MARSH. *Major-General Stanley*: FRANK MOULAN. *Edward, a Sergeant of Police*: WILLIAM DANFORTH. *Mabel*: VIVIAN HART. *Kate*: NINA DEAN. *Edith*: MARGARET DAUM. *Isabel*: Frances Baviello. *Ruth*: VERA ROSS.
Chorus of Pirates, Police and General Stanley's Daughters: Emily Marsh, Margaret Walker, Marion Castleray, Marie Valez, Eleanor Gilmore, Frances Baviello, Ione Haals, Madeline de Souter, Gertrude Waldon, Mildred Burke, Alma Tollefsen, Grace Garnett, Elfrida Andabel, Jean Talcott, Vera Muller, Marion Ross, Mildred Mercer, Ruth Manners, Jane Rondthaler, Helene Bush, Jean Matus, Edith Gibson, Joann Boekholtz, Adele Drury. Frederick Rudin, William Venturo, Rudolph Wagner, George Ebert, John Muccio, Roger Ingham, Don Becker, Alfred Drake, Solon West, Serge Ury, John Cosby, Robert Irving, George Rogers, Jay Amiss, John Albert, Siegfried Langer.

THE YEOMEN OF THE GUARD,
1935.07   or, The Merryman and His Maid

A Revival of the Comic Opera in Two Acts[7]. Libretto by by William S. Gilbert. Music by Arthur Sullivan. Staged by R. H. Burnside. Settings by Eugene Dunkel. Costumes by Brooks Costume Company, from sketches by Billie Livingston. Musical conductor, Louis Kroll. Produced by Lodewick Vroom. Opened 29 July 1935 at the Adelphi Theatre and closed 3 August 1935 after 8 performances; re-opened 26-28 August 1935 for 4 additional performances, closing 28 August 1935 after 12 performances total in repertory.

CAST: *Sir Richard Cholmondeley*: Bertram Peacock. *Colonel Fairfax*: HOWARD MARSH. *Sergeant Meryll*: HERBERT L. WATEROUS. *Leonard Meryll*: GEORGE ROGERS. *Jack Point*: FRANK MOULAN. *Wilfred Shadbolt*: WILLIAM DANFORTH. *Elsie Maynard*: MARGARET DAUM. *Phoebe Meryll*: VIVIAN HART. *Dame Carruthers*: VERA ROSS. *Kate*: Eleanor Gilmore. *First Yeoman*: George Ebert. *Second Yeoman*: William Venturo. *First Citizen*: Alfred Drake. *Headsman*: John Cosby.
Chorus of Yeomen of the Guard, Gentlemen, Citizens, etc.: Emily Marsh, Margaret Walker, Marion Castleray, Marie Valez, Eleanor Gilmore, Frances Baviello, Ione Haals, Madeline de Souter, Gertrude Waldon, Mildred Burke, Alma Tollefsen, Grace Garnett, Elfrida Andabel, Jean Talcott, Vera Muller, Marion Ross, Mildred Mercer, Ruth Manners, Jane Rondthaler, Helene Bush, Jean Matus, Edith Gibson, Joann Boekholtz, Adele Drury. Frederick Rudin, William Venturo, Rudolph Wagner, George Ebert, John Muccio, Roger Ingham, Don Becker, Alfred Drake, Solon West, Serge Ury, John Cosby, Robert Irving, George Rogers, Jay Amiss, John Albert, Siegfried Langer.

THE GONDOLIERS,
1935.08   or, The King of Barataria

A Revival of the Comic Opera in Two Acts[8]. Libretto by William S. Gilbert. Music by Arthur Sullivan. Staged by R. H. Burnside. Settings by Eugene

Dunkel. Costumes by Brooks Costume Company, from sketches by Billie Livingston. Musical conductor, Louis Kroll. Produced by Lodewick Vroom. Opened 5 August 1935 at the Adelphi Theatre, closing 10 August 1935 after 8 performances; reopened 29-31 August 1935 for 4 additional performances, and closed 31 August 1935 after 12 performances total in repertory.

CAST: *The Duke of Plaza-Toro*: FRANK MOULAN. *Luiz*: Walter Andrews. *Don Alhambra Del Bolero*: WILLIAM DANFORTH. *Marco Palmieri*: HOWARD MARSH. *Giuseppe Palmieri*: BERTRAM PEACOCK. *Antonio*: George Rogers. *Francesco*: William Venturo. *Giorgio*: John Cosby. *Annibale*: Solon West. *The Duchess of Plaza-Toro*: VERA ROSS. *Casilda*: Margaret Daum. *Gianetta*: VIVIAN HART. *Tessa*: PEGGY STRICKLAND. *Fiametta*: Frances Baviello. *Vittoria*: Edith Gibson. *Giulia*: Eleanor Gilmore. *Inez*: Ione Anne Haals.
Chorus of Gondoliers, Contadine, Men-at-Arms, Heralds and Pages: Margaret Walker, Marion Castleray, Marie Valez, Eleanor Gilmore, Frances Baviello, Madeline de Souter, Gertrude Waldon, Mildred Burke, Alma Tollefsen, Grace Garnett, Elfrida Andabel, Jean Talcott, Vera Muller, Marion Ross, Mildred Mercer, Ruth Manners, Jane Rondthaler, Jean Matus, Edith Gibson, Joann Boekholtz, Adele Drury. Frederick Rudin, William Venturo, Rudolph Wagner, George Ebert, John Muccio, Roger Ingham, Don Becker, Alfred Drake, Solon West, Serge Ury, John Cosby, Robert Irving, George Rogers, Jay Amiss, Francis Clarke, Siegfried Langer.

TRIAL BY JURY
1935.09

A Revival of the Comic Opera in One Act[9]. Libretto by William S. Gilbert. Music by Arthur Sullivan. Staged by R. H. Burnside. Settings by Eugene Dunkel. Costumes by Brooks Costume Company, from sketches by Billie Livingston. Musical conductor, Louis Kroll. Produced by Lodewick Vroom. Opened 12 August 1935 at the Adelphi Theatre, closing 17 August 1935 after 8 performances; reopened 2 September and closed 4 September 1935 after 4 additional performances, for a total of 12 performances in repertory.

CAST: *The Learned Judge*: FRANK MOULAN. *Foreman of the Jury*: HERBERT L. WATEROUS. *The Defendant*: HOWARD MARSH. *Counsel for the Plaintiff*: BERTRAM PEACOCK. *Usher*: WILLIAM DANFORTH. *Counsel for Defense*: George Rogers. *Plaintiff*: VIVIAN HART.
Jurors: Frederick Rudin, William Venturo, Rudolph Wagner, George Ebert, John Muccio, Roger Ingham, Don Becker, Alfred Drake, George Stevens, Serge Ury, John Cosby, Robert Irving. *Bridesmaids*: Margaret Walker, Marion Castleray, Marie Valez, Eleanor Gilmore, Frances Baviello, Ione Haals, Madeline de Souter, Gertrude Waldon, Mildred Burke, Alma Tollefsen, Grace Garnett, Elfrida Andabel, Jean Talcott, Vera Muller, Marion Ross, Mildred Mercer, Helene Bush, Jean Matus, Edith Gibson, Joann Boekholtz, Adele Drury.
followed by

H.M.S. PINAFORE,
1935.10   or, The Lass That Loved a Sailor

A Revival of the Comic Opera in Two Acts[10]. Libretto by William S. Gilbert. Music by Arthur Sullivan. Staged by R. H. Burnside. Settings by Eugene Dunkel. Costumes by Brooks Costume Company, from sketches by Billie Livingston. Musical conductor, Louis Kroll. Produced by Lodewick Vroom. Opened 12 August 1935 at the Adelphi Theatre, closing 17 August 1935 after 8 performances; re-opened 2-4 September 1935 for 4 additional performances, for a total of 12 performances in repertory.

CAST: *The Rt. Hon. Sir Joseph Porter, K.C.B.*: FRANK MOULAN. *Captain Corcoran, Commander of the H.M.S. Pinafore*: BERTRAM PEACOCK. *Ralph Rackstraw, Able Seaman*: HOWARD MARSH. *Dick Deadeye, Able Seaman*: WILLIAM DANFORTH. *Bill Bobstay, Boatswain*: Herbert L. Waterous. *Josephine, the Captain's Daughter*: MARGARET DAUM. *Little Buttercup, Mrs. Cripps, a Portsmouth Bum-Boat Woman*: VERA ROSS. *Hebe, Sir Joseph's First Cousin*: Dene Dickens. *Midshipmen*: Royce Perez, Ramon Perez. *Bob Becket*: John Cosby. *Sergeant of Marines*: George Stevens.
Sailors, Marines: Frederick Rudin, William Venturo, Rudolph Wagner, George Ebert, John Muccio, Roger Ingham, Don Becker, Alfred Drake, Serge Ury, John Cosby, Robert Irving, George Rogers, Jay Amiss, Francis Clarke, Siegfried Langer. *First Lord's Sisters, His Cousins, His Aunts*: Margaret Walker, Marion Castleray, Marie Valez, Eleanor Gilmore, Frances Baviello, Ione Haals, Madeline de Souter, Gertrude Waldon, Mildred Burke, Alma Tollefsen, Grace Garnett, Elfrida Andabel, Jean Talcott, Vera Muller, Marion Ross, Mildred Mercer, Helene Bush, Jean Matus, Edith Gibson, Joann Boekholtz, Adele Drury.

---

[6]First presented in New York 31 December 1879 at the Fifth Avenue Theatre for 91 performances in two engagements. For Synopsis of Scenes and Musical Numbers, see original 1879 production.
[7]First presented in New York 17 October 1888 at the Casino Theatre for 100 performances. For Synopsis of Scenes and Musical Numbers, see original 1888 production.
[8]Originally presented in New York 7 January 1890 at Park Theatre for 103 performances. For Synopsis of Scenes and Musical Numbers, see original 1890 production.

[9]First presented in New York 15 November 1875 at the Eagle Theatre for 8 performances. For Synopsis of Scenes and Musical Numbers, see original 1875 production.
[10]Originally presented in New York 15 January 1879 at the Standard Theatre for 175 performances. For Synopsis of Scenes and Musical Numbers, see original 1879 production.

1935.11

SMILE AT ME

A Musical Laugh Tour (Musical Revue) in Two Acts, 33 Scenes. Sketches and lyrics by Edward J. Lambert. Music by Gerald Dolin and Edward J. Lambert. Staged by Frank Merlin. Dances and ensembles created by Paul Lorenz. Costumes by Dorothy Van Winkle. Settings by Karl Amend. Music direction, Gerald Dolin. Orchestrations by Gerald Dolin, Joe Jordan, LeRoy Harris, Paul Hill. Produced by Harold K. Berg. Opened 23 August 1935 at the Fulton Theatre and closed 14 September 1935 after 27 performances.

CAST: JACK OSTERMAN, EDDIE BRUCE, RUTH EDELL, HAL THOMPSON, AVIS ANDREWS, EDWARD J. LAMBERT, DOROTHY MORRISON, JESSE WOLK, Gene Fontaine, Ivan Bankoff, Beth Cannon, Dean Wheeler, Dorothy Davis, Betty Fontaine, Paul Mears, Poppy Mears, Georges Vito, Irene Piri, Paul Dessez, Frank Kimball, Hugh Ellsworth, Jose Shalita, Riana De Bori, Harry Peterson, Jean Carroll, Cynthia Carlin.

Ensemble: Helene Darnell, Madeline Eubanks, Frances Hyatt, Gene Svesson, Blanche Klages, Jeanette Biesantz, Waverly N. Lambert, Ann Bendal, Jeanne Huson, Tina Marie Jensen, Mitzi Garner, Nikki Petell.

ACT 1

Scene 1

"Here and There"
> H. Thompson, D. Morrison, Ensemble
>> *Scene*: Starting Our Tour.

Scene 2

Mr. Jack Osterman Appears on the Scene

Scene 3

At Geneva
> *The Secretary of the United States Treasury*: E. Bruce. *The French Diplomat*: P. Dessez. *The Swedish Diplomat*: F. Kimball. *The Austrian Diplomat*: H. Ellsworth. *The Spanish Diplomat*: J. Shelita. *The Italian Diplomat*: G. Vito. *The English Diplomat*: H. Thompson.

Scene 4

"Fiesta in Madrid"
> J. Wolk, G. Fontaine
>> *Scene*: In Spain.
>> *Danced by* R. De Bori, J. Carroll, J. Shalita, F. Kimball, H. Ellsworth, H. Peterson, Ensemble.

Scene 5

Mr. Jack Osterman Has a Few Words to Say

Scene 6

Tobacco Juice
> *Scene*: On Tobacco Road.
>> *Rube*: E. Bruce. *Sada*: D. Wheeler. *Ella May*: D. Morrison. *Jitters*: E. J. Lambert. *The Preacher Woman*: R. Edell. *Gov*: P. Dessez. *Grandma*: I. Piri. *Myrtle*: B. Fontaine. *Two Men from Up No'th*: F. Kimball, H. Peterson.

Scene 7

"Smile at Me"
> H. Thompson, G. Fontaine, Ensemble
> (*Music by* Edward J. Lambert.)
>> *Scene*: In a Garden of Love.

Scene 8

The Old Proverb
> *Scene*: In the North Woods.
>> *The Man*: E. Bruce. *The Girl*: D. Morrison.

Scene 9

"Tired of the South"
> A. Andrews
>> *Scene*: In Mississippi.
>> *Danced by* Ensemble.

Scene 10

Children of Today
> *Scene*: In the Bronx.
>> *The Mother*: D. Wheeler. *Jennie*: R. Edell. *The Father*: E. J. Lambert. *Rosamund*: I. Piri. *Shirley*: D. Morrsion.

Scene 11

At the Ballet
> I. Bankoff, B. Cannon

Scene 12

The Kiss of Death
> *Danced by* G. Vito, I. Piri, Ensemble
>> *Scene*: In Fantasy.

Scene 13

Is Not in the Revue on Account of a Lot of Superstitious Actors

Scene 14

"Dancing Moe"
> *Scene*: In Paris.
>> *The Girl*: E. Edell. *The Gigolo*: E. J. Lambert. *The Gendarmes*: H. Peterson, F. Kimball. *The Flower Girl*: B. Fontaine.

Scene 15

Life Begins at Four (*by* Jack Osterman.)
> *Scene*: In Hollywood.
>> *Charles Gaemmle, Jr.*: J. Osterman. *His Secretary*: C. Carlin. *His Wife*: R. Edell.

Scene 16

At a Concert
> E. J. Lambert, D. Wheeler

Scene 17

"Goona Goona"
> A. Andrews
>> *Scene*: In the South Sea Islands.
>> *The Witch Doctor*: H. Ellsworth. *The Groom*: Paul Mears. *The Bride*: Poppy Mears. *Native Girls*: Ensemble. *Drummers*: Sami Lovan, Dori Pinto, Mike Tido, John Ramo.

Scene 18

"There's a Broadway Up in Heaven"[11]
> J. Osterman, Company
>> *Scene*: A Greater Broadway.

ACT 2

Scene 1

"I'm Dreaming While We're Dancing"
> J. Wolk, G. Fontaine
>> *Scene*: At West Point.
>> *Danced by* J. Carroll, J. Shalita, Ensemble Girls, West Point Cadets.

Scene 2

"Doing the Truck"
> A. Andrews
>> *Scene*: In Harlem.
>> *Danced by* P. Mears.

Scene 3

Modern Version
> *Scene*: On the United Actors Lot.
>> *Mr. Von Sternheim*: E. Bruce. *Mr. Bark Cable*: P. Dessez. *Mr. Fishbowl*: E. J. Lambert. *The "Yes Man"*: I. Bankoff. *Miss June Lovely*: D. Wheeler. *Script Girl*: R. De Bori. *Assistant Director*: G. Vito. *Camera Man*: J. Shalita. *Assistant Camera Man*: H. Ellsworth. *Mr. Hemingway*: F. Kimball. *Roman Soldiers*: C. Carlin, D. Davis, J. Carrol, B. Fontaine.

Scene 4

"You're a Magician"
> H. Thompson, D. Morrison, Ensemble
>> *Scene*: In the Land of Magic.

Scene 5

A Silent Announcement[12]
> D. Davis

Scene 6

At the Psycho-Analyst's Office[13]
> *The Psycho-Analyst*: E. Bruce. *The Lady*: B. Fontaine.

Scene 7

At a Maternity Hospital[14]
> *The Mother*: D. Morrison. *The Father*: F. Kimball. *The Nurse*: R. Edell. *The Kid*: A Doll.

Scene 8

At the Surgeon's Office
> *The Surgeon*: J. Shalita. *The Patient*: C. Carlin.

---

[11]Dropped after the opening.
[12]Dropped after the opening.
[13]Dropped after the opening.
[14]Dropped after the opening.

Scene 9

"Calcutta"

A. Andrews

Scene: In India.

Danced by G. Vito, I. Piri. *Oriental Dancer*: R. De Bori. *Hostess*: Poppy Mears. *Beggar*: F. Kimball. *Cafe Proprietor*: I. Bankoff. *The Drunk*: J. Shalita. *Cigarette Girl*: G. Fontaine. *Natives, Tourists, etc.*

Scene 10

On the Veldt

E. J. Lambert

Scene 11

"Caribbeana"

J. Wolk

Scene: On the Shores of Honduras.

Danced by Paul Mears, Poppy Mears, G. Vito, H. Ellsworth, F. Kimball, Ensemble.

Scene 12

A Dog's Life[15]

Scene: In front of an apartment house in Brooklyn.

Lulu: R. Edell. *Fifi*: I. Piri. *The Young Married Man*: H. Ellsworth. *The Young Married Woman*: D. Davis. *The Lover*: P. Dessez. *His Lady Friend*: B. Fontaine.

Scene 13

Is Not in the Revue on Account of a Superstitious Management

Scene 14

"I Love to Flutter"

E. Bruce, Ensemble, Male Ballet

Scene: At the Acropolis.

Scene 15

"Is This the End?"

J. Osterman

(*Music and Lyrics by* Grace Lambert.)

Scene 16

Back in America

Entire Company

1935.12   # AT HOME ABROAD

A Musical Holiday (Revue) in Two Acts, 26 Scenes. Sketches by Howard Dietz, (Marc Connelly, Dion Titheradge, Raymond Knight, Reginald Gardiner). Based on an idea by Raymond Knight. Music by Arthur Schwartz. Lyrics by Howard Dietz. Staged by Vincente Minnelli. Dialogue staged by Thomas Mitchell. Dances staged by Gene Snyder and Harry Losee. Settings and costumes by Vincente Minnelli. Music director, Al Goodman. Orchestral conductor, Charles Drury. Orchestrations by (Robert) Russell Bennett, David Raksin, Hans Spialek, Donald Walker, Phil Walsh, Russell Wooding. Vocal arrangements by Charles Henderson. Produced by the Messrs. Shubert. Opened 19 September 1935 at the Winter Garden, moved 20 January 1936 to the Majestic Theatre, and closed 7 March 1936 after 198 performances.

<u>CAST</u>: BEATRICE LILLIE, ETHEL WATERS, HERB WILLIAMS, ELEANOR POWELL, REGINALD GARDINER, PAUL HAAKON, EDDIE FOY, JR., VERA ALLEN, NINA WHITNEY, JAMES MacCOLL, Woods Miller, Roy Campbell's Continentals (Frank Baker, Cliff Billings, Neville Landor, Arnold Lenhart, Fred Locke, Joseph Meyer, John Payne, Craige Stevens), The 6 Spirits of Rhythm (Theodore Bonn, Douglas Daniels, Wilbur Daniels, Ernest Meyers, Virgil Scoggins, Leo Watson), Sue Hastings' Marionettes, Andre Charise, Woods Miller, Julie Jenner, Gene Martel, The Eton Boys.

Ladies of the Ensemble: Joanna Allen, Mary Bay, Regina Beck, Helen Bennett, Hazel Boffinger, Mildred Borst, Jane Burks, Mary Ann Carr, Jean Carson, Geri Chopin, Helen Ecklund, Peggy Gallimore, Marjorie Gayle, Pearl Harris, Helen Hannen, Julie Jenner, Jane Lane, Rose Lieder, June McNulty, Polly Rose, Claire Scott, Anne St. George, Sally Warren, Mildred Webb, Ruth White.

ACT 1

Scene 1

The Nightmare

The Sleeper: H. Williams. *American Characters*: Sue Hastings' Marionettes. *Voices*: V Allen, J. MacColl.

---

[15]Dropped after the opening.

Scene 2

"Get Away from It All"

The 6 Spirits of Rhythm, The Continentals, Ladies of the Ensemble

Scene 3

The Survey (*by* Marc Connelly)

Scene: The Pier of the *S. S. Magnificent*.

Otis P. Hatrick: H. Williams. *Henrietta Hatrick*: V. Allen. *Jackson*: J. MacColl. *Mr. Clee*: R. Gardiner.

Scene 4

"That's Not Cricket"

E. Powell, Eton Boys

Scene 5

Dinner Napkins (*Adapted from a scene by* Dion Titheridge)

Scene: A London Store.

Mrs. Blogden Blagg: B. Lillie. *Clerk*: R. Gardiner. *Mr. Martingale*: E. Foy, Jr. *Mr. Coldwater*: J. MacColl.

Scene 6

"Hottentot Potentate"

E. Waters, The 6 Spirits of Rhythm

Scene 7

The Gigolo Business

Scene: A hotel room on the Riviera.

Otis: H. Williams. *Henrietta*: V. Allen. *Rene*: R. Gardiner. *Flo Flo*: J. Jenner.

Scene 8

"Paree"

B. Lillie

Scene 9

"Farewell, My Lovely"

W. Miller, The Continentals

(*Danced by*) P. Haakon, N. Whitney, A. Charise, G. Martel, Ladies of the Ensemble.

Scene 10

The Audience Waits

Scene: A dressing room of the Imperial Ballet.

Babushka: V. Allen. *Sonia*: B. Lillie. *Doubletchek*: R. Gardiner. *Pilnik*: E. Foy, Jr. *Otisovitch*: H. Williams. *Kameroff*: J. MacColl.

Scene 11

"The Lady With the Tap"

W. Miller, The Continentals

Danced by E. Powell, Ladies of the Ensemble.

Scene 12

Trains (*by* Reginald Gardiner)

R. Gardiner

Scene 13

"Thief in the Night"

E. Waters

Scene 14

"O Leo!"

B. Lillie, H. Williams, Ensemble

ACT 2

Scene 1

"Love Is a Dancing Thing"

W. Miller, The Continentals

(*Danced by*) P. Haakon, N. Whitney, Ladies of the Ensemble

Scene 2

"The Toast of Vienna"

B. Lillie, The Continentals

Scene 3

Homesick Clinic (*by* Raymond Knight)

Scene: Brussels.

Otis: H. Williams. *Dr. Cook*: R. Gardiner. *Aide*: J. MacColl. *Policeman*: W. Miller. *Subway Guard*: E. Foy, Jr. *Pedestrians, Stenographers, etc.*

Scene 4

"What a Wonderful World"

E. Powell, Sue Hastings' Marionettes, W. Miller, The Continentals, Pedestrians

Scene 5

"You May Be Far Away from Me"
(*Dialogue under music by* William Yates Brown.)
He: B. Lillie. *She*: R. Gardiner.

Scene 6

"The Steamboat Whistle"
E. Waters, The 6 Spirits of Rhythm, Ensemble
Scene: Jamaica, West Indies.

Scene 7

The Resourceful Vocalist
R. Gardiner

Scene 8

"Get Yourself a Geisha"
Ladies of the Ensemble Plus (B. Lillie)

Scene 9

Death in the Afternoon
Toreador: P. Haakon. *Attendants*: A. Charise, G. Martel. *Duenna*: V. Allen.
Betrothed: N. Whitney. *Guard*: J. Payne. *Matadors*: The Continentals.

Scene 10

Two in a Bar (*by* Dion Titheridge)
Millicent Peabody: B. Lillie. *The Young Man*: R. Gardiner. *The Woman*: V.
Allen. *The Musician*: E. Foy, Jr. *A Man*: J. MacColl.

Scene 11

"Got a Bran' New Suit"
E. Waters, E. Powell

Scene 12

"Pomp and Circumstance"
Entire Company

PORGY AND BESS

1935.13

An American Folk Opera in Three Acts, 9 Scenes. Libretto by DuBose
Heyward, adapted from the play "Porgy" by Dorothy and DuBose Heyward,
and the novel "Porgy" by DuBose Heyward. Music by George Gershwin.
Lyrics by DuBose Heyward and Ira Gershwin. Directed by Rouben
Mamoulian. Settings by Sergei Soudeikine. (Costumes by Theatre Guild
Workroom.) Music director, Alexander Smallens, Alexander Steinert (alt.).
(Orchestrations by George Gershwin.) Choral director, Eva Jessye.
Produced by the Theatre Guild. Opened 10 October 1935 at the Alvin
Theatre and closed 25 January 1936 after 124 performances.

CAST (in order of appearance): *Mingo*: FORD L. BUCK. *Clara*: ABBIE
MITCHELL. *Sportin' Life*: JOHN W. BUBBLES. *Jake*: EDWARD MATTHEWS.
Maria: GEORGETTE HARVEY. *Annie*: Olive Ball. *Lily*: HELEN DOWDY. *Serena*:
RUBY ELZY. *Robbins*: Henry Davis. *Jim*: Jack Carr. *Peter*: Gus Simons. *Porgy*: TODD
DUNCAN. *Crown*: WARREN COLEMAN. *Bess*: ANNE BROWN. *Detective*:
Alexander Campbell. *Two Policemen*: Harold Woolf, Burton McEvilly. *Undertaker*:
John Garth. *Frazier*: J. ROSAMUND JOHNSON. *Mr. Archdale*: George Lessey.
Nelson: Ray Yeates. *Strawberry Woman*: HELEN DOWDY. *Crab Man*: Ray Yeates.
Coroner: George Carleton.
Residents of Catfish Row, Fisherman, Children, Stevedores, etc.: THE EVA JESSYE
CHOIR: Catherine Jackson Ayres, Lillian Cowan, Sara Daigeau, Darlean Duval, Kate
Hall, Altonell Hines, Louisa Howard, Harriet Jackson, Rosalie King, Assotta Marshall,
Wilnette Mayers, Sadie McGill, Massie Patterson, Annabelle Ross, Louise Twyman,
Helen R. White, Musa Williams, Reginald Beane, Caesar Bennett, G. Harry Bolden,
Edward Broadnax, Carroll Clark, Joseph Crawford, John Diggs, Leonard Franklin,
John Garth, Joseph James, Clarence Jacobs, Allen Lewis, Jimmie Lightfoot, Lycurgus
Lockman, Henry May, Junius McDaniel, Arthur McLean, William O'Neil, Robert
Raines, Andrew Taylor, Leon Threadgill, Jimmie Waters, Robert Williams, Ray Yeates.
Choral Conductor: Eva Jessye.
Children: Naida King, Regina Williams, Enid Wilkins, Allen Tinney, William
Tinney, Herbert Young.
The Charleston Orphans' Band: Sam Anderson, Eric Bell, Le Verria Belton,
Benjamin Brown, Claude Christian, Shedrack Dobson, David Ellis, Clarence Smith,
John Strachan, George Tait, Allen Tinney, William Tinney, Charles Williams, Herbert
Young.

Act 1, Scene 1: Catfish Row, Charleston, South Carolina. A summer evening in the
recent past. *Scene 2*: Serena's Room. The following night.

Act 2, Scene 1: Catfish Row. A month later. *Scene 2*: A Palmetto Jungle. Evening of the
same day. *Scene 3*: Catfish Row. Before dawn, a week later. *Scene 4*: Serena's Room.
Dawn of the following day.

Act 3, Scene 1: Catfish Row. The next night. *Scene 2*: Catfish Row. Early morning.
Scene 3: Catfish Row. Five days later.

ACT 1[16]

Scene 1

Lullaby, "Summer Time"
A. Mitchell

"A Woman Is a Sometime Thing"
E. Matthews, Ensemble

Entrance of Porgy: "They Pass By Singing"
T. Duncan

Scene 2

"Gone, Gone, Gone!"
Ensemble

"Overflow"
Ensemble

Arioso, "My Man's Gone Now"
R. Elzy, Ensemble

Train Song, "Leavin' Fo' De Promis' Lan'"
A. Brown, Ensemble

ACT 2

Scene 1

Rowing Song, "It Takes a Long Pull to Get There"
E. Matthews, Fishermen

"I Got Plenty o' Nuttin'"
T. Duncan

Divorce Scene, "Woman to Lady"
T. Duncan, A. Brown, J. R. Johnson, Ensemble

Duet, "Bess, You Is My Woman Now"
T. Duncan, A. Brown

Picnic Song, "Oh, I Can't Sit Down"
Charleston Orphan's Band

Scene 2

"It Ain't Necessarily So"
J. W. Bubbles, Ensemble

Duet, "What You Want With Bess?"
W. Coleman, A. Brown

Scene 3

"Time and Time Again"
R. Elzy, Ensemble

Street Cries, Strawberry Woman, Crab Man.

Duet, "I Loves You, Porgy"
A. Brown, T. Duncan

Scene 4

"Oh, de Lawd Shake de Heaven"
Ensemble

"A Red Headed Woman"
W. Coleman, Ensemble

"Oh, Doctor Jesus"
Principals, Ensemble

ACT 3

Scene 1

"Clara, Don't You Be Downhearted"
Ensemble

Scene 2

"There a Boat That's Leavin' Soon for New York"
J. W. Bubbles, A. Brown

Scene 3

Trio, "Where's My Bess"
T. Duncan, R. Elzy, H. Dowdy

"I'm On My Way"
T. Duncan, Ensemble

---

[16]Original Program Note: "As the music is continuous, for the convenience
of those interested in remembering individual numbers, we list the following." (Editor's note: A more complete music listing follows the original program listing).

The following comprehensive vocal listing (including recitative performed but not individually listed in the program)[17]:

ACT 1

Scene 1

Lullaby, "Summer Time"[18]
A. Mitchell

(Seems like these bones don't give me nothin' but box-cars tonight . . .)
E. Matthews, J. W, Bubbles, F. L. Buck

(A man's got a right to play . . . /"Summer Time"[19] reprise)
H. Davis, J. Carr, E. Matthews, A. Mitchell, Crap Shooters

"A Woman Is a Sometime Thing"[20]
E. Matthews, Ensemble

(Here come de honey man . . .)
G. Simons

(Hello, Peter . . .)
All

Entrance of Porgy: "They Pass By Singing"[21]
T. Duncan

(Crap Game Fugue[22], Here comes Big Boy . . . , "A Woman Is a Sometime Thing" reprise)
F. L. Buck, E. Matthews, J. Carr, W. Coleman, T. Duncan, R. Elzy, A. Brown, H. Davis, G. Simons, G. Harvey, Ensemble

Scene 2

"Gone, Gone, Gone!"[23]
Ensemble

"Overflow"[24]
Ensemble

(Um! A saucer burying set-up, I see . . .)
A. Campbell, R. Elzy, H. Dowdy, G. Simons, T. Duncan

(You're a damn liar . . . , "Gone, Gone, Gone" reprise)
A. Campbell, H. Woolf, G. Simons, G. Harvey, T. Duncan, E. Matthews, All

Arioso, "My Man's Gone Now"[25]
R. Elzy, Ensemble

(How de saucer stan' now my sister . . .)
J. Garth, R. Elzy, E. Matthews, T. Duncan

Train Song, "Leavin' Fo' De Promis' Lan'"[26]
A. Brown, Ensemble

ACT 2

Scene 1

Rowing Song, "It Takes a Long Pull to Get There"[27]
E. Matthews, Fishermen

(Mus' be you mens forgot about de picnic . . . .)
O. Ball, E. Matthews, A. Mitchell

"I Got Plenty o' Nuttin'"
T. Duncan, (Chorus)

Divorce Scene, "Woman to Lady"[28]
T. Duncan, A. Brown, J. R. Johnson, Ensemble

(Dey's a Bukra comin' . . .)
G. Lessey, A. Mitchell, R. Elzy, F. L. Buck, E. Matthews

('Lo Bess, goin' to picnic? . . .)
J. W. Bubbles, A. Brown, T. Duncan

Duet, "Bess, You Is My Woman Now"
T. Duncan, A. Brown

Picnic Song, "Oh, I Can't Sit Down"[29]
Charleston Orphan's Band

(What's de matter wid you, sister? . . . /"I Got Plenty o' Nuttin'" reprise)
G. Harvey, A. Brown, T. Duncan

Scene 2

"It Ain't Necessarily So"[30]
J. W. Bubbles, Ensemble
(*Dance specialty* interpolation: J. W. Bubbles.)

(Here there! Hold yo' holt. I's acomin' . . .)
G. Harvey

(Crown, I got something to tell you . . .)
A. Brown, W. Coleman

Duet, "What You Want With Bess?"[31]
W. Coleman, A. Brown

Scene 3

(Honey, dat's all de breakfast I got time for . . . /"It Takes a Long Pull to Get There"[32]

(reprise)
E. Matthews, R. Yeates, J. Carr, G. Harvey, Men

(Well, if it ain't ole Peter! . . .)
G. Harvey, G. Simons, A. Brown, T. Duncan, R. Elzy

"Time and Time Again"[33]
R. Elzy, Ensemble

Street Cries[34]

Strawberry Woman
(H. Dowdy)

Crab Man
(R. Yeates)

(Now de time, oh Gawd, now de time . . .)
T. Duncan, A. Brown

Duet, "I Loves You, Porgy"
A. Brown, T. Duncan

(Why you been out on that wharf so long, Clara? . . .)
G. Harvey, A. Mitchell

Scene 4

"Oh, de Lawd Shake de Heaven"[35]
Ensemble

(Oh, dere's somebody knockin' at de do' . . .)
G. Simons, H. Dowdy, F. L. Buck, G. Harvey, Ensemble

(You is a nice parcel of Christians . . .)
W. Coleman, R. Elzy, A. Brown

(Here, cut dat out! Stop it! . . .)
W. Coleman

"A Red Headed Woman"[36]
W. Coleman, Ensemble

"Oh, Doctor Jesus"
Principals, Ensemble

ACT 3

Scene 1

"Clara, Don't You Be Downhearted"[37]
Ensemble

(You low-lived skunk, ain't you got no shame . . . /"Summer Time" reprise)
G. Harvey, J. W. Bubbles, A. Brown

---

[17]Prepared from original piano vocal score (Gershwin Publishing Corporation; Random House, New York, 1935), with consultation from David Hummel of the Archives of the American Musical, and "The Life and Times of 'Porgy and Bess'" by Hollis Alpert (Alfred A. Knopf, New York, 1990).
[18]Lyrics by DuBose Heyward.
[19]Lyrics by DuBose Heyward.
[20]Lyrics by DuBose Heyward.
[21]Lyrics by DuBose Heyward.
[22]Lyrics by DuBose Heyward.
[23]Lyrics by DuBose Heyward.
[24]Lyrics by DuBose Heyward.
[25]Lyrics by DuBose Heyward.
[26]Lyrics by DuBose Heyward.
[27]Lyrics by DuBose Heyward.
[28]Lyrics by DuBose Heyward.

[29]Lyrics by Ira Gershwin.
[30]Lyrics by Ira Gershwin.
[31]Lyrics by DuBose Heyward.
[32]Lyrics by DuBose Heyward.
[33]Lyrics by DuBose Heyward.
[34]Lyrics by DuBose Heyward.
[35]Lyrics by DuBose Heyward.
[36]Lyrics by Ira Gershwin.
[37]Lyrics by DuBose Heyward.

Scene 2

(Wait for us at the corner, Al . . .)
> A. Campbell, O. Ball, H. Dowdy, G. Carleton

(We swear to dat, Boss . . .)
> Women, A. Campbell, O. Ball, H. Dowdy, G. Carleton

(Of course, you're the goat man . . .)
> G. Carleton, T. Duncan, A. Campbell, A. Brown, J. W. Bubbles

(I can't look at Crown's face . . .)
> T. Duncan, H. Woolf, A. Brown, J. W. Bubbles

"There a Boat That's Leavin' Soon for New York"[38]
> J. W. Bubbles, A. Brown

Scene 3

(Occupational Humoresque/Good mornin' sistuh![39] . . . /Sure to go to heaven/How are you dis mornin'? . . .)
> Ensemble, Children

(It's Porgy comin' home . . .)
> F. L. Buck, T. Duncan, H. Dowdy, Ensemble

(Jus' you wait til dat gal see me . . .)
> T. Duncan

Trio, "Where's My Bess"[40]
> T. Duncan, R. Elzy, H. Dowdy

(Where Bess gone? . . .)
> T. Duncan, F. L. Buck, G. Harvey, R. Elzy

"I'm On My Way"[41]
> T. Duncan, Ensemble

1935.14

JUBILEE

A Musical Comedy in Two Acts, 22 Scenes. Book by Moss Hart. Music and lyrics by Cole Porter. Supervised, staged and lighted by Hassard Short. Dialogue directed by Monty Woolley. Dances created by Albertina Rasch. Settings by Jo Mielziner. Costumes by Irene Sharaff and Connie DePinna. Orchestra conducted by Frank Tours. Assistant musical director, Richard Baravelle. Orchestrations by (Robert) Russell Bennett. Produced by Sam H. Harris and Max Gordon. Opened 12 October 1935 at the Imperial Theatre and closed 7 March 1936 after 169 performances.

CAST: *The King*: MELVILLE COOPER. *The Queen*: MARY BOLAND. *Prince James*: CHARLES WALTERS. *Princess Diana*: MARGARET ADAMS. *Prince Peter*: MONTGOMERY CLIFT. *Prince Rudolph*: JACKIE KELK. *Lord Wyndham*: RICHIE LING. *Eric Dare*: DEREK WILLIAMS. *Karen O'Kane*: JUNE KNIGHT. *Eva Standing*: MAY BOLEY. *Charles Rausmiller, Mowgli*: MARK PLANT. *Mrs. Watkins*: Jane Evans. *Laura Fitzgerald*: OLIVE REEVES-SMITH. *A Sandwich Man*: Charles Brokaw. *Professor Rexford*: Ralph Sumter. *The Beach Widow*: Dorothy Fox. *Cabinet Minister*: Leo Chalzell. *Cabinet Minister*: Charles Brokaw. *Lifeguard*: Don Douglas. *Announcer*: Albert Amato. *Master of Ceremonies*: Harold Murray. *The Drunk*: Jack Edwards. *The Usher*: Ted Fetter. *Keeper of Zoo*: Leo Chalzell.
> *The Satellites*: Girls: Betty Allen, Wyn Cahoon, Jacqueline Franc, Janice Joyce, Kay Sloan, Katherine Howard, Erika Zaranov. Boys: Albert Amato, Tom Curley, Vernon Hammer, Harold Murray, Sid Salzer, Castle Williams.
> *The Pages*: Donald Brown, Evelyn Eaton, Warren Eaton, Patricia Roe, Alice Fitzsimmons, Raymond Roe, John Roemele. *The Girls*: Virginia Allen, Dorothy Atkins, Jeannette Bradley, Kay Cameron, Helen Cole, Miriam Curtis, Denise Denning, Rose Gale, Dorothy Graves, Marion Heemsath, Joyce Johnson, Adele Jurgens, Helene Louise, Patricia Martin, Austra Neiman, Wilma Roelof, Tanya Sanina, Peggy Seel, Rose Tyrrell, Elsa Walbridge, Finette Walker, Janice Winter. *The Boys*: Bruce Barclay, Robert Burns, Jack Donaldson, George Herndon, Buddy Hertelle, Jay Hunter, James Keogan, Leslie Kingdon, Robert Lewis, Jules Mann, Philip Mann, Jack Millard, John Moore, Mickey Moore, Fred Nay, Michael James, David Preston, Victor Pullman, David Arnold, Bob Schultz, Vernon Tanner, Norman Van Emburgh, Gil White, Gilbert Wilson, Jack Whitney. *The Martinique Orchestra*: Reuben Cohen, James Flood, Wilbur Kurz, Seymour Mann, Joseph Pergola, Jack Rosenmerkel.

Act 1, Scene 1: The Throne Room of the Palace. *Scene 2*: Ante Room in the Palace. *Scene 3*: Nicodemus Bar. *Scene 4*: The Municipal Park. *Scene 5*: The Street. *Scene 6*: The Acme Motion Picture Theatre. *Scene 7*: The Stage Door. *Scene 8*: Café Martinique. *Scene 9*: Prime Minister's Library. *Scene 10*: Eva's Sitting Room. *Scene 11*: The Swimming Pool. *Scene 12*: Karen's Boudoir. *Scene 13*: The Hall of Eva's House. *Scene 14*: The Ballroom of Eva's House.

Act 2, Scene 1: Breakfast Room at Feathermore. *Scene 2*: The Beach Wagons at Rockwell Beach. *Scene 3*: The Beach. *Scene 4*: Along the Cliffs. *Scene 5*: The Zoo. *Scene 6*: The Zoo Garden. *Scene 7*: Ante Room in the Palace. *Scene 8*: The Throne Room of the Palace.

ACT 1[42]

Scene 1

"Our Crown" (National Anthem)
> Entire Company

"We're Off to Feathermore"
> M. Cooper, M. Boland, C. Walters, M. Adams

Scene 2

"Why Shouldn't I"
> M. Adams

Scene 3

Entrance of Eric
> The Satellites

"The Kling-Kling Bird on the Divi-Divi Tree"
> D. Williams

"When Love Comes Your Way"
> D. Williams, M. Adams

Scene 4

"What a Nice Municipal Park"
> The Satellites
> *Danced by* J. Whitney, Boys, Girls.

Scene 6

"When Me, Mowgli, Love"
> M. Plant

Scene 8

"Begin the Beguine"
> J. Knight
> *Danced by* J. Knight, C. Walters. (*Dance routine arranged by* Tony De Marco.)

Scene 10

Recitative
> M. Boley, The Satellites

"My Most Intimate Friend"
> M. Boley

Scene 12

"A Picture of Me Without You"
> J. Knight, C. Walters

Scene 13

"Ev'rybod-ee Who's Anybod'ee"
> The Satellites

Scene 14

Masque, "The Judgement of Paris"
> *Danced by* J. Knight

"Swing that Swing"
> Entire Company

ACT 2

Scene 1

"Sunday Morning, Breakfast Time"
> The Footmen

"Mr. and Mrs. Smith"
> M. Boland, M. Cooper, C. Walters, M. Adams, J. Knight, M. Boley, D. Williams, M. Plant

Scene 2

"Gay Little Wives"
> The Satellites

Scene 3

Opening Dance
> Ensemble

---

[38] Lyrics by Ira Gershwin.
[39] Lyrics by DuBose Heyward.
[40] Lyrics by Ira Gershwin.
[41] Lyrics by DuBose Heyward.

---

[42] Added during the run to Act 1:
> "Gather Ye Autographs" (Scene 7)
> The Satellites
> "My Loulou" (Scene 8, before "Begin the Beguine")
> Ensemble

Dance

D. K. Fox

"Me and Marie"

M. Cooper, M. Boland

Scene 4

"When Love Comes Your Way" (reprise)

M. Adams

Scene 5

"Just One of Those Things"

J. Knight, C. Walters

Scene 7

"Our Crown"(reprise)

The Guardsmen

Scene 8

Jubilee Presentation

Entire Company

1935.15   JUMBO

A Musical Comedy in Two Acts, 3 Scenes. Libretto (book) by Ben Hecht and Charles MacArthur. Music by Richard Rodgers. Lyrics by Lorenz Hart. Staged by John Murray Anderson. Book directed by George Abbott. Settings by Albert Johnson. Equestrian, acrobatic and aerial ballets by Allan K. Foster. Costumes by Raoul Pene du Bois. Orchestrations by Adolph Deutsch, Murray Cutter, Joseph Nussbaum, Hans Spialek, Conrad Salinger. Choral arrangement by Charles Henderson. Rhythmic movement and dance impressions by Marjery Fielding. Additional costumes and masks designed by Wynn and James Reynolds. Produced by Billy Rose. Opened 16 November 1935 at the Hippodrome and closed 18 April 1936 after 233 performances.

CAST (in order of appearance): *Mr. Ball:* BOB LAWRENCE. *Mr. Jellico:* A. P. KAYE. *First Artist:* Tom Lomas. *Second Artist:* Fred Spear. *"Poodles":* POODLES HANNEFORD. *John A. Considine:* ARTHUR SINCLAIR. *First Razorback:* Ray Miller. *Mickey Considine:* GLORIA GRAFTON. *Matthew Mulligan:* William J. McCarthy. *Matt Mulligan, Jr.:* DONALD NOVIS. *Second Razorback:* Dave Adams. *United States Marshal:* GEORGE WATTS. *Claudius B. Bowers:* JIMMY DURANTE. *Flanagan:* Henry LaMarr. *Auctioneer:* Willard Dashiell. *Little Girl:* Sybil Elaine. *Chief of Police:* Donald Black. *Mr. Piper:* Philip Wood. *Sweeney:* Gene Greenlaw. *McCarthy:* Walter Lewis. *Reilly:* John Kuebler. *Jumbo:* "BIG ROSIE." PAUL WHITEMAN AND HIS ORCHESTRA.

Circus Specialties: A. ROBINS, Grace Elizabeth Hanneford, Arthur la Fleur, Takayama, William Ferry, Barbette, Minnie LaPell, Helen Harvey, Victoria Miller, Margaret Brooks, Camilla's Birds, Stanley's Bears, Dr. Ostermeier and His "Doheos," Allen Bennett, Jack Barnes, Albert Dewbeery, William Selig, Joseph Caplan, Margaret Donohue, Robert Reano, Sonny Lang, William Brooks, Claude Ratliff, William Freeman, Karl Kosicsky, Litri Wagner, Frances Van Ritter, France and LaPell, the Lomas Troupe, Helen Brown, Edna Lee, Frances McMasters, Dave Ballard, Josie DeMotte, Tom Breen, Charles de Camo, Lenze Duo, The Nagyfys, Jim Mandy, Olivette, Tyana, Harry Jackson, Sr., Mary Jackson, Harry Jackson, Jr., Arthur Sherwood, Ed and Helen LaNole, The Stonleys, The Kimris, Menagerie from John T. Benson's Wild Animal Farm.

The Show Girls: Anita Arden, Aina Constant, Madeline Ecklund, Maurine Holmes, Mildred Hughes, Carlotta Mann, Gayle Mellott, Julie Sterling, Ethel Summerville. *The Dancers:* Evelyn Bonefine, Dorothy Bradshaw, Violet Carson, Gloria Claire, Vyna Dale, Betty De Elmo, Margaret Donahue, Virginia Donahue, Joan Gray, Tilda Getze, Billie Joyce, Patricia Knight, Charlotte Lorraine, Lela Manor, Lila Manor, Edwina Steele. *The Allan K. Foster Girls:* Nancy Antoine, Florence Blair, Mickey Elbert, Vivian Francis, Mona Gray, Betty Harris, Dorothy Keller, Gladys Lorraine, Josephine Martin, Kathryn McDonald, Virginia Moore, Lillian Sherry, Gwen Stader, Barbara Stuart, Dorothy Warren, Effie Winter, Mae Winter. *Henderson's Singing Razorbacks:* David Adams, Edward Angelry, Allen Bennett, William Parker, Theodore Daniels, Daniel Dansby, Lipman Duckat, Lynn Eldredge, Philip Eppens, William Freeman, Roger Gerry, Eugene Greenlaw, Julius Johnson, Robert Johnson, Joseph Kaplan, John Kuebler, Henry LaMarr, Jack Leslie, Walter Lewis, Rudolph Mattson, Ray Miller, J. H. Pendergast, Jack Philips, Claude Ratliff, Carol Tolle, Howard Urbach, Herbert Waldman, Merrit Wells, Solon West, Arnold Wilson, Clifford Whitcomb, Victor Young[43].

Act 1: John Considine's Wonder Show. Morning. Rehearsal.

Act 2, Scene 1: Considine's Tent, same as Act 1. Several weeks later. *Scene 2:* Considine and Mulligan's Combined Circus. Several weeks later.

ACT 1

"Over and Over Again"

B. Lawrence, Henderson Razorbacks

---

[43]Not the famous composer and conductor of the period.

A Circus Rehearsal: The Ringmaster: P. Hanneford. *The Bareback Rider:* G. E. Hanneford. *The Iron-Jaw Man:* A. la Fleur. *The Juggler:* Takayama. *The Whip Snapper:* H. Jackson, Jr. *The Clown:* A. Robins. *The Contortionist:* W. Ferry. *The Wire-Walker and Aerialist:* Barbette. *The Chair Juggler:* T. Kline. *The Loop-the-Loop Girl:* M. LaPell. *The Trapeze Girls:* H. Harvey, V. Miller. *The Girl in the Cannon:* M. Brooks. Camilla's Birds, Stanley's Bears, The Allan K. Foster Girls.

"The Circus Is on Parade"

Henderson's Razorbacks, Artists of the Circus

"The Most Beautiful Girl in the World"

D. Novis, G. Grafton

Musical Ride by the Allan K. Foster Girls, D. Ostermeier's Doheos.

"Laugh"

J. Durante, A. Robins

The Golfer: A. Bennett. *The Koo-Koo:* J. Barnes. *The Horse:* A. Dewberry. *The Woodpecker:* W. Selig. *The Kangaroo:* J. Caplan, M. Donahue. *The See-Saw:* R. Miller. *The Rube:* E. Greenlaw. *The Four-armed Man:* W. Ferry. *The Cop:* R. Reano. *The Man in the Fish Bowl:* S. Lang. *The Upside-down Man:* W. Brooks. *The Elephant:* C. Ratliff, W. Freeman, K. Kosicsky. Allan K. Foster Girls.

"My Romance"

D. Novis, G. Grafton

"Little Girl Blue"

G. Grafton

The Child: S. Elaine. *The Coachman:* K. Kosicsky. *The Postillons:* L. Wagner, H. Brooks. *The Mistress of the Ring:* F. Van Ritter. *The Clown:* A. Robins. *The Juggler:* Takayama. *The Aerialists:* France and LaPell. *The Iron-jaw Man:* A. la Fleur. *The Stilt Men:* The Lomas Troupe. *The Iron-jaw Girls:* H. Brown, H. Harvey, V. Miller, L. Wagner, E. Lee, F. McMasters. *And Tight-Rope Walkers, Tumblers, Silver Grooms, Crystal Clowns, and the Razerbacks.*

ACT 2

Scene 1

"The Song of the Roustabouts"

The Razorbacks

"Women"

J. Durante, Barbette, Allan K. Foster Girls, Dancers

"Memories of Madison Square Garden" (When the Circus Played the Garden)

(Ensemble)

P. T. Barnum: W. Dashiel. *The Giant:* D. Ballard. *General Tom Thumb:* K. Kosicsky. *The Bareback Rider:* J. DeMotte. *The Juggler:* T. Breen. *The Dog Trainer:* C. de Camo. *The Acrobats:* Lenze Duo. *The Frog:* W. Ferry. *The Fire-eaters:* The Nagyfys. *The Iron-Skull Man:* J. Mandy. *The Punching Bag Artist:* Olivette. *The Strong Woman:* Tyana. *The Man on the Tables:* J. Pickford. *On the Revolving Ladders:* E. LaNole, Helen LaNole. *The Axe-Thrower:* H. Jackson, Sr. *The Target:* M. Jackson. *The Whipsnapper:* H. Jackson, Jr. *The Aerialist:* A. Sherwood. *The Slide for Life Girl:* T. Kline.

Scene 2

"Diavolo"

B. Lawrence, The Razorbacks, The Stonleys, The Kimris

"The Circus Wedding" (finale/reprises)

Entire Company, The Menagerie

1935.16   MOTHER

A Play with Music in Three Acts, 18 Scenes. Play ("Die Mutter," original German book, lyrics) by Bertolt Brecht. Based on the novel of the same name by Maxim Gorki. Music by Hans Eisler. Translated by Paul Peters. Directed by Victor Wolfson. Settings designed by Modecai Gorelik. Lighting by Charles Friedman. Music director, Jerome Moross. Costumes by Fania Mindell. Produced by the Theatre Union, Inc. Opened 19 November 1935 at the Civic Repertory Theater and closed 15 December 1935 after 31 performances.

CAST (in order of appearance): *The Mother, Pelagea Vlasova:* HELEN HENRY. *Pavel Vlasov:* John Boruff. *Anton:* Tony Ross. *Andrei Maximovitch Nachodka:* Herbert Rudley. *Ivan Vesovchikov:* Martin Wolfson. *Masha:* Hester Sondergaard. *A Policeman:* Lee J. Cobb. *The Inspector:* James MacDonald. *Gatekeeper:* Charles Niemeyer. *Karpow:* Lester Lonergan, Jr. *Workers:* James MacDonald, Stanley G. Wood, Herbert Rudley. *Smilgin:* Lee J. Cobb. *The Teacher, Nicolai Ivanovich Vesovchikov:* Stanley G. Wood. *Sostakovich:* Lester Lonergan, Jr. *Women:* Frances Bavier, Hester Sondergaard. *A Prison Guard:* Tony Ross. *Yegor Luchin:* Herbert Rudley. *Scab:* Charles Niemeyer. *Butcher, Vasil Yefimovich:* Lee J. Cobb. *The Butcher's Wife:* Millicent Green. *The Landlady, Vera Stefanovna:* Frances Bavier. *Lydia Antonovna:* Frances Bavier. *Another Tenant:* Hester Sondergaard. *A Doctor:* James MacDonald. *Other Workers:* Guy Smith, Jr., Robert Miller, Bradley Louis Roberts. *At the pianos:* Jerome Moross, Alex North.

The action takes place in the cities of Tversk and Rostov, Russia, 1907-1917.

Act 1, Scene 1: The home of Pelagea Vlasova, Tversk. *Scene 2*: The same. *Scene 3*: At the gate of the Sukhlinov Works. *Scene 4*: Inside the yard of the Sukhlinov Works. *Scene 5*: The home of Pelagea Vlasova. *Scene 6*: A Street.

Act 2, Scene 1: The home of Nicolai Ivanov Vesovchikov, the teacher, in Rostov. *Scene 2*: The same. *Scene 3*: The same. *Scene 4*: The same. *Scene 5*: The prison. *Scene 6*: A country road. *Scene 7*: The kitchen of the Smirnoff Farms.

Act 3, Scene 1: The home of the teacher. *Scene 2*: The same. *Scene 3*: The same. *Scene 4*: A street-corner. *Scene 5*: A street.

ACT 1

"The Song of the Question"

"The Song of the Answer"

"The Whole Loaf"

ACT 2

"In Praise of Socialism"

"In Praise of Learning"

"A Song for Prison"

"In Praise of Vlasova"

ACT 3

"The Third Thing"

"The Death of a Comrade"

"The Party is in Danger"

"'Never' Becomes 'Today'"

1935.17   MAY WINE

A Musical Play in Two Acts, 15 Scenes. Book by Frank Mandel. Based on the novel "The Happy Alienist" by Wallace Smith, suggested by the story related by Eric von Stroheim. Music by Sigmund Romberg. Lyrics by Oscar Hammerstein II. Staged by José Ruben. Settings by Raymond Sovey. Costumes by Kay Morrison. Music director, Robert (Emmett) Dolan. Orchestrations by Don Walker; Additional orchestrations by (Robert) Russell Bennett. Produced by Laurence Schwab. Opened 5 December 1935 at the St. James Theatre and closed 6 June 1936 after 213 performances.

CAST (in order of appearance): *Professor Johann Volk*: WALTER SLEZAK. *Inspector Schnorrheim*: ROY GORDON. *Sergeant*: Tomes Chapman. *Policemen*: Edward Gallaway, Leonard Berry, Chester Herman. *Willi Zimmerkopf*: ROBERT SLOANE. *Baron Kuno Adelhorst*: WALTER WOOLF KING. *Herr Schmidt*, barber: Carlo Conte. *Hans*, assistant: Victor Casmore. *Gypsy*: Marie Louise Quevli. *Musicians*: Bela Loblov, Charles Palloy. *Father* (Herr Schrammel): Mitchell Harris. *Mother* (Frau Schrammel): Inga Hill. *Son*: Radley Collins. *Daughter*: Marian Huntley. *Waiter*: Maury Tuckerman. *The Lovers*: Earle MacVeigh, Betty Kerr. *Mr. Whalley*: Mitchell Harris. *Waiter*: Maury Tuckerman. *Marie—Baroness von Schlewitz*: NANCY McCORD. *Page Boy*: Radley Collins. *Box Holders*: Tomes Chapman, Devona Doxie, Lee Childs. *Vera Huber*, Volk's assistant: Patricia Calvert. *Strollers*: Flora Laney, Leonard Berry, Clifford Menz. *Josef*, clarinet player: ROBERT C. FISCHER. *Uncle Pishka*: LEO G. CARROLL. *Mr. Runtschli*, of "Die Wochende": Earle MacVeigh. *Old Couple*: Jessie Graham, Leonard Berry. *Dancers*: JACK COLE, ALICE DUDLEY. *Kathi*, maid at Hotel Schildersturn: Inga Hill. *Friedl*, Willie's model: VERA VAN. *Pawnbroker*: Victor Casmore. *Dr. Von Schlager*: Mitchell Harris. *Dr. Herbst*: Leonard Berry. *Dr. Karpis*: Carlo Conte. *Newsboy*: Radley Collins.

Act 1, Scene 1: Professor Volk's Living Room. The month of May. *Scene 2*: A Barber Shop. *Scene 3*: A Prater Café. *Scene 4*: The Benefit Performance. *Scene 5*: Marie's Room. *Scene 6*: Volk's Living Room. *Scene 7*: The Railroad Station. *Scene 8*: Hotel Schildersturn, Bridal Suite.

Act 2, Scene 1: Bridal Suite. *Scene 2*: Willi Zimmerkopf's Studio. *Scene 3*: Volk's Living Room. *Scene 4*: The Club "Florida." *Scene 5*: Professor Volk's Study. *Scene 6*[44]: A Pawn Shop, (a) A Conference Room, (b) A Street. *Scene 7*: Volk's Living Room.

ACT 1

Scene 1

"Something in the Air of May"

W. Slezak

Scene 2

"Interlude in a Barber Shop"

W. Slezak, W. W. King

Scene 3

"A Chanson in the Prater"

W. Slezak, N. McCord, M. Harris, I. Hill

Scene 4

"A Doll Fantasy"

N. McCord

Scene 5

"You Wait and Wait and Wait"

N. McCord, W. W. King

Scene 6

"I Built a Dream Today (One Day)"

W. Slezak, W. W. King, R. C. Fischer

Scene 7

"Dance, My Darlings"

N. McCord, Singing Ensemble

Dance Interlude

J. Cole, A. Dudley

Scene 8

Finale Act 1

N. McCord, W. W. King

ACT 2

Scene 1

"Always Be a Gentleman"

N. McCord, W. W. King

Scene 2

"I Built a Dream (One Day)" (reprise)

R. C. Fischer

Scene 4

"Somebody Ought To Be Told"

V. Van

Scene 5

"Something New Is in My Heart"

N. McCord

Dance Interlude

J. Cole, A. Dudley

Scene 6

"(Just) Once Around the Clock"

V. Van, W. W. King, L. G. Carroll

Scene 7

"Something New Is in My Heart" (reprise)

N. McCord

1935.18   GEORGE WHITE'S SCANDALS (1936)

A Musical Revue in Two Acts, 25 Scenes[45]. Dialogue (sketches) by George White, William K. Wells, Howard A. Shiebler, (A. Dorian Otvos). Lyrics by Jack Yellen. Music by Ray Henderson. Conceived and directed by George White. Dances by Russell Markert. Settings by Russell Patterson and Walter Jagemann. Costumes by Charles LeMaire. Orchestra director, Tom Jones. Orchestrations by (Robert) Russell Bennett and Conrad Salinger. Produced by George White. Opened 25 December 1935 at the New Amsterdam Theatre and closed 28 March 1936 after 110 performances.

CAST: RUDY VALLEE, BERT LAHR, WILLIE HOWARD, EUGENE HOWARD, GRACIE BARRIE, CLIFF EDWARDS, JANE COOPER, HAL FORDE, Estelle Jayne, Sam, Ted & Ray, Richard Lane, the Stanley Twins, (Jimmy) Shea and (Gus) Raymond, Ann Laxton, Harold Willard, Apollo Quartette, Alice Carleton, Edna Page, Verna Long. Edgar Battler, Roy Williams, James Langford, Frank Leonard.

THE GEORGE WHITE GIRLS: Peggy Moseley, Lois Eckhart, Claire McQuillen, Jean Gale, Vivian Porter, Helene Miller, Bert Foth, Alma Saunders, Eleanor LoVette, Prudence Hayes, Roslyn Shaw, Louise Clement, Flo Ward, Myrna Waverly, Dorothea Jackson, Rusty Anderson, Marjorie Dorman, Renee Johnson, Dolores Devito, Dorothy Reed, Eleanor Witt, Louise Arthur, Marjorie Conradi, Jean Mills, Peggy Bady, Laura Shevlin, Paula Manners, Charlotte Mount, Helen Dernell, Helen Saty, Polly Sturgis, Eleanor Low, Jesse Reed, Ann Collins, Grace Gillern, Audrey Hayes, June Tempest,

---

[44]Scene dropped shortly after opening.

[45]The twelfth in the series of musical revues produced by George White beginning in 1919.

Jane Oliver, Sally Weant, Bee Allen, Mona O'Neil, Edna Jans, Hazel Williams, Frances Dane, Ernette DuVal, Betty Shaw, Josephine Carr, Betty Hall, Paulette Gwynne. *Show Girls*: Fay Long, Florette DuElk, Patsy Ruth, Nancy Lewis, Ann Budick, Vera Devine, Ernette Muesseler.

ACT 1

Scene 1

Tune In on the World's First Television Broadcast
A. Laxton, V. Long

"Anything Can Happen"
G. Barrie
(*Lyrics by* Jack Yellen and Ballard McDonald.) *Announcer*: R. Lane.

Scene 2

"Life Begins at Sweet Sixteen"
G. Barrie
Peggy Joyce: L. Eckhart. *Mamie Simple McPherson*: H. Miller. *Mrs. Vandernuts*: E. Jayne. *Mae West*: G. Barrie. *Senator*: H. Forde. *Pride*: C. McQuillen. And the George White Girls.

Scene 3

Commercially Speaking
Mr. N. B. Cee: B. Lahr. *Mrs. N. B. Cee*: E. Jayne. *Abie*: C. Edwards.

Scene 4

Jane Cooper and the George White Girls

Scene 5

A Slight Case of Murder
Lawyer: E. Howard. *Client*: W. Howard. *Wife*: E. Jayne. *Stenographer*: C. McQuillen.

Scene 6

"Cigarette"
H. Willard, L. Eckhart, the George White Girls

Scene 7

A Blessed Event
Lord Tottingham: H. Forde. *Lord Marleybone*: B. Lahr. *Butler*: R. Lane.

Scene 8

"I'm the Fellow Who Loves You"
R. Vallee, G. Barrie, B. Lahr, W. Howard, L. Eckhart, P. Moseley, Apollo Quartete

Scene 9

"Truckin' in My Tails"
J. Cooper, Show Girls, George White Girls

Scene 10

Journey's End (*by* A. Dorian Otvos and George White)
Warden: H. Forde. *McGee*: W. Howard. *Stanford*: R. Lane. *Trusty*: H. Willard. *Guard*: V. Elliott. *Reporters*: J. Langford, R. Williams, F. Leonard.

Scene 11

Selassie and His Army
Sam, Ted and Ray

Scene 12

Mind Over Matter
Psychoanalyst: H. Forde. *Ambrose*: B. Lahr. *Nurse*: C. McQuillen. *Wife*: E. Jaynes.

Scene 13

Brother Sublime and His "Pied Piper of Harlem"
a. *A Street in Harlem*.
Brother Sublime: R. Vallee. *Pied Piper*: E. Battler. *Pedestrians*: R. Williams, J. Langford, N. Lewis, A. Budik, H. Miller, E. page, A. Carleton, V. Devine, F. Long, J. Cooper.
b. *Reefer Smoking Den, 7th Avenue*.
Policy Man: R. Lane. *Reefer Girls*: L. Shevlin, J. Mills, P. Bady, J. Gale, L. Eckhart, G. Gillern.
c. *The Black Cat Club, Lenox Avenue*.
Doorman: F. Leonard. *Cabaret Girls*: R. Anderson, A. Saunders, R. Johnson, C. McQuillan, E. Lovett, D. Reed.
d. *Upper Broadway*.
A Harlem Girl: G. Barrie.
e. *Cotton Exchange, Wall Street*.
f. *Cotton Plantation*.
Southern Colonels: H. Forde, H. Willard. *Southern Belles*: A. Laxton, V. Long, P. Ruth, V. Devine, E. Meuseler.
g. *Finale*
Entire Company

ACT 2

Scene 1

Relief Headquarters, New York City: "Boondoggling"
Announcer: R. Lane. *Taxi Driver*: B. Foth. *5 and 10 Salesgirl*: V. Porter. *Stenographer*: C. McQuillen. *Lady of the Evening*: J. Gale. *A White Wing*: L. Shevlin. *Plumber*: P. Moseley. And the George White Girls. *Mussolini*: W. Howard.

Scene 2

"The Buxom Mrs. Bascom"
C. Edwards, B. Lahr

Scene 3

The French Lesson
Announcer: R. Lane. *Professor*: W. Howard.

Scene 4

"May I Have My Gloves"
R. Vallee, P. Moseley, the George White Girls

Scene 5

Chrysanthemum Gardens
"I've Got to Get Hot"
G. Barrie
Proprietor: R. Lane.

Scene 6

The Stanley Twins

Scene 7

Rudy Vallee
["The (Daring Young) Man on the Flying Trapeze"
(*Music and Lyrics by* Walter O'Keefe.)]

Scene 8

Soup
Professor Von Kluck: B. Lahr. *Nurse*: L. Eckhart. *Radio Announcer*: H. Forde.

Scene 9

Willie and Eugene Howard in their famous version of "Rigoletto."
Assisted by A. Carleton, E. Page.

Scene 10

"Anything Can Happen" (reprise)
R. Vallee, G. Barrie, the George White Girls

Scene 11

The Year 2036
Announcer: R. Lane.
a. Henry the Eighth. *Henry*: C. Edwards. *Catherine*: E. Jayne.
b. Ponce de Leon. *De Leon*: B. Lahr. *Follower*: H. Forde.
c. Napoleon. *Napoleon*: E. Howard. *Josephine*: H. Miller.
d. Kate Smith. *Kate Smith*: E. Page.
e. Ukelele Ike. *Ukelele Ike*: C. Edwards.
f. Al Jolson. *Al Jolson*: W. Howard.
g. *A Fellow from Maine*: R. Vallee.

Scene 12

Finale
Entire Company

CONTINENTAL VARIETIES
OF 1936

1935.19

A New Edition of the International Vaudeville Revue in Two Acts, 13 Scenes[46]. Musical arrangements by Georges Tabet. Produced by Henry Carson. Opened 26 December 1935 at the Masque Theatre and closed 31 December 1935 after 9 performances.

CAST: LUCIENNE BOYER, (Jacques) PILS [Pills] and (Georges) TABET, GEORGES-ANDRÉ MARTIN, HELEN GRAY and PAAL and LEIF ROCKY, KING LAN CHEW, IZA VOLPIN'S CONTINENTAL ENSEMBLE.
Louise Marleau (Piano for King Lan Chew); Walter Kayaloff (Piano for Helen Gray, Paal and Leif Rocky, and Georges-André Martin).

ACT 1

Scene 1

A few words of introduction
G. Martin

---

[46]Previous Editions 1 and 2 presented in New York 3 October 1934 at the Little Theatre for 77 performances with a different cast.

Scene 2
  Hungarian Selection
    Iza Volpin's Continental Ensemble
Scene 3
  American Rhythm; Proximity
    H. Gray, Paal, L. Rocky
Scene 4
  Songs from their repertoire (see below)
    Pills and Tabet
Scene 5
  Chinese Actor (Traditional melody); Burmese Figurine (Native Melody)
    King Lan Chew
Scene 6
  Songs from her repertoire (see below)
    L. Boyer
ACT 2
Scene 1
  Georges-André Martin
Scene 2
  Gypsy Pot-Pourri
    Iza Volpin's Continental Ensemble
Scene 3
  Georges-André Martin . . . and his dancing fingers
Scene 4
  Phantasm (George Gershwin); Corvocado (Darius Milhaud)
    King Lan Chew
Scene 5
  Songs from their repertoire
    Pills and Tabet
Scene 6
  Impressions of Musical Comedy
    H. Gray, Paal, L. Rocky
Scene 7
  Songs from her repertoire
    L. Boyer
  Repertoire for Lucienne Boyer:
  "I Found a Bit of Paris"
    (*Music by* Jean Delettre. *Lyrics by* Stella Unger.)
  "L'Hôtel des amours faciles"
    (*Music by* Raoul Moretti. *Lyrics by* Maurice Aubret.)
  "En se regardant" (Dancing with my Dream)
    (*Music by* Jean Delettre. *Lyrics by* Pierre Bayle-Silverman.)
  "(This Is the) Kiss of Romance"
    (*Music by* Jean Delettre. *Lyrics by* Mitchell Parish.)
  "Si petite" (So Small)
    (*Music by* Gaston Claret. *Lyrics by* Pierre Bayle.)
  "Parlez-moi d'amour" (Speak to Me of Love)
    (*Music and Lyrics by* Jean Lenoir.)
  "Mon ami le vent"
    (*Music by* Jean Delettre. *Lyrics by* Alain Dhurtal.)
  "Depart" (Leave)
    (*Music by* Jean Delettre. *Lyrics by* Maurice Aubret.)
  "Dans la fumée" (In the Smoke)
    (*Music and Lyrics by* Jean Bos.)
  "Attends" (Wait)
    (*Music by* Jean Lenoir. *Lyrics by* Jacques-Charles.)
  "Parle-moi d'autre chose" (Speak to Me of Something Else)
    (*Music by* Jean Delettre. *English Lyrics by* Mitchell Parish.)
  "Les Gueuses" (The Streetwalkers)
    (*Music and Lyrics by* Vincent Scotto.)
  "Viens danser quand même" (Dancing with My Darling)
    (*Music by* Jean Delettre. *Lyrics by* Jamblan and Mitchell Parish.)
  "Moi, j'crache dans l'eau" (I Spit in the Water)
    (*Music and Lyrics by* Jean Tranchant.)
  "Ne dis pas toujours" (Don't Say Always)
    (*Music and Lyrics by* Jean Lenoir.)

"(Mais) Si tu pars" (If You Leave)
  (*Music by* Ted Grouya. *Lyrics by* Le Pointe.)
"Prenez mes roses" (Bring Me Roses)
  (*Music and Lyrics by* H. Champfleury.)
"It's a Thrill All Over Again"
  (*Music by* Jean Delettre. *Lyrics by* Stella Unger.)
"Des mots nouveaux" (I Need New Words)
  (*Music by* Jean Delettre. *Lyrics by* Maurice Aubret.)
"Parlez-moi d'amour" (Speak to Me of Love)
  (*Music and Lyrics by* Jean Lenoir.)
"(Dans) Le petit café du coin"
  (*Music by* Jean Bos. *Lyrics by* Pierre Bayle.)
"La voyageuse"
  (*Music by* Jean Delettre. *Lyrics by* Maurice Aubret.)
"Hands Across the Table"
  (*Music by* Jean Delettre. *Lyrics by* Mitchell Parish.)
"Un amour comme le nôtre" (A Love Like Ours)
  (*Music by* Borel-Clerc. *Lyrics by* Vincent Telly.)
"Le train du rêve"
  (*Music by* Jean Lenoir. *Lyrics by* Maurice Aubret.)
"Youp et Youp"
  (*Music by* Vincent Scotto. *Lyrics by* Bertal-Maubon.)

Repertoire for Pills and Tabet:
"Couches dans le foin"
  (*Music by* Mireille. *Lyrics by* Jean Nohain.)
"Le vieux château"
  (*Music by* Mireille. *Lyrics by* Jean Nohain.)
"La fille de Lévy"
  (*Music and Lyrics by* Georges Tabet.)
"27, Rue des Acacias"
  (*Music by* Mireille. *Lyrics by* Jean Nohain.)
"Le petit théâtre"
  (*Music by* Mireille. *Lyrics by* Jean Nohain.)
"Un cabanon près de Toulon"
  (*Music by* Georges Tabet. *Lyrics by* Jean Nohain.)
"La petite île" (with English chorus)
  (*Music by* Mireille. *Lyrics by* Jean Nohain.)
"Ici l'on pêche"
  (*Music and Lyrics by* Jean Tranchant.)
"Aux îles Hawai"
  (*Music by* Pascal Bastia. *Lyrics by* Jean Bastia.)
"C'est gentil quand on y passe"
  (*Music by* Mireille. *Lyrics by* Jean Nohain.)
"Femmes"
  (*Music by* Mary Myram. *Lyrics by* Jamblan.)
"Gwendoline"
  (*Music by* Christiane Verger. *Lyrics by* Jamblan.)
"Toi c'est moi"
  (*Music by* Moïses Simon. *Lyrics by* Albert Willemetz.)
"Nous serons toujours heureux"
  (*Music by* Georges Tabet. *Lyrics by* Ellis.)
"Little Dreams"
  (*Music by* Jean Delettre. *Lyrics by* Mitchell Parish.)
"Two in a Crowd"
  (*Music by* Jean Delettre. *Lyrics by* Stella Unger.)
"Let me draw you a picture"
  (*Music by* Jean Delettre. *Lyrics by* Robinson.)
Music Around the World
  (arr. by Pills-Tabet. *Lyrics by* Arthur Swanstrom.)
"New York-Paris"
  (*Music by* Pearl Lippmann. *Lyrics by* Arthur Lippmann.)
"Adam and Eve"
  (*Music by* Pearl Lippmann. *Lyrics by* Arthur Lippmann.)
"We Own a Haunted Castle"
  (*Music by* Mireille. *Lyrics by* Jean Nohain.)

1936.01 THE ILLUSTRATORS' SHOW

A Musical Revue in Two Acts, 31 Scenes[47]. Music mostly by Irving Actman. Lyrics mostly by Frank Loesser. (Additional music by Edgar Fairchild, Charlotte Kent, Frederick Loewe, Bernece Kazounoff, Michael H. Cleary. Additional lyrics by Milton Pascal, Charlotte Kent, Earl Crooker, Nat and Max Lief, Carl Randall. Sketches by Harry Evans, Max Liebman, Hi Alexander, Frank Gabrielson, David Lesan, Kenneth Webb, Donald Blackwell, Napie Moore, Otto Soglow.) Dances and musical numbers staged by Carl Randall. Sketches staged by Allen Delano. Music directed by Gene Salzer. Settings by Arne Lundborg from designs by (many members of) the Society of Illustrators. Costumes by Carl Sidney. Curtain design by Russell Patterson. Produced by Tom Weatherly. Opened 22 January 1936 at the 48th Street Theatre and closed 25 January 1936 after 5 performances.

CAST: HELEN LYND, EARL OXFORD, NIELA GOODELLE, GOMEZ & WINONA, OTTO SOGLOW, O. Z. WHITEHEAD, Elizabeth Houston, Dan Harden, Robert Berry, Fred Cooper, Joe Donatella, Norman Lind, Edward Mowen, William Houston.

Exquisite American Beauties (Girls): Phyllis Cameron, Claire Carroll, Dorothy Chilton, Connie Crowell, Betty Gillette, Harriette Howell, Helen Hudson, Betty Lee, Patricia Martin, Frances Nevins, Sondra Roy, Lorraine Teatom, Dorothy Waller, Davenie Watson.

ACT 1

Scene 1

Fred Cooper

Scene 2

And Now the Girls
(*Setting from a Design by* Rube Goldberg.)

Scene 3

"I Want to Play With the Girls"
D. Harden, Girls
(*Music by* Edgar Fairchild. *Lyrics by* Milton Pascal.)

Scene 4

Studio House Warming (*by* Harry Evans. *Setting from a design by* Dean Cornwell.)
Mary Lou Carter: H. Lynd. *Mr. Oxford*: E. Oxford.

Scene 5

Otto Soglow and Phyllis Cameron

Scene 6

"Let's Talk About the Weather"
E. Houston, D. Harden, Girls
(*Music and Lyrics by* Charlotte Kent.)

Scene 7

Post Haste (*by* Max Liebman and Hi Alexander)
Customer: H. Lynd. *Clerk*: D. Harden.

Scene 8

"Just For Tonight"
N. Goodelle
(*Music and Lyrics by* Charlotte Kent.)

Scene 9

Remote Patrol
First Big Business Man: F. Cooper. *Second Big Business Man*: N. Lind. *Third Big Business Man*: W. Houston. *Applicant*: D. Harden.

Scene 10

"Park Avenue's Going to Town"
Girls
(*Music by* Edgar Fairchild. *Lyrics by* Milton Pascal.)

Scene 11

Matter of Form (*by* Frank Gabrielson and David Lesan)
Operator: H. Lynd. *Customer*: O. Soglow.

Scene 12

"If You Didn't Love Me"
N. Goodelle, E. Oxford
(*Music by* Irving Actman. *Lyrics by* Frank Loesser.)

Scene 13

At the Doctor's (*by* Kenneth Webb)
Dr. Stedman: F. Cooper. *Mr. Ohashi*: O. Soglow. *Mrs. Ohashi*: D. Watson.

Scene 14

"I Like to Go to Strange Places"
H. Lynd
(*Music by* Irving Actman. *Lyrics by* Frank Loesser. *Setting from a design by* Dr. Suess.)

Scene 15

"Bang the Bell Rang"
(*Music by* Irving Actman. *Lyrics by* Frank Loesser. *Setting from a design by* Arne Lundborg.)
Girl at Bar: N. Goodelle. *Bartender*: E. Mowen. *Man at Bar*: E. Oxford. *Cigarette Girl*: E. Houston. *Bellboy*: D. Harden. *First Coin Machine Player*: N. Lind. *Second Coin Machine Player*: W. Houston. *Third Coin Machine Player*: R. Berry. *Hat Check Girl*: B. Gillette.

Scene 16

Enchantment (*by* Donald Blackwell. *Setting designed by* Arne Lundborg.)
Announcement: E. Houston. *Hildegarde*: H. Lynd. *Prince*: E. Oxford.

Scene 17

O. Z. Whitehead

Scene 18

"A Waltz Was Born in Vienna"
N. Goodelle, E. Oxford
(*Music by* Frederick Loewe. *Lyrics by* Earl Crooker. *Setting designed by* Arne Lundborg.)
Danced by Gomez and Winona

ACT 2

Scene 1

In Front of the Theatre
The Entire Cast
(*Setting from a design by* Harry Beckhoff.)
Danced by J. Donatello

Scene 2

High and Wide (*by* Hi Alexander)
Customer: N. Goodelle. *Clerk*: H. Lynd.

Scene 3

"I'm You"
E, Houston, D. Harden, Girls
(*Music by* Irving Actman. *Lyrics by* Frank Loesser.)

Scene 4

Tragedy in Scotland (*by* Napier Moore. *Setting from a design by* Ben Dale.)
Barman: E. Mowen. *First Scotchman*: F. Cooper. *Second Scotchman*: N. Lind. *Third Scotchman*: R. Berry. *Stranger*: E. Oxford.

Scene 5

"Give Me Wild Trumpets"
N. Goodelle
(*Music by* Irving Actman. *Lyrics by* Frank Loesser.)

Scene 6

Helen Lynd and the Girls
(*Music by* Bernece Kazounoff.)

Scene 7

"Hello Ma" (*Setting from a design by* Forrest Haring.)
(*Music by* Michael H. Cleary. *Lyrics by* Nathaniel and Max Lief.)
New Champ: E. Oxford. *Old Champ*: E. Mowen. *Radio Announcer*: R. Berry. *Referee*: N. Lind. *Old Champ's Second*: D. Harden. *Autograph Hunters, Managers, Picture Scout and Other Chislers*: (Cast).

Scene 8

Hereafter (*by* Max Liebman and Hi Alexander)
Mrs. Trevor: H. Lynd. *Professor*: F. Cooper. *Voice of Mr. Trevor*: R. Berry.

Scene 9

"I Love a Polka So"
E. Houston, D. Harden, Girls
(*Music by* Bernece Kazounoff. *Lyrics by* Carl Randall. *Setting from a design by* Harry Beckhoff.)

---

[47]Originally assembled by the Society of Illustrators; expanded and revised by Tom Weatherly.

Scene 10

"Wherefore Art Thou Juliet"
H. Lynd
(*Music and Lyrics by* Charlotte Kent.)

Scene 11

The Little King (*by* Otto Soglow. *Setting from a design by* Otto Soglow.)
The Strikers: H. Howell, B. Gillette, F. Nevins, D. Watson, C. Carroll, P. Martin. *The Little King*: O. Soglow. *The Major Domo*: F. Cooper. *The Bell Ringer*: E. Mowen. *Simon Legree*: N. Lind. *First Slave Girl*: C. Crowell. *Second Slave Girl*: H. Hudson. *Third Slave Girl*: P. Cameron.

Scene 12

Gomez and Winona

Scene 13

Finale
Entire Company
(*Music by* Irving Actman. *Lyrics by* Frank Loesser and Carl Randall.)

1936.02   ZIEGFELD FOLLIES (1936)

A Musical Revue in Two Acts, 24 Scenes[48]. Sketches by David Freedman. Lyrics by Ira Gershwin. Music by Vernon Duke. Staged by John Murray Anderson and Edward Clarke Lilley. Modern dances staged by Robert Alton. Ballets directed by George Balanchine. Settings and costumes by Vincente Minnelli. Additional costumes designed by Raoul Pene du Bois. Music director, John McManus. Orchestrations by Hans Spialek; additional orchestrations by Conrad Salinger, (Robert) Russell Bennett, Don Walker. Produced by Mrs. Florenz Ziegfeld [Billie Burke] (and the Messrs. Shubert). Opened 30 January 1936 at the Winter Garden and closed 9 May 1936 after 115 performances; re-opened a return engagement 14 September 1936 (see entry in following season) at the Winter Garden and closed 19 December 1936 after additional 112 performances. Total for both engagements: 227 performances.

CAST: FANNIE BRICE, JOSEPHINE BAKER, BOB HOPE, GERTRUDE NIESEN, HUGH O'CONNELL, HARRIET HOCTOR, EVE ARDEN, JUDY CANOVA, CHERRY PREISSER, JUNE PREISSER, JOHN HOYSRADT, The Nicholas Brothers (Harold and Fayard), Duke McHale, Rodney McLennan, Stan Kavanagh, George Church, Ben Yost's (California) Varsity Eight (George Enz, Thomas Gleason, Paul Nelson, William Quentmyer, Riques Tanzi, Everett West, Irving West, Ben Yost).
The Show Girls: Vera Haal, Lyn Leslie, Ula Love, Mary Alice Moore, Jane Moxon, Eileen O'Driscoll, Jessica Pepper, Gloria Pierre, Isabel Pulsford, Peggy Quinn, Ethel Thorsen. *The Corps de Ballet*: Evelyn Dale, Althea Elder, Stella Clausen, Georgia Hiden, Frances Rands, Didi Skoug, Marie Vanneman. *The Dancers*: Vicki Belling, Florine Callahan, Dorothy Daly, Maxine Darrell, Nancy Dolan, Helene Fromson, Gay Hoff, Irene Kelly, Elena Marano, Helene Marchand, Betty McMahon, Jean Moorhead, Cornelia Rogers, Marian Semler, Thelma Shearon, Marlyn Stuart, Peggy Thomas. *The Boys*: Gene Ashley, Milton Barnet, Herman Belmonte, Prescott Brown, Edward Browne, Tom Draper, Howard Morgan, Willem Van Loon.

ACT 1

Scene 1

"Time Marches On"
R. McLennan, Ben Yost's Varsity Eight
(*Music by* Vernon Duke. *Lyrics by* Ira Gershwin.)
The Tableau: The Girl in White: J. Pepper. *The Girl in Green*: I. Pulsford. *The Girl in Blue*: L. Leslie. *The Girl in Yellow*: E. Thorsen. *The Girls in the Mirror*: J. Moxon, E. O'Driscoll. *The Nymphs*: V. Haal, M. A. Moore, U. Love, P. Quinn.

Scene 2

"He Hasn't a Thing Except Me"
F. Brice

Scene 3

"(My) Red Letter Day"
C. Preisser, J. Preisser, D. McHale, Ensemble
(*Costumes designed by* Raoul Pene du Bois.)

Scene 4

Of Thee I Spend
Scene: Office of the F.S.A. *Rexford Givewell*: B. Hope. *Miss Gherkin*: E. Arden. *John D. Littlefeller*: H. O'Connell. *Charles G. Clawes*: J. Hoysradt.

[48]The twenty-third in the annual series of revues first originated by Florenz Ziegfeld beginning in 1907.

Scene 5

"(Island in the) West Indies"
G. Niesen, Ben Yost's Varsity Eight
The Conga danced by J. Baker, Ensemble. *Drummers*: J. Sastere, J. Ramos.
(*Costumes designed by* Raoul Pene du Bois.)

Scene 6

The Sweepstakes Ticket
Scene: A small apartment uptown. *Norma Shaeffer*: F. Brice. *Messenger Boy*: D. McHale. *Monty Shaeffer*: H. O'Connell. *Mr. Martin*: J. Hoysradt.

Scene 7

"Words Without Music" (A Surrealist Ballet) (*Staged by* George Balanchine)
The Singer: G. Niesen. *The Dancer*: H. Hoctor. *The Figures in Green*: M. Barnett, G. Church, T. Draper. *The Figures in Black*: G. Ashley, E. Browne, P. Brown, H. Morgan. *The Figure With the Light*: W. Van Loon. And the Corps de Ballet.

Scene 8

"The Economic Situation" (Aren't You Wonderful!)
E. Arden, The Twelve Economists (Show Girls)

Scene 9

"Fancy! Fancy!"
(*Sketch and Lyrics by* Ira Gershwin. *Music by* Vernon Duke.)
Zuleika: F. Brice. *Sir Robert*: B. Hope. *Sir Henry*: J. Hoysradt.

Scene 10

"Night Flight" (*Staged by* George Balanchine.)
Danced by H. Hoctor

Scene 11

Baby Snooks Goes to Hollywood
Scene: A Stage in a Hollywood Studio.
Mrs. Higgins: E. Arden. *Director*: B. Hope *Baby Snooks*: F. Brice. *Cameraman*: G. Church *Clark Gable*: R. McLennan *Joan Crawford*; J. Moxon. *Photographer*: R. Davis. *Official*: J. Hoysradt.

Scene 12

"Maharanee" (At the Night Races in Paris)
J. Baker, R. McLennan, Ensemble

Scene 13

The Nicholas Brothers

Scene 14

"The Gazooka"
(*Sketch by* David Freedman and Ira Gershwin. *Music by* Vernon Duke. *Lyrics by* Ira Gershwin.)
A Super-Special Musical Photoplay Starring Ruby Blondell and Bing Powell with a Large Cast of Supporting Players.
The Cast: Conductor: R. Davis. *Father*: J. Hoysradt. *Mother*: J. Canova. *Bing Powell*: B. Hope. *Aviator*: D. McHale. *Ruby Blondell*: F. Brice. *Casting Agent*: G. Church. *Dolores Del Morgan*: G.Niesen. *Producer*: H. O'Connell. *Scene 1*: A Railway Station. *Scene 2*: A Casting Office. "It's a Different World" *sung by* B. Hope, F. Brice. *Scene 3*: Backstage. *Scene 4*: "The Gazooka" in Techniquecolor on the Wildescope Screen. *Sung by* Entire Film Cast.

ACT 2

Scene 1

"(That) Moment of Moments"
G. Niesen, R. McLennan
(*Music by* Vernon Duke. *Lyrics by* Ira Gershwin.)
Scene: The Foyer of an Opera House in the 'Sixties.
The Ballerina: H. Hoctor *The Grand Duke*: H. Belmonte. Ben Yost's Varsity Eight., Ensemble.

Scene 2

"Sentimental Weather"
C. Preisser, J. Preisser, D. McHale
(*Costumes designed by* Raoul Pene du Bois.)

Scene 3

Amateur Night
Scene: A Broadcasting Studio.
Major Bones: H. O'Connell. *Attendant*: R. Davis. *Juggler*: S. Kavanagh. *Elvira Mackintosh*: J. Canova. *Lady De Vere*: E. Arden. *Myrtle Oppenshaw*: F. Brice.

Scene 4

Stan Kavanagh

Scene 5
  The Voice of Friendship (*by* Ogden Nash)
    B. Hope, the Twelve Undecided
Scene 6
  "5 A.M." (*Staged by* George Balanchine.)
    J. Baker
      The Shadows: G. Ashley, M. Barnett, G. Church, W. Van Loon.
Scene 7
  "I Can't Get Started With You"
    B. Hope, E. Arden, Ensemble
Scene 8
  "Modernistic Moe"
    F. Brice
Scene 9
  The Petrified Elevator
    Operator: B. Hope. *Evangelist*: H. O'Connell. *Banker*: J. Hoysradt. *Winston*: E. West. *Alice*: G. Niesen. *Doctor*: R. Tanzi. *Pickpocket*: W. Quentmeyer. *Tax Collector*: R. Davis. *Allan*: R. McLennan. *Mistress*: L. Leslie. *Anxious Girl*: J. Canova. *Husband*: G. Church. *Girl*: J. Moorhead.
Scene 10
  "Dancing to Our Score"
    R. McLennan, E. Arden, Ben Yost's Varsity Eight, Entire Company

MURDER IN THE OLD RED BARN

1936.03

A Melodrama with Songs in Four Acts, 11 Scenes. (Based on anonymous Victorian texts. Written by John Latimer.) Original music by Richard Lewine. Original lyrics by Jean-Treville [John] Latouche. (Settings by Frank Ambos and Stephen Golding.) Produced by Harry Bannister and John Krimsky, in association with Lucius Beebe[49]. Opened 1 February 1936 at the American Music Hall and closed 2 January 1937 after 337 performances.[50]

CAST: *Tim Robbin*: M. Manisoff. *William Corder*: RICHARD RAUBER. *Marten*: STAPLETON KENT. *Maria Marten*: MARIANNE COWAN. *Ishmael*: ROBERT VIVIAN. *Anne Marten*: Gertrude Keith. *Dame Marten*: JUDITH ELDER. *First Barker*: Alfred L. Rigali. *Second Barker*: HARRY MEEHAN. *Pharosee*: LESLIE LITOMY. *Mark*: George Jones. *Servant*: George Spelvin.

Act 1, Scene 1: Exterior of Marten's Cottage. *Scene 2*: Polestead Village Green. *Scene 3*: Single Tree. *Scene 4*: Interior of Cottage.

Act 2, Scene 1: A Secret Part of the Wood, a Gypsy Camp. *Scene 2*: Another Part of the Wood.

Act 3, Scene 1: Marten's Kitchen. *Scene 2*: Interior of the Red Barn.

Act 4, Scene 1: Drawing Room, William Corder's Home in London. *Scene 2*: A Prison Cell. *Scene 3*: The Execution.

ACT 1 Interlude
  The Cancan Volunteers, featuring Ann Suter and the American Music Hallettes
  Harry Meehan, the Irish Thrush
  ["When Irish Eyes Are Smiling" (from THE ISLE OF DREAMS)
    (*Music by* Ernest R. Ball. *Lyrics by* Chauncey Olcott and George Graff, Jr.)]
  "Not on Your Tintype"
    L. Litomy
  Pope and Thompson, Jugglers and Washboard Musicians

Act 2 Interlude
  Soubrette de Resistance, Ann Suter
  "Skating in the Bois"
    The Comets

Act 3 Interlude
  "Don't Throw Me Out of the House, Father"
    The American Music Hallettes
  That Quartette—George Jones, Aubrey Pringle, Johnny Burns, Al Duke:
    ["Annie Laurie," White Wings," "A Bicycle Built for Two," "Down Went McGinty."]
  The Six Danwills (Gymnasts)

---

[49]Later in the run producers were billed as John and Jerrold Krimsky.
[50]Performed seven nights a week, no matinees.

Finale: ["Happy Days Are Here Again" (from CHASING RAINBOWS, film)
  Music by Milton Ager. *Lyrics by* Jack Yellen.)]
  (Entire Company)

THE MIKADO, or, The Town of Titipu

1936.04

A Revival of the Comic Opera in Two Acts[51]. Libretto by William S. Gilbert. Music by Arthur Sullivan. Staged by Frank Moulan. Settings designed by Franklyn Ambos. Costumes designed by Billie Livingston. Musical conductor, J. Albert Hurley. Produced by S. M. Chartok. Opened 10 April 1936 at the Majestic Theatre, closing 18 April 1936 after 8 performances; re-opened 11-18 May 1936 at the Majestic Theatre for an additional 8 performances, for a total of 16 performances in repertory.

CAST: *The Mikado of Japan*: WILLIAM DANFORTH. *Nanki-Poo*: ROY CROPPER. *Ko-Ko*: FRANK MOULAN. *Pooh-Bah*: HERBERT L. WATEROUS. *Pish-Tush*: GEORGE HIROSE. *Yum-Yum*: VIVIAN HART. *Pitti-Sing*: FRANCES BAVIELLO. *Peep-Bo*: DENE DICKENS. *Katisha*: VERA ROSS.
  Ladies of the Mikado's Suite: Jane Ann Edwards, Dorothy Forsythe, Geraldine Bork, Marion Ross. *The Mikado's Bodyguards*: Joseph Olney, Norman Van Emburgh, David Milton, John Willard. *Chorus of School Girls, Nobles, Guards and Coolies*: Evelyn Adler, Elfrida Anabel, Mildred Burke, Kay Curl, Margaret Henzel, Emily Marsh, Celia Schiffrin, Gertrude Waldon, Georgia Dieter, Edith Maison, Jean Matus, Frances Wade, Bruce Barclay, August Loring, Joseph Olney, Paul Curtis, LeRoy McLean, David Milton, John Moore, John Cardini, Siegfried Langer, Joseph Scandur.

ON YOUR TOES

1936.05

A Musical in Two Acts, 13 Scenes. Book by Richard Rodgers, Lorenz Hart and George Abbott. Music by Richard Rodgers. Lyrics by Lorenz Hart. Staged by Worthington Miner (and George Abbott). Choreography by George Balanchine. Settings by Jo Mielziner. Costumes by Irene Sharaff. Music director, Gene Salzer. Orchestrations by Hans Spialek. Supervised and produced by Dwight Deere Wiman. Opened 11 April 1936 at the Imperial Theatre, moved 9 November 1936 to the Majestic Theatre, and closed 23 January 1937 after 315 performances.

CAST (in order of appearance): *Phil Dolan II*: Dave Jones. *Lil Dolan*: Ethel Hampton. *Phil Dolan III*: Tyrone Kearney. *Call Boy*: Beau Tilden. *Lola*: Betty Jane Smith. *Phil Dolan III*: RAY BOLGER. *Frankie Frayne*: DORIS CARSON. *Sidney Cohn*: David Morris. *Vera Barnova*: TAMARA GEVA. *Anushka*: Mae Noble. *Peggy Porterfield*: LUELLA GEAR. *Sergei Alexandrovitch*: MONTY WOOLLEY. *Konstantine Morrosine*: Demetrios Vilan. *Snoopy*: William Wadsworth. *Mischka*: Valery Streshnev. *Vassilli*: Robert Sidney. *Dimitri*: Basil Galahoff. *Leon*: Harold Haskin. *Call Boy*: Bob Long. *A Singer*: Earle MacVeigh. *A Waiter*: William Baker. *Stage Manager*: Harry Peterson. *A Policeman*: George Young. *First Thug*: Nick Dennis. *Second Thug*: Louis Walsh. *At the Duo-Pianos*: EDGAR FAIRCHILD and ADAM CARROLL. (*Featured Dancer*: George Church.)
  Ladies of the Ballet: May Block, Jill Christie, Dorothy Denton, Eleanor Fiata, Dorothy Hall, Joan Keena, Isabelle Kimpal, Gertrude Magee, Marie Monnig, Ursula Seiler, Betty Jane Smith, Alma Wertley. *Gentlemen of the Ballet*: William Baker, Edward Brinkman, Fred Danieli, Basil Galahoff, Harold Haskin, Julian Mitchell, Jack Quinn, Valery Streshnev. *Ladies of the Ensemble*: Libby Bennett, Enes Early, Marjorie Fisher, Gloria Franklin, Grace Kaye, Betty Lee, Frances Nevins, Carol Renwick, Patsey Schenck, Drucilla Strain, Dorothy Thomas, Davenie Watson, Amy Weber. *Gentlemen of the Ensemble*: William Broder, Henry Dick, Dave Jones, Robert Forsythe, Russ Milton, Harry Peterson, Beau Tilden, George Young.

Act 1, Scene 1: A Vaudeville Stage, sixteen years ago. *Scene 2*: The Vaudeville Dressing Room. *Scene 3*: A Classroom of Knickerbocker University, WPA Extension. *Scene 4*: Vera's Apartment, the next morning. *Scene 5*: Central Park, night. *Scene 6*: A Green Room, Cosmopolitan Opera House, the next evening. *Scene 7*: A Dressing Room, Cosmopolitan Opera House. *Scene 8*: "La Princesse Zenobia" Ballet, Cosmopolitan Opera House.

Act 2, Scene 1: A Planetarium Roof Garden. *Scene 2*: The Stage of the Cosmopolitan Opera House. *Scene 3*: The Green Room, a week later. *Scene 4*: "Slaughter on Tenth Avenue" Ballet. *Scene 6*: The Stage of the Cosmopolitan Opera House.

---

[51]First presented in New York 20 July 1885, 17-29 August 1885 at the Union Square and Henry Miner's People's Theatres for 22 performances. Presented 19 August 1885 at the Fifth Avenue Theatre by Richard D'Oyly Carte for 250 performances. For Synopsis of Scenes and Musical Numbers, see original 1885 D'Oyly Carte production.

ACT 1

Scene 1

"Two A Day for Keith"
D. Jones, E. Hampton, T. Kearney

Scene 3

"The Three B's"
R. Bolger, Ensemble

"It's Got To Be Love"
D. Carson, R. Bolger

Scene 4

"Too Good for the Average Man"
L. Gear, M. Woolley

Scene 5

"There's a Small Hotel"
D. Carson, R. Bolger

Scene 6

"The Heart Is Quicker Than the Eye"
L. Gear, R. Bolger

Scene 8

"La Princesse Zenobia" Ballet
Princess Zenobia: T. Geva. *Beggar*: D. Vilan. *Old Prince*: W. Baker. *Young Prince*: G. Church.

ACT 2

Scene 1

"Quiet Night"
E. MacVeigh, Ensemble

"Glad To Be Unhappy"
D. Carson, D. Morris

Scene 2

"On Your Toes"
D. Carson, R. Bolger, D. Morris, Ensemble

Scene 4

"Slaughter on Tenth Avenue" Ballet
Hoofer: R. Bolger. *Strip Tease Girl*: T. Geva. *Big Boss*: G. Church.

Scene 5

(Finale)
(Entire Company)

(GUS EDWARDS') BROADWAY SHO-WINDOW

1936.06

A Revusical-Vaudeville in Two Acts, 15 Scenes. Sketches and lyrics by Eugene Conrad. Music by Gus Edwards. Additional music and lyrics by Ted Fetter, Howard Johnson, Richard Lewine and Leo Edwards. (Staged by Gus Edwards). Settings by Clark Robinson. Costumes designed by William Weaver. Dances by Bill Powers. Orchestrations by Arthur Gutman. Produced by Gus Edwards. Opened 12 April 1936 at the Broadway Theatre and closed 24 April 1936 after 28 performances.

CAST: Ed "Scooter" Lowry, Armida, Mark Plant, Milton Charleston, Joe Cook, Jr., Al Verdi, Billy Ambrose, Ruth Ambrose, Danny Drayson, Hal Forde, Jay Golden, Larry Rich, Jr., Haline Frances, Bob Easton, Myra Lott, Mary Louise Harper, Ann Metzger, Joe Dorris, Gerald Phillips, Ondee Odette, Bill Bailey, Selma Marlowe, Roslyn Golden, Gretchen Kimmel, Constance Grandall, The Three Robbins, Fabello's Orchestra.
Sixteen Sweet Sixteens: DeBold Twins, Dorothy Stone, Connie Lusby, Janee Rich, Bertrice Grey, Barbara Coswell, Jane Miller, Joan Alexander, Gail Andrews, Lynne Carter, Aileen Barry, Evelyn Marsh, Marion Volk, Jean Scott, Bobette Walker.

ACT 1

Scene 1

Romance of Vaudeville
H. Forde

Scene 2

Sixteen Sweet Sixteens
J. Rich, C. Lusby, J. Alexander, M. Lott

Scene 3

Three Robbins

Scene 4

Ed Lowry, assisted by Mary Louise Harper

Scene 5

"The Vandal of Music"
A. Verdi, T. Lee

Scene 6

Dead Head (with apologies to Sidney Kingsley, author of "Dead End")
Hicky: S. Lowry. *Goofy*: M. Charleston. *Tummy*: J. Cook, Jr. *Spot*: J. Golden. *Angie*: L. Rich, Jr. *Stew*: H. Frances. *Milty and Oiv*: Deutch Twins. *Doorman*: B. Easton. *Lena*: M. Lott. *Nancy*: M. L. Harper. *Gay*: A. Metzger. *'Baby Face'*: E. Lowry. *Junk*: J. Dorris. *Gee Men*: B. Ambrose, G. Phillips. And Poverty Row Boys and Girls, Luxury Lane Girls.

"Poverty Row"
E. Lowry

Scene 7

A chip of a Star with Evelyn Graves
B. Easton, O. Odette

Scene 8

Armida of Stage, Screen and Radio

Dance
S. Marlowe, 8 Rhumbettes

Scene 9

Following Famous Footsteps: "Hitch Your Wagon to a Star"
E. Lowry
Jack Donahue: J. Cook, Jr. *Will Mahoney*: D. Drayson. *Bill Robinson*: Bill Bailey. *Ginger Rogers*: R. Ambrose. *Fred Astaire*: B. Ambrose. *Eleanor Powell*: S. Marlowe. *Ray Bolger*: J. Dorris.

ACT 2

Scene 1

Spring: "Spring Is in the Air"
M. Plant
Danced by Sixteen Sweet Sixteens, R. Ambrose, B. Ambrose, S. Marlowe.

Scene 2

Three Nonchalants

Scene 3

Mr. Ed Guswards presents a very dramatic episode 'Hollywood Folly's.' Staged by Mr. Guthrie McConrad. Set by Clark von Robinson.
Mr. Stonemile: M. Charleston. *Mr. Von Strongheart*: E. Lowry. *Mme. Secretary*: A. Metzger. *Miss Valoose*: Mlle. Armida. *Mr. Icemiller*: M. Plant. *Mrs. Columnist*: H. Frances. *Miss Katie Heartburn*: M. L. Harper. *Mr. Jawn Borrowmore*: J. Dorris. *Miss Greeta Grabbo*: E. Graves.

Scene 4

Mark Plant: The "Mowgli" of 'Jubilee'

Scene 5

Talent on Trial
Judge: E. Lowry. *Balieff*: M. Charleston. *Court Clerk*: B. Easton. *Jury*: Sixteen Sweet Sixteens. *Spectators*: R. Golden, G. Kimmel, C. Grandall, A. Metzger, E. Graves, M. L. Harper. *Prisoners*: Vaudevillians.

Scene 6

Exit March
Fabello's Orchestra

SUMMER WIVES

1936.07

A Comedy with Music in Three Acts, 4 Scenes. Play by Mark Linder and Dolph Singer. Music by Sam Morrison. Lyrics by Dolph Singer. Staged by Ira Hards. Settings by Mabel A. Buell. (Conductor, Sid Sayre.) Produced by Jack Linder and D. S. Wolfson. Opened 13 April 1936 at the Mansfield Theatre and closed 18 April 1936 after 8 performances.

CAST (in order of appearance): *Gertie*: Linda Lee Hill. *Mike Chisley*: CHARLES DALE. *Mel Tone*: Eddie Yubell. *Molly La Rue*: Helen Charleston. *Helen La Mott*: Miriam Battista. *Barney*: Phil Arnold. *Benny*: Ben Marks. *Sammy*: Harold Kahn. *Murray Lowen*: JOE SMITH. *Jennie Green*: ANNETTE HOFFMAN. *Joe Wilder*: Clarence Rock. *Fred Bernhard*: MILTON DOUGLAS. *Dan McGillicuddy*: Morgan Conway. *Minna Salmon*: Mary Douglas. *Mrs. Roslyn Berg*: GERTRUDE MUDGE. *Betty Pratt*: Jane Walsh. *Mrs. Mortimer Rich*: Fay Martin. *Mr. Mortimer Rich*: Herbert Warren. *Jacob Adelman*: Daniel Makarenko. *Max*: Jack Huntley. *Page Boy*: Seymour Linder. *Laura*: Gloria Cook. *Jack Archibald*: Jhoreck Rai. Syd Sayre and His Orchestra.
Guests, Firemen, Bell Boys, etc.: Jack Hassler, Robert Turner, William B. Newgard, John Wheeler, Max Beck, Jack Zero, Debby Dare, Bassine Alfaux, Marjorie Joyce, Bertha Mack, Jeanne Temple, Alma Ross, Roslyn Kay, Freya Schorr, Herbert Ritter Lynne, Saul Daniel.

Act 1: Mike Chisley's Booking Agency, Times Square, New York City. June.

Act 2: Porch of Lowen-Green Country Club. Afternoon in early September.

Act 3, Scene 1: Lover's Lane, Lowen-Green Country Club. *Scene 2*: Social Hall, Lowen-Green Country Club. Labor Day Eve.

ACT 1

"Lowen-Green Country Club, I Love You"

ACT 2

"My Love Carries On"

"Us on a Bus"

(*Music by* Vee Lawnhurst. *Lyrics by* Tot Seymour.)

"Play Me an Old-Time Two-Step"

ACT 3

"I Wrote a Song for You"

"Mickey"

"Chatterbox"

THE PIRATES OF PENZANCE,
1936.08   or, The Slave of Duty

A Revival of the Comic Opera in Two Acts[52]. Libretto by William S. Gilbert. Music by Arthur Sullivan. Staged by Frank Moulan. Settings designed by Franklyn Ambrose. Costumes designed by Billie Livingston. Musical conductor, J. Albert Hurley. Produced by S. M. Chartok. Opened 20 April 1936 at the Majestic Theatre and closed 25 April 1936 after 8 performances in repertory.

<u>CAST</u>: *Richard*, a Pirate King: HERBERT L. WATEROUS. *Samuel*: JOHN EATON. *Frederic*: ROY CROPPER. *Major-General Stanley*: FRANK MOULAN. *Edward*, a Sergeant of Police: WILLIAM DANFORTH. *Mabel*: VIVIAN HART. *Kate*: DENE DICKENS. *Edith*: FRANCES BAVIELLO. *Isabel*: Gertrude Waldon. *Ruth*: VERA ROSS.

Chorus of Pirates, Police and General Stanley's Daughters: Jane Ann Edwards, Dorothy Forsythe, Geraldine Bork, Marion Ross, Evelyn Adler, Elfrida Anabel, Mildred Burke, Kay Curl, Margaret Henzel, Emily Marsh, Celia Schiffrin, Gertrude Waldon, Georgia Dieter, Edith Maison, Jean Matus, Frances Wade. Joseph Olney, Norman Van Emburgh, David Milton, John Willard, Bruce Barclay, August Loring, Paul Curtis, LeRoy McLean, John Moore, John Cardini, Siegfried Langer, Joseph Scandur.

1936.09   TRIAL BY JURY

A Revival of the Comic Opera in One Act[53]. Libretto by William S. Gilbert. Music by Arthur Sullivan. Staged by Frank Moulan. Settings designed by Franklyn Ambrose. Costumes designed by Billie Livingston. Musical director, J. Albert Hurley. Produced by S. M. Chartok. Opened 27 April 1936 at the Majestic Theatre and closed 2 May 1936 after 8 performances; reopened 18 May 1936 at the Majestic Theatre, closing 23 May 1936 after 8 additional performances, for a total of 16 performances in repertory.

<u>CAST</u>: *The Learned Judge*: FRANK MOULAN. *Foreman of the Jury*: HERBERT L. WATEROUS. *The Defendant*: ROY CROPPER. *Counsel*: JOHN EATON. *Usher*: WILLIAM DANFORTH. *Plaintiff*: VIVIAN HART.

Jurors: Joseph Olney, Norman Van Emburgh, David Milton, John Willard, Bruce Barclay, August Loring, Paul Curtis, LeRoy McLean, John Moore, John Cardini, Siegfried Langer, Joseph Scandur, Francis Clarke, John Muccio. *Bridesmaids*: Jane Ann Edwards, Dorothy Forsythe, Geraldine Bork, Marion Ross, Evelyn Adler, Elfrida Anabel, Mildred Burke, Kay Curl, Margaret Henzel, Emily Marsh, Celia Schiffrin, Gertrude Waldon, Georgia Dieter, Edith Maison, Jean Matus, Frances Wade.

H.M.S. PINAFORE,
1936.10   or, The Lass That Loved a Sailor

A Revival of the Comic Opera in Two Acts[54]. Libretto by William S. Gilbert. Music by Arthur Sullivan. Staged by Frank Moulan. Settings designed by

Franklyn Ambos. Costumes designed by Billie Livingston. Musical director, J. Albert Hurley. Produced by S. M. Chartok. Opened 27 April 1936 at the Majestic Theatre and closed 2 May 1936 after 8 performances; reopened 18 May 1936 at the Majestic Theatre, closing 23 May 1936 after 8 additional performances. Total: 16 performances in repertory.

<u>CAST</u>: *The Rt. Hon. Sir Joseph Porter, K.C.B.*: FRANK MOULAN. *Captain Cocoran*, Commander of the *H.M.S. Pinafore*: JOHN EATON. *Ralph Rackstraw*, Able Seaman: ROY CROPPER. *Dick Deadeye*, Able Seaman: WILLIAM DANFORTH. *Bill Bobstay*, Boatswain: Herbert L. Waterous. *Josephine*, the Captain's Daughter: MARGARET DAUM. *Little Buttercup*, Mrs. Cripps, a Portsmouth Bum-Boat Woman: VERA ROSS. *Hebe*, Sir Joseph's First Cousin: Dene Dickens.

Sailors, Marines: Joseph Olney, Norman Van Emburgh, David Milton, John Willard, Bruce Barclay, August Loring, Paul Curtis, LeRoy McLean, John Moore, John Cardini, Siegfried Langer, Joseph Scandur, Francis Clarke, John Muccio. *First Lord's Sisters, His Cousins, His Aunts*: Jane Ann Edwards, Dorothy Forsythe, Geraldine Bork, Marion Ross, Evelyn Adler, Elfrida Anabel, Mildred Burke, Kay Curl, Margaret Henzel, Emily Marsh, Celia Schiffrin, Gertrude Waldon, Georgia Dieter, Edith Maison, Jean Matus, Frances Wade.

IOLANTHE,
1936.11   or, The Peer and the Peri

A Revival of the Comic Opera in Two Acts[55]. Libretto by William S. Gilbert. Music by Arthur Sullivan. Staged by Frank Moulan. Settings designed by Franklyn Ambos. Costumes designed by Billie Livingston. Musical director, J. Albert Hurley. Produced by S. M. Chartok. Opened 4 May 1936 at the Majestic Theatre and closed 9 May 1936 after 8 performances in repertory.

<u>CAST</u>: *The Lord Chancellor*: FRANK MOULAN. *Earl of Mountararat*: BERTRAM PEACOCK. *Earl Tolloller*: ROY CROPPER. *Private Willis*: HERBERT L. WATEROUS. *Strephon*: JOHN EATON. *Queen of the Fairies*: VERA ROSS. *Iolanthe*: DENE DICKENS. *Celia*: Frances Baviello. *Leila*: Georgina Dieter. *Fleta*: Gertrude Waldon. *Phyllis*: VIVIAN HART.

Chorus of Fairies, Earls, Viscounts, Lords, Peers: Jane Ann Edwards, Dorothy Forsythe, Geraldine Bork, Marion Ross, Evelyn Adler, Elfrida Anabel, Mildred Burke, Kay Curl, Margaret Henzel, Emily Marsh, Celia Schiffrin, Edith Maison, Jean Matus, Frances Wade. Joseph Olney, Norman Van Emburgh, David Milton, John Willard, Bruce Barclay, August Loring, Paul Curtis, LeRoy McLean, John Moore, John Cardini, Siegfried Langer, Joseph Scandur, Francis Clarke, John Muccio.

1936.12   NEW FACES OF 1936

A Musical Revue in Two Acts, 39 Scenes[56]. (Production conceived by Leonard Sillman.) Sketches by Mindret Lord, Everett Marcy, (Edwin Meiss, Irvin Graham, Leonard Sillman, Homer Fickett, Joseph Alger, Mort Lewis). Music by Alexander Fogarty, Irving Graham, (Forman Brown, Joseph Meyer, Muriel Pollack, Bud Harris). Lyrics by June Sillman, Edwin Gilbert, (Bickley Reichner, Everett Marcy, Edward Heyman, Jean Southern, Lawrence Harris). Staged and supervised by Leonard Sillman. Sketches directed by Anton Bundsmann. Dances by Ned McGurn. Music directed by Ray Kavanagh. Settings and costumes by Stewart Chaney. Lighting by (Abe) Feder. Orchestrations by Hans Spialek, David Raksin. Produced by Leonard Sillman. Opened 19 May 1936 at the Vanderbilt Theatre and closed 7 November 1936 after 193 performances.

<u>CAST</u>: Imogene Coca, Jack Smart, Helen Craig, Marion Pierce, Karl Swenson, Billie Haywood, Cliff Allen, Robert Bard, Tom Rutherfurd, Jack and June Blair, Marsha Norman, Gerry Probst, Jean Bellows, Mischa Pompianov, Irene Moore, Nancy Noland, Eleanor Bunker, Elizabeth Wilde, Ralph Blane, George Byron, Ione Reed, Bea Thrift, Edna Russell, Arthur Hughes, Owen Stewart, Robert Burton, Gloria Rondell, Harry Smith, Winnie Johnson, Stretch Johnson, Robert Johnson, Rose Dexter, William Chandler, Van Johnson, Nancy Wetherell, Dorothy Chilton, Indus Hollingsworth, Grace Milliman, Joyce Worth, Marion Martin.

ACT 1[57]

---

[52]First presented in New York 31 December 1879 at the Fifth Avenue Theatre for 91 performances in two engagements. For Synopsis of Scenes and Musical Numbers, see original 1879 production.

[53]First presented in New York 15 November 1875 at the Eagle Theatre for 8 performances. For Synopsis of Scenes and Musical Numbers, see original 1875 production.

[54]Originally presented in New York 15 January 1879 at the Standard Theatre for 175 performances. For Synopsis of Scenes and Musical Numbers, see original 1879 production.

[55]First presented in New York 25 November 1882 at the Standard Theatre for 105 performances. For Synopsis of Scenes and Musical Numbers, see original 1882 production.

[56]The second in the series of revues conceived by Leonard Sillman as a showcase for new talent. The first was produced in 1934.

[57]During the run, Martin Jones took over as producer, and the Duncan Sisters (Rosetta and Vivian), Charles Kemper were added to the cast. The following material was added to the show during the run:

Scouting a Rumor (*by* Norman Zeno, Martin Jones, Leonard Sillman)

Scout Leader: Mildred Todd. *Mrs. Hoover*: E. Wilde. *Mrs. Roosevelt*: G. Probst. *Girl Scouts*: B. Thrift, I. Reed, E. Russell. *The Mayor*: C. Kemper.

Scene 1

Introduction to "New Faces"
M. Norman, G. Probst, G. Byron, T. Rutherfurd
(*Music by* Martha Caples. *Lyrics by* Nancy Hamilton.)

Scene 2

"New Faces"
(*Music by* Alexander Fogarty. *Lyrics by* Edwin Gilbert.)
H. Craig, M. Pierce, I. Moore, E. Wilde, G. Probst, E. Bunker, N. Wetherell, D. Chilton, G. Milliman. K. Swenson, R. Bard, T. Rutherfurd, A. Hughes, J. Blair, O. Stewart, R. Burton, W. Chandler, V. Johnson.

Scene 3

The Wolf of Wall Street (*by* Edwin Gilbert)
Mr. Stonewall: J. Smart. *Miss Young*: G. Probst. *Mr. Brown*: R. Bard. *Miss Jones*: E. Wilde.

Scene 4

"Slap My Face"
N. Noland
(*Music by* Alexander Fogarty. *Lyrics by* Edwin Gilbert.)
Danced by J. Blair, W. Johnson, B. Johnson, D. Chilton, N. Wetherell, G. Milliman, J. Worth, O. Stewart, H. Smith, V. Johnson, W. Chandler.

Scene 5

Little Dove (*by* Mindret Lord)
Introduced by J. Bellows. *Comrade Itchalova*: H. Craig. *Comrade Sonavitch*: K. Swenson. *Comrade Mazorsky*: R. Bard. *Comrade Dostoievsky*: A. Hughes. *Comrade Pushky*: R. Burton. *Comrade Rubitch*: J. Smart.

Scene 6

"There Is a Santa Claus"
R. Blane, N. Noland, E. Wilde, R. Bard, J. Bellows, W. Chandler
(*Music by* Irving Graham. *Lyrics by* Bickley Reichner.)
Dancers: N. Wetherell, D. Chilton, G. Williams, J. Worth, J. Blair, I. Hollingsworth. *Girl in Beard*: M. Pierce.

Scene 7

"On Your Toes" (burlesque)
I. Coca, T. Rutherfurd, R. Burton, R. Bard

Scene 8

"Lottie of the Literati"
(*Music by* Alexander Fogarty. *Lyrics by* Edwin Gilbert.)

Fred and Ginger
Jack and June Blair

"My Last Affair" (from NEW FACES OF 1934)
B. Haywood, C. Allen
(*Music and Lyrics by* Haven Johnson.)

Valiant Is the Word for Carrie
I. Coca, T. Rutherfurd, R. Burton, R. Bard

"Do-Nuts"
The Duncan Sisters, Entire Company
(*Music by* the Rev. Hines Rubel (Hal Raynor). *Lyrics by* June Sillman. *Arranged by* the Duncan Sisters.)

"Spain, Spain, Spain"
The Duncan Sisters
(*Music and Lyrics by* Harry Clark and the Duncan Sisters.)

Five Star Final (*by* June Sillman and Viola Brothers Shore)
Mr. Dionne: C. Kamper. *Mrs Dionne*: E. Wilde. *Agent*: R. Blane. *Guard*: R. Burton. *Mrs. William Randolph Heart*: M. Todd. *Nurses*: J. Bellows, D. Chilton. *Policemen*: R. Bard, Frank Gagen, V. Johnson, Ray Clarke.

Pelleas and Melisande (*by* Martin Jones, Desmond Hallaran, Leonard Sillman)
Introduction: R. Burton. *Melisande*: E. Wilde. *Pelleas*: T. Rutherfurd.

Radio Auditions (*by* Billy K. Wells)
The Duncan Sisters

Gridiron Ghosts (*by* Ken Nichols and Charles Kemper)
Grange: C. Kamper. *Booth*: R. Clarke. *Carideo*: R. Bard.

"My Sixty-Second Romance" (from FOOLS RUSH IN)
B. Haywood, C. Allen
(*Music by* Bud Harris. *Lyrics by* Lawrence Harris.)
Danced by W. Johnson, B. Johnson.

Two Queens (*Written by* James Rennie. *Music by* Harold Duncan.)
Elizabeth: R. Duncan. *Mary, Queen of Scots*: V. Duncan. *Sir Walter Raleigh*: C. Kemper. *Bothwell*: R. Bard.

Lottie: H. Craig. *Hostess*: G. Probst. *First Young Lady*: E. Bunker. *First Author*: O. Stuart. *Second Young Lady*: N. Noland. *Third Young Lady*: J. Bellows. *Authoress*: N. Wetherell. *Critics*: G. Byron, H. Smith, R. Burton. *Butler*: W. Chandler. *Young Ladies*: M. Norman, D. Chilton. *Sinclair Lewis*: V. Johnson. *Fannie Hurst*: V. Johnson. *Clifford Odets*: M. Pierce. *George Jean Nathan*: K. Swenson. *Cecil Beaton*: R. Bard. *Ernest Hemingway*: T. Rutherfurd. *Second Author*: A. Hughes. *Samuel Goldwyn*: M. Pompianov.

Scene 9

"New Faces" (reprise)
Danced by Jack Blair

Scene 10

Keeping the Code (*by* Edwin Meiss)
Bystander: I. Coca. *Tony Benelli*: M. Parks. *Sergeant*: T. Rutherfurd. *Policeman*: A. Hughes. *Reporter*: H. Smith.

Scene 11

"My Love Is Young"
K. Mayfield
(*Music by* Irving Graham. *Lyrics by* Bickley Reichner.)
Danced by I. Moore, M. Pompianov.

Scene 12

Gypsy Tea Kettle (*by* Irving Graham)
I. Coca

Scene 13

The Other Woman (*by* Mindret Lord)
Fay: H. Craig. *Dolores*: E. Bunker. *Maid*: B. Thrift. *George*: K. Swenson.

Scene 14

"Off to the Deacon"
N. Noland, G. Byron, G. Rondell
(*Music by* Robert Sour. *Lyrics by* June Sillman.)
Danced by Jack and June Blair. *Dancers*: D. Chilton, I. Hollingsworth, J. Worth, G. Milliman, O. Stewart, H. Smith, V. Johnson, W. Chandler.

Scene 15

Cinderella's Night Out (*by* Everett Marcy and Leonard Sillman)
Cinderella: I. Coca. *Fairy Godmother*: M. Martin. *Cinderella's Sisters*: M. Pierce, E. Wilde.

Scene 16

Private Lives (*by* Everett Marcy)
Introduced by H. Craig. *Otto*: J. Smart. *Meyer*: K. Swenson.

Scene 17

"Miss Mimsey"
I. Coca
(*Music and Lyrics by* Irving Graham. *Ballet Music by* Alexander Fogarty.)
Miss Mimsey: I. Moore. *Students*: N. Wetherell, D. Chilton, I. Hollingsworth, J. Worth, G. Milliman.

Scene 18

"Too, Too, Too!"
(*Music by* Irving Graham. *Lyrics by* Everett Marcy.)
Introduced by M. Pierce, G. Probst, E. Bunker. *Noël Coward*: R. Bard. *Cole Porter*: T. Rutherfurd. *Moss Hart*: R. Burton.

Scene 19

A Marriage Is Arranged (*by* Mindret Lord)
The Lady: M. Pierce. *The Maid*: E. Wilde. *The Butler*: A. Hughes. *Prince Wilhelm of Baden-Baden*: Frederic Wilhelm[58].

Scene 20

Co-Respondent Unknown
I. Coca, T. Rutherfurd, R. Burton, R. Bard

Scene 21

"It Must Be Religion"
B. Haywood, C. Allen, R. Dexter
(*Music and Lyrics by* Forman Brown.)
Danced by S. Johnson, W. Johnson, R. Johnson. *Colonel Cadwallader*: J. Smart. *Jasmine Lou*: N. Noland. *Guests*: I. Coca, R. Blane, T. Rutherfurd, E. Wilde, G. Byron, D. Chilton, H. Smith, O. Stewart, I. Hollingsworth, R. Burton, J. Bellows, M. Pierce, G. Milliman, V. Johnson, J. Worth, W. Chandler, I. Moroe, A. Hughes.

ACT 2
Scene 1

"Tonight's the Night With You"

---

[58]Pseudonym for an unidentified member of the cast.

M. Norman, G. Byron
(*Music by* Alexander Fogarty. *Lyrics by* June Sillman.)
Danced by Jack and June Blair. *Dancers*: D. Chilton, N. Wetherell, J. Worth, G. Milliman, O. Stewart, H. Smith, V. Johnson, W. Chandler. *People on Beach*: G. Probst, E. Bunker, E. Russell, N. Noland, I. Hollingsworth, J. Bellows, R. Bard, T. Rutherford, R. Burton, A. Hughes, R. Blane, B. Haywood, C. Allen.

Scene 2

Manana (*by* Mindret Lord)
Bride: E. Bunker. *Groom*: T. Rutherfurd.

Scene 3

Marian Never Looked Lovelier (*by* Everett Marcy)
Louella Parsing: E. Wilde. *Radio Announcer*: R. Burton.

Scene 4

"You'd Better Go Now"
N. Noland, T. Rutherfurd
(*Music by* Irving Graham. *Lyrics by* Bickley Reichner.)

Scene 5

"It's High Time I Got the Low Down on You"
R. Dexter, W. Johnson, S. Johnson, B. Johnson
(*Music by* Joseph Meyer. *Lyrics by* Edward Heyman.)

Scene 6

Idiot's Delight (burlesque)
I. Coca, T. Rutherfurd, R. Burton, R. Bard

Scene 7

"We Shreik of Chic" ("Chi Chi")
H. Craig
(*Music by* Irving Graham. *Lyrics by* June Sillman.)
Mannequins: J. Bellows, M. Martin, G. Milliman, M. Pierce. *"Esquire"*: R. Bard.

Scene 8

Dinner at 7:30 (*by* Homer Fickett and Joseph Alger)
Mrs. Morgan: G. Probst. *Mr. Morgan*: T. Rutherfurd. *Professor Wertz*: K. Swenson. *Maid*: M. Pierce. *Old Man*: R. Blane.

Scene 9

"Love Is a Dancer"
M. Norman, G. Byron
(*Music by* Muriel Pollac. *Lyrics by* Jean Southern.)
Modern Dancers: I. Moore, M. Pompianov. *Tap Dancers*: Jack and June Blair. *Figures on Pedestal*: N. Wetherell, O. Stewart. *Ballet*: D. Chilton, J. Worth, G. Milliman, W. Chandler, V. Johnson, H. Smith.

Scene 10

The Show Must Go On, or, Why Vaudeville Never Came Back (*by* Edwin Gilbert)
Introduced by J. Bellows.
B. Thrift, E. Russell, I. Reed

Scene 11

Entertainment Night at the Cosmopolitan Chess Club (*by* Mindret Lord)
Chairman: T. Rutherfurd. *Entertainer*: J. Blair. *Bearded Man*: A. Hughes. *Man*: K. Swenson. *Members of the Chess Club*: O. Stewart, R. Bard, R. Blane.

Scene 12

"Off to the Deacon" (reprise)
Danced by W. Johnson, B. Johnson

Scene 13

Women in the White House (*by* Mort Lewis)
Introduced by J. Bellows. *Madame President*: J. Smart. *Secretary*: A. Hughes. *Postmistress General*: R. Burton. *Secretary of the Navy*: R. Bard. *French Ambassador*: K. Swenson.

Scene 14

"Your Face Is So Familiar"
R. Blane
(*Music by* Alexander Fogarty. *Lyrics by* Edwin Gilbert.)
Introduced by I. Coca, T. Rutherfurd. *Danced by* I. Coca, O. Stewart. *Boys*: R. Burton, H. Smith, W. Chandler, V. Johnson.

Scene 15

"I Was a Gyp in Egypt"
B. Haywood, C. Allen
(*Music by* Bud Harris. *Lyrics by* Lawrence Harris.)

Scene 16

Call It a Day
I. Coca, T. Rutherfurd, R. Burton, R. Bard

Scene 17

"Give Me a Song I Can Whistle"
G. Rondell, R. Blane
(*Music by* Alexander Fogarty. *Lyrics by* June Sillman.)

Scene 18

Finale
Entire Company

1936–1937 SEASON

Ethel Merman and Bob Hope in RED, HOT AND BLUE (Photo: Vandamm Studio)
Billy Rose Theatre Collection, New York Public Library for the Performing Arts

1936–1937 SEASON

THE MIKADO,
1936.13   or, The Town of Titipu

A Revival of the Comic Opera in Two Acts[1]. Libretto by William S. Gilbert. Music by Arthur Sullivan. Scenery and costumes designed by Charles Ricketts. Musical director, Isidore Godfrey. Produced by the D'Oyly Carte Opera Company. Opened 20 August 1936 at the Martin Beck Theatre and closed 2 January 1937 after 28 performances in repertory.

CAST: *The Mikado of Japan*: DARRELL FANCOURT. *Nanki-Poo*: DEREK OLDHAM. *Ko-Ko*: MARTYN GREEN. *Pooh-Bah*: SYDNEY GRANVILLE. *Pish-Tush*: LESLIE RANDS. *Go-To*: Radley Flynn. *Yum-Yum*: SYLVIA CECIL. *Pitti-Sing*: MARJORIE EYRE. *Peep-Bo*: ELIZABETH NICKELL-LEAN. *Katisha*: EVELYN GARDINER. *Chorus of School Girls, Nobles, Guards and Coolies.*

TRIAL BY JURY
1936.14

A Revival of the Comic Opera in One Act[2]. Libretto by William S. Gilbert. Music by Arthur Sullivan. Musical director, Isidore Godfrey. Produced by the D'Oyly Carte Opera Company. Opened 31 August 1936 at the Martin Beck Theatre and closed 26 December 1936 after 20 performances in repertory.

CAST: *The Learned Judge*: SYDNEY GRANVILLE. *Counsel for the Plaintiff*: Leslie Rands. *The Defendant*: ROBERT WILSON. *Foreman of the Jury*: T. Penry Hughes. *Usher*: Richard Walker. *Associate*: C. William Morgan. *The Plaintiff*: ANN DRUMMOND-GRANT. *First Bridesmaid*: Kathleen Naylor. *Chorus of Jurymen, Bridesmaids and Public.*

followed by

THE PIRATES OF PENZANCE,
1936.15   or, The Slave of Duty

A Revival of the Comic Opera in Two Acts[3]. Libretto by William S. Gilbert. Music by Arthur Sullivan. Costumes designed by Charles Ricketts. Musical director, Isidore Godfrey. Produced by the D'Oyly Carte Opera Company. Opened 31 August 1936 at the Martin Beck Theatre and closed 26 December 1936 after 20 performances in repertory.

CAST: *Major-General Stanley*: MARTYN GREEN. *The Pirate King*: DARRELL FANCOURT. *Samuel*: RICHARD WALKER. *Frederic*: JOHN DEAN. *Sergeant of Police*: SYDNEY GRANVILLE. *Mabel*: BRENDA BENNETT. *Edith*: MARJORIE EYRE. *Kate*: ELIZABETH NICKELL-LEAN. *Isabel*: Kathleen Naylor. *Ruth*: EVELYN GARDINER. *Chorus of Pirates, Police and General Stanley's Daughters.*

THE GONDOLIERS,
1936.16   or, The King of Barataria

A Revival of the Comic Opera in Two Acts[4]. Libretto by William S. Gilbert. Music by Arthur Sullivan. Scenery and costumes by Charles Ricketts.

[1]First presented in New York 20 July, 10-29 August 1885 at the Union Square and People's Theatres for 22 performances. First authorized production presented 19 August 1885 at the Fifth Avenue Theatre by Richard D'Oyly Carte for 250 performances. For Synopsis of Scenes and Musical Numbers, see 19 August 1885 D'Oyly Carte production.
[2]First presented in New York 15 November 1875 at the Eagle Theatre for 8 performances. For Synopsis of Scenes and Musical Numbers, see original 1875 production.
[3]First presented in New York 31 December 1879 at the Fifth Avenue Theatre for 91 performances in two engagements. For Synopsis of Scenes and Musical Numbers, see original 1879 production.
[4]Originally presented in New York 7 January 1890 at Park Theatre for 103 performances. For Synopsis of Scenes and Musical Numbers, see original 1890 production.

Musical director, Isidore Godfrey. Produced by the D'Oyly Carte Opera Company. Opened 7 September 1936 at the Martin Beck Theatre and closed 23 December 1936 after 20 performances in repertory.

CAST: *The Duke of Plaza-Toro*: MARTYN GREEN. *Luiz*: John Dean. *Don Alhambra Del Bolero*: SYDNEY GRANVILLE. *Marco Palmieri*: DEREK OLDHAM. *Antonio*: Richard Dunn. *Francesco*: Robert Wilson. *Giorgio*: Radley Flynn. *Annibale*: Frank Steward. *The Duchess of Plaza-Toro*: EVELYN GARDINER. *Casilda*: Brenda Bennett. *Gianetta*: SYLVIA CECIL. *Tessa*: MARJORIE EYRE. *Fiametta*: Ann Drummond-Grant. *Vittoria*: Elizabeth Nickell-Lean. *Giulia*: Margery Abbott. *Inez*: Josephine Curtis. *Chorus of Gondoliers, Contadine, Men-at-Arms, Heralds and Pages.*

ZIEGFELD FOLLIES
1936.17   (1936-1937)

A Return Engagement of the Musical Revue in Two Acts, 24 Scenes[5]. Sketches by David Freedman. Lyrics and additional sketches by Ira Gershwin. Music by Vernon Duke. Additional songs by Bob Rothberg and Joseph Meyer, Tot Seymour and Vee Lawnhurst, Edward Heyman and Harold Spina, Richard Jerome and Walter Kent, Edgar Leslie and Joe Burke. Sketches directed by Edward Clarke Lilley and Edward D. Dowling. Settings and costumes by Vincent Minnelli. Additional costumes designed by Raoul Pene du Bois. Orchestrations by Hans Spialek. Additional orchestrations by Conrad Salinger, (Robert) Russell Bennett, Don Walker, Bill Vodery[6]. Produced by Mrs. Florenz Ziegfeld [Billie Burke] (and the Messrs. Shubert). Opened 14 September 1936 at the Winter Garden and closed 19 December 1936 after 112 performances.

CAST: FANNIE BRICE, BOBBY CLARK, JANE PICKENS, RUTH HARRISON, ALEX HARRISON, CHERRY PREISSER, JUNE PREISSER, STAN KAVANAGH, GYPSY ROSE LEE, CASS DALEY, HUGH CAMERON, MARVIN LAWLER, JAMES FARRELL, BEN YOST'S VARSITY EIGHT (Del Arden, Joseph Frederic, Sidney Greene, George Herman, Melton Moore, Paul Nelson, William Quentmeyer, Ben Yost).
   Show Girls: Edelia Alvarez, Florence Baker, Betty Banister, Mary Bickes, Cristine Beau Mar, Julie Bryan, Irmgard Erik, Marjory Ezequelle, Diane Hunter, Virginia Langdon, Linda Lee, Sylvia Marsh, Erminie Randolph, Shirley Stevens. *Dancing Girls*: Ann Anderson, Gloria Arden, Mary Bay, Vicki Belling, Helen Bennett, Hiawana Booth, Betty Boyce, Florine Callahan, Virginia Collins, Jyll Egger, Helene Fromson, Kay Gable, Rita Horgan, Georgette Lampsi, Artheda Lane, Dionis Little, Evelyn Low, Beth Meredith, Mae Merrick, Joan Myles, Jo Raskin, Ruth Rathbun, Clare Scott, Terry Shannon, Marie Vanneman. *Dancing Boys*: Henning Irgens, Fay Lentz, Bernard Pearce, Eddie Wells.

ACT 1
Scene 1
  "Time Marches On"
    J. Farrell, Ben Yost's Varsity Eight
    (*Music by* Vernon Duke. *Lyrics by* Ira Gershwin.)
      The Tableau: The Girl in White: V. Langdon. *The Girl in Green*: J. Bryan. *The Girl in Blue*: I. Erik. *The Girl in Yellow*: D. Hunter. *The Girls in the Mirror*: L. Lee, E. Randolph. *The Nymphs*: E. Alvarez, F. Baker, M. Bicks, C. Beau Mar. *Danced by* the Ziegfeld Follies Girls.
Scene 2
  "He Hasn't a Thing Except Me"
    F. Brice
    (*Music by* Vernon Duke. *Lyrics by* Ira Gershwin.)
Scene 3
  "You Don't Love Right"[7]
    C. Daley, Show Girls, Ben Yost's Varsity Eight
    (*Music by* Vee Lawnhurst. *Lyrics by* Tot Seymour.)
    Danced by the Dancing Girls, Boys.
Scene 4
  Cherry and June Preisser and Marvin Lawler[8]

[5]Originally produced in New York 30 January 1936 at the Winter Garden for 115 performances; this revised edition subsequently toured. The twenty-third in the series of musical revues first produced by Florenz Ziegfeld in 1907.
[6]Not previously credited in the January 1936 production.
[7]Added material not in previous January 1936 production.
[8]Added material not in previous January 1936 production.

Scene 5

Of Thee I Spend[9]
Scene: Office of the F.S.A.
Rexford Givewell: B. Clark. *Miss Gherkin*: G. R. Lee. *John D. Littlefeller*: H. Cameron. *Charles G. Clawes*: W. Quentmeyer.

Scene 6

"(Isle in the) West Indies"
J. Pickens, Ben Yost's Varsity Eight
(*Music by* Vernon Duke. *Lyrics by* Ira Gershwin.)
The Conga danced by R. Harrison, A. Fisher, Ensemble.

Scene 7

The Sweepstakes Ticket[10]
Scene: A small apartment uptown.
Norma Shaeffer: F. Brice. *Messenger Boy*: M. Lawler. *Monty Shaeffer*: B. Clark. *Mr. Martin*: H. Cameron.

Scene 8

"The Economic Situation" (Aren't You Wonderful!)
G. R. Lee, Economists (Show Girls)
(*Music by* Vernon Duke. *Lyrics by* Ira Gershwin.)

Scene 9

"Midnight Blue"[11]
J. Pickens, J. Farrell
(*Music by* Edgar Burke. *Lyrics by* Joe Burke.)
Danced by R. Harrison, A. Fissher, Dancing Girls.

Scene 10

"Fancy! Fancy!"
(*Sketch and Lyrics by* Ira Gershwin. *Music by* Vernon Duke.)
Zuleika: F. Brice. *Sir Robert*: B. Clark. *Sir Henry*: H. Cameron.

Scene 11

"Harlem Waltz"[12]
C. Daley, B. Yost, W. Quentmeyer, D. Arden, J. Frederic
(*Music and Lyrics by* Richard Jerome and Walter Kent.)
Danced by C. Preisser, J. Preisser, Show Girls, Dancing Girls, Men.

Scene 12

Baby Snooks Goes to Hollywood
Scene: A Stage in a Hollywood Studio. *Mrs. Higgins*: G. R. Lee. *Director*: B. Clark. *Baby Snooks*: F. Brice. *Cameraman*: B. Yost. *Clark Gable*: J. Farrell. *Joan Crawford*; V. Langdon. *Photographer*: B. Pearce. *Official*: H. Cameron.

Scene 13

("The Fine Art of Strip Teasing"[13])
G. R. Lee
(*Music and Lyrics by* Edwin Gilbert.)

Scene 14

"The Gazooka"
(*Sketch by* David Freedman and Ira Gershwin. *Music by* Vernon Duke. *Lyrics by* Ira Gershwin.)
A Super-Special Musical Photoplay Starring Ruby Blondell and Bing Powell with a Large Cast of Supporting Players.
The Cast: Pilot: G. Spelvin. *Father*: J. Farrell. *Mother*: C. Daley. *Bing Powell*: B. Clark. *Ruby Blondell*: F. Brice. *Casting Agent*: W. Quentmeyer. *Dolores Del Morgan*: G. R. Lee. *Producer*: H. Cameron. *Dance Director*: M. Lawler. *Minster*: S. Kavanagh. And C. Preisser, J. Preisser, M. Lawler, Ben Yost's Varsity Eight, Show Girls, Dancing Girls, Boys.
Scene 1: A Railway Station. *Scene 2*: A Casting Office. "It's a Different World" *sung by* B. Clark, F. Brice. *Scene 3*: Backstage. *Scene 4*: "The Gazooka" in Techniquecolor on the Wildescope Screen. *Sung by* Entire Film Cast.

ACT 2

Scene 1

"(That) Moment of Moments"
(*Music by* Vernon Duke. *Lyrics by* Ira Gershwin.)
Scene: The Foyer of an Opera House in the 'Sixties.
The Young Lady: J. Pickens. *The Young Man*: J. Farrell. *The Ballerina*: R. Harrison. *The Grand Duke*: A. Fisher. *The Belles*: Show Girls. *The Beaux*: Ben Yost's Varsity Eight. And the Corps de Ballet.

Scene 2

"Sentimental Weather"
C. Preisser, J. Preisser, M. Lawler
(*Music by* Vernon Duke. *Lyrics by* Ira Gershwin.)

Scene 3

Dr. Fradler's Dilemma[14]
Mrs. Bigley: M. Leach. *Nurse*: G. R. Lee. *Dr. Fradler*: B. Clark. *Mrs. Phoebe Schwartz*: F. Brice.

Scene 4

"Words Without Music" (A Surrealist Ballet)
J. Pickens
(*Music by* Vernon Duke. *Lyrics by* Ira Gershwin.)
Danced by R. Harrison, A. Fisher, Corps de Ballet.

Scene 5

"Modernistic Moe"
F. Brice
(*Music by* Vernon Duke. *Lyrics by* Ira Gershwin, Billy Rose.)

Scene 6

"I Can't Get Started With You"
B. Clark, G. R. Lee, Show Girls, Ben Yost's Varsity Eight
(*Music by* Vernon Duke. *Lyrics by* Ira Gershwin.)

Scene 7

"Ridin' the Rails"[15]
Ben Yost's Varsity Eight
(*Music by* Harold Spina. *Lyrics by* Edward Heyman.)

Scene 8

Amateur Night
Scene: A Broadcasting Studio.
Major Bones: B. Clark. *Attendant*: B. Yost. *Juggler*: S. Kavanagh. *Elvira Mackintosh*: C. Daley. *Lady De Vere*: G. R. Lee. *Myrtle Oppenshaw*: F. Brice.

Scene 9

Stan Kavanagh[16]

Scene 10

Finale
F. Brice, B. Clark, Entire Company

THE YEOMEN OF THE GUARD,
1936.18   or The Merryman and His Maid

A Revival of the Comic Opera in Two Acts[17]. Libretto by William S. Gilbert. Music by Arthur Sullivan. Scenery and costumes by Charles Ricketts. Musical director, Isidore Godfrey. Produced by the D'Oyly Carte Opera Company. Opened 14 September 1936 at the Martin Beck Theatre and closed 19 December 1936 after 20 performances in repertory.

CAST: *Sir Richard Cholmondeley*: Leslie Rands. *Colonel Fairfax*: DEREK OLDHAM. *Sergeant Meryll*: DARRELL FANCOURT. *Leonard Meryll*: Robert Wilson. *Jack Point*: MARTYN GREEN. *Wilfred Shadbolt*: SYDNEY GRANVILLE. *First Yeoman*: Bernard Maher. *Second Yeoman*: Mansel Dyer. *First Citizen*: C. William Morgan. *Second Citizen*: Frank Steward. *Elsie Maynard*: Sylvia Cecil. *Phoebe Meryll*: Marjorie Eyre. *Dame Carruthers*: Evelyn Gardiner. *Kate*: Margery Abbott. *Chorus of Yeomen of the Guard, Gentlemen, Citizens, etc.*

IOLANTHE,
1936.19   or, The Peer and the Peri

A Revival of the Comic Opera in Two Acts[18]. Libretto by William S. Gilbert. Music by Arthur Sullivan. Dresses by George Sheringham. Musical direc-

---

[9]Added material not in previous January 1936 production.
[10]Added material not in previous January 1936 production.
[11]Added material not in previous January 1936 production.
[12]Added material not in previous January 1936 production.
[13]Added material not in previous January 1936 production.

[14]Added material not in previous January 1936 production.
[15]Added material not in previous January 1936 production.
[16]Added material not in previous January 1936 production.
[17]First presented in New York 17 October 1888 at the Casino Theatre for 100 performances. For Synopsis of Scenes and Musical Numbers, see original 1888 production.
[18]First presented in New York 25 November 1882 at the Standard Theatre for 105 performances. For Synopsis of Scenes and Musical Numbers, see original 1882 production.

tor, Isidore Godfrey. Produced by D'Oyly Carte Opera Company. Opened 21 September 1936 at the Martin Beck Theatre and closed 30 December 1936 after 20 performances in repertory.

CAST: *The Lord Chancellor:* MARTYN GREEN. *Earl of Mountararat:* DARRELL FANCOURT. *Earl Tolloler:* DEREK OLDHAM. *Private Willis:* SYDNEY GRANVILLE. *Strephon:* LESLIE RANDS. *Queen of the Fairies:* EVELYN GARDINER. *Iolanthe:* ELIZABETH NICKELL-LEAN. *Celia:* Ann Drummond-Grant. *Leila:* Ivy Sanders. *Fleta:* Kathleen Naylor. *Phyllis:* BRENDA BENNETT. *Chorus of Dukes, Marquises, Earls, Viscounts, Barons and Fairies.*

1936.20

COX AND BOX

A Revival of the Triumviretta in One Act[19]. Libretto by F. C. Burnand, based on Maddison Morton's farce "Box and Cox." Music by Arthur Sullivan. Setting by William Nicholson. Musical director, Isidore Godfrey. Produced by the D'Oyly Carte Opera Company. Opened 28 September 1936 at the Martin Beck Theatre and closed 21 November 1936 after 16 performances in repertory.

CAST: *Cox:* RICHARD DUNN. *Box:* JOHN DEAN. *Bouncer:* Richard Walker.

followed by

H.M.S. PINAFORE,
1936.21
or, The Lass That Loved a Sailor

A Revival of the Comic Opera in Two Acts[20]. Libretto by William S. Gilbert. Music by Arthur Sullivan. Ladies' costumes designed by George Sheringham. Musical director, Isidore Godfrey. Presented by the D'Oyly Carte Opera Company. Opened 28 September 1936 at the Martin Beck Theatre and closed 21 November 1936 after 16 performances in repertory[21].

CAST: *The Rt. Hon. Sir Joseph Porter, K.C.B.:* MARTYN GREEN. *Captain Corcoran:* LESLIE RANDS. *Ralph Rackstraw:* DEREK OLDHAM. *Dick Deadeye:* DARRELL FANCOURT. *Bill Bobstay:* Richard Walker. *Bob Becket:* Radley Flynn. *Josephine:* Sylvia Cecil. *Hebe:* Marjorie Eyre. *Little Buttercup:* EVELYN GARDINER. *First Lord's Sisters, His Cousins, His Aunts, Sailors, Marines, etc.*

1936.22

WHITE HORSE INN

A Musical Comedy in Three Acts, 23 Scenes. (Original German) Book (from the German singspiel-operette) by Hans Müller, suggested by a play "Im weissen Rössl" by Oskar Blumenthal and Gustav Kadelburg. (Original German lyrics by Robert Gilbert.) American adaptation by David Freedman. Music by Ralph Benatzky. Lyrics by Irving Caesar. Additional musical numbers by Robert Stolz, Irving Caesar, Norman Zeno and Will Irwin, Richard Fall, Jára Benes, Vivian Ellis, Eric Coates, (Adam Gelbtrunk). Play produced and staged by Erik Charell. Scenery and costumes by Professor Ernst Stern. Modern costumes by Irene Sharaff. Dances by Max Rivers. Lighting and special effects by Eugene Braun. Music direction by Victor Baravalle. Orchestrations by Hans Spialek. Musical adviser: Adam Gelbtrunk. Presented by Laurence Rivers, Inc. [Rowland Stebbins]. Opened 1 October 1936 at the Center Theatre and closed 10 April 1937 after 223 performances.

CAST (in order of appearance): *Pepi,* the Milkmaid: Reverelly. *Piccolo:* Tommy Gavin. *Hanni,* the Postwoman: Marie Marion. *Head Forester (Polman):* Oscar Ragland. *Zenzi,* the Goat Girl: Eleanor Bauman. *Cook's Guide:* Albert Mahler. *Franz,* a Waiter: Floyd Carnaby. *Leopold,* the Head Waiter: WILLIAM GAXTON. *Katarina Vogelhuber,* Proprietress of the White Horse Inn: KITTY CARLISLE. *The Honeymooners:* Mary Sutherland, Hal Voeth. *Captain of the Steamboat:* Grover White. *William McGonigle:* BILLY WHITE. *Natalie,* his daughter: CAROL STONE. *Donald Hutton:* ROBERT HALLIDAY. *Alpine Rose Hotel Porter:* Milton Gill. *Professor Hinzelman:* FREDERICK GRAHAM. *Gretel,* his Daughter: MELISSA MASON. *Sylvester S. Somerset, Jr.:* BUSTER WEST. *The Mayor:* Robert Williamson.

Schoolmaster Pimperl: Nelson Clifford. *Proprietor of Esplanade Hotel:* Howard Warriner. *Proprietor of Alpine Rose Inn:* Norman Van Emburgh. *Proprietor of the Black Bull:* Anthony Marvin. *Proprietor of the Golden Beer:* Jack Millard. *Farmer Thomas:* Maurice Carr. *Farmer Waldman:* John Barry. *Butcher Smith:* Martin LeRoy. *Baker Kaufman:* John Albert. *Farmer Christensen:* Ed Smith. *Miss Katzenjammer:* Almira Sessions. *The Emperor:* ARNOLD KORFF. *Katterl,* his Valet de Chambre: Ernst Robert.

Girls in the Ensemble: Betsy Berkeley, Maude Carroll, Phyllis Cameron, Helene Dernelle, Eleanor DeWitte, Valerie Eaton, Sonia Efron, Margie Evans, Dionne Farrelle, Wendy Greene, Lorraine Harris, Frances Hyatt, Loraine Latham, Velma Lord, Patricia Martin, Florence Menges, Mildred Patterson, Klara Buester, Adelaide Raleigh, Evelyn Sather, Ruth Shaw, Sonia Sorel, Georgina Yaeger, Luba Matiuk, Olga Schwenker, Mary Sutherland, Charlotte Lorraine, Evelyn Bonefine, Carol Crowell, Maxine Martin, Marion Harvey, Audrey Elliott, Tilda Getze, Ruth Rostyn, Evan Beatty, Betty Pope, Gloria Whitney, Ruth Roberts, Janice Winter, Frances Hayes. *Boys in the Ensemble:* George Gorst, Bill Chandler, William Bull, Clark Leston, Joseph Wirag, Mel Kacher, Gene Gally, Sid Gordon, Ed Hall, Billy Hale, Harry Quinn, Carl Trees, Edwin Gale, James Babbitt, Maurice Kelly, Edward Brown, Kenneth Weaver, Jack Voeth, Mickey Moore, Jack Barnes, Edwin Hackett, Buddy Hertelle, Charles Chavez, Bill Pollock, Harold Murray, Thomas Blayney, Edwin Sims, Jules Mann, Gene Kavanaugh, Paul Shobat, Floyd Cornaby, Jack Rogers, Paul Moore, Ed Smith, Herbert Rissman, Jack Millard, Winton Sears, Hal Voeth. *Singing Ensemble:* Penny Banks, Ruth Dawson, Geraldine Hamilton, Mae Muth, Florence Keezel, Lillian Sullivan, Gladys Haverty, Emily Marsh, Nina Verde, Esta Elman, Geraldine Bork, Anne Francis, Flora Laney, Norman Van Emburgh, Maurice Carr, Arthur de Voss, John Albert, Fred Locke, Arthur Vann, Howard Warriner, Alfred Drake, Martin LeRoy, Anthony Marvin, Morrie Siegel, John Barry. *Children:* Marguerite Lodge, Eleanor Bauman, Babs Rossiter, Dorothy Lodge, June Meier, Diane Chase, Dorothy Richel, Myra Green, Dorothy Joan Palmer, Gratia Landley, Virginia Lodge, Joe Shaughnessy, Leo Freedman, Joe Brown, Jr., Marvin Atkin, Walter Elliott, Anton Lonek, Billy Entenmann, Billy Lichtenberger, Joseph McCarthy.

Act 1, Scene 1: Early Morning outside the White Horse Inn. *Scene 2:* The White Horse Inn. *Scene 3:* The Forest. *Scene 4:* The Cow Shed. *Scene 5:* The Garden Restaurant. *Scene 6:* The White Horse Inn.

Act 2, Scene 1: Market Day in the Village. *Scene 2:* The White Horse Inn. *Scene 3:* The Railway Station. *Scene 4:* The Solarium. *Scene 5:* The Forest. *Scene 6:* An Alpine Plateau. *Scene 7:* The Forest. *Scene 8:* The Town Hall. *Scene 9:* The Forest. *Scene 10:* Welcome on the Landing Stage.

Act 3, Scene 1: Next Morning at the White Horse Inn. *Scene 2:* The Forest. *Scene 3:* A Tyrolean Wine Garden. *Scene 4:* The Forest. *Scene 5:* On the Hill Top. *Scene 6:* The Forest. *Scene 7:* A Summer Night at the White Horse Inn; A Trip Around the Lake on the Steamboat passing the Wine Garden, The Alpine Plateau, and The Village Fair.

ACT 1
"Arrival of Tourists"
    Singing Ensemble, Children
"Leave It to Katarina"
    K. Carlisle, Ensemble
    (*Music by* Jára Benes.)
"I Cannot Live Without Your Love"
    W. Gaxton, K. Carlisle
"Arrival of Steamboat"
    Ensemble
"White Horse Inn"
    K. Carlisle, R. Halliday, Ensemble
Spade Ballet
    Dairymaids
"Cowshed Rhapsody"
    Ensemble
    (*Music by* Adam Gelbtrunk.)
The Cow: L. Matiuk, O. Schwenker.
"Blue Eyes"
    R. Halliday, C. Stone, Ensemble
    (*Music by* Robert Stolz.)
"Rain Finale"
    Entire Company

ACT 2
"Market Day in the Village"
    K. Carlisle, W. Gaxton, Market Vendors
"Goodbye, Au Revoir, Auf Wiedersehn"
    W. Gaxton, Waiters
    (*Music by* Eric Coates, adapted from his "Knightsbridge March.")
"High Up on the Hills"
    K. Carlisle, B. House, Reverelly, Tyrolean Dancers, Ensemble

---

[19] First presented as COX AND BOX, or The Long-Lost Brothers in New York 14 August 1879 at the Standard Theatre for 48 performances. For Synopsis of Scenes and Musical Numbers, see original 1879 production.
[20] Originally presented in New York 15 January 1879 at the Standard Theatre for 175 performances. For Synopsis of Scenes and Musical Numbers, see original 1879 production.
[21] Settings, men's costumes, lighting uncredited.

"I Would Love to Have You Love Me"
    B. West, M. Mason, Ensemble
    (*Music by* Gerald Marks. *Lyrics by* Irving Caesar, Sammy Lerner.)

Alpine Symphony
    Reverelly, Tyrolean Dancers, Ensemble
    (*Music by* Adam Gelbtrunk.)

"Welcome on the Landing Stage"
    Entire Company

ACT 3

"Serenade to the Emperor"
    Serenaders

"We Prize Most the Things We Miss"
    K. Carlisle

"The Waltz of Love"
    Serenader, R. Halliday, C. Stone, Ensemble
    (*Music by* Richard Fall.)

Finale
    Entire Company

PATIENCE,
or, Bunthorne's Bride

1936.23

A Revival of the Comic Opera in Two Acts[22]. Libretto by William S. Gilbert. Music by Arthur Sullivan. Ladies' dresses designed by George Sheringham. Musical director, Isidore Godfrey. Produced by the D'Oyly Carte Opera Company. Opened 5 October 1936 at the Martin Beck Theatre and closed 30 November 1936 after 12 performances in repertory.

CAST: *Colonel Calverley*: DARRELL FANCOURT. *Major Murgatroyd*: Frank Steward. *Lieut. The Duke of Dunstable*: John Dean. *Reginald Bunthorne*: MARTYN GREEN. *Archibald Grosvenor*: Leslie Rands. *Mr. Bunthorne's Solicitor*: Wynn Dyson. *The Lady Angela*: Marjorie Eyre. *The Lady Saphir*: Elizabeth Nickell-Lean. *The Lady Ella*: Brenda Bennett. *The Lady Jane*: Evelyn Gardiner. *Patience*: SYLVIA CECIL. *Chorus of Rapturous Maidens and Officers of the Dragoon Guards.*

PRINCESS IDA,
or, Castle Adamant

1936.24

A Revival of the Comic Operetta in Three Acts[23]. Libretto by William S. Gilbert. Music by Arthur Sullivan. Costumes designed by Percy Anderson. Musical director, Isidore Godfrey. Produced by the D'Oyly Carte Opera Company. Opened 12 October 1936 at the Martin Beck Theatre and closed 5 December 1936 after 12 performances in repertory.[24]

CAST: *King Hildebrand*: SYDNEY GRANVILLE. *Hilarion*: DEREK OLDHAM. *Hilarion's Two Friends*: Cyril: John Dean. *Florian*: Leslie Rands. *King Gama*: MARTYN GREEN. *His Sons*: Arac: DARRELL FANCOURT. *Guron*: Richard Walker. *Scythius*: Radley Flynn. *Princess Ida*, Gama's Daughter: SYLVIA CECIL. *Lady Blanche*, Professor of Abstract Science: Evelyn Gardiner. *Lady Psyche*, Professor of Humanities: Ann Drummond-Grant. *Melissa*, Lady Blanche's Daughter: Marjorie Eyre. *Sacharissa*: Kathleen Naylor. *Chloe*: Marjorie Abbott. *Ada*: Elsie Winnall. *Soldiers, Courtiers, Girl Graduates, Daughters of the Plough, etc.*

RUDDIGORE,
or, The Witch's Curse

1936.25

A Revival of the Comic Opera in Two Acts[25]. Libretto by William S. Gilbert. Music by Arthur Sullivan. Conducted by Isidore Godfrey. Produced by the D'Oyly Carte Opera Company. Opened 22 October 1936 at the Martin Beck Theatre and closed 16 December 1936 after 8 performances in repertory.

[22]First presented in New York 22 September 1881 at the Standard Theatre for 177 performances. For Synopsis of Scenes and Musical Numbers, see original 1881 production.
[23]Originally presented in New York City 11 February 1884 at the Fifth Avenue Theatre for 48 performances. For Synopsis of Scenes and Musical Numbers, see original 1884 production.
[24]Scenery and lighting uncredited.
[25]First presented in New York 21 February 1887 at the Standard Theatre for 53 performances. For Synopsis of Scenes and Musical Numbers, see original 1887 production. Costumes, settings and lighting uncredited.

CAST: *Sir Ruthven Murgatroyd*: MARTYN GREEN. *Richard Dauntless*: JOHN DEAN. *Sir Despard Murgatroyd*: Sydney Granville. *Old Adam Goodheart*: Radley Flynn. *Sir Roderic Murgatroyd*: DARRELL FANCOURT. *Rose Maybud*: Brenda Bennett. *Mad Margaret*: MARJORIE EYRE. *Dame Hannah*: Evelyn Gardiner. *Zorah*: Ann Drummond-Grant. *Ruth*: Kathleen Naylor. *Chorus of Officers, Ancestors, Professional Bridesmaids, etc.*

RED, HOT AND BLUE

1936.26

A Musical Comedy in Two Acts, 10 Scenes. Book by Howard Lindsay and Russel Crouse. Music and lyrics by Cole Porter. Staged by Howard Lindsay. Dances and ensembles by George Hale. Settings by Donald Oenslager. Costumes by Constance Ripley. Orchestral arrangements, (Robert) Russell Bennett. Orchestra directed by Frank Tours. Produced by Vinton Freedley. Opened 29 October 1936 at the Alvin Theatre and closed 10 April 1937 after 183 performances.

CAST (in order of appearance): *Reporters*: Geoffrey Errett, Karl Kohrs, Bill Houston, Norman Lind, Eleanor Wallace, Arnita Wallace. *Deputy Warden Mulligan*: LEW PARKER. *Warden of Larks Nest Prison*: FORREST ORR. *"Nails" O'Reilly Duquesne*: ETHEL MERMAN. *"Policy" Pinkle*: JIMMY DURANTE. *Vivian*: VIVIAN VANCE. *Anne Westcott*: DOROTHY VERNON. *Grace*: GRACE HARTMAN. *Lucille*: Lucille Johnson. *Cecile*: Cecile Carey. *Kay*: Kay Picture. *Irene*: Ethelyne Holt. *Betty*: Betty Allen. *"Fingers"*: PAUL HARTMAN. *Bob Hale*: BOB HOPE. *Sonny Hadley*: THURSTON CRANE. *Peaches La Fleur*: POLLY WALTERS. *"Ratface" Dugan*: Bill Benner. *"Sure-Thing" Simpson*: Prentiss Davis. *"Flap-Ears" Metelli*: Leo Schippers. *"Louie the Louse"*: Bernard Jannsen. *Mrs. Peabody*: May Abbey. *Tiny*: Anne Wolf. *Louella*: Jeanette Owens. *Senator Musilovitch*: Lew Parker. *Senator Malvinsky*: Robert Leonard. *Senator O'Shaughnessy*: Forrest Orr. *Senator Del Grasso*: Houston Richards. *Sergeant-at-Arms*: Norman Lind. *First Expressman*: Geoffrey Erritt. *Second Expressman*: Karl Kohrs. *Girl*: Gloria Clare. *First Marine*: Frank Archer. *Second Marine*: Bruce Covert. *Decorator*: Houston Richards.

Debutantes: Marquita Nicolai, Evelyn Kelly, Ruth Ernst, Annette Nine, Eve Sorel, Helen Hudson, Jessica Pepper. *Guests*: Ruth Bond, Jeannette Bradley, Dorothy Jackson, Jean Scott, Dorothy Schwank, Stella Bailey, Charleen Tucker, Nancy Lee, Althea Elder, Prudence Hayes, Peggy Oden, Mary Joan Martin, Grace Gillern, Ruth Gormley, Marguerite James, Muriel Downey, June Le Roy, Hazel Nevin, Frances Stewart, Gloria Clare, Beverly Hosier, Joanne Allen.

Act 1, Scene 1: The Warden's Office at Larks Nest Prison. *Scene 2*: Mrs. Duquesne's Penthouse in New York City. *Scene 3*: A Street Corner in Washington, D.C. *Scene 4*: A Committee Room in the Senate. *Scene 5*: Lottery Headquarters. *Scene 6*: Pinkle's Bedroom in the Dolly Madison House. *Scene 7*: Garden of the Dolly Madison House.

Act 2, Scene 1: A Room in the White House. *Scene 2*: A Courtyard in the Marine Barracks. *Scene 3*: The White House Lawn.

ACT 1

"At Ye Olde Coffee Shoppe in Cheyenne"
    Reporters, Prison Band

Opening: "It's a Great Life"/"Perennial Debutantes"
    Guests, Debutantes

"Ours"
    D. Vernon, T. Crane, G. Hartman, P. Hartman, Girls

"Down in the Depths on the 90th Floor"
    E. Merman

"Carry On"
    T. Crane, Reporters, Muggs

"You've Got Something"
    B. Hope, E. Merman

"It's De-Lovely"
    E. Merman, B. Hope

"A Little Skipper from Heaven Above"
    J. Durante, Muggs and Reporters

Specialty Dance
    G. Hartman, P. Hartman

"Five Hundred Million"
    V. Vance, B. Allen, Debutantes, Guests

"Ridin' High"
    E. Merman, Ensemble
        Specialty Dance: K. Picture.

ACT 2

Opening: "We're About to Start Big Rehearsin'"
    Debutantes

"Hymn to Hymen"
    Guests

"What a Great Pair We'll Be"
D. Vernon, T. Crane, P, Hartman, G. Hartman, Ensemble

"You're a Bad Influence on Me"[26]
E. Merman

"Red, Hot and Blue"
E. Merman, Ensemble

Finale
Entire Company

1936.27 FORBIDDEN MELODY

A Musical in Two Acts, 11 Scenes. Book and lyrics by Otto Harbach. Music by Sigmund Romberg. Staged by Macklin Megley. Dialogue directed by José Ruben. Music directed by Robert (Emmett) Dolan. Settings by Sergei Soudeikine. Gowns and costumes by Ten Eyck. Orchestrations by Donald Walker. Produced by Jack Kirkland and Sam H. Grisman. Opened 2 November 1936 at the New Amsterdam Theatre and closed 28 November 1936 after 32 performances.

CAST (in order of appearance): *Thedor*, Leader of Gypsy Band: Bela Lublov. *Tosk*, a maitre d'hotel: LEO CHALZEL. *Kuzdu*, a singer: DANIEL HARRIS. *Katcha*, a singer: LILLION CLARK. *Alexis Constantine*: Charles Bryant. *Doma*: JOSEPH GREEN-WALD. *Gregor Fiorescu*: CARL BRISSON. *A Waiter*: Herman Williams. *Colonel Geza*: ARTHUR VINTON. *Madame Geza*: RUTH WESTON. *Nicholas Constantine*: JACK SHEEHAN. *Rozsa*, his wife: June Havoc. *Elene Constantine*: RUBY MERCER. *Mitzi*, a dancer: Nitza Vernille. *Yanczi*, another dancer: Helen Gray. *Butler*: Tomes Chapman. *Frederic*: Harry Raine. *A Streetwalker*: Mary Louise Quevli. *A Policeman*: Leo Chalzel. *A Girl*: Dolores Flanders. *Another Girl*: Muriel Muth. *Captain Fedovitch*: Gladstone Waldrip. *Lieut. Czenyi*: Clark Kramer.

Ladies of the Ensemble: Judith Gales, Beulah Blake, Betty Kerr, Jewel Marie Markham, Rita Joan Hume, Dolores Flanders, Muriel Muth, Dorothy Forsythe, Fay Hope, Joy Hampton, Marie (Louise) Quevli, Wadeeha Atiyeh, Virginia Cole, Mildred Newton. *Gentlemen of the Ensemble*: Tomes Chapman, Alexander Ancharoff, George Magis, Bruce Barclay, Jack Leslie, William Dunn, Mitchell Cowan, Jerry O'Rourke, Gladstone Waldrip, Herman Williams, Harry Raine.

Act 1, Scene 1: A Private Dining Room at the Hotel Roumania, Bucharest. 1 April 1930. Three o'clock in the morning. *Scene 2*: Elene's Dressing Room at the National Variety Theatre, Budapest. Some time later. *Scene 3*: A performance on the Stage of National Variety Theatre. Immediately thereafter. *Scene 4*: Backstage, directly after the performance. *Scene 5*: Elene's Villa, Budapest. The next night.

Act 2, Scene 1: A Street outside Hotel Buda, Budapest. Later that night. *Scene 2*: The Gate looking into the Garden of the Hotel Buda. Immediately following. *Scene 3*: The Royal Suite in the Hotel Buda, immediately following. *Scene 4*: Backstage of the National Variety Theatre, 3 days later. *Scene 5*: Elene's Dressing Room at the National Variety Theatre. 5 June 1930. *Scene 6*: Gardens of the Roumanian Embassy in Budapest. Six o'clock next Tuesday.

ACT 1

Opening
B. Lublov, Gypsy Band

"Bucharest"
L. Clark, D. Harris

"Lady in the Window"
L. Clark, D. Harris, Gypsy Band

"Just Hello"
C. Brisson, L. Clark, D. Harris, Gypsy Singers, Gypsy Band

"Moonlight and Violins"
R. Weston, C. Brisson

"Lady in the Window" (reprise)
C. Brisson, Ensemble, Gypsy Band

"Two Ladies and a Man"
R. Mercer, Ensemble, Gypsy Band

"You Are All I've Wanted"
C. Brisson

"Waltz Fantasie"
N. Vernille, C. Brisson

"Waltz Fantasie" (reprise)
C. Brisson

---

[26] Replaced during the run by:
"The Ozarks Are Calling Me Home"
E Merman

"How Could a Fellow Want More"
J. Havoc, J. Sheehan

"No Use Pretending"
R. Mercer, C. Brisson

"Hear the Gypsies Playing"
R. Mercer, Gypsy Band

"Just Hello" (reprise)
C. Brisson

Finale, Act 1
R. Mercer, C. Brisson

ACT 2

"Shadows"
L. Clark, Ensemble

"When a Girl Forgets to Scream"
C. Brisson

"Blame It All on the Night"
R. Mercer, C. Brisson

"Moonlight and Violins" (reprise)
R. Mercer, C. Brisson

"You Are All I've Wanted" (reprise)
C. Brisson

"No Use Pretending" (reprise)
R. Mercer, L. Clark

Dance
C. Brisson, H. Gray

Finale, Act 2
Entire Company

1936.28 JOHNNY JOHNSON

A Legend (Play) with Music in Three Acts, 13 Scenes. Play (book, lyrics) by Paul Green. Music by Kurt Weill. Staged by Lee Strasberg. Settings by Donald Oenslager. Costumes by Paul Du Pont. Music director, Lehman Engel. Orchestrations by Kurt Weill. Produced by The Group Theatre. Opened 19 November 1936 at the 44th Street Theatre and closed 16 January 1937 after 68 performances.

CAST (in order of speaking): *The Mayor*: BOB [Robert] LEWIS. *The Editor*: TONY [Gerrit] KRABER. *Minny Belle Tompkins*: PHOEBE BRAND. *Grandpa Joe*: ROMAN BOHNEN. *A Photographer*: WILL LEE. *A Boy*: Curt Conway. *Johnny Johnson*: RUSSELL COLLINS. *Anguish Howington*: GROVER BURGESS. *Aggie Tompkins*: SUSANNA SENIOR. *Captain Valentine*: SANFORD MEISNER. *Dr. McBray*: LEE J. COBB. *Private Patrick O'Day*: Curt Conway. *Sergeant Jackson*: ART SMITH. *A Camp Doll*: Eunice Stoddard. *Corporal George*: ALBERT VAN DEKKER [Albert Dekker]. *Private Fairfax*: William Challee. *Private Goldberger*: WILL LEE. *Private Harwood*: TONY (Gerrit) KRABER. *Private Kearns*: ELIA KAZAN. *Private Svenson*: Herbert Ratner. *A West Point Lieutenant*: JOSEPH PEVNEY. *An English Sergeant*: LUTHER ADLER. *Johann Lang*: JULES [John] GARFIELD. *A French Nurse*: PAULA MILLER. *An Orderly*: Paul Mann. *A Doctor*: Art Smith. *A Sister from the O.D.S.D.L.D.*: Ruth Nelson. *Chief of the Allied High Command*: MORRIS CARNOVSKY. *His Majesty*, a King: Orrin Jannings. *Belgian Major-General*: LUTHER ADLER. *British Commander-in-Chief*: John Most. *A French Major-General*: LEE J. COBB. *French Premier*: BOB [Robert] LEWIS. *American Commander-in-Chief*: ROMAN BOHNEN. *Scottish Colonel*: Thomas C. Kennedy. *A Liaison Office*: Jack Saltzman. *American Priest*: Alfred Saxe. *German Priest*: Paul Mann. *Military Policeman*: Herbert Ratner. *Dr. Mahodan*: MORRIS CARNOVSKY. *His Secretary*: Kate Allen. *Dr. Frewd*: ELIA KAZAN. *Brother Thomas*: Art Smith. *Brother Claude*: ROMAN BOHNEN. *Brother George*: LEE J. COBB. *Brother William*: Curt Conway. *Brother Hiram*: ALBERT VAN DEKKER. *Brother Jim*: Robert Joseph. *Brother Theodore*: TONY [Gerrit] KRABER. *Brother Henry*: LUTHER ADLER. *A Doctor*: William Challee. *An Attendant*: Herbert Ratner. *Anguish Howington, Jr.*: Eddie Ryan. *Soldiers*: Peter Ainsley, James Blake, Judson Hall.

Act 1, Scene 1: A Hilltop in a small town. April, 1917. *Scene 2*: The Tompkins Home. Several nights later. *Scene 3*: Recruiting Office No. 596,673. The next day. *Scene 4*: A Camp Drill-ground. A week later.

Act 2, Scene 1: A Front-line Trench. Several weeks later. *Scene 2*: A Churchyard. An hour later. *Scene 3*: The Hospital. A week later. *Scene 4*: The Chateau de Cent Fontaines, somewhere behind enemy lines. The same night. *Scene 5*: The edge of a great battlefield. The same night, just before dawn. *Scene 6*: No Man's Land.

Act 3, Scene 1: Superintendent's Office, State Hospital. A month later. *Scene 2*: The forensic arena in the House of Balm. Ten years later. *Scene 3*: A Street, Today.

ACT 1[27]

"Over in Europe"
    B. Lewis, Villagers
"Democracy's Call"
    P. Brand, B. Lewis, Villagers
"Up Chickamauga Hill"
    R. Bohnen
"Johnny's Melody"
    R. Collins
"Aggie's Sewing Machine Song"
    S. Senior
"O, Heart of Love"
    P. Brand
"Farewell, Goodbye"
    P. Brand
"Captain Valentine's Tango"
    S. Meisner
"Song of the Goddess"
    R. Collins

ACT 2

"Song of the Wounded Frenchmen"
    Soldiers
"Tea Song"
    A. Smith, English Soldiers
"Cowboy Song" (Oh, the Rio Grande)
    T. Kraber
Johnny's Dream
    P. Brand
"Song of the Guns"
    Soldiers
Music of the Stricken Redeemer
    Orchestra

ACT 3

"Mon Ami, My Friend"
    P. Miller
"The Allied High Command"
    M. Carnovsky, L. Adler, J. Most, L. J. Cobb, R. Bohnen
The Laughing Generals
    O. Jannings, M. Carnovsky, L. Adler, J. Most, L. J. Cobb, R. Bohnen
The Battle (No Man's Land)
    Orchestra
"In Times of War and Tumults"
    A. Saxe, P. Mann
Johnny's Arrest and Homecoming
    Orchestra
"The Psychiatry Song"
    M. Carnovsky
"How Sweetly Friendship Binds"
    A. Smith, R. Bohnen, L. J. Cobb, C. Conway, A. Van Dekker, R. Joseph, T. Kraber, L. Adler
"Hymn to Peace"
    A. Smith, R. Bohnen, L. J. Cobb, C. Conway, A. Van Dekker, R. Joseph, T. Kraber, L. Adler
"Johnny's Song" (Listen to My Song)
    R. Collins

1936.29 TONIGHT AT EIGHT-THIRTY

Nine One-Act plays with music (performed in 3 separate programs). Plays, music and lyrics by Noël Coward. Directed by Noël Coward. Settings by Gladys E. Calthrop. Miss Lawrence's costumes designed by Hartnell, Berkeley Square. Music director, John McManus. Produced by John C. Wilson. Opened 24 November 1936 at the National Theatre and closed 9 March 1937 after 118 performances.

---

[27]Musical numbers not listed in program. Song list prepared from published playscript, JOHNNY JOHNSON: The Biography of a Common Man (Samuel French, New York, 1937).

FIRST BILL
(24 November 1936)

HANDS ACROSS THE SEA
    A Comedy in 1 Scene.

CAST: *Walters*: MOYA NUGENT. *Lady Maureen Gilpin*, Piggie: GERTRUDE LAWRENCE. *Com. Peter Gilpin, R.N.*: NOËL COWARD. *Lieut. Commander Alastair Corbett, R.N.*: EDWARD UNDERDOWN. *Mrs. Wadhurst*: JOYCE CAREY. *Mr. Wadhurst*: ALAN WEBB. *Mr. Burnham*: Kenneth Carten. *The Hon. Clare Wedderburn*: Joan Swinstead. *Major Gosling*, Bogey: Anthony Pelissier.

Set: Drawing Room of the Gilpins' Flat in London. Present Day.

THE ASTONISHED HEART
    A Play in 6 Scenes.

CAST: *Barbara Faber*: JOYCE CAREY. *Susan Birch*: Joan Swinstead. *Tim Verney*: Anthony Pelissier. *Ernest*: EDWARD UNDERDOWN. *Sir Reginald French*: ALAN WEBB. *Leonora Vail*: GERTRUDE LAWRENCE. *Christian Faber*: NOËL COWARD.

Set: Drawing Room of the Fabers' Flat in London.

Scene 1: Late afternoon. November 1935. *Scene 2*: Late afternoon. November 1934. *Scene 3*: Midnight. January 1935. *Scene 4*: Dawn. April 1935. *Scene 5*: Evening. November 1935. *Scene 6*: Late afternoon. November 1935.

RED PEPPERS
    An Interlude with Music.

CAST: *Lily Pepper*: GERTRUDE LAWRENCE. *Geoge Pepper*: NOËL COWARD. *Alf*: Kenneth Carten. *Bert Bentley*: Anthony Pelissier. *Mr. Edwards*: ALAN WEBB. *Mabel Grace*: JOYCE CAREY.

Set: The Stage and Dressing Room of the Palace of Varieties in one of the smaller English provincial towns. Saturday Night. Present Day.

MUSICAL NUMBERS
    "Has Anyone Seen Our Ship?"
        G. Lawrence, N. Coward
    "Men About Town"
        G. Lawrence, N. Coward

SECOND BILL
(27 November 1936)

WE WERE DANCING
    A Comedy (with Music) in 2 Scenes.

CAST: *Ippaga*: Kenneth Carten. *George Davies*: EDWARD UNDERDOWN. *Eva Blake*: MOYA NUGENT. *Louise Charteris*: GERTRUDE LAWRENCE. *Karl Sandys*: NOËL COWARD. *Clara Bethel*: JOYCE CAREY. *Hubert Charteris*: ALAN WEBB. *Major Blake*: Anthony Pelissier.

Scene 1: Veranda at the Country Club at Samolo. Evening. *Scene 2*: The same. Early morning.

MUSICAL NUMBER
    "We Were Dancing"
        N. Coward

FUMED OAK
    An Unpleasant Comedy in 2 Scenes.

CAST: *Doris Gow*: GERTRUDE LAWRENCE. *Mrs. Rockett*, her mother: JOYCE CAREY. *Elsie*, daughter of Doris and Henry Gow: MOYA NUGENT. *Henry Gow*: NOËL COWARD.

Set: Sitting Room of the Gows' House in South London. The Present.

Scene 1: Morning. *Scene 2*: Evening.

SHADOW PLAY
    A Play with Music.

CAST: *Lena*: MOYA NUGENT. *Victoria Gayforth*: GERTRUDE LAWRENCE. *Martha Cunningham*: JOYCE CAREY. *Simon Gayforth*: NOËL COWARD. *Hodge*: Kenneth Carten. *A Young Man*: Anthony Pelissier. *George Cunningham*: ALAN WEBB. *Sibyl Heston*: Joan Swinstead. *Michael Doyle*: EDWARD UNDERDOWN.

Set: The Gayforths' House in Mayfair. The present.

MUSICAL NUMBERS
    "Then"
        N. Coward, G. Lawrence
    "Play, Orchestra, Play!"
        N. Coward, G. Lawrence
    "You Were There"
        N. Coward, G. Lawrence

THIRD BILL
(30 November 1936)

WAYS AND MEANS
A Comedy in 3 Scenes.

CAST: *Stella Cartwright*: GERTRUDE LAWRENCE. *Toby Cartwright*: NOËL COWARD. *Gaston*: Kenneth Carten. *Lord Chapworth*, Chaps: ALAN WEBB. *Olive Lloyd-Ransome*: Joan Swinstead. *Princess Elena Krassiloff*: MOYA NUGENT. *Murdoch*: Anthony Pelissier. *Nanny*: JOYCE CAREY. *Stevens*: EDWARD UNDERDOWN.

Set: A Bedroom in the Lloyd-Ransomes' House, Villa Zephyre, Cote d'Azur.

Scene 1: 11:30 on a July morning. The present. *Scene 2*: 1:30 A.M. the following morning. *Scene 3*: Two hours later.

STILL LIFE
A Play in 5 Scenes.

CAST: *Laura Jesson*: GERTRUDE LAWRENCE. *Myrtle Bagot*: JOYCE CAREY. *Beryl Waters*: MOYA NUGENT. *Young Man*: Charles Peters. *Stanley*: Kenneth Carten. *Albert Godby*: ALAN WEBB. *Alec Harvey*: NOËL COWARD. *Bill*: EDWARD UNDERDOWN. *Johnnie*: Anthony Pelissier. *Mildred*: Betty Hare. *Dolly Messiter*: Joan Swinstead.

Set: The refreshment room of Milford Junction Station. Present day.

Scene 1: 5:25 on an evening in April. *Scene 2*: July. *Scene 3*: October. *Scene 4*: 9:45 on an evening in December. *Scene 5*: Between 5 and 5:30 on an afternoon in March.

FAMILY ALBUM
A Comedy of Manners to Music.

CAST: *Jasper Featherways*: NOËL COWARD. *Jane*, his wife: GERTRUDE LAWRENCE. *Lavinia Featherways*: JOYCE CAREY. *Richard Featherways*: EDWARD UNDERDOWN. *Harriet Winter*: Joan Swinstead. *Charles Winter*: Anthony Pelissier. *Emily Valance*: MOYA NUGENT. *Edward Valance*: Kenneth Carten. *Burrows*: ALAN WEBB.

Set: The Drawing Room of the Featherways' House in Kent on an Autumn evening in the year 1860.

MUSICAL NUMBERS
"Here's a Toast"
    N. Coward, G. Lawrence, Cast
"Hearts and Flowers"
    G. Lawrence, N. Coward

BLACK RHYTHM

1936.30

A Sepia Swing Musical Comedy in Two Acts, 10 Scenes. Book, music and lyrics by Donald Heywood. Directed by Earl Dancer and Donald Heywood. Musical director, Donald Heywood. Produced by Earl Dancer and J. H. Levey. Opened 19 December 1936 at the Comedy Theatre and closed 24 December 1936 after 6 performances.[28]

CAST: *Jenny*: JENI LeGON. *Laura*: MAUDE RUSSELL. *Mr. Heydon*: William Walker. *Cornbread*: Alex Lovejoy. *Babe*: BABE MATTHEWS. *David Songbird*: WALTER RICHARDSON. *Rhythm*: AVON LONG. *Mr. Feinstein*: Franklin Klien. *Dusty*: JOE BYRD. *Bodidly*: SPEEDY WILSON. *Eva*: GENEVA WASHINGTON. *Slim*: Eddie Baer. *Eugene*: John Foss. *Toby*: Sammy Gardner. *Swing*: Sinclair Brooks. *Chichi*: Walder Davis. *Money*: Clarence Albright. *Joe Michaels*: Eddie Matthews. *Wardrobe Sal*: Ina Duncan. *Van Bugg*: Woodrow Wilson. *Sonny*: Barrington Guy.

Chorus: Wen Talbott Choir. *Dance Ensemble*: Savoy Lindy Hoppers. Cotton Club Boys, Rhythmettes, Black Rhythm Swingsters.

Ladies of the Ensemble: Edith Sykes, Mary Lou Murphy, Connie Jackson, Marion Dow, Mildred Hubert, Ruby Richard, Jackie Lewis, Dede Rogers, Lillian Hitchinson, Neauchanter Nerhune, Thelma Prince, Peggy Sheppard, Bertye Baker, Ronny Hutchinson, Nita Berry, Sonia Whitfield, Constance Thompson, Vivian Garnette.

Act 1: A Rehearsal Hall in Harlem.

Act 2: Back Stage.

ACT 1
Scene 1
    "Truckers Ball"
        S. Gardner, Ensemble
    Ventriloquist Bit, Magician Bit
        J. Byrd, E. Baer

"Bow Down Sinners"
    W. Richardson, Choir
Preacher Bit
    J. Byrd
Scene 2
    Getting Money
        A. Lovejoy, C. Albright, W. Davis, M. Russell, J. Byrd
    Dance Novelty (Audition)
        W. Wilson
Scene 3
    Signing Contract
        F. Klien, E. Matthews, W. Walker
Scene 4
    Cleaning Up
        J. Byrd, S. Wilson
Scene 5
    "Back in Circulation"
        Black Rhythm Swingsters, Lindy Hoppers, Rhythmettes, Choir
ACT 2
Scene 1
    Last Minute Rehearsals
        W. Wilson, J. Byrd, E. Baer
    "Orchids"
        W. Richardson
    Pianoisms
        S. Brooks
Scene 2
    "Here 'Tis"
        J. LeGon, Rhythmettes
Scene 3
    "Black Rhythm"
        G. Washington, A. Long
Scene 4
    "Doin' the Toledo"
        B. Matthews
Scene 5
    "Emaline"
        B. Guy, J. LeGon, M. Russell, B. Matthews, G. Washington, Ensemble
    Finale
        Entire Company

THE SHOW IS ON

1936.31

A Musical Revue in Two Acts, 24 Scenes. Entire production conceived, staged and designed by Vincente Minnelli. Sketches by David Freedman. "Mr. Gielgud Passes By" by Moss Hart. Music and lyrics mostly by Vernon Duke and Ted Fetter. Additional music and lyrics by Hoagy Carmichael and Stanley Adams, Howard Dietz and Arthur Schwartz, George and Ira Gershwin, E. Y. Harburg and Harold Arlen, Herman Hupfeld, Will Irwin and Norman Zeno, Richard Rodgers and Lorenz Hart. Sketches directed by Edward Clarke Lilley. Dances and principals' numbers staged by Robert Alton. Orchestrations and orchestra conducted by Gordon Jenkins. Additional orchestrations by (Robert) Russell Bennett and Hans Spialek. Produced by the Messrs. Shubert. Opened 25 December 1936 at the Winter Garden and closed 17 July 1937 after 236 performances; re-opened a return engagement 18 September 1937 at the Winter Garden, and closed 2 October 1937 after 17 performances. Total: 253 performances.

CAST: BEATRICE LILLIE, BERT LAHR, REGINALD GARDINER, MITZI MAYFAIR, PAUL HAAKON, GRACIE BARRIE, CHARLES WALTERS, VERA ALLEN, ROBERT SHAFER, JACK McCAULEY, Evelyn Thawl, Ralph Riggs, Marie Carroll, Roy Campbell's Continentals.

Girls: Marion Allen, Hazel Bofinger, Mary Ann Carr, Dorothy Daly, Doris Donaldson, Helen Ecklund, Claire Ellis, Peggy Gallimore, Ruth Greeley, Pearl Harris, Irene Kelly, Jerrie Koban, Jane Lane, Gertrude Medwin, June McNulty, Jean Moorhead, Marion Murray, Mary Phillips, Polly Rose, Sherry Stuart, Marie Vaughn, Mildred Webb. *Continentals*: John Edwards, Robert Herring, Arnold Lenhart, Gifford Nash, Paul Owen, Richard Satterfield. *Dancers*: Gene Ashley, Kenneth Bostock, Hugh Ellsworth, Harry Mack, Fred Nay, Mortimer O'Brien, Bob Pitts, Mischa Pompianov,

---

[28]Costumes, settings uncredited.

Harry Rogue, Willem Van Loon. *Children*: Evelyn Mills, Warren Mills. (Also: Duke Williams, Andre Charise, Marie Carrol.)

ACT 1

Scene 1

"Prologue"

(*Music by* Arthur Schwartz. *Lyrics by* Howard Dietz.)
The Angels of the Show: The Continentals. *Shakespeare*: R. Gardiner. *Cleopatra*: M. Murray. *Marc Antony*: M. Pompianov. *Fan Bearer*: D. Williams. *Rosencranz*: W. Van Loon. *Guildenstern*: M. O'Brien. *Shylock*: R. Riggs. *Romeo*: P. Owen. *Juliet*: M. Carroll. *The Three Witches*: P. Harris, P. Gallimore, J. McNulty. *The Broth*: H. Bofinger. *Desdemona*: V. Allen. *Maid*: P. Rose. *Othello*: R. Satterfield. *Brutus*: G. Nash. *Caesar's Ghost*: H. Rogue. *Ophelia*: E. Thawl. *King Lear*: J. McCauley.

Scene 2

"The Show Is On"

G. Barrie

(*Music by* Hoagy Carmichael. *Lyrics by* Ted Fetter.)
Danced by Girls' Ensemble.

Scene 3

Titania (*by* David Freedman)

Ronald Traylor: B. Lahr. *Prime Minister*: R. Gardiner. *Sybil Hutchins*: V. Allen.

Scene 4

"Now"

G. Barrie, R. Shafer

(*Music by* Vernon Duke. *Lyrics by* Ted Fetter.)
Danced by P. Haakon, E. Thawl, Girls and Boys.

Scene 5

"(There's) Rhythm (in That Heart of Mine)"

(*Music by* Richard Rodgers. *Lyrics by* Lorenz Hart.)
Go Go Benuti: B. Lillie. *Al Fleegle*: R. Gardiner.

Scene 6

"What Has He Got?"

M. Mayfair, C. Walters, Ensemble

(*Music by* Vernon Duke. *Lyrics by* Ted Fetter.)

Scene 7

Mr. Gielgud Passes By (*by* Moss Hart)

Scene: The Empire Theatre, New York City. (1) The Star's Dressing Room. (2) The Audience.
John Gielgud: R. Gardiner. *His Manager*: J. McCauley. *His Valet*: R. Riggs. *Stage Manager*: W. Van Loon. *Niesa*: V. Allen. *Fanny*: M. Carroll. *Irate Gentleman*: G. Nash. *Mrs. Slemp*: B. Lillie.

Scene 8

"Song of the Woodman"

B. Lahr

(*Music by* Harold Arlen. *Lyrics by* E. Y. Harburg.)

Scene 9

"Casanova"

G. Barrie

(*Music by* Vernon Duke. *Lyrics by* Ted Fetter. *Ballet Music by* Vernon Duke. *Choreography by* Harry Losee.)
Casanova: P. Haakon. *His Major Domo*: K. Bostock. *His Secretary*: H. Ellsworth. *His Valet*: M. Pompianov. *His Mistress*: J. Koban. *His Maid*: M. Webb. *The Cardinal*: M. O'Brien. *The Doge of Venice*: W. Van Loon. *The Grand Duchess*: M. A. Carr. *The Grand Duke*: A. Charise. *The Modern Girl*: E. Thawl.

Scene 10

Box Office (*by* David Freedman)

Scene: A Theatre Lobby, possibly on 52nd Street.
Treasurer: B. Lillie. *Brooks Hall*: J. McCauley. *Mrs. Smith*: V. Allen. *Mr. Brentwood*: R. Riggs. *A Critic*: B. Lahr.

Scene 11

Strawcuffsky

Written and performed by R. Gardiner

Scene 12

"Long As You've Got Your Health"

G. Barrie

(*Music by* Will Irwin. *Lyrics by* E. Y. Harburg, Norman Zeno.)
Danced by M. Mayfair, C. Walters, Ensemble.

Scene 13

"Buy Yourself a Balloon"

B. Lillie

(*Music and Lyrics by* Herman Hupfeld.)
Page Girl: H. Bofinger.

Scene 14

Tovarich[29] (*by* David Freedman)

Scene: A House in Washington, D.C.
Mihael: B. Lahr. *Tatiana*: V. Allen. *Mrs. Jackson*: M. Carroll. *Mr. Jackson*: R. Riggs. *A Visitor*: J. McCauley.

Scene 15

"Parade Night"

R. Shafer, the Continentals

(*Music by* Will Irwin. *Lyrics by* Norman Zeno.)

"Cakewalk"

Danced by M. Mayfair, P. Haakon, Ensemble

(*Music by* Will Irwin. *Lyrics by* Norman Zeno.)
Simon Legree: A. Charise. *Malcolm St. Clair*: C. Walters. *Skeggs*: R. Riggs. *Aunt Ophelia*: V. Allen. *Lawyer Marks*: H. Ellsworth. *Topsy*: P. Harris. *Little Eva*: E. Thawl. *Uncle Tom*: F. Nay. *Chloe*: W. Van Loon. *Eliza*: G. Barrie.

ACT 2

Scene 1

"By Strauss"

G. Barrie, R. Shafer

(*Music by* George Gershwin. *Lyrics by* Ira Gershwin.)
Danced by M. Mayfair, Ensemble.

Scene 2

"Woof"

B. Lahr

(*Music by* Will Irwin. *Lyrics by* Norman Zeno.)

Scene 3

The Reading of the Play (*by* David Freedman)

Scene: A Theatre Greenroom in the 90s.
Mlle. Leonore: B. Lillie. *Flyde Twitch*: R. Gardiner. *The Producer*: R. Riggs. *Armand*: J. McCauley. *Alphonse*: W. Van Loon. *Pierre*: A. Charise. *Warren Bruce*: M. O'Brien. *Supporting Cast*: V. Allen, M. Carrol, H. Bofinger.

Scene 4

"Little Old Lady"

M. Mayfair, C. Walters, Girls

(*Music by* Hoagy Carmichael. *Lyrics by* Stanley Adams.)

Scene 5

Taxes! Taxes!! (*by* David Freedman)

Scene: A Government Office.
Bert Larrimore: B. Lahr. *Mr. Higgins*: R. Gardiner. *Crunch*: R. Riggs.

Scene 6

"Josephine Waters"

B. Lillie, G. Ashley, W. Van Loon, F. Nay, M. Pompianov

(*Music by* Harold Arlen. *Lyrics by* E. Y. Harburg. *Dance Music by* Vernon Duke.)

Scene 7

"The Show Goes On" (reprise)

G. Barrie, Girls

Scene 8

Burlesque (*by* David Freedman)

Announced by R. Gardiner. *Scene 1*: Broadway and 42nd Street. *Putty Nose*: B. Lahr. *The Straight Man*: J. McCauley. *First Girl*: J. Lane. *Second Girl*: J. Koban. *A Strip Teaser*: B. Lillie. *Scene 2*: The Beaux Arts Ball. *Major Domo*: R. Riggs. *Madame Pompadour*: I. Kelly. *Queen Elizabeth*: G. Medwin. *Sir Walter Raleigh*: P. Owen. *Third Girl*: H. Ecklund. *The Spirit of '76*: D. Donaldson, P. Gallimore, M. Murray. *Fan Dancers*: M. Allen, H. Bofinger, D. Daley, J. Moorehead, M. Phillips, S. Stuart.

Scene 9

"Epilogue"

B. Lillie, B. Lahr, Entire Company

(*Music by* Vernon Duke. *Lyrics by* Ted Fetter.)

1936.31 THE SHOW IS ON

(Credits same as above.) Re-opened a return engagement 18 September 1937 at the Winter Garden and closed 2 October 1937 after 17 performances prior to tour.

---

[29]A burlesque of the play by Jacques Deval and its American adaptation by Robert E. Sherwood.

CAST: WILLIE HOWARD, EUGENE HOWARD, CHIC YORK, ROSE KING, CHARLES (Cookie) BOWERS, JOHN McCAULEY, JACK GOOD, TERRY LAWLOR, ROY CROPPER, Lyda Sue Leeds, Marcella Swanson, Demetrios Vilan, Mildred Webb, Dave Mallen, Ruth Scheim, John Englert.

Girls: Marion Allen, Gloria Arden, Muriel Baker, Hazel Bofinger, Letitia Bring, June Burde, Mary Ann Carr, Ruth Dennis, June Clifford Grey, Wendy Greene, Pearl Harris, Vivian Howe, Barbara Hunter, Jerrie Koban, Gertrude Medwin, Jean Moorhead, Della Muir, Marion Murray, Polly Rose, Clare Scott, Laurie Shevlin, Peggy Thomas, Edith Wallace. THE CONTINENTALS: John Edwards, Robert Herring, Arnold Lenhart, Gifford Nash, Paul Owen, Richard Satterfield. *Dancers*: Gene Ashley, James Babbitt, Jack Barratt, Kenneth Bostock, Edward Browne, Hugh Ellsworth, Robert Pitts, Mischa Pompianov, Harry Rogue, Frank Thompson. *Children*: Evelyn Mills, Warren Mills.

ACT 1

Scene 1

"Prologue"

(*Music by* Arthur Schwartz. *Lyrics by* Howard Dietz.)
The Angels of the Show: The Continentals. *Shakespeare*: J. McCauley. *Cleopatra*: M. Murray. *Marc Antony*: M. Pompianov. *Fan Bearer*: D. Williams. *Rosencranz*: K. Bostock. *Guildenstern*: A. Lenhart. *Shylock*: J. Barrett. *Romeo*: P. Owen. *Juliet*: P. Rose. *The Three Witches*: P. Harris, B. Hunter, M. Baker. *The Broth*: H. Bofinger. *Desdemona*: M. Swanson. *Othello*: R. Satterfield. *Brutus*: J. Edwards. *Caesar's Ghost*: H. Rogue. *Ophelia*: M. Webb. *King Lear*: D. Mallen.

Scene 2

"The Show Is On"

T. Lawlor
(*Music by* Hoagy Carmichael. *Lyrics by* Ted Fetter.)
Danced by Girls' Ensemble.

Scene 3

"(There's) Rhythm (in That Heart of Mine)"

(R. King)
(*Music by* Richard Rodgers. *Lyrics by* Lorenz Hart.)
Go Go Benuti: R. King. *Al Fleegle*: J. McCauley.

Scene 4

"Now"

T. Lawlor, R. Cropper
(*Music by* Vernon Duke. *Lyrics by* Ted Fetter.)
Danced by D. Vilan, M. Webb, Girls and Boys.

Scene 5

Taxes! Taxes!! (*by* David Freedman)

Scene: A Government Office. *Bert Larrimore*: W. Howard. *Mr. Higgins*: E. Howard. *Crunch*: D. Mallen.

Scene 6

"What Has He Got?"

L. S. Leeds, J. Good, Ensemble
(*Music by* Vernon Duke. *Lyrics by* Ted Fetter.)

Scene 7

Mr. Gielgud Passes By (*by* Moss Hart)

Scene: The Empire Theatre, New York City. (1) The Star's Dressing Room. (2) The Audience.
John Gielgud: J. McCauley. *His Manager*: C. York. *His Valet*: D. Mallen. *Stage Manager*: R. Herring *Niesa*: M. Swanson. *Usher*: R. Satterfield. *Fanny*: P. Rose. *Irate Gentleman*: G. Nash. *Mrs. Slemp*: R. King.

Scene 8

A Lesson in French[30]

Professor Pierre Ginsburg: W. Howard. *Radio Announcer*: E. Howard.

Scene 9

"Casanova"

T. Lawlor
(*Music by* Vernon Duke. *Lyrics by* Ted Fetter. *Ballet Music by* Vernon Duke. *Choreography by* Harry Losee.)
Casanova: D. Vilan. *His Major Domo*: K. Bostock. *His Secretary*: H. Ellsworth. *His Valet*: H. Rogue. *His Mistress*: J. Koban. *His Maid*: J. Moorhead. *The Cardinal*: G. Ashley. *The Doge of Venice*: J. Barrett. *The Grand Duchess*: M. A. Carr. *The Grand Duke*: A. Charise. *The Modern Girl*: M. Webb.

Scene 10

Charles "Cookie" Bowers[31]

Scene 11

"Long As You've Got Your Health"

T. Lawlor
(*Music by* Will Irwin. *Lyrics by* E. Y. Harburg, Norman Zeno.)
Danced by L. S. Leeds, J. Good, R. Scheim, J. Englert, Ensemble.

Scene 12

"Buy Yourself a Balloon"

R. King
(*Music and Lyrics by* Herman Hupfeld.)
Page Girl: H. Bofinger.

Scene 13

Tovarich (*by* David Freedman)

Scene: A House in Washington, D.C.
Mihael: W. Howard. *Tatiana*: M. Swanson. *Mrs. Jackson*: P. Rose. *Mr. Jackson*: D. Mallen. *A Visitor*: J. McCauley.

Scene 14

"Parade Night"

E. Howard, the Continentals
(*Music and Lyrics by* Norman Zeno and Will Irwin.)

"Cakewalk"

Danced by M. Webb, D. Vilan, Ensemble
(*Music and Lyrics by* Norman Zeno and Will Irwin.)
Simon Legree: A. Charise. *Malcolm St. Clair*: J. Good. *Skeggs*: D. Mallen. *Aunt Ophelia*: P. Thomas. *Lawyer Marks*: H. Ellsworth. *Topsy*: C. Scott. *Little Eva*: E. Mills. *Uncle Tom*: E. Browne. *Chloe*: G. Ashley. *Eliza*: T. Lawlor.

ACT 2

Scene 1

"By Strauss"

T. Lawlor, R. Cropper
(*Music by* George Gershwin. *Lyrics by* Ira Gershwin.)
Danced by L. S. Leeds, Ensemble.

Scene 2

"Song of the Woodman"

W. Howard
(*Music by* Harold Arlen. *Lyrics by* E. Y. Harburg.)

Scene 3

The Reading of the Play (*by* David Freedman)

Scene: A Theatre Greenroom in the 90s
Mlle. Leonore: R. King. *Flyde Twitch*: J. McCauley. *The Producer*: D. Mallen. *Armand*: A. Charise. *Alphonse*: P. Owen. *Pierre*: C. York. *Warren Bruce*: A. Lenhart. *Supporting Cast*: M. Swanson, P. Rose, H. Bofinger.

Scene 4

"Little Old Lady"

L. S. Leeds, J. Good, Girls
(*Music by* Hoagy Carmichael. *Lyrics by* Stanley Adams)

Scene 5

Animals Past and Present[32]

Announced by J. McCauley. *Prof. Stanislouse McCupcake*: C. York. *Miss Abernathy*: R. King.

Scene 6

Burlesque (*by* David Freedman)

Scene 1: Broadway and 42nd Street.
Announced by J. McCauley. *Putty Nose*: W. Howard. *The Straight Man*: E. Howard. *First Girl*: J. Moorhead. *Second Girl*: J. Koban. *A Strip Teaser*: R. King.
Scene 2: The Beaux Arts Ball. *Major Domo*: D. Mallen. *Madame Pompadour*: D. Muir. *Queen Elizabeth*: G. Medwin. *Sir Walter Raleigh*: P. Owen. *Third Girl*: M. Murray. *The Spirit of '76*: M. Baker, J. C. Grey, L. Breng. *Fan Dancers*: M. Allen, P. Thomas, M. A. Carr, L. Shevlin, V. Howe, H. Bofinger.

Scene 7

"Epilogue"

W. Howard, E. Howard, R. King, C. York, Entire Company

1937.01   # THE ETERNAL ROAD

A Biblical Spectacle in a Prologue, Three Acts, 12 Scenes. (Original German "Der Weg der Verheissung") Text by Franz Werfel, adapted for the

---

[30]New material not performed in the show's first engagement.
[31]New material not performed in the show's first engagement.

---

[32]New material not performed in the show's first engagement.

American stage by William A. Drake from a translation by Ludwig Lewisohn. Music by Kurt Weill. Staged by Max Reinhardt, assisted by Francesco von Mendelssohn, Harry Horner and Charles Alan. Dances directed by Benjamin Zemach. Settings, costumes and lighting by Norman Bel Geddes. Musical director, Isaac Van Grove. Associate musical director and conductor, Harry Horner. Produced by Meyer W. Weisgal and Crosby Gaige. Opened 7 January 1937 at the Manhattan Opera House and closed 15 May 1937 after 153 performances.

CAST (in order of appearance): *Prologue. The Rabbi*: Myron Taylor. *The Adversary*: SAM JAFFEE [Jaffe]. *The Timid Soul*: Mark Schweid. *The Rich Man*: Anthony Blair. *The Estranged One*: Harold Johnsrud. *The Estranged One's Son*: SIDNEY LUMET. *President of the Congregation*: David A. Leonard. *First Pious Man*: Robert Harrison. *Second Pious Man*: Charles Adler. *Third Pious Man*: Baruch Lumet. *Fourth Pious Man*: Leslie Austen. *Fifth Pious Man*: Bennett Challis. *Sixth Pious Man*: Cassius C. Quimby. *Seventh Pious Man*: Harry Hammill. *Eighth Pious Man*: Hal Kingsley. *Ninth Pious Man*: Kurt Kasznar. *Fanatic*: Roger De Koven. *Adversary's Follower*: Abner Biberman. *Watchman*: David Kurlan. *Elders*: Al Clifford, Charles Homer, Gustav Stryker. *Boys of the Congregation*: Nat L. Mintz, Howard Sherman, Dickie Van Patten. *Jesse—A Young Man*: Herbert Rudley. *The Alien Girl*: Olive Deering. *An Ancient*: Charles Hale. *Synagogue Choir*: Antoinette Allen, Ruth Virginia Lewis, Eva Ortman, Angela Schopp, Eleanor Searle, Molly Taylor, Michael Bataeff, Albert Cazentre, Carroll Howes, Lucien Rutman, Harold Sternberg, Sam Sternberg, James Spivak, Sol Tisman. *Voice of God*: Ben Cutler.

Act 1. ABRAHAM: *Abraham*: Thomas Chalmers. *Sarah*: Bertha Kunz-Baker. *Isaac*: Dickie Van Patten. *Eliezer*: Carl Formes. *The White Angel*: John Uppman. *First Dark Angel*: Edward Kane. *Second Dark Angel*: Ben Cutler. *Voice of a Cherub*: Tommy Mott. JACOB AND RACHEL. *Jacob*: Ralph Jameson. *Rachel*: Sarah Osnath-Halevy. JOSEPH AND HIS BROTHERS. *Joseph*: Earl Weatherford. *Reuben*: Robert Warren Bentley. *Shimon*: Noel Cravat. *Levi*: Paul Hammond. *Judah*: Joseph Macaulay. *Issachar*: Starr West Jones. *Zebulon*: Kurt Kasznar. *Dan*: Carl Formes. *Naphtali*: Edward Fisher. *Gad*: Leonard Mence. *Asher*: Edward Vermonti. *The Trader Angels*: Edward Kane, Ben Cutler, John Uppman, Albert Cazentre, Harold Sternberg. JOSEPH IN EGYPT. *Benjamin*: Walter Elliott. *The Steward*: Blake Scott. *The Juggler*: Florence Meyer.

Act 2. MOSES IN EGYPT. *Moses*: Samuel Goldenberg. *Miriam*: Lotte Lenya. *The Taskmaster*: Raymond Miller. *A Hebrew Slave*: Paul Marion. *Aaron*: Noel Cravat. *Elders of Israel*: Leslie Austen, Edward Fisher, Carl Formes, Harry Hammill, Starr West Jones, Kurt Kasznar, Leonard Mence, Cassius C. Quimby, Gustv Stryker, Edward Vermonti. IN THE WILDERNESS. *The Adversary's Follower*: Benjamin Zemach. *The Priestess of the Golden Calf*: Florence Meyer. *Joshua*: Robert Bentley. *White Angels*: Edward Kane, John Uppman. *The Angel of Death*: Joseph Macaulay. *Soul of Moses*: Tommy Mott.

Act 3. RUTH. *Ruth*: Katherine Carrington. *Naomi*: Bertha Kunz-Baker. *Boaz*: Ralph Jameson. *Head Reaper*: Kurt Kasznar. *Dancers at the Wedding*: Lil Liandre, Janet Janov, Frances Hellman, Ruth Nisenson. SAUL. *King Saul*: Walter Gilbert. *Samuel*: Bennett Challis. *Jonathan*: Hal Kingsley. *David*: Earl Weatherford. *A Henchman*: Fred Barrie. *David's Comrade*: Paul Hammond. *The Witch of Endor*: Lotte Lenya. DAVID. *King David*: Earl Weatherford. *Bath-Sheba*: Rosamund Pinchot. *Uriah*: Raymond Miller. *The Dark Angel*: Joseph Macaulay. *A Courtier*: Fred Barrie. *A Sentinel*: Starr West Jones. *The Ghost of Ruth*: Katherine Carrington. SOLOMON. *King Solomon*: John Uppman. THE SYNAGOGUE. *The Ghost of Rachel*: Sarah Osnath-Halevy. *The Voice*: Tommy Mott. *The King's Messenger*: Starr West Jones.

Dancers: Maia Airoff, Herbert Alani, Louise Allen, Nelson Barclift, Ida Bildner, Sophie Brent, Eva Dainova, Henry Day, Marguerite de Anquera, William Elliott, Blanche Evan, Jules Flier, Elizabeth Friend, Marie Guttman, Anita Gorin, Frances Hellman, William Howell, Janet Janov, Lil Liandre, Victorie Moussaieff, Alexander Lazuk, Lou Lief, Paul Leon, Betty Lind, William M. Miller, Ruth Nisenson, Doris Ostroff, Mary Perrine, Ruth Ross, Ethel Selwyn, Sylvia Shane, Marian Siwek, Ruth Stromberg, Lydia Tarnova, Maxene Trevor. *Servants, Slaves, Soldiers, Israelites, Reapers, Archers, Bride's Maids, Priests, etc.*: Misses Bernbaum, Bliss, Boone, Castle, Coates, Cooper, Cubitt, Curtiss, Druce, Heller, Hellman, Kubert, Lester, Lyons, Paduit, Petcheski, Quimby, Reilly Dewey, Romaine, Saunders, Seranne, Woodfin. Messrs. Adams, Alsop, Arndt, Bowden, Brock, Brooke, Budd, Burns, Beech, Chain, Clarke, Berwick, Dassori, Davis, Fuente, Dickens, Donahue, Ferguson, Firestone, H. Fisher, J. C. Fisher, Foote, Frank, Gardner, Gompers, B. Gordon, S. Gordon, Graves, Gray, Grimshaw, Haas, Halperin, Hare, Heure, Hinkley, Holmes, Jovanovitsch, Johnson, Kosoff, Leffler, Loeb, Lynch, Mahra, Martin, Merrill, Michael, Morgan, Murray, Nason, Nelson, O'Connell, Prince, Putnam, Rand, Reppetti, Richards, Rowland, Samuylow, Schein, Seymour, Shannon, Sheehy, Shem, Sherry, Shipman, Simons, Slocum, Stange, Stevens, Sullivan, Tandberg, Thomas, Thompson, Thoir, Waxman, Zwrit.

Prologue: A Synagogue.

Act 1, Scene 1: Abraham. *Scene 2*: Jacob and Rachel. *Scene 3*: Joseph and His Brothers. *Scene 4*: Joseph in Egypt.

Act 2, Scene 1: Moses in Egypt. *Scene 2*: In the Wilderness.

Act 3, Scene 1: The Synagogue. *Scene 2*: Ruth. *Scene 3*: Saul. *Scene 4*: David. *Scene 5*: Solomon. *Scene 6*: The Synagogue.

MUSICAL NUMBERS[33]
"Promise"
"Song of Miriam"
"The Dance of the Golden Calf"
"Song of Ruth"
"David's Psalm"
"The March to Zion"
"Duet of Rachel and Jacob"
"Sacrifice of Isaac"
"Story of Joseph"
Finale, Act 2 (Moses' Death)

1937.02   NAUGHTY NAUGHT '00

A Musical Drama of Life at Yale in Three Acts, 10 Scenes. Book by John Van Antwerp [Jerrold Krimsky]. Music by Richard Lewine. Lyrics by Ted Fetter. Directed by Morgan Lewis. Settings by Eugene Dunkel. Costumes by Eaves. Music director, Howard Johnson. Orchestrations by Ben Ludlow. Produced by John and Jerrold Krimsky. Opened 23 January 1937 at the American Music Hall and closed 30 May 1937 after 128 performances.[34]

CAST (in order of appearance): *P. deQuincy Devereux*: ALEXANDER CLARK. *Spunky*: Percy Helton. *Frank Plover*: BARTLETT ROBINSON. *Jack Granville*: LESLIE LITOMY. *Stub*: Phil Eppens. *Fred*: Howard Fischer. *Claire Granville*: ELEANOR PHELPS. *Jim Pawling*: Alan Handley. *Joe*: Lee Berkman. *Tom*: Douglas Rowland. *Bartender*: HARRY MEEHAN. *Tough*: Isham Keith. *Cathleen*: Gerrie Worthing. *Pugsy*: Howard Sullivan. *A Student*: Kermit Love.
Gibson Girls: Eleanora Dixon, Anna Erskine, Julie Hartwell, Jane Hammond, Barbara Hunter, Lucille Rich.

Act 1, Scene 1: Yale Campus. *Scene 2*: Frank and Jack's Dormitory Room.

Act 2, Scene 1: Frank and Jack's Dormitory Room. *Scene 2*: Moriarty's Saloon. *Scene 3*: Railroad Station, New Haven.

Act 3, Scene 1: Boathouse near Thames. *Scene 2*: The River Bank. *Scene 3*: Boathouse near Thames. *Scene 4*: The River Bank. *Scene 5*: At the Race.

ACT 1
Scene 1
"Goodbye Girls, Hello Yale"
   Freshmen
Scene 2
"Naughty-Naught"
   Seniors
"Love Makes the World Go Round"
   E. Phelps, B. Robinson, Chorus
ACT 2
Scene 1
"Love Makes the World Go Round" (reprise)
   E. Phelps
Scene 2
"Zim Zam Zee"
   G. Worthing, Men
Scene 3
"Pull the Boat for Eli"
   Students, Girls
Olio: "Coney-by-the-Sea"
ACT 3
Scene 5
Finale
   Entire Company

---

[33]Musical numbers not listed in program. Above list prepared from published text (Viking Press, New York, 1936). Lyrics for the Rachel scene, the Goliath Ballad and the Witch of Endor scene by Charles Alan.
[34]Performed seven nights a week, no matinees. Played a return engagement 24 January 1939 at the American Music Hall for 42 performances.

FREDERIKA

1937.03

An Operetta in Three Acts, a Prologue and 5 Scenes. Music by Franz Lehár. (Original German libretto to "Friederike" by Ludwig Herzer and Fritz Löhner-Beda.) American adaptation[35] by Edward Eliscu. Entire production supervised and staged by Hassard Short. Settings by Watson Barratt. Costumes by William Weaver. Choreography by Chester Hale. Musical director, Hilding Anderson. Orchestrations by Hilding Anderson and William Challis. Trio Dance, Acts 1 and 2 arranged by George Dobbs. Produced by the Messrs. Shubert. Opened 4 February 1937 at the Imperial Theatre and closed 1 May 1937 after 95 performances.

CAST (in order of appearance): *Prologue: Miss Hotchkiss:* EDITH GRESHAM. *Mrs. Thorne:* EDITH KING. *Mr. Linker:* George Dobbs. *Mrs. Linker:* Mary Jane Barrett. *Jessica Thorne:* Mildred Schroeder. *Arthur Benson:* William Newgord. *Dr. Bauer:* Wheeler Dryden. *Guide:* Fred Sherman.
Play: Parson Brion: J. Arthur Young. *Magda Brion:* Rose Winter. *Salomea:* DORIS PATSTON. *Postillion:* Fred Sherman. *Countess Scholl:* Ulita Torgerson. *Frederika:* HELEN GLEASON. *Students* (6): *Jung-Stilling:* GEORGE DOBBS. *Meyer:* CHARLES COLUMBUS. *Engelbach:* William Newgord. *Lenz:* ERNEST TRUEX. *Weyland:* GEORGE TRABERT. *Goethe:* DENNIS KING. *Herr Gruenwald:* Earl McDonald. *Captain Knebel:* ARTHUR VINTON. *Countess Hahn:* EDITH KING. *Liselotte:* Diana Gaylen. *Lackey:* Wesley Bender. *Count Hahn:* Wheeler Dryden. *Hortense:* Mary Jane Barrett. *Karl August, Duke of Weimar:* Ralph Magelsson. (*Premiere Danseuse:* Alyce Chapell.)
Girls: Marvel Conheney, Marilyn Duane, Mary Rhodes, Dorothy Forsythe, Clara Waring, Katherine von den Knesebeck, Dolly Miller, Patricia Caron, Alicia Parnahay, Bette Davis. *Boys:* Roger Gerry, Lipman Duckat, Frederick Ratliff, Ted Daniels, Gene Greenlaw, William Parker, Walter Lewis, Jack Phillips, George Sampson, Wesley Bender. *Dancers:* Betty Gour, Harriet Henning, Frances Rands, Joan Engel, Dorothy Hess, Nancy Knott, Mae Sigler, James Ryan, Vernon Hammer, Edward Murray, Jack Barrett, Todd Bolender, B. Batleroff [Boris Butleroff], Sonny Quinn.

Act 1, Scene 1: Prologue. Ante Room, Palace at Weimer. *Time, the present. Scene 2:* The Parsonage at Sesenheim, 1771.

Act 2: Countess Scholl's Salon, Strasburg. The following year.

Act 3, Scene 1: Goethe's Study. Eight years later. *Scene 2:* The Parsonage. The next evening.

ACT 1
"Out in the Sun"
    D. Patston, C. Columbus, G. Dobbs, Ensemble
"I Asked My Heart"
    H. Gleason
"Rising Star"
    D. King, G. Trabert, Ensemble
"One"
    H. Gleason, Girls
"Rose in the Heather"
    D. King
Finale

ACT 2
Ballet—"The Shepherd"
    A. Chapell
"Stormy Love"
    H. Gleason, G. Trabert, Ensemble
"A Word to Remind You"
    D. King, Girls
"One" (reprise)
    D. King, H. Gleason
"Jealousy Begins at Home"
    D. Patston, G. Dobbs, C. Columbus, Ensemble
"Why Did He Kiss My Heart Awake?"
    H. Gleason
Finale

ACT 3
Interlude—"The Bane of Man"
    E. Truex, C. Columbus, G. Dobbs, W. Newgord
"One" (reprise)
    H. Gleason
Finale

---

[35]An earlier English adaptation by Adrian Ross and Harry Pepper was presented in London in 1930.

BABES IN ARMS

1937.05

A Musical Comedy in Two Acts, 14 Scenes. Book by Richard Rodgers and Lorenz Hart. Music by Richard Rodgers. Lyrics by Lorenz Hart. Staged by Robert Sinclair. Choreography by George Balanchine. Settings by Raymond Sovey. Costumes by Helene Pons. Music director, Gene Salzer. Orchestrations by Hans Spialek. Produced and supervised by Dwight Deere Wiman. Opened 14 April 1937 at the Sam S. Shubert Theatre, moved 25 October 1937 to the Majestic Theatre, and closed 18 December 1937 after 289 performances.

CAST (in order of appearnce): *Maizie LaMar:* Ethel Intropidi. *Dan LaMar:* Jere Delaney. *Val LaMar:* RAY HEATHERTON. *Nat Blackstone:* George E. Mackay. *Emma Blackstone:* Aileen Poe. *Marshall Blackstone:* Alfred Drake. *Billie Smith:* MITZI GREEN. *Sheriff Reynolds:* George Watts. *Gus Fielding:* Rolly Pickert. *Booker Vanderpool:* Kenneth Wilkins. *Pinkie:* Bob Fishelson. *Lee Calhoun:* Dana Hardwick. *Sam Reynolds:* Ray McDonald. *Dolores Reynolds:* Grace McDonald. *Lincoln Vanderpool:* LeRoy James. *Peter:* DUKE McHALE. *Baby Rose:* WYNN MURRAY. *Ivor DeQuincy:* HAROLD NICHOLAS. *Irving DeQuincy:* FAYARD NICHOLAS. *Rene Flambeau:* Aljan de Loville. *Phil McCabe:* Alvin Kerr. *Dr. Snyder:* George E. Mack. *Bobby:* Bobby Lane. *Elenore:* Elenore Tennis. *At the Steinways:* (Edgar) FAIRCHILD and (Adam) CARROLL.

The Gang (playing themselves): Gloria Franklin, Mitzi Dahl, Jean Owens, Ted Gary, Don Liberto, Libby Bennett, Verna Cedars, Mickey Herson, Marjorie Jane, Betty Lee, Connie Leslie, Audrey Palmer, Claire Harvey, Davenie Watson, Stella Clausen, Tania Clell, Eleanore Fiata, Georgia Hiden, Gedda Petry, Ursula Seiler. Roy Adler, Buddy Allen, Mickey Alvarez, Jay Bee, Jack Stanton, Dan Dailey, Bronson Dudley, Alex Courtney, Clifton Darling, James Gillis, Robert Rounseville.

In Lee Calhoun's Follies: The Singer: WYNN MURRAY. *The Child:* Douglas Perry. *The High Priest:* ALFRED DRAKE. *The Priestess:* Elenore Tennis. *The Nubians:* THE NICHOLAS BROTHERS (Harold, Fayard). *The Acrobat:* Bobby Lane. *The Specialty Dancers:* MITZI GREEN, DUKE McHALE.

Act 1, Scene 1: The Kitchen of the LaMars' House, Seaport, Long Island. *Scene 2:* A Street. *Scene 3:* The Oscar W. Hemingway Post of the American Legion. *Scene 4:* A Discarded Railway Box Car. *Scene 5:* The Calhoun Living Room. *Scene 6:* The Back Door of the LaMar House. *Scene 7:* The Stage of the Old Barn Theatre. *Scene 8:* The Wings of the Old Barn Theatre. *Scene 9:* The Stage of the Old Barn Theatre (during "Lee Calhoun's Follies").

Act 2, Scene 1: A Stable on the Work Farm. *Scene 2:* Ballet, "Peter's Journey." *Scene 3:* The LaMars' Field. *Scene 4:* A Bedroom in the LaMar House. *Scene 5:* Solarium of Seaport Yacht Club.

ACT 1
Scene 1
"Where or When"
    M. Green, R. Heatherton
Scene 2
"Babes in Arms"
    M. Green, R. Heatherton, A. Drake, The Gang
Scene 3
"I Wish I Were in Love Again"
    G. MacDonald, R. Pickert
Scene 4
"All Dark People"
    Nicholas Brothers
Scene 5
"Way Out West"
    W. Murray, A. Courtney, C. Darling, J. Gillis, R. Rounseville
Scene 8
"My Funny Valentine"
    M. Green
Scene 9
"Johnny One-Note"
    W. Murray, The Gang

ACT 2
Scene 1
"Imagine"
    W. Murray, A. Courtney, C. Darling, J. Gillis, R. Rounseville
"All at Once"
    M. Green, R. Heatherton
Scene 2
"Peter's Journey" (Ballet)
    The Prince: D. McHale. *His Attendants:* K. Wilkins, L. James. *Rockefeller:* R.

[AU: Change order of Blonde Marie and Babes in Arms? Their catlog numbers, respectively, are 1937.04 and 1937.05, but you have Blonde Marie coming second.]

Pickert. *The Mermaid*: E. Tennis. *Greta Garbo*: G. Petry. *Marlene Dietrich*: U. Seiler. *Clark Gable*: T. Gary.

Scene 3

"The Lady Is a Tramp"
    M. Green

Scene 5

"You Are So Fair"
    G. MacDonald, R. Pickert, T. Gary, M. Dahl, D. McHale, J. Owens

Finale
    (Entire Company)

1937.04   BLONDE MARIE

A Dance Comedy in Two Acts, 8 Scenes. Story and staging by Trudi Schoop. Music by Paul Schoop. Costumes by Oscar Schlemmer. At the two Steinway pianos, Lothar Perl and Paul Schoop. Produced by Sol Hurok. Opened 27 April 1937 at the Longacre Theatre and closed 2 May 1937 after 8 performances.

CAST: TRUDI SCHOOP and Her Company: Katta Sterna, Otto Ulbricht, Meta Krahn, Edith Carola, Ralph Ray, Werner Herrmann, Marti Muffler, Marin Raae, Didi Lederer, Hilde Palmer, Niels Bjorn Larsen, Jenny Graf, Ellen Liy, Gitta Wallerstein.

Act 1, Scene 1: The Meyer Home. *Scene 2*: A Night Club. *Scene 3*: A Rehearsal Hall. *Scene 4*: A Beauty Parlor. *Scene 5*: The Premiere of the Operetta, Blonde Marie.

Act 2, Scene 1: The Villa. *Scene 2*: The Portrait Painter's Studio. *Scene 3*: The Picture Exhibition.

ACT 1

Scene 1

    Mrs. Meyer: K. Sterna. *Mr. Meyer*: O. Ulbricht. *Their Daughter*: M. Krahn. *The Servant Girl*: T. Schoop. *The Guests*: E. Carola, R. Ray, W. Herrmann.

Scene 2

    The Landlady: M. Muffler. *The Waitress*: T. Schoop. *Chorus Ladies*: E. Carola, M. Raae, D. Lederer, H. Palmer. *Card Players*: N. B. Larsen, W. Herrmann, J. Graff. *The Loving Couple*: E. Liy, G. Wallerstein. *The Celebrated Tenor*: R. Ray. *Two Fakirs (genuine)*: M. Krahn, O. Ulbricht.

Scene 3

    The Director: O. Ulbricht. *The Manager*: N. B. Larsen. *The Pianist*: G. Wallerstein. *The Dancer*: M. Raae. *The Tenor*: R. Ray. *The Singer*: E. Carola. *The Hoarse Soubrette*: M. Krahn. *Chorus Girl*: T. Schoop. *Chorus Singers*.

Scene 4

    The Hairdresser: K. Sterna. *The Assistants*: E. Liy, M. Raae, O. Ulbricht, N. B. Larsen. *The Customers*: M. Krahm, E. Carola. *Marie, a Lady*: T. Schoop.

Scene 5

Blonde Marie, an operetta with music by Paul Schoop.

    A Vengeful Princess: K. Sterna. *An Officer of the Guards*, tenor: R. Ray. *Eleano, his fiancée*, singer: *The Lieutenant*, buffo: O. Ulbricht. *Blonde Marie*, soubrette: T. Schoop. *The Dancer*: M. Raae. *Chorus, Guards, Ballet*.

ACT 2

Scene 1

    Marie: T. Schoop. *Her Husband*: O. Ulbricht. *Their Child*: M. Raae. *Governess*: G. Wallerstein. *Nurse*: M. Krahn. *Butler*: W. Herrmann. *Maid*: D. Lederer. *The Young Painter*: N. B. Larsen. *The Exclusive Guests*.

Scene 2

    Marie, the Mother: T. Schoop. *Her Child*: M. Raae. *The Young Painter*: N. B. Larsen.

Scene 3

    Marie: T. Schoop. *Her Husband*: O. Ulbricht. *The Young Painter*: N. B. Larsen. *Newspaper Men*: E. Carola, G. Wallerstein, W. Herrmann, R. Ray, N. B. Larsen. *Spectators*.

1937.06   ORCHIDS PREFERRED

A Musical Comedy in Two Acts, 11 Scenes. Book and lyrics by Fred Herendeen. (Based on his play "Taxi Fare.") Music by Dave Stamper. (Additional music and lyrics by Henry Russell and Morry Olsen.) Staged by Alexander Leftwich. Dances by Robert Sanford. Settings by Frederick Fox. Costumes by Jenkins. Music director, Louis Gress. Orchestrations by Paul Sprosty. Produced by Charles H. Abramson. Opened 11 May 1937 at the Imperial Theatre and closed 15 May 1937 after 7 performances.

CAST (in order of appearance): *Gertrude Devereaux*: HILDA KNIGHT. *Violet Manning*: FRANCES THRESS. *Billie*: Doris Vinton. *Elsie*: Elsie Edwards. *Margie*: Margie Conradi. *Sally*: Lillian Carson. *Edithe*: Violet Carson. *Sunny*: Lucille Rich. *Marion Brown*: VICKI CUMMINGS. *Bubbles Wilson*: EDDIE FOY, JR. *Bobbie*: James Babbitt. *Doorman*: William Chalmers. *Penelope Halchester*: Celia Krebs. *Evangeline Landreth*: Julie Sterling. *Henry Warrenton*: Jack Clifford. *Hortense Chatfield*: Frew Donald. *Mary Ann Miller*: Audrey Elliott. *Lillian Mahoney*: BENAY VENUTA. *Chauffeur*: Bill Pillick. *Footman*: Jack Curry. *Helene Windsor*: Fay Long. *Goldie*: Phyllis Avery. *Dr. Sommers*: Bob Borger. *Dorothy Charters*: Verna Long. *Teddy Barber*: Henry Russell. *Henry Monroe*: Bob Rice. *Eve*: Verda Twiford. *Eva*: Dilys Miles. *Evy*: Helen Martin. *June*: Joanne. *July*: Jules Walton. *Richard Hope, Jr.*: John Donaldson. *Elmer Traum*: JACK WHITTRIDGE. *Elizabeth Hope*: Helen Leftwich. *Richard Hope, Sr.*: LESLIE AUSTIN. (And THE MEN OF GOTHAM.)

Act 1, Scene 1: A Suite in the Waldmore. *Scene 2*: The Motor Entrance. *Scene 3*: A Corridor of the Crystal Bar. *Scene 4*: The Crystal Bar. *Scene 5*: The Corridor. *Scene 6*: Dick's Apartment.

Act 2, Scene 1: The Walk in the Waldmore. *Scene 2*: A Passageway. *Scene 3*: The Solarium. *Scene 4*: The Emergency Exit. *Scene 5*: The Gardens.

ACT 1

"I'm Leaving the Bad Girls for Good"
    E. Foy, Jr.

"Selling a Song"
    B. Venuta

"Sub-Debs' First Fling"
    Joanne, J. Walton

"The Dying Swan"
    J. Whittridge

"The Three R's"
    Men of Gotham
    (*Music and Lyrics by* Henry Russell and Morry Olsen.)

"A Million Dollars"
    V. Cummings, L. Austin

"Eddy-Mac"
    B. Venuta, E. Foy, Jr.

"A Boy, a Girl, a Moon"
    V. Cummings, L. Austin

ACT 2

"Strictly Confidential"
    E. Foy, Jr., J. Whittridge

"Minsky"
    Men of Gotham
    (*Music and Lyrics by* Henry Russell and Morry Olsen.)
    "Minsky" (reprise)
    B. Venuta, E. Foy, Jr.

"A Boy, a Girl, a Moon" (reprise)
    V. Cummings, L. Austin

"My Lady's Hand"
    V. Cummings, J. Whittridge

"Man About Town"
    H. Knight

"Paying Off"
    E. Foy, Jr., Pages

"The Echo of a Song"
    Men of Gotham, Joanne, J. Walton

"What Are You Going to Do About Love?"
    B. Venuta

"A Million Dollars" (reprise)
    Entire Company

1937.07   SEA LEGS

A Nautical Musical (Comedy) in Two Acts. Book and lyrics by Arthur Swanstrom. Based on the play "The Cat Came Back" by Lawrence E. Johnson, Beula King (and Avery Hopwood). Music by Michael H. Cleary. Book staged by Bertram Harrison. Dances staged by Johnny Mattison. Settings by Mabel Buell. Costumes by Brooks, Jay-Thorp, Charles Chrisdie Company, Grace Acuri. Lighting by Alfred Cheney Johnston. Music director, Frank Cork. Orchestrations by Joseph Jordan. Produced by Albert Bannister and J. Edmund Byrne. Opened 18 May 1937 at the Mansfield Theatre and closed 29 May 1937 after 15 performances.

CAST (in order of appearance): *Captain Nordstrom* of the Yacht *'Pixie'*: CHARLES KING. *Mrs. Alice Wytcherly*, the owner: MARY SARGENT. *George W. Tuttle*, a wealthy suitor: WALTER N. GREAZA. *Val Tuttle, Jr.*, his nephew: DEREK FAIRMAN. *Mildred*, Mrs. Wytcherly's maid: ROSIE MORAN. *James McCracken*, the ship's steward: ROSCOE ATES. *Bill Halliday*, a stowaway: CHARLES COLLINS. *Isobel West*, Mrs. Wytcherly's niece: KATHRYN MAYFIELD. *Barbara Deeds*, an artist: DOROTHY STONE. *Deedee*, a girl friend: Deedee. *Pat*, ditto: Patricia Knight.

Ben Yost's Catalina Eight: Dave Sorin, Al Terry, Henry Rudisell, Robert Arnold, Earl Mason, Park Caperton, George Henry Jerstad, Arthur Craig. *The Girls*: Deedee, Patricia Knight, Ronnie Beck, Mary Brent, Jeane Beryl, Althea Elder, Rita Carmen, Maude Carroll, Lynne Carter, Lorraine Latham, Patricia Martin, Barbara Mailman, Helen Sanford, Patsy Schenck, Willis Stiles, Diane Wentworth, Georgina Yaeger.

Act 1: Sun Deck of the Yacht *Pixie* lying off Catalina Island. Friday at Noon.

Act 2: Same. The following evening.

ACT 1

"Off on a Week-End Cruise"
　　C. King, M. Sargent, Sailors, Guests

"The Opposite Sex"
　　C. King, Deedee, P. Knight, Girls

Specialty
　　R. Moran

"Infatuation"
　　C. Collins, K. Mayfield, Ben Yost's Catalina Eight, Girls

"A Dark Stranger"
　　D. Stone, Ben Yost's Catalina Eight

"Looks Like Love Is Here to Stay"
　　R. Ates, R. Moran

"Ten O'Clock Town"
　　C. Collins, D. Stone, Girls, Ben Yost's Catalina Eight

"Chasing Henry"
　　Entire Company

"Ten O'Clock Town" (reprise)
　　Entire Company

ACT 2

"Infatuation" (reprise)
　　Ben Yost's Catalina Eight

"Catalina"
　　C. King, Deedee, P. Knight, Girls, Ben Yost's Catalina Eight

"Touched in the Head and Smitten in the Heart"
　　C. Collins, D. Stone

"Wake Me Up a Star"
　　K. Mayfield, Ben Yost's Catalina Eight, Ballet, Deedee

"The Opposite Sex" (reprise)
　　C. Collins

Finale
　　Entire Cast

George M. Cohan, Austin Marshall, and Joy Hodges in I'D RATHER BE RIGHT (Photo: Vandamm Studio)   Billy Rose Theatre Collection, New York Public Library for the Performing Arts

1937–1938 SEASON

1937.08   THE CRADLE WILL ROCK

A Play in Music (Musical Drama) in One Act, 10 Scenes[1]. Book, music and lyrics by Marc Blitzstein. Directed by Orson Welles. Conductor, Lehman Engel. Piano, Marc Bliztstein. Sets and costumes by Ed Schruers[2]. Lighting by (Abe) Feder. Produced by the WPA Federal Theatre Project 891 (John Houseman, producer). Opened 16 June 1937 at the Venice Theatre and closed 1 July 1937 after 19 performances. Re-opened 5 December 1937 at the Mercury Theatre for 4 Sunday evening performances; transferred 3 January 1938 to the Windsor Theatre under the commercial auspices of Sam H. Grisman[3], moved 28 February 1938 to the Mercury Theatre, and closed 9 April 1938 after 108 performances.

CAST (in order of appearance): *The Moll*: OLIVE STANTON. *A Gent*: George Fairchild. *A Dick*: Guido Alexander. *A Cop*: Robert Worth. *Members of the Liberty Committee (6)*: *Editor Daily*: Bert Weston. *Prexie*: Hansford Wilson. *Yasha*: Edward Fuller. *Dauber*: Warren Goddard. *Doctor Specialist*: Frank Marvel. *Reverend Salvation*: Edward Hemmer. *Druggist*: JOHN ADAIR. *Mr. Mister*: WILL GEER. *Mrs. Mister*: PEGGY COUDRAY. *Junior Mister*: Hiram Sherman. *Sister Mister*: Dulce Fox. *Maid*: Josephine Heatham. *Steve*: Howard Bird. *Bugs*: Geoffrey Powers. *Gus*: George Fairchild. *Sadie*: Marion Grant Rudley. *Larry*: HOWARD DA SILVA. *Professor Trixie*: Hiram Sherman. *Professor Scoot*: George Smithfield. *Reporters*: Robert Hopkins, Huntley Weston, Jack Mealy. *Ella Hammer*: BLANCHE COLLINS.

Chorus: Henry Colker, Rose Cooper, Georgia Empey, Harriet Flammang, Mary Kukawski, Donald MacMillan, Jane D. Madison, Lillian Sheldon, Paul Varro, Ann Voorhees, Wallace Acton, Peter Barbier, Cora Burler, Solomon Goldstein, Edith Groome, Don Harwood, Frank Kelly, Paula Laurence, Elizabeth Malone, Aurelia Molnar, Walter Palm, Myron Paulson, Louis Pennewell, Helena Rapport, Henry Russelle, Nina Salama, Bernard Savage, Harry Singer, Raymond Tobin, Charles Uday, Richie White, Jay Wilson.

(*Scene*: Steeltown, U.S.A. during a union drive.)

Scene 1: Streetcorner. *Scene 2*: Nightcourt. *Scene 3*: Mission. *Scene 4*: Lawn of Mr. Mister's Home. *Scene 5*: Drugstore. *Scene 6*: Hotellobby. *Scene 7*: Nightcourt. *Scene 8*: Facultyroom. *Scene 9*: Dr. Specialist's Office. *Scene 10*: Nightcourt.

MUSICAL NUMBERS[4]

Scene 1

   "Moll's Song" (I'm Checkin' Home Now)
      O. Stanton

   "Moll and Gent"
      O. Stanton, G. Fairchild

   "Moll and Dick"
      O. Stanton, G. Alexander

Scene 2

   "Moll and Druggist"
      O. Stanton, J. Adair

   "Oh, What a Filthy Night Court!"
      B. Weston, H. Wilson, E. Fuller, W. Goddard, F. Marvel, E. Hemmer

Scene 3

   "Mrs. Mister and Reverend Salvation"
      P. Coudray, E. Hemmer

---

[1]No intermission for Venice Theatre performances; for Windsor Theatre run an intermission was added after Scene 6.

[2]Sets and costumes billed but not used.

[3]For the commercial transfer, the cast remained the same except for the following changes: *Cop*: Robert Farnsworth. *Reverend Salvation*: Charles Niemeyer. *Dauber*: Jules Schmidt. *President Prexy*: LeROI OPERTI. *Professor Scoot*: Charles Niemeyer. *Mr. Mister*: RALPH McBANE. *Junior Mister*: Maynard Holmes. Also the following additional role: *Clerk, Reporter, Professor Mamie*: MARC BLITZSTEIN. *Chorus* (reduced in number to the following): Larri Lauria, Lilia Hallums, Harry Carter, Alma Dixon, Ralph Ranson, Robert Clarke, Billi Bodkin, Josephine Heathman, Lucile Schly.

[4]Scene and Song list prepared from published text (Random House, New York, 1938), as they do not appear in the programs.

Scene 4

   "Croon Spoon"
      H. Sherman, D. Fox

   "The Freedom of the Press"
      B. Weston, W. Geer

   "Let's Do Something"
      H. Sherman, D. Fox

   "Honolulu"
      E. Hemmer, H. Sherman, W. Geer, D. Fox

Scene 5

   "Drugstore Scene"
      J. Adair, H. Bird, G. Powers

   "Gus and Sadie Love Song"
      G. Fairchild, M. G. Rudley

Scene 6

   "The Rich"
      E. Fuller, W. Goddard

   "Ask Us Again"
      E. Fuller, W. Goddard, P. Coudray

   "Art for Art's Sake"
      E. Fuller, W. Goddard

Scene 7

   "Nickel Under the Foot"
      O. Stanton

   "Leaflets"
      H. da Silva

   "The Cradle Will Rock"
      H. da Silva

Scene 8

   "Faculty Room Scene"
      W. Geer, H. Wilson, H. Sherman, L. Badia, G. Smithfield

Scene 9

   "Doctor and Ella"
      B. Collins

   "Joe Worker"
      B. Collins

Scene 10

   Finale/"The Cradle Will Rock" (reprise)
      H. da Silva, Ensemble

1937.09   SWING IT

A Musical Comedy in Two Acts, 24 Scenes. Book by Cecil Mack [R. C. MacPherson]. Music by Milton Reddie and Eubie Blake. Lyrics by Milton Reddie and Cecil Mack. Staged by Cecil Mack and Jack Mason. Scenery designed by Walter Walden and Victor Zanoff. Costumes by Maxine and Alexander Jones. Dances and ensembles by Benny Johnson and Miriam Schiller. Music direction and orchestrations by Lorenzo Calduel [Caldwell], assisted by Harry Ferguson and Paul Heimberger. Produced by the Variety Unit of the WPA Federal Theatre Project (Frank Merlin, producer). Opened 22 July 1937 at the Adelphi Theatre and closed 1 September 1937 after 36 performances[5].

CAST: *Jake Frye*, Captain of the *Liza Jane* : EDWARD FRYE. *Gabby*, First Mate of the *Liza Jane* : GEORGE BOOKER. *Skadmoose*, First Deckhand of the *Liza Jane* : Ernest Mickens. *Miranda*, Frye's Best Half: Blanche Young. *Nate Smith*, Captain of the *Susan Belle* : Walter Crumbley. *Bud*, First Mate of the *Susan Belle* : Joe Loomis. *Sadie*, Captain Smith's Daughter: FRANCES EVERETT. *Mame*, A Gal from Memphis: GENORA ENGLISH. *Ginger*, Heading for Harlem: JAMES MORDECAI. *Steve*, A Gambling Man: Sonny Thompson. *Bob*, Steve's Partner: SHERMAN DIRKSON. *Rusty*: Henry Jines. *Dusty*: James Green. *Chin Chin*, Chinese Cook: Al Young. *Su San*, A Chinese Girl: Dorothy Turner. *Jamaica Joe*, Hot-Corn Man: John Fortune. *"Mom" Brown*, Fried-Chicken Vendor: Cora Parks. *Smoky*, Proprietor of the Cockroach Cafe: Richard Webb. *Sonny*, Smokey's Yes Man: Leo Bailey. *Gladys*, Cabaret Queen: OLENA WILLIAMS. *Ethel*, An Entertainer: MARION BRANTLEY. *Bill*, A Piano Plunker: Norman Barksdale. *Swipes*, Bartender: Lawrence Lomax. *Flatfut*, Levee Cop: Frank Jackson. *Sheriff*: Al Young. *Jasper*, Plantation Foreman: JAMES BOXWELL. *Amy*, Harlem Society Reporter: Anita Bush.

---

[5]Performed six nights a week, no matinees.

Roustabouts, River Gobs, Plantation Workers, Hoofers, Harmonizers: Ladies'
Ensemble: Ollie Schoonmaker, Dorothy Turner, Dorothy Gee, Frederika Phoenix,
Grace Driver, Fannie Suber, Ruth LaMarr, Roberta Lowery, Viola Smith, Edna Ricks,
Goldie Martien, Mabel Hamilton, Edna Deas, Bennie Johnson, Bobby Jackson. *Mens'*
Ensemble: Joe Northern, Herbert Brown, Ralph Northern, James B. McRiley, Sam
Owens, George St. Clair, Frank Jackson, Cliff Carter, Ed Hall, Nat Wilson, J. Flash
Riley, Allen George, Billy Young.

Act 1: A small river-town in the South in the present. *Scene 1*: Levee. *Scene 2*: Another
Part of the Levee. *Scene 3*: Levee. *Scene 4*: Sunflower Lane. *Scene 5*: In Front of the
Cockroach Cafe. *Scene 6*: Inside the Cafe. *Scene 7*: In Front of the Cockroach Cafe.
Scene 8: A Country Road. *Scene 9*: The Plantation. *Scene 10*: A Country Road. *Scene
11*: Another Part of the Levee. *Scene 12*: Levee.

Act 2: A Showboat anchored in the Harlem River, New York City. *Scene 1*: The Stage of
the Showboat. *Scene 2*: The Deck of the Showboat. *Scene 3*: The Stage of the
Showboat. *Scene 4*: Dance Specialty. *Scene 5*: Before the Curtain. *Scene 6*: The Stage
of the Showboat. *Scene 7*: The Deck of the Showboat. *Scene 8*: Dance Specialty. *Scene
9*: Before the Curtain. *Scene 10*: Behind the Curtain. *Scene 11*: Specialty. *Scene 12*:
Finale on Stage of Showboat.

ACT 1

Spiritual
J. Northern, H. Brown, R. Northern, J. McRiley

"Jollification" (Dance)
S. Owens, G. St. Clair, Ensemble

"The Susan Belle and *The Liza Jane"*
G. Booker, Ensemble

"What Do I Want With Love?"
J. Mordecai
Eight Levee Chicks: O. Schoonmaker, D. Turner, D. Gee, F. Phoenix, G.
Driver, F. Suber, R. LaMarr, R. Lowery.

"If You Want to Know Who We Are" (Travesty à la Mikado)
F. Jackson, R. Northern, J. Northern, E. Mickens, L. Lomax, C. Carter, J.
McRiley, E. Hall, J. Boxwell, N. Barksdale

"It's the Truth in Me"
G. English, N. Wilson, H. Brown, N. Barksdale, J. Riley, A. George, B. Young

"Blah-Blah-Blah-Blah"
E. Frye, G. Booker

"Ain't We Got Love"
F. Everett, S. Dirkson, Dancing and Singing Ensembles

"Old Time Swing"
M. Brantley

"Shine"
J. Nortern, R. Northern, J. McRiley, H. Brown
(*Music by* Ford T. Dabney. *Lyrics by* Cecil Mack, Lew Brown.)

Dancing Waiter (Specialty)
H. Brown

"Green and Blue"
O. Williams

"By the Sweat of Your Brow"
J. Boxwell, Ensemble

"I Believe" (Spiritual)
Ensemble

"By the Sweat of Your Brow" (reprise)

"Captain, Mate and Crew"
E. Frye, G. Booker, Mens' Ensemble

Finale—"Farewell Dixieland"
Entire Company

ACT 2

"Sons and Daughters of the Sea"
R. Northern, E. Mickens, Singing Ensemble, Eight Dancing Girls led by B.
Johnson

Singing and Dancing Specialty
L. Bailey, R. Webb

"Levee Ladies"
Ensemble

Rhapsody in Rhythm
N. Wilson

"Huggin an' Muggin'"
G. English, J. Mordecai, Dancing and Singing Ensemble

"The Conspirators"
W. Crumbley, J. Loomis, A. Young

"Down With Frye"
W. Crumbley, J. Loomis, A. Young

"I Praise Sue"
J. Loomis

"Spirit of Rhythm"
B. Johnson

Jungle Episode

"Jungle Swing"
J. Boxwell

"Jungle Love"
Ensemble
Jungle Princess: F. Everett. *Her Suitor*: J. Riley. *Her Rival*: D. Turner. *Jungle
Maids*: O. Schoonmaker, D. Gee, F. Phoenix, R. Lowery, R. LaMarr, G.
Driver. *Jungle Warriors*: E. Hall, C. Carter, F. Jackson, L. Lomax. *Jungle
Drummers*: C. Johnson, R. Northern, J. Northern, N. Barksdale. *Jungle
Dancers*: H. Brown, A. George, E. Mickens, B. Young.

"Rhythm Is a Racket"
W. Thompson, S. Dirkson

Grand Finale—"Swing Wedding"
Master of Ceremonies: J. Mordecai. *First Groom*: S. Dirkson. *First Bride*: F.
Everett. *Father of the Bride*: W. Crumbley. *Aunts of the Groom*: G. Martien, M.
Hamilton, E. Ricks, V. Smith, C. Parks, B. Jackson. *Uncles of the Bride*: C.
Carter, J. McRiley, F. Jackson, E. Hall, L. Lomax, E. Mickens. *Groom's Men*: B.
Young, N. Barksdale, A. George, H. Brown, R. Northern, S. Owens.
Bridesmaids: D. Gee, G. Driver, R. Lowery, R. LaMarr, O. Schoonmaker. *The
other Bride and Groom (Chinese Variety)*: D. Turner, A. Young. *Another Bride
and Groom*: C. Johnson, J. Northern. *'She' Who Gives the Bride Away*: A. Bush.
He Who Ties the Knots: E. Frye. *Guests at the Wedding*: The Audience.

1937.10   # VIRGINIA

A Musical Play in Two Acts, 15 Scenes. Book by Laurence Stallings and
Owen Davis. Music by Arthur Schwartz. Lyrics by Albert Stillman. Staged
by Leon Leonidoff. Book directed by Edward Clark Lilley. Dances by
Florence Rogge. Music supervised by Don Voorhees. Settings by Lee
Simonson. Costumes by Irene Sharaff. Orchestrations by Ardon Cornwall,
Hans Spialek, Phil Wall, Will Vodery, Maurice Baron. Vocal arrangements
by Lee Montgomery and Ken Christie. Produced by the Center Theatre
under the direction of John Kenneth Hyatt. Opened 2 September 1937 at
the Center Theatre and closed 23 October 1937 after 60 performances.

CAST (in order of appearance): *Lady Agatha*: MONA BARRIE. *Captain Somerset,
A.D.C. to the Governor*: GORDON RICHARDS. *Captain Boyd*, of the Virginia
Rangers: LANSING HATFIELD. *Sir Guy Carleton*: DENNIS HOEY. *Fortesque*, of
Drury Lane: GENE LOCKHART. *Minnie Fortesque*: BERTHA BELMORE. *Sylvia
Laurence*: ANNE BOOTH. *Miranda*: AVIS ANDREWS. *Daphne*: Helen Carroll.
Phyllis: Esta Elman. *Major-Domo*: Tom Tempest. *His Excellency, Governor of the
Colony*: NIGEL BRUCE. *Scipio*: JOHN W. BUBBLES. *Hannibal*: FORD L. BUCK.
Colonel Richard Fairfax, of the Virginia Rangers: RONALD GRAHAM. *Stage
Doorman*: Tom Tempest. *Prima Ballerina of Drury Lane*: PATRICIA BOWMAN.
Premier Dancer of Drury Lane: Valia Valentinoff. *Town Crier*: Herbert Garstin. *A
Patriot*: John Ravold. *Players of the Fair*: *Puppet Master*: George Prentice. *Fire-eater*:
Ajax. *Jugglers*: James Evans and Company. *Children of the Gentry*: Peggy Romano,
Doris Fischer, Billy Redfield, Charles Timpson. *Slave Children*: Bubblesette Leacock, Clarence Beasley,
Charles Timpson.
Corps du Ballet: Virginia Browning, Tania Clell, Gail Grant, Marie Grimaldi,
Hermione Hawkinson, Poly Iven, Lo Iven, Eleanor James, Nora Kaye, Anna
Lazarevich, Thalia Mara, Margaret Miller, Charlotte Mount, Doris Newcomb, Muriel
Pack, Martha Pacina, Margaret Rogers, Nina Sabatini, Irene Soussanin, Adrienne
Toner, Grace Walsh, Alma Wertley, Katherine Wilson, Irene Zambelli, Margaret
Haynes, Milton Barnette, Boris Butleroff, Leon Fokine, Val Gueral, George Kiddon,
Fyodor Nazinoff, David Preston, Harold Taub, David Worth. *Girls' Ensemble*:
Elizabeth Andrews, Martha Adamson, Margaret Benton, Alice Berwald, Geraldine
Bork, Helen Carroll, Mable Downs, Janice Dremann, Esta Elman, Marie Fox, Margo
Gavin, Gladys Haverty, Leona Krauss, Doris Moore, Mae Muth, Eunice Northup,
Marion Raber, Rosa Rubinstein, Sylvia Stone, Tatyanna, Gladys Vincent. *Boys'
Ensemble*: James Allison, Nelson Ames, Gene Archer, Bruce Barclay, John Barry,
George Beach, Max Benson, G. Congreve, Don Cortez, Ranolds Dupler, John Eldon,
Gordon Felts, Herbert Goff, Ed. Galloway, Norman Jackson, Karl Kohrs, Robert
Landine, Linn Ledford, Anthony Marvin, Joseph Meyer, Bruce Rogers, Joseph
Scandur, Tom Scott, Winton Sears, Morrie Siegel, Ed Smith, Howard Warriner. *Will
Vodery's Negro Choir*: Katie Hall, Louisa Howard, Zelda Shelton, Mabel Howard,
Bruce Howard, Sally Ellis, Lola Hayes, Charlotte Junius, Viola Anderson, Maude
Simmons, Laura Duncan, James Lillard, Henry Davis, John Diggs, Charles Welch,
W. W. Whitfield, Lewis White, Robert Raines, Ray Giles, Jack Carr, Gus Simons,
Maurice Ellis.

Act 1, Scene 1: Wharf at Yorktown, Virginia, 1775. *Scene 2*: Street in Williamsburg.
Scene 3: Outside the Raleigh Tavern. *Scene 4*: Gates of the Governor's Palace. *Scene 5*:
Slave Quarters. *Scene 6*: Ballroom in the Palace. *Scene 7*: Palace Garden.

Act 2, Scene 1: A Country Fair. The next day. *Scene 2*: Stage Door. *Scene 3*: Sylvia's Dressing Room. *Scene 4*: Fortesque's Dressing Room. *Scene 5*: Green Room in the Theatre. *Scene 6*: At the Play. *Scene 7*: Slave Quarters. *Scene 8*: Daphne's Room, Raleigh Tavern.

ACT 1

"Virginia"
L. Hatfield, Ensemble

"We Had to Rehearse"
Ensemble

"An Old Flame Never Dies"
A. Booth, Ensemble
(*Lyrics in collaboration with* Laurence Stallings.)

"Send One Angel Down"
A. Andrews, Choir

"We Had to Rehearse" (reprise)
Ensemble

"My Bridal Gown"
A. Booth
(*Lyrics in collaboration with* Laurence Stallings.)

"Good and Lucky"
J. W. Bubbles, A. Andrews, F. L. Buck

"It's Our Duty to the King"
N. Bruce, Ensemble

"If You Were Someone Else"
R. Graham, Ensemble

"Goodbye Jonah"
J. W. Bubbles, Choir

"An Old Flame Never Dies" (reprise)
R. Graham, A. Booth, M. Barrie

"My Heart Is Dancing"
A. Booth, P. Bowman, Ensemble

ACT 2[6]

"Meet Me at the Fair"
Ensemble

"If You Were Someone Else"[7] (reprise)
R. Graham, A. Booth

"Why Must I Play the Lady?"[8]
M. Barrie, Girls

"You and I Know"
A. Booth, R. Graham
(*Lyrics in collaboration with* Laurence Stallings.)

"Fee-Fie-Fo-Fum"
Girls

"I'll Be Sittin' in De Lap o' De Lord"
A. Andrews, J. W. Bubbles, F. L. Buck, Choir

"You and I Know" (reprise)
R. Graham, A. Booth

"Virginia" (reprise)
Entire Company

1937.11   A HERO IS BORN

An Extravaganza in Two Acts. Play by Theresa Helburn. Based on a fairy tale by Andrew Lang. Music by A. Lehman Engel. Lyrics by Agnes Morgan. Staged by Agnes Morgan. Settings by Tom Adrian Cracraft. Costumes by Alexander Jones. Music direction and orchestrations, Alexander Saron. Production supervised by Edward Goodman. Produced by the WPA Federal Theatre Project. Opened 1 October 1937 at the Adelphi Theatre and closed 27 November 1937 after 50 performances[9].

<u>CAST</u> (in order of appearance): *A Servant*: Delancey Cleveland. *Another*: Anthony Grey. *Chief Steward*: EDWARD FORBES. *Another Servitor*: T. Greenway. *And Another*: Lewis McMichael. *Still Another*: Louis Cruger. *One More*: Jack Shipman. *And the Last*: John McCormack. *Alfredo, a Page*: Jack Egan. *Antonio, Another*: John Christian. *Nicolo, Another*: Dvaid Resnikoff. *Chief Cook*: RAYMOND SOUTHWICK.

[6]During the run Act 2, Scenes 3-5 dropped.
[7]Dropped during the run.
[8]Dropped during the run.
[9]Performed Tuesday-Saturday evenings, and a Saturday matinee.

First Under Cook: James Coyle. *Second Under Cook*: Clarence Kane. *A Herald*: Donald Stewart. *H.M.Queen of Pantouflia*: MARGARET WYCHERLEY. *H.M. The King*: FREDERIC TOZERE. *A Retainer of Baron Grouchogg*: John McNulty. *A Courier from the Duke of Kinbabbles*: Alfred Allegro. *The Fairy of Flame*: Isabel Marlyn. *The Rainbow Fairy*: Camelia Campbell. *The Golden Fairy*: Jennie Wren. *The Star Fairy*: Louise Swanson. *The Silver Fairy*: Jane Jonson. *The Purple Fairy*: Elizabeth Bilencova. *The Fairy of the Sword*: Eleanora Barrie. *The Bubble Fairy*: Mary Roth. *The White Fairy*: Beatrice Olson. *The Gray Fairy*: Elinor Flynn. *The Armored Fairy*: Ione Bright. *The Fairy of Le Rouge et Noir*: Lilian Steele. *The Blue Fairy*: Eleanor Benedikt. *The Black Fairy*: Minnie Stanley. *The Royal Nurses*: Agnes Williams, Frances Ritchie. *A Gentleman of Uncertain Age (Time)*: WALTER BURKE. *Tony*: William Vaughan. *Lady Kathleena*: MARJORIE BROWN. *Lady Molinda*: HELEN MORROW. *H.R.H. Prince Prigio*: BEN STARKIE. *Zoroaster*: WILLIAM PHELPS. *Ladies and Gentlemen and Servants of the Court*: Alfred Allegro, Eleanor Benedikt, Elizabeth Bilencova, Ione Bright, Camelia Campbell, Delancey Cleveland, John Christian, Elinor Flynn, Toccoa Lander, Anthony Grey, Jane Jonson, Robert Lowe, Seymour Malmude, John McCormack, Lewis McMichael, John McNulty, Albert McWilliams, Frances Ritchie, David Resnikoff, Ethel Reynolds, Mary Roth, Sylvia St. John, Jack Shipman, Lillian Shrewsbury, Louise Swanson.

Two Pranksters: David Enton, Tom Greenway. *A Gourmet*: Muni Diamond. *His Crony*: Sidney Williams. *Paterfamilias*: C. McLean Savage. *Mater Familiar*: Lillian Steele. *Their Son*: Paul Jacchia. *Their Daughter*: Jennie Wren. *A Gentleman Who Should Know Better*: George Probert. *A Lady Who Does*: Beatrice Olson. *Gaston, The Proprietor*: JOHN FARMAN. *His Waiters*: Raymond Southwick, Clarence Kane, Louis Cruger. *His Chef*: Clay Cody. *First Young Buck*: Ronald Brogan. *Second Under Cook*: Jack Egan. *Third Young Buck*: Donald Stewart. *Baron Grouchogg*: Doan Borup. *Lady Rosalind*: DRUE LEYTON. *Viscount Piffle*: Harry Redding. *Lady Piffledown*: Janet Rathbun. *Lord Kelso*: GEORGE LeSOIR. *Count Piffledown*: Robert Bruce. *An Inebriated Patron*: Charles Henderson. *Gossiping Guests*: Ione Bright, Delancey Cleveland, Beatrice Olson, Toccoa Lander, Alfred Allegro, Jane Jonson, Donald Stewart, Louis Cruger, Claire Lillis, Frances Ritchie, Ethel Reynolds, Louise Swanson, C. McLean Savage, Eleanora Barrie, Ronald Brogan, Paul Jacchia, Mary Roth, Anthony Grey, James Bradleigh, Eleanor Benedikt, Raymond Southwick, Jack Shipman, Muni Diamond, John Christian, Sylvia St. John, Seymour Malmude, Jennie Wren, Clarence Kane, Jack Egan, Viola Swayne, Hugh Banks, Camelia Campbell, Lillian Shrewsbury, Agnes Williams.

A Guest Who Loves Dancing: Elinor Flynn. *Her Singing Escort*: JOHN FARMAN. *Thomas Benson*: Harry Sothern. *William*: Walter Burke. *A Footman*: Albert McWilliams. *Duchess of Kinbabbles*: Mary Berkeley. *Duke of Kinbabbles*: David Resnikoff. *Lord Chief Justice*: Charles Henderson. *A Manservant*: Peter Byrne. *An Unexpected Visitor*: James Coyle. *His Brother*: William Phelps. *Other Guests*: Elizabeth Bilencova, Camelia Campbell, Isabel Marlyn, Lewis McMichael, John McNulty, Sidney Williams. *Orchestral Trio*: Marie Valdez, June Victor, Mollie Hakim.

Place: Kingdom of Pantoufflia. *Time*: Unimportant.

Act 1, Scene 1: The Christening. Once Upon a Time. *Scene 2*: The Interim. *Scene 3*: The Robbery. Twenty years later. *Scene 4*: The Discovery. *Scene 5*: The Birth.

Act 2, Scene 1: The Research. *Scene 2*: The Experiment. *Scene 3*: The Approach. *Scene 4*: The Resolution.

ACT 1

Scene 1

"Tra la la"
E. Forbes, D. Cleveland, A. Grey, T. Greenway, L. McMichael, L. Cruger, J. Shipman, J. McCormack, J. Egan, J. Christian, P. Jacchia, D. Resnikoff

"Matters Culinary"
R. Southwick, J. Coyle, C. Kane

"Fiddle Dee Dee"
F. Tozere, M. Wycherly

"The Royal March"
F. Tozere, M. Wycherly, Servants

"Music in the Air"
I. Marlyn, C. Campbell, J. Wren, L. Swanson, J. Jonson, E. Bilencova, E. Barrie, M. Roth, B. Olson, E. Flynn, I. Bright, L. Steele, E. Benedikt, M. Stanley

"Magic Gifts"
I. Marlyn, C. Campbell, J. Wren, L. Swanson, J. Jonson, E. Bilencova, E. Barrie, M. Roth, B. Olson, E. Flynn, I. Bright, L. Steele, E. Benedikt, M. Stanley, M. Valdez, J. Victor, M. Hakim

"Christening Music"
Orchestra

Scene 2

"A Question of Gait"
W. Burke, Men's Ensemble
(*Lyrics by* Thomas Burke.)

Scene 3

"Woe Is Me"
H. Morrow, M. Brown

"Feline Wisdom"
W. Phelps
"Off to Gluckstein"
The Pantoufflian Court
"Keeping Priglio Company"
Orchestra
Scene 4
"Keeping Priglio Company" (reprise)
Orchestra
Scene 5
"The Secret of Success"
J. Farman
"We Believe"
D. Leyton, B. Starkie
ACT 2
Scene 2
"Combat"
The Elements
Scene 3
"A Love-Lorn Maid"
E. Forbes
"They Say"
Gossiping Guests
"The Best Dance of All"
J. Farman
Scene 4
"The Best Dance of All" (reprise)
J. Farman, Gossiping Guests
"The Song of Priglio"
Guests of Lord Kelso
"Important Announcement"
F. Tozere
"Hurrah for Life"
Guests of Lord Kelso
"Priglio Don't Know"
F. Tozere, H. Morrow, M. Brown, J. Coyle, W. Phelps
"The Last Word"
D. Leyton

ACT 1
Scene 1
"Hose Boys"
Blue Bird Boys, Red Heart Boys
Scene 3
"The Fireman's Flame"
C. Gillespie, Ensemble
Fire Belles Gallop
Pony Ballet
Scene 6
"Doin' the Waltz"
G. Coppin, Ensemble
"We're Off"
Blue Bird Boys
OLIOS
Harry Meehan, the Irish Thrush and Singing Waitresses: Dale Carter, Audrey Edmonds, Mildred Kent, Mary Thomas, Dorothy White, Helen Spina, Virginia Deane, Wilma Davis.
ACT 2
Scene 1
"Do My Eyes Deceive Me"
C. Rogers, B. Cutler, Ensemble
Scene 3
"Mother Isn't Getting Any Younger"
H. Meehan
Scene 5
"It's a Lovely Night on the Hudson River"
B. Cutler, C. Rogers, Ensemble
OLIOS
Singing Waitresses
ACT 3
Scene 2
"I Like the Nose on Your Face"
R. Lieder, I. Keith, Ensemble
Scene 5
Finale
Ensemble

1937.12 THE FIREMAN'S FLAME

A Musical Melodrama in Three Acts, 16 Scenes. Book by John Van Antwerp [Jerrold Krimsky]. Lyrics by Ted Fetter. Music by Richard Lewine. (Staged by John and Jerrold Krimsky.) Musical numbers staged by Morgan Lewis. Settings by Eugene Dunkel. Ladies' costumes and special effects by Kermit Love. Music director, Al Evans. Orchestrations, Ben Ludlow. Community singing directed by Leslie Litomy. Produced by John and Jerrold Krimsky. Opened 9 October 1937 at the American Music Hall and closed 30 April 1938 after 204 performances.

CAST (in order of appearance): *Napoleon Markham*, foreman of the Red Hearts: ALAN HANDLEY. *Miss Snodgrass*: Anna Erskine. *Miss Cabot*: Julie Hartwell. *Harry Howard*, a volunteer fireman: BEN CUTLER. *Moze*, a Bluebird Hose Boy: HARRY MEEHAN. *Nozzle*, a Bluebird Hose Boy: ISHAM KEITH. *Mrs. Howard*, Harry's Mother: CYNTHIA ROGERS. *Jenny*: ROSE LIEDER. *Daphne Vanderpool*, an heiress: CYNTHIA ROGERS. *Adolphus Vanderpool*, her foster father: PHILIP BOURNEUF. *Vesta Violet*, alias Mrs Prestongrange: GRACE COPPIN. *Bedlington*: Sellwyn Myers. *Bowery B'hoy*: Bruce Gordon. *Policeman*: Lee Burke. *Rensselaer*: George Stinchfeld. *Mayor Wickham*: Howard Fischer.
Fire Belles: Anna Erskine, Margaret Ballentine, Eleanora Dixon, Jo Ann Lee, Julie Hartwell, Honey Sinclaire, Christie Gillespie. *Red Heart and Blue Bird Volunteers*: Lee Burke, Bruce Gordon, George Stinchfield, Sellwyn Myer, James Hayes, Remington Olmstead, Howard Fischer.

Act 1, Scene 1: Outside the Firehouse. *Scene 2*: Garret Room. *Scene 3*: Outside the Firehouse. *Scene 4*: A Street in Front of the Vanderpool Mansion. *Scene 5*: Room inside of the Vanderpool Mansion. *Scene 6*: Fireman's Ball at the Academy of Music.

Act 2, Scene 1: Acker, Merrill and Condit's Soda Parlor. *Scene 2*: Room inside Vanderpool Mansion. *Scene 3*: Inside Firehouse. *Scene 4*: Office of Vanderpool and Izzard, Wall Street. *Scene 5*: The Battery.

Act 3, Scene 1: Office of Vanderpool and Izzard, Wall Street. *Scene 2*: Outside the Vanderpool Mansion. *Scene 3*: Inside the Firehouse. *Scene 4*: Panorama of Broadway. *Scene 5*: Street in Front of the Vanderpool Mansion.

1937.13 I'D RATHER BE RIGHT

A Musical Revue[10] in Two Acts. Book by George S. Kaufman and Moss Hart. Music by Richard Rodgers. Lyrics by Lorenz Hart. Book staged by George S. Kaufman. Setting by Donald Oenslager. Costumes by Irene Sharaff. Modern clothes by John Hambleton. Choreography by Charles Weidman. Modern Dances staged by Ned McGurn. (Conductor, Dave Allman.) Produced by Sam H. Harris. Opened 2 November 1937 at the Alvin Theatre, moved 23 May 1938 to the Music Box Theatre and closed 9 July 1938 after 290 performances.

CAST (in order of appearance): *Peggy Jones*: JOY HODGES. *Phil Barker*: AUSTIN MARSHALL. *The President of the United States*: GEORGE M. COHAN. *His Secretary*: Ralph Glover. *The Postmaster General*: Paul Parks. *The Secretary of the Treasury*: TAYLOR HOLMES. *The Secretary of State*: MARION GREEN. *The Secretary of Labor*: Bijou Fernandez. *The Secretary of the Navy*: David Allman. *The Secretary of Commerce*: Al Atkins. *The Secretary of Agriculture*: Robert Bleck. *The Secretary of War*: Jack Mills. *The Secretary of the Interior*: Charles McLoughlin. *The Attorney-General*: Robert Less. *The Chief Justice*: JOHN CHERRY. *James B. Maxwell*: FLORENZ AMES. *Federal Theatre Director*: Joseph Macaulay. *Social Service Messenger*: Georgie Tapps. *The President's Mother*: Marie Louise Dana. *A Butler*: Joseph Allen. *The Judge's Girl*: Mary Jane Walsh. *Sistie*: Evelyn Mills. *Buzzie*: Warren Mills. *Tony*: JOSEPH MACAULAY. *Joe*: Joe Verdi. *The Acrobats*: Jack Reynolds, Sol Black. Dave Allman's Band.
Singing Girls: Virginia Berger, Cecil Carey, Ruth Clayton, Geraldine Hamilton, Linda Kellogg, Marie Nash, Erminie Randolph, Jane Richardson, Emily Stephenson, Mary Jane Walsh. *Singing Boys*: Charles Bywater, Len Frank, John Fulco, Joe Granville, Jack Kearney, Jack Leslie, William Marel, John McQuade, Bob Spencer,

---

[10]Though billed as a Musical Revue in playbills, this show is most often referred to as a musical comedy.

Norman Van Emburgh, Herbert Wood. *Dancing Girls*: Jeanette Bradley, Jeanette Lee, Eleanor Dewitt, Kate Fredric, Ruth Gormley, Georgette Lampsi, Velma Lord, Lili Mann, Austra Neiman, Tina Rigat, Patsy Schenck, Betty Schlaffer, Clarise Sitomer, Dorothy Waller. *Dancing Boys*: Jack Barnes, Don Cater, Martin Fair, Jay Hunter, Beau Tilden, Edward Harrington, Robert Howard, Fred Nay.

Acts 1 and 2: Central Park, New York. 4 July.

ACT 1

"A Homogeneous Cabinet"
(Cabinet Members)

"Have You Met Miss Jones?"
J. Hodges, A. Marshall

"Take and Take and Take"
M. J. Walsh, Ensemble
Danced by I. McBride, Ensemble.

"Spring in Vienna"[11]
J. Macaulay
Danced by M. Sande, J. Whitney, Ensemble.

"A Little Bit of Constitutional Fun"
M. J. Walsh, Ensemble

"Sweet Sixty-Five"
J. Hodges, A. Marshall
Danced by G. Tapps, J. Whitney.

"We're Going to Balance the Budget"
G. M. Cohan, Company

ACT 2

"American Couple"[12] (Ballet)
The Girl: M. Sande. *The Mother*: I. McBride. *The Boy*: G. Tapps. *The Father*: F. Nay. *The Minstrel*: J. Barnes. *A Flower Girl*: C. Sitomer. *A Photographer*: J. Whitney. *Best Man*: E. Harrington. *The Nurse*: J. Bradley. *The Teacher*: L. Mann. *The Son*: W. Mills. *Ringmaster*: J. Whitney. *Clown*: M. Fair. *Bareback Rider*: A. Neiman. *A Seal*: D. Carter. *Another Mother*: T. Rigat. *Another Father*: J. Granville. *The Son*, grown up: G. Tapps. *His Girl*: M. Sande.

"Labor Is the Thing"
F. Ames, Ensemble

"I'd Rather Be Right"
J. Hodges, A. Marshall, M. J. Walsh, G. M. Cohan, Ensemble

"Off the Record"
G. M. Cohan

"A Baby Bond"
T. Holmes

1937.14

PINS AND NEEDLES

A Musical Revue in Two Acts, 19 Scenes[13]. Sketches by Arthur Arent, Marc Blitzstein, Emanuel Eisenberg, Charles Friedman, Harold J. Rome and David Gregory. Music and lyrics mostly by Harold J. Rome. Staged by Charles Friedman. Settings by Sointu Syrjala. Dance direction by Gluck Sandor. Choreography by Benjamin Zemach. Pianos, Earl Robinson and Harold J. Rome. Produced by International Ladies Garment Workers' Union Players. Opened 27 November 1937 at the Labor Stage Theatre; Second edition (PINS AND NEEDLES 1939) opened 20 April 1939, moved 26 June 1939 to the Windsor Theatre; renamed PINS AND NEEDLES 1939 in August 1939, renamed PINS AND NEEDLES 1940 in September 1939; Third edition (NEW PINS AND NEEDLES) opened 25 November 1939, and closed 22 June 1940 after a total of 1108 performances.

CAST: Lydia Annucci, Sol Babchin, Sadie Bershadsky, Anne Brown, Rose Czitron, Vincent Dazieri, Sam Dratch, Zitta Edinburgh, Al Eben, Anthony Fazio, Tillie Feldman, Irene Fox, Julius Frankel, Sandra Gelman, Eugene Goldstein, Hyman Goldstein, Enzo Grassi, Nettie Harary, Hattie Hausdorf, Lynne Jaffee, Harry Kadison, Hyman Kaplan, Rose Kaufman, Bella Kinburn, Elias Levine, Al Levy, May Martin, Murray Modick, Bettie Morrison, Miriam Morrison, Jean Newman, Rose Newmark, Olive Pearman, Joseph Roth, Ruth Rubinstein, Fred Schmidt, Moe Schreier, Paul Seymour, Isaac Sides, Sidney Sklar, Mae Spiegel, Millie Weitz, Beatty Uretsky.

[11]Title changed to "Spring In Milwaukee" in May 1938.

[12]Dropped shortly after opening, replaced with:
"What's It All About"
G. Tapps, Ensemble

[13]First produced in New York 11 June 1936 at the Labor Stage Studios. In May 1938, direction credited to Robert H. Gordon; dances directed by Adele Jerome. Special vocal work by Arthur Lessack. By November 1939, all sketches credited to Joseph Schrank.

Act 1[14]

Scene 1

"First Impression"
Entire Company
(*Music by* Harold Rome. *Lyrics by* Harold Rome and Charles Friedman.)

[14]New material was frequently introduced during the run of the show; the following list, though by no means complete, is representative of the changes:

"Lesson in Etiquette" (Added by September 1938)
The Expert: L. Jaffee. *Pickets*: S. Gelman, E. Grassi, F. Schmidt, A. Levy, I. Sides, R. Rubinstein, I. Fox, E. Golddstein, T. Feldman, N. Harary, R. Newmark.

One Third of a Mitten (*by* Emanuel Eisenberg and Jay Williams)(Added by September 1938)

"The Great White Way Turns Pink" (Added by September 1938)
(*Music by* Lee Wainer. *Lyrics by* John Latouche.)

"Lorelei on the Rocks" (Added December 1938)
(*Music by* Berenice Kazounoff. *Lyrics by* John Latouche.)

Die Lorelei: B. Gould. *A Storm Trooper*: F. Schmidt.

"Papa Lewis, Mama Green" (added 30 January 1939)
(*Pantomime and Dance Staged by* Felicia Sorel.)

Mama: A. Eben. *Papa*: H. Clark. *Children*: M. Weitz, A. Fazio.

"Back to Work" (added by February 1939)
Joe: Al Eben. *Strikers*: Entire Company.

"Britannia Rules the Waves" (added April 1939)
(*Music by* Berenice Kazounoff. *Sketch and Lyrics by* Arnold B. Horwitt and John Latouche.)

The Prime Minister: F. Schmidt. *The Secretary of State for Foreign Affairs*: A. Eben. *The Secretary of State for War*: Hy Gardner. *The First Lord of the Admiralty*: B. Gould. *The German Envoy*: H. Clark. *The Japanese Envoy*: M. Modick. *Miss Beamish*: A. Brown.

"The Red Mikado" (added late April 1939)
(*Book and Lyrics by* Joseph Schrank and Harold J. Rome, with apologies to Gilbert & Sullivan. *Vocal Direction by* Simon Rady.)

Lord High Executioner: H. Clark. *Flunky*: M. Modick. *Three Little Maids*: N. Harray, Alma Charmat, Ida Mandel. *Wandering Minstrel*: B. Gould. *Gilbert*: A. Eben. *Sullivan*: H. Gardner. *I.L.G.W.U. Titi-Pu Chorus*: Entire Company.

"I've Got the Nerve to Be in Love" (added April 1939)
(*Pantomime and Dance Staged by* Felicia Sorel. *Music Arranged by* Baldwin Bergersen.)

Girl: Ruth Elbaum. *Boy*: A. Levy.

"Cream of Mush" (added April 1939)
(*Sketch by* Joseph Schrank. *Music and Lyrics by* Harold J. Rome.)

Lem Godfrey: P. Seymour. *Dan Scotti*: A. Eben. *Pete*: Sol Israel. *Mr. Price*: H. Gardner. *Mr. Perkins*: H. Clark. *J. Drexel Weller*: M. Modick. *Mr. Black*: B. Gould.

"Mene Mene Tekel" (added August 1939)
Dorothy Harrison

"The Harmony Boys" (added June 1939)
(*Sketch by* Joseph Schrank. *Music and Lyrics by* Harold J. Rome.)

Coggie: A. Eben. *Bob*: B. Gould. *Fritzie*: H. Clark.

Paradise Mislaid (*Sketch by* Joseph Schrank.) (added by September 1939)
Jake: A. Eben. *Papa*: A. Saxe. *Minnie*: M. Weitz. *The Janitor*: B. Gould. *"Stupie"*: S. Israel. *Max*: P. Seymour. *Moe*: H. Clark. *Becky*: R. Kaufman. *The Nurse*: A. Charmat. *Lucille*: Ella Gerber. *The Moving Man*: A. Fazio. *Jack Smith*: A. Levy.

"Bertha, the Sewing Machine Girl," or "It's Better With a Union Man" (added November 1939)
(*Sketch by* Joseph Schrank. *Music and Lyrics by* Harold J. Rome. *Dance by* Katherine Dunham.)

The Singing Waiter: H. Clark. *Bertha*: E. Gerber. *Ted Trueblue*: B. Gould. *Harold Hotfoot*: M. Modick. *Ensemble*: N. Harary, A. Charmat, Dorothy Tucker, Elise Bregman, R. Kaufman, Ida Mandel, Jean Nicita, Perry Stone, S. Israel, Archie Savage, Don Meyer, A. Levy.

"We Sing America" (added November 1939)
Entire Company

"What This Party Needs" (added 2 November 1939)
(*Sketch by* Joseph Schrank. *Music by* Harold J. Rome. *Lyrics by* Harold J. Rome and Arthur Kramer.)

Bill: S. Israel. *Mack*: Wally Castellano. *First Graybeard*: B. Gould. *Second Graybeard*: H. Clark. *Third Graybeard*: H. Gardner.

Scene 2

"Why Sing of Skies Above?" (Sing Me a Song of Social Significance)

Boys: P. Seymour, E. Grassi, A. Levy, H. Goldstein, F. Schmidt. Girls: M. Weitz, I. Fox, L. Jaffee, R. Rubinstein, N. Harary.

Scene 3

Mussolini Handicap (by Arthur Arent)

Mussolini: A. Eben. Four Prize Winners: T. Feldman, A. Brown, R. Newmark, S. Gelman.

Scene 4

"Public Enemy No. 1"

R. Rubinstein

Scene 5

The General Is Unveiled

(Staged by Benjamin Zemach. Ballet Music by Harold Rome.)
General: H. Kadison. Speaker: B. Kinburn. Secretary: R. Kaufman. Invited Guests: L. Annucci, S. Bershadsky, R. Czitron, Z. Edinburgh, H. Hausdorf, B. Morrison, M. Morrison, J. Newman, B. Uretsky.

The Women's Auxiliary assembles to unveil the statue of a famous general on his birthday. In the middle of a stirring address by Mr. Warmonger, the general comes to life and does as he has always done: set man against man. When he resumes his granite self, he leaves behind him a chastened and thoughtful group.

Scene 6

"We'd Rather Be Right"

(Sketch by David Gregory. Music by Harold Rome. Lyrics by Arthur Kramer.)
First 100% American: P. Seymour. Second 100% American: H. Goldstein. Third 100% American: A. Eben. Boy: I. Sides.

"When I Grown Up" (The "G Man" Song)(added for NEW PINS AND NEEDLES tour)

B. Gould

"Sitting on Your Status Quo"

Dorothy Harrison, Ensemble

"Oh, Give Me the Good Old Days" (added by March 1940)

M. Weitz

International Situation (Sketch by Joseph Schrank.)

Don Meyer

"Pity the Poor Millionaire"

(Music and Lyrics by Harold J. Rome.)

"Stay Out, Sammy" (added by March 1940)

Mother: D. Harrison. Sammy: Talley Beatty.

Poker Players (Sketch by Joseph Schrank)(NEW PINS AND NEEDLES tour)

Adolf: B. Gould. Phui: M. Modick. Joe: H. Clark. Benny: A. Eben. French General: D. Mann.

Let 'Em Eat Guns (Sketch by Joseph Schrank.)(added for NEW PINS AND NEEDLES tour)

A Lecturer: H. Clark. The Exhibit: B. Gould.

"History Eight to the Bar" (added for NEW PINS & NEEDLES tour)

(Music and Lyrics by Harold J. Rome.)
Professor: D. Harrison. Students: Sherman Edwards, A. Charmat, E. Bregman, T. Fazio, L. Morrison, Sylvia Cahn, A. Levy, E. Gerber, W. Castellano, J. Nicita.

"Alone on the Lone Prairie" (added for NEW PINS AND NEEDLES tour)

B. Gould
(Music and Lyrics by Harold J. Rome.)

"The Pluto Boys" (added for NEW PINS AND NEEDLES tour)

(Music and Lyrics by Harold J. Rome.)
Girl: E. Bregman. Imp: Gene Barry. First Demon: Daniel Mann. Second Demon: B. Gould. Third Demon: H. Clark.

1+1=1 (added to NY run briefly, NEW PINS AND NEEDLES tour)

(Sketch by Joseph Schrank.)
Announcer: G. Barry. Judge: B. Gould. Professor: D. Mann. Boy: Sherman Edwards. Girl: Jean Nicita. Expert: A. Saxe. Man on Street: S. Israel. Vendor: A. Fazio. Mother: E. Gerber. Daughter: M. Weitz. Citizen: Don Meyer. Miss Dewberry: Ida Mandel. Shady Fellow: M. Modick. Passerby: A. Levy.

Scene 7

The Little Red Schoolhouse (by Emanuel Eisenberg)

Schmaltz: F. Schmidt. Bernadette: A. Levy. Mildred: R. Rubinstein. Lena: I. Fox. Boss: S. Dratch. Union Man: M. Modick.

Scene 8

"Sunday in the Park"

Papa: S. Dratch. Mama: M. Spiegel. Boy: R. Rubinstein. Girl: L. Jaffee. Cop: H. Kaplan. Balloon Man: S. Sklar. Vendor: M. Schreier. Couple: N. Harary, E. Grassi. Man With Carriage: A. Eben. Lonesome Guy: J. Roth. Park Attendant: M. Modick. Radical: P. Seymour. Man on Bench: F. Schmidt. Passersby: A. Levy, I. Fox, R. Newmark, S. Gelman, I. Sides, T. Feldman.

Scene 9

"Dear Beatrice Fairfax" (Nobody Makes a Pass at Me)

M. Weitz

Scene 10

"Economics 1"

(Sketch by Charles Friedman. Music and Lyrics by Harold Rome.)
The Stray: R. Rubinstein. Doorman: M. Modick. Stage Manager: G. Cameron. Banker: P. Seymour. Manufacturer: A. Levy. Wholesaler: F. Schmidt. Retailer: E. Goldstein. Consumer: H. Goldstein.

Scene 11

"Men Awake"

Entire Company, Dance Group
(Prelude Suggested by a Poem of Langston Hughes. Conceived and Staged by Benjamin Zemach.)
Singers: A. Fazio, M. Schreier.

ACT 2

Scene 1

"It's Not Cricket to Picket"

L. Jaffee, Company

Scene 2

"Vassar Girl Finds Job" (Chain Store Daisy)

R. Rubinstein

Scene 3

"F. T. P. (Federal Theatre Project) Plowed Under" (by Marc Blitzstein)

Mr. Bureaucrats: A. Eben. Mrs. Clubhouse: A. Brown. Mr. Zealous: M. Modick. Mr. Stallalong: P. Seymour. Mr. Hippity Bloomberg: J. Roth. Guards: I. Sides, E. Goldstein, F. Schmidt, H. Goldstein.

Scene 4

"What Good Is Love?"

N. Harary

Scene 5

"One Big Union for Two" (Dance Routine by Gluck Sandor.)

Girls: N. Harary, R. Newmark, L. Jaffee, R. Rubinstein, I. Fox. Boys: A. Levy, E. Grassi, F. Schmidt, E. Goldstein, H. Goldstein.

Scene 6

"Four Little Angels of Peace"

Eden: H. Goldstein. Mussolini: A. Eben. Japanese: M. Modick. Hitler: P. Seymour.

Scene 7

"Slumming Party" (Doing the Reactionary)

(Monologue, Music and Lyrics by Harold Rome. Dance Routine by Gluck Sandor.)
Mrs. Dalrymple III: A. Brown. Her Protege: N. Harary. Her Nephew: A. Levy. Her Aunt: S. Gelman. Her Uncle: S. Babchin. Her Chauffeur: F. Schmidt.

Scene 8

"We've Just Begun"

Entire Company
(Music by Harold Rome. Lyrics by Harold Rome and Charles Friedman.)

1937.15 # HOORAY FOR WHAT!

A Musical Comedy in Two Acts, 15 Scenes. Conceived by E. Y. Harburg. Book by Howard Lindsay and Russel Crouse. Music by Harold Arlen. Lyrics by E. Y. Harburg. Book staged by Howard Lindsay. Dances directed by Robert Alton. Settings by Vincente Minnelli. Costumes by Raoul Pene du Bois. Orchestrations by Don Walker; additional orchestrations by Joseph Glover, Conrad Salinger, Paul Sterrett. Music director, Robert Emmett Dolan. Singing ensemble coached by Kay Thompson. Vocal arrangements,

Kay Thompson and Hugh Martin. Special effects by Ferry Corwey, Harry LaMore, George Hanlon, Langdon McCormack. Staged and supervised by Vincente Minnelli. Produced by the Messrs. Shubert. Opened 1 December 1937 at the Winter Garden and closed 21 May 1938 after 200 performances.

CAST (in order of appearance): *The Mayor*: LEO CHALZEL. *Gracie*: Gracie Reilly. *Little Girl*: Carol Wanderman. *First Tough*: FRANKLYN FOX. *Second Tough*: AL BARON. *Mr. Harriman*: WILL FERRY. *Annabel Lewis*: JUNE CLYDE. *Breezy Cunningham*: JACK WHITING. *Chuckles*: ED WYNN. *Daniel*: Charles Senna. *Department Heads*: Sidney Salzer, Mickey Moore, Anthony Albert. *Benjamin Benedict*: ROBERT SHAFER. *Stephanie Stephanovich*: VIVIAN VANCE. *Marechal DuVal*: MARCEL ROSSEAU. *Generalissimo Di Gregorio*: CHARLES SENNA. *Admiral Sir Basil Entwhistle*: FRANKLYN FOX. *Herr Zingaroff*: LEO CHALZEL. *Benjy*: ROBERT SHAFER. *Manager*: Castle Williams. *A Spy*: Ralph Blane. *Marshall Dinkelspiel*: ARTHUR KAY. *Comrade Popikoff*: DON POPIKOFF. *The Voice of Conscience*: ARTHUR KAY. (Principal Dancers: PAUL HAAKON, RUTHANNA BORIS.) *Specialties*: THE FIVE REILLYS, THE BRIANTS, SUE HASTINGS' MARIONETTES, AL GORDON'S DOGS, Leon Polinsky.

Singing Ensemble: Peggy Badey, Bidda Blakely, Constance Carr, Carrol Clarke, Beverly Hosier, Meg Mundy, Dagmar Nilsson, Wynelle Patterson, Barbara Towne, Virginia Vonne, Armonce Wilkins. Ralph Blane, William Chandler, Harold Cook, Ford Crane, Frank Howard, Hugh Martin, John Smedberg, Castle Williams. *Dancing Ensemble*: Joanna Allen, Marjorie Baglin, Dorothy Bird, Florine Callahan, Maxine Darrell, Louisa DeForrest, Helene Ecklund, Peggy Gallimore, Helen Hannan, Rita Horgan, Evelyn Laurie, Mary Joan Martin, Mary Meyer, Evelyn Moser, Mary Anne Parker, Jo Raskin, Ruth Shaw, Virginia Smith, Marie Vanneman. Anthony Albert, Joel Friend, Philip Gordon, William Hawley, Mickey Moore, Edward Murray, William Pillick, Sidney Salzer.

Act 1, Scene 1: The Fourth of July in Sprinkle, Indiana. *Scene 2*: The South Road. *Scene 3*: The Harriman Munitions Factory. *Scene 4*: Chuckles' Laboratory. *Scene 5*: A Balustrade in Geneva. *Scene 6*: The Peace Ball. *Scene 7*: Corridor of the Grand Hotel de L'Espionage. *Scene 8*: Room No. 711. *Scene 9*: A Corridor. *Scene 10*: The Peace Conference.

Act 2, Scene 1: The Munitions Salon. *Scene 2*: A Peaceful Orchard near Geneva. *Scene 3*: Hero Ballet" *Scene 4*: A Bomb-Proof Dugout. *Scene 5*: Finale.

ACT 1

Scene 1

"Hooray For What!"
  Citizens of Sprinkle (Ensemble)

Scene 2

"God's Country"
  J. Whiting, The Reillys, Singing and Dancing Ensembles

Scene 3

"I've Gone Romantic on You"
  J. Whiting, J. Clyde

Scene 4

"Moanin' in the Mornin'"
  V. Vance, Singing Spies

Scene 5

"Viva for Geneva"
  International Colony (Ensemble)

Scene 6

"Life's a Dance"
  R. Shafer
    Danced by P. Haakon, R. Boris, The Internationals.

Scene 9

"Napoleon's a Pastry"
  J. Whiting, J. Clyde
    Danced by the Reillys.

Scene 10

"Down With Love"
  J. Whiting, J. Clyde, V. Vance, Ensemble

ACT 2

Scene 1

"A Fashion Girl"
  R. Blane, Singers
    Presented by J. Whiting. *Modeled by* the Girls, Boys, E. Wynn, the Briants.

"The Night of the Embassy Ball"
  V. Vance

Scene 2

"In the Shade of the New Apple Tree"

J. Whiting, J. Clyde, R. Blane, H. Cook, H. Martin, J. Smedberg. *Danced by* The Reillys[15], J. Whiting, the Girls.

Scene 3

Hero Ballet
  Danced by P. Haakon, P. Gordon, the Corps de Ballet.
    (Ballet Music by Harold Arlen. *Choreography by* Agnes de Mille.)

Scene 5

Finale
  E. Wynn, Entire Company

1937.15 BETWEEN THE DEVIL

A Musical Comedy in Two Acts, 13 Scenes. Book and lyrics by Howard Dietz. Music by Arthur Schwartz. Production staged by Hassard Short. Book staged by John Hayden. Dances and principals' numbers arranged by Robert Alton. Music direction by Don Voorhees. Settings by Albert Johnson. Costumes by Kiviette. Orchestra directed by Don Bryan. Orchestrations by Ardon Cornwall, Phil Wall, Hans Spialek, Conrad Salinger. Production co-supervised by Edward Duryea Dowling. Produced by the Messrs. Shubert. Opened 22 December 1937 at the Imperial Theatre and closed 12 March 1938 after 93 performances.

CAST (in order of appearance): *Peter Anthony, Pierre Antoine*: JACK BUCHANAN. *Natalie Rives*: EVELYN LAYE. *Harry Morley*: WILLIAM KENDALL. *Freddie Hill*: CHARLES WALTERS. *Claudette Gilbert*: ADELE DIXON. *Gaston*: Noel Cravat. *Maney, the Butler*: Ralph Sumter. *Marie, French Maid*: Natasha Dana. *THE TUNE TWISTERS*: Andy Love, Jack Lathrop, Bob Wacker. *Waiter*: Albert Amato. *Bartenders*: Ward Tallman, Vernon Hammer. *Annabelle Scott*: VILMA EBSEN. *Raymond Maurois, Prefect of Police*: Jules Epailly. *English Policeman*: Maurice Kelly.

THE DEBONAIRS: Harold Murray, Jack Voeth, Harold Voeth, Maurice Kelly, Buddy Hertelle, Edward Gale. *The Lady Guests*: Bunny Waters, Jessica Pepper, Joyce Duskin, Tilda Getze, Kay Cameron, Virginia Daly, Ruth Joseph, Helen Hudson, Dorothy Compton, Lee Stephenson, Loretta Dennison, Linda Lee. *The Gentlemen Guests*: Albert Amato, Ward Tallman, Vernon Hammer, Jack Richards, Frank Gagen, Erick Brotherson.

Act 1, Scene 1: A Roof Terrace off a hotel ballroom in London. *Scene 2*: The Anthonys' Drawing Room, the following forenoon. *Scene 3*: Claudette's Apartment in Paris, the same night. *Scene 4*: A Bar off a London Restaurant, the next day. *Scene 5*: The Entrance to Natalie's London House. *Scene 6*: The Anthony's Drawing Room, the following Sunday night.

Act 2, Scene 1: The Drawing Room. *Scene 2*: The Entrance to Natalie's House. *Scene 3*: Natalie's Bedroom, that night. *Scene 4*: A Street in Paris. *Scene 5*: Claudette's Apartment. *Scene 6*: The Foyer to the Hotel Ballroom, London, months later. *Scene 7*: The Roof Terrace.

ACT 1

Scene 1

"I See Your Face Before Me"
  E. Laye

"I See Your Face Before Me" (reprise)
  A. Dixon

"The Night Before the Morning After"
  C. Walters, the Debonairs

Scene 2

"Don't Go Away, Monsieur"
  A. Dixon, J. Buchanan

"Experience"
  J. Buchanan

"Five O'Clock"
  V. Ebsen, the Debonairs

Scene 3

"The Cocktail"
  Ensemble

"Triplets"
  A. Love, J. Lathrop, B. Wacker (Tune Twisters)

Scene 4

"Fly By Night"
  Ensemble

"You Have Everything"
  C. Walters, V. Ebsen

---

[15]Specialty staged by John Pierce.

Scene 5

"Bye Bye Butterfly Lover"
E. Laye, the Debonairs, Boys
"Celina Couldn't Say No"
A. Dixon, E. Laye, Ensemble

ACT 2

Scene 1

"Front Page News"
Ensemble
"Why Did You Do It?"
E. Laye, Ensemble

Scene 2

"By Myself"
J. Buchanan

Scene 4

The Uniform
Dance Created and Performed by the Debonairs

Scene 5

"The Gendarme"
J. Buchanan, A. Dixon
"The Gendarme" (reprise)
A. Dixon, J. Epailly

Scene 6

"I'm Against Rhythm"
C. Walters, V. Ebsen

Scene 7

Finale
J. Buchanan, E. Laye, A. Dixon, Entire Company

1937.17   ## THREE WALTZES

A Musical Play in Three Acts, 12 Scenes. Book by Clare Kummer and Rowland Leigh. Adapted from the Swiss operette "Drei Walzer" by Paul Knepler and Armin Robinson. (Lyrics by Clare Kummer.) Music after Johann Strauss, Sr. (Act 1), after Johann Strauss, Jr. (Act 2), by Oscar Straus (Act 3). (All music adapted by Oscar Straus.) Staged and directed by Hassard Short. Dances by Chester Hale. Settings by Watson Barratt. Costumes by Connie de Pinna. Orchestra conducted by Harold Levey. Produced by the Messrs. Shubert. Opened 25 December 1937 at the Majestic Theatre and closed 9 April 1938 after 122 performances.

CAST (in order of appearance) *Act 1—Vienna: Herr Baltramini*: Ralph Bunker. *Kalliwoda*: Ivy Scott. *Marie Hiller*: KITTY CARLISLE. *Karl Brenner*: GLENN ANDERS. *Sebastien*: Len Mence. *Countess Von Hohenbrunn*: MARGUERITA SYLVA. *Egon Von Hohenbrunn*: Harry Mestayer. *Herbert von Hohenbrunn*: Alfred Kappeler. *Feliz McDonald*: Earl McDonald. *Leopold Von Hohenbrunn*: Charlie Arnt. *Field Marshall Count Maximilian Von Hohenbrunn*: George Baxter. *Count Rudolph Von Honebrunn*: MICHAEL BARTLETT. *Herr Diffinger*: Wheeler Dryden. *Lilli*: Ruth MacDonald. *Orderly*: William Newgord.
Scandal Girls (Ladies Ensemble): Dolly Miller, Sylvia Liggett, Anita Arden, Kay York, Lila Royce, Diana Rutherford, Alice McWhorter, Dana Doran, Frances Rands, Jayne Manners. *Ballet Girls*: Wanda Cochran, Paula Kaye, Joan Engel, Marion Broske, Jean Sharpe, June Sharpe, Ellen Gibb, Dorothy Hardy. *Eight Officers (8 Men of Manhattan)*: Roger Gerry, Fred Ratliffe, William Parker, Gene Greenlaw, Lipman Duckat, Ted Daniels, Jack Phillips, Walter Lewis. *Ballet Boys*: Boris Butleroff, Michael Mann, Milton Barnett, Barry Gunn, Harold Taub, David Preston, Richard D'Arcy, Mischa Pompianov.
Act 2—Paris: Charlotte Hiller, Marie Hiller's Daughter: KITTY CARLISLE. *Conductor*: Truman Gaige. *Andre Coroit*, Baritone at the Theatre: Ralph Magelssen. *Manager*: Alfred Kappeler. *Author*: Ralph Bunker. *Reporter*: Earl McDonald. *Karl Brenner*: GLENN ANDERS. *Lilli Castelli*: Ruth MacDonald. *Steffi Castelli*, Lilli's Daughter: Rosie Moran. *Baron Delauncey*: Victor Morley. *Viscount Reve Duval*: John Barker. *Count Otto Von Hohenbrunn*, Rudolph's Son: MICHAEL BARTLETT. *Leopold Von Hohenbrunn*: Charlie Arnt. *Barmaid*: Adele Rich. *Marquise de Campo*: Marion Pierce. *Willi*: Fred Sherman. *Baroness de Launey*: ANN ANDERS. *Louis*, a waiter at Maxim's: Wheeler Dryden. *Page Boy*: William Newgord. *Gendarme*: David Preston. *Dr. Cavaneau*: George Baxter.
Act 3—England: Sackville, Film Director: George Baxter. *W. Wagstaff Wolf*, of Hollywood: Louis Sorin. *Miss Waring*, Script Girl: Adele Rich. *Cameraman*: Alfred Kappeler. *Franzi Coroit Hiller*, Grand-daughter of Marie Hiller: KITTY CARLISLE. *Trevor*: Earl McDonald. *Freddie*: Fred Sherman. *Karl Brenner*: GLENN ANDERS. *Max*, Count Von Hohenbrunn, Rudolph's Grandson: MICHAEL BARTLETT. *Musical Director*: Wheeler Dryden. *Lilli Castelli*: Ruth MacDonald. *Counterman at the Commissary*: Len Mence. *Leo*, an Actor: Truman Gaige.

Act 1, Scene 1: Rehearsal Room, Kaerntner Theatre, Vienna. 1865. *Scene 2*: A Salon in the Countess Von Hohenbrunn's Palace. *Scene 3*: Marie's Living Room.

Act 2, Scene 1: Back Stage, Theatre Varieties, Paris. 1900. *Scene 2*: Before the Curtain of the Theatre. *Scene 3*: The Bar of the Theatre. *Scene 4*: Cafe Maxime. Later that same night. *Scene 5*: A Private Dining Room at Maxime's. The same night. *Scene 6*: Charlotte's Dressing Room at the Theatre. Two weeks later.

Act 3, Scene 1: Denham-Buckinghamshire Films Ltd. Studio, England. 1937. *Scene 2*: A Section of the Studio Cafeteria. *Scene 3*: Finale—The Three Waltzes.

ACT 1

Scene 1

Opening
R. Bunker, Ballet Girls
"Springtime"
K. Carlisle, 8 Men of Manhattan

Scene 2

"My Heart Controls My Head"
K. Carlisle

Scene 3

Sextette
M. Sylva, H. Mestayer, A. Kappler, E. MacDonald, C. Arnt, G. Baxter
"Springtime (Is in the Air)"
M. Bartlett
Finaletto
M. Sylva, H. Mestayer, A. Kappler, E. MacDonald, C. Arnt, G. Baxter

Scene 4

"Vienna Gossip"
Ensemble

Scene 5

"My Heart Controls My Head" (reprise)
K. Carlisle
"Do You Recall" (duet)
K. Carlisle, M. Bartlett
Finale/"Springtime" (reprise)
M. Bartlett

ACT 2

Scene 1

Finale 'Duc de Rivoli' Operetta—"Champagne"
K. Carlisle, R. Magelssen, Ensemble

Scene 3

"To Live Is To Love"
K. Carlisle
"The Only One"
M. Bartlett

Scene 4

"Paree"
K. Carlisle, Ensemble, Ballet Girls
"I'll Can-Can All Day"
R. Moran
The Can-Can
The Can-Can Girls

Scene 5

"To Live Is To Love" (reprise)(duet)
K. Carlisle, M. Bartlett

Scene 6

"Scandal"
M. Pierce, A. Kappeler, R. Bunker, Ensemble

Scene 7

Finale "Duc de Rivoli"
K. Carlisle, R. Magelssen, Ensemble

ACT 3

Scene 1

"The History of Three Generations of Chorus Girls"
Ladies Ensemble
Opening: Ballet Rehearsal
Ballet Girls
Radetzky March
Dancing Girls

"Our Last Waltz Together" (duet)
  K. Carlisle, M. Bartlett

Scene 2

"The Olden Days"
  G. Anders, 8 Men of Manhattan

Scene 3

Finale—The Three Waltzes: The Waltz of Today, the Waltz of 1900, the Waltz of 1865
  K. Carlisle, M. Bartlett, Corps de Ballet, Ensemble

1938.01

RIGHT THIS WAY

A Musical Comedy in Two Acts, 10 Scenes. Book and lyrics by Marianne Brown Waters. Additional dialogue by Parke Levy and Allen Lipscott. Music by Brad Greene. Additional music and lyrics by Sammy Fain and Irving Kahal. Staged by Bertram Robinson. Ballet music and interludes by Fabian Storey. Musical director, Max Meth. Dances staged by Marjery Fielding. Settings by Nat Karson. Costumes by Miles White. Orchestrations by Hans Spialek, Maurice DePackh, Claude Austin. Entire production supervised by Alice Alexander. Produced by Alice Alexander. Opened 5 January 1938 at the 46th Street Theatre and closed 15 January 1938 after 15 performances.

CAST (in order of appearance): *Bomboski*: Leonard Elliott. *Lissa*, the maid: Leona Stephens. *Mimi Chester*: TAMARA [DRASIN]. *Jeff Doane*: GUY ROBERTSON. *Josie Huggins*: BLANCHE RING. *Flora Baldwin*: LEONA POWERS. *James Withington*: Milton Parson. *The Girl*: April. *The Boy*: Jack Williams. *Spaulding*: JOE E. LEWIS. *Phil Doane*: Henry Arthur. *Judy March*: THELMA WHITE. *Butlers*: Jack Gilchrist, Joey Raye. *Mimi's Assistant*: Dorothea Jackson. *Comptesse De Marco*: Dorothy Maris. *Peasant Vendor*: Leona Stephens. *Sam*: Joey Ray. *The Four Toppers (The Collegians)*: Leon Lawrence, John Lewis, Hal Hoha, Theodore Scott. *Ladies of the Ensemble*: Christine Bromley, Maude Carroll, Violet Carson, Ginger Dixon, Virginia Grimes, Frances Holmes, Dorothea Jackson, Catherine O'Neal, Dorothy Speicher, Zynaid Spencer, Charlotte Stoll, Edith Stromberg, Florence Ward. *Gentlemen of the Ensemble*: Nelson Barclift, William Cope, Charles Curran, James Cushman, Hugh Ellsworth, Robert Gompers, Clark Leston, Jack Riley, Harris Woodford.

Act 1, Scene 1: Mimi's Studio in Paris. *Scene 2*: Pier in Le Havre. *Scene 3*: Sun-Porch of Mimi's and Jeff's Home in Massachusetts, a year later. *Scene 4*: Exterior of Symphony Hall, Boston. *Scene 5*: Garden of Mimi's and Jeff's Home. After the concert.

Act 2, Scene 1: Mimi's Hat Salon, Paris. A few months later. *Scene 2*: A Street in Paris. Later the same night. *Scene 3*: A Market Place, dawn. *Scene 4*: Street in Paris. *Scene 5*: Mimi's Studio, the next morning.

ACT 1

Opening—"Paree"
  L. Elliott, Ensemble

"I Love the Way We Fell in Love"
  G. Robertson, Tamara
  (*Music by* Sammy Fain. *Lyrics by* Irving Kahal.)

"Doughnuts and Coffee"
  April, J. Williams, Ensemble
  (*Music by* Sammy Fain. *Lyrics by* Irving Kahal.)

"It's Great to be Home Again"
  J. Williams, the Collegians
  (*Music by* Sammy Fain. *Lyrics by* Irving Kahal.)

"He Can Dance"
  H. Arthur, T. White, the Collegians
  (*Music by* Sammy Fain. *Lyrics by* Irving Kahal.)

"I Can Dream, Can't I?"
  Tamara
  (*Music by* Sammy Fain. *Lyrics by* Irving Kahal.)

Ballet
  April, Guests

"Song in the Night"
  G. Robertson

ACT 2

"Soapbox Sillies"
  L. Elliott, Ensemble

"Don't Listen to Your Heart"
  Tamara

"Tip Your Hat"
  B. Ring, the Boys

"Paree" (reprise)
  Ensemble

"You Click With Me"
  H. Arthur, T. White, Ensemble

"Doughnuts and Coffee" (reprise)
  April, J. Williams

"I'll Be Seeing You"
  Tamara
  (*Music by* Sammy Fain. *Lyrics by* Irving Kahal.)

"You Click With Me" (reprise)
  J. Williams

"Right This Way"
  G. Robertson, Tamara

Finale
  Entire Company

1938.02

NO MORE PEACE

An Anti-War Comedy with Music in Two Acts, 7 Scenes. Original play "Nie wieder Friede" by Ernst Toller translated from the German by Edward Crankshaw. Lyrics by W. H. Auden. Music composed and arranged by Max Hirschfield. Production by Charles Hopkins. Scene from the design by The Experimental Theatre, Vassar College, and loaned courtesy of Mr. Lester Lang, director. Costumes by Ben Edwards, Brooks Costume Co. Lighting by (Abe) Feder. Produced by the Federal Theatre Project. Opened 25 January 1938 at the Maxine Elliott Theatre and closed 12 February 1938 after 4 performances in repertory.

CAST (in order of appearance): *Napoleon*: Douglas Cambell. *St. Francis*: Jay Velie. *The Angel*: Norma Downey. *Noah*, an unemployed worker: GEORGE McSWEENEY. *Samuel*, a Commissionaire: Dann Malloy. *Lot*, Emissary from League of Nations: Gene Webber. *Laban*, Banker in Dunkelstein: W. O. McWATTERS. *David*, a Schoolmaster; later Minister for Propaganda and Enlightenment: ERFORD GAGE. *Jacob*, a Brazilian; Rachel's fiance: John Randolph. *Rachel*, Daughter of Laban: LEONORE SORSBY. *The Fat Man*: Gordon Burby. *The Little Man*: John Giasi. *The Thin Man*: Robert Youmans. *Cain*, a Hairdresser, later Wartime Dictator: FRANK DALY. *Sarah*, Rachel's Old Nurse: May Kelly. *Doctor*: Wayland Strong. *Socrates*: CHARLES BERRE. *Warder*: Harry Clifton.

Children and Alternates at the Party: Barbara Tindall, Betty Hicks, Dick Richardson, Peter Seip, Jean Rankin, Howard Tindall, Mary Nicholson, Ann Roberts, William Millar, Alex Warden, Sinclair Martine. *Guests at the Party*: Ruth Masters, Sonia Shand, Irene Taylor, Murray Lindsley, Lee Carney, Robert Youmans, Wayland Strong, Edward Hankel, Victor Casmore, John Giasi, Harry Clifton, Florence Carrette, Rose MacDonald. *Peace Procession Band*: Harry Cutton (Drum Major), Messrs. Balsam, DeMilt, Samuelson, Spedick (Bandsmen).

Act 1, Scene 1: Olympus. *Scene 2*: The City Hall in Dunkelstein.

Act 2, Scene 1: Olympus. *Scene 2*: Cell in the Dunkelstein Prison. *Scene 3*: Olympus. *Scene 4*: The City Hall in Dunkelstein. *Scene 5*: Olympus.

ACT 1[16]

Scene 2

"Peace Song"
  E. Gage, Children's Choir

"Financier's Song"
  W. O. McWatters, G. Burby, J. Giasi, R. Youmans

"The Last War"
  W. O. McWatters, G. McSweeney, Chorus

"War Song"
  E. Gage, Children's Choir

"Dictator's Song"
  F. Daly

ACT 2

Scene 2

"Noah's Song"
  G. McSweeney

Duet (The Wisdom of This World)
  C. Berre, G. McSweeney

---

[16]Musical Numbers do not appear in program, but are reprinted from the published text (Farrar & Rinehart, Inc., New York, 1937); music credited to Herbert Murrill. Added to New York run:

"The Heavens Are Telling"
  (*Music by* Ludwig van Beethoven.)

"The International"
  (*Music by* P. Degeiter.)

Scene 4

    "Spy Song"
        W. O. McWatters, G. Burby, J. Giasi, R. Youmans

    "Socrates' Song"
        C. Berre

    "Rachel's Song"
        L. Sorsby

    "Peace Song" (reprise)
        Children's Choir

1938.03   SHOWING OFF

A Musical Revue in Two Acts, 13 Scenes. Music and lyrics by Eubie Blake, Milton Reddie, Matt Shelvey. Directed by William Sully. Scenic design by Maurette Renwick. Costumes by Charles Hawkins. Orchestra directed by Benjamin Roberts. Music supervised by Walter Travers. Produced by the Federal Theatre Project (Matt Shelvey, producer). Opened 1 February 1938 at the 49th Street Theatre and closed 5 February 1938 after 5 performances.

CAST: Harry Kohler, The Hanlon Brothers; Leddy, Stemsky, Wong and Leddy; Sheer and Dick Ferguson; The Four Aces, Marcel Fallet, Gallo and Maley, Ray Denton, Stan Stanley and Benson, Lew Edwards, Jimmy Donnelly, Charles Dalton, Billy Richie, James Howell, Joe Morris, Paul O'Neill, William Renaud, Eddie Mazier, Nick Hufford, Wallace Bradley, Gertrude Downey, Henry Barnes, Iris Collins, Lillian Broderick, Talbot Kenny, Betty Washington.
    Girls: Ruth Sherman, Nina Morsch, Lulu Craven, Helen Mack, Josephine Martino, Julie Steger, Jo Davidson. *Boys*: Walter Reddick, Paul Parrinelli, Bob Cloy, Bob Rhodes, Arthur Hartley, Nick Dale.

ACT 1

Scene 1

    Theatrical Booking Office
        Harry Kohler, Artist's Agent, looking for a new show, portrays for you some of the difficulties of show business.

Scene 2

    The Hanlon Brothers
        Two men of very few words try to help the agent out by acting as masters of ceremony.

Scene 3

    Leddy, Stemski, Wong and Leddy
        Four Clowns have fun moving furniture

Scene 4

    Sheer and Ferguson
        Dance à la Taps

Scene 5

    Four Aces
        Songs as you like 'em

Scene 6

    Hanlon Brothers and Nora
        They do it with mirrors-but Nora's a doll.

Scene 7

    Marcel Fallet
        She plays the violin—and How!

Scene 8

    Gallo and Maley
        "A Hup an' Downa"

Scene 9

    Step This Way
        (*Staged and Directed by* Matt Shelvey. *Orchestra directed by* Eddie Black.)
    Opening—"On Top"
        Entire Ensemble
      b) Meeting the Ladies (*Music, Lyrics and Dance by* Matt Shelvey.)
        The Boys: C. Dalton, J. Donnelly. *The Girls*: R. Sherman, N. Morsch, L. Craven, H. Mack.
      c) A Run Around
        Stanley, Benson, Sawyer
      d) Television—A Satire on the Commercial Radio Broadcast (*by* Matt Shelvey)
        The Broadcaster: L. Edwards. *The Husband*: J. Donnelly. *The Lover*: C. Dalton. *The Wife*: R. Sherman.
      e) With the Harmonica
        R. Denton
      f) "Sweetness of Love"

        (*Music and Lyrics by* Eubie Blake and Milton Reddie.)
      1) B. Cloy, J. Martino.
      2) *Dancer*: J. Steger. *Whistler*: T. Kenny.
      3) "The Waltz"
        L. Broderick, T. Kenny, B. Washington and *Voice Group*: B. Cloy, J. Martino, B. Rhodes, A. Hartley, N. Dale.
      g) Burlesque Ballet
        Stanley and Benson
      h) "Run Away from Home"
        J. Donnelly, I. Collins
        (*Music, Lyrics, Dances by* Matt Shelvey.)
        Four of a Kind: C. Dalton, W. Reddick, P. Parrinelli, J. White. *Dance Group*: C. Dalton, J. Donnelly, W. Reddick, J. White, P. Parrinelli, L. Craven, Cole, N. Morsch, R. Sherman, H. Mack, Cartier.

ACT 2

Scene 1

    Ray Denton—He also dances.

Scene 2

    Billy Richie: Try this on your velocipede. This clown on a bicycle has made Kings and Queens laugh the world over. Other featured artists with Mr. Richie are Wallace Bradley, Gertrude Downey, Henry Barnes.

Scene 3

    Stan Stanley: He's the tops in his particular specialty.

Scene 4

    The All-American Minstrels (*Directed by* Wesley Frazer.)
        Opening Chorus and Tambourine Drill
        Mr. James Howell introduces our first edition of end men: Joe Morris and Paul O'Neill.
    "Eccentricities"
        D. Ferguson
    Song
        W. Renaud
    Our second edition of end men: Eddie Mazier and Nick Hufford.
    Song and Dance
        P. O'Neill
    Song
        E. Mazier
    Song
        N. Hufford
    Song
        J. Morris
    Grand Finale
        Entire Company

1938.04   WHO'S WHO

A Musical Revue in Two Acts, 28 Scenes. Assembled and staged by Leonard Sillman. Music mostly by Baldwin Bergersen, James Shelton, Irvin Graham and Paul McGrane. Lyrics mostly by June Sillman, Irvin Graham and James Shelton. Sketches mostly by Leonard Sillman and Everett Marcy. Technically supervised by Macklin Megley. Scenery by Mercedes. Costumes by Billi Livingston. Orchestra directed by Earl Busby. Musical arrangements by Richard Du Page. Produced by Elsa Maxwell. Opened 1 March 1938 at the Hudson Theatre and closed 19 March 1938 after 23 performances.

CAST: IMOGENE COCA, JUNE SILLMAN, MICHAEL LORING, LOTTE GOSLAR, RAGS RAGLAND, MILDRED TODD, EDNA RUSSELL, JAMES SHELTON, MARA ALEXANDER, JACK BLAIR, JUNE BLAIR, ELISABETH WILDE, LEONE SOUSA, Peter Renwick, Joseph Beale, Jody S. Gilbert, Remi Martel, Chet O'Brien, Mort O'Brien, Jane Luther, Jean Luther, Bowen Charleton [Sonny Tufts], Johnnie Tunsill, Bobby Johnson, Jimmy Banner, Jeanne Bergersen, Beatrice Graham, Kirk Alyn. Ray Clarke, Ruth Gruette, Chick Gagnon, Prudence Hayes, Vincent Gardiner, Claire Winston, Henrietta Boyd, Ida Bildner, Betty Lind, Doris Ostroff, Ruth Ross, Ethel Selwyn.

ACT 1

Scene 1

    Prologue (*by* Everett Marcy and Leonard Sillman)
        The Actress: I. Coca. *Artist*: J. Beale. *Magician*: P. Renwick. *Producer*: R. Ragland. *Backer*: M. Loring.

Scene 2

    "Who's Who"
        (*Music by* Baldwin Bergersen. *Lyrics by* June Sillman.)

Mr. Drew: M. Loring. *Walter Winchell*: J. Shelton. *Girl Friday*: J. Sillman. *Cholly Knickerbocker*: B. Charleton. *Madame Flutterby*: M. Todd. And K. Alyn, J. Bergersen, J. Blair, R. Clarke, R. Gruette, C. Gagnon, P. Hayes, Jane Luther, Jean Luther, R. Martel, C. O'Brien, M. O'Brien, E. Russell, V. Gardiner, C. Winston. *Ice Breaker*: R. Ragland, P. Renwick, J. Beale.

Scene 3

"Skiing at Saks"

I. Coca

(*Music and Lyrics by* Irvin Graham.)

Scene 4

"Sunday Morning in June"

Introduced by L. Sousa

(*Music by* Paul McGrane. *Lyrics by* Neville Fleeson.)

Boy: Jack Blair. *Girl*: June Blair. K. Alyn, J. Bergersen, R. Clarke, J. Gilbert, B. Graham, R. Gruette, C. Gagnon, P. Hayes, C. O'Brien, M. O'Brien, B. Charleton, C. Winston, V. Gardiner.

Scene 5

Art Film (*by* Irvin Graham)

The Man: M. Loring. *The Woman*: E. Wilde. *The Other Woman*: M. Alexander. *Narrator*: R. Ragland.

Scene 6

Of Mice and Men

Introduced by the Editress of Readers Digest: E. Wilde. *Lennie*: B. Charleton.

Scene 7

"Croupier"

M. Loring, J. Sillman

(*Music by* Baldwin Bergersen. *Lyrics by* June Sillman.)

The Croupier: P. Renwick. *The Players*: K. Alyn, J. Bergersen, J. Gilbert, R. Gruette, C. Gagnon, R. Martel, C. O'Brien, M. O'Brien, J. Shelton, L. Sousa, B. Charleton, C. Winston, V. Gardiner.

Scene 8

Cartoon Specialty

Danced by B. Johnson, J. Banner

Scene 9

Our Town (*by* Thomas McKnight and Mort Lewis)

The Narrator: I. Coca. *The Guest*: R. Ragland.

Scene 10

Intoxication (*Music by* Jarolslav Jezek.)

Danced by L Goslar

Scene 11

"I Dance Alone"

J. Sillman

(*Music and Lyrics by* James Shelton. *Dance staged by* Chet O'Brien.)

Introduced by J. Bergersen, K. Alyn, J. Blair, V. Gardner, B. Graham, R. Gruette, C. Gagnon, P. Hayes. *Danced by* J. Sillman, R. Martel. *Specialty*: Jane and Jean Luther, C. O'Brien, M. O'Brien.

Scene 12

We Lunts in Wisconsin (*by* Everett Marcy and Leonard Sillman)

The Butler: P. Renwick. *Lynn*: M. Todd. *Alfred*: J. Shelton. *Members of the Household*: Jane Luther, H. Boyd, J. Beale, R. Clarke.

Scene 13

"Rinka Tinka Man"

E. Russell, J. Tunsill

(*Music by* Lew Kesler. *Lyrics by* June Sillman. *Danced staged by* Lew Kesler.)

Rinka Tinka Man: B. Johnson. *Policeman*: R. Clarke. *Sailor*: K. ALyn. *Young Couple*: Jack and June Blair. *Street Cleaner*: M. O'Brien. *Lady of the Streets*: P. Hayes. *Dowager*: J. S. Gilbert. *Vagrant*: V. Gardner. *Governess*: C. Winston. *Little Girl*: H. Boyd. *Cameraman*: C. O'Brien. *Nurse*: Jane Luther. *Candy Vendor*: R. Martel. *Office Girl*: R. Gruette. *Roue*: C. Gagnon. *Artist*: Jean Luther. *Chorus Girl*: J. Bergersen.

Scene 14

Whither America? (*by* Luther B. Davis and H. John Friedman)

The Secretary: J. Sillman. *The Switchboard Operator*: M. Alexander. *The Fakir*: J. Beale. *Introduction*: E. Wilde. *Written by* Everett Marcy.

Scene 15

"I Must Waltz"

I. Coca

(*Music by* Baldwin Bergersen. *Lyrics by* Irvin Graham. *Danced staged by* Lew Kesler and Morgan Lewis.)

Assisted by K. Alyn, R. Clarke, C. Gagnon, V. Gardner, R. Martel, C. O'Brien, M. O'Brien, B. Charleton. *Shag Dancers*: J. Bergersen, H. Boyd, R. Gruette, Jane Luther, June Luther, C. Winston.

Scene 16

Jones Beach (*by* Mort Lewis)

Introduced by L. Sousa. *An Agent*: C. O'Brien. *An Actor*: R. Ragland. *A Butler*: J. Beale. *A Lady*: L. Sousa.

Scene 17

"Dusky Debutante"

M. Loring

(*Music by* Baldwin Bergersen. *Lyrics by* June Sillman.)

Introduced by R. Ragland, J. Beale, P. Renwick, I. Coca. *The Butler*: K. Alyn. *The Dowagers*: M. Alexander, E. Wilde, C. Winston. *The Mother*: J. Bergersen. *The Mother*: J. S. Gilbert. *The Father*: M. Loring. *Ethel Waters*: J. Tunsill. *Josephine Baker*: J. Sillman. *Louis Armstrong*: J. Banner. *Cab Calloway*: B. Charleton. *The Minnie Moochers*: I. Bildner, B. Lind, D. Ostroff, R. Ross, E. Selwyn. *Abercrombie*: B. Johnson. *Guests*: H. Boyd, R. Clarke, R. Gruette, C. Gagnon, P. Hayes, Jane and June Luther, R. Martel, Chet and Mort O'Brien, V. Gardner.

ACT 2

Scene 1

"Girl With the Paint on Her Face"

J. Sillman

(*Music and Lyrics by* Irvin Graham.)

Announcer: C. O'Brien. *Millicent Van Sycle*: J. Sillman. *Specialty Dancer*: H. Boyd. *Acrobats*: I. Bildner, B. Lind, D. Ostroff, R. Ross, E. Selwyn. *Beef Trust*: H. Boyd, J. Gilbert, B. Graham, R. Gruette, P. Hayes, Jane and June Luther, L. Sousa, M. Todd, E. Wilde, J. Bergersen, C. Winston. *Candy Vendors*: R Clarke, V. Gardner. *Men in the Boxes*: K. Alyn, J. Blair, C. Gganon, M. Loring, R. Martel, M. O'Brien, J. Shelton, B. Charleton.

Scene 2

Shadow Dance

Danced by I. Coca, R. Ragland

Scene 3

"It's You I Want"

(*Music by* Paul McGrane. *Lyrics by* Al Stillman.)

Agitator: C. O'Brien. *Woman Picket*: M. Alexander. *Girl*: J. S. Gilbert. *The Dictators*: B. Charleton, R. Martel.

Song

M. Loring, E. Russell

Snow White and Burgess Meredith

(*Dialogue by* Irvin Graham. *Incidental Music by* Paul McGrane.)

SnowWhite: June Blair. *Burgess Meredith*: Jack Blair.

Scene 4

Forgive Us Odets (*by* Lawrence Riley)

Introduced by E. Wilde. *Comrade Cyril*: P. Renwick. *Comrade Stuyvesant*: B. Charleton. *Comrade Alicia*: M. Todd. *Comrade Vanderpoel*: J. Shelton. *The Woman in Red*: M. Alexander. *Joe*: M. Loring. *Fellow Members*: B. Graham, R. Gruette, C. Gagnon, R. Martel, C. O'Brien, C. Winston, L. Sousa, E. Wilde, V. Gardner.

Scene 5

Why Vaudeville Didn't Come Back

(*by* Rags Ragland. *Edited by* Everett Marcy and Leonard Sillman.)

Introduction: J. Beale, P. Renwick. *The Girl*: L. Sousa. *The Man*: R. Ragland.

Scene 6

Virgin

Dance by L. Goslar

Scene 7

"I Must Have a Dinner Coat"

J. Shelton

(*Music and Lyrics by* James Shelton.)

Danced by K. Alyn, J. Bergersen, Jane and June Luther, Chet and Mort O'Brien.

Scene 8

Zwei Herzen in 6 7/8 Time

(*by* Luther B. Davis, Leonard Sillman, Rags Ragland)

The Producer: R. Ragland. *The Actress*: I. Coca.

Scene 9

"Let Your Hair Down (With a Bang)"

J. Sillman

(*Music by* Baldwin Bergersen. *Lyrics by* June Sillman.)

Scene 10

Letting Her Hair Down

I. Coca

Scene 11
  Finale
    Entire Company
    Introduced by R. Ragland, I. Coca.

1938.05   I MARRIED AN ANGEL

A Musical Comedy in Two Acts, 11 Scenes. Book by Richard Rodgers and Lorenz Hart adapted from the Hungarian musical play "Angyalt vettem feleségül" by János Vaszary. Music by Richard Rodgers. Lyrics by Lorenz Hart. Staged by Joshua Logan. Settings by Jo Mielziner. Costumes by John Hambleton. Bird, Snow and Roxy Ballet costumes designed by Alice Halicka. Choreography by George Balanchine. Music directed by Gene Salzer. Orchestrations by Hans Spialek. Produced by Dwight Deere Wiman. Opened 11 May 1938 at the Sam S. Shubert Theatre and closed 25 February 1939 after 338 performances.

CAST (in order of appearance): *Major Domo:* David Jones. *Two Guests:* The Dunham Brothers. *Olga Madayn:* Hene Damur. *General Lucash:* Morton L. Stevens. *Guest:* Arthur Kent. *Peter Mueller:* CHARLES WALTERS. *Count Willy Palaffi:* DENNIS KING. *Countess Peggy Palaffi:* VIVIENNE SEGAL. *Anna Murphy:* AUDREY CHRISTIE. *Angel:* VERA ZORINA. *Justice of the Peace:* Arthur Kent. *Valet de Chambre:* David Jones. *Femme de Chambre:* Marie L. Quevli. *Modiste:* Ruth Urban. *First Vendeuse:* Janis Dremann. *Second Vendeuse:* Marcella Howard. *Harry Mischka Szigetti:* WALTER SLEZAK. *Duchess of Holstein-Kuhhoff:* Katherine Stewart. *First Clerk:* David Jones. *Second Clerk:* Arthur Kent. *First Stenographer:* Barbara Towne. *Second Stenographer:* Sylvia Stone. *Lucinda:* Marie L. Quevli. *Clarinda:* Janis Dremann. *Philomena:* Marcella Howard. *Rosalina:* Barbara Towne. *Seronella:* Sylvia Stone. *Arabella:* Diana Gaylen. *Florabella:* Althea Elder. *Premier Danseur:* Charles Laskey. *At the Harp:* Casper Reardon.

Ladies of the Ballet: Genevieve Cooke, Ronnie Cunningham, May Block, Marion Davison, Eleanor Fiata, Petra Gray, Ruth Haidt, Isabelle Kimpal, Nancy Knott, Evelyn Lafferty, Sonia Larina, Bobby Howell, Beatrice Lynn, Maria Monnig, Gedda Petry, Shirley F. Shaffer, Betty Jane Smith, Alma Wertley, (E.) Virginia Williams. *Gentlemen of the Ballet:* Milton Barnett, Edward Brinkmann, Boris Butleroff, Harold Haskin, Michael Mann, Jack Quinn, Nicolai Popov, Harold Taub, Nicolas Vasilieff.

Act 1, Scene 1: Willy's Salon, a spring evening. *Scene 2:* Willy's Study, later that evening. *Scene 3:* Bedroom in a Paris Hotel. The Next evening, the next morning. *Scene 4:* Honeymoon Ballet. *Scene 5:* Willy's Study, noon, one month later. *Scene 6:* Willy's Salon, immediately after.

Act 2, Scene 1: Palaffi's Brothers' Bank, five minutes to four that afternoon. *Scene 2:* Angel's Boudoir, that evening. *Scene 3:* Harry's Salon, later that evening. *Scene 4:* Dream of Roxy's Music Hall. *Scene 5:* Harry's Salon, six o'clock the next morning.

ACT 1
Scene 1
  "Did You Ever Get Stung?"
    D. King, V. Segal, C. Walters
Scene 3
  "I Married an Angel"
    D. King
  Musical Interlude—"The Modiste"
    D. King, V. Zorina, R. Urban, J. Dremann, M. Howard
Scene 4
  Honeymoon Ballet
    V. Zorina, D. King, C. Laskey, Corps de Ballet
Scene 5
  "I'll Tell the Man in the Street"
    V. Segal, W. Slezak
Scene 6
  "How to Win Friends and Influence People"
    A. Christie, C. Walters, Ensemble
  Finale
    D. King, V. Segal, V. Zorina
ACT 2
Scene 1
  "Spring Is Here"
    D. King, V. Segal
Scene 2
  Musical Interlude—"Angel Without Wings"
    V. Zorina, M. L. Quevli, J. Dremann, M. Howard, B. Towne, S. Stone, D. Gaylen, A. Elder

"A Twinkle in Your Eye"
  V. Segal
Scene 3
  "I'll Tell the Man in the Street" (reprise)
    W. Slezak
  "At the Roxy Music Hall"
    A. Christie
Scene 4
  Roxy's Music Hall
    Danced by Cast, Ensemble
Scene 5
  Finale
    Entire Company

1938.06   THE TWO BOUQUETS

An Operetta in Three Acts. Book and lyrics by Eleanor and Herbert Farjeon. (Music by approximately uncredited 20 Victorian composers.) Staged by Marc Connelly. Music directed by Macklin Morrow. Settings by Robert Barnhart. Consultant on Victorian décor, Allen Saalburg. Costumes by Raoul Pene du Bois. Dances staged by Leslie French. Associate producer, Béla Blau. Produced by Marc Connelly. Opened 31 May 1938 at the Windsor Theatre and closed 16 July 1938 after 55 performances.

CAST (in order of appearance): *Kate Gill:* MARCY WESTCOTT. *Laura Rivers:* PATRICIA MORISON. *Mrs Gill:* VIOLA ROCHE. *Mr. Gill:* LEO G. CARROLL. *Edward Gill:* LESLIE FRENCH. *Amelia:* ENID MARKEY. *Albert Porter:* ALFRED DRAKE. *Julian Bromley:* WINSTON O'KEEFE. *Flora Grantley:* Jane Archer. *Bella Manchester:* JOAN WETMORE. *Patty Moss:* GABRIELLE BRUNE. *George:* ROBERT CHISHOLM.

Guests, Thespians and Regatteers: Jane Archer, Helen Carroll, Elsie Eyre, Harriette Henning, Doris Moore, Ronnie Raymond, Margaret Stewart, Erika Zaranova, Robert Arnold, James Burrell, Burr Crandall, Sanders Draper, Tony Kraber, Robert Rounseville, Tom Scott, John Tyers.

Act 1: The Conservatory at Mr. Mrs. Gill's in Twickenham. A June evening.

Act 2: The Gardens of the Gill house. Late that night.

Act 3: The River Bank at Twickenham. The following day.

ACT 1
"Fly Forth, O Gentle Dove" (I Sent a Letter to My Love)
  M. Westcott
  (*Music by* M. Pinsuti.)
"Fly Forth, O Gentle Dove" (reprise)
  M. Westcott
"The Course of Nature"
  L. G. Carroll
"Albert Porter"
  P. Morison
"A Little Champagne for Papa"
  L. French, M. Westcott, P. Morison
"A Health to Dear Mama"
  L. G. Carroll, M. Westcott, P. Morison, L. French
"Varsovienne"
  Ensemble
"The Bashful Lover"
  A. Drake
  (*Music by* C. Moulton.)
"Ah, How Capricious"
  W. O'Keefe
"The White and the Pink"
  L. French
"The Man You Love"
  P. Morison, M. Westcott
"Dearest Miss Flo"
  L. French, J. Archer
"Dearest Miss Flo"
  L. French, J. Wetmore
"She Loves Thee"
  P. Morison
Polka
  Principals, Ensemble

Galop
Principals, Ensemble
Recitative
V. Roache
Finale
Principals, Ensemble
ACT 2
"Juanita"
M. Westcott, P. Morison, Ensemble
"Sweet Blossoms"
P. Morison, M. Westcott
(*Music* by M. Pinsuti.)
"Young Girls and Young Men"
V. Roache
"The Youth Who Sows"
L. French, P. Morison
"Kissing" (recitative)
A. Drake
"I'll Tell Papa"
M. Westcott, P. Morison
"Git on de Boat, Chillun"
G. Brune, R. Chisholm, Men
"She Did the Fandango"
R. Chisholm, G. Brune, Men
"I Wish I Was in Texas"
L. G. Carroll
"Pretty Patty Moss"
G. Brune

"Yes or No"
A. Drake, W. O'Keefe, L. G. Carroll, M. Westcott, P. Morison, G. Brune, R. Chisholm, Men
"Dearest Miss Bell"
L. French
Finale
Principals, Men
ACT 3
"Oh, the Regatta"
Ensemble
"Toddy's the Drink for Me"
R. Chisholm
(*Music* from an Old Irish Folk Song.)
"Oh, the Regatta" (reprise)
Ensemble
"When I Was But a Bounding Boy"
L. G. Carroll
"Against the Stream"
A. Drake, W. O'Keefe
"How Can We Bring the Old Folk Round"
A. Drake, L. French, G. Brune, W. O'Keefe
Rain Chorus
Ensemble
"What Can I Do?"
W. O'Keefe, A. Drake, M. Westcott, P. Morison
"Her Lily-White Hand"
W. O'Keefe, A. Drake, L. G. Carroll
Finale— "The Fireworks"
Principals, Ensemble

1938–1939 SEASON

William Gaxton and Victor Moore in LEAVE IT TO ME (Photo: Vandamm Studio)
Billy Rose Theatre Collection, New York Public Library for the Performing Arts

1938–1939 SEASON

YOU NEVER KNOW

A Musical Play in Two Acts, 11 Scenes. Book by Rowland Leigh. (Adapted from the Viennese operetta "Bei Kerzenlicht" by Robert Katscher and Karl Farkas. Based on the play "By Candlelight" by Siegfried Geyer.) Music and lyrics by Cole Porter. Additional lyrics, and book directed by Rowland Leigh. Dances by Robert Alton. Costumes by Jenkins, Wilma, Veronica, Brooks, Charles LeMaire. Settings by Albert Johnson and Watson Barratt. (Additional music and lyrics by Edwin Gilbert, Alex Fogarty, Robert Katscher and Dana Suesse.) Orchestra directed by John McManus. Orchestrations by Hans Spialek. Additional orchestrations by Claude Austin, Maurice DePackh, Minati Salta and Don Walker. Produced by Messrs. Shubert in association with John Shubert. Opened 21 September 1938 at the Winter Garden and closed 26 November 1938 after 78 performances.

CAST (in order of appearance): *Gaston:* CLIFTON WEBB. *Baron Ferdinand de Romer:* REX O'MALLEY. *Chauffeur:* Eddie Gale. *Ida Courtney:* TOBY WING. *Maria:* LUPE VELEZ. *Henri Baltin:* Charles Kemper. *Mme. Baltin,* Jeanne Montaigne: LIBBY HOLMAN. *Headwaiter:* Roger Stearns. *Louis:* Wesley Bender. *Geoffrey:* Dan Harden. *General Carruthers:* Truman Gaige. *Comptroleur:* Ray Dennis. THE DEBONAIRS: Edwin Gale, Buddy Hertelle, Harold Murray, Paul Pierce, Harold Voeth, Jack Voeth. *Specialties:* GRACE and PAUL HARTMAN, JUNE PREISSER.

Showgirls: Cynthia Cavanaugh, Dorothy Compton, Jacqueline Dahlia, Virginia Daly, Natasha Dana, Barbara Elliott, Tilde Getze, Chris Gustafson, Billie Hill, Helen Hudson, Alice McWhorter, Mildred Riley, Lee Stephenson, Arlene Stone, Ellen Taylor. *Dancers:* Joanna Allen, Helen Bennett, Marion Broske, Mary Ann Carr, Louise De Forrest, Enes Early, Helen Ecklund, Grace Gillern, Irene Kelly, Edith Lambot, Mary Ann O'Brien, Mildred Ramey. *Boys:* Wesley Bender, Gus Schirmer, Jr., Ray Dennis, Robert Smith, Jack Richards.

The entire action of the play takes place one summer evening.

Act 1, Scene 1: Baron de Romer's Home, Paris. *Scene 2:* Madame Baltin's Boudoir. *Scene 3:* The Foyer of the Club Bali. *Scene 4:* The Club Bali. *Scene 5:* Baron de Romer's Home. *Scene 6:* Outside Madame Baltin's House. *Scene 7:* Baron de Romer's Home.

Act 2, Scene 1: A Swimming Pool adjoining Baron de Romer's. *Scene 2:* Gare de Lyon. *Scene 3:* Outside Madame Baltin's Home. *Scene 4:* Baron de Romer's Home.

ACT 1
Scene 1

"I Am Gaston"
C. Webb
"Au Revoir, Cher Baron"
Ensemble
"By Candlelight"
C. Webb, R. O'Malley
(*Music by* Robert Katscher. *Lyrics by* Rowland Leigh.)
"Maria"
C. Webb
"Maria" (dance reprise)
C. Webb, J. Morehead, Ensemble

Scene 2

"You Never Know"
L. Holman

Scene 3

"Ladies' Room"
The Debonairs, Ensemble
(*Music by* Alex Fogarty. *Lyrics by* Edwin Gilbert.)

Scene 4

"What Is That Tune?"
L. Holman
"For No Rhyme or Reason"
T. Wing, C. Kemper, the Debonairs, Ensemble
Danced by the Hartmans.

Scene 5

"Alpha to Omega"
C. Webb, L. Velez
"By Candlelight" (reprise)
C. Webb, L. Velez

Scene 6

"Don't Let It Get You Down"
J. Preisser, D. Harden, the Debonairs, Ensemble

Scene 7

"What Shall I Do?"
L. Velez
(*Lyrics by* Rowland Leigh.)

ACT 2
Scene 1

"Let's Put It to Music"
J. Preisser, D. Harden, the Hartmans, Ensemble
(*Music by* Alex Fogarty. *Lyrics by* Edwin Gilbert.)
"At Long Last Love"
C. Webb

Scene 2

"Take Yourself a Trip"
Ensemble
(*Music by* Alex Fogarty. *Lyrics by* Edwin Gilbert.)
"Yes, Yes, Yes"
T. Wing, Ensemble
"Gendarme"
Danced by the Debonaires
(*Music by* Robert Katscher. *Lyrics by* Rowland Leigh.)

Scene 3

"No (You Can't Have My Heart)"
L. Holman, C. Webb
(*Music and Lyrics by* Dana Suesse.)

Scene 4

"Good Evening, Princess"
C. Webb, L. Velez
Finale
Entire Company

HELLZAPOPPIN'

A Vaudeville Revue in Two Acts, 27 Scenes. Assembled by Ole Olsen and Chic Johnson. Music and lyrics by Sammy Fain and Charles Tobias. Additional dialogue and business by Tom McKnight. Staged by Edward Duryea Dowling. Costumes by Veronica and Mahieu. Musical supervision by Harold Stern. Associate conductor, Edward A. Hunt. Vocal arrangements, Phil Ellis. Produced by Ole Olsen and Chic Johnson, (Messrs. Shubert). Opened 22 September 1938 at the 46th Street Theatre, moved 28 November 1938 to the Winter Garden, moved 25 November 1941 to the Majestic Theatre, and closed 17 December 1941 after 1404 performances. (Subsequent editions detailed immediately following).

CAST: OLE OLSEN [John Siguard Olsen], CHIC JOHNSON [Harold Ogden Johnson], (Dewey) BARTO and (George) MANN, HAL SHERMAN, THE RADIO ROGUES (Jimmy Hollywood, Eddie Bartell, Sidney Chatton), RAY KINNEY and THE ALOHA MAIDS (Leiomini Wood, Napua Wood), WALTER NILSSON, THE CHARIOTEERS (William Williams, Edward Jackson, Ira Williams, Jimmy Sherman, Howard Daniels), BETTYMAE and BEVERLY CRANE, THEO HARDEEN, SHIRLEY WAYNE, Dorothy Thomas, Bonnie Reed, Sidney Dean, Mel Reed, Roberta and Ray, Stormy Bergh, Happy Moore, Billy Adams, Whitey's Steppers, Sidney Gibson, Dippy Diers, Bobby Barry, J. C. Olsen, Henry Howe, John Callahan, The Starlings (Cyril Roodney, June Winters), Catharine Johnson, Mary Sutherland, Joe Wong.

Ensemble: Phyllis McBride, Helen Felix, Claire Katkin, Evelyn Deffon, Mary Barth, Dorothy Thomas, Helene Ecklund, Virginia Collins, Sally Bond, Evelyn Albright, Kay Wilson, Margaret Bacon, Dawn Greenwood, Blanche Poston, Elaine Caruso, Naomi Libby, Madeline O'Hara, Karl Lynn, Phyllis Lake, Evelyn Laurie, Jean Beryl, Regina Lewis, Marjorie Conrad, Renee Havel, Margie Young. Adolph Gudel, William Chandler, Philip Johnson, Fuzzy Lentz, Frank Sheppard, Ned Coupland.

ACT 1[1]
Scene 1

"Hellz-a-poppin"
Ensemble

---

[1]Added during run:
Murdered by the Critics (performed and dropped 6 October 1938)

Scene 2

  Trans-Continental
    O. Olsen, C. Johnson

Scene 3

  "Fuddle dee Duddle" (Funny Little Tune)
    B. Reed, M. Reed
      Danced by Bettymae Crane, Beverly Crane, Ensemble.

Scene 4

  "A Bedtime Story"
    O. Olsen, C. Johnson

Scene 5

  Holmes and Hawkshaw
    Inspector Guiness: O. Olsen. *Inspector Hennessey*: C. Johnson. *Maid*: M. Reed.
    Mrs. Ifingprattle: D. Thomas. *Mr. Ifingprattle*: E. Partell. *Gangster*: W. Nilsson.
    Murderer: J. Hollywood. *Salesman*: S. Gibson. *Meadows*: S. Chatton.

Scene 6

  "Strolling Thru the Park"—Gay Nineties
    O. Olsen, C. Johnson
      The Cycling Girls: M. Barth, S. Bond, V.Collins, E. Deffon, C. Katkin, P.
      McBride.

Scene 7

  Walter Nilsson (unicyclist)

Scene 8

  Ole Olsen presents Dippy Diers and his straightjacket

Scene 9

  Before the Curtain: O. Olsen.
  The Maternity Ward
    Dr. Bringem: D. Barto. *Butch*: B. Barry. *The Baby*: G. Mann.

Scene 10

  Before the Curtain: O. Olsen.
    Wall Street
      First Victim: S. Gibson. *Second Victim*: B. Barry. *Third Victim*: H. Sherman.
      Fourth Victim: H. Moore.

Scene 11

  "Abe Lincoln"
    The Charioteers
      (*Music and Lyrics by* Earl Robinson and Alfred Hayes.)

Scene 12

  A Cabinet Meeting
    Chancellor: O. Olsen. *Minister of War*: S. Dean. *Minister of Finance*: J. C.
    Olsen. *Minister of Navy*: H. Howe. *Secretary of Foreign Affairs*: J. Callahan.
    Orderly: J. Hollywood. *An American*: C. Johnson.

Scene 13

  "Shaganola"
    B. Reed, M. Reed
      Danced by Roberta and Ray, Ensemble.

Scene 14

  The Radio Rogues (impressions)
    J. Hollywood, E. Bartell, S. Chatton

Scene 15

  Who's the Dummy?
    O. Olsen, C. Johnson, E. Bartell, S. Chatton, D. Thomas

Scene 16

  Shirley Wayne (comedy fiddler)

Scene 17

  Olsen and Johnson (comedy dialogue)

Scene 18.

  Billy Adams (dancer)

Scene 19

  "It's Time to Say Aloha"
    C. Roodney, J. Winters
      Danced by R. Kinney, Aloha Maids, Ensemble. *Lena* (who looks for Oscar):
      C. Johnson.
  Intermission Interlude with Dippy Diers

ACT 2

Scene 1

  "Harem on the Loose"

Scene 2

  The Magic Hour
    O. Olsen, C. Johnson, T. Hardeen

Scene 3

  The Charioteers (male quartet)
  ["Ol' Man Mose'"]
    (*Music and Lyrics by* Louis Armstrong and Zilner T. Randolph.]

Scene 4

  Hal Sherman (pantomime, dance, comedy)

Scene 5

  Pep Talk
    O. Olsen

Scene 6

  "When You Look in Your Looking Glass"
    C. Roodney, J. Winters
    (*Music by* Paul Mann and Stephen Weiss. *Lyrics by* Sam M. Lewis.)
      Danced by Bettymae Crane, Beverly Crane, Ensemble. *Specialty by* D.
      Barto, G. Mann.

Scene 7

  Audience Participation
    O. Olsen, C. Johnson, D. Barto, G. Mann, H. Sherman, Roberta, Bergh and
    Moore, J. C. Olsen, B. Barry, M. Sutherland, J. Wong, H. Howe, S. Gibson, J.
    Callahan

Scene 8

  Finale—"It's Time to Say Aloha" (reprise)
    O. Olsen, C. Johnson, D. Barto, G. Mann, H. Sherman, Radio Rogues, W.
    Nilsson, T. Hardeen, Reed Sisters, Bettymae and Beverly Crane, C. Roodney, J.
    Winters, Ensemble

1938.08   # THE NEW HELLZAPOPPIN'

New Edition of the Vaudeville Revue in Two Acts, 25 Scenes. Book (sketches) by Olsen and Johnson. Music and lyrics by Sammy Fain and Charles Tobias. Production staged by Edward Duryea Dowling. Dances arranged by Gae Foster. Costumes designed by Joan Personette. Musical supervision, Harold Stern. Associate conductor, Edward A. Hunt. Consultant on production to Olsen and Johnson, Tom Greene. Produced by Olsen and Johnson. Opened 11 December 1939 as part of HELLZAPOPPIN'S continuous run.

CAST: (Ole) OLSEN and (Chic) JOHNSON, (Dewey) BARTO and (George) MANN, CHARLES WITHERS, THE RADIO ROGUES (Jimmy Hollywood, Eddie Bartell, Sidney Chatton), HAL SHERMAN, WALTER NILSSON, THE CHARIOTEERS (William Williams, Edward Jackson, Ira Williams, Jimmy Sherman, Howard Daniels), BETTYMAE and BEVERLY CRANE, THEO HARDEEN, SHIRLEY WAYNE, Gene Meredith, Catharine Johnson, Bonnie and Mel Reed, Stephen Olsen, Syd Dean, Al Downing, Bobby Barry, John Callaghan, Doug Geoffrey, Jim Collins, Sidney Gibson, Syd Dean, Ruth Faber, The Starlings (Cyril Roodney, June Winters), Stormy Bergh, Happy Moore, Gae Foster, Mary Sutherland, Joe Wong, Milton Stern.
  Ensemble: Phyllis McBride, Helen Felix, Claire Katkin, Mary Barth, Dorothy Thomas, Helene Ecklund, Sally Bond, Evelyn Albright, Kay Wilson, Margaret Bacon, Dawn Greenwood, Blanche Poston, Elaine Caruso, Naomi Libby, Madeline O'Hara, Kary Lynn, Phyllis Lake, Evelyn Laurie, Jean Beryl, Regina Lewis, Renee Havel, Margie Young, Helen Beck. Adolph Gudel, William Chandler, Philip Johnson, Fuzzy Lentz, Frank Sheppard, Eddie Murray.

ACT 1[2]

Scene 1

  "Hellz-a-poppin"
    Ensemble

---

[2] Added during run:
  "Any Bonds For Sale? (Any Bonds Today?)"
    The Charioteers
    (*Music and Lyrics by* Irving Berlin.)
  Added for subsequent 1943 edition and national tour:
  "Scarecrow"
    Kim Loo Sisters
    (*Music and Lyrics by* Sammy Fain and Charles Tobias)
  Draft Board (*by* Olsen and Johnson)
    Lew Parker, Jackie Gleason, etc.
  "Where To"
    Kim Loo Sisters

Sit-Downer: G. Meredith.

Scene 2

"I Tank I Go Home"
O. Olsen, C. Johnson
Lena: C. Johnson.

Scene 3

"Mosquito"
B. Reed, M. Reed
Danced by Bettymae Crane, Beverly Crane, Ensemble.

Scene 4

"A Bedtime Story"
O. Olsen, C. Johnson

Scene 5

The Time of Their Lives
Ole: O. Olsen. *Chic*: C. Johnson. *Guest*: S. Olsen. *Boy*: S. Dean.
Photographer: A. Downing.

Scene 6

Bridal Street—"Gay Nineties"
O. Olsen, C. Johnson
The Cycling Girls: M. Barth, S. Bond, B. Poston, D. Thomas, C. Katkin,
P. McBride.

Scene 7

"Up High"
W. Nilsson

Scene 8

Ole Olsen presents Dippy Diers and his straightjacket

Scene 9

"We Won't Let It Happen Here"
The Charioteers
(*Music and Lyrics by* Don George and Teddy Hall.)

Scene 10

Withers' Opry (by arrangement with C. B. Maddock)
The Old Opry House Manager: C. Withers.

The Storm
First Boy: F. Lentz. *Second Boy*: B. Barry. *Third Boy*: W. Chandler.
Fourth Boy: A. Downing. *The Lost Traveller*: C. Johnson.

Crossing the Baltic
Dictators: J. Callaghan, D. Geoffrey, J. Collins.

The Return of the Cossacks
Ninatochka: C. Johnson. *Vladimir Mamlock*: O. Olsen. *The Problem Child*: ?.
The Town Crier: S. Gibson.

Episode at Bunker Hill.
Paul Revere: O. Olsen. *Private Gams*: S. Dean. *Patrick Henry*: S. Olsen. *Chief
Odessa*: C. Johnson.

An Hour or So With Orson Welles: S. Olsen.

Public Enemy at Doorway of Hell
Gangster Moll: R. Faber. *Filthy McNaety*: C. Johnson. *Big Nick Gat*:
O. Olsen.

Scene 11

"Balloon"
C. Roodney, J. Winters
Danced by Bettymae and Beverly Crane, Ensemble.

Scene 12

Barto and Mann in 'Variations'

Scene 13

The Radio Rogues
J. Hollywood, E. Bartell, S. Chatton

(*Music and Lyrics by* Sammy Fain and Charles Tobias)

"Hellzapoppin Polka"
L. Parker, J. Gleason
(*Music and Lyrics by* Ole Olsen and Jay Levenson)

"I Pledge Allegiance"
The Commandos
(*Music and Lyrics by* Sammy Fain and Charles Tobias)

"Latin With the Patent Leather Hair"
Kim Loo Sisters

Scene 14

Shirley Wayne

Scene 15

"Boomps-a-Daisy"
O. Olsen, C. Johnson, Bettymae & Beverly Crane, Ensemble
(*Music and Lyrics by* Annette Mills.)

Scene 16

Olsen and Johnson

Scene 17

Billy Adams

Scene 18

"When McGregor Sings Off Key"
B. Reed, M. Reed
Danced by S. Wayne, S. Bergh, H. Moore, Ensemble. *Staged by*
Gae Foster.

ACT 2

Scene 1

"Scarem Harem"

Scene 2

"Now You See It—Now You Don't"
O. Olsen. C. Johnson, T. Hardeen, Company

Scene 3

The Charioteers
["Over the Rainbow" (from THE WIZARD OF OZ film, by permission
of MGM)
(*Music by* Harold Arlen. *Lyrics by* E. Y. Harburg.)]

Scene 4

Hal Sherman

Scene 5

"Havana For a Night" (Vereda Tropical)
M. Reed, B. Reed, C. Roodney, J. Winters
(*Music by* Gonzalo Curiel. *Lyrics by* Oscar Hammerstein II.)
Danced by Bettymae and Beverly Crane, F. Sheppard, W. Chandler,
Ensemble, D. Barto, G. Mann.

Scene 6

"Surpise Party"
O. Olsen, C. Johnson, D. Barto, G. Mann, C. Withers, H. Sherwood, J.
Johnson, Berg, Moore, J. C. Olsen, B. Barry, M. Sutherland, J. Wong, S.
Gibson, J. Callaghan, A. Downing, M. Stern

Scene 7

Finale—"Now Comes the Time"
O. Olsen, C. Johnson, D. Barto, G. Mann, C. Withers, H. Sherman, the Radio
Rogues, W. Nilsson, T. Hardeen, the Reed Sisters, Bettymae and Beverly Crane,
C. Roodney, J. Withers, Entire Ensemble

1938.09

SING OUT THE NEWS

A Musical Revue in Two Acts, 21 Scenes. Sketches by Charles Friedman,
(George S. Kaufman and Moss Hart). Music and lyrics by Harold J. Rome.
Staged by Charles Friedman. Dances by Ned McGurn, Dave Gould,
(Charles Walters). Settings by Jo Mielziner. Costumes by John Hambleton.
Orchestrations by Hans Spialek. Ballet music by Will Irwin. Music director,
Max Meth. Produced by Max Gordon in association with George S.
Kaufman and Moss Hart. Opened 24 September 1938 at the Music Box
Theatre and closed 7 January 1939 after 105 performances.

CAST: PHILIP LOEB, HIRAM SHERMAN, MARY JANE WALSH, WILL GEER,
DOROTHY FOX, REX INGRAM, MICHAEL LORING, GINGER MANNERS,
LESLIE LITOMY, JOEY FAYE, DAISY BERNIER, BURTON PIERCE,
CHRISTINA LIND, CHARLES LAWRENCE, Jean Peters, Kathryn Lazell, Jimmy
Lydon, Eleanor Eberle, Jane Frazer, June Allyson, Thelma Lee, Madelyn White, THE
VIRGINIANS (Bruce Rogers, Edwin Smith, Bruce Barclay, Howard Warriner,
Ranolds Dupler, Tomas Mitchell, John Barry, Edward Galloway), Lewis and Van,
Ethel Remey, Ben Ross.

Lillyn Brown, Henrietta Lovelace, Jackie Petty, Ethel Brown, Musa Williams,
Maude Simmons, Sadie McGill, Hazel Scott, Sally Ellis, Lucille Wilson,
Mae Williamson, Elizabeth Dozier, Miriam Franklin, Georgia Jarvis, Rosalind
Gordon, Wanda Macy, Shirley Macy, Jackie Petty, Fred Deming, Joel Friend, Chick
Gagnon, Michael Moore, Fred Nay, Bernard Pearce, Harry Woodford, Cecil Jackson,

John Benton. Add Bates, William Tinney, Allen Tinney, Ray Harrison, Herbert Sumpter, Richard Huey, Ben Wailes, Clarence Wheeler, George Jones, Jr., Gus Jones, Traverse Crawford, Ortho Gaines, Harry Lewis, Elmaurice Miller, James Lillard, Carrington Lewis, Emmett Matthews, Warren Coleman, Louie Williams, Grant Timmons, Sonny Timmons, Allen Tinney.

ACT 1

Scene 1

Time—The Present

Introduced by H. Sherman
M. J. Walsh, G. Manners, D. Bernier, C. Lind, M. Franklin, T. Lee, G. Jarvis, J. Fraser, J. Allyson, E. Eberle, M. White, R. Gordon, K. Lazell. M. Loring, E. Smith, B. Barclay, J. Barry, D. King, H. Warriner, T. Mitchell, E. Galloway, R. Dupler, B. Rogers.

Scene 2

I Married a Republican

Ed: P. Loeb. *Jim*: W. Geer. *Charlie*: L. Litomy. *Mac*: C. Lawrence. *John W. Angel*: H. Sherman. *Meyerowitz*: J. Faye. *Angels*: The Virginians.

Scene 3

"How Long Can Love Keep Laughing?"

The Boy: M. Loring. *The Girl*: C. Lind. *Professor*: G. Manners. *Class of 1938*: K. Lazell, T. Lee, M. Franklin, J. Allyson, M. White, G. Jarvis, J. Frazer, E. Eberle. F. Nay, B. Pearce, J. Friend, F. Deming, C. Gagnon, J. Benton, H. Woodford, B. Norris, M. Moore.

Scene 4

Up, Fiorello!

Mayor LaGuardia: P. Loeb. *First Policeman*: B. Ross. *Second Policeman*: R. Dupler. *Magistrate*: L. Litomy. *Reporter*: M. Moore. *Slot Machine Man*: C. Lawrence. *Boy*: J. Lydon. *Second Boy*: H. Sumpter. *Mayor's Secretary*: C. Lind. *Policemen*: The Virginians.

Scene 5

"Just an Ordinary Guy"

First Couple: D. Bernier, L. Litomy. *Second Couple*: G. Manners, J. Faye. *Third Couple*: M. J. Walsh, M. Loring.

Scene 6

"One of These Fine Days"

Singer: B. Wailes. *Quartette*: T. Crawford, O. Gaines, H. Lewis, E. Miller. *Passersby*: M. Williamson, E. Dozier, L. Wilson. *Old Woman*: L. Holmes. *The Belle*: H. Scott. *Plain Clothes Man*: C. Lawrence. *Second Plain Clothes Man*: J. Barry. *Policeman*: R. Dupler. *Man in Window*: J. Lillard. *Bartender*: W. Coleman. *Dandy*: L. Williams. *Twins*: Estelle and Elizabeth McDowell. *Fortune Teller*: M. Simmons. *First Boy*: W. Tinney. *Second Boy*: A. Tinney. *Kids*: R. Harrison, H. Sumpter. *Neighbor*: L. Brown. *Girl*: E. Brown. *Another Neighbor*: M. Williams. *Iceman*: A. Bates. *Man With Baby Carriage*: R. Huey. *His Wife*: S. Ellis. *His Children*: B. Holmes, W. Macy, S. Macy. *Jim's Wife*: S. Cain. *Gambling Woman*: S. McGill. *Deacon*: George Jones, Jr. *Drunk*: Gus Jones. *Drunk's Wife*: H. Lovelace. *Their Daughter*: J. Petty. *First Gangster*: E. Mathews. *Second Gangster*: C. Lewis. *Jim*: R. Ingram. *Passersby*: G. Timmons, S. Timmons, P. Patterson, J. Petty. *Old Man*: W. Brown. *Trumpet Player*: C. Wheeler.

Scene 7

Gone With the Revolution

W. S. Van Dyke: W. Geer. *Norma*: M. J. Walsh. *Robert Morley*: H. Sherman. *Tyrone Power*: M. Loring. *Script Girl*: D. Bernier. *Assistant to Van Dyke*: B. Ross. *Cameraman*: C. Gagnon. *Maid*: E. Dozier. *A Writer*: C. Lawrence. *Another Writer*: L. Litomy. *L. B.*: P. Loeb.

Scene 8

"Peace and the Diplomat"

(*Ballet Music by* Will Irwin. *Staged by* Charles Walters.)
Peace: D. Fox. *Diplomat*: B. Pierce. *Colleagues*: J. Friend, F. Nay, M. Moore, B. Pearce.

Scene 9

Cafe Society

Lucille: M. J. Walsh. *Chester*: L. Litomy. *Janet*: G. Manners. *Tom*: M. Loring. *Hal*: H. Sherman. *Stephina*: D. Bernier. *Newsboy*: J. Lydon. *Photographer*: J. Benton.

Scene 10

Congressional Minstrels

Mr. Speaker: W. Geer. *Gentleman from Virginia*: P. Loeb. *Gentleman from Vermont*: H. Sherman. *President's Messenger*: M. J. Walsh. *Ways and Means Committee*: M. Loring, L. Litomy, C. Lawrence, J. Faye. *Minstrels*: G. Manners, D. Bernier, C. Lind, E. Eberle, J. Allyson, M. Franklin, G. Jarvis, R. Gordon, K. Lazell, T. Lee, M. White, D. King, J. Frazer. F. Deming, J. Friend, C. Gagnon, M. Moore, F. Nay, B. Pearce, H. Woodford, C. Jackson, J. Benton, B. Norris, The Virginians.

ACT 2

Scene 1

"Tell Me, Pretty Maiden" (Modern Florodora Girl)
M. J. Walsh, the Florodora Girls, the Virginians, Boys of Today

Scene 2

"Plaza 6-9423"
H. Sherman

Scene 3

A Liberal Education

Father: W. Geer. *Junior*: J. Faye. *Assisted by* the Maypole Dancers and the Marchers.

Scene 4

Sing Ho for Private Enterprise

First Tycoon: W. Geer. *Second Tycoon*: L. Litomy. *Third Tycoon*: P. Loeb. *Fourth Tycoon*: C. Lawrence. *Debutantes*: M. Franklin, E. Eberle.

Scene 5

"My Heart Is Unemployed"

M. J. Walsh, M. Loring
Dance Interlude by D. Fox, B. Pierce. *Assisted by* the Boys and Girls. (*Ballet Music by* Will Irwin.)

Scene 6

"Yip Ahoy, or Adrift on the Old Prairie"
P. Loeb
Pete: J. Faye.

Scene 7

Man of the Year ("Franklin D. Roosevelt Jones")

Mr. Jones: R. Ingram. *The Jones Family*: L. Brown, H. Lovelace, J. Petty. *Guests*: E. Brown, M. Williams, A. Bates, W. Tinney, A. Tinney, R. Harrison, H. Sumpter, R. Huey, B. Wailes, C. Wheeler, George Jones, Jr., Gus Jones, T. Crawford, O. Gaines, H. Lewis, E. Miller, M. Simmons, J. Lillard, S. McGill, C. Lewis, H. Scott, S. Cain, S. Ellis, E. Matthews, W. Coleman, L. Watson, M. Williamson, E. Dozier, L. Williams.

Scene 8

The F.L.O.P. Plan

Secretary: C. Lawrence. *Groucho Marx*: P. Loeb. *Chico Marx*: L. Litomy. *Harpo Marx*: J. Faye. *Mrs. Rittenhouse*: E. Remey. *A Girl*: G. Manners.

Scene 9

"Entre Nous"
M. J. Walsh

Scene 10

International Mountain Climbers

Chamberlain: H. Sherman. *Stalin*: L. Litomy. *Daladier*: M. Loring. *Benes*: C. Lawrence. *Hitler*: W. Geer. *Mussolini*: B. Ross. *Hirohito*: J. Faye.

Scene 11

"We've Got the Song"
Entire Company
Uncle Sam: P. Loeb.

1938.10 # KNIGHTS OF SONG

A Musical Excursion into the Lives of Gilbert and Sullivan (Musical Play) in Two Acts, 12 Scenes. Book by Glendon Allvine, based on a story by Glendon Allvine and Adele Gutman Nathan[3]. Staged by Oscar Hammerstein II. Gilbert and Sullivan musical excerpts staged by Avalon Collard. Settings by Raymond Sovey. Costumes by Kate Lawson. Orchestra directed by George Hirst. Orchestrations furnished by Tams-Witmark Music Library; additional orchestrations by Harold Sanford. Produced by Laurence Schwab. Opened 17 October 1938 at the 51st Street Theatre and closed 29 October 1938 after 16 performances.

CAST (in order of appearance): *Harris*: Victor Beecroft. *William Schwenk Gilbert*: NIGEL BRUCE. *Arthur Seymour Sullivan*: JOHN MOORE. *Richard D'Oyly Carte*: REGINALD BACH. *McManus*: JOHN ADAIR. *Wardrobe Woman*: Shirley Gale. *Mrs. Gilbert*: Rosalind Ivan. *Maid*: Carrie Glenn. *Mrs. Cynthia Bradley*: NATALIE HALL. *His Royal Highness, Albert Edward, Prince of Wales*: MONTY WOOLLEY. *Oscar Wilde*: ROBERT CHISHOLM. *George Bernard Shaw*: WINSTON O'KEEFE. *Sarah Burnside*: Martha Roberts. *Vera Tracy*: Shannon Dean. *Mary Lou Simmons*: Eva Paul.

---

[3]A fictional account of the Gilbert and Sullivan collaboration. Music by Arthur Sullivan. Lyrics by William S. Gilbert.

Butler: Robert Collins. *Her Majesty, Queen Victoria*: MOLLY PEARSON. *Flunkey*: Leonard Rocky. *His Grace, the Archbishop of Canterbury*: HENRY MOWBRAY. *Ponsonby*: Orlo Rexford. *Lady-in-Waiting*: Dorothy Johnson. *Times Reporter*: Gladstone Waldrip. *Herald Reporter*: Norman Gray. *Tribune Reporter*: David Showalter. *Organ Grinder*: Burr Crandall. *James Caldwell Bradley*: Bruce Evans. *Union Delegate*: William Foran. *Clara*: Myrtis Jackson. *Thomas*: Everett West. *Lord Ansel*: David Showalter. *James McNeill Whistler*: Charles Atkin. *Perkins*: Bruce Evans. *David, Grandson of Edward VII*: Edward Ryan, Jr.

Characters in Excerpts from Gilbert and Sullivan Comic Operas: "Pinafore" *Sir Joseph Porter*: Ralph Bunker. *Cousin Hebe*: Shirley Dale. *Corcoran*: Earle MacVeigh. *Josephine*: Myrtis Jackson. *Buttercup*: Mary Dyer. *Ralph*: Everett West. *Dick Deadeye*: Orlo Rexford. *Bosum*: George Vaughan. *Mate*: Laurence Siegle. *Midshipmate*: Martha Burnett. "Pirates of Penzance" *Pirate King*: Laurence Siegel. *Mabel*: Shirley Dale. *Ruth*: Mary Dyer. *Major General*: Ralph Bunker. *Samuel*: Earle MacVeigh. *Frederic*: Everett West. *Edith*: Annamary Dickey. *Kate*: Myrtis Jackson. *Isabelle*: Martha Burnett. "The Mikado" *Nanki-Poo*: Everett West. *Katisha*: Mary Hoppel. *Pish-Tush*: Orlo Rexford. *Pitti-Sing*: Annamary Dickey. *Yum-Yum*: Shirley Dale. *Peep-Bo*: Martha Burnett. The Command Performance: *Three Little Maids from "The Mikado"*: Annamary Dickey, Shirtey Dale, Vera Deane. *Judge from "Trial By Jury"*: Ralph Bunker. *Dame Carruthers from "Yeomen of the Guard"*: Mary Hoppel. *Patience from "Patience"*: Myrtis Jackson. *Marco from "The Gondoliers"*: Everett West.

Ensemble: George Vaughan, Anthony Ferrara, Leonard Rockey, Edward Hayes, Paul Davin, Karl Holly, Jay Amiss, Remington Olmstead, Jr., Freeman Bloodgood, Laurence Siegel, Bob Collins, Angus Cairns, Gladstone Waldrip, Earl Ashcroft, Norman Gray, Norman Crandall. Davie Gladstone, Virginia Cole, Sally Hadley, Beulah Blake, Sandra Nova, Lois Kirk, Ruth Wenton, Vera Dean, Betty Sparks, Emily Marsh, Dorothy Johnson, Ann Francis.

Act 1, Scene 1: Stage of the Opera Comique, London, 1878. Dress Rehearsal of "Pinafore." *Scene 2*: Upstairs Library of Gilbert's London Home. A Sunday evening a few months later. *Scene 3*: Mrs. Bradley's Drawing Room. An hour later. *Scene 4*: Queen Victoria's Private Reception Room, Windsor Castle. A few days later. *Scene 5*: A steamship dock in Lower New York. 5 November 1879. *Scene 6*: Dress Rehearsal of "The Pirates of Penzance" on the stage of the Fifth Avenue Theatre, New York, 30 December 1879.

Act 2, Scene 1: Arthur Sullivan's Study. 1883. *Scene 2*: Mrs. Bradley's Drawing Room. New Year's Eve, 1889. *Scene 3*: D'Oyly Carte's Office in the Savoy Theatre, London. June, 1900. *Scene 4*: Stage of Savoy Theatre. Finale of Act I of "The Mikado" revival, same evening. *Scene 5*: The King's Private Reception Room in Windsor Castle. 15 July 1907. *Scene 6*: Grand Ballroom, Windsor Castle. Same afternoon.

ACT 1

"Over the Bright Blue Sea" (H.M. S. Pinafore)
Singing Girls

"Sir Joseph's Berge Is Seen" (H.M. S. Pinafore)
Singing Men and Girls

"Now Give Three Cheers" (H.M. S. Pinafore)
R. Bunker, E. MacVeigh, S. Dale

"When I Was a Lad" (H.M. S. Pinafore)
R. Bunker, S. Dale, Ensemble

Finale, Act 2, "H.M. S. Pinafore"
E. MacVeigh, R. Bunker, S. Dale, M. Jackson, E. West, O. Rexford, Ensemble

"Ring the Merry Bells" (H.M. S. Pinafore)
N. Hall, E. MacVeigh, R. Bunker, Guests

"I Was a Pale Young Curate Then" (The Sorcerer)
R. Chisholm

"Merry Young Heart" (The Sorcerer)
N. Hall, J. Moore

"When I, Good Friends" (Trial By Jury)
J. Moore

"Onward Christian Soldiers"
N. Hall

Opening Chorus, "The Pirates of Penzance"
E. MacVeigh, Pirates

"Oh, Is There Not One Maiden Breast" (The Pirates of Penzance)
E. West, Singing Girls

"Poor Wandering One" (The Pirates of Penzance)
S. Dale, Singing Girls

"Policeman's Song" (The Pirates of Penzance)
(Sergeant, Policeman)

Finale, Act 2, "The Pirates of Penzance"
L. Siegel, R. Bunker, M. Dyer, S. Dale, A. Dickey, M. Jackson, E. West, E. MacVeigh, N. Hall, Ensemble

ACT 2

"Happy With Winged Feet" (Ivanhoe)
M. Jackson, E. West

"None Shall Part Us" (Ivanhoe)
N. Hall, J. Moore

"The Flowers That Bloom in the Spring" (The Mikado)
N. Hall, J. Moore

"Am I Alone?" (Patience)
R. Chisholm

"The Moon and I" (The Mikado)
N. Hall

"Finale, Act 1, "The Mikado"
M. Hoppel, E. West, S. Dale, A. Dickey, M. Burnett, O. Rexford, Ensemble

Command Performance:

"Three Little Maids from School" (The Mikado)
S. Dale, V. Deane, A. Dickey

"I Am a Judge" (Trial By Jury)
R. Bunker, Ensemble

"The Screw May Twist" (The Yeomen of the Guard)
M. Hoppel, Ensemble

"For I Am Blithe" (Patience)
M. Jackson

"Take a Pair of Sparkling Eyes" (The Gondoliers)
E. West

Finale—"Bow Bow" (Iolanthe)
Principals, Ensemble

1938.11   KNICKERBOCKER HOLIDAY

A Musical Comedy in Two Acts, 3 Scenes. Book and lyrics by Maxwell Anderson. (Inspired by Washington Irving's "Knickerbocker History of New York.") Music by Kurt Weill. Staged by Joshua Logan. Settings by Jo Mielziner. Costumes by Frank Bevan. Dances by Carl Randall and Edwin Denby. Music director, Maurice de Abravanel. Orchestrations by Kurt Weill. Produced by the Playwrights' Company. Opened 19 October 1938 at the Ethel Barrymore Theatre, moved 13 February 1939 to the 46th Street Theatre, and closed 11 March 1939 after 168 performances.

CAST (in order of appearance[4]): *Washington Irving*: RAY MIDDLETON. *Anthony Corlear*: HARRY MEEHAN. *Tienhoven*: MARK SMITH. *Vanderbilt*: GEORGE WATTS. *Roosevelt*: FRANCIS PIERLOT. *DePeyster*: CHARLES ARNT. *DeVries*: JOHN E. YOUNG. *Van Rensselaer*: JAMES PHILLIPS. *Van Cortlandt, Jr.*: Richard Cowdery. *Tina Tienhoven*: JEANNE MADDEN. *Brom Broeck*: RICHARD KOLLMAR. *Tenpin*: CLARENCE NORDSTROM. *Schermerhorn*: HOWARD FREEMAN. *Pieter Stuyvesant*: WALTER HUSTON. *General Poffenburgh*: Donald Black. *Mistress Schermerhorn*: Edith Angold.

Citizens of New Amsterdam: Helen Carroll, Jane Brotherton, Carol Deis, Robert Arnold, Bruce Hamilton, Ruth Mamel, William Marel, Margaret MacLaren, Robert Rounseville, Rufus Smith, Margaret Stewart, Erika Zaranova, William Wahlert. *Soldiers*: Albert Allen, Matthias Ammann, Dow Fonda, Warde Peters. *Fighters*: The Algonquins.

Act 1: Washington Irving's Study, 1809; The Battery. A morning in 1647.

Act 2, Scene 1: Interior of the jail. Evening of the same day. *Scene 2*: The Battery. The following day.

ACT 1

Introduction
R. Middleton

"Clackety-Clack"
R. Middleton, Girls

"It's a Law"[5]
M. Smith, Council

"There's Nowhere to Go But Up"
R. Kollmar, C. Nordstrom, Ensemble

"It Never Was You"
R. Kollmar, J. Madden

"How Can You Tell an American?"
R. Kollmar, R. Middleton

---

[4]Council Members included the characters Anthony Corlear, Tienhoven, Vanderbilt, Roosevelt, DePeyster, DeVries, Van Rensselaer, Van Cortlandt Jr., Schermerhorn.
[5]Replaced during run by:
"Hush-Hush"
Roosevelt (George Watts), Ensemble

"Will You Remember Me?"
R. Kollmar, J. Madden, Ensemble

"One Touch of Alchemy"
W. Huston, Ensemble

"The One Indispensable Man"
W. Huston, M. Smith

"Young People Think About Love"
J. Madden, R. Kollmar, Ensemble

"September Song"
W. Huston

Finale
W. Huston, Ensemble

ACT 2

Scene 1

"Ballad of the Robbers"
R. Middleton

"We Are Cut in Twain"
R. Kollmar, J. Madden

Prologue to Scene 2—"There's Nowhere to Go But Up" (reprise)
R. Middleton

Scene 2

"To War!"
W. Huston, Council, Male Ensemble

"Our Ancient Liberties"
M. Smith, H. Meehan, Council

"Romance and Musketeer"
Ensemble

"The Scars"
W. Huston, Ensemble

Dance of the Algonquins
The Algonquins

"Dirge for a Soldier"
Ensemble

"Ve Vouldn't Gonto Do It"
Ensemble

Finale
W. Huston, R. Middleton, R. Kolmar, Ensemble

1938.12 THE GIRL FROM WYOMING

A Musical Burlesque in Three Acts, 13 Scenes. Book by John Van Antwerp [John Krimsky]. Music by Richard Lewine. Lyrics by Ted Fetter. Book staged by Robert Ross. Dances staged by John Pierce. Settings by Eugene B. Dunkel. Costumes by Peggy Clark. Music director, Al Evans. Orchestrations by Ben Ludlow. Produced by John and Jerrold Krimsky. Opened 29 October 1938 at the American Music Hall and closed 21 January 1939 after 86 performances.

CAST (in order of appearance): *Ben Longwood*: PHILIP HUSTON. *Mrs. Longwood*: Nellie Thorne. *Sheriff Peters*: Billy M. Greene. *Sleepy, a cowboy*: TONY KRABER. *Rusty*: Duncan Baldwin. *Marcy Desmond*: GEORGE PETRIE. *Alkali, a prospector*: Donald MacDonald. *The Girl from Wyoming*: JUNE WALKER. *Chiquori*: Anne Hunter. *Pedro*: JAMES RUSSO. *Bartender*: Jack Goldie.
Cowboys: Bruce Gordan, Duncan Baldwin, Walter Reed Smith, Alfred Brower, Jack Riley, Norman Barcliff. *Cowgirls*: Sherrard Pollard, Mary LaRoche, Jackie Susanne [Jacqueline Susann], Ruth Mann, Polly Smiley, Irene Mann.

Act 1, Scene 1: A Sitting Room in Boston's Back Bay. *Scene 2*: A Western Plain. *Scene 3*: Main Street of El Reno, Nevada. *Scene 4*: Desmond's Elysian Fields Saloon.

Act 2, Scene 1: Western Plain. *Scene 2*: The Prairie at Night. *Scene 3*: Western Plain. *Scene 4*: Desmond's Elysian Fields Saloon.

Act 3, Scene 1: Main Street of El Reno. *Scene 2*: Interior of Mountain Cabin. *Scene 3*: Western Plain. *Scene 4*: Mountain Pass. *Scene 5*: A Gulch.

ACT 1

Scene 1

"Boston in the Spring"
P. Huston, Ensemble

Scene 3

"Ride Cowboy Ride"
Cowboys, Cowgirls

"Hats Off"
G. Petrie, D. MacDonald, B. Greene, Cowboys

Scene 4

"Manuelo"
A. Hunter

"The Dying Cowboy" (Take My Bridgework Back to Mother)
D. MacDonald, G. Petrie, B. Greene, T. Kraber

ACT 2

Scene 1

"Lullaby of the Plain"
Cowboys

Scene 2

"Our Home"
P. Huston, Girl, Entire Company

Scene 4

"Stay East, Young Man"
Cowboys, Cowgirls

"Boston in the Spring" (reprise)
Boston Girls

Finaletto Act 2 (Dream Sequence)

ACT 3

Scene 2

"Kickin' the Corn Around"
Entire Company

Scene 5

Finale
Entire Company

1938.13 LEAVE IT TO ME

A Musical Comedy in Two Acts, 14 Scenes. Book by Samuel and Bella Spewack. (Based on their play "Clear All Wires.") Music and lyrics by Cole Porter. Staged by Samuel Spewack. Dances and ensembles by Robert Alton. Settings by Albert Johnson. Costumes by Raoul Pene du Bois. Music director, Robert Emmett Dolan. Orchestrations by Donald J. Walker. Produced by Vinton Freedley. Opened 9 November 1938 at the Imperial Theatre, closing 15 July 1939 for vacation after 291 performances; re-opened September 4 1939 at the Imperial Theatre for 16 additional performances, closing 16 September 1939 after a total of 307 performances.

CAST (in order of appearance): *First Secretary*: Ruth Bond. *Second Secretary*: Beverly Hosier. *Buckley Joyce Thomas*: WILLIAM GAXTON. *First Reporter*: William Lilling. *Second Reporter*: Walter Monroe. *Dolly Winslow*: MARY MARTIN. *J.H. Brody*: Edward H. Robins. *Mrs. Goodhue*: SOPHIE TUCKER. *Mrs. Goodhue's Daughters*: April, Mildred Chenaval, Ruth Daye, Audrey Palmer, Kay Picture. *Reporter*: Chett Bree. *Photographer*: George E. Mack. *French Conductor*: Walter Armin. *Chauffeur*: James W. Carr. *Alonzo P. Goodhue*: VICTOR MOORE. *Secretaries to Mr. Goodhue*: Gene Kelly, Maurice Kelly, Roy Ross, Jack Seymour, Jack Stanton, Walter B. Long, Jr. *Prince Alexander Tomofsky*: Eugene Sigaloff. *Jerry Granger*: Dean Carlton. *Colette*: TAMARA [DRASIN]. *Kostya*: Joseph Kallini. *Peasant*: Peter Lopouhin. *Sozanoff*: Alexander Asro. *Military Attaché*: John Eliot. *Naval Attaché*: John Panter. *Secretaries*: Roy Ross, Jack Seymour. *Decorators*: Michael Forbes, Thomas Jafollo. *Waiter*: Don Cortez. *German Ambassador*: Hans Hansen. *French Ambassador*: Walter Armin. *Latvian Minister*: Peter Lopouhin. *British Ambassador*: J. Colville Dunn. *Italian Ambassador*: Thomas Jafollo. *Japanese Ambassador*: George E. Mack. *Mackenzie*: Charles Campbell. *Graustein*: Matthew Vodnoy. *Folkin*: Ivan Izmailov. *Secretary*: Stanton Bier. *Foreign Minister*: Alexis Bolan. *Stalin*: Walter Armin.
The Buccaneers: Don Cortez, John Eliot, Michael Forbes, Eddie Heisler, Tom Jafolla, William Lilling, Walter Monroe, John Panter. *Guests*: Monica Bannister, Adele Jergens, Ruth Joseph, Evelyn Kelly, Viva Selwood, Frances Tannehill, Evelyn Bonefine. *Les Girls*: Vickie Belling, Dorothy Benson, Ruth Bond, Pearl Harris, Beverly Hosier, Dorothea Jackson, Nancy Lee, June LeRoy, Evelyn Moser, Mary Ann Parker, Barbara Pond, Jean Scott, Lawrie Shevlin, Zynaid Spencer, Marie Vanneman, Marie Vaughan.

Act 1, Scene 1: City Room of the Paris and Chicago *World-Tribune*. *Scene 2*: Gare de l'Est, Paris. *Scene 3*: A Park in Moscow. *Scene 4*: Anteroom in the American Embassy, Moscow. *Scene 5*: Goodhue's Bedroom in the Embassy. *Scene 6*: Thomas' Hotel Suite in Moscow. *Scene 7*: Red Square.

Act 2, Scene 1: Red Square, two weeks later. *Scene 2*: A Droshka. *Scene 3*: The Anteroom. *Scene 4*: A Steppe. *Scene 5*: Drawing Room in the Embassy. *Scene 6*: The Park. *Scene 7*: Railroad Station, Moscow.

ACT 1

"How Do You Spell Ambassador?"
Reporters

"We Drink to You, J. H. Hardy"
W. Gaxton, Guests

"Vite, Vite, Vite"
Porters, Girls

"I'm Taking the Steps to Russia"
S. Tucker, April, M. Chenaval, R. Daye, A. Palmer, K. Picture, G. Kelly, M. Kelly, R. Ross, J. Seymour, J. Stanton, W. B. Long, Les Girls

"Get Out of Town"
Tamara

"When It's All Said and Done"
W. Gaxton, M. Martin, Les Girls

"Most Gentlemen Don't Like Love"
S. Tucker, April, M. Chenaval, R. Daye, A. Palmer, K. Picture, G. Kelly, M. Kelly, R. Ross, J. Seymour, J. Stanton, W. B. Long

"Comrade Alonzo"
Ensemble

ACT 2

Opening
Ensemble

"From Now On"
W. Gaxton, Tamara

"I Want to Go Home"
V. Moore

"My Heart Belongs to Daddy"
M. Martin

"Tomorrow"
S. Tucker, Ensemble

"Far, Far Away"
W. Gaxton, Tamara

"From the U.S.A. to the U.S.S.R."
V. Moore, S. Tucker, April, M. Chenaval, R. Daye, A. Palmer, K. Picture

Finale
Entire Company

1938.14 THE BOYS FROM SYRACUSE

A Musical Comedy in Two Acts, 9 Scenes. Book by George Abbott. Based on William Shakespeare's play "The Comedy of Errors." Music by Richard Rodgers. Lyrics by Lorenz Hart. Directed by George Abbott. Scenery and lighting by Jo Mielziner. Costumes by Irene Sharaff. Choreography by George Balanchine. Music director, Harry Levant. Orchestrations by Hans Spialek. Produced by George Abbott. Opened 23 November 1938 at the Alvin Theatre and closed 10 June 1939 after 235 performances.

CAST (in order of appearance): *The Masks*: Robert Sidney, Harry Peterson. *Singing Policeman*: Bob Lawrence. *Another Policeman*: James Wilkinson. *Antipholus of Ephesus*: RONALD GRAHAM. *Dromio of Ephesus*: TEDDY HART. *Dancing Policeman*: George Church. *Tailor*: Clifford Dunstan. *Tailor's Apprentice*: Burl Ives. *Antipholus of Syracuse*: EDDIE ALBERT. *Dromio of Syracuse*: JIMMY SAVO. *Merchant of Syracuse*: Byron Shores. *Duke of Ephesus*: Carroll Ashburn. *Aegeon*: John O'Shaughnessy. *Luce*: WYNN MURRAY. *Adriana*: MURIEL ANGELUS. *Luciana*: MARCY WESTCOTT. *Sorcerer*: Owen Martin. *Courtezan*: BETTY BRUCE. *Secretary to Courtezan*: Heidi Vosseler. *Angelo*: John Clarke. *First Maid*: Florine Callahan. *Second Maid*: Claire Wolf. *Third Maid*: Alice Craig. *Merchant of Ephesus*: Clifford Dunstan. *Seeress*: Florence Fair.

Singers: Grace Albert, Laura Kellogg, Dolores Anderson, Armonce Wilkins, Marguerite Benton, Margaret Walsh, James Wilkinson, Joseph Scandor, Joe Granville, Herbert Wood. *Dancers*: Libby Bennett, Ruth Brady, Renee Cettel, Stella Clausen, Alice Craig, Bee Farnum, Ruth Gormly, Claire Harvey, Lita Lede, Connie Leslie, Vivien Moore, Florine Callahan, Mildred Solly, Anna Mae Tesslo, Davenie Watson, Betty De Elmo, Claire Wolf, Micky Alvarez, Sidney Gordon, Dan Karty, Tommy Lynch, Jack Malis, Edwin Mills, Harry Peterson, Joe Harris, Lee Tannen, Beau Tilden, Robert Howard, (Buddy Douglas).

Act 1, Scene 1: Before the Temple of Justice in Ephesus. *Scene 2*: Inside the House of Antipholus of Ephesus. *Scene 3*: A Square in Ephesus. *Scene 4*: Inside the House of Antipholus of Ephesus. *Scene 5*: Street outside the House of Antipholus of Ephesus.

Act 2, Scene 1: Street outside the House of Antipholus of Ephesus. *Scene 2*: A Square in Ephesus. *Scene 3*: Inside the House of Antipholus of Ephesus. *Scene 4*: A Square in Ephesus.

ACT 1

Forward
R. Sidney, H. Peterson

Scene 1

"I Had Twins"
B. Lawrence, J. Wilkinson, Ensemble

"Dear Old Syracuse"
J. Savo, E. Albert
Danced by E. Albert, A. Craig, V. Moore, L. Lede, Dancers.

"What Can You Do With a Man?"
W. Murray, T. Hart

Scene 2

"Falling in Love (With Love)"
M. Angelus, Ladies

Scene 3

"(The) Shortest Day of the Year"
R. Graham, D. Anderson, Policemen
Danced by B. Bruce, H. Vosseler, G. Church.

Scene 4

"This Can't Be Love"
M. Westcott, E. Albert

Scene 5

"Let Antipholus In"
Entire Company

ACT 2

Scene 1

"Ladies of the Evening"
B. Lawrence, J. Wilkinson, Policemen, Courtezans
Danced by H. Vosseler, G. Church.

"He and She"
W. Murray, J. Savo

"You Have Cast Your Shadow (On the Sea)"
M. Westcott, E. Albert

Scene 2

"Come With Me"
B. Lawrence, R. Graham, J. Wilkinson, J. Clarke, Singers

"Big Brother"
T. Hart

The Ballet
Danced by J. Savo, E. Albert, B. Douglas, H. Vosseler, R. Howard, W. Murray, Dancers.

Scene 3

"Sing for Your Supper"
M. Angelus, M. Westcott, W. Murray, Ladies
Danced by B. Bruce, Ensemble. (*Trio Arrangement by* Hugh Martin.)

Scene 4

"Oh, Diogenes"
W. Murray
Danced by G. Church, B. Bruce, Ensemble.

Happy Ending (Finale)
Entire Company

1938.15 GREAT LADY

A Biography[6] with Music (A Musical Play) in Two Acts, 14 Scenes. Book and lyrics by Earle Crooker and Lowell Brentano. Music by Frederick Loewe. Staged by Bretaigne Windust. Settings by Albert R. Johnson. Choreography by William Dollar. Costumes by Lucinda Ballard and Scott Wilson. Orchestrations by Hans Spialek. Music director, John Fredhoven. Produced by Dwight Deere Wiman and J. H. Del Bondio by arrangement with Frank Crumit. Opened 1 December 1938 at the Majestic Theatre and closed 17 December 1938 after 20 performances.

CAST (in order of appearance): *Office Boys*: Anthony Albert, Fernando Alonso, Basil Galahoff. *Stenographers*: Hortense Kharklin, Charlotte Sumner, Muriel Gratton, Joan Mann. *Managing Editor*: Edward Kane. *Bill Adams*: William Chambers. *Sub-Editor*:

---

[6]Suggested by the life of Eliza Jumel.

Frederick Schweppe. *Eliza Bowen*, later Elsa de la Croix: NORMA TERRIS. *Jailer*: William Mende. *Pierre de Moreau*: SHEPPERD STRUDWICK. *Rene Lorraine*: Jules Epailly. *Captain Jacques*: JOSEPH MACAULAY. *Freelove Clark*: HELEN FORD. *Nicky Clark*: Edward Craven. *Waitress*: June Forrest. *Floorwalker*: Andre Eglevsky. *Waiter*: John Young. *Stephen Jumel*: TULLIO CARMINATI. *Madame Colette*: IRENE BORDONI. *Prologue*: JOSEPH MACAULAY. *Organ Grinder*: Willliam Mende. *Poor Girl*: Leda Anchutina. *Rich Boy*: Annabelle Lyon. *First Admirer*: Basil Galahoff. *Second Admirer*: Anthony Albert. *Third Admirer*: Russell Protopoff. *Jonathan*: Robert Shanley. *Elizabeth Clark*: Jeanne Elkins. *Maid*: Katherine Mayfield. *A Doctor*: William Fariss. *A Minister*: Frederick Schweppe. *A Caretaker*: John Young. *Butler*: Walter Cassel. *First Assistant Dressmaker*: Katherine Mayfield. *Second Assistant Dressmaker*: Beverly Kirk. *Decazes*: Gage Clark. *Major Domo*: Walter Cassel. *Marquise*: Grace Manvini. *A Duchess*: Isabel Girard. *A Countess*: Doris Moore. *Louis XVIII*: Robert Greig. *Housekeeper*: Christine Johnson. *Maid*: Dorothy Kirsten. *Premier Danseur*: ANDRE EGLEVSKY. *Premier Danseuses*: LEDA ANCHUTINA, ANNABELLE LYON.

Ladies of the Ballet: Alice [Alicia] Alonso, Tania Clell, Dorothy Denton, Muriel Gratton, Hermione Darrell, Holly Howard, Nora Kaye, Hortense Kharklin, Albia Kavan, Joan Mann, Mary McDonnell, Yvonne Patterson, Lillian Reilly, Doris Jane Solly, Libby Starks, Charlotte Sumner, Olga Suarez, Margaret Vasilieff, Vera Volkenau. *Gentlemen of the Ballet*: Anthony Albert, Fernando Alonso, Arthur Frederix, Basil Galahoff, Paul Godkin, Edward Hedges, Jay Martinez, Russell Protopoff, Richard Reed, Jerome Robbins, Newcomb Rice.

Act 1, Scene 1: (a) Offices of *"Live"* Magazine, New York, 1939. (b) Managing Editor's Office. *Scene 2*: The Stocks, Providence, R.I., 1793. *Scene 3*: Clark's Ordinary, Providence. Immediately after. *Scene 4*: (a) Pierre's Room in Bordeaux. Six months later. (b) The same. Six months later. *Scene 5*: Madame Colette's Dressmaking Shop. *Scene 6*: Jumel's Suite in a Paris Hotel. *Scene 7*: John Street Theatre, New York, 1804. *Scene 8*: A Carriage Ride. A month later. *Scene 9*: Elsa's Boudoir, New York. Two weeks later.

Act 2, Scene 1: (a) Drawing Room, Jumel Mansion, New York, 1939. (b) The same, 1814. *Scene 2*: Madame Colette's Dressmaking Shop. Six months later. *Scene 3*: (a) Cabin Aboard the *"Elsa."* Some time later. (b) Elsa's Reverie. (c) Six hours later. *Scene 4*: A Room in the Jumel House in Paris. Some time later. *Scene 5*: Drawing Room, Jumel Mansion, New York, 1852.

ACT 1
Scene 2
"A Promenade"
    N. Terris
Scene 3
"Sweet William"
    H. Ford, J. Macaulay, Ensemble
"I Have Room in My Heart"
    N. Terris, S. Strudwick
Scene 4
"Why Can't This Night Last Forever?"
    N. Terris
Scene 5
Ballet
    A. Eglevsky, A. Lyon, L. Anchutina, N. Terris, Corps de Ballet
Scene 6
"May I Suggest Romance?"
    I. Bordoni
"In the Carefree Realm of Fancy"
    N. Terris, T. Carminati
Scene 7
"To Whom It May Concern"
    N. Terris
"I Have Room in My Heart" (reprise)
    N. Terris, S. Strudwick
Scene 8
"Though Tongues May Wag"
    N. Terris, T. Carminati, Ensemble
Scene 9
Finale (Act 1)
    N. Terris, T. Carminati, H. Ford, S. Strudwick, E. Craven, Ensemble
ACT 2
Scene 1
"Keep Your Hand on Your Heart"
    T. Carminati
Scene 2
"And So Will You"
    I. Bordoni

"The Little Corporal"
    S. Strudwick, Ensemble
Scene 3
"Sisters Under the Skin"
    H. Ford, Gentlemen of the Ballet
"There Had to Be the Waltz"
    N. Terris, S. Strudwick, Ensemble
        (a) The Waltz: *Napoleon*: R. Schultz. Corps de Ballet.
        (b) Pas de Sept: H. Howard, A. Kavan, Y. Patterson, N. Kaye, O. Suarez, H. Kahrklin, D. J. Solly.
        (c) Pas de Trois and Variations: L. Anchutina, A. Lyon, A. Eglevsky.
Scene 4
"I Never Saw a King Before"
    H. Ford, E. Craven, Ensemble
Scene 5
"Madame Is At Home"
    C. Johnson, K. Mayfield, B. Kirk, J. Forrest, D. Kirsten
Finale
    Entire Company

1938.16

PINOCCHIO

An Extravaganza with Music in Three Acts, 9 Scenes. Book and lyrics adapted by Yasha Frank from the Italian "Adventures of Pinocchio" by Carlo Collodi. Music by Eddison von Ottenfeld and Armando Loredo. Staged by Yasha Frank. Choreography by Alexandra Mamlet. Settings by Perry Watkins. Lighting by Moe Hack. Costumes by James Cochrane. Properties and special effects by Stephen Jan Tichacek. Military dance routine by Harry Miller. Special musical arrangements by I. L. Epstein. WPA Federal Theatre Orchestra Conductor, Aaron Pressman. Associate producer, Matt Shelvey. Produced by Morris Ankrum for the WPA Federal Theatre. Opened 23 December 1938 at the Ritz Theatre and closed 30 June 1939 after 197 performances.

CAST (in order of appearance): *Gepetto*: ALLAN FRANK. *His Cat*: ETTORE MAG-GIONI. *Town Crier*: Emil Hirsch. *Mice*: Jean Harper, Phyllis Reed. *Young Father*: Vito Scotti. *Pinocchio*: EDWIN MICHAELS. *Juggler*: Archie Onri. *Tumbler*: Anthony J. Salo. *Grandpa*: Bill Swan. *Puppeteers*: Ernest Moore, Elizabeth Roberts. *Marionette*: Gabrielle Duval. *Warrior Puppet*: George Cohan. *Rag Doll*: HELEN GALUBACK. *Hansel and Gretel*: Phyllis Reed, Mary Shannon. *Beggar Women*: Anya Kubert, Francena Scott. *Blue Haired Fairy Queen*: Georgiana Brand. *The Cat*: SAM LEWIS. *The Fox*: EDWARD LALOR. *Jolly Coachman*: Robert Williamson. *Ringmaster*: David Manning. *The General*: Hans Schweng. *Pinocchio, the Mule*: Mickey Kane. *The Maestro*: Sam Lewis. *The Fireman*: Sherman Dirkson. *Mlle. Fifi*: Kohana. *Capt. Fried Meatty*: Harry Duncan. *Lion*: Phil Dwyer. *Ship Figurehead*: Christiani. *Male Goldfish*: Kohana. *Female Goldfish*: Elizabeth Reydova. *Blind Woman*: Elaine Eldridge. *Baker's Daughter*: PHYLLIS REED.

Villagers: Sonia Raskov, Myrna Westcott, Adele Newald, Sarah Kyles, Yasha Yakolev, Bill Swan, Phil Dwyer, Albert Pizzoni, Doxie Thomas, Anne Wheeler, Arthur Keith, Bill Swan. *School Children*: Jean Harper, Katherine Shaelton, Rozsa Leone, Greta Karnot, Phyllis Reed, Frances Hess. *Boobies*: James Kelo, James Leddy, Stephen Leddy, Joe Melino, Will Smith, Albert Pizzoni. *Military*: Fred Gibson, Archie Savage, Arnold Wiley, Ollie Simmons, Max Burns. *Phoolharmonic Orchestra*: Sherman Dirkson, Sam Lazar, Albert Edwards, Jack Gropper, Joseph Palkowich, Waddel Thompson, Frances Heaton, Nicoli Mascariello, Vincent Castelli. *Calliope Quartet*: Ralph Northern, Joseph Northern, James Rielly, Herbert Brown. *Clowns*: Jack Toder, H. Weinberg, Will Smith, Arthur Keith, Albert Pizzoni, George Cohan, Pete Gimmarino. *Animals*: Joe Cooper, Albert Grant, Theodore Gross, Attilio Salzano, Pat McCullough, Frederick Giulano. *Mermaids*: Frances Hess, Greta Karnot, Sylvia Lipton, Katherine Shaelton, Mary Zaretsky, Marlyne Tobin, Celia Fisher, Jean Harper.

Act 1, Scene 1: Gepetto's Workshop, Italy. Long ago. *Scene 2*: A Street. *Scene 3*: A Marionette Stage.

Act 2, Scene 1: A Fork in the Road. *Scene 2*: The Land of the Boobies. *Scene 3*: Under the Big Top.

Act 3, Scene 1: The Bottom of the Sea. A Year later. *Scene 2*: Within the Whale. *Scene 3*: Gepetto's Cottage. The next day.

ACT 1
"Pinocchio"
    A. Frank
"Lullaby"
    A. Frank
        Offstage Voices: P. Reed, R. Northern, J. Northern, J. Reilly, H. Brown.

ACT 2

"Cat and Fox Song"
    S. Lewis, E. Lalor, E. Michaels
"Song of the Jolly Coachman"
    R. Williamson
        Assisted by J. Kelo, J. Leddy, S. Leddy, J. Melino.

ACT 3

"Lullaby" (reprise)
    P. Reed, A. Frank

1938.17

BLOSSOM TIME

A Revival of the Operetta in Three Acts[7]. Book and lyrics by Dorothy Donnelly, adapted from the Viennese original ("Das Dreimäderlhaus") of A.M. Willner and Heinz Reichert. Music by Franz Schubert, adapted by Sigmund Romberg. Staged by Edward Scanlon. Settings by Watson Barratt. Orchestra directed by Pierre DeReeder. Produced by the Messrs. Shubert. Opened 26 December 1938 at the 46th Street Theatre and closed 10 January 1939 after 19 performances.[8]

CAST (in order of appearance): *Kuppelweiser*: Neville Landor. *Vogel*, tenor at the Royal Opera: Allen Raymond. *Flower Girl*: Betti Davis. *Von Schwindt*, a painter: Joseph Toner. *Bellabruna*, Countess Sharntoff: CHARLOTTE LANSING. *Count Sharntoff*, the Danish Ambassador: WHEELER DRYDEN. *Schubert*: EVERETT MARSHALL. *Mitzi, Fritzi, Kitzi*, daughters of Christian Kranz: MARY McCOY, Marjorie Ford, Gracie Worth. *Erkman*, suitor of Fritzi: Ernest Goodheart. *Binder*, suitor of Kitzi: Burt Raeburn. *Domeyer*, restaurant proprietor: JOHN WHEELER. *Christian Kranz*, court jeweler: DOUGLAS LEAVITT. *Baron Schober*, a Viennese socialite: ROY CROPPER. *Rosi*, Bellabruna's maid: Virginia Vonne. *Mrs. Kranz*: ZELLA RUSSELL. *Emmy*, Kranz's maid: Alyce Chapelle. *Novotney*, a private detective: HARRY K. MORTON. *Mrs. Coburg*, Schubert's housekeeper: Ruth Lockwood. *Danseuse*: Alyce Chapelle.

Singing Girls: Dimples Reide, Mary Russell, Jane McKenzie, Virginia Vonne, Jeannette Gorman, Marvel Conheeny, Dolly Miller, Laura Gustafson, Florence Keezel. *Singing Boys*: Daniel Meduri, William Langley, Henry Becker, Sylvan Nathan, Chisholm Beach, John Tauro, William Bligh, Frederick Buckley.

1938.18

EVERYWHERE I ROAM

A Play with Music in Three Acts, 29 Scenes. Play by Arnold Sundgaard and Marc Connelly. Songs by Fred Stewart. Staged by Marc Connelly. Production (settings, costumes, lighting) designed by Robert Edmund Jones. Choral arrangements and direction by Lehman Engel. Dances staged by Felicia Sorel. Produced by Marc Connelly and Béla Blau (by arrangement with Robert Porterfield's Barter Theatre). Opened 29 December 1938 at the National Theatre and closed 7 January 1939 after 13 performances.

CAST (in order of appearance): *Schoolmistress*: Vera Deane. *Jeremy*: Royce Blackburn. *Samuel*: Ormond Lydon. *Prudence*: May Grimes. *Pupils*: Dorothy Littlejohn, Kathleen Slagle, Frank Westbrook. *The Man*: DEAN JAGGER. *The Wife*: KATHERINE EMERY. *Johnny Appleseed*: NORMAN LLOYD. *Clinton*: Robert Collins. *Barrel Rollers*: Phil Brown, William Howell, William Matons, Charles Clarke, Robert Breen. *Jim*: PAUL HUBER. *Lady*: Joan Wetmore. *Gentleman*: Erik Walz. *Little Boy*: Royce Blackburn. *Sandman*: Frank Maxwell. *Jay*: ARTHUR BARNETT. *Mayor*: Earl Weatherford. *Martyrs*: Robert Breen, Frank Maxwell, Frank Westbrook, William Howell, James Burrell, Peggy Anne Holmes. *Continental Soldier*: Phil Brown. *Cyrus*: ROBERT PORTERFIELD. *Joseph*: Robert H. Harvey. *Pete*: Tony Kraber. *Jacob*: Bill Benner. *Voice of the Steel Caller*: Fred Stewart. *Map*: Kathleen Slagle. *Swedish Girl*: Kalita Humphries. *Swedish Boy*: Douglas Stark. *Norwegian Girl*: Hannah Lee Childs. *Norwegian Boy*: Judson Best Hall. *Danish Girl*: Camilla Hull. *Danish Boy*: John Dickens. *Train Announcer*: Meredith Johnston. *Train Guards*: Charles S. Clarke, Jon Urban, Robert Collins. *Jim Jr.*: Jay Owen, Jr. *Jay Jr.*: Fred Lawrence. *Joe*: John A. Kennedy. *Travel Agent*: Earl Weatherford. *Accountant*: Robert Collins. *Gloria*: Camilla Hull. *Perry*: Judson Best Hall. *Decorator*: William Howell. *Process Server*: Frank Maxwell.

Singers: Vera Deane, Annamary Dickey, Anne Francis, Eleanor Knapp, Dorothy Johnson, Louise Virden, James Burrell, Charles S. Clarke, Robert Collins, Meredith Johnston, Laurence Siegle, Jon Urban, Earl Weatherford. *Dancers*: Dorothy Bird, Jennifer Chatfield, Peggy Anne Holmes, Kathleen Slagle, Robert Breen, Phil Brown, James G. Burrell, William Howell, William Matons, Frank Maxwell, Erik Walz, Frank Westbrook. *Country Folks and City People*: Emily Boileau, Louise Lamont, Mary Liles,

Jane Huntington, Becky White, Ford Bowman, David Evans, Melchior Ferrer, Jaimie Heron.

Act 1, Scene 1: Schoolroom, 1833. *Scene 2*: The Prairie. *Scene 3*: Varick Street, New York, 1838. *Scene 4*: The same. *Scene 5*: The Prairie. *Scene 6*: Virginia. *Scene 7*: The Prairie.

Act 2, Scene 1: The Prairie. *Scene 2*: Scandinavia. *Scene 3*: Depot, St. Paul. *Scene 4*: The Prairie. *Scene 5*: New York, Christmas, 1926. *Scene 6*: At a mailbox. *Scene 7*: New York, New Year's Eve, 1927.

Act 3, Scene 1: Travel Agency and Business Office. *Scene 2*: The Farm. *Scene 3*: The Wife's Room. *Scene 4*: The Man's Room. *Scene 5*: Lecture Hall. *Scene 6*: The Club. *Scene 7*: The Wife's Room. *Scene 8*: The Man's Room. *Scene 9*: The Picnic. *Scene 10*: The Storm. *Scene 11*: In front of the Capitol, Washington. *Scene 12*: Marching to New York. *Scene 13*: A Graveyard. *Scene 14*: Home of the Man and Wife. *Scene 15*: The Prairie.

1938.19

POLICY KINGS

A Musical Comedy in Two Acts, 6 Scenes. Book and lyrics by Michael Ashwood. Music by James P. Johnson. Staged by Winston Douglass. Dances arranged by Jimmy Payne. Musical arrangements, Ken Macomber. Musical director, James P. Johnson. Produced by Michael Ashwood. Opened 30 December 1938 at the Nora Bayes Theatre and closed 31 December 1938 after 3 performances.

CAST: *Small Fry*: BILLY CUMBY. *Buddy*: FRANKIE JAXSON. *Street Player*: Ray Sneed, Jr. *Small Fry's Girl*: WILLOR GUILFORD. *Preacher, Court Attendant*: Monte Norris. *Newsboys*: Kenneth Mitchell, Ray Sneed, Herbert Evans, Arthur Moore. *Policeman*: Robert Mason. *Barracuda*: Norman Astwood. *Shoe Shine Boy*: George Jenkins. *Santa Clara*: Enid Raphael. *Blind Man, Dumb Head*: Edward Davis. *Dream Book Players*: Cora Green, Nettie Perry. *Master of Ceremonies, Defense Attorney*: Niles Wells. *Rhumba Dancer*: Bessie DeSaussure. *Acrobatic Dancer*: Irene Cort. *Broom Dancer*: Herbert Evans. *Buddy's Wife*: Margie Ellison. *Judge*: Henry Drake. *Prosecutor*: Cora Green. *Attorney for the Defense*: Niles Wells. *Mr. Scat and the Interpreter*: Roland Gillis, Edward Davis. And the Mary Bruce Dancers.

Act 1, Scene 1: A Street in Harlem today. *Scene 2*: A Harlem Alley. *Scene 3*: Cabaret Life in Harlem.

Act 2, Scene 1: A Policy Bank in Harlem. *Scene 2*: A Flat in Harlem. *Scene 3*: A Court Scene in Harlem.

MUSICAL NUMBERS[9]
    Prologue
    Court House Sequence
    "Deed I Do Do Blues"
    "Dewey Blues"
    "Harlem Number Man"
    "Harlem Woogie"
    "Havin' a Ball"
        (*Lyrics by* Andy Razaf.)
    "(I'm) Gonna Hit the Numbers Today"
    "News News"
    "Radium Numbers"
    "To Do What We Like"
    "Walkin' My Baby Back Home"
        C. Green
    "We Like to Play Numbers"
    "You, You, You!" (Nobody Jes You You)
        C. Green

1939.01

TRIAL BY JURY

A Revival of the Comic Opera (Dramatic Cantata) in One Act[10]. Libretto by William S. Gilbert. Music by Arthur Sullivan. Musical director, Isidore Godfrey. Produced by the D'Oyly Carte Opera Company. Opened 5

---

[7]Originally presented in New York 29 September 1921 at the Ambassador Theatre for 592 performances. For Synopsis of Scenes and Musical Numbers, see original 1921 production.
[8]Costumes, lighting uncredited.

[9]Not in performance order. No program available.
[10]First presented in New York 15 November 1875 at the Eagle Theatre for 8 performances. For Synopsis of Scenes and Musical Numbers, see original 1875 production.

January 1939 at the Martin Beck Theatre and closed 4 March 1939 after 11 performances in repertory.[11]

CAST: *The Learned Judge*: WILLIAM SUMNER. *Counsel for the Plaintiff*: LESLIE RANDS. *The Defendant*: LEONARD OSBORN. *Foreman of the Jury*: T. Penry Hughes. *Usher*: RICHARD WALKER. *Associate*: C. WILLIAM MORGAN. *The Plaintiff*: MARGERY ABBOTT. *First Bridesmaid*: Maysie Dean.

followed by

THE PIRATES OF PENZANCE,
1939.02   or, The Slave of Duty

A Revival of the Comic Opera in Two Acts[12]. Libretto by William S. Gilbert. Music by Arthur Sullivan. Musical director, Isidore Godfrey. Produced by the D'Oyly Carte Opera Company. Opened 5 January 1939 at the Martin Beck Theatre and closed 4 March 1939 after 11 performances in repertory.[13]

CAST: *Major General Stanley*: MARTYN GREEN. *The Pirate King*: DARRELL FANCOURT. *Samuel*: Richard Walker. *Frederic*: JOHN DEAN. *Sergeant of Police*: SYDNEY GRANVILLE. *Mabel, Edith, Kate, Isabel*, General Stanley's Daughters: HELEN ROBERTS, MARJORIE EYRE, IVY SANDERS, Maysie Dean. *Ruth*: EVELYN GARDINER. *Chorus of Pirates, Police and General Stanley's Daughters*.

THE MIKADO,
1939.03   or, The Town of Titipu

A Revival of the Comic Opera in Two Acts[14]. Libretto by William S. Gilbert. Music by Arthur Sullivan. Musical director, Isidore Godfrey. Produced by the D'Oyly Carte Opera Company. Opened 9 January 1939 at the Martin Beck Theatre and closed 11 March 1939 after 15 performances in repertory.[15]

CAST: *The Mikado of Japan*: DARRELL FANCOURT. *Nanki-Poo*: JOHN DUDLEY. *Ko-Ko*, Lord High Executioner of Titipu: MARTYN GREEN. *Pooh-Bah*, Lord High Everything Else: SYDNEY GRANVILLE. *Pish-Tush, Go-To*, Noble Lords: Leslie Rands, Radley Flynn. *Yum-Yum, Pitti-Sing, Peep-Bo*, three sisters, wards of Ko-Ko: VIOLA WILSON, MARJORIE EYRE, MAYSIE DEAN. *Katisha*: EVELYN GARDINER. *Chorus of School Girls, Nobles, Guards and Coolies*.

IOLANTHE,
1939.04   or, The Peer and the Peri

A Revival of the Comic Opera in Two Acts[16]. Libretto by William S. Gilbert. Music by Arthur Sullivan. Musical director, Isidore Godfrey. Produced by the D'Oyly Carte Opera Company. Opened 12 January 1939 at the Martin Beck Theatre and closed 9 March 1939 after 11 performances in repertory.[17]

CAST: *The Lord Chancellor*: MARTYN GREEN. *Earl of Mountararat*: DARRELL FANCOURT. *Earl Tolloller*: JOHN DEAN. *Private Willis* of the Grenadier Guards: SYDNEY GRANVILLE. *Strephon*, an Arcadian Shepherd: LESLIE RANDS. *Queen of the Fairies*: EVELYN GARDINER. *Iolanthe*, a Fairy, Strephon's Mother: MAR-

---

JORIE EYRE. *Celia, Leila, Fleta*, Fairies: Margery Abbott, Ivy Sanders, Maysie Dean. *Phyllis*, an Arcadian Shepherdess and Ward in Chancery: HELEN ROBERTS, VIOLA WILSON (alt.). *Chorus of Dukes, Marquises, Earls, Viscounts, Barons and Fairies*.

1939.05   ## COX AND BOX

A Revival of the Triumviretta in One Act[18]. Libretto by F. C. Burnand, based on Maddison Morton's farce "Cox and Box." Music by Arthur Sullivan. Musical director, Isidore Godfrey. Produced by the D'Oyly Carte Opera Company. Opened 16 January 1939 at the Martin Beck Theatre and closed 8 March 1939 after 12 performances in repertory.[19]

CAST: *Cox*: WILLIAM SUMNER. *Box*: JOHN DEAN. *Bouncer*: RICHARD WALKER.

followed by

H.M.S. PINAFORE,
1939.06   or, The Lass That Loved a Sailor

A Revival of the Comic Opera in Two Acts[20]. Libretto by William S. Gilbert. Music by Arthur Sullivan. Musical director, Isadore Godfrey. Produced by the D'Oyly Carte Opera Company. Opened 16 January 1939 at the Martin Beck Theatre and closed 8 March 1939 after 12 performances in repertory[21].

CAST: *The Rt. Hon. Sir Joseph Porter, K.C.B.*, First Lord of the Admiralty: MARTYN GREEN. *Captain Corcoran*, Commanding the *H.M.S. Pinafore*: CHARLES DORNING. *Ralph Rackstraw*, Able Seaman: THOMAS ROUND. *Dick Deadeye*, Able Seaman: DARRELL FANCOURT, Radley Flynn, alt. *Bill Bobstay*, Bo'sun's Mate: Richard Walker. *Bob Beckett*, Carpenter's Mate: Radley Flynn, Donald Harris (alt.). *Josephine*, the Captain's Daughter: HELEN ROBERTS. *Hebe*, Sir Joseph's First Cousin: Joan Gillingham. *Little Buttercup*, a Portsmouth Bumboat Woman: ELLA HALMAN. *First Lord's Sisters, his Cousins, his Aunts, Sailors, Marines, etc.*

1939.07   ## SET TO MUSIC

A Musical Revue in Two Acts, 19 Scenes. Sketches, music and lyrics by Noël Coward. Settings and costumes by Gladys E. Calthrop. Orchestrations by Hans Spialek. Music director, John McManus. Directed by Noël Coward. Produced by John C. Wilson. Opened 18 January 1939 at the Music Box Theatre and closed 6 May 1939 after 129 performances.

CAST: BEATRICE LILLIE, RICHARD HAYDN, EVA ORTEGA, PENELOPE DUDLEY WARD, HUGH FRENCH, GLADYS HENSON, BRONSON DUDLEY, MOYA NUGENT, MAIDIE ANDREWS, Angus Menzies, Kenneth Carten, Anthony Pelissier, Laura Duncan, Florence Britton, Ray Dennis, Tilda Getze, Anna Jackson, Sarah Burton, Anne Graham, Rosemary Lomax, Laura Douglas, Ruby Green, Leonard Gibson, Sanders Draper, Carol Louise Wanderman, Robert Shackelton, Victor Cutrer, John Mathews, Gilbert Wilson, Mary Ann Carr.
  Ensemble: Toni Sorel, Helen Bennett, Helene Hudson, Verna Long, Ann Eden, Tilda Getz, Sylvia Dale, Anne Graham, Hilda Knight, Laurie Douglas.

ACT 1
Scene 1
"A Fragonard Impression"
  Singer: E. Ortega. *Lisette*: M. A. Carr. *Tiger Plon Plon*: L. Gibson. *La Marquise De Sauriole* (Maman): M. Andrews. *Monsieur L'Abbe*: S. Draper. *Blanche*: P. D. Ward. *Germaine*: M. Nugent. *Eugenie*: R. Lomax. *Marguerite*: S. Burton. *Giselle*: B. Lillie.
Scene 2
"Three Little Debutantes" (from WORDS AND MUSIC, London)
  A. Jackson, L. Duncan, R. Green

---

[11]No credits for scenery, costumes or lighting.
[12]First presented in New York 31 December 1879 at the Fifth Avenue Theatre for 91 performances in two engagements. For Synopsis of Scenes and Musical Numbers, see original 1879 production.
[13]No credits for scenery, costumes or lighting.
[14]First presented in New York 20 July, 10-29 August 1885 at the Union Square and People's Theatres for 22 performances. First authorized production presented 19 August 1885 at the Fifth Avenue Theatre by Richard D'Oyly Carte for 250 performances. For Synopsis of Scenes and Musical Numbers, see 19 August 1885 D'Oyly Carte production.
[15]No credits for scenery, costumes or lighting.
[16]First presented in New York 25 November 1882 at the Standard Theatre for 105 performances. For Synopsis of Scenes and Musical Numbers, see original 1882 production.
[17]No credits for scenery, costumes or lighting.

[18]First presented in New York as COX AND BOX, or The Long-Lost Brothers, 14 August 1879 at the Standard Theatre for 48 performances. For Synopsis of Scenes and Musical Numbers, see original 1879 production.
[19]No credits for scenery, costumes or lighting.
[20]First presented in New York 15 January 1879 at the Standard Theatre for 175 performances. For Synopsis of Scenes and Musical Numbers, see original 1879 production.
[21]No credits for scenery, costumes or lighting.

[AU:Naughty Naugh, 1939.10, is listed in catalog but does not appear here. Add?]

Scene 3

"Mad About the Boy" (from WORDS AND MUSIC, London)
  (a) *Outside a London Cinema*
  (b) *A Society Woman*: P. D. Ward. *Her Friend*: R. Lomax.
  (c) *A Housemaid*: G. Henson.
  (d) *A Girl of the Town*: L. Duncan.
  (e) *A School Girl*: B. Lillie. *Her Younger Sister*: M. Nugent.

Scene 4

"The Stately Homes of England" (from OPERETTE, London)
  H. French, A. Menzies, K. Carten, A. Pelissier

Scene 5

"(I'm So) Weary of It All"
  Lord Bitchette: R. Dennis. *Daisy, a dresser*: G. Henson. *Elmer Von Robespierre*: R. Shackelton. *Henry Beardworth*: A. Pelissier. *Marion Day*: B. Lillie.

Scene 6

"Children of the Ritz" (from WORDS AND MUSIC, London)
  E. Ortega, Ensemble

Scene 7

Madame Dines Alone
  Mrs. John Illsworth-Poindexter: B. Lillie. *Withers*: R. Haydn.

Scene 8

"Never Again"
  E. Ortega, H. French
  (*Special Arrangement by* Will Irwin.)
  Dancers: R. Shackelton, K. Carten, V. Cutrer.

Scene 9

"Midnight Matinee"
  (a) *Viscountess Hogan*: F. Britton. *Lady Millicent Headley*: S. Burton. *The Marchioness of Lemworth*: M. Andrews. *The Hon. Mrs. Douglas Draycott*: M. Nugent. *Miss Esme Ponting*: R. Lomax. *Miss Spence*: G. Henson. *The Lady Westmorsham*: P. D. Ward. *Mrs. F. N. J. Wilson*: T. Getze.
  (b) *Greek Chorus*: Ensemble.
  (c) *Mr. Stuart Ingleby*, Announcer: R. Haydn. *Mrs. Rowntree*, Organizer: B. Lillie. *Viscountess Hogan, as Diane De Poitiers*: F. Burton. *Lady Millicent Headley, as Cleopatra*: S. Burton. *The Marchioness of Lemworth, as Nell Gwynn*: M. Andrews. *The Hon. Mrs. Douglas Draycott, as Salome*: M. Nugent. *Miss Esme Ponting, as a Court Lady*: R. Lomax. *Miss Eleanor Sherrell, as a Court Lady*: A. Graham. *Miss Rebecca Mosenthorpe, as a Court Lady*: L. Douglas. *Lady Patricia Gainton, as a Page*: C. L. Wanderman. *The Hon. Julian Forrage, as a Page*: J. Mathews. *Miss Spence, as Joan of Arc*: G. Henson. *The Lady Westmorsham, as Lady Blessington*: P. D. Ward. *Mrs. F. N. J. Wilson, as Lady Godiva*: T. Getze. *Angels*: M. A. Carr, T. Sorel. *Lord Ackle*: S. Draper.

ACT 2

Scene 1

"Children of the Ritz" (reprise)
  E. Ortega, Ensemble

Scene 2

"Three White Feathers"
  She: B. Lillie. *He*: H. French.

Scene 3

Fish Mimicry (*by* Richard Haydn)
  Edwin Carp: R. Haydn.

Scene 4

"Three Little Debutantes" (reprise)
  A. Jackson, L. Duncan, R. Green

Scene 5

"(I've Been to a) Marvelous Party"
  B. Lillie

Scene 6

"The Stately Homes of England" (reprise)
  H. French, A. Menzies, K. Carten, A. Pelissier

Scene 7

Secret Service
  The Countess: B. Lillie. *Madame Moule*: G. Henson. *Lizi*: M. Nugent. *Leopold Rosen*: A. Menzies. *First Officer*: R. Haydn. *Second Officer*: H. French. *Maurice*: V. Cutrer. *Jittono*: K. Carten. *Fritz*: R. Dennis. *Serge*: S. Draper. *Ivan*: G. Wilson. *A Spanish Lady*: E. Ortega. *Masha*: F. Britton. *Luba*: S. Burton. *Sasha*: R. Shackelton. *Lorette*: M. A. Carr.

Scene 8

"Three Little Debutantes" (reprise)
  A. Jackson, L. Duncan, R. Green

Scene 9

"The Party's Over Now" (from WORDS AND MUSIC, London)
  P. D. Ward, H. French
  Danced by B. Dudley.

Scene 10

Finale
  Entire Company

THE GONDOLIERS,
1939.08   or, The King of Barataria

A Revival of the Comic Opera in Two Acts[22]. Libretto by William S. Gilbert. Music by Arthur Sullivan. Musical director, Isidore Godfrey. Produced by the D'Oyly Carte Opera Company. Opened 19 January 1939 at the Martin Beck Theatre and closed 10 March 1939 after 12 performances in repertory.[23]

CAST: *The Duke of Plaza-Toro*, a Grandee of Spain: MARTYN GREEN. *Luiz*, his attendant: RICHARD DUNN. *Don Alhambra Del Bolero*, The Grand Inquisitor: SYDNEY GRANVILLE. *Marco Palmieri, Giuseppe Palmieri, Antonio, Francesco, Giorgio*, Venetian Gondoliers: JOHN DUDLEY, LESLIE RANDS, William Sumner, Leonard Osborn, Radley Flynn. *Annibale*: T. Penry Hughes. *The Duchess of Plaza Toro*: EVELYN GARDINER. *Casilda*, her daughter: MARGERY ABBOTT. *Gianetta*: HELEN ROBERTS, Viola Wilson (alt.). *Tessa*: MARJORIE EYRE. *Fiametta*: Marjorie Flinn. *Vittoria*: Ivy Sanders. *Giulia*: Maysie Dean . *Inez*, the King's Foster-Mother: Ella Halman. *Chorus of Gondoliers, Contadine, Men-at-Arms, Heralds and Pages.*

THE YEOMEN OF THE GUARD,
1939.09   or, The Merryman and His Maid

A Revival of the Comic Opera in Two Acts[24]. Libretto by William S. Gilbert. Music by Arthur Sullivan. Musical director, Isidore Godfrey. Produced by the D'Oyly Carte Opera Company. Opened 23 January 1939 at the Martin Beck Theatre and closed 6 March 1939 after 11 performances in repertory.[25]

CAST: *Sir Richard Cholmondeley*: Leslie Rands. *Colonel Fairfax*: JOHN DEAN. *Sergeant Meryll*: DARRELL FANCOURT. *Leonard Meryll*: Thomas Hancock. *Jack Point*: MARTYN GREEN. *Wilfred Shadbolt*: SYDNEY GRANVILLE. *First Yeoman*: Leonard Osborn. *Second Yeoman*: Mansel Dyer. *First Citizen*: C. William Morgan. *Second Citizen*: William Sumner. *Elsie Maynard*: HELEN ROBERTS. *Phoebe Meryll*: Marjorie Eyre. *Dame Carruthers*: EVELYN GARDINER. *Kate*: Margery Abbott. *Chorus of Yeomen of the Guard, Gentlemen, Citizens, etc.*

PATIENCE,
1939.11   or, Bunthorne's Bride

A Revival of the Comic Opera in Two Acts[26]. Libretto by William S. Gilbert. Music by Arthur Sullivan. Musical director, Isadore Godfrey. Produced by the D'Oyly Carte Opera Company. Opened 26 January 1939 at the Martin Beck Theatre and closed 7 March 1939 after 4 performances in repertory.[27]

---

[22]First presented in New York 7 January 1890 at Park Theatre for 103 performances. For Synopsis of Scenes and Musical Numbers, see original 1890 production.
[23]No credits for scenery, costumes or lighting.
[24]Originally presented in New York 17 October 1888 at the Casino Theatre for 100 performances. For Synopsis of Scenes and Musical Numbers, see original 1888 production.
[25]No credits for scenery, costumes or lighting.
[26]First presented in New York 22 September 1881 at the Standard Theatre for 177 performances. For Synopsis of Scenes and Musical Numbers, see original 1881 production.
[27]No credits for scenery, costumes or lighting.

CAST: *Colonel Calverley*: DARRELL FANCOURT. *Major Murgatroyd*: William Sumner. *Lieut. the Duke of Dunstable*: JOHN DEAN. *Reginald Bunthorne, a Fleshly Poet*: MARTYN GREEN. *Archibald Grosvenor, an Idyllic Poet*: LESLIE RANDS. *Mr. Bunsthorne's Solicitor*: Wynn Dyson. *The Lady Angela, The Lady Saphir, The Lady Ella, The Lady Jane, Rapturous Maidens*: MARJORIE EYRE, IVY SANDERS, Margery Abbott, EVELYN GARDINER. *Patience, a Dairy Maid*: VIOLA WILSON. *Chorus of Rapturous Maidens and Officers of the Dragoon Guards.*

1939.12

ONE FOR THE MONEY

A Musical Revue in Two Acts, 21 Scenes. Sketches and lyrics by Nancy Hamilton. Music by Morgan Lewis. Entire production devised, directed and lighted by John Murray Anderson. Musical numbers staged by Robert Alton. Sketches staged by Edward Clarke Lilley. Settings and costumes by Raoul Pene du Bois. Music director, Ray Kavanaugh. Orchestrations by Hans Spialek. Produced by Gertrude Macey and Stanley Gilkey in association with Robert F. Cutler. Opened 4 February 1939 at the Booth Theatre and closed 27 May 1939 after 132 performances.

CAST: NANCY HAMILTON, BRENDA FORBES, RUTH MATTESON, GRACE McDONALD, FRANCES COMSTOCK, PHILIP BOURNEUF, ALFRED DRAKE, NELL O'DAY, GENE KELLY, ROBERT SMITH, DON LOPER, MAXINE BARRAT, NADINE GAE, KEENAN WYNN, GEORGE LLOYD, (JOHN) WILLIAM ARCHIBALD.

ACT 1[28]

Scene 1

An Ordinary Family
The Father: P. Bourneuf. *The Mother*: N. Hamilton. *The Sister*: N. O'Day. *The Brother*: A. Drake. *The Maid*: B. Forbes. *The Friends*: R. Matteson, R. Smith, D. Loper, M. Barrat, K. Wynn, F. Comstock, W. Archibald, G. McDonald, G. Kelly, N. Gae, G. Lloyd.

Scene 2

The First To Go
Michael Tunbridge: R. Smith. *Sylvia Tunbridge*: R. Matteson.

Scene 3

At the Drop of a Hat
The Bride: N. O'Day. *The Groom*: A. Drake. *The Best Man*: G. Kelly.

Scene 4

Parlor Game
Mrs. Jamison: R. Matteson. *Mr. Jamison*: R. Smith. *Bettina Hansen*: N. O'Day. *Mr. Fuller*: A. Drake. *Mrs. Marbury*: F. Comstock. *Mr. Marbury*: P. Bourneuf.

Scene 5

Adorable Little Star
Bebe Baiser: B. Forbes. *Her Manager*: D. Loper. *The Reporters*: K. Wynn, P. Bourneuf, G. Kelly, G. Lloyd, W. Archibald, R. Smith, A. Drake.

Scene 6

"I Only Know"
F. Comstock, A. Drake
Officer in Charge of Bureau of Missing Persons: P. Bourneuf.

Scene 7

My Day
First Lady: N. Hamilton. *Her Secretaries*: N. O'Day, M. Barrat, G. McDonald, N. Gae.

Scene 8

"Rhapsody"
R. Matteson, A. Drake
(*Vocal Arrangements and Musical Continuity by* Hugh Martin.)
Danced by D. Loper and M. Barrat ("Valse" variation), G. McDonald and G. Kelly ("Syncopated" variation), N. Gae and W. Archibald ("Modern" variation.)

Scene 9

The Five Kings
Orson Welles: A. Drake. *First King*: K. Wynn. *Second King*: R. Smith. *Third King*: P. Bourneuf. *Fourth King*: G. Lloyd. *Fifth King*: D. Loper.

---

[28] Added during the run:
"I Hate Spring"
N. Hamilton
(*Music by* Martha Caples. *Lyrics by* Nancy Hamilton.)

Scene 10

The Story of the Opera
Marilyn: N. Hamilton. *The Waiter*: G. Lloyd. *Lucy Timpkin*: M. Barrat.

Scene 11

"Teeter Totter Tessie"
G. McDonald, G. Kelly, Company
(*Suggested by* Morgan Lewis.)

ACT 2

Scene 1

Give Us the Days
W.P.A. Worker: K. Wynn. M. Barrat, F. Comstock, B. Forbes, N. Gae, N. Hamilton, R. Matteson, G. McDonald, N. O'Day.

Scene 2

All the World's Awheel
Madame President: N. O'Day. *Mr. Ernest Sprockett*: P. Bourneuf.

Scene 3

"A Little Bit Delighted With the Weather"
R. Matteson, R. Smith
Danced by N. Gae.

Scene 4

"Once Upon a Time"
F. Comstock, A. Drake
Guide: G. Lloyd. *The Emperor*: K. Wynn. *The Empress*: R. Matteson. *The Princess*: G. McDonald. *The Archduke*: D. Loper. *The Archduchess*: M. Barrat. *First Lady in Waiting*: N. O'Day. *Second Lady in Waiting*: N. Gae. *First Officer*: W. Archibald. *Aide de Camp*: R. Smith.

Scene 5

Gene Kelly (dance specialty)

Scene 6

Search Me
Customs Inspector: K. Wynn. *Matron*: F. Comstock. *Kitty Kingsley*: N. O'Day. *Elsie Whipple*: B. Forbes.

Scene 7

"Send a Boy"
The Manager: A. Drake. *Western Union Boys*: G. Kelly, G. Lloyd, W. Archibald, K. Wynn, D. Loper. *The Clients*: G. McDonald, N. Gae, N. O'Day, R. Matteson, M. Barrat. *Danced by* D. Loper, M. Barrat.

Scene 8

"The Yoo Hoo Blues"
N. Hamilton

Scene 9

The Quaint Companion
Dick McQuade: P. Bourneuf. *Barbara McQuade*: R. Matteson. *Miss Bickleford*: B. Forbes. *Emerson*: R. Smith.

Scene 10

"Kiss Me and We'll Both Go Home"
Company

1939.13

STARS IN YOUR EYES

A Musical Comedy in Two Acts. Book by J.P. McEvoy. Music by Arthur Schwartz. Lyrics by Dorothy Fields. Staged by Joshua Logan. Settings by Jo Mielziner. Costumes by John Hambleton. Choreography by Carl Randall. Music director, Al Goodman. Orchestrations by Hans Spialek, Donald J. Walker, Al Goodman. Produced by Dwight Deere Wiman. Opened 9 February 1939 at the Majestic Theatre and closed 27 May 1939 after 127 performances.

CAST (in order of appearance): *Assistant Director*: TED GARY. *Second Assistant Director*: Davis Cunningham. *Third Assistant Director*: Edward Kane. *Fourth Assistant Director*: Robert Shanley. *Fifth Assistant Director*: DAN DAILEY, JR. *Sixth Assistant Director*: ROGER STEARNS. *First Girl*: Edith Grant. *Second Girl*: Thekla Horn. *Third Girl*: Nancy Wiman. *Wardrobe Woman*: Johanne Hoven. *Carpenter*: DAVID MORRIS. *Fourth Girl*: Frances Rands. *Electrician*: Anthony Albert. *Soundman*: RENNIE McEVOY. *Babe*: DAWN ROLAND. *Wilder*: CLINTON SUNDBERG. *Cameraman*: Walter Wagner. *Assistant Soundman*: Ambrose Costello. *Fifth Girl*: Phyllis Roque. *Sixth Girl*: Natasha Dana. *Dancing Girl*: NORA KAYE. *Leading Man*: WALTER CASSEL. *Script Girl*: Gloria Clare. *Bess*: MILDRED NATWICK. *Jeanette Adair*: ETHEL MERMAN. *Voice Coach*: MARY WICKES. *Maid*: Kathryn Mayfield. *Bill*: JIMMY DURANTE. *Jockey*: Basil Galahoff. *Darrow*: Robert Ross. *John Blake*:

RICHARD CARLSON. *Tata*: TAMARA TOUMANOVA. *Dawson*: Richard Barbee. *Photographers*: Walter Cassel, Edward Kane, Davis Cunningham, Robert Shanley. *Russian Consul*: Russel Protopoff. *French Consul*: Dwight Godkin. *Italian Consul*: Fernando Alonso. *English Consul*: David Morris. *German Consul*: Ambrose Costello. *Watchman*: Ambrose Costello.

Ladies of the Ballet: Alicia Alonzo, Peggy Conrad, Maria De Galanta, Jane Everett, Gail Grant, Marion Haynes, Thekla Horn, Johanne Hoven, Marjorie Johnstone, Nora Kaye, Maria Karniloff [Karnilova], Frances Rands, Audrey Reynolds, Olga Suarez, Margaret Vasilieff, Mary Jane Williams. *Gentlemen of the Ballet*: Anthony Albert, Fernando Alonso, Paul Alvin, Savva Andreieff, Dwight Godkin, Basil Galahoff, George Kiddon, Russel Protopoff, Richard Reed, Newcombe Rice, Jerome Robbins.

Acts 1 and 2: Sound Stage "7" of the Monotone Picture Corporation, Hollywood, California.

ACT 1

"Places, Everybody"
  Company
"One Brief Moment"
  W. Cassel, P. Godkin, Ensemble
"This Is It"
  E. Merman, W. Cassel, E. Kane, R. Shanley, D. Cunningham
"All the Time"
  R. Carlson, T. Toumanova
"Self Made Man"
  J. Durante
"Okay for Sound"
  R. McEvoy, D. Roland, Ensemble
"A Lady Needs a Change"
  E. Merman
"Terribly Attractive"
  J. Durante, M. Natwick
"Just a Little Bit More"
  E. Merman
Night Club Ballet
  T. Toumanova, T. Gary, D. Dailey, Ensemble
Finale
  E. Merman, Ensemble

ACT 2

"As of Today"
  R. McEvoy, F. Rands, M. Wickes, R. Stearns, K. Mayfield, D. Morris, B. Hunter, D. Dailey, Ensemble
"He's Goin' Home"
  J. Durante, Ensemble
"I'll Pay the Check"
  E. Merman
"Never a Dull Moment"
  D. Roland, T. Gary, D. Dailey, R. McEvoy, A. Westphal, Ensemble
"This Is It" (reprise)
  E. Merman
Court Ballet
  T. Toumanova, Corps de Ballet, W. Cassel, E. Kane, R. Shanley, D. Cunningham
"It's All Yours"
  E. Merman, J. Durante
Finale
  Entire Company

(LEW LESLIE'S)
BLACKBIRDS OF 1939

1939.14

A Harlem Rhapsody (Musical Revue) in Two Acts, 21 Scenes. (Sketches by Lew Leslie, Nat Dorfman, Fred H. Finklehoffe, John Monks, Jr.) Lyrics by Johnny Mercer. Additional lyrics by Mitchell Parish, Dorothy Sachs, Irving Taylor. Music by Rube Bloom. Additional music by (George Gershwin,) Sammy Fain, Louis Haber, Vic Mizzy. Entire show conceived and staged by Lew Leslie. Settings by Mabel A. Buell. Costumes by Frances Feist. Dances by Eugene Van Grona. Orchestrations by Ferde Grofé, Ken Macomber. Vocal arrangements, J. Rosamund Johnson. Produced by Lew Leslie. Opened 11 February 1939 at the Hudson Theatre and closed 18 February 1939 after 9 performances.

CAST: LENA HORNE, HAMTREE HARRINGTON, DEWEY 'PIGMEAT' MARKHAM, TIM MOORE, BOBBY EVANS, JOE BYRD, RALPH BROWN, LAURENE HINES, KATE HALL, NORMAN and BLAKE (Norman McConny and Atta Blake), TAPS MILLER, Joyce Beasley, Lorenza Roberson.

Van Grona's Swing Ballet: Hazel Spence, Wahneta Talley, Violet Gray, Hettie Stephens, Elizabeth Thompson, BERYL CLARKE, Lavinia Williams, Marion Brown, Beryl Murray, Verona Blackburn, Dorothy Jones, Edith Ross, Edith Hurd, Mary Tennant, Williard Taylor, Renu Roma. AL BLEDGER, Coleman Hill.

J. Rosamund Johnson's Choir: *Sopranos*: KATE HALL, Marian Coleman, Zelda Shelton, Louisa Howard, Marguerite Robinson. *Altos*: Ruthena Matson, Jennie Taylor, Rosetta Crawford, Rosalie King, Leona Avery. *Tenors*: Walter Hilliard, Charles Welch, Gaylord Caldwell, James Logan, Richard Grant, Jerry Laws. *Baritones and Basses*: Frank Riley, Gilbert Adkins, Larri Lauria, Horatio Edwards, Robert Clarke. *Blackbirds Beauties*: Catherine Stevenson, Mae Francis, Thelma Walton, Billie French, Rosetta Williams, Edna Slatten. *Dancing Chorus*: Baby Simmons, Marion Egber, Marie Robinson, Cleo Hayes, Evelyn Sheppard, Muriel Cook, Madelyn Donable, Lucia Moses, Juanita Boisseau, Eva Bradley, Peggy Sheppard, Gladys Clayton. *Whitey's Lindy Hoppers*: Norma Miller, George Greenidge, Mickey Jones, William Downes, Gladys Crowder, Shorty Eddie, Joyce James, Joe Daniels, Ann Johnson, Billy Williams. (*Specialty*: Dr. Sausage and His Five Pork Chops.)

ACT 1

Scene 1

"Children of the Earth"
  Van Grona's Negro Swing Ballet

Scene 2

"Rhapsody in Blue"
  J. Rosamund Johnson's Choir
  (*Music by* George Gershwin.)

Scene 3

Do We Sell Numbers?
  Scene: Street in Harlem; Office of the N. P. A.
    Rufus: D. Markham. *Sam*: H. Harrington. *Police Lieutenant*: F. Riley. *Runner*: J. Laws. *Numbers Player*: T. Miller. *Newboy*: N. McConny. *Spectators, Onlookers, etc.*

Scene 4

"Name It and It's Yours"
  L. Horne, B. Evans, Blacbird Beauties
  (*Music by* Abner Silver and Sammy Fain. *Lyrics by* Mitchell Parish.)

Scene 5

"Jo Jo, the Cannibal Kid" (from BLACKBIRDS OF 1936, London)
  L. Hines
  (*Music by* Rube Bloom. *Lyrics by* Johnny Mercer.)
    Barker: H. Harrington. *Danced by* T. Miller, J. Beasley, Dancing Chorus.

Scene 6

Broadminded—Year 1950
  The Wife: L. Horne. *The Husband*: D. Markham. *Luke*: B. Evans. *Sam*: H. Harrington.

Scene 7

Norman and Blake

Scene 8

Harlem Bridge
  Jasper: T. Moore. *Romeo*: H. Harrington. *Rufus*: J. Byrd. *Bill*: F. Riley. *The Kibitzer*: D. Markham.

Scene 9

"Thursday"
  L. Horne, B. Evans, T. Miller, R. Crawford
  (*Music by* Louis Haber. *Lyrics by* Dorothy Sachs.)

Scene 10

Mr. Leslie's Version of "Frankie and Johnny" ('She Done Him Wrong')
  (from BLACKBIRDS OF 1936, London)
    Scene 1: A Barroom in Harlem. *Scene 2*: A Courtroom.
    Frankie: L. Williams. *Johnny*: B. Evans. *Bartender*: T. Miller. *Customer*: C. Hill. *District Attorney*: C. Welch. *Defense Lawyer*: F. Riley. *Judge*: R. Clarke. *Court Clerk*: J. Laws. *Jury and Spectators*: J. Rosamund Johnson's Choir.

Scene 11

Concentrating on Food
  Sam: H. Harrington. *Rufus*: D. Markham. *Preacher*: F. Riley. *First Housewife*: L. Howard. *Second Housewife*: R. King.

Scene 12

"Swing Struck"
L. Horne, B. Evans
(*Music by* Vic Mizzy. *Lyrics by* Irving Taylor.)
Assisted by J. Rosamund Johnson's Choir, Van Grona's Swing Ballet and Blackbirds Dancing Chorus, Blackbirds Beauties, Norman and Blake, R. Brown, T. Miller, Whitey's Lindy-Hoppers.

ACT 2

Scene 1

Krum Elbow (*by* Dorothy Sachs and Louis Haber)
Father Devine: D. Markham. *Salesman*: H. Harrington. *Secretary*: F. Riley. *Husband*: C. Welch. *Saleslady*: R. Crawford.

Scene 2

"Dixie Isn't Dixie Any More" (from BLACKBIRDS OF 1936, London)
L. Hines
(*Music by* Rube Bloom. *Lyrics by* Johnny Mercer.)

Scene 3

Harlem Spiritualism
Yogi Selassie: D. Markham. *Caesar*: H. Harrington. *Minnie*: E. Ross. *Brother Johnson*: F. Riley.

Scene 4

The Black Pirates
Pirate Chief: R. Brown. *Pirates*: J. Beasley, N. McConny, A. Blake.

Scene 5

"You're So Indifferent"
L. Horne
(*Music by* Sammy Fain. *Lyrics by* Mitchell Parish.)

Scene 6

The Jam Session
Dr. Sausage and His Five Pork Chops

Scene 7

"I Did It for the Red, White and Blue"
T. Moore, R. King
(*Music by* Rube Bloom. *Lyrics by* Johnny Mercer.)

Scene 8

"Shake Your Bluesies With Dancing Shoesies"
L. Horne
(*Music by* Louis Haber. *Lyrics by* Dorothy Sachs.)
Assisted by J. Rosamund Johnson Choir, Van Grona's Swing Ballet, Dancing Chorus.

Scene 9

Finale
Entire Company

1939.15   THE SWING MIKADO

The Chicago Federal Theatre "Swing" adaptation of the Gilbert and Sullivan operetta in Two Acts. Conceived by Harry Minturn. Book and lyrics by William S. Gilbert. Music by Arthur Sullivan. Swing orchestration by Charles Levy. Swing arrangements by Gentry Warden. Conceived and staged by Harry Minturn. Dances by Sammy Dyer, assisted by Hazel Davis. Vocal direction by Viola Hill. Music directed by Edward Wurtzebach. Settings by Clive Rickabaugh. Costumes by John Pratt. Lighting by Oscar Ryan. General supervision by George Jackson, Emil Neiglick and Margaret Rand. Produced by the WPA Federal Theatre. Opened 1 March 1939 at the New Yorker Theatre, closing 29 April 1939 after 62 performances; re-opened under the auspices of The Marolin Corporation (Bernhard Ulrich, Melvin Ericson) 1 May 1939 at the 44th Street Theatre, closing 20 May 1939 after 24 additional performances, for a total of 86 performances.

CAST: *Nanki-Poo*: MAURICE COOPER. *Pish-Tush*: Lewis White. *Ko-Ko*: HERMAN GREENE. *Pooh-Bah*: WILLIAM FRANKLIN. *Yum-Yum*: GLADYS BOUCREE. *Pitti-Sing*: Frankie Fambro. *Peep-Bo*: Mabel Carter. *Katisha*: MABEL WALKER. *The Mikado*: EDWARD FRACTION.
Chorus of Girls, Nobles, Guards of Natives: Dancers: Asa Barnes, Jack Wright, James Harris, Martin Logan, Paul Bradley, Percy Grace, Alfred Bean, John Bean, James Smith, Woody Wilson. Alice Biddix, Beatrice Yancy, Eddie Mae Nance, Geraldine Clark, Lulubelle Mosby, Alice Brooks, Clara Strickland, Deloise Alexander, Lillian Falls, Marion Brooks, Wilma Bowen. *Quintet*: Ashto Gorham, George Bateman, James Arnold, William Carr, William Burns. *Oarsmen*: James Arnold, Joseph Clarke, Samuel

Clark, John Hughes, Scott Manning, Raymond Lowe. *Fan-Bearers*: William Carr, William Burns. *Body-Guards*: Ashton Gorham, George Bateman. *Chorus of Women*: Alice Biddix, Beulah Nance, Clara Strickland, Elvira Johnson, Geraldine Clark, Hettie Reed, Lillian Falls, Marion Brooks, Rose Long, Tillie Johnson, Vivian Parker, Alice Brooks, Beatrice Yancy, Clara Brown, Deloise Alexander, Georgia Carpenter, Helen Howard, Isabel Futrell, Lulubelle Mosby, Margaret Cross, Rebecca Jones, Vivian Morrison, Wilma Bowen, Mercedes Taliaferro. *Chorus of Men*: Abie Crawford, Albert Standley, Ashton Gorham, Harry Jones, Emmet Richardson, Ernest Woodson, Irwin Richardson, James Arnold, John Hughes, Lloyd Cabbell, Martin Lucas, Paul Williams, Raymond Lowe, Samuel Clark, Shelby Nichols, Willard Gregg, William Burns, Albert Glenn, Asa Barnes, Charles Johnson, Ernest Roberts, George Bateman, Harry Mitchell, Jack Wright, James Harris, Joseph Clark, Martin Logan, Paul Bradney, Percy Grace, Robert Montgomery, Scott Manning, Theodore Ward, William Carr, Woody Wilson.

Act 1: A Coral Island in the Pacific.

Act 2: The Town meeting place on the Island.

ACT 1

Opening Chorus
Male Chorus

"A Wandering Minstrel"
M. Cooper, Male Chorus
Dancers: J. Wright, P. Bradley, J. Smith.

"Our Great Mikado"
L. White, Male Chorus

"Young Man Despair"
W. Franklin, L. White, M. Cooper

"Behold the Lord High Executioner"
H. Greene, Male Chorus

"I've Got a Little List"
H. Greene, Male Chorus

"Three Little Maids from School"
G. Boucree, F. Fambro, M. Carter, Girls Chorus

"So Pardon Us"
G. Boucree, F. Fambro, M. Carter, W. Franklin, L. White, Girls Chorus

"Were You Not to Ko-Ko Plighted"
G. Boucree, M. Cooper

"I Am So Proud"
H. Greene, W. Franklin, L. White

Finale Act 1
M. Cooper, L. White, H. Greene, W. Franklin, G. Boucree, F. Fambro, M. Carter, M. Walker, Ensemble

ACT 2

"Braid the Raven Hair"
F. Fambro, Girls Chorus

"Moon Song" (The Moon and I)
G. Boucree, Quintet

"Madrigal"
G. Boucree, F. Fambro, M. Cooper, L. White

"Here's a How-de-do"
G. Boucree, M. Cooper, H. Greene

"The Mikado"
M. Walker, E. Fraction

"I'm the Emperor of Japan"
E. Fraction, Chorus

"The Criminal Cried"
H. Greene, F. Fambro, W. Franklin

"A Is Happy"
E. Fraction, W. Franklin, F. Fambro, H. Greene, M. Walker

"Flowers That Bloom in the Spring"
F. Fambro, H. Greene, M. Walker, W. Franklin, M. Cooper, Dancers, Quintet, E. Johnson

"Titwillow"
H. Greene

"There Is Beauty in the Bellows of the Blast"
M. Walker, H. Greene

Finale Act 2
Principals, Ensemble

1939.16 FRANK FAY VAUDEVILLE

A Vaudeville Revue in Two Acts, 14 Scenes. (Assembled and directed by Frank Fay.) Settings designed by Hjalmar Hermanson. Costumes for the Chester Hale Girls designed by John Booth and Billy Livingston. Orchestra directed by Tom Jones. Produced by Frank Fay. Opened 2 March 1939 at the 44th Street Theatre and closed 19 April 1939 after 60 performances.

CAST: ELSIE JANIS, EVA LeGALLIENNE, FRANK FAY, JOE SMITH, CHARLES DALE, THE MERRY-MACS (Helen Carroll, George McMichael, Joe McMichael, Ted McMichael), FRED HILLEBRAND, George Hanneford and Family, Avis Andrews, Glen Pope, The Debutantes, Richard Waring, Flo Mayo, Johnny Barnes, Pedro & Luis, Rose Kessner, Nino Verela, Harry Hines, Chester Hale's Dancing Girls (incl. Helen Leitche).

ACT 1
Scene 1

George Hanneford and Family (Equestrienne Act)

Scene 2

Avis Andrews (Singer)["Begin the Beguine", etc.]

Scene 3

Frank Fay (Emcee, Comedy, Song)

Scene 4

Glen Pope (Magician)

Scene 5

The Debutantes (Park Avenue's Own)

Scene 6

Smith and Dale (Doctor Kronkheit Skit)

Scene 7

The Merry-Macs (Swing vocals)

Scene 8

Eva LeGallienne in (William Shakespeare's) 'Romeo and Juliet'
Juliet: E. LeGallienne. *Romeo*: R. Waring. *Staged by* Robert Milton.

ACT 2
Scene 1

Flo Mayo (Trapeze Act)

Scene 2

Chester Hale's Dancing Girls (16)
Specialty: H. Leitche.

Scene 3

Elsie Janis (Noel Cravat at the piano)("The Good Old Days — So What?")
(Impressions of Helen Hayes, Beatrice Lillie, George M. Cohan, Will Rogers, Will Rogers, Ethel Barrymore, John Barrymore, Sarah Bernhardt.)

Scene 4

Johnny Barnes (Tap dancer)

Scene 5

Frank Fay (Abel Baer at the piano)

Scene 6

Pedro & Luis (Rope from balcony to stage), Fred Hillebrand (Comedy), Rose Kessner (Comedy and Dance), Nino Verela (Operatic singing), Harry Hines, (Corinne Doyle, strip-tease).

1939.17 THE HOT MIKADO

A Swing Version of the Gilbert and Sulivan Operetta in Two Acts. Book and lyrics by William S. Gilbert. Music by Arthur Sullivan. Swing orchestrations by Charles L. Cooke. Entire production, book and ensembles staged by Hassard Short. Choral direction by William Parson. Dance arrangements by Truly McGee. Settings and costumes by Nat Karson. Orchestra conducted by William Parson. Produced by Michael Todd. Opened 23 March 1939 at the Broadhurst Theatre and closed 3 June 1939 after 85 performances.[29]

CAST: *Nanki-Poo*: ROBERT PARRISH. *Pish-Tush*: James A. Lillard. *Ko-Ko*: EDDIE GREEN. *Pooh-Bah*: MAURICE ELLIS. *Yum-Yum*: GWENDOLYN REYDE. *Pitti-Sing*: Frances Brock. *Peep-Bo*: ROSETTA LeNOIRE. *Messenger Boy*: Freddie Robinson. *Katisha*: ROSA BROWN. *The Mikado*: BILL ROBINSON. *Red Cap*: Vincent Shields.

Singing Girls: Alyce Ajaye, Fay Banks, Ethel Brown, Alice Carter, Maggie Carter, May Daniels, Vivian Eley, Marie Fraser, Marion Hairston, Ethel Harper, Pearl Harrison, Bruce Howard, Julie Hunter, Irene Johnson, Massie Patterson, Idelle Pemberton, Edna Rickes, Ann Simmons, Theresa Stone, Geneva Washington, Waldine Williams, Mary Young, Ethlynn Edmonson, Josephine Hall. *Singing Boys*: Charlie Banks, Lemuel Bullock, William Barber, Russell Carrington, Archie Cross, Travers Crawford, John Diggs, Leslie Grey, Otho Gains, Marshall Haley, John Jackson, Harry Lewis, Elmaurice Miller, Walter Mosby, Maynard Sandridge, Vincent Shields, Larry Seymour, Harold Slappy, Clyde Turner, Anthon Taylor, Ben Wailles, Roy White, Moke Wilson. *Dancing Girls*: Ronetta Batson, Valerie Black, Mitzi Coleman, Elaine Dash, Elizabeth Dozier, Claudie Haward, Sylvia Lee, Jackie Lewis, Cleo Law, Pearl McCormack, Ruby Richards, Mary Robinson. *Jitterbug Girls*: Gladys Croder, Geneva Davis, Belle Hill, Connie Hill, May Miller, Mildred Pollard. *Jitterbug Boys*: Eddie Davis, Leon James, Walter Johnson, Lee Lyons, Albert Minne, Russell Williams. *"Tap-a-Teers"*: Louis Brown, Jules Adger, Ernest Frazier, Fred Heron, Chick Lee, Eddie Morton. *Guards*: Sam Brown, Vincent Anderson, Willie Dinkins, Gershon Meyers, John Williams, Luther Williams. *Quartette*: Travers Crawford, Otho Gains, Harry Lewis, Elmaurice Miller.

Acts 1 and 2: Somewhere in Japan.

ACT 1
"If You Want to Know Who We Are"
Ensemble

"A Wandering Minstrel"
R. Parrish, Male Chorus, "Tap-a-Teers"

"Our Great Mikado"
J. Lillard, Male Chorus, "Tap-a-Teers"

"Young Man Despair"
M. Ellis, J. Lillard, R. Parrish

"Behold the Lord High Executioner"
E. Green, Male Chorus

"I've Got a Little List"
E. Green, Male Chorus

"Comes a Train of Little Ladies"
Girls' Chorus

"Three Little Maids"
G. Reyde, F. Brock, R. LeNoire, "Tap-a-Teers," Dancing Girls, Jitterbugs

"So Pardon Us"
G. Reyde, F. Brock, R. LeNoire, M. Ellis, J. Lillard, Girls' Chorus

"Were You Not to Ko-Ko Plighted?"
G. Reyde, R. Parrish

Finale Act 1
R. Parrish, E. Green, J. Lillard, M. Ellis, G. Reyde, F. Brock, R. LeNoire, R. Brown, Entire Ensemble

ACT 2
"Braid the Raven Hair"
Ensemble

"The Moon and I"
G. Reyde, The Harmoneers

"Here's a How-de-do"
G. Reyde, R. Parrish, E. Green

"The Mikado"
B. Robinson, R. Brown, Entire Ensemble

"I'm the Emperor of Japan"
B. Robinson, R. Brown

"My Object All Sublime"
B. Robinson

"Flowers That Bloom in the Spring"
F. Brock, G. Reyde, R. Parrish, M. Ellis, E. Green

Dance
"Tap-a-Teers," Dancing Girls, Jitterbugs

Dance
B. Robinson, Dancers

"I, Living I"
R. Brown

"Titwillow"
E. Green

Finale Act 2
Entire Company

---

[29]Subsequently transferred to the New York World's Fair for an extended run.

1939.18

MEXICANA

A Musical Revue Extravaganza in Two Acts, 27 Scenes. Staged under the general supervision of Celestino Gorostiza, Director of the Department of Fine Arts of Mexico. Musical supervisors, Eduardo Hernandez Moncada and Mario Ruiz. Dance supervisor, Gluck Sandor. Scenic supervsior, Julio Castellanos. Costume supervision, Agustin Lazo. Lighting by Eddie Dowling. Conductor, Paul Baron. Presented by the Republic of Mexico. Opened 21 April 1939 at the 46th Street Theatre and closed 20 May 1939 after 35 performances.

CAST: Graziella Parraga (Commentator), Rosita Rios, Carmen Molina, Elisa, Maria Luisa Lopez, Estela, Eva Perez Caro, Chucha Camacho, Lila Kiwa, Marissa Flores, Beatriz Ramos, Cuates Castilla, The Trio Nacional, Vicente Gomez, Tito Coral, Enrique Pastor, José Molina, José Luis Tapia, Rene, Rolando, Amparo Arozamena, Rafael Gutierrez, José Fernandez, Victor Novaro, Consuelo Solorzano, Trio Lina, Gustavo Aponte, Carlos Backman, Eduardo Hernandez Moncada.

Composers: Silvestre Revueltas, Tata Nacho, José Zabre Marroquin, Candelario Huizar, José Rolon, Blas Galindo, Alfonso Esparza Oteo, Luis Sandi. *Authors:* Agustin, Lazo, Xavier Villaurrutia, Celestino Gorostiza, Octavio G. Barreda, Rafael F. Munoz, Julio Bracho, Miguel Barveiller. *Choreographers:* José Fernandez, Rafael Diaz, Eva Perez Caro, Dick Schreurs. *Scene and Costume Designers:* Agustin Lazo, Julio Castellanos, Carlos Orozco, Carlos Merida, Manuel Fontanals, Gabriel Fernandez Ledesma.

ACT 1

Scene 1

"Ecos de Ayer" (Echoes of Yesterday)
 A cavalcade of the development of Mexican music and dance from the earliest Aztec times down to today.
 (a) Primitive Dance, (b) Dance of the Reindeer, (c) War Dance, (d) "Areito," Dance of the Aztec Nobles, (e) War Dance between Aztecs and Spaniards.

Scene 2

"Nocturnal" (Song)
 R. Rios, T. Corral
 Played by V. Gomez.

Scene 3

Oaxaquena
 Dance by the Trio Mixteco: C. Molina, E. Pastor, J. Molina.

Scene 4

"Yunuen" (The Legend of the Fisherman)
 On the island of Yunuen in the Lake of Patzcuaro, the fishermen are starving. A mysterious monster fish is devouring or frightening away the smaller fish, and the people have no food. A brave young man offers to go and kill the monster. The entire village gathers on the shore to pray and watch for his return, performing a ritual dance to bring him luck. On his victorious return, the populace celebrates, and the hero marries his sweetheart.
 The Bride: Elisa. *The Bridegroom:* R. Gutierrez. *An Old Man:* J. L. Tapia. *The Fish:* J. Molina.

Scene 5

Dance
 Rolando

Scene 6

"Mexicana" (Song)
 C. Castilla, M. L. Lopez, C. Solorzano, Trio Nacional

Scene 7

La Cucarachita (Dance)
 Trio Lina

Scene 8

La Mulata de Cordoba (The Mulatto of Cordoba)
 In the tropical city of Cordoba in Mexico, a beautiful mulatto has the gift of disappearing at will. She flirts with all the men, but only to baffle and exasperate them. When she is sought in Cordoba, she happens to be in Mexico City; and when she is sought in Mexico City, she happens to be in Cordoba. Accused of being a witch, she is delivered to the Tribunal of the Inquisition and condemned to be burnt at the stake. While in prison, though, she paints a caravel on the wall, embarks on it, and escapes.
 The Mulatto: Estela. *Her Suitor:* Rene.

Scene 9

Munecos de Petate (Straw Dolls) (Dance)
 Trio Lina

Scene 10

"Vereda Tropical" (Song)
 R. Rios, T. Coral

Scene 11

Un Velorio (The Wake)
 Death in Mexico is only an accident. A wake, therefore, is not necessarily a mourning ceremony. Like the ancient pagans, the Mexican Indians turn it into a fiesta. They drink, they sing, they dance. Even supernatural beings join the party—at least in the imagination of the participants—to fight for the soul of the departed.
 The Corpse: Rolando. *The Devil-Woman:* A. Arozamena. *The Widow:* C. Camacho. *A Friend:* E. P. Caro. *A Child:* L. Kiwa.

Scene 12

"La Farruca"
 V. Gomez

Scene 13

"Bulerias"
 V. Gomez
 Danced by J. Fernandez, M. Flores.

Scene 14

A Wedding in Tehuantepec
 In tropical Tehuantepec, love and passion are fiery like the sun and the climate. Lovers can not mate freely on account of the severity of parental authority. Wedding arrangements and ceremonies are so wrapped up in tradition that love is often tinged with tragedy. Sometimes, though, the call of the flesh is so strong that the young lovers take their fate into their own hands, and the young man carries his beloved off to the mountains. Since possession is ten-tenths of the Mexican marriage law, they return to receive the blessings of the entire village.
 The Bride: B. Ramoz. *Her Lover:* T. Coral. *The Bridegroom:* V. Novaro. *The Families of the Bride and Bridegroom:* J. L. Tapia, E. P. Caro, G. Aponte, C. Camacho.

ACT 2

Scene 1

Pinatas (Puppets)
 At a country fair, the vendors of the pinatas, Mexican dolls, have a dream about the puppets in their booths. By night, all of the doll characters come to life to live a tragedy of love and death like actual human beings.
 The Devil: G. Alvarez. *Serving Maid:* C. Avila. *Death:* F. Leon. *The Torero:* E. Salas. *The Soldier:* F. Ibarra.

Scene 2

"Pajarillo Embrujado" (Song)
 C. Castilla, M. L. Lopez, C. Solorzano

Scene 3

Dance
 Rolando

Scene 4

"La Morena" (Song)
 Las Serranitas and Los Huescas

Scene 5

Patio de Vecindad (In a Tenement House)
 A cross section of life in the densely populated tenement houses of Mexico. Widely contrasting character types reveal their inner personality in the manner of a Mexican 'Street Scene.'
 The Girl Without Stockings: C. Molina. *Serving Wench:* Elisa. *Peddler:* Lee. *Rent Collector:* G. Aponte. *A Gigolo:* C. Backman. *Policeman:* E. Pastor. *Street Vendor:* C. Camacho.

Scene 6

"Dime Que Si" (Song)
 R. Rios, T. Coral
 Danced by M. Flores.

Scene 7

"Limpiabotas" (Song)
 C. Castilla

Scene 8

Dance
 Rene, Estela

Scene 9

"Jota Aragonesa"
 V. Gomez

Scene 10

Los Viejitos (The Dance of the Little Old Men)

Scene 11

Goyescas (Dance)
J. Fernandez, M. Flores

Scene 12

Jarana (Dance of Yucatan)

Scene 13

Finale: (a) The Bottle Dance, (b) Jarabe Tapatio, a Dance, (c) Trio Mixteco.

1939.19   SING FOR YOUR SUPPER

A Musical Revue in Two Acts, 20 Scenes. Compiled and directed by Harold Hecht. Sketches by David Lesan, Turner Bullock. Additional material by Charlotte Kent and John Latouche. Lyrics by Robert Sour, (Hector Troy[30]). Music by Lee Wainer and Ned Lehac, (Earl Robinson). Production numbers staged by H. Gordon Graham. Sketches staged by Robert H. Gordon. Dance routines by Ned McGurn. Choreography and ensembles by Anna Sokolow. Settings by Herbert Andrews. Costumes by Mary Merrill. Lighting by Feder. Music director, Fred Hott. Orchestrations, Walter Paul. Assistant producer, Robert Sour. Produced by WPA Federal Theatre. Opened 24 April 1939 at the Adelphi Theatre and closed 30 June 1939 after 60 performances.

<u>CAST</u>: GORDON CLARKE, PEGGY COUDRAY, PAULA LAURENCE, COBY RUSKIN, GENORA ENGLISH, BOWEN [Sonny] TUFTS, JAMES MORDECAI, CARL CHAPIN, HANSFORD WILSON, BIDDA BLAKELEY, EDWARD FULLER, VIRGINIA BOLEN, Carol Coult, Allan Tinney, Muni Diamond, Richard Finlayson, Edith Groome, Louise Kelly, William Britten, Theodora Peck, Paul Jacchia, Edwin Wittner, John Campbell, William Tinney, Frank Newton, Rufus Finlayson, Edwin Cooper, Theresa Alvarez, Arthur Donaldson, Edward LeDuc, William Myron, Lee Wainer.

Ensemble: Choral: Spencer Barnes, Willis Bradley, Bonnie Clark, William Clayton, Eva Connell, Leon Diggs, Ethel Drayton, James Eakins, Estelle Ehrlich, Genora English, Walter Franklyn, Trudy Goodrich, Edward Gutter, Joseph Hall, Lena Halsey, Harry Hart, Rosyln Harvey, Edward Hemmer, Roy Holland, Vivian Holt, Minnie Hylton, Augustina Josephs, Louise Kelly, Adele Leo, Walter LeRoy, Alex Lovejoy, Muriel McCrory, Ruby Meyers, Ernest Pavano, Alice Ramsey, Clarence Redd, Emma Sealey, Maurice Siegel, Violet Smith, Ruth Thompson, Virgil VanCleve, Muriel Watts, George Whittington. *Modern Dance*: Joseph Belsky, Naomi Bodine, Mann Brown, Marjorie Church, John Connolly, William Elliott, Lily Verne, William Garrett, Julia Lane, Israel Lansky, Ray Lieb, Eve Lord, Virginia Mansfield, Anne Marcus, Martin Michel, Lou Rosen, Attilio Salzano, Georgette Schneer, Maurice Silvers, Sidney Stark. *Negro Tap*: J. Mae Batie, John Berry, Doris Bramble, William Brown, Lenore Cobb, George DeFour, St. Clair Dotson, Hilaria Friend, Dorothy Gee, Iris Griffith, Theresa Jentry, Ruth LaMarr, Ruth Lindsay, Blue McAllister, James Mordecai, Samuel Owens, Andre Pampleton, Rose Poindexter, Libby Robinson, Elsie Sealy, Lee Speaks, Dorothy Turner, Allen Williams, Costello Woolridge.

ACT 1

Scene 1

Opening

Scene: Federal Theatre. *Uncle Sam*: G. Clarke. *Hennery*: P. Jacchia. *Actors, Stagehands, Musicians, etc.*

Scene 2

"Sing for Your Supper"
(*Music by* Ned Lehac. *Lyrics by* Robert Sour.)
"At Long Last"
(*Music by* Lee Wainer. *Lyrics by* Robert Sour.)
V. Bolen, B. Blakely, R. Poindexter, R. Harvey, E. Fuller, E. Whittner, C. Ruskin, H. Hart, B. Tufts, P. Laurence, Entire Company

Scene 3

Peace at Any Price (*by* David Lesan and Turner Bullock)
Grover Whalen: C. Chapin. *Secretary*: P. Coudray. *Members of Grover Whalen's Staff.*

Scene 4

We Didn't Know It Was Loaded (*by* Charlotte Kent)
Watts: H. Hart. *Marconi*: C. Coult. *Orville Wright*: W. LeRoy. *Gutenberg*: H. Wilson. *Mr. Wong*: C. Ruskin.

[30]Alias for Harold Rome.

Scene 5

"Opening Night"
G. English
(*Music by* Lee Wainer. *Lyrics by* Robert Sour.)
Scene: (a) Outside the Casino Roof Garden, Ninth Avenue and 34th Street, 22 April 1900, at the opening of "Clorindy," the first all-Negro musical attraction in New York that was not just a minstrel show. The Cake-walk is supposed to have been first introduced in this production. (b) In the Theatre.
Specialty Dancers: W. Tinney, A. Tinney, Rufus Finalyson, Richard Finlayson, Entire Negro Ensemble.

Scene 6

Ping Pong on the Pacific (*by* David Lesan)
Admiral Stuffit: C. Chapin. *Lieutenant*: E. Fuller. *Quartermaster*: C. Ruskin.

Scene 7

"A Tisket A Tax It":
(*Music by* Lee Wainer. *Lyrics by* Robert Sour.)
"Bonnie Banks"
H. Hart, C. Coult, C. Ruskin, M. Diamond, J. Campbell
(b) "How Can We Swing It?"
P. Laurence
(c) "Oh, Boy Can We Deduct"
E. Fuller
Assisted by the Ensemble.

Scene 8

"Legitimate"
V. Bolen
(*Music by* Lee Wainer. *Lyrics by* John Latouche.)

Scene 9

"The Last Waltz"
Modern Dance Group
(*Composed and Arranged by* Alex North.)

Scene 10

We Go to the Theatre to Be Amused (*by* Charlotte Kent)
The Men: C. Ruskin, C. Chapin, E. Fuller. *The Girls*: L. Verne, E. Groome, T. Alvarez.

Scene 11

"Young Man With a Horn"
P. Laurence
(*Music by* Lee Wainer. *Lyrics by* Robert Sour.)
Young Man: F. Newton. *Quartette*: V. Smith, G. English, A. Joseph, C. Woolridge.

Scene 12

"Papa's Got a Job"
(*Music by* Ned Lehac. *Lyrics by* Robert Sour and Hector Troy.)
Trudy: T. Goodrich. *Mother*: L. Kelly. *Grandpa*: A. Donaldson. *Sister*: R. Harvey. *Brother*: P. Jacchia. *Older Sister*: B. Blakeley. *Landlord*: E. Cooper. *Prominent Citizen*: I. Lansky. *Papa*: E. LeDuc. And the Ensemble.

ACT 2

Scene 1

"Lucky"
G. English, C. Woolridge, J. Mordecai
(*Music by* Lee Wainer. *Lyrics by* Robert Sour.)
Specialty Dancers: W. Tinney, A. Tinney, Rufus Finlayson, Richard Finlayson. Entire Negro Ensemble.

Scene 2

"Imagine My Finding You Here"
B. Tufts, B. Blakeley
(*Music by* Ned Lehac. *Lyrics by* Robert Sour.)
Assisted by Choral Group, Ensemble.

Scene 3

"Perspiration"
(*Music by* Lee Wainer. *Lyrics by* John Latouche.)
Composer: L. Wainer. *Will*: M. Diamond. *Bill*: C. Ruskin. *Tessie*: P. Laurence. *Bessie*: V. Bolen. *Mr. Bankbook*: C. Coult. *Mr. Zipper*: E. Fuller. *Musician*: E. LeDuc. *Stagehand*: W. Britten. *Company Union members, pickets, etc.*

Scene 4

"Her Pop's a Cop"
(*Music by* Ned Lehac. *Lyrics by* Irving Crane and Phil Conwit.)
Girl: V. Bolen. *Boy*: C. Chapin. *Pop*: H. Wilson. *Cops*: W. Franklyn, W. LeRoy, E. Pavano, M. Siegel, W. Myron. *Policemen, Girls, etc.*

Scene 5

"Dirge"

H. Wilson

(*Music and Lyrics by* Charlotte Kent.)

Quartette: W. Franklyn, E. Gutter, J. Eakins, G. Whittington. *Assisted by* Choral Group.

Scene 6

Code for Actors (*by* Jack Murray)

Announcer: P. Coudray. *Timekeeper*: W. Britten. *First Wife*: V. Bolen. *First Lover*: C. Coult. *Second Lover*: W. Myron. *Second Wife*: T. Peck. *Third Lover*: M. Diamond. *First Husband*: B. Tufts. *Fourth Lover*: W. LeRoy. *Second Husband*: C. Ruskin. *Fifth Lover*: E. Whittner. *Third Husband*: E. Hemmer. *Third Wife*: B. Blakeley. *Fourth Wife*: P. Laurence.

Scene 7

"Leaning on a Shovel"

(*Music by* Lee Wainer. *Lyrics by* John Latouche.)

W.P.A. Workers: C. Chapin, E. Fuller, C. Ruskin, H. Wilson. *Dream Girl*: V. Bolen.

Scene 8

"Ballad of Uncle Sam" (Ballad for Americans)

Entire Company

(*Music by* Earl Robinson. *Lyrics by* John Latouche.)

Uncle Sam: G. Clarke. *Hennery*: P. Jacchia.

THE DEVIL AND DANIEL WEBSTER

1939.20

A Musical Folk Play (Opera) in One Act[31]. Book and lyrics by Stephen Vincent Benét. Adapted from his own short story of the Faust legend. Music by Douglas Moore. Staged by John Houseman. Conductor, Fritz Kitzinger. Music director, Lee Pattison. Chorus under the direction of May Valentine. Production designed and lighted by Robert Edmund Jones. Choreography by Eugene Loring. Associate producer, Richard Aldrich. Produced by the American Lyric Theatre in association with The League of Composers. Robert Edmund Jones, Managing director. Opened 18 May 1939 at the Martin Beck Theatre and closed 26 May 1939 after 5 performances in repertory. (Preceded by the ballet-document "Filling Station," Music by Virgil Thomson, choreography by Lew Christiansen, presented by The Ballet Caravan, Lincoln Kirstein, Director.)

CAST (in order of appearance): *Jabez Stone*: John Gurney. *Mary Stone*: NANCY McCORD, BETTINA HALL (alt.). *Daniel Webster*: LANSING HATFIELD, RICHARD HALE (alt.). *Mr. Scratch*: GEORGE RASELY. *The Fiddler*: Fred Stewart. *Justice Hathorne*: Clair Kramer. *Clerk of the Court*: Edward Marshall.

Jurymen: *Simon Girty*: Ernice Lawrence. *King Philip*: Philip Whitfield. *Teach*: Lawrence Siegle. *Walter Butler*: Don Lee. *Smeet*: W. H. Mende. *Dale*: Paul Roberts. *Morton*: James Chartrand. Jay Amiss, Karl Holly, Alan Stewart, James Gillis, Frank Chamberlain.

Wedding Guests, Men and Women of Cross Corners, New Hampshire: *Old Man*: Lee Couch. *Old Woman*: Alice Tobin. *School Teacher*: Telete Lester. Ross Lockwood, Beulah Blake, Angela Chope, Frances Earnest, Dorothy Essig, Geraldine Hamilton, Cathryn Harvey, Helen Mastelle, Helen Oliver, Eunice Northrup, Janet Joyce, Fannie Shiff, Elinor Waldron, Jean Watson, Marjorie Williamson.

Scene: Cross Corners, New Hampshire in the 1840s.

SUSANNA, DON'T YOU CRY

1939.21

A Musical Romance in Two Acts, 8 Scenes. Book by Sarah Newmeyer and Clarence Loomis. Based on melodies of Stephen Foster. (All music and lyrics by Stephen Foster[32].) Special arrangement of the minstrel scene and last act finale by Hans Spialek. Staged by José Ruben. Music director, Lee Pattison. Conductor, Andre Polah. Production designed and lighted by Robert Edmund Jones. Chorus under the direction of May Valentine.

---

[31]No individual musical numbers listed.

[32]Program note: The twenty-nine Stephen Foster songs in the play are presented exactly as Foster wrote them, words and music. In the case of "Dear Friends and Gentle Hearts," that title was discovered in Foster's wallet after his death, scribbled on a piece of paper. Clarence Loomis has written the words and music for that particular song.

Produced by the American Lyric Theatre in association with The League of Composers. Robert Edmund Jones, Managing Director. Opened 22 May 1939 at the Martin Beck Theatre and closed 27 May 1939 after 5 performances in repertory.

CAST (in order of appearance): *Brian Tolliver*: RALPH MAGELSSON, LANSING HATFIELD (BP). *Susan Eliot*: BETTINA HALL. *Carter Reynolds*: MICHAEL BARTLETT. *Eulalie Bland*: HOPE MANNING. *Judge Bland*: George Lessey. *Mrs. Bland*: Merle Maddern. *Grandfather*: John Kirk. *Cato*: J. Louis Johnson. *Lem*: Robert Clarke. *Grandmother, Ghost*: Helen Mastelle. *First Houseman*: Jonathan Brice. *Second Houseman*: James Armstrong. *Angie*: AVIS ANDREWS. *A Young Composer*: Richard Clark. *Stage Doorman*: Peter Chambers. *Jeb Martin*: Lawrence Bolton. *Jonathan Lamphrey*: Richard Hale. *Jeannie June*: Helen Renee. *Bradley*: Frank Chamberlin. *Mrs. Stoddard*: Mary Perry. *Mary Lou*: Helen Mestelle. *Randy*: Paul Roberts.

Minstrels: Jay Amiss, Peter Chambers, Lee Couch, Clair Kramer, Edward Marshall, W. H. Mende, Paul Roberts, Philip Whitfield. *Chorus*: *Women*: Belulah Blake, Angela Chope, Frances Ernest, Dorothy Essig, Isabel Gerard, Geraldine Hamilton, Kathryn Harvey, Janice Joyce, Telete Lester, Eunice Northrup, Helen Oliver, Caryl Crane, Alice Tobin, Elinor Waldon, Jean Watson, Marjorie Williamson. *Men*: James Chartrand, James Gillis, Karl Holly, Ernice Lawrence, Donald Lee, Ross Lockwood, Lawrence Siegle, Allen Stewart.

HALL JOHNSON CHOIR: *Women*: Leona Avery, Marguerite Avery, Mabel Bergen, Maudina Brown, Viola Drake, Ruth Gibbs, Winfred Gordon, Claudia Hall, Charlotte Junius, Mildred Lassiter, Juanita Polk, Claudia Reilly, Benveta Washington. *Men*: Oscar Brooks, Leslie Coles, George Dickson, Edward Edmonson, Louis Gilbert, Edgar Hall, George Hall, Wyer Handy, Adolph Henderson, Walter Keyes, Luther Saxon, William Vaughan, Ray Yeates. *Boys*: Trevor Bannister, Roland Wheatle, Jr., Newman Odon.

Act 1, Scene 1: Judge Bland's Plantation Home near Covington, Kentucky, Christmas Eve, 1851. *Scene 2*: Eulalie and Susan's Bedroom. A few hours later. *Scene 3*: The Stage of the Melodeon Theatre, Cincinnati. The following day. *Scene 4*: Judge Bland's Plantation Home. Three days later. *Scene 5*: The Levee. Next morning, shortly after dawn.

Act 2, Scene 1: Ballroom of the Eliot Hotel, San Francisco, April, 1861. *Scene 2*: Mrs. Stoddard's Boarding House, New York City. Late afternoon in May, 1865. *Scene 3*: Before the Bland Plantation home. Two days later.

ACT 1

"Ah, May the Red Rose Live Alway"

R. Magelssen

"(Oh!) Susanna, Don't You Cry"

R. Magelssen, Chorus

"Turn Not Away"

M. Bartlett, B. Hall

"Under the Willow She's Sleeping"

H. Manning, Hall Johnson Choir

"Eulalie"

H. Manning, Hall Johnson Choir

"The Voice of Bygone Days"

Hall Johnson Choir

"(Oh) Lemuel"

A. Andrews

"Go Down to the Cotton Fields"

R. Clark

"Beautiful Dreamer"

M. Bartlett

"Open Thy Lattice, Love"

L. Couch, Chorus

"Come Where My Love Lies Dreaming"

Valentine Chorus

"Sweet Emerald Isle"

R. Magelssen

"Where Shall I Turn?"

B. Hall

"Somebody's Coming to See Me Tonight"

H. Manning

"Gentle Annie"

H. Manning, Hall Johnson Choir

"Glendy Burke"

Hall Johnson Octette

"Angeline"

A. Andrews, R. Clarke, Hall Johnson Choir

Finale
  Entire Company
ACT 2
  "Ring de Banjo"
    R. Hale, Minstrels
  "Sweet Summertime"
    M. Bartlett
  "My Old Kentucky Home"
    R. Hale, Minstrels
  "Some Folks Do"
    Minstrels
  "Lemuel" (reprise)
    Minstrels
  "Camptown Races"
    Minstrels
  "Louisiana Belle"
    R. Hale, Minstrels, A. Andrews

"Farewell, My Eulalie"
  R. Hale
"Why Have My Loved Ones Gone?"
  B. Hall
"Dear Friends and Gentle Hearts"
  B. Hall, R. Clark
  (*Music and Lyrics by* Clarence Loomis.)
"Soft Be Thy Slumbers"
  Hall Johnson Choir
"We'll Put for the South"
  Hall Johnson Choir
"Village Bells"
  A. Andrews, Hall Johnson Choir
"(I Dream of) Jeannie With the Light Brown Hair"
  M. Bartlett
Finale
  Entire Company

Shirley Ross and Jack Haley in HIGHER AND HIGHER (Photo: Lucas and Monroe)
Billy Rose Theatre Collection, New York Public Library for the Performing Arts

1939–1940 SEASON

1939.22   THE STREETS OF PARIS

A Musical Revue in Two Acts, 29 Scenes. Sketches by Tom McKnight, Charles Sherman, S. Jay Kaufman, (Mitchell Hodges, Edward Duryea Dowling, James LaVer, Frank Eyton and Lee Brody). Music by James [Jimmy] McHugh. Lyrics by Al Dubin. Additional numbers by Harold J. Rome. Production directed and lighted by Edward Duryea Dowling. Costumes by Irene Sharaff. Dances and ensembles staged by Robert Alton. Scenery designed by Lawrence L. Goldwasser. Consultant on production, Jean Le Seyeux. Orchestra conducted by John McManus. Stage directed by Dennis Murray. Orchestral arrangements by Hans Spialek. Vocal arrangements directed by Hugh Martin. Produced by the Messrs. Shubert in association with Olsen and Johnson. Opened 19 June 1939 at the Broadhurst Theatre and closed 10 February 1940 after 274 performances.[1]

<u>CAST</u>: BOBBY CLARK, LUELLA GEAR, BUD ABBOTT and LOU COSTELLO, CARMEN MIRANDA, DELLA LIND, YVONNE BOUVIER, JEAN SABLON, DELLA LIND, MONS. "Think A Drink" HOFFMAN, YVONNE BOUVIER, GLORIA GILBERT, JO and JEANNE READINGER, GOWER (Champion) and JEANNE (Tyler), MARGARET IRVING, JOHN McCAULEY, THE HYLTON SISTERS (Margo, Kate, Evelyn), WARD and VAN, BEN DOVA, BILLY BRANCH, RAMON VINAY, MAGDA KARI, CHARLES LaTORRE, BUDDY ROBERTS, LINCOLN WILMERTON.

Mesdemoiselles: Barbara Beech, Frances O'Day, Maxine Martin, Mildred Hughes, Aina Constant, Bernice Smith, Lillian Lillemy, Nancy Lewis, Mary Ann, Lynda Grey, Margaret Hall, Nancy Lewis, Alice Anthony, Billy Aubrey, Trudy Burke, Flora Bowes, Betty Bartley, Lucie Chandler, Shannon Dean, Enes Early, Jackie Gateley, Peggy Gallimore, Marguerite James, Edith Lambot, Olive Nicolson, Leona Olsen, Mary Ann O'Brien, Tony Stuart.
Messieurs: Richard D'Arcy, Hugh Ellsworth, Arthur Grahl, Henning Irgens, Frederic Nay, Hugh Martin, Michael Moore, Mischa Pompianov, Edward Wells.

ACT 1
Scene 1

Theatre Marigny Dressing Room
> *The Callboy*: Himself. *The Costumer*: Himself. *The Wardrobe Mistress*: Herself. *The Girls*: Themselves.

Scene 2

"The Streets of Paris"
> *Les Beautés*: A. Constant, B. Beech, L. Grey, M. Hughes, M. Hall, N. Lewis, M. Martin, F. O'Day. And Passersby on the Streets of Paris.

Scene 3

The Ensemble Speaks—
> *Mesdemoiselles*: A. Anthony, B. Aubrey, T. Burke, F. Bowes, B. Bartley, M. Ann, L. Chandler, S. Dean, E. Early, J. Gately, P. Gallimore, M. James, E. Lambot, O. Nicolson, L. Olsen, M. A. O'Brien, T. Stuart. *Messieurs*: R. D'Arcy, H. Ellsworth, A. Grahl, H. Irgens, F. Nay, H. Martin, M. Moore, M. Pompianov, E. Wells.

Scene 4

In Paris (*by* S. Jay Kaufman)
> *Scene*: The Terrace of the Café de la Paix in Paris.
> *The First Woman*: L. Gear. *The Second Woman*: M. Irving. *The Waiter*: J. McCauley.

Scene 5

Abbott and Costello in 'Customs'

Scene 6

"Thanks for the Francs"
> J. Sablon, Hylton Sisters
> *Les Deputés*: H. Martin, M. Moore, F. Nay, M. Pompianov. *La Jeune Fille Americaine*: J. Tyler. *Le Fils Americain*: G. Champion. *La Mere Americaine*: M. Ann. *Le Pere Americain*: H. Ellsworth. *L'Apache*: R. D'Arcy. *Danced by* Jo Readinger, Jeanne Readinger, Dancing Girls.

Scene 7

The Photographer (*by* Tom McKnight and Edward Duryea Dowling)

> *Scene*: A photographer's studio in Paris.
> *The Model*: B. Beech. *The Photographer's Assistant*: C. LaTorre. *Mr. Satterthwaite Chalmers*: J. McCauley. *Mrs. Satterthwaite Chalmers*: L. Gear. *The Photographer*: B. Clark.

Scene 8

"Danger in the Dark"
> D. Lind, R. Vinay
> *Danced by* Jo Readinger, Jeanne Readinger, H. Ellsworth, F. Nay, E. Wells, Dancing Girls and Boys.

Scene 9

The Queen of Paris (*by* James LaVer)
> *Scene*: Paris. The boudoir of a grand cocotte.
> *Odette de Brioche*: L. Gear. *The Cadet*: J. Sablon.

Scene 10

"Three Little Maids"
> Hylton Sisters

Scene 11

"Is It Possible?"
> B. Clark, D. Lind
> *Scene*: A Moment in Montmarte.
> *The Girl*: M. Kari. *The Man*: B. Branch. *The Apaches*: B. Roberts, L. Wilmerton, Show Girls and Boys.

Scene 12

Abbott and Costello 'On the Boulevard'

Scene 13

"Doin' the Chamberlain"
> L. Gear
> *Danced by The Duchess*: J. Tyler. *The Duke*: G. Champion. And Dancing Girls and Boys.

Scene 14

Water—Water (*by* Tom McKnight and Charles Sherman)
> *Scene*: The French Sahara.
> *Gonzales*: J. McCauley. *Grombach*: B. Branch. *La Tour*: C. LaTorre. *Smith*: B. Clark.

Scene 15

"Rendezvous Time in Paris"
> J. Sablon, Y. Bouvier
> *The Girls in Chartreuse*: A. Anthony, L. Chandler, S. Dean, E. Early, J. Gateley, M. James, E. Lambot, O. Nicolson. *'Blanc'*: B. Beech, M. Moore. *'Blond'*: F. O'Day, F. Nay. *'Brun'*: L. Grey, A. Grahl. *'Noir'*: M. Hughes, H. Ellsworth. *'Rouge'*: M. Martin, H. Martin. *'Argent'*: A. Constant, E. Wells. ' ': M. Hall, N. Lewis, H. Irgens. And M. 'Think a Drink' Hoffman. *The Assistants*: B. Smith, L. Lillemy.

Scene 16

The Convict's Return (*by* Frank Eyton)
> *Scene*: A French theatre in the early 1890s.
> *Announced by*: J. Sablon. *Marie*: L. Gear. *Her Father*: B. Clark. *Michel*: B. Clark. *Armand*: B. Clark. *The Warden*: B. Clark.

Scene 17

Ben Dova

Scene 18

"South American Way"
> C. Miranda, R. Vinay, Hylton Sisters, D. Lind, Show Girls
> *Danced by* C. Miranda, Jo Readinger, Jeanne Readinger, G. Champion, J. Tyler, Dancing Girls and Boys.

ACT 2
Scene 1

"History Is Made at Night"
> Y. Bouvier
> (*Music and Lyrics by* Harold Rome.)
> *Avec le Soldat*: L. Grey. *Avec le Roi*: B. Beech. *Avec les Enfants*: M. Martin. *Avec les Vieux*: N. Lewis. *Avec le Chien*: M. Hall. *Avec le Gros*: F. O'Day. *Avec les Hillbillies*: M. Hughes. *Avec les Bêtes Noires*: A. Constant. And les Girls.

Scene 2

A Noël Coward Custom (*by* Lee Brody)
> *Scene*: Cannes, beautiful Cannes.
> *Announced by*: J. Sablon. *The Man*: B. Clark. *First Girl*: M. Irving. *Second Girl*: L. Gear.

Scene 3

"We (Can) Live on Love"/"We Haven't Got a Pot to Cook In"
> J. Sablon, Y. Bouvier
> *Danced by* G. Champion, J. Tyler, G. Gilbert.

---

[1] Subsequently presented by Michael Todd 11 May 1940 at the New York World's Fair Hall of Music in truncated 70-minute form on a 4 shows-per-day basis. Cast included Abbott & Costello, Gypsy Rose Lee, Milton Watson, Hylton Sisters, Dell O'Dell, Frank & Jean Hubert, Magda and Billy Brach & Co., Peggy Alexander, Enis Beyer, Joseph Lyons.

Scene 4

"Robert the Roué (from Reading, Pa.)"
B. Clark, et Ses Beautés

Scene 5

Rest Cure
Scene: A French Health Resort.
The Searcher: L. Costello. *The Manager*: B. Abbott. *The Nurse*: M. Irving.
The Doctor: J. McCauley. *The Apaches*: M. Moore, B. Roberts. *The Horticulturist*: F. O'Day. *The Strollers*: H. Ellsworth, M. Martin. *The Palmist*: E. Wells. *The Fruiterer*: B. Beech.

Scene 6

Ward and Van (harp and violin burlesque)

Scene 7

The Spy (*by* Tom McKnight)
Scene: An hotel in Paris.
Mr. Migglesworth: B. Clark. *Mrs. Migglesworth*: L. Gear. *The Bell-hop*: L. Wilmerton. *Yvonne*: Y. Bouvier. *The Gendarmes*: J. McCauley, E. Wells.

Scene 8

"Reading, Writing and a Little Bit of Rhythm"
Hylton Sisters
Scene: Graduation day at l'École de Jeunes Filles.
Danced by Jo Readinger, Jeanne Readinger, G. Champion, J. Tyler. (The sweet girl graduates and the austere professors)

Scene 9

"Three Little Maids"—Later
Hylton Sisters

Scene 10

That's Music (*by* Charles Sherman)
Scene: A Music Shop in Paris.
Capi: B. Abbott. *Marcel*: L. Costello. *Mr. Prout*: B. Clark.

Scene 11

Finale—"The French Have a Word For It"
B. Clark, L. Gear, B. Abbott, L. Costello, C. Miranda, J. Sablon, Entire Company
(*Music and Lyrics by* Harold Rome.)

1939.23   FROM VIENNA

A Musical Revue in Two Acts, 13 Scenes. (Sketches and lyrics by Lothar Metzl, Werner Michel, Hans Weigel, Jura Soyfer, Peter Hammerschlag, David Greggory, Jimmy Berg. English adaptations by John Latouche, Werner Michel, Eva Franklin, Hugo Hauff, David Gregory. Music by Werner Michel, Walter Drix, Otto Andreas and Jimmy Berg.) Staged by Herbert Berghof. Supervised by Charles Friedman. Settings by Donald Oenslager. Costumes by Irene Sharaff. Lighting by Hassard Short. Musical director, Otto Andreas. Choreographed by Lotte Goslar. Speech and voice training, Arthur Lessack. At the pianos: Hans Herberth and Henry Vanicelli. Produced by The Refugee Artists Group. Opened 20 June 1939 at the Music Box Theatre and closed 26 August 1939 after 79 performances.

CAST: Illa Roden, Paul Lindenberg, Elizabeth Neumann, Fred Lorenz, Nelly Franck, Henry Werbeck, Maria Pichler, Kurt Reichert, Hedy Pitt, Walter Martin, Katherine Mattern, John Banner, Fred Essler, Lothar Rewalt, Karl Mueller, Fritz Ebers.

ACT 1

Scene 1

Opening
Entire Company
(*Lyrics by* Lothar Metzl and Werner Michel. *Music by* Werner Michel.)

Scene 2

"Musical Day"
(*by* Hans Weigel. *English Version by* Werner Michel. *Music by* Walter Drix.)
The Father: P. Lindenberg. *The Mother*: E. Neumann. *The Daughters*: N. Franck, I. Roden. *Maid*: M. Pichler. *Grocery-boy*: K. Reichert. *Teacher*: F. Lorenz. *Pupil*: H. Pitt. *Secretary*: K. Mattern. *Waiter*: W. Martin. *Doctor*: J. Banner. *Guests*: Members of the Company.

Scene 3

"Journey to Paradise"
(*by* Jura Soyfer. *English Version by* John Latouche. *Music by* Otto Andreas.)
On the Dock
Tony: P. Lindenberg. *Annie*: I. Roden. *Pop*, a Beggar: F. Lorenz. *A Couple*: M. Pichler, H. Werbeck. *Joe Gadget*: F. Essler. *Harry*: K. Reichert. *Apparitions*: Members of the Company.

Scene 4

The Practical Inventor
Benjamin Franklin: W. Martin. *Tony*: P. Lindenberg. *Annie*: I. Roden. *Joe Gadget*: F. Essler.

Scene 5

The Scientist
Judges: L. Rewalt, W. Martin, K. Reichert. *Prosecutor*: H. Werbeck. *Defense Attorney*: H. Berghof. *Galileo*: F. Lorenz. *Professor Teufelsdreck*: K. Mueller. *Guard*: F. Ebers. *Tony*: P. Lindenberg. *Annie*: I. Roden. *Joe Gadget*: F. Essler.

Scene 6

The Explorer
Sailor: J. Banner. *Tony*: P. Lindenberg. *Annie*: I. Roden. *Joe Gadget*: F. Essler. *Columbus*: L. Rewalt. *Speaker*: K. Reichert.

Scene 7

The Craftsman
Gutenberg: W. Martin. *Apprentice*: H. Werbeck. *Tony*: P. Lindenberg. *Annie*: I. Roden. *Joe Gadget*: F. Essler.

Scene 8

Garden of Eden
Doorman: J. Banner. *Tony*: P. Lindenberg. *Annie*: I. Roden. *Joe Gadget*: F. Essler. *People*: Members of the Company.

ACT 2

Scene 1

"Salzburg Puppet Show" (*by* Lothar Metzl)
(*English Version by* Werner Michel and Eva Franklin. *Music by* Otto Andreas.)
Peasant: F. Lorenz. *His Wife*: M. Pichler. *The Noble Outlaw*: F. Essler. *The Young Lady of the Castle*: K. Mattern. *The Noble Outlaw's Heart*: W. Martin. *The Dragon*: J. Banner.

Scene 2

"Little Ballerina" (*German Lyrics by* Peter Hammerschlag. *English Lyrics by* Werner Michel and Hugo Hauff. *Music by* Jimmy Berg.)
The Little Ballerina: I. Roden.

Scene 3

English in Six Easy Lessons (*by* Lothar Metzl and Werner Michel)
The Newcomer: F. Lorenz. *Customs Officer*: H. Werbeck. *Subway Passenger*: J. Banner. *Reception Clerk*: N. Franck. *Bell-boy*: K. Reichert. *Hotel Detective*: L. Rewalt. *Girl*: M. Pichler. *Guest in the Cafeteria*: P. Lindenberg. *Passerby*: W. Martin.

Scene 4

"From Vienna"
Entire Company
(*Music and Lyrics by* Lothar Metzl and Werner Michel.)

Scene 5

"Final Song"
Entire Company
(*English Lyrics by* David Greggory. *Music and German Lyrics by* Jimmy Berg.)

1939.24   YOKEL BOY

A Musical Comedy in Two Acts, 19 Scenes. (Book written and production supervised by Lew Brown.) Music and lyrics by Lew Brown, Charles Tobias and Samuel H. Stept. Staged by Lew Brown. Orchestra conducted by Al Goodman. Dances staged by Gene Snyder. Scenery designed by Walter Jagemann. Costumes designed by Frances Feist. Produced by Lew Brown. Opened 6 July 1939 at the Majestic Theatre and closed 6 January 1940 after 208 performances.

CAST: *Elmer Whipple*: BUDDY EBSEN. *Judy*: JUDA CANOVA. *Tiny*: DIXIE DUNBAR. *"Punko" Parks*: PHIL SILVERS. *Spud*: JACKIE HELLER. *Mary Hawkins*: LOIS JANUARY. *Cliff Hawkins*: RALPH RIGGS. *Blacksmith*: MARK PLANT. *Mr. Rubbish*: LEW HEARN. *Grandpa Hawkins, Mayor*: CHARLES ALTHOFF. *Mrs. Hawkins*: ALMIRA SESSIONS. *Annie*: ANN CANOVA. *Hank*: ZEKE CANOVA. *Jimmy Powell*: RALPH HOLMES. *Sheriff*: BEN ROBERTS. *Angelina Bouchet*: Helene Standish. *Gateman*: Sidney Salzer. *Another Gateman*: Jack Richards. *Assistant to "Punko" Parks*: Ray Clarke. *Doorman*: Dick Langdon. *Marie*: Ruth Rathbun.

Ladies of the Ensemble: Lorraine Belore, June Blake, Helen Cole, Marguerite De Coursey, Glorianna King, Maxine Moore, Helene Standish. *Yokel Girls*: Irene Austin, Kalli Barton, Jeanne Bergersen, Pamela Clifford, Muriel Cole, Helen Dell, Jane Everett, Margaret Fitz-Patrick, Miriam Franklyn, Marjorie Johnstone, Grace Kaye, Katheryn Lazell, Jeanette Lee, Velma Lord, Marion Lulling, Alice Malteur, Joan Mann, Gloria Martin, Mary Joan Martin, Dorothy Matthews, Frances Rands, Ruth Rathbun, Tina Rigat, Renee Russell, Natalie Wynn. *Minute Men from Lexington*: James Burrell, Charles Clarke, Philip Crosbie, Roy Johnston, F. Richard Moors, Joseph Peterson, Louis Salmon, Donald Showalter, Turnley Walker, Harold Woodward. *Yokel Boys*: Bob Beh, Dick Langdon, Eddie Murray, Jack Richards, Sidney Salzer, Phil Shaw.

Act 1, Scene 1: Hawkins' Farm, Town of Lexington, Massachusetts at the present time. *Scene 2*: Behind the Hawkins' Barn. *Scene 3*: Entrance Gate, Colossal Picture Studios, Hollywood. *Scene 4*: Mary's Dressing Room. *Scene 5*: Sound Stage of Colossal Pictures. *Scene 6*: Juke Joint. *Scene 7*: Outside Sound Stage. *Scene 8*: Finale—"Uncle Sam's Lullaby."

Act 2, Scene 1: Hollywood and Vine Street, Hollywood, California. *Scene 2*: Elmer's Living Quarters. *Scene 3*: Projection Room. *Scene 4*: Entrance to Projection Room, Colossal Pictures. *Scene 5*: The Hawkins' Living-room, Hollywood. *Scene 6*: Entrance to the Trocadero, Hollywood. *Scene 7*: The Trocadero. *Scene 8*: Airport. *Scene 9*: Airplane Flight from Hollywood to Lexington. *Scene 10*: Parachute. *Scene 11*: Hawkins' Farm, Town of Lexington, Massachusetts.

ACT 1

"Lem and Sue"
    J. Canova, D. Dunbar, Yokel Boys and Girls

"I Know I'm Nobody"
    B. Ebsen

"For the Sake of Lexington"
    Entire Company

"Comes Love"
    J. Canova
        Danced by D. Dunbar, Yokel Girls.

"It's Me Again"
    D. Dunbar, Minute Men

"Let's Make Memories Tonight"
    L. January, Minute Men
        Danced by Yokel Girls.

"(Time for) Jukin'"
    J. Canova
    (*Music by* Walter Kent.)
        Danced by B. Ebsen, Yokel Boys and Girls.

Grandpa Hawkins
    C. Althoff

"Uncle Sam's Lullaby"
    M. Plant, Minute Men, Entire Ensemble

ACT 2[2]

"Hollywood and Vine"
    J. Burrell, Minute Men
        Danced by Yokel Girls.

"Catherine the Great"
    J. Canova, the Royal Bodyguards

"The Ship Has Sailed"
    L. January

Dance
    B. Ebsen, D. Dunbar

"I Can't Afford to Dream"
    M. Plant
        Danced by Yokel Girls.

Specialty
    J. Canova, A. Canova, Z. Canova

(Finale) "Lem and Sue," "Comes Love," "Uncle Sam's Lullaby" (reprises)
    Entire Company

GEORGE WHITE'S
SCANDALS (1939)

1939.25

A Musical Revue in Two Acts, 25 Scenes[3]. Dialogue (sketches) by Matt Brooks, Eddie Davis and George White. Music by Smmy Fain. Lyrics by

---

[2]During NY run the following was interpolated into Act 2 after "I Can't Afford to Dream" Dance:

"Beer Barrel Polka"
    Minute Men
    (*Music by* Jaromir Vejvoda. *Lyrics by* Lew Brown. *Original Czech lyrics to* "Skoda Lasky" *by* Vasek Zeman and Wladimir A. Timm.)

Added for subsequent tour:

"If I Feel This Way Tomorrow"
    Cass Daley (Judy)
    (*Music by* Ray Henderson. *Lyrics by* Lew Brown.)

Specialty
    C. Daley

[3]The thirteenth and last in the series of musical revues conceived by George White. The series began in 1919.

Jack Yellen. Conceived and staged by George White. Dialogue directed by William K. Wells. Scenery designed by Albert Johnson. Costumes designed by Charles LeMaire. Dances by George White. Dialogue directed by William K. Wells. Additional lyrics by Herb Magidson. Orchestrations by Hans Spialek, Don Walker, Lew Harris, Ted Royal. Orchestra conducted by Charles Drury. Produced by George White. Opened 28 August 1939 at the Alvin Theatre, moved 6 November 1939 to the Hollywood Theatre, and closed 9 December 1939 after 120 performances.

CAST: WILLIE HOWARD, EUGENE HOWARD, THE THREE STOOGES (Moe Howard, Curley Howard, Larry Fine), HARRY STOCKWELL, BEN BLUE, ELLA LOGAN, ANN MILLER, VICTOR ARDEN & HIS ORCHESTRA, MARTHA BURNETT, RAYMOND [Ray] MIDDLETON, BILLY RAYES, JACK WILLIAMS, COLLETTE LYONS, THE KIM LOO SISTERS (Alice, Bubbles, Margaret, Jenee), HAROLD WHALEN, The Knight Sisters (Betsy, Kitty), Craig Mathues, Frederick B. Manatt, Ross Wyse, Jr., James French.

THE GEORGE WHITE GIRLS: Barbara Lenton, LOIS ANDREW, BETTY ALLEN, CHRISTINE FORSYTHE, Dorothy Stanton, Marie Kelly, Lois Kent, Bonnie Bennett, Lillian Walsh, Florette DuElk, Miriam Franklin, Jane Hatfield, Dorothy Koster, Rhoda Long, Amy Collins, Fay Renault, Peggy Graham, Ginger Johnson, Jane Dixon, Fran English, Olga Gorey, Peggy Kirk, Georgia Jarvis, Mary King, Phyllis Dawn, Kay Buckley, Frances Neal, Loretta Kane, Marie Brady, Myra Weldon, Ella Windell, Constance Snow, Marji Beeler, Mary Carroll, Cece Ames, Mary Francis, Amelia Gentry, Prudence Hayes, Rose Marie Magrill, Betty Nielson, Lois Palmer, Dorothy Reed, Paula Rudolph, Gloria Scott, Helen Wishart, Mae Britton, Susan Carewe, June Curtis.

ACT 1

Scene 1

Scandals Day at the Fair (The Fairs—East and West)
    Grover Whalen: R. Middleton. *Mayor LaGuardia*: R. Wyse. *Sam Trylon*: W. Howard. *Max Perisphere*: E. Howard. *Lady from Havana*: D. Koster. *Amazon*: F. DuElk. *Lady in Ice*: F. Neal. *Dove Lady*: R. M. Magrill. The George White Girls.

Scene 2

Theatre Quiz
    Prof Quiz: B. Rayes.
        Quiz No. 1: *Woman*: J. Mann. *Man*: C. Mathues.
        Quiz No. 2: *Man*: J. French.
        Quiz No. 3: *Boy*: C. Mathues. *Girl*: J. Mann.
        Quiz No. 4: *Boy*: B. Rayes. *Friend*: C. Mathues.
        Quiz No. 5: *Man*: C. Mathues. *Girl*: J. Mann.

Scene 3

"Are You Having Any Fun?"
    E. Logan, Kim Loo Sisters, The Three Stooges, Girls

Scene 4

Tel-U-Vision
    Business Man: W. Howard. *Salesman*: E. Howard. *The Wife*: C. Lyons. *The Friend*: H. Whalen. *Iceman*: J. French.

Scene 5

"A Hat Like That"[4]
    A. Miller, J. Williams

Scene 6

The Stand In
    Bawdry: L. Fine. *Director*: M. Howard. *The Stand-In*: C. Howard. *Mexican Pete*: R. Middleton.

Scene 7

"Smart Little Girls"
    B. Allen, L. Andrew, V. Shea, D. Koster, K. Buckley, R M. Magrill, F. DuElk, B. Lenton, A. Gentry.

"Three Smart Girls"
    The Three Stooges

Scene 8

Yokel Boy
    Barker: H. Whalen. *Yokel Boy*: B. Blue. *Hostess*: C. Lyons.

Scene 9

"Our First Kiss"
    C. Mathues, L. Andrew, Girls

Scene 10

Columnist at Home
    Mrs. Winchell: C. Lyons. *Walter Winchell*: W. Howard. *Maid*: J. Mann.

---

[4]Dropped during the run.

Scene 11

"The Mexiconga"
> E. Logan, A. Miller, Kim Loo Sisters, Girls
> (*Lyrics by* Jack Yellen and Herb Magidson.)

Scene 12

Curb Your Dog
> W. Howard, The Three Stooges, L. Andrew, D. Koster, K. Buckley, B. Lenton, F. Neal

Scene 13

Ross Wyse, Jr., and June Mann

Scene 14

Tin Pan Alley
> *Song Plugger*: R. Middleton. *Music Teacher*: E. Logan. *Customer*: W. Howard. *"My Old Kentucky Home"*: M. Burnett. *"Old Man River"*: C. Mathues. The Girls and Entire Company.

ACT 2

Scene 1

"Good Night, My Beautiful"
> H. Stockwell, M. Burnett
> *Danced by* Girls, Knight Sisters.

Scene 2

Get It Wholesale
> *Sam Zucker*: E. Howard. *Willie Winn*: W. Howard.

Scene 3

Ann Miller[5] (Tap Specialty)

Scene 4

Madame DuBarry
> *Madame DuBarry*: C. Lyons. *Maid*: B. Allen. *Robert Taylor*: M. Howard. *Tyrone Power*: L. Fine. *Walt Disney*: C. Howard.

Scene 5

"In Waikiki"
> E. Logan
> *Danced by* C. Forsythe, Girls.

Scene 6

Harvest Moon Winners
> *Jitterbugs*: B. Allen, L. Andrew. *Minuet*: B. Blue, C. Lyons, H. Whalen.

Scene 7

There Must Be a Union
> *Mrs. Murphy*: B. Allen. *Mr. Murphy*: W. Howard. *John L. Lewis*: E. Howard. *Policeman*: F. B. Manatt.

Scene 8

Billy Rayes

Scene 9

"Good Night, My Beautiful"
> As Gypsy Rose Lee would present it.

Scene 10

The Three Stooges[6]
> M. Howard, C. Howard, L. Fine

Scene 11

"The Song's For Free"
> E. Logan, Entire Company

1939.26

THE STRAW HAT REVUE

A Musical Revue in Two Acts, 24 Scenes. Conceived and staged by Max Liebman. Music and lyrics by Sylvia Fine and James Shelton, (Glenn Bacon.) Sketches mostly by Max Liebman, (Samuel Locke). Settings by Edward Gilbert. Choreography by Jerome Andrews. Orchestra directed by

---

[5]When Ann Miller left the show, her specialty was replaced by:
> "Something I Dreamed Last Night"
>> E. Logan
>> (*Lyrics by* Jack Yellen and Herb Magidson.)

[6]When the Three Stooges left the show, their specialty in Act 2 was replaced by:
> Quartette from "Rigoletto" (sketch)
>> W. Howard, E. Howard, Edna Page, Alice Charlton

Edward A. Hunt. Produced by The Straw Hat Company (Harry Kaufman, the Messrs. Shubert). Opened 29 September 1939 at the Ambassador Theatre and closed 2 December 1939 after 75 performances.

CAST: IMOGENE COCA, DANNY KAYE, JAMES SHELTON, ALFRED DRAKE, LEE BRODY, ROBERT BURTON, RUTHANNA BORIS, DOROTHY BIRD, LEON BARTE, META MATA and OTTO HARI, ALBIA KAVAN, JEROME ANDREWS, Lilli Sandan, Herbert Shepard, Gertrude Goldsmith, Jerome Robbins, Dolores Granafei, Pancho Scordi, Nana Matisse, Vera Volkenau, William Bales, Maude Davis, Richard Reed, Nan Rae, Bronson Dudley, Marjorie Moffet, Henriette Henning.

ACT 1

Scene 1

"Crashing Thru"
> Entire Company
> (*Music and Lyrics by* Sylvia Fine.)

Scene 2

Danger, Author at Work (*by* Max Liebman)
> *Playwright*: A. Drake. *He*: D. Kaye. *She*: I. Coca.

Scene 3

Dance of the Fakir
> M. Mata, O. Hari

Scene 4

Child Star (*by* Sylvia Fine)
> *Dolly Dimple*: I. Coca. *Script Man*: R. Burton. *Director*: A. Drake. *Cameraman*: H. Shepard.

Scene 5

"Four Young People"
> A. Drake, D. Bird, J. Andrews, A. Kavan
> (*Music and Lyrics by* James Shelton.)

Scene 6

"Trampling on Life"
> R. Burton, I. Coca, J. Shelton
> (*by* Max Liebman and James Shelton. *Special Music by* Glenn Bacon.)

Scene 7

"Anatole of Paris"
> D. Kaye, Models
> (*Music and Lyrics by* Sylvia Fine.)

Scene 8

Scarecrow
> L. Sandan

Scene 9

Wolf of Wall Street (*by* Samuel Locke)
> *Minister*: J. Shelton. *Bride*: G. Goldsmith. *Father*: R. Burton. *Jo Jo*: D. Kaye. *Right-hand Man*: A. Drake. *Left-hand Man*: H. Shepard. *Bridesmaids*: H. Henning, N. Matisse. *Secretary*: V. Volkenau.

Scene 10

Piano and Lute (*Special Music by* Glenn Bacon.)
> *Ballet Dancers*: R. Boris, A. Kavan, V. Volkenau, H. Henning, L. Barte, R. Reed. *Modern Dancers*: D. Bird, W. Bales, J. Robbins.

Scene 11

"The Swingaroo Trio"
> I. Coca, R. Burton, D. Kaye
> (*Music and Lyrics by* Sylvia Fine.)

Scene 12

The Acrobats
> M. Mata, O. Hari

Scene 13

"The Great Chandelier"
> (*Book by* Max Liebman. *Music and Lyrics by* Sylvia Fine.)
> *Vanderveer*: R. Burton. *Secretary*: H. Shepard. *Bruce Benson*: J. Shelton. *Mario*: D. Kaye. *Mary Sue Ann*: I. Coca. *Trixie*: L. Brady. Boys, Girls.

ACT 2

Scene 1

The Water Sprite
> *The Sprite*: I. Coca. *The Poet*: L. Barte. *Sea Nymphs*: A. Kavan, V. Volkenau, H. Henning, R. Boris.

Scene 2

Three Little Hicks
> D. Kaye, J. Shelton, R. Burton

Scene 3

Crazy Cactus
> R. Boris, B. Dudley

Scene 4

Two Cups of Coffee (*by* Max Liebman)
Pinker: R. Burton. *Lapidus*: H. Shepard. *Waiter*: D. Kaye.

Scene 5

"Our Town"[7]
(*Dialogue, Music and Lyrics by* James Shelton.)
Singer and Commentator: J. Shelton. *Elinor Kimball*: A. Kavan. *Bank Clerk*: R. Reed. *Miss Wheeler*: G. Goldsmith. *Fowler Kids*: R. Boris, J. Robbins. *Ann Thompson*: H. Henning. *Judge Reed*: R. Burton. *Tom Stafford*: P. Scordi. *Mary Turner*: D. Granafei. *My Girl*: D. Bird.

Scene 6

The Debutante
M. Moffett

Scene 7

An Evening at Carnegie Hall
Music-lovers: L. Brody, A. Drake. *Nicolai*: D. Kaye.

Scene 8

Table for Two (*by* Max Liebman)
He: R. Burton. *She*: I. Coca. *Waiter*: H. Shepard.

Scene 9

The Roving Reporter
The Reporter: N. Rae. *Mrs. Stanislous Waterfall*: M. Davis.

Scene 10

"Soused American Way"
A. Drake
(*Music and Lyrics by* Sylvia Fine.)
Three Hicks: R. Burton, D. Kaye, J. Shelton. *Saramba*: I. Coca. *Dancers*: P. Scordi, D. Granafei, Entire Company.

Scene 11

Finale
Entire Company

1939.27 TOO MANY GIRLS

A Musical Comedy in Two Acts, 10 Scenes. Book by George Marion, Jr. Music by Richard Rodgers. Lyrics by Lorenz Hart. Staged by George Abbott. Dances by Robert Alton. Settings by Jo Mielziner. Costumes by Raoul Pene du Bois. Orchestra conducted by Harry Levant. Orchestrations by Hans Spialek. Vocal arrangements by Hugh Martin. Produced by George Abbott. Opened 18 October 1939 at the Imperial Theatre, moved 22 April 1940 to the Broadway Theatre, and closed 18 May 1940 after 249 performances.

<u>CAST</u> (in order of appearance): *Mrs. Tewksbury*: IVY SCOTT. *Manuelito*: DESI ARNAZ. *Clint Kelley*: RICHARD KOLLMAR. *First Co-Ed*: Mildred Law. *Second Co-Ed*: Leonor Sola. *Third Co-Ed*: La Verne Lupton. *Fourth Co-Ed*: Diane Sinclair. *Fifth Co-Ed*: Key Taylor. *Sixth Co-Ed*: Vera Fern. *Jojo Jordan*: EDDIE BRACKEN. *Al Terwilliger*: HAL LEROY. *Harvey Casey*: CLYDE FILLMORE. *Mr. Lister*: HANS ROBERT. *Consuelo Casey*: MARCY WESTCOTT. *Sheriff Andaluz*: BYRON SHORES. *Eileen Eilers*: MARY JANE WALSH. *Tallulah Lou*: LEILA ERNST. *Sue*: Mildred Law. *Student*: Van Johnson. *Co-Ed*: Libby Bennett. *Pepe*: DIOSA COSTEL-LO. *Beverly Waverly*: JAMES MacCOLL. *Deputy Sheriff*: Willis Duncan. *Cowboy*: Edison Rice. *Hawker*: Harry Jackson.

Co-Eds: Marjorie Baglin, Libby Bennett, Betty Boyce, Sondra Barrett, Florine Callahan, Renee Cettel, Marge Ellis, Betty De Elmo, Louise De Forrest, Lita Lede, Jeanette Lavis, Amarilla Morris, Charlene Harkins, Mildred Patterson, Dorothy Poplar, Mildred Solly, Olga Suarez, Anna-Mae Tesslo, Davenie Watson, Claire Wolf. *Dancers*: Alice Craig, Vera Fern, Mildred Law, LaVerne Lupton, Leonor Sola, Diane Sinclair, Key Taylor. *Student Quartet*: *First Robin Hood*: Robert Arnold. *Second Robin Hood*: James Wilkinson. *Third Robin Hood*: Ramolo Di Spirito. *Fourth Robin Hood*: William Mende. *Students*: John Beton, Bob Howard, Randolph Hughes, Vernon Hammer, Herb Lurie, Clarence Jaeger, Van Johnson, Harold Young, Russ Milton, Jack Riley, Harry Pedersen, Bob Shaw.

Act 1, Scene 1: The Road to the Hunted Stag. *Scene 2*: The Hunted Stag, an Old Colonial Tavern near Skohegan, Maine. Late summer. *Scene 3*: Gate in Front of Pottawatomie College, Stop Gap, New Mexico, before term begins. *Scene 4*: Campus of Pottawatomie College, evening. *Scene 5*: Campus of Pottawatomie College, a few days later.

Act 2, Scene 1: A Road Near the College. *Scene 2*: The Belfry of Pottawatomie College. *Scene 3*: A Rock in the Desert. *Scene 4*: The Campus, evening. *Scene 5*: The Campus, next day.

ACT 1

Scene 1

"Heroes in the Fall"
J. Wilkinson, Squad

---

[7]A burlesque of the play of the same name by Thornton Wilder.

Scene 2

"Tempt Me Not"
D. Arnaz, R. Kollmar, M. Law, L. Sola, L. Lupton, D. Sinclair, K. Taylor, V. Fern
Danced by H. LeRoy, M. Law, All.

"My Prince"
M. Westcott

"Pottawattomie"
C. Fillmore, H. Robert

Scene 3

"Pottawattamie" (reprise)
Male Quartette, Ensemble

"'Cause We Got Cake"
M. J. Walsh
Danced by Specialty Girls, Co-Eds, Students.

Scene 4

"Love Never Went to College"
M. Westcott, R. Kollmar

"Spic and Spanish"
D. Costello
Danced by Specialty Girls, Ensemble.

"I Like to Recognize the Tune"
E. Bracken, M. Westcott, M. J. Walsh, R. Kollmar, H. LeRoy

Scene 5

"Look Out"
M. J. Walsh, Company
Danced by D. Costello, D. Arnaz, Company.

ACT 2

Scene 1

"The Sweethearts of the the Team"
M. J. Walsh, Co-Eds

Scene 2

"She Could Shake the Maracas"
D. Costello, D. Arnaz

Scene 3

"I Didn't Know What Time It Was"
M. Westcott, R. Kollmar

Scene 4

"Spic and Spanish" (reprise)
D. Costello, M. Westcott, M. J. Walsh, H. LeRoy, R. Kollmar, E. Bracken, D. Arnaz, L. Ernst
Danced by Dancing Girls, Boys.

"Too Many Girls"
D. Arnaz
Danced by Specialty Girls, Co-Eds.

Scene 5

"Give It Back to the Indians"
M. J. Walsh
Danced by H. LeRoy, Students.

1939.28 VERY WARM FOR MAY

A Musical Comedy in Two Acts, 7 Scenes. Book and lyrics by Oscar Hammerstein II. Music by Jerome Kern. Staged by Vincente Minnelli. Dances staged by Albertina Rasch and Harry Loose. Book directed by Oscar Hammerstein II. Settings and costumes by Vincente Minnelli. Orchestrations by (Robert) Russell Bennett. Musical director, Robert Emmett Dolan. Produced by Max Gordon. Opened 17 November 1939 at the Alvin Theatre and closed 6 January 1940 after 59 performances.

<u>CAST</u> (in order of appearance): *William Graham*: DONALD BRIAN. *Jackson*: Avon Long. *May Graham*: GRACE McDONALD. *Johnny Graham*: JACK WHITING. *Kenny*: RAY MAYER. *Raymond Sibley*: Robert Shackleton. *Sonny Spofford*: RICHARD QUINE. *Liz Spofford*: FRANCES MERCER. *Lowell Pennyfeather*: Max Showalter. *Ogden Quiler*: HIRAM SHERMAN. *Jethro Hancock*: William Torpey. *Winnie Spofford*: EVE ARDEN. *Beamish*: Len Mence. *Schlessinger*: Seldon Bennett. *Electrician*: Bruce Evans.

Members of the Ogdon Quiler Progressive Workshop: *Susan*: Vera Ellen. *Smoothy*: DON LOPER. *Honey*: MAXINE BARRAT. *Mr. Pratt*: Frank Egan. *Jane*: EVELYN THAWL. *Sylvia*: Kate Friedlich. *Mr. Magee*: Peter Chambers. *Miss Wasserman*: Virginia Card. *Miss Hyde*: Kay Picture. *Walter*: Walter Long. *Carroll*: HOLLACE SHAW. *Charles*: Ralph Stuart. *Pam*: Pamela Randell. *Alice*: Mary Louise Quevli. *Helen*: Helena Bliss. *Dolores*: Dolores Anderson. *Beulah*: Beulah Blake. *Andre*: Andre

Charise. *Louis*: Louis Hightower. *Sally*: Sally Craven. *Jack*: Jack Seymour. *Webb*: Webb Tilton. *Peter*: Jack Wilson. *Bill*: William Collins. *Eleanor*: Eleanor Eberle. *Helen*: Helen Donovan. *Rudy*: Rudy Miller. *Ethel*: Ethel Lynn. *June*: June Allyson. *Claire*: Claire Harvey. *Billie*: Billie Wirth [Worth]. *Miriam*: Miriam Franklyn.

Alvin's Orchestra: MATTY MALNECK'S ORCHESTRA. *Alvin*, Violin: Matty Malneck. *O'Cedar*, Accordion: Milton Delugg. *Homer*, Trumpet: Charles Marlowe. *Marshall*, Guitar: Marshall Fisher. *Ralph*, Drums: Ralph Hansell. *Joseph*, Harp: Joseph Quintelle. *Jean*, Piano: Jean Plummer. *Russ*, Bass: Russ Morhoff.

Act 1, Scene 1: The Graham home, Great Neck, Long Island. An afternoon in May. *Scene 2*: Winnie's Barn. That night.

Act 2, Scene 1: Terrace, Winnie's House. A month later. *Scene 2*: A corner of Winnie's barn theatre. *Scene 3*: Stage of Winnie's barn theatre—dress rehearsal. *Scene 4*: Corner of Winnie's barn theatre. *Scene 5*: Stage of Winnie's barn theatre—during the performance.

ACT 1
Scene 1
"In Other Words, Seventeen" (Duettino)
   G. MacDonald, D. Brian
Stop Dance, Finaletto
   A. Long
Scene 2
Characterization
   H. Sherman
Babbling Brook Dance
   K. Picture.
"All the Things You Are"
   H. Sherman, F. Mercer, H. Shaw, R. Stuart
Winnie's Audition (William Tell Overture by Gioacchino Rossini)
   E. Arden
     Accordionist, M. Delugg.
(Harlem Boogie Woogie)
   (Dancing Boys and Girls)
May Tells All
   G. MacDonald
"Heaven in My Arms"
   J. Whiting, F. Mercer, H. Shaw
   Danced by E. Thawl, S. Craven, K. Friedlich.
Finaletto, "In Other Words, Seventeen" (reprise)
   E. Arden

ACT 2
Scene 1
"That Lucky Fellow"
   R. Shackleton
Gavotte; "L'histoire de Madame de la Tour"
   H. Shaw, V. Card, E. Thawl, A. Charise
"That Lucky Lady"
   G. McDonald
The Strange Case of Adam Standish
   H. Sherman
"In the Heart of the Dark"
   H. Shaw
Ballet Peculiaire
   W. Long, M. Barrat
Scene 2
Audition ("Swing Low, Sweet Chariot" and "All the Things You Are")
   Matty Malneck's Orchestra
Dance
   G. McDonald
"In the Heart of the Dark" (reprise)
   F. Mercer
Scene 3
"The Deer and the Park Avenue Lady"
   Danced by A. Charise, K. Picture
"All in Fun"
   F. Mercer, J. Whiting
Schottische Scena
   J. Whiting, G. McDonald
Scene 4
"All the Things You Are" (reprise)
   R. Mayer

Scene 5
  Dance Da Da
  Lady in Red
    K. Friedlich
  The Blackbird and the Lady in White
    D. Loper, M. Barrat
  "All in Fun" (reprise)
    F. Mercer, J. Whiting
  Interlude (Liebestraum)
    G. McDonald, R. Quine
  Finale
    Company

1939.29   **SWINGIN' THE DREAM**

A Musical (Comedy) Variation in Two Acts, 3 Scenes. Book by Gilbert Seldes and Erik Charell, adapted from "A Midsummer Night's Dream" by William Shakespeare. Music by Jimmy Van Heusen. Lyrics by Eddie de Lange. Staged by Erik Charell. Dialogue directed by Philip Loeb. Dances by Agnes de Mille. Jitterbugs by Herbert White. Swing choir by Lyn Murray. Scenery after Walt Disney's cartoons designed by Herbert Andrews and Walter Jageman. Costumes by Herbert Andrews. Music supervised by Benny Goodman and Don Voorhees. Vocal arrangements by Lynn Murray. Orchestrations by Phil Wall, Herb Guigley, Ardon Cornwell, Fletcher Henderson. Musical director, Don Voorhees. Produced by Erik Charell in association with Jean Rodney. Opened 29 November 1939 at the Center Theatre and closed 9 December 1939 after 13 performances.

CAST (in order of appearance): *Majordomo*: HERMAN GREEN. *Theodore*, Governor of Louisiana: JOSEPH HOLLAND. *Polly*, his fiancee: RUTH FORD. *Crimson*, her friend: CATHERYN LAUGHLIN. *Egbert*, cousin of Theodore: GEORGE LeSOIR. *Gloria*, Egbert's daughter: ELEANOR LYNN. *Cornelius*, First Secretary to the Governor: THOMAS COLEY. *Alexander*, Second Secretary to the Governor: BOYD CRAWFORD. *Helena*, Gloria's cousin: DOROTHY McGUIRE. *Starveling*, the tailor: NICODEMUS. *Quince*, the Midwife: JACKIE MABLEY. *Snug*, the Cleaner: GERARD DE LA FONTAINE. *Snout*, the Steeple-jack: TROY BROWN. *Flute*, the Iceman: OSCAR POLK. *Bottom*, the Fireman: LOUIS ARMSTRONG. *Peaceful Pearl*, the Cook: ALBERTA PERKINS. *Puck*: BUTTERFLY McQUEEN. *First Pixie*: Vivian Dandridge. *Second Pixie*: Dorothy Dandridge. *Third Pixie*: Etta Dandridge. *Titania*, Queen of the Pixies: MAXINE SULLIVAN. *Drummer Boy*: Sunny Payne. *Oberon*. King of the Pixies: JUAN HERNANDEZ.

Players in the Opera 'Pyramus and Thisbe': Prologue (Quince): JACKIE MABLEY. *Pyramus (Bottom)*: LOUIS ARMSTRONG. *Thisbe (Flute)*: Oscar Polk. *Wall (Snout)*: Troy Brown. *Moon (Starveling)*: NICODEMUS. *Lion (Snug)*: Gerald de la Fontaine. *Cupid*: BILL BAILEY.

THE BENNY GOODMAN SEXTET: BENNY GOODMAN (Clarinet), Lionel Hampton (Vibraharp), Fletcher Henderson (Piano), Charles Christian (Guitar), Arthur Bernstein (Bass), Nick Fatool (Drums).

BUD FREEMAN & THE SUMMA CUM LAUDE: Bud Freeman (Saxophone), Max Kaminsky (Cornet), Peewee Russell (Clarinet), Eddie Condon (Guitar), Brad Gowan (Valve Trombone), Dave Bowman (Piano), Sidney Catlett (Drums).

Specialties: BILL BAILEY (Dancer), THE DANDRIDGE SISTERS (Dorothy, Etta, Vivian), THE RHYTHMETTES (Alberta Perkins, Cora Parks, Anna Mae Fritz). THE DEEP RIVER BOYS (George Lawson, Harry Douglas, Vernon Gardner, Edward Ware).

Gardeners, Servants and People from the Governor's Plantation: Ensemble: *Singers*: Jean Daniels, Laura Duncan, Ethel Harper, Ersalyn Hayes, Irene Johnson, Gladys Madden, Josephine Ortego, Belle Powell, Muriel Rahn, Winnie Scott, Carol Wright, Jessie Zachary. Warren Coleman, Harry Douglas, Charles Ford, Vernon Gardner, John Garth III, George Lawson, Emmett Matthews, George W. Nixon, Kelsey Pharr, James Sparks, Edward Ware, Charles Willis. *Dancers*: Clemie Collinwood, Muriel Cook, Edith Hurd, Lawaune Kennard (Ingram), Cleo Law, Lora Pierre, Ruby Richards, Naomi Waller, Bernice Willis. Frank Bell, Al Bledger, Anthony Fleming, King Johnson, Martin Logan, Jr., Ray Saunders, Ollie Simmons, Lloyd Storey. *Jitterbugs*: Dottiemae Johnson and Frank Manning, Beatrice Elam and George Greeninge, Wilda Crawford and Wiliam Downes, Joyce Boyd and Joseph Daniels, Wilhelmina Moore and Billy Williams, Anne Johnson and Thomas Lee, Norma Miller and Thomas Washington, Lucille Middleton and Joe Riddick, Emily McCloud and Samuel Pierce, Frances Jones, and James Outlaw, Hilda Bess and Richard Bess, Joyce James and Leroy Jones, Arlyne Evans and Lonnie Jenkins. *Children*: Alice Coles, Elizabeth Dozier, Eadie Edwards, Hazel Ferguson, Celestine Fuller, Priscilla Richshard. Raymond Harrison, Clifford E. Johnson, Elwood Robinson, Herbert Sumpter, Sylvester Taylor, Randolph Willis.

Place: New Orleans, the Athens of the Southland.

Time: About 1890 at the birth of Swing.

Act 1: The Governor's Summer Residence, New Orleans, 1890.

Act 2, Scene 1: Voodoo Ward. *Scene 2*: Governor's Summer Residence.

ACT 1

"Spring Song"
Deep River Boys, Ensemble
(*Music by* Jimmy Van Heusen and Benny Goodman, based on Felix Mendelssohn.)
"Peace, Brother"
Deep River Boys, Ensemble
"There's Gotta Be a Weddin'"
L. Armstrong, O. Polk, T. Brown, J. Mabley, Nicodemus, G. de la Fontaine, the Rhythmettes, Stable Boys, Kitchen Maids
"Peace, Brother" Finale
L. Armstrong, O. Polk, Nicodemus, T. Brown, J. Mabley, G. de la Fontaine, Deep River Boys, Ensemble

ACT 2
Scene 1

"Swingin' a Dream"
Jitterbugs, Dandridge Sisters
"Moonland"
M. Sullivan, Deep River Boys, Ensemble
Comedy Dance
J. Hernandez, Male dancers
"Love's a Riddle"
M. Sullivan, Dandridge Sisters, Deep River Boys, Ensemble
(*Arranged by* Alec Wilder[8].)
Dream Dance
B. Bailey, Dancing Girls
"Darn That Dream"
M. Sullivan, L. Armstrong, B. Bailey, Dandridge Sisters, the Rhythmettes, Deep River Boys, Ensemble
"Jumpin' at the Woodside"
Jitterbugs
(*Music by* William "Count" Basie.)
"Swingin' a Dream" (reprise)
M. Sullivan, Deep River Boys, Ensemble
"Pick-a-Rib"
The Benny Goodman Sextette
(*Music by* Benny Goodman.)

Scene 2

"Wedding March"
J. Holland and his party, Deep River Boys, Ensemble
(*Music by* Felix Mendelssohn.)
The Opera "Pyramus and Thisbe"[9]
J. Mabley, L. Armstrong, O. Polk, T. Brown, Nicodemus, G. de la Fontaine, B. Bailey
"Jumpin' at the Woodside" (reprise)
(*Music by* William "Count" Basie.)
"Pick-a-Rib"
(*Music by* Benny Goodman.)
"St. Louis Blues"
(*Music and Lyrics by* W. C. Handy.)
"Ain't Misbehavin'" (from HOT CHOCOLATES, 1929)
(*Music by* Thomas "Fats" Waller and Harry Brooks. *Lyrics by* Andy Razaf.)
"I Can't Give You Anything But Love" (from BLACKBIRDS OF 1928)
(*Music by* Jimmy Hugh. *Lyrics by* Dorothy Fields.)
"Moonglow" (from BLACKBIRDS OF 1934, London)
(*Music and Lyrics by* Will Hudson, Eddie DeLange and Irving Mills.)
"Hold Tight-Hold Tight (Want Some Sea Food, Mama)"
(*Music and Lyrics by* Leonard Kent, Edward Robinson, Leonard Ware, Jerry Brandow, Willie Spotswood.)
"My Melancholy Baby"
(*Music by* Ernie Burnett. *Lyrics by* George A. Norton.)
"Christopher Columbus"
(*Music by* Leon Berry. *Lyrics by* Andy Razaf.)
"Way Down Yonder in New Orleans"
(*Music by* (Henry Creamer and Turner Layton, as arranged by) Count Basie.)
"The Dipsy Doodle"
(*Music and Lyrics by* Larry Clinton.)

"Ol' Man Mose"
(*Music and Lyrics by* Louis T. Armstrong and Zilner T. Randolph.)
"Jeepers Creepers" (from GOING PLACES, film)
(*Music by* Harry Warren. *Lyrics by* Johnny Mercer.)
"Oh, You Crazy Moon"
(*Music by* James Van Heusen. *Lyrics by* Johnny Burke.)
"The Flat Floot Floogie"
(*Music and Lyrics by* Slim Gaillard, Slam Stewart, Bud Green.)
"Down by the Old Mill Stream"
(*Music and Lyrics by* Tell Taylor.)
"Big John's Special"
(*Music by* Horace Henderson.)
"Rachel's Dream"
(*Music by* Benny Goodman.)
"Dinah" (from AFRICANA, 1927[10])
(*Music by* Harry Akst. *Lyrics by* Sam M. Lewis and Joe Young.)
"Flying Home"
(*Music by* Benny Goodman, Lionel Hampton.)
"Rose Room" (from ZIEGFELD MIDNIGHT FROLIC, 1918)
(*Music by* Art Hickman. *Lyrics by* Harry Williams.)
"Sugarfoot Stomp"
(*Music by* Joseph "King" Oliver. *Lyrics by* Walter Melrose.)
Finale
Principals, Ensemble

1939.30 ## DUBARRY WAS A LADY

A Musical Comedy in Two Acts, 10 Scenes. Book by Herbert Fields and Buddy G. DeSylva. Music and lyrics by Cole Porter. Book staged by Edward MacGregor. Dances by Robert Alton. Settings and costumes by Raoul Pene du Bois. Orchestra conducted by Gene Salzer. Orchestral arrangements by Hans Spialek. Additional arrangements by (Robert) Russell Bennett and Ted Royal. Choral arrangements by Hugh Martin. Produced by Buddy G. DeSylva. Opened 6 December 1939 at the 46th Street Theatre, moved 21 October 1940 to the Royale Theatre, and closed 12 December 1940 after 408 performances.

CAST (in order of their appearance): In New York City: *Jones*: Hugh Cameron. *Bill Kelly*: Walter Armin. *Harry Norton*: CHARLES WALTERS. *Alice Barton*: BETTY GRABLE. *Florian*: Harold Cromer. *Louis Blore*: BERT LAHR. *Vi Hennessey*: Jean Moorehead. *May Daly*: ETHEL MERMAN. *Alex Barton*: RONALD GRAHAM. *Ann Barton*: Kay Sutton. *Manuel Gomez*: Tito Renaldo. *Charley*: BENNY BAKER. *Four Internationals*: Douglas Hawkins, Peter Holliday, Robert Herring, Carl Nicholas. *Starlets of the Club Petite*: Ann Todd: Geraldine Spreckels. *Molly Wincor*: Betty Allen. *Sigana Sigan*: Ann Graham. *Ruth Frederic*: Janice Carter. *Peggy Brown*: Jacqueline Franc. *Mary Gray*: Marguerite Benton.

At Versailles: *Le Duc de Choiseul*: Hugh Cameron. *Mme. La Duchesse de Grammont*: Kay Sutton. *Mme. La Comtesse DuBarry*: ETHEL MERMAN. *Mme. La Marquise Alisande de Vernay*: BETTY GRABLE. *Captain of King's Guard*: CHARLES WALTERS. *Zamore*: Harold Cromer. *His Most Royal Majesty, the King of France, Louis XV*: BERT LAHR. *His Royal Highness, the Dauphin of France*: BENNY BAKER. *Mme. La Duchesse de Villardell*: Jean Moorehead. *Cosette*: Audrey Palmer. *Rene*: Jack Stanton. *Pierre*: Roy Ross. *Gateman*: Carl Nicholas. *Docteur Michel*: Walter Armin. *Henri*: Johnny Barnes. *Dames de la Coeur*: Mme. La Duchesse du Coeur Flottant: Geraldine Spreckels. *Mme. La Marquise du Pont l'Eveque*: Betty Allen. *Mme. La Comtesse de Camembert*: Ann Graham. *La Princesse Gruyere*: Janis Carter. *La Baronne de Brie*: Jaqueline Franc. *Mme. La Vicomtesse de Rocquefort*: Marguerite Benton.

Dancing Girls: Stella Clauson, Nina Wayler, Marion Harvey, Tilda Getze, Nancy Knott, Jane Sprowl, Helen Bennett, Edyth Turgell, Barbara Pond, Evelyn Bonefine, Ruth Bond, Patricia Knight, Adele Jergens[11], Francis Krell, Gloria Martin, Beverly Hosier, Gloria Arden, Marie Vannemen, Virginia Cheneval. *Dancing Boys*: Gene Ashley, Boris Butleroff, Joel Friend, Russell Georgiev, Stanley Grill, Mel Kacher, Don Liberto, Tito Renaldo, Lewis Turner, Paul Thorne.

Act 1, Scene 1: The Club Petite, New York. *Scene 2*: Washroom at the Club Petite. *Scene 3*: The Gardens of the Petite Trianon. (Versailles.) *Scene 4*: DuBarry's Bed Chamber. *Scene 5*: The Outer Hall—Night. *Scene 6*: A Salon at the Petite Trianon.

Act 2, Scene 1: A Pavilion in the Gardens of the Petite Trianon. *Scene 2*: The Outer Hall. *Scene 3*: A Room in the Royal Apartment. *Scene 4*: The Club Petite, New York.

---

[8]Other sources credit Alec Wilder and Jimmy Van Heusen as co-composers
[9]The opera was comprised of interpolated jazz standards not by Messrs. Van Heusen and DeLange. List is not in performance order.

[10]Introduced by Ethel Waters in the Plantation Revue in 1925, which she repeated for AFRICANA in 1927 and BLACKBIRDS OF 1930, on Broadway.
[11]Later well-known as a film actress.

ACT 1

    Opening (Where's Louie?)
        Ensemble

    "Ev'ry Day's a Holiday"
        C. Walters, B. Grable, Ensemble

    "It Ain't Etiquette"
        B. Lahr, J. Moorehead

    "When Love Beckoned"
        E. Merman

    "Come On In"
        E. Merman, Ensemble

    Dance
        B. Grable, C. Walters

    "Dream Song"
        D. Hawkins, P. Holliday, R. Herring, C. Nicholas

    "Mesdames and Messieurs"
        Dames de la Coeur

    "Gavotte"
        B. Grable, Ensemble

    "But in the Morning, No!"
        E. Merman, B. Lahr

    "Do I Love You"
        R. Graham, E. Merman

    (reprise)
        E. Merman, H. Cromer

    Danse Victoire
        J. Barnes

    Danse Erotique
        A. Palmer, Courtiers

    "DuBarry Was a Lady"
        Entire Company

ACT 2

    Danse Tzigane
        B. Grable, R. Ross, J. Stanton, Ballet

    "Give Him the Oo-La-La"
        E. Merman

    "Well, Did You Evah!"
        B. Grable, C. Walters

    Danse
        A. Palmer, J. Stanton, R. Ross

    "It Was Written in the Stars"
        R. Graham, Ensemble

    "L'Après Midi d'un Boeuf"
        B. Baker, H. Cromer

    "Katie Went to Haiti"
        E. Merman, Ensemble

    (reprise)
        R. Graham, E. Merman

    "Friendship"
        E. Merman, B. Lahr

    Finale
        Company

1939.31   # FOLIES BERGÈRE

A French Vaudeville Revue in One Act, 15 Scenes. Dances directed by George Moro. Costumes by Irene Karinsky, from the sketches of Freddy Wittop and Erté. Settings by Raymond Deshays, Bertin, Lavignac & Pellegry and Grosbois & Lambert. Musical director, Vincent Travers. Produced by Clifford C. Fischer. Opened 25 December 1939 at the Broadway Theatre and closed 11 February 1940 after 121 performances.

CAST: Joyce Claxton, Gil Lamb, Michele Magnin, Malcia, Florence Spencer, Iris Wayne, Betty Brite, Karin Zoska, Lucienne and Ashour, Andree Lorrain, The Robenis, The Menciassis, Fred Sanborn, Harald and Lola, Andre, Roberton, Malo, Leopold, Les Shyrettos, Juliette, Lorrain, Barsley, Wayne, Lime Trio, Little Fred and His Football Dogs, Lalage, Nita Carol, Tino Crisa, Steve Geray, Charles Laurence, Porges, Reid, Devorne, Olga, Usedom, Arys, Crocher, Fahy, Evan, Gilbe, Savory, Wester, Leroi, Dare, Grait, Margot, Normande, Jacques, Gorovenko, Betty, Reid, De St. Gilles, Porte, Lucy, Marie, Demar, Julie, Runk, Eve, Kisselef, Yvonne, Brown, Landerson, Fabian, Lavigne, Serves, Anita.

Can-Can Dancers: Natalie Reau, Helene Schley, Manya Wyshinska, Paula Vandervelde, Madeleine Caule, Violette Christian, Charlotte Cairns, Cissie Nolande, Muriel Brunzelle, Dolores Samson, Francoise Schley, Lillian Chemin, Virginie Pirson, Elyse Pirson.

Scene 1

    Prologue-Illusion de Paris
        Masters of Ceremony: Andre, Roberton. *Illusion of Dancing*: Porges, Reid, Malo. *Hand Illusion*: Devorne, Olga, Usedom. *Naughty Illusion*: Arys, Crocher, Evan, Gilbe, Savory, Wester. *Illusion of Youth*: Malcia, Leroi, Dare, Grait, Margot, Normande, Jacques, Gorovenko, Betty. *Specialty*: Karin Zoska. *The Jazz Leader*: Leopold. *The Cymbalums*: Dare, Reid, Grait, De St. Gilles, Brite, Normande, Spencer, Leroi, Wester, Porte, Arys, Margot. *The Tambourins*: Olga, Devorne, Wayne, Crocher, Fahy, Gorovenko, Betty, Jacques, Lucy, Marie, Demar, Julie. *The Flexatones*: Savory, Usedom, Runk, Porges, Evan. *The Ladies in Blue*: Eve, Kisselef, Yvonne, Brown, Landerson, Magnin. *England's Glamour Girl*: Joyce. *The Girl With the Balloons*: Fabian.

Scene 2

    Specialty
        Les Shyrettos

Scene 3

    For a Man
        The Furs: *The Astrakan*: Porges. *The Monkey*: Olga. *The Beaver*: Fabian. *The Seal*: Runk. *The Foxes*: Brown. *The Chichilla*: Landerson. *The Mink*: Joyce. *The Ermine*: Eve. *The Little Fur*: Juliette. *The Dresses*: Crocher, Kisselef, Wester, Fahy, Devorne, Yvonne. *Mademoiselle Paris*: A. Lorrain. *The Gigolos*: Malo, Andre. *The Crazy Girls*: Barsley, Wayne. *The Maids*: Normande, Dare, Jacques, Gilbe, Gorovenko, Porte, Margot, Lavigne. *The Fighters*: Wayne, Barsley, Malo.

Scene 4

    Specialty
        Lime Trio

Scene 5

    The French Can-Can
        The Underskirts of 1890: Savory, Landerson, Eve, Olga, Runk, Brown, Joyce, Kisselef, Usedom, Devorne, Porges, Yvonne, Crocher, Magnin, Fabian, Evan, Gilbe, Demar, Wester, Margot, Gorovenko, Grait, Lavigne, Arys, Anita, Betty, Julie, Dare, Porte, Fahy, De St. Gilles, Jacques, Normande. *The Specialty Dancers*: B. Brite, I. Wayne, F. Spencer. The Folies Bergère Can-Can Dancers.

Scene 6

    Specialty
        Little Fred and His Football Dogs

Scene 7

    Le Charmeur de Serpents
        The Folies Bergère Can-Can Dancers

Scene 8

    Specialty (snake dance)
        Harald and Lola

Scene 9

    Apaches
        The Gigolettes: Leroi, Dare, Margot, Grait, Normande, Porte, Fahy, Gorovenko, Jacques, Gilbe, Reid, Lavigne, Demar, Julie. *The Apaches*: Savory, Usedom, Runk, Brite, Spencer, Yvonne, Porges, Wester, Kisselef, Serves, Anita. *The Loafers*: Roberton, Magnin, Malcia. *The Policemen*: Leopold, Andre. *The Couple*: Lucienne & Ashour.

Scene 10

    Specialty
        Lalage

Scene 11

    Algeria
        The Foreign Lady: N. Carol. *The Gigolo*: Leopold. *The Waiter*: Roberton. *The Cheik*: Malo. *The Favorites*: Fabian, Eve. *The Snake Charmer*: Andre. *The Slave Driver*: Ashour. *The Slave*: De St. Gilles. *The Carpet Sellers*: Betty, Arys, Gilbe, Anita. *The Orange Merchants*: Runk, Usedom, Savory, Brown. *The Lemon Merchants*: Landerson, Yvonne, Kisselef, Joyce. *The Dancer*: Fahy. *The White Dancers*: Dare, Leroi, Porte, Normande, Jacques, Gorovenko, Grait, Margot. *The Girls from the Casbah*: Crocher, Porges, Wester, Devorne. *The Jumpers*: The Robenis. *Two Women*: Evan, Reid. *Two Men*: Olga, Magnin. *An Old Arab*: T. Crisa. *The Bootblack*: Malcia. *The Camel*: The Menciassis. *The Little Camels*: Jacques, Dare, Porte, Grait, Gilbe, Gorovenko, De St. Gilles, Margot, Leroi, Betty, Normande, Demar.

Scene 12

    Specialty
        S. Geray

Scene 13

    Bird of the Night

        The Bird: T. Crisa. *The Girl*: Malcia. *The Wings*: Leroi, Dare, Grait, Gorovenko, Normande, Porte, Jacques, Fahy, Margot, Anita, Gilbe, Demar. *The Veils*: Crocher, Arys, Usedom, Savory, Reid, Evans, Yvonne, Magnin.

Scene 14

    Specialty

        Fred Sanborn and his famous Xylophone
        Assisted by C. Laurence.

Scene 15

    Finale—Nobility of France

        The Herald: Leroi. *The Lackeys*: Wester, Normande. *The Pages*: Arys, Demar. *The Countess*: Eve. *The Viscountess*: Olga. *The Baroness*: Kisselef. *The Marquise*: Fabian. *The Duchess*: Runk. *The Princess*: Brown. *The Kings and Queens of the Show*: Entire Company.

1940.01 — JOHN HENRY

A Music Drama in Two Acts, 11 Scenes. Book and lyrics by Roark Bradford. Music by Jacques Wolfe. (Staged by Anthony Brown and Charles Friedman.) Choral direction by Leonard dePaur [Depaur]. Music directed by Don Voorhees. Settings by Albert Johnson. Costumes by John Hambleton. Production under the musical supervision of Leonard dePaur. Orchestrations by Charles Cooke and Hans Spialek. Produced by Sam Byrd in association with Fred Mitchell. Opened 10 January 1940 at the 44th Street Theatre and closed 15 January 1940 after 7 performances.

CAST (in order of appearance): *Blind Lemon*: JOSHUA WHITE. *Julie Ann's Mamma*: Henrietta Lovelace. *Julie Anne's Papa*: George Jones, Jr. *Julie Ann*: RUBY ELZY. *Old Aunt Dinah*: MINTO CATO. *Hell Buster*: ROBERT HARVEY. *Man Named Sam*: JOE ATTLES. *Ruby*: MUSA WILLIAMS. *John Henry*: PAUL ROBESON. *Deaf Man*: James Lightfoot. *A Rouster*: Ray Yeates. *Floyd*: Lloyd Howlett. *Nud*: J. DeWITT SPENCER. *Mate*: Alexander Gray. *Walking Boss*: Kenneth Spencer. *Poor Selma*: MYRA JOHNSON. *Pimps Quartette*: Merritt Smith, Wyer Owens Handy, Louis Gilbert, William Woolfolk. *Fancy Ladies' Octette*: Eva Vaughan, Alyce Carter, Mattie Washington, Benveneta Washington, Alice White, Ruth Gibbs, Marie Fraser, Mildred Lassiter. *Bad Stacker Lee*: JOE ATTLES. *Billie Bob Russell*: ALEXANDER GRAY. *Carrie*: Benveneta Washington. *Lead Heaver*: Ray Yeates. *Reader*: Merritt Smith. *First Caller*: Louis Gilbert. *Second Caller*: William Woolfolk. *Mink Eye*: J. DeWITT SPENCER. *Roustabout*: C. W. Scott.

Workers, Their Wives, etc.: James Armstrong, Loena Avery, Ernest Baskette, Ella Belle Davis, Oscar Brooks, Maudina Brown, Jonathan Brice, Alyce Carter, George Dickson, John Diggs, Nora Evans, Marie Fraser, Samuel A. Floyd, Ruth Gibbs, Louis Gilbert, Samuel Gary, James B. Gordon, Edgar Hall, Claudia Hall, Kate Hall, Wyer Owens Handy, Lloyd Howlett, George Kennedy, Mildred Lassiter, James Lightfoot, Sadie McGill, Massie Patterson, Bayard Rustin, C. W. Scott, Ernest Shaw, Anne Simmons, Maude Simmons, Randall Steplight, Eva Vaughan, Charles Welch, Benveneta Washington, Mattie Washington, Alice White, Frederick Wilkerson, William Woolfolk, Ray Yeates.

Act 1, Scene 1: In front of Julie Ann's House in the Black River Country. *Scene 2*: On the road to the Black River Landing. *Scene 3*: The Black River Landing. *Scene 4*: Aunt Dinah's Cabin. *Scene 5*: The Corner of Third and Bird Streets, Argenta. *Scene 6*: The Canebrake. *Scene 7*: The Yeller Dog Railroad.

Act 2, Scene 1: The Yeller Dog Supper Camp. *Scene 2*: A Moving Steamboat on the Mississippi. *Scene 3*: Mink Eye's Saloon, back of town in New Orleans. *Scene 4*: The Black River Landing.

ACT 1

Scene 1

    "I'm Singing About a Man"
        J. White

    "How Come I'm Born Wid a Hook in My Hand"
        P. Robeson

Scene 2

    "All the People on the Levee"
        P. Robeson, Chorus

Scene 3

    "Ya Gotta Bend Down"
        J. White, Chorus

    "How Come I'm Born Wid a Hook in My Hand" (reprise)
        P. Robeson

    "Coonjine"
        Chorus

Scene 4

    "Jaybird"
        M. Cato, P. Robeson

    "Got a Head Like a Rock"
        P. Robeson

Scene 5

    "Whiffer's Song"
        J. White

    "Stingaree Song"
        M. Johnson

    "Bad, Bad Stacker Lee"
        J. Attles

    "Careless Love"[12]
        R. Elzy

Scene 6

    "I've Trampled All Over"
        R. Elzy, P. Robeson

Scene 7

    "Caught Ole Blue"
        J. White, Chorus

    "The Captain's Song"
        A. Gray

    "Old John Henry"/"Po' Lil' Frenchie"
        P. Robeson, Men

    "Workin' on de Railroad"
        P. Robeson, Men

    "High Ballin'"
        Chorus

ACT 2

Scene 1

    "Where Did You Get Dem High Heeled Shoes?"
        J. White

    "Let De Sun Sink Down"
        B. Washington, Chorus

Scene 2

    "Ship of Zion"
        Chorus

    "No Bottom"
        Chorus

    "Lullaby"
        R. Elzy

Scene 3

    "Take Me a Drink of Whiskey"
        J. Attles, M. Williams

    "Sundown in My Soul"
        P. Robeson

    "I'm Gonna Git Down on My Knees"
        R. Harvey, Chorus

    "I Want Jesus to Walk With Me"
        R. Harvey, Chorus

Scene 4

    "I'm Born in the Country"
        P. Robeson

    "Now You Talks Mighty Big in the Country"
        J. Attles, Chorus

    "So Stand Back, All You Bullies"
        P. Robeson

    "Ship of Zion" (reprise)
        Chorus

    "I Don't Care Where They Buried My Body"
        Chorus

    "He Went to the East"
        Chorus

1940.02 — EARL CARROLL'S VANITIES (1940)

A Musical Revue in Two Acts, 50 Scenes[13]. (Assembled by Earl Carroll.) Lyrics by Dorcas Cochran. Music by Charles Rosoff. (Additional lyrics by

---

[12] Traditional blues, often credited to W. C. Handy and Spencer Williams.

[13] The eleventh and last in the series of Vanities musical revues conceived and produced by Earl Carroll on Broadway, beginning in 1923. Subsequent editions were presented in Los Angeles in the 1940s.

Mitchell Parish; additional music by Peter DeRose, Nacio Herb Brown.) Directed by Earl Carroll. Dances by Eddie Prinz. Settings and costumes by Jean LeSeyeux. Orchestra directed by Lionel Newman. Produced by Earl Carroll. Opened 13 January 1940 at the St. James Theatre and closed 3 February 1940 after 25 performances.

CAST: NORMAN LAWRENCE, SUSAN MILLER, PUDDY SMITH, JERRY LESTER, Prof. (Michael) LAMBERTI, NIRSKA, GARY STONE, JOHNNY WOODS, BERYL WALLACE, YGOR and TANYA, Loe, Westerlund and Milheim (Clarence Loe, Babe Westerlund, Don Milheim), Herbert Adams, Cass-Owen, Topsy, Walter Norris, Muriel Barr, The Four Hot Shots, The Three Nonchalants, Dorothy Barrett, Marylyn Stewart, Lela Moore, Betty Stuart, Ann Adams, Janet Atwater, Dale Wells, Ann Lynne, Yolande Donlan, Lorraine Gresh.

THE MOST BEAUTIFUL GIRLS IN THE WORLD: Muriel Barr, Kathleen Barclay, Joy Barlow, Mary Lou Bennett, Harriet Bennett, Anne Callahan, Jeanne Carroll, Carolyn Crumley, Florence Cubitt, Mary Daniels, Madeline Elliott, Jeanne Francis, Katherine Grey, Rose Heitner, Bonnie Kildare, Roberta Lee, Patricia Lee, Dolores Loesch, Virginia Maples, Mildred Morris, Diana Mumby, Gwynne Norys, Lola Patten, Kay Pines, Bebe Porter, Rosemary Randall, Dorothe Small, Lanita Smith, Marna Stansell, Louise Wohl, Barbara Walters, Meriam Weller, Dale Wentworth, Lillian Girard, Susanne Jeanne.

ACT 1

Scene 1

The Earl Carroll Theatre, Hollywood
  C.B.S. Announcer: N. Lawrence. *N.B.C. Announcer*: G. Stone.

Scene 2

Beauty on Parade

Scene 3

"The Lady Has Oomph"
  The Oomph Girls
  B. Wallace, assisted by M. Barr, H. Bennett, V. Maples, J. Francis, R. Heitner, P. Lee, B. Walters, J. Carroll.

Scene 4

"Angel"
  S. Miller
  (*Music by* Peter De Rose. *Lyrics by* Mitchell Parish.)

Scene 5

Cascade of Plumes
  The Most Beautiful Girls in the World

Scene 6

Jerry Lester (comedy)

Scene 7

Union Eyes[14]
  The Wife: B. Wallace. *The Lover*: N. Lawrence. *The Husband*: J. Lester.

Scene 8

The Little Broadcast (radio sketch)
  J. Woods

Scene 9

"Charming"
  S. Miller, N. Lawrence

Scene 10

The Golden Garden (Dance)
  B. Wallace

Scene 11

Cigarettes in the Moonlight

Scene 12

Specialty (dance duo)
  Ygor and Tanya

Scene 13

Fun in One
  J. Lester, Topsy

Scene 14

The Corset Shop
  Salesman: J. Lester. *Secretary*: Topsy. *Customer*: D. Milheim. *First Model*: P. Lee. *Second Model*: V. Maples. *Third Model*: M. Barr. *Fourth Model*: J. Carroll. *Premiere Model*: B. Wallace. *Another Customer*: C. Loe. *Still Another Customer*: B. Westerlund. (Corsets created by Hollywood Maxwell.)

Scene 15

The Three Nonchalants (acrobatic trio with dialogue)

Scene 16

Announcement
  B. Wallace

Scene 17

"The Starlit Hour"
  G. Stone, S. Miller, N. Lawrence, J. Carroll, M. Stewart
  (*Music by* Peter De Rose. *Lyrics by* Mitchell Parish.)

Scene 18

Fantasy of Feathers
  Gold Bird: P. Lee. *Black Bird*: B. Porter. *Flamingo*: J. Francis. *Hitlerio*: M. Stansell. *Blue Bird*: B. Stewart. *Swan*: H. Bennett. *Ostrich*: M. Barr. *Fire Bird*: B. Walters. And the Crystal Ball Girls.

Scene 19

Harmony
  Three Lovely Ladies

Scene 20

The Dance of Light
  Nirska
  (Butterfly Dance originated by Nirska.)

Scene 21

Announcement
  Miss Hollywood: M. Daniels. *Miss Los Angeles*: M. Stewart.

Scene 22

Musician Extraordinaire (xylophone specialty)
  P. Lamberti
  Stanley Livingston: Loe, Westerlund and Milheim. *Blue Allure*: Illustrated by R. Heitner. *San Francisco Bay*: J. Woods.

Scene 23

"Westward Ho!"
  S. Miller
  Three Hitch Hikers: B. Wallace, M. Barr, V. Maples.

Scene 24

Along the Road
  The Roller Skaters: P. Owen, P. Smith. *Wholly Rollers*: Cass-Owen, Topsy. *The Cyclists*: J. Francis, C. Loe, B. Westerlund. *The Hicyclist*: P. Lamberti. *Bantam Auto*: J. Woods. *Grand Person*: J. Lester.

Scene 25

Camera, Lights, Action
  N. Lawrence, G. Stone

Scene 26

"American Bolero"
  (*Music by* Nacio Herb Brown.)
  Blue Tambourines: M. Daniels, M. Morris, G. Norys, B. Kildare, D. Loesch, D. Barrett, K. Barclay, M. Stewart, L. Moore. *Gold Tambourines*: R. Randall, M. Elliott, J. Barlow, H. Bennett, M. Stansell, J. Francis, B. Walters, P. Smith, B. Stuart. *Green Tambourines*: R. Lee, A. Adams, D. Mumby, M. Barr, J. Carroll, V. Maples, P. Lee, B. Porter, Ygor and Tanya. *Red Tambourines*: J. Atwater, D. Wells, A. Lynne, D. Barrett, Y. Donlan, L. Gresh, K. Pines, R. Heitner, B. Wallace.

Scene 27

Tapping the Tom Toms
  The Four Hot Shots

Scene 28

Grand Finale

ACT 2[15]

Scene 1

"Can the Can-Can"
  S. Miller

Scene 2

Can-Can Girls
  R. Heitner, V. Maples, M. Bar, J. Frances, H. Bennett, B. Walters, P. Lee, D. Barrett.

---

[14]Dropped during the run.

---

[15]Added during the run to Act 2, after The Fortune Teller:
  Wishing (previously Act 1, Scene 22)
    Prof. Lamberti
    Blue Allure: R. Heitner.

Scene 3

Gay Paree

Scene 4

Isle of Capri

J. Lester

Scene 5

The Interrupted Broadcast

J. Woods

Needle Salesman: D. Milheim. *Palmist*: P. Lamberti.

Scene 6

"I Want My Mama"

J. Woods, B. Wallace, the Patticake Girls, P. Lamberti

(*Music by* Jararaca Paiva, Vicente Paiva. *Lyrics by* Al Stillman. *Original Brazilian lyrics to* "Mama Yo Quiero" *by* the composers[16].)

(The audience is invited to play patticake with the Carroll Beauties.)

Scene 7

Hot Feet

The Four Hot Shots

Scene 8

Mandalay

J. Lester

First Chinaman: W. Norris. *Second Chinaman*: H. Adams.

Scene 9

Pretty Thing

Ted Lewis: J. Lester. *Beautiful Hawaii*: B. Wallace.

Scene 10

"Angel" (reprise)(Special arrangement by Grace Saxon.)

S. Miller

Scene 11

Beauty Empanelled

Parade of Loveliness: The Girls.

Scene 12.

Lovers' Lane

First Bench: B. Wallace, N. Lawrence. *Second Bench*: M. Barr, G. Stone.

Scene 13

Dance of the Lovers (*Created by* L. Moore.)

L. Moore

Scene 14

Announcement

M. Daniels, M. Stewart

Scene 15

The Fortune Teller

The Wife: S. Miller. *The Husband*: Prof. Lamberti. *The Seer*: J. Woods.

Scene 16

The Glamour Parlor

Scene 17

Specialty

Cass-Owen, Topsy, J. Lester

Scene 18

"Song of the Sarong"

S. Miller, G. Stone, 36 Tahitian Ladies

Scene 19

Moon of Pepiti

Scene 20

Flaming Maracas

A Vision in Radium

Scene 21

Messin' Around (*Written by* Archie Bleyer.)

Scene 22

Grand Finale

Entire Company

1940.03 TWO FOR THE SHOW

A Musical Revue in Two Acts, 20 Scenes. Sketches and lyrics by Nancy Hamilton. Music by Morgan Lewis. Entire production devised, staged and lighted by John Murray Anderson. Sketches directed by Joshua Logan. Dances by Robert Alton. Orchestra directed by Ray Kavanaugh. Settings by Raoul Pene du Bois. Orchestrations by Hans Spialek and Don Walker. Vocal arrangements by Harold Cooke. Produced by Gertrude Macy and Stanley Gilkey. Opened 8 February 1940 at the Booth Theatre and closed 25 May 1940 after 124 performances.

CAST: EVE ARDEN, RICHARD HAYDN, BRENDA FORBES, BETTY HUTTON, EUNICE HEALEY, NADINE GAE, KEENAN WYNN, Richard Smart, Frances Comstock, Alfred Drake, Tommy Wonder, Kathryn Kimber, Robert Smith, William Archibald, Austine McDonnell, Willard Gary, Dean Norton, Virginia Bolen.

ACT 1

Scene 1

The Show's the Thing

The Patient: K. Wynn. *The Nurse*: B. Forbes. *A Visitor*: E. Arden. *Other Visitors*: V. Bolen, F. Comstock, N. Gae, E. Healey, B. Hutton, K. Kimber, W. Archibald, A. Drake, W. Gary, R. Smith, T. Wonder. *The Doctor*: R. Smart. *The New Arrival*: R. Haydn.

Scene 2

The Guess-It Hour

Radio Announcer: R. Smith. *Assistant Announcer*: R. Smart. *Clifton Sharp*: A. Drake. *Bessie Bee Keesee*: F. Comstock. *Mrs. Lily Higgens*: B. Forbes. *George T. Barnswallow*: K. Wynn.

Scene 3

"Calypso Joe"

B. Hutton

Danced by N. Gae, W. Gary, E. Healey, T. Wonder. *Calypso Joe*: W. Archibald.

Scene 4

"This 'Merry' Christmas"

B. Forbes

Scene 5

The Age of Innocence (*by* Richard Haydn)

Aunt Lucy: F. Comstock. *Betty*: B. Hutton. *First Scout*: R. Smith. *Second Scout*: T. Wonder. *The Scout from Over-Seas*: R. Haydn.

Scene 6

"That Terrible Tune"

R. Smith, W. Gary, E. Healey, T. Wonder, R. Smart

Danced by N. Gae.

Scene 7

"Destry Has Ridden Again"

Director: K. Wynn. *Assistant Director*: W. Archibald. *Cameraman*: R. Smith. *Piano Player*: A. Drake. *Una*: K. Kimber. *Destry*: D. Norton. *A Maid*: V. Bolen. *Make-Up Expert*: R. Smart. *Marlene*: E. Arden.

Scene 8

"How High the Moon"

F. Comstock, A. Drake

Scene: A Blackout in London. *An Air Raid Warden*: D. Norton. *A "Lady" of the Town*: K. Kimber. *A Diplomat*: R. Smart. *A Young Girl*: V. Bolen. *An Aviator*: R. Smith. *The Costermongers*: E. Healey, T. Wonder. *"Danse Macabre"*: N. Gae, W. Archibald.

Scene 9

Painless Distraction

Dr. Fifer: K. Wynn. *Miss Smith*, his assistant: V. Bolen. *Mrs. Bullock*: E. Arden.

Scene 10

"A House With a Little Red Barn"

K. Kimber, R. Smart

Swung by B. Hutton, R. Smith. *Danced by* "Soft Shoe": N. Gae. "Hot Foot": T. Wonder.

Scene 11

Cookery[17] (*by* Richard Haydn)

Mr. Carp: R. Haydn. *Introduced by* K. Wynn.

Scene 12

"The All-Girl Band"

A. Drake, W. Archibald, W. Gary, D. Norton, R. Smart, R. Smith, T. Wonder, K. Wynn

The Owner of the Band: K. Wynn. *The Leader of the Band*: E. Arden. *Members of the International All-Girl Band*: *Miss Hungary*: F. Comstock. *Miss American Indian*: N. Gae. *Miss Norway*: K. Kimber. *Miss France*: V. Bolen. *Miss England*: B. Forbes. *Miss Ireland*: B. Hutton. *Miss Scotland*: E. Healey. *The Mayor*: R. Haydn.

---

[16]Previously used in THE STREETS OF PARIS.

[17]Similar or same sketch introduced in SET TO MUSIC as Fish Mimicry.

ACT 2
Scene 1

"Where Do You Get Your Greens?"
The Man in the Stocks: R. Haydn. *The Cries of London*: "*Sweet Lavender*" sung by F. Comstock. "*Cherry Ripe*" sung by K. Kimber. "*Strawberries*" sung by V. Bolen. *Tinker*: R. Smart. *Tailor*: W. Archibald. *Soldier*: R. Smith. *Sailor*: T. Wonder. *Rich Man*: A. Drake. *The King*: K. Wynn. *Mistress Nell*: E. Healey.

Scene 2

Little Miss Muffett
Little Miss Muffett: B. Hutton. *The Spider*: K. Wynn.

Scene 3

To a Skylark
Adele: N. Gae. *Mrs. Brewster*: B. Forbes. *Miss Torrence*: E. Arden. *Tony*: A. Drake.

Scene 4

"At Last It's Love"
K. Kimber, R. Smart
Scene: The Make-Believe Ballroom. *Dancers in the Make-Believe Ballroom*: V. Bolen, N. Gae, E. Healey, B. Hutton, W. Archibald, A. Drake, R. Smith, T. Wonder. *The Lady of the Favors*: F. Comstock. *The Late-Comer*: W. Gary. (The Jitter Dance by B. Hutton, T. Wonder. Waltz Variation by T. Wonder, partner.)

Scene 5

"Song of Spain"
The Infanta: B. Forbes. *Courtiers*: F. Comstock, R. Haydn.

Scene 6

"Fool for Luck"
K. Kimber, R. Smith, B. Hutton
Danced by N. Gae, W. Gary, E. Healey, T. Wonder.

Scene 7

Out of This World
Herbert: R. Haydn. *Miss Caruthers*: E. Arden. *Madame Charlotte*: B. Forbes.

Scene 8

"Goodnight, Mrs. Astor" (Finale)
Entire Company

1940.04

REUNION IN NEW YORK

A Musical Revue in Two Acts, 23 Scenes. Conceived by Lothar Metzl and Werner Michel. (Sketches by Carl Don, Richard Alma, Richard Holden and Hans Lefebre.) Music mostly by André Singer, Werner Michel. Lyrics by David Greggory, Berenece Kazounoff. (Additional music by Bert Silving and M. Cooper Paul; additional lyrics by Peter Barry and Stewart Arthur.) Staged by Herbert Berghof and Ezra Stone. Settings by Harry Horner. Costumes by Lester Polakov. Dances and choreography by Lotte Goslar. Speech training by Arthur Lessac. (Musical directors, Hans Herberth, George Heinz.) Production supervised by Ezra Stone and Marc Daniels. Produced by The American Viennese Group, Inc. Opened 21 February 1940 at the Little Theatre and closed 4 May 1940 after 89 performances.

CAST: HERBERT BERGHOF, KLAUS BRILL, NELLY FRANCK, LOTTE GOSLAR, NELL HYRT, CHARLOTTE KRAUSS, VILMA KURER, PAUL LINDENBERG, FRED LORENZ, WALTER MARTIN, KATHERINE MATTERN, ELISABETH NEUMANN, HENRY PEEVER, MARIA PICHLER, LOTHAR REWALT, BERT SILVING, EDGAR VINCENT, TRUDE WEIL, LEO WEITH.
Annie Desser, Anthony Scott, Maria Temple, Liesl Paul, Herman Walter, Peter Koch, Emery Gondor. *At the Pianos*: Hans Herberth, George Heinz. *Violin*: Bert Silving. *Accordion*: Stanley Forbes.

ACT 1
Scene 1

Hereinspaziert
Drop in for a bit at our Viennese wine-garden. *Musical Arrangement*: Bert Silving. *Host*: L. Weith. *Hostess*: L. Paul. *Waiter*: A. Scott. *Salami Man*: H. Walter. *Waitress*: A. Desser. *Hat-check Girl*: C. Krauss. *Violinist*: B. Silving. *Cartoonist*: E. Gondor. *Lady*: M. Temple. *Guide*: P. Koch.

Scene 2

"At the Rail"
(*Dialogue and lyrics by* Lothar Metzl and Werner Michel. *Music by* Werner Michel.)
The Viennese Group: K. Brill, N. Franck, N. Hyrt, V. Kurer, P. Lindenberg, F. Lorenz, K. Mattern, W. Martin, E. Neumann, M. Pichler, H. Peever, L. Rewalt, E. Vincent.

Scene 3

English in Six Easy Lessons (*by* Lothar Metzl and Werner Michel)
The Stranger: F. Lorenz. *Customs Officer*: H. Peever. *Hotel Secretary*: N. Franck. *Bell-boy*: K. Brill. *Detective*: L. Rewalt. *Passenger*: E. Vincent. *Girl in the Park*: M. Pichler. *Customer in Cafeteria*: P. Lindenberg. *Passerby*: W. Martin.

Scene 4

Woodsprite (satirical dance)
L. Goslar

Scene 5

Borderline (*by* Richard Alma, Lothar Metzl and Werner Michel)
Paul, a Farmer: P. Lindenberg. *Milina*, his wife: M. Pichler. *Officer of Pushia*: H. Peever. *Officer of Kushia*: L. Rewalt. *Carol*, Milna's brother: K. Brill.

Scene 6

"Stars in Your Eyes"[18]
C. Krauss
(*Music by* Fritz Kreisler. *Lyrics by* Dorothy Fields.)

Scene 7

"Keep Laughing"
K. Mattern, W. Martin
(*Music and Lyrics by* Lothar Metzl and Werner Michel.)

Scene 8

"Where Is My Homeland?"
V. Kurer, M. Pichler, N. Franck
(*German by* Lothar Metzl. *English by* Werner Michel and Auguste Spectorsky. *Music by* Nelly Franck.)

Scene 9

The Pillmaker
F. Lorenz

Scene 10

Waltz Mania (Satirical dance)
L. Goslar

Scene 11

"Oratorium Salzburgiensis"[19]
([Sketch and Lyrics] *by* Lothar Metzl and Werner Michel. *Music by* A. Singer.)
Narrator: E. Vincent. *Mayor of Salzburg*: H. Peever. *Cats*: N. Franck, E. Neumann. *The New Mayor*: P. Lindenberg. *Trio*: V. Kurer, K. Mattern, H. Peever. K. Brill, N. Hyrt, F. Lorenz, W. Martin, L. Rewalt, A. Scott, L. Weith.

ACT 2
Scene 1

"Blitz-Carmen"
(*by* Lothar Metzl and Werner Michel with Richard Holden and Hans Lefebre. *Musical Arrangement by* A. Singer.)
Don José, a New York Cop: E. Vincent. *A Couple*: F. Lorenz, C. Krauss. *Carmen*, a Cigarette Girl: K. Mattern. *Two-Ton Tony of New Jersey*: P. Lindenberg. *Two Magistrates*: W. Martin, L. Rewalt. *The District Attorney*: H. Peever.

Scene 2

Modern Art (*by* Carl Don)
Guides: V. Kurer, F. Lorenz.

Scene 3

"Dachau"
H. Berghof
(*German by* Jura Soyfer. *English by* Milton Hindus. *Music by* André Singer.)

Scene 4

"A Character in Search of a Character"
(*Lyrics by* David Greggory. *Music by* Berenece Kazounoff.)
The Writer: H. Peever. *The Character*: V. Kurer.

Scene 5

Chorus Girls
L. Goslar, N. Hyrt
(*Musical Arrangement courtesy of* Benny Goodman.)

Scene 6

"Shooting Gallery"
(*Lyrics by* Lothar Metzl and Werner Michel. *Music by* André Singer.)

[18]Replaced during run with:
"A Party With My Memories"
C. Krauss
(*Lyrics by* Lothar Metzl and Werner Michel. *Music by* Werner Michel.)
[19]The authors thank Mr. Edwin Kalser for the valuable suggestions he contributed to this number.

Cupid: N. Franck. *Franz*: E. Vincent. *Marie*. V. Kurer. *Baron Kalafati*: H. Peever. *Track Walker*: F. Lorenz.

Scene 7

"The Only Time of Day"

P. Lindenberg

(*Lyrics by* Richard Holden and Lothar Metzl. *Music by* André Singer.)

Scene 8

"I'm Going Crazy With Strauss"

V. Kurer

(*Lyrics and Music by* Peter Barry and Werner Michel.)

Scene 9

Vienna-Berlin Express (after an old Viennese folk tale)

Travelers: P. Lindenberg, F. Lorenz. *An Officer*: W. Martin.

Scene 10

Ain't Love Awful? (*by* David Greggory)

Lieutenant: L. Rewalt. *The Girls*: V. Kurer, K. Mattern, M. Pichler. *The Boys*: P. Lindenberg, F. Lorenz, E. Vincent. *General*: W. Martin.

Scene 11

The Spinster

L. Goslar

Scene 12

"A Party With Our Memories"

The Company

(*Dialogue and Lyrics by* Lothar Metzl and Werner Michel. *Music by* Werner Michel.)

1940.05 THEATRE OF THE PICCOLI

A Musical Revue (with Puppets) in Two Acts, 12 Scenes, from Italy[20]. Conceived by Vittorio Podrecca. Settings designed by Bruno Angoletta. Costumes designed by Caramba of Scala Theatre Department, Milan. Director of orchestra, Angelo Canarutto. Produced by Cheryl Crawford. Opened 21 March 1940 at the Majestic Theatre and closed 6 April 1940 after 30 performances.

CAST: VITTORIO PODRECCA, Augusto Galli (baritone), Agostino Guidi (tenor), Emma Lattuada (soprano), Lia Podrecca (coloratura soprano), Antonio Quaglia (tenor), Mario Serangeli (baritone), Alma Zatti (soprano), Irma Zappata (soprano), Dario Zani (baritone), Rosa Giovonelli.

ACT 1

Scene 1

Prologue

V. Podrecca

Scene 2

Piccoli Jazz Band

Scene 3

Tallerino and Canellone (Athletes)

Scene 4

Cinderella: Four Scenes from the Famous Fairy Tale by Perrault and Cahin.

Music by Jules Massenet. *Scenery designed by* Grassi and Lefay.

Cinderella: E. Lattuada. *Noemi*: A. Zatti. *The Fairy*: L. Podrecca. *Pandolfo*: D. Zana. *Madame Haltiere*: I. Zappata. *Dorothy*: R. Giovonelli. *The Prince Charming*: N. Quaglia. *The King*: M. Serangeli. Supported by Gnomes, Servants, Ladies and Gentlemen of the King's Court and Pages.

Scene a: Cinderella's Home. *Scene b*: The King's Palace. *Scene c*: The Enchanted Coach. *Scene d*: The Magic Tree.

Scene 5

Bil-Bal-Bul (The Little Acrobat)

Scene 6

Clowns with Heads and Without

Scene 7

Latin American Revue

a. Rancherita (Argentina Music by Buerrero and Lomuto)

b. Mexico (Estrellita, Music by Ponce; Jarabe Tapatio, Popular Dance)

---

[20]This company previously appeared on Broadway as THE MARI-ONETTE PLAYERS, 20 September 23 1923 at the Fulton Theatre, for 16 performances; as THE PICCOLI OF VITTORIO PODRECCA, 22 December 1932 at the Hudson Theatre, 141 performances, returning 8 January 1934 to the Lyrics Theatre for an additional 45 performances.

c. Cuban Nights (Amor de mi Bohio, Music by Brito; Rhumba (Congo Alegre) by Matamoros.

ACT 2

Scene 1

Waltztime (*Music by* Franz Schubert and Johann Strauss.)

a. Wine and Song

b. Interlude

c. The Voice of Spring

L. Podrecca

d. Finale

Scene 2

Men, Birds and Monkeys

Scene 3

Aria from "Pagliacci" by Ruggero Leoncavallo

A. Guidi

Scene 4

Hollywood Party

Scene 5

The Concert Party introducing again to New York the World Famous Piccoli Pianist:

(*Music by* Franz Liszt, etc. etc.)

Specialty Number—Miss Skinny Liz

L. Podrecca

1940.06 HIGHER AND HIGHER

A Musical Comedy in Two Acts, 8 Scenes. Book by Gladys Hurlbut and Joshua Logan, based on an idea by Irvin Pincus. Music by Richard Rodgers. Lyrics by Lorenz Hart. Staged by Joshua Logan. Dances by Robert Alton. Settings by Jo Mielziner. Costumes by Lucinda Ballard. Orchestra conducted by Al Goodman. Orchestrations by Hans Spialek. Produced by Dwight Deere Wiman. Opened 4 April 1940 at the Sam S. Shubert Theatre, closing 15 June 1940 after 84 performances; re-opened 5 August 1940 at the Sam S. Shubert Theatre, closing 24 August 1940 after 24 additional performances, for a total of 108 performances.

CAST (in order of appearance): *Hilda O'Brien*: Eva Condon. *Byng*: Robert Chisholm. *Dottie*: Billie Worth. *Miss Whiffen*: Hilda Spong. *Sandy Moore*: SHIRLEY ROSS. *Zachary Ash*: JACK HALEY. *Mike O'Brien*: LEE DIXON. *Minnie Sorenson*: MARTA EGGERT. *Scullery Maid*: Mary Louise Quevli. *Three Nursemaids*: Gloria Hope, Hollace Shaw, Jane Richardson. *Soda Jerker*: Robert Rounseville. *Ladies' Maid*: Marie Nash. *First Cop*: Robert Shanley. *Cops*: Joe Scandur, Richard Moore. *Footman*: Carl Trees. *Patrick O'Toole*: LEIF ERICKSON. *Ellen*: Janet Fox. *Truckmen*: Robert Rounseville, Joe Scandur. *Snorri*: Fin Olsen. *Sharkey*: Himself. *The Handyman*: Frederic Nay. *The Cat*: Ted Adair. *The Frog*: Lyda Sue. *The Bat*: Sigrid Dagnie. *Coachman*: Frederic Nay. *The Gorilla*: Joseph Granville. *Purity*: Jane Ball.

Singing Girls: Kay Duncan, Gloria Hope, Marie Nash, Marie Louise Quevli, Jane Richardson, Hollace Shaw. *Singing Boys*: William Geery, Joseph Granville, Richard Moore, Robert Rounseville, Joe Scandur, Robert Shanley. *Specialty Girls*: June Allyson, Irene Austin, Jane Ball, Ronnie Cunningham, Sigrid Dagnie, Eleanor Eberle, Vera Ellen, Miriam Franklin, Marguerite James, Kay Picture, Lyda Sue. *Specialty Boys*: Ted Adair, Cliff Ferre, Bunnie Hightower, Louis Hightower, Michael Moore, Frederic Nay, Burton Pierce, Harry Rogue, Jack Seymour, Billy Skipper, Jr., Carl Trees.

Act 1, Scene 1: Section of Ballroom, New York Hotel. *Scene 2*: The Kitchen, Drake Mansion, New York. *Scene 3*: Deborah Drake's Bedroom. *Scene 4*: The Kitchen, Drake Mansion.

Act 2, Scene 1: The Kitchen. *Scene 2*: Zacky's Room. *Scene 3*: The Old Carriage House. *Scene 4*: Section of Ballroom, New York Hotel.

ACT 1

Scene 2

"A Barking Baby Never Bites"

J. Haley, S. Ross

"From Another World"

M. Eggert, J. Haley, S. Ross, E. Condon, R. Chisholm, Company

Scene 3

"Mornings at Seven"

L. Dickson, B. Worth, Ensemble

"Nothing But You"

M. Eggert, L. Erickson, Singers

Scene 4

"Disgustingly Rich"

J. Haley, S. Ross, L. Dixon, E. Condon, R. Chisholm, H. Spong, B. Worth, Ensemble

ACT 2

Scene 1

"Blue Monday"
R. Chisholm, H. Shaw, M. L. Quevli, M. Nash, Ensemble

"Ev'ry Sunday Afternoon"
M. Eggert, L. Erickson

"Lovely Day for a Murder"
L. Dixon, B. Worth, Ensemble

Scene 2

"How's Your Health"
J. Haley, M. Eggert, L. Erickson

"It Never Entered My Mind"
S. Ross

Scene 3

"I'm Afraid"
J. Haley, S. Ross, Specialty Girls and Boys

"I'm Afraid" (development)
S. Ross, J. Fox, L. Dixon, R. Chisholm, E. Condon, R. Shanley, Company

Scene 4

Finale
Entire Company

1940.07 ## KEEP OFF THE GRASS

A Musical Revue in Two Acts, 30 Scenes. Sketches by Mort Lewis, Parke Levy, Alan Lipscott, S. Jay Kaufman, (Norman) Panama and (Melvin) Frank, (Reginald Beckwith). Music by James [Jimmy] McHugh. Lyrics by Al Dubin, (Howard Dietz). Choreography by George Balanchine. Book directed and production lighted by Edward Duryea Dowling. (Production under the supervision of Harry Alvin Kaufman.) Settings and costumes by Nat Karson. Orchestra conducted by John McManus. Orchestrations by Hans Spialek and Don Walker. Vocal arrangements by Anthony R. Morelli. Miss O'Brien's arrangements by Art Wilson. Stage directed by Fred deCordova. Produced by the Messrs. Shubert. Opened 23 May 1940 at the Broadhurst Theatre and closed 29 June 1940 after 44 performances.

CAST: JIMMY DURANTE, RAY BOLGER, JANE FROMAN, ILKA CHASE, BETTY BRUCE, NAN RAE, MAUDE DAVIS, LARRY ADLER, VIRGINIA O'BRIEN, JOHN McCAULEY, SUNNIE O'DEA, JACK GLEASON, THE DeTUSCANS (Joanna, Bela), José Limon, Daphne Vane, Robert Shackleton, Sid Walker, Peanuts Bohn, Hal Neiman, Emmet Kelly, Margery Moore, La Motte Dodson's Monkeys, The Toreadors, Henry Dick, Saint Subber, LaMott Dodson.

The Morelli Singers: Esta Elman, Virginia Burke, Martha Burnett, Imogen Carpenter, Lynn Lawrence, Jane Starner, Aileen Stone, Sylvia Stone, Frances Tannehill. *Dancing Young Ladies:* Billie Bernice, Mimi Berry, Gloria Clare, Harriet Clarke, Margie Dale, Helen Devlin, Gloria Gaffey, Peggy Gallimore, June Leroy, Ann Lass, Peggy Littlejohn, Mary Joan Martin, Lois Martin, Jane Gray Petri, Mimi Walthers. *Dancing Young Men:* Ray Arnett, John Coy, Fred Deming, Jerry [Jerome] Robbins, Jerry Shepherd, Bob Sidney, Lee Tannen, Don Weissmuller.

ACT 1[21]

Scene 1

"The Cabby's Serenade"
J. Gleason, B. Sidney, P. Bohn, H. Neiman, E. Kelly, S. Walker

Scene 2

"This Is Spring" (Spring)
J. Froman, the Morelli Singers
Danced by J. Limon, D. Vane, M. Moore, Dancing Ladies.

Scene 3

Virginia O'Brien ("Spring")

Scene 4

The Tree Doctor (*by* Mort Lewis)
Dr. Bush: J. McCauley. *Commissioner:* H. Neiman. *Dr. Kildare:* J. Durante. *Dr. Gillespie:* P. Bohn. *Dr. Cyclops:* S. Walker. *Dr. Watson:* R. Shackleton. *Dr. Christian:* J. Gleason.

Scene 5

"Crazy As a Loon"
R. Bolger, S. O'Dea
Harmonica accompaniment by Larry Adler.

Scene 6

Romantique (*by* Mort Lewis and Reginald Beckwith)
She: I. Chase. *He:* J. McCauley.

Scene 7

"A Fugitive from Esquire"
(*Lyrics by* Howard Dietz.)
The Fugitive: J. Durante. *The Valets:* H. Neiman, S. Wlaker, J. Gleason, P. Bohn.

Scene 8

"I'll Applaud (You) With My Feet"
B. Bruce, Dancing Ladies and Men

Scene 9

The Fountain (*by* Mort Lewis)
Thirsty Man: R. Bolger. *Thirsty Woman:* I. Chase. *The Cop:* J. Gleason. *Park Attendant:* H. Neiman. *Bootblack:* S. Subber. *Park Strollers:* R. Shackleton, P. Bohn, L. Lawrence, E. Elman, I. Carpenter, F. Tannehill, A. Stone, B. Sidney.

Scene 10

"Two in a Taxi"
(*Lyrics by* Howard Dietz)
The Girl: J. Froman. *The Boy:* R. Shackleton.

Scene 11

"The Old Park Bench"
J. Gleason, L. Adler, P. Bohn, H. Neiman, E. Kelly, S. Walker
(*Lyrics by* Howard Dietz.)

Scene 12

Misinformation, Please (*by* Parke Levy and Alan Lipscott)
Announcer: L. Dodson. *Clifton Fadiman:* J. Durante. *Dorothy Thompson:* Blondie. *F.P.A.:* Jiggs. *John Kieran:* Slats. *Oscar Levant:* Louie. *Joe DiMaggio:* Tony. *Ann Sheridan:* Patsy. *Gypsy Rose Lee:* Percy.

Scene 13

"A Latin Tune, a Manhattan Moon, and You"
R. Bolger, B. Bruce, Morelli Singers
Danced by R. Bolger, B. Bruce, J. Limon, D. Vane, M. Moore, The Toreadors, Dancing Ladies and Men.

Scene 14

Life With Mother[22] by Parke Levy and Alan Lipscott)
Hostess: F. Tannehill. *John:* J. Gleason. *Elliot:* R. Shackleton. *Franklin Jr.:* J. McCauley. *James:* S. Walker. *Franklyn Sr.:* J. Durante. *Eleanor:* I. Chase. *Porters:* J. Coy, S. Subber. *Western Union Boy:* P. Bohn. *Waitresses:* L. Lawrence, M. Walthers, A. Stone. *The Boss:* H. Neiman.

Scene 15

Larry Adler

Scene 16

"Rhett, Scarlett & Ashley"
J. Durante, R. Bolger, I. Chase

Scene 17

"Clear Out of This World"
J. Froman, R. Shackleton, Morelli Singers
Danced by J. Limon, D. Vane, M. Moore, Dancing Ladies and Men.

Scene 18

Virginia O'Brien ("Clear Out of This World")

ACT 2

Scene 1

"Look Out for My Heart"
J. Froman, R. Shackleton, Morelli Singers
Scene: Armour Wing at the Metropolitan Museum.
Fencing Specialty: The de Tuscans. *Danced by* B. Bruce, J. Limon, Dancing Ladies.

Scene 2

Museum Piece (*by* S. J. Kaufman and Mort Lewis)
Guide: J. Durante. *Art Lovers:* I. Chase, J. Gleason, P. Bohn, R. Shackleton, S. Walker, E. Kelly, H. Neiman, S. Subber.

Scene 3

"(I'm an) Old Jitterbug"
R. Bolger, S. O'Dea
Danced by R. Bolger, S. O'Dea, M. Moore, the Old Jitterbugs.

---

[21]Song order revised during the run.

---

[22]A burlesque of the play by Howard Lindsay and Russel Crouse. Dropped during the run.

Scene 4

Virginia O'Brien ("Old Jitterbug")

Scene 5

Birds

The Lecturer: N. Rae. *The Interloper*: M. Davis. *Bird Lovers*: E. Elman, L. Lawrence, F. Tannehill, A. Stone, I. Carpenter, M. Burnett.

Scene 6

"I'm in the Mood"[23]

J. Froman
Danced by B. Bruce, D. Vane, J. Limon, H. Dick.

Scene 7.

Shakespeare's-a-Poppin (*by* Mort Lewis)
Billings: J. McCauley. *White*: H. Neiman. *McSwindle*: J. Durante. *First Gravedigger*: P. Bohn. *Juliet*: I. Chase. *Tybalt*: J. Gleason. *Playgoer*: M. Davis.

Scene 8

"Raffles"

(*Music by* Vernon Duke.)
Danced by R. Bolger, B. Bruce, D. Vane, M. Moore, Dancing Ladies and Men.

Scene 9

"The Old Park Bench"[24] (reprise)

Scene 10

Hormones (*by* Norman Panama and Melvin Frank)
Mulligan: J. Durante. *The Tiger*: R. Bolger. *A Salesman*: J. Gleason.

Scene 11

Virginia O'Brien (specialty)

Scene 12

"This Is Winter"—Finale

J. Froman
Danced by R. Bolger, J. Limon, D. Vane, M. Moore, Entire Company.

1940.08

LOUISIANA PURCHASE

A Musical Comedy in Two Acts, 15 Scenes. Book by Morrie Ryskind based on a story by Buddy G. De Sylva. Music and lyrics by Irving Berlin. Book staged by Edgar MacGregor. Ballets by George Balanchine. Dances by Carl Randall. Costumes and scenery by Tom Lee. Musical direction, Robert Emmett Dolan. Orchestral arrangements by (Robert) Russell Bennett. All vocal arrangements by Hugh Martin. Produced by Buddy G. DeSylva. Opened 28 May 1940 at the Imperial Theatre and closed 14 June 1941 after 444 performances.

CAST (in order of appearance): *Secretary*: Georgia Carroll. *Sam Liebowitz*: John Eliot. *Col. Davis D. Davis, Sr.*: Robert Pitkin. *Abner*: NICODEMUS. *Col. Davis D. Davis, Jr.*: Ray Mayer. *Dean Manning*: RALPH RIGGS. *Police Captain Whitfield*: Edward H. Robins. *Jim Taylor*: WILLIAM GAXTON. *Beatrice*: CAROL BRUCE. *Lee Davis*: NICK LONG, JR. *Emmy-Lou*: April Ames. *Marina Van Linden*: VERA ZORINA. *Madame Bordelaise*: IRENE BORDONI. *Senator Oliver P. Loganberry*: VICTOR MOORE. *Alphonse*: Charles La Torre. *The Martins*: Hugh Martin, Ralph Blane, Jo Jean Rogers, Phyllis Rogers. *The Buccaneers*: John Panter, John Eliot, Don Cortez, James Phillips. *Premier Danseur*: Charles Laskey.

Louisiana Belles: Georgia Carroll, Marion Rosamund, Judy Ford, Patricia Lee, Veva Selwood, Edith Luce. *Dancing Girls*: Helen Vincent, Dorothy Hall, Petra Gray, Rosemary Sankey, Anitra Upton, Betty Luster, Nancy Knott, Aleen Stewart, Althea Elder, Grace Gillern, Jean Scott, Zynade Spencer, Doris York, Mary Ganley, Leona Olsen, Dorothy Jeffers, Dorothy Barrett, May Hartwig, Virginia Morris. *Dancing Boys*: Harvey Mack, Charlie Curran, Clark Eggleston, James Leland, Douglas Dean [Deane], George Hunter, Jack McClendon, Kenneth Whelan, Henry Lahee, Richard Reed, Nicolai Popov, Dwight Godwin, Harold Haskins, Hubert Bland, Ned Coupland.

Act 1, Scene 1: Lawyer's Office. *Scene 2*: Library of Jefferson Davis Club. *Scene 3*: Street Scene. *Scene 4*: Madame Bordelaise's Café. *Scene 5*: A Park. *Scene 6*: Private Room, Madame Bordelaise's Café. *Scene 7*: Street Scene. *Scene 8*: Mardi Gras Ball.

Act 2, Scene 1: Mardi Gras Ball. *Scene 2*: A Park. *Scene 3*: A Wood. *Scene 4*: Street Scene. *Scene 5*: Senator Loganberry's Hotel Apartment. *Scene 6*: Near the Capitol. *Scene 7*: The State Capitol, Baton Rouge.

ACT 1

(Opening: "The Letter")
(J. Eliot)

"Apologia"
G. Carroll, J. Eliot, Ensemble

"Sex Marches On"
W. Gaxton, R. Pitkin, R. Mayer, R. Riggs, E. H. Robins

"Louisiana Purchase"
C. Bruce, the Martins, the Buccaneers, Ensemble

"Tomorrow Is a Lovely Day"
I. Bordoni

"Louisiana Purchase" (reprise)
C. Bruce, A. Ames, N. Long, the Martins, Ensemble

"Outside of That I Love You"
W. Gaxton, V. Zorina

"You're Lonely and I'm Lonely"
V. Zorina, V. Moore

Dance
Nicodemus

"(Dance with Me) Tonight at the Mardi Gras"
The Martins

Queen of the Mardi Gras: V. Zorina. *Premier Danseur*: C. Laskey. *Queen of the Creoles*: V. Zorina.

Finale
Entire Company

ACT 2

Opening
Ensemble

"Latins Know How"
I. Bordoni, Ensemble

"What Chance Have I (with Love)?"
V. Moore

"The Lord Done Fixed Up My Soul"
C. Bruce, Nicodemus, the Buccaneers, Ensemble

"Fools Fall in Love"
W. Gaxton, V. Zorina

"Old Man's Darling—Young Man's Slave?" (Ballet)
Marina: V. Zorina. *Spirit of Jim Taylor*: C. Laskey. *Spirit of Senator Loganberry*: H. Haskins.

"You Can't Brush Me Off"
A. Ames, N. Long, the Martins

Finale
Entire Company

---

[23]Dropped during the run and replaced by:
"Toscanini, Stokowski and Me"
Conducted by J. Durante
Assisted by J. Gleason, N. Nieman, L. Adler, P. Bohn, S. Walker.
[24]Dropped during the run.

1940–1941 SEASON

Gertrude Lawrence (and mannequin) in LADY IN THE DARK (Photo: Vandamm Studio)
Billy Rose Theatre Collection, New York Public Library for the Performing Arts

1940–1941 SEASON

1940.09

WALK WITH MUSIC

A Musical Comedy in Two Acts, 11 Scenes. Book by Guy Bolton, Parke Levy and Alan Lipscott. Based on the comedy "Three Blind Mice" by Stephen Powys. Lyrics by Johnny Mercer. Music by Hoagy Carmichael. Book staged by R. H. Burnside. Dance collaboration, Anton Dolin and Herbert Harper. Costumes by Tom Lee. Settings by Watson Barratt. Orchestra under the direction of Joseph Littau. Production under the supervision of Rowland Leigh. Produced by Ruth Selwyn (in association with the Messrs. Shubert). Opened 4 June 1940 at the Ethel Barrymore Theatre and closed 20 July 1940 after 55 performances.

<u>CAST</u> (in order of appearance): *Pamela Gibson*: KITTY CARLISLE. *Rhoda Gibson*: MITZI GREEN. *Carrie Gibson*: BETTY LAWFORD. *Henry Trowbridge*: LEE SULLIVAN. *Steve Harrington*: ART JARRETT. *Wing D'Hautville*: DONALD BURR. *Polly Van Zile*: FRANCES WILLIAMS. *Conrad Harrington*: MARTY MAY. *Bellboy*: TED GARY. *Chesterfield*: Troy Brown. *House Detective*: Barrie O'Daniels. *Stuart Hobson*: WILLIAM CASTLE. (*Featured Dance Satirists*: ALICE DUDLEY, KENNETH BOSTOCK.) *THE MODERNAIRES*: Ralph Brewster, Bill Conway, Harold Dickinson, Chuck Goldstein.

Glamour Girls: Connie Constant, Althea Gary, Linda Lee Griffith, Betty Lynn, Maxine Martin, Renee Russell. *Dancing Girls*: Billie Bernice, Nancy Chaplin, Muriel Cole, Nona Feid, Christie Gillespie, Georgia Jarvis, Terry Kelly, Ruth Maitland, Eleanor Parr, Sylvia diSalvo, Lorraine Todd, Jean Trybon. *Dancing Boys*: Larry Baker, Frank Gagon, Phil King, Zoli Parks, Bob Pitts, Jack Richards.

Act 1, Scene 1: The Ethel Barrymore Theatre. *Scene 2*: Gibson Farmhouse, East Gilead, New Hampshire. *Scene 3*: Modiste Shop, New York, *Scene 4*: Station Platform, Jacksonville, Florida. *Scene 5*: Gibson Patio, Hotel Alcazar, Palm Beach. *Scene 6*: Pathway along Lake Worth, Palm Beach. *Scene 7*: Pam Gibson's Bedroom. *Scene 8*: A Palm Beach Night Club, New Year's Eve.

Act 2, Scene 1: Gibson Patio, Hotel Alcazar, Palm Beach. *Scene 2*: Airport, Miami. *Scene 3*: Outside the Hotel Rio, near Havana.

ACT 1

"Greetings, Gates"
  Ensemble
"Today I Am a Glamour Girl"
  K. Carlisle, M. Green, B. Lawford, Glamour Girls, Ensemble
"Even If I Say It Myself"
  D. Burr, Modernaires, Ensemble
"I Walk With Music"
  K. Carlisle, D. Burr, Glamour Girls, Ensemble
"Ooh, What You Said"
  M. Green, Modernaires, T. Gary
"Everything Happens to Me"
  F. Williams
"Wait 'Till You See Me in the Morning"
  K. Carlisle, A. Jarrett
"I Walk With Music" (reprise)
  K. Carlisle
"Break It Up, Cinderella"
  M. Green, F. Williams, M. May, T. Gary, Modernaires, Glamour Girls, Ensemble

ACT 2

"Smile for the Press"
  K. Carlisle, D. Burr, A. Jarrett, Modernaires, Glamour Girls
"Friend of the Family"
  K. Carlisle, A. Jarrett, D. Burr
"Way Back in 1939 A.D."
  M. Green, M. May, Dudley and Bostock, Ensemble
"How Nice for Me"
  K. Carlisle
"Everything Happens to Me"[1] (reprise)
  S. Fetchit
"What'll They Think of Next"
  M. Green, A. Jarrett
"Today I Am a Glamour Girl" (reprise)
  A. Jarrett, M. May, D. Burr

---

[1]Dropped during the run.

"The Rhumba Jumps"
  F. Williams, Modernaires, Glamour Girls, Ensemble
"Ooh, What You Said" (reprise)
  M. Green, M. May
Finale
  Entire Company

1940.10

HOLD ON TO YOUR HATS

A Musical Comedy in Two Acts, 13 Scenes. Book by Guy Bolton, Matt Brooks and Eddie Davis. Music by Burton Lane. Lyrics by E. Y. Harburg. Book staged by Edgar MacGregor. Dances by Catherine Littlefield. Music directed by Al Goodman. Settings by Raoul Pene du Bois. Lighting by Feder. Orchestral arrangements by Hans Spialek and Don Walker. Vocal arrangements by Joseph Lilley. Entire production under the personal supervision of George Hale. Produced by Al Jolson and George Hale. Opened 11 September 1940 at the Sam S. Shubert Theatre and closed 1 February 1941 after 158 performances.

<u>CAST</u> (in order of appearance): *Sierra*: Margaret Irving. *"Slim"*: GIL LAMB. *"Lon"*: George Church. *Pete*: JACK WHITING. *Mamie*: MARTHA RAYE. *First Dudette*: "Jinx" Falkenburg. *Second Dudette*: Joyce Matthews. *Third Dudette*: Thea Pinto. *Sheriff*: Lew Eckles. *Fernando*: ARNOLD MOSS. *Lone Rider*: AL JOLSON. *Radio Announcer*: John Randolph. *"Shep" Martin*: Joe Stoner. *"Old Man" Hawkins*: Marty Drake. *"Concho"*: BERT GORDON. *Sound Effects*: George Maran. *"Dinky"*: RUSS BROWN. *Shirley*: EUNICE HEALY. *Luis*: Sid Cassel. *Pedro*: Will Kuluva. *Rita*: "Jinx" Falkenburg. *The Tanner Sisters*: Martha Tanner, "Mickey" Tanner, Betty Tanner. *THE RADIO ACES*: Marty Drake, Lou Stoner, Joe Stoner. *The Ranchettes*: Margie Greene, Anita Jakobi, Iris Wayne, Janis Williams.

Dudettes: Janet Moore, Betty Jane Hess, Jean Ellis, Joyce Matthews, Thea Pinto, Ruthe Reid, Francesca Sims, Dorothy Wygal. *Dancing Girls*: Marjorie Baglin, Betty Boyce, Flora Bowes, Renee Cettel, Grace DeVita, Constance Dowling, Betty Ford, Jackie Gately, Betty Gavin, Marion Lulling, Joanne Marshall, Dorothy Thomas, Myra Weldin, Claire Wolf. *Dancing Boys*: Albert Amato, Alan Bandler, Frank Carey, Arthur Grahl, Randolph Hughes, Clarence Jaeger, Dave Jones, Herb Lurie, George Miller, Russ Milton, Bill Rettie, Jack Smith.

Act 1, Scene 1: Route "66." *Scene 2*: Exterior of Sunshine Valley Rancho. *Scene 3*: Stage of Radio Station, WMCA, New York. *Scene 4*: Studio of Radio Station, WMCA, New York. *Scene 5*: Reception Room of Radio Station, WMCA, New York. *Scene 6*: Corridor of Radio Station, WMCA, New York. *Scene 7*: Pioneer Week at Sunshine Valley.

Act 2, Scene 1: Lounge of Alamo Hotel, Mexico. *Scene 2*: Patio of Sunshine Valley Rancho. *Scene 3*: El Marihuana Cafe. *Scene 4*: Street Scene. *Scene 5*: Broadcast at Sunshine Valley. *Scene 6*: Lobby of Sunshine Valley Rancho.

ACT 1

"Way Out West Where the East Begins"
  Tanner Sisters, Radio Aces, Boys
"Hold Onto Your Hats"
  M. Raye, Ranchettes, Ensemble
"Walkin' Along Mindin' My Business"
  A. Jolson
"The World Is In My Arms"
  J. Whiting, E. Healy, Ranchettes, Tanner Sisters, Radio Aces, Ensemble
"Would You Be So Kindly"
  A. Jolson, M. Raye, Ranchettes, Ensemble
Dance
  G. Lamb
"Life Was Pie for the Pioneer"
  M. Raye, G. Church, Boys
"Don't Let It Get You Down"
  J. Whiting, E. Healy, R. Brown, G. Lamb, M. Irving, Radio Aces, Tanner Sisters, Ensemble
"Don't Let It Get You Down" (reprise)
  A. Jolson, E. Healy
Finale—"There's a Great Day Coming, Mañana"
  A. Jolson, Ensemble

ACT 2

Opening—"Then You Were Never in Love"
  G. Church, Radio Aces, Ranchettes, Ensemble
Dance
  G. Church
"Down on the Dude Ranch"
  A. Jolson, B. Gordon, M. Raye

"She Came, She Saw, She Canned"
    M. Raye, A. Jolson, Ranchettes, Ensemble
"The World Is in My Arms" (reprise)
    E. Healy, Radio Aces, Boys
"Old-Timer"
    A. Jolson, Boys
Specialty
    G. Lamb
Broadcast
    A. Jolson
["Swanee" (added to SINBAD, tour)
    (*Music by* George Gershwin. *Lyrics by* Irving Caesar.)
"April Showers" (from BOMBO)
    (*Music by* Louis Silvers. *Lyrics by* Buddy G. DeSylva.)
"You Made Me Love You"
    (*Music by* James V. Monaco. *Lyrics by* Joseph McCarthy.)
"Sonny Boy" (from THE SINGING FOOL, film)
    (*Music and Lyrics by* Al Jolson, Buddy G. DeSylva, Lew Brown, Ray
    Henderson.)
"My Mammy" (from SINBAD)
    (*Music by* Walter Donaldson. *Lyrics by* Sam M. Lewis and Joe Young.)]
Finale
    Entire Company

THE GONDOLIERS,

1940.11 or, The King of Barataria

A Revival of the Comic Opera in Two Acts[2]. Libretto by William S. Gilbert. Music by Arthur Sullivan. Stage direction by Charles Alan. Dances arranged by Felicia Sorel. Settings by Samuel Leve. Musical direction by Joseph S. Daltry. The Lyric Opera Company production produced by Joseph Daltry and Herman Levin. Opened 30 September 1940 at the 44th Street Theatre and closed 19 October after 11 performances in repertory.[3]

CAST: *The Duke of Plaza-Toro,* a Grandee of Spain: FRANK KIERMAN. *Luiz,* his attendant: WALTER TIBBETTS. *Don Alhambra Del Bolero,* The Grand Inquisitor: PAUL REED. *Marco Palmieri, Giuseppe Palmieri, Antonio, Francesco, Giorgio,* Venetian Gondoliers: ALLEN STEWART, WILLIAM GEERY, James Pease, Frederick Loadwick, Ernest Eames. *Annibale:* Robert Eckles. *The Duchess of Plaza Toro:* CATHERINE JUDAH. *Casilda,* her daughter: MARJORIE KING. *Gianetta:* MIRIAM BENTLEY. *Tessa:* Kathleen Killcoyne. *Fiametta:* Janet Webb. *Vittoria:* Anne Dawson. *Giulia:* Carol Wolfe. *Inez,* the King's Foster-Mother: Anna Handzlik.

Chorus of Gondoliers, Contadine, Men-at-Arms, Heralds and Pages: Sibyl Baubre, Reta Baum, Lillian Bennett, Jeanette Bittner, Jane Bivins, Agnes Cassidy, Marilois Ditto, Marie Fox, Dean Gehring, Kathryn Lewis, Regina McMahon, Ellen Merrill, Mary Margaret Merrill, Dorothea Mueller, Mary Ten Eyck, Phyllis Rand, Mary Roche, Avonelle Schaffer, Gabrielle Winship, Carlton Bentley, Ernest Brown, William Calvin, James Chartrand, Robert de Lany, Thomas Donahue, Clifford Jackson, Michael Kozak, Charles Latterner, Glenn Martyn, Dana Maddocks, Sidney Morton, Rupert Pole, Leonard Stocker, Frank Stone, Evans C. Thornton.

1940.12 BOYS AND GIRLS TOGETHER

A Musical Revue in Two Acts, 26 Scenes. Talk (sketches) by Ed Wynn and Pat C. Flick. Music by Sammy Fain. Lyrics by Jack Yellen and Irving Kahal. Entire production created, produced and staged by Ed Wynn. Choreography by Albertina Rasch. Settings designed and painted by William Oden Waller. Costumes designed by Irene Sharaff, executed by Veronica. Musical director, John McManus. Orchestrations by Hans Spielac [Spialek]. Additional arrangements by (Robert) Russell Bennett and Don Walker. Choral numbers by Al Siegal. Produced by Ed Wynn (The Perfect Fool). Opened 1 October 1940 at the Broadhurst Theatre and closed 15 March 1941 after 191 performances.

CAST: ED WYNN, THE DEMARCOS (Tony, Renée), JANE PICKENS, DAVE APOLLON, JERRY COOPER, THE SIX WILLYS (Rosita, Hermina, Ebe, Eugene, Ersilio, Willie), LUCIENNE and ASHOUR, PAUL LA VARRE, WALTER LONG, EDNA SEDGEWICK, DICK and DOT REMY, MARJORIE KNAPP, SALLY CRAVEN, FLORENCE FOSTER, Frank La Varre, Kay Paulsen, Al Baron, Mira

Stephans, Jack Conover, Phyllis Colt, Dorothy Koster, Lynn Lawrence, Marjorie Knapp, Iris Marshall, Dell Parker, Ione Smith, Drucilla Strain.
    Dancing Girls: Billie Bernice, Betty Bartley, Trudy Burke, Eleanor Brown, Maude Carroll, Gloria Costa, Patricia Deering, Adair Dollar, Helen Devlin, Gloria Gaffey, Georgia Jarvis, Eleanore Marek, Mary Joan Martin, Hazel Nevin, Mary Ann Parker, Jane Petri, Davenie Watson.

ACT 1
Scene 1
    A Few Boys
        Express Boy: A. Baron. *Storage Boy:* P. La Varre. *Moving Boy:* Eugene Willy. *Helping Boy:* F. La Varre.
Scene 2
    The Boy
        E. Wynn
Scene 3
    Some Girls and a Boy
        A Singing Girl: M. Knapp. *A Dancing Boy:* W. Long. *A Dancing Girl:* E. Sedgewick.
    "Liable to Catch On"
        M. Knapp
        Danced by W. Long, E. Sedgewick, Dancing Girls.
Scene 4
    The Boy
        E. Wynn
        Another Boy: W. Long. *A Bunch of Boys:* J. McManus, Orchestra. *A Call Boy:* J. Connover. *Two More Boys:* Musicians.
Scene 5
    The Leading Girl
        J. Pickens
        The Boy: E. Wynn.
    Song ["Tschaikowski"[4]]
        J. Pickens
Scene 6
    The Boy
        E. Wynn
Scene 7
    The "Cocktail Hour Girls"
        Miss "St. Regis": D. Koster. *Miss "Waldorf-Astoria":* D. Strain. *Miss "Stork Club":* L. Lawrence. *Miss "El Morocco":* M. Stephans. *Miss "Monte Carlo":* I. Marshall. *Miss "Rainbow Room":* I. Smith. *Miss "Persian Room":* D. Parker. *The Leading Boy:* J. Cooper. *The Boy:* E. Wynn.
Scene 8
    Two Boys and a Girl
        The Leading Boy: J. Cooper. *The Leading Girl:* J. Pickens. *The Boy:* E. Wynn.
    "Such Stuff as Dreams Are Made Of"
        J. Cooper, J. Pickens
        (*Lyrics by* Irving Kahal.)
Scene 9
    Dream Girls
        Night Girl: S. Craven. *A Dream Girl:* F. Foster. *Other Dream Girls:* Dancing Girls.
Scene 10
    Four Boys and a Girl
        The "Police" Boy: E. Wynn. *A Taxi Boy:* W. Long. *A Nurse Girl:* D. Koster. *Two Odd Boys:* P. La Varre, F. La Varre.
Scene 11
    A Charming Boy and Girl—The Charm Bracelet
        What Boy and Girl?: The De Marcos. *The Boy:* E. Wynn.
    A Dance
        The DeMarcos
Scene 12
    The Boy
        E. Wynn
Scene 13
    Some New Boys and Girls
        Lots of Girls: Dancing Girls. *A Stout Girl:* Dot Remy. *A Helping Boy:* Dick

---

[2]Originally presented in New York 7 January 1890 at Park Theatre for 103 performances. For Synopsis of Scenes and Musical Numbers, see original 1890 production.
[3]No credits for costumes or lighting in programs.

[4]Not the Kurt Weill-Ira Gershwin song introduced in LADY IN THE DARK.

Remy. *A French Girl*: Lucienne. *A French Boy*: Ashour. *A Dancing Boy*: W. Long. *A Dancing Girl*: S. Craven. *A Persistent Girl*: F. Foster. *The Boy*: E. Wynn.

Scene 14

Boys and Girls Together
A Latin Girl: J. Pickens. *A Sailor Boy*: W. Long. *A Spicy Girl*: E. Sedgewick. *Two Dazzling Dancing Girls*: S. Craven, F. Foster. *A Red Hot Pepper Boy and Girl*: The De Marcos. *Eight Cactus Flower Girls*: D. Koster, D. Strain, L. Lawrence, M. Stephans, I. Marshall, I. Smith, K. Paulsen, D. Parker.

Scene 15

Sixteen "Down Mexico Way" Girls
Dancing Girls

Scene 16

Eight Conga Girls

Scene 17

The Boy
E. Wynn

"The Latin in Me"
J. Pickens
(*Lyrics by* Jack Yellen.)
Danced by the De Marcos, W. Long, E. Sedgewick, S. Craven, F. Foster, Conga Girls, Dancing Girls.

Scene 18

Finale of Act 1

ACT 2

Scene 1

The Boy
E. Wynn

Scene 2

Three Boys and Three Girls
Eugene, Ersilio, Willie, Hermina, Ebe, Rosita: The Six Willys. *The Boy*: E. Wynn.

Scene 3

A Boy and Five Girls
The Singing Boy: J. Cooper. *The Dancing Girl*: E. Sedgewick. *Other Girls*: E. Marek, E. Brown, B. Bernice, P. Deering.

"I Want to Live (as Long as You Love Me)"
J. Cooper
(*Lyrics by* Jack Yellen.)

Scene 4

A Girl and Two Boys
The Leading Boy: J. Cooper. *The Leading Girl*: J. Pickens. *The Boy*: E. Wynn.

Scene 5

Boys and Girls Together
A Tom Boy: M. Knapp. *A Rube Boy*: W. Long. *A Rube Girl*: E. Sedgewick. *A Bad Girl*: S. Craven. *A Bad Boy*: F. Foster. *A Boy and Girl*: The De Marcos.

Scene 6

Four Boys
One Boy: D. Apollon. *Another Boy*: F. LaVarre. *The Boy*: E. Wynn. *A Wise Boy*: A. Baron.

Scene 7

Five Girls and the Boy
One Girl: D. Strain. *Another Girl*: K. Paulsen. *A Girl*: M. Stephans. *One More Girl*: L. Lawrence. *The Leading Girl*: J. Pickens. *The Boy*: E. Wynn.

Scene 8

Boys and Girls Together
The Leading Boy: J. Cooper. *The Dancing Boy*: W. Long. *The Leading Girl*: J. Pickens. *A French Boy and Girl*: Lucienne & Ashour. *A Great Boy*: D. Apollon. *A Ballet Girl*: S. Craven. *A Blonde Girl*: F. Foster. *A Little Girl*: M. Knapp. *Some Boy and Some Girl*: The De Marcos. *The Dancing Girl*: E. Sedgewick. *Three Boys and Three Girls*: The Six Willys. *The Boy*: E. Wynn. Dancing Girls, Cocktail Hour Girls.

"The Sun Will Be Up in the Morning"
J. Cooper, Boys and Girls
(*Lyrics by* Jack Yellen.)
Danced by the De Marcos, W. Long, E. Sedgewick, S. Craven, F. Foster, Boys, Girls.
TO THE AUDIENCE
GOOD NIGHT — BOYS AND GIRLS
I HOPE YOU LIKED US.
ED WYNN

THE MIKADO,
1940.13   or, The Town of Titipu

A Revival of the Comic Opera in Two Acts[5]. Libretto by W. S. Gilbert. Music by Arthur Sullivan. Musical direction by Joseph S. Daltry. Stage direction by Charles Alan. Settings by Samuel Leve. Dances arranged by Felicia Sorel. The Lyric Opera Company production produced by Joseph Daltry and Herman Levin. Opened 3 October 1940 at the 44th Street Theatre and closed 17 October 1940 after 7 performances in repertory. [6]

CAST: *The Mikado of Japan*: WALTER TIBBETTS. *Nanki-Poo*: CHARLES LATTERNER. *Ko-Ko, Lord High Executioner of Titipu*: FRANK KIERMAN. *Pooh-Bah, Lord High Everything Else*: ROBERT ECKLES. *Pish-Tush, Noble Lord*: Leonard Stocker. *Yum-Yum, Pitti-Sing, Peep-Bo, three sisters, wards of Ko-Ko*: MIRIAM BENTLEY, DEAN GEHRING, MARY ROCHE. *Katisha*: CATHERINE JUDAH.

Chorus of School Girls, Nobles, Guards and Coolies: Sibyl Baubre, Reta Baum, Lillian Bennett, Jeanette Bittner, Jane Bivins, Agnes Cassidy, Anne Dawson, Marilois Ditto, Marie Fox, Anna Handzlik, Kathleen Killcoyne, Marjorie King, Kathryn Lewis, Regina McMahon, Ellen Merrill, Mary Margaret Merrill, Dorothea Mueller, Mary Ten Eyck, Phyllis Rand, Avonelle Schaffer, Janet Webb, Gabrielle Winship, Carol Wolfe, Carlton Bentley, Ernest Brown, William Calvin, James Chartrand, Robert de Lany, Thomas Donahue, Ernest Eames, William Geery, Clifford Jackson, Michael Kozak, Frederick Loadwick, Glenn Martyn, Dana Maddocks, Sidney Morton, James Pease, Rupert Pole, Paul Reed, Allen Stewart, Frank Stone, Evans C. Thornton.

1940.14   TRIAL BY JURY

A Revival of the Comic Opera in One Act[7]. Libretto by William S. Gilbert. Music by Arthur Sullivan. Musical direction by Joseph S. Daltry. Stage direction by Charles Alan. Settings by Samuel Leve. Dances arranged by Felicia Sorel. The Lyric Opera Company production produced by Joseph Daltry and Herman Levin. Opened 7 October 1940 at the 44th Street Theatre and closed 15 October 1940 after 6 performances in repertory.[8]

CAST: *Learned Judge*: FRANK STONE. *Foreman of the Jury*: PAUL REED. *The Defendant*: ALLEN STEWART. *Counsel for the Plaintiff*: LEONARD STOCKER. *Usher*: ERNEST EAMES. *Plaintiff*: MARY ROCHE.

Chorus of Bridesmaids: Jane Bivins, Dean Gehring, Kathryn Lewis, Ellen merrill, Avonelle Schaffer, Janet Webb. *Jury, Spectators*: Sibyl Baubre, Reta Baum, Lillian Bennett, Jeanette Bittner, Agnes Cassidy, Marilois Ditto, Marie Fox, Regina McMahon, Mary Margaret Merrill, Dorothea Mueller, Mary Ten Eyck, Phyllis Rand, Mary Roche, Gabrielle Winship, Carlton Bentley, Ernest Brown, William Calvin, James Chartrand, Robert de Lany, Thomas Donahue, Clifford Jackson, Michael Kozak, Charles Latterner, Glenn Martyn, Dana Maddocks, Sidney Morton, Rupert Pole, Leonard Stocker, Frank Stone, Evans C. Thornton.

THE PIRATES OF PENZANCE,
1940.15   or, The Slave of Duty

A Revival of the Comic Opera in Two Acts[9]. Libretto by William S. Gilbert. Music by Arthur Sullivan. Musical direction by Joseph S. Daltry. Stage direction by Charles Alan. Settings by Samuel Leve. Dances arranged by Felicia Sorel. The Lyric Opera Company production produced by Joseph Daltry and Herman Levin. Opened 7 October 1940 at the 44th Street Theatre and closed 15 October 1940 after 6 performances in repertory.[10]

CAST: *Major General Stanley*: FRANK KIERMAN. *The Pirate King*: WALTER TIBBETTS. *Samuel, his Lieutenant*: Sydney Morton. *Frederick, the Pirate Apprentice*: CARLTON BENTLEY. *Sergeant*: ROBERT ECKLES. *Mabel, Edith, Kate, Isabel, General Stanley's Daughters*: JANET WEBB, MIRIAM BENTLEY, KATHRYN LEWIS, Ellen Merrill. *Ruth, Pirate Maid-of-all-work*: ANNE DAWSON.

---

[5]First presented in New York 20 July, 10-29 August 1885 at the Union Square and People's Theatres for 22 performances. First authorized production presented 19 August 1885 at the Fifth Avenue Theatre by Richard D'Oyly Carte for 250 performances. For Synopsis of Scenes and Musical Numbers, see 19 August 1885 D'Oyly Carte production.
[6]No credits for costumes or lighting in programs.
[7]First presented in New York 15 November 1875 at the Eagle Theatre for 8 performances. For Synopsis of Scenes and Musical Numbers, see original 1875 production.
[8]No credits for costumes or lighting in programs.
[9]First presented in New York 31 December 1879 at the Fifth Avenue Theatre for a total of 91 performances in two engagements. For Synopsis of Scenes and Musical Numbers, see original 1879 production.
[10]No credits for costumes or lighting in programs.

Chorus of Pirates, Police and General Stanley's Daughters: Sibyl Baubre, Reta Baum, Lillian Bennett, Jeanette Bittner, Jane Bivins, Agnes Cassidy, Anne Dawson, Marilois Ditto, Marie Fox, Anna Handzlik, Catherine Judah, Kathleen Killcoyne, Marjorie King, Kathryn Lewis, Regina McMahon, Ellen Merrill, Mary Margaret Merrill, Dorothea Mueller, Mary Ten Eyck, Phyllis Rand, Avonelle Schaffer, Janet Webb, Gabrielle Winship, Carol Wolfe, Carlton Bentley, Ernest Brown, William Calvin, James Chartrand, Robert de Lany, Thomas Donahue, Ernest Eames, Clifford Jackson, Michael Kozak, Frederick Loadwick, Glenn Martyn, Dana Maddocks, Sidney Morton, James Pease, Rupert Pole, Paul Reed, Allen Stewart, Frank Stone, Evans C. Thornton.

1940.16

IT HAPPENS ON ICE

An Ice Skating Revue in Two Acts, 19 Scenes. (Assembled by Sonja Henie and Arthur Wirtz.) Music by Vernon Duke, Fred E. Ahlert and Peter deRose. Lyrics by Al Stillman and Mitchell Parish. Staged and devised by Leon Leonidoff. Choreography by Catherine Littlefield, assisted by Robert Linden. Music directed by Erno Rapee. Music conducted by David Mendoza. Setting, costumes and lighting by Norman Bel Geddes. Produced by Sonart Productions Inc. Opened 10 October 1940 at the Center Theatre, closing 8 March 1941 for vacation after 180 performances; re-opened 4 April 1941 for an additional 96 performances, and closed 14 June 1941 after 276 performances total. Second Edition opened 15 July 1941 at the Center Theatre and closed 26 April 1942 after 386 performances. Performance total for First and Second Editions: 662. (For Second Edition, see detail following First Edition)

CAST: JOE COOK, HEDI STENUF, CALEY SISTERS (Dorothy, Hazel), LE VERNE, JO ANN DEAN, MARY JANE YEO, LLOYD (Skippy) BAXTER, GENE BERG, CLARENCE SENNA, DR. A. DOUGLAS NELLES, THE FOUR BRUISES (Sid Spaulding, Geoffe Stevens, Montey Stott, Buster Grace). Vocals: JOAN EDWARDS, FELIX KNIGHT, JACK KILTY, THE BUCCANEERS.

Theckla Horn, Edwina Blades, Louise Clark, Janet Hester, Audrey Butler, Lynn Clare, Eileen Thompson, Helen Thompson, Dorothy Chandler, Lillian Oldham, Trudy Schneider, Pearl Joseph, Ethel Stout, Gweneth Butler, Mancy Mae Woodbury, Hertha Grossman, Kay Corcoran, Angela Carson, Gladys Gooding, Eileen Brokaw, Margo Miller, Peggy Fahy, Louise Clark, Bernice Loughborough, Ruth Noland, Jeanne Berman, May Judels, Patsy O'Day, Charlotte Weitzel, Florence Rohr, Reszka Law, Shirley Barney. Fred Marshall, Neil Rose, Ian Grey, Jack Reese, Lyle Clark, Scott Edwards, Charles Hain, Albert McNulty, Edmund Rudink, Tex Mangrum, Meryl Baxter, Stan Skidmore, Kenny Williams, Arthur Erickson, Rudy Richards, John Dunaway, Charles Storey, Charles Cavanaugh, Donald Arthur, Leon Kosofsky, John Anderson, Arthur Nelles, George Dewey, Marion Eddy, Gene Winchester, Paul Castle, Ronnie Roberts, Neil Rose, James Wright, Fred Marshall, Howard Bissell, Charles Senna, Bill Dewey, Andy McBann, Rawdon Barnes, William Hanston, The Ice Age Quartet (Orville Race, William Lilling, Roy Barnes, William Houston).

ACT 1[11]

Scene 1

Wintertime

Policeman: F. Marshall. *Scamps*: N. Rose, I. Grey, J. Reese. *Novice Skaters*: T. Horn, L. Clark, L. Clark, S. Edwards, J. Hester, C. Hain, A. Butler, A. McNulty. *Expert Skaters*: L. Clare, E. Rudink, E. Thompson, T. Mangrum, H. Thompson, M. Baxter, D. Chandler, S. Skidmore. *Nursemaid*: L. Oldham. *Two Small Girls*: T. Schneider, P. Joseph. *Balloon Man*: K. Williams. *Show Off*: G. Berg. *Two Admiring Girls*: J. Dean, M. J. Yeo. *Their Partners*: A. Erickson, R. Richards. *Cocottes*: E. Stout, G. Butler, E. Blades. *Flower Girls*: N. M. Woodbury, H. Grossman. *A Gracious Lady*: K. Corcoran. *Footman*: J. Dunaway *Three Laughing Girls*: A. Carson, G. Gooding, E. Brokaw. *Footman*: C. Storey. *A Roue*: C. Cavanaugh. *Footman*: D. Arthur. *A Mother*: M. Miller. *Child*: P. Fahy. *The Father*: L. Kosofsky. *Footman*: J. Anderson. *Musician*: A. Nelles.

Scene 2

Joe Cook's Fountain in the Park

(*Devised and written by* Joe Cook in collaboration with Bud Pearson, Lester White.) *Proprietor*: J. Cook. *His Assistant*: C. Senna. *Customers*: G. Dewey, M. Eddy, G. Winchester, W. Lilling, G. Stevens, M. Stott, P. Castle.

Scene 3

"Between You, Me and the Lamp Post"

J. Edwards, F. Knight

(*Music and Lyrics by* Al Stillman and Fred E. Ahlert.) *Lamp Posts*: S. Edwards, J. Anderson, C. Storey, E. Rudink, T. Mangrum, M. Baxter, L. Kosofsky, C. Hain, L. Clark, A. Erickson, C. Cavanaugh, R. Richards.

Sailors: D. Arthur, N. Rose, J. Wright, A. McNulty, J. Reese, F. Marshall. *Girls*: E. Stout, P. Fahy, L. Clark, J. Hester, H. Thompson, B. Loughborough. *A Park Bench*: M. Miller, K. Corcoran, D. Chandler. *Another Bench*: R. Noland, J. Berman, G. Gooding. *A Ladies' Maid*: M. Judels. *A Statue*: L. Oldham, E. Thompson, T. Horn. *Chauffeur*: S. Skidmore. *A Dog*: P. Castle. *Drunks*: G. Stevens, B. Grace.

Scene 4

Curlilocks and the Three Bears ('*Pavanne*' *by*: Morton Gould.)

Curlilocks: M. J. Yeo. *Father Bear*: A. Nelles. *Mother Bear*: K. Williams. *Baby Bear*: P. Castle.

Scene 5

Legend of the Lake

Butterflies: E. Blades, G. Butler, T. Horn, P. O'Day, L. O'Day, L. Oldham, E. Brokaw, A. Butler. *Hunters*: T. Mangrum, N. Rose, I. Grey, F. Marshall, D. Arthur, J. Reese, L. Clark, S. Skidmore, E. Rudink, M. Baxter, A. McNulty, S. Edwards, C. Hain, A. Erickson. *Kabalo*: L. Kosofsky. *The Prince*: L. Baxter. *The Princess*: H. Stenuf. *Swans*: N. M. Woodbury, H. Grossman, E. Stout, E. Thompson, J. Hester, R. Noland, D. Chandler, M. Miller, L. Clark, L. Clare, P. Fahy, C. Weitzel, K. Corcoran, T. Schneider, A. Carson, F. Rohr.

Scene 6

As I See It

J. Cook, with assistance of C. Senna

(*Devised and written by* Joe Cook in collaboration with Bud Pearson, Lester White.) *Introducing the Absent-Minded Professor*: A. Nelles.

Scene 7

Fast Colors[12]

(*Music by* Raymond Scott.)

Acrobatic Specialty Skaters: L. O'Day, H. Thompson, E. Stout, J. Hester, E. Brokaw, A. Carson, T. Horn, K. Corcoran, R. Noland, L. Clark, P. O'Day, L. Clare, B. Loughborough, F. Rohr, P. Fahy, M. Judels, P. Joseph, E. Thompson, M. J. Yeo, J. Dean.

Scene 8

"The Moon Fell in the River"

J. Edwards, F. Knight

(*Music and Lyrics by* Mitchell Parish and Peter DeRose.) *With* G. Butler, T. Schneider, C. Weitzel, N. M. Woodbury, H. Grossman, D. Chandler, M. Miller, D. Caley, H. Caley, G. Berg, M. Baxter.

Scene 9

Captain Cook at the North Pole

(*Devised and written by* Joe Cook in collaboration with Bud Pearson, Lester White.)

President of the Arctic Club: M. Eddy. *The Lecturer*: J. Cook. *His Shadow*: C. Senna. *Tourists*: G. Dewey, W. Lilling. *Vendor*: W. Houston. *Bathing Girl*: E. Blades. *Eskimos*: O. Race, G. Winchester, G. Stevens, M. Stott, S. Spaulding, B. Grace, A. Nelles, P. Castle.

Scene 10

"Don't Blow That Horn, Gabriel"

(*Music and Lyrics by* Al Stillman, Vernon Duke and Will Hudson.) *Deacons*: R. Barnes, W. Lilling, W. Hanston, O. Race. *Sinners*: M. Judels, L. Oldham, R. Noland, R. Law, F. Rohr, J. Berman, K. Corcoran, A. Butler, T. Horn, G. Gooding, B. Loughborough, S. Barney, P. Fahy, P. Joseph, L. O'Day, P. O'Day, N. Rose, J. Reese, F. Marshall, A. Erickson, C. Storey, L. Kosofsky, D. Arthur, K. Williams, A. McNulty, S. Edwards, C. Hain, J. Wright, C. Cavanaugh, J. Anderson, L. Clark, R. Richards. *In the Groove*: J. Dean, G. Berg. *Sister Susie*: LeVerne. *Gabriel*: J. Kilty. *St. Pete*: F. Knight. *Angels*: E. Brokaw, A. Carson. *Cherub*: P. Castle.

ACT 2

Scene 1

Your Presence Requested (R.S.V.P.)

"Long Ago"

J. Edwards

(*Music and Lyrics by* Al Stillman and Vernon Duke.) *Major-Domo*: G. Berg. *Blackamoors*: P. O'Day, J. Berman, K. Corcoran, L. Oldham, J. Dunaway, J. Anderson, R. Richards, L. Kosofsky. *Host*: L. Baxter. *Hostess*: E. Blades. *Maids*: T. Horn, L. O'Day, E. Brokaw, A. Carson. *Hostess' Friends*: H. Grossman, N. M. Woodbury. *Guests*: J. Hester, R. Noland, D. Chandler, M. Miller, L. Clark, L. Clare, E. Thompson, H. Thompson, P. Fahy, C. Weitzel, E. Stout, T. Schneider, P. Joseph, A. Butler. T. Mangrum, N. Rose, F. Marshall, I. Grey, D. Arthur, J. Reese, L. Clark, S. Skidmore, E. Rudink, M. Baxter, A. McNulty, S. Edwards, C. Hain, C. Storey, A. Erickson, C. Cavanaugh.

---

[11]During run, the following sketch was added:

Horning In

(*Devised and written by* Joe Cook in collaboration with Bud Pearson, Lester White.) *With* J. Cook. *Reindeer*: S. Spaudling, M. Stott, J. Dunaway, R. Lafond, P. Castle. *Vegetable Man*: C. Senna.

[12]Replaced during run with the number:

Hielo Caliente.

Scene 2

Two of a Kind
(*Music by* Fred E. Ahlert.)D. Caley, H. Caley

Scene 3

Chief Cook and His Arctic Indians
J. Cook
(*Devised and written by* Joe Cook in collaboration with Bud Pearson, Lester White.)
The Indians: G. Dewey, B. Dewey, A. McBann. *A Half Breed*: C. Senna.

Scene 4

Coquette
H. Stenuf, L. Baxter, A. McNulty, S. Edwards, L. Clark, E. Rudink

Scene 5

"So What Goes"
J. Edwards
(*Music and Lyrics by* Al Stillman and Fred E. Ahlert.)
With J. Dean, G. Berg, assisted by G. Gooding, A. Butler, B. Loughborough, F. Rohr, K. Corcoran, T. Horn, A. Carson, P. Fahy, P. O'Day, J. Berman, L.O'Day, J. Hester, H. Thompson, E. Brokaw, R. Law, R. Noland. M. Baxter, D. Arthur, J. Reese, R. Richards, S. Skidmore, F. Marshall, J. Anderson, T. Mangrum, C. Cavanaugh, A. Erickson, C. Hain, K. Williams, L. Kosofsky, I. Grey, J. Dunaway, N. Rose.

Scene 6

The 1941 Version of the Fuller Construction Symphony Orchestra
(*Devised and written by* Joe Cook in collaboration with Bud Pearson, Lester White.)
William Lilling introducing Maestro Joe Cook and his sterling group of musicians, including G. Dewey, B. Dewey, P. Castle, G. Winchester, A. McBann, C. Senna.

Scene 7

The Ice Has "It" ('*Bellita*' by Morton Gould.)
LeVerne

Scene 8

The Glamour Girls
The Four Bruises

Scene 9

"What's on the Penny"
J. Kilty, J. Edwards, F. Knight, The Buccaneers
(*Music and Lyrics by* Al Stillman and Fred E. Ahlert.)
The Girls: L. O'Day, P. Fahy, E. Brokaw, J. Hester, R. Noland, B. Loughborough, T. Schneider, G. Gooding, E. Stout, D. Chandler, L. Clark, A. Carson, L. Clare, P. O'Day, F. Rohr, T. Horn, M. Miller, H. Thompson, E. Thompson, K. Corcoran. *The Boys*: R. Richards, C. Storey, N. Rose, I. Grey, L. Kosofsky, H. Bissell, L. Clark, C. Cavanaugh, A. McNulty, J. Dunaway, S. Edwards, J. Wright, D. Arthur, S. Skidmore, E. Rudink, J. Anderson, T. Mangrum, M. Baxter, C. Hain, A. Erickson. *Drum Major*: K. Williams. *With* LeVerne, H. Stenuf, L. Baxter, D. Caley, H. Caley, G. Berg, J. Dean, M. J. Yeo, E. Blades, A. Nelles, G. Butler, M. Judels, P. Castle, H. Grossman, N. M. Woodbury.
(*Staged by* Gene Snyder.)
With J. Dean, G. Berg, assisted by K. Corcoran, L. Clare, P. Fahy, P. Joseph, N. M. Woodbury, J. Hester, T. Horn, S. Barney, B. Loughborough, R. Noland, L. O'Day, P. O'Day, F. Rohr, E. Stout, E. Thompson, H. Thompson. J. Anderson, Don Arthur, Ray Lafond, I. Grey, L. Clark, S. Edwards, A. Erickson, Temme Ellis, L. Kosofsky, T. Mangrum, R. Richards, N. Rose, E. Rudink, S. Skidmore, K. Williams, J. Wright. *Guests*: D. Chandler, Audrey Butler, J. Berman, H. Grossman, M. Miller, L. Oldham, T. Schneider, C. Weitsel. M. Baxter, H. Bissell, C. Cavanaugh, J. Dunaway, F. Marshall, J. Reese, C. Storey, A. Nelles.

IT HAPPENS ON ICE

1940.16   (Second Edition)

An Ice Skating Revue in Two Acts, 23 Scenes. (Assembled by Sonja Henie and Arthur Wirtz.) Staged by Leon Leonidoff and Gene Snyder. Choreography by Gene Snyder and Catherine Littlefield. Music conducted by David Mendoza, Jack Pfeiffer. Sets and costumes by Norman Bel Geddes; additional costumes by Willa Kim. Skating Direction by May Judels. Produced by Sonart Productions Inc. Opened 15 July 1941 at the Center Theatre and closed 26 April 1942 after 386 performances. Performance total for First and Second Editions: 662.

CAST: HEIDI STENUF, SKIPPY BAXTER, BETTY ATKINSON, GENE BERG, MARY JANE YEO, DOROTHY CALEY, CHARLES HAIN, JO ANN DEAN, EDWINA BLADES FRITZ DIETL, FREDDIE TRENKLER, HELGA and INGE BRANDT, ALEX HURD, A. DOUGLAS NELLES, TOMY LEE,

CHARLIE SLAGLE, THE FOUR BRUISES (Sid Spaulding, Geoffe Stevens, Monte Stott, Buster Grace). *Vocals*: June Forrest, Jack Kilty, Dorothy Allan.
Charlotte Weitzel, Audrey Butler, Trudy Schneider, Marta Dietl, Bernice Loughborough, Florence Rohr, Kay Corcoran, Ethel Stout, Corrynne Church, Irene Church, Muriel Pack, Patsy O'Day, Lucille O'Day, Helen Thompson, Ruth Noland, Iris Gordon, Janet Hester, Pearl Joseph, Daphne Poole, Rona Thaell, Dorothy Chandler, Nancy Mae Woodbury, Jeanne Berman, Herta Grossman, May Judels. Meryl Baxter, Donald Arthur, Leon Kosofsky, Noel Coffey, Scott Edwards, Jimmy Sisk, Neil Rose, Charles Cavanaugh, James Wright, John Van Doren, Jim Dunaway, Jimmy Hawley, Stanley Skidmore, Temme Ellis, Rudy Richards, Edmund Rudink, Raymond Berg, Paul Castle, Arthur Erickson, Thomas DePauw, Tommy Lee, Robert Coffman, Cliff Thael, John Anderson, Tex Mangrum, John Joliffe.

ACT 1[13]

Scene 1

"So What Goes"
D Allan
(*Music and Lyrics by* Al Stillman and Fred E. Ahlert.)
J. A. Dean, G. Berg, C. Weitzel, A. Butler, B. Loughborough, F. Rohr, K. Corcoran, E. Stout, C. Church, I. Church, M. Pack, P. O'Day, L. O'Day, H. Thompson, R. Noland, I. Gordon, P. Joseph, D. Poole. D. Arthur, R. Richards, J. Jolliffe, J. Sisk, J. Anderson, T. Mangrum, C. Cavanugh, A. Erickson, J. Wright, J. Van Doren, L. Kosofsky, J. Dunaway, N. Rose, J. Hawley, S. Skidmore, T. Ellis, S. Edwards.

Scene 2

Buster Grace

Scene 3

"Between You, Me and the Lamp Post"
J. Forrest, J. Kilty
(*Music and Lyrics by* Al Stillman and Fred E. Ahlert.)
Lamp Posts: J. Anderson, C. Cavanaugh, S. Edwards, N. Coffey, T. Ellis, T. Mangrum, E. Rudink, J. Hawley, J. Wright, R. Berg, S. Skidmore, J. Dunaway. *Chauffeur*: C. Hain. *A Ladies' Maid*: M. Judels. *A Dog*: P. Castle. *Sailors*: D. Arthur, R. Richards, L. Kosofsky, J. Jolliffe, J. Sisk, J. Van Doren. *Flappers*: B. Loughborough, H. Thompson, .E. Stout, M. Pack, C. Church, I. Gordon. *Majorette*: B. Atkinson.

Scene 4

Curlilocks and the Three Bears ('*Pavanne*' by Morton Gould.)
Curlilocks: M. J. Yeo. *Father Bear*: M. Baxter. *Mother Bear*: J. Sisk. *Baby Bear*: P. Castle.

Scene 5

Legend of the Lake
Butterflies: E. Blades, R. Thaell, I. Gordon, P. O'Day, L. O'Day, A. Butler, M. Dietl. *Kabalo*: G. Berg. *Hunters*: T. Mangrum, J. Hawley, R. Richards, J. Sisk, D. Arthur, T. Ellis, S. Edwards, E. Rudink, N. Coffey, J. Van Doren, J. Wright, J. Jolliffe, L. Kosofsky, S. Skidmore, J. Anderson. *Swans*: H. Grossman, E. Thompson, D. Chandler, N. M. Woodbury, M. Pack, J. Berman, K. Corcoran, J. Hester, B. Loughborough, M. Miller, R. Noland, T. Schneider, H. Thompson, C. Weitzel, C. Church, F. Rohr, P. Joseph, M. Judels. *Prince*: S. Baxter. *Princess*: H. Stenuf.

Scene 6

Horseplay
The Bruises
Horse: M. Stott, S. Spaulding. *Inebriate*: G. Stevens.

Scene 7

"The Moon Fell in the River"
J. Forrest, J. Kilty
(*Music and Lyrics by* Mitchell Parish and Peter De Rose.)
With M. J. Yeo, J. A. Dean, G. Berg, M. Baxter.

Scene 8

The Bouncing Ball of Ice
F. Trenkler

Scene 9

Adagio
B. Atkinson, C. Hain

Scene 10

Wintertime
Policeman: L. Kosofsky. *Scamps*: N. Rose, R. Richards. *Governess and Children*: J. Berman, T. Schneider, P. Joseph. *Flower Girls*: J. A. Dean, M. J. Yeo. *Balloon*

---

[13]Following a royalty dispute, a new musical score replaced the existing songs during run:
"Better Late Than Never"
P. Stewart

Man: J. Wright. *A Roué*: C. Cavanaugh. *Small Boy*: P. Castle. *His Sister*: R. Noland. *Gracious Lady*: K. Corcoran. *Laughing Girls*: M. Dietl, L. O'Day. *Accordion Player*: T. Lee. *Cocottes*: E. Blades, E. Stout, I. Church. *The Young Ladies*: N. M. Woodbury, H. Grossman, C. Weitzel, A. Butler, E. Thompson, D. Chandler, B. Loughborough, D. Poole, C. Church, P. O'Day, M. Pack. *A Mother*: C. Church. *Father*: J. Van Doren. *Child*: I. Gordon. *Their Footman*: J. Anderson. *The Young Gentlemen*: M. Baxter, S. Edwards, J. Dunaway, A. Erickson, J. Jolliffe, N. Coffey, T. Mangrum, E. Rudink, J. Sisk, D. Arthur, S. Skidmore. *Footmen*: T. Ellis, J. Hawley, R. Berg.

ACT 2

Scene 1

Hielo Argentine
D. Allen
J. A. Dean, G. Berg, K. Corcoran, I. Church, D. Poole, P. Joseph, J. Berman, C. Weitzel, C. Church, M. Pack, B. Loughborough, R. Noland, L. O'Day, P. O'Day, F. Rohr, E. Stout, E. Thompson, H. Thompson, J. Anderson, T. Mangrum, S. Edwards, R. Berg, D. Arthur, T. Ellis, A. Erickson, L. Kosofsky, R. Richards, N. Rose, E. Rudink, J. Van Doren, J. Wright, N. Coffey, J. Dunaway, J. Sisk.

Scene 2

Heidi Stenuf

Scene 3

Skating on High
F. Dietl

Scene 4

Your Presence Requested (R.S.V.P.)
"Long Ago"
J. Forrest, J. Kilty
(*Music and Lyrics by* Al Stillman and Vernon Duke.)
Major-Domo: G. Berg. *Maids*: M. Pack, L. O'Day, M. J. Yeo, M. Judels. *Host*: S. Baxter. *Hostess*: E. Blades. *Hostess' Friends*: H. Grossman, E. Stout. *Guests*: C. Church, D. Chandler, H. Thompson, E. Thompson, F. Rohr, T. Schneider, B. Loughborough, R. Noland, I. Gordon, K. Corcoran, P. O'Day, A. Butler, C. Weitzel, P. Joseph, T. Mangrum, J. Anderson, J. Wright, A. Erickson, M. Baxter, E. Rudink, J. Jolliffe, R. Richards, E. Rudink, N. Rose, N. Coffey, S. Edwards, D. Arthur, J. Sisk, S. Skidmore, C. Cavanaugh, J. Van Doren.

Scene 5

The Skating Scamps
T. Lee, C. Slagle

Scene 6

Rhythm on the Ice
Le Verne

Scene 7

Down South
Topsy: F. Trenkler. *Simon Legree*: F. Dietl.

Scene 8

Noel
H. Stenuf, S. Baxter, S. Edwards, E. Rudink, T. Ellis, N. Coffey

Scene 9

The Glamour Girls
The Four Bruises

Scene 10

"What's on the Penny"
J. Kilty, J. Forrest, D. Allan
(*Music and Lyrics by* Al Stillman and Fred E. Ahlert.)
The Entire Company: *Drum Majorette*: B. Atkinson. *Partner*: C. Hain. *With* N. M. Woodbury, H. Grossman, M. Judels, M. J. Yeo, P. Castle, A. Nelles, E. Blades, H. Stenuf, C. Thaell, R. Thaell, T. Lee, C. Slagle, J. A. Dean, G. Berg, F. Dietl, F. Trenkler, Le Verne, H. Stenuf, S. Baxter, G. Stevens, B. Grace, S. Spaulding, M. Stott. *The Girls*: J. Berman, A. Butler, C. Church, I. Church, K. Corcoran, D. Chandler, I. Gordon, M. Dietl, P. Joseph, B. Loughborough, D. Poole, R. Noland, L. O'Day, P. O'Day, M. Pack, T. Schneider, E. Thompson, H. Thompson, C. Weitzel, E. Stout. *The Boys*: M. Baxter, N. Rose, A. Erickson, R. Richards, L. Kosofsky, J. Hawley, S. Edwards, C. Cavanaugh, T. Ellis, J. Dunaway, N. Coffey, J. Wright, D. Arthur, J. Van Doren, J. Anderson, T. Mangrum, S. Skidmore, J. Sisk, R. Berg.
(*Music by* John Gerald. *Lyrics by* David Greggory.)
J. A. Dean, G. Berg, assisted by C. Weitzel, T. Schneider, B. Loughborough, F. Rohr, K. Corcoran, E. Stout, C. Church, I. Church, M. Pack, P. O'Day, L. O'Day, H. Thompson, R. Noland, J. Hester, P. Joseph, D. Poole, D. Arthur, R. Richards, J. Sisk, N. Rose, C. Cavanaugh, E. Marshall, J. Wright, J. Van Doren, J. Dunaway, J. Hawley, S. Skidmore, T. Ellis.

"The Lonely Lamp"
J. Forrest, J. Kilty

(*Music by* John Gerald. *Lyrics by* David Greggory.)
Lamp Posts: W. Stack, C. Cavanaugh, L. Clark, T. Ellis, E. Rudink, J. Wright, R. Berg, J. Dunaway. *Chauffeur*: S. Skidmore. *A Ladies' Maid*: M. Judels. *A Dog*: P. Castle. *Sailors*: N. Rose, J. Hawley, J. Sisk. *Flappers*: B. Loughborough, H. Thompson, R. Noland, M. Pack, C. Church, J. Hester. *Majorette*: B. Atkinson.

"Tonight We Love"
J. Forrest, J. Kilty
(*Tschaikowsky Concerto in B Flat Minor adapted by* Ray Austin and Freddy Martin. *Lyrics by* Bobby Worth.)
D. Caley, F. Dietl, M. J. Yeo, M. Baxter.

"Cubana"
P. Stewart
(*Music and Lyrics by* Joe Linz and Pembroke Davenport.)
J. A. Dean, K. Corcoran, I. Church, D. Poole, P. Joseph, J. Berman, C. Weitzel, C. Church, M. Pack, B. Loughborough, R. Noland, L. O'Day, P O'Day, F. Rohr, E. Stout, E. Thompson, H. Thompson, B. Kling, C. Cavanaugh, R. Berg, D. Arthur, T. Ellis, N. Rose, E. Rudink, J. Van Doren, J. Wright, L. Clark, J. Dunaway, J. Sisk.

"The Waltz of Memory"
J. Forrest, J. Kilty
(*Music and Lyrics by* John Burger and Pierre Norman.)
{Published music does not credit P. Norman.}
Major-Domo: G. Berg. *Maids*: M. Pack, L. O'Day, M. J. Yeo, M. Judels. *Host*: S. Baxter. *Hostess*: E. Blades. *Hostess' Friends*: H. Grossman, N. M. Woodbury. *Guests*: C. Church, D. Chandler, H. Thompson, E. Thompson, F. Rohr, T. Schneider, B. Loughborough, R. Noland, J. Hester, K. Corcoran, P. O'Day, E. Stout, C. Weitzel, P. Joseph, R. berg, J. Wright, J. Hawley, M. Baxter, E. Rudink, L. Clark, D. Arthur, J. Sisk, S. Skidmore, C. Cavanaugh, J. Van Doren, N. Rose.

"The Waiter and the Porter and the Upstairs Maid" (from BIRTH OF THE BLUES film)
Brandt Sisters
(*Music and Lyrics by* Johnny Mercer.)

"I Am an American"
J. Kilty, J. Forrest, P. Stewart, Entire Company
(*Music and Lyrics by* Leonard Whitcup, Ira Schuster and Paul Cunningham)
Drum Majorette: B. Atkinson. With N. M. Woodbury, H. Grossman, M. Judels, M. J. Yeo, P. Castle, A. Nelles, E. Blades, C. Thaell, R. Thaell, C. Slagle, J. A. Dean, H. Stenuf, S. Baxter, G. Stevens, B. Grace, S. Spaulding, M. Stott, C. Lynne, F. Dietl, D. Caley, A. Hurd, M. Baxter, R. Richards.

1940.17

CABIN IN THE SKY

A Musical Play (Fantasy) in Two Acts, 9 Scenes. Book by Lynn Root. (Based on a story "Little Joe" by Lynn Root.) Music by Vernon Duke. Lyrics by John Latouche. Entire Production Staged by George Balanchine. Dialogue directed by Albert Lewis. Music directed by Max Meth. Settings and costumes by Boris Aronson. Orchestrations by Domenico Savino, Charles Cooke, Fud Livingston, Nathan Van Cleve. Vocal arrangements by Hugh Martin. Produced by Albert Lewis in association with Vinton Freedley. Opened 25 October 1940 at the Martin Beck Theatre and closed 8 March 1941 after 156 performances.

CAST (in order of appearance): *Georgia Brown*: KATHERINE DUNHAM. *Dr. Jones*: Louis Sharp. *Brother Green*: J. ROSAMUND JOHNSON. *Lily*: Georgia Burke. *Petunia Jackson*: ETHEL WATERS. *Lucifer, Jr.*: REX INGRAM. *"Little Joe" Jackson*: DOOLEY WILSON. *Imps*: Archie Savage, Jieno Moxzer, Rajah Ohardieno, Alexander McDonald. *The Lawd's General*: TODD DUNCAN. *Fleetfoot*: Milton Williams. *John Henry*: J. Louis Johnson. *Dude*: Al Moore. *First Henchman*: Earl Sydnor. *Second Henchman*: Earl Edwards. *Third Henchman*: Maurice Ellis. *Devil's Messenger*: Al Stokes. *Messenger Boy*: Wilson Bradley. *Domino Johnson*: Dick Campbell.

Katherine Dunham Dancers: Claude Brown, Talley Beatty, Rita Christiana, Lucille Ellis, Lawaune Kennard [Ingram], Roberta McLaurin, Alexander McDonald, Jiene Moxzer Harris, Rajah Ohardieno, Evelyn Pilcher, Carmencita Romero, Edith Ross, Archie Savage, Lavinia Williams, Thomas Woosley, J. Emanuel Vanderhans, Candido Vicenti. *J. Rosamund Johnson Singers*: Wilson Bradley, Rebecca Champion, Helen Dowdy, Clarence Jacobs, Ella MacLashley, Fradye Marshall, Arthur McLean, Louis Sharp, Eulabel Riley, Al Stokes, Laura Vaughns.

Act 1, Scene 1: Exterior of the Jacksons' home, somewhere in the South. Night. *Scene 2*: Little Joe's Bedroom. *Scene 3*: The Jacksons' Backyard. One month later. *Scene 4*: The Head Man's Office in Hades. Three months later. *Scene 5*: The Jacksons' Front Porch.

Act 2, Scene 1: The Jacksons' Backyard. One month later. *Scene 2*: Exterior of John Henry's Cafe. One month later. *Scene 3*: John Henry's Cafe. *Scene 4*: At the Pearly Gates.

ACT 1

"The General's Song"
> T. Duncan, Saints

"Pay Heed"
> T. Duncan, Saints

"Taking a Chance on Love"
> E. Waters

"Cabin in the Sky"
> E. Waters, D. Wilson

"Holy Unto the Lord"
> E. Waters, D. Wilson, J. R. Johnson, Churchmembers

"Dem Bones"
> E. Waters, H. Dowdy, Churchmembers

"Do What You Wanna Do"
> R. Ingram, A. Savage, J. Moxzer, R. Ohardieno, A. McDonald

"Taking a Chance on Love" (reprise)
> E. Waters, D. Wilson

ACT 2

"Fugue"
> T. Duncan, Saints

"My Old Virginia Home on the Nile"
> E. Waters, D. Wilson

Egyptian Ballet (Vision)
> The Dunham Dancers

"Love Me Tomorrow"
> K. Dunham, D. Wilson

"Love Turned the Light Out"
> E. Waters

Lazy Steps
> The Dunham Dancers

Boogy Woogy
> The Dunham Dancers

"Honey in the Honeycomb"
> K. Dunham, Boys

"Savannah"
> E. Waters

Dance
> E. Waters, A. Savage

Finale

1940.18   'TIS OF THEE

An Intimate Revue in Two Acts, 25 Scenes. Sketches by Sam Locke. Music by Alex North and Al Moss. Lyrics by Alfred Hayes. Additional music and lyrics by David Greggory, Peter Barry and Richard Lewine. Choreography by Esther Junger. Settings by Carl Kent. Musical direction by Alex Saron. Entire production conceived and directed by Nat Lichtman. Produced by Nat Lichtman. Opened and closed 26 October 1940 at Maxine Elliott's Theatre after 1 performance.[14]

CAST: GEORGE LLOYD, ESTHER JUNGER, JERRY MUNSON, JANE HOFFMAN, MERVYN NELSON, VAN KIRK, LAURA DUNCAN, JACK BERRY, CAPPELLO and BEATRICE, Vivian Block, Daniel Nagrin, Virginia Burke, Paul Roberts, Arno Tanny, Alfred Hayes, Ray Harrison, Jan Zerfing, Saida Gerard, Bram Vandenberg, Susan Remos, Alfred and Reese, Frank Rogier, Sherle Hartt.

ACT 1

Scene 1

"You've Got Something to Sing About"
> Entire Company
> (*Music by* Al Moss. *Lyrics by* Alfred Hayes.)

Scene 2

Case 305 (*by* Sam Locke)
> M. Nelson, S. Hartt

Scene 3

Darryl Zanuck Carries On (*by* Sam Locke)
> *Narrator*: P. Roberts. *Tyrone Power*: J. Berry. *Alice Faye*: J. Hoffman. *Jean Hersholt*: A. Tanny. *Sonya Henie*: V. Block. *Abe Lincoln*: A. Hayes. *Nurse*: V. Burke.

Scene 4

"Lupe"
> A. Moss, A. Tanny, F. Rogier
> (*Music by* Alex North. *Lyrics by* Alfred Hayes. *Choreography by* Esther Junger.)
> *Lupe*: E. Junger. *Dancers*: J. Zerfing, S. Remos, S. Gerard, R. Harrison, D. Nagrin, B. Vandenberg.

Scene 5

Hymn to a Stuffed Shirt (*by* Sam Locke)
> *Mr. Williamson*: J. Munson. *Miss Cavendish*: J. Hoffman. *Davenport*: V. Kirk.

Scene 6

"What's Mine Is Thine"
> V. Burke, G. Lloyd
> (*Music by* Al Moss. *Lyrics by* Alfred Hayes.)

Scene 7

"(Brooklyn Baseball) Cantata" (saga of the diamond)
> (*Music by* George Kleinsinger. *Lyrics by* Mike Stratton.)
> *Umpire*: G. Lloyd. *Announcer*: J. Berry. *Baseball Hero*: J. Munson. *His Girl*: V. Block. *Gangsters*: P. Roberts, D. Nagrin. *The Mob*: The Company.

Scene 8

Case 306 (*by* Sam Locke)
> M. Nelson, S. Hartt

Scene 9

"After Tonight"
> L. Duncan
> (*Music by* Al Moss. *Lyrics by* Alfred Hayes.)

Scene 10

Prison Reformer (*by* Sam Locke)
> *Chairlady*: J. Zerfing. *Mrs. Smiggins*: J. Hoffman.

Scene 11

Going South (*by* Sam Locke)
> *Clancy*: J. Berry. *Salesmen*: P. Roberts, A. Tanny. *Customer*: M. Nelson.

Scene 12

Nerve Center (*by* George Lloyd)
> G. Lloyd

Scene 13

"Noises in the Street"
> (*Music by* Richard Lewine. *Lyrics by* David Greggory and Peter Barry.)
> *Street Musician*: M. Nelson. *Garbage Collector*: V. Kirk. *Doorman*: J. Munson.

Scene 14

"'Tis of Thee"
> Entire Company
> (*Music by* Alex North. *Lyrics by* Alfred Hayes.)

ACT 2

Scene 1

"Barroom Ballads or Virtue Rides Again"
> (*Music by* Alex North. *Choreography by* Esther Junger.)
> *Gambler's Mistress*: E. Junger. *Gambler*: D. Nagrin. *The Stranger*: B. Vandenberg. *Prospector*: R. Harrison. *Lady in Green*: S. Remos. *Lady in Plaid*: J. Zerfing. *Lady in Purple*: S. Gerard. *Waiter*: G. Lloyd. *Drunk*: M. Nelson. *Reformer*: J. Hoffman.

Scene 2

Imagination (*by* David Greggory and Peter Barry)
> *The Doctor*: A. Tanny. *Mr. Peabody*: V. Kirk.

Scene 3

Who Killed Vaudeville?
> M. Nelson, S. Hartt

Scene 4

"The Lady"
> V. Burke, A. Tanny
> (*Music by* Elsie Peters. *Lyrics by* Alfred Hayes.)

Scene 5

Telepathic Television (*by* David Greggory and Sam Locke)
> *Danced by* Cappello and Beatrice. *Commentator*: J. Berry.

Scene 6

Case 307 (*by* Sam Locke)
> M. Nelson, S. Hartt

Scene 7

"Hawaiian Ritual"
> (*Music by* Al Moss. *Lyrics by* David Greggory.)

---

[14]Costumes and lighting uncredited.

Chieftain: J. Munson. *Maidens*: S. Hartt, J. Hoffman, V. Burke, S. Gerard, S. Remos, J. Zerfing.

Scene 8

"The Rhythm Is Red an' White an' Blue"
L. Duncan, Alfred and Reese
(*Music by* Al Moss. *Lyrics by* David Greggory.)

Scene 9

Life Covers Completely (*by* Sam Locke)
Mr. Creep: M. Nelson. *Mrs. Creep*: S. Hartt. *Reporter*: J. Berry. *Photographers*: J Munson, A. Hayes. *Second Reporter*: A. Tanny.

Scene 10

String
G. Lloyd

Scene 11

"Tomorrow"
F. Rogier, Entire Company
(*Music by* Alex North. *Lyrics by* Alfred Hayes.)

1940.19 PANAMA HATTIE

A Musical Comedy in Two Acts, 13 Scenes. Book by Herbert Fields and Buddy G. DeSylva. Music and lyrics by Cole Porter. Book staged by Edgar MacGregor. Dances by Robert Alton. Settings and costumes by Raoul Pene du Bois. Orchestra conducted by Gene Salzer. Orchestral arrangements by (Robert) Russell Bennett, Hans Spialek and Don Walker. Vocal arrangements by Lynn Murray. Accompanist to Miss Merman, Lew Kesler. Produced by Buddy G. DeSylva. Opened 30 October 1940 at the 46th Street Theatre and closed 3 January 1942 after 501 performances.

CAST (in order of appearance): *Mrs. Gonzales*: Cochita. *Mac*, Bartender of Tropical Shore: Eppy Pearson. *Three Sailors from S. S. Idaho* : *Skat Briggs*: PAT HARRINGTON. *Windy Deegan*: FRANK HYERS. *Woozy Hogan*: RAGS RAGLAND. *Chiquita*: Nadine Gay. *Fruit Peddler*: Linda Griffith. *Four Soldiers*: *Tim*: Roger Gerry. *Tom*: Raymond Baine. *Ted*: Ted Daniels. *Ty*: Lipman Duckat. *Hattie Maloney*: ETHEL MERMAN. *Leila Tree*: PHYLLIS BROOKS. *Mildred Hunter*: Elaine Shepard. *Kitty Belle Randolph*: Ann Graham. *Nick Bullett*: JAMES DUNN. *Florrie*: BETTY HUTTON. *Geraldine Bullett*, Nick's Daughter, Jerry: JOAN CARROLL. *Vivian Budd*: ARTHUR TREACHER. *First Stranger*: Al Downing. *Second Stranger*: Frank DeRoss. *Mike*: Jack Donahue. *Whitney Randolph*: James Kelso.

Singing Girls: Janis Cater, Ann Graham, Marguerite Benton, Vera Dean. *Dancing Girls*: June Allyson, Irene Austin, Jane Ball, Mimi Berry, Betsy Blair, Lucille Bremer, Nancy Chaplin, Kathlyn Coulter, Ronnie Cunningham, Marriane Cude, Doris Dowling, Vera Ellen, Miriam Franklyn, Marguerite James, Pat Likely, Mary McDownell, Renee Russell, Audrey Westphal. *Dancing Boys*: Jack Baker, Cliff Ferre, Fred Nay, Harry Rogue, Jack Riley, Billy Skipper, Art Stanley, Carl Trees, Don Weissmuller.

Act 1, Scene 1: The Santa-Ana Plaza—Panama City. Morning. *Scene 2*: The Bar of The Tropical Shore. Afternoon of the same day. *Scene 3*: A Street in Panama. Evening of the same day. *Scene 4*: Yard of Nick's Cottage in the Canal Zone. Next morning. *Scene 5*: The Esplanade—Panama City. Evening of the same day. *Scene 6*: The Patio of Admiral Tree's Home. Following Sunday afternoon.

Act 2, Scene 1: The Santa-Ana Plaza—Panama City. Monday night. *Scene 2*: Room in a Barn Outside Panama City. Midnight Monday. *Scene 3*: A Street in Panama. Next day. *Scene 4*: Yard of Nick's Cottage in the Canal Zone. Wednesday afternoon. *Scene 5*: Control House—Canal Zone. Late in same afternoon. *Scene 6*: Street in Panama City. Friday noon. *Scene 7*: Patio of Admiral Tree's Home. Friday afternoon.

ACT 1

Opening (A Stroll on the Plaza Sant' Ana)
Singing Girls, Boys, Ensemble

"Join It Right Away"
R. Ragland, P. Harrington, F. Hyers

Specialty
N. Gae, L. Hightower, R. Hightower, Ensemble

"Visit Panama"
E. Merman, 4 Men of Manhattan, R. Russell, Ensemble

"American Family"
J. Carter, A. Downing, J. Allyson

"My Mother Would Love You"
E. Merman, J. Dunn

"I've Still Got My Health"
E. Merman, Ensemble

"I've Still Got My Health" (reprise)
Ensemble

Specialty
C. Ferre, M. Franklin

"Fresh As a Daisy"
B. Hutton, P. Harrington, F. Hyers

"Welcome to Jerry"
Singing Girls, Boys, Ensemble

Specialty
C. D'Antonio, L. Hightower, R. Hightower

"Let's Be Buddies"
E. Merman, J. Carroll

"They Ain't Done Right by Our Nell"[15]
B. Hutton, A. Treacher

Specialty
E. Pearson, N. Gae

"I'm Throwing a Ball Tonight"
E. Merman, Ensemble

Conga
E. Merman, N. Gae, L. Hightower, R. Hightower

ACT 2

Opening

"I Detest a Fiesta"
Singing Girls, Boys, Ensemble

Specialty Dance
R. Cunningham, J. Baker

"Who Would Have Dreamed"
J. Carter, L. Duckat

"Make It Another Old-Fashioned Please"
E. Merman

"All I've Got to Get Now Is My Man"
B. Hutton, Ensemble

Street Scene
Dancer: C. D'Antonio.

"You Said It"
E. Merman, A. Treacher, R. Ragland, F. Hyers, P. Harrington

"Who Would Have Dreamed" (Waltz reprise)
N. Gae, L. Hightower, R. Hightower, Ensemble

"Let's Be Buddies" (reprise)
E. Merman, J. Carroll

"God Bless the Women"
R. Ragland, F. Hyers, P. Harrington

Finale
Entire Company

1940.20 MUM'S THE WORD

An Entertainment in Two Acts, 10 Scenes, a Prologue and an Epilogue, as imagined by Jimmy Savo. Music by Chopin, Beethoven, Mussorsky, Gluck and a great many others 'tampered with' by Mr. Savo. Staged by Al Webster. Verbal annotations by Hiram Sherman. Produced by Jimmy Savo. Opened 5 December 1940 at the Belmont Theatre and closed 14 December 1940 after 12 performances.

CAST: JIMMY SAVO, Hiram Sherman, (unidentified stooge).

SKETCHES
Swedish Idyll
Old-Fashioned Girl
Singsong Mother Goose (Chinese singer parody)
Bourgeois Gentilhomme
The Emergency Call (The Hospital Porter's Big Chance)
Engagement at Sea
Washerwoman in Love
Chestnut Man
Deep South Fever
When Jokes Were Young

MUSICAL NUMBERS[16]
"Ol' Man River" (from SHOWBOAT)
(*Music by* Jerome Kern. *Lyrics by* Oscar Hammerstein II.)
"River, Stay 'Way from My Door"
(*Music by* Harry Woods. *Lyrics by* Mort Dixon.)

---

[15]Dropped after the opening.
[16]Not in performance order.

"Did You Ever See a Dream Walking?" (from the film SITTING PRETTY)
  (*Music by* Harry Revel. *Lyrics by* Mack Gordon.)
"Blue Moon"
  (*Music by* Richard Rodgers. *Lyrics by* Lorenz Hart.)
"The Song of the Flea" (Chanson de la Puce from the opera LA DAMNATION DE FAUST)
  (*Music by* Hector Berlioz.)

1940.21   MEET THE PEOPLE

A Musical Revue in Two Acts, 31 Scenes. Sketches by Ben and Sol Barzman, Mortimer Offner, Edward Eliscu, Danny Dare, Henry Blankfort, Bert Lawrence, Sid Kuller, Ray Golden, Milt Gross, Mike Quin and Arthur Ross. Music by Jay Gorney. Lyrics by Henry Myers. Staged by Danny Dare. Sketches directed by Mortimer Offner. Revue editor, Edward Eliscu. Settings by Frederick Stover. Costumes by Gerda Vanderneers and Kate Lawson. Lighting by Roy Holmes. Orchestra directed by Archie Bleyer. Orchestrations by Charles Miller, Archie Bleyer, George Bassman, David Raksin. Miss Colby's special arrangements by Art Wilson. Produced by The Hollywood Theatre Alliance. Opened 25 December 1940 at the Mansfield Theatre and closed 10 May 1941 after 160 performances.

CAST: Doodles Weaver, Nanette Fabares [Fabray], Peggy Ryan, Jack Gilford, Jack Albertson, Marion Colby, Robert Nash, Virginia Bryan, Fay McKenzie, Elizabeth Talbot-Martin, Marie DeForest, Jack Williams, Jack Boyle, Robert Davis, Eddie Johnson, Lois Paul, Angus Hopkins, Barney Phillips, Beverly Weaver, Sue Robin, Ted Arkin, Norman Lawrence, Dorothy Roberts, Beryl Carew, Jack Boyle, Kenneth Patterson, Patricia Brilhante, Michael Doyle, Josephine Del Mar, Rafe Eisenberg.

ACT 1[17]
Scene 1

The Legend of Sleeping Beauty
  (*by* Ben and Sol Barzman. *Music by* George Bassman.)
  Princess: F. McKenzie. *Prince Charming*: B. Phillips. *Ladies in Waiting*: M. Colby, P. Brilhante, B. Carew, N. Fabares, S. Robin, M. DeForest, V. Bryan, L. Paul. *First Newsboy*: E. Johnson. *Second Newsboy*: T. Arkin. *Gangster*: J. Boyle. *Policeman*: A. Hopkins. *Fuehrer*: K. Patterson. *Picket*: R. Davis. *State Trooper*: M. Doyle. *Radical*: D. Roberts. *The Spirit of California*: R. Eisenberg. *Rosasharn*: B. Weaver. *Chef*: R. Nash. *An Evangelist*: E. Talbot-Martin. *College Graduate*: J. Gilford. *School Girl*: P. Ryan. *Man With Radio*: J. Albertson. *Sailor*: D. Weaver. *Salesman*: J. Williams. *Stenographer*: J. Del Mar.

---

[17]Subsequent to its New York run, on tour and in Hollywood, the following material was added (does not include THE NEW MEET THE PEOPLE):
  Washington Run-Around
    (Senate in Session sketch without the song)
  It Shouldn't Happen to a Dog
    (*by* Edward Eliscu and William Copeland)
  Design for Earning a Living (includes:)
  "Voulez-vous, Mrs. Yifnif?"
    (*Music by* Jay Gorney. *Lyrics by* Henry Myers.)
  The Higher Education
    (*by* Searle Kramer)
  "No Lookin' Back"
    (*Music by* Jay Gorney. *Lyrics by* Henry Myers, Edward Eliscu.)
  "Mr. Capra Goes to Town"
    (*Music by* Jay Gorney. *Lyrics by* Henry Myers.)
  I Am an Artist
    (*by* Henry Myers)
  The Battle of the Century
    (*by* Mortimer Offner and Edward Eliscu, from an idea by Danny Dare)
  With Zanuck in Darkest Washington
    (*by* Henry Blankfort and Bert Lawrence)
  The Last Anschluss
    (*by* Arthur Rose)
  "Statement of Policy"
    (*Music by* Jay Gorney. *Lyrics by* Henry Myers.)
  "The Old Waltz"
    (*Music by* Jay Gorney. *Lyrics by* Henry Myers.)
  Libby Street
    (author not credited)

Scene 2
"Meet the People"
  The Cast
Scene 3
Inquiring Reporter
  (*by* Mortimer Offner and Edward Eliscu, from an idea by Danny Dare)
  The Inquirer: J. Albertson. *First American*: K. Patterson. *Second American*: A. Hopkins. *Innocent Bystanders, etc.*
Scene 4
"Senate in Session"
  The President: D. Weaver. *Junior Senator*: J. Boyle. *Senior Senator*: A. Hopkins. *Senators*: R. Nash, E. Johnson, B. Phillips. *Secretaries*: P. Brilhante, M. DeForest, P. Ryan. *Jitterbusters*: D. Roberts, T. Arkin.
Scene 5
"The Stars Remain"
  She: B. Carew. *He*: R. Davis. *Dancer*: M. DeForest. *Another She*: M. Colby.
Scene 6
The Unwritten Law
  (*by* Ben and Sol Barzman)
  Her: N. Fabares. *Him*: J. Albertson. *George*: K. Patterson.
Scene 7
"Union Label"
  (*Lyrics by* Henry Myers and Edward Eliscu.)
  First Girl: F. McKenzie. *Prince Charming*: B. Phillips. *First Boy*: J. Williams. *Second Girl*: P. Ryan. *Second Boy*: E. Johnson. *Boys and Girls*
Scene 8
Elizabeth Talbot-Martin
Scene 9
The Lecture
  (*by* Henry Blankfort and Danny Dare)
  Chairman: R. Nash. *Novelist*: K. Patterson. *Members of Company Union*: R. Davis, P. Brilhante, E. Johnson, P. Ryan, J. Gilford, N. Fabares, T. Arkin, D. Roberts, A. Hopkins.
Scene 10
Jack Williams
Scene 11
The Dictator at Home
  (*by* Henry Blankfort and Bert Lawrence)
  Pa: J. Albertson. *Ma*: D. Roberts. *Ray*: F. McKenzie. *Fay*: V. Bryan. *Kay*: M. Colby.
Scene 12
"Hurdy Gurdy Verdi"
  N. Fabares
  (*Music by* Giuseppe Verdi.)
Scene 13
"(It's) The Same Old South"
  (*Lyrics by* Edward Eliscu.)
  Mr. Mason: E. Johnson. *Mr. Dixon*: J. Albertson.
Scene 14
"The Bill of Rights" (Congress Shall Make No Law)
  Professor: B. Phillips. *Students and Co-eds.*
Scene 15
How Movies Are Made
  (*by* Milt Gross)
  Patron: J. Gilford. *Banker*: A. Hopkins. *Producer*: E. Johnson. *Writer*: T. Arkin. *Director*: J. Albertson. *Exhibitor*: K. Patterson. *Cashier*: M. DeForest.
The Movie Fan
  (*by* Jack Gilford)
Scene 16
"American Plan"
  P. Ryan, A. Hopkins
  The General: B. Phillips. The Entire Cast.

ACT 2
Scene 1
"Let's Steal a Tune from Offenbach"
  (*Music based on* Offenbach's "Orpheus")
  Chopin: A. Hopkins. *Beethoven*: R. Nash. *Tschaikowsky*: J. Boyle. *Debussy*: E. Johnson. *Ravel*: B. Phillips. *Sigmund, a Composer*: R. Davis. *His Girl Friend*: F. McKenzie. *Offenbach*: T. Arkin. *Spirit of Music*: P. Brilhante.

Scene 2

Doodles Weaver

Scene 3

"(There Was) A Fellow and a Girl"
(*Sketch and Lyric by* Edward Eliscu.)
Jane: S. Robin. *Bill*: J. Williams. *The Boss*: M. Doyle.

Scene 4

Marion Colby

Scene 5

Have You Had Any Good Dreams Lately?
(*by* Mortimer Offner and Henry Myers)
Nurse: F. McKenzie. *Doctor*: K. Patterson. *Patient*: J. Gilford. *Visitor*: M. DeForest.

Scene 6

Elizabeth Talbot-Martin, with Jack Albertson

Scene 7

"No Lookin' Back"
M. Doyle
(*Lyrics by* Henry Myers and Edward Eliscu.)

Scene 8

Fancy Footwork
P. Ryan
First Footworker: P. Brilhante. *Second Footworker*: J. Boyle.

Scene 9

Light Meat or Dark
(*by* Mike Quin)
Bongo: B. Phillips. *Wowzy*: K. Patterson.

Scene 10

"In Chichicastenango" (In Chi-Chi-Castenango)
La Chiquita: J. Del Mar. *Americans*: R. Davis, D. Weaver. *Guatemalans*: F. McKenzie, M. Colby, P. Brilhante, P. Ryan, S. Robin, D. Roberts, N. Fabares, B. Weaver, M. DeForest, L. Paul, E Johnson, T. Arkin, J. Boyle, J. Williams, R. Nash.

Scene 11

It's All Right, Joe
(*by* Ben and Sol Barzman)
Joe: J. Albertson. *First Radio Voice*: A. Hopkins. *Joe's Wife's Voice*: D. Roberts. *Radio Voices*: E. Johnson, J. Boyle, R. Davis, B. Phillips, F. McKenzie, N. Fabares, R. Nash, D. Weaver, E. Talbot-Martin. *The Hot Water Bottle*: By Itself.

Scene 12

"Elmer's Wedding Day"
M. Colby
(*Music and Lyrics by* Sid Kuller and Ray Golden.)
Dowager: N. Fabares. *Town Dude*: J. Gilford. *Uncle*: R. Nash. *Maiden Aunt*: E. Talbot-Martin. *Brat*: V. Bryan. *Village Idiot*: T. Arkin. *His Yes-Man*: D. Weaver. *Elmer's Sister*: M. DeForest. *Elmer's Brother*: J. Boyle. *Elmer's Pa*: R. Davis. *Elmer's Ma*: L. Paul. *Zeke, the Town Musician*: A. Hopkins. *First Maid-in-Waiting*: F. McKenzie. *Second Maid-in-Waiting*: P. Ryan. *Third Maid-in-Waiting*: B. Weaver. *Fourth Maid-in-Waiting*: S. Robin. *Fifth Maid-in-Waiting*: B. Carew. *Sixth Maid-in-Waiting*: D. Roberts. *Elmer Brown, in person*: E. Johnson. *Eliza May, his bride*: P. Brilhante. *Parson*: J. Williams. *Elmer's Landlord*: K. Patterson. *Elmer's Boss*: M. Doyle. *Banker*: B. Phillips.

Scene 13

Doodles Weaver

Scene 14

All This and Hollywood Too
(*by* Arthur Ross)
J. R.: K. Patterson. *Joe*: A. Hopkins. *Marilyn*: F. McKenzie.

Scene 15

Finale
Entire Cast

1940.22

PAL JOEY

A Musical Comedy in Two Acts, 12 Scenes. Book by John O'Hara based on his novel of the same name. Music by Richard Rodgers. Lyrics by Lorenz Hart. Staged by George Abbott. Dances directed by Robert Alton. Settings and lighting by Jo Mielziner. Costumes by John Koenig. Orchestra conductor, Harry Levant. Orchestrations by Hans Spialek. Produced by George Abbott. Opened 25 December 1940 at the Ethel Barrymore Theatre, closing

16 August 1941 after 270 performances; re-opened 1 September 1941 at the Sam S. Shubert Theatre, moved 21 October 1941 to the St. James Theatre, and closed 29 November 1941 after 104 additional performances, for a total of 374 performances.

CAST (in order of speaking): *Joey Evans*: GENE KELLY. *Mike Spears*: Robert J. Mulligan. *The Kid*: Sondra Barrett. *Gladys*: JUNE HAVOC. *Agnes*: Diane Sinclair. *Linda English*: LEILA ERNST. *Valerie*: Amarilla Morris. *Albert Doane*: Stanley Donen. *Vera Simpson*: VIVIENNE SEGAL. *Escort*: Edison Rice. *Terry*: Jane Fraser. *Victor*: Van Johnson. *Ernest*: John Clarke. *Stagehand*: Jerry (Jerome) Whyte. *Max*: Averell Harris. *The Tenor (Louis)*: Nelson Rae. *Melba Snyder*: JEAN CASTO. *Waiter*: Dummy Spelvin. *Ludlow Lowell*: JACK DURANT. *Commissioner O'Brien*: James Lane. *Assistant Hotel Manager*: Cliff Dunstan. *Specialty Dancer*: Shirley Paige.

Dancing Girls: Claire Anderson, Sondra Barrett, Alice Craig, Louise de Forrest, Enez Early, Tilda Getze, Charlene Harkins, Frances Krell, Janet Davis, Amarilla Morris, Olive Nicolson, Mildred Patterson, Dorothy Poplar, Diane Sinclair, Mildred Solly, Jeanne C. Trybom, Marie Vanneman. *Dancing Boys*: Adrian Anthony, John Benton, Milton Chisholm, Stanley Donen, Henning Irgens, Van Johnson, Howard Ledig, Michael Moore, Albert Ruiz.

Act 1, Scene 1: Night Club in Chicago's South Side. *Scene 2*: Pet Shop. *Scene 3*: The Night Club. *Scene 4*: Vera's and Joey's Rooms. *Scene 5*: The Night Club. *Scene 6*: Tailor Shop. *Scene 7*: Joey Looks into the Future.

Act 2, Scene 1: Chez Joey. *Scene 2*: Joey's Apartment. *Scene 3*: Chez Joey. *Scene 4*: Joey's Apartment. *Scene 5*: Pet Shop.

ACT 1

Scene 1

"You Musn't Kick It Around"
G. Kelly, J. Havoc, D. Sinclair, S. Barrett, Chorus Girls, Waiters

Scene 2

"I Could Write a Book"
G. Kelly, L. Ernst

Scene 3

"Chicago"
M. Moore, Chorus Girls

"That Terrific Rainbow"
J. Havoc, V. Johnson, Girls

Scene 4

"Love Is My Friend"[18]
V. Segal

Scene 5

"Happy Hunting Horn"
G. Kelly, J. Fraser, Chorus Girls, Boy Friends

Scene 6

"Bewitched, Bothered and Bewildered"
V. Segal

Scene 7

Joey Looks into the Future (Ballet)
G. Kelly, S. Paige, Company

ACT 2

Scene 1

"The Flower Garden of My Heart"
J. Havoc, N. Rae, S. Paige, Ensemble

"Zip"
J. Casto

"Plant You Now, Dig You Later"
J. Durant, J. Havoc, Ensemble
(*Vocal Arrangement by* Hugh Martin.)

Scene 2

"In Our Little Den (of Iniquity)"
V. Segal, G. Kelly

Scene 3

"Do It the Hard Way"
J. Durant, J. Havoc, C. Anderson, Ensemble

Scene 4

"Take Him"
V. Segal, L. Ernst, G. Kelly

"Bewitched" (reprise)
V. Segal

---

[18]Replaced shortly after the opening by new lyric, "What Is a Man?"

Scene 5

"I Could Write a Book" (reprise)
G. Kelly

1940.23 ALL IN FUN

A Musical Revue in Two Acts, 25 Scenes. Sketches by Virginia Faulkner, Charles Sherman, Everett Marcy. Music and lyrics by Baldwin [Beau] Bergerson, June Sillman, John Rox. Additional music and lyrics by Will Irwin and S K. Russel. Staged by Leonard Sillman. Additional direction by John Murray Anderson. Dances by Marjorie Fielding. Settings by Edward Gilbert. Costumes by Irene Sharaff. Orchestra directed by Ray Kavanaugh. Orchestral arrangements by Charles L. Cooke and Hilding Anderson. Vocal arrangements by Pembroke Davenport. Produced by Leonard Sillman. Opened 27 December 1940 at the Majestic Theatre and closed 28 December 1940 after 3 performances.

<u>CAST</u>: BILL ROBINSON, IMOGENE COCA, PERT KELTON, WYNN MURRAY, RED MARSHALL, Walter Cassel, Paul Gerrits, Marie Nash, David Morris, Don Loper, Maxine Barrat, Bill Johnson, Anita Alvarez, William Archibald, Candido Botelho.
Specialty Dancers: Kirk Alyn, Henry Dick, Mildred Law, Jack Whitney, Ray Long, Puk Paaris, Nancy Noel, Orpha Dickey, Christopher Curtis, Dorothy Dennis, Beverly Whitney. *The Men of a Chord*: Bob Ogelsby, Bob Herring, Peter Holliday, Ed Platt. *Dance Ensemble*: Anna Marie Barrie, Eleanor Fairchild, Jane Fears, Betty Hull, Jane Johnstone, Peggy Littlejohn, Theresa Mason, Gertrude Nicols, Roberta Ramon, Miriam Seabold, Dorothy Speicher, Natalie Wynn. Fred Demming, Hugh Ellsworth, Frank Milton, David Preston.

ACT 1
Scene 1

"It's All in Fun"
C. Curtis, B. Johnson
(*Music by* Baldwin Bergersen. *Lyrics by* S. K. Russel.)
Danced by A. M. Barrie, E. Fairchild, J. Fears, B. Hull, J. Johnstone, M. Law, P. Littlejohn, G. Nicols, R. Ramon, M. Seabold, D. Speicher, N. Wynn, F. Deming, H. Dick, H. Ellsworth, R. Long, D. Preston, J. Whitney.
Scene 2

Roll Out the Record
(*by* Virginia Faulkner)
Dorothy Tom-Tom: P. Kelton. *Miss Pindicle*: O. Dickey.
Scene 3

"Where Can I Go From You?"
W. Murray, B. Johnson, B. Robinson
(*Music by* Baldwin Bergersen. *Lyrics by* Virginia Faulkner.)
The Dancers: M. Law, H. Dick.
Scene 4

Slowly I Turn
The Derelict: I. Coca. *The Samaritan*: R. Marshall. *The Bride*: D. Dennis. *The Groom*: K. Alyn.
Scene 5

"Love and I"
M. Nash, W. Cassel
(*Music by* Baldwin Bergersen. *Lyrics by* Irvin Graham and June Sillman.)
The Dancers: D. Loper, M. Barrat.
Scene 6

Red Rails in the Sunset
Announced by K. Alyn. *Passenger*: R. Marshall. *Conductor*: D. Morris. *Bride*: M. Nash. *Groom*: B. Johnson. *Brakeman*: F. Milton. *French Girl*: P. Kelton.
Scene 7

"April in Harrisburg"
M. Nash
(*Music by* Baldwin Bergersen. *Lyrics by* Virginia Faulkner.)
(a) Dance Divertissement
J. Whitney, A. Alvarez, D. Preston
(b) Cake Walk
B. Robinson
Scene 8

Neurosis Peddler
(*by* Virginia Faulkner and Everett Marcy)
P. Gerrits
Scene 9

"Machine Age"
(*Special Music by* Glen Bacon.)
Danced by I. Coca, K. Alyn, H. Ellsworth, D. Preston, J. Whitney.

Scene 10

"Just Strollin'"
B. Robinson
Scene 11

"That Man and Woman Thing"
W. Archibald
(*Music by* Baldwin Bergersen. *Lyrics by* John Rox.)
Danced by A. Alvarez, W. Archibald.
Scene 12

Manhattan Transfer
(*by* Virginia Faulkner and Everett Marcy. *Suggested by* Albert Lewis.)
Scene: A Room in a New York Hotel.
Announced by P. Gerrits. *Jen*: P. Kelton. *Esther*: I. Coca. *Bert*: D. Morris. *Ralph*: R. Marshall.
Scene 13

"It's a Big, Wide Wonderful World"
W. Murray, W. Cassel, Company
(*Music and Lyrics by* John Rox.)

ACT 2
Scene 1

"How Did It Get So Late So Early?"
M. Nash, B. Johnson, The Men of a Chord
(*Music by* Will Irwin. *Lyrics by* June Sillman.)
Danced by D. Loper, M. Barrat. *Headwaiter*: R. Long.
Scene 2

Pert Kelton. *Accompanist*: Stuart Ross.
Scene 3

"Young Man With a Reefer"
(*Ballet Music by* Baldwin Bergersen.)
Danced by B. Robinson. *The Apparition*: T. Mason.
Scene 4

"Where's the Boy I Saved for a Rainy Day?"
W. Murray
(*Music by* Baldwin Bergersen. *Lyrics by* John Rox.)
Scene 5

A Matter of Principle
(*by* Charles Sherman. *Directed by* Edward Clarke Lilley)
Scene: A Roadside Diner. *Counterman*: R. Marshall. *Mr. Jones*: D. Morris. *Mrs. Jones*: P. Kelton.
Scene 6

"My Memories Started With You"
B. Johnson, D. Dennis, Men of a Chord
(*Music by* Baldwin Bergersen. *Lyrics by* June Sillman.)
Danced by H. Dick, M. Law, F. Demming, Ensemble.
Scene 7

Morning After of a Faun
Nymph: I. Coca. *Faun*: W. Archibald. *Two Nymphs*: E. Fairchild, M. Seabold.
Scene 8

Paul Gerrits, assisted by Puk Paaris.
Scene 9

Dr. Killjoy's Dilemma
Dr. Killjoy: D. Morris. *Patient*: F. Milton. *Nurse*: O. Dickey. *Sufferer*: R. Marshall.
Scene 10

"Macumba"
W. Murray
(*Music by* Baldwin Bergersen. *Lyrics by* June Sillman.)
Danced by A. Alvarez, W. Archibald.
L'Heuere Bleu
(*by* Virginia Faulkner)
Mrs. Burton: I. Coca. *Waiter*: D. Morris. *Newsboy*: H. Dick. *Cigarette Girl*: N. Wynn. *Flower Girl*: P. Kelton. *Photographer*: O. Dickey. *Professor Mazotto*: F. Milton. *Don Carlos*: K. Alyn.
Brazil
The Singer: C. Botelho.
Scene 11

Bill Robinson
Scene 12

"Quittin' Time"
W. Murray, Entire Company
(*Music and Lyrics by* John Rox.)

1941.01

NO FOR AN ANSWER

A Musical Play (Opera) in Two Acts, 20 Scenes. Book, music and lyrics by Marc Blitzstein. Directed by W. E. Watts. Musical direction, Marc Blitzstein. Director of chorus, Trude Rittman. Costumes, Maxine Geiser. Accompanist, Norman Cazden. Produced by a Committee, (James D. Proctor (Chairman), Bennett Cerf, John Henry Hammond Jr., Lillian Hellman, Lincoln Kirstein, Arthur Kober, Herman Shumlin). Opened 5 January 1941 at the Mecca Auditorium and closed 19 January 1941 after 3 Sunday evening performances.

CAST (in order of appearance): *Cutch,* Choral Director of the Diogenes Social Club: CHARLES POLACHECK. *Nick Kyriakos,* Chairman of the Diogenes Club: MARTIN WOLFSON. *Members of the Diogenes Social Club (8): Emanuel:* Ben Ross. *Gertie Phorylles:* Eda Reis. *Francie:* NORMA GREEN. *Gina Tonieri:* HESTER SONDERGAARD. *Alex:* Charles Mendick. *Steve:* Martin Ritt. *Bulge:* CURT CONWAY. *Mery:* Ellen Merrill. *Another Club Member:* George Fairchild. *Clara Carver Chase* : OLIVE DEERING. *Paul Chase:* LLOYD GOUGH. *Joe Kyriakos,* Nick's son: ROBERT SIMON. *Max Kraus,* a lawyer: Alfred Ryder. *Bobby, Jimmy* (Entertainers at the Pillbox Bar): Carol Channing, Coby Ruskin. *Mike:* BERT CONWAY. *First Cop:* Martin Andrews. *Second Cop:* Paul Kwartin. *Customer:* Carlton H. Bentley. *Waiter:* Paul Kwartin. *Two Monktowners:* Carlton H. Bentley, Rupert Pole. *Filling Station Attendant:* Ben Yaffee. *Commissioner of Public Safety:* Rupert Pole. *Board Supervisor:* Carlton H. Bentley.

Chorus: Members of Diogenes Club, People at Demonstration, People in Pillbox Bar: Martin Andrews, Arthur Atkins, Carlton H. Bentley, George Fairchild, Anna Handzlik, Nettie Harary, Agnes Ives, Adele Jerome, Dorothy Johnson, Michael Kozak, Paul Kwartin, Emily Marsh, Elaine Perry, Rupert Pole, Marion Rudley, Diana Selzer, Leonard Stocker.

The action takes place in and around the Diogenes Social Club at Crest Lake, a summer resort in the eastern United States. The time is mid-September, 1939, after the summer season is over.

Act 1, Scene 1: The Diogenes Social Club and Nick's Lunchcounter. Friday evening. *Scene 2:* The Counter. *Scene 3:* The Club. *Scene 4:* Pillbox Bar. *Scene 5:* The Club and Counter. Saturday afternoon. *Scene 6:* Pillbox Bar. Saturday night. *Scene 7:* The Counter. Sunday afternoon. *Scene 8:* The Club. *Scene 9:* The Counter. *Scene 10:* The Club. Monday morning.

Act 2, Scene 1: The Club. Monday, early evening. *Scene 2:* Courthouse steps. (Flashback to the afternoon.) *Scene 3:* Pillbox Bar. Monday evening. *Scene 4:* The Club. Monday night. *Scene 5:* Pillbox Bar. *Scene 6:* Paul's Bedroom. Later that night. *Scene 7:* The Counter. Thursday evening. *Scene 8:* The Club. *Scene 9:* A Filling Station. *Scene 10:* Road by the Club.

ACT 1[19]
 "The Song of the Bat"
  C. Polacheck, Chorus
 "Take the Book"
  C. Polacheck, Chorus
 "Gina"
  H. Sondergaard
 "Secret Singing"
  L. Gough, O. Deering
 "Dimples"
  C. Ruskin, C. Channing
 "Fraught"
  C. Channing, C. Ruskin
 "Francie"
  R. Simon, N. Green
 "No For an Answer"
  R. Simon, Chorus

ACT 2
 "Penny Candy"
  C. Conway
 "Mike"
  B. Conway
 "The Purest Kind of Guy"
  C. Conway
 "Nick"
  M. Wolfson

---

[19]Musical numbers not listed in program; list prepared from recordings and biography (Mark the Music: The Life and Work of Marc Blitzstein, by Eric A. Gordon (St. Martin's Press, New York, 1989).

 "Make the Heart Be Stone"
  Chorus
 "No For an Answer" (reprise)
  M. Wolfson, Chorus

1941.02

NIGHT OF LOVE

A Musical Play in Three Acts, 6 Scenes. Book and lyrics by Rowland Leigh. Adapted from the play "Tonight or Never" by Lili Hatvany. Music by Robert Stolz. Orchestration by George Lessner. Staged by Barrie O'Daniels. Settings by Watson Barratt. Costumes by Ernest Schrapps. Orchestra under the direction of Joseph Littau. Produced by the Messrs. Shubert. Opened 7 January 1941 at the Hudson Theatre and closed 11 January 1941 after 7 performances.

CAST: *Cleo De Francine:* Dorothy Sargent. *Madi Linden:* MARTHA ERROLLE. *Rubero:* Frank Hornaday. *Rudig:* Harrison Dowd. *Call Boy:* George Spelvin. *Count Albert De Gronac:* ROBERT CHISHOLM. *Nella Vago:* HELEN GLEASON. *Andor:* Jack Blair. *Lisel:* Melissa Mason. *Marchesa Sangiovani:* MARGUERITE NAMARA. *The Young Man:* JOHN LODGE. *Tilly:* Jann Moore. *Waiter:* Noel Cravat. *Ensemble.*

Act 1: Nella's Dressing Room, Lucerne Opera House. One morning in June.

Act 2, Scene 1: A Corner of the Public Dining Room, Hotel Royale. The same evening. *Scene 2:* Sitting Room of the Marchesa's Suite—Hotel Royale.

Act 3, Scene 1: Nella's Dressing Room—Opera House. The next day. *Scene 2:* The Foyer of the Opera House. *Scene 3:* Nella's Home.

ACT 1
 "My Loved One" (Aria)
  M. Errolle, F. Hornaday
 "Chiquitin Trio"
  M. Errolle, D. Sargent, F. Hornaday
 Musical Scene and Aria "I'm Thinking of Love"
  H. Gleason, H. Dowd, M. Errolle
 "I'm Thinking of Love" (reprise)
  F. Hornaday
 Musical Scene
  H. Gleason, R. Chisholm
 "The One Man I Need"
  H. Gleason
 Dance
  M. Mason, J. Blair
 Finale "Tonight or Never"
  H. Gleason, M. Mason, H. Dowd

ACT 2
 "Serenade for You"
  H. Gleason, J. Lodge
 Melodrama
 "Serenade for You" (reprise)
  J. Moore
 "Without You" (Duet)
  H. Gleason, J. Lodge
 Finale—"Tonight or Never" (reprise)
  H. Gleason, J. Lodge

ACT 3
 Reprise
  H. Gleason, M. Mason
 Musical Scene
  H. Gleason, R. Chisholm
 "Loosen Up" (Duet)
  M. Mason, J. Blair
 Reprise
  H. Gleason, M. Mason
 "Streamlined Pompadour"
  M. Errolle
 Finale
  Ensemble
 "Chiquitin" (reprise) and Finale
  Ensemble

1941.03

CRAZY WITH THE HEAT

A Musical Revue in Two Acts, 25 Scenes. (Sketches by Sam E. Werris, Arthur Sheekman, Mack Davis, Max Liebman and Don Herold.) Music and lyrics mostly by Irvin Graham. Additional music by Rudi Revil. Staged by Kurt Kasznar. Sketches staged by Arthur Sheekman. Settings and lighting by Albert Johnson. Costumes by Lester Polakov and Maria Humans. Choreography by Catherine Littlefield. Musical arrangements and orchestrations by Jacques Dallin. Vocal arrangements by Pete King. Some production ideas by Luther Davis, John Cleveland, Kay Kenney. Additional dialogue by Arthur Stander and Sydney Zelinka. Sketches for Willie Howard under supervision of Eugene Howard. Produced by Kurt Kasznar. Opened 14 January 1941 at the 44th Street Theatre, closing 18 January 1941 after 7 performances; re-opened with revised cast and material (see detail below) 30 January 1941 under the auspices of Ed Sullivan, re-staged by Lew Brown, at the 44th Street Theatre, and closed 19 April 1941 after 92 additional performances, for a total of 99 performances.

<u>CAST</u>: WILLIE HOWARD, LUELLA GEAR, GRACIE BARRIE, RICHARD KOLLMAR, LUBA [Lubov] ROSTOVA, CARL RANDALL, MARIE NASH, BETTY KEAN, DON CUMMING, Marion Bailey, Evelyn Bonfine, Harriet Clark, Eleanor Dawn, Hildegarde Halliday, Wilma Horner, Helen Hudson, Frances O'Day, Irene Reilly, Helenita Riordan, Jean Stanton, Edna Ward, Kay York, Paul Bartels, Raymond Burr, Bobby Busch, Harold Gary, Ted Gary, Harry Hale, William Howell, Philip King, David Rollins, Stapleton Kent, Eddie Eddy, Bobby Lane, Frank Cucksey, Philip Gordon. The Coronets (Quartette): Frances Williams[20], Vera Deane, Thomas Mitchell, Robert Evans.

Dancing Ensemble: Kathryn Lazell, Marion Warnes, Billie Dee, Ruth Neslie, Doris Call, Susan Scott, Rae McGregor, Lois Gerard, Roberta Ogg, Marion Warness, Pamela Clifford, Aileen Read, Barbara Bernard, Dale Priest, Matthew Bocchino, Hal Anthony, Philip Gordon, Remi Martel.

ACT 1

Scene 1

"This Way Out"

Footmen: D. Rollins, H. Hale, P. Bartels, R. Burr, W. Howell, P. King. *Madame*: M. Nash. *First Lady*: L. Rostova. *Madame's Entourage*: The Coronets. *Ladies in the House of Revue*: M. Bailey, H. Hudson, J. Stanton, E. Dawn, E. Bonefine, I. Reilly, H. Riordan, F. O'Day. And Dancing Ensemble.

Scene 2

Man About Town

C. Randall

Scene 3

"It Should Happen to Me"

(*Music by* Elsie Thompson. *Lyrics by* Richard Kollmar.)

She: G. Barrie. *He*: R. Kollmar. And Dancing Ensemble.

Scene 4

Call For Herbert Tilson

(*by* Sam [Snag] E. Werris)

Herbert Tilson: W. Howard. *Alice Tilson, his wife*: M. Nash. *Jack, his friend*: H. Gary. *Announcer*: B. Busch. *Neighbor*: H. Halliday.

Scene 5

"Sascha's Got a Girl"

(*Music and Lyrics by* Irvin Graham.)

The Tattletale: G. Barrie. *Sascha*: T. Gary. *Sascha's Girl*: B. Kean. *Animals*: *Zebra*: E. Bonefine. *Zebra*: H. Hudson. *Mama Monkey*: E. Ward. *Papa Monkey*: B. Lane. *Their Offspring*: F. Cucksey. *Active Lion*: R. Burr. *Passive Lion*: D. Rollins. *The Girls and Boys*: Dancing Ensemble.

Scene 6

Mental Giant

(*by* H. I. Phillips)

The Wife: L. Gear. *The Husband*: W. Howard.

Scene 7

Ted Gary

Scene 8

"Some Day"

(*Music by* Rudi Revil. *Lyrics by* Kurt Kasznar and Carl Kent.)

Sailor: R. Kollmar. In the Vision:

"Il Pleurait"

(*Music by* Rudi Revil. *Lyrics by* Maurice Vandair.)

La Jeune Fille Des Fleurs: L. Rostova. *Gendarme*: D. Rollins. *La Blonde*: H. Clark. *Le Maquereau*: T. Mitchell. *Le Musicien*: B. Evans. *Le Garcon*: A. Kelly.

L'Assistante: V. Deane. *Boulanger*: B. Busch. *L'Homme Cachouette*: E. Eddy. *L'Acrobat*: R. Burr. *Son Amie*: F. Williams. *Les Dames de la Rue*: I. Reilly, J. Stanton, E. Bonefine, H. Hudson. *Les Apaches*: B. Lane, E. Ward. *Les Touristes*: S. Kent, W. Howell, K. Lazell.

Scene 9

Butcher Boy

(*by* Mack Davis)

Patient: W. Horner. *Doctor*: H. Gary. *Patient's Sister*: V. Allen. *Butcher Boy*: W. Howard.

Scene 10

"Time of Your Life"

(*Music by* William Provost. *Lyrics by* Pete Kite Smith.)

The Maid: G. Barrie. *The Lady in Red*: B. Kean. Dancing Boys and F. Cucksey.

Scene 11

Life Without Father

(*by* Robert Marko)

Mother: L. Gear. *Maid*: J. Hoffman. *Father*: W. Howard. *John*: R. Kollmar. *Whitney*: H. Gary. *Harlan*: P. Gordon. *Junior*: B. Busch. *Cousin Gladys*: W. Horner. *Rodney*: B. Lane.

Scene 12

Don Cumming

Scene 13

Morning Mist

(*by* Sam E. Werris)

Announcer: L. Gear. *Ivan Roushinska*: W. Howard. *Attendant*: D. Cumming. And Corps de Ballet.

Scene 14

"(You Should Be) Set to Music"

(*Music and Lyrics by* Irvin Graham.)

The Bride: M. Nash. *The Groom*: R. Kollmar. *The Bridesmaids*: J. Stanton, H. Hudson, H. Riordan, M. Bailey, F. O'Day, E. Bonefine, I. Reilly, E. Dawn. *The Groom's Friends*: T. Mitchell, B. Evans, R. Burr, D. Rollins.

Scene 15

Announcement to the Audience

(*by* Don Herold)

Announcer: L. Gear.

Scene 16

"Crazy With the Heat"

(*Music by* Rudi Revil. *Lyrics by* Irvin Graham.)

Debutante: G. Barrie. *Crazy With Their Feet*: B. Kean, C. Randall. *Quartette*: The Coronets. *Doorman at Shapiro's*: H Hale. *Doorman at Cabana*: D. Rollins. *Doorman at Typhoon*: S. Kent. *Doorman at Zombie*: A. Kelly. *Shapiro's Eight Weaknesses*: M. Bailey, H. Hudson, I. Reilly, J. Stanton, E. Dawn, H. Riordan, E. Bonefine, F. O'Day. And Dancing Ensemble.

ACT 2

Scene 1

No Smoking

The Ushers: R. Burr, D. Rollins, H. Hale, T. Mitchell, B. Evans. *The Audience*: M. Bailey, H. Hudson, I. Reilly, J. Stanton, E. Dawn, H. Riordan, K. York, F. O'Day, P. Bartels, D. Priest, P. King, M. Boccino, H. Anthony, P. Gordon, R. Martel. *The Victim*: B. Busch. *The Announcer*: L. Gear.

Scene 2

"(With a) Twist of the Wrist"

(*Music and Lyrics by* Irvin Graham.)

Svengali: R. Kollmar. *Trilby*: G. Barrie. *Assistant Magician*: B. Busch. *Wire Walkers*: B. Kean, T. Gary. *Four Flying Aces*: The Coronets. And Dancing Ensemble.

Scene 3

A Voice of Experience

(*by* Arthur Sheekman)

Professor Willie: W. Howard. *Announcer*: B. Busch. *Attendant*: D. Rollins. *First Couple*: W. Horner, A. Kelly. *A Woman*: J. Hoffman. *Strange Case*: H. Gary.

Scene 4

"Yacht Song"

L. Gear

(*Music and Lyrics by* Walter Nones.)

Scene 5

Fightin' for the Funnies

B. Lane, E. Ward

Scene 6

"Wine From My Slipper" (Inspired by Toulouse-Lautrec)

Ballerina: L. Rostova. *Singer*: M. Nash. *Seducer*: P. King. *Ladies of the Can-Can*:

---

[20]Not the same Frances Williams appearing this season in WALK WITH MUSIC, or earlier in GEORGE WHITE'S SCANDALS, EVERYBODY'S WELCOME, etc.

B. Dee, B. Bernard, R. Neslie, A. Read, R. Ogg, M. Warness, D. Call, P. Clifford, S. Scott, L. Girard, K. Lazell, R. McGregor, The Ensemble.
Note: Toulouse-Lautrec's paintings are a brilliant mirror of nineteenth century Paris ... in this whirlpool of music, art, poetry and boundless luxury, the fragile and satiric Toulouse-Lautrec lived and created. The cafés and the Moulin Rouge were his home, studio and recreation, bringing to him all that was Paris: the peals of feminine laughter, kicking black-clad legs of can-can girls and ludicrous roués. So engrossed was he in his surroundings that a stream of paintings, lithographs and sketches poured forth, reproducing in uncanny mastership the grace and charm—the ugliness and flippancy—of that period.

Scene 7

Betty Kean

Scene 8

Music Hath Charms

>(*by* Max Liebman)
>*Alice*: W. Horner. *Charles*: R. Kollmar. *Singer*: W. Howard. *Professor*: H. Gary.

Scene 9

"(You Should Be) Set to Music" (reprise)—Finale

>Entire Company

CRAZY WITH THE HEAT

1941.03 (revised)

Re-opened 30 January 1941 as a Musical Revue in Two Acts, 26 Scenes. New sketches written and staged by Lew Brown. Additional dialogue by Arthur Stander and Sydney Zelinka.[21]

CAST: WILLIE HOWARD, LUELLA GEAR, GRACIE BARRIE, CARLOS RAMIREZ, BETTY KEAN, TIP, TAP and TOE, TED GARY, DON CUMMING, MARY RAYE and NALDI, DIOSA COSTELLO, Victor Borge, Ward and Lane, Vivienne Allen, Marion Bailey, Evelyn Bonefine, Eleanor Dawn, Jane Hoffman, Wilma Horner, Helen Hudson, Irene Reilly, Jean Stanton, Helenita Riordan, Frances O'Day, Frances Williams. Hal Anthony, Matthew Boccino, Harold Gary, Philip Gordon, Harry Hale, Al Kelly, Stapleton Kent, Philip King, Remi Martel, Dale Priest, David Rollins, Matthew Smith.

ACT 1[22]

Scene 1

That Intimate Touch

>*by* Don Herold)
>*Announcer*: L. Gear.

Scene 2

No Smoking

>*The Ushers*: D. Rollins, H. Hale. *The Audience*: M. Bailey, H. Hudson, I. Reilly, J. Stanton, E. Dawn, H. Riordan, F. O'Day, D. Priest, P. King, M. Boccino, H. Anthony, P. Gordon, R. Martel. *The Victim*: B. Busch. *The Announcer*: L. Gear.

Scene 3

"(With a) Twist of the Wrist"

>(*Music and Lyrics by* Irvin Graham.)
>*Svengali*: T. Gary. *Trilby*: G. Barrie. *Assistant Magician*: B. Busch. *Twister of the Wrister*: D. Cumming. Dancing Ensemble.

Scene 4

Lonely Hearts

>(*Written and staged by* Matt Brooks)
>*Lonely Heart*: W. Howard. *Cop*: H. Gary. *Doctor*: M. Smith. *Orderly*: D. Rollin. *Woman*: J. Hoffman.

Scene 5

Betty Kean

---

[21]All other production credits as above, except Pete King no longer credited for vocal arrangements.
[22]During the second run, the production underwent further revision. Added were:

Lamb Chops

>(*by* Mack Davis)(Act 1, before "Some Day")
>*Butcher Boy*: W. Howard. *Doctor*: D. Rollins. *Sister*: V. Allen. *Woman*: W. Horner.
>Adele Gerard (Swing harpist)(cast addition)

Grauman's Chinese Theatre

>(Act 2, after Call for Herbert Tilson)
>*Autograph Fan*: Kathryn Lazell. *Movie Star*: M. Smith. *Orator*: W. Howard.
>*Audience*: A. Kelly.

Mental Giant

>(*by* H. I. Phillips)(Act 2, after Grauman's Chinese Theater)
>*Wife*: L. Gear. *Husband*: W. Howard.

Scene 6

"Interpretation in C Minor"[23]

>*Professor*: V. Borge. *Singer*: F. Williams.

Scene 7

"Yes, My Darling Daughter"

>(*Music and Lyrics by* Jack Lawrence.)
>*Daughter*: G. Barrie.

Scene 8

Tip, Tap and Toe[24]

Scene 9

"Some Day"

>(*Music by* Rudi Revil. *Lyrics by* Kurt Kasznar and Carl Kent.)
>*S.S. Normandie Sailor*: C. Ramirez.

Scene 10

Morning Mist

>(*by* Sam E. Werris)
>*Announcer*: L. Gear. *Ivan Roushinska*: W. Howard. And Corps de Ballet.

Scene 11

Ward and Lane[25]

Scene 12

A Voice of Experience

>(*by* Arthur Sheekman)
>*Professor Willie*: W. Howard. *Announcer*: B. Busch. *First Couple*: W. Horner, A. Kelly. *A Woman*: J. Hoffman. *Strange Case*: H. Gary.

Scene 13

"Crazy With the Heat"

>G. Barrie
>(*Music by* Rudi Revil. *Lyrics by* Irvin Graham.)
>*Dancer*: D. Costello. *Conga Line*: Ensemble.

ACT 2

Scene 1

"Les Rendezvous des Artists" (The Bal Tabarin in Paris in the '90s)

>Inspired by Toulouse Lautrec's famous paintings. *Created and danced by* Mary Raye and Naldi. *Paul Geraldy*: M. Smith. *Maid*: V. Allen. *Les Jeunes et Filles*: Dancing Ensemble.

Scene 2

Carlos Ramirez[26]

Scene 3

Size 9 ?[27]

>(*Written and Staged by* Lew Brown.)
>*The Customer*: L. Gear. *Her Husband*: S. Kent. *The Assistant Manager*: M. Smith. *Saleslady*: F. O'Day. *Tiny*: D. Cumming.

Scene 4

"Time of Your Life"

>(*Music by* William Provost. *Lyrics by* Pete Kite Smith.)
>*The Maid*: G. Barrie. *The Lady in Red*: B. Kean.

Scene 5

Call for Herbert Tilson

>(*by* Sam E. Werris)
>*Herbert Tilson*: W. Howard. *Alice Tilson, his wife*: J. Hoffman. *Jack, his friend*: H. Gary. *Announcer*: B. Busch. *Neighbor*: V. Allen.

Scene 6

Don Cumming[28]

Scene 7

"Sascha's Got a Girl"

>(*Music and Lyrics by* Irvin Graham.)
>*The Tattletale*: G. Barrie. *Sascha*: T. Gary. *Sascha's Girl*: B. Kean. *Animals*: Leo Lion, Leota Lion, Rudy Rooster: Tip, Tap and Toe. *The Girls and Boys*: Dancing Ensemble.

Scene 8

Announcement to the Audience

>L. Gear

---

[23]Dropped during the run.
[24]Dropped during the run.
[25]Dropped during the run.
[26]Dropped during the run.
[27]Dropped during the run.
[28]Dropped during the run.

Scene 9

Music Hath Charm
(*by* Max Liebman)
Alice: W. Horner. *Charles*: M. Smith. *Singer*: W. Howard. *Professor*: H. Gary.

Scene 10

Ted Gary

Scene 11

"(You Should Be) Set to Music"
(*Music and Lyrics by* Irvin Graham.)
The Bride: G. Barrie. *The Groom*: C. Ramirez. *The Bridesmaids*: J. Stanton, H. Hudson, H. Riordan, M. Bailey, F. O'Day, E. Bonefine, I. Reilly, E. Dawn.

Scene 12

Mary Raye and Naldi

Scene 13

"(You Should Be) Set to Music" (reprise)—Finale
Entire Company

LADY IN THE DARK

1941.04

A Musical Play in Two Acts, 7 Scenes. Book by Moss Hart. Music by Kurt Weill. Lyrics by Ira Gershwin. Production and lighting by Hassard Short. Play staged by Moss Hart. All musical sequences staged by Hassard Short. Settings by Harry Horner. Costumes by Irene Sharaff; gowns by Hattie Carnegie. Choreography by Albertina Rasch. Musical direction by Maurice Abravanel. All Orchestrations and vocal arrangements by Kurt Weill. Produced by Sam H. Harris. Opened 23 January 1941 at the Alvin Theatre, closing 15 June 1941 for vacation after 162 performances. Re-opened 2 September 1941 at the Alvin Theatre, and closed 30 May 1942 after 305 additional performances, for a total of 467 performances.

CAST (in order of appearance): *Dr. Brooks*: Donald Randolph. *Miss Bowers*: Jeanne Shelby. *Liza Elliott*: GERTRUDE LAWRENCE. *Miss Foster*, secretary, also maid: EVELYN WYCKOFF. *Miss Stevens*: Ann Lee. *Maggie Grant*: Margaret Dale. *Alison Du Bois*: Natalie Schafer. *Russell Paxton*, also chauffeur: DANNY KAYE. *Charley Johnston*: MACDONALD CAREY. *Randy Curtis*: VICTOR MATURE. *Joe*, an office boy: Ward Tallmon. *Tom*, an office boy: Nelson Barclift. *Kendall Nesbitt*: BERT LYTELL. *Helen*, a model: Virginia Peine. *Ruthie*, a model: Gedda Petry. *Carol*, a model: Patricia Deering. *Marcia*, a model: Margaret Westberg. *Ben Butler*: Dan Harden. *Barbara*: Eleanor Eberle. *Jack*: Davis Cunningham.

The Albertina Rasch Dancers: Dorothy Bird, Audrey Costello, Patricia Deering, June MacLaren, Beth Nichols, Wana Wenerholm, Margaret Westberg, Jerome Andrews, Nelson Barclift, George Bockman, Andre Charise, Fred Hearn, Yaroslav Kirov, Parker Wilson. *The Singers*: Catherine Conrad, Jean Cumming, Carol Deis, Hazel Edwards, Gedda Petry, June Rutherford, Florence Wyman, Davis Cunningham, Max Edwards, Len Frank, Gordon Gifford, Manfred Hecht, William Marel, Larry Siegle, Harold Simmons. *The Children*: Anne Bracken, Sally Ferguson, Ellie Lawes, Joan Lawes, Jacqueline Macmillan, Lois Volkman, Kenneth Casey, Warren Mills, Robert Mills, Robert Lee, George Ward, William Welch.

Act 1, Scene 1: Dr. Brooks' Office. *Scene 2*: Liza Elliott's Office. *The same day. Scene 3*: Dr. Brooks' Office. *The next day. Scene 4*: Liza Elliott's Office. *Late that afternoon.*

Act 2, Scene 1: Liza Elliott's Office. *Late the following afternoon. Scene 2*: Dr. Brooks' Office. *Later that evening. Scene 3*: Liza Elliott's Office. *A week later.*

ACT 1

Scene 1

"Oh Fabulous One in Your Ivory Tower"
Liza Elliott's Serenaders
"The World's Inamorata"
G. Lawrence, E. Wyckoff
"One Life to Live"
G. Lawrence, D. Kaye
"Girl of the Moment"
Ensemble
"It Looks Like Liza"
Entire Company

Scene 2

Mapleton High Chorale
High School Graduates
"This Is New"
V. Mature, G. Lawrence
"The Princess of Pure Delight"
G. Lawrence, Children

"This Woman at the Altar"
Entire Company

ACT 2

Scene 1

"The Greatest Show on Earth"
D. Kaye, Ensemble
Dance of the Tumblers
Albertina Rasch Dancers
"The Best Years of His Life"
M. Carey, V. Mature
"Tschaikowsky"
D. Kaye, Ensemble
"The Saga of Jenny"
G. Lawrence, Jury, Ensemble

Scene 2

"My Ship"
G. Lawrence

LIBERTY JONES

1941.05

A Play with Music (Allegory) in Three Acts, 5 Scenes. Play by Philip Barry. Music by Paul Bowles. Staged by John Houseman. Dances directed by Lew Christiansen. Settings and costumes designed by Raoul Pene du Bois. Orchestra under the direction of Daniel Mendelsohn. Production under the supervision of Theresa Helburn and Lawrence Langner. Produced by the Theatre Guild. Opened 5 February 1941 at the Sam S. Shubert Theatre and closed 22 February 1941 after 22 performances.

CAST: *Liberty Jones*: NANCY COLEMAN. *Liberty's Uncle*: William Lynn. *Liberty's Aunt*: Martha Hodge. *Commander Tom Smith*: JOHN BEAL. *Dick Brown*: Tom Ewell. *Harry Robinson*: Howard Freeman. *Nurse Cotton*: Katherine Squire. *Nurse Maggie*: IVY SCOTT. *Singers*: Juanita Hall Choir.

The Two Reporters: Don Glenn, Crahan Denton. *The Two Dancers*: Lew Christiansen, Elise Reiman. *The Three Shirts*: Victor Thorley, Louis Polan, Richard Sanders. *The Four Doctors, The Committee of Four, The Four Policemen*: Norman Lloyd, Murray O'Neill, Allan Frank, William Mende. *The Five Singers*: William Castle, Roy Johnston, Eva Burton, Ruth Gibbs, Alyce Carter. *The Seven Friends*: Lew Christensen, Joseph Anthony, Vincent Gardner, Craig Mitchell, William Castle, Roy Johnston, Jack Parsons. *The Eleven Friends*: Elise Reiman, Bedelia Falls, Caryl Smith, Honora Harwood, Ellen Morgan, Helen Kramer, Barbara Brown, Constance Dowling, Eva Burton, Ruth Gibbs, Alyce Carter.

Act 1: Bedroom-Sitting Room in Samuel Bunting's Roof Apartment overlooking Rock Creek Park, Washington, D.C.

Act 2, Scene 1: The Park. *Scene 2*: The Roof Terrace.

Act 3, Scene 1: The Park. *Scene 2*: The Roof Terrace.

ACT 1[29]

Close Your Two Eyes
I. Scott

ACT 2

Scene 1

Nurse and Intern Ballet
Doctors, Reporters

Scene 2

Close Your Two Eyes (reprise)
Male Voice

ACT 3

Scene 1

Sleep Walk
Women's Voices

Scene 2

Wedding Cake Song
I. Scott
Wedding Song
Ushers, Bridesmaids
Waltz (instrumental)
Wedding Guests

---

[29]No song titles in program; song list prepared from production typescript.

Edith Meiser, Vivian Vance, Danny Kaye, and Eve Arden in LET'S FACE IT (Photo: Vandamm Studio)
Billy Rose Theatre Collection, New York Public Library for the Performing Arts

1941–1942 SEASON

BEST FOOT FORWARD

1941.06

A Musical Comedy in Two Acts, 16 Scenes. Book by John Cecil Holm. Music and lyrics by Hugh Martin and Ralph Blane. Staged by George Abbott. Dances directed by Gene Kelly. Settings and lighting by Jo Mielziner. Costumes by Miles White. Orchestra conductor, Archie Bleyer. Orchestrations by Donald Walker and Hans Spialek. Overture by Robert Russell Bennett. Produced by George Abbott. Opened 1 October 1941 at the Ethel Barrymore Theatre and closed 4 July 1942 after 326 performances.

CAST (in order of appearance): *Dutch Miller*: JACK JORDAN, JR. *Fred Jones*: Lou Wills, Jr. *Freshman*: Richard Dick. *Junior*: Danny Daniels. *Hunk Hoyt*: KENNETH BOWERS. *Satchel Moyer*: Bobby Harrell. *Goofy Clark*: Lee Roberts. *Chuck Green*: TOMMY DIX. *Dr. Reeber*: Fleming Ward. *Old Grad*: Stuart Langley. *Minerva*: JUNE ALLYSON. *Ethel*: VICTORIA SCHOOLS. *Miss Delaware Water Gap*: BETTY ANN NYMAN. *Blind Date*: NANCY WALKER. *Bud Hooper*: GIL STRATTON, JR. *Professor Lloyd*: Roger Hewlett. *Waitress*: Norma Lehn. *Jack Haggerty*: MARTY MAY. *Gale Joy*: ROSEMARY LANE. *Chester Billings*: Vincent York. *Helen Schlessinger*: MAUREEN CANNON. *Prof. Williams*: Robert Griffith.

Dancing Girls: Frances Bryan, Marianne Cude, Dorothy Eden, Bee Farnum, Mary Ganly, Ann Guier, Kay Guier, Rhoda Hoffman, Terry Kelly, Kaye Popp, Rosemary Schaefer, Rose Marie Schiller, Lenore Thomas, Doris York. *Singing Girls*: Eileen Barton, Peggy Ellis, Peggy Anne Ellis, Barbara Grant, Carol Horton, Beverly Hosier, Betty McCloskey, Elaine Miller, Penny Porter, Renee Rochelle, Marilyn Ross, Audrey Sperling. *Dancing Boys*: Buddy Allen, Wilbur Baron, Gil Johnson, Kenneth Buffett, Danny Daniels, Richard Dick, Stanley Donen, Perry Jubelirer, Billy Parsons, George Staisey, Buddy Styles, Elmer Vernon, Art Williams. *Singing Boys*: Van Atkins, John Balian, Harvey Gould, Eugene Martin.

Act 1, Scene 1: The Gymnasium. *Scene 2*: Room at the Eagle House. *Scene 3*: Room in Boys' Dormitory. *Scene 4*: Hall Outside Girls' Cot Room. *Scene 5*: Room at the Eagle House. *Scene 6*: Girls' Cot Room. *Scene 7*: Hall Outside Girls' Cot Room. *Scene 8*: The Gymnasium.

Act 2, Scene 1: The Gymnasium. *Scene 2*: Room in Boys' Dormitory. *Scene 3*: Exterior of Dormitory. *Scene 4*: The Gymnasium. *Scene 5*: Hall. *Scene 6*: Room at the Eagle House. *Scene 7*: Hall. *Scene 8*: The Gymnasium.

ACT 1

Scene 1

"Don't Sell the Night Short"
J. Allyson, N. Walker, Students, Girls

"Three Men on a Date"
G. Stratton, J. Jordan, K. Bowers
The Dancer: B. A. Nyman. *The Gay Blades*: S. Donen, B. Allen, A. Williams. *The Tap Dancers*: G. Staisey, L. Roberts, D. Daniels. *The Acrobats*: G. Johnson, B. Harrell, B. Parsons.

Scene 2

"That's How I Love the Blues"
R. Lane, M. May

Scene 4

"The Three B's"
V. Schools, J. Allyson, N. Walker
The Jury: C. Horton, B. Hosier, P. Ellis, E. Miller, P. Porter, E. Barton.

"Everytime" (Ev'ry Time)
M. Cannon

Scene 5

"The Guy Who Brought Me"
R. Lane, M. May, G. Stratton, J. Jordan, K. Bowers

Scene 6

"I Know You By Heart"
G. Stratton

Scene 7

"Shady Lady Bird"
M. Cannon, Students

Scene 8

"Shady Lady Bird" (reprise)
M. Cannon, Ensemble

ACT 2

Scene 1

"Buckle Down, Winsocki"
T. Dix, S. Langley, Chorus

Scene 3

"My First Promise"
V. Schools, Singers

Scene 4

"What Do You Think I Am?"
J. Allyson, K. Bowers, Chorus
The Acrobats: B. Harrell, G. Johnson.

Scene 7

"Just a Little Joint With a Juke Box"
N. Walker, K. Bowers

Scene 8

"Where Do You Travel?"
M. May, M. Cannon, B. A. Nyman, Singers
Danced by B. A. Nyman, Dancers.

"Everytime" (reprise)
R. Lane

"I'd Gladly Trade"
R. Lane, Entire Comnpany

VIVA O'BRIEN

1941.07

An Aquamusical (Musical Comedy) in Two Acts, 14 Scenes. Book by William K. and Eleanor Wells. Lyrics by Raymond Leveen. Music by Marie Grever. Directed by Robert Milton. Settings by Clark Robinson. Comedy scenes directed by William K. Wells. Dances by Chester Hale. Costumes by John N. Booth, Jr. Orchestral arrangements by Charles L. Cook and staff. Vocal arrangements by Leonard De Paur. Produced by John J. Hickey, Chester Hale and Clark Robinson. Opened 9 October 1941 at the Majestic Theatre and closed 25 October 1941 after 20 performances.

CAST (in order of speaking): *Jeeves*: Cyril Smith. *Emilio Morales*: MILTON WATSON. *Betty Dayton*: Ruth Clayton. *Manuel Estrada*: Roberto Bernardi. *Lupita Estrada*: VICTORIA CORDOVA. *Tom*: HAROLD DIAMOND. *Dick*: HUGH DIAMOND. *Harry*: TOM DIAMOND. *J. Foster Adams*: Edgar Mason. *Professor Sherwood*: JOHN (LESLIE) CHERRY. *Mrs. Sherwood*: Ann Dere. *Señor Estrada*: Adelina Roatina. *Pedro Gonzales*: GIL GALVAN. *Don José O'Brien*: RUSS BROWN. *Carol Sherwood*: MARIE NASH. *Gateman*: Hugh Diamond. *Maria*: Mara Lopez. *Dolores*: Tanya Knight. *Ramon*: Rudy Williams. *Juan*: Joe Frederic. *Native Carrier*: PETER DESJARDINS. *Zambrano*: James Phillips. *Boatman*: Joe Frederic. *Vicente, a Matador*: GIL GALVAN. *Rani*: Tony (Oswald) Labriola. *Ship's First Officer*: Cyril Smith. *Secretary of Mexican Consulate*: Terry La Franconi. *The Divers*: Peter Desjardins, Ray Twardy, Betty O'Rourke.

Male Singers: Terry La Franconi, Fred Kuhnly, Michael Singer, Frank E. Stafford. *The Four Grand Quartette*: Carter Ferris, Joe Frederic, Jack Leslie, Rudy Williams. *The Senoritas*: Deena Clark, Helena Goudvis, Diana Johnstone, Athalia Ponsell. *Ballet*: Patty Barker, Ann Marie Barrie, Marilyn Brandberg, Marjorie Castle, Muriel Cole, Jill De Sio, Carol Estes, Jane Fears, Dolores Goodman, Helen Grayson, Betti Heart, Audrey Kent, Roberta Ogg, June Reynolds, Charlotte Sumner, Jean Van Buskirk, Betty Yaeger.

Act 1, Scene 1: Swimming Pool on the J. Foster Adams Estate, Miami Beach, Florida. *Scene 2*: Airport, Pan-American Airways, Miami. *Scene 3*: Interior of Airliner. *Scene 4*: South of the Border. *Scene 5*: La Casa De Estrada, Merida, Mexico. *Scene 6*: Edge of the Forest, Yucatan. *Scene 7*: The Sacred Pool.

Act 2, Scene 1: Street in Merida, Mexico. *Scene 2*: Edge of the Forest, Yucatan. *Scene 3*: The Floating Gardens of Xochimilco, Mexico. *Scene 4*: Plaza del Toros, Mexico City. *Scene 5*: Deck of a Cruise Ship. *Scene 6*: Walking the Plank. *Scene 7*: Swimming Pool on Adams Estate, Miami Beach.

ACT 1

"Mozambamba"
J. Cherry, R. Clayton, Girls

"Don José O'Brien"
R. Brown

"Mood of the Moment"
M. Nash, M. Watson, Girls, Four Grand Quartette

"Mood of the Moment" (reprise)
M. Nash, M. Watson

"Mexican Bad Men"
Harold Diamond, Hugh Diamond, T. Diamond

"Carinito"
V. Cordova, Ensemble

"Broken Hearted Romeo"
R. Brown

"Wrap Me in Your Sarape"
  M. Nash, M. Watson, Ensemble
"Mood of the Moment" (reprise)
  M. Watson
"Yucatana"
  R. Clayton, Four Grand Quartette
"Ritual Dance
  G. Galvan, M. Lopez, T. Knight
The Rain Ballet
  Ensemble

ACT 2
"Our Song"
  M. Nash, Senoritas, Ballet
"El Matador Terrifico"
  V. Cordova
"How Long?"
  M. Nash, M. Watson
Matador Dance
  G. Galvan, Ensemble
"To Prove My Love"
  R. Brown, V. Cordova
"To Prove My Love" (reprise)
  V. Cordova, R. Brown
The Sailors
  Harold Diamond, Hugh Diamond, T. Diamond
Finale
  Ensemble

1941.08   LET'S FACE IT

A Musical Comedy in Two Acts, 9 Scenes. Book by Herbert and Dorothy Fields. Based on the play "The Cradle Snatchers" by Russell Medcraft and Norma Mitchell. Music and lyrics by Cole Porter. Staged by Edgar MacGregor. Dances and ensembles by Charles Walters. Music directed by Max Meth. Settings by Harry Horner. Costumes by John Harkrider. Orchestral arrangements by Hans Spialek, Donald J. Walker, and Ted Royal[1]. Produced by Vinton Freedley[2]. Opened 29 October 1941 at the Imperial Theatre, closing 18 July 1942 after 303 performances for a month's vacation; re-opened 17 August 1942 at the Imperial Theatre, and closed 20 March 1943 after 244 additional performances, for a total of 547 performances.

CAST (in order of appearance): *Madge Hall*: Marguerite Benton. *Helen Marcy*: Helene [Helena] Bliss. *Dorothy Crowthers*: Helen Devlin. *Anna*: Kalita Humphreys. *Winnie Potter*: MARY JANE WALSH. *Mrs. Fink*: Lois Bolton. *Mrs. Wigglesworth*: Margie Evans. *Another Maid*: Sally Bond. *Maggie Watson*: EVE ARDEN. *Julian Watson*: JOSEPH MACAULAY. *Nancy Collister*: VIVIAN VANCE. *George Collister*: James Todd. *Cornelia Abigail Pigeon*: EDITH MEISER. *Judge Henry Clay Pigeon*: FRED IRVING LEWIS. *Molly Wincor*: Marion Harvey. *Margaret Howard*: Beverly Whitney. *Ann Todd*: Jane Ball. *Phillip*, a selectee: Henry Austin. *Jules*, another selectee: Tony Caridi. *Eddie Hilliard*: JACK WILLIAMS. *Frankie Burns*: BENNY BAKER. *Muriel McGillicuddy*: SUNNIE O'DEA. *Jean Blanchard*: NANETTE FABRAY. *Lieutenant Wiggins*: Houston Richards. *Jerry Walker*: DANNY KAYE. *Gloria Gunther*, a hostess at Service Club: Betty Moran. *Sigana Earle*: Miriam Franklin. *Master of Ceremonies*: William Lilling. *Private Walsh*: Fred Nay. *Dance Team*: MARY PARKER, BILLY DANIEL. *Mrs. Wiggins*: Kalita Humphreys.
Royal Guards: TOMMY GLEASON, Ollie West, Roy Russell, Ricki Tanzi, Henry Austin, Toni Caridi. *Vocalists*: Marguerite Benton, Helene Bliss, Janice Joyce, Beverly Whitney, Lisa Rutherford, Frances Williams. *Guests*: Billie Dee, Mary Ann Parker, Sally Bond, Jane Ball, Peggy Carroll, Sondra Barrett, Jean Scott, Jean Trybom, Marilynn Randels, Marion Harvey, Miriam Franklin, Peggy Littlejohn, Pat Likely, Zynaid Spencer, Renee Russell, Pamela Clifford, Edith Turgell. *Selectees*: Garry Davis, George Florence, Fred Deming, Dale Priest, Mickey Moore, Jack Riley, Joel Friend, Fred Nay, Frank Ghegan, Randolph Hughes.

Act 1, Scene 1: The Alicia Allen Milk Farm on Long Island. *Scene 2*: The Service Club at Camp Roosevelt, L.I. *Scene 3*: A part of the Parade Grounds at Cap Roosevelt. *Scene 4*: Mrs. Watson's Summer Home at Southampton, Long Island.

Act 2, Scene 1: Mrs. Watson's Home. *Scene 2*: The Boathouse of Hollyhock Inn. *Scene 3*: The Hollyhock Inn Gardens. *Scene 4*: Exterior of the Inn. *Scene 5*: The Service Club at Camp Roosevelt.

ACT 1
"Milk, Milk, Milk"
  Guests at Milk Farm
"A Lady Needs a Rest"
  E. Arden, V. Vance, E. Meiser
"Jerry, My Soldier Boy"
  M. J. Walsh, Guests
"Let's Face It"
  T. Gleason, the Royal Guards
"Farming"
  D. Kaye, B. Baker, J. Williams, S. O'Dea, N. Fabray, Ensemble
"Ev'rything I Love"
  D. Kaye, M. J. Walsh
"Ace in the Hole"
  M. J. Walsh, S. O'Dea, N. Fabray, Ensemble
"You Irritate Me So"
  N. Fabray, J. Williams
"Baby Games"
  D. Kaye, E. Arden, B. Baker, E. Meiser, V. Vance, J. Williams
"A Fairy Tale"[3]
  D. Kaye
  (*Music and Lyrics by* Sylvia Fine and Max Liebman.)
"Rub Your Lamp"
  M. J. Walsh, Ensemble
"Cuttin' a Rug"(Specialty Dance)
  M. Parker, B. Daniel

ACT 2
"I've Got Some Unfinished Business With You"
  M. J. Walsh, N. Fabray, S. O'Dea, H. Devlin, B. Moran, J. Macaulay, J. Todd, F. I. Lewis.
"Let's Not Talk About Love"
  D. Kaye, E. Arden
"A Little Rumba Numba"
  T. Gleason, M. Benton, the Royal Guards
Specialty Dance
  M. Parker, B. Daniel
"I Hate You, Darling"
  V. Vance, J. Todd, M. J. Walsh, D. Kaye
"Melody in Four F"[4]
  D. Kaye
  (*Music and Lyrics by* Sylvia Fine and Max Liebman.)
Finale
  Entire Company

1941.09   HIGH KICKERS

A Musical Comedy in Two Acts, a Prologue and 17 Scenes. Book by George Jessel, Bert Kalmar and Harry Ruby from a suggestion by Sid Silvers. Music and lyrics by Bert Kalmar and Harry Ruby. Book directed by Edward Sobel. Dances by Carl Randall. Music directed by Val Ernie. Entire production (costumes, sets, lights) designed, created and supervised by Nat Karson. Produced by Alfred Bloomingdale (and George Jessel). Opened 31 October 1941 at the Broadhurst Theatre and closed 28 March 1942 after 171 performances.

CAST: *In the Prologue: The Candy Spieler*: Billy Vine. *High Kickers Chorus*: Themselves. *Two American Showgirls*: Joyce Mathews, Rose Teed. *Schultz*: JOE MARKS. *George M. Krause, Sr.* , Kelly: GEORGE JESSEL. *Sophia*: Mary Marlow. *The Doctor*: Rollin Bauer. *George M. Krause, Jr.*: Dick Monahan. *The Stylish Four*: Bob Shaw, Bob Bay, Harold Young, Victor Griffin. *Mamie*: BETTY BRUCE.
In the Play: Sophie Tucker: Herself (SOPHIE TUCKER). *George M. Krause, Jr.*: GEORGE JESSEL. *S. Kaufman Hart*: Jack Mann. *Kitty McKay*: LOIS JANUARY.

---

[1]Vocal arrangements for "Ace in the Hole," "A Lady Needs a Rest," "Ev'rything I Love" by Lyn Murray and Carley Mills. Vocal arrangements for the Royal Guards by Miss Edna Fox.
[2]Program note: Mr. Freedley acknowledges his indebtedness to Ed Forman for his helpful suggestions.

[3]After Danny Kaye left the show and was replaced by José Ferrer, "A Fairy Tale" was dropped.
[4]After Danny Kaye left the show and was replaced by José Ferrer, "Melody in Four F" was dropped, and replaced by "It Aint Etiquette" (from DUBARRY WAS A LADY) .

Jimmy Wilberforce: LEE SULLIVAN. *Frank Whipple*: Franklyn Fox. *Mayor John Wilberforce*: Chick York. *Hortense Wilberforce*: Rose King. *Chief of Police*: Jack Howard. *Betty*: BETTY BRUCE. *Stuart Morgan Dancers*: Themselves. *Betty Jane*: Betty Jane Smith. *The Pianist*: Ted Shapiro. *A Stage Hand*: Chaz Chase.

Showgirls: Sunny Ainsworth, Barbara Brewster, Gloria Brewster, Lucille Casey, Bonita Edwards, Eleanor Hall, Joyce Mathews, Betty Stewart, Rose Teed. *Dancing Girls*: Jean Anthony, Helen Barrie, Stephanie Cekan, Marilyn Hale, Frances Hammond, Ann Helm, Ellen Howard, Marjorie Jackson, Dorothy Jeffers, Mary-Robin Marlow, Ray McGregor, Bobby Prieser, Helen Spruill, Marion Warnes. *Boys*: Bob Bay, Bob Shaw, Harry Mack, Victor Griffin, Harold Young, Donald Weissmuller.

Act 1, Scene 1: Inside Piners Burlesque Theatre — Year 1910. *Scene 2*: The High Kickers in Paris. *Scene 3*: A Dressing Room in the Cellar. *Scene 4*: Dancing Time Away. *Scene 5*: Stage Door of a Theatre in Chambersville, U.S.A. — Year 1941. *Scene 6*: Backstage. *Scene 7*: The Opening Night. *Scene 8*: In Panama. *Scene 9*: Sophie Tucker's Dressing Room. *Scene 10*: The Strip.

Act 2, Scene 1: Courtroom in Chamberville. *Scene 2*: On the Street Outside the Court. *Scene 3*: Hotel Lobby. *Scene 4*: Boudoir of Mrs. Wilberforce. *Scene 5*: Specialty — Chaz Chase. *Scene 6*: Outside the Mayor's Estate. *Scene 7*: In the Garden.

ACT 1

Opening Chorus
"My Sweetheart Mamie"
B. Bruce, Quartette
"Didn't Your Mother Tell You Nothing"
S. Tucker
"You're on My Mind"
L. January, L. Sullivan
"Army and Navy Song" (Specialty)
S. Tucker
(*Music and Lyrics by* Jack Yellen.)
Opening Chorus
Specialty
G. Jessel
"Panic in Panama"
L. January, B. Bruce, Ensemble
Strip

ACT 2
"The Girls"
B. Bruce
"Memories"
G. Jessel
"Time to Sing"
L. January, L. Sullivan, D. Weissmuller, Ensemble
"I Got Something"
S. Tucker
"Cigarettes"
B. Bruce, Ensemble
"Waltzing in the Moonlight"
L. January, L. Sullivan, Ensemble
Stuart Morgan Dancers[5]
"Some of These Days"
S. Tucker
(*Music and Lyrics by* Shelton Brooks.)
Bits of What You've Heard (Finale)
Entire Company

1941.10 LA VIE PARISIENNE

A Revival of the Comic Opera in Three Acts, 4 Scenes[6]. Music by Jacques Offenbach. New English book by Felix Brentano and Louis Verneuil after the French original by Henri Meilhac and Ludovic Halévy. New lyrics by Marion Farquhar. Directed by Felix Brentano. Choreography by Igor Schwezoff. Settings and costumes designed by Marco Montedoro. Conductor, Antal Dorati. Chorus master, Herbert Winkler. Produced by the New Opera Company. Opened 5 November 1941 at the 44th Street Theatre and closed 11 November 1941 after 7 performances in repertory.

CAST: *Comte Raoul de Gardefeu*, a rich nobleman (also *Pompa de Mataodres*): RALPH MAGELSSEN. *Baron Bobinet*, his friend: JOHN TYERS. *Metella*, famous opera singer: CAROLINA SEGRERA. *Mr. Hutchinson*, an American millionaire: CLIFFORD NEWDAHL. *Evelyn*, his daughter: RUBY MERCER. *Jackson*, trainer of Mr. Hutchinson's race horses: GEORGE RASELY. *Gabrielle*, a modiste: ANN LIPTON. *Gontran*, a man about town: Hugh Thompson. *Georges*, head of the Dubois Theatrical Agency: Norman Roland. *Gaston*, employee of the Dubois Agency: Leon Lischiner. *Alphonse*, Gardefeu's butler: Paul Best. *Dancing Master*: Igor Schwezoff. *Railroad employees, travelers, tradespeople, servants, waiters, guests at the Café Anglais, etc.*:

Chorus: Vivian Bower, Louise Fearney, Marie Fox, Josephine Griffin, Meta Hartog, Marion Ross, Dorothy Starner, Dorothy Hartigan, Mary David, Dean Mundy, Alice Philipp, Margaret Ormos, Anna Steck, Carol York, Cynthia Rose, Mary McKenna, Virginia Syms. Sam Adams, Hans Gareis, Hans Kuhn, Nathaniel Sprinzena, Elton Plowman, Eric Rautens, Franc Alden, Bertram Briess, John Reiff, Roneo Rim, Boris Voronovsky, Ludlow White, Anthony Scott, Leland Goodwin. *Ballet*: Maria Azrova, Phyllis Le Gassie, Julia Horvath, Sonia Orlova, Serge Ismailoff, Remington Olmsted, Miriam Oreck, George Grant, Angelo Rovida, Joan Schille, Edwina Seaver, Gemze de Lappe, Jack Abbott, Arlene Garver, Betty Nitsch.

The action takes place in Paris in the spring of 1866.

Act 1: Entrance hall of the Gare Saint-Lazare between 4 and 5 P.M.

Act 2, Scene 1: Salon at Gardefeu's house, in late afternoon. Three days later. *Scene 2*: "Grande Seize," the famous private banquet room at the fashionable "Cafe Anglais," the following evening.

Act 3: Later the same night at Gardefeu's Salon.

ACT 1[7]
Train Arrival (Porter! Yes, sir! Porter! Here, sir!)
Chorus
Train Arrival (reprise)
J. Tyers, R. Magelssen, C. Segrera, H. Thompson, Chorus
Metella's Entrance (But why? Wait a moment please)
C. Segrera
Duet (Fighting with you on any ground)
J. Tyers, R. Magelssen
Jackson's Song (But for women my life would be sweeter than honey)
G. Rasely, Chorus
Trio (All her monuments and treasures)
R. Magelssen, C. Newdahl, R. Mercer
Finale (From the train, with its visitors)
R. Magelssen, Chorus

ACT 2
Scene 1
Duet (Do you come from America?)
G. Rasely, A. Lipton
Evelyn's Aria ("The Heart of Every Girl")
R. Mercer
Ensemble (Then you are sure you'll play the game)
R. Magelssen, G. Rasely, A. Lipton, Tradespeople
Metella's Aria (My dear do you remember)
C. Segrera
Finale, Scene 1 (Here we come! Our thirst is pernicious)
R. Magelssen, A. Lipton, C. Newdahl, Tradespeople
Scene 2
Bobinet's Serenade (A dreaming world is waiting)
J. Tyers
Gabrielle's Song (She sallies out, she runs about)
A. Lipton, C. Newdahl, Girls
Hutchinson's Song (To the ladies of Paree)
C. Newdahl
Ensemble (Oh, his coat! The back is torn in two)
C. Segrera, G. Rasely, C. Newdahl, A. Lipton, J. Tyers, Chorus
Finale, Scene 2 (Hurrah! Hurrah!)
A. Lipton, C. Newdahl, C. Segrera, J. Tyers, Chorus

ACT 3
Gardefeu's Aria (Oh you were a picture of loveliness)
R. Magelssen

---

[5]Acrobatic dance specialty in which three husky men toss a little girl.
[6]First presented in New York in English 18 March 1884 at the Bijou Theatre in a version (LA VIE) by H. B. Farnie for 50 performances.

[7]No individual musical numbers listed in program. Musical Numbers taken from production typescript and published libretto (Fred Rullman, Inc., New York, 1941).

Duet (My dear—let me explain!)
  R. Mercer, R. Magelssen
Finale (I am mellow)
  Entire Company
Solo (You have seen la vie, la vie Parisienne)
  C. Segrera

1941.11   SONS O' FUN

A Vaudeville Revue in Two Acts, a Prologue and 27 Scenes. Fun (sketches)
by Ole Olsen [John Siguard Olsen], Chic Johnson [Harold Ogden
Johnson]. Music and lyrics by Jack Yellen and Sam E. [Sammy] Fain.
Additional music and lyrics by Jay Levison [Livingston] and Ray Evans[8].
Staged and lighted by Edward Duryea Dowling. Entire production super-
vised by Harry Kaufman. Dances and ensemble directed by Robert Alton.
Settings by Raoul Penc du Bois. Additional fun by Hal Block. Orchestra
direction, John McManus. Vocal arrangements by Pembroke Davenport.
Orchestrations by Domenico Savino. Arrangements by Domenico Savino
and Charles C. Cooke. Produced by the Messrs. Shubert. Opened 1
December 1941 at the Winter Garden, moved to the 46th Street Theatre 29
March 1943, and closed 9 August 1943 after 742 performances.

CAST: OLE OLSEN, CHIC JOHNSON, CARMEN MIRANDA, ELLA LOGAN,
FRANK LIBUSE, JOE BESSER, ROSARIO (Perez) & ANTONIO (Ruiz), THE
PITCHMEN (Al Ganz, Al Meyers). LIONEL KAYE, (Paul) WALTON & (Michael)
O'ROURKE, VALENTINOFF, MARGOT BRANDER, James Little, Ben Beri, Kitty
Murray, Ivan Kirov, Vilma Josey, Stanley Ross, Milton Charleston, Richard Craig,
Martha Rawlins, Catherine Johnson, Eddie Davis, (William) Moran & (Al) Wiser
[Weiser], Parker & Porthole, Carter & Bowie, The Statler Twins (Jane, Jean), The
Mullen Twins, The Crystal Twins, The Blackburn Twins (Royce, Ramon), H. Magna
& Sprenger. *The Biltmorettes*: Edna Isenburg, Joan Baker, Beverly Sweet.
  Ensemble: Joan Baker, Trudy Burke, Ronda Dale, Shannon Dean, Georgia Francis,
Margaret Gairaud, Amelia Gentry, Barbara Hull, Gloria Koster, Kay Lazell, Joan
Martin, Virginia McCurdy, Jean Moorehead, Carol Murphy, Olive Nicholson,
Eleanor Parr, Eileen Shirley, Diane Sinclair, Winifred Seeley. Al Anthony, Tony
Barrett, Phil Clavedetscher, William Hawley, Henning Irgens, Jack McClendon, Peter
Nielson, Albert Ruiz, Carl Trees.

BEFORE THE SHOW
  Fun on the Stage—Olsen & Johnson's Fun House
    Cast: The Audience.
  Fun in the Audience
    Head Usher: F. Libuse.
  Fun in the Orchestra Pit—The Simp-phony Orchestra
    Conductor: F. Libuse.

ACT 1
Scene 1
  "The Joke's On Us"
    (*Interpolated dance music by* Will Irwin.)
    Stagehands, Usherettes, Chorus Girls, Vendors: Girls, Boys. *Scrubladies*: D.
    Gautier, D. Tompkins, B. Evans. *The Attendants*: K. Murray, E. Davis.
Scene 2
  Those Sons O' Fun
    O. Olsen, C. Johnson
    With F. Libuse, J. Besser, J. Howes, G. Winchester, A. Meyers, A. Ganz, P.
    Walton, M. Rawlins, D. Gautier, B. Moran, J. Little, S. Renna, E. D'Amato, B.
    Evans, E. Parr, M. Charleston.
Scene 3
  "It's a New Kind of Thing"
    E. Logan
    Couple: D. Sinclair, I. Kirov. *Maid*: K. Murray. *Jivers*: G. Francis, Blackburn
    Twins, J. Moorehead, Ensemble.
Scene 4
  Fun in One—with Ole Olsen
    Bowler: J. Keno. *Lena*: C. Johnson. *Maestro*: F. Libuse.
Scene 5
  A Quiet Night in the Country—with Chic Johnson
    And O. Olsen, E. Logan, F. Libuse, J. Besser, J. Little
Scene 6
  More Fun in One
    O. Olsen, M. Charleston, J. Little, C. Johnson, H. Magna, H. Papajohn

---

[8]Livingston and Evans' songs are not identified in the program.

Scene 7
  The Olsen & Johnson Mystery Hour
Scene 8
  Meditation
    Divorcee: S. Dean. *Husband*: O. Olsen. *Dumbo*: C. Johnson.
Scene 9
  The Pitchmen—Al Ganz and Al Meyers, featuring the Sing-a-tina.
Scene 10
  Induction Center
    Captain: O. Olsen. *Sergeant*: J. Little. *Navy Man*: M. Charleston. *Volunteer*: D.
    Tompkins. *Conscientious Objector*: C. Johnson. *Army Hostess*: E. Shirley.
    Rookie: J. Besser.
Scene 11
  "Happy in Love"
    E. Logan
    With The Blackburn Twins, The Crystal Twins, The Mullen Twins, The Statler
    Twins, D. Sinclair, I. Kirov, S. Dean, Valentinoff, K. Murray, E. Davis, Magna
    & Sprenger, Dancing Girls and Boys.
Scene 12
  Moment Musicale
    At the Baby Grand: F. Libuse. *Soloist*: M. Brander. *Valet*: E. D'Amato.
Scene 13
  Some More Fun in One
    O. Olsen, M. Charleston, J. Little, J. Keno, J. Besser, V. McCurdy, C. Johnston,
    G. Crystal
Scene 14
  Porthole and Poopdeck
    Porthole: A Dummy. *Poopdeck*: C. Johnson. *The Master Mind*: O. Olsen.
Scene 15
  "Thank You, South America"
    Hattie: E. Logan. *Little Girl*: H. Magna. *The Dancer*: Valentinoff. *Los
    Chavalillos*: Rosario and Antonio.
Scene 16
  "Thank You, North America"[9]
    C. Miranda, Her Caballeros da Lua
    (*Dance music by* Will Irwin.)
INTERMISSION
    Call Boy: F. Libuse. *Artists, Indians, F.B.I. Men. Piano Duet*: F. Carter, A.
    Bowie.

ACT 2
Scene 1
  "It's a Mighty Fine Country We Have Here"
    Sheriff: E. Logan. *LittleNell*: D. Sinclair. *Her Maw and Paw*: W. Seeley, D.
    Gautier. *Two Bandits*: Valentinoff, I. Kirov. *Madame la Rue*: S. Dean.
Scene 2
  Hellzapoppin' Night in Buckeye, Arizona
    Deadeye Dick: C. Johnson. *Gentleman Jim*: O. Olsen. *Mexican Pete*: S. Renna.
    Cowboy Joe: J. Besser. *Black Mike*: M. Charleston. *Prospectors*: Moran and
    Weiser. *An Admiral*: D. Tompkins. *Bartender*: J. Little.
Scene 3
  "Hi-Ho, The Hoe-Down Way"
    (*Lyrics by* Irving Kahal.)
    Every Man for Himself.
Scene 4
  Lena
    C. Johnson
Scene 5
  Walton & O'Rourke (puppet act)
Scene 6
  "Manuelo"
    C. Miranda, Her Caballeros da Lua
    (*Lyrics by* Irving Kahal.)
    Scene: A Cockfight, the Canary Islands. *Gypsies*: Rosario and Antonio. *Fighters*:
    Valentinoff (The Vanquished), Ivan Kirov (The Victor), Entire Ensemble.

---

[9]After Carmen Miranda departed the cast, Rosario and Antonio took over
the Act 1 closing spot with "Los Chavalillos" (Gypsy Dance), "Malaguena"
and "La Cancion de la Flores" (Love at First Sight) composed by Sylvio
Masciarelli.

Scene 7
  "Tete à Tete"
    C. Miranda, O. Olsen, C. Johnson
Scene 8
  Those Umbrella Men
    F. Libuse, J. Besser
Scene 9
  Fun in Bed—with Olsen & Johnson
Scene 10
  Olsen & Johnson's Surprise Party
    The Daffy Auctioneer: L. Kaye.
Scene 11
  "Let's Say Goodnight with a Dance" (Finale)
    R. Craig, T. Burke
    Danced by Valentinoff, J. Moorehead.

1941.12   SUNNY RIVER

A Musical in Two Acts, 8 Scenes. Book and lyrics by Oscar Hammersein II. Music by Sigmund Romberg. Book staged by Oscar Hammerstein II. Dances by Carl Randall. Settings by Stewart Chaney. Costumes by Irene Sharaff. Musical conductor, Jacob Schwartzdorf [Jay Blackton]. Production supervised by John Murray Anderson. Produced by Max Gordon. Opened 4 December 1941 at the St. James Theatre and closed 3 January 1942 after 36 performances.

<u>CAST</u> (in order of appearance): *Children:* Carol Renee, Joan Shepherd, Edwin Bruce Moldow. *Old Henry:* Richard Huey. *Aristide:* Oscar Polk. *Gabriel Gervais:* Ainsworth Arnold. *Mother Gervais:* Ivy Scott. *Jean Gervais:* BOB LAWRENCE. *Jim:* Donald Clark. *Harry:* George Holmes. *Emil:* Gordon Dilworth. *Emma:* Vicki Charles. *Lolita:* ETHEL LEVEY. *George Marshall:* Dudley Clements. *Judge Pope Martineau:* Frederic Persson. *Marie Sauvinet:* MURIEL ANGELUS. *Daniel Marshall:* TOM EWELL. *Cecilie Marshall:* HELEN CLAIRE. *Madeleine Caresse:* Joan Roberts. *Martha:* Peggy Alexander. *Harlequin:* Jack Riano. *Columbine:* Miriam LaVelle. *Achille Caresse:* WILLIAM O'NEAL. *The Drunk:* Howard Freeman. *The Doctor:* Kenneth Tobey.
  Ensemble: Barbara Barton, Henni Brooks, Betty Gilpatrick, Lodema Legg, Gwen Mann, Ann Morlowe, Helen Marshall, Mariquita Moll, May Muth, Ethel Taylor, Stephanie Turash, Helen Wagner. James Allison, Jay Amiss, Russ Anderson, Alfredo Costello, Edward Dunbar, William Hearne, William Hogue, Philip Jones, John Marshall, Byron Milligan, Robert Ormiston, Fred Perrone, Michael Sigel, Roy Williams, Buddy Worth.

Pictorial Overture: Levee Street, New Orleans. Late afternoon, 1806.

Act 1, Scene 1: Patio of the Café des Oleandres. That evening. *Scene 2:* Upstairs Sitting Room in the home of M. and Mme. Jean Gervais. 1811. *Scene 3:* Jean's Dressing Room. Immediately after. *Scene 4:* Reception hall in Gervais home. Midnight, the same day.

Act 2, Scene 1: Patio of the Café des Oleandres. One o'clock, next morning. *Scene 2:* Levee Street. An hour later. *Scene 3:* Patio of the Café des Oleandres. An afternoon in 1815.

PICTORIAL OVERTURE
  "Symphonic Pantomime"
    Ensemble
  "My Girl and I"
    B. Lawrence

ACT 1
  "Call It a Dream"
    M. Angelus, Ensemble
  "It Can Happen to Anyone"
    M. Angelus, Ensemble
  "The Butterflies and Bees"
    T. Ewell, V, Charles, E. Levey, D. Clements, F. Persson
  "Along the Winding Road"
    M. Angelus, B. Lawrence
  Finaletto
    M. Angelus, E. Levey, T. Ewell, V. Charles, Ensemble
  Interlude
  "Bundling"
    T. Ewell
  "Along the Winding Road"
    B. Lawrence
  "Can You Sing?"
    M. Angelus, Ensemble

  "Making Conversation"
    M. Angelus, H. Claire, Ensemble
  "The Butterflies and the Bees" (reprise)
    T. Ewell, J. Roberts
  "Let Me Live Today"
    M. Angelus, B. Lawrence, Ensemble

ACT 2
  "Bow-Legged Sal"
    Ensemble
  "Sunny River"
    E. Levey, Ensemble
  "Call It a Dream" (reprise)
    M. Angelus, Ensemble
  "The Duello"
    W. O'Neal, T. Ewell
  "She Got Him"
    J. Roberts, V. Charles, W. O'Neal, T. Ewell, Ensemble
  "My Girl and I" (reprise)
    B. Lawrence
  "Time Is Standing Still"
    M. Angelus, B. Lawrence
  "Let Me Live Today" (reprise)
    B. Lawrence, M. Angelus, Male Ensemble
  Finaletto
    B. Lawrence, H. Freeman
  Finale Ultimo
    M. Angelus, H. Claire, E. Levey

1941.13   BANJO EYES

A Musical Comedy in Two Acts, 12 Scenes. Book by Joe Quillan and Izzy Elinson. Based on the play "Three Men on a Horse" by John Cecil Holm and George Abbott. Music by Vernon Duke. Lyrics by John Latouche. Additional lyrics by Harold Adamson. Staged and lighted by Hassard Short. Book directed by Albert Lewis. Dances by Charles Walters. Settings by Harry Horner. Costumes and gowns by Irene Sharaff. Orchestra directed by Ray Sinatra. Orchestrations supervised by Domenico Savino. (Musical) Arrangements by Domenico Savino, Charles L. Cooke and staff. Vocal arrangements by Buck [Clay] Warnick. All musical sequences staged by Hassard Short. The DeMarcos' arrangements by Alan Moran. Produced by Albert Lewis. Opened 25 December 1941 at the Hollywood Theatre and closed 12 April 1942 after 126 performances.

<u>CAST</u> (in order of appearance): *Miss Clark:* Jacqueline Susann. *Mr. Carver:* E. J. Blunkall. *Erwin Trowbridge:* EDDIE CANTOR. *Sally Trowbridge:* JUNE CLYDE. *Harry, the Bartender:* Richard Rober. *Charlie:* Bill Johnson. *Ginger:* Virginia Mayo. *The DeMarcos:* TONY and SALLY DeMARCO. *Patsy:* LIONEL STANDER. *Frankie:* RAY MAYER. *Mabel:* AUDREY CHRISTIE. *Tommy:* Tommy Wonder. *The General:* John Ervin. *The Captain:* James Farrell. *The Filly:* Ronnie Cunningham. *"Banjo Eyes":* Mayo and Morton. *The Quartette:* George Richmond, Phil Shafer, Doug Hawkins, George Lovesee. And Mayo, Morton and Virginia; Lynn, Royce and Vanya; Gloria Gilbert.
  Singing Show Girls: Ann Graham, Linda Griffeth, Adele Jurgens, Doris Kent, Florence Foster, Miriam Gwinn, Helene Hudson, Sherry Shadburne, Shirl Thomas. *Dancing Girls:* Betty Boyce, Norma Brown, Pamela Clifford, Kay Coulter, Doris Dowling, Kate Friedlich, Peggy Holmes, Mitzi Haynes, Leona Olsen, June Reynolds, Tina Rigat, Puddy Smith, Margie Young, Mimi Walthers, Evelyn Weiss, Audrey Westphal, Virginia Howe. *Boys:* Ray Arnett, Clark Eggleston, Arthur Grahl, Ray Harrison, Dick Irving, Ray Johnson, Rayford Malone, Jack Nagle, Remi Martell, John McCord, Bill Skipper, Ray Weamer, Carl Eberle, Lynn Malone, Joseph Malvin.

Act 1, Scene 1: The Display Salon of Carver Greeting Card Co. *Scene 2:* The Bar in a Midtown Hotel. *Scene 3:* Mabel's Room, in the same hotel. *Scene 4:* The Dream Pastures. *Scene 5:* Mabel's Room.

Act 2, Scene 1: The Bar. *Scene 2:* Erwin's Home, Jackson Heights. *Scene 3:* The Dream Pastures. *Scene 4:* Erwin's Home. *Scene 5:* Camp Dixon. *Scene 6:* The Clubhouse, Belmont Park. *Scene 7:* The Grandstand, Belmont Park.

ACT 1
  Opening
    E. J. Blunkall, Girls, Boys
  The Greeting Cards:
  "Birthday Card"
    H. Hudson, S. Shadburne, S. Thomas

"Valentine's Day Card"
B. Bailey

"Easter Greetings"
L. Giffith

"Merry Christmas"
Quartette

"Mother's Day"
F. Foster

"I'll Take the City"
E. Cantor, Boys, Girls

"The Toast of the Boys at the Post"
A. Christie, Quartette
(*Music and Lyrics by* George Sumner.)

"I've Got to Hand It to You"
B. Bailey, Dancers

"A Nickel to My Name"
B. Johnson, Quartette, Singing Girls

Dance
The De Marcos

"Who Started the Rhumba?"
E. Cantor, Mayo and Morton

Dance
R. Cunningham

"It Could Only Happen in the Movies"
E. Cantor, A. Christie
(*Lyrics by* Harold Adamson.)

ACT 2

Make With the Feet"
A. Christie, the De Marcos
(*Lyrics by* Harold Adamson.)

Dance
Lynn, Royce and Yanya

"We're Having a Baby (My Baby and Me)"
E. Cantor, J. Clyde
(*Lyrics by* Harold Adamson.)

"Banjo Eyes"
Ensemble

Dance
G. Gilbert

"The Yanks Are on the March Again"[10]
J. Farrell, Boys

"Not a Care in the World"
B. Johnson, Ensemble

Dance
The De Marcos

Eddie Cantor Medley
E. Cantor

Finale
Entire Company

"We Did It Before, (We'll Do It Again)"
E. Cantor, J. Farrell, Boys
(*Music by* Cliff Friend. *Lyrics by* Charles Tobias.)

1942.01 ## THE LADY COMES ACROSS

A Musical Comedy in Two Acts, 12 Scenes. Book by Fred Thompson and Dawn Powell. Music by Vernon Duke. Lyrics by John Latouche. Book directed by Romney Brent. Choreography by George Balanchine. Settings and costumes by Stewart Chaney. Musical director, Jacques Rabiroff. Orchestrations supervised by Domenico Savino. (Musical) Arrangements by Domenico Savino, Charles L. Cooke and staff. Production under the supervision of Morrie Ryskind. Produced by George Hale in association with Charles R. Rogers and Nelson Seabra[11]. Opened 9 January 1942 at the 44th Street Theatre and closed 10 January 1942 after 3 performances.

---

[10]Replaced during the run by:
"We Did It Before, (We'll Do It Again)
E. Cantor, J. Farrell, Boys
(*Music by* Cliff Friend. *Lyrics by* Charles Tobias.)
[11]Program note: Mr. Hale gratefully acknowledges the assistance of Edgar MacGregor and Charles Walters.

CAST (in order of appearance): *Jill Charters*: EVELYN WYCKOFF. *Tony Patterson*: RONALD GRAHAM. *Otis Kibber*: JOE E. LEWIS. *Elmer James*: Morton L. Stevens. *Mary*: Betty Douglas. *Alberto Zorel*: Stiano Braggiotti. *Four Shoppers*: THE MARTINS [Hugh Martin, Ralph Blane, Jo Jean Rogers, Phyllis Rogers]. *Mrs. Riverdale*: RUTH WESTON. *Campbell*: GOWER (Champion). *Kay*: JEANNE (Tyler). *Babs Appleway*: WYNN MURRAY. *Ernie Bustard*: MISCHA AUER. *Baroness Helstrom*: Helen Windsor. *Ballerina Comique*: Eugenia Delarova. *Ballerina*: Lubov Rostova. *The Phantom Lover*: Marc Platt. *Autograph Seekers, Reporters, Guests, etc.*

Models: Betty Douglas, Evelyn Carmel, Patricia Donnelly, Judith Ford, Dorothy Partington, Arline Harvey, Joan Smith, Drucilla Strain. *Dancing Ensemble*: Betty Apple, Mary Ann Crawford, Betty De Elmo, June Graham, Babs (Barbara) Heath, Phyllis Hill, Bettilu Ismailoff, Hortense Kharklin, Lorraine Latham, Edith Laumer, Claire Loring, Marian Lulling, Marjorie (Margery) Moore, Elise Reiman, Aleen Stuart, Olga Suarez, Dorothy Thomas. Clarence Jaeger, Joseph Johnson, Roy Marshall, Bob Norris, Harry Pedersen, Peter Kite Smith, Zachary Solov, Ken (Kenneth) Whelan.

Act 1, Scene 1: A Railroad Station. *Scene 2*: Jill's Room in a Hotel. *Scene 3*: The Blue Room at Chez Zoral. *Scene 4*: The Red Room at Chez Zorel. *Scene 5*: The Red Room.

Act 2, Scene 1: At Mrs. Riverdale's Estate. *Scene 2*: On Way to the Bathing Pavilion. *Scene 3*: Bathing Pavilion at Mrs. Riverdale's. *Scene 4*: After the Party. *Scene 5*: A Bedroom at Mrs. Riverdale's. *Scene 6*: The Garden Scene. *Scene 7*: A Railroad Station.

ACT 1

Scene 1
"Three Rousing Cheers"
Souvenir Hunters, Autograph Seekers, Reporters

Scene 2
"Feeling Lucky Today"
E. Wyckoff, J. E. Lewis

Scene 3
"Modes in Manhattan"
Models, Photographers

"You Took Me By Surprise"
E. Wyckoff, R. Graham, the Martins

"Hit the Ramp"
W. Murray, M. Auer, Ensemble

"February"
J. E. Lewis
(*Music and Lyrics by* Danny Shapiro, Jerry Seelen and Lester Lee.)

"Eenie Meenie Minee Mo"
M. Auer, W. Murray, J. E. Lewis, R. Weston

Scene 4
"Tango"
M. Auer, E. Delarova, Ensemble

"Tango" (reprise)
E. Wyckoff, J. E. Lewis, M. Auer, Ensemble

ACT 2

Scene 1
"Lady"
R. Graham, the Models, G. Champion, J. Tyler, Ensemble

"The Queen of the Opera"
R. Weston

"Coney Island Ballet"
E. Delarova, L. Rostova, M. Platt

Scene 2
"This Is Where I Came In"
W. Murray, G. Champion, J. Tyler

Scene 3
"You Can't Get the Merchandise"
J. E. Lewis
(*Music and Lyrics by* Danny Shapiro and Lester Lee.)

Scene 4
"Summer Is a Comin' In"
The Martins, Ensemble

Scene 5
"Daybreak"
E. Wyckoff, M. Platt

Scene 6
(reprise)

H.M.S. PINAFORE,
or The Lass That Loved a Sailor

1942.02

A Revival of the Comic Opera in Two Acts[12], (preceded by 'The Green Table', a Dance Drama in 8 Scenes by Kurt Jooss, performed by the Jooss Ballet Dance Theatre). Libretto by William S. Gilbert. Music by Arthur Sullivan. Staged by R. H. Burnside. Musical director, Louis Kroll. Produced by the Boston Comic Opera Company (R. H. Burnside, Producing director). Opened 21 January 1942 at the St. James Theatre and closed 14 March 1942 after 18 performances in repertory[13].

CAST: *The Rt. Hon. Sir Joseph Porter, K.C.B.*, First Lord of the Admiralty: FLORENZ AMES. *Captain Corcoran*, Commanding the *H.M.S. Pinafore*: BERTRAM PEACOCK. *Ralph Rackstraw*, Able Seaman: MORTON BOWE. *Dick Deadeye*, Able Seaman: ROBERT PITKIN. *Bill Bobstay*, Bo'sun's Mate: Frederic Persson. *Bob Becket*, Carpenter's Mate: Edward Platt. *Tommy Tucker*, Midshipmate: Arthur Henderson. *Josephine*, the Captain's Daughter: KATHLEEN ROCHE. *Hebe*, Sir Joseph's First Cousin: Margaret Roy. *Little Buttercup*, a Portsmouth Bumboat Woman: HELEN LANVIN.

First Lord's Sisters, his Cousins, his Aunts: Beatrice Babush, Phyllis Blake, Mary Lou Bartholomew, Ruth Carrigan, Margaret Fischer, Sally Hadley, Lillian Konniver, Florence Keezel, Mary Lundon, Vera Muller, Edith Maison, Lillian Purdue, Doris Pantoplas, Rosylin Ross, Sylvia Singer, Marie Valdez, Natalie Winston, Victoria Mayer. *Sailors, Marines*: William Berman, William Burgess, Robert Curi, Joseph Dunkley, Allan Lowell, Joseph Monte, Edward Marsh, Anthony Pitre, Edward Platt, Morris Rohr, Otto Simanek, Larry Shindel, John Wheeler, Carl Wolf.

PORGY AND BESS

1942.03

A Revival of the Folk Opera in Three Acts, 9 Scenes[14]. Book by DuBose Heyward, adapted from the play "Porgy" by DuBose and Dorothy Heyward. Music by George Gershwin. Lyrics by DuBose Heyward and Ira Gershwin. Directed by Robert Ross. Chorus directed by Eva Jessye. Settings by Herbert Andrews. Costumes supervised by Paul du Pont. Conductor, Alexander Smallens. Produced by Cheryl Crawford in association with John J. Wildberg. Opened 22 January 1942 at the Majestic Theatre and closed 26 September 1942 after 286 performances.

CAST (in order of appearance): *Maria*: GEORGETTE HARVEY. *Lily*: Helen Dowdy. *Annie*: Catherine Ayers. *Clara*: HARRIET JACKSON. *Jake*: EDWARD MATTHEWS. *Sportin' Life*: AVON LONG. *Mingo*: Jimmy Waters. *Robbins*: Henry Davis. *Serena*: RUBY ELZY. *Jim*: Jack Carr. *Peter*: Robert Ecton. *Porgy*: TODD DUNCAN. *Crown*: WARREN COLEMAN. *Bess*: ANNE BROWN. *First Policeman*: John Demmigar. *Second Policeman*: Paul Du Pont. *Detective*: Gibbs Penrose. *Undertaker*: John Garth. *Frazier*: J. Rosamund Johnson. *Nelson*: William Bowers. *Strawberry Woman*: Helen Dowdy. *Crab Man*: William Woolfolk. *Coroner*: Al West.

Residents of Catfish Row, Fishermen, Children, Stevedores, etc.: THE EVA JESSYE CHOIR: Eva Jessye, Lillian Cowan, Gladys Goode, June Hawkins, Louisa Howard, Alma Hubbard, Rosalie King, Assota Marshall, Sadie McGill, Annabelle Ross, Musa Williams, John Diggs, Leslie Gray, Jerry Laws, Arthur MacLean, William McDaniel, William Smith, Charles Welch, Lawrence Whisonant.

Children: Harvey McGill, Granville Williams, Lorraine Williams, Rosalie King, Naida King, Patricia Rice, Osbert Chevers.

THE MIKADO,
or, The Town of Titipu

1942.04

A Revival of the Comic Opera in Two Acts[15], (preceded by the Jooss Ballet Theatre in a ballet program of "The Seven Heroes" and "A Ball in Old Vienna"). Libretto by William S. Gilbert. Music by Arthur Sullivan. Staged by R. H. Burnside. Musical director, Louis Kroll. Produced by Boston Opera Company (R. H. Burnside, Producing director). Opened 3 February 1942 at the St. James Theatre and closed 14 March 1942 after 19 performances in repertory.[16]

CAST: *The Mikado of Japan*: ROBERT PITKIN. *Nanki-Poo*, his son, disguised as a wandering minstrel in love with Yum-Yum: MORTON BOWE. *Ko-Ko*, Lord High Executioner of Titipu: FLORENZ AMES. *Pooh-Bah*, Lord High Everything Else: BERTRAM PEACOCK. *Pish-Tush*, Noble Lord: Frederic Persson. *Yum-Yum, Pitti-Sing, Peep-Bo*, three sisters, wards of Ko-Ko: KATHLEEN ROCHE, MARY ROCHE, MARGARET ROY. *Katisha*: HELEN LANVIN. *Chorus of School Girls, Nobles, Guards and Coolies*: Boston Opera Company Ensemble[17].

OF V WE SING

1942.05

A Musical Revue in Two Acts, 24 Scenes. (Sketches by Al Geto, Sam D. Locke, Mel Tolkin. Music by Alex North, George Kleinsinger, Ned Lehack [Lehak], Beau Bergersen, Lou Cooper, Toby Sacher. Lyrics by Alfred Hayes, Lewis Allen, Roslyn Harvey, Mike Stratton, Bea Goldsmith, Joe Barian, Arthur Zipser.) Staged by Perry Bruskin. Music directed by Lou Cooper. Dances directed by Susanne Remos. At the Two Pianos, Lou Cooper and Saul Davis. Drapes and curtains by Harry Schumer. Produced by American Youth Theatre in association with Alexander (H.) Cohen and Lennie Hatten. Opened 11 February 1942 at the Concert Theatre and closed 25 April 1942 after 76 performances[18].

CAST: PHIL LEEDS, BETTY GARRETT, CURT CONWAY, ADELE JEROME, LEE BARRIE, JOHN WYNN, BUDDY YARUS, ROBERT SHARRON, SUSANNE REMOS, DANIEL NAGRIN, PERRY BRUSKIN, ELEANOR BAGLEY, LETTY STEVER, Mary Titus, John Flemming, Connie Baxter, Ann Garlan, Byron Milligan.

ACT 1

Scene 1

"You Can't Fool the People"
    Entire Company
    (*Music by* George Kleinsinger. *Lyrics by* Alfred Hayes.
    Coda Lou Cooper.)

Scene 2

News Story
    P. Leeds, A. Jerome

Scene 3

NBC Goes to Broadcast (*by* Sam D. Locke)
    Announcer: C. Conway. *Monsieur Jacquelon*: P. Leeds. *Maid*:
    E. Bagley. *News Announcer*: R. Sharron. *Recruiting Officer*: B. Yarus.
    Mayor: P. Bruskin. *Mayor's Assistant*: L. Stever. *Second Announcer*:
    J. Wynn. *Trio*: B. Garrett, L. Barrie, A. Jerome. *Third Announcer*:
    D. Nagrin. *Kaltincuff*: J. Wynn.

Scene 4

"Sisters Under the Skin"
    L. Barrie, B. Garrett, A. Jerome
    (*Music by* Beau Bergersen. *Lyrics by* Sylvia Marks.)

Scene 5

Rhumba
    Danced by and choreographed by S. Remos, D. Nagrin

Scene 6

"Don't Sing Solo"
    B. Garrett
    (*Music by* George Kleinsinger. *Lyrics by* Roslyn Harvey.)

Scene 7

One Way Passage (*by* Sam Locke)
    Angel: P. Leeds. *Senator*: C. Conway.

---

[12]Originally presented in New York 15 January 1879 at the Standard Theatre for 175 performances. For Synopsis of Scenes and Musical Numbers, see original 1879 production.
[13]Settings, costumes, lighting uncredited.
[14]First produced in New York 10 October 1935 at the Alvin Theatre for 124 performances. For Synopsis of Scenes and Musical Numbers, see original 1935 production. According to Hollis Alpert in his volume "The Life and Times of Porgy and Bess" (Alfred A. Knopf, New York, 1990), Alexander Smallens reorchestrated the score for 27 musicians, down from the production's original 44. For this production, note the following program changes:
    Crap Game Fugue ("Roll Them Bones") restored to Act 1, Scene 1.
    "Where's My Bess?" no longer a trio, but a solo for T. Duncan (Porgy).

---

[15]First presented in New York 20 July, 10-29 August 1885 at the Union Square and People's Theatres for 22 performances. First authorized production presented 19 August 1885 at the Fifth Avenue Theatre by Richard D'Oyly Carte for 250 performances. For Synopsis of Scenes and Musical Numbers, see 19 August 1885 D'Oyly Carte production.
[16]Settings, costumes, lighting uncredited.
[17]For personnel detail see H.M.S. PINAFORE revival above, 21 January 1942.
[18]Previously produced as V FOR VICTORY, a semi-professional revue in September 1941 at the Malin Studio Theatre, New York.

Scene 8
"Red, White and Blues"
J. Fleming
(*Music and Lyrics by* Lewis Allan.)
Scene 9
Mother Love (*by* Mel Tolkin)
P. Leeds, B. Yarus
Scene 10
"Brooklyn (Baseball) Cantata" (from 'TIS OF THEE)
(*Music by* George Kleinsinger. *Lyrics by* Mike Stratton.)
Announcer: C. Conway. *Umpire*: P. Leeds. *Drunk*: J. Wynn. *Pinch Hitter*: B.
Yarus. *Girl Friend*: E. Bagley. And Company.
Scene 11
"Take a Poem"
R. Sharron
(*Music by* George Kleinsinger. *Poem by* Norman Corwin.)
Scene 12
"Victory Conga"
Entire Company
(*Music and Lyrics by* Mel Tolkin.)

ACT 2
Scene 1
"Priorities"
Entire Company
(*Music by* Lou Cooper. *Lyrics by* Roslyn Harvey.)
Scene 2
News Story (Again)
P. Leeds, A. Jerome
Scene 3
Ivan the Terrible (*by* Al Geto)
Technician: P. Bruskin. *Announcer*: J. Wynn. *Hitler*: P. Leeds. *Ivan*, off-stage
voice: B. Yarus.
Scene 4
"Queen Esther"
B. Garrett, Chorus
(*Music by* George Kleinsinger. *Lyrics by* Beatrice Goldsmith.)
Scene 5
Hy'a Joe (*by* Al Geto)
C. Conway, P. Leeds
Scene 6
"Gertie, the Stool Pigeon's Daughter"
E. Bagley
(*Music by* Ned Lehack [Lehak]. *Lyrics by* Joe Darion.)
Gertie: L. Stever. *Bartender*: C. Conway. And Company.
Scene 7
"You've Got to Appease With a Strip Tease"
P. Leeds, A. Jerome, L. Barrie
(*Music by* Toby Sacher. *Lyrics by* Lewis Allan.)
Scene 8
Belinda Blue (*by* Sam Locke)
Master of Ceremonies: C. Conway. *Movie Star*: B. Garrett. *Ushers*: R. Sharron,
B. Yarus. And Company.
Scene 9
"We Have a Date"
(*Music by* Lou Cooper. *Lyrics by* Roslyn Harvey.)
First Couple: D. Davis, N. Lawrence.
Second Couple: C. Baxter, R. Sharron.
Third Couple: L. Barrie, B. Yarus.
Scene 10
"Juke Box"
(*Music by* Alex North. *Lyrics by* Alfred Hayes.)
Hep Cat: P. Leeds. *Proprietor*: J. Fleming. *Waitress*: B. Garrett.
Dancers: S. Remos, D. Nagrin, A. Jerome, L. Barrie, B. Yarus, P. Bruskin,
J. Wynn.
Scene 11
Prologue to Finale
R. Sharon
(*Music by* Lou Cooper. *Poem*: Walt Whitman.)

Scene 12
"Of V We Sing"
Entire Company
(*Music by* Lou Cooper. *Lyrics by* Arthur Zipser.)

THE PIRATES OF PENZANCE,
1942.06 or, The Slave of Duty

A Revival of the Comic Opera in Two Acts[19], (preceded by the Jooss Ballet
Theatre in a ballet program "The Prodigal Son"). Libretto by William S.
Gilbert. Music by Arthur Sullivan. Staged by R. H. Burnside. Musical direc-
tor, Louis Kroll. Produced by Boston Opera Company (R. H. Burnside,
Producing director). Opened 17 February 1942 at the St. James Theatre and
closed 14 March 1942 after 11 performances in repertory.[20]

CAST: *The Pirate King*: BERTRAM PEACOCK. *Samuel*, his Lieutenant: Frederic
Persson. *Frederic*, the Pirate Apprentice: MORTON BOWE. *Major General Stanley*.
FLORENZ AMES. *Sergeant of Police*: ROBERT PITKIN. *Mabel, Edith, Kate, Isabel*,
General Stanley's Daughters: KATHLEEN ROCHE, MARY ROCHE, MARGARET
ROY, Marie Valdez. *Ruth*, Pirate Maid-of-all-work: HELEN LANVIN. *Chorus
of Pirates, Police and General Stanley's Daughters*: Boston Opera Company
Ensemble[21].

IOLANTHE,
1942.07 or, The Peer and the Peri

A Revival of the Comic Opera in Two Acts[22], (preceded by the Jooss Ballet
Theatre in a program of ballet.) Libretto by William S. Gilbert. Music by
Arthur Sullivan. Staged by R. H. Burnside. Musical director, Louis Kroll.
Produced by Boston Opera Company (R. H. Burnside, Producing director).
Opened 23 February 1942 at the St. James Theatre and closed 14 March
1942 after 5 performances in repertory.[23]

CAST: *The Lord Chancellor*: FLORENZ AMES. *Earl of Mountararat*: ROBERT
PITKIN. *Lord Tolloller*: MORTON BOWE. *Private Willis*, of the Grenadier Guards:
Frederic Persson. *Strephon*, an Arcadian Shepherd: PHILLIP TULLY. *Queen of the
Fairies*: HELEN LANVIN. *Iolanthe*, a Fairy, Strephon's Mother: MARGARET ROY.
Celia, Fleta, Fairies: Mary Roche, Marie Valdez. *Phyllis*, an Arcadian Shepherdess and
Ward in Chancery: KATHLEEN ROCHE. *Chorus of Dukes, Marquises, Earls,
Viscounts, Barons and Fairies*: Boston Opera Company Ensemble.[24]

1942.08 ## TRIAL BY JURY

A Revival of the Comic Opera in One Act[25], (preceded by the Jooss Ballet
Theatre in a program of ballet.) Libretto by William S. Gilbert. Music by
Arthur Sullivan. Staged by R. H. Burnside. Musical director, Louis Kroll.
Produced by Boston Opera Company (R. H. Burnside, Producing director).
Opened 28 February 1942 at the St. James Theatre and closed 14 March
1942 after 7 performances in repertory.[26]

CAST: *Judge*: FLORENZ AMES. *First Bridesmaid*: MARY ROCHE. *Counsel for the
Plaintiff*: BERTRAM PEACOCK. *The Defendant*: PHILLIP TULLY. *Foreman of the
Jury*: FREDERIC PERSSON. *Usher*: ROBERT PITKIN. *Chorus of Jurymen,
Bridesmaids and Public*: Boston Opera Company Ensemble[27].

---

[19]First presented in New York 31 December 1879 at the Fifth Avenue
Theatre for a total of 91 performances in two engagements. For Synopsis of
Scenes and Musical Numbers, see original 1879 production.
[20]Settings, costumes, lighting uncredited.
[21]For personnel detail see H.M.S. PINAFORE revival above, 21 January
1942.
[22]First presented in New York 25 November 1882 at the Standard Theatre
for 105 performances. For Synopsis of Scenes and Musical Numbers, see
original 1882 production.
[23]Settings, costumes, lighting uncredited.
[24]For personnel detail see H.M.S. PINAFORE revival above, 21 January
1942.
[25]First presented in New York 15 November 1875 at the Eagle Theatre for
8 performances. For Synopsis of Scenes and Musical Numbers, see original
1875 production.
[26]Settings, costumes uncredited.
[27]For personnel detail see H.M.S. PINAFORE revival above, 21 January
1942.

THE GONDOLIERS,
1942.09 or, The King of Barataria

A Revival of the Comic Opera in Two Acts[28]. (preceded by the Jooss Ballet Theatre in a program of ballet). Libretto by William S. Gilbert. Music by Arthur Sullivan. Staged by R. H. Burnside. Musical director, Louis Kroll. (Produced by Boston Opera Company (R. H. Burnside, Producing director). Opened 3 March 1942 at the St. James Theatre and closed 14 March 1942 after 3 performances in repertory.[29]

CAST: *The Duke of Plaza-Toro*, a Grandee of Spain: FLORENZ AMES. *Luiz*, his attendant: PHILLIP TULLY. *Don Alhambra Del Bolero*, The Grand Inquisitor: ROBERT PITKIN. *Marco Palmieri, Giuseppe Palmieri, Antonio, Francesco, Giorgio*, Venetian Gondoliers: MORTON BOWE, BERTRAM PEACOCK, Edward Platt, Lawrence Shindel, Frederic Persson. *The Duchess of Plaza Toro*: HELEN LANVIN. *Casilda*, Her Daughter: MARGARET ROY. *Gianetta, Tessa, Fiametta, Vittoria, Giulia*, Contadine: KATHLEEN ROCHE, MARY ROCHE, Marie Valdez, Phyllis Blake, Mary Lundon. *Inez*, The King's Foster-Mother: Florence Keezel. *Chorus of Gondoliers, Contadine, Men-at-Arms, Heralds and Pages*: Boston Opera Company Ensemble[30].

PRIORITIES OF 1942
1942.10

A Variety Revue in Two Acts, 14 Scenes. (Assembled by Clifford C. Fischer.) Ensemble Music and lyrics by Marjery Fielding and Charles Barnes. Choreography by Marjery Fielding. Music directed by Lou Forman. Produced by Clifford C. Fischer by arrangement with the Messrs. Shubert. Opened 12 March 1942 at the 46th Street Theatre and closed 6 September 1942 after 353 performances.[31]

CAST: LOU HOLTZ, WILLIE HOWARD, PHIL BAKER, PAUL DRAPER, JOAN MERRILL, HAZEL SCOTT, Helen Reynolds Skaters (8), The (Three) Nonchalants, The Barrys (Fred, Elaine), Gene Sheldon and Loretta Fischer, Diane Denise, Joe Morris, Johnny Masters and Rowena Rollins, Lari and Conchita , Beverly Lane. Al Kelly, Lora Saunders, Charles Senna, John Leopold, Calvin Jackson (Piano). *Versailles Beauties*: Hazel Baker, Michelle Magnin, Mary Lou Savage, Patricia Donnelly, Lillian O'Donnell, Margaret Lane, Sheila Herman, Trudy Byers, Lee Loprete, Sonia Tanya, Murnai Pins, Lorayne Lloyd, Helen Wenzel, Gail Hereford, Helen Beck, Aleita Albert, Lee Mayer, Joan Dare, Carol Gordon.

ACT 1

Scene 1

"Vaudeville Is Back"
Versailles Beauties

Scene 2

Helen Reynolds Skaters

Scene 3

The Nonchalants

Scene 4

Willie Howard, assisted by A. Kelly, L. Saunders, C. Senna, J. Leopold.

Scene 5

Joan Merrill:
["Blues in the Night" (from film of the same name)
(*Music by* Harold Arlen. *Lyrics by* Johnny Mercer.)]

Scene 6

Phil Baker, with Diane Denise.

Scene 7

Hazel Scott:
["Dark Eyes"
(*Music by* A. Salama.)
"Tea for Two" from NO, NO, NANETTE
(*Music by* Vincent Youmans. *Lyrics by* Irving Caesar.)]

Scene 8

Brazilian Rhythms
Lari and Conchita, D. Denise, Versailles Beauties

Scene 9

Lou Holtz (joined by Willie Howard, Phil Baker)

ACT 2

Scene 1

"I Waltzed With a Major"
Barrys, D. Denise, Versailles Beauties

Scene 2

Gene Sheldon and Loretta Fischer

Scene 3

Paul Draper, with Calvin Jackson at the Piano

Scene 4

Willie Howard, assisted by L. Saunders (Voice of Experience sketch)

Scene 5

Finale
Entire Company

JOHNNY 2 X 4
1942.11

A Novelty Melodrama in Three Acts, 4 Scenes. Play by Rowland Brown. Special material written by Frank Dolan. Staged by Anthony Brown. Choreography by Douglas Dean. Costumes designed by Rose Bogdanoff. Setting by Howard Bay. Music director, Merle Pitt. Produced by Rowland Brown. Opened 16 March 1942 at the Longacre Theatre and closed 9 May 1942 after 65 performances.

CAST (in order of their appearance): *Creepy*: Lester Lonergan, Jr. *Pete*: Lew Eckles. *Bottles*: YEHUDI WYNER. *Mike Maloney*: Ralph Chambers. *Johnny 2 X 4*: JACK ARTHUR. *THE YACHT CLUB BOYS*: Charles Adler, George Kelly, Rodney McLennan, Don Richards. *Coaly Lewis*: BARRY SULLIVAN. *Bettle-Puss*: Bert Reed. *Mary Collins*: EVELYN WYCKOFF. *Dutch*: Jack Lambert. *Martin*: Arthur L. Sachs. *Grandmother*: Ann Brodie. *Mabel*: HELEN HEIGH. *Knuckles Kelton*: HARRY BELAVER. *Butch*: MARIE AUSTIN. *Rudy Denton*: Douglas Dean. *Burns*: Sam Raskyn. *The B Girls*: Marianne O'Brien, Irene Collett, Josi Johnson, Muriel Cole. *Ohio Customer*: Eddie Hodges. *Midal*: BERT FROHMAN. *Apples*: LEONARD SUES. *Billy the Booster*: James La Curto. *Harry*, a waiter: Al Durant. *Cigarette Girl*: MONICA LEWIS. *Maxine*: Karen Van Ryn. *Dot*: Wilma Drake. *Jerry Sullivan*: Russel Conway. *Kean*: Thom Conroy.

Bakery Man, Meat Man, Bodyguards and Guests: John Harvey, Syl Lamont, Charles L. Douglass, Chester Adams, John Stark, Jack Parsons, William Sharon, Paul Clare, Victor Finney, Joseph Martel, James Falon, Stephen Morrow, Carmen Costi, Michel Spreder, William Forester, Eleanor Swayne, Carolyn Cromwell, Bea Barclay, Nancy Clark, Jordie McLean, Mary Martin[32], Eleanor Pryne, Ellwin Evans, Betty [Lauren] Bacall, Virginia Wyckoff, Maxine Sheppard, Ruth Maitland.

The Scenes of the play take place in the "Johnny 2 x 4" Club in Greenwich Village. *Time*: 1926-1936.

Act 1, Scene 1: Five o'clock in the afternoon. *Scene 2*: Later that night.

Act 2: The Lush Days.

Act 3: After Repeal.

ACT 1

Liszt's Tarantella (*Music by* Franz Liszt.)
Y. Wyner

"Close Your Eyes"
E. Wyckoff
(*Music and Lyrics by* Bernice Petkere.)

"Mother" (M-O-T-H-E-R, a Word That Means the World to Me)
J. Arthur
(*Music by* Theodore F. Morse. *Lyrics by* Howard Johnson.)

Chopin
Y. Wyner

"Ace in the Hole"
J. Arthur
(*Music and Lyrics by* George D. Mitchell and James E. Dempsey.)

"Down by the O-HI-O" (from ZIEGFELD FOLLIES OF 1920)
M. Austin
(*Music by* Abe Olman. *Lyrics by* Jack Yellen.)

"Solitude"
L. Sues
(*Music by* Duke Ellington. *Lyrics by* Eddie DeLange and Irving Mills.)

---

[28]Originally presented in New York 7 January 1890 at Park Theatre for 103 performances. For Synopsis of Scenes and Musical Numbers, see original 1890 production.
[29]Settings, costumes, lighting uncredited.
[30]For personnel detail see H.M.S. PINAFORE revival above, 21 January 1942.
[31]Performed twice daily, with three shows on Saturdays and Sundays. No credits for scenery or costumes.

---

[32]Not the same Mary Martin who first appeared in LEAVE IT TO ME.

"The Customer's Always Right"
  The Yacht Club Boys
"Deep Night"
  E. Wyckoff
  (*Music by* Charlie Henderson. *Lyrics by* Rudy Vallee.)

ACT 2

"(Between the) Devil and the Deep Blue Sea" (from
RHYTHMANIA)
  M. Lewis
  (*Music by* Harold Arlen. *Lyrics by* Ted Koehler.)
"It's Been a Whole Year"
  The Yacht Club Boys
"I Want a Girl (Just Like the Girl That Married Dear Old Dad)"
  M. Austin
  (*Music by* Harry Von Tilzer. *Lyrics by* William Dillon.)
"Hill and Dale"
  The Yacht Club Boys
"Blue Prelude"
  L. Sues
  (*Music and Lyrics by* Joe Bishop and Gordon Jenkins.)
"We Were Lucky Together"
  E. Wyckoff
  (*Music and Lyrics by* Gladys Shelley and Harry Archer.)

1942.12 KEEP 'EM LAUGHING

A Variety Revue in Two Acts, 16 Scenes. (Assembled and staged by Clifford C. Fischer.) Settings and draperies by Frank W. Stevens. Produced by Clifford C. Fischer by arrangement with the Messrs. Shubert. Opened 24 April 1942 at the 44th Street Theatre and closed 28 May 1942 after 77 performances.

CAST: WILLIAM GAXTON, VICTOR MOORE, PAUL and GRACE HARTMAN, HILDEGARDE, JACK COLE AND HIS DANCERS (trio including Virginia Millar), ZERO MOSTEL, Stuart Morgan Dancers, The Bricklayers, Fred Sanborn, Miriam La Velle, Kitty Mattern, Shirley Paige, Peggy French, Jack Tyler, George E. Mack, Charles Lawrence, PHIL ROMANO and His Orchestra.

Al White Beauties: Alice Anthony, Paddy Barker, Eleanor Broun, Marji Beeler, Rita Berry, Cece Eames, Michael Neale, Isabel Rolfe, Lucy Lewis, Ellen Taylor, June Peiter, Edith Stromberg, Norma Richter, Kay Paige, Emily Fabian, Pinto, Ruth Joseph, Vera Devine.

ACT 1

Scene 1

  Al White Beauties

Scene 2

  Miriam La Velle (Acrobatic dancing)

Scene 3

  The Bricklayers (Dog Act)

Scene 4

  Sketch (*by* L. Metzl and W. Michel)
    Kitty Mattern

Scene 5

  Authoritis (*by* Arthur Pierson.)
    W. Gaxton, P. French, J. Tyler, G. E. Mack

Scene 6

  Victor Moore in "Change Your Act, or Back to the Woods," assisted by S. Paige and Company. The action takes place after the opening performance in a metropolitan vaudeville theatre when no audience is present.

Scene 7

  Jack Cole and His Dancers (East Indian Dances)
    (*Music by* Raymond Scott and Albert Ketelby.)

Scene 8

  Fred Sanborn, assisted by C. Lawrence:
    ("Poet and Peasant Overture," *Music by* Franz von Suppé, on xylophone.)

Scene 9

  Gay Nineties—Al White Beauties

Scene 10

  The Hartmans (Ballroom dancing routine)

ACT 2

Scene 1

  Rainbow—Al White Beauties

Scene 2

  Stuart Morgan Dancers[33]

Scene 3

  Zero Mostel (Impressions of Jimmy Durante, Charles Boyer, Adolph Hitler, a Roseland Jitterbug, and a US Senator from the South)

Scene 4

  Hildegarde, with Leo Kahn at the piano
    ["A Pink Cocktail for a Blue Lady"
    (*Music by* Ben Oakland. *Lyrics by* Herb Magidson.)
    "I Said No" (from SWEATER GIRL film)
    (*Music by* Jule Styne. *Lyrics by* Frank Loesser.)
    "There's Something About a Soldier" (from SOLDIERS OF THE KING film)
    (*Music and Lyrics by* Noel Gay.)
    Lizst Swing number
    "Not a Care in the World" (from BANJO EYES)
    (*Music by* Vernon Duke. *Lyrics by* John Latouche.)]

Scene 5

  Gaxton and Moore—A Small Purchase (not Louisiana)
    (*Sketch by* Eddie Davis, followed by a medley of their hits from FIFTY MILLION FRENCHMEN, OF THEE I SING, ANYTHING GOES, LOUISIANA PURCHASE.)

Scene 6

  Finale

1942.13 HARLEM CAVALCADE

A Vaudeville Revue in Two Acts, 18 Scenes. Entire production designed and staged by Ed Sullivan and Noble Sissle. Dances by Leonard Harper. Costumes by Veronica. Music directed by Bill [Will] Vodery. Produced by Ed Sullivan. Opened 1 May 1942 at the Ritz Theatre and closed 23 May 1942 after 49 performances[34].

CAST: NOBLE SISSLE, THE PETERS SISTERS (Mattye, Ann Virginia Vee), MOKE & POKE, FLOURNOY MILLER, TIM MOORE and JOE BYRD, UNA MAE CARLISLE, RED and CURLEY, (Monty) HAWLEY and (Johnny) LEE, POPS & LOUIE, THE MILLER BROTHERS and LOIS, 5 CRACKERJACKS, WINI and BOB JOHNSON, THE (4) GINGERSNAPS, AMANDA RANDOLPH, TOM FLETCHER, JIMMIE DANIELS, GARLAND WILSON, DELTA RHYTHM BOYS[35], Edward Steele, Jesse Crior, Maude Russell.

The 16 Harper Harlemaniacs: Claudia Heyward (captain), Bee Williamson, June DeCuir, Julia Rogers, Jackie Bass, Cleo Hayes, Alyce Bishop, Olive Prince, Frances Jackson, Rusty Stanford, Mabel Garrett, Ruby Richards, Carolyne Rich, Ferebee Purnell, Nickey O'Daniel, Jackie Lewis.

ACT 1

Scene 1

  "Bandana Days" (from SHUFFLE ALONG)
    Crackerjacks, A. Randolph, J. Crior, T. Fletcher, Harlemaniacs
    (*Music by* Eubie Blake. *Lyrics by* Noble Sissle.)

Scene 2

  Pops & Louie (drums, dancing)

Scene 3

  John Doe Meets John Law
    M. Hawley, J. Lee

Scene 4

  "Interlude in Harlem"
    J. Daniels
    Pianists: G. Wilson, E. Steele. *Dancers:* Harlemaniacs. *Quartet:* Gingersnaps.

Scene 5

  Red and Curley (drums, dancing)

Scene 6

  Midnight Sonata (Shivers in the Cemetery at Twelve)[36]
    T. Moore, J. Byrd

---

[33]Acrobatic dance specialty in which three husky men toss a little girl.
[34]Performed twice daily, and three times daily on Saturday and Sunday.
[35]Some, but not all, opening night reviewers remarked upon the specialty of the Delta Rhythm Boys in Act 2 which does not appear in programs.
[36]Sketch about air raid wardens stationed in a cemetery.

Scene 7

   The Peters Sisters (A Ton of Harmony and Rhythm)
     ["Embraceable You" (from GIRL CRAZY)
     Music by George Gershwin. *Lyrics by* Ira Gershwin.)]

Scene 8

   His Honor, the Jedge
     The Jedge: T. Moore. *The Bailiff*: J. Byrd. *The Lawyer*: M. Russell. *Court Clerk*: J. Crior. *The Killer*: F. Miller. *The Number Runner*: J. Lee.

Scene 9

   Finale—in which the Peters Sisters introduce "Pushin' the Sand," Harlem's newest dance, with Moke & Poke (dancing comics) as partners, and the 16 Harlemaniacs as sand pushers. The boy and girl are Wini Johnson and Brother Bob.

ACT 2[37]

Scene 1

   "I'm Just Wild About Harry" (from SHUFFLE ALONG)
     N. Sissle, Harlemaniacs
     (*Music by* Eubie Blake. *Lyrics by* Noble Sissle.)

Scene 2

   Pops & Louie

Scene 3

   Una Mae Carlisle ["Walking By the River," others written by her]

Scene 4

   Drafting an Answer
     F. Miller

Scene 5

   "Melody in Sepia"

Scene 6

   Another Policy Game—An Afterpiece with F. Miller, J. Lee, T. Moore, J. Byrd, A. Randolph, The Gingersnaps.

Scene 7

   Miller Brothers and Lois (Dance trio)

Scene 8

   Noble Sissle
     [Specialty included "I'm Just Wild About Harry" (reprise), new patriotic song about the unknown soldier]

Scene 9

   Finale

1942.14

TOP-NOTCHERS

A Variety Revue in Two Acts, 17 Scenes[38]. (Assembled by Clifford C. Fischer.) Produced by Clifford C. Fischer by arrangement with the Messrs. Shubert. Opened 29 May 1942 at the 44th Street Theatre and closed 20 June 1942 after 48 performances.[39]

<u>CAST</u>: GRACIE FIELDS, ARGENTINITA, AL TRAHAN, WALTER O'KEEFE, "THINK-A-DRINK" HOFFMAN, GRACE and PAUL HARTMAN, PILAR LÓPEZ, A. ROBINS, THE BRICKLAYERS, ZERO MOSTEL, JACK STANTON, SIX WILLYS, MARGUERITE ADAMS, EVELYN BROOKS, AL WHITE BEAUTIES, FEDERICO REY, Carlos Montoya, Pablo Miquel, Benigno Medina, PHIL ROMANO's Orchestra.

Al White Beauties: Alice Anthony, Paddy Barker, Eleanor Broun, Marji Beeler, Rita Berry, Cece Eames, Michael Neale, Isabel Rolfe, Lucy Lewis, Ellen Taylor, June Peiter, Edith Stromberg, Norma Richter, Kay Paige, Emily Fabian, Pinto, Ruth Joseph, Vera Devine.

ACT 1

Scene 1

   Al White Beauties

Scene 2

   Jack Stanton (Singing, dancing)

Scene 3

   The Six Willys (Jugglers)

Scene 4

   Walter O'Keefe (Comedy)

Scene 5

   The Bricklayers (Dog act)

Scene 6

   A. Robins (Clown)

Scene 7

   Zero Mostel (Impressions of Jimmy Durante, Charles Boyer, Adolph Hitler, a Roseland Jitterbug, and a US Senator from the South)

Scene 8

   Walter O'Keefe (Radio Quiz)

Scene 9

   The Hartmans (Ballroom Dancing Routine)

Scene 10

   Gracie Fields, with Ingolf Dahl at the piano
     ["The Sweetest Song in the World"
     (*Music and Lyrics by* Harry Parr-Davies.)
     "Kerry Dances"
     (*Music and Lyrics by* James L. Molloy.)
     "Turn 'Erbert's Face to the Wall, Mother"
     (*Music and Lyrics by* Ronald Hill.)
     "Scotch Boy's Birthday"
     "The Biggest Aspidistra in the World"
     (*Music and Lyrics by* Thomas Connor, W. G. Haines and James S. Hancock.)
     "London Pride"
     (*Music and Lyrics by* Noël Coward.)
     "The Yanks Are Coming Again"
     (*Music and Lyrics by* Lew Pollack and Tony Stern.)]

ACT 2

Scene 1

   Al White Girls

Scene 2

   Jack Stanton and Evelyn Brooks (Singing, dancing)

Scene 3

   Walter O'Keefe (LaGuardia comedy song)

Scene 4

   Al Trahan, assisted by Marguerite Adams (Comedy routine with piano)

Scene 5

   Argentinita ("Inca Indian Ritual Dance," "Malaguena," "El Huayno"), Pilar López, Federico Rey, Carlos Montoya, Pablo Miquel, Benigno Medina.

Scene 6

   "Think-a-Drink" Hoffman

Scene 7

   Finale ("The Yanks Are Coming" reprise)

---

[37]On opening night, Jesse Crior performed a shoeshine song to close the intermission, and Ed Sullivan made an appearance.
[38]A revised version of KEEP 'EM LAUGHING which played the 44th Street Theatre 24 April-28 May 1942 for 77 performances.
[39]Performed twice daily, with an additional show Sunday at 5:30P.M. Settings, costumes, musical direction uncredited.

1942–1943 SEASON

Ray Bolger and Bertha Belmore in BY JUPITER (Photo: Vandamm Studio)
Billy Rose Theatre Collection, New York Public Library for the Performing Arts

1942–1943 SEASON

1942.15
BY JUPITER

A Musical Comedy in Two Acts, 5 Scenes. Book by Richard Rodgers and Lorenz Hart. Based on the play "The Warrior's Husband" by Julian F. Thompson. Music by Richard Rodgers. Lyrics by Lorenz Hart. Staged by Joshua Logan. Dances by Robert Alton. Settings and lighting by Jo Mielziner. Costumes by Irene Sharaff. Orchestra under the direction of Johnny Green. Orchestral arrangements by Don Walker. Vocal arrangements by Johnny Green and Buck [Clay] Warnick. Produced by Dwight Deere Wiman and Richard Rodgers in association with Richard Kollmar. Opened 3 June 1942 at the Sam S. Shubert Theatre and closed 12 June 1943 after 427 performances.

CAST (in order of appearance): *Achilles*: Bob Douglas. *A Herald*: Mark Dawson. *Agamemnon*: Robert Hightower. *Buria*: Jayne Manners. *First Sentry*: Martha Burnett. *Second Sentry*: Rose Inghram. *Third Sentry*: Kay Kimber. *Sergeant*: Monica Moore. *Caustica*: Maidel Turner. *Heroica*: MARGARET BANNERMAN. *Pomposia*: BERTHA BELMORE. *First Boy*: Don Liberto. *Second Boy*: Tony Matthews. *Third Boy*: William Vaux. *Hippolyta*: BENAY VENUTA. *Sapiens*: RAY BOLGER. *Antiope*: CONSTANCE MOORE. *A Huntress*: Helen Bennett. *An Amazon Dancer*: Flower Hujer. *Theseus*: RONALD GRAHAM. *Homer*: Berni Gould. *Minerva*: Vera-Ellen. *Slaves*: Robert Hightower, William Hightower. *Amazon Runner*: Wana Wenerholm. *Hercules*: Ralph Dumke. *Penelope*: Irene Corlett. *First Camp Follower*: Vera-Ellen. *Second Camp Follower*: Ruth Brady. *Third Camp Follower*: Helen Bennett. *Fourth Camp Follower*: Joyce Ring. *Fifth Camp Follower*: Rosemary Sankey.

Girls of the Ensemble: Helen Bennett, Ruth Brady, Betty Jo Creager, June Graham, Babs (Barbara) Heath, Janet Lavis, Virginia Meyer, Marjorie (Margery) Moore, Mary Virginia Morris, Beth Nichols, Dorothy Poplar, Bobby Priest, Joyce Ring, Rosemary Sankey, Toni Stuart, Olga Suarez, Wana Wenerholm. *Boys of the Ensemble*: Ray Koby, Don Liberto, Michael Mann, Tony Matthews, George Schwalbe, William Silvers, Ken (Kenneth) Whelan, Robert Wilson, William Vaux.

Act 1, Scene 1: A Greek Camp, a week's march from Pontus. *Scene 2*: A Terrace of Hippolyta's Palace in Pontus, two days later.

Act 2, Scene 1: Before Hippolyta's Tent, afternoon, a week later. *Scene 2*: The Greek Camp, the same night. *Scene 3*: Inside Theseus' Tent, immediately after.

ACT 1
Scene 1
"For Jupiter and Greece"
B. Douglas, M. Dawson, Greek Warriors
Scene 2
The Amazons
Danced by M. Moore, Amazon Warriors
"Jupiter Forbid"
B. Venuta, M. Burnett, R. Inghram, K. Kimber, M. Moore
Danced by R. Hightower, W. Hightower, F. Hujer, Ensemble.
"Life With Father"
R. Bolger
"Nobody's Heart Belongs to Me"
C. Moore
"The Gateway of the Temple of Minerva"
R. Graham, Ensemble
"Life With Father" (reprise)
B. Belmore, R. Bolger
"Here's a Hand"
R. Graham, C. Moore
"No, Mother, No"
R. Bolger, Ensemble
ACT 2
Scene 1
"The Boy I Left Behind Me"
J. Manners, Ensemble
"Nobody's Heart Belongs to Me" (reprise)
R. Bolger
"Ev'rything I've Got"
R. Bolger, B. Venuta
"Bottoms Up"
M. Dawson, B. Venuta, C. Moore, B. Gould, B. Douglas, Vera-Ellen, F. Hujer, R. Hightower, W. Hightower, Ensemble

"Careless Rhapsody"
C. Moore, R. Graham
Finaletto
R. Bolger, B. Venuta, B. Belmore, Ensemble
Scene 2
"Ev'rything I've Got" (reprise)
B. Venuta
Scene 3
"Wait Till You See Her"
R. Graham, Ensemble
"Now That I've Got My Strength"
R. Bolger, I. Corlett, Vera-Ellen, Ensemble
Finale
Entire Company

1942.16
LAUGH, TOWN, LAUGH

A Vaudeville Revue in Two Acts, 14 Scenes. (Assembled, staged and directed by Ed Wynn.) Gowns for Miss Froman by Valentina and Saks Fifth Avenue. Gowns for Misses Schramm, Graham and Kirk designed by Ernest Schrapps. Scenery by Frank W. Stevens. Produced by Ed Wynn. Opened 22 June 1942 at the Alvin Theatre and closed 25 July 1942 after 65 performances.

CAST: ED WYNN, JANE FROMAN, CARMEN AMAYA, (JOE) SMITH & (CHARLES) DALE, SEÑOR WENCES, RED DONOHUE and UNO, HERMANOS WILLIAMS TRIO, HECTOR and PALS[1] with MARION, KEN DAVIDSON, HUGH FORGIE, EMIL COLEMAN and His Orchestra, Eleanore Schramm, Ann Graham, Gene Wright, Gene Ashley, The Herzogs, Jerry Brannon.
Carmen Amaya Gypsy Flamenco Troupe: Antonía, Léonor, José and Paco, with Sabicas, guitarist.
The Volga Singers: Nicholas Vasilieff (director), Stephen Slepushkui, Leonid Troyitsky, Andrew Gregorioff, Boris Belostozky, Michael Greben, Veacheslav Mamonuff, Sasha Kuroschkin.

ACT 1
Scene 1
It Begins With Ed Wynn (as the nimble mountain-goat leaps from crag to crag, so will he leap from act to act.)
Passersby: E. Schramm, A. Graham, G. Wright, G. Ashley.
Scene 2.
And now Vaudeville (incl. 'The Mighty Nimrod' with Ed Wynn)
Scene 3
From Australia, the Herzogs, famous international aerialists
Scene 4
From Russia, the Volga Singers ("Volga Boatman," etc.)
Scene 5
From Portugal[2], Señor Wences, a Gentleman of Originality
Scene 6
From the U.S.A., Jane Froman, America's Leading Lady of Song:
["Sleepy Lagoon"
(*Music by* Eric Coates. *Lyrics by* Jack Lawrence.)
"I'm Breathless"
"One Dozen Roses"
(*Music by* Dick Jurgens and Walter Donovan. *Lyrics by* Roger Lewis and Country Washburn.)
"Three Little Sisters" (from PRIVATE BUCKAROO film)
(*Music and Lyrics by* Irving Taylor and Vic Mizzy.)
"Don't Sit Under the Apple Tree (with Anyone Else But Me)" (from PRIVATE BUCKAROO film)
(*Music by* Sam Stept. *Lyrics by* Lew Brown and Charles Tobias.)]
Scene 7
From Ireland, Red Donohue and Uno, The Rookie Drives to Camp
Scene 8
From Spain, Carmen Amaya and Her Gypsy Flamenco Troupe with Sabicas

---

[1]Hector's Pals were a dog act.
[2]Señor Wences hailed originally from Spain, not Portugal; the program billing was adjusted in view of Spain's wartime alliance with the Nazis, according to Anthony Slide in his Encyclopedia of Vaudeville.(Greenwood Press, Westport, Connecticut, 1994).

ACT 2

Scene 1

From Argentina, Hermanos Williams Trio, a Latin-American Interlude

Scene 2

A Little Bit of Fun (Ed Wynn and Jane Froman in Bicycle Piano routine) [incl. "Tea for Two," *Music by* Vincent Youmans.]

Scene 3

From Great Britain, Ken Davidson, World Champion Exhibitionist, and from Canada, Hugh Forgie, His Opponent, Professional Badminton Champions, and Jerry Brannon, Sports Announcer.

Scene 4

From "The Sidewalks of New York," the famous Character Comedy Stars, Joe Smith and Charles Dale (Originators of the Avon Comedy Four), in their Famous Skit, 'Dr. Kronkheit.'

Scene 5

From Here, There and Everywhere, Hector and Pals, with Marion.

Scene 6

And That's Vaudeville

1942.17 THE CHOCOLATE SOLDIER

A Revival of the Operetta in Three Acts[3]. Original Viennese libretto by ("Der tapfere Soldat") Rudolph Bernauer and Leopold Jacobson, based on George Bernard Shaw's "Arms and the Man." Music by Oscar Straus. American book and lyrics by Stanislaus Stange. Staged by John Pierce. Book directed by José Ruben. Settings by E. B. Dunkel Studios. Costumes by Paul Dupont. Musical director, Joseph S. Tushinsky. Special ballet music composed and scored by Murray Rumsey and Carl Weber. Produced by Joseph S. Tushinsky and Hans Bartsch. Opened 23 June 1942 at Carnegie Hall and closed 12 July 1942 after 24 performances.

CAST: *Nadina*: HELEN GLEASON. *Aurelia*: Frances Comstock. *Mascha*: Doris Patson. *Lieutenant Bummerli*: ALLAN JONES. *Capt. Massakroff*: Detmar Poppen. *Colonel Casimir Popoff*: A. Russell Slagle. *Major Alexius Spiridoff*: Michael Fitzmaurice. *Ballerina*: Tashamira. *Premier Dancer*: Peter Birch.

Singers: Joan Benoit, Harriet Borger, Irene Carroll, Tonya Cherney, Jean Cumming, Mary LaRoche, Katherine Lester, Emily Marsh, Mae Muth, Marvel Skeels, Mildred Talbot, Joan Wheatley. Jimmy Allison, Ray Cook, Robert Curi, Joseph Monte, Carl Nelson, Nat Schultz, Larry Shindel, Ben Siegel, Gene Stern, Richard Torigi, Robert Tower, Paul L. Wendel. *Dancers*: Harriet Adler, Kay Alton, Deanne Benmore, Marie Grey, Virginia Harriot, Emily Jewell, Audrey Kent, Anna Konstance, Ann Kus, Marion Lynn, Ruth Mann, Eileen McBride, Donna Mission, Mary Lou Reed, Arleen Robinson, Grace Rudder, Judy Sargent. Lief Argo, Dan Denton, Eddie Howland, Peter Kite Smith, Richard Audré, Nicolai Fatula, Irving Rappeé, John Schindehette.

1942.18 STAR AND GARTER

A Burlesque Revue in Two Acts, 21 Scenes. (Assembled by Michael Todd.) Music and lyrics by Irving Berlin, Al Dubin, Will Irwin, Harold J. Rome, Lester Lee, Irving Gordon, Alan Roberts, Harold Arlen, Frank McCue, Doris Tauber, Dorival Caymmi, Jerry Seelen, Jerome Brainin, Johnny Mercer, Sis Wilner, Al Stillman. Staged and lighted by Hassard Short. Dances directed by Al White, Jr. Settings by Harry Horner. Costumes by Irene Sharaff. Orchestra conducted by Raymond Sinatra. Orchestrations by Raymond Sinatra and Lionel Rand. Vocal arrangements by Raymond Sinatra. Produced by Michael Todd. Opened 24 June 1942 at the Music Box Theatre and closed 4 December 1943 after 609 performances.[4]

CAST: BOBBY CLARK, GYPSY ROSE LEE, PROF. LAMBERTI, GEORGIA SOUTHERN, PAT HARRINGTON, CARRIE FINNELL, JUANITA RIOS, Marjorie Knapp, (George) Wayne and (Glenn) Marlin, Lynn, Royce and Vanya, Gil Maison, LaVerne Lupton, Richard Rober, Eppy (Tiny) Pearson, Joe Lyons, (Bill) Skipper and Kate (Frederick), Frank Price, Leticia, Victoria Schools, Frank and Jean Hubert, The Hudson Wonders (Ray and Geraldine Hudson), Artie Conroy, Dorothy Bigby.

Dancing Girls: Sunny Wright, Puddy Smith, Frances Hammond, Virginia Howe, Terry Lasky, Lorraine Latham, Janice Wallace, June Powers, Ruthe Reid, Jo Ann

Flanagan, June MacLaren, Mimi Berry, Charlotte Lorraine, Betty Lee, Gloria Anderson, Margaret Kayes. *Show Girls*: June Sitarr, Andrea Mann, Helene Hudson, Audrey Westphal, Cynthia Cavanaugh, Lynn Powers, Adele Jurgens, Iris Marshall, Mary Lawrence, Ruth Josephs. *Singers*: Helen Price, Nina Dean, Carol Deis, Bob Lenn, Helen McCartney, Bill Marel, Richard Finney, Lipman Dukat.

ACT 1

Scene 1

"Star and Garter Girls"
   G. R. Lee, The Star and Garter Girls
   (*Music by* Lester Lee. *Lyrics by* Jerry Seelen.)

Scene 2

The Sacred Gherkin
   Mr. Wise: J. Lyons. *Biff*: G. Maison. *Boff*: P. Harrington. *First Girl*: J. Rios. *Second Girl*: G. Hudson.

Scene 3

"Clap Your Hands"
   G. Sothern

Scene 4

That Merry Wife of Windsor
   (Stolen from William Shakespeare by Bobby Clark.)
   Jennie Windsor: G. R. Lee. *Andrew*: B. Clark. *Gus*: J. Lyons. *Victor Windsor*: E. Pearson.

Scene 5

Gil Maison (and His Racketeers—Doggone Nonsense)

Scene 6

"Les Sylphides Avec la Bumpe"
   (*Music and Lyrics by* Irving Gordon, Alan Roberts and Jerome Brainin.)
   Premier Dancer: B. Skipper. *Premiere Danseuse*: K. Friedlich. *La Bumpe*: L. Lupton. *Second Premier Dancer*: Wayne. *Third Premier Dancer*: Marlin. With the Star and Garter Corps de Ballet.

Scene 7

Wayne and Marlin

Scene 8

"In the Malamute Saloon" (As it might have been)
   (*Music by* Will Irwin.)
   The "Ragtime" Kid: P. Harrington. *The Bartender*: E. Pearson. *Dangerous Dan McGrew*: J. Lyons. *The Lady that's known as "Lou"*: G. R. Lee. A Miner: B. Clark.

Scene 9

"The Bunny"[5]
   M. Knapp, Star and Garter Girls
   (*Music and Lyrics* by Harold Rome.)
   Danced by the Hudson Wonders.

Scene 10

Prof. Lamberti, assisted by D. Bigby.

Scene 11

"The Girl on the Police Gazette" (from ON THE AVENUE, film)
   F. Price
   (*Music and Lyrics by* Irving Berlin.)
   The Girl on the Police Gazette: G. R. Lee.

ACT 2

Scene 1

"For a Quarter"
   (*Music by* Lester Lee. *Lyrics by* Jerry Seelen.)
   The Candy Butchers: B. Clark, P. Harrington, E. Pearson.

Scene 2

The Harem
   The Dancer: Leticia. *The Sultan*: G. Marlin. *The Favorite Wife*: C. Finnell. And Star and Garter Girls.
   "Don't Take on More Than You Can Do"
   (*Words and Music by* Irving Gordon, Alan Roberts and Jerome Brainin.)

Scene 3

Frank and Jean Hubert

---

[3]First produced in New York 13 September 1909 at the Lyric Theatre for 296 performances. For Synopsis of Scenes and Musical Numbers, see original 1909 production. For this production, "Never Was There Such a Lover" and "The Chocolate Soldier" were dropped. The Letter Song (Solo and Duet) were combined as one in the program.
[4]Sketches not credited.

[5]Replaced during the run of the show:
   "Money"
      M. J. Knapp, Girls
      (*Music and Lyrics by* Harold J. Rome.)
      Danced by the Hudson Wonders.

Scene 4

"I Can't Strip to Brahms"
    G. R. Lee
    (*Written by* Gypsy Rose Lee.)

Scene 5

"Blues in the Night" (from film of the same name)
    (*Music by* Harold Arlen. *Lyrics by* Johnny Mercer.)
    Ladies of the Night: Show Girls. *The Evening Breeze*: Leticia.

Scene 6

"Robert the Roué" (from STREETS OF PARIS)
    B. Clark, Star and Garter Girls
    (*Music by* Jimmy McHugh. *Lyrics by* Al Dubin.)

Scene 7

Aired in Court
    Court Clerk: J. Lyons. *Judge Gabby*: B. Clark. *District Attorney*:
    R. Rober. *Gloria Pinkee*: G. L. Lee. *Council for the Defense*:
    E. Pearson. *William Abernathy*: P. Harrington. *Court Recorder*:
    G. Maison.

Scene 8

"I Don't Get It"
    M. Knapp
    (*Music by* Doris Tauber. *Lyrics by* Sis Wilner.)
    Danced by L. Lupton.

Scene 9

Lynn, Royce and Vanya[6]

Scene 10

"Brazilian Nuts"
    J. Rios, Entire Company
    (*Music by* Dorival Caymmi. *Lyrics by* Al Stillman.)

Finale
    Nurse: G. R. Lee. *Doctor*: D. Rober. *Patient*: B. Clark. *Gangsters*: Dave Jones,
    Frank Coletti. *Another Patient*: E. Pearson. *Another Patient*: P. Harrington.
    Woman Patient: G. Sothern. *A Barber*: G. Maison. *The Persian*: J. Lyons. *A Girl*:
    D. Bigby.

1942.19

STARS ON ICE

An Ice Skating Revue in Two Acts, 28 Scenes. Production by Sonart
Productions, William H. Burke, Executive director. Staged by Catherine
Littlefield. Music by Paul McGrane and Paul Van Loan. Lyrics by Al
Stillman. Skating direction, May Judels. Musical conductor, David
Mendoza. Choreography by Catherine Littlefield. Settings designed
and created by Bruno Maine. Costumes by Lucinda Ballard. Lighting by
Eugene Braun. Musical arrangements by Paul Van Loan. Produced by
Sonja Henie and Arthur M. Wirtz. Opened 2 July 1942 at the Center
Theatre and closed for vacation 16 May 1943 after 427 performances;
Second Edition (detail immediately following) opened 24 June 1943 and
closed 16 April 1944 after 403 performances. Total for both editions: 830
performances.

CAST: CAROL LYNNE, SKIPPY BAXTER, TWINKLE WATTS, DOROTHY
CALEY, MARY JANE YEO, HELGE and INGE BRANDT, FRITZ DIETL,
EDWINA and CLIFF THAELL, MAYITA MONTEZ, BOB and PEGGY WHIGHT,
HERTHA GROSSMAN, ALEX HURD, PAUL CASTLE, RUDY RICHARDS, PAUL
DUKE, FREDDIE TRENKLER, THE FOUR BRUISES (SID SPAULDING,
CHARLES SLAGLE, MONTE STOTT, BUSTER GRACE), A. DOUGLAS
NELLES, 3 ROOKIES (Neil Rose, Rudy Van Dyke, Meryl Baxter), Donald Arthur,
Edwina Blades, Marta Dietl, Karen Lane, Geoff Stevens. *Vocals*: VIVIENNE ALLEN,
JACK KILTY.
    Girls: Patsy O'Day, Irene Church, Peggy Gordon, Jeanne Berman, Kay Corcoran,
Edith Kandel, Jean Conrad, Daphne Pool, Ruth Noland, Bing Stott, Corrynne
Church, Muriel Pack, Janet Hester, Karen Lane, Irene Abitz, Trudy Schneider, Billie
Kling, Lucille O'Day, Sharlee Munster, Pearl Joseph, Vera Papa, Helen Bull, Dorothy
Chandler, Florence Rohr, Eileen Thompson, Helen Thompson. *Boys*: Peter Fenton,
James Wright, Arthur Meehan, Bob Coffman, Adolph Davidson, Kurt Fishman,
Lyle Clark, Jerry Decker, Ted Bruenn, James Carter, William Taft, Thomas DePauw,
Bob Petrillo, Ray Koby, Rob Wilson, Leonard Muncaster, Stan Skidmore, Clarence
Anderson, Walter Hedberg, Fred Thompson, James Sisk, Bruce Clark, Will
Stikarowski, G. W. Bennett.

---

[6]Replaced during the run of the show:
    Crazy House

ACT 1

Scene 1

"Stars on Ice"
    J. Kilty
    Ladies of the Ensemble: I. Abitz, J. Berman, H. Bull, J. Conrad, I. Church, C.
    Church, D. Chandler, K. Corcoran, P. Gordon, J. Hester, P. Joseph, B. Kling,
    E. Kandel, K. Lane, R. Noland, P. O'Day, D. Poole, M. Pack, B. Stott, T.
    Schneider, E. Thompson, F. Rohr, H. Thompson.

Scene 2

Speed Kings
    T. DePauw, R. Van Dyke, J. Carter, P. Fenton, J. Wright, C. Cavanaugh, R.
    Coffman, S. Skidmore, A. Davidson, B. Wilson, L. Clark, K. Fishman, A.
    Meehan, T. Bruenn, R. Petrillo, F. Thompson, J. Sisk, W. Stikarowski, B. Clark,
    G. W. Bennett.

Scene 3

Fun in the Park
    Nurse: M. Stott. *Sailor*: C. Slagle. *Brat*: P. Castle.

Scene 4

Two of a Kind
    H. Brandt, I. Brandt

Scene 5

Little Miss Muffet
    Little Miss Muffet: T. Watts. *Spider and Prince Charming*: M. Baxter.
    Mushrooms: P. Gordon, E. Kandel, J. Conrad, K. Lane, S. Munster, V. Papa.

Scene 6

"Juke Box Saturday Night"
    V. Allen, M. J. Yeo, A. Nelles, R. Richards, P. Castle
    (*Music by* Paul McGrane. *Lyrics by* Al Stillman.)
    Girls: M. Pack, K. Corcoran, P. O'Day, L. O'Day, P. Joseph, B. Kling, B. Stott,
    H. Bull, J. Hester, D. Chandler, D. Poole, R. Noland, K. Lane, T. Schneider,
    E. Thompson, C. Church, I. Abitz, J. Berman, I. Church, F. Rohr. *Boys*: R.
    Richards, R. Coffman, F. Thompson, W. Taft, T. DePauw, C. Cavanugh, P.
    Fenton, K. Fishman, B. Petrillo, S. Skidmore, W. Hedberg, R. Van Dyke, J. Sisk,
    W. Stikarowski, E. Taylor, R. Lippman, R. berg, J. Wright, G. W. Bennett.

Scene 7

A Maid, a Cat and a Kitten
    M. J. Yeo, N. Rose, P. Castle
"The Cavalier Cat"
    M. J. Yeo

Scene 8

South of the Border
    M. Pack, J. Wright

Scene 9

Skating Around in Circles
    G. Owen

Scene 10

The Chase
    Fox: R. Richards. *Girls*: R. Noland, T. Schneider, P. Joseph, L. O'Day,
    K. Corcoran, D. Chandler, C. Church, B. Kling, H. Bull, J. Hester, M. Pack,
    P. O'Day, B. Stott, E. Thompson, I. Abitz, F. Rohr. *Boys*: J. Carter, W. Taft,
    F Thompson, H. Altinger, D. Brower, A. Davidson, P. Fenton, T. DePauw, R.
    Van Dyke, R. Coffman, C. Cavanaugh, S. Skidmore, K. Fishman, T. Bruenn,
    J. Donahue, J. Kenny. *Grooms*: R. Koby, J. Decker, G. Verden, A. Meehan.

Scene 11

Symphony in Smoke
    P. Duke

Scene 12

Playtime Pranks
    N. Rose, R. Van Dyke, M. Baxter

Scene 13

Russian Steppes
    C. Lynne
    Cossacks: A. Meehan, R. Koby, J. Decker, C. Anderson.

Scene 14

Hijinx
    B. Grace, C. Slagle

Scene 15

Jack Frost Reverie
"Little Jack Frost"
    V. Allen

Jack Frost: S. Baxter. *Snow Queen*: H. Grossman. *Babies*: T. Watts, P. Castle. *Mother*: P. Gordon. *Five Palette Boys*: R. Van Dyke, F. Thompson, T. DePauw, J. Wright, B. Petrillo. *Snowflakes*: L. O'Day, M. Pack, P. Joseph, H. Bull, R. Noland, B. Kling, C. Church, I. Abitz, I. Church, P. O'Day, E. Thompson, K. Lane, H. Thompson, D. Chandler, B. Stott, K. Corcoran, T. Schneider, J. Conrad, J. Berman, D. Poole, S. Skidmore, K. Fishman, D. Brower, R. Coffman, C. Cavanaugh, B. Petrillo, P. Fenton, A. Davidson, J. Carter, J. Decker, H. Altinger, G. Verden, T. Bruenn, J. Kenny, C. Anderson, B. Wilson.

ACT 2

Scene 1

Pan-Americana: "Estrillita" (*Music by* Ponce.)
    Castanet Group: *Piano Accordion*: M. J. Yeo, M. Pack, R. Richards, H. Bull, K. Fishman. *Girls*: P. Gordon, E. Thompson, J. Berman, E. Kandel, K. Corcoran, D. Chandler, D. Poole, J. Hester, B. Stott, K. Lane, P. Joseph, T. Schneider, I. Church, I. Abitz, C. Church, B. Kling, J. Conrad, F. Rohr, B. O'Dell. *Boys*: J. Wright, B. Petrillo, R. Koby, T. Bruenn, J. Decker, J. Carter, A. Meehan, D. Brower, F. Thompson, R. Van Dyke, T. DePauw, B. Wilson, C. Cavanaugh, A. Davidson, L. Clark, P. Fenton, J. Donahue, H. Altinger, J. Kenny, C. Anderson. *Samba*: M. Montez. *Rhumba*: T. Watts, P. Castle.

Scene 2

The Gaucho
    G. Owen

Scene 3

Ballroom Satire
    S. Skidmore, W. Taft

Scene 4

Elevated Antics
    B. Grace, C. Slagle

Scene 5

Autumn Leaves: "Like a Leaf Falling in the Breeze"
    J. Kilty, M. J. Yeo
    (*Music by* James Littlefield.)
    The Girl: M. J. Yeo. *Chrysanthemum*: C. Lynne. *The Wind*: S. Baxter. *Autumn Leaves*: M. Pack, K. Corcoran, R. Noland, E. Thompson, J. Berman, H. Bull, C. Church, P. O'Day, P. Gordon, L. O'Day, T. Schneider, D. Poole, I. Abitz, D. Chandler, P. Joseph, I. Church, B. Stott, F. Rohr, J. Conrad.

Scene 6

Up and Over
    A. Hurd

Scene 7

Double in Blues
    H. Brandt, I. Brandt

Scene 8

The Three Rookies
    N. Rose, R. Van Dyke, M. Baxter

Scene 9

Gin Rummy: "Gin Rummy, I Love You"
    V. Allen, J. Kilty
    Players: M. J. Yeo, W. Taft. *The Joker*: N. Rose. *The Deck*: Ensemble.

Scene 10

Poetry of Motion
    B. Whight, P. Whight

Scene 11

Smart Set: "You're Awfully Smart"
    V. Allen, J. Kilty
    Girls and Boys: K. Corcoran, B. Coffman, P. Josephs, A. Davidson, L. O'Day, F. Thompson, M. Peck, J. Wright, P. Gordon, L. Clark, J. Hester, J. Donahue, D. Poole, K. Fishman, S. Munster, J. Carter, J. Berman, H. Altinger, H. Bull, D. Brower, D. Chandler, C. Cavanaugh, E. Thompson, B. Wilson, F. Rohr, G. Verden, R. Noland, B. Petrillo, T. Schneider, T. Bruenn, P. O'Day, A. Meehan, B. Stott, R. Van Dyke, I. Church, P. Fenton, I. Abitz, W. Taft, B. Kling, T. DePauw.

Scene 12

Maids-a-Miss
    Four Bruises (S. Spaulding, C. Slagle, M. Stott, B. Grace)

Scene 13

Victory Ball: "Big Broad Smile"
    V. Allen, J. Kilty
    (*Music by* Paul McGrane. *Lyrics by* Al Stillman.)
    Girl Principals: H. Brandt, I. Brandt, H. Grossman, C. Lynne, M. Montez, P. Whight, M. J. Yeo. *Boy Principals*: B. Whight, R. Van Dyke, S. Baxter, M.

Baxter, P. Castle, P. Duke, B. Grace, A. Hurd, A. Nelles, N. Rose, S. Spaulding, M. Stott, C. Slagel, G. Owen, R. Richards. *Girls*: P. O'Day, I. Church, P. Gordon, J. Berman, K. Corcoran, E. Kandel, J. Conrad, D. Pool, R. Noland, B. Stott, C. Church, M. Pack, J. Hester, K. Lane, I. Abitz, T. Schneider, B. Kling, L. O'Day, S. Munster, P. Joseph. *Boys*: P. Fenton, J. Wright, A. Meehan, D. Brower, B. Coffman, A. Davidson, K. Fishman, L. Clark, J. Decker, T. Bruenn, J. Carter, W. Taft, T. DePauw, B. Petrillo, J. Donahue, H. Altinger, G. Verden, R. Koby, R. Wilson, L. Muncaster.

STARS ON ICE

1942.19   (Second Edition)

An Ice Skating Revue in Two Acts, 21 Scenes. Second Edition opened 24 June 1943 and closed 16 April 1944 after 403 performances.[7]

CAST: FREDDIE TRENKLER, CAROL LYNNE, GEOFFE STEVENS, JAMES WRIGHT, JIMMY SISK, MAY JUDELS, AUDREY PEPPE, HERTHA GROSSMAN, CLAIRE WILKINS, RUDY RICHARDS, PAUL CASTLE, PAUL DUKE, JAMES CAESAR, HAZEL CALEY, DOROTHY CALEY, PEGGY WHIGHT, FRITZ DIETL, MURIEL PACK, BILLE DePAUW, ROBERT PAYNE, Claire Wilkins, Ragna Ray, Robert Ballard, Joe Shillen. *Vocals*: VIVIENNE ALLEN, LEWIS APPLETON, MAX CONDON, RAND SMITH, Robert Brink.
    Girls: Helen Thompson, Michel Winters, Lucille Risch, Joyce Brownell, Jean Conrad, Nona MacDonald, Lucille O'Day, Sharlee Munster, Karen Lane, Dorothy Chandler, Vera Papa, Marcia Mae Buhl, Alice Farrar, Betty Timanus, Pearl Marshall, Barbara Johnson, Scotty Robertson, Edith Kandel, Eileen Thompson, Bernice O'Dell, Eloise Christina, Janet Rose, Elizabeth Cravens, Betty Timanus, Helen Dutcher, Virginia Litz, Michel Winters. *Boys*: Jerry Kerman, Alfred Kutchey, Julian Appley, Fred Hirschfeld, Arnold Reubens, Jack Raffloer, Joachim Dietl, Bernard Feldman, Arthur Meehan, Fred Kaufman, Arnold Shoda, Richard Brower, Bain Lightfoot, Alex Lindgren, James Kenny, George Wagner, Jack Roach, James Carter, William Carvel, James Partridge, Harper Flaherty.

ACT 1

Scene 1

"Put Your Cares on Ice"
    V. Allen, L. Appleton, M. Condon, R. Smith
    (*Music and Lyrics by* James Littlefield.)
    Ladies of the Ensemble: L. Risch, M. Barry, P. Joseph, L. O'Day, B. Stott, V. Papa, J. Rose, I. Abitz, H. Dutcher, J. Brownell, E. Cravens, M. Winters, M. M. Buhl, J. Conrad, H. Thompson, K. Lane, R. Ray, B. O'Dell, D. Chandler, J. Berman, B. Timanus, A. Farrar, B. Johnson, S. Robertson. *Show Girls*: V. Litz, E. Kandel, E. Thompson, P. Marshall. *Boys of the Ensemble*: J. Dietl, B. Lightfoot, A. Shoda, F. Kaufman, J. Kerman, A. Kutchey, A. Reubens, J. Roach, W. Carvel, G. Wagner, J. Apley, F. Hirschfeld.

Scene 2

Waltz in Swingtime
    B. DePauw, R. Payne

Scene 3

South of the Border
    M. Pack, H. Flaherty

Scene 4

The Chase
    Fox: J. Kenny. *Girls*: L. Risch, A. Farrar, N. MacDonald, J. Rose, L. O'Day, B. Stott, E. Thompson, E. Kandel, P. Joseph, E. Cravens, J. Brownell, I. Abitz, R. Ray, D. Chandler, M.M. Buhl, S. Robertson. *Boys*: J. Apley, R. Brower, C. Storey, F. Kaufman, G. Decker, F. Hirschfeld, B. Lightfoot, B. Feldman, J. Sisk, J. Shillen, C. Cavanaugh, J. Raffloer, J. Carter, W. Carvel, A. Lindgren, G. Wagner. *Grooms*: P. Marshall, J. Conrad, H. Dutcher, H. Thompson.

Scene 5

Symphony in Smoke
    P. Duke, assisted by V. Litz

Scene 6

The Dancing Lesson
    Dancing Master: G. Stevens. *The Brat*: P. Castle. *Mother*: J. Berman. *Girls*: B. DePauw, B. Stott, P. Joseph, D. Chandler, E. Thompson, M. Winters.

Scene 7

Russian Steppes
    Cossack Princess: C. Lynne. *Cossacks*: J. Conrad, P. Marshall, E. Kandel, N. MacDonald.

Scene 8

"Juke Box Saturday Night"

---

[7]Production credits same as above, except: Costumes by Paul Dupont. Songs individually credited.

V. Allen, L. Appleton, M. Condon, R. Smith
(*Music by* Paul McGrane. *Lyrics by* Al Stillman.)
With C. Wilkins, C. Cavanaugh, P. Castle, R. Richards.

Scene 9

Bouncing Ball of Ice
F. Trenkler

Scene 10

Jack Frost Reverie: "Little Jack Frost"
V. Allen
Mother: V. Litz. *Baby*: A. Peppe. *Snow Queen*: H. Grossman. *Jack Frost*: J. Wright.

ACT 2

Scene 1

Pan-Americana: "Estrillita" (*Music by* Ponce.)
Castanet Group: M. Pack, E. Cravens, J. Kenny, C. Wilkins. *Girls*: I. Abitz, J. Berman, J. Brownell, H. Dutcher, P. Joseph, E. Kandel, K. Lane, H. Thompson, B. O'Dell, V. Papa, E. Thompson, N. MacDonald, M. Winters, S. Munster, E. Cravens, J. Sturgeon, P. Marshall, B. Timanus, B. Johnson. *Boys*: A. Meehan, B. Feldman, J. Dietl, A. Rubens, F. Hirschfeld, G. Decker, A. Shoda, J. Kerman, A. Kutchey, J. Raffloer, C. Storey, H. Flaherty, A. Lindgren, G. Wagner, J. Carter, W. Carvel, J. Roach, J. Shillen, J. Partridge. *Samba*: M. Judels. *Rhumba*: C. Wilkins, R. Richards.

Scene 2

Poetry in Motion
P. Whight, R. Ballard

Scene 3

Elevated Antics
F. Dietl

Scene 4

Pied Piper of Rhythm
R. Richards, *assisted by* C. Wilkins, R. Ray

Scene 5

Autumn Leaves
"Like a Leaf Falling in the Breeze"
R. Brink, L. Appleton, M. Condon
(*Lyrics by* Al Stillman. *Music by* James Littlefield.)
The Girl: A. Peppe. *Chrysanthemum*: C. Lynne. *The Wind*: J. Wright. *Autumn Leaves*: M. Barry, D. Chandler, J. Sturgeon, L. O'Day, I. Abitz, B. DePauw, L. Risch, E. Thompson, J. Berman, J. Rose, J. Brownell, M. Pack, E. Cravens, J. Conrad, M.M. Buhl, N. MacDonald, B. Timanus, H. Dutcher, E. Christina, A. Farrar.

Scene 6

Over the Top
J. Caesar

Scene 7

Two of a Kind
H. Caley, D. Caley

Scene 8

The Three Kilties
J. Sisk, J. Shillen, G. Stevens

Scene 9

Valse Elegante: "You Must be a Part of a Dream"
M. Condon
(*Music by* Marten Lowell. *Lyrics by* James Littlefield.)
Girl: H. Grossman. *Two Couples*: C. Wilkins, F. Dietl, A. Peppe, R. Payne.

Scene 10

There's One in Every Camp
The One: F. Trenkler. *Sergeant*: C. Storey. *Roookies*: G. Decker, J. Sisk, C. Cavanaugh.

Scene 11

Victory Ball
"Big Broad Smile"
V. Allen, L. Appleton, M. Condon, R. Smith
(*Music by* Paul McGrane. *Lyrics by* Al Stillman.)
Featured and Principal Skaters: C. Lynne, M. Judels, H. Grossman, P. Castle, A. Peppe, M. Pack, J. Caesar, P. Whight, F. Dietl, J. Wright, R. Richards, C. Wilkins, R. Ray, R. Payne, B. DePauw, G. Stevens, J. Sisk, F. Trenkler, H. Caley, D. Caley. *Girls*: H. Thompson, M. Winters, L. Risch, J. Brownell, J. Conrad, N. MacDonald, L. O'Day, S. Munster, K. Lane, D. Chandler, V. Papa, M. M. Buhl, A. Farrar, B. Timanus, P. Marshall, B. Johnson, S. Robertson, E. Kandel, E. Thompson, B. O'Dell. *Boys*: Jerry Kerman, Alfred Kutchey, Julian Appley, Fred Hirschfeld, Arnold Reubens, Jack Raffloer, Joachim Dietl, Bernard

Feldman, Arthur Meehan, Fred Kaufman, Arnold Shoda, Richard Brower, Bain Lightfoot, Alex Lindgren, James Kenny, George Wagner, Jack Roach, James Carter, William Carvel, James Partridge, Harper Flaherty.

1942.20

THIS IS THE ARMY

A Musical Revue in Two Acts, 13 Scenes. (Conceived by Irving Berlin.) Music and lyrics by Irving Berlin. Staged by Staff Sergeant Ezra Stone. Dances directed by Private Robert Sidney and Corporal Nelson Barclift. Orchestra directed by Corporal Milton Rosenstock. Settings and costumes by Private John Koenig. Additional direction by Private Joshua Logan. Military formations by Corporal Chester O'Brien. Dialogue for Minstrel Show by Private Jack Mendelsohn, Pfc. Richard Burdick, Private Tom McDonnell. Musical arrangements for dances by Private Melvin Pahl. Produced by Uncle Sam for the benefit of the Army Emergency Relief Fund. Opened 4 July 1942 at the Broadway Theatre and closed 26 September 1942 after 113 performances.

CAST: STAFF SERGEANT EZRA STONE, SERGEANT IRVING BERLIN (1917), Private Stewart Churchill, Corporal Earl Oxford, Private William Horne, Private Jules Oshins, Pfc. Fred Kelly, Pfc. Leander Berg, Pfc. Joe Cook Jr., Private Anthony Ross, Private Robert Moore, Corporal Philip Truex, Private Hayden Rorke, Private William Pillich, Private Juss Addiss, Private Robert Sidney, Private Robert Shanley, Private Derek Fairman, Private Gary Merrill, Private Louis de Milhau, Private Ralph Margelssen, Private Ray Goss, Private Alan Manson, Private Larry Weeks, Sergeant Dick Bernie, Private Hank Henry, Private Pinkie Mitchell, Sergeant John Mendes, Pfc. James McColl, Private Ross Elliott, Private Leonard Berchman, The Allon Trio, Pfc. Louis Salmon, Sergeant Arthur Steiner, Private Samuel Carr, Private Belmonte Cristiani, Private Claude Watson, Corporal James A. Cross, Private Richard Irving, Private William Wykoff, Private Tileston Perry, Private Marion Brown, Private Joe Bush, Private Arthur Atkins, Sergeant Alan Anderson, Private Richard Reeves, Private Howard Brooks, Private Norman Van Emburgh, Private William Roerich, Private Burl Ives, Private Robert Kinne. *Yip, Yip, Yaphankers*: Peter O'Neill, Peter J. Burns, Dan Healy, John Murphy, Jack Riano, Harold Kennedy.

ACT 1

Scene 1

A Military Minstrel Show
First Interlocutor: Private G. Merrill. *Captain*: Private R. Magelssen. *Guards*: Private T. Perry, Private E. O'Connor.

a. Opening Chorus
Minstrel Men

b. "This Is the Army"
Selectees, Minstrel Men
Selectees: Privates R. Elliot, N. Sassi, H. Jones, C. Blake, S. Robin, W. Roerick, S. Saloman, K. Bates, H. Beller. *Guards*: Private J. Draper, Corporal C. O'Brien. *Second Interlocutor*: Private A. Manson.

c. "I'm Getting Tired So I Can Sleep"
Private W. Horne
Octette: Sergeant Z. Arthur, Corporal J. Burrell, Privates O. Race, J. Farrell, T. Chetlin, W. Collier, E. Lippy, D. McCray. *End Man*: Sergeant R. Bernie.

d. "My Sergeant and I"
Private P. Mitchell
End Man: Pfc. J. MacColl, assisted by Private L. Berchman. *Messenger*: Pfc. L. Salmon.

e. "I Left My Heart at the Stage Door Canteen"
Corporal E. Oxford, Company
Guards: Pfc. L. Salmon, Private R. Elliot. *Third Interlocutor*: Corporal P. Truex. *End Men*: Private J. Oshins, Sergeant E. Stone.

f. "The Army's Made a Man Out of Me"
Sergeant E. Stone, Corporal P. Truex, Private J. Oshins

g. "Mandy" (from YIP, YIP, YAPHANK)
(*Dance directed by* Pfc. F. Kelly.)
Banjoists: Privates S. Carr, C. Watson. *Mandy*: Private R. Irving. *Her Boy Friend*: PFC. F. Kelly. *Mandy Girls*: Privates L. Gengo, N. Sassi, C. Reade, E. Jarvis, J. Lenny, S. Sirois. *Mandy Boys*: Privates S. Lamarca, F. Deming, J. Wojcikowski, B. Sterner, P. King, H. Prael.

Scene 2

A Military Vaudeville Show

a. Pages
Privates R. Goss, W. Pillich

b. Kitchen Police
Privates L. Weeks, H. Henry

c. Inspection
Sergeant J. Mendes, Private R. Elliot

d. Manoeuvers
   The Allon Trio, Sergeant A. Steiner, Pfc. L. Berg, Privates B. Cristiani, P. Mitchell

Scene 3
Ladies of the Chorus (from YIP, YIP, YAPHANK)
   Girls: Privates B. Ives, A. Manson, A. Lane, R. Moore, A. Ross, S. Farnworth, L. Weill, S. Robin. *Boys*: Privates E. O'Connor, S. Salomon, R. Browning, K. Bates, R. Reeves, J. Draper, A. Bandler, D. Longo.

Scene 4
"That Russian Winter"
   Private J. Oshins
   Specialty danced by Private L. Berchman. *Girls*: Corporal N. Barclift, Private R. Sidney, Private C. Jaeger. *Boys*: Private C. Reade, Pfcs. G. Berg, F. Kelly, Privates F. Deming, J. Wojcikowski, M. Kelly, R. Irving, P. King, W. Pillich, A. Steiner, C. Ferre. *Ensemble*: B. Stermer, H. Prael, C. Reade, R. Goss, C. Gagnon, W. Lynch, R. Langdon, S. Salzberg, B. Howell, T. Cappy.

Scene 5
"What the Well Dressed Man in Harlem Will Wear"
   Sergeants. C. Turner, J. Brodmax, Corporals O. Johnson, A. Hatchett, G. Anderson, E. Allen, Privates J. Riley, R. Culley, S. Ramos, G. Watson
   Specialities: Corporal J. A. Cross, Privates M. Brown, W. Wyckoff.

Scene 6
Finale Act 1
   Entire Company
   This Is the Army Quartet: Privates T. Perry, A. Ross, J. Bush, H. Henry. *Stage Manager*: Sergeant A. Anderson. *Shore Policemen*: Privates H. Rorke, J. Addiss, H. Brooks.

ACT 2
Scene 1
Stage Door Canteen
   (*Dialogue and Direction by* Pfc. James MacColl.)
   Jane Cowl: Private A. Manson. *Sergeant*: Sergeant E. Stone. *Joe Cook*: Pfc. J. Cook, Jr. *Vera Zorina*: Corporal N. Barclift. *Noel Coward*: Private H. Rorke. *Gypsy Rose Lee*: Private J. Oshins. *Lynn Fontanne*: Private T. Perry. *Alfred Lunt*: Pfc. J. MacColl. *Eileen*: Corporal P. Truex. *Soldier*: Corporal E. Oxford. *Hostesses*: Privates A. Bandler, S. Farnworth, C. Jaeger, W. Roerick, F. Kapner, J Draper, N. Stuart, A. Whitley, L. Gengo, H. Montgomery, L. Weill, C. Blake, Cpls. C. O'Brien. *Stage Door Canteen Soldiers*: V. Campbell, S. Tamber, R. Burdick, J. Mendelsohn, D. Fairman, M. Grubman, H. Ecconomou, Sergeant Z. Arthur, J. Bush, W. Collier, T. Chetlin, L. Fried, B. Frank, F. D'Elia, R. Goss, L. Hawkins, H. Hoha, B. Ives, A. Ross, R. Magelssen, A. Canzano, J. Wiggins, R. Browning, S. Churchill, H. Rosenblatt, O. Race, M. Newman, M. Rogers, R. Reeves, M. Goodis, W. Horne, A. Atkins, S. Benson, C. Bacior, M. Fiorella, L. Salmon, D. Schoenfeld, B. Welansky, G. Simini, I. Albert, W. O'Harr, H. Horowitz, J. C. Dempsey.

Scene 2
"I'm Getting Tired So I Can Sleep" (reprise)
   Corporal N. Barclift, Privates R. Sidney, M. Kelly, Corporal C. O'Brien

Scene 3
"American Eagle" and "Head in the Clouds"
   Air Corps
   (*Written at the request of, and dedicated to* Lieutenant General Henry H. Arnold.)
   Soloist: Private R. Shanley.

Scene 4
"Aryans Under the Skin"
   Japs: Corporal P. Truex, Privates R. Moore, P. Mitchell, A. Atkins. *Germans*: Privates R. Reeves, N. Van Emburgh, B. Ives, R. Kinne.

Scene 5
"A Soldier's Dream"
   Private S. Churchill
   Sergeant: Sergeant A. Steiner. *Soldiers*: Pfc. F. Kelly, Privates W. Howell, H. Ecconomu, M. Kelly, J. Wojcikowski, F. Deming, C. Ferre. *Gypsy Violinists*: Pfc. L. Salmon, Private W. Roerick. *Valets*: Privates S. Salzberg, R. Langdon, W. Lynch, S. Farnworth, D. Fairman, H. Montgomery, A. Whitley. *Waitresses*: Privates L. Gagnon, H. Prael, B. Goss, B. Sterner, R. Irving, W. Pillich, B. Dutton. *Dream Girls*: Corporal N. Barclift, Privates J. Johnson, C. Jaeger, R. Sidney, P. King, L. Berg, F. Hearn.

Scene 6
"Oh, How I Hate to Get Up in the Morning" (from YIP, YIP, YAPHANK and ZIEGFELD FOLLIES OF 1919)
   I. Berlin, Yip Yip Yaphankers
   Yip Yip Yaphankers: P. O'Neill, P. J. Burns, D. Healy, J. Murphy, J. Riano, H. Kennedy. *Introduced by* Private G. Merrill.

Scene 7
"This Time"
   Entire Company

1942.21 **THE MERRY WIDOW**

A Revival of the Operetta in Three Acts[8]. Original Viennese libretto ("Die Lustige Witwe") by Victor Léon and Leo Stein after "L'Attaché d'Ambassade" by Henri Meilhac. Music by Franz Lehár. English lyrics by Adrian Ross. Staged by John Pierce and Felix Brentano. Artistic supervision by Richard Eichberg. Music directed by Joseph S. Tushinsky. Costumes and gowns designed by Eaves Costume Company. Produced by Joseph S. Tushinsky and Hans Bartsch. Opened 15 July 1942 at Carnegie Hall and closed 16 August 1942 after 39 performances.[9]

CAST: *St. Brioche*: Michael Fitzmaurice. *Natalie*: Elizabeth Houston. *Camille de Jolidon*: FELIX KNIGHT. *Cascada*: George Mitchell. *Olga*: Elaine Ellis. *Novakovich*: Neil Fitzgerald. *Khadja*: Roy M. Johnston. *Nish*: John Cherry. *Baron Popoff*: EDDIE GARR. *Sonia*: HELEN GLEASON. *Prince Danilo*: WILBUR EVANS. *Madame Khadja*: Harriet Borger. *Head Waiter*: Carl Nelson. *Zo Zo*: Diana Corday. *Premier Dancer*: Peter Birch. *Singers*: [same as THE CHOCOLATE SOLDIER above].

1942.22 **THE NEW MOON**

A Revival of the Operetta in Two Acts, 4 Scenes[10]. Book and lyrics by Oscar Hammerstein II, Frank Mandel and Laurence Schwab. Music by Sigmund Romberg. Staged by John Pierce. Music directed by Joseph Tushinsky. Produced by Joseph S. Tushinsky. Opened 18 August 1942 at Carnegie Hall and closed 6 September 1942 after 24 performances.[11]

CAST (in order of appearance): *Julie*: Doris Patson. *Beaunoir*: GEORGE LEONARD. *Captain Duval*: GENE BARRY. *Vicomte Ribaud*: MARCEL JOURNET. *Fouchette*: Carl Nelson. *Robert Misson*: WILBUR EVANS. *Alexander*: TEDDY HART. *Besac*: Paul Reed. *Jacques*: George Mitchell. *Marianne Beaunoir*: RUBY MERCER. *Philippe*: EVERETT WEST. *Spanish Dancer*: Viola Essenova. *Clotilde*: HOPE EMERSON. *Première Danseuse*: Viola Essen. *Premier Dancer*: Peter Birch. *Singers*: [same as THE CHOCOLATE SOLDIER above].

1942.23 **NEW PRIORITIES OF 1943**

A Variety Revue in Two Acts, 16 Scenes[12]. (Assembled by Clifford C. Fischer.) Music and lyrics by Lester Lee and Jerry Seelen. Staged by Jean Le Seyeux. Dances directed by Truly McGee. Scenery supervised by Edouard Halouze. Costumes by Mahieu. Musical director, Lou Forman. Produced by Clifford C. Fischer by arrangement with the Messrs. Shubert. Opened 15 September 1942 at the 46th Street Theatre and closed 11 October 1942 after 54 performances.[13]

CAST: HARRY RICHMAN, BERT WHEELER, CAROL BRUCE, HANK LADD, HENNY YOUNGMAN, JOHNNY BURKE, THE BRICKLAYERS, THE RADIO ACES, SALLY KEITH, HARRISON and FISHER, IMOGEN CARPENTER, The Acromaniacs, Francetta Malloy, Ted Adair, Dorothy Partington, The Priorettes.
   Dancing Priorettes: Vela Ceres, Paddy Barker, Ruth Ryder, Olga Roberts, Norma Holt, Shirley Gordon, Mary Jane Pieter, Toni Traub, Carmelita Lanza, Betty De Elmo, Xenia Astafieva, Molly Pierson, Lee Mayer. *Priorette Show Girls*: Beatrice Ratcliffe, Roy Standish, Lucille Casey, Mary Siem, Theo Willis, Pamela De Vorne.

ACT 1
Scene 1
"It's Mental"
   The Priorettes
   (*Music and Lyrics by* Lester Lee and Jerry Seelen.)

---

[8]Originally produced in New York 21 October 1907 at the New Amsterdam Theatre for 416 performances. For Synopsis of Scenes and Musical Numbers, see original 1907 production.
[9]English book uncredited. Scenery uncredited.
[10]Originally produced in New York 19 September 1928 at the Imperial Theatre for 509 performances. For Synopsis of Scenes and Musical Numbers, see original 1928 production.
[11]Settings, costumes, lighting uncredited.
[12]A successor to the previous season's PRIORITIES OF 1942 which opened 12 March 1942 at the 46th Street Theatre for 353 performances.
[13]Performed nightly, plus 5 matinees weekly.

Scene 2

The Acromaniacs (Acrobats)

Scene 3

Henny Youngman (Monologue)

Scene 4

Johnny Burke (Monologue about going to France with the AEF)

Scene 5

The Bricklayers (Dog Act)

Scene 6

Carol Bruce:
["St. Louis Blues" *Music and Lyrics by* W. C. Handy.
Medley from LOUISIANA PURCHASE, *Music and Lyrics by* Irving Berlin.
George Gershwin Medley]

Scene 7

Bert Wheeler and Hank Ladd, with Francetta Malloy.

Scene 8

Harry Richman, with Jack Golden at the piano:
["I Love a Parade" (from GEORGE WHITE'S MUSIC HALL VARIETIES;
introduced in RHYTHMANIA, Cotton Club revue)
(*Music by* Harold Arlen. *Lyrics by* Ted Koehler.)
"Puttin' on the Ritz" (from PUTTIN' ON THE RITZ film)
(*Music and Lyrics by* Irving Berlin.)]

Scene 9

"Heigh Ho, Tra, La, La, La"
C. Bruce, I. Carpenter
(*Music and Lyrics by* Lester Lee and Jerry Seelen.)

Scene 10

"Song of the WAAC's"
S. Keith
(*Music and Lyrics by* Lester Lee and Jerry Seelen.)

ACT 2

Scene 1

Harrison and Fisher (Dancers—'Amphitryon '39')

Scene 2

Henny Youngman

Scene 3

"I Like Your Style"
H. Richman, T. Adair, D. Partington
(*Music and Lyrics by* Lester Lee and Jerry Seelen.)

Scene 4

Bert Wheeler

Scene 5

The Radio Aces

Scene 6

Finale

1942.24 SHOW TIME

A Variety Show in Two Acts. (Assembled by Fred F. Finklehoffe.) Musical director, Walter Guterson. Produced by Fred F. Finklehoffe. Opened 16 September 1942 at the Broadhurst Theatre and closed 3 April 1943 after 342 performances.[14]

CAST: GEORGE JESSEL, JACK HALEY, ELLA LOGAN, THE DeMARCOS (Tony, Renee), LUCILLE NORMAN, BOB WILLIAMS, CON COLLEANO, THE BERRY BROTHERS, OLSEN and SHIRLEY.

ACT 1

Mr. George Jessel is our conferencier, a noun imported twenty years ago to describe the activities of M. Nikita Balieff as he committed assault and battery on the language in an attempt to inform the customers what was going on in his Russian vaudeville, "Chauve Souris." Freely translated into pure Broadway conferencier means "master of ceremonies," an identification worn thin through abuse. (Jessel: Salute to the Good Old Days, Telephone Conversation with Ma, Czechoslovakian Slide Lecturer, Professor Labbamacher)

In the first fraction of this performance our conferencier, Mr. Jessel, will introduce Jack Haley (operatic version of "Chattanooga Choo-Choo," letter from the draft board sketch), Lucille Norman (singer), Olsen and Shirley (contortionists), Con Colleano (high-wire dancer) and the DeMarcos (dancers).

Then, with a nod to custom, an intermission.

ACT 2

Resuming after this interval, Mr. Jessel will present Ella Logan, the Glasgow grenade:

"Strip Polka"
(*Music and Lyrics by* Johnny Mercer.)
"Something I Dreamed Last Night" (from GEORGE WHITE'S SCAN-DALS 1939)
(*Music by* Sammy Fain. *Lyrics by* Herb Magidson and Jack Yellen.)
"Shady Side of the Street"
"(It's a Long Way to) Tipperary" (interpolated into CHIN CHIN)
(*Music and Lyrics by* Jack Judge and Harry H. Williams.)
"I'll Take the High Note" (from HI YA, GENTLEMEN!)
(*Music by* Johnny Green. *Lyrics by* Harold Adamson.)]

Mr. Haley again, the dancing Berry Brothers and Bob Williams (dog act).

1942.25 WINE WOMEN AND SONG

A Revue-Vaudeville-Burlesque Show in Two Acts, 19 Scenes. (Supervised by Max Liebman.) Ensembles by Truly McGee. Orchestra directed by Murray Friedman. Decor by Frederick Fox. (Produced by Lee Shubert, I.H. Herk and Max Liebman.) Opened 28 September 1942 at the Ambassador Theatre and closed 3 December 1942 after 150 performances.[15]

CAST: MARGIE HART, JIMMY SAVO, The Wesson Brothers (Eugene, Richard), Pinky Lee, Herbie Faye, Marian Miller, Isabelle Brown, Noel Toy, Don Ritz Favorettes, Murray Briscoe, Evelyn Farney, Ruth Mason, Billy and Buster Burnell, Murray White.
Dancing Chorus: Elita Albert, Rita Carmen, Maude Carroll, Muriel Cole, Dolores Goodman, Virginia Grimes, Lucy Lewin, Sylvia Mettler, Tola Nelson, Gloria Page, Lenore Thall, Gail Vaughn. *Show Girls:* Patsy Ann, Connie Constant, Bobbe Jason, Margaret Lane, Kay Mallah, Pat Marlan, Florence Moore, Rene Stahl.

ACT 1

Scene 1

"This Is Not a Play by Saroyan"
M. Hart, Girls
(*Music and Lyrics by* Irvin Graham.)

Scene 2

Queen of Quiver
M. Miller

Scene 3

Shore Leave
P. Lee, M. White, M. Hart

Scene 4

Noel Toy (Oriental Fan Dance)

Scene 5

Confidential Loan
H. Faye, M. Briscoe, R. Mason, E. Wesson

Scene 6

Don Ritz Favorettes

Scene 7

52nd Street
J. Savo, M. Hart, M. Briscoe, M. White

Scene 8

It's Smart to be Stupid
H. Faye, R. Mason

Scene 9

Strawberry Blonde
Don Ritz Favorettes, B. and B. Burnell, Girls

---

[14]Direction, costumes, settings uncredited. Performed nightly, plus 5 matinees weekly.

[15]Performed twice daily, with 3 performances Saturdays and Sundays.

Scene 10
Wesson Brothers (Impersonators, President and Mrs. Roosevelt sing)
Scene 11
Jitterbug Wedding
B. and B. Burnell, R. Wesson
ACT 2
Scene 1
Starry Night
M. White, I. Brown, Girls
Scene 2
Taking Her Home
H. Faye, M. Hart
Scene 3
New York Cowboy
M. White, E. Farney, Girls
Scene 4
Hands Off (Strip tease)
I. Brown
Scene 5
Jimmy Savo
["River, Stay Away from My Door"
(*Music by* Harry Woods. *Lyrics by* Mort Dixon.)]
Scene 6
Margie Hart (Strip tease), asssisted by Don Ritz Favorettes
Song by Irvin Graham.
Scene 7
Jivin' Around
P. Lee, M. Briscoe, Girls
Scene 8
Finale
Entire Company

1942.26   # LET FREEDOM SING

A Musical Revue in Two Acts, 24 Scenes. Sketches by Sam Locke. Music and lyrics mostly by Harold Rome. Additional music and lyrics by Earl Robinson, Marc Blitzstein, Lou Cooper, Roslyn Harvey, Walter Kent, (John Latouche, Hy Zaret, Jack Gerald, David Greggory, Jay Gorney, Henry Myers, Edward Eliscu and Lewis Allen). Staged by Joseph C. Pevney. Settings by Herbert Andrews. Costumes by Paul duPont. Dance direction by Dan Eckley. Musical direction by Lou Cooper. Musical arrangements by Morton Gould and Phil Lang. Orchestra directed by David Mordecai. Produced by Youth Theatre. Opened 5 October 1942 at the Longacre Theatre and closed 10 October 1942 after 8 performances.

<u>CAST</u>: MITZI GREEN, BERNI GOULD, LEE SULLIVAN, BETTY GARRETT, PHIL LEEDS, MORDECAI [Morty] BAUMAN, Jane Johnstone, Jack Baker, Margie Jackson, Bob Davis, Joan Dexter, Marion Warnes, Jules Racine, Ethel Sherman, Bill Randall, Lois Girard, Harry Mack, Sally Gracie, Remi Martel, Ruth Cavanaugh, Pat Shibley, Buddy Yarus, Molly Hoban.

ACT 1[16]
Scene 1
"Ring Up the Curtain"
(*Music and Lyrics by* Harold Rome.)
Scene 2
"It's Fun to Be Free"
Entire Company
(*Music and Lyrics by* Harold Rome.)
Scene 3
Tactics
First Man: B. Gould. *Second Man*: P. Leeds.

---

[16]The following sketches were added for the subsequent tour:
Ivan the Terrible
(*by* Al Geto)
N.B.C. Goes to War
(*by* Sam Locke)
Hy'a Joe
(*by* Al Geto). [This may be same as Tactics, above.]

Scene 4
"The Lady Is a WAAC"
M. Green
(*Music and Lyrics by* Harold Rome.)
Danced by J. Johnstone, M. Jackson, M. Warnes, E. Sherman, L. Girard, P. Shibley.
Scene 5
A Night in Washington
Landlady: B. Garrett. *Mr. Dwerp*: P. Leeds. *Jenkins*: R. Martel. *Judd*: B. Gould. *Smith*: B. Yarus. *Secretary*: M. Jackson. *Leon Henderson*: H. Mack. *Seantor*: M. Bauman. *Spy*: J. Dexter. *F.B.I. Man*: J. Baker. *Dollar a Year Men*: J. Racine, B. Davis. *Congressman*: B. Randall.
Scene 6
"I Did It for Defense"
M. Green
(*Music and Lyrics by* Harold Rome.)
Scene 7
"We Have a Date"
J. Dexter, L. Sullivan
(*Music by* Lou Cooper. *Lyrics by* Roslyn Harvey.)
Danced by J. Johnstone, J. Baker, Company.
Scene 8
"Be Calm"
(*Music and Lyrics by* Harold Rome.)
Chairlady: B. Garrett. *Senator*: B. Gould. *Attendants*: J. Racine, B. Davis.
Scene 9
Congress
First Senator: J. Baker. *Second Senator*: M. Bauman.
Scene 10
"History Eight to the Bar"
(*Music and Lyrics by* Harold Rome. *Staged by* Robert H. Gordon.)
Teacher: B. Garrett. *Students*: Ensemble.
Scene 11
Mitzi Green
Scene 12
"Little Miss Victory Jones"
L. Sullivan, Entire Company
(*Music and Lyrics by* Harold Rome.)

ACT 2
Scene 1
"Give a Viva!"
B. Garrett, Entire Company
(*Music and Lyrics by* Harold Rome.)
Scene 2
How Do I Get There? (*by* Al Gheto)
First Man: B. Gould. *Second Man*: P. Leeds.
Scene 3
"The Little Things We Like"
M. Green, L. Sullivan
(*Music by* Lou Cooper. *Lyrics by* Roslyn Harvey.)
Scene 4
"Flowers in Bloom"
P. Leeds
(*Music by* Jack Gerald. *Lyrics by* David Greggory.)
Scene 5
Women in Uniform
Captain Flagg: B. Garrett. *Sergeant Squirt*: M. Green. *Blotto*: B. Gould. *WAAC Girls*: J. Johnstone, M. Jackson, M. Warnes, E. Sherman, L. Girard, P. Shibley.
Scene 6
Blackout Blackout
B. Yarus, M. Bauman, R. Cavanaugh, R. Martel, H. Mack, M. Hoban, B. Randall, L. Girard, S. Gracie
Scene 7
"The House I Live In"
M. Bauman
(*Music by* Earl Robinson. *Lyrics by* Lewis Allen.)
Scene 8
"Grandpa Guerrila"
M. Green, Entire Company
(*Music by* Walter Kent. *Lyrics by* Hy Zaret. *Choreography by* Ken Whelan.)

Scene 9

"Johnny Is a Hoarder"
(*Music and Lyrics by* Harold Rome. *Staged by* Robert H. Gordon.)
Johnny: P. Leeds. *Janie*: B. Garrett.

Scene 10

"Mittel Europa"
B. Gould, J. Baker, H. Mack, R. Martel, J. Racine
(*Music and Lyrics by* Jay Gorney, Henry Myers, Edward Eliscu.)

Scene 11

"Fraught" (from NO FOR AN ANSWER)
M. Green, P. Leeds
(*Music and Lyrics by* Marc Blitzstein.)

Scene 12

"Of the People Stomp" (from THE LITTLE DOG LAUGHED)
B. Garrett, Entire Company
(*Music and Lyrics by* Harold Rome.)

1942.27   COUNT ME IN

An All-American Musical Comedy in Two Acts, 16 Scenes. Book by Walter Kerr, Leo Brady (and Nancy Hamilton.) Music and lyrics by Ann Ronell. Book staged by Robert Ross. Production supervised by Harry Kaufman. Musical numbers staged by Robert Alton. Settings by Howard Bay. Costumes by Irene Sharaff. Orchestrations by (Robert) Russell Bennett. Orchestra conducted by John McManus. Special orchestral arrangements by Hans Spialek and Don Walker. Vocal arrangements by Buck [Clay] Warnick. Produced by the Messrs. Shubert, Ole Olsen and Chic Johnson in association with Richard Krakeur and W. Horace Schmidlapp[17]. Opened 8 October 1942 at the Ethel Barrymore Theatre and closed 28 November 1942 after 61 performances.

<u>CAST</u>: CHARLES BUTTERWORTH, LOUELLA GEAR, HAL LeROY, JUNE PREISSER, MARY HEALY, GOWER (Champion) and JEAN (Tyler), MELISSA MASON, ALICE DUDLEY, MILTON WATSON, THE ROSS SISTERS (Betsy, Vicki, Dixie), THE RHYTHMAIRES (Robert Bay, Don Weissmuller, Robert Shaw, Victor Griffin), JOHN McCAULEY, JOE E. MARKS, ALFRED LATELL, DON RICHARDS, Willard Woolsey, William Sharon, Willis Claire, Whitner Bissell, Gibbs Penrose, Jack Lambert, Lew Eckles, Stanley Jessup.
Singing Girls: Julie Colt, Jean Darling, Agnes Kane, Cornelia Kilbourn, Johanna Gillman, Olga Novosel, Marian Sumetz, Alice Tyrell. *Dancing Girls*: Jean Arthur, Carolyn Ayers, Mary Alice Bigham, Kay Coulter, Dorothy Griffin, Cookie Kley, June Kim, Kay Lewis, Claire Loring, Bubbles Mandel, Dolores Milan, Janie New, Jeane Owens, Margaret Ryan, Elizabeth Ryan, Nina Starkey, Pay Weakley, Marie Wilson. *Dancing Boys*: Leonard Adriance, Jim Barron, Vincent Carbone, Danny Daniels, Charles Julian, William O'Shay, Jack Riley, Harry Rogue, Joe Viggiano.

ACT 1
PAPA'S TRIBULATION
Scene 1

"All-Out Bugle Call"
Rhythmaires, Singing Girls, Dancing Girls and Boys

Scene 2

Life With the Brandywines
Scene: Somewhere in Connecticut.
Priscilla, the maid: M. Mason. *Sherry Brandywine*: M. Healy. *Teddy Roosevelt Brandywine*: G. Champion. *Alvin York Brandywine*: H. LeRoy. *Mama*: L. Gear. *Papa*: C. Butterworth. *Radio Voice*: J. McCauley.

"The Way My Ancestors Went"
C. Butterworth
General Brandywine, Revolutionary War: R. Bay. *Captain Brandywine*, War of 1812: D. Weissmuller. *Lieutenant Brandywine*, Civil War: R. Shaw. *Private Brandywine*: Spanish-American War: V. Griffin. *Cadet Brandywine*: W. Woolsey. *Aunt Carrie Brandywine*: A. Dudley.

Scene 3

On Duty With Alvin
Scene: 24th and Bleak.
Alvin: H. LeRoy. *Tommy*: J. Preisser. *Papa*: C. Butterworth. *Alvin's Girlfriends*: Themselves.

<hr>

[17]Sketches for slides for Papa's illustrated lecture drawn by Eric Ericson. Papa at age of one posed by Baby Farrell. Management extends sincere thanks to Lester Lee and Jerry Seelen.

"Someone in the Know"
J. Preisser, H. LeRoy
Three Little Girls: Ross Sisters. *Dancers*: H. Rogue, Girls, Boys.

Scene 4

On Duty With Mama
Scene: History, A.
Mama: L. Gear. *The W.A.A.P.'s*: Singing Girls. *Marianne*: D. Griffin. *Hilda & Hulda*: M. Ryan, E. Ryan. *Olga*: M. A. Bigham. *Dolores*: B. Mandl. *Lotus*: J. Kim. *Papa*: C. Butterworth.

"On Leave for Love"
L. Gear

Scene 5

On Duty With Sherry
Scene: First Aid Class.
Sherry: M. Healy. *Janie*: J. New. *Jean*: J. Arthur. *Carolyn*: C. Ayers. *Papa*: C. Butterworth. *Nurse*: A. Dudley. *Bandagers*: Ross Sisters. *Dr. Heart*: M. Watson. *Sad Eyes*: A. Latell.

"You've Got It All"
M. Healy, M. Watson

Scene 6

On Duty With Ted—"O.K.—1-A"
Scene: Induction Center.
First Examiner: J. McCauley. *Second Examiner*: W. Sharon. *Third Examiner*: W. Claire. *First Draftee*: W. Bissell. *Second Draftee*: G. Penrose. *Third Draftee*: J. Lambert. *Fourth Draftee*: J. E. Marks. *Fifth Draftee*: H. Rogue. *Sixth Draftee*: D. Daniels. *Runner*: W. Woolsey. *Ted*: G. Champion. *Papa*: C. Butterworth.

Scene 7

"Why Do They Always Say They're the Fair Sex?"
D. Richards, Rhythmaires, Singing Girls
Scene: Alvin's Post.
Danced by G. Champion, J. Tyler, Girls, Boys.
Tommy: J. Preisser. *Alvin*: H. LeRoy. *Sherry*: M. Healy. *Dr. Heart*: M. Watson. *Papa*: C. Butterworth. *Mama*: L. Gear. *Aides*: J. Darling, A. Kane. *Sad Eyes*: A. Latell.

Scene 8

Scene: At Papa's Map Office.
Papa: C. Butterworth. *Tommy*: J. Preisser. *Alvin*: H. LeRoy. *F.B.I. Men*: L. Eckles, G. Penrose, S. Jessup. *Sherry*: M. Healy. *Dr. Heart*: M. Watson. *Ted*: G. Champion. *Mama*: L. Gear.

"We're Still on the Map" (*Choreographic Music by* Will Irwin.)
Singers: M. Healy, M. Watson. *Coordinator*: D. Richards. *The West*: M. Mason, The Rhythmaires. *The North*: M. Healy, M. Watson, J. McCauley, A. Latell. *The South*: G. Champion, J. Tyler, G. Penrose, W. Woolsey. *The Southwest*: L. Gear, R. Brasno, Rhythmaires. *Dancers*: H. LeRoy, J. Preisser, Rhythmaires, Girls, Boys.

ACT 2
PAPA'S TRIUMPH
Scene 1

Papa's Warning
Scene: Australia.
American Announcer: W. Claire. *Australian Announcer*: W. Bissell. *Ted*: G. Champion. *Richard*: D. Richards.

"Ticketyboo"
D. Richards, Singing Girls
Danced by A. Dudley, G. Champion, J. Tyler, Girls, Boys.
Ticketyboo: A. Latell. *Ickety Ticketyboo*: R. Brasno.

Scene 2

Papa's Internment
Scene: Somewhere in Virginia.
Four Japs: Rhythmaires. *Mr. Moto*: J. E. Marks. *Chinese Laundrymen*: G. Penrose, J. Lambert. *Sergeant*: J. McCauley. *Papa*: C. Butterworth.

"Who Is General Staff?"
J. E. Marks, Rhythmaires

Scene 3

On Manoeuvres With Mama
Sergeant Brandywine: L. Gear. *Pvt. Sweeney*: A. Tyrell. *Susy Phillips*: J. Colt. *Wilma*: O. Novosel. *Myrtle*: M. A. Bigham. *Pvt. Vanderhoff*: C. Kley. *Pvt. McMullen*: J. Arthur. *Pvt. Simpson*: D. Griffin. *Pvt. Hamilton*: M. Sumetz. *Tommy*: J. Preisser. *Sad Eyes*: A. Latell.

"Why Do They Say They're the Fair Sex?" (reprise)
Danced by H. LeRoy

Scene 4

"The Woman of the Year" (*Choreographic Music by* Will Irwin.)
> *The Singers*: M. Healy, Singing Girls. *Columbia*: A. Dudley. *The Dancers*:
> Rhythmaires, Girls, Boys.

Scene 5

Papa's Recapture
> *Priscilla*: M. Mason. *Lowell Cabot, U.S.N.*: W. Bissell. *Benny The Gut, U.S.N.*:
> J. Lambert. *Sherry*: M. Healy. *Dr. Heart*: M. Watson. *Papa*: C. Butterworth.
> *Mama*: L. Gear. *Alvin*: H. LeRoy. *Tommy*: J. Preisser. *Three F.B.I. Men*: L.
> Eckles, G. Penrose, S. Jessup.

"You've Got It All" (reprise)
> M. Healy, M. Watson

Scene 6

"On Leave for Love"
> M. Mason, W. Bissell, J. Lambert

Scene 7

Papa's Investigation
> *Scene*: Washington, D.C.
> *First Officer*: J. McCauley. *Second Officer*: W. Claire. *Third Officer*: W. Sharon.
> *F.B.I. Men*: L. Eckles, G. Penrose, S. Jessup. *Papa*: C. Butterworth. *Alvin*: H.
> LeRoy.

Scene 8

Papa's Return
> *Scene*: The Village Green Canteen.

Finale
> Entire Company

OY IS DUS A LEBEN!

1942.28

(Oh, What a Life!)

A Musical Cavalcade in Two Acts, a Prologue and 9 Scenes, in Yiddish
and English. Book by Jacob Kalich. (Based on the life of Molly Picon
and Jacob Kalich.) Lyrics by Molly Picon. Music by Joseph Rumshinsky.
Staged by Jacob Kalich. Dances directed by David Lubritsky. Settings by
Harry Gordon Bennett. Produced by Edwin A. Relkin. Opened 12 October
1942 at the Molly Picon Theatre[18] and closed 6 February 1943 after 139
performances.

CAST (in order of appearance): *Prologue. Theater*: Leon Gold. *Achashverosh*: David
Lubritsky. *Vaschti*: Jennie Casher. *Vaizuso*: ESTA SALTZMAN. *Broder Zinger*: Sam
Levine, S. Steinberg, L. Yachson, H. Lieberman. *Jacob P. Adler*: Boris Auerbach.
David Kessler: IZIDOR CASHER. *Sigmund Mogilesco*: Sam Kasten. *Boris Thomashefsky*:
Michael Wilenski. *Bessie Thomashefsky*: Tillie Rabinowitz. *Keni Lipzin*: Celia Pearson.
Bertha Kalich: Rose Greenfield.
  In the Play. Molly, a stage-struck girl: MOLLY PICON. *Mr. Kay*, a youth with the-
atrical ambitions: JACOB KALICH. *Mrs. Picon*, a wardrobe mistress: Dora Weissman.
Ziggie, a former undertaker now a manager: IZIDOR CASHER. *Rosalia*, a theatrical
nightingale: ANNA APPEL. *Misha*, her son, an actor with a future: LEON GOLD. *A
Comedian*: Sam Kasten. *Sylvia*, an actress: ESTA SALTZMAN. *Nadya*, a chorine:
Jennie Casher. *Zelda*, sells knishes at the theatre: Tillie Rabinowitz. *Rebbitzen*, Kay's
mother: Rosa Greenfield. *Schlome*, Kay's step-father: Charles Cohan. *Zalmyn*,
Rebbitzen's lazy son-in-law: David Lubritsky. *Getzel*, a sexton: Boris Auerbach. *Chayeh-
Sura*: Rebecca Weintraub. *Two Romanian policemen*: Morris Friedman, Samuel
Mlanock. *Judah, Israel*, two refugee children: Sam Milman, Herbert Cohen.

Prologue: The Yiddish Theatre of Yesteryear.

Act 1, Scene 1: Stage of Arch Street Theatre, Philadelphia, 1912. *Scene 2*: Grand Opera
House, Boston, 1918. *Scene 3*: Onstage, prior to curtain rise. Eight weeks later. *Scene 4*:
First performance of "Molly Dolly" at the Grand Opera House. Scene of play takes
place on a farm in the Catskills.

Act 2, Scene 1: The first performance of "Schmendrick" at Teater Cel mare (Royal
Theatre), Bucharest, Romania, 1923. *Scene 2*: A Little Town in Galicia, Poland.
Several weeks later. *Scene 3*: The home of Mr. Kay's Mother. *Scenes 4 and 5*: The
Molly Picon Theatre.

MUSICAL NUMBERS[19]

"Oy, Is Dus a Leben!"

"I Don't Want to Be A Man"
> M. Picon

1942.29

BEAT THE BAND

A Musical Comedy in Two Acts, 14 Scenes. Book by George Marion, Jr.
and George Abbott. Music by Johnny Green. Lyrics by George Marion, Jr.
Dances by David Lichine. Settings by Sam Leve. Costumes by Freddy
Wittop. Orchestrations by Donald Walker. Orchestra conductor, Archie
Bleyer. Staged by George Abbott. Produced by George Abbott. Opened 14
October 1942 at the 46th Street Theatre and closed 12 December 1942 after
68 performances.

CAST (in order of appearance): *Buster da Costa*: ROMO VINCENT. *Veronica*:
Joan Caulfield. *Hugo Dillingham*: JERRY LESTER. *Willow Willoughby*: Toni
Gilman. *Mr. Pirosch*: Ralph Bunker. *Princess*: EUNICE HEALY. *Damon Dillingham*:
JACK WHITING. *Doorman*: James Lane. *Drummer*: LEONARD SUES. *Trumpet
Player*: JOHNNY MACK. *Band Girl*: EVELYN BROOKS. *Mamita*: JUANITA
JUAREZ. *Querida*: SUSAN MILLER. *Don Domingo*: Averell Harris. *First Detective*:
Brian Connaught. *Second Detective*: Marc Platt. *Hotel Manager*: Cliff Dunstan. *Bell
Girl*: Doris Dowling. *Hotel Owner*: John Clarke.
  Dancing Girls: Dorothy Barrett, Tessie Corrano, Eileen Devlin, Doris Dowling,
Marilyn Hightower, Rhoda Hoffman, Muriel Hunt, Terry Kelly, Margaret Long, Mary
MacDonnell, Frances Martone, Judy O'Brien, Ellen Taylor, Mimi Walthers, Doris
York. *Singing Girls*: Kathleen Canes, Anita Dillon, Dolores Gaylord, Rosalind
Madison, Leonore Rae, Roberta Welch, Nellihew Winger, Beverly Whitney. *Dancing
Boys*: Jack Allen, Richard Andre, Larry Baker, Bob Copsey, Stanley Donen, Sidney
Gordon, Harold Haskins, Herb Lurie, Robert McKernan.
  Damon Dillingham's Band: Johnny Mack (*drums*); Leonard Sues, Steady Nelson,
Clarence Willard (*trumpets*); Ford Leary, Spud Murphy (*trombones*); Pete Pumiglio
(*clarinet*); Dave Harris (*tenor sax*); Dick Kissinger (*bass*); David LeWinter (*piano*).

Act 1, Scene 1: A Theatrical Agent's Office. *Scene 2*: The Terrace, one week later. *Scene
3*: The Apartment. *Scene 4*: Theatrical Agent's Office, one week later. *Scene 5*: The
Terrace. *Scene 6*: The Apartment.

Act 2, Scene 1: A Corridor. *Scene 2*: The Apartment. *Scene 3*: The Lobby of the Savoy-
Perkins Hotel, Washington, D.C. *Scene 4*: The Boiler-Room of the Savoy-Perkins
Hotel. *Scene 5*: The Lobby. *Scene 6*: A Peach Orchard Outside of Washington, D.C.
Scene 7: The Lobby . *Scene 8*: Opening Night of The Boiler-Room Cafe.

ACT 1

Scene 1

"Down Through the Agents"
> R. Vincent, Wiman Girls, Cole Porter Girls,
> Script Girls, Bistro Girls, Ballet Boys, Male Quartet,
> Saroyan Boy

Scene 2

"Free, Cute and Size Fourteen"
> J. Lester, E. Healy
> *Danced by* Ensemble and E. Healy.

Scene 3

"Song of Two Islands"
> S. Miller

"Keep It Casual"
> J. Whiting, S. Miller
> *Danced by* J. Mack, Dancing Girls and Boys.

"Proud of You"
> J. Whiting

Scene 4

"Break It Up"
> R. Vincent, Damon Dillingham's Band

Trumpet Solo
> L. Sues

Scene 6[20]

"Let's Comb Beaches"
> J. Whiting, S. Miller

The Swimmers
> D. York, M. Platt, Ensemble

"America Loves a Band"
> S. Miller, J. Whiting, E. Healy, R. Vincent,
> J. Juarez, J. Lester, Ensemble, Damon Dillingham's
> Band

---

[18]Previously known as Jolson's 59th Street Theatre. Costumes, lighting
uncredited.
[19]Musical numbers not listed in programs.

[20]Added during run to Scene 6 between The Swimmers and "America
Loves a Band":
  "The Hula Girl"
> L. Rae

ACT 2

Scene 1

"The Afternoon of a Phoney"
R. Vincent, Clients
Danced by E. Healy, M. Platt.

Scene 2

"Men"
J. Juarez, S. Miller

Scene 4

"(The) Steam Is On the Beam"
E. Healy, E. Brooks, J. Whiting, R. Vincent, L. Sues,
J. Mack, M. Hightower, L. Baker, Damon Dillingham's Band, Ensemble

Scene 5

"I'm Physical, You're Cultured"
J. Lester, T. Gilman

Scene 6

"Every Other Heartbeat"
S. Miller, J. Whiting, L. Sues, Singing Girls

Scene 8

"The Four Freedoms—Calypso"
J. Juarez, J. Whiting, J. Lester, R. Vincent, Entire Company

The Encore
S. Miller

THE TIME, THE PLACE AND THE GIRL

1942.30

A Musical Comedy in Two Acts. Book by Will Morrissey and John Neff. Based on the original version[21] by Will M. Hough, Frank R. Adams and Joe Howard. Lyrics by William B. Friedlander. Music by Joe Howard. Staged by William B. Friedlander. Choreography by Carl Randall. Musical director, Louis Katzman. Settings by Karl Amend. Costumes by Paul duPont. Orchestrations and vocal arrangements by Louis Katzman. Produced by Georges D. Gersene. Opened 21 October 1942 at the Mansfield Theatre and closed 31 October 1942 after 13 performances.

CAST (in order of appearance): *Mrs. Talcott*: EVELYN CASE. *Molly Kelly*: VICKIE CUMMINGS. *Joe Howard*: JOE HOWARD. *A Guide*: James Philips. *A Patient*: Robert Douglas. *Tom Cunningham*: LEE SULLIVAN. *Johnny Hicks*: "RED" MARSHALL. *Mr. Duval*: ROLFE SEDAN. *An Attendant*: Fred Kuhnly. *Lawrence Farnham*: RICHARD WORTH. *Margaret Howard*: IRENE HILDA. *Willie Talcott*: DUKE NORMAN. *A Policeman*: James Phillips. *Ballerina*: RAE McGREGOR.

Nurses, Guests, Boarding School Girls, Sanitarium Attendants, Patients, Inmates, etc.: THE BUCCANEERS: James Phillips, Wilson Lang, Fred Kuhnly, Robert Douglas. THE SOPHISTI-KIDS: Irene Carrol, May Muth, Terry Saunders, Doris Pare, Jimmy Allison, Ray Cook, Gene Stern, Andrew Thurston. *Specialty Dancers*: Kendrick Coy, Alfred Weber. *The Girls*: Olga Alexandrova, Kay Dowd, Rhoda Gerard, Sheila Herman, Marion Lulling, Peggy Lynn, Ruth Mitchell, Dorothy Ostrander, Connie Sheldon, Dot Sloane, Fanette Stalle, Dorothy Stirwalt, Helen Zurad.

Act 1: Grounds of the Sanitarium and Hotel of the famous Keeley Cure in the Mountains of Virginia. Afternoon.

Act 2: Grounds of the Sanitarium. Evening of the same day.

ACT 1

"There's a Little Man on My Shoulder"
The Buccaneers, The Sophisti-Kids, Ensemble
Danced by D. Norman.

"Ocarina"
E. Case, The Sophisti-Kids, The Buccaneers

"Travelling Man"
R. Worth, The Buccaneers, The Sophisti-Kids

"Something in My Eye"
I. Hilda, Dancing Ensemble
(*Music and Lyrics by* Joe Howard, Randolph and Britten)

"Dr. Keeley"
V. Cummings, R. Marshall

"Will-o'-the-Wisp"
E. Case, The Sophisti-Kids

Danced by R. McGregor, K. Coy, W. Weber, Ensemble. Dance Sequence transcribed by Borris Kogan.

Dance
D. Norman

"A Penny for Your Thoughts, Junior Miss"
I. Hilda, L. Sullivan, The Sophisti-Kids
(*Vocal Arrangements by* Borris Kogan.)
Danced by Dancing Girls.

"The Custom of Dressing for Dinner" (Finale Act 1)
E. Case, Entire Ensemble
Danced by R. McGregor, K. Coy, W. Weber.

ACT 2

"The Custom of Dressing for Dinner" (reprise)

"Work Eight Hours"
L. Sullivan, Entire Company

"Treason"
I. Hilda, R. Worth

"Rations"
V. Cummings, R. Marshall, Dancing Ensemble

"I Can't Get Along With You"
I. Hilda, L. Sullivan

Song Hits
J. Howard

ROSALINDA

1942.31

An Operetta in a Prologue and Three Acts. Adapted from the Max Reinhardt version of "Die Fledermaus."[22] Music by Johann Strauss. American book by Gottfried Reinhardt and John Meehan, Jr. Lyrics by Paul Kerby. Conducted by Eric Wolfgang Korngold. Dances by George Balanchine. Staged by Felix Brentano. Settings by Oliver Smith. Costumes by Ladislas Czettel. Lighting by Jean Rosenthal. (Produced under the supervision of Max Reinhardt.) Produced by Lodewick Vroom for the New Opera Company. Opened 28 October 1942 at the 44th Street Theatre, moved 24 May 1943 to the Imperial Theatre, moved 4 October 1943 to the 44th Street Theatre, moved 15 November 1943 to the 46th Street Theatre, and closed 22 January 1944 after 521 performances.

CAST (in order of appearance): *Alfredo Allevano*: Everett West. *Gabriel Von Eisenstein*: RALPH HERBERT. *Adele*: VIRGINIA MacWATTERS. *Rosalinda Von Eisenstein*: DOROTHY SARNOFF, Frances McCann (matinees). *Blint*: Leonard Stocker. *Falke*: GENE BARRY. *Dr Frank*: PAUL BEST. *Fifi*: Shelley Winter [Winters]. *Prince Orlofsky*: OSCAR KARLWEIS. *Aide de Camp*: Edwin Fowler. *Frosch*: LOUIS SORIN. *Premier Dancer*: José Limon. *Première Danseuse*: Mary Ellen.

Ladies of the Ensemble: Nina Alen, Thelma Altman, Betty Baker, Xenia Baker, Nancy Baskerville, Jeanne Beauvais, Lillian C. Bennett, Betty Billings, Diana Corday, Anne Dawson, Camille Fischelli, Lucy Marshall, Frances McCann, Joan O'Neill, Dorothy Ramsey, Loretta Schere, Joan Wheatley, Jane Whyte. *Gentlemen of the Ensemble*: Marden Bate, Edwin Fowler, David Goldstein, Harold Gordon, William Herne, Alfred Kunz, Lawrence Lieberman, Alfred D. Morgan, Benjamin Siegel, Robert Tower, Bernard Tunisse, George V. Vincent, Alan Winston.
Ballet: Lillian Lanese, Yvonne Patterson, Phyllis Hill, Joyce Hill, Elise Reiman, Betty Lou Reed, Yvonne Tibor, Anne (Anna) Wiman, Julia Horvath, Sonya (Sonia) Orlova, Douglas Caudy (Coudy), Todd Bolender, Herbert Bliss, Jack Gansaert (Gansert), Edward Bigelow, Jean Faust, Simon Sadoff, William Dollar (ballet master).

The action takes place in a summer resort, near Vienna, in the year 1890.

Prologue: Outside Von Eisenstein's House.

Act 1: Living-Room of Von Eisenstein's House. A few hours later.

Act 2: Ballroom at Prince Orlofsky's Palace. A few hours later.

Act 3: The Warden's Office at Local Jail. 6 A.M. the following morning.

PROLOGUE[23]

Adele's Letter Song
V. MacWatters

Alfredo's Serenade
E. West

---

[21]Originally produced in New York 5 August 1907 for 32 performances. With the exception of the Song Hits Medley, no songs in this revival appeared in the original 1907 production.

[22]Original Viennese libretto by Carl Haffner and Richard Genée, based on "Le Reveillon" by Henri Meilhac and Ludovic Halévy.
[23]Musical Numbers do not appear in program, but are taken from the published musical score.

ACT 1
  Trio
    D. Sarnoff, R. Herbert, L. Stocker
  Recitative
    R. Herbert
  Second Recitative
    D. Sarnoff
  Duet
    G. Barry, R. Herbert
  "Rosalinda, Love of Mine"
    E. West
  Third Recitative
    R. Herbert, V. MacWatters, D. Sarnoff
  Trio
    R. Herbert, V. MacWatters, D. Sarnoff
  Strip Tease Duet
    D. Sarnoff, V. MacWatters
  Duet
    E. West, D. Sarnoff
  Drinking Song
    E. West
  Finale Act 1

ACT 2
  Introductory Chorus
    Guests
  Parlando Chorus
    Guests
  Falke's Song ("Chacun à son gout")
    G. Barry
  Marquis Song ("Laughing Song")
    O. Karlweis
  Czardas
    D. Sarnoff, G. Barry
  Watch Duet
    D. Sarnoff, R. Herbert
  Ballet ("Wine, Women and Song")
    Ensemble
  Drinking Song
    Entire Company
  Merci
    Entire Company
  Brother Mine
    Entire Company
  Finale Act 2
    Entire Company

ACT 3
  "Rosalinda, Love of Mine" (reprise)
    E. West
  Dream Pantomime
    P. Best, L. Sorin
  Audition Song
    V. MacWatters
  Duet
    P. Best, R. Herbert
  Trio
    E. West, D. Sarnoff, R. Herbert
  Finale Act 3
    Entire Company

1942.32   LA VIE PARISIENNE

A Return Engagement of the Comic Opera in Three Acts, 4 Scenes[24]. Music by Jacques Offenbach. New English book by Felix Brentano and

---

[24]This version previously presented 5 November 1941 at the 44th Street Theatre for 7 performances. For Synopsis of Scenes and Musical Numbers, see previous 1941 production. First presented in New York in English 18 April 1883 at the Bijou Theatre in a version (LA VIE) by H. B. Farnie.

Louis Verneuil after the original libretto to the French opéra-bouffe by Henri Meilhac and Ludovic Halévy. New lyrics by Marion Farquhar. Additional dialogue by Frank Torloff and Leo Riskin. Directed by Felix Brentano. Settings and costumes designed by Marco Montedoro. Musical direction by Paul Breisach. Produced by the New Opera Company. Opened 10 November 1942 at the Broadway Theatre and closed 7 December 1942 after 17 performances in repertory.

CAST (in order of appearance): *Station Master*: Stanley Carlson. *Comte Raoul de Gardefeu*, a rich nobleman: DONALD BURR. *Baron Bobinet*, his friend: WILBUR EVANS. *Jackson*, trainer of Mr. Hutchinson's race horses: PAUL REED. *Metella*, famous opera singer: CAROLINA SEGRERA. *Gontran*, a man about town: Paul Kwartin. *Evelyn*, his daughter: VIRGINIA CARD. *Mr. Hutchinson*, an American millionaire: HUGH THOMPSON. *Gabrielle*, a modiste: ANDZIA KUZAK. *Alphonse*, Gardefeu's butler: Paul Kwartin. *Tradespeople*: Mary Davis, Cynthia Rose, Josephine Griffin. *Revolutionary*: Stanley Carlson.

    Chorus: Mary David, Josephine Griffin, Margaret Ormos, Cynthia Rose, Freda Starr, Carol Yorke, Alice Philipps, Julia Beoletto, Marian Ross, Maria Orleos, Marie Fox, Zadah Guerian, Meta Hartog, Louise Fearney, Patricia Neway, Elsa Fiore. Hans Kuhn, Elton Plowman, Eric Rautens, Nathaniel Sprinzena, Samuel Adams, Carter Farriss, Franz George, Roger Hill, Bertram Breiss, Walter Graf, Romeo Rim, Boris Brown, Ludlow White, Sebastian Engelberg, Tony Gardell, Raymond Pach.

    Ballet: Anne Barlow, Margit DeKova, Arlene Garver, Pauline Goddard, Georgia Hiden, Miriam Oreck, Mary Jane Shea, Beatrice Tompkins, Jane (Jayne) Ward, Nora White, Baret Cummings, Nicholas Magallanes, Frank (Francisco) Moncion, Stanley Zompakos. *Première Danseuse*: Gisella Caccialanza.

1942.33   ONCE OVER LIGHTLY

A Musical Play in a Prologue and Two Acts. (Libretto) Americanized from Beaumarchais' "The Barber of Seville" by László Halász. Original music of Gioacchino Rossini (from the opera "Il Barbiere di Siviglia"). Dialogues and solos by Louis Garden. Additional dialogue by Robert Pierpont Forshaw. Staged by Robert H. Gordon. Ensembles by George Mead. Settings by Richard Rychtarik. Costumes by Eaves. Lighting by Century Lighting. Conductor, László Halász. Produced by Saul Colin in association with Henry Leiser. Opened 19 November 1942 at the Alvin Theatre and closed 22 November 1942 after 6 performances.

CAST: *Figaro*: IGOR GORIN, John De Surra. *Rosina*: GRACE PANVINI, Frances Watkins. *Almaviva*: FELIX KNIGHT, Robert Marshall. *Don Basilio*: CARLOS ALEXANDER, Harold Kravitt. *Dr. Bartolo*: RICHARD WENTWORTH, Carlos Alexander. *Bertha*: Ardelle Warner. *Fiorella*: Myron Szandrowsky, Nord Vernellj.

    Musicians and Soldiers: Van Atkins, Max Birnbaum, Dick Bracken, Anthony Musarra, Frank E. Price, Martin Stewart.

Prologue: A Street in Seville, dawn.

Act 1: A room in Dr. Bartolo's home, later that day.

Act 2: Dr. Bartolo's home, several hours later.

PROLOGUE
  "Dawn Is Approaching"
    F. Knight
  "I'm the Most Popular Barber in Town"
    I. Gorin
  Duet
    F. Knight, I. Gorin

ACT 1
  "When a Maiden Must Decide"
    G. Panvini
  "Slander's Whisper"
    C. Alexander
  "I'm a Man of Reputation"
    R. Wentworth

ACT 2
  "When You Find a Man of Forty"
    A. Warner

1942.34   NEW FACES OF 1943

New Shoes (A Musical Revue) in Two Acts, 33 Scenes[25]. Book and lyrics by John Lund. Music by Lee Wainer. Additional lyrics and sketches by June

---

[25]The Third in the series of revues conceived by Leonard Sillman as a showcase for new talent. The first was produced in 1934.

Carroll and J. B. Rosenberg. Sketches directed by Lawrence Hurdle. Choreography by Charles Weidman and John Wray. Settings and costumes designed by Edward Gilbert. Lighting consultant, Carlton Winkler. Orchestra directed by Lee Wainer. Production supervised by Leonard Sillman. Produced by Leonard Sillman. Opened 22 December 1942 at the Ritz Theatre and closed 13 March 1943 after 94 performances.

CAST: Leonard Sillman, Diane Davis, Irwin Corey, Dorothy Dennis, Kent Edwards, Laura Deane Dutton, Tony Farrar, Doris Dowling, Ralph Lewis, Ilsa Kevin, John Lund, Marie Lund, Robert Weil, Alice Pearce, Hie Thompson, Ann Robinson, Mervyn Nelson, Bernard West, Blanche Fellows, Evelyn Brooks, Diane Davis.

ACT 1[26]

Scene 1

Opening
(*Music by* Lee Wainer. *Lyrics by* John Lund.)
The Producer: L. Sillman. *Mr. Priddis*: J. Lund. *The Stagehand*: K. Edwards. *The Showgirl*: D. Dowling. *The Dancers*: I. Kevin, T. Farrar, D. Davis, H. Thompson. *The Comics*: M. Nelson, B. West.

Scene 2

"We'll Swing It Through!"
Entire Company
(*Music by* Lee Wainer. *Lyrics by* John Lund.)

Scene 3

Cue Says—Go!
(*by* John Lund, J. B. Rosenberg)
Miss Cue: M. Lund. *Lecturer at Museum of Modern Art*: A. Pearce. *At the Automat*: E. Brooks, K. Edwards, J. Lund, D. Davis, B. West, A. Pearce. *At the Colony*: L. Sillman, K. Edwards. *At Star & Garter*: B. Fellows, B. West. *At Life With Father*: D. Davis, H. Thompson, B. West, K. Edwards. *At the Copacabana*: B. West, R. Lewis, E. Brooks.

Scene 4

"Animals Are Nice"
(*Music by* Lee Wainer. *Lyrics by* J. B. Rosenberg.)
The Pony: E. Brooks. *The Flamingo*: I. Kevin. *The Tiger*: H. Thompson. *The Skunk*: T. Farrar. *The Cat*: D. Dowling. *The Deer*: D. Davis. *The Donkey*: K. Edwards. *Tap Specialty*: H. Thompson.

Scene 5

Welles of Loneliness
(*by* John Lund, Sidney Carrol)
The Psychiatrist: K. Edwards. *The Producer*: J. Lund. *The Director*: L. Sillman. *The Writer*: B. West. *The Actor*: R. Lewis.

Scene 6

"Richard Crudnut's Charm School"
(*Music by* Lee Wainer. *Lyrics by* June Carroll, John Lund.)
Heddy Schwarz: A. Pearce. *Basil*: M. Lund. *Miss Farafield*: I. Kevin. *Elizabeth*: E. Brooks. *Dorothy*: M. Lund. *Helena*: D. Davis. *Mr. Beecher*: K. Edwards. *Physical Instructor*: R. Lewis. *Dancing Master*: H. Thompson.

Scene 7

Showgirl
D. Dowling

Scene 8

Quiet Zone
(*by* John Lund, J. B. Rosenberg)
Orderly: H. Thompson. *Receptionist*: M. Lund. *Dr. Scalpel*: J. Lund. *Dr. Forceps*: I. Kevin. *Dr. Clystra*: R. Lewis. *Expectant Father*: M. Nelson. *Emergency Case*: L. Sillman. *Interne*: T. Farrar. *Nurse*: D. Davis.

Scene 9

"Love, Are You Raising Your Head?"
(*Music by* Lee Wainer. *Lyrics by* June Carroll.)
The Girl: E. Brooks. *The Man*: R. Lewis. *The Dancers*: I. Kevin, H. Thompson.

Scene 10

Reprise
A. Robinson

Scene 11

Far Above Angustora's Bitters
(*by* John Lund)
Professor: J. Lund. *Binion*: M. Nelson. *Bunion*: L. Sillman. *Manion*: B. West. *Olsen*: T. Farrar.

[26]Added during run:
The Assembly Line
(*by* Charles Sherman)
Manager: B. West. *Secretary*: B. Fellows. *Mr. Jones*: M. Nelson.

Scene 12

"Yes, Sir, I've Made a Date"
(*Music by* Lee Wainer. *Lyrics by* J. B. Rosenberg.)
The Boy: H. Thompson. *The Girl*: D. Davis. *The Boy's Parents*: M. Lund, J. Lund. *The Girl's Parents*: E. Brooks, R. Lewis.

Scene 13

Showgirl
D. Dowling

Scene 14

The Skin of Your Life
(*by* John Lund)
Introduction, the Showgirl: D. Dowling. *Mordkin*: M. Nelson. *Bodkin*: K. Edwards. *Barber*: R. Lewis. *Groyn*: J. Lund. *Julie*: I. Kevin. *Messenger*: B. West. *Cathartics*: H. Thompson. *Gorilla*: H. Thompson. *Drunken Woman*: M. Lund.

Scene 15

Tony Farrar (*Choreography by* Tony Farrar)

Scene 16

Travel, Travel, Toil and Travel
(*by* Sidney Carrol)
Ed: R. Lewis. *Joe*: J. Lund. *Lady*: A. Pearce.
"Radio City, I Love You"
(*Music by* Lee Wainer. *Lyrics by* June Carroll.)

Scene 17

"Land of Rockefellera"
(*Music by* Lee Wainer. *Lyrics by* John Lund.)
Lieutenant: K. Edwards. *Tourist*: A. Pearce. *Dowager*: M. Lund. *Captain*: J. Lund. *Mature*: B. West. *Sergeant*: L. Sillman. *Lieutenant Lipschitz*: M. Nelson. *Tourists and Guides*.

Scene 18

Mervyn Nelson

Scene 19

"Shoes"
E. Brooks, A. Robinson, I. Kevin, H. Thompson, Entire Company
(*Music by* Will Irwin. *Lyrics by* June Carroll.)

ACT 2

Scene 1

"Shoes" (reprise)
Entire Company

Scene 2

"Back to Bundling"
L. Sillman, H. Thompson, D. Dowling, D. Davis, M. Lund, R. Lewis, K. Edwards, T. Farrar. *Tap Specialty*: H. Thompson.
(*Music by* Lee Wainer. *Lyrics by* Dorothy Sachs.)

Scene 3

Showgirl
D. Dowling

Scene 4

Help Wanted
(*by* J. B. Rosenberg, Nannie Foster)
Miss Swerk: M. Lund. *Miss Swenson*: I. Kevin. *Mrs. Astor*: D. Davis. *The Marquise*: A. Pearce. *Flunkeys*: H. Thompson, K. Edwards.

Scene 5

Bernard West

Scene 6

Whither America!
Switchboard Operator: D. Davis. *Typist*: M. Lund. *Swami*: L. Sillman.

Scene 7

"Hey, Gal!"
(*Music by* Will Irwin. *Lyrics by* June Carroll.)
The Gal: I. Kevin. *The Singers*: K. Edwards, E. Brooks, H. Thompson, R. Lewis, J. Lund.

Scene 8

Nearsighted Bullfighter
T. Farrar

Scene 9

Vacation Sketch
(*by* Charles Sherman and Harry Young)
Manager: B. West. *Secretary*: B. Fellows. *Mr. Jones*: M. Nelson.

Scene 10

Ten Percenters
(*Dialogue and Music by* Lee Wainer.)
A Voice: J. Lund. *An Agent*: M. Nelson. *A Band Leader*: K. Edwards.
A Hoofer: H. Thompson. *A Torch Singer*: I. Kevin. *A Comic*:
B. West.

Scene 11

"Well, Well!"
A. Robinson, Entire Company
(*Music by* Lee Wainer. *Lyrics by* June Carroll.)

Scene 12

Reprise
D. Davis

Scene 13

The Star's the Thing (Tea for Three)
(*by* John Lund, William Callanan, Bus Davis)
Scoggins: M. Lund. *Wigby*: L. Sillman. *Millicent*: A. Pearce. *Bolingbroke*: R.
Lewis. *Strangeways*: B. West.

Scene 14

Musical Chairs—Finale
Entire Company

1942.35   YOU'LL SEE STARS

A Musical Comedy Biography of Gus Edwards in Two Acts, 11 Scenes. Book and lyrics by Herman Timberg. Music by Leo Edwards. Dialogue staged by Herman Timberg and Dave Kramer. Dances directed by Eric Victor. Jessel choreographer, Sam Carlton. Art director, Perry Watkins. Costumes by Eaves. Musical supervison by Harold Stern. Musical director, Charles S. Sanford. Musical arrangers, Adam Carroll and Bernard Weissman. Produced by Dave Kramer. Opened 29 December 1942 at the Maxine Elliott Theatre and closed 2 January 1943 after 4 performances.

CAST (in order of appearance): *Gus Edwards*: ALAN RAY. *Cuddles*: PHYLLIS BAKER. *Georgie Price*: BUDDY SWAN. *Eddie Cantor*: JACKIE GREEN. *George Jessel*: JACKIE MICHAELS. *Walter Winchell*: IRVING FREEMAN. *Groucho Marx*: LOU DAHLMAN. *Herman Timberg*: ARNOLD STANG. *Willie Hammerstein*: JOHN STUART BREITER. *Harpo Marx*: GEORGE LYONS. *Chico Marx*: SAL LaPORTA. *Zeppo Marx*: EUGENE MARTIN. *Ray Bolger*: Eric Victor. *Bob Williams*: Ronny Carver. *Johnny Boston Beans Perry*: Gordon King. *Biff Dugan*: Jack Matis. *Yasha Kasha*: Maurice Doner. *Mary Jones*: Norma Shea. *Hildegarde*: PATRICIA BRIGHT. *The Tough Kid*: Jack Matis. *Lola Lane*: Renee Rochelle. *Joseph Kelly*: RONNY CARVER. *Maggie Grabenheimer*: NORMA SHEA. *Sassie Little*: Arlene Robinson. *Martha, the School Teacher*: JOAN BARRIE. *Tony Zuccini*: Sal La Porta. *Biff Dugan*: Jack Matis. *Yasha Kasha*: Maurice Doner. *Daisy Fair*: Edith Russell. *Vera Nutty*: Pat Marshall. *Hazel Nulty*: Betty Mae Lee. *Ima Hog*: Claire Harvey. *Patrick Levi*: Arnold Stang. *Ura Hog*: Peggy Fisher. *Freshie Buttinsky*: HONEY MURRAY. *Tommy Tatters*: George Lyons. *Carl Dachshundt*: Don Marshall. *Rajah*: Iris Karyl. *Dokes*: Maurice Doner. *Radio Announcer*: John Stuart Breiter. *Sue*: Audrey Burkes. *Judy Williams*: NORMA SHEA. *Jack*: Don Marshall.

Girls: Iris Karyl, Edith Russell, Peggy Fisher, Betty Mae Lee, Pat Marshall, Claire Harvey, Arlene Robinson, Dorothy Dale, Harriet Greene, Honey Murray. *Boys*: Don Marshall, Jack Matis, Gordon King, Sal LaPorta, Eugene Martin.

Act 1, Scene 1: Gus Edwards' Music Publishing Co. Yesterday. *Scene 2*: Hammerstein's Stage Door. *Scene 3*: Bare Stage of Hammerstein's. *Scene 4*: Schoolroom. *Scene 5*: Princess Rajah. *Scene 6*: Hammerstein's Stage Door. *Scene 7*: Hotel Astor Living Room—Five years later.

Act 2, Scene 1: Walgreen's. Today. *Scene 2*: Madison Square Garden. *Scene 3*: Backstage. *Scene 4*: Finale.

ACT 1
Scene 1

"Future Stars"
A. Ray

Scene 4

"America"
Entire Company
"Time and Time Again"
J. Barrie
"(By the Light of the) Silvery Moon" (from ZIEGFELD FOLLIES OF 1909)
H. Murray, Company
(*Music by* Gus Edwards. *Lyrics by* Edward Madden.)
"It Could Happen, It's Possible"
R. Carver, N. Shea

Scene 6

"All You Have to Do Is Stand There"
I. Freeman, L. Dahlman, N. Shea, E. Victor

Scene 7

"Dancing on a Rainbow"
E. Martin, Boys, Girls
Harp Solo: G. Lyons.

ACT 2
Scene 1

"Jelly Beans at Walgreen's"
H. Murray, Boys, Girls
"Betcha I Make Good"
N. Shea, P. Marshall, Company

Scene 2

"Swinging the Bhumba"
R. Rochelle
Danced by A. Robinson, D. Marshall, Boys, Girls.
"What a Pretty Baby You Are"
P. Bright

Scene 4

"Readin', Writin' and 'Rhythmatic" (School Days)
N. Shea, Entire Company
(*Music by* Gus Edwards. *Lyrics by* Will D. Cobb.)

1943.01   SOMETHING FOR THE BOYS

A Musical Comedy in a Prologue and Two Acts, 12 Scenes. Book by Herbert and Dorothy Fields. Music and lyrics by Cole Porter. Staged and lighted by Hassard Short. Book directed by Herbert Fields. Dances by Jack Cole. Settings by Howard Bay. Costumes by Billy Livingston. Orchestra conducted by William Parson. Orchestrations by Hans Spialek, Don Walker, (Robert) Russell Bennett, Ted Royal. Choral arrangements by William Parson. Produced by Michael Todd. Opened 7 January 1943 at the Alvin Theatre and closed 8 January 1944 after 422 performances.

CAST (in order of appearance): *Chiquita Hart*: PAULA LAURENCE. *Roger Calhoun*: JED PROUTY. *Harry Hart*: ALLEN JENKINS. *Blossom Hart*: ETHEL MERMAN. *Staff Sergeant Rocky Fulton*: BILL JOHNSON. *Sergeant Laddie Green*: Stuart Langley. *Mary-Frances*: BETTY GARRETT. *Betty-Jean*: BETTY BRUCE. *Corporal Burns*: BILL CALLAHAN. *Micheala*: Anita Alvarez. *Lois, Lucille*: Barnes Twins (Lois, Lucille). *Lieutenant Colonel S. D. Grubbs*: Jack Hartley. *Mr. Tobias Twitch*: William Lynn. *Sergeant Carter*: Remi Martel. *Melanie Walker*: Frances Mercer. *Burke*: Walter Rinner. *Mrs. Grubbs*: Madeleine Clive.

Dancing Girls: Alice Anthony, May Block, Jean Coyne, Betty Deane, Patricia Deering, Ruth Godfrey, Dolores Goodman, Betty Heather, Margie Jackson, Jean Owens, Leslie Shannon, Ethel Sherman, Puddy Smith, Nina Starkey, Patricia Welles, Helen Wenzel, June Wieting. *Dancing Boys*: Stanley Catron, Bob Davis, Benny DeSio, Jerry Florio, Albert Gaeta, Aaron Gobetz, Ray Harrison, David Mann, Remi Martel, Paul Martin, Duncan Noble, Ricky Riccardi, William Vaux, Joe Viggiano, William Weber, Lou Will, Jr., Parker Wilson. *Singing Boys*: Jimmy Allison, Joseph Bell, Alan Fleming, Richard Harvey, Buddy Irving, Art Lambert, Bruce Lord, Paul Mario, John W. Mayo, Joseph Monte, Walter Rinner, Murvyn Vye.

Prologue, Set 1: Chiquita's Dressing Room in The Piccadilly Club, Kansas City. *Set 2*: 6th Ave. at 50th Street, New York City. *Set 3*: An Assembly Line in a Defense Plant, Newark, New Jersey.

Act 1, Scene 1: Alamo Plaza, San Antonio, Texas. (Army Day.) *Scene 2*: Near the P.X. at Kelly Field. *Scene 3*: The Patio of the Old Hart Estate, near San Antonio. (Next morning.) *Scene 4*: A Crossroads. (Night.) *Scene 5*: Patio of the New Hart Estate. (Three weeks later.)

Act 2, Scene 1: The Alamo Plaza. (Noon of the following day.) *Scene 2*: The Terrace of Col. Grubbs' Home (on the Post.) *Scene 3*: The Crossroads. *Scene 4*: The Cadet Club at the Texas Hotel, San Antonio. *Scene 5*: The Corridor of Texas Hotel. *Scene 6*: An Army Plane. (Later that night.) *Scene 7*: The Cadet Club at the Texas Hotel, San Antonio. (Later.)

PROLOGUE

Announcement of Inheritance
J. Prouty, P. Laurence, A. Jenkins, E. Merman

ACT 1
Scene 1

"See That You're Born in Texas"
Ensemble

"When My Baby Goes to Town"
B. Johnson
Dance by A. Alvarez, Ensemble.
"Something for the Boys"
E. Merman, Boys
"When We're Home on the Range"[27]
E. Merman, P. Laurence, A. Jenkins
Scene 2
"Could It Be You?"
B. Johnson, Boys
Scene 3
"Hey, Good Lookin'"
E. Merman, B. Johnson
"Hey, Good Lookin'" (reprise)
B. Bruce, B. Callahan, Girls, Boys
Scene 4
"He's a Right Guy"
E. Merman
Scene 5
Assembly Line
A. Jenkins, B. Garrett, B. Bruce, Girls
"The Leader of a Big Time Band"
E. Merman
Dance by B. Callahan, Ensemble.

ACT 2
Scene 1
"I'm in Love With a Soldier Boy"
B. Garrett, Girls, Boys
"There's a Happy Land in the Sky"[28]
E. Merman, P. Laurence, A. Jenkins, W. Lynn, B. Johnson
Scene 3
"He's a Right Guy" (reprise)
E. Merman
Scene 4
"Could It Be You?" (Waltz reprise)
B. Johnson, Ensemble
"By the Mississinewa"[29]
E. Merman, P. Laurence
Square Dance
Ensemble
Scene 5
Dance
P. Laurence, Boys
Scene 6
Finale
E. Merman, Entire Company

1943.02   FOR YOUR PLEASURE

A Dance Vaudeville in Four Parts, 13 Scenes. (Assembled by George M. Gatts.) Produced and staged by Frank Veloz. Orchestra directed by Jerry Shelton. Yolanda's and Susan Miller's gowns by Katherine Kuhn. Presented by George M. Gatts. Opened 5 February 1943 at the Mansfield Theatre and closed 13 February 1943 after 11 performances.

CAST: (FRANK) VELOZ and YOLANDA (CASAZZA), SUSAN MILLER, VINCENTE GOMEZ, BILL GARY, AL and LEE REISER, THE GOLDEN GATE QUARTET (Willie Johnson, Orlandus Wilson, Clyde Riddick, Henry Owens), JERRY SHELTON.

Scene 1
Al and Lee Reiser

PART 1
Scene 2.
Veloz and Yolanda:
"Moonlight Madonna"
(*Music by* Zdenek Fibich.)
"Darktown Strutters' Ball"
(*Music and Lyrics by* Shelton Brooks.)
"Carnival"
(*Music by* Ann Ronell.)
Scene 3
Bill Gary (Tap Dancer)
Scene 4
Vincente Gomez (Guitarist)

PART 2
Scene 5
Veloz and Yolanda:
Caprice
(*Music by* Schonberger.)
Rhumba (Son)
(*Music by* J. Fernandez.)(Cuba)
"Dance of Mistakes"
(*Music by* Frank Veloz.)
Scene 6
The Golden Gate Quartet:
["I'm Listenin', Lord," "Stalin Wasn't Stallin'," and a 'Timber' number]
Scene 7
Veloz and Yolanda
Chiapenecas (Mexican Folk Dance)

INTERMISSION
Scene 8
Al and Lee Reiser (Duo-pianists)
Scene 9
Bill Gary (Tap Dancer)
Gitanerias
(*Music by* Ernesto Lecuona.)
Capriccio Espagnole
(*Music by* Nikolai Rimsky-Korsakoff.)

PART 3
Scene 10
Veloz and Yolanda:
Blue Danube
(*Music by* Johann Strauss.)
The Maxixa
(*Music by* Philipo Mendez.)
Minuet
(*Music by* S. Henry.)
Scene 11
Susan Miller (Singer):
["Brazil," "You'd Be So Nice to Come Home To," "Summertime."]
Scene 12
Jerry Shelton (Accordionist)

PART 4
Scene 13
Veloz and Yolanda:
Three Easy Lessons
(*Music by* Frank Veloz.)
Alexander's Ragtime Band
(*Music by* Irving Berlin.)
Samba
(*Music by* Arroyo.)
Tango Yolanda
(*Music by* Frank Veloz.)

---

[27]Staged by Lew Kessler.
[28]Staged by Lew Kessler.
[29]Staged by Lew Kessler.

1943.03

LADY IN THE DARK

A Return Engagement of the Musical Play in Two Acts, 7 Scenes[30]. Book by Moss Hart. Music by Kurt Weill. Lyrics by Ira Gershwin. Play staged by Moss Hart. Production (direction) and lighting by Hassard Short. Choreography by Albertina Rasch. Settings by Harry Horner. Costumes by Irene Sharaff. Gowns by Hattie Carnegie. Musical direction by Maurice Abravanel. Produced by Sam H. Harris. Opened 27 February 1943 at the Broadway Theatre and closed 15 May 1943 after 83 performances.

CAST (in order of appearance): *Dr. Brooks*: RICHARD HALE. *Miss Bowers*: Jeanne Shelby. *Liza Elliott*: GERTRUDE LAWRENCE. *Miss Foster*: Gedda Petry. *Miss Stevens*: Adrienne Moore. *Maggie Grant*: MARGARET DALE. *Alison du Bois*: ANN LEE. *Russell Paxton*: ERIC BROTHERSON. *Charley Johnson*: HUGH MARLOWE. *Randy Curtis*: WILLARD PARKER. *Joe*: Edward Browne. *Tom*: Walter Stane. *Kendall Nesbitt*: JOHN LESLIE. *Helen*: Helene Young. *Ruthie*: Rose Marie Elliott. *Carol*: Margaret Gibson. *Marcia*: Christine Horn. *Liza's Father*: Nicholas Saunders. *Ben Butler*: Lee Bergere. *Barbara*: Jane Irving. *Jack*: Lynn Alden. *Soloists*: Arthur Davies, Warren Jones, Byron Milligan.

The Albertina Rasch Dancers: Rita Charise, Anne Helm, Joan Lee, June MacLaren, Christine Horn, Margaret Gibson, Alla Shishkina, Edward Browne, Richard D'Arcy, Nikolai Fatula, John Scott, Walter Stane, Scott Merrill, George Martin. *The Mapleton High Glee Club*: Adelaide Abbot, Florence White, Ingeborg Bransen, Jean Cumming, Joyce Doncaster, Rose Marie Elliott, Jane Irving, Lynn Alden, Ken Black, Jack Collins, Arthur Davies, Warren Jones, Byron Milligan, Fred Perrone, Edwin Ziegler, Matthew Ferrugio. *The Children*: Bonnie Baker, Anne Bracken, Phyllis De Bus, Sally Ferguson, Louise Pearl, Janice Smith, Edward Tappa, Robert Allen, William Welch.

1943.04

OKLAHOMA!

A Musical Comedy in Two Acts, 6 Scenes. Book and lyrics by Oscar Hammerstein II. Music by Richard Rodgers. Based on the play "Green Grow the Lilacs" by Lynn Riggs. Staged by Rouben Mamoulian. Dances directed by Agnes de Mille. Orchestrations by (Robert) Russell Bennett. Music directed by Jacob Schwartzdorf [Jay Blackton]. Settings by Lemuel Ayers. Costumes by Miles White. Production under the supervision of Lawrence Langner and Theresa Helburn. Produced by The Theatre Guild. Opened 31 March 1943 at the St. James Theatre and closed 29 May 1948 after 2212 performances[31].

CAST (in order of appearance): *Aunt Eller*: BETTY GARDE. *Curly*: ALFRED DRAKE. *Laurey*: JOAN ROBERTS. *Ike Skidmore*: Barry Kelley. *Fred*: Edwin Clay. *Slim*: Herbert Rissman. *Will Parker*: LEE DIXON. *Jud Fry*: HOWARD DaSILVA. *Ado Annie Carnes*: CELESTE HOLM. *Ali Hakim*: JOSEPH BULOFF. *Gertie Cummings*: Jane Lawrence. *Ellen*: KATHARINE SERGAVA. *Kate*: Ellen Love. *Sylvie*: Joan McCracken. *Armina*: Kate Friedlich. *Aggie*: Bambi Linn. *Andrew Carnes*: RALPH RIGGS. *Cord Elam*: Owen Martin. *Jess*: George Church. *Chalmers*: MARC PLATT. *Mike*: Paul Shiers. *Joe*: George S. Irving. *Sam*: Hayes Gordon.

Singers: Elsie Arnold, Harvey Brown, Suzanne Lloyd, Ellen Love, Dorothea MacFarland, Virginia Oswald, Faye Smith, Vivienne Simon. John Baum, Edwin Clay, Hayes Gordon, George S. Irving, Arthur Ulisse, Herbert Rissman, Paul Shiers, Robert Penn. *Dancers*: Diana Adams, Margit DeKova, Bobby Barrentine, Nona Feid, Rhoda Hoffman, Maria Harriton, Kate Friedlich, Bambi Linn, Joan McCracken, Vivian Smith, Billie Zay. Kenneth Buffet, Jack Dunphy, Gary Fleming, Eddie Howland, Ray Harrison, Erik Kristen, Kenneth LeRoy.

Time: Just after the Turn of the Century. *Place*: Indian Territory (now Oklahoma).

Act 1, Scene 1: The Front of Laurey's Farm House. *Scene 2*: The Smoke House. *Scene 3*: A Grove on Laurey's Farm.

Act 2, Scene 1: The Skidmore Ranch. *Scene 2*: Skidmore's Kitchen Porch. *Scene 3*: The Back of Laurey's Farm House.

ACT 1
Scene 1

"Oh, What a Beautiful Mornin'"
   A. Drake
"The Surrey With the Fringe on Top"
   A. Drake, J. Roberts, B. Garde
"Kansas City"
   L. Dixon, B. Garde, Boys
"I Can't Say No"
   C. Holm

"Many a New Day"
   J. Roberts, Girls
   Danced by J. McCracken (The Girl Who Falls Down), K. Friedlich, M. DeKova.
"It's a Scandal! It's an Outrage!"
   J. Buloff, Boys, Girls
"People Will Say We're in Love"
   A. Drake, J. Roberts

Scene 2

"Poor Jud"
   A. Drake, H. da Silva
"Lonely Room"
   H. da Silva

Scene 3

"Out of My Dreams"
   J. Roberts, Girls
"Laurey Makes Up Her Mind" Ballet
   Laurey: K. Sergava. *Curly*: M. Platt. *Jud*: G. Church. *The Child*: B. Linn. *Jud's Post Cards*: J. McCracken, K. Friedlich, M. DeKova. *Laurey's Friends*: R. Hoffman, R. Schaeffer, N. Feid, M. Hamilton, D. Adams, B. Zay. *Cowboys*: G. Fleming, E. Kristen, J. Dunphy, R. Harrison, K. LeRoy, E. Howland, K. Buffet. *Other Post Cards*: B. Barrentine, V. Smith.

ACT 2
Scene 1

"The Farmer and the Cowman"
   R. Riggs, B. Garde, A. Drake, L. Dixon, C. Holm, E. Clay, Ensemble
   Danced by M. Platt.
"All er Nothin'"
   C. Holm, L. Dixon
   Danced by J. McCracken, K. Friedlich.

Scene 2

"People Will Say We're in Love" (reprise)
   A. Drake, J. Roberts

Scene 3

"Oklahoma"
   A. Drake, J. Roberts, B. Garde, P. Shiers, E. Clay, Ensemble
"Oh, What a Beautiful Mornin'" (reprise)
   J. Roberts, A. Drake, Ensemble
Finale
   Ensemble

1943.05

ZIEGFELD FOLLIES (OF 1943)

A Musical Revue in Two Acts, 24 Scenes[32]. Music by Ray Henderson. Lyrics by Jack Yellen. (Sketches by Lester Lee, Jerry Seelen, Bud Pearson, Les White, Joseph Erens, Charles Sherman, Harry Young, Lester Lawrence, Baldwin Bergersen, Ray Golden, Sid Kuller, William Wells and Harold Rome. Additional music by Dan White, lyrics by Buddy Burston.) Entire production devised and staged by John Murray Anderson. Supervised by Harry A. Kaufman. Dialogue directed by Arthur Pierson and Fred deCordova. Orchestra directed by John McManus. Scenery by Watson Barratt. Costumes by Miles White. Dances directed by Robert Alton. Orchestrations by Don Walker. Stage management by Fred deCordova. Produced by the Messrs. Shubert in association with Alfred Bloomingdale and Lou Walters by arrangement with Billi Burke Ziegfeld. Opened 1 April 1943 at the Winter Garden, moved 25 January 1944 to the Imperial Theatre, and closed 22 July 1944 after 553 performances.

CAST: MILTON BERLE, ILONA MASSEY, ARTHUR TREACHER, JACK COLE, SUE RYAN, TOMMY WONDER, NADINE GAE, DEAN MURPHY, Christine Ayers, The Rhythmaires (Robert Bay, Don Weissmuller, Robert Shaw, Victor Griffin),, Jack McCauley, Imogen Carpenter, Jay Martin, Katherine Meskill, Bil and Cora Baird, Arthur Maxwell, Charles Senna, The Jansleys, Ben Yost's Vi-Kings (Edward Hayes, Manfred Hecht, Howard Jackson, Robert Rippy, Edmund [Bob] Lyndeck, Theodore Teddick), Ray Long, Mary Ganley, Patricia Hall, Penny Edwards, Dixie Roberts, Rebecca Lee, Virginia Miller, Ruth Rowan, Jerry Jansley.

Ziegfeld Follies Show Girls: Bea Bailey, Doris Brent, Veronica Burnes, Josine Cagle, Betty Douglas, Eleanor Hall, Yvonne Kummer, Renee Riley, Betty Stuart, Rose Teed. *Dancing Girls*: Carolyn Ayres, Mary Alice Bingham, Virginia Cheneval, Skippy Cekan,

---

[30]Originally produced in New York 25 January 1941 at the Alvin Theatre for 467 performances. For Synopsis of Scenes and Musical Numbers, see original 1941 production. Total for all engagements: 550 performances.
[31]Including 44 special matinees for the armed forces.

---

[32]The twenty-fourth in the annual series of revues originated by Florenz Ziegfeld beginning in 1907.

Grace DeWitt, Gretchen Houser, Marilyn Hightower, Jerry Koban, Kay Lewis, Bubbles Mandel, Mary McDonnell, Janie New, Marianne O'Brien, Rosaleen Simpson, Ila Marie Wilson, Mimi Walthers, Doris York. *Messrs.*: Jim Barron, Bob Copsy, Ray Cook, David Gray, Arthur Grahl, Bruce Davison, Howard Ludwig, Michael Pober, Tom Smith.

ACT 1

Scene 1

Prologue

(*by* Jerry Seelen and Lester Lee) N. Gae, T. Wonder, I. Carpenter, J. Martin

Vignette (after Cole Porter)

C. Ayres, M. Ganley, D. Roberts, M. Pober, P. Edwards, J. Barron, H. Ludwig, Ben Yost's Vi-Kings

Vignette (after Ernest Hemingway)

The Hero: J. McCauley. *Bellringer*: J. Jansley.

Vignette (after William Saroyan)

A Character: M. Hecht. *Another Character*: C. Senna. *Still Another Character*: B. Baird.

Vignette (after Irving Berlin)

Show Girls, Dancing Girls, Messrs.

Scene 2

Something for the Berles

(M. Berle)

Scene 3

"Thirty Five Summers Ago"

I. Massey, J. Martin, Show Girls, Yost's Vi-Kings

Scene 4

Good God Godfrey[33]

(*by* Bud Pearson and Les White)

Mr. Tappan: J. McCauley. *Mrs. Tappan*: K. Meskill. *Godfrey*: A. Treacher.

Scene 5

"This Is It"

A. Maxwell, I. Carpenter

Danced by N. Gae, P. Edwards, P. Hall, D. Roberts, M. Ganley, Dancing Girls and Boys, the Rhythmaires, T. Wonder.

Scene 6

Counter Attack

(*by* Charles Sherman and Harry Young)

Cecil: M. Berle. *Mr. Andrews*: J. McCauley. *Mrs. Andrews*: S. Ryan.

Scene 7

"The Wedding of a Solid Sender"

(*Composed and Arranged by* Baldwin Bergersen. *Choreography by* Jack Cole.)

The Groom: J. Cole. *The Bride*: R. Lee. *Bridesmaids*: V. Miller, R. Rowan. *Congregation*: C. Ayres, M. McDonnell, M. Walthers, M. Hightower.

Scene 8

The Merchant of Venison

(*by* Lester Lee and Jerry Seelen)

J. Pierswift Armour: M. Berle.

Scene 9

"Love Songs Are Made in the Night"

I. Massey, J. Martin

Romantic Ballet: N. Gae, the Rhythmaires. *Rhythmic Ballet*: C. Ayres, R. Long, Ensemble.

Scene 10

Sue Ryan (Specialty)

(*Music by* Dan White. *Lyrics by* Buddy Burston.)

Scene 11

Ben Yost's Vi-Kings

Scene 12

"Come Up and Have a Cup of Coffee"

A. Maxwell, I. Carpenter, Ben Yost's Vi-Kings, Show Girls

Danced by D. Roberts, M. Ganley, P. Hall, P. Edwards, The Rhythmaires, Dancers, N. Gae, T. Wonder.

Scene 13

Loves-A-Poppin

(*by* Ray Golden and Sid Kuller)

Introduction by K. Meskill. *Gertrude Olsen*: I. Massey. *Perry Johnson*: M. Berle. *Crumpet*: A. Treacher.

Scene 14

Carmen in Zoot

Prologue: J. Martin, I. Carpenter.

"The Saga of Carmen"

S. Ryan

A Fortune Teller: C. Ayres. *A Smuggler*: R. Long. *The Bull*: N. Gae. *A Toreador*: T. Wonder. *Michala*: I. Massey. *Don José*: A. Treacher. *Matadors*: The Rhythmaires. *Carmen*: S. Ryan. *Picadors*: Ben Yost's Vi-Kings. *Escamillo*: M. Berle. Entire Company.

ACT 2

Scene 1

"Swing Your Lady, Mr. Hemingway"

S. Ryan, R. Long, The Rhythmaires,

C. Ayres, D. Brent, J. McCauley, M. Hightower, N. Gae, T. Wonder, Ensemble

Scene 2

The Jansleys

Scene 3

Once a Butler—[34]

(*by* Lester Lawrence)

Himself: A. Treacher. *His Wife*: K. Meskill. *Mr. Smith*: J. McCauley.

Scene 4

Dean Murphy

Scene 5

"Back to the Farm"

S. Ryan, C. Ayres, Show Girls

(*Music by* Dan White. *Lyrics by* Buddy Burston.)

Scene 6

Mr. Grant Goes to Washington

(*by* Joseph Erens)

Charlie Grant: M. Berle. *Mary Grant*: K. Meskill. *Bell Boy*: C. Senna. *Hotel Manager*: J. McCauley.

Scene 7

Bil and Cora Baird (Marionettes)

Scene 8

"Hindu Serenade"

I. Massey, J. Martin

Danced by J. Cole, R. Lee, V. Miller, R. Rowan.

Scene 9

"The Micromaniac"

M. Berle

(*Music and Lyrics by* Harold Rome.)

Scene 10

"Hold That Smile"

N. Gae, T. Wonder, J. Martin, I. Carpenter

Danced by M. Ganley, M. Berle, I. Massey, A. Treacher, Entire Company.

---

[33]Dropped during the run.

[34]Dropped during the run.

Mary Martin in ONE TOUCH OF VENUS
Billy Rose Theatre Collection, New York Public Library for the Performing Arts

1943–1944 SEASON

1943.06 ## THE STUDENT PRINCE

A Revival of the Operetta in a Prologue and Four Acts, 5 Scenes[1]. Book and lyrics by Dorothy Donnelly. (Based on the play "Old Heidelberg" by Rudolf Bleichmann, adapted from "Alt-Heidelberg" by Wilhelm Meyer-Förster.) Music by Sigmund Romberg. Direction by J.J. Shubert. Choreography by Ruthanne Boris. Settings by Watson Barratt. Costumes by Stage Costumes, Inc. Orchestra under the direction of Fred Hoff. Produced by the Messrs. Shubert. Opened 8 June 1943 at the Broadway Theatre and closed 2 October 1943 after 153 performances.

CAST (in order of their appearance): *First Lackey*: Colin Harvey. *Second Lackey*: Larry O'Dell. *Third Lackey*: Jonathan Reed. *Fourth Lackey*: John McCarthy. *Fifth Lackey*: Stanley Turner. *Sixth Lackey*: Merrill Moorman. *Prime Minister von Mark*: WILLIAM PRINGLE. *Dr. Engel*, the Prince's Tutor: EVERETT MARSHALL. *Prince Karl Franz*: FRANK HORNADAY. *Ruder*, Landlord of Inn of Three Gold Apples: Walter Johnson. *Gretchen*, Maid at the Inn: ANN PENNINGTON. *Toni*, a waiter: Nathaniel Sack. *Detlef*, a student leader: Roy Barnes. *Von Asterberg*, another student leader: Lyndon Crews. *Lucas*, another student leader: Daniel De Paolo. *Kathie*, niece of Ruder: BARBARA SCULLY. *Lutz*, valet to the Prince: DETMAR POPPEN. *Hubert*, the valet's valet: Jesse M. Cimberg. *Grand Duchess Anastasia*: NINA VARELA. *Princess Margaret*, fiancée of Prince Karl Franz: HELENE ARTHUR. *Captain Tarnitz*: Raymond Jacquemont. *Countess Leyden*, lady-in-waiting to the Princess: Helene Le Berthon. *Rudolph*, cousin of Kathie: Herman Magidson. *Captain of the Guard*: Jack Richards.
Ladies of the Ensemble: Judy Turnbull, Phyllis Manning, Gloria Hope, Marilyn Merkt, Harriet Williams, Elaine Haslett, Page Morton, Shirley Gordon, Carol Hunter, Jacqueline Max, Helene Le Berthon, Gale Sterling, Marvel Conheeny. *Gentlemen of the Ensemble*: Lewis Pierce, Fred Catania, Jack Richards, Eugene Gadol, Roland Power, Colin Harvey, Stanton Barrett, Paul Campbell, Steve Wilson, Dale Spangler, Andrew Thurston, George T. Miller, Jonathan Reed, Warren Dunning, Robert Lauren, John McCarthy, James Growner, Merrill Moorman, Stanley Turner, Eden Burrows, Herman Magidson, Larry O'Dell, Charles M. Perry.

1943.07 ## EARLY TO BED

A Musical Comedy in Two Acts, 9 Scenes. Book and lyrics by George Marion, Jr. Music by Thomas "Fats" Waller. Staged by Richard Kollmar[2]. Dances staged by Robert Alton. Scenery by George Jenkins. Costumes by Miles White. Orchestrations by Don Walker. Orchestra directed by Archie Bleyer. Vocal arrangements by Buck [Clay] Warnick. Special ballet music composed and arranged by Baldwin Bergersen. Production supervised by Alfred Bloomingdale. Produced by Richard Kollmar. Opened 17 June 1943 at the Broadhurst Theatre and closed 13 May 1944 after 382 performances.

CAST (in order of appearance): *Opal*: Ruth Webb. *Bartender*: Anthony Blair. *O'Connor*: John Lund. *Gardener*: David Bethea. *Gendarme*: Maurice Ellis. *Lily Ann*: JENI LeGON. *Mayor*: RALPH BUNKER. *Marcella*: Louise Jarvis. *Pauline*: Choo Choo Johnson. *Interlude*: Peggy Cordrey. *Jessica*: MARY SMALL. *Butch*: Eleanor Boleyn. *Duchess*: Helen Bennett. *Minerva*: Honey Murray. *Caddy*: Harold Cromer. *Madame Rowena*: MURIEL ANGELUS. *Isabella*: Angela Greene. *Pooch*: BOB HOWARD. *Pablo*: GEORGE ZORITCH. *El Magnifico*: RICHARD KOLLMAR. *Lois*: JANE DEERING. *Wilbur*: Jimmy Gardiner. *Coach*: George Baxter. *Eileen*: JANE KEAN. *Charlotte*: Charlotte Maye. *Burt*: Burt Harger. *Naomi*: Evelyn Ward. *Charles*: Charles Kraft. *Junior*: Harrison Muller. *Admiral Saint-Cassette*: Franklyn Fox. *Radio representation of President Roosevelt's voice*: Dean Murphy.

[1]First produced in New York as THE STUDENT PRINCE IN HEIDELBERG 2 December 1924 at the Jolson Theatre for 608 peformances. For Synopsis of Scenes and Musical Numbers, see original 1924 production. For this production, "Farmer Jacob" (Opening Act 2) was dropped and replaced by:
"I've Never Heard About Love"
E. Marshall, Students
For this production, "Farewell, Dear" was dropped and replaced by:
"Golden Days" (reprise)
E. Marshall
"Deep in My Heart" (reprise)
F. Hornaday, B. Scully
[2]Direction initially uncredited. Kollmar's directorial credit added late in New York run.

Pigeons: Deanne Benmore, Helen Bennett, Eleanor Boleyn, Marianne Cude, Kay Dowd, Marge Ellis, Claire Loring, Virginia McGraw, Dolores Milan, Olive Nicolson, Helen Osborne, June Reynolds, Olga Roberts, Isabel Rolfe, Jean Scott, Toni Stuart, Evelyn Ward. *Track Team*: George Hunter, Thomas Kenny, Charles Kraft, John Martin, Harrison Muller, Tom Powers, Robert Trout, Jack Wilkins.

Act 1, Scene 1: A Bar in New York City. *Scene 2*: Villa of the Angry Pigeon, Martinique. Daybreak. *Scene 3*: A Corridor. Later that morning. *Scene 4*: Bedroom of the Royal Suite. *Scene 5*: Villa of the Angry Pigeon. Still later that morning.

Act 2, Scene 1: Again the Bar, New York City. *Scene 2*: Corridor of the Angry Pigeon. That afternoon. *Scene 3*: The Angry Pigeon. That evening. *Scene 4*: Tradesmen's Entrance to the Angry Pigeon. That night. *Scene 5*: The Angry Pigeon. Later that afternoon.

ACT 1
"A Girl Who Doesn't Ripple When She Bends"
M. Small, H. Murray, H. Cromer, Girls
"There's a Man in My Life"
M. Angelus
"Me and My Old World Charm"
R. Kollmar
"Supple Couple"
M. Small, J. LeGon, B. Howard, R. Kollmar
"Slightly Less Than Wonderful"
J. Deering, G. Zoritch
"Slightly Less Than Wonderful" (reprise)
J. LeGon, B. Howard, H. Cromer, D. Bethea, M. Ellis
"This Is So Nice (It Must Be Illegal)"
M. Angelus, R. Kollmar
"Hi-De-Ho High"
B. Howard, J. Le Gon, H. Cromer, D. Bethea, M. Ellis, E. Ward, C. Kraft, Ensemble
"The Ladies Who Sing With the Band"[3]
M. Small, M. Angelus, J. Kean, J. Deering
"There's "Yes" in the Air"
R. Kollmar, M. Small, J. Kean,
J. Deering, G. Zoritch, B. Harger, C. Maye, H. Murray, Ensemble
ACT 2
"Get Away, Young Man"
J. Kean, H. Muller, C. Kraft, J. Gardiner, Ensemble
"Long Time No Song"
R. Kollmar, M. Angelus
"Early to Bed"
M. Small, J. Deering, G. Zoritch, B. Harger, C. Maye, H. Cromer, Ensemble
"There's a Man in My Life" (reprise)
M. Angelus
"When the Nylons Bloom Again"
B. Howard, J. LeGon
Finale
Entire Company

1943.08 ## THE VAGABOND KING

A Revival of the Musical Play in Four Acts[4]. Book and lyrics by Brian Hooker and Russell Janney. Based on Justin McCarthy's play "If I Were King," adapted from the novel by R. H. Russell. Music by Rudolf Friml. Staged by George Ermoloff. Costumes by James Reynolds. Scenery by Raymond Sovey. Orchestrations and music direction by Joseph Majer. Dances directed by Igor Schwezoff. Produced by Russell Janney. Opened 29 June 1943 at the Sam S. Shubert Theatre and closed 14 August 1943 after 56 performances.

CAST (in order of appearance): *Rene de Montigny*: Artells Dickson. *Casin Cholet*: Bert Stanley. *Jehan Le Loup*: George Karle. *Margot*: Jann Moore. *Isabeau*: Evelyn Wick. *Jehanneton*: Rosalind Madison. *Huguette du Hamel*: ARLINE THOMSON.

[3]Interpolations: "Jim," "You Made Me Love You," "Love Is the Sweetest Thing," "Wanting You," "Love Me or Leave Me," "All of Me," "Love, Your Magic Spell Is Everywhere," "That Old Black Magic," "I Want My Mama," "Oh, Johnny, Oh," "What Is This Thing Called Love?"
[4]Originally presented in New York 21 September 1925 at the Casino Theatre for 511 performances. For Synopsis of Scenes and Musical Numbers, see original 1925 production.

Guy Tabarie: WILL H. PHILBRICK. *Tristan L'Hermite*: Douglas Gilmore. *Louis XI*: JOSÉ RUBEN. *Francois Villon*: JOHN BROWNLEE. *Katherine de Vaucelles*: FRANCES McCANN. *Thibaut d'Aussigny*: Ben Roberts. *Captain of Scotch Archers*: Charles Henderson. *An Astrologer*: Franz Bendtsen. *Lady Mary*: TERI KEANE. *Noel of Anjou*: Dan Gallagher. *Oliver Le Dain*: Curtis Cooksey. *Herald of Burgundy*: Earl Ashcroft. *The Queen*: Betty Berry. *The Hangman*: Craig Newton. *The Cardinal*: Vincent Henry. *Premier Dancers*: Julia Harvath, Dorothee Littlefield, Peter Birch. *The Two Dice Players*: Kenneth Sonnenberg, Birger Hallderson.

Corps de Ballet: Franca Baldwin, Sally Sheppard, Carlye Ramey, Patricia Leith, Muriel Bruenig, Anna Jacqueline, Ginee Richardson, Davide Daniel. *Ladies of the Ensemble*: Ruth Barber, Muriel Blane, Zola Palmer, Helen Carlson, Claire Wells, Ann Garland, Betty Berry, Doris Blake, Linda Kay, Katrina VanOss, Rosalind Madison, Iris Howard, Helen George, Evelyn Wick, Mary David, Shirley Conklin, Mary Burns, Bernice Hoffman, Joan Barrie, Mary Ellen Bright.

Gentlemen of the Ensemble: Frederick Langford, Vincent Henry, Charles Arnold, Robert Kimberly, Kenneth Sonnenberg, Chris Gerard, Earle Ashcroft, Al Bartolet, William Gephart, Jay Patrick, Birger Halldorson, George Walker, Norvel Campbell, Max Plagmann, Ernest Pavano, Geoge Beach, Otto Simetti, Jerry Madden, Graham Alexander, Jerry Clayton, Harry Nordin, Charles Trott.

1943.09   THE MERRY WIDOW

A Revival of the Operetta in a Prologue and Three Acts[5]. Music by Franz Lehár. Original Viennese libretto ("Die Lustige Witwe") by Victor Léon and Leo Stein after "L'Attaché d'Ambassade" by Henri Meilhac. New musical version by Robert Stolz. New book by Sidney Sheldon and Ben Roberts. New lyrics by Adrian Ross and Robert Gilbert. Special lyrics by Robert Gilbert. Production directed and staged by Felix Brentano. Music directed by Robert Stolz. Choreography by George Balanchine. Scenery by Howard Bay. Costumes by Walter Florell. Produced by Yolanda Mero-Irion for The New Opera Company. Opened 4 August 1943 at the Majestic Theatre and closed 6 May 1944 after 322 performances.

<u>CAST</u> (in order of appearance): *The King*: KARL FARKAS. *Popoff*: MELVILLE COOPER. *Jolodon*: Robert Field. *Natalie*: RUTH MATTESON. *Olga Bardini*: Ethelyne Holt. *General Bardini*: RALPH DUMKE. *Novakovich*: Gene Barry. *Cascada*: Alex Alexander. *Khadja*: Arnold Spector. *Guests*: Josephine Griffin, Mark Farrington. *Nish*: David Wayne. *Sonia Sadoya*: MARTA EGGERTH. *Prince Danilo*: JAN KIEPURA. *Clo-Clo*: LISETTE VEREA. *Lo-Lo*: Wana Allison. *Frou-Frou*: Bobbie Howell. *Do-Do*: Babs Heath. *Premiere Danseuses*: LUBOV ROUDENKO, MILADA MLADOVA. *Premier Dancer*: CHRIS VOLKOFF. *Headwaiter*: KARL FARKAS.

Ladies of the Ensemble: Janie Janvier, Doris Pape, Birute Ramoska, Renee Rochelle, Peggy Turnley, Marya Woczeska, Frances Yeend, Marie Fox, Arline Carmen, Josephine Griffin, Florence McGovern, Irene Jordan. *Gentlemen of the Ensemble*: Jerome Cardinale, Frank Finn, John Harrold, Robert La Marr, Albert Schiller, Nathaniel Sprinzena, Edward Visca, Mark Farrington, Nicholas Torzs, Robert Tower, Alan Vaughan, Dennis Dengate. *Ballet*: Wana Allison, June Graham, Babs (Barbara) Heath, Bobbie Howell, Zoya Leporska, Jayne (Jane) Ward, David Adhar, Alan Banks, Nicholas Magallenes, Frank (Francisco) Moncion, Stanley Zompakos, James Starbuck. *Lackies*: Morgan Kendall, George Buzante, Eddie Dane.

Prologue, Act 1: The Marsovian Embassy in Paris. A summer evening in the Year 1906.

Act 2: Grounds of Sonia's House, near Paris. The following evening.

Act 3: Maxim's Restaurant, Paris. Later that same evening.

ACT 1

"A Dutiful Wife"
   R. Matteson, R. Field

"In Marsovia"
   M. Eggerth, R. Dumke, A. Alexander, Male Chorus

"Maxim's"
   J. Kiepura

Polka
   L. Roudenko, J. Starbuck

Finale
   J. Kiepura, M. Eggerth, M. Cooper, R. Dumke, A. Alexander, Ensemble

ACT 2

"Vilia"
   M. Eggerth

Marsovian Dance
   M. Mladova, C. Volkoff, Corps de Ballet

"The Pavilion"
   J. Kipeura

"The Women"
   a) M. Cooper, R. Dumke, R. Field, D. Wayne, A. Spector, G. Barry, A. Alexander.
   b) Same as above, with J. Graham, B. Heath.
   c) J. Griffin, R. Rochelle, A. Carmen, M. Woczeska, D. Pape, J. Janvier.

"I Love You So"
   J. Kiepura, M. Eggerth
   Danced by M. Mladova, C. Volkoff, Corps de Ballet.

Finale
   Entire Company

ACT 3

"The Girls at Maxim's"
   L. Verea
   Danced by L. Roudenko, Ballet Girls.

"Kuiawiak" (Kujawiak)
   J. Kiepura
   (*Music by* Henri Wieniawski. *Lyrics by* W. Eiger and Jan Kiepura. Arranged by and sung in Polish by Jan Kiepura.)

"I Love You So" (reprise)
   J. Kiepura, M. Eggerth

Finale
   Entire Company

1943.10   RUN LITTLE CHILLUN

A Revival of the Folk Drama with Music in Two Acts, 6 Scenes[6]. Book and music by Hall Johnson. Staged by Clarence Muse. Supervised by Lew Cooper. Music directed by Hall Johnson. Choreography by Felicia Sorel. Settings and costumes by Perry Watkins. Produced by Lew Cooper in association with Meyer Davis and George Jessel. Opened 11 August 1943 at the Hudson Theatre and closed 26 August 1943 after 16 performances.

<u>CAST</u> (in order of appearance): *Sister Mattie Fullilove*: Bessie Guy. *Sister Flossie Lou Little*: BERTHA POWELL. *Sister Mahalie Cockletree*: Rosalie King. *Sister Judy Ann Hicks*: Maggie Carter. *Sister Lulu Jane Hunt*: Eloise Uggams. *Sister Susie May Hunt*: Eva Vaughan. *Brother Esau Redd*, Chairman Deacon Board: Robert Harvey. *Brother Bartholomew Little*: Wardell Saunders. *Brother Goliath Simpson*: William O. Davis. *Brother Jeremiah Johnson*: Randall Steplight. *Brother George W. Jenkins*: Elijah Hodges. *Ella Jones*: Helen Dowdy. *Jeems Jackson*: Edwin Roche. *Bessiola*: Mariam Burton. *Organist*: Awilda Frazier. *The Rev. Sister Luella Strong*: Olive Ball. *Rev. Jones*, Pastor of the Hope Baptist Church: Louis Sharp. *Jim*, Son of Rev. Jones: Caleb Petersen. *"Charlie"*, Mail Carrier: CHARLES HOLLAND. *Sulumai*: Edna Mae Harris. *Mary Lou Mack*: Violet McDowell. *Elder Tongola*, Leader of "Pilgrims of the New Day": Service Bell. *Brother Moses*, Young Priest of the Pilgrims: P. Jay Sidney. *Mother Kanda*, Daughter of Tongola: Maude Simmons. *Sister Mata*, Priestess of the Pilgrims: FREDYE MARSHALL. *Brother Jo-Ba*, Herald of Joy: Walter Mosby. *Mag*, Sulamai's Mother: Gertrude Saunders. *Belle* of Toomer's Bottom: Viola Anderson. *Mame* of Toomer's Bottom: Myrtl Anderson. *Sue Scott* of Toomer's Bottom: Lulu B. King. *Sexton of the Hope Baptist Church*: Adolph Henderson. *Brother Absalom Brown*: Roger Alford. *Blind Man*: Clarence Harris. *"Run, Little Chillun'"* Singer: Charles Holland. *Soloist*: INEZ MATTHEWS.

Dancers: Olive Gordon, Roxie Foster, Norma Miller, Norma Ross, Nyoka Pleasant, Robert Lopez, Joseph Noble, Geraldine Prillerman, Mabel Hart, Enid Williams, James Riley, Alfred Bledger, Lillian Roberts, Frank Green, Joan Smith, Bill O'Neill, Dorothy Williams, Garfield Ritter. *Novitiates of 'Pilgrims of the New Day'*: James Jones, Roger Alford, Wardell Saunders, Andrew Taylor, W. O. Davis, Elijah Hodges. *Young People's Choir*: Ruth Collins, Howard Carter, Miriam Burton, Eddie Roche. *Rhythm Beaters*: Thornton Cherokee, Martin James, Means Mases, Sylvanna Cole, John Alele, Okey Lawson.

Act 1, Scene 1: The Parlor of Rev. Jones' House. Somewhere in the South. *Scene 2*: Fork of the Road. *Scene 3*: The New Day Pilgrims Meeting.

Act 2, Scene 1: The Back Porch of Sulumai's House in Toomer's Bottom. Evening, three days later. *Scene 2*: Fork of the Road. Same evening. *Scene 3*: Interior of Hope Baptist Church. Same evening.

ACT 1[7]

Scene 1

"Church in the Dale"
   The Choir

---

[5]Original New York production opened 21 October 1907 at the New Amsterdam Theatre for 416 performances.

[6]Original New York production opened 1 March 1933 at the Lyric Theatre for 126 performances.

[7]Also performed: "The Star-Spangled Manner" in an arrangement by Hall Johnson.

Scene 2

"Bye and Bye"
"Song of the Hill"
Solos by C. Holland
(*Composed by* Hall Johnson.)

Scene 3

"Processional"/"Credo"/"Moon-Music"/"Tongola Dance Music"
Solos by F. Marshall, I. Matthews
(*Composed by* Hall Johnson.)

ACT 2
Scene 2

"I Can't Stay Here by Myself"
Solo by B. Powell
"Song of the Hill"
Solo by C. Holland

Scene 3

"Steal Away"/"Amazing Grace"/"Oh, Jesus, Come Dis-a-Way"/"Done Written Down-a My Name"/"I'll Never Turn Back No Mo'"/"Oh, My Lovin' Brother"/"Do You Love My Lord?"/"Great Gettin' Up Mornin'"/"Nobody Knows de Trouble I See"
The Choir
"Run Little Chillun"
(*Composed by* Hall Johnson.)
"So Glad"/"Return, Oh Holy Dove"/"Lord, Oh Have Mercy on Me"
The Choir

1943.11 # CHAUVE-SOURIS 1943

A New Edition of the Russian Musical Revue in Two Acts, 18 Scenes[8]. Music compiled and arranged by Gleb Yellin. English lyrics by Irving Florman. Settings and costumes by Serge Soudeikine. Staged by Michel Michon. Choreography by Vecheslav Swoboda and Boris Romanoff. (Comedy director, Michael Dalamatoff.) Entire production devised and supervised by Leon Greanin. Produced by Leon Greanin, by arrangement with Mme. Nikita Balieff. Opened 12 August 1943 at the Royale Theatre and closed 21 August 1943 after 12 performances.

CAST: MARUSIA SAVA, ZINAIDA ALVERS, VERA PAVLOVSKA, TATIANA POBERS, JEANNE SOUDEIKINA, DANIA KRUPSKA, GEORGIANA BANNISTER, NORMA SLAVINA, GEORGES DOUBROVSKY, MICHAEL DALAMATOFF, SIMEON KARAVAEFF, MICHEL MICHON, ARCADI STOYANOVSKY (Stoianovsky), JACK GANSERT (Gansaert), VLADIMIR LAZAREV, LEO RESNICKOFF, ARSEN TARPOFF, LEO VLASSOFF, NICOLAS DONTZOFF, GEORGE YURKA.

Florence Berline, Cyprienne Gabelman, Audrey Keane, Olga Nicolaeva, Blanche Sanborska, Fern Sironi, Norma Slavina, Nicolas Yourovsky, Sergei Zdanoff, Lev Xanoff.

ACT 1
Scene 1

"Russian Shawls" (Songs of Babi with greetings from Russia)
(*Lyrics by* Michel Michon.)
J. Soudeikina, M. Sava, Z. Alvers, G. Bannister, V. Pavlovska, T. Pobers.

Scene 2

"The Parade of the Wooden Soldiers"
A. Stoyanovsky, J. Gansert, F. Berline, C. Gabelman, A. Keane, D. Krupska, B. Saborska, F. Sironi, N. Slavina
(*Music by* Leon Jessel. *Setting by* S. Soudeikine after Georgy Narbout.)

Scene 3

"Victory Parade"
M. Dalamatoff, N. Dontzoff, G. Doubrovsky, L. Resnickoff, A. Tarpoff, L. Vlassoff, G. Yurka.

Scene 4

"Song of the Flea"
(*Music by* Modest Moussorgsky.)
Mephistopheles: G. Doubrovsky.

Scene 5

Trepak (Folk Dance)

(*Choreography by* B. Roumanoff.)
C. Gabelman, A. Keane, D. Krupska, B. Sanbornska, F. Sironi, S. Karavaeff, J. Gansert

Scene 6

"Love in the Ranks" (The Daughter of the Regiment in Old St. Petersburg)
(*Music by* Alexei Archangelsky. *Staged by* B. Roumanoff. *Scenery and Costumes by* S. Soudeikine after Nicola Benois.)
The Daughter of the Regiment: V. Pavlovska. *The Corporal*: A. Stoyanovsky. *The Lieutenant*: A. Tarpoff. *The Captain*: M. Michon. *The Major*: G. Doubovsky. *The General*: M. Dalmatoff.

Scene 7

The Nightingale
Danced by N. Slavina
(*Music by* Alexander Alabieff-Liszt. *Choreography by* V. Swoboda.)

Scene 8

"The WAC and the Sniper"
(*Lyrics and Music for the Sniper Song by* I. Florman. *Staged by* R. Boris)
The WAC: G. Bannister. *The Sniper*: V. Pavlovska.

Scene 9

"Hobo-Genius Chorus in 4F"
G. Doubrovsky, N. Dontzoff, S. Karavaeff, M. Michon, L. Resnickoff, A. Stoyanovsky, A. Tarpoff, L. Vlassoff, G. Yurka, under the leadership of M. Dalmatoff.

Scene 10

"Song of Chauve-Souris 1943"
V. Pavlovska

Scene 11

Harvest Festival (Inspired by contemporary Russian composers)
(*Choreography by* V. Swoboda.)
"Song of the Fields"
(*Music by* Lev Knipper.)
"United Nations"
(*Music by* Dimitri Shostakovich.)Z. Alvers, G. Doubrovsky
"Balalaikas"
(*Music by* H. Dounaevsky[9].)
"Oh, My Heart!"
(*Music by* H. Dounaevsky.)M. Sava
"Strolling Home"
(*Music by* Vladimir Zakharoff.)
"Electric Lights Come to the Village"
J. Soudeikina
(*Music by* Dimitri. Shostakovich and Vladimir Sakharoff.)
M. Sava, Z. Alvers, G. Bannister, F. Berline, C. Gabelman, A. Keane, D. Krupska, V. Pavlovska, T. Pobers, B. Sanbornska, F. Sironi, N. Slavina, J. Soudeikina, O. Nicolaeva. M. Dalmatoff, G. Doubrovsky, N. Dontzoff, J. Gansert, S. Karavaeff, V. Lazarev, M. Michon, L. Resnickoff, A. Stoyanovsky, A. Tarpoff, L. Vlassoff, G. Yurka, N. Yourovsky, S. Zdanoff, L. Xanoff.

ACT 2
Scene 1

"The Gypsies" (Original Gypsy Romances)
(*Songs arranged by* Mme. Nastia Poliakova.)
First Gypsy Soloist: M. Sava. *Second Gypsy Soloist*: Z. Alvers. *Third Gypsy Soloist*: T. Pobers. *Minstrel*: M. Michon. *Hussar*: G. Doubrovsky. *Gypsies*: G. Bannister, J. Soudeikina, C. Gabelman, F. Berline, L. Resnickoff, N. Dontzoff, A. Tarpoff, L. Vlasoff, G. Yurka. Chorus under the leadership of M. Dalmatoff.

Scene 2

Polka
(*Choreography by* V. Swoboda.)A. Keane, N. Slavinia, J. Gansert

Scene 3

"Romances of Tchaikovsky"
Z. Alvers, V. Pavlovska
Peter Ilich Tchaikovsky: M. Michon.

Scene 4

Katinka's Birthday ("Katinka Is Sweet Sixteen")
(*Lyrics by* Michon and Robbins. *Katinka's Polka by* B. Romanoff.)
Katinka: D. Krupska. *Mother*: J. Soudeikina. *Father*: L. Vlassof. *Aunt*: G. Bannister. *Bridegroom*: A. Tarpoff. *Uncle*: A. Stoyanovsky. *Portrait*: G. Doubrovsky. *Statue*: M. Michon. *Little Brother*: B. Sanbornska.

---

[8]Original New York production of CHAUVE-SOURIS opened 1 February 1922 at the 49th Street Theatre for 520 performances in 4 different editions. Original productions conceived by Nikita Balieff.

---

[9]Most likely the popular Russian composer Isaak Iosifovich Dunayevsky.

Scene 5

    A Russian Sailor in New York
      The Sailor: S. Karavaeff.

Scene 6

    Night Idyl
      (*Staged by* Mme. E. Balieff. *Setting by* S. Soudeikine after Nicholas Remisoff.)
      The Boy: M. Sava. *The Girl*: A. Stoyanovsky. *Musical Echoes*: J. Soudeikina,
      G. Bannister, S. Karavaeff, L. Resnickoff. *Accordionist*: N. Dontzoff. *Guitarist*:
      G. Yurka.

Scene 7

    Wedding in Ukraine (Original Ukrainian folk songs and dances)
      (*Choreography for* Hopak by B. Romanoff.)
      Bride: V. Pavlovska. *Groom*: V. Lazarev. *Mother*: J. Soudeikina. *Father*: M.
      Dalmatoff. *First Best Man*: S. Karavaeff. *Second Best Man*: M. Michon. *Priest*:
      G. Doubrovsky. *Bridesmaids, Neighbors, Friends and Guests*: Entire Company.

BLOSSOM TIME

1943.12

A Revival of the Operetta in Three Acts[10]. (American) Book and lyrics by Dorothy Donnelly. Adapted from the Viennese (singspiel "Das Dreimäderlhaus") by A. M. Willner and H. Reichert, based on a novel "Schwammerl" by Rainer H. Bartsch. Music adapted and augmented by Sigmund Romberg from the melodies of Franz Schubert selected and arranged by Heinrich Berté. Staged by J. J. Shubert. Choreography by Carthay. Settings by Watson Barratt. Costumes by Stage Costumes, Inc. Music directed by Pierre de Reeder. Produced by the Messrs. Shubert. Opened 4 September 1943 at the Ambasssador Theatre and closed 9 October 1943 after 47 performances.

CAST: *Franz Schubert*: ALEXANDER GRAY. *Christian Kranz*: DOUG LEAVITT. *Baron Schober*: ROY CROPPER. *Scharntoff*: ROBERT CHISHOLM. *Mitzi*: BARBARA SCULLY. *Fritzi*: Adelaide Bishop. *Kitzi*: Loraine Manners. *Bellabruna*: Helene Arthur. *Flower Girl*: Helen Thompson. *Mrs. Kranz*: ZELLA RUSSELL. *Greta*: JACQUELINE SUSANN. *Rosie*: Helena LeBerthon. *Mrs. Coburg*: Pamela Dow. *Vogel*: Roy Barnes. *Von Schwindt*: George Mitchell. *Kuppelweiser*: Nord Cornell. *Novotny*: HARRY K. MORTON. *Domeyer*: Walter Johnson. *Erkman*: George Beach. *Binder*: John O'Neill. *Waitress*: Alice Drake. *Waiter*: Walter Johnson. *Prima Ballerina*: Monna Montes.

Flower Girls and Bridesmaids: Gloria Sterling, Marcella Markham, Edith Vincent, Jay Flower, V. Stowe. *Ballet Girls*: Jacqueline Jacoby, Aura Vainio, Virginia Meyer, Mary Grey, Frances Spelz, Greta Borjosen, Lola Balser.

LAUGH TIME

1943.13

A Vaudeville Revue in Two Acts. Orchestra under the direction of Lou Forman. Ethel Waters accompanied on piano by Reginald Beane. Produced by Paul Small and Fred Finklehoffe. Opened 8 September 1943 at the Sam S. Shubert Theatre, moved 17 October 1943 to the Ambassador Theatre, and closed 20 November 1943 after 126 performances.

CAST: FRANK FAY, ETHEL WATERS, BERT WHEELER, JANE and ADAM DiGATANO, (Ford Lee) BUCK and (John W.) BUBBLES, ADRIANA and CHARLY, LUCIENNE and ASHOUR, JERRI VANCE, WARREN JACKSON, THE BRICKLAYERS.

The Messrs. Small and Finklehoff have never conceded the *corpus delicti*. They have disbanded the pallbearers, halted the requiem, on the laudable suspicion that "Laugh Time" will demonstrate that the burial of vaudeville, circa 1932, was premature.

In the first fraction of this fracas Frank Fay will introduce, sporadically, Adriana and Charly (trampoline act), Buck and Bubbles, the Bricklayers (Leonard Gautier's dog act), the DiGatanos (ballroom dancers). Early in the exercises he will explain a few of his theories about cosmic problems, later will conspire with Bert Wheeler in something that defies Roget. Lest the conventions be outraged, an intermission will follow.

After the recess Bert Wheeler will be found on the rostrum (sandwich monologue). On his flight Mr. Fay will successively introduce Ethel Waters ["Cabin in the Sky," "Am I Blue?," "Stormy Weather," "Heat Wave," "Dinah" and "Taking a Chance on Love"] and Lucienne and Ashour (Apache Dance), then pause to give, what in ye olde Palace days was yclept, "his specialty." At the peak of this confusion will come the finale, without benefit of spiral stairway, adagio dancer or chorus girl symbolizing the Four Freedoms.

---

[10]First presented in New York 29 September 1921 at the Ambassador Theatre for 592 performances. For Synopsis of Scenes and Musical Numbers, see original 1921 production.

1943.14

MY DEAR PUBLIC

A Revusical Story in Two Acts, 11 Scenes. Book by Irving Caesar and Charles [Chuno] Gottesfeld. Music and lyrics by Irving Caesar, Sam Lerner and Gerald Marks. Staged by Edgar MacGregor. Dances directed by Felicia Sorel. Assistant dance director, Henry LeTang. Choreography supervised by Loretta Jefferson. Settings by Albert Johnson. Costumes by Lucinda Ballard. Lighting by Al Alloy. Vocal arrangements by Buck [Clay] Warnick. Orchestrations by Hans Spialek and Ted Royal. Music directed by Harry Levant. Produced by Irving Caesar. Opened 9 September 1943 at the 46th Street Theatre and closed 16 October 1943 after 45 performances.

CAST (in order of appearance): *Walters*: DAVID BURNS. *Tapps*: GEORGIE TAPPS. *Jean*: NANETTE FABRAY. *Daphne Drew*: ETHEL SHUTTA. *Barney Short*: WILLIE HOWARD. *Renee*: Renee Russell. *Louise*: Louise Fisk. *Mitzi*: Mitzi Perry. *Byron Burns*: ERIC BROTHERSON. *Lulu*: Sherle North. *Gordon*: Gordon Gifford. *Playwright*: William Nunn. *Gus Wagner*: Jesse White. *Kelly*: Al Kelly. *Rose Brown*: Rose Brown. *Announcer*: Dave Hamilton. *Ruth*: Janice Wallace. *Edith*: Edith Laumer.

Crandall Sisters (Truda, Mickey, Heather), the Harmoneers (Dave Hamilton, Louise Rose, Bill Jones, Michael Kojak), Monica Boyer, Lee Varrett, Marlynn Arden, Heather Crandall, Della Lorrie, Harry Day, Helene and her violin, Marlynn Arden.

Girls: Renee Russell, Marilyn Johnson, Zynaid Spencer, Ann Middleton, Betty Burns, Virginia Stevens, Janice Wallace, Joan Sommers, Mitzi Perry, Edith Laumer, Louise Fiske, Marjorie Gaye, Betty Leighton, Jean Cooke, Dorothy Thomas, Billie Ferguson, Robin Marlowe, Vivian Newell, Dorothy Hyatt, Lorene Gray, Ginger Lynne. *Boys*: Jack Lyons, Richard Andre, Paul Vincent, Ernie DiGennaro, Larry Evers, William Hunter, William Lundy.

Act 1, Scene 1: Backstage. *Scene 2*: Inside Barney Short's Office. *Scene 3*: Private Room in the Crystal Hill Hospital. *Scene 4*: Backstage. *Scene 5*: Private Room in the Crystal Hill Hospital. *Scene 6*: Backstage.

Act 2, Scene 1: LaGuardia Field. *Scene 2*: Barney Short's Office. *Scene 3*: Backstage. *Scene 4*: Jean's Dressing Room. *Scene 5*: Finale.

ACT 1

  Opening—"Feet on the Sidewalk"
    G. Tapps, N. Fabray,
    T. Crandall, M. Crandall, M. Boyer, the Harmoneers, Boys and Girls
    (*Music and Lyrics by* Sammy Lerner and Gerald Marks.)

  "My Dear Public"
    G. Gifford, S. North, J. White, M. Boyer, L. Varrett,
    M. Arden, Crandall Sisters, the Harmoneers

  "Last Will and Testament"
    E. Brotherson

  "Little Gamins"
    E. Shutta, Ensemble

  "(This Is) Our Private Love Song"
    E. Brotherson, N. Fabray, Helene and her violin

  "My Spies Tell Me"
    D. Burns, S. North, Crandall Sisters

  "Color Line" (There Ain't No Color Line Around the Rainbow)
    R. Brown

  "If You Want a Deal With Russia"
    W. Howard

  "May All Our Children Have Rhythm"
    G. Tapps, N. Fabray, Crandall Sisters, the Harmoneers, D. Lorrie, H. Day,
    Girls and Boys

ACT 2

  "Pipes of Pan Americana"
    G. Gifford, the Harmoneers, M. Boyer, D. Lorrie, H. Day, Boys and Girls

  "Rhumba Jake"
    W. Howard, E. Shutta

  "Lulu"
    D. Burns, S. North

  "Love Is Such a Cheat"
    E. Shutta, the Harmoneers, Helene and her violin
    (*Music and Lyrics by* Irving Caesar, Gerald Marks and Irma Hollander.)

  Enesco's Rumanian Rhapsody No. 1 (Ballet)
    M. Arden, Helene, Boys and Girls

  "I Love to Sing the Words"
    N. Fabray, G. Tapps, Boys and Girls

  "(This Is) Our Private Love Song" (reprise)

  Finale
    Entire Company

1943.15

PORGY AND BESS

A Return Engagement of the Revival of the Musical Play in Three Acts, 7 Scenes[11]. Book by DuBose Heyward, adapted from the play "Porgy" by DuBose and Dorothy Heyward. Music by George Gershwin. Lyrics by DuBose Heyward and Ira Gershwin. Directed by Robert Ross. Chorus directed by Eva Jessye. Settings by Herbert Andrews. Costumes by Paul du Pont. Produced by Cheryl Crawford in association with John J. Wildberg. Opened 13 September 1943 at the 44th Street Theatre and closed 2 October 1943 after 24 performances.

CAST (in order of appearance): *Maria*: GEORGETTE HARVEY. *Lily*: Catherine Ayers. *Annie*: Musa Williams. *Clara*: HARRIET JACKSON. *Jake*: EDWARD MATTHEWS. *Sportin' Life*: AVON LONG. *Mingo*: Jerry Laws. *Robbins*: Henry Davis. *Serena*: Alma Hubbard. *Jim*: William C. Smith. *Peter*: George Randol. *Porgy*: TODD DUNCAN. *Crown*: WARREN COLEMAN. *Bess*: ETTA MOTEN. *Policeman*: Kenneth Konopka. *Detective*: Richard Bowler. *Undertaker*: Coyal McMahon. *Lawyer Frazier*: Charles Welch. *Nelson*: Charles Colman. *Strawberry Woman*: Catherine Ayers. *Crab Man*: Edward Tyler. *Coroner*: Don Darcy.
Residents of Catfish Row, Fishermen, Children, Stevedores, etc.: THE EVA JESSYE CHOIR: Virginia Girvin, Gladys Goode, Eulabel Riley, Louisa Howard, Assota Marshall, Sadie McGill, Annabelle Ross, Zelda Shelton, Eloise Uggams, Musa Williams, John Diggs, Leslie Gray, Jerry Laws, William C. Smith, Harold Desverney, Velda Shelton, Roger Aeford, Charles Coleman, Coyal McMahon, Edward Tyler, William O'Neal. *Children*: Robert Tucker, Ruthetta Anderson, Kenneth Tucker, Thomas Tucker, Douglas Rice, Patricia Rice.

1943.16

BRIGHT LIGHTS OF 1944

A Intimate Musical Revue in Two Acts, 18 Scenes. Sketches by Norman Anthony and Charles Sherman. Additional dialogue by Joseph Erens. Music by Jerry Livingston. Lyrics by Mack David. Staged by Dan Eckley. Dances directed by Truly McGee. Settings and costumes by Perry Watkins. Lighting by Al Alloy. Orchestra directed by Max Meth. Associate conductor, Murray Kellner. Musical arrangements by (Robert) Russell Bennett, Hans Spialek and Ted Royal. Produced by Alexander H. Cohen in association with Martin Poll and Joseph Kipness. Opened 16 September 1943 at the Forrest Theatre and closed 18 September 1943 after 4 performances.

CAST: JAMES BARTON, FRANCES WILLIAMS, JOE SMITH and CHARLES DALE [Smith & Dale], BUDDY CLARK, JAYNE MANNERS, BILLIE WORTH, JERE McMAHON, RENEE CARROLL, John A. Lorenz, Cece Eames, Sollen Burry, Dave Leonard, Don Roberts, Russell Morrison, Elaine Miller, Kathryn Barton, Mimi Lynne, JOHN KIRBY'S ORCHESTRA.
The Royal Guards: Thomas Gleason, Arthur Barry, John Hamill, Carleton Male.
The Dancing Girls: Janet Joy, Betty de Elmo, Darlene Francys, Murnai Pins, Rose Marie Magrill.

ACT 1
Scene 1

Outside Sardi's
Cop: J. A. Lorenz. *Out of Towner*: C. Eames.

Scene 2

Inside Sardi's
The Boy: J. McMahon. *The Girl*: B. Worth. *First Waiter*: J. Smith. *Second Waiter*: C. Dale. *Levy*: S. Burry. *Farquardt*: D. Leonard. *Marquardt*: D. Roberts.
"Haven't We Met Before?"
B. Worth, J. McMahon

Scene 3

James Barton (Specialty):
"Damned Ole Jeeter"[12]
(*Music and Lyrics by* Dick Leibert and George Blake.)
"I Can't Give You Anything But Love" (from BLACKBIRDS OF 1928)
(*Music and Lyrics by* Jimmy McHugh and Dorothy Fields.)

Scene 4

Inside Sardi's
Mr. Potts: R. Morrison. *Miss Miller*: E. Miller. *Renee Carroll*: Herself. *Buddy Clark*: Himself.

---

[11]First presented in New York 10 October 1935 at the Alvin Theatre for 124 performances; revived 22 January 1942 at the Majestic Theatre for 286 performances. For Synopsis of Scenes and Musical Numbers, see original 1935 production and 1942 revival.
[12]Inspired by Barton's role of Jeeter in the long running success TOBACCO ROAD.

"You'd Better Dance"
B. Worth, J. McMahon
"Thoughtless"
B. Clark

Scene 5

Punxsutawney, Pa.
"Don't Forget the Girl from Punxsutawney"
J. Manners, Royal Guards, Chorus

Scene 6

The Pest
(*by* James Barton)
The Pest: J. Barton. *Gert*: K. Barton. *Charlie*: J. A. Lorenz.

Scene 7

"That's Broadway"
F. Williams
(*Music and Lyrics by* Gene Herbert and Teddy Hall.)

Scene 8

John Kirby and His Orchestra

Scene 9

Inside Sardi's
"We're Having Our Fling"
Entire Company

ACT 2
Scene 1

"Back Bay Beat"
F. Williams, J. Kirby Orchestra, Dancing Girls

Scene 2

The Royal Guards

Scene 3

"Your Face Is Your Fortune"
J. McMahon, B. Worth, F. Williams, B. Clark, Dancing Girls

Scene 4

"Yes, I Love You Honey"
J. Barton, J. Kirby Orchestra
(*Music and Lyrics by* James. P. Johnson.)

Scene 5.

Smith & Dale

Scene 6

"Frankie and Johnny"
F. Williams
Frankie: J. Manners. *Johnny*: J. Barton. *Nellie Bly*: M. Lynne. Ensemble.

Scene 7

Jere McMahon

Scene 8

The Trio
"A Lick, and a Riff, and a Slow Bounce"
F. Williams, J. Manners, B. Worth
(*Music and Lyrics by* Norman Zeno and Al Scofield.)

Scene 9

Finale
Entire Company

1943.17

TROPICAL REVUE

A Dance Revue in Three Acts, 8 Scenes. (Conceived,) Choreographed and staged by Katherine Dunham. Costumes and settings by John Pratt. Production and lighting by Dale Wasserman. Orchestra under the direction of Albert Arkuss. Choral direction: Helen Dowdy. Suggestions on minstrel tunes and dances by Lawrence Deas and Clarence Muse. Produced by Sol Hurok. Opened 19 September 1943 at the Martin Beck Theatre, moved 16 November 1943 to the Forrest Theatre, and closed 4 December 1943 after 87 performances.

CAST: KATHERINE DUNHAM, LEONARD WARE TRIO. *THE DUNHAM DANCERS*: ROGER (Rajah) OHARDIENO, LUCILLE ELLIS, TOMMY GOMEZ, LAVINIA WILLIAMS, LaVERNE FRENCH, SYVILLA FORT, Claude Marchant, Lawaune (Kennard) Ingram, Lenwood Morris, Maria Montiero, Vanoye Aikens, Ramona Erwin, Andre Drew.

Drums: Gaucho Vanderhans, Cándido Vicenty. *First piano*: Albert Arkuss. *Second piano*: Raul Barragan.

ACT 1[13]

Scene 1

Primitive Rhythms

(a) Rara Tonga (*Music by* Paquita Anderson.)
> This is a Melanesian folk story in terms of dance. The Chosen Woman, performs a love dance expressing joy and pride in her beauty. The God enters and chooses her for his own, to the annoyance of The Jealous Husband, who, for his audacity, is turned into a snake. After the tale is finished, there is general merriment.
> *The Chosen Woman*: L. Williams. *The God*: R. Ohardieno. *The Jealous Husband*: T. Gomez. (*Narrator*: K. Dunham.)

(b) Tempo-Son
> *Possessed Dancer*: L. Ellis.

(c) Tempo-Bolero
> L. Williams, T. Gomez, Group
> (*Music by* Paquita Anderson.)

Scene 2

Rumba Suite

(a) Concert Rumba
> K. Dunham, S. Fort, L. Williams, C. Marchant, T. Gomez
> (*Music by* Morejon.)

(b) Rumba With a Little Jive Mixed In
> L. Ellis, L. French, C. Marchant
> (*Music by* Andre.)

(c) Brazilian Carnival Macumba
> K. Dunham, L. Morris, A. Drew, L. French, T. Gomez

(d) Santos Ritual (Dance)
> S. Fort, R. Ohardieno

(e) Mexican Rumba (From the "Rumba Symphony")
> K. Dunham, T. Gomez, Group
> (*Music by* Harl MacDonald.)

ACT 2

Scene 1

Rites de Passage
> (*Music based on a Haitian theme by* Paquita Anderson. *Percussion by* Gaucho.)
> This can best be characterized as the set of rituals surrounding the transition of an individual or group of individuals from one life crisis to another. The ritual period, often at once both sacred and dangerous, is under the guidance of the elders of the community; the entire community joins in this critical transition so that the individual may, in a changed status, have a complete rejoining with the society. The rites dealt with here do not concern any specific community nor any authentic series of rituals. They were created to try and capture in abstraction the emotional body of any primitive community and to project this intense, even fearful personal experience, under the important change in status and the reaction of the society through this period.

(a) The Fertility Ritual—here associated with marriage or mating.
> *Maiden in the Community*: L. Williams. *Man in the Community*: L. French.

(b) Male Puberty Ritual
> *Boy Initiate*: T. Gomez. *Warrior*: R. Ohardieno.
> The passing from boyhood to manhood by means of formal initiations. The first section portrays the boy's isolation and his vision of becoming a warrior. In the second section, masked men of the community, led by the warrior who has appeared in the boy's vision, come to take him to the formal initiation. He is both eager and afraid.

(c) Death Ritual
> *Matriarch*: K. Dunham.
> The wives of a chief mourn his death. Through the intervention of the matriarch the defeat of death is accomplished, and the life cycle continued in the ceremonial ritual of fecundation.

(d) Rhythm Interlude
> L. Ellis, Gaucho, Candido

Scene 2

"Bahiana"
> K. Dunham, R. Ohardieno, C. Marchant, T. Gomez, L. Morris
> (*Music by* Don Alfonso.)

---

[13]The program changed substantially during the run, and the running order was revised. Dropped were: Tempo-Son, Tempo-Bolero, Concert Rumba, Brazilian Carnival Macumba; Rhythm Interlude.

Scene 3

Tropics—Shore Excursion
> (*Music by* Paquita Anderson. *Percussion by* Gaucho.)
> *Woman With the Cigar*: K. Dunham. (*Dockhand*: R. Ohardieno.)

ACT 3

Scene 1

Plantation Dances from "Br'er Rabbit an' de Tah Baby"

Strutters' Ball
> H. Dowdy, Singers

Square Dance, Juba, Jennie Cooler, Palmer House, Pas Mala, Ballin' de Jack, Strut and Cakewalk
> Corps de Ballet
> *Interlocutor*: K. Dunham. *Field Hands*: C. Marchant, T. Gomez, R. Ohardieno, L. Morris, V. Aikens. *Couple from Memphis*: S. Fort, L. French.

Scene 2

Leonard Ware Trio

Scene 3

Le Jazz Hot

(a) Variations on the theme Boogie Woogie
> L. Ellis, Group
> (*Music by* Meade Lux Lewis, Albert Ammons and Smith.)

(b) Barrel House (Florida Swamp Shimmy)
> K. Dunham, R. Ohardieno
> (*Music by* Meade Lux Lewis and Albert Ammons.)

(c) Honky-Tonk Train
> (*Music by* Meade Lux Lewis.)
> *"Cokey" Brakeman*: L. French. *Lady Passenger*: L. Ellis.

Added were:

"Cuban Slave Lament" (Act 1)
> *The Singer*: B. Capo. *The Possessed Dancer*: L. Ellis.

"Moorish Bolero" (Act 1)
> L. Williams, T. Gomez and Group
> (*Music by* Paquita Anderson.)

"Para Que Tu Ver" (Act 1)
> B. Capo

Choro (A 19th Century Brazilian Quadrille) (Act 1)
> K. Dunham, S. Fort, C. Marchant, T. Gomez
> (*Music by* Gogliano.)

Street Scene—Port au Prince (Act 2)
> L. Ellis, Gaucho, Candido

Added for subsequent tour:

Callate ("Sh-be Quiet")
> K. Dunham, R. Ohardieno, L. Morris, V. Aikens
> (*Music by* Candido Vicenty.)

Promenade—Havana 1910
> K. Dunham, Company, Bobby Capo, Helen Dowdy Quartet
> (*Music by* Mercedes Navarro.)

1943.18

HAIRPIN HARMONY

A Musical Farce in Two Acts. Book, music and lyrics by Harold Orlob. Staged by Dora Maugham. Setting by Donald Oenslager. Costumes by Mahieu. Lighting by Jeannette Hackett. Orchestrations by Arthur Norris. Production supervised by Mack Hilliard. Produced by Harold Orlob. Opened 1 October 1943 at the National Theatre and closed 2 October 1943 after 3 performances.

CAST (in order of appearance): *Bill Heller*: LENNIE KENT. *Howard Swift*: CARLYLE BLACKWELL. *Chet Warren*: GIL JOHNSON. *Reenie Franton*: MAUREEN CANNON. *Jackie Stevens*: TERI KEANE. *Evelyn*: KAREN CONRAD. *Betty*: GAY GAYNOR. *June*: BARBARA CLAWSON. *Ruth*: DORIS CLAWSON. *Sue*: DOROTHY CLAWSON. *Cobalt, Looseknit*: Smiles & Smiles. *Racey Corday*: Irene Corlett. *Rev. Dr. Brown*: Don Valentine. *Buddy Roc*: VING MERLIN. *Mrs. Warren*: Margaret Irving. *Inspector*: David Leonard. *State Trooper*: Clair Kramer.

Hairpin Harmonettes: *Piano*: Rochelle Kritchmar. *Violin*: Esther Shure. *Violin*: Esther Rabiroff. *Harp and Viola*: Suzanne Sprecher. *Bass*: Thelma Fitch. *Drums and Violin*: Julia Goldman. *Saxophone*: Nadine Winstead. *Saxophone*: L'Ana Hyams. *Saxophone*: Muriel Burns. *Trumpet*: Leona May Smith. *Trumpet*: Elvira Rohl. *Trombone*: Elaine Fitch.

Acts 1 and 2: Lucy Warren's Home. Summer afternoon and evening.

ACT 1

Opening
Hairpin Harmonettes
"Hairpin Harmony"
M. Cannon, Clawson Triplets
"You're the Reason"
G. Johnson, M. Cannon, Clawson Triplets, Smiles
"What-a-Ya-Say"
L. Kent, G. Johnson, M. Cannon, T. Keane, Clawson Triplets
"I'm Tickled Pink"
T. Keane, Clawson Triplets
"I'm a Butter Hoarder"
G. Johnson
"Without a Sponsor"
L. Kent, Clawson Triplets
Danced by K. Conrad.
Tango
K. Conrad

ACT 2

Trumpet Solo
L. M. Smith
"You're the Reason" (reprise)(Violin Solo)
V. Merlin
Dance
K. Conrad
"I Can Be Like Grandpa"
G. Johnson, M. Cannon
"Without a Sponsor" (reprise)
M. Cannon, G. Johnson
"That's My Approach to Love"
T. Keane, L. Kent
Violin Solo
V. Merlin
"Piccaninny Pic"
Smiles & Smiles
"That's My Approach to Love" (reprise)
T. Keane, L. Kent, Clawson Triplets
"What Do the Neighbors Say?"
M. Cannon, T. Keane, K. Conrad, G. Gaynor, Clawson Triplets
Finale—"You're the Reason" (reprise)
Entire Company

1943.19 ONE TOUCH OF VENUS

A Musical Comedy in Two Acts, 11 Scenes. Book by S. J. Perelman and Ogden Nash, suggested by F. Anstey's [Thomas Anstey Guthrie] story "The Tinted Venus." Music by Kurt Weill. Lyrics by Ogden Nash. Staged by Elia Kazan. Dances by Agnes de Mille. Musical director, Maurice Abravanel. Settings by Howard Bay. Costumes designed by Paul duPont and Kermit Love. Miss Martin's gowns from Mainbocher. Musical arrangements and orchestrations by Kurt Weill. Produced by Cheryl Crawford in association with John Wildberg. Opened 7 October 1943 at the Imperial Theatre, moved 24 January 1944 to the 46th Street Theatre, and closed 10 February 1945 after 567 performances.

CAST (in order of appearance): *Whitelaw Savory*: JOHN BOLES. *Molly Grant*: PAULA LAURENCE. *Taxi Black*: TEDDY HART. *Stanley*: Harry Clark. *Rodney Hatch*: KENNY BAKER. *Venus*: MARY MARTIN. *Mrs. Moats*: Florence Dunlap. *Store Manager*: Sam Bonnell. *Bus Starter*: Lou Wills, Jr. *Sam*: Zachary A. Charles. *Mrs. Kramer*: Helen Raymond. *Gloria Kramer*: RUTH BOND. *Police Lieutenant*: Bert Freed. *Rose*: Jane Hoffman. *Zuvelti*: Harold Stone. *Dr. Rook*: Johnny Stearns. *Anatolians*: Sam Bonnell, Matthew Farrar. *Premier Danseuse*: SONO OSATO.

Singers: Jane Davies, Beatrice Hudson, Rose Marie Elliot, Julie Jefferson, Willa Robbins, Betty Spain. Lynn Alden, Arthur Davies, Matthew Farrar, Jeffrey Warren

Dancers: Nelle Fisher, Ruth Harte, Jinx Heffelfinger, Jean Houloose, Ann Hutchinson, Pearl Lang, Allyn Ann McLerie, Lavina Nielsen, Ginee Richardson, Patricia Schaeffer, Kirsten Valbor, Carle Eberle, William Garrett, Ralph Linn, Duncan Noble, Kevin Smith, William (Bill) Weber, Lou Wills, Jr., Parker Wilson.

Act 1, Scene 1: Main Gallery of the Whitelaw Savory Foundation of Modern Art. *Scene 2*: Rodney's Room. *Scene 3*: Arcade of N.B.C. Building, Radio City. *Scene 4*: Waiting Room of the Mid-City Bus Terminal. *Scene 5*: The Roof of the Museum. *Scene 6*: Rodney's Barber Shop. *Scene 7*: The Roof of the Museum.

Act 2, Scene 1: Savory's Bedroom. *Scene 2*: The Tombs. *Scene 3*: A Hotel Room. *Scene 4*: Main Gallery of the Foundation.

ACT 1

Scene 1
"New Art Is True Art"
J. Boles, Chorus
"One Touch of Venus"
P. Laurence, Girls
Scene 2
"How Much I Love You"
K. Baker
"I'm a Stranger Here Myself"
M. Martin
Scene 3
"Forty Minutes for Lunch" Ballet
Danced by M. Martin, S. Osato, P. Birch, Dancers.
"West Wind"
J. Boles
Scene 4
"Way Out West in Jersey"
H. Raymond, H. Raymond, R. Bond, K. Baker
Danced by R. Bond, L. Wills, Jr.
Scene 5
"Foolish Heart"
M. Martin
Danced by S. Osato, R. Pagent.
Scene 6
"The Trouble With Women"
K. Baker, J. Boles, T. Hart, H. Clark
"Speak Low"
M. Martin, K. Baker
Scene 7
"Dr. Crippen"
J. Boles, Dancers

ACT 2

Scene 1
"Very, Very, Very"
P. Laurence
Scene 2
"Speak Low" (reprise)
K. Baker, M. Martin
"Catch Hatch"
J. Boles, P. Laurence, et al
Scene 3
"That's Him"
M. Martin
"Wooden Wedding"
K. Baker
"Venus in Ozone Heights" Ballet
Venus: M. Martin. *Children*: R. Harte, J. Houloose, R. Linn, L. Wills, Jr. *Shy Girls*: D. Adams, A. A. McLerie. *The Head Nymph*: S. Osato. *The Jumping Nymphs*: N. Fisher, K. Valbor, P. Lang. *The Aviator and His Girl*: K. Smith, P. Schaeffer. *Gods*: R. Pagent, P. Birch. *Fauns, Nymphs, Satyrs, Gods*.
Scene 4
Finale
K. Baker

1943.20 ARTISTS AND MODELS (OF 1943)

A Musical Revue in Two Acts, 18 Scenes[14]. Music and lyrics by Dan Shapiro, Milton Pascal and Phil Charig. Dialogue by Lou Walters, Don Ross and Frank Luther. Dialogue directed by John Kennedy. Choreography by Natalie Kamarova, assisted by Lauretta Jefferson. Settings by Watson

---

[14]The sixth and last in the series of musical revues; the previous five editions from 1923-30 were produced by the Messrs. Shubert.

Barratt. Costumes by Kathryn Kuhn. Orchestra conducted by Max Meth. Vocal arrangements by Buck [Clay] Warnick. Orchestrations by Hans Spialek, Ted Royal, Don Walker, Emil Gerstenberger, Charlie Cooks. Entire production conceived and staged by Lou Walters. Produced by Lou Walters and Don Ross in association with E. M. Loew and Michael Redstone. Opened 5 November 1943 at the Broadway Theatre and closed 27 November 1943 after 28 performances.

CAST: JANE FROMAN, JACKIE GLEASON, FRANCES FAYE, MARTY MAY, COLLETTE LYONS, BILLY NEWELL, THE RADIO ACES (Joe and Lou Stoner, Marty Drake), NICK LONG, CAROL KING, THE PETERS SISTERS (Mattye, Ann, Virginia), HAROLD & LOLA, WORTH SISTERS (Toni, Mimi), BEN YOST, DON SAXON, MAYLA, MILDRED LAW, THREE BUSINESSMEN OF RHYTHM and PEARL, BILLIE BOZE, BARBARA BANNISTER, BEN YOST SINGERS (Octet), MARY RAYE & NALDI, Harp Ensemble (Helen Thomas, Margaret Ross, Catherine Johnk, Ann Roberts).
Specialty Dancers: Sheila Bond, Gloria LeRoy, Jeanne Blanche, Lee Loprete, Mullen Sisters, Gertrude Erdey, Betty Jane Hunt, Patsy Lu Rains, Mary-Jo Ball. *Dancing Girls*: Ellen Taylor, Maureen Cunningham, Wynn Stanley, Lillian Moore, Edna Ryan, Helen Heller, Grace de Witt, Frances Gardner. *Ballet Girls*: Carmelita Lanza, Virginia Harriot, Jane Sproule, Patti Robins, Irene Vernon, Nancy Newton, Didi Foret, Margret Neil, Leandra Hines, Anita Divine. *Models*: Iris Amber, Gail Banner, Nancy Callahan, Ruth Dexter, Lana Holmes, Jackie Jordan, Joan Myles, Velvet Knight (Mira Stephans). *Aerial Ballet*: Chat Chilvers, Betty Hackett, Corinne Rose, Florence Walsh. *Yost Octet*: Albert Cazentre, William Hogue, Alfred Jimenez, Arthur Laurent, Jack Leslie, Fred Peters, Jack Paddock, Torine Rella. *Ballet Boys*: Charles Beckman, Joseph Hahn, Harold Haskins, Slava Toumina [Sviatoslav Toumine].

ACT 1
Scene 1

"Parade of Models"
Velvet Night: M. Stephans. *Golden Day*: N. Callahan. *My Sin*: J. Jordan. *Midnight Madness*: J. Myles. *Melody Mood*: R. Dexter. *Star Saphire*: G. Banner. *Tempest Topaz*: L. Holmes. *Amber Glow*: I. Amber. *Bridal Blush*: H. Heller. *Coral Crown*: E. Ryan. *Blithe Harbor*: L. Moore. *Rose Bloom*: G. DeWitt. *Blue Heaven*: M. Cunningham. *Dusky Dawn*: P. Robins. *Radiant Ruby*: C. Lanza.

Scene 2

Prologue in which Jackie Gleason, Marty May and Billy Newell explain the Proceedings.

Scene 3

Minstrelsy
"Way Up North in Dixieland"
M. May, J. Gleason, B. Newell, Radio Aces,
3 Businessmen, Peters Sisters, Minstrel Men, Minstrel Girls,
Ensemble
"Swing Low, Sweet Harriet"
J. Froman

Scene 4

Burlesque
Candy Butcher: J. Gleason.
"How'ja Like to Take Me Home"
C. Lyons
Strip Tease
Worth Sisters
Pages: Mullen Twins.
Taken for a Ride:
Boze-O-Snider: J. Gleason. *Sliding Willie Weston*: M. May. *Mike Specks*: B. Newell. *Gypsy Rose Corio*: C. Lyons. *Margie Smart*: B. Boze. *Georgia Sudden*: B. Bannister.

Scene 5

Hollywood
The Road to Manasooris (A Super-Duper Epic in Technicolor)
Virgin Princess: Mayla. *Chief Danasooris*: J. Gleason. *Beachcomber*: D. Saxon. *Kay Townsend*: M. Law. *Margie (Boo-Boo) Le May*: C. Lyons. *Bob Stevens*: N. Long. *Girls of Manasooris*: B. Boze, B. Bannister, G. DeWitt. *Schwartzersooris*: Peters Sisters. *Captain of Marines*: B. Yost.
"Isle of Manasooris"
Mayla, Island Beauties
"Sears Roebuck"
J. Gleason, C. Lyons
Lover's Tryst Narrative
Mayla

Dance of the Cobra
Harold & Lola
Scene 6
Resume for Latecomers
M. May
Scene 7
Concert
F. Faye, Harps in Swing (Harp Ensemble)
Scene 8
Vaudeville
"North Dakota, South Dakota Moon"
J. Gleason, M. May, B. Newell
Scene 9
"My Heart Is on a Binge Again"
J. Froman
Scene 10
"New York Heartbeat" Ballet
(*Music by* Mons. Georges F. Kamaroff. *Staging and Choreography by* Mme. Natalie Kamarova.)
N. Long, Worth Sisters, Mayla, 3 Businessmen of Rhythm & Pearl, Yost Singers, Corps de Ballet, Dancing Girls, Specialty Girls, American Beauties.
Ballerina: C. King. *Dancer*: S. Toumine.

ACT 2
Scene 1
Circus
Equestriennes: S. Bond, J. Blanche, G. Erdey, L. Loprete. *Jungle Denizens*: M. Stephans, R. Dexter, L. Holmes, I. Amber, J. Myles, J. Jordan, G. Banner, N. Callahan. *Ponies*: Ballet, Dancing Girls. *Birds of Paradise*: Worth Sisters. *Carnivori*: B. J. Hunt, Mullen Sisters, P. LuRains. *Clowns*: Yost Octet. *Aerial Ballet*: C. Chilvers, B. Hackett, C. Rose, F. Walsh. *Trainer—Lion Tamer*: J. Hahn, M. Law.
Scene 2
Questionnaire
(*Special material by* Bud Burtson.)
"What Does the Public Want"
Radio Aces
Scene 3
Specialty
G. LeRoy
Scene 4
Revue
"You Are Romance"
J. Froman, D. Saxon, Yost Octet,
Dancers, Specialty Girls, Ballet Boys, Mary Raye & Naldi
"Blowing My Top"
N. Long, D. Saxon, M. Law, Specialty Girls
Scene 5
Afternoon Tea
C. Lyons
Scene 6
Drama
Submarine U Boat X37
Captain Anchluss: J. Gleason. *Lieutenant Eingamacht*: B. Newell. *Bystander*: M. May. *Seamen*: L. Stoner, M. Drake. *Boatswain*: J. Stoner. *Stowaway*: B. Boze.
Scene 7
"Let's Keep It That Way"
J. Froman
(*Music by* Abner Silver. *Lyrics by* Milton Berle and Ervin Drake.)
Scene 8
Finale (Every Show Has One)
(Entire Company)

1943.21

WHAT'S UP

A Musical Comedy in Two Acts, 9 Scenes. Book by Alan Jay Lerner and Arthur Pierson. Music by Frederick Loewe. Lyrics by Alan Jay Lerner. Book directed by Robert H. Gordon. Settings by Boris Aronson. Costumes by Grace Houston. Orchestra directed by Will Irwin. Orchestrations by Van Cleave. Vocal arrangements by Bobby Tucker. Lighting by Al Alloy. Production staged by George Balanchine. Produced by Mark Warnow. Opened 11 November 1943 at the National Theatre and closed 4 January 1944 after 63 performances.

CAST (in order of appearance): *Jayne*: Mary Roche. *Susan*: Pat Marshall. *Eleanor*: Mitzi Perry. *Margaret*: Lynn Gardner. *Harriet Spinner*: Claire Meade. *Pamela*: Honey Murray. *Louise*: Sondra Barrett. *Martha*: Sara Macon. *May*: Marjorie Beecher. *Jennifer*: Phyllis Hill. *Doctor*: Frank Kreig. *Sgt. Willie Klink*: LARRY DOUGLAS. *Captain Robert Lindsay*: Rodney McLennan. *Sgt. Henry Wagner*: Jack Baker. *Second Lt. Murray Bacchus*: Robert Bay. *First Lt. Ed. Anderson*: DON WEISSMULLER. *Sgt. Moroney*: JOHNNY MORGAN. *Judy*: Helen Wenzel. *Sgt. Dick Benham*: WILLIAM TABBERT. *Virginia Miller*: GLORIA WARREN. *Rawa of Tanglinia*: JIMMY SAVO. *Sgt. Jimmy Stevenson*: Kenneth Buffett.

Act 1, Scene 1: The Living Room. Afternoon. *Scene 2*: The Men's Bedroom. That night. *Scene 3*: The Girls' Bedroom. *Scene 4*: The Living-room.

Act 2, Scene 1: The Rumpus Room. *Scene 2*: The Rawa's Bedroom. *Scene 3*: The Living Room. *Scene 4*: The Linen Closet. *Scene 5*: The Living Room.

ACT 1

Scene 1

"Miss Langley's School for Girls"
    M. Roche, Girls

"From the Chimney to the Cellar"
    M. Roche, Girls

"You've Got a Hold on Me"
    L. Gardner, L. Douglas

Scene 2

"A Girl Is Like a Book"
    R. McLennan

Scene 3

"Joshua"
    L. Gardner
    Danced by the Girls, Fliers.

Scene 4

"Three Girls in a Boat"
    J. Gardner, M. Roche, P. Marshall

Ballet
    J. Savo, P. Hill

"How Fly Times"
    L. Douglas, W. Tabbert, Fliers
    Danced by D. Weissmuller.

"My Last Love"
    M. Roche, L. Douglas, L. Gardner, J. Morgan, W. Tabbert

ACT 2

Scene 1

"You Wash and I'll Dry"
    L. Gardner, L. Douglas, P. Marshall, R. Bay
    Danced by S. Barrett, K. Buffett, H. Murray.
    Duo by M. Beecher, R. McLennan.

"You Wash and I'll Dry" (reprise)
    G. Warren

Scene 3

"The Ill-Tempered Clavichord"
    M. Roche, P. Marshall
    Danced by Fliers, Girls. *Specialty by* R. Bay.

"You've Got a Hold on Me" (reprise)
    G. Warren, W. Tabbert, Fliers, Girls
    Danced by P. Hill, J. Baker.

Scene 5

Finale
    Entire Company

1943.22   A CONNECTICUT YANKEE

A Revival of the Musical Comedy in Two Acts, a Prologue, 5 Scenes and an Epilogue[15]. Book by Herbert Fields. Adapted from Mark Twain's novel "A Connecticut Yankee in King Arthur's Court." Music by Richard Rodgers.

---

[15]Originally produced in New York 3 November 1927 at the Vanderbilt Theatre for 418 performances. Dropped from the original for this revival: "A Ladies' Home Companion," "Nothing's Wrong," "The Sandwich Men," and "Evelyn, What Do You Say?"

Lyrics by Lorenz Hart. Orchestrations by Don Walker. Directed by John C. Wilson. Orchestra directed by George Hirst. Vocal arrangements by Buck [Clay] Warnick. Dances directed by William Holbrook and Al White, Jr. Production (settings, costumes, lighting) by Nat Karson. Produced by Richard Rodgers. Opened 17 November 1943 at the Martin Beck Theatre and closed 11 March 1944 after 135 performances.

CAST (in order of appearance): *In Hartford: Lieutenant Kenneth Kay, U.S.N.*: Robert Byrn. *Judge Thurston Merrill*: John Cherry. *Admiral Arthur K. Arthur, U.S.N.*: ROBERT CHISHOLM. *Ensign Gerald Lake, U.S.N.*: CHESTER STRATTON. *Ensign Allan Gwynn, U.S.N.*: Jere McMahon. *Lieutenant Martin Barrett, U.S.N.*: DICK FORAN. *Captain Lawrence Lake, U.S.N.*: Stuart Casey. *Lieutenant Fay Merrill, W.A.V.E.*: VIVIENNE SEGAL. *Corporal Alice Courtleigh, W.A.C.*: Julie Warren.
In Camelot: Sir Kay, The Seneschal: Robert Byrn. *Martin*: DICK FORAN. *The Demoiselle Alisande La Courtelloise, Sandy*: Julie Warren. *Arthur, King of Britain*: ROBERT CHISHOLM. *Queen Guinevere*: Katherine Anderson. *Sir Lancelot of the Lake*: Stuart Casey. *Sir Galahad, his son*: CHESTER STRATTON. *Angela, Hand-maiden to Queen Morgan Le Fay*: Mimi Berry. *Queen Morgan La Fay*: VIVIENNE SEGAL. *Sir Gawain*: Jere McMahon. *Mistress Evelyn La Rondelle*: VERA-ELLEN.
Dancing Girls: Dorothy Blute, Carole Burke, Eleanore Eberle, Bee Farnum, Virginia Gorski, Janet Joy, Rose Marie Magrill, Frances Martone, Mary McDonnell, Beth Nichols, Murnai Pins, Dorothy Poplar, Joyce Ring, Rosemary Sankey, Helen Vent, Violetta Weems, Doris York. *Dancing Boys*: Tad Bruce, Buster Burnell, Pittman Corry, Frank de Winters, Bob Gari, William Hunter, Hal Loman, William Lundy, Jack Lyons.
Singing Girls: Marjorie Cowen, Toni Hart, Linda Mason, Martha Emma Watson. *Singing Boys*: Lester Freedman, Vincent Henry, Craig Holden, Wayne McIntyre.

Prologue: A Banquet Hall of a Hotel in Hartford, 1943.

Act 1, Scene 1: On the Road to Camelot, 543 A.D. *Scene 2*: Courtyard of King Arthur's Castle.

Act 2, Scene 1: Corridor of Royal Factory. Three Months Later. *Scene 2*: On the Road from Camelot. *Scene 3*: The Palace of Queen Morgan La Fay.

Epilogue: A Banquet Hall of a Hotel in Hartford, 1943.

ACT 1

Prologue

"This Is My Night to Howl"[16]
    V. Segal, Ensemble

"My Heart Stood Still"
    D. Foran, J. Warren

Scene 1

"Thou Swell"
    D. Foran, J. Warren

Scene 2

"At the Round Table"
    The Company

"On a Desert Island"
    C. Stratton, Vera-Ellen, J. McMahon, Ensemble

"To Keep My Love Alive"[17]
    V. Segal

"My Heart Stood Still"
    D. Foran, J. Warren

Finale

ACT 2

Scene 1

"Ye Lunchtime Follies"[18]
    C. Stratton, Ensemble

"Can't You Do a Friend a Favor?"[19]
    V. Segal, D. Foran

"Thou Swell" (reprise)
    D. Foran, J. Warren

"I Feel at Home With You"
    C. Stratton, Vera-Ellen, J. McMahon, Ensemble

Scene 2

"You Always Love the Same Girl"[20]
    D. Foran, R. Chisholm

---

[16]Added for this production.
[17]Added for this production.
[18]Added for this production.
[19]Added for this production.
[20]Added for this production.

Scene 3

"The Camelot Samba"[21]
J. McMahon, Ensemble

Epilogue

Finale
The Company

1943.23 WINGED VICTORY

A Drama with Music in Two Acts, 17 Scenes. Play by Moss Hart. Original music and musical arrangements by Sergeant David Rose. Directed by Moss Hart. Music directed by Sergeant David Rose. Choral Direction by Second Lieutenant Leonard de Paur. Settings by Sergeant Harry Horner. Costumes by Sergeant Howard Shoup. Lighting by Sergeant Abe Feder. Executive director Army Air Forces Show, Lieutenant Colonel Dudley S. Dean. Produced by the U.S. Army Air Forces for the benefit of Army Emergency Relief. Opened 20 November 1943 at the 44th Street Theatre and closed 20 May 1944 after 212 performances.

CAST (in order of appearance): *Allan Ross*: Corporal Mark Daniels. *Frankie Davis*: Private Dick Hogan. *Danny (Pinky) Scariano*: Private Don Taylor. *Dorothy Ross*: Phyllis Avery. *Mrs. Ross*: Virginia Hammond. *Whitey*: Private Red Buttons. *Fred Cassidy*: Private Bert Hicks. *Eddie Borden*: Pfc. Kenneth Forbes. *Tommy Gregg*: Private William Nash. *Ronny Meade*: Sergeant Kevin McCarthy. *Sergeant Casey*: Private Elliot Sullivan. *Bobby Grills*: Private Barry Nelson. *Irving Miller*: Pfc. Edmond O'Brien. *Dave Anderson*: Sergeant Rune Hultman. *Sergeant Everett*: Sergeant Edward Reardon. *Major Halper*: Private Alan Baxter. *Lieutenant Jules Hudson*: Private Whitner Bissell. *Captain Elkton*: Private Grant Richards. . *Captain Payne*: Corporal Edward Ashley. *Captain Speer*: Private Henry Rowland. *Lieutenant Johnson*: First Lieutenant William Neil. *Peter Clark*: Private Harry Lewis. *Lieutenant McCarthy*: Private Paul Kaye. *Henry Larsen*: Private John Elliott. *A.L. Simpson*: Sergeant Gilbert Frye. *Ed Slater*: Sergeant Frank Kane. *Russell Chandler*: Corporal Russell W. Drewes. *Gordon Williams*: Private Hayes Gordon. *Mark Walton*: Corporal Don Richards. *Al Black*: Sergeant Daniel Scholl. *Gilbert Paxton*: Private John R. Kearney. *Bob Chapman*: Private Stuart Langley. *Jim Gardner*: Sergeant Robert Willey. *Mr. Gardner*: Pfc. Anthony Ross. *Mrs. Gardner*: Laura Pierpont. *Lieutenant Stevens*: Private Michael Harvey. *Ed Ried*: Private Kent Morrison. *Sally*: Mary Lenhardt. *Jane*: Jean McCoy. *Captain McIntyre*: Corporal Gary Merrill. *Dick Talbert*: Sergeant David Calvin. *Nick Bush*: Private Cy Perkins. *Gordon Cantrell*: Corporal Ira Cirker. *Mack Hall*: Pfc. Edward McMahon. *Sid Marshall*: Sergeant David Durston. *Ralph Stevens*: Private James Engler. *Leo Nadler*: Pfc. Donald Hammer. *David Michaelson*: Pfc. Thomas Dillon. *Colonel Gibney*: Private Phillip Bourneuf. *Lieutenant Thompson*: Sergeant George Reeves. *Jerry Ellison*: Private Walter Reed. *Russ Coleman*: Sergeant Zeke Manners. *George Morse*: Private Ray Merrill. *Sid Green*: Corporal Jerry Hilliard Adler. *Fred Kelly*: Pfc. Ray McDonald. *Lee*: Sergeant Victor Young. *Chaplain*: Corporal Fred Cotton. *Lieutenant Reynolds*: Second Lieutenant Gilbert Herman. *Colonel Ross*: Private Damian O'Flynn. *Lieutenant Sperry*: Sergeant Ray Middleton. *Lieutenant Rayburn*: First Lieutenant George Hoffman. *Charles Jordan*: Captain Raye Bidwell. *The Mayor*: Capt. Sidney Bassler. *Mr. Grills*: Sergeant Joseph Meyer. *Helen*: Elisabeth Fraser. *Mrs. Grills*: Genevieve Frizzell. *The Minister*: Private Richard Beach. *Barker*: Private George Petrie. *Milhauser*: Private Alfred Ryder. *Adams*: Private Karl Malden. *O'Brien*: Sergeant Peter Lind Hayes. *Gleason*: Pfc. Martin Ritt. *Ruth*: Olive Deering. *Radio Announcer*: Srgeant John Ademy. *Glenn Barrows*: Private Archie Robbins. *Paul Conway*: Private Jack Powell, Jr. *Miguel Lopez*: S/Sergeant Sascha Brastoff. *Sam Preston*: Private Henry Slate. *Harry Preston*: Private Jack Slate. *Colonel Blakely*: Second. Lieutenant Donald Beddoe. *Corporal Regan*: Private John Tyers. *Jack Browning*: Private Barry Mitchell. *Miss Aldridge*: Mary Cooper. *Doctor Baker*: Private Lee J. Cobb. *Milton Benson*: Private Michael Duane.

Army Air Forces Personnel portraying Soldiers, Civilians, Aviation Students, Mechanics and Pilots. Civilian Members of the "Winged Victory" Cast Portraying WACS, Soldiers' Wives and Mothers. Choral Group.

Act 1, Scene 1: The Back Porch of the Ross Home, Mapleton, Ohio. *Scene 2:* A Barrack Street. *Scene 3:* An Examination Room. *Scene 4:* A Washroom. *Scene 5:* An Academic Board Meeting Room. *Scene 6:* A Classification Room. *Scene 7:* The Entrance Gates at Classification Center. *Scene 8:* A Hangar. *Scene 9:* A Clearing in Desert. *Scene 10:* A Parade Ground.

Act 2, Scene 1: The Grill's Farmhouse in Oregon. *Scene 2:* A Flying Field. *Scene 3:* A Bedroom in a Barrack. *Scene 4:* A Hotel Room in Oakland, California. *Scene 5:* An Island in the South Pacific. *Scene 6:* A Nearby Landing Field. *Scene 7:* Winged Victory.

[21]Added for this production.

ACT 1[22]

Scene 2

"Gee Mom, I Want to Go Home"
Air Force Men

"When the War Is Over"
Air Force Men
(*Music by* Carmen Dragon. *Lyrics by* Jerome Lawrence and Robert E. Lee.)

"Mademoiselle from Armentieres"[23] (Hinky Dinky Parlay Voo)
Air Force Men

Scene 12

"The Army Air Corps"
Air Force Men
(*Music and Lyrics by* Robert Crawford.)

"Auld Lang Syne" (Anon.)
Air Force Men

ACT 2

Scene 5

Yuletide Follies:

"Pennsylvania Polka"
3 G. I. 'Andrews Sisters'
(*Music and Lyrics by* Lester Lee and Zeke Manners.)

"Chica Chica Boom Chic" (from THAT NIGHT IN RIO film)
G. I. 'Carmen Miranda'
(*Music by* Harry Warren. *Lyrics by* Mack Gordon.)

"Silent Night"
A Corporal
(*Music and Lyrics by* Joseph Mohr and Franz Gruber.)

Scene 7

"Winged Victory"
Air Force Men

1943.24 CARMEN JONES

A Musical Play in Two Acts, 5 Scenes. Book and lyrics by Oscar Hammerstein II[24]. Based on Henri Meilhac and Ludwig Halévy's operatic adaptation of Prosper Merimée's novel "Carmen." Music by Georges Bizet. Staging, lighting and color schemes of entire production by Hassard Short. Libretto directed by Charles Friedman. New orchestral arrangements by Robert Russell Bennett. Settings designed by Howard Bay. Costumes designed by Raoul Pene du Bois. Choreography by Eugene Loring. Choral direction by Robert Shaw. Orchestra conducted by Joseph Littau. Produced by Billy Rose. Opened 2 December 1943 at the Broadway Theatre and closed 10 February 1945 after 503 performances.

[22]Two songs appear in program; complete song list prepared from production manuscript. Also performed:

"My Dream Book of Memories"
(*Music and Lyrics by* David Rose.)

"The Whiffenpoof Song"
(*Special Lyrics by* Moss Hart.)
(*Music and Lyrics by* Meade Minnigerode, George S. Pomeroy, Tod B. Galloway.)

[23]A popular World War I song variously claimed by Harry Wincott, also arranged by Sergeant Red Rowley and Lieutenant Gitz Rice.

[24]Author's note: "Believing Carmen to be a perfect wedding of story and music, we have adhered, as closely as possible, to its original form. All the melodies—with a very few minor exceptions—are sung in their accustomed order. The small deviations we have made were only those which seemed honestly demanded by a transference of 'Carmen' to a modern American background.

"In our elimination of the recitatif passages, we are not taking as great a liberty as may be supposed. Bizet and his collaborators originally wrote 'Carmen' with spoken dialogue scenes between the airs that were sung. The work was intended for theatres of average size, like the Opera Comique in Paris (where it is played today as a dialogue opera).

"'Carmen' was not converted to a 'grand opera' until after Bizet's death. The music set to the dialogue is not his music. It was written by Ernest Guiraud."Oscar Hammerstein II

CAST (in order of appearance): *Corporal Morrell*: Napoleon Reed or Robert Clarke. *Foreman*: Robert Clarke or George Willis. *Cindy Lou*: CARLOTTA FRANZELL or ELTON J. WARREN. *Sergeant Brown*: JACK CARR. *Joe*: LUTHER SAXON or NAPOLEON REED. *Carmen*: MURIEL SMITH or MURIEL RAHN. *Sally*: Sibol Cain. *T-Bone*: Edward Roche. *Tough Kid*: William Jones. *Drummer*: COSY [Cozy] COLE. *Bartender*: Melvin Howard. *Waiter*: Edward Christopher. *Frankie*: JUNE HAWKINS. *Myrt*: JESSICA RUSSELL. *Rum*: EDWARD LEE TYLER. *Dink*: DICK MONTGOMERY. *Husky Miller*: GLENN BRYANT. *Mr. Higgins*: P. JAY SIDNEY. *Miss Higgins*: Fredye Marshall. *Photographer*: Alford Pierre. *Card Players*: Urylee Leonardos, Ethel White, Sibol Cain. *Dancing Girl*: Ruth Crampton. *Poncho*: William Dillard. *Dancing Boxers*: Sheldon B. Hoskins, Randolph Sawyer. *Bullet Head*: Melvin Howard. *Referee*: Tony Fleming, Jr. *Soldiers*: Robert Clarke, William Woolfolk, George Willis, Elijah Hodges.

Soldiers, Factory Workers, Socialites: Viola Anderson, Lee Allen, William Archer, Miriam Burton, Sibol Cain, Clarice Crawford, Ruth Crumpton, Robert Clarke, Anne Dixon, Marguerite Duncan, Richard DeVaultier, George Dosher, William Davis, Awilda Frasier, Elijah Hodges, Melvin Howard, Clarence Jones, Elsie Kennedy, Fredye Marshall, Maithe Marshall, Bertha Powell, Alford Pierre, Fred Randall, Chauncey Reynolds, Edward Roche, Randall Steplight, Andrew Taylor, Harold Taylor, Ethel White, George Willis, Urylee Leonardos, Oliver Busch, Mary Graham, Mattie Washington, Willie May Bourne, Mildred Saffold.

Dancers: Valerie Black, Al Bledger, Posie Flowers, Tony Fleming Jr., J. Prioreau Gray, Frank Green, Erona Harris, Mable Hart, Sheldon B. Hoskins, Rhoda Johnson, Richard James, Dorothy McNichols, Vera McNichols, Betty Nichols, Frank Neal, Joel A. Noble, Boll O'Neil, Evelyn Pilcher, Edith Ross, J. Flash Riley, Randolph Sawyer, Randolph Scott, Royce Wallace, Dorothy Williams, Edward Christopher, Carmencita Romero, Daniel Lloyd.

Children: Gilbert Irvis, Oliver Hamilton, LeRoy Westfall, Carlos Van Puten, Delano Vanterpool, James Holman, L. Drayton, E. Drayton, David Lee, Melvin Duncan, James Scott, John Richards.

Time: The Present.

Act 1, Scene 1: Outside a Parachute factory near a Southern Town. *Scene 2*: A Nearby Roadside, immediately after. *Scene 3*: Billy Pastor's Café, three weeks later.

Act 2, Scene 1: Terrace of the Meadowland Country Club, Southside of Chicago, two weeks later. *Scene 2*: Outside a Sport Stadium, one week later.

ACT 1

Scene 1

Opening Scene
N. Reed, C. Franzell, Workmen

"Lift 'Em Up and Put 'Em Down"
Street Boys

"Honey Gal o' Mine"
Workers

"Good Luck, Mr. Flyin' Man"
Ensemble, Dancers

"Dat's Love"
M. Smith, Ensemble

Scene: Joe and Cindy Lou

"You Talk Just Like My Maw" (Duet)
L. Saxon, C. Franzell

Finale Scene 1
M. Smith, L. Saxon, J. Carr, S. Cain, Ensemble

"Carmen Jones Is Goin' to Jail" (Entr' Scene)
Ensemble

Scene 2

"Dere's a Café on de Corner"
M. Smith, L. Saxon

Finaletto and Entr' Scene

Scene 3

"Beat Out Dat Rhythm on a Drum"
J. Russell, C. Cole, Dancers, Ensemble

"Stan' Up and Fight"
G. Bryant

"Whizzin Away Along de Track" (Quintet)
E. L. Tyler, D. Montgomery, J. Russell, J. Hawkins, M. Smith

Scene: Carmen and Joe

"Dis Flower"
L. Saxon

"If You Would Only Come Away" (Duet)
M. Smith, L. Saxon

Finale Act 1

ACT 2

Scene 1

"De Cards Don't Lie"
J. Hawkins, J. Russell, Card Players

"Dat Ol' Boy"
M. Smith

"Poncho De Panther From Brazil"
J. Hawkins, J. Russell, G. Bryant, E. L. Tyler, Ensemble

Ballet Divertissement

"My Joe"
C. Franzell

Finale Scene 1
M. Smith, L. Saxon, C. Franzell, G. Bryant, E. L. Tyler, D. Montgomery, J. Hawkins, J. Russell

Scene 2

"Get Yer Program for de Big Fight"
Ensemble

"Dat's Our Man"
Ensemble

Scene: Joe and Carmen

Finale

1944.01 JACKPOT

A Musical Comedy in Two Acts, 10 Scenes. Book by Guy Bolton, Sidney Sheldon and Ben Roberts. Music by Vernon Duke. Lyrics by Howard Dietz. Directed by Roy Hargrave. Dances by Lauretta Jefferson. Ballet directed by Charles Weidman. Music directed by Max Meth. Settings by Raymond Sovey and Robert Edmond Jones. Costumes by Kiviette. Vocal arrangements by Buck [Clay] Warnick. Orchestral arrangements by Hans Spialek, (Robert) Russell Bennett and Vernon Duke. Produced by Vinton Freedley. Opened 13 January 1944 at the Alvin Theatre and closed 11 March 1944 after 69 performances.

CAST (in order of appearance): *Peggy*: Althea Elder. *Billie*: Billie Worth. *Mr. Dill*: Morton L. Stevens. *Bill Bender*: Ben Lackland. *Nancy Parker*: MARY WICKES. *Sally Madison*: NANETTE FABRAY. *Dexter De Wolf*: Houston Richards. *Edna*: Jacqueline Susann. *Hedy*: Helena Goudvis. *Hawley*: John Kearny. *Assistant Bartender*: Walter Monroe. *Jerry Finch*: JERRY LESTER. *Winkie Cotter*: BENNY BAKER. *Hank Trimble*: ALLAN JONES. *Girl*: Flower Hujer. *Reporter*: Bill Jones. *Tot Patterson*: Althea Elder. *Sergeant Naylor*: Wendell Corey. *Sgt. Maguire*: BETTY GARRETT. *Helen Westcott*: Frances Robinson. *Sniper*: Bob Beam. *First Marine*: John Hamil. *Second Marine*: Bill Jones. *Edith*: Edith Turgell. *Accordionist*: Eva Barcinska. *Monica*: Drucilla Strain. *Pat*: Pat Ogden. *Betty*: Betty Stuart. *Sherry*: Sherry Shadburne. *Mary Lou*: Mary Louise Meade. *Connie*: Connie Constant. *Nurse*: Billie Worth. (*Specialty Dancers*: Don Liberto, Peter Hamilton, Florence Lessing.)

Hostesses: Cece Eames, Virginia Barnes, Diane Chase, Gene Cooke, Billie Dee, Marion Harvey, Marion Lulling, Edith Laumer, Dorothy G. Thomas, Dorothy Matthews, Aileen Reed, Ellen Taylor, Sally Tepley, Edith Turgell, Jeanne C. Trybom, Lorraine Todd, Georginia E. Yeager. *Vocalists*: Fague Springman, Robert Beam, George Frank, Mario Pichler, Bill Jones, Michael Kozak, Roger E. Miller, John Hamill. *Marines*: Ray Cook, Lawrence Evers, Bob Ferguson, T.C. Jones, Jack McCaffrey, Robert Sullivan, Joe Wismak, Frank Westbrook.

Act 1, Scene 1: Assembly Room of Duff and Dill Engine Corporation. *Scene 2*: Hawley's Bar. *Scene 3*: A Broadcasting Studio. *Scene 4*: Recreation Room, Priscilla Manor, Turtle Beach, South Carolina. *Scene 5*: A Cornfield. *Scene 6*: The Recreation Room, Priscilla Manor, Turtle Beach, South Carolina.

Act 2, Scene 1: Garden of the Priscilla Manor. *Scene 2*: Bedroom of the Bridal Suite. *Scene 3*: The Balcony. *Scene 4*: Garden of the Priscilla Manor—the next day.

ACT 1

"The Last Long Mile"
N. Fabray, A. Elder, B. Worth, Factory Workers

"Blind Date"
N. Fabray, Workers

"I Kissed My Girl Goodbye"
A. Jones, Marines

"A Piece of a Girl"
A. Jones, J. Lester, B. Baker

"My Top Sergeant"
J. Lester, B. Garrett, Boys

"Sugar Foot"
    B. Garrett, M. Wickes, J. Lester, B. Baker, Ensemble
    Specialty Dance: D. Liberto.
"I Kissed My Girl Goodbye" (reprise)
    Marines
"What Happened?"
    N. Fabray, A. Jones
"Sugar Foot" (reprise)
    B. Garrett, J. Lester, B. Baker
"Grist for De Mille"
    (*Staged by* Charles Weidman.)
    M. Wickes, Ensemble
    Cowboy: P. Hamilton. *Nymph*: F. Lessing. *Pagan Girl*: F. Hujer.

ACT 2
Opening
    E. Barcinska
"He's Good for Nothing But Me"
    B. Garrett, Ensemble
    Danced by D. Liberto, B. Worth, A. Elder. (*Staged by* Charles Weidman.)
"What's Mine Is Yours"
    J. Lester, B. Baker
"What Happened?" (reprise)
    A. Jones
"It Was Nice Knowing You"
    N. Fabray, A. Jones
"Nobody Ever Pins Me Up"
    M. Wickes, Ensemble
"One Track Mind"
    A. Jones
    Danced by F. Lessing, P. Hamilton.
"There Are Yanks"
    B. Garrett, Ensemble
Finale
    Entire Company

1944.02

MEXICAN HAYRIDE

A Musical Comedy in Two Acts, 10 Scenes. Book by Herbert and Dorothy Fields. Music and lyrics by Cole Porter. Staged by Hassard Short. Book directed by John Kennedy. Dances by Paul Haakon. Sets by George Jenkins. Costumes by Mary Grant. Orchestra directed by Harry Levant. Orchestrations by (Robert) Russell Bennett and Ted Royal. Choral Arrangements by William Parson. Produced by Michael Todd. Opened 28 January 1944 at the Winter Garden, moved 18 December 1944 to the Majestic Theatre, and closed 17 March 1945 after 481 performances.

CAST (in order of appearance): *Mrs. Augustus Adamson*: Jean Cleveland. *Lombo Campos*: GEORGE GIVOT. *Eadie Johnson*: EDITH MEISER. *Augustus, Jr.*: Eric Roberts. *Mr. Augustus Adamson*: William A. Lee. *Joe Bascom*, alias Humphrey Fish: BOBBY CLARK. *Montana*: JUNE HAVOC. *Picadors*: Horton Henderson, Jerry Sylvon. *Billy*: BILL CALLAHAN. *Dagmar Marshak*: LUBA MALINA. *Henry A. Wallace*: Byron Halstead. *José*, head-waiter: Raul Reyes. *Lolita Cantine*: CORINNA MURA. (*A. C. Blumenthal*: Larry Martin.) *Tillie Leeds*: Lois Bolton. *Lydia Toddle*: Virginia Edwards. *Carol, Ex-King of Roumania*: Arthur Gondra. *Mme. Lupescu*: Dorothy Durkee. *Miguel Correres*: SERGIO DeKARLO. *David Winthrop*: WILBUR EVANS. (*Bolero*: Alfonso Pedroza.) *Chief of Police*: Richard Bengali. *Lottery Boy*: Hank Wolff. *Mrs. Molly Wincor*: Jeanne Shelby. *First Merchant*: Raul Reyes. *Second Merchant*: Horton Henderson. *Third Merchant*: Hen Hernandez. *Fourth Merchant*: Jerry Sylvon. *Fifth Merchant*: Bobby Lane. *Woman Vendor*: Claire Anderson. *Lottery Girl*: Eva Reyes. *Paul*: PAUL HAAKON. *Eleanor*: Eleanor Tennis. *Lillian*: Marjory Leach. *Senor Martinez*: David Leonard.

Show Girls: Anita Arden, Cynthia Cavanaugh, Mildred Hughes, Andrea Mann, Nancy Callahan, Martha McKinney, Candy Jones, Gail Banner. *Singing Girls*: Jean Cummings, Lydia Fredericks, Perdita Hanson, Barbara Jevne, Grace Martin, Rose Marie Patane, Naomi Sanders. *Dancing Girls*: Margaret Cuddy, Malka Farber, Marjorie Gaye, Janet Gaylord, Peggy Holmes, Audrey Howell, Dorothy Hyatt, Alicia Krug, Ramona Lang, Dean Mylas, Vera Teatom, Aura Vainio, Betty Williams. *Dancing Boys*: Richard Andre, Thor Bassoe, Aleks Bird, John Conrad, Edmund Howland, Joey Gilbert, James Lanphier, Ted Lund, Jimmy Russell, Eric Schepard, Pat Vecchio, Leonard Bushong, Donald Powell. *Singing Boys*: Morton Beck, Danny Leeds, James Mate, Roy Mantelman, Tony Montell, Gar Moore, Armando Sisto, Robert Tavis. *Mariachi Players*: Manuel San Miguel, Frank Guzzardo, Ben Hernandez. *Children*: Jimmy Dutton, Louis Altmark, Hank Wolf, Francine Hernandez.

Act 1, Scene 1: The Plaza de Toros, Mexico, D.F. *Scene 2*: The Bedroom De la Reforma Hotel. *Scene 3*: The Bar at Ciro's. *Scene 4*: A Street in the Merced Market. *Scene 5*: An Outdoor Corridor of the National Palace. *Scene 6*: Terrace of the Palace at Chepultepec.

Act 2, Scene 1: Xochimilco. *Scene 2*: A Gas Station (on the Paseo de la Reforma). *Scene 3*: Taxco. *Scene 4*: Terrace of the Palace at Chepultepec.

ACT 1
Scene 1
    Entrance of Montana
        Principals, Girls and Boys
    Dance
        (*Directed by* Dan Eckley.)
        Girls, Boys
    Dance
        (*Directed by* Dan Eckley.)
        B. Callahan
Scene 3
    "Sing to Me, Guitar"
        C. Mura, Ensemble, Hermanos Williams Trio
    "The Good-Will Movement"
        W. Evans, Ensemble
    Dance
        (*Directed by* Virginia Johnson and Dan Eckley.)
        M. Nita, B. Callahan, Girls and Boys
    "The Good-Will Movement" (reprise)
        W. Evans, Girls
Scene 4
    "I Love You"
        W. Evans
    Dance
        P. Haakon, E. Tennis
    "I Love You" (reprise)
        W. Evans
Scene 5
    "There Must Be Someone For Me"
        J. Havoc
Scene 6
    "Carlotta"
        C. Mura, Ensemble
    Dance
        Girls and Boys
    "Girls"
        (*Directed by* Lew Kesler.)
        B. Clark, Girls

ACT 2
Scene 1
    "What a Crazy Way to Spend Sunday"
        Girls and Boys
    Dance
        B. Lane, C. Anderson
Scene 2
    "Abracadabra"
        (*Directed by* Lew Kesler.)
        J. Havoc, Boys
    "I Love You" (reprise)
        W. Evans
Scene 3
    Dance
        Girls and Boys, the Mariachi Players
    Dance
        P. Reyes, E. Reyes
    "Count Your Blessings"
        J. Havoc, B. Clark, G. Givot
Scene 4
    Toreador Ballet
        P. Haakon, Ensemble
    Finale
        Entire Company

1944.03

PORGY AND BESS

A Return Engagement of the Revival of the Musical Play in Three Acts, 7 Scenes[25]. Book by DuBose Heyward adapted from the play "Porgy" by DuBose and Dorothy Heyward. Music by George Gershwin. Lyrics by DuBose Heyward and Ira Gershwin. Staged by Robert Ross. Chorus directed by Eva Jessye. Settings by Herbert Andrews. Costumes by Paul du Pont. Produced by Cheryl Crawford in association with John J. Wildberg. Opened 7 February 1944 at the New York City Center, closing 19 February 1944; re-opened 28 February 1944 and closed 8 April 1944 after a total of 64 performances.

CAST (in order of appearance): *Maria*: Georgette Harvey. *Lily*: Catherine Ayers. *Annie*: Musa Williams. *Clara*: Harriet Jackson. *Jake*: Edward Matthews. *Sportin' Life*: AVON LONG. *Mingo*: Jerry Laws. *Robbins*: Henry Davis. *Serena*: Alma Hubbard. *Jim*: William C. Smith. *Peter*: George Randol. *Porgy*: WILLIAM FRANKLIN, Edward Matthews, alt. *Crown*: WARREN COLEMAN. *Bess*: ETTA MOTEN. *Policeman*: Kenneth Konopka. *Detective*: Richard Bowler. *Undertaker*: Coyal McMahon. *Lawyer Frazier*: Charles Welch. *Nelson*: Charles Colman. *Strawberry Woman*: Catherine Ayers. *Crab Man*: Leslie Gray. *Coroner*: Don Darcy.

Residents of Catfish Row, Fishermen, Children, Stevedores, etc.: THE EVA JESSYE CHOIR: Frances Brock, Olive Ball, Gladys Goode, Eulabel Riley, Louisa Howard, Assota Marshall, Sadie McGill, Annabelle Ross, Zelda Shelton, Eloise Uggams, Musa Williams, John Diggs, Leslie Gray, Jerry Laws, William C. Smith, Harold Desverney, Roger Alford, Charles Colman, Coyal McMahon, William O'Neal. *Children*: Robert Tucker, Ruthetta Anderson, Kenneth Tucker, Thomas Tucker, Douglas Rice, Patricia Rice.

1944.04

THE MIKADO,
or The Town of Titipu

A Revival of the Comic Opera in Two Acts[26]. Libretto by William S. Gilbert. Music by Arthur Sullivan. Music director, Louis Kroll. Produced by The Gilbert and Sullivan Opera Company (R. H. Burnside, director). Opened 11 February 1944 at the Ambassador Theatre and closed 26 March 1944 after 13 performances in repertory.[27]

CAST: *The Mikado of Japan*: ROBERT PITKIN. *Nanki-Poo, his son, disguised as a wandering minstrel in love with Yum-Yum*: JAMES GERARD or ALLEN STEWART. *Ko-Ko, Lord High Executioner of Titipu*: FLORENZ AMES. *Pooh-Bah, Lord High Everything Else*: ROBERT ECKLES. *Pish-Tush*: Bertram Peacock. *Go-To*: Lewis Pierce. *Yum-Yum*: KATHLEEN ROCHE. *Pitti-Sing*: KATHRYN REECE. *Peep-Bo*: MARIE VALDEZ. *Katisha*: CATHERINE JUDAH.

Chorus of Nobles and Coolies: John Dewey, David Bogart, F. Chester MaDan, Edwin Marsh, Walter George, Joseph Filos, Tom Bennett, Gerald Bercier, August Loring, Edward Bird, Barry Lyndall, Larry Odell. *Schoolgirls, etc.*

1944.05

TRIAL BY JURY

A Revival of the Comic Opera in One Act[28]. Libretto by William S. Gilbert. Music by Arthur Sullivan. Music director, Louis Kroll. Produced by The Gilbert and Sullivan Opera Company (R. H. Burnside, director). Opened 14 February 1944 at the Ambassador Theatre and closed 14 March 1944 after 11 performances in repertory.[29]

CAST: *Judge*: FLORENZ AMES. *Plaintiff*: KATHRYN REECE. *Counsel for Plaintiff*: BERTRAM PEACOCK. *Defendant*: FRANK MURRAY. *Foreman of the Jury*: Robert Eckles. *Usher*: Robert Pitkin. *Chorus of Jurymen, Bridesmaids and Public.*

1944.06

H.M.S. PINAFORE,
or, The Lass That Loved a Sailor

A Revival of the Comic Opera in Two Acts[30]. Libretto by William S. Gilbert. Music by Arthur Sullivan. Music director, Louis Kroll. Produced by The Gilbert and Sullivan Opera Company (R. H. Burnside, director). Opened 14 February 1944 at the Ambassador Theatre and closed 14 March 1944 after 11 performances in repertory[31].

CAST: *The Rt. Hon. Sir Joseph Porter, K.C.B.*: FLORENZ AMES. *Captain Corcoran*: BERTRAM PEACOCK. *Ralph Rackstraw*: JAMES GERARD. *Dick Deadeye*: ROBERT PITKIN. *Bill Bobstay*: Robert Eckles. *Bob Becket*: Frank Murray. *Tommy Tucker*: Master Arthur Henderson. *Josephine*: KATHLEEN ROCHE. *Cousin Hebe*: Marie Valdez. *Little Buttercup*: CATHERINE JUDAH.

First Lord's Sisters, His Cousins, His Aunts: Virginia Tyre, Athena Pappas, Flo Keezel, Helen Prentiss, Lillian Koniver, Edith Sterling, Louise King, Helen Jayson, Ruth Cumming, Doris Parker, Victoria Mayer, Charlotte Kremla, Jean Davis, Mary Lundon. *Sailors, Marines*: John Dewey, David Bogart, F. Chester MaDan, Edwin Marsh, Walter George, Joseph Filos, Tom Bennett, Gerald Bercier, August Loring, Edward Bird, Barry Lyndall, Larry Odell.

1944.07

COX AND BOX

A Revival of the Triumviretta in One Act[32]. Libretto by F. C. Burnand, based on J. Madison Morton's farce "Box and Cox." Music by Arthur Sullivan. Music director, Louis Kroll. Produced by The Gilbert and Sullivan Opera Company (R. H. Burnside, director). Opened 17 February 1944 at the Ambassador Theatre and closed 19 March 1944 after 10 performances in repertory[33].

CAST: *James John Cox*: ALLEN STEWART. *John James Box*: FLORENZ AMES. *Sergeant Bouncer*: ROBERT ECKLES.

1944.08

THE PIRATES OF PENZANCE,
or, The Slave of Duty

A Revival of the Comic Opera in Two Acts[34]. Libretto by William S. Gilbert. Music by Arthur Sullivan. Music director, Louis Kroll. Produced by The Gilbert and Sullivan Opera Company (R. H. Burnside, director). Opened 17 February 1944 at the Ambassador Theatre and closed 19 March 1944 after 10 performances in repertory.[35]

CAST: *The Pirate King*: ROBERT ECKLES. *Samuel*: BERTRAM PEACOCK. *Frederic*: ALLEN STEWART or JAMES GERARD. *Major General Stanley*: FLORENZ AMES. *Sergeant of Police*: ROBERT PITKIN. *Mabel*: KATHLEEN ROCHE. *Edith*: KATHLEEN REECE. *Kate*: MARIE VALDEZ. *Isabel*: Mary Lundon. *Ruth*: CATHERINE JUDAH.

Chorus of Pirates, Police: John Dewey, David Bogart, F. Chester MaDan, Edwin Marsh, Walter George, Joseph Filos, Tom Bennett, Gerald Bercier, August Loring, Edward Bird, Barry Lyndall, Larry Odell, Harry Marlatt. *General Stanley's Wards*: Virginia Tyre, Athena Pappas, Flo Keezel, Helen Prentiss, Lillian Koniver, Edith Sterling, Louise King, Helen Jayson, Ruth Cumming, Doris Parker, Victoria Mayer, Charlotte Kremla, Jean Davis, Lousie Miller, Maxine Masseretto, Lucille Benon.

1944.09

THE GONDOLIERS,
or, The King of Barataria

A Revival of the Comic Opera in Two Acts[36]. Libretto by William S. Gilbert. Music by Arthur Sullivan. Music director, Louis Kroll. Produced by The

---

[25]First presented in New York 10 October 1935 at the Alvin Theatre for 124 performances; revived 22 January 1942 at the Majestic Theatre for 286 performances, 13 September 1943 at the 44th Street Theatre for 24 performances. For Synopsis of Scenes and Musical Numbers, see original 1935 production and 1942 revival.
[26]First presented in New York 20 July, 10-29 August 1885 at the Union Square and People's Theatres for 22 performances. First authorized production presented 19 August 1885 at the Fifth Avenue Theatre by Richard D'Oyly Carte for 250 performances. For Synopsis of Scenes and Musical Numbers, see 19 August 1885 D'Oyly Carte production.
[27]Costumes, settings, lighting uncredited.
[28]First presented in New York 15 November 1875 at the Eagle Theatre for 8 performances. For Synopsis of Scenes and Musical Numbers, see original 1875 production.
[29]Costumes, settings, lighting uncredited.

[30]Originally presented in New York 15 January 1879 at the Standard Theatre for 175 performances. For Synopsis of Scenes and Musical Numbers, see original 1879 production.
[31]Costumes, settings, lighting uncredited.
[32]First presented in New York as COX AND BOX, or, The Long-Lost Brothers 14 August 1879 at the Standard Theatre for 48 performances. For Synopsis of Scenes and Musical Numbers, see original 1879 production.
[33]Settings, costumes, lighting uncredited.
[34]First presented in New York 31 December 1879 at the Fifth Avenue Theatre for a total of 91 performances in two engagements. For Synopsis of Scenes and Musical Numbers, see original 1879 production.
[35]Costumes, settings, lighting uncredited.
[36]Originally presented in New York 7 January 1890 at Park Theatre for 103 performances. For Synopsis of Scenes and Musical Numbers, see original 1890 production.

Gilbert and Sullivan Opera Company (R. H. Burnside, director). Opened 21 February 1944 at the Ambassador Theatre and closed 17 March 1944 after 4 performances in repertory.[37]

CAST: *The Duke of Plaza-Toro*: FLORENZ AMES. *Luiz*: ROLAND PARTRIDGE. *Don Alhambra Bolero*: ROBERT PITKIN. *Marco Palmieri*: ALLEN STEWART. *Giuseppe Palmieri*: LEWIS PIERCE. *Antonio*: Frank Murray. *Francesco*: Edwin Marsh. *Giorgio*: Robert Eckles. *The Duchess of Plaza Del Toro*: CATHERINE JUDAH. *Casilda*: MARIE VALDEZ. *Gianetta*: KATHLEEN ROCHE. *Tessa*: KATHRYN REECE. *Fiametta*: Virginia Tyre. *Giulia*: Mary Lundon. *Vittoria*: Jean Davis. *Inez*: Florence Keezel. *Chorus of Gondoliers, Contadine, Men-at-Arms, Heralds and Pages.*

IOLANTHE,
1944.10   or, The Peer and the Peri

A Revival of the Comic Opera in Two Acts[38]. Libretto by William S. Gilbert. Music by Arthur Sullivan. Music director, Louis Kroll. Produced by The Gilbert and Sullivan Opera Company (R. H. Burnside, director). Opened 22 February 1944 at the Ambassador Theatre and closed 21 March 1944 after 6 performances in repertory.[39]

CAST: *The Lord Chancellor*: FLORENZ AMES. *Earl of Mountararat*: ROBERT PITKIN. *Earl Tolloller*: ALLEN STEWART. *Private Willis*: ROBERT ECKLES. *Strephon*: LEWIS PIERCE. *Queen of the Fairies*: CATHERINE JUDAH. *Iolanthe*: KATHRYN REECE. *Celia*: Mary Lundon. *Fleta*: Marie Valdez. *Phyllis*: KATHLEEN ROCHE.

Chorus of Peers: John Dewey, David Bogart, F. Chester MaDan, Edwin Marsh, Walter George, Joseph Filos, Tom Bennett, Gerald Bercier, August Loring, Edward Bird, Barry Lyndall, Larry Odell, Harry Marlatt. *Fairies*: Virginia Tyre, Athena Pappas, Flo Keezel, Helen Prentiss, Lillian Koniver, Edith Sterling, Louise King, Helen Jayson, Ruth Cumming, Doris Parker, Victoria Mayer, Charlotte Kremla, Jean Davis, Lousie Miller, Maxine Masseretto, Lucille Benon.

PATIENCE,
1944.11   or, Bunthorne's Bride

A Revival of the Comic Opera in Two Acts[40]. Libretto by William S. Gilbert. Music by Arthur Sullivan. Music director, Louis Kroll. Produced by The Gilbert and Sullivan Opera Company (R. H. Burnside, director). Opened 25 February 1944 at the Ambassador Theatre and closed 24 March 1944 after 4 performances in repertory.[41]

CAST: *Colonel Calverley*: ROBERT PITKIN. *Major Murgatroyd*: Bertram Peacock. *Lieut. the Duke of Dunstable*: ROLAND PARTRIDGE. *Reginald Bunthorne*: FLORENZ AMES. *Mr. Bunsthorne's Solicitor*: Frank Murray. *Archibald Grosvenor*: ALLEN STEWART. *The Lady Angela*: KATHRYN REECE. *The Lady Saphir*: MARIE VALDEZ. *The Lady Ella*: MARY LUNDON. *The Lady Jane*: CATHERINE JUDAH. *Patience*: KATHLEEN ROCHE. *Chorus of Rapturous Maidens and Officers of the Dragoon Guards.*

RUDDIGORE,
1944.12   or, The Witch's Curse

A Revival of the Comic Opera in Two Acts[42]. Libretto by William S. Gilbert. Music by Arthur Sullivan. Music director, Louis Kroll. Produced by The Gilbert and Sullivan Opera Company (R. H. Burnside, director). Opened 2 March 1944 at the Ambassador Theatre and closed 25 March 1944 after 4 performances in repertory.[43]

CAST: MORTALS: *Sir Ruthven Murgatroyd*: FLORENZ AMES. *Richard Dauntless*: ALLEN STEWART or ROLAND PATRIDGE. *Sir Despart Murgatroyd*: ROBERT

PITKIN. *Old Adam Goodheart*: Robert Eckles. *Rose Maybud*: KATHLEEN ROCHE. *Mad Margaret*: MARIE VALDEZ. *Dame Hannah*: CATHERINE JUDAH. *Zorah*: Kathryn Reece. *Ruth*: Mary Lundon.
GHOSTS: *Sir Rupert Murgatroyd*: Lewis Pierce. *Sir Jasper Murgatroyd*: Walter George. *Sir Lionel Murgatroyd*: August Loring. *Sir Conrad Murgatroyd*: Edwin Marsh. *Sir Desmond Murgatroyd*: Chester MaDan. *Sir Gilbert Murgatroyd*: Joseph Filos. *Sir Melvin Murgatroyd*: David Bogart. *Sir Roderic Murgatroyd*: BERTRAM PEACOCK.

THE YEOMEN OF THE GUARD,
1944.13   or, The Merryman and His Maid

A Revival of the Comic Opera in Two Acts[44]. Libretto by William S. Gilbert. Music by Arthur Sullivan. Music director, Louis Kroll. Produced by The Gilbert and Sullivan Opera Company (R. H. Burnside, director). Opened and closed 3 March 1944 at the Ambassador Theatre after 2 performances in repertory.[45]

CAST: *Sir Richard Cholmondeley*: BERTRAM PEACOCK. *Colonel Fairfax*: JAMES GERARD. *Sergeant Meryll*: ROBERT ECKLES. *Leonard Meryll*: Allen Stewart. *Jack Point*: FLORENZ AMES. *Wilfred Shadbolt*: ROBERT PITKIN. *The Headsman*: Walter George. *First Yeoman*: Frank Murray. *Second Yeoman*: Lewis Pierce. *First Citizen*: Chester MaDan. *Second Citizen*: Gus Loring. *Elsie Maynard*: KATHLEEN ROCHE. *Phoebe Meryll*: KATHRYN REECE. *Dame Carruthers*: CATHERINE JUDAH. *Kate*: MARIE VALDEZ. *Chorus of Yeomen of the Guard, Gentlemen, Citizens.*

FOLLOW THE GIRLS
1944.14

A Musical Comedy in Two Acts, 9 Scenes. Book by Guy Bolton and Eddie Davis. Additional dialogue by Fred Thompson. Music and lyrics by Dan Shapiro, Milton Pascal and Phil Charig. Production devised and staged by Harry Delmar. Orchestra directed by Will Irwin. Dances and ensembles by Catherine Littlefield. Settings and lighting by Howard Bay. Costumes by Lou Eisele. Orchestral arrangements by Joe Glover, Charles Cook, Van Cleeve, Walter Paul, Bobby Haggart, Julian Work, George Leeman, Ernie Watson, Cornell Tannassy. Produced by Dave Wolper in association with Albert Borde[46]. Opened 8 April 1944 at the New Century Theatre, moved 12 June 1944 to the 44th Street Theatre, moved 4 June 1945 to the Broadhurst Theatre, and closed 18 May 1946 after 888 performances.

CAST (in order of appearance): *Yokel Sailor*: Bill [William] Tabbert. *Doorman*: Ernest Goodhart. *First Girl Fan*: Terry Kelly. *Second Girl Fan*: Rae MacGregor. *Bob Monroe*: FRANK PARKER. *Anna Viskinova*: IRINA BARONOVA. *Goofy Gale*: JACKIE GLEASON. *Seaman Pennywhistle*: Frank Kreig. *Catherine Pepburn*: Geraldine Stroock. *Sailor Val*: VAL VALENTINOFF. *Marine*: Charles Conaway, Jr. *Bubbles LaMarr*: GERTRUDE NIESEN. *Cigarette Girl*: Kathryn Lazell. *Spud Doolittle*: TIM HERBERT. *Dinky Riley*: BUSTER WEST. *Peggy Baker*: DOROTHY KELLER. *Phyllis Brent*: TONI GILMAN. *Dan Daley*: Robert Tower. *Petty Officer Banner*: LEE DAVIS. *Capt. Hawkins*: WALTER LONG. *Archie Smith*: Frank Kreig. *Felix Charrel*: VAL VALENTINOFF. *Officer Flanagan*: George Spaulding. *Flirtatious Miss*: Dell Parker. *Dance Team in Canteen*: THE DiGATANOS (Jayne, Adam).

Dancing Girls: Lillian Moore, Rae MacGregor, Ruth Rathbun, Renee Russell, Kathryn Lazell, Ruthe Reid, Nancy Newton, Mitzi Perry, Lee Mayer, Virginia Harriot, Virginia Conrad, Edna Ryan, Terry Kelly, Sherri Phillips, Myra Weldon, Patricia Matin, Merritta Moore. *Dancing Boys*: Roy Andrews, Dave Pullman, François Brouillard, George J. Sabo, Jr., Ben Piazza, Bob Emmett, Walter Hastings, Ray Hamilton, Arthur Randy, Danny Aiello, Albert Bahr, Don Miraglia, Erik Kristen, Henry Tatler, Ken Tibbetts, Herbert Ross. *Singing Men*: Bernard Kovler, Robert Thomas, Bill [William] Tabbert, Richard Harvey, Frank Touhey, Larry Lieberman, Larry Mayo, George Lambrose, John O'Neill, Charles Marten. *Show Girls*: Ruth Joseph, Dorothea Pinto, Norma Amigo, Joan Myles, Dell Parker, Dorothy Wygal, June Sitar, Kay Crespi.

Act 1, Scene 1: Outside Spotlight Canteen, evening, August 1943. *Scene 2*: Inside Spotlight Canteen, same evening. *Scene 3*: Outside Naval Training Station, Great Neck, Long Island, next day. *Scene 4*: Trophy Room, Great Neck Estate.

Act 2, Scene 1: Flower Garden, Great Neck Estate. *Scene 2*: Room in House, midnight. *Scene 3*: Navy Park, Great Neck, next day. *Scene 4*: Good Ship *Lady Luck.*, four weeks later. *Scene 5*: Inside Spotlight Canteen, next night.

---

[37]Costumes, settings uncredited.
[38]First presented in New York 25 November 1882 at the Standard Theatre for 105 performances. For Synopsis of Scenes and Musical Numbers, see original 1882 production.
[39]Costumes, settings, lighting uncredited.
[40]First presented in New York 22 September 1881 at the Standard Theatre for 177 performances. For Synopsis of Scenes and Musical Numbers, see original 1881 production.
[41]Costumes, settings, lighting uncredited.
[42]First presented in New York 21 February 1887 at the Standard Theatre for 53 performances. For Synopsis of Scenes and Musical Numbers, see original 1887 production.
[43]Costumes, settings uncredited.

[44]First presented as RUDDYGORE in New York 17 October 1888 at the Casino Theatre for 100 performances. For Synopsis of Scenes and Musical Numbers, see original 1888 production.
[45]Costumes, settings, lighting uncredited.
[46]Program note: The producer is indebted to Fred Thompson for his assistance in the direction of the book.

ACT 1

"At the Spotlight Canteen"
Soldiers, Sailors, Marines

"Where You Are"
F. Parker, I. Baranova

"You Don't Dance"
D. Keller, V. Valentinoff, Boys and Girls

"Strip Flips Hip"[47]
G. Niesen, Boys

"Thanks for a Lousy Evening"
T. Herbert, D. Keller, B. West

"You're Perf"
G. Niesen, J. Gleason, Boys and Girls

Dance
I. Baranova

"Twelve O'Clock and All Is Well"
G. Niesen

"Out for No Good"
B. West

Dance
D. Keller

"You Don't Dance" (Waltz reprise)
Boys and Girls

Dance
The DiGatanos

"Where You Are" (reprise)
F. Parker, I. Baranova

Flamingo Dance
I. Baranova

"Follow the Girls"
G. Niesen, Entire Company

ACT 2

"John Paul Jones"
F. Parker, Boys and Girls

Dance
V. Valentinoff, Boys and Girls

"Where You Are" (reprise)
F. Parker, I. Baranova

"I Wanna Get Married"
G. Niesen, Bridesmaids

"Today Will Be Yesterday Tomorrow"
F. Parker, Marines

"You're Perf" (reprise)
Boys and Girls

Dance
I. Baranova

Specialty Dance
T. Herbert, D. Keller

"A Tree That Grows in Brooklyn"
G. Niesen, J. Gleason, T. Herbert, B. West

Finale
Entire Company

1944.15   ALLAH BE PRAISED!

A Musical Comedy in Two Acts, 9 Scenes. Book and lyrics by George Marion, Jr. Music by Don Walker and Baldwin [Beau] Bergersen. Staged by Robert H. Gordon and Jack Small. Choreography by Jack Cole. Production design and lighting by George Jenkins. Costumes by Miles White. Orchestra conducted by Ving Merlin. Vocal arrangements by Don Walker. Produced by Alfred Bloomingdale. Opened 20 April 1944 at the Adelphi Theatre and closed 6 May 1944 after 20 performances.

CAST (in order of appearance): *Caswell*: Jack Albertson. *Receptionist*: Helen Bennett. *Tex O'Carroll*: EDWARD ROECKER. *Clerk*: Sheila Bond. *Citizen*: JOEY FAYE. *Abdul*: Sid Stone. *Bulbul*: Jack Albertson. *Carol O'Carroll*: MARY JANE WALSH. *Roberta*: Marge Ellis. *Paula*: Lee Joyce. *Doris*: Mary McDonnell. *Tubaga*: ANITA

ALVAREZ. Emir: JOHN HOYSRADT. *Zarah*: MILADA MLADOVA. *Youssouf*: JOEY FAYE. *Nij O'Carroll*: PITTMAN CORRY. *Dulcy Robot*: Marge Jackson. *Beatrice*: BEATRICE KRAFT. *Evelyne*: EVELEYNE KRAFT. *Marcia Mason Moore*: PATRICIA MORISON. *Mimi McSlump*: JAYNE MANNERS. *Matron*: Helen Bennett. *Merchant*: Tom Powers. *Girls About Teheran*: Eleanor Hall, Louise Jarvis.

Trainees: Lee Joyce, Susan Scott, Marge Ellis, Mari Lynn, Natalie Wynn, Barbara Neal, Alice Anthony, Olga Suarez, Margie Jackson, Mary McDonnell, Dorothy Bird, Ila Marie Wilson, Grace Crystal, Gloria Crystal, Hazel Roy, Muriel Breunig, Pat Welles.

Photographers: Mischa Pompianov, Ray Arnett, Jr., Remi Martel, Jack Baker, Jacy McCord, Johnny Oberon, Tom Powers, Jack L. Nagle, William Lundy, Forrest Boncher.

Act 1, Scene 1: Bureau of Missing Persons, New York, 20 February 1948. *Scene 2*: The Minarets of Sultanbad, 29 February 1948. *Scene 3*: The Emir's Palace—Siesta time. *Scene 4*: The Palace Gardens—Twilight, a few hours later. *Scene 5*: The Emir's Palace—the same evening.

Act 2, Scene 1: The Minarets of Sultanbad—Later that night. *Scene 2*: Harem Sleeping Porch. *Scene 3*: Hollywood, California. *Scene 4*: Harem Sleeping Porch.

ACT 1

"Persian Way of Life"
M. J. Walsh

Dance
A. Alvarez, M. McDonnell

"Allah Be Praised"
E. Roecker

Dance (*Staged by* Dan Eckley.)
S. Bond, P. Corry

"What's New in New York"
M. J. Walsh

"Leaf in the Wind"
P. Morison

Dance
E. Kraft, B. Kraft

"Katinka to Eva to Frances"
J. Hoysradt

Dance
A. Alvarez

"Let's Go Too Far"
E. Roecker, P. Morison

Dance
M. Mladova, P. Corry

Finaletto and Ballet
Entire Company

ACT 2

"Getting Oriental Over You"
M. J. Walsh

Dance
S. Bond, M. Mladova, B. Kraft, E. Kraft

"Let's Go Too Far" (reprise)
J. Faye, J. Manners

"Secret Song"
P. Morison, E. Roecker

"Sunrise on Sunset"
E. Roecker

Finale
Entire Company

1944.16   HELEN GOES TO TROY

An Operetta in Two Acts, 13 Scenes. Book by Gottfried Reinhardt and John Meehan, Jr., based on Gottfried Reinhardt's version of Jacques Offenbach's "La Belle Hélène." Music by Jacques Offenbach. New musical version by Eric Wolfgang Korngold[48]. Lyrics by Herbert Baker. Staged by Herbert Graf.

---

[47]Dropped late in the run. Albert Borde later became sole producer during the run at the Broadhurst.

[48]A (Program) Note about the score: Erich Wolfgang Korngold, conductor and musical collaborator of Max Reinhardt's production of "La Belle Hélène" in Berlin, Vienna and London, not only rearranged and reorchestrated the original Offenbach score, but also interpolated 14 newly adapted numbers into the Helen music, taken from more or less forgotten Offenbach operettas (including "La Périchole," "Geneviève de Brabant," "Doctor Ox," "Le Roi Carotte," and "Robinson Crusoe"). Substituting

Choreography by Leonide Massine. Dialogue directed by Melville Cooper. Choral director, Irving Landau. Orchestra conducted Eric Wolfgang Korngold. Production design and lighting by Robert Edmund Jones. Costumes by Ladislas Czettel. Produced by Yolanda Mero-Irion for The New Opera Company. Opened 24 April 1944 at the Alvin Theatre and closed 16 July 1944 after 97 performances.

CAST (in order of appearance): *Philocomus*, Assistant Seer: GEORGE RASELY. *Calchas*, High Priest of Jupiter: RALPH DUMKE. *Helen*, Queen of Sparta: JARMILA NOVOTNA, Lillian Anderson. *Orestes*, Helen's Nephew: DONALD BUKA. *Parthenis*, a Courtesan: Doris Blake. *Laela*, Another Courtesan: Phyllis Hill. *Paris*, Prince of Troy: WILLIAM HORNE, Joseph Laderoute. *Discordia*, Goddess of Mischief: Rose Inghram. *Minerva*, Goddess of Wisdom: Doris Blake. *Juno*, Wife of Jupiter: Rosalind Nadell. *Venus*, Goddess of Love and Beauty: Peggy Corday. *Policeman*: Michael Mann. *White Wing*: John Guelis. *Ajax the First*, King of Small Nation: Jesse White. *Ajax the Second*, Another King, His Twin Brother: Alfred Porter. *Menelaus*, King of Sparta: ERNEST TRUEX. *Agamemnon*, Another King, Menelaus' Brother: Gordon Dilworth. *Achilles*, Another King: Hugh Johnson. *Lady-in-Waiting*: Jane Kiser. *Premier Danseuses*: Katia Geleznova, Kathryn Lee, Nancy Mann. *Premier Dancers*: Michael Mann, John Guelis, George Chaffee.

Ladies of the Ensemble: Johnsie Bason, Peggy Blatherwick, Louise Fagg, Elizabeth Giacobbe, Eleanor Jones, Nancy Kenyon, Jeanne Stephens, Virginia Beeler, Anne Bolyn, Louise Newton, Maria Orelo, Matilda Strazza, Betty Tucker, Leona Vanni. *Gentlemen of the Ensemble*: Sam Adams, George Crawford, William Golden, John Gould, Vincent Henry, Robert Marco, Edwin Alberian, Paul Campbell, Robert Kirland, Seymour Osborne, Gordon Richards, Irving Strull.

Ballet: Galina Razoumova, Lee Lauterbur, Rickey Soma, Edwina Seaver, Jane Kiser, Claire Pasch, Katherine Clark, Ricia Orkina, Nina Frenkin, Nicholas Beriozoff, Sviatoslav Toumine, Todd Bolender, David Adhar, Ricardo Sarroga.

Act 1, Scene 1: The Temple of Jupiter in Sparta. *Scene 2*: Mount Ida. *Scene 3*: The Temple of Jupiter in Sparta. *Scene 4*: A Street in Sparta. *Scene 5*: The Temple of Jupiter in Sparta.

Act 2, Scene 1: Helen's Bath in Palace. *Scene 2*: King's Private Banquet Hall. (Bacchanale.) *Scene 3*: A Road near Sparta. *Scene 4*: Helen's Boudoir. *Scene 5*: Outside Palace Door. *Scene 6*: Helen's Boudoir. *Scene 7*: Corridor in the Palace. *Scene 8*: Main Banquet Hall.

ACT 1

Scenic Overture: Antiquity Awakes
Danced by M. Mann, J. Guelis, K. Lee, E. Seaver, Ballet

Scene 1

"Come to the Sacrifice"
G. Rasely, Chorus

"Where Is Love?"
J. Novotna, J. Kiser, Ladies in Waiting

"Tsing-la-la"
D. Buka, R. Dumke, P. Hill, D. Blake, G. Rasely, Chorus, Ballet

"Take My Advice"
J. Novotna, D. Buka

Scene 2

"The Shepherd Song"
W. Horne

"The Judgement of Paris"
W. Horne, R. Inghram, D. Blake, R. Nadell, P. Corday

Scene 3

"What Will the Future Say?"
R. Dumke

Scene 4

"Extra! Extra!"
G. Rasely, M. Mann, Chorus, Ballet

Ajax 1 and Ajax 2

---

these Offenbach melodies for some wilted music pieces of the original score, he kept only the best known ones such as Helen's entrance-air, Orestes' Tsinglala, The Judgement, The Dream-Duet, the Concert-Overture and, of course, the Finales.

For the New York production Mr. Korngold added two other important numbers: "What Will the Future Say" (A 6/8 serenade from the "Bridge of Sighs," changed into a modern fox trot tempo) and, for Jarmila Novotna, the best known and most beloved melody Offenbach ever wrote, the "Barcarole" from the "Tales of Hoffman," which, incidentally, was originally composed for another Offenbach opera ("Die Rheinnixen," produced in Vienna), and which was inserted into "The Tales of Hoffman" after the death of Offenbach.

"Sweet Helen"
J. Novotna, W. Horne

Scene 5

Entrance of the Kings
Entire Company

First Finale:
Entire Company

Introduction of the Kings; Dance of Procreation; Opera Parody; Go to Naxos.

ACT 2

Prologue to Second Act
R. Inghram

Scene 1

Dance of the Ladies in Waiting
K. Gleleznova, Ballet

"Love at Last"
J. Novotna

Scene 2

"Bring on the Concubines"
Cast and Chorus

Waltz and Can-Can
D. Blake, K. Lee, D. Buka, Ballet

"If Menelaus Only Knew It"
J. White, A. Porter, E. Truex, G. Dilworth, H. Johnson, R. Dumke, Chorus

Drinking Song and Dance
W. Horne, J. White, A. Porter, E. Truex, G. Dilworth, H. Johnson, R. Dumke, K. Lee, M. Mann, J. Guelis, Ballet

Scene 3

Reprise
E. Truex

Scene 4

"Is It a Dream?"
J. Novotna, W. Horne

Scene 6

"A Little Chat"
D. Buka, G. Dilworth, E. Truex, Chorus

"Advice to Husbands"
J. Novotna, Chorus

Scene 7

Grecian Frieze
Entire Company

Scene 8

"Come With Me"
J. Novotna, W. Horne, E. Truex, Company

Second Finale
Entire Company

THE NEW MOON

1944.17

A Revival of the Operetta in Three Acts, 8 Scenes[49]. Book by Oscar Hammerstein II, Frank Mandel and Laurence Schwab. Music by Sigmund Romberg. Lyrics by Oscar Hammerstein II. Staged by José Ruben. Choreography by Charles Weidman. Settings by Oliver Smith. Musical director, Charles Blackman. Produced by Perry Frank for the Belmont Operetta Company. Opened 17 May 1944 at the New York City Center and closed 24 June 1944 after 45 performances.

CAST (in order of appearance): *Julie*: ELIZABETH HOUSTON. *M. Beaunoir*: Laurence Hays. *Captain Duval*: George Mitchell. *Vicomte Ribaud*: HAROLD GORDON. *Fouchette*: Carl Nelson. *Robert*: EARL WRIGHTSON. *Alexander*: JOHNNY MORGAN. *Besac*: Hamilton Benz. *Jacques*: Frederick Poller. *Marianne Beaunoir*: DOROTHY KIRSTEN. *Doorkeeper of Tavern*: William Sutherland. *Tavern Proprietor*: Ludlow White. *A Spaniard*: Peter Hamilton. *A Dancer*: Zoya Leporsky. *Philippe*: JOHN HAMILL. *Clotilde Lombaste*: DOROTHY RAMSEY. *Emile*: Hail Carnegie. *Brunet*: Vaughn Trinnier. *Latouche*: Ralph Sassano. *Gervais*: John Scott. *A Sailor*: George Bruno. *Admiral De Jean*: Dick Todd.

---

[49]First presented in New York 19 September 1928 at the Imperial Theatre for 509 performances. For Synopsis of Scenes and Musical Numbers, see original 1928 production.

Guests, Servants, Sailors, Pirates: Ladies: Harriet Oniell, Jeanne Gordon, Jeanne Beauvais, Molly Consley, Elline Walther, Lucille Barton, Alice Richmond, Donna Gardner, Villetta Russell, Margit Fisher, Martha King, Betty Leighton, Ann Jackson, Virginia Barnes, Patricia Leith, Ann Winters, Roberta Casell, Zoya Leporsky. *Gentlemen:* William Sydenstricker, John Jackson, Vaughn Trinnier, Ludlow White, G. Raymond Breit, John P. Sheridan, Jerry Davenport, Carl Nelson, William Sutherland, John Scott, Ralph Sessano, Kenneth Renner, Joe Monte, Everett S. Anderson, John Duane, David Raher, Aaron Girard

1944.18

DREAM WITH MUSIC

A Musical Fantasy in Two Acts, 14 Scenes. Book by Sidney Sheldon, Dorothy Kilgallen and Ben Roberts. Music by Clay Warnick[50]. Lyrics by Edward Eager. Staged by Richard Kollmar. Choreography by George Balanchine. Tap routines directed by Henry LeTang. Orchestra conducted by Max Meth. Settings by Stewart Chaney. Costumes by Miles White. Orchestral arrangements by (Robert) Russell Bennett, Hans Spialek, Ted Royal and Clay Warnick. Vocal arrangements by Clay Warnick. Produced by Richard Kollmar. Opened 18 May 1944 at the Majestic Theatre and closed 10 June 1944 after 28 performances.

<u>CAST</u>: *In Reality: Ella:* BETTY ALLEN. *Marian:* JOY HODGES. *Dinah:* VERA ZORINA. *Western Union Boy:* ALEX ROTOV. *Michael:* RONALD GRAHAM. *Robert:* ROBERT BRINK.

In the Dream: Scheherazade: VERA ZORINA. *Jasmin:* JOY HODGES. *Sultan:* ROBERT BRINK. *Wazier:* ALEX ROTOV. *Mispah:* Marcella Howard. *Hispah:* Janie Janvier. *Rispah:* LOIS BARNES. *Tispah:* LUCILLE BARNES. *Fispah:* Jane Hetherington. *Kispah:* Donna Devel. *Aladdin:* RONALD GRAHAM. *Rug Merchant:* Ray Cook. *Perfume Merchant:* Robert Beam. *Fakir:* Michael Kozak. *Candy Salesman:* Bill Jones. *Musical Instrument Merchant:* John Panter. *Snake Charmer:* Byron Milligan. *Sand Diviner:* RALPH BUNKER. *Sinbad:* LEONARD ELLIOTT. *Mrs. Sinbad:* BETTY ALLEN. *Genie:* DAVE BALLARD. *Guards:* JERRY ROSS, Larry Evers, Bill Weber, Parker Wilson. *The Little One:* DOROTHY BABB. *The Blonde One:* Dee Turnell. *First Hot One:* SUNNY RICE. *Second Hot One:* DIXIE ROBERTS. *The Slender One:* MAVIS MIMS. *The Tall One:* DOLORES MILAN. *The One With the Pug Nose:* TARI VANCE. *The Twins:* LOIS and LUCILLE BARNES. *Day:* PETER BIRCH. *Night:* SUNNY RICE. *Mrs. Panda:* DIXIE ROBERTS. *Mr. Panda:* RALPH BUNKER. *Lion:* PETER BIRCH. *Rabbit:* Donna Devel. *Mr. Owl:* Byron Milligan. *Mrs. Owl:* Marcella Howard. *Unicorn:* Bill Jones. *Mrs. Lion:* Janie Janvier. *Penguin:* Bill Weber. *Wolf:* Ray Cook. *Ermine:* LUCILLE BARNES. *Lamb:* DOROTHY BABB. *I. J.:* Robert Beam. *Mrs. Fox:* Jane Hetherington. *Leopard:* LOIS BARNES. *Monkey:* JERRY ROSS. *Tiger:* Michael Kozak. *Mouse:* BUDDY DOUGLAS. *Aladdin's Aide:* Bill Weber. *Chinese Masseur:* JERRY ROSS.

Tap Specialists: SUNNY RICE, MAVIS MIMS, DIXIE ROBERTS, DOROTHY BABB, TARI VANCE, DOLORES MILAN. *Corps de Ballet:* Jacquline Cezanne, Betty Claire, Dorothy De Molina, Georgia Hiden, Carmelita Lanza, Margaret Murray, Toni Stuart, Dee Turnell. Larry Evers, Jerry Ross, Bill Weber, Parker Wilson. *Singers:* Lois Barnes, Lucille Barnes, Donna Devel, Jane Hetherington, Marcella Howard, Janie Janvier. Robert Beam, Ray Cook, Bill Jones, Michael Kozak, Byron Milligan, John C. Panter. *The Caryatids:* Mae Francis, Beatrice Griffith, Roseler Joynes, Rosemary Mitchell, Gladys Pollard, Bonita Purdue.

Act 1, Scene 1: Dinah's Apartment. *Scene 2:* The Palace of Shariar, King of the Indies. *Scene 3:* A Street in Bazaars of Bagdad. *Scene 4:* Sinbad's Garden. *Scene 5:* A Corridor in Sinbad's House. *Scene 6:* The Magic Carpet. *Scene 7:* In the Clouds.

Act 2, Scene 1: Aladdin's Forest—China. *Scene 2:* Aladdin's Game Preserve. *Scene 3:* The Corridor in Sinbad's House. *Scene 4:* Aladdin's Palace. *Scene 5:* The Corridor in Sinbad's House. *Scene 6:* The Palace of Shariar. *Scene 7:* Dinah's Apartment.

ACT 1

Scheherezade's Dance
    V. Zorina, Singing Ensemble

"Be Glad You're Alive"
    J. Hodges, Singing Ensemble, A. Rotov, P. Birch, Dancing Ensemble

"I'm Afraid I'm in Love"
    R. Brink

"Baby, Don't Count on Me"
    R. Graham, Singing Ensemble

"Give, Sinbad, Give"
    L. Elliott, Singing Ensemble

"I'll Take the Solo"
    B. Allen, Tap Specialty Girls, Barnes Twins, Ballet

"Love at Second Sight"
    J. Hodges, R. Brink

"Relax and Enjoy It"
    V. Zorina, J. Hodges, R. Brink, B. Allen, L. Elliott

"Come With Me"
    R. Graham, V. Zorina

"Battle of the Genie"
    A. Rotov, D. Ballard, L. Evers, J. Ross, B. Weber, P. Wilson

"Mr. and Mrs. Wrong"
    B. Allen, L. Elliott

"Ballet in the Clouds"
    V. Zorina, P. Birch, S. Rice, Corps de Ballet, Singing Ensemble

ACT 2

"The Lion and the Lamb"
    D. Devel, Ensemble

"Mouse Meets Girl"
    V. Zorina, B. Douglas

"Baby, Don't Count on Me" (reprise)
    S. Rice

"Love at Second Sight" (reprise)
    J. Hodges

"The Moon Song"
    R. Graham

"Woman Against the World"
    V. Zorina, J. Ross, Barnes Twins, Tap Specialty Girls, Singing Girls

"The Ballet"
    L. Elliott

"Dinah's Nightmare"
    Entire Company

---

[50]The music is based on themes from: Saint-Saëns' Violin Concerto in B Minor, Rimsky-Korsakoff's "Scheherezade," Schubert's Ninth Symphony, Beethoven's Seventh Symphony, Weber's "Oberon," Grieg's Piano Concerto, Beethoven's First Symphony, Borodin's "Prince Igor," Moussorgsky's "Night on Bald Mountain," Wagner's "Ride of the Valkyries," Chopin's Twenty-Four Preludes, Gluck's "Ballet Suite," Schumann's Piano Concerto, Dvorak's "New World Symphony, Haydn's First Symphony, and Tschaikowsky's Nutcracker Suite.

Betty Comden and Adolph Green in ON THE TOWN (Photo: Vandamm Studio)
Billy Rose Theatre Collection, New York Public Library for the Performing Arts

1944–1945 SEASON

1944.19

TAKE A BOW

A Variety Show in Two Acts, 15 Scenes. Staged by Wally Wanger. Dancers directed by Marjery Fielding. Costumes designed by Ben Wallace, executed by Madame Berthe. Scenery by Kaj Velden. Orchestra conducted by Ray Kavanaugh. Produced by Lou Walters. Opened 15 June 1944 at the Broadhurst Theatre and closed 24 June 1944 after 12 performances.

CAST: CHICO MARX, (Alan) CROSS and (Henry) DUNN, MARY RAYE & NALDI, THE MURTAH SISTERS (Kate-Ellen, Jean, Onriett), GENE SHELDON, JAY C. FLIPPEN, PAT ROONEY, "Think-a-Drink" HOFFMAN, THE (4) WHITSON BROTHERS, JOHNNY MACK, LORETTA FISCHER. *MARJERY FIELDING DANCERS*: Gloria Riley, Helen Simpson, Dede Barrington, Amita Artega, Kathryn Reed, Rae Hardin.

Ladies of the Ensemble: Elaine Singer, Bee Farnum, Kay Popp, Doris Call, Rosemary Ryan, June Powers, Betty Francys, Marion Kay, Darlene Zito, Betty Baussher, Charlotte Lorraine, Elaine Meredith.

ACT 1

Scene 1

"Take a Bow"
Marjorie Fielding Dancers
(*Music by* Ted Murray. *Lyrics by* Benny Davis.)
The Master of Ceremonies: J. C. Flippen. *The Man in the Box*: C. Marx.

Scene 2

The Whitson Brothers (Acrobatics)

Scene 3

Gene Sheldon (Banjo) with Loretta Fischer

Scene 4

Johnny Mack and Show Girls

Scene 5

Don't Play With Strangers (Card game sketch from THE COCOANUTS)
C. Marx, G. Sheldon

Scene 6

Cross & Dunn (Song Stylists)
At the piano: Newman Fear.

Scene 7

Let's Reminisce
P. Rooney, Marjery Fielding Dancers
["The Daughter of Rosie O'Grady"
(*Music by* Walter Donaldson. *Lyrics by* Monty C. Brice.)]

Scene 8

'Think-a-Drink' Hoffman

ACT 2

Scene 1

"The Hollywood Jump"
Marjery Fielding Dancers

Scene 2

Interlude with Gene Sheldon (Classical dance burlesque, etc.)

Scene 3

"A Study in Black and White"
Marjery Fielding Dancers

Scene 4

"Poetry in Motion" (Ballroom Dance)
Mary Raye & Naldi

Scene 5

The Murtah Sisters in a cycle of their inimitable songs

Scene 6

Chico Marx and his piano

Scene 7

Finale
(Whitson Brothers, J. C. Flippen, Company)

1944.20

HATS OFF TO ICE

A Skating Icetravaganza (Musical Revue) in Two Acts, 23 Scenes. Music and lyrics by James Littlefield and John Fortis. Staged by Catherine Littlefield. Settings designed and created by Bruno Maine. Costumes by Grace Houston. Lighting effects by Eugene Braun. Choreography by Catherine Littlefield, assisted by Dorothie Littlefield. Skating direction by May Judels. Musical conductor, David Mendoza. Musical arrangements by Paul Van Loan. Executive director, William H. Burke. Produced by Sonja Henie and Arthur M. Wirtz. Opened 22 June 1944 at the Center Theatre, vacationed 6-29 May 1945, and closed 27 April 1946 after 890 performances.

CAST: FREDDIE TRENKLER, CAROL LYNNE, LUCILLE PAGE, CALEY SISTERS, BRANDT SISTERS, GOFFE STEVENS, RUDY RICHARDS, JAMES CAESAR, PAUL CASTLE, JEAN STURGEON, CLARE WILKINS, ROBERT and GRETLE UKSILA, PEGGY WHIGHT & BOB BALLARD, JIMMY SISK, JOE SHILLEN. *Vocals*: PAT MARSHALL, THE TOP HATTERS (Andrei Kristopher, John Patteson, Everett Anderson), DAN LORING ROGERS.

Ensemble: Nancy Adamack, Katherine Arnaiz, Margaret Barry, Jean Conrad, Kay Corcoran, Helen Carter, Jeanne Crystall, Helen Dutcher, Alice Farrar, Janet Hester, Barbara Johnson, May Judels, Edith Kandel, Billy Kling, Annette Lawrence, Virginia Litz, Marian Lulling, Sharlene Munster, Roth Noland, Berenice O'Dell, Jane Petri, Ragna Ray, Lucille Risch, Lela Rolontz, Theresa Rothacker, Jane Sakovich, Bing Stott, Sally Tepley, Dorothy Thomas, Eileen Thompson, Helen Thompson, Clare Wilkins, Michelle Winters. Julian Apley, James Black, William Campbell, James Carter, William Carvel, Jere Decker, Manuel Del Toro, Joachim Dietl, Bernard Feldman, Harper Flaherty, Fred Griffith, Gordon Harris, Gordon Holley, Fred Kaufman, James Kenny, Garry Kerman, Alfred Kutchy, Alex Lindgren, Arthur Meheen, Robert Payne, Bert Pegram, Robert Petrillo, Jack Raffloer, John Roach, Charlie Storey, Tom Travers, George Wagner, Harvey Wolfers.

ACT 1

Scene 1

"Hats Off to Ice"
P. Marshall, D. L. Rogers, Top Hatters
Octette: B. Stott, J Hester, B. Johnson, C. Wilkins, J. Carter, H. Flaherty, A. Lindgren, J. Roach. *Ladies of the Ensemble*: K. Arnaiz, N. Adamack, M. Barry, J. Conrad, H. Carter, J. Crystal, H. Dutcher, E. Kandel, B. Kling, M. Lulling, A. Lawrence, S. Munster, K. Corcoran, R. Noland, B. O'Dell, J. Petri, T. Rothacker, L. Rolontz, R. Ray, J. Sakovich, D. Thomas, S. Tepley, E. Thompson, H. Thompson, M. Winters. *Gentlemen of the Ensemble*: J. Black, W. Campbell, W. Carvel, M. Del Toro, J. Decker, J. Dietl, G. Harris, F. Kaufman, G. Kerman, A. Kutchy, B. Pegram, G. Holley, H. Wolfers, G. Wagner, T. Travers, A. Meheen.

Scene 2

Little Red Riding Hood
J. Sturgeon
Woodchoppers: J. Kenny, R. Payne. *Wolf*: B. Feldman.

Scene 3

Double Vision
H. Brandt, I. Brandt

Scene 4

Nautical Nonsense
Olive Oil: G. Uksila. *Pop-Eye*: R. Uksila.

Scene 5

"Love Will Always Be the Same"
P. Marshall, D. L. Rogers
King: F. Griffith. *Queen*: V. Litz. *Princess*: B. Johnson. *Prince*: H. Flaherty. *Black Prince*: C. Storey. *Heralds*: A. Farrar, J. Hester, L. Risch, B. Stott, R. Noland. *Handmaidens*: K. Corcoran, M. Barry, R. Ray, E. Thompson. *Knights*: J. Apley, W. Carvel, M. Del Toro, G. Kerman, J. Kenny, A. Kutchy, A. Lindgren, G. Wagner.

Scene 6

Sophisticated Lady
L. Page
Boys: J. Carter, C. Cavanaugh, J. Dietl, B. Feldman, R. Payne, J. Raffloer, J. Roach, H. Wolfers.

Scene 7

Goddess of the Hunt
Diana: C. Lynne. *Maidens*: K. Corcoran, B. Johnson, V. Litz, E. Thompson.

Scene 8

The Skating Rileys
Mother: V. Litz. *Father*: F. Griffith. *Sweetheart*: J. Sturgeon. *Junior*: P. Castle.

Scene 9

The Boogie Bachelor

883

Bachelor: R. Richards. *Chorines*: R. Ray, A. Farrar. *Debs*: J. Hester, B. Stott. *Herself*: C. Wilkins.

Scene 10

They've Got What It Takes:

"You've Got What It Takes"

P. Marshall, D. L. Rogers

Girls: K. Arnaiz, N. Adamack, M. Barry, J. Conrad, H. Carter, J. Crystall, H. Dutcher, E. Kandel, B. Kling, M. Lulling, A. Lawrence, V. Litz, S. Munster, R. Noland, B. O'Dell, J. Petri, T. Rothacker, L. Rolontz, J. Sakovich, D. Thomas, S. Tepley, E. Thompson, H. Thompson, M. Winters. *Boys*: J. Black, W. Carvel, M. Del Toro, J. Dietl, G. Harris, J. Kenny, F. Kaufman, G. Kerman, A. Kutchy, A. Meehan, B. Pegram, G. Holley, R. Payne, G. Wagner, T. Travers, J. Decker. *Swingtime*: D. Caley, H. Caley.

Scene 11

Bouncing Ball of the Ice

F. Trenkler

Lovelies: B. Johnson, V. Litz, S. Munster, E. Thompson.

Scene 12

Slavic Rhapsody

The Flame: C. Lynne. *Gypsy Girls*: J. Hester, B. Johnson, C. Wilkins. *Gypsy Boys*: J. Carter, H. Flaherty, J. Raffloer, J. Roach. *Peasant Girls*: K. Arnaiz, N. Adamack, M. Barry, J. Conrad, H. Carter, K. Corcoran, J. Crystall, H. Dutcher, E. Kandel, B. Kling, M. Lulling, A. Lawrence, S. Munster, R. Noland, B. O'Dell, J. Petri, T. Rothacker, L. Rolontz, R. Ray, J. Sakovich, D. Thomas, S. Tepley, H. Thompson, M. Winters. *Peasant Boys*: W. Campbell, W. Carvel, J. Decker, J. Dietl, B. Feldman, G. Harris, J. Kenny, F. Kaufman, G. Kerman, A. Kutchy, A. Meheen, G. Holley, H. Wolfers, R. Payne, G. Wagner, T. Travers.

ACT 2

Scene 1

"Isle of the Midnight Rainbow"

P. Marshall, D. L. Rogers, Top Hatters

Drum Dancer: C. Wilkins. *Mayor*: G. Stevens. *Warriors*: J. Kenny, C. Storey, R. Petrillo. *Native Boys*: A. Lindgren, G. Holley. *Hulka Dancers*: A. Farrar, J. Hester, R. Ray, L. Risch, B. Stott, K. Arnaiz, N. Adamack, M. Barry, J. Conrad, H. Carter, H. Dutcher, E. Kandel, M. Lulling, A. Lawrence, S. Munster, R. Noland, B. O'Dell, J. Petri, T. Rothacker, L. Rolontz, J. Sakovich, D. Thomas, S. Tepley, H. Thompson, M. Winters, K. Corcoran. *Boys*: J. Black, W. Campbell, W. Carvel, M. Del Toro, J. Dietl, G. Harris, G. Kerman, A. Kutchey, A. Meheen, B Pegram, H. Wolfers, G. Wagner, T. Travers, J. Apley, C. Cavanaugh.

Scene 2

Russian Rhythm

D. Caley, H. Caley

Scene 3

Over the Jumps

J. Caesar

Scene 4

Pathway to the Stars

"With Every Star"

P. Marshall, Ladies of the Ensemble

Scene 5

Out of the Blue

P. Whight, R. Ballard

Scene 6

The Lazy Q: "Headin' West"

D. L. Rogers, Top Hatters

Cowgirls: J. Hester, A. Farrar, R. Ray, L. Risch, B. Stott. *Twins*: H. Brandt, I. Brandt. *Cowhand*: G. Stevens. *The Horse*: J. Shillen, J. Sisk. *Tenderfoot*: L. Page. *Cowboys*: J. Kenny, R. Payne, B. Feldman.

Scene 7

A Persian Legend

Prince Iskander, seeking the flower of immortality, implores the Genii to bring him to the Gates of Paradise. Therein resides the Peri—Guardian of the Flower.

Prince: F. Griffith. *Genii*: J. Caesar. *Peri*: C. Lynne. *Attendants of the Prince*: K. Arnaiz, H. Carter, B. O'Dell, T. Rothacker, J. Sakovich, M. Winters. *Odalisques*: C. Wilkins, J. Hester, S. Tepley, A. Farrar, B. Stott, R. Ray, L. Risch, D. Thomas, H. Thompson, R. Noland, J. Petri, M. Lulling, A. Lawrence, E. Thompson, E. Kandel, M. Barry. H. Dutcher, L. Rolontz, S. Munster, J. Conrad, N. Adamack. *Boys*: J. Kenny, F. Kaufman, R. Payne, J. Apley, G. Kerman, J. Dietl, T. Travers, G. Holley, G. Harris, H. Wolfers, J. Raffloer, J. Decker, M. Del Toro, B. Pegram, J. Black.

Scene 8

Shore Leave

G. Stevens, J. Shillen, J. Sisk

Pin Up Girls: M. Barry, R. Noland, H. Thompson.

Scene 9

Cocktail Time in Rio

Caballero: R. Richards. *Octette Girls*: J. Hester, B. Stott, B. Johnson, C. Wilkins. *Octette Boys*: J. Carter, H. Flaherty, A. Lindgren, J. Roach. *Show Girls*: E. Kandel, H. Dutcher, M. Barry, S. Tepley, M. Lulling, V. Litz. *Boys and Girls of the Ensemble.*

Scene 10

G.I. Nuisance

The Nuisance: F. Trenkler. *Sergeant*: C. Storey. *Squad*: C. Cavanaugh, J. Shillen, J. Sisk.

Scene 11

"Here's Luck"

P. Marshall, D. L. Rogers, Top Hatters

The Ensemble: H. Brandt, I. Brandt, D. Caley, H Caley, M. Judels, C. Lynne, L. Page, J. Sturgeon, G. Uksila, P. Whight, C. Wilkins, J. Caesar, P. Castle, R. Richards, J. Shillen, J. Sisk, G. Stevens, F. Trenkler, R. Uksila, F. Griffith.

1944.21 # SONG OF NORWAY

An Operetta in Two Acts, 7 Scenes. Book by Milton Lazarus from a play by Homer Curran. Based on the life and music of Edvard Grieg. Musical adaptation and lyrics by Robert Wright and George Forrest. Orchestral and choral arrangements and musical direction by Arthur Kay. Choreography and singing ensembles staged by George Balanchine. Production designed by Lemuel Ayres. Settings supervised by Carl Kent. Costumes designed by Robert Davison. Piano soloist: Louis Teicher. Lighting by Howard Bay. Book direction by Charles K. Freeman. Produced by Edwin Lester. Opened 21 August 1944 at the Imperial Theatre, moved to the Broadway Theatre 15 April 1946 and closed 7 September 1946 after 860 performances.

CAST (in order of appearance): *Rikard Nordraak*: ROBERT SHAFER. *Sigrid*: Janet Hamer. *Einar*: Kent Edwards. *Eric*: William Carroll. *Gunnar*: Gerald Matthews. *Grima*: Patti Brady. *Helga*: Jackie Lee. *Nina Hagerup*: HELENA BLISS. *Edvard Grieg*: LAWRENCE BROOKS. *Father Grieg*: WALTER KINGSFORD. *Father Nordraak*: Philip White. *Mother Grieg*: IVY SCOTT. *Freddy*: JAMES STARBUCK. *Inn Keeper*: Lewis Bolyard. *Count Peppi Le Loup*: SIG ARNO. *Louisa Giovanni*: IRRA PETINA. *Members of the Faculty*: Ewing Mitchell, Audrey Guard, Paul dePoyster. *Frau Professor Norden*: Doreen Wilson. *Elvera*: Sharon Randall. *Hedwig*: Karen Lund. *Greta*: Gwen Jones. *Marghareta*: Ann Andre. *Hilda*: Elizabeth Bockoven. *Miss Anders*: Sonia Orlova. *Henrik Ibsen*: Dudley Clements. *Tito*: James Starbuck. *Waitresses at Tito's*: Adda Pourmel, Rosine Sedova. *Maestro Pisoni*: Robert Bernard. *Butler*: Cameron Grant. *Adelina*: Dorothie Littlefield. *Signora Eleanora*: Barbara Boudwin. *Children*: Sylvia Allen, Shannon Randolph. *The Maiden Norway*: Olga Suarez. *The Minstrel*: Roland Guerard.

Dancing Peasants, Employees at Tito's, the Ballet of the Teatro Royale, and Characters of the Fantasy by the Artist Personnel of the Ballet Russe de Monte Carlo (Sergei J. Denham, Director): Roland Guerard, Olga Suarez, James Starbuck, Dorothie Littlefield, Sonia Orlova, Sviatoslav Toumine, Betty Burge, Adda Pourmel, Rosine Sedova, Jeanne Jones, Carlye Ramey, Jean Faust, Anna Wiman, Marjorie Castle, Toni Stuart, Gloria Stone, Harold Haskin, Milton Feher, Yura Radine, Nat Stoudenmire, Francis Kiernan, Robert Bernoff, Erik Kristen.

Singing Peasants, Guests and Faculty at Copenhagen and Guests at the Villa Pinchio by the Singing Ensemble of the Los Angeles and San Francisco Civic Light Opera: *Girls*: Ann Andre, Elizabeth Bockoven, Barbara Boudwin, Mary Bradley, Shirley Conklin, Kaye Connors, Audrey Dearden, Audrey Guard, Leone Hall, Gwen Jones, Karen Lund, Sharon Randall, Margaret Ritter, Mary Walker, Doreen Wilson. *Boys*: Robert Bailes, Lewis E. Bolyard, Frank Brenneman, John Chaloupka, Paul dePoyster, Cameron Grant, Larry Haynes, Hal Horton, Raymond Keast, Hal McMurrin, Arthur Waters, Maurice Winthrop, Stanley Wolfe, Walter Young.

Act 1, Scene 1: Troldhaugen (Hill of the Trolls)—just outside the town of Bergen Norway. Midsummer's Eve—in the 1860's. *Scene 2*: A Square on the outskirts of Bergen.

Act 2, Scene 1: Copenhagen—Reception Room of the Royal Conservatory. One year later. *Scene 2*: Rome—Tito's Chocolate Shop. One year later. *Scene 3*: Rome—Ballroom of the Villa Pincio. *Scene 4*: Troldhaugen—Interior of the Grieg Home. Some time later. *Scene 5*: The Song of Norway.

ACT 1

Scene 1

Prelude

Orchestra

"The Legend" (Adapted from the A-Minor Concerto)
R. Shafer
"Hill of Dreams" (also from the A-Minor Concerto)
H. Bliss, L. Brooks, R. Shafer

Scene 2

In the Holiday Spirit {Spring Dance; Halling}
Dancing Peasants
"Freddy and His Fiddle" (from "Norwegian Dance" {and "Halling" in
D-Major})
K. Edwards, J. Hamer, J. Starbuck & Singing Townspeople
"Now" (from Waltz Op. 12, No. 2 and the Violin Sonata No 2 in G-
Major)
I. Petina, Townspeople
"Strange Music" (from "Nocturne" and "Wedding in Troldhaugen")
L. Brooks, H. Bliss
"Midsummer's Eve" (from "'Twas on a Lovely Eve in June" and
"Scherzo")
R. Shafer, I. Petina
"March of the Trollgers" (The Cake Lottery)
Entire Ensemble
(from "Mountaineers' Song," "Halling" in C Minor, and "March of the
Dwarfs")
Finale of Act 1:
a. "Hymn of Betrothal" ("To Spring")
I. Scott, Villagers
b. "Strange Music" (reprise)
L. Brooks, H. Bliss, Chorus
c. "Midsummer's Eve" (reprise)
R. Shafer, H. Bliss, Chorus

ACT 2
Scene 1

Introduction: ("Papillon")
"Bon Vivant"
—Part I (from "Water Lily")
L. Brooks & Girls
—Part II (from "The Brook of Haugtussa Cycle")
S. Arno, L. Brooks, S. Orlova, Girls
"Three Loves" (from "Albumblatt" and "Poeme Erotique")
I. Petina, L. Brooks
Finaletto:
a. "Down Your Tea"
I. Petina, Faculty, Guests
b. "Nordraak's Farewell" ("Springtide")
R. Shafer
c. "Three Loves" (reprise)
I. Petina, H. Bliss, Ensemble

Scene 2

Chocolate Pas des Trois (from "From Monte Pincio" and "Rigaudon")
J. Starbuck, Employees

Scene 3

"Waltz Eternal" (from "Waltz Caprice")
Ladies, Gentlemen
"Peer Gynt" (Ballet of the Italian Opera)
Solvejg's Melody
Hall of the Dovre King
Anitra's Dance
"I Love You" (from "Ich Liebe Dich")
H. Bliss

Scene 4

"At Christmastime" (from "Woodland Wanderings")
W. Kingsford, I. Scott, H. Bliss
"Midsummer's Eve" (reprise)
L. Brooks, H. Bliss
"Strange Music" (reprise)
L. Brooks

Scene 5

"The Song of Norway" (from A-Minor Piano Concerto)

L. Brooks
Beyond—
Far beyond the span and space of all place North,
And before—
Oh long before the face of time fell upon the fjord,
The mountains loved the sky,
The sun knew the earth,
And the land bore spring.
And there, in that far-off time
And full upon Spring's flowing breast
Children danced. Even Norway danced.

1944.22

STAR TIME

A Vaudeville Show in Two Acts. Orchestra under the direction of Waldemar Guiterson. Produced by Paul Small. Opened 12 September 1944 at the Majestic Theatre and closed 9 December 1944 after 120 performances.[1]

CAST: LOU HOLTZ, BENNY FIELDS, TONY and SALLY DeMARCO, SHIRLEY DENNIS, JIMMY and MILDRED MULCAY, THE WHITSON BROTHERS, ARMAND CORTEZ, FRANCINE BORDEAU, GEORGE PROSPERY, THE BERRY BROTHERS.

Lou Holtz, valiant at the barricades when the Palace capitulated, will open the services with some unilateral conversation (Sam Lapidus stories, "O Sole Mio," "Me and My Gal"), then wax rhapsodic over the Whitson Brothers (acrobats) and Jimmy and Mildred Mulcay (harmonica players). In his capacity of regisseuer the later-day Balieff will then give a brief sales talk for Shirley Dennis, identified by time-conscious producer Small, in his more Gallic moments, as une chaude chanteuse (Showboat selection, incl. "Ol' Man River"). Miss Dennis behind him, Mr. Holtz will undertake to unravel a French drama, not by Moliere ('Napoleon and Josephine', performed by A. Cortez, F. Bordeau, G. Prospery). Once the DeMarcos (ballroom dancing) have scorched the groundcloth, Mr. Holtz will conclude the first fraction of the fracas with an address in which he will touch on life, love and the cosmos.

Then there'll be an intermission, just as in "Othello."

Guess who's on the stage when the curtain goes up again? Right! He'll keep talking until the dancing Berry Brothers overpower him (Pogo Dance). Benny Fields, another Palace alumnus, then takes over ("Lullaby of Broadway," "Over There"), inevitably joined by Mr. H. in a scuffle over a piano. After the Paul Small Art Players have tattered an aria, there will come a saturnalia, or something, which beggars description.

1944.23

BLOOMER GIRL

A Musical in Two Acts, 10 Scenes. Book by Sig Herzig and Fred Saidy[2]. Based on a play[3] by Lilith and Dan James. Music by Harold Arlen. Lyrics by E.Y. Harburg. Settings and lighting by Lemuel Ayres. Costumes by Miles White. Book directed by William Schorr. Dances by Agnes deMille. Musical director, Leon Leonardi. Orchestrations by Russell Bennett. Production staged by E.Y. Harburg. Produced by John C. Wilson in association with Nat Goldstone. Opened 5 October 1944 at the Sam S. Shubert Theatre and closed 27 April 1946 after 657 performances.

CAST (in order of appearance): *Serena*: MABEL TALIAFERRO. *Octavia*: Pamela Randall. *Lydia, Julia, Phoebe, Delia (The Applegate Daughters)*: Claudia Jordan, Toni Hart, Arlene Anderson, Nancy Douglass. *Daisy*: JOAN McCRACKEN. *Horatio*: MATT BRIGGS. *Gus*: John Call. *Evelina*: CELESTE HOLM. *Joshua Dingle*: Robert Lyon. *Herman Brasher, Ebeneezer Mimms, Wilfred Thrush, Hiram Crump*, Sons-in-law: Victor Bender, Joe E. Marks, Vaughn Trinnier, Dan Gallagher. *Dolly*: MARGARET DOUGLASS. *Jeff Calhoun*: DAVID BROOKS. *Paula*: Matilda Strazza. *Prudence*: Eleanor Jones. *Hetty*: Terry Saunders. *Betty*: Eleanor Winter. *Hamilton Calhoun*: Blaine Cordner. *Pompey*: DOOLEY WILSON. *Sheriff Quimby*: Charles Howard. *First Deputy*: John Byrd. *Second Deputy*: Joseph Florestano. *Third Deputy*: Ralph Sessano. *Augustus*: Hubert Dilworth. *Alexander*: Richard Huey. *State Official*: John Byrd. *Governor Newton*: Butler Hixon.

Vocal Ensemble: Eleanor Jones, Matilda Strazza, Harriet Hall, Terry Saunders, Alice Richmond, Eleanor Winter. Ralph Sessano, Ray Cook, Henry Roberts, Byron Milligan, Joseph Florestano, Alan Gilbert.

---

[1]Scenery, costumes, lighting and direction uncredited.
[2]Authors' note: The incidents in the story of "Bloomer Girl" are entirely fictional, and the characters are not intended to portray any persons living or dead.
[3]Unproduced.

Dancers: Peggy Holmes, Dorothy Hill, Betty Low, Carmelita Lanza, Elena Karina, Joan Mann, Phyllis Gehrig, Theresa Gushurst, Emy St. Just, Lidija Franklin, Kathleen O'Brien. Art Partington, Jack L. Nagle, Frank DeWinters, James Mitchell, William Weber, Jack Starr, Arthur Grahl.

The action takes place in Cicero Falls, a small Eastern manufacturing town, in the spring of 1861.

Act 1, Scene 1: The conservatory of the Applegate mansion. *Scene 2*: The Applegate bathroom, half hour later. *Scene 3*: The Lily, a few hours later. *Scene 4*: Hedge outside Applegate estate, the following Saturday afternoon. *Scene 5*: The Yellow Pavilion, that evening. *Scene 6*: Applegate garden, a few minutes later.

Act 2, Scene 1: The village green, next day. *Scene 2*: Corridor of the town jail, the next morning. *Scene 3*: Stage of the Cicero Falls Opera House, that night. *Scene 4*: The Conservatory of the Applegate mansion. Morning, a week later.

ACT 1

Scene 1
    "When the Boys Come Home"
        M. Taliaferro, P. Randell, C. Jordan, T. Hart, A. Anderson, N. Douglass
    "Evelina"
        D. Brooks, C. Holm
    "Welcome Hinges"
        M. Taliaferro, M. Briggs, P. Randell, C. Jordan,T. Hart, A. Anderson, N. Douglass, R. Lyon, V. Bender,J. Marks, V. Trinnier, D. Gallagher, C. Holm, D. Brooks

Scene 2
    "Farmer's Daughter"
        R. Lyon, V. Bender, J. Marks, V. Trinnier, D. Gallagher

Scene 3
    "It Was Good Enough for Grandma"
        C. Holm, the Bloomer Girls
    Dance Specialty
        J. McCracken, Dancers
    "The Eagle and Me"
        D. Wilson
    "Right As the Rain"
        D. Brooks, C. Holm

Scene 4
    "T'morra', T'morra'"
        J. McCracken

Scene 5
    "Rakish Young Man With the Whiskers"
        C. Holm, D. Brooks

Scene 6
    "Pretty As a Picture"
        Male Ensemble
    Waltz
        The Waltzers: L. Franklin, J. Mitchell, J. Mann, T. Gushurst, K. O'Brien, P. Gehrig, R. Darcy, A. Grahl, W. Weber, A. Partington.
    Style Show Ballet
        Principals, Dancers

ACT 2

Scene 1
    "Sunday in Cicero Falls"
        (*Staged by* Agnes deMille.)Principals, Company

Scene 2
    "I Got a Song"
        R. Huey, H. Dilworth, D. Wilson
    "Lullaby"
        C. Holm

Scene 3
    "Simon Legree"
        J. Florestano
    "Liza Crossing the Ice"
        Ensemble
        Dance by E. St. Just.
    "I Never Was Born"
        J. McCracken
    "Man For Sale"
        A. Gilbert

Scene 4
    Civil War Ballet
        Dancers
        Woman in black and red: B. Low. *Girl in rose*: L. Franklin. *Her soldier*: J. Mitchell.
    "The Eagle and Me"(reprise)
        Ensemble
    "When the Boys Come Home"(reprise)
        Entire Company

1944.24   THE MERRY WIDOW

A Return Engagement of the Operetta in Three Acts[4]. New book by Sidney Sheldon and Ben Roberts. (Original Viennese libretto to "Die Lustige Witwe" by Victor Léon and Leo Stein after "L'Attaché d'Amabassade" by Henri Meilhac.) Music by Franz Lehár. New musical version by Robert Stolz. Lyrics by Adrian Ross. Special lyrics by Edward Gilbert. Production directed by Felix Brentano. Choreography by George Balanchine. Scenery by Howard Bay. Costumes by Walter Florell. Conductor, Fritz Zweig. Produced by Yolanda Mero-Irion (The New Opera Company Production). Opened 7 October 1944 at the New York City Center and closed 4 November 1944 after 32 performances.

CAST (in order of appearance): *The King*: John Harrold. *Popoff*: KARL FARKAS. *Jolidon*: Nils Landin. *Natalie*: XENIA BANK. *Olga Bardini*: Lucy Hillary. *General Bardini*: GORDON DILWORTH. *Novakovich*: Alan Vaughan. *Cascada*: Dennis Dengate. *Khadja*: Alfred Porter. *Guests*: Connie Clark, Ward Richard. *Nish*: NORMAN BUDD. *Sonia Sadoya*: MARTA EGGERTH. *Prince Danilo*: JAN KIEPURA. *Clo-Clo*: LISETTE VEREA. *Lo-Lo*: Annette Norman. *Frou-Frou*: Mary Broussard. *Do-Do*: Babs Heath. *Margot*: Alice Borbus. *Jou-Jou*: Teddi Sanders. *Premiere Danseuses*: BABS HEATH, NINA POPOVA. *Premier Dancer*: JACK GANSERT. *Gaston*: John Harrold.

    Ladies of the Ensemble: Connie Clark, Irene Gans, Leona Vanni, Georgette Rolandez, Maxine Schraeder, Jan Rankin, Doris Parker, Dorothy Ramsay, Katherine Borron, Beatrice Gordon, Mary Rankin. *Gentlemen of the Ensemble*: Alfred Morgan, George Karle, Joseph Monte, Ward Richard, Joseph Bellafiore, Louis Fried, Colin Harvey, Stanton Barrett, Jon Carlson.

    Ballet: Mary Broussard, Teddi Sanders, Alice Borbus, Rita Charise, Barbara Gaye, Annette Norman, Alice Tisen, Aleks Bird, Jeffrey Longe, Stanley Zompakos, Terry Townes, Ernest Richman, Bruce Laffey, Charles Chartier.

1944.25   ROBIN HOOD

A Revival of the Comic Opera in Three Acts[5]. Book and lyrics by Harry B. Smith. Music by Reginald deKoven. Staged by R. H. Burnside in its original form as played by the famous Bostonians. Scenery by United Studios. Costumes by Veronica. Orchestra under the direction of Roger P. Vené. Produced by R.H. Burnside (and the Messrs. Shubert). Opened 7 November 1944 at the Adelphi Theatre and closed 18 November 1944 after 15 performances.

CAST: *Robert of Huntington*, afterward Robin Hood: ROBERT FIELD. *Sheriff of Nottingham*: GEORGE LIPTON. *Sir Guy of Gisborne*, his ward: FRANK FARRELL. *Little John*: HAROLD PATRICK. *Will Scarlett*: WILFRED GLENN. *Friar Tuck*: JERRY ROBBINS[6]. *Allan-a-Dale*: EDITH HERLICK. *Lady Marian Fitzwalter*, a ward of the Crown, afterward Maid Marian: BARBARA SCULLY. *Dame Durden*, a widow: Zamah Cunningham. *Annabel*, her daughter: Margaret Spencer.

    Milkmaids: Lucille Barton, Virginia Chestnutt, Susan Corey, Frances Joslyn, Helena Koslowsky, Gloria Marshall, Margaret McKenna, Beatrice Miller, Wanda Owen, Jane Riehl, Ruth Simas, Doris Sward.

    Sheriff's Men: Edgar Joseph, Philip Lowry, William Nuss, Raymond Vincent. *King's Men*: Roy Ballard, Tom Kelly, Stanley Turner, Louis Vern. *Villagers and Archers*: Gerda Christensen, Frances Fleming, Florence Hurst, Adele Jakiel, Ethel Johnson, Gloria Laflin, Jean Lawrence, Jeanne Lee, Jane Moses, Arlene Ross, Jane Shelby,

---

[4]This new version first presented in New York 4 August 1943 at the Majestic Theatre for 321 performances. Original New York production opened 21 October 1907 at the New Amsterdam Theatre for 416 performances. For Synopsis of Scenes and Musical Numbers, see 1943 production. In this production, "The Girls at Maxim's" which previously appeared at the Opening of Act 3 was replaced by a French song "Ya de la Joie" written and performed by Lisette Verea, danced by Nina Popova and Ballet Girls.

[5]First presented in New York 28 September 1891 at the Standard Theatre for two engagements of 35 and 42 performances.

[6]Not to be confused with the choreographer Jerome Robbins.

Norine Winters. *Villagers and Outlaws*: Lee Edwards, Herman Glazer, Stven Kent, Jerry Madeira, Gerry Sherwood, Dale Sommer, Milton Vaughn, Melville Veitch, Allan Whitman.

Scene: England at the time of Richard I.

Act 1: A Market Place in Nottingham.

Act 2: Sherwood Forest.

Act 3: Courtyard of the Sheriff's Castle.

ACT 1

Introduction and Opening Chorus
  Chorus
"The Milkmaid's Song"
  Milkmaids
"Come the Bowmen in Lincoln Green"
  R. Field
"My Dream Has Come True"
  R. Field, B. Scully
"I Am the Sheriff of Nottingham"
  F. Farrell, G. Lipton, Chorus
"Churning"
  G. Lipton, F. Farrell, B. Scully
Finale

ACT 2

"It Takes Nine Tailors to Make a Man"
  W. Glenn, Ensemble
"Brown October Ale"
  H. Patrick, Chorus
"Oh Promise Me"
  E. Herlick
"The Tinker Song"
  G. Lipton, F. Farrell, Tinkers
"See the Little Lambkins Play"
  Sextette
"The Forest Song"
  B. Scully
"The Serenade"
  R. Field
The Scena–"Revenge Is Mine"
  E. Herlick, W. Glenn, R. Field, B. Scully
Finale

ACT 3

"The Armorer's Song"
  W. Glenn
"When a Maiden Weds"
  M. Spencer
"The Legend of the Chimes"
  E. Herlick, Chorus
Quintette
  M. Spencer, Z. Cunningham, F. Farrell, G. Lipton, J. Robbins
Finale

1944.26 THE GYPSY BARON

A Revival of the Comic Opera in Three Acts and a Prologue[7]. Music by Johann Strauss. (Original Viennese libretto to "Der Ziegeunerbaron" by Ignaz Schnitzer based on the story "Saffi" by Mór Jókai. First American adaptation by Sydney Rosenfeld.) Libretto revised and adapted into English by George Mead. Stage director, William Wymetal. Dialogue director, Jessie Royce Landis. Ballet choreographer, Helen Playova. Sets by H. A. Condell. Conductor, Laszlo Halasz. Produced by the New York City Opera. Opened 14 November 1944 at the New York City Center, and closed 10 December 1944 after 20 performances in repertory. Returned 15-28 April 1945 to the New York City Center for 4 additional performances. Total for both engagements this season: 24 performances.[8]

[7]First presented in New York 15 February 1886 at the Casino Theatre for 86 performances.
[8]Costumes and lighting uncredited. No individual songs listed in program.

CAST: *Barinkay*: WILLIAM HORNE. *Saffi*: POLYNA STOSKA, MARGUERITE PIAZZA. *Czipra*: ALICE HOWLAND, ELIZABETH WYSOR. *Arsena*: MARGUERITE PIAZZA, MARJORIE KING. *Zsupan*: STANLEY CARLSON, EMILE RENAN. *Ottokar*: THOMAS HAYWARD, ARTHUR OLISSE. *Carnero*: PAUL DENNIS, EMILE RENAN (alt). *Count Homonnay*: CARLTON GAULD. *Solo Dancers*: RUTH HARRIS (Czardas and Waltz), TASHAMIRA (Gypsy Dances). *Villagers, Gypsies, Gussars, Vivandieres, Soldiers, Citizens, Town-folk.*

Time: 19th Century. *Prologue*: A Ballroom in the Royal Palace in Budapest.

Act 1: A remote region of the Transylvanian countryside.

Act 2: The following morning. A gypsy encampment around the ruins of Barinkay's castle.

Act 3: A public square in Vienna.

1944.27 SADIE THOMPSON

A Musical Play in Two Acts, 3 Scenes. Book by Howard Dietz and Rouben Mamoulian, based on the short story by Somerset Maugham and the play "Rain" by John Colton and Clemence Randolph. Music by Vernon Duke. Lyrics by Howard Dietz. Dances by Edward Caton. Setting by Boris Aronson. Costumes by Motley.[9] All vocal arrangements by Vernon Duke. Choral ensembles trained by Millard Gibson. Orchestra conductor, Charles G. Sanford. Musical arrangements by Charles Cooke, Walter Eiger, John Klein, Joseph Glover, Irving Landau, Julian Work and Vernon Duke. Entire production directed by Rouben Mamoulian. Produced by A. P. Waxman. Opened 16 November 1944 at the Alvin Theatre and closed 6 January 1945 after 60 performances.

CAST (in order of appearance): *Joe Horn*: Ralph Dumke. *Corporal Hodgson*: DANIEL COBB. *Private Griggs*: NORMAN LAWRENCE. *Sergeant Tim O'Hara*: JAMES NEWILL. *Ameena, Horn's Wife*: Grazia Narciso. *Honeypie*: BEATRICE KRAFT. *Mrs. Alfred Davidson*: Zolya Talma. *Cicely St. Clair*: Doris Patson. *Lao Lao*: Remington Olmsted. *Sadie Thompson*: JUNE HAVOC. *Quartermaster Bates*: WALTER BURKE. *Reverend Alfred Davidson*: LANSING HATFIELD. *Polynesian Girl*: Milada Mladova. *Polynesian Boy*: Chris Volkoff. *Marines and Natives.*
  Singers: Ann Browning, Arlene Carmen, Paula Carpino, Molly Cousley, Ethel Greene, Marilyn Merkt, Dorris Moore, Linda White. Jimmy Allison, Anthony Amato, Adolph Anderson, John [Jack] Cassidy, Harold Bayne, Delmar Horstmann, Robert Lawrence, Alan Noel.
  Dancers: Vivian Cherry, Toni Darnay, Andrea Downing, Mary Grey, Lil Liandre, Virginia Meyer, Theodora Roosevelt, Anna Scarpova, Alla Shishkina, Ruth Sobotka. Fred Bernaski, Bob Gari, T.C. Jones, William Lundy, Mischa Pompianov, William Vaux, John Ward, William Hunter. (*Featured female dancer*: Vanessi.)

Act 1, Scene 1: Trader Joe Horn's Hotel-Store in Pago-Pago, in the South Seas. *Scene 2*: The Jungle.

Act 2: Trader Joe Horn's Hotel-Store.

ACT 1

Polynesian Scene
"Barrel of Beads"
  N. Lawrence, B. Kraft
"If You Can't Get the Love You Want"
  J. Havoc
"When You Live on an Island"
  J. Newill, Choral Ensemble
"Poor as a Church Mouse"
  J. Havoc
Jungle Dance (a)
  B. Kraft, Natives
Jungle Dance (b)
  M. Mladova, C. Volkoff, Natives
"The Love I Long For"
  J. Havoc, J. Newill
Dance to the Sun God
  R. Olmsted, Vanessi, Natives
"Garden in the Sky"
  L. Hatfield

ACT 2

"Dancing Lesson"
  D. Patson, Native Girls

[9]Except for Miss Havoc's which are from studies by Azadia Newman for her painting of 'Sadie Thompson.'

"Siren of the Tropics"
B. Kraft, W. Burke, N. Lawrence, D. Cobb
"Life's a Funny Present"
J. Havoc
"Born All Over Again"
L. Hatfield

1944.28   RHAPSODY

An Operetta in Two Acts, 6 Scenes. Book by Leonard Louis Levinson and Arnold Sundgaard. Based on an original story by A.N. Nagler. Music by Fritz Kreisler. Musical adaptation and arrangements by (Robert) Russell Bennett. Lyrics by John Latouche. Additional lyrics by (Robert) Russell Bennett and Blevins Davis. Book and choreography staged by David Lichine. Settings by Oliver Smith. Costumes by Frank Bevan. Lighting by Stanley McCandless. Musical director, Fritz Mahler. Produced by Blevins Davis in association with Lorraine Manville Dresselhuys. Opened 22 November 1944 at the New Century Theatre and closed 2 December 1944 after 13 performances.

CAST (in order of appearance): *Lotzi Hugenhaugen*: JOHN CHERRY. *Lili Hugenhausen*: GLORIA STORY. *Charles Eckert*: JOHN HAMILL. *Frau Tina Hugenhaugen*: BERTHA BELMORE. *Ilse Bonen*: PATRICIA BOWMAN. *Greta*, a maid: Mildred Jocelyn. *Casanova*: EDDIE MAYEHOFF. *Madame Boticini*: ROSEMARIE BRANCATO. *Demi-Tasse*: Mister Johnson. *Ivan*: George Zoritch. *Sonya*: Alexandra Denisova. *Emperor Francis I*: George Young. *Empress Maria Theresa*: ANNAMARY DICKEY. *Captain of the Palace Guard* Randolph Symonette. *Rickshaw Man*: Nicolas Beriozoff. *The Dandy*: Jerry Ross. *Jailer*: Robert W. Kirland.
Court Octette: Barbara Jevne, Muriel O'Malley, Lucille Shea, Camille Fischelli, Carl Anders, William Hearne, Gordon Gaines, Gar Moore. *Maywine Octette*: Angela Carabella, Evelyn Keller, Mildred Jocelyn, Nina Allen, John Henson, Thomas LoMonaco, Harry Ward, Rudy Rudisill.
Rhapsody Double Quintette: Betty Baker, Bette Van, Stephanie Turash, Ella Mayer, Maxine Dorelle, Lewis Rose, Robert Marco, Tony Coffaro, Robert W. Kirland, Rudolph Bain. *Musical Ensemble trained by* Fritz Mahler, assisted by Herbert Winkler.
Corps de Ballet: Adele Bodroghy, Leslie Cater, Joan Collonette, Joan Hansen, Betty Jayne, Jane Kiser, Irene Larson, Kirra Lehachova, Marina Lvova, Cecile Mann, Ann Mauldlin, Dorothy Scott, Pat Sims, Sally Sorvo, Yvonne Tibor, Janie Ward, Betty Yeager. *Boys*: Charles Bockman, Jack Donald Claus, Walter Roberts, Igor Storojeff.

Time: Reign of Maria Theresa. The action takes place from noon to midnight on the Emperor's birthday. *Place*: Vienna.

Act 1, Scene 1: Music Room of the Hugenhaugen Home. *Scene 2*: Gardens of the Schoenbrunn Palace. *Scene 3*: Maywine Pavilion Outside Vienna.

Act 2, Scene 1: The Jail. *Scene 2*: Apartment of Casanova in the Palace. *Scene 3*: The Ballroom of the Schoenbrunn Palace.

ACT 1
"They're All the Same"
E. Mayehoff, P. Bowman,
Misses Allen, Carabella, Fischelli, Lvova, Mayer, Tibor, Turash, Ward
"My Rhapsody"
G. Story, J. Hamill
"Scherzo"
R. Brancato
"Heaven Bless Our Home"
G. Young
"The World is Young Again"
A. Dickey, Ladies of the Court
Presentation
A. Dickey, G. Young, R. Brancato, R. Symonette, Ensemble
Chinese Porcelain Ballet
P. Bowman, G. Zoritch, N. Beriozoff, Ladies of the Corps de Ballet
"To Horse"
R. Brancato, E. Mayehoff, B. Belmore, J. Cherry
The Dandy's Polka
J. Ross
May Wine Polka
Corps de Ballet, Ensemble
"Take Love"
G. Story, J. Hamill, Ensemble
The Hunt
P. Bowman, Corps de Ballet, Ensemble
The Roulette Game
A. Denisova, assisted by N. Beriozoff, Corps de Ballet, Ensemble

"Song of Defiance"
J. Hamill, Ensemble
ACT 2
"Because You're Mine"
J. Hamill
"When Men Are Free"
J. Hamill, Ensemble
"Happy Ending"
A. Dickey
"Rosemarin"
R. Brancato
"Caprice Viennois"
A. Dickey, G. Young
Midnight Ballet
P. Bowman, G. Zoritch, A. Denisova, Corps de Ballet
Finale
Entire Company

1944.29   SEVEN LIVELY ARTS

An Entertainment (Musical Revue) in Two Acts, 22 Scenes. Music and lyrics by Cole Porter. Staged and lighted by Hassard Short. Miss Lillie's sketches by Moss Hart. Doc Rockwell's comments by Ben Hecht. Scenery by Norman Bel Geddes. Dances and songs directed by Jack Donohue. Costumes by Mary Grant; modern gowns by Valentina. Choral group trained by Robert Shaw. Orchestra conducted by Maurice Abravanel. Sketches directed by Philip Loeb. Ballet choreography by Anton Dolin. Orchestral arrangements by (Robert) Russell Bennett, Ted Royal and Hans Spialek. Produced by Billy Rose[10]. Opened 7 December 1944 at the Ziegfeld Theatre and closed 12 May 1945 after 182 performances.

CAST: BEATRICE LILLIE, BERT LAHR, BENNY GOODMAN, ALICIA MARKOVA, ANTON DOLIN, DOC ROCKWELL, Nan Wynn, Jere McMahon, Paula Bane, Billie Worth, Bill (William) Tabbert, Dolores Gray, Albert Carroll, Michael Barrett, Dennie Moore, Thomas Kenny, Edward Hackett, King Ross, Robert Austin, Teddy Wilson, Red Norvo, Morey Feld, Sid Weiss, Mary Roche.
Ladies of Fashion: Savona King, Jean Colleran, Alma Holt, Cissy Smith, Truly Barbara, Viki Maulsby, Gwen Shirey, Susan Blanchard, Adrian Storms, Paddy Ellerton, Gayle Mellott, Temple Texas. (Selected with the assistance of Harry Conover).
Corps de Ballet: Franca Baldwin, Virginia Barnes, John Bregg, Angelina Buttignol, Phyllis Brown, Evangeline Collis, Margarita de Valera, Bettye Durrence, Adriana Favalaro, Louise Ferrand, Jerry Florio, Nina Frenkin, Helen Gallagher, Arlene Garver, Mimi Gomber, Edward Hackett, Jean Harris, Ray Johnson, Harriet Katzman, Thomas Kenny, Lee Lauterbur, Constance Love, Richard Martini, Paul Olson, Michael Pober, Lester Russon.
Singers: Robert Austin, Johnsie Bason, Charlotte Bruce, Irene Carroll, Nina Dean, Rose Marie Elliott, Paul Fairleagh, Vincent Henry, Bob Herring, Raynor Howell, Stella Hughes, Jimmy Kane, Robert Kimberly, Mary Ann Krejci, Ethel Madson, John Mathews, Helen Molveau, Louise Newton, Richmond Page, Allen Sharp, Gordon Taylor, William Utely, Martha Emma Watson.
Page Boys: Charles Franklin Beck, Sonny Cavell, Alan Grossman, Barry Laffin, Buddy Millard, Dickie Millard, Donald Rose.
ACT 1
Overture: "Frahngee-Pahnee"
Scene 1
"Big Town"
Mr. Audience: D. Rockwell. *The Young Hopefuls* (in order of appearance) *Painter*: N. Wynn. *Tap Dancer*: J. McMahon. *Radio Singer*: P. Bane. *Ballet Dancer*: B. Worth. *Playwright*: B. Tabbert. *Movie Actress*: D. Gray. *Stage Actress*: M. Roche. Ensemble.
Scene 2
"Is It the Girl (or Is It the Gown)?"
D. Gray, Ladies of Fashion
Scene 3
Local Boy Makes Good
(*by* George S. Kaufman)
Scene: A Theatrical Producer's Office.
The Secretary: B. Worth. *The Producer*: A. Carroll. *The Agent*: M. Barrett. *The Stagehand*: B. Lahr.

---

[10]Producer's note: Salvador Dali has painted a surrealist conception of the Seven Lively Arts. The pictures are on exhibition in the downstairs lounge.

Scene 4

"Ev'ry Time We Say Goodbye"
The Girl: N. Wynn. *The Boy*: J. McMahon. Ensemble.

Scene 5

There'll Always Be an England
(*by* Moss Hart)
Scene: An English garden which has been turned into an outdoor canteen.
Lady Carlton: D. Moore. *Lady Agatha Pendleton*: B. Lillie. *First Soldier*: T. Kenny. *Second Soldier*: E. Hackett. *Colonel Charteris*: A. Carroll. *Third Soldier*: M. Barrett.

Scene 6

"Only Another Boy and Girl"
The Girl: M. Roche. *The Boy*: B. Tabbert. *Fragonard in Pink*: B. Lillie, B. Lahr, Ensemble.

Scene 7

"Wow-ooh-wolf!"
N. Wynn, D. Gray, M. Roche

Scene 8

Ticket for the Ballet
(*by* Moss Hart)
Scene: The Lobby of a Theatre.
The Customer: B. Lillie. *The Box Office Man*: M. Barrett. *The Manager*: A. Carroll. *A Man in the Line*: K. Ross.

Scene 9

"Drink"
B. Lahr, Male Ensemble

Scene 10

"When I Was a Little Cuckoo"
B. Lillie

Scene 11

"Billy Rose Buys the Metropolitan Opera House!"
B. Goodman, T. Wilson, R. Norvo, M. Feld, S. Weiss, Ensemble
Toreador Dance by J. McMahon.

ACT 2[11]

Scene 1

"Scene de Ballet" (Excerpts)
(*Music by* Igor Stravinsky. *Choreography by* Anton Dolin.)
Danced by A. Markova, A. Dolin, Corps de Ballet.

Scene 2

Song
B. Lillie

Scene 3

The Great Man Speaks
(*by* Charles Sherman)
Scene: A Doctor's Office.
The Nurse: B. Worth. *The Doctor*: A. Carroll. *The Patient*: B. Lahr.

Scene 4

Weber's Concertina for Clarinet
B. Goodman

Scene 5

"Frahngee-Pahnee"
B. Tabbert, Ensemble
"Dancin' to a Jungle Drum" (Let's End the Beguine)
B. Lillie

Scene 6

"Hence It Don't Make Sense"
N. Wynn, M. Roche, D. Gray, B. Worth
Danced by J. McMahon, B. Worth.

Scene 7

Heaven on Angel Street
(*by* Moss Hart)
Scene: The Living-room in Angel Street.

---

[11]Added during the course of the run:
"The Band Started Swinging a Song"(Act 2, Scene 7)
N. Wynn
"The Big Parade"
Ensemble

Mr. Manningham: A. Dolin. *Mrs. Manningham*: B. Lillie. *Mr. Clarence Day*: B. Lahr. *Mrs. Day*: D. Moore. *Dude Lester*: M. Barrett. *Jeeter Lester*: A. Carroll. *George Jean Nathan*: R. Austin. *The Maid*: B. Worth.

Scene 8

"Is It the Girl (or Is It the Gown)?" (reprise)
M. Roche
Lecture by D. Rockwell.

Scene 9

Pas de Deux
Danced by A. Markova, A. Dolin

Scene 10

"They All Made Good"
D. Rockwell, Young Hopefuls

Scene 11

Finale
D. Rockwell, Entire Company

1944.30 # LAFFING ROOM ONLY

A Revue in Two Acts, 24 Scenes. Book by Olsen and Johnson and Eugene Conrad. Music and lyrics by Burton Lane. Staged by John Murray Anderson. Dances by Robert Alton. Production designed by Stewart Chaney. Costumes designed by Billy Livingston. Comedy directed by Edward Cline. Orchestra under the direction of John McManus. General director for Olsen and Johnson, David Murray. Assistant to John Murray Anderson, Arnold Saint Subber. Production supervised by Harry Kaufman. Produced by the Messrs. Shubert, Olsen and Johnson. Opened 23 December 1944 at the Winter Garden and closed 14 July 1945 after 233 performances.

CAST: OLE OLSON (John Siguard Olsen), CHIC JOHNSON (Harold Ogden Johnson), FRANK LIBUSE, BETTY GARRETT, WILLIE WEST and (TED) McGINTY, MATA & HARI, MARGOT BRANDER, ETHEL OWEN, WILLIAM ARCHIBALD, KATHRYN LEE, PAT BREWSTER, ETHEL OWEN, IDA JAMES, LOU WILLS, JR., O'Donnell Blair, Bruce Evans, Robert Breton, Harry Burns, Penny Edwards, Billy Young, Joe Young, Charles Senna, Ernest D'Amato, Kenny Buffett, Frances Henderson, Jean Moorhead, Shannon Dean, Catherine Johnson, (Tom) McKee & (Sam) Kramer, Virginia Barrett, Dippy Diers, Stanley Stevens, Lee Joyce, Rhythm Red, Eddie Vincent with Chico & Coco, Stanley, Gus and John Stevens, Mary La Roche.
Singing Ensemble (The Glee Club): Ruth Cottingham, Johanna Gillman, Betty Gilpatrick, Jocelyn McIntyre, Lewis Appleton, George Beach, Gerard Bercier, Gene Bone, Francis Cooke, Burk Esaias, John Ferguson, Jerry Gilbert, James Kovach, Allan Leonard, Roger Miller, Fred Peters, Andrew Ratousheff, Roy Russell, Edward Saunders, Otto Simanek, Tommy Thompson.
Corps de Ballet: May Block, Jean Bortz, Lillian Cross, Dotty Dee, Eloise Farmer, Virginia Gorski, Gae Hess, Penny Holt, Gretchen Houser, Elana Keller, Marjorie Johnstone, Lee Joyce, Eleanor Leaman, Jennie Lewis, Patricia Lenn, Marcia Maier, June Walker, Susan West, Doris York. Ray Arnett, Forrest Bonshire, Ronny Chetwood, Norman Drew, Jack Pierce, Kenneth Peterson, J. C. McCord, Budd Rogers, Herbert Ross.

BEFORE THE SHOW
In the lobby: D. Diers, W. West, H. Burns. *In the audience*: F. Libuse.

ACT 1

"Overture"
The conductor: F. Libuse. *Stage Manager*: C. Senna. *Company Manager*: F Peters.

Scene 1

The Russian Arts Players
Anna: C. Johnson. *Sonya*: M. LaRoche. *Count Dimitri Resluvsky*: R. Breton. *Prince Vasiloff*: B. Evans.

Scene 2

"Hooray for Anywhere"
P. Brewster, The Glee Club
Danced by Dance Ensemble.

Scene 3

Olsen & Johnson

Scene 4

The White House
Guests and Tourists: F. Libuse, M. Brander, P. Brewster, C. O'Donnell, J. Young, S. Dean, C. Senna, H. Burns, S. Evans, E. D'Amato, B. Young, J. Moorhead, P. Edwards, B. Evans, F. Henderson, B. Gilpatrick, D. York, L. Joyce, and Olsen and Johnson.

Scene 5

"Go Down to Boston Harbor"

B. Garrett
Danced by K. Lee, W. Archibald, J. C. McCord. *British Soldiers*: N. Drew,
H. Ross, R. Chetwood, K. Peterson. *Conspirators*: E. Keller, J. C. McCord.
Girl Patriots: G. Hess, M. Maier, L. Cross, E. Leaman, E. Farmer, Corps de
Ballet. *General Duquesne*: C. Johnson. Corps de Ballet. (*Ballet Music by*
Alan Moran.)

Scene 6

The Russian Art Players

Colonel: B. Evans. *Firing Squad*: F. Cooke, J. Ferguson, J. Gilbert.

Scene 7

Mata & Hari

Scene 8

An Apartment in 1980

Real Estate Agent: O. Olsen. *Mr. Tenant*: C. Johnson. *Mrs. Tenant*: E. Owen.
Miner: F. Libuse, S. Stevens, G. Stevens, J. Stevens, D. Diers, J. Lewis, A.
Ratousheff, H. Burns, B. Young, S. West, B. Evans, S. Dean, P. Brewster, C.
Senna, T. McGinty, E. Vincent with Chico & Coco.

Scene 9

"Moments Musicales"

Harpist: F. Libuse. *Soprano*: M. Brander. *Flutist*: T. McKee.
Cellist: S. Kramer.

Scene 10

"Stop That Dancing"

B. Garrett
The Sailor: W. Archibald. *In Central Park*: P. Holt, J. Pierce. *On Broadway*:
E. Leaman, R. Chetwood, L. Cross, H. Ross. *In Greenwich Village*: F.
Henderson, F. Bonshire, G. Hess, J.C. McCord, M. Maier. *At El Morocco*:
P. Edwards, K. Buffett, M. Johnstone, V. Gorski, M. Block, D. Dee. *In Harlem*:
G. Houser, K. Peterson, R. Arnett, L. Joyce. The Glee Club, Corps de Ballet.

Scene 11

Pocatello, Idaho

O. Olsen, J. Young, C. Johnson

Scene 12

The Russian Art Players

Scene 13

The Ghost Train (A Night on a Union Pacific Pullman)

Olsen and Johnson, O. Blair, E. D'Amato, B. West, F. Peters, T. McKee,
V. Barrett, S. Dean, T. Fletcher, B. Young, J. Young, J. Moorhead, P. Edwards,
S. West, H. Burns, J. Lewis, F. Henderson, P. Brewster, E. Owens, C. Senna,
R. Russell.

Scene 14

"This Is As Far As I Go"

B. Garrett, R. Arnett, F. Bonshire,
R. Chetwood, N. Drew, K. Peterson, J. Pierce, J. C. McCord, B. Rogers, H. Ross

Scene 15

Willie West and McGinty

Scene 16

Stanley Stevens and "Big Boy"

Scene 17

"Fussin', Feudin' and Fightin'" (Feudin' and Fightin')

P. Brewster, Glee Club
Danced by K. Lee, W. Archibald, Corps de Ballet. *Mother Hatfield*: E. Leaman.
Grandmother: J. Walker. *Daughter*: K. Lee. *Father*: H. Ross. *Uncles*: R.
Chetwood, N. Drew. *McCoy Son*: W. Archibald. *Maw McCoy*: E. Owen. *Child*:
J. Moorhead. *Neighbors*: S. Stevens, V. Barrett, B. Young. *Judge*: B. Evans.
Bridegroom: O. Olsen. *Paw*: H. Burns. *Bride*: C. Johnson. *Sons*: R. Breton, C.
Senna, E. D'Amato.

"Gotta Get Joy"

Entire Company
In the Box: F. Libuse, M. Brander, V. Barrett, A. Ratousheff, D. Diers.

ACT 2
Scene 1

"Got That Good Time Feelin'" (Mississippi)

I. James, the Glee Club
Danced by The Ballerina: K. Lee. *The Beau*: K. Buffett. *The Suitor*: R.
Chetwood. Corps de Ballet.

Scene 2

The Piano Movers

O. Olsen, C. Johnson, O. Blair

Scene 3

Lou Wills, Jr.

Scene 4

"Sunny California"

B. Garrett
Danced by the Hollywood Star: P. Edwards. *The Hollywood Producer*:
W. Archibald. *The Cameraman*: L. Appleton. *Chauffeur*: R. Red. Ensemble,
The Olympic Team, Mata & Hari.

Scene 5

In the Radio Station

A Radio Announcer: O. Olsen. *The Sound Man*: C. Johnson. The Glee Club,
E. Owen, B. Young, J. Young, C. Senna, J. Moorhead, S. Dean, J. Lewis, A.
Ratousheff, T. Fletcher, S. West, V. Barrett, B. Evans, T. McKee, G. Houser.

Scene 6

"The Hellzapoppin' Polka"

Danced by V. Barrett, R. Cottingham, J. Moorhead, D. York, S. Dean, B.
Gilpatrick, J. Gillman, M. LaRoche, J. McIntyre, P. Holt, S. West, J. Lewis,
F. Henderson.

Scene 7

"The Steps of the Capitol"

B. Garrett, P. Brewster, the Glee Club

1944.31   TROPICAL REVUE

A Return Engagement of the Revue in Two Acts, 16 Scenes[12]. (Conceived,)
Choreographed and staged by Katherine Dunham. Costumes and settings
by John Pratt. Stage direction and lighting by Dale Wasserman. Musical
director, conductor and pianist, Martin Gabowitz. Choral direction, Helen
Dowdy. Produced by Sol Hurok. Opened 26 December 1944 at the New
Century Theatre and closed 13 January 1945 after 24 performances.

CAST: KATHERINE DUNHAM. *The Dunham Dancers*: Roger Ohardieno, Tommy
Gomez, Talley Beatty, Claude Marchant, Lenwood Morris, Vanoye Aikens, Andre
Drew, Eddy Clay. Lucille Ellis, Syvilla Fort, Lavinia Williams, Lawaune Ingram,
Ramona Erwin, Ora Lee, Richardena Jackson, Dolores Harper, Gloria Mitchell.
Singers: Bobby Capo, Dowdy Quartet (Helen Dowdy, Rosalie King, Howard Carlos,
Oliver Busch). *Drums*: Oscar Estrada, Julio Mendez, Cándido Vicenty.

ACT 1
Scene 1

"Rara Tonga"

(*Music by* Paquita Anderson.)
The Chosen Woman: R. Erwin. *The God*: R. Ohardieno. *The Jealous Husband*:
T. Gomez. *Narrator*: K. Dunham.
A folk tale of the Polynesian people on the island of Rara Tonga in the South
Pacific. The Chosen Woman, proud of her beauty, is taken over by The God
to the annoyance of The Jealous Husband, who, for his audacity, is turned into
a snake.

Scene 2

"Cuban Slave Lament"

The Singer: B. Capo. *The Possessed Dancer*: L. Ellis.

Scene 3

"Moorish Bolero"

L. Williams, T. Gomez and Group
(*Music by* Paquita Anderson.)

Scene 4

"Choro" (A 19th Century Brazilian Quadrille)

K. Dunham, S. Fort, L. Morris, T. Beatty
(*Music by* Vadico Gogliano.)
(Alternate for Miss Dunham: L. Ingram.)

Scene 5

"Rumba With a Little Jive Mixed In"

L. Ellis, V. Aikens, C. Marchant
(*Music by* Andre.)

Scene 6

"Bahiana" (A Brazilian Song)

K. Dunham, R. Ohardieno, V. Aikens, T. Beatty, T. Gomez
(*Music by* Don Alfonso.)

---

[12]Katherine Dunham and her company previously appeared on Broadway
with a different repertoire 19 September 1943 at the Martin Beck Theatre
for 87 performances.

Scene 7

"Tropics"

(*Music by* Paquita Anderson.)
Woman With the Cigar: K. Dunham. *Dockhand*: R. Ohardieno.

Scene 8

"Para Que Tu Veas"

B. Capo

Scene 9

"Promenade—Havana 1910"

K. Dunham, Company. B. Capo, Dowdy Quartet
(*Music by* Mercedes Navarro.)

ACT 2

Scene 1

"L'Ag'Ya"

(*Music by* Robert Sanders. *Orchestration by* Martin Gabowitz.)
From an original story by Katherine Dunham. The scene is Vauclin, a tiny 18th century fishing village in Martinique. Loulouse loves and is loved by Alcide. Julot, the villain, repulsed by Loulouse and filled with hatred and desire for revenge, decides to seek the aid of the king of the zombies. Deep in the jungle, Julot fearfully seeks the lair of the zombies and witnesses their strange rites which bring back the dead to life. Frightened, but remembering his purpose, Julot pursues Roi Zombie and obtains the "cambois," powerful love charm, from him. The following evening: it is a day of gaiety, opening with the stately Creole Mazurka, or "Mazouk," and moving into the uninhibited excitement of the Beguine. Into this scene enters Julot, horrifying the villagers when he exposes his coveted "cambois." Even Alcide is under its spell. Now begins the Majumba, love dance of ancient Africa. As Loulouse falls more and more under the charm, Alcide suddenly defies its power, breaks loose from the villages who protect him, and challenges Julot to the Ag'Ya, fighting dance of Martinique. In L'Ag'Ya and its ending are the climax and the consummation of the forces loosed in magic and superstition.
Loulouse: K. Dunham. *Alcide*: V. Aikens. *Julot*: C. Marchant, T. Gomez (alternate). *Roi Zombie*: R. Ohardieno. *Porteresses, vendors, fishermen, zombies, townspeople of Vauclin*: Dunham Company.

Scene 2

Street Scene—Port au Prince

L. Ellis, O. Estrada, J. Mendez

Scene 3

"Strutters' Ball"

H. Dowdy, R. King, H. Carlos, O. Busch

Scene 4

"Cakewalk"

S. Fort, V. Aikens, Ensemble

Scene 5

"Barrel House" (A Florida Swamp Shimmy)

K. Dunham, R. Ohardieno
(*Music by* Meade Lux Lewis and Albert Ammons.)

Scene 6

"Flaming Youth, 1927"

(*Music by* "Brad" Gowans.)
Blues Singer: H. Dowdy. *Kansas City Woman*: L. Ellis. *Snakehips Tucker*: T. Gomez.

Black Bottom, Charleston, Mooch and Fishtail

L. Ingram, C. Marchant, Ensemble

Scene 7

Finale

Dunham Dancers

1944.32   SING OUT, SWEET LAND!

A Salute to American Folk and Popular Music (Musical Revue) in Two Acts, 13 Scenes. Written by Walter Kerr. Production staged by Leon Leonidoff. Music arranged and conducted, and special music written by Elie Siegmeister. Book directed by Walter Kerr. Dances and numbers directed by Doris Humphrey and Charles Weidman. Settings by Albert Johnson. Costumes by Lucinda Ballard. Verse chorus directed by Arthur Lessac. Production under the supervision of Lawrence Langner and Theresa Helburn. Produced by the Theatre Guild. Opened 27 December 1944 at the International Theatre and closed 24 March 1945 after 102 performances.

<u>CAST</u>: ALFRED DRAKE, BURL IVES, BIBI OSTERWALD, ALMA KAYE, PHILIP COOLIDGE, JACK McCAULEY, ROBERT PENN, JAMES WESTERFIELD,

PETER HAMILTON, IRENE HAWTHORNE, ETHEL MANN, Ellen Love, Jules Racine, William Sharon, Ted Tiller, Irene Jordan, Adrienne Gray, Charles Hart, Juanita Hall, Christine Karner, Lawrence Gilbert, Sam Greene, Pat Newman, Peggy Campbell, Dorothy Baxter, Morty Halpern, Ruth Tyler, George Cassidy.

Vocal Ensemble: Dorothy Baxter, Cathleen Chambers, Marjorie Chandler, Carol Hall, Irene Jordan, Selma Rogoff, Phyliss Wilcox, Maria Wilde. George Cassidy, Charles Ford, Lawrence Gilbert, Sam Green, Calvin Harris, Edwin Marsh, Fred Rivetti, Ludlow White, Fred Kohler.

Dancers: Peggy Campbell, Roberta Cassell, Margaret Cuddy, Ann S. Halprin, Christine Karner, Ethel Mann, Patricia Newman, Miriam Pandor, Frances Rainer, Harriett Roeder, Helen Waggoner, Ann Williams. Kendrick Coy, Joseph Gifford, Joseph Landis, Robert Mayo, Joseph Precker, Sam Steen, Bill Summer, Bill Weaver.

Verse Chorus: Morty Halpern, Ellen Love, Dorothy Baxter, Carol Hall, Irene Jordan, Christine Karner, Ethel Mann, Patricia Newman, Frances Rainer, George Cassidy, Joseph Gifford, Sam Green, Robert Mayo, Fred Rivetti, Ludlow White.

Spiritual Ensemble (coached by Juanita Hall): Juanita Hall, Rhoda Boggs, Claretta Freeman, Massine Patterson. Hercules Armstrong, Harry Bolden, Oscar Brooks, James Gordon, Virtes Reese, Wilson Woodbeck, William Sol.

ACT 1

Scene 1

Puritan New England

Parson Killjoy: P. Coolidge. *Charity Wouldlove*: E. Love. *Priscilla*: A. Kaye. *Puritan*: R. Penn.

"Who Is the Man"

(Puritan Hymn) Vocal Ensemble

"As I Was Going Along"

A. Drake
(*Music and Lyrics by* Elie Siegmeister and Edward Eager based on folk music.)

Scene 2

A New England Town

The Patriot: J. McCauley. *His Daughter*: A. Kaye.

"Way Down the Ohio"

(Folk song, author unknown)
A. Drake

Scene 3

Illinois Wilderness

Fiddler: B. Ives. *Bear*: J. Racine. *Bill*: T. Tiller. *Mary Jane*: I. Jordan. *Mary Jane's Father*: P. Coolidge. *Farm Girl*: A. Gray. *Farm Woman*: B. Osterwald. *Mohee*: A. Kaye.

Mountain Whipporwill

(*by* Stephen Vincent Benet)
Recited by A. Drake

Country Dance

Dancing Ensemble
(*Staged by* Charles Weidman)

"When I Was Single"

(Folk song, author unknown)
B. Osterwald

"Foggy, Foggy Dew"

(Folk song, author unknown)
B. Ives

"Hardly Think I Will"

(Folk song, author unknown)
A. Gray, T. Tiller

"The Devil and the Farmer's Wife"

(Folk song, author unknown)
A. Drake, Ensemble

"Little Mohee"

(Kentucky Mountain Ballad, author unknown)
A. Drake, A. Kaye

Scene 4

The Oregon Trail

First Man: R. Penn. *Second Man*: C. Hart. *Third Man*: J. Racine. *Tough Woman*: E. Love. *Big Bear of a Man*: J. Westerfield.

Oregon Trail

(*by* James Marshall)
Recited by E. Love, Verse Chorus

"Oh Susannah"

(*Music and Lyrics by* Stephen Foster.)
Vocal Ensemble

"Springfield Mountain"

(author unknown)
A. Drake

Scene 5

The South

Watermelon Woman: J. Hall.

"Hammer Ring"
(Work Chant, author unknown)
Spiritual Ensemble

"Watermelon Cry"
(author unknown)
J. Hall

"You Better Mind"
(Spiritual, author unknown)
Spiritual Ensemble

"Didn't My Lord Deliver Daniel"
(Spiritual, author unknown)
Spiritual Ensemble

Scene 6

Mississippi Boat

Johnny: J. McCauley. *Frankie*: A. Kaye. *Frankie's Mother*: E. Love. *Trasker*: R. Penn. *Bonaforte*: B. Ives. *Bartender*: T. Tiller. *Captain*: C. Hart. *Sheriff*: P. Coolidge. *Nellie Bly*: C. Karner. *Specialty Dancers*: D. Gray, I. Hawthorne.

"The Roving Gambler"
(Ballad, author unknown)
J. McCauley, A. Kaye, E. Love

"Louisiana Gals"
(Minstrel song, *Music and Lyrics by* Cool White.)

"Camptown Races"
(*by* Stephen Foster)Vocal Ensemble
Danced by D. Gray, I. Hawthorne, Dancing Ensemble.
(*Staged by* C. Weidman.)

"Frankie and Johnny"
(Folk song, author unknown) (*Staged by* Walter Kerr.)
B. Ives, A. Kaye, J. McCauley, P. Coolidge, C. Karner, T. Tiller

"Polly Wolly Doodle"
(Folk song, author unknown)
Company
(*Staged by* Doris Humphrey.)

ACT 2

Scene 1

Civil War Campfire

First Soldier: B. Ives. *Lieutenant*: P. Coolidge. *Corporal*: T. Tiller

"Captain Jinks"
(Civil War song, author unknown)
Male Ensemble

"Blue Tail Fly"
(Civil War song, author unknown)
B. Ives

"Marching Down This Road"
(Folk song, author unknown)
A. Drake, B. Ives

Scene 2

Railroad Station, Texas

Yard Boss: J. Westerfield. *Mrs. Casey Jones*: B. Osterwald. *Her Daughters*: P. Newman, P. Campbell, D. Baxter. *Old Timer*: M. Halpern. *Jolly Tramp* B. Ives. *Gentleman Tramp*: J. McCauley. *Sad Tramp*: R. Penn. *Fat Tramp*: C. Hart.

"Casey Jones"
B. Osterwald, J. Westerfield, M. Halpern
(*Music by* Eddie Newton. *Lyrics by* T. Lawrence Seibert.)

"Rock Candy Mountain"
(Hobo song, author unknown)
B. Ives

"I Have Been a Good Boy"
(Folk song, author unknown)
J. McCauley

"Wanderin'"
(Hobo song, author unknown)
A. Drake

"Hallelujah, I'm a Bum"
(Hobo song, *words by* Joe Hill)
A. Drake

Jesse James
(*by* William Rose Benet)
Recited by M. Alpern, Verse Chorus
(*Staged by* Charles Weidman.)

Scene 3

City Park

Daisy: A. Kaye. *Jack*: T. Tiller. *Villain*: P. Coolidge. *Policeman*: B. Ives.

"While Strolling Through the Park"
Vocal Ensemble
(*Music and Lyrics by* Ed Haley)

"Bicycle Built for Two"
A. Kaye, T. Tiller
(*Music and Lyrics by* Harry Dacre.)

"Heaven Will Protect the Working Girl"
(from TILLIE'S NIGHTMARE)
A. Kaye, T. Tiller
(*Music by* A. Baldwin Sloane. *Lyrics by* Edgar Smith.)

"Hot Time in the Old Town Tonight"
A. Drake, B. Ives, A. Kaye, T. Tiller
(*Music by* Theodore H. Metz. *Lyrics by* Joe Hayden.)

Scene 4

Five O'Clock Whistle
(*Choreography by* Doris Humphrey.)
Blues Singer: R. Tyler. *Bluecoat*: J. Racine. *Bluejeans*: P. Hamilton. *Bluenose*: P. Coolidge. *Red Light Girl*: E. Mann.

"Trouble, Trouble"
(Blues, author unknown)
R. Tyler

"By the (Beautiful) Sea"
(*Music by* Harry Carroll. *Lyrics by* Harold R. Atteridge.)

"Come, Josephine (in My Flying Machine)"
(*Music by* Fred Fisher. *Lyrics by* Alfred Bryan.)

"Maxixe" (Dance)
Dancing Ensemble
(*Music and Lyrics by* William Tracey and Ray Walker.)

"Funny Bunny Hug"
A. Drake
(*Music and Lyrics by* Dave Ringle, William Tracey and Ray Walker.)

"Temptation Rag"
(*Music and Lyrics by* Louis Weslyn and Henry Lodge.)

"Hey, Mr. Bossman"
R. Tyler
(Jail song, *Music and Lyrics by* Elie Siegmeister.)

"Basement Blues"
R. Tyler, Spiritual Ensemble
(Early blues by W. C. Handy.)
Danced by Dancing Ensemble.

"Some of These Men"
(Blues, author unknown)
R. Tyler, Ensemble

Scene 5

Speakeasy Night Club
(Dance numbers staged by Charles Weidman.)
Tycoon: J. McCauley. *Maxie*: B. Osterwald. *Bartender*: C. Hart. *Trigger*: J. Westerfield. *Baby*: A. Kaye. *Drunk*: J. Racine. *Police Chief*: W. Sharon. *Specialty Dancers*: P. Hamilton, I. Hawthorne.

"I Got Rhythm" (from GIRL CRAZY)
Dancing Ensemble
(*Music by* George Gershwin. *Lyrics by* Ira Gershwin)

"At Sundown"
(*Music and Lyrics by* Walter Donaldson.)

"My Blue Heaven" (from ZIEGFELD FOLLIES OF 1927)
A. Drake
(*Music by* Walter Donaldson. *Lyrics by* Richard Whiting.)

"Yes, Sir, That's My Baby"
B. Osterwald
(*Music by* Walter Donaldson. *Lyrics by* Gus Kahn.)

"The Charleston" (from RUNNIN' WILD)
P. Hamilton, I. Hawthorne, Dancing Ensemble
(*Music and Lyrics by* Cecil Mack and James P. Johnson.)

Scene 6

Aircraft Carrier

Boatswain: B. Ives. *Tom*: T. Tiller. *Dick*: L. Gilbert. *Harry*: G. Cassidy. *George*: S. Green. *Murph*: R. Penn. *Aide*: C. Harris. *Commander*: P. Coolidge.

"Sea Chanty"
B. Ives
"Where"
A. Drake
(*Music by* James Mundy. *Lyrics by* Edward Eager.)

Scene 7
Finale
(*Staged by* Doris Humphrey.)
"More Than These"
A. Drake, Entire Company
(*Music by* James Mundy. *Lyrics by* Edward Eager.)

1944.33 ON THE TOWN

A Musical Comedy in Two Acts, 17 Scenes. Book and lyrics by Betty Comden & Adolph Green. Book based on an idea by Jerome Robbins. Additional lyrics by Leonard Bernstein. Music by Leonard Bernstein. Musical numbers and choreography staged by Jerome Robbins. Production designed by Oliver Smith. Costumes designed by Alvin Colt. Musical director, Max Goberman. Technical director, Peggy Clark. Lighting by Sam Amdurs. Orchestrations by Leonard Bernstein, Hershy Kay, Don Walker, Elliot Jacoby and Ted Royal. Production directed by George Abbott. Produced by Oliver Smith and Paul Feigay. Opened 28 December 1944 at the Adelphi Theatre, moved 5 June 1945 to the 44th Street Theatre, moved 30 July 1945 to the Martin Beck Theatre, and closed 2 February 1946 after 462 performances.

CAST (in order of appearance): (*First*) *Workman*: Marten Sameth. *Second Workman*: Frank Milton. *Third Workman*: Herbert Greene. *Ozzie*: ADOLPH GREEN. *Chip*: CRIS ALEXANDER. *Sailor*: Lyle Clark. *Gabey*: JOHN BATTLES. *Andy*: Frank Westbrook. *Tom*: Richard D'Arcy. *Flossie*: Florence MacMichael. *Flossie's Friend*: Marion Kohler. *Bill Poster*: Larry Bolton. *Little Old Lady*: Maxine Arnold. *Policeman*: Lonny Jackson. *S.Uperman*: Milton Taubman. *Hildy*: NANCY WALKER. *Policeman*: Roger Treat. *Figment*: Remo Bufano. *Claire*: BETTY COMDEN. *Highschool Girl*: Nellie Fisher. *Sailor in Blue*: Richard D'Arcy. *Maude P. Dilly*: Susan Steell. *Ivy*: SONO OSATO. *Lucy Schmeeler*: Alice Pearce. *Pitkin*: ROBERT CHISHOLM. *Master of Ceremonies*: Frank Milton. *Singer*: Frances Cassard. *Waiter*: Herbert Greene. *Spanish Singer*: Jeanne Gordon. *The Great Lover*: RAY HARRISON. *Conductor*: Herbert Greene. *Bimmy*: Robert Lorenz.

Dancers: Barbara Gaye, Lavina Nielsen, Atty Vandenberg, Dorothy McNichols, Cyprienne Gabelman, Jean Handy, Virginia Miller, Nelle Fisher, Royce Wallace, Allyn Ann McLerie, Malka Farber, Aza Bard, Ray Harrison, Frank Neal, Carle Eberle, James Flashe Riley, Ben Piazza, Douglas Matheson, Duncan Noble, Frank Westbrook, John Butler, Richard D'Arcy, Lyle Clark, (Don Weissmuller).

Singers: Frances Cassard, Jeanne Gordon, Lila King, Frances Lager, Marion Kohler, Dorothy Johnson, Regina Owens, Shirley Ann Burton, Frank Milton, Roger Treat, Martin Sameth, Benjamin Trotman, Milton Taubman, Herbert Greene, Lonny Jackson, Melvin Howard, Sam Adams, Robert Lorenz.

Act 1, Scene 1: Brooklyn Navy Yard. *Scene 2*: Subway. *Scene 3*: Street. *Scene 4*: Miss Turnstiles. *Scene 5*: A Taxi. *Scene 6*: Museum. *Scene 7*: Outside the Park. *Scene 8*: Corridor of Carnegie Hall. *Scene 9*: Carnegie Hall (Madame Dilly's Studio). *Scene 10*: Claire's Apartment. *Scene 11*: Hildy's Apartment. *Scene 12*: Times Square.

Act 2, Scene 1: Night Clubs, (a) Diamond Eddie's, (b) Congacabana, (c) Slam-Bang. *Scene 2*: Gabey in the Playground of the Rich. *Scene 3*: The Subway. *Scene 4*: Coney Island. *Scene 5*: Navy Yard.

ACT 1
"I Feel Like I'm Not Out of Bed (Yet)"
M. Sameth
"New York, New York"
J. Battles, C. Alexander, A. Green
"Miss Turnstiles" (Ballet)
Danced by S. Osato, Messrs. Westbrook, Clark, Butler, Noble, Weissmuller, D'Arcy.
"Come Up to My Place"
N. Walker, C. Alexander
"I Get Carried Away"
B. Comden, A. Green, Dance Ensemble
"Lonely Town"
J. Battles, Chorus
Danced by N. Fisher, R. D'Arcy and Ballet.
"Do, Re, Do"
S. Steell, S. Osato, Girls
Danced by S. Osato.

"I Can Cook Too"
N. Walker
"Lucky to Be Me"
J. Battles, Chorus
"Sailors on the Town" (Times Square Ballet)
Danced by Dance Ensemble
Penny Arcade Boy: D. Weissmuller.
ACT 2[13]
"So Long"
Girls
"I'm Blue"
F. Cassard, J. Gordon
"You Got Me"
N. Walker, B. Comden, A. Green, C. Alexander
"I Understand" (Ballet)
Danced by S. Osato, R. Harrison, Entire Dance Ensemble.
"Some Other Time"
B. Comden, A. Green, N. Walker, C. Alexander
"New York, New York" (reprise)
L. Clark, F. Milton, D. Weissmuller, Entire Company

1945.01 A LADY SAYS YES

A Musical in Two Acts, a Prologue and 6 Scenes. Book by Clayton Ashley [Maxwell Maltz]. Music by Fred Spielman and Arthur Gershwin. Lyrics by Stanley Adams. Musical ensembles and dances by Boots McKenna. Ballets by Natalie Kamarova. Scenery by Watson Barratt. Costumes by Lou Eisele. Lighting by William Thomas. Orchestra directed by Ving Merlin. Musical arrangements by Irving Riskin, Paul Shelley, Ralph Lane, Frank Denning and Ving Merlin. Produced by J.J. Shubert in association with Clayton Ashley. Opened 10 January 1945 at the Broadhurst and closed 25 March 1945 after 87 performances.

CAST (1945): *First Nurse*: Helene Le Berthon. *Licetta*: SUE RYAN. *Second Nurse*: Jackson Jordan. *Third Nurse*: Blanche Grady. *Doctor*: Jack Albertson. *Scapino*: BOBBY MORRIS. *Ghisella*: CAROLE LANDIS. *Hilegarde*: JACQUELINE SUSANN. *Lt. Anthony Caufield U.S.N.R.*: ARTHUR MAXWELL. *Dr. Gaspare*: Earl McDonald. *Isabella*: Martha King. *Captain Gordon*: Pittman Corry.

CAST (1545): *Captain Desiri*: Pittman Corry. *Francesca*: Helene Le Berthon. *Rosa*: Blanche Grady. *Carmela*: Jackson Jordan. *Dr. Bartoli*: Jack Albertson. *Isabella*: Martha King. *Scapino*: BOBBY MORRIS. *Anthony Gaspare*: ARTHUR MAXWELL. *Christine*: CHRISTINE AYRES. *Hildegarde*: JACQUELINE SUSANN. *Licetta*: SUE RYAN. *Gaspare*: Earl McDonald. *Killer Pepoli*: Fred Catania. *Second*: Al Klein. *Pantaloon*: Steve Mills. *Ghisella*: CAROLE LANDIS. *Page Boy*: Francelia Schmidt. (*Judges*: Messrs. Allen, Blowe, Aco, Booth, Miller, Wells. *Chambermaids*: Misses Cella, Schmidt, Schmidt, Swanson, Meredith, Lee.)

Ladies of the Ensemble: Maika Beranova, Doris Brent, Jan Brooks, Jane Cleaveland, Betty Greene, Lola Kendrick, Marguerite Kimball, Pat Leslie, Candace Montgomery, Cecilia Nielsen, Shirley Norman, Olivia Russell, Exilona Savre, Fredi Sears, Tiigra, Eileen K. Upton.

Dancers: Burnie Brady, Fena Cella, Madeleine Detry, Sheila Herman, Albertina Horstmann, Jacqueline Jones, Jacqueline Karsh, Carol Keyser, Virginia Lee, Patricia Leith, Jeanne Lewis, Elaine Meredith, Cammy O'Brien, Susan Pearce, Desirée Rockafellow, Francelia Schmidt, Helen Schmidt, Helen Schmidt, Alice Swanson. Lucas Aco, Jack Allen, Peyton Blowe, Corbett Booth, Dick Hayes, Eddie Miller, Joseph O. Paz, Eddie Wells, (Tatiana Grantzeva.)

Prologue: Scene 1: Waiting Room of a Hospital, 1945. *Scene 2*: The Operating Room.

Act 1, Scene 1: A Street in Venice, 1545. *Scene 2*: Ghisella's Bedroom.

Act 2, Scene 1: Street in Venice, 1545. *Scene 2*: Garden of the Emperor of China. *Scene 3*: Hospital Laboratory, 1945. *Scene 4*: A Garden Party, Washington D.C.

PROLOGUE
Opening Chorus—"Viva Vitamins"
Ensemble
A Lesson in Terpsichore
C. Ayres, B. Morris
ACT 1
"You're the Lord of Any Manor"
Ensemble

---

[13]Added during run in Act 2 before "Gabey in the Playground of the Rich": "Subway to Coney Island" (dance sequence)

"Take My Heart With You"
  M. King, A. Maxwell
  Danced by P. Corry, T. Grantzeva, Ensemble.
"Without a Caress"
  C. Landis, Ladies of the Ensemble
"I Wonder Why You Wander"
  S. Ryan, B. Morris, Ensemble
"I Don't Care What They Say About Me"
  A. Maxwell. Ensemble
"A Hop, A Skip, A Jump, A Look"
  Judges
"A Pillow for His Royal Head"
  Chambermaids
  Danced by R. Cunningham.
Dance
  C. Ayres
"Don't Wake Them Up Too Soon"
  C. Landis, Ladies of the Ensemble
Finaletto
  Entire Company

ACT 2
Opening - Carnival Dance
  P. Corry, R. Cunningham, Ensemble
"You're More Than a Name and an Address"
  C. Landis, A. Maxwell
"Brooklyn U.S.A."
  S. Ryan
  (*Music and Lyrics by* Will Morrissey.)
Chinese Ballet
  (*Music by* George Kamaroff.)
  Boy: P. Corry. *Princess:* T. Grantzeva. *Emperor:* L. Aco. *Slave Girl:* V. Lee.
  Executioner: A. Klein. *Gong Girls:* Misses F. Schmidt, H. Schmidt, Swanson.
  Monkeys: Misses Brady, Lewis, Leith. *Commentator:* B. Morris.
"I'm Setting My Cap for a Throne"
  C. Landis
"Leave us let things alone like they was"
  S. Ryan
  (*Music by* Harold Cohen. *Lyrics by* Bud Burton.)
"It's the Girl Everytime, It's the Girl"
  A. Maxwell, Ladies of the Ensemble
"You're More Than a Name and an Address"(reprise)
  C. Landis, A. Maxwell
Finale
  Entire Company

1945.02   ## LA VIE PARISIENNE

A Return Engagement of the Opéra-bouffe in Three Acts, 4 Scenes[14]. New English version by Felix Brentano and Louis Verneuil. (Original French libretto by Henri Meilhac and Ludovic Halévy.) Music by Jacques Offenbach. New musical version by Antal Dorati. Lyrics by Marian Farquhar. Staged by Ralph Herbert. Choreography by Leonide Massine. Costumes designed by Ladislas Czettel. Scenery designed by Richard Rychtarik. Conductor: Antal Dorati. Choral director, Irving Landau. Assistant conductor, Dr. Otto Hertz. Curtain by Marco Montedoro. Produced by Yolanda Mero Irion (The New Opera Company). Opened 12 January 1945 at the New York City Center and closed 10 February 1945 after 37 performances.

CAST (in order of appearance): *Stationmaster:* Philip George. *Policeman:* Roy Ballard. *Newsboy:* Irene E. Sherrock. *Flower Girl:* Loretta Schere. *Comte Raoul de Gardefeu*, a rich nobleman: BRIAN LAWRENCE. *Baron Bobinet*, his friend: EDWARD ROECKER. *Metella*, a famous opera singer: MARION CARTER. *Gontran*, a man about town: Lee Edwards. *Jackson*, trainer of Mr. Hutchinson's race

horses: David Morris. *Evelyn*, Mr. Hutchinson's daughter: LILLIAN ANDERSON. *Mr. Hutchinson*, an American millionaire: ARTHUR NEWMAN. *Premier Danseuses:* Anna Istomina, Elena Kramarr. *Premier Dancer:* James Lyons. *Custom Inspectors:* Nicholas J. Insardi, Sylvan Evans. *Gabrielle*, a modiste: Frances Watkins. *Alphonse*, Gardefeu's butler: Lee Edwards. *Delivery People:* George Bakos, Doris M. Sward, Bonnie Murray, Jeanette Weise.

Chorus: Louise Barnhart, Charlotte Cheney, June Dunn, Patricia Glennon, Rosalind Guest, Jean Mary Lawrence, Millicent Lewis, Bonnie Murray, Flora Previn, Loretta Schere, Irene E. Sherrock, Doris M. Sward, Jeannette Weise, Mary Lou Wallace, George Bakos, Roy Ballard, Salvatore Cosentino, William Peen Bradford, Sylvan Evans, Nicholas J. Insardi, John J. Girt, William G. Schwarz, Barkev Vartanyan, Philip George. *Ballet:* Jeanne Reeves, Jane Kiser, Irene Larson, Aline Dubois, Gloria Morgan, Jane Rattinger, Kirra LeHachova, Deanne Benmore, Elmer Maddox, Julian Mitchell, Stephen Billings, Rex Harrower. *Railroad Employees, Travelers, Tradespeople, Servants, Waiters, Guests at the Cafe Anglais, etc.*

1945.03   ## UP IN CENTRAL PARK

A Musical Comedy in Two Acts, 11 Scenes. Book by Herbert and Dorothy Fields. Music by Sigmund Romberg. Lyrics by Dorothy Fields. Book staged by John Kennedy. Dances by Helen Tamiris[15]. Settings and lighting by Howard Bay. Costumes by Grace Houston and Ernest Schraps. Orchestra directed by Max Meth. Orchestrations by Don Walker. Produced by Michael Todd. Opened 27 January 1945 at the New Century Theatre, moved 11 June 1945 to the Broadway Theatre, and closed 13 April 1946 after 504 performances.

CAST (in the order of appearance): *A Laborer:* Bruce Lord. *Danny O'Cahane:* Walter Burke. *Timothy Moore:* CHARLES IRWIN. *Bessie O'Cahane:* BETTY BRUCE. *Rosie Moore:* MAUREEN CANNON. *John Matthews of the New York Times:* WILBUR EVANS. *Thomas Nast of Harper's Weekly:* Maurice Burke. *William Dutton:* John Quigg. *Andrew Munroe:* Robert Field. *Vincent Peters:* Paul Reed. *Mayor A. Oakey Hall:* Rowan Tudor. *Richard Connolly, Comptroller of the City of New York:* George Lane. *Peter Sweeney, Park Commissioner:* Harry Meehan. *William Marcy Tweed, Grand Sachem of Tammany Hall:* NOAH BEERY, SR. *Butler:* Herman Glazer.*Mildred Wincor:* Lydia Fredericks. *Joe Stewart:* FRED BARRY. *Porter:* Harry Matlock. *Lotta Stevens:* Delma Byron. *Fanny Morris:* Kay Griffith. *Clara Manning:* Martha Burnett. *James Fisk, Jr.:* Watson White. *Daniel:* Daniel Nagrin. *Governess:* Louise Holden. *First Child:* Ann Hermann. *Second Child:* Joan Lally. *Third Child:* Janet Lally. *Fourth Child:* Mary Alice Evans. *Headwaiter:* John Quigg. *Page Boy:* Henry Capri.*Arthur Finch:* Wally Coyle. *Ellen Lawrence:* ELAINE BARRY. *Bicycle Rider:* Stnaley Schimmel. *George Jones:* Guy Standing, Jr. *Bagpipe Players:* Isobel Glasgow, James McFadden, Thomas Lorimer. *Newsboys:* Kenneth Casey, Teddy Casey. *Organ Grinders:*William Nuss, Charles Wood.

Singing Men: Phil Lowry, Charles W. Wood, Jerome Cardinale, Kenneth Renner, Leonard Daye, Stanley Turner, Bruce Lord, Bob Woodward, James Caputo, William Nuss, Rudy Rudisill, Harry Matlock, Sidney Paul, William Sydenstricker. *Dancers:* Daniel Nagrin, Saul Bolasini, George Bockman, Henri Capri, Wally Coyle, Payne Converse, Gregor Taksa.

Singing Girls: Martha Burnett, Beatrice Lind, Mildred Jocelyn, Elyse Jahoda, Lillian Horn, Claire Saunders, Rose Marie Patane, Donna Hughes, Lydia Fredericks, Joan Gladding. *Dancers:* Wana Allison, Joan Dubois, Margaret Gibson, Miriam Kornfield, Rebecca Lee, Ruth Lowe, Peggy Ann Nilsson, Hazel Roy, Evelyn Shaw, Gloria Stevens, Natalie Wynn.

Act 1, Scene 1: A Site in Central Park. June 1870. *Scene 2:* The Park Commissioner's Temporary Office in Central Park. July 1870. *Scene 3:* The Lounge of the Stetson Hotel (formerly McGowan's Pass Tavern), Christmas Eve 1870. *Scene 4:* The Bird House in the Central Park Zoo. Next day. *Scene 5:* The Central Park Gardens. February 1871.

Act 2, Scene 1: The Annual Tammany Hall Outing (July 1871). *Scene 2:* Office of George Jones, Owner of the New York Times, later that day. *Scene 3:* Central Park West. Next day at noon. *Scene 4:* The Stetson Hotel. The same afternoon. *Scene 5:* The Mall in Central Park. 4 July 1872. *Scene 6:* The Bandstand in the Mall. That evening.

ACT 1
Scene 1
"Up from the Gutter"
  B. Bruce
"Up from the Gutter" (reprise)
  B. Bruce, M. Cannon, W. Burke, C. Irwin

---

[14]First presented in New York in English 18 April 1883 at the Bijou Theatre in a version by H. B. Farnie. This adaptation previously presented in New York 5 November 1941 at the 44th Street Theatre for 7 performances, and 10 November 1942 at the Broadway Theatre for 17 performances. For Synopsis of Scenes and Musical Numbers, see original 1941 production.

[15]Musical Numbers: "Carrousel in the Park," "Rip Van Winkle," "The Fireman's Bride" and reprise "The Big Back Yard" and "Finaletto" staged by Miss Tamiris; all other principals' and singing ensemble numbers staged by Lew Kesler.

Dance
B. Bruce, M. Cannon, W. Burke, C. Irwin, Singers, Dancers
"Carrousel in the Park"
M. Cannon
"It Doesn't Cost You Anything to Dream"
B. Bruce, W. Evans
"It Doesn't Cost You Anything to Dream" (reprise)
B. Bruce, M. Cannon, W. Evans

Scene 2
"Boss Tweed"
N. Beery, R. Tudor, G. Lane, H. Meehan, R. Field, P. Reed,
C. Irwin, Men

Scene 3
Opening
Singing Girls, Boys
"When She Walks in the Room"
W. Evans
"Currier and Ives"
M. Cannon, F. Barry
Dance
M. Cannon, F. Barry, D. Nagrin, Dancers
"Close As Pages in a Book"
B. Bruce, W. Evans
"Rip Van Winkle"
B. Bruce, M. Cannon, N. Beery, W. Evans, F. Barry, P. Reed,
Singers, Dancers
Dance
D. Nagrin, Dancers

Scene 4
"Close As Pages in a Book" (reprise)
W. Evans

Scene 5
Opening
Dancers
"The Fireman's Bride"
B. Bruce, M. Cannon, F. Barry, D. Nagrin, Dancers
"The Fireman's Bride" (reprise)
Principals, Singing Girls, Boys

ACT 2
Scene 1
"When the Party Gives a Party"
Singing Girls, Boys, P. Reed, R. Tudor,
R. Field, H. Meehan, C. Irwin, W. Burke
Maypole Dance
The Dancers
Specialty
F. Barry, E. Barry
"The Big Back Yard"
W. Evans, Singing Girls, Boys
"April Snow"
B. Bruce, W. Evans
Finaletto
Dancers, Singing Girls, Boys

Scene 4
"The Birds and the Bees"
B. Bruce, M. Cannon, C. Irwin, W. Burke

Scene 5
Specialty
M. Cannon

Scene 6
"The Big Back Yard" (reprise)
Orchestra
"Close As Pages in a Book" (reprise)
B. Bruce, W. Evans
Finale
Entire Company

1945.04 THE FIREBRAND OF FLORENCE

A Musical in Two Acts, 9 Scenes. Book by Edwin Justus Mayer and Ira Gershwin. Music by Kurt Weill. Lyrics by Ira Gershwin. Based on the play "The Firebrand" by Edwin Justus Mayer. Settings and lighting by Jo Mielziner. Costumes by Raoul Pene du Bois. Choreography and singing ensembles by Catherine Littlefield. Musical director, Maurice Abravanel. All musical arrangements and orchestrations by Kurt Weill. Book directed by John Haggott. Staged by John Murray Anderson. Produced by Max Gordon. Opened 22 March 1945 at the Alvin Theatre and closed 28 April 1945 after 43 performances.

CAST (in order of appearance): *Hangman*: Randolph Symonette. *Tartman*: Don Marsahll. *Souvenir Man*: Bert Freed. *Maffio*: Boyd Heathen. *Arlecchino*: JEAN GUELIS. *Columbina*: Norma Gentner. *Pierot*: Eric Kristen. *Flomina*: Diane Merloff. *Pantalone*: Hubert Bland. *Fiorinetta*: Mary Alice Bingham. *Gelfomino*: Kenneth LeRoy. *Rosania*: Mary Grey. *Dottore*: William Vaux. *Magistrate*: Marion Green. *(Benvenuto) Cellini*: EARL WRIGHTSON. *Captain of the Guard*: Charles Sheldon. *Ottaviano*: Ferdi Hoffman. *Ascanio*: James Dobson. *Emelia*: GLORIA STORY. *Angela*: BEVERLY TYLER. *Marquis*: Paul Best. *Duke*: MELVILLE COOPER. *Page*: Billy Williams. *Duchess*: LOTTE LENYA. *Major-Domo*: Walter Graf. *Clark of the Court*: Alan Noel. *Models*: Yvette Heap, Doris Blake, Marya Iversen, Gedda Petry, Rose Marie Elliot, Perdita Chandler. *Apprentices*: John [Jack] Cassidy, Lynn Alden, Walter Rinner, Frank Stevens.

Soldiers, Promenaders, Courtiers: Misses Suzie Baker, Joan Bartels, Lisa Bert, Angela Carabella, Jean Crone, Gay English, Donna Gardner, Frances Joslyn, Julie Jefferson, Lily Paget, Stephanie Turash, Evelyn Ward; Messrs. John Henson, Frank Stevens, Paul Mario, Eric Sander, Gayne Sullivan, Edwin Alberian, Jimmy Allison, Ray Bessmer, Tony Coffaro, Thomas La Monaco, Ralph Lee, William Sutherland. *Duchess' sedan chair bearers*: George McDonald, Walter Korman.

Act 1, Scene 1: A Public Square in Florence. Time: 1535. *Scene 2*: Cellini's Workshop. *Scene 3*: The City Gates. *Scene 4*: The Garden of the Summer Palace.

Act 2, Scene 1: Cellini's Workshop. *Scene 2*: Outside the City Palace. *Scene 3*: A Loggia in the City Palace. *Scene 4*: The Grand Council Chamber at the Palace. *Scene 5*: The Palace of the King of France.

ACT 1
Scene 1
"Song of the Hangman"
R. Symonette, Two Assistants
"Come to Florence"(Civic Song)
R. Symonette, Chorale Ensemble,
J. Guelis, N. Gentner, Commedia Dell' Arte Dancers
"My Lords and Ladies" (Aria)
E. Wrightson, Apprentices, Choral Ensemble
"There Was Life, There Was Love, There Was Laughter" (Farewell Song)
E. Wrightson, Choral Ensemble

Scene 2
"You're Far Too Near Me"(Love Song)
B. Tyler, E. Wrightson
"Alessandro the Wise"(The Duke's Song)
M. Cooper, Choral Ensemble
"I Am Happy Here" (Finaletto)
M. Cooper, F. Hoffman, E. Wrightson,
B. Tyler, P. Best, G. Story, Choral Ensemble

Scene 3
"Sing Me Not a Ballad" (The Duchess' Song)
L. Lenya, 4 Courtiers

Scene 4
"When the Duchess Is Away" (Madrigal)
C. Sheldon, M. Cooper, G. Story , Choral Ensemble
"There'll Be Life, Love and Laughter" (Love Song)
E. Wrightson, B. Tyler
"I Know Where There's a Cozy Nook" (Trio)
M. Cooper, B. Tyler, E. Wrightson
"The Nighttime Is No Time for Thinking" (Night Music)
G. Story, M. Cooper, B. Tyler, Choral Ensemble
"Dizzily, Busily" (Tarantella)
G. Story, Choral Ensemble, J. Guelis, N. Gentner, Commedia Dell' Arte Dancers
Finale
Entire Company

ACT 2

Scene 1

"You're Far Too Near Me" (reprise)
B. Tyler, E. Wrightson

"The Little Naked Boy" (Cavatina)
B. Tyler, Female Choral Ensemble

"My Dear Benvenuto" (Letter Song)
E. Wrightson, B. Tyler

Scene 2

"Just in Case" (March of the Soldiers of the Duchy)
C. Sheldon, Soldiers of the Duchy

Scene 3

"A Rhyme for Angela" (Ode)
M. Cooper, Poets, Ladies in Waiting

Scene 4

Procession
R. Symonette, Vendors, Apprentices, Models, Clerks

"The World Is Full of Villains" (Chant of Law and Order)
M. Cooper, Clerks, Magistrates, Choral Ensemble

"You Have to Do What You Do Do" (Trial By Music)
E. Wrightson,
M. Cooper, P. Best, L. Lenya, F. Hoffman, M. Green,
Choral Ensemble

"Love Is My Enemy" (Duet)
E. Wrightson, B. Tyler

"The Little Naked Boy" (reprise)
L. Lenya, B. Tyler

Scene 5

"Come to Paris"(Civic Song)
P. Best, Two Ladies of Paris, Choral Ensemble

Finale—

Gigue
The Commedia Dell' Arte Dancers

Sarabande
Choral Ensemble

"There'll Be Life, Love and Laughter"
Entire Ensemble

1945.05

CAROUSEL

A Musical Play in Two Acts, a Prelude and 9 Scenes. Book and lyrics by Oscar Hammerstein II. Based on Ferenc Molnár's play "Liliom" as adapted by Benjamin F. Glazer. Music by Richard Rodgers. Production directed by Rouben Mamoulian. Dances by Agnes de Mille. Settings by Jo Mielziner. Costumes by Miles White. Production supervised by Lawrence Langner and Theresa Helburn. Musical director, Joseph Littau. Ballet piano arrangements by Trude Rittman. Orchestrations by Don Walker. Produced by the Theatre Guild. Opened 19 April 1945 at the Majestic Theatre and closed 24 May 1947 after 890 performances.

CAST (in order of appearance): *Carrie Pipperidge*: JEAN DARLING. *Julie Jordan*: JAN CLAYTON. *Mrs. Mullin*: JEAN CASTO. *Billy Bigelow*: JOHN RAITT. *Bessie*: Mimi Strongin. *Jessie*: Jimsie Somers. *Juggler*: Lew Foldes. *First Policeman*: Robert Byrn. *David Bascombe*: Franklyn Fox. *Nettie Fowler*: CHRISTINE JOHNSON. *June Girl*: Pearl Lang. *Enoch Snow*: ERIC MATTSON. *Jigger Craigin*: Murvyn Vye. *Hannah*: ANNABELLE LYON. *Boatswain*: PETER BIRCH. *Arminy*: Connie Baxter. *Penny*: Marilyn Merkt. *Jennie*: Joan Keenan. *Virginia*: Ginna Moise. *Susan*: Suzanne TaFel. *Jonathan*: Richard H. Gordon. *Second Policeman*: Larry Evers. *Captain*: Blake Ritter. *First Heavenly Friend (Brother Joshua)*: Jay Velie. *Second Heavenly Friend*: Tom McDuffie. *Starkeeper*: Russell Collins. *Louise*: BAMBI LINN. *Carnival Boy*: ROBERT PAGENT. *Enoch Snow, Jr.*: Ralph Linn. *Principal*: Lester Freedman.
   Singers: Martha Carver, Iva Withers, Anne Calvert, Connie Baxter, Glory Wills, Josephine Collins, Marilyn Merkt, Joan Keenan, Ginna Moise, Beatrice Miller, Suzanne TaFel. Verlyn Webb, Joseph Bell, Robert Byrn, Tom Duffey, Blake Ritter, Charles Leighton, Louis Freed, Niel Chirico, Lester Freedman, Richard H. Gordon, John Harrold.
   Dancers: Pearl Lang, Andrea Downing, Margaret Cuddy, Polly Welch, Diane Chadwick, Ruth Miller, Lee Lauterbur, Margaretta De Valera, Lynn Joelson, Sonia Joroff, Elena Salamatova, Marjory Svetlik. Ernest Richman, Tom Avera, Larry Evers, Ralph Linn, Tony Matthews, David Adhar.

Time: 1873-1888

Prelude: An Amusement Park on the New England Coast. May.

Act 1, Scene 1: A tree-lined path along the shore. A few minutes later. *Scene 2*: Nettie Fowler's Spa on the ocean front. June.

Act 2, Scene 1: On an island across the bay. That night. *Scene 2*: Mainland waterfront. An hour later. *Scene 3*: Up there. *Scene 4*: Down here. On a beach. Fifteen years later. *Scene 5*: Outside Julie's cottage. *Scene 6*: Outside a schoolhouse. Same day.

PRELUDE

Waltz Suite: "Carousel" (Carousel Waltz)
Orchestra

ACT 1

Scene 1

"You're a Queer One, Julie Jordan"
J. Darling, J. Clayton

"When I Marry Mister Snow"
J. Darling

"If I Loved You"
J. Raitt, J. Clayton

Scene 2

"June Is Bustin' Out All Over"
C. Johnson, J. Darling, Ensemble

Dance
Dancing Ensemble, led by P. Lang

"When I Marry Mr. Snow"(reprise)
J. Darling, E. Mattson, Girls

"When the Children Are Asleep"
E. Mattson, J. Darling

"Blow High, Blow Low"
M. Vye, J. Raitt, Male Chorus

Hornpipe Dance
Led by A. Lyon, P. Birch

"Soliloquy"
J. Raitt

Finale

ACT 2

Scene 1

"This Was a Real Nice Clambake"
J. Darling, C. Johnson, J. Clayton, E. Mattson, Ensemble

"Geraniums in the Winder"
E. Mattson

"There's Nothin' So Bad for a Woman"
M. Vye, Ensemble

"What's the Use of Wond'rin'"
J. Clayton

Scene 2

"You'll Never Walk Alone"
C. Johnson

Scene 3

"The Highest Judge of All"
J. Raitt

Scene 4

Ballet (Billy Makes a Journey)
Louise: B. Linn. *A Younger Miss Snow*: A. Lyon. *The Brothers and Sisters Snow*: M. de Valera, L. Joelson, S. Joroff, P. Welch, D. Chadwick. *Badly Brought Up Boys*: R. Linn, E. Richman. *A Young Man Like Billy*: R. Pagent. *A Carnival Woman*: P. Lang, *Members of the Carnival Troupe*: R. Pagent, P. Lang, A. Downing, L. Evers, L. Lauterbur, T. Matthews, M. Svetlik, D. Ahdar, M. Cuddy, T. Avera.

Scene 5

"If I Loved You"(reprise)
J. Raitt

Scene 6

"You'll Never Walk Alone"(reprise)
Company

Finale

1945.06

CARMEN JONES

A Return Engagement of the Musical Play in Two Acts, 5 Scenes[16]. Book and lyrics by Oscar Hammerstein II. Based on Meilhac and Halevy's adaptation of Prosper Merimée's "Carmen." Music by Georges Bizet. Staging, lighting and color schemes of entire production by Hassard Short. Libretto directed by Charles Friedman. New orchestral arrangements by Robert Russell Bennett. Settings designed by Howard Bay. Costumes designed by Raoul Pene du Bois. Choreography by Eugene Loring. Choral direction by Robert Shaw. Orchestra conducted by David Mordecai. Produced by Billy Rose. Opened 2 May 1945 at the New York City Center and closed 19 May 1945 after 21 performances.

CAST (in order of appearance): *Corporal Morrell*: Robert Clarke. *Foreman*: George Willis. *Cindy Lou*: ELTON J. WARREN, CARLOTTA FRANZELL. *Sergeant Brown*: JACK CARR. *Joe*: NAPOLEON REED, LaVERN HUTCHERSON. *Carmen*: MURIEL SMITH, INEZ MATTHEWS. *Sally*: Sibol Cain. *T-Bone*: Edward Roche. *Tough Kid*: Carlos Van Putten. *Drummer*: JOE SKINS. *Bartender*: Maithe Marshall. *Waiter*: Edward Christopher. *Myrt*: JUNE HAWKINS. *Frankie*: THERESA MERRITTE. *Rum*: JOHN BUBBLES. *Dink*: FORD BUCK. *Boy*: Bill O'Neil. *Girl*: Erona Harris. *Husky Miller*: GLENN BRYANT. *Soldiers*: Robert Clarke, Randall Steplight, George Willis, Elijah Hodges. *Mr. Higgins*: George Spelvin. *Miss Higgins*: Fredye Marshall. *Photographer*: George Willis. *Card Players*: Urylee Leonardos, Doris Brown, Sibol Cain. *Dancing Girl*: Audrey Vanterpool. *Poncho*: Elijah Hodges. *Dancing Boxers*: Sheldon B. Hoskins, Randolph Sawyer. *Bullet Head*: Lee Allen. *Referee*: Tony Fleming, Jr.

Soldiers, Factory Workers, Socialites: Anne Dixon, Urylee Leonardos, Fredye Marshall, Doris Brown, Ida Johnson, Mattie Washington, Margaret Eley, Elsie Kennedy, Mary Graham, Sibol Cain, Clarice Crawford, Ruth Crumpton, Lee Allen, Robert Clarke, Elijah Hodges, Randall Steplight, Maithe Marshall, Chauncey Reynolds, Edward Roche, Richard de Vaultier, George Willis, Clarence Jones, Andrew J. Taylor, Harold Taylor.

Dancers: Evelyn Pilcher, Edith Ross, Dorothy McDavid, Hedye Brown, Carmencita Romero, Westleen Foster, Posie Flowers, Audrey Graham, Erona Harris, Mabel Hart, Rhoda Johnson, Vera McNichols, Edith Hurd, Randolph Sawyer, Charles Williams, Daniel Lloyd, Walter Smith, Edward Christopher, Ivan Gittens, Gilbert Rivera, Tony Fleming, Clifton Gray, Sheldon Hoskins, Smalls Boykins, Joseph Noble, Bill O'Neil.

Children: Lawrence Drayton, Jr., Earl Drayton, Gilbert Irvis, Albert Smith, Carlos Van Patten, James Holeman, Melba Evelyn Hawkins, Roger Smith.

1945.07

BLUE HOLIDAY

A Variety Show in Two Acts, 14 Scenes. Music and lyrics by Al Moritz. Staged by Monroe (Moe) B. Hack, (Jed Harris). Production designed and supervised by Perry Watkins. Choral direction by Hall Johnson. Costumes by Kasia. Orchestra under the direction of Billy Butler. "Fiji Island" and "Voodoo in Haiti" numbers created and staged by Katherine Dunham. Produced by Irvin Shapiro and Doris Cole. Opened 21 May 1945 at the Belasco Theatre and closed 26 May 1945 after 8 peformances.

CAST: ETHEL WATERS, JOSH WHITE, WILLIE BRYANT, TIMMIE ROGERS, MARY LOU WILLIAMS, Josephine Premice, Lillian Fitzgerald, The Chocolateers, The Three Poms, Evelyn Ellis, Mildred Smith.

THE KATHERINE DUNHAM DANCERS: Leaders: Lavinia Williams, Talley Beatty, Florence Moriles, Roxie Foster. *Dancers*: Wilbur Bradley, Teppy Fletcher, Jesse Hawkins, Victoria Henderson, Richard James, Eartha Kitt, Alvaleta Hudson, Albert Popwell, Eugene Robinson, Joe Smith, J. DeWitt Spencer, John Weaver, Enid Williams.

THE HALL JOHNSON CHOIR: Laura Adamson, James Armstrong, Olive Ball, Mable Bergen, Maudiva Brown, William Davis, Bessie Guy, Lola Hayes, Willie Mays, Ruthena Matson, Violet McDowell, Massie Patterson, Bertha Powell, George Rayston, Jessie Williams, Robert Woodland.

ACT 1

Scene 1

"The Star Spangled Banner"
  Hall Johnson Choir

"Blue Holiday"
  L. Fitzgerald
  (*Music and Lyrics by* Al Moritz.)

Scene 2

Willie Bryant (Master of Ceremonies/Comedian)

Scene 3

The Three Poms (Dancers)

Scene 4

"Voodoo in Haiti"
  J. Premice, Katherine Dunham Dancers
Chant
  (*Choreography by* Katherine Dunham.)
  Hall Johnson Choir

Scene 5

Timmie Rogers (Comedian)

Scene 6

Miss Ethel Waters in scenes from the play "Mamba's Daughters" by Dubose and Dorothy Heyward, courtesy of Guthrie McClintic.
  Hagar: E.Waters. *Gilly Bluton*: W. Bryant. *Mamba*: E. Ellis. *Lissa*: M. Smith.

"Sleeptime Lullaby"
  (E. Waters)
  (*Music and Lyrics by* Al Moritz.)

Scene 7.

Josh White:
"Hard Time Blues"
  (*Music and Lyrics by* Josh White and Warren Cuney.)
"Evil-Hearted Man"
  (*Traditional Song, arranged by* Josh White.)
"The House I Live In"
  (*Music and Lyrics by* Lewis Allan and Earl Robinson.)
"(I'm Gonna Move to the) Outskirts of Town"
  (*Music and Lyrics by* William Weldon and Andy Razaf.)
"One Meat Ball"
  (*Music by* Lou Singer. *Lyrics by* Hy Zaret.)

Scene 8

"Free and Equal Blues"
  (J. White, T. Rogers, Hall Johnson Choir)
  (*Music by* Earl Robinson. *Lyrics by* E.Y. Harburg.)

ACT 2

Scene 1

"Fiji Island"
  Katherine Dunham Dancers
  Featured: L. Williams (R. Foster, alt.), T. Beatty.
  (*Music by* Herbert Kingsley. *Choreography by* Katherine Dunham.)

Scene 2

Mary Lou Williams
  (Boogie Woogie Piano Medley of her own compositions, "Limehouse Blues," and a Duke Ellington Medley)

Scene 3

Josephine Premice: Haitian Songs and Dances:
  "Philomene, The Lazy Girl," "Angelico," "Nibo—Carnival"

Scene 4

The Hall Johnson Choir
  (*Choral Arrangements by* Hall Johnson.)
"I Got a Mule," (Traditional Song)
"Fare Ye Well" (Traditional Spiritual)
"Saint Louis Blues"
  (*Music and Lyrics by* W.C. Handy.)

Scene 5

The Chocolateers (Dancers)

Scene 6

Miss Ethel Waters with Marian Roberts at the piano.
["Stormy Weather" (from COTTON CLUB PARADE, 23rd edition)
  (*Music by* Harold Arlen. *Lyrics by* Ted Koehler.)
"Happiness Is Just a Thing Called Joe" (from CABIN IN THE SKY film)
  (*Music by* Harold Arlen. *Lyrics by* E. Y. Harburg.)]

---

[16]First presented in New York 2 December 1943 at the Broadway Theatre for 503 performances. For Synopsis of Scenes and Musical Numbers see original 1943 production.

MEMPHIS BOUND

1945.08

A Musical Comedy in Two Acts, Ten Scenes. Book by Albert Barker and Sally Benson (with gratitude to W.S. Gilbert and Sir Arthur Sullivan[17]). Music and lyrics by Don Walker and Clay Warnick. Production directed by Robert Ross. Dances by Al White, Jr. Scenery designed and lighted by George Jenkins. Costumes designed by Lucinda Ballard. Conductor, Charles Sanford. Orchestrations by Don Walker. Vocal arrangements by Clay Warnick. Assistant to Mr. Ross, Eva Jessye. Orchestrations to Mr. Robinson's dances by Ted Royal. Additional vocal arrangements by Rene deKnight. Production under the personal supervision of Vinton Freedley. Produced by John Wildberg[18]. Opened 24 May 1945 at the Broadway Theatre, moved 11 June 1945 to the Belasco Theatre, and closed 23 June 1945 after 36 performances.

CAST (in order of their appearance): *Hector*: William C. Smith. *Melissa Carter* (Aunt Mel): EDITH WILSON. *Chloe*: ANN ROBINSON. *Roy Baggott*: BILLY DANIELS. *Mrs. Paradise*: ADA BROWN. *Lily Valentine*: SHEILA GUYS. *Penny Paradise*: IDA JAMES. *Henny Paradise*: THELMA CARPENTER. *Mr. Finch*: FRANK WILSON. *Winfield Carter* (Windy): AVON LONG. *Pilot Meriwether* (Pops): BILL ROBINSON. *Timmy*: Timothy Grace. *Sheriff McDaniels*: Oscar Plante. *Eulalia*: Joy Merrimore. *Sarabelle*: Harriet Jackson. *Bill*: Charles Welch. *Gabriel*: William Dillard. *Cherubs*: Georgia Ann Timmons, Marliene Strong. *DELTA RHYTHM BOYS*: Traverse Crawford, Rene DeKnight, Carl Jones, Kelsey Pharr, Lee Gaines.

Members of the Calliboga Social Drama Center: Lee Eberle, Ethel White, Joy Merrimore, Eulabel Riley, Nell Plante, Marion Bruce, Harriet Jackson, Mary Lewis, Muriel Watkins. John Diggs, Leslie Gray, William C. Smith, Oscar Plante, Roy White, William Archer, David Perry, Rodesta Timmons, Lulling Williams, Charles Welch, Theodore Brown, William Dillard.

Dancing Girls: Sophia Miller, Louise Patterson, Lula Hill, Bethesta Williamson, Laure Catherell, Mitzi Coleman, Clarice Cook, Eleanor Brown, Mimi Williams, Jacqueline Petty, Jackie Lewis, Joan Cooper, Charlotte Saunders, Libby Parker. *Dancing Boys*: Prince Hall, William Chapman, Toni Thompson, Morton Brown, Wilson Young, Abe Moore, Charles Keith, John Smith, Andre Drew.

Children: Georgia Ann Timmons, Jeanne Petti, June Fussell, Marliene Strong, Richard Reed, Neils LeRoy, Timothy Grace, James Worden.

Place: Near Calliboga, Tennessee. *Time*: The Present.

Act 1, Scene 1: Deck of the *Calliboga Queen*. *Scene 2*: A Street. *Scene 3*: A Cell in Calliboga Jail. *Scene 4*: "H.M.S. Pinafore" aboard the *Calliboga Queen*.

Act 2, Scene 1: The Village Square. *Scene 2*: The Street. *Scene 3*: The Cell. That Night. *Scene 4*: The Trial. *Scene 5*: The Cell. Next morning. *Scene 6*: The Street. *Scene 7*: "Pops" Meriwether in the rest of "Pinafore."

ACT 1

"Big Old River"
    Ensemble
"Stand Around the Band"
    A. Long, Delta Rhythm Boys, Ensemble
"Old Love and Brand New Love"
    B. Daniels, A. Long, S. Guys
"Growing Pains"
    B. Robinson
"We Sail the Ocean Blue"
    Sailors
"I'm Called Little Buttercup"
    A. Brown, Delta Rhythm Boys
"A Maiden Fair to See"
    B. Daniels, Sailors
"I Am the Captain of the Pinafore"
    A. Long, Sailors
"Sorry Her Lot"
    S. Guys, I. James, T. Carpenter
"Over the Bright Blue Sea"
    Ensemble
"I Am the Monarch of the Sea"
    B. Robinson, Ensemble
"The Ruler of the Queen's Navee"
    B. Robinson

"The Nightingale, the Moon and I"
    B. Daniels
Finale
    Ensemble

ACT 2

"The Gilbert & Sullivan Blues"
    A. Robinson
"Farewell, My Own"
    B. Robinson, B. Daniels, the Beer Garden Four
"Fair Moon"
    A. Long, Delta Rhythm Boys, Ensemble
"Love or Reason"
    S. Guys, I. James, T. Carpenter
"Things Are Seldom What They Seem"
    B. Robinson, A. Long
"Trial By Jury"
    B. Robinson, A. Long, E. Wilson, F. Wilson, W. Dillard, Ensemble
"The Nightingale, the Moon and I" (reprise)
    B. Daniels, S. Guys, Ensemble
"Old Love and Brand New Love" (reprise)
    Delta Rhythm Boys, Ensemble
"A-Many Years Ago"
    A. Brown & Delta Rhythm Boys
"Ring the Merry Belles"
    B. Robinson
Finale
    Entire Company

HOLLYWOOD PINAFORE,
or the Lad Who Loved a Salary

1945.09

A Musical Comedy in Two Acts. Based on W. S. Gilbert and Arthur Sullivan's "H.M.S. Pinafore." Book and lyrics revised by George S. Kaufman, with deepest apologies to William S. Gilbert. Music by Arthur Sullivan[19]. Directed by George S. Kaufman. Production supervised by Arnold Saint Subber. Ballet by Antony Tudor. Settings and lighting by Jo Mielziner. Ensemble dances by Douglas Coudy. Modern costumes by Kathryn Kuhn; period costumes by Mary Percy Schenck. Musical conductor: George Hirst. Ballet orchestrated by Hans Spialek. Additional orchestrations by Stephen Jones. Choral assistant, Silas Engum. Produced by Max Gordon in association with Meyer Davis. Opened 31 May 1945 at the Alvin Theatre and closed 14 July 1945 after 52 performances.

CAST: *Joseph W. Porter*, head of Pinafore Pictures: VICTOR MOORE. *Mike Corcoran*, a director: GEORGE RASELY. *Ralph Rackstraw*, a writer: GILBERT RUSSELL. *Dick Live-Eye*, an agent: WILLIAM GAXTON. *Brenda Blossom*, a star: ANNAMARY DICKEY. *Louhedda Hopsons*, a columnist: SHIRLEY BOOTH. *Bob Beckett*, a press agent: RUSS BROWN. *Miss Hebe*, Mr. Porter's secretary: MARY WICKES. *Miss Gloria Mundi*: Diana Corday. *Miss Beverly Wilshire*: Pamela Randell. *Little Miss Peggy*: Ella Mayer. *Doorman*: Dan De Paolo. *Secretaries*: Jackson Jordan, Eleanor Prentiss, Drucilla Strain. *Guard*: Ernest Taylor. *Actors, Actresses, Assistant Directors, Cameramen, Technicians, etc.*

Singers: Sally Billings, Florence George, Jane Hansen, Lucy Hillary, Josephine Lambert, Margaret McKenna, Candace Montgomery, Jeanne North, Annette Sorell, Mary Williams, Dean Campbell, Harold Cole, Jack Collins, Charles Dubin, Silas Engum, Howard Hoffman, Barry Kent, James Mate, John Mathews, Larry Stuart, Jeffrey Warren.

Dancers: Eleanor Boleyn, Helene Constantine, Barbara (Babs) Heath, Virginia Meyer, Ann Newland, Mary Alice Bingham, John Butler, Ronny Chetwood, Stanley Herbert, Shaun O'Brien, Jack Purcell, Regis Powers.

Scene: The Pinafore Pictures Studio, Hollywood.

Act 1: Morning. *Act 2*: Night.

ACT 1[20]

"Simple Movie Folk"
    D. Corday, P. Randell, E. Mayer, Girls, Ensemble

---

[17]Drawn freely from TRIAL BY JURY and H.M.S. PINAFORE.
[18]Mr. Wildberg and everyone connected with "Memphis Bound" gratefully acknowledge the invaluable aid which Harry Wagstaff Gribble has contributed to every phase of this production.

[19]HOLLYWOOD PINAFORE has brazenly borrowed a single number from "The Pirates of Penzance." Other music by Arthur Sullivan is also heard during Mr. Tudor's Ballet.
[20]Musical Numbers not listed in program; detail secured from production manuscript.

"Little Butter-Up"
    S. Booth
"An Agent's Lot Is Not a Happy One"
    W. Gaxton
"A Maiden Often Seen"
    G. Russell, P. Randell, Ensemble
"I'm a Big Director at Pinafore"
    G. Rasely, Ensemble
"Here on the Lot"
    A. Dickey
"Joe Porter's Car is Seen"
    Male Chorus, Ensemble
"I Am the Monarch of the Joint"
    V. Moore, M. Wickes, Ensemble
"When I Was a Lad"
    V. Moore, Ensemble
"A Writer Fills the Lowest Niche"
    R. Brown, G. Russell, E. Taylor, Ensemble
"Never Mind the Why and Wherefore"
    W. Gaxton, Ensemble
"Refrain, Audacious Scribe"/"Proud Lady, Have Your Way"
    G. Russell, A. Dickey, M. Wickes, Ensemble
"Can I Survive This Overbearing?" (Finale Act 1)
    W. Gaxton, A. Dickey, M. Wickes, G. Russell, R. Brown, Ensemble

ACT 2
    "Fair Moon"
        G. Rasely

"I Am the Monarch of the Joint" (reprise)
    V. Moore, M. Wickes, Ensemble
Ballet Interlude: "Success Story"
    V. Essen
    Other Little Maids: B. Heath, H. Constantine. *Talent Scout*: R. Powers.
    Her True Love: R. Chetwood. *Two More Boys*: S. O'Brien, J. Purcell. *Armand,*
    the Movie Hero: J. Butler. *Director*: S. Herbert. *Studio Assistants*: E. Boleyn,
    A. Newland, V. Butler.
"Hollywood's a Funny Place"
    S. Booth, V. Moore
"To Go Upon the Stage"
    A. Dickey
"He Is a Movie Man"
    V. Moore, W. Gaxton, Ensemble
"The Merry Maiden and the Jerk"
    W. Gaxton, V. Moore
"Carefully on Tiptoe Stealing"
    A. Dickey, G. Russell, W. Gaxton, G. Rasely, Ensemble
"Pretty Daughter of Mine"
    G. Rasely, G. Russell, M. Wickes, V. Moore, W. Gaxton, Ensemble
"Farewell, My Own"
    G. Russell, A. Dickey, M. Wickes, V. Moore, S. Booth, R. Brown,
    Ensemble
"This Town I Now Must Shake"
    S. Booth, Ensemble
Finale Act 2
    Entire Company

1945–1946 SEASON

Ethel Merman and Bert Freed in ANNIE GET YOUR GUN (Photo: Vandamm Studio)
Billy Rose Theatre Collection, New York Public Library for the Performing Arts

1945–1946 SEASON

CONCERT VARIETIES

An Entertainment in Two Acts, 13 Scenes. (Production assembled by Billy Rose.) Orchestra conducted by Pembroke Davenport. Technical director: Carlton Winckler. Produced by Billy Rose. Opened 1 June 1945 at the Ziegfeld Theatre and closed 28 June 1945 after 36 performances.

CAST: KATHERINE DUNHAM and COMPANY, ZERO MOSTEL, DEEMS TAYLOR, JEROME ROBBINS and COMPANY, ROSARIO and ANTONIO, IMOGENE COCA, EDDIE MAYEHOFF, AMMONS, JOHNSON & SIDNEY CATLETT, SALICI PUPPETS, NESTOR CHAYRES.
Dunham Dancers: Vanoye Aikens, Talley Beatty, Eddy Clay, La Verne French, Tommy Gomez, Lenwood Morris, Roger Ohardieno, Lucille Ellis, Syvilla Fort, Dolores Harper, Richardena Jackson, Ora Leak, Gloria Mitchell. *Drummers*: (Cándido) Vicenty, (La Rosa) Estrada, (Julio) Mendez.
Robbins Dancers: Janet Reed, John Kriza, Michael Kidd, Muriel Bentley, Rozsika Sabo (courtesy of Ballet Theatre), Bettina Rosay, Erik Kristen. *Piano*: Tibor Krizma.

ACT 1

Deems Taylor explains

Scene 1

Salici Puppets

Scene 2

Eddie Mayehoff (Comedian)

Scene 3

'Caprice Espagnol' (Spanish Dance)
Rosario and Antonio
(*Music by* Nikolai Rimsky-Korsakov.)

Scene 4

Nestor Chayres (Lyric tenor from Mexico)

Scene 5

'Dansa Ritual del Fuego'(Fire Dance)
Rosario and Antonio
(*Music by* Manuel de Falla.)
This is a dance taken from the Spanish ballet, 'El Amor Brujo,' the ritual fire dance. The Evil Spirit sets out to dominate the Fire Spirit; a struggle ensues, and, of course, the Fire Spirit conquers and kills the Evil Spirit.

Scene 6

Imogene Coca (Comedienne)

Scene 7

'Interplay'
(*Ballet by* Jerome Robbins. *Music by* Morton Gould. *Decor and Costumes by* Carl Kent.)
"Interplay" is a ballet based on dance games. There is the interplay of the dancers among themselves. There is the interplay of classic ballet steps and the contemporary spirit with which they are danced. There is the interplay of the dancers and the orchestra, and finally there is, in the orchestra itself, the interplay of the piano and the other instruments. On stage and in the orchestra there is a play between the classic and jazz elements. The music is by Morton Gould, "American Concertette," a short piano concerto, premiered in April, 1943, by José Iturbi and the N.B.C. Symphony. It is in four movements marked 1-with drive and vigor, 2-gavotte, 3-blues, 4-very fast.
I. Free Play
J. Robbins, Company
II. Horse Play
J. Robbins
III. By Play
J. Reed, J. Kriza
IV. Team Play
Full Company

ACT 2

Scene 8

Katherine Dunham and Her Dance Company
Callate (Brazil)
(*Music by* Cándido Vicenty.)
K. Dunham, Vicenty, V. Aikens, R. Ohardieno, E. Clay

Rhumba (Mexico)
(*Music by* Harl MacDonald.)
K. Dunham, T. Beatty, Ensemble
Tropics (Martinique)
(*Music by* Paquita Anderson.)
K. Dunham, R. Ohardieno, Entire Company

Scene 9

'Dance Divertissement'
I. Coca, W. Archibald

Scene 10

Albert Ammons, Pete Johnson and Sidney Catlett (Duo-piano, percussion)

Scene 11

Zero Mostel (Comedy, impressions)

Scene 12

'Canasteros de Triana' (Flirtation Dance)
Rosario and Antonio
(*Music by* Curritos-Matos-Villacanas.)
A fire, a gypsy camp, boy woos girl and succeeds—an old Spanish custom. Silvio Masciarelli, musical director. G. Villarino, guitarist.

Scene 13

Finale

MARINKA

A Romantic Musical in Two Acts, 12 Scenes. Book by George Marion Jr. and Karl Farkas[1]. Music by Emmerich Kalman. Lyrics by George Marion Jr. Staged by Hassard Short. Dances and ballet by Albertina Rasch. Settings by Howard Bay. Costumes by Mary Grant. Orchestra under the direction of Ray Kavanaugh. Orchestrations by Hans Spialek. Produced by Jules J. Leventhal and Harry Howard. Opened 18 July 1945 at the Winter Garden, moved 1 October 1945 to the Ethel Barrymore Theatre, and closed 8 December 1945 after 165 performances.

CAST: *Nadine*: Ruth Webb. *Countess von Diefendorfer*: Elaine Walther. *Bratfisch*: ROMO VINCENT. *Crown Prince Rudolph*: HARRY STOCKWELL. *Count Lobkowitz*: TAYLOR HOLMES. *Naval Lieutenant*: Noel Gordon. *Count Hoyos*: Paul Campbell. *Francis*: Leonard Elliott. *Tilly*: Ronnie Cunningham. *Marinka*: JOAN ROBERTS. *Madame Sacher*: ETHEL LEVEY. *Countess Landovska*: LUBA MALINA. *Waiter*: Jack Leslie. *Lietenant Baltatky*: Bob Douglas. *Emperor Franz Josef*: REINHOLD SCHUNZEL. *Countess Huebner*: Adrienne Gray. *Sergeant Negulegul*: Michael Barrett. *Lieutenant Palafy*: Jack Gansert.
Ladies of the Ensemble: Suzie Baker, Ethel Madsen, Jane Riehl, Gloria A. Tromara, Elline Walther, Donna Gardner, Lois Eastman. *Gentlemen of the Ensemble*: Jimmy Allison, Paul Campbell, John [Jack] Cassidy, Richard Clemens, Edwin Craig, Noel Gordon, Lynn Alden, Vincent Henry.
Dancing Girls: Tessie Carrano, Muriel Bruenig, Aline DuBois, Phoebe Engel, Marie Fazzin, Albertina Horstmann, Ann Hutchinson, Jeanne Lewis, Thea Lind, Franca Baldwin, Judy Sargent, Nathalie Kelpouska, Alla Shishkina, Aura Vainio, Betty Williams, Carol Keyser, Anna Scarpova. *Dancing Boys*: Stanley Zompakos, Robert Armstrong, Lee Michael, Edmund Howland, Ted Lund, George Tomal, John Begg, Francisco Xavier.

Act 1, Scene 1: An Open Air Movie Theatre in Connecticut. A June evening, the present. *Scene 2*: Gardens of the Imperial Palace of Schoenbrunn. Time: A Summer Night in 1888. *Scene 3*: Bratfisch's Cab. *Scene 4*: Living-room of the Lodge of Mayerling. *Scene 5*: A Street in Vienna. *Scene 6*: Red Room of the Sache Restaurant. *Scene 7*: The Gardens at Schoenbrunn.

Act 2, Scene 1: The Austro-Hungarian Border, 1888. *Scene 2*: Budapest. A Corner of the Parade Ground. *Scene 3*: Gardens of the Imperial Palace of Schoenbrunn. *Scene 4*: Mayerling. Time: A January Evening, 1889. *Scene 5*: An Open Air Movie Theatre in Connecticut. A June evening, the present.

ACT 1[2]

Scene 1

"One Touch of Vienna"
R. Vincent, Girls

---

[1]Inspired by Claude Anet's book "Mayerling."
[2]Added to Act 1, Scene 4 during run:
"I Admit" (Rudolph's Narrative)
H.Stockwell

901

Scene 2
    Ballet
        R. Cunningham, Ballet Girls
    "The Cab Song"
        R. Vincent, R. Cunningham, L Vincent
    "My Prince Came Riding"
        J. Roberts, Debutantes
    "If I Never Waltz Again"
        J. Roberts, H. Stockwell
Scene 3
    "The Cab Song" (reprise)
        R. Cunningham, E. Walther, Debutantes
Scene 4
    "Turn on the Charm"
        R. Vincent
    "One Last Love Song"
        J. Roberts, H. Stockwell
Scene 5
    "Old Man Danube"
        R. Vincent, Officers
Scene 6
    Hungarian Dance
        R. Cunningham, J. Gansert, Dancers
    "Czardas"
        L. Malina, Officers
Scene 7
    "Sigh by Night"
        J. Roberts, H. Stockwell
Scene 8
    "One Last Love Song" (reprise)
        J. Roberts, H. Stockwell
Scene 9
    "Paletas" (Dance)
        J. Gansert, Dancers
ACT 2
Scene 2
    "Treat a Woman Like a Drum"
        J. Roberts, R. Cunningham, R. Vincent, L. Elliott, J. Gansert
    Dance
        Ballerinas, Sailors
    "Shah"
        L. Malina
    "Young Man Danube"
        L. Elliott, R. Cunningham, J. Gansert, Ensemble
Scene 3
    "Turn on the Charm" (reprise)
        J. Roberts, H. Stockwell
Scene 4
    "Sigh by Night" (reprise)
        J. Roberts, H. Stockwell
Scene 5
    Finale—"One Last Love Song"
        J. Roberts, H. Stockwell, Entire Company

1945.12 MR. STRAUSS GOES TO BOSTON

A Romantic Comedy with Music in Two Acts, 9 Scenes. Book by Leonard L. Levinson. Based on an original story by Alfred Gruenwald and Geza Herczeg[3]. Music by Robert Stolz. Lyrics by Robert Sour. Choreography by George Balanchine. Production designed by Stewart Chaney. Costumes by Walter Florell. Conductor, Robert Stolz. Orchestrations by George Lessner. Production staged and directed by Felix Brentano. Produced by Felix Brentano. Opened 6 September 1945 at the New Century Theatre and closed 16 September after 12 performances.

---

[3]Any similarity between "Mr. Strauss Goes to Boston" and actual history is coincidental.

CAST (in order of appearance): *Dapper Dan Pepper*: RALPH DUMKE. *Policeman McGillicuddy*: Brian O'Mara. *Inspector Gogarty*: Don Fiser. *First Reporter*: Dennis Dengate. *Second Reporter*: Larry Gilbert. *Third Reporter*: Joseph Monte. *Pepi*: FLORENCE SUNDSTROM. *Bellhop*: Frank Finn. *Johann Strauss*: GEORGE RIGAUD. *Elmo Tilt*: EDWARD J. LAMBERT. *Hotel Manager*: Lee Edwards. *Brook Whitney*: VIRGINIA MacWATTERS. *A Waiter*: Paul Mario. *Mrs. Dexter*: Lailye Tenen. *Mrs. Blakely*: Rose Perfect. *Mr. Whitney*: Sydney Grant. *Mrs. Taylor*: Arlene Dahl. *Mrs. Hastings*: Selma Felton. *Mrs. Iverson*: Marie Barova. *Mrs. Byrd*: Cecile Sherman. *Butler*: John Oliver. *Tom Avery*: JAY MARTIN. *A Photographer*: John Harrold. *Earl*: Brian O'Mara. *Hetty Strauss*: RUTH MATTESON. *Man in Overalls*: Paul Mario. *Aide to President*: Lee Edwards. *President Grant*: Norman Roland. *Solo Dancers*: HAROLD LANG, Babs Heath, Margit DeKova.

Ladies and Gentlemen of Singing Ensemble: Nancy Baskerville, Jeanne Beauvais, Arlene Carmen, Doris Elliott, Alma Fernandez, Lucy Hillary, Olga Pavlova, Mia Stenn, Mary Lou Wallace, Dennis Dengate, Lee Edwards, Frank Finn, Larry Gilbert, John Harrold, Philip Harrison, Paul Mario, Joseph Monte, John Oliver, Brian O'Mara.

Corps de Ballet: Mary Burr, Jacqueline Cezanne, Sylvia de Penso, Andrea Downing, Helen Gallagher, Arlene Garver, Mary Grey, Fiala Mraz, Virginia Poe, Stephen Billings, Paul Olson, William Sarazen, Tilden Shanks, Terry Townes.

Act 1, Scene 1: The Lobby of the Grand Palace Hotel. New York City, 16 June 1872. *Scene 2*: Corridor in the Hotel. Immediately after. *Scene 3*: Sitting-room of Strauss' Suite. A few minutes later. *Scene 4*: Off to Boston. *Scene 5*: Drawing-room of the Whitney Home in Boston. Two weeks later. *Scene 6*: Reception in honor of Johann Strauss.

Act 2, Scene 1: Bedroom of Johann Strauss at the Governor Winthrop House. A few hours later. *Scene 2*: The Balcony of the Governor Winthrop House. The next morning. *Scene 3*: Along the Charles River. Evening of the Fourth of July.

ACT 1
Scene 1
    "Can Anyone See"
        Ensemble
Scene 2
    Radetzky March-Fantasie[4]
        Dancing Girls
    "For the Sake of Art"
        R. Dumke, Reporters, Girls
Scene 3
    Laughing Waltz
        V. MacWatters
Scene 4
    "Mr. Strauss Goes to Boston"
        R. Dumke, F. Sundstrom, E. J. Lambert
Scene 5
    "Down With Sin"
        R. Dumke, E.J. Lambert, Boston Ladies
    "Who Knows?"
        V. MacWatters
Scene 6
    "Midnight Waltz"[5]
        Danced by B. Heath, H. Lang, Corps de Ballet
    "Into the Night"
        J. Martin
    Coloratura Waltz[6]
        V. MacWatters
    "The Gossip Polka"[7]
        Ensemble
        Danced by B. Heath, H. Lang, Corps de Ballet.
ACT 2
Scene 1
    Dream Scene
        Ensemble
    "Going Back Home"
        R. Matteson

---

[4]Musical arrangements of Johann Strauss' melodies by Robert Stolz and George Lessner.

[5]Musical arrangements of Johann Strauss' melodies by Robert Stolz and George Lessner.

[6]Musical arrangements of Johann Strauss' melodies by Robert Stolz and George Lessner.

[7]Musical arrangements of Johann Strauss' melodies by Robert Stolz and George Lessner.

Scene 2

"You Never Know What Comes Next"
F. Sundstrom

"Mr. Strauss Goes to Boston" (reprise)
G. Rigaud, R. Matteson, R. Dumke

"You Never Know What Comes Next" (reprise)
Danced by H. Lang.

Scene 3

"Into the Night" (reprise)
J. Martin, Ensemble
Ballet danced by H. Lang, M. DeKova, Corps de Ballet.

"What's a Girl Supposed to Do"
V. MacWatters, J. Martin

"The Grand and Glorious Fourth"
Ensemble
Ballet danced by H. Lang, H. Gallagher, Corps de Ballet.

"Who Knows?" (reprise)
V. MacWatters

Waltz Finale[8]
Entire Company

1945.13

CARIB SONG

A Musical Play of the West Indies in Two Acts, 13 Scenes. Book by William Archibald[9]. Music by Baldwin Bergersen. Lyrics by William Archibald. Book directed by Mary Hunter. Choreography by Katherine Dunham. Production staged by Katherine Dunham and Mary Hunter. Scenery designed and lighted by Jo Mielziner. Costumes designed by Motley. Musical direction, Pembroke Davenport. Orchestrations by Ted Royal. Produced by George Stanton. Opened 27 September 1945 at the Adelphi Theatre and closed 27 October 1945 after 36 performances.

CAST (in order of appearance): *The Singer*: HARRIET JACKSON. *The Friends*: Eulabel Riley, Mary Lewis. *The Fat Woman*: Mable Sanford Lewis. *The Tall Woman*: Mercedes Gilbert. *The Husband*: WILLIAM FRANKLIN. *The Fisherman*: AVON LONG. *The Woman*: KATHERINE DUNHAM. *The Fishwoman*: Elsie Benjamin. *The Madras Seller*: Byron Cuttler. *The Shango Priest*: La Rosa Estrada. *The Boy Possessed by a Snake*: Tommy Gomez. *The Leaders of the Shango Dancers*: Vanoye Aikens, Lucille Ellis.

The Village Friends: Lucille Ellis, Roxie Foster, Lawaune Ingram, Richardena Jackson, Eartha Kitt, Ora Leak, Mary Lewis, Gloria Mitchell, Eulabel Riley, Priscilla Stevens, Enid Williams, James Alexander, Eddy Clay, Norman Coker, Byron Cutler, John Diggs, Jesse Hawkins, Julio Mendez, Lenwood Morris, Eugene Lee Robinson, William C. Smith, Charles Welch.

Katherine Dunham Dancers: Lucille Ellis, Lenwood Morris, Tommy Gomez, Vanoye Aikens, Lawaune Ingram. Richardena Jackson, Gloria Mitchell, Ora Leak, Eddy CLay, Byron Cuttler, James Alexander, Roxie Foster, Eugene Robinson, Eartha Kitt, Jesse Hawkins, Enid Williams. *Native Drummers*: La Rosa Estrada, Julio Mendez, Norman Coker.

Singing Ensemble (under the direction of Baldwin Bergersen): Mary Lewis, Eulabel Riley, Priscilla Stevens, John Diggs, William C. Smith, Charles Welch.

The entire action takes place in a West Indian Village.

Act 1, Scene 1: The Wake. *Scene 2*: Early Morning by the River. *Scene 3*: The New House. *Scene 4*: The Corn Sorting. *Scene 5*: The Lie. *Scene 6*: The Road to the Shango. *Scene 7*: The Shango.

Act 2, Three months later. *Scene 1*: Market. Dry Season. *Scene 2*: "Today I Is So Happy" *Scene 3*: The Forest at Night. *Scene 4*: "Go to Church Sunday" *Scene 5*: "Wash Clothes Monday" *Scene 6*: The Rain Comes.

---

[8]Musical arrangements of Johann Strauss' melodies by Robert Stolz and George Lessner.

[9]*Author's note on the West Indies*: The lives of West Indian natives often find expression in dances that, while being uninhibited, have certain ritual foundations. For instance, a wake in the West Indies is held in order to entertain the spirit of the departed rather than to mourn for it. At the Shango, a ritual which is based on West African religious practices in combination with Catholic elements (the word Shango meaning Saint John the Baptist), the people often go into a trance. A particular "spirit" is invited which on "possessing" the body governs its movements. The "spirits" of vodoun are numerous; one of the most important is Damballa, one of whose signs is the snake.

ACT 1

Scene 1

"Go Sit by the Body" (Chant)
The Company

Legba
C. Welch, Company

"This Woman"
W. Franklin, W. C. Smith, C. Welch, Company

Scene 2

"Water Movin' Slow"
W. Franklin

Scene 3

"Basket, Make a Basket"
K. Dunham
Dancers: L. Ellis, L. Ingram, R. Jackson, T. Gomez, L. Morris, V. Aikens. *Singers*: E. Kitt, M. Lewis, E. Riley, P. Stevens, J. Diggs, J. Hawkins, W. C. Smith, C. Welch.

Scene 4

Congo Paillette
K. Dunham, Company

"Woman Is a Rascal"
A. Long, W.C. Smith, C. Welch

Scene 5

"A Girl She Can't Remain"
K. Dunham, L. Estrada, B. Cuttler, J. Alexander

Scene 7

Shango Ritual
L. Estrada, T. Gomez, K. Dunham, A. Long, V. Aikens, Company

ACT 2

Scene 1

Market Song
M. Lewis, Company

"Sleep, Baby, Don't Cry"
H. Jackson

Things Remembered
K. Dunham, L. Ellis, R. Jackson, O. Leak,
L. Estrada, L. Ingram, V. Aikens, G. Mitchell, L. Morris

Scene 2

"Today I Is So Happy"
W. Franklin

"Can't Stop the Sea"
J. Diggs

Scene 3

Forest at Night
K. Dunham, L. Morris, V. Aikens, J. Alexander, B. Cuttler, T. Gomez

Scene 4

"You Know, Oh Lord"
W. Franklin

"Go to Church Sunday"
Company

Scene 5

"Go Down to the River"
P. Stevens, E. Riley, M. Lewis, M. S. Lewis

Washerwomen Dance
L. Ingram, L. Ellis, R. Foster, R. Jackson, E. Kitt, O. Leak,
G. Mitchell, E. Williams

"Oh, Lonely One"
K. Dunham, H. Jackson

1945.14

POLONAISE

A Musical in Two Acts, 9 Scenes. Book by Gottfried Reinhardt and Athony Veiller. Music by Frederic Chopin. (Musical) Adaptations and original numbers by Bronislaw Kaper. Lyrics by John LaTouche. Choreography by David Lichine. Book directed by Stella Adler. Settings by Howard Bay. Costumes by Mary Grant. Orchestrations by Don Walker. Musical director, Max Goberman. Choral director, Irving Landau. Produced by W. Horace Schmidlapp, in association with Harry Bloomfield. Opened 6 October 1945 at the Alvin Theatre, moved 3 December 1945 to the Adelphi Theatre, and closed 12 January 1946 after 113 performances.

CAST: *Captain Adams*: John V. Schmidt. *General Washington*: Josef Draper. *Colonel Hale*: Martin Lewis. *General Thaddeus Kosciusko*: JAN KIEPURA. *Sergeant Wacek Zapolski*: CURT BOIS. *Private Tompkins*: Sidney Lawson. *Private Skinner*: Arthur Lincoln. *Private Motherwell*: Martin Cooke. *Marisha*: Marta Eggerth. *Wladek*: Rem Olstead. *Tecla*: Tatiana Riabouchinska. *General Boris Volfoff*: HARRY BANNISTER. *Count Casimir Zaleski*: Josef Draper. *Peniatowski*: Lewis Appleton. *Kollontaj*: Andrew Thurston. *Potocki*: Gary Green. *Countess Luwika Zaleski*: ROSE INGHRAM. *Blacksmith*: Martin Cooke. *Butcher*: Larry Beck. *Priest*: Larry O'Dell. *Pianist*: Zadel Skolovsky. *King Stanislaus Augustus*: James MacColl. *Count Gronski*: Walter Appler. *Princess Margarita*: Candy Jones. *Princess Lydia*: Leta Mauree. *Princess Lania*: Sherry Shadburne. *Princess Anna*: Martha Emma Watson. *Peasant Girl*: Betty Durrence. *"Exchange of Lovers"—The Princess*: Ruth Riekman. *The Prince*: Shawn O'Brien. *The Highwayman*: Sergei Ismaeloff. *The Page*: Amalia Valez. *The Ballerinas*: Jean Harris, Virginia Barnes, Adele Bodroghy, Joan Collenette.

Singers: Eileen Ayers, Joan Bartels, Marjorie Chandler, Jean Cumming, Ann Dennis, Leigh Hoffmna, Mary McQuade, Mary Woodley, Barbara Barlow, Jeanette Weiss. Lewis Appleton, Oakley Bailey, Larry Beck, Oliver Boersma, Martin Cooke, Gary Green, Raynor C. Howell, Arthur Lincoln, Sidney Lawson, Laryy O'Dell, John Schmidt, Otto Simanek, Andrew Thurston, Michael Vertzilous, Tony Montell.

Dancers: Virginia Barnes, May Block, Adele Bodroghy, Jane Collenette, Betty Durrence, Jean Harris, Pamela Kastner, Alicia Krug, Dorothy Love, Ruthanna [Ruth] Mitchell, Ruth Riekman, Dorothy Scott, Amalia Velez. Hubert Bland, Jay Dowd, Jerry Florio, Sergei Ismaeloff, Martin Kraft, Tangi Nicelli, Shaun O'Brien, Martin Schneider, Marc West.

Act 1, Scene 1: The Ramparts, West Point, 1783. *Scene 2*: The Waterfront — New York. *Scene 3*: A Hayfield near Cracow, Poland. Some time later. *Scene 4*: The Road to the Manor House.

Act 2, Scene 1: The Royal Palace, Warsaw. A few weeks later. *Scene 2*: A Street in Warsaw. *Scene 3*: The Battle of Macijowice. *Scene 4*: Volkoff's Headquarters. After the Battle. *Scene 5*: The Waterfront — Philadelphia. Some time later.

ACT 1
Scene 3

"Autumn Bells"
   M. Eggerth, R. Olmsted, Peasants
"Laughing Bells"
   T. Riabouchinska, C Bois
   (*Music by* Bronislaw Kaper.)
"O Heart of My Country" (from Chopin's Nocturne in E Flat)
   J. Kiepura
"Stranger"
   M. Eggerth
   (*Music by* Bronislaw Kaper.)
Scene 5
"Au Revoir, Soldier"
   R. Inghram
   (*Music by* Bronislaw Kaper.)
"Meadow-lark" (from Chopin's Mazurka in B Flat)
   J. Kiepura, Peasants
"Mazurka" (Various themes of Chopin)
   T. Riabouchinska, R. Olmsted, Peasants
"Hay, Hay, Hay"
   C. Bois
Scene 7
"Just for Tonight" (from Chopin's Etude in E)
   J. Kiepura, M. Eggerth
"Moonlight Soliloquy" (Chopin's Nocturne in F Sharp Major)
   T. Riabouchinska
Finale (from the Polonaise in A Flat and the Revolutionary Etude by Chopin)

ACT 2[10]
Scene 1
"Gavotte" (from Chopin's Variations on a French Air)
   Courtiers
"Exchange of Lovers" (Various Themes of Chopin)
   Corps de Ballet
"Polonaise" (Chopin's Polonaise in A Flat)
   Z. Skolovsky

---

[10]Added to Act 2, Scene 1 during the run at the Alvin.
"An Imperial Conference"
   J. MacColl, W. Appler, L. Mauree

Scene 2
"Now I Know Your Face By Heart" (from Chopin's Waltz in D Flat)
   J. Kiepura, M. Eggerth
"The Next Time I Care"
   R. Inghram
   (*Music by* Bronislaw Kaper.)
Scene 3
"Tecla's Mood" (Various themes of Chopin)
   T. Riabouchinska, Girls
"Motherhood"
   C. Bois, C. Jones, L. Mauree, S. Shadburne, M.E. Watson
   (*Music by* Bronislaw Kaper.)
"Wait for Tomorrow" (various themes of Chopin)
   J. Kiepura
Scene 4
"I Wonder as I Wander"
   M. Eggerth
   (from Waltz in A Minor and Fantasie Impromptu by Chopin)
Scene 5
Battle Ballet (Four Chopin Etudes)
   Corps de Ballet
   Spirit of the Flag: T. Riabouchinska. *Spirit of the Soldier*: R. Olmsted. *Bugler*: S. Ismaeloff. *Drummer*: H. Bland.
Scene 6
"Just for Tonight" (reprise)
   J. Kiepura, M. Eggerth
Scene 7
"Wait for Tomorrow" (reprise)
   J. Kiepura
Finale

1945.15

THE GYPSY BARON

A Return Engagement of the Revival of the Comic Opera in Three Acts and a Prologue[11]. (Original German libretto by Ignaz Schnitzer based on the story "Saffi" by Mór Jókai. First American adaptation by Sydney Rosenfeld.) Music by Johann Strauss. Libretto revised and adapted into English by George Mead. Settings by H. A. Condell. Staged by Leopold Sachse. Choreographed by Carl Randall. Conductor, Laszlo Halasz. Musical director, Julius Rudel. Produced by the New York City Opera. Opened 6 October 1945 at the New York City Center and closed 10 November 1945 after 4 performances in repertory.

CAST: *Barinkay*: GORDON DILWORTH. *Czipra*: ENID SZANTHO. *Saffi*: BRENDA LEWIS. *Zsupan*: GEORGE LIPTON. *Arsena*: HELEN GEORGE. *Ottokar*: JOHN HARROLD, NATHANIEL SPRINZEMA (alt.). *Carnero*: HERBERT NORVILLE. *Count Homonnay*: GRANT GARNELL. *Ensemble*: New York City Opera Chorus.

1945.16

THE RED MILL

A Revival of the Musical in Two Acts, 3 Scenes[12]. Music by Victor Herbert. Original book and lyrics by Henry Blossom. (Book revisions by Milton Lazarus.) Additional lyrics by Forman Brown. Stage direction by Billy Gilbert. Dances staged by Aida Broadbent. Scenic and lighting supervision by Adrian Awan. Scene sketches by Arthur Lonergan, Richard Jackson. Costumes by Walter Israel. New orchestrations and dance arrangements by Edward Ward. Orchestra under the direction of Edward Ward. Vocal numbers staged by George Cunningham. Choral direction by William Tryoler. Produced by Paula Stone and Hunt Stromberg, Jr.[13] Opened 16 October 1945 at the Ziegfeld Theatre, moved 24 December 1945 to the 46th Street Theatre, and closed 18 January 1947 after 531 performances.

---

[11]This production previously presented 14 November 1944 at the New York City Center for 11 performances. For Synopsis of Scenes and Musical Numbers, see previous 1944 engagement. Original English language version first presented in New York 15 February 1886 at the Casino Theatre for 86 performances.
[12]First produced in New York 24 September 1906 at the Knickerbocker Theatre for 274 performances.
[13]Miss Stone and Mr. Stromberg express grateful appreciation to Edwin Lester for his invaluable assistance in the preparation of this production.

CAST (in order of appearance): *Town Crier*: BILLY GRIFFITH. *Willem*: HAL PRICE. *Franz*: GEORGE MEADER. *Tina*: DOROTHY STONE. *Bill-Poster*: Tom Halligan. *Flora*: Hope O'Brady. *Lena*: Lois Potter. *Dora*: Mardi Bayne. *The Burgomaster*: FRANK JAQUET. *A Sailor*: Thomas Spengler. *Juliana*: LORNA BYRON. *Con Kidder*: MICHAEL O'SHEA. *Kid Conner*: EDDIE FOY, JR. *Gretchen*: ANN ANDRE. *Hendrik Van Damn*: ROBERT HUGHES. *Gaston*: CHARLES COLLINS. *Pennyfeather*: BILLY GRIFFITH. *Madame La Fleur*: ODETTE MYRTIL. *Georgette*: Phyllis Bateman. *Suzette*: Nony Franklin. *Fleurette*: Kathleen Ellis. *Nanette*: Jacqueline Ellis. *Lucette*: Patricia Gardner. *Yvette*: Joan Johnston. *The Governor*: Edward Dew.

Singing Ensemble: Mardi Bayne, Jane Bender, Phyllis Bateman, Betty Bursher, Charlotte Christman, Kathleen Ellis, Jacqueline Ellis, Betty Fadden, Nony Franklin, Betty Galavan, Patricia Gardner, Carol Johnston, Joan Johnston, Hope O'Brady, Lois Potter, Patsy Tingstrom. Lloyd R. Bell, Gordon Boelzner, Pete Civello, Kenneth Davies, Tom Decker, Jack Garland, Elton Howard, Leland Ledford, Wally Mohr, Tom Spengler, Calvin Swihart, Michael King.

Ballet Ensemble: Dorothy Bauer, Elaine Corbett, Gloria DeWard, June Fitzpatrick, Irene Hall, Georgia Reed, Doris Walcott, Patricia Sims, Mildred Ann Mauldin, Donna Birock, Barbara Penland, Barbara Hallstone, Jackie Lindberg, Jacqueline Dupont, Shirley Glickman. *Ballet Soloists*: Mildred Ann Mauldin, Dorothy Bauer, Pat Sims, Tom Halligan, Elton Howard.

Time: About 1900. *Place*: Katwyk-ann-Zee, Holland.

Act 1: The Inn at the Red Mill. (Lonergan.)

Act 2, Scene 1: A Neighborhood Street. *Scene 2*: Home of the Burgomaster. (Jackson.)

ACT 1

Opening Chorus
 Village Girls, Boys, Artists
"Mignonette"
 D. Stone, Boys, Dancing Girls
"Whistle It"
 M. O'Shea, E. Foy Jr., D. Stone
"Isle of Our Dreams"
 A. Andre, R. Hughes
The Dancing Lesson
 C. Collins, Ballet Ensemble
"In Old New York"
 M. O'Shea, E. Foy Jr., Dancers
"When You're Pretty and the World Is Fair"
 O. Myrtil, B. Griffith, Ensemble
"Moonbeams" and Finale
 A. Andre, R. Hughes, Ballet Ensemble, D. Stone, C. Collins, F. Jaquet, Ensemble

ACT 2

Opening:
"Why the Silence?"
 Boys and Girls
"Legend of the Mill"
 L. Byron, Ensemble, Ballet Ensemble
 Pas de Deux: Princess: D. Bauer. *Sailor*: E. Howard. *King*: T. Halligan.
"Every Day Is Ladies' Day With Me"
 E. Dew, Male Chorus, P. Bateman, N. Franklin, K. Ellis, J. Ellis, P. Gardner, J. Johnston
"I Want You to Marry Me"
 A. Andre, R. Hughes
"Al Fresco"
 D. Stone, C. Collins
"Because You're You"
 E. Dew, L. Byron, Dancing Boys and Girls
"Romanza?"
 E. Foy Jr., O. Myrtil
"Wedding Bells"
 Guests, Bridesmaids, E. Dew, O. Myrtil, L. Byron, F. Jaquet, A. Andre, R. Hughes
Finale
 Entire Company

1945.17 THE GIRL FROM NANTUCKET

A Musical Comedy in Two Acts, a Prologue and 14 Scenes. Book by Paul Stanford and Harold Sherman. Based on a story by Fred Thompson and

Bernie Giler. Music by Jacques Belasco. Lyrics by Kay Twomey. Additional music and lyrics by Hughie Prince and Dick Rogers. Additional dialogue by Hy Cooper. Book directed by Edward Clarke Lilley. Production staged by Henry Adrian. Choreography by Val Raset. Settings and lighting by Albert Johnson. Costumes by Lou Eisele. Production assistant, Harry Howell. Musical director, Harry Levant. Vocal and orchestral arrangements by Jacques Belasco. Additional arrangements by Ted Royal. Produced by Henry Adrian. Opened 8 November 1945 at the Adelphi Theatre and closed 17 November 1945 after 12 performances.

CAST (in order of appearance): *Michael Nicolson*: BOB KENNEDY. *Betty Ellis*: ADELAIDE BISHOP (eves.), PAT McCLARNEY (mats.) *Tom Andrews*: GEORGE L. HEADLEY. *Ann Ellis*: MARION NILES. *Dodey Ellis*: JANE KEAN. *Keziah Getchel*: HELEN RAYMOND. *Judge Peleg*: John Robb. *Captain Matthew Ellis*: BILLY LYNN. *Dick Oliver*: JACK DURANT. *Enrico Nicoletti*: Richard Clemens. *The Corporation: the Four Buccaneers*: Paul Shiers, John Panter, Don Cortez, Joseph Cunneff. *Roy, Caleb and several other fellows*: JOHNNY EAGER. *Mary*: Connie Sheldon. *Dance Specialists*: KIM and KATHY GAYNES. *Solo Dancer*: TOM LADD. (Featured *Dancers*: RAPPS and TAPPS.)

The Nantucket Guides: Claire Weidener, Deanne Benmore, Marilyn Pendry, Mary Bernice Brady, Madeline Detry, Gloria Evans, Lee Joyce, Zelda Allen, Fran Celia, Kay Popp, Louise Harris, Arleen Frank, Sylvia Mehler. *The Vacationists*: Bettina Theyer, Ruth Vrana, Jeanne North, Geraldine Willier, Harriet Pegors, Linda Hayes. *The Townfolk*: Jean D'Arcy, Doris Claire, Rita Rallis, Lee Dennis, Vicky Raaf, Jerry Daily, Sherry Stevens, Francis Pruitt, Temple Texas, Norma Hetzler, Panette Piper, Francis Kiernan, Allan Waine, Mischa Pompianov, Randolf Hughes. *The Fishermen*: Erno Czako, Gerald Scima, Robert Vaden, Neal Towner, Jack Riley, T.C. Jones, Terry Dawson.

Prologue: An Apartment House in New York City.

Act 1, Scene 1: Office of the Nantucket Steamship Company. *Scene 2*: Nantucket Pier. *Scene 3*: Mike and Dick's Apartment in New York City. *Scene 4*: Nantucket Pier. *Scene 5*: Whalers' Bar. *Scene 6*: Outside the Nantucket Museum, a week later. *Scene 7*: Inside the Museum. The following night. *Scene 8*: Old Nantucket.

Act 2, Scene 1: Nantucket Pier. The following day. *Scene 2*: Mike and Chick's Bungalow in Nantucket. *Scene 3*: Keziah's Beach. Her Home. *Scene 4*: Outside the Museum. *Scene 5*: Inside the Museum. *Scene 6*: Nantucket Square.

ACT 1

"I Want to See More of You"
 A. Bishop, B. Kennedy
"Take the Steamer to Nantucket"
 Vacationists, Guides
 Dance Specialty by Kim Gaynes, Kathy Gaynes, M. Niles.
"What's He Like?"
 A. Bishop, J. Kean, Girls
"What's a Sailor Got?"
 B. Lynn, Ensemble
"Magnificent Failure"
 J. Durant
 (*Music and Lyrics by* Hughie Prince and Dick Rogers; arrangements by Sam Medoff.)
"Hurray for Nicoletti"
 J. Durant, Entire Ensemble
 (*Lyrics by* Kay Twomey and Burt Milton.)
 Dance Specialty by M. Niles, Rapps and Tapps.
"When a Hick Chick Meets a City Slicker"
 J. Kean, J. Durant
 (*Lyrics by* Burt Milton.)
"Your Fatal Fascination"
 A. Bishop, B. Kennedy, Kim Gaynes, Kathy Gaynes, M. Niles, Ensemble
"Let's Do and Say We Didn't"
 J. Kean, Girls
 (*Music and Lyrics by* Hughie Prince and Dick Rogers; arrangements by Sam Medoff.)
"Nothing Matters"
 C. Sheldon, Girls
 Dance Specialty by Rapps and Tapps.
"Sons of the Sea"
 G. L. Headley, Fishermen
Whalers' Ballet—A Page from Old Nantucket.
 Monologue written by Mary Carroll, spoken by G. L. Headley. *The Sea*: Kathy Gaynes. *The Whale*: Kim Gaynes. *Tom, the Fisherman*: T. Ladd.

ACT 2

"Isn't It a Lovely View?"
 A. Bishop, Vacationists

"Isn't It a Lovely View?"(reprise)
  A. Bishop
"From Morning Till Night"
  A. Bishop. B. Kennedy
"I Love That Boy"
  J. Kean, J. Durant
"From Morning Till Night"(reprise)
  B. Kennedy
"Hammock in the Blue"
  A. Bishop, B. Kenned, Ensemble
"Boukra Fill Mish Mish"
  B. Lynn, T. Ladd, Ensemble
Dance Specialty
  J. Durant, B. Lynn
Reprise
Finale

1945.18 ARE YOU WITH IT?

A Musical Comedy in Two Acts, 19 Scenes. Book by Sam Perrin and George Balzer Adapted from the novel "Slightly Perfect" by George Malcolm-Smith. Music by Harry Revel. Lyrics by Arnold B. Horwitt. Musical numbers staged by Jack Donohue. Directed by Edward Reveaux. Settings designed and lighted by George Jenkins. Costumes by Willa Kim from sketches by Raoul Pene du Bois. Musical director, Will Irwin. Vocalizations supervised and arranged by H. Clay Warnick. Orchestrations by Joe Glover, Hans Spialek, Ted Royal, Don Walker, Walter Paul. Produced by Richard Kollmar and James W. Gardiner. Opened 10 November 1945 at the New Century Theatre, moved 30 April 1946 to the Sam S. Shubert Theatre, and closed 29 June 1946 after 267 performances.

CAST (in order of their speaking): *Marge Keller*: Jane Dulo. *Mr. Bixby*: Sydney Boyd. *Mr. Mapleton*: Johnny Stearns. *Wilbur Haskins*: JOHNNY DOWNS. *Vivian Reilly*: JOAN ROBERTS. *Policeman*: Duke McHale. *"Goldie"*: LEW PARKER. *Bartender*: LOU WILLS, JR. *Carter*: Lew Eckles. *Snake Charmer's Daughter*: Jeanne Coyne. *Cicero*: BUNNY BRIGGS. *Cleo*: JUNE RICHMOND. *A Barker*: Johnny Stearns. *Balloon Seller*: Mildred Jocelyn. *Bunny La Fleur*: DOLORES GRAY. *Sally Swivelhips*: Diane Adrian. *Georgetta*: BUSTER SHAVER. *Olive*: OLIVE (SHAVER). *George*: GEORGE (SHAVER). *Richard*: RICHARD (SHAVER). *Strong Man*: Ray Arnett. *Aerialist*: Kathryn Lee. *Office Boy*: Hal Hunter. (*Quartette*:) *First Musician*: Lou Hurst. *Second Musician*: David Lambert. *Third Musician*: Jerry Duane. *Fourth Musician*: Jerry Packer.

Girls: Dorothy Bennett, Vivian Cook, Jeanne Coyne, Dorothy Drew, Cece Eames, Suzanne Graves, Beth Green, Penny Holt, Gretchen Houser, Jo Ann Kavanaugh, Charlotte Lorraine, Pat Marlowe, June Morrison, Kay Popp, Renee Russell, Bette Valentine, Doris York. *Boys*: Jimmy Allen, Ray Arnett, Bill Julian, John Laverty, John Martin, Don Miraglia, Tommy Morton, George Thornton, Eddie Vale.

Act 1, Scene 1: A Boarding House in Hartford, Conn. at 7:45 on a summer morning. *Scene 2*: Bushnell Park, Hartford, a moment later. *Scene 3*: Office of the Nutmeg Insurance Company. *Scene 4*: Bushnell Park, a few minutes later. *Scene 5*: Joe's Bar-Room. *Scene 6*: Behind the tent of the "Plantation Minstrels." *Scene 7*: The Midway — "Acres of Fun." *Scene 8*: Behind the Minstrel Tent. *Scene 9*: Two Train Compartments. *Scene 10*: Behind the Tent. *Scene 11*: The Midway.

Act 2, Scene 1: Office of the Nutmeg Insurance Company. *Scene 2*: Behind the Tent. *Scene 3*: "Acres of Fun" in Worcester. *Scene 4*: The Tent. *Scene 5*: The Train. *Scene 6*: Carter's Office on the Train. *Scene 7*: Inside the Midway Frolics Tent. *Scene 8*: The Midway.

ACT 1
  "Five More Minutes in Bed"
    J. Dulo, Ensemble
    Dance: K. Lee.
  "Nutmeg Insurance"
    J. Downs, J. Dulo, S. Boyd, J. Stearns, Ensemble
  "Slightly Perfect"
    J. Roberts, J. Downs
  "When a Good Man Takes to Drink"
    J. Roberts, D. McHale
  "When a Good Man Takes to Drink"(reprise)
    J. Roberts, D. McHale, L. Wills, Jr.
  "Poor Little Me"
    J. Richmond
  "Are You With It?"
    D. Gray, Quartette, Ensemble

"This Is My Beloved"
    J. Roberts, J. Downs
  "Slightly Slightly"
    O. Shaver, G. Shaver, R. Shaver
    Dance: B. Shaver, O. Shaver.
  "Vivian's Reverie"
    K. Lee, R. Arnett, Circus Performers
    (*Music adapted by* Will Irwin from themes by Harry Revel.)
ACT 2
  "Send Us Back to the Kitchen"
    J. Dulo, Girls
    Dance: H. Hunter.
  "Here I Go Again"
    J. Roberts, Quartette
  "You Gotta Keep Saying 'No'"
    D. Gray
  "Just Beyond the Rainbow"
    J. Richmond, Ensemble
    Dance: B. Briggs.
  "In Our Cozy Little Cottage of Tomorrow"
    D. Gray, L. Parker
  Finale
    Entire Company

1945.19 THE DAY BEFORE SPRING

A Musical in Two Acts, 9 Scenes. Book and lyrics by Alan Jay Lerner. Music by Frederick Loewe. Book directed by Edward Padula. Orchestrations by Harold Byrns. Vocal arrangements by Frederick Loewe. Sets by Robert Davison. Costumes by Miles White. Ballets and musical ensembles by Anthony Tudor. Production staged by John C. Wilson. Musical director, Maurice Abravanel. Produced by John C. Wilson. Opened 22 November 1945 at the National Theatre and closed 14 April 1946 after 165 performances.

CAST (in order of appearance): *Katherine Townshend*: IRENE MANNING. *Peter Townshend*: JOHN ARCHER. *Bill Tompkins*: Bert Freed. *May Tompkins*: Lucille Benson. *Alex Maitland*: BILL JOHNSON. *Marie*: Karol Loraine. *Lucille*: Bette Anderson. *Leonore*: Lucille Floetman. *Marjorie*: Estelle Loring. *Susan*: Arlouine Goodjohn. *Anne*: Betty Jean Smythe. *Gerald Barker*: TOM HELMORE. *Joe McDonald*: Don Mayo. *Harry Scott*: Robert Field. *Eddie Warren*: Dwight Marfield. *Christopher Randolph*: PATRICIA MARSHALL. *Katherine* (in the book): MARY ELLEN MOYLAN. *Alex* (in the book): HUGH LAING. *Voltaire*: Paul Best. *Plato*: Ralph Glover. *Freud*: Hermann Leopoldi.

Vocal Ensemble: Nina Dean, Arlouine Goodjohn, Karol Loraine, Estelle Loring, Bette Anderson, Lucille Floetman, Shirley Dean, Betty Jean Smythe. Ernest Taylor, Jeffrey Warren, Alfred Sukey, Tommy Matthews, Robert Lussier, Paul Mario, Kenny McCord, Bernard Tunis.

Dancers: Janice M. Cioffi, Mattlyn Gevurtz, Isabel Mirrow, June Morris, Eva Soltesz, Eleanor Treiber, Sonja Tyven. Bruce Cartwright, Ronny Chetwood, Erik Kristen, Jack Miller, Frank Westbrook, Richard Astor.

The action of the play takes place within twenty-four hours on a day—and night—in June.

Act 1, Scene 1: The Townshends' apartment, New York City. *Scene 2*: Harrison. *Scene 3*: A path near Harrison. *Scene 4*: Rotunda of Harrison Library. *Scene 5*: A corridor. *Scene 6*: Harrison.

Act 2, Scene 1: A Harrison resident house. *Scene 2*: The roadside. *Scene 3*: Harrison.

ACT 1
Scene 1
  "The Day Before Spring"
    I. Manning
  The Invitation
    B. Freed
Scene 2
  "God's Green World"
    B. Johnson, Ensemble
    A girl: E. Treiber. *A boy*: R. Chetwood. *Another boy*: J. Miller.
  "You Haven't Changed at All"
    I. Manning, B. Johnson
Scene 3
  "My Love Is a Married Man"
    P. Marshall

Scene 4

"The Day Before Spring" (reprise)
I. Manning, B. Johnson

Ballet of the book according to Alex
Katherine: M. E. Moylan. *Alex*: H. Laing.

Scene 5

Katherine receives advice
H. Leopoldi, R. Glover, P. Best

Scene 6

Finale
I. Manning, Ensemble

ACT 2

Scene 1

"Friends to the End"
B. Freed, D. Mayo, R. Field, T. Helmore, Alumni

"A Jug of Wine"
P. Marshall

The Book
Narrated by J. Archer

"I Love You This Morning"
I. Manning, B. Johnson

"The Day Before Spring" (reprise)
B. Johnson, I. Manning

"Where's My Wife?"
J. Archer, Ensemble

Scene 2

"This Is My Holiday"
I. Manning

Ballet of the book according to Gerald
Katherine: M. E. Moylan. *Alex*: H. Laing.

Scene 3

Finale
Principals, Company

1945.20 BILLION DOLLAR BABY

A Musical Play of the Terrific Twenties in Two Acts, 22 Scenes. Book and lyrics by Betty Comden and Adolph Green. Music by Morton Gould. Production directed by George Abbott. Choreography and musical numbers staged by Jerome Robbins. Settings designed by Oliver Smith. Costumes designed by Irene Sharaff. Lighting by George Schaff. Musical director, Max Goberman. Orchestrations by Morton Gould, Philip J. Lang, Allan Small. Musical assistants, George Davis, Trudy Rittman. Assistant to Jerome Robbins, Anita Alvarez. Technical director, Peggy Clark. Technical advisor on marathons, June Havoc. Produced by Paul Feigay and Oliver Smith. Opened 21 December 1945 at the Alvin Theatre and closed 29 June 1946 after 220 performances.

CAST (in order of appearance): *Ma Jones*: EMILY ROSS. *Pa Jones*: William David. *Esme*: SHIRLEY VAN. *Neighbors*: Maria Harriton, Eddie Hodge, Howard Lenters, Douglas Deane, Helen Gallagher, Beverly Hosier. *Champ Watson*: DANNY DANIELS. *Photographer*: Anthony Reed. *Reporter*: Alan Gilbert. *Maribelle Jones*: JOAN McCRACKEN. *Newsboys*: Stefan Gierasch, Richard Thomas. *Master of Ceremonies*: Thomas Hume. *Miss Texas*: Althea Elder. *Georgia Motley*: MITZI GREEN. *Violin Player*: Tony Gardell. *Jerry Bonanza*: DON DeLEO. *Dapper Welch*: DAVID BURNS. *Rocky Barton*: WILLIAM TABBERT. *Cigarette Girl*: Jeri Archer. *Waiter*: David Thomas. *M.M. Montague*: ROBERT CHISHOLM. *Marathon M.C.*: Alan Gilbert. *Chorines*: Joan Mann, Lorraine Todd, Virginia Gorski, Virginia Poe, Helen Gallagher, Maria Harriton. *Comic*: Douglas Deane. *Danny*: Tony Gardell. *J.C. Creasy*: Horace Cooper. *Art Leffenbush*: Eddie Hodge. *Rodney Gender*: Thomas Hume. *Watchman*: Robert Edwin. *Rocky (who dances)*: JAMES MITCHELL. *Policeman*: Howard Lenters.

Dancers: Jacqueline Dodge, Helen Gallagher, Virginia Gorski, Maria Harriton, Ann Hutchinson, Cecille Mann, Joan Mann, Virginia Poe, Lorraine Todd, Lucas Aco, Allan Waine, Douglas Deane, Fred Hearne, Joe Landis, Arthur Partington, Bill Sumner.

Singers: Peggy Ann Ellis, Jeri Archer, Future Fulton, Lynne Gammon, Doris Hollingsworth, Beverly Hosier, Sydney Wylie, Betty Saunders, Thelma Stevens, Beth Shea, Tony Caffaro, Tony Gardell, Ray Morrissey, Franklin Powell, Anthony Reed, David Thomas, Philip La Torre.

Time: 1928-1929

Act 1, Scene 1: Staten Island Living-room. *Scene 2*: Atlantic City Boardwalk. *Scene 3*: Staten Island Living-room. *Scene 4*: Staten Island Ferry. *Scene 5*: Front of Speakeasy.

Scene 6: Chez Georgia. *Scene 7*: Georgia's Dressing Room. *Scene 8*: Staten Island Living-room. *Scene 9*: Street. *Scene 10*: Dapper's Apartment. *Scene 11*: The Marathon. *Scene 12*: Dapper's Apartment. *Scene 13*: Backstage of the Jollities. *Scene 14*: On stage Jollities.

Act 2, Scene 1: A Funeral. *Scene 2*: Porch of the Plaza Hotel, Palm Beach. *Scene 3*: Entrance to Marathon. *Scene 4*: The Marathon. *Scene 5*: Entrance to Marathon. *Scene 6*: Maribelle's Bedroom. *Scene 7*: Church Vestry. *Scene 8*: Wedding.

ACT 1

Scene 2

"Million Dollar Smile" (Billion Dollar Baby)
The Radio

"Who's Gonna Be the Winner?"
J. McCracken, A. Elder, B. Hoiser,
B. Saunders, D. Hollingsworth, Bathing Beauties

Scene 3

"Dreams Come True"
J. McCracken, J. Mitchell, F. Hearne, B. Skipper

Scene 5

"Charleston"
Cop: A. Partington. *3 Flappers*: V. Gorski, H. Gallagher, L. Todd. *Rich Girl*: J. Mann. *Playboy*: F. Hearne. *A Timid Girl*: A. Hutchinson. *Good Time Charlie*: B. Skipper. *Collegiates*: V. Poe, D. Deane. *Younger Generation*: B. Sumner, M. Harriton. *Older Generation*: J. Dodge, J. Landis. *Two Gangsters*: L. Aco, A. Waine. *Two Bootleggers*: A. Reed, A. Gilbert.

Scene 6

"Broadway Blossom"
M. Green

"Speaking of Pals"
D. Burns, D. DeLeo, D. Thomas, T. Gardell, W. Tabbert, Ensemble

Scene 7

"There I'd Be"
M. Green, R. Chisholm

Scene 8

"One Track Mind"
S. Van, D. Daniels

Scene 10

"Bad Timing"
W. Tabbert, J. McCracken

Scene 11

"The Marathoners"
Dance Ensemble

Scene 14

"A Lovely Girl"
M. Green, J. McCracken, Jollities Beauties

ACT 2

Scene 1

"Funeral Procession"
The Mob

Scene 2

"Havin' a Time"
M. Green

Scene 4

"The Marathon Dance"
D. Daniels

Scene 5

"Faithless"
R. Chisholm, J. McCracken

Scene 6

"I'm Sure of Your Love"
W. Tabbert

"A Life With Rocky"
J. McCracken
The Wealthy Ones: J. Dodge, D. Deane. *Rocky*: J. Mitchell. *Two Cops*: J. Landis, A. Waine. *Passerby*: A. Partington. *Bartender*: F. Hearne. *Two Thugs*: L. Aco, B. Sumner. *Their Molls*: J. Mann, L. Todd. *Leader of Thugs*: B. Skipper.

Scene 8

"The Wedding"
Entire Company

1946.01 ## SHOWBOAT

A Revival of the Musical Play in Two Acts, 15 Scenes[14]. Music by Jerome Kern. Book and lyrics by Oscar Hammerstein II[15]. Based on the novel of the same name by Edna Ferber. Staged by Hassard Short. Book directed by Oscar Hammerstein II. Dances by Helen Tamiris. Settings by Howard Bay. Costumes by Lucinda Ballard. Musical director, Edwin McArthur. Orchestrations by Robert Russell Bennett. Choral director, Pembroke Davenport. Associate, William Vodery. Produced by Jerome Kern and Oscar Hammerstein II[16]. Opened 5 January 1946 at the Ziegfeld Theatre and closed 4 January 1947 after 418 performances.

CAST (in order of their appearance): *Windy*: Scott Moore. *Steve*: Robert Allen. *Pete*: Seldon Bennett. *Queenie*: HELEN DOWDY. *Parthy Ann Hawkes*: ETHEL OWEN. *Captain Andy*: RALPH DUMKE. *Ellie*: COLETTE LYONS. *Frank*: BUDDY EBSEN. *Rubber Face*: Francis Mahoney. *Julie*: CAROL BRUCE. *Gaylord Ravenal*: CHARLES FREDERICKS. *Vallon*: Ralph Chambers. *Magnolia*: JAN CLAYTON. *Joe*: KENNETH SPENCER. *Backwoodsman*: Howard Frank. *Jeb*: Duncan Scott. *Sal*: Pearl Primus. *Sam*: LaVerne French. *Fatima*: Jean Reeves. *Old Sport*: Willie Torpey. *Strong Woman*: Paula Kaye. *Congress of Beauties* (8); *Spanish*: Andrea Downing. *Italian*: Vivian Cherry. *French*: Janice Bodenhoff. *Scotch*: Elana Keller. *Greek*: Audrey Keane. *English*: Marta Becket. *Russian*: Olga Lunick. *Indian*: Eleanor Boleyn. *Dahomey Queen*: Pearl Primus. *Ata*: Alma Sutton. *Mala*: Claude Marchant. *Bora*: Talley Beatty. *Landlady*: Sara Floyd. *Ethel*: Assota Marshall. *Sister*: Sheila Hogan. *Mother Superior*: Iris Manley. *Kim* (child): Alyce Mace. *Jake*: Max Showalter. *Jim*: Jack Daley. *Man with Guitar*: Thomas Bowman. *Doorman at Trocadero*: William C. Smith. *Lottie*: Nancy Kenyon. *Dolly*: Lydia Fredericks. *Sally*: Bettina Thayer. *Kim* (in her twenties): JAN CLAYTON. *Old Lady on Levee*: Frederica Slemons. *Jimmy Craig*: Charles Tate.

Singers: Girls: Carmine Alexandria, Grace Brenton, Clarise Crawford, Lydia Fredericks, Adah Friley, Marion Hairston, Katie Hall, Marion Holvas, Jean Jones, Frances Joslyn, Charlotte Junius, Assota Marshall, Linda Mason, Eulabel Riley, Agnes Sundgren, Bettina Thayer, Fannie Turner, Ethel Brown White, Evelyn Wick. *Boys*: Jerome Addison, Gilbert Adkins, William Bender, Thomas Bowman, Robert Bulger, Glenn Burris, Edward Chappel, William Cole, Erno Czako, Richard Di Silvera, John Garth III, Hayes Gordon, George H. Hall, Thomas Jordan, Robert Kimberly, James Lapsley, Albert McCary, William McDaniel, Bowling H. Mansfield, Walter Mosby, Clarence Redd, Paul Shiers, William C. Smith, William Sol, Rodester Timmons, David Trimble.

Dancers: Girls: Marta Becket, Elmira Jones Bey, Janice Bodenhoff, Eleanor Boleyn, Vivian Cherry, Andrea Downing, Betty Jane Geiskopf, Carol Harriton, Vickie Henderson, Audrey Keane, Elana Keller, Ora Leak, Olga Lunick, Jeane Reeves, Alma Sutton, Viola Taylor, Yvonne Tibor. *Boys*: Talley Beatty, Terry Dawson, LaVerne French, Eddie Howland, Gerard Leavitt, Claude Marchant, William Miller, Nick Nadeau, Joseph Nash, Stanley Simmons, William Weber, Henry Wessel, Francisco Xavier. *Captain*: Paula Kaye.

Act 1, Scene 1: The Levee at Natchez on the Mississippi. In the 1880s. *Scene 2*: Kitchen pantry of the "Cotton Blossom." Five minutes later. *Scene 3*: Auditorium and stage of the "Cotton Blossom." One hour later. *Scene 4*: Box-office, on foredeck. Three weeks later. *Scene 5*: Auditorium and stage during the 3rd Act of "The Parson's Bride" that night. *Scene 6*: The top deck. Later that night. *Scene 7*: The Levee at Greenville. Next morning.

Act 2, Scene 1: The Midway Plaisance, Chicago World's Fair, 1893. *Scene 2*: A room on Ontario Street, 1904. *Scene 3*: Rehearsal room, Trocadero Music Hall. A few days later. *Scene 4*: St. Agatha's Convent. About the same time. *Scene 5*: Trocadero Music Hall. Just before midnight. New Year's Eve 1905. *Scene 6*: Stern of the Show Boat, 1927. *Scene 7*: Top deck of the "Cotton Blossom." That night. *Scene 8*: Levee at Greenville. The next night.

ACT 1

"Cotton Blossom"
  Entire Ensemble
Show Boat Parade and Ballyhoo
  R. Dumke, Show Boat Troupe, Townspeople

---

[14]First presented in New York 27 December 1927 at the Ziegfeld Theatre for 572 performances.
[15]Book revisions by Oscar Hammerstein II.
[16]Producers' note: Mr. Kern and I have kept the libretto and score of "Show Boat" substantially as they were when originally written in 1927. We have eliminated one "front scene" and three minor musical numbers. We have added one new song in the last scene of the play, "Nobody Else But Me." This takes the place of a series of imitations of stars of the Twenties performed in this spot by the original Magnolia, Miss Norma Terris. I am particularly anxious to point out that the lyric for "Bill" was written by P.G. Wodehouse. Although he has always been given credit in the prgram, it has frequently been assumed that since I wrote all of the other lyrics for "Show Boat," I also wrote this one, and I have had praise for it which belonged to another man.—Oscar Hammerstein II

"Only Make Believe"
  C. Fredericks, J. Clayton
"Ol' Man River"
  K. Spencer, Stevedores
"Can't Help Lovin' Dat Man"
  C. Bruce, H. Dowdy, J. Clayton, K. Spencer, Quartette
"Life Upon the Wicked Stage"
  C. Lyons
Dance: "No Gems, No Roses, No Gentlemen"
  C. Lyons, Stage Door Admirers
"Ballyhoo"
  H. Dowdy, Ensemble
Dance: "No Shoes"
  P. Primus, L. French, Theatregoers
"You Are Love"
  J. Clayton, C. Fredericks
Finale
  Entire Ensemble
Levee Dance:
  C. Marchant, T. Beatty, L. French, Levee Dancers.

ACT 2
"At the Fair"
  Sightseers, Barkers, Ushers
Dance: "Congress of Beauties"
  Beauties, Ushers
"Why Do I Love You?"
  J. Clayton, C. Fredericks, R. Dumke, E. Owen, Ensemble
Waltz
  A. Keane, C. Fredericks, Couples
"In Dahomey"
  Dahomey Village
(a) Dance of the Dahomeys, (b) Avenue A Release
  P. Primus, A. Sutton, C. Marchant, T. Beatty, and the Bewitched
"Bill"
  C. Bruce
  (*Lyrics by* P.G. Wodehouse.)
"Can't Help Lovin' Dat Man" (reprise)
  J. Clayton
Service and Scene Music, St. Agatha's Convent
"Only Make Believe" (reprise)
  C. Fredericks
"Goodbye, My Lady Love" Cake Walk
  B. Ebsen, C. Lyons
  (*Music and Lyrics by* Joe Howard.)
Magnolia's Debut in Trocadero Music Hall: "After the Ball"
  J. Clayton
  (*Music and Lyrics by* Charles K. Harris.)
"Ol' Man River" (reprise)
  K. Spencer
"You Are Love" (reprise)
  C. Fredericks
"Nobody Else But Me"[17]
  J. Clayton
Dance 1927:
  J. Clayton, C. Tate, Flappers, Cake Eaters, Levee Dancers
Finale
  Entire Company

1946.02 ## THE WOULD-BE GENTLEMAN

An Adaptation (by Bobby Clark) of Moliere's comedy "Le Bourgeois Gentilhomme" in Two Acts. Staged by John Kennedy. Scenery by Howard Bay. Costumes by Irene Sharaff. Music adapted from the original Jean Baptiste Lully score by Jerome Moross; music for Miss Harrison and Mr. Fisher by Cosme McMoon[18]. Incidental dances staged by Miss Harrison and Mr. Fisher. Produced by Michael Todd. Opened 7 January 1946 at the Booth Theatre and closed 16 March 1946 after 77 performances.

---

[17]Newly written for the 1946 revival, just prior to Kern's death.
[18]Musical numbers not listed in the program.

CAST (in the order in which they speak): *Music Master*: DONALD BURR. *Dancing Master*: ALEX FISHER. *Criquet*: Fred Werner. *Nicole*: ANN THOMAS. *Marcel*: Rand Elliott. *Baptiste*: Albert Henderson. *Monsieur Jordain*: BOBBY CLARK. *Madamoiselle Valere*: RUTH HARRISON. *Singers*: Constance Brigham, Mary Godwin, Lewis Pierce. *Madame Jourdain*: EDITH KING. *Fencing Master*: EARL MacVEIGH. *Philosopher*: Frederic Persson. *Count Dorante*: GENE BARRY. *Lucille Jourdain*: ELEANORE WHITNEY. *Covielle*: LEONARD ELLIOTT. *Cleonte*: JOHN HEATH. *Tailor*: LeRoi Operti. *Raymond*, the tailor's apprentice: Lester Towne. *Marquise Dorimene*: JUNE KNIGHT. *Musicians*: Max Tartasky, James Nassy, Eric Silberman, Gregory Bemko, David Gindin.

Act 1: Drawing-room in Monsieur Jordain's House in Paris -circa 1670.

Act 2: Same as Act One. Immediately following.

1946.03

THE DESERT SONG

A Revival of the Musical Play in Two Acts, 8 Scenes[19]. Book by Otto Harbach, Oscar Hammerstein II and Frank Mandel. Music by Sigmund Romberg. Lyrics by Otto Harbach and Oscar Hammerstein II. Directed by Sterling Holloway. Ballets by Aida Broadbent. Orchestra under the direction of Waldemar Guterson. Scenery designed by Boris Aronson. Lighting by Nels Petersen. Produced by Russell Lewis and Howard Young. Opened 8 January 1946 at the New York City Center and closed 16 February 1946 after 46 performances.

CAST (in order of appearance): *Mindar*: Edward Wellman. *Sid El Kar*: RICHARD CHARLES. *Ahmed*: Keith Gingles. *Omar*: Jack Saunders. *Hassi*: Thayer Roberts. *Pierre Birabeau* (Red Shadow): WALTER CASSEL. *Benjamin Kidd*: JACK GOODE. *Sentinel*: William Bower. *Captain Paul Fontaine*: WILTON CLARY. *Sergeant Le Verne*: Joseph Claudio. *Sergeant De Boussac*: Antonio Rovano. *Azuri*: CLARISSA. *Edith*: TAMARA PAGE. *Susan*: SHERRY O'NEIL. *Mardi*: Barbara Bailey. *Florette*: Bettina Orth. *Yvonne*: Maria Taweel. *Margot Bonvalet*: DOROTHY SANDLIN. *General Birabeau*: LESTER MATTHEWS. *Clementina*: JEAN BARTEL. *Harem Guard*: Richard Hughes. *Ali Ben Ali*: GEORGE BURNSON. *Nogi*: Louis DeMagnus. *Riff Runner*: Paul Ruth.

French Girls, Natives and Ladies of the Harem: Joan Bishop, Lillian Bloch, Beth Alba Cushing, Georgine Dwyer, Florette Hillier, Rosemary Leisen, Doris Luff, Suzette Meredith, Tamara Page, Margaret Smitherum, Helen Vey, June Walks. *Riffs and French Legionnaires*: William Bower, Fred Butterworth, Warren Christian, Arthur Couture, John Donaty, Charles Fries, Louis DeMagnus, Dean Etmund, Keith Gingles, Sterling P. Hall, Richard Hughes, Joseph Malpasuto, Allan Mars, Antonio Rovano, Paul Ruth, Russell Sanders, W. Vernon Sanders, Harvey Sauber, Jack Saunders, Walter Swanson, Edward Wellman, Stanley Wolfe.

Dancing Girls: Barbara Bailey, Natalie Carr, Rita Currier, Jean Caples, Barbara Downie, Lynn Hunt, Betina Orth, Dorothy Jean Sheppard, Betty Slabe, Marie Taweel.

Time: 1925. *Place*: North Africa.

Act 1, Scene 1: Hiding Place of the Red Shadow in the Riff Mountains. Evening.

Scene 2: Garden outside General Birabeau's Villa. Before dawn, next day. *Scene 3*: Inside General Birabeau's Villa. That afternoon.

Act 2, Scene 1: The Desert Retreat of Ali Ben Ali. Afternoon of the following day. *Scene 2*: The Corridor to the Bath. *Scene 3*: The Room of the Silken Couch. *Scene 4*: The Edge of the Desert. *Scene 5*: General Birabeau's Villa. Two days later.

ACT 1
Scene 1
Prelude and Opening ("High on a Hill")
  Chorus
"The Riff Song" (Ho!)
  W. Cassel, R. Charles, Riffs
"Margot"
  W. Clary, Soldiers
Scene 2
"I'll Be a Buoyant Girl"
  S. O'Neil, T. Page, Ballet
Scene 3
Opening ("Why Did We Marry Soldiers?")
  Girls
"French Military Marching Song"
  D. Sandlin, Girls, Soldiers
"Romance"
  D. Sandlin
"Then You Will Know"
  D. Sandlin, W. Cassel, Ensemble

"I Want a Kiss"
  D. Sandlin, W. Clary, W. Cassel, Chorus
"Tropics"[20]
  J. Goode, S. O'Neil
"The Desert Song"
  D. Sandlin, W. Cassel
"Morocco Dance of Marriage"[21]
  Clarissa, R. Charles, Dancing Girls
"The Desert Song" (reprise)
  W. Cassel, D. Sandlin

ACT 2
Scene 1
Opening–"My Little Castagnet"
  Harem Girls
"Song of the Brass Key"
  J. Bartel, Girls
Spanish Dance
  Dancing Girls
"One Good Boy Gone Wrong"
  J. Goode, J. Bartel
"Eastern and Western Love"
  W. Cassel, R. Charles, G. Burnson, Men
"Let Love Go"
  G. Burnson
"One Flower (Grows Alone) in Your Garden"
  R. Charles
"One Alone"
  W. Cassel
Scene 2
En Route à la Bain[22]
  Damsels of the Harem
Scene 3
"The Saber Song"
  D. Sandlin, W. Cassel
Finalette
  W. Cassel, D. Sandlin
Scene 4
"Farewell"
  W. Cassel, Riffs
Scene 5
Opening
  L. Matthews, Girls
"The Tropics"[23] (reprise)
  J. Goode, S. O'Neil, Dancing Girls
Finale

1946.04

NELLIE BLY

A Musical Comedy in Two Acts, 18 Scenes. Book by Joseph Quillan. Music by James Van Heusen. Lyrics by Johnny Burke. Musical supervision, Joseph Lilley. Choreography by Edward Caton and Lee Sherman. Dialogue directed by Edgar MacGregor. Orchestra under the direction of Charles Drury. Entire production designed and lighted by Nat Karson. Orchestrations by Ted Royal and Elliott Jacoby. Choral direction by Simon Rady. Produced by Nat Karson and Eddie Cantor. Opened 21 January 1946 at the Adelphi Theatre and closed 2 February 1946 after 16 performances.

CAST (in order of appearance): *Pulitzer*: WALTER ARMIN. *Bennett*: EDWARD H. ROBINS. *Newsboy*: William O'Shay. *Frank Jordan*: WILLIAM GAXTON. *Ferry Captain*: Fred Peters. *Deckhand*: Harold Murray. *Phineas T. Fogarty*: VICTOR MOORE. *First Reporter*: ROBERT STRAUSS. *Murphy*: ARTELLS DIXON. *Wardheeler*: Jack Voeth. *Second Reporter*: Larry Stuart. *Third Reporter*: Eddy diGenova. *Nellie Bly*: JOY HODGES. *Battle Annie*: BENAY VENUTA. *Steward*: Larry Stuart. *Honeymoon Couple*: Doris Sward, Jack Voeth. *French Girl*: Drucilla Strain. *Grisette*: LUBOV ROUDENKO. *French Dandy*: JACK WHITNEY. *French Mayor*: WALTER ARMIN. *Santos Dumont*: Fred Peters. *Reporters*: THE DEBONAIRS. *Czar*: WALTER

---

[19]First presented in New York 30 November 1926 at the Casino Theatre for 471 performances.

[20]Not in the original production.
[21]Not in the original production.
[22]Not in the original production.
[23]Not in the original production.

ARMIN. *Russian Captain*: Fred Peters. *First Sheik*: ROBERT STRAUSS. *Second Sheik*: Edward H. Robins. *Third Sheik*: Larry Stuart. *Official*: Harold Murray. *Copygirl*: Suzie Baker.

Members of the Choir: *Girls*: Marjorie Anderson, Suzie Baker, Johnsie Bason, Jeannine Burke, Betty deCormier, Margaret Lide, Betty Spain, Drucilla Strain, Ruth Strickland, Doris Sward, Julie van Dusen. *Boys*: Eddy diGenova, William Golden, Bernard Griffin, Alfred Homan, Karl Newart, Merrill Shea, Larry Stuart.

Dancing Ensemble: *Girls*: Charlotte Bergmeier, Faith Dane, Mimi Gomber, Mary Grey, Sandra Scott, Dorothy Jeffers, Nathalie Kelepovska, Terry Lasky, Michael Neale, Nancy Newton, Mitzi Perry, Rita Barry, Ronan York. *Boys*: Ed Dragon, Bob Gari, William O'Shay, Jack Richards, William Segar, Kenny Springer.

Act 1, Scene 1: Barclay Street Ferry Slip, New York, 1889. *Scene 2*: In Front of ferry House at Barclay Street. *Scene 3*: Battle Annie's Saloon. *Scene 4*: City Hall Square. *Scene 5*: Steamship Pier in Hoboken. *Scene 6*: The After Deck. *Scene 7*: Stateroom the S.S. Augusta Victoria. *Scene 8*: At Gates of Paris Exposition. *Scene 9*: Paris Exposition.

Act 2, Scene 1: City Room of the New York Herald. *Scene 2*: Stratosphere. *Scene 3*: Public Square, Moscow. *Scene 4*: Street in Aden. *Scene 5*: The Pass. *Scene 6*: Street in Aden. *Scene 7*: Somewhere in Texas. *Scene 8*: In Transit. *Scene 9*: Barclay Street Ferry Slip.

ACT 1

"There's Nothing Like Travel"
  Ensemble, V. Moore
"All Around the World"
  W. Gaxton, J. Hodges
"Fogarty the Great"
  V. Moore, Fogarty Boosters
"That's Class"
  B. Venuta
"Nellie Bly"
  Nellie Bly Social Club
"Nellie Bly"/"Fogarty the Great" (reprise)
  Ensemble
"May the Best Man Win"
  Entire Cast
"How About a Date?"
  S. Baker, J. Bason, S. Scott, D. Strain, the Debonairs
"You Never Saw That Before"
  B. Venuta
"L'Exposition Universalle"
  L. Roudenko, J. Whitney, Ensemble
"Sky High"
  W. Gaxton, J. Hodges, Ensemble

ACT 2

"No News Today"
  The Debonairs, N.Y. Herald Employees
"Choral Russe"
  W. Armin, Officers, Guards, Muscovites
"Just My Luck"
  W. Gaxton, J. Hodges, Ensemble
"Aladdin's Daughter"
  B. Venuta
"Start Dancing"
  W. Gaxton, B. Venuta, L. Roudenko, J. Whitney, Ensemble
"Harmony"
  W. Gaxton, V. Moore
Finale
  Entire Company

1946.05   LUTE SONG

A Love Story With Music in Three Acts, 17 Scenes. Book by Sidney Howard and Will Irwin from the famous Chinese play "Pi-Pa-Ki." Music by Raymond Scott. Lyrics by Bernard Hanighen. Directed by John Houseman. Choreography by Yeichi Nimura. Scenery, costumes and lighting by Robert Edmond Jones. Miss Martin's costumes designed by Valentina. Musical director, Eugene Kusmiak. Orchestrations by Raymond Scott. Produced by Michael Myerberg. Opened 6 February 1946 at the Plymouth Theatre and closed 8 June 1946 after 142 performances.

CAST (in order of their appearance): *The Manager, The Honorable Tschang*: CLARENCE DERWENT. *Tsai-Yong, the Husband*: YUL BRYNNER. *Tsai, the father*: AUGUSTIN DUNCAN. *Madame Tsai, the Mother*: MILDRED DUNNOCK. *Tchao-ou-Niang, the Wife*: MARY MARTIN. *Prince Nieou, the Imperial Preceptor*: McKAY MORRIS. *Princess Nieou-chi, his daughter*: HELEN CRAIG. *Si-Tchun,*

a Lady in Waiting: Nancy Davis. *Waiting Women*: Pamela Wilde, Sydelle Sylovna. *Hand Maidens*: Blanche Zohar, Mary Ann Reeve. *Youen-Kong, the Steward*: REX O'MALLEY. *A Marriage Broker*: Diane De Brett. *A Messenger*: Jack Amoroso. *The Imperial Chamberlain*: RALPH CLANTON. *The Food Commissioner*: Gene Galvin. *First Clerk*: Charles Leavitt. *Second Clerk*: Bob Turner. *First Applicant*: Tom Emlyn Williams. *Second Applicant*: Michael Balir. *Imperial Guards*: John Robert Lloyd, John High. *Imperial Attendants*: Gordon Showalter, Ronald Fletcher. *The Genie*: Ralph Clanton. *The White Tiger*: Lisa Maslova. *The Ape*: Lisan Kay. *Phoenix Birds*: Lisa Maslova, Lisan Kay. *Li-Wang*: Charles Leavitt. *Priest of Amida Buddha*: Tom Emlyn Williams. *A Bonze*: Gene Galvin. *Two Lesser Bonzes*: Joseph Camiolo, Leslie John. *A Rich Man*: John High. *A Little Boy*: Donald Rose. *The Lion*: Walter Stane, Alberto Vecchio. *Children*: Mary Ann Reeve, Blanche Zohar, Teddy Rose. *A Secretary*: Michael Blair.

Travellers on the North Road, Beggars, Guards, Attendants, Gods, and others: Mary Burr, Arlene Garver, Sydelle Sylvona, Pamela Wilde, Alan Banks, Victor Burset, Jack Amoroso, Joseph Camiolo, Jack Cooper, Ronald Fletcher, John High, John Robert Lloyd, Lang Page, Bernard Pisarski, Leslie John, Gordon Showalter, Walter Stane, Alberto Vecchio.

Act 1, Scene 1: The House of Tsai in the Village of Tchin-lieou. *Scene 2*: The North Road leading to the Capitol. *Scene 3*: The Gate to the Palace of the Voice of Jade. *Scene 4*: The House of Tsai in the Village of Tchin-lieou. *Scene 5*: Gardens of the Palace of Prince Nieou.

Act 2, Scene 1: Gardens of the Palace of Prince Nieou. *Scene 2*: A Public Granary in the Village of Tchin-lieou. *Scene 3*: Gardens of the Palace of Prince Nieou. *Scene 4*: The House of Tsai in the Village of Tchin-lieou. *Scene 5*: Market Place - Street of the Hair Buyers. *Scene 6*: A Burial Place in the Village of Tchin-lieou.

Act 3, Scene 1: Gardens of the Palace of Prince Nieou. *Scene 2*: The North Road leading to the Capitol. *Scene 3*: In the Palace. *Scene 4*: The Temple of Amidha Buddha. *Scene 5*: A Street in the Capitol. *Scene 6*: The Blue Pavilion in the Palace of Prince Nieou.

ACT 1

Introduction to Act 1
"Mountain High, Valley Low"
  M. Martin, Y. Brynner
North Road
Imperial March
"Monkey See, Monkey Do"
  M. Martin
"Where You Are"
  M. Martin
Eunuch Scene
Marriage Music

ACT 2

Introduction to Act 2
"Willow Tree"
  Y. Brynner
Beggars Music
"Vision Song"
  M. Martin, Y. Brynner
Chinese Market Place and "Bitter Harvest"
  M. Martin
Dirge Song
Genie Music

ACT 3

Introduction to Act 3
Phoenix Dance
"Mountain High, Valley Low" (reprise)
  M. Martin
Lion Dance
Imperial March (reprise)
"Lute Song"
  M. Martin

1946.06   THE DUCHESS MISBEHAVES

A Frolicsome Musical Comedy in Two Acts, 8 Scenes. Book and lyrics by Gladys Shelley. Music by Dr. Frank Black. Additional dialogue by Joe Bigelow. Staged by Martin Manulis. Musical numbers and dances staged by George Tapps. Production supervised by Chet [Chester] O'Brien. Production (settings) designed by A. A. Ostrander. Costumes by Willa Kim. Lighting by Carlton Winckler. Orchestrations by Don Walker. Vocal arrangements by Clay Warnick. Orchestra under the direction of Charles Sandford. Produced by A. P. Waxman. Opened 13 February 1946 at the Adelphi Theatre and closed 16 February 1946 after 5 performances.

CAST (in order of appearance in Carlton's Department Store): *Woman*: Grace Hale. *Franchot*: Buddy Ferraro. *First Sister*: ELENA BOYD. *Second Sister*: MILDRED BOYD. *Third Sister*: EDITH BOYD. *Butterfly*: PENNY EDWARDS. *Paul*: LARRY DOUGLAS. *Fitzgerald*: JAMES MacCOLL. *Woonsocket*: JOEY FAYE. *First Girl*: Gail Adams. *Second Girl*: Ethel Madson. *Miss Kiester*: PAULA LAURENCE. *Crystal Shalimar*: AUDREY CHRISTIE. *Reporter*: Al Downing. *Neville Goldglitter*: Philip Tonge.

(In Spain) *Pablo*: LARRY DOUGLAS. *Amber*: Grace Hayle. *Goya*: JOEY FAYE. *Model*: Joanne Jaap. *Roberto*: JAMES MacCOLL. *Duchess of Alba*: AUDREY CHRISTIE. *Mariposa*: PENNY EDWARDS. *Barber*: Paul Marten. *Manicurist*: Joanne Jaap. *Tailor*: Ken Martin. *Ass't Tailor*: Bernie Williams. *Messenger*: Buddy Ferraro. *First Student*: Victor Clark. *Second Student*: Jess Randolph. *Duke of Alba*: PHILIP TONGE. *Ladies in Waiting*: THE BOYD TRIPLETS. *Queen of Spain*: PAULA LAURENCE. *A Model*: Norma Kohane. *Matador*: GEORGE TAPPS. *Jose*: Al Downing. *Dancer*: Mata Monteria. *The Woman*: Jean Handzlik. *Her Man*: GEORGE TAPPS.

Models: Joanne Jaap, Norma Kohane, Ann Miller, Lillian Moore. *Singing Girls*: Gail Adams, Adele Lulince, Ethel Madson, Jane Riehl. *Singing Boys*: Victor Clark, Vincent Henry, Jerry O'Rourke, Jess Randolph.

Dancing Girls: Jane Atwood, Trudy Cirrito, Theo Denis, Helen Devlin, Gertrude Gibbons, Eleanore Gregory, Freddie Grey, Janet Joy, Beverly Joyce, Mary Jane Kersey, Anna Konstance, Dorothy Matthews, Marilyn Pendry. *Dancing Boys*: Dan Karry, Walter Koremin, Paul Marten, Anthony Starman, Merritt Thompson, Bernie Williams.

Time: The Present.

Act 1, Scene 1: Carlton's Department Store, Art Section. *Scene 2*: Goya's Studio. In Spain. *Scene 3*: A Street in Madrid. *Scene 4*: Outside the Fiesta Grounds.

Act 2, Scene 1: Public Square in Madrid. *Scene 2*: A Side Street. *Scene 3*: Goya's Studio. *Scene 4*: Carlton's Department Store.

ACT 1

Scene 1
   "Art"
      J. MacColl
      Danced by G. Tapps, Ensemble.
Scene 2
   "My Only Romance"
      L. Douglas, Singing Girls, Dancing Girls
   "Broadminded"
      J. Faye, Showgirls
   "I Hate Myself in the Morning"
      A. Christie, Students
   "Men"
      P. Laurence, Boyd Triplets
Scene 3
   "Couldn't Be More in Love"
      L. Douglas, P. Edwards
Scene 4
   "Dance of the Matador"
      ('Ritual Fire Dance' music by Manuel De Falla.)
      G. Tapps
   "Ole' Ole'"
      J. Faye, Ensemble
   "Katie Did in Madrid"
      A. Christie, Singers, Dancing Boys and Girls

ACT 2

Scene 1
   "Morning in Madrid"
      Entire Ensemble
   "Lost"
      The Woman: J. Handzlik. *Her Man*: G. Tapps.
   "Honeymoon Is Over"
      P. Laurence, P. Edwards, Dancers
Scene 2
   "Nuts"
      A. Christie
   "Fair Weather Friends"
      L. Douglas, P. Edwards
Scene 3
   "The Nightmare"
      J. Faye, P. Laurence, A. Christie, Dancers, Singers

Scene 4
   "Art" (reprise)
      Entire Company

1946.07   ## THREE TO MAKE READY

A Musical Revue in Two Acts, 21 Scenes. Sketches and lyrics by Nancy Hamilton. Music by Morgan Lewis. Entire production devised and staged by John Murray Anderson. Sketches directed by Margaret Webster. Dances and musical numbers staged by Robert Sidney. Production designed by Donald Oenslager. Costumes by Audre. Orchestra conducted by Ray M. Kavanaugh. Orchestrations by (Robert) Russell Bennett, Charles L. Cooke, Elliott Jacoby, Ted Royal, Hans Spialek, Walter Paul. Musical continuity by Melvin Pahl. Vocal arrangements by Joe Moon. Produced by Stanley Gilkey and Barbara Payne. Opened 7 March 1946 at the Adelphi Theatre, moved to the Broadhurst Theatre 20 May 1946, and closed 14 December 1946 after 327 performances.

CAST: RAY BOLGER, BRENDA FORBES, ROSE INGHRAM, GORDON MacRAE, BIBI OSTERWALD, HAROLD LANG, JANE DEERING, Garry Davis, ALTHEA ELDER, MEG MUNDY, ARTHUR GODFREY[24], Joe Johnson, Carleton Carpenter, Mary Alice Bingham, Martin Kraft, Mary McDonnell, Jack Purcell, Edythia Turrnell, Irwin Charles, Candace Montgomery, Jimmy Venable, Iris Linde, Jim Elsegood.

ACT 1

Scene 1
   "It's a Nice Night for It"
      G. MacRae
      Wardrobe Mistress: B. Osterwald. *Stage Manager*: G. Davis. *Stagehand*: C. Carpenter. *Ballerina*: J. Deering. *Ballet Dancer*: H. Lang. With M. A. Bingham, A. Elder, M. McDonnell, C. Montgomery, M. Mundy, E. Turnell, I Charles, J. Jonson, M. Kraft, J. Purcell, J. Venable.
Scene 2
   Post Mortem
      He: R. Bolger. *She*: R. Inghram. *Alexandre Bernier*: G. Davis. *Bellboy*: C. Carpenter.
Scene 3
   Arthur Godfrey
Scene 4
   "There's Something on My Program"
      Juliet: J. Deering. *Romeo*: H. Lang. *The Nurse*: M. Mundy. *The Capulets*: M. McDonnell, E. Turnell, M.A. Bingham, A. Elder. *The Montagues*: J. Venable, J. Purcell, M. Kraft, J. Jonson.
Scene 5
   The Shoe on the Other Foot
      Lady: B. Forbes. *Salesman*: R. Bolger.
Scene 6
   "Tell Me the Story"
      R. Inhgram, G. MacRae
Scene 7
   "The Old Soft Shoe"
      R. Bolger
      Jitterbugs: M. McDonnell, J. Purcell. *Samba Dancers*: M. A. Bingham, J. Jonson.
Scene 8
   The Russian Lesson
      Mrs. Budge: R. Inghram. *Mrs. Wattrous*: B. Osterwald. *Mrs. Pellobie*: M. Mundy. *Miss Umstedder*: B. Forbes.
Scene 9
   "Barnaby Beach"
      G. MacRae, A. Elder
      Danced by J. Deering, H. Lang.
Scene 10
   Arthur Godfrey
Scene 11
   Cold Water Flat (Housing Shortage)
      Jo: R. Bolger. *Mary*: R. Inghram.

---

[24]Once Arthur Godfrey was forced to leave the show due to physical exhaustion, Garry Davis was reassigned his roles and solo spot. Added was:
   "Hot December" (to Act 1)
      B. Osterwald

Scene 12
Arthur Godfrey

Scene 13
"Wisconsin" or "Kenosha Canoe" ([Burlesque of OKLAHOMA!] with a
bow to Richard Rodgers and Oscar Hammerstein II.)
Auntie Plum: B. Osterwald. *Clyde Griffiths:* R. Bolger. *Roberta:* R. Inghram.
June Alden: J. Deering. *Ido Wanny:* B. Forbes. *Mr. Snow:* G. MacRae. *Yellow
Belly:* G. Davis. *Judge:* I. Charles.

Scene 14
"Kenosha Canoe Ballet"
Danced by H. Lang, Cowboys, Children, Strumpets

ACT 2
Scene 1
"If It's Love"
R. Inghram, G. MacRae
Danced by R. Bolger, A. Elder, M. McDonnell, M.A. Bingham, E. Turnell, J.
Deering.

Scene 2
The Story of the Opera (from ONE FOR THE MONEY)
Marilyn: B. Forbes. *Lucy:* B. Osterwald. *Waiter:* M. Kraft.

Scene 3
"A Lovely Lazy Kind of Day"
A. Godfrey
Danced by R. Bolger. *Milkmaid:* B. Osterwald.

Scene 4
"And Why Not I?"
B. Forbes

Scene 5
The Sad Sack (based on the character created by Sgt. George Baker)
The Sack: R. Bolger. *Sergeant:* G. Davis. *Joe:* J. Jonson. *Goldbricks:* I. Charles.
Slug: C. Carpenter. *Lieutenant:* H. Lang. *M.P.:* M. Kraft. *Captain:* A. Godfrey.
Colonel: A. Godfrey. *General:* A. Godfrey. *Sleeper:* J. Venable. *Greeley:* J.
Purcell.

Scene 6
Ray Bolger

Scene 7
Finale
Entire Company

1946.08 ST. LOUIS WOMAN

A Musical Play in Three Acts, 12 Scenes. Book by Arna Bontemps and
Countee Cullen. Based on the novel "God Sends Sunday" by Arna
Bontemps. Music by Harold Arlen. Lyrics by Johnny Mercer. Production
directed by Rouben Mamoulian. Settings and costumes by Lemuel Ayers.
Dances by Charles Walters. Musical director, Leon Leonardi. Orchestrations by Ted Royal, Allan Small, Menotti Salta, Walter Paul. Choral
arrangements by Leon Leonardi. Produced by Edward Gross. Opened 30
March 1946 at the Martin Beck Theatre and closed 6 July 1946 after 113
performances.

CAST (in order of speaking): *Badfoot:* Robert Pope. *Little Augie:* HAROLD
NICHOLAS. *Barney:* FAYARD NICHOLAS. *Lila:* JUNE HAWKINS. *Slim:* Louis
Sharp. *Butterfly:* PEARL BAILEY. *Della Green:* RUBY HILL. *Biglow Brown:*
REX INGRAM. *Ragsdale:* Elwood Smith. *Pembroke:* Merritt Smith. *Jasper:* Charles
Welch. *The Hostess:* Maude Russell. *Drum Major:* J. Mardo Brown. *Mississippi:*
Milton J. Williams. *Dandy Dave:* Frank Green. *Leah:* JUANITA HALL. *Jackie:* Joseph
Eady. *Celestine:* Yvonne Coleman. *Piggie:* Herbert Coleman. *Joshua:* Lorenzo Fuller.
Mr. Hopkins: Milton Wood. *Preacher:* Creighton Thompson. *Waiter:* Carrington Lewis.
Choral Group: Olive Ball, Rhoda Boggs, Miriam Burton, Rosalie King, Maude
Russell, Zelda Shelton, Lori Wilson, J. Mardo Brown, John Diggs, Leon Edwards,
Lorenzo Fuller, Theodore Hines, Jerry Laws, Arthur Lawson, Merritt Smith, Charles
Welch.
Dancers: Rita Garrett, Dorothea Greene, Gwendolyn Hale, Betty Nichols,
Marguerite Roan, Royce Wallace, Enid Williams, Theodore Allen, Smalls Boykins,
Norman DeJoie, Frank Green, Lonny Reed, Arthur Smith, George Thomas.

The action takes place in St. Louis, 1898.

Act 1, Scene 1: A stable, early afternoon of a day in August. *Scene 2:* Biglow's bar, late
afternoon, the same day. *Scene 3:* Outside Barney's room, at twilight. *Scene 4:* A ballroom, evening of the same day.

Act 2, Scene 1: Augie's and Della's home, late afternoon, the following week. *Scene 2:*
The alley. *Scene 3:* Funeral Parlor.

Act 3, Scene 1: Augie's and Della's home, early evening. *Scene 2:* The alley. *Scene 3:*
The bar. *Scene 4:* The stable. *Scene 5:* Street corner close to the race track.

ACT 1
"Li'l Augie Is a Natural Man"("Sweeten' Water")
R. Pope
"Any Place I Hang My Hat Is Home"
R. Hill
"I Feel My Luck Comin' Down"
H. Nicholas
"(I Had Myself a) True Love"
J. Hawkins
"Legalize My Name"
P. Bailey
"Cakewalk Walk Your Lady"
Drum Major: J. M. Brown. *Quartet:* R. Boggs, R. King, R. Pope, M.J. Williams.
Competing Couples: 1. B. Nichols, S. Boykins. 2. R. Garrett, T. Allen. 3.
D. Greene, M. Wood. 4. R. Wallace, L. Reed. 5. G. Hale, N. DeJoie. 6.
E. Williams, G. Thomas. 7. P. Bailey, F. Nicholas. 8. R. Hill, H. Nicholas.

ACT 2
"Come Rain or Come Shine"
R. Hill, H. Nicholas
"Chinquapin Bush"
Children
"We Shall Meet to Part, No Never"
H. Coleman
"Lullaby"
R. Hill
"Sleep Peaceful, (Mr. Used-Te-Be)"
J. Hawkins
Funeral Scene: "Leavin' Time"
Choral Group

ACT 3
"Come Rain or Come Shine" (reprise)
R. Hill
"(It's) A Woman's Prerogative"
P. Bailey
"Ridin' on the Moon"
H. Nicholas, Ensemble
"Least That's My Opinion"
R. Pope
"Racin' Form"
J. Hall
"Come On, Li'l Augie"
Ensemble
Finale
Entire Company

1946.09 CARMEN JONES

A Return Engagement of the Musical Play in Two Acts, 5 Scenes[25]. Book
and lyrics by Oscar Hammerstein II. Based on Henri Meilhac and Ludovic
Halevy's adaptation of Prosper Merimée's "Carmen." Music by Georges
Bizet. Staging, lighting and color schemes of entire production by Hassard
Short. Libretto directed by Charles Friedman. New orchestral arrangements
by Robert Russell Bennett. Settings designed by Howard Bay. Costumes
designed by Raoul Pene du Bois. Choreography by Eugene Loring. Choral
direction by Robert Shaw. Orchestra conducted by David Mordecai.
Produced by Billy Rose. Opened 7 April 1946 at the New York City Center
and closed 4 May 1946 after 32 performances.

CAST (in order of appearance): *Corporal Morrell:* Robert Clarke. *Foreman:* George
Willis. *Cindy Lou:* ELTON J. WARREN or COREANIA HAYMAN. *Sergeant Brown:*
JACK CARR. *Joe:* NAPOLEON REED or LeVERN HUTCHERSON. *Carmen:*
MURIEL SMITH or URYLEE LEONARDOS. *Sally:* Sibol Cain. *T-Bone:* Edward
Roche. *Tough Kid:* James May. *Drummer:* OLIVER COLEMAN. *Bartender:* Andrew J.
Taylor. *Waiter:* Edward Christopher. *Myrt:* RUTH CRUMPTON. *Frankie:* THERESA

[25]First presented 2 December 1943 at the Broadway Theatre for 503 performances. For Synopsis of Scenes and Musical Numbers see original 1943
production.

MERRITTE. *Rum*: JOHN BUBBLES. *Dink*: FORD BUCK. *Boy*: Bill O'Neil. *Girl*: Erona Harris. *Husky Miller*: GLENN BRYANT. *Soldiers*: Robert Clarke, Randall Steplight, George Willis, Elijah Hodges. *Mr, Higgins*: JACK CARR. *Miss Higgins*: Fredye Marshall. *Photographer*: Harold Taylor. *Card Players*: Fredye Marshall, Doris Brown, Sibol Cain. *Waiter*: Richard De Vaultier. *Dancing Girl*: Audrey Vanterpool. *Poncho*: Frank Palmer. *Dancing Boxers*: Sheldon B. Hoskins, Randolph Sawyer. *Bullet Head*: George Willis. *Referee*: George Spelvin.

Soldiers, Factory Workers, Socialites: Anne Dixon, Etta May Curry, Fredye Marshall, Doris Brown, Ida Johnson, Mattie Washington, Margaret Eley, Elsie Kennedy, Mary Graham, Sibol Cain, Adelaide Boatner, Lee Allen, Robert Clarke, Elijah Hodges, Randall Steplight, Andrey Vantepool, John Kelly, Chauncey Reynolds, Edward Roche, Richard de Vaultier, George Willis, Clarence Jones, Andrew J. Taylor, Harold Taylor.

Dancers: Evelyn Pilcher, Edith Ross, Dorothy McDavid, Hedye Brown, Posie Flowers, Audrey Graham, Erona Harris, Rita Christiani, Margaret Scott, Mable Hart, Rhoda Johnson, Vera McNichols, Edith Hurd, Randolph Sawyer, Alonzo Hodo, Lester Goodman, Rudolph Crier, Edward Christopher, Ivan Gittens, Albert Rivera, Clifton Gray, Sheldon B. Hoskins, Joseph Noble, Bill O'Neil, James Truitte, Edmond Woodard.

Children: Jenkins Hightower, Payton Hightower, James May, Albert Smith, Ralph May, Jack Hightower, Bobby May, Roger Smith.

1946.10

CALL ME MISTER

A Musical Revue in Two Acts, 23 Scenes. Sketches by Arnold Auerbach. Music and lyrics by Harold Rome. Production directed by Robert H. Gordon. Dances by John Wray. Musical direction by Lehman Engel. Scenery by Lester Polakov. Costumes by Grace Houston. Lighting by Carlton Winkler. Musical arrangements by Ben Ludlow, Julian Work, Charles Huffine. Choral arrangements by Lehman Engel. Produced by Melvyn Douglas and Herman Levin. Opened 18 April 1946 at the National Theatre, moved 21 July 1947 to the Majestic Theatre, moved 6 October 1947 to the Plymouth Theatre, and closed 10 January 1948 after 734 performances.

<u>CAST</u>: BETTY GARRETT, JULES MUNSHIN, BETTY LOU HOLLAND, BILL CALLAHAN, PAULA BANE, DANNY SCHOLL, MARIA KARNILOVA, DAVID NILLO, LAWRENCE WINTERS, Robert Baird, Joan Bartels, Harry Clark, Joe Calvan, Chandler Cowles, Fred Danieli, Virginia Davis, Alex Dunaeff, Bettye Durrence, Peter Fara, Ruth Feist, Shellie Filkins, Kate Friedlich, Ward Carner, Darcy Gardener, Betty Gilpatrick, George Hall, Bruce Howard, George S. Irving, Tommy Knox, Henry Lawrence, Sid Lawson, Betty Lorraine, Rae MacGregor, Howard Malone, Alan Manson, William Mende, Marjorie Oldroyd, Doris Parker, Patricia Penso, Paula Purnell, Roy Ross, Evelyn Shaw, Edward Silkman, Kevin Smith, Alvis Tinnin, Eugene Tobin, Glen Turnbull.

ACT 1

Scene 1

"Opening Number"

Sergeant: J. Munshin. *Soldiers*: B. Callahan, H. Clark, C. Cowles, W. Garner, G. Hall, A. Manson, D. Scholl, L. Winters. *Sailors*: R. Baird, A. Dunaeff, H. Lawrence, S. Lawson, W. Mende, E. Silkman, A. Tinnin, E. Tobin. *Canteen Girls*: B. Durrence, K. Friedlich, S. Filkins, D. Gardner, B. Lorraine, R. MacGregor, P. Penso, E. Shaw. *Marines*: J. Calvan, F. Danieli, T. Knox, H. Malone, D. Nillo, R. Ross, K. Smith, G. Turnbull.

Scene 2

"Going Home Train"

Ex-GIs: B. Callahan, H. Clark, C. Cowles, W. Garner, G. Hall, A. Manson, D. Nillo, D. Scholl, L. Winters, R. Baird, H. Lawrence, S. Lawson, W. Mende, E. Silkman, A. Tinnin, E. Tobin, G. Turnbull, J. Calvan, F. Danieli, A. Dunaeff, T. Knox, R. Ross.

Scene 3

Welcome Home

Bill Wilson: G. Turnbull. *A Soldier*: H. Clark. *Mr. Charles Wilson*: G. S. Irving. *Mrs. Josephine Wilson*: B. Garrett. *Lottie*: E. Shaw. *Wally Wilson*: J. Calvan.

Scene 4

Love Story, Chapter I. Three Thousand Miles Apart.

"Along With Me"

The Boy: D. Scholl. *His Mates*: R. Baird, H. Lawrence, S. Lawson, W. Mende, E. Silkman, A. Tinnin, E. Tobin. *The Girl*: P. Bane. *Her Co-Workers*: J. Bartels, V. Davis, R. Feist, B. Gilpatrick, B. Howard, M. Oldroyd, D. Parker, P. Purnell.

Scene 5

The Army Way

Sam: A. Manson. *Soldier*: T. Knox. *Capt. Baines*: G. S. Irving. *Paul Revere*: G. Hall. *Master Sergeant*: H. Clark. *Corporal*: B. Callahan. *Dental Officer*: S. Lawson. *Insurance Officer*: G. Turnbull. *Hygiene Officer*: R. Ross.

Scene 6

"Surplus Blues"

A Waitress: B. Garrett.

Scene 7

Love Story, Chapter II. He remembers.

"The Drugstore Song"

The Boy: D. Scholl. *Ballet*: *The Girl*: M. Karnilova. *The Boy*: D. Nillo. *Pop Higgins*: G. Turnbull. *First Couple*: B. Lorraine, H. Malone. *Second Couple*: K. Friedlich, F. Danieli. *Trio*: S. Filkins, P. Penso, J. Calvan.

Scene 8

Off We Go

(co-authored with Arnold B. Horwitt)

Ted: R. Ross. *Lou*: G. S. Irving. *Mulvey*: H. Clark. *Grover*: J. Munshin. *Dover*: A. Manson. *Stover*: G. Hall. *Menu Girl*: M. Oldroyd. *Canape Girl*: B. Gilpatrick. *Cigarette Girl*: J. Bartels. *Mac*: S. Lawson. *Merryweather*: C. Cowles. *Plover*: G. Turnbull. *General*: W. Garner.

Scene 9

"The Red Ball Express"

Truck Driver: L. Winters. *Other Truck Drivers*: R. Baird, W. Mende, E. Silkman, A. Tinnin. *Foreman*: R. Ross.

Scene 10

"Military Life" (The Jerk Song)

The Sailor: H. Clark. *The Soldier*: C. Cowles. *The Marine*: J. Munshin. *The Wave*: B. Garrett. *The Wac*: B. Gilpatrick. *The Tenderneck*: E. Shaw.

Scene 11

"Call Me Mister"

The Marine: B. Callahan. *Floorwalker*: J. Munshin. *Customers*: B. Garrett, B. L. Holland. *Sales Clerks*: J. Bartels, V. Davis, R. Feist, B. Gilpatrick, B. Howard, M. Oldroyd, D. Parker, P. Purnell, R. Baird, G. S. Irving, H. Lawrence, S. Lawson, W. Mende, E. Silkman, A. Tinnin, E. Tobin. *Underwear Models*: B. Durrence, S. Filkins, R. MacGregor, P. Penso. *The WACs*: K. Friedlich, D. Gardner, B. Lorraine, E. Shaw. *The GIs*: J. Calvan, T. Knox, H. Malone, R. Ross. *The Civilians*: F. Danieli, A. Dunaeff, K. Smith, P. Fara.

ACT 2

Scene 1

"Yuletide, Park Avenue"

The Grandmother: B. Garrett. *The Butler*: W. Mende. *The Uncle*: G. S. Irving. *The Sister*: M. Oldroyd. *Her Husband*: E. Tobin. *The Brother*: R. Baird. *His Wife*: B. Gilpatrick. *The Father*: E. Silkman. *The Mother*: V. Davis. *The Young Sister*: B. L. Holland. *The Lieutenant, j.g.*: C. Cowles.

Scene 2.

Jules Munshin[26]

Scene 3

Love Story, Chapter III. She Dreams.

"When We Meet Again"

The Girl: P. Bane. *Ballet*: *The Girl*: M. Karnilova. *The Boy*: D. Nillo. *The Girls*: K. Friedlich, S. Filkins, D. Gardner, B. Lorraine, R. MacGregor, P. Penso. *The Boys*: J. Calvan, F. Danieli, A. Dunaeff, H. Malone, R. Ross.

Scene 4

Once Over Lightly

(co-authored with Arnold B. Horwitt)

Mike: J. Munshin. *Ted*: W. Garner. *Barber*: H. Clark.

Scene 5

"The Face on the Dime"

A Man: L. Winters.

Scene 6

A Home of Our Own

Mrs. Winthrop: B. Garrett. *Arthur Benson*: S. Lawson. *A Soldier*: A. Manson. *A Young Husband*: G. S. Irving. *A Young Wife*: B. Gilpatrick. *A Captain*: C. Cowles. *Lucille*: B. L. Holland. *Bill*: B. Callahan. *Lucille's Mother*: V. Davis. *Lucille's Father*: H. Clark. *Applicants*: J. Bartels, R. Feist, B. Howard, M. Oldroyd, D. Parker, P. Purnell, R. Baird, H. Lawrence, W. Mende, E. Silkman, A. Tinnin, E. Tobin.

Scene 7

Dance Specialty

B. L. Holland, B. Callahan

Scene 8

Love Story, Chapter IV, Together.

---

[26]When Jules Munshin left the show, the following was sketch added to replace his special material:

America's Square Table of the Air (Round Table of the Air)

Announcer: CARL REINER. *Lieut. Gen. Thomas Judson*: Ralph Stanley. *Rear Admiral Frank A. Mooney*: G. S. Irving. *General K. B. Jones*: H. Clark.

"His Old Man"
> *The Girl:* P. Bane. *The Boy:* D. Scholl.

Scene 9

"South America, Take It Away"
> *The Hostess:* B. Garrett. *Her Partners:* C. Cowles, F. Danieli, H. Malone, A. Manson.

Scene 10

South Wind
> *Senator Burble:* J. Munshin. *Representative Snide:* H. Clark. *Representative Gumble:* G. Hall. *Senator Dibble:* G. S. Irving. *G.I. Joe:* C. Cowles.

Scene 11

"The Senators' Song"
> H. Clark, G. Hall, J. Munshin

Scene 12

Finale
> *Entire Company*
> *The Veteran:* C. Cowles.

THE PIRATES OF PENZANCE,
1946.11   or, The Lass That Loved a Sailor

A Revival of the Comic Opera in Two Acts[27]. Libretto by William S. Gilbert. Music by Arthur Sullivan. Staged by Eugene Bryden. Choreographed by Igor Schwezoff. Settings by H. A. Condell. Music directed by Julius Rudel. Produced by Laszlo Halasz. Opened 12 May 1946 in repertory at the New York City Center and closed 31 May 1946 after 4 performances in repertory; returned 20 September–12 October 1946 to the New York City Center for 3 additional performances in repertory, with substantially the same cast.

CAST: *Pirate King:* GEAN GREENWELL, JAMES PEASE. *Samuel,* his lieutenant: HUBERT NORVILLE. *Frederic,* Pirate apprentice: JOHN HAMILL. *Ruth,* Pirate Maid-of-all-work: CATHERINE JUDAH. *Major-General Stanley:* JOHN DUDLEY. *Major General Stanley's Daughters: Mabel:* VIRGINIA MacWATTERS. *Edith:* SUSAN GRISKA. *Kate:* LENORE PARKER. *Isabel:* Mary Polynach. *Sergeant of Police:* EMILE RENAN. *Chorus of Pirates, Police, and General Stanley's Daughters:* Ensemble.

ANNIE GET YOUR GUN
1946.12

A Musical in Two Acts, 10 Scenes. Music and lyrics by Irving Berlin. Book by Herbert and Dorothy Fields. Directed by Joshua Logan. Sets and lighting by Jo Mielziner. Dances by Helen Tamiris. Costumes by Lucinda Ballard. Orchestra directed by Jay S. Blackton. Orchestrations by Philip J. Lang, (Robert) Russell Bennett, Ted Royal. Vocal arrangements by Joe Moon. Piano arrangements by Helmy Kresa. Produced by Richard Rodgers and Oscar Hammerstein II. Opened 16 May 1946 at the Imperial Theatre and closed 12 February 1949 after 1147 performances.

CAST (in order of appearance): *Little Boy:* Warren Berlinger. *Little Girl:* Mary Ellen Glass. *Charlie Davenport:* MARTY MAY. *Iron Tail:* DANIEL NAGRIN. *Yellow Foot:* Earl Sauvain. *Mac* (Property Man): Cliff Dunstan. *Cowboys:* Rob Taylor, Bernard Griffin, Jack Pierce. *Cowgirls:* Mary Grey, Evelyn Giles. *Foster Wilson:* ART BARNETT. *Coolie:* Beau Tilden. *Dolly Tate:* LEA PENMAN. *Winnie Tate:* BETTY ANNE NYMAN. *Tommy Keeler:* KENNY BOWERS. *Frank Butler:* RAY MIDDLETON. *Girl With Bouquet:* Katrina Van Oss. *Annie Oakley:* ETHEL MERMAN. *Minnie,* Annie's Sister: Nancy Jean Raab. *Jessie,* Another Sister: Camilla DeWitt. *Nellie,* Another Sister: Marlene Cameron. *Little Jake,* Her Brother: Clifford Sales. *Harry:* Don Liberto. *Mary:* Ellen Hanley. *Col. Wm.F. Cody,* Buffalo Bill: WILLIAM O'NEAL. *Mrs. Little Horse:* Alma Ross. *Mrs. Black Tooth:* Elizabeth Malone. *Mrs. Yellow Foot:* Nellie Ranson. *Trainman:* John Garth III. *Waiter:* Leon Bibb. *Porter:* Clyde Turner. *Riding Mistress:* Lubov Roudenko. *Major Gordon Lillie,* Pawnee Bill: GEORGE LIPTON. *Chief Sitting Bull:* HARRY BELAVER. *Mabel:* Mary Woodley. *Louise:* Ostrid Lind. *Nancy:* Dorothy Richards. *Timothy Gardner:* Jack Byron. *Andy Turner:* Earl Sauvain. *Clyde Smith:* Victor Clarke. *John:* Rob Taylor. *Freddie:* Robert Dixon. *The Wild Horse,* Ceremonial Dancer: DANIEL NAGRIN. *Pawnee's Messenger:* Milton Watson. *Major Domo:* John Garth III. *First Waiter:* Clyde Turner. *Second Waiter:* Leon Bibb. *Mr. Schuyler Adams:* Don Liberto. *Mrs. Schuyler Adams:* Dorothy Richards. *Dr. Percy Ferguson:* Bernard Griffin. *Mrs. Percy Ferguson:* Marietta Vore. *Debutante:* Ruth Vrana. *Mr. Ernest Henderson:* Art Barnett. *Mrs. Ernest Henderson:* Truly Barbara. *Sylvia Potter-Porter:* Marjorie

Crossland. *Mr. Clay:* Rob Taylor. *Mr. Lockwood:* Fred Rivett. *Girl in Pink:* Jet MacDonald. *Girl in White:* Mary Grey.

Singing Girls: Truly Barbara, Ellen Hanley, Ostri Lind, Jet MacDonald, Dorothy Richards, Ruth Strickland, Katrina Van Oss, Marietta Vore, Ruth Vrana, Mary Woodley. *Singing Boys:* Jack Byron, Victor Clarke, Robert Dixon, Bernard Griffin, Marvin Goodis, Vincent Henry, Don Liberto, Fred Rivett, Earl Sauvain, Rob Taylor.

Dancing Girls: Franca Baldwin, Tessie Carrano, Madeleine Detry, Cyprienne Gabelman, Barbara Gaye, Evelyn Giles, Mary Grey, Harriet Roeder. *Dancing Boys:* Jack Beaber, John Begg, Michael Maule, Duncan Noble, Jack Pierce, Paddy Stone, Ken Whelan, Parker Wilson.

Act 1, Scene 1: The Wilson House, a summer hotel on the outskirts of Cincinnati, Ohio. July. *Scene 2:* A Pullman Parlor in an Overland Steam Train. Six weeks later. *Scene 3:* The Fair Grounds at Minneapolis, Minnesota. A few days later. *Scene 4:* The Arena of the Big Tent. *Scene 5:* A Dressing-room Tent. The same day. *Scene 6:* The Arena of the Big Tent. Later that night.

Act 2, Scene 1: The Deck of a Cattle Boat. Eight months later. *Scene 2:* Ballroom of the Hotel Brevoort. The next night. *Scene 3:* Aboard a Ferry. En route to Governor's Island. Next morning. *Scene 4:* Governor's Island. Near the Fort. Immediately following.

ACT 1

"(Colonel) Buffalo Bill"
> M. May, Ensemble

"I'm a Bad, Bad Man"
> R. Middleton, Girls
> *Danced by* D. Noble, P. Stone, P. Wilson, Ensemble.

"Doin' What Comes Naturally"
> E. Merman, N. J. Raab, C. DeWitt, M. Cameron, C. Sales, A. Barnett

"The Girl That I Marry"
> R. Middleton

"You Can't Get a Man With a Gun"
> E. Merman

"(There's No Business Like) Show Business"
> W. O'Neal, M. May, R. Middleton, E. Merman

"They Say It's Wonderful"
> R. Middleton, E. Merman

"Moonshine Lullaby"
> E. Merman, Trio

"I'll Share It All With You"[28]
> B. A. Nyman, K. Bowers

Ballyhoo
> *Danced by* L. Roudenko, Show People

"Show Business" (reprise)
> E. Merman

"My Defenses Are Down"
> R. Middleton, Boys

Wild Horse Ceremonial Dance
> *Danced by* D. Nagrin, Braves, Maidens

"I'm an Indian Too"
> E. Merman

Adoption Dance
> E. Merman, D. Nagrin, Braves

ACT 2

"(I Got) Lost in His Arms"
> E. Merman, Ensemble

"Who Do You Love, I Hope?"
> B. A. Nyman, K. Bowers
> *Danced by* B. A. Nyman, K. Bowers, Ensemble.

"(I Got the) Sun in the Morning"
> E. Merman, Ensemble
> *Danced by* L. Roudenko, D. Nagrin, Show People.

"They Say It's Wonderful" (reprise)
> E. Merman, R. Middleton

"The Girl That I Marry" (reprise)
> R. Middleton

"Anything You Can Do"
> E. Merman, R. Middleton

"Show Business" (reprise)
> Entire Company

---

[27] First presented in New York 31 December 1879 at the Fifth Avenue Theatre for a total of 91 performances in two engagements. For Synopsis of Scenes and Musical Numbers, see original 1879 production.

[28] Tap dance devised by Harry King.

AROUND THE WORLD IN EIGHTY DAYS

A Musical Extravaganza in Two Acts, 34 Scenes. Book by Orson Welles, adapted from the novel of the same name by Jules Verne. Music and lyrics by Cole Porter. Choreography by Nelson Barclift. Settings by Robert Davison. Costumes by Alvin Colt. Circus arranged by Barbette. Musical director, Harry Levant. Orchestrations by (Robert) Russell Bennett and Ted Royal. Film editor, Irving Lerner. Produced by Orson Welles (A Mercury Production). Opened 31 May 1946 at the Adelphi Theatre and closed 3 August 1946 after 75 performances.

CAST (in order of appearance): A *Bank Robber*: BRAINERD DUFFIELD. A *Police Inspector*: GUY SPAULL. *Dick Fix*, a Copper's Knark: ORSON WELLES. *London Bobbies*: Nathan Baker, Jack Pitchon, Myron Speth, Gordon West. A *Lady*: Genevieve Sauris. *Mr. Phileas Fogg*: ARTHUR MARGETSON. *Avery Jevity*, the First Earl of Cravenshaw: STEFAN SCHNABEL. *Molly Muggins*, an Irish Nursemaid: JULIE WARREN. *Passepartout*, a Yankee manservant to Fogg: LARRY LAURENCE. *Mr. Benjamin Cruett-Spew*: BRAINERD DUFFIELD. *Mr. Ralph Runcible*: GUY SPAULL. *Sir Charles Mandiboy*: BERNARD SAVAGE. *Lord Updditch*: Billy Howell. A *Servingman*: Bruce Cartwright. *Another Servingman*: Gregory McDougall. A *Station Attendant*: Billy Howell. *Meerahlah*, a dancer: DOROTHY BIRD. *Two Dancing Fellas*: Lucas Aco, Myron Speth. *The British Consul, in Suez*: BERNARD SAVAGE. *An Arab Spy*: STEFAN SCHNABEL. *A Second Arab Spy*: BRAINERD DUFFIELD. *Snake Charmers*: Eddy diGenova, Victor Savidge, Stanley Turner. *A Fakir*: Lucas Aco. *Maurice Goodpile*, Conductor on the Great Indian Peninsula R.R.: GUY SPAULL. *A Sikh*: Spencer James. *Mrs. Aouda*, an Indian Princess: MARY HEALY. *A High Priest*: Arthur Cohen. *Various Sinsister Chinese*: Phil King, Billy Howell, Lucas Aco, Nathan Baker. *Lee Toy*: Jackie Cezanne. *Two Daughters of Joy*: Lee Morrison, Nancy Newton. *Mr. Oka Saka*, Proprietor of the Oka Saka Circus: BRAINERD DUFFIELD. *Circus Artists*: The Foot Jugglers: The Three Kanasawa. *The Rolling Globe Lady*: Adelaide Corsi. *The Contortionist*: Miss Lu. *The Hand Balancer*: Ishikawa. *The Aerialists*: Mary Broussard, Lee Vincent, Patricia Leith, Virginia Morris. *Assistants*: Billy Howell, Lucas Aco, Gregory McDougall, Myron Speth. *The Slide for Life*: Ray Goody. *Roustabouts*: Jack Pitchon, Tony Montell. *Clowns*: Mother: STEFAN SCHNABEL. *Father*: Nathan Baker. *Child*: Bernie Pisarski. *Bride*: Cliff Chapman. *Groom*: LARRY LAURENCE. *Minister*: Arthur Cohen. *Policeman*: Jack Cassidy. *Monkey Man*: Eddy diGenova. *Kimona Man*: Allan Lowell. *Firemen*: Bruce Cartwright, Gordon West. *Dragon*: Daniel DePaolo. *An Attendant*: Stanley Turner. *A Bartender*: Eddy diGenova. *Mexican Dancers*: DOROTHY BIRD, Bruce Cartwright. *Lola*, the proprietress of a Cafe: VICTORIA CORDOVA. *Sol*, a station master in San Francisco: BRAINERD DUFFIELD. *Sam, a stagecoach driver*: Billy Howell. *Jim*, a railroad conductor of the Central Pacific R.R.: James Aco. *Jake*, a railroad engineer: Spencer James. *A Medicine Man of the Ojibiway*: STEFAN SCHNABEL. *Other Medicine Men*: George Spelvin, Billy Howell. *Jail Guard*: Allan Lowell.

Singing Gentlemen: Kenneth Bonjukian, Jack Cassidy, Arthur Cohen, Eddy diGenova, Allan Lowell, Tony Montell, Daniel de Paolo, Jack Pitchon, Victor Savidge, Stanley Turner. *Dancing Gentlemen*: Lucas Aco, Nathan Baker, Bruce Cartwright, Billy Howell, Phil King, Gregory McDougall, Myron Speth, Gordon West.

Singing Ladies: Florence Gault, Natalie Greene, Arline Hanna, Marion Kohler, Rose Marie Patane, Genevieve Sauris, Gina Siena, Drucilla Strain. *Dancing Ladies*: Mary Broussard, Jackie Cezanne, Elinor Gregory, Patricia, Leith, Virginia Morris, Lee Morrison, Nancy Newton, Miriam Pandor, Virginia Sands, Lee Vincent.

Act 1, Scene 1: Movies. *Scene 2*: Interior of Jevity's Bank, London, England. *Scene 3*: Movies. *Scene 4*: Hyde Park. *Scene 5*: A London Street. *Scene 6*: Mr. Fogg's Flat in London. *Scene 7*: A Street before the Whist Club. *Scene 8*: The Card Room of the Whist Club. *Scene 9*: Fogg's Flat. *Scene 10*: The Charing Cross Railroad Station. *Scene 11*: Suez, Egypt. *Scene 12*: The End of Railway Tracks in British India. *Scene 13*: The Great Indian Forest. *Scene 14*: The Pagoda of Pilagi. *Scene 15*: A Jungle Encampment in the Himalayas. *Scene 16*: Aboard the S.S. Tankadere on the China Sea. *Scene 17*: Movies. *Scene 18*: A Street of Evil Repute in Hong-Kong. *Scene 19*: Interior of an Opium Hell in the same city. *Scene 20*: The Oka Saka Circus, Yokohama, Japan.

Act 2, Scene 1: Movies. *Scene 2*: Lola's, a low place in Lower California. *Scene 3*: The Railroad Station in San Francisco. *Scene 4*: Movies. *Scene 5*: A Passenger Car on the Central Pacific Highway-Somewhere in the Rocky Mountains. *Scene 6*: The Perilous Pass at Medicine Bow. *Scene 7*: A Water Stop on the Banks of the Republican River. *Scene 8*: The Peak of Bald Mountain. *Scene 9*: The Harbor, Liverpool, England. *Scene 10*: The Gaol in Liverpool. *Scene 11*: A Cell in the Liverpool Gaol. *Scene 12*: A Street in London. *Scene 13*: Outside the London Whist Club. *Scene 14*: Grand Tableau.

ACT 1

Scene 4
"Look What I Found"
J. Warren, L. Laurence

Scene 6
"There He Goes, Mr. Phileas Fogg"
A. Margetson, L. Laurence

Scene 7
"There He Goes, Mr. Phileas Fogg" (reprise)
A. Margetson, L. Laurence, Dancers, Singers

Scene 11
"Meerahlah"
Singing Boys
(Suez) Dance
D. Bird, Dancers

Scene 13
"Suttee Procession"
M. Healy, Dancers, Singers

Scene 14
Dance
Dancers

Scene 16
"Sea Chantey"
Singing Boys
"Should I Tell You I Love You?"
M. Healy

Scene 19
"Pipe Dreaming"
L. Laurence, Singing Chorus

Scene 20
"Oka Saka Circus"
Circus Performers

ACT 2

Scene 2
Dance
D. Bird, B. Cartwright, J. Cezanne, Dancers
"If You Smile at Me"
V. Cordova
"Pipe Dreaming" (reprise)
L. Laurence
"If You Smile at Me" (reprise)
J. Warren

Scene 8
"Wherever They Fly the Flag of Old England"
A. Margetson, Singing Girls
"The Marine's Hymn"
M. Healy, Singing Boys

Scene 11
"Should I Tell You I Love You?" (reprise)
M. Healy

Scene 14
Finale
Entire Company

Joan McCracken in BLOOMER GIRL
Billy Rose Theatre Collection, New York Public Library for the Performing Arts

1946–1947 SEASON

1946.14 ICETIME

An Ice Skating Revue in Two Acts, 22 Scenes. Music and lyrics by James Littlefield and John Fortis. Production by Sonart Productions. Executive director, Arthur M. Wirtz. Production director, William H. Burke. Staged by Catherine Littlefield. Settings designed and created by Edward Gilbert. Costumes by Lou Eisele and Billy Livingston. Choreography by Catherine Littlefield, assisted by Dorothie Littlefield. Lighting effects by Eugene Braun. Skating direction by May Judels. Musical conductor, David Mendoza. Musical arrangements by Paul Van Loan. Produced by Sonja Henie and Arthur M. Wirtz. Opened 20 June 1946 at the Center Theatre and closed 12 April 1947 after 405 performances.

CAST: JOAN HYLDOFT, FREDDIE TRENKLER, THE BRUISES (Monty Stott, Geoffe Stevens, Sid Spaulding), BRANDT SISTERS (Helga, Inga Brandt), BOB and FLORENCE BALLARD, (Buster) GRACE and (Charles) SLAGLE, BOB and FLORENCE, FRITZ DIETL, PAUL CASTLE, CLAIRE DALTON, JAMES CAESAR, JACK REESE, PATRICK KAZDA, JAMES CARTER. Vocals: JAY MARTIN, DENISE BRIAULT, SHIRLEY WEBER, RICHARD CRAIG.

Ensemble: Helen Carter, Charles Cavanaugh, Grace Church, Jinx Clark, Kay Corcoran, Helen Dutcher, Walli Hackman, John Kasper, Patrick Kazda, Marion Lulling, Edward McDonald, Ann Michel, Sharlee Munster, Berenice Odell, Buck Pennington, Ragna Ray, Jack Reese, Jerry Rehfield, Lucille Risch, Jean Sakovich, Joe Shillen, Jimmie Sisk, Bing Stott, Sally Tepley, Eileen Thompson, Cissy Trenholm, John Walsh. Ellen Barkey, Grace Bleckman, Babette George, Gloria Haupt, Edith Kandel, Patricia Lemaire, Marion Lulling, Marvette Mosic, Blach Poston, Lela Rolontz, Theresa Rothacker, Evelyn Smith, Beth Stevens, Edward Brandstetter, Edward Berry, Ray Blow, Charles Caminiti, Gere Decker, Robert Fitzgerald, Gordon Holley, Dan Hurley, Buddy Jones, Garry Kerman, William Knapp, Kenneth Leslie, Arthur Meehan, Jack Millikan, Gus Patrick, Kenneth Parker, Leonard Stofka, Jack Strand, Fred Thompson, James Trenholm, Wallace Van Sickle.

ACT 1
Scene 1

Winter Holiday: "Song of the Silver Blades"
R. Craig, D. Briault, S. Weber
Ladies of the Ensemble: E. Barkey, K. Corcoran, H. Dutcher, B. George, G. Haupt, W. Hackman, E. Kandel, P. Lemaire, M. Mosic, S. Munster, A. Michel, B. Odell, B. Poston, T. Rothacker, B. Stevens, E. Thompson. *Gentlemen of the Ensemble:* E. Brandstetter, E. Berry, G. Decker, R. Fitzgerald, D. Hurley, B. Jones, G. Kerman, W. Knapp, K. Leslie, E. McDonald, A. Meehan, J. Millikan, G. Patrick, K. Parker, L. Stofka, J. Trenholm.

Scene 2

Holiday Inn Octette (Skating Lesson/Ski Lesson)
Instructor and Partner: F. Dietl, C. Trenholm. B. Stott, J. Carter, J. Clark, J. Walsh, G. Church, C. Cavanaugh, J. Sakovich, J. Sisk.

Scene 3

Mary, Mary Quite Contrary: "Mary, Mary"
R. Craig
Butterfly: H. Carter. *Cat:* J. Reese. *Mary's Mother:* J. Kasper. *Mary:* F. Ballard. *Rabbit:* B. Pennington. *Bee:* J. Shillen. *Boy with Flowers:* P. Kazda.

Scene 4

Setting the Pace
Ladies of the Ensemble: E. Barkey, G. Bleckman, G. Church, K. Corcoran, H. Dutcher, B. George, G. Haupt, W. Hackman, E. Kandel, P. Lemaire, M. Lulling, M. Mosic, S. Munster, A. Michel, B. Odell, B. Poston, L. Rolontz, R. Ray, T. Rothacker, B. Stott, B. Stevens, C. Trenholm, E. Thompson, S. Tepley. *Gentlemen of the Ensemble:* E. Berry, E. Brandstetter, R. Blow, C. Cavanaugh, C. Caminiti, G. Decker, R. Fitzgerald, D. Hurley, B. Jones, G. Kerman, J. Kenny, W. Knapp, K. Leslie, E. McDonald, A. Meehan, J. Millikan, G. Patrick, K. Parker, J. Strand, L. Stofka, J. Trenholm, F. Thompson, W. Van Sickle, G. Holley.

Scene 5

Precision Plus
F. Dietl, J. Carter
Ladies of the Ensemble: E. Barkey, K. Corcoran, H. Dutcher, B. George, G. Haupt, W. Hackman, E. Kandel, P. Lemaire, M. Mosic, S. Munster, A. Michel, B. Odell, B. Poston, T. Rothacker, B. Stevens, E. Thompson. *Gentlemen of the Ensemble:* E. Brandstetter, E. Berry, G. Decker, R. Fitzgerald, D. Hurley, B. Jones, G. Kerman, W. Knapp, K. Leslie, E. McDonald, A. Meehan, J. Millikan, G. Patrick, K. Parker, L. Stofka, J. Trenholm.

Scene 6

Old King Cole: "Old King Cole"
R. Craig, D. Briault, S. Weber
Footmen: J. Walsh, C. Cavanaugh. *King:* J. Kasper. *First Fiddler:* B. Pennington. *Second Fiddler:* C. Dalton. *Third Fiddler:* P. Castle.

Scene 7

Light and Shadow
H. Brandt, I. Brandt

Scene 8

Zouaves
B. Grace, C. Slagle, J. Sisk, J. Shillen

Scene 9

Sherwood Forest
Robin Hood's Band: J. Clark, J. Sakovich, G. Church. *Robin Hood:* J. Caesar. *Cavalier:* R. Ballard. *Countess:* B. Stott.

Scene 10

The Nutcracker
Father: C. Cavanugh. *Mother:* K. Corcoran. *Children:* B. Odell, E. Smith, K. Leslie. *Nutcracker:* P. Castle. *Candy Prince:* J. Rehfield. *Tutu Girls:* G. Bleckman, H. Dutcher, E. Kandel, G. Haupt, P. Lemaire, M. Lulling, M. Mosic, B. Poston, L. Rolontz, R. Ray, T. Rothacker, B. Stevens, C. Trenholm, E. Thompson, S. Tepley. *Candy Fairy:* J. Hyldoft, E. Berry, E. Brandstetter, R Blow, C. Cavanaugh, C. Caminiti, G. Decker, R. Fitzgerald, G. Kerman, J. Kenny, K. Leslie, J. Millikan, G. Patrick, J. Strand, F. Thompson, W. Van Sickle, G. Holley. *Dance Chinoise:* L. Risch, H. Carter, B. Pennington. *Trepak:* J. Reese. *Waltz of the Flowers:* Tutu Girls, K. Corcoran, W. Hackman, S. Munster, A. Michel.

Scene 11

Bouncing Ball of the Ice
F. Trenkler
Policeman: J. Shillen. *Nursemaid:* J. Clark.

Scene 12

When the Minstrels Come to Town
R. Craig, D. Briault, S. Weber
"Mandy" and "Cuddle Up"
J. Martin
Drummer Boy: E. McDonald. *Banner Bearers:* D. Hurely, G. Kerman. *Head Interlocutor:* J. Walsh. *Interlocutors:* J. Kasper, J. Carter, P. Kazda, J Rehfield. *Sambo, Bones, Tambo, Jones:* B. Grace, C. Slagle, J. Sisk, B. Pennington. *Banjo Boys:* E. Berry, E. Brandstetter, R. Blow, C. Cavanaugh, C. Caminiti, G. Decker, R. Fitzgerald, W. Knapp, K. Leslie, A. Meehan, J. Millikan, G. Patrick, K. Parker, J. Strand, F. Thompson, W. Van Sickle. *Tambourine Girls:* E. Barkey, G. Bleckman, G. Church, B. George, G. Haupt, W. Hackman, P. Lemaire, M. Lulling, S. Munster, B. Odell, B. Poston, T. Rothacker, J. Sakovich, C. Trenholm, B. Stevens, S. Tepley. *Lillian Russell:* C. Dalton. *Can Can Girls:* G. Bleckman, E. Barkey, G. Church, K. Corcoran, H. Dutcher, E. Kandel, P. Lemaire, M. Lulling, M. Mosic, S. Munster, A. Michel, B. Odell, B. Poston, L. Rolontz, R. Ray, B. Stott, J. Sakovich, C. Trenholm, E. Thompson, S. Tepley.

ACT 2
Scene 1

Cossack Lore
R. Craig, D. Briault, S. Weber
Princes: P. Kazda, J. Rehfield. *Nobles:* R. Blow, C. Caminiti, G. Decker, R. Fitzgerald, D. Hurley, B. Jones, W. Knapp, J. Millikan, L. Stofka, J. Trenholm. *Court Pages:* H. Carter, L. Risch. *Grooms:* J. Clark, R. Ray, B. Stott, J. Sakovich. *Cossacks:* J. Carter, J. Kasper, B. Pennington, J. Walsh. *Gypsy Girls:* E. Barkey, K. Corcoran, H. Dutcher, B. George, W. Hackman, E. Kandel, P. Lemaire, M. Lulling, M. Mosic, S. Munster, A. Michel, B. Odell, B. Poston, L. Rolontz, T. Rothacker, B. Stevens, E. Thompson, S. Tepley. *Ivan:* J. Caesar.

Scene 2

Divertissement
E. Kenny, J. Kenny

Scene 3

"Lovable You"
J. Martin. J. Clark, H. Dutcher, M. Lulling, S. Munster, J. Sakovich, E. Thompson, S. Tepley, J. Hyldoft

Scene 4

Double Vision
H. Brandt, I. Brandt
Escorts: J. Walsh, J. Rehfield.

Scene 5

Garden of Versailles

Les Faunes: J. Kasper, B. Pennington, J. Reese, P. Castle. *Peintre*:
P. Kazda. *Mademoiselle*: C. Dalton. *Madame Jeanne*: F. Dietl. *Academy
of Madame Jeanne*: E. Barkey, G. Bleckman, G. Church, J. Clark,
K. Corcoran, H. Dutcher, B. George, G. Haupt, W. Hackman, E. Kandel,
P. Lemaire, M. Lulling, M. Mosic, S. Munster, A. Michel, B. Odell,
B. Poston, L. Rolontz, T. Rocthacker, J. Sakovich, B. Stevens, C. Trenholm,
E. Thomson, S. Tepley. *Les Amoureux*: F. Ballard, R. Ballard.

Scene 6

Those Good Old Days

L. Risch, J. Sisk, J. Clark, J. Walsh, C. Dalton, J. Rehfiled, H. Carter, J. Carter
The Sport: J. Reese.

Scene 7

Higher and Higher

B. Grace, C. Slagle

Scene 8

The Dream Waltz: ("Her Dream Man")

J. Martin, D. Briault, S. Weber
Jivers: B. Odell, R. Ray, J. Kenny, B. Pennington, J. Kasper. *Dream
Girl*: J. Hyldoft. *Hussars*: J. Carter, P. Kazda, J. Rehfield, J. Walsh.
Waltz Girls: E. Barkey, G. Bleckman, G. Church, K. Corcoran,
J. Clark, H. Dutcher, B. George, W. Hackman, E. Kandel, P. Lemaire,
M. Lulling, M. Mosic, S. Munster, A. Michel, B. Poston, L. Rolontz,
R. Ray, T. Rothacker, B. Stott, J. Sakovich, B. Stevens, C. Trenholm,
E. Thompson, S. Tepley. *Yellow Hussars*: E. Brandstetter, R. Blow,
C. Cavanaugh, C. Caminiti, G. Decker, R. Fitzgerald, G. Kerman,
W. Knapp, J. Millikan, G. Patrick, J. Strand, L. Stofka, J. Trenholm,
F. Thompson, W. Van Sickle, G. Holley. *Her Dream Man*: F. Dietl.

Scene 9

The Bruises

M. Stott, G. Stevens, S. Spalding

Scene 10

Finale

(Company)

TIDBITS OF 1946

1946.15

An Intimate Musical Entertainment in Two Acts, 17 Scenes, based on The
Youth Theatre Revue[1]. Sketches written and directed by Sam Locke.
Orchestra directed by Phil Romano. Produced by Arthur Klein in association with Henry Schumer. Opened 8 July 1946 at the Plymouth Theatre and
closed 13 July 1946 after 8 performances.[2]

CAST: JOEY FAYE, MURIEL GAINES, LEE TRENT, JOSEF MIRAIS and
MIRANDA, CARMEN and ROLANDO, EDDY MANSON, ROBERT
MARSHALL, JOSHUA SHELLEY, JOSEPHINE BOYER, JACK DIAMOND, THE
DEBONAIRS.

ACT 1

Scene 1

Apologia

L. Trent

Scene 2

Harmonica Days

E. Manson

Scene 3

"Hi Havana!" (Dance)

Carmen and Rolando
Bongo Boy: Candido.

Scene 4

On the Veld (South African folk songs)

J. Mirais and Miranda

Scene 5

Psychiatry in Technicolor

Dr. Serutan Pimento: J. Faye. *Miss Fortescue Wimpy*: J. Boyer. *The Oedipus Rex*:
J. Diamond. *Mr. Pickling*: J. Shelley.

---

[1]First presented in New York the week of 20 May 1946 at the Barbizon-
Plaza Theatre.
[2]Settings and costumes uncredited.

Scene 6

So It Goes at the Met (Opera burlesque)

R. Marshall

Scene 7

In a Jeep

J. Faye, J. Diamond

Scene 8

"I'm the Belle of the Ballet"

J. Boyer

Scene 9

"Step This Way" (Dance Quintet)

The Debonairs

ACT 2

Scene 1

"On the Way to Sloppy Joe's" (Dance)

Carmen, Rolando, Candido

Scene 2

A Few Moments with Lee Trent (Comedian)

Scene 3

The Man Who Came to Heaven

The Angel: J. Faye. *The Congressman*: J. Shelley.

Scene 4

Capetown Capers (South African folk songs)

J. Mirais and Miranda

Scene 5

Never Kill Your Mother on Mother's Day

(*by* Mel Tolkin)L. Trent, J. Shelley

Scene 6

The Lass With the Delicate Air (Singer-dancer)

M. Gaines

Scene 7

Meet Me on Flugle Street

J. Faye, J. Diamond

Scene 8

Finale

(Company)

YOURS IS MY HEART

1946.16

An Operetta in Three Acts. Book and Lyrics by Ira Cobb and Karl Farkas.
Based on "The Land of Smiles" (the romantic operette "Das Land des
Lächelns," with German libretto by Ludwig Herzer and Fritz Löhner,
adapted from "Die gelbe Jacke" by Victor Léon). Music by Franz Lehár.
Entire production staged by Theodore Bache. Dialogue direction by
Monroe Manning. Dances by Henry Shwarze. Scenery and costumes by H.
A. Condell. Lighting by Milton Lowe. Musical director, George Schick.
Musical adaptation by Felix Guenther. Presented in association with
Continental Music Publishing Co., Inc. Produced by Arthur Spitz. Opened
5 September 1946 at the Sam S. Shubert Theatre and closed 5 October
1946 after 36 performances.

CAST (in order of appearance): *Guy*: Monroe Manning. *Lucille*: Helene Whitney.
Lou: Jane Mackle. *Pierre*: Harold Lazaron. *Fernand D'Orville*: ALEXANDER
D'ARCY. *Yvonne*: Natalye Green. *Fifi*: Dorothy Karrol. *Marie*: Jane Heisey. *Archibald
Mascotte*, Impressario: SAMMY WHITE. *Claudette Vernay, Prima Donna*: STELLA
ANDREVA. *Butler*: Harvey Kier. *Prince Sou Chong*: RICHARD TAUBER. *Huang
Wei, Chinese Ambasssador*: Edward Groag. *Prince Tschang*, Sou Chong's Uncle:
Arnold Spector. *Hsi Fueng, Minister of Finance*: FRED KEATING. *Princess Mi*, Sou
Chong's Sister: LILLIAN HELD. *Master of Ceremonies*: Albert Schoengold. *High
Priest*: Fred Briess. *Li Tsi, Chinese Bride*: Beatrice Eden. *Solo Dancers*: Trudy Goth,
Henry Schwarze, Wayne Lamb, Alberto Feliciano. *Guests, Maids, Servants, Dancers,
Mandarins, etc.*

Ladies of the Dance Ensemble: Elfi Duke, Helen Farrell, Eleanore Gregory,
Mary Kane, Athena Kellar, Sonia Levanskaya, Sondra Lipton, Margaret McCallion,
Carol Percy, Gloria Stevens, Estelle Tamus, Edythe A. Uden, Joanna Vischer,
Geraldine Wyss.

Ladies and Gentlemen of the Singing Ensemble: Natalye Green, Jean Heisey, Julie
Jefferson, Dorothy Karrol, Phyllis Lockard, Jane Mackle, Helene Whitney, Isabella
Wilson, Edward Budana, Harry Kiery, Harold Lazaron, Scotty Miller, Frank Price,
Albert Shoengold.

Act 1: Drawing-room of Claudette Vernay's Paris apartment. About 1900.

Act 2: Hall in Sou Chong's Palace in Peiping, six weeks later.

Act 3: Room in Sou Chong's Palace, the following day.

ACT 1

Music Box and Waltz
Ensemble

"Goodbye, Paree"
A. D'Arcy, Ensemble

"Free As the Air"
S. Andreva, Ensemble

"Chinese Melody"
S. Andreva

"Patiently Smiling"
R. Tauber

"A Cup of China Tea"
S. Andreva, R. Tauber

"Upon a Moonlight Night in May"
R. Tauber, Ensemble

Finale
S. Andreva, R. Tauber

ACT 2

Chinese Ceremony
Entire Ensemble

Master of Ceremonies
H. Shwarze

Sword Dance
W. Lamb, A. Feliciano

Dance of the Girls
Dance Ensemble

Chinese Puppet Dance
T. Goth, Dance Ensemble

"Love, What Has Given You This Magic Power?"
S. Andreva, R. Tauber

"Men of China"
L. Held, Dance Ensemble

"Chingo-Pingo"
L. Held, A. D'Arcy, Ensemble

"Yours Is My Heart Alone"
R. Tauber

Wedding Ceremony
Entire Ensemble

Finale
S. Andreva, R. Tauber

ACT 3

"Upon a Moonlight Night in May" (reprise)
S. Andreva, T. Goth, Ensemble

"Paris Sings Again"
S. Andreva
(*Music by* Paul Durant.)

Opium Ballet
H. Schwarze, S. White, A. D'Arcy, Dance Ensemble

"Ma Petite Cheri"
L. Held, A. D'Arcy

Finale
S. Andreva, L. Held, R. Tauber, S. White, A. D'Arcy

1946.17

A FLAG IS BORN

A Pageant in One Act. Play by Ben Hecht. Music by Kurt Weill. Staged by Luther Adler. Choreography by Zamira Gon. Music arranged by Isaac Van Grove. Settings by Robert Davison. Costumes by John Boyt. Lighting supervised by George Gebhardt. Musical director, Isaac Van Grove. Orchestrations by Rudolf Goehr. In charge of production, Julius J. Leventhal. Produced by the American League for a Free Palestine. Opened 5 September 1946 at the Alvin Theatre, moved 5 October 1946 to the Adelphi Theatre, moved 22 October 22 1946 to the Music Box Theatre, moved 19 November 1946 to the Broadway Theatre, and closed 15 December 1946 after 120 performances.

CAST (in order of appearance): *Speaker*: QUENTIN REYNOLDS. *Tevya*: PAUL MUNI. *Zelda*: CELIA ADLER. *David*: MARLON BRANDO. *The Singer*: Mario Berini. *Saul*: GEORGE DAVID BAXTER. *Old One*: Morris Samuylow. *Middle Aged One*: David Manning. *Young One*: John Baragrey. *David the King*: William Allyn. *Solomon*: GREGORY MORTON. *American Statesman*: JONATHAN HARRIS. *Russian Statesman*: Yasha Rosenthal. *First English Statesman*: TOM EMLYN WILLIAMS. *Second English Statesman*: Jefferson Coates. *French Statesman*: Frederick Rudin. *First Soldier*: STEVE HILL. *Second Soldier*: JONATHAN HARRIS. *Third Soldier*: HAROLD GARY.

Supers: William Berg, Randolph Jones, Nick Ferber, Jack Wesley, Allen Lindstrom, Vincent Beck, Jo Davidson, Charles Feurman, George Anderson, Martin Leavitt, Solomon Goldstein, Jack Sloane, Harry Moses, Gilbert Leigh, Jack Buxbaum, Jim Flynn, Norman Kilroy, Jules Preuss, Thomas Arena, Rudoph McKool, Joe Bernard, Daniel Moskowitz, Carl Shelton, Robert Weston, Bill Reid, Ray Johnson, Jim Davidson, Pearl Sugerman, Natalie Norwick, Rona Christie, Selma Stern, Michael Kazaras, Terry Becker, Paul Firestone, Peggy Strange, Steve Graves, Don Sacks, Eileen Ayres.

Dancers: Evangeline Collis, Anne Wayne, Lillian Ekman, Evelyn Leeds, Anne Widman, Ruth Harris, Audrey Eden, Pearl Borchard, Lee Morrison, Lillian Fisher, Maybelle Lama, Sophia Babert, Virginia Gilchrist, Shirley King, Rosalind Posnick, Jeanne Belkin, Miriam Levy.

Choir: Paul Mario, Elton Plowman, Joseph Hill, William Durkin, Carl Manning, Allen Lowell, Nicholas Torzs, Richard Monte.

MUSICAL SELECTION[3]

Prelude, Lament, Tevya Music, Wandering, Partisan Theme, Religious Prayer, Theme PP, Kol Nidre, Trumpets/Fanfare/Rhythm, King David Theme, The Lord Is My Shepherd, Fanfares/Rhythm, Rozinkas und mandlen, Chant, Solomon's Song of Songs, Fanfares and Medley (Punishment Fits the Crime/Give My Regards to Broadway/Marseillaise/Red Army March), Drums, Russian March, Wandering Theme, Rozinkas und mandlen (reprise), Lament, Partisan Theme, Prelude/Patriotic Themes (reprise), Wandering (reprise), Laughter Themes, Partisan Theme Finale.

1946.18

GYPSY LADY

An Operetta in Two Acts, 8 Scenes. Music by Victor Herbert. Book by Henry Myers, created to re-introduce melodies from "The Fortune Teller" and "The Serenade," by arrangement with Ella Herbert Bartlett. Musical adaptation and direction, orchestration and choral arrangements by Arthur Kay. Stage direction and new lyrics by Robert Wright and George Forrest. Vocal numbers staged by Lew Kessler. Dance direction by Aida Broadbent. Scenic designs by Boris Aronson. Costume designs by Miles White. Lighting and technical supervision by Adrian Awan. Produced by Edwin Lester. Opened 17 September 1946 at the New Century Theatre and closed 23 November 1946 after 79 performances.

CAST (in order of appearance): *Baron Pettibois*: CLARENCE DERWENT. *Yvonne*: KAYE CONNOR. *Fresco*: JACK GOODE. *Musetta*: HELENA BLISS. *Sergeant of Gendarmes*: Edmund Dorsay. *The Great Alvarado*: JOHN TYERS. *Valerie, Marquise of Roncevalle*: DOREEN WILSON. *Imri*: VAL VALENTINOFF. *Rudolfo*: William Bauer. *Boris*: MELVILLE COOPER. *Roszika*: PATRICIA SIMS. *Sandor*: GEORGE BRITTON. *Andre, Marquis of Roncevalle*: GILBERT RUSSELL. *Stephan, Duke of Roncevalle*: JOSEPH MACAULAY. *The Undecided Mademoiselle*: Suzanne Meredith. *M. Guilbert Armand*: Bert Hillner. *Majordomo*: Harvey Shahan.

Young Ladies of the Academy, Gypsies, Guests, Maids and Mannikins: Jeanne Bal, Phyllis Bateman, Mardi Bayne, Betty Brusher, Marydee Buscher, Dorothy Coulter, Beth Alba Cushing, Betty Galavan, Florette Hillier, Rosemary Leisen, Suzette Meredith, Dani Nelson, Bernice Saunders, Nelda Scarsella, Peggy Weakland, Helen Wysatt.

Gypsies, Gentlemen, Bellboys, Waiters: James Andrews, George Dempsey, Paul De Poyster, Ray Drakely, Dean Etmund, Max Hart, Bert Hillner, Elton Howard, William James, Dale Johnson, Richard Scott, Robert Searles, Harvey Shahan, Ray Smith, John Stamford, Stanley Wolfe. *Dancing Gypsies and Ballet*: Barbara Bailey, Lyza Baugher, Donna Biroc, Florence Brundage, Jean Marie Caples, Kathleen Cartmill, Elaine Corbett, Marietta Elliott, Mitzi Gerber, Irene Hall, Judy Landon, Joan Larkin, Betty Orth, Patricia Sims, Betty Slade, Maria Taweel.

Act 1, Scene 1: Baron Pettibois' Academy of Theatre Arts. An afternoon early in summer in France, about 1900. *Scene 2*: The Gypsy Camp. At sunset the same day. *Scene 3*: The Baron's Garden. The next day.

_____

[3]Individual musical numbers not listed in program; music list prepared from production typescript.

Act 2, Scene 1: A Suite in a Paris Hotel. A few weeks later. Scene 2: Roof of the Hotel overlooking Montmartre. The same evening. Scene 3: Terrace of the Chateau de Roncevalle. A fortnight later. Scene 4: Cupid's Cupola. Later that night. Scene 5: The Road. Dawn.

ACT 1

Scene 1

"On a Wonderful Day Like Today"
Young Ladies of the Academy
"The Facts of Life Backstage"
J. Goode, K. Connor, Young Ladies
The Serenade: "I Love You, I Adore You"
J. Tyers, D. Wilson
"Interlude"
H. Bliss, J. Tyers
"On a Wonderful Day Like Today" (reprise)
Young Ladies

Scene 2

"Life Is a Dirty Business"
Gypsy Men
"My Treasure"
G. Britton, Gypsy Men
"Romany Life"
H. Bliss, Gypsies
(Original lyrics by Harry B. Smith.)

Scene 3

"Pantomime"
J. Goode
"The World and I"
G. Russell, J. Tyers, Girls from Paris
"Piff Paff"
J. Macaulay, D. Wilson, G. Russell
"Andalusia Bolero"
V. Valentinoff, P. Sims, Gypsies
"Keepsakes"
J. Tyers, D. Wilson
Finale
J. Tyers, H. Bliss, C. Derwent, J. Goode, G. Britton, Gypsies

ACT 2

Scene 1

"Young Lady a la Mode"
J. Tyers, H. Bliss, J. Goode, K. Connor, B. Hillner, Bellboys, Maids, Mannikins

Scene 2

"Springtide"
G. Russell, H. Bliss

Scene 3

Ballet Divertissement
Ballet Company
"My First Waltz"
H. Bliss, G. Russell, J. Tyers, J. Goode, Ensemble
"Reality"
M. Cooper, J. Goode, C. Derwent
"Gypsy Love Song"
G. Britton
(Original lyrics by Harry B. Smith.)
"Piff Paff"
J. Macaulay, J. Tyers, G. Russell, D. Wilson, J. Goode, Guests

Scene 4

"Springtide" (reprise)
G. Russell
"Serenade" (reprise)
J. Tyers

Scene 5

"Romany Life" (Finale)
Ensemble

1946.19

NAUGHTY NAUGHT

A Revival of the Musical Drama of Life at Yale in Three Acts, 10 Scenes[4]. Book by John Van Antwerp [Jerrold Krimsky]. Music by Richard Lewine. Lyrics by Ted Fetter. Directed by Ted Fetter. Dances by Ray Harrison. Physical production (settings) conceived and lighted by Kermit Love. Costumes by Robert Moore. Music director, Richard Lewine. Orchestra direction and arrangements by Leroy Anderson. Produced by Paul Killiam in association with Oliver Rea. Opened 19 October 1946 at the American Music Hall and closed 2 November 1946 after 21 performances.

CAST (in order of appearance): P. DeQuincy Devereux: JOHN CROMWELL. Spunky: Teddy Hart. Frank Plover: LEONARD HICKS. Jack Granville: KENNETH FORBES. Stub: Shepard Curelop. Fred: King Taylor. Claire Granville: OTTILIE KRUGER. Jim Pawling: Marshall Jamison. Joe: Roy Wolvin. Tom: Len Smith, Jr. Bartender: GEORGE SPELVIN. Cathleen: Virginia Barbour. Pugsy: L. A. Nicoletti.
Naughty Naughty Girls: Aza Bard, Helen Franklin, Dorothy Hill, Rhoda Johannson, Diane Renay, Mildred Roane.

Act 1, Scene 1: Yale Campus. Scene 2: Frank and Jack's Dormitory Room.

Act 2, Scene 1: Frank and Jack's Dormitory Room. Scene 2: Moriarity's Saloon.

Act 3, Scene 1: New Haven Railroad Station. Scene 2: Boathouse near Thames. Scene 3: The River Bank. Scene 4: Boathouse near Thames. Scene 5: The River Bank. Scene 6: At the Race.

ACT 1

Scene 1

"Goodbye Girls, Hello Yale"
Freshmen

Scene 2

"Naughty-Naught"
Seniors
"Mother Isn't Getting Any Younger"
T. Hart
"When We're in Love"
O. Kruger, L. Hicks, Company
Olio: Myrtle Dunedin (Unicyclist Extraordinary)

ACT 2

Scene 1

"When We're in Love" (reprise)
O. Kruger

Scene 2

"Zim Zam Zee"
V. Barbour, Men
Olios:
Maxine and Bobby (A Man and His Dog)
"Coney-by-the-Sea"
V. Barbour, K. Taylor, Company
Ullaine Malloy (Aerialist Supreme)

ACT 3

Scene 1

"What's Good About Good Morning?"
Crewmen
"Pull the Boat for Eli"
Students, Girls

Scene 2

"Just Like a Woman"
J. Cromwell, Men

Scene 5

Finale
Entire Company

---

[4]Originally produced in New York as NAUGHTY NAUGHT '00 23 January 1937 at the American Music Hall for 173 performances.

1946.20 ## PARK AVENUE

A Musical Comedy in Two Acts. Book by Nunnally Johnson and George S. Kaufman. (Based on the short story "Holy Matrimony" by Nunnally Johnson as published in the *Saturday Evening Post* in 1933). Music by Arthur Schwartz. Lyrics by Ira Gershwin. Book directed by George S. Kaufman. Dances and musical numbers by Helen Tamiris. Production supervised by Arnold Saint Subber. Settings and lighting by Donald Oenslager. All gowns, except Miss Corbett's, designed by Tina Leser; Miss Corbett's gowns by Mainbocher. Vocal direction and musical adaptation for dances by Clay Warnick. Musical conductor, Charles Sanford. Orchestrations by Don Walker. Produced by Max Gordon. Opened 4 November 1946 at the Sam S. Shubert Theatre and closed 4 January 1947 after 72 performances.

CAST: *Carlton*: Byron Russell. *Ned Scott*: RAY McDONALD. *Madge Bennett*: MARTHA STEWART. *Ogden Bennett*: ARTHUR MARGETSON. *Mrs. Sybil Bennett*: LEONORA CORBETT. *Charles Crowell*: ROBERT CHISHOLM. *Mrs. Elsa Crowell*: MARTHE ERROLLE. *Reggie Fox*: CHARLES PURCELL. *Mrs. Myra Fox*: RUTH MATTESON. *Richard Nelson*: RAYMOND WALBURN. *Mrs. Betty Nelson*: MARY WICKES. *Ted Woods*: Harold Mattox. *Mrs. Laura Woods*: Dorothy Bird. *James Meredith*: William Skipper. *Mrs. Beverly Meredith*: Joan Mann. *Mr. Meachem*: David Wayne. *Freddie Coleman*: Wilson Smith. *Carole Benswanger*: Virginia Gordon. *Brenda Stokes*: Adelle Rasey. *Brenda Follansbee*: Sherry Shadburne. *Brenda Follansbee-Stokes*: Carol Chandler. *Brenda Follansbee-Stokes-Follansbee*: Betty Ann Lynn. *Brenda Cadwallader*: Kyle MacDonnell. *Brenda Stuyvesant*: Eileen Coffman. *Brenda Cathcart*: June Graham. *Brenda Cathcart-Cathcart*: Betty Low. *Brenda Kerr*: Virginia Morris. *Brenda Ker-Ker-Ker*: Judi Blacque. *Brenda Quincy Adams*: Gloria Anderson. *Brenda Wright, Jr., Sr., III*: Margaret Gibson.

The action takes place in the Home of Mrs. Ogden Bennett. Long Island.

Act 1: The Terrace. Lunch Time.

Act 2: The drawing-room. Dinner Time.

ACT 1

"Tomorrow Is the Time"
   D. Bird, Bridesmaids
"For the Life of Me"
   R. McDonald, M. Stewart
Dance
   R. McDonnell, M. Stewart, W. Skipper, H. Mattox, Bridesmaids
"The Dew Was on the Rose"
   L. Corbett, A. Margetson, C. Purcell, R. Walburn, R. Chisholm
"Don't Be a Woman If You Can"
   M. Wickes, M. Errolle, R. Matteson
"Sweet Nevada"
   L. Corbett, D. Wayne
Dance In the Courtroom:
   Plaintiffs: D. Bird, J. Mann, B. Low. *Judge*: D. Wayne.
   Court Attendants: W. Skipper, H. Mattox. *Other Plaintiffs*:
   All "Brendas".
"There's No Holding Me"
   M. Stewart, R. McDonald
"The Dew Was on the Rose" (reprise)
   L. Corbett, A. Margetson
"There's Nothing Like Marriage for People"
   Entire Company

ACT 2

"Hope for the Best"
   Bridesmaids, H. Mattox, W. Skipper
"My Son-in-Law"
   L. Corbett, M. Stewart, R. Walburn
"Land of Opportunities"
   A. Margetson, R. Walburn, C. Purcell, R. Chisholm
Dance
   D. Bird, J. Mann, All "Brendas"
"Goodbye to All That"
   M. Stewart, R. McDonald
Dance: "Echo"
   H. Mattox, D. Bird, W. Skipper, J. Mann, Bridesmaids
Finale
   Entire Company

1946.21 ## BAL NEGRE

A Native Music and Dance Revue in Three Acts, 6 Scenes. Directed and choreographed by Katherine Dunham. Costumes by John Pratt. Orchestra under the direction of Gilberto Valdes. Advisor on Ragtime Material, Tom Fletcher. Vocal arrangement on Chocounne and Ragtime Medley, Reginald Beane. Musical arrangement and orchestration on Ragtime Medley by Billy Butler. Produced by Nelson L. Gross and Daniel Melnick. Opened 7 November 1946 at the Belasco Theatre and closed 22 December 1946 after 54 performances.

CAST: KATHERINE DUNHAM, LUCILLE ELLIS, LENWOOD MORRIS, LAWAUNE INGRAM, VANOYE AIKENS, James Alexander, Ronnie Aul, Wilber Bradley, Byron Cuttler, Eddy Clay, Roxie Foster, Dolores Harper, Jesse Hawkins, Richardena Jackson, Eartha Kitt, Gloria Mitchell, Eugene Robinson, Othella Strozier, Syvilla Fort (Guest Artist). *Sans-Souci Singers*: JEAN LEON DESTINÉ, EARTHA KITT, ROSALIE KING, Mary Lewis, Miriam Burton, Gordon Simpson, Ricardo Morrison. *Drummers*: La Rosa Estrada, Cándido Vicenty, Julio Mendez.

ACT 1

Overture:
Ylenko-Ylembe
   (*Music by* Gilberto Valdes.)
   E. Kitt, J. L. Destiné, M. Burton, Sans-Souci Singers
Congo Paillette—Haitian Corn Sorting Ritual (Native Air)
   K. Dunham, L. Morris, Company
Katherine Dunham has devised an overture to be seen as well as heard. Ylenke-Ylembe, written by the brilliant young composer-conductor, Gilberto Valdes, is a vocal and orchestral combination which emphasizes unrestrained Afro-Cuban themes. The second half of the overture, Congo Paillette, is based on a native Haitian air.

Scene 1
Motivos:
   a. Rhumba
      (*Music by* Gilberto Valdes.)
      L. Ellis, E. Kitt, O. Strozier
   b. Son (Cuban Slave Lament)
      J. Hawkins
      Possessed Dancer: D. Harper.
   c. Nanigo
      (*Music by* Gilberto Valdes.) L. Estrada, V. Aikens, Company
   d. Choro
      (*Music by* Vadico Gogliano.) (A 19th Century Brazilian Quadrille)
      G. Mitchell, R. Jackson, W. Bradley, R. Aul
   e. La Comparsa
      (*Music by* Ernesto Lecuona.)
      K. Dunham, V. Aikens, B. Cuttler, J. Alexander
      Alone in the deserted streets in the early morning hours after carnival, a woman encounters three men. She believes that one may be her husband.
Scene 2
Haitian Roadside
   (*Music by* Paquita Anderson, Gilberto Valdes.)
"Soleil, O" (Invocation)
   J. L. Destiné, Male Quartet
"Apollon" (Carnival Meringue)
   J. L. Destiné
"Chocounne"
   K. Dunham
On the dusty roads of Haiti many things happen in the late afternoon.
   Peddler with the guitar: C. Vicenty. *Other peddlers*: L. Estrada, B. Cuttler, J. Mendez, J. Alexander. *Traveling priest*: J. L. Destiné. *Market girls*: L. Ingram, G. Mitchell. *Carnival kings*: L. Morris, J. L. Destiné. *Chacoon*: K. Dunham. *Market people and wayside travelers*.
Scene 3
Shango (Ritual and Dance)
   (*Music by* Baldwin Bergerson.)
   The Shango priest: L. Estrada. *The boy possessed by a snake*: J. L. Destiné. *The leaders of the Shango dancers*: L. Ellis, E. Clay.

ACT 2

Scene 1

L'Ag'ya

(*Music by* Robert Sanders.) (From an original story by Katherine Dunham.) *Loulouse*: K. Dunham. *Alcide*: V. Aikens. *Julot*: W. Bradley. *Roi Zombie*: L. Morris. *Porteresses, vendors, fishermen, townspeople of Vauclin.*

The scene is Vauclin, a tiny eighteenth century fishing village in Martinique. Loulouse loves and is desired by Alcide. Julot, the villain, repulsed by Loulouse and filled with hatred and desire for revenge, decides to seek the aid of the king of the zombies. Deep in the jungle, Julot fearfully seeks the lair of the zombies and witnesses their strange rites which bring the dead back to life. Frightened, but remembering his purpose, Julot pursues Roi Zombie and obtains the "cambois," powerful love charm from him. The following evening: It is a time of gaiety, opening with the stately Creole Mazurka or "Mazouk" and moving into the uninhibited excitement of the Beguine. Into this scene enters Julot, horrifying the villagers when he exposes the coveted "cambois." Even Alcide is under its spell. Now begins the Majumba, love dance of ancient Africa. As Loulouse falls more and more under the charm, Alcide suddenly defies its powers, breaks loose from the villagers, who protect him, and challenges Julot to the Ag'ya, the fighting dance of Martinique. In L'Ag'ya and its ending is the climax of the forces loosed in magic and superstition.

ACT 3

Scene 1

Nostalgia:

a. Ragtime Medley ("Chong," "Under the Bamboo Tree," "Ragtime Cowboy," "Oh, You Beautiful Doll," "Alexander's Ragtime Band.")
   R. King, Sans-Souci Singers
   Dancers: L. Ellis, L. Morris, Company in the Waltz, Fox-trot, Ballin' the Jack, Tango, Maxixe, Turkey Trot.

b. Blues
   (*Music by* Floyd Smith.)K. Dunham, V. Aikens

c. Flaming Youth . . . 1927
   (*Music by* "Brad" Gowans)R. King
   Kansas City Woman: L. Ellis.

Charleston, Black Bottom, Mooch, Fishtail and Snake Hips
   L. Ingram, W. Bradley, Company

Scene 2

Finale:

Sans-Souci Singers and the Dunham Company

Havana 1910

(*Music by* Mercedes Navarro.)

Para Que Tu Veas

(*Music by* Bobby Capo.)J. L. Destiné
Entertainer: K. Dunham. *Two Lady Tourists*: R. Jackson, D. Harper.

1946.22   IF THE SHOE FITS

A Musical Comedy in Two Acts, a Prologue and 13 Scenes. (Based on the "Cinderella" legend by Perrault.) Book by June Carroll and Robert Duke. Music by David Raksin. Lyrics by June Carroll. Book direction by Eugene Bryden. Choreography by Charles Weidman. Settings by Edward Gilbert. Costumes by Kathryn Kuhn. Tap routines by Don Liberto. Production manager, Archie Thompson. Musical director, Will Irwin. Orchestrations, (Robert) Russell Bennett. Additional orchestrations by Ted Royal, Hans Spialek, Walter Paul, Joseph Glover. Vocal director, Joe Moon. Entire production supervised by Leonard Sillman. Produced by Leonard Sillman. Opened 5 December 1946 at the New Century Theatre and closed 21 December 1946 after 20 performances.

<u>CAST</u> (in order of appearance): *Town Crier*: ROBERT PENN. *Singing Attendant*: Eugene Martin. *Dancing Attendant*: Billy Vaux. *Broderick*: JACK WILLIAMS. *Acrobatic Attendants*: Jane Vinson, Paula Dee. *Cinderella*: LEILA ERNST. *Mistress Spratt*: JODY GILBERT. *Delilah, Thais*, her daughters: MARILYN DAY, SHERLE NORTH. *The Butcher Boy*: Richard Wentworth. *First Undertaker*: Don Mayo. *Second Undertaker*: Walter Kattwinkel. *Lorelei*: Gail Adams. *Lilith*: Eileen Ayers. *First Lawyer*: Harvey Braun. *Second Lawyer*: Stanley Simmons. *Lady Eve*: FLORENCE DESMOND. *Herman*: JOE BESSER. *Four Sprites*: Vincent Carbone, Harry Rogers, Allen Knowles, Fred Bernaski. *First Troubadour*: William Raines. *Second Troubadour*: Ray Morrissey. *Third Troubadour*: Richard Wentworth. *Their Arranger*: FIN OLSEN. *Major Domo*: YOUKA TROUBETZKOY. *Lady Guinevere*: Eleanor Jones. *Lady Persevere*: Dorothy Karroll. *Dame Crackle*: Chloe Owen. *The Baker*: Ray Cook. *Dame Crumple*: Joyce White. *Dame Crinkle*: Jean Olds. *Prince*

Charming: EDWARD DEW. *Widow Willow*: ADRIENNE. *Kate*: BARBARA PERRY. *King Kindly*: EDWARD LAMBERT. *His Magnificence, The Wizard*: FRANK MILTON. *Court Dancer*: Vincent Carbone. *Sailor*: Richard D'Arcy. *His Sweethearts*: Marcia Maier, Marybly Harwood.
Corps de Ballet: Paula Dee, Yvette Fairhill, Jean Harris, Marybly Harwood, Marcia Maier, Ruth Ostrander, Audrey Peters, Gloria Smith, Jane Vinson. Fred Bernaski, George Drake, Vincent Carbone, Allen Knowles, Roy Marshall, Harry Rogers, Billy Vaux.

The story takes place during the Middle Ages in one of those mythical kingdoms known only to writers of musical comedies, in this case, "The Kingdom of Nicely."

Act 1, Prologue. Scene 1: Town Gate. *Scene* 2: Cinderella's Kitchen. *Scene* 3: Palace Gate. *Scene* 4: Ballroom. *Scene* 5: Ante-room of Palace. *Scene* 6: Ballroom.

Act 2, Scene 1: Town Gate. *Scene* 2: Cinderella's Kitchen. *Scene* 3: Palace Gate. *Scene* 4: Village Street. *Scene* 5: Palace Gate. *Scene* 6: Ante-room. *Scene* 7: Village Street. Finale.

ACT 1

Prologue

R. Penn

Scene 1

"Start the Ball Rollin'"
   J. Williams
   Danced by J. Williams, Corps de Ballet.

Scene 2

"I Wish"
   L. Ernst

"Start the Ball Rollin'"(reprise)
   J. Gilbert, M. Day, S. North

"I Wish" (reprise)
   L. Ernst

"In the Morning"
   F. Desmond

Scene 3

"Come and Bring Your Instruments"
   F. Olsen, W. Rains, R. Wentworth, R. Morrisey

Scene 4

"Night After Night"
   E. Jones
   Danced by B. Perry, Corps de Ballet.

"Every Eve"
   E. Dew, E. Lambert

"With a Wave of My Hand"
   F. Desmond, L. Ernst
   Danced by Good Girls: J. Harris, M. Harwood, A. Peters.
   Bad Girls: M Maier, Y. Fairhill, G. Smith.

Scene 5

"Am I a Man or a Mouse?"
   J. Besser

"I'm Not Myself Tonight"
   L. Ernst, E. Dew, B. Perry, F. Desmond

Scene 6

"Three Questions"
   F. Desmond, L. Ernst, F. Milton
   Danced by B. Perry, V. Carbone.

Entr'acte [sung]
   E. Jones, E. Martin

ACT 2

Scene 1

"If the Shoe Fits"
   F. Milton, Citizens
   Danced by the Corps de Ballet.

Scene 2

"I Wish" (reprise)
   E. Dew

"In the Morning" (reprise)
   F. Desmond, J. Besser, L. Ernst

Scene 3

"What's the Younger Generation Coming To?"
   E. Lambert, Entourage

Scene 4

"Have You Seen the Countess Cindy?"
E. Dew, Citizens

"This Is the End of the Story"
L. Ernst
Danced by R. D'Arcy, M. Maier, M. Harwood.

Scene 5

"I Took Another Look"
B. Perry, J. Williams

Scene 6

"I Want to Go Back to the Bottom of the Garden"
F. Desmond

"This Is the End of the Story" (reprise)
E. Dew, J. Williams

Scene 7

"My Business Man"
Adrienne

Finale
Entire Company

TOPLITZKY OF NOTRE DAME

1946.23

A Musical Comedy in Two Acts, a Prologue and 8 Scenes. Book and lyrics by George Marion, Jr. Music by Sammy Fain. Additional Dialogue and Lyrics by Jack Barnett. Staged by José Ruben. Dances and musical numbers staged by Robert Sidney. Settings by Edward Gilbert. Costumes by Ken Barr. Musical director, Leon Leonardi. Vocal and choral arrangements by Leon Leonardi. Orchestral arrangements by Allan Small, Lewis Raymond, Menotti Salta. Assistant dance director, Ted Cappy. Produced by William Cahn. Opened 26 December 1946 at the New Century Theatre and closed 15 February 1947 after 60 performances.

CAST (in order of appearance): *Army Angel*: PHYLLIS LYNNE. *Recording Angel*: CANDACE MONTGOMERY. *Lionel*: HARRY FLEER. *Angelo*: WARDE DONOVAN. *Mrs. Strutt*: DORIS PATSTON. *Betty*: MARION COLBY. *Dodo*: ESTELLE SLOAN. *McCormack*: GUS VIAN. *Roger*: WALTER LONG. *Toplitzky*: J. EDWARD BROMBERG. *Bobby, a girl*: BETTY JANE WATSON. *Mailman*: ROBERT BAY. *Leary*: FRANK MARLOWE. *Patti*: PHYLLIS LYNNE. *Male Quartet*: Oliver Boersma, John Frederick, Eugene Kingsley, Chris Overson.

Dancers: *Girls*: Priscilla Callan, Ann Collins, Helen Devlin, Cece Eames, Jessie Fullum, Joan Kananaugh, Pat Marlowe, Mollie Pearson, Frances Wyman. *Boys*: George Andrew, Gene Banks, Charles Dickson, Case Jaeger, Thomas Kenny, Anthony Starman, Rodney Strong, Joe Wagner, John Wilkins.

Act 1, Prologue: Heaven. *Scene 1*: Toplitzky's Tavern, New York City, a September day. *Scene 2*: A field on the Jersey shore, late afternoon. *Scene 3*: Toplitzky's Tavern, later that day. *Scene 4*: Toplitzky's Terrace, a late afternoon in October.

Act 2, Scene 1: Toplitzky's Tavern, the day before the Big Game. *Scene 2*: Toplitzky's Terrace. Evening, same day. *Scene 3*: Going to the Big Game. *Scene 4*: Yankee Stadium. Army-Notre Dame Game.

ACT 1[5]

"Let Us Gather at the Goal Line"
W. Donovan, Company

"Baby, Let's Face It"
W. Long
Dance: W. Long, E. Sloan, Boys and Girls.

"Let Us Gather at the Goal Line"(reprise)
J. E. Bromberg, G. Van

"I Want to Go to City College"
F. Marlowe, M. Colby, Boys and Girls

"Love Is a Random Thing"
B. J. Watson

"Common Sense"
J. E. Bromberg

"Love Is a Random Thing" (reprise)
W. Donovan

"A Slight Case of Ecstasy"
W. Long, E. Sloan, F. Marlowe, P. Lynne
Dance: W. Long, Girls, Boys.

Finale
B. J. Watson, Company

ACT 2

"Wolf Time"
M. Colby, P. Lynne
Dance: E. Sloan, Girls, Boys.

"McInerney's Farm"
G. Van

"You Are My Downfall"
W. Donovan, B. J. Watson
Dance: Boys, Girls, W. Long, E. Sloan.

"All American Man"
P. Lynne, E. Sloan, M. Colby, F. Marlowe, G. Van, J. E. Bromberg
Dance: R. Bay, Boys, Girls.

Finale
Entire Company

BEGGAR'S HOLIDAY

1946.24

A Musical Comedy in Two Acts, 13 Scenes. Book and lyrics by John LaTouche. Based on "The Beggar's Opera" by John Gay. Music by Duke Ellington. Book directed by Nicholas Ray. Production designed by Oliver Smith. Costumes designed by Walter Florell. Technical supervision and lighting by Peggy Clark. Choreography by Valerie Bettis. Musical director, Max Meth. Orchestrations under the personal supervision of Billy Strayhorn. Vocal arrangements by Crane Calder. Produced by Perry Watkins and John R. Sheppard, Jr. Opened 26 December 1946 at the Broadway Theatre and closed 29 March 1947 after 108 performances.

CAST (in order of appearance): *The Pursued*: Tommy Gomez. *Cop*: Archie Savage. *Policemen*: Herbert Ross, Lucas Hoving. *Plainclothesman*: Albert Popwell. *The Lookout*: Marjorie Bell. *Macheath*: ALFRED DRAKE. *The Cocoa Girl*: MARIE BRYANT. *Jenny*: BERNICE PARKS. *Dolly Trull*: Lavinia Nielsen. *Betty Doxy*: Leonne Hall. *Tawdry Audrey*: Tommie Moore. *Mrs. Trapes*: Doris Goodwin. *Annie Coaxer*: Royce Wallace. *Baby Mildred*: Claire Hale. *Minute Lou*: Nina Korda. *Trixy Turner*: Malka Farber. *Bessie Buns*: Elmira Jones-Bey. *Flora, the Harpy*: Enid Williams. *The Horn*: Bill Dillard. *Highbinder*: Jack Bittner. *O'Heister*: Gordon Nelson. *The Foot*: Perry Bruskin. *Gunsel*: Archie Savage. *Fingersmith*: Stanley Carlson. *Strip*: Lucas Hoving. *Mooch*: Perry Bruskin. *The Eye*: Pan Theodore. *Wire Boy*: Paul Godkin. *The Other Eye*: Tommy Gomez. *Slam*: Albert Popwell. *The Caser*: Douglas Henderson. *Two Customers*: Gordon Nelson, Hy Anzell. *A Drunk*: Lewis Charles. *Bartender*: Herbert Ross. *Careless Love*: AVON LONG. *Polly Peachum*: JET MacDONALD. *Black Marketeer*: Gordon Nelson. *Mrs. Peachum*: Dorothy Johnson. *Hamilton Peachum*: ZERO MOSTEL. *Chief Lockit*: Rollin Smith. *Lucy Lockit*: MILDRED SMITH. *Blenkinsop*: Pan Theodore. *The Girl*: Marjorie Belle. *The Boy*: Paul Godkin.

The Dancers: Paul Godkin, Marjorie Belle, Malka Farber, Doris Goodwin, Claire Hale, Elmira Jones-Bey, Lavinia Nielsen, Royce Wallace, Enid Williams, Tommy Gomez, Lucas Hoving, Albert Popwell, Herbert Ross, Archie Savage.

Mac's Gang: Stanley Carlson, Lewis Charles, Gordon Nelson, Bill Dillard, Jack Bittner, Perry Bruskin.

Act 1, Scene 1: Exterior of Miss Jenny's. *Scene 2*: Interior of Miss Jenny's. *Scene 3*: Exterior of Miss Jenny's. *Scene 4*: At Hamilton Peachum's. *Scene 5*: A Street. *Scene 6*: A Hobo Jungle—Two days later.

Act 2, Scene 1: The Street. *Scene 2*: Chief Lockit's Office. *Scene 3*: The Jail. *Scene 4*: The Street. *Scene 5*: Jenny's Bedroom. *Scene 6*: Under the Bridge. *Scene 7*: Finale.

ACT 1

"Inbetween"[6]
M. Smith

The Chase
T. Gomez, H. Ross, L. Hoving

"When You Go Down By Miss Jenny's"
Citizens, Girls

---

[5]"The Notre Dame Victory March" was composed by the Rev. Michael J. Shea; the lyric by John F. Shea. "The Notre Dame Hike Song" was composed by Joseph Casastana and Vincent F. Fagan.

[6]Dropped during the run.

"I've Got Me"
 A. Drake
"TNT"
 M. Bryant
"Take Love Easy"
 B. Parks
"I Wanna Be Bad"
 A. Long
"Rooster Man"[7]
 B. Parks
"When I Walk With You"
 J. MacDonald, A. Drake
Wedding Ballet
"I've Got Me" (reprise)
 First Girl
"The Scrimmage of Life"
 D. Johnson, Z. Mostel, M. Smith
"Ore from a Gold Mine"
 D. Johnson, Z. Mostel
Finaletto
 J. MacDonald, D. Johnson, Z. Mostel
"When I Walk With You" (reprise)
 A. Drake, J. MacDonald
"Tooth and Claw"
 Mac's Gang
"Maybe I Should Change My Ways"
 A. Drake
"The Wrong Side of the Railroad Tracks"
 M. Bryant, A. Long, B. Dillard
"Tomorrow Mountain"
 A. Drake et al

ACT 2
"Brown Penny"[8]
 M. Smith
 (Lyrics based on poem by William Butler Yeats.)
Chorus of Citizens
 Ensemble
"Tooth and Claw" (reprise)
 Z. Mostel, Reporters
"Lullaby for Junior"
 B. Parks
"Quarrel for Three"
 J. MacDonald, M. Smith, A. Drake
"Fol-de-rol-rol"
 A. Drake
"Women, Women, Women"
 Prisoners
"Women, Women, Women" (reprise)
 M. Bryant, A. Long
"When I Walk With You" (reprise)
 A. Drake
Ballet
"The Hunted"
 A. Drake
Finale
 A. Drake, B. Parks, J. MacDonald, M. Smith et al

1947.01 # BLOOMER GIRL

A Return Engagement of the Musical Comedy in Two Acts, 10 Scenes[9]. Book by Sig Herzig and Fred Saidy. Based on a play by Lilith and Dan

---

[7]Dropped during the run.
[8]Dropped during the run.
[9]First presented 5 October 1944 at the Sam S. Shubert Theatre for 657 performances. For Synopsis of Scenes and Musical Numbers, see original 1944 production.

James. Music by Harold Arlen. Lyrics by E.Y. Harburg. Book directed by William Schorr. Production staged by E.Y. Harburg. Dances by Agnes deMille. Settings and Lighting by Lemuel Ayers. Costumes by Miles White. Musical director, Jerry Arlen. Orchestration by Robert Russell Bennett. Produced by John C. Wilson in association with Nat Goldstone. Opened 6 January 1947 at the New York City Center and closed 15 February 1947 after 48 performances.

CAST (in order of appearance): *Serena*: MABEL TALIAFERRO. *The Five Applegate Daughters*: *Octavia*: Holly Harris. *Lydia*: Ellen Leslie. *Julia*: Dorothy Cothran. *Phoebe*: Claire Stevens. *Delia*: Calire Minter. *Daisy*: Peggy Campbell. *Horatio*: MATT BRIGGS. *Gus*: John Call. *Evelina*: NANETTE FABRAY. *The Five Sons-in-Law*: *Wilfred Thrush*: Byron Milligan. *Joshua Dingle*: Carlos Sherman. *Ebeneezer Mimms*: Lester Towne. *Herman Brasher*: Victor Bender. *Hiram Crump*: Walter Russell. *Dolly*: OLIVE REEVES-SMITH. *Jeff Calhoun*: DICK SMART. *Paula*: LIly Paget. *Prudence*: Noella Pelloquin. *Hetty*: Alice Ward. *Pompey*: HUBERT DILWORTH. *Sheriff Quimby*: Joe E. Marks. *First Deputy*: Edward Chapel. *Second Deputy*: Ralph Sassano. *Third Deputy*: Donald Green. *Hamilton Calhoun*: John Byrd. *State Official*: John Byrd. *Governor Newton*: Sidney Bassler. *Augustus*: Arthur Lawson.

 Vocal Ensemble: Lily Paget, Noella Pelloquin, Gloria Rudsdil, Alice Ward, Elaine Harrington, Claudia Campbell, Edward Chapel, Donald Green, Robert Patterson, Richard Spencer, Hugh Holt, Ralph Sassano.

 Dancers: Margit Dekova, Emy St. Just, Virginia Bosler, Patricia O'Bryrne, Jean Kinsella, Ruth Mitchell, Susan Stewart, Cecile Bergman, Eleanor Snyder, Ruthanne Welsh, Patricia Gianinoto, Scott Merrill, Arthur Grahl, Paul Olson, David Raher, Frank Reynolds, John Martin, Ray Johnson.

1947.02 # STREET SCENE

A Dramatic Musical in Two Acts, 3 Scenes. Book by Elmer Rice from his play of the same name. Music by Kurt Weill. Lyrics by Langston Hughes. Directed by Charles Friedman. Scenery and lighting by Jo Mielziner. Costumes by Lucinda Ballard. Dances by Anna Sokolow. Musical director, Maurice Abravanel. Musical arrangements and orchestrations by Kurt Weill. Produced by Dwight Deere Wiman and the Playwrights' Company. Opened 9 January 1947 at the Adelphi Theatre and closed 17 May 1947 after 148 performances.

CAST (in order of appearance): *Abraham Kaplan*: Irving Kaufman. *Greta Fiorentino*: Helen Arden. *Carl Olsen*: Wilson Smith. *Emma Jones*: HOPE EMERSON. *Olga Olsen*: Ellen Repp. *Shirley Kaplan*: Norma Chambers. *Henry Davis*: Creighton Thompson. *Willie Maurrant*: Peter Griffith. *Anna Maurrant*: POLYNA STOSKA, Bette Van (alt.) *Sam Kaplan*: BRIAN SULLIVAN. *Daniel Buchanan*: Remo Lota. *Frank Maurrant*: NORMAN CORDON. *George Jones*: David E. Thomas. *Steve Sankey*: Lauren Gilbert. *Lippo Fiorentino*: SYDNEY RAYNER. *Jennie Hildebrand*: Beverly Janis. *Second Graduate*: Zosia Gruchala. *Third Graduate*: Marion Covey. *Mary Hildebrand*: Juliana Gallagher. *Charlie Hildebrand*: Bennett Burrill. *Laura Hildebrand*: Elen Lane. *Grace Davis*: Helen Ferguson. *First Policeman*: Ernest Taylor. *Rose Maurrant*: ANNE JEFFREYS. *Harry Easter*: Don Saxon. *Mae Jones*: Sheila Bond. *Dick McGann*: Danny Daniels. *Vincent Jones*: Robert Pierson. *Dr. John Wilson*: Edwin G. O'Connor. *Officer Harry Murphy*: Norman Thomson. *A Milkman*: Russell George. *A Music Pupil*: Joyce Carrol. *City Marshall James Henry*: Randolph Symonette. *Fred Cullen*: Paul Lilly. *An Old Clothes Man*: Edward Reichert. *An Interne*: Roy Munsell. *An Ambulance Driver*: John Sweet. *First Nursemaid*: Peggy Turnley. *Second Nursemaid*: Ellen Carleen. *A Married Couple*: Bette Van, Joseph E. Scandur.

 Passersby, Neighbors, Children, etc.: Aza Bard, Ellen Carleen, Joyce Carrol, Marion Covey, Diana Donne, Bessie Franklin, Zosia Gruchala, Juanita Hall, Beverly Janis, Elen Lane, Marie Leidal, Sasha Pressman, Biruta Ramoska, Peggy Turnley, Bette Van. Larry Baker, Tom Barragan, Mel Bartell, Victor Clarke, Russell George, Bobby Horn, Bernard Kovler, Roy Munsell, Edwin G. O'Connor, Edward Reichert, Joseph E. Scandur, John Sweet, Ernest Taylor, Wilson Woodbeck.

Act 1: An evening in June. A sidewalk in New York City.

Act 2, Scene 1: The following morning. *Scene 2*: Afternoon of the same day.

ACT 1
"Ain't It Awful, the Heat?"
 H. Arden, H. Emerson, E. Repp, I. Kaufman, W. Smith, Neighbors
"I Got a Marble and a Star"
 C. Thompson
"Get a Load of That"
 H. Emerson, H. Arden, E. Repp
"When a Woman Has a Baby"
 R. Lota, H. Arden, H. Emerson, P. Stoska
"Somehow I Never Could Believe"
 P. Stoska

"Get a Load of That"
    H. Emerson, H. Arden, D. E. Thomas,
    W. Smith
"Ice Cream"
    S. Rayner, H. Emerson, H. Arden, C. Thompson, D. E. Thomas, W. Smith,
    E. Repp
"Let Things Be Like They Always Was"
    N. Cordon
"Wrapped in a Ribbon and Tied in a Bow"
    B. Janis, Neighbors
"Lonely House"
    B. Sullivan
"Wouldn't You Like to be on Broadway?"
    D. Saxon
"What Good Would the Moon Be?"
    A. Jeffreys
"Moon-Faced, Starry-Eyed"
    D. Daniels, S. Bond
"Remember That I Care"
    B. Sullivan, A. Jeffreys

ACT 2
Scene 1
"Catch Me If You Can"
    B. Burrill, J. Gallagher, P. Griffith, Children
"There'll Be Trouble"
    N. Cordon, P. Stoska, A. Jeffreys
"A Boy Like You"
    P. Stoska
"We'll Go Away Together"
    B. Sullivan, A. Jeffreys
"The Woman Who Lived Up There"
    Ensemble
Scene 2
"Lullaby"
    Nursemaids
"I Loved Her, Too"
    N. Cordon, A. Jeffreys, Ensemble
"Don't Forget the Lilac Bush"[10]
    B. Sullivan, A. Jeffreys
"Ain't It Awful, the Heat? (reprise)
    H. Arden, H. Emerson, E. Repp, I. Kaufman

1947.03   FINIAN'S RAINBOW

A Musical (Satire) in Two Acts, 10 Scenes. Book by E. Y. Harburg and Fred Saidy. Music by Burton Lane. Lyrics by E. Y. Harburg. Directed by Bretaigne Windust. Choreography and musical numbers by Michael Kidd. Scenery and lighting by Jo Mielziner. Costumes by Eleanor Goldsmith. Orchestrations by Robert Russell Bennett and Don Walker. Vocal arrangements by Lyn Murray. Dance music arrangements by Trude Rittman. Orchestra conducted by Ray Charles. Produced by Lee Sabinson and William R. Katzell. Opened 10 January 1947 at the 46th Street Theatre and closed 2 October 1948 after 725 performances.

CAST (in order of appearance): *Sunny,* Harmonica Player: Sonny Terry. *Buzz Collins:* Eddie Bruce. *Sheriff:* Tom McElhany. *First Sharecropper:* Alan Gilbert. *Second Sharecropper:* Robert Eric Carlson. *Susan Mahoney:* ANITA ALVAREZ. *Henry:* Augustus Smith, Jr. *Finian McLonergan:* ALBERT SHARPE. *Sharon McLonergan:* ELLA LOGAN. *Woody Mahoney:* DONALD RICHARDS. *Third Sharecropper:* Ralph Waldo Cummings. *Og, a Leprechaun:* DAVID WAYNE. *Howard:* William Greaves. *Senator Billboard Rawkins:* Robert Pitkin. *First Geologist:* Lucas Aco. *Second Geologist:* Nathaniel Dickerson. *Diane:* Diane Woods. *Jane:* Jane Earle. *John,* the Preacher: Roland Skinner. *Fourth Sharecropper:* Maude Simmons. *Mr. Robust:* Arthur Tell. *Mr. Shears:* Royal Dano. *First Passion Pilgrim Gospeller:* Jerry Laws. *Second Passion Pilgrim Gospeller:* Lorenzo Fuller. *Third Passion Pilgrim Gospeller:* Louis Sharp. *First Deputy:* Michael Ellis. *Second Deputy:* Robert Eric Carlson. *Third Deputy:* Harry Day. *Other Children:* Norma Jane Marlowe, Elayne Richards.

---
[10]The poem "When Lilacs Last in the Dooryard Bloomed" referred to above was written by Walt Whitman.

Dancers: Freda Flier, Annabelle Gold, Eleanore Gregory, Ann Hutchinson, Erona Harris, Anna Mitten, Kathleen Stanford, Lavinia Williams. Lucas Aco, Harry Day, Daniel Lloyd, J.C. McCord, Frank Neal, Arthur Partington, James Flash Riley, Don Weissmuller.
THE LYN MURRAY SINGERS: Arlene Anderson, Connie Baxter, Carroll Brooks, Lyn Joi, Mimi Kelly, Dolores Martin, Marijane Maricle, Maude Simmons. Robert Eric Carlson, Ralph Waldo Cummings, Nathaniel Dickerson, Alan Gilbert, Theodore Hines, Morty Rappe, William Scully, Roland Skinner.

Act 1, Scene 1: The Meetin' Place. Rainbow Valley, Missitucky. *Scene 2:* The same. That night. *Scene 3:* The Colonial Estate of Senator Billboard Rawkins. The next morning. *Scene 4:* The Meetin' Place. Following day. *Scene 5:* A Path in the Woods. *Scene 6:* The Meetin' Place. Next morning.

Act 2, Scene 1: Rainbow Valley. A few weeks later. *Scene 2:* A Wooded Section of the Hills. *Scene 3:* The Meetin' Place. *Scene 4:* Just Before Dawn.

ACT 1
Scene 1
"This Time of the Year"
    Singing Ensemble
Dance
    A. Alvarez, Dance Ensemble
"How Are Things in Glocca Morra?"
    E. Logan
"Look to the Rainbow"
    E. Logan, Singing Ensemble
Dance
    A. Sharpe, A. Alvarez, D. Weissmuller, Dance Ensemble
Scene 2
"Old Devil Moon"
    E. Logan, D. Richards
Scene 4
"How Are Things in Glocca Morra?" (reprise)
    E. Logan
"Something Sort of Grandish"
    E. Logan, D. Wayne
"If This Isn't Love"
    E. Logan, D. Richards, Singing Ensemble
    Dance: A. Alvarez. *Two Couples:* A. Mitten, J. C. McCord, A. Gold, L. Aco. *The Uninitiated:* E. Gregory, A. Partington. *The Tentative Two:* A. Hutchinson, H. Day. *The Intense Pair:* A. Gold, J. C. McCord. *The Exuberant Ones:* F. Flier, D. Weissmuller. *Triangle:* K. Stanford, J. F. Riley, L. Williams. *Another Couple:* E. Harris, F. Neal.
"Something Sort of Grandish" (reprise)
    D. Wayne
Scene 6
"Necessity"
    D. Martin, M. Simmons, A. Anderson, B. Anderson,
    L. Joi, M. Kelly, C. Brooks, M. Maricle, A. Gilbert
"(That) Great Come-and-Get-It-Day"
    E. Logan, D. Richards, Singing Ensemble
    Dance: Dance Ensemble.

ACT 2
Scene 1
"When the Idle Poor Become the Idle Rich"
    E. Logan, Singing Ensemble
    Dance: J. C. McCord, K. Stanford, F. Neal, L. Williams,
    A. Hutchinson, F. Flier, A. Partington, J. F. Riley, D. Weissmuller,
    A. Gold, L. Aco, A. Mitten
"Old Devil Moon" (reprise)
    E. Logan, D. Richards
Dance of the Golden Crock
    A. Alvarez, accompanied by S. Terry
Scene 2
("Fiddle Faddle")
    D. Wayne
"The Begat"
    R. Pitkin, J. Laws, L. Fuller, L. Sharp
Scene 3
"Look to the Rainbow" (reprise)
    E. Logan, D. Richards, Singing Ensemble

Scene 4

    "When I'm Not Near the Girl I Love"
        D. Wayne, A. Alvarez

    "If This Isn't Love" (reprise)
        Entire Ensemble

    Finale
        Entire Company

1947.04   # SWEETHEARTS

A Revival of the Operetta in Two Acts[11]. Music by Victor Herbert. Original book by Harry B. Smith and Fred De Gresac. Lyrics by Robert B. Smith. Book revisions by John Cecil Holm. Production staged by John Kennedy. Ensembles by Catherine Littlefield. Choreography by Theodore Adolphus. Scenery designed by Peter Wolf. Costumes created by Michael Lucyk. Musical arrangements by Robert Russell Bennett. Musical director, Harry S. Levant. Vocal direction by Pembroke Davenport. Produced by Paula Stone and Michael Sloane. Opened 21 January 1947 at the Sam S. Shubert Theatre and closed 27 September 1947 after 288 performances.

<u>CAST</u> (in order of appearance): *Daughters (6): Doreen*: Marcia James, *Corinne*: Nony Franklin, *Eileen*: Janet Medlin, *Pauline*: Betty Ann Busch, *Kathleen*: Martha Emma Watson, *Nadine*: Gloria Lind. *Gretchen*: Eva Soltesz. *Hilda*: Mureil Bruenig. *Lt. Karl*: ROBERT SHACKLETON. *Dame Lucy*: MARJORIE GATESON. *Peasants*: Rober Reeves, Raynor Howell. *Liane*: JUNE KNIGHT. *Mikel Mikleoviz*: BOBBY CLARK. *Sylvia*: GLORIA STORY. *Prince Franz*: MARK DAWSON. *Peter*: Richard Benson. *Hans*: Ken Arnold. *Baron Petrus von Tromp*: PAUL BEST. *Hon. Butterfield Slingsby*: ANTHONY KEMPLE-COOPER. *Prima Ballerina*: Janice Cioffi. *Adolphus, Homberg, Footmen*: John Anania, Cornell MacNeil. *Ambassadors*: Robert Feyti, Louis DeMangus. *Captain Laurent*: Tom Perkins.

    Singing Ensemble: Ella Mayer, Florence Gault, Peggy Gavan, Getrude Hild, Nora Neal, Lillian Shelley, LaVernn Yotti, Alice Arnold, Marjorie Wellock. Richard Benson, Phil Crosbie, Louis DeMangus, Arnold Knippenburg, Wilbur Nelson, Robert Reeves, Charles Wood, Raynor Howell, Robert Feyti, Tom Perkins, Frank Whitemore.

    Dancing Ensemble: Jeanette Tannan, Aura Vainio, Bernice Brady, Ingrid Secretan, Connie Wege, Marie Louise Forsyth, Olivia Cardone, Jeanne Lewis, Dorothea Weidner, Alma Lee, Sally Sorvo. James Russell, Bruce Cartwright, Peter Holmes, John Ward.

Act 1: Village Square in Zilania.

Act 2: The Palace.

ACT 1

    Opening "Iron, Iron"
        The Daughters

    "On Parade"
        R. Shackleton, Daughters, Singing Ensemble

    "Sweethearts"
        G. Story, Daughters, Singing Ensemble

    "For Every Lover Must Meet His Fate"
        M. Dawson, Daughters, Singing Ensemble

    "Game of Love"
        R. Shackleton, Daughters, Ballet Ensemble
        Pas de Deux danced by: Coquette: E. Soltesz. Cavalier:
        B. Cartwright. *Strong Minded Girl*: A. Vainio.
        Impetuous Fellow: J. Russell. *The Romantic Girl*: J. Cioffi.
        The Poet: P. Holmes. *The Martial Maid*: O. Cardone.
        The Soldier: J. Ward.

    "The Angelus"
        G. Story, Singing Ensemble

    "Jeanette and Her Little Wooden Shoes"
        B. Clark, J. Knight,
        A.K. Cooper, P. Best, Ballet Ensemble

    Finale Act 1
        M. Dawson, G. Story, B. Clark, J. Knight,
        R. Shackleton, P. Best, M. Gateson, Daughters,
        Singing Ensemble

---

[11]First presented in New York 8 September 1913 at the New Amsterdam Theatre for 136 performances.

ACT 2

    Opening
        J. Cioffi

    "Pretty As a Picture"
        B. Clark, Male Chorus, Ballet Ensemble

    "Land of My Own Romance"
        G. Story, M. Dawson

    "I Might Be Your Once-in-a-While"
        J. Knight, R. Shackleton
        Danced by J. Russell (Lt. Karl), B. Cartwright (Von Tromp),
        P. Holmes (Slingsby).

    "Pilgrims of Love"
        B. Clark, R. Shackleton, P. Best, A. K. Cooper, J. Anania, C. MacNeil

    Finale
        Entire Company

1947.05   # MAURICE CHEVALIER

An Evening of Songs and Impressions in Two Acts. Accompanied by Irving Actman. Produced by Arthur Lesser. Opened 10 March 1947 at the Henry Miller's Theatre and closed 19 April 1947 after 46 performances.

ACT 1

    "La marche de menilmontant"
        (*Music by* B. Clerc. *Lyrics by* M. Voudair.)

    "La leçon de piano"
        (*Music by* Henri Betti. *Lyrics by* M. Voudair.)

    American Medley:

    "You Brought a New Kind of Love to Me" (from THE BIG POND, film)
        (*Music by* Sammy Fain. Lyrics by Irving Kahal and
        Pierre Norman.)

    "My Love Parade" (from THE LOVE PARADE, film)
        (*Lyrics by* Clifford Grey. *Music by* Victor Schertzinger.)

    "Hello, Beautiful"
        (*Music and Lyrics by* Walter Donaldson.)

    "Baby"
        (*Music by* Jimmy McHugh. *Lyrics by* Dorothy Fields.)

    "Mimi" (from LOVE ME TONIGHT film)
        (*Music by* Richard Rodgers. *Lyrics by* Lorenz Hart; *French lyrics by*
        André Hornez.)

    "Vingt ans"
        (*Music by* Marc Fontenoy. *Lyrics by* Maurice Chevalier.)

    "A Barcelone"
        (*Music by* Henri Betti. *Lyrics by* Maurice Chevalier.)

ACT 2

    "Weeping Willie"
        (*Music by* Rudi Révil. *Lyrics by* R. Pirosch.)

    "Quai de Bercy"
        (*Music by* Alstone. *Lyrics by* Maurice Chevalier.)

    "Mandarinade"
        (*Music by* Henri Betti. *Lyrics by* Pierre Gilbert,
        Maurice Chevalier.)

    "Place Pigalle"
        (*Music by* Alstone. *French lyrics by* Maurice Chevalier.
        English lyrics by R. Pirosch.)

    "La symphonie des smelles de bois"
        (*Music by* Anonymous. *Lyrics by* Maurice Chevalier.)

    Encore:

    "Louise" (from INNOCENTS OF PARIS, film)
        (*Music by* Richard A. Whiting. *Lyrics by* Leo Robin.)

    "Just a Bum" (Ma Pomme)
        (Ch. Borel-Clerc)

    "Valentine" (from INNOCENTS OF PARIS, film)
        (*Music by* Henri Christiné. *French Lyrics by* Albert Willemetz;
        English Lyrics by Herbert Reynolds.)

1947.06 THE CHOCOLATE SOLDIER

A Revival of the Operetta in Three Acts[12]. Music by Oscar Straus. (Original German) Libretto ('Der tapfere Soldat') by Rudolph Bernauer and Leopold Jacobson. (Based on "Arms and the Man" by George Bernard Shaw.) American version by Stanislaus Stange. Revised book by Guy Bolton. Book revisions and additional lyrics by Bernard Hanighen. Directed by Felix Brentano. Settings and lighting by Jo Mielziner. Costumes by Lucinda Ballard. Choreography by George Balanchine. Orchestrations and musical direction by Jay Blackton. Produced by J. H. Del Bondio and Hans Bartsch for the Delvan Company. Opened 12 March 1947 at the New Century Theatre and closed 10 May 1947 after 69 performances.

CAST (in order of appearance): *Nadia*: FRANCES McCANN. *Mascha*: GLORIA HAMILTON. *Aurelia*: MURIEL O'MALLEY. *Bumerli*: KEITH ANDES. *Massakroff*: HENRY CALVIN. *Popoff*: BILLY GILBERT. *Alexius*: ERNEST McCHESNEY. *Stefan, a servant*: Michael Mann. *Katrina, a servant*: Anna Wiman. *Premiere Danseuse*: MARY ELLEN MOYLAN. *Premier Dancer*: FRANCISCO MONCION.

Singing Ensemble: Elizabeth Bockoven, Eileen Coffman, Catherine Chambers, Peggy Ferris, Adah Friley, Lucy Hillary, Frances Joslyn, Jeanne Koumarian, Josephine Lambert, Terry Saunders, Grace Varik, Evelyn Wick. Jack Anderson, John Duffy, Craig Reynolds, Walter Kelvin, Allan Lowell, Richard Monte, Richmond Page, Harvey Sauber, Stan Simmonds, Karl Sittler, King Taylor, Bill E. Thompson.

Ballet Ensemble: Barbara Heath, Lillian Lenase, Eleanor Miller, Virginia Poe, Yvonne Tibor, Anna Wiman, Marjorie Winters. Hubert Bland, Harold Haskins, Brooks Jackson, Michael Mann, Shaun O'Brien, George Reich, Walter Stane.

Act 1: Nadina's bedroom in Popoff's house, situated in a small town in Bulgaria. Autumn, last century.

Act 2: The courtyard of the Popoff house. An afternoon in spring. A year later.

Act 3: The same. That evening.

ACT 1

"We Are Marching Through the Night"
  Men's Ensemble

"Lonely Women"
  F. McCann, M. O'Malley, G. Hamilton

"My Hero"
  F. McCann

"The Chocolate Soldier"
  F. McCann, K. Andes

"Sympathy"
  K. Andes, F. McCann

"Seek the Spy"
  H. Calvin, F. McCann, G. Hamilton, M. O'Malley, K. Andes, Men's Ensemble

Finale
  M. O'Malley, G. Hamilton, F. McCann

ACT 2

"Bulgaria Victorious"
  Singing Ensemble

"Thank the Lord the War Is Over"
  E. McChesney, G. Hamilton, B. Gilbert, M. O'Malley, Singing Ensemble

Slavic Dance[13]
  M. E. Moylan, F. Moncion, Corps de Ballet

"After Today"[14]
  E. McChesney, F. McCann

"Forgive"
  F. McCann, K. Andes

"Tale of the Coat"
  B. Gilbert, F. McCann, M. O'Malley, G. Hamilton, E. McChesney, K. Andes

"Falling in Love"
  K. Andes, F. McCann

Finale Act 2
  Entire Company

ACT 3

Waltz Ballet
  M. E. Moylan, F. Moncion, Corps de Ballet

"Just a Connoisseur"[15]
  B. Gilbert, K. Sittler, J. Anderson, E. Coffman, T. Saunders, B. Heith, M. Winters

"The Letter Song"
  F. McCann, K. Andes

"After Today"[16] (reprise)/"That Would Be Lovely"
  E. McChesney, G. Hamilton

"After Today Gala Polka"[17]
  M. E. Moylan, F. Moncion, Corps de Ballet

Finale
  Entire Company

1947.07 BRIGADOON

A Musical Play in Two Acts, a Prologue and 11 Scenes. Book and lyrics by Alan Jay Lerner. Music by Frederick Loewe. Dance and musical numbers by Agnes deMille[18]. Staged by Robert Lewis. Scenery designed by Oliver Smith. Costumes designed by David Ffolkes. Lighting by Peggy Clark. Musical director, Franz Allers. Vocal arrangements by Frederick Loewe. Orchestrations by Ted Royal. Produced by Cheryl Crawford. Opened 13 March 1947 at the Ziegfeld Theatre and closed 31 July 1948 after 581 performances.

CAST (in order of appearance): *Tommy Albright*: DAVID BROOKS. *Jeff Douglas*: GEORGE KEANE. *Archie Beaton*: Elliott Sullivan. *Harry Beaton*: JAMES MITCHELL. *Fishmonger*: Bunty Kelley. *Angus MacGuffie*: Walter Scheff. *Sandy Dean*: Hayes Gordon. *Andrew MacLaren*: Edward Cullen. *Fiona MacLaren*: MARION BELL. *Jean MacLaren*: Virginia Bosler. *Meg Brockie*: PAMELA BRITTON. *Charlie Dalrymple*: LEE SULLIVAN. *Maggie Anderson*: Lidija Franklin. *Mr. Lundie*: WILLIAM HANSEN. *Sword Dancers*: Roland Guerard, George Drake. *Frank*: John Paul. *Jane Ashton*: Frances Charles. *Bagpipers*: James MacFadden, Arthur Horn. *Stuart Dalrymple*: Paul Anderson. *MacGregor*: Earl Redding.

Townsfolk of Brigadoon: *Singers*: Kay Borron, Wanda Cochran, Lois Eastman, Lydia Fredericks, Jeanne Grant, Margaret Hunter, Linda Mason, Virginia Oswald, Eleanore Parker, Shirley Robbins, Faye Elizabeth Smith, Betty Templeton. Delbert Anderson, Arthur Carroll, Hayes Gordon, Michael Raymond, Mark Kramer, Robert Lussier, Tommy Matthews, Keny McCord, Earl Redding, John Schmidt, Paul Valin, Jeff Warren.

Dancers: Ann Friedland, Helen Gallagher, Phyllis Gehrig, Lidija Franklin, Dorothy Hill, Bunty Kelley, Ina Kurland, Olga Lunick, Mary Martinet, Kirsten Valbor. Forrest Bonshire, George Drake, Richard D'Arcy, Roland Guerard, Kenneth LeRoy, Charles McCraw, Stanley Simmons, Alan Waine, William Weber, Nathan Baker.

Act 1, Scene 1: A forest in the Scottish Highlands, about five on a May morning. *Scene 2*: A road in Brigadoon, then the village square—MacConnachy Square—later the same morning. *Scene 3*: An open shed, about noon. *Scene 4*: The MacLaren House, mid-afternoon. *Scene 5*: Outside the house of Mr. Lundie. *Scene 6*: The churchyard, dusk.

Act 2, Scene 1: A forest inside Brigadoon, later at night. *Scene 2*: A road in Brigadoon. *Scene 3*: The glen, immediately after. *Scene 4*: A bar in New York City, four months later. *Scene 5*: The forest—same as Act 1, Scene 1—three days later.

PROLOGUE

"Once in the Highlands"
  Chorus

ACT 1

Scene 1

"Brigadoon"
  Chorus

Scene 2

"Down on MacConnachy Square"
  H. Gordon, P. Britton, Townsfolk

---

[12]First presented in New York 13 September 1909 at the Lyric Theatre for 296 performances.
[13]Arranged and adapted by Jay Blackton from Oscar Straus melodies.
[14]Arranged and adapted by Jay Blackton from Oscar Straus melodies.

[15]Arranged and adapted by Jay Blackton from Oscar Straus melodies.
[16]Arranged and adapted by Jay Blackton from Oscar Straus melodies.
[17]Arranged and adapted by Jay Blackton from Oscar Straus melodies.
[18]Program note: Agnes de Mille was assisted in her research on Scotch dances by James Jamison.

"Waitin' for My Dearie"
   M. Bell, Girls
"I'll Go Home With Bonnie Jean"
   L. Sullivan, Townsfolk
   Dance: L. Franklin, J. Mitchell, Fishmongers, Townsfolk.
"The Heather on the Hill"
   D. Brooks, M. Bell
Scene 3
"The Love of My Life"
   P. Britton
Scene 4
"Jeannie's Packing Up"
   Girls
"Come to Me, Bend to Me"
   L. Sullivan
   Dance: V. Bosler, Dancers.
"Almost Like Being in Love"
   D. Brooks, M. Bell
Scene 6
"The Wedding Dance"
   V. Bosler, L. Sullivan, Dancers
"The Sword Dance"
   J. Mitchell, Sword Dancers, Dancers

ACT 2
Scene 1
"The Chase"
   Men of Brigadoon
Scene 2
"There But For You Go I"
   D. Brooks
Scene 3
"My Mother's Weddin' Day"
   P. Britton, Townsfolk
Funeral Dance
   L. Franklin
"From This Day On"
   D. Brooks, M. Bell
Scene 4
"Come to Me, Bend to Me" (reprise)
   M. Bell
"The Heather on the Hill" (reprise)
   M. Bell
"I'll Go Home With Bonnie Jean" (reprise)
   L. Sullivan
"From This Day On" (reprise)
   D. Brooks, M. Bell
"Down on MacConnachy Square" (reprise)
   Townsfolk
Scene 5
Finale

1947.08 BAREFOOT BOY WITH CHEEK

A Musical Comedy in Two Acts, 15 Scenes. Book by Max Shulman (from his novel of the same name). Music by Sidney Lippman. Lyrics by Sylvia Dee. Scenery and lighting by Jo Mielziner. Costumes by Alvin Colt. Choreography by Richard Barstow. Vocal arrangements by Hugh Martin. Orchestrations by Philip Lang. Musical director, Milton Rosenstock. Production staged by George Abbott. Produced by George Abbott. Opened 3 April 1947 at the Martin Beck Theatre and closed 5 July 1947 after 108 performances.

CAST: *Roger Hailfellow*: JACK WILLIAMS. *Shyster Fiscal*: RED BUTTONS. *Van Varsity*: Ben Murphy. *Charlie Convertible*: Loren Welch. *Freshman*: Patrick Kingdon. *Asa Hearthrug*: BILLY REDFIELD. *Eino Fflliikkiinnenn*: Benjamin Miller. *Noblesse Oblige*: BILLIE LOU WATT. *Clothilde Pfefferkorn*: ELLEN HANLEY. *Yetta Samovar*: NANCY WALKER. *Professor Schultz*: PHILIP COOLIDGE. *Peggy Hepp*: SHIRLEY VAN. *Kermit McDermott*: JERRY AUSTEN. *Boris Fiveyearplan*: Solen Burry. *Play-wright*: Marten Sameth. *Bartender*: James Lane. *Muskie Pike*: TOMMY FARRELL.

First Band Member: Harris Gondell. *Second Band Member*: Nathaniel Frey.
   Dancers: Jean Marie Caples, June Graham, Mary Bly Harwood, Louisa Lewis, Marcia Maier, Audrey Peters, Doris York, Leonard Claret, Douglas Deane, Ray Kirchner, John Laverty, David Neuman, Tommy Randall.
   Singers: Betty Abbott, Adrienne Aye, Mary Lee Carrell, Carol Coleman, Beverly Fite, Nell Foster, Marion Kohler, Gay Laurence, Abbe Marshall, Ellen Martin, Jean Sincere, Pamela Ward, James Bowie, Harvey Braun, Dean Campbell, Robert Edwin, Nathaniel Frey, Harris Gondell, John Leslie, Ray Morrissey, Robert Paul Neukum, Alfred Porter, Walter Rinner, Marten Sameth.

Act 1, Scene 1: Alpha Cholera Fraternity House on the Campus of the University of Minnesota. *Scene 2*: College Corridor. *Scene 3*: Class Room. *Scene 4*: Corridor. *Scene 5*: Campus Publications Office. *Scene 6*: The Sty. *Scene 7*: Street. *Scene 8*: The Knoll. *Scene 9*: Street. *Scene 10*: Alpha Cholera Fraternity House.

Act 2, Scene 1: Alpha Cholera Fraternity House. *Scene 2*: Street. *Scene 3*: The Knoll. *Scene 4*: Polling Place. *Scene 5*: Alpha Cholera Fraternity House.

ACT 1
"A Toast to Alpha Cholera"
   Fraternity Men
"We Feel Our Man Is Definitely You"
   R. Buttons, J. Williams, Fraternity Men
"The Legendary Eino Fflliikkiinnen"
   B. Miller, B. Redfield, Fraternity Men
"Too Nice a Day to Go to School"
   J. Austen, S. Van, L. Welch, B. Murphy, Students
   Specialty Dance: J. Graham, L. Claret. *Puppy Love*: E. Martin, J. Laverty.
"I Knew I'd Know"
   E. Hanley
"I'll Turn a Little Cog"
   N. Walker, B. Redfield, L. Welch, B. Murphy, J. Leslie, R. Neukum, Students
   Danced by J. Graham, M. B. Harwood, L. Claret, D. Deane, R. Kirchner.
"Who Do You Think You Are?"
   J. Austen, B. Redfield, Students
"Everything Leads Right Back to Love"
   E. Hanley, B. Redfield
"Little Yetta's Gonna Get a Man"
   N. Walker
"Alice in Boogieland"
   T. Farrell, S. Van, R. Buttons, J. Williams
   Quartet: B. Fite, H. Braun, D. Campbell, B. Abbott. *Danced by* Students.
   Dance Specialty: S. Van, L. Claret.

ACT 2
"After Graduation Day"
   L. Welch, Students
"There's Lots of Things You Can Do With Two (But Not With Three)"
   N. Walker, R. Buttons, B.L. Watt, J. Williams, B. Redfield, T. Farrell, L. Claret, D. Deane, M. B. Harwood, Students
"The Story of the Carrot"
   B. Redfield, B. Miller
"When You Are Eighteen"
   E. Hanley
"Star of the North Star State"
   Students
"I Knew I'd Know" (reprise)
   E. Hanley
"It Couldn't Be Done (But We Did It)"
   Entire Company

1947.09 ALICE IN WONDERLAND and THROUGH THE LOOKING GLASS

A Revival of the Fantasy in Two Acts[19]. Adapted from the books by Lewis Carroll for the stage by Eva LeGallienne and Florida Freibus, based on the

[19]First presented in New York 12 December 1932 at the Civic Repertory Theatre for 127 performances. For Synopsis of Scenes and Musical Numbers see original 1932 production.

John Tenniel drawings. Music by Richard Addinsell. Scenery designed by Robert Rowe Paddock. Costumes by Noel Taylor. Masks and marionettes by Remo Bufano. Orchestra conducted by Tibor Kozma. Choreography by Ruth Wilson. Entire production devised and directed by Eva LeGalliennne. Produced by Rita Hassan and the American Repertory Theatre (Cheryl Crawford, Managing director). Opened 5 April 1947 at the International Theatre, moved 28 May 1947 to the Majestic Theatre, and closed 28 June 1947 after 97 performances.

CAST (Part One) in order of appearance: Alice: BAMBI LINN. White Rabbit: William Windom, Julie Harris. Mouse: Henry Jones. Dodo: John Straub. Lory: Angus Cairns. Eaglet: Arthur Keegan. Crab: Don Allen. Duck: Eli Wallach. Caterpillar: Theodore Tenley. Fish Footman: Ed Woodhead. Frog Footman: Robert Rawlings. Duchess: Raymond Greenleaf. Cook: Don Allen. Cheshire Cat: Donald Keyes. March Hare: Arthur Keegan. Mad Hatter: RICHARD WARING. Dormouse: Don Allen. 2 of Spades: Eli Wallach. 5 of Spades: Robert Rawlings. 7 of Spades: Donald Keyes. Queen of Hearts: John Becher. King of Hearts: Euegne Stuckman. Knave of Hearts: Frederick Hunter. Gryphon: Jack Manning. Mock Turtle: Angus Cairns. 3 of Clubs: John Behney. 5 of Clubs: Bart Henderson. 7 of Clubs: John Straub. 9 of Clubs: Thomas Grace. Hearts: Don Allen, Robert Carlson, Michel Corhan, Will Davis, Robert Leser, Gerald McCormack, Walter Neal, James Rafferty, Dan Scott, Charles Townley.

(Part Two) Red Chess Queen: MARGARET WEBSTER. Train Guard: John Straub. Gentleman Dressed in White Paper: William Windom. Goat: Don Allen. Beetle Voice: Donald Keyes. Gnat Voice: Cavada Humphrey. Gentle Voice: Angus Cairns. Other Voices: Mary Alice Moore, Eli Wallach. Tweedledum: Robert Rawlings. Tweedledee: Jack Manning. White Chess Queen: EVA LE GALLIENNE. Sheep: Theodore Tenley. Humpty Dumpty: Henry Jones. White Knight: PHILIP BOURNEUF. Horse: Will Davis, Charles Townley. Old Frog: Donald Keyes. Shrill Voice: Angus Cairns. Singers: Eloise Roehm, Mara Lunden.

Marionettes worked by Michel Corhan, Thomas Grace, Bart Henderson, Cavada Humphrey, Robert Leser, Mary Alice Moore, Walter Neal, James Rafferty, Charles Townley, under the direction of A. Spolidoro.

THE TELEPHONE and THE MEDIUM

1947.10

A Double Bill of Two Operas, 3 Scenes[20]. Music and libretto by Gian-Carlo Menotti. Staged by the composer. Settings and costumes by Horace Armistead. Lighting by Jean Rosenthal. Musical director, Emanuel Balaban. Produced by Chandler Cowles and Efrem Zimbalist, Jr. in association with Edith Lutyens. Opened 1 May 1947 at the Ethel Barrymore Theatre and closed 1 November 1947 after 212 performances.

ACT 1

THE TELEPHONE (or "L'Amour à Trois"). A Comic Opera curtain raiser in One Act.

The action takes place in Lucy's apartment and a telephone booth around the corner.
    CAST: Lucy: MARILYN COTLOW. Ben: FRANK ROGIER.

ACT 2

THE MEDIUM. A Tragic Opera in 2 Scenes [Acts].

The action takes place in Madame Flora's parlor in our time.

Act 1: Evening. Act 2: Evening, a few days later.
    CAST: Monica: EVELYN KELLER. Toby, a Mute: LEO COLEMAN. Madame Flora (Baba): MARIE POWERS. Mrs. Gobineau: BEVERLY DAME. Mr. Gobineau: FRANK ROGIER. Mrs. Nolan: CATHERINE MASTICE.

MUSICAL NUMBERS[21]
"Where, Oh Where"
"Behold the King of Baylon"
"Where Have You Been All Night?"
"We Had a House in France"
"Mother, Mother"
"Are You There?"
"Doodly, Doodly"
"Are You Happy?"

"Mummy, Mummy, Dear"
"You Must Not Cry for Me"
"But Why Be Afraid?"
"I Know Now!"
"The Sun Has Fallen"
"Up in the Sky"
"Monica, Monica"
"Toby"
"Good Evening, Madame Flora"
"Could That Be?"
"Please Let Us Have Our Seance, Madame Flora"
"You Cannot Send Him Away"
"Am I Afraid?"
"Oh, Black Swan"

UP IN CENTRAL PARK

1947.11

A Return Engagement of the Musical Comedy in Two Acts, 11 Scenes[22]. Book by Herbert and Dorothy Fields. Music by Sigmund Romberg. Lyrics by Dorothy Fields. Book staged by John Kennedy. Dances by Helen Tamiris[23]. Settings and lighting by Howard Bay. Costumes by Grace Houston and Ernest Schraps. Orchestra directed by William Parson. Orchestrations by Don Walker. Stage supervised by Sammy Lambert. Produced by Michael Todd. Opened 19 May 1947 at the New York City Center and closed 31 May 1947 after 16 performances.

CAST (in order in which they speak): A Laborer: Orens Dabbs. Danny O'Cahane: WALTER BURKE. Timothy Moore: Russ Brown. Bessie O'Cahane: BETTY BRUCE. Rosie Moore: MAUREEN CANNON. John Matthews of the New York Times: EARLE MacVEIGH. Thomas Nast of Harper's Weekly: GUY STANDING, JR. Andrew Munroe: James Judson. William Dutton: John Quigg. Vincent Peters: PAUL REED. Mayor A. Oakey Hall: Rowan Tudor. Richard Connolly, Comptroller of the City of New York: George Lane. Peter Sweeney, Park Commissioner: Harry Meehan. William Marcy Tweed, Grand Sachem of Tammany Hall: MALCOLM LEE BEGGS. Butler: Dick Hughes. Maid: Louise Holden. Second Maid: Eve Harley. Mildred Wincor: Lillian Withington. Joe Stewart: JACK STANTON. Porter: John Thorne. Lotta Stevens: June MacLaren. Fanny Morris: Janet Roland. Clara Manning: Lilias MacLellan. James Fisk, Jr.: Jack Howard. George: George Bockman. The Gnome: Kenneth Owen. Governess: Louise Holden. First Child: Joanne Lally. Second Child: Janet Lally. Head Waiter: John Quigg. Arthur Finch: Wally Coyle. George Jones, Owner of the New York Times: Rowan Tudor. Newsboy: Hobart Streiford. Organ Grinders: Edward Pate, Kenneth Owen.

Dancing Ensemble: Betty Lou Bolles, Marjory Bradford, Rita Charise, Isabelle Chase, Virginia Conwell, Spicy Gillen, Ruth Lowe, Gloria Michaels, Sheila Reilly, Joanne Stone, Patsy Wymore. George Bockman, Captain; Robert Billheimer, Ray Arnett, Wally Coyle, Kenneth Owen, Dick Trevorrah, Louis Yetter.

Singing Ensemble: Mary Allen, Eloise Anderson, Betty Halperin, Eve Harvey, Shirley Neumann, Janet Roland, Lillian Withington, Mary Jane Woerner, Martha Wright. Will Bigelow, Oren Dabbs, Joseph Fazio, Dick Hughes, Russ Jondreau, Calvin Marsh, William Nuss, Edward Pate, Sidney Paul, Hobart Streiford, John Throne, Bernard Zwarg.

ICETIME OF 1948

1947.12

A Musical Icetravaganza (Revue) in Two Acts, 22 Scenes[24]. Music and lyrics by James Littlefield and John Fortis. Production by Sonart Productions. Executive director, Arthur M. Wirtz. Production director, William H. Burke. Staged by Catherine Littlefield. Choreography by Catherine Littlefield, assisted by Dorothie Littlefield. Settings designed and created by Bruno Maine and Edward Gilbert. Costumes by Lou Eisele, Billy

---

[20]Originally presented 18 February 1947 at the Heckscher Theatre Off-Broadway for a limited run; previously commissioned and presented in New York at Columbia University, New York City, 8 May 1946.
[21]Musical Numbers not listed in the program; list prepared from libretto and published score (G. Schirmer, New York, 1947).

[22]First presented 27 January 1945 at the New Century Theatre for 504 performances. For Synopsis of Scenes and Musical Numbers, see original 1945 production.
[23]"Carousel in the Park," "Rip Van Winkle," "The Fireman's Bride," "The Big Back Yard" (reprise), "Finaletto" staged by Helen Tamiris; all other principals' and singing ensemble numbers staged by Lew Kesler.
[24]A First Edition of the revue ICETIME was presented 20 June 1946 at the Center Theatre for 405 performances.

Livingston and Katherine Kuhn. Lighting effects by Eugene Braun. Skating direction by May Judels. Musical conductor, David Mendoza. Musical arrangements by Paul Van Loan. Produced by Sonja Henie and Arthur M. Wirtz. Opened 28 May 1947 at the Center Theatre and closed 3 April 1948 after 422 performances.

CAST: SKIPPY BAXTER, JOAN HYLDOFT, FREDDIE TRENKLER, JOE JACKSON, JR., THE BRUISES (Monty Stott, Geoffe Stevens, Sid Spaulding), BRANDT SISTERS (Helga, Inge), FRED GRIFFITH, FRITZ DIETL, JAMES CAESAR, JAMES CARTER, CLAIRE DALTON, PAUL CASTLE, BUSTER GRACE, JIMMIE SISK, LOU FOLDS. *Vocals*: NOLA FAIRBANKS, RICHARD CRAIG, MELBA WELCH.

Ensemble: Julian Apley, Peggy Bauer, Pauline Beevor, Edward Berry, Evelyn Biderman, Grace Bleckman, Ray Blow, Edward Brandstetter, Charles Caminiti, William Carvel, Charles Cavanaugh, Kay Corcoran, Nicholas Dantos, Helen Dutcher, Leonard Edwards, Arthur Erickson, Alice Farrar, Kurt Fishman, Louis Glessman, Walli Hackman, Pat Harrington, Rose Holder, Dan Hurley, Garry Keran, John Kasper, Lorraine Lanthier, Patricia LeMaire, Kenneth Leslie, Sheri Lynn, Marge Mahne, Ernest Mann, Robert Martina, Arthur Meehan, John Melendez, Marvette Mosic, Doris Nelson, Berenice Odell, Ken Parker, Gus Patrick, James Paul, Priscilla Paulson, Buck Pennington, Blanche Poston, Ragna Ray, Jerry Rehfield, Gerri Richardson, Lucille Risch, Rusty Rodgers, Lela Rolontz, Theresa Rothacker, Ruth Russell, Sandy Quitne, Jean Sakovich, Joe Shillen, Charles Slagle, Beth Stevens, Cissy Trenholm, Eileen Thompson, James Toth, James Trenholm, Janet Van Sickle, Wally Van Sickle, John Walsh.

ACT 1

Scene 1

"Breaking the Ice"

N. Fairbanks, R. Craig, M. Welch
(*Music by* Paul McGrane. *Lyrics by* Al Stillman.)
Ladies of the Ensemble: P. Bauer, P. Beevor, H. Dutcher, P. Harrington, R. Holder, W. Hackman, L. Lanthier, S. Lynn, P. LeMaire, M. Mahne, M. Mosic, D. Nelson, B. Odell, P. Paulson, B. Poston, R. Rodgers, R. Russel, L. Rolontz, R. Ray, G. Richardson, T. Rothacker, B. Stevens, E. Thompson. *Gentlemen of the Ensemble*: J. Apley, E. Berry, E. Brandstetter, R. Blow, W. Carvel, N. Dantos, L. Edwards, S. Edwards, A. Erickson, K. Fishman, L. Glessmna, D. Hurley, G. Keran, K. Leslie, R. Martina, J. Melendez, A. Meehan, G. Patrick, K. Parker, J. Paul, S. Quitne, J. Toth, J. Trenholm, W. Van Sickle.

Scene 2.

Precision Plus

J. Carter, J. Rehfield, J. Walsh, C. Caminiti, C. Dalton, G. Bleckman, J. Sakovich, C. Trenholm

Scene 3.

Curlylocks and the Three Bears

Curlylocks: A. Farrar. *Papa Bear*: J. Sisk. *Mama Bear*: J. Shillen. *Baby Bear*: P. Castle.

Scene 4

Mountain Echoes

K. Corcoran, J. Kasper

Scene 5

Cossack Lore

Tartar Princess: C. Trenholm. *Princes*: J. Rehnfield, J. Walsh. *Cossacks*: R. Blow, C. Caminiti, F. Griffith, B. Pennington, J. Trenholm, W. Van Sickle. *Nobles*: J. Apley, W. Carvel, N. Dantos, L. Edwards, S. Edwards, A. Erickson, E. Mann, J. Paul, S. Quitne, J. Toth. *Gypsy Girls*: P. Bauer, P. Beevor, E. Biderman, H. Dutcher, P. Harrington, R. Holder, W. Hackman, L. Lanthier, S. Lynn, P. Paulson, P. Lemaire, M. Mosic, B. Odell, G. Richardson, R. Russell, L. Rolontz, T. Rothacker, B. Stevens, E. Thompson. *Court Pages*: G. Bleckman, A. Farrar.

Scene 6

Design in Rhythm

F. Dietl, J. Carter

Scene 7

Bit of Old Erin

Colleens: G. Bleckman, K. Corcoran, J. Sakovich, C. Trenholm. *Carpenter*: E. Berry. *Bricklayer*: E. Brandstetter.

Scene 8

Light and Shadow

H. Brandt, I. Brandt

Scene 9

Toss Up

L. Folds

Scene 10

The Nutcracker

Father: J. Kasper. *Mother*: K. Corcoran. *Children*: B. Odell, B. Stevens, K. Leslie. *Nutcracker*: P. Castle. *Tutu Girls*: P. Bauer, P. Beevor, E. Biderman, H. Dutcher, W. Hackman, R. Holder, P. Lemaire, M. Mahne, M. Mosic, B. Poston, R. Rodgers, L. Rolontz, D. Nelson, P. Paulson, T. Rothacker, E. Thompson. *Prince*: S. Baxter. *Candy Fairy*: J. Hyldoft. *Boys*: W. Carvel, J. Decker, L. Edwards, S. Edwards, L. Glessman, D. Hurley, G. Kerna, E. Mann, R. Martina, J. Melnedez, A. Meehan, G. Patrick, K. Parker, J. Paul, J. Toth, W. Van Sickle. *Dance Chinoise*: R. Ray, B. Odell, B. Pennington. *Waltz of the Flowers*: *Girls*: P. Bauer, P. Beevor, G. Bleckman, K. Corcoran, H. Ducther, E. Thompson, L. Rolontz, W. Hackman, P. Harrington, L. Lanthier, M. Mosic, R. Holder, P. Lemaire, S. Lynn, M. Mahne, D. Nelson, G. Richardson, R. Rodgers, T. Rothacker, R. Russell.

Scene 11

Man of Distinction

J. Jackson, Jr.

Scene 12

When the Minstrels Come to Town

"Mandy," "Cuddle Up"

R. Craig, N. Fairbanks, M. Welch
Drummer Boy: G. Keran. *Banner Bearers*: N. Dantos, J. Trenholm. *Head Interlocutor*: J. Walsh. *Interlocutors*: J. Kasper, W. Van Sickle, C. Caminiti, J. Rehfield. *Sambo, Bones, Tambo, Jones*: E. Brandstetter, E. Berry, B. Grace, J. Shillen. *Banjo Boys*: J. Apley, R. Blow, W. Carvel, J. Decker, S. Edwards, L. Glessman, D. Hurley, K. Leslie, E. Mann, R. Martina, J. Melendez, A. Meehan, G. Patrick, S. Quitne, J. Paul, J. Toth. *Tambourine Girls*: P. Bauer, P. Beevor, E. Biderman, P. Harrington, R. Holder, S. Lynn, P. Lemaire, M. Mahne, D. Nelson, B. Odell, P. Paulson, B. Poston, G. Richardson, T. Rothacker, R. Russell, B. Stevens. *Lillian Russell*: C. Dalton. *Can Can Girls*: P. Bauer, P. Beevor, E. Biderman, K. Corcoran, H. Dutcher, W. Hackman, R. Holder, L. Lanthier, S. Lynn, P. Lemaire, M. Mosic, D. Nelson, B. Odell, B. Poston, G. Richardson, L. Rolontz, R. Ray, J. Sakovich, C. Trenholm.

ACT 2

Scene 1

The Dream Waltz: ("Her Dream Man")

R. Craig
Jivers: R. Odell, R. Ray, J. Shillen, J. Kasper, E. Brandstetter. *Dream Girl*: J. Hyldoft. *Hussars*: J. Carter, J. Rehfield, J. Walsh, C. Caminiti. *Waltz Girls*: P. Bauer, P. Beevor, E. Biderman, K. Corcoran, H. Dutcher, R. Holder, W. Hackman, P. Harrington, L. Lanthier, S. Lynn, P. Lemaire, M. Mahne, M. Mosic, D. Nelson, P. Paulson, R. Ray, G. Rothacker, R. Rodgers, R. Russell, L. Rolontz, T. Rothacker, B. Stevens, E. Thompson. *Yellow Hussars*: J. Apley, R. Blow, W. Carvel, J. Decker, L. Edwards, S. Edwards, A. Erickson, L. Glessman, D. Hurley, G. Keran, E. Mann, J. Melendez, K. Parker, G. Patrick, S. Quitne, J. Trenholm. *Her Dream Man*: S. Baxter.

Scene 2

Zouaves

B. Grace, P. Castle, B. Pennington, J. Sisk

Scene 3

Double Vision

H. Brandt, I. Brandt
Escorts: J. Walsh, C. Caminiti.

Scene 4

"Garden of Versailles"

R. Craig
Le Faun: P. Castle. *Les Amoureux*: C. Dalton, F. Griffith. *Court Ladies*: P. Bauer, P. Beevor, E. Biderman, G. Bleckman, H. Dutcher, R. Holder, W. Hackman, P. Harrington, S. Lynn, P. Lemaire, M. Mahne, M. Mosic, D. Nelson, B. Odell, P. Paulson, B. Poston, R. Rodgers, R. Russell, L. Rolontz, R. Ray, A. Farrar, G. Richardson, T. Rothacker, B. Stevens.

Scene 5

Over the Top

J. Caesar

Scene 6

Setting the Pace

Ladies of the Ensemble: P. Bauer, P. Beevor, E. Biderman, A. Boykin, K. Corcoran, H. Dutcher, W. Hackman, R. Holder, L. Lanthier, P. Lemaire, S. Lynn, M. Mahne, M. Mosic, D. Nelson, B. Odell, P. Paulson, R. Rodgers, R. Russell, L. Rolontz, R. Ray, G. Richardson, T. Rothacker, B. Stevens, E. Thompson. *Gentlemen of the Ensemble*: J. Apley, E. Berry, E. Brandstetter, R. Blow, W. Carvel, K. Fishman, N. Dantos, J. Decker, S. Edwards, A. Erickson, L. Glessman, D. Hurley, G. Keran, K. Leslie, E. Mann, R. Martina, J. Melendez, A. Meehan, G. Patrick, K. Parker, J. Paul, S. Quitne, J. Toth, J. Trenholm.

Scene 7

"Lovable You"
R. Craig
(*Skating Solo*:) J. Hyldoft.

Scene 8

Style on Steel
S. Baxter

Scene 9

The Bruises
M. Stott, G. Stevens, S. Spaulding

Scene 10

Finale
(Company)

Lisa Kirk and John Battles in ALLEGRO (Photo: Vandamm Studio)
Billy Rose Theatre Collection, New York Public Library for the Performing Arts

1947.13 LOUISIANA LADY

A Musical Comedy in Two Acts, 9 Scenes. Book by Isaac Green, Jr. and Eugene Berton. Based on the play "Creoles" by Samuel Shipman and Kenneth Perkins. Music and lyrics by Monte Carlo and Alma Sanders. Staged by Edgar MacGregor. Dances and musical numbers staged by Felicia Sorel. Settings by Watson Barratt. Costumes supervised by Frank Thompson. Lighting by Leo Kerz. Musical director, Hilding Anderson. Orchestrations by Hans Spialek and Robert Russell Bennett. Choral arrangements by Hilding Anderson. Produced by Hall Shelton. Opened 2 June 1947 at the New Century Theatre and closed 4 June 1947 after 4 performances.

CAST (in order of speaking): *El Gato*: RAY JACQUEMOT. *Joe*: LOU WILLS, JR. *Michel*: Val Buttignol. *Sarah*: Tina Prescott. *Corrine*: Ann Lay. *Germaine*: Patti Hall. *Annette*: Angela Carabella. *Suzanne*: Patti Kingsley. *Yvonne*: Ann Viola. *Marie-Louise*: EDITH FELLOWS. *Charley*: Howard Blaine. *Christophe*: Bert Wilcox. *Hugo*: Lee Kerry. *Geneveive*: Isabella Wilson. *Madame Corday*: MONICA MOORE. *Pierre*: Gil Cass. *Marquet*: Robert Kimberly. *Merluche*: GEORGE BAXTER. *Alphonse*: CHARLES JUDELS. *Celeste*: Bertha Powell. *A Drunk*: George Roberts. *Hoskins*: Berton Davis. *Janet*: Frances Keyes. *Golondrina*: VICTORIA CORDOVA. *Lieutenant Mason*: Patrick Meany. *Judge Morgan*: Bert Wilcox.

Singing Ensemble: Angela Carabella, Patti Hall, Frances Keyes, Patti Kingsley, Ann Lay, Tina Prescott, Ann Viola, Isabella Wilson, Gil Cass, Berton Davis, Ken Emery, Gerald Griffin Jr., George Baxter, Robert Kimberly, Michael Landau, Patrick Meany.

Ballet Ensemble: Aleta Buttignol, Karlyn DeBoer, Louise Harris, Anzia Kubicek, Terry Miele, Nancy Milton, Helen Osborne, Ruth Ostrander, Daniel Buberniak, Val Buttignol, Kenneth Davis, Robert DeVoye, Tony Matthews, Ralph Williams, Raoul Celeda.

Act 1, Scene 1: A Levee in New Orleans—April 1830. *Scene 2*: A Study in Miss Browne's Finishing School—Sunday Afternoon. *Scene 3*: The Parlor of the Casino De Luxe of Mme. Corday—The following evening. *Scene 4*: A Garden. *Scene 5*: The Parlor—A few minutes later.

Act 2, Scene 1: Canal Street. *Scene 2*: The Cucaracha Cafe. *Scene 3*: A Street. *Scene 4*: The Garden.

ACT 1

"Gold, Women and Laughter"
 R. Jacquemot, Men
"That's Why I Want to Go Home"
 E. Fellows
"Men About Town"
 M. Moore, Ensemble
"That's Why I Want to Go Home" (reprise)
 E. Fellows
"Just a Bit Naive"
 E. Fellows, R. Jacquemot
"The Cuckoo-Cheena"
 V. Cordova, L. Wills Jr., Ensemble
Dance
 H. Osborne, L. Harris, T. Matthews, Ensemble
"I Want to Live—I Want to Love"
 E. Fellows
Ballet
 Corps de Ballet
 Classic Trio: R. Ostrander, K. Davis, R. De Voye.
"The Night Was All to Blame"
 R. Jacquemot
"Beware of Lips That Say, 'Cherie'"
 M Moore
"Louisiana Holiday"
 R. Jacquemot, V. Cordova, Ensemble
Finale, Act 1
 The Company

ACT 2

"It's Mardi Gras"
 Ensemble, Corps de Ballet

Specialty
 K. Davis
"No, No, Mam'selle"
 R. Jacquemot, Girls
"When You Are Close to Me"
 E. Fellows, R. Jacquemot
"When You Are Close to Me" (reprise)
 E. Fellows
Mardi Gras Dance
 L. Wills, Jr.
"No One Cares for Dreams"
 M. Moore. Ensemble, Ballet
"Mammy's Little Baby"
 B. Powell
Finale
 The Company

1947.14 MUSIC IN MY HEART

A Romantic Musical Play in Two Acts, 7 Scenes. Book by Patsy Ruth Miller. Melodies by (Pyotor Ilyich) Tchaikovsky, adapted by Franz Steininger. Lyrics by Forman Brown. Staged and lighted by Hassard Short. Choreography by Ruth Page. Scenery and costumes by Alvin Colt. Book directed by Hassard Short. Musical director, Franz Steininger. Orchestrations by Hans Spialek. Choral arrangements by Clay Warnick. Co-producer, June Winslow. Produced by Henry Duffy. Opened 2 October 1947 at the Adelphi Theatre, suspended 3-11 January 1948, and closed 24 January 1948 after 124 performances.

CAST (in order of appearance): *Girl*: Dorothy Etheridge. *Boy*: Nannon Millis. *Stage Manager*: Harold Norman. *Tatiana Kerskaya*: VIVIENNE SEGAL. *Mischa*: George Lambrose. *Desiree Artot*: MARTHA WRIGHT. *Maurice Cabanne*: JAN MURRAY. *Capt. Nicholas Gregorovitch*: CHARLES FREDERICKS. *Ivan Petrofski*: JAMES STARBUCK. *Natuscha*: DOROTHY ETHERIDGE. *Gypsy*: JEAN HANDZLIK. *Joseph*: Robert Hayden. *Princess Katherine Dolgoruki*: DELLA LIND. *Lady in Waiting*: Martha Flynn. *Olga*: Pauline Goddard. *Messenger of the Tsar*: Edward White. *Sonya*: Jeanne Shelby. *Vera Remisova*: OLGA SUAREZ. *Lord Chamberlain*: Ralph Glover. *Prima Ballerina*: OLGA SUAREZ. *Premier Danseur*: NICHOLAS MAGALLANES.

Ballet: Dorothy Bauer, Iris Burton, Barbara Cole, Nancy Falk, Mary Haywood, Ann Hubbell, Clara Knox, Sheila Lawrence, Nannon Millis, Carol Nelson, Nina Popova, Yvonne Tibor, Marjorie Winters. James Barron, Robert Cadwallader, Ronald Chetwood, Charles Dickson, Charles L. Grasse, Jack Miller, Nicolai Polajenko.

Vocal Ensemble: Dorthea Berthelsen, Anne Marie Biggs, Eleanor Burrow, Audrey Dearden, Jane Flynn, Martha Flynn, Joyce Homire, Joan Kibrig, Barbara Weaver, Kathleen Zaranova. Jack Cassidy, Peter Hagen, Bernie Koveler, Allan Lowell, Harold Norman, Robert Rippy, Michael Risk, John Vanderhoof, Frank Whitmore.

Stagehands Footmen, Claque, etc.: Jack Cassidy, Peter Hagen, Bernie Koveler, Robert Rippy, Michael Risk.

Act 1, Scene 1a.: Ballet Rehearsal. *Scene 1b.*: Stage of the Odeon Theatre, St. Petersburg. *Scene 2*: The Cafe Samovar—A few weeks later.

Act 2, Scene 1: Nikki's Country House—A month later. *Scene 2*: Road to St. Petersburg—That night. *Scene 3*: Foyer of Imperial Opera House—A few weeks later. *Scene 4*: Stage of Imperial Opera House—A few minutes later. (a) Ballet—"Beauty and the Beast," (b) "Love Song." *Scene 5*: Backstage of Imperial Opera House.

ACT 1

Scene 1a.

"Unrequited Love, or The Storm" (Ballet)
 Ballet Ensemble
 Girl: D. Etheridge. *Boy*: N. Millis. This ballet to music by Rossini typifies the Italian style of dancing and the Italian music in vogue in Russia before the success of Tchaikovsky's first ballets.

Scene 1b.

"Flower Waltz"
 M. Wright

Scene 2

"Natuscha"
 J. Starbuck, D. Etheridge, Ensemble
"Love Is a Game for Soldiers"
 C. Fredericks

"Stolen Kisses"
D. Lind, C. Fredericks
"No! No! No!"
V. Segal, J. Murray
"While There's a Song to Sing"
M. Wright, Ensemble
"The Balalaika Serenade"
J. Handzlik
"Danse Arabe"
P. Goddard
"Trepak"
Ensemble
"I Am Enchanted" (Finale)
M. Wright, C. Fredericks, Ensemble

ACT 2

Scene 1
"Gossip"
J. Starbuck, D. Etheridge, Ballet Ensemble
"Once Upon a Time"
M. Wright, C. Fredericks
"Three's a Crowd"
M. Wright, D. Lind, C. Fredericks

Scene 2
"Song of the Troika"
M. Wright, C. Fredericks

Scene 3
"The Ballerina's Story"
V. Segal
"Song of the Claque"
J. Murray

Scene 4a
"Beauty and the Beast" (Ballet)
The Beauty: O. Suarez. *The Beast*: N. Magallanes.

Scene 4b
"Love Song"
M. Wright

Scene 5
"Love Is the Sovereign of My Heart"
M. Wright, C. Fredericks
Finale

1947.15 UNDER THE COUNTER

A Comedy with Music in Two Acts, 4 Scenes. Play by Arthur Macrae. Music by Manning Sherwin. Lyrics by Harold Purcell. Directed by Jack Hulbert. Dances arranged by Jack Hulbert and John Gregory. Decor by Clifford Pember. Orchestra under the direction of Harry Levant. Orchestrations by Ben Frankel. Produced by Lee Ephraim in association with the Messrs. Shubert. Opened 3 October 1947 at the Sam S. Shubert Theatre and closed 25 October 1947 after 27 performances.

CAST (in order of appearance): *Eva*: Winnifred Hindle. *Detective Inspector Baxter*: Francis Roberts. *Mike Kenderdine*: BALLARD BERKELEY. *Tim Garret*: THORLEY WALTERS. *Jo Fox*: CICELY COURTNEIDGE. *Mr. Burroughs*: GEORGE STREET. *Zoe Tritton*: Glen Alyn. *Kitty*: Ingrid Forrest. *Sir Alec Dunne*: WILFRID HYDE WHITE. *Lt. Cmdr. Hugo Conway, RNVR*: JOHN GREGORY. *Mr. Appleyard*: Frederick Farley.

The Play takes place in Jo Fox's House in London.

Act 1: Monday Afternoon. *Act 2, Scene 1*: Wednesday Morning. *Scene 2*: Thursday Evening. *Act 3*: Friday Morning.

MUSICAL NUMBERS
"Everywhere"
The Girls
"No-one's Tried to Kiss Me"
T. Walters, Girls

"The Moment I Saw You"
C. Courtneidge, T. Walters
"Let's Get Back to Glamour"
C. Courtneidge, Girls
"Ai Yi Yi"
C. Courtneidge, J. Gregory, Girls
"The Moment I Saw You" (reprise)
C. Courtneidge, T. Walters

1947.16 HIGH BUTTON SHOES

A Musical Comedy in Two Acts, 15 Scenes. Book by Stephen Longstreet, adapted from his novel "The Sisters Liked Them Handsome." Music by Jule Styne. Lyrics by Sammy Cahn. Settings by Oliver Smith. Costumes by Miles White. Lighting by Peggy Clark. Orchestrations by Philip Lang. Musical direction, Milton Rosenstock. Vocal arrangements, Bob Martin. Ballet music by Jule Styne. Dances and staging by Jerome Robbins. Production directed by George Abbott. Produced by Monte Proser and Joseph Kipness. Opened 9 October 1947 at the New Century Theatre, moved 22 December 1947 to the Sam S. Shubert Theatre, moved 18 October 1948 to the Broadway Theatre, and closed 2 July 1949 after 727 performances.

CAST: *Harrison Floy*: PHIL SILVERS. *Mr. Pontdue*: JOEY FAYE. *Uncle Willie*, mama's brother: Paul Godkin. *Henry Longstreet*: JACK McCAULEY. *General Longstreet*, gramp: Clay Clement. *Stevie Longstreet*: Johnny Stewart. *Fran*, mama's sister: LOIS LEE. *Sara Longstreet*, mama: NANETTE FABRAY. *Nancy*, the maid: Helen Gallagher. *Hubert Ogglethorpe* (Oggle): MARK DAWSON. *Shirley Simpkins*: Carole Coleman. *Elmer Simpkins*: Nathaniel Frey. *Elmer Simpkins, Jr.*: Donald Harris. *Coach*: Tom Glennon. *Mr. Anderson*: William David. *A Boy at the Picnic*: Arthur Partington. *His Playmate*: Sondra Lee. *A Popular Girl*: Jacqueline Dodge. *Her Friend*: Raul Celada. *A Betting Man*: George Spelvin. *Another Betting Man*: Howard Lenters.

Corps de Ballet: Jean Marie Caples, Jacqueline Dodge, Evelyn Giles, Christine Karner, Elena Lane, Sondra Lee, Kay Lewis, Louisa Lewis, Audrey Peters, Gloria Smith, Eleonore Trieber. Vincent Carbone, Evans Davis, Fred Hearn, Ray Kirchner, Tommy Morton, Arthur Partington, William Peirson, Kenneth Spaulding, William Sumner, Roy Tobias, Don Weissmuller.

Singers: Nancy Babcock, Gloria Casper, Estelle Gardner, Ronnie Hartmann, Dorothy Karrol, Hannah O'Leary, Fay Moore, Helene Whitney. Edward Cole, Ray Cook, Erno Czako, John Dennis, Nathaniel Frey, Neil Harwood, Edward Hayes, Ben Murphy.

Act 1, Scene 1: Kokomo and Points East. *Scene 2*: Living-room of the Longstreet Home, New Brunswick, N.J. Early Autumn, 1913. *Scene 3*: Redmond Street. *Scene 4*: Near the Stadium. *Scene 5*: The Longstreet Living-room. *Scene 6*: Road to the Picnic. *Scene 7*: "Longstreetville."

Act 2, Scene 1: Atlantic City—the Bathhouses. *Scene 2*: The Beach. *Scene 3*: The Bathhouses. *Scene 4*: Redmond Street, New Brunswick. *Scene 5*: The Longstreet Living-room. *Scene 6*: The Road. *Scene 7*: The Stadium. *Scene 8*: The Longstreet Garden.

ACT 1

Scene 1
"He Tried to Make a Dollar"
E. Cole, R. Cook, J. Dennis, E. Hayes

Scene 2
"Can't You Just See Yourself in Love With Me?"
M. Dawson, L. Lee

Scene 3
"There's Nothing Like a Model T"[1]
P. Silvers, Company

Scene 4
"Next to Texas, I Love You"
M. Dawson, L. Lee
Dance
Girls, Boys
"Security"
N. Fabray, L. Lee, Singing Girls

---

[1]Choral Arrangement by Hugh Martin.

Scene 5

Tango
H. Gallagher, P. Godkin

"Bird Watcher's Song"
N. Fabray, Singing Girls

Scene 6

"Get Away for a Day in the Country"
J. McCauley, J. Stewart, Singers

A Summer Incident
A Boy: A. Partington. *His Playmate*: S. Lee.
A Popular Girl: J. Dodge.
Her Friend: R. Celada.

Scene 7

"Papa, Won't You Dance With Me?"
N. Fabray, J. McCauley, Girls, Boys

Finaletto
Entire Company

ACT 2

Scene 1

"On a Sunday By the Sea"
Singers

Scene 2

Mack Sennett Ballet
Bathing Beauties: A. Peters, J. M. Caples, V. Gorski, J. Graham, E. Lane,
G. Smith, E. Treiber. *Life Guard*: E. Davis. *The Twins*: B. Hyatt, T. Stuart,
F. Hearn, D. Weissmuller. *Crooks*: R. Celada, J. Dodge, S. Lee. *Chief of Police*:
W. Sumner. *Cops*: V. Carbone, L. Claret, R. Kirchner, T. Morton, W. Pierson.

Scene 4

"You're My Girl"
M. Dawson, L. Lee

Scene 5

"I Still Get Jealous"
N. Fabray, J. McCauley

Scene 6

"You're My Boy"
P. Silvers, J. Faye

Scene 7

"Nobody Ever Died for Dear Old Rutgers"
P. Silvers, M. Dawson, Singing Boys

Scene 8

"Castle Walk"[2]
Danced by N. Fabray, J. McCauley
"He Tried to Make a Dollar" (reprise)
Entire Company

1947.17   ALLEGRO

A Musical Play in Two Acts. Book and lyrics by Oscar Hammerstein II.
Music by Richard Rodgers. Direction and choreography by Agnes de Mille.
Settings and lighting by Jo Mielziner. Costumes by Lucinda Ballard. Pro-
duction supervised by Lawrence Langner and Theresa Helburn. Orchestra-
tions by Robert Russell Bennett. Orchestra directed by Salvatore Dell'Isola.
Choral director, Crane Calder. Director of choral speech, Josephine Callan.
Music for the dances arranged by Trude Rittman. Produced by the Theatre
Guild. Opened 10 October 1947 at the Majestic Theatre and closed 10 July
1948 after 315 performances.

<u>CAST</u> (in order of appearance): *Marjorie Taylor*: ANNAMARY DICKEY. *Dr. Joseph
Taylor*: WILLIAM CHING. *Mayor*: Edward Platt. *Grandma Taylor*: MURIEL
O'MALLEY *Joey's Friends*: Ray Harrison, Frank Westbrook. *Jennie Brinker*: ROBERTA
JONAY. *Principal*: Robert Byrn. *Mabel*: Evelyn Taylor. *Bicycle Boy*: Stanley Simmons.
Georgie: Harrison Muller. *Hazel*: KATHRYN LEE. *Charlie Townshend*: JOHN
CONTE. *Joseph Taylor, Jr.*: JOHN BATTLES. *Miss Lipscombe*: Susan Svetlik. *Cheer
Leaders*: Charles Tate, Sam Steen. *Coach*: Wilson Smith. *Ned Brinker*: PAUL PARKS.
English Professor: David Collyer. *Chemistry Professor*: William McCully. *Greek

Professor: Raymond Keast. *Philosophy Professor*: Robert Bryn. *Shakespeare Student*:
Susan Svetlik. *Betram Woolhaven*: Ray Harrison. *Molly*: Katrina Van Oss. *Beulah*:
Gloria Wills. *Minister*: Edward Platt. *Millie*: Julie Humphries. *Dot*: Sylvia Karlton.
Addie: Patricia Bybell. *Dr. Bigby Denby*: LAWRENCE FLETCHER. *Mrs. Mulhouse*:
Frances Rainer. *Mrs. Lansdale*: Lily Paget. *Jarman, a butler*: Bill Bradley. *Maid*: Jean
Houloose. *Emily*: LISA KIRK. *Doorman*: Tom Perkins. *Brook Lansdale*: Stephen
Chase. *Buckley*: Wilson Smith.
Singers: Mary O'Fallon, Charlotte Howard, Lily Paget, Helen Hunter, Sylvia
Karlton, Christina Lind, Gay Lawrence, Josephine Lambert, Julie Humphries, Patricia
Bybell, Yolanda Renay, Devida Stewart, Nanette Vezina, Mia Stenn, Lucille Udovick.
Glen Scandur, Gene Tobin, Walter Kelvin, Bernard Green, David Collyer, Joseph
Caruso, Tommy Barragan, Victor Clarke, Edward Platt, Robert Reeves, Wilson Smith,
James Jewell, David Poleri, Robert Neukum, Raymond Keast, Wesley Swails, Clarence
Hall, Blake Ritter, Ralph Patterson, Robert Byrn, William McCully, Robert Arnold.
Dancers: Jean Tachau, Evelyn Taylor, Mariane Oliphant, Patricia Gianinoto,
Andrea Downing, Jean Houloose, Therese Miele, Frances Rainer, Susan Svetlik, Ruth
Ostrander, Patrcia Barker. Ralph Linn, Harrison Muller, Stanley Simmons, Charles
Tate, Frank Westbrook, Edward Weston, Ralph Williams, Sam Steen.

The story starts in 1905 on the day Joseph Taylor, Jr., is born, and follows his life to his
thirty-fifth year. The three major locations of action are:

Act 1: His home town and his college town. *Act 2*: A large city.

ACT 1

"Joseph Taylor, Jr."
Entire Ensemble

"I Know It Can Happen Again"
M. O'Malley

"One Foot, Other Foot"
Singing Ensemble, Ballet Ensemble
Specialists: K. Lee, P. Barker, R. Herget.

"A Fellow Needs a Girl"
W. Ching, A. Dickey

Freshman Dance
Ensemble
As They Imagine They Are: E. Taylor, H. Muller.

"A Darn Nice Campus"
J. Battles
Cheerleaders: S. Steen, C. Tate.

"The Purple and the Brown"
The Freshmen

"So Far"
G. Wills

"You Are Never Away"
W. Ching, R. Jonay, Vocal Chorus

"What a Lovely Day for the Wedding"
Singing Ensemble, P. Parks

"It May Be a Good Idea for Joe"
J. Conte

Wedding
Relatives, Guests of the Bride and Groom

"To Have and To Hold"
Singing Ensemble

"Wish Them Well"
Singing Ensemble

ACT 2

"Money Isn't Everything"
R. Jonay, K. Lee, P. Bybell, J. Humphries, S. Karlton

Hazel Dances
K. Lee

"Yatata, Yatata, Yatata"
J. Conte, Ensemble

"The Gentleman Is a Dope"
L. Kirk

"Allegro"
L. Kirk, J. Conte, J. Battles, Singing Ensemble, K. Lee,
Ballet Ensemble

"Come Home"
A. Dickey

Finale
Entire Company

---

[2]Dance originally created by Vernon and Irene Castle.

EDITH PIAF

1947.18   and Her Continental Entertainers

A Revue in Two Acts, 6 Scenes. Produced by Clifford C. Fischer. Opened 30 October 1947 at the Playhouse and closed 6 December 1947 after 44 performances.

CAST: EDITH PIAF, LES COMPAGNONS DE LA CHANSON (Joseph Frachon, Guy Bourguignon, Hubert Lancelot, Gerard Sabbat, Paul Buissonneau, Jean-Louis Jaubert [director], Jean Alber, March Herrand, Fred Mella); GEORGES ANDRE MARTIN (Conferencier), GEORGE and TIM DORMONDE, LES CANOVA, LYDA ALMA and VANNI FLEURY, Dorrit Merrill (Announcer).

ACT 1

Scene 1

Lyda Alma and Vanni Fleury (Hellenic Dancers from Greece)

Scene 2

George and Tim Dormonde (Scientific Nonsense from Sweden)

Scene 3

Les Canova (Poetry in Motion from Italy)

Scene 4

Georges Andre Martin (Digital Dancing)

Scene 5

Les Compagnons de la Chanson (French Voices in Satiric Ballads):
Song About the Bear
"My lover must stay in bed or he may catch a cold"
"The Duel"—an opera in two acts
"Au Claire de Lune"—as rendered by a Jazz Band, a Russian Choir, and Symphony Orchestra

ACT 2

Edith Piaf, Chanteuse
"De l'autre côte de la rue"
"La marice"
"Je n'en connais pas la fin"
"L'accordeoniste"
    (*Music and Lyrics by* Michel Emer.)
"Monsieur St. Pierre"
"C'est toujours la même histoire"
"J'ai dansé avec l'amour"
"Mon homme"
    (*Music by* Maurice Yvain. *Lyrics by* Albert Willemetz and Jacques Charles.)
"(Mon) Legionnaire"
    (*Music and Lyrics by* Marguerite Monnot, Asso.)
"Les cloches"
    (*Music by* Vincent Scotto. *Lyrics by* Decaye.)

CARIBBEAN CARNIVAL

1947.19

A Calypso Musical Revue in Two Acts, 22 Scenes. Music and lyrics by Samuel L. Manning and Adolph Thenstead. Directed by Samuel L. Manning. Associate director, Col. John J. Hirshman. Additional choreography by Claude Marchant. Costumes designed by Lou Eisele. Scenery painted by Jules Laurent Studios. Orchestra conducted and orchestrations by Ken Macomber. Drum rhythms composed by Mario Costillo. Produced by Adolph Thenstead. Opened 5 December 1947 at the International Theatre and closed 13 December 1947 after 11 performances.

CAST: PEARL PRIMUS, JOSEPHINE PREMICE, CLAUDE MARCHANT, THE DUKE OF IRON [Cecil Anderson], SAM MANNING, SMITH KIDS, PAMELA WARD, TRIO CUBANA, Peggy Watson, Eddie Talifferro.
Calypso Dancers: Gem Bolling, Dorothy Graham, Eloise Hill, Curtis James, Andrew King, Paul Meeres, Lillie Peace, Charles Queenan, Bernard Taylor, Mildred Thomas, Alex Young.
Claude Marchant Dance Group: Billie Allen, Jacqueline Hairston, Marjorie James, Donald Curtis, James Brown.
Singing Ensemble: Helen Carr, Clara Hubbard, Dorothy Macdavid, Wahnetta San, Fannie Turner, Clifton Gray, Louis Sterling, Fred Thomas.

Drummers: Alphonse Cimber, Bernard Taylor, Paul Meeres.
Ensemble: Padjet Fredericks, William Johnson, Jerry Meeres, Wahne Ha San, Helen Tinsley.

ACT 1

Scene 1

Overture—Fantasia Calypso
    Orchestra

Scene 2

Carnival in Trinidad
    Sergeant Squashie: S. Manning. *Press Photographer:* P. Ward. *A Native:* E. Talifferro.

Scene 3

"America the Great," "Marabella," "Pretty"
    Duke of Iron, J. Premice, P. Watson, E. Talifferro
    Each year the carnival spirit takes possession of everyone on the quaint little island of Trinidad, and the population swarms to the public places to make merry—and say just what they have been thinking about their neighbors, through the age old medium of Calypso, as in the case of Marabella.

Scene 4

Native Songs
    Smith Kids

Scene 5

Native Dances:
    (*Choreography by* Claude Marchant.)
    a. Enlloro (Voodoo Moon)
        (*Music by* Morales-Blanco.)
    b. Canto de las Palmas (Chant of the Palms)
        (*Music by* Paquita Anderson.)
        The Claude Marchant Group, featuring C. Marchant, B. Allen

Scene 6

Trio Cubana

Scene 7

Bribe for an Officer
    S. Manning, P. Ward

Scene 8

Firefly Dance
    E. Hill, Dancers
    Fireflies of the Bayou, scattered by a bat, return in friendliness.

Scene 9

Love in the Dark (comedy skit)
"Love Love Love"

Scene 10

"Anything Goes When You Sing Calypso"
    P. Ward

Scene 11

Market Scene—Finale
    Smith Kids, Washerwoman, Duke of Iron, Claude Marchant and Group

ACT 2

Scene 1

"Rookombay" (Voodoo Night)
    P. Primus
    (*Choreography by* Pearl Primus. Chant music for "Rookombay" by Duke of Iron.)
"Don't Stop the Carnival" (Calypso)
    Company

Scene 2

"Hold 'em, Joe" (Calypso)
    Fat Woman: P. Watson. *Donkey:* A. Young. *Singers:* Smith Kids.

Scene 3

"Rookombay" (Shango Calypso)
    (*Choreography by* Pearl Primus. Chant music for "Rookombay" by Duke of Iron.)
    Serpent Totem: C. James. *Guards:* A. Young, C. James, P. Fredericks. *Singer:* F. Thomas. *Shango Woman:* P. Primus.

Dancers: G. Bolling, D. Graham, E. Hill, L. Peace, M. Thomas, C. James, A. King, C. Queenan, A. Young, P. Fredericks. *Chorus*: H. Carr, C. Hubbard, D. Macdavid, W. San, F. Turner, C. Gray, L. Sterling, F. Thomas.

Scene 4

"Cleaning Up Song"
H. Carr, F. Thomas, Company

Scene 5

"Teas for Two"
G. Bolling, C. James

Scene 6.

"Tamboule" (Stick Fight)
A. Young, C. James

Scene 7

Exultation
Shango Woman: P. Primus.

Scene 8

At Bay
(*Music by* Camilla DeLeon.)
Guards: A. Young, C. James, P. Fredericks. *Shango Woman*: P. Primus.

Scene 9

Celebration
Women Possessed: E. Hill, D. Graham. *Man Possessed*: C. Queenan. *Shango Woman*: P. Primus. *Drummers*: A. Cimber, B. Taylor, P. Meeres.

Scene 10

Sam Manning, Pamela Ward.

Scene 11

Native Cafe Scene; Finale
J. Premice, Entire Company

1947.20   ANGEL IN THE WINGS

An Intimate Musical Revue in Two Acts, 19 Scenes. Words (lyrics) and music by Bob Hilliard and Carl Sigman. Sketches by Hank Ladd, Ted Luce and The Hartmans. Production staged by John Kennedy. Choreography by Edward Noll. Settings and lighting by Donald Oenslager. Costumes by Julia Sze. Musical arrangements by David Mann and Fred Barovick. Musical director, Phil Ingalls. Produced by Marjorie and Sherman Ewing. Opened 11 December 1947 at the Coronet Theatre and closed 4 September 1948 after 308 performances.

CAST: THE HARTMANS (Grace, Paul), HANK LADD, NADINE GAE, PETER HAMILTON, ROBERT STANTON, VIOLA ROCHE, JOHNNY BARNES, ELAINE STRITCH, EILEEN BARTON, Patricia Jones, Bill McGraw, Janet Gaylord, Alan Green.

ACT 1

Scene 1

The Hartmans

Scene 2

Hank Ladd

Scene 3

"Long Green Blues"
H. Ladd
Dancers: N. Gae, P. Hamilton.

Scene 4

Up Early With the Upjohns
Nettie: G. Hartman. *Horace*: P. Hartman. *Wilford*: R. Stanton. *Charlie*: J. Barnes. *Lula Belle*: E. Stritch.

Scene 5

"Holler Blue Murder"
E. Barton

Scene 6

Reminiscences
H. Ladd

Scene 7

Professor De Marco and Company
The Hartmans

Scene 8

"Breezy"
P. Jones, B. McGraw
Dancers: N. Gae, P. Hamilton.

Scene 9

Swingeasy
The Killer: H. Ladd. *Lefty*: R. Stanton. *The Kid*: J. Barnes. *The Stranger*: P. Hartman. *Three "Gone Cats"*: V. Roche, J. Gaylord, A. Green.

Scene 10

"Civilization" (Bongo, Bongo, Bongo)
E. Stritch

Scene 11

Apoliagia
H. Ladd

Scene 12

The Glamorous Ingabord
Headwaiter: B. McGraw. *Mrs. Tidworth*: V. Roche. *Mr. Tidworth,III*: R. Stanton. *Mrs. Blodgett*: G. Hartman. *Mr. Blodgett*: P. Hartman. *Waiter*: J. Barnes. *Ingabord*: E. Stritch.

ACT 2

Scene 1

"Tambourine"
E. Barton
Danced by: J. Barnes. *Assisted by*: H. Ladd.

Scene 2

Trailer Trouble
George: P. Hartman. *Charlie*: J. Barnes. *Ruth*: G. Hartman. *Milly*: E. Stritch. *Lt. Jackson*: R. Stanton. *Joe*: B. McGraw.

Scene 3

"If It Were Easy to Do"
E. Barton
Danced by: N. Gae, P. Hamilton.

Scene 4

The Serious Note
H. Ladd

Scene 5

"(The) Thousand Islands Song" (I Left My Love on One of the Thousand Islands)
H. Ladd
Florence: N. Gae.

Scene 6

The Salina Select Garden Club
Mrs. Schultz: V. Roche. *Mrs. Hutchinson*: G. Hartman. *Dr. Hutchinson, W.T.*: P. Hartman.

Scene 7

"The Big Brass Band from Brazil"
Entire Company

1947.21   THE CRADLE WILL ROCK

A Revival of the Play in Music in One Act, 10 Scenes[3]. Play and music by Marc Blitzstein. Staged by Howard DaSilva. Orchestra conducted by Leonard Bernstein[4]. Produced by Michael Myerberg. Opened 26 December 1947 at the Mansfield Theatre, closed 11 January 1948 after 21 perform-

---

[3] First presented 16 June 1937 at the Venice Theatre for 19 performances, subsequently at the Mercury and Windsor Theatres for 112 performances. For Synopsis of Scenes and Musical Numbers see original 1937 production. Unlike the original, this revival was performed without intermission. This revival was inspired by the success of the New York City Symphony production at the New York City Center 24-25 November 1947.

[4] For the Broadway Theatre transfer, succeeded by Howard Shanet.

ances; re-opened 28 January 1948 under the auspices of David Lowe at the Broadway Theatre and closed 7 February 1948 after 13 additional performances, for a total of 34 performances.

CAST: *Moll*: ESTELLE LORING. *Gent*: Edward S. Bryce. *Dick*: Jesse White. *Cop*: Taggart Casey. *Reverend Salvation*: Harold Patrick. *Editor Daily*: Brooks Dunbar. *Yasha*: Jack Albertson. *Dauber*: Chandler Cowles. *President Prexy*: Howard Blaine. *Professor Trixie*: Leslie Litomy. *Professor Mamie*: Edmund Hewitt. *Professor Scoot*: Ray Fry. *Doctor Specialist*: Robert Pierson. *Harry Druggist*: DAVID THOMAS. *Mr. Mister*: WILL GEER. *Mrs. Mister*: VIVIAN VANCE. *Junior Mister*: Dennis King, Jr. *Sister Mister*: Jo Hurt. *Steve*: Stephen West Downer. *Sadie Polock*: Marie Leidal. *Gus Polock*: Walter Scheff. *Bugs*: Edward S. Bryce. *Larry Foreman*: ALFRED DRAKE. *Ella Hammer*: MURIEL SMITH. *Attendant's Voice*: Hazel Shermet. *First Reporter*: Rex Coston. *Second Reporter*: Gil Houston. *Clerk*: Howard Shanet.

Chorus: Lucretia Anderson, Robert Burr, John Fleming, Michael Pollock, Germaine Poulin, Napoleon Reed, Gwen Ward.

THE MIKADO,
1947.22 or, The Town of Titipu

A Revival of the Comic Opera in Two Acts[5]. Libretto by William S. Gilbert. Music by Arthur Sullivan. Scenery and costumes designed by Charles Ricketts. Directed by Anna Bethell. Musical director, Isidore Godfrey. Assistant, Alan E. Ward. Produced by the D'Oyly Carte Opera Company. Opened 29 December 1947 at the New Century Theatre, closing 3 January 1948; reopened 16-21 February 1948, and 5-24 April 1948 for a total of 40 performances in repertory

CAST: *The Mikado of Japan*: DARRELL FANCOURT. *Nanki-Poo*, his son, disguised as a wandering minstrel in love with Yum-Yum: THOMAS ROUND. *Ko-Ko*, Lord High Executioner of Titipu: MARTYN GREEN. *Pooh-Bah*, Lord High Everything Else: RICHARD WATSON. *Pish-Tush*, *Go-To*, Noble Lords: Charles Dorning, Peter Pratt. *Yum-Yum*, *Pitti-Sing*, *Peep-Bo*, three sisters, wards of Ko-Ko: MARGARET MITCHELL, MARIAN SMITH, JOAN GILLINGHAM. *Katisha*: ELLA HALMAN. *Chorus of School Girls, Nobles, Guards and Coolies.*

TRIAL BY JURY
1948.01

A Revival of the Comic Opera in One Act[6]. Libretto by William S. Gilbert. Music by Arthur Sullivan. Costumes designed by George Sheringham. Directed by Anna Bethell. Musical director, Isidore Godfrey. Produced by the D'Oyly Carte Opera Company. Opened 5 January 1948 at the Century Theatre and closed 10 January 1948; re-opened 8 March 1948 and closed 13 March 1948 after 16 performances in repertory.[7]

CAST: *The Learned Judge*: RICHARD WATSON. *Counsel for the Defendant*: CHARLES DORNING. *The Defendant*: LEONARD OSBORN. *Foreman of the Jury*: Radley Flynn. *Usher*: RICHARD WALKER. *Associate*: C. WILLIAM MORGAN. *The Plaintiff*: GWYNETH CULLIMORE. *First Bridesmaid*: Enid Walsh. *Chorus of Jurymen, Bridesmaids and Public.*

THE PIRATES OF PENZANCE,
1948.02 or, The Slave of Duty

A Revival of the Comic Opera in Two Acts[8]. Libretto by William S. Gilbert. Music by Arthur Sullivan. Costumes designed by George Sheringham. Directed by Anna Bethell. Musical director, Isidore Godfrey. Produced by D'Oyly Carte Opera Company. Opened 5 January 1948 at the New Century

Theatre, closing 10 January 1948; re-opened 8-13 March 1948, for a total of 16 performances in repertory.[9]

CAST: *The Pirate King*: DARRELL FANCOURT, RICHARD WATSON, alt. *Major General Stanley*: MARTYN GREEN. *Samuel*, his Lieutenant: Richard Dunn. *Frederic*, the Pirate Apprentice: THOMAS ROUND. *Sergeant of Police*: RICHARD WALKER. *Mabel, Edith, Kate, Isabel*, General Stanley's Daughters: HELEN ROBERTS, JOYCE WRIGHT (DENISE FINDLAY, alt.), JOAN GILLINGHAM, Enid Walsh. *Ruth*, Pirate Maid-of-all-work: ELLA HALMAN. *Chorus of Pirates, Police and General Stanley's Daughters.*

IOLANTHE,
1948.03 or, The Peer and the Peri

A Revival of the Comic Opera in Two Acts[10]. Libretto by William S. Gilbert. Music by Arthur Sullivan. Costumes designed by Norman Wilkinson. Directed by Anna Bethell. Musical director, Isidore Godfrey. Produced by the D'Oyly Carte Opera Company. Opened 12 January 1948 at the New Century Theatre, closing 17 January 1948; re-opened 29 March-3 April 1948 for a total of 16 performances in repertory.

CAST: *The Lord Chancellor*: MARTYN GREEN. *Earl of Mountararat*: RICHARD DUNN, (RICHARD WALKER, alt.) *Earl Tolloller*: LEONARD OSBORN. *Private Willis* (of the Grenadier Guards): RICHARD WALKER, (RICHARD WATSON, alt.) *Strephon*, an Arcadian Shepherd: CHARLES DORNING. *Queen of the Fairies*: ELLA HALMAN. *Iolanthe*, a Fairy, Strephon's Mother: DENISE FINDLAY. *Celia, Leila, Fleta*, Fairies: Gwyneth Cullimore, Joan Gillingham, Patricia Hadfield. *Phyllis*, an Arcadian Shepherdess and Ward in Chancery: MARGARET MITCHELL. *Chorus of Dukes, Marquises, Earls, Viscounts, Barons and Fairies.*

MAKE MINE MANHATTAN
1948.04

A Musical Revue in Two Acts, 22 Scenes. Sketches and lyrics by Arnold B. Horwitt. Music by Richard Lewine. Sketches directed by Max Liebman. Choreography by Lee Sherman. Settings by Frederick Fox. Costumes by Morton Hack. Musical director, Charles Sanford. Orchestrations by Ted Royal. Vocal supervision by Lois Moseley. Musical continuity for dances by Mel Pahl. Produced by Joseph M. Hyman. Opened 15 January 1948 at the Broadhurst Theatre and closed 8 January 1949 after 429 performances.[11]

CAST: SID CAESAR, DAVID BURNS, SHEILA BOND, JOSHUA SHELLEY, KYLE MacDONNELL, JACK KILTY, DANNY DANIELS, NELLE FISHER, RAY HARRISON, ELEANOR BAGLEY, MAX SHOWALTER, Richard Arnold, Perry Bruskin, Louise Berrand, Wayne Lamb, Sterling Mace, Joseph Melvin.

Dancers: Anne Feris, Annabelle Gold, Rhoda Johannson, Phyllis Mayo, Marta Nita, Dolores Novins, Willis Brunner, Tony Charmoli, Hal Loman, Tommy Morton, Skip Randall, Rudy Tone, Betty Lind. *Singers*: Stephanie Augustine, Joy Carroll, Jean Jones, Barbara Weaver, Larry Carr, Ed Chappel, Biff McGuire.

ACT 1[12]

Scene 1

"Anything Can Happen in New York"

---

[5]First presented in New York 20 July, 10-29 August 1885 at the Union Square and People's Theatres for 22 performances. First authorized production presented 19 August 1885 at the Fifth Avenue Theatre by Richard D'Oyly Carte for 250 performances. For Synopsis of Scenes and Musical Numbers, see 19 August 1885 D'Oyly Carte production.
[6]First presented in New York 15 November 1875 at the Eagle Theatre for 8 performances. For Synopsis of Scenes and Musical Numbers, see original 1875 production.
[7]Scenery uncredited.
[8]First presented in New York 31 December 1879 at the Fifth Avenue Theatre for a total of 91 performances in two engagements. For Synopsis of Scenes and Musical Numbers, see original 1879 production.

[9]Scenery uncredited.
[10]First presented in New York 25 November 1882 at the Standard Theatre for 105 performances. For Synopsis of Scenes and Musical Numbers, see original 1882 production.
[11]Program note: "Make Mine Manhattan" gratefully thanks Moss Hart for his valued suggestions.
[12]Once Bert Lahr joined the show during its run replacing Sid Caesar, the following material was added:

Doctors Don't Tell. (Act 1)
  (*by* Matt Brooks)
  Scene: Doctor's Office in Mid-town Manhattan.
  Nurse: J. Jones. *Mr. Smith*: Jack Albertson. *Doctor*: B. Lahr.

"Schrafft's" (Act 1)
  B. Lahr

Income Tax (Act 2)
  (*by* David Freedman)
  Higgins: J. Albertson. *Gruncher*: Bob Gallagher. *Clarkson*: B. Lahr.

"Song of the Woodman" (from THE SHOW IS ON)(Act 2)
  B. Lahr
  (*Music and Lyrics by* Harold Arlen and E. Y. Harburg)

M. Showalter, E. Bagley, S. Augustine, J. Carroll, J. Jones, L. Carr, E. Chappel, B. McGuire
Danced by N. Fisher, H. Loman, A. Feris, L. Ferrand, A. Gold, R. Johnstone, B. Lind, P. Mayo, D. Novins, W. Brunner, T. Charmoli, W. Lamb, T. Morton, S. Randall, R. Tone.

Scene 2

First Avenue Gets Ready
   (*by* Arnold B. Horwitt and Max Liebman)
   Scene: Kelly's First Avenue Diner.
   Kelly: D. Burns. *Mamie*: S. Bond. *A Delegate*: S. Caesar. *His Aide*: P. Bruskin.
   Another Delegate: S. Caesar. *Still Another Delegate*: S. Caesar. *Ukrainian*:
   R. Arnold. *Slovanian*: E. Chappel. *Roumanian*: J. Melvin.

Scene 3

"Phil the Fiddler"
   J. Kilty
   Phil: R. Harrison. *Passers-by*: B. McGuire, D. Novins, B. Lind, A. Feris,
   A. Gold. *Ballroom Dancers*: S. Augustine, R. Johannson, P. Mayo, W. Brunner,
   S. Randall, R. Tone. *The Heroine*: N. Fisher. *The Villain*: T. Morton. *The
   Horses*: T. Cahrmoli, H. Loman. *The Billionaire*: J. Shelley. *The Lackeys*:
   L. Carr, B. McGuire, M. Showalter.

Scene 4

"Movie House in Manhattan"
   E. Bagley

Scene 5

Any Resemblance . . . . .
   Scene: Office of the Daily Gazette.
   Blodgett: S. Caesar. *Bassett*: D. Burns. *Jukes*: J. Shelley.

Scene 6

"Talk to Me"
   S. Bond, D. Daniels

Scene 7

"Traftz"
   J. Shelley

Scene 8

"I Don't Know His Name"
   Scene: Roof-tops in Manhattan.
   The Boy: J. Kilty. *The Girl*: K. MacDonnell.

Scene 9

"The Good Old Days"
   S. Caesar, D. Burns
   (*Lyrics by* Arnold B. Horwitt and Ted Fetter.)
   The Girls: S. Bond, E. Bagley.

Scene 10

Once Over Lightly
   In front of the theatre: D. Burns, E. Bagley, Dancers.
   Mother: P. Mayo. *Father*: P. Bruskin. *Mother-in-law*: J. Jones. *Great Aunt*:
   R. Johannson. *Second Cousin*: E. Bagley. *Herman W. Willoughby, Jr.*: S. Caesar.
   Bessie Bricker: S. Bond. *Nurse*: N. Fisher. *Patient*: M. Showalter. *The Choir*:
   J. Shelley, J. Kilty, K. MacDonnell, S. Augustine, J. Carroll, B. Weaver,
   B. McGuire, E. Chappel, L. Carr. *The Dancers*: A. Feris, A. Gold, B. Lind,
   D. Novins, T. Charmoli, T. Morton, S. Randall, R. Tone.

Scene 11

Penny Gum Machine
   (*by* Allan Roberts, Sid Caesar, Max Liebman)S. Caesar

Scene 12

"Saturday Night in Central Park"
   K. MacDonnell, E. Bagley, M. Showalter, Singers
   Dance Variations: A. Gold, T. Charmoli, R. Tone, H. Loman, P. Mayo, D.
   Novins, W. Brunner, S. Bond, N. Fisher, D. Daniels, R. Harrison.

ACT 2

Scene 1

"Ringalevio"
   J. Shelley
   First Ringleader: T. Morton. *Second Ringleader*: R. Tone. *Sissy*: D. Daniels.
   Dancers.

Scene 2

"Noises in the Street"
   (*Lyrics by* Peter Barry, David Gregory, Arnold B. Horwitt.)
   Taxi Driver: D. Burns. *Milkman*: M. Showalter. *Street Cleaner*:
   S. Caesar. *Street Digger*: P. Bruskin. *Newsboy*: J. Shelley.

Scene 3

"I Fell in Love With You"
   K. MacDonnell, J. Kilty
   Scene: Overlooking the East River.
   Danced by: N. Fisher, R. Harrison.

Scene 4

"My Brudder and Me"
   S. Bond, D. Daniels

Scene 5

Hollywood Heads East
   (*by* Arnold B. Horwitt and Max Liebman)
   The Mayor: M. Showalter. *Eddie*: J. Shelley. *Mr. Bigelow*: S. Caesar.
   The Actress: K. MacDonnell. *The Actor*: J. Kilty. *Photographer*:
   B. McGuire. *Assistant Photographer*: P. Bruskin. *Make-up Girl*: S. Augustine.
   Mr. Rappaport: D. Burns.

Scene 6

"Gentleman Friend"
   S. Bond, H. Loman, Dancers
   Scene: Union Square.

Scene 7

"Subway Song"
   J. Shelley
   The Girl: R. Johannson.

Scene 8

Full Fathom Five
   (*by* Arnold B. Horwitt and Sylvia Rosales)
   Scene: A Pen Shop in Manhattan.
   The Salesman: M. Showalter. *The Customer*: D. Burns.
   The Model: J. Jones. *The Clerks*: L. Carr, E. Chappel, S. Mace,
   B. McGuire.

Scene 9

A Night Out
   (*by* Max Liebman)S. Caesar

Scene 10

"Glad to Be Back"
   Entire Company
   Scene: Grand Central Station.

COX AND BOX

1948.05

A Revival of the Triuviretta in One Act[13]. Libretto by F. C. Burnand, based on Maddison Morton's farce "Box and Cox." Music by Arthur Sullivan. Directed by Anna Bethell. Musical director, Isidore Godfrey. Opened 19 January 1948 at the New Century Theatre, closing 24 January 1948; re-opened 23-28 February 1948 for a total of 16 performances in repertory.[14]

CAST: *Cox*, a Journeyman Hatter: RICHARD DUNN. *Box*, a Journeyman Printer: LEONARD OSBORN. *Bouncer*, their Landlord: RICHARD WALKER.

H.M.S. PINAFORE,
1948.06   or, The Lass That Loved a Sailor

A Revival of the Comic Opera in Two Acts[15]. Libretto by William S. Gilbert. Music by Arthur Sullivan. Directed by Anna Bethell. Designed and painted by Joseph and Paul Harker. Ladies' costumes designed by George Sheringham. Musical director, Isidore Godfrey. Presented by D'Oyly Carte Opera Company. Opened 19 January 1948 at the New Century Theatre, closing 24 January 1948; re-opened 23-28 February 1948 for a total of 16 performances in repertory.

---

[13]First presented in New York as COX AND BOX, or The Long-Lost Brothers 14 August 1879 at the Standard Theatre for 48 performances. For Synopsis of Scenes and Musical Numbers, see original 1879 production.
[14]Scenery and costumes uncredited.
[15]Originally presented in New York 15 January 1879 at the Standard Theatre for 175 performances. For Synopsis of Scenes and Musical Numbers, see original 1879 production.

CAST: *The Rt. Hon. Sir Joseph Porter, K.C.B.,* First Lord of the Admiralty: MARTYN GREEN. *Captain Corcoran,* Commanding the *H.M.S. Pinafore:* CHARLES DORNING. *Ralph Rackstraw* (Able Seaman): THOMAS ROUND. *Dick Deadeye,* Able Seaman: DARRELL FANCOURT, (Radley Flynn, alt.) *Bill Bobstay,* Bo'sun's Mate: Richard Walker. *Bob Beckett,* Carpenter's Mate: Radley Flynn, (Donald Harris, alt.) *Josephine,* the Captain's Daughter: HELEN ROBERTS. *Hebe,* Sir Joseph's First Cousin: Joan Gillingham. *Little Buttercup,* a Portsmouth Bumboat Woman: ELLA HALMAN. *First Lord's Sisters, his Cousins, his Aunts, Sailors, Marines, etc.*

THE GONDOLIERS,
1948.07 or, The King of Barataria

A Revival of the Comic Opera in Two Acts[16]. Libretto by William S. Gilbert. Music by Arthur Sullivan. Scenery and costumes by Charles Ricketts. Directed by Anna Bethell. Musical director, Isidore Godfrey. Produced by D'Oyly Carte Opera Company. Opened 26 January 1948 at the New Century Theatre, closing 31 January 1948; re-opened 1-6 March 1948 for a total of 16 performances in repertory.

CAST: *The Duke of Plaza-Toro,* a Grandee of Spain: MARTYN GREEN. *Luiz,* his attendant: THOMAS ROUND. *Don Alhambra Del Bolero,* The Grand Inquisitor: RICHARD WATSON. *Marco Palmieri, Giuseppe Palmieri, Antonio, Francesco, Giorgio,* Venetian Gondoliers: LEONARD OSBORN, CHARLES DORNING, Eric Hutson, Thomas Hancock, Radley Flynn. *Annibale:* Richard Dunn. *The Duchess of Plaza Del Toro:* ELLA HALMAN. *Casilda,* Her Daughter: MARGARET MITCHELL. *Gianetta, Tessa, Fiametta, Vittoria, Giulia,* Contadine: GWYNETH CULLIMORE, DENISE FINDLAY, Enid Walsh, Joan Gillingham, Laura Crombie. *Inez,* The King's Foster-Mother: Caryl Fane. *Chorus of Gondoliers, Contadine, Men-at-Arms, Heralds and Pages.*

LOOK MA, I'M DANCIN'
1948.08

A Musical Comedy in Two Acts, 13 Scenes. Conceived by Jerome Robbins. Music and lyrics by Hugh Martin. Book by Jerome Lawrence and Robert E. Lee. Direction and choreography by George Abbott and Jerome Robbins. Settings by Oliver Smith. Costumes by John Pratt. Musical director, Pembroke Davenport. Orchestrations by Don Walker. Ballet arrangements by Trude Rittman. Vocal arrangements by Hugh Martin. Produced by George Abbott. Opened 29 January 1948 at the Adelphi Theatre and closed 10 July 1948 after 188 performances.

CAST (in order of speaking): *Wotan:* DON LIBERTO. *Larry:* LOREN WELCH. *Dusty Lee:* ALICE PEARCE. *Ann Bruce:* JANET REED. *Snow White:* VIRGINIA GORSKI. *Eddie Winkler:* HAROLD LANG. *Tommy:* TOMMY RALL. *F. Plancek:* ROBERT H. HARRIS. *Tanya Drinskaya:* KATHARINE SERGAVA. *Vladimir Luboff:* ALEXANDER MARCH. *Lily Malloy:* NANCY WALKER. *Mr. Gleeb:* James Lane. *Mr. Ferbish:* Eddie Hodge. *Tanya's Partner:* Raul Celada. *Bell Boy:* Dean Campbell. *Stage Manager:* Dan Sattler. *Suzy:* SANDRA DEEL. (Additional Ballet performers featured in 'Mademoiselle Marie' ballet: Herbert Ross, Gisella Svetlik, Leonard Claret, Charles Dickson, Richard D'Arcy, Forrest Bonshire, Bruce Cartwright, Ina Kurland, Marybly Harwood, Virginia Conwell.)
  Members of the Russo-American Ballet Company: Margaret Banks, Mary Broussard, Julie Curtis, Clare Duffy, June Graham, Nina Frenkin, Priscilla Hathaway, Douglas Luther, Bettye McCormack, Gloria Patrice, James Pollack, Dottie Pyren, Walter Rinner, Herbert Ross, Marten Sameth, Water Stane, Robert Tucker.

Act 1, Scene 1: Pennsylvania Station, New York City. *Scene 2:* On tour. *Scene 3:* A rehearsal hall. Joplin, Missouri. *Scene 4:* On tour. *Scene 5:* Hotel room. Amarillo, Texas. *Scene 6:* Outside a Theatre. Phoenix, Arizona. *Scene 7:* Stage door of the Philharmonic Auditorium. Los Angeles. *Scene 8:* Back stage of the Philharmonic. *Scene 9:* Stage of the Philharmonic.

Act 2, Scene 1: A railroad platform. Glendale, California. Early the next morning. *Scene 2:* A Pullman car. *Scene 3:* On tour. *Scene 4:* A theatre basement. Des Moines, Iowa.

ACT 1
Scene 1
  "Gotta Dance"
    H. Lang, Company
Scene 3
  "I'm the First Girl"
    N. Walker, Corps de Ballet

Scene 4
  "I'm Not So Bright"
    L. Welch
    Danced by J. Reed, H. Lang.
Scene 5
  "I'm Tired of Texas"
    N. Walker, Company
  "Tiny Room"
    L. Welch
Scene 6
  "The Little Boy Blues"
    V. Gorki, D. Liberto
Scene 9
  "Mademoiselle Marie" Ballet
    (*Music by* Trude Rittman.)
    Mademoiselle Marie, a young bride: N. Walker. *Her Beloved:* H. Ross. *Attendants:* V. Gorski, G. Svetlik. *Messenger:* T. Rall. *Innkeeper:* E. Kristen. *Servant:* W. Stane. *Jacques:* C. Dickson. *Igor:* R. D'Arcy. *Adolph:* R. Celada. *Archie:* F. Bonshire. *Serfs:* L. Claret, B. Cartwright, I. Kurland, M. Harwood, V. Conwell. Corps de Ballet.

ACT 2
Scene 1
  "Jazz"
    D. Liberto, N. Walker, Company
  "The New Look"
    A. Pearce
Scene 2
  "If You'll Be Mine"
    N. Walker, D. Campbell, P. Hathaway, S. Deel, L. Welch, A. Pearce, J. Pollack
  "Pajama Dance"
    The Company
Scene 3
  "Shauny O'Shay"
    V. Gorski, D. Liberto
Scene 4
  Pas de Deux from "Swan Lake"
    J. Reed, H. Lang
    (*Music by* Pyotor Ilyich Tchaikovsky.)
  "The Two of Us"
    N. Walker, H. Lang, Co-workers

THE YEOMEN OF THE GUARD,
1948.09 or, The Merryman and His Maid

A Revival of the Comic Opera in Two Acts[17]. Libretto by William S. Gilbert. Music by Arthur Sullivan. Directed by Anna Bethell. Scenery and costumes by Peter Goffin. Musical director, Isidore Godfrey. Produced by D'Oyly Carte Opera Company. Opened 2 February 1948 at the New Century Theatre, closing 7 February 1948; reopened 22-27 March 1948, and closed after a total of 16 performances in repertory.

CAST: *Sir Richard Cholmondeley,* Lieutenant of the Tower: RICHARD WATSON. *Colonel Fairfax* under sentence of death: LEONARD OSBORN. *Sergeant Meryll* of the Yeomen of the Guard: DARRELL FANCOURT, (Radley Flynn, alt.) *Leonard Meryll,* his Son: Thomas Hancock. *Jack Point,* a Strolling Jester: MARTYN GREEN. *Wilfred Shadbolt,* Head Jailor and Assistant Tormentor: RICHARD WALKER. *First Yeoman:* Rhys Thomas. *Second Yeoman:* Richard Dunn. *First Citizen:* C. William Morgan. *Second Citizen:* Peter Pratt. *Elsie Maynard,* a Strolling Player: HELEN ROBERTS. *Phoebe Meryll,* Sergeant Meryll's Daughter: JOAN GILLINGHAM. *Dame Carruthers,* Housekeeper to the Tower: ELLA HALMAN. *Kate,* her Niece: GWYNETH CULLIMORE. *Chorus of Yeomen of the Guard, Gentlemen, Citizens, etc.*

---

[16]Originally presented in New York 7 January 1890 at Park Theatre for 103 performances. For Synopsis of Scenes and Musical Numbers, see original 1890 production.

[17]First presented in New York 17 October 1888 at the Casino Theatre for 100 performances. For Synopsis of Scenes and Musical Numbers, see original 1888 production.

PATIENCE,

1948.10
or, Bunthorne's Bride

A Revival of the Comic Opera in Two Acts[18]. Libretto by William S. Gilbert. Music by Arthur Sullivan. Scenery and Aesthetic Maidens' costumes designed by George Sheringham; Costumes of the Everyday Girls by Hugo Rombold. Directed by Anna Bethell. Musical director, Isidore Godfrey. Produced by D'Oyly Carte Opera Company. Opened 9 February 1948 at the New Century Theatre and closed 14 February 1948; reopened 15-20 March 1948, closing after a total of 16 performances in repertory.

CAST: *Colonel Calverley*: DARRELL FANCOURT, (RICHARD WALKER, alt.) *Major Murgatroyd*: C. William Morgan. *Lieutenant the Duke of Dunstable*: LEONARD OSBORN. *Reginald Bunthorne*, a Fleshly Poet: MARTYN GREEN. *Archibald Grosvenor*, an Idyllic Poet: CHARLES DORNING. *Mr. Bunsthorne's Solicitor*: Milton Rees. *The Lady Angela, The Lady Saphir, The Lady Ella, The Lady Jane*, Rapturous Maidens: JOAN GILLINGHAM, GWYNETH CULLIMORE, Muriel Harding, ELLA HALMAN. *Patience*, a Dairy Maid: MARGARET MITCHELL, (HELEN ROBERTS, alt.) *Chorus of Rapturous Maifdens and Officers of the Dragoon Guards.*

1948.11
TONIGHT AT 8:30

A Revival of the Series of Triple Bills with Music[19]. Plays and music by Noël Coward, presented in 2 bills. Directed by Noël Coward. Dances by Richard Barstow. Miss Lawrence's gowns by Hattie Carnegie; all other costumes under the supervision of James Morgan. (Settings, costumes) Designed by George Jenkins. Musical director, Frank Tours. Produced by Homer Curran, Russell Lewis and Howard Young. Opened 20 February 1948 at the National Theatre and closed 13 March 1948 after 26 performances (13 performances each bill).

First Bill presented Mondays, Thursday, Saturday evenings, Wednesday matinees:

WAYS AND MEANS

A Light Comedy in 3 Scenes
CAST: *Stella Cartwright*: GETRUDE LAWRENCE. *Toby Cartwright*: GRAHAM PAYN. *Gaston*: Booth Colman. *Lord Chapworth* (Chaps): William Roerick. *Olive Lloyd-Ransome*: SARAH BURTON. *Princess Elena Krassiloff*: VALERIE COSSART. *Murdoch*: PHILIP TONGE. *Manny*: NORAH HOWARD. *Stevens*: Rhoderick Walker.

FAMILY ALBUM

A Victorian Comedy with Music
CAST: *Jasper Featherways*: GRAHAM PAYN. *Jane*, his wife: GERTRUDE LAWRENCE. *Lavinia*, his sister: SARAH BURTON. *Harriet*, his sister: NORAH HOWARD. *Emily*, his sister: VALERIE COSSART. *Richard*, his brother: William Roerick. *Charles Winter*, Harriet's husband: Rhoderick Walker. *Edward Valance*, Emily's husband: Booth Colman. *Burrows*: PHILIP TONGE.

RED PEPPERS

An Interlude with Music
CAST: *Lily Pepper*: GERTRUDE LAWRENCE. *George Pepper*: GRAHAM PAYN. *Alf*: Booth Colman. *Bert Bentley*: Rhoderick Walker. *Mr. Edwards*: PHILIP TONGE. *Mabel Grace*: NORAH HOWARD.

Second Bill, presented Tuesday, Wednesday, Friday evenings, Saturday Matinees:

HANDS ACROSS THE SEA

A Light Comedy in 1 Scene
CAST: *Walters*: SARAH BURTON. *Lady Maureen Gilpin*, Piggy: GERTRUDE LAWRENCE. *Commander Peter Gilpin, R.N.*, her husband: GRAHAM PAYN. *Lieut. Commdr. Alastair Corbett, R.N.*: William Roerick.

---

[18]First presented in New York 22 September 1881 at the Standard Theatre foi 177 performances. For Synopsis of Scenes and Musical Numbers, see original 1881 production.
[19]First produced in New York 24 November 1936 at the National Theatre for 118 performances. Originally a series of 9 Short Plays presented in 3 bills, including "The Astonished Heart," "We Were Dancing," and "Still Life" not presented here.) For Synopsis of Scenes, see original 1936 production. The Overture contains "Dance Little Lady" and "A Room With a View" from THIS YEAR OF GRACE, "Someday I'll Find You" from PRIVATE LIVES, "You Were There" from SHADOW PLAY, and "I'll Follow My Secret Heart" from CONVERSATION PIECE.

Mrs. Wadhurst: VALERIE COSSART. *Mr. Wadhurst*: PHILIP TONGE. *Mr. Burnham*: Booth Colman. *The Hon. Clare Wedderburn*: NORAH HOWARD. *Major Gosling*: Rhoderick Walker.

FUMED OAK

An Unpleasant Comedy in 2 Scenes
CAST: *Doris Gow*: GERTRUDE LAWRENCE. *Mrs. Rockett*, her mother: NORAH HOWARD. *Elsie*, daughter of Doris and Henry Gow: VALERIE COSSART. *Henry Gow*: PHILIP TONGE.

SHADOW PLAY

A Fantasy with Music
CAST: *Lena*: VALERIE COSSART. *Victoria Gayforth*: GERTRUDE LAWRENCE. *Martha Cunningham*: NORAH HOWARD. *Simon Gayforth*: GRAHAM PAYN. *Hodge*, Dresser: Booth Colman. *Sibyl Heston*: SARAH BURTON. *Michael Doyle*: William Roerick. *A Young Man*: Rhoderick Walker. *George Cunningham*: PHILIP TONGE.

1948.12
MAURICE CHEVALIER

An Evening of Songs and Impressions (One Man Show) in Two Acts. Accompanied by Irving Actman. Produced by Arthur Lesser. Opened 29 February 1948 at the John Golden Theatre and closed 28 March 1948 after 33 performances.

ACT 1

"J'ai du ciel dans mon chapeau"
  (*Music by* Alstone. *Lyrics by* Maurice Chevalier.)
"It's Good to Fall in Love"
  (*Music by* George Van Parys. *Lyrics by* Robert Piroshe.)
"Mandarinade"
  (*Music by* H. Betti. *Lyrics by* Pierre Gilbert, Maurice Chevalier.)
"Mimi"
  (*Music by* Richard Rodgers. *Lyrics by* Maurice Chevalier.)
"A Barcelone"
  (*Music by* Henri Betti. *Lyrics by* Maurice Chevalier.)

ACT 2

"Fox a poil dur"; "Arthur"
  (*Music and Lyrics by* Fred Pearly.)
"Quai de Bercy"
  (*Music by* Alstone. *Lyrics by* Louis Poterat, Maurice Chevalier.)
"Weeping Willie"
  (*Music by* Revil. *Lyrics by* Robert Piroshe, Maurice Chevalier.)
"Priere"
  (*Music by* Alstone. *Lyrics by* Maurice Chevalier.)
"Place Pigalle"
  (*Music by* Alstone. *Lyrics by* Robert Piroshe.)
"La Symphonie des smelles de bois"
  (*Music by* Anonymous. *Lyrics by* Maurice Chevalier.)
Encore: "Louise," "Just a Bum," "Valentine."

1948.13
HOLIDAY ON BROADWAY

A Variety Revue in Two Acts, 9 Scenes. Produced by Al Wilde. Opened 27 April 1948 at the Mansfield Theatre and closed 1 May 1948 after 6 performances.

CAST: BILLIE HOLIDAY, SLAM STEWART TRIO (John Collins, guitar; Beryl Booker, piano; Slam Stewart, bass), COZY COLE, BOBBY TUCKER QUINTET, WYATT and TAYLOR (piano and organ).

ACT 1

Scene 1

"I Got Rhythm," "Lover," "You Were Meant for Me"
  Wyatt and Taylor

Scene 2

Show Tunes:
  Billie Holiday with the Bobby Tucker Quintet
"Easy to Love" (from BORN TO DANCE film)
  (*Music and Lyrics by* Cole Porter.)
"Lover Man (Oh, Where Can You Be?)"
  (*Music and Lyrics by* Jimmy Davis, Roger "Ram" Ramirez, Jimmy Sherman.)

"Lover Come Back to Me" (from THE NEW MOON)
  (*Music by* Sigmund Romberg. *Lyrics by* Oscar Hammerstein II.)
"Them There Eyes"
  (*Music and Lyrics by* Maceo Pinkard, William Tracey, Doris Tauber.)
"Strange Fruit"
  (*Music and Lyrics by* Lewis Allan.)

Scene 3
"Play, Fiddle, Play"
  The Slam Stewart Trio

Scene 4
Billie Holiday with the Bobby Tucker Quintet: Mood Songs

ACT 2
Scene 1
Cozy Cole on the Drums

Scene 2
Wyatt and Taylor

Scene 3
The Slam Stewart Trio

Scene 4
"You're Driving Me Crazy" (from SMILES)
  (*Music and Lyrics by* Walter Donaldson.)
"I Cover the Waterfront" (from film of the same name)
  (*Music by* Johnny Green. *Lyrics by* Edward Heyman.)
"Lovin' Man, Where Can You Be?"
"Billie's Blues"
  Billie Holiday with the Bobby Tucker Quintet

Scene 5
Finale

1948.14

INSIDE U.S.A.

A Musical Revue in Two Acts, 18 Scenes. Sketches by Arnold Auerbach, Moss Hart and Arnold B. Horwitt. Suggested by John Gunther's book of the same name. Music by Arthur Schwartz. Lyrics by Howard Dietz. Additional sketch material by Arnold Auerbach. Dances and musical numbers staged by Helen Tamiris. Sketches directed by Robert H. Gordon. Production designed by Lemuel Ayers. Costumes by Eleanor Goldsmith. Miss Lillie's costumes and gowns by Castillo. Orchestrations by Robert Russell Bennett. Musical conductor, Jay Blackton. Incidental music for dances, Genevieve Pitot. Production associate, Victor Samrock. Produced by Arthur Schwartz. Opened 30 April 1948 at the New Century Theatre, moved 23 August 1948 to the Majestic Theatre, and closed 19 February 1949 after 339 performances.

CAST: BEATRICE LILLIE, JACK HALEY, JOHN TYERS, VALERIE BETTIS, HERB SHRINER, ERIC VICTOR, ESTELLE LORING, LEWIS NYE, JANE LAWRENCE, CARL REINER, WILLIAM LeMASSENA, Thelma Carpenter, Albert Popwell, Joan Mann, J. C. McCord.
  Ensemble: Rod Alexander, Talley Beatty, Mary Lou Boyd, Beverlee Bozeman, Jack Cassidy, Michael Charnley, Ronald Chetwood, Jacqueline Fisher, Court Fleming, Bob Hamilton, Holly Harris, Jim Hawthorne, Randell Henderson, Alfred Homan, Pat Horn, Norma Larkin, Mara Lynn, Dorothy MacNeil, Nanon Mills, John Mooney, Betty Nichols, Hilde Palmer, Richard Reed, George Reich, Ricky Riccardi, Thomas Rieder, Michael Risk, Boris Runanin, Dorothy Scott, Sherry Shadburne, Raymond Stephens, Gloria Stevens, Royce Wallace.

ACT 1
Scene 1
"Inside U.S.A."
  Entire Company

Scene 2
Leave My Pulse Alone
  Scene: The Jones' Living-room. Any Town, Coast-to-Coast.
  Lottie, the maid: E. Loring. *First Pollster*: C. Reiner. *Mrs. Jones*: J. Lawrence.
  Mr. Jones: J. Haley. *Second Pollster*: L. Nye. *Mary*, the daughter: B. Bozeman.
  Third Pollster: W. LeMassena.

Scene 3
"Come, O Come"
  Singing Ensemble
  Pittsburgh Choral Director: B. Lillie.

Scene 4
Forty Winks
  (*by* Arnold B. Horwitt and Arnold Auerbach)
  Scene: Regal-Plaza Hotel. Miami Beach.
  Mr. Bemis: J. Haley. *Hotel Manager*: W. LeMassena. *Bellboy*: L. Nye. *Prof. Poultergeist*: C. Reiner.

Scene 5
"Blue Grass"
  T. Carpenter
  Scene: Churchill Downs, Kentucky.
  Danced by Her Boy Friend: A. Popwell. *His Friend*: J.C. McCord.
  Bookies, Spectators, Jockeys: R. Alexander, T. Beatty, B. Bozeman,
  M. Charnley, R. Chetwood, J. Fisher, B. Hamilton, H. Harris,
  P. Horn, N. Larkin, M. Lynn, D. MacNeil, J. Mann, N. Mills,
  J. Mooney, B. Nichols, R. Reed, G. Reich, R. Riccardi,
  T. Reider, B. Runanin, D. Scott, S. Shadburne, G. Stevens,
  R. Wallace.

Scene 6
A Song to Forget
  (*by* Arnold Auerbach)
  Scene: In front of a movie theatre. Chillicothe, Ohio.
  Miss Twitchell: B. Lillie. *Frederic Chopin*: C. Reiner. *A Butler*:
  W. LeMassena. *Mme. Lapis de Lazuli*: B. Lillie. *Franz Liszt*:
  J. Tyers. *Peter Ilyitch Tschiakowsky*: L. Nye.

Scene 7
"Rhode Island Is Famous for You"
  J. Haley, E. Loring

Scene 8
"Haunted Heart"
  J. Tyers
  Danced by: V. Bettis, J. C. McCord, G. Reich, R. Alexander.
  Scene: San Francisco Waterfront.

Scene 9
"Massachusetts Mermaid"
  B. Lillie

Scene 10
A Feller from Indiana[20]
  H. Shriner

Scene 11
"First Prize at the Fair"
  Scene: Fair Grounds, Kenosha County. Wisconsin.
  Ticket Seller: W. LeMassena. *First Couple*: J. Lawrence,
  R. Stephens. *Second Couple*: E. Loring, J. Hawthorne. *Third Couple*: B. Lillie, J. Haley. *Caller*: E. Victor. *Contestants and Spectators*: Entire Company.

ACT 2
Scene 1
"At the Mardi Gras"
  B. Lillie
  Scene : New Orleans.
  Six Swains: J. Cassidy, J. Hawthorne, A. Homan, T. Rieder, M. Risk,
  R. Stephens. *Danced by*: R. Alexander, T. Beatty, R. Riccardi,
  B. Bozeman, M. Charnley, R. Chetwood, R. Hamilton, P. Horn,
  M. Lynn, J. Mann, J.C. McCord, N. Mills, B. Nichols, A. Popwell,
  R. Reed, G. Reich, B. Runanin, D. Scott, G. Stevens, R. Wallace.
  (*Masks by* John Robert Lloyd.)

Scene 2
School for Waiters
  (*by* Arnold Auerbach, *suggested by* George S. Kaufman)

----

[20]For subsequent national tour, replaced by:
  All Over the Map
    (*by* Joseph Stein and Will Glickman)
    J. Haley

Scene: Schoolroom for Waiters. New York City.
Girl: J. Mann. *Man*: C. Reiner. *Professor*: J. Haley. *Herman*: L. Nye.
Girl Diner: J. Lawrence. *Her Escort*: W. LeMassena. *Another Diner*:
C. Reiner. *His Companions*: H. Harris, H. Palmer. *Captain of Waiters*:
R. Chetwood. *Student Waiters*: R. Alexander, C. Fleming, R Reed,
G. Reich, B. Runanin.

Scene 3

"My Gal Is Mine Once More"
J. Tyers
Scene: A street in Jackson Hole. Wyoming.
Groom: J. Tyers. *Bride*: E. Loring. *Minister*: C. Reiner. *Cowboy
with Rope*: J.C. McCord. *Townspeople*: M L. Boyd, B. Bozeman,
J. Cassidy, J. Hawthorne, N. Larkin, M. Lynn, D. MacNeil, J. Mann,
J.C. McCord, J. Mooney, T. Rieder, M. Risk, D. Scott, S. Shadburne,
R. Stephens, G. Stevens.

Scene 4

Better Luck Next Time
(*by* Moss Hart)
Scene: Miss Shelton's dressing-room. Just Off Broadway.
Mary Shelton: J. Lawrence. *Gladys*, her maid: B. Lillie. *The Stage
Manager*: R. Henderson.

Scene 5

"Tiger Lily" (A tabloid ballet conceived by Helen Tamiris.)
Scene: Chicago.
Tiger Lily: V. Bettis. *Doctor Zilmore*: E. Victor. *Detectives*: R. Alexander,
R. Hamilton, J.C. McCord, R. Reed. *Prosecuting Attorney*: R. Alexander.
Defense Attorney: R. Chetwood. *Jury*: T. Beatty, M. Charnley,
R. Hamilton, J.C. McCord, B. Runanin. *Judge*: C. Reiner. *Newspaper
Readers and Spectators*: B. Bozeman, J. Cassidy, J. Fisher, C. Fleming,
H. Harris, J. Hawthorne, A. Homan, P. Horn, N. Larkin, W. LeMassena,
M. Lynn, N. Mills, J. Mooney, B. Nichols, G. Reich, R. Reed,
R. Riccardi, T. Rieder, M. Risk, D. Scott, S. Shadburne, R. Stephens,
G. Stevens, R. Wallace.

Scene 6

"We Won't Take It Back"
B. Lillie, J. Haley
Scene: Railroad Station. Albuquerque, New Mexico.
Tourists: A. Homan, J. Lawrence, W. LeMassena, C. Reiner, L. Nye,
H. Palmer.

Scene 7

Finale
Entire Company

1948.15

HOLD IT!

A Musical Comedy in Two Acts, 14 Scenes. Book by Matt Brooks and Art
Arthur. Music by Gerald Marks. Lyrics by Sam Lerner. Dances and musical
numbers staged by Michael Kidd. Directed by Robert E. Perry. Settings by
Edward Gilbert. Costumes by Julia Sze. Orchestra conducted by Clay
Warnick. Orchestrations by Hans Spialek and Ted Royal. Vocal arrange-
ments by Clay Warnick. Ballet arrangements by Irma Jurist. Produced by
Sammy Lambert. Opened 5 May 1948 at the National Theatre and closed
12 June 1948 after 46 performances.

<u>CAST</u> (in order of appearance): *Usherettes*: Wana Allison, Gloria Benson, Janet
Bethel, Penny Carroll, Kathryne Mylroie, Helena Schurgot. *Rodney Trent*: Bob
Shawley. *Mrs. Simpkins*: Ruth Saville. *Mr. Simpkins*: Douglas Rutherford. *Mrs.
Blandish*: Helen Wenzel. *Mr. Blandish*: Budd Rogers. *"Sarge" Denton*: LARRY
DOUGLAS. *Bobby Manville*: JOHNNY DOWNS. *Helen*, Stage Manager: Helen
Wenzel. *Jack*: Jack Warner. *Chuck*: Bob Evans. *"Judge" Rogers*: KENNY BUFFETT.
Sid: Sid Lawson. *Jessica Dale*: JET McDONALD. *Pamela Scott*: PATRICIA
WYMORE. *Millie Henderson*: ADA LYNNE. *Budd*: Budd Rogers. *Bernie*: Bob
Bernard. *"Dinky" Bennett*: "RED" BUTTONS. *Paul*: Paul Lyday. *George Monopolis*:
Douglas Chandler. *Penny*: Penny Carroll. *Mr. Jenkins*: PAUL REED. *Joe*: Tom
Bowman. *Charlie Blake*: PAT McVEY. *Headwaiter*: Douglas Rutherford. *Mrs. Jollop*,
House Mother: Ruth Saville. *O'Brien*: Scott Lewis. *Martin*: Martin Kraft. *Reporters*:
Budd Rogers, Sid Lawson, Helena Schurgot. *Felix Dexter*: JOHN KANE. *Anne Green*:
Ruth Saville.

Singing Ensemble: Gloria Benson, Penny Carroll, Kathryn Mylroie, Helena
Schurgot, Tom Bowman, Sid Lawson, Budd Rogers, Frank Stevens. *Dancing
Ensemble*: Onna White (Captain), Wana Allison, Janet Bethel, Margit DeKova, Helen
Kramer, Barbara McCutcheon, Elena Salamatova, Yvonne Tibor, Helen Wenzel, John
Begg, Bob Bernard, Jack Claus, Robert Cadwallader, Robert Evans, Martin Kraft,
Vernon Lusby, Paul Lyday.

Act 1, Scene 1: Lobby of Lincoln University Auditorium. The present. *Scene 2*: Stage
of University Auditorium. Immediately following. *Scene 3*: The Tasty Toasty. The
following day. *Scene 4*: The Campus Walk. Nine days later. *Scene 5*: The Tasty Toasty.
The following day. *Scene 6*: The Tasty Toasty. The following evening. *Scene 7*: The
Campus Walk. Same night. *Scene 8*: Lobby of the Pink Angel Night Club. Later that
night.

Act 2, Scene 1: Outside of Sorority House. Later that night. *Scene 2*: The Sorority
Dormitory. Immediately following. *Scene 3*: The Campus Walk. The following
afternoon. *Scene 4*: The Tasty Toasty. Later the same day. *Scene 5*: Outside of Sorority
House. A few minutes later. *Scene 6*: Living-room of Dexter's Hotel Suite. That night.

ACT 1

Opening
W. Allison, G. Benson, J. Bethel, P. Carroll, K. Mylroie,
H. Schurgot
"Heaven Sent"
L. Douglas, J. Downs, Boys
Dance
Dancing Ensemble
"Buck in the Bank"
J. Downs, J. McDonald, Singing Ensemble
Dance
J. Downs
"Always You"
J. Downs, J. McDonald
"About Face"
L. Douglas, J. Downs, R. Buttons, K. Buffett, Singing Ensemble
Dance
J. Downs, R. Buttons, K. Buffett, Dancing Ensemble
"Fundamental Character"
A. Lynne, R. Buttons
"Hold It!"
J. Downs, J. McDonald, R. Buttons,
A. Lynne, P. Wymore, K. Buffet, Singing Ensemble
Dance
P. Wymore
"Nevermore"
J. McDonald
"Roll 'Em"
L. Douglas, J. McDonald, A. Lynne, P. Wymore, Singing Ensemble
(Music for Hollywood Sequence by Irma Jurist.)
'Continued Next Week': *Star*: J. McDonald. *Stand-in*: A. Lynne. *Director*:
L. Douglas.
'Operation 'X'': *Doctor*: V. Lusby. *Patient*: J. Claus. *Nurses*: E. Salamatova,
J. Bethel, W. Allison, H. Kramer.
'Saga of Roaring Gulch': *The Kid*: J. Warner. *TheGal*: M. DeKova.
The Boss: M. Kraft. *Bartender*: P. Lyday. *Dance Hall Girls*: B. McCutcheon,
Y. Tibor. *Cowboys*: R. Evans, R. Cadwallader, B. Bernard.
'Arsenic and Old Araby': *Sultan*: B. Rogers. *Favorite*: J. McDonald.
Out of favor Trio: W. Allison, H. Wenzel, O. White. *Out of favor Duo*:
M. DeKova, B. McCutcheon. *Vessel Bearers*: E. Salamatova, Y. Tibor.
Message Bearers: J. Claus, B. Bernard. *Attendants*: H. Kramer, J. Bethel.
Sinbad: M. Kraft.

ACT 2

"So Nice Having You"
A. Lynne, Entire Ensemble
Dance
Dancing Ensemble
"Down the Well"
L. Douglas, J. McDonald
"You Took Possession of Me"
P. Wymore, K. Buffett
Dance
Dancing Ensemble
"Always You" (reprise)
J. Downs
"Friendly Enemy"
A. Lynne, R. Buttons
"Hold It!" (reprise)
Entire Company
Finale
Entire Company

1948.16

SALLY

A Revival of the Musical Comedy in Two Acts, 7 Scenes[21]. Music by Jerome Kern. (Revised) Book by Guy Bolton.[22] Lyrics by P.G. Wodehouse and Clifford Grey. Dances and musical numbers by Richard Barstow. Settings and lighting by Stewart Chaney. Costumes by Henry Mulle. Production staged by Billy Gilbert. Orchestra conducted by David Mordecai. Musical supervision by Pembroke Davenport. Orchestrations by Robert Russell Bennett. Additional orchestrations by Philip J. Lang. Production associates, David Lowe, Sue Davidson. Produced by Hunt Stromberg, Jr. and William Berney[23]. Opened 6 May 1948 at the Martin Beck Theatre and closed 5 June 1948 after 36 performances.

CAST (in order of appearance): *Nadina*: Gloria Sullivan. *The Young Waiter*: Charles Wood. *The Old Waiter*: Holger Sorenson. *Otis Hooper*: JACK GOODE. *Rosie*: KAY BUCKLEY. *Lily Bedlington*: BIBI OSTERWALD. *Shendorf*: HENRY CALVIN. *Mickey Sinclair*: ROBERT SHACKLETON. *Sally*: BAMBI LINN. *The Grand Duke Constantine*: WILLIE HOWARD. *Mrs. Vischer Van Alstyn*: Kathryn Cameron. *Toto*: Lucy Hillary. *Olga*: Andrea Mann.

Singers: Lucy Hillary, Ruth Johnston, Andrea Mann, Audrey Guard, Jean Olds, Eila Brynn, Gloria Haydn, Gloria Sullivan. Charles Wood, John George, Lynn Alden, Richard Oneto, Holger Sorenson, Steve Coleman, Hank Roberts, Brian Otis. *Dancers*: Aura Vainio, Marcella Dodge, Mary Alice Bingham, Carmina Cansino, Gretchen Houser, Karlyn DeBoer, Carol Lee, Marcia Maier, Dolores Nevins, Jo McCann. Tommy Randall, Lee Lindsey, Dusty McCaffrey, Joe Vilane, Frank Reynolds, Garry Fleming, Jack Miller, Jimmy Russell.

Time: The Early 1920s.

Act 1, Scene 1: Shendorf's Cafe in Greenwich Village. *Scene 2*: The Long Island garden of Mrs. Van Alstyn.

Act 2, Scene 1: The Church Around the Corner. *Scene 2*: The Kitchen of Shendorf's Cafe. *Scene 3*: "The Follies." *Scene 4*: Backstage. *Scene 5*: The Church Around the Corner.

ACT 1

"Down Here in Greenwich Village"
Ensemble
"Bungalow in Quogue"
K. Buckley, J. Goode
"Look for the Silver Lining"
B. Linn, R. Shackleton
"Looking All Over for You"
Principals, Ensemble
"Tulip Time in Sing Sing"
W. Howard, Waiters
"The Whippoorwill Waltz"
Ensemble
Dancers: J. Russell, A. Vainio.
"The Siren Song"
B. Linn, R. Shackleton, Ensemble
"Cleopatra"
B. Osterwald
"Wild Rose"
B. Linn, R. Shackleton, Male Ensemble

ACT 2

"The Church Around the Corner"
K. Buckley, J. Goode
Sailors: T. Randall, D. McCaffrey. *Sailors' Girl Friend*: C. Cansino. *Old Man*: J. Vilane. *His Bride*: G. Houser. *Lovesick Couple*: M. A. Bingham, J. Miller.
"Dear Little Girl"
R. Shackleton, B. Linn
"Look for the Silver Lining" (reprise)
B. Linn, W. Howard

---

[21]Originally presented in New York 21 December 1920 at the New Amsterdam Theatre for 570 performances.
[22]Based on an unproduced libretto "The Little Thing" by Bolton and Wodehouse.
[23]The producers wish to express appreciation for assistance to Miss Catherine Littlefield and Morey Amsterdam.

"Reaching for Stars"
B. Linn, Ensemble
Finale
Entire Company

1948.17

BALLET BALLADS

Three One-Act Dance Plays written by John Latouche. Composed by Jerome Moross. Directed by Mary Hunter. Choral and musical director, Hugh Ross. Associate conductor, Gerard Samuel. Choreographers: Katherine Litz, Paul Godkin, Hanya Holm. Pianists: John Lesko, Jr. and Mordecai Sheinkman. Production devised, designed and lighted by Nat Karson. Women's costumes for "Susanna" and "Davey Crockett" by Ted Cohen. Production Committee: Cheryl Crawford, James Grow, Alexander Kirkland. Produced by Nat Karson under the Sponsorship of the American National Theatre and Academy (ANTA) The Experimental Theatre, Inc. Opened 9 May 1948 at the Maxine Elliott's Theatre, closing after a limited run of 6 performances; transferred under the auspices of T. Edward Hamilton and Alfred R. Stern 18 May 1948 to the Music Box Theatre and closed 10 July 1948 after 62 performances. Total for both engagements: 68 performances.

CAST: BARBARA ASHLEY, PAUL GODKIN, RICHARD HARVEY, TED LAWRIE, ROBERT LENN, KATHERINE LITZ, SONO OSATO, SHEILA VOGELLE, Olga Lunick, Carl Luman, William A Myers.

Dance Ensemble: Ellen R. Albertini, Cecille Bergman, Nora Bristow, John Castello, Mary Ann Cousins, Margaret Cuddy, Beau Cunningham, Barbara Downie, Richard Goltra, Sandra Lipton, Iona McKenzie, Rosa Rolland, Jack Warren Konzl, James R. Nygren, Frank Seabolt, Walter Stane, Spencer Teakle, Sharry Traver, Robert Trout, William Weaver, Charles Yongue.

Singing Ensemble: *Sopranos*: Arlouine Goodjohn (alternate), Barbara Lewis, Frances Joslyn, Marian C. Covey, Dea Carrol, Manya Kanty. *Altos*: Carol Nason, Ethel Madsen, Getrude Lockaway, Jane Flynn, Estelle Moss, Joan Bartels (alternate), Betty Abbott. *Tenors*: Harold Michener, M.R. Rich (alternate), Farrold Stevens, Eddie Varrato, Douglas Martin, Kenneth Renner. *Basses*: Bernard Zwarg (alternate), Robert Baird, David Vogel (alternate), Lorin Barrett, Arthur Friedman (alternate), William Ambler (alternate).

ACT 1: SUSANNA AND THE ELDERS
Choreography by Katherine Litz.

CAST: *The Parson*: RICHARD HARVEY. *Susanna* (The Dancer): KATHERINE LITZ. *Susanna* (The Singer): SHEILA VOGELLE. *The Cedar from Lebanon*: Sharry Traver. *The Little Juniper Tree*: Ellen B. Albertini. *The Handmaidens*: Margaret Cuddy, Barbara Downie. *The Elder* (Moe): Frank Seabolt. *The Elder* (Joe): Robert Trout. *The Angel*: James R. Nygren. *The Ladies and Gentlemen of the Congregation*: Singing Ensemble.

Scene: A revival meeting. The Parson takes his sermon from the story of Susanna and The Elders as found in the Apocrypha.

MUSICAL NUMBER[24]
"Susanna and the Elders"
R. Harvey, S. Vogelle, Ensemble

ACT 2: WILLIE THE WEEPER
Choreography by Paul Godkin.

CAST: *Cocaine Lil*: SONO OSATO. *Singing Willie*: ROBERT LENN. *Dancing Willie*: PAUL GODKIN. The Singing Ensemble.
Dancers: Cecille Bergman, Nora Bristow, Mary Ann Cousins, Sandra Lipton, Iona McKenzie, Rosa Rolland, Jack Warren Konzl, James R. Nygren, William Weaver, Walter Stane, Richard Goltra, Charles Yongue.

Scene: The action takes place in Willie's untidy mind. *Episode 1*: Rich Willie. *Episode 2*: Lonely Willie. *Episode 3*: Famous Willie. *Episode 4*: Baffled Willie. *Episode 5*: Super-Willie. *Episode 6*: Self-sufficient Willie. *Episode 7*: Lover Willie.

MUSICAL NUMBERS
"I've Got Me" (Episode 6)
R. Lenn
"Oh, Oh, Baby" (Episode 7)
R. Lenn, Ensemble

---

[24]The production was entirely "through-sung" and "through-danced;" the individual numbers listed below were not listed in programs, but were published and/or recorded separately.

ACT 3: THE ECCENTRICITIES OF DAVEY CROCKETT (as told by himself)
Choreography by Hanya Holm.

CAST: *Davey Crockett*: TED LAWRIE. *Sally Ann*: BARBARA ASHLEY. *Indian Chief*: Lorin Barrett. *A Backwoodsman*: Carl Luman. *The Mermaid*: Betty Abbott. *The Comet*: Olga Lunick. *Brown Bear*: William A. Myers. *Ghost Bear*: Robert Baird. *John Oldham* sung by William Ambler, danced by John Castello. *Ann Hutchinson* sung by Gertrude Lockaway, danced by Sharry Traver. *Nathaniel Bacon* sung by Eddie Varrato, danced by Frank Seabolt. *Grace Sherwood* sung by Arlouine Goodjohn, danced by Barbara Downie. *Nathaniel Turner* sung by Arthur Friedman, danced by Beau Cunningham. *President Andrew Jackson*: Harold Michener. *Friends and Neighbors*: The Singing Ensemble.

Dancers: Ellen R. Albertini, Margaret Cuddy, Barbara Downie, Sharry Traver, Beau Cunningham, John Castello, Frank Seabolt, Robert Trout, Spencer Teakle.

MUSICAL NUMBERS
"My Yellow Flower"
B. Ashley
"Riding on the Breeze"
T. Lawrie
The people assemble to celebrate the memory of Davey Crockett. In terms of his own tall tales they recall his exploits; his youth, courtship, and marriage; how he built a living house in the wilderness; how he fought the Indian Wars; how he hooked a Mermaid; how he saved the world from Halley's Comet; how he went to Congress and left it; how he died at the Alamo and became a legend.

Nanette Fabray and Ray Middleton in LOVE LIFE (Photo: Sarony)
Billy Rose Theatre Collection, New York Public Library for the Performing Arts

SLEEPY HOLLOW

1948.18

A Musical Play in Two Acts, 11 Scenes. Based on Washington Irving's "Legend of Sleepy Hollow." Book and lyrics by Russell Maloney and Miriam Battista; additional lyrics by Ruth Hughes Aarons. Music by George Lessner. Suggested by Nicholas Bela. Production directed by John O'Shaughnessy. Settings and lighting by Jo Mielziner. Musical numbers and dances staged by Anna Sokolow. Costumes by David Ffolkes. Musical director, Irving Actman. Orchestrations by Hans Spialek, Ted Royal and George Lessner. Choral arrangements by Elie Siegmeister. Produced by Lorraine Lester[1]. Opened 3 June 1948 at the St. James Theatre and closed 12 June 1948 after 12 performances.

<u>CAST</u> (in order of appearance): *Ike*: William Ferguson. *Roelf*: Larry Robbins. *Mrs. Van Brunt*: Laura Pierpont. *Mrs. Van Tassel*: RUTH McDEVITT. *Mrs. Van Ripper*: Jean Handzlik. *Wilhelmina*: ELLEN REPP. *Mr. Van Brunt*: Bert Wilcox. *Mr. Van Tassel*: Tom Hoier. *Mr. Van Ripper*: Morley Evans. *Jacob Van Tassel*: Bobby [Robert] White. *Willie Van Twiller*: Walter Butterworth. *Hans Van Ripper*: Alan Shay. *Martin Van Horsen*: Richard Rhoades. *Stuyveling Van Doorn*: Lewis Scholle. *Teena*: Doreen Lane. *Hilda*: Robin Sloane. *Greta*: Sylvia Lane. *Brom "Bones" Van Brunt*: HAYES GORDON. *Katrina Van Tassel*: BETTY JANE WATSON. *Hendrick*: WARD GARNER. *Eva*: MARY McCARTY. *Luther*: Russel George. *Ichabod Crane*: GIL LAMB. *Annie*: Margery Oldroyd. *Lena*: Peggy Ferris. *Nick*: Franklin Wagner. *Piet*: Shaun O'Brien. *Balt*: Ray Drakeley. *Walt*: JAMES STARBUCK. *Chris*: John Ward. *Bertha*: Margaret Ritter. *Margaret*: Jo Sullivan. *Elizabeth*: Kaja Sumdsten. *Jenny*: Ann Dunbar. *Mr. Van Hooten*: Ken Foley. *Joost*: John Russel. *Conscience*: Ty Kearney. *Indian*: Kenneth Remo. *Cotton Mather*: William Mende. *The Lady from New Haven*: DOROTHY BIRD.

Village Girls Who Dance: Aza Bard, Clara Courdery, Ann Dunbar, Kate Friedlich, Saida Gerrard, Carmella Guiterrez, Margaret McCallion, Kaja Sumdsten. *Village Boys Who Dance*: Alex Dunaeff, Don Farnworth, Jay Lloyd, Remi Martel, Joseph Milan, Shaun O'Brien, Franklin Wagner, John Ward.

Village Girls Who Sing: Ilona Albok, Joan Barrett, Peggy Ferris, Deda LaPetina, Margery Oldroyd, Margaret Ritter, Janice Sprei, Jo Sullivan. *Village Boys Who Sing*: Ray Drakeley, William Ferguson, Ken Foley, Russell George, Vincent Lubrano, William Mende, Larry Robbins, John Russel.

Village Children: Walter Butterworth, Doreen Lane, Sylvia Lane, Richard Rhoades, Lewis Francis Scholle, Alan Shay, Robin Sloane.

The play takes place in the autumn of 1795 in the village of Sleepy Hollow, up by the Tappan Zee on the east bank of the Hudson River.

Act 1, Scene 1: The Churchyard at the Crossroads of the Village. Noontime. *Scene 2*: The River Bank. The following morning. *Scene 3*: The Schoolroom in a Clearing. Later that morning. *Scene 4*: The Kitchen of the Van Tassel House. The following morning. *Scene 5*: The River Bank. Several days later. *Scene 6*: The Churchyard. Sunday evening.

Act 2, Scene 1: The Van Tassel Barn. A few days later. *Scene 2*: The Attic Room in Eva's House. That night. *Scene 3*: The Kitchen of the Van Tassel House. The following night. *Scene 4*: The Churchyard. That night. *Scene 5*: The Churchyard. The following morning.

ACT 1

Scene 1
"Time Stands Still"
  Villagers
"I Still Have Plenty to Learn"
  H. Gordon
"Ask Me Again"
  B. J. Watson
"I Still Have Plenty to Learn" (reprise)
  H. Gordon, B. J. Watson
"Never Let Her Go"
  Villagers
"There's History to Be Made"
  G. Lamb
  (*Lyrics by* Russell Maloney, Miriam Battista and Ruth Hughes Aarons.)
Scene 2
"Here and Now"
  H. Gordon, B. J. Watson

[1]Program note: The Management gratefully acknowledges the assistance of Marc Connelly.

Dance
  D. Bird, J. Starbuck
Scene 3
"Why Was I Born on a Farm?"
  M. McCarty
  (*Lyrics by* Ruth Hughes Aarons.)
"If"
  G. Lamb
Scene 4
"My Lucky Lover"
  J. Watson, E. Repp, M. McCarty, Sleepy Hollow Girls
"A Musical Lesson"
  G. Lamb
Scene 5
"You've Got That Kind of a Face"
  W. Garner, M. McCarty
  (*Lyrics by* Russell Maloney, Miriam Battista and Ruth Hughes Aarons.)
Couple Dance
  First Couple: C. Courdery, J. Lloyd. *Second Couple*: A. Bard, J. Milan. *Third Couple*: K. Friedlich, A. Dunaeff. *Girl with a flower*: K. Sundstrom.
Scene 6
"I'm Lost"
  H. Gordon
  (*Lyrics by* Ruth Hughes Aarons.)
"Goodnight"
  Villagers
"The Englishman's Head"
  E. Repp, H. Gordon, Villagers

ACT 2

Scene 1
"Pedro, Ichabod"
  H. Gordon, J. Starbuck, Village Boys
"Poor Man"
  G. Lamb
  (*Lyrics by* Russell Maloney, Miriam Battista and Ruth Hughes Aarons.)
"The Things That Lovers Say"
  B. J. Watson
"I'm Lost" (reprise)
  H. Gordon
Scene 2
"Ichabod"
  T. Kearney, K. Remo, W. Mende
Dance
  D. Bird
Scene 3
Bourée
  Village Dancers
Scene 4
Headless Horseman Ballet
  G. Lamb, Village Dancers
Scene 5
"The Gray Goose"
  B. White, Ensemble

HOWDY, MR. ICE

1948.19

A Musical Ice-travaganza in Two Acts, 20 Scenes. Music and lyrics by Al Stillman and Alan Moran. Production by Sonart Productions, Inc. Executive director, Arthur M. Wirtz. Production director, William H. Burke. Staged by Catherine Littlefield. Settings designed and created by Bruno Maine. Costumes by Billy Livingston and Katherine Kuhn. Choreography by Catherine Littlefield, assisted by Dorothie Littlefield. Lighting effects by Eugene Braun. Skating direction by May Judels. Musical conductor, David Mendoza. Musical arrangements by Paul Van Loan. Produced by

Sonja Henie and Arthur M. Wirtz. Opened 24 June 1948 at the Center Theatre and closed 23 April 1948 after 404 performances.

CAST: SKIPPY BAXTER, ELLEN SEIGH, THE BRUISES, THE PRESTONS (Mickee, Paul), JINX CLARK, HARRISON THOMSON, RUDY RICHARDS, PAUL CASTLE, TRIXIE, JAMES SISK, BUSTER GRACE, JOHN KASPER, BUCK PENNINGTON, CISSY TRENHOLM, JOHN WALSH, FREDDIE TRENKLER. *Vocals*: NOLA FAIRBANKS, DICK CRAIG, FRED MARTELL, WILLIAM DOUGLAS.

Skaters: Margaret Barry, Peggy Bauer, Josephine Belluccia, Dorothy Bergman, Evelyn Biderman, Ann Boykin, Bernice Deane, Helen Dutcher, Walli Hackman, Pat Harrington, Gloria Haupt, Lynne Immes, Joan King, Pat Lemaire, Ann Liff, Marjorie Mahne, Marvette Mosic, Doris Nelson, Priscilla Paulson, Ragna Ray, Gerri Richardson, Rusty Rodgers, Lela Rolontz, Theresa Rothacker, Betty Smith, Eileen Thompson, Catherine Webber. Eddie Berry, Ray Blow, Nicholas Dantos, Gerry Decker, Arthur Erickson, Kurt Fischman, Louis Glessman, Ray Hendrickson, Dan Hurley, George Kramser, Gene Leff, Kenneth Leslie, Robert Lewis, Ernest Mann, Mickey Meehan, John Melendez, Ken Parker, Gus Patrick, James Paul, Sandy Quitne, Leonard Stofka, William Taft, James Toth, Wally Van Sickle, William Waldron, Harvey Weber.

ACT 1

Scene 1

"In the Pink"

> N. Fairbanks, R. Craig, W. Douglas, F. Martell
> *Girls*: P. Bauer, J. Belluccia, E. Biderman, A. Boykin, B. Deane, W. Hackman, G. Haupt, J. King, P. Lemaire, M. Mahne, M. Mosic, D. Nelson, P. Paulson, R. Ray, G. Richardson, R. Rodgers, T. Rothacker, B. Stevens, C. Webber. *Boys*: J. Apley, R. Blow, G. Decker, K. Fischman, L. Glessman, R. Hendrickson, D. Hurley, J. Pasul, S. Quitne, L. Stofka, S. Stofka, W. Taft, J. Toth, W. Van Sickle, W. Waldron. *Showgirls*: M. Barry, D. Bergamnn, H. Dutcher, P. Harrington, L. Rolontz, E. Thompson.

Scene 2

Dynamic Duo

> C. Trenholm, J. Walsh

Scene 3

Landscape Artists

> E. Berry, J. Melendez

Scene 4

Celebration

a. Easter:

> *Lilies*: M. Barry, D. Bergmann, H. Dutcher, W. Hackman, L. Rolontz, E. Thompson. *Daffodils*: P. Bauer, E. Biderman, A. Boykin, B. Deane, P. Harrington, J. King, P. Lemaire, M. Mosic, D. Nelson, G. Richardson, T. Rothacker, B. Stevens. *Chicks*: J. Belluccia, G. Haupt, M. Mahne, P. Paulson, R. Rodgers, C. Webber.

b. Fourth of July:

> *Yankee Doodle Dandies*: J. Apley, R. Blow, G. Decker, N. Dantos, K. Fischmann, L. Glessman, R. Hendrickson, D. Hurley, G. Kramser, R. Lewis, J. Paul, S. Quitne, L. Stofka, S. Stokfa, J. Toth, W. Waldren.

c. The Prestons.

d. Thanksgiving:

> *Pilgrims*: K. Corcoran, J. Kasper. *Turkeys*: K. Leslie, K. Parker, G. Patrick, W. Taft.

e. "Yuletide"

> N. Fairbanks, R. Craig, W. Douglas, F. Martel
> *Townsfolk*: M. Barry, P. Bauer, D. Bergmann, E. Biderman, G. Bleckman, A. Boykin, B. Deane, H. Dutcher, W. Hackman, P. Harrington, J. King, P. Lemaire, M. Mosic, D. Nelson, R. Ray, G. Richardson, L. Rolontz, T. Rothacker, B. Stevens, J. Apley, R. Blow, G. Decker, N. Dantos, K. Fischman, L. Glessman, R. Hendrickson, D. Hurley, G. Kramser, R. Lewis, E. Mann, J. Paul, S. Quitne, L. Stofka, S. Stofka, J. Toth, W. Van Sickle, W. Waldron. *Santa Claus*: A. Erickson.

Scene 5

Precision Plus

> H. Thomson, R. Richards

Scene 6

Safari

> *Hunters*: B. Brace, B. Pennington, J. Sisk. *Lion*: E. Berry.

Scene 7

Trinidad Wharf

"Plenty More Fish in the Sea"

> N. Fairbanks, R. Craig, W. Douglas, F. Martel

Calypso Pete: R. Richards. *Tropical Siren*: C. Trenholm. *Islanders*: M. Barry, P. Bauer, J. Belluccia, D. Bergman, G. Bleckman, A. Boykin, B. Deane, H. Dutcher, W. Hackman, P. Harrington, Joan King, P. Lemaire, M. Mahne, M. Mosic, D. Nelson, P. Paulson, R. Ray, R. Rodgers, T. Rothacker, B. Stevens, R. Blow, C. Caminiti, G. Decker, N. Dantos, A. Erickson, K. Fischman, L. Glessman, G. Kramser, K. Leslie, R. Lewis, E. Mann, J. Melendez, K. Parker, J. Paul, G. Patrick, S. Quitne, L. Stofka, S. Stofka, J. Toth, W. Waldren.

Scene 8

Mercury

> *Mercury*: S. Baxter. *Pandora*: J. Clark. *Maidens*: K. Corcoran, L. Rolontz, E. Thompson.

Scene 9

Trixie

> *Assistant*: L. Stofka.

Scene 10

"48 States"

> D. Craig, F. Martel, W. Douglas
> *Inquiring Reporter*: R. Craig. *Matron*: N. Fairbanks. *Chorine*: K. Corcoran. *Schoolgirls*: D. Nelson, T. Rothacker. *Newsboy*: P. Castle. *Ensemble*: M. Barry, P. Bauer, J. Belluccia, D. Bergman, E. Biderman, G. Bleckman, A. Boykin, B. Deane, H. Dutcher, W. Hackman, P. Harrington, G. Haupt, J. King, P. Lemaire, M. Mahne, M. Mosic, P. Paulson, R. Ray, G. Richardson, R. Rodgers, L. Rolontz, B. Stevens, E. Thompson, C. Webber, J. Apley, R. Blow, C. Caminiti, G. Decker, N. Dantos, A. Erickson, K. Fischman, L. Glessman, R. Hendrickson, D. Hurley, K. Leslie, R. Lewis, E. Mann, J. Melendez, K. Parker, J. Paul, G. Patrick, S. Quitne, L. Stofka, S. Stofka, W. Taft, J. Toth, W. Van Sickle, W. Waldron. *Golden Eagle*: E. Seigh. *Pilots*: B. Grace, J. Kasper, J. Sisk, J. Walsh.

ACT 2

Scene 1

The Sleeping Beauty

The Princess' Birthday.

> *Princess Aurora*: J. Clark. *King*: A. Erickson. *Queen*: K. Corcoran. *Maids of Honor*: J. Belluccia, G. Bleckman, B. Deane, G. Haupt, J. King, M. Mosic, D. Nelson, P. Paulson, R. Ray, R. Rodgers, T. Rothacker, B. Stevens. *Prince from the East*: R. Richards. *Prince from the West*: B. Pennington. *Prince from the North*: J. Farris. *Prince from the South*: J. Walsh. *Guards*: J. Melendez, J. Toth.

A Remote Tower.

> *Wicked Fairy*: J. Kasper. *Good Fairy*: C. Trenholm.

The Forest.

> *Prince Desire*: H. Thomson. *The Archers*: J. Apley, R. Blow, C. Caminiti, E. Mann, J. Paul, G. Patrick.

The Sleeping Castle.

> *Ladies in Waiting*: M. Barry, E. Biderman, H. Dutcher, W. Hackman, P. Harrington, E. Thompson. *Courtiers*: P. Bauer, D. Bergman, A. Boykin, P. Lemaire, M. Mahne, G. Richardson, L. Rolontz, C. Webber, G. Decker, K. Fischman, L. Glessman, D. Hurley, R. Lewis, L. Stofka, S. Stofka, W. Van Sickle.

Scene 2

Highland Laddies

> P. Castle, B. Grace, B. Pennington, J. Sisk

Scene 3

The Bluebirds

> E. Seigh, S. Baxter

Scene 4

"The Cradle of Jazz"

> R. Craig, W. Douglas, N. Fairbanks, F. Martell
> *Rhythm Man*: R. Richards. *Cocottes*: E. Biderman, R. Ray, R. Rodgers. *Blues Boys and Girls*: J. Belluccia, A. Boykin, P. Lemaire, M. Mosic, G. Richardson, B. Stevens, R. Blow, L. Glessman, D. Hurley, E. Mann, G. Patrick, L. Stofka. *Cakewalkers*: P. Bauer, T. Rothacker, C. Caminiti, J. Farris. *Strutters*: K. Fischman, R. Lewis, J. Paul, S. Stofka, W. Van Sickle, W. Waldren. *Mr. Strut*: J. Walsh. *Flappers*: J. King, D. Nelson, P. Paulson, C. Webber. *Kampus Kids*: K. Corcoran, J. Kasper. *Boogie Woogie*: M. Barry, D. Bergmann, H. Dutcher, W. Hackman, L. Rolontz, E. Thompson, G. Decker, N. Dantos, G. Kramser, K. Parker, S. Quitne, J. Toth. *Jitterbugs*: M. Mahne, G. Haupt, E. Berry, A. Erickson.

Scene 5

Flirtation Lesson

Mam'zelle: M. Preston. *Bellhop*: P. Preston.

Scene 6

In the Dark

"I Only Wish I Knew"

N. Fairbanks, F. Martell

Sweethearts: J. Clark, K. Corcoran, C. Trenholm, J. Farris, H. Thomson, J. Walsh. *Ladies of the Ensemble*: M. Barry, P. Bauer, J. Belluccia, D. Bergmann, E. Biderman, G. Bleckman, B. Deane, H. Dutcher, W. Hackman, P. Harrington, G. Haupt, J. King, P. Lemaire, M. Mahne, D. Nelson, P. Paulson, R. Ray, G. Richardson, R. Rodgers, L. Rolontz, T. Rothacker, B. Stevens, E. Thompson, C. Webber.

Scene 7

Variations on a Romantic Theme

Beguine: S. Baxter. *Valse*: E. Seigh.

Scene 8

Fireman, Save That Tramp

Chief: A. Erickson. *Firemen*: B. Grace, B. Pennington, J. Sisk. *Tramp*: F. Trenkler.

Scene 9

"The World's Greatest Show"

N. Fairbanks, R. Craig, W. Douglas, F. Martell

Ringmaster: H. Thomson. *Clowns*: N. Dantos, K. Fischman, L. Glessman, R. Hendrickson, G. Kramser, K. Leslie, J. Melendez, K. Parker, S. Stofka, W. Taft, J. Toth, W. Waldren. *Elephant Girls*: P. Bauer, J. Belluccia, G. Haupt, P. Paulson, R. Ray, C. Webber. *Tumblers*: J. Apley, R. Blow, C. Caminiti, E. Mann, J. Paul, G. Patrick. *Trainer*: C. Trenholm. *Gold Leopards*: E. Biderman, B. Deane, P. Harrington, J. King, D. Nelson, G. Richardson. *Trainer*: J. Walsh. *Black Panthers*: M. Barry, D. Bergamnn, W. Hackman, M. Mosic, T. Rothacker, E. Thompson. *Giant*: B. Grace. *Giantess*: R. Rodgers. *Snake Charmer*: K. Corcoran. *Mammy Mine*: P. Castle. *Ranee*: P. Bauer, M. Mahne. *Rajah*: R. Richards. *Aerialists*: J. Clark, A. Boykin, H. Dutcher, P. Lemaire, B. Stevens, J. Farris, J. Kasper. *Acrobats*: M. Preston, P. Preston. *Trixie*. *Equestrienne Horses*: G. Decker, D. Hurley, R. Lewis, S. Quitne. *Cowboys*: E. Berry, B. Pennington. *Billy the Kid*: S. Baxter. *Strongman*: A. Erickson. *Freddie Trenkler*: Himself.

Scene 10

Finale

1948.20   SHOWBOAT

A Return Engagement of the Revival of the Musical Comedy in Two Acts, 15 Scenes[2]. Music by Jerome Kern. Book and lyrics by Oscar Hammerstein II. Staged by Hassard Short. Based on the novel by Edna Ferber. Dances by Helen Tamiris. Settings by Howard Bay. Costumes by Lucinda Ballard. Musical director, David Mordecai. Orchestrations by Robert Russell Bennett. Book directed by Oscar Hammerstein II. Produced by Jerome Kern[3] and Oscar Hammerstein II. Opened 7 September 1948 at the New York City Center and closed 18 September 1948 after 16 performances.

CAST (in order of their appearance): *Windy*: George Spellman. *Steve*: Fred Brookins. *Pete*: Gerald Prosk. *Queenie*: HELEN DOWDY. *Parthy Ann Hawkes*: RUTH GATES. *Captain Andy*: BILLY HOUSE. *Ellie*: CLARE ALDEN. *Frank*: SAMMY WHITE.

---

[2]This revival first presented in New York 5 January 1946 at the Ziegfeld Theatre for 418 performances. Book revisions by Oscar Hammerstein II. Original New York production opened 27 December 1927 at the Ziegfeld Theatre for 572 performances. For Synopsis of Scenes and Musical Numbers, see 1946 revival. Note following changes for this production:

"Life Upon the Wicked Stage" (Act 1) replaced by "I Might Fall Back on You" (S. White, C. Alden).

Olio Dance (S. White) added after "Life Upon the Wicked Stage."

Dance: Congress of Beauties (Act 2) dropped.

"Why Do I Love You?" Waltz dropped; Service and Scene Music, St. Agatha's Convent dropped.

"Nobody Else But Me" and "Dance 1927" dropped.

[3]A posthumous credit conceived at the time of the 1946 revival.

Rubber Face: Gordon Alexander. *Julie*: CAROL BRUCE. *Gaylord Ravenal*: NORWOOD SMITH. *Vallon*: Fred Ardath. *Magnolia*: PAMELA CAVENESS. *Joe*: WILLIAM C. SMITH. *Backwoodsman*: Howard Frank. *Jeb*: Gerald Prosk. *Sam*: LaVerne French. *Sal*: Gloria Smith. *Barker*: Walter Russell. *Fatima*: Sylvia Myers. *Sport*: Robert Fleming. *Dahomey King*: La Verne French. *Landlady*: Sara Floyd. *Ethel*: Assota Marshall. *Sister*: Sheila Hogan. *Mother Superior*: Lorraine Waldman. *Kim, child*: Alyce Mace. *Jake*: King Brill. *Jim*: Seldon Bennett. *Man With Guitar*: Albert McCary. *Doorman at Trocadero*: Walter Mosby. *Lottie*: Sara Dillon. *Dolly*: Elaine Hume. *Sally*: Janet Van Derveer. *Old Lady on Levee*: Ann Lloyd.

Singers: *Girls*: Sybol Cain, Clarice Crawford, Sara Dillon, Betty Graeber, Marion Hairston, Kate Hall, Elaine Hume, Charlotte Junius, Assota Marshall, Sylvia Myers, Eleyn Paul, Eulabel Riley, Dee Sherman, Janet Vanderveer, Lorraine Waldman. *Boys*: Jerome Addison, Gilbert Adkins, Gordon Alexander, Ivory Bass, Henry Davis, William Cole, Clarence Jones, Albert McCary, Walter Mosby, Walter Russell, William Sol, Charles Welch, Leo Norman, Robert Flavelle, Francis Fleming, Henry Hamilton. *Dancers*: *Girls*: Eloise Hill, Evelyn Pilcher, Gloria Smith, Alma Sutton. *Boys*: Isaiah Clark, James Hunt, Reginald Ridgley, George Thomas, James Fields.

1948.21   HILARITIES

A Vaudeville Revue in Two Acts, 20 Scenes. Conceived by Ken Robey. Sketches by Sidney Zelinka, Howard Harris, Morey Amsterdam. Music and lyrics by Buddy Kaye, Stanley Arnold and Carl Lampl. Supervised by Mervyn Nelson. Dances arranged by George Tapps. Scenes by Crayon. Special musical arrangements by Elliot Jacoby. Musical director, Ruby Zwerling. Produced by Ken Robey and Stan Zucker. Opened 9 September 1948 at the Adelphi Theatre and closed 18 September 1948 after 14 performances.

CAST: MOREY AMSTERDAM, BETTY JANE WATSON, GEORGE TAPPS, CONNIE SAWYER, LARRY DOUGLAS, Gali Gali, Gil Maison, Raul and Eva Reyes, Al Kelly, Gerald Austen, Sid Stone, The Calgarys (Andre, Steve), Nancy Andrews, Mazzone and the Abbott Dancers, The Holloway Sisters, Harold and Lola, The Herzogs, Enid Williams, Connie Stevens, Mitzi Novelle, Victoria Crandall, Moreland Kortkam.

ACT 1

"Showtime"

B. J. Watson, M. Novelle, L. Douglas, G. Austen, C. Stevens, Calgary Brothers, E. Williams, R. and E. Reyes, Entire Company

Your host, Morey Amsterdam, and others

The Man and the Snake

Harold and Lola

The Pitchman

S. Stone

"Rise and Shine"

G. Austen, C. Stevens, C. Sawyer, N. Andrews, M. Novelle, M. Amsterdam

The Holloway Sisters

Gali Gali

The Bridegroom

M. Amsterdam, L. Douglas, G. Austen, Calgary Brothers

"Where in the World"

B. J. Watson, L. Douglas, G. Tapps

The Lost Weekend

Calgary Brothers

George Tapps, assisted by V. Crandall and M. Kortkam

Morey Amsterdam and his cello

ACT 2

About Politics

M. Amsterdam, A. Kelly

"'Tis the Luck of the Irish"

B. J. Watson, G. Austen, N. Andrews, M. Novelle, L. Douglas, G. Tapps, the Holloway Sisters

The Herzogs

Vaudeville Hoofer

G. Tapps

Great New Talent

C. Stevens

One Man's Menagerie

G. Maison

"Rio de Janeiro"
  N. Andrews, G. Austen, L. Douglas, the Holloway Sisters, R. and E. Reyes
The Entrance of the Adelphi Theatre
  M. Amsterdam, Entire Company

1948.22 SMALL WONDER

A Musical Revue in Two Acts, 20 Scenes. Sketches by Charles Spaulding, Max Wilk, George Axelrod, Louis Laun. Music by Baldwin Bergersen and Albert Selden. Lyrics by Phyllis McGinley and Billings Brown. Directed by Burt Shevelove. Choreographed by Gower Champion. Scenery and lighting by Ralph Alswang. Costumes by John Derro. Orchestrations by Ted Royal. Orchestra conducted by William Parson. Vocal arrangements by Herbert Greene. Produced by George Nichols III. Opened 15 September 1948 at the Coronet Theatre and closed 8 January 1949 after 134 performances.

CAST: Tom Ewell, Alice Pearce, Mary McCarty, Marilyn Day, Hayes Gordon, Tommy Rall, J. C. McCord, Joan Mann, Jonathan Lucas, Kate Friedlich, Chandler Cowles, Alan Ross, Mort Marshall, Virginia Oswald, Jack Cassidy, Joan Diener, Evelyn Taylor, Bill Ferguson, Devida Stewart.

ACT 1

Scene 1
  "Count Your Blessings"
    Entire Company
    (*Music by* Baldwin Bergersen. *Lyrics by* Phyllis McGinley.)

Scene 2
  The Normal Neurotic
    T. Ewell

Scene 3
  "The Commuters' Song" (Between the 5:08 and the 8:01)
    M. Day, A. Ross
    (*Music by* Baldwin Bergersen. *Lyrics by* Phyllis McGinley.)

Scene 4
  "Ballad for Billionaires"
    (*Music by* Albert Selden. *Lyrics by* Billings Brown [Burt Shevelove].)
    Junior: C. Cowles. *Pop*: M. Marshall. *Louise van Steele*: M. McCarty. *Clint LaRue*: H. Gordon.

Scene 5
  "No Time"
    (*Music by* Baldwin Bergersen. *Lyrics by* Phyllis McGinley. Musical development for dance by Richard Priborsky.)
    First variation: J. Lucas, K. Friedlich. *Second variation*: T. Rall, E. Taylor. *Third variation*: J. C. McCord, J. Mann.

Scene 6
  The Human Body
    T. Ewell

Scene 7
  "Flaming Youth"
    M. McCarty
    (*Music by* Albert Selden. *Lyrics by* Billings Brown [Burt Shevelove].)

Scene 8
  D-e-m-ocracy
    The Normal Neurotic: T. Ewell. *The Wife*: A. Pearce. *The Husband*: M. Marshall.

Scene 9
  "Show Off"
    T. Rall, M. Day
    (*Music by* Albert Selden. *Lyrics by* Billings Brown [Burt Shevelove]. Musical development for dance by Richard Priborsky.)

Scene 10
  I Could Write a Book
    The Normal Neurotic: T. Ewell.
    1. *Mom*: A. Pearce. *Joey*: J. Lucas. *Gabby*: J. Mann.
    2. *Eddie*: C. Cowles. *Dolores*: M. Day.
    3. *Joy Polloi*: M. McCarty. *Czar Nicholas*: M. Marshall.

Scene 11
  "Badaroma"

J. C. McCord, Entire Company
(*Music by* Albert Selden. *Lyrics by* Billings Brown [Burt Shevelove]).

ACT 2

Scene 1
  "Nobody Told Me"
    (*Music by* Baldwin Bergersen. *Lyrics by* Phyllis McGinley.)
    The Bride: J. Diener. *The Groom*: H. Gordon. *The Maid of Honor*: D. Stewart. *The Best Man*: A. Ross. *The Mother*: A. Pearce. *The Bridesmaids*: M. McCarty, M. Day, V. Oswald. *The Ushers*: J. Lucas, J. Cassidy, B. Ferguson.

Scene 2
  The Civilized Thing
    (by Richard F. Maury)T. Ewell

Scene 3
  "Pistachio"
    A. Pearce, M. Marshall
    (*Music and Lyrics by* Mark Lawrence.)

Scene 4
  "When I Fall in Love"
    M. Day
    (*Music and Lyrics by* Albert Selden. Musical development for dance by Richard Priborsky.)
    Danced by J. Lucas, K. Friedlich. *Assisted by* J. Mann, E. Taylor, T. Rall, J. C. McCord.

Scene 5
  (This Is an Adv.)
    The Normal Neurotic: T. Ewell.

Scene 6
  "Saturday's Child"
    M. McCarty
    (*Music by* Baldwin Bergersen. *Lyrics by* Phyllis McGinley.)

Scene 7
  "William McKinley High"
    M. Day, J. Lucas, T. Rall, J. Cassidy, C. Cowles, M. Marshall, A. Ross
    (*Music by* Albert Selden. *Lyrics by* Billings Brown [Burt Shevelove].)

Scene 8
  The Happy Ending
    1. *Small Boy*: T. Ewell. *Nina*: J. Mann.
    2. *Maurice*: T. Ewell. *Beryl*: A. Pearce. *Elvira*: K. Friedlich.
    3. *Nick*: T. Ewell. *The Kid*: M. McCarty. *Her Brother*: T. Rall. *Tony Akimbo*: J. Cassidy.
  "From A to Z"
    M. McCarty, J. Cassidy, the Megalo-Golden-Mania Girls
    (*Music by* Albert Selden. *Lyrics by* Billings Brown [Burt Shevelove].)

Scene 9
  "Just an Ordinary Guy"
    V. Oswald, Entire Company
    (*Music by* Albert Selden. *Lyrics by* Phyllis McGinley, Billings Brown [Burt Shevelove].)

1948.23 HEAVEN ON EARTH

A Musical Comedy in Two Acts, 10 Scenes. Book and lyrics by Barry Trivers. Music by Jay Gorney. Entire production supervised by Eddie Dowling. Directed and lighted by John Murray Anderson. Dances and lyric numbers staged by Nick Castle. Settings and costumes by Raoul Pene du Bois. Vocal arrangements and direction by Hugh Martin. Musical arrangements by (Robert) Russell Bennett and Don Walker. Musical direction, Clay Warnick. Added lyrics by Norman Zeno. Musical adaptation for dances by Alan Morand. Produced by Monte Proser in association with Ned. C. Kitwack. Opened 16 September 1948 at the New Century Theatre and closed 25 September 1948 after 12 performances.

CAST (in order of appearance): *James Aloysius McCarthy*: PETER LIND HAYES. *Friday*: DODROTHY JARNAC. *Punchy*: DANNY DRAYSON. *Fannie Frobisher*: Caren Marsh. *Florabelle Frobisher*: Ruth Merman. *Mrs. Frobisher*: Nina Varella. *Commissioner Frobisher*: IRWIN COREY. *Officer Clabber*: CLAUDE STROUD. *John Bowers*: ROBERT DIXON. *Mary Brooks*: BARBARA NUNN. *The Lovers*: JUNE GRAHAM, RICHARD D'ARCY. *Lieut. Sullivan*: WYNN MURRAY. *Officer Jonesy*:

DOROTHY KELLER. *Officer Blandings*: Betty George. *Sailor*: BILLY PARSONS. *H.H. Hutton*: DAVID BURNS. *Magistrate Kennedy*: DICK BERNIE. *Sailor with Trumpet*: STEVE CONDOS. *Officer O'Brien*: Bert Sheldon. *Radio Engineeer*: Jack Russell. *Slim*: Remi Martel. *Dippy*: Jack Russell. *Butch*: Bill Hogue.

Dancers: Lisa Ayres, Cece Eames, Babette George, Gretchen Houser, Marguerite James, Carol Lee, Dorothy Love, Caron Marsh, Ruth Merman, Gloria Sickling, Alice Swanson, Evelyn Ward. Harold Drake, Ernie DiGennaro, Dante DiPaolo, Ray Johnson, Red Knight, Remi Martel, Jack Mattis, Don Powell, Frank Reynolds, Jack Whitney, Jack Wilkins.

Singers: Angela Castle, Julie Curtis, Betty George, Pearl Hacker, Ellen McCown, Jean Olds, Dottie Pyren, Lucille Udovick. Dean Campbell, John Gray, Bill Hogue, Doug Luther, Vincent Van Lynn, Jack Russell, Bert Sheldon, Curt Stafford.

The action of the play takes place in New York City on the first day of spring.

Act 1, Scene 1: Central Park. Noon. *Scene 2*: The Housing Commissioner's Office. That afternoon. *Scene 3*: Central Park. That afternoon. *Scene 4*: The Hutton Home of Tomorrow. That evening.

Act 2, Scene 1: Central Park. Next morning. *Scene 2*: A Cell Block in the Park Jail. That morning. *Scene 3*: Police Court in the Park Jail. That morning. *Scene 4*: Fifth Avenue. Immediately afterwards. *Scene 5*: Interior of Hutton Home. Late that day. *Scene 6*: Central Park. Immediately afterwards.

ACT 1

"In the Back of a Hack"
> P. L. Hayes, B. George, P. Hacker, D. Luther, D. Campbell

"Anything Can Happen"
> Full Company

"So Near and Yet So Far"
> B. Nunn, R. Dixon
> *Lovers Dance*: J. Graham, R. D'Arcy.

"Don't Forget to Dream"
> P. L. Hayes

"Bench in the Park"
> W. Murray, D. Keller, B. Parsons, D. Drayson, Dancing Ensemble

"The Letter"
> P. L. Hayes, D. Jarnac

"Push a Button in a Hutton"
> D. Burns, J. Whitney, Singing and Dancing Ensemble

"Home Is Where the Heart Is"
> B. Nunn, R. Dixon, Singing Ensemble

"Apple Jack"[4]
> W. Murray, S. Condos, D. Keller, D. Jarnac, Singing and Dancing Ensemble

"Wedding in the Park"
> P. L. Hayes, B. Nunn, R. Dixon

"Heaven on Earth"
> B. Nunn, R. Dixon, J. Graham, R. D'Arcy

Finale
> Full Company

ACT 2

"What's the Matter with Our City?"
> P. L. Hayes, Full Company

"So Near and Yet So Far" (reprise)
> B. Nunn, R. Dixon

"(You're the) First Cup of Coffee in the Morning"[5]
> W. Murray, C. Stroud, D. Keller, B. Parsons, S. Condos, Singing and Dancing Ensemble

Gift Number
> P. L. Hayes, C. Stroud, J. Whitney Quartette, Ensemble

Musical Tour of the City
> P. L. Hayes, C. Stroud

Finale
> P. L. Hayes, Entire Company

---

[4]Vocal arrangements by Bus [Buster] Davis.
[5]Vocal arrangements by Bus [Buster] Davis.

1948.24

MAGDALENA

A Musical Adventure in Two Acts, 9 Scenes. Book by Frederick Hazlitt Brennan and Homer Curran. Music by Heitor Villa-Lobos. Pattern and lyrics by Robert Wright and George Forrest. Directed by Jules Dassin. Settings and lighting by Howard Bay. Costumes by (Irene) Sharaff. Choreography by Jack Cole. Musical direction by Arthur Kay. Choral direction by Robert Zeller. Produced by Edwin Lester. Presented by Homer Curran. Opened 20 September 1948 at the Ziegfeld Theatre and closed 4 December 1948 after 88 performances.

CAST (in order of appearance): *Padre Josef*: GERHARD PECHNER. *Manuel*: Peter Fields. *Solis*: Melva Niles. *Ramon*: Henry Reese. *Maria*: DOROTHY SARNOFF. *Pedro*: JOHN RAITT. *Major Blanco*: Ferdinand Hilt. *Doctor Lopez*: Carl Milletaire. *General Carabana*: HUGO HAAS. *Chanteuse*: Betty Huff. *Cigarette Girl*: Christine Matsios. *Zoggie*: John Schickling. *Danseuse*: Lorraine Miller. *Teresa*: IRRA PETINA. *The Old One*: Gene Curtsinger. *Chico*: Patrick Kirk. *Juan*: Leonard Morganthaler. *Conchita*: Betty Brusher. *Major Domo*: Roy Raymond. *Bailadora*: Marie Groscup. *Bailador*: Matt Mattox.

Singers: Lucy Andonian, Marion Begin, Jean Bishop, Betty Brusher, Trudy DeLuz, Sofia Derue, Jeanne Eisen, Vera Ford, Martha Flynn, Audrey Guard, Betty Flannagan, Phyllis Kramer, Gwenn LaKind, Christine Matsios, Theresa Piper, Mary Wood. Ralph Angell, Arthur Brey, Stephen Esail, Kahler Flock, Tommy Gleason, John Huck, Robert Hudson, John King, Ross Lynch, Joe Mazzzolini, Roy Raymond, Stanley Rose, Leonard Taylor.

Dancers: Libby Burke, Rita Charise, Norma Doggett, Marie Groscup, Judy Landon, Mary Menzies, Lorraine Miller, Joan Morton, Sue Remos, Dale Lefler, Matt Mattox, Bill Miller, Verne Miller, Michael Sandin, Michael Scrittorale, Ralph Smith, Paul Steffen, Robert Thompson. *Assistants to Jack Cole*: Gweneth Verdun [Gwen Verdon], George Martin. *Captain of the Dancers*: Matt Mattox.

Children: Fred Cuelar, Peter De Bear, Patrick Kirk, Rosarita Varela.

Soldiers and Servants: Ralph Graves, Robert Meser, Maurice Monte, Arthur Veiga.

Time: About 1912.

Act 1, Scene 1: The courtyard of Padre Josef's chapel near the Magdalena River. *Scene 2*: A private dining room in the Little Black Mouse Cafe in Paris. Two weeks later. *Scene 3*: The boat landing at the Muzo Village. Ten days later. *Scene 4*: At the Shrine of the Madonna. The same evening.

Act 2, Scene 1: At the Singing Tree. A few hours later. *Scene 2*: The kitchen of General Carabana's hacienda. The next afternoon. *Scene 3*: Terrace of the General's hacienda. That evening. *Scene 4*: The floor of a canyon near the General's hacienda. A few minutes later. *Scene 5*: The chapel courtyard. The next morning.

ACT 1

Scene 1

"The Jungle Chapel"

"Women Weaving"
> Ensemble, G. Pechner

"Petacal"
> M. Niles, H. Reese, Dancers, Ensemble

"The Seed of God"
> G. Pechner, Dancers, Ensemble

"The Omen Bird" (Teru, Teru)
> D. Sarnoff, Dancers, Ensemble

"My Bus and I"
> J. Raitt, Ensemble

"The Emerald"
> D. Sarnoff, J. Raitt

Scene 2

"The Civilized People"
> H. Haas, L. Miller, J. Schickling, Ensemble

"Food For Thought"
> I. Petina, Ensemble

"Colombia Calls"

"Come to Colombia"
> I. Petina, H. Haas, Ensemble

"Plan It by the Planets"
> I. Petina, J. Schickling, Ensemble

"Bon Soir, Paris"
> I. Petina

"Travel, Travel, Travel"
> I. Petina, H. Haas, F. Hilt, J. Schickling, Ensemble

Scene 3

"Magdalena"

951

"Magdalena"
  G. Curtsinger
"The Broken Pianolita"
  M. Mattox, N. Doggett, Dancers, Ensemble
"The Festival"
"Greeting"
  Children
"River Song"
  D. Sarnoff, Ensemble
"Chivor Dance"
  Dancers
"My Bus and I" (reprise)
  J. Raitt, I. Petina, F. Hilt, Children

Scene 4

"The Forbidden Orchid"
  D. Sarnoff, J. Raitt

ACT 2

Scene 1

"Ceremonial"
  M. Groscup, N. Doggett, L. Miller, G. Curtsinger, Dancers, Ensemble
"The Singing Tree"
  H. Reese, M. Niles, Ensemble
"Lost"
  D. Sarnoff, J. Raitt
"Freedom!"
  J. Raitt, Ensemble

Scene 3

"Vals de Espana"
  M. Groscup, M. Mattox, Dancers
"The Emerald" (reprise)
  J. Raitt
"Piece de Resistance"
  I. Petina, H. Haas

Scene 4

"The Broken Bus"
  J. Raitt

Scene 5

"The Seed of God"
  G. Pechner, D. Sarnoff, J. Raitt, H. Reese, M. Niles, Ensemble

1948.25 # LOVE LIFE

A Vaudeville in Two Acts, 16 Scenes. Book and lyrics by Alan Jay Lerner. Music by Kurt Weill. Directed by Elia Kazan. Choreography by Michael Kidd. Scenery designed by Boris Aronson. Costumes designed by Lucinda Ballard. Musical director, Joseph Littau. Lighting by Peggy Clark. Musical arrangements and orchestrations by Kurt Weill. Produced by Cheryl Crawford. Opened 7 October 1948 at the 46th Street Theatre and closed 14 May 1949 after 252 performances.

CAST: *The Magician*: JAY MARSHALL. *Susan*: NANETTE FABRAY. *Sam*: RAY MIDDLETON. *Mary Jo*: Holly Harris. *Tim*: Evans Thornton. *George Crockett*: David Thomas. *Jonathan Anderson*: Gene Tobin. *Charlie Hamilton*: VICTOR CLARKE. *Will*: Mark Kramer. *Hank*: Robert Byrn. *Ben*: Lenn Dale. *Child*: Vincent Gugleotti. *Elizabeth Cooper*: CHERYL ARCHER. *Johnny Cooper*: JOHNNY STEWART. *Walt*: Evans Thornton. *Three Tots*: Rosalie Alter, Vincent Gugleotti, Lenn Dale. *Trapeze Artist*: ELLY ARDELTY. *Two women soloists*: Lily Paget, Faye Elizabeth Smith. *Hobo*: JOHNNY THOMPSON. *Entertainer*: Virginia Conwell. *Harvey*: David Thomas. *Boylan*: VICTOR CLARKE. *Slade*: Larry Robbins. *Leffcourt*: David Collyer. *William Taylor*: LYLE BETTGER. *Madrigal Leader*: David Thomas. *Punch*: Arthur Partington. *Judy*: Barbara McCutcheon. *Lawyer*: Forrest Bonshire. *Judge*: Jules Racine. *Bell Hop*: Ed Phillips. *Correspondent*: Vida Brown. *Lawyer*: Frank Westbrook. *Flighty Pair*: Melissa Hayden, Ed Phillips. *Speedy Pair*: Pat Hammerlee, Bill Bradley. *Child*: Virginia Conwell. *Father*: Michael Maule. *Mother*: Wanna Allison. *Interlocutor*: VICTOR CLARKE. *Miss Horoscope*: Holly Harris. *Miss Mysticism*: Carolyn Maye. *Mr. Cynic*: David Thomas. *Girl*: Josephine Lambert. *Girl*: Marie Leidal. *Miss Ideal Man*: Sylvia Stahlman.
  Quartette: John Diggs, Joseph James, James Young, William Veasey. *The Go-Getters*: David Collyer, VICTOR CLARKE, David Thomas, Robert Byrn, Jules Racine, Gene Tobin, Mark Kramer, Larry Robbins.

Singers: Holly Harris, Josephine Lambert, Peggy Turnley, Marie Leidal, Sylvia Stahlman, Carol Maye, Lily Paget, Dorothea Berthelson, Faye E. Smith, David Collyer, VICTOR CLARKE, David Thomas, Robert Byrn, Evans Thornton, Gene Tobin, Mark Kramer, Larry Robbins. *Dancers*: Paula Lloyd, Melissa Hayden, Pat Hammerlee, Wanna Allison, Virginia Conwell, Barbara McCutcheon, Ed Phillips, Bill Bradley, Frank Westbrook, Arthur Partington, Forrest Bonshire, Michael Maule, Vida Brown, Robert Tucker.

Act 1, Scene 1: The Magician. *Scene 2*: The Cooper Family. Outside the Cooper Home, Mayville, 1791. *Scene 3*: Eight Men. *Scene 4*: The Farewell. Outside the Cooper Home, Mayville. April 1821. *Scene 5*: Quartette. *Scene 6*: The New Baby. The Bedroom of the Cooper House. September, 1857. *Scene 7*: The Three Tots and a Woman. *Scene 8*: My Kind of Night. The Porch and Living-room of the Cooper Home. The early 1890s. *Scene 9*: Love Song. *Scene 10*: The Cruise. The Main Dining-room of an Ocean Liner. In the 1920s.
Act 2, Scene 1: Radio Night. The Living-room of the Cooper's New York Apartment. The present time. *Scene 2*: Madrigal Singers. *Scene 3*: Farewell Again. *Scene 4*: "Punch and Judy Get a Divorce." *Scene 5*: A Hotel Room. *Scene 6*: "The Minstrel Show."

ACT 1

Scene 2

"Who Is Samuel Cooper?"
  H. Harris, D. Thomas, G. Tobin, V. Clarke, R. Byrn, Women
"My Name Is Samuel Cooper"
  R. Middleton
"Here I'll Stay"
  N. Fabray, R. Middleton

Scene 3

"Progress"
  The Go-Getters

Scene 4

"I Remember It Well"
  N. Fabray, R. Middleton
"Green-Up Time"
  N. Fabray, Men and Women
"Green-Up Time" Dance
  A. Partington, Dancers

Scene 5

"Economics"
  Quartette

Scene 7

"Mother's Getting Nervous"
  R. Alter, V. Gugleotti, L. Dale

Scene 8

"My Kind of Night"
  R. Middleton
"Women's Club Blues"
  N. Fabray, Women
Dance
  Dancers

Scene 9

"Love Song"
  J. Thompson

Scene 10

"I'm Your Man"
  R. Middleton, L. Robbins, V. Clarke, D. Thomas, D. Collyer

ACT 2

Scene 2

"Ho, Billy O!"
  Madrigal Singers

Scene 3

"I Remember It Well" (reprise)
  R. Middleton, N. Fabray
"Is It Him or Is It Me"
  N. Fabray

Scene 4

"Punch and Judy Get a Divorce" Ballet
  Dancers

Scene 5

"This Is the Life"
R. Middleton

Scene 6

"Here I'll Stay" (reprise)
V. Clarke
"Minstrel Parade"
Minstrels
"Madame Zuzu"
H. Harris, C. Maye
"Taking No Chances"
D. Thomas
"Mr. Right"
N. Fabray, S. Stahlman

1948.26 WHERE'S CHARLEY?

A Musical Comedy in Two Acts, 9 Scenes. Book by George Abbott. Based on the play "Charley's Aunt" by Brandon Thomas. Music and lyrics by Frank Loesser. Dances directed by George Balanchine, assisted by Fred Danielli. Sets and costumes by David Ffolkes. Vocal arrangements and direction by Gerry Dolin. Orchestrations by Ted Royal, Hans Spialek, Phil Lang. Musical director, Max Goberman. Production directed by George Abbott. Produced by Cy Feuer and Ernest H. Martin in association with Gwen Rickard. Opened 11 October 1948 at the St. James Theatre and closed 9 September 1950 after 792 performances[6].

CAST (in order of appearance): *Brassett*: John Lynds. *Jack Chesney*: BYRON PALMER. *Charley Wykeham*: RAY BOLGER. *Kitty Verdun*: DORETTA MORROW. *Amy Spettigue*: ALLYN McLERIE. *Wilkinson*: Edgar Kent. *Sir Francis Chesney*: PAUL ENGLAND. *Mr. Spettigue*: HORACE COOPER. *A Professor*: Jack Friend. *Donna Lucia D'Alvadorez*: JANE LAWRENCE. *Photographer*: James Lane. *Patricia*: Marie Foster. *Reggie*: Douglas Deane.

Dancers: Mary Alice Bingham, Vicki Barrett, Geraldine Delaney, Marge Ellis, Marie Foster, Marcia Maier, Nina Starkey, Susan Stewart, Toni Stuart, Douglas Deane, George Enke, John Friend, Bobby Harrell, Dusty McCaffrey, Walter Rinner, Bill Weber, Gordon West, Ken Whelan. *Singers*: Rae Abruzzo, Jane Judge, Ruth McVane, Betty Oakes, Eleanor Parker, Katharine Reeve, Gloria Sullivan, Irene Weston, Robert Baird, James Bird, Dan Gallagher, Bob Held, Cornell McNeil, Stowe Phelps, William Scully, Ernest Taylor.

The action takes place at St. Olde's College, Oxford University, 1892.

Act 1, Scene 1: A Room at Oxford University. *Scene 2*: A Street. *Scene 3*: The Garden. *Scene 4*: Where the Nuts Come From!

Act 2, Scene 1: The Garden. *Scene 2*: A Street. *Scene 3*: Where the Ladies Go. *Scene 4*: A Garden Path. *Scene 5*: The Ballroom.

ACT 1

Scene 1

"The Years Before Us"
Students
"Better Get Out of Here"
R. Bolger, A. McLerie, D. Morrow, B. Palmer

Scene 2

"The New Ashmolean Marching Society and Students' Conservatory Band"
B. Palmer, A. McLerie, D. Morrow, B. Harrell, Student, Young Ladies

Scene 3

"My Darling, My Darling"
B. Palmer, D. Morrow
"Make a Miracle"
R. Bolger, A. McLerie
"Serenade With Asides"
H. Cooper
"Lovelier Than Ever"
J. Lawrence, P. England, Students, Young Ladies

---

[6]Played a return engagement 29 January 1951 at the Broadway Theatre, and closed 10 March 1951 after 56 performances. See separate entry in 1950-51 season for detail.

"The Woman in His Room"
A. McLerie

Scene 4

"Pernambuco"
R. Bolger, A. McLerie, the "Pernambucans"

ACT 2

Scene 1

"Where's Charley?"
B. Palmer, C. McNeil, S. Phelps, Students, Young Ladies

Scene 2

"Once in Love With Amy"
R. Bolger

Scene 3

"The Gossips"
J. Judge, M. Foster, R. Abruzzo, B. Oakes, K. Reeves,
G. Sullivan, E. Parker, M A. Bingham, I. Weston, R. McVane, G. Delaney

Scene 4

"At the Red Rose Cotillion"
B. Palmer, D. Morrow, Guests
Dance
R. Bolger, A. McLerie

Scene 5

Finale
Entire Company

1948.27 MY ROMANCE

A Musical Play in Three Acts, Prologue and Epilogue. Book and lyrics by Rowland Leigh. Adapted from Edward Sheldon's play "Romance." Music by Sigmund Romberg. Staged by Rowland Leigh. Ensembles by Frederic N. Kelly. Settings by Watson Barratt. Costumes by Lou Eisele. Musical director, Roland Fiore. Orchestrations by Don Walker. Produced by the Messrs. Shubert. Opened 19 October 1948 at the Sam S. Shubert Theatre, moved 29 November 1948 to the Adelphi Theatre and closed 8 January 1949 after 95 performances.

CAST (in order of appearance): *Bishop Armstrong* (Tom): LAWRENCE BROOKS. *Suzette Armstrong*: JOAN SHEPARD. *Alice*: Marion Bradley. *Miss Potherton*: Hildegarde Halliday. *Harry Armstrong*: William Berrian. *Cornelius Van Tuyl*: MELVILLE RUICK. *Susan Van Tuyl*: HAZEL DAWN, JR. *Percival Hawthorne-Hillary*: Tom Bate. *Mrs. DeWitt*: Barbara Patton. *Veronica DeWitt*: Gail Adams. *Octavia Fotheringham*: LUELLA GEAR. *Sir Frederick Putman*: REX EVANS. *Lady Putman*: DORIS PATSTON. *Rupert Chandler*: Melton Moore. *Vladimir Luccachevitch*: NAT BURNS. *Miss Joyce*: Natalie Norman. *Bertie Wessel*: Lawrence Weber. *Georgianna Curtright*: Verna Epperly. *Margaret Fears*: Mary Jane Sloan. *Lawrence Riley*: Andy Aprea. *Thyra Winslow*: Lou Maddox. *DeWitt Bodeen*: Donald Crocker. *Rosella*: ALLEGRA VARRON. *Mme. Marguerita Cavallini* (Rita): ANNE JEFFREYS. *Charlotte Armstrong*: Madeline Holmes. *Tosatti*, the Organ Grinder: Tito Coral. *First Maid*: Edith Lane. *Second Maid*: Patricia Boyer. *Page Boy*: Norval Tormsen.

Other Guests: Martha Burnett, June Reimer, Muriel Birkhead, Harold Ronk, LeRoy Bush.

Prologue: Bishop Armstrong's Library in the Rectory attached to St. Giles Church, New York City. The present.

Act 1: Home of Cornelius Van Tuyl. New York City. 1898.

Act 2: Rectory, St. Giles Church. Six weeks later.

Act 3: Mme. Cavallini's Suite at Brevoort House. Four hours later.

Epilogue: Bishop Armstrong's Library. The present.

PROLOGUE

"Souvenir"
L. Brooks

ACT 1

"1898"
Ensemble
"Debutante"
H. Dawn, Jr., G. Adams, Ensemble

"Written in Your Hand"
    H. Dawn, Jr., L. Brooks
"Millefleurs"
    A. Jeffreys
"Love and Laughter"
    A. Jeffreys, L. Brooks
"From Now Onward"
    A. Jeffreys, L. Brooks
"Little Emmaline"
    L. Gear
"Aria"
    A. Jeffreys

ACT 2
"Desire"
    L. Brooks
"Polka"
    G. Adams, B. Patton, Ensemble
"If Only"
    A. Jeffreys
"Bella Donna"
    T. Coral, A. Jeffreys, Ensemble
"Paradise Stolen"
    A. Jeffreys, L. Brooks
"In Love With Romance"
    A. Jeffreys, L. Brooks
Finaletto
    L. Brooks

ACT 3
"Waltz Interlude"
    A. Varron
Musical Scene
    A. Jeffreys, L. Brooks
"Prayer"
    A. Jeffreys

EPILOGUE
Finale
    A. Jeffreys, L. Brooks

1948.28 AS THE GIRLS GO

A Musical Comedy in Two Acts, 21 Scenes. Book by William Roos. Music by Jimmy McHugh. Lyrics by Harold Adamson. Staged and designed by Howard Bay. Dances by Hermes Pan. Costumes designed by Oleg Cassini. Orchestra conducted by Max Meth. Orchestrations by Ted Royal. Vocal direction and arrangements by Hugh Martin. Produced by Michael Todd. Opened 13 November 1948 at the Winter Garden, suspended 9 July 1949[7], re-opened 14 September 1949 at the Broadway Theatre and closed 14 January 1950 after 420 performances.

CAST (in order of appearance): *Waldo Wellington*: BOBBY CLARK. *Lucille Thompson Wellington*: IRENE RICH. *Kenny Wellington*: BILL CALLAHAN. *Mickey Wellington*: BETTY LOU BARTO. *Tommy Wellington*: Donny Harris. *Guard*: John Sheehan. *Kathy Robinson*: BETTY JANE WATSON. *Barber*: HOBART CAVANAUGH. *White House Visitor*: John Brophy. *Miss Swenson*: Cavada Humphrey. *Butler*: Curt Stafford. *Daughters of the Boston Tea Party*: Claire Grenville, Claire Louise Evans, Lois Bolton, Marjorie Leach. *Floyd Robinson*: Douglas Luther. *Diane*: Mildred Hughes. *Photographer*: Kenneth Spaulding. *Ross Miller*: Jack Russell. *Daphne*: Dorothea Pinto. *Photographer*: William Reedy. *Blinky Joe*: DICK DANA. *Darlene*: Rosemary Williamson. *Secret Service Men*: George Morris, John Sheehan. *Secret Service Women*: Gregg Sherwood, Truly Barbara. *Children*: Marlene Cameron, Pauline Hahn, Norma Marlowe, Jonathan Marlowe, Clifford Sales, Eugene Steiner. *Secretary*: Ruth Thomas. *President of Potomac College*: Douglas Luther. *Première Danseuse*: KATHRYN LEE.
    Dancing Ensemble: Jeanette Acquillina, Carmina Cansino, Arline Castle, Babs Claire, Jessie Elliott, Yvette Fairhill, Christina Frerichs, Petty Ann Jackson, Margaret Jeanne Klein, Frances Krell, Pat Marlowe, Ila McAvoy, Toni Parker, Joyce Reedy, Diane Sinclair, Norma Thornton. James Brock, Charles Chartier, Peter Conlow, James

Elsegood, William Reedy, Bobby Roberts, Joseph Schenck, Eugene Schwab, Kenneth Spaulding, Larry Villani.
    Singing Ensemble: Barbara Davis, Lydia Fredericks, Betty George, Pearl Hacker, Abbe Marshall, Ellen McCowan, Judy Sinclair, Jo Sullivan. Bob Burkhardt, Dean Campbell, John Gray, Douglas Luther, George Morris, Jack Russell, John Sheehan, Curt Stafford.
    Show Girls: Truly Barbara, Pat Gaston, Mildred Hughes, Mickey Miller, Dorothea Pinto, Gregg Sherwood, Ruth Thomas, Rosemary Williamson.

Act 1, Scene 1: The Roxy Theatre, 20 January 1953. *Scene 2*: The Truman Balcony, early in the morning. *Scene 3*: The White House Barber Shop, the following morning. *Scene 4*: The White House Grounds, immediately after. *Scene 5*: The Chartreuse Room in the White House, that spring. *Scene 6*: A Corridor in the White House, the following afternoon. *Scene 7*: The Rumpus Room, immediately after. *Scene 8*: A Hotel Room. *Scene 9*: The White House Grounds, the next afternoon; A Newspaper Office; A Boudoir. *Scene 10*: The American Cannes Beach Club. *Scene 11*: A Corridor in the White House. *Scene 12*: The White House Barber Shop, that evening. *Scene 13*: Kathy's Bedroom, that night; A Telephone Company Switchboard; Kenny's Bedroom. *Scene 14*: The Lobby of the Mayfair Hotel, later. *Scene 15*: The Union Depot, Washington, D.C., the next afternoon.

Act 2, Scene 1: The Union Depot, Washington, D.C., that night. *Scene 2*: The Campus Inn, later. *Scene 3*: A Street in Washington, later, at night. *Scene 4*: The Chartreuse Room in the White House, Sunday Breakfast, 3 June. *Scene 5*: The College Campus, the next morning. *Scene 6*: The Gold Room in the White House, later, in the evening.

ACT 1
"As the Girls Go"
    B. Clark, Girls
"Nobody's Heart But Mine"
    B. J. Watson, B. Callahan
"Brighten Up and Be a Little Sunbeam"
    B. Clark, Children
"Rock, Rock, Rock"
    B. Callahan, B. J. Watson
"It's More Fun Than a Picnic"
    B. L. Barto, Children
"American Cannes"
    B. Clark, Girls
"You Say the Nicest Things, Baby"
    B. J. Watson, B. Callahan, Singing Girls
"I've Got the President's Ear"
    B. Clark, Girls
"Holiday in the Country"
    Entire Company

ACT 2
"There's No Getting Away From You"[8]
    B. J. Watson, Singing, Dancing Ensemble
Dance
    K. Lee, K. Spaulding, Dance Ensemble
"Lucky in the Rain"
    B. Callahan, B. J. Watson, Ensemble
Dance
    K. Lee, B. Callahan
"Father's Day"
    B. Clark, I. Rich, B. Callahan, B. L. Barto, D. Harris
"It Takes a Woman To Get a Man"
    B. Clark, Ensemble
"You Say The Nicest Things, Baby" (reprise)
    B. Clark, I. Rich
Finale
    Entire Company

1948.30 LEND AN EAR

An Intimate Musical Revue in Two Acts, 17 Scenes. Sketches, music and lyrics by Charles Gaynor. Additional sketches by Joseph Stein and Will Glickman. Directed by Hal Gerson. Choreography by Gower Champion.

---

[7]Performances suspended due to Bobby Clark's illness.

[8]Vocal arrangement by Buster Davis.

Costumes, settings and lighting by Raoul Pene DuBois. Musical direction by George Bauer. Orchestrations by Clare Grundman. Duo pianists, George Bauer, Dorothy Freitag. Additional musical arrangements by George Bauer. Vocal arrangements by D. Freitag. Production staged by Gower Champion. Produced by William R. Katzell, Franklin Gilbert and William Eythe. Opened 16 December 1948 at the National Theatre, moved 22 February 1949 to the Broadhurst Theatre, moved 10 October 1949 to the Sam S. Shubert Theatre, moved 31 October 1949 to the Mansfield Theatre, and closed 21 January 1950 after 460 performances.

CAST: Yvonne Adair, Anne Renee Anderson, Dorothy Babbs, Carol Channing, Al Checco, Robert Dixon, William Eythe, Nancy Franklin, Antoinette Guhlke, George Hall, Gloria Hamilton, Bob Herget, Beverly Hosier, Jenny Lou Law, Arthur Maxwell, Tommy Morton, Gene Nelson, Bob Scheerer, Jeanine Smith, Lee Stacy, Larry Stewart.

ACT 1

Scene 1

"After Hours"
  The Company

Scene 2

"Give Your Heart a Chance to Sing"
  The Girl: D. Babbs. *The Boys*: R. Dixon, A. Maxwell, B. Herget, T. Morton, B. Scheerer.

Scene 3

"Neurotic You and Psychopathic Me"
  The Nurse: L. Stacy. *The Patient*: A. R. Anderson. *The Doctor*: W. Eythe.

Scene 4

"I'm Not in Love"
  The Boss Who Dictates: A. Maxwell. *The Secretary Who Sings*: Y. Adair. *The Bosses Who Dance*: G. Nelson, T. Morton, B. Scheerer.

Scene 5

Power of the Press
  Husband: G. Hall. *Wife*: C. Channing.

Scene 6

"Friday Dancing Class"
  G. Hamilton, B. Hosier, J. Smith, A. Maxwell, R. Dixon, L. Stewart
  Henry Jones: B. Scheerer. *His Mother*: C. Channing. *His Friends*: A. Checco, B. Herget. *Miss Bridey*: J. L. Law. *The Girl*: D. Babbs. *The Dancing Class*: L. Stacy, A. Guhlke, N. Franklin, G. Nelson, B. Herget, T. Morton.

Scene 7

"Ballade"
  A. R. Anderson

Scene 8

"When Someone Loves You"
  G. Hamilton, R. Dixon
Dance
  A. Guhlke, G. Nelson

Scene 9

The Missing Road Company:
  Announcer: W. Eythe.
"The Gladiola Girl"
  Cast of Characters: *Rosalie*: G. Hamilton. *Larry Van Patten*: W. Eythe. *Ginger O'Toole*: Y. Adair. *Skiddy Tyres*: G. Hall. *Policeman*: B. Herget. *Girls*: D. Babbs, A.R. Anderson, C. Channing, L. Stacy. *Boys*: B. Scheerer, A. Checco, T. Morton, A. Maxwell.

Act 1
  Scene: A Garden in Bronxville.
  "Join Us in a Cup of Tea"
    Boys, Girls
  "Where Is the She For Me"
    W. Eythe, Girls
  "I'll Be True to You"
    G. Hamilton, W. Eythe
  "Doin' the Old Yahoo Step"
    Y. Adair, Chorus
  Finaletto
    Y. Adair, Chorus

Act 2
  Scene: Skiddy's Estate on Long Island.

Opening: "A Little Game of Tennis"
    Boys, Girls
  "In Our Teeny Little Weeny Nest"
    G. Hamilton, W. Eythe
  Finale
    Full Company

ACT 2

Scene 1

"Santo Domingo"
  The Travel Agent: A. Maxwell. *The Tourist*: Y. Adair. *Santo Domingans*: The Company.

Scene 2

"I'm On the Lookout"
  G. Hamilton

Scene 3

"Three Little Queens of the Silver Screen"
  L. Stacy, A. R. Anderson, C. Channing

Scene 4

"Molly O'Reilly"
  J. Smith, G. Hamilton, B. Hosier, R. Dixon, A. Maxwell, L. Stewart
  Danced by B. Scheerer, D. Babbs.

Scene 5

All the World's
  Announcer: A. Maxwell. *Mr. Playgoer*: W. Eythe. *Mrs. Playgoer*: C. Channing. *A Bartender*: G. Hall.

Scene 6

"Who Hit Me?"
  Y. Adair
  Danced by G. Nelson.

Scene 7

Words Without Song
  Announcer: A. Maxwell. *The Countess*: C. Channing. *Mathilda*: A. R. Anderson. *Alberto*: G. Hall. *The Count*: W. Eythe. *The Chorus*: A. Guhlke, L. Stacey, B. Hosier, J. L. Law, B. Herget, A. Checco, T. Morton, L. Stewart.

Scene 8

"Finale"
  The Company

THE TELEPHONE
and THE MEDIUM

1948.29

A Revival of the Double Bill of Two Operas[9]. Libretto and music by Gian-Carlo Menotti. Staged by the composer. Settings and costumes by Horace Armistead. Lighting by Jean Rosenthal. Musical director, Emanuel Balaban. Produced by the New York City Center by arrangement with Chandler Cowles and Efrem Zimbalist, Jr. and Edith Lutyens. Opened 7 December 1948 at the New York City Center and closed 1 January 1949 after 40 performances.

THE TELEPHONE (or "L'Amour A Trois")

A Comic Opera curtain raiser in One Act.

  CAST: *Lucy*: MARIA D'ATTILI. *Ben*: PAUL KING.

THE MEDIUM

A Tragic Opera in Two Acts. The action takes place in Madame Flora's parlor in our time.

  CAST: *Monica*: EVELYN KELLER, DERNA DE LYS (alt.). *Toby*, a Mute: LEO COLEMAN *Madame Flora* (Baba): MARIE POWERS, Margery Mayer (alt.). *Mrs. Gobineau*: BEVERLY DAME, MARIA D'ATTILI (alt.). *Mr. Gobineau*: PAUL KING. *Mrs. Nolan*: VIRGINIA BEELER.

---

[9]Originally produced in New York 1 May 1947 at the Ethel Barrymore Theatre for 212 performances. For Synopsis of Scenes and Musical Numbers, see original 1947 production.

1948.31 THE RAPE OF LUCRETIA

A Music Drama (Opera) in Two Acts, 4 Scenes. Book by Ronald Duncan. Music by Benjamin Britten. Scenery and costumes designed by John Piper, courtesy of the English Opera Group. Costume supervision by Frank Thompson. Lighting by Peggy Clark. Vocal director, John Daggett Howell. Entire production staged by Agnes de Mille. Musical director and conductor, Paul Breisach. Assistant conductor, Walter Taussig. Produced by Marjorie and Sherman Ewing, and Giovanni Cardelli. Opened 29 December 1948 at the Ziegfeld Theatre and closed 16 January 1949 after 23 performances[10].

CAST (in order of speaking): *The Male Chorus*: EDWARD KANE[11], DONALD CLARKE[12]. *The Female Chorus*: BRENDA LEWIS[13], PATRICIA NEWAY[14]. *Collatinus*, A Roman General: HOLGER SORENSEN[15], EDWIN STEFFE[16]. *Junius*, A Roman General: EMILE RENAN. *Tarquinius*, An Etruscan Prince: GEORGE (Giorgio) TOZZI[17], ANDREW GAINEY[18]. *Lucretia*, Wife of Collatinus: KITTY CARLISLE[19], BELVA KIBLER[20]. *Bianca*, Lucretia's Nurse: VIVIAN BAUER[21], EUNICE ALBERTS[22]. *Lucia*, Lucretia's Maid: MARGUERITE PIAZZA[23], ADELAIDE BISHOP[24]. *Roman Woman*: Lidija Franklin. *Two Etruscan Soldiers*: Kazimir Kokic, Lucas Hoving. *Roman Man*: Robert Pagent. *Roman Youth*: Stanley Simmons. *A Prostitute*: Bunty Kelley.

Time: Rome, 509 B.C.

Act 1, Scene 1: The Generals' tent in the camp outside Rome. *Scene 2*: Lucretia's house in Rome, the same evening.

Act 2, Scene 1: Lucretia's bedroom. That night. *Scene 2*: Lucretia's house, the next morning.

1948.32 KISS ME, KATE

A Musical Comedy in Two Acts, 16 Scenes. Book by Sam [Samuel] and Bella Spewack. (Suggested by William Shakespeare's "The Taming of the Shrew.") Music and lyrics by Cole Porter. Choreography by Hanya Holm. Settings and costumes by Lemuel Ayers. Lighting by Al Alloy. Musical director, Pembroke Davenport. Orchestrations by Robert Russell Bennett. Incidental ballet music arranged by Genevieve Pitot. Production staged by John C. Wilson. Produced by Saint Subber and Lemuel Ayers. Opened 30 December 1948 at the New Century Theatre, moved 31 July 1950 to the Sam S. Shubert Theatre and closed 28 July 1951 after 1077 performances. [25]

CAST (in order of appearance): *Fred Graham*: ALFRED DRAKE. *Harry Trevor*: THOMAS HOIER. *Lois Lane*: LISA KIRK. *Ralph*, Stage Manager: Don Mayo. *Lilli Vanessi*: PATRICIA MORISON. *Hattie*: ANNABELLE HILL. *Paul*: LORENZO FULLER. *Bill Calhoun*: HAROLD LANG. *First Man*: HARRY CLARK. *Second Man*: JACK DIAMOND. *Stage Doorman*: Bill Lilling. *Harrison Howell*: Denis Green. *Specialty Dancers*: Fred Davis, Eddie Sledge.
"*Taming of the Shrew*" Players: *Bianca* (Lois Lane): LISA KIRK. *Baptista* (Harry Trevor): THOMAS HOIER. *Gremio* (First Suitor): Edwin Clay. *Hortensio* (Second Suitor): Charles Wood. *Lucentio* (Bill Calhoun): HAROLD LANG. *Katharine* (Lilli Vanessi): PATRICIA MORISON. *Petruchio* (Fred Graham): ALFRED DRAKE. *Haberdasher*: John Castello. *Tailor*: Marc Breaux.
Singing Ensemble: Peggy Ferris, Christine Matsios, Joan Kibrig, Gay Laurence, Ethel Madsen, Helen Rice, Matilda Strazza, Tom Bole, George Cassidy, Herb Fields, Noel Gordon, Allan Lowell, Stan Rose, Charles Wood. *Dancing Ensemble*: Ann Dunbar, Shirley Eckl, Jean Houloose, Doreen Oswald, Janet Gaylord, Gisella Svetlik,

Jean Tachau, Marc Breaux, John Castello, Victor Duntiere, Tom Hansen, Paul Olson, Glen Tetley, Rudy Tone.

Act 1, Scene 1: Stage of the Ford Theatre, Baltimore. *Scene 2*: The Corridor Backstage. *Scene 3*: Dressing-rooms, Fred Graham and Lilli Vanessi. *Scene 4*: Padua. *Scene 5*: Street Scene, Padua. *Scene 6*: Backstage. *Scene 7*: Fred and Lilli's Dressing-rooms. *Scene 8*: Exterior Church.

Act 2, Scene 1: Theatre Alley. *Scene 2*: Before the Curtain. *Scene 3*: Petruchio's House. *Scene 4*: The Corridor Backstage. *Scene 5*: Fred and Lilli's Dressing-rooms. *Scene 6*: The Corridor Backstage. *Scene 7*: Backstage. *Scene 8*: Baptista's Home.

ACT 1

Scene 1
  "Another Op'nin', Another Show"
    A. Hill, Singing Ensemble
    Danced by Dancing Ensemble.

Scene 2
  "Why Can't You Behave"
    L. Kirk

Scene 3
  "Wunderbar"
    P. Morison, A. Drake

Scene 4
  "So in Love"
    P. Morison

Scene 5
  "We Open in Venice"
    A. Drake, P. Morison, L. Kirk, H. Lang

Scene 6
  Dance
    Dancing Ensemble
  "Tom, Dick or Harry"
    L. Kirk, H. Lang, E. Clay, C. Wood
  Specialty Dance
    H. Lang
  "I've Come to Wive It Wealthily in Padua"
    A. Drake, Singing Ensemble
  "I Hate Men"
    P. Morison
  "Were Thine That Special Face"
    A. Drake
    Danced by S. Eckl, Dancing Girls.

Scene 7
  "I Sing of Love"
    L. Kirk, H. Lang, Singing Ensemble

Scene 8
  Finale—"Kiss Me, Kate"
    P. Morison, A. Drake, Singing Emsemble
  Tarantella
    L. Kirk, H. Lang, Dancing Ensemble

ACT 2

Scene 1
  "Too Darn Hot"
    L. Fuller, F. Davis, E. Sledge
    Danced by F. Davis, E. Sledge, H. Lang, Dancing Ensemble.

Scene 3
  "Where Is the Life That Late I Led?"
    A. Drake

Scene 4
  "Always True to You (in My Fashion)"
    L. Kirk

Scene 6
  "Bianca"
    H. Lang, Singing Girls
    Danced by H. Lang, Dancing Girls.

---

[10]Peformed as an opera with no individual musical numbers listed.
[11]Wednesday, Friday, Sunday evenings, Saturday matinees.
[12]Tuesday, Thursday, Saturday evenings, Sunday matinees.
[13]Wednesday, Friday, Sunday evenings, Saturday matinees.
[14]Tuesday, Thursday, Saturday evenings, Sunday matinees.
[15]Wednesday, Friday, Sunday evenings, Saturday matinees.
[16]Tuesday, Thursday, Saturday evenings, Sunday matinees.
[17]Wednesday, Friday, Sunday evenings, Saturday matinees.
[18]Tuesday, Thursday, Saturday evenings, Sunday matinees.
[19]Tuesday-Sunday evenings.
[20]Saturday and Sunday matinees.
[21]Wednesday, Friday, Sunday evenings, Saturday matinees.
[22]Tuesday, Thursday, Saturday evenings, Sunday matinees.
[23]Wednesday, Friday, Sunday evenings, Saturday matinees.
[24]Tuesday, Thursday, Saturday evenings, Sunday matinees.
[25]Played a return engagement 8 January 1952 at the Brooadway Theatre for 8 performances. For detail, see 1951-52 season.

"So in Love" (reprise)
   A. Drake

Scene 7

"Brush Up Your Shakespeare"
   H. Clark, J. Diamond

Scene 8

"I Am Ashamed That Women Are So Simple"
   P. Morison
Finale
   A. Drake, P. Morison, Company

1949.01 ALONG FIFTH AVENUE

A Musical Revue in Two Acts, 24 Scenes. Sketches by Charles Sherman and Nat Hiken. Music by Gordon Jenkins. Lyrics by Tom Adair. Additional music and lyrics by Richard Stutz, Milton Pascal and Nat Hiken. Scenery by Oliver Smith. Costumes by David Ffolkes. Vocal coaching by Robert Lenn. Musical and vocal arrangements by Gordon Jenkins. Musical director, Irving Actman. Dances and musical numbers staged by Robert Sidney. Produced by Arthur Lesser. Opened 13 January 1949 at the Broadhurst Theatre, moved 21 February 1949 to the Imperial Theatre, and closed 18 June 1949 after 180 performances.[26]

CAST: NANCY WALKER, JACKIE GLEASON, HANK LADD, CAROL BRUCE, DONALD RICHARDS, VIOLA ESSEN, JOHNNY COY, VIRGINIA GORSKI, JUDYTH BURROUGHS, Joyce Mathews, Dick Bernie, George S. Irving, Zachary Solov, Lee Krieger, Wallace Seibert, Louise Kirtland.
   Singing Ensemble: Joan Coburn, Gloria Hayden, Candace Montgomery, Tina Prescott, Dorothy Pyren, Lucille Udovick, Ted Allison, Leonard Claret, Bob Neukum, Ken Renner, Bert Sheldon. *Dancing Ensemble*: Franca Baldwin, Tessie Carrano, Shellie Farrell, Marian Horosko, Gretchen Houser, Carol Nelson, Janet Sayers, Harry Asmus, Ted Cappy, Dante DiPaolo, Howard Malone, Walter Stane.

ACT 1

Scene 1

"Fifth Avenue"
   V. Gorski, Company

Scene 2

Sweet Surrender
   (*by* Nat Hiken)
   Miss Herkimer: N. Walker. *Mr. Farquarhar*: G. S. Irving. *Mr. Higgins*: D. Bernie.

Scene 3

"The Best Time of Day"
   C. Bruce, D. Di Paolo, B. Neukum, K. Renner, B. Sheldon

Scene 4

"A Window on the Avenue"
   (*Music by* Gordon Jenkins.)
   Window Dresser: Z. Solov. *Girls*: S. Farrell, M. Horosko, G. Houser. *Boys*: H. Asmus, H. Malone, W. Seibert.

Scene 5

"If This Is Glamour!"
   N. Walker
   (*Music by* Richard Stutz. *Lyrics by* Rick French.)

Scene 6

The Fifth Avenue Label
   (*by* Charles Sherman)
   Nurse: J. Mathews. *Doctor*: D. Bernie. *Ambulance Driver*: L. Krieger. *Patient*: J. Gleason. *Insurance Adjuster*: G. S. Irving. *Models*: T. Allison, K. Renner, W. Stane.

Scene 7

"Skyscraper Blues"
   D. Richards

Girl: V. Essen. *Boy*: Z. Solov. *Lovers*: M. Horosko, W. Seibert. *Young Girls*: F. Baldwin, S. Farrell. *Street Walkers*: T. Carrano, G. Houser, J. Sayers. *Men*: H. Asmus, D. DiPaolo, W. Stane.

Scene 8

   Hank Ladd

Scene 9:

"I Love Love in New York"
   Scene: Washington Square.
   Hurdy-gurdy Man: L. Krieger. *First Couple*: C. Bruce, D. Richards. *Second Couple*: V. Gorski, J. Coy. *Girls*: F. Baldwin, S. Farrell, M. Horosko, G. Houser, C. Nelson, J. Sayers. *Boys*: H. Asmus, D. DiPaolo, H. Malone, W. Seibert, Z. Solov, W. Stane.

Scene 10

"The Fugitive from Fifth Avenue"
   (*Music by* Richard Stutz. *Lyrics by* Nat Hiken.)
   Captain: L. Krieger. *Legionnaires*: T. Allison, D. Bernie, G. S. Irving. *The Fugitive*: J. Gleason.

Scene 11

   Hank Ladd

Scene 12

"Santo Dinero"
   N. Walker, V. Essen, Z. Solov, W. Seibert, L. Krieger, Singing, Dancing Ensembles
   (*Music by* Richard Stutz. *Lyrics by* Milton Pascal.)

ACT 2

Scene 1

"In the Lobby"
   Singing and Dancing Ensembles

Scene 2

What's in the Middle?
   (*by* Charles Sherman)
   Counter Girl: N. Walker. *Customer*: J. Gleason.
   Other Customers: D. Bernie, L. Claret, L. Krieger.
   Manager: G. S. Irving. *Assistant Counter Girl*: J. Mathews.
   Assistant Manager: B. Sheldon.

Scene 3

"Weep No More"
   C. Bruce

Scene 4

Mr. Rockefeller Builds His Dream House
   (*by* Mel Tolkin and Max Liebman)
   Guide: L. Krieger. *Visitors*: Singing Ensemble.
   Gentleman: H. Ladd.

Scene 5

"Challenge"
   (*Music by* Mel Pahl and Richard Stutz.)
   Hoofer: J. Coy. *Ballerina*: V. Essen.

Scene 6

"Chant D'Amour" (Irving)
   N. Walker
   (*Lyrics by* Nat Hiken.)

Scene 7

"Vacation in the Store"[27]
   Trio: G. Hayden, C. Montgomery, T. Prescott. And N. Walker, J. Gleason, C. Bruce, D. Richards, J. Coy, V. Gorski, Z. Solov, L. Krieger, W. Seibert, Company.

Scene 8

   Hank Ladd

Scene 9

"Call It Applefritters"
   Music by Richard Stutz. *Lyrics by* Milton Pascal.)
   Boy: H. Ladd. *Girl*: C. Bruce.

---

[26]Director uncredited. Program note: The Management acknowledges the assistance of Charles Friedman.

[27]Courtesy of Lord & Taylor.

Scene 10

Murder on Fifth Avenue

(*by* Charles Sherman)
Detective: D. Bernie. *Philip Ashton*: D. Richards.
Mrs. Schuyler: J. Mathews. *Butler*: T. Allison.
Inspector Maloney: J. Gleason. *Daisy*: N. Walker.
Mrs. Ashton: L. Kirtland. *Dr. Brown*: G. S. Irving.

Scene 11

"A Trip Doesn't Care at All"

(*Music by* Philip Kadison, *Lyrics by* Thomas Howell)
Pam: J. Burroughs. *Chris*: D. Richards.

Scene 12

Finale—"Fifth Avenue" (reprise)

(Entire Company)

1949.02

ALL FOR LOVE

A Musical Revue in Two Acts, 22 Scenes. Music and lyrics by Allan Roberts and Lester Lee. Sketch editor, Max Shulman. Production staged by Edward Reveaux. Choreography and musical numbers by Eric Victor. Scenery by Edward Gilbert. Costumes by Billy Livingston. Musical direction by Clay Warnick. Orchestrations by Ted Royal, Don Walker, (Robert) Russell Bennett, Hans Spialek. Produced by Sammy Lambert and Anthony Brady Farrell. Opened 22 January 1949 at the Mark Hellinger Theatre and closed 7 May 1949 after 121 performances.

CAST: GRACE and PAUL HARTMAN, BERT WHEELER, PATRICIA WYMORE, MILADA MLADOVA, DICK SMART, LENI LYNN, KATHRYNE MYLROIE, MILTON FROME, PAUL REED, BUDD ROGERSON, JUNE GRAHAM, RICHARD D'ARCY, Peter Gladke, Robert Shawley.

Singing Ensemble: Gloria Benson, Ann Blackburn, Ruth Edberg, Arlyne Frank, Marilyn Frechette, Janie Janvier, Helen Schurgot, Thomas Bowman, Arthur Carroll, Cary Conway, John Henson, Sid Lawson, Frank Stevens.

Dancing Ensemble: Janet Bethel, Norma Doggett, Jean Handzlik, Carol Lee, Tiny Shimp, Yvonne Tibor, Prue Ward, Helen Wenzel, Onna White, Verne Rogers, Jack Warner.

ACT 1

Scene 1

"All for Love"

Singing Girls and Boys, Dancing Girls and Boys

Scene 2

Fashion Expert

(*by* Jane Bishir)
Manager of Blatz Department Store: M. Frome. *Renee Mulfinger*: G. Hartman.
Signor Pignatelli: P. Hartman.

Scene 3

"My Baby's Bored"

P. Wymore, B. Rogerson

Scene 4

Morris, My Son

(*by* Billy K. Wells)
Foreword: B. Wheeler. *Withers*: M. Frome. *Ivy*: J. Janvier. *Lord Malcolm Twonkey*: B. Wheeler. *Olive*: P. Wymore.

Scene 5

"The Big Four"

(*Music paraphrased by* Peter Howard Weiss.)
Producer: M. Frome. *First Secretary*: C. Lee. *Second Secretary*: P. Ward.
Office Boy: J. Warner. *Agents*: F. Stevens, C. Conway, S. Lawson,
T. Bowman. *Jerry Redbreast*: E. Kristen. *Aggie Dee*: T. Shimp.
Mr. X. Jackson: P. Gladke. *Ellen LaMouris*: O. White. Dancing
Girls and Boys.

Scene 6

Isolde

(*by* Ted Luce, Grace and Paul Hartman)
Treadwell: P. Hartman. *Barton*: B. Wheeler. *Isolde*: G. Hartman.
Wagernick: D. Smart.

Scene 7

"Why Can't It Happen Again"

K. Mylroie
(*Music by* Michael Elmer. *Lyrics by* Sammy Gallop.)

Scene 8

"My Heart's in the Middle of July"

D. Smart, L. Lynn

Specialty Dance

P. Wymore, B. Rogerson, Dancing, Singing Ensembles

Scene 9

Lament

B. Wheeler

Scene 10

"It's a Living"

G. Hartman, P. Hartman

Scene 11

"Benjamin B. O'Dell"

Boy: D. Smart. *Girl*: L. Lynn. *Policeman*: M. Frome. *Captain*: B. Wheeler.
Chambermaid: G. Hartman. *Purser*: P. Hartman. *Sailors*: B. Thompson, P.
Gladke. *Balloon-man*: B. Shawley. *Little Girl*: J. Graham. *Little Boy*: R. D'Arcy.
P. Wymore, M. Mladova, K. Mylroie, B. Rogerson, Dancing and Singing
Ensembles.

ACT 2

Scene 1

"Prodigal Daughter"

(*Ballet Music by* Peter Howard Weiss.)
Dorothy, Crystal: J. Graham. *First Man in Her Life*: R. D'Arcy. *Honky-Tonk
Girls*: Y. Tibor, H. Wenzel, T. Shimp, J. Bethel, N. Doggett. *Jewel*: M. Mladova.
Shadow: O. White. And Singing and Dancing Ensembles.

Scene 2

Message to Our Sponsor

B. Wheeler

Scene 3

Sea Diver

(*by* J. Bishir)
Professor Pisces Beebe: P. Hartman. *Mrs. Beebe*: G. Hartman. *Sailor*: D. Smart.

Scene 4

"Run to Me, My Love"

L. Lynn, D. Smart

Scene 5

Mary Maggie O'Neil

(*by* Ted Luce, Grace and Paul Hartman)
Make-up Girl: J. Janvier. *Chief Peterson*: B. Wheeler. *Sonya*: J. Handzlik. *LeRoy*:
M. Frome. *Mary Maggie McNeil*: G. Hartman. *Cameramen*: C. Conway, S.
Lawson. *Hobart Havermill*: P. Hartman. *Make-up Girl*: M. Frechette. *Wardrobe
Man*: J. Henson. *Boy*: B. Shawley.

Scene 6

"No Time for Love"

P. Wymore, Be-Bop Boys

Scene 7

Flying Mare

(*by* Max Shulman)
Gus, first wrestler: P. Reed. *Al*, second wrestler: A. Carroll. *McNulty*: M. Frome.
Harold Minafee: B. Wheeler. *Georgeius Georgia*: V. Rogers. *Referee*: R. D'Arcy.
Seconds: J. Henson, B. Shawley.

Scene 8

"(A) Dreamer With a Penny"

D. Smart

Scene 9

"The Farrell Girl"

B. Rogerson, Boys

Scene 10

"Oh, How Fortunate You Mortals Be"

K. Mylroie

Scene 11
Finale
Entire Company

1949.03

CAROUSEL

A Revival of the Musical Play in Two Acts, Prelude and 8 Scenes[28]. Book and lyrics by Oscar Hammerstein II. Based on Ferenc Molnar's play "Liliom" as adapted by Benjamin F. Glazer. Music by Richard Rodgers. Production directed by Rouben Mamoulian. Danced by Agnes de Mille. Settings by Joe Mielziner. Costumes by Miles White. Production supervised by Lawrence Langner and Theresa Helburn. Musical director, Frederick Dvonch. Orchestrations by Don Walker. Produced by the Theatre Guild. Opened 25 January 1949 at the New York City Center, moved to the Majestic Theatre 22 February 1949, and closed 5 March 1949 after 49 performances.

CAST (in order of appearance): *Carrie Pipperidge*: MARGOT MOSER. *Julie Jordan*: IVA WITHERS, Jean Rogers (alt.). *Mrs. Mullin*: LOUISE LARABEE. *Billy Bigelow*: STEPHEN DOUGLASS, Warren Harr (alt.). *First Policeman*: Kenneth Knapp. *David Bascombe*: Ross Chetwynd. *Nettie Fowler*: CHRISTINE JOHNSON. *June Girl*: Mavis Ray. *Enoch Snow*: ERIC MATTSON. *Jigger Craigin*: MARIO DE LAVAL. *Hannah*: DUSTY WORRALL. *Boatswain*: KENNETH MacKENZIE. *Arminy*: Bobra Suiter. *Penny*: Evelyne Ross. *Jennie*: Audrey Sabetti. *Virginia*: Jean Rogers. *Susan*: Ruth Devorin. *Second Policeman*: Richmond Page. *Captain*: Warren Harr. *Heavenly Friend (Brother Joshua)*: Jay Velie. *Starkeeper*: Calvin Thomas. *Louise*: DIANE KEITH. *Carnival Boy*: KENNETH MacKENZIE. *Enoch Snow, Jr.*: Anthony Aleo. *Principal*: Kenneth Knapp.

Singers: Lonna Phillips, Jean Rogers, Edith Fitch, Evelyne Ross, Audrey Sabetti, Grace Bruns, Bobra Suiter, Ruth Devorin. Robert Davis, Richmond Page, Jerry Lucas, Warren Harr, Kenneth E. Knapp, Joseph Milly, Charles Scott, Anthony Aleo, Charles E. Wood, Jr.

Dancers: Karl Krauter, Lila Popper, Hazel Patterson, Shirley Andahazy, Jane Burroughs, Mildred Ferguson, Virginia Harris, Hilda Wagner, Meredith Baylis, Yolanda Novak. Lorand Andahazy, Stanley Herbert, Hubert Bland, Raymond Dorian, Joseph Camiolo, Martin Schneider, Marvin Krauter.

1949.04

SOUTH PACIFIC

A Musical Play in Two Acts, 23 Scenes. Book by Oscar Hammerstein II and Joshua Logan. Adapted from James A. Michener's novel "Tales of the South Pacific." Music by Richard Rodgers. Lyrics by Oscar Hammerstein II. Book and musical numbers staged by Joshua Logan. Scenery and lighting by Jo Mielziner. Costumes by Motley. Musical director, Salvatore Dell'Isola. Orchestrations by Robert Russell Bennett. Produced by Richard Rodgers and Oscar Hammerstein II in association with Leland Hayward and Joshua Logan. Opened 7 April 1949 at the Majestic Theatre, closing 16 May 1953 for a 6-week tour in Boston, resuming 29 June 1953 at the Broadway Theatre, and closed 16 January 1954 after 1925 performances.

CAST (in order of appearance): *Ngana*: Barbara Luna. *Jerome*: Michael DeLeon or Noel De Leon. *Henry*: Richard Silvera. *Ensign Nellie Forbush*: MARY MARTIN. *Emile de Becque*: EZIO PINZA. *Bloody Mary*: JUANITA HALL. *Bloody Mary's Assistant*: Musa Williams. *Abner*: Archie Savage. *Stewpot*: Henry Slate. *Luther Billis*: MYRON McCORMICK. *Professor*: Fred Sadoff. *Lt. Joseph Cable, U.S.M.C.*: WILLIAM TABBERT. *Capt. George Brackett, U.S.N.*: MARTIN WOLFSON. *Cmdr. William Harbison, U.S.N.*: HARVEY STEPHENS. *Yeoman Herbert Quale*: Alan Gilbert. *Sgt. Kenneth Johnson*: Thomas Gleason. *Seabee Richard West*: Dickinson Eastham. *Seabee Morton Wise*: Henry Michel. *Seaman Tom O'Brien*: Bill Dwyer. *Radio Operator Bob McCaffrey*: Biff McGuire. *Marine Cpl. Hamilton Steeves*: Jim Hawthorne. *Staff Sgt. Thomas Hassinger*: Jack Fontan. *Seaman James Hayes*: Beau Tilden. *Lt. Genevieve Marshall*: Jacqueline Fisher. *Ensign Dinah Murphy*: Rosyln Lowe. *Ensign Janet MacGregor*: Sandra Deel. *Ensign Cora MacRae*: Bernice Saunders. *Ensign Sue Yaeger*: Pat Northrop. *Ensign Lisa Minelli*: Gloria Meli. *Ensign Connie Walewska*: Mardi Bayne. *Ensign Pamela Whitmore*: Evelyn Colby. *Ensign Bessie Noonan*: Helena Schurgot. *Liat*: BETTA St. JOHN. *Marcel, Henry's Assistant*: Richard Loo. *Lt. Buzz Adams*: Don Fellows. *Islanders, Sailors, Marines, Officers*: Mary Ann Reeve, Chin Yu, Alex Nichol, Eugene Smith, Richard Loo, William Ferguson.

The action takes place on two islands in the South Pacific, during World War II.

---

[28]Original production opened 19 April 1945 at the Majestic Theatre for 890 performances. For Synopsis of Scenes and Musical Numbers, see original 1945 production.

Act 1, Scene 1: Emile de Becque's Plantation Home. *Scene 2*: Another Part of the Island. *Scene 3*: The Edge of a Palm Grove Near the Beach. *Scene 4*: The Company Street. *Scene 5*: Inside the Island Commander's Office. *Scene 6*: The Company Street. *Scene 7*: The Beach. *Scene 8*: Inside the Island Commander's Office. *Scene 9*: Another Part of the Island. *Scene 10*: Interior of Native Hut on Bali Ha'i. *Scene 11*: Near the Beach of Bali Ha'i. *Scene 12*: Emile's Terrace.

Act 2, Scene 1: The Stage during a Performance of "The Thanksgiving Follies." *Scene 2*: In Back of the Stage. *Scene 3*: The Stage. *Scene 4*: In Back of the Stage. *Scene 5*: The Communications Office. *Scene 6*: Another Part of the Island. *Scene 7*: The Communications Office. *Scene 8*: The Company Street. *Scene 9*: The Beach. *Scene 10*: The Company Street. *Scene 11*: Emile's Terrace.

ACT 1
Scene 1
"Dites-Moi"
    B. Luna, M. De Leon or N. De Leon
"A Cockeyed Optimist"
    M. Martin
("Twin Soliloquies")
    M. Martin, E. Pinza
"Some Enchanted Evening"
    E. Pinza
("Dites-Moi") (reprise)
    B. Luna, M. De Leon or N. De Leon
Scene 2
"Bloody Mary (Is the Girl I Love)"
    Sailors, Seabees, Marines
Scene 3
"There Is Nothin' Like a Dame"
    M. McCormick, Sailors, Seabees, Marines
"Bali Ha'i"
    J. Hall
Scene 7
"I'm Gonna Wash That Man Right Outa My Hair"
    M. Martin, Nurses
("Some Enchanted Evening") (reprise)
    E. Pinza, M. Martin
"(I'm in Love With) A Wonderful Guy"
    M. Martin, Nurses
Scene 9
("Bali Ha'i")(reprise)
    French Girls
Scene 10
"Younger Than Springtime"
    W. Tabbert
Scene 11
("Bali Ha'i")(reprise)
    French Girls
Scene 12
Finale
    M. Martin, E. Pinza

ACT 2
Scene 1
Soft Shoe Dance (Opening Act 2)
    Nurses, Seabees
Scene 2
"Happy Talk"
    J. Hall
("Younger Than Springtime")(reprise)
    W. Tabbert
Scene 3
"Honey Bun"
    M. Martin, M. McCormick
Scene 4
"You've Got to Be Carefully Taught"
    W. Tabbert

"This Nearly Was Mine"
E. Pinza

Scene 9

"Some Enchanted Evening" (reprise)
M. Martin

Scene 10

("Honey Bun") (reprise)
Sailors, Seabees, Marines

Scene 11

Finale
(M. Martin, E. Pinza, B. Luna, M. De Leon or N. De Leon)

1949.05 HOWDY, MR. ICE OF 1950

A Ice Skating Revue in Two Acts, 22 Scenes. Lyrics and music by Al Stillman and Alan Moran. Production by Sonart Productions, Inc. Executive Director, Arthur M. Wirtz. Production director, William H. Burke. Staged by Catherine Littlefield. Settings designed and created by Bruno Maine. Costumes by Grace Houston, Billy Livingston and Katherine Kuhn. Choreography by Catherine Littlefield, assisted by Dorothie Littlefield. Lighting effects by Eugene Braun. Skating direction by May Judels. Musical conductor, David Mendoza. Musical arrangements by Paul Van Loan. Produced by Sonja Henie and Arthur M. Wirtz. Opened 26 May 1949 at the Center Theatre and closed 15 April 1950 after 430 performances.

CAST: SKIPPY BAXTER, EILEEN SEIGH, HARRISON THOMSON, THE BRUISES (Monty Stott, Geoffe Stevens, Sid Spaulding), THE PRESTONS (Mickee, Paul), JINX CLARK, EDDIE BERRY, SID KROFFT, PAUL CASTLE, TRIXIE [Martha Escoe LaRue], BUSTER GRACE, JOHN KASPER, BUCK PENNINGTON, CISSY TRENHOLM, ART ERICKSON, JOHN WALSH. Vocals: NOLA FAIRBANKS, DICK CRAIG, FRED MARTELL, BILL DOUGLAS.
Skaters: Margaret Berry, Peggy Bauer, Josephine Belluccia, Dorothy Bergman, Evelyn Biderman, Ann Bovkin, Bernice Deane, Helen Dutcher, Walli Hackman, Pat Harrington, Gloria Haupt, Lynne Immes, Joan King, Pat Lemaire, Ann Liff, Marjorie Mahne, Marvette Mosic, Doris Nelson, Priscilla Paulson, Ragna Ray, Gerri Richardson, Rusty Rodgers, Lela Rolontz, Theresa Rothacker, Betty Smith, Jean Sturgeon, Eileen Thompson, Catherine Weber. Stanley Belliveau, Fred Brennen, Gerry Decker, Nicholas Dantos, Ralph Evans, John Farris, Kurt Fischman, Peter Fernandez, Louis Glessman, Ray Henderson, Dan Hurley, John Kasmarsik, James Kelly, Gary Keran, Ken Leslie, Ed McDonald, Frank Meyer, Kenneth Parker, James Patridge, Gus Patrick, James Paul, Stephen Stofka, William Taft, James Toth, Dan Touhy, Wally Van Sickle, William Waldren, William Wallenborn.

ACT 1

Scene 1

"Big City"
N. Fairbanks, B. Douglas, D. Craig, F. Martell
Girls: M. Barry, P. Bauer, J. Belluccia, D. Bergman, E. Biderman, A. Boykin, B. Deane, H. Dutcher, P. Harrington, G. Haupt, L. Immes, J. King, P. Lemaire, A. Liff, M. Mahne, M. Mosic, D. Nelson, P. Paulson, G. Richardson, L. Rolontz, T. Rothacker, B. Smith, E. Thompson, C. Webber. *Boys*: S. Belliveau, G. Decker, N. Dantos, R. Evans, K. Fischman, P. Fernandez, L. Glessman, R. Hendrickson, D. Hurley, J. Kasmarsik, G. Keran, B. Lee, H. Pope, E. McDonald, F. Meyer, K. Parker, G. Patrick, L. Stofka, S. Stofka, W. Taft, J. Toth, D. Tuohy, W. Wadren, W. Wallenborn.

Scene 2

At Your Service

"We're the Doormen of New York"
D. Craig, F. Martell, B. Douglas
Doormen: B. Grace, B. Pennington, J. Farris.

Scene 3

Man About Town
Man: E. Berry. *Policeman*: A. Erickson.

Scene 4

"Hearts Aglow"
N. Fairbanks, B. Douglas, D. Craig, F. Martell
Pair: C. Trenholm, J. Walsh. *Cupids*: M. Barry, E. Biderman, G. Bleckman, H. Dutcher, W. Hackman, L. Rolontz, T. Rothacker, E. Thompson. *Desires*: P. Bauer, J. Belluccia, B. Dean, P. Harrington, G. Haupt, L. Immes, J. King, P. Lemaire, A. Liff, M. Mahne, M. Mosic, D. Nelson, P. Paulson, R. Ray, G. Richardson, B. Smith, C. Webber. *Beaux*: G. Decker, N. Dantos, P. Fernandez,

L. Glessman, R. Hendrickson, D. Hurley, J. Kasmarsik, G. Keran, J. Paul, G. Patrick, L. Stofka, S. Stofka, J. Toth, D. Tuohy, W. Van Sickle, W. Waldren.

Scene 5

Puppet Artistry (presented by Sid Krofft)

Scene 6

The Prestons

Scene 7

On High
B. Grace, J. Sturgeon, R. Rodgers
"You Was"
N. Fairbanks, F. Martell

Scene 8

The Cradle of Jazz
"Rocked in the Cradle of Jazz"
B. Douglas, D. Craig
Rhythm Man: B. Pennington. *Cocottes*: E. Biderman, D. Nelson, G. Haupt. *Blues Boys and Girls*: J. Belluccia, A. Boykin, P. Leamire, M. Mosic, P. Paulson, G. Richardson, D. Hurley, B. Lee, J. Kasmarsik, L. Stofka, W. Taft, D. Tuohy. *Cakewalkers*: B. Bauer, T. Rothacker, J. Farris, L. Glessman. *Strutters*: P. Fernandez, R. Hendrickson, G. Patrick, J. Paul, S. Stofka, W. Van Sickle. *Mr. Strut*: J. Walsh. *Flappers*: B. Deane, P. Harrington, J. King, A. Liff, B. Smith, C. Webber. *Kampus Kids*: R. Ray, J. Kasper. *Boogie Woogie*: M. Barry, D. Bergman, H. Dutcher, W. Hackman, L. Rolontz, E. Thompson, G. Decker, N. Dantos, K. Leslie, E. McDonald, K. Parker, J. Toth. *Jitterbugs*: M. Mahne, A. Erickson.

Scene 9

Mercury
Mercury: S. Baxter. *Pandora*: J. Clark. *Maidens*: W. Hackman, L. Rolontz, E. Thompson.

Scene 10

Bouncing Ball of the Ice
F. Trenkler
Seeress: J. Farris.

Scene 11

"48 States"
D. Craig
Inquiring Reporter: D. Craig. *Matron*: N. Fairbanks. *Schoolgirls*: T. Rothacker, J. Sturgeon. *Ladies and Gentlemen of the Ensemble*: M. Barry, P. Bauer, J. Belluccia, D. Bergman, E. Biderman, A. Boykin, B. Deane, H. Dutcher, W. Hackman, P. Harrington, G. Haupt, L. Immes, J. King, A. Liff, M. Mahne, M. Mosic, P. Paulson, R. Ray, G. Richardson, L. Rolontz, B. Smith, E. Thompson, C. Webber, S. Belliveau, G. Decker, R. Evans, P. Fernandez, L. Glessman, R. Hendrickson, D. Hurley, J. Kasmarsik, G. Keran, B. Lee, K. Leslie, E. McDonald, F. Meyer, K. Parker, J. Paul, G. Patrick, H. Pope, S. Stofka, W. Taft, J. Toth, D. Tuohy, W. Van Sickle, W. Waldren, W. Wallenborn. *Golden Eagle*: E. Seigh. *Pilots*: B. Grace, J. Kasper, J. Sisk, J. Walsh.

ACT 2

Scene 1

The Sleeping Beauty

The Princess' Birthday:
Princess Aurora: J. Clark. *King*: A. Erickson. *Queen*: E. Thompson. *Maids of Honor*: J. Belluccia, E. Biderman, G. Bleckman, B. Deane, G. Haupt, L. Immes, J. King, A. Liff, M. Mosic, D. Nelson, P. Paulson, R. Ray, T. Rothacker. *Prince from the East*: W. Van Sickle. *Prince from the West*: B. Pennington. *Prince from the North*: J. Farris. *Prince from the South*: J. Walsh. *Guards*: F. Meyer, W. Wallenborn.

A Remote Tower:
Wicked Fairy: J. Kasper. *Good Fairy*: C. Trenholm.

The Forest:
Prince Desire: H. Thomson. *The Archers*: D. Hurley, J. Paul, G. Patrick, L. Stofka, S. Stofka, W. Waldren.

The Sleeping Castle:
Ladies in Waiting: M. Barry, E. Biderman, H. Dutcher, W. Hackman, P. Harrington, B. Smith. *Courtiers*: P. Bauer, D. Bergman, A. Boykin, P. Lemaire, M. Mahne, G. Richardson, L. Rolontz, C. Webber, G. Decker, R. Evans, P. Fernandez, L. Glessman, G. Keran, H. Pope, W. Taft, D. Touhy.

Scene 2

In Every Port
Sailors: B. Grace, E. Berry, B. Pennington. *Mermaid*: R. Rodgers. *Little Brown Girl*: J. Sturgeon. *Monkey*: K. Leslie.

Scene 3

Romantic Variations

Valse: E. Seigh. *Beguine*: S. Baxter.

Scene 4

Trinidad Wharf

"Plenty More Fish in the Sea"

N. Fairbanks, B. Douglas, D. Craig, F. Martell

Calypso Pete: J. Walsh. *Tropical Siren*: C. Trenholm. *Islanders*: M. Barry, P. Bauer, J. Belluccia, D. Bergman, G. Bleckman, A. Boykin, B. Deane, H. Dutcher, P. Harrington, L. Immes, J. King, P. Lemaire, M. Mahne, M. Mosic, D. Nelson, P. Paulson, R. Ray, T. Rothacker, B. Smith, C. Webber, S. Belliveau, R. Evans, G. Decker, N. Dantos, P. Fernandez, L. Glessman, R. Hendrickson, G. Keran, B. Lee, F. Meyer, K. Parker, J. Paul, G. Patrick, H. Pope, S. Stofka, W. Taft, J. Toth, D. Tuohy, W. Van Sickle, W. Waldren.

Scene 5

Trixie, assisted by L. Stofka.

Scene 6

Flirtation

Mam'zelle: M. Preston. *Bellhop*: P. Preston.

Scene 7

The Bluebirds

E. Seigh, S. Baxter

Scene 8

Reflections in the Dark

Ladies of the Ensemble

"If I Only Knew"

N. Fairbanks, F. Martell

Scene 9

The Bruises

M. Stott, G. Stevens, S. Spaulding

Scene 10

"The World's Greatest Show"

N. Fairbanks, B. Douglas, D. Craig, F. Martell

Ringmaster: H. Thomson. *Clowns*: S. Belliveau, N. Dantos, P. Fernandez, J. Kasmarsik, L. Glessman, R. Hendrickson, G. Keran, K. Leslie, E. McDonald, F. Meyer, K. Parker, L. Stofka, W. Taft, W. Waldren. *Elephant Girls*: G. Haupt, P. Lemaire, A. Liff, P. Paulson, R. Ray, C. Webber. *Tumblers*: R. Evans, B. Lee, J. Paul, G. Patrick, D. Tuohy, W. Van Sickle. *Trainer*: C. Trenholm. *Gold Leopards*: E. Biderman, B. Deane, P. Harrington, J. King, D. Nelson, G. Richardson. *Trainer*: J. Walsh. *Black Panthers*: M. Barry, D. Bergman, W. Hackman, M. Mosic, T. Rothacker, G. Bleckman. *Giant*: B. Grace. *Giantess*: R. Rodgers. *Snake Charmer*: J. Sturgeon. *Ranee*: P. Bauer, M. Mahne. *Rajah*: B. Pennington. *Aerialists*: J. Clark, J. Belluccia, B. Smith, H. Dutcher, L. Immes, J. Farris, J. Kasper. *Acrobats*: M. Preston, P. Preston. *Trixie. Equestrienne*: E. Seigh. *Horses*: P. Fernandez, W. Wallenborn, D. Hurley, J. Toth. *Cowboys*: E. Berry, J. Sisk. *Billy the Kid*: S. Baxter. *Strongman*: A. Erickson.

Scene 11

Finale

1949–1950 SEASON

Carol Channing in GENTLEMEN PREFER BLONDES (Photo: Maurice Seymour)
Billy Rose Theatre Collection, New York Public Library for the Performing Arts

1949–1950 SEASON

1949.06   FUNZAPOPPIN'

A Vaudeville Revue in Two Acts, 20 Scenes. Conceived by Ole Olsen [John Siguard Olsen], Chic Johnson [Harold Ogden Johnson] and Arthur M. Wirtz. Executive director, Arthur M. Wirtz. Assistant executive director, William H. Burke. Music and lyrics by Ole Olsen, Chic Johnson, Chuck Gould and Perry Martin. Choreography and staging by Catherine Littlefield, assisted by Carl Littlefield. Musical director, Jack Pfeiffer. Musical arrangements by Paul Van Loan. Settings, properties designed by Becker Brothers Studios. Directed by Olsen and Johnson. Produced by Arthur M. Wirtz. Opened 30 June 1949 at Madison Square Garden and closed 31 July 1949 after 37 performances.

CAST: OLE OLSEN, CHIC JOHNSON, MARTY MAY, NIRSKA, GLORIA GILBERT, CLARK BROTHERS, THE CHORALEERS, GLORIA SHORT, WILLIAM [Bill] HAYES, JUNE JOHNSON, J. C. OLSEN, THE BERRY BROTHERS, RAY DORIAN, The Three Jigsaws, Six Mighty Atoms, Lee Barrie, Lou Barrison, Shirley Ann Basso, Irene Billings, Chiampi, Red Breen, Eugenie Carlson, Frank Cook, Dixon & Dugan, Frank Harty, Baron Hopper, John Howes, Jack Joyce, Billy Kay, Happy Kellems, Joe Madden, Helen Magna, Maurice Millard, Pat Moran, Andy Ratouscheff, Shorty Renna, Russ Sobey, Georges Suzanne, Andy Wollandi.

The Choraleers: Audrey Calib, Mignon Chappell, Nora Dee, Norma Hawkins, Jacqueline Paul, Rita Stevans, Carl Bryson, Lynford Cautz, Ward Ohrman, Fred Smythe, Alan Stone, John Tantillo.

The Ensemble: Anna Andrews, Shirley Ann Basso, Sonya Besant, Iris Burton, Marie Camadeca, Connie Codilis, Celeste Cowan, Georgine Darcy, Juanita M. Eastman, Norma Ek, Dolores Frazzini, Juanita Given, Caroline Grant, Barbara C. Greaves, Joyce Harley, Nancy Heck, Jeanette Heller, Betty Kallas, Marion Kallas, Joy Kerber, May Kirby, Florence Leighton, Eleanor Lynne, Dorothy Macy, Beverly McNichols, June Miller, Candace Monte, Sharon O'Neill, Joyce O'Rourke, Nancy O'Rourke, Billy Patridge, Victoria Risch. Inger Van Jepmond, Dawn Zarlinga, Raymond Dorian, Albert Fiorella, Phillip Gerard, Joseph Kaminski, Jack Tygett.

Prelude
    J. C. Olsen, M. May

ACT 1
Scene 1
    "Oh, What a Nite for a Party"
    (Music and Lyrics by Olsen and Johnson and Chuck Gould.)
    B. Hayes, Choraleers, J. C. Olsen, O. Olsen, C. Johnson
Scene 2
    Bedlam
      O. Olsen, C. Johnson, Company
Scene 3
    Dancing Feet
      Berry Brothers
Scene 4
    Men About Town
      O. Olsen, C. Johnson
Scene 5
    "Jungle Rhythm"
      B. Hayes, P. L. Taylor Trio,
      Mighty Atoms, Choraleers, Dancing and Singing Boys and Girls
Scene 6
    Perjury in Pittsburgh
      O. Olsen, C. Johnson, M. May, J. Johnson, J. Howes
Scene 7
    Daisies Won't Tell
      The 36 Precisionists
Scene 8
    Baby Sitters
      O. Olsen, C. Johnson, J. Johnson, J. C. Olsen, Little People
    "I'd Like to Be a Baby Sitter for a Baby Like You"
    (Music and Lyrics by Olsen and Johnson and Perry Martin.)
Scene 9
    Here Comes Cookie
      F. Cook

Scene 10
    "It's a Great Wide Wonderful World"
    (a) Bridal Party
      J. Johnson, B. Hayes
    (b) Venice
      Choraleers
    (c) East India
      G. Short, R. Dorian
    (d) Berry Brothers in Harlem
Scene 11
    "Swing on the Corner"
    (Music and Lyrics by Olsen and Johnson and Chuck Gould.)
Finale
    O. Olsen, C. Johnson, Entire Company

ACT 2
Scene 1
    The Good Old West: "Six Gun Joe from Cicero"
    O. Olsen, C. Johnson, M. May, J. C. Olsen, J. Johnson, Company
    (Music and Lyrics by Olsen and Johnson and Chuck Gould.)
    (a) Street Scene, (b) Saloon Interior, (c) Along to the Arctic, (d) Back to the Bar
Scene 2
    Marty May
Scene 3
    The Barber Shop
      O. Olsen, C. Johnson, M. May, J. Johnson, Company
Scene 4
    Ballet Beautiful
      G. Gilbert
Scene 5
    The Escape Artist
      C. Johnson
Scene 6
    Foolin' Around
      O. Olsen, C. Johnson, J. C. Olsen
Scene 7
    "Hoe Down" (The audience is in the act.)
Scene 8
    Give Away Time
Scene 9
    Jam Session
      F. Cook, R. Sobey (tap Dancer), Berry Brothers,
      H. Magna (miniature Miranda), J. C. Olsen, A. Ratsoucheff,
      P. Moran (tumbler), L. Barrison (stilt dancer), J. Joyce (one-legged dancer)
Scene 10
    Finale—"Funzapoppin'"
      O. Olsen, C. Johnson, Entire Company
    (Music and Lyrics by Olsen and Johnson and Chuck Gould)

1949.07   CABALGATA

A Spanish Musical Cavalcade (Revue) in Two Acts, 19 Scenes[1]. Produced and directed by Daniel Cordoba. Musical director, Ramon Bastida. Choreography by Daniel Cordoba. Settings by Luis Marquez. Costumes by Daniel Cordoba. Musical arrangements and orchestrations by Ramon Bastida. Presented by Sol Hurok. Opened 7 July 1949 at the Broadway Theatre and closed 10 September 1949 after 76 performances.

CAST: *Dancers*: CARMEN VAZQUEZ, PEPITA MARCO, FLORIANA ALBA, PILAR CALVO, AUREA REYES, JOSE TOLEDANO, PACO FERNANDEZ, JULIE TOLEDO, SEBASTIAN CASTRO, FERNANDO VARGAS, Violeta Carrillo, Maria Castan, Pepita Durango, Conchita Escobar, Carmen Gamez, Luisa Garcia, Paloma Larios, Zenia Lopez, Teresa Martinez, Catalina Maytorena, Elba Ocaiza, Pepita Ramirez, Gracia Rios, Rocio Santisteban, Malena Telmo, Armonia Villa, Andres

---

[1]Title changed to A NIGHT IN SPAIN during the run and for subsequent tour.

Aguirre, Carlos Castro, Gustavo Delgado, Raul Izquierdo, Gustavo Garzon, Guillermo Marin, Fernando Marti, Rene Ochoa, Luis Riestra, Ricardo Solano, Jose Valois, Juan Villarias.

Singers: MIGUEL HERRERO, ROSA DeAVILA, ENRIQUE BARRERA, VICTOR TORRES, RAFAEL HERNAN.

Concert Pianist: JOSE CORTES. *Guitars*: PACO MILLET, MANUEL MEDINA.

ACT 1

"The Wedding of Luis Alonso"
(*Music by* Gerónimo Giménez y Bellido.)

Scene 1

A Garden in Valencia.

Vignette of the customs of the region.

1. "Song of Valencia"
(*Music by* Giner.)
2. "Women of Valencia"
(*Music by* Bastida.)
3. Regional Dances (popular)
Dancers: P. Marco, F. Alba, A. Reyes, J. Toledano, J. Toledo, S. Castro, Corps de Ballet. *Singers*: R. de Avila, E. Barrera, R. Hernan.

Scene 2

"Zambra" (Gypsy Dance)
(*Music by* Soutullo and Juan Vert y Carbonell.)
P. Calvo, P. Fernandez

Scene 3

"Petenera"—A woman is tortured by stigma.
(*Music by* Manuel Quiroga.)
Dancer: C. Vazquez. *Singer*: M. Herrero. *Guitars*: P. Millet, M. Medina.

Scene 4

"Salmantina"—Provincial dance.
(*Music by* Monreal.)
P. Marco

Scene 5

Dance School—Seville in the period of 1840.
Rivalry between the classical and popular schools of dance.
(*Music by* Latorre.)
F. Alba, P. Calvo, A. Reyes, P. Fernandez, S. Castro, Corps de Ballet

Scene 6

"Tanguillo"—Three Flamenco Boys (popular)
Dancers: J. Toledano, J. Toledo, F. Vargas. *Guitars*: P. Millet, M. Medina.

Scene 7

"Asturias" (Castenet Dance)
((*Music by* Isaac Albéniz.)
C. Vazquez

Scene 8

Three Popular Songs
(*Music by* Manuel deFalla.)
R. de Avila assisted at the piano by J. Cortes
1. "Castellana" (Dance)
F. Vargas, L. Garcia
2. "La Nana" (Dance)
F. Alba
3. "El Pano Muruno" (Dance)
J. Toledano, P. Fernandez

Scene 9

An Inn in Seville—Vignette
1. "Fandangos" (popular)
P. Calvo, F. Vargas, Corps de Ballet
2. Jealousy
(*Music by* Manuel Quiroga.)
C. Vazquez, M. Herrero
3. The Shellfish Vendor (popular)
P. Fernandez
4. "La Chunga"
(*Music by* Monreal.)
P. Marco, J. Toledo
5. The Bootblack (popular)
J. Toledano

6. "Espanola"
(*Music by* Pablo Luna y Carné.)
R. de Avila
7. "Alegrias": Dance of Cadiz (popular)

ACT 2

Scene 1

Glory and Blood—Madrid at the time of Goya (1808).
The joy and tragedy of bullfighting.
(*Music by* Francisco Asenjo Barbieri.)
Arrival at the Bull Ring; Girls and Toreadors; The Bullfight; Tragedy; Road to Glory
Dancers: P. Marco, A. Reyes, J. Toledano, P. Fernandez, J. Toledo, S. Castro, F. Vargas, Corps de Ballet. *Singers*: M. Herrero, R. de Avila, E. Barrera, V. Torres, R. Hernan.

Scene 2

Sevilla—Dance
(*Music by* Isaac Albéniz.)
C. Vargas

Scene 3

"Jota"
(*Music by* Joaquín Larregla.)
Piano solo by J. Cortes

Scene 4

Madrid 1900—Mazurka
(*Music by* Frederico Chueca and Joaquin Valverde.)
F. Alba, J. Toledo

Scene 5

Los Piconeros—Andalucia
(*Music by* Manuel Quiroga.)
Singer: M. Herrero. *Dancers*: P. Calvo, J. Toledano, P. Fernandez.

Scene 6

Galician Airs—Vignette
1. Dawn
(*Music by* Caballero.)
2. Song of the Washerwomen (popular)
3. Farewell of the Emigrant
(*Music by* Amadeo Vives.)
4. Song of the Fishermen (popular)
5. "La Muniera" dance
(*Music by* Amadeo Vives.)
Dancers: F. Alba, P. Marco, A. Reyes, J. Toldeo, S. Castro, F. Vargas, Corps de Ballet. *Singers*: R. de Avila, E. Barrera.

Scene 7

Andaluza
(*Music by* Enrique Granados y Campiña.)
C. Vazquez, J. Toledano, P. Fernandez

Scene 8

Popular Songs
Singer: M. Herrero. *Guitars*: P. Millet, M. Medina.

Scene 9

Classic Bolero—18th Century (popular)
A. Reyes, S. Castro

Scene 10

"Rondalla Aragonesa"—Vignette
1. Popular Songs
2. Serenaders
(*Music by* Monreal.)
3. Dance of the "Ribbon-Pole"
4. "Jota"
(*Music by* Tomás Bretón y Hernández .)
Dancers: P. Marco, A. Reyes, J. Toledo, S. Castro, Corps de Ballet. *Singers*: E. Barrera, V. Torres, R. Hernan. *Guitars*: P. Millet, M. Medina.

Finale

1949.08

MISS LIBERTY

A Musical Comedy in Two Acts, 12 Scenes. Music and lyrics by Irving Berlin. Book by Robert E. Sherwood. Directed by Moss Hart. Dances and musical numbers staged by Jerome Robbins. Settings and lighting by Oliver Smith. Costumes by Motley. Musical director, Jay Blackton. Orchestrations by Don Walker. Dance arrangements, Genevieve Pitot. Vocal arrangements by Jay Blackton. Piano arrangements, Helmy Kresa. Produced by Irving Berlin, Robert E. Sherwood and Moss Hart. Opened 15 July 1949 at the Imperial Theatre and closed 8 April 1950 after 308 performances.

CAST (in order of appearance): *Maisie Dell*: MARY McCARTY. *The Herald Reader*: Rowan Tudor. *James Gordon Bennett*: CHARLES DINGLE. *Horace Miller*: EDDIE ALBERT. *Police Captain*: Evans Thornton. *The Mayor*: Donald McClelland. *French Ambassador*: Emile Renan. *Carthwright*: Sid Lawson. *Joseph Pulitzer*: PHILIP BOURNEUF. *The Sharks*: Bill Bradley, Allen Knowles, Kazimir Kokic, Robert Pagent. *Bartholdi*: HERBERT BERGHOF. *The Models*: Stephanie Augustine, Trudy DeLuz, Marilyn Frechette. *Monique Dupont*: ALLYN McLERIE. *The Boy*: TOMMY RALL. *The Girl*: Maria Karnilova. *The Acrobats*: Virginia Cowell, Joe Milan, Eddie Phillips. *Strong Man*: Kazimir Kokic. *The Countess*: ETHEL GRIFFIES. *A Lover*: Ed Chappel. *His Girl*: Helene Whitney. *A Gendarme*: Rober Penn. *A Lamplighter*: Johnny V. R. Thompson. *Another Lamplighter*: TOMMY RALL. *A Socialite*: Marilyn Frechette. *An Actress*: Helene Whitney. *A Minister*: Ed Chappel. *An Admiral*: Robert Patterson. *The Boys*: Bob Kryl, Ernest Laird. *The Mother*: Elizabeth Watts. *The Policeman*: Evans Thornton. *The Brothers*: Lewis Bolyard, David Collyer. *The Train*: Eddie Phillips, Erik Kristen, Joseph Milan. *Reception Delegation*: Dolores Goodman, Virginia Conwell, Fred Hearn, Bob Tucker, Allen Knowles. *A Maid*: Gloria Patrice. *The Dandy*: TOMMY RALL. *Ruby*: Maria Karnilova. *A Sailor*: Eddie Phillips. *His Girl*: Dolores Goodman. *Richard K. Fox*: Donald McClelland. *The Judge*: Erik Kristen. *A Policeman*: Robert Patterson. *Immigration Officer*: Evans Thornton. *A Boy*: William Calhoun.

Singers: Stephanie Augustine, Irene Carroll, Trudy DeLuz, Marilyn Frechette, Estelle Gardner, Norma Larkin, Yolanda Renay, Helene Whitney. Lewis Bolyard, Ed Chappel, David Collyer, Billy Hogue, Sid Lawson, Robert Patterson, Robert Penn, John Sheehan, Evans Thornton. *Dancers*: Virginia Conwell, Coy Dare, Norma Doggett, Dolores Goodman, Patricia Hammerlee, Norma Kaiser, Gloria Patrice, Janice Rule, Tiny Shimp. Bill Bradley, Fred Hearn (Captain), Allen Knowles, Kazimir Kokic, Erik Kristen, Joe Milan, Robert Pagent, Eddie Phillips, Bob Tucker. *Newsboys*: William Calhoun, Ronald Kane, Bob Kryl, Ernest Laird, Kevin Mathews, Rusty Slocum.

Act 1, Scene 1: Printing House Square. *Scene 2*: Bartholdi's Studio in Paris. *Scene 3*: Bennett's Office. *Scene 4*: Under a Paris Bridge.

Act 2, Scene 1: Cabin on the RMS "Aurania." *Scene 2*: The Waterfront. *Scene 3*: North River Dock. *Scene 4*: On Tour. *Scene 5*: Salon in the Fifth Avenue Hotel. *Scene 6*: Walhalla Hall. (The Policeman's Ball) *Scene 7*: Castle Garden. *Scene 8*: Finale.

ACT 1
"Extra, Extra"
   Newsboys, Ensemble
"What Do I Have to Do to Get My Picture Took?"
   M. McCarty, E. Albert, Dancers
"The Most Expensive Statue in the World"
   P. Bourneuf, C. Dingle, D. McClelland, Singers, Dancers
"A Little Fish in a Big Pond"
   E. Albert, M. McCarty, B. Bradley, A. Knowles, K. Kokic, R. Pagent
"Let's Take an Old-Fashioned Walk"
   E. Albert, A. McLerie, Singers, Dancers
"Homework"
   M. McCarty
"Paris Wakes Up and Smiles"
   J. V. R. Thompson, A. McLerie, Ensemble
"Only for Americans"
   E. Griffies, E. Albert, Singers, Dancers
"Just One Way to Say I Love You"
   E. Albert, A. McLerie
ACT 2
"Miss Liberty"
   Entire Company
"The Train"
   A. McLerie, E. Phillips, E. Kristen, J. Milan
   (*Dance Arrangement by* Trudi Rittman.)
"You Can Have Him"
   M. McCarty, A. McLerie
"The Policeman's Ball"
   M. McCarty, T. Rall, Ensemble
"Homework" (reprise)
   M. McCarty
"Follow the Leader Jig"
   Ensemble

"Me and My Bundle"
   E. Albert, A. McLerie, Company
"Falling Out of Love Can Be Fun"
   M. McCarty
"Give Me Your Tired, Your Poor"
   A. McLerie, Singers
   (*Lyric by* Emma Lazarus from the poem "The New Colossus.")

KEN MURRAY'S BLACKOUTS OF 1949

1949.09

A Vaudeville Revue in Two Acts, 20 Scenes. Entire show conceived, produced and directed by Ken Murray. Musical director, Bert Shefter. Special dialogue and comedy material by Royal Foster. Gowns designed by Betty Colburn Kreisel. Musical arrangements, A. M. Courage. Setting, Ben Tipton; Sky background, Leo Atkinson. Electric traveling sign, Imagineering. Presented by David W. Siegel. Opened 6 September 1949 at the Ziegfeld Theatre and closed 15 October 1949 after 51 performances.

CAST: KEN MURRAY, NICK LUCAS, PAT WILLIAMS, GEORGE BURTON, OWEN McGIVENEY, JACK MULHALL, HARRIS and SHORE, LES ZORIS (Claudine Baudin, Robert Gross), MILTON CHARLESTON, PEG LEG BATES, SHELTON BROOKS, D'Vaughn Pershing, Charles Nelson, Alphonse Berge, Dot Remy, Elizabeth Walters, Irene Kaye, Hightower and Ross, Al Mardo, Danny Duncan, Danny Alexander, Joe Wong.
The Enchanters: Darla Hood, Bob Decker, Val Ground, Sheldon Disrud, Bob Wollter. *The Glamourlovelies*: LoRayne Anderson, Phyllis Applegate, Consuelo Cezon, Bettye Meade, Jean Marshall, Joan Morley, Crystal White, Joy Windsor, The Corbett Twins (Jean, JoAnn). *The Elderlovelies*: Rose DeHaven, Ethel Getty, Mabel Hart, Sally Hale, Perle Kincaid, Mattie Kennedy, Julia Wright, Mable Butterworth. *Miss 1949*: Darla Hood.

ACT 1
Scene 1
"Hollywood and Vine"
   (*Music and Lyrics by* Charles Henderson and Royal Foster.)
   Movie Extra: J. Morley. *Woman in Slacks*: M. Hart. *Twins*: Corbett Twins.
   Peter, the Hermit: D. Duncan. *Newsboy*: B. Decker. *Broadway Playboy*:
   B. Wollter. *Maharajah*: V. Grund. *Prospector*: S. Disrud. *Miss Iowa*:
   D. Hood. *Veronica*: I. Kaye. *Plaza Doorman*: S. Brooks. *Bette Davis*:
   C. Cezon. *Chinese Laundryman*: J. Wong. *Shoe Shine Boy*:
   D. Alexander. *Strolling Couple*: B. Ross, M. Charleston. *Sailor*:
   R. Hightower.
Scene 2
Now and Then
   Glamourlovelies, Elderlovelies
Scene 3
Introducing Your Host—Ken Murray
Scene 4
Pat Williams
Scene 5
Three Idle Rumors
Scene 6
Ecstasy in F
   Harris and Shore
Scene 7
Shelton Brooks
Scene 8
Bridal Night
   Groom: J. Mulhall. *Bride*: J. Marshall. *Bell-Hop*: D. Alexander.
   Bridesmaids: I. Kaye, B. Ross, J. Morley. *Hotel Guest*: K. Murray.
Scene 9
Jungle Fantasy with Les Zoris
   Vocal Specialty: The Enchanters. *Dance Specialty*: C. White.
   Jungle Man: R. Gross. *Leopard*: C. Baudin. *Girls of the Forest*:
   The Glamourlovelies.
Scene 10
D'Vaughn Pershing
Scene 11
Charles Nelson

Scene 12

Burton's Birds

America's Most Outstanding Novelty Act, introducing "Bill & Coo," the stars of Ken Murray's Academy Award film.

ACT 2

Scene 1

Al Mardo—"This shouldn't happen to a man."

Scene 2

"Blackouts' Television Newsreel

Scene 3

"The New Look"—Alphonse Berge

Models: L. Anderson, J. Morley, C. White, C. Cezon, J. Windsor, J. Marshall, B. Meade, P. Applegate, C. Twins. Maid: E. Walters.

Scene 4

Nick Lucas

Scene 5

Owen McGiveney—The World's Greatest Quick-Change Artist[2] in a page from "Oliver Twist."

Scene: Sike's Garret. Time: An hour before dawn.
Monks, Nancy, Fagin, Bill Sikes,The Artful Dodger: O. McGiveney.

Scene 6

Nautical Moments

Pirates: The Glamourlovelies. Long John Silver: P. L. Bates.

Scene 7

'Blackouts of 1949' Sports Parade

Archery: B. Meade. Ice-Skating: D. Hood. Cowgirl: L. Anderson. Golf: J. Morley. Baseball: C. Cezon. Hunting: C. Twins. Skiing: J. Marshall. Swimming: P. Applegate. Fishing: J. Windsor.

Scene 8

Finale

THE MIKADO,
1949.10 or The Town of Titipu

A Revival of the Comic Opera in Two Acts[3]. Libretto by W. S. Gilbert. Music by Arthur Sullivan. Musical director, Lehman Engel. Directed by S. M. Chartok. Scenery and lighting by Ralph Alswang. Costumes by Peggy Morrison. Production manager, Lewis Pierce. Produced by S. M. Chartok. Opened 4 October 1949 at the Mark Hellinger Theatre and closed 8 October 1949 after 7 performances.

CAST: Nanki-Poo: MORTON BOWE. Pish-Tush: EARLE MacVEIGH. Pooh-Bah: ROBERT ECKLES. Ko-Ko: RALPH RIGGS. Yum-Yum: KATHLEEN ROCHE. Pitti-Sing: BEVERLY JANIS. Peep-Bo: ELAINE MALBIN. The Mikado of Japan: JOSEPH MACAULAY. Katisha: JEAN HANDZLIK. Go-To: Craig Timberlake.

Nobles and Schoolgirls: Joyce Carroll, Dolores de Puglia, Natalye Green, Patricia Hall, Annabelle Lee, Marie Petek, Trudy Prager, Elsa Shannon, Martha Aleson, Phyllis Blake, Dorothy Johnson, Helen Stanton, Mia Stenn, Stanley Ames, Thomas Batten, Joseph Caruso, Anthony Cerami, Edwin Easter, Frank Gagliardi, Joseph Mazzolini, James Vitale, Howard Andricola, William Diehl, Samuel Lirkman, Mathew Powers, John Salter, Glen Scander, Jack Shannon, Craig Timberlake. Guards and Flower Girls: Donald Crocker, Robert Fisher, John Ieto, Richard Posten, Marjorie Day, Virginia Huie, Margaret Salter, Miramar Stewart.

THE PIRATES OF PENZANCE,
1949.11 or, The Slave of Duty

A Revival of the Comic Opera in Two Acts[4]. Libretto by William S. Gilbert and Arthur Sullivan. Musical director, Lehman Engel. Directed by S. M.

[2]Program note: Mr. McGiveney is the only artist alive offering this type of entertainment.
[3]First presented in New York 20 July, 10-29 August 1885 at the Union Square and People's Theatres for 22 performances. First authorized production presented 19 August 1885 at the Fifth Avenue Theatre by Richard D'Oyly Carte for 250 performances. For Synopsis of Scenes and Musical Numbers, see 19 August 1885 D'Oyly Carte production.
[4]First presented in New York 31 December 1879 at the Fifth Avenue Theatre for a total of 91 performances in two engagements. For Synopsis of Scenes and Musical Numbers, see original 1879 production.

Chartok. Scenery and lighting by Ralph Alswang. Costumes by Peggy Morrison. Production manager, Lewis Pierce. Produced by S. M. Chartok. Opened 10 October 1949 at the Mark Hellinger Theatre and closed 15 October 1949 after 8 performances.

CAST: Samuel: EARLE MacVEIGH. Frederic: MORTON BOWE. Ruth: JEAN HANDZLIK. Richard, The Pirate King: JOSEPH MACAULAY. Kate: BEVERLY JANIS. Edith: ELAINE MALBIN. Isabel: Marie Petek. Mabel: KATHLEEN ROCHE. Major General Stanley: RALPH RIGGS. Edward, Sergeant of Police: ROBERT ECKLES.

General Stanley's Wards: Joyce Carroll, Dolores de Puglia, Natalye Green, Patricia Hall, Annabelle Lee, Trudy Prager, Elsa Shannon, Martha Aleson, Phyllis Blake, Regina Burger, Laura Byola, Inez Harris, Dorothy Johnson, Helen Stanton, Mia Stenn. Pirates and Policemen: Stanley Ames, Thomas Batten, Joseph Caruso, Anthony Cerami, Edwin Easter, Frank Gagliardi, Joseph Mazzolini, James Vitale, Howard Andricola, William Diehl, Samuel Lirkman, Mathew Powers, John Salter, Glen Scander, Jack Shannon, Craig Timberlake.

1949.12 ## TOUCH AND GO

An Intimate Musical Revue in Two Acts, 19 Scenes. Sketches and lyrics by Jean and Walter Kerr. Music by Jay Gorney. Chorography by Helen Tamiris. Directed by Walter Kerr. Production designed by John Robert Lloyd. Orchestrations by Don Walker. Musical director, Antonio Morelli. Lighting by Peggy Clark. Ballet music by Genevieve Pitot. Vocal arrangements by Antonio Morielli. Produced by George Abbott. Opened 13 October 1949 at the Broadhurst Theatre, moved 27 February 1950 to the Broadway Theatre, and closed 18 March 1950 after 176 performances.

CAST: KYLE MacDONNELL, NANCY ANDREWS, GEORGE HALL, DICK SYKES, MURIEL O'MALLEY, PEGGY CASS, JONATHAN LUCAS, HELEN GALLAGHER, PEARL LANG, DANIEL NAGRIN, LEWIS NYE.

Ensemble: Mary Anthony, Eleanor Boleyn, Art Carroll, Lydia Fredericks, Arlyne Frank, Nat (Nathaniel) Frey, Pearl Hacker, David Lober, Greb Lober, Ilona Murrai, Carl Nicholas, Ray Page, Beverly Purvin, Merritt Thompson, Dorothy Scott, Richard Reed, George Reich, Larry Robbins, Willliam Sumner, Beverly Tassoni, Bobby Trelease, Parker Wilson, Mara Lynn.

ACT 1

Scene 1

"An Opening for Everybody"

Theatregoers: G. Hall, H. Gallagher, J. Lucas, Company.

Scene 2

"This Had Better Be Love"

N. Andrews, D. Sykes

Scene 3

Gorilla Girl

Director: G. Hall. Assistant Director: A. Carroll. Miss Hilton: K. MacDonnell. Skeets: J. Lucas. Trainer: L. Nye. Cameraman: N. Frey.

Scene 4

"American Primitive" (Funny Little Old World)

M. O'Malley

Father: A. Carroll. Daughter: H. Gallagher. Danced by P. Lang, D. Nagrin, G. Lober, D. Lober, R. Reed, W. Sumner, B. Tassoni, M. Thompson, D. Scott, P. Wilson.

Scene 5

"Highbrow, Lowbrow"

D. Sykes, J. Lucas, L. Robbins

Scene 6

Disenchantment

Muffins: G. Hall. Old Gent, Pippy: D. Sykes. Moonbeam: P. Cass. Newsboy: W. Sumner. Papa: L. Nye. Pilgrim: L. Robbins.

Scene 7

"Easy Does It"

The Girl: H. Gallgher. The Man: D. Nagrin. The Other Man: D. Lober. The Girl Friends: E. Boleyn, G. Lober. The Company.

Scene 8

"Be a Mess"

Olivia: P. Cass. Barbara: N. Andrews. Jane: K. MacDonnell.

Scene 9

"Broadway Love Song"

P. Lang, J. Lucas

Scene 10

"It'll Be All Right in a Hundred Years"

Boy: A. Carroll. *Girl*: K. MacDonnell.

Scene 11

Great Dane A-Comin'

King: R. Page. *Queen*: N. Andrews. *Hamlet*: D. Sykes. *Laertes*: D. Nagrin. *Ophelia*: K. MacDonnell. *Polonius*: G. Hall. The Company.

ACT 2
Scene 1

"Wish Me Luck"

N. Andrews

Croupier: D. Lober. *Danced by* the Company.

Scene 2

What It Really Was Like

First Aide: N. Frey. *Second Aide*: L. Nye. *General*: D. Sykes. *Malloy*: L. Robbins. *C O.*: G. Hall. *Kerrigan*: J. Lucas.

Scene 3

"Under the Sleeping Volcano"

The Singers: P. Hacker, L. Fredericks, A. Frank, B. Purvin. *Carita's Sister*: I. Murrai. *Carita*: P. Lang. *Felipe*: D. Nagrin. *Francesco*: D. Lober. *Villagers*: D. Scott, E. Boleyn, B. Tassoni, G. Lober, W. Sumner, P. Wilson, M. Thompson, R. Reed, G. Reich.

Scene 4

"Men of the Water-Mark"

A. Carroll, N. Frey, G. Hall, C. Nicholas, L. Nye, L. Robbins

Scene 5

"Mr. Brown, Miss Dupree"

Miss Dupree: K. MacDonnell. *Mama*: M. O'Malley. *Mr. Brown*: J. Lucas. *Danced by* M. Anthony, I. Murrai, B. Tassoni, D. Scott, D. Lober, R. Reed, G. Reich, M. Thompson.

Scene 6

"Miss Platt Selects Mate"

N. Andrews

Scene 7

Cinderella

Stepmother: M. O'Malley. *Neighbor*: H. Gallagher. *First Sister*: N. Andrews. *Second Sister*: P. Cass. *Cinderella*: K. MacDonnell. *Newsboy*: J. Lucas. *Prince*: L. Nye. *Page*: L. Robbins.

Scene 8

Finale

The Company

1949.13 TRIAL BY JURY

A Revival of the Comic Opera in One Act[5]. Libretto by William S. Gilbert. Music by Arthur Sullivan. Musical director, Lehman Engel. Directed by S. M. Chartok. Scenery and lighting by Ralph Alswang. Costumes by Peggy Morrison. Production manager, Lewis Pierce. Produced by S. M. Chartok. Opened 17 October 1949 at the Mark Hellinger Theatre and closed 22 October 1949 after 8 performances.

CAST: *Usher*: Robert Eckles. *Defendant*: MORTON BOWE. *Counsel*: EARLE MacVEIGH. *Barrister*: Howard Andriola. *Judge*: RALPH RIGGS. *First Bridesmaid*: Joyce Carroll. *Second Bridesmaid*: Marie Petek. *Third Bridesmaid*: Natalye Green. *Foreman of the Jury*: Craig Timberlake. *Plaintiff*: ELAINE MALBIN. *Gentlemen of the Jury, etc.*

H.M.S. PINAFORE,
1949.14 or, The Lass That Loved a Sailor

A Revival of the Comic Opera in Two Acts[6]. Libretto by W S Gilbert. Music by Arthur Sullivan. Musical director, Lehman Engel. Directed by S. M.

[5]First presented in New York 15 November 1875 at the Eagle Theatre for 8 performances. For Synopsis of Scenes and Musical Numbers, see original 1875 production.
[6]Originally presented in New York 15 January 1879 at the Standard Theatre for 175 performances. For Synopsis of Scenes and Musical Numbers, see original 1879 production.

Chartok. Scenery and lighting by Ralph Alswang. Costumes by Peggy Morrison. Production manager, Lewis Pierce. Produced by S. M. Chartok. Opened 17 October 1949 at the Mark Hellinger Theatre and closed 22 October 1949 after 8 performances.

CAST: *Little Buttercup*: JEAN HANDZLIK. *Tommy Tucker*: Marie Petek. *Bill Bobstay*: Robert Eckles. *Dick Deadeye*: JOSEPH MACAULAY. *Ralph Rackstraw*: MORTON BOWE. *Captain Corcoran*: EARLE MacVEIGH. *Josephine*: KATHLEEN ROCHE. *The Rt. Hon. Sir Joseph Porter*: RALPH RIGGS. *Cousin Hebe*: Beverly Janis. *Bob Becket*: Craig Timberlake.

First Lord's Sisters, his Cousins, his Aunts, Sailors, Marines, etc.: Dolores de Puglia, Patricia Hall, Annabelle Lee, Trudy Prager, Elsa Shannon, Martha Aleson, Phyllis Blake, Regina Burger, Laura Byola, Inez Harris, Dorothy Johnson, Helen Stanton, Mia Stenn. *Pirates and Policemen*: Stanley Ames, Thomas Batten, Joseph Caruso, Anthony Cerami, Edwin Easter, Frank Gagliardi, Joseph Mazzolini, James Vitale, Howard Andricola, William Diehl, Samuel Lirkman, Mathew Powers, John Salter, Glen Scander, Jack Shannon, Craig Timberlake.

1949.15 LOST IN THE STARS

A Musical Tragedy in Two Acts, 20 Scenes. Words (book, lyrics) by Maxwell Anderson. Music by Kurt Weill. Based on the novel "Cry, the Beloved Country" by Alan Paton. Production directed and supervised by Rouben Mamoulian. Settings by George Jenkins; Johannesburg backdrop by Horace Armistead. Costumes by Anna Hill Johnstone. Conducted by Maurice Levine. Musical arrangements and orchestrations by Kurt Weill. Choral group trained by Maurice Levine. Produced by the Playwrights' Company. Opened 30 October 1949 at the Music Box Theatre and closed 1 July 1949 after 281 performances.

CAST (in order of appearance): *Leader*: FRANK ROANE. *Answerer*: Joseph James. *Nita*: Elayne Richards. *Grace Kumalo*: Gertrude Jeanette. *Stephen Kumalo*: TODD DUNCAN. *The Young Man*: Lavern French. *The Young Woman*: Mable Hart. *James Jarvis*: LESLIE BANKS. *Edward Jarvis*: Judson Rees. *Arthur Jarvis*: John Morley. *John Kumalo*: WARREN COLEMAN. *Paulus*: Charles McRae. *William*: Ray Allen. *Jared*: William C. Smith. *Alex*: Herbert Coleman. *Foreman*: Jerome Shaw. *Mrs. M'Kize*: Georgette Harvey. *Hlabeni*: William Marshall. *Eland*: Charles Grunwell. *Linda*: SHEILA GUYSE. *Johannes Pafuri*: Van Prince. *Matthew Kumalo*: WILLIAM GREAVES. *Absalom Kumalo*: JULIAN MAYFIELD. *Rose*: Gloria Smith. *Irina*: INEZ MATTHEWS. *Policeman*: Robert Byrn. *White Woman*: Biruta Ramoska. *White Man*: Mark Kramer. *The Guard*: Jerome Shaw. *Burton*: John W. Stanley. *The Judge*: Guy Spaull. *Villager*: Robert McFerrin.

Singers: Sibol Cain, Alma Hubbard, Elen Longone, June McMechen, Biruta Ramoska, Christine Spencer, Constance Stokes, Lucretia West, LaCoste Brown, Robert Byrn, Joseph Crawford, Russell George, Joseph James, Mark Karmer, Moses LaMar, Paul Mario, Robert McFerrin, William C. Smith, Joseph Theard.

Time: The Present. *Opening*: Ndotsheni—a small village in South Africa. *Act 1, Scene 1*: Stephen Kumalo's Home. *Scene 2*: The Railroad Station. *Scene 3*: Johannesburg. John Kumalo's Tobacco Shop. *Scene 4*: The Search: (1) The factory Office, (2) Mrs. M'Kize's House, (3) Hlabeni's House, (4) Parole Office. *Scene 5*: Stephen's Shantytown Lodging. *Scene 6*: A Dive in Shantytown. *Scene 7*: Irina's Hut in Shantytown. *Scene 8*: Kitchen in Arthur Jarvis' Home. *Scene 9*: Arthur Jarvis' Library. *Scene 10*: Street. *Scene 11*: Prison. *Scene 12*: Stephen's Shantytown Lodging.

Act 2, Scene 1: Johannesburg. John Kumalo's Tobacco Shop. *Scene 2*: Stephen's Prayer. *Scene 3*: Arthur Jarvis' Doorway. *Scene 4*: Irina's Hut in Shantyown. *Scene 5*: The Courtroom. *Scene 6*: Prison Cell. *Scene 7*: Ndotsheni. Stephen's Chapel. *Scene 8*: Stephen Kumalo's Home.

ACT 1
Opening

"The Hills of Ixtapo"

F. Roane, Singers

Scene 1

"Thousands of Miles"

T. Duncan

Scene 2

"Train to Johannesburg"

F. Roane, Singers

Scene 4

"The Search"

T. Duncan, F. Roane, Singers

Scene 5

"The Little Grey House"

T. Duncan, Singers

Scene 6

"Who'll Buy?"
S. Guyse
Danced by L. French, M. Hart.

Scene 7

"Trouble Man"
I. Matthews

Scene 8

"Murder in Parkwold"
Singers

Scene 10

"Fear"
Singers

Scene 12

"Lost in the Stars"
T. Duncan, Singers

ACT 2

Opening

"The Wild Justice"
F. Roane, Singers

Scene 2

"O Tixo, Tixo, Help Me"
T. Duncan

Scene 4

"Stay Well"
I. Matthews

Scene 6

"Cry, the Beloved Country"
F. Roane, Singers

Scene 7

"Big Mole"
H. Coleman

"A Bird of Passage"
R. McFerrin, Singers

Scene 8

"Thousands of Miles" (reprise)
Singers

1949.16 # REGINA

A Musical Drama (Opera) in Two Acts, Prologue and 4 Scenes. Written and composed by Marc Blitzstein. Based on the play "The Little Foxes" by Lillian Hellman. Production directed by Robert Lewis. Dances by Anna Sokolow. Musical director, Maurice Abravanel. Settings designed by Horace Armistead. Costumes designed by Aline Bernstein. Lighting by Charles Elson. Orchestrations by Marc Blitzstein. Produced by Cheryl Crawford in association with Clinton Wilder. Opened 31 October 1949 at the 46th Street Theatre and closed 17 December 1949 after 56 performances.

CAST (in order of appearance): *Addie,* Cook: LILLYN BROWN. *Cal,* Butler: WILLIAM WARFIELD. *Alexandra Giddens,* Regina's Daughter: PRISCILLA GILLETTE. *Chinkypin:* PHILIP HEPBURN. *Jazz:* WILLIAM DILLARD (trumpet). *Angel Band:* Bernard Addison (banjo), Buster Bailey (clarinet), Rudy Nichols (traps), Benny Morton (trombone). *Regina Giddens:* JANE PICKENS. *Birdie Hubbard,* Oscar's Wife: BRENDA LEWIS. *Oscar Hubbard,* Regina's Brother: DAVID THOMAS. *Leo Hubbard,* Oscar's Son: RUSSELL NYPE. *Marshall:* DONALD CLARKE. *Ben Hubbard,* Regina's Brother: GEORGE LIPTON. *Belle,* Maid: Clarisse Crawford. *Pianist:* Marion Carley. *Violinist:* Alfred Bruning. *Horace Giddens,* Regina's Husband: WILLIAM WILDERMAN. *Manders:* Lee Sweetland. *Ethelinda:* Peggy Turnley.

Townspeople: Ellen Carleen, Earl MacDonald, Robert Anderson, Kay Borron, Kayton Nesbitt, Sara Carter, Keith Davis, Barbara Moser, Karl Brock, Isabelle Felder, Derek MacDermott. *Dancers:* Wana Allison, Joan Engel, Barbara Ferguson, Kate Friedlich, Gisella Weidner, Onna White; Leo Guerrard, Robert Hanlin, Regis Powers, Boris Runanin, Walter Stane, John Ward.

Prologue: Late morning in Spring, 1900, the Alabama town of Bowden, veranda of the Giddens home. *Act 1, Scene 1:* Living-room of the Giddens home, the same evening. *Scene 2:* The same, a week later. Evening. *Scene 3:* Ballroom and veranda of the Giddens home, later the same night.

Act 2: Living-room of the Giddens home, the next afternoon.

PROLOGUE[7]

Prologue [includes "Naught's a Naught"]
L. Brown, W. Warfield, W. Dillard, P. Gillette

ACT 1

Scene 1

Birdie
B. Lewis

Small Talk
J. Pickens, D. Clarke, R. Nype, D. Thomas, P. Gillette, G. Lipton

Goodbyes
D. Thomas, J. Pickens, D. Clarke, B. Lewis

Big Rich
D. Thomas, G. Lipton, J. Pickens, B. Lewis

I Don't Know
J. Pickens, G. Lipton, D. Thomas

My, My
D. Thomas, G. Lipton, J. Pickens

Away
J. Pickens, G. Lipton

"The Best Thing of All"
J. Pickens, G. Lipton

"What Will It Be"
P. Gillette

Birdie and Zan
B. Lewis, P. Gillette

Scene 2

Oh, Addie, where are you?
J. Pickens

"Deedle-doodle"
R. Nype

These cee-gars what you looking for, son?
D. Thomas, R. Nype, J. Pickens

Horace's entrance
W. Wilderman, L. Brown, P. Gillette

Greetings
W. Wilderman, L. Brown, J. Pickens, D. Thomas, R. Nype, G. Lipton, B. Lewis

Horace and Regina [includes "Summer Day"]
W. Wilderman, J. Pickens

The Business
W. Wilderman, R. Nype, J. Pickens, G. Lipton, P. Gillette, D. Thomas

Scene 3

Sing Hubbard
Chorus

"Chinkypin"
W. Dillard

"Blues"
L. Brown, B. Lewis

Waltz
J. Pickens

Gallop
J. Pickens, G. Lipton, Chorus

ACT 2

Rain Quartet ["Make a Quiet Day," "Consider the Rain," "Certainly, Lord"]
B. Lewis, P. Gillette, W. Wilderman, L. Brown, W. Dillard, Chorus

Birdie's Aria ["Lionnet"]
B. Lewis

Horace and Regina
W. Wilderman, J. Pickens

Regina's Aria
J. Pickens, W. Wilderman

Melodrama
G. Lipton, D. Thomas, R. Nype, J. Pickens

---

[7] Musical Numbers not listed in program. Following list prepared from the published libretto with production cuts.

"Greedy Girl"
  J. Pickens, G. Lipton
Horace's Death
  J. Pickens, G. Lipton, D. Thomas, P. Gillette
Finale [includes "Certainly, Lord"]
  J. Pickens, P. Gillette, W. Dillard, Chorus

1949.17 TEXAS, LI'L DARLIN'

A Musical Comedy in Two Acts, a Prelude and 10 Scenes. Book by John Whedon and Sam Moore. Music by Robert Emmett Dolan. Lyrics by Johnny Mercer. Staged by Paul Crabtree. Choreography by Al White, Jr. Scenery and lighting by Theodore Cooper. Costumes by Eleanor Goldsmith. Orchestra under the direction of Will Irwin. Orchestrations by Robert Russell Bennett. Produced by Studio Productions, Inc. and Anthony Brady Farrell Productions. Opened 25 November 1949 at the Mark Hellinger Theatre, vacationed 15 July-21 August 1950, and closed 9 September 1950 after 293 performances.

CAST (in order of appearance): *Harvey Small*: LORING SMITH. *John Baxter Trumbull*: Charles Bang. *Parker Stuart Eliot*: Alden Aldrich. *William Dean Benson, Jr.*: Edward Platt. *Frothingham Fry*: Ned Wertimer. *Brewster Ames II*: FREDD WAYNE. *The Three Coyotes*: The Texas Rhythm Boys: (*Bunkhouse*: Eddy Smith. *Muleshoes*: Bill Horan. *Fred*: Joel McConkey.) *Hominy Smith*: KENNY DELMAR. *Dogie Smith*: BETTY LOU KEIM. *Amos Hall*: Dante Di Paolo. *Sherm*: Cameron Andrews. *Duane Fawcett*: William Ambler. *Branch Pedley*: RAY LONG. *Delia Pratt*: Ronnie Hartmann. *Red*: Merrill Hilton. *Jo Ann Woods*: Elyse Weber. *Calico Munson*: Dorothy Love. *Rebecca Bass*: Carol Lee. *Sally Tucket*: Ruth Ostrander. *Sue Crocket*: Doris Schmitt. *Sarah Boone*: Arleen Ethane. *Belle Cooper*: Yvonne Tibor. *Dallas Smith*: MARY HATCHER. *Easy Jones*: DANNY SCHOLL. *Sam*: JARED REED. *Melissa Tatum*: KATE MURTAH. *Three Little Maids*: Elyse Weber, Carol Lee, Dorothy Love. *Three Prospectors*: Elliott Martin, Edmund Hall, Carl Conway. *Stan*: Edmund Hall. *Herb*: Ralph Patterson. *Jack Prow*: Bob Bernard. *Harry Stern*: Joey Thomas. *Cowboys*: Ray Long, Dante Di Paolo, Merrill Hilton. *Oil Workers*: Jack Purcell, Carol Lee, Tommy Maier. *Drum Majorette*: Jacqueline James. *Cheer Leader*: Elyse Weber. *Football Player*: Edmund Hall. *Texas Rangers*: Charles Bang, Ralph Patterson, Edward Platt, William Ambler. *Voice of "Trend"*: Edward Platt. *"Trend" Secretaries*: Jacqueline James, Ronnie Hartmann, Elyse Weber, Dorothy Mary Richards, Marion Lauer, B. J. Keating. *Guard*: Ray Long. *Radio Announcer*: Charles Bang. *Engineer*: Alden Aldrich. *Joe Raker*: Cameron Andrews. *Neighbors*: Elliott Martin, Patricia Jennings, Carl Conway, Lloyd Knight, Jo Gibson, Muriel Bullis. (Ensemble not listed.)

Time: The Present. *Prelude*: The Office of Harvey Small in New York City.

Act 1, Scene 1: Hominy Smith's Mansion. *Scene 2*: Down the Road a piece. *Scene 3*: Hominy's Back Yard. *Scene 4*: God's Country.

Act 2, Scene 1: "The Trend of the Times." *Scene 2*: Hominy's Headquarters at the Fair. *Scene 3*: Another Part of the Fair. *Scene 4*: On the Midway. *Scene 5*: Dallas' Dressing Tent. *Scene 6*: The Ballroom of the Hotel Pioneer.

ACT 1
Scene 1
  "Whoopin' and a-Hollerin'"
    B. L. Keim, K. Delmar, Texas Rhythm Boys
  "Texas, Li'l Darlin'"
    K. Delmar, Ensemble
  "They Talk a Different Language" (The Yodel Blues)
    M. Hatcher, K. Delmar, Texas Rhythm Boys
  "A Month of Sundays"
    M. Hatcher, D. Scholl
Scene 2
  "Down in the Valley"
    E. Weber, C. Lee, D. Love, E. Martin, E. Hall, C. Conway
Scene 3
  "Hootin' Owl Trail"
    D. Scholl, B. L. Keim, Ensemble
  "They Talk a Different Language" (reprise)
    M. Hatcher, Ensemble
  "The Big Movie Show in the Sky"
    D. Scholl, Ensemble
  "Horseshoes Are Lucky"
    D. Scholl
  "The Big Movie Show in the Sky" (reprise)
    J. Reed, D. Scholl, Ensemble

Scene 4
  "Love Me, Love My Dog"
    K. Delmar, D. Scholl, Ensemble

ACT 2
Scene 1
  "Take a Crank Letter"
    Secretaries
Scene 2
  "Politics"
    K. Delmar, L. Smith
Scene 3
  "Ride 'em, Cowboy"
    M. Hatcher
Scene 4
  Square Dance
    R. Long, K. Delmar, M. Hatcher, Ensemble
  "Take a Crank Letter" (reprise)
    F. Wayne, Secretaries
Scene 5
  "Affable, Balding Me"
    M. Hatcher, F. Wayne
  "A Month of Sundays" (reprise)
    M. Hatcher, D. Scholl
  "Whichaway'd They Go?"
    M. Hatcher, J. Reed, B. L. Keim, Friends
Scene 6
  "It's Great to Be Alive"
    D. Scholl, Ensemble

1949.18 GENTLEMEN PREFER BLONDES

A Musical Comedy in Two Acts, 12 Scenes. Book by Joseph Fields and Anita Loos, based on her novel of the same name. Music by Jule Styne. Lyrics by Leo Robin. Dances and musical ensembles by Agnes de Mille. Production (sets) designed by Oliver Smith. Costumes designed by Miles White. Musical direction by Milton Rosenstock. Musical arrangements by Don Walker. Vocal direction and arrangements by Hugh Martin. Lighting by Peggy Clark. Music for dances arranged by Trude Rittmann. Entire production staged by John C. Wilson. Produced by Herman Levin and Oliver Smith. Opened 8 December 1949 at the Ziegfeld Theatre and closed 15 September 1951 after 740 performances.

CAST (in order of speaking): *Dorothy Shaw*: YVONNE ADAIR. *A Steward*: Jerry Craig. *Lorelei Lee*: CAROL CHANNING. *Gus Esmond*: JACK McCAULEY. *Frank, George* (of the Olympic Team): Robert Cooper, Eddie Weston. *Sun Bathers*: Pat Donohue, Marjorie Winters. *Lady Phyllis Beekman*: RETA SHAW. *Sir Francis Beekman*: REX EVANS. *Mrs. Ella Spofford*: ALICE PEARCE. *Deck Stewards*: Bob Burkhradt, Shelton Lewis. *Henry Spofford*: ERIC BROTHERSON. *An Olympic*: Curt Stafford. *Josephus Gage*: GEORGE S. IRVING. *Deck Walkers*: Fran Keegan, Junior Standish. *Bill*, a Dancer: PETER BIRCH. *Gloria Stark*: ANITA ALVAREZ. *Pierre*, a Steward: Bob Neukum. *Taxi Driver*: Kazimir Kokic. *Leon*, a Valet: Peter Holmes. *Robert Lemanteur*: MORT MARSHALL. *Louis Lemanteur*, his son: HOWARD MORRIS. *A Flower Girl*: Nicole France. *Maitre d'Hotel*: Crandall Diehl .*Zizi*: Judy Sinclair. *Fifi*: Hope Zee. *Coles and Atkins*: HONI COLES and CHOLLY ATKINS. *The Tenor*: William Krach. *Policeman*: William Diehl. *Headwaiter*: Kazimir Kokic. *Mr. Esmond, Sr.*: IRVING MITCHELL.

Show Girls: Pat Donohue, Anna Rita Duffy, Fran Keegan, Annette Kohl, Junior Standish, Marjorie Winters. *Singing Ensemble*: Angela Castle, Joan Coburn, Ellen McCown, Candy Montgomery, Judy Sinclair, Lucille Udovick, Beverly Jane Weston, Hope Zee, Bob Burkhardt, Jerry Craig, William Diehl, William Krach, Shelton Lewis, Bob Neukum, Curt Stafford, David Vogel. *Dancing Ensemble*: Suzanne Ames, Floreence Baum, Nicole France, Pauline Goddard, Pattty Ann Jackson, Alicia Krug, Mary Martinet, Caren Preiss, Evelyn Taylor, Norma Thornton, Polly Ward, Prue Ward, Helen Wood, Charles Basile, Bill Bradley, Rex Cooper, Robert Cooper, Crandall Diehl, Aristide J. Ginoulias, Peter Holmes, John Laverty, Eddie Weston.

Time: 1924.

Act 1, Scene 1: The French Line Pier in New York. A Midnight Sailing. *Scene 2*: The Sun Deck of the *Ile de France*. Third day out. *Scene 3*: The Boat Deck. The same day. *Scene 4*: Lorelei's Suite on the *Ile de France*. Later that day. *Scene 5*: Paris. The Place Vendome. One week later. *Scene 6*: Champs de Mars—Under the Eiffel Tower. Same

Day. *Scene 7*: The Place Vendome. Later that day. *Scene 8*: The Ritz Hotel in Paris—Lorelei's Suite. That evening.

Act 2, Scene 1: The Pre-Catelan in the Bois. The same evening. *Scene 2*: A Street in Paris. Later that evening. *Scene 3*: The Ritz Hotel in Paris. Lorelei's Suite. Three A.M. the next morning. *Scene 4*: The Central Park Casino, New York, Ten days later.

ACT 1

Scene 1

"It's High Time"
Y. Adair, Ensemble

"Bye, Bye Baby"
J. McCauley, C. Channing

"Bye, Bye Baby" (reprise)
J. McCauley, Ensemble

Scene 2

"A Little Girl from Little Rock"
C. Channing

"I Love What I'm Doing"
Y. Adair

Dance
P. Birch, Y. Adair, Ensemble

Scene 4

"Just a Kiss Apart"
E. Brotherson

The Practice Scherzo
A. Alvarez

"It's Delightful Down in Chile"
R. Evans, C. Channing, Show Girls, Male Ensemble

Scene 5

"Sunshine"
E. Brotherson, Y. Adair

Scene 6

"In the Champs de Mars"
Ensemble

Dance
A. Alvarez, K. Kokic

Scene 7

"Sunshine" (reprise)
Ensemble

Scene 8

"I'm A'Tingle, I'm A'Glow"
G. S. Irving

"House on Rittenhouse Square"
Y. Adair

"You Say You Care"
E. Brotherson

Finaletto
C. Channing, Ensemble

ACT 2

Scene 1

"Bye, Bye Baby" (reprise)
Dancing Ensemble

"Mamie Is Mimi"
A. Alvarez, H. Coles, C. Atkins

"Coquette"
W. Krach, Show Girls

Scene 2

"Diamonds Are a Girl's Best Friend"
C. Channing

Scene 3

"You Say You Care" (reprise)
Y. Adair, E. Brotherson

"Gentlemen Prefer Blondes"
C. Channing, J. McCauley

"Homesick Blues"
C. Channing, Y. Adair, J. McCauley, E. Brotherson, A. Pearce, G. S. Irving

Scene 4

"Keeping Cool With Coolidge"
Y. Adair, P. Birch, Ensemble

"Button Up With Esmond"
C. Channing, Show Girls, Ensemble

Finale:

"Gentlemen Prefer Blondes" (reprise)
C. Channing, J. McCauley, Ensemble

"Bye, Bye Baby" (reprise)
Entire Company

1950.01   # HAPPY AS LARRY

A Musical in Two Acts, 7 Scenes. Book and lyrics by Donagh MacDonagh. Music by Mischa and Wesley Portnoff. (Based on the play of the same name by Donagh MacDonagh.) Staged by Burgess Meredith. Choreography by Anna Sokolow. Musical director, Franz Allers. Scenery and costumes by Motley. Orchestrations by Rudolph Goehr and Charles Cook. Vocal arrangements by Herbert Greene. Mobiles by Alexander Calder. Produced by Leonard Sillman. Opened 6 January 1950 at the Coronet Theater and closed 7 January 1950 after 3 performances.

CAST (in order of appearance): *First Tailor*: Maurice Edwards. *Third Tailor*: Frank Milton. *Fourth Tailor*: Harry Allen. *Fifth Tailor*: Henry Calvin. *Sixth Tailor*: William Hogue. *Seventh Tailor*: Jack Warner. *Eighth Tailor*: Fin Olsen. *Second Tailor*: Himself. *Larry*: BURGESS MEREDITH. *The Widow*: MARGUERITE PIAZZA. *The Grave-digger*: Ralph Hertz. *Mrs. Larry*: BARBARA BARRY. *The Doctor*: GENE BARRY. *Seamus*, a Local Pharmacist: IRWIN COREY. *Clotho, Lachesis, Atropos*, Three Fates: Mara Kim, Diane Sinclair, Royce Wallace.

The action of the play takes place anywhere, anytime.

Act 1, Scene 1: A casual tailor shop. *Scene 2*: A restless graveyard. *Scene 3*: Interior, the house of Larry. *Scene 4*: Space.

Act 2, Scene 1: Exterior, the house of Larry. *Scene 2*: Interior, the house of Larry. *Scene 3*: The tailor shop.

ACT 1

Opening, "No One Loves Me"
Second Tailor

"Without a Stitch"
M. Edwards, F. Milton, H. Allen,
H. Calvin, W. Hogue, J. Warner, F. Olsen, Second Tailor

"Now and Then"
B. Meredith

"October"
M. Piazza

"Mrs. Larry, Tell Me This"
G. Barry, B. Perry

"A Cup of Tea"
B. Meredith, B. Perry, M. Piazza, I. Corey, G. Barry

"He's With My Johnny"
M. Piazza

"And So He Died"
M. Edwards, F. Milton, H. Allen,
H. Calvin, W. Hogue, J. Warner, F. Olsen, Second Tailor

"Three Old Ladies from Hades"
M. Kim, D. Sinclair, R. Wallace

Dance of the Fates
J. Warner, M. Kim, D. Sinclair, R. Wallace

ACT 2

"It's Pleasant and Delightful"
G. Barry

"The Dirty Dog"
M. Edwards, F. Milton, H. Allen,
H. Calvin, W. Hogue, J. Warner, F. Olsen, Second Tailor

"The Flatulant Ballad"
I. Corey

"The Loyalist Wife"
B. Perry

"Oh, Mrs. Larry"
M. Edwards, F. Milton, H. Allen,
H. Calvin, W. Hogue, J. Warner, F. Olsen, Second Tailor, B. Perry

"Give the Doctor the Best in the House"
M. Edwards, F. Milton, H. Allen,
H. Calvin, W. Hogue, J. Warner, F. Olsen, Second Tailor

"The Doctors Dance"
M. Edwards, F. Milton, H. Allen,
H. Calvin, W. Hogue, J. Warner, F. Olsen, Second Tailor

"Double Murder, Double Death"
H. Calvin, M. Piazza

"He's a Bold Rogue"
B. Perry, M. Piazza, M. Edwards, F. Milton, H. Allen,
H. Calvin, W. Hogue, J. Warner, F. Olsen, Second Tailor

"I Remember Her"
B. Meredith

"The Tobacco Blues"
M. Piazza, B. Meredith

Finale
B. Meredith, M. Edwards, F. Milton, H. Allen,
H. Calvin, W. Hogue, J. Warner, F. Olsen, Second Tailor

1950.02 ALIVE AND KICKING

A Musical Revue in Two Acts, 21 Scenes. Sketches by Ray Golden, I.A.L. Diamond, Henry Morgan, Jerome Chodorov, Joseph Stein, Will Glickman, Mike Stuart. Music by Hal Borne, Irma Jurist and Sammy Fain. Lyrics by Paul Francis Webster and Ray Golden. Additional music and lyrics by Sonny Burke, Leonard Gershe, Billy Kyle, Sid Kuller, Leo Schumer. Special music and lyrics by Harold Rome. Choreography by Jack Cole. Settings and costumes by Raoul Pene du Bois. Lighting by Mason Arvold. Orchestra conducted by Irving Actman. Musical direction and vocal arrangements by Lehman Engel. Orchestral arrangements by George Bassman. Production directed by Robert H. Gordon. Produced by William R. Katzell and Ray Golden. Opened 17 January 1950 at the Winter Garden and closed 25 February 1950 after 46 performances.

CAST: DAVID BURNS, LENORE LONERGAN, JACK GILFORD, CARL REINER, JACK COLE AND HIS DANCERS, Margery Oldroyd, Sam Kirkham, Arthur Maxwell, Jack Cassidy, Jack Russell, Marie Groscup, Dolores Starr, Laurel Shelby, Louise Kirtland, June Brady, Ray Stephens, Patricia Bybell, Rex Thompson, Bobby Van, Mickey Deems, Earl William, Gwen Verdon, Eve Lynn, Jessie Elliott.
Singers: Rae Abruzzo, Margaret Baxter, Madelaine Chambers, Fay de Witt, Sylvia Chaney, Jean Bal, Bryn Corey, Graham Lee, Jay Harnick. *Dancers*: Velerie Camille, Ruth Davis, Jean Harris, George Bockman, Kenneth Davis, Marc Hertsens, Paul Olson, Jack Miller, Dolores Starr.

ACT 1
Scene 1

"Alive and Kicking"
R. Abruzzo, M. Baxter, J. Brady, P. Bybell, M. Chambers,
F. de Witt, M. Oldroyd, L. Shelby, L. Kirtland, S. Chaney, J. Bal, B. Corey,
J. Cassidy, A. Maxwell, S. Kirkham, G. Lee, R. Stephens, E. Williams,
J. Harnick
(*Music by* Hal Borne. *Lyrics by* Ray Golden and Sid Kuller. *Vocal Arrangements by* George Bassman.)
Milkman: B. Van. *The Girl*: D. Starr. *Danced by* V. Camille, R. Davis, J. Harris,
G. Bockman, K. Davis, M. Hertsens, P. Olson, J. Miller.

Scene 2

"Pals of the Pentagon"
(*Sketch by* Ray Golden and I.A.L. Diamond. *Music and Lyrics by* Harold Rome.)
Undersecretary: J. Russell. *Army*: D. Burns. *Navy*: C. Reiner. *Airforce*: M. Deems. *Secretary*: E. Lynn.

Scene 3

"I Didn't Want Him"
J. Brady
(*Music by* Irma Jurist. *Lyrics by* Leonard Gershe.)
Danced by J. Cole, G. Verdon.

Scene 4

"What a Delightful Day"
(*Music by* Irma Jurist. *Lyrics by* Leonard Gershe.)
Introduction by C. Reiner. *Madrigal Trio*: J. Gilford, M. Oldroyd,
M. Chambers.

Scene 5

Meet the Authors
(*by* Jerome Chodorov)

Chairwoman: L. Kirtland. *Dr. Hiram Flick*: C. Reiner. *Viola Tremaine*:
L. Lonergan. *Dr. Allen Drawbridge*: D. Burns. *Waiter*: S. Kirkham.

Scene 6

"A World of Strangers"
A. Maxwell, P. Bybell
(*Music by* Sammy Fain. *Lyrics by* Paul Francis Webster and
Ray Golden.)

Scene 7

"Abou Ben Adhem"
(*Music and Lyrics by* Ray Golden, adapted from the poem by Leigh Hunt.
Original Dance Music by Billy Kyle.)
Sergeant: J. Russell. *Boy*: R. Thompson. *Trio*: S. Kirkham, J. Cassidy,
R. Stephens. *Abou*: J. Cole. *Abou's Wife*: G. Verdon. *Angel*: M. Groscup.
Danced by V. Camille, J. Harris, D. Starr, G. Bockman, M. Hertsens,
P. Olson, J. Miller.

Scene 8

"Cry, Baby"
L. Lonergan, R. Abruzzo, L. Shelby
(*Music and Lyrics by* Harold Rome.)

Scene 9

I Never Felt Better
(*by* Joseph Stein and Will Glickman)
Wife: L. Kirtland. *Barney*: J. Gilford. *Charlie*: C. Reiner.

Scene 10

"One Word Led to Another"
B. Van
(*Music by* Hal Borne. *Lyrics by* Ray Golden.)

Scene 11

Calypso Celebration: "Love It Hurts So Good"
L. Lonergan
(*Music and Lyrics by* Harold Rome. *Dance Music by* Billy Kyle.)
Danced by J. Cole, G. Verdon, M. Groscup.
Singers: J. Cassidy, S. Kirkham, G. Lee, J. Russell, R. Stephens, E. William,
J. Harnick, R. Abruzzo, M. Baxter, P. Bybell, M. Chambers, F. de Witt, E. Lynn,
M. Oldroyd, L. Shelby, L. Kirtland, S. Chaney, J. Bal, B. Corey. *Dancers*:
G. Bockman, K. Davis, M. Hertsens, P. Olson, J. Miller, V. Camille, R. Davis,
J. Harris, D. Starr.

ACT 2
Scene 1

"Building Going Up"
A. Maxwell, Singers
(*Music by* Sammy Fain. *Lyrics by* Paul Francis Webster and Ray Golden.)
Singers: R. Abruzzo, M. Baxter, J. Brady, P. Bybell, M. Chambers, F. de Witt,
E. Lynn, M. Oldroyd, L. Shelby, L. Kirtland, S. Chaney, J. Bal, B. Corey, J.
Cassidy, S. Kirkham, G. Lee, J. Russell, R. Stephens, E. William, J. Harnick,
R. Thompson.

Scene 2

"My Day of Rest"
M. Deems
(*Music and Lyrics by* Lucille Kallen, Max Liebman and Mickey Deems.)

Scene 3

Hippocrates Hits the Jackpot
(*by* Henry Morgan and Joseph Stein)
First Man: J. Cassidy. *Dr. Walsh*: C. Reiner. *First Nurse*: L. Shelby. *Woman*: L.
Kirtland. *Patient*: M. Deems. *Dr. Frisbee*: D. Burns. *Announcer*: J. Brady. *Second
Nurse*: F. de Witt. *Anesthetist*: R. Stephens.

Scene 4

"Propinquity"
J. Russell
(*Music by* Sonny Burke. *Lyrics by* Paul Francis Webster and Ray Golden.)
Danced by J. Cole, G. Verdon. *Singers*: J. Cassidy, G. Lee, S. Kirkham,
M. Oldroyd, M. Chambers, R. Abruzzo. *Dancers*: M. Groscup, V. Camille,
R. Davis, J. Harris, D. Starr, G. Bockman, K. Davis, M. Hertsens, P. Olson,
J. Miller.

Scene 5

"I'm All Yours"
(*Music by* Leo Schumer. *Lyrics by* Mike Stuart and Ray Golden.)
Agnes: J. Elliott. *George*: B. Van.

Scene 6

Once Upon a Time
(*by* Joseph Stein and Will Glickman)
Director: C. Reiner. *Floogelman*: J. Gilford. *Miss Honeysuckle*: L. Lonergan.
Mike: M. Deems.

Scene 7

"One Two Three"

E. William, P. Bybell, G. Lee, R. Abruzzo
(*Music by* Sonny Burke. *Lyrics by* Paul Francis Webster and Ray Golden.)
Danced by G. Verdon, M. Groscup, V. Camille, R. Davis, J. Harris, D. Starr, G. Bockman, K. Davis, M. Hertsens, P. Olson, J. Miller.

Scene 8

"French With Tears"

L. Lonergan
(*Music and Lyrics by* Harold Rome.)

Scene 9

"Cole Scuttle Blues"

Danced by J. Cole, G. Verdon, M. Groscup
(*Music by* Billy Kyle.)

Scene 10

Finale

Entire Company

1950.03   DANCE ME A SONG

A Musical Revue in Two Acts, 25 Scenes. Songs by James Shelton. Additional numbers by Herman Hupfeld, Albert Hague, Maurice Valency and Bud Gregg. Sketches by Jimmy Kirkwood and Lee Goodman, George Oppenheimer and Vincente Minnelli, Marya Mannes, Robert Anderson, James Shelton, Wally Cox. Staged by James Shelton. Settings and lighting by Jo Mielziner. Choreography by Robert Sidney. Costumes by Irene Sharaff. Orchestrations by Robert Russell Bennett. Musical direction, Tony Cabot. Produced by Dwight Deere Wiman in association with Robert Ross. Opened 20 January 1950 at the Royale Theatre and closed 18 February 1950 after 35 performances.

CAST: JOAN McCRACKEN, MARION LORNE, ANN THOMAS, BOB SCHEERER, WALLY COX, (Bob) FOSSE and (Mary-Ann) NILES, JIMMY [James] KIRKWOOD, LEE GOODMAN, ERIK RHODES, Babe Hines, Tina Prescott, Cliff Ferre, Alan Ross, Heidi Krall, Robert B. Sola, Hope Foye, Cynthia Rogers, Donald Saddler, Biff McGuire, Tony Albert and Silver.

Dancing Ensemble: Francine Bond, Carmina Cansino, Marilyn Gennaro, June Graham, Marian Horosko, Don Little, Dusty McCaffrey, Scott Merrill, Douglas Moppert.

ACT 1

Scene 1

A Pair for Tonight

(*by* James Shelton, based on an idea by Jo Mielziner)
Man: T. Albert. *Wife:* C. Rogers. *Taxi Driver:* D. Saddler. *Driller:* C. Ferre. *Phone Man:* S. Merrill.

Scene 2

Average Family

Cook: B. Hines. *Son-in-Law:* E. Rhodes. *Grandmother:* M. Lorne. *Sister Kate:* A. Thomas. *Mother:* T. Prescott. *Uncle:* W. Cox. *Sons:* A. Ross, J. Kirkwood, B. Scheerer. *Dog:* Silver.

Scene 3

"It's the Weather"

B. McGuire, T. Prescott, B. Fosse, C. Ferre, S. Merrill, M. Niles, F. Bond
Danced by: B. Fosse, M. Niles, D. Saddler, J. Graham, supported by C. Cansino, F. Bond, M. Horosko, D. McCaffrey, S. Merrill, D. Moppert.

Scene 4

She's No Lady

(*by* James Shelton and Cynthia Rogers)
Judoee: B. McGuire. *Judoer:* A. Thomas.

Scene 5

A Woman's Place[8]

Salesman: E. Rhodes. *Sleeping Beauty:* J. . Graham.

Scene 6

"Glee Club"

H. Krall, A. Thomas, F. Bond, C. Rogers, W. Cox, A. Ross, E. Rhodes, B. McGuire, J. Kirkwood, S. Merrill.

[8]After opening, replaced by:

Inspection

(*by* Wally Cox)
P.F.C.: W. Cox.

Scene 7

"Strange New Look"

Farmer: B. McGuire. *Nellie:* J. McCracken. *City Slicker:* B. Scheerer.

Scene 8

Buck and Bobbie

(*by* Lee Goodman and Jimmy Kirkwood)
Buck: L. Goodman. *Bobbie:* J. Kirkwood. *Secretary:* A. Thomas.

Scene 9

"I'm the Girl"

H. Foye

Scene 10

The Lunts Are the Lunts Are the Lunts

(*by* Robert Anderson)
Alfred: A. Ross. *Lynn:* J. McCracken.

Scene 11

"Matilda"

Matilda: J. Graham. *Hilda:* M. Niles. *Butler:* B. Scheere. *Servants:* F. Bond, M. Gennaro, C. Cansico, M. Horosko, S. Merrill, D. Moppert, D. Little, D. McCaffrey.

Scene 12

"Love"

B. Hines

Scene 13

"Documentary"

(*Narration written by* James Shelton. *Music by* Bud Gregg. *Monologue written by* Wally Cox.)
Narrator: E. Rhodes. *Dufo's Friend:* W. Cox. *Girl:* T. Prescott. *Dufo:* B. Fosse. *Policeman:* S. Merrill. *A Woman:* H. Foye. *Children:* F. Bond, M. Gennaro, D. McCaffrey. *Drunkard:* D. Saddler. *Cora Cox:* C. Rogers.

ACT 2

Scene 1

"One Is a Lonely Number"

(*Music by* Albert Hague. *Lyrics by* Maurice Valency.)
Girl: H. Krall. *Boy:* A. Ross. And the Company.

Scene 2

Texas

Girl: A. Thomas. *Two Cowboys:* B. Scheerer, C. Ferre.

Scene 3

"The Folks at Home"

(*Sketch by* George Oppenheimer and Vincente Minnelli. *Music and Lyrics by* James Shelton.)
Mad Scientist: J. Kirkwood. *Idiot Servant:* W. Cox. *Vampire:* T. Prescott. *Mad Professor:* E. Rhodes. *Frankenstein:* B. McGuire. *Crone:* L. Goodman. *Marion:* M. Lorne. *Harpo Marx:* B. Fosse. *Highboy:* R. Sola. *Blonde Maiden:* M. Horosko. *George Washington:* D. McCaffrey. *Mr. McIntosh:* D. Moppert.

Scene 4

"My Little Dog Has Ego"

(*Music and Lyrics by* Herman Hupfeld.)
Boy: B. Scheerer. *Dog:* Silver.

Scene 5

The Board Meeting[9]

(*by* Marya Mannes)
Chairman: E. Rhodes. *Mason:* A. Ross. *Bates:* C. Ferre. *Tilpin:* B. McGuire. *Knight:* J. Kirkwood. *A Visitor:* S. Merrill.

Scene 6

"Lilac Wine"

H. Foye
Danced by J. Graham, D. Saddler.

Scene 7

"Paper!" (Ballet)

Newspaper Boy: B. McGuire. *Girl:* J. McCracken. *The Rake:* C. Ferre. *Boy Friend:* D. Saddler. And the Company.

[9]After opening, replaced by:

Operation Cumulus

(*by* Lee Goodman and Jimmy Kirkwood)
Colonel: L. Goodman. *Merriweather:* W. Cox. *Abercrombie:* J. Kirkwood. *Pilots:* S. Merrill, D. Saddler.)

Scene 8

Hello from Hollywood

Written and performed by L. Goodman, J. Kirkwood.

Scene 9

"How Little Adam Knew"

The Serpent: T. Prescott. *Eve*: M. Niles. *Adam*: B. Fosse.

Scene 10

It's His Money

(*by* Wally Cox)

Counterman: W. Cox. *Customer*: B. McGuire. *Owner*: D. Saddler.

Scene 11

"Dance Me a Song"

The Boys: C. Ferre, B. Fosse, B. Scheerer. *The Girl*: J. McCracken. And the Company.

Scene 12

Finale

The Company

1950.04   ARMS AND THE GIRL

A Musical in Two Acts, 10 Scenes. Book by Herbert and Dorothy Fields, Rouben Mamoulian. Based on the play "The Pursuit of Happiness" by Lawrence Langner and Armina Marshall. Lyrics by Dorthy Fields. Music by Morton Gould. Production directed by Rouben Mamoulian. Dances by Michael Kidd. Settings designed by Horace Armistead. Costumes by Audre. Musical conductor, Frederick Dvonch. Orchestrations by Morton Gould and Philip J. Lang. Production under the supervision of Theresa Helburn and Lawrence Langner. Produced by the Theatre Guild in association with Anthony Brady Farrell. Opened 2 February 1950 at the 46th Street Theatre and closed 27 May 1950 after 134 performances.

CAST (in order of appearance): *Connecticut*: PEARL BAILEY. *Franz*: GEORGES GUÉTARY. *Jo Kirkland*: NANETTE FABRAY. *Thad Jennings*: Seth Arnold. *Two Sons of Liberty*: Andrew Aprea, Victor Young. *Town Crier*: William J. McCarthy. *Captain Aaron Kirkland*: FLORENZ AMES. *Drummer*: Jerry Miller. *Sergeant*: Norman Weise. *Prudence Kirkland*: EDA HEINEMAN. *Comfort Kirkland*: Lulu Belle Clarke. *Ben*: Sterlign Hall. *Matthew*: Joseph Caruso. *A Militiaman*: Peter Miceli. *Abigail*: Mimi Cabanne. *Betsy*: Joan Keenan. *Colonel Mortimer Sherwood*: JOHN CONTE. *Aide to General Curtis*: Daniel O'Brien. *General Lucius Curtis*: Cliff Dunstan. *John*: Paul Fitzpatrick. *David*: Philip Rodd. *Aide to General Washington*: Robert Rippy. *General George Washington*: Arthur Vinton.

Dancers: Barbara Ferguson, Annabelle Gold, Maria Harriton, Barbara McCutcheon, Patricia Muller, Onna White, Fern Whitney. Edmund Balin, Peter Gennaro, William Inglis, Robert Josias, Arthur Partington, Marc West, Lou Yetter. Singers: Mimi Cabanne, Katherine Hennig, Joan Keenan, Mary O'Fallon, Shirley Robbins, Patricia Rogers, Helen Stanton, Bettina Thayer. Howard Andreola, Andrew Aprea, Joseph Caruso, Sterling Hall, Peter Miceli, Daniel O'Brien, Frederick Olsson, Robert Rippy, Donald Thrall, William Thunhurst, Norman Weise, Victor Young.

Act 1, Scene 1: The Hayloft of Thad Jennings' Barn, Ridgefield, Connecticut, 1776. *Scene 2*: The Village Green. A few hours later. *Scene 3*: Behind the Kirkland Barn. Immediately following. *Scene 4*: The Meeting House. The same evening. *Scene 5*: Outside the Meeting House. *Scene 6*: The Parlor of the Kirkland Home.

Act 2, Scene 1: The Kirkland Parlor. *Scene 2*: The Boston Post Road. Early the next morning. *Scene 3*: Behind the Kirkland Barn. *Scene 4*: The Village Green.

ACT 1

"A Girl With a Flame"

N. Fabray

"That's What I Told Him Last Night"

F. Ames, Girls

"I Like It Here"

G. Guétary

"That's My Fella"

N. Fabray

Danced by A. Partington, B. McCutcheon, and *First Two Couples*: F. Whitney, M. Harriton, W. Inglis, E. Balin. *Whittler and Girl*: M. West, A. Gold. *Deacon*: L. Yetter. *Siren*: O. White. *Butterfly Catcher and Girl*: P. Gennaro, P. Muller. *The Pursued*: R. Josias. *Patient One*: S. Robbins.

"A Cow and a Plough and a Frau"

G. Guétary

"Nothin' for Nothin'"

P. Bailey

"He Will Tonight"

N. Fabray, Girls

"Don't Talk"

J. Conte

"Plantation in Philadelphia"

N. Fabray, G. Guétary, P. Bailey, J. Conte, Company

Danced by Boys and Girls.

"You Kissed Me"

N. Fabray

ACT 2

"Don't Talk" (reprise)

J. Conte

"I'll Never Learn"

N. Fabray, G. Guétary

"There Must Be Something Better Than Love"

P. Bailey

"She's Exciting"

G. Guétary

"Mister Washington! Uncle George!"

Boys and Girls

"A Cow and a Plow and a Frau" (reprise)

N. Fabray, G. Guétary

1950.05   THE CONSUL

A Musical Drama in Three Acts, 6 Scenes by Gian-Carlo Menotti. Orchestra directed by Lehman Engel. Musical coordination by Thomas Schippers. Settings by Horace Armistead. Lighting by Jean Rosenthal. Production by Bill Butler. Costumes by Grace Houston. Dreams choreography by John Butler. Entire production staged by Gian-Carlo Menotti. Produced by Chandler Cowles and Efrem Zimbalist, Jr. Opened 15 March 1950 at the Ethel Barrymore Theatre and closed 4 November 1950 after 269 performances.

CAST: (in order of appearance): *John Sorel*: CORNELL MacNEIL. *Magda Sorel*: PATRICIA NEWAY; VERA BRYNER (alt.) *The Mother*: MARIE POWERS. *Chief Police Agent*: LEON LISHNER. *First Police Agent*: Chester Watson. *Second Police Agent*: Donald Blackey. *The Secretary*: GLORIA LANE. *Mr. Kofner*: GEORGE JONGEYANS [Gaynes]. *The Foreign Woman*: MARIA MARLO. *Anna Gomez*: Maria Andreassi. *Vera Boronell*: Lydia Summers. *Nika Magadoff*: ANDREW McKINLEY. *Assan*: Francis Monachino. *Voice on the Record*: Mabel Mercer.

The action takes place somewhere in Europe.

Act 1, Scene 1: The Home, early morning. *Scene 2*: The Consulate, later the same day.

Act 2, Scene 1: The Home, in the evening, a month later. *Scene 2*: The Consulate, a few days later.

Act 3, Scene 1: The Consulate, late afternoon, several days later. *Scene 2*: The Home, that night.

MUSICAL NUMBERS[10]

"Tu Reviendras"

"Now, O Lips, Say Goodbye"

"In Endless Waiting Rooms"

"Lullaby" (Sleep My Love)

"Oh, What a Lovely Dance"

"To This We've Come"

"All the Documents Must be Signed"

"Death's Frontiers Are Opened"

1950.06   GREAT TO BE ALIVE!

A Musical Comedy in Two Acts, 14 Scenes. Book by Walter Bullock and Sylvia Regan. Music by Abraham Ellstein. Lyrics by Walter Bullock.

---

[10]Performed as an opera without individual songs or arias listed.

Directed by Mary Hunter. Dances and musical numbers staged by Helen Tamiris. Settings, costumes and lighting by Stewart Chaney. Orchestrations by Robert Russell Bennett and Donald J. Walker. Musical director, Max Meth. Music for ballets for Abraham Ellstein. Arrangements for "Headin' for a Weddin'," "Dreams Ago," and "The Riddle" by Genevieve Pitot. Vocal arrangements by Crane Calder. Produced by Vinton Freedley in association with Anderson Lawler and Russell Merkert. Opened 23 March 1950 at the Winter Garden and closed 6 May 1950 after 52 performances.

CAST (in order of appearance): *Bonnie*: BAMBI LINN. *Prudence*: Betty Low. *Albert*: ROD ALEXANDER. *Jake*: J. C. McCord. *Maybelle*: Aleen Buchanan. *Kitty*: VALERIE BETTIS. *Crumleigh*: Jay Marshall. *Butch*: Earl Oxford. *Leslie Butterfield*: VIVIENNE SEGAL. *Carol*: MARTHA WRIGHT. *Vince*: MARK DAWSON. *Woodrow Twigg*: STUART ERWIN. *Mimsey*: Marjorie Peterson. *Sandra*: Jeanne Bal. *Freddie*: Russell Nype. *Blodgett*: LULU BATES. *Jonathan*: David Nillo. *The Minister*: Ken Carroll. *O'Brien*: Don Kennedy. *Rafferty*: Paul Reed.

Dancers: Eleanor Fairchild, Eleanore Gregory, Barbara Heath, Ann Hutchinson, Norma Kaiser, Janice Rule, Chuck Brenner, Ted Cappy, Roscoe French, David Nillo, Harry Rogers, Swen Swenson. *Singers*: Leigh Allen, Jeanne Bal, Virginia Curtis, Ruth McVayne, Joyce Mitchell, Julia Williams, Fred Bryan, Ken Carroll, Ed Gombos, John Juliano, Russell Nype, Robert Wallace.

Act 1, Scene 1: The Reception Hall of an old Pennsylvania Mansion—Before dawn. *Scene 2*: The Reception Hall—A few weeks later. *Scene 3*: Exterior of the Mansion. *Scene 4*: The Reception Hall—Midnight. *Scene 5*: Exterior of the Mansion. *Scene 6*: The Reception Hall—A moment later.

Act 2, Scene 1: The Garden—Afternoon of the same day. *Scene 2*: Exterior of the Mansion. *Scene 3*: The Reception Hall—Later that day. *Scene 4*: Exterior of the Mansion. *Scene 5*: A Corner of the Library. *Scene 6*: The Reception Hall—Midnight. *Scene 7*: Exterior of the Mansion. *Scene 8*: The Reception Hall—The following morning.

ACT 1

"When the Sheets Come Back from the Laundry"
V. Bettis, B. Linn, B. Low, A. Buchanan, R. Alexander, J. C. McCord, J. Marshall, Dancers

"It's a Long Time Till Tomorrow"
M. Wright, M. Dawson

"Headin' for a Weddin'"
S. Erwin, V. Bettis, B. Linn, B. Low, A. Buchanan, R. Alexander, J. C. McCord, J. Marshall, Dancers

"Redecorate"
E. Oxford

"What a Day!"
M. Wright, M. Dawson, L. Bates, V. Curtis, R. Nype, Guests

"Call It Love"
M. Wright, M. Dawson

"There's Nothing Like It"
L. Bates

"Dreams Ago"
M. Wright, M. Dawson

(a) Waltz
B. Linn, R. Alexander

(b) The Story of Kitty
V. Bettis, D. Nillo, Dancers

"From This Day On"
Entire Company

ACT 2

"Who Done It?"
V. Curtis, R. Nype, D. Kennedy, P. Reed, L. Bates, Guests

"Blue Day"
M. Wright

"That's a Man Everytime"
V. Segal, M. Peterson, V. Curtis, Bridesmaids

"You Appeal to Me"
V. Segal, S. Erwin

"Who Done It?" (reprise)
L. Bates

"Let's Have a Party"
V. Bettis, B. Low, J. C. McCord, Dancers

"Call It Love" (reprise)
M. Wright, M. Dawson

"Thank You, Mrs. Butterfield"
Wedding Guests

Finale
Entire Company

KATHERINE DUNHAM AND HER COMPANY

1950.07

A Dance Revue in Three Parts, Prologue and 10 Scenes. Choreography and direction by Katherine Dunham. Costumes by John Pratt. Orchestra under the direction of Vadico Gogliano. Produced by Sol Hurok. Opened 19 April 1950 at the Broadway Theatre and closed 20 May 1950 after 38 performances.

CAST: KATHERINE DUNHAM, VANOYE AIKENS, LUCILLE ELLIS, LENWOOD MORRIS, WILBERT BRADLEY, CLAUDE MARCHANT, DOLORES HARPER, Wilbert Bradley, Miriam Burton, Eddy Clay, Edward Hawkins, Eloise Hill, Rosalie King, Jon Lei, Julie Robinson, Gordon Simpson, Anna Smith, Frances Taylor, Jacqueline Walcott.

First Pianist: Dorothea Freitag. *Drummers*: Julio Mendez, La Rosa Estrada.

PROLOGUE[11]

Scene 1

AFRIQUE (Native Air)
K. Dunham, M. Burton, R. King, G. Simpson, Corps de Ballet, Singers, Drummers

"The ladies are lovely, and the men are handsome and strong."

PART 1

BRAZILIAN SUITE

"Maracatu" (Brazilian Indian Rhythm; folk air.)
L. Ellis, J. Walcott, J. Lei

Scene 2

Choros (*Music by* Vadico Gogliano.)

a. A Brazilian 19th Century Quadrille
D. Harper, L. Morris, J. Robinson, W. Bradley

b. (Second Choro)
K. Dunham, D. Harper, L. Morris, J. Robinson, W. Bradley

c. (Third Choro)
K. Dunham, D. Harper, L. Morris, J. Robinson, W. Bradley

Scene 3

Adeus Terras
(*Music adapted by* Vadico Gogliano-Nardini.)
G. Simpson, M. Burton, R. King

Rio de Janeiro; the Avenida do Mongue section on a Saturday night. The singer leads the return of the men from the coffee plantations.

Scene 4

Batacuda
(*Music by* Don Alfonso.) K. Dunham, Men of the Company
A group of waterfront loafers flirt with a woman from the Bahia region.

Scene 5

VERACRUZIANA
(*Music by* Dorothea Freitag & Foster; adapted by Vadico Gogliano-Nardini.)
Musicians: L. Estrada, J. Mendez. *The Family from Yucatan*: R. King, G. Simpson, F. Taylor. A *"Tacos" Vendor*: M. Burton. *"The Rat"*: W. Bradley. *The Cuckold*: L. Morris. *The Veracruziana*: K. Dunham. *"Bamba" dancers of the village*: L. Ellis, D. Harper, J. Robinson, Corps de Ballet.

PART 2

Scene 1

Nostalgia
(*Music arranged by* Beane.) R. King, Sans-Souci Singers

Scene 2

Flaming Youth
(*by* "Brad" Gowans)

---

[11]Effective 8 May 1950, "Tropics," "Rites de Passage" and "Shango" were substituted for "Afrique," "Nostalgia" and "Barrelhouse."

Blues Singer: R. King. *Kansas City Woman*: L. Ellis.
And D. Harper, W. Bradley, L. Morris in the Charleston, Black Bottom, Mooch, Fishtail and Snakehips.

Scene 3

Barrelhouse

(*Music by* Stacy.)K. Dunham, V. Aikens

Florida Swamp Shimmy.

Scene 4

Jazz in Five Movements

(*Music by* Dorothea Freitag.)

a. Tango

J. Robinson, J. Lei

b. Jitterbug

D. Harper, J. Walcott, L. Morris

c. Stomp

L. Ellis

d. Blues

K. Dunham

e. Rondo

K. Dunham and her company

PART 3

Scene 1

"L'Ag'Ya"

(*Music by* Robert Sanders, Original Story by Katherine Dunham.)
Alcide: V. Aikens. *Julot*: W. Bradley. *Loulouse*: K. Dunham. *Roi Zombie*: L. Morris. *Porteresses, vendors, fishermen, townspeople of Vauclin*: Dunham Company.

The scene is Vauclin, a tiny 18th century fishing village in Martinique. Loulouse loves and is loved by Alcide. Julot, the villain, repulsed by Loulouse and filled with hatred and desire for revenge, decides to seek the aid of the king of the zombies. Deep in the jungle, Julot fearfully seeks the lair of the zombies and witnesses their strange rites which bring back the dead to life. Frightened, but remembering his purpose, Julot pursues Roi Zombie and obtains the "cambois," powerful love charm, from him. The following evening : it is a day of gaiety, opening with the stately Creole Mazurka, or "Mazouk," and moving into the uninhibited excitement of the Beguine. Into this scene enters Julot, horrifying the villagers when he exposes his coveted "cambois." Even Alcide is under its spell. Now begins the Majumba, love dance of ancient Africa. As Loulouse falls more and more under the charm, Alcide suddenly defies its power, breaks loose from the villages who protect him, and challenges Julot to the Ag'Ya, fighting dance of Martinique. In L'Ag'Ya and its ending are the climax and the consummation of the forces loosed in magic and superstition.

1950.08   PETER PAN

A Revival of the Play in Three Acts, 7 Scenes and an Epilogue[12]. Play by James M. Barrie with new songs by Leonard Bernstein. Production staged by John Burrell. Associate director, Wendy Toye. Scenery and lighting by Ralph Alswang. Costumes by Motley. Musical conductor, Ben Steinberg. Orchestrations by Hershy Kaye. Music coordination and arrangements, Trude Rittman. Flying effects arranged and apparatus installed by Kirby's Flying Ballet. Produced by Peter Lawrence and Roger L. Stevens. Opened 24 April 1950 at the Imperial Theatre, moved 3 October 1950 to the St. James Theatre, and closed 27 January 1951 after 320 performances.

<u>CAST</u> (in order of appearance): *Nana*: Norman Shelly. *Michael*: Charles Taylor. *Mrs. Darling*: PEG HILLIAS. *John*: Jack Dimond. *Wendy*: MARCIA HENDERSON. *Mr. Darling*: BORIS KARLOFF. *Peter Pan*: JEAN ARTHUR. *Liza*: Gloria Patrice. *Tottles*: Lee Barnett. *Slightly*: Richard Knox. *Curly*: Philip Hepburn. *The Twins*: Charles Brill, Edward Benjamin. *Nibs*: Buzzy Martin. *Captain Hook*: BORIS KARLOFF. *Starkey*: David Kurlan. *Smee*: JOE E. MARKS. *Jukes*: Will Scholz. *Cecco*: Nehemiah Persoff. *Mullins*: Harry Allen. *Noodler*: John Dennis. *Cookson*: William Marshall. *Whibbles*: Vincent Beck. *The Crocodile*: Norman Shelly. *Tiger Lily*: Gloria Patrice. *Big Chief Panther*: Ronnie Aul.
Indians: Kenneth Davis, Norman DeJoie, Loren Hightower, Jay Riley, William Sumner. *Mermaids*: Stephanie Augustine, Eleanor Winter. *Pirates*: Alf Mason: Kenneth Davis. *Canary Robb*: William Sumner. *Flash McCready*: Jay Riley.

Act 1: The Nursery.

Act 2, Scene 1: The Never Land. *Scene 2*: The Mermaids' Lagoon. *Scene 3*: The Home Under the Ground.

Act 3, Scene 1: The Pirate Ship. *Scene 2*: Under the Sea. *Scene 3*: The Nursery. *Epilogue*: The Treetops.

ACT 1

"Who Am I?"

M. Henderson

ACT 2

"The Pirate Song"

B. Karloff, Pirates

"Never Land"

S. Augustin, E. Winter

"My House"

M. Henderson

"Peter, Peter"

M. Henderson

ACT 3

"The Plank"

B. Karloff, Pirates

1950.09   TICKETS, PLEASE!

An Intimate Musical Revue in Two Acts, 21 Scenes. Sketches by Harry Herrmann, Edmund Rice, Jack Roche and Ted Luce. Music and lyrics by Lyn Duddy, Joan Edwards, Mel Tolkin, Lucille Kallen and Clay Warnick. Directed by Mervyn Nelson. Choreography by Joan Mann. Settings designed by Ralph Alswang. Costumes designed by Peggy Morrison. Musical conductor, Phil Ingalls. Incidental music by Phil Ingalls and Hal Hastings. Orchestrations by Ted Royal. Produced by Arthur Klein. Opened 27 April 1950 at the Coronet Theatre, moved 30 October 1950 to the Mark Hellinger Theatre, and closed 25 November 1950 after 245 performances.

<u>CAST</u>: THE HARTMANS (Grace and Paul), JACK ALBERTSON, DOROTHY JARNAC, PATRICIA BRIGHT, TOMMY WONDER, ROGER PRICE, BILL NORVAS AND THE UPSTARTS (Dee Arlen, Larry Kert, Ronnie Edwards, Phyllis Cameron), Stuart Wade, Midge Parker, Mildred Hughes.

ACT 1

Scene 1

Prologue

G. Hartman, P. Hartman, M. Hughes

Scene 2

"Tickets, Please!"

B. Norvas and the Upstarts

(*Music and Lyrics by* Mel Tolkin, Lucille Kallen and Clay Warnick.)

Scene 3

Roller Derby

J. Albertson, G. Hartman, P. Hartman

Scene 4

"Washington Square"

S. Wade

(*Music and Lyrics by* Mel Tolkin, Lucille Kallen and Clay Warnick.)
Danced and Choreographed by D. Jarnac. *Artist*: J. Albertson.

Scene 5

"Darn It, Baby, That's Love"

J. Albertson, P. Bright

(*Music and Lyrics by* Joan Edwards and Lyn Duddy.)

Scene 6

Roger Price[13]

Scene 7

"The Ballet Isn't Ballet Any More"

P. Bright

(*Music and Lyrics by* Jack Weinstock, Willie Gilbert and Herb Hecht.)

---

[12]First presented in New York 6 November 1905 at the Empire Theatre for 223 performances.

[13]Roger Price monologues written by himself. After Price departed the show, 2 untitled monologues by Len Stern were performed by cast replacements Gabe [Gabriel] Dell and Norman Abbott.

Scene 8

Les Ballets
G. Hartman, P. Hartman, R. Price, B. Norvas and the Upstarts

Scene 9

"Restless"
M. Parker
(*Music and Lyrics by* Joan Edwards and Lyn Duddy.)
Danced by T. Wonder.

Scene 10

A Senate Investigation
R. Price, J. Albertson, P. Bright, G. Hartman, P. Hartman

Scene 11

"You Can't Take It With You"
P. Bright, J. Albertson, G. Hartman
(*Music and Lyrics by* Joan Edwards and Lyn Duddy.)

Scene 12

Drama—The Plot Is Always the Same
The Author: R. Price. *The Thespians:* G. Hartman, P. Hartman, J. Albertson, P. Bright, D. Jarnac, T. Wonder, M. Hughes, B. Norvas and the Upstarts, M. Parker, S. Wade.

ACT 2
Scene 1

"Back at the Palace"
P. Hartman, J. Albertson
(*Music and Lyrics by* Mel Tolkin, Lucille Kallen and Clay Warnick. *Additional lyrics by* Jack Fox.)

Scene 2

"Symbol of Fire"
S. Wade
(*Music and Lyrics by* Mel Tolkin, Lucille Kallen and Clay Warnick.)
Danced by G. Hartman, P. Hartman, T. Wonder, B. Norvas, L. Kert, R. Edwards.

Scene 3

"(Television's) Tough on Love"
P. Bright
(*Music and Lyrics by* Joan Edwards and Lyn Duddy.)

Scene 4

Mister Proggle
G. Hartman, P. Hartman

Scene 5

"The Moment I Looked in Your Eyes"
S. Wade, M. Hughes
(*Music and Lyrics by* Joan Edwards and Lyn Duddy.)

Scene 6

"Spring Has Come"
(*Music by* Mel Tolkin and Max Liebman.)
Danced by D. Jarnac, T. Wonder, J. Albertson, B. Bright, B. Norvas and the Upstarts.

Scene 7

Roger Price

Scene 8

"Maha Roger"
B. Norvas and the Upstarts
(*Music and Lyrics by* Mel Tolkin, Lucille Kallen and Clay Warnick.)

Scene 9

Maha the Great
G. Hartman, P. Hartman, B. Norvas and the Upstarts, M. Hughes

1950.10   # BRIGADOON

A Revival of the Musical Play in Two Acts, 11 Scenes[14]. Book and lyrics by Alan Jay Lerner. Music by Frederick Loewe. Dance and musical numbers by Agnes de Mille. Staged by Robert Lewis. Scenery designed by Oliver

---

[14]Original production opened 13 March 1947 at the Ziegfeld Theatre for 581 performances. For Synopsis of Scenes and Musical Numbers, see original 1947 production.

Smith. Costumes designed by David Ffolkes. Vocal arrangements by Frederick Loewe. Orchestrations by Ted Royal. Lighting by Peggy Clark. Orchestra and chorus under the direction of Ignace Strasfogel. Produced by Cheryl Crawford. Opened 2 May 1950 at the New York City Center and closed 21 May 1950 after 24 performances.

CAST (in order of appearance): *Tommy Albright:* PHIL HANNA. *Jeff Douglas:* PETER TURGEON. *Sandy Dean:* Douglas Rideout. *Archie Beaton:* Thaddeus Clancy. *Fishmonger:* Elizabeth Logue. *Harry Beaton:* JAMES JAMIESON. *Angus MacGuffie:* Angus Cairns. *Andrew MacLaren:* Donald McKee. *Fiona MacLaren:* VIRGINIA OSWALD. *Jean MacLaren:* ANN DEASY. *Meg Brockie:* SUSAN JOHNSON. *Charlie Dalrymple:* JEFF WARREN. *Maggie Anderson:* Virginia Richardson. *Mr. Lundie:* FRED STEWART. *Stuart Dalrymple:* James Schlader. *Sword Dancers:* Wayne Sheridan, James White. *Bagpiper:* James McFadden. *Frank:* Angus Cairns. *Jane Ashton:* Winifred Ainslee.
Townsfolk of Brigadoon: Singers: Sylvia Chaney, Elizabeth Early, Margaret Hunter, Grayce Spence, Bobra Suiter, Eileen Turner, Lorraine Waldman, Dorothy Zurn. Robert Busch, Arthur Carroll, Walter Kelvin, Louis Polacek, Earl Redding, Douglas Rideout, James Schlader, Stanley Simmonds. *Dancers:* Meredith Baylis, Janice Boyd, Betty Buday, Barbara Davenport, Julie Hiller, Elizabeth Logue, Barbara McClarin, Yolanda Novak. William Harris, Lloyd Malenfant, William Narcy, Glenn Olson, Robert Scoble, Wayne Sheridan, James White, Joseph Wiley.

1950.11   # THE LIAR

A Musical in Two Acts, 7 Scenes. Book by Edward Eager and Alfred Drake. Based on the play of the same name by Carlo Goldoni. Music by James Mundy. Lyrics by Edward Eager. Directed by Alfred Drake. Musical sequences staged by Hanya Holm. Setting and lighting by Donald Oenslager. Costumes designed by Motley. Musical director, Lehman Engel. Orchestrations by Lehman Engel and Ben Ludlow, Jr. Swordplay staged by Leslie Litomy. Produced by Dorothy Willard and Thomas Hammond. Opened 18 May 1950 at the Broadhurst Theatre and closed 27 May 1950 after 12 performances.

CAST (in order of appearance): *Innkeeper:* Walter F. Appler. *Innkeeper's Wife:* JEAN HANDZLIK. *Servingwench:* Lee Wilcox. *Servingmen:* Leonardo Cimino, Martin Balsam. *Woman at Window:* May Muth. *Fiori:* Margery Oldroyd. *Vino:* David Collyer. *Vegetabili:* Marybelle Norton. *Letter Carrier:* Leslie Litomy. *Urchin:* William Myers. *Captain of the Venetian Guards:* ROBERT PENN. *Guards:* Edward Bryce, William Hogue, Laurence Weber, Walter Matthau. *Lelio Bisognosi:* WILLIAM EYTHE. *Arlecchino:* JOSHUA SHELLEY. *Brighella:* RUSSELL COLLINS. *Florindo Pallido:* GLENN BURRIS. *Rosaura Balanzoni:* BARBARA MOSER. *Beatrice Balanzoni:* KAREN LINDGREN. *Ottavio Ossimorsi:* STANLEY CARLSON. *Colombina:* PAULA LAURENCE. *Pantalone Bisognosi:* MELVILLE COOPER. *Doctor Balanzoni:* PHILIP COOLIDGE. *Cleonice Anselmi:* BARBARA ASHLEY.

Place: Venice. *Time:* Spring in the Sixteenth Century. The entire action takes place within twenty-four hours.

Act 1, Scene 1: The Square. *Scene 2:* The Inn. *Scene 3:* The Doctor's House. *Scene 4:* The Square.

Act 2, Scene 1: The Square. *Scene 2:* The Doctor's House. *Scene 3:* The Square.

ACT 1
Scene 1

"March of the Guards"
R. Penn, Guards

"The Ladies' Opinion"
J. Handzlik, M. Muth, L. Wilcox, M. Oldroyd, M. Norton

"You've Stolen My Heart"
G. Burris

"The Liar's Song"
W. Eythe, J. Shelley

"Supper Trio"
W. Eythe, J. Shelley, S. Carlson

"Truth"
P. Laurence, J. Shelley, W. Eythe, B. Moser, K. Lindgren

Scene 3

"Lackaday"
B. Moser, G. Burris

"Stop Holding Me Back"
S. Carlson, Company

Scene 4

"What's in a Name"
B. Moser, W. Eythe

Finale

ACT 2
Scene 1
  "Women's Work"
    P. Laurence, J. Handzlik, L. Wilcox, M. Muth
    (*Music by* Lehman Engel.)
  "Spring"
    P. Laurence, R. Collins
  "Stomachs and Stomachs"
    J. Shelley
  "A Jewel of a Duel"
    R. Penn, B. Moser, K. Lindgren,
    P. Laurence, M. Cooper, P. Coolidge, W. Eythe, J. Shelley
  "Out of Sight, Out of Mind"
    W. Eythe, Company

Scene 2
  "Lackaday" (reprise)
    B. Moser, G. Burris
  "A Plot to Catch a Man In"
    Company
Scene 3
  "Out of Sight, Out of Mind" (reprise)
    B. Ashley
  "Funeral March"
    Company
  "'Twill Never Be the Same"
    B. Ashley
  Finale

1950–1951 SEASON

Gertrude Lawrence and Yul Brynner in THE KING AND I (Photo: Vandamm Studio)
Billy Rose Theatre Collection, New York Public Library for the Performing Arts

1950–1951 SEASON

MICHAEL TODD'S PEEP SHOW

1950.12

A Musical Revue in Two Acts, 23 Scenes. Sketches by Bobby Clark, H. I. Phillips, William Roos, Billy K. Wells. Music by Bhumibol [Phumiphon Aduldet, King of Thailand], Sammy Fain, Herb Magidson, Harold Rome, Raymond Scott, Sammy Stept, Jule Styne. Lyrics by Harold Rome, Bob Hilliard, Dan Shapiro, Chakraband [Chancellor of Thailand]. Dances by James Starbuck. Scenery by Howard Bay. Costumes by Irene Sharaff. Scenes directed by Mr. Robert Edwin Clark, Esq. (Bobby Clark). Staged and lighted by Hassard Short. Orchestra conducted by Clay Warnick. Musical arranger, Mel Pahl. Vocal Arrangements, Clay Warnick. Musical supervision by Jack Saunders. Orchestrations by Ken Hopkins and Irwin Kostal. Produced by Michael Todd. Opened 28 June 1950 at the Winter Garden and closed 25 February 1951 after 278 performances.

CAST: LINA ROMAY, LILLY CHRISTINE, CLIFFORD GUEST, PEIRO BROTHERS, CORRINE & TITO VALDEZ, SHANNON DEAN, JUNE ALLEN, CHRISTINE & MOLL, MYRTILL & PACAUD, LINDA BISHOP, LES FARCEURS, (THOMAS) 'BOZO' SYNDER, 'RED' MARSHALL, 'HI WILBERFORCE' CONLEY, (BEN) 'SPIKE' HAMILTON, (JACK) 'PEANUTS' MANN, DICK 'GABBY' DANA.

The Peepers: Charlotte Bergmeier, Penny Davidson, Glen Grayson, Bucy, Hegyi, June Kirby, Barbara Leslie, Rosemarie Lynn, Mickey Miller, Mira Stefen, Gwenna Lee Smith, Jeanne Tyler, Rosemary Williamson. *Ladies and Gentlemen of the Ensemble*: Jan Arnold, Lisa Ayres, Wendy Bartlett, Lynn Bernay, Gloria Danyl, Audrey Dearden, Bettina Edwards, Carol Hendricks, Christina Frerichs, Frances Krell, Jill Melford, Leila Martin, Ronny Oatley, Elsie Rhodes, Kaja Sundsten, Jackie Tapp, Mary Thomas, Valarie Wallace, Ruth Vernon, Fern Whitney, Ronan York, Hubert Bland, James Brock, Garry Fleming, Edward Gambos, Vincent Henry, Robert Davis, Ralph Linn, John Juliano, Frank Reynolds.

ACT 1
Scene 1
"The Model Hasn't Changed"
(*Music and Lyrics by* Harold Rome.)
Singer: L. Bishop. *The Keyhole Girl*: M. Donn.
Ladies of the Ensemble.

Scene 2
Street Scene
R. Marshall, H. W. Conley, P. Mann, B. Snyder,
D. G. Dana, J. Allen, S. Dean, L. Bishop

Scene 3
"You've Never Been Loved"
L. Romay, Peiro Brothers, Ensemble
(*Music by* Sammy Stept. *Lyrics by* Dan Shapiro.)

Scene 4
Friendly Neighbors
(*by* Billy K. Wells)
First Wife: L. Romay. *First Husband*: P. Mann.
Second Wife: S. Dean. *Second Husband*: R. Marshall.
Policeman: D. G. Dana.

Scene 5
"Got What It Takes"
Ladies Ensemble
(*Music by* Sammy Stept. *Lyrics by* Dan Shapiro.)

Scene 6
The Shades of Night

Scene 7
Minnie
Wife: C. Moll. *Husband*: H. W. Conley.
Second Husband: D. G. Dana.
Detective: S. Hamilton.

Scene 8
"Desire"
(*Music by* Raymond Scott.)
The Cat Girl: L. Christine. Ladies Ensemble.

Scene 9
Clifford Guest and Lester[1]

Scene 10
Midway[2]
Barker: D. G. Dana. *First Rube*: R. Marshall. *Second Rube*: B. Snyder. *Slicker*: P. Mann. *Third Rube*: H. W. Conley. *Passerby*: S. Dean. *Joseph Paige*: S. Hamilton.

Scene 11
Clifford Guest

Scene 12
"Ballet Burlesque"
Ballerina: J. Allen, L. Bishop, Ensemble.

Scene 13
"I Hate a Parade"
H. W. Conley, R. Marshall, B. Snyder, P. Mann, D. G. Dana
(*Music and Lyrics by* Harold Rome.) *Danced by* J. Moll.

Scene 14
"Blue Night"
A. Carroll, Ensemble
(*Music by* Bhumibol. *Lyrics by* Chakraband.)
The Idols: Myrtill and Pacaud.

ACT 2
Scene 1
"Stay With the Happy People"
L. Romay, Ensemble
(*Music by* Jule Styne. *Lyrics by* Bob Hilliard.)

Scene 2
Love Nest[3]
Proprietor: D. G. Dana. *Wilbur Winterbottom*: H. W. Conley. *Mlle. Dagmar Pepper*: L. Romay. *Banker*: R. Marshall. *Butler*: S. Hamilton.

Scene 3
"Violins From Nowhere"
A. Carroll, Ensemble
(*Music by* Sammy Fain. *Lyrics by* Herb Magidson.)
(*Danced by*) Corrine, T. Valdez

Scene 4
"Pocketful of Dreams"
R. Marshall, P. Mann, B. Snyder, H. W. Conley
(*Music and Lyrics by* Harold Rome.)

Scene 5
Cocktails at Five (parody of "The Cocktail Party")
Mrs. Irvington Irving: S. Dean. *Beechum*: P. Mann. *First Paperhanger*: S. Hamilton. *Second Paperhanger*: B. Snyder. *Mr. Irvington Irving*: D. G. Dana. *Waldo Bromley*: H. W. Conley. *Lydia Fitz-Hugh*: L. Bishop. *Dr. C C. Chedder*: R. Marshall. *Guest*: C. Guest.

Scene 6
"Gimme the Shimmy"
(*Music and Lyrics by* Harold Rome.)
The Charleston: G. Fleming, R. Linn, J. Brock, F. Reynolds, G. Danyl, C. Frerichs, F. Whitney, L. Bernay.

Scene 7
The Castle Walk
(*Danced by*) Corrine, T. Valdez

---

[1]When Clifford Guest and Lester departed the show, their solo spots were taken over by the Maxwells (Max Kitson, Lou Sachse) and Dick Dana, respectively.
[2]During run, replaced by:
Lower Eight
Conductor: D. G. Dana. *First Passenger*: R. Marshall. *Second Passenger*: B. Snyder. *Absolm (and eight wives)*: A. Albin. *Candy Butcher*: S. Hamilton. *First Sailor*: C. Chartier. *Second Sailor*: L. Villani. *First Couple*: S. Dean, R. Towers. *Third Passenger*: J. P. Mann. *Second Couple*: H. W. Conley, R. Williamson. *Fourth Passenger*: L. Bishop.
[3]During run, replaced by:
Dentist
Dentist: J. P. Mann. *First Patient*: A. Albin. *Nurse*: L. Bishop. *Second Patient*: R. Marshall.

Scene 8

The Shimmy
L. Romay
(*Danced by*) L. Christine.

Scene 9

Finale
Entire Company

THE TELEPHONE
and THE MEDIUM

1950.13

A Revival of Two Musical Plays (Operas)[4]. Libretto and music by Gian-Carlo Menotti. Designed and lighted by William Riva. Staged by Gian-Carlo Menotti. Musical director, William McDermott. Produced by David Heilweil and Derrick Lynn-Thomas in association with Chandler Cowles. Opened 19 July 1950 at the Arena and closed 14 October 1950 after 102 performances.

THE TELEPHONE

A Comic Opera in One Act.

<u>CAST</u>: *Lucy*: EDITH GORDON. *Ben*: PAUL KING.

THE MEDIUM

A Tragic Opera in Two Acts.

<u>CAST</u>: *Monica*: EVELYN KELLER, Derna De Lys (alt.). *Toby*: LEO COLEMAN. *Madame Flora*: ZELMA GEORGE. *Mrs. Gobineau*: DERNA DE LYS, Edith Gordon, (alt.). *Mr. Gobineau*: Paul King. *Mrs. Nolan*: Dorothy Staiger.

1950.14

PARDON OUR FRENCH

A Musical Revue in Two Acts, 19 Scenes. Sketches by Ole [John Siegford] Olsen and Chic [Harold Ogden] Johnson. Music by Victor Young. Lyrics by Edward Heyman. Additional music by Harry Sukman. Additional lyrics by Olsen and Johnson. Musical numbers and choreography by Ernst and Maria Matray. Musical director, Harry Sukman. Scenery by Albert Johnson. Costumes by Jack Mosser. Orchestral and choral arrangements by Al Woodbury, Ruby Raskin, Fran Frey. Produced by Olsen and Johnson. Opened 5 October 1950 at the Broadway Theatre, vacationed 17-24 December 1950, and closed 6 January 1951 after 100 performances.[5]

<u>CAST</u>: OLE OLSEN, CHIC JOHNSON, DENISE DARCEL, MARTY MAY, JUNE JOHNSON, BILL SHIRLEY, HELENE STANLEY, PATRICIA DENISE, J. C. OLSEN, GEORGE ZORITCH, LUBOV ROUDENKO, FAY DE WITT, NINA VARELA, Billy Kay, Phil Terry, Chickie Johnson, Maurice Millard, Leo Anthony, Richard Clayton, Six Mighty Atoms (Charles Young, Teddy Kiss, Jack Zlik, Steve Kochanski, Ivor Boden, George Day), Robert Rossellat, Howard Joslin, The Konyots (Robert, Marion), John Ciampa, David Collyer, Les Huit Chanteuses.
Showgirls: Orlando Merdene, Helene Perry, Cynthia Cavanaugh, Felice Ingersoll, Sandra Insel, Jackson Jourdan, Diana Laye, Millicent Roy, June St. Clair, Helen L. Thompson. *Dancers*: Joan Bonomo, Iris Burton, Gloria Braun, Pepper Cole, Christine Petersen, Salli Sorvo, Gloria Stone, Joy Walker, Carolyn Wells, Edward Andrews, Richard Cahill, Fred Curt, Phil Gerard, Jack Monts, George Tomal, Brahm van den Berg, Richard Wyatt. *Singers*: Margot Carmen, Cecile Descant, Bunny Lane, Joan Rodgers, Stacey Scott, Robert Arnold, Walter Russell, Harry Snow.

ACT 1[6]

Scene 1

"Pardon Our French"
(*Music by* Harry Sukman. *Lyrics by* Olsen and Johnson.)
The Stage Hand: P. Terry. *The Newsboy*: F. Curt. *The Dandies*: R. Rossellat, R. Wyatt. *Ladies in Red*: C. Petersen, J. Walker. *The Post Card Vendor*: P. Gerard. *The Tourists*: R. Cahill, C. Wells, P. Cole. *The Apaches*: G. Stone, B. v.d. Berg. *The Waiters*: J. Monts, G. Tomal. *The Shadow Dancer*: G. Zoritch. And Dancers, Singers.

Scene 2

Street Scene
Themselves: Olsen and Johnson. *The Quizzer*: J. Johnson. *The Quizzed*: B. Shirley. *The Little Mother*: C. Johnson. *The Pleader*: P. Terry. *The Model*:

S. Insel. *The Winner*: M. Roy. *The Vendor*: B. Kay. *The Penn-Staters*: M. Millard, C. Young. *The Shady Characters*: I. Boden, J. Zlik. *The Whiz*: G. Day. *The Chasers*: J. Burton, C. Petersen, G. Braun.

Scene 3

No. 96 Rue Blondell
The Boy: L. Anthony. *The Girl*: D. Darcel. *The Maid*: J. Johnson. *The Friend*: C. Johnson. *Another Friend*: R. Rossellat. *The Patrons*: Olsen and Johnson. *The Watchers*: D. Collyer, N. Varela, J. C. Olsen.

Scene 4

"There's No Man Like a Snowman"
H. Stanley
School Girls: G. Braun, P. Cole, C. Petersen, S. Sorvo, G. Stone, J. Walker, C. Wells *Snowmen*: R. Cahill, F. Curt, R. Rossellat, G. Tomal, B. v.d. Berg, R. Wyatt, S. Kochansky, C. Young.

Scene 5

Life of a Salesman
Salesmen: M. May, B. Shirley, P. Terry. *Click, Click*: C. Johnson. *Man in Hiding*: G. Day.

Scene 6

"I Ought to Know More About You"
F. DeWitt, B. Shirley, Les Huit Chanteuses
The Columnists: C. Wells, R. Clayton. *The Wife*: N. Varela. *The Husband*: B. Kay. *The Man in Red*: F. Curt. *The Man from Home*: G. Tomal. *The Chaste*: M. Olive. *The Reporter*: R. Konyot.

Scene 7

An Evening with Marie Antoinette
Maid: H. Stanley. *Marie*: J. Johnson. *Gentlemen Callers*: L. Anthony, R. Wyatt, B. Shirley. *Pages*: B. Kay, L. Anthony. *Trumpeters*: S. Insel, M. Roy. *Louis XVI*: Chic Johnson. *His Other Self*: P. Terry. *His Shadow*: C. Young. *Lord Calvert*: W. Russell. *Soldiers*: G. Day, I. Boden, C. Young, S. Kochansky, T. Kiss, J. Zlik. *The Victor*: M. May. *Ladies of the Court*: Chickie Johnson, M. Roy, M. Millard.

Scene 8

The Konyots
The Models: C. Cavanaugh, F. Ingersoll, J. Jourdan, D. Laye, J. St. Clair, H. L. Thompson. *The Voice*: S. Scott.

Scene 9

"Venezia and Her Three Lovers"
(*A Ballet by* Ernst Matray.)
Prologue: The Lovers: G. Zoritch, R. Cahill, B. v.d. Berg. *The Gondolier*: C. Johnson. *Ballet: Venezia*: P. Denise. *The Taylor*: R. Rossellat. *The First Lover*: G. Zoritch. *The Second Lover*: R. Cahill. *The Third Lover*: B. v.d. Berg. *The Drunkard*: P. Terry.

Scene 10

Marty May

Scene 11

"A Face in the Crowd"
B. Shirley
First Policeman: G. Zoritch. *The Seeker*: B. Shirley. *Also Seeking*: J. Johnson. *The Face*: P. Denise. *The Apache Chief*: L. Anthony. *Second Policeman*: D. Collyer. *The Strollers*: J. Bonomo, M. Carmen, B. Lane. *Other Apaches*: R. Cahill, R. Rossellat, P. Gerard, R. Wyatt, P. Terry. *The Hunters*: C. Johnson, M. May. *The Whistler*: J. C. Olsen. *The Whiz*: G. Day. *The Sinister One*: L. Anthony. *The Shaker*: P. Terry. *The Street Cleaner*: R. Rossellat. *The Loser*: J. Johnson. *The Pages*: I. Boden, C. Young, T. Kiss, S. Kochansky. *The Ballerina*: P. Denise. *Corps de Ballet*: J. Bonomo, G. Braun, C. Cole, C. Petersen, S. Sorvo, G. Stone, J. Walker, C. Wells.

ACT 2

Scene 1

"I'm Gonna Make a Fool Out of April"
(B. Shirley, H. Stanley)
The Girls with Umbrellas: G. Stone, P. Cole, J. Walker, C. Wells. *The Gendarmes*: R. Rossellat, B. v.d. Berg, R. Wyatt, R. Cahill. *Boy*: B. Shirley. *Girl*: H. Stanley. *Parisiennes*: Chickie Johnson, F. De Witt, C. Descant, M. Carmen, B. Lane, J. Rodgers, S. Scott, S. Sorvo, G. Braun, H. Talbot, J. Bonomo, I. Burton, F. Ingersoll, S. Insel, D. Laye, M. Roy, J. St. Clair, H. Thompson. *Parisians*: P. Gerard, E. Andrews, R. Arnold, D. Collyer, W. Russell, H. Snow, L. Anthony, G. Tomal, P. Terry, J. Monts.

Scene 2

"The Flower Song"
Chic Johnson, M. May

Scene 3

Tourist Service
The Visiting Rotarians: Chic Johnson, M. May. *Miss Information*: J. Johnson.

---

[4]Originally presented in New York 1 May 1947 at the Ethel Barrymore Theatre for 211 performances. For Synopsis of Scenes, see original 1947 production.
[5]Direction uncredited.
[6]First produced in New York City January 18-28 1950 at the Brander Matthews Theatre, Columbia University for 10 performances.

The Counterman: D. Collyer. *Beauty on a Binge*: M. Millard. *The Petite Girl*: Chickie Johnson. *Big John*: R. Arnold. *Little John*: I. Boden. *Along Came Laughing Water*: J. C. Olsen. *Mr. Pop-Up*: P. Terry. *Mr. Lack-lustre*: B. Kay. *Mr. Mystery*: J. Ciampa.

Scene 4

"Dolly from the Follies Bergere"
D. Darcel
(*Music by* Harry Sukman. *Lyrics by* Olsen and Johnson.)
The Bluebeards: F. Curt, G. Tomal, B. v.d.Berg. *The Midinettes*: M. Carmen, Chickie Johnson, B. Lane.

Scene 5

A Night on the *Ile de France*
The Passenger: Chic Johnson. *The Purser*: L. Anthony. *Mrs. Tacit*: J. Johnson. *The Tourists*: P. Terry, B. Kay, J. C. Olsen, M. Millard, I. Boden, G. Day, S. Kochanski, C. Young.

Scene 6

"The Polker Polka"
The Gentleman: B. Shirley. *The Pages*: I. Boden, S. Kochansky. *The Gamblers*: E. Andrews, R. Cahill, F. Curt, J. Monts, R. Rossellat, G. Tomal, B. v.d. Berg, R. Wyatt. *The Ladies of the Casino*: J. Bonomo, G. Braun, P. Cole, C. Petersen, G. Stone, S. Sorvo, J. Walker, C. Wells. *The Polka Dancers*: L. Roudenko, G. Zoritch. *The Lady in Ricksha*: J. Johnson. And Les Huit Chanteuses and Showgirls.

Scene 7

Olsen and Johnson and Nina Varela

Scene 8

Finale
Entire Company

1950.15   CALL ME MADAM

A Musical Comedy in Two Acts, 13 Scenes. Book by Howard Lindsay and Russel Crouse. Music and lyrics by Irving Berlin. Directed by George Abbott. Dances and musical numbers staged by Jerome Robbins. Scenery and costumes by Raoul Pene du Bois. Miss Merman's dresses by Main Bocher. Musical director, Jay Blackton. Orchestrations by Don Walker. Additional orchestrations by Joe Glover. Dance music arrangements by Genevieve Pitot and Jesse Meeker. Produced by Leland Hayward. Opened 12 October 1950 at the Imperial Theatre and closed 3 May 1952 after 644 performances.

<u>CAST</u> (in order of appearance): *Mrs. Sally Adams*: ETHEL MERMAN. *The Secretary of State*: Geoffrey Lumb. *Supreme Court Justice*: OWEN COLL. *Congressman Wilkins*: Pat Harrington. *Henry Gibson*: William David. *Kenneth Gibson*: RUSSELL NYPE. *Senator Gallagher*: RALPH CHAMBERS. *Secretary to Mrs. Adams*: Jeanne Bal. *Butler*: William Hail. *Senator Brockbank*: Jay Velie. *Cosmo Constantine*: PAUL LUKAS. *Pemberton Maxwell*: ALAN HEWITT. *Clerk*: Stowe Phelps. *Hugo Tantinnin*: E A. KRUMSCHMIDT. *Sebastian Sebastian*: HENRY LASCOE. *Princess Maria*: GALINA TALVA. *Court Chamberlain*: Willaim David. *A Maid*: Lily Paget. *Grand Duchess Sophie*: Lilia Skala. *Grand Duke Otto*: OWEN COLL. *Principal Dancers*: Tommy Rall, Muriel Bentley, Arthur Partington, Norma Kaiser. *The 'Potato Bugs'*: Ollie Engebretsen, Richard Fjellman.

Singers: Rae Abruzzo, Jeanne Bal, Trudy DeLuz, Lydia Fredericks, Estelle Gardner, Ruth McVayne, Lily Paget, Noella Peloquin, Helene Whitney, Aristede Bartis, Nathaniel Frey, William Hail, Albert Linville, Robert Penn, Tom Reider, John Sheehan, Stanley Simmonds, Ray Stephens. *Dancers*: Shellie Farrell, Nina Frenkin, Patricia Hammerlee, Barbara Heath, Norma Kaiser, Virginia LeRoy, Kirsten Valbor, Fred Hearn, Allan Knowls, Kenneth LeRoy, Ralph Linn, Douglas Moppert, Arthur Partington, Bobby Tucker, William Weslow.

The play is laid in two mythical countries. One is called Lichtenburg, the other the United States of America. Neither the character of Mrs. Sally Adams, nor Miss Ethel Merman, resembles any other person alive or dead.

Act 1, Scene 1: Office of the Secretary of State. Scene 2: Sally's Living-room in Washington. Scene 3: Public Square in Lichtenburg. Scene 4: Reception Room in the American Embassy. Scene 5: Public Square in Lichtenburg. Scene 6: The Lichtenburg Fair. Scene 7: A Corridor at the Palace. Scene 8: Sally's Sitting-room at the Embassy.

Act 2, Scene 1: The Public Square. Scene 2: The Embassy Garden. Scene 3: The Public Square. Scene 4: Sally's Sitting-room. Scene 5: Sally's Living-room in Washington.

ACT 1
Scene 2

"Mrs. Sally Adams"
The Company

Scene 3

"The Hostess With the Mostes' on the Ball"
E. Merman

"Washington Square Dance"
E. Merman, Company

Scene 4

"Lichtenburg"
P. Lukas, Singers

Scene 5

"Can You Use Any Money Today?"
E. Merman

"Marrying For Love"
P. Lukas, E. Merman

Scene 6

"The Ocarina"
G. Talva, R. Linn, O. Engebretson, R. Fjellman, Company

"It's a Lovely Day Today"
R. Nype, G. Talva

"It's a Lovely Day Today" (reprise)
R. Nype, N. Kaiser, A. Partington, Company

Scene 8

"The Best Thing For You (Would Be Me)"
E. Merman, P. Lukas

ACT 2
Scene 1

"Lichtenburg" (reprise)
P. Lukas, Singers

Scene 2

"Something To Dance About"
E. Merman, T. Rall, M. Bentley, N. Kaiser, A. Partington, Company

"Once Upon a Time Today"
R. Nype

Scene 3

"They Like Ike"
P. Harrington, R. Chambers, J. Velie

Scene 4

"You're Just in Love"
E. Merman, R. Nype

"The Best Thing For You (Would Be Me)" (reprise)
E. Merman, P. Lukas

"It's a Lovely Day Today" (reprise)
R. Nype, G. Talva

Scene 5

"Mrs. Sally Adams" (reprise)
The Company

Finale
E. Merman, Company

1950.16   THE BARRIER

A Musical Drama in Two Acts, 3 Scenes[7]. Book and lyrics by Langston Hughes. (Based on his play "Mulatto.") Music by Jan Meyerowitz. Choreography by Charles Weidman and Doris Humphrey. Setting by H. A. Condell. Conductor, Herbert Zipper. Staged by Doris Humphrey. Produced by Michael Myerberg and Joel Spector. Opened 2 November 1950 at the Broadhurst Theatre and closed 4 November 1950 after 4 performances.[8]

<u>CAST</u>: *William*: Lorenzo Herrera. *Sally*: Charlotte Holloman. *Livonia*: Dolores Bowman. *Maid*: Reri Grist. *Houseman*: John Diggs. *Sam*: Laurence Watson. *Talbot*: Victor Thorley. *Col. Thomas Norwood*: LAWRENCE TIBBETT. *Cora Lewis*: MURIEL RAHN. *Fred Higgins*: Richard Dennis. *Bert*: WILTON CLARY. *Plantation Storekeeper*: Robert Tankersley. *Undertaker*: Jesse Jacobs. *Assistant to the Undertaker*: Stuart Hodes. *Young Norwood*, sung by LAWRENCE TIBBETT, danced by Marc Breaux. *Young Cora*, sung by Charlotte Holloman, danced by Josephine Keene. *The Bride*: Helene Ellis.

The action takes place in a rural Georgia community between noon and night of a hot summer day.

---

[7]First produced in New York City January 18-28 1950 at the Brander Matthews Theatre, Columbia University for 10 performances.
[8]Costumes uncredited.

Act 1: The Living room at Albamar, Thomas Norwood's plantation, noon.

Act 2, Scene 1: The same, late afternoon. *Scene 2*: That night.

ACT 1[9]

"September Sunlight"
L. Herrera, C. Holloman

"City Theme"
D. Bowman

"But, Colonel Tom"
M. Rahn, L. Tibbett

"I Just Wanted to Tell You Goodbye"
C. Holloman, L. Tibbett

"Little Girl Goodbye"
Negroes

"You Should Have Married Again"
R. Dennis

"Help Me, Lawd"
M. Rahn, L. Herrera

"It's a Wonderful Day"
W. Clary

"You Are Not Your Father's Son"
M. Rahn, W. Clary

ACT 2

Scene 1

"Flesh of My Flesh, Bone of My Bone"
L. Tibbett

"Trio"
M. Rahn, W. Clary, L. Tibbett

"My Father's Own House"
L. Tibbett, W. Clary, M. Rahn

"Damn You, Colonel Tom!"
M. Rahn

Scene 2

"I Don't Want to Die"
L. Watson

"The First Time I Was Yours in the Dark"
M. Rahn

"And From the Earth a Sweetness Rose"
C. Holloman, L. Tibbett

"Go to Sleep"
C. Holloman

Finale ("Mercy, Lawd")
M. Rahn, W. Clary

1950.17   GUYS AND DOLLS

A Musical Fable (Comedy) in Two Acts, 17 Scenes. Book by Jo Swerling and Abe Burrows. Based on a story ("The Idyll of Miss Sarah Brown") and characters by Damon Runyon. Music and lyrics by Frank Loesser. Dances and musical numbers staged by Michael Kidd. Settings and lighting by Jo Mielziner. Costumes by Alvin Colt. Musical director, Irving Actman. Orchestral arrangements by George Bassman and Ted Royal. Vocal arrangements and direction by Herbert Greene. Staged by George S. Kaufman. Produced by Cy Feuer and Ernest H. Martin. Opened 24 November 1950 at the 46th Street Theatre and closed 28 November 1953 after 1200 performances.

CAST (in order of appearance): *Nicely-Nicely Johnson*: STUBBY KAYE. *Benny Southstreet*: Johnny Silver. *Rusty Charlie*: Douglas Deane. *Sarah Brown*: ISABEL BIGLEY. *Arvide Abernathy*: PAT ROONEY, SR. *Mission Band* (3): *Calvin*: Margery Oldroyd. *Agatha*: Paul Migan. *Priscilla*: Christine Matsios. *Harry the Horse*: Tom Pedi. *Lieut. Brannigan*: Paul Reed. *Nathan Detroit*: SAM LEVENE. *Angie the Ox*: Tony Gardell. *Miss Adelaide*: VIVIAN BLAINE. *Sky Masterson*: ROBERT ALDA. *Joey Biltmore*: Bern Hoffman. *Mimi*: Beverly Tassoni. *General Matilda B. Cartwright*: Netta Packer. *Big Jule*: B. S. Pully. *Drunk*: Eddie Phillips. *Waiter*: Joe Milan.

Dancers: Wana Allison, Geraldine Delaney, Barbara Ferguson, Lee Joyce, Marcia Maier, Beverly Tassoni, Ruth Vernon, Onna White, Forrest Bonshire, Peter Gennaro, Joe Milan, Eddie Phillips, Harry Lee Rogers, Bud Schwab, Merritt Thompson. *Singers*: Beverly Lawrence, Christine Matsios, Charles Drake, Bern Hoffman, Carl Nicholas, Don Russell, Hal Saunders, Earle Styres.

Act 1, Scene 1: Broadway. *Scene 2*: Interior of the Save-a-Soul Mission. *Scene 3*: A Phone Booth. *Scene 4*: The Hot Box. *Scene 5*: Off Broadway. *Scene 6*: Exterior of the Mission. Noon, the next day. *Scene 7*: Off-Broadway. *Scene 8*: Havana, Cuba. *Scene 9*: Outside Cafe El Cubano. Immediately following. *Scene 10*: Exterior of Mission.

Act 2, Scene 1: The Hot Box. *Scene 2*: The West Forties. *Scene 3*: The Crap Game. *Scene 4*: Off Broadway. *Scene 5*: Interior of Save-a-Soul Mission. *Scene 6*: Near Times Square. *Scene 7*: Broadway.

ACT 1

Scene 1

Opening ("Runyonland")
Ensemble

"Fugue for Tinhorns"
S. Kaye, J. Silver, D. Deane

"Follow the Fold"
I. Bigley, P. Rooney, M. Oldroyd, P. Migan, C. Matsios

"The Oldest Established"
S. Levene, S. Kaye, J. Silver, Ensemble

"Travelling Light"[10]
R. Alda, S. Levene

Scene 2

"I'll Know"
I. Bigley, R. Alda

Scene 4

"A Bushel and a Peck"
V. Blaine, Hot Box Girls

"Adelaide's Lament"
V. Blaine

Scene 5

"Guys and Dolls"
S. Kaye, J. Silver
Guy and Doll: P. Gennaro, B. Lawrence.

Scene 8

"Havana"
B. Ferguson, Ensemble

Scene 9

"If I Were a Bell"
I. Bigley

Scene 10

"My Time of Day"
R. Alda

"I've Never Been in Love Before"
R. Alda, I. Bigley

ACT 2

Scene 1

"Take Back Your Mink"
V. Blaine, Hot Box Girls

"Adelaide's Lament" (reprise)
V. Blaine

Scene 2

"More I Cannot Wish You"
P. Rooney, Sr.

Scene 3

"The Crap Game Dance" (Crapshooters' Dance)
Ensemble

"Luck Be a Lady"
R. Alda, Crap Shooters

Scene 4

"Sue Me"
S. Levene, V. Blaine

---

[9]No individual Musical Numbers listed in the program. Song list prepared from orchestra score.

[10]Dropped shortly after opening, and not performed with any subsequent revivals.

Scene 5

"Sit Down, You're Rockin' the Boat"
S. Kaye, Ensemble
"Follow the Fold" (reprise)
Mission Meeting Group

Scene 6

"Marry the Man Today"
V. Blaine, I. Bigley

Scene 7

"Guys and Dolls" (reprise)
Entire Company

1950.18 ## LET'S MAKE AN OPERA

A Musical Novelty (Double Bill) in Two Acts, 5 Scenes. Book and lyrics by Eric Crozier. Music by Benjamin Britten. Staged by Marc Blitzstein. Musical director and conductor, Norman Del Mar. Scenery and lighting by Ralph Alswang. Costumes by Aline Bernstein. Produced by Peter Lawrence and the Show-of-the-Month Club. Opened 13 December 1950 at the John Golden Theatre and closed 16 December 1950 after 5 performances[11].

CAST: *The Play (Act 1)*: ROSALIND NADELL, Paul Carter, Claire Richard, JO SULLIVAN, *Angela Adamides, Frank Catal,* ARLYNE FRANK, RANDOLPH SYMONETTE, *Mario Santamaria, Lawrence Young,* RAWN SPEARMAN, *Norman Del Mar*: Themselves.

The Opera (Act 2) ("The Little Sweep"): *Big Bob,* Sweep-master: RANDOLPH SYMONETTE. *Clem,* His Apprentice: RAWN SPEARMAN. *Sammy,* the New Sweep-Boy: Lawrence Young. *Miss Baggott,* Housekeeper at Iken Hall: ROSALIND NADELL. *Rowan,* Nursery Maid to the Woodbridge Cousins: ARLYNE FRANK. *Children at Iken Hall (3): Juliet:* JO SULLIVAN. *Gay:* Frank Catal. *Sophie:* Claire Richard. *Woodbridge Cousins (3): Tina:* Angela Adamides. *Hughie:* Paul Carter. *Johnny:* Mario Santamaria. *Tom,* Coachman: RANDOLPH SYMONETTE. *Alfred,* Gardener: RAWN SPEARMAN.

Act 1, Scene 1: Rosalind's home. An autumn evening. *Scene 2:* Stage of the School Auditorium. Before Dress Rehearsal.

Act 2, Scene 1: Nursery at Iken Hall, England, 1810. A January morning. *Scene 2:* A few minutes later. *Scene 3:* The following morning.

1950.19 ## BLESS YOU ALL

A Musical Revue in Two Acts, 19 Scenes. Sketches by Arnold Auerbach. Music and lyrics by Harold Rome. Dances and musical ensembles staged by Helen Tamiris. Production (scenery) designed by Oliver Smith. Costumes designed by Miles White. Musical direction and vocal arrangements by Lehman Engel. Orchestrations by Don Walker. Lighting by Peggy Clark. Ballet music composed and arranged by Mischa and Wesley Portnoff, Don Walker. Entire production staged by John C. Wilson. Produced by Herman Levin and Oliver Smith. Opened 14 December 1950 at the Mark Hellinger Theatre and closed 24 February 1951 after 84 performances.

CAST: JULES MUNSHIN, MARY McCARTY, PEARL BAILEY, VALERIE BETTIS, JANE HARVEY, BYRON PALMER, LEE BARNETT, GARRY DAVIS, ROBERT CHISHOLM, GENE BARRY, DONALD SADDLER, CHARLENE HARRIS, NOEL GORDON.

Show Girls: Blanche Grady, Jill Melford, Kris Nodland, Gloria Olson, Dell Parker, Madelyn Remini, Gwenna Lee Smith, Jeane Williams. *Singing Ensemble:* Jane Carlyle, Geraldine Hamburg, Betsy Holland, Dorothy Richards, Irene Riley, Eileen Turner, Grace Varik, Margaret Wright, Fred Bryan, Clive Dill, Gordon Edwards, Noel Gordon, Ray Morrissey, Kenny Smith, William Sutherland, Norval Tormsen. *Dancing Ensemble:* Eleanor Boleyn, Carlene Carroll, Dorothy Etheridge, Sage Fuller, Elmira Jones-Bey, Billie Kirpich, Vera Lee, Ilona Murai, Emy St. Just, Helen Wenzel, Richard D'Arcy, Joseph Gifford, Donald McKayle, Joe Nash, Philip Nasta, Bertram Ross, Richard Reed, John Sandal, Swen Swenson, Parker Wilson.

ACT 1
Scene 1

"Bless You All"
J. Munshin, M. McCarty, P. Bailey, V. Bettis, Ensemble

Scene 2

"Do You Know a Better Way to Make a Living?"
J. Munshin, Showgirls

---

[11]No individual music numbers listed. Act 2 performed as an Opera.

Scene 3

Southern Fried Chekhov
Colonel Jasper Oglethorpe: G. Davis. *Emmaline,* his wife: C. Harris. *Marmaduke,* his son: G. Edwards. *Marybelle,* his daughter: M. McCarty. *The Publisher:* G. Barry.
"Don't Wanna Write About the South"
M. McCarty, G. Davis, C. Harris, G. Edwards

Scene 4

"I Can Hear It Now"
J. Harvey
The Poor Girl: D. Etheridge. *The Poor Boy:* D. Reed. *The Rich Girl:* E. Boleyn. *The Rich Boy:* D. Saddler. *Dancing Couples:* C. Caroll, S. Fuller, V. Lee, I. Murai, E. St. Just, H. Wenzel, S. Swenson, J. Gifford, P. Nastra, B. Ross, J. Sandal, P. Wilson.

Scene 5

"When"
P. Bailey
A Boy: J. Nash. *A Girl:* E. Jones-Bey.

Scene 6

Back to Napoli
Benson: R. Chisholm. *Miss Kane:* C. Harris. *Jaroslav:* G. Davis. *Laszlo:* G. Barry. *The Ladies:* G. L. Smith, D. Parker, J. Melford, J. Williams. *Enrico Bonzo:* J. Munshin. *The Children:* L. Barnett, B. Kirpich, C. Dill, I. Riley, B. Holland, R. Morrissey.

Scene 7

"Little Things Meant So Much to Me"
M. McCarty

Scene 8

"A Rose Is a Rose"
J. Harvey, B. Palmer
The Rose: V. Bettis. *The Musicos:* J. Gifford, D. Reed, B. Ross. *The Mobile:* D. Saddler. *The Sleeping Boy:* J. Nash. *A Piece of Sculpture:* E. Jones-Bey. *The Revelers:* I. Murai, H. Wenzel, P. Wilson.

Scene 9

"Love Letter to Manhattan"
B. Palmer

Scene 10

TV Over the White House
Announcer: G. Barry. *Joseph Gabriel Blow:* J. Munshin. *Jane Blow:* M. McCarty. *Their Son:* L. Barnett.
a) "Love That Man"
J. Munshin, Ensemble
b) Breakfast with Joe and Jane
c) "Just a Little White House"
J. Munshin, M. McCarty, L. Barnett
d) Somewhere Up There
George Washington: N. Gordon. *Abe Lincoln:* G. Davis. *Teddy Roosevelt:* R. Chisholm.
e) "Voting Blues"
V. Bettis
f) Stop the Politics!
J. Munshin, M. McCarty
Miss Strong Constitution: D. Parker. *Miss Natural Resources:* J. Williams. *Miss International Peace:* K. Nodland. *Miss Federal Water Power:* G. L. Smith.
g) Finale
J. Munshin, Entire Ensemble

ACT 2
Scene 1

"Summer Dresses"
B. Palmer, Ensemble
The Mannequin: G. L. Smith. *Morning Dresses:* J. Williams, B. Grady, S. Fuller, E. St. Just. *Cocktail Dresses:* J. Melford, G. Olson, E. Boleyn, V. Lee, B. Kirpich. *Evening Dresses:* K. Nodland, D. Parker, M. Remini, C. Carroll, I. Murai, H. Wenzel. *Stock Boys:* B. Ross, S. Swenson.

Scene 2

The Cold War
Bill Slade: J. Munshin. *The Druggist:* G. Davis.

Scene 3

"Take Off the Coat"
J. Harvey

Scene 4

The Nobbiest Hobby

An Art Enthusiast: J. Munshin. *A Clergyman*: R. Chisholm.
Aunty: M. Wright. *Doctor Smith*: N. Gordon. *Grandma*: C. Harris. *A Nursemaid*: G. Varik. *A Good Humor Man*: G. Barry. *A Dowager*:
G. Hamburg. *An Old Fisherman*: G. Edwards. *A Pretty Young Girl*:
E. Turner. *A Lifeguard*: R. Morrissey. *A Schoolgirl*: I. Riley. *Bathers*:
G. Olson, M. Remini, K. Nodland, J. Melford, B. Grady, D. Parker,
G. L. Smith, J. Williams.

Scene 5

"The Desert Flame"

(*Music by* Don Walker.)

Desert Flame: V. Bettis. *Monsieur le Commandant*: P. Wilson.
Gendarmes: J. Gifford, D. McKayle, J. Nash, P. Nasta, D. Reed,
B. Ross. *Pepe Le Koko*: R. D'Arcy. *Houris*: E. Boleyn, D. Etheridge,
B. Kirpich, V. Lee, I. Murai, E. St. Just, H. Wenzel. *The Texan*:
D. Saddler. *Native Drummers*: J. Comadore, O. Smith. *The Toturers*:
J. Sandal, S. Swenson. *Singing Houris*: E. Turner, G. Varik, M. Wright.
Scene a: A Street in Morocco. *Scene b*: A Cafe in Morocco. *Scene c*:
Desert Flame's Bedroom. *Scene d*: The Execution Grounds.

Scene 6

Peter and the P.T.A.

Mrs. Weatherby (Peter): M. McCarty. *Mr. Fothergill*: G. Davis.
Wendy: L. Barnett. *Captain Hook*: R. Chisholm. *The Pirates*:
J. Carlyle, B. Holland, D. Ricahrds, F. Bryan, C. Dill, K. Smith,
W. Sutherland, N. Tormsen.

Scene 7

"You Never Know What Hit You When It's Love"

P. Bailey

Scene 8

"The Roaring 20's Strike Back"

J. Munshin, M. McCarty

Scene 9

Finale

Entire Company

OUT OF THIS WORLD

1950.20

A Musical in Two Acts, a Prologue and 18 Scenes. Book by Dwight Taylor and Reginald Lawrence[12]. Music and lyrics by Cole Porter. Choreography by Hanya Holm. Settings and costumes by Lemuel Ayers. Musical director, Pembroke Davenport. Orchestrations by Robert Russell Bennett. Dance music arranged by Genevieve Pitot. Incidental music arranged by Trudi Rittman. Entire production staged by Agnes de Mille. Produced by (Arnold) Saint Subber and Lemuel Ayers[13]. Opened 21 December 1950 at the New Century Theatre and closed 5 May 1951 after 157 performances.

CAST (in order of appearance): *Mercury*: WILLIAM REDFIELD. *Jupiter*: GEORGE JONGEYANS [Gaynes]. *Helen*: PRISCILLA GILLETTE. *Waiter*: Frank Milton. *Art O'Malley*: WILLIAM EYTHE. *Night*: JANET COLLINS. *Vulcania*: Peggy Rea. *Juno*: CHARLOTTE GREENWOOD. *Chloe*: BARBARA ASHLEY. *Niki Skolianos*: DAVID BURNS. *Strephon*: RAY HARRISON.

Singing Ensemble: Barbara Weaver, Shirley Prior, Enid Hall, Nola Fairbanks, B. J. Keating, Lois Monroe, John Schickling, John Schmidt, Richard Curry, Ken Ayers, Orrin Hill, Robert Baird, Joe Hill, Leo Kayworth, Michael Kingsley. *Dancing Ensemble*: Gisella Svetlik, Virginia Bosler, Eleanor Fairchild, Joan Engel, Joan Kruger, Jacqueline Sager, Glen Tetley, David Nillo, Stanley Simmons, Paul Lyday, Eric Kristen, Barton Mumaw, Jan Kovac, Doria Avila.

Prologue: Curtain. *Act 1, Scene 1*: Jupiter's Portico. *Scene 2*: New York Bar. *Scene 3*: Curtain of Night. *Scene 4*: Great Hall—Olympus. *Scene 5*: Road to Athens. *Scene 6*: Arcadia Inn. *Scene 7*: Colonnade. *Scene 8*: Inn Tavern. *Scene 9*: Arcadia Inn.

Act 2, Scene 1: Mt. Olympus. *Scene 2*: Curtain of Night. *Scene 3*: Arcadia Inn. *Scene 4*: Colonnade. *Scene 5*: Bedroom. *Scene 6*: Curtain of Night. *Scene 7*: Mountain Shrine. *Scene 8*: Another Part of the Forest. *Scene 9*: Arcadia Inn and Heaven.

ACT 1

Scene 1

"I Jupiter, I Rex"

G. Jongeyans, Ensemble

Scene 2

"Use Your Imagination"

W. Redfield, P. Gillette

Scene 4

"Hail, Hail, Hail"

P. Rea, W. Redfield, Ensemble

"I Got Beauty"

C. Greenwood, Ensemble

Scene 6

"Maiden Fair"

Ensemble

"Where, Oh, Where"

B. Ashley
Danced by Boys, Girls.

"I Am Loved"

P. Gillette

Scene 7

"They Couldn't Compare to You"

W. Redfield, Singing Girls, Dancing Girls

Scene 8

"What Do You Think About Men?"

P. Gillette, B. Ashley, C. Greenwood

Scene 9

Dance

J. Collins

"I Sleep Easier Now"

C. Greenwood

Ballet

J. Collins, R. Harrison, Dancing Ensemble

ACT 2

Scene 1

"Climb Up the Mountain"

C. Greenwood, D. Burns, Company

Scene 3

"No Lover for Me"

P. Gillette

Scene 4

"Cherry Pies Ought to Be You"

W. Redfield, B. Ashley, C. Greenwood, D. Burns

Scene 5

"I Am Loved" (reprise)

P. Gillette

Scene 6

"Hark to the Song of the Night"

G. Jongeyans

Scene 7

Dance

R. Harrison, B. Ashley, Ensemble

Scene 8

"Nobody's Chasing Me"

C. Greenwood

Dance

Ensemble

Scene 9

"Use Your Imagination" (reprise)

Entire Company

WHERE'S CHARLEY?

1951.02

A Return Engagement of the Musical Comedy in Two Acts, 9 Scenes[14]. Book by George Abbott. Based on the play "Charley's Aunt" by Brandon Thomas. Music and lyrics by Frank Loesser. Dances directed by George

---

[12]Based on the Amphitryon legend.
[13]Program note: Messrs. Subber and Ayers gratefully wish to acknowledge the [directorial] assistance of Mr. George Abbott.

[14]First produced in New York 11 October 1948 at the St. James Theatre for 792 performances. For Synopsis of Scenes and Musical Numbers, see original 1948 production.

Balanchine. Sets and costumes by David Ffolkes. Vocal arrangements and direction by Herbert Greene. Orchestrations by Ted Royal, Hans Spialek, (Phil Lang). Musical director, Edward Scott. Production directed by George Abbott. Produced by Cy Feuer and Ernest H. Martin in association with Gwen Rickard. Opened 29 January 1951 at the Broadway Theatre and closed 10 March 1951 after 56 performances.

CAST (in order of appearance): *Brassett*: John Lynds. *Jack Chesney*: ROBERT SHACKLETON. *Charley Wykeham*: RAY BOLGER. *Kitty Verdun*: BETTY OAKES. *Amy Spettigue*: ALLYN McLERIE. *Wilkinson*: James Lane. *Sir Francis Chesney*: PAUL ENGLAND. *Mr. Spettigue*: HORACE COOPER. *Donna Lucia D'Alvadorez*: ROSE INGHRAM. *Photographer*: James Lane. *Patricia*: Irene Weston. *Reggie*: Ralph Lowe.

Dancers: Donna Beaumont, Arun Evans, Ann Lee Hudson, Virginia McClamroch, Nancy Pearson, Gretchen Winnecke, James Capp, Ray Johnson, Jack Konzal, Maurice Phillips, Reggie Powers, Victor Reilley. *Singers*: Michele Burke, Dorothy Juden, Helen Moore, Ann Richards, Lita Terris, Irene Weston, Paty Wilkes, Jennifer Woods, Forrest Carter, John Decker, John Fortna, Ralph Lowe, Gerald Lynch, Gene Scott, Ernest Taylor, Paul Wolff.

THE MIKADO,
1951.01 or, The Town of Titipu

A Revival of the Comic Opera in Two Acts[15]. Libretto by William S. Gilbert. Music by Arthur Sullivan. Directed by Eleanor Evans. Scenery and costumes designed by Charles Ricketts. Orchestra directed by Isidore Godfrey. Produced by the D'Oyly Carte Opera Company. Opened 29 January 1951 at the St. James Theatre and closed 3 February 1951 after 8 performances.

CAST: *The Mikado of Japan*: DARRELL FANCOURT. *Nanki-Poo*: NEVILLE GRIF-FITHS. *Ko-Ko*: MARTYN GREEN. *Pooh-Bah*: RICHARD WATSON. *Noble Lords (2)*: *Pish-Tush*: ALAN STYLER. *Go-To*: Donald Harris. *Three Sisters, Wards of Ko-Ko*: *Yum-Yum*: MARGARET MITCHELL. *Pitti-Sing*: JOAN GILLINGHAM. *Peep-Bo*: JOYCE WRIGHT. *Katisha*: ELLA HALMAN. *Chorus of School Girls, Nobles, Guards and Coolies.*

TRIAL BY JURY
1951.03

A Revival of the Comic Opera in One Act[16]. Libretto by William S. Gilbert. Music by Arthur Sullivan. Directed by Eleanor Evans. Scenery designed by Joseph and Phil Harker. Ladies' costumes designed by George Sheringham. Orchestra directed by Isidore Godfrey. Produced by the D'Oyly Carte Opera Company. Opened 5 February 1951 at the St. James Theatre and closed 10 February 1951 after 8 performances.

CAST: *The Learned Judge*: RICHARD WATSON. *Counsel for the Plaintiff*: ALAN STYLER. *The Defendant*: LEONARD OSBORN. *Foreman of the Jury*: DONALD HARRIS. *Usher*: RADLEY FLYNN. *Associate*: Ivor Emmanuel. *The Plaintiff*: ENID WALSH. *First Bridesmaid*: Joyce Wright. *Chorus of Jurymen, Bridesmaids and Public.*

H.M.S. PINAFORE,
1951.04 or, The Lass That Loved a Sailor

A Revival of the Comic Opera in Two Acts[17]. Libretto by William S. Gilbert. Music by Arthur Sullivan. Directed by Eleanor Evans. Scenery designed by Joseph and Phil Harker. Orchestra directed by Isidore Godfrey. Produced by the D'Oyly Carte Opera Company. Opened 5 February 1951 at the St. James Theatre and closed 10 February 1951 after 8 performances.[18]

---

[15]First presented in New York 20 July, 10-29 August 1885 at the Union Square and People's Theatres for 22 performances. First authorized production presented 19 August 1885 at the Fifth Avenue Theatre by Richard D'Oyly Carte for 250 performances. For Synopsis of Scenes and Musical Numbers, see 19 August 1885 D'Oyly Carte production.

[16]First presented in New York 15 November 1875 at the Eagle Theatre for 8 performances. For Synopsis of Scenes and Musical Numbers, see original 1875 production.

[17]Originally presented in New York 15 January 1879 at the Standard Theatre for 175 performances. For Synopsis of Scenes and Musical Numbers, see original 1879 production.

[18]Costumes uncredited.

CAST: *The Rt. Hon. Sir Joseph Porter, K.C.B., First Lord of the Admiralty*: MARTYN GREEN. *Captain Corcoran, Commander of the H.M.S. Pinafore*: ERIC THORNTON. *Ralph Rackstraw, Able Seaman*: NEVILLE GRIFFITHS. *Dick Deadeye, Able Seaman*: DARRELL FANCOURT. *Bill Bobstay, Boatswain*: Donald Harris. *Bob Becket*: Radley Flynn. *Josephine, the Captain's Daughter*: MURIEL HARDING. *Hebe, Sir Joseph's First Cousin*: Joan Gillingham. *Little Buttercup, Mrs. Cripps, a Portsmouth bum-boat woman*: ELLA HALMAN. *First Lord's Sisters, His Cousins, His Aunts, Sailors, Marines, etc.*

JOTHAM VALLEY
1951.05

A Story That Actually Happened (Musical Play) in Two Acts, 6 Scenes. Book and lyrics by Cecil Broadhurst. Music by Cecil Broadhurst, Frances Hadden, Will Reed. Direction and production by Howard Reynolds in association with Lena Ashwell. Musical direction by Will Reed and George Fraser. Dances by June Day and Christine Nowell. Sets designed by Erling Roberts. Lighting by Louis Fleming. Produced by Moral Re-Armament. Opened 6 February 1951 at the 48th Street Theatre, moved 19 February 1951 to the Coronet Theatre, and closed 3 March 1951 after 31 performances.[19]

CAST [in order of appearance]: *Nielson*: Scoville Wishard. *'Joth' Jotham*: LELAND HOLLAND. *Spindle*: Cecil Broadhurst. *The Waggle Kids*: David Allen, Valerie Exton, June Day, TOM KENNEDY, Christine Nowell. *Jennifer*: ILENE GODFREY. *Mrs. Whipple*: MARION CLAYTON. *Miss Hubbard*: PHYLLIS KONSTAM. *Widow Waggle*: ELSA PURDY. *The Four Cowhands*: *Moose*: Dwight Boileau. *Slugger*: Frank McGee. *Smokey*: Ron Roberts. *Sundown*: Howard Boyd. *Mart Billings*: Bill Stubbs. *Jack*: Jack Currie. *Seth Jotham*: DICK STOLLERY. *Murray Wilkins*: Scoville Wishard. *Will*: Robert Anderson. *The Judge*: Eugene Bedford. *Sarah*: Greta Stollery.

Twicklehampton School Girls: Valerie Exton, Rosemary Pinsent, Leone Exton, Molly Corner, Sally Hore-Ruthven, Nancy Hore-Ruthven, Juliet Rodd, Clare Meynell, Christine Nowell, Barbara Jardine. *Their Teacher*: June Day. *Jotham Valley's Ladies Aid*: Marion Clayton, Phyllis Konstam, Mabel Curtis, Nancy Curtis, Janet Binns, Mary Jane Broadhurst, Leone Exton, Ruth Ridgway, Rea Zimmerman. *Chorus Ensemble*: Cyril Beall, Ben Trotter, Hope Kitchen, Walter Farmer, Florence Farmer, Eric Millar, Vere James, Ivor Sharp, Carol Ann Beal, Phyllis Limburg, Eleanor Crary, Hugh Nowell, Helen Hunter, Aage Anderson, Harold Sack, Ken Twitchell, Jr., Ed MacRae, Frank Sherry, Norman Schwab.

The action of the play takes place over a period of one week.

Act 1, Scene 1: Jotham's Ranch House in the Sierra Country. *Scene 2*: A Cafe in Town. *Scene 3*: The Jotham Reservoir.

Act 2, Scene 1: Outside the County Court House. *Scene 2*: Widow Waggle's Kitchen. *Scene 3*: Jotham's Ranch House.

ACT 1
Scene 1
   "Wonder Why?"
      L. Holland
   "Nuthin' Like a Celebration"
      The Neighbors
   "There's a Certain Kind o' Jingle to My Spurs"
      D. Boileau, F. McGee, R. Roberts, H. Boyd
   "I'm the Luckiest Girl Alive"
      I. Godfrey, Neighbors
   "When I Point My Finger at My Neighbor"
      C. Broadhurst, Cowhands
   "Nothing's Ever Quite Like This"
      I. Godfrey, E. Purdy
   "Twickenham School for Girls"
      School Girls
   "Have You Heard?"
      M. Clayton, Gossip Chorus
Scene 3
   "There's a Certain Kind o' Jingle to My Spurs" (reprise)
      D. Boileau, F. McGee, R. Roberts, H. Boyd
   "Wonder Why?" (reprise)
      L. Holland

---

[19]Costumes uncredited.

ACT 2

Scene 2

"When I Grow Up"
The Waggle Kids

"The Omelet Song"
E. Purdy, The Waggle Kids, Cowhands

Scene 3

"Somewhere in the Heart of a Man"
L. Holland, C. Broadhurst, I. Godfrey

"Change in a Home on the Range"
L. Holland, I. Godfrey

"Look to the Mountains"
L. Holland, I. Godfrey, Neighbors

Finale
The Whole Valley (Entire Company)

THE GONDOLIERS,
1951.06 or, The King of Barataria

A Revival of the Comic Opera in Two Acts[20]. Libretto by William S. Gilbert. Music by Arthur Sullivan. Directed by Eleanor Evans. Orchestra directed by Isidore Godfrey. Produced by the D'Oyly Carte Opera Company. Opened 12 February 1951 at the St. James Theatre and closed 14 February 1951 after 4 performances.[21]

CAST: *The Duke of Plaza-Toro*: MARTYN GREEN. *Luiz*: HENRY GOODIER. *Don Alhambra Del Bolero*: RICHARD WATSON. *Marco Palmieri*: LEONARD OSBORN. *Giuseppe Palmieri*: ALAN STYLER. *Antonio*: Peter Pratt. *Francesco*: Thomas Hancock. *Giorgio*: Radley Flynn. *Annibale*: Stanley Youngman. *The Duchess of Plaza-Toro*: ELLA HALMAN. *Casilda*: MARGARET MITCHELL. *Gianetta*: MURIEL HARDING. *Tessa*: JOAN GILLINGHAM. *Fiametta*: Enid Walsh. *Vittoria*: Ceinwen Jones. *Giulia*: Joyce Wright. *Inez*: Caryl Fane. *Chorus of Gondoliers, Contadine, Men-at-Arms, Heralds and Pages.*

IOLANTHE,
1951.07 or, The Peer and the Peri

A Revival of the Comic Opera in Two Acts[22]. Libretto by William S. Gilbert. Music by Arthur Sullivan. Directed by Eleanor Evans. Fairy costumes designed by Norman Wilkinson. Orchestra directed by Isidore Godfrey. Produced by the D'Oyly Carte Opera Company. Opened 15 February 1951 at the St. James Theatre and closed 17 February 1951 after 4 performances.[23]

CAST: *The Lord Chancellor*: MATYN GREEN. *Earl of Mountararat*: ERIC THORNTON. *Earl Tolloler*: LEONARD OSBORN. *Private Willis*: RICHARD WATSON. *Strephon*: ALAN STYLER. *Queen of the Fairies*: ELLA HALMAN. *Iolanthe*: JOAN GILLINGHAM. *Celia*: Enid Walsh. *Leila*: Joyce Wright. *Fleta*: Henrietta Steytler. *Phyllis*: MARGARET MITCHELL. *Chorus of Dukes, Marquises, Earls, Viscounts, Barons and Fairies.*

1951.08 ## COX AND BOX

A Revival of the Triumviretta in One Act[24]. Libretto by F. C. Burnand, based on Maddison Morton's farce "Box and Cox." Music by Arthur

Sullivan. Directed by Eleanor Evans. Orchestra directed by Isidore Godfrey. Produced by the D'Oyly Carte Opera Company. Opened 19 February 1951 at the St. James Theatre and closed 24 February 1951 after 8 performances.

CAST: *Cox, a Journeyman Hatter*: ALAN STYLER. *Box, a Journeyman Printer*: LEONARD OSBORN. *Bouncer, their Landlord*: ERIC THORNTON.

THE PIRATES OF PENZANCE,
1951.09 or, The Slave of Duty

A Revival of the Comic Opera in Two Acts[25]. Libretto by William S. Gilbert. Music by Arthur Sullivan. Directed by Eleanor Evans. Orchestra directed by Isidore Godfrey. Produced by the D'Oyly Carte Opera Company. Opened 19 February 1951 at the St. James Theatre and closed 24 February 1951 after 8 performances.

CAST: *Major General Stanley*: MARTYN GREEN. *The Pirate King*: DARRELL FANCOURT. *Samuel, his Lieutenant*: Donald Harris. *Frederic, the Pirate Apprentice*: NEVILLE GRIFFITHS. *Sergeant of Police*: RICHARD WATSON. *Mabel, Edith, Kate, Isabel, General Stanley's Daughters*: MURIEL HARDING, JOAN GILLINGHAM. JOYCE WRIGHT, Enid Walsh. *Ruth, Pirate Maid-of-all-work*: ELLA HALMAN. *Chorus of Pirates, Police and General Stanley's Daughters.*

1951.10 ## RAZZLE DAZZLE

A Musical Revue in Two Acts, 18 Scenes. Sketches and lyrics by Mike Stewart. Music by Leo Schumer, Shelley Mowell, James Reed Lawlor, Bernice Kroll, Irma Jurist. Directed by Edward Reveaux. Choreography by Nelle Fisher; associate choreographer, Jerry Ross. Musical direction and dance arrangements by James Reed Lawlor. Production (costumes, sets) designed by William Riva. Musical arrangements by Herbert Schutz. Produced by David Heilweil and Derrick Lynn-Thomas in association with Madeline Capp and Greer Johnson. Opened 19 February 1951 at the Arena and closed 24 February 1951 after 8 performances.

CAST: JAMES JEWELL, JET MacDONALD, LEE GOODMAN, BOB HERGET, DOROTHY GREENER, KATE FRIEDLICH, JANE WHITE, PETER CONLOW, FLORI WAREN, FRANK REYNOLDS, JEAN SINCERE, CHRISTINE KARNER, BARBARA HAMILTON, JAMES HARWOOD, Cris Goodyear, Robert H. Baron, Bill Newey. *At the Pianos*: James Reed Lawlor, Herbert Schutz. *Percussion*: Irwin Cooper.

ACT 1

Scene 1

"What's a Show"
(*Music by* Shelley Mowell.)
Ringmaster: J. Jewell. *Acrobat*: K. Friedlich. *Clown*: D. Greener. *Equestrienne*: F. Waren. *Romeo*: F. Reynolds. *Juliet*: J. MacDonald. *Girl With Roses*: J. Sincere. *Sweethearts*: C. Karner, B. Herget. *Girl With Hat*: B. Hamilton. *Riveter*: J. Harwood. *Texan*: L. Goodman. *Kid*: C. Goodyear. *Keystone Cop*: P. Conlow. *Girl With Shoulders*: J. White.

Scene 2

M.G.M.
The Girl: D. Greener.

Scene 3

"Sign Here"
(*Music by* Leo Schumer.)
Wife: J. Sincere. *Husband*: J. Harwood. *Owner*: L. Goodman. *Rufus McBain*: F. Reynolds. *McBain Sisters*: K. Friedlich, C. Karner. *Boyfriends*: P. Conlow, B. Herget. *Beth*: F. Waren.

Scene 4

"Then I'm Yours"
J. MacDonald, J. Jewell
(*Music by* Leo Schumer.)

---

[20]Originally presented in New York 7 January 1890 at Park Theatre for 103 performances. For Synopsis of Scenes and Musical Numbers, see original 1890 production.
[21]Costumes and scenery uncredited.
[22]First presented in New York 25 November 1882 at the Standard Theatre for 105 performances. For Synopsis of Scenes and Musical Numbers, see original 1882 production.
[23]Scenery uncredited.
[24]First presented in New York as COX AND BOX, or The Long-Lost Brothers 14 August 1879 at the Standard Theatre for 48 performances. For Synopsis of Scenes and Musical Numbers, see original 1879 production.

[25]First presented in New York 31 December 1879 at the Fifth Avenue Theatre for a total of 91 performances in two engagements. For Synopsis of Scenes and Musical Numbers, see original 1879 production.

Scene 5

All About Bambi—Part 1

A. Dressing Room

Bambi: B. Hamilton. *Girl*: D Greener.

B. "The Wages of Sin"—1925

(*Music by* James Reed Lawlor.)

Waiter: R. H. Baron. *Boy*: F. Reynolds. *Bunny Girl*: C. Karner. *Nell's Date*: B. Herget. *Little Nell*: K. Friedlich. *Nell's Father*: J. Harwood. *Nell's Mother*: F. Waren. *Bambi*: B. Hamilton.

Scene 6

"N.Y.C."

(*Music by* Leo Schumer.)

Girl: J. Sincere. *Scarecrow*: P. Conlow.

Scene 7

Magic in the Woods

The Author: L. Goodman.

Scene 8

"Haven't We Met Before?"

(*Music by* Irma Jurist.)

The Producer: J. Harwood. *First Lady*: J. White. *Second Lady*: J. Sincere. *Visitor*: B. Hamilton.

Scene 9

"What a Way to Make a Living"

J. MacDonald, L. Goodman

(*Music by* Leo Schumer.)

Scene 10

All About Bambi—Part 2

A. Dressing Room

Bambi: B. Hamilton. *Girl*: D Greener.

B. "Frivolity Frolics"—1930

(*Music by* Leo Schumer.)

Singer: J. Harwood. *Girls*: K. Friedlich, C. Karner, F. Waren, J. MacDonald, J. Sincere. *Stripper*: J. White. *Bambi*: B. Hamilton.

ACT 2

Scene 1

"Catch Me If You Can"

(*Music by* Shelley Mowell.)

The Girl: J. MacDonald. *The Men*: P. Conlow, B. Herget, F. Reynolds.

Scene 2

"You're Only Young Once or Twice"

(*Music by* Bernice Kroll.)

Girl: C. Karner. *Boy*: J. Jewell.

Scene 3

All About Bambi—Part 3

A. The Stage

Bambi: B. Hamilton. *Girl*: D Greener. *Stage Manager*: B. Herget. *Actor*: L. Goodman.

B. Love on Shrove Tuesday—1939

Diantha: B. Hamilton. *Maid*: D. Greener. *Gregory*: L. Goodman. *Butler*: J. Harwood.

Scene 4

"The Light Fantastic"

(*Music by* James Reed Lawlor.)

The Witch: F. Waren. *Narrator*: J. Harwood.

Scene 5

Grace Fogarty

Girl: D. Greener.

Scene 6

"Someone"

J. White

(*Music by* Shelley Mowell. *Danced by* K. Friedlich, B. Herget.)

Scene 7

All About Bambi—Part 4

A. Dressing Room

Actor: L. Goodman. *Girl*: D. Greener. *Stage Manager*: J. Jewell.

B. "Two Hearts in Gypsy Time"—1951

(*Music by* Shelley Mowell.)

Dancer: P. Conlow. *Flowergirl*: K. Friedlich. *Innkeeper*: J. Harwood. *Girls*: J. Sincere, J. White, C. Karner, F. Waren. *Waiters and Students*: C. Goodyear, B. Newey, J. Jewell, R. H. Baron. *Rupert*: F. Reynolds. *Prince Stanislaus*: L. Goodman. *Zaza*: D. Greener. *Gypsy*: B. Hamilton.

Scene 8

Finale

Entire Company

1951.11   THE GREEN PASTURES

A Revival of the Fable (with Music) in Two Acts, 17 Scenes[26]. Play by Marc Connelly. Based on Roark Bradford's Southern Sketches "Ol' Man Adam an' His Chillun." (Costumes, scenery, lighting) Designed by Robert Edmund Jones. Directed by Marc Connelly. Choir directed by Hall Johnson[27]. Produced by The Wigreen Company in association with Harry Fromkes. Opened 15 March 1951 at the Broadway Theatre and closed 21 April 1951 after 44 performances.

CAST (in order of appearance):*Mr. Deshee*: JOHN MARRIOTT. *Myrtle*: Joyce Gissentanner. *First Boy*: Philip Hepburn. *Second Boy*: Pierre Dillard. *Randolph*: Ernest Bloomfield. *Carlisle*: Philip Brinson. *First Cook*: William Veasey. *A Voice*: William McDaniel. *Second Cook*: Alma L. Hubbard. *First Man Angel*: AVON LONG. *First Mammy Angel*: Ethel Purnello. *A Stout Angel*: ANNA MAE RICHARDSON. *A Slender Angel*: MARGARET WILLIAMS. *Archangel*: William O. Davis. *Teacher Angel*: Courtenaye Olden. *Gabriel*: OSSIE DAVIS. *God*: WILLIAM MARSHALL. *Choir Leader*: Rodger Alford. *Custard Maker*: JAMES FULLER. *Adam*: WILLIAM DILLARD. *Eve*: MILROY INGRAM. *Cain*: VAN PRINCE. *Zeba*: VINIE BURROWS. *Cain the Sixth*: VAN PRINCE. *Boy Gambler*: Philip Hepburn. *Gamblers*: James Fuller, George Hill, John Rainey, George Royston, Robert McFerrin. *Voice in Shanty*: ANNA MAE RICHARDSON. *Noah*: ALONZO BOSAN. *Noah's Wife*: ALMA L. HUBBARD. *Shem*: Robert McFerrin. *First Woman*: MILROY INGRAM. *Second Woman*: ANNA MAE RICHARDSON. *Third Woman*: Tina Marshall. *First Man*: JOHN BOUIE. *Flatfoot*: RANDOLPH SAWYER. *Ham*: AVON LONG. *Japheth*: JAMES FULLER. *First Cleaner*: MARGARET WILLIAMS. *Second Cleaner*: ANNA MAE RICHARDSON. *Abraham*: ALONZO BOSAN. *Isaac*: Robert McFerrin. *Jacob*: JOHN BOUIE. *Moses*: JOHN MARRIOTT. *Zipporah*: MILROY INGRAM. *Aaron*: William Veasey. *A Candidate Magician*: Rodger Alford. *Pharaoh*: JOHN BOUIE. *A General*: George O. Willis. *A Concubine*: Courtenaye Olden. *A Manicurist*: Tina Marshall. *First Wizard*: William O. Davis. *Head Magician*: AVON LONG. *Joshua*: VAN PRINCE. *Scoutsmaster of Ceremonies*: Randolph Sawyer. *King of Babylon*: AVON LONG. *The King's Favorites*: Hope Foye, Yvonne Jiggets, Jumel Jones, MILROY INGRAM, Courtenaye Olden. *Prophet*: William Veasey. *High Preist*: JOHN BOUIE. *His Guest*: Tina Marshall. *Corporal*: Calvin Dash. *Hezdrel*: WILLIAM DILLARD. *Second Officer*: Robert McFerrin.

The Children: Patricia Bloomfield, Beatrice Edwards, Joyce Gissentanner, Dierdre Greenway, Marcia Titus, Mary Young, Ernest Bloomfield, Eugene Bloomfield, Philip Brinson, Jimmie Burton, Pierre Dillard, Philip Hepburn, Robert Titus.

The Choir: *Director*: Hall Johnson. *Assistant Director*: Louvinia White. *Sopranos*: Mabel Bergen, Maudine Brown, Miriam Burton, Hope Faye, Louise Hawthorne, Alma L. Hubbard, Oci Johnson, Madeline Preston, Louvinia White. *Altos*: Alice Ajaye, Leona Avery, Willie Mays, Louise Parker, Ethel Purnelllo. *Tenors*: Rodger Alford, Lawson Bates, Calvin Dash, William O. Davis, Curtis Hawkins, William McDaniel, Robert McFerrin, George Royston. *Baritones*: Alonzo Jones, John H. Rainey, Beecher Wilson. *Bassos*: Jack Carr, George Hill, William Veasey, George O. Willis.

1951.12   THE KING AND I

A Musical Play in Two Acts, 17 Scenes. Book and lyrics by Oscar Hammerstein II. Based on the novel "Anna and the King of Siam" by Margaret Landon. Music by Richard Rodgers. Settings and lighting by Jo Mielziner. Costumes designed by Irene Sharaff. Choreography by Jerome Robbins. Orchestrations by Robert Russell Bennett. Musical director, Frederick Dvonch. Directed by John van Druten. Produced by Richard Rodgers and Oscar Hammerstein II. Opened 29 March 1951 at the St. James Theatre and closed 20 March 1954 after 1246 performances.

---

[26]First presented in New York 26 February 1930 at the Mansfield Theatre for 640 performances. For Synopsis of Scenes and Musical Numbers, see original 1930 production. For this revival, Act 1, Scenes 5, 6 and 7 were revised and combined as two scenes; total scenes reduced from 18 to 17. Added to Act 1 (before "I Want To Be Ready"): "Welcome Table."

[27]All choral arrangements used have been written especially for "The Green Pastures" by Hall Johnson.

CAST (in order of appearance): *Captain Orton*: Charles Francis. *Louis Leonowens*: Sandy Kennedy. *Anna Leonowens*: GERTRUDE LAWRENCE. *The Interpreter*: Leonard Graves. *The Kralahome*: John Juliano. *The King*: YUL BRYNNER. *Phra Alack*: Len Mence. *Tuptim*: DORETTA MORROW. *Lady Thiang*: DOROTHY SARNOFF. *Prince Chulalongkorn*: Johnny Stewart. *Princess Ying Yaowalak*: Baayork Lee. *Lun Tha*: LARRY DOUGLAS. *Sir Edward Ramsay*: Robin Craven.

Princesses and Princes: Crisanta Cornejo, Andrea Del Rosario, Margie James, Barbara Luna, Nora Baez, Corinne St. Denis, Bunny Warner, Rodolfo Cornejo, Robert Cortazal, Thomas Griffen, Alfonso Maribo, James Maribo, Orlando Rodriguez. *The Royal Dancers*: Jamie Bauer, Lee Becker, Mary Burr, Gemze de Lappe, Shellie Farrell, Marilyn Gennaro, Evelyn Giles, Ina Kurland, Nancy Lynch, Michiko, Helen Murrielle, Prue Ward, Dusty Worrall, Yuriko. *Wives*: Stephanie Augustine, Marcia James, Ruth Korda, Suzanne Lake, Gloria Marlowe, Carolyn Maye, Helen Merritt, Phyllis Wilcox. *Amazons*: Geraldine Hamburg, Maribel Hammer, Norma Larkin, Miriam Lawrence. *Priests*: Duane Camp, Joseph Caruso, Leonard Graves, Jack Matthews, Ed Preston. *Slaves*: Doris Avila, Raul Celada, Beau Cunningham, Tommy Gomez.

The action takes place in and around the King's Palace, Bangkok, Siam (Thailand). *Time*: Early 1860s.

Act 1, Scene 1: Deck of the *Chow Phya* as it approaches Bangkok. *Scene 2*: A Palace Corridor. *Scene 3*: The King's Study in the Palace. *Scene 4*: In the Palace Grounds. *Scene 5*: The Schoolroom. *Scene 6*: A Palace Corridor. *Scene 7*: Anna's Bedroom. *Scene 8*: A Palace Corridor. *Scene 9*: The King's Study.

Act 2, Scene 1: The Schoolroom. *Scene 2*: In the Palace Grounds. *Scene 3*: The Theatre Pavilion. *Scene 4*: The King's Study. *Scene 5*: In the Palace Grounds. *Scene 6*: A Room in Anna's House. *Scene 7*: A Palace Corridor. *Scene 8*: The King's Study.

ACT 1

Scene 1

"I Whistle a Happy Tune"
   G. Lawrence, S. Kennedy

Scene 3

"My Lord and Master"
   D. Morrow

"Hello, Young Lovers!"
   G. Lawrence

"(March of) The Royal Siamese Children"
   (*Acted by*) G. Lawrence, Y. Brynner, Wives, Children

Scene 4

"A Puzzlement"
   Y. Brynner

Scene 5

"The Royal Bangkok Academy"
   G. Lawrence, Children

"Getting to Know You"
   G. Lawrence, Wives, Children, Michiko

"We Kiss in a Shadow"
   D. Morrow, L. Douglas

Scene 6

"A Puzzlement" (reprise)
   J. Stewart, S. Kennedy

Scene 7

"Shall I Tell You What I Think of You?"
   G. Lawrence

"Something Wonderful"
   D. Sarnoff

Scene 9

Finale
   Entire Company

ACT 2

Scene 1

"Western People Funny"
   D. Sarnoff, Wives

Scene 2

"I Have Dreamed"
   L. Douglas, D. Morrow

"Hello, Young Lovers!" (reprise)
   G. Lawrence

Scene 3

"The Small House of Uncle Thomas" — Ballet
   Narrator: D. Morrow. *Uncle Thomas*: D. Worrall. *Topsy*: I. Kurland. *Little Eva*: S. Farrell. *Eliza*: Yuriko. *King Simon*: G. DeLappe. *Angel*: Michiko. *Royal Dancers*: J. Bauer, L. Becker, M. Burr, M. Gennaro, E. Giles, M. James, N. Lynch, H. Murielle, P. Ward, C. St. Denis. *Musicians*: D. Avila, R. Celada, B. Cunningham. *Drummer*: T. Gomez.

Scene 4

("Song of the King")
   (Y. Brynner)

"Shall We Dance?"
   G. Lawrence, Y. Brynner

Scene 8

("I Whistle a Happy Tune") (reprise)
   (G. Lawrence)

Finale
   Entire Company

1951.13   MAKE A WISH

A Musical Comedy in Two Acts, 19 Scenes. Book by Preston Sturges, (Abe Burrows). Based on the play "A jo tündér" (The Good Fairy) by Ferenc Molnár. Music and lyrics by Hugh Martin. Dances and musical ensembles by Gower Champion. Settings and costumes by Raoul Pene du Bois. Musical direction by Milton Rosenstock. Vocal arrangements by Hugh Martin. Orchestrations by Phil Lang and Allan Small. Vocal direction by Buster Davis. Dance music arranged by Richard Pribor. Entire production staged by John C. Wilson. Produced by Harry Rigby and Jule Styne with Alexander H. Cohen. Opened 18 April 1951 at the Winter Garden and closed 14 July 1951 after 102 performances.

CAST: *Dr. Didier*: EDA HEINEMANN. *Dr. Francel*: PHIL LEEDS. *Janette*: NANETTE FABRAY. *Ricky*: HAROLD LANG. *Poupette*: HELEN GALLAGHER. *Policeman*: Howard Wendell. *Marius Frigo*: MELVILLE COOPER. *Paul Dumont*: STEPHEN DOUGLASS. *The Madam*: MARY FINNEY. *Felix Labiche*: LeRoi Operti. *Sales Manager*: Howard Wendell. *SYLVIA MANON TRIO*: Sylvia Manon, Ray Borden, Victor Voley.

Singers: Mary Harmon, Carol Hendricks, Anne Humphrey, Janie Janvier, Beverly McFadden, Ellen Martin, Claire Mitchell, Peggy O'Hara, Rica Owen, Dean Campbell, Robert Davis, Edward Gombos, David Huenergardt, Douglas Luther, Don McKay, Michael Mason, Robert Shaver, David Vogel. *Dancers*: Aleen Buchanan, Lynn Joelson, Margaret Jeanne, Lida Koehring, Carol Lee, Charlotte Ray, Sue Scott, Thelma Tadlock, Norma Thornton, Gene Bayliss, Dick Crowley, Ray Dorian, John Laverty, Jack Purcell, Ernie Preston, Richard Reed, Kenneth Urmston, Ken Whelan.

The action takes place on the Left Bank of Paris.

Act 1, Scene 1: A Museum. *Scene 2*: A Street. *Scene 3*: Café Victor. *Scene 4*: A Street. *Scene 5*: A Dressing Room. *Scene 6*: Folies Labiche Curtain. *Scene 7*: Folies Labiche. *Scene 8*: Outside of Folies Labiche. *Scene 9*: A Street. *Scene 10*: The Students Ball.

Act 2, Scene 1: A Courtyard. *Scene 2*: Hallway of Paul's Apartment. *Scene 3*: Paul's Apartment. *Scene 4*: A Street. *Scene 5*: Galerie Napoléon Department Store. *Scene 6*: A Street. *Scene 7*: Mr. Frigo's Apartment. *Scene 8*: A Street. *Scene 9*: A Courtyard.

ACT 1

Scene 1

"The Tour Must Go On"
   D. Campbell, Girls, Boys

"I Wanna Be Good 'n Bad"
   N. Fabray, Girls

Scene 2

The Time Step
   N. Fabray, H. Gallagher, H. Lang

Scene 3

"(You're Just) What I Was Warned About"
   N. Fabray

"Who Gives a Sou?"
   N. Fabray, S. Douglass, H. Gallagher, H. Lang

Scene 6

"Folies Labiche Overture (Hello, Hello, Hello)"
   Folies Chorus

Scene 7

"Tonight You Are in Paree"
N. Fabray, Girls, Boys

Scene 8

"When Does This Feeling Go Away?"
S. Douglass

Scene 9

"Suits Me Fine"
H. Gallagher, H. Lang

Scene 10

Students Ball
Girls, Boys

"Paris, France"
Entire Company

ACT 2

Scene 1

"That Face!"
H. Gallagher, H. Lang, Girls, Boys

Scene 3

"Make a Wish"
N. Fabray

Scene 4

"I'll Never Make a Frenchman Out of You"
H. Gallagher, H. Lang

Scene 5

"Over and Over"
N. Fabray, Boys

The Sale (Ballet)
A. Buchanan, Sylvia Manon Trio, R. Dorian, H. Wendell, Girls, Boys

Scene 6

"Over and Over" (reprise)
H. Gallgher, H. Lang

"Who Gives a Sou?" (reprise)
N. Fabray, S. Douglass

Scene 8

"Take Me Back to Texas With You"
N. Fabray, H. Gallagher, H. Lang

Scene 9

"Suits Me Fine" (reprise)
Girls, Boys

Finale—"Make a Wish"
N. Fabray, Entire Company

1951.14 A TREE GROWS IN BROOKLYN

A Musical in Two Acts, 21 Scenes. Book by Betty Smith and George Abbott. Based on the novel of the same name by Betty Smith. Music by Arthur Schwartz. Lyrics by Dorothy Fields. Scenery and lighting by Jo Mielziner. Costumes by Irene Sharaff. Choreography by Herbert Ross. Musical supervision by Jay Blackton. Musical arrangements (orchestrations) by Joe Glover, Robert Russell Bennett. Musical director, Max Goberman. Production directed by George Abbott. Produced by George Abbott in association with Robert Fryer. Opened 19 April 1951 at the Alvin Theatre and closed 8 December 1951 after 270 performances.

CAST (in order of appearance): *Willie*: Billy Parsons. *Allie*: Joe Calvan. *Hildy*: Dody Heath. *Della*: Beverly Purvin. *Petey*: LOU WILLS, JR. *Katie*: MARCIA VAN DYKE. *Aloysius*: Jordan Bentley. *Johnny Nolan*: JOHNNY JOHNSTON. *Cissy*: SHIRLEY BOOTH. *Harry*: NATHANIEL FREY. *Max*: Bruno Wick. *Mae*: Ruth Amos. *Moriarty*: Roland Wood. *Annie*: Claudia Campbell. *Old Clothes Man*: Harland Dixon. *Florence*: Janet Parker. *Edgie*: Donald Duerr. *Francie*: NOMI MITTY. *Junior*: Howard Martin. *Swanswine*: Albert Linville. *Hick*: Alan Gilbert. *Judge*: Harland Dixon. *Salesman*: Art Carroll. *Girls in Mae's Place*: Beverly Purvin, Claudia Campbell, Jane Copeland, Marta Beckett, Mary Statz, Dorothy Hill. *Maudie*: Celine Flanagan.

Dancers: Marta Beckett, Dorothy Hill, Mary Statz, Doris Wright, Oleg Briansky, Val Buttignol, Donn [Donald] Driver, Dick Price. *Singers*: Elaine Barrow, Claudia Campbell, Jane Copeland, Jeanne Grant, Beverly Purvin, Beverly Jane Welch, Eleanor Williams, Art Carroll, Delbert Anderson, Johnny Ford, James McCracken, John Mooney, Feodore Tedick, Kenneth Utt. *Children*: John Connoughton, Donald Duerr, Celine Flanagan, Buzzie Martin, Howard Martin, Patti Milligan, Janet Parker.

Act 1, Scene 1: A Street in Brooklyn on a Saturday, nearly 50 years ago. *Scene 2*: Around the corner, a few minutes later. *Scene 3*: Cissy's House, a few weeks later. *Scene 4*: On the corner, early next morning. *Scene 5*: Max's Furniture Store, the same morning. *Scene 6*: On the way to Katie's, a year later. *Scene 7*: The Nolan Kitchen, a year later. *Scene 8*: On the Street. *Scene 9*: Cissy's House. *Scene 10*: A Sidewalk. *Scene 11*: Up on the Roof.

Act 2, Scene 1: The Courtyard, 12 years later. *Scene 2*: The Nolan Kitchen. *Scene 3*: A Street Corner. *Scene 4*: Mae's Place. *Scene 5*: A Dark and Deserted Street. *Scene 6*: The Nolan Kitchen. *Scene 7*: An Empty Street fronting a Vacant Lot. *Scene 8*: The Nolan Kitchen. A Somber Autumn Day. *Scene 9*: In the Street. Late June. *Scene 10*: The Courtyard.

ACT 1

Scene 1

"Payday"
The Company

"Mine Til Monday"
J. Johnston, D. Heath, Company

Scene 2

"Mine 'Til Monday" (reprise)
J. Bentley, D. Heath, L. Wills, Jr., J. Calvan, B. Parsons

Scene 3

"Make the Man Love Me"
M. Van Dyke, J. Johnston

"I'm Like a New Broom"
J. Johnston, Friends

Scene 4

"I'm Like a New Broom" (reprise)
J. Johnston, Friends

Scene 5

"Look Who's Dancing"
M. Van Dyke, S. Booth, J. Johnston, J. Calvan,
B. Parsons, L. Wills, Jr., M. Statz, I. McKenzie, D. Wright, M. Becket

Scene 6

("Look Who's Dancing") (reprise)
Friends

Scene 7

("Make the Man Love Me") (reprise)
M. Van Dyke

Scene 8

"Love Is the Reason"
S. Booth, J. Kilbrig, D. Heath, B. Purvin, E. Williams

"Mine Next Monday"
J. Bentley, D. Heath

Scene 10

"If You Haven't Got a Sweetheart"
J. McCracken, Company

Scene 11

"I'll Buy You a Star"
J. Johnston, Company

ACT 2

Scene 1

"That's How It Goes"
H. Dixon, C. Flanagan, J. Parker, Company

"He Had Refinement"
S. Booth

Scene 2

"Growing Pains"
J. Johnston, N. Mitty

"Is That My Prince?"
S. Booth, A. Linville

Scene 5

Halloween (Ballet)[28]
J. Johnston, L. Wills, Jr., J. Calvan, B. Parsons, Dancers, Children, Singers

---

[28]For subsequent national tour replaced by "The Raffle Ballet."

Scene 6

"Don't Be Afraid"
J. Johnston

"I'm Like a New Broom" (reprise)
J. Johnston

Scene 7

"Love Is the Reason" (reprise)
S. Booth, N. Frey

Scene 9

"Look Who's Dancing" (reprise)
N. Frey, Children

Scene 10

"If You Haven't Got a Sweetheart" (reprise)
The Company

1951.15   FLAHOOLEY

A Musical Comedy in Two Acts, 17 Scenes. Book by E. Y. Harburg and Fred Saidy. Music by Sammy Fain. Lyrics by E. Y. Harburg. Dances and musical numbers staged by Helen Tamiris. Scenery and lighting by Howard Bay. Costumes designed by David Ffolkes. Book directed by E. Y. Harburg and Fred Saidy. Musical director, Maurice Levine. Orchestrations by Ted Royal. Choral numbers arranged and directed by Maurice Levine. Special material for Yma Sumac by Moises Vivanco. Dance music arranged by Freda Miller. Produced by Cheryl Crawford in association with Messrs. Harburg and Saidy. Opened 14 May 1951 at the Broadhurst Theatre and closed 17 June 1951 after 40 performances.

CAST (in order of appearance): *A March of Time Voice*: Stanley Carlson. *Clyde*: Bil Baird. *Mirabelle*: Cora Baird. *Sandy*: BARBARA COOK. *Sylvester*: JEROME COURTLAND. *Griselda*: Fay DeWitt. *Switchboard Operators*: Vicki Barrett, Jane Fischer, Laurel Shelby, Tafi Towers, Urylee Leonardos, Annaliese Widman. *K. T. Pettigrew*: EDITH ATWATER. *Board of Director (6)*: *Quimsby*: Stanley Carlson. *Peabody*: Ted Thurston. *Evans*: Rowan Tudor. *Farquarson*: Richard Temple. *Lovingham*: Andrew Aprea. *Hastings*: Edgar Thompson. *The Voice on the P.A.*: Tafi Towers. *B. G. Bigelow*: ERNEST TRUEX. *Miss Buckley*: Marilyn Ross. *Clayfoot Trowbridge*: Rowan Tudor. *Fowzi, the Younger Arab*: Nehemiah Persoff. *El-Akbar, the Elder Arab*: Louis Nye. *Najla*: YMA SUMAC. *Buyers*: Lee Ballard, Ray Cook, Clifford Fearl, Franklin T. Syme, Laurel Shelby. *Abou Ben Atom*: IRWIN COREY. *Elsa Bullinger*: Lulu Bates. *Citizens of Capsulanti*: Norval Tormsen, Ray Cook, Clifford Fearl, Sheldon Ossosky. *Arabs*: Stanley Carlson, Andrew Aprea, Ted Thurston, Rowan Tudor. *Doctor Smith*: Franklin T. Syme. *Nurse*: Laurel Shelby. *Flahooley*: Elizabeth Logue. *Radio Voice*: Edgar Thompson. THE BIL BAIRD MARIONETTES.

Singers: Vicki Barrett, Carol Donn, Urylee Leonardos, Laurel Shelby, Lois Shearer, Tafi Towers, Andrew Aprea, John Anderson, Lewis Bolyard, Ray Cook, Clifford Fearl, Franklin T. Syme, Norval Tormsen, Edgar Thompson. *Dancers*: Sara Aman, Jane Fischer, Annaliese Widman, Normand Maxon, Joe Nash, Sheldon Ossosky, James M. Tarbutton. *Marionette Operators*: Bil Baird, Cora Baird, Carl Harms, Franz Farkas. *Puppet Singing Voices*: *Mirabelle, Cinderella, Poodle*: Lois Shearer. *Clyde, F.D.R.*: John Anderson. *Hen*: Carl Donn. *Rhino*: Ted Thurston. *Cat*: Fay DeWitt. *Lincoln*: Stanley Carlson. *Lion*: Franz Fazakas. *Tom Payne*: Carl Harms.

Act 1, Scene 1: B. G. Bigelow, Inc. *Scene 2*: A Section of the Puppet Laboratory. *Scene 3*: Telephone Room. *Scene 4*: The Board Room. *Scene 5*: Bigelow's Toyland Bazaar. *Scene 6*: The Bigelow Hall of Fame (Showroom to you). *Scene 7*: The Puppet Laboratory. *Scene 8*: (Najla's Specialty.) *Scene 9*: Bigelow's Inner Sanctum.

Act 2, Scene 1: B. G. Bigelow, Inc. *Scene 2*: City Hall Sqaure. *Scene 3*: B. G. Bigelow Inc. *Scene 4*: Bigelow's Bagdad. *Scene 5*: Hospital Waiting-Room. *Scene 6*: Abou's Hospital Room. *Scene 7*: "Sing the Merry." *Scene 8*: Main Street—Capsulanti.

ACT 1

Scene 2

"You Too Can Be a Puppet"
Puppet Singers

"Here's to Your Illusions"
B. Cook, J. Courtland

Scene 5

"B. G. Bigelow, Inc."
Ex.cutives, Personnel

Demonstration Dances
S. Aman, J. Nash, S. Ossosky, A. Widman, J. Fisher, V. Barrett

"Najla's Song"[29]
Y. Sumac

"Who Says There Ain't No Santa Claus?"
J. Courtland, B. Cook, Executives, Personnel

Scene 6

"Flahooley"
F. DeWitt, M. Ross, Executives, Personnel
Danced by Toy Band: *Big Drum*: J. Nash. *Clarinet*: J. M. Tarbutton. *Accordion*: J. Anderson. *Tuba*: S. Ossosky. *Glockenspiel*: N. Maxon.

Scene 7

"The World Is Your Balloon"
B. Cook, J. Courtland, Puppet Singers

"He's Only Wonderful"
B. Cook, J. Courtland

Scene 8

Arabian for "Get Happy"[30]
Y. Sumac, I. Corey, N. Persoff, L. Nye

Scene 9

"Jump, Little Chillun'"
Ensemble

ACT 2

Scene 2

"Spirit of Capsulanti"
M. Ross, Townspeople

"Happy Hunting"
L. Bates, M. Ross, F. DeWitt, Townspeople

Scene 4

"Enchantment"[31]
Y. Sumac

"Scheherezade"
Arabs, Executives

Scene 6

"Come Back, Little Genie"
B. Cook

"The Springtime Cometh"
I. Corey
Danced by E. Logue.

Scene 7

"Sing the Merry"
F. DeWitt, J. Anderson, C. Fearl, R. Cook, N. Tormsen, F. T. Syme, L. Bolyard

Scene 8

Finale
Entire Company

1951.16   OKLAHOMA!

A Return Engagement of the Musical Play in Two Acts, 6 Scenes[32]. Book and lyrics by Oscar Hammerstein II. Music by Richard Rodgers. Based on the play "Green Grow the Lilacs" by Lynn Riggs. (Original) Production directed by Rouben Mamoulian. Dances by Agnes de Mille. Production reproduced by Jerome Whyte. Settings by Lemuel Ayers. Costumes by Miles White. Orchestra directed by Peter Laurini. Orchestrations by (Robert) Russell Bennett. Production under the supervision of Lawrence Langner and Theresa Helburn. Produced by The Theatre Guild. Opened 29 May 1951 at the Broadway Theatre and closed 28 July 1951 after 72 performances.

CAST (in order of appearance): *Aunt Eller*: MARY MARLO. *Curly*: RIDGE BOND, Warren Schmoll (alt.). *Laurey*: PATRICIA NORTHROP, Patricia Johnson (alt.). *Cord*

---

[29]Special material for Yma Sumac by Moises Vivanco.
[30]Special material for Yma Sumac by Moises Vivanco.
[31]Special material for Yma Sumac by Moises Vivanco.
[32]Originally produced in New York 31 March 1943 at the St. James Theatre for 2,212 performances. For Synopsis of Scenes and Musical Numbers, see original 1943 production.

Elam: Owen Martin. *Fred*: Warren Schmoll. *Will Parker*: WALTER DONAHUE. *Jud Fry*: HENRY CLARKE. *Ado Annie Carnes*: JACQUELINE SUNDT. *Ali Hakim*: JERRY MANN. *Gertie Cummings*: Patricia Johnson. *Kate*: Judy Rawlings. *Armina*: Jeanne Parsons. *'Child in Pigtails'*: Patricia Barker. *'Girl Who Falls Down'*: Audree Wilson. *Andrew Carnes*: DAVE MALLEN. *'Laurey' in the Ballet*: Claire Pasch. *'Curly' in the Ballet*: Philip Cook. *'Jud' in the Ballet*: Valentin Froman. *Slim*: John Addis. *Mike*: Charles Scott.

Dancers: Edmund Gasper, Glenn Forbes, Joseph Ribeau, George Stecher, Edmund Howland, Peyton Townes, Harry Asmus, Betty Gour, Carmen Froman, Nancy Milton, Marquita Living, Jeanne Parsons, Audree Wilson, Josephine Andrews, Jean Bledsoe, Muriel Ives, Patricia Brooks, Patricia Barker. *Singers*: Charles Scott, Warren Schmoll, Robert Early, James Fox, Donald Swenson, John Addis, George Cayley, Beth Johnson, Dolores Kempner, Enid Little, Virginia Walker, Judy Rawlings, Sara Jane Wilson, Jeannine Cowles.

NEW FACES OF 1952

Billy Rose Theatre Collection, New York Public Library for the Performing Arts

1951–1952 SEASON

1951.17   COURTIN' TIME

A Musical Comedy in Two Acts, 9 Scenes. Book by William Roos. Based on the play "The Farmer's Wife" by Eden Philpotts. Music and lyrics by Don Walker and Jack Lawrence. Entire production staged by Alfred Drake. Dances staged by George Balanchine. Scenery and lighting by Ralph Alswang. Costumes by Saul Bolasni. Music and vocal arrangements by Don Walker. Musical director, Bill Jonson. Produced by James Russo and Michael Ellis in association with Alexander H. Cohen. Opened 14 June 1951 at the National Theatre, moved 2 July 1951 to the Royale Theatre, and closed 14 July 1951 after 37 performances.

CAST (in order of appearance): *Nell Rilling*: GLORIA PATRICE. *Cathy Rilling*: GLORIA HAMILTON. *Laura*: Mary O'Fallon. *George Mullins*: PETER CONLOW. *Samuel Rilling*: JOE E. BROWN. *Carl Stevens*: THEODOR UPPMAN. *Fred Lawson*: David E. Thomas. *Araminta*: BILLIE WORTH. *Harriet Hearn*: EFFIE AFTON. *Mr. Hearn*: JOSEPH SWEENEY. *Theresa Tapper*: CARMEN MATHEWS. *Louisa Windeatt*: KATHERINE ANDERSON. *Polly*: May Muth. *Sadie*: Rosemary Kuhlmann. *Millie*: Teddy Taverner. *Larry Walton*: EARL WILLIAM. *The Brat*: Patricia Poole.

Singing Ensemble: Betty Jane Cocho, Peggy Gavan, Glynn Hill, Joan Keenan, Rosemary Kuhlmann, May Muth, Mary O'Fallon, Teddy Tavenner, Walter Brandin, Michael T. Carolan, John Michael King, Michael Kingsley, Charles Rule, Robert Strobel, John Taliaferro, Lawrence Weber. *Dancing Ensemble*: Patricia Casey, Audrey Keane, Mary Martinet, Patricia Poole, Frances Sorenson, Elsa Van Horne, Edward Andrews, Hubert Bland, Peter Deign, William Maguire, Lou Yetter, Charles Zulkeski.

Act 1, Scene 1: Samuel Rilling's Farm, Maine, 1898. *Scene 2*: Louisa Windeatt's Apiary. *Scene 3*: The Parlor of the Rilling Home. *Scene 4*: The Post Office and General Store. *Scene 5*: Theresa Tapper's Garden.

Act 2, Scene 1: Samuel Rilling's Farm. *Scene 2*: The Rilling Kitchen. *Scene 3*: The Road to the Station. *Scene 4*: The Railroad Station.

ACT 1

"Today at Your House, Tomorrow at Mine"
    J. E. Brown, T. Uppman, D. E. Thomas, P. Conlow, Male Ensemble
       Danced by G. Patrice, P. Conlow, Ensemble.
"Fixin' for a Long, Cold Winter"
    J. E. Brown, B. Worth
"Araminta to Herself"
    B. Worth
"An Old-Fashioned Glimmer in Your Eye"
    B. Worth, G. Hamilton, Girls
"Goodbye, Dear Friend, Goodbye"
    G. Hamilton, E. William
"The Wishbone Song"
    B. Worth, G. Hamilton, E. William, G. Patrice, P. Conlow, T. Uppman, Ensemble
"Smile Awhile"
    B. Worth
"The Wishbone Song" (reprise)
       Danced by G. Patrice, P. Conlow
"Too Much Trouble"
    J. E. Brown
"Choose Your Partner"
    G. Patrice, G. Hamilton, E. William, T. Uppman, Singing Ensemble
       Danced by G. Patrice, P. Conlow, Ensemble
"I Do, He Doesn't"
    B. Worth
"Golden Moment"
    C. Mathews, J. E. Brown
"I Do, He Doesn't" (reprise)
    B. Worth

ACT 2

"Johnny Ride the Sky"
    T. Uppman, G. Hamilton, Singing Ensemble
"Johnny and the Puckwudgies[1]" (Ballet)
    (*At the Concert Grand*: Dorothea Freitag.)
    P. Conlow (Johnny-Ride-the-Sky), G. Patrice, Dancing Ensemble

---

[1]Puckwudgies are Maine pixies often accused of tampering with the weather.

"The Sensible Thing to Do"
    B. Worth, E. William
"The Wishbone Song" (reprise)
    B. Worth, G. Hamilton, E. William, G. Patrice, P. Conlow
"Masculinity"
    K. Anderson, C. Mathews, E. Afton
"Maine Will Remember the Maine"
    E. William, T. Uppman, J. Sweeney, Male Ensemble
"Heart in Hand"
    J. E. Brown, B. Worth
Finale
    Entire Company

1951.18   SEVENTEEN

A Musical Comedy in Two Acts, 11 Scenes. Book by Sally Benson. Based on the novel of the same name by Booth Tarkington. Music by Walter Kent. Lyrics by Kim Gannon. Staged and lighted by Hassard Short. Book directed by Richard Whorf. Dances and musical numbers by Dania Krupska. Scenery by Stewart Chaney. Costumes by David Ffolkes. Musical arrangements by Ted Royal. Choral arrangements by Crane Calder. Dance music arrangements by Jess Meeker. Musical director, Vincent Travers. Produced by Milton Berle, Sammy Lambert, Bernie Foyer. Opened 21 June 1951 at the Broadhurst Theatre and closed 24 November 1951 after 180 performances.

CAST (in order of appearance): *Genesis*: MAURICE ELLIS. *Johnnie Watson*: JOHN SHARPE. *Willie Baxter*: KENNETH NELSON. *Jane Baxter*: BETTY JANE SEAGLE. *Bert*: Greg O'Brien. *Charlie*: Jim Moore. *Dave*: Bill Reilly. *Joe Bullitt*: DICK KALLMAN. *Lester*: Richard France. *Darrell*: Darrell Notara. *Don*: Bob Bakanic. *Lola Pratt*: ANN CROWLEY. *Mrs. Baxter*: DORIS DALTON. *May Parcher*: ELLEN McCOWN. *Emmie*: HELEN WOOD. *Ida*: Carol Cole. *Madge*: Bonnie Brae. *Sue*: Elizabeth Pacetti. *Jenny*: Sherry McCutcheon. *Nan*: Joan Bowman. *Mr. Baxter*: FRANK ALBERTSON. *Mr. Parcher*: KING CALDER. *Mrs. Parcher*: PENNY BANCROFT. *George Crooper*: HARRISON MULLER. *Mr. Genesis*: ALONZO BOSAN. *Porter*: Joseph James.

Singers: Margaret Baxter, Dorothy Manko, Jenne Shea, Paula Stewart, Stan [Stanley] Grover, Henry Lawrence, Bill Nuss, Ray Thomas.

Act 1, Scene 1: The Baxters' House, Indianapolis, 1907. *Scene 2*: A Path. *Scene 3*: Willie's Room. *Scene 4*: The Parchers' House. *Scene 5*: A Path. *Scene 6*: The Baxters' House.

Act 2, Scene 1: The Woods. *Scene 2*: Harper Road. *Scene 3*: Willie's Room. *Scene 4*: The Parchers' Lawn. *Scene 5*: The Railroad Station.

ACT 1
Scene 1
    "Weatherbee's Drug Store"
       D. Kallman, B. Bakanic, R. France, J. Moore,
       D. Notara, B. Reilly, J. Sharpe
    "This Was Just Another Day"
       A. Crowley, K. Nelson
Scene 2
    "Things Are Gonna Hum This Summer"
       A. Crowley, E. McCown, H. Wood,
       D. Kallman, J. Sharpe, J. Moore, B. Brae, R. France, Friends
Scene 3
    "How Do You Do, Miss Pratt?"
       K. Nelson
Scene 4
    "Summertime Is Summertime"
       H. Wood, R. France, E. McCown, D. Kallman, Friends
    "Reciprocity"
       A. Crowley, B. Bakanic, J. Moore, R. France, B. Reilly, D. Notara, J. Sharpe
Scene 5
    "Ode to Lola"
       E. McCown, H. Wood, J. Bowman, B. Brae, C. Cole, S. McCutcheon, E. Pacetti
Scene 6
    "Headache and Heartache"
       D. Dalton, F. Albertson
    "OO-OOO-OOO, What You Do to Me"
       H. Muller

ACT 2

Scene 1

"The Hoosier Way"
H. Muller, H. Wood, R. France, J. Moore, C. Cole, Friends

"I Could Get Married Today"
K. Nelson, M. Ellis, A. Bosan

"After All, It's Spring"
E. McCown, D. Kallman, Friends

Scene 4

"If We Only Could Stop the Old Town Clock"
A. Crowley, K. Nelson, H. Muller, D. Kallman, E. McCown, H. Wood, Friends

Scene 5

"After All, It's Spring" (reprise)
The Company

TWO ON THE AISLE

1951.19

A Musical Revue in Two Acts, 20 Scenes. Music by Jule Styne. Sketches and lyrics by Betty Comden and Adolph Green. Musical numbers staged by Ted Cappy. Settings and lighting by Howard Bay. Costumes by Joan Personette. Orchestrations by Philip J. Lang. Dance music arranged by Genevieve Pitot. Vocal arrangements and orchestra conducted by Herbert Greene. Entire production directed by Abe Burrows. Produced by Arthur Lesser. Opened 19 July 1951 at the Mark Hellinger Theatre and closed 15 March 1952 after 276 performances.

CAST: BERT LAHR, DOLORES GRAY, ELLIOT REID, COLETTE MARCHAND, J. C. McCord, Kathryne Mylroie, Stanley Prager, Robert Gallagher, Larry Laurence, Alan LeRoy, Richard Gray, Gordon Hamilton, Patricia Tobin.
Singers: Marion Lauer, Leila Martin, Beverly McFadden, Leslie Parry, Peggy Reiss, Carol Sawyer, Joanne Spiller, Julie Williams, John Allen, Arthur Arney, Fred Bryan, Buford Jasper, Walter Kelvin, John Raye, Arthur Rubin. *Dancers*: Jeannett Aquilina, Margery Beddow, Betty Buday, Gloria Danyl, Dorothy Etheridge, Doris Goodwin, Vera Lee, Jane Mason, Bob Emmett, Jerry Fries, John Kelly, Paul Lyday, Victor Reilley, Frank Reynolds. *Showgirls*: Gregg Evans, Rosemary Kittelton, Dell Parker, Mira Stefan, Jeanne Tyler, Charlotte Van Lein.

ACT 1

Scene 1

"Show Train"
Conductors: S. Prager, R. Gallagher, L. Laurence, A. Rubin, W. Kelvin. And Ladies and Gentlemen of the Ensemble.

Scene 2

"Hold Me Tight" (Hold Me—Hold Me—Hold Me)
(D. Gray)
First Suitor: F. Reynolds. *Second Suitor*: J. Kelly. *Third Suitor*: B. Emmett. *Maid*: J. Aquilina. *The Girl*: D. Gray.

Scene 3

Highlights from the World of Sports
Producer: A. LeRoy. *Announcer*: E. Reid. *Cameramen*: R. Gray, R. Gallagher. *Lefty Hogan*: B. Lahr.

Scene 4

"East River Hoe Down" (Here She Comes Now)
(Ensemble)
Danced by J. C. McCord, V. Lee, Ladies and Gentlemen of the Ensemble.

Scene 5

"There Never Was a Baby Like My Baby"
(D. Gray)
Wife: D. Gray. *Husband*: E. Reid. *Danced by* J. C. McCord, assisted by G. Danyl, M. Beddow, J. Mason, J. Kelly, F. Reynolds.

Scene 6

Space Brigade
Hodgkins: R. Gray. *Hotchkiss*: L. Laurence. *Hitchcock*: R. Gallagher. *Captain Universe*: B. Lahr. *Higgins*: S. Prager. *Radio Voice*: W. Kelvin. *Queen Chlorophyl*: K. Mylroie. *Denizens of Venus*: F. Reynolds, J. Kelly, A. Arney, J. Raye, V. Reilley.

Scene 7

"If You Hadn't, But You Did"
(D. Gray)
The Girl: D. Gray. *The Other Woman*: G. Danyl. *The Man*: B. Emmett.

Scene 8

"The Clown"
B. Lahr
Assisted by V. Lee, G. Danyl, D. Parker, M. Stefan.

Scene 9

The Guide Book
Three Urchins: F. Reynolds, V. Reilly, J. Kelly. *The Girl*: C. Marchand. *The Lovers*: P. Lyday, B. Buday. *Traveller*: B. Emmett. *The American*: J. C. McCord. *Assisted by* J. Mason, J. Aquilina, M. Beddow, J. Fries.

Scene 10

Here's What You Said
E. Reid

Scene 11

"Catch Our Act" (Vaudeville Ain't Dead)
Two Vaudevillians: B. Lahr, D. Gray.

Scene 12

"At the Met"
Siegfried: B. Lahr. *Brünnhilde*: D. Gray. *The Dragon*: S. Prager. *Danced by* C. Marchand. *Assisted by* Ladies and Gentlemen of the Ensemble.

ACT 2

Scene 1

"Everlasting"
K. Mylroie, F. Bryan
Danced by D. Etheridge, J. Fries. *Assisted by* Ladies and Gentlemen of the Ensemble.

Scene 2

Schneider's Miracle
(by Nat Hiken and William Friedberg)
Schneider: B. Lahr. *Mrs. Higgleston*: P. Tobin. *Piper*: S. Prager. *Miss Flaherty*: K. Mylroie. *Inspector*: R. Gallagher. *Man on Bench*: A. LeRoy. *Little Girl*: J. Aquilina. *Policeman*: R. Gray. *Passersby*: J. Allen, L. Martin, F. Reynolds, W. Kelvin.

Scene 3

"Give a Little, Get a Little Love"
D. Gray, Ladies and Gentlemen of the Ensemble

Scene 4

Didy Dolls
B. Lahr
Ladies of the Ensemble: D. Parker, M. Stefan, C. Van Lein, G. Evans, R. Kittleton, J. Tyler. *Voice*: A. Rubin.

Scene 5

Triangle
(1) *Hubby*: E. Reid. *Wifey*: D. Gray. *Lovey*: B. Lahr. (2) *Husband*: E. Reid. *Wife*: D. Gray. *Close Friend*: B. Lahr. (3) *He*: E. Reid. *She*: D. Gray. *Him*: B. Lahr.

Scene 6

Dog Show
(*Choreographed by* Ruthanna Boris.)
Judge: B. Emmett. *Russian Wolfhounds*: G. Evans, R. Kittelton, D. Parker, M. Stefan, J. Tyler, C. Van Lein. *Their Trainer*: J. Fries. *Pekinese*: D. Etheridge. *Her Trainer*: P. Lyday. *Cocker Spaniels*: G. Danyl, J. Mason. *Their Trainer*: V. Reilley. *Dalmatians*: B. Buday, D. Goodwin. *Their Trainer*: J. Kelly. *French Poodle*: C. Marchand. *Her Manager*: G. Hamilton.

Scene 7

"How Will He Know?"
(D. Gray)
Mr. Murdock: B. Lahr. *Miss Travers*: D. Gray.

Scene 8

Finale
B. Lahr, D. Gray, C. Marchand, Entire Company

BAGELS AND YOX

1951.20

An American-Yiddish Revue in Two Acts, 13 Scenes. Songs by Sholom Secunda and Hy Jacobson. Additional lyrics by Millie Alpert. Lighting by Bruno Maine. Orchestra conducted by Irv Carroll, with Curt Bell at the piano. Musical arrangements by Jerome Goldstein. Produced by Al Beckman and John Pransky in association with the Brandt Theatres. Opened 12 September 1951 at the Holiday Theatre and closed 12 February 1952 after 204 performances.[2]

CAST: BARTON BROTHERS (Murray, Eddie, Paul), MARY FORREST, LOU SAXON, LARRY ALPERT, RICKIE LAYNE and VELVEL, Marty Drake, Ricki Fields, Ina Lerner, Paula Stevens, Johnny Conrad, Dian Lund, Audrey Barfoot, Tibby Rayburn, Patrice Helene, Jan Howard.

[2]Direction, scenery and costumes uncredited.

ACT 1

Scene 1

Prologue

Scene 2

"Bagels and Yox"
L. Saxon, Barton Brothers, M. Drake,
L. Alpert, R. Layne, M. Forrest, R. Fields, I. Lerner, P. Stevens

Scene 3

"Such a Good Looking Boy"
R. Layne and Velvel

Scene 4

J. Conrad, D. Lund, A. Barfoot, T. Rayburn, J. Hansen

Scene 5

A Song in Any Language
M. Forrest

Scene 6

Yox, Yox and Yox
Barton Brothers

ACT 2

Scene 1

"Chi-Ri-Bim"
Entire Cast

Scene 2

"Sholom Aleichem"
L. Saxon

Scene 3

"Inimitably Yours"
P. Helene, J. Howard

Scene 4

Culture From Carnegie Hall
M. Drake

Scene 5

Who Needs It?
L. Alpert

Scene 6

"Let's Dance a Frailichs"
Barton Brothers, M. Drake, L. Alpert, L. Saxon, R. Layne

Scene 7

Finale—"Bagels and Yox" (reprise)
Entire Company

1951.21   BORSCHT CAPADES

An English-Yiddish Musical Revue in Two Acts, 14 Scenes. Entire production directed by Mickey Katz. Settings and lighting by Charles Elson. Costumes by Natalie Barth Walker. Special music for dances by Joseph Rumshinsky. Choreography by Ted Adair. Orchestra directed by Max Pollack. Produced by Hal Zeiger. Opened 17 September 1951 at the Royale Theatre and closed 2 December 1951 after 90 performances.

CAST: MICKEY KATZ, PHIL FOSTER, JOEL KAYE, DAVE BARRY, RAASCHE, THE BARRY SISTERS (Claire, Merna), PATSY ABBOTT, JACK HILLIARD, ALAN SHACKNER.

Ted Adair Dancers: Sonia Levkova, Harold Lawrence, Carmen Montoya, Faye Keith, Carol Chanson, Troubles Weithorn, Eddie Andrews, Peter Holmes, Carey Leverett, Vincent Morino, Max Solomon.

ACT 1

Scene 1

Yiddish Square Dance
M. Katz, Dancers

Scene 2

"Yiddish Mule Train"
M. Katz, Band

Scene 3

"Lighting of the Sabbath Candles"
Raasche, Dancers
(*Special Choreography by* Belle Didjah.)

Scene 4

Raasche (Israeli Melodies and Folk-songs)

Scene 5

"Geshray of de Vilde Katchke"
M. Katz, Band

Scene 6

Jack Hilliard (Singer)

Scene 7

Alan Shackner

Scene 8

(Yiddish Swing)
Barry Sisters

Scene 9

(He Grows in Brooklyn)(Comedy)
P. Foster

Scene 10

From Israel to Egypt
J. Hilliard, Barry Sisters, Dancers
a) On the Nile, b) Shepherd Fantasy, c) Dance Chassidic, d) Israeli Hora

ACT 2

Scene 1

Olio of Yiddish Music America Loves Best
M. Katz, Band

Scene 2

(From Sunset Boulevard to Lindy's)(Comedy, Song)
P. Abbott

Scene 3

(Professor of 'Fractured Yiddish')
D. Barry

Scene 4

Finale

1951.22   MUSIC IN THE AIR

A Revival of the Musical Comedy in Two Acts, 8 Scenes[3]. Book and lyrics by Oscar Hammerstein II. (Book revisions by Oscar Hammerstein II.) Music by Jerome Kern. Staged by Oscar Hammerstein II. Production (scenery, costumes) designed by Lemuel Ayers. Musical director, Maurice Levine. Orchestrations by Robert Russell Bennett. Produced by Reginald Hammerstein. Opened 8 October 1951 at the Ziegfeld Theatre and closed 24 November 1951 after 56 performances.

CAST (in order of appearance): *Mrs. Pflugfelder*: Julie Kelety. *Tila*: Marybeth Fitzpatrick. *Herman*: Richard Case. *Karl Reder*, the Schoolmaster: MITCHELL GREGG. *Burgomaster*: Hal Frye. *Sieglinde Lessing*: LILLIAN MURPHY. *Dr. Walther Lessing*, the Music Teacher: CHARLES WINNINGER. *Schmidt*: Carlo Corelli. *Priest*: Milton Watson. *Pflugfelder*: Walter Born. *Ernst Weber*: Conrad Nagel. *Uppmann*: Guy Spaull. *Marthe*: Terry Saunders. *Frieda Hatzfeld*: JANE PICKENS. *Bruno Mahler*: DENNIS KING. *Waiter*: John M. King. *Zoo Attendant*: Waldorf. *Anna*: Norah Howard. *Porter*: James Beni. *Kirschner*: Richard Bishop. *Lilli*: Muriel O'Malley. *Sophie*: Julie Kelety. *Assistant Stage Manager*: John M. King. *Lawyer Baum*: Gordon Alexander. *Barmaid*: Biruta Ramoska. *Willi*: James Beni. *Frau Schreimann*: Jean Ellsperman. *Frau Moeller*: Susan Steell.

Various Characters of Edendorf and Zurich: *Women*: Madelaine Chambers, Jean Ellsperman, Joan Keenan, Julie Kelety, Rosemary Kuhlman, Sheila Mathews, Grace Olsen, Biruta Ramoska, Marjorie Samsel, Helen Stanton, Susan Steell. *Men*: Gordon Alexander, Robert Baird, James Beni, Walter Born, Robert Busch, Carlo Corelli, Charles Dunn, Warren Galjour, Robert Gilson, John M. King, William Krach, Frederick Olsson, Fred Rivetti, Donald Thrall. *Children*: Richard Case, Marybeth Fitzpatrick, Georgianna Catal, Mary Hoyer, Charles Lee Saari.

The Action takes place in Switzerland.

Act 1, Scene 1: Etude. A Schoolroom in Edendorf. Morning. *Scene 2*: Impromptu. Ernst Weber's office in Zurich. Three days later.

Act 2, Scene 1: Sonata. The zoo. That afternoon. *Scene 1a*: Interlude. *Scene 2*: Caprice. Sieglinde's hotel room. That night. *Scene 3*: Rhapsody. A star-dressing room. Four

---

[3]First presented in New York 8 November 1932 at the Alvin Theatre for 342 performances.

weeks later. *Scene 4*: Intermezzo. Stage and orchestra pit. About an hour later. *Scene 5*: Humoresque. The star dressing-room. Later, the same night. *Scene 6*: Rondo. Three weeks later.

ACT 1[4]

Dr. Lessing's Chorale:

"Melodies of May"
Choral Society

"I've Told Every Little Star"
M. Gregg, L. Murphy, Choral Society

"Prayer"
Schoolroom Ensemble

"There's a Hill Beyond a Hill"
Walking Club

"I've Told Every Little Star" (reprise)
L. Murphy

Bruno's Play:

"I'm Coming Home"
D. King

"I'm Alone"
J. Pickens

"I Am So Eager"
D. King, J. Pickens

Finaletta
T. Saunders, C. Nagel, C. Winninger

ACT 2

"One More Dance"
D. King

"Night Flies By"
J. Pickens

"When the Spring Is in the Air"
L. Murphy, M. O'Malley, C. Winninger

"In Egern on Tegern See"
M. O'Malley

"The Song Is You"
D. King

"The Song Is You" (reprise)
J. Pickens, D. King

"We Belong Together"
Edendorf Ensemble

1951.23

TOP BANANA

A Musical Comedy in Two Acts, 15 Scenes. Book by Hy Kraft. Music and lyrics by Johnny Mercer. Settings and lighting by Jo Mielziner. Dances by Ron Fletcher. Costumes by Alvin Colt. Musical director, Harold Hastings. Vocal arrangements and direction, Hugh Martin. Orchestrations by Don Walker. Dance music arranged by Lee Pockriss. Production directed by Jack Donohue. Production associate, Harry Zevin. Produced by Paula Stone and Mike Sloane. Opened 1 November 1951 at the Winter Garden and closed 4 October 1952 after 350 performances.

CAST (in order of appearance): *Danny*: Eddie Hanley. *Script Girl*: Eve Hebert. *Bubble Girls*: Beverly Weston, Sara Dillon. *Vic Davis*: JACK ALBERTSON. *Tommy*: BOB SCHEERER. *Walter*: Walter Dare Wahl. *Jerry Biffle*: PHIL SILVERS. *Cliff Lane*: LINDY DOHERTY. *Moe*: HERBIE FAYE. *Pinky*: JOEY FAYE. *Betty Dillon*: ROSE MARIE. *Sally Peters*: JUDY LYNN. *A Man*: Johnny Trama. *Elevator Operator*: Sara Dillon. *Models*: Marion Burke, Basha Regis. *Sales Girls*: Joy Skylar, Polly Ward, Florence Baum, Eve Hebert. *Customers*: B. J. Keating, Joan Fields, Laurel Shelby, Doug Luther, Betsy Holland. *Russ Wiswell*: Zachary A. Charles. *Mr. Parker*: BRADFORD HATTON. *Announcer*: Dean Campbell. *Featured Dancers*: Hal Loman, Joan Fields. *TV Technician*: Ken Harvey. *Miss Pillsbury*: Betsy Holland. *Dr. LeRoy*: Doug Luther. *Stagehand*: Don Covert. *Ted (Sport) Morgan*: Himself. *Dance Team*: Bob Scheerer, Polly Ward. *Juggler*: Claude Heater. *Photographers*: Don Covert, Ken Harvey, Herb Fields, Don McKay. *A Passing Girl*: Mary Harmon. *The Widow*: Judy Sinclair. *Magician's Assistant*: Basha Regis. "*Bubbles*": Gloria Smith.

Dancers: Florence Baum, Eve Hebert, Vivian Smith, Joy Skylar, Gloria Smith, Thelma Tadlock, Polly Ward, Nikki Cellini, Bill Joyce, John Laverty, George Marci, Walter Stane, Bill Summer, Ken Urmston. *Singers*: Marian Burke, Sara Dillon, Mary

Harmon, Betsy Holland, B. J. Keating, Laurel Shelby, Judy Sinclair, Beverly Weston, Dean Campbell, Don Covert, Herb Fields, Ken Harvey, Claude Heater, Bob Kole, Doug Luther, Don McKay.

Act 1, Scene 1: TV Studio. *Scene 2*: Dressing Room, early next morning. *Scene 3*: The Gown Shop, MacCracken's Store. *Scene 4*: In Front of Elevator. *Scene 5*: The Book Department. *Scene 6*: Interior of Elevator. *Scene 7*: The Fitting Room. *Scene 8*: TV Studio.

Act 2, Scene 1: TV Studio. *Scene 2*: 40 W. 82nd Street. *Scene 3*: Vignettes. *Scene 4*: Dressing Room. *Scene 5*: Top Banana. *Scene 6*: Dressing Room. *Scene 7*: TV Studio.

ACT 1

"The Man of the Year This Week"
Ensemble

"You're So Beautiful That—"
L. Doherty

"Top Banana"
P. Silvers, J. Albertson, L. Doherty, J. Faye, H. Faye

"Elevator Song"
Ensemble

"Hail to MacCracken's"
Ensemble

"Only If You're in Love"
L. Doherty, J. Lynn

"My Home Is in My Shoes"
B. Scheerer, Ensemble

"I Fought Every Step of the Way"[5]
R. Marie

"O.K. for TV"
P. Silvers, J. Albertson, J. Lynn, J. Faye, H. Faye, E. Hanley, Z. Charles

"Slogan Song"
P. Silvers, R. Marie, J. Albertson, J. Lynn, L. Doherty, R. Scheerer, J. Faye, H. Faye, E. Hanley, Z. Charles, B. Hatton

"Meet Miss Blendo"
Entire Company

ACT 2

"Sans Souci"[6]
R. Marie, H. Loman, J. Fields, Ensemble

"A Dog Is a Man's Best Friend"
P. Silvers, T. Morgan, the Grenadiers

"That's For Sure"[7]
L. Doherty, J. Lynn, Ensemble

"A Word Is Day"
P. Silvers, R. Marie

"Top Banana Ballet"
P. Silvers, Ensemble

Finale
Entire Company

1951.24

PAINT YOUR WAGON

A Musical Play in Two Acts, 17 Scenes. Book and lyrics by Alan Jay Lerner. Music by Frederick Loewe. Dances and musical ensembles by Agnes de Mille. Scenery designed by Oliver Smith. Costumes by Motley. Orchestra and chorus conducted by Franz Allers. Lighting by Peggy Clark. Orchestrations by Ted Royal. Music for dances arranged by Trude Rittman. Production associate, Bea Lawrence. Entire production directed by Daniel Mann. Produced by Cheryl Crawford. Opened 12 November 1951 at the Sam S. Shubert Theatre and closed 19 July 1952 after 289 performances.

CAST (in order of appearance): *Walt*: Bert Matthews. *Jennifer Rumson*: OLGA SAN JUAN. *Salem Trumbull*: Ralph Bunker. *Jasper*: Ted Thurston. *Ben Rumson*: JAMES BARTON. *Steve Bullnack*: RUFUS SMITH. *Pete Billings*: James Mitchell. *Cherry*: Kay Medford. *Jake Whippany*: Robert Penn. *Mike Mooney*: John Randolph. *Doctor Newcomb*: David Thomas. *Sing Yuy*: Tom Ai. *Lee Zen*: Chun-Tao Cheng. *Edgar Crocker*: Richard Aherne. *Sandy Twist*: Jared Reed. *Reuben Sloane*: Gordon Dilworth. *Julio Valveras*: TONY BAVAAR. *Jacob Woodling*: Josh Wheeler. *Elizabeth Woodling*:

---

[4]Dropped from original 1932 production for this revival: "And Love Was Born," Bubble Dance, Act 2 reprises of "I've Told Every Little Star" and "I'm Alone."

---

[5]Orchestrated by Bill Finnigan.
[6]Orchestrated by Bill Finnigan.
[7]During run, replaced by:

"Be My Guest"
L. Doherty, J. Lynn, Ensemble

MARIJANE MARICLE. *Sarah Woodling*: Jan Sherwood. *Dutchie*: Bert Matthews. *Carmellita*: Lorraine Havercroft. *Yvonne Sorel*: GEMZE DE LAPPE. *Suzanne Duval*: MARY BURR. *Elsie*: Gisella Svetlik. *Raymond Janney*: Gordon Dilworth. *Rocky*: James Tarbutton. *Joe*: Norman Weise. *Sam*: Delbert Anderson.

Singers: Delbert Anderson, John Anderson, Gino Baldi, Edward Becker, Jack Dabdoub, John Faulkner, Robert Flavelle, John Schickling, John Schmidt, John Spach, Newton Sullivan, Feodor Tedick, David Thomas, Edgar Thompson, Ted Thurston, Norman Weise. *Dancers*: Mary Burr, Tamara Chapman, Gemze de Lappe, Joan Djorup, Katia Geleznova, Dorothy Hill, Stuart Hodes, Jean Houloose, Carmelita Lanza, Robert Morrow, Ilona Murai, Paul Olson, Dick Price, Charlotte Ray, Mavis Ray, Frederick Schaeffen, John Smolko, Gisella Svetlik, James Tarbutton.

Act 1, Scene 1: A Hilltop in Northern California. A Spring evening, 1853. *Scene 2*: Outside Salem's Store, Rumson. Evening, four months later. *Scene 3*: Outside Rumson's Cabin. Evening, two months later. *Scene 4*: Rumson's Cabin, immediately following. *Scene 5*: A Hill near Rumson Town, two nights later. *Scene 6*: Dutchie's Saloon, the following Sunday. *Scene 7*: Outside Rumson's Cabin, later that night. *Scene 8*: Julio's Cabin, later that night. *Scene 9*: The diggin's, the next morning. *Scene 10*: The Square, immediately following.

Act 2, Scene 1: Jake's Palace, October , 1855. *Scene 2*: The diggin's, two months later. *Scene 3*: Rumson's Cabin, two days later. *Scene 4*: A Street in Rumson, the next night. *Scene 5*: Jake's Palace, that night. *Scene 6*: A hill near Rumson, the following dawn. *Scene 7*: Rumson Square, the following spring.

ACT 1[8]

Scene 1
"I'm On My Way"
R. Smith, R. Penn, J. Randolph, C. Cheng, T. Ai, J. Reed, R. Aherne, G. Dilworth, Miners

Scene 2
"Rumson"
R. Penn

"What's Goin' On Here?"
O. San Juan

"I Talk to the Trees"
T. Bavaar, O. San Juan

"They Call the Wind Maria"
R. Smith, Miners
Danced by J. Mitchell, Miners.

Scene 4
"I Still See Elisa"
J. Barton

"How Can I Wait?"
O. San Juan

Scene 5
"Trio"
M. Maricle, J. Sherwood, J. Wheeler

Scene 6
"Rumson" (reprise)
R. Penn

"In Between"
J. Barton

"Whoop-Ti-Ay!"
J. Barton, M. Maricle, Miners

Scene 8
"How Can I Wait?" (reprise)
O. San Juan, T. Bavaar

"Carino Mio"
T. Bavaar, O. San Juan

Scene 9
"There's a Coach Comin' In"
Miners

Scene 10
Finaletto
Danced by the Fandangos and Miners

---

[8]Revised for subsequent national tour into Two Acts, 15 Scenes. "Wand'rin' Star" opened Act 1, and in its place in Act 2 a new song was added:

"Take the Wheels Off the Wagon"
Burl Ives (Ben Rumson)

ACT 2

Scene 1
"Hand Me Down That Can O' Beans"
R. Penn, Miners

Rope Dance
Fandangos, J. Mitchell, G. de Lappe

Can-can
Danced by M. Burr, J. Tarbutton, Fandangos, Miners

"Another Autumn"
T. Bavaar
Danced by G. de Lappe, J. Mitchell.

Scene 2
"Movin'"
Miners

"I'm On My Way" (reprise)
Miners

Scene 3
"All for Him"
O. San Juan

"(I Was Born Under a) Wand'rin' Star"
J. Barton

Scene 4
"I Talk to the Trees" (reprise)
O. San Juan

Scene 5
"Strike!"
R. Smith, T. Thurston, R. Penn

Scene 6
"Wand'rin' Star" (reprise)
R. Penn, R. Smith, J. Reed, Miners

Scene 7
Finale

1952.01

PAL JOEY

A Revival of the Musical Comedy in Two Acts, 12 Scenes[9]. Book by John O'Hara based on his collected short stories of the same name. Music by Richard Rodgers. Lyrics by Lorenz Hart. Dances and musical numbers staged by Robert Alton. Settings by Oliver Smith. Costumes by Miles White. Lighting by Peggy Clark. Musical director, Mex Meth. Orchestrations by Don Walker. Dance arrangements by Oscar Kosarin. Production associate, Emil Katzka. Book directed by David Alexander. Entire production supervised by Robert Alton. Produced by Jule Styne and Leonard Key in association with Anthony Brady Farrell. Opened 2 January 1952 at the Broadhurst Theatre and closed 18 April 1953 after 542 performances.

CAST (in order of appearance): *Mike*: JACK WALDRON. *Joey Evans*: HAROLD LANG. *Kid*: Helen Wood. *Gladys*: HELEN GALLAGHER. *Agnes*: Janyce Ann Wagner. *Mickey*: Phyllis Dorne. *Diane*: Frances Krell. *Dottie*: Lynn Joelson. *Sandra*: Eleanor Boleyn. *Adele*: Rito Tanno. *Francine*: Gloria O'Malley. *Linda*: PAT NORTHROP. *Vera Simpson*: VIVIENNE SEGAL. *Valerie*: Barbara Nichols. *Waiter*: George Martin. *Amarilla*: Thelma Tadlock. *Ernest*: Gordon Peters. *Victor*: Robert Fortier. *Delivery Boy*: Barry Ryan. *Stage Manager*: Clarke Gordon. *Louis*, the Tenor: Lewis Bolyard. *Melba*: ELAINE STRITCH. *Ludlow Lowell*: LIONEL STANDER. *O'Brien*: T. J. Halligan.

Dancers: Eleanor Boleyn, Bonnie Brae, Phyllis Dorne, Eleanor Fairchild, Jean Goodall, Patty Ann Jackson, Lynn Joelson, Helene Keller, Frances Krell, Ina Learner, Ethel Martin, June McCain, Gloria O'Malley, Thelma Tadlock, Rita Tanno, Norma Thornton, Janyce Ann Wagner, Harry Asmus, Hank Brunjes, Peter Holmes, Ray Kyle, George Martin, Buzz Miller, David Neuman, Stanley Simmons, George Vosburgh.

---

[9]Originally produced in New York 25 December 1940 at the Ethel Barrymore Theatre for 374 performances. For Synopsis of Scenes and Musical Numbers, see original 1940 production. For this and all subsequent revivals "What Is a Man" permanently replaced "Love Is My Friend" in Act 1, Scene 4; "Do It the Hard Way" moved from Scene 3 to Scene 4 in Act 2. In its place in Scene 3 appears A Dance Rehearsal, performed by Boys and Girls, which is called "Morocco" set to the music of "Chicago."

1952.02

KISS ME, KATE

A Return Engagement of the Musical Comedy in Two Acts, 16 Scenes[10]. Music and lyrics by Cole Porter. Book by Sam [Samuel] and Bella Spewack. (Based on William Shakespeare's "The Taming of the Shrew.") Choreography by Hanya Holm. Settings and costumes by Lemuel Ayers. Lighting by Al Alloy. Musical director, George Hirst. Orchestrations by Robert Russell Bennett. Incidental ballet music arranged by Genevieve Pitot. Production staged by John C. Wilson. Produced by (Arnold) Saint Subber and Lemuel Ayers. Opened 8 January 1952 at the Broadway Theatre and closed 13 January 1952 after 8 performances.

CAST (in order of appearance): *Fred Graham*: ROBERT WRIGHT. *Harry Trevor*: NAT BURNS. *Lois Lane*: MARILYN DAY. *Ralph*, Stage Manager: Emory Bass. *Lilli Vanessi*: HOLLY HARRIS. *Hattie*: LILLYAN BROWN. *Paul*: BOBBY JOHNSON. *Bill Calhoun*: FRANK DERBAS. *Cab Driver*: Max Hart. *Stage Doorman*: Bruce Laffey. *First Man*: HANK HENRY. *Second Man*: SPARKY KAYE. *Harrison Howell*: Lionel Ince. *Specialty Dancers*: Charles Cook, Ernest Brown.

"Taming of the Shrew" Players: *Bianca* (Lois Lane): MARILYN DAY. *Baptista* (Harry Trevor): NAT BURNS. *Gremio* (First Suitor): Jim Howard. *Hortensio* (Second Suitor): Alfred Homan. *Lucentio* (Bill Calhoun): FRANK DERBAS. *Katharine* (Lilli Vanessi): HOLLY HARRIS. *Petruchio* (Fred Graham): ROBERT WRIGHT. *Haberdasher*: Jan Kovac.

Singing Ensemble: Jean Cannon, Sylvia Chaney, Marilyn Hanson, Louise Hoffman, Janey Medlin, Pat Sayers, Bobra Suitor, Charles Adrian, Emory Bass, Frank Green, Joseph Gregory, Max Hart, Alfred Homan, Edward Whitman. *Dancers*: Esta Beck, Naomi Boneck, Doris Atkinson, Albertina Horstmann, Claire Mallardy, Julie Marlowe, Florence Miller, Charles Arnett, Harold Drake, Bill Harris, Jay Kleindorf, Jan Kovac, Roland Landry, Jess Ramirez.

1952.03

COME OF AGE

A Revival of the Play in Music and Words (Dramatic Fantasy) in Three Acts, a Prologue and 5 Scenes[11]. Play (book and lyrics) by Clemence Dane. Music by Richard Addinsell. Directed by Guthrie McClintic. Settings by Raymond Sovey from designs by James Reynolds. Miss Anderson's costumes by Valentina; other costumes by Noel Taylor. Orchestra director, Macklin Marrow. Produced by the New York City Center Theatre Company (George Schaefer, Artistic director). Opened 23 January 1952 at the New York City Center and closed 10 February 1952 after 24 performances.

CAST: *A Boy*: ROBERT BROWN. *A Shadow of Death*: ROBERT HARRISON. *A Woman*: JUDITH ANDERSON. *Man*: MELVILLE RUICK. *A Close Friend*: Marian Seldes. *Friends of the Woman*: Ethel Colt, Richard Barbee, June Jollie, James Noble, Lita Dal Porto, Stephen Reese, Muriel Rahn, James Bronson, Barbara Torrance, Gerry Jedd, Phoebe Mackaye, Peter Brandon, Bill Krach, Jacqueline deWit. *An Entertainer*: MURIEL RAHN. *Singer for the Woman*: MURIEL RAHN. *Singer for River Music*: Beverly Hosier. *Singer for the Boy*: Thomas Motto. *Pianists*: George Bauer, Jack Eisenberg.

1952.04

PARIS '90

A Solo Musical Revue in Three Acts, 14 Scenes. (Sketches) by Cornelia Otis Skinner. Music and lyrics by Kay Swift. Directed by Alden S. Blodget. Settings and lighting by Donald Oenslager. Costumes designed by Helene Pons. Musical director, Nathaniel Shilkret. Orchestrations by Robert Russell Bennett. Produced by Alden S. Blodget. Opened 4 March 1952 at the Booth Theatre, moved 21 April 1952 to the John Golden Theatre, and closed 17 May 1952 after 87 performances.

CAST: CORNELIA OTIS SKINNER.

ACT 1: Champs Elysees
Scene 1
The 'Nou-Nou': "Champs Elysees Polka"
Scene 2
A Fashionble Parisienne: "Chatterbox"

Scene 3
La Duchesse de Vertpres: "Cortege for a Nobleman"
Scene 4
La Belle Conchita: " La Belle Conchita"
Scene 5
The New Woman: "Lady on a Tandem Bicycle"

ACT 2: Left Bank
Scene 1
Niche in a Portal of Notre Dame: "Moonlight on Notre Dame"
Scene 2
The Laundress: "The Laundress"
"Turn My Little Millwheel"
(*Music by* Paul Delmet. *Lyrics by* Kay Swift.)
Scene 3
A Boston School Teacher: "From a Window on the Seine"
Scene 4
A Woman of Virtue: "The Enchantress"
"Lend Me a Bob Till Monday"
Scene 5
A Professor's Wife: "Lament"
"With My Sabots" (March; traditional)

ACT 3: Montmartre; Friends of Toulouse-Lautrec:
Scene 1
"La Goulue," "Can-Can," "Calliope"
Scene 2
A Lion Tamer of The Medrano Circus: "Calliope" (instrumental reprise)
Scene 3
Berthe La Sourde ("Deaf Bertha"): "The Waltz I Heard in a Dream"
a. In the Parlor: "Fughetta"
b. On the Seine: "The House Where I Was Born . . ."
Scene 4
Yvette Guilbert: Yvette
"Saint Lazare"
(*Music by* Aristede Bruant. *Lyrics by* Kay Swift.)
"Madame Arthur"
(*Music by* Yvette Guilbert. *Lyrics by* Kay Swift.)

1952.05

THREE WISHES FOR JAMIE

A Musical Play in Two Acts, 19 Scenes. Book by Charles O'Neal and Abe Burrows. Based on the novel "The Three Wishes of Jamie McRuin" by Charles O'Neal. Music and lyrics by Ralph Blane. Settings by George Jenkins. Costumes by Miles White. Lighting by (Abe) Feder. Orchestral arrangements, Robert Russell Bennett. Conductor, Joseph Littau. Choral arrangements by William Ellfeldt. Choreography by Ted Cappy. Entire production directed by Abe Burrows. Produced by Albert Lewis and Arthur Lewis. Opened 21 March 1952 at the Mark Hellinger Theatre, moved 27 May 1952 to the Plymouth Theatre, and closed 7 June 1952 after 92 performances.

CAST (in order of appearance): *Tim Shanahan*: ROBERT HALLIDAY. *Nora*: Michele Burke. *McCaffrey*: Wilton Clary. *Bridgie Quinn*: Marie Gibson. *Tirsa Shanahan*: CHARLOTTE RAE. *Owen Roe Tavish*: BERT WHEELER. *Jamie McRuin*: JOHN RAITT. *Power O'Malley*: WALTER BURKE. *Maeve Harrigan*: ANNE JEFFREYS. *Randal Devlin*: JEFF MORROW. *Aunt Bid*: Grania O'Malley. *Jess Proddy*: ROYAL DANO. *Big Patrick*: Wilton Clary. *Shiel Harrigan*: MALCOLM KEEN. *Dennis O'Ryan*: PETER CONLOW. *Father Kerrigan*: RALPH MORGAN. *Kevin*: Billy Chapin. *Sheriff Haines*: Dick Foote.

Principal Dancers: Sandra Zell, George Foster. *Dancers*: Doris Atkinson, Estelle Aza, Ann Deasy, Mary Haywood, Elizabeth Logue, Mildred Ann Mauldin, Janet Sayers, Buddy Bryan, James Capp, Don [Donald] Driver, Jerry Newby, Greg O'Brien, Joe Stember, Robert St. Clair. *Singers*: Leigh Allen, Marion Baird, Michele Burke, Marie Gibson, Joan Kilbrig, Nancy Price, June Reimer, Ann Richards, Tafi Towers, Robert Baird, Jerry Cardoni, Clifford Fearl, Robert Lamont, Richard Scott, Donald Thrall, Richard Vine. *Children*: *Kenneth Francis*: Pud Flanagan. *Johnny Finley*: Jackie Scholle. *Sorley Boy Donner*: Alfred Catal. *Little Patrick*: Martin Walker.

Act 1, Scene 1: The McRuin cottage in the Province of Connacht. The West Coast of Ireland—1896. *Scene 2*: A road. Immdiately following. *Scene 3*: The Camp of Shiel Harrigan's horse traders. The State of Georgia. *Scene 4*: A lane in the Forest. *Scene 5*:

---

[10]First produced in New York 30 December 1948 at the New Century Theatre for 1077 performances. For Synopsis of Scenes and Musical Numbers, see original 1948 production.

[11]First presented in New York 12 January 1934 at the Maxine Elliott Theatre for 35 performances. For Synopsis of Scenes and Musical Numbers, see original 1934 production.

Outside Power O'Malley's shop in Atlanta. *Scene 6:* A lane near Harrigan's camp. *Scene 7:* Maeve Harrigan's tent. *Scene 8:* A lane. The next morning. *Scene 9:* The ritual tent.

Act 2, Scene 1: Harrigan's camp. Two years later. *Scene 2:* Tirsa's tent. *Scene 3:* A lane. *Scene 4:* The cook tent. *Scene 5:* A lane. *Scene 6:* Maeve's tent. *Scene 7:* A lane. That evening. *Scene 8:* The deep forest. *Scene 9:* A lane. A few days later. *Scene 10:* The camp. Immediately following.

ACT 1[12]

"The Wake"
R. Halliday, C. Rae, B. Wheeler, Mourners

"The Girl That I Court in My Mind"
J. Raitt

"My Home's a Highway"
A. Jeffreys, Horse Traders

"We're for Love"
B. Wheeler, Horse Traders, Women of the Camp

"My Heart's Darlin'"
J. Raitt

"Goin' On a Hayride"
J. Raitt, A. Jeffreys, Boys, Girls

"Love Has Nothing to Do With Looks"
C. Rae, R. Halliday, B. Wheeler
(*Lyrics by* Charles Lederer.)

"My Heart's Darlin'" (reprise)
A. Jeffreys, J. Raitt

"I'll Sing You a Song"
C. Rae, R. Halliday, P. Conlow, B. Wheeler, Dennis' Brothers

"It Must Be Spring"
A. Jeffreys, Brides and Bridesmaids

"Wedding March"—Finale
Entire Company

ACT 2

"The Army Mule Song"
J. Raitt, Men and Women of the Camp

"What Do I Know?"
A. Jeffreys

"Expectant Father"
Danced by P. Conlow
(*Choreography by* Herbert Ross. *Special Music by* Lee J. Pockriss.)

"It's a Wishing World"
A. Jeffreys, J. Raitt

"Trottin' to the Fair"
J. Raitt, R. Halliday, P. Conlow, Men and Women of the Camp
(*Choreography by* Eugene Loring.)

"Love Has Nothing to Do With Looks" (reprise)
C. Rae, P. Conlow

"April Face"
B. Wheeler, A. Jeffreys, J. Raitt

"It's a Wishing World"—Finale
Entire Company

1952.06 FOUR SAINTS IN THREE ACTS

A Revival of the Opera in Four Acts, and a Prelude[13]. Libretto by Gertrude Stein. Music by Virgil Thomson. Book direction by Maurice Grosser. Choreography by William Dollar. Scenery and costumes by Paul Morrison after original models by Florine Stettheimer. Artistic and musical direction, Virgil Thomson. Associate conductor and choral director, William Jonson. Produced by The American National Theatre and Academy (Managing director, Robert Whitehead) in asssociation with Ethel Linder Reiner. Opened 16 April 1952 at the Broadway Theatre and closed 27 April 1952 after 15 performances.

---

[12]Added during run to Act 1, after "The Girl That I Court in My Mind":
"Women's Work"
Women of the Camp
[13]First presented in New York 20 February 1934 at the 44th Street Theatre for 48 performances. For Synopsis of Scenes, see original 1934 production. No individual musical numbers listed.

CAST (in order of appearance): *St. Stephen:* Clyde Turner. *St. Settlement:* Martha Flowers. *St. Plan:* Calvin Dash. *St. Sara:* Doris Mayes. *Commere:* ALTONELL HINES. *Compere:* ELWOOD SMITH. *St. Theresa I:* INEZ MATTHEWS. *St. Theresa II:* BETTY LOU ALLEN. *St. Ignatius:* EDWARD MATTHEWS. *St. Cecilia:* LEONTYNE PRICE. *St. Electra:* Ida Johnson. *St. Jan:* George Goodman. *St. Chavez:* RAWN SPEARMAN. *St. Eustace:* Charles Colman. *St. Vincent:* Rayfield Du Bard.

Male Saints: Rayfield Du Bard, George Goodman, Charles Colman, William Hughes, Hugh Hurd, Kelsey Pharr, George Royston, Jesse Williams, Nat Wright, Ned Wright, James Young, Curtis Hawkins. *Female Saints:* Adelaide Boatner, Yvonne Cummings, Billie Daniel, Gloria Davey, Olga James, Ida Johnson, Vera Little, Mary Robbs, Dorothy Ross, Mae Wilaims, Gloria Wynder. *Dancers:* Billie Allen, Robert Curtis, Carolyn Jorrin, Louis Johnson, Arthur Mitchell, Helen Taitt.

1952.07 OF THEE I SING

A Revival of the Musical Comedy in Two Acts, 11 Scenes[14]. Book by George S. Kaufman and Morrie Ryskind. Music by George Gershwin. Lyrics by Ira Gershwin. Directed by George S. Kaufman. Musical numbers and ensembles staged by Jack Donohue. Settings by Albert Johnson. Costumes by Irene Sharaff. Lighting by Peggy Clark. Musical director, Maurice Levine. Musical supervision and vocal direction, David Craig. Orchestrations, Don Walker. Dance arrangements by David Baker. Production associates, William Tiernan, Charles F. Spaulding. Production coordinator, Ann Noyes. Produced by Chandler Cowles and Ben Segal. Opened 5 May 1952 at the Ziegfeld Theatre and closed 5 July 1952 after 72 performances.

CAST: *Francis X. Gilhooley:* J. PAT O'MALLEY. *Louis Lippman:* ROBERT F. SIMON. *Chambermaid:* Louise Carlyle. *Matthew Arnold Fulton:* LORING SMITH. *Senator Carver Jones:* HOWARD FREEMAN. *Senator Robert E. Lyons:* DONALD FOSTER. *Alexander Throttlebottom:* PAUL HARTMAN. *John P. Wintergreen:* JACK CARSON. *Beauty Contestant:* Jean Bartel. *Mary Turner:* BETTY OAKES. *Sam Jenkins:* JONATHAN LUCAS. *Diana Devereaux:* LENORE LONERGAN. *Emily Benson:* JOAN MANN. *Announcer:* Mort Marshall. *Vladimir Vidovitch:* Abe Stein. *Yussef Yussevitch:* Bob Oran. *The Chief Justice:* JACK WHITING. *Guide:* JACK WHITING. *A Sightseer:* Parker Wilson. *The French Ambassador:* FLORENZ AMES. *Chief Senate Clerk:* Mort Marshall. *Senator from Massachusetts:* JACK WHITING. *Attache:* Tom Wells. *Chief Flunkey:* Al McGranary. *Flunkies:* Al McGranary, Michael King, Ken Ayers.

Singers: Claudia Campbell, Louise Carlyle, Helen Rice, Jeanne Schlegel, Joanne Spiller, Gloria Van Dorpe, Ken Ayers, Norman Clayton, Warren Galjour, Jay Harnick, Keith Kaldenberg, Joe Kerrigan, Michael King, Willaim Krach, James McCracken, Larry Weber. *Dancers:* Vicki Barrett, Betty Buday, Georgine Darcy, Peggy Merber, Pat Stanley, Crandall Diehl, J. Corkey Geil, Skeet Guenther, Frank Seabolt, Bob Tucker, Parker Wilson. *Showgirls:* Arlene Anderson, Joan Bartel, Gregg Evans, Charlotte Foley, Dorothy Richards, Siri, Jeanne Tyler, Charlotte Van Lein.

1952.08 SHUFFLE ALONG

A Revival of the Musical Comedy in Two Acts, 9 Scenes[15]. Revised book by Flournoy Miller and Paul Gerard Smith. Music by Eubie Blake. Lyrics by Noble Sissle. Additional music and lyrics by Joseph Meyer and Floyd Huddleston. Directed by Paul Gerard Smith. Choreography by Henry LeTang. Settings by Albert Johnson. Costumes by Waldo Angelo. Orchestrations by Charles E. Cooke. Vocal arrangements by Claude Garreau. Entire production devised and staged by George Hale. Produced by Irving Gaumont in association with Grace Rosenfield. Opened 8 May 1952 at the Broadway Theatre and closed 10 May 1952 after 4 performances.

CAST (in order of appearance): *Bugler:* William Dillard. *Sergeant Rocky Mason:* James E. Wall. *Corporal Betty Lee:* THELMA CARPENTER. *Lieutenant Jim Crocker:* AVON LONG. *Colonel Alexander Popham:* EARL SYDNOR. *Major Joseph Gantt:* William McDaniel. *Captain Frederick Graham:* T. S. Krlgarin. *Sergeant Lucy Duke:* DELORES MARTIN. *Corporal Louie Bauche:* Leslie Scott. *Captain Henry Gaillard:* NAPOLEON REED. *Private Cyphus Brown:* FLOURNOY MILLER. *Private Longitude Lane:* HAMTREE HARRINGTON. *Chaplain:* Laurence Watson. *Mable:* Mable Lee. *Fifeto:* Henry Sherwood. *Rosa Pasini:* Louise Woods. *SS Trooper:* Harro Meller. *Laura Popham:* Urylee Leonardos. *Sergeant Mabel Powers:* Marie Young.

---

[14]First presented in New York 26 December 1931 at the Music Box Theatre for 441 performances. For Synopsis of Scenes and Musical Numbers, see original 1931 production. Added to Act 2, Scene 1, after "Hello, Good Morning":
"Mine" (from LET 'EM EAT CAKE)
J. Carson, B. Oakes
[15]Originally presented in New York 23 May 1921 at Daly's 63rd Street Theatre for 484 performances.

Margie: Sara Lou Harris. *NOBLE SISSLE*: Himself. *EUBIE BLAKE*: Himself. *Principal Dancers*: Mable Lee, Arleigh Peterson. (*Featured Dancer*: Eddie Rector.)

Dancing Group: Wini Benson, Mildred Clemons, Katherine Davidson, Tempy Fletcher, Delores Harper, Erona Harris, Roberta Harris, Marie Kenney, Celise King, Sophie Miller, Ruth Mosley, Jackie Petty, Estelle Price, Sterling Bough, Smalls Boykin, Bill Del Campo, Harold Gordon, Stefhan Maroud, James McMillan, Carson Moore, Joel Nobel, Leigh Parham, Conrad Pringle, Lew Smith, James A. Smith. *Models*: Sara Lou Harris, Lois Kibler, Courteney Olden. *Singing Group*: Barbara Jai, Freddy Marshall, Rosalie Maxwell, Audrey Vanderpool, Louise Woods, Marie Young, William Dillard, George Fischer, T. S. Krlgarin, William McDaniel, Henry Pierre, Leslie Scott, Rhodesta Timmons.

Act 1, Scene 1: Castle del Vezzio. Northern Italy, the spring of 1945. *Scene 2*: An Alpine Pass. *Scene 3*: The Clutterhorn. *Scene 4*: A Street in Genoa. *Scene 5*: Cafe Fifeto.

Act 2, Scene 1: Le Salon de Madame Lucy. New York City, the following Spring. *Scene 2*: A Street in New York. *Scene 3*: Popham's Office. *Scene 4*: Pier 17.

ACT 1

"Jive Drill"
W. Dillard, J. E. Wall, Ensemble

"Bitten by Love"
T. Carpenter, A. Long, Ensemble
(*Music by* Joseph Meyer. *Lyrics by* Floyd Huddleston.)

"Falling"
D. Martin, N. Reed

"I'm Just Wild About Harry"
D. Martin, N. Reed, Ensemble

"City Called Heaven—Juba-lee"
L. Watson, Ensemble

"Bongo-Boola"
M. Lee, W. Dillard, Drummer, Ensemble

"Swanee Moon"
T. Carpenter, Singers
Danced by E. Rector.

"Love Will Find a Way"
D. Martin, A. Long, L. Scott, L. Woods, Singers

"Rhythm of America"
D. Martin, Entire Company

ACT 2

"It's the Gown That Makes the Gal That Makes the Guy"
Ensemble
(*Lyrics by* Joan Javitts.)

"You Can't Overdo a Good Thing"
D. Martin, Models
(*Music by* Joseph Meyer. *Lyrics by* Floyd Huddleston.)

"My Day"
A. Long, GIs
(*Music by* Joseph Meyer. *Lyrics by* Floyd Huddleston.)

"Give It Love"
T. Carpenter, WACs
(*Music by* Joseph Meyer. *Lyrics by* Floyd Huddleston.)

Farewell With Love
D. Martin

"Here 'Tis"
M. Lee
(*Music by* Joseph Meyer. *Lyrics by* Floyd Huddleston.)

"Reminiscing"
N. Sissle, E. Blake

Finale
Entire Company

(LEONARD SILLMAN'S) NEW FACES OF 1952

1952.09

A Musical Revue in Two Acts, 27 Scenes[16]. Words and music mostly by Ronny Graham, June Carroll, Arthur Siegel, Sheldon Harnick, Michael Brown, (Francis Lemarque, Herbert Farjeon, Alan Melville, Elisse Boyd). Sketches mostly by Ronny Graham, Melvin [Mel] Brooks, (Peter De Vries, Roger Price, Luther Davis, John Cleveland, Paul Lynde, Alan Melville).

---

[16]The Fourth in the series of revues conceived by Leonard Sillman as a showcase for new talent. The first was produced in 1934.

Entire production devised and staged by John Murray Anderson. Choreography and staging of musical numbers by Richard Barstow. Sketches directed by John Beal. Scenery by Raoul Pene du Bois. Costumes by Thomas Becher. Musical director, Anton Coppola. Orchestral arrangements, Ted Royal. Production supervised by Leonard Sillman. Produced by Leonard Sillman[17]. Opened 16 May 1952 at the Royale Theatre and closed 28 March 1953 after 365 performances.

CAST: Virginia Bosler, Allen Conroy, Alice Ghostley, Eartha Kitt, Paul Lynde, Jimmy Russell, June Carroll, Virginia deLuce, Ronny Graham, Joe Lautner, Bill Mullikin, Robert Clary, Michael Domenico, Patricia Hammerlee, Carol Lawrence, Carol Nelson, Rosemary O'Reilly.

ACT 1[18]

Scene 1
"Opening"
Entire Company
(*Music and Lyrics by* Ronny Graham. *Dialogue by* Peter DeVries.)
Reader: R. Graham.

Scene 2
Crazy, Man!
(*by* Ronny Graham and Roger Price)
Counsellor Holly: P. Lynde. *Senator Marble*: J. Lautner. *Senator Hutchinson*: B. Mullikin. *A Policeman*: J. Russell. *Dazz Rocco*: R. Graham.

Scene 3
"Lucky Pierre"
(*Music and Lyrics by* Ronny Graham.)
Girls: V. de Luce, P. Hammerlee, R. O'Reilly. *Pierre*: R. Clary. *Reporter*: B. Mullikin.

Scene 4
"Guess Who I Saw Today?"
J. Carroll
(*Music by* Murray Grand. *Lyrics by* Elisse Boyd.)

Scene 5
"Restoration Piece"
(*Dialogue and Lyrics by* June [Alan] Melville. *Music by* Arthur Siegel.)
Introduced by V. deLuce. *Lady Sylvia Malpractice*: A. Ghostley. *Simple*: P. Hammerlee. *Sir Solemnity Sourpuss*: P. Lynde. *Sir Militant Malpractice*: J. Lautner.

Scene 6
"Love Is a Simple Thing"
R. O'Reilly, R. Clary, E. Kitt, J. Carroll
(*Music by* Arthur Siegel. *Lyrics by* June Carroll.)
Danced by V. Bosler, A. Conroy (First Couple), C. Nelson, J. Russell (Second Couple), C. Lawrence, M. Domenico (Third Couple).

Scene 7
"Boston Beguine"
A. Ghostley
(*Music and Lyrics by* Sheldon Harnick.)

Scene 8
"The Bard and the Beard"
(*Dialogue by* Ronny Graham. *Music by* Arthur Siegel. *Lyrics by* June Carroll. *Additional Lyrics by* Sheldon Harnick.)
Introduced by V. deLuce. *Miss Leigh*: J. Carroll. *Sir Laurence*: R. Graham. *Call Boy*: B. Mullikin. *Maid*: R. O'Reilly.

Scene 9
"Nanty Puts Her Hair Up"
(*Music by* Arthur Siegel. *Lyrics by* Herbert Farjeon.)
Nanty: V. Bosler. *Father*: J. Lautner. *Mother*: A. Ghostley. *Brother*: B. Mullikin. *Highlander*: A. Conroy.

Scene 10
Oedipus Goes South
(*by* Ronny Graham)R. Graham
Introduced by V. de Luce.

Scene 11
"Time for Tea"
(J. Carroll, A. Ghostley)

---

[17]Subsequent national tour presented by Walter P. Chrysler, Jr.
[18]Recurrent throughout the show:
"He Takes Me Off His Income Tax"
V. deLuce
(*Music by* Arthur Siegel. *Lyrics by* June Carroll.)